160Z388

Current Law

CASE CITATOR 1998 - 2001

Sweet & Maxwell
A THOMSON COMPANY

AUSTRALIA
LBC Information Services
Sydney

CANADA and USA
Carswell
Toronto

NEW ZEALAND
Brooker's
Auckland

SINGAPORE and MALAYSIA
Sweet & Maxwell Asia
Singapore and Kuala Lumpur

CurrentLaw

CASE CITATOR
1998 - 2001

SWEET & MAXWELL

EDITORIAL TEAM
Catherine Collins
Susan Kilgallon
Colette Rybicki
Martin Syrett
Nina Taylor
Alix Robinson
Chris Jowett

PRODUCTION TEAM
Roger Greenwood
Debra Wade

LONDON
SWEET & MAXWELL

EDINBURGH
W. GREEN

2002

Published in 2002 by
Sweet & Maxwell Limited of
100 Avenue Road, Swiss Cottage, London NW3 3PF.
Typeset by Sweet & Maxwell Ltd, Mytholmroyd, Hebden Bridge, West Yorkshire.
Printed by The Bath Press, Bath, Avon.

A CIP catalogue record for this book is available from the British Library.

ISBN This Volume only 0 421 795506
With Year Book and Legislation Citator 0 421 795107

No forests were destroyed to make this product; only farmed timber was used and re-planted.

ISBN 0-421-79550-6

9 780421 795501

CONTENTS

i

PREFACE

The Sweet & Maxwell Current Law Service

The Current Law Service began in 1947 and provides a comprehensive guide to developments in case law, primary legislation and secondary legislation in the UK and mainland Europe. The Current Law Service presently consists of the Monthly Digests, the Year Book, Current Law Statutes, the Statute Citator, the Statutory Instrument Citator, the Case Citator, Current Law Week and European Current Law.

Also available is the Current Legal Information CD Rom, which contains an archive of Year Books dating back to 1947, the present year's accumulated Monthly Digests and the English and Scottish Case Citators from 1947 to the current month, as well as a range of other Sweet & Maxwell current awareness products such as the Current Law Legislation Citators, Legal Journals Index and Financial Journals Index.

The Case Citators

The Current Law Case Citators comprise three volumes covering the years 1947-1976, 1977-1997 and 1998-2001. Together they provide a comprehensive reference guide to case law after 1946.

How to use the Citators

When searching for a case, users should consult the most recent citator volume first, since it provides the most comprehensive and authoritative information. The current volume contains a cumulative guide to the complete history of cases digested or judicially considered from 1998 (inclusive). For earlier case law not considered since 1998, users should consult either the two previous citator volumes (1977-1997 and 1947-1976) or the Current Legal Information CD Rom.

The material in this volume is arranged in alphabetical order in three sections:

English Citator
Scottish Citator
Ships' Names Index

The details in each entry can be used on a number of different levels, including identifying law report series in which a full report of a case can be found, the judicial history of a case and the location of an abstract of a case within a Current Law Yearbook. The following information is provided:

(a) The full name of any case reported between 1947 and 2001

Cases are listed alphabetically by the first party's name, giving the most recent Current Law Year Book paragraph reference to the appropriate digest. Most references have a year before the paragraph number, eg 01/**239** alludes to the 2001 Year Book, paragraph 239. If no year is given, the case is contained in the Current Law Consolidation 1947-1951. (For Scotland see the Scottish Year Books 1948-1951)

(b) An extensive list of references to the law reports and journals reporting each case

Each entry gives details about one case, beginning with the case name and any joined cases or other names by which the case might be known, followed by the reports in descending order of authority and the court in which the case was heard. Where cases go on to an appellate court, the entry states whether the higher court affirmed or reversed the decision of the lower court.

(c) The judicial history of a case

If a case has been applied, considered, approved, distinguished, overruled, etc., since it was decided, Current Law Year Book references to digests of cases in which the judicial consideration took place are provided. These references are in normal type while the paragraph number of the actual digest of each case is given in bold.

(d) Details of Scottish cases

Part II of the Citator contains details of cases decided or judicially considered in the Scottish Courts. References to English cases judicially considered in Scotland are also included in this part, so subscribers wishing to follow the full history of an English case should consult both parts of the Citator. Scottish cases published in English Law Reports are included in both the Scottish and English sections.

(e) Ships' Names Index

This is an alphabetical listing of all ships' names and their law report citations to assist where only the ship's name is known by the user. The official party names for these cases will be located in the main body of the Citator.

Whilst every effort has been made to ensure that details of cases in this citator are correct, there may be occasions when a citation is wrong. The editor would be grateful for notification of any errors to enable them to be rectified on the database from which this volume was derived.

Case Citator Editor
Sweet & Maxwell Ltd
The Hatchery
Hall Bank Lane
Mytholmroyd, Hebden Bridge
West Yorkshire
HX7 5HQ
email: CaseCitatorEditor@sweetandmaxwell.co.uk

TABLE OF ABBREVIATIONS

Court Abbreviations

1 Div = First Division
2 Div = Second Division
AAT = Administrative Appeals Tribunal (Australia)
Adm Ct = Admiralty Court
Admin Ct = Administrative Court
Afr Comm HPR = African Commission on Human and Peoples Rights
AG = Amtsgericht (Germany)
AGO = Advocate Generals Opinion
App (B) = Cour d'Appel (Belgium)
App (I) = Corte di Appello (Italy)
Ar Pag = Areios Pagos (Greece)
ArbG = Arbeitsgericht (Germany)
ARRS = Afdeling Rechtspraak van de Raad van State (NL)
AsTic Mah = Asliye Ticaret Mahkemesi (Turkey)
Aud = Audiencia Provincial (Spain)
BAG = Bundesarbeitsgericht (Germany)
Bd of Trade = Board of Trade
BezG = Bezirksgericht (Switzerland)
BFH = Bundesfinanzhof (Germany)
BG = Bundesgericht (Switzerland)
BGH = Bundesgerichtshof (Germany)
BKA = Bundeskartellamt (Germany)
BPG = Bundespatentgericht (Germany)
BRB = Burgerlijke Rechtbank (Belgium)
BsozG = Bundessozialgericht (Germany)
BverfG = Bundesverfassungsgericht (Germany)
BverwG = Bundesverwaltungsgericht (Germany)
C Adm A = Cour Administrative d'Appel (Belgium/France)
C Concurrence = Conseil de la Concurrence (Belgium/France)
C Cost = Corte Costituzionale (Italy)
C d'A = Cour d'Appel (France/Luxembourg)
CA = Court of Appeal
CAEW = Central Authority for England and Wales
Cass = Cour de Cassation (Belgium/France/Luxembourg)
CC = County Court
CCA = Court of Criminal Appeal
CCAT = Competition Commission Appeal Tribunal
CCC = Central Criminal Court
CCP = Court of Common Pleas
CE = Conseil d'Etat (Belgium/France)
CEC = Commission of the European Communities
Cent Crim Ct = Central Criminal Court (Ireland)
CFA = Court of Final Appeal
CFI = Court of First Instance
CFI (HK) = Court of First Instance of the High Court (Hong Kong Special Administrative Region)
CFI (Phl) = Court of First Instance (Philippines)
Ch D = Chancery Division
CICA = Criminal Injuries Compensation Authority
CICAP = Criminal Injuries Compensation Appeals Panel
CICB = Criminal Injuries Compensation Board
Circ Ct = Circuit Court (Ireland)
CJ = Court of Justice
CJ (Gen Div) (Ont) = Ontario Court of Justice (General Division)
CMAC = Courts Martial Appeal Court
CollvB = College van Beroep voor het Bedrijfsleven (NL)
Comm Cartels = Commission des Cartels (Switzerland)

Comm Conc = Commission de la Concurrence (France)
Comm Ct = Commercial Court
Comm Tributaria PG = Commissione Tributaria di Primo Grado (Italy)
Comm Tributaria SG = Commissione Tributaria di Secondo Grado (Italy)
Comp Auth = Competition Authority (Ireland)
Cons Const = Conseil Constitutionnel (France)
Cons Ct = Consistory Court
Cons Stato = Consiglio di Stato (Italy)
Const Ct = Constitutional Court
Cour d'Arb = Cour d'Arbitrage (Belgium)
CP = Court of Protection
CPD = Common Pleas Division
CRC = Commission Federale de Recours en Matiere de Contributions (Switzerland)
Crim CA = Criminal Court of Appeal (Ireland)
CRvB = Centrale Raad van Beroep (Netherlands)
CS = Court of Session
CSJ = Cour Superieure de Justice (Luxembourg)
Ct Sup = Corte Suprema de Justicia (Argentina)
DC = Divisional Court
DR = District Registry
EAT = Employment Appeal Tribunal
EC Council = European Council
Eccl Ct = Court of Ecclesiastical Causes Reserved
ECHR = European Court of Human Rights
ECJ = European Court of Justice
ED = Eparhiako Dikastrio (Cyprus)
EFTA = EFTA Court of Justice
Epit Antag = Epitropi Antagonismou (Greece)
EPO = European Patent Office
ES = Eidgenossisches Steuerrekurskommission (Switzerland)
ET = Employment Tribunal
Eur Comm HR = European Commission on Human Rights
Ex Chamber = Court of Exchequer Chamber
Ex Ct = Court of Exchequer
Ex Div = Extra Division
Fam Ct = Family Court
Fam Div = Family Division
Fed CA = Federal Court of Appeal
Fed Ct = Federal Court
Fed HC = Federal High Court
FG = Finanzgericht (Germany)
GC = Giudice Conciliatore (Italy)
HC = High Court
HCJ = High Court of Justiciary
HD = Hogsta Domstolen (Finland/Sweden)
HerrR = Herredsrett (Norway)
HFD = Hogsta forvaltningsdomstolen (Finland)
HL = House of Lords
HO = Hovioikeus/Hovratt (Finland)
Hof = Gerechtshof (Netherlands)
HR (DK) = Hojesteret (Denmark)
HR (N) = Hoyesterett (Norway)
HR (NL) = Hoge Raad (NL)
HR (Swe) = Hovratt (Sweden)
HR Ch = Human Rights Chamber for Bosnia and Herzegovina
HvB = Hof van Beroep (Belgium)
HvC = Hof van Cassatie (Belgium)

TABLE OF ABBREVIATIONS

IA Comm HR = Inter American Commission on Human Rights
IACHR = Inter American Court of Human Rights
IAT = Immigration Appeal Tribunal
ICC = International Chamber of Commerce, Arbitration Tribunal
ICJ = International Court of Justice
ICTA Tr = Tribunal constituted under the Income and Corporation Taxes Act 1988 s.706
IH = Inner House
IT = Industrial Tribunal
It Cass = Corte di Cassazione (Italy)
JP = Juge de Paix (Belgium)
JPI = Juzgado de Primera Instancia (Spain)
KBD = Kings Bench Division
KG (Ger) = Kammergericht (Germany)
KG (Swi) = Kassationsgericht (Switzerland)
KHO = Korkein Hallinto-Oikeus (Finland)
KKO = Korkein Oikeus (Finland)
KO = Kihlakunnanoikeus/Haradsratt (Finland)
Ktg = Kantongerecht (Netherlands)
Lab Ct = Labour Court (Ireland)
LArbG = Landesarbeitsgericht (Germany)
LCD = Lord Chancellors Department
Legf Bir = Legfelsobb Birosag (Hungary)
LG (A) = Landesgericht (Austria)
LG (Ger) = Landgericht (Germany)
LJ in Lunacy = Lords Justices sitting in Lunacy
LR = Lagmannsrett (Norway)
LSozG = Landessozialgericht (Germany)
LVAC = Lands Valuation Appeal Court
LVT = Leasehold Valuation Tribunal
MC = Magistrates Court
MCLC = Mayor's and City of London Court
MD = Marknadsdomstolen (Sweden)
Merc Ct = Mercantile Court
MMC = Monopolies and Mergers Commission
MR = Markedsradet (Norway)
Nat Ct = National Court
NI Comm = National Insurance Commissioner
NIRC = National Industrial Relations Court
NO = Naringsfrihetotombudsman (Swe)
NS CR = Nejvyssi soud Ceske republiky (Czech Republic)
ObG = Obergericht (Switzerland)
ODEI = Office of the Director of Equality Investigations (Ireland)
OGH = Oberster Gerichtshof (Austria)
OH = Outer House
OHIM = Office for Harmonization in the Internal Market
Okr Sod = Okrozno Sodisce (Slovenia)
OL = Ostre Landsret (Denmark)
OLG = Oberlandesgericht (Austria/Germany)
OPM = Oberster Patent- und Markensenat (Austria)
OR = Official Referee
OVG = Oberverwaltungsgericht (Germany)
Pat App Tr = Patents Appeal Tribunal
Pat Ct = Patents Court
Pat Val Apel Pad = Patentu Valdes Apelacijas Padome (Latvia)
PC = Privy Council
PCA = Parliamentary Commissioner for Administration
PCC = Patents County Court
PDAD = Probate, Divorce & Admiralty Division
PO = Patent Office
Prer Ct = Prerogative Court
Pret = Pretura (Italy)
PVO = Plant Variety Office
PVST = Plant Varieties & Seeds Tribunal

QB = Court of Queens Bench
QBD = Queens Bench Division
RB (B) = Tribunal de Premiere Instance (Belgium)
RB (NL) = Arrondissementsrechtbank (Netherlands)
RDAT = Registered Designs Appeal Tribunal
Refugees Status Apps = Refugees Status Appeals Authority (New Zealand)
Rel = Tribunal de Relacao (Portugal)
RP Comm = Restrictive Practices Commission (Ireland)
RPC = Restrictive Practices Court
RR = Regeringsratten (Sweden)
RvK = Rechtbank van Koophandel (Belgium)
Ry & Canal Comm = Railway and Canal Commision
Ry Rates Tr = Railway Rates Tribunal
SENT = Special Educational Needs Tribunal
SH = So- og Handelsret (Denmark)
Sh Ct = Sheriff Court
Sh Pr = Sheriff Principal
Solicitors Disc Ctte (SC) = Solicitors Discipline (Scotland) Committee
SozG = Sozialgericht (Germany)
Sp Comm = Special Commissioners
Sp Imm App Comm = Special Immigration Appeals Commission
Spec Crim Ct = Special Criminal Court (Ireland)
SS Comm = Social Security Commissioner
Sup Ct = Supreme Court
Sup Trib = Supremo Tribunal de Justica (Portugal)
Sup Trib Admin = Supremo Tribunal Administrativo (Portugal)
Sym Ep = Symvoulio tis Epikrateias (Greece)
T&CC = Technology & Construction Court
TAR = Tribunale Amministrativo (Italy)
TMR = Trade Marks Registry
Tr = Tribunal
TR = Tingsratt (Sweden)
Transport Arb Tr = Transport Arbitration Tribunal
Trib = Tribunale (Italy)
Trib Ad = Tribunal Administratif (France)
Trib Civil = Tribunal Civil (Belgium)
Trib Comm = Tribunal de Commerce (Belgium/France)
Trib Comp = Tribunal de Defensa de la Competencia (Spain)
Trib Const = Tribunal Constitucional (Spain)
Trib Corr = Tribunal Correctionnel (France)
Trib Correct = Tribunal Correctionnel (Belgium)
Trib d'Arr = Tribunal d'Arrondissement (Luxembourg)
Trib Fed = Tribunal Federal (Switzerland)
Trib Gde Inst = Tribunal de Grande Instance (Belgium/France)
Trib Police = Tribunal de Police (France)
Trib Prem Inst = Tribunal de Premiere Instance (Monaco)
Trib Sup = Tribunal Supremo (Spain)
Trib Travail = Tribunal du Travail (Belgium)
UN CAT = UN Committee Against Torture
UN CERD = UN Committee on the Elimination of Racial Discrimination
UN HRC = UN Human Rights Committee
V&D Tr = VAT and Duties Tribunal
VAC = Valuation Appeal Court
VfGH = Verfassungsgerichtshof (Austria)
VGH = Verwaltungsgericht (Germany/Switzerland)
Visje Sod = Visje Sodisce (Slovenia)
VL = Vestre Landsret (Denmark)
VrS = Vrchni soud (Prague)
VT = Valuation Tribunal
VwGH = Verwaltungsgerichtshof (Austria)
Yrg = Yargitay (Turkey)

TABLE OF ABBREVIATIONS

Jurisdiction Abbreviations

A = Austria
Abu = Abu Dhabi (United Arab Emirates)
ACT = Australian Capital Territory
Afg = Afghanistan
AI = Ascension Island (St Helena)
AL = Albania
Ald = Alderney
Alg = Algeria
Alta = Alberta
And = Andorra
Ang = Anguilla
Ango = Angola
Ant = Antigua and Barbuda
Arg = Argentina
Arm = Armenia (CIS)
Aus = Australia
Aze = Azerbaijan (CIS)
B = Belgium
Bah = Bahamas
Bahr = Bahrain
Bang = Bangladesh
Bar = Barbados
BC = British Columbia
BEL = Belarus (CIS)
Ben = Benin
Ber = Bermuda
BF = Burkina Faso
BG = British Guiana
BH = British Honduras
Bhu = Bhutan
BIH = Bosnia Herzegovina
Bol = Bolivia
Bots = Botswana
Bru = Brunei
Bul = Bulgaria
Bur = Burundi
BVI = British Virgin Islands
Bze = Belize
Bzl = Brazil
Camb = Cambodia
Camn = Cameroon
Can = Canada
Canary I = Canary Islands (Spain)
Cape = Cape of Good Hope
CAR = Central African Republic
Cey = Ceylon
CI = Cayman Islands
CIS = Commonwealth of Independent States
Com = Comoros
Con = Congo
Cook I = Cook Islands
CR = Costa Rica
CV = Cape Verde
Cy = Cyprus
CZ = Czech Republic
Dji = Djibouti
DK = Denmark
Dom = Dominica
DomR = Dominican Republic
Dub = Dubai
EA = Eastern Africa
EC = European Communities
Ecu = Ecuador
Egy = Egypt
EIS = El Salvador
EqG = Equatorial Guinea
Eri = Eritrea

Eth = Ethiopia
EU = European Union
EW = Estonia
F = France
FI = Falkland Islands
Fin = Finland
FL = Lichtenstein/Liechtenstein
FMS = Federated Malay States
FRY = Yugoslavia
Gab = Gabon
Gam = Gambia, The
GBi = Guinea Bissau
Geo = Georgia (CIS)
Ger = Germany
Gha = Ghana
Gib = Gibraltar
Gld = Greenland (Denmark)
GR = Greece
Gren = Grenada
Gua = Guatemala
Gue = Guernsey
Gui = Guinea
Guy = Guyana
H = Hungary
HK = Hong Kong
Hon = Honduras
HR = Croatia
I = Italy
Ind = India
Indo = Indonesia
IoM = Isle of Man
Irl = Ireland
IS = Iceland
Isr = Israel
Ivo = Ivory Coast
Jam = Jamaica
Jer = Jersey
Jor = Jordan
Jpn = Japan
Kaz = Kazakhstan (CIS)
Ken = Kenya
Kir = Kiribati
Kuw = Kuwait
Kyr = Kyrgyzstan (CIS)
LA = Latvia
Leb = Lebanon
Les = Lesotho
Libe = Liberia
LT = Lithuania
Lux = Luxembourg
M = Malta
Mace = Macedonia
Mad = Madagascar
Made = Madeira (Portugal)
Mal = Malaysia
Man = Manitoba
Mar = Martinique
Marshall I = Marshall Islands (Micronesia)
Mau = Mauritius
MC = Monaco
Mex = Mexico
Mic = Micronesia
Mnegro = Montenegro (Yugoslavia)
Mnia = Mauritania
Mol = Moldova (CIS)
Mong = Mongolia
Mor = Morocco

Moz = Mozambique
Mrat = Montserrat
Mves = Maldives
Mwi = Malawi
Mya = Myanmar
N = Norway
Nam = Namibia
NAnt = Netherlands Antilles
Nau = Nauru
NB = New Brunswick
Nfld = Newfoundland
NI = Northern Ireland
Nic = Nicaragua
Nig = Nigeria
NK = North Korea
NL = Netherlands
NS = Nova Scotia
NSW = New South Wales
NT = Northern Territory
NWT = North West Territories
NZ = New Zealand
Oman = Oman
Ont = Ontario
P = Portugal
Pak = Pakistan
Pal = Palestine
Pan = Panama
Par = Paraguay
PEI = Prince Edward Island
Phl = Philippines
Pl = Pitcairn Islands (New Zealand)
PL = Poland
PNG = Papua New Guinea
Poly = Polynesia
PR = Puerto Rico
PRC = China
Qat = Qatar
Qld = Queensland
Que = Quebec
RF = Russian Federation
Rho = Rhodesia
RI = Rhode Island
RO = Romania
Rwa = Rwanda
SA = South Africa
Sask = Saskatchewan
Saudi = Saudi Arabia
SAus = South Australia
SC = Scotland
Sen = Senegal
Serb = Serbia (Yugoslavia)
Sey = Seychelles
Sing = Singapore
SK = South Korea
SL = Sierra Leone

Slo = Slovakia
Slove = Slovenia
Smld = Somaliland
Sol = Solomon Islands
Som = Somalia
Sp = Spain
SrL = Sri Lanka
StC = Saint Christopher and Nevis
StH = St Helena
StL = Saint Lucia
StV = Saint Vincent and the Grenadines
Sud = Sudan
Sur = Surinam
Swa = Swaziland
Swe = Sweden
Swi = Switzerland
Tai = Taiwan
Taj = Tajikistan (CIS)
Tan = Tanzania
Tas = Tasmania
TCI = Turks and Caicos Islands
TDC = Tristan Da Cunha (St Helena)
Thai = Thailand
Tka = Tanganyika
Ton = Tonga
TR = Turkey
Trin = Trinidad and Tobago
Tun = Tunisia
Turkn = Turkmenistan (CIS)
Tuv = Tuvalu
UAE = United Arab Emirates
Ug = Uganda
UK = United Kingdom
UK-Irl = UK - Ireland (pre 1922)
UKEW = England and Wales
UKR = Ukraine (CIS)
UN = United Nations
Uru = Uruguay
US = United States
Uzb = Uzbekistan (CIS)
Van = Vanuatu
Ven = Venezuela
VI = Virgin Islands
Vic = Victoria
Viet = Vietnam
WA = Western Australia
WI = West Indies
Wind = Windward Islands
WS = Western Samoa
WSah = Western Sahara
YT = Yukon Territory
Zai = Zaire
Zam = Zambia
Zim = Zimbabwe

Law Report/Journal Abbreviations

A.2d = Atlantic Reporter 2nd
A.B.C. = Australian Bankruptcy Cases
A.C. = Appeal Cases
A.C.D. = Administrative Court Digest
A.C.L.C. = Australian Company Law Cases
A.C.L.R. = Australian Company Law Reports
A.C.S.R. = Australian Companies and Securities Reports
A.C.T.R. = Australian Capital Territory Reports
A.D. = Appellate Division Reports (NY)
A.D.2d = Appellate Division Reports 2nd (NY)

A.F.T.R. = American Federal Tax Reports
A.I.R. All. = All India Reporter, Allahabad Series
A.I.R. Bom. = All India Reporter, Bombay Series
A.I.R. Delhi = All India Reporter, Delhi Series
A.I.R. Mad. = All India Reporter, Madras Series
A.I.R. P.C. = All India Reporter, Privy Council Series
A.I.R. S.C. = All India Reporter, Supreme Court Series
A.L.J. = Australian Law Journal
A.L.J.R. = Australian Law Journal Reports
A.L.M.D. = Australian Legal Monthly Digest
A.L.R. = Australian Law Reports

TABLE OF ABBREVIATIONS

A.L.R. = American Law Reports

A.L.R. (C.N.) = Argus Law Reports, Current Notes (Australia)

A.L.R. Fed. = American Law Reports Federal

A.L.R.2d = American Law Reports 2nd

A.L.R.3d = American Law Reports 3rd

A.M.C. = American Maritime Cases

A.R. = Alberta Reports

A.T.C. = Annotated Tax Cases

Ad. & El. = Adolphus & Ellis' Reports

Adam = Adam's Justiciary Reports (Scotland)

Add. = Addams' Ecclesiastical Reports

Admin. L.R. = Administrative Law Reports

All E.R. = All England Law Reports

All E.R. (Comm) = All England Law Reports (Commercial Cases)

All E.R. (EC) = All England Law Reports (European Cases)

All E.R. Rep. = All England Law Reports Reprints

All N.L.R. = All Nigeria Law Reports

Am.Dec. = American Decisions

Am.Rep. = American Reports

Am.St.Rep. = American State Reports

Amb. = Ambler's Chancery Reports

And. = Anderson's Common Pleas Reports

Ark. = Arkley's Justiciary Reports (Scotland)

Asp. = Aspinall's Maritime Cases (1870-1940)

Atk. = Atkyn's Chancery Reports

B. & Ad. = Barnewall and Adolphus King's Bench Reports

B. & Ald. = Barnewall and Alderson King's Bench Reports

B. & C. = Barnewall and Cresswell King's Bench Reports

B. & C.R. = Reports of Bankruptcy and Companies (Winding up) Cases (1918-41)

B. & S. = Best and Smith's Queen's Bench Reports

B.C.C. = British Company Law Cases

B.C.L.C. = Butterworths Company Law Cases

B.C.L.R. = British Columbia Law Reports

B.H.R.C. = Butterworths Human Rights Cases

B.L.G.R. = Butterworths Local Government Reports

B.L.R. = Building Law Reports

B.M.L.R. = Butterworths Medico Legal Reports

B.P.I.R. = Bankruptcy and Personal Insolvency Reports

B.R. = Bankruptcy Reporter

B.T.C. = British Tax Cases

B.V.C. = British VAT Cases

B.W.C.C. = Butterworths Workmen's Compensation Cases

Bank. L.R. = Banking Law Reports

Bankr.Ct.Dec. = Bankruptcy Court Decisions (CRR)

Barnes = Barnes' Notes of Cases in Common Pleas

Beat. = Beatty's Irish Chancery Reports

Beav. = Beavan's Rolls Court Reports

Bell C.C. = Bell's Crown Cases Reserved

Bing. = Bingham's Common Pleas Reports

Bing. N.C. = Bingham, New Cases, English Common Pleas

Binn. = Binney's Reports (U.S.A.)

Bli. = Bligh's House of Lords Reports

Bli. N.S. = Bligh's House of Lords Reports, New Series

Bos. & P. = Bosanquet and Puller's Common Pleas Reports

Bos. & P.N.R. = Bosanquet and Puller's New Reports, Common Pleas

Bott P.L. = Bott's Poor Law Cases

Br. & Col. Pri. Cas. = British and Colonial Prize Cases

Bro. C.C. = W. Brown's Chancery Reports

Bro. P.C. = J. Brown's Parliamentary Cases

Brod. & Bing. = Broderip and Bingham's Common Pleas Reports

Broun = Broun's Justiciary Reports (Scotland)

Brown. & Lush. = Browning and Lushington's Admiralty Reports

Brownl. = Brownlow and Goldesborough's Common Pleas Reports

Bulst. = Bulstrode's King's Bench Reports

Bunb. = Bunbury's Exchequer Reports

Burr. = Burrow's King's Bench Reports, tempore Mansfield

C. Rob. = Christopher Robinson's Admiralty Reports

C.B. = Common Bench Reports (Manning)

C.B. N.S. = Common Bench Reports (Manning), New Series

C.C.C. = Canadian Criminal Cases

C.C.C. (2d) = Canadian Criminal Cases, 2nd Series

C.C.C. (3d) = Canadian Criminal Cases, 3rd Series

C.C.L. = Canadian Current Law

C.C.L. Rep. = Community Care Law Reports

C.C.L.R. = Consumer Credit Law Reports

C.C.L.T. = Canadian Cases on the Law of Torts

C.C.P.A. = Court of Customs & Patent Appeals Reports

C.E.C. = European Community Cases

C.I.L.L. = Construction Industry Law Letter

C.I.L.R. = Cayman Islands Law Reports

C.L.C. = Commercial Law Cases

C.L.R. = Commonwealth Law Reports

C.M.L. Rev. = Common Market Law Review

C.M.L.R. = Common Market Law Reports

C.M.L.R. D = Common Market Law Reports Restrictive Practices Supplement

C.M.L.R. M = Common Market Law Reports Merger Decisions

C.O.D. = Crown Office Digest

C.P. Rep. = Civil Procedure Reports

C.P.C. (2d) = Carswell's Practice Cases, Second Series

C.P.C. (3d) = Carswell's Practice Cases, Third Series

C.P.L. = Current Property Law (1952-53)

C.P.L.R. = Civil Practice Law Reports

C.P.R. = Canadian Patent Reporter

C.P.R. (2d) = Canadian Patent Reporter, 2nd Series

C.P.R. (3d) = Canadian Patent Reporter, 3rd Series

C.P.R. (4th) = Canadian Patent Reporter, 4th Series

C.R. = Criminal Reports (Canada)

C.R. N.S. = Criminal Reports (New Series) (Canada)

C.S. = Rapports Judiciaires de Quebec, Cour Superieure

CJ C.A.R. = Colorado Appellate Report

Cab. & Ell. = Cababe and Ellis' Queen's Bench Reports

Cal. = California Reports

Cal. Daily Op. Serv. = California Daily Opinion Service

Cal.3d = California Reports 3rd

Cal.4th = California Reports, 4th Series

Cal.Rptr.2d = California Reporter 2d (West's)

Camp. = Campbell's Nisi Prius Reports

Can. B.R. = Canadian Bar Review

Car. & K. = Carrington and Kirwan's Nisi Prius Reports

Car. & M. = Carrington and Marshman's Nisi Prius Reports

Car. & P. = Carrington and Payne's Nisi Prius Reports

Cart. = Carter's Common Pleas Reports

Ch. = Chancery Division

Ch. Cas. = Cases in Chancery

Chit. = Chitty's King's Bench Practice Reports

Civ. = New York District Court transcript

TABLE OF ABBREVIATIONS

Cl. & F. = Clark and Finnelly's House of Lords Reports

Clark's Rep. = Clark's Reports (Jamaica)

Clay. = Clayton's Reports and Pleas of Assises at Yorke

Clunet = Journal du Droit International (France)

Co. Rep. = Coke's King's Bench Reports

Coll. = Collyer's Chancery Cases, tempore Bruce

Com. = Comyn's Reports, King's Bench

Com. Cas. = Commercial Cases

Com. L.R. = Commercial Law Reports

Comb. = Comberbach's King's Bench Reports

Comp. A.R. = Competition Appeal Reports

Con. L.R. = Construction Law Reports

Const. L.J. = Construction Law Journal

Coop. t. Cott. = Cooper's Chancery Reports, tempore Cottenham

Costs L.R. = Costs Law Reports

Costs L.R. (Core Vol.) = Costs Law Reports, Core Volume

Coup. = Couper's Justiciary Reports (Scotland)

Cowp. = Cowper's King's Bench Reports

Cox = Cox's Chancery Reports

Cox C.C. = Cox's Criminal Cases

Cox Eq. Cas. = Cox's Equity Cases

Cr. & J. = Crompton and Jervis' Exchequer Reports

Cr. & M. = Crompton and Meeson's Exchequer Reports

Cr. & Ph. = Craig and Phillip's Chancery Reports

Cr. App. R. = Criminal Appeal Reports

Cr. App. R. (S.) = Criminal Appeal Reports (Sentencing)

Cr. M & R. = Crompton, Meeson and Roscoe's Exchequer Reports

Cr. S. & P. = Craigie, Stewart and Paton's Scottish Appeal Cases

Cranch = Cranch's United States Supreme Court Reports

Crim. L.R. = Criminal Law Review

Cro. Eliz. = Croke's King's Bench Reports, tempore Elizabeth

Cro. Jac. = Croke's King's Bench Reports, tempore James

Curt. = Curteis' Ecclesiastical Reports

D. = Dunlop, Bell and Murray's Reports, Session Cases, 2nd series (Scotland)

D. & R. = Decisions and Reports of the European Commission of Human Rights

D. (H.L.) = Dunlop's Session Cases, 2nd Series (House of Lords cases, Scotland)

D.L.R. = Dominion Law Reports

D.L.R. (2d) = Dominion Law Reports (2d)

D.L.R. (3d) = Dominion Law Reports (3d)

D.L.R. (4th) = Dominion Law Reports (4th)

D.R.A. = De-rating Appeals

Daily Telegraph = Daily Telegraph

De G. = De Gex's Bankruptcy Reports

De G. & J. = De Gex and Jones' Chancery Reports

De G. & Sm. = De Gex and Smales Chancery Reports

De G.F. & J. = De Gex, Fisher and Jones' Chancery Reports

De G.J. & S. = De Gex, Jones and Smith's Chancery Reports

De G.M. & G. = De Gex, Macnaghten and Gordons' Chancery Reports

Dea. & Sw. = Deane and Swabey's Ecclesiastical Reports

Deac. & Ch. = Deacon and Chitty's Bankruptcy Reports

Dears. = Dearsley's Crown Cases Reserved

Dears. & B. = Dearsley and Bell's Crown Cases Reserved

Den. = Denison and Pearce's Crown Cases Reserved

Dick. = Dickens' Chancery Reports

Disc. L.R. = Discrimination Law Reports

Dods. = Dodson's Admiralty Reports

Doug. K.B. = Douglas' King's Bench Reports

Dow = Dow's House of Lords Cases

Dowl. & L. = Dowling and Lowndes' Bail Court Reports

Dowl. & Ry. K.B. = Dowling and Ryland's King's Bench Reports

Dowl. N.S. = Dowling's Bail Court Reports, New Series

Dowl. Pr. Cas. = Dowling's Bail Court Practice Cases

Dr. & War. = Drury and Warren's Irish Chancery Reports

Drew. = Drewry's Chancery Reports, tempore Kindersley

Drew. & Sm. = Drewry and Smales' Chancery Reports

Dyer = Dyer's King's Bench Reports

E.A. = East African Law Reports

E.A.C.A. = Law Reports of the Court of Appeals for Eastern Africa

E.A.T.C. = East African Tax Cases

E.B.L.R. = Electronic Business Law Reports

E.C.C. = European Commercial Cases

E.C.D.R. = European Copyright and Design Reports

E.C.D.R. CN = European Copyright and Design Reports Case Notes

E.C.R. = European Court Reports

E.C.R. IA = European Court Reports

E.G. = Estates Gazette

E.G.C.S. = Estates Gazette Case Summaries

E.G.D. = Estates Gazette Digest of Cases

E.G.L.R. = Estates Gazette Law Reports (Bound Volume)

E.H.L.R. = Environmental Health Law Reports

E.H.L.R. Dig. = Environmental Health Reports Digest Pages

E.H.R.R. = European Human Rights Reports

E.H.R.R. CD = European Human Rights Reports, Commission Decisions

E.L.R. = Education Law Reports

E.M.L.R. = Entertainment and Media Law Reports

E.N.P.R. = European National Patent Reports

E.P.O.R. = European Patent Office Reports

E.P.O.R. A = European Patent Office Reports

E.P.O.R. B = European Patent Office Reports

E.P.O.R. C = European Patent Office Reports

E.P.T. Leaflet = Excess Profits Tax Leaflet

E.R. = English Reports

E.T.M.R. = European Trade Mark Reports

E.T.M.R. CN = European Trade Mark Reports Case Notes

ERC = Environment Reporter Cases (BNA)

EWCA Civ = Court of Appeal (Civil)

EWCA Crim = Court of Appeal (Criminal)

EWHC = High Court

EWHC Admin = High Court (Administrative Court)

East = East's Term Reports, King's Bench

East P.C. = East's Pleas of the Crown

Ed. C.R. = Education Case Reports

Ed. Law Rep. = Education Law Reporter

Edw. = Edward's Admiralty Reports

El. & Bl. = Ellis and Blackburn's Queen's Bench Reports

El. & El. = Ellis and Ellis' Queen's Bench Reports

El. Bl. & El. = Ellis, Blackburn and Ellis' Queen's Bench Reports

Emp. L.R. = Employment Law Reports

TABLE OF ABBREVIATIONS

Employee Benefits Cas. = Employee Benefits Cases
Env. L.R. = Environmental Law Reports
Env. L.R. D = Environmental Law Reports Digest Pages
Envtl. L. Rep. = Environmental Law Reporter (ELR) (cases only)
Eq. Cas. Abr. = Abridgment of Cases in Equity
Esp. = Espinasse's Nisi Prius Reports
Eu. L.R. = European Law Reports
Ex. = Exchequer Reports (Welsby, Hurlstone and Gordon)
Ex. C.R. = Canada Law Reports, Exchequer Court

F. = Federal Reporter (U.S.A.)
F. & F. = Foster and Finlason's Nisi Prius Reports
F. (Ct. of Sess.) = Faculty Decisions, Court of Session (Scotland)
F. (H.L.) = Fraser's Session Cases, 5th Series (House of Lords, Scotland)
F. (J.) = Fraser's Session Cases, 5th Series (Justiciary cases, Scotland)
F.2d = Federal Reporter, 2nd Series (U.S.A.)
F.3d = Federal Reporter, 3rd Series (U.S.A.)
F.C. = Canada Law Reports, Federal Court
F.C.R. = Family Court Reporter
F.L.R. = Family Law Reports
F.R.D. = Federal Rules Decisions (U.S.A.)
F.S.R. = Fleet Street Reports
F.Supp. = Federal Supplement (U.S.A.)
F.Supp.2d = Federal Supplement, Second Series
F.T.L.R. = Financial Times Law Reports
Fam. = Family Division
Fam. L.R. = Family Law Reports (Scottish)
Fam. Law = Family Law
Fed. L.R. = Federal Law Reports (Australia)
Fed. R. Evid. Serv. = Federal Rules of Evidence Service (Callaghan's)
Fed. Sec. L. Rep. P = Federal Securities Law Reports (CCH)
Fed.R.Serv.2d = Federal Rules Service 2nd (Callaghan's)
Fed.R.Serv.3d = Federal Rules Service 3rd (Callaghan's)
Fed.Sent.R. = Federal Sentencing Reporter
Fin. L.R. = Financial Law Reports
Financial Times = Financial Times
Fla. L. Weekly Fed. S = Florida Law Weekly, United States Supreme Court
Fost. = Foster's Crown Cases
Freem. Ch. = Freeman's Chancery Reports

G.W.D. = Green's Weekly Digest (Scottish)
GRUR = Gewerblicher Rechtsschutz und Urheberrecht
Ga. = Georgia Reports
Giff. = Giffard's Chancery Reports
Gilb. K.B. = Gilbert's Cases in Law and Equity
Gl. & J. = Glyn and Jameson's Bankruptcy Reports
Gould. = Gouldsborough's King's Bench Reports
Guardian = Guardian

H. Bl. = H. Blackstone's Common Pleas Reports
H.B.R. = Hansell's Bankruptcy Reports (1915-17)
H.K. Cases = Hong Kong Cases
H.K.L.R. = Hong Kong Law Reports
H.K.L.R.D. = Hong Kong Law Reports and Digest
H.L. Cas. = Clark's House of Lords Cases
H.L.R. = Housing Law Reports
H.R.C.D. = Human Rights Case Digest
H.R.L.R. = Human Rights Law Reports - UK Cases
Hag. Adm. = Haggard's Admiralty Reports

Hag. Con. = Haggard's Consistorial Reports
Hag. Ecc. = Haggard's Ecclesiastical Reports
Hardres = Hardres' Exchequer Reports
Hare = Hare's Chancery Reports
Hem. & M. = Hemming and Miller's Chancery Reports
Het. = Hetley's Reports
Hob. = Hobart's Reports (Common Pleas and King's Bench)
Hodg. = Hodges' Common Pleas Reports
Holt K.B. = Holt's King's Bench Reports
Holt N.P. = F Holt's Nisi Prius Reports
Hous. L.R. = Housing Law Reports (Scottish)
How. = Howard's United States Supreme Court Reports
Hume = Hume's Session Cases (Scotland)
Hurl. & C. = Hurlstone and Coltman's Exchequer Reports
Hurl. & N. = Hurlstone and Norman's Exchequer Reports

I.C.L.R. = Irish Common Law Reports, Second Series (1850-66)
I.C.R. = Industrial Cases Reports
I.H.R.R. = International Human Rights Reports
I.L.Pr. = International Litigation Procedure
I.L.R. = International Law Reports
I.L.R.M. = Irish Law Reports Monthly
I.L.T. = Irish Law Times
I.L.T.R. = Irish Law Times Reports
I.N.L.R. = Immigration and Nationality Law Reports
I.P.D. = Intellectual Property Decisions
I.P.L.R. = Industrial Property Law Reports (India)
I.P.R. = Intellectual Property Reports (Australia)
I.R. = Irish Reports
I.R. C.L. = Irish Reports, Common Law
I.R.L.R. = Industrial Relations Law Reports
I.T.C. = Srinivasan's Reports of Income Tax Cases (India)
I.T.C.L.R. = IT & Communications Law Reports
I.T.E.L.R. = International Trust and Estate Law Report
I.T.L. Rep. = International Tax Law Reports
I.T.R. = Industrial Tribunal Reports
ITRD = International Trade Reporter Decisions (BNA)
Ill.2d = Illinois Reports, 2nd Series
Ill.Dec. = Illinois Decisions
Imm. A.R. = Immigration Appeal Reports
Ind. = Indiana Reports
Ind. Cas. = Indian Cases
Ind. L.R. = Indian Law Reports
Ind. L.R. All. = Indian Law Reports, Allahabad Series
Ind. L.R. Cal. = Indian Law Reports, Calcutta Series
Ind. L.R. Mad. = Indian Law Reports, Madras Series
Ind. L.R. Pat. = Indian Law Reports, Patna Series
Independent = Independent
Info. T.L.R. = Information Technology Law Reports
Ir. Ch. R. = Irish Chancery Reports (1850-66)
Ir. Eq. = Irish Reports, Equity (1866-77)
Ir. Eq. R. = Irish Equity Reports, First Series (1838-50)
Ir. Jur. Rep. = Irish Jurist Reports
Ir. L.J. = Irish Law Journal
Ir. L.R. = Irish Law Reports
Irvine = Irvine's High Court and Circuit Courts of Justiciary Reports (Scotland)

J. & Lat. = Jones and LaTouche's Irish Chancery Reports (1844-46)
J. Bridg. = Sir John Bridgman's Reports
J.C. = Justiciary Cases (Scotland)
J.J. = Jersey Judgments
J.L.R. = Jamaica Law Reports

xi

TABLE OF ABBREVIATIONS

J.P. = Justice of the Peace Reports

J.P. Rep. = Local Government Review Reports

J.P.I. Law = Journal of Personal Injury Law

J.P.I.L. = Journal of Personal Injury Litigation

J.P.L. = Journal of Planning & Environment Law

J.P.N. = Justice of the Peace Notes of Cases

Jac. & W. = Jacob and Walker's Chancery Reports

Jebb. & Sym. = Jebb and Syme's Queen's Bench Reports (Ireland, 1838-41)

Jer. L.R. = Jersey Law Reports

John. = Johnson's Chancery Reports

John. & H. = Johnson and Hemmings Chancery Reports

Jones = Sir Thomas Jones' King's Bench Reports

Jur. = Jurist

Jur. N.S. = Jurist, New Series

K.B. = Kings Bench

K.I.R. = Knight's Industrial Law Reports

Kay & J. = Kay and Johnson's Vice Chancellors Reports

Keen = Keen's Rolls Court Reports

Kn. = Knapp's Privy Council Appeal Cases

Ky. = Kentucky Reports

L. & T.R. = Landlord and Tenant Reports

L.D.B. = Legal Decisions Affecting Bankers

L.Ed. = Lawyers' Edition, United States Supreme Court Reporter

L.Ed.2d = Lawyers' Edition 2nd Series, United States Supreme Court Reporter

L.G. Rev. = Local Government Review

L.G.L.R. = Local Government Law Reports

L.G.R. = Local Government Reports

L.G.R.A. = Local Government Reports of Australia

L.J. = Law Journal (Newspaper)

L.J. Bcy. = Law Journal Reports, Bankruptcy (1832-80)

L.J. C.P. = Law Journal Reports, Common Pleas (1831-75)

L.J. Ch. = Law Journal Reports, Chancery (1831-1946)

L.J. Ex. = Law Journal Reports, Exchequer (1831-75)

L.J. K.B. = Law Journal Reports, King's Bench (1831-1946)

L.J. M.C. = Law Journal Reports, Magistrates Cases (1831-96)

L.J. N.C. = Law Journal, Notes of Cases

L.J. N.C.C.R. = Law Journal, County Court Reports (1934-47)

L.J. N.S. = Law Journal Reports, New Series (1832-1946)

L.J. O.S. = Law Journal Reports, Old Series (1822-31)

L.J. P. = Law Journal Reports, Probate, Divorce and Admiralty (1875-1946)

L.J. P. & M. = Law Journal Reports, Probate, Divorce and Matrimonial (1858-59, 1866-75)

L.J. P.C. = Law Journal Reports, Privy Council (1831-1946)

L.J. P.M. & A. = Law Journal Reports, Probate, Matrimonial and Admiralty (1860-65)

L.J. Q.B. = Law Journal Reports, Queen's Bench (1831-1946)

L.J.R. = Law Journal Reports (1947-49)

L.M.C.L.Q. = Lloyd's Maritime and Commercial Law Quarterly

L.R. A. & E. = Admiralty and Ecclesiastical Cases (1865-75)

L.R. App. Cas. = Appeal Cases (1875-90)

L.R. C.C.R. = Crown Cases Reserved

L.R. C.P. = Common Pleas (1865-75)

L.R. C.P.D. = Common Pleas Division (1875-80)

L.R. Ch. App. = Chancery Appeals (1865-75)

L.R. Ch. D. = Chancery Division (1875-90)

L.R. Eq. = Equity Cases

L.R. Ex. = Exchequer (1865-75)

L.R. Ex. D. = Exchequer Division (1875-80)

L.R. H.L. = English and Irish Appeals (1866-75)

L.R. Ind. App. = Indian Appeals

L.R. Ir. = Ireland

L.R. P. & D. = Probate and Divorce (1865-75)

L.R. P.C. = Privy Council

L.R. P.D. = Probate Division (1875-90)

L.R. Q.B. = Queen's Bench (1865-75)

L.R. Q.B.D. = Queen's Bench Division (1875-90)

L.R. R.P. = Restrictive Practices (1958-72)

L.R. Sc. = Scotch and Divorce Appeals

L.R.B. = Law Reports of the Bahamas

L.R.C. = Law Reports of the Commonwealth

L.R.C. (Const) = Law Reports of the Commonwealth (Constitutional & Administrative Reports)

L.R.L.R. = Lloyd's Reinsurance Law Reports

L.R.R.M. (BNA) = Labor Relations Reference Manual (BNA)

L.S.G. = Law Society Gazette

L.T. = Law Times (1859-1965)

L.T. O.S. = Law Times (Old Series) (1843-59)

L.T.R. = Law Times Reports (1859-1947)

Lab.Cas. P = Labor Cases (CCH)

Lat. = Latch's King's Bench Reports

Ld. Raym. = Lord Raymond's King's Bench Reports

Le. & Ca. = Leigh and Cave's Crown Cases Reserved

Leach = Leach's Cases in Crown Law

Lee = Lee's Ecclesiastical Reports

Lee temp Hard. = Lee's King's Bench Cases tempore Hardwicke

Leo. = Leonard's Reports

Lev. = Levinz's King's Bench and Common Pleas Reports

Lewin = Lewin's Crown Cases Reserved

Ll. L. Pr. Cas. = Lloyd's List Prize Cases (1914-24)

Ll. L. Pr. Cas. (N.S.) = Lloyd's List Prize Cases, Second Series (1939-53)

Ll. L. Rep. = Lloyd's List Law Reports (1919-50)

Lloyd's List = Lloyd's List

Lloyd's Rep. = Lloyd's Law Reports (1951-)

Lloyd's Rep. Bank. = Lloyd's Law Reports Banking

Lloyd's Rep. I.R. = Lloyd's Law Reports, Insurance & Reinsurance

Lloyd's Rep. Med. = Lloyd's Law Reports Medical

Lloyd's Rep. P.N. = Lloyd's Law Reports Professional Negligence

Lofft = Lofft's King's Bench Reports

Lush. = Lushington's Admiralty Reports

Lutw. = Lutwyche's Entries and Reports, Common Pleas

M. = Macpherson's Session Cases, 3rd Series (Scotland)

M. & S. = Maule and Selwyn's King's Bench Reports

M. & W. = Meeson and Welsby's Exchequer Reports

M. (H.L.) = Macpherson's Session Cases, 3rd Series (House of Lords cases, Scotland)

M.C.C. = MacGillivray's Copyright Cases

M.L.J. = Malaysian Law Journal

M.P.L.R. = Municipal and Planning Law Reports (Canada)

M.P.R. = Maritime Provinces Reports (Canada)

M.R. = Mauritius Reports

TABLE OF ABBREVIATIONS

Mac. & G. = Macnaghten and Gordon's Chancery Reports
Macq. = Macqueen's Scottish Appeal Cases
Madd. = Maddock's Chancery Reports
Man. & G. = Manning and Granger's Common Pleas Reports
Man. Law = Managerial Law
Mans. = Manson's Bankruptcy and Companies Winding up Cases (1894-1913)
Manx L.R. = Manx Law Reports
Masons C.L.R. = Masons Computer Law Reports
Masons C.L.R. Rep. = Masons Computer Law Reports Reprints (Case Digests, 1994-97)
Mass. = Massachusetts Reports
Med. L.R. = Medical Law Reports
Media L. Rep. = Media Law Reporter (BNA)
Mer. = Merivale's Chancery Reports
Misc. = New York Miscellaneous Reports
Misc.2d = Miscellaneous Reports, 2nd Series (New York)
Mod. = Modern Reports
Mol. = Molloy's Chancery Reports (Ireland, 1927-31)
Mont. D. & De G. = Montagu, Deacon and De Gex Bankruptcy Reports
Moo. K.B. = Moore's King's Bench Reports
Moo. P.C. = Moore's Privy Council Cases
Moo. P.C. N.S. = Moore's Privy Council Cases, New Series
Mood. & R. = Moody and Robinson's Nisi Prius Reports
Mood. C.C. = Moody's Crown Cases Reserved
Mor. Dic. = Morison's Dictionary of Decisions (Scotland)
Morr. = Morrell's Bankruptcy Reports
Mos. = Moseley's Chancery Reports
My. & C. = Mylne and Craig's Chancery Reports
My. & K. = Mylne and Keen's Chancery Reports

N.B. Eq. = New Brunswick Equity Reports
N.B.R. = National Bankruptcy Register Reports
N.B.R. 2d = New Brunswick Reports, 2nd Series
N.C. = Notes of Cases, Ecclesiastical and Maritime (ed. Thornton)
N.E. = North Eastern Reporter (U.S.A.)
N.E.2d = North Eastern Reporter 2nd
N.H. = New Hampshire Reports
N.I. = Northern Ireland Law Reports
N.I.J.B. = Northern Ireland Judgment Bulletin
N.I.L.Q. = Northern Ireland Legal Quarterly
N.J. = New Jersey Reports
N.L.J. = New Law Journal
N.L.J. Rep. = New Law Journal Reports
N.L.R. = New Law Reports (Sri Lanka)
N.P.C. = New Property Cases
N.R. = National Reporter (Canada)
N.S.R. 2d = Nova Scotia Reports, 2nd Series
N.S.W.L.R. = New South Wales Law Reports
N.S.W.R. = New South Wales Reports (1960-70)
N.W. = North Western Reporter (U.S.A.)
N.W.2d = North Western Reporter, 2nd Series (U.S.A.)
N.Y. = New York Reports
N.Y.2d = New York Reports, 2nd Series
N.Y.S. = New York Supplement Reporter
N.Y.S.2d = New York Supplement Reporter, 2nd Series
N.Z.L.R. = New Zealand Law Reports
NDLR P = National Disability Law Reporter
Nev. & M.K.B. = Neville and Manning's King's Bench Reports
New Rep. = New Reports

Nfld. & P.E.I.R. = Newfoundland and Prince Edward Island Reports

O'M. & H. = O'Malley and Hardcastle's Election Cases (1869-1929)
O.F.L.R. = Offshore Financial Law Reports
O.J. E.P.O. = Official Journal of the European Patent Office
O.L.R. = Ontario Law Reports (1901-30)
O.P.L.R. = Occupational Pensions Law Reports
O.R. = Ontario Reports (1882-1900, 1931-)
O.R. (2d) = Ontario Reports, 2nd Series
O.R. (3d) = Ontario Reports, 3rd Series
Owen = Owen's King's Bench and Common Pleas Reports

P. = Pacific Reporter (U.S.A.)
P. = Probate
P. & C.R. = Property, Planning and Compensation Reports
P. & C.R. D = Property and Compensation Reports Digest Pages
P.Wms. = Peere Williams Chancery Reports
P.2d = Pacific Reporter, 2nd Series (U.S.A.)
P.A.D. = Planning Appeal Decisions
P.C.C. = Palmer's Company Cases
P.I.Q.R. P = Personal Injury and Quantum Reports
P.I.Q.R. Q = Personal Injury and Quantum Reports
P.L.C.R. = Planning Law Case Reports
P.L.R. = Planning Law Reports
P.N.G.L.R. = Papua New Guinea Law Reports
P.N.L.R. = Professional Negligence and Liability Reports
P.T. Leaflet = Profits Tax Leaflet
Pal. L.R. = Palestine Law Reports
Park on Ins. = Park on Insurance, 8th ed.
Pat. = Paton's Scottish Appeals, House of Lords
Peake = Peake's Nisi Prius Reports
Peake Add. Cas. = Peake's Additional Cases
Pens. App. R. = Pensions Appeal Reports
Pens. L.R. = Pensions Law Reports
Perry & K. = Perry and Knapp's Election Cases
Ph. = Phillip's Chancery Reports
Phil. Ecc. = Phillimore's Ecclesiastical Reports
Plow. = Plowden's Commentaries
Pop. = Sir John Popham's Reports
Prec. Ch. = Precedents in Chancery
Price = Price's Exchequer Reports

Q.B. = Queens Bench
Q.J.P. = Queensland Justice of the Peace Reports
Q.L.J. = Queensland Law Journal Reports (1897-1901)
Q.R. = Quantum Reports (Kemp & Kemp)
Q.S.R. = Queensland State Reports (1902-57)
Q.W.N. = Queensland Law Reporter and Weekly Notes (1908-72)
Qd. R. = Queensland State Reports (1958-)

R. = Retties Session Cases, 4th Series (Scotland)
R. & I.T. = Rating and Income Tax Reports
R. (H.L.) = Retties Session Cases, 4th Series (House of Lords cases, Scotland)
R. (J.) = Retties Session Cases, 4th Series (Justiciary cases, Scotland)
R.A. = Rating Appeals
R.C.N. = Rating Case Notes
R.F.L. = Reports of Family Law (Canada)
R.I.C.S. = Royal Institution of Chartered Surveyors, Scottish Lands Valuation Appeal Reports

TABLE OF ABBREVIATIONS

R.J.Q. B.R. = Rapports Judiciares de Quebec, Cour du Banc du Roi (1875-91)

R.L.R. = Road Law Reports

R.P.C. = Reports of Patent Cases

R.P.R. = Real Property Reports (Canada)

R.R.C. = Ryde's Rating Cases

R.T.R. = Road Traffic Reports

R.V.R. = Rating and Valuation Reporter

RICO Bus.Disp.Guide = RICO Business Disputes Guide (CCH)

Ram. = Ramanathan's Reports, Sri Lanka

Re. L.R. = Reinsurance Law Reports

Recueil = Recueil de la Jurisprudence de la Cour (ECJ)

Rep. L.R. = Reparation Law Reports (Scottish)

Rep. L.R. (Quantum) = Reparation Law Reports, Quantum Cases (Scottish)

Rob. = Robinson's Scottish Appeal Cases, House of Lords

Rob. Ecc. = Robertson's Ecclesiastical Reports

Roll. Abr. = Rolle's Abridgment des Plusieurs Cases

Russ. = Russell's Chancery Reports

Russ. & M. = Russell and Mylne's Chancery Reports

Russ. & Ry. = Russell and Ryan's Crown Cases Reserved

Russ. Cr. = Russell on Crime

Ry. & M. = Ryan and Moody's Nisi Prius Reports

S. = Shaw's Session Cases, 1st Series (Scotland)

S.A. = South African Law Reports

S.A. (A.D.) = South African Law Reports (Appellate Division)

S.A. (T.P.D.) = South African Law Reports (Transvaal Provincial Division)

S.A.C.R. = South African Criminal Law Reports

S.A.L.J. = South African Law Journal

S.A.S.R. = South Australian State Reports

S.C. = Session Cases (Scotland)

S.C. (H.L.) = Session Cases (House of Lords cases, Scotland)

S.C. (J.) = Session Cases (Justiciary 1907-16, Scotland)

S.C. (P.C.) = Session Cases (Privy Council Cases, Scotland)

S.C. (S.A.) = Supreme Court Reports (South Africa)

S.C.C.R. = Scottish Criminal Case Reports

S.C.C.R. (Supp.) = Scottish Criminal Case Reports Supplement

S.C.L.R. = Scottish Civil Law Reports

S.C.R. = Canada Law Reports, Supreme Court

S.Ct. = Supreme Court Reporter

S.E. = South Eastern Reporter (U.S.A.)

S.E.2d = South Eastern Reporter, 2nd Series (U.S.A.)

S.J. = Solicitors Journal (Old)

S.J.L.B. = Solicitors Journal Law Brief

S.L.C.R. = Scottish Land Court Reports

S.L.C.R. App. = Scottish Land Court Reports (Appendix)

S.L.L.P. = Scottish Licensing Law and Practice

S.L.R. = Scottish Law Reporter (1865-1924)

S.L.T. = Scots Law Times

S.L.T. (Land Ct) = Scots Law Times (Land Court Reports)

S.L.T. (Land Ct.) = Scots Law Times (Land Ct)

S.L.T. (Lands Tr) = Scots Law Times (Lands Tribunal Reports)

S.L.T. (Lands Tr.) = Scots Law Times (Lands Tr)

S.L.T. (Lyon Ct) = Scots Law Times (Lyon Court Reports)

S.L.T. (Lyon Ct.) = Scots Law Times (Lyon Ct)

S.L.T. (Notes) = Scots Law Times (Notes)

S.L.T. (P.L.) = Scots Law Times (Poor Law Reports)

S.L.T. (Sh Ct) = Scots Law Times (Sheriff Court Reports)

S.L.T. (Sh Ct.) = Scots Law Times (Sheriff Court)

S.L.T. (Sh. Ct.) = Scots Law Times (Sheriff Court)

S.N. = Session Notes

S.R. (N.S.W.) = New South Wales State Reports (1901-)

S.S.L.R. = Straits Settlements Law Reports (Malaysia)

S.T.C. = Simons Tax Cases

S.T.C. (S.C.D.) = Simons Tax Cases: Special Commissioners Decisions

S.T.I. = Simon's Tax Intelligence

S.W.2d = South Western Reporter, 2nd Series (U.S.A.)

Salk. = Salkeld's King's Bench Reports

Sask. R. = Saskatchewan Reports

Saund. = Saunder's King's Bench Reports

Sc. Jur. = Scottish Jurist

Sch. & L. = Schoales and Lefroy's Irish Chancery Reports

Scotsman = Scotsman

Scott N.R. = Scott's New Common Pleas Reports

Sel. Cas. Ch. = Select Cases in Chancery, tempore King

Sess. Cas. K.B. = Session Cases touching settlements (England, 1710-48)

Sh. App. = Shaw's Scottish Appeal Cases, House of Lords

Sh. Ct. Rep. = Scottish Law Review, Sheriff Court Reports (1885-1963)

Shaw = Shaw's Justiciary Cases (Scotland)

Ship. Gaz. = Shipping Gazette

Sid. = Siderfin's King's Bench Reports

Sim. = Simon's Vice Chancellors Reports

Sim. & St. = Simon and Stuart's Vice Chancellor's Reports

Sim. N.S. = Simon's Vice Chancellors Reports, New Series

Skin. = Skinner's King's Bench Reports

Sm. & G. = Smales and Giffard's Chancery Reports

Smith & B. = Smith and Batty's King's Bench Reports (Ireland, 1824-25)

Smith L.C. = Smith's Leading Cases on Various Branches of the Law

Sneed (TN) = Sneed's Tennessee Reports

So.2d = Southern Reporter, 2nd Series (U.S.A.)

Sol. = The Solicitor

Sp. Ecc. & Ad. = Spink's Ecclesiastical and Admiralty Reports

St. Tr. = Cobbett and Howell's State Trials

St. Tr. (N.S.) = MacDonnell's State Trials, New Series

Stark. = Starkie's Nisi Prius Reports

Str. = Strange's King's Bench Reports

Sw. & Tr. = Swabey and Tristram's Reports

Sw. Admr. = Swabey's Admiralty Reports

Swans. = Swanston's Chancery Reports

Syme = Syme's Justiciary Reports (Scotland)

T. Raym. = Sir Thomas Raymond's King's Bench Reports

T.C. = Tax Cases

T.C.L.R. = Technology and Construction Law Reports

T.L.R. = Times Law Reports

T.R. = Taxation Reports (1939-81)

T.S. = Transvaal Supreme Court Reports (South Africa)

Tang. L.R. (R.) = Tanganyika Law Reports

Tas. R. = Tasmanian Reports (1979-)

Tas. S.R. = Tasmanian State Reports (1941-98)

Taunt. = Taunton's Common Pleas Reports

TABLE OF ABBREVIATIONS

Tenn. = Tennessee Reports
Term Rep. = Durnford and East's Term Reports
Times = Times
TNS = transcript reference number not specified
Tr. Consist. J. = Tristram's Consistory Judgments
Tr. L. = Trading Law
Tr. L.R. = Trading Law Reports
Traff. Cas. = Traffic Cases
Trin. L.R. = Trinidad Law Reports
Turn. & R. = Turner and Russell's Chancery Reports
Tyr. = Tyrwhitt's Exchequer Reports

U.C.R. = Upper Canada Reports
U.K.C.L.R. = UK Competition Law Reports
U.K.H.R.R. = United Kingdom Human Rights Reports
U.K.T. = UK Transcripts
U.S. = United States Supreme Court Reports
U.S.App.D.C. = United States District Court for the District of Columbia
U.S.P.Q. = United States Patent Quarterly (BNA)
U.S.P.Q.2d = United States Patent Quarterly 2nd (BNA)
UCC Rep.Serv. = Uniform Commercial Code Reporting Service (Callaghan's)
UKHL = House of Lords
UKIAT = Immigration Appeal Tribunal
UKPC = Privy Council
UKPC D = Privy Council (Devolution)
USLW = United States Law Week

V. & B. = Vesey and Beames' Chancery Reports
V. & D.R. = Value Added Tax and Duties Reports
V.A.T.T.R. = Value Added Tax Tribunal Reports
V.L.R. = Victorian Law Reports (1875-1956)
V.R. = Victorian Reports (1957 -)

Va. = Virginia Reports
Vaugh. = Vaughan's Common Pleas Reports
Vent. = Ventris' King's Bench Reports
Vern. = Vernon's Chancery Reports

Ves. Jr. = Vesey Junior's Chancery Reports
Ves. Sen. = Vesey Senior's Chancery Reports

W. & S. = Wilson and Shaw's Scottish Appeal Cases, House of Lords
W. Jones = Sir William Jones' Reports
W. Rob. = W. Robinson's Admiralty Reports
W.A.C.A. = West African Court of Appeal Reports
W.A.L.R. = Western Australian Law Reports (1875-1956)
W.A.R. = Western Australian Reports (1957-)
W.I.R. = West Indian Reports
W.L.R. = Weekly Law Reports
W.N. = Weekly Notes (1866-1952)
W.N. (N.S.W.) = Weekly Notes, New South Wales
W.P.A.R. = War Pensions Appeal Reports
W.P.C. = Webster's Patent Cases
W.R. = Weekly Reporter (1853-1906)
W.T.L.R. = Wills & Trusts Law Reports
W.W.R. = Western Weekly Law Reports (Canada)
Wall. = Wallace's United States Supreme Court Reports
Wheat. = Wheaton's Supreme Court Reports (U.S.A.)
White = White's Justiciary Reports (Scotland)
Will. Woll. & Dav. = Willmore, Wollaston and Davison's Queen's Bench Reports
Willes = Willes' Common Pleas Reports
Wilm. = Wilmot's Notes and Opinions, King's Bench
Wils. K.B. = Wilson's King's Bench Reports
Wm. Bl. = W. Blackstone's King's Bench Reports
Wms. Saund. = William's Notes to Saunders' Reports

Y. & C. Ch. = Younge and Collier's Chancery Cases
Y. & C. Ex. = Younge and Collier's Exchequer Reports
Y. & J. = Younge and Jervis' Exchequer Reports
Y.B. = Year Books
Y.B. (R.S.) = Year Books, Rolls Series
Y.B. (S.S.) = Year Books, Selden Society
Yer. = Yerger's Tennessee Reports

Z.L.R. = Zimbabwe Law Reports

CURRENT LAW
PART I
CASE CITATOR 1998-2001 (ENGLAND)

The Current Law Case Citator comprises in a single table:
(i) Full case name of cases reported in 1998-2001
(ii) The judicial history of any case of whatever date which has been considered, applied, overruled, etc., in 1998-2001
Note: Figures appearing in bold type indicate the paragraph in the Current Law Year Book at which the case is digested

1-800 Flowers Inc *v.* Phonenames Ltd; *sub nom* 800-FLOWERS Trade Mark [2001]
EWCA Civ 721; [2001] 2 Costs L.R. 286; (2001) 24(7) I.P.D. 24042; (2001)
98(28) L.S.G. 42; *Times,* July 9, 2001, CA; affirming [2000] E.T.M.R. 369;
[2000] F.S.R. 697, Ch D . . . . *Digested,* 01/**4044**
1st Indian Cavalry Club Ltd *v.* Customs and Excise Commissioners [1998] S.T.C. 293;
1998 S.C. 126; 1998 S.L.T. 554; 1998 S.C.L.R. 47; [1998] B.T.C. 5030; [1998]
B.V.C. 58; 1997 G.W.D. 38-1976, Ex Div . . . . *Digested,* 98/**6218**

3M/Reformatio in peius (G01/99) [2001] E.P.O.R. 50, EPO (Enlarged Bd App) . . . . . . *Digested,* 01/**3897**

10 ROYAL BERKSHIRE POLO CLUB Trade Mark see Polo Lauren Co's Trade Mark Application
11 Donegall Square West, Belfast, Re see Campbells (Caterers) Ltd *v.* Scottish Provident
Institution

26 Clarendon Villas, Hove (Trusts Affecting), Re see Copeland *v.* Houlton

100 Old Broad Street *v.* Sidley [1999] E.G.C.S. 65, CA
134 Shirland Road Management Co Ltd *v.* Lester [1997] 2 E.G.L.R. 207; [1997] 49 E.G.
141, LVT . . . . *Digested,* 98/**3635**
183 Day Rule, Re (BK-98/02743) 3 I.T.L. Rep. 631, Hof (Den Haag)

800-FLOWERS Trade Mark see 1-800 Flowers Inc *v.* Phonenames Ltd

1406 Pub Co Ltd *v.* Hoare [2001] 23 E.G.C.S. 154, Ch D
1986 Budget (C34/86), Re; *sub nom* Council of Ministers of the European
Communities (Germany, France and United Kingdom intervening) *v.* European
Parliament (C34/86) [1986] E.C.R. 2155; [1986] 3 C.M.L.R. 94; *Times,* July 4,
1986, ECJ. . . . . *Digested,* 86/**1396**:
Followed, 00/2374: *Referred to,* 86/1395

A (A Child), Re see A (A Child) *v.* Sefton MBC
A (A Child) (Adoption: Agreement: Procedure), Re; *sub nom* A (A Child) (Adoption:
Consent), Re [2001] 2 F.L.R. 455; [2001] 2 F.C.R. 174; [2001] Fam. Law 648,
CA . . . . *Digested,* 01/**2530**
A (A Child) (Adoption: Consent), Re see A (A Child) (Adoption: Agreement: Procedure), Re
A (A Child) (Adoption of a Russian Child), Re [2000] 1 F.L.R. 539; [2000] 1 F.C.R. 673;
[2000] Fam. Law 596; (2000) 164 J.P.N. 644, Fam Div . . . . *Digested,* 00/**2433**
A (A Child) (Application for Judicial Review), Re; O (A Child) (Application for Judicial
Review), Re [2001] N.I. 454, CA (NI)
A (A Child) (Change of Name), Re see W (A Child) (Illegitimate Child: Change of Surname),
Re
A (A Child) (Contact: Separate Representation), Re; *sub nom* A *v.* A; A (A Child)
(Separate Representation in Contact Proceedings), Re [2001] 1 F.L.R. 715;
[2001] 2 F.C.R. 55; *Times,* February 28, 2001, CA. . . . . *Digested,* 01/**2589**
A (A Child) (Mental Health of Mother), Re [2001] EWCA Civ 162; [2001] 1 F.C.R. 577, CA

A (A Child) (Non Accidental Injury: Medical Evidence), Re; *sub nom* A (A Child) (Retinal Haemorrhages: Non Accidental Injury), Re [2001] 2 F.L.R. 657; [2001] 3 F.C.R. 262; [2001] Fam. Law 735, Fam Div

A (A Child) (Permission to Remove Child from Jurisdiction: Human Rights), Re; *sub nom* G-A (A Child), Re [2000] 2 F.L.R. 225; [2001] 1 F.C.R. 43; [2000] U.K.H.R.R. 572; [2000] Fam. Law 706, CA . . . . *Digested,* 00/**2485**

A (A Child) (Retinal Haemorrhages: Non Accidental Injury), Re see A (A Child) (Non Accidental Injury: Medical Evidence), Re

A (A Child) (Secure Accommodation Order), Re [2001] Fam. Law 806, Fam Div

A (A Child) (Separate Representation in Contact Proceedings), Re see A (A Child) (Contact: Separate Representation), Re

A (A Child) *v.* DPP (2000) 164 J.P. 317; [2000] Crim. L.R. 572; (2001) 165 J.P.N. 44; *Times,* March 29, 2000, QBD . . . . *Digested,* 00/**1080**

A (A Child) *v.* Governors of King Edwards School, Bath (Unreported, August 20, 1999), CC (Bath) [*Ex rel.* Withy King Solicitors, 5-6 Northumberland Buildings, Queen Square, Bath] . . . . *Digested,* 00/**4222**

A (A Child) *v.* Milupa Ltd [2000] 4 Q.R. 8, CC (Stourbridge) [*Ex rel.* Richard Gregory, Barrister, 24 The Ropewalk, Nottingham] . . . . *Digested,* 00/**1659**

A (A Child) *v.* Sefton MBC; *sub nom* A (A Child), Re [2000] E.L.R. 639, QBD . . . . *Digested,* 01/**2040**

A (A Child) *v.* Shorrock (Unreported, March 19, 2001), QBD [*Ex rel.* Sinton & Co Solicitors, 5 Osborne Terrace, Newcastle Upon Tyne] . . . . *Digested,* 01/**4466**

A (A Child) *v.* Westminster Society for People with Learning Disabilities (Unreported, October 13, 1999), CC (Central London) [*Ex rel.* David Levene & Co Solicitors, Bedford House, 125-133 Camden High Street, London] . . . . *Digested,* 00/**1667**

A (A Minor) (Abduction: Non-Convention Country), Re see JA (A Minor) (Child Abduction: Non-Convention Country), Re

A (A Minor) (Child of the Family), Re [1998] 1 F.L.R. 347; [1998] 1 F.C.R. 458; [1998] Fam. Law 14, CA . . . . *Digested,* 98/**2465**

A (A Minor) (Children: 1959 UN Declaration), Re; *sub nom* A (A Minor) (Residence Order), Re [1998] 1 F.L.R. 354; [1998] 2 F.C.R. 633; [1998] Fam. Law 72, CA . *Digested,* 97/**447**

A (A Minor) (Holiday in a Non-Convention Country) see A (Security for Return to Jurisdiction), Re

A (A Minor) (Residence Order), Re see A (A Minor) (Children: 1959 UN Declaration), Re

A (A Minor) *v.* Ellwood (Unreported, January 15, 1999), CC (Bury St Edmunds) [*Ex rel.* Amanda Drane, Barrister, 4 King's Bench Walk, Temple, London] . . . . *Digested,* 99/**1617**

A (A Minor) *v.* Leeds City Council (Unreported, March 2, 1999), CC (Leeds) [*Ex rel.* Levi & Co Solicitors, 33 St Pauls Street, Leeds] . . . . *Digested,* 99/**3977**

A (A Minor) *v.* Severn Trent Water Plc (Unreported, June 17, 1998), CC (Nottingham) [*Ex rel.* Nelsons Solicitors, Pennine House, 8 Stanford Street, Nottingham] . . . . *Digested,* 99/**1458**

A (A Minor) *v.* Sullivan (1999) 99(5) Q.R. 8, CC (Oxford) [*Ex rel.* Paul McGrath, Barrister, 1 Temple Gardens, Temple, London] . . . . *Digested,* 99/**1595**: *Applied,* 00/1580

A (Abduction: Habitual Residence), Re [1998] 1 F.L.R. 497; [1998] 3 F.C.R. 617; [1998] Fam. Law 244, Fam Div . . . . *Digested,* 98/**2382**

A (Adoption: Mother's Objections), Re [2000] 1 F.L.R. 665; [2000] Fam. Law 393, Fam Div
. . . . *Digested,* 00/**2428**

A (Application for Leave), Re [1998] 1 F.L.R. 1; [1999] 1 F.C.R. 127; [1998] Fam. Law 71, CA
. . . . *Digested,* 98/**2454**

A (Children) (Conjoined Twins: Medical Treatment) (No.1), Re; *sub nom* A (Children) (Conjoined Twins: Surgical Separation), Re [2001] Fam. 147; [2001] 2 W.L.R. 480; [2000] 4 All E.R. 961; [2001] 1 F.L.R. 1; [2000] 3 F.C.R. 577; [2000] H.R.L.R. 721; [2001] U.K.H.R.R. 1; 9 B.H.R.C. 261; [2000] Lloyd's Rep. Med. 425; (2001) 57 B.M.L.R. 1; [2001] Crim. L.R. 400; [2001] Fam. Law 18; (2000) 150 N.L.J. 1453; *Times,* October 10, 2000; *Independent,* October 3, 2000, CA; affirming [2001] Fam. Law 16, Fam Div . . . . *Digested,* 00/**3246**

A (Children) (Conjoined Twins: Medical Treatment) (No.2), Re [2001] 1 F.L.R. 267; [2001] 1 F.C.R. 313; [2001] Fam. Law 100; *Times,* November 15, 2000, CA . . . . *Digested,* 00/**2513**

A (Children) (Conjoined Twins: Surgical Separation), Re see A (Children) (Conjoined Twins: Medical Treatment) (No.1), Re

A (Children) (Contact: Expert Evidence), Re; *sub nom* A (Children) (Family Proceedings: Expert Witnesses), Re [2001] 1 F.L.R. 723; [2001] 98(16) L.S.G. 32; (2001) 151 N.L.J. 224; *Times,* February 27, 2001; *Independent,* March 19, 2001 (C.S), Fam Div . . . . *Digested,* 01/**2621**

A (Children) (Education), Re see A (Children) (Specific Issue Order: Parental Dispute), Re

A (Children) (Family Proceedings: Expert Witnesses), Re see A (Children) (Contact: Expert Evidence), Re

A (Children) (Interim Care Order), Re [2001] 3 F.C.R. 402; (2001) 165 J.P.N. 968, Fam Div

A (Children) (Specific Issue Order: Parental Dispute), Re; *sub nom* A (Children) (Education), Re [2001] 1 F.L.R. 121; [2001] 1 F.C.R. 210; [2001] Fam. Law 22, CA . . . . *Digested,* 01/**2588**

A (CICA: Quantum: 2000), Re [2000] 6 Q.R. 6, CICA (London) [*Ex rel.* Abigail Sheppard, Barrister, 4 Brick Court, Temple, London] . . . . *Digested,* 00/**1525**

A (Contact: Domestic Violence), Re [1998] 2 F.L.R. 171; [1999] 1 F.C.R. 729; [1998] Fam. Law 456, Fam Div. . . . . *Digested,* 98/**2422**

A (Disclosure of Medical Records to GMC), Re [1998] 2 F.L.R. 641; [1999] 1 F.C.R. 30;
(1999) 47 B.M.L.R. 84; [1998] Fam. Law 586; *Times*, August 21, 1998, Fam Div   *Digested*, 98/**2479**

A (Medical Treatment: Male Sterilisation), Re see A (Mental Patient: Sterilisation), Re

A (Mental Patient: Sterilisation), Re; *sub nom* A (Medical Treatment: Male Sterilisation),
Re; R-B (A Patient) *v.* Official Solicitor; RB (Male Patient: Sterilisation), Re
[2000] 1 F.L.R. 549; [2000] 1 F.C.R. 193; [2000] Lloyd's Rep. Med. 87; (2000)
53 B.M.L.R. 66; [2000] Fam. Law 242; (2000) 97(2) L.S.G. 30; *Times*, March
15, 2000, CA . . . .   *Digested*, 00/**2780**

A (Protection from Offenders Regulations), Re [1999] 1 F.L.R. 697; [1999] 3 F.C.R. 620;
[1999] Fam. Law 89, Fam Div . . . .   *Digested*, 99/**2354**

A (Security for Return to Jurisdiction), Re; *sub nom* A (A Minor) (Holiday in a Non-
Convention Country) [1999] 2 F.L.R. 1, Fam Div . . . .   *Digested*, 99/**2385**

A *v.* A see A (A Child) (Contact: Separate Representation), Re

A *v.* A (A Child) (Removal from Jurisdiction) (1980) 1 F.L.R. 380, CA . . . .   *Applied*, 01/2596

A *v.* A (Ancillary Relief); B *v.* B (Ancillary Relief) [2000] 1 F.L.R. 701; [2000] 1 F.C.R.
577; [2000] Fam. Law 470, Fam Div . . . .   *Digested*, 00/**480**

A *v.* A (Children: Shared Residence Order) [1994] 1 F.L.R. 669; [1995] 1 F.C.R. 91;
[1994] Fam. Law 431; (1994) 158 J.P.N. 817; *Times*, February 23, 1994;
Independent, February 14, 1994 (C.S), CA . . . .   *Digested*, 95/**3561**:
                                                   Applied, 95/3563, 96/604, 96/616, 01/2666

A *v.* A (Duxbury Calculations); *sub nom* A *v.* A (Elderly Applicant: Lump Sum) [1999]
2 F.L.R. 969; [1999] 3 F.C.R. 433; [1999] Fam. Law 752, Fam Div . . . .   *Digested*, 00/**2525**

A *v.* A (Elderly Applicant: Lump Sum) see A *v.* A (Duxbury Calculations)

A *v.* A (Financial Provision) [1998] 2 F.L.R. 180; [1998] 3 F.C.R. 421; [1998] Fam.
Law 393, Fam Div . . . .   *Digested*, 98/**2469**

A *v.* A (Forum Conveniens) [1999] 1 F.L.R. 1; [1999] 3 F.C.R. 376; [1998] Fam. Law
735, Fam Div . . . .   *Digested*, 99/**2405**

A *v.* A (Maintenance Pending Suit: Provision for Legal Costs) see A *v.* A (Maintenance
Pending Suit: Provision for Legal Fees)

A *v.* A (Maintenance Pending Suit: Provision for Legal Fees); *sub nom* A *v.* A
(Maintenance Pending Suit: Provision for Legal Costs) [2001] 1 W.L.R. 605;
[2001] 1 F.L.R. 377; [2001] 1 F.C.R. 226; [2001] Fam. Law 96; (2000) 97(44)
L.S.G. 45; (2000) 144 S.J.L.B. 273; *Times*, November 14, 2000; *Independent*,
December 11, 2000 (C.S), Fam Div. . . . .   *Digested*, 00/**2528**

A *v.* Australia 4 B.H.R.C. 210, UN HRC . . . .   *Digested*, 98/**3210**

A *v.* B see E *v.* E

A *v.* B (A Firm) HQ0101837, QBD . . . .   *Subsequent proceed-*
                                           ings, 01/4415

A *v.* B (A Firm) see A *v.* B Plc

A *v.* B (Copyright: Diary Pages) [2000] E.M.L.R. 1007, Ch D . . . .   *Digested*, 01/**3851**

A *v.* B Ex p. News Group Newspapers Ltd; *sub nom* Chessington World of Adventures
Ltd *v.* Reed (Restricted Reporting Order) [1998] I.C.R. 55; [1998] I.R.L.R. 56;
Times, July 4, 1997, EAT. . . . .   *Digested*, 97/**2212**:
                                           Considered, 98/2166

A *v.* B Plc; *sub nom* A *v.* B (A Firm); A2/2001/2086, CA; reversing [2001] 1 W.L.R.
2341; (2001) 98(41) L.S.G. 34; (2001) 145 S.J.L.B. 235; *Times*, November 2,
2001; *Independent*, November 16, 2001, QBD. . . . .   *Digested*, 01/**4415**

A *v.* Broadmoor Hospital Authority, *Independent*, October 9, 2000 (C.S), QBD

A *v.* Denmark (1996) 22 E.H.R.R. 458, ECHR . . . .   *Considered*, 98/3135

A *v.* Kirklees MBC; *sub nom* R. *v.* Kirklees MBC Ex p. A (A Child) [2001] EWCA Civ
582; [2001] B.L.G.R. 448; [2001] E.L.R. 657; *Times*, May 1, 2001, CA; affirming
CO/193/2000, QBD . . . .   *Digested*, 01/**2018**

A *v.* L (Contact) [1998] 1 F.L.R. 361; [1998] 2 F.C.R. 204; [1998] Fam. Law 137, Fam
Div . . . .   *Digested*, 98/**2418**

A *v.* Lambeth LBC see R. (on the application of A) *v.* Lambeth LBC

A *v.* M (Family Proceedings: Publicity) [2000] 1 F.L.R. 562; [2000] 1 F.C.R. 1; [2000]
Fam. Law 26, Fam Div. . . . .   *Digested*, 00/**2517**

A *v.* Minister for Immigration and Ethnic Affairs 2 B.H.R.C. 143; [1998] I.N.L.R. 1, HC
(Aus) . . . .   *Digested*, 97/**2934**:
                                           Approved, 97/2851

A *v.* N (Committal: Refusal of Contact); *sub nom* N (A Minor), Re [1997] 1 F.L.R. 533;
[1997] 2 F.C.R. 475; [1997] Fam. Law 233; (1997) 161 J.P.N. 698, CA . . . .   *Digested*, 97/**416**:
                                           Applied, 98/2420

A *v.* National Blood Authority (No.1); *sub nom* Hepatitis C Litigation, Re [2001] 3 All
E.R. 289; [2001] Lloyd's Rep. Med. 187; (2001) 60 B.M.L.R. 1; *Times*, April 4,
2001; *Daily Telegraph*, April 3, 2001, QBD . . . .   *Digested*, 01/**2933**

A *v.* Norway 3 I.T.L. Rep. 90, HR (N)

A *v.* Scottish Ministers; D *v.* Scottish Ministers; R *v.* Scottish Ministers [2001] UKPC
D5; 2001 S.L.T. 1331; 2001 G.W.D. 33-1312; *Times*, October 29, 2001;
Independent, December 17, 2001 (C.S), PC (Sc); affirming 2001 S.C. 1; 2000
S.L.T. 873; [2000] H.R.L.R. 450; [2000] U.K.H.R.R. 439; 8 B.H.R.C. 590; 2000
G.W.D. 22-864; *Times*, June 21, 2000, 1 Div . . . .   *Digested*, 01/**6707**

A v. United Kingdom [1998] 2 F.L.R. 959; [1998] 3 F.C.R. 597; (1999) 27 E.H.R.R. 611; 5 B.H.R.C. 137; [1998] Crim. L.R. 892; [1998] H.R.C.D. 870; [1998] Fam. Law 733; *Times*, October 1, 1998, ECHR . . . . *Digested*, 98/**3065**:
Applied, 01/3459: *Considered*, 01/1147

A v. Y (Child's Surname) [1999] 2 F.L.R. 5; [1999] 1 F.C.R. 577; [1999] Fam. Law 443, Fam Div . . . . *Digested*, 99/**2376**

A De Bloos Sprl v. Bouyer SA (C14/76) [1976] E.C.R. 1497; [1977] 1 C.M.L.R. 60, ECJ *Digested*, 77/**1280**:
Applied, 92/3944, 94/5037: *Considered*, 89/3014, 00/739: *Followed*, 01/802

A Fairhurst & Son v. Secretary of State for the Environment, Transport and the Regions (1999) 96(39) L.S.G. 40, QBD . . . . *Digested*, 00/**4434**

A Fulton Co Ltd v. Grant Barnett & Co Ltd [2001] R.P.C. 16; (2001) 24(1) I.P.D. 24003, Ch D . . . . *Digested*, 01/**3861**

A Health Authority v. X (Discovery: Medical Conduct) (No.1) see A Health Authority v. X (No.1)

A Health Authority v. X (No.1); *sub nom* A Health Authority v. X (Discovery: Medical Conduct) (No.1) [2001] EWCA Civ 2014, CA; affirming [2001] 2 F.L.R. 673; [2001] 2 F.C.R. 634; [2001] U.K.H.R.R. 1213; [2001] Lloyd's Rep. Med. 349; (2001) 61 B.M.L.R. 22; [2001] Fam. Law 653; *Independent*, June 25, 2001 (C.S.), Fam Div

A Irrevocable Trust, Re (1999-2000) 2 I.T.E.L.R. 482, HC (Cook I)

A Local Authority v. A (A Mother and Child) see C (Legal Aid: Preparation of Bill of Costs), Re

A Meredith Jones & Co Ltd v. Vangemar Shipping Co Ltd (The Apostolis) (No.2) [2000] 2 Lloyd's Rep. 337; [2000] C.L.C. 1488, CA; reversing [1999] 2 Lloyd's Rep. 292, QBD (Comm Ct) . . . . *Digested*, 00/**4711**

A Schroeder Music Publishing Co Ltd v. Instone (formerly Macaulay); *sub nom* Instone (formerly Macaulay) v. A Schroeder Music Publishing Co Ltd [1974] 1 W.L.R. 1308; [1974] 3 All E.R. 616; 118 S.J. 734, HL; affirming [1974] 1 All E.R. 171, CA . . . . *Digested*, 74/**1270**:
Applied, 74/1268, 75/434, 77/375, 84/388, 91/444, 00/2114: *Followed*, 01/951

A Straume (UK) Ltd v. Bradlor Developments Ltd [2000] B.C.C. 333; (2000) 2 T.C.L.R. 409; *Times*, June 29, 1999, Ch D . . . . *Digested*, 99/**3270**

A&C Supplies Ltd, Re; *sub nom* Sutton (Removal of Liquidator), Re [1998] B.C.C. 708; [1998] 1 B.C.L.C. 603; [1998] B.P.I.R. 303; (1997) 94(43) L.S.G. 29; *Times*, November 3, 1997, Ch D . . . . *Digested*, 97/**3065**

A&D Maintenance & Construction Ltd v. Pagehurst Construction Services Ltd (2000) 16 Const. L.J. 199, QBD (T&CC) . . . . *Digested*, 01/**863**

A&J Fabrications (Batley) Ltd v. Grant Thornton (A Firm) (No.1) [1999] B.C.C. 807; [1998] 2 B.C.L.C. 227; [2000] Lloyd's Rep. P.N. 565, Ch D . . . . *Digested*, 98/**3300**

A&J Fabrications (Batley) Ltd v. Grant Thornton (A Firm) (No.2) [2000] B.P.I.R. 1; [1999] Lloyd's Rep. P.N. 863; [1999] P.N.L.R. 811; [1999] 96(31) L.S.G. 41; (1999) 143 S.J.L.B. 213; *Times*, August 5, 1999, Ch D . . . . *Digested*, 99/**4023**

A-M v. A-M (Divorce: Jurisdiction: Validity of Marriage) see M v. M (Divorce: Jurisdiction: Validity of Marriage)

A's Application for Judicial Review, Re [2001] N.I. 335, QBD (NI)

A's Curator Bonis v. Criminal Injuries Compensation Board see P's Curator Bonis v. Criminal Injuries Compensation Board

A/S D/S Svendborg v. Awada [1999] 2 Lloyd's Rep. 244, QBD (Comm Ct) . . . . *Digested*, 99/**488**

A2B Radio Cars v. Customs and Excise Commissioners [1998] B.V.C. 2025, V&DTr

AA Insurance Services Ltd v. Customs and Excise Commissioners [1999] B.V.C. 2330; [1999] V. & D.R. 361, V&DTr . . . . *Digested*, 00/**5299**

Aadan v. Brent LBC [2000] C.P. Rep. 17; (2000) 32 H.L.R. 848; *Times*, December 3, 1999 ; *Independent*, December 20, 1999 (C.S.), CA . . . . *Digested*, 00/**366**

Aannamaersbedrijf PK Kraaijveld BV v. Gedeputeerde Staten van Zuid-Holland (C72/95) [1997] All E.R. (E.C.) 134; [1996] E.C.R. I-5403; [1997] 3 C.M.L.R. 1; [1997] Env. L.R. 265, ECJ . . . . *Digested*, 97/**2319**:
Applied, 01/4700: *Followed*, 99/2161

Aannemersbedrijf Gebroedes van Leeuwen BV v. Netherlands (32602/96) (2000) 29 E.H.R.R. CD96, ECHR

Aaro Forsman OY's European Trade Mark Application [2000] E.T.M.R. 142, KHO (Fin)

Aaron v. Okoye [1998] 2 Costs L.R. 6, CA. . . . . *Digested*, 00/**451**

AB (CICB: Quantum: 1998), Re (Unreported, October 23, 1997), CICB (Birmingham) [*Ex rel*. John Harvey, Barrister, 4 King's Bench Walk, Temple, London] . . . . *Digested*, 98/**1514**

AB v. CD [2001] I.R.L.R. 808, Ch D

AB v. John Wyeth & Brother Ltd (No.4) [1994] P.I.Q.R. P109; [1994] 5 Med. L.R. 149; (1993) 18 B.M.L.R. 38; (1994) 91(4) L.S.G. 45; (1994) 138 S.J.L.B. 12; *Times*, December 1, 1993; *Independent*, December 15, 1993, CA . . . . *Digested*, 95/**3882**:
Distinguished, 99/1394

AB v. South West Water Services Ltd; Gibbons v. South West Water Services Ltd [1993] Q.B. 507; [1993] 2 W.L.R. 507; [1993] 1 All E.R. 609; [1993] Env. L.R. 266; [1993] P.I.Q.R. P167; (1993) 143 N.L.J. 235; [1992] N.P.C. 146; *Times*, November 26, 1992; *Independent*, November 18, 1992, CA; reversing [1992] 4 All E.R. 574; [1993] Env. L.R. 176; [1992] P.I.Q.R. P224; (1992) 142 N.L.J. 897; *Times*, May 8, 1992; *Independent*, May 15, 1992, QBD. . . . .   *Digested*, 93/**1598**:
                        Considered, 96/2606, 97/3798: *Followed*, 00/824, 00/5112:
                                           Overruled, 01/1512
AB Bank v. Inspector of Taxes [2000] S.T.C. (S.C.D.) 229; [2000] S.T.I. 754, Sp Comm .   *Digested*, 00/**4939**
Abacus (CI) Ltd v. Al-Sabah see Grupo Torras SA v. Al-Sabah (No.6)
Abacus Trust Co (Isle of Man) Ltd v. National Society for the Prevention of Cruelty to Children; *sub nom* Abacus Trust Co (Isle of Man) Ltd v. NSPCC [2001] S.T.C. 1344; [2001] W.T.L.R. 953; (2000-01) 3 I.T.E.L.R. 846; [2001] S.T.I. 1225; (2001) 98(35) L.S.G. 37; *Times*, September 25, 2001, Ch D . . . .   *Digested*, 01/**5532**
Abacus Trust Co (Isle of Man) Ltd v. NSPCC see Abacus Trust Co (Isle of Man) Ltd v. National Society for the Prevention of Cruelty to Children
Abada v. Gray (1998) 40 B.M.L.R. 116, CA . . . .   *Digested*, 98/**3915**
Abadeh v. British Telecommunications Plc [2001] I.C.R. 156; [2001] I.R.L.R. 23, EAT
Abala v. Surrey Oaklands NHS Trust (Unreported, July 23, 1999), MCLC [*Ex rel.* Thompsons Solicitors, Congress House, Great Russell Street, London] . . . .   *Digested*, 00/**527**
ABB Lummus Global Ltd v. Keppel Fels Ltd (formerly Far East Levingston Shipbuilding Ltd) [1999] 2 Lloyd's Rep. 24, QBD (Comm Ct) . . . .   *Digested*, 99/**240**
ABB Power Construction Ltd v. Norwest Holst Engineering Ltd (2000) 2 T.C.L.R. 831; 77 Con. L.R. 20; (2001) 17 Const. L.J. 246, QBD (T&CC) . . . .   *Digested*, 01/**859**:
                                           Followed, 01/6287
ABB Zantingh Ltd v. Zedal Building Services Ltd [2001] B.L.R. 66; (2001) 3 T.C.L.R. 19; 77 Con. L.R. 32; (2001) 17 Const. L.J. 255; [2001] 5 E.G.C.S. 166, QBD (T&CC) . . . .   *Digested*, 01/**877**
Abbey Life Assurance Co Ltd v. Colclough (Inspector of Taxes) see HSBC Life (UK) Ltd v. Stubbs (Inspector of Taxes)
Abbey Life Assurance Co Ltd v. Tansell see MHC Consulting Services Ltd v. Tansell
Abbey National Building Society v. Cann [1991] 1 A.C. 56; [1990] 2 W.L.R. 833; [1990] 1 All E.R. 1085; [1990] 2 F.L.R. 122; (1990) 22 H.L.R. 360; (1990) 60 P. & C.R. 278; (1990) 87(17) L.S.G. 32; (1990) 140 N.L.J. 477; *Times*, March 30, 1990, HL; affirming [1989] 2 F.L.R. 265; (1989) 57 P. & C.R. 381; [1989] Fam. Law 314; *Times*, March 15, 1989, CA. . . . .   *Digested*, 90/**707**:
                  Applied, 94/4028, 96/4953, 01/4867: *Considered*, 93/2538, 96/5031,
                                         97/4258: *Followed*, 90/706
Abbey National Mortgages Plc v. Powell (1999) 78 P. & C.R. D16, CA
Abbey National Plc v. Boscawen see Boscawen v. Bajwa
Abbey National Plc v. Clive Travers & Co [1999] Lloyd's Rep. P.N. 753; [1999] P.N.L.R. 819, CA . . . .   *Digested*, 99/**3801**
Abbey National Plc v. Customs and Excise Commissioners [1997] V. & D.R. 224, V&DTr . . . .   *Digested*, 98/**4932**
Abbey National Plc v. Customs and Excise Commissioners (C408/98) [2001] 1 W.L.R. 769; [2001] All E.R. (EC) 385; [2001] S.T.C. 297; [2001] E.C.R. I-1361; [2001] 2 C.M.L.R. 28; [2001] C.E.C. 80; [2001] B.T.C. 5481; [2001] B.V.C. 581; [2001] S.T.I. 244; *Times*, March 13, 2001, ECJ (5th Chamber) . . . .   *Digested*, 01/**5586**:
                                           Considered, 01/5585
Abbey National Plc v. David Prosser & Co [2001] P.N.L.R. 15, Ch D . . . .   *Digested*, 01/**4268**
Abbey National Plc v. Formoso [1999] I.R.L.R. 222, EAT. . . . .   *Digested*, 99/**2115**
Abbey National Plc v. Frost [1999] 1 W.L.R. 1080; [1999] 2 All E.R. 206; [1999] Lloyd's Rep. P.N. 301; [1999] E.G.C.S. 16; [1999] N.P.C. 13; *Times*, February 5, 1999; *Independent*, February 10, 1999, CA; reversing [1998] 2 All E.R. 321; (1998) 95(16) L.S.G. 23; (1998) 148 N.L.J. 444; (1998) 142 S.J.L.B. 108; [1998] N.P.C. 40; [1998] N.P.C. 44; *Times*, March 19, 1998, Ch D . . . .   *Digested*, 99/**529**
Abbey National Plc v. Lee see Lloyds TSB General Insurance Holdings Ltd v. Lloyds Bank Group Insurance Co Ltd
Abbey National Plc v. Moss [1994] 1 F.L.R. 307; [1994] 2 F.C.R. 587; (1994) 26 H.L.R. 249; [1994] Fam. Law 255; [1993] N.P.C. 153; *Times*, November 30, 1993, CA . . . .   *Digested*, 95/**2214**:
                                Applied, 98/4356: *Considered*, 97/4268
Abbey National Plc v. Sayer Moore [1999] E.G.C.S. 114; *Times*, August 30, 1999, Ch D   *Digested*, 99/**479**
Abbey National Plc v. Tufts [1999] 2 F.L.R. 399; [1999] Fam. Law 542; [1999] E.G.C.S. 24, CA. . . . .   *Digested*, 99/**4388**
Abbot (John), Re see Licence Holder, Re
Abbotsley Golf & Squash Club Ltd v. Customs and Excise Commissioners [1997] V. & D.R. 355, V&DTr . . . .   *Digested*, 00/**5313**
Abbott v. Bayley (2000) 32 H.L.R. 72; [1999] L. & T.R. 267; (1999) 77 P. & C.R. D44, CA . . . .   *Digested*, 99/**3651**
Abbott v. Minister for Lands [1895] A.C. 425, PC (Aus) . . . .   *Applied*, 71/**1877**:
                                         Considered, 99/4582
Abbott v. Strong [1998] 2 B.C.L.C. 420; *Times*, July 9, 1998, Ch D . . . .   *Digested*, 98/**3922**

ABC Cars v. PSA Finance Plc (Unreported, July 4, 2000), CC (Winchester) [*Ex rel.* Nicholas Preston, Barrister, 8 Bell Yard, London] . . . . *Digested,* 00/**2561**
Abdel Bary, Re see R. (on the application of Al-Fawwaz) v. Governor of Brixton Prison
Abdel Bary v. Governor of Brixton Prison see R. (on the application of Al-Fawwaz) v. Governor of Brixton Prison
Abdoulaye v. Regie Nationale des Usines Renault SA (C218/98) [1999] E.C.R. I-5723; [2001] 2 C.M.L.R. 18; [2001] I.C.R. 527; [1999] I.R.L.R. 811; *Times,* October 20, 1999, ECJ (5th Chamber) . . . . *Digested,* 99/**2114**
Abdulaziz v. United Kingdom (A/94); Cabales v. United Kingdom (9473/81); Balkandali v. United Kingdom (9474/81) (1985) 7 E.H.R.R. 471, ECHR; affirming in part (1984) 6 E.H.R.R. 28, Eur Comm HR . . . . *Applied,* 90/5327,
94/5927, 95/2724, 98/3154, 98/3229: *Followed,* 98/3218, 01/3616:
Referred to, 98/5998
Abdulhayoglu's Patent Application [2000] R.P.C. 18, PO . . . . *Digested,* 00/**433**
Abdulla v. Harwood (Unreported, May 17, 2001), CC (Birkenhead) [*Ex rel.* DLA Solicitors, 101, Barbirolli Square, Manchester] . . . . *Digested,* 01/**499**
Abdullah v. Shropshire CC see R. v. Barnet LBC Ex p. Shah (Nilish)
Abdullah M Fahem & Co v. Mareb Yemen Insurance Co [1997] 2 Lloyd's Rep. 738, QBD (Comm Ct) . . . . *Digested,* 98/**239**
Abedi v. Penningtons [2000] 2 Costs L.R. 205; (2000) 150 N.L.J. 465, CA
Abedin v. Karim (Unreported, June 25, 2001), CC [*Ex rel.* Elizabeth Darlington, Barrister, 5 Pump Court, Temple, London] . . . . *Digested,* 01/**535**
Aberdeen DC v. Emslie & Simpson Ltd 1995 S.C. 264; *Times,* March 10, 1995, 1 Div . . . *Followed,* 98/4178
Abermeadow Ltd (No.1), Re; *sub nom* Secretary of State for Trade and Industry v. Pollock; Secretary of State for Trade and Industry v. Berry; No.003494 of 1995D, QBD . . . . *Digested,* 98/**681**
Abermeadow Ltd (No.2), Re; *sub nom* Berry v. Secretary of State for Trade and Industry [2001] B.C.C. 724; [2000] 2 B.C.L.C. 824, Ch D . . . . *Digested,* 01/**713**
Ablack v. Inner London Education Authority see R. v. Barnet LBC Ex p. Shah (Nilish)
Ableway Ltd v. Customs and Excise Commissioners see Ableway Ltd v. Inland Revenue Commissioners
Ableway Ltd v. Inland Revenue Commissioners; *sub nom* Ableway Ltd v. Customs and Excise Commissioners [2001] S.T.I. 1527, Sp Comm
ABN Amro Holding NV's Application (R 190/1999-3) [2001] E.T.M.R. 8, OHIM (3rd Bd App) . . . . *Digested,* 01/**3995**
Abnett (known as Sykes) v. British Airways Plc see Sidhu v. British Airways Plc
Abouzaid v. Mothercare (UK) Ltd, *Times,* February 20, 2001, CA . . . . *Digested,* 01/**920**
Abraham v. Commissioner of Police of the Metropolis; *sub nom* Abrahams v. Commissioner of Police of the Metropolis [2001] 1 W.L.R. 1257; (2001) 98(5) L.S.G. 37; (2001) 145 S.J.L.B. 20; *Times,* December 21, 2000, CA . . . . *Digested,* 01/**42**
Abraham v. Thompson [1997] 4 All E.R. 362; [1997] C.L.C. 1377; (1997) 94(37) L.S.G. 41; (1997) 141 S.J.L.B. 217; *Times,* August 19, 1997, CA; reversing [1997] C.L.C. 1370; (1997) 94(23) L.S.G. 27; (1997) 141 S.J.L.B. 114; *Times,* May 15, 1997; *Independent,* June 9, 1997 (C.S.), Ch D . . . . *Digested,* 97/**562**:
Considered, 98/411, 99/546: *Distinguished,* 00/436: *Followed,* 99/417
Abrahams v. Abrahams Trustee in Bankruptcy see Abrahams v. Trustee in Bankruptcy of Abrahams
Abrahams v. Commissioner of Police of the Metropolis see Abraham v. Commissioner of Police of the Metropolis
Abrahams v. Performing Right Society Ltd [1995] I.C.R. 1028; [1995] I.R.L.R. 486; *Times,* June 5, 1995; *Independent,* May 25, 1995, CA . . . . *Digested,* 95/**1981**:
Distinguished, 98/2205
Abrahams v. Trustee in Bankruptcy of Abrahams; *sub nom* Abrahams v. Abrahams Trustee in Bankruptcy [1999] B.P.I.R. 637; [2000] W.T.L.R. 593; (1999) 96(31) L.S.G. 38; *Times,* July 26, 1999 ; *Independent,* October 4, 1999, Ch D . . . . *Digested,* 99/**4959**
Abrahamsson v. Fogelqvist (C407/98) [2000] E.C.R. I-5539; [2000] I.R.L.R. 732, ECJ (5th Chamber) . . . . *Digested,* 00/**2170**
Abrasive Technology NA Inc's European Patent No.0280657 (2000) 23(1) I.P.D. 23005, EPO (Technical Bd App)
Abraxas Computer Services Ltd v. Rabin Leacock Lipman [2000] E.G.C.S. 70; [2000] N.P.C. 63, QBD
ABSOLUT Trade Mark (I ZB 45/96) [2001] E.T.M.R. 3, BGH (Ger)
Absolute Rentals Ltd v. Gencor Enterprises Ltd (2001) 17 Const. L.J. 322, QBD (T&CC)
ABSOLUTE Trade Mark see Mitutoyo Corp's Trade Mark Application
Abu Dhabi National Tanker Co v. Product Star Shipping (The Product Star) (No.2) [1993] 1 Lloyd's Rep. 397; *Times,* December 29, 1992, CA; reversing [1991] 2 Lloyd's Rep. 468, QBD (Comm Ct) . . . . *Digested,* 93/**3597**:
Considered, 98/3410
Abuki v. Attorney General of Uganda 3 B.H.R.C. 199, Const Ct (Ug) . . . . *Digested,* 98/**3108**
AC Egerton Ltd's European Patent (No.0683925) (1999) 22(2) I.P.D. 22022, PO
AC Egerton Ltd's Patent Application (2000) 23(9) I.P.D. 23075, PO
ACADEMY Trade Mark; *sub nom* Tritonstyle Ltd's Application for Revocation (No.1301046) [2000] R.P.C. 35; (1999) 22(7) I.P.D. 22072, Appointed Person . . . *Digested,* 00/**3792**

Academy Trading Ltd v. Greece (30342/96) (2001) 33 E.H.R.R. 44, ECHR
Accinauto SA v. Commission of the European Communities (T176/95) [1999] E.C.R.
    II-1635; [2000] 4 C.M.L.R. 67, CFI . . . .   *Digested*, 00/**718**
Accountancy Personnel v. Worshipful Company of Salters [1972] E.G.D. 461; (1972)
    116 S.J. 240; *Times*, March 8, 1972 . . . .   *Digested*, 72/**1964**:
                                               Considered, 00/3892
Accountant v. Inspector of Taxes [2000] S.T.C. (S.C.D.) 522; [2000] S.T.I. 1518, Sp
    Comm . . . .   *Digested*, 01/**5314**
ACE Insurance SA-NV (formerly Cigna Insurance Co of Europe SA NV) v. Zurich Insurance
    Co [2001] EWCA Civ 173; [2001] 1 All E.R. (Comm) 802; [2001] 1 Lloyd's
    Rep. 618; [2001] C.L.C. 526; [2001] I.L.Pr. 41; [2001] Lloyd's Rep. I.R. 504;
    (2001) 98(8) L.S.G. 46; *Times*, February 27, 2001, CA; affirming [2000] 2 All
    E.R. (Comm) 449; [2000] 2 Lloyd's Rep. 423; [2001] I.L.Pr. 23; *Times*,
    September 6, 2000, QBD (Comm Ct) . . . .   *Digested*, 01/**814**
Ackbar v. CF Green & Co Ltd [1975] Q.B. 582; [1975] 2 W.L.R. 773; [1975] 2 All E.R.
    65; [1975] 1 Lloyd's Rep. 673; 119 S.J. 219, QBD. . . . .   *Digested*, 75/**1962**:
                               Considered, 89/2342, 92/2829, 98/541
Acme Industry Co Ltd v. Council of the European Union (T48/96) [1999] E.C.R. II-
    3089; [1999] 3 C.M.L.R. 823, CFI (5th Chamber) . . . .   *Digested*, 00/**2346**
Acorn Management Services Ltd v. Customs and Excise Commissioners [2001] B.V.C.
    2388, V&DTr
Acquaviva v. France (19248/91) (2001) 32 E.H.R.R. 7, ECHR . . . .   *Considered*, 97/2809
Actual Services Ltd, Re see Licence Holder, Re
Acturus Properties Ltd v. Attorney General (2000-01) 3 I.T.E.L.R. 360, Royal Ct (Jer) . .   *Digested*, 01/**1047**
AD2000 Trade Mark [1997] R.P.C. 168; (1997) 20(3) I.P.D. 20029, Appointed Person .   *Digested*, 97/**4895**:
                                      Applied, 99/3572: *Considered*, 00/3758
Adagio Properties Ltd v. Ansari [1998] 2 E.G.L.R. 69; [1998] 35 E.G. 86; [1998]
    E.G.C.S. 9; (1998) 95(5) L.S.G. 30, CA . . . .   *Digested*, 98/**3616**
Adair v. National Trust for Places of Historic Interest or Natural Beauty [1998] N.I. 33;
    [1997] N.P.C. 162; [1999] Env. L.R. D5; *Times*, December 19, 1997, Ch D (NI) . .   *Digested*, 98/**5179**
Adam v. Ward [1917] A.C. 309, HL . . . .   *Applied*, 80/1715,
    81/1657, 89/2251: *Approved*, 83/2204: *Cited*, 99/1629: *Considered*, 65/2269,
           95/3133: *Disapproved*, 64/2136: *Distinguished*, 90/2916, 91/2320
Adam v. Woking BC [2000] R.V.R. 329, Lands Tr . . . .   *Digested*, 01/**3441**
Adam & Co International Trustees Ltd v. Theodore Goddard (A Firm) [2000] W.T.L.R.
    349; (1999-2000) 2 I.T.E.L.R. 634; (2000) 97(13) L.S.G. 44; (2000) 144
    S.J.L.B. 150; *Times*, March 17, 2000, Ch D . . . .   *Digested*, 00/**5267**
Adam & Partners Ltd, Re see Inland Revenue Commissioners v. Adam & Partners Ltd
Adam Phones Ltd v. Goldschmidt [1999] 4 All E.R. 486; [2000] C.P. Rep. 23; [2000]
    F.S.R. 163; (1999) 22(11) I.P.D. 22110; *Times*, August 17, 1999 ; *Independent*,
    July 22, 1999, Ch D . . . .   *Digested*, 99/**12**
Adami v. Lincoln Grange Management Ltd (1998) 30 H.L.R. 982; [1998] 1 E.G.L.R.
    58; [1998] 17 E.G. 148; [1997] E.G.C.S. 182; (1998) 95(3) L.S.G. 25; (1998)
    142 S.J.L.B. 37; [1997] N.P.C. 180; *Times*, December 22, 1997, CA . . . .   *Digested*, 98/**3655**
Adams, Re see Adams Ex p. Griffin, Re
Adams (Francis Christopher) (Deceased), Re see Adams v. Lewis
Adams v. Associated Newspapers Ltd; Associated Newspapers Ltd v. Northumbrian
    Fine Foods Plc [1999] E.M.L.R. 26, CA . . . .   *Digested*, 99/**1633**
Adams v. Attridge 98/MTC/1088, QBD. . . . .   *Digested*, 99/**2005**
Adams v. Cape Industries Plc [1990] Ch. 433; [1990] 2 W.L.R. 657; [1991] 1 All E.R.
    929; [1990] B.C.C. 786; [1990] B.C.L.C. 479, CA; affirming *Times*, June 23,
    1988; *Independent*, June 21, 1988, Ch D . . . .   *Digested*, 90/**3684**:
             Applied, 98/2212, 01/705: *Considered*, 97/880: *Followed*, 96/1666
Adams v. Dorset Ambulance NHS Trust (Unreported, November 11, 1999), CC
    (Southampton) [*Ex rel.* Allan Gore, Barrister, 12 King's Bench Walk, Temple,
    London] . . . .   *Digested*, 00/**1475**
Adams v. Lewis; *sub nom* Adams (Francis Christopher) (Deceased), Re [2001]
    W.T.L.R. 493, Ch D . . . .   *Digested*, 01/**5156**
Adams v. London Improved Motor Coach Builders Ltd [1921] 1 K.B. 495; [1920] All
    E.R. Rep. 340, CA; affirming [1920] 3 K.B. 82, KBD . . . .   *Applied*, 73/2671,
            83/590, 84/553: *Distinguished*, 47-51/7790: *Followed*, 99/383, 99/3757
Adams v. Rhymney Valley DC (2001) 33 H.L.R. 41; (2001) 3 L.G.L.R. 9; [2000]
    Lloyd's Rep. P.N. 777; [2001] P.N.L.R. 4; [2000] 3 E.G.L.R. 25; [2000] 39 E.G.
    144; [2000] E.G.C.S. 94; (2000) 150 N.L.J. 1231; [2000] N.P.C. 83; *Times*,
    August 11, 2000; *Independent*, October 23, 2000 (C.S), CA . . . .   *Digested*, 00/**4283**
Adams v. Trustees of the Michael Batt Charitable Trust see Batt v. Adams
Adams v. Young [2001] N.P.C. 38; 2001 G.W.D. 3-127, OH
Adams & Wade Ltd v. Minister of Housing and Local Government (1967) 18 P. & C.R.
    60, QBD . . . .   *Digested*, 67/**3850**:
                                    Applied, 71/11500, 01/4714
Adams Ex p. Griffin, Re; *sub nom* Adams, Re (1879) L.R. 12 Ch. D. 480, CA . . . .   *Considered*, 64/205,
                                            00/4562
Adams-Eden Furniture Ltd v. Kansa General International Insurance Co Ltd [1997] 6
    Re. L.R. 352, CA (Man). . . . .   *Digested*, 98/**3939**

Adams's Application for Judicial Review, Re [2001] N.I. 1, CA (NI) . . . .   *Digested*, 01/**5878**
Adamson *v.* Waveney DC [1997] 2 All E.R. 898; (1997) 161 J.P. 787; (1997) 161 J.P.N.
    1118; [1997] 8 S.L.L.P. 17; *Times*, February 24, 1997, QBD . . . .   *Digested*, 97/**3422**:
                                       Followed, 98/4865
Adan *v.* Newham LBC; *sub nom* Newham LBC *v.* Adan [2001] EWCA Civ 1916;
    [2001] N.P.C. 185, CA
Adan (Hassan Hussein) *v.* Secretary of State for the Home Department; *sub nom*
    Secretary of State for the Home Department *v.* Adan (Hassan Hussein); R. *v.*
    Secretary of State for the Home Department Ex p. Adan (Hassan Hussein);
    Nooh *v.* Secretary of State for the Home Department; Lazarevic *v.* Secretary of
    State for the Home Department; Radivojevic *v.* Secretary of State for the Home
    Department [1999] 1 A.C. 293; [1998] 2 W.L.R. 702; [1998] 2 All E.R. 453;
    [1998] Imm. A.R. 338; [1998] I.N.L.R. 325; (1998) 95(18) L.S.G. 33; (1998)
    148 N.L.J. 552; [1998] 142 S.J.L.B. 139; *Times*, April 6, 1998, HL; reversing
    [1997] 1 W.L.R. 1107; [1997] 2 All E.R. 723; 2 B.H.R.C. 65; [1997] Imm. A.R.
    251; [1997] I.N.L.R. 1; *Times*, March 7, 1997; *Independent*, March 12, 1997, CA . .   *Digested*, 98/**3241**:
                Applied, 99/3183: *Considered*, 00/3319: *Followed*, 00/6491, 01/3639:
                                       Not followed, 01/3694
Adcock *v.* Cooperative Insurance Society Ltd [2000] Lloyd's Rep. I.R. 657; *Times*,
    April 26, 2000, CA . . . .   *Digested*, 00/**3518**
Addax Ltd *v.* Arcadia Petroleum Ltd [2000] 1 Lloyd's Rep. 493, QBD (Comm Ct) . . . . .   *Digested*, 00/**1466**
Addis *v.* Gramophone Co Ltd [1909] A.C. 488, HL . . . .   *Applied*, 57/567,
           75/1088, 76/875, 85/1145, 85/1282, 87/1303, 92/1514, 95/1976, 99/2149:
           Considered, 97/2190, 98/2106, 01/2253: *Distinguished*, 47-51/9801, 70/894,
                                   97/2192: *Followed*, 66/9533, 67/3114
Addison *v.* Denholm Ship Management (UK) Ltd [1997] I.C.R. 770; [1997] I.R.L.R.
    389, EAT . . . .   *Digested*, 97/**2276**:
                                       Considered, 00/5007
Addison *v.* Kenward (Unreported, October 26, 1998), CC (Woolwich) [*Ex rel.*
    Jonathan Hough, Barrister, 1 Temple Gardens, London] . . . .   *Digested*, 99/**2498**
Addou *v.* Land Nordrhein Westfalen (C180/99) see Khalil *v.* Bundesanstalt fur Arbeit
    (C95/99)
Adedayo *v.* Secretary of State for the Home Department (Unreported, April 16, 1997),
    IAT . . . .   *Considered*, 98/3182
Adekeye *v.* Post Office (No.2); *sub nom* Post Office *v.* Adekeye [1997] I.C.R. 110;
    [1997] I.R.L.R. 105; (1996) 93(46) L.S.G. 29; (1996) 140 S.J.L.B. 262; *Times*,
    December 3, 1996, CA; affirming [1995] I.C.R. 540; [1995] I.R.L.R. 297; *Times*,
    February 23, 1995, EAT . . . .   *Digested*, 97/**2245**:
                               Applied, 01/2322: *Followed*, 99/2112
Adeshola *v.* Southwark LBC (Unreported, August 4, 1998), MC [*Ex rel.* Cliona
    Papazian, Barrister, Warwick House Chambers, 8 Warwick Court, Grays Inn,
    London] . . . .   *Digested*, 98/**2249**
Adham *v.* Bank of Credit and Commerce International SA (No.1) see El Jawhary *v.*
    Bank of Credit and Commerce International SA (No.1)
ADI (UK) Ltd *v.* Firm Security Group Ltd [2001] EWCA Civ 971; [2001] 3 C.M.L.R. 8;
    [2001] I.R.L.R. 542, CA; reversing EAT/11/99, EAT . . . .   *Digested*, 01/**2338**
Adidas AC *v.* Famco NV [1998] E.T.M.R. 616, Trib Comm (Brussels)
Adidas AG (C223/98), Re; *sub nom* Adidas AG's Reference (C223/98) [1999] E.C.R.
    I-7081; [1999] 3 C.M.L.R. 895; [1999] E.T.M.R. 960; [2000] F.S.R. 227, ECJ
    (5th Chamber) . . . .   *Digested*, 00/**2340**
Adidas AG's Reference (C223/98) see Adidas AG (C223/98), Re
Administration des Douanes *v.* Gondrand Freres SA (169/80) [1981] E.C.R. 1931, ECJ
    (3rd Chamber) . . . .   *Followed*, 99/5005
Administrative Proceedings Concerning AFS Intercultural Programs Finland RY (C237/97)
    [1999] E.C.R. I-825; [2000] 1 C.M.L.R. 845; *Times*, March 4, 1999, ECJ (5th
    Chamber) . . . .   *Digested*, 99/**3822**
Administrators of the Estate of Caton *v.* Couch (Inspector of Taxes) see Couch
    (Inspector of Taxes) *v.* Administrators of the Estate of Caton
Adobe Systems Inc *v.* Kaajamaa (KKO 1999: 115) [2001] E.C.D.R. 1, KKO (Fin)
Adoko *v.* Jemal, *Times*, July 8, 1999, CA. . . . .   *Digested*, 99/348
Adoption Application (96 AO 147), Re (Unreported, January 31, 1997), CC . . . .   *Considered*, 00/2434
ADT *v.* United Kingdom (35765/97) [2000] 2 F.L.R. 697; (2001) 31 E.H.R.R. 33; 9
    B.H.R.C. 112; [2000] Crim. L.R. 1009; [2000] Fam. Law 797; *Times*, August 8,
    2000, ECHR . . . .   *Digested*, 00/**3251**
ADT Auctions Ltd *v.* Secretary of State for the Environment, Transport and the Regions
    [2000] J.P.L. 1155; [2000] Env. L.R. D32, QBD . . . .   *Digested*, 00/**4459**
Adur DC *v.* Courcha (2001) 16 P.A.D. 85, Planning Inspector
Adur DC *v.* Secretary of State for the Environment, Transport and the Regions [2000]
    1 P.L.R. 1; *Independent*, November 1, 1999 (C.S.), CA; reversing [1999] P.L.C.R.
    295, QBD . . . .   *Digested*, 99/**4174**
ADVANCED SEMICONDUCTOR PRODUCTS/Limiting (G01/93) [1995] E.P.O.R. 97, EPO
    (Enlarged Bd App) . . . .   *Applied*, 00/3600:
                        Considered, 00/3602: *Referred to*, 99/3472

Advanced Specialist Treatment Engineering Ltd v. Cleveland Structural Engineering
   (Hong Kong) Ltd; *sub nom* Cleveland Structural Engineering (Hong Kong) Ltd v.
   Advanced Specialist Treatment Engineering Ltd [2000] 1 W.L.R. 558; [2000] 2
   All E.R. (Comm) 189; *Times*, February 7, 2000, QBD (Comm Ct) . . . .   *Digested*, 00/**219**
Advanced Technology Structures Ltd v. Cray Valley Products Ltd [1993] B.C.L.C. 723;
   Times, December 29, 1992, CA . . . .   *Digested*, 93/**3100**:
                         Applied, 94/3598: *Not followed*, 96/682: *Overruled*, 98/375
Advantage Healthcare (T10) Ltd, Re see Grove v. Advantage Healthcare (T10) Ltd
Advocate General for Scotland v. MacDonald; *sub nom* Secretary of State for Defence
   v. MacDonald; MacDonald v. Ministry of Defence 2001 S.L.T. 819; 2001 S.C.L.R.
   795; [2001] I.R.L.R. 431; 2001 G.W.D. 19-731, Ex Div; reversing [2001] 1 All
   E.R. 620; [2001] I.C.R. 1; [2000] I.R.L.R. 748; [2001] H.R.L.R. 5; *Independent*,
   November 27, 2000 (C.S), EAT . . . .   *Digested*, 01/**6475**:
                                              Considered, 01/2315

Advocate General for Scotland v. Mann see Secretary of State for Scotland v. Mann
AE v. Special Educational Needs Tribunal [1999] E.L.R. 341, QBD . . . .   *Digested*, 00/**1952**
AE Beckett & Sons (Lyndons) Ltd v. Midland Electricity Plc [2001] 1 W.L.R. 281; (2001)
   98(5) L.S.G. 37; (2001) 145 S.J.L.B. 15; *Times*, January 10, 2001; *Daily
   Telegraph*, January 9, 2001, CA; reversing1997 A 1817, QBD . . . .   *Digested*, 01/**4489**
AE/Pistons (T570/91) [2000] E.P.O.R. 360, EPO (Technical Bd App) . . . .   *Digested*, 00/**3634**
AEA Technology Plc's Patent Application (1998) 21 (11) I.P.D. 21122, PO
AEG KABEL/Cable outer sheath (T118/84) [1999] E.P.O.R. 186, EPO (Technical Bd App)
AEG (UK) Ltd v. Logic Resource Ltd [1996] C.L.C. 265, CA . . . .   *Considered*, 00/4710
AEG Telefunken AG v. Commission of the European Communities (107/82R) [1982]
   E.C.R. 1549, ECJ. . . . .   *Followed*, 01/2451
Aegean Sea Traders Corp v. Repsol Petroleo SA (The Aegean Sea) [1998] 2 Lloyd's
   Rep. 39; [1998] C.L.C. 1090, QBD (Comm Ct) . . . .   *Digested*, 98/**4409**
AEI Rediffusion Music Ltd v. Phonographic Performance Ltd (Costs); *sub nom*
   Phonographic Performance Ltd v. AEI Rediffusion Music Ltd (Costs) [1999] 1
   W.L.R. 1507; [1999] 2 All E.R. 299; [1999] C.P.L.R. 551; [1999] E.M.L.R. 335;
   [1999] R.P.C. 599; (1999) 22(5) I.P.D. 22046; (1999) 96(12) L.S.G. 33; (1999)
   143 S.J.L.B. 97; *Times*, March 3, 1999; *Independent*, February 24, 1999, CA;
   affirming [1999] E.M.L.R. 129; (1998) 21(12) I.P.D. 21130, Ch D; reversing
   [1998] E.M.L.R. 459, Copyright Tr . . . .   *Digested*, 99/**3456**:
                         Considered, 00/396, 00/457, 01/470: *Followed*, 01/460
AEI Rediffusion Music Ltd v. Phonographic Performance Ltd (No.1); *sub nom*
   Phonographic Performance Ltd v. AEI Rediffusion Music Ltd [1998] Ch. 187;
   [1997] 3 W.L.R. 982; [1997] 3 All E.R. 560; [1998] E.M.L.R. 270; [1997] R.P.C.
   729; (1997) 94(29) L.S.G. 29; *Times*, July 14, 1997, Ch D . . . .   *Digested*, 97/**3564**
AEI Rediffusion Music Ltd v. Phonographic Performance Ltd (No.2) [1998] E.M.L.R.
   240; [1998] R.P.C. 335, Copyright Tr . . . .   *Digested*, 98/**3435**:
                                 Considered, 99/3449, 00/3581
AEM (Avon) Ltd v. Bristol City Council [1999] B.L.G.R. 93; [1998] R.A. 89; [1998]
   E.G.C.S. 31, QBD. . . . .   *Digested*, 98/**4320**
Aeolian Shipping SA v. ISS Machinery Services Ltd (The Aeolian); *sub nom* ISS
   Machinery Services Ltd v. Aeolian Shipping SA (The Aeolian) [2001] EWCA Civ
   1162; [2001] 2 Lloyd's Rep. 641; [2001] C.L.C. 1708, CA
AERAZUR/Parachute (T986/92) [1999] E.P.O.R. 21, EPO (Technical Bd App)
Aeroports de Paris v. Commission of the European Communities (C82/01)); *sub nom*
   Aeroports de Paris v. Commission of the European Communities (T128/98)
   [2000] E.C.R. II-3929; [2001] 4 C.M.L.R. 38, CFI (3rd Chamber) . . . .   *Digested*, 01/**761**
Aeroports de Paris v. Commission of the European Communities (T128/98) see
   Aeroports de Paris v. Commission of the European Communities (C82/01))
Aerts v. Belgium (2000) 29 E.H.R.R. 50; 5 B.H.R.C. 382; (2000) 53 B.M.L.R. 79;
   [1998] H.R.C.D. 749, ECHR . . . .   *Digested*, 99/**3094**
AFFINITY Trade Mark see Telecom Securicor Cellular Radio Ltd's Trade Mark Application
   (No.1588293/4)
Affish BV v. Rijksdienst (C183/95) [1997] E.C.R. I-4315, ECJ . . . .   *Followed*, 00/2638
Affleck v. Newcastle Mind [1999] I.C.R. 852; [1999] I.R.L.R. 405, EAT . . . .   *Digested*, 99/**2034**
Afovos Shipping Co SA v. R Pagnan & Fratelli (The Afovos) [1983] 1 W.L.R. 195;
   [1983] 1 All E.R. 449; [1983] 1 Lloyd's Rep. 335; [1983] Com. L.R. 83; (1983)
   127 S.J. 98, HL; affirming [1982] 1 W.L.R. 848; [1982] 3 All E.R. 18; [1982] 1
   Lloyd's Rep. 562; [1982] Com. L.R. 128; 126 S.J. 242, CA; reversing [1980] 2
   Lloyd's Rep. 469, QBD (Comm Ct) . . . .   *Digested*, 83/**3414**:
                                Applied, 00/870: *Considered*, 82/2873
Afrika v. Cape Plc see Lubbe v. Cape Plc (No.2)
Afro Continental Nigeria v. Meridian Shipping Co SA (The Vrontados) [1982] 2 Lloyd's
   Rep. 241; (1982) 79 L.S.G. 954; 126 S.J. 331, CA . . . .   *Digested*, 82/**2597**:
                Applied, 86/2725: *Considered*, 98/586: *Referred to*, 84/2745
Afunyah (Mary) v. Secretary of State for the Home Department; *sub nom* R. v.
   Secretary of State for the Home Department Ex p. Afunyah (Mary) [1998] Imm.
   A.R. 201, CA. . . . .   *Digested*, 98/**3231**

Afzal v. Ford Motor Co Ltd; Caldwell v. Wiggins Teape Fine Papers Ltd; Green v. British
    Gas (North Eastern) Plc; Willingham v. Kimberley Clark Ltd; Featherstone v.
    Ideal Standard Ltd; Joyce v. Ford Motor Co Ltd; Kavanagh v. Ideal Standard Ltd;
    Sokhal v. Ford Motor Co Ltd [1994] 4 All E.R. 720; [1994] P.I.Q.R. P418;
    (1994) 144 N.L.J. 935; Times, July 6, 1994; Independent, June 16, 1994, CA . . .   Digested, 95/**3897**:
            Applied, 95/4217, 95/4220, 97/570: Cited, 95/3981: Considered, 95/3978,
                95/4215, 95/4216, 95/4218, 95/4219, 95/4221, 96/707, 98/404, 98/453,
                98/457, 99/537, 00/445: Followed, 96/732: Referred to, 97/569
AG Securities v. Vaughan; Antoniades v. Villiers [1990] 1 A.C. 417; [1988] 3 W.L.R.
    1205; [1988] 3 All E.R. 1058; (1989) 21 H.L.R. 79; (1989) 57 P. & C.R. 17;
    [1988] 47 E.G. 193; (1989) 86(1) L.S.G. 39; (1988) 138 N.L.J. Rep. 325;
    (1988) 132 S.J. 1638; Times, November 11, 1988, HL; reversing [1988] 2 W.L.R.
    689; [1988] 2 All E.R. 173; (1988) 20 H.L.R. 212; (1988) 56 P. & C.R. 168;
    [1988] 06 E.G. 112; (1988) 85(7) L.S.G. 38; (1988) 138 N.L.J. Rep. 23; (1988)
    132 S.J. 301, CA . . . .   Digested, 89/**2145**:
            Applied, 00/3928, 01/4808: Cited, 00/311: Considered, 89/2144, 89/2146,
                89/2147, 89/2148, 90/2815, 92/2655, 01/4150: Distinguished, 92/2752:
                        Followed, 98/3664: Referred to, 95/3018
AGA Estate Agencies, Re [1986] P.C.C. 358; Times, June 4, 1986, Ch D . . . .   Digested, 87/**338**:
                                    Applied, 98/5521: Considered, 00/5956
Agard v. Jetha (Unreported, October 18, 1999), CC (Bow) [Ex rel. Nicholas Preston,
    Barrister, Bracton Chambers, 8 Bell Yard, London] . . . .   Digested, 00/**2581**
Agecrest Ltd v. Gwynedd CC [1998] J.P.L. 325; [1996] N.P.C. 106, QBD . . . .   Digested, 98/**4235**
Ager v. Ager [1998] 1 W.L.R. 1074; [1998] 1 All E.R. 703; [1998] 1 F.L.R. 506; [1998]
    3 F.C.R. 355; [1998] Fam. Law 253; Times, January 6, 1998; Independent,
    January 19, 1998 (C.S.), CA . . . .   Digested, 98/**430**
AGF Belgium SA v. European Economic Community (C191/94) [1996] E.C.R. I-1859;
    [1998] R.T.R. 27, ECJ . . . .   Digested, 98/**2332**
Agfa AG v. Ilford [1960] R.P.C. 108 . . . .   Digested, 60/**3218**:
                                                            Considered, 99/3576
Aggeliki Charis Compania Maritima SA v. Pagnan SpA (The Angelic Grace) [1995] 1
    Lloyd's Rep. 87, CA; affirming [1994] 1 Lloyd's Rep. 168, QBD (Comm Ct) . . . .   Digested, 94/**4066**:
            Applied, 98/239: Considered, 97/880, 99/733, 99/745, 99/4441, 01/950
Agip (Africa) Ltd v. Jackson [1991] Ch. 547; [1991] 3 W.L.R. 116; [1992] 4 All E.R.
    451; (1991) 135 S.J. 117; Times, January 9, 1991; Financial Times, January 18,
    1991, CA; affirming [1990] Ch. 265; [1989] 3 W.L.R. 1367; [1992] 4 All E.R.
    385; (1989) 86(3) L.S.G. 34; (1990) 134 S.J. 198; Times, June 5, 1989, Ch D . .   Digested, 92/**2039**:
            Applied, 96/421, 00/4316: Considered, 90/4259, 91/3379, 95/3601, 00/520
Agip SpA v. Direct Tax Office of Milan (4612/97) 1 I.T.L. Rep. 451, Comm Tributaria PG
    (I)
AGN (Adoption: Foreign Adoption), Re see N (A Child) (Adoption: Foreign Guardianship),
    Re
Agnew v. Inland Revenue Commissioner see Brumark Investments Ltd, Re
Agnew v. Lansforsakringsbolagens AB [2001] 1 A.C. 223; [2000] 2 W.L.R. 497;
    [2000] 1 All E.R. 737; [2000] 1 All E.R. (Comm) 321; [2000] C.L.C. 848;
    [2001] I.L.Pr. 25; [2000] Lloyd's Rep. I.R. 317; (2000) 97(9) L.S.G. 39; (2000)
    144 S.J.L.B. 109; Times, February 23, 2000, HL; affirming [1997] 4 All E.R.
    937; [1997] L.R.L.R. 671; [1998] C.L.C. 390; [1998] I.L.Pr. 231, CA; affirming
    [1996] 4 All E.R. 978; [1996] L.R.L.R. 392; [1997] C.L.C. 245; [1997] 6 Re.
    L.R. 33, QBD (Comm Ct) . . . .   Digested, 00/**767**
Agodzo v. Bristol City Council [1999] 1 W.L.R. 1971; [2000] E.H.L.R. Dig. 96; Times,
    June 9, 1999, CA . . . .   Digested, 99/**427**
Agopoff, Re (188273) 3 I.T.L. Rep. 42, CE (F)
Agora Srl v. Ente Autonomo Fiera Internazionale di Milano (C223/99); Excelsior SNC
    di Pedrotti Bruna & C v. Ente Autonomo Fiera Internazionale di Milano (C260/
    99) [2001] All E.R. (EC) 769; [2001] E.C.R. I-3605; [2001] 3 C.M.L.R. 12;
    Times, June 26, 2001, ECJ . . . .   Digested, 01/**695**
Agreement between Football Association Premier League Ltd, Football Association Ltd,
    Football League Ltd and their respective Member Clubs, Re see Televising Premier
    League Football Matches, Re
Agreement relating to the Supply of Services facilitating the Broadcasting on Television of
    Premier League Football Matches, Re see Televising Premier League Football
    Matches, Re
AGREVO/Triazole sulphonamides (T939/92) [1996] E.P.O.R. 171, EPO (Technical Bd App)
                                                            Applied, 98/3477
Agricultural Tyres & Wheels v. Customs and Excise Commissioners [2000] S.T.I. 111,
    V&DTr
Agrila Ltd v. Rating and Valuation Commissioner see Rating and Valuation
    Commissioner v. Agrila Ltd
Agriplant Services Ltd (In Liquidation), Re [1997] B.C.C. 842; [1997] 2 B.C.L.C. 598, Ch D
                                                            Digested, 98/**3330**
Agroexport Entreprise d'Etat pour le Commerce Exterieur v. Goorden Import Cy SA NV
    [1956] 1 Lloyd's Rep. 319, QBD . . . .   Digested, 56/**351**:
                                                            Applied, 00/892

Agrokor AG *v.* Tradigrain SA [2000] 1 Lloyd's Rep. 497, QBD (Comm Ct) . . . .   *Digested,* 00/**3848**
Agros Trading Co Ltd *v.* Glencore Grain Ltd see Glencore Grain Ltd *v.* Agros Trading Co
    Ltd
Agrosin Pty Ltd *v.* Highway Shipping Co Ltd (The Mata K) [1998] 2 Lloyd's Rep. 614;
    [1998] C.L.C. 1300, QBD (Comm Ct) . . . .   *Digested,* 99/**4415**
Aher-Waggon GmbH *v.* Germany (C389/96) [1998] E.C.R. I-4473; [1999] 2 C.M.L.R.
    589, ECJ (5th Chamber) . . . .   *Digested,* 99/**2221**
Ahlstrom (A) OY *v.* Commission of the European Communities (C89/85); *sub nom*
    Wood Pulp Cartel (C89/85), Re [1993] E.C.R. I-1307; [1993] 4 C.M.L.R. 407;
    Financial Times, April 6, 1993, ECJ (5th Chamber) . . . .   *Digested,* 93/**4254**:
                                                                   Considered, 98/726
Ahmad *v.* Ahmad [1999] 1 F.L.R. 317; [1998] Fam. Law 732, CA . . . .   *Digested,* 99/**2419**
Ahmad (Mariam) *v.* Secretary of State for the Home Department; *sub nom* R. *v.*
    Secretary of State for the Home Department Ex p. Simba; R. *v.* Secretary of
    State for the Home Department Ex p. Ahmad (Mariam); Simba *v.* Secretary of
    State for the Home Department [1999] Imm. A.R. 356, CA . . . .   *Digested,* 00/**3285**
Ahmed *v.* Austria (1997) 24 E.H.R.R. 278; [1998] I.N.L.R. 65, ECHR . . . .   *Digested,* 97/**2764**
Ahmed *v.* Cardiff CC (Unreported, December 17, 1999), CC (Cardiff) [*Ex rel.* Helen
    Gower, Barrister, Old Square Chambers, Hanover House, 47 Corn Street,
    Bristol] . . . .   *Digested,* 00/**1744**
Ahmed *v.* Customs and Excise Commissioners [1998] B.V.C. 2171, V&DTr . . . .   *Digested,* 98/**4968**
Ahmed (t/a Lister Fisheries) *v.* Customs and Excise Commissioners [1999] S.T.C. 468;
    [1999] B.T.C. 5193; [1999] B.V.C. 205, QBD . . . .   *Digested,* 99/**5025**
Ahmed *v.* DPP [1998] R.T.R. 90, QBD . . . .   *Digested,* 97/**1137**
Ahmed *v.* Habib Bank Ltd see Habib Bank Ltd *v.* Ahmed
Ahmed *v.* Hussein (Unreported, October 5, 1999), CC (Central London) [*Ex rel.*
    Philippa Daniels, Barrister, Fleet Chambers, Mire House, 44-46 Fleet Street,
    London] . . . .   *Digested,* 99/**434**
Ahmed *v.* Leicester City Council see Ahmed *v.* Nicholls
Ahmed *v.* McLeod 1998 J.C. 242; 1999 S.L.T. 762; 1998 S.C.C.R. 486; [2000] R.T.R.
    201; 1998 G.W.D. 27-1391, HCJ Appeal . . . .   *Digested,* 98/**5695**:
                                                                   Followed, 00/1201
Ahmed *v.* Nicholls; *sub nom* Ahmed *v.* Leicester City Council [2000] E.H.L.R. 182;
    Times, March 29, 2000; *Independent,* May 15, 2000 (C.S.), QBD . . . .   *Digested,* 00/**967**
Ahmed (Iftikhar) *v.* Secretary of State for the Home Department; *sub nom* Secretary of
    State for the Home Department *v.* Ahmed (Iftikhar) [2000] I.N.L.R. 1; *Times,*
    December 8, 1999, CA . . . .   *Digested,* 00/**3313**
Ahmed (Naseer) *v.* Secretary of State for the Home Department; *sub nom* R. *v.*
    Secretary of State for the Home Department Ex p. Ahmed (Parveen); R. *v.*
    Secretary of State for the Home Department Ex p. Ahmed (Naseer); R. *v.*
    Secretary of State for the Home Department Ex p. Barrow (Buba); Ahmed
    (Parveen) *v.* Secretary of State for the Home Department; Barrow *v.* Secretary of
    State for the Home Department [2000] Imm. A.R. 370, CA. . . . .   *Digested,* 00/**3327**
Ahmed (Parveen) *v.* Secretary of State for the Home Department see Ahmed (Naseer)
    v. Secretary of State for the Home Department
Ahmed *v.* Southwark LBC (1999) 31 H.L.R. 286, CA . . . .   *Digested,* 99/**3675**
Ahmed *v.* United Kingdom [1999] I.R.L.R. 188; (2000) 29 E.H.R.R. 1; 5 B.H.R.C. 111;
    (1999) 1 L.G.L.R. 94; [1998] H.R.C.D. 823; *Times,* October 2, 1998, ECHR . . . .   *Digested,* 98/**3087**
Ahnee *v.* DPP [1999] 2 A.C. 294; [1999] 2 W.L.R. 1305; (1999) 143 S.J.L.B. 149, PC
    (Mau) . . . .   *Digested,* 99/**757**:
                                                                   Applied, 01/837
AIB Finance Ltd *v.* Alsop; *sub nom* AIB Finance Ltd *v.* Debtors [1998] 2 All E.R. 929;
    [1998] Lloyd's Rep. Bank. 102; [1998] B.C.C. 780; [1998] 1 B.C.L.C. 665;
    [1998] B.P.I.R. 533; (1998) 95(14) L.S.G. 22; (1998) 142 S.J.L.B. 108; *Times,*
    March 11, 1998, CA; affirming [1997] 4 All E.R. 677; [1997] 2 B.C.L.C. 354;
    [1997] B.P.I.R. 559; [1997] N.P.C. 46; *Times,* April 10, 1997, Ch D . . . .   *Digested,* 98/**3342**:
                                                Considered, 98/322, 01/**4855**
AIB Finance Ltd *v.* Debtors see AIB Finance Ltd *v.* Alsop
AIB Group (UK) Ltd *v.* Martin see AIB Group (UK) Plc (formerly Allied Irish Banks Plc
    and AIB Finance Ltd) *v.* Martin
AIB Group (UK) Plc (formerly Allied Irish Bank Plc and AIB Finance Ltd) *v.* Gold see AIB
    Group (UK) Plc (formerly Allied Irish Banks Plc and AIB Finance Ltd) *v.* Martin
AIB Group (UK) Plc (formerly Allied Irish Bank Plc and AIB Finance Ltd) *v.* Martin see AIB
    Group (UK) Plc (formerly Allied Irish Banks Plc and AIB Finance Ltd) *v.* Martin
AIB Group (UK) Plc (formerly Allied Irish Banks Plc and AIB Finance Ltd) *v.* Martin; *sub*
    nom AIB Group (UK) Ltd *v.* Martin; AIB Group (UK) Plc (formerly Allied Irish
    Bank Plc and AIB Finance Ltd) *v.* Martin; AIB Group (UK) Plc (formerly Allied
    Irish Bank Plc and AIB Finance Ltd) *v.* Gold [2001] UKHL 63; [2001] N.P.C. 183;
    Times, December 17, 2001, HL; affirming [2000] 2 All E.R. (Comm) 686;
    [2000] Lloyd's Rep. Bank. 385; (2000) 97(28) L.S.G. 34; (2000) 97(30)
    L.S.G. 42, CA; affirming (2000) 97(28) L.S.G. 34; (2000) 97(30) L.S.G. 42,
    Pat Ct . . . .   *Digested,* 00/**2606**
AIB Group (UK) Plc *v.* Hennelley Properties Ltd see Allied Irish Bank Group (UK) Plc *v.*
    Hennelly Properties Ltd

Aid to French Newspapers, Re (C18/84) see Commission of the European Communities v. France (C18/84)

Aiden Shipping Co Ltd v. Interbulk Ltd (The Vimeira) (No.2) [1986] A.C. 965; [1986] 2 W.L.R. 1051; [1986] 2 All E.R. 409; [1986] 2 Lloyd's Rep. 117; (1986) 130 S.J. 429, HL; reversing [1985] 1 W.L.R. 1222; [1985] 3 All E.R. 641; [1986] 1 Lloyd's Rep. 107; (1985) 82 L.S.G. 3529; (1985) 135 N.L.J. 1165; (1985) 129 S.J. 812; *Financial Times*, October 16, 1985, CA; reversing [1985] 2 Lloyd's Rep. 377, QBD (Comm Ct) . . . . *Digested*, 86/**2606**:
Applied, 86/978, 87/2991, 89/2243, 89/2938, 91/2819, 92/3454, 93/49, 94/3591, 95/3994, 96/710: *Considered*, 88/296, 90/3604, 90/3615, 91/2823, 92/2535, 92/2570, 93/3153, 93/3175, 94/3579, 96/940, 97/607, 97/3113, 99/390, 01/1817: *Followed*, 96/3541, 99/392, 99/417

AIG Europe (UK) Ltd v. Anonymous Greek Co of General Insurances see AIG Europe (UK) Ltd v. Ethniki

AIG Europe (UK) Ltd v. Ethniki; *sub nom* AIG Europe (UK) Ltd v. Anonymous Greek Co of General Insurances; Anonymous Greek Co of General Insurances v. AIG Europe (UK) Ltd [2000] 2 All E.R. 566; [2000] 1 All E.R. (Comm) 65; [2000] C.L.C. 446; [2000] I.L.Pr. 426; [2000] Lloyd's Rep. I.R. 343, CA; affirming [1998] 4 All E.R. 301; [1999] Lloyd's Rep. I.R. 221, QBD (Comm Ct) . . . . *Digested*, 00/**3515**

AIG Europe SA v. QBE International Insurance Ltd [2001] 2 All E.R. (Comm) 622; [2001] 2 Lloyd's Rep. 268; [2001] C.L.C. 1259; *Times*, June 22, 2001, QBD (Comm Ct) . . . . *Digested*, 01/**3838**

Aiken v. Stewart Wrightson Members Agency Ltd [1996] 2 Lloyd's Rep. 577; [1997] 6 Re. L.R. 79, CA; affirming [1995] 1 W.L.R. 1281; [1995] 3 All E.R. 449; [1995] 2 Lloyd's Rep. 618; *Times*, March 8, 1995, QBD (Comm Ct) . . . . *Digested*, 96/**3589**:
Cited, 00/4657: *Considered*, 00/4656

Ailsa Craig Fishing Co Ltd v. Malvern Fishing Co Ltd (The Strathallan); Malvern Fishing Co Ltd v. Ailsa Craig Fishing Co Ltd (The Strathallan) [1983] 1 W.L.R. 964; [1983] 1 All E.R. 101; [1983] 1 Lloyd's Rep. 183 (Note); 1982 S.C. (H.L.) 14; 1982 S.L.T. 377; (1983) 80 L.S.G. 2516; (1983) 127 S.J. 508, HL; affirming 1981 S.L.T. 130, 1 Div . . . . *Digested*, 83/**3440**:
Applied, 83/3314, 95/5569, 00/895: *Considered*, 82/403

Aimo-Boot v. Fabre [1999] E.T.M.R. 55, Trib Gde Inst (Paris) . . . . *Digested*, 99/**3549**

Ainsbury v. Millington [1987] 1 W.L.R. 379; [1987] 1 All E.R. 929; (1987) 84 L.S.G. 1241; (1987) 131 S.J. 361, HL; affirming [1986] 1 All E.R. 73; [1986] 1 F.L.R. 331, CA . . . . *Digested*, 87/**2886**:
Applied, 01/430: *Considered*, 93/1928, 93/3933, 94/3273, 95/3575: *Followed*, 94/2195: *Referred to*, 00/557

Aintree Hospital Trust v. UNISON see RCO Support Services Ltd v. UNISON

Air Canada v. Basra [2000] I.R.L.R. 683; *Independent*, April 3, 2000 (C.S.), EAT

Air Canada v. Secretary of State for Trade (No.2) [1983] 2 A.C. 394; [1983] 2 W.L.R. 494; [1983] 1 All E.R. 910, HL; affirming [1983] 2 W.L.R. 494; [1983] 1 All E.R. 161; (1983) 127 S.J. 205; *Times*, September 25, 1982, CA; reversing 126 S.J. 709, QBD . . . . *Digested*, 83/**2936**:
Applied, 91/2857, 91/2944, 94/5239, 00/329: *Followed*, 97/466

Air Ecosse Ltd v. Civil Aviation Authority 1987 S.C. 285; 1987 S.L.T. 751; (1987) 3 B.C.C. 492, 2 Div . . . . *Digested*, 87/**4041**:
Not applied, 99/3280: *Not followed*, 00/3432

Air Express v. Ansett Transport Industries Pty; *sub nom* Ansett Transport Industries (Operations) Pty v. Halton (1979-1981) 146 C.L.R. 249; (1981) 33 A.L.R. 578, HC (Aus) . . . . *Considered*, 89/3026, 99/440

Air France v. Commission of the European Communities (T2/93) [1994] E.C.R. II-323; *Financial Times*, May 31, 1994, CFI (1st Chamber) . . . . *Digested*, 94/**4775**:
Applied, 98/2311

Air France v. Saks 470 U.S. 392, US Ct . . . . *Applied*, 01/5385

Air India v. Wiggins [1980] 1 W.L.R. 815; [1980] 2 All E.R. 593; (1980) 71 Cr. App. R. 213; 124 S.J. 478, HL; reversing [1980] 1 W.L.R. 102; [1980] 1 All E.R. 192; (1980) 70 Cr. App. R. 58; [1980] Crim. L.R. 44; (1979) 123 S.J. 718, DC . . . . . . *Digested*, 80/**523**:
Followed, 98/687

Air Jamaica Ltd v. Charlton; Air Jamaica Ltd v. Goodall; Air Jamaica Ltd v. Philpotts; Air Jamaica Ltd v. Clarke [1999] 1 W.L.R. 1399; [1999] O.P.L.R. 11; [1999] Pens. L.R. 247; (1999-2000) 2 I.T.E.L.R. 244, PC (Jam) . . . . *Digested*, 99/**4958**:
Applied, 01/4631

Air Jamaica Ltd v. Clarke see Air Jamaica Ltd v. Charlton

Air Jamaica Ltd v. Goodall see Air Jamaica Ltd v. Charlton

Air Jamaica Ltd v. Philpotts see Air Jamaica Ltd v. Charlton

AIR PRODUCTS AND CHEMICALS/Air separation (T307/95) [1998] E.P.O.R. 389, EPO (Technical Bd App)

Airbus Industrie GIE *v.* Patel [1999] 1 A.C. 119; [1998] 2 W.L.R. 686; [1998] 2 All E.R. 257; [1998] 1 Lloyd's Rep. 631; [1998] C.L.C. 702; [1999] I.L.Pr. 238; (1998) 95(18) L.S.G. 32; (1998) 148 N.L.J. 551; (1998) 142 S.J.L.B. 139; *Times*, April 6, 1998, HL; reversing [1997] 2 Lloyd's Rep. 8; [1997] C.L.C. 197; [1997] I.L.Pr. 230; (1996) 93(36) L.S.G. 35; (1996) 140 S.J.L.B. 214; *Times*, August 12, 1996, CA; reversing [1996] I.L.Pr. 465; (1996) 93(24) L.S.G. 26; *Times*, May 21, 1996, QBD . . . . *Digested*, 98/**755**:
Considered, 00/758

Airedale NHS Trust *v.* Bland [1993] A.C. 789; [1993] 2 W.L.R. 316; [1993] 1 All E.R. 821; [1993] 1 F.L.R. 1026; [1994] 1 F.C.R. 485; [1993] 4 Med. L.R. 39; [1993] Fam. Law 473; (1993) 143 N.L.J. 199; *Times*, February 5, 1993; *Independent*, February 5, 1993; *Guardian*, February 5, 1993, HL; affirming (1992) 142 N.L.J. 1755; *Times*, December 10, 1992; *Independent*, December 10, 1992, CA; affirming (1992) 142 N.L.J. 1648; *Times*, November 23, 1992; *Independent*, November 20, 1992, Fam Div . . . . *Digested*, 93/**2712**:
Applied, 94/3015, 94/3850, 95/4266, 01/2934: *Considered*, 94/1004, 95/4104, 97/2593, 97/6070, 98/958, 00/3246, 01/2662, 01/2935:
Distinguished, 97/5783: *Followed*, 98/2650, 98/2651, 01/3571

Airey *v.* Ireland (No.1) (A/32) (1979-80) 2 E.H.R.R. 305, ECHR . . . . *Considered*, 98/3154, 01/3439

Airways Pension Scheme, Re see Stevens *v.* Bell
Ait-Mouhoub *v.* France (2000) 30 E.H.R.R. 382; [1998] H.R.C.D. 976, ECHR . . . . *Digested*, 01/**3545**
Aitken *v.* Independent Insurance Co Ltd 2001 S.L.T. 376; 2001 G.W.D. 2-101, OH . . . . . *Digested*, 01/**6720**
Aitken's Trustee *v.* Aitken see Kerr *v.* Aitken
AJ and MA Levy's Trade Mark Application (Extension of Time) [1999] R.P.C. 291, Appointed Person . . . . *Digested*, 99/**3525**:
Considered, 00/3792

AJ and MA Levy's Trade Mark Application (Referral of Appeal) [1999] R.P.C. 358, Appointed Person . . . . *Digested*, 99/**3527**
Ajeh, Re (Unreported, August 30, 1996), IAT . . . . *Distinguished*, 01/3595
Ajinomoto Co Inc *v.* Council of the European Union (C76/98); *sub nom* Ajinomoto Co Inc *v.* Council of the European Union (T159/94); NutraSweet Co *v.* Council of the European Union (T160/94); NutraSweet Co *v.* Council of the European Union (C77/98) [2001] E.C.R. I-3223; [2001] 2 C.M.L.R. 40, ECJ (6th Chamber) [1997] E.C.R. II-2461; [2001] E.C.R. I-3223, AGO; affirming . . . . *Digested*, 01/**2509**
Ajinomoto Co Inc *v.* Council of the European Union (T159/94) see Ajinomoto Co Inc *v.* Council of the European Union (C76/98)
Ajlan & Bros Trade Mark Application see Ajlan Bin Abdullaziz Al-Ajlan & Bros Co's Trade Mark Application
Ajlan Bin Abdullaziz Al-Ajlan & Bros Co's Trade Mark Application; *sub nom* Ajlan & Bros Trade Mark Application [2000] E.T.M.R. 710, Appointed Person . . . . *Digested*, 00/**3762**
Ajodha *v.* Trinidad and Tobago; Chandree *v.* Trinidad and Tobago; Fletcher *v.* Trinidad and Tobago; Noreiga *v.* Trinidad and Tobago [1982] A.C. 204; [1981] 3 W.L.R. 1; [1981] 2 All E.R. 193; (1981) 73 Cr. App. R. 129; [1981] Crim. L.R. 555; 125 S.J. 305, PC (Trin) . . . . *Digested*, 81/**415**:
Applied, 88/558, 97/1094, 00/907: *Considered*, 84/585, 85/557, 85/563, 85/564, 87/614

AK (A Child) (Secure Accommodation Order), Re [2000] N.I. 205; [2000] 1 F.L.R. 317; [2000] 3 F.C.R. 289; [2000] Fam. Law 613, Fam Div (NI) . . . . *Digested*, 00/**5534**
AK (Adult Patient) (Medical Treatment: Consent), Re [2001] 1 F.L.R. 129; [2001] 2 F.C.R. 35; (2001) 58 B.M.L.R. 151; [2000] Fam. Law 885, Fam Div . . . . *Digested*, 01/**2934**
Aka *v.* Turkey (19639/92) (2001) 33 E.H.R.R. 27; [1998] H.R.C.D. 866, ECHR
Akai Pty Ltd *v.* People's Insurance Co Ltd [1998] 1 Lloyd's Rep. 90; [1997] C.L.C. 1508; [1999] I.L.Pr. 24, QBD (Comm Ct) . . . . *Digested*, 98/**771**:
Considered, 00/3516

Akbar (t/a Mumtaz Paan House) *v.* Customs and Excise Commissioners [1998] B.V.C. 2157; [1998] V. & D.R. 52, V&DTr . . . . *Digested*, 98/**4887**
Akbar (t/a Mumtaz Paan House) *v.* Customs and Excise Commissioners [2000] S.T.C. 237; [2000] B.T.C. 5081; [2000] B.V.C. 88; [2000] S.T.I. 124, QBD . . . . *Digested*, 00/**5280**
Akbarali *v.* Brent LBC see R. *v.* Barnet LBC Ex p. Shah (Nilish)
Akdivar *v.* Turkey (1997) 23 E.H.R.R. 143; 1 B.H.R.C. 137, ECHR . . . . *Digested*, 97/**2770**:
Applied, 98/3077, 98/3240, 99/3085, 99/3086

Akelis *v.* Normand 1997 S.L.T. 136, HCJ Appeal . . . . *Digested*, 97/**6400**:
Applied, 99/960

Akewushola *v.* Immigration Officer (Heathrow) see Akewushola *v.* Secretary of State for the Home Department
Akewushola *v.* Secretary of State for the Home Department; *sub nom* Akewushola *v.* Immigration Officer (Heathrow) [2000] 1 W.L.R. 2295; [2000] 2 All E.R. 148; [1999] Imm. A.R. 594; [1999] I.N.L.R. 433; *Times*, November 3, 1999, CA . . . . . *Digested*, 99/**3210**:
Applied, 01/3600, 01/3663: *Followed*, 00/3382

Akhbari *v.* Secretary of State for the Home Department [2000] Imm. A.R. 436, CA . . . . *Digested*, 00/**3300**
Akhtar *v.* Grout (1998) 162 J.P. 714; (1998) 162 J.P.N. 786, QBD . . . . *Digested*, 99/**3550**

13

Akhtar (Tahzeem) *v.* Immigration Appeal Tribual; *sub nom* R. *v.* Immigration Appeal Ex
p. Akhtar (Tahzeem) [1991] Imm. A.R. 326; *Times*, December 4, 1990, CA . . . . .   *Digested*, 92/**2412**:
                                                                                      Followed, 98/3234
Akhuemonkhan *v.* Secretary of State for the Home Department [1998] I.N.L.R. 265,
IAT . . . .   *Digested*, 98/**3181**:
                                                                                      Followed, 00/3279
Akkus *v.* Turkey (2000) 30 E.H.R.R. 365, ECHR . . . .   *Digested*, 01/**3458**
Akman *v.* Oberkreisdirektor des Rheinisch Bergischen Kreises (C210/97) [1998]
E.C.R. I-7519; [2001] 1 C.M.L.R. 17, ECJ (6th Chamber)
AKP *v.* United Kingdom see IJL *v.* United Kingdom
Akpre *v.* Immigration Appeal Tribunal see R. *v.* Immigration Appeal Tribunal Ex p. Akpre
Akrami *v.* Customs and Excise Commissioners [1999] V. & D.R. 51, V&DTr . . . .   *Digested*, 00/**4974**
Aksoy *v.* Turkey (1997) 23 E.H.R.R. 553; 1 B.H.R.C. 625, ECHR . . . .   *Digested*, 97/**2824**:
                                               Applied, 98/3162: *Followed*, 98/3073
Aktiebolaget Volvo *v.* Heritage (Leicester) Ltd [2000] E.T.M.R. 940 (Note); [2000]
F.S.R. 253, Ch D   *Digested*, 99/**3553**
Aktielselkabet Dampskibsselskabel Svendborg *v.* Mobil North Sea Ltd see
Aktieselskabet Dampskibsselskabet Svendborg *v.* Mobil North Sea Ltd
Aktieselskabet Dampskibsselskabet Svendborg *v.* Mobil North Sea Ltd; *sub nom*
Aktielselkabet Dampskibsselskabel Svendborg *v.* Mobil North Sea Ltd;
Aktieselskabet Dampskibsselskabet Svendorg *v.* Mobil North Sea Ltd [2001] 2
All E.R. (Comm) 553; [2001] 2 Lloyd's Rep. 127, QBD (Comm Ct) . . . .   *Digested*, 01/**4914**
Aktieselskabet Dampskibsselskabet Svendorg *v.* Mobil North Sea Ltd see
Aktieselskabet Dampskibsselskabet Svendborg *v.* Mobil North Sea Ltd
AKZO Chemie BV *v.* Commission of the European Communities (C62/86) [1991]
E.C.R. I-3359; [1993] 5 C.M.L.R. 215; [1994] F.S.R. 25; *Times*, October 7, 1991,
ECJ (5th Chamber) . . . .   *Digested*, 91/**3834**:
                                               Applied, 97/854: *Followed*, 98/716
Akzo Nobel NV's European Patent (No.189958) see Fort Dodge Animal Health Ltd *v.* Akzo
Nobel NV
AL BASSAM Trade Mark [1995] R.P.C. 511, CA; affirming [1994] R.P.C. 315, Ch D . . .   *Digested*, 95/**4945**:
                                                                                      Referred to, 00/3766
Al-Adsani *v.* United Kingdom (No.1) (35763/97) (2000) 29 E.H.R.R. CD99, ECHR
Al-Adsani *v.* United Kingdom (No.2) (35763/97), *Times*, November 26, 2001, ECHR
Al-Amiry *v.* Manchester City Council (Unreported, June 26, 1998), CC (Manchester)
[*Ex rel.* Christopher Limb, Barrister, Young Street Chambers, 38 Young Street,
Manchester] . . . .   *Digested*, 98/**444**
Al-Ani *v.* Shubber, *Times*, April 28, 1999, CA . . . .   *Digested*, 99/**371**
Al-Fawwaz, Re see R. (on the application of Al-Fawwaz) *v.* Governor of Brixton Prison
Al-Fawwaz *v.* Governor of Brixton Prison see R. (on the application of Al-Fawwaz) *v.*
Governor of Brixton Prison
Al-Fayed *v.* Secretary of State for the Home Department see R. *v.* Secretary of State
for the Home Department Ex p. Al-Fayed (No.2)
Al-Fayed *v.* United Kingdom (A/294-B) (1994) 18 E.H.R.R. 393; *Times*, October 11,
1994; *Independent*, October 6, 1994; *Guardian*, September 26, 1994, ECHR . . . .   *Digested*, 95/**2622**:
                                               Applied, 98/3156, 00/2212, 01/5652
Al-H (Rashid) *v.* F (Sara) [2001] EWCA Civ 186; [2001] 1 F.L.R. 951; [2001] 1 F.C.R.
385; *Times*, March 2, 2001, CA . . . .   *Digested*, 01/**2676**
Al-Ibraheem *v.* Bank of Butterfield International (Cayman) Ltd (2000-01) 3 I.T.E.L.R. 1,
Grand Court (CI) . . . .   *Digested*, 01/**5520**
Al-Kishtaini *v.* Shanshal; *sub nom* Shanshal *v.* Al-Kishtaini [2001] EWCA Civ 264;
[2001] 2 All E.R. (Comm) 601; [2001] Lloyd's Rep. Bank. 174; (2001) 98(17)
L.S.G. 38; *Times*, March 8, 2001, CA; reversing *Times*, June 16, 1999, QBD . . . . .   *Digested*, 01/**4123**
Al-Midani *v.* Al-Midani; Al-Midani *v.* Kayal [1999] 1 Lloyd's Rep. 923; [1999] C.L.C.
904, QBD (Comm Ct) . . . .   *Digested*, 99/**249**
Al-Midani *v.* Kayal see Al-Midani *v.* Al-Midani
Al-Naimi (t/a Buildmaster Construction Services) *v.* Islamic Press Agency Inc; *sub nom*
Al-Naimi (t/a Buildmaster Construction Services) *v.* Islamic Press Services Inc
[2000] 1 Lloyd's Rep. 522; [2000] C.L.C. 647; [2000] B.L.R. 150; (2000) 2
T.C.L.R. 499; 70 Con. L.R. 21; *Times*, March 16, 2000, CA; affirming [1999]
C.L.C. 212; (2000) 2 T.C.L.R. 160, QBD (T&CC) . . . .   *Digested*, 00/**234**
Al-Naimi (t/a Buildmaster Construction Services) *v.* Islamic Press Services Inc see Al-
Naimi (t/a Buildmaster Construction Services) *v.* Islamic Press Agency Inc
Al-Sabah *v.* Al-Hawaz see Al-Sabah *v.* Ali
Al-Sabah *v.* Ali; *sub nom* Al-Sabah *v.* Al-Hawaz; Al-Sabah *v.* Brickwood; A3/1999/
0374, A3/1999/0375, CA; reversing [1999] E.G.C.S. 11; (1999) 96(5) L.S.G.
38; *Independent*, January 27, 1999, Ch D . . . .   *Digested*, 99/**4361**
Al-Sabah *v.* Brickwood see Al-Sabah *v.* Ali
Al-Sabah *v.* Grupo Torras SA see Grupo Torras SA *v.* Al-Sabah (No.5)
Al-Wazir *v.* Islamic Press Agency Inc (Interest); *sub nom* Islamic Press Agency *v.* Al-
Wazir [2001] EWCA Civ 1276; [2001] N.P.C. 130; *Times*, October 4, 2001, CA;
affirming Ch.1995-A-4562, Ch D . . . .   *Digested*, 01/**4871**
Alabaster *v.* Woolwich Plc A1/2000/2013 EATRF, CA [2000] I.C.R. 1037; [2000]
I.R.L.R. 754; *Times*, April 19, 2000, EAT . . . .   *Digested*, 00/**2165**

Alain Bernardin et Cie v. Pavilion Properties Ltd [1967] F.S.R. 341; [1967] R.P.C. 581,
Ch D . . . .   *Digested*, 67/**3948**:
     Applied, 73/2491: *Considered*, 73/3324: *Not followed*, 77/3042, 77/3050,
     98/3518

Alan Glaves International Ltd v. Customs and Excise Commissioners [2000] B.V.C.
2019, V&DTr

Alan Wibberley Building Ltd v. Insley [1999] 1 W.L.R. 894; [1999] 2 All E.R. 897;
(1999) 78 P. & C.R. 327; [1999] 2 E.G.L.R. 89; [1999] 24 E.G. 160; [1999]
E.G.C.S. 66; (1999) 96(21) L.S.G. 39; (1999) 143 S.J.L.B. 146; [1999] N.P.C.
54; (1999) 78 P. & C.R. D19; *Times*, April 30, 1999, HL; reversing [1998] 1
W.L.R. 881; [1998] 2 All E.R. 82; [1998] 2 E.G.L.R. 107; [1998] 29 E.G. 111;
(1997) 94(45) L.S.G. 28; (1997) 141 S.J.L.B. 249; [1997] N.P.C. 160; *Times*,
November 24, 1997, CA. . . . .   *Digested*, 99/**4352**

Albany International BV v. Stichting Bedrijfspensioenfonds Textielindustrie (C67/96)
[1999] E.C.R. I-5751; [2000] 4 C.M.L.R. 446, ECJ [1999] E.C.R. I-5751, AGO .   *Digested*, 00/**2357**:
     Joined proceedings, 00/2358, 00/2359

Albert v. Albert [1997] 2 F.L.R. 791; [1998] 1 F.C.R. 331; [1996] B.P.I.R. 233; [1998]
Fam. Law 17, CA . . . .   *Digested*, 95/**418**

Albert v. Belgium (A/58); Le Compte v. Belgium (A/58) (1983) 5 E.H.R.R. 533,
ECHR . . . .   *Applied*, 98/3128,
     98/3131, 99/3093: *Considered*, 96/3123: *Explained*, 01/4761:
     Not followed, 01/3425

Albert v. Gooda Walker Ltd see Deeny v. Gooda Walker Ltd (No.2)
Albert v. Tse Wai Chun Paul see Tse Wai Chun Paul v. Albert
Albon v. Inland Revenue Commissioners [1998] S.T.C. 1181; 1998 S.C. 934; 1999 S.L.T.
814; 71 T.C. 174; [1999] B.T.C. 138; 1998 G.W.D. 28-1441, Ex Div . . . .   *Digested*, 99/**6458**

Albon v. Railtrack Plc; *sub nom* Basildon DC v. Railtrack Plc [1998] E.H.L.R. 83;
[1998] N.P.C. 21; *Times*, February 27, 1998, QBD . . . .   *Digested*, 98/**2295**

Alboni v. Ind Coope Retail Ltd [1998] I.R.L.R. 131, CA . . . .   *Digested*, 98/**2232**:
     Followed, 99/2104

Albright & Wilson UK Ltd v. Biachem Ltd [2001] EWCA Civ 301; [2001] 2 All E.R.
(Comm) 537; [2001] C.L.C. 1023, CA; affirming 1997-A-No.1506, QBD. . . . . . .   *Digested*, 01/**939**

ALCAN/Aluminium alloys (T22/89) [1999] E.P.O.R. 347, EPO (Technical Bd App) . . . .   *Digested*, 99/**3484**

Alcatel Austria AG v. Bundesministerium fur Wissenschaft und Verkehr (C81/98) [1999]
E.C.R. I-7671; (2000) 2 T.C.L.R. 894, ECJ (6th Chamber) . . . .   *Digested*, 01/**2518**

Alcatel Submarine Networks Ltd v. Customs and Excise Commissioners [1999] V. &
D.R. 179, V&DTr . . . .   *Digested*, 00/**4947**

Alchemea Ltd, Re [1998] B.C.C. 964, Ch D . . . .   *Digested*, 99/**606**

Alcoa Minerals of Jamaica Inc v. Broderick [2000] 3 W.L.R. 23; [2000] B.L.R. 279;
(2000) 2 T.C.L.R. 850; [2000] Env. L.R. 734; (2000) 144 S.J.L.B. 182; *Times*,
March 22, 2000, PC (Jam) . . . .   *Digested*, 00/**1467**

ALCOA/Aluminium lithium alloys (T86/95) [2000] E.P.O.R. 54, EPO (Technical Bd App)

     Digested, 00/**3648**

Alcock v. Chief Constable of South Yorkshire; *sub nom* Jones v. Wright; Penk v. Wright;
Jones v. Chief Constable of South Yorkshire; Copoc v. Chief Constable of South
Yorkshire [1992] 1 A.C. 310; [1991] 3 W.L.R. 1057; [1991] 4 All E.R. 907;
[1992] P.I.Q.R. P1; (1992) 89(3) L.S.G. 34; (1991) 141 N.L.J. 166; (1992) 136
S.J.L.B. 9; *Times*, November 29, 1991; *Independent*, November 29, 1991;
Guardian, December 11, 1991, HL; affirming [1991] 3 All E.R. 88; *Times*, May 6,
1991; *Independent*, May 10, 1991; *Guardian*, May 9, 1991, CA; affirming [1991] 2
W.L.R. 814; [1991] 1 All E.R. 353; (1990) 140 N.L.J. 1717, QBD . . . .   *Digested*, 92/**3250**:
     Applied, 92/3253, 93/2972, 95/6157, 98/3938, 00/531, 01/5352, 01/6665:
     Considered, 95/3682, 97/2615, 98/4035, 99/4059, 00/4213, 00/4220,
     00/6598

Aldavon Co Ltd v. Deverill [1999] 2 E.G.L.R. 69; [1999] 32 E.G. 92, CC (Bromley) . . . .   *Digested*, 99/**3692**

Alder (CICA: Quantum: 2000), Re [2001] 3 Q.R. 16, CICAP [*Ex rel.* Stuart Nicol, Barrister,
Bridewell Chambers, 2 Bridewell Place, London] . . . .   *Digested*, 01/**1678**

Alderson v. North Herefordshire Trust, CC (Hereford) [*Ex rel.* James Hassall, Barrister,
Guildhall Chambers, 22-26 Broad Street, Bristol] . . . .   *Digested*, 01/**641**

Aldrich v. Norwich Union Life Insurance Co Ltd [1998] C.L.C. 1621; [1999] Lloyd's
Rep. I.R. 276, Ch D

Aldrich v. Norwich Union Life Insurance Co Ltd (formerly Norwich Union Life
Insurance Society); *sub nom* Norwich Union Life Insurance Society v. Qureshi;
Norwich Union Life Insurance Co Ltd v. Qureshi [1999] 2 All E.R. (Comm) 707;
[1999] C.L.C. 1963; [2000] Lloyd's Rep. I.R. 1; *Times*, August 13, 1999, CA;
affirming [1998] C.L.C. 1605; [1999] Lloyd's Rep. I.R. 263, QBD (Comm Ct) . .   *Digested*, 99/**3396**

Aldridge v. Edwards [2000] C.P.L.R. 349; *Times*, March 28, 2000, CA . . . .   *Digested*, 00/**596**

Aldwyck Housing Association v. Cunningham (Unreported, May 15, 2000), CC (Luton)
[*Ex rel.* Richard Colbey, Barrister, Francis Taylor Building, Temple, London] . . . . .   *Digested*, 00/**52**

Alec Lobb Garages Ltd v. Total Oil Great Britain Ltd [1985] 1 W.L.R. 173; [1985] 1 All
   E.R. 303; [1985] 1 E.G.L.R. 33; (1985) 273 E.G. 659; (1985) 82 L.S.G. 45;
   (1985) 129 S.J. 83, CA; affirming [1983] 1 W.L.R. 87; [1983] 1 All E.R. 944;
   (1983) 133 N.L.J. 401; 126 S.J. 768, Ch D . . . .   *Digested*, 85/**397**:
                  Applied, 01/4876: *Cited*, 93/2496, 95/3016: *Considered*, 94/2765, 94/2766:
                                                                      Followed, 91/1728
Aleksandr Marinesko and Quint Star, The [1998] 1 Lloyd's Rep. 265, QBD (Adm Ct) . . .   *Digested*, 98/**4418**
Ales Auto SA v. Automobiles Citroen SA [1999] E.C.C. 216, Cass (F). . . . .   *Digested*, 99/**669**
Alex Lawrie Factors Ltd v. Mander Fashions (Unreported, July 26, 2000), CC
   (Leicester) [*Ex rel.* Sunil Iyer, Barrister, Bracton Chambers, Bell Yard, London] . .   *Digested*, 01/**508**
Alex Lawrie Factors Ltd v. Morgan [2001] C.P. Rep. 2; *Times*, August 18, 1999, CA. . . .   *Digested*, 99/**310**
Alex Lawrie Receivable Financing Ltd v. Penge (Unreported, February 2, 1998), CC
   (Central London) [*Ex rel.* Paul Brant, Barrister, Oriel Chambers, Upper Ground
   Floor, 5 Covent Garden, Liverpool, L2 8UD] . . . .   *Digested*, 98/**391**
Alex Pirie and Son's Application, Re see Pirie's Application, Re
Alexander v. Arts Council of Wales [2001] EWCA Civ 514; [2001] 1 W.L.R. 1840;
   [2001] 4 All E.R. 205; [2001] E.M.L.R. 27; (2001) 98(22) L.S.G. 35; (2001)
   145 S.J.L.B. 123; *Times*, April 27, 2001; *Independent*, April 27, 2001, CA . . . . . .   *Digested*, 01/**1827**:
                                                                      Considered, 01/1821
Alexander v. Chief Adjudication Officer [1998] E.L.R. 455, CA
Alexander v. Home Office see Alexander v. Secretary of State for the Home
   Department
Alexander v. Hyland (Unreported, September 18, 2000), CC (Newcastle) [*Ex rel.* Mark
   Beesley, Barrister, 7 Harrington Street, Liverpool] . . . .   *Digested*, 01/**893**
Alexander v. Immigration Appeal Tribunal see R. v. Immigration Appeal Tribunal Ex p.
   Alexander
Alexander v. Lambeth LBC (Unreported, December 14, 1999), CC (Lambeth) [*Ex rel.*
   Jon Holbrook, Barrister, 2 Garden Court, London] . . . .   *Digested*, 00/**3931**
Alexander v. Midland Bank Plc; Lancaster v. Midland Bank Plc; Mulholland v. Midland
   Bank Plc; Osler v. Midland Bank Plc; Rolfe v. Midland Bank Plc [2000] I.C.R.
   464; [1999] I.R.L.R. 723, CA. . . . .   *Digested*, 00/**2984**
Alexander v. Rayson [1936] 1 K.B. 169; 114 A.L.R. 357, CA . . . .   *Applied*, 47-51/1751,
          47-51/5327, 47-51/5378, 47-51/5609, 47-51/7929, 53/1004, 59/542, 78/3048,
          87/432, 88/437: *Approved*, 01/676: *Considered*, 54/1809, 57/998, 61/7207,
                70/144, 71/640, 75/2662, 87/1826: *Distinguished*, 53/3754, 55/1148,
                                                                      55/1502, 60/956
Alexander v. Royal Hotel (Caithness) Ltd; *sub nom* Alexander v. Taylor 2001 S.L.T. 17;
   [2001] 1 E.G.L.R. 6; [2001] 16 E.G. 148; 2000 G.W.D. 33-1258, Ex Div . . . .   *Digested*, 01/**6737**
Alexander v. Secretary of State for the Home Department; *sub nom* Alexander v.
   Home Office [1988] 1 W.L.R. 968; [1988] 2 All E.R. 118; [1988] I.C.R. 685;
   [1988] I.R.L.R. 190; (1988) 85(40) L.S.G. 45, CA; reversing (Unreported,
   December 20, 1984), CC (Southampton) . . . .   *Digested*, 88/**1295**:
                  Applied, 96/2606, 98/2099: *Approved*, 98/5150: *Considered*, 00/2181
Alexander v. Standard Telephones & Cables Ltd (No.1); Wall v. Standard Telephones &
   Cables Ltd (No.1) [1990] I.C.R. 291; [1990] I.R.L.R. 55. . . . .   *Digested*, 91/**1622**
Alexander v. Standard Telephones & Cables Ltd (No.2); Wall v. Standard Telephones &
   Cables Ltd (No.2) [1991] I.R.L.R. 286 . . . .   *Digested*, 91/**1620**:
                                                                      Applied, 98/2107: *Followed*, 98/2110
Alexander v. Taylor see Alexander v. Royal Hotel (Caithness) Ltd
Alexandrou v. Oxford [1993] 4 All E.R. 328; (1991) 3 Admin. L.R. 675; (1991) 155
   L.G. Rev. 566; *Times*, February 19, 1990, CA . . . .   *Digested*, 94/**3384**:
                  Distinguished, 96/4442, 99/3972, 00/4204, 00/4210
Alf Vaughan & Co Ltd (In Receivership) v. Royscot Trust Plc [1999] 1 All E.R. (Comm.)
   856, Ch D . . . .   *Digested*, 99/**847**
Alfa Laval Cheese Systems Ltd v. Wincanton Engineering Ltd [1990] F.S.R. 583, Ch D .   *Followed*, 99/3437
AlfaTel's Trade Mark Application [2001] E.T.M.R. CN6, VrS (Prague)
Alfadda v. Fenn [1999] I.L.Pr. 390, US Ct
Alford v. Superior Developments Ltd see Longlands Farm, Re
Alford v. Thompson (Valuation Officer) [2001] R.V.R. 32, Lands Tr
Alford v. West Bromwich Building Society see Investors Compensation Scheme Ltd v.
   West Bromwich Building Society (No.1)
Alfred C Toepfer v. Continental Grain Co [1974] 1 Lloyd's Rep. 11; (1973) 117 S.J. 649,
   CA; affirming [1973] 1 Lloyd's Rep. 289, QBD (Comm Ct) . . . .   *Digested*, 73/**3027**:
                                                       Applied, 00/892: *Approved*, 84/403
Alfred C Toepfer International GmbH v. Societe Cargill France; *sub nom* Toepfer
   International GmbH v. Societe Cargill France [1998] 1 Lloyd's Rep. 379; [1998]
   C.L.C. 198; *Times*, December 26, 1997, CA [1997] 2 Lloyd's Rep. 98, QBD
   (Comm Ct) . . . .   *Digested*, 98/**761**

Alfred Crompton Amusement Machines Ltd *v.* Customs and Excise Commissioners (No.2) [1974] A.C. 405; [1973] 3 W.L.R. 268; [1973] 2 All E.R. 1169; 117 S.J. 602, HL; affirming [1972] 2 Q.B. 102; [1972] 2 W.L.R. 835; [1972] 2 All E.R. 353; 116 S.J. 198, CA; reversing [1972] 2 All E.R. 353; 115 S.J. 587; *Times,* July 16, 1971, QBD . . . . *Digested,* 73/**2642**:
Applied, 77/2324, 81/**1965**: *Considered,* 80/2131, 81/2142, 82/2551, 86/1519, 87/1688, 88/1593, 91/2863, 99/337: *Followed,* 76/1203, 98/**4879**

Alfred Dunhill Ltd *v.* Diffusion Internationale de Maroquinerie de Prestige Sarl [2001] C.L.C. 949, QBD . . . . *Digested,* 01/**812**

Alfred McAlpine Construction Ltd *v.* Panatown Ltd (No.1); *sub nom* Panatown Ltd *v.* Alfred McAlpine Construction Ltd [2001] 1 A.C. 518; [2000] 3 W.L.R. 946; [2000] 4 All E.R. 97; [2000] C.L.C. 1604; [2000] B.L.R. 331; (2000) 2 T.C.L.R. 547; 71 Con. L.R. 1; [2000] E.G.C.S. 102; (2000) 97(38) L.S.G. 43; (2000) 150 N.L.J. 1299; (2000) 144 S.J.L.B. 240; [2000] N.P.C. 89; *Times,* August 15, 2000, HL; reversing [1998] C.L.C. 636; 88 B.L.R. 67; 58 Con. L.R. 46; (1998) 14 Const. L.J. 267; [1998] E.G.C.S. 19; [1998] N.P.C. 17; *Times,* February 11, 1998, CA . . . . *Digested,* 00/**864**:
Cited, 99/1417

Alfred McAlpine Construction Ltd *v.* Panatown Ltd (No.2) [2001] EWCA Civ 485; 76 Con. L.R. 224, CA. . . . . *Digested,* 01/**875**
Alfred McAlpine Homes (Yorkshire) Ltd *v.* Kirklees MBC (2000) 79 P. & C.R. 352, QBD . . . . . *Digested,* 00/**4528**
Alfred McAlpine Homes Northumbria Ltd *v.* Darlington BC; Alfred McAlpine Homes Northumbria Ltd *v.* Yuill Developments Ltd; Yuill Developments Ltd *v.* Darlington BC [1999] J.P.L. 53; [1998] E.G.C.S. 105, QBD . . . . *Digested,* 99/**4225**
Alfred McAlpine Homes Northumbria Ltd *v.* Yuill Developments Ltd see Alfred McAlpine Homes Northumbria Ltd *v.* Darlington BC
Alfred McAlpine Plc *v.* BAI (Run-Off) Ltd [2000] 1 All E.R. (Comm) 545; [2000] 1 Lloyd's Rep. 437; [2000] C.L.C. 812; (2001) 3 T.C.L.R. 5; 69 Con. L.R. 87; [2000] Lloyd's Rep. I.R. 352, CA; affirming [1998] 2 Lloyd's Rep. 694; [1998] C.L.C. 1145; (1999) 1 T.C.L.R. 92; 66 Con. L.R. 57, QBD (Comm Ct) . . . . *Digested,* 00/**3532**
Algemene Maatschappij voor Investering en Dienstverlening NV (AMID) *v.* Belgium (C141/99) [2000] E.C.R. I-11619; 3 I.T.L. Rep. 201; [2000] S.T.I. 1735, ECJ (6th Chamber)
Alghile *v.* Westminster City Council [2001] EWCA Civ 363; (2001) 33 H.L.R. 57; *Times,* March 9, 2001, CA . . . . *Digested,* 01/**3436**
Algie *v.* Eastern Health and Social Services Board [2000] N.I. 181, QBD (NI) . . . . *Digested,* 00/**5437**
Ali *v.* Courtaulds Textiles Ltd [1999] Lloyd's Rep. Med. 301; (2000) 52 B.M.L.R. 129; *Times,* May 28, 1999, CA. . . . . *Digested,* 99/**465**:
Applied, 01/4460: *Followed,* 01/603

Ali (t/a Bengal Brasserie) *v.* Customs and Excise Commissioners [2001] S.T.I. 574, V&DTr
Ali *v.* McDonagh see Triesman *v.* Ali
Ali (Ifzal) *v.* Secretary of State for the Home Department see R. *v.* Secretary of State for the Home Department Ex p. Ali (Ifzal)
Ali *v.* Switzerland (1999) 28 E.H.R.R. 304; [1998] H.R.C.D. 774, ECHR . . . . *Digested,* 99/**3104**
Ali *v.* Westminster City Council; Nairne *v.* Camden LBC [1999] 1 W.L.R. 384; [1999] 1 All E.R. 450; (1999) 31 H.L.R. 349; [1998] N.P.C. 135; *Times,* September 16, 1998; *Independent,* July 30, 1998, CA . . . . *Digested,* 98/**3003**
Ali Enus *v.* Tower Hamlets LBC (Unreported, September 25, 1997), CC (Central London) [*Ex rel.* Maurice Rifat, Barrister, Verulam Chambers, Peer House, Verulam Street, London] . . . . *Digested,* 98/**2987**
Ali Shipping Corp *v.* Shipyard Trogir [1999] 1 W.L.R. 314; [1998] 2 All E.R. 136; [1998] 1 Lloyd's Rep. 643; [1998] C.L.C. 566; *Independent,* January 26, 1998 (C.S.), CA . . . . *Digested,* 98/**240**
Ali-Sheikh Bahai *v.* Rashidian see Bahai *v.* Rashidian
Alimport *v.* Soubert Shipping Co Ltd [2000] 2 Lloyd's Rep. 447, QBD (Comm Ct) . . . . *Digested,* 00/**4679**
Alipour *v.* Ary; *sub nom* Alipour *v.* UOC Corp (No.1); UOC Corp (No.1), Re; Company (No.002180 of 1986), Re [1997] 1 W.L.R. 534; [1997] B.C.C. 377; [1997] 1 B.C.L.C. 557; *Times,* December 18, 1996, CA . . . . *Digested,* 97/**3088**:
Considered, 97/3101

Alipour *v.* UOC Corp (No.1) see Alipour *v.* Ary
Alipour *v.* UOC Corp (No.2) see UOC Corp (No.2), Re
Alitalia Linee Aeree Italiane SpA *v.* Commission of the European Communities (T296/97) [2001] All E.R. (EC) 193; [2000] E.C.R. II-3871, CFI (3rd Chamber) . . . . . . *Digested,* 01/**787**
All Saints Church, Ecclesall, Re, *Times,* June 8, 1998, Cons Ct. *Digested,* 98/**1789**
All Saints with St Nicholas Church, Icklesham *v.* Customs and Excise Commissioners [2000] S.T.I. 198, V&DTr
All-in-One Design & Build Ltd *v.* Motcomb Estates Ltd (2000) 144 S.J.L.B. 219; *Times,* April 4, 2000; *Independent,* April 10, 2000 (C.S.), QBD (T&CC) [*Ex rel.* Michael Black Q.C., Barrister, 22 Old Buildings, Lincoln's Inn, London] . . . . *Digested,* 00/**1453**
Allan *v.* Morrison [1900] A.C. 604, PC (NZ) . . . . *Considered,* 01/**5167**
Allard Holdings Ltd, Re [2001] 1 B.C.L.C. 404, Ch D . . . . *Digested,* 01/**3747**

Allcard v. Skinner (1887) L.R. 36 Ch. D. 145, CA . . . . *Applied*, 52/1485,
70/1145, 70/1706, 73/419, 74/1691, 81/1251, 82/285, 83/1361.b, 85/396,
86/426, 87/456, 01/4880: *Considered*, 60/1802, 88/1733, 89/1829:
Distinguished, 77/1207: *Followed*, 97/4270

Allen, Re see Debtor (No.367 of 1992), Re
Allen v. Amalgamated Construction Co Ltd (C234/98) [2000] All E.R. (EC) 97;
[1999] E.C.R. I-8643; [2000] 1 C.M.L.R. 1; [2000] C.E.C. 18; [2000] I.C.R.
436; [2000] I.R.L.R. 119; *Times*, December 10, 1999, ECJ (5th Chamber). . . . . . *Digested*, 00/**2233**
Allen v. Bloomsbury HA [1993] 1 All E.R. 651; [1992] P.I.Q.R. Q50; [1992] 3 Med.
L.R. 257, QBD. . . . . *Digested*, 93/**1416**:
Applied, 01/4464: *Considered*, 00/1450
Allen v. BREL Ltd C97/1097, QBD. . . . . *Digested*, 00/**454**
Allen v. British Rail Engineering Ltd (BREL) [2001] EWCA Civ 242; [2001] I.C.R. 942;
[2001] P.I.Q.R. Q10, CA; affirming C970197, QBD. . . . . *Digested*, 01/**4448**
Allen v. Drake (Unreported, December 3, 1998), CC (Poole) [*Ex rel.* Nicholas Moss,
Barrister, 1 Temple Gardens, Temple, London] . . . . *Digested*, 99/**422**
Allen v. Elmbridge BC [1999] B.L.G.R. 65; *Times*, May 20, 1998, QBD . . . . *Digested*, 98/**2857**
Allen v. Gulf Oil Refining Ltd [1981] A.C. 1001; [1981] 2 W.L.R. 188; [1981] 1 All E.R.
353; [1981] J.P.L. 353; 125 S.J. 101, HL; reversing [1980] Q.B. 156; [1979] 3
W.L.R. 523; [1979] 3 All E.R. 1008; [1979] J.P.L. 674; 123 S.J. 737, CA . . . . . . *Digested*, 81/**2003**:
Applied, 92/4130: *Considered*, 93/432, 00/4293: *Followed*, 92/4197
Allen v. Home Office, CC (Central London) [*Ex rel.* Alexander Bastin, Barrister, 2nd
Floor, Francis Taylor Building, Temple, London] . . . . *Digested*, 01/**1524**
Allen v. Mohammed (Unreported, December 10, 1998), CC (Sheffield) [*Ex rel.* Law
Partnership Solicitors, City Plaza, 2 Pinfold Street, Sheffield]. . . . . *Digested*, 99/**1405**
Allen v. Rochdale BC [2000] Ch. 221; [2000] 2 W.L.R. 182; [1999] 3 All E.R. 443;
(2000) 80 P. & C.R. 1, CA . . . . *Digested*, 99/**4953**
Allen v. Sir Alfred McAlpine & Sons Ltd; Bostic v. Bermondsey & Southwark Group
Hospital Management Committee; Sternberg v. Hammond [1968] 2 Q.B. 229;
[1968] 2 W.L.R. 366; [1968] 1 All E.R. 543; 112 S.J. 49; 112 S.J. 72, CA . . . . . . *Digested*, 68/**3104**:
Applied, 69/2846, 69/3838, 69/3840, 71/9211, 72/2811, 74/2143, 74/2944,
76/1614, 77/1802, 81/1966, 93/3336, 94/3693, 95/3889, 98/4023:
Considered, 68/3107, 68/3112, 69/2925, 69/3841, 70/2269, 70/2350,
71/8609, 82/2461, 89/3071, 92/3609, 92/3610, 93/3334, 93/3338,
94/3788, 95/3887: *Distinguished*, 68/3114, 68/3115, 71/114, 72/114,
73/2647: *Explained*, 81/119: *Followed*, 68/3109, 68/3116, 69/2840, 98/3363

Allen v. Unigate Dairies Ltd see Ridehalgh v. Horsefield
Allen v. West Yorkshire Probation Service Community Service Organisation [2001]
EWHC Admin 2; (2001) 165 J.P. 313; (2001) 165 J.P.N. 267; *Times*, February
20, 2001; *Independent*, February 12, 2001 (C.S), QBD . . . . *Digested*, 01/**1098**
Allen v. Whittle (Unreported, February 29, 2000), CC (Croydon) [*Ex rel.* Philip
Goddard, Barrister, 4 King's Bench Walk, 2nd Floor, Temple, London] . . . . *Digested*, 00/**425**
Allen & Hanburys Ltd's (Salbutamol) Patent [1987] R.P.C. 327, CA . . . . *Digested*, 87/**2803**:
Applied, 98/3458
Allen's Application, Re [1998] N.I. 46, QBD (NI) . . . . *Digested*, 99/**5174**:
Applied, 99/5215

Allerdale BC v. Cumbria Wind Farms Ltd (2000) 15 P.A.D. 833, Planning Inspector
Allergan Inc v. Sauflon Pharmaceuticals Ltd; Sauflon Pharmaceuticals Ltd v. Allergan
Inc (2000) 23(4) I.P.D. 23030; (2000) 98(8) L.S.G. 37; *Times*, March 15, 2000;
Independent, March 13, 2000 (C.S), Pat Ct . . . . *Digested*, 00/**3682**
Alles Wird Teurer see TELEKOM Trade Mark
Alleyne-Forte v. Attorney General of Trinidad and Tobago [1998] 1 W.L.R. 68; [1998]
R.T.R. 75; (1997) 141 S.J.L.B. 238, PC (Trin) . . . . *Digested*, 98/**3107**
Alliance against the Birmingham Northern Relief Road v. Secretary of State for the
Environment, Transport and the Regions (No.1) see R. v. Secretary of State for
the Environment, Transport and the Regions Ex p. Alliance Against the
Birmingham Northern Relief Road (No.1)
Alliance against the Birmingham Northern Relief Road v. Secretary of State for the
Environment, Transport and the Regions (No.2) see R. v. Secretary of State for
the Environment, Transport and the Regions Ex p. Alliance against the
Birmingham Northern Relief Road (No.2)
Alliance & Leicester Building Society v. Dhanoa see Alliance & Leicester Building
Society v. Edgestop Ltd (Application for Leave)
Alliance & Leicester Building Society v. Dhanoa see Alliance & Leicester Building
Society v. Edgestop Ltd
Alliance & Leicester Building Society v. Edgestop Ltd; Alliance & Leicester Building
Society v. Dhanoa; Alliance & Leicester Building Society v. Samra [1999] Lloyd's
Rep. P.N. 868, Ch D . . . . *Digested*, 00/**1455**

Alliance & Leicester Building Society v. Edgestop Ltd (Application for Leave); Alliance & Leicester Building Society v. Dhanoa; Alliance & Leicester Building Society v. Samra; Mercantile Credit Co Ltd v. Lancaster; Alliance & Leicester Building Society v. Hamptons; LTA 94/5856/B, CA; affirming [1993] 1 W.L.R. 1462; [1994] 2 All E.R. 38; [1994] 2 E.G.L.R. 229; [1993] E.G.C.S. 93; [1993] N.P.C. 79, Ch D . . . . *Digested,* 95/**2828**: *Applied,* 00/5108

Alliance & Leicester Building Society v. Hamptons see Alliance & Leicester Building Society v. Edgestop Ltd (Application for Leave)

Alliance & Leicester Building Society v. Samra see Alliance & Leicester Building Society v. Edgestop Ltd (Application for Leave)

Alliance & Leicester Building Society v. Samra see Alliance & Leicester Building Society v. Edgestop Ltd

Alliance & Leicester Plc v. Hamer (Inspector of Taxes) [2000] S.T.C. (S.C.D.) 332; [2000] S.T.I. 1010, Sp Comm . . . . *Digested,* 00/**4932**

Alliance & Leicester Plc v. Harrison Robertshaw [1999] E.G.C.S. 149, Ch D

Alliance & Leicester Plc v. Lewis (1999) 96(7) L.S.G. 37, CA

Alliance & Leicester Plc v. Paul Robinson & Co (Leave to Appeal) [2000] C.P. Rep. 3, CA . . . . *Digested,* 99/**357**

Alliance & Leicester Plc v. Slayford [2001] 1 All E.R. (Comm) 1; [2001] C.P. Rep. 52; [2001] B.P.I.R. 555; (2001) 33 H.L.R. 66; [2000] E.G.C.S. 113; (2000) 97(41) L.S.G. 41; (2000) 150 N.L.J. 1590; [2000] N.P.C. 102; (2001) 81 P. & C.R. D10; *Times,* December 19, 2000, CA . . . . *Digested,* 01/**4839**

Alliance Paper Group Plc v. Prestwich (No.1) [1996] I.R.L.R. 25, Ch D . . . . *Digested,* 96/**2602**

Alliance Paper Group Plc v. Prestwich (No.2), *Times,* December 11, 1997, CA . . . . *Digested,* 98/**2191**

Alliance Perpetual Building Society v. Belrum Investments Ltd [1957] 1 W.L.R. 720; [1957] 1 All E.R. 635; 101 S.J. 406, Ch D . . . . *Digested,* 57/**2759**: *Applied,* 57/2236: *Considered,* 68/608: *Distinguished,* 98/49

Allianz Versicherungs AG v. Fortuna Co Inc (The Baltic Universal); *sub nom* Versicherungs AG v. Fortuna Co Inc [1999] 1 W.L.R. 2117; [1999] 2 All E.R. 625; [1999] 1 Lloyd's Rep. 497; [1999] C.L.C. 258, QBD (Comm Ct) . . . . *Digested,* 99/**4456**

Allied Carpets Group Ltd v. Customs and Excise Commissioners [1998] S.T.C. 894; [1998] B.T.C. 5306; [1998] B.V.C. 304; *Independent,* June 15, 1998 (C.S.), QBD . . . . *Digested,* 98/**4974**

Allied Carpets Group Plc v. Nethercott [2001] B.C.C. 81, QBD . . . . *Digested,* 01/**729**

Allied Domecq Leisure Ltd v. Cooper (1999) 163 J.P. 1; [1999] Crim. L.R. 230; (1999) 163 J.P.N. 14; *Times,* October 13, 1998, QBD . . . . *Digested,* 98/**841**

Allied Domecq Plc, Re [2000] B.C.C. 582; [2000] 1 B.C.L.C. 134, Ch D . . . . *Digested,* 00/**682**

Allied Domecq Plc v. Customs and Excise Commissioners (C305/97) see Royscot Leasing Ltd v. Customs and Excise Commissioners (C305/97)

Allied Domecq Plc v. Customs and Excise Commissioners (Withdrawal of Reference) see Royscot Leasing Ltd v. Customs and Excise Commissioners (Withdrawal of Reference)

Allied Domecq Retailing Ltd v. Williams (Valuation Officer) see Williams (Valuation Officer) v. Scottish & Newcastle Retail Ltd

Allied Domecq Spirits & Wine Ltd v. Murray McDavid Ltd 1998 S.C. 354; 1999 S.L.T. 157; [1998] E.T.M.R. 61; [1997] F.S.R. 864; 1997 G.W.D. 35-1816; *Times,* December 9, 1997, OH . . . . *Digested,* 98/**6021**

Allied Dunbar Assurance Plc v. Homebase Ltd; *sub nom* Homebase Ltd v. Allied Dunbar Assurance Plc; A3/2001/1021, CA [2001] 16 E.G.C.S. 146; (2001) 98(17) L.S.G. 40; [2001] N.P.C. 76, Ch D

Allied Finance and Investments Ltd v. Haddock & Co [1983] N.Z.L.R. 22 . . . . *Considered,* 99/4046

Allied Irish Bank Group (UK) Plc v. Hennelly Properties Ltd; *sub nom* AIB Group (UK) Plc v. Hennelley Properties Ltd; B2/2000/2219, CA; affirming [2000] E.G.C.S. 63; *Times,* June 7, 2000; *Independent,* June 26, 2000 (C.S), Ch D . . . . *Digested,* 00/**4665**

Allied Irish Bank Plc v. Ashford Hotels Ltd; Ashford Hotels Ltd v. Higgins [1997] 3 All E.R. 309; [1998] B.C.C. 440, CA . . . . *Digested,* 97/**3048**

Allied London & Scottish Properties Plc v. Riverbrae Construction Ltd 2000 S.L.T. 981; [1999] B.L.R. 346; (2000) 2 T.C.L.R. 398; 68 Con. L.R. 79; 1999 G.W.D. 27-1265; *Times,* November 11, 1999, OH . . . . *Digested,* 99/**5781**

Allied London Property Investment Ltd v. Secretary of State for the Environment (1996) 72 P. & C.R. 327; [1997] J.P.L. 199; [1996] E.G.C.S. 52; [1996] N.P.C. 42; *Times,* March 28, 1996, QBD . . . . *Digested,* 96/**4803**: *Not followed,* 98/4209, 00/4502

Allied Maples Group Ltd v. Simmons & Simmons [1995] 1 W.L.R. 1602; [1995] 4 All E.R. 907; [1996] C.L.C. 153; 46 Con. L.R. 134; [1955-95] P.N.L.R. 701; (1995) 145 N.L.J. 1646; [1995] N.P.C. 83, CA . . . . *Digested,* 96/**4489**: *Applied,* 97/3832, 98/1447, 98/3604, 00/4266, 00/4276: *Considered,* 95/1843, 96/4482, 96/4505, 97/3839, 97/3903, 97/4264: *Not applied,* 01/537: *Referred to,* 97/3917

Allied Marine Transport v. Vale do Rio Doce Navegacao SA (The Leonidas D); Vale do
  Rio Doce Navegacao SA v. Ocean Freighters Corp [1985] 1 W.L.R. 925; [1985]
  2 All E.R. 796; [1985] 2 Lloyd's Rep. 18; (1985) 82 L.S.G. 2160; (1985) 129
  S.J. 431, CA; reversing [1984] 1 W.L.R. 1; [1983] 3 All E.R. 737; [1983] 2 Lloyd's
  Rep. 411; (1983) 127 S.J. 729, QBD (Comm Ct) . . . .   *Digested*, 85/**110**:
                    Applied, 84/94, 87/133: *Considered*, 86/90, 87/147: *Distinguished*, 98/3675
Allison, Re see R. v. Bow Street Metropolitan Stipendiary Magistrate Ex p. United
  States (No.2)
Allium SA v. Alfin Inc [2001] E.C.C. 35, Cass (F)
Allonby v. Accrington and Rossendale College; Allonby v. Education Lecturing
  Services; Allonby v. Department for Education and Employment [2001] EWCA
  Civ 529; [2001] 2 C.M.L.R. 27; [2001] I.C.R. 1189; [2001] I.R.L.R. 364; [2001]
  Emp. L.R. 613; [2001] E.L.R. 679; [2001] Pens. L.R. 185; *Times*, April 3, 2001,
  CA; reversing in part EAT/1300/97, EAT/1080/98, EAT/1081/98, EAT . . . .   *Digested*, 01/**2319**
Allonby v. Department for Education and Employment see Allonby v. Accrington and
  Rossendale College
Allonby v. Education Lecturing Services see Allonby v. Accrington and Rossendale
  College
Alloy Surcharge, Re (IV/35.814) [1998] 4 C.M.L.R. 973, CEC
Allridge (Builders) Ltd v. Grand Actual Ltd 55 Con. L.R. 91, QBD (OR) . . . .   *Digested*, 98/**800**
Allt-Yr-Yn and Caerleon Enterprises & Services Ltd v. Customs and Excise
  Commissioners see University of Wales College, Newport v. Customs and Excise
  Commissioners
Alman v. Approach Housing Ltd [2001] 1 B.C.L.C. 530; [2001] B.P.I.R. 203, Ch D . . . .   *Digested*, 01/**3787**
Almare Societa di Navigazione SpA v. Derby & Co Ltd (The Almare Prima) [1989] 2
  Lloyd's Rep. 376, QBD (Comm Ct) . . . .   *Digested*, 90/**204**
Almond v. Ash Bros & Heaton see Dawkins (Valuation Officer) v. Ash Bros & Heaton
  Ltd
Almond (Valuation Officer) v. Heathfield Laundry (Birmingham) Ltd; Cushing (t/a
  Fakenham Steam Laundry) v. Webber (Valuation Officer) (No.2) [1960] 1 W.L.R.
  1339; [1960] 3 All E.R. 700; 125 J.P. 75; 59 L.G.R. 25; 7 R.R.C. 49; 53 R. & I.T.
  718; 104 S.J. 1056, CA; reversing 52 R. & I.T. 772; [1959] J.P.L. 869, Lands Tr . .   *Digested*, 60/**2687**:
                                    Applied, 00/5678: *Previous proceedings*, 60/2669.110
Alnwick DC v. Secretary of State for the Environment, Transport and the Regions
  (2000) 79 P. & C.R. 130; [1999] 4 P.L.R. 43; [2000] J.P.L. 474; (1999) 96(32)
  L.S.G. 35; (1999) 96(34) L.S.G. 35, QBD . . . .   *Digested*, 00/**4492**
Alpha Steel Ltd v. Commission of the European Communities (14/81) [1982] E.C.R.
  749, ECJ. . . . .   *Digested*, 83/**1410**:
                                                                          Distinguished, 00/724
Alpine Bulk Transport Co Inc v. Saudi Eagle Shipping Co Inc (The Saudi Eagle) [1986] 2
  Lloyd's Rep. 221, CA . . . .   *Digested*, 87/**3044**:
                    Applied, 93/3203, 98/513: *Considered*, 94/2765, 96/757, 96/4984, 00/502:
                                                              Followed, 96/756, 98/514
Alpine Investments BV v. Minister van Financien (C384/93) [1995] All E.R. (EC) 543;
  [1995] E.C.R. I-1141; [1995] 2 B.C.L.C. 214; [1995] 2 C.M.L.R. 209; *Times*, June
  16, 1995, ECJ . . . .   *Digested*, 95/**641**:
                    Considered, 96/1074, 00/4165: *Distinguished*, 99/3191: *Followed*, 98/3855
Alt Landscapes, Re [1999] B.P.I.R. 459, Ch D   *Digested*, 99/**3300**
Altan-Evans v. Leicester LEA [1998] E.L.R. 237; [1997] C.O.D. 113, QBD . . . .   *Digested*, 97/**2131**
Altecnic Ltd v. Reliance Water Controls Ltd see Altecnic Ltd's Trade Mark Application
  (No.2126884)
Altecnic Ltd's Trade Mark Application (No.2126884); *sub nom* Altecnic Ltd v. Reliance
  Water Controls Ltd; Reliance Water Controls Ltd v. Altecnic Ltd; CAREMIX Trade
  Mark [2001] EWCA Civ 1928, CA; reversing [2001] R.P.C. 37, Ch D; reversing
  [2001] R.P.C. 13, TMR . . . .   *Digested*, 01/**4045**
Aluflet SA v. Vinave Empresa de Navegacao Maritima Lda (The Faial) [2000] 1 Lloyd's
  Rep. 473, QBD (Adm Ct) . . . .   *Digested*, 00/**4693**
ALUMINIUM-WERKE/Deep-drawn aluminium container (T591/90) [1998] E.P.O.R. 56,
  EPO (Technical Bd App)
Alusign Ltd's Application for Settlement of Terms of a Licence of Right (1998) 21 (1) I.P.D.
  21010, PO
AM v. SPV see AM v. WC
AM v. WC; AM v. SPV [1999] I.C.R. 1218; [1999] I.R.L.R. 410, EAT. . . . .   *Digested*, 99/**2120**
Amalgamated Investment & Property Co Ltd (In Liquidation) v. Texas Commerce
  International Bank Ltd [1982] Q.B. 84; [1981] 3 W.L.R. 565; [1981] 3 All E.R.
  577; [1982] 1 Lloyd's Rep. 27; [1981] Com. L.R. 236; 125 S.J. 623, CA;
  affirming [1981] 2 W.L.R. 554; [1981] 1 All E.R. 923; [1981] Com. L.R. 37; 125
  S.J. 133, QBD (Comm Ct) . . . .   *Digested*, 81/**1273**:
                    Applied, 84/3161, 86/44, 86/1883, 88/1371, 89/1531, 94/4047, 96/1229:
                    Considered, 82/421, 85/407, 93/2456, 96/3694, 97/1005, 01/410:
                    Followed, 97/3171: *Not followed*, 96/1230: *Referred to*, 82/1145
Amann v. Switzerland (2000) 30 E.H.R.R. 843, ECHR . . . .   *Digested*, 01/**3585**:
                                                        Considered, 00/921: *Distinguished*, 01/980
Amaron Ltd, Re (No.1) see Secretary of State for Trade and Industry v. Lubrani (No.1)

Amaron Ltd, Re (No.2) see Secretary of State for Trade and Industry *v.* Lubrani (No.2)

Amatyakul *v.* Olding (1997) 97(5/6) Q.R. 11, CC (Canterbury) . . . .   *Digested*, 98/**1599**

AMAZE COLLECTION Trade Mark [1999] R.P.C. 725, TMR . . . .   *Digested*, 99/**3590**

Amazon.com Inc *v.* Barnesandnoble.com Inc [2001] E.B.L.R. 47, US Ct

Amazon.com Inc *v.* Citi Services Inc [2001] E.T.M.R. 95, Protodikeio (Athens)

AMB Imballaggi Plastici Srl *v.* Pacflex Ltd [1999] 2 All E.R. (Comm) 249; [1999] C.L.C. 1391; [2000] E.C.C. 381; [1999] Eu. L.R. 930; (1999) 18 Tr. L.R. 153; (1999) 96(27) L.S.G. 34; *Times*, July 8, 1999, CA; affirming (1999) 17 Tr. L.R. 557, QBD (Merc Ct) . . . .   *Digested*, 99/**109**

Ambase Corp *v.* Commissioner of Internal Revenue 3 I.T.L. Rep. 834, US Ct

Ambassador Life Co Ltd, Re see Hill Samuel Life Assurance Ltd, Re

Amber *v.* Stacey [2001] 1 W.L.R. 1225; [2001] 2 All E.R. 88; [2001] C.P. Rep. 26; [2001] C.P.L.R. 37; (2001) 3 T.C.L.R. 20; [2001] 2 Costs L.R. 325; (2000) 150 N.L.J. 1755; *Daily Telegraph*, November 28, 2000, CA . . . .   *Digested*, 01/**503**: *Applied*, 01/502

Amber Valley BC *v.* Fretwell (1999) 14 P.A.D. 407, Planning Inspector

Ambler *v.* Bolton (1872) L.R. 14 Eq. 427, Ct of Chancery . . . .   *Considered*, 92/108, 99/4092

Amec Civil Engineering Ltd *v.* Cheshire CC [1999] B.L.R. 303, QBD (T&CC) . . . .   *Digested*, 99/**793**

Amec Developments Ltd *v.* Jury's Hotel Management (UK) Ltd (2001) 82 P. & C.R. 22; [2001] 1 E.G.L.R. 81; [2001] 07 E.G. 163; [2000] E.G.C.S. 138; [2000] N.P.C. 125, Ch D . . . .   *Digested*, 01/**1549**

Amec Process & Energy Ltd *v.* Stork Engineers & Contractors BV (Costs Order) [2000] B.L.R. 70, QBD (T&CC). . . . .   *Digested*, 00/**458**

Amec Process & Energy Ltd *v.* Stork Engineers & Contractors BV (Preliminary Issues) 68 Con. L.R. 17, QBD (T&CC) . . . .   *Digested*, 00/**817**

Amerada Hess *v.* Rome (2000) 97(10) L.S.G. 36; (2000) 144 S.J.L.B. 126; *Times*, March 15, 2000, QBD . . . .   *Digested*, 00/**565**

Amerada Hess Ltd *v.* Inland Revenue Commissioners; *sub nom* Inland Revenue Commissioners *v.* Amerada Hess Ltd [2001] S.T.C. 420; 73 T.C. 488; [2001] B.T.C. 8003; [2001] S.T.I. 283; *Times*, March 20, 2001, Ch D; affirming [2000] S.T.C. (S.C.D.) 397; [2000] S.T.I. 1239, Sp Comm . . . .   *Digested*, 01/**5294**

American Air Liquide Inc *v.* Internal Revenue Commissioner 3 I.T.L. Rep. 249, US Ct

American Cyanamid Co *v.* Ethicon Ltd [1975] A.C. 396; [1975] 2 W.L.R. 316; [1975] 1 All E.R. 504; [1975] F.S.R. 101; [1975] R.P.C. 513; 119 S.J. 136, HL; reversing [1974] F.S.R. 312, CA . . . .   *Digested*, 75/**2640**: *Applied*, 75/445, 75/2453, 76/317, 76/2116, 76/2155, 76/2156, 76/2157, 76/2806, 77/375, 77/885, 77/1097, 77/2307, 77/2346, 81/2164, 83/2987, 84/2644, 84/3529, 84/3554, 85/1791, 85/2054, 85/2058, 87/1296, 87/3023, 87/3037, 88/1620, 88/2656, 89/1729, 91/3463, 91/4030, 92/4143, 93/1734, 93/2356, 93/3264, 93/3278, 93/3285, 93/3799, 96/791, 96/3816, 97/4888, 98/3471, 98/3511, 99/686, 01/567: *Considered*, 75/319, 76/276, 77/413, 77/1787, 79/1656, 80/1354, 80/2152, 82/3280, 83/481, 83/2969, 83/2973, 83/3605, 83/3796, 84/420, 84/1903, 84/3553, 85/1881, 86/2646, 87/1295, 87/2768, 87/3035, 87/3039, 88/1245, 88/2146, 88/2871, 88/2872, 88/3559, 89/1408, 89/1468, 89/3688, 90/3697, 91/2885, 91/4032, 92/4422, 94/3046, 96/2709, 96/4566, 97/631, 97/4882, 98/437, 99/5082, 01/570, 01/772, 01/2462: *Distinguished*, 76/2160, 86/2648, 86/3285, 87/3027, 88/3398, 91/2886, 93/2470: *Explained*, 84/2656: *Followed*, 91/2694, 92/4134, 97/868, 97/3873, 98/3445: *Not followed*, 77/2213

AMERICAN CYANAMID/Melamine derivatives (T279/93) [1999] E.P.O.R. 88, EPO (Technical Bd App)

American Express Europe Ltd *v.* Adamson see Olympia & York Canary Wharf Ltd (No.1), Re

American Home Products Corp *v.* Novartis Pharmaceuticals UK Ltd [2001] R.P.C. 8; (2000) 23(10) I.P.D. 23080, CA; reversing [2000] R.P.C. 547; (2000) 23(2) I.P.D. 23010, Pat Ct

American Home Products Corp *v.* Novartis Pharmaceuticals UK Ltd (Application for Disclosure); *sub nom* American Home Products Corp *v.* Novartis Pharmaceuticals UK Ltd (No.2) [2001] EWCA Civ 165; [2001] F.S.R. 41; (2001) 24(4) I.P.D. 24021, CA; reversing (2001) 24(2) I.P.D. 24010, Pat Ct . . . .   *Digested*, 01/**3866**

American Home Products Corp *v.* Novartis Pharmaceuticals UK Ltd (No.2) see American Home Products Corp *v.* Novartis Pharmaceuticals UK Ltd (Application for Disclosure)

American Home Products Corp's Trade Mark Application [2001] E.T.M.R. 51, PO (Irl)

AMERICAN HOME PRODUCTS/Canine coronavirus (T977/93) [2001] E.P.O.R. 36, EPO (Technical Bd App) . . . .   *Digested*, 01/**3938**

American Leaf Blending Co Sdn Bhd *v.* Director General of Inland Revenue [1979] A.C. 676; [1978] 3 W.L.R. 985; [1978] 3 All E.R. 1185; [1978] S.T.C. 561; [1978] T.R. 243; 122 S.J. 641, PC (Mal). . . . .   *Digested*, 79/**270**: *Cited*, 98/4622

American Power Conversion Corp's Trade Mark Application [2001] E.T.M.R. CN9, PO

American Screw Co's Application, Re [1959] R.P.C. 344 . . . . *Digested*, 60/**3220**:
                                           Considered, 98/3534: *Followed*, 94/4496

Amersham Pharmacia Biotech AB *v.* Amicon Ltd [2001] EWCA Civ 1042; (2001) 24(12) I.P.D. 24078, CA; affirming (2001) 24(2) I.P.D. 24011, Pat Ct

Amersham Pharmacia Biotech UK Ltd (Community Trade Mark Application No.846691) (2000) 23(10) I.P.D. 23082, OHIM (1st Bd App)

AMGEN/Fresh ground of opposition (T736/95) [2001] E.P.O.R. 55, EPO (Technical Bd App) . . . . *Digested*, 01/**3892**

Amgulf Polymers & Chemicals Ltd *v.* Owners of the Athinoula [2001] 2 All E.R. (Comm) 821; [2001] C.L.C. 935, QBD (Adm Ct) . . . . *Digested*, 01/**670**:
                                           Applied, 01/664

Amin *v.* Hussain (Unreported, August 17, 1998), CC (Accrington) [*Ex rel.* David Bridgman, Barrister, 1 Serjeant's Inn, Fifth Floor, Fleet Street, London] . . . . *Digested*, 98/**533**:
                                           Overruled, 99/431

Amin *v.* Hussain (Appeal to Circuit Judge) (Unreported, January 29, 1999), CC (Burnley) [*Ex rel.* David Bridgman, Barrister, 1 Serjeant's Inn, Fifth Floor, Fleet Street, London]. . . . . *Digested*, 99/**431**

Ammerlaan Agro Projecten BV *v.* Les Serres de Cosquerou [1999] I.L.Pr. 627, Cass (F)

Amministrazione delle Finanze dello Stato *v.* Marine Insurance Consultants Srl (C280/96) see Ansaldo Energia SpA *v.* Amministrazione delle Finanze dello Stato (C279/96)

Amministrazione delle Finanze dello Stato *v.* San Giorgio SpA (C199/82) [1983] E.C.R. 3595; [1985] 2 C.M.L.R. 658, ECJ . . . . *Digested*, 85/**1433**:
                               Applied, 95/5067, 96/2803, 00/2406

Amministrazione delle Finanze dello Stato *v.* Simmenthal SpA (No.2) (106/77); *sub nom* Italian Tax and Revenue Administration *v.* SA Simmenthal, Monza (Italy) (106/77) [1978] E.C.R. 629; [1978] 3 C.M.L.R. 263; *Times*, March 13, 1978, ECJ . . . . *Digested*, 78/**1299**:
                           Applied, 98/4972: *Considered*, 91/4030, 94/2766

Amoabeng *v.* El-Sawy Travel Ltd (Unreported, November 17, 1999), CC (Bow) [*Ex rel.* Anna Short, Barrister, Halton House, 20-23 High Holborn, London] . . . . *Digested*, 00/**4047**

Amoah *v.* Barking and Dagenham LBC (2001) 82 P. & C.R. D6, Ch D

Amoco (UK) Exploration Co *v.* British American Offshore Ltd (Disclosure of Documents) [2000] C.P. Rep. 51, QBD (Comm Ct) . . . . *Digested*, 00/**313**

Amoco (UK) Exploration Co *v.* British American Offshore Ltd (Service of Process) [1999] 2 All E.R. (Comm) 201; [1999] 2 Lloyd's Rep. 772; [2001] I.L.Pr. 15, QBD (Comm Ct). . . . . *Digested*, 99/**527**

Amoco (UK) Exploration Co *v.* Imperial Chemical Industries Plc (ICI) see Amoco (UK) Exploration Co *v.* Teesside Gas Transportation Ltd

Amoco (UK) Exploration Co *v.* Teesside Gas Transportation Ltd; Amoco (UK) Exploration Co *v.* Imperial Chemical Industries Plc (ICI) [2001] UKHL 18; [2001] 1 All E.R. (Comm) 865, HL. . . . . *Digested*, 01/**4552**

AMOCO/Thermoplastic polymers (T749/89) [1998] E.P.O.R. 295, EPO (Technical Bd App)

Amonoo *v.* Grant (1999) 96(1) L.S.G. 25, QBD

Amoo-Gottfried *v.* Legal Aid Board, *Independent*, December 8, 2000, CA . . . . *Digested*, 01/**4229**

AMP (UK) Plc *v.* Barker [2001] Pens. L.R. 77; [2001] W.T.L.R. 1237; (2000-01) 3 I.T.E.L.R. 414, Ch D . . . . *Digested*, 01/**4595**

Ampleforth Abbey Trust *v.* Customs and Excise Commissioners [1999] B.V.C. 2083, V&DTr

AMR (Adoption: Procedure), Re [1999] 2 F.L.R. 807; [1999] 3 F.C.R. 734; [1999] Fam. Law 684, Fam Div. . . . . *Digested*, 00/**2436**:
                                           Considered, 00/2434

AMS *v.* Child Support Officer [1998] 1 F.L.R. 955; [1998] 2 F.C.R. 622; [1998] Fam. Law 388, CA . . . . *Digested*, 98/**2470**

Amstrad Plc *v.* Seagate Technology Inc 86 B.L.R. 34; [1998] Masons C.L.R. Rep. 1, QBD. . . . . *Digested*, 98/**4384**

Amuur *v.* France (1996) 22 E.H.R.R. 533, ECHR . . . . *Digested*, 97/**2766**:
                                   Applied, 01/3620: *Considered*, 00/3248

Anacon Corp Ltd *v.* Environmental Research Technology Ltd [1994] F.S.R. 659, Ch D . *Digested*, 95/**852**:
                                         Considered, 97/1030, 98/3416

ANC Ltd *v.* Clark Goldring & Page Ltd [2001] B.C.C. 479; [2001] B.P.I.R. 568; *Times*, May 31, 2000, CA. . . . . *Digested*, 00/**859**

Ancare New Zealand Ltd *v.* Fort Dodge New Zealand Ltd see Ancare New Zealand Ltd's Patent, Re

Ancare New Zealand Ltd's Patent, Re; *sub nom* Ancare New Zealand Ltd *v.* Fort Dodge New Zealand Ltd; 32 of 2001, PC (NZ); affirming [2001] R.P.C. 20, CA (NZ). . . *Digested*, 01/**3967**

Ancell & Ancell *v.* McDermott [1993] 4 All E.R. 355; [1993] R.T.R. 235; (1994) 6 Admin. L.R. 473; (1995) 159 L.G. Rev. 389; (1993) 90(11) L.S.G. 46; (1993) 143 N.L.J. 363; (1993) 137 S.J.L.B. 36; [1994] J.P.I.L. 78; *Times*, February 4, 1993; *Independent*, February 18, 1993, CA; reversing *Times*, February 17, 1992, QBD. . . . . *Digested*, 93/**2958**:
                                           Distinguished, 99/3972

Anchor Brewhouse Developments *v.* Jaggard see Marcel *v.* Commissioner of Police of the Metropolis

Anchor Foods Ltd v. Customs and Excise Commissioners (Inspection of Documents)
[1998] V. & D.R. 108, V&DTr . . . .   *Digested,* 00/**5359**
And So To Bed Ltd v. Dixon [2001] F.S.R. 47, Ch D
Anderson v. British Coal Corp, *Times,* February 8, 1993, QBD . . . .   *Digested,* 93/**1753**:
                                                                                                       Applied, 99/2074
Anderson v. Dalkeith Engineering (In Receivership) [1985] I.C.R. 66; [1984] I.R.L.R.
429, EAT. . . . .   *Digested,* 85/**1263**:
                                              Disapproved, 98/2213: *Not followed,* 87/1416
Anderson v. Dundee City Council 2000 S.L.T. (Sh Ct) 134; 1999 S.C.L.R. 518; 1999
Hous. L.R. 82; [2000] E.H.L.R. Dig. 96; 1999 G.W.D. 1-52, Sh Ct (Tayside) . . . .   *Digested,* 99/**6379**
Anderson v. Eastlea Training Centre (Unreported, June 4, 2001), CC (Clerkenwell) [*Ex
rel.* Pattinson & Brewer, Solicitors, 30 Great James Street, London] . . . .   *Digested,* 01/**3306**
Anderson v. Forth Valley Health Board 1998 S.L.T. 588; 1998 S.C.L.R. 97; (1998) 44
B.M.L.R. 108; 1998 Rep. L.R. 3; 1997 G.W.D. 39-2016, OH . . . .   *Digested,* 98/**6115**:
                                                 Applied, 00/1464: *Considered,* 00/4200
Anderson v. Halifax Plc [2000] N.I. 1, Ch D (NI) . . . .   *Digested,* 00/**5532**
Anderson v. Hyde (t/a Hyde Property Services) [1996] N.I. 304; [1996] 2 B.C.L.C.
144; *Times,* May 2, 1996, CA (NI) . . . .   *Digested,* 96/**6205**
Anderson v. Ministry of Defence see Ministry of Defence v. Wheeler
Anderson v. Pringle of Scotland Ltd 1998 S.L.T. 754; [1998] I.R.L.R. 64; 1997 G.W.D.
40-2033; *Times,* May 18, 1998, OH . . . .   *Digested,* 98/**5814**:
                                                                                                    Considered, 99/6033
Anderson Berry, Re; Harris v. Griffith [1928] Ch. 290, CA . . . .   *Followed,* 63/1590,
                                                                                                               99/3227
Andersson v. Sweden (C321/97) [1999] E.C.R. I-3551; [2000] 2 C.M.L.R. 191, ECJ . .   *Digested,* 00/**2380**
Andersson (Anne-Marie) v. Sweden (1998) 25 E.H.R.R. 722, ECHR. . . . .   *Digested,* 99/**3119**
Anderton v. Clwyd CC see Phelps v. Hillingdon LBC
Anderton v. Clwyd CC [2001] C.P. Rep. 110, QBD . . . .   *Digested,* 01/**643**
Anderton v. Clwyd CC (Disclosure of Records) [1999] E.L.R. 1, CA; reversing [1998]
E.L.R. 533, QBD . . . .   *Digested,* 99/**4010**:
                                                    Subsequent proceedings, 00/1947
Anderton v. Granulators Ltd (Unreported, May 20, 1998), CC (Oldham) [*Ex rel.*
Pannone & Partners Solicitors, 123 Deansgate, Manchester] . . . .   *Digested,* 99/**1468**
Anderton & Rowland v. Rowland, *Times,* November 5, 1999, QBD (Merc Ct) . . . .   *Digested,* 99/**845**
Andre Cayman Islands Trading Co v. Stolt Nielson BV (The Sun Sapphire) [2000] C.L.C.
156, QBD (Comm Ct) . . . .   *Digested,* 00/**4700**
Andre et Cie SA v. Universal Bulk Carriers Ltd see Universal Bulk Carriers Pte Ltd v.
Andre et Cie SA
Andrea Merzario Ltd v. Internationale Spedition Leitner Gesellschaft GmbH [2001]
EWCA Civ 61; [2001] 1 All E.R. (Comm) 883; [2001] 1 Lloyd's Rep. 490; [2001]
C.L.C. 643; (2001) 98(9) L.S.G. 41; (2001) 145 S.J.L.B. 54; *Times,* February
27, 2001; *Daily Telegraph,* February 13, 2001, CA; affirming 1999 Folio 1256, QBD
(Comm Ct) . . . .   *Digested,* 01/**5419**
Andreae v. Selfridge & Co Ltd [1938] Ch. 1, CA. . . . .   *Applied,* 53/2812:
                                 Considered, 62/2774, 00/4293: *Distinguished,* 98/4041
Andreas Stihl AG & Co's Trade Mark Application [2001] R.P.C. 12, TMR . . . .   *Digested,* 01/**4042**
Andreou v. Institute of Chartered Accountants in England and Wales [1998] 1 All E.R.
14, CA . . . .   *Digested,* 98/**98**
Andrew v. Bellman (Unreported, March 16, 2000), CC (Watford) [*Ex rel.* Nicholas
Preston, Barrister, Bracton Chambers, 8 Bell Yard, London] . . . .   *Digested,* 00/**576**
Andrew v. Kounnis Freeman [1999] 2 B.C.L.C. 641; [2000] Lloyd's Rep. P.N. 263, CA .   *Digested,* 00/**4205**
Andrew Grant Services Ltd v. Watton (Inspector of Taxes) see Grant v. Watton
(Inspector of Taxes)
Andrews (Thomas Charles), Re [1999] 1 W.L.R. 1236; [1999] 2 All E.R. 751; [2000] C.P.
Rep. 30; [1999] 2 B.C.L.C. 442; [1999] 2 Costs L.R. 133; (1999) 96(14) L.S.G. 31;
(1999) 143 S.J.L.B. 105; *Times,* March 19, 1999; *Independent,* March 3, 1999,
CA . . . .   *Digested,* 99/**971**
Andrews v. Barkers & Stonehouse Ltd, CC (Willesden) [*Ex rel.* Nigel Ffitch, Barrister,
Phoenix Chambers, Gray's Inn, London] . . . .   *Digested,* 01/**891**
Andrews v. Barkers & Stonehouse Ltd (Quantum) [2001] 5 Q.R. 17, CC (Willesden)
[*Ex rel.* Nigel Ffitch, Barrister, Phoenix Chambers, Gray's Inn, London] . . . .   *Digested,* 01/**1793**
Andrews (t/a BA Contractors) v. Bradshaw [2000] B.L.R. 6; *Times,* October 11, 1999,
CA . . . .   *Digested,* 99/**223**
Andrews v. Brewer; *sub nom* Brewer v. Andrews (1998) 30 H.L.R. 203; [1997]
E.G.C.S. 19, CA . . . .   *Digested,* 98/**3596**:
                                                                                                    Considered, 98/3598
Andrews v. Initial Cleaning Services Ltd [2000] I.C.R. 166; (1999) 96(33) L.S.G. 31;
Times, August 18, 1999, CA . . . .   *Digested,* 99/**1377**
Andrews v. Law Society of British Columbia (1989) 56 D.L.R. (4th) 1, Sup Ct (Can). . .   *Followed,* 98/2124

Andrews (Deceased) *v.* Lewisham and Guys Mental Health NHS Trust; *sub nom* Harris (Personal Representatives of Andrews (Deceased)) *v.* Lewisham and Guys Mental Health NHS Trust; Lewisham and Guys Mental Health NHS Trust *v.* Andrews (Deceased) [2000] 3 All E.R. 769; [2000] I.C.R. 707; [2000] I.R.L.R. 320; (2000) 97(15) L.S.G. 40; (2000) 144 S.J.L.B. 159; *Times*, March 28, 2000; *Independent*, March 29, 2000, CA; reversing [1999] I.C.R. 774; [1999] I.R.L.R. 407; [1999] Disc. L.R. 143; *Times*, April 21, 1999, EAT . . . . *Digested*, 00/**2130**

Andrews *v.* Russell (Valuation Officer) [2001] R.A. 333, Lands Tr

Andrews *v.* Secretary of State for Health (Damages Assessments); *sub nom* Creutzfeldt-Jakob Disease Litigation (No.9), Re; CJD Litigation (No.9), Re (2000) 54 B.M.L.R. 111, QBD . . . . *Digested*, 00/**4196**

Andrews *v.* Secretary of State for the Environment, Transport and the Regions [2000] P.L.C.R. 366; [2000] J.P.L. 1080 (Note), QBD . . . . *Digested*, 00/**4496**

Andronicou *v.* Cyprus (1998) 25 E.H.R.R. 491; 3 B.H.R.C. 389; [1998] Crim. L.R. 823, ECHR . . . . *Digested*, 98/**3157**

Anduff Carwash Ltd *v.* Attwood (Inspector of Taxes) see Attwood (Inspector of Taxes) *v.* Anduff Car Wash Ltd

Aneco Reinsurance Underwriting Ltd (In Liquidation) *v.* Johnson & Higgins Ltd; *sub nom* Aneco Reinsurance Underwriting Ltd *v.* Johnson & Higgs Ltd [2001] UKHL 51; [2001] 2 All E.R. (Comm) 929, HL; affirming [2000] 1 All E.R. (Comm) 129; [1999] C.L.C. 1918; [2000] Lloyd's Rep. I.R. 12; [2000] Lloyd's Rep. P.N. 1; [2000] P.N.L.R. 152, CA; affirming in part [1998] 1 Lloyd's Rep. 565; *Times*, November 14, 1997, QBD (Comm Ct) . . . . *Digested*, 00/**4252**

Aneco Reinsurance Underwriting Ltd *v.* Johnson & Higgs Ltd see Aneco Reinsurance Underwriting Ltd (In Liquidation) *v.* Johnson & Higgins Ltd

Angestelltenbetriebsrat der Wiener Gebietskrankenkasse *v.* Wiener Gebietskrankenkasse (C309/97) [1999] E.C.R. I-2865; [1999] 2 C.M.L.R. 1173; [2000] I.C.R. 1134; [1999] I.R.L.R. 804; *Times*, May 20, 1999, ECJ . . . . *Digested*, 99/**2069**

Anglesey CBC *v.* Walker (2001) 16 P.A.D. 4, Planning Inspector

Anglia Hastings & Thanet Building Society *v.* House & Son [1955-95] P.N.L.R. 209, QBD

Anglian Water Services Ltd *v.* Crawshaw Robbins & Co Ltd [2001] B.L.R. 173; [2001] N.P.C. 32, QBD . . . . *Digested*, 01/**933**

Anglo American Insurance Co Ltd, Re [2001] 1 B.C.L.C. 755, Ch D (Companies Ct) . . . *Digested*, 01/**3748**

Anglo Group Plc *v.* Winther Browne & Co Ltd; *sub nom* Winther Brown & Co Ltd *v.* Anglo Group Plc 72 Con. L.R. 118; [2000] I.T.C.L.R. 559; [2000] Masons C.L.R. 13; (2000) 144 S.J.L.B. 197, QBD (T&CC)

Anglo Leasing Plc *v.* Pascoe [1997] C.C.L.R. 69, CA . . . . *Digested*, 98/**622**

Anglo-Moravian Hungarian Junction Railway Co Ex p. Watkin, Re (1875-76) L.R. 1 Ch. D. 130, CA . . . . *Applied*, 99/3311

Anglo-Soviet Shipping Co Ltd *v.* Beldis, The see Beldis, The

Anglodent Co *v.* Customs and Excise Commissioners [2001] S.T.I. 262, V&DTr

Angonese *v.* Cassa di Risparmio di Bolzano SpA (C281/98) [2000] All E.R. (EC) 577; [2000] E.C.R. I-4139; [2000] 2 C.M.L.R. 1120; [2000] C.E.C. 374, ECJ . . . . . . *Digested*, 00/**2387**

Angora Trust, Re see Rosewood Trust Ltd *v.* Schmidt

Anheuser Busch Inc *v.* Budejovicky Budvar Narodni Podnik see BUDWEISER Trade Marks

Anheuser Busch Inc *v.* Budejovicky Budvar Narodni Podnik [2001] E.T.M.R. 7, BG (Swi)

Anheuser-Busch Inc *v.* Budejovicky Budvar NP (t/a Budweiser Budvar Brewery) [1984] F.S.R. 413; (1984) 81 L.S.G. 1369; (1984) 128 S.J. 398, CA . . . . *Digested*, 84/**3528**: *Applied*, 98/3518: *Considered*, 96/3638, 97/4905: *Not followed*, 90/4320: *Referred to*, 95/4945

Aniagwu *v.* Hackney LBC; Aniagwu *v.* Owens [1999] I.R.L.R. 303, EAT . . . . *Digested*, 99/**2099**: *Distinguished*, 00/2128

Aniagwu *v.* Owens see Aniagwu *v.* Hackney LBC

Anisminic Ltd *v.* Foreign Compensation Commission (No.2) [1969] 2 A.C. 147; [1969] 2 W.L.R. 163; [1969] 1 All E.R. 208; (1968) 113 S.J. 55; *Times*, December 18, 1968, HL; reversing [1968] 2 Q.B. 862; [1967] 3 W.L.R. 382; [1967] 3 All E.R. 986; 111 S.J. 374, CA; reversing [1969] 2 A.C. 223, QBD . . . . *Digested*, 69/**1866**: *Applied*, 70/2778, 74/3742, 78/2324, 79/19, 80/1639, 84/447, 92/2435, 93/2167, 96/4839, 00/5979, 01/81: *Considered*, 68/1909, 70/2436, 84/3464.A, 84/3483, 85/2791, 85/3415, 86/950, 88/2417, 88/3418, 89/3626, 90/4424, 94/1896, 96/2508: *Distinguished*, 76/19, 92/2740, 92/3464, 94/5367: *Explained*, 80/273: *Not applied*, 92/163, 93/63: *Referred to*, 92/6511

Anker & Jerome *v.* J&J Securities (Unreported, January 8, 1999) . . . . *Considered*, 00/514

Anker-Petersen *v.* Anker-Petersen [2000] W.T.L.R. 581, Ch D . . . . *Digested*, 01/**5533**

Ankerl *v.* Switzerland (17748/91) (2001) 32 E.H.R.R. 1, ECHR . . . . *Followed*, 98/3125

Anklagemyndigheden (Public Prosecutor) *v.* PM Poulsen and Diva Navigation (C286/90) [1992] E.C.R. I-6019, ECJ . . . . *Digested*, 93/**4314**: *Referred to*, 99/3555

Ankrah *v.* DPP [1998] R.T.R. 169 (Note), QBD

Anley Maritime Agencies Ltd, Re [1999] Eu. L.R. 97, QBD (NI) . . . . *Digested*, 99/**5150**

24

Annable v. Southern Derbyshire HA see Heil v. Rankin
Annable v. Southern Derbyshire HA (Costs) see Heil v. Rankin (Costs)
ANNE FRANK Trade Mark [1998] E.T.M.R. 687; [1998] R.P.C. 379,TMR. . . . .   *Digested*, 98/**3437**
Annibaldi v. Sindaco del Comune di Guidonia (C309/96) [1997] E.C.R. I-7493;
    [1998] 2 C.M.L.R. 187, ECJ (1st Chamber)
Annodeus Ltd v. Gibson, *Times*, March 3, 2000, Ch D . . . .   *Digested*, 00/**614**:
                                                                                                    Applied, 01/664

Anns v. Merton LBC; *sub nom* Anns v. Walcroft Property Co Ltd [1978] A.C. 728;
    [1977] 2 W.L.R. 1024; [1977] 2 All E.R. 492; 75 L.G.R. 555; (1977) 243 E.G.
    523; (1988) 4 Const. L.J. 100; [1977] J.P.L. 514; (1987) 84 L.S.G. 319; (1987)
    137 N.L.J. 794; 121 S.J. 377, HL; affirming [1976] Q.B. 882; [1976] 2 W.L.R.
    512; 74 L.G.R. 374; (1976) 241 E.G. 311; 120 S.J. 216, CA; reversing (Unreported,
    October 24, 1975), HC. . . . .   *Digested*, 77/**2030**:
                            Applied, 78/1550, 78/2067, 79/213, 79/1865, 79/2570, 80/198, 81/1837,
                               81/1849, 81/1859, 81/1860, 81/3409, 82/339, 82/2134, 82/4055, 83/2531,
                                     83/2535, 83/2538, 83/2746, 84/2337, 84/3044, 85/952, 85/1603,
                               85/2303, 86/210, 87/241, 87/242, 87/2579, 87/2857, 87/3153, 88/2442,
                            90/5493, 95/3452, 99/274: *Cited*, 00/4232: *Considered*, 80/1878, 82/2266,
                                     84/2298, 84/2300, 84/2566, 85/2305, 85/3549, 86/2252, 86/2259,
                                     86/4338, 87/2580, 87/2586, 87/2591, 87/3466, 88/2418, 88/2433,
                               88/2435, 88/2438, 88/2444, 88/2457, 88/2465, 88/3409, 88/3410,
                            89/259, 89/469, 89/2564, 89/2566, 90/3270, 94/2278, 94/3749, 94/4517,
                               94/5335, 95/3659, 95/3681, 95/4189: *Distinguished*, 78/1547, 83/2523,
                               87/2709.a, 92/3197: *Followed*, 78/2062, 80/1879, 82/766, 82/2125,
                               82/2133: *Not followed*, 86/2274: *Overruled*, 76/1873, 90/3288, 91/2661:
                                     Referred to, 78/2074, 79/1866, 79/1884, 83/2521, 87/3582
Anns v. Walcroft Property Co Ltd see Anns v. Merton LBC
ANON/Appointment of Professional Representative (J17/98) [2001] E.P.O.R. 7, EPO
    (Legal Bd App) . . . .   *Digested*, 01/**3894**
Anonima Petroli Italiana SpA and Neste Oy v. Marlucidez Armadora SA (The Filiatra
    Legacy) [1991] 2 Lloyd's Rep. 337, CA; reversing [1990] 1 Lloyd's Rep. 354;
    Times, November 21, 1989, QBD (Comm Ct) . . . .   *Digested*, 92/**3920**:
                                                                                                    Considered, 00/329
Anonymous Greek Co of General Insurances v. AIG Europe (UK) Ltd see AIG Europe
    (UK) Ltd v. Ethniki
Anraj Fish Products Industries Ltd v. Hyundai Merchant Marine Co Ltd [2000] I.L.Pr.
    717, Fed Ct (Can) . . . .   *Digested*, 01/**4902**
Ansalda Energia SpA v. Amministrazione delle Finanze dello Stato (C279/96) see
    Ansaldo Energia SpA v. Amministrazione delle Finanze dello Stato (C279/96)
Ansaldo Energia SpA v. Amministrazione delle Finanze dello Stato (C279/96); *sub nom*
    Ansalda Energia SpA v. Amministrazione delle Finanze dello Stato (C279/96);
    Amministrazione delle Finanze dello Stato v. Marine Insurance Consultants Srl
    (C280/96); GMB Srl v. Amministrazione delle Finanze dello Stato (C281/96)
    [1998] E.C.R. I-5025; [1999] 2 C.M.L.R. 776, ECJ.   *Digested*, 99/**2227**
Anscomb v. Secretary of State for the Environment, Transport and the Regions see R.
    (on the application of Anscomb) v. Secretary of State for the Environment,
    Transport and the Regions
Ansell (Inspector of Taxes) v. Brown [2001] S.T.C. 1166; 73 T.C. 338; [2001] B.T.C. 381;
    [2001] S.T.I. 847; (2001) 98(31) L.S.G. 37; *Times*, June 20, 2001, Ch D . . . . . .   *Digested*, 01/**5242**
Ansen, Re see R. v. Liverpool Magistrates Court Ex p. Ansen
Ansett Transport Industries (Operations) Pty v. Halton see Air Express v. Ansett Transport
    Industries Pty
Anson (t/a Party Planners) v. Trump; *sub nom* Lady Elizabeth Anson (t/a Party
    Planners) v. Trump [1998] 1 W.L.R. 1404; [1998] 3 All E.R. 331; *Times*, May 8,
    1998; *Independent*, May 6, 1998, CA; reversing in part1994-A-2188, QBD . . . .   *Digested*, 98/**516**
Ansys Inc v. Lim; *sub nom* Ansys Inc v. Lim Thuan Khee [2001] E.C.D.R. 24; [2000]
    Masons C.L.R. 25, CA; affirming [2000] I.T.C.L.R. 532; [1999] Masons C.L.R.
    135, Ch D . . . .   *Digested*, 00/**889**
Ansys Inc v. Lim Thuan Khee see Ansys Inc v. Lim
Antaios Compania Naviera SA v. Salen Rederierna AB (The Antaios) [1985] A.C. 191;
    [1984] 3 W.L.R. 592; [1984] 3 All E.R. 229; [1984] 2 Lloyd's Rep. 235; (1984)
    81 L.S.G. 2776; (1984) 128 S.J. 564, HL; affirming [1983] 1 W.L.R. 1362;
    [1983] 3 All E.R. 777; [1983] 2 Lloyd's Rep. 473; [1983] Com. L.R. 262; (1983)
    127 S.J. 730, CA . . . .   *Digested*, 84/**96**:
                            Applied, 86/1909, 90/193, 90/2850, 92/2745, 98/807, 00/874, 01/332:
                               Considered, 85/2602, 86/91, 86/92, 86/1907, 86/2711, 87/146, 89/104,
                                     90/180, 91/201, 91/203, 91/2269, 92/2721, 94/2760: *Referred to*, 87/2216
Antec International Ltd v. South Western Chicks (Warren) Ltd [1998] F.S.R. 738;
    (1998) 21(6) I.P.D. 21062; (1998) 95(18) L.S.G. 32; *Times*, April 8, 1998;
    Independent, March 31, 1998, Ch D . . . .   *Digested*, 98/**3515**:
                                                                                                    Referred to, 99/3593
Anthogyr v. Biolase Technology Inc (97/02362) [2001] E.N.P.R. 7, C d'A (Paris)
Anthony v. Donges [1998] 2 F.L.R. 775; [1998] Fam. Law 666; *Times*, July 22, 1998,
    Ch D . . . .   *Digested*, 98/**4596**

Anthony v. Ellis & Fairbairn [2000] 2 Costs L.R. 277, QBD
Anthony v. Wright (Discontinuance: Costs) Ch-1992-A-9581, Ch D . . . .   *Digested*, 98/**427**
Anthony v. Wright (Investments: Auditing) [1995] B.C.C. 768; [1995] 1 B.C.L.C. 236;
   Independent, September 27, 1994, Ch D . . . .   *Digested*, 96/**4484**:
                                     Distinguished, 99/4013: *Followed*, 98/4000
Antiphon AB's Application [1984] R.P.C. 1, Pat Ct . . . .   *Followed*, 87/2775,
                                                 99/3469
Antiquesportfolio.com Plc v. Rodney Fitch & Co Ltd [2001] E.C.D.R. 5; [2001]
   E.B.L.R. 20; [2001] F.S.R. 23; (2000) 23(11) I.P.D. 23092; (2000) 97(30)
   L.S.G. 41; *Times*, July 21, 2000, Ch D . . . .   *Digested*, 00/**3577**
Antonelli v. Allen [2001] Lloyd's Rep. P.N. 487, Ch D . . . .   *Digested*, 01/**4267**
Antonelli v. Allen (Costs), *Times*, December 8, 2000, Ch D . . . .   *Digested*, 01/**456**
Antonelli v. Secretary of State for Trade and Industry [1998] Q.B. 948; [1998] 2
   W.L.R. 826; [1998] 1 All E.R. 997; [1998] Admin. L.R. 75; [1998] 1 E.G.L.R. 9;
   [1998] 14 E.G. 133; [1998] C.O.D. 178; (1997) 94(35) L.S.G. 35; (1997) 141
   S.J.L.B. 198; [1997] N.P.C. 123; *Times*, October 3, 1997; *Independent*, October
   14, 1997, CA; affirming [1996] 2 E.G.L.R. 229; [1995] C.O.D. 334; [1995]
   N.P.C. 68, QBD . . . .   *Digested*, 97/**82**
Antonelli v. Wade Gery Farr see Ridehalgh v. Horsefield
Antoni and Alison's Application [1998] E.T.M.R. 460, OHIM (2nd Bd App) . . . .   *Considered*, 00/3789:
                                       Distinguished, 00/3750
Antoniades v. Villiers see AG Securities v. Vaughan
Antoniades v. Wong see Full Cup International Trading Ltd, Re
Antonio Munoz y Cia SA v. Frumar Ltd [1999] 3 C.M.L.R. 684; [1999] F.S.R. 872;
   (1999) 22(6) I.P.D. 22053; *Times*, April 2, 1999, Ch D . . . .   *Digested*, 99/**2606**
Antoniou (t/a Sackville Fisheries) v. Customs and Excise Commissioners [2001] S.T.I.
   1119, V&DTr
Anya v. University of Oxford [2001] EWCA Civ 405; [2001] I.C.R. 847; [2001]
   I.R.L.R. 377; [2001] Emp. L.R. 509; [2001] E.L.R. 711; *Times*, May 4, 2001, CA;
   reversing EAT/739/98, EAT . . . .   *Digested*, 01/**2298**
Anyanwu v. South Bank Student Union see Anyanwu v. South Bank Students Union
Anyanwu v. South Bank Students Union; *sub nom* Anyanwu v. South Bank Student
   Union [2001] UKHL 14; [2001] 1 W.L.R. 638; [2001] 2 All E.R. 353; [2001]
   I.C.R. 391; [2001] I.R.L.R. 305; [2001] E.L.R. 511; (2001) 98(21) L.S.G. 39;
   (2001) 151 N.L.J. 501; (2001) 145 S.J.L.B. 110; *Times*, March 27, 2001;
   Independent, March 28, 2001, HL; reversing [2000] 1 All E.R. 1; [2000] I.C.R.
   221; [2000] I.R.L.R. 36; [2000] E.L.R. 229; (1999) 96(43) L.S.G. 34; (1999)
   143 S.J.L.B. 271; *Times*, November 4, 1999 ; *Independent*, December 13, 1999
   (C.S.), CA . . . .   *Digested*, 01/**2300**:
                                         Followed, 01/3492
AO v. Italy (22534/93) (2001) 29 E.H.R.R. CD92, ECHR
AOM Minerve SA v. INPI [2001] E.T.M.R. CN18, C d'A (Paris)
AOOT Kalmneft v. Glencore International AG see Kalmneft JSC v. Glencore
   International AG
Aoudia (CICB: Quantum: 2000), Re [2000] 5 Q.R. 6, CICB (London) [*Ex rel*. Prince Evans
   Solicitors, 77 Uxbridge Road, London] . . . .   *Digested*, 00/**1581**
AP v. Switzerland (1998) 26 E.H.R.R. 541, ECHR . . . .   *Digested*, 99/**3141**
Aparau v. Iceland Frozen Foods Plc (No.2) [2000] 1 All E.R. 228; [2000] I.C.R. 341;
   [2000] I.R.L.R. 196; (1999) 96(45) L.S.G. 31; *Times*, November 11, 1999, CA . . .   *Digested*, 99/**2054**
Aparta Hotels Caledonia SA v. Watson see Watson v. First Choice Holidays & Flights Ltd
Apis v. Slovakia (399754/98) (2001) 29 E.H.R.R. CD105, ECHR
Apis AS v. Fantazia Kereskedelmi KFT (No.1) [2001] 1 All E.R. (Comm) 348, QBD
   (Comm Ct) . . . .   *Digested*, 01/**342**:
                                        Referred to, 01/4043
Apollinaris Co's Trade Marks (No.1) [1891] 1 Ch. 1, CA. . . . .   *Referred to*, 01/4043
Apollo Cleaning Services Ltd, Re see Richards v. Lundy
Appeal (No. 2000/11) (Children: Video Evidence), Re [2001] N.I. 358, CA (NI)
Appellant v. Inspector of Taxes [2001] S.T.C. (S.C.D.) 21; [2001] S.T.I. 171, Sp Comm . . .   *Digested*, 01/**5259**
Apple and Pear Development Council v. Customs and Excise Commissioners (102/86)
   [1988] 2 All E.R. 922; [1988] S.T.C. 221; [1988] E.C.R. 1443; [1988] 2
   C.M.L.R. 394; *Times*, March 11, 1988, ECJ (6th Chamber) . . . .   *Digested*, 88/**1572**:
             Applied, 88/3637, 89/3771, 90/4626, 91/3666, 91/3667, 91/5666, 92/4545,
             92/4552, 93/4091, 93/4093, 94/4606, 00/5326: *Distinguished*, 88/3619,
                               89/3745, 97/5006: *Referred to*, 95/5095
Apple Computer Inc v. Apple Leasing and Industries, Sup Ct (Ind) . . . .   *Applied*, 98/3521
Appleby v. Chief Adjudication Officer, *Times*, August 5, 1999, CA . . . .   *Digested*, 99/**4583**
Appleby v. Walsall HA [1999] Lloyd's Rep. Med. 154, QBD . . . .   *Digested*, 99/**467**
Appleby Bowers v. Customs and Excise Commissioners [2001] S.T.C. 185; [2001]
   B.T.C. 5301; [2001] B.V.C. 341; [2000] S.T.I. 1652, Ch D; reversing [2000] S.T.I.
   1500, V&DTr . . . .   *Digested*, 01/**5604**
Applegarth v. Secretary of State for the Environment, Transport and the Regions
   [2001] EWHC Admin 487; [2001] 27 E.G.C.S. 486, QBD (Admin Ct)
Appleton v. Great Yarmouth BC [2001] 3 Q.R. 17, CC (Norwich) [*Ex rel*. Anthony Bate,
   Barrister, East Anglian Chambers, 15 The close, Norwich, Norfolk] . . . .   *Digested*, 01/**1695**

Appleton v. JB Taxis (Unreported, September 22, 1999), CC (Bolton) [*Ex rel.* Timothy
White, Barrister, 15 Winckley Square, Preston] . . . . *Digested,* 00/**1696**
Applications Pursuant to r.7.28 of the Insolvency Rules 1986, Re see Austintel Ltd, Re
Applied Implants Technology Ltd v. Lufthansa Cargo AG [2000] 1 All E.R. (Comm)
958; [2000] 2 Lloyd's Rep. 46; [2001] C.L.C. 771; (2000) 97(22) L.S.G. 43;
Times, May 17, 2000, QBD (Comm Ct) . . . . *Digested,* 00/**5156**
Applin v. Race Relations Board [1975] A.C. 259; [1974] 2 W.L.R. 541; [1974] 2 All
E.R. 73; 72 L.G.R. 479; 118 S.J. 311, HL; affirming [1973] Q.B. 815; [1973] 2
W.L.R. 895; [1973] 2 All E.R. 1190; 117 S.J. 417, CA . . . . *Digested,* 74/**19**:
Applied, 75/597, 78/1180, 79/1060, 79/1061, 00/3200: *Considered,* 83/1265
Approval of a Merger, Re [1998] E.C.C. 482, OGH (A)
Apps v. Weldtite Products Ltd [2001] F.S.R. 39; [2001] E.C.D.R. CN3, Ch D . . . . *Digested,* 01/**3860**
Aprile Srl v. Amministrazione delle Finanze dello Stato (C228/96) [2000] 1 W.L.R.
126; [1998] E.C.R. I-7141, ECJ . . . . *Digested,* 00/**2345**:
Applied, 00/2406
Apse v. Newcastle upon Tyne City Council [1999] R.V.R. 284, Lands Tr . . . . *Digested,* 00/**4436**
APV ANHYDRO/Granulation by spray drying (T79/96) [2001] E.P.O.R. 40, EPO (Technical
Bd App) . . . . *Digested,* 01/**3939**
APV Pasilac AS v. Tetra Laval Holdings & Finance SA (B250593) [2001] E.N.P.R. 10,
OL (DK)
Aquarius Financial Enterprises Inc v. Lloyd's Underwriters (The Delphine) [2001] 2
Lloyd's Rep. 542; (2001) 151 N.L.J. 694, QBD (Comm Ct) . . . . *Digested,* 01/**3824**
Aquator Shipping Ltd v. Kleimar NV (The Capricorn 1) [1998] 2 Lloyd's Rep. 379, QBD
(Comm Ct) . . . . *Digested,* 98/**230**
Arab African Energy Corp v. Olie Producten Nederland BV [1983] 2 Lloyd's Rep. 419;
[1983] Com. L.R. 195, QBD (Comm Ct) . . . . *Digested,* 83/**139**:
Applied, 00/217

Arab Bank Plc v. Browne see Arab Bank Plc v. John D Wood (Commercial) Ltd
Arab Bank Plc v. John D Wood (Commercial) Ltd; Arab Bank Plc v. Browne [2000] 1
W.L.R. 857; [2000] Lloyd's Rep. I.R. 471; [2000] Lloyd's Rep. P.N. 173; [1999]
E.G.C.S. 133; (1999) 96(47) L.S.G. 30; (2000) 144 S.J.L.B. 6; [1999] N.P.C.
134; *Times,* November 25, 1999, CA; reversing [1998] E.G.C.S. 34, QBD . . . . . . *Digested,* 99/**3410**
Arab Bank Plc v. Zurich Insurance Co; Banque Bruxelles Lambert SA v. Zurich
Insurance Co [1999] 1 Lloyd's Rep. 262; [1998] C.L.C. 1351, QBD (Comm Ct) . . *Digested,* 99/**3382**
Arab Business Consortium International Finance & Investment Co v. Banque Franco-
Tunisienne [1997] 1 Lloyd's Rep. 531, CA; affirming [1996] 1 Lloyd's Rep. 485,
QBD (Comm Ct) . . . . *Digested,* 97/**713**:
Not followed, 98/587
Arab Monetary Fund v. Hashim (Unreported, March 21, 1997) . . . . *Applied,* 99/16
Arab Monetary Fund v. Hashim (No.8) (1994) 6 Admin. L.R. 348; *Times,* May 4, 1993;
Independent, April 30, 1993, CA; affirming [1989] 1 W.L.R. 565; [1989] 3 All
E.R. 466; (1989) 133 S.J. 749; *Times,* January 16, 1989, Ch D . . . . *Digested,* 95/**3938**:
Considered, 95/3112, 99/3796: *Referred to,* 93/3211
Arab Monetary Fund v. Hashim (Stay of Taxation Pending Appeal) (Unreported, March
25, 1994), CA . . . . *Considered,* 98/476
Aran Caterers Ltd v. Gilbert [2001] N.P.C. 139, Ch D
Arathoon v. Southend on Sea BC (Unreported, February 1, 2001), CC (Southend) [*Ex
rel.* Shoosmiths Solicitors, Quantum house, Basing View, Basingstoke, Hants] . . *Digested,* 01/**475**
Aratra Potato Co Ltd v. Egyptian Navigation Co (The El Amria) [1981] 2 Lloyd's Rep.
119; [1981] Com. L.R. 136, CA; affirming [1980] 1 Lloyd's Rep. 390, QBD (Adm
Ct) . . . . *Digested,* 81/**2198**:
Applied, 83/387, 93/454, 00/760: *Considered,* 85/1291, 97/872, 97/881:
Followed, 98/771
Aratra Potato Co Ltd v. Taylor Joynson Garrett [1995] 4 All E.R. 695; (1995) 145 N.L.J.
1402, QBD . . . . *Digested,* 96/**3920**:
Disapproved, 98/3714
Arbeiterwohlfahrt der Stadt Berlin EV v. Botel (C360/90) [1992] E.C.R. I-3589; [1992]
3 C.M.L.R. 446; [1992] I.R.L.R. 423; *Financial Times,* June 9, 1992, ECJ (6th
Chamber) . . . . *Digested,* 92/**4836**:
Applied, 99/2085: *Cited,* 94/2013, 95/2095: *Considered,* 95/2052, 96/2629:
Distinguished, 96/2574
Arbeitsgemeinschaft Deutscher Rundfunkanstalten (ARD) v. Pro Sieben Media AG
(C6/98) [2000] All E.R. (EC) 3; [1999] E.C.R. I-7599; [1999] 3 C.M.L.R. 769;
[2000] C.E.C. 59; [2000] E.M.L.R. 349, ECJ (6th Chamber) . . . . *Digested,* 00/**4165**
Arbiter Group Plc v. Gill Jennings & Every [2001] R.P.C. 4; [2000] Lloyd's Rep. P.N.
669; [2000] P.N.L.R. 680, CA; affirming [1999] R.P.C. 686; [2000] Lloyd's
Rep. P.N. 367; [2000] P.N.L.R. 1, Ch D . . . . *Digested,* 00/**4215**
Arbitration between Cogstad & Co and H Newsum Sons & Co Ltd, Re see CT Cogstad & Co
(The SS Lord) v. H Newsum Sons & Co Ltd
Arbitration between Mahmoud and Ispahani, Re see Mahmoud and Ispahani, Re
Arbitration between Stewardson Stubbs & Collett Pty Ltd and Bankstown Municipal
Council, Re [1965] N.S.W.R. 161, Sup Ct (NSW) . . . . *Followed,* 98/811
Arbitrators Institute of New Zealand Inc v. Legal Services Board [1995] 2 N.Z.L.R. 202,
HC (NZ) . . . . *Applied,* 98/3100

Arbuthnot Latham Bank Ltd *v.* Trafalgar Holdings Ltd; Chishty Coveney & Co *v.* Raja
  [1998] 1 W.L.R. 1426; [1998] 2 All E.R. 181; [1998] C.L.C. 615; *Times,* December
  29, 1997, CA . . . .   *Digested,* 98/**619**:
                         Applied, 00/608: *Considered,* 98/611, 00/344, 00/4656, 01/671:
                                                         Followed, 98/3363, 00/348
Arbuthnott *v.* Fagan; Deeny *v.* Gooda Walker Ltd (Agency Agreement: Construction)
  [1996] L.R.L.R. 135; [1995] C.L.C. 1396; *Independent,* October 1, 1993, CA . . .   *Digested,* 96/**3583**:
                                            Applied, 00/3447: *Followed,* 99/3315
Arbuthnott *v.* Fagan (Discovery) [1996] L.R.L.R. 143; *Independent,* July 11, 1994
  (C.S.), CA . . . .   *Digested,* 96/**3585**:
                                                              Considered, 98/340
Archangel *v.* Lambeth LBC see Lambeth LBC *v.* Archangel
Archer *v.* Archer [1999] 1 F.L.R. 327; [1999] 2 F.C.R. 158; [1999] Fam. Law 141;
  (1998) 95(46) L.S.G. 34; *Times,* November 23, 1998, CA . . . .   *Digested,* 98/**2445**
Archer *v.* Hickmotts see Northern Rock Building Society *v.* Archer
Archital Luxfer Ltd *v.* Henry Boot Construction Ltd [1981] 1 Lloyd's Rep. 642, QBD . . .   *Digested,* 81/**90**:
                                                              Applied, 01/346
ARCO Chemie Nederland Ltd *v.* Minister van Volkshuisvesting, Ruimtelijke Ordening en
  Milieubeheer (C418/97); *sub nom* Epon (C419/97), Re; Vereniging Dorpsbelang
  Hees *v.* Directeur van de Dienst Milieu en Water van de Provincie Gelderland
  (C419/97) [2000] E.C.R. I-4475; [2001] Env. L.R. D6, ECJ . . . .   *Considered,* 01/2413
ARCO/Miscible polyblend (T685/91) [1999] E.P.O.R. 237, EPO (Technical Bd App)
ARCO/Polymer compositions (T939/90) [1999] E.P.O.R. 227, EPO (Technical Bd App)
Arctic Engineering (No.2), Re [1986] 1 W.L.R. 686; [1986] 2 All E.R. 346; [1986] P.C.C. 1;
  (1986) 83 L.S.G. 1895; (1985) 130 S.J. 429, Ch D . . . .   *Digested,* 86/**344**:
                                                              Considered, 99/2189
Ards Autopoint, Ards Shopping Centre, Newtownards, Re see Save Service Stations Ltd *v.*
  Ravenseft Properties Ltd
Ards BC *v.* Northern Bank Ltd [1994] N.I. 121, CA (NI).   *Digested,* 00/**5438**
ARGE Gewasserschutz *v.* Bundesministerium fur Land- und Forstwirtschaft (C94/99)
  [2000] E.C.R. I-11037; *Times,* January 9, 2001, ECJ . . . .   *Digested,* 01/**2514**
Argento *v.* Italy (1999) 28 E.H.R.R. 719, ECHR. . . . .   *Digested,* 00/**3220**
Argos Distributors Ltd *v.* Customs and Excise Commissioners (C288/94) [1997] Q.B.
  499; [1997] 2 W.L.R. 477; [1996] S.T.C. 1359; [1996] E.C.R. I-5311; [1996] 3
  C.M.L.R. 569; [1996] C.E.C. 963; [1997] B.V.C. 64; *Times,* November 18, 1996;
  Independent, November 25, 1996 (C.S.), ECJ (6th Chamber) . . . .   *Digested,* 96/**5909**:
              Applied, 99/6472: *Distinguished,* 00/5364, 01/5614: *Followed,* 97/4980:
                         Joined proceedings, 96/5908: *Referred to,* 00/5317
Argyle Motors (Birkenhead) Ltd *v.* Birkenhead Corp [1975] A.C. 99; [1974] 2 W.L.R.
  71; [1974] 1 All E.R. 201; 72 L.G.R. 147; (1974) 27 P. & C.R. 122; (1973) 118 S.J.
  67; *Times,* December 13, 1973, HL; affirming [1973] 2 W.L.R. 487; [1973] 1 All
  E.R. 866; 71 L.G.R. 205; (1973) 25 P. & C.R. 32; (1972) 117 S.J. 125; *Times,*
  December 23, 1972, CA; affirming 70 L.G.R. 202; (1972) 23 P. & C.R. 47, Ch D
  . . . .   *Digested,* 74/**374**:
                                            Considered, 93/427: *Followed,* 98/4040
Argyll Training Ltd *v.* Sinclair [2000] I.R.L.R. 630, EAT
ARI/Clauses (T490/90) [1998] E.P.O.R. 44, EPO (Technical Bd App)
Aries Tanker Corp *v.* Total Transport Ltd (The Aries) [1977] 1 W.L.R. 185; [1977] 1 All
  E.R. 398; [1977] 1 Lloyd's Rep. 334; 121 S.J. 117, HL; affirming [1976] 2 Lloyd's
  Rep. 256, CA . . . .   *Digested,* 77/**2741**:
                        Applied, 78/2704, 79/2429, 83/302, 84/273, 95/4212, 96/5741:
              Considered, 78/100, 86/1594, 87/199, 87/2911, 88/186, 89/3409, 98/3324:
                         Distinguished, 79/2438, 88/3260, 94/4078, 96/5302
Arif *v.* Secretary of State for the Home Department see Secretary of State for the
  Home Department *v.* Arif
Arioso Sarl *v.* Bibliotheque Nationale [1998] E.C.C. 133, C d'A (Paris)
Aristoc Ltd *v.* Rysta Ltd; *sub nom* Rysta Ltd's Application [1945] A.C. 68; (1945) 62
  R.P.C. 65, HL; reversing (1943) 60 R.P.C. 87, CA . . . .   *Applied,* 55/2780:
                        Considered, 74/2765, 92/4429, 93/3990, 94/4488, 98/3537:
                        Explained, 92/4426: *Followed,* 78/2953, 95/4937, 00/3774
Ariyo *v.* Sovereign Leasing Plc [1998] B.P.I.R. 177; *Times,* August 4, 1997, CA . . . .   *Digested,* 97/**3030**
Arkin *v.* Borchard Lines Ltd (Costs) [2001] C.P. Rep. 108; (2001) 151 N.L.J. 970, QBD
  (Comm Ct) . . . .   *Digested,* 01/**469**
Arkin *v.* Borchard Lines Ltd (Preliminary Issue) [2000] U.K.C.L.R. 495; [2000] Eu.
  L.R. 232, QBD (Comm Ct) . . . .   *Digested,* 00/**721**
Arklow Investments Ltd *v.* Maclean [2000] 1 W.L.R. 594; (2000) 144 S.J.L.B. 81, PC
  (NZ) . . . .   *Digested,* 00/**2323**
Arlidge *v.* Secretary of State for the Environment [1998] J.P.L. 116; [1997] E.G.C.S.
  93, CA . . . .   *Digested,* 98/**4206**:
                                                              Applied, 00/4529

Armagas Ltd *v.* Mundogas SA (The Ocean Frost) [1986] A.C. 717; [1986] 2 W.L.R. 1063; [1986] 2 All E.R. 385; [1986] 2 Lloyd's Rep. 109; (1986) 83 L.S.G. 2002; (1986) 130 S.J. 430, HL; affirming [1985] 3 W.L.R. 640; [1985] 3 All E.R. 795; [1985] 1 Lloyd's Rep. 1; (1984) 81 L.S.G. 2169; (1984) 129 S.J. 362, CA . . *Digested*, 86/**37**:
Applied, 89/55, 94/537, 95/763, 99/456: *Considered*, 93/64, 94/106
Armitage *v.* Johnson see HM Prison Service *v.* Johnson
Armitage *v.* Nurse (Assessment of Costs) [2000] 2 Costs L.R. 231, Ch D
Armitage *v.* Nurse (Exclusion Clauses) [1998] Ch. 241; [1997] 3 W.L.R. 1046; [1997] 2 All E.R. 705; (1997) 74 P. & C.R. D13; *Times*, March 31, 1997; *Independent*, April 11, 1997, CA; affirming [1995] N.P.C. 110; *Independent*, July 3, 1995 (C.S.), Ch D . . . . *Digested*, 97/**4940**:
Applied, 00/5253: *Considered*, 00/5268
Armitage *v.* South Oxfordshire DC [1998] 2 P.L.R. 89; [1998] 2 E.G.L.R. 121; [1998] 26 E.G. 158; [1998] E.G.C.S. 50; [1998] N.P.C. 38; [1998] N.P.C. 42, QBD . . . . *Digested*, 98/**4245**
Armitage *v.* West Bromwich Building Society see Investors Compensation Scheme Ltd *v.* West Bromwich Building Society (No.1)
Armstrong (A Minor) *v.* Gharhdaghi (Unreported, June 17, 1998), CC (Central London) [*Ex rel.* Andrew G Stafford, Barrister, 4 King's Bench Walk, Temple, London] . . . . *Digested*, 98/**1610**
Armstrong *v.* Bernard Campbell & Co [1998] N.I. 320, Ch D (NI) . . . . *Digested*, 99/**5421**
Armstrong *v.* British Coal Corp QBENF 97/1578/C, CA . . . . *Digested*, 98/**2842**
Armstrong *v.* Pearcy (Unreported, October 26, 1999), CC (Bury) [*Ex rel.* Simon McCann, Barrister, Deans Court Chambers, 24 St John Street, Manchester] . . . *Digested*, 00/**2570**
Armstrong *v.* Scarborough HA (1999) 99(6) Q.R. 3; (1999) 99(3) Q.R. 5, QBD [*Ex rel.* Tim Hirst, Barrister, 40 Park Cross Street, Leeds, W Yorkshire] . . . . *Digested*, 99/**1434**
Arnold *v.* DPP [1999] R.T.R. 99; *Independent*, June 23, 1997 (C.S.), QBD . . . . *Digested*, 97/**4351**
Arnold *v.* Greenwich LBC (Unreported, October 9, 1997), QBD [*Ex rel.* Jon Holbrook, Barrister, Two Garden Court, Middle Temple] . . . . *Digested*, 98/**3618**
Arnold *v.* National Westminster Bank Plc (No.1) [1991] 2 A.C. 93; [1991] 2 W.L.R. 1177; [1991] 3 All E.R. 41; (1991) 62 P. & C.R. 490; [1991] 2 E.G.L.R. 109; [1991] 30 E.G. 57; [1991] E.G.C.S. 49; (1991) 135 S.J. 574; *Times*, April 26, 1991, HL; affirming [1990] Ch. 573; [1990] 2 W.L.R. 304; [1990] 1 All E.R. 529; (1990) 59 P. & C.R. 389; [1990] 01 E.G. 58; (1990) 87(7) L.S.G. 35; (1990) 134 S.J. 1010; *Times*, November 20, 1989; *Independent*, November 24, 1989, CA; affirming [1989] Ch. 63; [1988] 3 W.L.R. 1229; [1988] 3 All E.R. 977; (1989) 58 P. & C.R. 175; [1988] 45 E.G. 106; (1988) 85(46) L.S.G. 41; (1988) 138 N.L.J. Rep. 218; (1988) 132 S.J. 1639; *Times*, July 11, 1988; *Independent*, July 7, 1988, Ch D . . . . *Digested*, 91/**1736**:
Applied, 90/180, 91/203, 94/3453, 95/3781, 97/487, 00/3772:
Considered, 96/2578, 97/766, 97/3886: *Distinguished*, 98/2162:
Followed, 99/370: *Referred to*, 94/2807
Arogol Co Ltd *v.* Rajah see Rajah *v.* Arogol Co Ltd
Arora *v.* Bose (1998) 76 P. & C.R. D1, CA
Aroso *v.* Coutts & Co [2001] W.T.L.R. 797, Ch D . . . . *Digested*, 01/**5517**
Arranmore Investment Co Ltd *v.* Inland Revenue Commissioners; Carnalea Investment Co *v.* Inland Revenue Commissioners [1973] S.T.C. 195; 48 T.C. 623; [1973] T.R. 151, CA (NI) . . . . *Digested*, 73/**1642**:
Applied, 01/5200: *Considered*, 99/4663
Arrow Nominees Inc *v.* Blackledge [2000] C.P. Rep. 59; [2000] 2 B.C.L.C. 167; *Times*, July 7, 2000; *Independent*, July 31, 2000 (C.S), CA; reversing [2000] 1 B.C.L.C. 709; *Times*, December 8, 1999, Ch D . . . . *Digested*, 00/**601**:
Considered, 01/2271
Arrowsmith *v.* Jenkins [1963] 2 Q.B. 561; [1963] 2 W.L.R. 856; [1963] 2 All E.R. 210; 127 J.P. 289; 61 L.G.R. 312; 107 S.J. 215, DC . . . . *Digested*, 63/**1614**:
Considered, 83/725: *Followed*, 98/2855
Arrowsmith *v.* United Kingdom (1981) 3 E.H.R.R. 218, Eur Comm HR . . . . *Applied*, 01/3481
Arsenal Football Club Plc *v.* Reed [2001] 2 C.M.L.R. 23; [2001] E.T.M.R. 77; [2001] R.P.C. 46; (2001) 24(6) I.P.D. 24037; *Times*, April 26, 2001; *Daily Telegraph*, April 17, 2001, Ch D . . . . *Digested*, 01/**4041**
Arsenal Football Club Plc *v.* Reed (Reference to European Court of Justice) [2001] E.T.M.R. CN12, Ch D
Arsenault-Cameron *v.* Government of Prince Edward Island 9 B.H.R.C. 90, Sup Ct (Can) . . . . *Digested*, 01/**836**
Arslan *v.* Turkey (23462/94) (2001) 31 E.H.R.R. 9, ECHR . . . . *Digested*, 01/**3475**
Artesian Residential Developments Ltd *v.* Beck; *sub nom* Artesian Residential Investments Ltd *v.* Beck [2000] Q.B. 541; [2000] 2 W.L.R. 357; [1999] 3 All E.R. 113; (2000) 32 H.L.R. 107; [1999] L. & T.R. 278; [1999] 2 E.G.L.R. 30; [1999] 22 E.G. 145; [1999] E.G.C.S. 46; [1999] N.P.C. 41, CA . . . . *Digested*, 99/**3710**
Artesian Residential Investments Ltd *v.* Beck see Artesian Residential Developments Ltd *v.* Beck
Arthur *v.* Attorney General [1999] I.C.R. 631; *Times*, March 18, 1999, EAT . . . . *Digested*, 99/**2075**
Arthur Average Association, Re see Arthur Average Association for British, Foreign and Colonial Ships, Re

Arthur Average Association for British, Foreign and Colonial Ships, Re; *sub nom* Arthur Average Association, Re; Arthur Average Association for British, Foreign, & Colonial Ships Ex p. Hargrove & Co, Re (1874-75) L.R. 10 Ch. App. 542, CA in Chancery . . . .   *Applied*, 54/2149:
                                                    Followed, 98/3308

Arthur Average Association for British, Foreign, & Colonial Ships Ex p. Hargrove & Co, Re see Arthur Average Association for British, Foreign and Colonial Ships, Re

Arthur JS Hall & Co *v.* Simons; *sub nom* Harris *v.* Scholfield Roberts & Hall; Barratt *v.* Ansell (t/a Woolf Seddon); Barratt *v.* Woolf Seddon; Cockbone *v.* Atkinson Dacre & Slack; Harris *v.* Scholfield Roberts & Hill [2000] 3 W.L.R. 543; [2000] 3 All E.R. 673; [2000] B.L.R. 407; [2000] E.C.C. 487; [2000] 2 F.L.R. 545; [2000] 2 F.C.R. 673; [2001] P.N.L.R. 6; [2000] Fam. Law 806; [2000] E.G.C.S. 99; (2000) 97(32) L.S.G. 38; (2000) 150 N.L.J. 1147; (2000) 144 S.J.L.B. 238; [2000] N.P.C. 87; *Times*, July 21, 2000; *Independent*, July 25, 2000, HL; affirming [1999] 3 W.L.R. 873; [1999] 1 F.L.R. 536; [1999] 2 F.C.R. 193; [1999] Lloyd's Rep. P.N. 47; [1999] P.N.L.R. 374; [1999] Fam. Law 215; [1998] N.P.C. 162; *Times*, December 18, 1998; *Independent*, December 18, 1998, CA; affirming [1998] 2 F.L.R. 679; [1999] P.N.L.R. 208; [1998] Fam. Law 524, QBD . . . .   *Digested*, 00/**4269**:
                  Applied, 00/597: *Cited*, 01/525: *Considered*, 01/4515

Arthur Rathbone Kitchens Ltd, Re [1998] B.C.C. 450; [1997] 2 B.C.L.C. 280; [1998] B.P.I.R. 1, Ch D (Companies Ct) . . . .   *Digested*, 98/**3306**:
                                                    Followed, 99/3338

Article 27 UK-Netherlands DTC, Re (32330) 1 I.T.L. Rep. 551, HR (NL)
Article 43 of Trusts (Jersey) Law 1984, Re [2001] W.T.L.R. 571, Royal Ct (Jer) . . . .   *Digested*, 01/**5535**
Artico *v.* Italy (A/37) (1981) 3 E.H.R.R. 1, ECHR . . . .   *Considered*, 01/3534,
                                                         01/6760

Artistic Upholstery Ltd *v.* Art Forma (Furniture) Ltd [1999] 4 All E.R. 277; [2000] F.S.R. 311; (1999) 22(12) I.P.D. 22118; *Times*, September 21, 1999, Ch D . . . . . .   *Digested*, 99/**3561**
Arun DC *v.* Mills [2001] N.P.C. 150, CA; affirming 000431, QBD
AS (Secure Accommodation Order), Re [1999] 1 F.L.R. 103; [1999] 2 F.C.R. 749; [1999] Fam. Law 20; (2000) 164 J.P.N. 27, Fam Div . . . .   *Digested*, 99/**2395**
AS Screenprinting Ltd *v.* British Reserve Insurance Co Ltd [1996] C.L.C. 1470; [1999] Lloyd's Rep. I.R. 430, CA . . . .   *Digested*, 99/**3397**
Asahi Kasei Kogyo KK's Application, Re [1991] R.P.C. 485; *Financial Times*, May 14, 1991, HL; reversing [1990] F.S.R. 546, CA . . . .   *Digested*, 92/**3275**:
                   Applied, 93/3028, 99/3518: *Referred to*, 93/3041, 94/3440
Asahi Medical Co Ltd *v.* Macopharma (UK) Ltd A3/2001/0263, CA; affirming (2001) 24(3) I.P.D. 24016, Pat Ct
Ascon Contracting Ltd *v.* Alfred McAlpine Construction Isle of Man Ltd 66 Con. L.R. 119; (2000) 16 Const. L.J. 316, QBD (T&CC) . . . .   *Digested*, 00/**826**
Ascot Commodities NV *v.* Northern Pacific Shipping (The Irini A) (No.1) [1999] 1 Lloyd's Rep. 196, QBD (Comm Ct) . . . .   *Digested*, 99/**4478**
Ascot Commodities NV *v.* Northern Pacific Shipping (The Irini A) (No.2) [1999] 1 Lloyd's Rep. 189, QBD (Comm Ct) . . . .   *Digested*, 99/**4426**
Ascot Wood Ltd *v.* Secretary of State for the Environment, Transport and the Regions [2000] P.L.C.R. 265, QBD . . . .   *Digested*, 00/**4519**
Asda Stores Ltd *v.* Croke (Unreported, December 20, 1999), CC (Brighton) [*Ex rel.* Sally Ann Smith, Barrister, Crown Office Row Chambers, Blenheim House, 120 Church Street, Brighton] . . . .   *Digested*, 00/**1493**
ASDA Stores Ltd *v.* Secretary of State for Scotland 1999 S.L.T. 503; 1998 S.C.L.R. 246; [1998] P.L.C.R. 233; 1998 G.W.D. 3-146, Ex Div; reversing 1997 S.L.T. 1286; 1997 S.C.L.R. 661; 1997 G.W.D. 10-439, OH . . . .   *Digested*, 98/**6151**:
                            Applied, 99/4266: *Distinguished*, 01/6855
Ash *v.* Lloyd's Corp [1993] I.L.Pr. 330; (1992) 9 O.R. (3d) 755, CA (Ont); affirming (1991) 6 O.R. (3d) 235, CJ (Gen Div) (Ont) . . . .   *Applied*, 01/817:
                                                    Followed, 00/740
Ashbridge Investments Ltd *v.* Minister of Housing and Local Government [1965] 1 W.L.R. 1320; [1965] 3 All E.R. 371; 129 J.P. 580; 63 L.G.R. 400; 109 S.J. 595, CA; reversing (1965) 109 S.J. 474 . . . .   *Digested*, 65/**522**:
       Applied, 65/532, 66/1535, 67/533, 71/1503, 74/3473, 75/3090, 82/3167,
       83/3662, 00/4445: *Considered*, 79/2608, 83/3649, 83/3745, 86/3259,
       86/3745, 88/385, 89/362, 89/363, 90/588, 92/452, 93/440, 96/4763:
                                      Distinguished, 67/3791, 68/3786
Ashburn Anstalt *v.* WJ Arnold & Co (No.1) [1989] Ch. 1; [1988] 2 All E.R. 147; (1988) 55 P. & C.R. 137; (1987) 284 E.G. 1375; (1988) 132 S.J. 416; *Times*, November 9, 1987, CA; affirming (1988) 55 P. & C.R. 13, Ch D . . . .   *Digested*, 88/**2061**:
       Applied, 92/2691, 00/3896: *Considered*, 90/719, 92/1798, 93/426, 93/1614,
               96/4995: *Distinguished*, 92/2688: *Followed*, 96/4953:
                                          Not followed, 99/4395

Ashby *v.* Secretary of State for the Environment [1980] 1 W.L.R. 673; [1980] 1 All E.R.
508; 78 L.G.R. 226; (1980) 40 P. & C.R. 362; [1980] J.P.L. 178; 124 S.J. 185,
CA; affirming 77 L.G.R. 222; (1979) 37 P. & C.R. 197; [1978] J.P.L. 761; 122 S.J.
524, QBD . . . . *Digested,* 80/**1330**:
Followed, 98/4217
Ashby *v.* Tolhurst [1937] 2 K.B. 242; [1937] 2 All E.R. 837, CA. . . . . *Applied,* 47-51/**4924**,
47-51/4934, 47-51/6685, 54/200, 54/582: *Considered,* 59/3033, 63/523,
66/571: *Followed,* 71/12556, 99/833
Ashdown *v.* Telegraph Group Ltd [2001] EWCA Civ 1142; [2001] 3 W.L.R. 1368;
[2001] 4 All E.R. 666; [2001] E.M.L.R. 44; [2001] H.R.L.R. 57; [2001]
U.K.H.R.R. 1242; (2001) 24(9) I.P.D. 24058; (2001) 98(33) L.S.G. 29; (2001)
145 S.J.L.B. 201; *Times,* August 1, 2001; *Independent,* July 20, 2001; *Daily
Telegraph,* July 24, 2001, CA; affirming [2001] Ch. 685; [2001] 2 W.L.R. 967;
[2001] 2 All E.R. 370; [2001] E.C.D.R. 21; [2001] E.M.L.R. 20; [2001] H.R.L.R.
30; [2001] R.P.C. 34; (2001) 98(8) L.S.G. 47; (2001) 151 N.L.J. 58; (2001)
145 S.J.L.B. 31; *Times,* February 6, 2001; *Independent,* February 26, 2001 (C.S),
Ch D . . . . *Digested,* 01/**3850**
Ashe (Trustee in Bankruptcy of Henry Samuel Mumford) *v.* Mumford (No.1) [2000]
B.P.I.R. 389; *Times,* March 7, 2000, QBD
Ashe (Trustee in Bankruptcy of Henry Samuel Mumford) *v.* Mumford (No.2); *sub nom*
Mumford *v.* Ashe [2001] B.P.I.R. 1; (2001) 33 H.L.R. 67; (2000) 97(43) L.S.G.
38; *Times,* November 15, 2000, CA. . . . . *Digested,* 00/**3941**
Ashfield DC *v.* Customs and Excise Commissioners [2001] S.T.C. 1706; [2001] S.T.I.
1662, Ch D; affirming [2001] S.T.I. 983, V&DTr
Ashford BC *v.* Propan Homes (2001) 16 P.A.D. 2, Planning Inspector
Ashford Hotels Ltd *v.* Higgins see Allied Irish Bank Plc *v.* Ashford Hotels Ltd
Ashingdane *v.* United Kingdom (A/93) (1985) 7 E.H.R.R. 528, ECHR; affirming
(1982) 4 E.H.R.R. 590, Eur Comm HR . . . . *Applied,* 99/3094
Ashmore *v.* British Coal Corp [1990] 2 Q.B. 338; [1990] 2 W.L.R. 1437; [1990] 2 All
E.R. 981; [1990] I.C.R. 485; [1990] I.R.L.R. 283, CA . . . . *Digested,* 90/**3542**:
Applied, 98/3385: *Followed,* 97/628: *Referred to,* 00/346
Ashmore *v.* Corp of Lloyd's (No.2) [1992] 2 Lloyd's Rep. 620; *Times,* July 17, 1992;
Independent, July 22, 1992, QBD (Comm Ct). . . . . *Digested,* 93/**2407**:
Considered, 01/3823
Ashouri *v.* Penfold (Unreported, October 22, 1999), CC (Southampton) [*Ex rel.* Vershal
Rehan, Barrister, 20 Lorne Park Road, Bournemouth] . . . . *Digested,* 00/**1722**
Ashraf *v.* Secretary of State for Social Security (1999) 96(48) L.S.G. 40; *Times,*
January 11, 2000, CA. . . . . *Digested,* 00/**4758**
Ashton, Re; *sub nom* R. *v.* Manchester Crown Court Ex p. DPP [1994] 1 A.C. 9;
[1993] 2 W.L.R. 846; [1993] 2 All E.R. 663; (1993) 97 Cr. App. R. 203; (1994)
6 Admin. L.R. 329; [1993] Crim. L.R. 959; (1993) 157 J.P.N. 362; (1993)
90(24) L.S.G. 40; (1993) 143 N.L.J. 687; (1993) 137 S.J.L.B. 144; *Times,* May 7,
1993; *Independent,* May 10, 1993; *Guardian,* May 7, 1993, HL; reversing [1992]
C.O.D. 444, QBD. . . . . *Digested,* 93/**15**:
Applied, 94/19, 00/2420: *Followed,* 96/1550
Ashton *v.* Chief Constable of West Mercia [2001] I.C.R. 67; *Times,* November 14,
2000, EAT . . . . *Digested,* 00/**2209**
Ashton *v.* DPP (1996) 160 J.P. 336; [1998] R.T.R. 45; *Times,* July 14, 1995;
Independent, July 10, 1995 (C.S.), QBD . . . . *Digested,* 95/**4416**
Ashton *v.* Securum Finance Ltd see Securum Finance Ltd *v.* Ashton (No.1)
Ashton-Hurst *v.* Carter (Unreported, July 22, 1998), CC (Bury) [*Ex rel.* Dibb Lupton
Alsop Solicitors, 101 Barbirolli Square, Manchester] . . . . *Digested,* 98/**604**
Ashurst *v.* Coe; *sub nom* Debtor (No.17 of 1998), Re [1999] B.P.I.R. 662; *Times,*
March 25, 1999; *Independent,* February 1, 1999 (C.S.), Ch D . . . . *Digested,* 99/**3251**
Ashurst *v.* Pollard; *sub nom* Pollard *v.* Ashurst [2001] Ch. 595; [2001] 2 W.L.R. 722;
[2001] 2 All E.R. 75; [2001] B.P.I.R. 131; (2001) 98(3) L.S.G. 42; (2000) 150
N.L.J. 1787; *Times,* November 29, 2000, CA; affirming [2000] 2 All E.R. 772;
[2001] I.L.Pr. 7; [2000] B.P.I.R. 347; [2000] 2 E.G.L.R. 29; [2000] 24 E.G. 171;
[2000] E.G.C.S. 18; [2000] N.P.C. 11; *Times,* March 16, 2000, Ch D . . . . *Digested,* 01/**3736**
Ashworth *v.* McKay Foods Ltd [1996] 1 W.L.R. 542; [1996] 1 All E.R. 705; [1996]
P.I.Q.R. P187; *Times,* November 16, 1995, CA . . . . *Digested,* 95/**4044**:
Applied, 01/433
Ashworth Frazer Ltd *v.* Gloucester City Council (Consent to Assignment) [2001] UKHL
59; [2001] 1 W.L.R. 2180; [2001] 46 E.G.C.S. 180; (2001) 98(45) L.S.G. 27;
(2001) 151 N.L.J. 1695; *Times,* November 12, 2001; *Independent,* November 13,
2001, HL; reversing in part (2000) 80 P. & C.R. 11; [2000] 1 E.G.L.R. 44; [2000]
12 E.G. 149; [2000] E.G.C.S. 3; *Times,* February 3, 2000 ; *Independent,*
January 20, 2000, CA; reversing *Times,* April 1, 1999, Ch D . . . . *Digested,* 01/**4185**
Ashworth Hospital Authority *v.* MGN Ltd; *sub nom* Ashworth Security Hospital *v.* MGN
Ltd [2001] 1 W.L.R. 515; [2001] 1 All E.R. 991; [2001] E.M.L.R. 11; [2001]
F.S.R. 33; (2001) 61 B.M.L.R. 48; (2001) 98(6) L.S.G. 46; (2001) 145 S.J.L.B.
20; *Times,* January 10, 2001; *Independent,* January 18, 2001; *Daily Telegraph,*
January 9, 2001, CA; affirming HQ 0000397, QBD . . . . *Digested,* 01/**4413**
Ashworth Security Hospital *v.* MGN Ltd see Ashworth Hospital Authority *v.* MGN Ltd

Asia Motor France SA *v.* Commission of the European Communities (C1/01); *sub nom*
Asia Motor France SA *v.* Commission of the European Communities (T154/98
R) (No.2) [2000] E.C.R. II-3453; [2001] 4 C.M.L.R. 6, CFI (5th Chamber) ....   *Digested*, 01/**2455**
Asia Motor France SA *v.* Commission of the European Communities (T154/98 R)
(No.2) see Asia Motor France SA *v.* Commission of the European Communities
(C1/01)
Asia Motor France SA *v.* Commission of the European Communities (T154/98 R) (No.1)
[1999] E.C.R. II-1703; [2001] 4 C.M.L.R. 5, CFI (5th Chamber) . . . .   *Digested*, 01/**2454**
Asia Motor France SA *v.* Commission of the European Communities (T7/92) [1993]
E.C.R. II-669; [1994] 4 C.M.L.R. 30; *Financial Times*, July 6, 1993, CFI (2nd
Chamber) . . . .   *Digested*, 93/**4259**:
                                          Followed, 00/715

Asianac International Panama SA and Transocean Transport Corp *v.* Transocean Ro-Ro-
Corp (The Seaspeed America) [1990] 1 Lloyd's Rep. 150, QBD (Adm Ct) . . . . .   *Digested*, 91/**2345**:
                                          Applied, 01/4946

Asker *v.* Turkey see Selcuk *v.* Turkey
Askew *v.* Governing Body of Clifton Middle School see Governing Body of Clifton
Middle School *v.* Askew
Askew-Page *v.* Page [2001] Fam. Law 794, CC (Bath)
Askey Computer Corp's European Trade Mark Application [2000] E.T.M.R. 214, KHO (Fin)
Askin *v.* Absa Bank Ltd [1999] I.L.Pr. 471; (1999) 96(13) L.S.G. 32; *Times*, February
23, 1999, CA. . . . .   *Digested*, 99/**719**
Aslam *v.* South Bedfordshire DC [2001] R.V.R. 65; (2001) 98(2) L.S.G. 42; *Times*,
January 18, 2001, CA; reversing [2000] R.V.R. 121, LandsTr . . . .   *Digested*, 01/**4660**
Aslam *v.* South Bedfordshire DC (Rate of Interest) [2001] EWCA Civ 515; [2001]
J.P.L. 1324 (Note), CA
Aslan *v.* Malta (29493/95) (2000) 29 E.H.R.R. CD106, ECHR
Aspen Property Investment Plc *v.* Ratcliffe [1997] 2 Costs L.R. 1, Ch D . . . .   *Digested*, 98/**473**
Aspex Visual Arts Trust *v.* Customs and Excise Commissioners [2000] S.T.I. 618, V&DTr
Aspinalls Club Ltd *v.* Halabi [1998] B.P.I.R. 322, Ch D . . . .   *Digested*, 98/**3289**
Aspro Travel Ltd *v.* Owners Abroad Group Plc [1996] 1 W.L.R. 132; [1995] 4 All E.R.
728; [1995] E.M.L.R. 501; *Times*, July 11, 1995; *Independent*, July 20, 1995, CA.   *Digested*, 96/**5665**:
                                          Not followed, 98/1772

ASRS Establishment Ltd (In Administrative Receivership and Liquidation), Re; *sub nom*
Lawrence *v.* Buchler; DQ Henriques Ltd *v.* Buchler; Buchler *v.* DQ Henriques
Ltd [2000] 2 B.C.L.C. 631, CA; affirming [2000] 1 B.C.L.C. 727; *Times*,
November 17, 1999, Ch D (Companies Ct) . . . .   *Digested*, 01/**733**
Assco Geruste GmbH *v.* Wilhelm Layher GmbH & Co KG (C392/98) see Parfums
Christian Dior SA *v.* Tuk Consultancy BV (C300/98)
Assedic Pas-de-Calais AGS *v.* Dumon (C235/95) [1998] E.C.R. I-4531; [1999] 2
C.M.L.R. 113, ECJ . . . .   *Digested*, 99/**2016**
Assenov *v.* Bulgaria (1999) 28 E.H.R.R. 652; [1998] H.R.C.D. 986, ECHR . . . .   *Digested*, 00/**3197**
Assessor for Glasgow *v.* Ron Wood Greetings Cards [2000] R.A. 271; 1999 G.W.D. 38-
1868, LVAC . . . .   *Digested*, 00/**6661**
Assessor for Highland and Western Isles Valuation Joint Board *v.* A; *sub nom* Assessor for
Highland and Western Isles Valuation Joint Board's Appeal (No.1), Re; Assessor
for Highland and Western Isles Valuation Joint Board *v.* Fraser 2001 S.C. 473;
[2001] R.V.R. 32; 2001 G.W.D. 1-72, 1 Div . . . .   *Digested*, 01/**6871**
Assessor for Highland and Western Isles Valuation Joint Board *v.* Fraser see Assessor for
Highland and Western Isles Valuation Joint Board *v.* A
Assessor for Highland and Western Isles Valuation Joint Board *v.* Macleod; *sub nom*
Assessor for Highland and Western Isles Valuation Joint Board's Appeal (No.2),
Re 2001 S.C. 476; 2001 S.L.T. 483; [2001] R.V.R. 33; 2001 G.W.D. 1-71, 1 Div . . .   *Digested*, 01/**6872**
Assessor for Highland and Western Isles Valuation Joint Board's Appeal (No.1), Re see
Assessor for Highland and Western Isles Valuation Joint Board *v.* A
Assessor for Highland and Western Isles Valuation Joint Board's Appeal (No.2), Re see
Assessor for Highland and Western Isles Valuation Joint Board *v.* Macleod
Assessor for Tayside Joint Valuation Board *v.* Joseph Johnston & Sons Ltd 2000 S.L.T.
308; [2000] R.A. 258; 1999 G.W.D. 37-1828, LVAC
Assicurazioni Generali SpA *v.* Commission of the European Communities (T87/96)
[1999] E.C.R. II-203; [2000] 4 C.M.L.R. 312, CFI (1st Chamber). . . . .   *Digested*, 00/**2368**
Assignment of a Consumer Credit Agreement, Re [2000] E.C.C. 280, BGH (Ger)
Associacao dos Refinadores de Acucar Portugueses (ARAP) *v.* Commission of the
European Communities (C321/99); *sub nom* Associacao dos Refinadores de
Acucar Portugueses (ARAP) *v.* Commission of the European Communities
(T82/96) ECJ [1999] E.C.R. II-1889; [1999] 2 C.M.L.R. 1411, CFI (4th
Chamber) . . . .   *Digested*, 99/**2278**
Associacao dos Refinadores de Acucar Portugueses (ARAP) *v.* Commission of the
European Communities (T82/96) see Associacao dos Refinadores de Acucar
Portugueses (ARAP) *v.* Commission of the European Communities (C321/99)
Associated British Ports *v.* Palmer see Associated Newspapers Ltd *v.* Wilson
Associated Bulk Carriers Ltd *v.* Koch Shipping Inc (The Fuohsan Maru) [1978] 2 All
E.R. 254; [1978] 1 Lloyd's Rep. 24; 7 B.L.R. 18; 122 S.J. 708, CA . . . .   *Digested*, 78/**2690**:
                         Applied, 84/132: *Considered*, 79/2141, 98/624: *Distinguished*, 88/2940

Associated Japanese Bank (International) Ltd v. Credit du Nord SA [1989] 1 W.L.R. 255; [1988] 3 All E.R. 902; [1989] Fin. L.R. 117; (1989) 86(8) L.S.G. 43; (1988) 138 N.L.J. Rep. 109; (1989) 133 S.J. 81, QBD . . . . *Digested,* 89/**430**:
Applied, 94/572, 01/954

Associated Newspapers Group v. Fleming (Inspector of Taxes); *sub nom* Fleming (Inspector of Taxes) v. Associated Newspapers Ltd [1973] A.C. 628; [1972] 2 W.L.R. 1273; [1972] 2 All E.R. 574; [1972] T.R. 87; 116 S.J. 446, HL; affirming [1972] Ch. 170; [1971] 3 W.L.R. 551; [1971] 2 All E.R. 1526; [1971] T.R. 189; 115 S.J. 773, CA; affirming [1970] 3 W.L.R. 809; [1971] 1 All E.R. 203; (1970) 49 A.T.C. 248; [1970] T.R. 233; 114 S.J. 809, Ch D . . . . *Digested,* 72/**1753**:
Applied, 01/5265

Associated Newspapers Group Plc v. News Group Newspapers Ltd [1986] R.P.C. 515, Ch D . . . . *Digested,* 87/**506**

Associated Newspapers Ltd v. London (North) Industrial Tribunal see R. v. London (North) Industrial Tribunal Ex p. Associated Newspapers Ltd

Associated Newspapers Ltd v. Northumbrian Fine Foods Plc see Adams v. Associated Newspapers Ltd

Associated Newspapers Ltd v. Wilson; *sub nom* Wilson v. Associated Newspapers Ltd; Associated British Ports v. Palmer [1995] 2 A.C. 454; [1995] 2 W.L.R. 354; [1995] 2 All E.R. 100; [1995] I.C.R. 406; [1995] I.R.L.R. 258; (1995) 92(17) L.S.G. 48; (1995) 145 N.L.J. 417; (1995) 139 S.J.L.B. 110; *Times,* March 31, 1995; *Independent,* April 5, 1995, HL; reversing [1993] I.R.L.R. 336; (1993) 137 S.J.L.B. 134; *Times,* May 5, 1993, CA; reversing [1992] I.C.R. 681; [1992] I.R.L.R. 440; *Times,* July 2, 1992, EAT. . . . . *Digested,* 95/**1990**:
Considered, 94/1999, 95/1989, 96/5730, 01/2324: *Referred to,* 96/2670

Associated Newspapers Property Ltd v. Drapers Co; *sub nom* Associated Newspapers Property Ltd v. Mystery of Drapers in the City of London [1997] 2 E.G.L.R. 88; [1997] 50 E.G. 84; [1997] E.G.C.S. 24; [1997] N.P.C. 27, CA; affirming [1995] N.P.C. 127, Ch D . . . . *Digested,* 98/**3685**

Associated Newspapers Property Ltd v. Mystery of Drapers in the City of London see Associated Newspapers Property Ltd v. Drapers Co

Associated Portland Cement Manufacturers (1900) Ltd v. Tolhurst see Tolhurst v. Associated Portland Cement Manufacturers (1900) Ltd

Associated Provincial Picture Houses Ltd v. Wednesbury Corp [1948] 1 K.B. 223; [1947] 2 All E.R. 680; 63 T.L.R. 623; 112 J.P. 55; 45 L.G.R. 635; [1948] L.J.R. 190; 177 L.T. 641; 92 S.J. 26, CA; affirming [1947] 1 All E.R. 498; [1947] L.J.R. 678, KBD . . . . *Digested,* 48/**8107**:
Applied, 59/3229, 60/3110, 64/1723, 64/2999, 67/3791, 68/3786, 70/2777, 72/2933, 75/17, 76/22, 77/2972, 77/3080, 78/1570, 78/2003, 78/3001, 79/2710, 80/311, 80/347, 80/1358, 80/1715, 81/396, 81/1657, 81/1797, 81/2237, 81/2710, 81/2716, 82/369, 82/3181, 83/359, 83/1795, 83/2235, 83/2258, 83/2288, 83/3761, 84/147, 84/1637, 84/2247, 84/2604, 85/17, 85/1112, 85/1626, 85/2029, 85/2212, 85/2502, 85/2728, 85/3450, 86/27, 86/1127, 86/1682, 86/2143, 87/1989, 87/2145, 88/36, 88/53, 88/57, 88/845, 89/898, 89/1367, 89/2298, 89/2396, 89/3764, 89/3823, 89/4022, 89/4276, 90/1175, 90/3042, 91/21, 91/63, 91/71, 91/1971, 91/3176, 92/55, 93/7, 93/865, 93/4058, 95/68, 95/2546, 95/3252, 95/4800, 96/4715, 98/1921, 98/4938: *Considered,* 68/3837, 70/1547, 70/2780, 76/1349, 79/2243, 80/121, 82/2383, 83/1724, 83/1935, 83/3045, 83/3745, 84/7, 84/246, 84/1578, 84/1705, 84/2210, 84/2756, 84/3231, 85/1107, 85/1117, 85/1149, 85/1615, 85/1702, 85/1725, 85/2079, 85/2233, 85/2791, 86/2017, 86/2022, 86/2068, 86/2164, 86/2169, 86/2181, 86/2217, 86/2678, 86/2938, 86/3745, 87/1286, 87/1773, 87/1920, 87/2463, 87/2518, 87/2522, 88/1, 88/6, 88/284, 88/385, 88/1867, 88/2016, 88/2226, 88/2760, 88/3089, 89/363, 89/1086, 89/2245, 90/9, 90/588, 90/1552, 90/3914, 90/3918, 91/55, 91/67, 91/464: *Distinguished,* 69/3447, 80/1365, 81/1721, 82/1987, 82/2880: *Followed,* 71/3831, 72/2062, 85/2594:
Overruled in part, 83/1908: *Referred to,* 92/5981

Associates Fleet Services Ltd v. Customs and Excise Commissioners [2001] S.T.I. 1276, V&DTr

Association France Nature Environnement v. French Minister for Planning and the Environment [2000] 3 C.M.L.R. 404, CE (F)

Association Generale des Journalistes Professionnels de Belgique v. SCRL Central Station [1998] E.C.C. 40, RB (Brussels)

Association Greenpeace France v. Ministere de l'Agriculture et de la Peche (C6/99) [2001] All E.R. (EC) 791; [2000] E.C.R. I-1651; [2001] 2 C.M.L.R. 45, ECJ . . . . *Digested,* 01/**2504**

Association Henri Langlois v. La Cinematheque Francaise [1999] E.C.C. 160, C d'A (Paris)

Association of British Travel Agents Ltd v. British Airways Plc [2000] 2 All E.R. (Comm) 204; [2000] 2 Lloyd's Rep. 209, CA; affirming [2000] 1 Lloyd's Rep. 169, QBD (Comm Ct) . . . . *Digested,* 00/**865**

Association of British Travel Agents Ltd v. Director General of Fair Trading see Institute of Independent Insurance Brokers v. Director General of Fair Trading

Association of Certified Public Accountants of Britain v. Secretary of State for Trade and
Industry [1998] 1 W.L.R. 164; [1997] B.C.C. 736; [1997] 2 B.C.L.C. 307;
(1997) 94(35) L.S.G. 33; (1997) 141 S.J.L.B. 128; *Times*, June 12, 1997, Ch D . .   *Digested*, 97/**803**

Association of Independent Radio Companies Ltd v. Phonographic Performance Ltd
[1993] E.M.L.R. 181; [1994] R.P.C. 143, Copyright Tr . . . .   *Digested*, 94/**623**:
    Applied, 99/3444: *Distinguished*, 00/3581

Association Ornithologique et Mammalogique de Saone-et-Loire v. French Minister for
Planning and the Environment [2000] 3 C.M.L.R. 399, CE (F)

Association Ornithologique et Mammalogique de Saone-et-Loire v. French Prime
Minister [2000] 3 C.M.L.R. 395, CE (F)

Associazione Italiana Calciatori v. Autorita Garante della Concorrenza e del Mercato see
Panini v. Autorita Garante della Concorrenza e del Mercato

Associazione Italiana Tecnico Economica del Cemento (AITEC) v. Commission of the
European Communities (T447/93) [1995] E.C.R. II-1971; *Financial Times*, July 11,
1995, CFI . . . .   *Digested*, 96/**3420**:
    Applied, 98/735

Assuranceforeningen Skuld v. International Oil Pollution Compensation Fund (No.1)
2000 S.L.T. 1333; 1999 G.W.D. 16-766; *Times*, June 14, 1999, OH . . . .   *Digested*, 99/**6442**

Assurances Generales de France (AGF) SA v. Rigaud [2001] E.C.C. 39, Cass (F)

Astec (BSR) Plc, Re [1999] B.C.C. 59; [1998] 2 B.C.L.C. 556, Ch D (Companies Ct) . .   *Digested*, 99/**646**

Asteris AE v. Commission of the European Communities (C97/86) [1988] E.C.R. 2181;
[1988] 3 C.M.L.R. 493, ECJ . . . .   *Digested*, 90/**2200**:
    Followed, 00/2374

Astilleros Zamacona SA v. Commission of the European Communities (T72/98)
[2000] E.C.R. II-1683; [2000] 3 C.M.L.R. 762, CFI (2nd Chamber) . . . .   *Digested*, 01/**790**

Astley v. Austrust Ltd [1999] Lloyd's Rep. P.N. 758, HC (Bar) . . . .   *Digested*, 99/**3984**

Astley v. Hart (t/a Top Shop) (Unreported, November 10, 1997), CC (Manchester) [*Ex
rel*. Group Legal Department, Royal & Sun Alliance, Manchester] . . . .   *Digested*, 98/**505**

Aston Cantlow and Wilmcote with Billesley Parochial Church Council v. Wallbank; *sub
nom* Wallbank v. Aston Cantlow and Wilmcote with Billesley Parochial Church
Council [2001] EWCA Civ 713; [2001] 3 W.L.R. 1323; [2001] 3 All E.R. 393; 4
I.T.L. Rep. 353; [2001] 21 E.G.C.S. 167; (2001) 98(22) L.S.G. 37; (2001)
98(25) L.S.G. 46; (2001) 145 S.J.L.B. 140; *Times*, June 15, 2001; *Independent*,
May 24, 2001, CA; reversing (2001) 81 P. & C.R. 14; [2000] 2 E.G.L.R. 149;
(2000) 97(17) L.S.G. 32; (2000) 144 S.J.L.B. 181; [2000] N.P.C. 33; *Times*,
March 30, 2000, Ch D . . . .   *Digested*, 01/**1844**

Astra Developments Ltd v. 3M Business Consultants Ltd 002886 of 1996, Ch D
(Companies Ct) . . . .   *Digested*, 98/**3326**

Astra Holdings Plc, Re; *sub nom* Secretary of State for Trade and Industry v. Anderson
[1999] B.C.C. 121; [1998] 2 B.C.L.C. 44; *Times*, January 13, 1998; *Times*,
December 31, 1997, Ch D . . . .   *Digested*, 98/**676**

Astra SA Insurance and Reinsurance Co v. Sphere Drake Insurance Ltd (formerly Sphere
Drake Insurance Plc, Sphere Insurance Plc and Odyssey Re (London) Ltd)
[2000] 2 Lloyd's Rep. 550, QBD (Comm Ct) . . . .   *Digested*, 00/**3558**

Astra SA Insurance and Reinsurance Co v. Yasuda Fire and Marine Insurance Co of
Europe Ltd [1999] C.L.C. 950, QBD (Comm Ct) . . . .   *Digested*, 99/**3423**:
    Considered, 00/3558

Astro Exito Navegacion SA v. WT Hsu (The Messiniaki Tolmi) [1984] 1 Lloyd's Rep.
266; (1984) 128 S.J. 265, CA; reversing [1983] 1 Lloyd's Rep. 666, QBD
(Comm Ct) . . . .   *Digested*, 84/**351**:
    Applied, 00/768

ASULAB/Fee reduction (G06/91) [1993] E.P.O.R. 231, EPO (Enlarged Bd App) . . . . .   *Followed*, 01/3917

Aswan Engineering Establishment Co v. Lupdine Ltd see M/S Aswan Engineering
Establishment Co v. Lupdine Ltd

AT & T Istel v. Tully (No.1) [1993] A.C. 45; [1992] 3 W.L.R. 344; [1992] 3 All E.R. 523;
(1992) 142 N.L.J. 1088; [1992] 136 S.J.L.B. 227; *Times*, July 24, 1992;
Independent, July 21, 1992, HL; reversing [1992] Q.B. 315; [1992] 2 W.L.R. 112;
[1992] 2 All E.R. 28; (1992) 89(2) L.S.G. 32; (1992) 142 N.L.J. 88; *Times*,
November 18, 1991, CA . . . .   *Digested*, 92/**3488**:
    Considered, 94/3660, 94/3679, 95/1196, 01/638

AT Poeton (Gloucester Plating) Ltd v. Horton; *sub nom* Poeton Industries Ltd v. Horton
[2000] I.C.R. 1208; [2001] F.S.R. 14; (2000) 23(8) I.P.D. 23060, CA . . . .   *Digested*, 01/**4064**

AT&T Corp v. Saudi Cable Co [2000] 2 All E.R. (Comm) 625; [2000] 2 Lloyd's Rep.
127; [2000] C.L.C. 1309; [2000] B.L.R. 293; *Times*, May 23, 2000, CA;
affirming [2000] 1 All E.R. (Comm) 201; [2000] 1 Lloyd's Rep. 22; [2000]
C.L.C. 220, QBD (Comm Ct) . . . .   *Digested*, 00/**223**

AT&T/Computer system (T204/93) [2001] E.P.O.R. 39, EPO (Technical Bd App) . . . .   *Digested*, 01/**3952**

AT&T/Dielectric deposition (T169/98) [2001] E.P.O.R. 29, EPO (Technical Bd App) . . .   *Digested*, 01/**3888**

Ata v. American Express Bank Ltd, *Times*, June 26, 1998, CA . . . .   *Digested*, 98/**379**

Ata v. Hellen [2000] 4 Q.R. 3, CC (Wandsworth) [*Ex rel*. Kevin Haven, Barrister, 2
Gray's Inn Square Chambers, Gray's Inn, London] . . . .   *Digested*, 00/**1497**

Atari Corp (UK) Ltd v. Electronics Boutique Stores (UK) Ltd [1998] Q.B. 539; [1998] 2
W.L.R. 66; [1998] 1 All E.R. 1010; (1997) 16 Tr. L.R. 529; (1997) 94(33) L.S.G.
27; (1997) 141 S.J.L.B. 168; *Times*, July 25, 1997, CA. . . . .   *Digested*, 97/**4476**

Athanassoglou v. Switzerland (27644/95) (2001) 31 E.H.R.R. 13, ECHR . . . . *Digested,* 01/**3542**
Athens Cape Naviera SA v. Deutsche Dampfschiffahrts-Gesellschaft Hansa AG (The
    Barenbels) [1985] 1 Lloyd's Rep. 528; (1985) 82 L.S.G. 1256, CA; affirming
    [1984] 2 Lloyd's Rep. 388, QBD (Comm Ct) . . . . *Digested,* 85/**3224**:
                                          Distinguished, 00/4741
Atherton (Inspector of Taxes) v. British Insulated and Helsby Cables Ltd see British
    Insulated and Helsby Cables Ltd v. Atherton (Inspector of Taxes)
Atherton v. Brooke see Lockwood (Deceased), Re
Athey v. Leonati [1999] Lloyd's Rep. Med. 458, CA (BC) . . . . *Digested,* 00/**4187**
Athinaiki Zithopiia AE v. Elliniko Dimosio (C294/99) see Athinaiki Zithopiia AE v.
    Greece (C294/99)
Athinaiki Zithopiia AE v. Greece (C294/99); *sub nom* Athinaiki Zithopiia AE v. Elliniko
    Dimosio (C294/99) [2001] B.T.C. 451; 4 I.T.L. Rep. 116, ECJ (5th Chamber)
Athukorale v. Attorney General of Sri Lanka 2 B.H.R.C. 610, Sup Ct (SrL) . . . . *Digested,* 98/**3083**
Atkin v. DPP (1989) 89 Cr. App. R. 199; (1989) 153 J.P. 383; [1989] Crim. L.R. 581;
    (1989) 153 J.P.N. 451, DC . . . . *Digested,* 90/**1156**:
                                  Distinguished, 97/1171, 99/906
Atkins v. DPP; *sub nom* DPP v. Atkins; Goodland v. DPP [2000] 1 W.L.R. 1427;
    [2000] 2 All E.R. 425; [2000] 2 Cr. App. R. 248; (2000) 97(13) L.S.G. 42;
    (2000) 144 S.J.L.B. 148; *Times,* March 16, 2000; *Independent,* April 17, 2000
    (C.S.), QBD . . . . *Digested,* 00/**993**
Atkins v. Hiscock (Unreported, January 16, 2001), CC (Bury) [*Ex rel.* Tim Grover,
    Barrister, 7 Harrington Street, Liverpool] . . . . *Digested,* 01/**617**
Atkinson (Inspector of Taxes) v. Dancer; Mannion (Inspector of Taxes) v. Johnston
    [1988] S.T.C. 758; 61 T.C. 598; (1988) 85(17) L.S.G. 50; *Times,* July 22, 1988,
    Ch D . . . . *Digested,* 89/**250**:
                Considered, 93/332, 94/357, 95/533, 96/436, 00/4923
Atkinson v. Whittle (Unreported, March 30, 1998), QBD [*Ex rel.* Michael Smith,
    Barrister, 6 Park Square, Leeds] . . . . *Digested,* 99/**1479**
Atlan v. INPI [2001] E.T.M.R. 88, C d'A (Paris)
Atlan v. United Kingdom (36533/97) [2001] Crim. L.R. 819; *Times,* July 3, 2001,
    ECHR . . . . *Digested,* 01/**988**
Atlanta AG v. Council of the European Union (C104/97 P) [1999] E.C.R. I-6983;
    [2001] 1 C.M.L.R. 20, ECJ (5th Chamber)
Atlantic & General Investment Trust Ltd v. Richbell Information Services Inc; *sub nom*
    Richbell Information Services Inc, Re [2000] B.C.C. 111; [2000] 2 B.C.L.C. 778;
    Times, January 21, 1999, Ch D . . . . *Digested,* 99/**3351**:
                             Previous proceedings, 99/3359
Atlantic Bar & Grill Ltd v. Posthouse Hotels Ltd (Costs) [2000] C.P. Rep. 32, Ch D . . . *Digested,* 00/**420**
Atlantic Computer Systems Plc, Re see Blackspur Group Plc (No.2), Re
Atlantic Computer Systems Plc (No.1), Re [1992] Ch. 505; [1992] 2 W.L.R. 367; [1992] 1 All
    E.R. 476; [1990] B.C.C. 859; [1991] B.C.L.C. 606; *Financial Times,* August 1,
    1990, CA; reversing [1990] B.C.C. 454; [1990] B.C.L.C. 729; *Financial Times,*
    June 13, 1990, Ch D (Companies Ct) . . . . *Digested,* 91/**2127**:
        Applied, 93/2325, 93/4812: *Considered,* 99/3349, 00/3432, 01/507, 01/733:
          Distinguished, 95/566, 96/400: *Followed,* 93/2314, 93/2315, 94/2591,
                     96/4916, 99/3267, 99/3358: *Referred to,* 90/514
Atlantic Computers Plc (In Administration), Re see British & Commonwealth Holdings Plc
    (In Administration) v. Barclays de Zoete Wedd Ltd (No.1)
Atlantic Lines & Navigation Co Inc v. Hallam Ltd (The Lucy) [1983] 1 Lloyd's Rep. 188,
    QBD (Comm Ct) . . . . *Digested,* 83/**1726**:
                                              Followed, 00/818
Atlas Wright (Europe) Ltd v. Wright see Wright v. Atlas Wright (Europe) Ltd
ATOTECH/Rehearing (T433/93) [1998] E.P.O.R. 135, EPO (Technical Bd App)
Atter v. Atkinson (1865-69) L.R. 1 P. & D. 665, Ct of Probate . . . . *Applied,* 01/**5167**:
                                   Not followed, 69/3662, 70/2935
Attorney General v. Arthur Andersen & Co (UK) [1989] E.C.C. 224; *Independent,*
    March 31, 1988, CA; affirming *Times,* October 13, 1987, QBD . . . . *Digested,* 88/**2929**:
                           Applied, 98/757: *Followed,* 97/3904
Attorney General v. Associated Newspapers Ltd [1998] E.M.L.R. 711; *Independent,*
    November 6, 1997, QBD . . . . *Digested,* 97/**23**
Attorney General v. Associated Newspapers Ltd [1999] C.O.D. 190, QBD
Attorney General v. B see Attorney General v. Barker (Civil Proceedings Order)
Attorney General v. Barker (Civil Proceedings Order); *sub nom* Attorney General v. B
    [2000] 1 F.L.R. 759; [2000] 2 F.C.R. 1; [2000] Fam. Law 400; (2000) 97(10)
    L.S.G. 37; *Times,* March 7, 2000, QBD . . . . *Digested,* 00/**631**:
                                           Applied, 01/92
Attorney General v. BBC; *sub nom* Dible v. BBC [1981] A.C. 303; [1980] 3 W.L.R. 109;
    [1980] 3 All E.R. 161; 78 L.G.R. 529; 124 S.J. 444, HL; reversing [1979] 3
    W.L.R. 312; [1979] 3 All E.R. 45; 78 L.G.R. 137; 123 S.J. 405, CA; affirming
    [1978] 1 W.L.R. 477; [1978] 2 All E.R. 731; 76 L.G.R. 386; 122 S.J. 180, QBD . . . *Digested,* 80/**2119**:
        Applied, 81/998, 82/2430, 84/207, 95/3956, 98/16: *Considered,* 82/460,
                  84/448, 85/441, 86/2760, 87/2429: *Referred to,* 82/397
Attorney General v. Benyon see Attorney General v. Beynon

Attorney General v. Beynon; *sub nom* Attorney General v. Benyon [1970] Ch. 1; [1969] 2 W.L.R. 1447; [1969] 2 All E.R. 263; (1969) 133 J.P. 349; 113 S.J. 468, Ch D .   *Digested,* 69/**1578**: *Applied,* 91/376: *Considered,* 98/4370

Attorney General v. Birmingham Post and Mail Ltd [1999] 1 W.L.R. 361; [1998] 4 All E.R. 49; [1999] E.M.L.R. 39; [1998] C.O.D. 432; (1998) 95(37) L.S.G. 36; *Times,* August 31, 1998, QBD. . . . .   *Digested,* 98/**19**: *Considered,* 99/19

Attorney General v. Blake [2001] 1 A.C. 268; [2000] 3 W.L.R. 625; [2000] 4 All E.R. 385; [2000] 2 All E.R. (Comm) 487; [2001] I.R.L.R. 36; [2000] E.M.L.R. 949; (2000) 23(12) I.P.D. 23098; (2000) 97(32) L.S.G. 37; (2000) 150 N.L.J. 1230; (2000) 144 S.J.L.B. 242; *Times,* August 3, 2000; *Independent,* November 6, 2000 (C.S), HL; affirming [1998] Ch. 439; [1998] 2 W.L.R. 805; [1998] 1 All E.R. 833; [1998] E.M.L.R. 309; (1998) 95(4) L.S.G. 33; (1998) 148 N.L.J. 15; (1998) 142 S.J.L.B. 35; *Times,* December 22, 1997; *Independent,* December 19, 1997, CA; reversing [1997] Ch. 84; [1996] 3 W.L.R. 741; [1996] 3 All E.R. 903; [1996] E.M.L.R. 382; [1996] F.S.R. 727; (1996) 19(7) I.P.D. 19066; *Times,* April 23, 1996, Ch D . . . .   *Digested,* 00/**797**: *Applied,* 00/2132

Attorney General v. Channel 4 Television see Attorney General v. Channel Four Television Co Ltd

Attorney General v. Channel Four Television Co Ltd; *sub nom* Attorney General v. Channel 4 Television [1988] Crim. L.R. 237, CA . . . .   *Digested,* 88/**666**: *Not followed,* 00/6031

Attorney General v. Corke [1933] Ch. 89, Ch D . . . .   *Applied,* 57/2579: *Considered,* 72/2528, 99/4066

Attorney General v. Covey; Attorney General v. Matthews *Times,* March 2, 2001, CA . . .   *Digested,* 01/**92**

Attorney General v. Flack [2001] A.C.D. 362, QBD (Admin Ct)

Attorney General v. Foley [2000] 2 All E.R. 609; [2000] C.P.L.R. 277; (2000) 97(13) L.S.G. 44; *Times,* March 7, 2000; *Independent,* April 17, 2000 (C.S.), CA . . . . . .   *Digested,* 00/**87**

Attorney General v. Gouriet see Gouriet v. Union of Post Office Workers

Attorney General v. Great Eastern Railway Co (1879-80) L.R. 5 App. Cas. 473, HL; affirming (1879) L.R. 11 Ch. D. 449, CA . . . .   *Applied,* 53/500, 54/2747, 61/3959, 62/1428, 62/2440, 71/1531, 72/2835, 94/60, 95/1173, 95/6406, 01/5642

Attorney General v. Greater Manchester Newspapers Ltd see Venables v. News Group International (Breach of Injunction)

Attorney General v. Growfar see Attorney General v. Times Newspapers Ltd

Attorney General v. Guardian Newspapers Ltd (Contempt) [1999] E.M.L.R. 904; *Independent,* July 30, 1999, QBD. . . . .   *Digested,* 99/**19**

Attorney General v. Guardian Newspapers Ltd (No.2); Attorney General v. Observer Ltd (No.2); Attorney General v. Times Newspapers Ltd (No.2) [1990] 1 A.C. 109; [1988] 3 W.L.R. 776; [1988] 3 All E.R. 545; [1989] 2 F.S.R. 181; (1988) 85(42) L.S.G. 45; (1988) 138 N.L.J. Rep. 296; (1988) 132 S.J. 1496; *Times,* October 14, 1988; *Independent,* October 14, 1988, HL; affirming [1988] 2 W.L.R. 805; (1988) 138 N.L.J. Rep. 47; (1988) 132 S.J. 566, CA; affirming *Times,* December 22, 1987, Ch D . . . .   *Digested,* 89/**3103**: *Applied,* 89/2900, 89/4740, 90/3099, 92/2791: *Considered,* 96/1219, 99/5990, 01/1057: *Followed,* 97/2040

Attorney General v. Harris see Harris v. Harris

Attorney General v. Jones (Fiona Elizabeth) [2000] Q.B. 66; [1999] 3 W.L.R. 444; [1999] 3 All E.R. 436; (1999) 11 Admin. L.R. 557; [1999] C.O.D. 297; (1999) 96(21) L.S.G. 39; (1999) 149 N.L.J. 720; (1999) 143 S.J.L.B. 148; *Times,* May 3, 1999; *Independent,* May 13, 1999, QBD . . . .   *Digested,* 99/**771**

Attorney General v. Jones (Marcus David) [1990] 1 W.L.R. 859; [1990] 2 All E.R. 636; [1990] C.O.D. 373, CA; affirming [1989] C.O.D. 546; *Independent,* March 23, 1989, QBD . . . .   *Digested,* 90/**3818**: *Considered,* 91/2790, 92/3389, 96/931, 99/573

Attorney General v. Kelsey see Attorney General v. Times Newspapers Ltd

Attorney General v. Leppard see Attorney General v. Times Newspapers Ltd

Attorney General v. Leveller Magazine Ltd; Attorney General v. National Union of Journalists; Attorney General v. Peace News Ltd [1979] A.C. 440; [1979] 2 W.L.R. 247; [1979] 1 All E.R. 745; (1979) 68 Cr. App. R. 342; [1979] Crim. L.R. 247; 123 S.J. 129, HL; reversing [1979] Q.B. 31; [1978] 3 W.L.R. 395; [1978] 3 All E.R. 731; [1978] Crim. L.R. 627; 122 S.J. 541, DC . . . .   *Digested,* 79/**2120**: *Applied,* 80/2120, 81/446, 87/679, 92/971, 92/1005, 94/5047, 98/75: *Considered,* 87/675, 88/692, 89/784, 91/868, 91/2819, 92/969, 92/3454, 93/736, 93/740, 94/1084, 94/3282, 94/3754, 95/3545, 97/5066: *Followed,* 95/144, 96/674: *Referred to,* 83/2353, 84/866

Attorney General v. Matthews see Attorney General v. Covey

Attorney General v. Morgan; Attorney General v. News Group Newspapers Ltd [1998] E.M.L.R. 294; *Independent,* July 17, 1997, QBD. . . . .   *Digested,* 97/**22**

Attorney General v. National Union of Journalists see Attorney General v. Leveller Magazine Ltd

Attorney General v. News Group Newspapers Ltd see Attorney General v. Morgan

Attorney General v. Newspaper Publishing Plc see Attorney General v. Times
    Newspapers Ltd
Attorney General v. Observer and Guardian Newspapers see Attorney General v. Times
    Newspapers Ltd
Attorney General v. Observer Ltd (No.2) see Attorney General v. Guardian Newspapers
    Ltd (No.2)
Attorney General v. Peace News Ltd see Attorney General v. Leveller Magazine Ltd
Attorney General v. Punch; *sub nom* Steen v. Attorney General; Attorney General v.
    Punch Ltd [2001] EWCA Civ 403; [2001] Q.B. 1028; [2001] 2 W.L.R. 1713;
    [2001] 2 All E.R. 655; [2001] E.M.L.R. 24; (2001) 98(21) L.S.G. 39; (2001)
    145 S.J.L.B. 101; *Times*, March 30, 2001; *Independent*, March 30, 2001; *Daily
    Telegraph*, April 3, 2001, CA; reversing in partTNS, QBD . . . .   *Digested*, 01/**18**
Attorney General v. Punch Ltd see Attorney General v. Punch
Attorney General v. SundayTelegraph see Attorney General v. Times Newspapers Ltd
Attorney General v. Times Newspapers Ltd [1974] A.C. 273; [1973] 3 W.L.R. 298;
    [1973] 3 All E.R. 54; 117 S.J. 617, HL; reversing [1973] Q.B. 710; [1973] 2
    W.L.R. 452; [1973] 1 All E.R. 815; 117 S.J. 188, CA; reversing [1972] 3 W.L.R.
    855; [1972] 3 All E.R. 1136; [1973] Crim. L.R. 38; 116 S.J. 885, QBD . . . .   *Digested*, 73/**2618**:
                            Applied, 72/2703, 73/2619, 78/2339, 79/2122, 81/2217, 86/2600,
                      87/3026.a, 88/666, 98/3094: *Approved*, 74/2143: *Considered*, 86/2598,
                                   88/771, 89/2915, 89/3108, 90/3588, 91/2805, 93/587:
                    Distinguished, 81/998, 82/2436, 95/3959: *Followed*, 77/2309
Attorney General v. Times Newspapers Ltd; *sub nom* Attorney General v. Observer and
    Guardian Newspapers; Attorney General v. Newspaper Publishing Plc; Attorney
    General v. Growfar; Attorney General v. Sunday Telegraph [1992] 1 A.C. 191;
    [1991] 2 W.L.R. 994; [1991] 2 All E.R. 398; (1991) 141 N.L.J. 528; (1991) 135
    S.J.L.B. 508; *Times*, April 12, 1991; *Independent*, April 23, 1991; *Guardian*, April
    12, 1991, HL; affirming *Times*, February 28, 1990, CA; affirming [1989] 1 F.S.R.
    457; *Times*, May 9, 1989 ; *Independent*, May 9, 1989 ; *Guardian*, May 9, 1989,
    Ch D . . . .   *Digested*, 91/**2809**:
                                    Considered, 95/1009, 96/27, 01/18
Attorney General v. Times Newspapers Ltd; *sub nom* Attorney General v. Kelsey;
    Attorney General v. Leppard [2001] EWCA Civ 97; [2001] 1 W.L.R. 885; [2001]
    E.M.L.R. 19; (2001) 98(9) L.S.G. 38; (2001) 145 S.J.L.B. 30; *Times*, January
    31, 2001; *Independent*, January 30, 2001, CA. . . . .   *Digested*, 01/**4414**
Attorney General v. Times Newspapers Ltd (No.2) see Attorney General v. Guardian
    Newspapers Ltd (No.2)
Attorney General v. Tod Heatley [1897] 1 Ch. 560, CA . . . .   *Applied*, 01/**4549**:
                                    Distinguished, 47-51/**6972**
Attorney General v. Unger [1998] 1 Cr. App. R. 308; [1998] E.M.L.R. 280;
    Independent, July 8, 1997, QBD . . . .   *Digested*, 97/**24**
Attorney General v. Wheen [2001] I.R.L.R. 91; (2001) 98(4) L.S.G. 49; *Times*, January
    23, 2001; *Independent*, January 29, 2001 (C.S), CA; affirming [2000] I.R.L.R.
    461, EAT . . . .   *Digested*, 01/**2275**
Attorney General ex rel Sutcliffe v. Calderdale MBC (1983) 46 P. & C.R. 399; [1983]
    J.P.L. 310, CA . . . .   *Digested*, 84/**3451**:
                       Applied, 85/2927: *Considered*, 86/2814, 00/4473: *Distinguished*, 87/3195
Attorney General ex rel Tilley v. Wandsworth LBC [1981] 1 W.L.R. 854; [1981] 1 All E.R.
    1162; (1981) 11 Fam. Law 119; 125 S.J. 148; *Times*, February 5, 1981, CA;
    affirming *Times*, March 21, 1980, Ch D . . . .   *Digested*, 81/**1304**:
                   Applied, 82/1906, 83/3147: *Considered*, 95/1885, 96/3042, 99/3049
Attorney General for Northern Ireland's Reference (No.3 of 2000) see Attorney General of
    Northern Ireland's Reference (No.3 of 2000), Re
Attorney General for Ontario v. M 7 B.H.R.C. 489, Sup Ct (Can) . . . .   *Digested*, 00/**3254**
Attorney General of Antigua and Barbuda v. Lake [1999] 1 W.L.R. 68; (1998) 142
    S.J.L.B. 279, PC (Ant) . . . .   *Digested*, 99/**3101**
Attorney General of Canada v. Ward [1997] I.N.L.R. 42; (1993) 103 D.L.R. (4th) 1;
    [1993] 2 S.C.R. 689, Sup Ct (Can) . . . .   *Digested*, 98/**3245**:
                      Applied, 99/3147: *Considered*, 96/3205, 96/3217, 97/2851
Attorney General of Gibraltar v. May [1999] 1 W.L.R. 998; *Times*, November 20, 1998,
    CA . . . .   *Digested*, 98/**888**
Attorney General of Hong Kong v. Humphreys Estate (Queen's Gardens) Ltd [1987]
    A.C. 114; [1987] 2 W.L.R. 343; [1987] 2 All E.R. 387; (1987) 54 P. & C.R. 96;
    (1987) 84 L.S.G. 574; (1987) 131 S.J. 194, PC (HK) . . . .   *Digested*, 87/**1443**:
                               Applied, 93/2456, 00/4670: *Considered*, 91/2686
Attorney General of Hong Kong v. Shimizu Corp (1998) 14 Const. L.J. 111, CA (HK) . . .   *Digested*, 98/**231**
Attorney General of Jamaica v. Williams [1998] A.C. 351; [1997] 3 W.L.R. 389; (1997)
    141 S.J.L.B. 162, PC (Jam). . . . .   *Digested*, 97/**1362**
Attorney General of New Zealand v. Horton [1999] 1 W.L.R. 1195; (1999) 143 S.J.L.B.
    149, PC (NZ) . . . .   *Digested*, 99/**4399**
Attorney General of Nigeria v. Abacha see Compagnie Noga d'Importation et
    d'Exportation SA v. Abacha (No.2)

Attorney General of Northern Ireland's Reference (No.1 of 1975), Re; *sub nom* Reference under s.48A of the Criminal Appeal (Northern Ireland) Act 1968 (No.1 of 1975), Re [1977] A.C. 105; [1976] 3 W.L.R. 235; [1976] 2 All E.R. 937; 120 S.J. 524, HL (NI) . . . . *Digested*, 76/**1917**:
Considered, 83/2691, 95/1282: *Distinguished*, 00/1022
Attorney General of Northern Ireland's Reference (Nos.1 and 2 of 1996), Re [1996] N.I. 456, CA (Crim Div)
Attorney General of Northern Ireland's Reference (No.1 of 1998), Re [1998] N.I. 232, CA (NI) . . . . *Digested*, 99/**5225**:
Considered, 99/5223

Attorney General of Northern Ireland's Reference (No.3 of 2000), Re; *sub nom* Attorney General for Northern Ireland's Reference (No.3 of 2000); R. *v.* Rogan (Gerard James) [2001] N.I. 367, CA (Crim Div) (NI)
Attorney General of Ontario *v.* Keller (1978) 86 D.L.R. (3d) 426, HC (Ont) . . . . *Digested*, 79/**2089**:
Followed, 98/3932

Attorney General of the Cayman Islands *v.* Wahr-Hansen [2001] 1 A.C. 75; [2000] 3 W.L.R. 869; [2000] 3 All E.R. 642; [2001] W.T.L.R. 345; (2000-01) 3 I.T.E.L.R. 72; *Times*, July 27, 2000, PC (CI) . . . . *Digested*, 00/**5256**
Attorney General of Trinidad and Tobago *v.* Phillip [1995] 1 A.C. 396; [1994] 3 W.L.R. 1134; [1995] 1 All E.R. 93; (1994) 91 (41) L.S.G. 43; (1994) 144 N.L.J. 1549; (1994) 138 S.J.L.B. 208; *Times*, October 11, 1994; *Independent*, October 19, 1994, PC (Trin) . . . . *Digested*, 95/**899**:
Followed, 01/1072

Attorney General of Trinidad and Tobago *v.* Tokai see DPP *v.* Tokai
Attorney General's Guidelines on the Acceptance of Pleas [2001] 1 Cr. App. R. 28, Court not applicable . . . . *Digested*, 01/**1175**
Attorney General's Reference (No.1 of 1980), Re [1981] 1 W.L.R. 34; [1981] 1 All E.R. 366; (1981) 72 Cr. App. R. 60; [1981] Crim. L.R. 41; (1980) 124 S.J. 881, CA (Crim Div)
Digested, 81/**447**:
Considered, 98/892

Attorney General's Reference (No.1 of 1982), Re [1983] Q.B. 751; [1983] 3 W.L.R. 72; [1983] 2 All E.R. 721; (1983) 77 Cr. App. R. 9; (1984) 148 J.P. 115; [1983] Crim. L.R. 534; (1983) 127 S.J. 377, CA (Crim Div) . . . . *Digested*, 83/**574**:
Considered, 00/952: *Distinguished*, 96/1473
Attorney General's Reference (No.2 of 1982), Re; *sub nom* Attorney General's Reference (No.2 of 1983), Re [1984] Q.B. 624; [1984] 2 W.L.R. 447; [1984] 2 All E.R. 216; (1984) 78 Cr. App. R. 131; [1985] Crim. L.R. 241; (1984) 81 L.S.G. 279; (1984) 128 S.J. 221, CA (Crim Div) . . . . *Digested*, 84/**958**:
Followed, 01/1084

Attorney General's Reference (No.2 of 1983), Re see Attorney General's Reference (No.2 of 1982), Re
Attorney General's Reference (No.1 of 1989), Re [1989] 1 W.L.R. 1117; [1989] 3 All E.R. 571; (1990) 90 Cr. App. R. 141; (1989) 11 Cr. App. R. (S.) 409; [1989] Crim. L.R. 923, CA (Crim Div) . . . . *Digested*, 91/**1138**:
Cited, 92/1300, 92/1301, 92/1304, 92/1419, 93/1186, 94/1275, 94/1286, 94/1330: *Considered*, 89/1037, 90/1207, 90/1393, 91/1193, 92/1162, 93/1269, 94/1272, 94/1340, 96/1794, 97/1443, 97/1454, 99/1192, 99/1193, 99/1304, 01/1352: *Distinguished*, 92/1376: *Referred to*, 95/1402
Attorney General's Reference (No.2 of 1989), Re; *sub nom* R. *v.* Major (Darren Mark) (1989) 11 Cr. App. R. (S.) 481; [1990] Crim. L.R. 212, CA (Crim Div) . . . . *Digested*, 91/**1208**:
Cited, 91/1214, 93/1278, 95/1468: *Considered*, 96/2060, 98/1307, 00/1137
Attorney General's Reference (No.4 of 1989), Re [1990] 1 W.L.R. 41; (1990) 90 Cr. App. R. 366; (1989) 11 Cr. App. R. (S.) 517; [1990] Crim. L.R. 438; *Times*, November 11, 1989, CA (Crim Div) . . . . *Digested*, 90/**1207**:
Applied, 96/2017, 97/1622: *Cited*, 92/1285, 92/1304, 93/1048, 93/1057, 93/1331, 94/1411: *Considered*, 91/1033, 92/1180, 92/1428, 93/1050, 96/2070, 96/2094, 99/1201, 99/1304, 99/1306, 00/1294: *Followed*, 96/1978
Attorney General's Reference (No.7 of 1989), Re; *sub nom* R. *v.* Thornton (Paul Anthony) (1990) 12 Cr. App. R. (S.) 1; [1990] Crim. L.R. 436; *Times*, January 16, 1990, CA (Crim Div) . . . . *Digested*, 91/**1194**:
Cited, 92/1378: *Considered*, 93/1268, 94/1337, 98/1353, 98/1354, 99/1309, 00/1402: *Referred to*, 95/1457
Attorney General's Reference (No.9 of 1989), Re; *sub nom* R. *v.* Lacey (Steven Lloyd) (1990) 12 Cr. App. R. (S.) 7; [1990] Crim. L.R. 437, CA (Crim Div) . . . . *Digested*, 91/**1214**:
Applied, 92/1399, 93/1101: *Cited*, 93/1274: *Considered*, 92/1155, 92/1392, 96/2060, 97/1596, 00/1137, 00/1421, 01/1400, 01/1478: *Followed*, 97/1699:
Referred to, 99/1331

Attorney General's Reference (No.1 of 1990), Re [1992] Q.B. 630; [1992] 3 W.L.R. 9; [1992] 3 All E.R. 169; (1992) 95 Cr. App. R. 296; (1992) 156 J.P. 593; [1993] Crim. L.R. 37; (1992) 156 J.P.N. 476; (1992) 89 (21) L.S.G. 28; (1992) 142 N.L.J. 563; *Times*, April 16, 1992; *Independent*, May 1, 1992, CA (Crim Div) . . . . *Digested*, 92/**615**:
Applied, 93/623, 94/658, 00/925, 01/1190: *Considered*, 93/619, 94/656, 95/900, 95/1052, 96/1599, 96/4859, 97/1276, 97/2566, 98/1063, 99/1037, 01/1119

Attorney General's Reference (No.17 of 1990), Re; *sub nom* R. *v.* Jones (Stephen John)
(1991) 92 Cr. App. R. 288; (1990) 12 Cr. App. R. (S.) 572; [1991] Crim. L.R.
487; *Times,* December 10, 1990, CA (Crim Div) . . . . *Digested,* 91/**1219**:
                    Considered, 93/1028, 93/1033, 94/1183: *Referred to,* 97/1435
Attorney General's Reference (Nos.19 and 20 of 1990), Re; *sub nom* R. *v.* McLoughlin
(George Gerrard); R. *v.* Clarke (Vincent) (1990) 12 Cr. App. R. (S.) 490; [1991]
Crim. L.R. 306, CA (Crim Div) . . . . *Digested,* 91/**1027**:
            Cited, 94/1186: *Considered,* 96/1737, 97/1417, 97/1420, 98/1128, 00/1413
Attorney General's Reference (Nos.21 and 22 of 1990), Re; *sub nom* R. *v.* Nuttall (Nathan
Matthew); R. *v.* Nuttall (Marcus Joel) (1991) 12 Cr. App. R. (S.) 648; [1991]
Crim. L.R. 487, CA (Crim Div) . . . . *Digested,* 92/**1456**:
                                                                  Considered, 98/1381
Attorney General's Reference (No.23 of 1990), Re; *sub nom* R. *v.* Mellor (Paul James)
(1990) 12 Cr. App. R. (S.) 575; [1991] Crim. L.R. 486, CA (Crim Div) . . . . *Digested,* 92/**1426**:
                            Considered, 98/1410, 01/1333: *Referred to,* 93/1183
Attorney General's Reference (No.8 of 1991), Re; *sub nom* R. *v.* Jepson (Lawrence)
(1992) 13 Cr. App. R. (S.) 360; [1992] Crim. L.R. 136, CA (Crim Div) . . . . *Digested,* 93/**1265**:
                                        Considered, 97/1444, 00/1400, 01/1463
Attorney General's Reference (No.11 of 1991), Re; *sub nom* R. *v.* Burnett (Edward Peter)
(1992) 13 Cr. App. R. (S.) 402; [1992] Crim. L.R. 135, CA (Crim Div) . . . . *Digested,* 93/**1057**:
                                                                  Considered, 99/1185
Attorney General's Reference (No.18 of 1991), Re (1992) 13 Cr. App. R. (S.) 624; [1992]
Crim. L.R. 455, CA (Crim Div) . . . . *Digested,* 93/**1264**:
                                                                  Considered, 99/1311
Attorney General's Reference (Nos.22 and 23 of 1991), Re; *sub nom* R. *v.* Jacques (Mark
John); R. *v.* Jacques (Richard Charles) (1992) 13 Cr. App. R. (S.) 592; [1992]
Crim. L.R. 382, CA (Crim Div) . . . . *Digested,* 93/**1281**:
                    Considered, 98/1328, 98/1372, 98/1376: *Referred to,* 93/1280
Attorney General's Reference (No.7 of 1992), Re; *sub nom* R. *v.* Khan (Jahan Zeb)
(1993) 14 Cr. App. R. (S.) 122; [1992] Crim. L.R. 679, CA (Crim Div) . . . . *Digested,* 93/**1278**:
                                                                  Considered, 00/1421
Attorney General's Reference (No.11 of 1992), Re; *sub nom* R. *v.* Howes (Robert Charles)
(1993) 14 Cr. App. R. (S.) 136; [1992] Crim. L.R. 677, CA (Crim Div) . . . . *Digested,* 93/**1056**:
                              Cited, 98/1232: *Considered,* 99/1225
Attorney General's Reference (No.19 of 1992), Re; *sub nom* R. *v.* McMorrow (Francis
Christopher) (1993) 14 Cr. App. R. (S.) 330; [1993] Crim. L.R. 83, CA (Crim
Div) . . . . *Digested,* 94/**1183**:
                              Considered, 98/1256: *Referred to,* 97/1435
Attorney General's Reference (No.22 of 1992), Re; *sub nom* R. *v.* Thomas (Steven Mark)
[1994] 1 All E.R. 105; (1993) 97 Cr. App. R. 275; (1993) 14 Cr. App. R. (S.)
435; [1993] Crim. L.R. 227, CA (Crim Div) . . . . *Digested,* 94/**1227**:
                                                                  Considered, 98/1171
Attorney General's Reference (No.32 of 1992), Re; *sub nom* R. *v.* N (Robert William)
(1994) 98 Cr. App. R. 206; (1994) 15 Cr. App. R. (S.) 149, CA (Crim Div) . . . . . *Considered,* 97/1454,
                                                                          00/1400
Attorney General's Reference (No.36 of 1992), Re; *sub nom* R. *v.* Hills (Gary William)
(1994) 15 Cr. App. R. (S.) 117, CA (Crim Div) . . . . *Considered,* 00/1424
Attorney General's Reference (No.5 of 1993), Re (1994) 15 Cr. App. R. (S.) 201, CA (Crim
Div) . . . . *Considered,* 96/1721,
                                                  97/1399, 97/1401, 00/1129, 00/1135
Attorney General's Reference (No.10 of 1993), Re; *sub nom* R. *v.* Bartley (Roger
Anthony) (1994) 15 Cr. App. R. (S.) 487; [1994] Crim. L.R. 233, CA . . . . *Digested,* 95/**1496**:
                                                                  Considered, 01/1326
Attorney General's Reference (No.11 of 1993), Re; *sub nom* R. *v.* Tovey (William Joseph)
(1994) 15 Cr. App. R. (S.) 490; [1994] Crim. L.R. 232, CA (Crim Div) . . . . *Digested,* 95/**1455**:
                                        Considered, 96/2041, 99/1311
Attorney General's Reference (No.12 of 1993), Re; *sub nom* R. *v.* Bigby (Wayne Edward)
(1994) 15 Cr. App. R. (S.) 424; *Times,* October 14, 1993, CA (Crim Div) . . . . *Digested,* 93/**1276**:
                                                                  Considered, 00/1423
Attorney General's Reference (Nos.14 and 24 of 1993), Re; *sub nom* R. *v.* Shepherd (Peter
James); R. *v.* Wernet (Robert Stewart) [1994] 1 W.L.R. 530; [1994] 2 All E.R.
242; (1994) 99 Cr. App. R. 39; (1994) 15 Cr. App. R. (S.) 640; [1994] R.T.R. 49;
(1994) 138 S.J.L.B. 23; *Times,* December 27, 1993, CA (Crim Div) . . . . *Digested,* 94/**1193**:
            Applied, 95/1319: *Approved,* 96/1836: *Considered,* 96/1756, 96/1757,
                96/1762, 96/1763, 96/1767, 96/1822, 96/1824, 96/1826, 96/1827, 96/1828,
                96/1829, 96/1835, 97/1662, 97/1668, 97/1669, 97/1671, 97/1673, 99/1326,
                00/1197, 00/1364: *Distinguished,* 96/1759: *Followed,* 96/1761, 97/1678:
                    Referred to, 94/1193.a, 95/1344, 97/1661, 97/1665, 97/1667
Attorney General's Reference (No.18 of 1993), Re; *sub nom* R. *v.* Kavanagh (Peter
Dennis) (1994) 15 Cr. App. R. (S.) 800, CA (Crim Div) . . . . *Digested,* 95/**1394**:
                                                                  Considered, 99/1185
Attorney General's Reference (No.19 of 1993), Re; *sub nom* R. *v.* Downey (Conor
Edward) (1994) 15 Cr. App. R. (S.) 760; [1994] Crim. L.R. 535, CA (Crim Div) . *Digested,* 95/**1448**:
        Considered, 00/1378: *Distinguished,* 97/1612: *Referred to,* 99/1110

Attorney General's Reference (No.20 of 1993), Re; *sub nom* R. *v.* Darah (Salam Ali) (1994) 15 Cr. App. R. (S.) 797, CA (Crim Div) . . . .   *Digested,* 95/**1495**:
                           Considered, 96/1920, 98/1410, 99/1373, 00/1266, 01/1338:
                                           Followed, 98/1408

Attorney General's Reference (No.2 of 1994), Re; *sub nom* R. *v.* Crook (Anthony Michael) (1995) 16 Cr. App. R. (S.) 117, CA (Crim Div) . . . .   *Digested,* 96/**2070**:
                      Cited, 97/1694: *Considered,* 00/1423: *Referred to,* 99/1331

Attorney General's Reference (No.3 of 1994), Re [1998] A.C. 245; [1997] 3 W.L.R. 421; [1997] 3 All E.R. 936; [1998] 1 Cr. App. R. 91; [1997] Crim. L.R. 829; (1997) 94 (36) L.S.G. 44; (1997) 147 N.L.J. 1185; (1997) 141 S.J.L.B. 189; *Times,* July 25, 1997; *Independent,* October 1, 1997, HL; affirming in part [1996] Q.B. 581; [1996] 2 W.L.R. 412; [1996] 2 All E.R. 10; [1996] 1 Cr. App. R. 351; [1996] 2 F.L.R. 1; (1996) 29 B.M.L.R. 99; [1996] Crim. L.R. 268; (1995) 145 N.L.J. 1777; (1996) 140 S.J.L.B. 20; *Times,* November 29, 1995; *Independent,* December 6, 1995, CA . . . .   *Digested,* 97/**1222**

Attorney General's Reference (No.3 of 1994) (Unduly Lenient Sentence), Re; *sub nom* R. *v.* Dacres (Robert Clive) (1995) 16 Cr. App. R. (S.) 176; [1994] Crim. L.R. 766, CA (Crim Div) . . . .   *Digested,* 96/**2060**:
                     Considered, 97/1454, 97/1596, 00/1340: *Followed,* 97/1699

Attorney General's Reference (No.6 of 1994), Re; *sub nom* R. *v.* Lee (Christopher) (1995) 16 Cr. App. R. (S.) 343; [1994] Crim. L.R. 951, CA (Crim Div) . . . .   *Considered,* 97/1692,
              98/1381, 99/1238, 99/1332, 00/1419, 01/1397: *Referred to,* 99/1340, 00/1336

Attorney General's Reference (No.7 of 1994), Re; *sub nom* R. *v.* Chadwick (Barry John) (1995) 16 Cr. App. R. (S.) 300; [1994] Crim. L.R. 954; *Times,* August 10, 1994, CA (Crim Div) . . . .   *Digested,* 94/**1319**:
                                       Considered, 01/1500

Attorney General's Reference (No.8 of 1994), Re; *sub nom* R. *v.* Asquith (Neil Henry) (1995) 16 Cr. App. R. (S.) 327; [1995] R.T.R. 54; [1994] Crim. L.R. 950, CA (Crim Div) . . . .   *Digested,* 95/**1345**:
                                       Considered, 99/1321

Attorney General's Reference (No.12 of 1994), Re; *sub nom* R. *v.* Dyke (Phillip) (1995) 16 Cr. App. R. (S.) 559, CA (Crim Div) . . . .   *Considered,* 99/1198

Attorney General's Reference (No.14 of 1994), Re; *sub nom* R. *v.* Walker (David) (1995) 16 Cr. App. R. (S.) 376; [1994] Crim. L.R. 955, CA (Crim Div) . . . .   *Considered,* 99/1373,
                                               00/1442

Attorney General's Reference (No.15 of 1994), Re (1995) 16 Cr. App. R. (S.) 593, CA (Crim Div) . . . .   *Considered,* 98/1299:
                                       Distinguished, 96/1978

Attorney General's Reference (No.16 of 1994), Re; *sub nom* R. *v.* Fairfax (Kenneth) (No.2) (1995) 16 Cr. App. R. (S.) 629, CA (Crim Div) . . . .   *Digested,* 96/**1737**:
              Considered, 97/1417, 97/1418, 98/1127, 98/1128, 00/1146, 00/1147

Attorney General's Reference (Nos.17 and 18 of 1994), Re; *sub nom* R. *v.* Chamberlain (Patrick Arthur); R. *v.* Chamberlain (Toby) (1995) 16 Cr. App. R. (S.) 418; [1994] Crim. L.R. 955, CA (Crim Div) . . . .   *Considered,* 97/1562,
                           97/1570, 98/1298: *Followed,* 97/1568

Attorney General's Reference (No.19 of 1994), Re; *sub nom* R. *v.* Arnold (Neil Terry) (1995) 16 Cr. App. R. (S.) 541, CA (Crim Div) . . . .   *Considered,* 99/1185

Attorney General's Reference (Nos.24 and 45 of 1994), Re; *sub nom* R. *v.* Rayner (Simon Nicholas); R. *v.* Wing (David) (1995) 16 Cr. App. R. (S.) 583; [1995] R.T.R. 119; [1995] Crim. L.R. 178; *Times,* October 31, 1994; *Independent,* November 28, 1994 (C.S.), CA (Crim Div) . . . .   *Digested,* 95/**1344**:
             Applied, 96/1824: *Considered,* 97/1666, 97/1680, 97/1689, 99/1326:
                                       Referred to, 96/1767

Attorney General's Reference (No.33 of 1994), Re; *sub nom* R. *v.* McIntosh (Stuart Robert) (1995) 16 Cr. App. R. (S.) 632; [1995] Crim. L.R. 179, CA (Crim Div) . .   *Digested,* 96/**1920**:
                                       Considered, 99/1243

Attorney General's Reference (No.35 of 1994), Re; *sub nom* R. *v.* H (Terence) (1995) 16 Cr. App. R. (S.) 635, CA (Crim Div) . . . .   *Digested,* 96/**1782**:
                                   Considered, 99/1195, 00/1280

Attorney General's Reference (No.39 of 1994), Re; *sub nom* R. *v.* Millard (Andrew Derek) (1995) 16 Cr. App. R. (S.) 763, CA (Crim Div) . . . .   *Digested,* 96/**1911**:
                                   Considered, 97/1575, 01/1337

Attorney General's Reference (No.41 of 1994), Re; *sub nom* R. *v.* O'Boyle (Michael James) (1995) 16 Cr. App. R. (S.) 792, CA (Crim Div) . . . .   *Digested,* 96/**1919**:
          Considered, 97/1552, 98/1410, 00/1266, 01/1324, 01/1329, 01/1338:
                Distinguished, 97/1724: *Followed,* 98/1408: *Referred to,* 97/1574

Attorney General's Reference (No.43 of 1994), Re; *sub nom* R. *v.* Smith (Robert) (1995) 16 Cr. App. R. (S.) 815, CA (Crim Div) . . . .   *Digested,* 96/**1734**:
             Considered, 98/1139, 98/1256, 99/1085: *Referred to,* 97/1435

Attorney General's Reference (No.44 of 1994), Re; *sub nom* R. *v.* Middleton (Steven Peter) [1996] 1 Cr. App. R. (S.) 256; *Times,* July 13, 1995, CA (Crim Div) . . . . . .   *Digested,* 95/**1449**:
                                   Considered, 99/1289, 00/1294

Attorney General's Reference (No.47 of 1994), Re; *sub nom* R. *v.* Smith (Robert John)
(1995) 16 Cr. App. R. (S.) 865, CA (Crim Div) . . . . *Digested,* 96/**1910**:
Considered, 97/1556, 97/1559, 97/1561, 97/1562, 98/1236:
Referred to, 97/1574

Attorney General's Reference (No.1 of 1995), Re; *sub nom* R. *v.* Henry (David James)
[1996] 1 Cr. App. R. (S.) 11, CA (Crim Div) . . . . *Digested,* 96/**1692**:
Considered, 97/1416, 97/1418, 98/1126, 98/1127, 98/1128, 00/1147:
Followed, 98/1129

Attorney General's Reference (No.2 of 1995), Re [1996] 3 All E.R. 860; [1997] 1 Cr. App. R.
72; [1996] Crim. L.R. 662, CA (Crim Div). . . . . *Digested,* 96/**1499**:
Considered, 99/1201

Attorney General's Reference (No.2 of 1995) (Unduly Lenient Sentence), Re; *sub nom* R.
v. S (David William) [1996] 1 Cr. App. R. (S.) 274; [1995] Crim. L.R. 835, CA
(Crim Div). . . . . *Digested,* 96/**1788**:
Considered, 99/1194, 00/1288

Attorney General's Reference (No.3 of 1995), Re; *sub nom* R. *v.* H (Cyril Arthur) [1996]
1 Cr. App. R. (S.) 26, CA (Crim Div) . . . . *Digested,* 96/**1775**:
Considered, 97/1453, 00/1395

Attorney General's Reference (Nos.11 and 12 of 1995), Re; *sub nom* R. *v.* Mitchinson
(Daniel Steven); R. *v.* Harling (Andrew Bentley) [1996] 1 Cr. App. R. (S.) 229,
CA (Crim Div). . . . . *Digested,* 96/**1922**:
Considered, 98/1128

Attorney General's Reference (Nos.14, 15 and 16 of 1995), Re; *sub nom* R. *v.* Ward
(Michael Grainger); R. *v.* Howarth (Jeremy John); R. *v.* Hendry (George) *Times,*
April 10, 1997, CA (Crim Div) . . . . *Digested,* 97/**1547**:
Subsequent proceedings, 00/3216, 01/717

Attorney General's Reference (No.28 of 1995), Re; *sub nom* R. *v.* Rook (Philip) [1996] 1
Cr. App. R. (S.) 410, CA (Crim Div). . . . . *Digested,* 96/**1967**:
Considered, 99/1243, 00/1323

Attorney General's Reference (No.29 of 1995), Re; *sub nom* R. *v.* Mighty (Daniel Ivor)
[1996] 2 Cr. App. R. (S.) 60, CA (Crim Div) . . . . *Digested,* 96/**2074**:
Considered, 99/1339, 00/1424

Attorney General's Reference (No.30 of 1995), Re; *sub nom* R. *v.* Law (Richard) [1996]
1 Cr. App. R. (S.) 364, CA (Crim Div) . . . . *Digested,* 96/**1826**:
Considered, 97/1673, 98/1364

Attorney General's Reference (Nos.32 and 33 of 1995), Re; *sub nom* R. *v.* Pegg (Shane
Robin); R. *v.* Martin (Mark Anthony) [1996] 2 Cr. App. R. (S.) 346, CA (Crim
Div) . . . . *Digested,* 97/**1421**:
Considered, 97/1700, 98/1132, 00/1414: *Referred to,* 97/1419

Attorney General's Reference (No.36 of 1995), Re; *sub nom* R. *v.* Dawson (Neil Andrew)
[1996] 2 Cr. App. R. (S.) 50; *Times,* November 24, 1995, CA (Crim Div). . . . . . . *Digested,* 95/**1442**:
Considered, 99/1306

Attorney General's Reference (No.38 of 1995), Re; *sub nom* R. *v.* Harvey (Michael)
[1996] 2 Cr. App. R. (S.) 103, CA (Crim Div) . . . . *Digested,* 96/**2069**:
Considered, 98/1328, 98/1372, 99/1239

Attorney General's Reference (No.39 of 1995), Re; *sub nom* R. *v.* Grey (Kenneth) [1996]
2 Cr. App. R. (S.) 125, CA (Crim Div) . . . . *Digested,* 96/**2000**:
Considered, 98/1405

Attorney General's Reference (No.40 of 1995), Re; *sub nom* R. *v.* Humberstone (Alan)
[1996] 2 Cr. App. R. (S.) 109, CA (Crim Div) . . . . *Digested,* 96/**1878**:
Considered, 99/1128

Attorney General's Reference (Nos.41 and 42 of 1995), Re; *sub nom* R. *v.* Edwards
(Vincent); R. *v.* Horton (Richard David) [1996] 2 Cr. App. R. (S.) 115, CA (Crim
Div) . . . . *Digested,* 96/**2057**:
Followed, 00/1341

Attorney General's Reference (Nos.44 and 46 of 1995), Re; *sub nom* R. *v.* Barthelmy
(Robert); R. *v.* Hobbs (Daniel) [1996] 2 Cr. App. R. (S.) 128, CA (Crim Div). . . . *Digested,* 96/**2058**:
Considered, 00/1338

Attorney General's Reference (Nos.62, 63 and 64 of 1995), Re; *sub nom* R. *v.* O'Halloran
(Paul Gerrard); R. *v.* Cameron (Clarence Raymond); R. *v.* Wood (Jane Leslie)
[1996] 2 Cr. App. R. (S.) 223, CA (Crim Div) . . . . *Digested,* 96/**2062**:
Considered, 00/1419

Attorney General's Reference (No.66 of 1995), Re; *sub nom* R. *v.* Ward (Adrian John)
[1996] 2 Cr. App. R. (S.) 371, CA (Crim Div) . . . . *Digested,* 97/**1706**:
Considered, 99/1238, 99/1332

Attorney General's Reference (No.66 of 1995), Re; *sub nom* R. *v.* Lloyd (David Russell)
[1996] 2 Cr. App. R. (S.) 373, CA (Crim Div) . . . . *Digested,* 97/**1662**:
Considered, 99/1326

Attorney General's Reference (Nos.72 and 73 of 1995), Re; *sub nom* R. *v.* Bernard
(Stanley); R. *v.* Harvey (Vernon) [1996] 2 Cr. App. R. (S.) 438, CA (Crim Div) . . *Considered,* 01/1479
Attorney General's Reference (No.5 of 1996), Re; *sub nom* R. *v.* D (Carl) [1996] 2 Cr.
App. R. (S.) 434, CA (Crim Div). . . . . *Digested,* 97/**1454**:
Considered, 99/1306, 00/1395

Attorney General's Reference (No.6 of 1996), Re; *sub nom* R. *v.* Kousourous (Adam)
   [1997] 1 Cr. App. R. (S.) 79, CA (Crim Div) . . . .   *Digested*, 97/**1674**:
                                                                                                                      Applied, 98/1278
Attorney General's Reference (No.10 of 1996), Re; *sub nom* R. *v.* Moore (John Michael)
   [1997] 1 Cr. App. R. (S.) 76, CA (Crim Div) . . . .   *Digested*, 97/**1414**:
                                                                                                           Considered, 98/1126, 98/1128
Attorney General's Reference (Nos.17 and 18 of 1996), Re; *sub nom* R. *v.* Iseton (Mark
   Andrew); R. *v.* Wardle (Lee) [1997] 1 Cr. App. R. (S.) 247, CA (Crim Div) . . . . . .   *Digested*, 97/**1667**:
                                                                                                                      Applied, 98/1278
Attorney General's Reference (Nos.26 and 27 of 1996), Re; *sub nom* R. *v.* Nazir (Jangeer);
   R. *v.* Ahmed (Naveed) [1997] 1 Cr. App. R. (S.) 243, CA (Crim Div). . . . .   *Digested*, 97/**1600**:
                                                                                                                  Considered, 99/1333
Attorney General's Reference (No.32 of 1996), Re; *sub nom* R. *v.* Whittaker (Steven Alan)
   [1997] 1 Cr. App. R. (S.) 261; [1996] Crim. L.R. 917; (1996) 93(38) L.S.G. 42;
   Times, July 24, 1996, CA (Crim Div) . . . .   *Digested*, 96/**1912**:
                                                 Considered, 98/1233, 98/1346, 98/1405, 99/1251, 99/1255, 99/1308:
                                                                                                                   Followed, 99/1254
Attorney General's Reference (No.33 of 1996), Re; *sub nom* R. *v.* Latham (Daniel
   George) [1997] 2 Cr. App. R. (S.) 10; [1997] Crim. L.R. 140; *Times*, November
   15, 1996; *Independent*, November 12, 1996, CA (Crim Div) . . . .   *Digested*, 97/**1622**:
                                                         Applied, 97/1163: *Considered*, 97/1623, 98/1288, 00/1267:
                                                                             Distinguished, 99/1259: *Followed*, 97/1621
Attorney General's Reference (No.35 of 1996), Re; *sub nom* R. *v.* Hoyle (Damien James)
   [1997] 1 Cr. App. R. (S.) 350, CA (Crim Div) . . . .   *Digested*, 97/**1401**:
                                                                                                                  Considered, 00/1135
Attorney General's Reference (No.36 of 1996), Re; *sub nom* R. *v.* Johnson (Jason Leon)
   [1997] 1 Cr. App. R. (S.) 363, CA (Crim Div) . . . .   *Digested*, 97/**1556**:
                                                                                                                  Considered, 99/1185
Attorney General's Reference (No.37 of 1996), Re; *sub nom* R. *v.* Hobday (David
   Thomas) [1997] 1 Cr. App. R. (S.) 304, CA (Crim Div) . . . .   *Digested*, 97/**1575**:
                                                                                                             Distinguished, 98/1407
Attorney General's Reference (No.39 of 1996), Re; *sub nom* R. *v.* Searle (Wayne Thomas)
   [1997] 1 Cr. App. R. (S.) 355, CA (Crim Div) . . . .   *Digested*, 97/**1692**:
                                                 Considered, 98/1381, 99/1332, 00/1419: *Referred to*, 00/1336
Attorney General's Reference (No.40 of 1996), Re; *sub nom* R. *v.* Robinson (Mark Leslie)
   [1997] 1 Cr. App. R. (S.) 357; [1997] Crim. L.R. 69, CA (Crim Div) . . . .   *Digested*, 97/**1540**:
                                                                                                                   Followed, 00/1135
Attorney General's Reference (No.51 of 1996), Re; *sub nom* R. *v.* G (Lee Eugene) (A
   Juvenile) [1997] 2 Cr. App. R. (S.) 248, CA (Crim Div) . . . .   *Digested*, 97/**1557**:
                                                                                                                  Considered, 99/1243
Attorney General's Reference (No.52 of 1996), Re; *sub nom* R. *v.* Anderson (Steven
   John) [1997] 2 Cr. App. R. (S.) 230, CA (Crim Div) . . . .   *Digested*, 97/**1718**:
                                                                                                                  Referred to, 00/1262
Attorney General's Reference (No.58 of 1996), Re; *sub nom* R. *v.* Jones (Karl David)
   [1997] 2 Cr. App. R. (S.) 233, CA (Crim Div) . . . .   *Digested*, 97/**1699**:
                                                                                                                  Considered, 01/1478
Attorney General's Reference (No.59 of 1996), Re; *sub nom* R. *v.* Grainger (Terence)
   [1997] 2 Cr. App. R. (S.) 250, CA (Crim Div) . . . .   *Digested*, 97/**1571**:
                                                                                                                  Considered, 99/1243
Attorney General's Reference (No.61 of 1996), Re; *sub nom* R. *v.* McGregor (Thomas
   Hunter) [1997] 2 Cr. App. R. (S.) 316, CA (Crim Div) . . . .   *Digested*, 97/**1399**:
                                                                                                                  Considered, 00/1129
Attorney General's Reference (Nos.62, 63, 64 and 65 of 1996), Re; *sub nom* R. *v.* Samuel
   (Michael Andrew); R. *v.* Beresford (Amanda Elizabeth); R. *v.* Jones (Jason
   Robert); R. *v.* Murphy (Karen Amanda) [1998] 1 Cr. App. R. (S.) 9, CA (Crim
   Div) . . . .   *Digested*, 97/**1658**:
                                                                                                                  Considered, 00/1378
Attorney General's Reference (No.66 of 1996), Re; *sub nom* R. *v.* Spencer (Simon)
   [1998] 1 Cr. App. R. (S.) 16, CA (Crim Div) . . . .   *Digested*, 97/**1689**:
                                                                                                           Considered, 99/1321, 00/1155
Attorney General's Reference (Nos.68 and 69 of 1996), Re; *sub nom* R. *v.* L (Gemma
   Gail) (A Juvenile); R. *v.* H (Grace M) (A Juvenile) [1997] 2 Cr. App. R. (S.) 280,
   CA (Crim Div) . . . .   *Digested*, 97/**1591**:
                                                                                                                  Considered, 98/1299
Attorney General's Reference (No.1 of 1997), Re; *sub nom* R. *v.* Wheeler (Glen); R. *v.*
   Wheeler (Ian) [1998] 1 Cr. App. R. (S.) 54, CA (Crim Div) . . . .   *Digested*, 97/**1402**:
                                                                                                           Considered, 00/1131, 00/1135
Attorney General's Reference (No.2 of 1997), Re; *sub nom* R. *v.* Hoffman (Neville
   Anthony); Attorney General's Reference (No.6 of 1997), Re [1998] 1 Cr. App. R.
   (S.) 27; [1997] Crim. L.R. 611, CA (Crim Div) . . . .   *Digested*, 97/**1621**:
                                                                                                                  Considered, 00/1267
Attorney General's Reference (No.4 of 1997), Re; *sub nom* R. *v.* Hetherington (Peter)
   [1998] 1 Cr. App. R. (S.) 96, CA (Crim Div) . . . .   *Digested*, 97/**1437**:
                                                                                                                  Considered, 98/1256

Attorney General's Reference (No.6 of 1997), Re see Attorney General's Reference (No.2 of 1997), Re

Attorney General's Reference (No.7 of 1997), Re; *sub nom* R. *v.* Fearon (Robert) [1998] 1 Cr. App. R. (S.) 268; [1997] Crim. L.R. 908, CA (Crim Div) . . . . *Digested*, 97/**1433**

Attorney General's Reference (Nos.8 and 9 of 1997), Re; *sub nom* R. *v.* Jewitt (Andrew Mark); R. *v.* Jewitt (Nicholas Ian) [1998] 1 Cr. App. R. (S.) 98, CA (Crim Div) . . *Digested*, 97/**1566**: *Considered*, 00/1267

Attorney General's Reference (No.10 of 1997), Re; *sub nom* R. *v.* S (L Gavin) (A Juvenile) [1998] 1 Cr. App. R. (S.) 147, CA (Crim Div) . . . . *Digested*, 97/**1691**

Attorney General's Reference (No.18 of 1997), Re; *sub nom* R. *v.* Cutler (Saul Roland) [1998] 1 Cr. App. R. (S.) 151, CA (Crim Div) . . . . *Digested*, 97/**1694**

Attorney General's Reference (Nos.19, 20, 21 and 22 of 1997), Re; *sub nom* R. *v.* Reeves (Steven); R. *v.* Marshall (Raymond Martin); R. *v.* Nixon (John William); R. *v.* Nixon (Thomas Agnew) [1998] 1 Cr. App. R. (S.) 164, CA (Crim Div) . . . . *Digested*, 98/**1197**: *Considered*, 99/1124

Attorney General's Reference (No.23 of 1997), Re; *sub nom* R. *v.* A (Amos) [1998] 1 Cr. App. R. (S.) 378, CA (Crim Div) . . . . *Digested*, 98/**1349**

Attorney General's Reference (No.24 of 1997), Re; *sub nom* R. *v.* B (Christian Darren) (A Juvenile) [1998] 1 Cr. App. R. (S.) 319, CA (Crim Div) . . . . *Digested*, 98/**1273**

Attorney General's Reference (No.25 of 1997), Re; *sub nom* R. *v.* Williams (Gwilyn Lloyd) [1998] 1 Cr. App. R. (S.) 310, CA (Crim Div) . . . . *Digested*, 97/**1583**: *Considered*, 01/1373

Attorney General's Reference (No.26 of 1997), Re; *sub nom* R. *v.* Thoms (Stephen); 9703583/S2, CA (Crim Div) . . . . *Digested*, 98/**1124**

Attorney General's Reference (No.29 of 1997), Re; *sub nom* R. *v.* Hayes (Darren); 97/ 4181/R2, CA (Crim Div) . . . . *Digested*, 98/**1128**

Attorney General's Reference (No.30 of 1997), Re; *sub nom* R. *v.* C (Danny Gerald) (A Juvenile) [1998] 1 Cr. App. R. (S.) 349, CA (Crim Div) . . . . *Digested*, 97/**1598**

Attorney General's Reference (No.33 of 1997), Re; *sub nom* R. *v.* McGinn (Philip Lee) [1998] 1 Cr. App. R. (S.) 352, CA (Crim Div) . . . . *Digested*, 97/**1551**

Attorney General's Reference (No.34 of 1997), Re; *sub nom* R. *v.* Reed (Peter David) [1998] 1 F.L.R. 515; [1998] Fam. Law 190; *Times*, November 20, 1997, CA (Crim Div) . . . . *Digested*, 97/**1450**: *Considered*, 98/1266, 00/1280, 00/1288

Attorney General's Reference (Nos.35 and 37 of 1997), Re; *sub nom* R. *v.* T (Timothy David) (A Juvenile); R. *v.* AA (A Juvenile) [1998] 1 Cr. App. R. (S.) 344, CA (Crim Div) . . . . *Digested*, 98/**1372**

Attorney General's Reference (No.36 of 1997), Re; *sub nom* R. *v.* Wilson (Mark Robert) [1998] 1 Cr. App. R. (S.) 365, CA (Crim Div) . . . . *Digested*, 98/**1129**: *Considered*, 00/1147

Attorney General's Reference (Nos.37 and 38 of 1997), Re; *sub nom* R. *v.* Angus (Jamie John); R. *v.* Davies (Hilton) [1998] 2 Cr. App. R. (S.) 48, CA (Crim Div) . . . . . . *Digested*, 98/**1126**

Attorney General's Reference (No.39 of 1997), Re; *sub nom* R. *v.* Chandler (Adrian Anthony) [1998] 2 Cr. App. R. (S.) 336, CA (Crim Div) . . . . *Digested*, 98/**1264**: *Considered*, 00/1300

Attorney General's Reference (Nos.40 to 42 of 1997), Re; R. *v.* Routledge (Wayne Christopher); R. *v.* Laycock (Christopher Martin); R. *v.* Pype (Michael James) [1998] 2 Cr. App. R. (S.) 151, CA (Crim Div) . . . . *Digested*, 98/**1118**

Attorney General's Reference (No.43 of 1997), Re; *sub nom* R. *v.* Beckham (Leigh Spencer); 9706499/R2, CA (Crim Div) . . . . *Digested*, 98/**1232**

Attorney General's Reference (No.44 of 1997), Re; *sub nom* R. *v.* H (Kevin Errol) (A Juvenile); R. *v.* Bunter (Kevin Leslie) [1998] 2 Cr. App. R. (S.) 105, CA (Crim Div) . . . . *Digested*, 98/**1381**: *Applied*, 00/1425: *Considered*, 00/1419, 01/1472: *Referred to*, 00/1336

Attorney General's Reference (No.46 of 1997), Re; *sub nom* R. *v.* Zaman (Afraz) [1998] 2 Cr. App. R. (S.) 338, CA (Crim Div) . . . . *Digested*, 98/**1409**

Attorney General's Reference (No.47 of 1997), Re; *sub nom* R. *v.* Oldsworth (Kenneth Anthony) [1998] 2 Cr. App. R. (S.) 68, CA (Crim Div). . . . . *Digested*, 98/**1127**: *Considered*, 00/1146

Attorney General's Reference (Nos.48 and 49 of 1997), Re; *sub nom* R. *v.* Day (Mark Allen); R. *v.* Drady (Elliott John) [1998] 2 Cr. App. R. (S.) 392, CA (Crim Div) . . *Digested*, 99/**1089**

Attorney General's Reference (No.50 of 1997), Re; *sub nom* R. *v.* V (David Victor) [1998] 2 Cr. App. R. (S.) 155, CA (Crim Div) . . . . *Digested*, 98/**1249**: *Considered*, 00/1287

Attorney General's Reference (No.51 of 1997), Re; *sub nom* R. *v.* O'Rourke (Peter Kevin) [1998] 2 Cr. App. R. (S.) 313, CA (Crim Div) . . . . *Digested*, 98/**1288**

Attorney General's Reference (No.53 of 1997), Re; *sub nom* R. *v.* Bunce (Mark Wayne); 97/7635/R2, CA (Crim Div) . . . . *Digested*, 98/**1177**

Attorney General's Reference (No.54 of 1997), Re; *sub nom* R. *v.* A (Timothy) [1998] 2 Cr. App. R. (S.) 324, CA (Crim Div) . . . . *Digested*, 98/**1266**: *Considered*, 00/1288

Attorney General's Reference (No.55 of 1997), Re; *sub nom* R. *v.* Dainty (Paul); 9708061/R2, CA (Crim Div) . . . . *Digested*, 98/**1307**

Attorney General's Reference (Nos.57, 58 and 59 of 1997), Re; *sub nom* R. *v.* Beveridge (Susan); R. *v.* McDonnell (Amanda); R. *v.* Jones (Lesley) [1999] 1 Cr. App. R. (S.) 31, CA (Crim Div) . . . . *Digested,* 99/**1262**
Attorney General's Reference (Nos.60 and 61 of 1997), Re [1998] 2 Cr. App. R. (S.) 330, CA (Crim Div) . . . . *Digested,* 98/**1299**
Attorney General's Reference (Nos.62 and 63 of 1997), Re; *sub nom* R. *v.* McMaster (Shane Anthony); R. *v.* Case (Danny David) [1998] 2 Cr. App. R. (S.) 300; *Times,* February 20, 1998, CA (Crim Div) . . . . *Digested,* 98/**1235**
Attorney General's Reference (Nos.64 and 65 of 1997), Re; *sub nom* R. *v.* O'Gorman (John); R. *v.* Hibbard (Terence) [1999] 1 Cr. App. R. (S.) 237, CA (Crim Div) . . . *Digested,* 99/**1145**
Attorney General's Reference (No.66 of 1997), Re; *sub nom* R. *v.* Roberts (Anthony Charles) [2000] 1 Cr. App. R. (S.) 149, CA (Crim Div) . . . . *Digested,* 00/**1133**:
Considered, 00/1130, 00/1132, 00/1134, 01/1214
Attorney General's Reference (No.67 of 1997), Re; *sub nom* R. *v.* Birch (Christopher Louis) [1998] 2 Cr. App. R. (S.) 420, CA (Crim Div) . . . . *Digested,* 98/**1410**
Attorney General's Reference (No.68 of 1997), Re; *sub nom* R. *v.* Willoughby (Matthew Overton); 9708523/R2, CA (Crim Div) . . . . *Digested,* 99/**1195**
Attorney General's Reference (No.1 of 1998), Re (1999) 163 J.P. 390; (1999) 163 J.P.N. 473; (1998) 95(37) L.S.G. 36; (1998) 142 S.J.L.B. 250; *Times,* October 2, 1998, CA (Crim Div) . . . . *Digested,* 98/**938**
Attorney General's Reference (No.2 of 1998), Re [2000] Q.B. 412; [1999] 3 W.L.R. 961; [1999] B.C.C. 590; (1999) 96(21) L.S.G. 37; (1999) 149 N.L.J. 746; *Times,* May 10, 1999; *Independent,* May 6, 1999, CA (Crim Div) . . . . *Digested,* 99/**613**
Attorney General's Reference (No.3 of 1998), Re [2000] Q.B. 401; [1999] 3 W.L.R. 1194; [1999] 3 All E.R. 40; [1999] 2 Cr. App. R. 214; (1999) 49 B.M.L.R. 124; [1999] Crim. L.R. 986; (1999) 96(19) L.S.G. 27; (1999) 149 N.L.J. 522; (1999) 143 S.J.L.B. 130; *Times,* May 10, 1999; *Independent,* May 17, 1999 (C.S.), CA (Crim Div) . . . . *Digested,* 99/**942**:
Approved, 00/982: *Considered,* 99/933
Attorney General's Reference (No.4 of 1998), Re; *sub nom* R. *v.* Ward (Mark Richard) [1998] 2 Cr. App. R. (S.) 388, CA (Crim Div) . . . . *Digested,* 98/**1407**
Attorney General's Reference (No.5 of 1998), Re; *sub nom* R. *v.* Davies (Paul Stewart) [1998] 2 Cr. App. R. (S.) 442, CA (Crim Div) . . . . *Digested,* 99/**1254**
Attorney General's Reference (No.6 of 1998), Re; *sub nom* R. *v.* Sheppard (Robert) [1998] 2 Cr. App. R. (S.) 423, CA (Crim Div) . . . . *Digested,* 99/**1298**
Attorney General's Reference (No.7 of 1998), Re; *sub nom* R. *v.* B; 98/0424/R2, CA (Crim Div) . . . . *Digested,* 98/**1256**
Attorney General's Reference (Nos.8, 9 and 10 of 1998), Re 98/0680/R2; 98/0682/R2; 98/0681/R2, CA (Crim Div) . . . . *Digested,* 98/**1378**
Attorney General's Reference (No.11 of 1998), Re; *sub nom* R. *v.* Were (Jon Bonville) [1999] 1 Cr. App. R. (S.) 145, CA (Crim Div) . . . . *Digested,* 99/**1321**:
Considered, 00/1155
Attorney General's Reference (No.12 of 1998), Re; *sub nom* R. *v.* M (Andrew) [1999] 1 Cr. App. R. (S.) 44, CA (Crim Div) . . . . *Digested,* 99/**1306**:
Considered, 99/1304
Attorney General's Reference (No.13 of 1998), Re; *sub nom* R. *v.* D (Mathew David) (A Juvenile) [1999] 1 Cr. App. R. (S.) 140, CA (Crim Div) . . . . *Digested,* 99/**1238**:
Referred to, 00/1336
Attorney General's Reference (No.14 of 1998), Re; *sub nom* R. *v.* McGregor (Lee James) [1999] 1 Cr. App. R. (S.) 205; [1998] Crim. L.R. 911, CA (Crim Div) . . . . *Digested,* 98/**1346**
Attorney General's Reference (No.15 of 1998), Re; *sub nom* R. *v.* Hewitt (Shaun Anthony) [1999] 1 Cr. App. R. (S.) 209, CA (Crim Div) . . . . *Digested,* 98/**1408**
Attorney General's Reference (No.16 of 1998), Re; *sub nom* R. *v.* Tunstall (Nicholas) [1999] 1 Cr. App. R. (S.) 149, CA (Crim Div) . . . . *Digested,* 99/**1325**
Attorney General's Reference (No.17 of 1998), Re; *sub nom* R. *v.* Stokes (Ellen Marie) [1999] 1 Cr. App. R. (S.) 407; (1999) 163 J.P. 279; [1999] Crim. L.R. 92; (1999) 163 J.P.N. 234; *Times,* October 12, 1998, CA (Crim Div) . . . . *Digested,* 98/**1383**
Attorney General's Reference (No.18 of 1998), Re; *sub nom* R. *v.* Wright (Ezra James) [1999] 1 Cr. App. R. (S.) 142, CA (Crim Div) . . . . *Digested,* 99/**1243**
Attorney General's Reference (No.19 of 1998), Re; *sub nom* R. *v.* Azad (Afran) [1999] 1 Cr. App. R. (S.) 275, CA (Crim Div) . . . . *Digested,* 99/**1185**
Attorney General's Reference (No.20 of 1998), Re; *sub nom* R. *v.* P (Gary) [1999] 1 Cr. App. R. (S.) 280, CA (Crim Div) . . . . *Digested,* 99/**1201**:
Considered, 00/1288
Attorney General's Reference (No.24 of 1998), Re; *sub nom* R. *v.* Pope (Michael Dean) [1999] 1 Cr. App. R. (S.) 278, CA (Crim Div) . . . . *Digested,* 99/**1373**:
Considered, 00/1443, 01/1329, 01/1333
Attorney General's Reference (No.25 of 1998), Re; *sub nom* R. *v.* H (David Lee) (A Juvenile) [1999] 1 Cr. App. R. (S.) 351, CA (Crim Div) . . . . *Digested,* 99/**1225**
Attorney General's Reference (No.27 of 1998), Re; *sub nom* R. *v.* H (Mahzer) [1999] 1 Cr. App. R. (S.) 259, CA (Crim Div) . . . . *Digested,* 99/**1309**:
Considered, 00/1402
Attorney General's Reference (No.29 of 1998), Re; *sub nom* R. *v.* B (Douglas) [1999] 1 Cr. App. R. (S.) 311, CA (Crim Div) . . . . *Digested,* 99/**1304**

Attorney General's Reference (Nos.30 and 31 of 1998), Re; *sub nom* R. *v.* C (Keith John) (A Juvenile); R. *v.* C (Gary Justin) (A Juvenile) [1999] 1 Cr. App. R. (S.) 200, CA (Crim Div) . . . . *Digested,* 99/**1224**
Attorney General's Reference (No.32 of 1998), Re; *sub nom* R. *v.* G (Roy) [1999] 1 Cr. App. R. (S.) 316, CA (Crim Div) . . . . *Digested,* 99/**1210**:
Considered, 00/1288
Attorney General's Reference (No.35 of 1998), Re; *sub nom* R. *v.* J (Vivian Sidney) [1999] 1 Cr. App. R. (S.) 400, CA (Crim Div) . . . . *Digested,* 99/**1208**
Attorney General's Reference (No.39 of 1998), Re; *sub nom* R. *v.* Shearn (Damien); 9303716/R2, CA (Crim Div) . . . . *Digested,* 99/**1339**
Attorney General's Reference (No.44 of 1998), Re; *sub nom* R. *v.* Haywood (James) [1999] 1 Cr. App. R. (S.) 458, CA (Crim Div) . . . . *Digested,* 99/**1266**
Attorney General's Reference (No.45 of 1998), Re; R. *v.* Sylvester (Jason William) [1999] 1 Cr. App. R. (S.) 461, CA (Crim Div) . . . . *Digested,* 99/**1311**
Attorney General's Reference (No.47 of 1998), Re; *sub nom* R. *v.* Gale (Stephen Allen) [1999] 1 Cr. App. R. (S.) 464, CA (Crim Div) . . . . *Digested,* 99/**1206**
Attorney General's Reference (No.48 of 1998), Re; *sub nom* R. *v.* Jones (Stephen Michael) [1999] 2 Cr. App. R. (S.) 48, CA (Crim Div) . . . . *Digested,* 99/**1332**
Attorney General's Reference (No.49 of 1998), Re; *sub nom* R. *v.* Chevelleau (David) [1999] 1 Cr. App. R. (S.) 396, CA (Crim Div) . . . . *Digested,* 99/**1162**
Attorney General's Reference (Nos.51 and 52 of 1998), Re; *sub nom* R. *v.* Gani (Saleem Ibrahim); R. *v.* Gani (Farouk); (Unreported, December 14, 1998), CA (Crim Div) . *Digested,* 99/**1168**
Attorney General's Reference (No.53 of 1998), Re; *sub nom* R. *v.* Sandford (Terence); R. *v.* Kelly (Edward) (No.1) [2000] Q.B. 198; [1999] 2 W.L.R. 1100; [1999] 2 All E.R. 13; [1999] 2 Cr. App. R. 36; [1999] 2 Cr. App. R. (S.) 176; [1999] 2 Cr. App. R. (S.) 185; [1999] Crim. L.R. 240; *Times,* December 29, 1998, CA (Crim Div) . . *Digested,* 99/**1249**:
Considered, 00/1267, 00/1347, 00/1358, 00/1393, 01/1470
Attorney General's Reference (No.54 of 1998), Re; *sub nom* R. *v.* W (Michael Paul) (A Juvenile) [2000] 1 Cr. App. R. (S.) 219, CA (Crim Div) . . . . *Digested,* 99/**1315**
Attorney General's Reference (No.56 of 1998), Re; *sub nom* R. *v.* M (Incest: Sentencing); 9805583/R2, CA (Crim Div) . . . . *Digested,* 99/**1193**
Attorney General's Reference (No.57 of 1998), Re; *sub nom* R. *v.* Kerswell (John William) [2000] 1 Cr. App. R. (S.) 422, CA (Crim Div) . . . . *Digested,* 00/**1130**:
Considered, 01/1214
Attorney General's Reference (Nos.59, 60 and 63 of 1998), Re; *sub nom* R. *v.* Goodwin (Frankie); R. *v.* JO'B (A Juvenile); R. *v.* TH (A Juvenile) [1999] 2 Cr. App. R. (S.) 128; [1999] Crim. L.R. 341; *Times,* December 28, 1998, CA (Crim Div) . . . . *Digested,* 99/**1371**:
Considered, 00/1322, 00/1323
Attorney General's Reference (No.61 of 1998), Re; *sub nom* R. *v.* W (RL); R. *v.* RLW [1999] 2 Cr. App. R. (S.) 226; [1999] Crim. L.R. 428, CA (Crim Div) . . . . *Digested,* 99/**1194**:
Considered, 99/1302
Attorney General's Reference (No.62 of 1998), Re; *sub nom* R. *v.* Onubogu (Godwin) [2000] 2 Cr. App. R. (S.) 286, CA (Crim Div) . . . . *Digested,* 00/**1294**
Attorney General's Reference (No.64 of 1998), Re; *sub nom* R. *v.* G (Christopher Ian) [1999] 2 Cr. App. R. (S.) 395, CA (Crim Div) . . . . *Digested,* 99/**1305**
Attorney General's Reference (No.67 of 1998), Re; *sub nom* R. *v.* Stephens (Vivian John) [1999] 2 Cr. App. R. (S.) 152, CA (Crim Div) . . . . *Digested,* 99/**1331**:
Considered, 01/1478
Attorney General's Reference (No.71 of 1998), Re; *sub nom* R. *v.* Anderson (Paul); Attorney General's Reference (No.71 of 1999), Re [1999] 2 Cr. App. R. (S.) 369; [1999] Crim. L.R. 587; *Independent,* March 22, 1999 (C.S.), CA (Crim Div) . . . . *Digested,* 99/**1256**
Attorney General's Reference (Nos.73 and 74 of 1998), Re; *sub nom* R. *v.* Clark (Henry George); R. *v.* Masters (Veronica Michelle); (Unreported, December 15, 1998), CA (Crim Div) . . . . *Digested,* 99/**1071**
Attorney General's Reference (No.75 of 1998), Re; *sub nom* R. *v.* JN [2000] 1 Cr. App. R. (S.) 102, CA (Crim Div) . . . . *Digested,* 99/**1310**
Attorney General's Reference (No.76 of 1998), Re; *sub nom* R. *v.* Kirkham (Gary) [1999] 2 Cr. App. R. (S.) 361, CA (Crim Div) . . . . *Digested,* 99/**1175**
Attorney General's Reference (Nos.78, 79 and 85 of 1998), Re; *sub nom* R. *v.* Russell (Robert John); R. *v.* O (Jason Patrick) (A Juvenile); R. *v.* M (Sarah Ruth) (A Juvenile) [2000] 1 Cr. App. R. (S.) 371, CA (Crim Div) . . . . *Digested,* 00/**1132**:
Considered, 00/1130, 01/1375
Attorney General's Reference (No.84 of 1998), Re; *sub nom* R. *v.* Hines (Malcolm) [1999] 2 Cr. App. R. (S.) 380, CA (Crim Div) . . . . *Digested,* 00/**1135**:
Distinguished, 01/1211
Attorney General's Reference (No.86 of 1998), Re; *sub nom* R. *v.* De St Aubin (Anthony) [2000] 1 Cr. App. R. (S.) 10, CA (Crim Div) . . . . *Digested,* 99/**1372**
Attorney General's Reference (No.87 of 1998), Re; *sub nom* R. *v.* G (Jayne Elizabeth); 9807453/R2, CA (Crim Div) . . . . *Digested,* 99/**1200**
Attorney General's Reference (No.88 of 1998), Re; R. *v.* Searson (Raymond Martin) [1999] 2 Cr. App. R. (S.) 346, CA (Crim Div) . . . . *Digested,* 99/**1258**
Attorney General's Reference (No.89 of 1998), Re; *sub nom* R. *v.* S (Paul William) [2000] 1 Cr. App. R. (S.) 49, CA (Crim Div) . . . . *Digested,* 00/**1157**

Attorney General's Reference (Nos.90 and 91 of 1998), Re; *sub nom* R. *v.* Smith (Peter) ;
R. *v.* Foley (Michael John) [2000] 1 Cr. App. R. (S.) 32, CA (Crim Div) . . . . . . *Digested,* 99/**1124**
Attorney General's Reference (No.92 of 1998), Re; *sub nom* R. *v.* Williams (Huw David)
[2000] 1 Cr. App. R. (S.) 13, CA (Crim Div) . . . . *Digested,* 99/**1177**
Attorney General's Reference (No.93 of 1998), Re; R. *v.* Sagoo (Permjit); R. *v.* Sagoo
(Harmeet); (Unreported, March 2, 1999), CA (Crim Div) . . . . *Digested,* 99/**1171**
Attorney General's Reference (No.95 of 1998), Re; *sub nom* R. *v.* Highfield (Kim) *Times,*
April 21, 1999, CA (Crim Div) . . . . *Digested,* 99/**1072**
Attorney General's Reference (No.1 of 1999), Re [2000] Q.B. 365; [1999] 3 W.L.R. 769;
[1999] 2 Cr. App. R. 418; (1999) 163 J.P. 769; (1999) 163 J.P.N. 1010; (1999)
96(26) L.S.G. 27; *Times,* July 6, 1999 ; *Independent,* July 12, 1999 (C.S.), CA
(Crim Div) . . . . *Digested,* 99/**966**
Attorney General's Reference (No.1 of 1999) (Unduly Lenient Sentence), Re; *sub nom* R. *v.*
Newberry (Colin Stewart) [1999] 2 Cr. App. R. (S.) 398, CA (Crim Div) . . . . . . *Digested,* 99/**1334**:
Considered, 00/1413, 00/1414
Attorney General's Reference (No.2 of 1999), Re [2000] Q.B. 796; [2000] 3 W.L.R. 195;
[2000] 3 All E.R.182; [2001] B.C.C. 210; [2000] 2 B.C.L.C. 257; [2000] 2 Cr. App.
R. 207; [2000] I.R.L.R. 417; [2000] Crim. L.R. 475; (2000) 97(9) L.S.G. 39; *Times,*
February 29, 2000, CA (Crim Div) . . . . *Digested,* 00/**980**
Attorney General's Reference (No.3 of 1999), Re; *sub nom* R. *v.* B [2001] 2 A.C. 91;
[2001] 2 W.L.R. 56; [2001] 1 All E.R. 577; [2001] 1 Cr. App. R. 34; [2001]
H.R.L.R. 16; [2001] Crim. L.R. 394; (2001) 98(7) L.S.G. 39; (2000) 150 N.L.J.
1889; (2001) 145 S.J.L.B. 8; *Times,* December 15, 2000; *Independent,*
December 19, 2000, HL; reversing [2000] 3 W.L.R. 1164; [2000] 4 All E.R. 360;
[2000] 2 Cr. App. R. 416; [2000] Crim. L.R. 994; (2000) 144 S.J.L.B. 222;
Times, June 16, 2000; *Independent,* June 9, 2000, CA (Crim Div) . . . . *Digested,* 01/**973**:
Applied, 01/718: *Followed,* 00/912
Attorney General's Reference (No.3 of 1999) (Unduly Lenient Sentence), Re; *sub nom* R.
v. Lynn (James) [1999] 2 Cr. App. R. (S.) 433; *Times,* May 18, 1999, CA (Crim
Div) . . . . *Digested,* 99/**1267**
Attorney General's Reference (No.4 of 1999), Re; *sub nom* R. *v.* Blundell (Jacqueline
Louise) (Unduly Lenient Sentence) [2000] 2 Cr. App. R. (S.) 5, CA (Crim Div) . *Digested,* 00/**1134**
Attorney General's Reference (No.6 of 1999), Re; *sub nom* R. *v.* Midda (Julian Ellery)
(Unduly Lenient Sentence) [2000] 2 Cr. App. R. (S.) 67, CA (Crim Div) . . . . *Digested,* 00/**1290**
Attorney General's Reference (No.8 of 1999), Re; *sub nom* R. *v.* A (Paul Eric) [2000] 1
Cr. App. R. (S.) 56, CA (Crim Div) . . . . *Digested,* 99/**1303**
Attorney General's Reference (No.14 of 1999), Re; *sub nom* R. *v.* Gosgombe (John Lee);
R. *v.* Goscombe (John Lee) [2000] 1 Cr. App. R. (S.) 174, CA (Crim Div) . . . . . . *Digested,* 99/**1338**
Attorney General's Reference (No.15 of 1999), Re; *sub nom* R. *v.* Thoburn (Neil Matthew)
[2000] 1 Cr. App. R. (S.) 128, CA (Crim Div) . . . . *Digested,* 99/**1246**
Attorney General's Reference (No.16 of 1999), Re; *sub nom* R. *v.* Harris (Timothy John);
R. *v.* Marsh (Peter Michael) [2000] 1 Cr. App. R. (S.) 524, CA (Crim Div) . . . . . . *Digested,* 00/**1364**
Attorney General's Reference (No.17 of 1999), Re; *sub nom* R. *v.* Taylor (David Alec)
[2000] 1 Cr. App. R. (S.) 215, CA (Crim Div) . . . . *Digested,* 99/**1155**
Attorney General's Reference (No.18 of 1999), Re; *sub nom* R. *v.* M (Andrew James)
[2000] 1 Cr. App. R. (S.) 246, CA (Crim Div) . . . . *Digested,* 99/**1301**
Attorney General's Reference (No.19 of 1999), Re; *sub nom* R. *v.* Kitchener (Marvine
Wayne) [2000] 1 Cr. App. R. (S.) 287, CA (Crim Div) . . . . *Digested,* 99/**1259**
Attorney General's Reference (No.21 of 1999), Re; *sub nom* R. *v.* N (Stephen James) (A
Juvenile) [2000] 1 Cr. App. R. (S.) 197, CA (Crim Div) . . . . *Digested,* 00/**1336**:
Considered, 01/1477
Attorney General's Reference (No.22 of 1999), Re; *sub nom* R. *v.* B (Brian Phillip) [2000]
1 Cr. App. R. (S.) 253, CA (Crim Div) . . . . *Digested,* 99/**1205**
Attorney General's Reference (No.23 of 1999), Re; *sub nom* R. *v.* PR [2000] 1 Cr. App.
R. (S.) 258, CA (Crim Div) . . . . *Digested,* 00/**1400**
Attorney General's Reference (No.24 of 1999), Re; *sub nom* R. *v.* F (Toby) [2000] 1 Cr.
App. R. (S.) 275, CA (Crim Div) . . . . *Digested,* 99/**1302**
Attorney General's Reference (No.25 of 1999), Re; *sub nom* R. *v.* Murphy (David Eric);
9902461/R2, CA (Crim Div) . . . . *Digested,* 99/**1074**
Attorney General's Reference (No.26 of 1999), Re; *sub nom* R. *v.* Gastinger (Neale
Arthur) [2000] 1 Cr. App. R. (S.) 394, CA (Crim Div) . . . . *Digested,* 00/**1194**:
Considered, 01/1263
Attorney General's Reference (No.27 of 1999), Re; *sub nom* R. *v.* Higgs (Christopher
David) [2000] 1 Cr. App. R. (S.) 237, CA (Crim Div) . . . . *Digested,* 00/**1441**
Attorney General's Reference (No.28 of 1999), Re; *sub nom* R. *v.* G (Alan Robert)
[2000] 1 Cr. App. R. (S.) 314, CA (Crim Div) . . . . *Digested,* 00/**1395**
Attorney General's Reference (No.29 of 1999), Re; *sub nom* R. *v.* J (Andrew) [2000] 1
Cr. App. R. (S.) 209, CA (Crim Div) . . . . *Digested,* 00/**1300**
Attorney General's Reference (No.34 of 1999), Re; *sub nom* R. *v.* Probert (Anthony
David) [2000] 1 Cr. App. R. (S.) 322, CA (Crim Div) . . . . *Digested,* 99/**1340**
Attorney General's Reference (No.35 of 1999), Re; *sub nom* R. *v.* S (David John) [2000]
1 Cr. App. R. (S.) 440, CA (Crim Div) . . . . *Digested,* 00/**1393**

Attorney General's Reference (Nos.36, 37, 38 and 39 of 1999), Re; *sub nom* R. *v.* Doughty (Barry Michael); R. *v.* Brignull (Sean); R. *v.* Hunt (James); R. *v.* Norris-Copson (Brian) [2000] 2 Cr. App. R. (S.) 303, CA (Crim Div) . . . . *Digested*, 00/**1230**

Attorney General's Reference (No.43 of 1999), Re; *sub nom* R. *v.* GGM [2000] 1 Cr. App. R. (S.) 398, CA (Crim Div). . . . . *Digested*, 00/**1287**: *Considered*, 01/1358

Attorney General's Reference (No.44 of 1999), Re; *sub nom* R. *v.* L (Stephen Peter) [2000] 1 Cr. App. R. (S.) 317, CA (Crim Div). . . . . *Digested*, 99/**1295**

Attorney General's Reference (No.46 of 1999), Re; *sub nom* R. *v.* M (Albert) [2000] 1 Cr. App. R. (S.) 310, CA (Crim Div) . . . . *Digested*, 99/**1199**

Attorney General's Reference (No.47 of 1999), Re; *sub nom* R. *v.* KB [2000] 1 Cr. App. R. (S.) 446, CA (Crim Div). . . . . *Digested*, 00/**1401**

Attorney General's Reference (No.48 of 1999), Re; *sub nom* R. *v.* Morton (Stephen Richard) [2000] 1 Cr. App. R. (S.) 472, CA (Crim Div) . . . . *Digested*, 00/**1181**

Attorney General's Reference (No.49 of 1999), Re; *sub nom* R. *v.* Hinchliffe (Allen Patrick) [2000] 1 Cr. App. R. (S.) 436, CA (Crim Div) . . . . *Digested*, 00/**1244**: *Considered*, 01/1312

Attorney General's Reference (No.51 of 1999), Re; *sub nom* R. *v.* DH [2000] 1 Cr. App. R. (S.) 407, CA (Crim Div) . . . . *Digested*, 00/**1404**

Attorney General's Reference (Nos.52, 53, 54 and 55 of 1999), Re; *sub nom* R. *v.* T (A Juvenile); R. *v.* L (A Juvenile); R. *v.* B (A Juvenile); R. *v.* J (A Juvenile) [2000] 1 Cr. App. R. (S.) 450, CA (Crim Div) . . . . *Digested*, 00/**1340**

Attorney General's Reference (No.56 of 1999), Re; *sub nom* R. *v.* Ward (Alan John) [2000] 1 Cr. App. R. (S.) 401, CA (Crim Div) . . . . *Digested*, 00/**1418**

Attorney General's Reference (Nos.57 and 58 of 1999), Re; *sub nom* R. *v.* L (Catherine Fiona) (A Juvenile); R. *v.* G (Joanne Rainey) (A Juvenile) [2000] 1 Cr. App. R. (S.) 502, CA (Crim Div). . . . . *Digested*, 00/**1338**

Attorney General's Reference (No.60 of 1999), Re; *sub nom* R. *v.* Thompson (Mark Anthony) [2000] 2 Cr. App. R. (S.) 449, CA (Crim Div)

Attorney General's Reference (No.61 of 1999), Re; *sub nom* R. *v.* B (Wayne) (A Juvenile) [2000] 1 Cr. App. R. (S.) 516, CA (Crim Div) . . . . *Digested*, 00/**1328**

Attorney General's Reference (No.64 of 1999), Re; *sub nom* R. *v.* L (Albert David) [2000] 1 Cr. App. R. (S.) 529, CA (Crim Div) . . . . *Digested*, 00/**1402**

Attorney General's Reference (No.65 of 1999), Re; *sub nom* R. *v.* W (Robert) [2000] 1 Cr. App. R. (S.) 554, CA (Crim Div) . . . . *Digested*, 00/**1291**

Attorney General's Reference (No.66 of 1999), Re; *sub nom* R. *v.* BW [2000] 1 Cr. App. R. (S.) 558, CA (Crim Div). . . . . *Digested*, 00/**1288**

Attorney General's Reference (No.67 of 1999), Re; *sub nom* R. *v.* Williams (Roxanne Diane) [2000] 2 Cr. App. R. (S.) 380, CA (Crim Div) . . . . *Digested*, 01/**1324**

Attorney General's Reference (No.68 of 1999), Re; *sub nom* R. *v.* Thomas (Nigel Wynn) [2000] 2 Cr. App. R. (S.) 50, CA (Crim Div) . . . . *Digested*, 00/**1423**

Attorney General's Reference (No.69 of 1999), Re; *sub nom* R. *v.* H (Bilal) (A Juvenile) [2000] 2 Cr. App. R. (S.) 53, CA (Crim Div) . . . . *Digested*, 00/**1322**

Attorney General's Reference (No.70 of 1999), Re; *sub nom* R. *v.* Rance (Richard) [2000] 2 Cr. App. R. (S.) 28, CA (Crim Div) . . . . *Digested*, 00/**1180**

Attorney General's Reference (No.71 of 1999), Re see Attorney General's Reference (No.71 of 1998), Re

Attorney General's Reference (No.71 of 1999), Re; *sub nom* R. *v.* AN [2000] 2 Cr. App. R. (S.) 83, CA (Crim Div) . . . . *Digested*, 00/**1392**

Attorney General's Reference (No.72 of 1999), Re; *sub nom* R. *v.* MG (Sex Offence: Registration); R. *v.* G (Sex Offence: Registration) [2000] 2 Cr. App. R. (S.) 79; *Times*, January 26, 2000, CA (Crim Div) . . . . *Digested*, 00/**1428**

Attorney General's Reference (No.73 of 1999), Re; *sub nom* R. *v.* C (Mark) [2000] 2 Cr. App. R. (S.) 209; [2000] Crim. L.R. 396, CA (Crim Div) . . . . *Digested*, 00/**1419**

Attorney General's Reference (No.74 of 1999), Re; *sub nom* R. *v.* Levitt (Darren Paul) [2000] 2 Cr. App. R. (S.) 150, CA (Crim Div) . . . . *Digested*, 00/**1421**

Attorney General's Reference (No.75 of 1999), Re; *sub nom* R. *v.* G (Wesley Stuart) (A Juvenile) [2000] 2 Cr. App. R. (S.) 146, CA (Crim Div) . . . . *Digested*, 00/**1323**

Attorney General's Reference (No.77 of 1999), Re; *sub nom* R. *v.* S (David Gealy) [1999] 2 Cr. App. R. (S.) 336, CA (Crim Div) . . . . *Digested*, 99/**1204**

Attorney General's Reference (No.77 of 1999), Re; *sub nom* R. *v.* T (John) [2000] 2 Cr. App. R. (S.) 250, CA (Crim Div) . . . . *Digested*, 00/**1280**: *Distinguished*, 01/1365

Attorney General's Reference (No.79 of 1999), Re; *sub nom* R. *v.* Branch (David) [2000] 2 Cr. App. R. (S.) 124, CA (Crim Div) . . . . *Digested*, 00/**1266**

Attorney General's Reference (Nos.80 and 81 of 1999), Re; *sub nom* R. *v.* Thompson (Wilfrid Frank); R. *v.* Rodgers (Andrew Campbell) [2000] 2 Cr. App. R. (S.) 138; [2000] Crim. L.R. 398, CA (Crim Div) . . . . *Digested*, 00/**1238**: *Applied*, 00/1085

Attorney General's Reference (No.82 of 1999), Re, *Independent*, February 28, 2000 (C.S.), CA (Crim Div). . . . . *Digested*, 00/**1427**

Attorney General's Reference (No.83 of 1999), Re; *sub nom* R. *v.* Blackwell (Warren Anthony) [2001] EWCA Crim 819; [2001] 2 Cr. App. R. (S.) 117, CA (Crim Div) . . . . *Digested*, 01/**1370**

Attorney General's Reference (No.84 of 1999), Re; *sub nom* R. *v.* Jennison (Colin Albert) [2000] 2 Cr. App. R. (S.) 213, CA (Crim Div) . . . . *Digested,* 00/**1438**

Attorney General's Reference (Nos.86 and 87 of 1999), Re; *sub nom* R. *v.* Webb (Robert Edward); R. *v.* Simpson (Moira) [2001] 1 Cr. App. R. (S.) 141; [2001] Crim. L.R. 58; *Times,* November 8, 2000; *Independent,* December 11, 2000 (C.S), CA (Crim Div) . . . . *Digested,* 00/**1186**

Attorney General's Reference (No.89 of 1999), Re; *sub nom* R. *v.* Farrow (Neil Jack) [2000] 2 Cr. App. R. (S.) 382, CA (Crim Div) . . . . *Digested,* 00/**1414**

Attorney General's Reference (No.90 of 1999), Re; *sub nom* R. *v.* Hutchinson (Jonathan) [2001] EWCA Crim 424; [2001] 2 Cr. App. R. (S.) 74, CA (Crim Div) . . . . *Digested,* 01/**1229**

Attorney General's Reference (No.1 of 2000), Re; *sub nom* R. *v.* JT (False Instruments) [2001] 1 W.L.R. 331; [2001] 1 Cr. App. R. 15; [2001] Crim. L.R. 127; *Times,* November 28, 2000; *Independent,* November 30, 2000, CA (Crim Div) . . . . . . *Digested,* 01/**1046**

Attorney General's Reference (No.1 of 2000) (Unduly Lenient Sentence), Re; *sub nom* R. *v.* Shioui (Rashid) [2000] 2 Cr. App. R. (S.) 340, CA (Crim Div) . . . . *Digested,* 00/**1147**

Attorney General's Reference (No.2 of 2000), Re; *sub nom* R. *v.* W [2001] 1 Cr. App. R. 36; (2001) 165 J.P. 195; [2001] Crim. L.R. 842; (2001) 165 J.P.N. 466; *Times,* November 23, 2000, CA (Crim Div) . . . . *Digested,* 00/**1106**

Attorney General's Reference (No.2 of 2000) (Unduly Lenient Sentence), Re; *sub nom* R. *v.* Hinds (Michael Joshua) [2001] 1 Cr. App. R. (S.) 9, CA (Crim Div) . . . . *Digested,* 01/**1304**

Attorney General's Reference (No.3 of 2000), Re; *sub nom* R. *v.* G (Entrapment); R. *v.* Loosley (Grant Spencer) (No.2); R. *v.* Loosely (Grant Spencer); R. *v.* Looseley (Grant Spencer) (No.2) [2001] UKHL 53; [2001] 1 W.L.R. 2060; [2001] 4 All E.R. 897; (2001) 98(45) L.S.G. 25; (2001) 145 S.J.L.B. 245; *Times,* October 29, 2001; *Independent,* November 2, 2001; *Daily Telegraph,* November 6, 2001, HL; reversing [2001] EWCA Crim 1214; [2001] 2 Cr. App. R. 26; [2001] H.R.L.R. 47; [2001] Crim. L.R. 645; *Times,* June 27, 2001; *Independent,* May 25, 2001, CA (Crim Div) . . . . *Digested,* 01/**992**

Attorney General's Reference (No.3 of 2000) (Unduly Lenient Sentence), Re; *sub nom* R. *v.* Hayles (George) [2001] 1 Cr. App. R. (S.) 26, CA (Crim Div) . . . . *Digested,* 01/**1327**

Attorney General's Reference (No.4 of 2000), Re; *sub nom* R. *v.* GC [2001] EWCA Crim 780; [2001] 2 Cr. App. R. 22; [2001] R.T.R. 27; [2001] Crim. L.R. 578; *Times,* March 27, 2001, CA (Crim Div) . . . . *Digested,* 01/**1031**

Attorney General's Reference (No.5 of 2000), Re [2001] EWCA Crim 1077; [2001] 2 C.M.L.R. 41; [2001] 3 P.L.R. 66; [2001] 23 E.G.C.S. 155; *Times,* June 6, 2001; *Independent,* June 18, 2001 (C.S), CA (Crim Div) . . . . *Digested,* 01/**2413**

Attorney General's Reference (No.6 of 2000), Re; *sub nom* R. *v.* Goldsmith (Simon) [2001] 1 Cr. App. R. (S.) 20; [2000] Crim. L.R. 701; *Times,* May 24, 2000, CA (Crim Div) . . . . *Digested,* 00/**1357**

Attorney General's Reference (No.7 of 2000), Re [2001] EWCA Crim 888; [2001] 1 W.L.R. 1879; [2001] 2 Cr. App. R.19; [2001] H.R.L.R. 41; [2001] B.P.I.R. 953; [2001] Crim. L.R. 736; (2001) 98(22) L.S.G. 35; (2001) 145 S.J.L.B.109; *Times,* April 12, 2001, CA (Crim Div) . . . . *Digested,* 01/**974**

Attorney General's Reference (Nos.7, 8, 9 and 10 of 2000), Re; *sub nom* R. *v.* K (Imran) (A Juvenile); R. *v.* S (Joe) (A Juvenile); R. *v.* P (Gareth) (A Juvenile); R. *v.* W (Lee) (A Juvenile) [2001] 1 Cr. App. R. (S.) 48; *Times,* June 15, 2000, CA (Crim Div) . *Digested,* 00/**1339**: *Applied,* 01/1476

Attorney General's Reference (Nos.11 and 12 of 2000), Re; *sub nom* R. *v.* T (James) (A Juvenile); R. *v.* F (Nicholas) (A Juvenile) [2001] 1 Cr. App. R. (S.) 10, CA (Crim Div) . . . . *Digested,* 00/**1342**

Attorney General's Reference (No.13 of 2000), Re; *sub nom* R. *v.* F (Frederick Joseph) [2001] 1 Cr. App. R. (S.) 25, CA (Crim Div) . . . . *Digested,* 01/**1455**

Attorney General's Reference (No.14 of 2000), Re; *sub nom* R. *v.* Boffey (Kevin Paul) [2001] 1 Cr. App. R. (S.) 16, CA (Crim Div). . . . . *Digested,* 00/**1443**: *Considered,* 01/1338

Attorney General's Reference (No.15 of 2000), Re; *sub nom* R. *v.* G (Richard) [2001] 1 Cr. App. R. (S.) 23, CA (Crim Div) . . . . *Digested,* 00/**1286**

Attorney General's Reference (No.16 of 2000), Re; *sub nom* R. *v.* Downey (Thomas) [2001] 1 Cr. App. R. (S.) 27, CA (Crim Div) . . . . *Digested,* 00/**1137**

Attorney General's Reference (No.16 of 2000), Re; *sub nom* R. *v.* Skittlethorpe (Stuart) [2001] 1 Cr. App. R. (S.) 42, CA (Crim Div) . . . . *Digested,* 00/**1420**

Attorney General's Reference (No.19 of 2000), Re; *sub nom* R. *v.* Stock (Mark Peter) [2001] 1 Cr. App. R. (S.) 11, CA (Crim Div) . . . . *Digested,* 01/**1222**

Attorney General's Reference (No.21 of 2000), Re; *sub nom* R. *v.* Hartwell (Nigel) [2001] 1 Cr. App. R. (S.) 50; [2000] Crim. L.R. 773, CA (Crim Div). . . . . *Digested,* 01/**1272**: *Considered,* 01/1264

Attorney General's Reference (No.21 of 2000) (Unduly Lenient Sentence), Re; *sub nom* R. *v.* Woodward (Paul) [2001] 1 Cr. App. R. (S.) 51, CA (Crim Div) . . . . *Digested,* 01/**1482**

Attorney General's Reference (No.23 of 2000), Re; *sub nom* R. *v.* Bullock (Richard) [2001] 1 Cr. App. R. (S.) 45; [2000] Crim. L.R. 772, CA (Crim Div) . . . . *Digested,* 01/**1461**

Attorney General's Reference (Nos.24 and 25 of 2000), Re; *sub nom* R. *v.* Mullings (Richard Wilbert); R. *v.* Edwards (Thomas) [2001] 1 Cr. App. R. (S.) 69, CA (Crim Div). . . . . *Digested,* 01/**1471**

Attorney General's Reference (No.26 of 2000), Re; *sub nom* R. *v.* Pearson (Geoffrey)
[2001] 1 Cr. App. R. (S.) 54, CA (Crim Div) . . . . *Digested,* 01/**1339**
Attorney General's Reference (No.28 of 2000), Re; *sub nom* R. *v.* S (John Ivor) [2001] 1
Cr. App. R. (S.) 90, CA (Crim Div) . . . . *Digested,* 01/**1364**
Attorney General's Reference (No.31 of 2000), Re; *sub nom* R. *v.* T (Leigh) (A Juvenile)
[2001] 1 Cr. App. R. (S.) 112, CA (Crim Div) . . . . *Digested,* 00/**1303**
Attorney General's Reference (No.32 of 2000), Re; *sub nom* R. *v.* CB; 2000/3359/R2,
CA (Crim Div) . . . . *Digested,* 00/**1282**
Attorney General's Reference (No.33 of 2000), Re; *sub nom* R. *v.* E (Nicholas) (A
Juvenile) [2001] 1 Cr. App. R. (S.) 102, CA (Crim Div) . . . . *Digested,* 00/**1324**
Attorney General's Reference (No.34 of 2000), Re; *sub nom* R. *v.* R (Darren) [2001] 1
Cr. App. R. (S.) 103, CA (Crim Div)
Attorney General's Reference (Nos.35 and 36 of 2000), Re; *sub nom* R. *v.* Henry
(Thomas Lashlie); R. *v.* Douglas (David) [2001] 1 Cr. App. R. (S.) 95, CA (Crim
Div) . . . . *Digested,* 01/**1476**
Attorney General's Reference (Nos.37 and 38 of 2000), Re; *sub nom* R. *v.* Fisher
(Malcolm); R. *v.* Thomson (Cameron Kirkwood); 2000/03478/R2, 2000/
03479/R2, CA (Crim Div) . . . . *Digested,* 00/**1425**
Attorney General's Reference (No.41 of 2000), Re; *sub nom* R. *v.* H (David John) [2001]
1 Cr. App. R. (S.) 107, CA (Crim Div) . . . . *Digested,* 01/**1362**
Attorney General's Reference (No.42 of 2000), Re; *sub nom* R. *v.* Pinkney (Dale) [2001]
1 Cr. App. R. (S.) 114, CA (Crim Div) . . . . *Digested,* 00/**1262**
Attorney General's Reference (No.43 of 2000), Re; *sub nom* R. *v.* Pacholok (Paul Stefan)
[2001] 1 Cr. App. R. (S.) 110, CA (Crim Div) . . . . *Digested,* 01/**1321**
Attorney General's Reference (No.44 of 2000), Re; *sub nom* R. *v.* Peverett (Robin)
[2001] 1 Cr. App. R. 27; [2001] 1 Cr. App. R. (S.) 132; (2001) 165 J.P. 93;
[2001] Crim. L.R. 60; *Times,* October 25, 2000, CA (Crim Div) . . . . *Digested,* 00/**1085**:
Distinguished, 00/1186

Attorney General's Reference (No.45 of 2000), Re; *sub nom* R. *v.* West (Stewart
Jonathan) [2001] 1 Cr. App. R. (S.) 119, CA (Crim Div) . . . . *Digested,* 00/**1416**
Attorney General's Reference (No.46 of 2000), Re; *sub nom* R. *v.* Dyson (Gerald Frank)
[2001] 1 Cr. App. R. (S.) 118, CA (Crim Div) . . . . *Digested,* 00/**1297**
Attorney General's Reference (No.47 of 2000), Re; *sub nom* R. *v.* Harvey (Calvin David)
[2001] 1 Cr. App. R. (S.) 134, CA (Crim Div) . . . . *Digested,* 01/**1214**
Attorney General's Reference (No.48 of 2000), Re; *sub nom* R. *v.* Johnson (Martin Clive)
[2001] 1 Cr. App. R. (S.) 123, CA (Crim Div) . . . . *Digested,* 00/**1413**
Attorney General's Reference (No.49 of 2000), Re; *sub nom* R. *v.* Louis (Terry) [2001] 1
Cr. App. R. (S.) 122, CA (Crim Div) . . . . *Digested,* 01/**1437**
Attorney General's Reference (No.56 of 2000), Re; *sub nom* R. *v.* Dickerson (Nigel Roy)
[2001] 1 Cr. App. R. (S.) 127, CA (Crim Div) . . . . *Digested,* 00/**1259**
Attorney General's Reference (No.58 of 2000), Re; *sub nom* R. *v.* Wynne (Anthony
Vincent) [2001] 2 Cr. App. R. (S.) 19, CA (Crim Div) . . . . *Digested,* 01/**1264**
Attorney General's Reference (No.60 of 2000), Re; *sub nom* R. *v.* DS [2001] 2 Cr. App.
R. (S.) 18, CA (Crim Div) . . . . *Digested,* 01/**1456**
Attorney General's Reference (No.61 of 2000), Re; *sub nom* R. *v.* Hooper (Jonathan
Andrew) [2001] 2 Cr. App. R. (S.) 11, CA (Crim Div) . . . . *Digested,* 01/**1337**
Attorney General's Reference (No.62 of 2000), Re; *sub nom* R. *v.* S (Daniel Edward) (A
Juvenile); 200004847/R2, CA (Crim Div) . . . . *Digested,* 00/**1341**
Attorney General's Reference (No.73 of 2000), Re; *sub nom* R. *v.* Brookes (Barry)
[2001] EWCA Crim 191, CA (Crim Div) . . . . *Digested,* 01/**1491**
Attorney General's Reference (No.77 of 2000), Re; *sub nom* R. *v.* EMW [2001] 2 Cr.
App. R. (S.) 17, CA (Crim Div) . . . . *Digested,* 01/**1366**
Attorney General's Reference (No.78 of 2000), Re; *sub nom* R. *v.* Jones (Jason) [2001]
EWCA Crim 2114, CA (Crim Div) . . . . *Digested,* 01/**1334**
Attorney General's Reference (No.80 of 2000), Re; *sub nom* R. *v.* Keegan (Anthony)
[2001] 2 Cr. App. R. (S.) 12, CA (Crim Div) . . . . *Digested,* 01/**1367**
Attorney General's Reference (No.81 of 2000), Re; *sub nom* R. *v.* Jacobs (Paul) [2001] 2
Cr. App. R. (S.) 16, CA (Crim Div) . . . . *Digested,* 01/**1331**
Attorney General's Reference (No.82 of 2000), Re; *sub nom* R. *v.* Vinnicombe (Stephen
Robin) [2001] EWCA Crim 65; [2001] 2 Cr. App. R. (S.) 60, CA (Crim Div) . . . . *Digested,* 01/**1502**
Attorney General's Reference (No.84 of 2000), Re; *sub nom* R. *v.* Francis (Ollrick Mark)
[2001] EWCA Crim 166; [2001] 2 Cr. App. R. (S.) 71, CA (Crim Div) . . . . *Digested,* 01/**1288**
Attorney General's Reference (No.86 of 2000), Re; *sub nom* R. *v.* Oliver (Michael Roger)
[2001] EWCA Crim 161, CA (Crim Div) . . . . *Digested,* 01/**1262**
Attorney General's Reference (No.88 of 2000), Re; *sub nom* R. *v.* Heighton (Mark
Kristian) [2001] EWCA Crim 68, CA (Crim Div) . . . . *Digested,* 01/**1335**
Attorney General's Reference (No.89 of 2000), Re; *sub nom* R. *v.* Jones (Neil Andrew)
[2001] EWCA Crim 137; [2001] 2 Cr. App. R. (S.) 65, CA (Crim Div) . . . . *Digested,* 01/**1202**
Attorney General's Reference (No.90 of 2000), Re; *sub nom* R. *v.* King (Michael) [2001]
EWCA Crim 697, CA (Crim Div) . . . . *Digested,* 01/**1495**
Attorney General's Reference (No.92 of 2000), Re; *sub nom* R. *v.* Jenkins (Ian) [2001]
EWCA Crim 411, CA (Crim Div) . . . . *Digested,* 01/**1204**
Attorney General's Reference (No.1 of 2001), Re; *sub nom* R. *v.* M (Arthur John) [2001]
EWCA Crim 766; [2001] 2 Cr. App. R. (S.) 105, CA (Crim Div) . . . . *Digested,* 01/**1365**

Attorney General's Reference (No.2 of 2001), Re; *sub nom* R. *v.* J (Unreasonable Delay) [2001] EWCA Crim 1568; [2001] 1 W.L.R. 1869; [2001] U.K.H.R.R. 1265; (2001) 98(32) L.S.G. 36; (2001) 145 S.J.L.B. 172; *Times*, July 12, 2001, CA (Crim Div). . . . .   *Digested*, 01/**1119**

Attorney General's Reference (No.2 of 2001) (Unduly Lenient Sentence), Re; *sub nom* R. *v.* F (Richard John) [2001] EWCA Crim 1015; [2001] 2 Cr. App. R. (S.) 121, CA (Crim Div). . . . .   *Digested*, 01/**1357**

Attorney General's Reference (No.3 of 2001), Re; *sub nom* R. *v.* Smith (Joanna Gay) [2001] EWCA Crim 847; [2001] 2 Cr. App. R. (S.) 122, CA (Crim Div) . . . .   *Digested*, 01/**1255**

Attorney General's Reference (No.5 of 2001), Re; *sub nom* R. *v.* C (Terence) [2001] EWCA Crim 771; [2001] 2 Cr. App. R. (S.) 106, CA (Crim Div) . . . .   *Digested*, 01/**1371**

Attorney General's Reference (No.13 of 2001), Re; *sub nom* R. *v.* Cole (John) [2001] EWCA Crim 721; [2001] 2 Cr. App. R. (S.) 112, CA (Crim Div) . . . .   *Digested*, 01/**1330**

Attorney General's Reference (No.15 of 2001), Re; *sub nom* R. *v.* J (David Graham) [2001] EWCA Crim 850; [2001] 2 Cr. App. R. (S.) 123, CA (Crim Div) . . . .   *Digested*, 01/**1484**

Attorney General's Reference (No.18 of 2001), Re; *sub nom* R. *v.* Edwards (Gareth Stephen) [2001] EWCA Crim 1037; [2001] 2 Cr. App. R. (S.) 120, CA (Crim Div) . . . .   *Digested*, 01/**1322**

Attorney General's Reference (Nos.19, 20 and 21 of 2001), Re; *sub nom* R. *v.* Byrne (Alan); R. *v.* Field (Jason); R. *v.* C (Craig) (A Juvenile) [2001] EWCA Crim 1432, CA (Crim Div). . . . .   *Considered*, 01/**1434**

Attorney General's Reference (No.23 of 2001), Re; *sub nom* R. *v.* Fielder (Paul Martin) [2001] EWCA Crim 1008; [2001] 2 Cr. App. R. (S.) 118, CA (Crim Div) . . . .   *Digested*, 01/**1211**

Attorney General's Reference (No.24 of 2001), Re; *sub nom* R. *v.* Y (Jayne Alison) [2001] EWCA Crim 894; [2001] 2 Cr. App. R. (S.) 124, CA (Crim Div) . . . .   *Digested*, 01/**1232**

Attorney General's Reference (No.25 of 2001), Re; *sub nom* R. *v.* Moran (Frank Adam); Moran, Re [2001] EWCA Crim 1770; [2001] S.T.C. 1309; [2001] B.T.C. 351; [2001] Crim. L.R. 825; [2001] S.T.I. 1142; (2001) 98(37) L.S.G. 38; (2001) 145 S.J.L.B. 218; *Times*, August 8, 2001, CA (Crim Div). . . . .   *Digested*, 01/**1111**

Attorney General's Reference (No.26a of 2001), Re; *sub nom* R. *v.* B (Malcolm Kevin) [2001] EWCA Crim 1288, CA (Crim Div) . . . .   *Digested*, 01/**1300**

Attorney General's Reference (No.29 of 2001), Re; *sub nom* R. *v.* Styring (Katrina) [2001] EWCA Crim 1491, CA (Crim Div) . . . .   *Digested*, 01/**1500**

Attorney General's Reference (No.30 of 2001), Re; *sub nom* R. *v.* Humphrey (Warren Martin) [2001] EWCA Crim 1319, CA (Crim Div). . . . .   *Digested*, 01/**1477**

Attorney General's Reference (Nos.33 and 34 of 2001), Re; *sub nom* R. *v.* Smith (Richard Peter); R. *v.* Curtis (Anthony John) [2001] EWCA Crim 1908, CA (Crim Div) . . .   *Digested*, 01/**1434**

Attorney General's Reference (No.36 of 2001), Re; *sub nom* R. *v.* Hall (Christopher James) [2001] EWCA Crim 1489, CA (Crim Div) . . . .   *Digested*, 01/**1312**

Attorney General's Reference (No.43 of 2001), Re; *sub nom* R. *v.* C-T (Ronnie) [2001] EWCA Crim 1275, CA (Crim Div) . . . .   *Digested*, 01/**1459**

Attorney General's Reference (No.46 of 2001), Re; *sub nom* R. *v.* Black (John William) [2001] EWCA Crim 2025, CA (Crim Div) . . . .   *Digested*, 01/**1373**

Attorney General's Reference (No.50 of 2001), Re; *sub nom* R. *v.* Hill (Catherine Louise) [2001] EWCA Crim 1475, CA (Crim Div) . . . .   *Digested*, 01/**1263**

Attorney General's Reference (No.51 of 2001), Re; *sub nom* R. *v.* MC [2001] EWCA Crim 1635, CA (Crim Div) . . . .   *Digested*, 01/**1463**

Attorney General's Reference (No.52 of 2001), Re; *sub nom* R. *v.* Lamoon (Johnathon Joe) [2001] EWCA Crim 1906, CA (Crim Div) . . . .   *Digested*, 01/**1501**

Attorney General's Reference (Nos.53, 54, 55, 56 and 57 of 2001), Re; *sub nom* R. *v.* SM (A Juvenile); R. *v.* T (Nathan) (A Juvenile); R. *v.* Bahashwan (Anis Said); R. *v.* Hussein (Mohammed); R. *v.* H (Robert James) (A Juvenile) [2001] EWCA Crim 1963, CA (Crim Div) . . . .   *Digested*, 01/**1399**

Attorney General's Reference (Nos.58 and 59 of 2001), Re; *sub nom* R. *v.* Mayhall (David John); R. *v.* Danter (Jason Conrad) [2001] EWCA Crim 2029, CA (Crim Div) . .   *Digested*, 01/**1490**

Attorney General's Reference (No.60 of 2001), Re; *sub nom* R. *v.* Ross-Duff (Alan William) [2001] EWCA Crim 2026, CA (Crim Div) . . . .   *Digested*, 01/**1483**

Attorney General's Reference (No.61 of 2001), Re; *sub nom* R. *v.* H (Steven Donald) [2001] EWCA Crim 1454, CA (Crim Div) . . . .   *Digested*, 01/**1408**

Attorney General's Reference (No.63 of 2001), Re; *sub nom* R. *v.* G (Jamie Andrew) (A Juvenile) [2001] EWCA Crim 1652, CA (Crim Div) . . . .   *Digested*, 01/**1429**

Attorney General's Reference (No.64 of 2001), Re; *sub nom* R. *v.* Little (David) [2001] EWCA Crim 2028, CA (Crim Div). . . . .   *Digested*, 01/**1426**

Attorney General's Reference (Nos.65 and 66 of 2001), Re; *sub nom* R. *v.* Smith (Colin Paul); R. *v.* Hope (Marc John) [2001] EWCA Crim 2406, CA (Crim Div) . . . . . .   *Digested*, 01/**1479**

Attorney General's Reference (No.67 of 2001), Re; *sub nom* R. *v.* Carpenter (Amber Louise) [2001] EWCA Crim 2027, CA (Crim Div) . . . .   *Digested*, 01/**1338**

Attorney General's Reference (No.68 of 2001), Re; *sub nom* R. *v.* Newbury (Stephen David) [2001] EWCA Crim 1803, CA (Crim Div).   *Digested*, 01/**1253**

Attorney General's Reference (No.70 of 2001), Re; *sub nom* R. *v.* Hardy (Richard Nicholas) [2001] EWCA Crim 2446, CA (Crim Div) . . . .   *Digested*, 01/**1261**

Attorney General's Reference (Nos.73 and 74 of 2001), Re; *sub nom* R. *v.* Walker (Deborah Alison); R. *v.* Siddique (Barbar) [2001] EWCA Crim 1923, CA (Crim Div) . . . .   *Digested*, 01/**1297**

Attorney General's Reference (No.75 of 2001), Re; *sub nom* R. *v.* Hochard (David Gaston) [2001] EWCA Crim 1928; *Daily Telegraph*, October 2, 2001, CA (Crim Div)

Attorney General's Reference (No.77 of 2001), Re; *sub nom* R. *v.* H (Bruce William) [2001] EWCA Crim 1909, CA (Crim Div) . . . . *Digested*, 01/**1361**

Attorney General's Reference (No.78 of 2001), Re; *sub nom* R. *v.* Martin (John Patrick) [2001] EWCA Crim 1798, CA (Crim Div) . . . . *Digested*, 01/**1478**

Attorney General's Reference (No.79 of 2001), Re; *sub nom* R. *v.* M (Douglas James) (A Juvenile) [2001] EWCA Crim 1925, CA (Crim Div) . . . . *Digested*, 01/**1400**

Attorney General's Reference (No.91 of 2001), Re; *sub nom* R. *v.* Jones (Anthony Russell) [2001] EWCA Crim 2135, CA (Crim Div) . . . . *Digested*, 01/**1273**

Attorney General's Reference (No.13 of 1995), Re; *sub nom* R. *v.* Eaglen (Timothy John) [1996] 1 Cr. App. R. (S.) 120; [1996] R.T.R. 1, CA . . . . *Digested*, 96/**1766**:
Considered, 00/1211

Attorney General's Reference (Nos.36 and 38 of 1998) see R. *v.* L (Deferred Sentence)

Attwood (Inspector of Taxes) *v.* Anduff Car Wash Ltd; *sub nom* Anduff Carwash Ltd *v.* Attwood (Inspector of Taxes) [1997] S.T.C. 1167; 69 T.C. 575; [1997] B.T.C. 454; *Independent*, July 21, 1997 (C.S.), CA; affirming [1996] S.T.C. 110; (1996) 140 S.J.L.B. 13; *Times*, December 11, 1995, Ch D . . . . *Digested*, 97/**1067**

Attwood *v.* Bovis Homes Ltd; *sub nom* Atwood *v.* Bovis Homes Ltd [2001] Ch. 379; [2000] 3 W.L.R. 1842; [2000] 4 All E.R. 948; (2001) 82 P. & C.R. 2; [2000] 3 E.G.L.R. 139; [2000] E.G.C.S. 54; (2000) 97(16) L.S.G. 43; (2000) 97(20) L.S.G. 46; *Times*, April 18, 2000, Ch D . . . . *Digested*, 00/**4632**

Attwood *v.* Woodward (Unreported, December 11, 1998), CC (Southend) [*Ex rel.* Nigel Brockley, Barrister, Bracton Chambers, 95a Chancery Lane, London] . . . . *Digested*, 99/**1573**

Atwall *v.* Leicester City Bus, CC (Leicester) [*Ex rel.* Richard Gregory, Barrister, 24 The Ropewalk, Nottingham] . . . . *Digested*, 01/**1583**

Atwell *v.* Michael Perry & Co; *sub nom* Atwell *v.* Perry & Co [1998] 4 All E.R. 65; [1998] P.N.L.R. 709; *Times*, July 27, 1998, Ch D . . . . *Digested*, 98/**4004**:
Distinguished, 99/3791

Atwell *v.* Perry & Co see Atwell *v.* Michael Perry & Co

Atwood *v.* Bovis Homes Ltd see Attwood *v.* Bovis Homes Ltd

Aubergine Enterprises Ltd *v.* Lakewood International Ltd A3/2001/0514, CA; affirming [2001] 10 E.G.C.S. 155; [2001] N.P.C. 37, Ch D

AUBEX/Pen nib (T713/91) [1999] E.P.O.R. 173, EPO (Technical Bd App)

Aubrey Investments Ltd *v.* DS Crawford Ltd (In Receivership) 1998 S.L.T. 628; 1997 G.W.D. 25-1273; *Times*, July 30, 1997, OH . . . . *Digested*, 98/**6032**

Auchincloss *v.* Agricultural & Veterinary Supplies Ltd; *sub nom* Auchinloss *v.* Agricultural & Veterinary Supplies Ltd [1999] R.P.C. 397; (1999) 22(1) I.P.D. 22003, CA; reversing in part [1997] R.P.C. 649; (1997) 20(8) I.P.D. 20074, Pat Ct . . . . *Digested*, 99/**3494**

Auchinloss *v.* Agricultural & Veterinary Supplies Ltd see Auchincloss *v.* Agricultural & Veterinary Supplies Ltd

Auckland Gas Co Ltd *v.* Inland Revenue Commissioner; *sub nom* Auckland Gas Co Ltd *v.* Inland Revenue Commissioner (New Zealand) [2000] 1 W.L.R. 1783; [2000] S.T.C. 527; 73 T.C. 266; [2000] B.T.C. 249; [2000] S.T.I. 914, PC (NZ) . . . . *Digested*, 00/**4929**

Auckland Gas Co Ltd *v.* Inland Revenue Commissioner (New Zealand) see Auckland Gas Co Ltd *v.* Inland Revenue Commissioner

Auckland Medical Aid Trust *v.* Commissioner of Police [1976] 1 N.Z.L.R. 485, Sup Ct (NZ) . . . . *Considered*, 01/3851

AUDI-MED Trade Mark; *sub nom* Audio Medical Devices Ltd's Trade Mark Application [1999] E.T.M.R. 1010; [1998] R.P.C. 863, TMR . . . . *Digested*, 99/**3587**:
Referred to, 99/3562

Audio Medical Devices Ltd's Trade Mark Application see AUDI-MED Trade Mark

Auditel, Re (IV/32.031) [1995] 5 C.M.L.R. 719, CEC . . . . *Applied*, 99/2231

Auditel *v.* Commission of the European Communities (T66/94) [1995] E.C.R. II-239 . . *Followed*, 99/2231

Aughton Ltd (formerly Aughton Group Ltd) *v.* MF Kent Services Ltd 57 B.L.R. 1; 31 Con. L.R. 60, CA . . . . *Digested*, 93/**152**:
Applied, 95/331, 00/3515: *Considered*, 98/242

Augustus Barnett & Son, Re [1986] P.C.C. 167; *Times*, December 7, 1985 . . . . *Digested*, 86/**301**:
Considered, 00/675

AUJOURD'HUI/Luxury foodstuff (T330/87) [2000] E.P.O.R. 265, EPO (Technical Bd App) . . . . *Digested*, 00/**3646**

Aumac Ltd's European Patent Application (No.94120537.9) see AUMAC/Designation of states in a divisional application (J22/95)

AUMAC/Designation of states in a divisional application (J22/95); *sub nom* Aumac Ltd's European Patent Application (No.94120537.9) (1998) 21(2) I.P.D. 21017, EPO (Legal Bd App)

Aurum Investments Ltd *v.* Avonforce Ltd (In Liquidation) (2001) 3 T.C.L.R. 21; 78 Con. L.R. 115; [2001] Lloyd's Rep. P.N. 285; (2001) 17 Const. L.J. 145, QBD (T&CC) . . . . *Digested*, 01/**4518**

Aurum Marketing Ltd (In Liquidation), Re see Secretary of State for Trade and Industry *v.* Aurum Marketing Ltd

Ausiello *v.* Italy (1997) 24 E.H.R.R. 568, ECHR . . . . *Digested*, 98/**3130**

AUSIMONT/Fee reduction (J21/98) [2001] E.P.O.R. 8, EPO (Legal Bd App) . . . .   *Digested*, 01/**3917**

Austin *v.* Zurich General Accident and Liability Insurance Co Ltd [1945] K.B. 250; (1945) 78 Ll. L. Rep. 185, CA; affirming [1944] 2 All E.R. 243; (1944) 77 Ll. L. Rep. 409, KBD . . . .   *Applied*, 70/1378, 79/1506: *Considered*, 00/1460: *Distinguished*, 52/1738

Austin Hall Building Ltd *v.* Buckland Securities Ltd [2001] B.L.R. 272; (2001) 3 T.C.L.R. 18; 80 Con. L.R. 115; (2001) 17 Const. L.J. 325; [2001] 25 E.G.C.S. 155, QBD (T&CC) . . . .   *Digested*, 01/**855**

Austin's Application for Judicial Review, Re [1998] N.I. 327, QBD (NI) . . . .   *Digested*, 99/**5436**

Austintel Ltd, Re; Applications Pursuant to r.7.28 of the Insolvency Rules 1986, Re; Creditnet Ltd, Re; Debtor Management Ltd, Re [1997] 1 W.L.R. 616; [1997] B.C.C. 362; [1997] 1 B.C.L.C. 233; [2000] B.P.I.R. 223; (1996) 93(43) L.S.G. 26; (1996) 140 S.J.L.B. 254; *Times*, November 11, 1996; *Independent*, November 25, 1996 (C.S.), CA; affirming [1996] 1 W.L.R. 1291; [1996] B.C.C. 444; [1996] 2 B.C.L.C. 133; (1996) 146 N.L.J. 916; *Times*, May 22, 1996, Ch D . . . .   *Digested*, 96/**3535**

Australia and New Zealand Banking Group Ltd *v.* Societe Generale [2000] 1 All E.R. (Comm) 682; [2000] Lloyd's Rep. Bank. 153; [2000] C.P. Rep. 71; [2000] C.L.C. 833, CA; affirming [1999] 2 All E.R. (Comm) 625; [2000] C.L.C. 161, QBD (Comm Ct). . . . .   *Digested*, 00/**361**

Australian Capital Television (Pty) Ltd *v.* Australia (1992) 177 C.L.R. 106, HC (Aus). . . .   *Applied*, 98/3094

Australian Competition Commission *v.* CG Berbatis Holdings Pty Ltd [2000] N.P.C. 98, Fed Ct (Aus) (Sgl judge)

Australian Knitting Mills *v.* Grant Ltd see Grant *v.* Australian Knitting Mills Ltd

Australian Securities Commission *v.* AS Nominees Ltd (1995) 133 A.L.R. 1 . . . .   *Followed*, 00/658

Australian Securities Commission *v.* Bank Leumi Le-Israel [1997] 6 Bank. L.R. 277, Fed Ct (Aus) (Sgl judge) . . . .   *Digested*, 98/**687**

Australian Steel & Mining Corp Pty Ltd *v.* Corben [1974] 2 N.S.W.L.R. 202 . . . .   *Approved*, 99/856

Austrian Garnishee Order, Re [1998] I.L.Pr. 248, OGH (A)

Austrian National Tourist Office *v.* Customs and Excise Commissioners [1998] B.V.C. 2284, V&DTr. . . . .   *Digested*, 98/**4957**

Autodesk Inc *v.* Dyason (No.1) [1992] R.P.C. 575; (1992) 173 C.L.R. 330; (1992) 104 A.L.R. 563, HC (Aus) . . . .   *Disapproved*, 01/3858: *Followed*, 98/3443

Autodesk Inc *v.* Dyason (No.2) [1993] R.P.C. 259; (1993) 111 A.L.R. 385, HC (Aus) . .   *Disapproved*, 01/3858

Autodesk SA, Re [1999] E.C.C. 1, C d'A (Paris)

Automec Srl *v.* Commission of the European Communities (T24/90) [1992] E.C.R. II-2223; [1992] 5 C.M.L.R. 431, CFI . . . .   *Digested*, 93/**4251**: *Applied*, 99/695: *Followed*, 00/2365, 01/786

Automobiles Peugeot SA *v.* Safari Senlis SA [2001] E.C.C. 26, C d'A (Paris)

Automotive Industry Action Group's Trade Mark Application (No.2103490) see AUTOMOTIVE NETWORK EXCHANGE Trade Mark

AUTOMOTIVE NETWORK EXCHANGE Trade Mark; *sub nom* Automotive Industry Action Group's Trade Mark Application (No.2103490) [1998] R.P.C. 885; (1998) 21 (10) I.P.D. 21115, Appointed Person . . . .   *Digested*, 99/**3572**

Autotrasporti Librandi SNC *v.* Cuttica Spedizione e Servizi Internazionali Srl (C38/97) [1998] E.C.R. I-5955; [1998] 5 C.M.L.R. 966, ECJ (2nd Chamber)

Autronic AG *v.* Switzerland (A/178) (1990) 12 E.H.R.R. 485; [1991] F.S.R. 55; *Times*, May 30, 1990, ECHR . . . .   *Digested*, 92/**2360**: *Applied*, 01/850

Auty *v.* British Rail Engineering Ltd (Unreported, September 26, 2000), CC (Sheffield) [*Ex rel.* Thompsons, Solicitors, Arundel House, 1 Furnival Square, Sheffield] . . . .   *Digested*, 01/**603**

Ava Leisure Ltd's Application for Judicial Review, Re see R. *v.* Department of the Environment for Northern Ireland Ex p. Ava Leisure Ltd

Availability to the public (G01/92) [1993] E.P.O.R. 241, EPO (Enlarged Bd App). . . . . .   *Applied*, 01/3938

Avalon Enterprises Ltd *v.* Secretary of State for the Environment, Transport and the Regions see R. (on the application of Elmbridge BC) *v.* Secretary of State for the Environment, Transport and the Regions

Avco Trust Plc *v.* Customs and Excise Commissioners [2000] B.V.C. 2090, V&DTr

Avco Trust Plc *v.* Hooker (Unreported, January 28, 1999), CC (Oxford) [*Ex rel.* Peter Sayer, Barrister, Gough Square Chambers, London] . . . .   *Digested*, 99/**2513**

Aventis Pharma AB *v.* Paranova Lakemedel AB [2001] E.T.M.R. 60, TR (Stockholm) . . .   *Considered*, 01/6728

Averill *v.* United Kingdom (36408/97) (2001) 31 E.H.R.R. 36; 8 B.H.R.C. 430; [2000] Crim. L.R. 682; *Times*, June 20, 2000, ECHR . . . .   *Digested*, 00/**3228**

Avery *v.* Gough (Unreported, October 27, 2000), CC (Cardiff) [*Ex rel.* Matthew White, Barrister, St. John's Chambers, Small Street, Bristol] . . . .   *Digested*, 01/**402**

Avgerinos (CICB: Quantum: 1999), Re (Unreported, May 18, 1999), CICB (Manchester) [*Ex rel.* Rowlands Solicitors, 3 York Street, Manchester] . . . .   *Digested*, 00/**1554**

Avilion Ltd's European Patent Application (T167/96) (1998) 21 (7) I.P.D. 21074, EPO (Technical Bd App)

AVIR/Green Glass (T301/94) [1999] E.P.O.R. 384, EPO (Technical Bd App) . . . .   *Digested*, 99/**3477**

Avis *v.* Newman see Cartwright, Re

Avis Enterprises *v.* Greece [1998] H.R.C.D. 767; (1998) 26 E.H.R.R. CD 21, ECHR

Avnet Inc *v.* Isoact Ltd [1997] E.T.M.R. 562; [1997-98] Info. T.L.R. 197; [1998] F.S.R. 16; (1997) 20(11) I.P.D. 20107, Ch D . . . .   *Digested*, 97/**4878**

Avon CC v. Hooper [1997] 1 W.L.R. 1605; [1997] 1 All E.R. 532; (1997-98) 1 C.C.L.
Rep. 366; *Times*, March 18, 1996, CA . . . .   *Digested*, 96/**3977**:
                                              Considered, 01/581: *Followed*, 98/1674
Avon CC v. Howlett [1983] 1 W.L.R. 605; [1983] 1 All E.R. 1073; [1983] I.R.L.R. 171;
81 L.G.R. 555; (1983) 133 N.L.J. 377; (1983) 127 S.J. 173, CA; reversing [1981]
I.R.L.R. 447 . . . .   *Digested*, 83/**1210**:
                Applied, 89/3755: *Considered*, 01/2434, 01/2440: *Distinguished*, 00/2331
Avon Insurance Plc v. Swire Fraser Ltd [2000] 1 All E.R. (Comm) 573; [2000] C.L.C.
665; [2000] Lloyd's Rep. I.R. 535, QBD (Comm Ct) . . . .   *Digested*, 01/**3844**
AW, Re see Whitbread (Habeas Corpus: Compulsory Admission), Re
AWA Ltd v. Daniels (formerly practising as Deloitte Haskins & Sells) [1955-95]
P.N.L.R. 727, CA (NSW)
Awadh v. Secretary of State for the Home Department [1997] I.N.L.R. 39, IAT . . . .   *Digested*, 98/**3171**
Awan, Re; *sub nom* Petitioning Creditor v. Awan (A Bankrupt) [2000] B.P.I.R. 241,
Ch D . . . .   *Digested*, 00/**3446**
Awoyemi (C230/97), Re see Criminal Proceedings against Awoyemi (C230/97)
Awua v. Brent LBC see R. v. Brent LBC Ex p. Awua
Awwad v. Geraghty & Co; *sub nom* Geraghty & Co v. Awwad [2001] Q.B. 570;
[2000] 3 W.L.R. 1041; [2000] 1 All E.R. 608; [2000] 1 Costs L.R. 105; [1999]
N.P.C. 148; *Independent*, December 1, 1999, CA . . . .   *Digested*, 00/**4002**
AXA Equity & Law Life Assurance Society Plc (No.1), Re; AXA Sun Life Plc (No.1), Re
[2001] 2 B.C.L.C. 447; (2001) 98(1) L.S.G. 23; *Times*, December 19, 2000, Ch D
                                                   Digested, 01/**3803**
AXA Equity & Law Life Assurance Society Plc (No.2), Re; Axa Sun Life Plc (No.2), Re
[2001] 1 All E.R. (Comm) 1010; [2001] 2 B.C.L.C. 447; (2001) 98(10) L.S.G. 43;
(2001) 145 S.J.L.B. 51; *Times*, January 31, 2001, Ch D . . . .   *Digested*, 01/**3804**
AXA Equity & Law Life Assurance Society Plc v. National Westminster Bank Plc [1998]
C.L.C. 1177, CA; affirming [1998] P.N.L.R. 433, Ch D . . . .   *Digested*, 98/**332**
Axa Insurance Co Ltd v. Swire Fraser Ltd (formerly Robert Fraser Insurance Brokers
Ltd) [2001] C.P. Rep. 17; [2000] C.P.L.R. 142; *Times*, January 19, 2000, CA. . . .   *Digested*, 00/**626**:
                                                   Cited, 00/350
AXA Reinsurance (UK) Ltd v. Field [1996] 1 W.L.R. 1026; [1996] 3 All E.R. 517; [1996]
2 Lloyd's Rep. 233; [1996] C.L.C. 1169; [1996] 5 Re. L.R. 184; (1996) 93(33)
L.S.G. 24; (1996) 146 N.L.J. 1093; (1996) 140 S.J.L.B. 155; *Times*, July 2, 1996,
HL; reversing [1996] 1 Lloyd's Rep. 26; [1995] 4 Re. L.R. 384; *Times*, October
10, 1995, CA . . . .   *Digested*, 96/**3599**:
                                                 Distinguished, 98/3405
AXA Sun Life Plc (No.1), Re see AXA Equity & Law Life Assurance Society Plc (No.1), Re
Axa Sun Life Plc (No.2), Re see AXA Equity & Law Life Assurance Society Plc (No.2), Re
Axis Genetics Plc's (In Administration) Patent, Re see Biosource Technologies Inc v. Axis
Genetics Plc (In Administration)
Axtell-Powell v. Labor (Unreported, June 13, 2000), CC (Barnet) [*Ex rel.* Giffen Couch
& Archer Solicitors, Bridge House, Bridge Street, Leighton Buzzard,
Bedfordshire] . . . .   *Digested*, 00/**589**
Aydin v. Turkey (23178/94) (1998) 25 E.H.R.R. 251; 3 B.H.R.C. 300, ECHR . . . .   *Digested*, 98/**3162**
Aylesbond Estates Ltd v. MacMillan (2000) 32 H.L.R. 1; [1999] L. & T.R. 127, CA . . . . .   *Digested*, 00/**3906**
Aylesbury v. Hale (Unreported, November 9, 1994) [*Ex rel.* Bryan Thomas, Barrister] . . .   *Digested*, 95/**1691**:
                                                 Considered, 00/1501
Aylesbury Vale DC v. Barlow (2000) 15 P.A.D. 725, Planning Inspector
Aylesbury Vale DC v. Matterson (1999) 14 P.A.D. 670, Planning Inspector
Aylesbury Vale DC v. North (1999) 14 P.A.D. 727, Planning Inspector
Aylwen v. Taylor Joynson Garrett (A Firm) [2001] EWCA Civ 1171; (2001) 98(29)
L.S.G. 40, CA; affirming [2001] P.N.L.R. 38, Ch D
Ayobiojo v. McGoldrick (1998) 76 P. & C.R. D26, CA
Ayres v. Evans [2000] B.P.I.R. 697, Fed Ct (Aus) (Full Ct) . . . .   *Digested*, 01/**3714**
Ayrshire Employers Mutual Association Ltd v. Inland Revenue see Inland Revenue
Commissioners v. Ayrshire Employers Mutual Insurance Association Ltd
Aytekin v. Turkey (22880/93) (2001) 32 E.H.R.R. 22; [1998] H.R.C.D. 882, ECHR
Ayuntamiento de Sevilla v. Recaudadores de Tributos de las Zonas Primera y Segunda
(C202/90) [1993] S.T.C. 659; [1991] E.C.R. I-4247; [1994] 1 C.M.L.R. 424,
ECJ (5th Chamber) . . . .   *Applied*, 98/**4905**
AZ (A Minor) (Abduction: Acquiescence), Re [1993] 1 F.L.R. 682; [1993] 1 F.C.R. 733, CA
                                                 Digested, 94/**3145**:
               Applied, 94/3146, 95/3430: *Considered*, 94/3156, 00/2440:
                                                 Followed, 97/387
Azad v. Entry Clearance Officer (Dhaka) [2001] Imm. A.R. 318; [2001] I.N.L.R. 109;
Daily Telegraph, January 30, 2001, CA . . . .   *Digested*, 01/**3696**
Azam v. Singleton [2001] 2 Q.R. 10, CC (Leeds) [*Ex rel.* Fox Hayes Solicitors, Bank
House, 150 Roundhay Road, Leeds] . . . .   *Digested*, 01/**1638**
Azienda Agraria Perda Rubia v. Cantina Soaciale Ogliastra [2001] E.T.M.R. CN16, Trib (I)
Azimi v. Newham LBC (2001) 33 H.L.R. 51, CA
Aziz v. Bethnal Green City Challenge Co Ltd [2000] I.R.L.R. 111, CA . . . .   *Digested*, 99/**2038**
Aziz v. Norman see Norman v. Ali (Limitation Period)

Aziz v. Trinity Street Taxis Ltd [1989] Q.B. 463; [1988] 3 W.L.R. 79; [1988] I.C.R. 534; [1988] I.R.L.R. 204; (1988) 132 S.J. 898, CA; affirming [1986] I.R.L.R. 435, EAT . . . . *Digested*, 88/**1300**:
Applied, 98/2183, 01/2302: *Considered*, 96/2614: *Doubted*, 99/2093
Azov Shipping Co v. Baltic Shipping Co (No.1) [1999] 1 All E.R. 476; [1999] 1 Lloyd's Rep. 68; [1998] C.L.C. 1240, QBD (Comm Ct) . . . . *Digested*, 99/**226**
Azov Shipping Co v. Baltic Shipping Co (No.2) [1999] 1 All E.R. (Comm.) 716; [1999] 2 Lloyd's Rep. 39; [1999] C.L.C. 624, QBD (Comm Ct) . . . . *Digested*, 99/**224**
Azov Shipping Co v. Baltic Shipping Co (No.3) [1999] 2 All E.R. (Comm) 453; [1999] 2 Lloyd's Rep. 159; [1999] C.L.C. 1425, QBD (Comm Ct) . . . . *Digested*, 99/**4452**

B, Re see R. v. BHB Community Healthcare NHS Trust Ex p. B
B (Abduction: Retention of Orphan Belarussian), Re [2001] Fam. Law 90, Fam Div
B (A Child) (Abduction: Acquiescence), Re [1999] 2 F.L.R. 818; [1999] 3 F.C.R. 557; [1999] Fam. Law 608, Fam Div. . . . . *Digested*, 00/**2440**
B (A Child) (Adoption by One Natural Parent to the Exclusion of Other), Re see B v. P (Adoption by Unmarried Father)
B (A Child) (Adoption: Natural Parent), Re see B v. P (Adoption by Unmarried Father)
B (A Child) (Adoption Order), Re [2001] EWCA Civ 347; [2001] 2 F.L.R. 26; [2001] 2 F.C.R. 89; [2001] Fam. Law 492; (2001) 165 J.P.N. 565; *Times*, March 23, 2001, CA. . *Digested*, 01/**2531**
B (A Child) (Interim Care Orders: Renewal), Re [2001] 2 F.L.R. 1217; [2001] Fam. Law 802; *Times*, June 28, 2001, Fam Div. . . . . *Digested*, 01/**2643**
B (A Child) (Sexual Abuse: Expert's Report), Re; *sub nom* B (A Child) (Sexual Abuse: Independent Expert), Re [2000] 1 F.L.R. 871; [2000] 2 F.C.R. 8; [2000] Fam. Law 479; (2000) 164 J.P.N. 624; *Times*, March 29, 2000, CA. . . . . *Digested*, 00/**2510**
B (A Child) (Sexual Abuse: Independent Expert), Re see B (A Child) (Sexual Abuse: Expert's Report), Re
B (A Child) (Sole Adoption by Unmarried Parent), Re see B v. P (Adoption by Unmarried Father)
B (A Child) (Split Hearings: Jurisdiction), Re [2000] 1 W.L.R. 790; [2000] 1 F.L.R. 334; [2000] 1 F.C.R. 297; [2000] Fam. Law 320; (2000) 164 J.P.N. 441; (1999) 96(48) L.S.G. 39; (2000) 144 S.J.L.B. 23; *Times*, January 18, 2000, CA . . . . *Digested*, 00/**2511**:
Distinguished, 01/403
B (A Child) v. B (Unreported, January 9, 2001), CC (Torquay) [*Ex rel.* Crosse & Crosse, Solicitors, 14, Southernhay West, Exeter] . . . . *Digested*, 01/**1739**
B (A Child) v. Butlins Ltd [2001] 4 Q.R. 15, CC (Liverpool) [*Ex rel.* Paul Simpson, Barrister, 2nd Floor, 14 Cook Street, Liverpool] . . . . *Digested*, 01/**1704**
B (A Child) v. Camden LBC [2001] P.I.Q.R. P9, QBD. . . . . *Digested*, 01/**4502**
B (A Child) v. D [2001] 3 Q.R. 11, CC (Manchester) [*Ex rel.* Philip Butler, Barrister, Deans Court Chambers, 24 St John Street, Manchester] . . . . *Digested*, 01/**1585**
B (A Child) v. DPP [2000] 2 A.C. 428; [2000] 2 W.L.R. 452; [2000] 1 All E.R. 833; [2000] 2 Cr. App. R. 65; [2000] Crim. L.R. 403; (2000) 97(11) L.S.G. 36; (2000) 144 S.J.L.B. 108; *Times*, February 25, 2000; *Independent*, April 10, 2000 (C.S.), HL; reversing [1999] 3 W.L.R. 116; [1998] 4 All E.R. 265; [1999] 1 Cr. App. R. 163; (1998) 148 N.L.J. 1177, QBD. . . . . *Digested*, 00/**1002**:
Applied, 00/5063, 01/1070
B (A Child) v. F (A Child) [2001] 1 Q.R. 8, CC (Nottingham) [*Ex rel.* Nelsons Solicitors, Pennine House, 8 Stanford Street, Nottingham] . . . . *Digested*, 01/**1599**
B (A Child) v. Gaskill [2001] 3 Q.R. 20, CC (Colchester) [*Ex rel.* David White, Barrister, 12 King's Bench Walk, London] . . . . *Digested*, 01/**1776**
B (A Child) v. Hall (Costs) (Unreported, February 2, 2001), CC (Leicester) [*Ex rel.* Barratts Solicitors, The Old Dairy, 67a Melton Road, West Bridgeford, Nottingham] . . . . *Digested*, 01/**500**
B (A Child) v. Hounslow LBC [2000] Ed. C.R. 680, QBD. . . . . *Digested*, 01/**2035**
B (A Child) v. Little (Unreported, June 30, 2000), CC (Halifax) [*Ex rel.* Rhodes Thain & Collinson Solicitors, 27 Harrison Road, Halifax] . . . . *Digested*, 01/**1740**
B (A Child) v. Littlewoods Plc (Unreported, October 19, 1999), CC (Cheltenham) [*Ex rel.* Davis Gregory Solicitors, 25 Rodney Road, Cheltenham, Gloucs] . . . . *Digested*, 00/**1547**
B (A Child) v. RP see B v. P (Adoption by Unmarried Father)
B (A Child) v. S Howell & Sons Transport [2001] 6 Q.R. 18, CC (Birmingham) [*Ex rel.* Stephen Garner, Barrister, 8 Fountain Court, Steelhouse Lane, Birmingham] . . . *Digested*, 01/**1735**
B (A Child) v. Secretary of State for Social Security [2001] EWCA Civ 498; [2001] 1 W.L.R. 1404; [2001] Lloyd's Rep. Med. 297; [2001] 98(22) L.S.G. 36; (2001) 145 S.J.L.B. 120; *Times*, May 3, 2001, CA. . . . . *Digested*, 01/**5047**
B (A Child: Property Transfer), Re; *sub nom* B (A Minor) (Consent Order: Property Transfer), Re [1999] 2 F.L.R. 418; [1999] 3 F.C.R. 266; [1999] Fam. Law 535; *Times*, May 10, 1999, CA . . . . *Digested*, 99/**2364**
B (A Minor), Re see F-B (Minors) (Leave to Appeal), Re
B (A Minor), Re see V-B (Abduction: Rights of Custody), Re
B (A Minor) (Abduction: Father's Rights), Re see W (Minors) (Abduction: Father's Rights), Re

B (A Minor) (Abduction: Rights of Custody), Re [1997] 2 F.L.R. 594; [1998] 2 F.C.R. 212;
    [1999] Fam. Law 451, CA . . . .   *Digested*, 97/**404**:
                    Considered, 99/2326
B (A Minor) (Adoption Order: Nationality), Re [1999] 2 A.C. 136; [1999] 2 W.L.R. 714;
    [1999] 2 All E.R. 576; [1999] 1 F.L.R. 907; [1999] 1 F.C.R. 529; [1999] Imm. A.R.
    277; [1999] I.N.L.R. 125; [1999] Fam. Law 374; (1999) 96(14) L.S.G. 32; (1999)
    143 S.J.L.B. 105; *Times*, March 15, 1999; *Independent*, March 22, 1999 (C.S.),
    HL; reversing [1998] 1 F.L.R. 965; [1998] 2 F.C.R. 357; [1998] Imm. A.R. 324;
    [1998] I.N.L.R. 505; [1998] Fam. Law 384; (1998) 95(14) L.S.G. 22; (1998)
    142 S.J.L.B. 108; *Times*, March 16, 1998, CA . . . .   *Digested*, 99/**2299**
B (A Minor) (Adoption: Parental Rights), Re; *sub nom* B (Adoption: Father's Objections),
    Re [1999] 2 F.L.R. 215; [1999] 3 F.C.R. 522; [1999] Fam. Law 440, CA . . . . . .   *Digested*, 99/**2301**
B (A Minor) (Confidential Evidence: Disclosure), Re see B (A Minor) (Disclosure of
    Evidence), Re
B (A Minor) (Consent Order: Property Transfer), Re see B (A Child: Property Transfer), Re
B (A Minor) (Contact: Stepfather's Hostility), Re see B (A Minor) (Contact: Stepfather's
    Opposition), Re
B (A Minor) (Contact: Stepfather's Opposition), Re; *sub nom* B (A Minor) (Contact:
    Stepfather's Hostility), Re [1997] 2 F.L.R. 579; [1998] 3 F.C.R. 289; [1997] Fam.
    Law 720; *Times*, July 9, 1997; *Independent*, June 25, 1997, CA . . . .   *Digested*, 97/**414**
B (A Minor) (Costs), Re; *sub nom* B (A Minor: Contact Orders), Re [1999] 2 F.L.R. 221;
    [1999] 3 F.C.R. 586, CA . . . .   *Digested*, 99/**2411**
B (A Minor) (Disclosure of Evidence), Re; *sub nom* B (A Minor) (Confidential Evidence:
    Disclosure), Re [1993] Fam. 142; [1993] 2 W.L.R. 20; [1993] 1 All E.R. 931;
    [1993] 1 F.L.R. 191; [1992] 2 F.C.R. 617; [1993] Fam. Law 26; *Times*, July 31,
    1992; *Independent*, September 29, 1992; *Independent*, August 3, 1992 (C.S.),
    CA . . . .   *Digested*, 93/**2747**:
            Applied, 99/2412: *Considered*, 94/3265, 95/3562, 96/474
B (A Minor) (Rejection of Expert Evidence), Re see B (Care: Expert Witnesses), Re
B (A Minor) (Residence Order: Reasons), Re see B v. B (Residence Order: Reasons for
    Decision)
B (A Minor) (Residence Order: Status Quo), Re [1998] 1 F.L.R. 368; [1998] 1 F.C.R. 549;
    [1998] Fam. Law 73, CA . . . .   *Digested*, 98/**2444**
B (A Minor) (Unmarried Father), Re see W (Minors) (Abduction: Father's Rights), Re
B (A Minor) (Wardship: Medical Treatment), Re [1981] 1 W.L.R. 1421; 80 L.G.R. 107; 125 S.J.
    608, CA . . . .   *Digested*, 81/**1790**:
             Considered, 82/3117, 90/3197, 91/2588: *Referred to*, 00/3246
B (A Minor) (Wardship: Sterilisation), Re [1988] A.C. 199; [1987] 2 W.L.R. 1213; [1987] 2
    All E.R. 206; [1987] 2 F.L.R. 314; 86 L.G.R. 417; [1987] Fam. Law 419; (1987) 151
    L.G. Rev. 650; (1987) 84 L.S.G. 1410; (1987) 137 N.L.J. 432; (1987) 131 S.J. 625,
    HL; affirming (1987) 137 N.L.J. 291, CA . . . .   *Digested*, 87/**2533**:
          Applied, 00/3246: *Considered*, 87/2426, 88/2276, 89/3044, 95/3578,
                   96/7002, 97/6266, 01/2662: *Distinguished*, 89/2496
B (A Minor) v. Dodd (Unreported, June 16, 1999), CC (Chelmsford) [*Ex rel.* Paul
    McGrath, Barrister, 1 Temple Gardens, Temple, London] . . . .   *Digested*, 99/**403**
B (A Minor) v. Knight [1981] R.T.R. 136, QBD . . . .   *Digested*, 82/**2756**:
                    Distinguished, 94/4000, 95/3726, 99/3414
B (A Minor) v. Mitchell (1999) 99(2) Q.R. 7, CC (Doncaster) [*Ex rel.* David S Dixon,
    Barrister, Sovereign Chambers, 25 Park Square, Leeds] . . . .   *Digested*, 99/**1598**
B (A Minor) v. Pleasure & Leisure Corp (Unreported, November 16, 1999), CC
    (Skegness) [*Ex rel.* Hodgkinsons Solicitors, The Old Manse, 14 Lumley Avenue,
    Skegness, Lincolnshire] . . . .   *Digested*, 00/**1617**
B (A Minor) v. Thanet DC (Unreported, May 7, 1998), CC (Canterbury) [*Ex rel.* A E
    Wyeth & Co Solicitors, Bridge House, High Street, Dartford, Kent] . . . .   *Digested*, 99/**3965**
B (A Minor: Contact Orders), Re see B (A Minor) (Costs), Re
B (Abduction: Children's Objections), Re; *sub nom* B (Abduction: Views of Children), Re
    [1998] 1 F.L.R. 667; [1998] 3 F.C.R. 260; [1998] Fam. Law 308, Fam Div. . . . .   *Digested*, 98/**2378**
B (Abduction: False Immigration Information), Re [2000] 2 F.L.R. 835; [2000] Fam. Law
    796, Fam Div . . . .   *Digested*, 01/**3666**
B (Abduction: Views of Children), Re see B (Abduction: Children's Objections), Re
B (Adoption by Unmarried Father), Re see B v. P (Adoption by Unmarried Father)
B (Adoption: Father's Objections), Re see B (A Minor) (Adoption: Parental Rights), Re
B (Agreed Findings of Fact), Re; *sub nom* B (Threshold Criteria: Agreed Facts), Re
    [1998] 2 F.L.R. 968; [1999] 2 F.C.R. 328; [1998] Fam. Law 583; (1999) 163
    J.P.N. 994, CA . . . .   *Digested*, 99/**2363**
B (Care: Expert Witnesses), Re; *sub nom* B (A Minor) (Rejection of Expert Evidence),
    Re [1996] 1 F.L.R. 667; [1996] 2 F.C.R. 272; [1996] Fam. Law 347; (1996) 160
    J.P.N. 684, CA . . . .   *Digested*, 97/**367**:
                                     Followed, 99/2351
B (Care Proceedings: Legal Representation), Re [2001] 1 F.L.R. 485; [2001] 1 F.C.R. 512;
    [2001] Fam. Law 180, CA . . . .   *Digested*, 01/**2570**
B (Care Proceedings: Notification of Father Without Parental Responsibility), Re see K
    (Care Proceedings: Joinder of Father), Re

B (Children) (Abduction: New Evidence), Re [2001] EWCA Civ 625; [2001] 2 F.C.R. 531, CA

B (Children) (Change of Name), Re seeW (A Child) (Illegitimate Child: Change of Surname), Re

B (Children) (Removal from Jurisdiction), Re [2001] 1 F.C.R. 108, CA . . . .   *Digested*, 01/**2595**

B (Children Act Proceedings: Issue Estoppel), Re see B (Minors) (Care Proceedings: Issue Estoppel), Re

B (CICB: Quantum: 1998), Re (1999) 99(2) Q.R. 5, CICB (York) [*Ex rel*. Nicola Saxton, Barrister, St Paul's Chambers, St Paul's House, 23 Park Square, Leeds] . . . .   *Digested*, 99/**1439**

B (CICB: Quantum: 1999), Re (1999) 99(6) Q.R. 6, CICB (Birmingham) [*Ex rel*. Glyn Ross Samuel, Barrister, St Philip's Chambers, Fountain Court, Steelhouse Lane, Birmingham] . . . .   *Digested*, 99/**1451**

B (CICB: Quantum: 1999), Re [2000] 1 Q.R. 6, CICB (Manchester) [*Ex rel*. Robert Lizar Solicitors, 159 Princess Road, Manchester] . . . .   *Digested*, 99/**1440**

B (CICB: Quantum: 2000), Re (Unreported, February 23, 2000), CICB (Durham) [*Ex rel*. Joseph PAP O'Brien, Barrister, Broad Chare Chambers, 33 Broad Chare, Newcastle-upon-Tyne] . . . .   *Digested*, 00/**1519**

B (Deceased), Re; *sub nom* Bouette *v.* Rose [2000] Ch. 662; [2000] 2 W.L.R. 929; [2000] 1 All E.R. 665; [2000] 1 F.L.R. 363; [2000] 1 F.C.R. 385; [2000] W.T.L.R. 403; [2000] Fam. Law 316; (2000) 150 N.L.J. 20; *Times*, February 1, 2000; *Independent*, February 14, 2000 (C.S.), CA; reversing [1999] Ch. 206; [1999] 2 W.L.R. 1115; [1999] 2 All E.R. 425; [1999] 2 F.L.R. 466; [1999] 2 F.C.R. 145; [1999] Fam. Law 303; (1999) 96(7) L.S.G. 36; *Times*, January 26, 1999, Ch D . . . .   *Digested*, 00/**4906**

B (Disclosure to Other Parties), Re [2001] 2 F.L.R. 1017; [2001] Fam. Law 798, Fam Div

B (Francis) (CICA: Quantum: 2000), Re (Unreported, November 3, 1999), CICA (Manchester) [*Ex rel*. Rowlands Solicitors, 3 York Street, Manchester] . . . .   *Digested*, 00/**1533**

B (Minors) (Abduction: Disclosure), Re; *sub nom* B (Minors: Abduction), Re [1995] 1 F.L.R. 774; [1995] 2 F.C.R. 601; [1995] Fam. Law 398, CA; affirming [1993] 1 F.L.R. 988; [1994] 1 F.C.R. 389; [1993] Fam. Law 450; *Times*, November 6, 1992, Fam Div. . . . .   *Digested*, 94/**3162**: *Followed*, 00/2450

B (Minors) (Care Proceedings: Evidence), Re see B (Minors) (Care Proceedings: Issue Estoppel), Re

B (Minors) (Care Proceedings: Issue Estoppel), Re; *sub nom* B (Minors) (Care Proceedings: Evidence), Re; B (Minors: Issue Estoppel), Re; B (Children Act Proceedings: Issue Estoppel), Re [1997] Fam. 117; [1997] 3 W.L.R. 1; [1997] 2 All E.R. 29; [1997] 1 F.L.R. 285; [1997] 1 F.C.R. 477; [1997] Fam. Law 235; (1997) 161 J.P.N. 358; (1996) 93(44) L.S.G. 30; (1996) 140 S.J.L.B. 252; *Times*, December 16, 1996; *Independent*, November 25, 1996 (C.S.), Fam Div . .   *Digested*, 96/**685**: *Considered*, 98/1981

B (Minors) (Care Proceedings: Practice), Re; *sub nom* CB and JB (Minors) (Care Proceedings: Guidelines), Re [1999] 1 W.L.R. 238; [1998] 2 F.L.R. 211; [1998] 2 F.C.R. 313; [1998] Fam. Law 454; *Times*, May 13, 1998, Fam Div . . . .   *Digested*, 98/**2401**: *Followed*, 99/2358

B (Minors) (Change of Surname), Re [1996] 1 F.L.R. 791; [1996] 2 F.C.R. 304; [1996] Fam. Law 346; (1996) 140 S.J.L.B. 28; *Times*, December 1, 1995, CA . . . .   *Digested*, 96/**516**: *Considered*, 98/2432

B (Minors) (Psychiatric Therapy for Parents), Re [1999] 1 F.L.R. 701; [1999] 3 F.C.R. 20; [1999] Fam. Law 206; (2000) 164 J.P.N. 502, CA . . . .   *Digested*, 98/**2408**: *Followed*, 99/2361

B (Minors) (Residence Order: Leave to Appeal), Re [1998] 1 F.L.R. 520; [1998] 3 F.C.R. 351; [1998] Fam. Law 258, CA . . . .   *Digested*, 98/**2442**

B (Minors: Abduction), Re see B (Minors) (Abduction: Disclosure), Re

B (Minors: Issue Estoppel), Re see B (Minors) (Care Proceedings: Issue Estoppel), Re

B (Threshold Criteria: Agreed Facts), Re see B (Agreed Findings of Fact), Re

B *v.* B (Adult Student: Liability to Support); *sub nom* B *v.* B (Financial Provision for Child) [1998] 1 F.L.R. 373; [1998] 1 F.C.R. 49; [1998] Fam. Law 131, CA . . . . .   *Digested*, 98/**2461**

B *v.* B (Ancillary Relief) see A *v.* A (Ancillary Relief)

B *v.* B (Divorce: Northern Cyprus) [2000] 2 F.L.R. 707; [2001] 3 F.C.R. 331; [2000] Fam. Law 701, Fam Div . . . .   *Digested*, 01/**2616**

B *v.* B (Financial Provision for Child) see B *v.* B (Adult Student: Liability to Support)

B *v.* B (Injunction: Restraint on Leaving Jurisdiction); *sub nom* B *v.* B (Passport Surrender: Jurisdiction) [1998] 1 W.L.R. 329; [1997] 3 All E.R. 258; [1997] 2 F.L.R. 148; [1997] 3 F.C.R. 262; [1997] Fam. Law 538; (1997) 94(14) L.S.G. 25; (1997) 141 S.J.L.B. 93; *Times*, April 1, 1997, Fam Div . . . .   *Digested*, 97/**639**

B *v.* B (Occupation Order) [1999] 1 F.L.R. 715; [1999] 2 F.C.R. 251; (1999) 31 H.L.R. 1059; [1999] Fam. Law 208; *Times*, January 5, 1999, CA . . . .   *Digested*, 99/**2440**

B *v.* B (Occupation Order: Mental Health) [1999] 1 F.L.R. 726; [1999] Fam. Law 209, CC (Oxford) [*Ex rel*. June Rodgers, Barrister, 2 Harcourt Buildings, Temple, London] . . . .   *Digested*, 99/**2437**

B *v.* B (Passport Surrender: Jurisdiction) see B *v.* B (Injunction: Restraint on Leaving Jurisdiction)

B *v.* B (Residence Order: Reasons for Decision); *sub nom* B (A Minor) (Residence Order: Reasons), Re [1997] 2 F.L.R. 602; [1998] 1 F.C.R. 409; [1997] Fam. Law 792; (1998) 162 J.P.N. 283; *Times*, June 6, 1997, CA. . . . .   *Digested*, 97/**448**

B *v.* B (Unmeritorious Applications) [1999] 1 F.L.R. 505; [1998] 3 F.C.R. 650; [1999] Fam. Law 217, Fam Div . . . .   *Digested*, 99/**2417**

B *v.* B (Wasted Costs Order) see B *v.* B (Wasted Costs: Abuse of Process)

B *v.* B (Wasted Costs: Abuse of Process); *sub nom* B *v.* B (Wasted Costs Order) [2001] 1 F.L.R. 843; [2001] 3 F.C.R. 724, Fam Div . . . .   *Digested*, 01/**539**

B *v.* Chief Constable of Avon and Somerset [2001] 1 W.L.R. 340; [2001] 1 All E.R. 562, QBD . . . .   *Digested*, 01/**87**:   *Applied*, 01/10

B *v.* Congdon [2001] 6 Q.R. 24, QBD [*Ex rel.* Richard Colbey, Barrister, Tanfield Chambers, Francis Taylor Building, Temple, London] . . . .   *Digested*, 01/**1813**

B *v.* France (A/232-C) [1992] 2 F.L.R. 249; (1993) 16 E.H.R.R. 1; [1992] Fam. Law 491; *Times*, March 31, 1992; *Guardian*, April 15, 1992, ECHR . . . .   *Digested*, 93/**2156**:   *Considered*, 98/3163

B *v.* Gloucestershire CC [1999] Ed. C.R. 446; [1998] E.L.R. 539, QBD . . . .   *Digested*, 99/**1894**

B *v.* H (Unreported, May 11, 2000), Fam Div [*Ex rel.* DA Pears, Barrister, Francis Taylor Building, Temple, London] . . . .   *Digested*, 00/**2521**

B *v.* Harrow LBC (No.1); *sub nom* F *v.* Harrow LBC; F *v.* Special Education Needs Tribunal; B *v.* Special Educational Needs Tribunal [2000] 1 W.L.R. 223; [2000] 1 All E.R. 876; [2000] 3 F.C.R. 1; [2000] B.L.G.R. 162; [2000] Ed. C.R. 188; [2000] E.L.R. 109; (2000) 97(6) L.S.G. 34; (2000) 144 S.J.L.B. 83; *Times*, January 28, 2000; *Independent*, February 2, 2000, HL; reversing [1998] 3 F.C.R. 231; [1999] B.L.G.R. 144; [1998] Ed. C.R. 176; [1998] E.L.R. 351; (1998) 42 B.M.L.R. 88; (1998) 95(17) L.S.G. 32; (1998) 142 S.J.L.B. 134; *Times*, March 26, 1998, CA; reversing [1998] Ed. C.R. 1; *Times*, December 29, 1997, QBD . . . .   *Digested*, 00/**1946**:   *Considered*, 98/1983

B *v.* Harrow LBC (No.2) [2000] Ed. C.R. 62; [2000] E.L.R. 1, QBD . . . .   *Digested*, 00/**1953**

B (A Beneficiary) *v.* Inland Revenue Commissioners 1 I.T.L. Rep. 705, Sp Comm

B *v.* Isle of Wight Council [1997] E.L.R. 279, QBD . . . .   *Digested*, 97/**2130**:   *Considered*, 99/1898

B *v.* J [1999] E.M.L.R. 490, QBD . . . .   *Digested*, 99/**1624**

B *v.* Luton and Dunstable NHS Trust [2001] 1 Q.R. 11

B *v.* MHA Ltd (Unreported, October 29, 1998), CC (Yeovil) [*Ex rel.* Jeremy Burns, Barrister, 17 Carlton Crescent, Southampton] . . . .   *Digested*, 99/**3681**

B *v.* Minister of Correctional Services (1999) 50 B.M.L.R. 206, Provincial Div (SA)

B *v.* P (Adoption by Unmarried Father); *sub nom* B (A Child) *v.* RP; B (A Child) (Adoption by One Natural Parent to the Exclusion of Other), Re; B (A Child) (Adoption: Natural Parent), Re; B (A Child) (Sole Adoption by Unmarried Parent), Re; B (Adoption by Unmarried Father), Re [2001] UKHL 70; 11 B.H.R.C. 702; *Times*, December 19, 2001, HL; reversing [2001] 1 F.L.R. 589; [2001] 1 F.C.R. 600; [2001] Fam. Law 174; *Daily Telegraph*, January 16, 2001, CA; reversing [2000] 2 F.L.R. 717; [2000] Fam. Law 695, Fam Div . . . .   *Digested*, 01/**2542**

B *v.* Queen, The [2000] 1 A.C. 45; [1999] 3 W.L.R. 1158; (1999) 143 S.J.L.B. 181; *Times*, May 11, 1999, PC (StC) . . . .   *Digested*, 99/**781**

B *v.* Secretary of State for the Home Department (Deportation: Proportionality) [2000] 2 C.M.L.R. 1086; [2000] Eu. L.R. 687; [2000] H.R.L.R. 439; [2000] U.K.H.R.R. 498; [2000] Imm. A.R. 478; [2000] I.N.L.R. 361; *Independent*, June 26, 2000 (C.S), CA . . . .   *Digested*, 00/**3345**

B *v.* Special Educational Needs Tribunal see B *v.* Harrow LBC (No.1)

B *v.* United Kingdom [2000] 1 F.L.R. 1; [2000] 1 F.C.R. 289; [2000] Fam. Law 88, ECHR . . . .   *Digested*, 00/**2453**

B *v.* United Kingdom (36337/97); P *v.* United Kingdom (35974/97) [2001] 2 F.L.R. 261; [2001] 2 F.C.R. 221; 11 B.H.R.C. 667; [2001] Fam. Law 506; *Times*, May 15, 2001, ECHR . . . .   *Digested*, 01/**2628**

B *v.* United Kingdom (Hearing in Private) (36337/97) [2000] 2 F.C.R. 97, ECHR . . . . .   *Digested*, 00/**3211**

B *v.* V (Children: Financial Provision: Unmarried Parents) (Unreported, April 12, 1999), CC (Croydon) [*Ex rel.* Nicola Rushton, Barrister, 5 Paper Buildings, Temple, London] . . . .   *Digested*, 99/**2427**

B and W (Children) (Threshold Criteria), Re see Lancashire CC *v.* B (A Child) (Care Orders: Significant Harm)

B Ex p. Moschi *v.* Inland Revenue Commissioners see Moschi, Re

B Liggett (Liverpool) Ltd *v.* Barclays Bank Ltd [1928] 1 K.B. 48, KBD . . . .   *Considered*, 86/153:   *Distinguished*, 00/272

B MBC *v.* H (Goodman Project: Concurrent Planning) [2000] Fam. Law 237, CC (Manchester)

B Mullan & Sons Contractors Ltd *v.* Ross see McLaughlin & Harvey Plc (In Liquidation), Re

B&H Manufacturing Co/Web-cutting apparatus (T166/91) [1999] E.P.O.R. 179, EPO (Technical Bd App)

B&I Line Plc *v.* Sealink Harbours Ltd (IV/34.174); B&I Line Plc *v.* Sealink Stena Ltd (IV/ 34.174) [1992] 5 C.M.L.R. 255, CEC . . . .   *Distinguished*, 99/5150

B&I Line Plc v. Sealink Stena Ltd (IV/34.174) see B&I Line Plc v. Sealink Harbours Ltd
  (IV/34.174)
B&Q Plc v. Central Scotland Assessor [2000] R.A. 205, LandsTr (Scot) . . . .   *Digested*, 00/**6665**
B&Q Plc v. Liverpool and Lancashire Properties Ltd (2001) 81 P. & C.R. 20; [2001] 1
  E.G.L.R. 92; [2001] 15 E.G. 138; [2000] E.G.C.S. 101; (2000) 97(39) L.S.G. 41;
  Times, September 6, 2000, Ch D . . . .   *Digested*, 00/**4634**
B-J (A Child) (Non Molestation Order: Power of Arrest), Re [2001] Fam. 415; [2001] 2
  W.L.R. 1660; [2001] 1 All E.R. 235; [2000] 2 F.L.R. 443; [2000] 2 F.C.R. 599;
  [2000] Fam. Law 807; *Independent*, July 4, 2000, CA . . . .   *Digested*, 00/**2544**
B-M (A Child) (Adoption: Parental Agreement), Re [2001] 1 F.C.R. 1, CA . . . .   *Digested*, 01/**2529**
BAA Plc v. Customs and Excise Commissioners; *sub nom* Customs and Excise
  Commissioners v. BAA Plc; CH/2001/APP/764, Ch D; affirming [2001] B.V.C.
  2405, V&DTr
Baars v. Inspecteur der Belastingdienst Particulieren/Ondernemingen Gorinchem
  (C251/98) [2000] E.C.R. I-2787; 2 I.T.L. Rep. 660, ECJ (5th Chamber)
Baba v. General Medical Council (2001) 62 B.M.L.R. 34, PC (UK)
Babanaft International Co SA v. Avant Petroleum Inc see Babanaft International Co SA
  v. Avanti Petroleum Inc (The Oltenia)
Babanaft International Co SA v. Avanti Petroleum Inc (The Oltenia); *sub nom* Babanaft
  International Co SA v. Avant Petroleum Inc [1982] 1 W.L.R. 871; [1982] 3 All E.R.
  244; [1982] 2 Lloyd's Rep. 99; [1982] Com. L.R. 104; [1983] E.C.C. 365;
  (1982) 79 L.S.G. 953; 126 S.J. 361, CA; affirming [1982] 1 Lloyd's Rep. 448;
  [1982] Com. L.R. 40, QBD (Comm Ct) . . . .   *Digested*, 82/**138**:
                   Applied, 93/2535, 01/4916: *Considered*, 91/2269, 92/2721, 92/3547, 95/491:
                                                       Distinguished, 83/135, 83/136
Babanaft International Co SA v. Bassatne [1990] Ch. 13; [1989] 2 W.L.R. 232; [1989]
  1 All E.R. 433; [1988] 2 Lloyd's Rep. 435; [1989] E.C.C. 151; (1988) 138 N.L.J.
  Rep. 203; (1989) 133 S.J. 46; *Times*, July 2, 1988; *Independent*, June 30,
  1988; *Financial Times*, July 6, 1988, CA; reversing [1988] 2 F.T.L.R. 116; (1988)
  138 N.L.J. Rep. 134; *Times*, May 5, 1988; *Independent*, May 11, 1988; *Financial
  Times*, May 9, 1988, Ch D . . . .   *Digested*, 89/**3024**:
                                    Applied, 88/2909, 88/2911, 89/3040, 89/3042, 92/3547:
                                                  Considered, 90/3744, 91/2921, 94/3740, 99/754
Babcock International Ltd v. National Grid Co Plc see Fairchild v. Glenhaven Funeral
  Services Ltd (t/a GH Dovener & Son)
Babic v. Thompson (1999) 96(2) L.S.G. 30; (1999) 96(3) L.S.G. 33, Ch D
Baby Dan AS v. Brevi Srl [1999] F.S.R. 377; (1998) 21 (12) I.P.D. 21134, Ch D . . . .   *Digested*, 99/**3462**
Bacchiocchi v. Academic Agency Ltd [1998] 1 W.L.R. 1313; [1998] 2 All E.R. 241;
  (1999) 78 P. & C.R. 276; [1998] L. & T.R. 151; [1998] 3 E.G.L.R. 157; (1998)
  95(12) L.S.G. 27; (1998) 142 S.J.L.B. 85; [1998] N.P.C. 25; (1998) 75 P. & C.R.
  D43; *Times*, March 3, 1998, CA . . . .   *Digested*, 98/**3603**:
                                                                        Distinguished, 00/3886
Baccus Srl v. Servicio Nacional del Trigo [1957] 1 Q.B. 438; [1956] 3 W.L.R. 948;
  [1956] 3 All E.R. 715; [1956] 2 Lloyd's Rep. 448; 100 S.J. 872, CA . . . .   *Digested*, 56/**6979**:
                                              Applied, 98/2233: *Considered*, 71/6115, 72/1824
BACH and BACH FLOWER REMEDIES Trade Marks; *sub nom* Healing Herbs Ltd v. Bach
  Flower Remedies Ltd; Bach Flower Remedies Ltd v. Healing Herbs Ltd [2000]
  R.P.C. 513; (2000) 23(3) I.P.D. 23022; (1999) 96(42) L.S.G. 42; *Times*,
  December 1, 1999, CA; affirming [1999] R.P.C. 1; (1998) 21 (9) I.P.D. 21097,
  Ch D . . . .   *Digested*, 00/**3755**:
                                                    Applied, 00/3791: *Considered*, 00/3705
Bach Flower Remedies Ltd v. Healing Herbs Ltd see BACH and BACH FLOWER
  REMEDIES Trade Marks
Bache v. Essex CC [2000] 2 All E.R. 847; [2000] I.C.R. 313; [2000] I.R.L.R. 251;
  (2000) 97(5) L.S.G. 33; (2000) 150 N.L.J. 99; *Times*, February 2, 2000 ;
  Independent, March 13, 2000 (C.S.), CA . . . .   *Digested*, 00/**2144**
Bachmann v. Belgium (C204/90) (No.1); *sub nom* Insurance Premiums, Re;
  Commission of the European Communities v. Belgium (C300/90) [1994] S.T.C.
  855; [1992] E.C.R. I-249; [1993] 1 C.M.L.R. 785, ECJ . . . .   *Digested*, 92/**4805**:
                                                          Applied, 95/2773, 98/4517
Bachy SA v. Belbetoes Fundacoes e Betoes Especiais LDA [1999] I.L.Pr. 743, Cass (F)
Back v. Wheat (Unreported, May 1, 1998), CC (Southampton) [*Ex rel.* Peter Rickson &
  Partners Solicitors, The Stock Exchange Building, 4 Norfolk Street, Manchester]   *Digested*, 98/**390**
Backer v. Secretary of State for the Environment [1983] 1 W.L.R. 1485; [1983] 2 All
  E.R. 1021; (1983) 46 P. & C.R. 357; [1983] J.P.L. 602; (1983) 127 S.J. 748,
  QBD . . . .   *Digested*, 83/**3650**:
                                                    Considered, 90/1153, 91/971, 98/4300
Backman v. R. 3 I.T.L. Rep. 647, Sup Ct (Can)
Bacon v. Cooper (Metals) Ltd [1982] 1 All E.R. 397, QBD . . . .   *Digested*, 82/**764**:
                                                    Applied, 89/1185: *Considered*, 01/1517
Bacon v. Howard Kennedy (A Firm) [1999] P.N.L.R. 1; [2000] W.T.L.R. 169, Ch D . . . .   *Digested*, 98/**4021**
Bacon v. Parmenter (2000) 80 P. & C.R. D43, CA

Badeck's Application (C158/97), Re [2000] All E.R. (EC) 289; [2000] E.C.R. I-1875; [2001] 2 C.M.L.R. 6; [2000] C.E.C. 218; [2000] I.R.L.R. 432; *Times*, March 31, 2000, ECJ . . . . *Digested*, 00/**2171**: *Considered*, 00/2170

Baden *v.* Societe Generale pour Favoriser le Developpement du Commerce et de l'Industrie en France SA [1993] 1 W.L.R. 509; [1992] 4 All E.R. 161, Ch D . . . . . *Digested*, 92/**214**: *Considered*, 90/1993, 99/2217, 00/2315: *Followed*, 94/558

Badfinger Music *v.* Evans [2001] W.T.L.R. 1, Ch D . . . . *Digested*, 01/**2436**

Badische Erfrischungs-Getranke GmbH & Co KG *v.* Land Baden-Wurttemberg (C17/96) [1997] E.C.R. I-4617; [1998] 1 C.M.L.R. 341; (1998) 42 B.M.L.R. 113, ECJ (1st Chamber) . . . . *Digested*, 98/**4990**

Baghbadrani *v.* Commercial Union Assurance Co Plc [2000] Lloyd's Rep. I.R. 94, QBD . . . . *Digested*, 00/**3525**

Baghdadi *v.* Sunderland (Unreported, August 27, 1999), CC (Tunbridge Wells) [*Ex rel.* Charles Bagot, Barrister, Harwicke Building, Lincoln's Inn, London] . . . . *Digested*, 00/**500**

Baghlaf Al Zafer Factory Co BR for Industry Ltd *v.* Pakistan National Shipping Co (No.1) [1998] 2 Lloyd's Rep. 229; [1998] C.L.C. 716; (1998) 95(2) L.S.G. 23; *Times*, December 17, 1997, CA . . . . *Digested*, 98/**765**

Baghlaf Al Zafer Factory Co BR for Industry Ltd *v.* Pakistan National Shipping Co (No.2) [2000] 1 Lloyd's Rep. 1; [2000] I.L.Pr. 82, CA. . . . . *Digested*, 00/**770**

Baghli *v.* France (34374/97) (2001) 33 E.H.R.R. 32, ECHR

Bagots Hutton & Co Ltd's Application (1916) 33 R.P.C. 357 . . . . *Referred to*, 00/3766

Bahaddar *v.* Netherlands (1998) 26 E.H.R.R. 278; [1998] H.R.C.D. 284, ECHR. . . . . . . *Digested*, 98/**3240**

Bahai *v.* Rashidian; *sub nom* Ali-Sheikh Bahai *v.* Rashidian [1985] 1 W.L.R. 1337; [1985] 3 All E.R. 385; (1985) 82 L.S.G. 2162; (1985) 135 N.L.J. 1033; (1985) 129 S.J. 777; *Times*, October 9, 1985, CA; affirming (1985) 82 L.S.G. 2162; (1985) 135 N.L.J. 677, HC . . . . *Digested*, 86/**2603**: *Considered*, 93/3153, 01/538

Baigent *v.* McCulloch; Baigent *v.* O'Hare 1998 S.L.T. 780; 1997 Rep. L.R. 107; 1997 G.W.D. 16-737, OH. . . . . *Digested*, 97/**5973**: *Subsequent proceedings*, 99/5991

Baigent *v.* O'Hare see Baigent *v.* McCulloch

Bailey *v.* Armes [1999] E.G.C.S. 21; (1999) 96(7) L.S.G. 37, CA. . . . . *Digested*, 99/**4003**

Bailey *v.* Asplin [1999] N.P.C. 10, CA

Bailey *v.* Barnes [1894] 1 Ch. 25, CA. . . . . *Followed*, 99/4389

Bailey *v.* Brigham (t/a Quinborne Ltd) [2001] 6 Q.R. 8, CC (Birmingham) [*Ex rel.* Cameron Brown, Barrister, 4 King's Bench Walk, 2nd Floor, Temple, London] . . . *Digested*, 01/**1631**

Bailey *v.* Chemical Recoveries Ltd (1997) 97(5/6) Q.R. 10, CC (Bristol) . . . . *Digested*, 98/**1534**

Bailey *v.* DPP (1999) 163 J.P. 518; (1998) 95(31) L.S.G. 36; (1998) 142 S.J.L.B. 198; *Times*, July 30, 1998, QBD. . . . . *Digested*, 98/**899**

Bailey *v.* HSS Alarms Ltd, *Times*, June 20, 2000, CA. . . . . *Digested*, 00/**4210**

Bailey *v.* IBC Vehicles Ltd [1998] 3 All E.R. 570; [1998] 2 Costs L.R. 46; (1998) 142 S.J.L.B. 126; *Times*, April 9, 1998, CA . . . . *Digested*, 98/**433**: *Considered*, 99/411

Bailey *v.* Knowsley BC (1999) 99(1) Q.R. 8, CC (Liverpool) . . . . *Digested*, 98/**1703**

Bailey *v.* Nynex Cablecomms (Unreported, April 24, 2001), CC (Altrincham) [*Ex rel.* Rowlands Solicitors, 3 York Street, Manchester] . . . . *Digested*, 01/**495**

Bailey *v.* Turner (Unreported, July 30, 1999), CC (Basildon) [*Ex rel.* Tim Kevan, Barrister, 1 Temple Gardens, Temple, London] . . . . *Digested*, 99/**395**

Baillie Lite Ltd *v.* Glasgow City Council 1999 S.C. 606; 2001 S.C.L.R. 331; [1999] 3 P.L.R. 64; 1999 G.W.D. 18-849, OH . . . . *Digested*, 99/**6402**

Bain *v.* Bowles [1991] I.R.L.R. 356; *Times*, April 24, 1991; *Independent*, April 29, 1991 (C.S.); *Daily Telegraph*, May 2, 1991, CA . . . . *Digested*, 91/**1945**: *Applied*, 99/2098

Bainbridge *v.* Hambleton DC (2000) 80 P. & C.R. 61; [2000] J.P.L. 796, QBD

Bainbrigge *v.* Browne (1880-81) L.R. 18 Ch. D. 188, Ch D . . . . *Applied*, 87/2544, 01/4880

Bains *v.* Patel, *Times*, May 20, 1983, CA. . . . . *Digested*, 83/**3053**: *Considered*, 99/430

Bainton *v.* General Dental Council, *Times*, October 17, 2000, PC (UK) . . . . *Digested*, 00/**2713**

Baird *v.* Cookstown DC [1998] N.I. 88, CA (NI) . . . . *Digested*, 99/**5282**

Baird *v.* Williams (Inspector of Taxes) [1999] S.T.C. 635; 71 T.C. 390; [1999] B.T.C. 228; (1999) 96(22) L.S.G. 35; (1999) 143 S.J.L.B. 148; *Times*, May 25, 1999, Ch D . . . . *Digested*, 99/**4731**

Baird Textile Holdings Ltd *v.* Marks & Spencer Plc; *sub nom* Baird Textiles Holdings Ltd *v.* Marks & Spencer Plc [2001] EWCA Civ 274; [2001] C.L.C. 999, CA; affirming 2000 Folio No. 22, QBD (Comm Ct) . . . . *Digested*, 01/**931**

Baird Textiles Holdings Ltd *v.* Marks & Spencer Plc see Baird Textile Holdings Ltd *v.* Marks & Spencer Plc

Bairstow *v.* Queens Moat Houses Plc; Marcus *v.* Queens Moat Houses Plc; Hersey *v.* Queens Moat Houses Plc; Porter *v.* Queens Moat Houses Plc [2001] EWCA Civ 712; [2001] 2 B.C.L.C. 531, CA; affirming [2000] B.C.C. 1025; [2000] 1 B.C.L.C. 549, QBD . . . . *Digested*, 00/**669**: *Previous proceedings*, 97/459

Bairstow v. Queens Moat Houses Plc (Admissibility) [1998] 1 All E.R. 343; *Times,*
October 23, 1997, CA . . . . *Digested,* 97/**459**:
Subsequent proceedings, 00/669
Bairstow v. Queens Moat Houses Plc (Assessment of Costs); Marcus v. Queens Moat
Houses Plc (Assessment of Costs); Hersey v. Queens Moat Houses Plc
(Assessment of Costs); Porter v. Queens Moat Houses Plc (Assessment of
Costs) [2001] C.P. Rep. 59, QBD . . . . *Digested,* 01/**487**
Bairstow v. Queens Moat Houses Plc (Costs); Marcus v. Queens Moat Houses Plc
(Costs); Hersey v. Queens Moat Houses Plc (Costs); Porter v. Queens Moat
Houses Plc (Costs) [2000] C.P. Rep. 44; *Independent,* February 14, 2000
(C.S.), QBD . . . . *Digested,* 00/**411**
Bajjawi v. NE Davies (Engineering) Ltd (In Receivership) [*Ex rel.* Andrew Ritchie,
Barrister, 9 Gough Square, London] . . . . *Digested,* 01/**1679**
Bajwa v. British Airways Plc; Wilson v. Mid Glamorgan CC; Whitehouse v. Smith
(Michael) [1999] P.I.Q.R. Q152; *Times,* July 1, 1999, CA . . . . *Digested,* 99/**1380**
Bajwa v. Secretary of State for the Home Department [2000] Imm. A.R. 364, CA . . . . . *Digested,* 00/**3283**
Bakcsi v. Finanzamt Furstenfeldbruck (C415/98) [2001] E.C.R. I-1831; [2001] S.T.I.
499; *Times,* March 22, 2001, ECJ . . . . *Digested,* 01/**5548**
Baker (A Minor) v. Williams (Unreported, April 27, 1998), CC (Winchester) [*Ex rel.* Guy
Opperman, Barrister, Winchester Chambers, 4 Peter Street, Winchester,
Hampshire] . . . . *Digested,* 98/**1499**
Baker v. Birmingham City Council see R. v. Birmingham City Council Ex p. Ireland
Baker v. Black Sea & Baltic General Insurance Co Ltd; *sub nom* Black Sea & Baltic
General Insurance Co Ltd v. Baker [1998] 1 W.L.R. 974; [1998] 2 All E.R. 833;
[1998] C.L.C. 820; [1998] Lloyd's Rep. I.R. 327; (1998) 95(23) L.S.G. 26;
(1998) 148 N.L.J. 782; (1998) 142 S.J.L.B. 171; *Times,* May 21, 1998, HL;
reversing in part [1996] L.R.L.R. 353; [1996] 5 Re. L.R. 202, CA; affirming
[1995] L.R.L.R. 261, QBD (Comm Ct) . . . . *Digested,* 98/**3407**
Baker v. Carrick [1894] 1 Q.B. 838, CA . . . . *Applied,* 99/1629:
Considered, 00/1760
Baker v. Courage & Co [1910] 1 K.B. 56, KBD . . . . *Applied,* 01/4153
Baker v. Francis [1997] P.I.Q.R. P155, CA . . . . *Digested,* 98/**528**
Baker v. Ian McCall International Ltd [2000] C.L.C. 189; [2001] Lloyd's Rep. I.R. 149,
QBD (Comm Ct) . . . . *Digested,* 00/**785**
Baker v. Kaye [1997] I.R.L.R. 219; (1998) 39 B.M.L.R. 12; *Times,* December 13, 1996,
QBD . . . . *Digested,* 98/**3930**:
Considered, 98/3931
Baker v. Market Harborough Industrial Cooperative Society; Wallace v. Richards
(Leicester) [1953] 1 W.L.R. 1472; 97 S.J. 861, CA . . . . *Digested,* 53/**2473**:
Applied, 54/2244, 66/4843, 69/2417, 73/2982, 77/2010, 86/1197:
Distinguished, 87/1337: *Followed,* 01/4465
Baker v. Queen, The [1975] A.C. 774; [1975] 3 W.L.R. 113; [1975] 3 All E.R. 55;
[1976] Crim. L.R. 49; 119 S.J. 491, PC (Jam) . . . . *Digested,* 75/**220**:
Applied, 81/1626: *Considered,* 01/5021
Baker v. Secretary of State for the Environment, Transport and the Regions [2001]
EWHC Admin 39; (2001) 82 P. & C.R. 24; [2001] J.P.L. 1299; [2001] N.P.C. 22,
QBD (Admin Ct) . . . . *Digested,* 01/**4692**
Baker v. Secretary of State for the Home Department [2001] U.K.H.R.R. 1275; *Daily
Telegraph,* October 9, 2001, Information Tr
Baker v. Secretary of State for Trade and Industry see Deaduck Ltd (In Liquidation), Re
Baker v. Sussex Police Authority (Unreported, July 9, 2001), CC (Eastbourne) [*Ex rel.*
Edwin Buckett, Barrister, 9 Gough Square, London] . . . . *Digested,* 01/**548**
Baker v. Tugwell (1998) 98(2) Q.R. 7, CC (Bath) . . . . *Digested,* 98/**1745**
Baker v. Willoughby [1970] A.C. 467; [1970] 2 W.L.R. 50; [1969] 3 All E.R. 1528; 7
K.I.R. 457; 114 S.J. 15, HL; reversing [1969] 2 W.L.R. 489; [1969] 2 All E.R. 549;
6 K.I.R. 5; (1968) 113 S.J. 37; *Times,* December 11, 1968, CA; reversing [1969]
1 Q.B. 38; [1968] 2 W.L.R. 1138; [1968] 2 All E.R. 236; 112 S.J. 234, QBD . . . . *Digested,* 70/**1862**:
Applied, 71/3255, 72/2531, 76/2671, 00/6163: *Cited,* 00/1482:
Considered, 70/599, 70/737: *Distinguished,* 78/718, 80/1885:
Doubted, 81/1835: *Followed,* 77/2011, 79/683, 98/6103
Baker Rasti Lari v. Armstel Shipping Corp (The Jay Bola) see Payabi v. Armstel
Shipping Corp (The Jay Bola)
Bakewell v. Bevan (Unreported, March 17, 2000), CC (Liverpool) [*Ex rel.* David
Knifton, Barrister, 7 Harrington Street, Liverpool] . . . . *Digested,* 00/**460**
Balabel v. Air India [1988] Ch. 317; [1988] 2 W.L.R. 1036; [1988] 2 All E.R. 246;
(1988) 138 N.L.J. Rep. 85; (1988) 132 S.J. 699, CA; reversing *Daily Telegraph,*
February 8, 1988, Ch D . . . . *Digested,* 88/**1594**:
Applied, 89/1932, 95/4114, 01/399: *Considered,* 90/3666.A, 94/1027,
99/879: *Followed,* 98/355
Balamoan v. Holden & Co (1999) 149 N.L.J. 898; *Independent,* June 15, 1999, CA . . . . *Digested,* 99/**4049**
Balamoody v. United Kingdom Central Council for Nursing, Midwifery and Health
Visiting (Professional Conduct), *Independent,* June 15, 1998 (C.S.), QBD . . . . . . *Digested,* 98/**2642**
Balchin v. Chief Constable of Hampshire [2001] EWCA Civ 538; *Times,* May 4, 2001,
CA . . . . *Digested,* 01/**1143**

Baldwin (Gordon George)'s UK Patent (No.2280345) [1998] R.P.C. 415; (1998) 21 (1)
  I.P.D. 21005, PO . . . . *Digested*, 98/**3476**
Baldwin (Gordon Lee)'s UK Patent (No.2280345) (2000) 23(2) I.P.D. 23012, PO
Baldwin v. Rusbridger [2001] E.M.L.R. 47; *Times*, July 23, 2001, QBD . . . . *Digested*, 01/**1832**
Baldwin v. Rusbridger (Application to Strike Out) HQ 9903195, QBD. . . . . *Subsequent proceed-
  ings*, 01/1832
Baldwin v. Torvale Group Ltd No.6536 of 97, Ch D . . . . *Digested*, 98/**3314**
Balfour v. Balfour [1919] 2 K.B. 571, CA. . . . . *Applied*, 47-51/**4571**,
  59/1470, 61/4038, 68/546, 69/517, 69/519: *Considered*, 70/1226, 00/888
Balfour v. Occupational Therapists Board (2000) 51 B.M.L.R. 69; *Times*, July 24, 1999,
  PC (UK) . . . . *Digested*, 99/**2086**
Balfour Beatty Building Ltd v. Chestermount Properties Ltd 62 B.L.R. 1; 32 Con. L.R.
  139; (1993) 9 Const. L.J. 117, QBD. . . . . *Digested*, 94/**335**:
  Considered, 00/232
Balfour Beatty Civil Engineering (t/a Balfour Beatty/Costain (Cardiff Bay Barrage) Joint
  Venture) v. Technical & General Guarantee Co Ltd [2000] C.L.C. 252; 68 Con.
  L.R. 180, CA . . . . *Digested*, 00/**819**
Balfron Trustees Ltd v. Petersen; *sub nom* Balfron Trustees Ltd v. Peterson [2001]
  I.R.L.R. 758; (2001) 151 N.L.J. 1180; *Independent*, October 29, 2001 (C.S), Ch
  D
Balfron Trustees Ltd v. Petersen (Stay Application); *sub nom* Balfron Trustees Ltd v.
  Peterson (Stay Application); HC0003601, Ch D . . . . *Digested*, 01/**665**
Balfron Trustees Ltd v. Peterson see Balfron Trustees Ltd v. Petersen
Balfron Trustees Ltd v. Peterson (Stay Application) see Balfron Trustees Ltd v. Petersen
  (Stay Application)
BALI Trade Mark (No.1) see Berlei (UK) Ltd v. Bali Brassiere Co Inc (No.1)
Balkanbank v. Taher (No.2) [1995] 1 W.L.R. 1056; [1995] 2 All E.R. 904; *Times*,
  December 1, 1994, CA. . . . . *Digested*, 94/**3550**:
  Considered, 98/326
Balkandali v. United Kingdom (9474/81) see Abdulaziz v. United Kingdom (A/94)
Ball v. Banner; Neill Clerk (A Firm) v. Healey & Baker; A3/2000/0246, CA; reversing
  [2000] Lloyd's Rep. P.N. 569; [2000] E.G.C.S. 36; (2000) 97(12) L.S.G. 45,
  Ch D . . . . *Digested*, 00/**4280**
Ball v. Eden Project Ltd [2001] E.T.M.R. 87; *Times*, June 6, 2001, Ch D . . . . *Digested*, 01/**725**
Ball v. Howells Transport (Unreported, February 2, 1999), CC (Oldham) [*Ex rel.*
  Horwich Farrelly Solicitors, National House, 36 St Ann Street, Manchester] . . . . *Digested*, 99/**1404**
Ball v. Norwich Union Fire Assurance Society LTA 98/7465/2, CA. . . . . *Digested*, 99/**350**
Ball v. Secretary of State for the Environment, Transport and the Regions [2000] 1
  P.L.R. 64; [2000] P.L.C.R. 299; (2000) 97(4) L.S.G. 34, QBD . . . . *Digested*, 00/**4447**
Ballantine v. Newalls Insulation Co Ltd [2001] I.C.R. 25; [2000] P.I.Q.R. Q327;
  (2000) 97(26) L.S.G. 36; *Times*, June 22, 2000; *Independent*, July 24, 2000
  (C.S), CA; reversing [2000] P.I.Q.R. Q57, QBD . . . . *Digested*, 00/**1471**
Ballard (Kent) Ltd v. Oliver Ashworth (Holdings) Ltd; *sub nom* Oliver Ashworth
  (Holdings) Ltd v. Ballard (Kent) Ltd [2000] Ch. 12; [1999] 3 W.L.R. 57; [1999] 2
  All E.R. 791; [1999] L. & T.R. 400; [1999] 2 E.G.L.R. 23; [1999] 19 E.G. 161;
  (1999) 96(16) L.S.G. 36; (1999) 149 N.L.J. 521; [1999] N.P.C. 36; *Times*, April
  1, 1999; *Independent*, March 26, 1999, CA; reversing [1998] 3 E.G.L.R. 60;
  [1998] 46 E.G. 190, Ch D . . . . *Digested*, 99/**3660**
Ballast Nedam Groep NV v. Belgium (C5/97) [1997] E.C.R. I-7549; 88 B.L.R. 32, ECJ . *Digested*, 99/**2275**
Ballast Plc v. Burrell Co (Construction Management) Ltd 2001 S.L.T. 1039; 2001
  S.C.L.R. 837; [2001] B.L.R. 529; 2001 G.W.D. 22-826; *Times*, October 9, 2001,
  OH . . . . *Digested*, 01/**6288**
Balli v. Mahmood (Unreported, February 8, 1999), CC (Brentford) [*Ex rel.* Nigel S
  Brockley, Barrister, Bracton Chambers, 95a Chancery Lane, London] . . . . *Digested*, 99/**1566**
Ballyedmond Castle Farms Ltd's Application, Re; DPP for Northern Ireland's Application for
  Judicial Review, Re [2000] N.I. 174, QBD (NI) . . . . *Digested*, 00/**5400**
Balmer-Schafroth v. Switzerland (1998) 25 E.H.R.R. 598, ECHR . . . . *Digested*, 98/**3156**:
  Applied, 01/3542
Balmoral Group Ltd v. CRP Marine Ltd [2000] F.S.R. 860, CA; affirming (1999) 22(1)
  I.P.D. 22001, Pat Ct . . . . *Digested*, 01/**3959**
Balmoral Group Ltd v. Rae, *Times*, January 25, 2000, EAT . . . . *Digested*, 00/**6218**
BALMORAL Trade Mark [1999] R.P.C. 297, Appointed Person. . . . . *Digested*, 99/**3581**:
  Referred to, 99/3542, 99/3562
Baltic Insurance Group v. Jordan Grand Prix Ltd see Jordan Grand Prix Ltd v. Baltic
  Insurance Group
Baltic Insurance Group v. Quay Financial Software see Jordan Grand Prix Ltd v. Baltic
  Insurance Group
Baltimore County Register of Wills v. Arrowsmith 4 I.T.L. Rep. 47, US Ct
Bamberski v. Krombach (C7/98); *sub nom* Krombach v. Bamberski (C7/98) [2001]
  Q.B. 709; [2001] 3 W.L.R. 488; [2001] All E.R. (EC) 584; [2000] E.C.R. I-1935;
  [2001] I.L.Pr. 36; *Times*, March 30, 2000, ECJ [1998] I.L.Pr. 681, BGH (Ger) . . *Digested*, 00/**784**:
  Applied, 00/782: *Followed*, 01/768
Ban Hin Lee Bank Bhd v. Sonali Bank, *Independent*, November 28, 1988 (C.S.), CA . . . *Followed*, 98/510
Banana v. Zimbabwe 8 B.H.R.C. 345, Sup Ct (Zim)

Banana Framework Agreement (C122/95), Re see Germany v. Council of the European Union (C122/95)

Banarsi Dass, Re see Ellora Industries v. Banarsi Dass & Ors

Banca Carige SpA v. Banco Nacional de Cuba see Banca Carige SpA Cassa di Risparmio di Genova e Imperio v. Banco Nacional de Cuba

Banca Carige SpA Cassa di Risparmio di Genova e Imperia v. Banco Nacional de Cuba see Banca Carige SpA Cassa di Risparmio di Genova e Imperio v. Banco Nacional de Cuba

Banca Carige SpA Cassa di Risparmio di Genova e Imperio v. Banco Nacional de Cuba; *sub nom* Banca Carige SpA Cassa di Risparmio di Genova e Imperia v. Banco Nacional de Cuba; Banco Nacional de Cuba, Re; Banca Carige SpA v. Banco Nacional de Cuba [2001] 1 W.L.R. 2039; [2001] 3 All E.R. 923; [2001] 2 Lloyd's Rep. 147; [2001] Lloyd's Rep. Bank. 203; [2001] 2 B.C.L.C. 407; [2001] B.P.I.R. 407; (2001) 98(23) L.S.G. 40; (2001) 145 S.J.L.B. 124; *Times,* May 18, 2001, Ch D (Companies Ct) . . . . *Digested,* 01/**376**

Bance Ltd's Licence of Right (Copyright) Application, Re [1996] R.P.C. 667, PO . . . . . *Digested,* 97/**1044**:
Considered, 01/3854: *Distinguished,* 00/3579

Banco de Fomento e Exterior SA v. Pechim (C66/97) [1997] E.C.R. I-3757; [1997] C.E.C. 1221, ECJ . . . . *Digested,* 98/**2319**

Banco de Portugal v. Waddell; *sub nom* Hooper, Re (1879-80) L.R. 5 App. Cas. 161, HL; affirming (1879) L.R. 11 Ch. D. 317, CA . . . . *Applied,* 01/3772

Banco de Portugal v. Waterlow & Sons Ltd; Waterlow & Sons Ltd v. Banco de Portugal [1932] A.C. 452; [1932] All E.R. Rep. 181, HL . . . . *Applied,* 71/3157,
76/332, 77/739, 78/2821, 82/764, 83/1074, 98/4384

Banco Exterior Internacional v. Mann [1995] 1 All E.R. 936; [1995] 1 F.L.R. 602; [1995] 2 F.C.R. 282; (1995) 27 H.L.R. 329; (1995) 145 N.L.J. 179; [1994] N.P.C. 150; *Times,* December 19, 1994; *Independent,* December 8, 1994, CA. . . . *Digested,* 95/**2443**:
Considered, 96/5032, 97/4240, 97/4243, 99/4390

Banco Nacional de Cuba, Re see Banca Carige SpA Cassa di Risparmio di Genova e Imperio v. Banco Nacional de Cuba

Banco Nacional de Cuba v. Cosmos Trading Corp [2000] B.C.C. 910; [2000] 1 B.C.L.C. 813, CA . . . . *Digested,* 00/**3499**

Banco Santander SA v. Banque Paribas see Banco Santander SA v. Bayfern Ltd

Banco Santander SA v. Bayfern Ltd; *sub nom* Banco Santander SA v. Banque Paribas [2000] 1 All E.R. (Comm) 776; [2000] Lloyd's Rep. Bank. 165; [2000] C.L.C. 906, CA; affirming [1999] 2 All E.R. (Comm) 18; [1999] Lloyd's Rep. Bank. 239; [1999] C.L.C. 1321; (1999) 96(26) L.S.G. 27; *Times,* June 29, 1999 ; *Independent,* June 21, 1999 (C.S.), QBD (Comm Ct) . . . . *Digested,* 00/**282**

Bancroft v. Harrogate HA [1997] 8 Med. L.R. 398, QBD . . . . *Digested,* 98/**3964**

Bandegani v. Norwich Union Fire Insurance Society Ltd CCRTI 99/0008/2, CA . . . . . . *Digested,* 01/**1550**

Bandeira v. Royal Society for the Prevention of Cruelty to Animals see Bandeira v. RSPCA

Bandeira v. RSPCA; *sub nom* Bandeira v. Royal Society for the Prevention of Cruelty to Animals (2000) 164 J.P. 307, QBD . . . . *Digested,* 00/**190**

Banfield McFarlane Evans Real Estate v. Hoffer [1977] 4 WW.R. 465, CA (Man) . . . . . *Digested,* 77/**39**

Bank Austria Trade Services Gesellschaft mbH v. Customs and Excise Commissioners [2001] S.T.I. 528, V&DTr

Bank fur Arbeit und Wirtschaft AG v. Office for Harmonisation in the Internal Market (Trade Marks and Designs) (OHIM) (T87/00) [2001] E.C.R. II-1259; [2001] C.E.C. 73; [2001] E.T.M.R. 68, CFI . . . . *Digested,* 01/**4007**

Bank of America v. Arnell [1999] Lloyd's Rep. Bank. 399, QBD (Comm Ct) . . . . *Digested,* 99/**278**

Bank of America National Trust and Savings Association v. Morris (Application to Strike Out) TNS, Ch D . . . . *Digested,* 00/**620**

Bank of America National Trust and Savings Association v. Taylor (The Kyriaki) [1992] 1 Lloyd's Rep. 484; *Financial Times,* May 24, 1991, QBD (Comm Ct) . . . . *Digested,* 92/**3976**:
Applied, 01/642

Bank of Baroda v. Dhillon [1998] 1 F.L.R. 524; [1998] 1 F.C.R. 489; (1998) 30 H.L.R. 845; [1998] Fam. Law 138; [1997] N.P.C. 145; *Times,* November 4, 1997, CA . . . *Digested,* 97/**4252**

Bank of Baroda v. Mahomed; *sub nom* Mahomed v. Bank of Baroda [1999] Lloyd's Rep. Bank. 14; [1999] C.L.C. 463; (1998) 95(47) L.S.G. 29; *Times,* December 10, 1998, CA . . . . *Digested,* 99/**269**

Bank of Baroda v. Panessar [1987] Ch. 335; [1987] 2 W.L.R. 208; [1986] 3 All E.R. 751; [1987] P.C.C. 165; (1987) 84 L.S.G. 339; (1986) 136 N.L.J. 963; (1987) 131 S.J. 21; *Times,* July 10, 1986, Ch D . . . . *Digested,* 87/**326**:
Applied, 99/504: *Followed,* 99/3324

Bank of Baroda v. Rayarel [1996] E.C.C. 157; [1995] 2 F.L.R. 376; [1995] 2 F.C.R. 631; (1995) 27 H.L.R. 387; [1995] Fam. Law 610; [1995] N.P.C. 6; *Times,* January 19, 1995, CA . . . . *Digested,* 96/**4967**:
Considered, 96/5032: *Distinguished,* 01/4878

Bank of Boston Connecticut (formerly Colonial Bank) *v.* European Grain & Shipping Ltd (The Dominique); *sub nom* Colonial Bank *v.* European Grain & Shipping Ltd [1989] A.C. 1056; [1989] 2 W.L.R. 440; [1989] 1 All E.R. 545; [1989] 1 Lloyd's Rep. 431; (1989) 86(11) L.S.G. 43; (1989) 133 S.J. 219, HL; reversing [1988] 3 W.L.R. 60; [1988] 3 All E.R. 233; [1988] 1 Lloyd's Rep. 215; [1988] 1 F.T.L.R. 327; (1988) 132 S.J. 896, CA; reversing [1987] 1 Lloyd's Rep. 239, QBD (Comm Ct) . . . . *Digested,* 89/**3409**: *Applied,* 01/941: *Considered,* 97/3871

Bank of China *v.* NBM LLC [2001] EWCA Civ 1933, CA; affirming [2001] 4 All E.R. 954; (2001) 151 N.L.J. 1034, QBD (Comm Ct)

Bank of Credit and Commerce International (Overseas) Ltd (In Liquidation) *v.* Ernst & Whinney see Bank of Credit and Commerce International (Overseas) Ltd (In Liquidation) *v.* Price Waterhouse (No.3)

Bank of Credit and Commerce International (Overseas) Ltd (In Liquidation) *v.* Habib Bank Ltd [1999] 1 W.L.R. 42; [1998] 4 All E.R. 753; [1998] 2 B.C.L.C. 459; [1999] B.P.I.R. 1; *Times,* July 20, 1998, Ch D . . . . *Digested,* 98/**510**

Bank of Credit & Commerce International (Overseas) Ltd (In Liquidation) *v.* Jan CH.1998-B-1572, Ch D (Companies Ct) . . . . *Digested,* 00/**520**

Bank of Credit and Commerce International (Overseas) Ltd (In Liquidation) *v.* Price Waterhouse (No.1) [1997] 4 All E.R. 108, Ch D . . . . *Digested,* 97/**920**

Bank of Credit and Commerce International (Overseas) Ltd (In Liquidation) *v.* Price Waterhouse (No.2) [1998] Lloyd's Rep. Bank. 85; [1998] B.C.C. 617; [1998] E.C.C. 410; [1998] P.N.L.R. 564; (1998) 95(15) L.S.G. 32; (1998) 142 S.J.L.B. 86; *Times,* March 4, 1998, CA; reversing [1997] B.C.C. 585; *Times,* February 10, 1997, Ch D . . . . *Digested,* 98/**3921**: *Applied,* 01/4538: *Considered,* 00/4216

Bank of Credit and Commerce International (Overseas) Ltd (In Liquidation) *v.* Price Waterhouse (No.3); Bank of Credit and Commerce International (Overseas) Ltd (In Liquidation) *v.* Ernst & Whinney [1998] Ch. 84; [1997] 3 W.L.R. 849; [1997] 4 All E.R. 781; [1997] 6 Bank. L.R. 216; [1998] B.C.C. 511; *Times,* June 25, 1997, Ch D . . . . *Digested,* 97/**316**: *Doubted,* 00/274

Bank of Credit and Commerce International (Overseas) Ltd (In Liquidation) *v.* Price Waterhouse (No.4) [1999] B.C.C. 351; *Times,* April 2, 1998, Ch D . . . . *Digested,* 98/**4001**

Bank of Credit and Commerce International (Overseas) Ltd *v.* Chief Labode Onadimaki Akindele [2001] Ch. 437; [2000] 3 W.L.R. 1423; [2000] 4 All E.R. 221; [2000] Lloyd's Rep. Bank. 292; [2000] B.C.C. 968; [2000] W.T.L.R. 1049; (1999-2000) 2 I.T.E.L.R. 788; (2000) 97(26) L.S.G. 36; (2000) 150 N.L.J. 950; *Times,* June 22, 2000; *Independent,* June 29, 2000, CA; affirming [1999] B.C.C. 669, Ch D . . . . *Digested,* 00/**2315**

Bank of Credit and Commerce International SA, Re see Morris *v.* Banque Arabe Internationale d'Investissement SA (No.2)

Bank of Credit and Commerce International SA (In Liquidation) (No.3), Re [1993] B.C.L.C. 1490, CA; affirming [1992] B.C.C. 83; [1993] B.C.L.C. 106, Ch D . . . . *Digested,* 94/**2649**: *Applied,* 01/3748

Bank of Credit and Commerce International SA (In Liquidation) (No.7), Re [1994] 1 B.C.L.C. 455, Ch D . . . . *Applied,* 99/**3283**: *Considered,* 00/3469

Bank of Credit and Commerce International SA (In Liquidation) (No.8), Re; *sub nom* Morris *v.* Rayners Enterprises Inc; Morris *v.* Agrichemicals Ltd [1998] A.C. 214; [1997] 3 W.L.R. 909; [1997] 4 All E.R. 568; [1998] Lloyd's Rep. Bank. 48; [1997] B.C.C. 965; [1998] 1 B.C.L.C. 68; [1998] B.P.I.R. 211; (1997) 94(44) L.S.G. 35; (1997) 147 N.L.J. 1653; (1997) 141 S.J.L.B. 229; *Times,* November 13, 1997, HL; affirming [1996] Ch. 245; [1996] 2 W.L.R. 631; [1996] 2 All E.R. 121; [1996] B.C.C. 204; [1996] 2 B.C.L.C. 254; (1996) 140 S.J.L.B. 36; *Times,* January 8, 1996, CA; affirming [1995] Ch. 46; [1994] 3 W.L.R. 911; [1994] 3 All E.R. 565; [1994] 1 B.C.L.C. 758; *Times,* March 22, 1994, Ch D . . . . *Digested,* 97/**3047**: *Considered,* 98/3314

Bank of Credit and Commerce International SA (In Liquidation) (No.13), Re; *sub nom* Morris *v.* State Bank of India [1999] B.C.C. 943, Ch D (Companies Ct) . . . . *Digested,* 99/**3322**

Bank of Credit and Commerce International SA *v.* Aboody [1990] 1 Q.B. 923; [1989] 2 W.L.R. 759; [1992] 4 All E.R. 955; [1990] 1 F.L.R. 354; [1989] C.C.L.R. 63; [1989] Fam. Law 435; (1988) 132 S.J. 1754, CA . . . . *Digested,* 89/**1829**: *Considered,* 94/3299, 94/3300, 95/2451, 97/4232: *Followed,* 96/5032, 98/4362: *Overruled,* 94/3293: *Referred to,* 95/2448, 96/4973

Bank of Credit and Commerce International SA *v.* Al-Kaylani [1999] I.L.Pr. 278, Ch D . . *Digested,* 99/**726**

Bank of Credit and Commerce International SA (In Liquidation) *v.* Ali (No.1) [2001] UKHL 8; [2001] 2 W.L.R. 735; [2001] 1 All E.R. 961; [2001] I.C.R. 337; [2001] I.R.L.R. 292; (2001) 98(15) L.S.G. 32; (2001) 151 N.L.J. 351; (2001) 145 S.J.L.B. 67; (2001) 145 S.J.L.B. 70; *Times,* March 6, 2001, HL; affirming [2000] 3 All E.R. 51; [2000] I.C.R. 1410; [2000] I.R.L.R. 398; *Times,* May 10, 2000, CA; reversing [1999] 2 All E.R. 1005; [1999] I.C.R. 1068; [1999] I.R.L.R. 226; (1999) 96(7) L.S.G. 35; (1999) 149 N.L.J. 53; *Times,* January 25, 1999, Ch D . . *Digested,* 01/**2228**

Bank of Credit and Commerce International SA (In Liquidation) v. Ali (No.2) [2000] C.C.L.R. 1, Ch D . . . . *Digested,* 00/**2594**

Bank of Credit and Commerce International SA (In Liquidation) v. Ali (No.3); *sub nom* BCCI SA v. Ali; Husain v. Bank of Credit and Commerce International SA; A3/ 2001/9016/CHANF, CA; affirming [1999] 4 All E.R. 83; [2000] I.C.R. 1354; [1999] I.R.L.R. 508; (1999) 96(30) L.S.G. 28; *Times,* June 30, 1999, Ch D . . . . *Digested,* 99/**2010**

Bank of Credit and Commerce International SA (In Liquidation) v. Ali (No.4) (1999) 149 N.L.J. 1734; *Times,* March 2, 2000, Ch D . . . . *Digested,* 00/**386**:
Considered, 01/470

Bank of Credit and Commerce International SA (In Liquidation) v. Ali (No.5); *sub nom* BCCI v. Ali [2000] 2 Costs L.R. 243, HC . . . . *Digested,* 01/**479**

Bank of Credit and Commerce International SA (In Liquidation) v. Ali (No.8); *sub nom* Bank of Credit and Commerce International SA (In Liquidation) v. Former Employees (2001) 151 N.L.J. 1852, Ch D

Bank of Credit and Commerce International SA v. Blattner (Unreported, November 20, 1986), CA (Crim Div) . . . . *Distinguished,* 00/2624

Bank of Credit and Commerce International SA (In Liquidation) v. Former Employees see Bank of Credit and Commerce International SA (In Liquidation) v. Ali (No.8)

Bank of Cyprus (London) Ltd v. Markou [1999] 2 All E.R. 707; [1999] 2 F.L.R. 17; (1999) 78 P. & C.R. 208; [1999] Fam. Law 385; [1999] E.G.C.S. 13; (1999) 96(6) L.S.G. 36; *Independent,* February 8, 1999 (C.S), Ch D . . . . *Digested,* 99/**2519**

Bank of East Asia Ltd v. Tsien Wui Marble Factory Ltd (1998) 14 Const. L.J. 189, HC (HK) . . . . *Digested,* 98/**3955**

Bank of Hindustan, China and Japan Ex p. Smith, Re (1867-68) L.R. 3 Ch. App. 125, CA in Chancery . . . . *Considered,* 01/507

Bank of India v. Mody (1998) 95(12) L.S.G. 29, Ch D

Bank of India v. Trans Continental Commodity Merchants Ltd (No.2) [1983] 2 Lloyd's Rep. 298, CA; affirming [1982] 1 Lloyd's Rep. 506; *Times,* October 27, 1981, QBD (Comm Ct) . . . . *Digested,* 83/**190**:
Considered, 99/849

Bank of Ireland v. AMCD (Property Holdings) Ltd [2001] 2 All E.R. (Comm) 894; [2001] N.P.C. 61, Ch D . . . . *Digested,* 01/**683**

Bank of Ireland v. Hollicourt (Contracts) Ltd see Hollicourt (Contracts) Ltd (In Liquidation) v. Bank of Ireland

Bank of Ireland Home Mortgages Ltd v. Bell [2001] 2 All E.R. (Comm) 920; [2001] 2 F.L.R. 809; [2001] 3 F.C.R. 134; [2001] B.P.I.R. 429; [2001] Fam. Law 805; [2000] E.G.C.S. 151, CA . . . . *Digested,* 01/**4870**

Bank of Ireland Home Mortgages Ltd v. Bissett (Unreported, June 23, 1999), CC (Northampton) [*Ex rel.* Ben Davey, Barrister, 11 Old Square, Lincoln's Inn, London] . . . . *Digested,* 99/**409**
Cited, 00/2624

Bank of New South Wales v. Brown (1983) 151 C.L.R. 514, HC (Aus) . . . .

Bank of New Zealand Officers Provident Fund Association Management Board v. Bank of New Zealand; *sub nom* Board of Management of the Bank of New Zealand Officers Provident Association v. Bank of New Zealand [1999] Pens. L.R. 117, HC (NZ) . . . . *Digested,* 99/**4143**

Bank of Scotland v. A Ltd [2001] EWCA Civ 52; [2001] 1 W.L.R. 751; [2001] 3 All E.R. 58; [2001] 1 All E.R. (Comm) 1023; [2001] Lloyd's Rep. Bank. 73; (2000-01) 3 I.T.E.L.R. 503; (2001) 98(9) L.S.G. 41; (2001) 151 N.L.J. 102; (2001) 145 S.J.L.B. 21; *Times,* February 6, 2001; *Independent,* January 23, 2001, CA; affirming [2000] Lloyd's Rep. Bank. 271; [2001] C.P. Rep. 14; *Times,* July 18, 2000; *Independent,* July 31, 2000 (C.S), Ch D . . . . *Digested,* 01/**370**

Bank of Scotland v. Bennett see Royal Bank of Scotland Plc v. Etridge (No.2)

Bank of Scotland v. Bennett [1999] Lloyd's Rep. Bank. 145; [1999] 1 F.L.R. 1115; [1999] 1 F.C.R. 641; (1999) 77 P. & C.R. 447; [1999] Fam. Law 307; [1999] E.G.C.S. 1; (1999) 96(3) L.S.G. 33, CA; reversing [1997] 1 F.L.R. 801; [1997] 3 F.C.R. 193; [1997] Fam. Law 477, Ch D . . . . *Digested,* 99/**4391**:
Overruled in part, 01/4880

Bank of Scotland v. Brunswick Developments (1987) Ltd (No.2) 1999 S.C. (H.L.) 53; 1999 S.L.T. 716; 2000 S.C.L.R. 30; 1999 G.W.D. 15-687; *Times,* May 5, 1999, HL; reversing 1997 S.C. 226; 1998 S.L.T. 439; 1997 S.C.L.R. 498; 1997 G.W.D. 16-716, 1 Div; affirming 1997 S.L.T. 48, OH . . . . *Digested,* 99/**5726**

Bank of Scotland v. Butcher [1998] N.P.C. 144, CA

Bank of Scotland v. Dunedin Property Investment Co Ltd (No.1) 1998 S.C. 657; 1999 S.L.T. 470; 1998 S.C.L.R. 531; 1998 G.W.D. 18-887; *Times,* September 24, 1998, 1 Div; reversing 1997 G.W.D. 17-761; *Times,* May 16, 1997, OH . . . . *Digested,* 98/**5864**

Bank of Scotland v. Grimes [1985] Q.B. 1179; [1985] 3 W.L.R. 294; [1985] 2 All E.R. 254; [1985] F.L.R. 322; [1985] Fam. Law 314; (1985) 82 L.S.G. 1857; (1985) 136 N.L.J. 411; (1985) 129 S.J. 331, CA . . . . *Digested,* 85/**2266**:
Applied, 01/4875: *Referred to,* 91/2795

Bank of Scotland v. Henry Butcher & Co [2001] 2 All E.R. (Comm) 691, Ch D . . . . *Digested,* 01/**4564**

Bank of Scotland v. Ladjadj; *sub nom* Ladjadj v. Bank of Scotland [2000] 2 All E.R. (Comm) 583, CA . . . . *Digested,* 00/**2610**

Bank of Scotland *v.* Seitz 1990 S.L.T. 584; 1990 S.C.L.R. 418; [1991] I.L.Pr. 426, IH;
affirming 1989 S.L.T. 641; 1989 S.C.L.R. 270, OH . . . . *Digested*, 90/**5353**:
Followed, 92/5933, 94/5960, 00/5927
Bankers Trust Co *v.* PT Jakarta International Hotels and Development [1999] 1 All E.R.
(Comm) 785; [1999] 1 Lloyd's Rep. 910; *Times*, May 10, 1999, QBD (Comm
Ct) . . . . *Digested*, 99/**239**
Bankers Trust Co *v.* Shapira [1980] 1 W.L.R. 1274; [1980] 3 All E.R. 353; 124 S.J. 480,
CA . . . . *Digested*, 80/**2136**:
Applied, 92/3483: *Considered*, 85/155, 86/1501, 86/1512, 91/781, 95/4131,
96/769, 99/3444: *Followed*, 93/3280, 94/3738
Bankers Trust New York Corp *v.* United States 3 I.T.L. Rep. 453, US Ct
Bankgesellschaft Berlin AG *v.* First International Shipping Corp Ltd [2001] C.P. Rep.
62, QBD (Adm Ct) . . . . *Digested*, 01/**560**
Bankrupt (457/2001), Re see Solomons *v.* Williams
Bankrupt Estate of Cirillo Ex p. Official Trustee in Bankruptcy (No.1), Re; *sub nom* Cirillo (A
Bankrupt) Ex p. Official Trustee in Bankruptcy, Re [1997] B.P.I.R. 166, Fed Ct
(Aus) (Sgl judge) . . . . *Digested*, 97/**3038**
Bankrupt Estate of Cirillo Ex p. Official Trustee in Bankruptcy (No.2), Re [1997] B.P.I.R. 574,
Fed Ct (Aus) (Full Ct) . . . . *Digested*, 98/**3267**
Bankruptcy Notice (No.171 of 1934), Re [1934] Ch. 431, CA. . . . . *Considered*, 57/208,
01/3780
Bankrupts (Nos.9587 and 9588 of 1994), Re see Judd *v.* Brown
Banks *v.* Chief Adjudication Officer see Stafford *v.* Chief Adjudication Officer
Banks *v.* Goodfellow (1869-70) L.R. 5 Q.B. 549, QB . . . . *Applied*, 47-51/10956,
47-51/10958, 01/5165, 01/5167
Banks *v.* Kokkinos [1999] 3 E.G.L.R. 133; [1998] E.G.C.S. 187; [1998] N.P.C. 171;
Times, January 19, 1999; *Independent*, January 18, 1999 (C.S.), Ch D . . . . *Digested*, 99/**3726**
Banks *v.* Tesco Stores Ltd [2000] 1 C.M.L.R. 400; [1999] I.C.R. 1141, EAT . . . . *Digested*, 00/**2164**
Banks *v.* Theatre Royal de la Monnaie (C178/97); *sub nom* Banks *v.* Theatre Royale de
la Monnaie (C178/97) [2000] Q.B. 865; [2000] 3 W.L.R. 1069; [2000] All E.R.
(EC) 324; [2000] 2 C.M.L.R. 754; [2000] C.E.C. 256; *Times*, April 5, 2000,
ECJ (5th Chamber) . . . . *Digested*, 00/**4817**
Banks *v.* Theatre Royale de la Monnaie (C178/97) see Banks *v.* Theatre Royal de la
Monnaie (C178/97)
Banks *v.* Woodhall Duckham Ltd (No.1) 95/7387/C, CA. . . . . *Digested*, 96/**2990**:
Considered, 01/4492
Banks *v.* Woodhall Duckham Ltd (No.2); *sub nom* Stathams (Wasted Costs Order), Re
[1997] P.I.Q.R. P464, CA . . . . *Digested*, 98/**500**
Bankway Properties Ltd *v.* Dunsford; *sub nom* Bankway Properties Ltd *v.* Penfold-
Dunsford; Dunsford *v.* Bankway Properties Ltd [2001] EWCA Civ 528; [2001] 1
W.L.R. 1369; [2001] L. & T.R. 27; [2001] 26 E.G. 164; [2001] 16 E.G.C.S. 145;
[2001] N.P.C. 74; *Times*, April 24, 2001, CA . . . . *Digested*, 01/**4150**
Bankway Properties Ltd *v.* Penfold-Dunsford see Bankway Properties Ltd *v.* Dunsford
Banner Homes Holdings Ltd (formerly Banner Homes Group Plc) *v.* Luff Developments
Ltd (No.1) [2000] 2 All E.R. 117; [2000] 2 B.C.L.C. 269; [2000] W.T.L.R. 473;
(1999-2000) 2 I.T.E.L.R. 525; [2000] E.G.C.S. 15; (2000) 97(6) L.S.G. 35;
(2000) 97(6) L.S.G. 37; (2000) 144 S.J.L.B. 83; (2000) 79 P. & C.R. D29;
Times, February 17, 2000; *Independent*, February 11, 2000, CA . . . . *Digested*, 00/**2327**
Banner Homes Holdings Ltd (formerly Banner Homes Group Plc) *v.* Luff Developments
Ltd (No.2) [2000] Ch. 372; [2000] 2 W.L.R. 772, CA . . . . *Digested*, 00/**2317**
Bannertown Developments Ltd *v.* Cotswold DC see Bannertown Developments Ltd *v.*
Secretary of State for the Environment, Transport and the Regions
Bannertown Developments Ltd *v.* Kimberley Securities Plc see Bannertown
Developments Ltd *v.* Secretary of State for the Environment, Transport and the
Regions
Bannertown Developments Ltd *v.* Secretary of State for the Environment, Transport and
the Regions; Bannertown Developments Ltd *v.* Cotswold DC; Bannertown
Developments Ltd *v.* Kimberley Securities Plc [1999] J.P.L. 1016, CA; reversing
[1999] J.P.L. 599; [1998] E.G.C.S. 12, QBD . . . . *Digested*, 00/**4524**
Bannister *v.* SGB Plc; *sub nom* Order 17, Rule 11 of the County Court Rules, Re [1998]
1 W.L.R. 1123; [1997] 4 All E.R. 129; [1997] P.I.Q.R. P165; (1997) 147 N.L.J.
685; *Times*, May 2, 1997, CA . . . . *Digested*, 97/**736**:
Applied, 00/606, 01/433: *Considered*, 97/737, 97/738, 97/750, 98/392,
98/394, 98/395, 98/397, 00/368
Banque Arabe Internationale d'Investissement SA *v.* Morris see Morris *v.* Banque Arabe
Internationale d'Investissement SA (No.2)

Banque Bruxelles Lambert SA v. Eagle Star Insurance Co Ltd; United Bank of Kuwait Plc v. Prudential Property Services Ltd; Nykredit Mortgage Bank Plc v. Edward Erdman Group Ltd; BNP Mortgages Ltd v. Key Surveyors Nationwide Ltd; BNP Mortgages Ltd v. Goadsby & Harding Ltd; Mortgage Express Ltd v. Bowerman & Partners (No.2) [1995] Q.B. 375; [1995] 2 W.L.R. 607; [1995] 2 All E.R. 769; [1995] L.R.L.R. 195; [1996] 5 Bank. L.R. 64; 73 B.L.R. 47; [1995] E.C.C. 398; [1996] 5 Re. L.R. 23; [1995] 1 E.G.L.R. 129; [1995] 12 E.G. 144; [1995] E.G.C.S. 31; (1995) 92(12) L.S.G. 34; (1995) 145 N.L.J. 343; (1995) 139 S.J.L.B. 56; [1995] N.P.C. 32; *Times*, February 21, 1995; *Independent*, February 24, 1995, CA; reversing in part [1995] L.R.L.R. 17; 68 B.L.R. 39; [1994] 32 E.G. 89; [1994] 31 E.G. 68; *Times*, March 7, 1994; *Independent*, April 4, 1994 (C.S.), QBD (Comm Ct) . . . .   *Digested*, 95/**1834**:
Applied, 95/2905, 95/3705, 96/3602, 96/4507, 96/4527, 01/965:
Considered, 94/3383, 95/3645, 95/4838, 96/2610, 96/4485, 96/4517,
99/4017, 00/4252: *Followed*, 96/4520, 96/4528: *Overruled*, 96/4519:
Referred to, 95/3696, 96/4497: *Subsequent proceedings*, 96/4510

Banque Bruxelles Lambert SA v. Zurich Insurance Co see Arab Bank Plc v. Zurich Insurance Co

Banque de France v. Societe Editions Catherine Audval [2001] E.C.C. 20, C d'A (Paris)

Banque Financiere de la Cite SA v. Parc (Battersea) Ltd [1999] 1 A.C. 221; [1998] 2 W.L.R. 475; [1998] 1 All E.R. 737; [1998] C.L.C. 520; [1998] E.G.C.S. 36; (1998) 95(15) L.S.G. 31; (1998) 148 N.L.J. 365; (1998) 142 S.J.L.B. 101; *Times*, March 2, 1998, HL; reversing CHANF 95/0221/B, CA . . . .   *Digested*, 98/**2521**:
Applied, 01/3793: *Cited*, 00/3550: *Referred to*, 00/1460

Banque Financiere de la Cite SA (formerly Banque Keyser Ullmann SA) v. Westgate Insurance Co (formerly Hodge General & Mercantile Co Ltd); *sub nom* Banque Keyser Ullmann SA v. Skandia (UK) Insurance Co; Skandia (UK) Insurance Co v. Chemical Bank; Skandia (UK) Insurance Co v. Credit Lyonnais Bank Nederland NV [1991] 2 A.C. 249; [1990] 3 W.L.R. 364; [1990] 2 All E.R. 947; [1990] 2 Lloyd's Rep. 377; (1990) 87(35) L.S.G. 36; (1990) 140 N.L.J. 1074; (1990) 134 S.J. 1265, HL; affirming [1990] 1 Q.B. 665; [1989] 3 W.L.R. 25; [1989] 2 All E.R. 952; [1988] 2 Lloyd's Rep. 513; [1989] Fin. L.R. 1; (1989) 133 S.J. 817; *Times*, August 24, 1988; *Independent*, August 19, 1988; *Financial Times*, August 12, 1988, CA; reversing [1987] 2 W.L.R. 1300; [1987] 2 All E.R. 923; [1987] 1 Lloyd's Rep. 69; [1987] Fin. L.R. 134; (1987) 84 L.S.G. 1965; (1987) 131 S.J. 775, QBD (Comm Ct) . . . .   *Digested*, 90/**2696**:
Applied, 90/3277, 90/4101, 96/4519, 99/3396, 00/4185:
Considered, 01/4490: *Followed*, 90/3281

Banque Keyser Ullmann SA v. Skandia (UK) Insurance Co see Banque Financiere de la Cite SA (formerly Banque Keyser Ullmann SA) v. Westgate Insurance Co (formerly Hodge General & Mercantile Co Ltd)

Banque National de Paris Plc v. Montman Ltd [2000] 1 B.C.L.C. 576; (1999) 96(32) L.S.G. 32; (1999) 143 S.J.L.B. 222; *Times*, September 7, 1999 ; *Independent*, October 18, 1999 (C.S.), Ch D (Companies Ct) . . . .   *Digested*, 99/**3262**

Bansal v. Cheema [2001] C.P. Rep. 6, CA . . . .   *Digested*, 00/**338**:
Applied, 00/481: *Followed*, 00/373

Barakot Ltd v. Epiette Ltd [1998] 1 B.C.L.C. 283, CA; reversing [1997] 6 Bank. L.R. 28; [1997] 1 B.C.L.C. 303, QBD . . . .   *Digested*, 98/**618**

Barber v. Guardian Royal Exchange Assurance Group (C262/88) [1991] 1 Q.B. 344; [1991] 2 W.L.R. 72; [1990] 2 All E.R. 660; [1990] E.C.R. I-1889; [1990] 2 C.M.L.R. 513; [1990] I.C.R. 616; [1990] I.R.L.R. 240; [1990] 1 P.L.R. 103; (1990) 140 N.L.J. 925; *Times*, May 18, 1990; *Independent*, May 23, 1990; *Financial Times*, May 25, 1990; *Guardian*, July 12, 1990, ECJ . . . .   *Digested*, 90/**1915**:
Applied, 91/1636, 91/1669, 92/1979, 93/1751, 94/4820, 94/4824, 95/1997,
95/1998, 95/2001, 98/2240, 98/4133, 01/2277, 01/2281: *Cited*, 92/1940,
92/1968, 94/2013, 95/2095, 00/4382: *Considered*, 93/3060, 94/1982,
94/4814, 94/4821, 94/4822, 94/4826, 95/2000, 95/2039, 95/2052,
96/2629, 96/4609, 97/5378, 01/4605: *Followed*, 00/2159:
Referred to, 97/2214, 97/3947

Barber v. RJB Mining (UK) Ltd [1999] 2 C.M.L.R. 833; [1999] I.C.R. 679; [1999] I.R.L.R. 308; (1999) 143 S.J.L.B. 141; *Times*, March 8, 1999; *Independent*, March 22, 1999 (C.S.), QBD . . . .   *Digested*, 99/**2072**

Barber v. Staffordshire CC [1996] I.C.R. 379; [1996] I.R.L.R. 209; (1996) 140 S.J.L.B. 43; *Times*, January 29, 1996; *Independent*, February 2, 1996, CA . . . .   *Digested*, 96/**2578**:
Applied, 97/2241, 01/2278: *Considered*, 98/2162, 98/2190

Barclay v. Dunlop Ltd see Carroll v. Fearon

Barclay v. Sweeney [1999] I.L.Pr. 288, C d'A (Paris) . . . .   *Digested*, 99/**712**

Barclays Bank Ltd v. Quistclose Investments Ltd; *sub nom* Quistclose Investments Ltd
v. Rolls Razor Ltd (In Voluntary Liquidation) [1970] A.C. 567; [1968] 3 W.L.R.
1097; [1968] 3 All E.R. 651; 112 S.J. 903, HL; affirming [1968] Ch. 540; [1968]
2 W.L.R. 478; [1968] 1 All E.R. 613; (1967) 118 N.L.J. 13; 112 S.J. 85; *Times*,
December 18, 1967, CA; reversing [1967] Ch. 910; [1967] 2 W.L.R. 1064;
[1967] 1 All E.R. 864; 111 S.J. 190, Ch D . . . . *Digested*, 68/**459**:
    Applied, 84/332, 87/345, 89/178, 94/489: *Considered*, 75/160, 79/153,
    94/2098, 95/2938, 99/294, 00/437, 01/3835: *Distinguished*, 68/3706,
        69/2281, 69/3367, 77/1205, 78/142, 95/4151
Barclays Bank Ltd v. WJ Simms Son & Cooke (Southern) Ltd [1980] Q.B. 677; [1980]
2 W.L.R. 218; [1979] 3 All E.R. 522; [1980] 1 Lloyd's Rep. 225; 123 S.J. 785,
QBD (Comm Ct) . . . . *Digested*, 79/**157**:
    Applied, 83/182, 99/292, 99/2218, 01/374: *Considered*, 83/447, 90/1993,
        90/3914, 90/3918, 00/2331: *Followed*, 97/319
Barclays Bank Plc v. Barclays Pension Funds Trustees Ltd see Barclays Bank Plc v.
Holmes
Barclays Bank Plc v. Bee [2001] EWCA Civ 1126; [2001] 37 E.G. 153; (2001) 98(34)
L.S.G. 40; (2001) 145 S.J.L.B. 206; (2001) 82 P. & C.R. D22; *Times*, August 3,
2001, CA . . . . *Digested*, 01/**4156**
Barclays Bank Plc v. Boulter [1999] 1 W.L.R. 1919; [1999] 4 All E.R. 513; [2000]
Lloyd's Rep. Bank. 29; [1999] C.P. Rep. 16; [1999] 2 F.L.R. 986; [1999] 3
F.C.R. 529; (2000) 32 H.L.R. 170; [1999] 3 E.G.L.R. 88; [1999] 49 E.G. 97;
[2000] Fam. Law 25; [1999] E.G.C.S. 121; (1999) 96(42) L.S.G. 41; (1999)
96(42) L.S.G. 44; (1999) 149 N.L.J. 1645; (1999) 143 S.J.L.B. 250; [1999]
N.P.C. 124; (2000) 79 P. & C.R. D1; *Times*, October 26, 1999; *Independent*,
October 26, 1999, HL; affirming [1998] 1 W.L.R. 1; [1997] 2 All E.R. 1002;
[1997] 2 F.L.R. 157; [1997] 3 F.C.R. 252; (1998) 30 H.L.R. 134; [1997] Fam.
Law 545; [1997] N.P.C. 63; (1997) 74 P. & C.R. D11; *Times*, April 25, 1997;
Independent, April 25, 1997, CA . . . . *Digested*, 99/**4377**
Barclays Bank Plc v. Brooks [1997] C.C.L.R. 60, QBD . . . . *Digested*, 98/**405**
Barclays Bank Plc v. Caplan [1998] 1 F.L.R. 532; (1999) 78 P. & C.R. 153; [1998] Fam.
Law 257; [1997] N.P.C. 164; *Times*, December 12, 1997, Ch D . . . . *Digested*, 98/**2525**
Barclays Bank Plc v. Coleman see Royal Bank of Scotland Plc v. Etridge (No.2)
Barclays Bank Plc v. Coleman [2001] Q.B. 20; [2000] 3 W.L.R. 405; [2000] 1 All E.R.
385; [2000] Lloyd's Rep. Bank. 67; [2000] 1 F.L.R. 343; [2000] 1 F.C.R. 398;
(2001) 33 H.L.R. 8; [2000] Fam. Law 245; [2000] E.G.C.S. 4; (2000) 97(3)
L.S.G. 37; (2000) 144 S.J.L.B. 42; [2000] N.P.C. 2; (2000) 79 P. & C.R. D28;
Times, January 5, 2000; *Independent*, February 21, 2000 (C.S.), CA . . . . *Digested*, 00/**4662**:
    Subsequent proceedings, 01/4880
Barclays Bank Plc v. Dean see Barclays Bank Plc v. Weeks Legg & Dean
Barclays Bank Plc v. Ellis [2001] C.P. Rep. 50; *Times*, October 24, 2000, CA . . . . *Digested*, 00/**573**
Barclays Bank Plc v. Eustice [1995] 1 W.L.R. 1238; [1995] 4 All E.R. 511; [1995] B.C.C.
978; [1995] 2 B.C.L.C. 630; (1995) 145 N.L.J. 1503; *Times*, August 3, 1995,
CA . . . . *Digested*, 96/**3510**:
    Applied, 01/398: *Considered*, 98/355, 98/356
Barclays Bank Plc v. Fairclough Building Ltd (No.1) [1995] Q.B. 214; [1994] 3 W.L.R.
1057; [1995] 1 All E.R. 289; 68 B.L.R. 1; 38 Con. L.R. 86; (1995) 11 Const. L.J.
35; [1995] E.G.C.S. 10; (1994) 91(25) L.S.G. 30; (1994) 138 S.J.L.B. 118;
Times, May 11, 1994, CA; reversing (1994) 10 Const. L.J. 48, QBD . . . . *Digested*, 95/**1571**:
    Applied, 98/2490: *Considered*, 99/3369
Barclays Bank Plc v. Goff [2001] EWCA Civ 635; [2001] 2 All E.R. (Comm) 847;
[2001] Lloyd's Rep. Bank. 189; (2001) 98(20) L.S.G. 45; [2001] N.P.C. 88,
CA . . . . *Digested*, 01/**4879**
Barclays Bank Plc v. Harris see Royal Bank of Scotland Plc v. Etridge (No.2)
Barclays Bank Plc v. Hendricks [1996] 1 F.L.R. 258; [1996] 1 F.C.R. 710; [1996]
B.P.I.R. 17; [1996] Fam. Law 148; *Independent*, November 3, 1995, Ch D . . . . . *Digested*, 95/**2365**:
    Applied, 98/4356
Barclays Bank Plc v. Henson; Barclays Bank Plc v. Stapleton [2000] B.P.I.R. 941, CA . . *Digested*, 01/**3719**
Barclays Bank Plc v. Holmes; Barclays Bank Plc v. Barclays Pension Funds Trustees Ltd
[2001] O.P.L.R. 37; [2000] Pens. L.R. 339, Ch D . . . . *Digested*, 01/**4625**
Barclays Bank Plc v. Kapur (No.2) [1995] I.R.L.R. 87; *Independent*, August 15, 1994
(C.S.), CA . . . . *Digested*, 95/**2028**:
    Followed, 01/5771
Barclays Bank Plc v. Kent CC; *sub nom* Kent CC v. Barclays Bank Plc (1998) 76 P. &
C.R. 1; [1998] 2 E.G.L.R. 14; [1998] 33 E.G. 76; [1998] R.V.R. 74, CA; reversing
[1996] N.P.C. 177, QBD . . . . *Digested*, 98/**434**
Barclays Bank Plc v. Layton Lougher & Co see Barclays Bank Plc v. Weeks Legg &
Dean
Barclays Bank Plc v. Miller [1990] 1 W.L.R. 343; [1990] 1 All E.R. 1040, CA . . . . *Digested*, 90/**3644**:
    Applied, 98/614: *Considered*, 97/761
Barclays Bank Plc v. NE Hopkin John & Co see Barclays Bank Plc v. Weeks Legg &
Dean

Barclays Bank Plc v. O'Brien [1994] 1 A.C. 180; [1993] 3 W.L.R. 786; [1993] 4 All E.R. 417; [1994] 1 F.L.R. 1; [1994] 1 F.C.R. 357; (1994) 26 H.L.R. 75; (1994) 13 Tr. L.R. 165; [1994] C.C.L.R. 94; [1994] Fam. Law 78; [1993] E.G.C.S. 169; (1993) 143 N.L.J. 1511; (1993) 137 S.J.L.B. 240; [1993] N.P.C. 135; *Times*, October 22, 1993; *Independent*, October 22, 1993, HL; affirming [1993] Q.B. 109; [1992] 3 W.L.R. 593; [1992] 4 All E.R. 983; [1993] 1 F.L.R. 124; [1993] 1 F.C.R. 97; (1993) 66 P. & C.R. 135; (1992) 11 Tr. L.R. 153; [1992] C.C.L.R. 37; [1993] Fam. Law 62; (1992) 89(27) L.S.G. 34; (1992) 142 N.L.J. 1040; (1992) 136 S.J.L.B. 175; [1992] N.P.C. 74; *Times*, June 3, 1992; *Independent*, June 17, 1992; *Financial Times*, June 10, 1992, CA . . . . *Digested*, 94/**3300**:
Applied, 94/3291, 94/3294, 94/3299, 95/2443, 95/2451, 96/419, 98/4363, 99/6431, 01/4878, 01/4880: *Cited*, 98/305, 00/4662, 01/2653: *Considered*, 94/276, 94/2246, 95/2196, 95/2444, 95/2446, 95/2448, 95/2449, 95/2452, 95/4659, 96/411, 96/4967, 96/4970, 96/4973, 97/4232, 97/4240, 97/4244, 99/3715, 99/4377, 00/2333, 00/4664, 00/6670, 01/669: *Disapproved*, 97/6087: *Distinguished*, 94/5914: *Explained*, 98/4358: *Followed*, 97/4238, 99/4390, 00/4273: *Not followed*, 94/5881, 95/5982, 96/6577: *Referred to*, 94/3290, 95/2447, 99/310
Barclays Bank Plc v. Pearson (Unreported, October 20, 1997), QBD [*Ex rel.* Toby Watkins, Barrister, 22 Old Buildings, Lincoln's Inn] . . . . *Digested*, 98/**613**
Barclays Bank Plc v. Prudential Assurance Co Ltd [1998] B.C.C. 928; [1998] B.P.I.R. 427; [1998] 1 E.G.L.R. 44; [1998] 10 E.G. 159; [1997] E.G.C.S. 131, Ch D . . . . . *Digested*, 98/**3651**
Barclays Bank Plc v. RBS Advanta [1997] E.T.M.R. 199; [1996] R.P.C. 307; (1996) 15 Tr. L.R. 262; (1996) 19(3) I.P.D. 19025; *Times*, February 8, 1996, Ch D . . . . *Digested*, 96/**3631**:
Considered, 98/3501, 98/3511: *Referred to*, 99/3587
Barclays Bank Plc v. Rivett [1999] 1 F.L.R. 730; [1998] 3 F.C.R. 304; (1997) 29 H.L.R. 893; [1999] Fam. Law 308; [1997] N.P.C. 18, CA . . . . *Digested*, 98/**4363**:
Distinguished, 97/4239
Barclays Bank Plc v. Stapleton see Barclays Bank Plc v. Henson
Barclays Bank Plc v. Stuart Landon Ltd [2001] EWCA Civ 140; [2001] 2 B.C.L.C. 316, CA
Barclays Bank Plc v. Taylor; Trustee Savings Bank of Wales and Border Counties v. Taylor [1989] 1 W.L.R. 1066; [1989] 3 All E.R. 563; [1989] Fin. L.R. 304; (1990) 87(4) L.S.G. 66; (1989) 133 S.J. 1372, CA . . . . *Digested*, 90/**251**:
Considered, 91/878, 92/981: *Followed*, 99/3952
Barclays Bank Plc v. Thomson [1997] 4 All E.R. 816; [1996] 5 Bank. L.R. 402; [1997] 1 F.L.R. 156; [1997] 1 F.C.R. 541; (1998) 75 P. & C.R. 5; [1997] Fam. Law 245; (1996) 146 N.L.J. 1778; [1996] N.P.C. 155; (1997) 73 P. & C.R. D21; *Independent*, November 15, 1996, CA. . . . . *Digested*, 96/**5032**
Barclays Bank Plc v. Weeks Legg & Dean; *sub nom* Barclays Bank Plc v. Dean; Barclays Bank Plc v. Layton Lougher & Co; Mohamed v. Fahiya; Barclays Bank Plc v. NE Hopkin John & Co [1999] Q.B. 309; [1998] 3 W.L.R. 656; [1998] 3 All E.R. 213; [1998] P.N.L.R. 729; (1999) 77 P. & C.R. 320; [1998] 3 E.G.L.R. 103; [1998] 40 E.G. 182; (1998) 95(25) L.S.G. 33; (1998) 95(21) L.S.G. 38; (1998) 142 S.J.L.B. 180; [1998] N.P.C. 89; (1998) 76 P. & C.R. D27; *Times*, June 15, 1998; *Independent*, June 3, 1998, CA; affirming [1996] 5 Bank. L.R. 162; [1996] E.C.C. 396; [1996] E.G.C.S. 29; [1996] N.P.C. 15; *Times*, February 28, 1996; *Independent*, February 26, 1996 (C.S.), QBD . . . . *Digested*, 98/**4374**:
Applied, 00/4263: *Considered*, 99/4379, 00/4281
Barclays Bank Trust Co Ltd v. McDougall [2001] W.T.L.R. 23; *Times*, August 3, 2000, Ch D . . . . *Digested*, 00/**5264**
Barclays Bank Trust Co Ltd v. Slack see Koeppler Will Trusts, Re
Barclays De Zoete Wedd Services Ltd v. Secretary of State for Social Security see Tullett & Tokyo Forex International Ltd v. Secretary of State for Social Security
Barclays Plc v. Villers; *sub nom* Villers v. Equitas Ltd; Villers v. Lovells (formerly Lovell White Durrant) [2000] 1 All E.R. (Comm) 357; [2000] C.L.C. 616; [2001] Lloyd's Rep. I.R. 162, QBD (Comm Ct) . . . . *Digested*, 00/**391**
Barder v. Barder see Barder v. Caluori
Barder v. Caluori; *sub nom* Barder v. Barder [1988] A.C. 20; [1987] 2 W.L.R. 1350; [1987] 2 All E.R. 440; [1987] 2 F.L.R. 480; [1988] Fam. Law 18; (1987) 84 L.S.G. 2046; (1987) 137 N.L.J. 497; (1987) 131 S.J. 776, HL; reversing [1987] Fam. 24; [1986] 3 W.L.R. 145; [1986] 2 All E.R. 918; [1987] 1 F.L.R. 18; [1986] Fam. Law 331; (1986) 83 L.S.G. 1996; (1986) 136 N.L.J. 561; (1986) 130 S.J. 524, CA . . . . *Digested*, 87/**1746**:
Applied, 92/2085, 95/2320, 95/2323, 96/2857: *Considered*, 94/2188, 96/2888, 97/2476, 99/370: *Followed*, 96/2868: *Referred to*, 95/2321
Bardetti (t/a Obertelli Quality Sandwiches) v. Customs and Excise Commissioners [2000] S.T.I. 1691, V&DTr
Barex Brokers Ltd v. Morris Dean & Co [1999] P.N.L.R. 344, CA . . . . *Digested*, 99/**4058**
Barings Futures (Singapore) PTE Ltd (In Liquidation) v. Mattar (No.1) see Barings Plc (In Liquidation) v. Coopers & Lybrand (No.1)
Barings Futures (Singapore) Pte Ltd (In Liquidation) v. Mattar (No.2) see Barings Plc (In Liquidation) v. Coopers & Lybrand (No.2)

Barings Plc (In Liquidation), Re; *sub nom* Hamilton *v.* Law Debenture Trustees Ltd
    [2001] 2 B.C.L.C. 159, Ch D
Barings Plc (No.1), Re see Secretary of State for Trade and Industry *v.* Baker (No.1)
Barings Plc (No.2), Re see Secretary of State for Trade and Industry *v.* Baker (No.2)
Barings Plc (No.3), Re see Secretary of State for Trade and Industry *v.* Baker (No.3)
Barings Plc (No.4), Re see Secretary of State for Trade and Industry *v.* Baker (No.4)
Barings Plc (No.5), Re see Secretary of State for Trade and Industry *v.* Baker (No.5)
Barings Plc (No.6), Re see Secretary of State for Trade and Industry *v.* Baker (No.6)
Barings Plc (In Liquidation) *v.* Coopers & Lybrand (No.1); *sub nom* Barings Futures
    (Singapore) PTE Ltd (In Liquidation) *v.* Mattar (No.1) [2000] 1 W.L.R. 2353;
    [2000] 3 All E.R. 910; [2000] Lloyd's Rep. Bank. 225; (2000) 150 N.L.J. 681;
    Times, May 17, 2000; *Independent*, May 10, 2000, CA . . . . *Digested*, 00/**274**
Barings Plc (In Liquidation) *v.* Coopers & Lybrand (No.2); Barings Futures (Singapore)
    Pte Ltd (In Liquidation) *v.* Mattar (No.2) [2001] Lloyd's Rep. Bank. 85; [2001]
    Lloyd's Rep. P.N. 379; [2001] P.N.L.R. 22; (2001) 98(13) L.S.G. 40; *Times*,
    March 7, 2001; *Daily Telegraph*, February 27, 2001, Ch D . . . . *Digested*, 01/**394**
Barings Plc (In Liquidation) *v.* Coopers & Lybrand (No.3) [2001] EWCA Civ 1163;
    [2001] C.P.L.R. 451; *Times*, October 19, 2001, CA . . . . *Digested*, 01/**439**
Barker, Re; *sub nom* Forrest *v.* Royal Trust Co (1958) 11 D.L.R. (2d) 146, Sup Ct (BC) . . *Digested*, 58/**3099**:
    Considered, 00/5263
Barker *v.* Lydon (Unreported, August 6, 2001), CC (Epsom) [*Ex rel.* Simon Brindle,
    Barrister, 199 Strand, London] . . . . *Digested*, 01/**1515**
Barker *v.* Wingo 407 U.S. 514, US Ct . . . . *Applied*, 98/3137:
    Considered, 91/604, 91/756, 91/761.a, 99/1037
Barking and Dagenham LBC *v.* Home Charm Retail see Stoke on Trent City Council *v.*
    B&Q (Retail) Ltd
Barking and Dagenham LBC *v.* Oguoko [2000] I.R.L.R. 179, EAT . . . . *Digested*, 00/**2150**
Barking and Dagenham LBC *v.* Saint; *sub nom* Saint *v.* Barking and Dagenham LBC
    (1999) 31 H.L.R. 620, CA [*Ex rel.* Jon Holbrook, Barrister, 2 Garden Court,
    Middle Temple, London] . . . . *Digested*, 98/**3045**:
    Considered, 01/4166
Barking and Dagenham LBC *v.* Stamford Asphalt Co Ltd 82 B.L.R. 25; 54 Con. L.R. 1;
    Times, April 10, 1997, CA . . . . *Digested*, 97/**934**:
    Applied, 01/865
Barking and Dagenham LBC *v.* Terrapin Construction Ltd [2000] B.L.R. 479; 74 Con.
    L.R. 100, CA . . . . *Digested*, 01/**876**
Barlow *v.* BOC Ltd see BOC Ltd *v.* Instrument Technology Ltd
Barlow *v.* Polly Peck International Finance Ltd see Polly Peck International Plc (In
    Administration) (No.4), Re
Barnard *v.* Mahiet and Macleod (Unreported, July 3, 1998), CC (Brighton) [*Ex rel.*
    Roger Pezzani, Barrister, Sussex Chambers, 9 Old Steine, Brighton, East
    Sussex] . . . . *Digested*, 98/**524**
Barnard *v.* Restormel BC [1998] 3 P.L.R. 27, CA . . . . *Digested*, 99/**4232**
Barnes *v.* Addy (1873-74) L.R. 9 Ch. App. 244; (1874) 22 W.R. 505; (1874) 43 L.J.
    Ch. 513; (1874) 30 L.T. 4, CA in Chancery. . . . . *Applied*, 68/3706,
    69/3367, 78/242, 80/279, 92/2039: *Considered*, 86/170:
    Distinguished, 66/11052, 98/4871
Barnes *v.* Chief Constable of Durham see Barnes *v.* DPP
Barnes *v.* Dowling (1881) 44 L.T. 809, QBD . . . . *Applied*, 00/3939
Barnes *v.* DPP; *sub nom* Barnes *v.* Chief Constable of Durham [1997] 2 Cr. App. R.
    505; (1998) 162 J.P. 126; (1998) 162 J.P.N. 121; *Times*, May 6, 1997, QBD . . . . . *Digested*, 97/**1154**:
    Considered, 97/1198
Barnes (t/a Barnes Thomas & Co) *v.* Leavesley; Barnes (t/a Barnes Thomas & Co) *v.*
    Taylors Solicitors [2001] I.C.R. 38; *Independent*, October 9, 2000 (C.S), EAT
Barnes *v.* Nayer, *Times*, December 19, 1986, CA . . . . *Digested*, 87/**3795**:
    Considered, 01/6045
Barnes *v.* Sheffield City Council (1995) 27 H.L.R. 719; [1995] N.P.C. 87, CA . . . . *Digested*, 96/**3104**:
    Applied, 99/3704: *Considered*, 98/4299: *Overruled*, 95/4234, 96/2781
Barnes (t/a Barnes Thomas & Co) *v.* Taylors Solicitors see Barnes (t/a Barnes Thomas &
    Co) *v.* Leavesley
Barnet LBC *v.* Ehrentreu (2000) 15 P.A.D. 696, Planning Inspector
Barnet LBC *v.* Hammersons UK Properties Plc (2000) 15 P.A.D. 512, Planning
    Inspector
Barnet LBC *v.* McCarthy & Stone Ltd see Barnet LBC *v.* Secretary of State for the
    Environment, Transport and the Regions
Barnet LBC *v.* Merritt (1998) 13 P.A.D. 154, Planning Inspector
Barnet LBC *v.* Michael Gerson (Investments) Ltd (2001) 16 P.A.D. 15, Planning
    Inspector
Barnet LBC *v.* Nothman (No.2) see Nothman *v.* Barnet LBC (No.2)
Barnet LBC *v.* Patel (1998) 13 P.A.D. 140, Planning Inspector
Barnet LBC *v.* Robin (1999) 2 C.C.L. Rep. 454, CA . . . . *Digested*, 00/**4180**
Barnet LBC *v.* Secretary of State for the Environment, Transport and the Regions
    [2001] J.P.L. 113 (Note), QBD

Barnet LBC *v.* Secretary of State for the Environment, Transport and the Regions; Barnet LBC *v.* McCarthy & Stone Ltd; C/01/1988, CA; reversing [2001] EWHC Admin 642, QBD (Admin Ct); reversing (2001) 16 P.A.D. 26, Planning Inspector

Barnet LBC *v.* Secretary of State for the Environment, Transport and the Regions (Change of Use) [1998] P.L.C.R. 305; [1998] E.G.C.S. 49, QBD . . . .   *Digested,* 99/**4181**

Barnet LBC *v.* Secretary of State for the Environment, Transport and the Regions (Retail Development) (1999) 78 P. & C.R. 179, QBD . . . .   *Digested,* 00/**4514**

Barnet LBC *v.* Smith see Hammersmith and Fulham LBC *v.* Monk

Barnett *v.* Brabyn (Inspector of Taxes) [1996] S.T.C. 716; 69 T.C. 133; *Times,* July 5, 1996, Ch D . . . .   *Digested,* 96/**3406**

Barnett *v.* Chief Constable of West Yorkshire (Unreported, April 24, 1998), CA [*Ex rel.* Force Solicitor, Police Headquarters, Laburnum Road, Wakefield] . . . .   *Digested,* 98/**1451**: *Considered,* 01/1524

Barnett *v.* Lintern (1998) 98(2) Q.R. 5, CC (Swindon) . . . .   *Digested,* 98/**1590**

Barney's Inc. *v.* CMC SA [2001] I.L.Pr. 47, Cass (F); reversing [1999] I.L.Pr. 386, C d'A (Paris)

Baron *v.* Lovell [1999] C.P.L.R. 630; [2000] P.I.Q.R. P20; *Times,* September 14, 1999, CA . . . .   *Digested,* 99/**520**: *Considered,* 00/500

Baron Holding Investments, Re see Baron Investments (Holdings) Ltd, Re

Baron Investments (Holdings) Ltd, Re; *sub nom* Baron Holding Investments, Re; Halstuk *v.* Venvil [2000] 1 B.C.L.C. 272; *Independent,* May 17, 1999 (C.S.), Ch D . . . . . .   *Digested,* 99/**3797**

Baroness Wenlock *v.* River Dee Co (No.3) (1888) L.R. 38 Ch. D. 534, CA; affirming (1887) L.R. 36 Ch. D. 674, Ch D . . . .   *Applied,* 01/**5642**

Barony of Moynihan, Re [2000] 1 F.L.R. 113; [2000] Fam. Law 21; *Times,* March 28, 1997, HL . . . .   *Digested,* 97/**4731**

Barr *v.* Matthews (2000) 52 B.M.L.R. 217, QBD . . . .   *Digested,* 00/**4189**

Barr & Stroud Ltd *v.* West of Scotland Water Authority [1998] Env. L.R. D5, OH

Barraclough *v.* Brown [1897] A.C. 615, HL . . . .   *Applied,* 64/1813, 82/1264, 82/2928, 84/2379, 87/2666, 98/281: *Considered,* 93/3391: *Distinguished,* 58/3343, 59/3260, 69/2896, 70/11

Barrass *v.* Harding [2001] 1 F.L.R. 138; [2001] 1 F.C.R. 297; [2000] W.T.L.R. 1071; [2000] Fam. Law 878, CA . . . .   *Digested,* 01/**5155**

Barratt *v.* Ansell (t/a Woolf Seddon) see Arthur JS Hall & Co *v.* Simons

Barratt *v.* Shaw & Ashton [2001] EWCA Civ 137; [2001] C.P. Rep. 57, CA . . . .   *Digested,* 01/**688**

Barratt *v.* Woolf Seddon see Arthur JS Hall & Co *v.* Simons

Barratt Homes Ltd *v.* Customs and Excise Commissioners [2000] B.V.C. 2257; [2000] S.T.I. 902, V&DTr

Barratt London Ltd *v.* South London Family Housing Association Ltd [2001] E.H.L.R. 1, QBD (T&CC) . . . .   *Digested,* 01/**868**

Barratt Manchester Ltd *v.* Bolton MBC [1998] 1 W.L.R. 1003; [1998] 1 All E.R. 1; [1998] C.L.C. 138; [1997] N.P.C. 142; *Times,* November 3, 1997, CA . . . .   *Digested,* 97/**757**

Barrell Enterprises, Re [1973] 1 W.L.R. 19, CA . . . .   *Applied,* 83/1245, 84/1242, 00/585, 01/582: *Considered,* 83/2901, 84/479, 85/1068, 86/1906

Barresi *v.* Acton & Borman Ltd (Unreported, May 15, 1998), CC (Wandsworth) [*Ex rel.* Cole & Cole Solicitors, Suffolk House, George Street, Croydon] . . . .   *Digested,* 98/**353**

Barret *v.* McCormack (2001-02) 4 I.T.E.L.R. 1, CA (Van)

Barret McKenzie *v.* Escada (UK) Ltd see Barrett McKenzie & Co Ltd *v.* Escada (UK) Ltd

Barrett *v.* Artts International (Unreported, July 9, 2001), CC (Cardiff) [*Ex rel.* Julian Reed, Barrister, 9 Park Place, Cardiff] . . . .   *Digested,* 01/**1518**

Barrett *v.* Cramp (1998) 98(3) Q.R. 6, CC (Cardiff) . . . .   *Digested,* 98/**1600**

Barrett *v.* Enfield LBC [2001] 2 A.C. 550; [1999] 3 W.L.R. 79; [1999] 3 All E.R. 193; [1999] 2 F.L.R. 426; [1999] 2 F.C.R. 434; (1999) 1 L.G.L.R. 829; [1999] B.L.G.R. 473; (1999) 11 Admin. L.R. 839; [1999] Ed. C.R. 833; (1999) 2 C.C.L. Rep. 203; [1999] P.I.Q.R. P272; (1999) 49 B.M.L.R. 1; [1999] Fam. Law 622; (1999) 96(28) L.S.G. 27; (1999) 143 S.J.L.B. 183; *Times,* June 18, 1999, HL; reversing [1998] Q.B. 367; [1997] 3 W.L.R. 628; [1997] 3 All E.R. 171; [1997] 2 F.L.R. 167; [1997] 3 F.C.R. 145; (1998) 10 Admin. L.R. 230; (1997) 37 B.M.L.R. 16; [1997] Fam. Law 534; *Times,* April 22, 1997, CA . . . .   *Digested,* 99/**3966**: *Applied,* 99/1889, 00/4212: *Considered,* 99/3967: *Distinguished,* 99/3963: *Followed,* 98/3944, 99/1765

Barrett *v.* Inntrepreneur Pub Co (GL) Ltd [2000] E.C.C. 106; [1999] E.G.C.S. 93, Ch D . . . .   *Digested,* 99/**682**

Barrett *v.* Lounova (1982) Ltd [1990] 1 Q.B. 348; [1989] 2 W.L.R. 137; [1989] 1 All E.R. 351; (1988) 20 H.L.R. 584; (1989) 57 P. & C.R. 216; [1988] 36 E.G. 184; (1989) 86(15) L.S.G. 39; (1989) 133 S.J. 121, CA . . . .   *Digested,* 88/**2082**: *Considered,* 99/3738, 01/4160

Barrett *v.* Ministry of Defence [1995] 1 W.L.R. 1217; [1995] 3 All E.R. 87; *Times,* January 13, 1995; *Independent,* January 3, 1995; *Guardian,* December 24, 1994, CA . . . .   *Digested,* 95/**3681**: *Followed,* 00/5626

Barrett v. Morgan [2000] 2 A.C. 264; [2000] 2 W.L.R. 284; [2000] 1 All E.R. 481;
(2001) 81 P. & C.R. 1; [2000] L. & T.R. 209; [2000] 1 E.G.L.R. 8; [2000] 06
E.G. 165; (2000) 97(6) L.S.G. 36; (2000) 144 S.J.L.B. 84; (2000) 79 P. & C.R.
D23; *Times*, January 28, 2000 ; *Independent*, March 13, 2000 (C.S.), HL;
reversing [1999] 1 W.L.R. 1109; [1998] 4 All E.R. 179; (1999) 78 P. & C.R. 17;
[1998] L. & T.R. 172; [1998] 3 E.G.L.R. 3; [1998] 50 E.G. 87; [1998] E.G.C.S.
107; (1998) 95(27) L.S.G. 26; (1998) 142 S.J.L.B. 230; [1998] N.P.C. 110;
(1998) 76 P. & C.R. D42; *Times*, July 13, 1998, CA; affirming [1997] 1 E.G.L.R. 1;
[1997] 12 E.G. 155, Ch D .... *Digested*, 00/**3871**
Barrett (Inspector of Taxes) v. Powell [1998] S.T.C. 283; [1998] 2 E.G.L.R. 117; [1998]
22 E.G. 155; 70 T.C. 432; [1998] B.T.C. 59; [1998] E.G.C.S. 17; (1998) 95(8)
L.S.G. 32; (1998) 142 S.J.L.B. 76; [1998] N.P.C. 15; *Times*, February 11, 1998,
Ch D .... *Digested*, 98/**4611**:
Considered, 00/4923
Barrett McKenzie & Co Ltd v. Escada (UK) Ltd; *sub nom* Barret McKenzie v. Escada
(UK) Ltd [2001] E.C.C. 50; [2001] Eu. L.R. 567; *Times*, May 15, 2001, QBD
Barrington v. Colbert (1998) 162 J.P. 642, QBD .... *Digested*, 98/**209**
Barrington v. Glass Glover Group Plc (Unreported, May 1, 1998), QBD [*Ex rel.* Antonis
Georges, Barrister, Martins Bank Buildings, 2nd Floor, 4 Water Street, Liverpool,
L2 3SP] .... *Digested*, 98/**1577**
Barrington Court Developments Ltd v. Barrington Court Residents Association [2001]
29 E.G. 128, Lands Tr .... *Digested*, 01/**4177**
Barrister (Wasted Costs Order) (No.1 of 1991), Re; *sub nom* H (A Barrister), Ex p. [1993]
Q.B. 293; [1992] 3 W.L.R. 662; [1992] 3 All E.R. 429; (1992) 95 Cr. App. R.
288; (1992) 142 N.L.J. 636; (1992) 136 S.J.L.B. 147; *Times*, May 6, 1992;
Independent, April 23, 1992; *Guardian*, May 6, 1992, CA (Crim Div) .... *Digested*, 92/**748**:
Applied, 94/3623, 00/1042, 01/540: *Cited*, 97/602: *Considered*, 94/3620,
98/1016, 99/422, 99/986, 99/987: *Followed*, 00/469
Barrister (Wasted Costs Order) (No.9 of 1999), Re (2000) 97(26) L.S.G. 36; *Times*, April
18, 2000, CA (Crim Div) .... *Digested*, 00/**4001**
Barristers (Wasted Costs Order: Criminal Proceedings) (No.5 of 1997), Re, *Times*,
September 7, 1999, CA (Crim Div) .... *Digested*, 99/**989**
Barros D'Sa v. University Hospital Coventry and Warwickshire NHS Trust; *sub nom*
Barros D'Sa v. Walsgrove Hospital NHS Trust; Barros D'Sa v. Walsgrave Hospital
NHS Trust [2001] EWCA Civ 983; [2001] I.R.L.R. 691; [2001] Lloyd's Rep.
Med. 442; (2001) 62 B.M.L.R. 39; *Daily Telegraph*, June 26, 2001, CA .... *Digested*, 01/**2244**
Barros D'Sa v. Walsgrave Hospital NHS Trust see Barros D'Sa v. University Hospital
Coventry and Warwickshire NHS Trust
Barros D'Sa v. Walsgrove Hospital NHS Trust see Barros D'Sa v. University Hospital
Coventry and Warwickshire NHS Trust
Barrow v. Bankside Members Agency Ltd; *sub nom* Barrow v. Bankside Underwriting
Management Ltd [1996] 1 W.L.R. 257; [1996] 1 All E.R. 981; [1996] 1 Lloyd's
Rep. 278; [1996] C.L.C. 413; [1996] 5 Re. L.R. 1; *Times*, November 10, 1995, CA;
affirming [1995] 2 Lloyd's Rep. 472; *Lloyd's List*, June 20, 1995 (I.D.), QBD
(Comm Ct) .... *Digested*, 95/**3894**:
Applied, 01/4678: *Considered*, 98/518: *Distinguished*, 97/461, 99/3952:
Followed, 99/1376
Barrow v. Bankside Underwriting Management Ltd see Barrow v. Bankside Members
Agency Ltd
Barrow (Terrence) v. Queen, The [1998] A.C. 846; [1998] 2 W.L.R. 957; (1998) 142
S.J.L.B. 133; *Times*, March 31, 1998, PC (Trin) .... *Digested*, 98/**1050**
Barrow v. Secretary of State for the Home Department see Ahmed (Naseer) v.
Secretary of State for the Home Department
Barrow Borough Transport Ltd, Re [1990] Ch. 227; [1989] 3 W.L.R. 858; [1989] B.C.L.C.
653; (1989) 86(42) L.S.G. 39; (1989) 133 S.J. 1513, Ch D .... *Digested*, 91/**2136**:
Considered, 00/3428
Barrs v. Bethell [1982] Ch. 294; [1981] 3 W.L.R. 874; [1982] 1 All E.R. 106; 81 L.G.R.
269; 125 S.J. 808, Ch D .... *Digested*, 81/**1626**:
Considered, 93/340, 94/369, 01/5021
Barry v. Ablerex Construction (Midlands) Ltd [2001] EWCA Civ 433; (2001) 98(22)
L.S.G. 35; *Times*, April 3, 2001, CA; reversing [2000] P.I.Q.R. Q263; *Times*,
March 30, 2000, QBD .... *Digested*, 01/**1546**:
Disapproved, 00/1492
Followed, 01/5509
Barry v. Adams (Unreported, October 15, 1907), Sup Ct (NSW)
Barry v. Barry [1992] Fam. 140; [1992] 2 W.L.R. 799; [1992] 3 All E.R. 405; [1992] 2
F.L.R. 233; [1992] Fam. Law 485, Fam Div .... *Digested*, 93/**1912**:
Overruled, 98/2467
Barry v. Bradshaw [2000] C.L.C. 455; [2000] I.L.Pr. 706, CA .... *Digested*, 00/**746**
Barry v. Davies (t/a Heathcote Ball & Co); *sub nom* Heathcote Ball & Co (Commercial
Auctions) Ltd v. Barry; Barry v. Heathcote Ball & Co (Commercial Auctions) Ltd
[2000] 1 W.L.R. 1962; [2001] 1 All E.R. 944; [2000] 3 E.G.L.R. 7; [2000] 47
E.G. 178; (2000) 97(39) L.S.G. 41; (2000) 150 N.L.J. 1377; (2000) 144 S.J.L.B.
249; *Times*, August 31, 2000, CA .... *Digested*, 00/**860**

Barry v. Heathcote Ball & Co (Commercial Auctions) Ltd see Barry v. Davies (t/a Heathcote Ball & Co)
Barry v. Midland Bank Plc [1999] 1 W.L.R. 1465; [1999] 3 All E.R. 974; [1999] I.C.R. 859; [1999] I.R.L.R. 581; (1999) 96(31) L.S.G. 36; (1999) 149 N.L.J. 1253; (1999) 143 S.J.L.B. 221; *Times*, July 23, 1999 ; *Independent*, October 25, 1999 (C.S.), HL; affirming [1998] 1 All E.R. 805; [1999] I.C.R. 319; [1998] I.R.L.R. 138; *Times*, December 29, 1997, CA; affirming [1997] I.C.R. 192; *Times*, October 25, 1996, EAT . . . . *Digested*, 99/**2117**
Barry v. News Group Newspapers Ltd see Clinton v. News Group Newspapers Ltd
Barry v. Phenix (Unreported, September 18, 1997), CC (Birkenhead) [*Ex rel.* Weightmans Solicitors, Richmond House, Liverpool] . . . . *Digested*, 98/**1464**
Barry Artist Ltd, Re see Secretary of State for Trade and Industry v. Forsyth
Barsby v. Harrison (Unreported, January 26, 1998), CC (Derby) [*Ex rel.* Neil Wylie, Barrister, King Charles House Chambers, Standard Hill, Nottingham] . . . .   *Digested*, 98/**1754**
Barthold v. Germany (A/90) (1985) 7 E.H.R.R. 383, ECHR . . . .   *Applied*, 01/**4409**
Bartholomew v. Hackney LBC [1999] I.R.L.R. 246, CA . . . .   *Digested*, 99/**2108**:
                                                                                                     Applied, 01/**2254**
Bartlam v. Evans see Evans v. Bartlam
Bartlett v. Barclays Bank Trust Co Ltd (No.2) [1980] Ch. 515; [1980] 2 W.L.R. 430; [1980] 2 All E.R. 92; 124 S.J. 221, Ch D . . . .   *Digested*, 80/**2403**:
                                 Applied, 80/2413, 81/2453, 86/2612, 99/4634: *Considered*, 01/**3726**
Barton v. County Natwest Ltd; *sub nom* County Natwest Ltd v. Barton [1999] Lloyd's Rep. Bank. 408; [1999] E.G.C.S. 103; (1999) 96(33) L.S.G. 31; *Times*, July 29, 1999, CA . . . .   *Digested*, 99/**856**
Barton v. DPP [2001] EWHC Admin 223; (2001) 165 J.P. 779; (2001) 165 J.P.N. 887, QBD (Admin Ct)
Barton v. London and North Western Railway Co (1888) L.R. 38 Ch. D. 144, CA. . . . . .   *Applied*, 55/**362**:
                                                                                                     Considered, 00/**5439**
Barton v. Saunders (Unreported, December 4, 1997), CC (Manchester) [*Ex rel.* Pannone & Partners Solicitors, 123 Deansgate, Manchester] . . . .   *Digested*, 98/**1437**
Barton Manufacturing Co Ltd, Re [1998] B.C.C. 827; [1999] 1 B.C.L.C 740, Ch D . . . . .   *Digested*, 99/**3307**
Barton Thompson & Co Ltd v. Stapling Machines Co [1966] Ch. 499; [1966] 2 W.L.R. 1429; [1966] 2 All E.R. 222; 110 S.J. 313, Ch D . . . .   *Digested*, 66/**1817**:
                                     Considered, 85/2604, 90/4032: *Followed*, 99/**3665**
Barvis v. Secretary of State for the Environment (1971) 22 P. & C.R. 710, QBD . . . .   *Digested*, 71/**11383**:
                                     Applied, 99/4171: *Considered*, 93/3827, 94/4326, 00/**4415**
Basch v. Stekel [2001] L. & T.R. 1; (2001) 81 P. & C.R. D1, CA
BASF AG v. Commission of the European Communities (T4/89) [1991] E.C.R. II-1523, CFI (1st Chamber) . . . .   *Digested*, 92/**4703**:
                                                                                                     Referred to, 00/**2376**
BASF AG v. Iticon Plc (C 98 0433 N) [2001] E.N.P.R. 2, Cass (B)
BASF AG v. Prasident des Deutschen Patentamts (C44/98); *sub nom* BASF AG v. President of the German Patent Office [1999] E.C.R. I-6269; [2001] 2 C.M.L.R. 21; (1999) 22 I.P.D. 22113; *Times*, October 12, 1999, ECJ (5th Chamber) . . . . . .   *Digested*, 99/**2249**
BASF AG v. President of the German Patent Office see BASF AG v. Prasident des Deutschen Patentamts (C44/98)
BASF AG's SPC Application [2000] R.P.C. 1, PO . . . .   *Digested*, 00/**3691**
BASF Coating AG v. Commission of the European Communities (T175/95) [1999] E.C.R. II-1581; [2000] 4 C.M.L.R. 33, CFI . . . .   *Digested*, 00/**719**
Basham (Deceased), Re [1986] 1 W.L.R. 1498; [1987] 1 All E.R. 405; [1987] 2 F.L.R. 264; [1987] Fam. Law 310; (1987) 84 L.S.G. 112; (1986) 130 S.J. 986, Ch D . . . . . .   *Digested*, 87/**1444**:
                                     Cited, 97/4736, 98/4585: *Distinguished*, 95/**2339**
Bashir v. Hanson (Unreported, July 9, 1999), CC (Birmingham) [*Ex rel.* Beachcroft Wansbroughs Solicitors, Somerset House, 37 Temple Street, Birmingham] . . . . .   *Digested*, 99/**418**
Bashir Mohamed Ltd v. Customs and Excise Commissioners [2000] S.T.I. 1723, V&DTr
Basildon DC v. Palmer (1998) 13 P.A.D. 707, Planning Inspector
Basildon DC v. Railtrack Plc see Albon v. Railtrack Plc
Basildon DC v. Secretary of State for the Environment, Transport and the Regions [2001] J.P.L. 1184, QBD (Admin Ct) . . . .   *Digested*, 01/**4708**
Basingstoke and Deane BC v. Barwood Developments Ltd see Basingstoke and Deane BC v. Secretary of State for the Environment
Basingstoke and Deane BC v. Secretary of State for the Environment; Basingstoke and Deane BC v. Barwood Developments Ltd (1998) 75 P. & C.R. 397, QBD . . . . . .   *Digested*, 98/**4232**
Baskaya v. Turkey (23536/94); Okcuoglu v. Turkey (24408/94) (2001) 31 E.H.R.R. 10, ECHR . . . .   *Digested*, 01/**3477**
Baskin Robbins Ice Cream Co v. Gutman [1976] F.S.R. 545, Ch D . . . .   *Digested*, 77/**415**:
                                                                                 Followed, 77/3050, 98/**3518**
Bass Holdings Ltd v. Brodie [1998] 1 E.G.L.R. 51; [1998] 14 E.G. 138, QBD . . . .   *Digested*, 98/**512**
Bass Taverns Ltd v. Burgess [1995] I.R.L.R. 596, CA . . . .   *Digested*, 96/**2669**:
                                                                                 Applied, 97/2259, 98/**2103**
Bassairi Ltd v. Camden LBC; *sub nom* Bassari Ltd v. Camden LBC [1999] L. & T.R. 45; [1998] E.G.C.S. 27, CA
Bassari Ltd v. Camden LBC see Bassairi Ltd v. Camden LBC
Bassetlaw DC v. JG Pears (Newark) Ltd (1999) 14 P.A.D. 322, Planning Inspector

Bassetlaw DC *v.* McIlwain (2000) 15 P.A.D. 404, Planning Inspector
Bassett Road Housing Association *v.* Gough (Unreported, April 20, 1998), CC (Central London) [*Ex rel.* Max Thorowgood, Barrister, Mitre Court Chambers, Temple, London] . . . . *Digested,* 98/**3653**
Bastick *v.* James Lane (Turf Accountants) [1979] I.C.R. 778, EAT . . . . *Digested,* 79/**896**:
Applied, 85/1158, 99/2024: *Approved,* 80/935
Bastik *v.* Yamaichi International Europe Ltd (Unreported, January 15, 1993), CA . . . . . . *Considered,* 98/2206
BAT Industries Plc, Re; *sub nom* BAT Industries Plc *v.* BAT Reconstructions Ltd; No.001165 of 1998, Ch D . . . . *Digested,* 98/**658**
BAT Industries Plc *v.* BAT Reconstructions Ltd see BAT Industries Plc, Re
Batchelor *v.* Kent CC (1990) 59 P. & C.R. 357; [1990] 1 E.G.L.R. 32; [1990] 14 E.G. 129; [1989] R.V.R. 181; [1990] J.P.L. 571; (1990) 154 L.G. Rev. 493; *Times,* August 17, 1989, CA; affirming (1988) 56 P. & C.R. 320; [1988] R.V.R. 158, Lands Tr . . . . *Digested,* 90/**582**:
Considered, 96/4832, 99/4192
Batchelor *v.* Marlow (No.1) [2001] R.T.R. 12; [2001] 1 E.G.L.R. 119; (2000) 97(23) L.S.G. 40; (2000) 97(21) L.S.G. 42; (2001) 81 P. & C.R. D6; *Times,* June 7, 2000, Ch D . . . . *Digested,* 00/**4630**
Batchelor *v.* Marlow (No.2) [2001] EWCA Civ 1051; (2001) 82 P. & C.R. 36; (2001) 98(28) L.S.G. 45; [2001] N.P.C. 111, CA; reversing HC-98-05394, Ch D
Bate *v.* Chief Adjudication Officer [1996] 1 W.L.R. 814; [1996] 2 F.C.R. 637; (1996) 93(22) L.S.G. 28; (1996) 146 N.L.J. 749; (1996) 140 S.J.L.B. 135; *Times,* May 17, 1996, HL; reversing [1995] 3 F.C.R. 145; *Times,* December 12, 1994; *Independent,* December 2, 1994, CA . . . . *Digested,* 96/**5470**:
Followed, 98/4511
Bateman *v.* Boyd (Unreported, December 4, 2000), CC (Southport) [*Ex rel.* Fletchers, 160-162 Lord Street, Southport, Merseyside] . . . . *Digested,* 01/**883**
Bateman *v.* Industrial Orthopaedic Society (1997) 97(5/6) Q.R. 12, QBD . . . . *Digested,* 98/**1762**
Bateman *v.* Lancashire CC [1999] 2 E.G.L.R. 203; [1999] R.V.R. 125, Lands Tr. . . . . *Digested,* 99/**4185**
Bater *v.* Bater see Bater *v.* Greenwich LBC
Bater *v.* Greenwich LBC; *sub nom* Bater *v.* Bater; Greenwich LBC *v.* Bater [1999] 4 All E.R. 944; [1999] 2 F.L.R. 993; [1999] 3 F.C.R. 254; (2000) 32 H.L.R. 127; [2000] L. & T.R. 1; [1999] Fam. Law 694; [1999] E.G.C.S. 111; (1999) 96(33) L.S.G. 30; [1999] N.P.C. 102; *Times,* September 28, 1999 ; *Independent,* October 25, 1999 (C.S.), CA . . . . *Digested,* 99/**2406**
Bates *v.* Croydon LBC [2001] EWCA Civ 134; [2001] C.P. Rep. 70; (2001) 33 H.L.R. 70, CA . . . . *Digested,* 01/**3439**
Bates *v.* Hotpoint Ltd (Unreported, August 28, 1998), CC (Coventry) [*Ex rel.* Weightmans Solicitors, Richmond House, 1 Rumford Place, Liverpool] . . . . *Digested,* 99/**2869**
Bates *v.* Leicester HA [1998] Lloyd's Rep. Med. 93, QBD . . . . *Digested,* 98/**548**
Bates *v.* Leicestershire HA [2001] 1 Q.R. 7
Bath and North East Somerset Council *v.* Toye (2001) 16 P.A.D. 1, Planning Inspector
Bath and North East Somerset DC *v.* Trustees of Bath Masonic Hall (2000) 15 P.A.D. 505, Planning Inspector
Bath and North East Somerset DC *v.* Warman [1999] Ed. C.R. 517; [1999] E.L.R. 81, QBD . . . . *Digested,* 99/**1832**:
Considered, 01/1986
Bath and Wells Diocesan Board of Finance *v.* Jenkinson [2001] W.T.L.R. 353; (2000) 97(38) L.S.G. 44; *Times,* September 6, 2000, Ch D . . . . *Digested,* 00/**295**
Bathampton Properties, Re [1976] 1 W.L.R. 168; [1976] 3 All E.R. 200; 120 S.J. 47, Ch D
Digested, 76/**272**:
Considered, 90/3746: *Followed,* 78/249, 00/3498: *Not followed,* 92/2570
Batley *v.* DPP, *Times,* March 5, 1998, QBD . . . . *Digested,* 98/**905**
Batmark Inc's Application [1998] E.T.M.R. 448, OHIM (1st Bd App)
Batt (CICA: Quantum: 2000), Re [2001] 3 Q.R. 12, CICAP [*Ex rel.* John Bassett, Barrister 5 Essex Court, London] . . . . *Digested,* 01/**1598**
Batt *v.* Adams; *sub nom* Adams *v.* Trustees of the Michael Batt Charitable Trust [2001] 32 E.G. 90; [2001] 21 E.G.C.S. 164, Ch D . . . . *Digested,* 01/**4844**
Battan Singh *v.* Amirchand [1948] A.C. 161; [1948] 1 All E.R. 152; [1948] L.J.R. 827, PC (Fiji) . . . . *Digested,*
47-51/**10958**:
Distinguished, 01/5167
Battersby *v.* Campbell (Inspector of Taxes) [2001] S.T.C. (S.C.D.) 189; [2001] S.T.I. 1498, Sp Comm
Battersea Freehold & Leasehold Property Co Ltd *v.* Wandsworth LBC (2001) 82 P. & C.R. 12; [2001] 19 E.G. 148; [2001] 12 E.G.C.S. 164; (2001) 98(20) L.S.G. 41; [2001] N.P.C. 50; *Times,* March 30, 2001, Ch D . . . . *Digested,* 01/**4841**
Bauman *v.* Fussell [1978] R.P.C. 485; *Times,* May 19, 1953, CA. . . . . *Digested,* 78/**349**:
Distinguished, 00/3577: *Referred to,* 00/3570
Baustahlgewebe GmbH *v.* Commission of the European Communities (C185/95 P); *sub nom* Baustahlgewebe GmbH *v.* Commission of the European Communities (T145/89) [1998] E.C.R. I-8417; [1999] 4 C.M.L.R. 1203; (1999) 18 Tr. L.R. 87, ECJ [1995] E.C.R. II-987, CFI . . . . *Digested,* 99/**2242**:
Followed, 01/768

Baustahlgewebe GmbH v. Commission of the European Communities (T145/89) see
Baustahlgewebe GmbH v. Commission of the European Communities (C185/95
P)

Bavage v. Southwark LBC (Unreported, October 15, 1998), CC (Lambeth) [*Ex rel.* A
Butler, Barrister, Second Floor, Francis Taylor Building, Temple, London] . . . .   *Digested,* 98/**3623**

Bavarian Lager Co Ltd v. Commission of the European Communities (T309/97) [1999]
E.C.R. II-3217; [1999] 3 C.M.L.R. 544; [1999] C.E.C. 543; *Times,* November
10, 1999, CFI (4th Chamber) . . . .   *Digested,* 99/**2239**

Bavin v. Ferguson see Classick v. Blazenby

Bavin v. NHS Trust Pension Agency [1999] I.C.R. 1192; [1999] O.P.L.R. 285, EAT

Bawden v. Gardner (1998) 98(6) Q.R. 3, CC (Central London) . . . .   *Digested,* 98/**1497**

Bawejem Ltd v. MC Fabrications Ltd [1999] 1 All E.R. (Comm.) 377; [1999] B.C.C.
157; [1999] 1 B.C.L.C. 174, CA . . . .   *Digested,* 99/**832**

Baxall Securities Ltd v. Sheard Walshaw Partnership; *sub nom* Blaxhall Securities Ltd v.
Sheard Walshaw Partnership; A1/2000/3460 QBENF, CA; reversing in part
[2001] C.L.C. 188; [2001] B.L.R. 36; (2001) 3 T.C.L.R. 8; 74 Con. L.R. 116;
[2001] Lloyd's Rep. P.N. 85; [2001] P.N.L.R. 9; (2001) 17 Const. L.J. 150; *Daily
Telegraph,* November 14, 2000, QBD (T&CC) . . . .   *Digested,* 01/**4509**

Baxendale v. British Fuels Ltd see Meade v. British Fuels Ltd

Baxendale v. British Fuels Ltd see Wilson v. St Helens BC

Baxter v. Bristol City Council [1998] E.L.R. 552; [1998] C.O.D. 458, CA (Crim Div) . . .   *Digested,* 99/**1895**

Baxter v. Camden LBC (No.1) [1998] Env. L.R. 270; (1998) 30 H.L.R. 501; [1998] 2
E.G.L.R. 29; [1998] 22 E.G. 150; [1997] E.G.C.S. 102; [1997] N.P.C. 97, CA . . .   *Digested,* 98/**3621**:
      Disapproved, 98/3622

Baxter v. Camden LBC (No.2) see Southwark LBC v. Mills

Baxter v. Camden LBC (No.2) [2001] Q.B. 1; [1999] 2 W.L.R. 566; [1999] 1 All E.R.
237; [1999] Env. L.R. 561; (1999) 31 H.L.R. 356; [1999] B.L.G.R. 239; [1999]
L. & T.R. 136; [1998] E.G.C.S. 157; (1998) 95(45) L.S.G. 41; (1999) 143 S.J.L.B.
11; [1998] N.P.C. 147; [1999] E.H.L.R. Dig. 205; *Times,* November 11, 1998, CA .   *Digested,* 98/**4044**:
      Subsequent proceedings, 99/3672

Baxter v. Chief Constable of the West Midlands, *Independent,* June 15, 1998 (C.S.),
QBD . . . .   *Digested,* 98/**1000**

Baxter International Inc v. Nederlands Produktielaboratorium voor
Bloedtransfusiapparatuur BV [1998] R.P.C. 250; (1997) 20(9) I.P.D. 20091, Pat
Ct. . . . .   *Digested,* 98/**3451**

BAXTER/Blood Extraction Method (T329/94) [1998] E.P.O.R. 363, EPO (Technical Bd
App)

Bayer AG v. Commission of the European Communities (T41/96) [2001] All E.R. (EC)
1; [2000] E.C.R. II-3383; [2001] 4 C.M.L.R. 4; [2001] I.C.R. 735; *Times,*
February 9, 2001, CFI (5th Chamber) . . . .   *Digested,* 01/**776**

Bayer AG's Application, Re [1999] I.L.Pr. 786, US Ct

Bayer Corp v. Octapharma Ltd (1999) 22(4) I.P.D. 22033, Pat Ct

Bayer Corp v. Octapharma Ltd (Costs) [1999] F.S.R. 926, Pat Ct . . . .   *Digested,* 00/**3673**

BAYER/Coating Composition (T574/88) [2001] E.P.O.R. 61, EPO (Technical Bd App)

BAYER/Diastereomers (T12/81) [1979-85] E.P.O.R. B308, EPO (Technical Bd App) . .   *Applied,* 00/3643

Bayerische Hypotheken- und Wechselbank AG v. Dietzinger (C45/96) [1998] 1 W.L.R.
1035; [1998] All E.R. (E.C.) 332; [1998] E.C.R. I-1199; [1998] 2 C.M.L.R. 499;
[1999] C.C.L.R. 1; *Times,* March 25, 1998, ECJ (5th Chamber) . . . .   *Digested,* 98/**828**

Bayerische Motorenwerke AG v. Deenik (C63/97); *sub nom* BMW AG v. Deenik (C63/
97) [1999] All E.R. (EC) 235; [1999] E.C.R. I-905; [1999] 1 C.M.L.R. 1099;
[1999] C.E.C. 159; [1999] E.T.M.R. 339, ECJ [1999] E.C.R. I-905; [1998]
E.T.M.R. 348, AGO . . . .   *Digested,* 99/**3554**:
      Considered, 99/3553: *Followed,* 01/4029

Baylis (Inspector of Taxes) v. Gregory see Craven (Inspector of Taxes) v. White
(Stephen)

Baylis (Gloucester) Ltd v. Bennett Construction (UK) Ltd see Secretary of State for the
Environment, Transport and the Regions v. Baylis (Gloucester) Ltd

Baynard v. Manchester City Council (Unreported, December 5, 1997), CC
(Manchester) [*Ex rel.* Barrie Searle, Barrister, 68 Quay Street, Manchester] . . . .   *Digested,* 98/**1694**

Baynham v. Kenmore (Unreported, December 15, 1997), CC (Leeds) [*Ex rel.* Andrew
McGrath, Barrister, Five Fountain Court, Steelhouse Lane, Birmingham] . . . . . .   *Digested,* 98/**1746**

Baynton v. Morgan (1889) L.R. 22 Q.B.D. 74, CA; affirming (1888) L.R. 21 Q.B.D.
101, QBD . . . .   *Applied,* 83/2061,
      84/1868, 84/1909, 84/1954, 85/1868, 93/2483: *Considered,* 92/497, 92/2758,
      98/3615: *Explained,* 74/356

Baynton v. Saurus General Engineers Ltd [2000] I.C.R. 375; [1999] I.R.L.R. 604, EAT .   *Digested,* 99/**2024**:
      Applied, 00/2129

Bayoil SA, Re; *sub nom* Seawind Tankers Corp v. Bayoil SA [1999] 1 W.L.R. 147;
[1999] 1 All E.R. 374; [1999] 1 Lloyd's Rep. 211; [1998] B.C.C. 988; [1999] 1
B.C.L.C. 62; (1998) 142 S.J.L.B. 251; *Times,* October 12, 1998, CA . . . .   *Digested,* 98/**3324**:
      Applied, 99/3351, 00/3486: *Considered,* 99/3254, 99/3350

Bayoil SA v. Seawind Tankers Corp (The Leonidas) [2001] 1 All E.R. (Comm) 392;
[2001] 1 Lloyd's Rep. 533; [2001] C.L.C. 1800, QBD (Comm Ct) . . . .   *Previous proceedings,*
      98/3324

Bayoumi v. Protim Services Ltd (1998) 30 H.L.R. 785; [1997] P.N.L.R. 189; [1996]
E.G.C.S. 187, CA . . . .   *Digested,* 97/**3767**
BayWa AG v. Bundesanstalt fur Landwirtschaftliche Marktordnung (146/81) [1982]
E.C.R. 1503, ECJ . . . .   *Digested,* 83/**1375**:
Followed, 00/170
Bazley v. Curry (1999) 174 D.L.R. (4th) 45 . . . .   *Considered,* 01/**5359**
BB v. France [1998] H.R.C.D. 853, ECHR
BBC v. British Satellite Broadcasting Ltd [1992] Ch. 141; [1991] 3 W.L.R. 174; [1991] 3
All E.R. 833; *Times,* January 22, 1991; *Daily Telegraph,* January 24, 1991, Ch D . .   *Digested,* 92/**575**:
Considered, 98/3422
BBC v. Farnworth [1998] I.C.R. 1116; *Times,* October 7, 1998, EAT . . . .   *Digested,* 98/**2185**
BBC v. Hearn [1977] 1 W.L.R. 1004; [1978] 1 All E.R. 111; [1977] I.C.R. 685; [1977]
I.R.L.R. 273; 121 S.J. 374, CA; reversing 121 S.J. 363; *Times,* May 20, 1977. . . . .   *Digested,* 77/**1097**:
Applied, 80/2752, 81/2818, 84/3554
BBC v. Ioannou; *sub nom* Ioannou v. BBC [1975] Q.B. 781; [1975] 3 W.L.R. 63;
[1975] 2 All E.R. 999; [1975] I.C.R. 265; [1975] I.C.R. 267; [1975] I.R.L.R. 184;
(1975) 10 I.T.R. 88; 18 Man. Law 19; 119 S.J. 337, CA; affirming [1974] I.C.R.
414; [1974] I.R.L.R. 77; (1974) 9 I.T.R. 213, NIRC . . . .   *Digested,* 75/**1091**:
Applied, 00/2244: *Considered,* 97/2198: *Distinguished,* 77/1140, 78/1127,
94/1919: *Not followed,* 78/1126, 79/1019
BBC v. K (A Child) see K (A Child) v. BBC
BBC v. Kelly-Phillips [1998] 2 All E.R. 845; [1998] I.C.R. 587; [1998] I.R.L.R. 294;
Times, April 24, 1998; *Independent,* April 22, 1998, CA; reversing [1998] I.C.R. 1;
[1997] I.R.L.R. 571, EAT . . . .   *Digested,* 98/**2151**:
Followed, 00/2244
BBC v. Talksport Ltd (No.1); *sub nom* British Broadcasting Corp v. Talksport Ltd [2001]
F.S.R. 6; (2000) 23(10) I.P.D. 23084; (2000) 97(27) L.S.G. 39; *Times,* June
29, 2000, Ch D . . . .   *Digested,* 00/**5120**
BBC Scotland v. Souster 2001 S.C. 458; [2001] I.R.L.R. 150; 2000 G.W.D. 40-1490,
Ex Div. . . . .   *Digested,* 01/**6473**
BBC Worldwide Ltd v. Pally Screen Printing Ltd [1998] F.S.R. 665; (1998) 21(5) I.P.D.
21053, Ch D . . . .   *Digested,* 98/**3421**:
Applied, 99/3442
BBC's Application, Re see R. v. Lees (William John)
BBC, Petitioners (No.1) 2000 J.C. 419; 2000 S.L.T. 845; 2000 G.W.D. 11-383; *Times,* April
11, 2000, HCJ . . . .   *Digested,* 00/**6117**
BBC, Petitioners (No.2) 2000 J.C. 521; 2000 S.L.T. 860; 2000 S.C.C.R. 533; [2000]
H.R.L.R. 423; 2000 G.W.D. 15-584; *Times,* June 13, 2000, HCJ Appeal . . . .   *Digested,* 00/**6116**
BC (A Minor) (Care Order: Appropriate Local Authority), Re [1995] 3 F.C.R. 598; (1996)
160 L.G. Rev. 13, Fam Div . . . .   *Digested,* 96/**485**:
Considered, 99/2352: *Followed,* 99/2312
BCCI v. Ali see Bank of Credit and Commerce International SA (In Liquidation) v. Ali
(No.5)
BCCI v. Morris see Morris v. Banque Arabe Internationale d'Investissement SA (No.2)
BCCI SA, Re see Malik v. Bank of Credit and Commerce International SA (In
Liquidation)
BCCI SA v. Ali see Bank of Credit and Commerce International SA (In Liquidation) v.
Ali (No.3)
BDG Roof Bond Ltd (In Liquidation) v. Douglas [2000] B.C.C. 770; [2000] 1 B.C.L.C.
401; [2000] Lloyd's Rep. P.N. 273; [2000] P.N.L.R. 397, Ch D . . . .   *Digested,* 00/**679**
BeA Fastening Systems Ltd v. Todd (Valuation Officer) [1999] R.A. 389, Lands Tr . . . . .   *Digested,* 00/**4607**
Beacham v. Shaw (Unreported, April 21, 1999), CC [*Ex rel.* Steven Ball, Barrister, 11
Old Square, Lincoln's Inn, London] . . . .   *Digested,* 99/**1474**
Beahan v. Stoneham QB 2000 PTA 0158, Ch D; reversing [2001] 2 Q.R. 8, CC
(Central London) [*Ex rel.* Richard JL Roberts, Barrister, Lamb Building, Temple,
London] . . . .   *Digested,* 01/**1589**
Beale v. Baland (Unreported, July 25, 2000), CC (Haywards Heath) [*Ex rel.* Timothy
Petts, Barrister, 12 Kings Bench Walk, London] . . . .   *Digested,* 01/**3830**
Beales (CICB: Quantum: 1997), Re (Unreported, November 3, 1997), CICB (London) [*Ex
rel.* Frank R. Moat, Barrister, 3 Pump Court, Temple, London] . . . .   *Digested,* 98/**1495**
Beaman v. ARTS [1949] 1 K.B. 550; [1949] 1 All E.R. 465; 65 T.L.R. 389; 93 S.J.
236, CA; reversing [1948] 2 All E.R. 89; 64 T.L.R. 285; [1948] W.N. 224, KBD .   *Digested,* 47-51/**9952**:
Applied, 58/1876, 58/1887, 58/3230, 65/2280: *Approved,* 71/6818:
Considered, 69/2098, 85/160, 01/3726
Bean v. Cowling Swift & Kitchin see Estill v. Cowling Swift & Kitchin
Beard v. Secretary of State for Social Security (C328/91) see Secretary of State for
Social Security v. Thomas (C328/91)
Beard v. United Kingdom (24882/94) (2001) 33 E.H.R.R. 19, ECHR . . . .   *Joined proceedings,*
01/4744
Bearman (A Bankrupt), Re see Saunders (A Bankrupt), Re
Beasley v. Buckinghamshire CC [1997] P.I.Q.R. P473, QBD . . . .   *Digested,* 98/**3941**
Beasley (Listing Officer) v. National Council of YMCAs [2000] R.A. 429, QBD
Beatham v. Carlisle Hospitals NHS Trust, *Times,* May 20, 1999, QBD . . . .   *Digested,* 99/**1419**

Beattie v. British Steel Plc (Unreported, March 6, 1997), CA . . . .   *Applied*, 99/464:
   Considered, 97/656
Beauchamp Estates v. Dantata see John D Wood & Co v. Dantata
Beaufont v. DPP [1998] R.T.R. 175, QBD
Beaufort Developments (NI) Ltd v. Gilbert-Ash (NI) Ltd [1999] 1 A.C. 266; [1998] 2
   W.L.R. 860; [1998] 2 All E.R. 778; [1998] N.I. 144; [1998] C.L.C. 830; 88
   B.L.R. 1; 59 Con. L.R. 66; (1998) 14 Const. L.J. 280; [1998] E.G.C.S. 85; (1998)
   95(24) L.S.G. 33; (1998) 95(31) L.S.G. 34; (1998) 148 N.L.J. 869; (1998)
   142 S.J.L.B. 172; [1998] N.P.C. 91; [1998] N.P.C. 93; *Times*, June 8, 1998, HL
   (NI); reversing [1997] N.I. 142; 83 B.L.R. 1; (1997) 13 Const. L.J. 321, CA (NI) . .   *Digested*, 98/**5055**:
   Applied, 00/815, 00/820: *Followed*, 99/792, 00/237
Beaulande v. Directeur des Services Fiscaux de Nantes (C208/91) [1996] S.T.C. 1111;
   [1992] E.C.R. I-6709; [1993] 1 C.M.L.R. 765, ECJ (4th Chamber) . . . .   *Digested*, 93/**4407**:
   Applied, 01/5276: *Followed*, 98/4944
Beaumartin v. France (A/296-B) (1995) 19 E.H.R.R. 485, ECHR . . . .   *Considered*, 98/3151
Beaumont v. Road-Night (Unreported, December 11, 2000), CC (Chichester) [*Ex rel.*
   George Ide Phillips, Solicitors, Lion House, 79 St Pancras, Chichester, West
   Sussex] . . . .   *Digested*, 01/**1540**
Beautimatic International Ltd v. Mitchell International Pharmaceuticals Ltd [1999]
   E.T.M.R. 912; [2000] F.S.R. 267; (1999) 22(10) I.P.D. 22100; *Times*, July 8,
   1999, Ch D . . . .   *Digested*, 99/**3559**
BEAUTY FREE SHOP Trade Mark [1999] E.T.M.R. 20, OHIM (Opposition Div) . . . .   *Digested*, 99/**3578**
Bechal v. Kitsford Holdings Ltd [1989] 1 W.L.R. 105; [1988] 3 All E.R. 985; [1989] 10
   E.G. 105; (1989) 86(14) L.S.G. 45; (1989) 133 S.J. 152, Ch D . . . .   *Digested*, 89/**477**:
   Considered, 98/4372
Beck v. Tropical Worldwide Holidays Ltd (Unreported, August 19, 1999), CC
   (Peterborough) [*Ex rel.* Winters Solicitors, 70A High Street, Huntingdon,
   Cambridgeshire] . . . .   *Digested*, 99/**1384**
Beck Foods Ltd, Re see Rees v. Boston BC
Beck Foods Ltd v. Boston Tax see Rees v. Boston BC
Beckenham UDC v. Wood (1896) 60 J.P. 490 . . . .   *Followed*, 00/2296
Becker v. Finanzamt Munster-Innenstadt (C8/81) [1982] E.C.R. 53; [1982] 1 C.M.L.R.
   499, ECJ . . . .   *Digested*, 82/**1333**:
   Applied, 89/1681, 91/3640, 98/2111, 99/4984, 00/5321: *Cited*, 00/5317
Becker Properties Ltd v. Garden Court NW8 Property Co Ltd [1998] 1 E.G.L.R. 121;
   [1998] 12 E.G. 135, Lands Tr. . . . .   *Digested*, 98/**3638**
Beckett v. United Kingdom see Lustig-Prean v. United Kingdom (No.1)
Beckett v. United Kingdom see Smith v. United Kingdom (No.1)
Beckford v. Queen, The [1988] A.C. 130; [1987] 3 W.L.R. 611; [1987] 3 All E.R. 425;
   (1987) 85 Cr. App. R. 378; [1988] Crim. L.R. 116; (1987) 84 L.S.G. 2192; (1987)
   137 N.L.J. 591; (1987) 131 S.J. 1122, PC (Jam) . . . .   *Digested*, 87/**825**:
   Applied, 94/1075, 96/1618, 00/1002: *Distinguished*, 90/1026, 91/867
Beckham v. Drake (1849) 2 H.L. Cas. 579; (1841) 9 M. & W. 79, HL . . . .   *Applied*, 47-51/26,
   47-51/102: *Considered*, 98/3285, 01/3732
Beckman v. Dynamco Whicheloe Macfarlane Ltd see Beckmann v. Dynamco
   Whicheloe Macfarlane Ltd
Beckman v. Inland Revenue Commissioners [2000] S.T.C. (S.C.D.) 59; [2000] S.T.I.
   162, Sp Comm . . . .   *Digested*, 00/**5024**
Beckmann v. Dynamco Whicheloe Macfarlane Ltd; *sub nom* Beckman v. Dynamco
   Whicheloe Macfarlane Ltd [2000] O.P.L.R. 245; [2000] Pens. L.R. 269, QBD. .   *Digested*, 00/**4404**
Becu (C22/98), Re see Criminal Proceedings against Becu (C22/98), Re
Becvar v. Jarvis Norfolk Hotel Ltd (Unreported, June 12, 1999), CC (Brighton) [*Ex rel.*
   Bunkers Solicitors, 7 The Drive, Hove, East Sussex] . . . .   *Digested*, 99/**833**
Beddoe, Re; *sub nom* Downes v. Cottam [1893] 1 Ch. 547, CA . . . .   *Considered*, 93/3322,
   94/2101, 94/2102, 95/2213: *Followed*, 75/2602, 98/484:
   Referred to, 77/2496, 78/1415
Bedford (A Minor) v. Dyson (Unreported, April 27, 1998), CC (Wandsworth) [*Ex rel.*
   T.D. Livingstone, Barrister, New Court, London] . . . .   *Digested*, 98/**1498**
Bedford BC v. De Montfort University (2001) 16 P.A.D. 88, Planning Inspector
Bedfordshire CC v. Fitzpatrick Contractors Ltd 62 Con. L.R. 64, QBD (T&CC) . . . .   *Digested*, 99/**838**
Bedfordshire CC v. Fitzpatrick Contractors Ltd (Interim Payment) [2001] B.L.R. 226;
   [2001] B.L.G.R. 397, QBD (T&CC)
Bedfordshire CC v. Redland Aggregates Ltd (1998) 13 P.A.D. 492, Planning Inspector
Beecham Group Plc v. Munro Wholesale Medical Supplies Ltd [2001] E.T.M.R. 29;
   2001 G.W.D. 1-67, OH . . . .   *Digested*, 01/**6728**
BEECHAM/Benzopyrans (T309/91) [1998] E.P.O.R. 11, EPO (Technical Bd App)
BEECHAM/Bioisosterism (T643/96) [1998] E.P.O.R. 18, EPO (Technical Bd App)
BEECHAM/Pharmaceutical composition (T69/94) [2000] E.P.O.R. 179, EPO (Technical
   Bd App) . . . .   *Digested*, 00/**3644**
Beechinor, Re see NHS Pensions Agency v. Pensions Ombudsman
Beedell v. West Ferry Printers Ltd [2001] EWCA Civ 400; [2001] C.P. Rep. 83; [2001]
   I.C.R. 962; *Times*, April 5, 2001, CA; affirming [2000] I.C.R. 1263; [2000]
   I.R.L.R. 650, EAT . . . .   *Digested*, 01/**427**

Beeforth v. Beeforth, *Times*, September 17, 1998, CA . . . . *Digested*, 98/**339**:
                                             Applied, 00/592: *Considered*, 99/569
Beegas Nominees Ltd v. BHP Petroleum Ltd; Beegas Nominees Ltd v. Sevington
   Properties Ltd; Sevington Properties Ltd v. Adams (1999) 77 P. & C.R. 14;
   [1998] L. & T.R. 190; [1998] 2 E.G.L.R. 57; [1998] 31 E.G. 96; [1998] E.G.C.S.
   60; [1998] N.P.C. 59, CA; affirming in partCH.1996-B-4162, Ch D . . . . *Digested*, 98/**3615**
Beegas Nominees Ltd v. Sevington Properties Ltd see Beegas Nominees Ltd v. BHP
   Petroleum Ltd
Beer v. Davies [1958] 2 Q.B. 187; [1958] 2 W.L.R. 920; [1958] 2 All E.R. 255; (1958)
   42 Cr. App. R. 198; 122 J.P. 344; 56 L.G.R. 261; 102 S.J. 383, DC . . . . *Digested*, 58/**2976**:
                                Considered, 70/2570: *Distinguished*, 59/2887, 66/11845, 99/3667:
                                                   Followed, 61/7797, 61/11196
Beer v. Germany (28934/95) (2001) 33 E.H.R.R. 3, ECHR . . . . *Digested*, 01/**3530**
Beer v. Higham see Higham (A Bankrupt), Re
Begley's Application, Re [1996] N.I. 1, QBD (NI)
Beguelin Import Co v. Import Export SA GL (C22/71) [1971] E.C.R. 949; [1972]
   C.M.L.R. 81, ECJ. . . . . *Digested*, 72/**1416**:
                                          Applied, 98/719
Begum v. Entry Clearance Officer (Dhaka) [2001] I.N.L.R. 115, CA . . . . *Digested*, 01/**3669**
Begum (Nipa) v. Tower Hamlets LBC; *sub nom* Tower Hamlets LBC v. Begum (Nipa)
   [2000] 1 W.L.R. 306; (2000) 32 H.L.R. 445; [2000] C.O.D. 31; (1999) 96(44)
   L.S.G. 41; (1999) 143 S.J.L.B. 277; [1999] N.P.C. 131; *Times*, November 9, 1999
   ; *Independent*, December 20, 1999 (C.S.), CA. . . . . *Digested*, 99/**3051**
Begum v. Ullah (Unreported, August 27, 1998), CC (Central London) [*Ex rel.* Andrew
   Ritchie, Barrister, 9 Gough Square, London] . . . . *Digested*, 98/**590**
Behluli v. Secretary of State for the Home Department see R. v. Secretary of State for
   the Home Department Ex p. Behluli
Beiersdorf AG's Community Trade Mark [2001] E.T.M.R. 19, OHIM (Cancellation Div) . . *Digested*, 01/**3991**
Beis v. Greece (1998) 25 E.H.R.R. 335, ECHR . . . . *Digested*, 98/**3077**
Bekol BV v. Terracina Shipping Corp (Unreported, July 13, 1988), HC . . . . *Approved*, 97/4499,
                                                                       98/4405
Beldis, The; *sub nom* Anglo-Soviet Shipping Co Ltd v. Beldis, The [1936] P. 51; (1935)
   53 Ll. L. Rep. 255, CA. . . . . *Applied*, 99/243
Beldjoudi v. France (A/234-A) (1992) 14 E.H.R.R. 801; *Times*, April 10, 1992, ECHR . . . *Digested*, 93/**2148**:
                                          Applied, 98/3152
Belfast Corp v. Goldring [1954] N.I. 107 . . . . *Applied*, 00/5658
Belfast Telegraph Newspapers Ltd's Application for Judicial Review, Re [2001] N.I.178, CA
   (NI) . . . . *Digested*, 01/**5652**
Belfast West Power Ltd v. Belfast Commissioners [1998] N.I. 347, CA (NI); affirming
   [1998] N.I. 112, Ch D (NI) . . . . *Digested*, 99/**5409**
Belgacom v. Benelux Trade Mark Office [2000] E.T.M.R. 286, App (Brussels)
Belgacom Skynet NV v. IFPI Belgium VZW see IFPI Belgium VZW v. Belgacom Skynet
   NV
Belgian Linguistic Case (No.1) (A/5) (1979-80) 1 E.H.R.R. 241, ECHR . . . . *Digested*, 81/**1087**:
                                          Applied, 01/4582
Belgian Linguistic Case (No.2) (A/6) (1979-80) 1 E.H.R.R. 252, ECHR . . . . *Digested*, 81/**1088**:
                                    Applied, 01/5745: *Considered*, 01/1899
Belgium v. Banque Indosuez (C177/96); Belgium v. European Community [1997]
   E.C.R. I-5659; [1998] 1 C.M.L.R. 653, ECJ
Belgium v. Commission of the European Communities (C75/97) [1999] E.C.R. I-3671;
   [2000] 1 C.M.L.R. 791, ECJ (6th Chamber) . . . . *Digested*, 00/**731**
Belgium v. Commission of the European Communities (C9/95) [1997] E.C.R. I-645;
   [1997] 3 C.M.L.R. 511, ECJ . . . . *Followed*, 00/2349
Belgium v. European Community see Belgium v. Banque Indosuez (C177/96)
Belgium v. Ghent Coal Terminal NV (C37/95) [1998] All E.R. (EC) 223; [1998] S.T.C.
   260; [1998] E.C.R. I-1; [1998] 1 C.M.L.R. 950; [1998] C.E.C. 137; [1998] B.T.C.
   5121; [1998] B.V.C. 139; *Times*, February 4, 1998, ECJ (2nd Chamber) . . . . *Digested*, 98/**4918**:
                                          Applied, 01/5577
Belgium v. Postlethwaite; *sub nom* R. v. Governor of Ashford Remand Centre Ex p.
   Postlethwaite; Postlethwaite, Re [1988] A.C. 924; [1987] 3 W.L.R. 365; [1987]
   2 All E.R. 985; (1987) 84 L.S.G. 2449; (1987) 137 N.L.J. 666; (1987) 131 S.J.
   1038, HL. . . . . *Digested*, 87/**1703**:
                                       Considered, 01/5783: *Followed*, 97/2439
Belgium v. Spain (C388/95) [2000] E.C.R. I-3123; [2000] E.T.M.R. 999, ECJ. . . . . *Digested*, 01/**2490**
Belgocodex SA v. Belgium (C381/97) [2000] S.T.C. 351; [1998] E.C.R. I-8153; [2001]
   1 C.M.L.R. 11; [2000] B.T.C. 5168; [2000] B.V.C. 211, ECJ (5th Chamber) . . . . . *Digested*, 00/**5305**
Belgolaise SA v. Rupchandani [1999] Lloyd's Rep. Bank. 116; (1998) 95(37) L.S.G. 36;
   (1998) 142 S.J.L.B. 252; *Times*, July 30, 1998, QBD (Comm Ct) . . . . *Digested*, 98/**14**
Belgrave International SA v. Nomura International Plc [2000] C.P. Rep. 5, QBD (Comm
   Ct) . . . . *Digested*, 00/**505**
Belgravia Property Co Ltd v. S&R (London) Ltd [2001] C.L.C. 1626; [2001] B.L.R.
   424, QBD (T&CC)
Bell (A Bankrupt), Re [1998] B.P.I.R. 26, Sup Ct (BC) . . . . *Digested*, 98/**3272**
Bell v. A Kings (Loft Extensions) Ltd see Bell v. Galynski

Bell v. DPP of Jamaica [1985] A.C. 937; [1985] 3 W.L.R. 73; [1985] 2 All E.R. 585; [1985] Crim. L.R. 738; (1985) 82 L.S.G. 2161; (1985) 129 S.J. 448, PC (Jam) . . . . . *Digested,* 85/**181**: *Applied,* 94/491, 01/1152: *Considered,* 91/604, 91/756, 91/761.a, 92/2353, 99/1037

Bell v. Dungannon Meats Ltd [1996] N.I. 603, QBD (NI)

Bell v. Galynski; Bell v. A Kings (Loft Extensions) Ltd [1974] 2 Lloyd's Rep. 13, CA . . . . *Digested,* 74/**819**: *Considered,* 98/4033

Bell v. General Accident Fire & Life Assurance Corp Ltd [1998] L. & T.R. 1; [1998] 1 E.G.L.R. 69; [1998] 17 E.G. 144; [1997] E.G.C.S. 174; [1997] N.P.C. 174, CA . . . *Digested,* 98/**3612**

Bell v. Lever Bros Ltd; *sub nom* Lever Bros Ltd v. Bell [1932] A.C. 161, HL; reversing [1931] 1 K.B. 557, CA . . . . *Applied,* 47-51/1785, 47-51/1786, 47-51/4202, 47-51/9247, 47-51/9254, 53/3290, 57/596, 80/592, 83/430, 88/449, 89/430, 91/408, 91/425: *Considered,* 47-51/4201, 47-51/8914, 68/3999, 69/1819, 99/2111: *Distinguished,* 66/1854, 68/2240, 83/1254

Bell v. Peter Browne & Co [1990] 2 Q.B. 495; [1990] 3 W.L.R. 510; [1990] 3 All E.R. 124; (1990) 140 N.L.J. 701, CA . . . . *Digested,* 91/**2343**: *Considered,* 93/2997, 94/2912, 00/2621

Bell v. Rycroft (Valuation Officer) [2000] R.A. 103, Lands Tr . . . . *Digested,* 00/**4603**

Bell v. Secretary of State for Defence [1986] Q.B. 322; [1986] 2 W.L.R. 248; [1985] 3 All E.R. 661; (1986) 83 L.S.G. 206; (1985) 135 N.L.J. 847, CA . . . . *Digested,* 86/**952**: *Applied,* 99/261: *Overruled,* 87/2569

Bell Atlantic Corp v. Bell Atlantic Communications Plc [1998-99] Info. T.L.R. 110, Ch D . . . . *Digested,* 99/**3556**

Bell's Application for Judicial Review, Re [2000] N.I. 245, QBD (NI). . . . . *Digested,* 00/**5396**

Bellefield Computer Services Ltd v. E Turner & Sons Ltd; Unigate (UK) Ltd v. E Turner & Sons Ltd [2000] B.L.R. 97; (2000) 2 T.C.L.R. 759; [2000] N.P.C. 9, CA; affirming [1999] N.P.C. 104, QBD. . . . . *Digested,* 00/**4227**

Bellet v. France (Unreported, December 4, 1995), ECHR. *Considered,* 00/3212

Bellinger v. Bellinger (Validity of Marriage: Transsexual) [2001] EWCA Civ 1140; [2001] 2 F.L.R. 1048; [2001] 3 F.C.R. 1; [2001] Fam. Law 807; (2001) 98(33) L.S.G. 30; (2001) 145 S.J.L.B. 207; *Times,* August 15, 2001, CA; affirming [2001] 1 F.L.R. 389; (2001) 58 B.M.L.R. 52; [2001] Fam. Law 107; *Times,* November 22, 2000; *Independent,* December 18, 2000 (C.S), Fam Div . . . . *Digested,* 01/**2652**

Bellintani v. European Atomic Energy Community (C65/74) see Porrini v. European Atomic Energy Community (C65/74)

Bellmex International (In Liquidation) v. British American Tobacco see Bellmex International Ltd (In Liquidation), Re

Bellmex International Ltd (In Liquidation), Re; *sub nom* Bellmex International (In Liquidation) v. British American Tobacco [2001] B.C.C. 253; [2001] 1 B.C.L.C. 91; (2000) 97(12) L.S.G. 42; (2000) 144 S.J.L.B. 133; *Times,* March 31, 2000, Ch D . . . . *Digested,* 00/**3469**

Bello v. Oakins [2000] R.V.R. 207, Lands Tr . . . . *Digested,* 00/**3898**

Bello v. Secretary of State for the Environment see Wendy Fair Markets Ltd v. Secretary of State for the Environment

Bellone v. Yokohama SpA (C215/97) [1998] E.C.R. I-2191; [1998] 3 C.M.L.R. 975, ECJ (1st Chamber) . . . . *Applied,* 00/116

Bellow Properties Ltd v. Trinity College Cambridge [2001] EWCA Civ 1386, CA; reversing [2000] E.G.C.S. 97, Ch D

Belmont Finance Corp v. Williams Furniture (No.2) [1980] 1 All E.R. 393, CA . . . . *Digested,* 80/**279**: *Applied,* 85/306: *Considered,* 00/2315

Belmont Olympic SA's Trade Mark Application [2000] E.T.M.R. 919, OHIM (Opposition Div) . . . . *Digested,* 01/**4054**

Belmont Riding Centre v. Secretary of State for the Environment, Transport and the Regions [2001] P.L.C.R. 12; [2001] J.P.L. 734 (Note); (2000) 97(41) L.S.G. 41, QBD (Admin Ct) . . . . *Digested,* 01/**4730**

Beloit Technologies Inc v. Valmet Paper Machinery Inc (No.2) [1997] R.P.C. 489; (1997) 20(6) I.P.D. 20051, CA; affirming [1995] R.P.C. 705; *Times,* May 12, 1995, Pat Ct . . . . *Digested,* 97/**3901**: *Applied,* 00/3639: *Referred to,* 98/3453, 00/3679

Beloit Technologies Inc's European Patent (T99/96) (1999) 22(1) I.P.D. 22005, EPO (Technical Bd App)

Belshaw v. Bush (1851) 11 C.B. 191 . . . . *Applied,* 99/2059

Belster Properties Ltd v. Secretary of State for the Environment, Transport and the Regions (1998) 95(23) L.S.G. 28, QBD

Belvedere Alberghiera Srl v. Italy [2000] R.V.R. 303, ECHR. . . . . *Digested,* 01/**4860**

Belvue (11834a) Unreported, IAT . . . . *Distinguished,* 00/3322

Belziuk v. Poland (2000) 30 E.H.R.R. 614; [1998] H.R.C.D. 362, ECHR . . . . *Digested,* 01/**3509**

Bem Dis A Turk Ticaret S/A TR v. International Agri Trade Co Ltd (The Selda) [1999] 1 All E.R. (Comm.) 619; [1999] 1 Lloyd's Rep. 729; [1999] C.L.C. 813, CA; affirming [1998] 1 Lloyd's Rep. 416; *Times,* December 13, 1997, QBD (Comm Ct) . . . . . . *Digested,* 99/**3618**

Ben Nevis v. Inland Revenue Commissioners (SC-281); *sub nom* X v. Inland Revenue Commissioners (SC-281) [2001] S.T.C. (S.C.D.) 144; [2001] S.T.I. 1108, Sp Comm

BEN-GIATH/EPO Communications (J32/97) [1999] E.P.O.R. 116, EPO (Legal Bd App)

BENAS DE BRIGANTE/Filing date (J15/98) [2001] E.P.O.R. 51, EPO (Legal Bd App) . . *Digested*, 01/**3891**
Bence Graphics International Ltd *v.* Fasson UK Ltd [1998] Q.B. 87; [1997] 3 W.L.R.
205; [1997] 1 All E.R. 979; [1997] C.L.C. 373; (1996) 93(40) L.S.G. 24; (1996)
146 N.L.J. 1577; (1996) 140 S.J.L.B. 227; *Times*, October 24, 1996, CA . . . . *Digested*, 96/**1196**:
Distinguished, 01/965
Benckiser Italia *v.* Henkel SpA see Benckiser NV *v.* Henkel SpA
Benckiser NV *v.* Henkel SpA; Benckiser Italia *v.* Henkel SpA [1999] E.T.M.R. 614, Trib
(Napoli)
BEND RESEARCH/Pest control (T691/91) [1998] E.P.O.R. 408, EPO (Technical Bd App)
Bendenoun *v.* France (A/284) (1994) 18 E.H.R.R. 54, ECHR . . . . *Digested*, 94/**2397**:
Applied, 98/3144, 99/3141
Benefoot UK Ltd *v.* Customs and Excise Commissioners [2001] S.T.I. 768, V&DTr
Benetton Sportsystem SpA's Application To Oppose [1999] E.T.M.R. 563, OHIM (2nd Bd
App) . . . . *Digested*, 00/**3738**
Benfield Greig Group Plc, Re see Nugent *v.* Benfield Greig Group Plc
Benford Ltd *v.* Cameron Equipment Ltd [1997] Eu. L.R. 334, HC . . . . *Digested*, 98/**718**
Benham *v.* United Kingdom (19380/92) (1996) 22 E.H.R.R. 293; *Times*, June 24,
1996; *Independent*, June 19, 1996, ECHR . . . . *Digested*, 96/**3155**:
Applied, 97/2765: *Cited*, 96/16: *Followed*, 00/3221
Benham's Will Trusts, Re [1995] S.T.C. 210; [1995] S.T.I. 186, Ch D . . . . *Not followed*, 99/4741
Beni-Felkai Mining Co Ltd, Re [1934] Ch. 406, Ch D *Applied*, 00/3467
Benincasa *v.* Dentalkit Srl (C269/95) [1998] All E.R. (EC) 135; [1997] E.C.R. I-3767;
[1997] E.T.M.R. 447; [1997] I.L.Pr. 559; *Times*, October 13, 1997, ECJ (6th
Chamber) . . . . *Digested*, 97/**888**:
Considered, 01/3838: *Distinguished*, 01/816
Benjamin (Valuation Officer) *v.* Anston Properties Ltd [1998] 2 E.G.L.R. 147; [1998] 19
E.G. 163; [1998] R.A. 53, Lands Tr . . . . *Digested*, 98/**4316**:
Distinguished, 00/6661
Benjamin *v.* Minister of Information and Broadcasting [2001] UKPC 8; [2001] 1 W.L.R.
1040; 10 B.H.R.C. 237; (2001) 145 S.J.L.B. 93, PC (Ang) . . . . *Digested*, 01/**838**
Benkessiouer *v.* France (26106/95) (2001) 33 E.H.R.R. 55; [1998] H.R.C.D. 814,
ECHR
Benmax *v.* Austin Motor Co Ltd [1955] A.C. 370; [1955] 2 W.L.R. 418; [1955] 1 All
E.R. 326; (1955) 72 R.P.C. 39; 99 S.J. 129, HL; affirming (1953) 70 R.P.C. 284,
CA; reversing (1953) 70 R.P.C. 143, Ch D . . . . *Digested*, 55/**2078**:
Applied, 73/2505, 77/1392, 85/1089, 93/2508, 94/2730, 00/660:
Approved, 66/8132: *Considered*, 59/77, 59/3917, 60/1958, 60/2603,
61/2987, 74/2785, 94/3439
Bennet *v.* Notley (Unreported, March 4, 1999), CC (Doncaster) [*Ex rel.* Ian Groom,
Barrister, Paradise Square Chambers, 26 Paradise Square, Sheffield] . . . . *Digested*, 99/**1575**
Bennett, Re see Harrington *v.* Bennett
Bennett *v.* Brinks Ltd (Unreported, July 23, 1999), CC (Leeds) [*Ex rel.* Horwich
Farrelly Solicitors, National House, 36 St Anne Street, Manchester] . . . . *Digested*, 99/**1378**
Bennett *v.* Commissioner of Police of the Metropolis (1998) 10 Admin. L.R. 245;
(1998) 162 J.P.N. 402; *Times*, October 24, 1997; *Independent*, October 20, 1997
(C.S.), Ch D . . . . *Digested*, 97/**4866**
Bennett *v.* Customs and Excise Commissioners (No.1) [1999] S.T.C. 248; [1999] B.T.C.
5109; [1999] B.V.C. 143, QBD; reversing [1997] V. & D.R. 155, V&DTr . . . . *Digested*, 99/**5005**
Bennett *v.* Customs and Excise Commissioners (No.2) [2001] S.T.C. 137; [2001]
H.R.L.R. 10; [2001] B.T.C. 5067; [2001] B.V.C. 124; [2001] S.T.I. 100; (2001)
98(13) L.S.G. 41; *Times*, February 27, 2001, Ch D; affirming [2000] B.V.C. 2334;
[2000] S.T.I. 1094, V&DTr . . . . *Digested*, 01/**5546**
Bennett *v.* Filmer [1998] B.P.I.R. 444, Ch D *Digested*, 99/**3326**
Bennett *v.* Greenland Houchen & Co [1998] P.N.L.R. 458, CA . . . . *Digested*, 98/**541**
Bennett *v.* Hewitt (Unreported, April 13, 2000), CC (Luton) [*Ex rel.* David Allen,
Barrister, 9 Bedford Row, London] . . . . *Digested*, 00/**1731**
Bennett (Paul James) *v.* HM Advocate 1995 S.L.T. 510; 1994 S.C.C.R. 902, HCJ
Appeal . . . . *Digested*, 95/**5744**:
Considered, 98/2353
Bennett *v.* Markham [1982] 1 W.L.R. 1230; [1982] 3 All E.R. 641; 81 L.G.R. 60; (1983)
2 Tr. L.R. 1; (1982) 79 L.S.G. 1176; 126 S.J. 511, DC . . . . *Digested*, 82/**3381**:
Distinguished, 98/841
Bennett Construction (UK) Ltd *v.* Baylis (Gloucester) Ltd see Secretary of State for the
Environment, Transport and the Regions *v.* Baylis (Gloucester) Ltd
Bennett Properties *v.* H&S Engineering (Unreported, October 14, 1998), QBD (Comm
Ct) [*Ex rel.* Jeffrey Terry, Barrister, 8 King Street, Manchester] . . . . *Digested*, 98/**3683**
Bensaid *v.* Secretary of State for the Home Department see R. *v.* Immigration Officer
Ex p. Bensaid
Bensaid *v.* United Kingdom (44599/98) (2001) 33 E.H.R.R. 10; 11 B.H.R.C. 297;
[2001] I.N.L.R. 325, ECHR
Benson *v.* Cummings (Unreported, July 22, 1999), CC (Plymouth) [*Ex rel.* Peter
Telford, Barrister, Devon Chambers, 3 St Andrews Street, Plymouth] . . . . *Digested*, 99/**2476**
Benson *v.* Northern Ireland Transport Board [1942] A.C. 520, HL . . . . *Cited*, 00/1022:
Considered, 89/3021, 90/3548

Bensusan v. Airtours Holidays Ltd (Unreported, January 25, 2001), CC (Brentford)
    [*Ex rel.* Sarah Tozzi, Barrister, Farrar's Building, Temple, London] . . . .   *Digested*, 01/**4277**
Bent v. High Cliff Developments Ltd (1999) 96(32) L.S.G. 35; (1999) 96(34) L.S.G.
    35, Ch D
Bentinck v. Associated Newspapers Ltd [1999] E.M.L.R. 556, QBD. . . . .   *Digested*, 99/**1627**
Bentinck Ltd v. Cromwell Engineering Co [1971] 1 Q.B. 324; [1970] 3 W.L.R. 1113;
    [1971] 1 All E.R. 33; [1971] R.T.R. 7; 114 S.J. 823, CA. . . . .   *Digested*, 71/**5304**:
                                                   Distinguished, 98/2515
Bentley Engineering Co v. Mistry [1979] I.C.R. 47; [1978] I.R.L.R. 437, EAT . . . .   *Digested*, 79/**990**:
                   Applied, 90/1975: *Considered*, 99/2138
Bentleys Estate Agents v. Granix [1989] 27 E.G. 93 . . . .   *Digested*, 89/**53**:
                                                   Considered, 01/112
Benzine en Petroleum Handelsmaatschappij BV v. Commission of the European
    Communities (C77/77) [1978] E.C.R. 1513; [1978] 3 C.M.L.R. 174; [1978] F.S.R.
    629, ECJ . . . .   *Digested*, 78/**1345**:
                                                 Distinguished, 00/713
Beresford (Harold), Re (1952) 36 Cr. App. R. 1, Assizes (Derby). . . . .   *Digested*, 52/**671**:
                               Approved, 99/1058: *Explained*, 54/2922
Berezovsky v. Forbes Inc (No.1); *sub nom* Berezovsky v. Michaels; Glouchkov v.
    Michaels; Glouchkov v. Forbes Inc [2000] 1 W.L.R. 1004; [2000] 2 All E.R. 986;
    [2001] I.L.Pr. 21; [2000] E.M.L.R. 643; (2000) 97(22) L.S.G. 44; (2000) 150
    N.L.J. 741; *Times*, May 16, 2000; *Independent*, May 18, 2000, HL; affirming
    [1999] I.L.Pr. 358; [1999] E.M.L.R. 278; *Times*, November 27, 1998, CA;
    reversing *Times*, January 19, 1998, QBD . . . .   *Digested*, 00/**769**:
                       Applied, 01/1825: *Distinguished*, 99/750
Berezovsky v. Forbes Inc (No.2) [2001] EWCA Civ 1251; [2001] E.M.L.R. 45, CA . . . .   *Digested*, 01/**1824**
Berezovsky v. Michaels see Berezovsky v. Forbes Inc (No.1)
Berg v. Loftus Road Plc (Unreported, February 1, 2001), CC (Central London) [*Ex rel.*
    Nigel Ffitch, Barrister, Phoenix Chambers, Gray's Inn, London] . . . .   *Digested*, 01/**1519**
Bergen, The (No.1) [1997] 1 Lloyd's Rep. 380; [1997] C.L.C. 444, QBD (Adm Ct). . . . .   *Digested*, 97/**4490**
Bergen, The (No.2) [1997] 2 Lloyd's Rep. 710, QBD (Adm Ct) . . . .   *Digested*, 98/**4398**
Bergens Tidende v. Norway (26132/95) (2001) 31 E.H.R.R. 16, ECHR . . . .   *Digested*, 01/**3472**
Berhe v. Secretary of State for the Home Department; *sub nom* R. v. Secretary of
    State for the Home Department Ex p. Berhe [2000] Imm. A.R. 463; *Times*, May
    26, 2000, CA . . . .   *Digested*, 00/**3334**
Berisha v. Secretary of State for the Home Department see R. v. Secretary of State for
    the Home Department Ex p. Elshani
Berkeley v. Fulham Football Club see Berkeley v. Secretary of State for the
    Environment, Transport and the Regions (No.2)
Berkeley v. Secretary of State for the Environment, Transport and the Regions (No.1)
    [2001] 2 A.C. 603; [2000] 3 W.L.R. 420; [2000] 3 All E.R. 897; [2001] 2
    C.M.L.R. 38; [2001] Env. L.R. 16; (2001) 81 P. & C.R. 35; [2000] 3 P.L.R. 111;
    [2001] J.P.L. 58; [2000] E.G.C.S. 86; [2000] N.P.C. 77; *Times*, July 7, 2000,
    HL; reversing [1999] 1 C.M.L.R. 945; [1998] Env. L.R. 741; [1998] 3 P.L.R. 39;
    [1998] P.L.C.R. 97; [1998] N.P.C. 18; *Times*, March 2, 1998, CA . . . .   *Digested*, 00/**4460**:
                   Considered, 01/4726: *Distinguished*, 00/4505
Berkeley v. Secretary of State for the Environment, Transport and the Regions (No.2);
    Berkeley v. Fulham Football Club *Times*, April 7, 1998, CA . . . .   *Digested*, 98/**4180**
Berkeley v. Secretary of State for the Environment, Transport and the Regions (No.3)
    [2001] EWCA Civ 1012; [2001] 3 C.M.L.R. 11; (2001) 98(30) L.S.G. 38; [2001]
    N.P.C. 107; *Times*, October 19, 2001; *Daily Telegraph*, July 10, 2001, CA;
    affirming [2001] Env. L.R. 32; [2001] J.P.L. 660, QBD (Admin Ct) . . . .   *Digested*, 01/**4700**
Berkeley Applegate (Investment Consultants) Ltd (No.2), Re (1988) 4 B.C.C. 279, DC .   *Digested*, 88/**363**:
                           Considered, 99/3269: *Referred to*, 97/3073
Berkeley Leisure Group Ltd v. Hampton [2001] EWCA Civ 1474; [2001] 42 E.G.C.S.
    137; [2001] N.P.C. 148, CA
Berkholz v. Finanzampt Hamburg Mitte-Altstadt (C168/84) [1985] E.C.R. 2251;
    [1985] 3 C.M.L.R. 667, ECJ (2nd Chamber) . . . .   *Digested*, 86/**1495**:
                   Applied, 01/5588: *Considered*, 96/5902, 97/5021
Berkoff v. Burchill [1996] 4 All E.R. 1008; [1997] E.M.L.R. 139; *Times*, August 9, 1996;
    Independent, October 4, 1996, CA . . . .   *Digested*, 96/**5681**:
                                              Distinguished, 99/1634
Berkshire and Oxfordshire Magistrates Courts Committee v. Gannon [2000] I.C.R. 1003;
    Times, May 10, 2000, QBD . . . .   *Digested*, 00/**2193**
Berkshire Capital Funding Ltd v. Street (2000) 32 H.L.R. 373; (1999) 78 P. & C.R. 321;
    [1999] 2 E.G.L.R. 92; [1999] 25 E.G. 191; (1999) 78 P. & C.R. D23; *Times*,
    May 27, 1999, CA . . . .   *Digested*, 99/**4381**
Berkshire CC v. Scott see R. v. Metropolitan Stipendiary Magistrate Ex p. London
    Waste Regulation Authority

Berlei (UK) Ltd v. Bali Brassiere Co Inc (No.1); *sub nom* BALI Trade Mark (No.1) [1969]
1 W.L.R. 1306; [1969] 2 All E.R. 812; [1969] F.S.R. 288; [1969] R.P.C. 472;
113 S.J. 720, HL; reversing [1968] F.S.R. 1; [1968] R.P.C. 426, CA; reversing
[1966] F.S.R. 8; [1966] R.P.C. 387, Ch D . . . . *Digested,* 69/**3565**:
Applied, 74/3830, 75/3432, 97/4893, 99/3537, 00/3770:
Considered, 72/3435, 93/3990, 96/5723, 98/3534, 98/3539, 98/3540:
Followed, 95/4946, 97/4899, 00/3774, 00/3786: *Referred to,* 00/3795
Berliner Industriebank AG v. Jost [1971] 2 Q.B. 463; [1971] 3 W.L.R. 61; [1971] 2 All
E.R. 1513; 115 S.J. 505, CA; affirming [1971] 1 Q.B. 278; [1970] 3 W.L.R. 743;
[1971] 2 All E.R. 117; 114 S.J. 492, QBD . . . . *Digested,* 71/**1589**
Berliner Kindl Brauerei AG v. Siepert (C208/98) [2001] All E.R. (EC) 673; [2000]
E.C.R. I-1741, ECJ (5th Chamber) . . . . *Digested,* 01/**2505**
Bermuda Cablevision Ltd v. Colica Trust Co Ltd [1998] A.C. 198; [1998] 2 W.L.R. 82;
[1997] B.C.C. 982; [1998] 1 B.C.L.C. 1; (1997) 141 S.J.L.B. 247; *Times,* October
31, 1997, PC (Ber) . . . . *Digested,* 97/**847**
Bermuda International Securities Ltd v. KPMG [2001] EWCA Civ 269; [2001] C.P. Rep.
73; [2001] C.P.L.R. 252; [2001] Lloyd's Rep. P.N. 392; (2001) 98(15) L.S.G.
33; (2001) 145 S.J.L.B. 70; *Times,* March 14, 2001, CA; affirming A1001/729,
QBD (Comm Ct) . . . . *Digested,* 01/**435**
Bernadone v. Pall Mall Services Group Ltd see Martin v. Lancashire CC
Bernadone v. Pall Mall Services Group Ltd [1999] I.R.L.R. 617; *Times,* August 2, 1999,
QBD . . . . *Digested,* 99/**2129**
Bernard v. Enfield LBC [2001] EWCA Civ 1831; [2001] N.P.C. 178; *Independent,*
December 12, 2001, CA
Bernard v. France (22885/93) (2000) 30 E.H.R.R. 808; [1998] H.R.C.D. 471, ECHR . . *Digested,* 01/**3538**
Bernasconi v. Nicholas Bennett & Co [2000] B.C.C. 921; [2000] B.P.I.R. 8; [2000]
Lloyd's Rep. P.N. 285; [1999] N.P.C. 132, Ch D . . . . *Digested,* 00/**4186**
Bernhard's Rugby Landscapes Ltd v. Stockley Park Consortium Ltd (1998) 14 Const.
L.J. 329, QBD (OR) . . . . *Digested,* 99/**791**
Bernini (MJE) v. Netherlands Ministry of Education and Science (C3/90) [1992]
E.C.R. I-1071, ECJ . . . . *Digested,* 92/**4767**:
Followed, 00/2389
Bernisse, The (No.1); Elve, The [1921] 1 A.C. 458; (1920) 5 Ll. L. Rep. 359, PC (UK); affirming
[1920] P. 1, PDAD . . . . *Considered,* 99/396:
Distinguished, 47-51/7988, 47-51/7993, 47-51/7997
Berridge v. Doncaster MBC [2000] J.P.L. 532; [1999] E.G.C.S. 67; (1999) 96(19)
L.S.G. 29, QBD . . . . *Digested,* 00/**4530**
Berrill (t/a Cobweb Antiques) v. Hill (Valuation Officer) [2000] R.A. 194, Lands Tr . . . . . *Digested,* 00/**4600**:
Considered, 01/4832
Berry v. British Transport Commission [1962] 1 Q.B. 306; [1961] 3 W.L.R. 450; [1961]
3 All E.R. 65; 105 S.J. 587, CA; reversing in part [1961] 1 Q.B. 149; [1960] 3
W.L.R. 666; [1960] 3 All E.R. 322; 104 S.J. 826, QBD . . . . *Digested,* 61/**5397**:
Applied, 01/478
Berry v. Calderdale HA [1998] Lloyd's Rep. Med. 179, CA . . . . *Digested,* 98/**557**
Berry (t/a Automotive Management Services) v. Customs and Excise Commissioners
[2000] S.T.I. 1382, V&DTr
Berry v. Newport BC (2001) 33 H.L.R. 19; [2000] 2 E.G.L.R. 26; [2000] N.P.C. 27,
CA . . . . *Digested,* 01/**3447**
Berry v. Secretary of State for Trade and Industry see Abermeadow Ltd (No.2), Re
Berry v. St Marylebone BC [1958] Ch. 406; [1957] 3 W.L.R. 1029; [1957] 3 All E.R.
677; 122 J.P. 59; 56 L.G.R. 144; 2 R.R.C. 292; 50 R. & I.T. 821; 101 S.J. 973, CA;
affirming [1957] 1 W.L.R. 495; [1957] 1 All E.R. 681; 121 J.P. 250; 55 L.G.R.
173; 1 R.R.C. 325; 50 R. & I.T. 146, Ch D . . . . *Digested,* 57/**2971**:
Applied, 57/2983, 58/2845: *Considered,* 01/3849: *Followed,* 59/2769
Berrycroft Management Co Ltd v. Sinclair Gardens Investments (Kensington) Ltd
(1997) 29 H.L.R. 444; (1998) 75 P. & C.R. 210; [1997] 1 E.G.L.R. 47; [1997] 22
E.G. 141; [1996] E.G.C.S. 143; [1996] N.P.C. 127; *Times,* September 30, 1996,
CA . . . . *Digested,* 97/**3331**
Berryman v. Hounslow LBC (1998) 30 H.L.R. 567; [1997] P.I.Q.R. P83; *Times,*
December 18, 1996, CA . . . . *Digested,* 97/**2726**
Bersey v. Evans (Unreported, February 8, 2001), CC (Aylesbury) [*Ex rel.* Marcus
Grant, Barrister, 1 Temple Gardens, London] . . . . *Digested,* 01/**886**
Bertelsmann AG v. Finanzamt Wiedenbruck (C380/99) [2001] S.T.C. 1153; [2001]
E.C.R. I-5163; [2001] 3 C.M.L.R. 13; [2001] C.E.C. 197; [2001] B.V.C. 403;
[2001] S.T.I. 1013, ECJ (6th Chamber) . . . . *Digested,* 01/**5599**
Berthon Boat Co Ltd v. Hood Sailmakers Ltd [2000] 1 E.G.L.R. 39; [2000] 08 E.G.
175, QBD [*Ex rel.* Mark Loveday, Barrister, Francis Taylor Building, 3rd Floor,
Temple, London] . . . . *Digested,* 99/**3664**
Berto v. Istituto Nazionale della Previdenza Sociale (C95/95) see Bonifaci v. Istituto
Nazionale della Previdenza Sociale (INPS) (C94/95)
Bertucci v. McDonalds Corp [1999] E.T.M.R. 742, Trib Gde Inst (Paris)
Beside BV v. Minister van Volkshuisvesting, Ruimtelijke Ordening en Milieubeheer
(C192/96) [1998] E.C.R. I-4029; [1999] 1 C.M.L.R. 4; [1999] Env. L.R. 328,
ECJ (6th Chamber) . . . . *Digested,* 99/**2196**

Besloten Vennootschaap met Beperkte Aansprakelijkheid Christine Le Duc BV *v.* De Vennootschap Onder Firma Erochique Enschede vof (33299 KG ZA 199 of 1999) [2001] E.C.D.R. 19, RB (NL)

Bessa Plus Plc *v.* Lancaster (1998) 30 H.L.R. 48; [1997] E.G.C.S. 42, CA . . . .   *Digested,* 97/**3252**

Bessant *v.* South Cone Inc see REEF Trade Mark

Bessenden Properties *v.* Corness [1974] I.R.L.R. 338, CA; affirming [1973] I.R.L.R. 365; [1974] I.T.R. 128, NIRC . . . .   *Digested,* 75/**1178**:
Applied, 00/2239: *Explained,* 76/1002

Best *v.* Charter Medical of England Ltd [2001] EWCA Civ 1588; (2001) 98(47) L.S.G. 27; *Times,* November 19, 2001, CA . . . .   *Digested,* 01/**659**

Best of Frank Sinatra/New York, New York (3 U 250/98; ZUM 1999, 853), Re [2001] E.C.D.R. 7, OLG (Hamburg)

Best Travel Ltd *v.* Customs and Excise Commissioners [1999] B.V.C. 2069, V&DTr

Besterman (Deceased), Re; *sub nom* Besterman *v.* Grusin [1984] Ch. 458; [1984] 3 W.L.R. 280; [1984] 2 All E.R. 656; [1984] Fam. Law 203; (1984) 81 L.S.G. 2699; (1984) 128 S.J. 515, CA . . . .   *Digested,* 84/**3671**:
Applied, 84/3670: *Considered,* 85/3646, 94/2160, 98/2469:
Followed, 96/5547

Besterman *v.* Grusin see Besterman (Deceased), Re

Bestley *v.* North West Water Ltd [1998] 1 E.G.L.R. 187, Lands Tr . . . .   *Digested,* 98/**4993**

Bestobell Paints Ltd *v.* Bigg [1975] F.S.R. 421; 119 S.J. 678, Ch D . . . .   *Digested,* 75/**1957**:
Applied, 92/1908, 92/4422, 98/3511: *Considered,* 92/4135, 95/3774:
Followed, 92/4134

Bestrustees *v.* Stuart [2001] Pens. L.R. 283, Ch D

Bestuur van de Nieuwe Algemene Bedrijfsvereniging *v.* Drake (C12/93) [1994] E.C.R. I-4337, ECJ. . . . .   *Digested,* 95/**4590**:
Applied, 97/4703, 98/4519

Bestway (Holdings) Ltd *v.* Luff (Inspector of Taxes) [1998] S.T.C. 357; 70 T.C. 512; [1998] B.T.C. 69; (1998) 95(13) L.S.G. 28; (1998) 142 S.J.L.B. 87; *Times,* March 4, 1998; *Independent,* March 2, 1998 (C.S.), Ch D . . . .   *Digested,* 98/**4599**

Beswick *v.* Beswick [1968] A.C. 58; [1967] 3 W.L.R. 932; [1967] 2 All E.R. 1197; 111 S.J. 540, HL; affirming [1966] Ch. 538; [1966] 3 W.L.R. 396; [1966] 3 All E.R. 1; 110 S.J. 507, CA; reversing [1965] 3 All E.R. 858; (1965) 116 N.L.J. 245, Chancery Ct of Lancaster . . . .   *Digested,* 67/**641**:
Applied, 69/543, 70/375, 77/1382, 85/300, 86/1864, 95/1990:
Considered, 67/643, 67/3478, 68/3160, 69/1456, 70/303, 70/1250, 71/1250,
71/1863, 71/5442, 72/522, 72/523, 74/821, 74/2992, 75/393, 75/2660,
75/3217, 76/2517, 79/341, 99/796: *Distinguished,* 68/963:
Followed, 68/1816, 69/1633

Beta Computers (Europe) Ltd *v.* Adobe Systems (Europe) Ltd 1996 S.L.T. 604; [1996] C.L.C. 821; [1997-98] Info. T.L.R. 73; [1996] F.S.R. 367; [1998] Masons C.L.R. Rep. 104, OH. . . . .   *Digested,* 96/**6703**

Beta Construction Ltd *v.* Channel Four Television Co Ltd [1990] 1 W.L.R. 1042; [1990] 2 All E.R. 1012; (1989) 139 N.L.J. 1561, CA. . . . .   *Digested,* 90/**2918**:
Applied, 00/510

Beth Johnson Housing Association Ltd *v.* Customs and Excise Commissioners [2001] S.T.I. 953, V&DTr

Betriebsrat der Bofrost Josef H Boquoi Deutschland West GmbH & Co KG *v.* Bofrost Josef H Boquoi Deutschland West GmbH & Co KG (C62/99) [2001] E.C.R. I-2579; [2001] I.R.L.R. 403, ECJ (6th Chamber)

Bettati *v.* Safety Hi-Tech Srl (C341/95) [1998] E.C.R. I-4355, ECJ . . . .   *Followed,* 01/2512

Bettison *v.* Langton; *sub nom* Bettison *v.* Penton [2001] UKHL 24; [2001] 2 W.L.R. 1605; [2001] 3 All E.R. 417; (2001) 82 P. & C.R. 37; [2001] 21 E.G.C.S. 166; (2001) 98(26) L.S.G. 44; (2001) 145 S.J.L.B. 141; [2001] N.P.C. 92; *Times,* May 30, 2001, HL; affirming [2000] Ch. 54; [1999] 3 W.L.R. 39; [1999] 2 All E.R. 367; [1999] E.G.C.S. 28; [1999] N.P.C. 20; *Times,* March 11, 1999, CA. . . . .   *Digested,* 01/**4849**

Bettison *v.* Penton see Bettison *v.* Langton

Bettridge *v.* Hoque (Unreported, October 30, 1998), CC (Southampton) [*Ex rel.* Amanda Gillet, Pupil Barrister, College Chambers, 19 Carlton Crescent, Southampton] . . . .   *Digested,* 99/**1579**

Betts *v.* Brintel Helicopters Ltd (t/a British International Helicopters); Betts *v.* KLM ERA Helicopters (UK) Ltd [1997] 2 All E.R. 840; [1998] 2 C.M.L.R. 22; [1997] I.C.R. 792; [1997] I.R.L.R. 361; (1997) 147 N.L.J. 561; *Times,* April 1, 1997, CA; reversing [1996] I.R.L.R. 45, QBD . . . .   *Digested,* 97/**2270**:
Applied, 00/2232: *Distinguished,* 99/2133: *Referred to,* 98/2220

Betts *v.* De Vitre see Neilson *v.* Betts

Betts *v.* KLM ERA Helicopters (UK) Ltd see Betts *v.* Brintel Helicopters Ltd (t/a British International Helicopters)

Betts *v.* Neilson see Neilson *v.* Betts

Betty's Cafes Ltd *v.* Phillips Furnishing Stores Ltd (No.1) [1959] A.C. 20; [1958] 2
W.L.R. 513; [1958] 1 All E.R. 607; 102 S.J. 228, HL; affirming [1957] Ch. 67;
[1956] 3 W.L.R. 1134; [1957] 1 All E.R. 1; 100 S.J. 946, CA; reversing [1956] 1
W.L.R. 678; [1956] 2 All E.R. 497; 100 S.J. 435, Ch D . . . . *Digested,* 58/**1818**:
    Applied, 60/1743, 61/4862, 62/1717, 63/1969, 69/2027, 78/1773, 86/1829,
    87/2124, 90/2772, 91/2209: *Considered,* 67/2242, 68/2190, 87/2129,
    87/2229, 88/2007, 88/2010, 89/2192, 89/2194, 90/120, 90/2829, 91/119,
    00/3904: *Followed,* 57/1945
BETTY'S KITCHEN CORONATION STREET Trade Mark [2000] R.P.C. 825, TMR . . . . . .   *Digested,* 01/**4024**
Bevan *v.* Pannell (Unreported, August 3, 1998), CC (Swindon) [*Ex rel.* David McHugh,
Barrister, Bracton Chambers, 2nd Floor, 95A Chancery Lane, London] . . . .   *Digested,* 98/**1708**
Bevan *v.* South Wales Fire Service (Unreported, January 19, 2000), CC (Cardiff) [*Ex
rel.* Andrew Arentsen, Barrister, 33 Park Place, Cardiff] . . . .   *Digested,* 00/**1745**
Bevan Ashford *v.* Geoff Yeandle (Contractors) Ltd (In Liquidation) [1999] Ch. 239;
[1998] 3 W.L.R. 172; [1998] 3 All E.R. 238; 59 Con. L.R. 1; [1998] 2 Costs L.R.
15; (1998) 95(16) L.S.G. 27; (1998) 148 N.L.J. 587; (1998) 142 S.J.L.B. 151;
[1998] N.P.C. 69; *Times,* April 23, 1998, Ch D . . . .   *Digested,* 98/**3712**
Bevan Investments Ltd *v.* Blackhall & Struthers (No.2) 11 B.L.R. 78; [1978] 2 N.Z.L.R.
97, CA (NZ) . . . .   *Digested,* 80/**188**:
    Distinguished, 00/6597
Beveridge *v.* KLM UK Ltd [2000] I.R.L.R. 765, EAT . . . .   *Digested,* 00/**2197**
Bevington *v.* Doyle (Unreported, February 15, 2000), CC (Milton Keynes) [*Ex rel.*
Amanda Drane, Barrister, 4 King's Bench Walk, 2nd Floor, Temple, London] . . . .   *Digested,* 00/**1706**
Bevis *v.* Tarmey (Unreported, July 19, 1993), CC (Walsall) [*Ex rel.* Michael W Halsall,
Solicitors] . . . .   *Digested,* 94/**3617**:
    Applied, 98/509: *Considered,* 97/542: *Distinguished,* 97/538:
    Followed, 96/2143, 98/424
Bewise Motors Co Ltd *v.* Hoi Kong Container Services Ltd [1998] 4 H.K. Cases 377,
CFA (HK) . . . .   *Applied,* 00/**4678**
Bewleys Ltd *v.* Customs and Excise Commissioners [2000] S.T.I. 271, V&DTr
Bewry *v.* Cumbria CC, *Times,* November 17, 1998, CA . . . .   *Digested,* 98/**2142**
Bexley LBC *v.* Cassin see Cassin *v.* Bexley LBC
Bexley LBC *v.* Secretary of State for the Environment, Transport and the Regions;
Sainsbury's Supermarkets Ltd *v.* Secretary of State for the Environment,
Transport and the Regions [2001] EWHC Admin 323; [2001] J.P.L. 1442 (Note);
[2001] 18 E.G.C.S. 172; (2001) 98(18) L.S.G. 46, QBD (Admin Ct)
Bexley LBC *v.* St James PCC (2000) 15 P.A.D. 435, Planning Inspector
Beyeler *v.* Italy (33202/96) (2001) 33 E.H.R.R. 52, ECHR
Beyers *v.* Secretary of State for the Environment, Transport and the Regions (2001) 82
P. & C.R. 5; [2001] J.P.L. 586, QBD . . . .   *Digested,* 01/**4769**
Beynon *v.* Customs and Excise Commissioners CH 2001/APP/010565, Ch D;
affirming [2001] B.V.C. 2331; [2001] S.T.I. 1323, V&DTr
Beynon *v.* Scadden [1999] I.R.L.R. 700, EAT . . . .   *Digested,* 00/**2148**
Bezicheri *v.* Italy (A/164) (1990) 12 E.H.R.R. 210, ECHR . . . .   *Applied,* 01/**4424**
BFI Holding BV *v.* Municipality of Arnhem (C360/96) see Gemeente Arnhem *v.* BFI
Holding BV (C360/96)
BG Plc *v.* O'Brien; *sub nom* Transco Plc (formerly BG Plc) *v.* O'Brien; A1/2001/1269,
CA; affirming [2001] I.R.L.R. 496; [2001] Emp. L.R. 697, EAT . . . .   *Digested,* 01/**2305**
Bhai *v.* Black Roof Community Housing Association Ltd [2001] 2 All E.R. 865;
(2001) 33 H.L.R. 55; (2000) 97(45) L.S.G. 41; [2000] N.P.C. 117; (2001) 81 P.
& C.R. D22; *Times,* November 14, 2000, CA . . . .   *Digested,* 00/**3907**
Bhanot *v.* South West London and St George's Mental Health NHS Trust [2000]
Lloyd's Rep. Med. 324, QBD . . . .   *Digested,* 01/**2928**:
    Applied, 01/2245: *Doubted,* 01/2892
Bhatt *v.* Chelsea and Westminster Healthcare NHS Trust (Defamation: Qualified
Privilege) 1997-B-17907, QBD . . . .   *Digested,* 98/**1782**
Bhatt *v.* Chelsea and Westminster Healthcare NHS Trust (Unfair Dismissal) A1/97/
1378, CA; affirming [1998] I.C.R. 576; [1997] I.R.L.R. 660; *Times,* October 24,
1997, EAT . . . .   *Digested,* 00/**2244**
Bhatti, Re (Unreported, September 24, 1997), CICB (London) [*Ex rel.* Kate Akerman,
Barrister, Regency Chambers, Peterborough] . . . .   *Digested,* 98/**1538**
Bhatti *v.* Barnet LBC (Unreported, July 23, 1999), CC (Edmonton) [*Ex rel.* AE Wyeth
& Co Solicitors, Bridge House, High Street, Dartford, Kent] . . . .   *Digested,* 99/**2891**
Bhavsar (CICB: Quantum: 2000), Re [2000] 3 Q.R. 6, CICB (Manchester) [*Ex rel.* Philip A
Butler, Barrister, Deans Court Chambers, 24 St John Street, Manchester] . . . . .   *Digested,* 00/**1584**
Bheekhun *v.* Stafford see Bheekhun *v.* Williams
Bheekhun *v.* Williams; Bheekhun *v.* Stafford [1999] 2 F.L.R. 229; [1999] Fam. Law
379, CA . . . .   *Digested,* 99/**4638**
Bhikha *v.* Leicester City Council see R. *v.* Wandsworth LBC Ex p. O
Bhimji *v.* Chatwani (No.2); *sub nom* Chatwani *v.* Bhimji [1992] 1 W.L.R. 1158; [1992]
4 All E.R. 912; [1992] B.C.L.C. 387, Ch D . . . .   *Digested,* 92/**3511**:
    Applied, 01/17
Bhogal *v.* Cheema see Debtor (No.325 of 1997), Re

Bhopal v. Walia (2000) 32 H.L.R. 302; [1999] L. & T.R. 461; [1999] E.G.C.S. 49;
(1999) 96(14) L.S.G. 33, CA . . . .   *Digested*, 00/**3879**
BHP Great Britain Petroleum Ltd v. Chesterfield Properties Ltd see BHP Petroleum Great
Britain Ltd v. Chesterfield Properties Ltd
BHP Petroleum Great Britain Ltd v. Chesterfield Properties Ltd; *sub nom* Chesterfield
Properties Ltd v. BHP Petroleum Great Britain Ltd; BHP Great Britain Petroleum
Ltd v. Chesterfield Properties Ltd [2001] EWCA Civ 1797; [2001] 50 E.G.C.S.
88; [2001] N.P.C. 174; *Independent*, December 6, 2001, CA; reversing in part
[2001] 3 W.L.R. 277; [2001] 2 All E.R. 914; [2001] L. & T.R. 28; [2001] 22 E.G.
155; [2001] 10 E.G.C.S. 158; (2001) 98(15) L.S.G. 32; (2001) 98(10) L.S.G.
46; (2001) 145 S.J.L.B. 76; [2001] N.P.C. 47; (2001) 82 P. & C.R. D11; *Times*,
March 30, 2001, Ch D . . . .   *Digested*, 01/**4173**
BHP Petroleum Ltd v. British Steel Plc [2000] 2 All E.R. (Comm) 133; [2000] 2 Lloyd's
Rep. 277; [2000] C.L.C. 1162; 74 Con. L.R. 63, CA; affirming [1999] 2 All E.R.
(Comm) 544; [1999] 2 Lloyd's Rep. 583, QBD (Comm Ct). . . . .   *Digested*, 00/**895**
Bhudia v. Gulvantessian [2001] 3 Q.R. 14, CC (Willesden) [*Ex rel.* David McIlroy,
Barrister, 3 Paper Buildings, Temple, London] . . . .   *Digested*, 01/**1759**
Bhullar v. McArdle [2001] EWCA Civ 510; (2001) 82 P. & C.R. 38; [2001] N.P.C. 75,
CA; reversing [1999] E.G.C.S. 84, Ch D . . . .   *Digested*, 01/**4846**
Bi v. Doud [2001] 5 Q.R. 11, CC (Rotherham) [*Ex rel.* Jinder S Boora, Barrister, 24
Ropewalk Chambers, Nottingham] . . . .   *Digested*, 01/**1748**
Bibby v. Chief Constable of Essex (2000) 164 J.P. 297; [2000] R.A. 384; (2001) 165
J.P.N. 44; *Times*, April 24, 2000; *Independent*, April 13, 2000, CA . . . .   *Digested*, 00/**950**
Bibby (Inspector of Taxes) v. Prudential Assurance Co Ltd; Oakes (Inspector of Taxes) v.
Equitable Life Assurance Society [2000] S.T.C. 459; 73 T.C. 235; [2000] B.T.C.
158; [2000] S.T.I. 751; (2000) 97(22) L.S.G. 46; *Times*, May 17, 2000;
Independent, June 19, 2000, Ch D . . . .   *Digested*, 00/**4942**
Bibby v. Stirling (1998) 76 P. & C.R. D36, CA
Bibi v. Chief Adjudication Officer [1998] 1 F.L.R. 375; [1998] 1 F.C.R. 301; [1997]
Fam. Law 793; (1997) 94(27) L.S.G. 22; (1997) 141 S.J.L.B. 162; *Times*, July 10,
1997, CA. . . . .   *Digested*, 97/**4705**
                                                        Digested, 00/**3358**
Bibi v. Entry Clearance Officer (Dhaka) [2000] Imm. A.R. 385, CA. . . . .
Biblical Archaeology Society v. Qimron [2001] E.C.D.R. 6, Sup Ct (Isr)
Bic Benelux SA v. Belgium (C13/96) [1997] E.C.R. I-1753; [1998] Env. L.R. 22, ECJ
(5th Chamber) . . . .   *Digested*, 98/**2266**
BICC Ltd v. Parkman Consulting Engineers see Parkman Consulting Engineers v.
Cumbrian Industrials Ltd
BICC Plc v. Burndy Corp [1985] Ch. 232; [1985] 2 W.L.R. 132; [1985] 1 All E.R. 417;
[1985] R.P.C. 273; (1984) 81 L.S.G. 3011; (1984) 128 S.J. 750, CA . . . .   *Digested*, 85/**2604**:
                         Applied, 94/504, 95/2827, 00/2326: *Considered*, 97/3366
BICC Plc v. Customs and Excise Commissioners [1998] B.V.C. 2120; [1998] V. & D.R.
224, V&DTr . . . .   *Digested*, 98/**4929**:
                                                      Considered, 00/**5310**
Bickel, Re (C274/96) see Criminal Proceedings against Bickel (C274/96)
Bickel v. Duke of Westminster [1977] Q.B. 517; [1976] 3 W.L.R. 805; [1976] 3 All E.R.
801; (1977) 34 P. & C.R. 22; [1976] J.P.L. 574; 120 S.J. 604, CA. . . . .   *Digested*, 78/**1763**:
                      Applied, 79/1644, 01/4185: *Considered*, 89/2152, 89/2154, 90/2871
Bickenhall Engineering Co Ltd v. Grandmet Restaurants Ltd [1995] 1 E.G.L.R. 110;
[1995] 10 E.G. 123; [1994] E.G.C.S. 146; [1994] N.P.C. 118, CA . . . .   *Digested*, 95/**3068**:
                                                       Followed, 01/4207
Bickley v. Bradley (Unreported, March 2, 2000), CC (Manchester) [*Ex rel.* Pannone &
Partners Solicitors, 123 Deansgate, Manchester] . . . .   *Digested*, 00/**1599**
Biddle v. Secretary of State for the Environment, Transport and the Regions [1999] 4
P.L.R. 31; [1999] J.P.L. 835, QBD . . . .   *Digested*, 99/**4202**
Bideaux, Re (95-1021) 3 I.T.L. Rep. 18, C Adm A (F)
Bielecki, Re see Sea Voyager Maritime Inc v. Bielecki (t/a Hughes Hooker & Co)
Bielecki v. Inland Revenue Commissioners [2001] B.P.I.R. 975, Ch D
Biesheuvel v. Birrell (No.2) [1999] P.I.Q.R. Q40, QBD . . . .   *Digested*, 99/**1397**
Bigden v. Lambeth LBC see Lambeth LBC v. Bigden
Biggar v. McLeod [1955-95] P.N.L.R. 144; [1978] 2 N.Z.L.R. 9, CA (NZ) . . . .   *Digested*, 79/**2111**
Biggin & Co Ltd v. Permanite Ltd [1951] 2 K.B. 314; [1951] 2 All E.R. 191; [1951] 2
T.L.R. 159; 95 S.J. 414, CA; reversing in part [1951] 1 K.B. 422; [1950] 2 All E.R.
859; (1950) 66 T.L.R. (Pt. 2) 944, KBD . . . .   *Digested*, 47-51/**2491**:
                 Applied, 53/3273, 84/3104, 99/1379, 99/1400, 00/826: *Considered*, 75/179,
                                         82/230, 99/244, 99/789: *Followed*, 84/3449, 85/3479
Biggin Hill Airport Ltd v. Bromley LBC [2001] EWCA Civ 1089; (2001) 98(33) L.S.G.
30; *Times*, August 13, 2001, CA; reversing (2001) 98(3) L.S.G. 42; [2000]
N.P.C. 130; *Times*, January 9, 2001, Ch D . . . .   *Digested*, 01/**5379**
Biggs v. Forrester Hyde IFA [2001] 1 Q.R. 13, CC (Gloucester) [*Ex rel.* Mark Garside,
Barrister, Victoria Chambers, 177 Corporation Street, Birmingham] . . . .   *Digested*, 01/**1790**

Biggs *v.* Somerset CC [1996] 2 C.M.L.R. 292; [1996] I.C.R. 364; [1996] I.R.L.R. 203; (1996) 146 N.L.J. 174; (1996) 140 S.J.L.B. 59; *Times*, January 29, 1996; *Independent*, February 1, 1996, CA; affirming [1995] I.C.R. 811; [1995] I.R.L.R. 452; *Times*, July 17, 1995, EAT . . . . *Digested*, 96/**2577**:
Applied, 97/2241, 98/2236, 98/5826: *Approved*, 96/2578:
Distinguished, 98/2195: *Referred to*, 96/2625, 97/2266
Bignell's Application, Re [1997] N.I. 36, CA (NI) . . . . *Digested*, 99/**5271**
Biguzzi *v.* Rank Leisure Plc [1999] 1 W.L.R. 1926; [1999] 4 All E.R. 934; [2000] C.P. Rep. 6; [1999] C.P.L.R. 675; [2000] 1 Costs L.R. 67; *Times*, October 5, 1999; *Independent*, October 13, 1999, CA . . . . *Digested*, 99/**367**:
Applied, 00/599, 00/625, 00/627, 01/621: *Cited*, 00/604:
Considered, 00/407, 00/608, 00/609, 01/671: *Followed*, 00/373, 00/626
Bijl *v.* General Medical Council [2001] UKPC 42; *Times*, October 24, 2001, PC (UK) . . . *Digested*, 01/**3287**
Bile *v.* Secretary of State for the Home Department (Unreported, August 19, 1996), IAT . . . . *Considered*, 98/3194
Biles *v.* Barking HA (Unreported, October 30, 1987), QBD [*Ex rel.* Margaret Puxon Q.C. and Andrew Buchan, Barrister] . . . . *Digested*, 88/**1103**:
Considered, 98/1630
BILFINGER/Sealing screen (T842/91) [1999] E.P.O.R. 192, EPO (Technical Bd App)
Bilka-Kaufhaus GmbH *v.* Weber von Hartz (C170/84) [1986] E.C.R. 1607; [1986] 2 C.M.L.R. 701; [1987] I.C.R. 110; [1986] I.R.L.R. 317, ECJ . . . . *Digested*, 87/**1633**:
Applied, 86/1190, 87/1325, 89/1626, 91/4077, 91/4078, 94/1981, 95/2048, 98/2240: *Approved*, 98/5807: *Considered*, 95/2052, 96/2629, 97/2214
Billingham (Inspector of Taxes) *v.* Cooper see Cooper *v.* Billingham (Inspector of Taxes)
Billingham (Inspector of Taxes) *v.* John [1998] S.T.C. 120; [1998] 1 F.L.R. 677; [1998] 1 F.C.R. 339; 70 T.C. 380; [1998] B.T.C. 18; [1998] Fam. Law 246; *Times*, December 22, 1997; *Independent*, December 1, 1997 (C.S.), Ch D . . . . *Digested*, 98/**4677**
Billington (CICB: Quantum: 1999), Re (Unreported, April 16, 1999), CICB (York) [*Ex rel.* ET Legard, Barrister, York Chambers, 14 Toft Green, York] . . . . *Digested*, 99/**1605**
Billows *v.* Hammond (Inspector of Taxes) [2000] S.T.C. (S.C.D.) 430; [2000] S.T.I. 1363, Sp Comm . . . . *Digested*, 01/**5188**
Billson *v.* Residential Apartments Ltd (No.1) [1992] 1 A.C. 494; [1992] 2 W.L.R. 15; [1992] 1 All E.R. 141; (1992) 24 H.L.R. 218; (1992) 63 P. & C.R. 122; [1992] 1 E.G.L.R. 43; [1992] 01 E.G. 91; (1992) 89(2) L.S.G. 31; (1992) 136 S.J.L.B. 10; *Times*, December 13, 1991; *Independent*, January 8, 1992, HL; reversing [1991] 3 W.L.R. 264; [1991] 3 All E.R. 265; (1991) 62 P. & C.R. 505; [1991] 1 E.G.L.R. 70; [1991] 19 E.G. 122; [1991] 18 E.G. 169; [1991] E.G.C.S. 17; *Times*, February 26, 1991, CA; affirming (1990) 60 P. & C.R. 392, Ch D . . . . *Digested*, 92/**2678**:
Applied, 92/2749, 92/3426, 94/2744, 95/2993: *Considered*, 92/2, 92/2682, 96/3778: *Followed*, 98/3652: *Not followed*, 96/3744
Billson *v.* Tristrem [2000] L. & T.R. 220, CA
Bilon *v.* WH Smith Trading Ltd; *sub nom* Harrow LBC *v.* WH Smith Trading Ltd; R. (on the application of Bilon) *v.* WH Smith Trading Ltd [2001] EWHC Admin 469; (2001) 165 J.P. 701; [2001] Crim. L.R. 850, QBD (Admin Ct)
Bim Kemi *v.* Blackburn Chemicals Ltd (No.1) [2001] EWCA Civ 457; [2001] 2 Lloyd's Rep. 93; [2001] C.L.C. 1166, CA . . . . *Digested*, 01/**941**
Bingham *v.* Guidera see Guidera's Estate, Re
Binions *v.* Evans [1972] Ch. 359; [1972] 2 W.L.R. 729; [1972] 2 All E.R. 70; 23 P. & C.R. 192; 116 S.J. 122, CA . . . . *Digested*, 72/**1996**:
Applied, 75/1093, 76/294, 79/1085, 82/1139, 00/3896:
Considered, 88/2042, 89/1516, 91/1721
Binks *v.* Avon HA see Binks *v.* Maken
Binks *v.* Maken; Binks *v.* Avon HA [1998] P.I.Q.R. P1, CA . . . . *Digested*, 98/**600**
Binnie *v.* Lancashire Saw Mill Co Ltd (Unreported, November 20, 1998), CC (Bolton) [*Ex rel.* Simpson Millar Solicitors, First Floor, Fastrack House, 64 Stramongate, Kendal, Cumbria] . . . . *Digested*, 99/**1403**
Binning Bros Ltd (In Liquidation) *v.* Thomas Eggar Verrall Bowles (A Firm) [1998] 1 All E.R. 409, CA . . . . *Digested*, 98/**632**
Bio Claire International Ltd *v.* Benelux Trade Marks Office [1998] E.T.M.R. 251, Hof (Den Haag)
Bio Medical Research Ltd (t/a Slendertone) *v.* Delatex SA [2000] I.L.Pr. 23, HC (Irl) . . *Digested*, 00/**741**
Bioforce GmbH *v.* Oberfinanzdirektion Munchen (C177/91) [1993] E.C.R. I-45, ECJ (4th Chamber) . . . . *Digested*, 93/**4236**:
Applied, 98/4613
Biogen Inc *v.* Medeva Plc [1997] R.P.C. 1; (1997) 38 B.M.L.R. 149; (1997) 20(1) I.P.D. 20001; *Times*, November 1, 1996, HL; affirming [1995] F.S.R. 4; [1995] R.P.C. 25; *Independent*, November 28, 1994 (C.S.), CA; reversing [1993] R.P.C. 475; *Times*, December 1, 1992, Pat Ct . . . . *Digested*, 96/**4549**:
Applied, 96/4554, 99/3518: *Considered*, 00/3599: *Distinguished*, 97/3890
Biogen Inc *v.* SmithKline Beecham Biologicals SA (C181/95) [1997] E.C.R. I-357; [1997] R.P.C. 833; (1997) 38 B.M.L.R. 94, ECJ (6th Chamber) . . . . *Digested*, 98/**3481**
Biogen Inc's European Patent (No.041313) (1998) 21 (4) I.P.D. 21040
BIOGEN/Hepatitis B virus (T886/91) [1999] E.P.O.R. 361, EPO (Technical Bd App) . . . *Digested*, 99/**3486**

BIOGEN/Human beta-interferon (T207/94) [1999] E.P.O.R. 451, EPO (Technical Bd App)

                     Digested, 00/**3625**

BIOGEN/Recombinant DNA (T301/87) [1990] E.P.O.R. 190, EPO (Technical Bd App) . *Applied*, 99/**3486**

Biosource Technologies Inc v. Axis Genetics Plc (In Administration); *sub nom* Axis Genetics Plc's (In Administration) Patent, Re [2000] B.C.C. 943; [2000] 1 B.C.L.C. 286; [2000] F.S.R. 448; (2000) 23(2) I.P.D. 23011; (1999) 96(45) L.S.G. 33; (1999) 143 S.J.L.B. 278; *Times*, November 25, 1999, Ch D . . . . *Digested*, 99/**3267**

Biotrading & Financing OY v. Biohit Ltd [1998] F.S.R. 109; (1997) 20(12) I.P.D. 20125, CA; affirming [1996] F.S.R. 393, Ch D . . . . *Digested*, 97/**1038**

Birch v. Aslam (Unreported, May 25, 2001), CC (Chelmsford) [*Ex rel.* William Latimer-Sayer, Barrister, Cloisters, 1 Pump Court, Temple, London] . . . . *Digested*, 01/**1532**

Birch v. DPP [2000] Crim. L.R. 301; *Independent*, January 13, 2000, QBD . . . . *Digested*, 00/**987**

Birchall v. Secretary of State for Education [1998] Eu. L.R. 609, EAT . . . . *Digested*, 99/**2094**

Bircham & Co Nominees (No.2) Ltd v. Worrell Holdings Ltd [2001] EWCA Civ 775; (2001) 82 P. & C.R. 34; [2001] 47 E.G. 149; [2001] 22 E.G.C.S. 153; [2001] N.P.C. 94, CA . . . . *Digested*, 01/**4858**

Birchview Ltd v. Customs and Excise Commissioners [1998] B.V.C. 2076, V&DTr

Bird v. British Celanese Ltd [1945] K.B. 336; [1945] 1 All E.R. 488, CA . . . . *Applied*, 98/**2207**

Bird v. Hadkinson [2000] C.P. Rep. 21; [1999] B.P.I.R. 653; *Times*, April 7, 1999, Ch D . *Digested*, 99/**3316**

Bird Precision Bellows Ltd, Re [1986] Ch. 658; [1986] 2 W.L.R. 158; [1985] 3 All E.R. 523; [1986] P.C.C. 25; (1986) 83 L.S.G. 36; (1986) 130 S.J. 51, CA; affirming [1984] Ch. 419; [1984] 2 W.L.R. 869; [1984] 3 All E.R. 444; (1984) 81 L.S.G. 187; (1984) 128 S.J. 348, Ch D . . . . *Digested*, 85/**309**:

               Considered, 85/308, 86/317, 00/688

Birds Eye Walls Ltd v. Roberts (C132/92) [1993] E.C.R. I-5579; [1993] 3 C.M.L.R. 822; [1994] I.C.R. 338; [1994] I.R.L.R. 29; *Times*, December 16, 1993, ECJ (2nd Chamber) . . . . *Digested*, 94/**4823**:

                   Considered, 01/4605

Birkett v. Acorn Business Machines Ltd [1999] 2 All E.R. (Comm) 429; (1999) 96(31) L.S.G. 35; *Times*, August 25, 1999, CA . . . . *Digested*, 99/**849**

Birkett v. Hayes [1982] 1 W.L.R. 816; [1982] 2 All E.R. 70; 126 S.J. 399, CA . . . . *Digested*, 82/**791**:

     Applied, 83/984, 00/1489: *Considered*, 84/2346: *Distinguished*, 84/1004, 85/942

Birkett v. James [1978] A.C. 297; [1977] 3 W.L.R. 38; [1977] 2 All E.R. 801; 121 S.J. 444, HL . . . . *Digested*, 77/**2410**:

    Applied, 78/2237, 78/2426, 79/2191, 81/113, 81/1966, 83/2209, 83/3068, 84/2739, 92/3495, 93/1764, 93/3336, 94/2902, 95/2963, 96/366, 96/900, 97/785, 00/616: *Considered*, 77/2407, 77/2408, 77/2411, 79/1663, 81/2201, 81/2880, 82/2461, 82/2553, 83/3073, 85/2683, 85/2728, 87/133, 87/2985, 88/2825, 88/2934, 89/2963, 89/3070, 89/3071, 91/184, 91/2971, 92/190, 92/2813, 92/3610, 92/3611, 93/3334, 94/3644, 94/3788, 94/3904, 97/489, 97/644, 97/759, 97/761, 97/1314, 97/3024, 98/611, 98/612, 98/613, 98/619, 00/348, 00/4656: *Disapproved*, 87/2903, 88/2937, 89/3075, 00/626: *Distinguished*, 77/2412, 78/1848, 78/2425, 80/2194, 81/868, 88/2838, 90/3644, 94/3635, 94/3792, 95/3888, 96/909, 98/614: *Followed*, 78/2423, 96/898, 97/1007, 99/3356: *Not followed*, 99/367: *Referred to*, 97/754, 97/1037, 00/605, 00/617

Birkett v. Technical Indexes Ltd [2001] 4 Q.R. 11, CC (Reading) [*Ex rel.* David McHugh, Barrister, Bracton Chambers, 8 Bell Yard, London] . . . . *Digested*, 01/**1608**

Birkett v. Vehicle Inspectorate; *sub nom* Birkett v. Wing; Fisher v. Dukes Transport (Craigavon) Ltd; Vehicle Inspectorate v. Dukes Transport Ltd (1997) 161 J.P. 805; [1998] R.T.R. 264; [1997] C.O.D. 410; *Times*, June 10, 1997, QBD . . . . *Digested*, 97/**4366**

Birkett v. Wing see Birkett v. Vehicle Inspectorate

Birkin v. Guardweald Ltd (In Liquidation) (1997) 29 H.L.R. 908, CA . . . . *Digested*, 98/**407**

Birkinshaw v. Nawaz [2001] 3 Q.R. 16, CC (Derby) [*Ex rel.* Nick Blake, Barrister, 24 The Ropewalk, Nottingham] . . . . *Digested*, 01/**1672**

Birmingham Citizens Permanent Building Society v. Caunt [1962] Ch. 883; [1962] 2 W.L.R. 323; [1962] 1 All E.R. 163; 106 S.J. 96, Ch D . . . . *Digested*, 62/**1938**:

    Applied, 67/3151, 68/2509, 82/2096, 96/5003: *Considered*, 68/608, 73/2209, 96/5002, 99/4386, 01/4875

Birmingham City Council v. Bourneville Village Trust (2000) 15 P.A.D. 35, Planning Inspector

Birmingham City Council v. Citilite 6's Ltd (1998) 13 P.A.D. 778, Planning Inspector

Birmingham City Council v. Equal Opportunities Commission (No.1) see R. v. Birmingham City Council Ex p. Equal Opportunities Commission (No.1)

Birmingham City Council v. H (Care Order) [1992] 2 F.L.R. 323; [1993] 1 F.C.R. 247 . . *Digested*, 93/**2773**

Birmingham City Council v. Laird (1999) 14 P.A.D. 271, Planning Inspector

Birmingham City Council v. Oakley see Oakley v. Birmingham City Council

Birmingham City Council v. Southside Veterinary Clinic (2001) 16 P.A.D. 13, Planning Inspector

Birmingham Corp v. Khan (Sarwar) see Birmingham Corp v. Minister of Housing and Local Government

Birmingham Corp v. Minister of Housing and Local Government; Birmingham Corp v. Khan (Sarwar); Birmingham Corp v. Ullah (Habib) [1964] 1 Q.B. 178; [1963] 3 W.L.R. 937; [1963] 3 All E.R. 668; 128 J.P. 33; 61 L.G.R. 623; (1964) 15 P. & C.R. 404; [1963] R.V.R. 712; 107 S.J. 812, DC . . . . *Digested,* 63/**3408**:
     Applied, 66/11835, 80/2631: *Considered,* 93/3860: *Explained,* 65/3796:
     Followed, 99/4173
Birmingham Corp v. Sowsbery (1969) 113 S.J. 877 . . . . *Digested,* 69/**890**:
     Cited, 00/350: *Considered,* 93/1582: *Distinguished,* 01/1535
Birmingham Corp v. Ullah (Habib) see Birmingham Corp v. Minister of Housing and Local Government
Birmingham Corp v. West Midland Baptist (Trust) Association Inc; *sub nom* West Midland Baptist (Trust) Association Inc v. Birmingham Corp [1970] A.C. 874; [1969] 3 W.L.R. 389; [1969] 3 All E.R. 172; (1969) 133 J.P. 524; 67 L.G.R. 571; (1969) 20 P. & C.R. 1052; 113 S.J. 606, HL; affirming [1968] 2 Q.B. 188; [1968] 2 W.L.R. 535; [1968] 1 All E.R. 205; (1968) 132 J.P. 127; (1968) 19 P. & C.R. 9; 111 S.J. 851; *Times,* October 30, 1967, CA; reversing (1967) 18 P. & C.R. 125; [1967] J.P.L. 161, Lands Tr. . . . . *Digested,* 69/**433**:
     Applied, 76/293, 79/297, 80/642, 86/337: *Considered,* 70/321, 71/1476,
     71/8934, 71/8984, 79/302, 80/304, 90/583, 90/584, 91/455, 91/3426,
     92/439, 92/449, 92/4178: *Distinguished,* 71/1521.9, 72/3642, 92/3678:
     Followed, 76/1882, 81/274.1, 81/3663, 84/341.12, 01/4661
Birmingham Midshires Building Society v. Infields (A Firm) 66 Con. L.R. 20; [1999] Lloyd's Rep. P.N. 874; [1999] E.G.C.S. 77, QBD (T&CC) . . . . *Digested,* 00/**4265**
Birmingham Midshires Building Society v. Wretham 63 Con. L.R. 93; [1999] Lloyd's Rep. P.N. 133; [1999] P.N.L.R. 685; [1999] 1 E.G.L.R. 69; [1999] 07 E.G. 138; [1998] E.G.C.S. 176, QBD (T&CC) . . . . *Digested,* 99/**481**
Birmingham Midshires Mortgage Services Ltd v. Ansell [1998] P.N.L.R. 237, Ch D . . . . *Digested,* 98/**355**
Birmingham Midshires Mortgage Services Ltd v. David Parry & Co; *sub nom* Hypo-Mortgage Services Ltd v. David Parry & Co [1997] E.G.C.S. 150; [1997] N.P.C. 153, CA; affirming 51 Con. L.R. 1; [1996] P.N.L.R. 494; [1996] E.G.C.S. 39, Ch D . . . . *Digested,* 96/**3914**:
     Applied, 01/4523
Birmingham Midshires Mortgage Services Ltd v. George Ide Phillips (A Firm) (Special Damages); *sub nom* Birmingham Midshires Mortgage Services Ltd v. Phillips (Special Damages) [1998] P.N.L.R. 468, Ch D . . . . *Digested,* 98/**1472**
Birmingham Midshires Mortgage Services Ltd v. Phillips (Special Damages) see Birmingham Midshires Mortgage Services Ltd v. George Ide Phillips (A Firm) (Special Damages)
Birmingham Midshires Mortgage Services Ltd v. Sabherwal (Equitable Interest) (2000) 80 P. & C.R. 256, CA. . . . . *Digested,* 00/**4658**
Birru v. Secretary of State for the Home Department [1998] Imm. A.R. 212, CA . . . . . . *Digested,* 98/**3169**
Birse v. HM Advocate; *sub nom* Birse v. MacNeill 2000 J.C. 503; 2000 S.L.T. 869; 2000 S.C.C.R. 505; 2000 G.W.D. 16-649; *Times,* June 28, 2000, HCJ Appeal . . *Digested,* 00/**6125**
Birse v. MacNeill see Birse v. HM Advocate
Birse Construction Ltd (formerly Peter Birse Ltd) v. Cooperative Wholesale Society Ltd (t/a CWS Engineering Group) see Cooperative Wholesale Society Ltd (t/a CWS Engineering Group) v. Birse Construction Ltd (formerly Peter Birse Ltd)
Birse Construction Ltd v. Haiste Ltd [1996] 1 W.L.R. 675; [1996] 2 All E.R. 1; [1996] C.L.C. 577; 76 B.L.R. 31; 47 Con. L.R. 162; [1996] P.N.L.R. 8; (1996) 93(2) L.S.G. 29; (1996) 140 S.J.L.B. 25; *Times,* December 12, 1995, CA; reversing 44 Con. L.R. 17, QBD . . . . *Digested,* 96/**5655**:
     Considered, 01/609, 01/946
Birse Construction Ltd v. St David Ltd (No.1) [2000] B.L.R. 57; 70 Con. L.R. 10, CA; reversing [1999] B.L.R. 194, QBD (T&CC) . . . . *Digested,* 00/**593**:
     Considered, 00/234
Birse Construction Ltd v. St David Ltd (No.2) 78 Con. L.R. 121, QBD (T&CC)
Bishop v. Berkshire HA [1999] P.I.Q.R. P92; [1999] Lloyd's Rep. Med. 16; (1999) 46 B.M.L.R. 67; *Independent,* October 26, 1998 (C.S.), QBD . . . . *Digested,* 98/**1474**:
     Distinguished, 99/1422
Bishop v. Bonham [1988] 1 W.L.R. 742; (1988) 4 B.C.C. 347; [1988] B.C.L.C. 656; [1988] F.L.R. 282; (1988) 132 S.J. 933, CA; reversing (1988) 4 B.C.C. 265, Ch D . . . . *Digested,* 88/**2388**:
     Explained, 01/4873
     Followed, 98/3623
Bishop v. Consolidated London Properties Ltd [1933] All E.R. Rep. 963, KBD . . . .
Bishop Auckland Local Board v. Bishop Auckland Iron and Steel Co Ltd (1882-83) L.R. 10 Q.B.D. 138, QBD . . . . *Applied,* 75/2459:
     Considered, 01/4550
Bishop Square Ltd (formerly Parinv (Hatfield) Ltd) v. Inland Revenue Commissioners see Parinv (Hatfield) Ltd v. Inland Revenue Commissioners
Bissell v. Cole CCRTF 96/1780/C, CA. . . . . *Digested,* 98/**4071**
Bistern Estate Trust's Appeal, Re [2000] 2 E.G.L.R. 91, Lands Tr . . . . *Digested,* 01/**4183**
Bitumen Mix Producers, Re [2000] E.C.C. 426, OGH (A)
BJ (Minors) (Care: Third Party Intervention), Re [1999] Fam. Law 613, CA

Black v. Braer Corp 1999 S.L.T. 1401; 1998 G.W.D. 29-1523; *Times*, October 12, 1998,
OH . . . .   *Digested*, 98/**5834**
Black v. Doncaster MBC [1999] 1 W.L.R. 53; [1998] 3 All E.R. 631; [1998] P.I.Q.R.
Q139; (1998) 95(29) L.S.G. 27; (1998) 142 S.J.L.B. 199; *Times*, July 14, 1998;
Independent, June 29, 1998 (C.S.), CA. . . . .   *Digested*, 98/**504**
Black v. Inspector of Taxes [2000] S.T.C. (S.C.D.) 540; [2000] S.T.I. 1521, Sp Comm. . .   *Digested*, 01/**5240**
Black v. Sumitomo Corp [2001] EWCA Civ 1819; *Independent*, December 13, 2001,
CA; reversing TNS, QBD (Comm Ct)
Black Country Housing Association Ltd v. Shand [1998] N.P.C. 92, CA
Black King Shipping Corp v. Massie (The Litsion Pride) [1985] 1 Lloyd's Rep. 437;
(1984) 134 N.L.J. 887, QBD (Comm Ct) . . . .   *Digested*, 85/**3208**:
Considered, 95/4533: *Not followed*, 90/4101, 96/3572, 01/3825:
Referred to, 97/3152

Black Sea & Baltic General Insurance Co Ltd v. Baker see Baker v. Black Sea & Baltic
General Insurance Co Ltd
Blackburn v. ARC Ltd [1998] Env. L.R. 469, QBD (OR) . . . .   *Digested*, 98/**4042**
Blacklock v. Swan Hunter Shipbuilders Ltd see Thompson v. Smiths Shiprepairers
(North Shields) Ltd
Blackman (A Debtor), Re see Oben v. Blackman
Blackpool and Fylde Aero Club Ltd v. Blackpool BC [1990] 3 All E.R. 25, CA . . . .   *Referred to*, 00/830
Blackshaw v. Lord [1984] Q.B. 1; [1983] 3 W.L.R. 283; [1983] 2 All E.R. 311, CA . . . . .   *Digested*, 83/**2204**:
Applied, 01/1823: *Considered*, 97/2036, 01/1831: *Followed*, 96/5680
Blackspur Group Plc, Re see Secretary of State for Trade and Industry v. Eastaway
Blackspur Group Plc (No.2), Re; *sub nom* Secretary of State for Trade and Industry v.
Davies (No.2); Atlantic Computer Systems Plc, Re; Secretary of State for Trade
and Industry v. Ashman [1998] 1 W.L.R. 422; [1998] B.C.C. 11; [1998] 1
B.C.L.C. 676; (1998) 95(1) L.S.G. 25; (1998) 142 S.J.L.B. 20; *Times*, December
9, 1997; *Independent*, November 21, 1997, CA; affirming [1997] 1 W.L.R. 710;
[1997] B.C.C. 488; [1997] 2 B.C.L.C. 96, Ch D . . . .   *Digested*, 97/**831**
Blackspur Group Plc (No.3), Re; *sub nom* Secretary of State for Trade and Industry v.
Davies (No.3); Secretary of State for Trade and Industry v. Eastaway
(Undertakings) [2001] EWCA Civ 1595, CA; affirming (2001) 98(26) L.S.G. 43;
(2001) 151 N.L.J. 889; (2001) 145 S.J.L.B. 155; *Times*, July 5, 2001, Ch D . . . .   *Digested*, 01/**719**
Blackstone Franks Investment Management Ltd v. Robertson; *sub nom* Robertson v.
Blackstone Franks Investment Management Ltd [1998] I.R.L.R. 376; *Times*, May
4, 1998, CA; affirming *Times*, November 12, 1996, EAT . . . .   *Digested*, 98/**2246**
Blackwell, Re see Blackwell v. Blackwell
Blackwell (A Minor) v. Macclesfield BC (Unreported, November 27, 1997), CC
(Warrington) [*Ex rel*. Weightmans Solicitors, Richmond House, 1 Rumford Place,
Liverpool] . . . .   *Digested*, 98/**598**
Blackwell v. Blackwell; *sub nom* Blackwell, Re [1929] A.C. 318; 67 A.L.R. 336, HL;
affirming [1928] Ch. 614, CA . . . .   *Applied*, 47-51/11014,
72/3168, 98/4589
Blackwell v. Evans (Valuation Officer) [2000] R.V.R. 248, Lands Tr . . . .   *Digested*, 00/**4597**
Blackwood Hodge Plc, Re [1997] B.C.C. 434; [1997] 2 B.C.L.C. 650; [1999] O.P.L.R. 179,
Ch D (Companies Ct) . . . .   *Digested*, 97/**850**
Bladet Tromso v. Norway (21980/93) (2000) 29 E.H.R.R. 125; 6 B.H.R.C. 599, ECHR . .   *Digested*, 00/**3190**:
Applied, 01/3474: *Followed*, 01/3472
Blaenau Gwent CBC v. JPM Ltd (2001) 16 P.A.D. 35, Planning Inspector
Blair v. Curran (1939) 62 C.L.R. 464, HC (Aus) . . . .   *Considered*, 96/853,
01/5509
Blair v. Vallely [2000] W.T.L.R. 615, HC (NZ) . . . .   *Digested*, 01/**5528**
Blake v. Barking and Dagenham LBC (1996) 30 H.L.R. 963; [1999] P.N.L.R. 171;
[1996] E.G.C.S. 145; [1996] N.P.C. 134; *Times*, November 1, 1996, QBD. . . . . . .   *Digested*, 96/**3766**
Blake v. Pensions Ombudsman [2000] O.P.L.R. 341, Ch D . . . .   *Digested*, 01/**4616**
Blakemore v. Heron Service Stations see Heron Service Stations v. Coupe
Blamey v. London Fire and Civil Defence Authority Unreported, HC . . . .   *Considered*, 01/1642
Blamire v. South Cumbria HA [1993] P.I.Q.R. Q1, CA. . . . .   *Digested*, 93/**1403**:
Applied, 99/1438: *Followed*, 97/1769: *Referred to*, 99/1449
Bland v. Ingram's Estates Ltd (No.2) see Bland v. Ingrams Estates Ltd (No.2)
Bland v. Ingrams Estates Ltd (No.1) [2001] Ch. 767; [2001] 2 W.L.R. 1638; [2001] L.
& T.R. 13; [2001] 24 E.G. 163; [2001] 4 E.G.C.S. 144; [2001] N.P.C. 5; *Times*,
January 18, 2001, CA; reversing [1999] 2 E.G.L.R. 49; [1999] 25 E.G. 185;
[1999] E.G.C.S. 54; [1999] N.P.C. 45; *Independent*, May 17, 1999 (C.S.), Ch D .   *Digested*, 01/**4187**:
Considered, 01/3746
Bland v. Ingrams Estates Ltd (No.2); *sub nom* Bland v. Ingram's Estates Ltd (No.2)
[2001] EWCA Civ 1088; [2001] 50 E.G. 92; (2001) 98(35) L.S.G. 35; [2001]
N.P.C. 115; *Times*, August 29, 2001, CA. . . . .   *Digested*, 01/**4186**
Bland v. Sparkes, *Times*, December 17, 1999, CA. . . . .   *Digested*, 00/**863**
Blasi v. Finanzamt Munchen I (C346/95) [1998] All E.R. (EC) 211; [1998] S.T.C. 336;
[1998] E.C.R. I-481; [1998] C.E.C. 408; [1998] B.T.C. 5188; [1998] B.V.C. 247,
ECJ (5th Chamber). . . . .   *Digested*, 98/**4897**

Blathwayt *v.* Baron Cawley [1976] A.C. 397; [1975] 3 W.L.R. 684; [1975] 3 All E.R. 625; 119 S.J. 795, HL . . . .
Digested, 75/**3572**:
Considered, 76/2492, 00/5271
Blaxhall Securities Ltd *v.* Sheard Walshaw Partnership see Baxall Securities Ltd *v.* Sheard Walshaw Partnership
Blayney (t/a Aardvark Jewellery) *v.* Clogau St Davids Gold Mines Ltd (2001) 24(10) I.P.D. 24064; [2001] E.C.D.R. CN5, Ch D
Bleakley *v.* Grimway (Unreported, November 17, 1997), CC (Plymouth) [*Ex rel.* David Caden, Barrister, King's Bench Chambers, 115 North Hill, Plymouth] . . . .
Digested, 98/**2499**:
Followed, 98/1461
Bleakley *v.* Home Office (Unreported, April 17, 2000), CC (Bolton) [*Ex rel.* Titus Gibson, Barrister, Oriel Chambers, 14 Water Street, Liverpool] . . . .
Digested, 00/**1684**
Bleis *v.* Ministere de l'Education Nationale (C4/91) [1991] E.C.R. I-5627; [1994] 1 C.M.L.R. 793, ECJ . . . .
Digested, 92/**4785**:
Applied, 99/5272, 01/5769
Blendhome Ltd (t/a Stanhill Court Hotel) *v.* Customs and Excise Commissioners [1999] B.V.C. 2280, V&DTr
Blenheim Leisure (Restaurants) Ltd (No.1), Re [2000] B.C.C. 554; (1999) 96(33) L.S.G. 29; [1999] N.P.C. 105; *Times*, August 13, 1999 ; *Independent*, November 8, 1999 (C.S.), CA . . . .
Digested, 99/**602**
Blenheim Leisure (Restaurants) Ltd (No.2), Re [2000] B.C.C. 821; (1999) 96(40) L.S.G. 42; (1999) 143 S.J.L.B. 248; *Times*, October 26, 1999, Ch D . . . .
Digested, 99/**603**
Blenheim Leisure (Restaurants) Ltd (No.3), Re (1999) 96(44) L.S.G. 40; *Times*, November 9, 1999, Ch D . . . .
Digested, 99/**453**
Blenheim Leisure (Restaurants) Ltd *v.* Westminster City Council (No.1) see Westminster City Council *v.* Blenheim Leisure (Restaurants) Ltd (No.1)
Blenkiron *v.* Turton (Unreported, June 21, 1999), CC (Kingston upon Hull) [*Ex rel.* Andrew M. Jackson & Co Solicitors, P.O. Box 47, Essex House, Manor Street, Hull] . . . .
Digested, 99/**1597**
Blexen *v.* G PercyTrentham Ltd 54 B.L.R. 37; 21 Con. L.R. 61; [1990] 42 E.G. 133, CA . .
Digested, 91/**188**:
Applied, 92/171, 93/163: *Considered*, 94/214, 97/270, 99/227
Blin *v.* Les Etablissements Doremus [1999] E.C.C. 543, C d'A (Amiens)
Bliss (Deceased), Re [2001] 1 W.L.R. 1973; (2001) 98(23) L.S.G. 41; (2001) 145 S.J.L.B. 122; *Times*, April 13, 2001, Ch D . . . .
Digested, 01/**5163**
Bliss (Valuation Officer) *v.* Lamb & Shirley Ltd; *sub nom* Lamb & Shirley Ltd *v.* Bliss (Valuation Officer) [2001] EWCA Civ 562; [2001] R.A. 99; [2001] 15 E.G.C.S. 137; [2001] N.P.C. 73; *Independent*, May 3, 2001, CA; affirming [1999] R.A. 373, LandsTr. . . . .
Digested, 01/**4822**
Bliss *v.* South East Thames RHA [1987] I.C.R. 700; [1985] I.R.L.R. 308, CA; reversing (1984) 134 N.L.J. 121; *Times*, December 13, 1983 . . . .
Digested, 87/**1303**:
Applied, 88/1044, 90/1524: *Considered*, 92/1514: *Not applied*, 01/1828
Bloom *v.* Gibbs (Unreported, August 12, 1999), CC (Rawtenstall) [*Ex rel.* Graham Leigh, Pfeffer & Co Solicitors, Maple House, Haymarket Street, Bury] . . . .
Digested, 99/**535**:
Not followed, 01/657
Bloomfield *v.* Roberts (Unreported, March 6, 1989), CC (Newbury) . . . .
Digested, 89/**2948**:
Approved, 92/3434: *Cited*, 00/466: *Considered*, 97/1789
Bloomfield *v.* Secretary of State for the Environment, Transport and the Regions [1999] 2 P.L.R. 79; [1999] E.G.C.S. 38, QBD . . . .
Digested, 99/**4241**
Bloor Construction (UK) Ltd *v.* Bowmer & Kirkland (London) Ltd [2000] B.L.R. 314; (2000) 2 T.C.L.R. 914, QBD (T&CC)
BLP Group Plc *v.* Customs and Excise Commissioners (C4/94); Swallowfield *v.* Customs and Excise Commissioners [1996] 1 W.L.R. 174; [1995] All E.R. (E.C.) 401; [1995] S.T.C. 424; [1995] E.C.R. I-983; [1995] 2 C.M.L.R. 750; [1995] B.V.C. 159; *Times*, April 17, 1995, ECJ (5th Chamber) [1994] S.T.C. 41; *Independent*, December 27, 1993 (C.S.), CA . . . .
Digested, 95/**5059**:
Applied, 00/5309, 01/5585: *Considered*, 96/5906, 98/4932, 99/5015:
Distinguished, 96/5869, 99/4994: *Followed*, 96/5866, 97/5003, 01/5606:
Referred to, 95/5047, 00/5337
Blue Circle Industries Plc *v.* Ministry of Defence; *sub nom* Ministry of Defence *v.* Blue Circle Industries Plc [1999] Ch. 289; [1999] 1 W.L.R. 295; [1998] 3 All E.R. 385; [1999] Env. L.R. 22; [1998] E.G.C.S. 93; [1998] N.P.C. 100; *Times*, June 16, 1998, CA; affirming [1997] Env. L.R. 341; (1998) 76 P. & C.R. 251; [1996] E.G.C.S. 190; (1997) 94(2) L.S.G. 25; (1997) 141 S.J.L.B. 11; [1996] N.P.C. 170; *Times*, December 11, 1996, Ch D . . . .
Digested, 98/**1416**
Blue Circle Industries Plc *v.* West Midlands CC [1994] 20 E.G. 149; [1994] R.V.R. 210, CA [1989] R.V.R. 34, LandsTr . . . .
Digested, 95/**671**:
Applied, 00/4431: *Referred to*, 00/552
Blue Nile Shipping Co Ltd *v.* Iguana Shipping & Finance Inc (The Happy Fellow) [1998] 1 Lloyd's Rep. 13; [1997] C.L.C. 1391; [1998] I.L.Pr. 440, CA; affirming [1997] 1 Lloyd's Rep. 130; [1997] C.L.C. 567, QBD (Adm Ct) . . . .
Digested, 98/**773**:
Considered, 00/738
Blue Note Enterprises Ltd, Re [2001] 2 B.C.L.C. 427, Ch D (Companies Ct) . . . .
Digested, 01/**703**
Blue Triangle Cars Ltd *v.* Phillips (Unreported, February 3, 2000), CC (Bristol) [*Ex rel.* Paul McGrath, Barrister, 1 Temple Gardens, Temple, London] . . . .
Digested, 00/**350**

Blueco Ltd's Application [1999] E.T.M.R. 394, OHIM (1st Bd App)
Bluestone Chemicals Ltd v. Environment Agency see Celtic Extraction Ltd (In Liquidation), Re
BLUEWATER/Admissibility (T156/90) [1994] E.P.O.R. 515, EPO (Technical Bd App) . .   *Followed*, 00/3617
Blume v. Spain (37680/97) (2000) 30 E.H.R.R. 632, ECHR . . . .   *Digested*, 01/**3562**
Blyth Valley BC v. Kwik Fit Properties Ltd (2000) 15 P.A.D. 230, Planning Inspector
Blythe Limited Partnership v. Customs and Excise Commissioners [1999] V. & D.R. 112,
    V&DTr. . . . .   *Digested*, 00/**5315**
BMBF (No.12) Ltd v. Harland & Wolff Shipbuilding & Heavy Industries Ltd [2001]
    EWCA Civ 862; [2001] 2 All E.R. (Comm) 385; [2001] 2 Lloyd's Rep. 227;
    [2001] C.L.C. 1552, CA; reversing [2001] C.L.C. 559, QBD (Comm Ct) . . . . . .   *Digested*, 01/**4947**
BMG Trading Ltd v. AS McKay Ltd [1998] I.L.Pr. 691, CA . . . .   *Considered*, 00/770
BMK v. Logue [1993] I.C.R. 601; [1993] I.R.L.R. 477, EAT . . . .   *Digested*, 93/**1725**:
                                                                                                        Not applied, 99/2145
BMW AG v. Deenik (C63/97) see Bayerische Motorenwerke AG v. Deenik (C63/97)
BMW (GB) Ltd v. Customs and Excise Commissioners [1997] S.T.C. 824; [1997] B.T.C.
    5273; [1997] B.V.C. 400; *Independent*, May 19, 1997 (C.S.), QBD . . . .   *Digested*, 97/**5009**:
                                                                                                        Applied, 00/5320
BMW/Non appealing party (G09/92) [1995] E.P.O.R. 169, EPO (Enlarged Bd App) . . .   *Applied*, 01/3920:
                                                    Explained, 01/3897: *Referred to*, 00/3607
BNP Mortgages Ltd v. Goadsby & Harding Ltd see Banque Bruxelles Lambert SA v. Eagle Star Insurance Co Ltd
BNP Mortgages Ltd v. Key Surveyors Nationwide Ltd see Banque Bruxelles Lambert SA v. Eagle Star Insurance Co Ltd
BNZ Finance Ltd v. Holland see BNZ Finance Ltd v. Inland Revenue Commissioner (New Zealand)
BNZ Finance Ltd v. Inland Revenue Commissioner (New Zealand); *sub nom* BNZ
    Finance Ltd v. Holland [1997] S.T.C. 1396; [1997] B.T.C. 555, PC (NZ) . . . .   *Digested*, 98/**4617**
Boafo v. Secretary of State for the Home Department see R. (on the application of Boafo) v. Secretary of State for the Home Department
Board of Governors of the National Heart and Chest Hospital v. Chettle (1998) 30 H.L.R.
    618; [1997] N.P.C. 130, CA . . . .   *Digested*, 98/**614**
Board of Management of the Bank of New Zealand Officers Provident Association v. Bank of New Zealand see Bank of New Zealand Officers Provident Fund Association Management Board v. Bank of New Zealand
Board of Management of Trim Joint District School v. Kelly; *sub nom* Trim Joint District
    School Board of Management v. Kelly [1914] A.C. 667, HL (UK-Irl) . . . .   *Applied*, 63/1818,
        63/2564, 79/2311, 00/4845: *Considered*, 70/1368: *Followed*, 47-51/11031
Board of Trade v. Owen; *sub nom* R. v. Owen (Henry Geoffrey); R. v. Seth-Smith
    (Patrick Sidney) [1957] A.C. 602; [1957] 2 W.L.R. 351; [1957] 1 All E.R. 411;
    (1957) 41 Cr. App. R. 11; 121 J.P. 177; 101 S.J. 186, HL; affirming [1957] 1 Q.B.
    174; [1956] 3 W.L.R. 739; [1956] 3 All E.R. 432; 120 J.P. 553; 100 S.J. 769,
    CCA; reversing in part [1956] 3 W.L.R. 252; (1956) 40 Cr. App. R. 103; 100 S.J.
    454, CCC . . . .   *Digested*, 57/**697**:
        Applied, 69/1453, 75/591, 81/1204, 83/574, 85/527: *Considered*, 72/590,
                                                            00/952: *Distinguished*, 68/652
Boardman v. Phipps; *sub nom* Phipps v. Boardman [1967] 2 A.C. 46; [1966] 3 W.L.R.
    1009; [1966] 3 All E.R. 721; 110 S.J. 853, HL; affirming [1965] Ch. 992; [1965]
    2 W.L.R. 839; [1965] 1 All E.R. 849; 109 S.J. 197, CA; affirming [1964] 1
    W.L.R. 993; [1964] 2 All E.R. 187; 108 S.J. 619, Ch D . . . .   *Digested*, 66/**11052**:
        Applied, 72/361, 72/487, 81/2624, 93/1834, 94/2083, 01/5525:
                Considered, 77/2708, 87/3552, 89/459, 90/487, 01/951
Boardman v. Portman [2001] EWCA Civ 1450, CA; affirming (2001) 3 L.G.L.R. 7,
    QBD . . . .   *Digested*, 01/**4806**
Bobin v. DPP [1999] R.T.R. 375, QBD . . . .   *Digested*, 00/**1202**
Bobo v. Spain (39293/98) (2001) 31 E.H.R.R. 50, ECHR. . . . .   *Digested*, 01/**3466**
BOC Group Plc v. Centeon LLC [1999] 1 All E.R. (Comm) 970; 63 Con. L.R. 104, CA;
    affirming [1999] 1 All E.R. (Comm) 53; [1999] C.L.C. 497, QBD (Comm Ct) . . .   *Digested*, 99/**647**
BOC Ltd v. Barlow see BOC Ltd v. Instrument Technology Ltd
BOC Ltd v. Instrument Technology Ltd; *sub nom* BOC Ltd v. Barlow; Barlow v. BOC Ltd
    [2001] EWCA Civ 854; [2001] 3 W.L.R. 1687; *Times*, July 10, 2001;
    Independent, June 15, 2001, CA; affirming HQ 000 4304, QBD. . . . .   *Digested*, 01/**390**
Bock v. Germany (A/150) (1990) 12 E.H.R.R. 247, ECHR . . . .   *Applied*, 98/3135
Boddaert v. Belgium (A/235D) (1993) 16 E.H.R.R. 242, ECHR . . . .   *Digested*, 93/**2135**:
                                                                                                        Considered, 01/3522
Boddington v. British Transport Police [1999] 2 A.C. 143; [1998] 2 W.L.R. 639; [1998]
    2 All E.R. 203; (1998) 162 J.P. 455; (1998) 10 Admin. L.R. 321; (1998) 148
    N.L.J. 515; *Times*, April 3, 1998, HL; affirming [1997] C.O.D. 3; (1996) 140
    S.J.L.B. 185; *Times*, July 23, 1996; *Independent*, July 12, 1996, QBD . . . .   *Digested*, 98/**89**:
                                                                                                        Followed, 01/81
Bodhu v. Hampshire AHA [1982] I.C.R. 200, EAT . . . .   *Digested*, 82/**1093**:
                                                    Approved, 84/1238: *Considered*, 99/2146
Boehringer Ingelheim KG v. Dowelhurst Ltd see Boehringer Ingelheim KG v. Swingward Ltd

Boehringer Ingelheim KG v. Dowelhurst Ltd (Defence Amendments) see Glaxo Group
    Ltd v. Dowelhurst Ltd (Defence Amendments)
Boehringer Ingelheim KG v. Dowelhurst Ltd (Infringement Action) see Glaxo Group Ltd
    v. Dowelhurst Ltd (Infringement Action)
Boehringer Ingelheim KG v. Swingward Ltd; Boehringer Ingelheim KG v. Dowelhurst
    Ltd; Glaxo Group Ltd v. Swingward Ltd; Glaxo Group Ltd v. Dowelhurst Ltd; Eli
    Lilly & Co v. Dowelhurst Ltd; SmithKline Beecham Plc v. Dowelhurst Ltd
    [2000] Eu. L.R. 660, CA . . . . *Digested*, 01/**2480**:
                                                    Previous proceedings, 00/3703
Boehringer Ingelheim KG v. Swingward Ltd (Defence Amendments) see Glaxo Group
    Ltd v. Dowelhurst Ltd (Defence Amendments)
Boehringer Ingelheim KG v. Swingward Ltd (Infringement Action) see Glaxo Group Ltd
    v. Dowelhurst Ltd (Infringement Action)
BOEHRINGER/Benzimidazolone (T1052/97) [2000] E.P.O.R. 538, EPO (Technical Bd
    App) . . . . *Digested*, 01/**3909**
BOEHRINGER/Reflection photometer (T416/86) [1989] E.P.O.R. 327, EPO (Technical Bd
    App) . . . . *Considered*, 00/3603
Bogdal v. Kingston upon Hull City Council [1998] R.A. 45, QBD . . . . *Digested*, 98/**4309**
Bogg v. Raper, *Times*, April 22, 1998, CA . . . . *Digested*, 98/**4592**:
                                                         Followed, 98/4874
Boissevain v. Weil [1950] A.C. 327; [1950] 1 All E.R. 728; 66 T.L.R. (Pt. 1) 771; 94 S.J.
    319, HL; affirming [1949] 1 K.B. 482; [1949] 1 All E.R. 146; 65 T.L.R. 197; 93
    S.J. 133, CA; reversing [1948] 1 All E.R. 893, KBD . . . . *Digested*, 47-51/**9891**:
                             Applied, 58/2943, 01/4123: *Distinguished*, 62/2619
Bolam v. Friern Hospital Management Committee [1957] 1 W.L.R. 582; [1957] 2 All
    E.R. 118; [1955-95] P.N.L.R. 7; 101 S.J. 357, QBD . . . . *Digested*, 57/**2431**:
           Applied, 67/2729, 83/2548, 83/2576, 84/2322, 84/2326, 85/2318,
           86/2278, 87/2601, 87/2605, 90/3279, 91/2654, 92/3213, 93/2999,
           94/3399, 95/3679, 97/3789, 97/3797, 99/3997, 00/2779, 00/4250,
           01/4513: *Approved*, 75/245: *Cited*, 00/4248, 00/4283: *Considered*, 88/2453,
                    89/3044, 93/2712, 94/1535, 94/3359, 95/3714, 96/3580:
            Distinguished, 74/265, 92/233, 93/233, 96/4469: *Followed*, 97/2142,
               98/3986, 99/789, 99/4056: *Not applied*, 99/3992, 99/3995
Boland v. Corby Towage (1999) 99(6) Q.R. 6, CC (Liverpool) [*Ex rel.* William Waldron,
    Barrister, Exchange Chambers, Pearl Assurance House, Derby Square,
    Liverpool] . . . . *Digested*, 99/**1506**
Bold v. Noon (Unreported, February 21, 2000), CC (Birkenhead) [*Ex rel.* Michael W
    Halsall Solicitors, 2 The Parks, Newton-le-Willows] . . . . *Digested*, 00/**1725**
Boldack v. East Lindsey DC (1999) 31 H.L.R. 41, CA . . . . *Digested*, 99/**3735**
BOLESTA/Power generator (T451/89) [1998] E.P.O.R. 333, EPO (Technical Bd App)
Boliden Ore & Metals Co v. Dawn Maritime Corp [2000] 1 Lloyd's Rep. 237, QBD
    (Comm Ct) . . . . *Digested*, 00/**483**
Bolitho (Deceased) v. City and Hackney HA [1998] A.C. 232; [1997] 3 W.L.R. 1151;
    [1997] 4 All E.R. 771; [1998] P.I.Q.R. P10; [1998] Lloyd's Rep. Med. 26; (1998)
    39 B.M.L.R. 1; [1998] P.N.L.R. 1; (1997) 94(47) L.S.G. 30; (1997) 141 S.J.L.B.
    238; *Times*, November 27, 1997, HL; affirming [1993] P.I.Q.R. P334; [1993] 4
    Med. L.R. 381, CA . . . . *Digested*, 97/**3789**:
          Applied, 98/3977, 99/3994, 01/4263, 01/4542: *Considered*, 98/3986:
              Distinguished, 98/3969: *Followed*, 98/3963, 99/3989
Bolkiah v. KPMG; *sub nom* HRH Prince Jefri Bolkiah v. KPMG [1999] 2 A.C. 222;
    [1999] 2 W.L.R. 215; [1999] 1 B.C.L.C. 1; [1999] P.N.L.R. 220; (1999) 149
    N.L.J. 16; (1999) 143 S.J.L.B. 35; *Times*, April 20, 1999; *Independent*, January
    12, 1999, HL; reversing [1999] 1 All E.R. 517; [1999] C.L.C. 175; (1998) 95(42)
    L.S.G. 33; (1998) 148 N.L.J. 1602; (1998) 142 S.J.L.B. 268; *Times*, October
    22, 1998; *Independent*, October 22, 1998, CA; reversing *Times*, September 25,
    1998, Ch D . . . . *Digested*, 99/**1**:
              Applied, 00/2504, 00/4008: *Considered*, 99/2, 99/3796, 00/4007:
                                            Followed, 00/2469
Bollard v. Simmonds (Unreported, August 10, 1998), CC (Reading) [*Ex rel.* Elaine
    Strachan, Barrister, 3 Paper Buildings, Temple, London] . . . . *Digested*, 98/**1604**
Bolnore Properties Ltd v. Cobb (1997) 29 H.L.R. 202; (1998) 75 P. & C.R. 127; [1996]
    E.G.C.S. 42; [1996] N.P.C. 37, CA . . . . *Digested*, 96/**3837**:
                                                Considered, 98/3682
Bolt v. Redman [*Ex rel.* Simon John, Barrister, 33 Park Place, Cardiff] . . . . *Digested*, 01/**1658**
Bolt & Nut Co (Tipton) Ltd v. Rowlands Nicholls & Co Ltd [1964] 2 Q.B. 10; [1964] 2
    W.L.R. 98; [1964] 1 All E.R. 137; 107 S.J. 909, CA. . . . . *Digested*, 64/**594**:
                                                Considered, 98/515
Bolton v. Insall see Gleaves v. Insall
Bolton v. Law Society [1994] 1 W.L.R. 512; [1994] C.O.D. 295; *Times*, December 8,
    1993, CA . . . . *Digested*, 94/**4220**:
                                   Applied, 98/3724: *Followed*, 97/3375
Bolton v. North Dorset DC (1997) 74 P. & C.R. 73; [1998] 1 P.L.R. 69; [1997] 2
    E.G.L.R. 180; [1997] 47 E.G. 132; [1997] R.V.R. 247; [1998] J.P.L. 71, Lands Tr . . *Digested*, 97/**4119**
Bolton v. Southern Electric Plc [1999] 1 E.G.L.R. 177; [2000] R.V.R. 233, Lands Tr . . . . . *Digested*, 99/**1998**

Bolton v. Stone; *sub nom* Stone v. Bolton [1951] A.C. 850; [1951] 1 All E.R. 1078; [1951] 1 T.L.R. 977; 50 L.G.R. 32; 95 S.J. 333, HL; reversing [1950] 1 K.B. 201; [1949] 2 All E.R. 851; 65 T.L.R. 683; 48 L.G.R. 107; 93 S.J. 710, CA; reversing [1949] 1 All E.R. 237, KBD. . . . . *Digested*, 47-51/**2316**:
Applied, 47-51/2551, 47-51/3978, 47-51/6863, 47-51/9605, 47-51/9855, 53/2524, 57/2376, 57/2416, 61/5875, 62/2033, 62/2083, 69/2400, 74/3364, 98/3994: *Considered*, 70/1067, 73/2306, 75/2291, 75/2324, 77/2146, 77/2597, 82/4057, 87/2597, 87/4737, 94/2278, 95/3659:
Distinguished, 66/3445

BOLTON BRADY/Shutter (T251/91) [1999] E.P.O.R. 16, EPO (Technical Bd App)
Bolton MBC v. Park Pit Landfill Ltd (2001) 16 P.A.D. 18, Planning Inspector
Bolton MBC v. Qasmi (1999) 77 P. & C.R. D36, CA
Bolton MBC v. Secretary of State for the Environment; *sub nom* R. v. Secretary of State for the Environment Ex p. Bolton MDC (1991) 61 P. & C.R. 343; [1991] J.P.L. 241, CA [1991] J.P.L. 32. . . . . *Digested*, 91/**94**:
Applied, 92/4318, 93/3840, 96/4764, 97/4130, 01/2038: *Considered*, 94/43, 96/4734, 96/4754, 97/4031, 97/4061: *Distinguished*, 99/4230:
Followed, 94/4400, 97/4125

Bolton MBC v. Tudor Properties Ltd; *sub nom* Tudor Properties Ltd v. Bolton MBC (2000) 80 P. & C.R. 537; [2000] R.V.R. 292; [2000] R.V.R. 348; [2000] J.P.L. 1307 (Note); [2000] N.P.C. 49, CA; affirming [2000] R.V.R. 94, LandsTr . . . . . . *Digested*, 00/**4426**
Bolton MDC v. Manchester Ship Canal Co see Bolton MDC v. Secretary of State for the Environment
Bolton MDC v. Secretary of State for the Environment; Bolton MDC v. Manchester Ship Canal Co; Bolton MDC v. Trafford Park Development Corp 94 L.G.R. 387; (1996) 71 P. & C.R. 309; [1995] J.P.L. 1043; (1996) 160 L.G. Rev. 361; [1995] E.G.C.S. 94; (1995) 139 S.J.L.B. 190; [1995] N.P.C. 99; *Times*, May 25, 1995; *Independent*, July 10, 1995 (C.S.), HL; reversing (1995) 69 P. & C.R. 324; [1994] 2 P.L.R. 42; [1994] E.G.C.S. 127; [1994] N.P.C. 104; *Times*, August 4, 1994, CA; reversing (1994) 67 P. & C.R. 333; [1993] E.G.C.S. 170, QBD . . . . . . *Digested*, 96/**4834**:
Applied, 96/4674, 97/4130, 01/4684: *Considered*, 96/4777, 97/4090:
Followed, 95/4886, 96/4753, 97/4122, 98/4222
Bolton MDC v. Trafford Park Development Corp see Bolton MDC v. Secretary of State for the Environment
Bolwell v. Redcliffe Homes Ltd [1999] I.R.L.R. 485; [1999] P.I.Q.R. P243; *Independent*, February 1, 1999 (C.S.), CA . . . . *Digested*, 99/**2035**
Bombay Official Assignee v. Shroff (1932) 48 T.L.R. 443, PC (Ind) . . . . *Applied*, 01/3778
BON MATIN Trade Mark [1989] R.P.C. 537, Ch D; affirming [1988] R.P.C. 553, TMR. . . *Digested*, 89/**3699**:
Referred to, 99/3544, 01/4063

Bonafonte v. GrupoTorras SA see GrupoTorras SA v. Al-Sabah (No.5)
Bond v. Leicester City Council [2001] EWCA Civ 1544; (2001) 98(47) L.S.G. 27; (2001) 145 S.J.L.B. 259; *Times*, November 23, 2001; *Independent*, November 1, 2001, CA . . . . *Digested*, 01/**3423**
Bond v. Livingstone & Co [2001] P.N.L.R. 30, QBD. . . . . *Digested*, 01/**589**
Bond v. United States 8 B.H.R.C. 584, US Ct
Bond van Adverteerders v. Netherlands (C352/85) [1988] E.C.R. 2085; [1989] 3 C.M.L.R. 113; *Times*, May 20, 1988, ECJ . . . . *Digested*, 91/**3985**:
Applied, 98/3856

Bonifaci v. Istituto Nazionale della Previdenza Sociale (INPS) (C94/95); Berto v. Istituto Nazionale della Previdenza Sociale (C95/95) [1997] E.C.R. I-3969; [1998] 1 C.M.L.R. 257; (1997) 94(34) L.S.G. 30, ECJ (5th Chamber)
Bonifacti v. Italy (C9/90) see Francovich v. Italy (C6/90)
Bonita Bryg v. Fuji Television Network Inc (Unreported, June 2, 1993), CC (Central London) [*Ex rel*. Howard Lederman, Barrister] . . . . *Digested*, 93/**1512**:
Considered, 98/1638
Bonnard v. Perryman [1891] 2 Ch. 269; [1891-94] All E.R. Rep. 965, CA . . . . *Applied*, 59/3338,
75/1950, 77/1787, 79/1656, 86/1990: *Considered*, 86/2598, 91/2885,
98/1773: *Distinguished*, 87/2298: *Followed*, 68/3133
Bonner-Williams v. Peter Lindsay Leisure Ltd [2001] 1 All E.R. (Comm) 1140, QBD (T&CC) . . . . *Digested*, 01/**3797**
Bonnington Castings Ltd v. Wardlaw; *sub nom* Wardlaw v. Bonnington Castings Ltd [1956] A.C. 613; [1956] 2 W.L.R. 707; [1956] 1 All E.R. 615; 1956 S.C. (H.L.) 26; 1956 S.L.T. 135; 54 L.G.R. 153; 100 S.J. 207, HL; affirming 1955 S.C. 320; 1955 S.L.T. 225, 1 Div . . . . *Digested*, 56/**3489**:
Applied, 57/360, 57/1420, 57/1421, 57/2004, 58/1324, 61/877, 61/3522, 62/1267.a, 72/2356, 73/2281, 74/2554, 88/2415, 96/2185, 96/4457, 01/4448: *Considered*, 58/2270, 87/2604, 94/3079, 00/5114
Bonomi SA v. Volvo Automobiles France SA [1999] E.C.C. 394, Cass (F)
BONUS GOLD Trade Mark [1998] R.P.C. 859, Appointed Person . . . . *Digested*, 99/**3589**
Bonz Group (Pty) Ltd v. Cooke [1994] 3 N.Z.L.R. 216, HC (Aus) . . . . *Applied*, 00/3572
Bonzel (T) v. Intervention Ltd (No.3) [1991] R.P.C. 553, Pat Ct . . . . *Digested*, 92/**3292**:
Applied, 00/3676: *Referred to*, 96/4557
Boodram v. Baptiste [1999] 1 W.L.R. 1709; *Times*, June 1, 1999, PC (Trin) . . . . *Digested*, 99/**1120**
Boodram v. Trinidad and Tobago [2001] UKPC 20; *Times*, May 15, 2001, PC (Trin) . . . . . *Digested*, 01/**1101**

Booker Aquaculture Ltd (t/a Marine Harvest McConnell) v. Secretary of State for
Scotland (Judicial Review) 2000 S.C. 9; [2000] U.K.H.R.R. 1; 1999 G.W.D. 30-
1435, 1 Div; reversing [1999] 1 C.M.L.R. 35; [1999] Eu. L.R. 54; 1998 G.W.D.
21-1089; *Times*, September 24, 1998, OH . . . . *Digested*, 00/**6301**
Booker Aquaculture Ltd (t/a Marine Harvest McConnell) v. Secretary of State for
Scotland (Reference to ECJ) [2000] Eu. L.R. 449, 1 Div . . . . *Digested*, 01/**6501**
Boote (Inspector of Taxes) v. Banco do Brasil SA [1997] S.T.C. 327; [1997] 6 Bank.
L.R. 127; 69 T.C. 333; [1997] B.T.C. 140; *Times*, January 28, 1997, CA; affirming
[1996] S.T.C. 339; *Times*, April 2, 1996, Ch D . . . . *Digested*, 97/**1075**
Booth v. Bradford MDC see Bradford MDC v. Booth
Booth v. United States [1999] I.R.L.R. 16, EAT . . . . *Digested*, 00/**2111**
Booth & Phipps Garages Ltd v. Milton (Unreported, October 1, 1999), CC (Oxford) [*Ex
rel.* Alexander Pelling, Barrister, New Court Chambers, 5 Verulam Buildings,
Gray's Inn, London] . . . . *Digested*, 00/**2601**
Boots Co Plc v. Customs and Excise Commissioners (C126/88) [1990] S.T.C. 387;
[1990] E.C.R. I-1235; [1990] 2 C.M.L.R. 731; *Times*, March 29, 1990, ECJ;
affirming [1988] S.T.C. 138; [1988] 1 C.M.L.R. 433, QBD; affirming [1987] 3
C.M.L.R. 609; [1986] V.A.T.T.R. 49, VAT Tr (London) . . . . *Digested*, 91/**3668**:
Considered, 00/5339: *Distinguished*, 98/4945, 01/5614
Boots the Chemist Ltd, Re see FA Wellworth & Co Ltd's Application, Re
Bord Telecom Eireann Plc's Trade Mark Application; *sub nom* Bord Telecom Erieann Plc's
Trade Mark Application [2001] E.T.M.R. 72, PO (Irl)
Bord Telecom Erieann Plc's Trade Mark Application see Bord Telecom Eireann Plc's Trade
Mark Application
Border Business Systems Ltd v. John (Unreported, July 9, 2001), Ch D [*Ex rel.* Mark
Beesley, Barrister, 7 Harrington Street, Liverpool] . . . . *Digested*, 01/**3724**
Bordin v. St Mary's NHS Trust [2000] Lloyd's Rep. Med. 287, QBD. . . . . *Digested*, 00/**1451**
Borealis AB (formerly Borealis Petrokemi AB and Statoil Petrokemi AB) v. Stargas Ltd
(The Berge Sisar) [2001] UKHL 17; [2001] 2 W.L.R. 1118; [2001] 2 All E.R. 193;
[2001] 1 All E.R. (Comm) 673; [2001] 1 Lloyd's Rep. 663; [2001] C.L.C. 1084;
(2001) 98(20) L.S.G. 43; (2001) 145 S.J.L.B. 93; *Times*, March 27, 2001, HL;
affirming [1999] Q.B. 863; [1998] 3 W.L.R. 1353; [1998] 4 All E.R. 821; [1998]
2 Lloyd's Rep. 475; [1998] C.L.C. 1589; *Times*, September 14, 1998, CA;
reversing [1997] 1 Lloyd's Rep. 642 (Note), QBD (Comm Ct) . . . . *Digested*, 01/**4948**:
Previous proceedings, 97/638
Borgers v. Belgium (A/214) (1993) 15 E.H.R.R. 92, ECHR . . . . *Digested*, 93/**2128**:
Applied, 97/2803, 98/3142: *Distinguished*, 00/6100
Borissov v. Secretary of State for the Home Department [1996] Imm. A.R. 524, CA . . . *Digested*, 97/**2849**:
Applied, 99/3147
Borland's Trustee v. Steel Bros & Co Ltd [1901] 1 Ch. 279, Ch D . . . . *Considered*, 01/3778
Borrowman v. West Lothian Council [1998] R.V.R. 53, Lands Tr. . . . . *Digested*, 98/**6137**
Borrows v. P McGuiness & Co (Unreported, January 17, 2001), CC (Stockport) [*Ex
rel.* Julian Orr, Barrister, Cobden House Chambers, 19 Quay Street,
Manchester] . . . . *Digested*, 01/**903**
Borthwick v. Elderslie Steamship Co Ltd (No.1) see Elderslie Steamship Co Ltd v.
Borthwick
Boscawen v. Bajwa; Abbey National Plc v. Boscawen [1996] 1 W.L.R. 328; [1995] 4
All E.R. 769; (1995) 70 P. & C.R. 391; (1995) 92(21) L.S.G. 37; (1995) 139
S.J.L.B. 111; *Times*, April 25, 1995; *Independent*, May 23, 1995, CA . . . . *Digested*, 95/**3601**:
Considered, 97/2380, 98/4355
Boss v. Kingston [1963] 1 W.L.R. 99; [1963] 1 All E.R. 177; [1962] 2 Lloyd's Rep. 431;
61 L.G.R. 109; 106 S.J. 1053, DC . . . . *Digested*, 63/**3074**:
Distinguished, 01/3829
Boss Group Ltd v. Boss France SA [1997] 1 W.L.R. 351; [1996] 4 All E.R. 970; [1996]
L.R.L.R. 403; [1996] C.L.C. 1419; [1996] I.L.Pr. 544; (1996) 146 N.L.J. 918;
Times, April 15, 1996, CA . . . . *Digested*, 96/**1110**:
Followed, 01/802
Bossa v. Ansett Worldwide Aviation Services; *sub nom* Bossa v. Nordstress Ltd; Bossa
v. Hall [1998] 2 C.M.L.R. 175; [1998] I.C.R. 694; [1998] I.R.L.R. 284; *Times*,
March 13, 1998, EAT . . . . *Digested*, 98/**2181**
Bossa v. Hall see Bossa v. Ansett Worldwide Aviation Services
Bossa v. Nordstress Ltd see Bossa v. Ansett Worldwide Aviation Services
Bostic v. Bermondsey & Southwark Group Hospital Management Committee see Allen
v. Sir Alfred McAlpine & Sons Ltd
Bostock v. Totham (Inspector of Taxes) [1997] S.T.C. 764; 69 T.C. 356; [1997] B.T.C.
257; *Independent*, April 21, 1997 (C.S.), Ch D . . . . *Digested*, 97/**1066**
Boston BC v. Rees see Rees v. Boston BC
Boston Capital Ltd v. Chee-A-Tow (Unreported, October 7, 1999), CC (Central
London) [*Ex rel.* Paul St J Letman, Barrister, 3 Paper Buildings, Temple, London] . . . *Digested*, 00/**3916**
Boston Deep Sea Fisheries v. Wilson see Hellyer Brothers Ltd v. McLeod
Boston Deep Sea Fishing & Ice Co v. Ansell (1888) L.R. 39 Ch. D. 339, CA . . . . *Applied*, 47-51/525,
47-51/3579, 47-51/5255, 72/2781: *Approved*, 66/4401, 67/1429:
Considered, 00/313: *Distinguished*, 74/39: *Followed*, 81/941:
Not applied, 70/901

Boston Scientific BV v. Cordis Corp (98/111) [2000] E.N.P.R. 87, Hof (Den Haag)
Boston Scientific Ltd v. Palmaz see Palmaz v. Boston Scientific BV
Botchett v. Chief Adjudication Officer (1999) 2 C.C.L. Rep. 121; (1996) 32 B.M.L.R.
   153; *Times*, May 8, 1996, CA . . . . *Digested*, 96/**5480**
Botlon MBC v. Trustees of Beaumont Estate (2000) 15 P.A.D. 112, Planning Inspector
Botta v. Italy (21439/93) (1998) 26 E.H.R.R. 241; 4 B.H.R.C. 81; (1999) 2 C.C.L. Rep.
   53; [1998] H.R.C.D. 302, ECHR. . . . . *Digested*, 98/**3154**
Botten v. Norway (16206/90) (2001) 32 E.H.R.R. 3, ECHR
Bottrill v. Secretary of State for Trade and Industry see Secretary of State for Trade and
   Industry v. Bottrill
Botu v. Brent LBC see Brent LBC v. Botu
Bouchelkia v. France (1998) 25 E.H.R.R. 686, ECHR . . . . *Digested*, 98/**3152**
Boucher v. R. (1955) 110 C.C.C. 263, Sup Ct (Can) . . . . *Applied*, 98/3116
Bouette v. Rose see B (Deceased), Re
Boughanemi v. France (1996) 22 E.H.R.R. 228, ECHR . . . . *Digested*, 96/**3131**:
                                                           Applied, 98/3152
Boughton v. Knight; Marston v. Knight (1872-75) L.R. 3 P. & D. 64, Ct of Probate . . . . . *Applied*, 53/1627,
                                                            01/5167
Boujlifa v. France (2000) 30 E.H.R.R. 419; [1998] H.R.C.D. 21, ECHR. . . . . *Digested*, 01/**3554**
Boukssid v. Secretary of State for the Home Department [1998] 2 C.M.L.R. 281;
   [1998] 2 F.L.R. 200; [1998] Imm. A.R. 270; [1998] I.N.L.R. 275; *Times*, March
   6, 1998, CA. . . . . *Digested*, 98/**3250**
Boulevard Land Ltd v. Secretary of State for the Environment, Transport and the
   Regions [1998] J.P.L. 983; [1998] E.G.C.S. 38, QBD . . . . *Digested*, 98/**4238**
Boultif v. Switzerland (54273/00) [2001] 2 F.L.R. 1228; (2001) 33 E.H.R.R. 50;
   [2001] Fam. Law 875, ECHR
Bounds v. Camden LBC (Unreported, March 23, 1999), CC (Central London) [*Ex rel.*
   Simon Brilliant, Barrister, Lamb Chambers, Lamb Building, Temple, London] . . . . *Digested*, 99/**3728**
Bourgoin SA v. Ministry of Agriculture, Fisheries and Food [1986] Q.B. 716; [1985] 3
   W.L.R. 1027; [1985] 3 All E.R. 585; [1986] 1 C.M.L.R. 267; [1985] 82 L.S.G.
   3435; *Times*, August 3, 1985, CA; reversing in part [1985] 1 C.M.L.R. 528;
   Times, October 4, 1984, QBD . . . . *Digested*, 86/**1437**:
                        Applied, 87/1473, 88/4, 95/4730: *Considered*, 87/20, 90/4316, 91/3411,
                                            92/2904, 94/2766, 96/5701, 99/4854
Bourlet v. Stagecoach East Kent Road Car Co Ltd [1999] P.I.Q.R. P43, CA . . . . *Digested*, 00/**476**
Bourne v. De Giles (Unreported, April 21, 1998), CC (Ashford) [*Ex rel.* Lee Evans,
   Barrister, Farrar's Building, Temple, London] . . . . *Digested*, 98/**494**
Bournemouth & Boscombe Athletic Football Club Co Ltd, Re [1998] B.P.I.R. 183, Ch D   *Digested*, 98/**3345**
Bournemouth BC v. BP Oil UK Ltd (1998) 15 P.A.D. 487, Planning Inspector
Bournemouth Council v. Orange Personal Communications Ltd (2001) 16 P.A.D. 17,
   Planning Inspector
Bourns Inc v. Raychem Corp see Raychem Corp's Patents
Bourns Inc v. Raychem Corp (No.1) (1997) 20(4) I.P.D. 20032, Ch D
Bourns Inc v. Raychem Corp (No.2); *sub nom* Raychem Corp's Patents, Re [1998]
   R.P.C. 31; (1997) 20(10) I.P.D. 20098, Pat Ct . . . . *Digested*, 98/**3477**
Bourns Inc v. Raychem Corp (No.3) [1999] 3 All E.R. 154; [1999] C.L.C. 1029; [1999]
   2 Costs L.R. 72; [1999] F.S.R. 641; (1999) 22(7) I.P.D. 22063; *Times*, May 12,
   1999; *Independent*, May 24, 1999 (C.S.), CA; affirming [1999] 1 All E.R. 908;
   [1999] 1 Costs L.R. 27; (1999) 22(2) I.P.D. 22014; (1998) 148 N.L.J. 1809;
   Times, November 26, 1998, Ch D . . . . *Digested*, 99/**321**
Bourns Inc v. Raychem Corp (No.4) [2000] C.P.L.R. 155; [2000] F.S.R. 841, CA . . . . . *Digested*, 00/**309**
Bouygues Offshore SA v. Caspian Shipping Co (No.1) [1996] 2 Lloyd's Rep. 140, QBD
   (Adm Ct) . . . . *Digested*, 96/**1079**:
                                               Subsequent proceedings, 98/4411
Bouygues Offshore SA v. Caspian Shipping Co (No.2) [1997] I.L.Pr. 472, CA [1997] 2
   Lloyd's Rep. 485, QBD (Adm Ct) . . . . *Digested*, 98/**756**
Bouygues Offshore SA v. Caspian Shipping Co (No.3) [1997] 2 Lloyd's Rep. 493;
   [1997] C.L.C. 1443, QBD (Adm Ct) . . . . *Digested*, 98/**764**:
                         Considered, 98/757: *Subsequent proceedings*, 98/4411
Bouygues Offshore SA v. Caspian Shipping Co (No.4); *sub nom* Caspian Basin
   Specialised Emergency Salvage Administration v. Bouygues Offshore SA (No.4);
   Ultisol Transport Contractors Ltd v. Bouygues Offshore SA (No.4) [1997] 2
   Lloyd's Rep. 507; [1997] C.L.C. 1463; (1997) 94(35) L.S.G. 35; *Times*, July 3,
   1997, QBD (Adm Ct) . . . . *Digested*, 97/**4513**:
                                               Subsequent proceedings, 98/4411
Bouygues Offshore SA v. Caspian Shipping Co (No.5); *sub nom* Ultisol Transport
   Contractors Ltd v. Bouygues Offshore SA (No.5) [1997] 2 Lloyd's Rep. 533;
   [1997] C.L.C. 1497, QBD (Adm Ct) . . . . *Digested*, 98/**757**:
                                              Subsequent proceedings, 98/4411

Bouygues Offshore SA v. Caspian Shipping Co (Nos.1, 3, 4 and 5); *sub nom* Caspian
    Basin Specialised Emergency Salvage Administration v. Bouygues Offshore SA
    (Nos.1, 3, 4 and 5); Ultisol Transport Contractors Ltd v. Bouygues Offshore SA
    (Nos.1, 3, 4 and 5) [1998] 2 Lloyd's Rep. 461; [1998] C.L.C. 1526; *Times*, August
    7, 1998, CA . . . .   *Digested*, 98/**4411**:
                              Previous proceedings, 96/1079, 97/4513, 98/757, 98/764
Bouygues UK Ltd v. Dahl-Jensen UK Ltd [2001] 1 All E.R. (Comm) 1041; [2001]
    C.L.C. 927; [2000] B.L.R. 522; (2001) 3 T.C.L.R. 2; 73 Con. L.R. 135; (2000)
    97(35) L.S.G. 36; *Times*, August 17, 2000, CA; affirming [2000] B.L.R. 49;
    (2000) 2 T.C.L.R. 308; 70 Con. L.R. 41; *Independent*, February 7, 2000 (C.S.),
    QBD (T&CC) . . . .   *Digested*, 00/**3489**:
                                                                              Followed, 01/6289
Bouzagou, Re see R. v. Governor of Ashford Remand Centre Ex p. Bouzagou
Bovis Construction Ltd v. Commercial Union Assurance Co Plc [2001] 1 Lloyd's Rep.
    416; [2001] Lloyd's Rep. I.R. 321; [2000] N.P.C. 133, QBD (Comm Ct)
Bovis Lend Lease Ltd (formerly Bovis Construction Ltd) v. Braehead Glasgow Ltd
    (formerly Braehead Park Retail Ltd) 71 Con. L.R. 208, QBD (T&CC) . . . .   *Digested*, 00/**862**
Bovis Lend Lease Ltd (formerly Bovis Construction Ltd) v. Saillard Fuller & Partners 77
    Con. L.R. 134, QBD (T&CC)
Bowater Windows Ltd v. Aspen Windows Ltd [1999] F.S.R. 759; (1999) 22(7) I.P.D.
    22066, Ch D . . . .   *Digested*, 99/**3445**
Bowden v. Lancashire CC [2001] B.L.G.R. 409, QBD . . . .   *Digested*, 01/**4470**
Bowden v. South West Water Services Ltd [1999] 3 C.M.L.R. 180; [1999] Eu. L.R.
    573; [1999] Env. L.R. 438, CA; reversing in part [1998] 3 C.M.L.R. 330; [1998]
    Eu. L.R. 418; [1998] Env. L.R. 445, QBD . . . .   *Digested*, 99/**2573**
Bowden v. South West Water Services Ltd (Leave to Appeal) [1998] Env. L.R. D15,
    CA
Bowden v. Tuffnells Parcels Express Ltd (C133/00); *sub nom* Bowden v. Tufnells
    Parcels Express Ltd (C133/00) [2001] All E.R. (EC) 865; [2001] 3 C.M.L.R. 52;
    [2001] I.R.L.R. 838; *Times*, October 15, 2001, ECJ (1st Chamber) [2001] 3
    C.M.L.R. 53; [2000] I.R.L.R. 560, EAT . . . .   *Digested*, 01/**2219**
Bowden v. Tuffnells Parcels Express Ltd (C133/00) see Bowden v. Tuffnells Parcels
    Express Ltd (C133/00)
Bowen v. Mills & Knight Ltd [1973] 1 Lloyd's Rep. 580, QBD . . . .   *Digested*, 73/**2315**:
                              Considered, 99/1414: *Disapproved*, 89/2939
                                                       Disapproved, 98/3159
Bowers v. Hardwick 478 U.S. 186, US Ct.
Bowers v. Levy (Unreported, September 10, 1998), CC (Woolwich) [*Ex rel.* A E Wyeth
    & Co Solicitors, Bridge House, High Street, Dartford, Kent] . . . .   *Digested*, 98/**1466**
Bowers v. Whellans (Unreported, April 28, 1998), CC (Norwich) [*Ex rel.* Fiona Baruah,
    Barrister, East Anglian Chambers, 57 London Street, Norwich] . . . .   *Digested*, 98/**486**
Bowling v. Smith (Unreported, March 17, 1998), CC (Chester) [*Ex rel.* Davies Wallis
    Foyster Solicitors, 5 Castle Street, Liverpool] . . . .   *Digested*, 98/**513**
Bowman v. United Kingdom (1998) 26 E.H.R.R. 1; 4 B.H.R.C. 25; [1998] H.R.C.D.
    273; *Times*, February 23, 1998, ECHR . . . .   *Digested*, 98/**3086**
Bown v. Gould & Swayne [1996] P.N.L.R. 130; [1996] N.P.C. 5, CA. . . . .   *Digested*, 96/**4498**:
                              Applied, 99/308: *Distinguished*, 99/4051
Box v. Barclays Bank Plc; Brown v. Barclays Bank Plc; Jacobs v. Barclays Bank Plc
    [1998] Lloyd's Rep. Bank. 185; (1998) 95(18) L.S.G. 33; [1998] N.P.C. 52;
    Times, April 30, 1998, Ch D . . . .   *Digested*, 98/**289**
Boy Scouts of America v. Dale 8 B.H.R.C. 535, US Ct
Boyce v. Secur Scan (UK) Ltd (Unreported, November 20, 1998), CC (Salisbury) [*Ex
    rel.* Toby Case, Barrister, 18 Carlton Crescent, Southampton] . . . .   *Digested*, 99/**1478**
Boyce v. Wyatt Engineering [2001] EWCA Civ 692; [2001] C.P. Rep. 87; [2001]
    C.P.L.R. 343; *Times*, June 14, 2001, CA.   *Digested*, 01/**676**
Boyd & Forrest v. Glasgow & South Western Railway Co 1915 S.C. 20 . . . .   *Considered*, 84/388,
                                                                                    01/3805
Boyd Line Management Services Ltd v. Ministry of Agriculture, Fisheries and Food
    (No.1) [1999] Eu. L.R. 44, CA . . . .   *Digested*, 99/**2565**
Boyd Line Management Services Ltd v. Ministry of Agriculture, Fisheries and Food
    (No.2) (1999) 96(18) L.S.G. 33; *Times*, May 19, 1999, CA. . . . .   *Digested*, 99/**2559**
Boyde v. Commissioner of Valuation for Northern Ireland VR/24/1999, Lands Tr (NI) . . .   *Digested*, 00/**5676**
Boyer v. Everard (Unreported, July 10, 2000), CC [*Ex rel.* Andrew M Jackson & Co,
    PO Box 47, Essex House, Manor Street, Hull] . . . .   *Digested*, 01/**1621**
Boyle v. Equal Opportunities Commission (C411/96) [1998] All E.R. (EC) 879; [1998]
    E.C.R. I-6401; [1998] 3 C.M.L.R. 1133; [1998] C.E.C. 1025; [1999] I.C.R. 360;
    [1998] I.R.L.R. 717; [1999] 1 F.L.R. 119; [1999] 1 F.C.R. 581; (2000) 52 B.M.L.R.
    169; [1998] O.P.L.R. 289; [1999] Pens. L.R. 103; *Times*, October 29, 1998,
    ECJ . . . .   *Digested*, 98/**2169**
Boyle v. Ford Motor Co Ltd; Melia v. Ford Motor Co Ltd; Porter v. Ford Motor Co Ltd;
    Wallace v. Ford Motor Co Ltd [1992] 1 W.L.R. 476; [1992] 2 All E.R. 228;
    Times, March 13, 1992, CA . . . .   *Digested*, 92/**3458**:
                                                                              Doubted, 99/353

Boyle v. Kodak [1969] 1 W.L.R. 661; [1969] 2 All E.R. 439; 6 K.I.R. 427; 113 S.J. 382,
  HL; reversing (1967) 3 K.I.R. 28, CA . . . . *Digested*, 69/**316**:
  Considered, 73/1460, 73/3709, 74/4247, 00/4228
Boyle v. Secretary of State for the Environment, Transport and the Regions [1999]
  J.P.L. 1096; (1999) 96(16) L.S.G. 37, QBD . . . . *Digested*, 00/**4490**
Boyle v. Walker see Walker v. Boyle
Boyle and Rice v. United Kingdom (A/131) (1988) 10 E.H.R.R. 425; *Times*, May 13,
  1988, ECHR . . . . *Digested*, 89/**1920**:
  Considered, 01/3542
Boyo v. Lambeth LBC [1994] I.C.R. 727; [1995] I.R.L.R. 50, CA . . . . *Digested*, 95/**2122**:
  Applied, 98/2098, 98/2206: *Considered*, 96/2522
Boys v. Chaplin; *sub nom* Chaplin v. Boys [1971] A.C. 356; [1969] 3 W.L.R. 322;
  [1969] 2 All E.R. 1085; [1969] 2 Lloyd's Rep. 487; 113 S.J. 608, HL; affirming
  [1968] 2 Q.B. 1; [1968] 2 W.L.R. 328; [1968] 1 All E.R. 283; 111 S.J. 968; *Times*,
  December 7, 1967, CA; affirming [1967] 3 W.L.R. 266; [1967] 2 All E.R. 665;
  111 S.J. 297, QBD . . . . *Digested*, 69/**469**:
  Applied, 76/2174, 92/477: *Considered*, 89/3528, 91/514, 92/1916, 94/4282,
  95/4724, 95/4736: *Explained*, 91/2841, 92/3456: *Followed*, 83/360,
  00/1463
Boys and Girls Welfare Society v. Customs and Excise Commissioners [1998] B.V.C.
  2070, V&DTr
Bozkurt, Re CO 3316/97, QBD . . . . *Referred to*, 00/1043
Bozkurt v. Thames Magistrates Court see R. (on the application of Bozkurt) v. Thames
  Magistrates Court
Bozzetti v. Invernizzi SpA (C179/84) [1985] E.C.R. 2301; [1986] 2 C.M.L.R. 246, ECJ . *Digested*, 86/**1306**:
  Applied, 99/704
BP Amoco Plc v. John Kelly Ltd [2001] N.I. 25; [2001] E.T.M.R. CN14, CA (NI);
  reversing [2001] F.S.R. 21, HC (NI) . . . . *Digested*, 01/**5881**
BP Australia Ltd v. Commissioner of Taxation of the Commonwealth of Australia (No.2)
  [1966] A.C. 224; [1965] 3 W.L.R. 608; [1965] 3 All E.R. 209; (1965) 44
  A.T.C. 312; [1965] T.R. 317; (1964) 37 A.L.J.R. 365, HC (Aus) . . . . *Digested*, 65/**1922**:
  Applied, 65/1924, 90/761, 00/4933: *Considered*, 88/534
BP BV v. W GmbH (2 U 122/95) [2000] E.N.P.R. 1, OLG (Dusseldorf)
BP Chemicals Ltd v. Commission of the European Communities (T11/95R) (No.2)
  [1998] E.C.R. II-3235; [1998] 3 C.M.L.R. 693, CFI
BP Chemicals Ltd v. Commission of the European Communities (T184/97) [2000]
  E.C.R. II-3145; [2000] 3 C.M.L.R. 1076, CFI (2nd Chamber) . . . . *Digested*, 01/**769**:
BP Chemicals Ltd v. Gillick [1995] I.R.L.R. 128, EAT . . . . *Cited*, 00/5528
BP Exploration Co (Libya) Ltd v. Hunt (No.2) [1983] 2 A.C. 352; [1982] 2 W.L.R. 253;
  [1982] 1 All E.R. 925; *Times*, February 5, 1981, HL; affirming [1981] 1 W.L.R.
  232; 125 S.J. 165, CA; affirming [1979] 1 W.L.R. 783; 123 S.J. 455, QBD . . . . . . *Digested*, 82/**406**:
  Applied, 00/3523: *Considered*, 87/3131, 88/121, 89/410:
  Distinguished, 84/1869: *Followed*, 84/3187: *Referred to*, 82/1145
BP Exploration Operating Co Ltd v. Chevron Shipping Co; *sub nom* BP Exploration
  Operating Co Ltd v. Chevron Transport (Scotland); BP Exploration Operating Co
  Ltd v. Chevron Tankers (Bermuda) Ltd; BP Exploration Operating Co Ltd v.
  Chevron Transport Corp [2001] UKHL 50; [2001] 3 W.L.R. 949; 2001 S.L.T.
  1394; 2001 S.C.L.R. 1029; (2001) 98(45) L.S.G. 26; (2001) 145 S.J.L.B. 244;
  2001 G.W.D. 33-1316; *Times*, October 19, 2001; *Independent*, December 3, 2001,
  HL; reversing 2000 S.L.T. 1374; 2000 S.C.L.R. 580; 2000 G.W.D. 14-559, 1
  Div; reversing in part 2000 S.L.T. 201; 1999 S.C.L.R. 438; 1999 G.W.D. 7-355;
  Times, May 6, 1999, OH . . . . *Digested*, 01/**6865**
BP Exploration Operating Co Ltd v. Chevron Tankers (Bermuda) Ltd see BP Exploration
  Operating Co Ltd v. Chevron Shipping Co
BP Exploration Operating Co Ltd v. Chevron Transport (Scotland) see BP Exploration
  Operating Co Ltd v. Chevron Shipping Co
BP Exploration Operating Co Ltd v. Chevron Transport Corp see BP Exploration
  Operating Co Ltd v. Chevron Shipping Co
BP Exploration Operating Co Ltd v. Inland Revenue Commissioners [2000] S.T.C.
  (S.C.D.) 466; [2000] S.T.I. 1433, Sp Comm . . . . *Digested*, 01/**5295**
BP Properties Ltd v. Buckler (1988) 55 P. & C.R. 337; (1987) 284 E.G. 375; (1987)
  137 N.L.J. 899, CA . . . . *Digested*, 88/**2155**:
  Applied, 01/578: *Followed*, 01/4842
BP Refinery (Westernpoint) Pty Ltd v. Shire of Hastings (1977) 180 C.L.R. 266; (1978)
  52 A.L.J.R. 20 . . . . *Applied*, 93/295,
  97/4845, 99/3447
BPR Ltd, Re [1998] B.C.C. 259, Ch D . . . . *Digested*, 98/**672**
Braathens Sverige AB v. Riksskatteverket (C346/97) [1999] E.C.R. I-3419; [2000] Env.
  L.R. D4, ECJ
Brabazon-Drenning v. United Kingdom Central Council for Nursing, Midwifery and
  Health Visiting [2001] H.R.L.R. 6; *Daily Telegraph*, November 28, 2000, QBD . . . *Digested*, 01/**3290**
Brabon, Re; *sub nom* Treharne v. Brabon [2000] B.C.C. 1171; [2001] 1 B.C.L.C. 11;
  [2000] B.P.I.R. 537; [2000] E.G.C.S. 38; [2000] N.P.C. 21, Ch D . . . . *Digested*, 00/**3450**

Bracco SpA Petition for Revocation, Re see General Hospital Corp's European Patent (No.222886)

Bracegirdle v. Cobley see Bracegirdle v. Oxley

Bracegirdle v. Oxley; Bracegirdle v. Cobley [1947] K.B. 349; [1947] 1 All E.R. 126; 63 T.L.R. 98; (1947) 111 J.P. 131; [1947] L.J.R. 815; 176 L.T. 187; 91 S.J. 27, KBD ... *Digested*, 47-51/**9026**: *Applied*, 47-51/6069, 47-51/6081, 47-51/7494, 47-51/8311, 56/7782, 75/2588, 78/417, 81/2347, 01/2422: *Considered*, 69/3441: *Distinguished*, 97/510: *Followed*, 73/2988, 74/3379

Bracken v. East Hertfordshire DC [2000] P.L.C.R. 434; [2000] C.O.D. 366; (2000) 97(19) L.S.G. 45; [2000] N.P.C. 52, QBD . . . . *Digested*, 01/**4690**

Brackenbrough's Community Trade Mark Application [2001] E.T.M.R. 39, OHIM (Opposition Div) . . . . *Digested*, 01/**3990**

Bracknell Forest LBC v. Barratt Thames Valley Ltd (2000) 15 P.A.D. 578, Planning Inspector

Bradburn v. Great Western Railway Co (1874-75) L.R. 10 Ex. 1, Ex Ct . . . . *Applied*, 47-51/2525, 47-51/2543, 47/2525, 63/2456, 66/8472, 71/3091, 71/3207, 72/836, 73/740, 79/2472: *Approved*, 69/906: *Considered*, 63/951, 99/793

Bradbury v. Hoolin [1998] N.P.C. 87, Ch D

Bradcrown Ltd, Re see Official Receiver v. Ireland

Braddock v. Tillotson's Newspapers Ltd [1950] 1 K.B. 47; [1949] 2 All E.R. 306; (1949) 65 T.L.R. 553; 93 S.J. 464, CA . . . . *Digested*, 47-51/**7458**: *Applied*, 47-51/7459, 47-51/7517, 53/1379, 53/2714, 53/2715: *Considered*, 01/634: *Distinguished*, 61/6677

Bradford & Bingley Building Society v. Boyce Evans Shepherd [1998] P.N.L.R. 250, Ch D . . . . *Digested*, 98/**569**

Bradford & Bingley Building Society v. Seddon (Hancock t/a Hancocks) [1999] 1 W.L.R. 1482; [1999] 4 All E.R. 217; [1999] Lloyd's Rep. P.N. 657; (1999) 96(15) L.S.G. 30; (1999) 143 S.J.L.B. 106; *Times*, March 30, 1999; *Independent*, March 17, 1999, CA . . . . *Digested*, 99/**351**: *Applied*, 00/624: *Considered*, 99/549

Bradford & Bingley Building Society v. Verdi see Leamington Spa Building Society v. Verdi

Bradford City Council v. Anderton 89 L.G.R. 681; [1991] R.A. 45; [1991] C.O.D. 313; (1991) 135 S.J. 251; *Times*, February 15, 1991; *Independent*, March 8, 1991; *Daily Telegraph*, February 21, 1991 . . . . *Digested*, 91/**2373**: *Considered*, 93/2636, 95/3206, 95/3207, 98/4308

Bradford City Council v. Bellway Homes Ltd (2001) 16 P.A.D. 58, Planning Inspector

Bradford MBC v. Dawson [1999] I.C.R. 312, EAT . . . . *Digested*, 99/**2140**

Bradford MDC v. Booth; *sub nom* Booth v. Bradford MDC (2000) 164 J.P. 485; (2001) 3 L.G.L.R. 8; [2000] C.O.D. 338; (2000) 164 J.P.N. 801; *Times*, May 31, 2000, QBD . . . . *Digested*, 00/**395**

Bradford MDC v. Glovers Garages Ltd (1998) 13 P.A.D. 735, Planning Inspector

Bradford MDC v. Yorkshire Water Services Ltd [2001] EWHC Admin 687; *Times*, November 15, 2001, QBD (Admin Ct). . . . . *Digested*, 01/**5633**

Bradford Third Equitable Benefit Building Society v. Borders [1941] 2 All E.R. 205, HL; reversing in part [1940] Ch. 202, CA; reversing in part [1939] Ch. 520, Ch D . . *Applied*, 01/5356

Bradford-Smart v. West Sussex CC A2/2001/0597, CA; affirming (2001) 3 L.G.L.R. 28; [2001] E.L.R. 138; (2000) 97(48) L.S.G. 37; *Times*, December 5, 2000, QBD . . . . *Digested*, 01/**1989**

Bradlaugh v. Gossett (1883-84) L.R. 12 Q.B.D. 271, QBD . . . . *Applied*, 60/2321, 71/6775: *Considered*, 99/5164

Bradley (Inspector of Taxes) v. London Electricity Plc (No.1) [1996] S.T.C. 231; 70 T.C. 155, Ch D . . . . *Digested*, 96/**5570**

Bradley (Inspector of Taxes) v. London Electricity Plc (No.2) [1996] S.T.C. 1054; [1996] E.G.C.S. 147; (1996) 93(37) L.S.G. 27; (1996) 140 S.J.L.B. 210; *Times*, August 1, 1996; *Independent*, October 14, 1996 (C.S.), Ch D . . . . *Digested*, 96/**5566**: *Considered*, 01/859

Bradley-Hole (A Bankrupt), Re [1995] 1 W.L.R. 1097; [1995] 4 All E.R. 865; [1995] B.C.C. 418; [1995] 2 B.C.L.C. 163; [1995] 2 F.L.R. 838; [1996] 2 F.C.R. 259; [1995] Fam. Law 673, Ch D . . . . *Digested*, 95/**428**: *Approved*, 99/3242: *Distinguished*, 96/3516, 96/3522

Bradley's Application, Re [1995] N.I. 192, QBD (NI)

Bradwin Ltd's Petition (formerly t/a Big Boppers Inn), Re [1997] N.I. 394, Ch D (NI) . . *Digested*, 99/**5402**

Brady v. Brady [1989] A.C. 755; [1988] 2 W.L.R. 1308; [1988] 2 All E.R. 617; (1988) 4 B.C.C. 390; [1988] B.C.L.C. 579; [1988] P.C.C. 316; [1988] 2 F.T.L.R. 181; (1988) 132 S.J. 820, HL; reversing (1987) 3 B.C.C. 535; [1988] B.C.L.C. 20; [1977] P.C.C. 434; [1987] 2 F.T.L.R. 414; (1987) 137 N.L.J. 898, CA . . . . *Digested*, 88/**347**: *Applied*, 98/706

Braham v. Golding (Unreported, November 26, 1997), CC (Bow) [*Ex rel.* Frank R. Moat, Barrister, 3 Pump Court, Temple, London] . . . . *Digested*, 98/**1595**

Braid v. Walsall MBC (1999) 78 P. & C.R. 94; [1998] E.G.C.S. 41; [1998] N.P.C. 35, CA . . . . *Digested*, 99/**3725**

Brain v. Ingledew Brown Bennison & Garrett (No.1) [1996] F.S.R. 341; (1996) 19(5) I.P.D. 19036, CA; reversing in part [1995] F.S.R. 552; *Independent*, April 18, 1995 (C.S.), Ch D . . . . *Digested*, 96/**4558**:
Applied, 98/3528: *Referred to*, 96/4550

Brain v. Ingledew Brown Bennison & Garrett (No.3); Brain v. Riso National Laboratory [1997] F.S.R. 511; (1997) 20(5) I.P.D. 20047, Ch D . . . . *Digested*, 97/**3917**:
Applied, 98/3528: *Followed*, 01/3966

Brain v. Riso National Laboratory see Brain v. Ingledew Brown Bennison & Garrett (No.3)

Brain v. Uddin (Unreported, May 18, 2000), CC (Birmingham) [*Ex rel.* James Morgan, Barrister, St Philip's Chambers, Fountain Court, Steelhouse Lane, Birmingham] . *Digested*, 00/**2583**:
Applied, 01/905

Braintree DC v. Barons (2000) 15 P.A.D. 667, Planning Inspector
Braintree DC v. Clark (Unreported, March 31, 1998), CA [*Ex rel.* Stephen Morley, Barrister, Bridewell Chambers, Ground Floor, 2 Bridewell Place, Temple, London] . . . . *Digested*, 98/**13**

Braithwaite, Re see Braithwaite v. Law Society
Braithwaite v. Doncaster MBC [2000] E.G.C.S. 42; (2000) 97(13) L.S.G. 45, QBD
Braithwaite v. Law Society; *sub nom* Braithwaite, Re [1998] P.N.L.R. 478, QBD . . . . . . *Digested*, 98/**3724**
Bramall v. DPP [1998] Masons C.L.R. 246, QBD . . . . *Digested*, 99/**884**
Bramelid v. Sweden (8588/79, 8589/79) (1983) 5 E.H.R.R. 249, Eur Comm HR . . . . . *Distinguished*, 01/3752
Branagan v. DPP; *sub nom* R. v. DPP Ex p. Branagan [2000] R.T.R. 235, QBD . . . . *Digested*, 00/**938**
Brandeis Brokers Ltd v. Black [2001] 2 All E.R. (Comm) 980; [2001] 2 Lloyd's Rep. 359, QBD (Comm Ct) . . . . *Digested*, 01/**333**
Brandeis Goldschmidt & Co Ltd v. Western Transport Ltd [1981] Q.B. 864; [1981] 3 W.L.R. 181; [1982] 1 All E.R. 28; [1981] F.S.R. 481; 125 S.J. 395, CA . . . . *Digested*, 81/**2654**:
Applied, 90/1527, 91/3408: *Considered*, 94/1758, 00/5107:
Distinguished, 90/4308

Brandenstein v. Finanzamt Dusseldorf-Mettmann (C323/99) see Fischer v. Finanzamt Burgdorf (C322/99)
Brandle (Johann) (E4/00), Re [2001] 2 C.M.L.R. 52, EFTA . . . . *Digested*, 01/**2500**
Brandon and Goold v. Murphy Bros [1983] I.R.L.R. 54, EAT . . . . *Digested*, 83/**1343**:
Applied, 98/2239
Brannan v. Airtours Plc, *Times*, February 1, 1999, CA . . . . *Digested*, 99/**3945**:
Distinguished, 01/4282

Brannigan v. Davison [1997] A.C. 238; [1996] 3 W.L.R. 859; 2 B.H.R.C. 395; (1996) 140 S.J.L.B. 231, PC (NZ) . . . . *Digested*, 97/**1168**:
Applied, 00/315

Branson v. Bower (No.1) [2001] EWCA Civ 791; [2001] E.M.L.R. 32, CA; affirming TS/ 01/0012, QBD . . . . *Digested*, 01/**1822**
Branson v. Bower (No.2) [2001] E.M.L.R. 33; *Times*, July 23, 2001, QBD . . . . *Digested*, 01/**1821**
Branston & Gothard Ltd, Re [1999] 1 All E.R. (Comm) 289; [1999] Lloyd's Rep. Bank. 251; [1999] B.P.I.R. 466, Ch D . . . . *Digested*, 99/**3304**
Branwhite v. Worcester Works Finance Ltd [1969] 1 A.C. 552; [1968] 3 W.L.R. 760; [1968] 3 All E.R. 104; 112 S.J. 758, HL . . . . *Digested*, 68/**1776**:
Applied, 92/487, 95/2459, 96/1173, 96/1193, 00/2600:
Distinguished, 94/500: *Followed*, 84/4180, 95/2458

Brass Band Instruments Ltd v. Boosey & Hawkes Plc (IV/32.279) [1988] 4 C.M.L.R. 67, CEC. . . . . *Digested*, 88/**1406**:
Applied, 99/666

Brasserie du Pecheur SA v. Germany (C46/93); R. v. Secretary of State for Transport Ex p. Factortame Ltd (No.4) (C48/93) [1996] Q.B. 404; [1996] 2 W.L.R. 506; [1996] All E.R. (E.C.) 301; [1996] E.C.R. I-1029; [1996] 1 C.M.L.R. 889; [1996] C.E.C. 295; [1996] I.R.L.R. 267; *Times*, March 7, 1996, ECJ. . . . . *Digested*, 96/**2803**:
Applied, 98/2321, 99/144, 99/2565, 00/2383, 01/5581: *Considered*, 96/101, 96/292, 96/2596, 96/5648, 97/80, 99/2259

Bratts Ltd v. Habboush [1999] N.P.C. 82, QBD
Bratty v. Attorney General of Northern Ireland [1963] A.C. 386; [1961] 3 W.L.R. 965; [1961] 3 All E.R. 523; (1962) 46 Cr. App. R. 1; 105 S.J. 865, HL. . . . . *Digested*, 61/**1839**:
Applied, 61/7782, 63/748, 68/3422, 74/654, 81/2346, 91/903:
Cited, 00/6026: *Considered*, 73/558, 83/618, 87/3266, 88/3071, 91/902, 93/925, 94/3944: *Followed*, 80/431: *Not applied*, 62/667

Braun GA v. Elbeka Electro BV [1998] E.T.M.R. 259, RB (Breda)
Bray v. Ford [1896] A.C. 44, HL . . . . *Applied*, 47-51/5211,
47-51/5692, 47-51/5696, 47-51/7783, 47-51/9422, 47-51/9429, 47-51/9431, 63/3169, 69/2160, 90/487: *Approved*, 66/11052: *Considered*, 85/1994, 87/2305, 88/2123, 95/2215, 01/2436

Braymist Ltd v. Wise Finance Co Ltd; *sub nom* Wise Finance Ltd v. Braymist Ltd; A3/ 2001/0704 CHANF, CA; affirming [2001] 11 E.G.C.S. 174; [2001] N.P.C. 55; *Times*, March 27, 2001, Ch D . . . . *Digested*, 01/**704**
Brazil v. Chief Constable of Surrey [1983] 3 All E.R. 537; (1983) 77 Cr. App. R. 237; (1984) 148 J.P. 22; [1983] Crim. L.R. 483; (1983) 127 S.J. 712, QBD . . . . *Digested*, 83/**2841**:
Considered, 85/3386, 91/3409, 01/4788

Brazil (Concrete) Ltd *v.* Amersham Rural DC 65 L.G.R. 365; 18 P. & C.R. 396; 202 E.G.
    413; (1967) 111 S.J. 497, CA; affirming 65 L.G.R. 207, DC . . . .   *Digested,* 67/**3856**:
                                                      Applied, 69/3445, 99/4220
Breadner *v.* Granville-Grossman [2001] Ch. 523; [2001] 2 W.L.R. 593; [2000] 4 All
    E.R. 705; [2000] W.T.L.R. 829; (1999-2000) 2 I.T.E.L.R. 812, Ch D . . . .   *Digested,* 01/**5508**
Breadner *v.* Granville-Grossman (Costs) [2001] W.T.L.R. 377, Ch D . . . .   *Digested,* 01/**5526**
Breckland DC *v.* Burroughes (1999) 14 P.A.D. 494, Planning Inspector
Breda Fucine Meridionali SpA (BFM) *v.* Commission of the European Communities
    (T126/96); Ente Partecipazioni e Finanziamento Industria Manifatturiera (EFIM)
    v. Commission of the European Communities (T127/96) [1998] E.C.R. II-3437;
    [1999] 1 C.M.L.R. 997, CFI (3rd Chamber) . . . .   *Digested,* 99/**705**
Breeden *v.* Lampard (Unreported, March 21, 1985), CA . . . .   *Considered,* 00/204
Breeze *v.* John Stacey & Sons Ltd [2001] N.P.C. 2, QBD
Breeze (Disclosure) *v.* John Stacey & Sons Ltd; *sub nom* Breeze *v.* John Stacy & Sons
    Ltd [2000] C.P. Rep. 77; (1999) 96(28) L.S.G. 27; *Times,* July 8, 1999 ;
    Independent, July 19, 1999 (C.S.), CA. . . . .   *Digested,* 99/**336**
Breeze *v.* John Stacy & Sons Ltd see Breeze (Disclosure) *v.* John Stacey & Sons Ltd
Brelec Installations Ltd, Re see Welsby *v.* Brelec Installations Ltd (In Liquidation)
Bremer Vulcan Schiffbau und Maschinenfabrik *v.* South India Shipping Corp see Bremer
    Vulcan Schiffbau und Maschinenfabrik *v.* South India Shipping Corp Ltd
Bremer Vulcan Schiffbau und Maschinenfabrik *v.* South India Shipping Corp Ltd; *sub
    nom* Bremer Vulcan Schiffbau und Maschinenfabrik *v.* South India Shipping
    Corp; Gregg *v.* Raytheon [1981] A.C. 909; [1981] 2 W.L.R. 141; [1981] 2 All E.R.
    289; [1981] 1 Lloyd's Rep. 253; [1981] Com. L.R. 19; [1981] E.C.C. 151; 125
    S.J. 114, HL; affirming [1980] 2 W.L.R. 905; [1980] 1 All E.R. 420; [1980] 1
    Lloyd's Rep. 255; 124 S.J. 396; *Times,* November 28, 1979, CA; affirming [1979]
    3 W.L.R. 905; [1979] 3 All E.R. 194; (1979) 76 L.S.G. 834; 123 S.J. 504, QBD . .   *Digested,* 81/**119**:
                Applied, 81/99, 81/106, 81/118, 82/139, 83/142, 88/131, 92/189, 94/2705,
                95/179: *Considered,* 80/2384, 81/113, 84/133, 85/116, 86/90, 87/133,
                87/147, 98/244, 01/5711: *Distinguished,* 93/151: *Referred to,* 80/2461, 81/79,
                81/281
Bremer Vulcan Verbund AG *v.* Commission of the European Communities (C63/95) see
    Germany *v.* Commission of the European Communities (C329/93)
Bremner (A Bankrupt), Re [1999] 1 F.L.R. 912; [1999] B.P.I.R. 185; [1999] Fam. Law 293,
    Ch D . . . .   *Digested,* 99/**3243**
Brennan (A Minor) *v.* Howell (Unreported, October 29, 1998), CC (Tunbridge Wells)
    [*Ex rel.* Cripps Harries Hall Solicitors, Seymour House, 11-13 Mount Ephraim
    Road, Tunbridge Wells, Kent] . . . .   *Digested,* 98/**1673**
Brennan (Inspector of Taxes) *v.* Deanby Investment Co Ltd; *sub nom* Deanby
    Investment Co Ltd *v.* Brennan (Inspector of Taxes) [2001] S.T.C. 536; 73 T.C.
    455; [2001] B.T.C. 205; [2001] S.T.I. 596, CA (NI); reversing [2000] S.T.C.
    (S.C.D.) 172; [2000] S.T.I. 587, Sp Comm . . . .   *Digested,* 01/**6037**
Brennan *v.* Home Office [2001] 4 Q.R. 14, CC (Liverpool) [*Ex rel.* Paul Simpson,
    Barrister, 2nd Floor, 14 Cook Street, Liverpool] . . . .   *Digested,* 01/**1728**
Brennan *v.* JH Dewhurst Ltd [1984] I.C.R. 52; [1983] I.R.L.R. 357, EAT . . . .   *Digested,* 84/**1270**:
                                      Considered, 98/2183
Brennan *v.* Lambeth LBC (1998) 30 H.L.R. 481, CA . . . .   *Digested,* 98/**3028**
Brennan *v.* United Kingdom (39846/98), *Times,* October 22, 2001, ECHR. . . . .   *Digested,* 01/**1163**
Brent LBC *v.* Botu; *sub nom* Botu *v.* Brent LBC (2001) 33 H.L.R. 14; [2000] E.G.C.S.
    34; (2000) 97(11) L.S.G. 40; (2000) 97(13) L.S.G. 43; (2000) 144 S.J.L.B. 148;
    [2000] N.P.C. 23, CA . . . .   *Digested,* 00/**3944**
Brent LBC *v.* Charles (1997) 29 H.L.R. 876, CA . . . .   *Digested,* 98/**3681**
Brent LBC *v.* Cronin (1998) 30 H.L.R. 43, CA . . . .   *Digested,* 98/**3062**
Brent LBC *v.* Griffin Housing Association Ltd (2001) 16 P.A.D. 3, Planning Inspector
Brent LBC *v.* Loftus Road Plc (2000) 15 P.A.D. 1, Planning Inspector
Brent LBC *v.* Marks (1999) 31 H.L.R. 343, CA . . . .   *Digested,* 99/**3711**
Brent LBC *v.* Patel [2001] 1 W.L.R. 897; [2001] B.L.G.R. 285; (2000) 97(48) L.S.G.
    36; *Times,* November 30, 2000, Ch D . . . .   *Digested,* 01/**3437**
Brent LBC *v.* Reynolds; *sub nom* Reynolds *v.* Brent LBC [2001] EWCA Civ 1843;
    [2001] 50 E.G.C.S. 89; [2001] N.P.C. 177; *Times,* December 18, 2001;
    Independent, December 7, 2001, CA
Brent LBC *v.* Sadiq see R. *v.* Brent LBC Ex p. Sadiq
Brent LBC *v.* Sebanjor; *sub nom* Sebanjor *v.* Brent LBC; Senbanjo *v.* Brent [2001] 1
    W.L.R. 2374; [2001] B.L.G.R. 339; *Times,* January 4, 2001, Ch D . . . .   *Digested,* 01/**3448**
Brent LBC *v.* Sharma (1993) 25 H.L.R. 257; [1992] N.P.C. 102, CA . . . .   *Digested,* 93/**2114**:
                                      Considered, 00/3894
Brent LBC *v.* Super Toughened Glass Ltd (2001) 16 P.A.D. 82, Planning Inspector
Brentjens Handelsonderneming BV *v.* Stichting Bedrijfspensioenfonds voor de Handel in
    Bouwmaterialen (C115/97) [1999] E.C.R. I-6025; [2000] 4 C.M.L.R. 566;
    [2001] I.C.R. 774, ECJ . . . .   *Digested,* 00/**2358**:
                            Joined proceedings, 00/2357, 00/2359
Brentwood BC *v.* BP Oil UK Ltd (1999) 14 P.A.D. 131, Planning Inspector
Brentwood BC *v.* External Resource Bureau (1999) 14 P.A.D. 382, Planning Inspector

Brentwood BC v. Hook see Brentwood BC v. Secretary of State for the Environment, Transport and the Regions (No.1)

Brentwood BC v. Secretary of State for the Environment, Transport and the Regions (No.1); Brentwood BC v. Hook (1999) 78 P. & C.R. 301; [1999] J.P.L. 528, QBD . . . . *Digested*, 99/**4212**

Brentwood BC v. Secretary of State for the Environment, Transport and the Regions (No.2) CO 1220/99, QBD . . . . *Digested*, 00/**4466**

Brera v. Ufficio Brevetti [2001] E.T.M.R. 44, Trib (Milano)

Bretagne Angleterre Irlande (BAI) v. Commission of the European Communities (T14/96) [1999] E.C.R. II-139; [1999] 3 C.M.L.R. 245, CFI (1st Chamber) . . . . *Digested*, 00/**725**

Brett v. Lewisham LBC [2000] B.L.G.R. 443, CA . . . . *Digested*, 00/**4230**

Brewer v. Andrews see Andrews v. Brewer

Brewer v. North Tees Health NHS Trust (Unreported, October 24, 1997), CC (Manchester) [*Ex rel.* Jones Maidment Wilson Solicitors, 5-7 Byrom Street, Manchester] . . . . *Digested*, 98/**555**

Brian D Pierson (Contractors) Ltd, Re; *sub nom* Penn v. Pierson [1999] B.C.C. 26; [2001] 1 B.C.L.C. 275; [1999] B.P.I.R. 18, Ch D (Companies Ct) . . . . *Digested*, 99/**3294**

Brice v. Coulthard, CC (Canterbury) [*Ex rel.* Nicholas Yell, Barrister, No.1 Serjeants' Inn, Fleet Street, London] . . . . *Digested*, 01/**1683**

Brick v. Colleys Professional Services [1999] Lloyd's Rep. P.N. 309, CA . . . . *Digested*, 99/**4055**

Brickenden v. London Loan & Savings Co [1934] 3 D.L.R. 465, PC (Can) . . . . *Applied*, 96/**3909**: *Considered*, 99/1401: *Not applied*, 97/3822

Bricom Holdings Ltd v. Inland Revenue Commissioners [1997] S.T.C. 1179; 70 T.C. 272; [1997] B.T.C. 471, CA; affirming [1996] S.T.C. (S.C.D.) 228, Sp Comm . . . . *Digested*, 97/**1072**

Bridge v. Deacons [1984] A.C. 705; [1984] 2 W.L.R. 837; [1984] 2 All E.R. 19; (1984) 81 L.S.G. 1291; (1984) 134 N.L.J. 723; (1984) 128 S.J. 263, PC (HK) . . . *Digested*, 84/**405**: *Considered*, 89/4674, 98/4024

Bridge Oil Ltd v. Owners and/or Demise Charterers of the Ship Guiseppe di Vittorio (No.1) (The Guiseppe di Vittorio) [1998] 1 Lloyd's Rep. 136; [1998] C.L.C. 149; (1997) 94(44) L.S.G. 35; (1997) 141 S.J.L.B. 223; *Times*, November 10, 1997, CA . . . . *Digested*, 97/**4491**

Bridge Oil Ltd v. Owners and/or Demise Charterers of the Ship Guiseppe di Vittorio (The Guiseppe di Vittorio) (No.2) [1998] 1 Lloyd's Rep. 661; [1998] C.L.C. 165, QBD (Adm Ct) . . . . *Digested*, 98/**4391**

Bridgeman v. Brown CCRTI 99/0977.B3, CA . . . . *Digested*, 00/**498**

Bridgend CBC v. Jones (t/a Shamrock Coaches) see R. v. Bridgend CBC Ex p. Jones (t/a Shamrock Coaches)

Bridgend CBC v. Persimmon Homes (Wales) Ltd (2000) 15 P.A.D. 488, Planning Inspector

Bridges v. Mees [1957] Ch. 475; [1957] 3 W.L.R. 215; [1957] 2 All E.R. 577; 101 S.J. 555, Ch D . . . . *Digested*, 57/**1906**: *Applied*, 65/2179, 66/6733, 01/4866: *Considered*, 84/2952, 85/3607

Bridgewater v. Griffiths [2000] 1 W.L.R. 524; [1999] 2 Costs L.R. 52; *Independent*, June 14, 1999 (C.S.), QBD . . . . *Digested*, 99/**380**

Bridisco Ltd v. Jordan see Parkfield Group Plc (In Liquidation), Re

Bridle v. Jones 1997-B-No.1259, QBD . . . . *Digested*, 98/**1777**

Bridle v. Secretary of State for the Environment, Transport and the Regions (2000) 97(44) L.S.G. 46, QBD (Admin Ct)

Briffet v. DPP see Briffett v. DPP

Briffett v. Crown Prosecution Service see Briffett v. DPP

Briffett v. DPP; *sub nom* Briffett v. Crown Prosecution Service; Briffet v. DPP [2001] EWHC Admin 841; *Times*, November 26, 2001, QBD (Admin Ct) . . . . *Digested*, 01/**83**

Brigden v. American Express Bank Ltd [2000] I.R.L.R. 94, QBD . . . . *Digested*, 00/**2117**

Briggs v. Baptiste [2000] 2 A.C. 40; [2000] 2 W.L.R. 574; *Times*, November 3, 1999, PC (Trin) . . . . *Digested*, 99/**3092**

Briggs v. Pitt-Payne [1999] Lloyd's Rep. Med. 1; (1999) 46 B.M.L.R. 132, CA . . . . *Digested*, 99/**471**

Brightlife Ltd, Re [1987] Ch. 200; [1987] 2 W.L.R. 197; [1986] 3 All E.R. 673; [1986] P.C.C. 435; (1987) 84 L.S.G. 653; (1987) 131 S.J. 132, Ch D . . . . *Digested*, 88/**306**: *Applied*, 00/3483: *Followed*, 91/2145, 92/2549, 93/2332

Brighton and Hove BC v. Ocean Coachworks (Brighton) Ltd [2001] Env. L.R. 4; [2000] E.H.L.R. 279; [2000] C.O.D. 277, QBD . . . . *Digested*, 00/**4286**

Brighton and Hove BC v. Sainsbury's Supermarkets Ltd (1999) 14 P.A.D. 48, Planning Inspector

Brighton and Hove Council v. Aquarium Entertainments Ltd (2000) 15 P.A.D. 552, Planning Inspector

Brij, The [2001] 1 Lloyd's Rep. 431, CFI (HK) . . . . *Digested*, 01/**4898**

Brikom Investments Ltd v. Carr; Brikom Investments Ltd v. Roddy; Brikom Investments Ltd v. Hickey [1979] Q.B. 467; [1979] 2 W.L.R. 737; [1979] 2 All E.R. 753; (1979) 38 P. & C.R. 326; (1979) 251 E.G. 359, CA . . . . *Digested*, 79/**1598**: *Applied*, 01/3855: *Considered*, 90/2775

Brikom Investments Ltd v. Hickey see Brikom Investments Ltd v. Carr

Brikom Investments Ltd v. Roddy see Brikom Investments Ltd v. Carr

Brill & Co v. Penn see Penn v. Bristol and West Building Society

Brillouet v. Hachette Magazines Ltd; *sub nom* Debtor (No.27 of 1990), Re [1996]
  B.P.I.R. 522, CA; affirming [1996] B.P.I.R. 518, Ch D . . . . *Digested*, 97/**3023**:
Approved, 00/**3434**
Brindle v. HW Smith (Cabinets) Ltd see HW Smith (Cabinets) Ltd v. Brindle
Brink's-MAT Ltd v. Elcombe [1988] 1 W.L.R. 1350; [1988] 3 All E.R. 188; [1989] 1
  F.S.R. 211; (1988) 132 S.J. 1555; *Independent*, June 25, 1987, CA . . . . *Digested*, 89/**3030**:
Applied, 89/3028, 91/48, 91/2884, 92/7, 92/574, 99/435, 01/591, 01/764:
Considered, 96/786, 98/522, 00/488
Brinkibon v. Stahag Stahl und Stahlwarenhandels GmbH; *sub nom* Brinkibon Ltd v.
  Stahag Stahl und Stahlwarenhandelsgesellschaft mbH [1983] 2 A.C. 34; [1982]
  2 W.L.R. 264; [1982] 1 All E.R. 293; [1982] 1 Lloyd's Rep. 217; [1982] Com.
  L.R. 72; [1982] E.C.C. 322; 126 S.J. 116, HL; affirming [1980] 2 Lloyd's Rep.
  556, CA . . . . *Digested*, 82/**388**:
Applied, 84/172, 85/3107, 01/801: *Considered*, 83/379: *Referred to*, 81/2193
Brinkibon Ltd v. Stahag Stahl und Stahlwarenhandelsgesellschaft mbH see Brinkibon v.
  Stahag Stahl und Stahlwarenhandels GmbH
Brinkmann Tabakfabriken GmbH v. Skatteministeiet (C319/96) [1998] E.C.R. I-5255;
  [1998] 3 C.M.L.R. 673, ECJ
Briody v. St Helens and Knowsley AHA [1999] Lloyd's Rep. Med. 185, CA . . . . *Digested*, 00/**515**
Briody v. St Helens and Knowsley AHA (Claim for Damages and Costs) [2001] EWCA
  Civ 1010; [2001] 2 F.L.R. 1094; [2001] 2 F.C.R. 481; (2001) 62 B.M.L.R. 1;
  [2001] Fam. Law 796; (2001) 98(33) L.S.G. 32; *Times*, August 14, 2001;
  Independent, July 3, 2001, CA; affirming [2000] 2 F.C.R. 13; [2000] P.I.Q.R.
  Q165; [2000] Lloyd's Rep. Med. 127; (2000) 53 B.M.L.R. 108; (2000) 97(5)
  L.S.G. 33; (2000) 144 S.J.L.B. 57; *Times*, March 1, 2000, QBD . . . . *Digested*, 01/**1520**
Briscoe, Re [1998] C.O.D. 402, QBD
Briscoe v. Lubrizol Ltd (No.1) [2000] I.C.R. 694; [2000] P.I.Q.R. P39; (1999) 96(41)
  L.S.G. 36; *Times*, November 5, 1999, CA. . . . . *Digested*, 99/**3400**
Briscoe v. Shattock [1999] 1 W.L.R. 432; (1999) 163 J.P. 201; [1999] E.H.L.R. 108;
  [1999] Crim. L.R. 396; [1999] C.O.D. 3; (1999) 193 J.P.N. 271; [1999] E.H.L.R.
  Dig. 105; *Times*, October 12, 1998, QBD . . . . *Digested*, 98/**218**
Bristol Airport Plc v. Powdrill; *sub nom* Paramount Airways Ltd (No.1), Re [1990] Ch.
  744; [1990] 2 W.L.R. 1362; [1990] 2 All E.R. 493; [1990] B.C.C. 130; [1990]
  B.C.L.C. 585; (1990) 87(17) L.S.G. 28, CA . . . . *Digested*, 90/**511**:
Applied, 92/2527, 94/278.a, 95/421, 99/3270, 00/3432:
Considered, 93/2315, 00/3428
Bristol and West Building Society v. Baden Barnes Groves & Co [2000] Lloyd's Rep.
  P.N. 788, Ch D . . . . *Digested*, 01/**4523**
Bristol and West Building Society v. Fancy & Jackson [1997] 4 All E.R. 582; [1997]
  N.P.C. 109, Ch D . . . . *Digested*, 98/**4027**:
Considered, 01/4529: *Followed*, 99/4036, 99/4379, 01/4528
Bristol and West Building Society v. Heath (Unreported, December 10, 1996) . . . . *Approved*, 98/330
Bristol and West Building Society v. May May & Merrimans (No.1) [1996] 2 All E.R. 801;
  [1996] P.N.L.R. 138; [1996] E.G.C.S. 69; (1996) 93(19) L.S.G. 30; (1996) 146
  N.L.J. 625; (1996) 140 S.J.L.B. 110; *Times*, April 26, 1996, Ch D . . . . *Digested*, 96/**3909**:
Applied, 98/4027: *Distinguished*, 97/3819
Bristol and West Building Society v. May May & Merrimans (No.2) [1998] 1 W.L.R. 336;
  [1997] 3 All E.R. 206; [1997] N.P.C. 31, Ch D . . . . *Digested*, 97/**1024**:
Approved, 99/3410: *Considered*, 98/333
Bristol and West Building Society v. Mothew (t/a Stapley & Co); *sub nom* Mothew v.
  Bristol and West Building Society [1998] Ch. 1; [1997] 2 W.L.R. 436; [1996] 4
  All E.R. 698; [1997] P.N.L.R. 11; (1998) 75 P. & C.R. 241; [1996] E.G.C.S. 136;
  (1996) 146 N.L.J. 1273; (1996) 140 S.J.L.B. 206; [1996] N.P.C. 126; *Times*,
  August 2, 1996, CA. . . . . *Digested*, 96/**4503**:
Applied, 97/3822, 97/3823, 98/859, 99/458, 00/2334: *Considered*, 97/3827,
98/2298, 99/3796, 00/649, 00/2323, 00/5270: *Followed*, 99/3814,
99/4037
Bristol and West Building Society v. Saunders see Saunders (A Bankrupt), Re
Bristol and West Building Society v. Trustee of the Property of John Julius Back (A
  Bankrupt); *sub nom* Melinek (A Bankrupt), Re [1998] 1 B.C.L.C. 485; [1997]
  B.P.I.R. 358; *Times*, April 10, 1997, Ch D . . . . *Digested*, 97/**3004**
Bristol and West Plc v. Bhadresa; Bristol and West Plc v. Mascarenhas [1999] C.P.L.R.
  209; [1999] 1 Lloyd's Rep. I.R. 138; [1999] Lloyd's Rep. P.N. 11; (1999) 96(1)
  L.S.G. 23; *Times*, November 23, 1998, Ch D . . . . *Digested*, 98/**462**
Bristol and West Plc v. Mascarenhas see Bristol and West Plc v. Bhadresa
Bristol City Council v. Aldi Stores Ltd (1998) 13 P.A.D. 575, Planning Inspector
Bristol City Council v. Dookwah [1999] E.L.R. 174, CA . . . . *Digested*, 99/**1748**
Bristol City Council v. Lovell [1998] 1 W.L.R. 446; [1998] 1 All E.R. 775; (1998) 30
  H.L.R. 770; [1999] L. & T.R. 66; [1998] R.V.R. 133; [1998] E.G.C.S. 29; (1998)
  95(14) L.S.G. 23; (1998) 95(9) L.S.G. 30; (1998) 148 N.L.J. 329; (1998) 142
  S.J.L.B. 116; [1998] N.P.C. 31; *Times*, February 27, 1998, HL; reversing (1997) 29
  H.L.R. 528; [1996] E.G.C.S. 140; [1996] N.P.C. 130, CA . . . . *Digested*, 98/**3055**:
Followed, 98/3056

Bristol City Council v. Mousah (1998) 30 H.L.R. 32, CA . . . . *Digested,* 98/**3044**:
Applied, 97/2669: *Distinguished,* 00/3925

Bristol Myers Squibb v. Paranova (C427/93); Eurim-Pharm Arzneimittel GmbH v.
Beiersdorf AG (C71/94); MPA Pharma v. Rhone-Poulenc (C232/94) [1996]
E.C.R. I-3457; [1997] 1 C.M.L.R. 1151; [1996] C.E.C. 716; [1996] E.T.M.R. 1;
[1997] F.S.R. 102; (1997) 34 B.M.L.R. 59, ECJ [1996] E.C.R. I-3457; [1996]
F.S.R. 225, AGO . . . . *Digested,* 97/**4879**:
Applied, 97/3892, 98/3506, 00/3706, 00/3709: *Cited,* 00/3703:
Considered, 98/3514, 98/3544, 99/3560: *Distinguished,* 98/3426:
Followed, 99/3558

Bristol Myers Squibb Co v. Baker Norton Pharmaceuticals Inc; Bristol Myers Squibb Co
v. Napro Biotherapeutics Inc [2000] E.N.P.R. 230; [2001] R.P.C. 1; (2001) 58
B.M.L.R. 121; (2000) 23(8) I.P.D. 23058; *Independent,* July 10, 2000 (C.S), CA;
affirming in part [1999] 1 C.M.L.R. 557; [2000] E.N.P.R. 57; [1999] R.P.C.
253; (1999) 49 B.M.L.R. 173; (1998) 21 (12) I.P.D. 21127, Pat Ct . . . . *Digested,* 00/**3677**:
Applied, 01/3902

Bristol Myers Squibb Co v. Baker Norton Pharmaceuticals Inc (Costs) [2001] EWCA
Civ 414; [2001] R.P.C. 45; (2001) 24(6) I.P.D. 24035; *Times,* April 26, 2001,
CA . . . . *Digested,* 01/**416**

Bristol Myers Squibb Co v. Napro Biotherapeutics Inc see Bristol Myers Squibb Co v.
Baker Norton Pharmaceuticals Inc
Bristol Myers Squibb Co v. Rhone Poulenc Rorer SA (T 7-1185-905) [2001] E.N.P.R. 1,
TR (Stockholm)
Bristol Myers Squibb Co v. Yew Tree Pharmaceuticals BV (97/914) [2000] E.N.P.R. 26,
Hof (Den Haag) . . . . *Applied,* 00/3677
Britannia Building Society v. Crammer [1997] B.P.I.R. 596, Ch D . . . . *Digested,* 98/**3310**
Britannia Building Society v. Pugh [1997] 2 F.L.R. 7; [1998] 2 F.C.R. 668; (1997) 29
H.L.R. 423; [1997] Fam. Law 478; [1996] E.G.C.S. 128; [1996] N.P.C. 113, CA . *Digested,* 97/**4241**
Britannia Distribution Co Ltd v. Factor Pace Ltd [1998] 2 Lloyd's Rep. 420, DR
(Manchester) . . . . *Digested,* 98/**3568**
Britannia Homes Centres Ltd, Re; *sub nom* Official Receiver v. McCahill; Company
Directors Disqualification Act 1986, Re [2001] 2 B.C.L.C. 63; (2000) 97(26)
L.S.G. 36; *Times,* June 27, 2000; *Independent,* July 24, 2000 (C.S), Ch D . . . . *Digested,* 00/**661**
Britax International GmbH v. Inland Revenue Commissioners see Lloyds UDT Finance
Ltd v. Chartered Finance Trust Holdings Plc
Britel Developments (Thatcham) Ltd v. Nightfreight (Great Britain) Ltd [1998] 4 All E.R.
432; [1998] N.P.C. 96, Ch D . . . . *Digested,* 99/**4367**
British Aerospace Plc v. Dee Howard Co [1993] 1 Lloyd's Rep. 368, QBD (Comm Ct) . . *Digested,* 93/**451**:
Applied, 01/647: *Considered,* 00/761
British Aerospace Plc v. Secretary of State for the Environment (1998) 75 P. & C.R.
486; [1997] N.P.C. 96, QBD . . . . *Digested,* 98/**4208**
British Airways (European Operations) Gatwick Ltd v. Moore see British Airways
(European Operations at Gatwick) Ltd v. Moore
British Airways (European Operations at Gatwick) Ltd v. Moore; *sub nom* British
Airways (European Operations) Gatwick Ltd v. Moore [2000] 2 C.M.L.R. 343;
[2000] I.C.R. 678; [2000] I.R.L.R. 296, EAT . . . . *Digested,* 00/**2161**
British Airways Pension Schemes, Re [2000] Pens. L.R. 311, Ch D . . . . *Digested,* 01/**506**
British Airways Plc v. Boyce 2001 S.C. 510; [2001] I.R.L.R. 157; 2000 G.W.D. 40-1489,
Ex Div . . . . *Digested,* 01/**6474**
British Airways Plc v. Commission of the European Communities (T371/94) [1998]
E.C.R. II-2405; [1998] 3 C.M.L.R. 429; [1998] C.E.C. 731, CFI (2nd Chamber) . *Digested,* 98/**736**
British Airways Plc v. Customs and Excise Commissioners see Customs and Excise
Commissioners v. British Airways Plc
British Airways Plc v. Customs and Excise Commissioners [2000] B.V.C. 2207; [2000]
S.T.I. 675, V&DTr
British Airways Plc v. Performing Right Society Ltd [1998] E.M.L.R. 556; [1998]
R.P.C. 581, Copyright Tr . . . . *Digested,* 98/**3436**
British Airways Plc v. Ryanair Ltd [2001] E.T.M.R. 24; [2001] F.S.R. 32; (2001) 24(3)
I.P.D. 24013, Ch D . . . . *Digested,* 01/**4023**
British Alcan Aluminium Plc v. Chiltern DC; *sub nom* British Alcan Aluminium Plc v.
Secretary of State for the Environment; Services Sound & Vision Corp v. Chiltern
DC (1999) 77 P. & C.R. 178, QBD . . . . *Digested,* 98/**4190**
British Alcan Aluminium Plc v. Secretary of State for the Environment see British Alcan
Aluminium Plc v. Chiltern DC
British American Cattle Co v. Caribe Farm Industries Ltd (In Receivership) [1998] 1
W.L.R. 1529; (1998) 142 S.J.L.B. 231; *Times,* September 17, 1998, PC (Bze) . . . . *Digested,* 98/**4375**
British American Tobacco Co Ltd v. Netherlands (A/331-A) (1996) 21 E.H.R.R. 409;
Times, December 11, 1995, ECHR . . . . *Digested,* 96/**4551**:
Applied, 98/3120, 98/3140

British American Tobacco International (Investments) Ltd v. Commission of the European
Communities (T111/00) [2001] 3 C.M.L.R. 60; [2001] C.E.C. 348, CFI
British & Commonwealth Holdings Plc (Nos.1 and 2), Re see British & Commonwealth
Holdings Plc (Joint Administrators) v. Spicer and Oppenheim

British & Commonwealth Holdings Plc (In Administration) v. Atlantic Computers Plc see
British & Commonwealth Holdings Plc (In Administration) v. Barclays de Zoete
Wedd Ltd (No.2)

British & Commonwealth Holdings Plc (In Administration) v. Barclays de Zoete Wedd Ltd
(No.1); *sub nom* Atlantic Computers Plc (In Administration), Re [1998] B.C.C.
200; *Times*, April 25, 1997, Ch D . . . . *Digested*, 98/**3307**

British & Commonwealth Holdings Plc (In Administration) v. Barclays de Zoete Wedd Ltd
(No.2); British & Commonwealth Holdings Plc (In Administration) v. Atlantic
Computers Plc; British & Commonwealth Holdings Plc (In Administration) v.
Spicer & Oppenheim; British & Commonwealth Holdings Plc (In Administration)
v. NM Rothschild & Sons Ltd [1999] 1 B.C.L.C. 86; (1998) 95(45) L.S.G. 41;
(1999) 143 S.J.L.B. 14; *Times*, November 13, 1998, Ch D . . . . *Digested*, 98/**340**

British & Commonwealth Holdings Plc (In Administration) v. NM Rothschild & Sons Ltd
see British & Commonwealth Holdings Plc (In Administration) v. Barclays de
Zoete Wedd Ltd (No.2)

British & Commonwealth Holdings Plc (In Administration) v. Spicer & Oppenheim see
British & Commonwealth Holdings Plc (In Administration) v. Barclays de Zoete
Wedd Ltd (No.2)

British & Commonwealth Holdings Plc (Joint Administrators) v. Spicer and Oppenheim;
sub nom British & Commonwealth Holdings Plc (Nos.1 and 2), Re [1993] A.C.
426; [1992] 3 W.L.R. 853; [1992] 4 All E.R. 876; [1992] B.C.C. 977; [1993]
B.C.L.C. 168; (1992) 142 N.L.J. 1611; *Times*, November 3, 1992, HL; affirming
[1992] Ch. 342; [1992] 2 W.L.R. 931; [1992] 2 All E.R. 801; [1992] B.C.C. 165;
[1992] B.C.C. 172; [1992] B.C.L.C. 641; *Times*, December 31, 1991, CA;
reversing [1991] B.C.C. 651; [1991] B.C.C. 658; [1992] B.C.L.C. 306; [1992]
B.C.L.C. 314; *Times*, November 8, 1991; *Financial Times*, November 6, 1991;
Financial Times, August 6, 1991, Ch D . . . . *Digested*, 93/**2317**:
　　　　　　Applied, 92/2557, 98/3308: *Considered*, 96/3472: *Followed*, 95/5555

British Anzani (Felixstowe) Ltd v. International Marine Management (UK) Ltd [1980]
Q.B. 137; [1979] 3 W.L.R. 451; [1979] 2 All E.R. 1063; (1980) 39 P. & C.R. 189;
(1978) 250 E.G. 1183; 123 S.J. 64, QBD . . . . *Digested*, 79/**1633**:
　　　　　　　　　　Considered, 92/2700, 93/2519, 94/2797, 99/3723

BRITISH BIOTECH/Heterocyclic compounds (T684/96) [2000] E.P.O.R. 190, EPO
(Technical Bd App) . . . . *Digested*, 00/**3602**

British Broadcasting Corp v. Talksport Ltd see BBC v. Talksport Ltd (No.1)

British Celanese Ltd v. Courtaulds Ltd (1935) 52 R.P.C. 171 . . . . *Approved*, 98/**3462**

British Coal Corp v. British Coal Staff Superannuation Fund Scheme Trustees [1995] 1
All E.R. 912; [1994] I.C.R. 537; *Times*, October 12, 1993, Ch D . . . . *Digested*, 95/**3805**:
　　　　　　　Considered, 95/2215: *Distinguished*, 01/4626

British Coal Corp v. Commission of the European Communities (T367/94) see National
Power Plc, Re (C151/97P(I))

British Coal Corp v. Keeble [1997] I.R.L.R. 336, EAT . . . . *Digested*, 97/**2266**:
　　　　　　　　　　　　　　　Applied, 98/2195

British Columbia College of Teachers v. Trinity Western University 10 B.H.R.C. 425, Sup
Ct (Can) . . . . *Digested*, 01/**3456**

British Columbia Development Corp v. Spun Cast Industries Ltd 5 B.C.L.R. 94 . . . . *Followed*, 00/**3482**

British Columbia Government & Service Employees Union v. British Columbia 7 B.H.R.C.
437, Sup Ct (Can) . . . . *Digested*, 00/**3253**

British Data Management Plc v. Boxer Commercial Removals Plc [1996] 3 All E.R. 707;
[1996] E.M.L.R. 349; *Times*, February 28, 1996, CA . . . . *Digested*, 96/**5663**:
　　　　　　　　　　　　　　　Followed, 01/659

British Eagle International Airlines Ltd v. Compagnie Nationale Air France [1975] 1
W.L.R. 758; [1975] 2 All E.R. 390; [1975] 2 Lloyd's Rep. 43; 119 S.J. 368, HL;
reversing in part [1974] 1 Lloyd's Rep. 429, CA; affirming [1973] 1 Lloyd's Rep.
414, Ch D . . . . *Digested*, 75/**320**:
　　　　Applied, 92/292, 97/5287: *Considered*, 99/3305, 01/3778:
　　　　　　Distinguished, 84/332, 93/289, 93/2319

British Fermentation Products Ltd v. Compair Reavell Ltd [1999] 2 All E.R. (Comm)
389; [1999] B.L.R. 352; (2000) 2 T.C.L.R. 704; 66 Con. L.R. 1, QBD (T&CC) . . *Digested*, 99/**843**

British Fuels Ltd v. Baxendale see Wilson v. St Helens BC

British Gas Plc v. Stockport MBC see Stockport MBC v. British Gas Plc

British Gas Services Ltd v. McCaull [2001] I.R.L.R. 60, EAT. *Digested*, 01/**2240**

British Gas Trading Ltd v. Data Protection Registrar [1997-98] Info. T.L.R. 393, Data
Protection Tr . . . . *Digested*, 99/**823**

British Home Stores Ltd v. Burchell [1980] I.C.R. 303; [1978] I.R.L.R. 379; (1978) 13
I.T.R. 560, EAT. . . . . *Digested*, 80/**1004**:
　　Applied, 80/1005, 80/1006, 82/113, 82/2856, 83/1348, 90/1929, 90/1975,
　　　　97/2286, 97/6017, 99/2139: *Approved*, 00/2237: *Considered*, 84/1304,
　　　　84/1312, 86/1266, 87/1395, 91/1696, 97/2289: *Referred to*, 89/1504,
　　　　　　　　　　　　　　　96/2656

British Horse Society Ltd v. Customs and Excise Commissioners [2000] B.V.C. 2062,
V&DTr

British Horseracing Board Ltd *v.* William Hill Organisation Ltd (No.2); *sub nom* British
   Horseracing Board Ltd *v.* William Hill Organization Ltd (No.2) [2001] EWCA Civ
   1268; (2001) 24(9) I.P.D. 24059, CA; reversing in part [2001] 2 C.M.L.R. 12;
   [2001] E.C.D.R. 20; [2001] E.B.L.R. 71; [2001] R.P.C. 31; (2001) 151 N.L.J. 271;
   Times, February 23, 2001; *Independent,* March 26, 2001 (C.S), Pat Ct. . . . .   *Digested,* 01/**3848**
British Horseracing Board Ltd *v.* William Hill Organization Ltd (No.2) see British
   Horseracing Board Ltd *v.* William Hill Organisation Ltd (No.2)
British Insulated and Helsby Cables Ltd *v.* Atherton (Inspector of Taxes); *sub nom*
   Atherton (Inspector of Taxes) *v.* British Insulated and Helsby Cables Ltd [1926]
   A.C. 205, HL; affirming [1925] 1 K.B. 421, CA . . . .   *Applied,* 47-51/**4727,**
                      53/1699, 53/1702, 54/1561, 59/1529: *Considered,* 64/1782, 65/1922,
                      65/1937, 85/462, 86/453: *Distinguished,* 47-51/4729, 47-51/4732, 53/1703,
                      00/4934: *Doubted,* 89/534
British Legion *v.* British Legion Club (Street) Ltd (1931) 48 R.P.C. 555 . . . .   *Applied,* 98/**3497:**
                      Considered, 97/4888
British Leyland (UK) Ltd *v.* Swift [1981] I.R.L.R. 91, CA . . . .   *Digested,* 81/**945:**
                      Applied, 82/1102, 83/1316, 83/1325, 97/2289: *Considered,* 83/1319,
                      00/2239
British Leyland Motor Corp Ltd *v.* Armstrong Patents Co Ltd [1986] A.C. 577; [1986] 2
   W.L.R. 400; [1986] 1 All E.R. 850; [1986] E.C.C. 534; [1986] F.S.R. 221;
   [1986] R.P.C. 279; (1986) 5 Tr. L.R. 97; (1986) 83 L.S.G. 974; (1986) 83 L.S.G.
   1971; (1986) 136 N.L.J. 211; (1986) 130 S.J. 203, HL; reversing [1984] 3
   C.M.L.R. 102; [1984] F.S.R. 591; (1984) 81 L.S.G. 2225; (1984) 128 S.J. 659,
   CA; affirming [1982] Com. L.R. 240; [1982] 3 C.M.L.R. 603; [1983] F.S.R. 50,
   Ch D . . . .   *Digested,* 86/**432:**
                      Considered, 84/440, 89/2822, 90/3465, 95/854, 96/1270, 96/4560,
                      97/1038, 97/1040, 99/3462: *Distinguished,* 92/456, 95/774, 99/3498:
                      Referred to, 94/3525, 95/3767, 97/1055
British Leyland Motor Corp Ltd *v.* TI Silencers Ltd (1979) [1980] 1 C.M.L.R. 598; [1979]
   F.S.R. 591, Ch D . . . .   *Digested,* 79/**349:**
                      Followed, 99/3498
British Leyland Motor Corp Ltd *v.* TI Silencers Ltd (1980) [1981] Com. L.R. 3; [1981] 2
   C.M.L.R. 75; [1981] F.S.R. 213, CA; reversing [1980] 2 C.M.L.R. 332; [1980]
   F.S.R. 400, Ch D . . . .   *Digested,* 81/**1039:**
                      Followed, 99/3498
British Midland *v.* Belgium see Zaventem Airport Landing Fees, Re
British Newspaper Printing Corp (North) *v.* Kelly [1989] I.R.L.R. 222, CA. . . . .   *Digested,* 90/**1893:**
                      Not followed, 00/2151
British Nursing Association *v.* Inland Revenue (National Minimum Wage Compliance
   Team) A1/2001/1908, CA; affirming [2001] I.R.L.R. 659, EAT. . . . .   *Digested,* 01/**2290**
British Petroleum Co Plc's Application [1999] E.T.M.R. 282, OHIM (2nd Bd App) . . . . .   *Digested,* 00/**3756**
British Phonographic Industry Ltd *v.* Mechanical Copyright Protection Society Ltd
   (No.2) [1993] E.M.L.R. 86, Copyright Tr. . . . .   *Digested,* 93/**583:**
                      Followed, 98/3436
British Railways Board *v.* Herrington; *sub nom* Herrington *v.* British Railways Board
   [1972] A.C. 877; [1972] 2 W.L.R. 537; [1972] 1 All E.R. 749; 116 S.J. 178, HL;
   affirming [1971] 2 Q.B. 107; [1971] 2 W.L.R. 477; [1971] 1 All E.R. 897; 114 S.J.
   954, CA (1970) 214 E.G. 561. . . . .   *Digested,* 72/**2344:**
                      Applied, 72/2343, 75/2006, 76/1649, 79/397, 84/2309, 84/2310, 96/4454,
                      99/4007: *Considered,* 72/2367, 75/2341, 79/1888, 80/1973, 85/2301,
                      94/2278, 95/3659, 96/5697: *Distinguished,* 74/2572, 75/2310
British Railways Board *v.* National Union of Railwaymen [1989] I.C.R. 678; [1989]
   I.R.L.R. 349; *Times,* June 21, 1989; *Independent,* June 21, 1989; *Guardian,* June
   21, 1989, CA; affirming *Times,* June 21, 1989; *Independent,* June 20, 1989,
   Ch D . . . .   *Digested,* 90/**4543:**
                      Applied, 98/2157
British Road Services Ltd *v.* Loughran [1996] N.I. 181; [1997] Eu. L.R. 166; [1997]
   I.R.L.R. 92, CA (NI). . . . .   *Digested,* 97/**5226**
British Shipbuilders *v.* VSEL Consortium Plc [1997] 1 Lloyd's Rep. 106; *Times,* February
   14, 1996, Ch D . . . .   *Digested,* 96/**1018:**
                      Followed, 98/3677
British Shoe Corp Ltd *v.* Customs and Excise Commissioners [1998] V. & D.R. 348,
   V&DTr. . . . .   *Digested,* 00/**5322**
British Sky Broadcasting Group Plc *v.* Customs and Excise Commissioners; *sub nom* R.
   v. Customs and Excise Commissioners Ex p. British Sky Broadcasting Group
   [2001] EWHC Admin 127; [2001] S.T.C. 437; [2001] B.T.C. 5123; [2001] B.V.C.
   198; [2001] S.T.I. 246, QBD (Admin Ct); affirming [2000] B.V.C. 2067; [1999] V.
   & D.R. 283, V&DTr. . . . .   *Digested,* 01/**5605**
British Sky Broadcasting Ltd *v.* Performing Right Society Ltd [1998] E.M.L.R. 193;
   [1998] R.P.C. 467; (1998) 21 (7) I.P.D. 21069, Copyright Tr . . . .   *Digested,* 98/**3434:**
                      Distinguished, 98/3436

British South Africa Co *v.* Companhia de Mocambique; *sub nom* Companhia de
Mocambique *v.* British South Africa Co; De Sousa *v.* British South Africa Co
[1893] A.C. 602; [1891-94] All E.R. Rep. 640, HL; reversing [1892] 2 Q.B. 358,
CA . . . . *Applied*, 90/609,
               99/731: *Approved*, 67/128: *Considered*, 97/901: *Distinguished*, 47-51/9453,
               47-51/9454, 47-51/9457, 47-51/9624, 47-51/10496: *Followed*, 78/286
British Steel Plc *v.* Commission of the European Community (T185/96) [1999] E.C.R.
II-2089; [1999] 3 C.M.L.R. 21, CFI (4th Chamber) . . . . *Digested*, 99/**704**
British Steel Plc *v.* Customs and Excise Commissioners (No.1) [1997] 2 All E.R. 366,
CA; reversing [1996] 1 All E.R. 1002, QBD . . . . *Digested*, 97/**1735**:
                                 Considered, 98/98
British Steel Plc *v.* Customs and Excise Commissioners (No.2), *Times*, May 12, 1999,
CA . . . . *Digested*, 99/**4687**
British Sugar Plc *v.* Commission of the European Communities (T204/98) see Tate &
Lyle Plc *v.* Commission of the European Communities (T202/98)
British Sugar Plc *v.* James Robertson & Sons Ltd [1997] E.T.M.R. 118; [1996] R.P.C.
281; (1996) 19(3) I.P.D. 19023; *Times*, February 17, 1996, Ch D . . . . *Digested*, 96/**5708**:
           Applied, 99/3544, 00/3791: *Considered*, 97/4906, 98/3537, 98/3538,
            99/3584, 99/3589, 00/3758: *Followed*, 98/3541: *Referred to*, 97/4891,
                 97/4895, 99/3542, 99/3566, 99/3581
British Sugar Plc *v.* Kirker [1998] I.R.L.R. 624; [1999] Disc. L.R. 87, EAT . . . . *Digested*, 98/**2122**
British Sugar Plc *v.* NEI Power Projects Ltd 87 B.L.R. 42; [1997-98] Info. T.L.R. 353;
[1998] I.T.C.L.R. 125; (1998) 14 Const. L.J. 365, CA; affirming [1997] C.L.C.
622; *Times*, February 21, 1997, QBD . . . . *Digested*, 97/**1751**
British Technology Group Ltd *v.* Boehringer Mannheim Corp (1998) 21(7) I.P.D. 21077,
Pat Ct
British Telecom Pension Scheme Trustees *v.* Clarke (Inspector of Taxes) see Clarke
(Inspector of Taxes) *v.* BT Pension Scheme Trustees
British Telecommunications, Re (T829/93) Unreported, EPO (Technical Bd App) . . . . . *Applied*, 01/3918
British Telecommunications Plc *v.* Bell Cable Media (Leeds) Ltd [2001] B.L.R. 343,
QBD (Merc Ct)
British Telecommunications Plc *v.* Central Valuation Officer [1998] R.V.R. 86, VT . . . . *Digested*, 98/**4311**
British Telecommunications Plc *v.* Customs and Excise Commissioners [2000] B.V.C.
2086, V&DTr
British Telecommunications Plc *v.* Deutsche Telekom AG (12 O (Kart) 428/96); *sub nom*
British Telecommunications Plc and Viag Interkom GmbH & Co KG *v.* Deutsche
Telekom AG and Atlas Deutschland Telekommunikationsdienste GmbH [1998] 2
C.M.L.R. 114, LG (Ger)
British Telecommunications Plc *v.* Deutsche Telekom AG (U (Kart) 34/96); *sub nom*
British Telecommunications Plc and Viag Interkom GmbH & Co KG *v.* Deutsche
Telekom AG and Atlas Deutschland Telekommunikationsdienste GmbH [1998] 2
C.M.L.R. 95, OLG (Ger)
British Telecommunications Plc *v.* Humber Bridge Board [2000] N.P.C. 144, Ch D
British Telecommunications Plc *v.* James Thomson & Sons (Engineers) Ltd [1999] 1
W.L.R. 9; [1999] 2 All E.R. 241; 1999 S.C. (H.L.) 9; 1999 S.L.T. 224; 1999
S.C.L.R. 126; [1999] B.L.R. 35; (1999) 1 T.C.L.R. 1; 61 Con. L.R. 1; [1999] 1
Lloyd's Rep. I.R. 105; [1999] Lloyd's Rep. I.R. 105; (1999) 96(4) L.S.G. 40;
(1999) 143 S.J.L.B. 28; [1998] N.P.C. 161; 1999 G.W.D. 1-47; *Times*, December
11, 1998, HL; reversing 1997 S.C. 59; 1997 S.L.T. 767; 1997 S.C.L.R. 228; 82
B.L.R. 1; 54 Con. L.R. 108; [1997] 6 Re. L.R. 325; 1997 Rep. L.R. 23; (1997) 13
Const. L.J. 332; 1997 G.W.D. 3-77; *Times*, January 28, 1997, 2 Div; affirming
49 Con. L.R. 163, OH . . . . *Digested*, 99/**5783**:
                                 Applied, 01/4469
British Telecommunications Plc *v.* Nextcall Telecom Plc (Trade Marks) [2000] C.P. Rep.
49; [2000] E.T.M.R. 943; [2000] F.S.R. 679; (2000) 23(5) I.P.D. 23037, Ch D
. . . . *Digested*, 00/**496**
British Telecommunications Plc *v.* Nottinghamshire CC [1999] Crim. L.R. 217; [1998]
E.G.C.S. 147; (1998) 148 N.L.J. 1601; *Independent*, November 2, 1998 (C.S.),
QBD . . . . *Digested*, 98/**2884**
British Telecommunications Plc *v.* One in a Million Ltd; Marks & Spencer Plc *v.* One in a
Million Ltd; Virgin Enterprises Ltd *v.* One in a Million Ltd; J Sainsbury Plc *v.* One
in a Million Ltd; Ladbroke Group Plc *v.* One in a Million Ltd [1999] 1 W.L.R.
903; [1998] 4 All E.R. 476; [1999] E.T.M.R. 61; [1997-98] Info. T.L.R. 423;
[1998] I.T.C.L.R. 146; [2001] E.B.L.R. 2; [1999] F.S.R. 1; [1998] Masons C.L.R.
165; (1998) 95(37) L.S.G. 37; (1998) 148 N.L.J. 1179; *Times*, July 29, 1998;
Independent, July 31, 1998, CA; affirming [1997-98] Info. T.L.R. 316; [1998]
I.T.C.L.R. 7; [1998] F.S.R. 265; (1997) 16 Tr. L.R. 554; [1998] Masons C.L.R.
116; (1998) 21(2) I.P.D. 21016; (1997) 147 N.L.J. 1809; *Times*, December 2,
1997, Ch D . . . . *Digested*, 98/**3520**:
         Considered, 98/3501, 00/3592, 01/5357: *Referred to*, 99/3587
British Telecommunications Plc *v.* RE Docwra Ltd (Unreported, January 24, 2001), CC
(Uxbridge) [*Ex rel.* Peter de Verneuil Smith, Barrister, 2 Temple Gardens,
London] . . . . *Digested*, 01/**1517**

British Telecommunications Plc v. Secretary of State for the Environment see R. v. Secretary of State for the Environment Ex p. British Telecommunications Plc

British Telecommunications Plc v. Sun Life Assurance Society Plc [1996] Ch. 69; [1995] 3 W.L.R. 622; [1995] 4 All E.R. 44; (1997) 73 P. & C.R. 475; [1995] 2 E.G.L.R. 44; [1995] 45 E.G. 133; (1995) 145 N.L.J. 1366; (1995) 139 S.J.L.B. 203; [1995] N.P.C. 140; *Times,* August 3, 1995; *Independent,* September 12, 1995, CA; affirming (1995) 69 P. & C.R. 305; [1994] 43 E.G. 158; [1994] E.G.C.S. 117, Ch D . . . . *Digested,* 96/**3817**: *Applied,* 98/3051, 98/3623

British Telecommunications Plc v. Williams [1997] I.R.L.R. 668, EAT . . . . *Digested,* 98/**2202**

British Telecommunications Plc and Viag Interkom GmbH & Co KG v. Deutsche Telekom AG and Atlas Deutschland Telekommunikationsdienste GmbH see British Telecommunications Plc v. Deutsche Telekom AG (12 O (Kart) 428/96)

British Telecommunications Plc and Viag Interkom GmbH & Co KG v. Deutsche Telekom AG and Atlas Deutschland Telekommunikationsdienste GmbH see British Telecommunications Plc v. Deutsche Telekom AG (U (Kart) 34/96)

British United Provident Association Ltd v. Customs and Excise Commissioners see BUPA Ltd v. Customs and Excise Commissioners

British Vacuum Cleaner Co Ltd v. New Vacuum Cleaner Co Ltd [1907] 2 Ch. 312, Ch D . *Followed,* 01/3877

British Waterways Board v. Norman (1994) 26 H.L.R. 232; [1994] C.O.D. 262; (1995) 159 J.P.N. 288; [1993] E.G.C.S. 177; [1993] N.P.C. 143; *Times,* November 11, 1993; *Independent,* November 29, 1993, QBD . . . . *Digested,* 94/**4216**: *Considered,* 01/1116: *Disapproved,* 98/3714

British Waterways Board v. Severn Trent Water Ltd [2001] EWCA Civ 276; [2001] 3 W.L.R. 613; [2001] 3 All E.R. 673; [2001] Env. L.R. 45; (2001) 98(16) L.S.G. 34; (2001) 98(13) L.S.G. 43; [2001] N.P.C. 53; *Times,* March 23, 2001; *Independent,* March 14, 2001, CA; reversing [2001] Ch. 32; [2000] 3 W.L.R. 1; [2000] 1 All E.R. 347; [2000] Env. L.R. 284; (1999) 96(42) L.S.G. 41; (1999) 143 S.J.L.B. 249; [1999] N.P.C. 120; *Times,* October 26, 1999; *Independent,* November 29, 1999 (C.S.), Ch D . . . . *Digested,* 01/**5632**

British Westinghouse Electric & Manufacturing Co Ltd v. Underground Electric Railways Co of London Ltd (No.2) [1912] A.C. 673, HL; reversing [1912] 3 K.B. 128, CA . *Applied,* 47-51/431, 53/3775, 55/2483, 56/936, 65/993, 69/3313, 70/748, 72/826, 78/312, 78/704, 79/658, 00/2566: *Approved,* 66/3146: *Considered,* 75/248, 79/849, 85/1860, 90/1564, 91/1503, 91/3194, 94/3438, 95/4510, 97/1808, 01/894: *Distinguished,* 90/1565: *Followed,* 93/1596, 95/3704, 97/3843

British-American Tobacco (Holdings) Ltd v. Fabriques de Tabac Reunies see HORIZON Trade Mark

Britten Norman Ltd (In Liquidation) v. State Ownership Fund of Romania [2000] Lloyd's Rep. Bank. 315; (2000) 97(30) L.S.G. 41; *Times,* August 3, 2000, Ch D . . . . *Digested,* 00/**279**

Broadbent (Deceased), Re; *sub nom* Imperial Cancer Research Fund v. Bradley [2001] EWCA Civ 714; [2001] W.T.L.R. 967; (2000-01) 3 I.T.E.L.R. 787; (2001) 98(28) L.S.G. 44; *Times,* June 27, 2001, CA . . . . *Digested,* 01/**5502**

Broadley (t/a Professional Haircare) v. Customs and Excise Commissioners [2000] S.T.I. 1273, V&DTr

Broadley v. Guy Clapham & Co [1994] 4 All E.R. 439; [1993] 4 Med. L.R. 328; *Times,* July 6, 1993; *Independent,* September 9, 1993, CA . . . . *Digested,* 94/**2907**: *Applied,* 00/4197: *Cited,* 97/668: *Considered,* 94/2908, 95/3171: *Distinguished,* 95/3169

Broadmoor Special HA v. R see Broadmoor Special Hospital Authority v. R

Broadmoor Special Hospital Authority v. R; *sub nom* Broadmoor Special HA v. R [2000] Q.B. 775; [2000] 1 W.L.R. 1590; [2000] 2 All E.R. 727; [2000] E.M.L.R. 245; [2000] Lloyd's Rep. Med. 65; (2000) 52 B.M.L.R. 137; (2000) 97(3) L.S.G. 36; (2000) 144 S.J.L.B. 48; *Times,* February 9, 2000 ; *Independent,* January 25, 2000, CA; affirming [1999] Q.B. 957; [1999] 2 W.L.R. 1006; [1999] C.O.D. 75; *Times,* October 15, 1998, QBD . . . . *Digested,* 00/**4177**: *Referred to,* 01/4413

Broads Authority v. Accorde Technology (2000) 15 P.A.D. 163, Planning Inspector

Broads Authority v. Secretary of State for the Environment, Transport and the Regions (2001) 81 P. & C.R. 3; [2001] P.L.C.R. 4; [2001] J.P.L. 115 (Note), QBD . . . . *Digested,* 01/**4713**

Broads Authority v. Withers (1998) 13 P.A.D. 353, Planning Inspector

Broadwater Manor School v. Davis (Unreported, January 8, 1999), CC (Worthing) [*Ex rel.* Harveys Solicitors, 96 Station Road, Liss, Hampshire] . . . . *Digested,* 99/**1801**

Broadway, Re Appeal of [1998] R.A. 71, Lands Tr. . . . . *Digested,* 98/**4330**

Broadway v. Clydesdale Bank Plc (No.1) 2000 G.W.D. 19-763; *Times,* September 12, 2000, OH . . . . *Digested,* 00/**6676**

Broadwith v. Chief Constable of Thames Valley [2000] Crim. L.R. 924, QBD . . . . *Digested,* 01/**1064**

Brobbey v. North Manchester Healthcare NHS Trust (Unreported, March 22, 2000), CC (Manchester) [*Ex rel.* Thompsons Solicitors, Acresfield, 8 Exchange Street, Manchester] . . . . *Digested,* 00/**2980**

Brobbey v. North Manchester Healthcare NHS Trust (Quantum) (Unreported, March 22, 2000), CC (Manchester) [*Ex rel.* Thompsons Solicitors, Acresfield, 8 Exchange Street, Manchester] . . . . *Digested,* 00/**1648**

Brocket Hall (Jersey) Ltd v. Clague (Unreported, March 26, 1998), CC (Luton) [*Ex rel.*
Catherine Brown, Barrister, 12 King's Bench Walk, Temple, London] . . . . *Digested*, 98/**4367**
Brockhouse Plc's Patent [1985] R.P.C. 332, PO. . . . . *Considered*, 98/3476
Brocklesby v. Armitage & Guest [2001] 1 All E.R. 172; [1999] Lloyd's Rep. P.N. 888;
[2000] P.N.L.R. 33; [2001] 1 E.G.L.R. 67; [2001] 14 E.G. 150, CA. . . . . *Digested*, 00/**4274**:
Applied, 00/4254, 01/630, 01/4520, 01/4535: *Considered*, 00/534
Brockwell v. Secretary of State for the Environment, Transport and the Regions [2001]
J.P.L. 998 (Note), QBD (Admin Ct)
Broderick v. Jones (Unreported, October 7, 1998), CC (Watford) [*Ex rel.* Alex
Glassbrook, Barrister, 1 Temple Gardens, Temple, London] . . . . *Digested*, 98/**421**
Broderip v. Salomon see Salomon v. Salomon & Co Ltd
Brogan v. United Kingdom (A/145-B) (1989) 11 E.H.R.R. 117; *Times*, November 30,
1988; *Independent*, November 30, 1988; *Guardian*, December 7, 1988, ECHR . . *Digested*, 88/**1804**:
Followed, 98/3073
Bromarin AB v. IMD Investments Ltd [1999] S.T.C. 301; [1999] B.T.C. 74, CA; reversing
[1998] S.T.C. 244; [1998] B.T.C. 3, Ch D . . . . *Digested*, 99/**4662**
Bromberg v. Bromberg [1962] 1 W.L.R. 1143; [1962] 3 All E.R. 289; 106 S.J. 592,
PDAD . . . . *Digested*, 62/**943**:
Considered, 99/2401
Bromiley v. United Kingdom (33747/96) (2000) 29 E.H.R.R. CD111, ECHR
Bromley LBC v. Bromley Youth Music Trust (2000) 15 P.A.D. 257, Planning Inspector
Bromley LBC v. Governors of Coopers School (1998) 13 P.A.D. 762, Planning
Inspector
Bromley LBC v. Morritt [2000] E.H.L.R. 24; (2000) 79 P. & C.R. 536; (1999) 78 P. &
C.R. D37, CA . . . . *Digested*, 00/**2296**
Bromley LBC v. Old Beccehamian Rugby Football Club (1998) 13 P.A.D. 109, Planning
Inspector
Bromley LBC v. Secretary of State for the Environment, Transport and the Regions;
Bromley LBC v. Tee [1999] J.P.L. 536, QBD . . . . *Digested*, 99/**4213**
Bromley LBC v. Secretary of State for the Environment, Transport and the Regions
[2001] EWHC Admin 561; (2001) 98(29) L.S.G. 40, QBD (Admin Ct)
Bromley LBC v. Special Educational Needs Tribunal (No.1) [1999] Ed. C.R. 704, QBD . . *Digested*, 99/**1898**
Bromley LBC v. Special Educational Needs Tribunal (No.2) [1999] 3 All E.R. 587;
(1999) 1 L.G.L.R. 970; [1999] B.L.G.R. 747; [1999] Ed. C.R. 907; [1999] E.L.R.
260; (1999) 2 C.C.L. Rep. 239; [1999] C.O.D. 409; *Times*, June 14, 1999 ;
Independent, June 17, 1999, CA; affirming (Unreported, December 18, 1998),
QBD . . . . *Digested*, 99/**1890**
Bromley LBC v. Spooner (1998) 13 P.A.D. 509, Planning Inspector
Bromley LBC v. Susannah [1999] Env. L.R. D13, CA . . . . *Applied*, 00/4616
Bromley LBC v. Tee see Bromley LBC v. Secretary of State for the Environment,
Transport and the Regions
Bromley Park Garden Estates Ltd v. Palmeiro see Palmeiro (Debtor No.3666 of 1999),
Re
Brompton v. AOC International Ltd [1997] I.R.L.R. 639, CA . . . . *Digested*, 98/**2206**:
Considered, 99/2013
Bromsgrove DC v. Banner (2001) 16 P.A.D. 32, Planning Inspector
Bromsgrove Medical Products Ltd (formerly Peterborough Pressure Castings Ltd) v.
Edgar Vaughan & Co Ltd [1997] 1 W.L.R. 1188; [1997] 2 All E.R. 56; [1998] 1
Costs L.R. 75; *Times*, January 25, 1997, QBD . . . . *Digested*, 97/**582**:
Considered, 98/464
Bronda v. Italy (22430/93) (2001) 33 E.H.R.R. 4; [1998] H.R.C.D. 641, ECHR . . . . *Digested*, 01/**3549**:
Referred to, 01/3525
Brook v. Faulkner (Unreported, February 10, 2000), CC (Chelmsford) [*Ex rel.* Michael
Morris, Barrister, 169 Temple Chambers, Temple Avenue, London] . . . . *Digested*, 00/**1597**
Brook v. Haringey LBC [1992] I.R.L.R. 478, EAT . . . . *Digested*, 92/**1975**:
Disapproved, 01/2319
Brook Lane Finance Co Ltd v. Bradley [1988] I.C.R. 423; [1988] I.R.L.R. 283, EAT. . . . *Digested*, 88/**1357**:
Followed, 98/2187: *Not followed*, 90/1949
Brookes v. Borough Care Services [1998] I.C.R. 1198; [1998] I.R.L.R. 636, EAT . . . . . *Digested*, 98/**2212**
Brookes v. Iddon (Unreported, October 19, 1999), CC (Llangefni) [*Ex rel.* Salmons
Solicitors, 336 Hartshill Road, Hartshill, Stoke on Trent, Staffs.] . . . . *Digested*, 00/**3917**
Brookes v. JP Coates (UK) Ltd [1984] 1 All E.R. 702; [1984] I.C.R. 158, QBD . . . . *Digested*, 84/**1012**:
Considered, 01/5651
Brookes v. T Elmes & Sons Ltd (Unreported, February 25, 1999), CC (Luton) [*Ex rel.*
Stuart R Yeung, Barrister, 22 Albion Place, Northampton] . . . . *Digested*, 99/**1596**
Brooks v. Civil Aviation Authority 2000 S.C. 565; 2000 S.L.T. 1386; [2000] O.P.L.R.
365; 2000 G.W.D. 24-918; *Times*, July 28, 2000, 1 Div . . . . *Digested*, 00/**6620**
Brooks v. Home Office [1999] 2 F.L.R. 33; (1999) 48 B.M.L.R. 109; *Times*, February
17, 1999, QBD . . . . *Digested*, 99/**3998**
Brooks v. Humphries (Unreported, May 30, 2001), CC (Basildon) [*Ex rel.* Robert Weir,
Barrister, Devereux Chambers, Devereux Court, London] . . . . *Digested*, 01/**557**
Brooks v. Olyslager Oms (UK) Ltd [1998] I.R.L.R. 590, CA . . . . *Digested*, 98/**2109**
Brooks v. Reliance Mutual Ltd (Unreported, November 3, 1997), CC (Ilford) [*Ex rel.*
Hodge Malek, Barrister, 4-5 Gray's Inn Square, Gray's Inn, London] . . . . *Digested*, 98/**364**

Brooks v. Secretary of State for Trade and Industry [1999] B.C.C. 232, EAT. . . . .   *Digested,* 99/**2100**
Brooks & Co v. Mortgage Corps Plc (1999) 77 P. & C.R. 355, CA . . . .   *Digested,* 99/**4379**
Broome (A Debtor), Re see Horrocks v. Broome
Broome v. Broome [1955] P. 190; [1955] 2 W.L.R. 401; [1955] 1 All E.R. 201; 99 S.J.
   114, PDAD . . . .   *Digested,* 55/**2114**:
                       Considered, 00/5392: *Distinguished,* 57/2791, 57/4249
Broome v. Cassell & Co Ltd (No.1) [1972] A.C. 1027; [1972] 2 W.L.R. 645; [1972] 1
   All E.R. 801; 116 S.J. 199, HL; affirming [1971] 2 Q.B. 354; [1971] 2 W.L.R. 853;
   [1971] 2 All E.R. 187; 115 S.J. 289, CA; affirming [1971] 1 All E.R. 262, QBD. . . .   *Digested,* 72/**2745**:
         Applied, 79/399, 84/1099, 87/1140, 90/2995, 92/1941, 94/5067, 96/1276,
         96/2606, 97/3798, 98/5150: *Considered,* 73/861, 74/2993, 77/336, 78/284,
         83/971, 84/1580, 88/1295, 89/2245, 90/1552, 96/5673, 97/2754:
         Distinguished, 92/1526, 93/1598, 01/1512: *Followed,* 97/3286, 00/824
Broomleigh Housing Association Ltd v. Hughes [1999] E.G.C.S. 134; *Times,* November
   26, 1999, Ch D . . . .   *Digested,* 00/**3951**
Brophy v. Dunphys Chartered Surveyors [1998] E.G.C.S. 37; (1998) 95(16) L.S.G. 23;
   (1998) 142 S.J.L.B. 109; *Times,* March 11, 1998, CA . . . .   *Digested,* 98/**610**
BROSELOW/Measuring tape (T77/92) [1998] E.P.O.R. 266, EPO (Technical Bd App)
Brother Industries Ltd v. Commission of the European Communities (C56/85); Brother
   Industries Ltd v. Council of Ministers of the European Communities (C250/85)
   [1988] E.C.R. 5655; [1988] E.C.R. 5683; [1990] 1 C.M.L.R. 792, ECJ (5th
   Chamber) . . . .   *Digested,* 91/**3741**
Brother Industries Ltd v. Council of Ministers of the European Communities (C250/85)
   see Brother Industries Ltd v. Commission of the European Communities (C56/
   85)
Brough v. Carty (Unreported, November 11, 1997), CC (Barnet) [*Ex rel.* Robert Jan
   Temmink, Barrister, 35 Essex Street, Temple, London] . . . .   *Digested,* 98/**1723**
Browell v. Goodyear, *Times,* October 24, 2000, Ch D . . . .   *Digested,* 00/**4310**
Brown (Christopher) v. Attorney General of Jamaica see Lewis v. Attorney General of
   Jamaica
Brown v. Barclays Bank Plc see Box v. Barclays Bank Plc
Brown v. Bennett [1999] B.C.C. 525; [1999] 1 B.C.L.C. 649, CA; affirming [1999]
   B.C.C. 91; [1998] 2 B.C.L.C. 97; *Times,* January 3, 1998, Ch D . . . .   *Digested,* 99/**3288**
Brown v. Bennett (Exchange of Skeleton Arguments), *Times,* June 13, 2000, Ch D . . . .   *Digested,* 00/**375**
Brown v. Bennett (Wasted Costs) (No.1) (2001) 151 N.L.J. 1733; (2001) 145 S.J.L.B.
   267; *Times,* November 21, 2001, Ch D . . . .   *Digested,* 01/**537**
Brown v. Bennett (Witness Summons), *Times,* November 2, 2000, Ch D . . . .   *Digested,* 00/**341**
Brown v. Classification Review Board 5 B.H.R.C. 619, Fed Ct (Aus) (Full Ct); affirming
   3 B.H.R.C. 72, Fed Ct (Aus) (Sgl judge) . . . .   *Digested,* 99/**3109**
Brown (Gordon) v. DPP (1998) 162 J.P. 333; (1998) 95(17) L.S.G. 30; (1998) 142
   S.J.L.B. 132; *Times,* March 26, 1998, QBD. . . . .   *Digested,* 98/**79**
Brown v. Ealing LBC see Brown v. Secretary of State for the Environment, Transport
   and the Regions
Brown v. EOM Construction Ltd (Unreported, July 19, 2000), CC (Bury) [*Ex rel.* David
   Calvert, Barrister, 68 Quay Street, Manchester] . . . .   *Digested,* 00/**1727**
Brown v. George (1999-2000) 2 I.T.E.L.R. 669, Fed Ct (Aus) (Full Ct)
Brown v. GIO Insurance Ltd [1998] C.L.C. 650; [1998] Lloyd's Rep. I.R. 201; (1998)
   95(9) L.S.G. 29; *Times,* February 18, 1998, CA . . . .   *Digested,* 98/**3405**
Brown v. Gloucester City Council [1998] 1 E.G.L.R. 95; [1998] 16 E.G. 137; [1997]
   E.G.C.S. 149; [1997] N.P.C. 154; (1998) 75 P. & C.R. D24; *Times,* December 20,
   1997, CA. . . . .   *Digested,* 98/**3674**:
                                               Applied, 01/4159
Brown v. Guardian Royal Exchange Assurance Plc [1994] 2 Lloyd's Rep. 325; (1994)
   91(9) L.S.G. 40; (1994) 138 S.J.L.B. 35; [1994] N.P.C. 8; *Times,* January 27,
   1994; *Independent,* February 11, 1994, CA . . . .   *Digested,* 96/**3616**:
                                            Considered, 00/4023
Brown v. Hicks (Unreported, January 28, 2000), CC (Basingstoke) [*Ex rel.* Amery-
   Parkes Solicitors, 12a London Street, Basingstoke, Hampshire] . . . .   *Digested,* 00/**389**
Brown v. KMR Services Ltd (Application for Expedited Appeal) see Unilever Plc v.
   Chefaro Proprietaries Ltd (Application for Expedited Appeal)
Brown v. Lewisham and North Southwark HA [1999] Lloyd's Rep. Med. 110; (1999)
   48 B.M.L.R. 96, CA; affirming [1998] Lloyd's Rep. Med. 265, QBD. . . . .   *Digested,* 99/**3986**
Brown v. Merchant Ferries Ltd [1998] I.R.L.R. 682, CA (NI) . . . .   *Digested,* 99/**2030**
Brown v. Owen [2000] 6 Q.R. 8, CC (Chichester) [*Ex rel.* Deputy District Judge
   Harvey, Harveys Solicitors, 96 Station Road, Liss, Hampshire]. . . . .   *Digested,* 00/**1595**
Brown v. Rentokil Ltd 1996 S.C. 415; 1996 S.L.T. 839; [1995] 2 C.M.L.R. 85; [1995]
   I.R.L.R. 211, Ex Div; affirming [1992] I.R.L.R. 302, EAT. . . . .   *Digested,* 96/**6958**:
           Distinguished, 96/2628, 97/2237: *Not followed,* 99/5283:
                              Subsequent proceedings, 98/2148
Brown v. Rentokil Ltd (C394/96) [1998] All E.R. (EC) 791; [1998] E.C.R. I-4185;
   [1998] 2 C.M.L.R. 1049; [1998] C.E.C. 829; [1998] I.C.R. 790; [1998] I.R.L.R.
   445; [1998] 2 F.L.R. 649; [1999] 1 F.C.R. 49; (1999) 48 B.M.L.R. 126; [1998]
   Fam. Law 597; *Times,* July 2, 1998, ECJ . . . .   *Digested,* 98/**2148**:
                        Applied, 99/2115: *Previous proceedings,* 92/1972

Brown v. Roberts [1965] 1 Q.B. 1; [1963] 3 W.L.R. 75; [1963] 2 All E.R. 263; [1963] 1 Lloyd's Rep. 314; 107 S.J. 666, QBD . . . . *Digested*, 63/**3071**:
Distinguished, 92/2889, 94/4000, 95/3726, 96/3615, 99/3414

Brown v. Saunders Valve Co Ltd (Unreported, April 8, 1997), CC (Cardiff) [*Ex rel.* Peter Brooks, Barrister, 9 Park Place, Cardiff] . . . . *Digested*, 98/**1626**

Brown v. Secretary of State for Scotland (C197/86) [1988] E.C.R. 3205; 1989 S.L.T. 402; [1988] 3 C.M.L.R. 403; *Times*, September 3, 1988, ECJ . . . . *Considered*, 95/4617, 01/2496

Brown v. Secretary of State for Social Security [1995] C.O.D. 260; *Times*, December 7, 1994, QBD. . . . . *Digested*, 94/**904**:
Disapproved, 99/873

Brown v. Secretary of State for the Environment, Transport and the Regions; Brown v. Ealing LBC [2000] J.P.L. 1081 (Note), QBD . . . . *Digested*, 00/**4448**

Brown v. Southall & Knight [1980] I.C.R. 617; [1980] I.R.L.R. 130, EAT . . . . *Digested*, 80/**1016**:
Considered, 98/2203

Brown v. Stott; *sub nom* Stott (Procurator Fiscal) v. Brown [2001] 2 W.L.R. 817; [2001] 2 All E.R. 97; 2001 S.C. (P.C.) 43; 2001 S.L.T. 59; 2001 S.C.C.R. 62; [2001] R.T.R. 11; [2001] H.R.L.R. 9; [2001] U.K.H.R.R. 333; 11 B.H.R.C. 179; (2001) 3 L.G.L.R. 24; (2001) 145 S.J.L.B. 100; 2000 G.W.D. 40-1513; *Times*, December 6, 2000; *Independent*, February 7, 2001 (C.S), PC (Sc); reversing 2000 J.C. 328; 2000 S.L.T. 379; 2000 S.C.C.R. 314; [2000] R.T.R. 394; [2000] U.K.H.R.R. 239; 2000 G.W.D. 6-237; *Times*, February 14, 2000, HCJ Appeal . . . *Digested*, 01/**6319**:
Applied, 01/972: *Considered*, 01/1237, 01/5291

Brown v. Thomson Tour Operations Ltd (Unreported, November 18, 1998), CC (Sheffield) [*Ex rel.* Peter Sayer, Barrister, Gough Square Chambers, London] . . . *Digested*, 99/**1412**

Brown v. TNT Express Worldwide (UK) Ltd see TNT Express Worldwide (UK) Ltd v. Brown

Brown v. United Kingdom see Laskey v. United Kingdom

Brown v. Williams (t/a Scholars Public House) [2001] 2 Q.R. 11, CC (Neath & Port Talbot) [*Ex rel.* Hutchinson Morris & LC Thomas Solicitors, 19 London Road, Neath] . . . . *Digested*, 01/**1698**

Brown & Co v. Watkins & Co (1885-86) L.R. 16 Q.B.D. 125, QBD . . . . *Not applied*, 99/327

Brown & Root Technology Ltd v. Sun Alliance and London Assurance Co Ltd [2001] Ch. 733; [2000] 2 W.L.R. 566; (1998) 75 P. & C.R. 223; [1997] 1 E.G.L.R. 39; [1997] 18 E.G. 123; (1997) 94(7) L.S.G. 29; (1997) 141 S.J.L.B. 38; [1996] N.P.C. 183; *Times*, January 27, 1997, CA; reversing [1996] Ch. 51; [1995] 3 W.L.R. 558, Ch D . . . . *Digested*, 97/**3301**

Brown Bayley's Steel Works, Re (1905) 21 T.L.R. 374 . . . . *Cited*, 99/603:
Followed, 73/339

Browne v. Anelay see Vehicle Inspectorate v. Anelay

Brownie Wills (A Firm) v. Shrimpton [1999] Lloyd's Rep. P.N. 39; [1999] P.N.L.R. 552, CA (NZ) . . . . *Digested*, 99/**4046**

Browning v. Tameside MBC see Tameside MBC v. Browning

Brownlow v. GH Marshall Ltd; *sub nom* GH Marshall Ltd, Re [2001] B.C.C. 152; [2000] 2 B.C.L.C. 655; *Independent*, March 20, 2000 (C.S.), Ch D . . . . *Digested*, 01/**747**

Brownrigg v. Gooda Walker Ltd see Deeny v. Gooda Walker Ltd (No.2)

Brownsville Holdings Ltd v. Adamjee Insurance Co Ltd (The Milasan) [2000] 2 All E.R. (Comm) 803; [2000] 2 Lloyd's Rep. 458, QBD (Comm Ct) . . . . *Digested*, 00/**4724**

Broxbourne BC v. Secretary of State for the Environment [1980] Q.B. 1; [1979] 2 W.L.R. 846; [1979] 2 All E.R. 13; 77 L.G.R. 381; (1979) 38 P. & C.R. 381; (1978) 249 E.G. 959; [1979] J.P.L. 308; 123 S.J. 34, QBD . . . . *Digested*, 79/**2609**:
Applied, 99/4220

Broxtowe BC v. Soar Robinson (2000) 15 P.A.D. 399, Planning Inspector

BRS Northern Ltd v. Templeheights Ltd [1998] 2 E.G.L.R. 182; [1997] E.G.C.S. 180; (1998) 95(1) L.S.G. 26; [1997] N.P.C. 181, Ch D . . . . *Digested*, 99/**3691**

Brualla Gomez de la Torre v. Spain (26737/95) (2001) 33 E.H.R.R. 57; [1998] H.R.C.D. 191, ECHR

Bruce (Malcolm) v. Customs and Excise Commissioners [2000] S.T.I. 1379, V&DTr

Brueton v. Farmiloe see Dolphin Showers Ltd v. Farmiloe

Brumant v. Boyle (Unreported, December 3, 1998), CC (Birmingham) [*Ex rel.* Paul Cain, Principal Solicitor, Litigation Unit, Eagle Star Insurance Co Ltd, Regency Suite, India Buildings, Water Steet, Liverpool] . . . . *Digested*, 99/**1406**

Brumarescu v. Romania (28342/95) (2001) 33 E.H.R.R. 35, ECHR

Brumarescu v. Romania (Just Satisfaction: Pecuniary Damages) (28342/95) (2001) 33 E.H.R.R. 36, ECHR

Brumark Investments Ltd, Re; *sub nom* Inland Revenue Commissioner v. Agnew; Agnew v. Inland Revenue Commissioner [2001] UKPC 28; [2001] 2 A.C. 710; [2001] 3 W.L.R. 454; [2001] Lloyd's Rep. Bank. 251; [2001] B.C.C. 259; [2001] 2 B.C.L.C. 188; *Independent*, July 16, 2001 (C.S); *Daily Telegraph*, June 12, 2001, PC (NZ); affirming [2000] 1 B.C.L.C. 353, CA (NZ) . . . . *Digested*, 01/**732**

Brunei Darussalam v. Bolkiah, *Times*, September 5, 2000, Ch D . . . . *Digested*, 00/**489**

Brunei LNG Sendirian Berhad v. Interbeton BV (1998) 14 Const. L.J. 117, CA (Bru) . . . . *Digested*, 98/**844**

Brunnhofer v. Bank der Osterreichischen Postsparkasse AG (C381/99) [2001] All E.R. (EC) 693; [2001] E.C.R. I-4961; [2001] 3 C.M.L.R. 9; [2001] I.R.L.R. 571; [2001] Emp. L.R. 1176; *Times*, July 9, 2001, ECJ (6th Chamber) . . . . *Digested*, 01/**2277**

Brunninghausen v. Glavanics (1999) 32 A.C.S.R. 294 . . . . *Considered*, 00/649

Bruns v. Colocotronis (The Vasso) [1979] 2 Lloyd's Rep. 412, QBD (Comm Ct) . . . . *Digested*, 80/**2496**: *Applied*, 00/5438

Brunsden v. Humphrey (1884-85) L.R. 14 Q.B.D. 141, CA; reversing (1882-83) L.R. 11 Q.B.D. 712, QBD . . . . *Applied*, 64/1370, 98/533: *Considered*, 99/431: *Disapproved*, 68/2639: *Distinguished*, 47-51/7913: *Followed*, 61/1377, 89/2724

Brunt v. Brunt (1872-75) L.R. 3 P. & D. 37, Ct of Probate . . . . *Considered*, 01/5167

Brush v. Bower Cotton & Bower; Business Mortgages (Midland) v. Brush; Business Mortgages Trust v. Brush; Business Mortgages (Midland) v. Trimvale; Brush v. OTS Equipment Financing [1993] 1 W.L.R. 1328; [1993] 4 All E.R. 741, QBD . . . *Digested*, 93/**3169**: *Considered*, 94/2154, 95/4019, 98/416

Brush v. OTS Equipment Financing see Brush v. Bower Cotton & Bower

Bruton v. Inland Revenue Commissioners; *sub nom* Debtor (No.647-SD-1999), Re [2000] B.P.I.R. 946; *Times*, April 10, 2000, Ch D . . . . *Digested*, 00/**3487**

Bruton v. London & Quadrant Housing Trust; *sub nom* Bruton v. Quadrant Housing Trust [2000] 1 A.C. 406; [1999] 3 W.L.R. 150; [1999] 3 All E.R. 481; (1999) 31 H.L.R. 902; [1999] L. & T.R. 469; [1999] 2 E.G.L.R. 59; [1999] 30 E.G. 91; [1999] E.G.C.S. 90; (1999) 96(28) L.S.G. 26; (1999) 149 N.L.J. 1001; (1999) 143 S.J.L.B. 195; [1999] N.P.C. 73; (1999) 78 P. & C.R. D21; *Times*, June 25, 1999, HL; reversing [1998] Q.B. 834; [1998] 3 W.L.R. 438; [1997] 4 All E.R. 970; [1997] 2 E.G.L.R. 91; [1997] 50 E.G. 87; [1997] E.G.C.S. 125; (1997) 147 N.L.J. 1385; [1997] N.P.C. 124; (1998) 75 P. & C.R. D1; *Times*, August 14, 1997, CA . . . . *Digested*, 99/**3698**

Bruton v. Quadrant Housing Trust see Bruton v. London & Quadrant Housing Trust

Brutus v. Cozens [1973] A.C. 854; [1972] 3 W.L.R. 521; [1972] 2 All E.R. 1297; (1972) 56 Cr. App. R. 799; [1973] Crim. L.R. 56; 116 S.J. 647, HL; reversing [1972] 1 W.L.R. 484; [1972] 2 All E.R. 1; 116 S.J. 217, QBD . . . . *Digested*, 72/**706**: *Applied*, 72/746, 73/602, 73/655, 74/2726, 79/2532, 91/974, 92/1129, 93/977, 93/4067, 98/4669: *Considered*, 82/632, 86/1238, 88/3243, 89/3395, 91/2373, 95/5116, 95/5119, 96/1506: *Distinguished*, 90/4372: *Followed*, 97/2863

Bryan v. Customs and Excise see R. v. Isleworth Crown Court Ex p. Marland

Bryan v. Euroguard Ltd (Unreported, July 16, 1998), CC (Pontefract) [*Ex rel*. Hartley and Worstenholme Solicitors, 1 Bank Street, Hemsworth, Pontefract] . . . . *Digested*, 98/**1537**

Bryan v. Maloney 74 B.L.R. 35; 51 Con. L.R. 29; (1995) 11 Const. L.J. 274, HC (Aus) . . *Digested*, 96/**4436**: *Followed*, 98/3924

Bryan v. United Kingdom (A/335-A) (1996) 21 E.H.R.R. 342; [1996] 1 P.L.R. 47; [1996] 2 E.G.L.R. 123; [1996] 28 E.G. 137; *Times*, December 8, 1995, ECHR . . . *Digested*, 96/**4707**: *Applied*, 98/3120, 01/4761: *Considered*, 01/855: *Distinguished*, 00/5841, 01/2269

Bryans v. Mount Vernon and Watford Hospitals Trust (Unreported, February 5, 1999), CC (Central London) [*Ex rel*. Allan Gore, Barrister, 12 King's Bench Walk, Temple, London] . . . . *Digested*, 99/**1543**

Bryant (CICA: Quantum: 2000), Re (Unreported, July 20, 2000), CICA (Cardiff) [*Ex rel*. Andrew Arentsen, Barrister, 33 Park Place, Cardiff] . . . . *Digested*, 01/**1684**

Bryant v. Housing Corp see Housing Corp v. Bryant

Bryant v. Portsmouth City Council; *sub nom* Portsmouth City Council v. Bryant [2000] E.H.L.R. 287; (2000) 32 H.L.R. 906; *Independent*, July 10, 2000 (C.S), CA . . . . *Digested*, 00/**3156**

Bryne v. South Sefton HA see Byrne v. Sefton HA

BS&N Ltd (BVI) v. Micado Shipping Ltd (Malta) (The Seaflower) (No.2) [2000] 2 All E.R. (Comm) 169; [2000] 2 Lloyd's Rep. 37; [2000] C.L.C. 802, QBD (Comm Ct) . . . . *Digested*, 00/**4702**

BS&N Ltd (BVI) v. Micado Shipping Ltd (Malta) (The Seaflower) (No.1) [2001] 1 All E.R. (Comm) 240; [2001] 1 Lloyd's Rep. 341; [2001] C.L.C. 421, CA; reversing [2000] C.L.C. 795, QBD (Comm Ct) . . . . *Digested*, 01/**4913**

BSE Trading Ltd v. Hands (1998) 75 P. & C.R. 138; [1996] 2 E.G.L.R. 214; [1996] E.G.C.S. 99; [1996] N.P.C. 86, CA . . . . *Digested*, 96/**3843**

BT3G Ltd v. Secretary of State for Trade and Industry see R. (on the application of BT3G Ltd) v. Secretary of State for Trade and Industry

BTG/Magnetic Field Screen (T473/98) [2001] E.P.O.R. 64, EPO (Technical Bd App)

BTR Plc, Re [1999] 2 B.C.L.C. 675, Ch D (Companies Ct) . . . . *Digested*, 00/**683**: *Subsequent proceedings*, 00/684

BTR Plc (Leave to Appeal), Re [2000] 1 B.C.L.C. 740, CA . . . . *Digested*, 00/**684**: *Previous proceedings*, 00/683

Bua International Ltd v. Hai Hing Shipping Co Ltd (The Hai Hing) [2000] 1 Lloyd's Rep. 300; [2000] C.P. Rep. 68; [2000] C.L.C. 603, QBD (Comm Ct) . . . . *Digested*, 00/**569**: *Applied*, 01/4946

Buchan v. Secretary of State for Employment; Ivey v. Secretary of State for Employment [1997] B.C.C. 145; [1997] I.R.L.R. 80, EAT . . . . *Digested*, 97/**2251**:
Considered, 98/5812, 99/2019, 99/2100: *Disapproved*, 98/2188:
Referred to, 99/2110

Buchanan v. Alba Diagnostics Ltd 2001 S.C.L.R. 307; [2001] R.P.C. 43; 2001 G.W.D. 6-234, 1 Div; affirming [2000] R.P.C. 367; 1999 G.W.D. 24-1170, OH . . . . *Digested*, 01/**6725**

Buchanan v. McLean see McLean v. Buchanan

Buchanan v. Milton [1999] 2 F.L.R. 844; (2000) 53 B.M.L.R. 176; [1999] Fam. Law 692, Fam Div . . . . *Digested*, 00/**4905**

Buchanan v. Moore-Pataleena see Moore v. Buchanan

Buchler v. DQ Henriques Ltd see ASRS Establishment Ltd (In Administrative Receivership and Liquidation), Re

Buchler v. Morphitis see Lawrence v. Buchler

Buchler v. Talbot see Leyland DAF Ltd, Re

Buck v. English Electric Co Ltd [1977] 1 W.L.R. 806; [1978] 1 All E.R. 271; [1977] I.C.R. 629; (1976) 121 S.J. 13; *Times*, November 25, 1976, QBD . . . . *Digested*, 77/**1802**:
Considered, 77/1803, 79/1671: *Disapproved*, 95/3174, 99/464

Buck v. Hamer (Unreported, October 29, 1998), CC (Central London) [*Ex rel*. Antonia Lyon, Barrister, 2nd Floor, Queen Elizabeth Building, Temple, London] . . . . *Digested*, 98/**1587**

Buckenham v. Dickinson [2000] W.T.L.R. 1083, QBD [*Ex rel*. Andrew Hogan, Barrister] . . . . *Digested*, 97/**4733**

Buckingham (Inspector of Taxes) v. Securities Properties [1980] 1 W.L.R. 380; [1980] S.T.C. 166; 53 T.C. 292; [1979] T.R. 415; 124 S.J. 17, Ch D . . . . *Digested*, 82/**473**:
Approved, 98/4600

Buckingham International Plc (In Liquidation) (No.2), Re; *sub nom* Mitchell v. Carter (No.2); Mitchell v. Buckingham International Plc (In Liquidation) [1998] B.C.C. 943; [1998] 2 B.C.L.C. 369, CA; affirming *Times*, November 20, 1997, Ch D . . . *Digested*, 99/**3305**:
Distinguished, 01/3750

Buckinghamshire CC v. Moran [1990] Ch. 623; [1989] 3 W.L.R. 152; [1989] 2 All E.R. 225; 88 L.G.R. 145; (1989) 58 P. & C.R. 236; (1989) 139 N.L.J. 257; (1989) 133 S.J. 849, CA; affirming 86 L.G.R. 472; (1988) 56 P. & C.R. 372; *Times*, March 2, 1988, Ch D . . . . *Digested*, 89/**449**:
Applied, 91/545, 94/567, 94/568, 01/4840: *Considered*, 91/546, 92/106, 97/4223

Buckinghamshire CC v. Secretary of State for the Environment, Transport and the Regions (2001) 81 P. & C.R. 25; [2001] 1 P.L.R. 38; [2001] P.L.C.R. 16; [2001] J.P.L. 496 (Note); *Times*, October 13, 2000, QBD . . . . *Digested*, 00/**4449**

Buckinghamshire CC v. Secretary of State for the Environment, Transport and the Regions (Enforcement Notice) [1998] 4 P.L.R. 19, QBD . . . . *Digested*, 99/**4203**

Buckinghamshire CC v. YJ Lovell & Son [1956] J.P.L. 196 . . . . *Digested*, 56/**1496**:
Distinguished, 01/952

Buckinghamshire Constabulary Widows and Orphans Fund Friendly Society (No.2), Re; *sub nom* Thompson v. Holdsworth [1979] 1 W.L.R. 936; [1979] 1 All E.R. 623; 122 S.J. 557, Ch D . . . . *Digested*, 79/**1346**:
Followed, 99/3561

Buckland v. Palmer [1984] 1 W.L.R. 1109; [1984] 3 All E.R. 554; [1985] R.T.R. 5; (1984) 81 L.S.G. 2300; (1984) 128 S.J. 565, CA . . . . *Digested*, 84/**2549**:
Considered, 97/688: *Distinguished*, 01/585: *Referred to*, 94/3773

Buckland v. Secretary of State for the Environment, Transport and the Regions; Smith (Thomas) v. Secretary of State for the Environment, Transport and the Regions; Evans (John) v. Secretary of State for the Environment, Transport and the Regions; Wychavon DC v. Smith (Siting of Caravans) [2001] EWHC Admin 524; [2001] 4 P.L.R. 34, QBD (Admin Ct)

Buckland v. Secretary of State for the Environment, Transport and the Regions (Bridleways) [2000] 1 W.L.R. 1949; [2000] 3 All E.R. 205; (2000) 80 P. & C.R. 206; [2000] 4 P.L.R. 16; [2000] E.G.C.S. 7; [2000] N.P.C. 3; *Times*, February 10, 2000; *Independent*, February 28, 2000 (C.S.), QBD . . . . *Digested*, 00/**4414**

Buckle v. Brown (Unreported, June 1, 1998), CC (Cardiff) [*Ex rel*. Andrew Arentsen, Barrister, 33 Park Place, Cardiff] . . . . *Digested*, 98/**1744**

Buckley v. Hudson Forge Ltd [1999] O.P.L.R. 249; [1999] Pens. L.R. 151, Ch D . . . . . . *Digested*, 99/**4146**

Buckley v. JJ O'Leary (Unreported, February 19, 1993), CC (Medway) . . . . *Digested*, 93/**2557**:
Not followed, 01/444

Buckley v. Law Society (Unreported, October 9, 1985), CA . . . . *Applied*, 00/4030

Buckley v. United Kingdom (1997) 23 E.H.R.R. 101; [1997] 2 P.L.R. 10; [1996] J.P.L. 1018; *Times*, October 9, 1996; *Independent*, October 10, 1996, ECHR . . . . *Digested*, 96/**4838**:
Considered, 99/4198

Bucknall v. Jepson (Unreported, September 9, 1998), CC (Leigh) [*Ex rel*. Steven Turner, Barrister, Park Lane Chambers, Park Lane House, 19 Westgate, Leeds] . . *Digested*, 98/**1456**

Bucks Printing Press Ltd v. Prudential Assurance Co 1988/FO/2354, QBD (Comm Ct) . *Digested*, 00/**880**

Buckton, Re Unreported . . . . *Considered*, 01/506

Buckton (Costs), Re; *sub nom* Buckton v. Buckton [1907] 2 Ch. 406, Ch D . . . . *Considered*, 98/481, 01/455, 01/5522

Buckton v. Buckton see Buckton (Costs), Re

Bud and Jet Ltd v. Warrington BC [2001] R.V.R. 22, Lands Tr . . . . *Digested*, 01/**4669**

Budd *v.* Bowditch (1998) 98(3) Q.R. 6, CC (Norwich) . . . .   *Digested,* 98/**1483**

Budd *v.* Colchester BC [1999] Env. L.R. 739; [1999] E.H.L.R. 347; [1999] B.L.G.R. 601; [1999] J.P.L. 717; (1999) 96(10) L.S.G. 32; (1999) 96(12) L.S.G. 34; (1999) 143 S.J.L.B. 96; [1999] N.P.C. 30; *Times,* April 14, 1999, CA; affirming [1997] Env. L.R.128; [1997] C.O.D. 36, QBD . . . .   *Digested,* 99/**2209**

Budd *v.* Fowler (Unreported, December 3, 1998), CC (Peterborough) [*Ex rel.* Winters Solicitors, 70A High Street, Huntingdon, Cambridgeshire] . . . .   *Digested,* 99/**4635**

Budejovicky Budvar Narodni Podnik *v.* Anheuser-Busch Inc see BUDWEISER Trade Marks

Budgens Stores Ltd *v.* Secretary of State for the Environment, Transport and the Regions [1998] E.G.C.S. 28, QBD

BUDWEISER Trade Marks; *sub nom* Anheuser Busch Inc *v.* Budejovicky Budvar Narodni Podnik; Budejovicky Budvar Narodni Podnik *v.* Anheuser-Busch Inc [2000] R.P.C. 906; (2000) 23(5) I.P.D. 23039; *Times,* March 14, 2000, CA; affirming [1998] R.P.C. 669; *Times,* May 20, 1998, Ch D . . . .   *Digested,* 00/**3767**

Buehler AG *v.* Chronos Richardson Ltd [1998] 2 All E.R. 960; [1998] R.P.C. 609; (1998) 21(7) I.P.D. 21076; (1998) 95(16) L.S.G. 25; (1998) 142 S.J.L.B. 133; *Times,* April 3, 1998, CA. . . . .   *Digested,* 98/**3456**

Bugdaycay *v.* Secretary of State for the Home Department; *sub nom* R. *v.* Secretary of State for the Home Department Ex p. Bugdaycay; Nelidow Santis *v.* Secretary of State for the Home Department; Norman *v.* Secretary of State for the Home Department; Musisi *v.* Secretary of State for the Home Department [1987] A.C. 514; [1987] 2 W.L.R. 606; [1987] 1 All E.R. 940; [1987] Imm. A.R. 250; (1987) 84 L.S.G. 902; (1987) 137 N.L.J.199; (1987) 131 S.J. 297, HL; affirming [1986] 1 W.L.R. 155; [1986] 1 All E.R. 458; [1986] Imm. A.R. 8; (1986) 83 L.S.G. 700; (1986) 130 S.J. 129; *Times,* November 12, 1985, CA; affirming *Times,* July 11, 1985, DC . . . .   *Digested,* 87/**1989**:

     Applied, 87/1926, 89/1951, 89/1954, 92/2402, 92/2450, 93/2233, 94/2452, 96/3220, 97/4111, 01/3421: *Cited,* 94/2498, 95/2695: *Considered,* 87/23, 87/1983, 88/14, 90/2572, 91/1965, 94/2455, 96/3236, 96/3278: *Followed,* 96/3300, 97/2929, 98/3196: *Referred to,* 89/1939, 95/2676

Bugeja *v.* Customs and Excise Commissioners (No.1) [1998] B.V.C. 2256, V&DTr . . . . .   *Digested,* 98/**4947**

Bugeja *v.* Customs and Excise Commissioners (No.2) see Littlewoods Organisation Plc *v.* Customs and Excise Commissioners

Bugeja *v.* Customs and Excise Commissioners (No.2) [2000] S.T.C. 1; [1999] B.T.C. 5431; [2000] B.V.C. 21, QBD; reversing in part [1998] B.V.C. 2306; [1998] V. & D.R. 392, V&DTr . . . .   *Digested,* 00/**5339**:

     Overruled, 01/**5556**

Bugg *v.* Customs and Excise Commissioners [1998] B.V.C. 2021, V&DTr

Bugg *v.* DPP; DPP *v.* Percy [1993] Q.B. 473; [1993] 2 W.L.R. 628; [1993] 2 All E.R. 815; (1993) 157 J.P. 673; [1993] 5 Admin. L.R. 633; [1993] Crim. L.R. 374; [1993] C.O.D. 8; (1993) 157 J.P.N. 329; (1993) 157 L.G. Rev. 621; *Times,* September 11, 1992; *Independent,* September 8, 1992, DC . . . .   *Digested,* 93/**2618**:

     Considered, 96/97, 97/4065, 97/4856: *Not followed,* 96/5688: *Overruled,* 98/89

Buhr *v.* Barclays Bank Plc [2001] EWCA Civ 1223; [2001] 31 E.G.C.S. 103; (2001) 98(31) L.S.G. 38; [2001] N.P.C. 124, CA

Buhus-Orwin *v.* Costa Smeralda Holidays Ltd (Unreported, August 16, 2001), MCLC [*Ex rel.* Matthew Chapman, Barrister, No.1 Serjeant's Inn, Fleet Street, London] .   *Digested,* 01/**4279**

Bulbul *v.* Secretary of State for the Home Department see Sepet *v.* Secretary of State for the Home Department

Bulk Trading Corp Ltd *v.* Zenziper Grains and Feed Stuffs; *sub nom* Zenziper Grains and Feed Stuffs *v.* Bulk Trading Corp Ltd [2001] 1 All E.R. (Comm) 385; [2001] 1 Lloyd's Rep. 357; [2001] C.L.C. 496; *Times,* January 23, 2001, CA . . . .   *Digested,* 01/**935**

Bull *v.* Devon AHA [1993] 4 Med. L.R. 117, CA . . . .   *Considered,* 01/4502

Bull *v.* Queen, The [1998] 1 W.L.R. 1523; (1998) 142 S.J.L.B. 158, PC (Bze) . . . .   *Digested,* 99/**1024**

Bull Information Systems Ltd *v.* Stedman see Reed *v.* Stedman

Bullas *v.* Public Trustee [1981] 1 N.S.W.L.R. 641, DC . . . .   *Considered,* 00/5263

Bullen *v.* Manufacturers Mutual Insurance Ltd [1999] C.L.C. 292, QBD (Comm Ct) . . .   *Digested,* 99/**494**

Bullivant Holdings Ltd *v.* Inland Revenue Commissioners [1998] S.T.C. 905; [1998] B.T.C. 234, Ch D . . . .   *Digested,* 98/**4604**

Bullrun Inc *v.* Inspector of Taxes [2000] S.T.C. (S.C.D.) 384; [2000] S.T.I. 1129, Sp Comm . . . .   *Digested,* 01/**5201**

Bulthuis-Griffioen *v.* Inspecteur der Omzetbelasting (C453/93) [1995] S.T.C. 954; [1995] E.C.R. I-2341; [1996] C.E.C. 3, ECJ . . . .   *Digested,* 96/**5880**:

     Followed, 97/4991: *Not followed,* 99/4986

Bulut *v.* Austria (17358/90) (1997) 24 E.H.R.R. 84, ECHR . . . .   *Digested,* 97/**2811**:

     Applied, 98/3123: *Considered,* 98/3146

Bulut *v.* Secretary of State for the Home Department [1999] Imm. A.R. 210, CA . . . . . .   *Digested,* 99/**3156**

Bumbesti, The; *sub nom* SC Rolinay Sea Star Srl *v.* Owners of the Bumbesti; SC Rolinay Sea Star Srl *v.* Compania de Navigatie Maritimie Petromin SA (The Bumbesti) [2000] Q.B. 559; [2000] 2 W.L.R. 533; [2000] 2 All E.R. 692; [1999] 2 All E.R. (Comm) 187; [1999] 2 Lloyd's Rep. 481; [1999] C.L.C. 1413; (1999) 96(28) L.S.G. 25; (1999) 143 S.J.L.B. 189; *Times,* July 12, 1999, QBD (Adm Ct) .... *Digested,* 99/**243**

Bunce *v.* Quinn (Unreported, March 5, 1997), CC (Stoke on Trent) [*Ex rel.* Sean Hale, Barrister, St Mary's Chambers, 50 High Pavement, Nottingham] .... *Digested,* 97/**568**:
Followed, 98/**595**

Bundesfinanzhof (II R 12/92) see Pipeline Case, The (II R 12/92)

Bundesknappschaft Bochum *v.* Brock (C68/69) [1970] E.C.R. 171; [1971] C.M.L.R. 55, ECJ .... *Digested,* 71/**4372**:
Applied, 00/**3582**

Bunge Corp *v.* Tradax Export SA [1981] 1 W.L.R. 711; [1981] 2 All E.R. 540; [1981] 2 Lloyd's Rep. 1; 125 S.J. 373, HL; affirming [1981] 2 All E.R. 524; [1980] 1 Lloyd's Rep. 294, CA; reversing [1979] 2 Lloyd's Rep. 477, QBD (Comm Ct) .... *Digested,* 81/**2433**:
Applied, 81/**2403**, 83/262, 90/628, 91/3188, 00/4723, 01/4913:
Considered, 89/415, 01/4911

Bunkate *v.* Netherlands (A/248-B) (1995) 19 E.H.R.R. 477, ECHR .... *Digested,* 95/**2637**:
Distinguished, 00/6090

Bunn *v.* BBC [1998] 3 All E.R. 552; [1998] E.M.L.R. 846; [1999] F.S.R. 70; (1998) 95(28) L.S.G. 31; (1998) 148 N.L.J. 979; *Times,* June 23, 1998, Ch D .... *Digested,* 98/**84**

Bunyan *v.* Vassor (Unreported, June 1, 2000), CC (Reading) [*Ex rel.* Matthew Brunning, Barrister, Wessex Chambers, 48 Queens Road, Reading, Berkshire] .. *Digested,* 00/**1705**

Bunzl *v.* Martin Bunzl International Ltd (2000) 150 N.L.J. 1076; *Times,* September 19, 2000, Ch D .... *Digested,* 00/**439**

BUPA Ltd *v.* Customs and Excise Commissioners; *sub nom* British United Provident Association Ltd *v.* Customs and Excise Commissioners [2001] B.V.C. 2353; [2001] S.T.I. 1509, V&DTr .... *Digested,* 01/**5588**

Burbridge *v.* Argos Distribution Plc (Unreported, April 20, 1998), CC (Bristol) [*Ex rel.* Jonathan Dingle, Barrister, South Western Chambers, 12 Middle Street, Taunton, TA1 1SH] .... *Digested,* 98/**1605**

Burca *v.* Parkinson (Inspector of Taxes) [2001] S.T.C. 1298; [2001] S.T.I. 1016, Ch D

Burden *v.* Foster [2001] 3 Q.R. 10, QBD .... *Digested,* 01/**1577**

Burdick *v.* Garrick (1869-70) L.R. 5 Ch. App. 233, CA in Chancery............... *Applied,* 96/4149:
Considered, 94/2086, 95/2203, 00/513

Burdis *v.* Livsey [2001] 1 W.L.R. 1751, QBD .... *Digested,* 01/**1527**

Burdle *v.* Secretary of State for the Environment [1972] 1 W.L.R. 1207; [1972] 3 All E.R. 240; 70 L.G.R. 511; (1972) 24 P. & C.R. 174; 116 S.J. 507, QBD .... *Digested,* 72/**3335**:
Applied, 82/3130, 89/3559, 90/4333, 97/4089, 99/4220:
Considered, 79/2608, 83/3649, 92/4172, 93/182, 93/3860, 96/4766,
01/4656: *Distinguished,* 83/3683

Bureau Europeen des Medias de l'Industrie Musicale (BEMIM) *v.* Commission of the European Communities (T114/92); Tremblay *v.* Commission of the European Communities (T5/93) [1995] E.C.R. II-147; [1995] E.C.R. II-185; [1996] 4 C.M.L.R. 305; [1996] E.M.L.R. 97; *Financial Times,* January 31, 1995, CFI (2nd Chamber) .... *Digested,* 95/**629**:
Applied, 99/695

Bureau Europeen des Unions de Consommateurs (BEUC) *v.* Commission of the European Communities (Interpretation: Admissibility Criteria) (T256/97) [2000] E.C.R. II-101; [2000] 1 C.M.L.R. 542, CFI (5th Chamber) .... *Digested,* 00/**2366**

Bureau Rik Decan-Business Research & Development NV (BRD) *v.* Belgium (C401/95) see Garage Molenheide BVBA *v.* Belgium (C286/94)

Burfoot (A Bankrupt), Re see Hill *v.* Alex Lawrie Factors Ltd

Burford UK Properties Ltd *v.* Forte Hotels (UK) Ltd (2001) 98(46) L.S.G. 37, Ch D

Burgemeester en Wethouders van Haarlemmerliede en Spaarnwoude *v.* Gedeputeerde Staten van Noord-Holland (C81/96) [1998] E.C.R. I-3923; [2001] 1 C.M.L.R. 29; [1999] Env. L.R. D7, ECJ (6th Chamber) .... *Digested,* 01/**4742**

Burgess *v.* Auger; Burgess *v.* Vanstock Ltd [1998] 2 B.C.L.C. 478, Ch D .... *Digested,* 99/**3285**

Burgess *v.* British Steel [2000] C.P. Rep. 48; [2000] P.I.Q.R. Q240; (2000) 97(5) L.S.G. 33; (2000) 144 S.J.L.B. 58; *Times,* February 29, 2000; *Independent,* March 13, 2000 (C.S.), CA..................................... *Digested,* 00/**422**

Burgess *v.* Electricity Sports & Social Club (Unreported, October 13, 1999), CC (Cardiff) [*Ex rel.* Bryan Thomas, Barrister, 33 Park Place, Cardiff] .... *Digested,* 00/**1683**

Burgess *v.* Florence Nightingale Hospital for Gentlewomen [1955] 1 Q.B. 349; [1955] 2 W.L.R. 533; [1955] 1 All E.R. 511; 99 S.J. 170, QBD .... *Digested,* 55/**736**:
Approved, 99/1381: *Distinguished,* 57/102, 57/110, 57/2861, 62/830, 63/918, 66/3228

Burgess *v.* Home Office see Burgess *v.* Secretary of State for the Home Department

Burgess *v.* Secretary of State for the Home Department; *sub nom* Secretary of State for the Home Department *v.* Burgess; Burgess *v.* Home Office [2001] 1 W.L.R. 93; [2001] A.C.D. 29; (2000) 97(47) L.S.G. 39; (2000) 144 S.J.L.B. 280; *Times,* November 14, 2000; *Independent,* November 6, 2000, CA .... *Digested,* 00/**1028**

Burgess *v.* Vanstock Ltd see Burgess *v.* Auger

Burgoyne's Trade Mark (1889) 6 R.P.C. 227 . . . . *Referred to,* 00/3766
Burke, Re; *sub nom* R. *v.* Governor of Brixton Prison Ex p. Burke [2001] 1 A.C. 422;
    [2000] 3 W.L.R. 33; [2000] 3 All E.R. 481; *Times,* June 16, 2000; *Independent,*
    July 24, 2000 (C.S), HL; affirming (1999) 149 N.L.J. 521; *Times,* April 15, 1999;
    Independent, March 22, 1999 (C.S.), QBD . . . . *Digested,* 00/**2424**
Burke *v.* DPP [1999] R.T.R. 387, QBD . . . . *Digested,* 00/**958**
Burke *v.* Royal Infirmary of Edinburgh NHS Trust 1999 S.L.T. 539; 1998 Rep. L.R. 87;
    1998 G.W.D. 20-1045; *Times,* June 8, 1998, OH . . . . *Digested,* 98/**5718**:
    Considered, 00/6169
Burke *v.* Royal Liverpool University Hospital NHS Trust [1997] I.C.R. 730, EAT . . . . *Digested,* 97/**2187**:
    Distinguished, 98/2107
Burke *v.* Thornton (Unreported, June 26, 2000), CC (Hastings) [*Ex rel.* Morgan Cole
    Solicitors, Apex Plaza, Forbury Road, Reading] . . . . *Digested,* 00/**311**
Burkett, Re see R. (on the application of Burkett) *v.* Hammersmith and Fulham LBC
Burman *v.* Mount Cook Land Ltd [2001] EWCA Civ 1712; [2001] 48 E.G.C.S. 128;
    (2001) 98(46) L.S.G. 37; [2001] N.P.C. 166; *Independent,* November 30, 2001,
    CA; reversing [2001] 1 E.G.L.R. 62; [2001] 10 E.G. 164, CC (Central London) . . *Digested,* 01/**4181**
Burn Stewart Distillers Plc *v.* Assessor for Lanarkshire Valuation Joint Board [2001] R.A.
    110; 2001 G.W.D. 20-780, Lands Tr (Scot) . . . . *Digested,* 01/**6877**
Burnell *v.* Christian Brothers of Ireland in Canada (In Liquidation) see Rowland *v.*
    Vancouver College Ltd
Burner *v.* Secretary of State for the Environment [1983] J.P.L. 459 . . . . *Digested,* 83/**3675**:
    Considered, 99/4176
Burns (A Minor) *v.* Doncaster HA (Unreported, October 20, 1997), CC (Doncaster) [*Ex
    rel.* Frank Allen Pennington, Solicitors, Hill House Chambers, 6/7 Regent
    Terrace, South Parade, Doncaster] . . . . *Digested,* 98/**1760**
Burns (CICB: Quantum: 1997), Re (Unreported, December 2, 1997), CICB (York) [*Ex rel.*
    Darren Finlay, Barrister and Gary Warriner Solicitor, Godloves, Russell House, 15
    St Paul's Street, Leeds] . . . . *Digested,* 98/**1540**
Burns *v.* Currell [1963] 2 Q.B. 433; [1963] 2 W.L.R. 1106; [1963] 2 All E.R. 297; 127
    J.P. 397; 61 L.G.R. 356; 107 S.J. 272, QBD . . . . *Digested,* 63/**3038**:
    Applied, 86/2956, 86/2966, 87/3295, 89/2755, 00/1000:
    Considered, 65/3439, 92/3820
Burns *v.* Davies [1999] Lloyd's Rep. Med. 215, QBD . . . . *Digested,* 99/**1424**:
    Followed, 00/1464
Burns *v.* General Accident Fire and Life Assurance Corp Plc see Burns *v.* Shuttlehurst
    Ltd
Burns *v.* Morton [2000] 1 W.L.R. 347; [1999] 3 All E.R. 646, CA . . . . *Digested,* 99/**4353**
Burns *v.* Sandwell MBC [1998] R.V.R. 97, Lands Tr . . . . *Digested,* 98/**4163**
Burns *v.* Shuttlehurst Ltd; *sub nom* Burns *v.* General Accident Fire and Life Assurance
    Corp Plc [1999] 1 W.L.R. 1449; [1999] 2 All E.R. 27; [1999] P.I.Q.R. P229;
    (1999) 96(6) L.S.G. 35; *Times,* January 12, 1999, CA . . . . *Digested,* 99/**324**
Burns Application for Judicial Review, Re see R. *v.* Attorney General for Northern Ireland
    Ex p. Burns
Burns Trustee *v.* Burns see Ritchie *v.* Burns
Burnside *v.* Emerson [1968] 1 W.L.R. 1490; [1968] 3 All E.R. 741; (1968) 132 J.P. 66;
    67 L.G.R. 467; 112 S.J. 565, CA . . . . *Digested,* 68/**1762**:
    Applied, 71/5265, 92/1524, 93/1391: *Approved,* 00/4237:
    Considered, 74/2584, 78/1547, 79/1361, 85/1598, 97/3785:
    Followed, 99/2889
Burr (t/a Penny's Place) *v.* Customs and Excise Commissioners [2001] S.T.I. 253, V&D Tr
Burr *v.* Eyre [1998] 2 E.G.L.R. 92; [1998] 20 E.G. 132, CC (Central London) . . . . *Digested,* 98/**3640**
Burrell (t/a The Firm) *v.* Customs and Excise Commissioners [1997] S.T.C. 1413; [1997]
    B.T.C. 5460; [1998] B.V.C. 3, QBD . . . . *Digested,* 98/**4938**
Burrells Wharf Freeholds Ltd *v.* Galliard Homes Ltd [2000] C.P. Rep. 4; (2000) 2
    T.C.L.R. 54; 65 Con. L.R. 1; [1999] 2 E.G.L.R. 81; [1999] 33 E.G. 82; [1999]
    N.P.C. 79, QBD (T&CC) . . . . *Digested,* 99/**315**
Burridge *v.* Stafford; Khan *v.* Ali [2000] 1 W.L.R. 927; [1999] 4 All E.R. 660; [1999]
    C.P.L.R. 645; [2001] 1 Costs L.R. 77; (1999) 149 N.L.J. 1474; *Times,* September
    14, 1999, CA . . . . *Digested,* 99/**3760**
Burroughes *v.* Abbott [1922] 1 Ch. 86, Ch D . . . . *Applied,* 55/848:
    Considered, 00/3912: *Distinguished,* 47-51/9380
Burrow *v.* Burrow [1999] 1 F.L.R. 508; [1999] 2 F.C.R. 549; [1999] Fam. Law 83,
    Fam Div . . . . *Digested,* 99/**2422**
Burrows *v.* Brent LBC [1996] 1 W.L.R. 1448; [1996] 4 All E.R. 577; [1997] 1 F.L.R.
    178; [1997] 2 F.C.R. 43; (1997) 29 H.L.R. 167; [1997] 1 E.G.L.R. 32; [1997] 11
    E.G. 150; [1997] Fam. Law 246; (1996) 93(43) L.S.G. 26; (1996) 146 N.L.J.
    1616; (1996) 140 S.J.L.B. 239; [1996] N.P.C. 149; *Times,* November 4, 1996;
    Independent, November 8, 1996, HL; reversing (1995) 27 H.L.R. 748; (1996) 72
    P. & C.R. 261; [1995] E.G.C.S. 128; [1995] N.P.C. 124; *Times,* July 21, 1995;
    Independent, August 22, 1995, CA . . . . *Digested,* 96/**3829**:
    Applied, 00/4297: *Considered,* 97/2713: *Distinguished,* 96/3834, 01/4146
Burrows *v.* Kingston upon Hull City Council [2000] 3 Q.R. 7, CC (Nottingham) [*Ex rel.*
    Andrew Hogan, Barrister, 24 The Ropewalk, Nottingham] . . . . *Digested,* 00/**1738**

Burrows *v.* Stevens (Unreported, June 16, 2000), CC (Watford) [*Ex rel.* Richard Miles, Barrister, 2 King's Bench Walk, Temple, London] . . . . *Digested,* 00/**2579**
Burrows *v.* University of York [1999] Ed. C.R. 586, Visitor (University) . . . . *Digested,* 99/**1935**
Burrows *v.* Vauxhall Motors Ltd; Mongiardi *v.* IBC Vehicles [1998] P.I.Q.R. P48; (1997) 94(47) L.S.G. 31; (1997) 147 N.L.J. 1723; (1997) 141 S.J.L.B. 237; *Times,* December 17, 1997, CA . . . . *Digested,* 98/**477**:
Distinguished, 98/441: *Followed,* 98/491
Burstein *v.* Times Newpapers Ltd (Costs) HQ 9902700, QBD . . . . *Digested,* 00/**408**
Burstein *v.* Times Newspapers Ltd [2001] 1 W.L.R. 579; [2001] E.M.L.R. 14; (2001) 98(8) L.S.G. 44; (2001) 145 S.J.L.B. 30; *Times,* January 31, 2001, CA; affirming 1999 TLQ (J) 1205, QBD . . . . *Digested,* 01/**1820**:
Considered, 01/1818
Burt *v.* Montague Wells (Unreported, July 26, 1999), CA . . . . *Applied,* 01/673
Burton *v.* Camden LBC [2000] 2 A.C. 399; [2000] 2 W.L.R. 427; [2000] 1 All E.R. 943; [2000] 1 F.C.R. 481; (2000) 32 H.L.R. 625; [2000] B.L.G.R. 289; [2000] L. & T.R. 235; [2000] 1 E.G.L.R. 49; [2000] 14 E.G. 149; [2000] E.G.C.S. 23; (2000) 97(9) L.S.G. 41; [2000] N.P.C. 16; (2000) 79 P. & C.R. D38; *Times,* February 23, 2000; *Independent,* February 25, 2000, HL; reversing [1998] 1 F.L.R. 681; [1998] 3 F.C.R. 254; (1998) 30 H.L.R. 991; [1998] Fam. Law 322; (1998) 95(4) L.S.G. 33; (1998) 142 S.J.L.B. 37; *Times,* January 15, 1998, CA . . *Digested,* 00/**3929**
Burton *v.* De Vere Hotels Ltd [1997] I.C.R. 1; [1996] I.R.L.R. 596; *Times,* October 3, 1996; *Independent,* November 4, 1996 (C.S.), EAT . . . . *Digested,* 96/**2587**:
Applied, 98/2194: *Considered,* 00/2206, 01/2316
Burton *v.* FX Music Ltd; Taube *v.* FX Music Ltd [1999] E.M.L.R. 826; *Times,* July 8, 1999 ; *Independent,* July 26, 1999 (C.S.), Ch D . . . . *Digested,* 99/**4963**
Burton *v.* Green [2001] 4 Q.R. 12, CC (Bristol) [*Ex rel.* Sarah Boyd, Barrister, Assize Court Chambers, Bristol] . . . . *Digested,* 01/**1655**
Burton Allton & Johnson Ltd *v.* Peck [1975] I.C.R. 193; [1975] I.R.L.R. 87, QBD . . . . . . *Digested,* 75/**1141**:
Applied, 00/6215: *Distinguished,* 84/1214, 85/1150
Burton Group Plc *v.* Rapps (Valuation Officer) [2000] R.V.R. 229, Lands Tr . . . . *Digested,* 00/**4580**
Bury *v.* British Gas Plc (Unreported, December 10, 1996), CC (Staines) [*Ex rel.* Ivor Collett, Barrister] . . . . *Digested,* 97/**599**:
Referred to, 98/438

Bus Employees Pension Trustees Ltd *v.* Harrod; *sub nom* NBC Pension Trustees Ltd *v.* Paddock; NBPF Pension Trustees Ltd *v.* Paddock [2000] Ch. 258; [1999] 3 W.L.R. 1260; [1999] 2 All E.R. 993; [1999] O.P.L.R. 113; [2000] Pens. L.R. 183; (1999) 96(14) L.S.G. 32; (1999) 143 S.J.L.B. 99; *Times,* May 6, 1999; *Independent,* March 8, 1999 (C.S.), Ch D . . . . *Digested,* 99/**4152**
Busby *v.* Draper (Unreported, April 18, 2001), CC (Stafford) [*Ex rel.* Lawrence Graham, Solicitors, 190 Strand, London] . . . . *Digested,* 01/**890**
Buscarini *v.* San Marino (24645/94) (2000) 30 E.H.R.R. 208; 6 B.H.R.C. 638, ECHR . . *Digested,* 00/**3195**
Bushbury Land Rover Ltd *v.* Bushbury Ltd [1997] F.S.R. 709, CA . . . . *Digested,* 98/**437**
Business City Express Ltd, Re [1997] B.C.C. 826; [1997] 2 B.C.L.C. 510, Ch D . . . . . . *Digested,* 98/**3297**
Business Computers International Ltd *v.* Registrar of Companies [1988] Ch. 229; [1987] 3 W.L.R. 1134; [1987] 3 All E.R. 465; (1987) 3 B.C.C. 395; [1987] B.C.L.C. 621; [1988] P.C.C. 16; (1988) 85(4) L.S.G. 35; (1987) 137 N.L.J. 758; (1987) 131 S.J. 1628, Ch D . . . . *Digested,* 87/**2582**:
Considered, 99/3953

Business Mortgages (Midland) *v.* Brush see Brush *v.* Bower Cotton & Bower
Business Mortgages (Midland) *v.* Trimvale see Brush *v.* Bower Cotton & Bower
Business Mortgages Trust *v.* Brush see Brush *v.* Bower Cotton & Bower
Bussey *v.* Chief Constable of Suffolk; *sub nom* Bussey *v.* DPP [1999] 1 Cr. App. R. (S.) 125; [1998] Crim. L.R. 908; *Independent,* June 8, 1998 (C.S.), QBD . . . . *Digested,* 98/**986**
Bussey *v.* DPP see Bussey *v.* Chief Constable of Suffolk
Butcher *v.* North West Water Ltd [1997] R.V.R. 287, Lands Tr . . . . *Digested,* 98/**4988**
Butcher *v.* Wolfe [1999] C.P.L.R. 112; [1999] B.L.R. 61; [1999] 1 F.L.R. 334; [1999] 2 F.C.R. 165; [1999] Fam. Law 80; [1998] E.G.C.S. 153; (1998) 95(48) L.S.G. 31; (1998) 95(43) L.S.G. 33; *Times,* November 9, 1998, CA . . . . *Digested,* 98/**414**
Butcher Robinson & Staples Ltd *v.* London Regional Transport (2000) 79 P. & C.R. 523; [1999] 3 E.G.L.R. 63; [1999] 36 E.G. 165; [1999] E.G.C.S. 71, QBD (T&CC) . . . . *Digested,* 99/**4068**
Butigan *v.* Negus-Fancey [2000] E.G.C.S. 67, QBD
Butland *v.* O'Connor (Unreported, April 12, 2000), CC (Portsmouth) [*Ex rel.* Daniel Jones, Barrister, Phoenix Chambers, Chancery Lane, Gray's Inn, London] . . . . . *Digested,* 00/**1708**
Butler *v.* Butler (No.2) [1998] 1 W.L.R. 1208; [1997] 2 All E.R. 822; [1997] 2 F.L.R. 321; [1997] 2 F.C.R. 300; [1997] Fam. Law 603; (1997) 94(12) L.S.G. 22; (1997) 147 N.L.J. 525; (1997) 141 S.J.L.B. 57; *Times,* March 6, 1997, CA . . . . . . *Digested,* 97/**2452**:
Considered, 97/2453
Butler *v.* DPP [2001] R.T.R. 28; [2001] Crim. L.R. 580; *Times,* February 14, 2001, QBD . *Digested,* 01/**990**
Butler *v.* Fareham BC (Unreported, June 26, 2000), CC (Southampton) [*Ex rel.* Robert Duddridge, Barrister, 2 Gray's Inn Square Chambers, London] . . . . *Digested,* 00/**3143**
Butler *v.* Pearce (Unreported, August 24, 2000), CC (Birkenhead) [*Ex rel.* Michael W Halsall, Solicitors, 2 The Parks, Newton-le-Willows] . . . . *Digested,* 00/**410**

Butlers Wharf Ltd, Re [1995] B.C.C. 717; [1995] 2 B.C.L.C. 43; *Times*, April 17, 1995, Ch D
    Digested, 95/**2833**:
    Applied, 01/3842

Butlin *v.* Butlin (Rectification) see Butlin's Settlement Trusts (Rectification), Re
Butlin's Settlement Trusts (Rectification), Re; *sub nom* Butlin *v.* Butlin (Rectification)
    [1976] Ch. 251; [1976] 2 W.L.R. 547; [1976] 2 All E.R. 483; (1975) 119 S.J. 794,
    Ch D . . . . *Digested*, 76/**2508**:
                      Applied, 98/4873, 01/5510: *Followed*, 01/4595
Butterfly Music Srl *v.* Carosello Edizioni Musicali e Discografiche Srl (CEMED) (C60/
    98) [1999] E.C.R. I-3939; [2000] 1 C.M.L.R. 587; [2000] C.E.C. 200; [2000]
    E.C.D.R. 1; [1999] E.M.L.R. 847, ECJ . . . . *Digested*, 00/**3582**
Butters *v.* Grimsby and Scunthorpe HA [1998] Lloyd's Rep. Med. 111, CA . . . . *Digested*, 98/**1630**
Butterworth *v.* Soutter [2000] B.P.I.R. 582, Ch D . . . . *Digested*, 01/**3717**
Butterworth *v.* Supplementary Benefits Commission see Crake *v.* Supplementary
    Benefits Commission
Buttes Gas and Oil Co *v.* Hammer (No.3); Occidental Petroleum Corp *v.* Buttes Gas and
    Oil Co (No.2) [1982] A.C. 888; [1981] 3 W.L.R. 787; [1981] 3 All E.R. 616;
    [1981] Com. L.R. 257; 125 S.J. 776; *Times*, October 31, 1981, HL; reversing
    [1981] Q.B. 223; [1980] 3 W.L.R. 668; [1980] 3 All E.R. 475; 124 S.J. 630,
    CA . . . . *Digested*, 81/**1473**:
                Applied, 87/3060, 95/2939, 96/3659: *Cited*, 93/3224: *Considered*, 84/2700,
               91/2860, 92/3479, 96/681, 96/1086, 98/3552, 99/723, 00/1756, 00/5107:
               Distinguished, 85/2651, 90/3689: *Not followed*, 88/1595, 89/1699
Buxton *v.* Equinox Design Ltd [1999] I.C.R. 269; [1999] I.R.L.R. 158; [1999] Disc.
    L.R. 133; *Times*, December 3, 1998, EAT . . . . *Digested*, 99/**2021**
Buxton *v.* Westmacott [1999] P.I.Q.R. Q115, CA. . . . . *Digested*, 00/**588**
Buzzacott *v.* Hill see Nulyarimma *v.* Thompson
BW (Care Orders), Re see Lancashire CC *v.* B (A Child) (Care Orders: Significant Harm)
Byblos Bank SAL *v.* Barrett see Byblos Bank SAL *v.* Rushingdale SA
Byblos Bank SAL *v.* Khudhairy see Byblos Bank SAL *v.* Rushingdale SA
Byblos Bank SAL *v.* Rushingdale SA; *sub nom* Rushingdale SA *v.* Byblos Bank SAL;
    Byblos Bank SAL *v.* Khudhairy; Byblos Bank SAL *v.* Barrett [1987] B.C.L.C. 232;
    [1986] P.C.C. 249, CA; affirming [1985] P.C.C. 342 . . . . *Digested*, 86/**2839.a**:
    Applied, 01/4872

Bybrook Barn Centre Ltd *v.* Kent CC see Bybrook Barn Garden Centre Ltd *v.* Kent CC
Bybrook Barn Garden Centre Ltd *v.* Kent CC; *sub nom* Bybrook Barn Centre Ltd *v.* Kent
    CC [2001] B.L.R. 55; [2001] Env. L.R. 30; (2001) 3 L.G.L.R. 27; [2001]
    B.L.G.R. 239; (2001) 98(14) L.S.G. 39; [2000] N.P.C. 135; *Times*, January 5,
    2001; *Daily Telegraph*, December 19, 2000, CA; reversing [2000] B.L.G.R. 302;
    [2000] 2 E.G.L.R. 63; [2000] 20 E.G. 158; [1999] E.G.C.S. 132; (1999) 96(44)
    L.S.G. 42; [1999] N.P.C. 138, QBD . . . . *Digested*, 01/**4547**
Bydand Ltd, Re [1997] B.C.C. 915; [1999] B.P.I.R. 843, Ch D (Companies Ct) . . . . *Digested*, 98/**3332**
Byers *v.* Brent LBC [1998] 98(3) Q.R. 7, QBD . . . . *Digested*, 98/**1645**
Byrne *v.* Anixter (UK) Ltd (Unreported, June 30, 2000), CC (Epsom) [*Ex rel.* Ivor
    Collett, Barrister, No.1 Serjeant's Inn, Fleet Street, London] . . . . *Digested*, 00/**370**
Byrne *v.* Conroy [1999] 2 C.M.L.R. 617, Sup Ct (Irl); affirming [1997] 1 C.M.L.R. 595,
    HC (Irl) . . . . *Digested*, 99/**2290**
Byrne *v.* Hall Pain & Foster [1999] 1 W.L.R. 1849; [1999] 2 All E.R. 400; 68 Con. L.R.
    110; [1999] Lloyd's Rep. P.N. 147; [1999] P.N.L.R. 565; [1999] 1 E.G.L.R. 73;
    [1999] 12 E.G. 165; (1999) 15 Const. L.J. 388; [1998] E.G.C.S. 182; (1999)
    96(5) L.S.G. 37; (1999) 143 S.J.L.B. 36; [1998] N.P.C. 164; *Times*, January 8,
    1999, CA . . . . *Digested*, 99/**477**:
    Applied, 01/4526
Byrne *v.* Inntrepreneur Beer Supply Co Ltd (Unreported, November 26, 1998), Ch D . . *Digested*, 99/**680**
Byrne *v.* Kunkel & Kunkel (Unreported, March 5, 1998), CC (Central London) [*Ex rel.*
    Alexander Hutton, Barrister, 6 Pump Court, Temple, London] . . . . *Digested*, 99/**3757**
Byrne *v.* Secretary of State for the Environment (1997) 74 P. & C.R. 420; [1998] J.P.L.
    122, QBD . . . . *Digested*, 98/**4165**
Byrne *v.* Sefton HA; *sub nom* Byrne *v.* South Sefton HA; Bryne *v.* South Sefton HA
    [2001] EWCA Civ 1904; (2001) 145 S.J.L.B. 268; *Times*, November 28, 2001,
    CA . . . . *Digested*, 01/**541**
Byrne *v.* South Sefton HA see Byrne *v.* Sefton HA
Byrne *v.* Tibsco Ltd see Courage Ltd *v.* Crehan (No.1)

C (A Child) (Abduction: Grave Risk of Physical or Psychological Harm) (No.1), Re; *sub nom*
    C (A Minor) (Child Abduction), Re [1999] 2 F.L.R. 478; [1999] 3 F.C.R. 510;
    [1999] Fam. Law 520; *Times*, May 14, 1999, CA . . . . *Digested*, 99/**2335**
C (A Child) (Abduction: Unmarried Father) see C (A Child) (Abduction: Wrongful
    Removal), Re
C (A Child) (Abduction: Wrongful Removal), Re; *sub nom* C (A Child) (Abduction:
    Unmarried Father) [1999] 2 F.L.R. 859; [1999] 3 F.C.R. 678; [1999] Fam. Law
    609, Fam Div . . . . *Digested*, 00/**2452**:
    Approved, 99/2327

C (A Child) (Care Order or Supervision Order), Re [2001] 2 F.L.R. 466; [2001] Fam. Law
    580, Fam Div . . . .   *Digested,* 01/**2567**
C (A Child) (Care Orders), Re [2001] EWCA Civ 810; [2001] 3 F.C.R. 381, CA
C (A Child) (HIV Testing), Re; *sub nom* C (A Minor) (HIV Test), Re [1999] 2 F.L.R. 1004;
    [2000] Fam. Law 16, CA [2000] Fam. 48; [2000] 2 W.L.R. 270; [1999] 3
    F.C.R. 289; (1999) 50 B.M.L.R. 283; *Times,* September 14, 1999, Fam Div . . . . .   *Digested,* 00/**2493**
C (A Child) (Leave to Remove from Jurisdiction), Re; *sub nom* C (A Child) (Removal from
    Jurisdiction), Re [2000] 2 F.L.R. 457; [2000] 2 F.C.R. 40; [2000] Fam. Law
    813, CA . . . .   *Digested,* 00/**2489**
C (A Child) (Removal from Jurisdiction), Re see C (A Child) (Leave to Remove from
    Jurisdiction), Re
C (A Child) (Secure Accommodation Order: Representation), Re; *sub nom* M (A Child)
    (Secure Accommodation Order), Re [2001] EWCA Civ 458; [2001] 2 F.L.R.
    169; [2001] 1 F.C.R. 692; [2001] Fam. Law 507; *Times,* April 5, 2001, CA;
    affirming [2001] 1 F.L.R. 857; [2001] Fam. Law 424, Fam Div . . . .   *Digested,* 01/**2672**
C (A Child) *v.* Bentham Country Club [2001] 4 Q.R. 13, CC (Cheltenham) [*Ex rel.* Davis
    Gregory, Solicitors, 25 Rodney Road, Cheltenham, Gloucestershire] . . . .   *Digested,* 01/**1788**
C (A Child) *v.* Carta [2001] 2 Q.R. 9, CC (Portsmouth) [*Ex rel.* Archna Dawar, Barrister,
    Assize Court Chambers, 14 Small Street, Bristol] . . . .   *Digested,* 01/**1620**
C (A Child) *v.* DPP [2001] EWHC Admin 453; (2001) 165 J.P. 806; [2001] Crim. L.R.
    671; (2001) 165 J.P.N. 810, QBD (Admin Ct)
C (A Child) *v.* Great Universal Stores Plc (Unreported, March 31, 2000), CC (Burnley)
    [*Ex rel.* Waddington & Son Solicitors, 28 Manchester Road, Burnley,
    Lancashire] . . . .   *Digested,* 00/**1649**
C (A Child) *v.* Imperial Design Ltd [2001] Env. L.R. 33, CA . . . .   *Digested,* 01/**4467**
C (A Child) *v.* Intatravel Group Plc [2001] 2 Q.R. 11, MCLC [*Ex rel.* Clyde & Co
    Solicitors, 51 Eastcheap, London] . . . .   *Digested,* 01/**1690**
C (A Child) *v.* Kitchen (Unreported, August 2, 2000), CC (Poole) [*Ex rel.* Lyons
    Davidson Solicitors, Victoria House, 51 Victoria Street, Bristol] . . . .   *Digested,* 00/**1562**
C (A Child) *v.* Leeds NHS Teaching; *sub nom* C (A Child) *v.* Leeds NHS Teaching
    National Trust [2000] 3 Q.R. 7, CC (Leeds) [*Ex rel.* Lupton Fawcett Solicitors,
    PO Box 121, Leeds] . . . .   *Digested,* 00/**1730**
C (A Child) *v.* Leeds NHS Teaching National Trust see C (A Child) *v.* Leeds NHS
    Teaching
C (A Child) *v.* London Underground Ltd (Unreported, March 9, 2000), CC (Central
    London) [*Ex rel.* Stephen Shay, Barrister, 1 King's Bench Walk, Temple, London] .   *Digested,* 00/**1612**
C (A Child) *v.* Nottingham City Council (Unreported, August 3, 2000), CC
    (Nottingham) [*Ex rel.* Matthew Chapman, Barrister, No. 1 Serjeants Inn, Fleet
    Street, London] . . . .   *Digested,* 00/**4231**
C (A Child) *v.* Peers (Unreported, November 26, 1999), CC (Leicester) [*Ex rel.* Andrew
    Skelly, Barrister, 1 Gray's Inn Square, London] . . . .   *Digested,* 00/**1715**
C (A Child) *v.* Plymouth City Council; *sub nom* Plymouth City Council *v.* C; C *v.*
    Plymouth CC [2000] 1 F.L.R. 875; [2000] 2 F.C.R. 289; [2000] Fam. Law 460;
    (2000) 97(15) L.S.G. 39; (2000) 144 S.J.L.B. 180; *Times,* March 21, 2000, CA .   *Digested,* 00/**2461**
C (A Child) *v.* Scott [2001] N.I. 48, CA (NI) . . . .   *Digested,* 01/**5743**
C (A Child) *v.* Scout Association [2001] 6 Q.R. 15, CC (Pontefract) [*Ex rel.* Hartley &
    Worstenholme, Solicitors, 20 Bank Street, Castleford] . . . .   *Digested,* 01/**1673**
C (A Child) *v.* Sefton MBC Independent Appeals Panel see R. (on the application of C
    (A Child)) *v.* Sefton MBC Independent Appeals Panel
C (A Child) *v.* Taylor (Unreported, January 12, 2000), CC (Nottingham) [*Ex rel.*
    Nelsons, Solicitors, Pennine House, 8 Stanford Street, Nottingham] . . . .   *Digested,* 00/**1545**
C (A Child) *v.* Thomson Tour Operations Ltd; *sub nom* C (A Child) *v.* Thomsons Tour
    Operators Ltd *Times,* October 20, 2000, CA [*Ex rel.* Berrymans Lace Mawer
    Solicitors, Salisbury House, London Wall, London] . . . .   *Digested,* 00/**4041**:
                                                                                            Followed, 01/4453
C (A Child) *v.* Thomsons Tour Operators Ltd see C (A Child) *v.* Thomson Tour Operations
    Ltd
C (A Child), Re; *sub nom* R. *v.* Croydon Youth Court Ex p. C (A Child) (2000) 164 J.P.
    693; [2001] Crim. L.R. 40; (2000) 164 J.P.N. 901; *Independent,* October 9,
    2000 (C.S), QBD
C (A Minor) (Abduction: Rights of Custody Abroad), Re see C *v.* C (A Minor) (Abduction:
    Rights of Custody Abroad)
C (A Minor) (Adoption: Freeing Order), Re; *sub nom* SC (A Minor), Re [1999] Fam. 240;
    [1999] 1 W.L.R. 1079; [1999] 1 F.L.R. 348; [1999] 1 F.C.R. 145; [1999] Fam.
    Law 11; (1999) 163 J.P.N. 771; (1998) 95(45) L.S.G. 37; (1998) 142 S.J.L.B.
    263; *Times,* October 26, 1998; *Independent,* November 9, 1998 (C.S.), Fam Div .   *Digested,* 98/**2366**
C (A Minor) (Adoption: Illegality), Re; *sub nom* C (A Minor) (Adoption: Legality), Re
    [1999] Fam. 128; [1999] 2 W.L.R. 202; [1999] 1 F.L.R. 370; [1998] 2 F.C.R.
    641; [1998] Fam. Law 724; (1998) 95(22) L.S.G. 28; (1998) 142 S.J.L.B. 151;
    Times, June 2, 1998, Fam Div. . . . .   *Digested,* 98/**2367**
C (A Minor) (Adoption: Legality), Re see C (A Minor) (Adoption: Illegality), Re
C (A Minor) (Adoption: Parental Agreement: Contact), Re [1993] 2 F.L.R. 260; [1994] 2
    F.C.R. 485; [1993] Fam. Law 612, CA . . . .   *Digested,* 94/**3087**:
                                                                 Considered, 98/2365, 00/2430, 01/2529

C (A Minor) (Care Proceedings: Disclosure), Re; *sub nom* EC (A Minor) (Care Proceedings: Disclosure), Re; EC (Disclosure of Material), Re [1997] Fam. 76; [1997] 2 W.L.R. 322; [1996] 2 F.L.R. 725; [1996] 3 F.C.R. 556; [1997] Fam. Law 160; *Times*, October 22, 1996, CA; reversing in part [1996] 2 F.L.R. 123; [1996] 3 F.C.R. 521; [1996] Fam. Law 603, Fam Div . . . . *Digested, 96/***1347**: *Considered,* 97/377, 98/2386, 00/7: *Followed,* 99/2349

C (A Minor) (Change of Surname), Re [1998] 2 F.L.R. 656; [1999] 1 F.C.R. 318; [1998] Fam. Law 659; *Times*, February 2, 1998, CA . . . . *Digested, 98/***2433**: *Considered,* 98/2431

C (A Minor) (Child Abduction), Re see C (A Child) (Abduction: Grave Risk of Physical or Psychological Harm) (No.1), Re

C (A Minor) (HIV Test), Re see C (A Child) (HIV Testing), Re

C (A Minor) (Interim Care Order: Residential Assessment), Re; *sub nom* C (A Minor) (Local Authority: Assessment), Re [1997] A.C. 489; [1996] 3 W.L.R. 1098; [1996] 4 All E.R. 871; [1997] 1 F.L.R. 1; [1997] 1 F.C.R. 149; [1997] Fam. Law 228; (1997) 161 J.P.N. 62; (1997) 94(1) L.S.G. 23; (1996) 146 N.L.J. 1777; (1997) 141 S.J.L.B. 12; *Times*, November 29, 1996; *Independent*, December 4, 1996, HL; reversing [1996] 2 F.L.R. 708; (1996) 93(39) L.S.G. 27; (1996) 140 S.J.L.B. 221; *Times*, October 3, 1996; *Independent*, November 11, 1996 (C.S.), CA . . . . *Digested,* 97/**365**: *Applied,* 98/2410: *Followed,* 98/2408, 99/2361

C (A Minor) (Local Authority: Assessment), Re see C (A Minor) (Interim Care Order: Residential Assessment), Re

C (A Minor) (Medical Treatment), Re; *sub nom* C (A Minor) (Withdrawal of Lifesaving Treatment), Re [1998] 1 F.L.R. 384; [1998] 1 F.C.R. 1; [1998] Lloyd's Rep. Med. 1; (1998) 40 B.M.L.R. 31; [1998] Fam. Law 135; *Independent*, December 11, 1997, Fam Div . . . . *Digested, 98/***2646**

C (A Minor) (Medical Treatment: Refusal of Parental Consent), Re see T (A Minor) (Wardship: Medical Treatment), Re

C (A Minor) (Withdrawal of Lifesaving Treatment), Re see C (A Minor) (Medical Treatment), Re

C (A Minor) *v.* Chief Constable of Hampshire (Unreported, November 6, 1998), CC (Southampton) [*Ex rel.* Bell Pope Solicitors, Ashley House, 5 Grosvenor Square, Southampton, Hampshire] . . . . *Digested, 99/***1462**

C (A Minor) *v.* Kay (1999) 99(2) Q.R. 7, CC (Bury) [*Ex rel.* Jonathan Thompson, Barrister, 8 King Street, Manchester] . . . . *Digested, 99/***1524**

C (A Minor) *v.* Thomson Tour Operations Ltd (Unreported, May 20, 1999), CC (Torquay) [*Ex rel.* Berrymans Lace Mawer Solicitors, Salisbury House, London Wall, London] . . . . *Digested, 99/***4005**

C (Adoption Notice), Re [1999] 1 F.L.R. 384; [1998] Fam. Law 725, Fam Div . . . . *Digested, 99/***2309**

C (Adult: Refusal of Medical Treatment), Re [1994] 1 W.L.R. 290; [1994] 1 All E.R. 819; [1994] 1 F.L.R. 31; [1994] 2 F.C.R. 151, Fam Div . . . . *Digested, 94/***3063**: *Considered,* 94/3850, 95/3535, 95/4266, 96/2979, 98/3890: *Referred to,* 94/3803

C (Care or Supervision Order), Re [1999] 2 F.L.R. 621; [1999] Fam. Law 750, Fam Div. *Digested, 99/***2396**

C (Children) (Residential Assessment), Re [2001] EWCA Civ 1305; [2001] 3 F.C.R. 164, CA

*Digested, 01/***2608**

C (CICA: Quantum: 2001), Re [2001] 5 Q.R. 10, CICA (Manchester) [*Ex rel.* Karim Sabry, Barrister, 8 King Street Chambers, Manchester] . . . . *Digested, 01/***1587**

C (CICB: Quantum: 1998), Re (1999) 99(6) Q.R. 4, CICB (London) [*Ex rel.* Jonathan Ashworth, Pupil Barrister, 6 King's Bench Walk, Temple, London] . . . . *Digested, 99/***1450**

C (CICB: Quantum: 1999), Re (Unreported, January 11, 1999), CICB (London) [*Ex rel.* Jonathan Ashworth, Pupil Barrister, 6 King's Bench Walk, Temple, London] . . . . *Digested, 99/***1445**

C (Contact: No Order for Contact), Re [2000] 2 F.L.R. 723; [2000] Fam. Law 699, Fam Div

*Digested, 01/***2586**

C (Disclosure), Re [1996] 1 F.L.R. 797; [1996] 3 F.C.R. 765; (1996) 160 J.P.N. 732, Fam Div

*Digested, 96/***508**: *Approved,* 99/2360

C (Enduring Power of Attorney), Re; *sub nom* Enduring Powers of Attorney Act 1985, Re [2001] W.T.L.R. 39, CA; affirming [2001] W.T.L.R. 33, Ch D . . . . *Digested, 01/***4445**

C (Legal Aid: Preparation of Bill of Costs), Re; *sub nom* A Local Authority *v.* A (A Mother and Child) [2001] 1 Costs L.R. 136; [2001] 1 F.L.R. 602; [2001] Fam. Law 260, CA

C (Minors) (Abduction: Consent), Re [1996] 1 F.L.R. 414; [1996] 3 F.C.R. 222; [1996] Fam. Law 266, Fam Div . . . . *Digested,* 96/**521**: *Applied,* 00/2439: *Followed,* 97/389, 99/2318

C (Minors) (Abduction: Grave Risk of Psychological Harm), Re; *sub nom* C (Minors) (Abduction: Habitual Residence), Re [1999] 1 F.L.R. 1145; [1999] 2 F.C.R. 507; [1999] Fam. Law 371; (1999) 96(10) L.S.G. 28; (1999) 143 S.J.L.B. 74; *Times*, February 23, 1999, CA. . . . . *Digested, 99/***2329**

C (Minors) (Abduction: Habitual Residence), Re see C (Minors) (Abduction: Grave Risk of Psychological Harm), Re

C (Minors) (Change of Surname), Re see PC (Change of Surname), Re

C (Minors) (Change of Surname), Re [1998] 1 F.L.R. 549; [1998] 2 F.C.R. 544; [1998] Fam. Law 250; (1997) 94(48) L.S.G. 29; (1998) 142 S.J.L.B. 20; *Times*, December 8, 1997, CA. . . . .   *Digested*, 98/**2432**
C (Power of Attorney), Re [2000] 2 F.L.R. 1; [2000] Fam. Law 467, CA. . . . .   *Digested*, 00/**74**
C (Privacy: Photographs) (1 BvR 653/96), Re 10 B.H.R.C. 131, BverfG (Ger)
C v. A Local Authority see C v. Flintshire CC (formerly Clwyd CC)
C v. Belgium (21794/93) (2001) 32 E.H.R.R. 2, ECHR. . . . .   *Applied*, 98/3152
C v. Buckingham CC see C v. Buckinghamshire CC
C v. Buckinghamshire CC; *sub nom* C v. Buckingham CC [1999] B.L.G.R. 321; [1999] E.L.R. 179; [1999] C.O.D. 227; *Times*, March 18, 1999; *Independent*, March 12, 1999, CA; affirming [1999] Ed. C.R. 430; [1998] E.L.R. 463; [1998] C.O.D. 279, QBD. . . . .   *Digested*, 99/**1896**:
Applied, 99/1899, 00/1955: *Considered*, 99/1894, 00/1948
C v. C (A Minor) (Abduction: Rights of Custody Abroad); *sub nom* C (A Minor) (Abduction: Rights of Custody Abroad), Re [1989] 1 W.L.R. 654; [1989] 2 All E.R. 465; [1989] 1 F.L.R. 403; [1989] F.C.R. 197; [1989] Fam. Law 228; (1989) 153 J.P.N. 236; (1989) 133 S.J. 660; *Times*, December 19, 1988; *Independent*, January 2, 1989 (C.S.), CA. . . . .   *Digested*, 89/**2437**:
Applied, 89/2491, 90/3155, 91/2522, 91/2527, 93/2789:
Considered, 95/3431, 95/3436, 95/3448, 96/534, 97/402:
Distinguished, 94/3151, 95/5533: *Followed*, 94/5440, 98/2383, 98/5842
C v. C (Application for Non Molestation Order: Jurisdiction) [1998] Fam. 70; [1998] 2 W.L.R. 599; [1998] 1 F.L.R. 554; [1998] 1 F.C.R. 11; [1998] Fam. Law 254; (1997) 94(47) L.S.G. 30; (1997) 141 S.J.L.B. 236; *Times*, December 16, 1997; *Independent*, November 27, 1997, Fam Div . . . .   *Digested*, 97/**2496**
C v. C (Custody: Affidavit) see C v. C (Privilege: Criminal Communications)
C v. C (Divorce: Stay of English Proceedings) [2001] 1 F.L.R. 624; [2001] Fam. Law 181, Fam Div . . . .   *Digested*, 01/**2610**
C v. C (Evidence: Privilege) see C v. C (Privilege: Criminal Communications)
C v. C (Privilege: Criminal Communications); *sub nom* C v. C (Evidence: Privilege); GC v. JC; C v. C (Custody: Affidavit) [2001] EWCA Civ 469; [2001] 3 W.L.R. 446; [2001] 2 F.L.R. 184; [2001] 1 F.C.R. 756; [2001] Fam. Law 496; *Times*, March 16, 2001; *Daily Telegraph*, March 20, 2001, CA . . . .   *Digested*, 01/**399**
C v. Congdon [2001] 6 Q.R. 24, QBD [*Ex rel.* Richard Colbey, Barrister, Tanfield Chambers, Francis Taylor Building, Temple, London]. . . . .   *Digested*, 01/**1814**
C v. Criminal Injuries Compensation Board see C, Petitioner
C (A Patient: Severe Head Injuries) v. Crisp (Unreported, June 7, 2000), QBD [*Ex rel.* Russell Jones & Walker, Solicitors, 4th Floor, Brazennose House, Brazennose Street, Manchester]. . . . .   *Digested*, 01/**1567**
C v. DPP [1999] C.O.D. 290, QBD
C (A Patient: Dependency) v. Ewin (Unreported, July 25, 2000), QBD [*Ex rel.* David Mason, Barrister, Milburn House Chambers, Floor A, Milburn House, Dean Street, Newcastle-upon-Tyne] . . . .   *Digested*, 00/**1520**
C (A Patient: Head Injuries) v. Ewin (Unreported, July 25, 2000), QBD [*Ex rel.* David Mason, Barrister, Milburn House Chambers, Floor A, Milburn House, Dean Street, Newcastle-upon-Tyne] . . . .   *Digested*, 00/**1510**
C v. F (Child Maintenance) see C v. F (Disabled Child: Maintenance Orders)
C v. F (Disabled Child: Maintenance Orders); *sub nom* C v. F (Child Maintenance) [1998] 2 F.L.R. 1; [1999] 1 F.C.R. 39; [1998] Fam. Law 389, CA; reversing [1998] 1 F.L.R. 151; [1997] 3 F.C.R. 405; [1998] Fam. Law 69; (1997) 161 J.P.N. 918, Fam Div. . . . .   *Digested*, 98/**2393**
C v. Flintshire CC (formerly Clwyd CC); *sub nom* C v. A Local Authority [2001] EWCA Civ 302; [2001] 2 F.L.R. 33; [2001] 1 F.C.R. 614; [2001] P.I.Q.R. Q9; [2001] Fam. Law 420; *Times*, March 13, 2001, CA . . . .   *Digested*, 01/**1547**
C v. G see G v. C (Residence Order: Committal)
C v. Greenwich LBC see C v. Special Educational Needs Tribunal
C v. Health Authority 1991 -C- 6714, QBD . . . .   *Digested*, 99/**4002**
C v. Lambeth LBC [1999] Ed. C.R. 933; [1999] E.L.R. 350; *Times*, May 27, 1999, QBD . . . .   *Digested*, 99/**1883**
C v. Newell [2001] 6 Q.R. 3, HC [*Ex rel.* Crosse & Crosse, Solicitors, 14 Southernhay West, Exeter] . . . .   *Digested*, 01/**1572**
C v. Plymouth CC see C (A Child) v. Plymouth City Council
C v. S (CICB: Quantum: 1997); *sub nom* C v. S (Damages: Sexual Abuse); (Unreported, November 14, 1997), CC (Norwich) [*Ex rel.* Ruth Blair, Barrister, 2 King's Bench Walk, Temple, London] . . . .   *Digested*, 98/**1508**
C v. S (Damages: Sexual Abuse) see C v. S (CICB: Quantum: 1997)
C v. S (Foetus: Unmarried Father) [1988] Q.B. 135; [1987] 2 W.L.R. 1108; [1987] 1 All E.R. 1230; [1987] 2 F.L.R. 505; [1987] Fam. Law 269; (1987) 84 L.S.G. 1410; (1987) 131 S.J. 624, CA. . . . .   *Digested*, 87/**2501**:
Considered, 99/5185
C v. S (Minors) (Abduction: Illegitimate Child) see J (A Minor) (Abduction: Custody Rights), Re

C *v.* S (Money Laundering: Discovery of Documents) (Practice Note); *sub nom*
Practice Note (CA: Money Laundering: Discovery of Documents) [1999] 1
W.L.R. 1551; [1999] 2 All E.R. 343; [1999] Lloyd's Rep. Bank. 26; (1998) 148
N.L.J.1723; *Times*, November 5, 1998, CA . . . .   *Digested*, 98/**69**:
                                                       Applied, 00/**491**
C *v.* Special Educational Needs Tribunal [1997] E.L.R. 390, QBD . . . .   *Digested*, 98/**1971**
C *v.* Special Educational Needs Tribunal; C *v.* Greenwich LBC [1999] Ed. C.R. 625;
[1999] E.L.R. 5, QBD . . . .   *Digested*, 99/**1884**
C *v.* United Kingdom (A/184) see Cossey *v.* United Kingdom (A/184)
C *v.* W (A Minor) (Contact: Leave to Apply) [1999] 1 F.L.R. 916; [1998] 1 F.C.R. 618;
[1999] Fam. Law 298, Fam Div . . . .   *Digested*, 98/**2453**
C and B (Children) (Care Order: Future Harm), Re; *sub nom* C and J (Children), Re
[2001] 1 F.L.R. 611; [2000] 2 F.C.R. 614; [2001] Fam. Law 253; (2000) 164
J.P.N. 940, CA . . . .   *Digested*, 00/**2460**
C & H Jefferson, Re [1998] N.I. 404, CA (NI) . . . .   *Digested*, 99/**5144**
C and J (Children), Re see C and B (Children) (Care Order: Future Harm), Re
C and V (Minors) (Contact: Parental Responsibility Order), Re [1998] 1 F.L.R. 392; [1998] 1
F.C.R. 52; [1998] Fam. Law 10; *Times*, June 30, 1997, CA . . . .   *Digested*, 97/**439**
C Evans & Son Ltd *v.* Spritebrand Ltd [1985] 1 W.L.R. 317; [1985] 2 All E.R. 415;
[1985] P.C.C. 109; [1985] F.S.R. 267; (1985) 82 L.S.G. 606; (1985) 129 S.J.
189, CA . . . .   *Digested*, 85/**3389**:
                     Considered, 98/3421: *Distinguished*, 93/5553: *Followed*, 92/3524:
                                        Referred to, 93/3041, 95/3755
C Inc Plc *v.* L [2001] 2 All E.R. (Comm) 446; [2001] 2 Lloyd's Rep. 459; [2001]
C.L.C. 1054; (2001) 151 N.L.J. 535; *Times*, May 4, 2001, QBD (Comm Ct) . . . . .   *Digested*, 01/**46**
C Itoh & Co Ltd *v.* Companhia De Navegacao Lloyd Brasileiro (The Rio Assu) (No.1)
[1999] 1 Lloyd's Rep. 201, QBD (Comm Ct) . . . .   *Digested*, 99/**752**
C Itoh & Co Ltd *v.* Companhia De Navegacao Lloyd Brasileiro (The Rio Assu) (No.2); C
Itoh & Co Ltd *v.* Republica Federativa Do Brasil (The Rio Assu) (No.2) [1999]
1 Lloyd's Rep. 115, CA . . . .   *Digested*, 99/**4421**
C Itoh & Co Ltd *v.* Republica Federativa Do Brasil (The Rio Assu) (No.2) see C Itoh &
Co Ltd *v.* Companhia De Navegacao Lloyd Brasileiro (The Rio Assu) (No.2)
C (Device) Trade Mark [1998] R.P.C. 439, TMR . . . .   *Digested*, 98/**3530**
C Van der Lely NV *v.* Bamfords Ltd [1964] R.P.C. 54, CA; reversing [1963] R.P.C. 368 .   *Digested*, 64/**2766**:
         Applied, 74/2786, 95/3750, 96/4568: *Considered*, 74/2748, 74/2781,
              95/3752, 95/3780, 98/3460: *Previous proceedings*, 59/2409, 63/2628
C Walton Ltd *v.* Harborough DC see C Walton Ltd *v.* Secretary of State for the
Environment, Transport and the Regions
C Walton Ltd *v.* Secretary of State for the Environment, Transport and the Regions; C
Walton Ltd *v.* Harborough DC [2001] J.P.L. 220 (Note); [2000] N.P.C. 66, CA;
affirming CO 575/99, QBD
C&G Homes Ltd *v.* Secretary of State for Health [1991] Ch. 365; [1991] 2 W.L.R. 715;
[1991] 2 All E.R. 841; (1991) 23 H.L.R. 145; (1991) 62 P. & C.R. 69; [1991] 06
E.G. 170; *Independent*, November 6, 1990, CA; reversing in part [1990] 1 W.L.R.
1272; (1990) 134 S.J. 1040, Ch D . . . .   *Digested*, 91/**3552**:
                                             Distinguished, 00/**5733**
C&V (Advice Line) Services Ltd *v.* Customs and Excise Commissioners [2001] B.V.C.
2639, V&D Tr
C, Petitioner; *sub nom* C *v.* Criminal Injuries Compensation Board 1999 S.C. 551; 1999
S.C.L.R. 992; 1999 G.W.D. 21-985; *Times*, June 3, 1999, OH . . . .   *Digested*, 99/**5614**
CA Pacific Finance Ltd (In Liquidation), Re [2000] 1 B.C.L.C. 494, CFI (HK) . . . .   *Digested*, 00/**690**
CA Sheimer (M) Sdn Bhd's Application (Opposition by Visa International Service
Association) [1999] E.T.M.R. 519, TMR. . . . .   *Digested*, 00/**3769**
CA Sheimer (M) Sdn Bhd's Trade Mark Application [2000] E.T.M.R. 1170 (Note); [2000]
R.P.C. 484, Appointed Person . . . .   *Digested*, 00/**3768**
Caba *v.* United States 3 I.T.L. Rep. 825, US Ct
Cabales *v.* United Kingdom (9473/81) see Abdulaziz *v.* United Kingdom (A/94)
Caballero *v.* United Kingdom (2000) 30 E.H.R.R. 643; [2000] Crim. L.R. 587; *Times*,
February 29, 2000, ECHR . . . .   *Digested*, 00/**3165**
CABANAS HABANA (Device) Trade Mark [2000] R.P.C. 26, TMR . . . .   *Digested*, 00/**3795**
Cable *v.* United Kingdom (2000) 30 E.H.R.R. 1032; *Times*, March 11, 1999, ECHR . . . . .   *Digested*, 99/**3091**
Cable and Wireless (Dominica) Ltd *v.* Marpin Telecoms and Broadcasting Co Ltd [2001]
1 W.L.R. 1123; 9 B.H.R.C. 486; *Times*, January 9, 2001, PC (Dom) . . . .   *Digested*, 01/**850**
Cable & Wireless Plc *v.* British Telecommunications Plc [1998] F.S.R. 383; (1998) 21 (4)
I.P.D. 21042, Ch D . . . .   *Digested*, 98/**3507**:
                                      Applied, 01/4023: *Followed*, 99/3535
Cable Television Broadcasts, Re see Commission of the European Communities *v.* Belgium
(C11/95)
Cabot Italiana SpA, Re (387) 1 I.T.L. Rep. 657, Comm Tributaria PG (I)
Cabot Safety Intermediate Corp's Three Dimensional Trade Mark Application [2001]
E.T.M.R. 85, OHIM (1st Bd App) . . . .   *Digested*, 01/**4000**
Cachia *v.* Faluyi [2001] EWCA Civ 998; [2001] 1 W.L.R. 1966; [2001] C.P. Rep. 102;
(2001) 98(29) L.S.G. 39; (2001) 145 S.J.L.B. 167; *Times*, July 11, 2001; *Daily
Telegraph*, July 3, 2001, CA . . . .   *Digested*, 01/**411**

Cadbury Schweppes Inc v. FBI Foods Ltd [2000] F.S.R. 491, Sup Ct (Can) . . . .　*Digested*, 00/**3567**
Cadbury Schweppes Plc v. Somji; *sub nom* Somji v. Cadbury Schweppes Plc [2001] 1
　W.L.R. 615; [2001] 1 B.C.L.C. 498; [2001] B.P.I.R. 172; (2001) 98(8) L.S.G.
　43; *Times*, January 16, 2001, CA; affirming [2000] B.P.I.R. 950, Ch D . . . .　*Digested*, 01/**3791**
Cadbury Schweppes Pty Ltd v. Pub Squash Co Pty Ltd [1981] 1 W.L.R. 193; [1981] 1
　All E.R. 213; [1981] R.P.C. 429; 125 S.J. 96, PC (Aus) . . . .　*Digested*, 81/**2789**:
　　　　　　　　　Applied, 98/3497: *Followed*, 97/4882, 99/3524
CADDIE Trade Mark see SA Ateliers Reunis Caddie v. Sarl Societe Nouvelle De Presse et
　De Communication
Cadger v. Vauxhall Motors Ltd (Unreported, March 28, 2000), CC (Central London)
　[*Ex rel.* Rowley Ashworth Solicitors, 247 The Broadway, Wimbledon, London] . .　*Digested*, 00/**2972**
Cadogan v. McCarthy & Stone (Developments) Ltd [2000] L. & T.R. 249; [1996]
　E.G.C.S. 94; [1996] N.P.C. 77; *Independent*, June 17, 1996 (C.S.), CA . . . .　*Digested*, 96/**3776**
Cadogan Estates Ltd v. McMahon [2001] 1 A.C. 378; [2000] 3 W.L.R. 1555; [2000] 4
　All E.R. 897; [2001] B.P.I.R. 17; (2001) 33 H.L.R. 42; [2001] L. & T.R. 2;
　[2001] 1 E.G.L.R. 47; [2001] 06 E.G. 164; [2000] E.G.C.S. 119; (2000) 97(43)
　L.S.G. 39; (2000) 97(44) L.S.G. 45; (2000) 150 N.L.J. 1625; (2000) 144
　S.J.L.B. 281; [2000] N.P.C. 110; (2001) 81 P. & C.R. D11; *Times*, November 1,
　2000, HL; affirming [1999] 1 W.L.R. 1689; [1999] B.P.I.R. 849; (2000) 32
　H.L.R. 433; [1999] L. & T.R. 481; [1999] 2 E.G.L.R. 67; [1999] 31 E.G. 92;
　[1999] E.G.C.S. 80; (1999) 96(22) L.S.G. 35; (1999) 96(23) L.S.G. 36; *Times*,
　June 1, 1999, CA . . . .　*Digested*, 00/**3921**
Cadogan Estates Ltd v. Morris see Viscount Chelsea v. Morris
Cadogan Estates Ltd v. Shahgholi [1999] 1 E.G.L.R. 189; [1998] R.V.R. 266, Lands Tr . .　*Digested*, 99/**3689**:
　　　　　　　　　　　　　　　　　　　　　　　　　　　　Applied, 99/3690
Cadogan Properties Ltd v. Mount Eden Land Ltd [1999] C.P.L.R. 476; [2000] I.L.Pr.
　722; [1999] N.P.C. 78, CA . . . .　*Digested*, 00/**568**
Cadwell v. Jackson [2001] B.P.I.R. 966, Ch D
Caerphilly CBC v. Stripp [2001] 2 C.M.L.R. 5; *Independent*, May 8, 2000 (C.S.), QBD　*Digested*, 01/**1092**
Caffoor (Trustees of the Abdul Gaffoor Trust) v. Income Tax Commissioner (Colombo);
　sub nom Gaffoor (Abdul) Trustees v. Ceylon Commissioner of Income Tax;
　Trustees of Abdul Gaffoor Trust v. Income Tax Commissioner, Colombo [1961]
　A.C. 584; [1961] 2 W.L.R. 794; [1961] 2 All E.R. 436; (1961) 40 A.T.C. 93;
　[1961] T.R. 97; 105 S.J. 383, PC (Cey) . . . .　*Digested*, 61/**4092**:
　　　　　　　　Applied, 01/5291: *Considered*, 66/5957, 70/158: *Followed*, 88/247
Caffrey's Application for Judicial Review, Re [2000] N.I. 17, QBD (NI) . . . .　*Digested*, 00/**5476**
Cahill May Roberts Ltd's Application for a Declaration of Invalidity; *sub nom* Medicine
　Shoppe International's Community Trade Mark [2000] E.T.M.R. 794, OHIM
　(Cancellation Div) . . . .　*Digested*, 01/**4020**
Cahm v. Ward & Goldstone [1979] I.C.R. 574, EAT . . . .　*Digested*, 79/**960**:
　　　　　　　　　　　　　　　　　　　　　　　　　　　　Approved, 99/2062
Cairnstores Ltd v. Aktiebolaget Hassle (2001) 24(8) I.P.D. 24052, Pat Ct . . . .　*Digested*, 01/**3969**
Caisse de Pension des Employes Prives v. Korde (C397/96) see Caisse de Pension des
　Employes Prives v. Kordel (C397/96)
Caisse de Pension des Employes Prives v. Kordel (C397/96); *sub nom* Caisse de
　Pension des Employes Prives v. Korde (C397/96) [1999] E.C.R. I-5959; *Times*,
　October 22, 1999, ECJ . . . .　*Digested*, 99/**4516**
Caisse Nationale d'Assurance Vieillesse des Travailleurs Salaries (CNAVTS) v. Thibault
　[1999] 1 C.M.L.R. 692, Cass (F) . . . .　*Previous proceedings*,
　　　　　　　　　　　　　　　　　　　　　　　　　　　　98/2150
Caisse Nationale d'Assurance Vieillesse des Travailleurs Salaries (CNAVTS) v. Thibault
　(C136/95); *sub nom* Thibault v. Caisse Nationale d'Assurance Vieillesse des
　Travailleurs Salaries (C136/95) [1998] All E.R. (EC) 385; [1998] E.C.R. I-2011;
　[1998] 2 C.M.L.R. 516; [1999] I.C.R. 160; [1998] I.R.L.R. 399; *Times*, May 13,
　1998, ECJ (6th Chamber) . . . .　*Digested*, 98/**2150**
Caisse Nationale des Monuments Historiques et des Sites v. Duret (t/a Transports Duret)
　[2000] E.C.C. 471, C d'A (Paris)
Caixa D'Estalvis y Pensions de Barcelona v. Namezero.com [2001] E.T.M.R. 107,
　Arbitration
Cakici v. Turkey (23657/94) (2001) 31 E.H.R.R. 5, ECHR . . . .　*Digested*, 01/**3569**
CAL-U-TEST Trade Mark [1967] F.S.R. 39, PO . . . .　*Digested*, 67/**3959**:
　　　　　　　　　Considered, 98/3500: *Subsequent proceedings*, 67/3961
Cala Homes (South) Ltd v. Alfred McAlpine Homes East Ltd (No.1) [1995] F.S.R. 818,
　Ch D . . . .　*Digested*, 96/**3632**:
　　　　　　　　　　　　　　　　　　　　　　　　　　　　Considered, 98/3431
Cala Homes (South) Ltd v. Chichester DC (Time Limits) [2000] C.P. Rep. 28; (2000)
　79 P. & C.R. 430; [1999] 4 P.L.R. 77; [2000] P.L.C.R. 205; (1999) 96(33)
　L.S.G. 33; *Times*, October 15, 1999, QBD . . . .　*Digested*, 99/**4269**
Calabar Properties Ltd v. Stitcher [1984] 1 W.L.R. 287; [1983] 3 All E.R. 759; (1984)
　11 H.L.R. 20; (1983) 268 E.G. 697; (1983) 80 L.S.G. 3163; (1983) 127 S.J. 785,
　CA . . . .　*Digested*, 84/**1892**:
　　　　　Applied, 84/1962, 86/1843, 88/2019, 93/2462: *Considered*, 87/2142,
　　　　　　　　89/2195, 90/2764: *Distinguished*, 89/2116, 99/3663
Calam Vale Ltd v. Customs and Excise Commissioners [2001] S.T.I. 254, V&DTr

Calcott v. JS Bloor (Measham) Ltd see JS Bloor (Measham) Ltd v. Calcott (No.1)

Calderbank v. Shields (Unreported, July 5, 2001), CC (Preston) [*Ex rel.* Lupton
Fawcett, Solicitors, Yorkshire House, Greek Street, Leeds] . . . .   *Digested,* 01/**620**

Calderon v. President of the Republic 6 B.H.R.C. 306, Sup Ct (CR)

Caldwell v. Wiggins Teape Fine Papers Ltd see Afzal v. Ford Motor Co Ltd

Cale v. Rhys Davis & Sons (Unreported, March 31, 1998), CC (Leeds) [*Ex rel.* Ison
Harrison & Co Solicitors, Duke House, 54 Wellington Street, Leeds] . . . .   *Digested,* 98/**509**

Caledonia Bureau Investment & Property v. Caffrey [1998] I.C.R. 603; [1998] I.R.L.R.
110, EAT . . . .   *Digested,* 98/**5825**

Caledonia North Sea Ltd v. British Telecommunications Plc see Caledonia North Sea Ltd
v. London Bridge Engineering Ltd

Caledonia North Sea Ltd v. BT Plc see Caledonia North Sea Ltd v. London Bridge
Engineering Ltd

Caledonia North Sea Ltd v. London Bridge Engineering Ltd; *sub nom* Caledonia North
Sea Ltd v. British Telecommunications Plc; Caledonia North Sea Ltd v. BT Plc;
Caledonia North Sea Ltd v. Norton (No.2) Ltd (In Liquidation); TNS, HL;
affirming 2000 S.L.T. 1123; [2000] Lloyd's Rep. I.R. 249; 2000 G.W.D. 3-84;
Times, February 8, 2000, 1 Div . . . .   *Digested,* 00/**6517**

Caledonia North Sea Ltd v. Norton (No.2) Ltd (In Liquidation) see Caledonia North Sea
Ltd v. London Bridge Engineering Ltd

Calfa, Re (C348/96) see Criminal Proceedings against Calfa (C348/96)

Calford v. Campbell [2000] 3 Q.R. 5, CC (Rawtenstall) [*Ex rel.* Paul Clark, Barrister,
Exchange Chambers, Pearl Assurance House, Derby Square, Liverpool] . . . . . .   *Digested,* 00/**1559**

Callagan v. Glasgow City Council see Callaghan v. Glasgow City Council

Callaghan v. Dominion Insurance Co Ltd [1997] 2 Lloyd's Rep. 541; *Times,* July 14,
1997, QBD . . . .   *Digested,* 97/**3139**:
                                              Distinguished, 00/530

Callaghan v. Glasgow City Council; *sub nom* Callagan v. Glasgow City Council [2001]
I.R.L.R. 724, EAT. . . . .   *Digested,* 01/**6463**

Callaghan v. Thompson QBENF 96/0890/C, CA . . . .   *Digested,* 98/**3360**

Callaghan (t/a Stage 3 Discotheque) v. Thompson [2000] C.L.C. 360; [2000] Lloyd's
Rep. I.R. 125, QBD (Comm Ct) . . . .   *Digested,* 00/**3511**

Callender v. Ray Braidwood & Sons (Unreported, October 14, 1998), CC (Salford) [*Ex
rel.* Edward Hutchin, Barrister, Bracton Chambers, 95A Chancery Lane,
London] . . . .   *Digested,* 99/**1408**

Callery v. Gray (No.1); Russell v. Pal Pak Corrugated Ltd (No.1) [2001] EWCA Civ 1117;
[2001] 1 W.L.R. 2112; [2001] 3 All E.R. 833; [2001] 2 Costs L.R. 163; [2001]
Lloyd's Rep. I.R. 743; [2001] P.I.Q.R. P32; (2001) 151 N.L.J. 1129; *Times,* July 18,
2001; *Independent,* July 24, 2001; *Daily Telegraph,* July 24, 2001, CA; reversing
in part [*Ex rel.* Amelans, Solicitors, Barlow House, 708-710 Wilmslow Road,
Manchester] . . . .   *Digested,* 01/**493**

Callery v. Gray (No.2); Russell v. Pal Pak Corrugated Ltd (No.2) [2001] EWCA Civ
1246; [2001] 1 W.L.R. 2142; [2001] 4 All E.R. 1; [2001] C.P.L.R. 501; [2001] 2
Costs L.R. 205; [2001] Lloyd's Rep. I.R. 765; (2001) 98(35) L.S.G. 33; (2001)
145 S.J.L.B. 204; *Times,* October 24, 2001, CA. . . . .   *Digested,* 01/**492**

Calorifique Ltd Ex p. Betts, Re see Sankey Furniture Ltd Ex p. Harding, Re

Caltex Trading Pte Ltd v. Metro Trading International Inc [2000] 1 All E.R. (Comm) 108;
[1999] 2 Lloyd's Rep. 724; [2000] C.L.C. 114, QBD (Comm Ct) . . . .   *Digested,* 00/**768**

Calveley v. Chief Constable of Merseyside; Worrall v. Chief Constable of Merseyside;
Park v. Chief Constable of Greater Manchester [1989] A.C. 1228; [1989] 2
W.L.R. 624; [1989] 1 All E.R. 1025; (1989) 153 L.G. Rev. 686; (1989) 86(15)
L.S.G. 42; (1989) 139 N.L.J. 469; (1989) 133 S.J. 456, HL; affirming [1989]
Q.B. 136; [1988] 3 W.L.R. 1020; [1988] 3 All E.R. 385; [1989] C.O.D. 229;
(1988) 138 N.L.J. Rep. 267; (1988) 132 S.J. 1244, CA . . . .   *Digested,* 89/**2863**:
                  Considered, 00/5117: *Distinguished,* 00/4229: *Followed,* 97/4150

Calver v. Westwood Veterinary Group [2001] P.I.Q.R. P11; [2001] Lloyd's Rep. Med.
20; (2001) 58 B.M.L.R. 194; [2001] Lloyd's Rep. P.N. 102, CA . . . .   *Digested,* 01/**4542**

Calvert, Re [1899] 2 Q.B. 145, QBD . . . .   *Applied,* 54/229,
                                                      01/592

Calvert (CICB: Quantum: 2000), Re (Unreported, December 14, 1999), CICB (London) [*Ex
rel.* James Laughland, Barrister, 1 Temple Gardens, Temple, London] . . . .   *Digested,* 00/**1539**

Calvin v. Carr [1980] A.C. 574; [1979] 2 W.L.R. 755; [1979] 2 All E.R. 440; 123 S.J.
112, PC (Aus) . . . .   *Digested,* 79/**14**:
                  Applied, 80/315, 80/2904, 89/1500: *Considered,* 87/3162, 95/3252,
             00/6628: *Distinguished,* 97/63: *Followed,* 91/43, 93/31: *Referred to,* 81/108

Cambridge v. Callaghan see Cambridge v. Motor Insurers Bureau

Cambridge v. Motor Insurers Bureau; *sub nom* Cambridge v. Callaghan [1998] R.T.R.
365; *Times,* March 21, 1997, CA . . . .   *Digested,* 97/**708**

Cambridge City Council v. Douglas [2001] Env. L.R. 41; [2001] E.H.L.R. 9; [2001]
J.P.L. 1003 (Note); (2001) 98(12) L.S.G. 44; [2001] N.P.C. 8, QBD (Admin Ct).   *Digested,* 01/**2426**

Cambridge City Council v. Secretary of State for the Environment; *sub nom* Secretary of State for the Environment v. Cambridge City Council 90 L.G.R. 275; (1992) 64 P. & C.R. 257; [1992] 1 E.G.L.R. 201; [1992] 21 E.G. 108; [1992] J.P.L. 644; [1992] E.G.C.S. 16; [1992] N.P.C. 17; *Times*, February 12, 1992, CA; reversing 89 L.G.R. 1015; (1991) 62 P. & C.R. 320; [1991] 1 E.G.L.R. 177; [1991] 9 E.G. 119; [1991] J.P.L. 428; *Times*, February 20, 1991, QBD . . . . *Digested*, 93/**3837**: *Followed*, 98/3609

Cambridge Water Co Ltd v. Eastern Counties Leather Plc; Cambridge Water Co Ltd v. Hutchings & Harding Ltd [1994] 2 A.C. 264; [1994] 2 W.L.R. 53; [1994] 1 All E.R. 53; [1994] 1 Lloyd's Rep. 261; [1994] Env. L.R. 105; [1993] E.G.C.S. 211; (1994) 144 N.L.J. 15; (1994) 138 S.J.L.B. 24; *Times*, December 10, 1993; *Independent*, December 10, 1993, HL; reversing [1993] Env. L.R. 287; [1992] N.P.C.147; *Times*, December 29, 1992, CA; reversing [1993] Env. L.R. 116; *Times*, October 23, 1991, QBD . . . . *Digested*, 94/**3410**:
Applied, 97/3864, 00/4289, 01/3800: *Considered*, 97/1032, 98/4042

Cambridge Water Co Ltd v. Hutchings & Harding Ltd see Cambridge Water Co Ltd v. Eastern Counties Leather Plc

Cambridgeshire CC v. JD [1999] 2 F.L.R. 42; [1999] 3 F.C.R. 613; [1999] Fam. Law 386; *Times*, October 26, 1998, CA . . . . *Digested*, 98/**17**

Camco International (Canada) Ltd v. Porodo (1997) 211 A.R. 71, QB (Alta) . . . . *Applied*, 00/**742**

Camden LBC v. Akanni (1997) 29 H.L.R. 845, CA . . . . *Digested*, 98/**3046**:
Applied, 99/3705: *Considered*, 01/4168: *Distinguished*, 01/4166

Camden LBC v. Alexandrou (No.1) (1997) 74 P. & C.R. D3, CA

Camden LBC v. Alexandrou (No.2) (1998) 30 H.L.R. 534; (1997) 74 P. & C.R. D33, CA . . . . *Digested*, 98/**3047**

Camden LBC v. Customs and Excise Commissioners [2001] S.T.I. 1228, V&DTr

Camden LBC v. Gilsenan (1999) 31 H.L.R. 81, CA . . . . *Digested*, 99/**3707**

Camden LBC v. Gunby [2000] 1 W.L.R. 465; [1999] 4 All E.R. 602; [2000] E.H.L.R. 33; (2000) 32 H.L.R. 572; [1999] 3 E.G.L.R. 13; [1999] 44 E.G. 147; (1999) 96(29) L.S.G. 30; (1999) 149 N.L.J. 1146; [2000] Env. L.R. D10; *Times*, July 12, 1999, QBD . . . . *Digested*, 99/**2152**

Camden LBC v. Kings College London (1998) 13 P.A.D. 16, Planning Inspector

Camden LBC v. Lahouasnia (Unreported, November 12, 1997), CC (Central London) [*Ex rel.* Dominic Preston Barrister, Luper Partnership Solicitors, Arden Chambers, London] . . . . *Digested*, 98/**3033**

Camden LBC v. Levene (2001) 16 P.A.D. 55, Planning Inspector

Camden LBC v. London Underground Ltd [2000] Env. L.R. 369; [2000] E.H.L.R. 101; (2000) 97(1) L.S.G. 25; [1999] N.P.C. 160; *Independent*, February 14, 2000 (C.S.), QBD . . . . *Digested*, 00/**4285**:
Distinguished, 01/2423

Camden LBC v. Mallett (2001) 33 H.L.R. 20, CA . . . . *Digested*, 01/**3438**

Camden LBC v. Marshall [1996] 1 W.L.R. 1345; (1998) 30 H.L.R. 173; (1997) 74 P. & C.R. 107; [1996] C.O.D. 472; (1996) 160 J.P. Rep. 967; [1996] E.G.C.S. 104; (1996) 140 S.J.L.B. 154; [1996] N.P.C. 97; *Times*, July 11, 1996; *Independent*, July 22, 1996 (C.S.), QBD . . . . *Digested*, 96/**3108**

Camden LBC v. McBride (Unreported, November 11, 1998), CC (Clerkenwell) [*Ex rel.* Jon Holbrook, Barrister, 2 Garden Court, MiddleTemple, London] . . . . *Digested*, 99/**3737**

Camden LBC v. Sonkor [2001] EWHC Admin 41; [2001] E.H.L.R. 21, QBD (Admin Ct) . *Digested*, 01/**4314**

Camdex International Ltd v. Bank of Zambia [1998] Q.B. 22; [1996] 3 W.L.R. 759; [1996] 3 All E.R. 431; [1996] C.L.C. 1477; *Times*, April 8, 1996, CA . . . . *Digested*, 96/**2904**

Camelot Group Plc v. Centaur Communications Ltd [1999] Q.B. 124; [1998] 2 W.L.R. 379; [1998] 1 All E.R. 251; [1998] I.R.L.R. 80; [1998] E.M.L.R. 1; (1997) 94(43) L.S.G. 30; (1997) 147 N.L.J. 1618; (1998) 142 S.J.L.B. 19; *Times*, October 30, 1997; *Independent*, October 28, 1997, CA; affirming [1997] E.M.L.R. 532; *Times*, July 15, 1997, QBD . . . . *Digested*, 97/**3595**:
Considered, 98/18

Camenzind v. Switzerland (21353/93) (1999) 28 E.H.R.R. 458; [1998] H.R.C.D. 180, ECHR . . . . *Digested*, 99/**3122**

Cameron (Deceased), Re; *sub nom* Phillips v. Cameron [1999] Ch. 386; [1999] 3 W.L.R. 394; [1999] 2 All E.R. 924; (1998-99) 1 I.T.E.L.R. 815; (1999) 96(16) L.S.G. 35; (1999) 149 N.L.J. 522; *Times*, April 2, 1999, Ch D . . . . *Digested*, 99/**4646**

Cameron v. Customs and Excise Commissioners [1999] B.V.C. 2091, V&DTr

Cameron v. Treasury Solicitor; *sub nom* O'Rourke (Deceased), Re [1996] 2 F.L.R. 716; [1997] 1 F.C.R. 188; [1996] Fam. Law 723, CA . . . . *Digested*, 96/**5551**:
Applied, 01/5155

Camilla Cotton Oil Co v. Granadex SA; Shawnee Processors Inc v. Granadex SA [1976] 2 Lloyd's Rep. 10, HL; reversing [1975] 1 Lloyd's Rep. 470; (1975) 119 S.J. 115, CA . . . . *Digested*, 76/**99**:
Applied, 84/99, 88/136, 98/3528: *Considered*, 85/2743: *Followed*, 97/890

Camiller v. Commissioner of Police of the Metropolis, *Times*, June 8, 1999, CA . . . . *Digested*, 99/**407**

Camm v. Camm (1983) 4 F.L.R. 577; (1983) 13 Fam. Law 112, CA . . . . *Digested*, 83/**1100**:
Applied, 95/2340: *Cited*, 00/2519: *Followed*, 95/2341

Camp v. Netherlands (28369/95) [2000] 3 F.C.R. 307; [2001] W.T.L.R. 513, ECHR . . . *Digested*, 01/**3555**

Campaign for the Protection of Rural Wales v. Secretary of State for Wales [2000] J.P.L.
1304 (Note); (2000) 97(16) L.S.G. 43, QBD . . . .   *Digested*, 01/**4687**
Campaign to Separate Church and State Ltd v. Minister for Education; *sub nom* CSCS v.
Minister for Education 4 B.H.R.C. 635, Sup Ct (Irl)
Campbell (A Minor) v. Nottingham City Council (1999) 99(1) Q.R. 8, CC (Nottingham)   *Digested*, 98/**1704**
Campbell v. Campbell (Financial Relief: Jurisdiction of County Court) [1997] 2 F.L.R.
609; [1998] 2 F.C.R. 123; [1997] Fam. Law 539, CA . . . .   *Digested*, 98/**2458**
Campbell v. Campbell (Financial Relief: Re-Trial) [1998] 1 F.L.R. 828; [1998] 3 F.C.R.
63; [1998] Fam. Law 394, CA . . . .   *Digested*, 98/**2466**
Campbell v. Chu (Unreported, March 19, 1999), CC (Willesden) [*Ex rel*. Adrian Iles,
Barrister, 5 Paper Buildings, Temple, London] . . . .   *Digested*, 99/**3654**:
                                                    Not followed, 00/3876
Campbell v. Edwards [1976] 1 W.L.R. 403; [1976] 1 All E.R. 785; [1976] 1 Lloyd's Rep.
522; 119 S.J. 845, CA . . . .   *Digested*, 76/**1533**:
                Applied, 78/325, 90/637, 92/419: *Considered*, 92/2740, 00/237:
                                Distinguished, 83/336, 01/264
Campbell v. Griffin [2001] EWCA Civ 990; [2001] W.T.L.R. 981; [2001] N.P.C. 102;
(2001) 82 P. & C.R. D23, CA . . . .   *Digested*, 01/**4859**
Campbell v. Mylchreest [1999] P.I.Q.R. Q17, CA; affirming [1998] P.I.Q.R. P20, QBD . .   *Digested*, 00/**1459**
Campbell v. Northern Ireland Housing Executive [1995] N.I. 167, CA (NI)
Campbell v. Secretary of State for the Home Department see R. v. Oxford Regional
Mental Health Tribunal Ex p. Secretary of State for the Home Department
Campbell v. United Kingdom see Fox v. United Kingdom (A/182)
Campbell v. United Kingdom (A/233A) (1993) 15 E.H.R.R. 137; *Times*, April 1, 1992;
Independent, April 16, 1992; *Guardian*, April 2, 1992, ECHR . . . .   *Digested*, 93/**2155**:
                                                 Considered, 00/3166
Campbell & Smith Construction Group Ltd v. Greenwood [2001] I.R.L.R. 588, EAT . . .   *Digested*, 01/**6478**
Campbell Court Property Ltd v. Secretary of State for the Environment, Transport and
the Regions see R. (on the application of Campbell Court Property) v. Secretary
of State for the Environment, Transport and the Regions
Campbells (Caterers) Ltd v. Scottish Provident Institution; *sub nom* 11 Donegall Square
West, Belfast, Re; BT/33/1998, Lands Tr. . . . .   *Digested*, 99/**5408**
Campina Melkunie BV v. Bureau Benelux des Marques (A98/2/14) [2001] E.T.M.R. 37,
CJ (Benelux)
Campion v. Bradley (Unreported, May 6, 1999), CC (Portsmouth) [*Ex rel*. Tim Petts,
Barrister, 12 King's Bench Walk, Temple, London] . . . .   *Digested*, 99/**1410**:
                                                 Considered, 00/545
Campomar SL's Community Trade Mark Application (102/1999) [2000] E.T.M.R. 50, OHIM
(Opposition Div) . . . .   *Digested*, 00/**3719**
Campsie Spring Scotland Ltd v. Assessor for Dunbartonshire, Argyll and Bute Valuation
Joint Board [2000] R.A. 401, Lands Tr (Scot) . . . .   *Digested*, 00/**6664**
Canada v. Schreiber 5 B.H.R.C. 145, Sup Ct (Can) . . . .   *Digested*, 99/**3123**:
                                                 Considered, 99/3139
Canada Steamship Lines Ltd v. King, The [1952] A.C. 192; [1952] 1 All E.R. 305;
[1952] 1 Lloyd's Rep. 1; [1952] 1 T.L.R. 261; 96 S.J. 72, HL . . . .   *Digested*, 52/**610**:
         Applied, 55/1174, 55/3036, 71/9949, 74/296, 74/447, 74/4063, 75/273,
               76/2987, 78/339, 78/3186, 80/359, 82/2909, 88/461, 90/636, 93/499,
                   94/540, 95/778, 96/1216, 99/836, 01/947: *Cited*, 99/3311:
        Considered, 68/2647, 72/489, 73/407, 79/2344, 81/304, 81/3603, 97/937,
              00/895, 00/5991: *Followed*, 94/4078, 96/5302: *Referred to*, 95/5571
Canada Trust Co v. Stolzenberg (No.1) [1997] 1 W.L.R. 1582; [1997] 4 All E.R. 983;
[1997] C.L.C. 1083; [1998] I.L.Pr. 30; *Times*, May 1, 1997; *Independent*, May 7,
1997, CA. . . . .   *Digested*, 97/**887**
Canada Trust Co v. Stolzenberg (No.2) (Mareva Injunction), *Times*, November 10, 1997;
Independent, October 13, 1997 (C.S.), Ch D . . . .   *Digested*, 97/**676**
Canada Trust Co v. Stolzenberg (No.2) [2000] 3 W.L.R. 1376; [2000] 4 All E.R. 481;
[2001] C.L.C. 118; [2001] I.L.Pr. 40; (2000) 97(42) L.S.G. 44; (2000) 150
N.L.J. 1537; (2000) 144 S.J.L.B. 256; *Times*, October 17, 2000; *Independent*,
October 17, 2000, HL; affirming [1998] 1 W.L.R. 547; [1998] 1 All E.R. 318;
[1998] C.L.C. 23; [1998] I.L.Pr. 290; *Times*, November 10, 1997, CA . . . .   *Digested*, 00/**744**:
                                             Followed, 98/584, 99/526
Canada Trust Co v. Stolzenberg (No.3) [1998] C.L.C. 1171; *Times*, May 14, 1998, CA . . .   *Digested*, 98/**317**
Canadian Pacific Ltd v. R. (1995) 125 D.L.R. (4th) 385, Sup Ct (Can) . . . .   *Applied*, 98/3108
Canadian Pacific Ltd v. R. 4 I.T.L. Rep. 588, CA (Can); affirming 3 I.T.L. Rep. 238, Tax
Ct (Can)
Canadian Shredded Wheat Co Ltd v. Kellogg Co of Canada Ltd [1938] 1 All E.R. 618;
(1938) 55 R.P.C. 125, PC (Can) . . . .   *Considered*, 74/3829:
                                                 Referred to, 99/3593
Canadian Transport Co v. Court Line [1940] A.C. 934, HL . . . .   *Applied*, 87/3444:
                                        Considered, 99/4430, 00/4711
Canaj v. Secretary of State for the Home Department see R. (on the application of
Vallaj) v. Special Adjudicator
Canal & Image UK Ltd v. Vanitymail Services Inc [2001] E.T.M.R. 40, Arbitration . . . . . .   *Digested*, 01/**3869**
Canal Plus SA v. SNC Television par Satellite [2001] E.C.C. 10, C d'A (Paris)

Canalside Housing Partnership v. Ali (Unreported, August 16, 2001), Ch D [*Ex rel.* Edward Francis, Barrister, Enterprise Chambers, Gold Square, Lincoln's Inn, London] . . . . *Digested*, 01/**4890**

Canary Wharf Contractors (DS6) Ltd v. Niagara Mechanical Services International Ltd (In Administration) see Niagara Mechanical Services International Ltd (In Administration), Re

Canbolat v. Secretary of State for the Home Department see R. v. Secretary of State for the Home Department Ex p. Canbolat

Cancer Research Campaign v. Ernest Brown & Co [1997] S.T.C. 1425; [1998] P.N.L.R. 592, Ch D . . . . *Digested*, 98/**4019**

Candler v. Crane Christmas & Co [1951] 2 K.B. 164; [1951] 1 All E.R. 426; [1951] 1 T.L.R. 371; 95 S.J. 171, CA . . . . *Digested*, 47-51/**6584**:
Applied, 61/518, 69/1998, 70/1493, 81/1837, 81/1860: *Considered*, 61/825,
70/1881, 71/8000, 89/2566, 00/4205: *Distinguished*, 62/2006:
Overruled, 63/2416

Candler v. Thomas (t/a London Leisure Lines) [1998] R.T.R. 214, CA . . . . *Digested*, 98/**4038**

Candy Rock Recording Ltd v. Phonographic Performance Ltd see Phonographic Performance Ltd v. Candy Rock Recording Ltd

Canea Catholic Church v. Greece (1999) 27 E.H.R.R. 521, ECHR . . . . *Digested*, 99/**3114**

Cank v. Broadyard Associates Ltd [2001] C.P. Rep. 47, CA . . . . *Digested*, 00/**373**

Canniffe v. East Riding of Yorkshire Council [2000] I.R.L.R. 555, EAT . . . . *Digested*, 00/**2120**

CANNON Trade Mark Application, Re [1998] E.T.M.R. 77, BGH (Ger)

Cannonquest Ltd, Re see Official Receiver v. Hannan

Canon Kabushiki Kaisha v. Green Cartridge Co (Hong Kong) Ltd [1997] A.C. 728; [1997] 3 W.L.R. 13; [1997] F.S.R. 817; (1997) 20(9) I.P.D. 20085; (1997) 141 S.J.L.B. 112; *Times*, May 1, 1997, PC (HK); reversing [1996] F.S.R. 874, CA (HK); reversing [1995] F.S.R. 877, HC (HK) . . . . *Digested*, 97/**1040**:
Applied, 99/3437

Canon Kabushiki Kaisha v. Metro Goldwyn Mayer Inc (C39/97) [1998] All E.R. (EC) 934; [1998] E.C.R. I-5507; [1999] 1 C.M.L.R. 77; [1998] C.E.C. 920; [1999] E.T.M.R. 1; [1999] F.S.R. 332; [1999] R.P.C. 117; *Times*, October 10, 1998, ECJ [1998] E.C.R. I-5507; [1998] E.T.M.R. 366, AGO . . . . *Digested*, 98/**3526**:
Applied, 00/3742, 00/3748, 01/3987, 01/4025, 01/4036:
Considered, 99/3531, 00/3728: *Followed*, 00/3701, 01/4029:
Not followed, 99/3544: *Referred to*, 01/4024

Cantabrica Coach Holdings Ltd v. Vehicle Inspectorate see Vehicle Inspectorate v. Cantabrica Coach Holdings Ltd

Canterbury City Council v. Lowe (2001) 33 H.L.R. 53; [2001] L. & T.R. 14, CA . . . . *Digested*, 01/**3440**

Cantor v. Cox (1975) 239 E.G. 121 . . . . *Digested*, 77/**1209**:
Disapproved, 99/4368

Cantor Fitzgerald International v. Callaghan [1999] 2 All E.R. 411; [1999] I.C.R. 639; [1999] I.R.L.R. 234; *Times*, January 25, 1999; *Independent*, January 26, 1999, CA . . . . *Digested*, 99/**2015**

Cantor Fitzgerald International v. Customs and Excise Commissioners see Customs and Excise Commissioners v. Cantor Fitzgerald International (C108/99)

Cantor Fitzgerald International v. Customs and Excise Commissioners (C108/99) see Customs and Excise Commissioners v. Mirror Group Plc (C409/98)

Cantor Fitzgerald International v. Tradition (UK) Ltd (Third Party Proceedings) (1998) 21 (12) I.P.D. 21131, Ch D

Cantor Fitzgerald International v. Tradition (UK) Ltd [2000] R.P.C. 95; [1999] Masons C.L.R. 157; (1999) 22(7) I.P.D. 22068; *Times*, May 19, 1999; *Independent*, May 5, 1999, Ch D . . . . *Digested*, 99/**3454**

Cantor Fitzgerald International v. Tradition (UK) Ltd (Costs) [2001] EWCA Civ 942; (2001) 24(9) I.P.D. 24057, CA; reversing1995-C-3477, Ch D

Cantrell (t/a Foxearth Lodge Nursing Home) v. Customs and Excise Commissioners [2000] S.T.C. 100; [2000] B.T.C. 5044; [2000] B.V.C. 82; [2000] S.T.I. 103, QBD . . . . *Digested*, 00/**5366**

Cantwell, Re (Unreported, October 22, 1998), CICB (London) [*Ex rel.* David Brounger, Barrister, Lamb Building, London] . . . . *Digested*, 99/**1463**

Cantwell v. Criminal Injuries Compensation Board [2001] UKHL 36; 2001 S.L.T. 966; 2001 G.W.D. 24-879; *Times*, July 16, 2001, HL; reversing 2000 S.C. 407; 2000 S.L.T. 956; 2000 G.W.D. 7-238, 1 Div; reversing 1998 G.W.D. 28-1395, OH. . . . . *Digested*, 01/**6413**

Caparo Industries Plc *v.* Dickman [1990] 2 A.C. 605; [1990] 2 W.L.R. 358; [1990] 1
All E.R. 568; [1990] B.C.C. 164; [1990] B.C.L.C. 273; [1990] E.C.C. 313; [1955-
95] P.N.L.R. 523; (1990) 87(12) L.S.G. 42; (1990) 140 N.L.J. 248; (1990) 134
S.J. 494; *Times,* February 12, 1990; *Independent,* February 16, 1990; *Financial
Times,* February 13, 1990; *Guardian,* February 15, 1990; *Daily Telegraph,* February
15, 1990, HL; reversing [1989] Q.B. 653; [1989] 2 W.L.R. 316; [1989] 1 All
E.R. 798; (1989) 5 B.C.C. 105; [1989] B.C.L.C. 154; [1989] P.C.C. 125; (1988)
138 N.L.J. Rep. 289; (1989) 133 S.J. 221; *Times,* August 8, 1988; *Independent,*
August 10, 1988; *Financial Times,* August 5, 1988; *Daily Telegraph,* August 26,
1988, CA; reversing in part (1988) 4 B.C.C. 144; [1988] B.C.L.C. 387, QBD. . . .   *Digested,* 90/**3266**:
Applied, 89/2540, 90/3254, 90/3265, 91/2650, 91/2652, 92/1915,
92/2605, 92/3201, 93/2953, 93/2982, 94/3335, 94/3352, 94/3365,
95/3668, 95/3686, 95/3701, 95/4519, 95/4730, 96/4440, 96/4484,
97/331, 97/3778, 97/3816, 98/3997, 99/3956, 99/3963, 99/3966, 99/4025,
99/5435, 00/679, 00/4201, 00/4246, 00/4249, 00/6162, 00/6586, 01/1509,
01/1989, 01/4462, 01/4464, 01/4541: *Cited,* 00/4218: *Considered,* 89/2538,
90/3315, 91/2657, 93/2044, 93/2958, 93/2983, 93/2997, 94/3345,
95/3452, 95/3652, 95/3921, 98/3951, 98/3999, 99/3953, 00/4205,
01/550: *Distinguished,* 91/2653: *Followed,* 90/3281, 93/5553, 97/424,
97/4087, 98/3930, 98/3987, 99/3959, 99/4015, 00/4219, 00/4224,
01/4470: *Referred to,* 92/6078, 94/6386, 95/5841, 99/4023
Cape & Dalgleish *v.* Fitzgerald TNS, HL; affirming [2001] Lloyd's Rep. P.N. 110, CA . . . .   *Digested,* 01/**656**
Cape Distribution Ltd *v.* O'Loughlin see O'Loughlin *v.* Cape Distribution Ltd
Cape Plc *v.* Iron Trades Employers Insurance Association Ltd [1999] P.I.Q.R. Q212,
QBD (Comm Ct) . . . .   *Digested,* 99/**3384**
Capek *v.* Lincolnshire CC [2000] I.C.R. 878; [2000] I.R.L.R. 590; (2000) 97(24)
L.S.G. 39; *Times,* June 7, 2000; *Independent,* June 15, 2000, CA . . . .   *Digested,* 00/**2149**
Capital and Counties Plc *v.* Hampshire CC; John Munroe (Acrylics) Ltd *v.* London Fire
and Civil Defence Authority; Church of Jesus Christ of Latter Day Saints (Great
Britain) *v.* West Yorkshire Fire and Civil Defence Authority; Digital Equipment Co
Ltd *v.* Hampshire CC [1997] Q.B. 1004; [1997] 3 W.L.R. 331; [1997] 2 All E.R.
865; [1997] 2 Lloyd's Rep. 161; (1997) 147 N.L.J. 599; (1997) 141 S.J.L.B. 92;
Times, March 20, 1997; *Independent,* April 10, 1997, CA; affirming [1996] 1
W.L.R. 1553; [1996] 4 All E.R. 336; (1996) 146 N.L.J. 1543; *Times,* April 26,
1996, QBD (OR) . . . .   *Digested,* 97/**3778**:
Applied, 97/3774: *Distinguished,* 99/3956, 00/4203, 00/4204:
Not followed, 97/3779: *Previous proceedings,* 96/4440, 96/4441
Capital & Suburban Properties Ltd *v.* Swycher [1976] Ch. 319; [1976] 2 W.L.R. 822;
[1976] 1 All E.R. 881; (1976) 32 P. & C.R. 101; [1976] J.P.L. 374; 120 S.J. 251,
CA . . . .   *Digested,* 76/**2864**:
Applied, 99/4008: *Distinguished,* 77/3151
Capital Prime Plus Plc *v.* Wills (1999) 31 H.L.R. 926, CA. . . . .   *Digested,* 00/**3882**
Capital Prime Properties Plc *v.* Worthgate Ltd (In Liquidation) [2000] B.C.C. 525;
[2000] 1 B.C.L.C. 647; [1999] E.G.C.S. 112, Ch D . . . .   *Digested,* 00/**3504**
Capital Trust Investments Ltd *v.* Radio Design TJ AB; *sub nom* Capital Trusts Investments
Ltd *v.* Radio Design TJ AB; A3/2001/0542, CA; affirming [2001] 3 All E.R.
756; [2001] 1 All E.R. (Comm) 1079; *Independent,* March 26, 2001 (C.S), Ch D
. . . .   *Digested,* 01/**345**
Capital Trusts Investments Ltd *v.* Radio Design TJ AB see Capital Trust Investments Ltd
v. Radio Design TJ AB
Capon *v.* DPP, *Independent,* March 23, 1998 (C.S.), QBD. . . . .   *Digested,* 98/**982**
Cappus *v.* Centre Regional de Transfusion Sanguine de Bordeaux [1999] E.C.C. 70,
Cass (F)
Car and Universal Finance Co Ltd *v.* Caldwell [1965] 1 Q.B. 525; [1964] 2 W.L.R. 600;
[1964] 1 All E.R. 290; 108 S.J. 15, CA; affirming [1963] 2 All E.R. 547; 107 S.J.
738, QBD . . . .   *Digested,* 64/**3286**:
Applied, 64/3288, 65/34: *Cited,* 00/2602: *Considered,* 70/1518, 74/3560
Car Wheel Rim Trade Mark Application, Re [1998] E.T.M.R. 584, BGH (Ger)
Carabalona *v.* Welsh (Unreported, June 21, 1999), CC (Coventry) [*Ex rel.* Alex
Glassbrook, Barrister, 1 Temple Gardens, Temple, London] . . . .   *Digested,* 99/**2475**
Caradon DC *v.* Beazer Homes Bridgwater (2001) 16 P.A.D. 48, Planning Inspector
Caradon DC *v.* Bussell see Caradon DC *v.* Paton
Caradon DC *v.* Cheeseman [2000] Crim. L.R. 190, QBD
Caradon DC *v.* Paton; Caradon DC *v.* Bussell (2001) 33 H.L.R. 34; [2000] 3 E.G.L.R.
57; [2000] 35 E.G. 132; [2000] E.G.C.S. 59; (2000) 97(22) L.S.G. 44; *Times,*
May 17, 2000; *Independent,* June 19, 2000, CA . . . .   *Digested,* 00/**4625**
Caradon DC *v.* Secretary of State for the Environment, Transport and the Regions
[2001] P.L.C.R. 18; [2001] J.P.L. 613 (Note), QBD . . . .   *Digested,* 01/**4722**
Caraher *v.* United Kingdom (24520/94) (2000) 29 E.H.R.R. CD119, ECHR
Caravelle Investments Ltd *v.* Martaban Ltd (The Cape Don) [2000] 1 Lloyd's Rep. 388,
Fed Ct (Aus) (Sgl judge) . . . .   *Digested,* 00/**752**

Card Protection Plan Ltd v. Customs and Excise Commissioners [2001] UKHL 4;
[2001] 2 W.L.R. 329; [2001] 2 All E.R. 143; [2001] 1 All E.R. (Comm) 438;
[2001] S.T.C. 174; [2001] 2 C.M.L.R. 2; [2001] B.T.C. 5083; [2001] B.V.C. 158;
[2001] S.T.I. 151; (2001) 98(9) L.S.G. 41; (2001) 145 S.J.L.B. 60; *Times*,
February 6, 2001, HL; reversing [1994] S.T.C. 199; [1994] 1 C.M.L.R. 756, CA;
affirming [1992] S.T.C. 797, QBD . . . .   *Digested*, 01/**5600**:
                    Applied, 94/4602: *Considered*, 98/4961: *Previous proceedings*, 99/4972:
                                    Referred to, 95/5039, 95/5093: *Subsequent proceedings*, 99/4972
Card Protection Plan Ltd v. Customs and Excise Commissioners (C349/96) [1999] 2
A.C. 601; [1999] 3 W.L.R. 203; [1999] All E.R. (E.C.) 339; [1999] S.T.C. 270;
[1999] E.C.R. I-973; [1999] 2 C.M.L.R. 743; [1999] C.E.C. 133; [1999] B.T.C.
5121; [1999] B.V.C. 155; *Times*, March 18, 1999, ECJ (6th Chamber) . . . .   *Digested*, 99/**4972**:
                    Applied, 00/5343, 00/5346, 00/5369: *Considered*, 01/5599:
                    Distinguished, 00/5294, 01/5564: *Followed*, 99/4983, 00/5344:
                                                     Subsequent proceedings, 01/5600
Carder v. Davies (1998) 76 P. & C.R. D33, CA
CARDIAC/Correction of mistake (J18/93) [1998] E.P.O.R. 38, EPO (Legal Bd App)
Cardiff CC v. Ahmed (2001) 16 P.A.D. 23, Planning Inspector
Cardiff CC v. Hopkins (1998) 13 P.A.D. 472, Planning Inspector
Cardiff CC v. Pendragon Construction Ltd (2000) 15 P.A.D. 752, Planning Inspector
Cardiff CC v. Pritchard (2000) 15 P.A.D. 344, Planning Inspector
Cardiff CC v. Railtrack Plc (2000) 15 P.A.D. 766, Planning Inspector
Cardiff CC v. Rombourne Ltd (2001) 16 P.A.D. 16, Planning Inspector
Cardiff Community Housing Association v. Customs and Excise Commissioners [2001]
B.V.C. 2112; [2001] S.T.I. 225, V&DTr . . . .   *Digested*, 01/**5617**
Cardiff Rating Authority v. Guest Keen Baldwin's Iron & Steel Co Ltd [1949] 1 K.B.
385; [1949] 1 All E.R. 27; 65 T.L.R. 159; (1949) 113 J.P. 78; 47 L.G.R. 159;
(1949) 152 E.G. 449; (1949) 42 R. & I.T. 2; [1949] L.J.R. 713; 93 S.J. 117, CA;
affirming [1948] 1 All E.R. 830; 64 T.L.R. 314, KBD . . . .   *Digested*, 47-51/**8289**:
                    Applied, 47-51/8288, 52/2887, 57/2957, 71/11383: *Considered*, 70/235,
                                                     93/3827, 94/4326, 99/4239, 00/4415
Cardinal Financial Investment Corp v. Central Bank of Yemen (No.1); *sub nom* Central
Bank of Yemen v. Cardinal Financial Investments Corp [2001] Lloyd's Rep. Bank.
1, CA; affirming 1999 Folio No.1195, QBD (Comm Ct) . . . .   *Digested*, 01/**2679**
Cardot v. France (A/200) (1991) 13 E.H.R.R. 853, ECHR . . . .   *Applied*, 98/3078
Cardservice International Inc v. McGee . . . .   *Considered*, 00/3591
Care First Partnership Ltd v. Roffey; *sub nom* Roffey v. Care First Partnership Ltd
[2001] I.C.R. 87; [2001] I.R.L.R. 85; (2000) 97(45) L.S.G. 41; *Times*, November
22, 2000; *Independent*, November 10, 2000, CA . . . .   *Digested*, 00/**2153**
Carecraft Construction Co Ltd, Re [1994] 1 W.L.R. 172; [1993] 4 All E.R. 499; [1993] B.C.C.
336; [1993] B.C.L.C. 1259, Ch D . . . .   *Digested*, 93/**374**:
                    Applied, 99/608: *Considered*, 96/977, 96/978, 97/828:
                    Distinguished, 97/829, 97/831: *Followed*, 99/624: *Referred to*, 01/3520
CAREMIX Trade Mark see Altecnic Ltd's Trade Mark Application (No.2126884)
Carflow Products (UK) Ltd v. Linwood Securities (Birmingham) Ltd (Inquiry as to
Damages) [1998] F.S.R. 691; (1998) 21 (7) I.P.D. 21072, Pat Ct. . . . .   *Digested*, 98/**3495**
Cargill v. PR Excavations (Unreported, November 16, 1999), QBD [*Ex rel*. Pannone &
Partners, Solicitors, 123 Deansgate, Manchester] . . . .   *Digested*, 00/**4228**
Cargill International SA v. Bangladesh Sugar & Food Industries Corp [1998] 1 W.L.R.
461; [1998] 2 All E.R. 406; [1998] C.L.C. 399; (1998) 95(3) L.S.G. 25; (1998)
142 S.J.L.B. 14; *Times*, December 10, 1997, CA; affirming [1996] 4 All E.R. 563;
[1996] 2 Lloyd's Rep. 524, QBD (Comm Ct) . . . .   *Digested*, 98/**846**:
                                                                             Considered, 97/994
Cargill International SA Antigua (Geneva Branch) v. Sociedad Iberica de Molturacion
SA; Sociedad Iberica de Molturacion SA v. Cargill International SA; SIMSA v.
Cargill International SA [1998] 1 Lloyd's Rep. 489; [1998] C.L.C. 231; (1998)
95(4) L.S.G. 33; (1998) 142 S.J.L.B. 34; *Times*, December 26, 1997, CA;
affirming *Times*, November 12, 1997, QBD (Comm Ct) . . . .   *Digested*, 98/**238**
Cargo Communication Sarl v. La Cite des Sciences et de l'Industrie [1999] E.T.M.R.
545, Trib Gde Inst (Paris)
Cargo of the Alfonsina, Re (C68/88) see Commission of the European Communities v.
Greece (C68/88)
Carillion Construction Ltd v. Felix (UK) Ltd [2001] B.L.R. 1; 74 Con. L.R. 144, QBD
(T&CC) . . . .   *Digested*, 01/**872**
Carillo v. Instituto Nacional de Empleo (C423/93) see Zabala Erasun v. Instituto
Nacional de Empleo (C422/93)
Carl v. Grosvenor Estate Belgravia [2000] 3 E.G.L.R. 79; [2000] 38 E.G. 195, Lands Tr .   *Digested*, 00/**3897**
CARL MAHR/Capacitive Displacement (T881/96) [2001] E.P.O.R. 63, EPO (Technical Bd
App)

Carl Zeiss Stiftung v. Rayner & Keeler Ltd (Authority to Institute Proceedings: Issue Estoppel); *sub nom* Carl Zeiss Stiftung v. Rayner & Keeler Ltd (No.2); Rayner & Keeler Ltd v. Courts & Co [1967] 1 A.C. 853; [1966] 3 W.L.R. 125; [1966] 2 All E.R. 536; [1967] R.P.C. 497; 110 S.J. 425, HL; reversing [1965] Ch. 596; [1965] 2 W.L.R. 277; [1965] 1 All E.R. 300; [1965] R.P.C. 141; 109 S.J. 51; *Times*, December 18, 1964; *Guardian*, December 18, 1964, CA; reversing [1964] R.P.C. 299, RPC .... *Digested*, 66/**1665**:
Applied, 86/2689, 87/1441: *Considered*, 70/798, 71/3476, 77/1212, 79/791, 80/2609, 85/1291, 90/610, 90/2860, 90/3686, 00/785: *Followed*, 96/853, 96/1102: *Previous proceedings*, 60/2469, 64/531, 64/532: *Referred to*, 95/6225: *Subsequent proceedings*, 68/3923, 69/3560

Carl Zeiss Stiftung v. Rayner & Keeler Ltd (No.2) see Carl Zeiss Stiftung v. Rayner & Keeler Ltd (Authority to Institute Proceedings: Issue Estoppel)

CARL ZEISS/Documents as filed (T382/94) [1998] E.P.O.R. 200, EPO (Technical Bd App)

Carless, Capel & Leonard v. F Pilmore Bedford & Sons; *sub nom* LIGHTHOUSE Trade Mark (1928) 45 R.P.C. 205 .... *Referred to*, 98/3500

Carlisle Golf Club v. Customs and Excise Commissioners see Keswick Golf Club v. Customs and Excise Commissioners

Carlsen v. Rasmussen [1999] 3 C.M.L.R. 854, HR (DK)

Carlson v. Rio Tinto Plc [1999] C.L.C. 551, QBD. .... *Digested*, 99/**718**

Carlson v. Townsend [2001] EWCA Civ 511; [2001] 1 W.L.R. 2415; [2001] 3 All E.R. 663; [2001] C.P. Rep. 86; [2001] C.P.L.R. 405; [2001] P.I.Q.R. P24; (2001) 62 B.M.L.R. 50; *Daily Telegraph*, April 24, 2001, CA .... *Digested*, 01/**629**

Carltona Ltd v. Commissioners of Works [1943] 2 All E.R. 560, CA .... *Applied*, 47-51/1530, 47-51/8203, 54/46, 61/7385, 68/3426, 69/276, 76/23, 76/279, 96/7374: *Considered*, 83/2708, 87/4112, 90/2585, 91/1981, 93/1662, 00/5396: *Distinguished*, 97/4123: *Followed*, 90/4713, 96/2961

Carlyle Finance Ltd v. Pallas Industrial Finance Ltd [1999] 1 All E.R. (Comm) 659; [1999] R.T.R. 281; [1999] C.C.L.R. 85, CA .... *Digested*, 99/**2517**:
Followed, 01/880

Carmarthenshire CC v. Lewis [1955] A.C. 549; [1955] 2 W.L.R. 517; [1955] 1 All E.R. 565; 119 J.P. 230; 53 L.G.R. 230; 99 S.J. 167, HL; affirming [1953] 1 W.L.R. 1439; [1953] 2 All E.R. 1403; 118 J.P. 51; 52 L.G.R. 13; 97 S.J. 831, CA; affirming [1953] 1 All E.R. 1025; 117 J.P. 231, Assizes .... *Digested*, 55/**2194**:
Applied, 00/4223: *Considered*, 70/1849, 99/5434

Carmichael v. National Power Plc [1999] 1 W.L.R. 2042; [1999] 4 All E.R. 897; [1999] I.C.R. 1226; [2000] I.R.L.R. 43; (1999) 96(46) L.S.G. 38; (1999) 143 S.J.L.B. 281; *Times*, November 23, 1999 ; *Independent*, November 25, 1999, HL; reversing [1998] I.C.R. 1167; [1998] I.R.L.R. 301; (1998) 95(19) L.S.G. 23; (1998) 142 S.J.L.B. 140; *Times*, April 2, 1998, CA .... *Digested*, 99/**2002**:
Considered, 01/2262

Carnahan v. Chief Constable of the Royal Ulster Constabulary [1998] N.I. 384, CA (NI) .... *Digested*, 99/**5141**

Carnalea Investment Co v. Inland Revenue Commissioners see Arranmore Investment Co Ltd v. Inland Revenue Commissioners

Carnarvon v. Villebois (1844) 13 M. & W. 313. .... *Considered*, 99/4953

Carnduff v. Rock [2001] EWCA Civ 680; [2001] 1 W.L.R. 1786; (2001) 98(25) L.S.G. 47; (2001) 145 S.J.L.B. 141; *Times*, May 30, 2001; *Independent*, July 2, 2001 (C.S); *Daily Telegraph*, May 22, 2001, CA .... *Digested*, 01/**4774**

Carnegie v. Barkers (of Malton) Ltd (Unreported, July 23, 1999), CC (York) [*Ex rel.* Edward Legard, Barrister, York Chambers, 14 Toft Green, York] .... *Digested*, 99/**1507**

Carnell v. A-B Aegon (Unreported, January 4, 2000), CC (Exeter) [*Ex rel.* Crosse & Crosse Solicitors, 14 Southernhay West, Exeter] .... *Digested*, 00/**1627**

Carpenter v. Customs and Excise Commissioners [1998] B.V.C. 2066, V&DTr

Carpenter v. Mid-Kent Healthcare Trust (Unreported, August 1, 2001), MCLC [*Ex rel.* Thompsons Solicitors, Congress House, Great Russell Street, London] .... *Digested*, 01/**524**

Carpoint SpA v. Microsoft Corp [2000] E.T.M.R. 802, Trib (Rome)

Carr v. Allen Bradley Electronics [1980] I.C.R. 603; [1980] I.R.L.R. 263, EAT .... *Digested*, 80/**932**:
Applied, 98/2167

Carr (Inspector of Taxes) v. Armpledge Ltd; Carr (Inspector of Taxes) v. Fielden & Ashworth Ltd [2000] S.T.C. 410; 72 T.C. 420; [2000] B.T.C. 182; [2000] S.T.I. 782; *Times*, May 24, 2000; *Independent*, July 3, 2000 (C.S), CA; reversing in part [1998] S.T.C. 999; [1998] B.T.C. 322; *Times*, October 12, 1998, Ch D ..... *Digested*, 00/**4911**

Carr (Inspector of Taxes) v. Fielden & Ashworth Ltd see Carr (Inspector of Taxes) v. Armpledge Ltd

Carr v. Hanson [2001] 4 Q.R. 12, CC (Worcester) [*Ex rel.* S Garner, Barrister, No.8 Chambers, Fountain Court, Steelhouse Lane, Birmingham] .... *Digested*, 01/**1786**

Carr v. IMI Plc (Unreported, March 25, 1999), CC (Northampton) [*Ex rel.* Benedict Leech, Barrister, 3 Paper Buildings, Temple, London] .... *Digested*, 99/**1609**

Carr v. Leeds City Council see Leeds City Council v. Carr

Carr-Glynn v. Frearsons [1999] Ch. 326; [1999] 2 W.L.R. 1046; [1998] 4 All E.R. 225; [1999] 1 F.L.R. 8; [1998] 3 F.C.R. 487; [1999] P.N.L.R. 13; [1998] Fam. Law 739; [1998] E.G.C.S. 128; (1998) 148 N.L.J. 1487; [1998] N.P.C. 136, CA; reversing [1997] 2 All E.R. 614; [1997] P.N.L.R. 343, Ch D . . . . *Digested*, 98/**4595**:
Applied, 01/4537: *Considered*, 00/4225

Carradine Properties Ltd v. DJ Freeman & Co [1999] Lloyd's Rep. P.N. 483; [1955-95] P.N.L.R. 219; (1989) 5 Const. L.J. 267; *Times*, February 19, 1982, CA . . . . *Digested*, 90/**3283**:
Applied, 88/2011: *Considered*, 98/4020

Carranza v. Argentina 4 B.H.R.C. 459, IACHR . . . . *Digested*, 98/**3148**

Carrick DC v. Falmouth Boat Construction Ltd (1998) 13 P.A.D. 238, Planning Inspector

Carrick Jewellery Ltd's Trade Mark Application (No. 2042882A) (2000) 23(8) I.P.D. 23067, TMR

Carrier Corp's Community Trade Mark Application [2000] E.T.M.R. 234, OHIM (3rd Bd App) . . . . *Digested*, 00/**3728**

Carrieres de Sainte-Marthe SA v. Caulet [2001] E.C.C. 28, Cass (F)

Carrimore Six Wheelers Ltd v. Inland Revenue Commissioners 26 T.C. 301 . . . . *Applied*, 01/5200:
Considered, 99/4663

Carrington (CICB: Quantum: 2000), Re [2000] 4 Q.R. 5, CICB (York) [*Ex rel.* Richard Gregory, Barrister, 24 The Ropewalk, Nottingham] . . . . *Digested*, 00/**1549**

Carrington v. Harwich Dock Co Ltd [1998] I.C.R. 1112; [1998] I.R.L.R. 567; *Times*, August 31, 1998, EAT . . . . *Digested*, 98/**2230**

Carrington Carr Ltd v. Leicestershire CC (1994) 158 J.P. 570; [1994] C.C.L.R. 14; [1993] Crim. L.R. 938; [1993] C.O.D. 441, DC . . . . *Digested*, 94/**946**:
Followed, 00/2677

Carrisi v. Jackson [2000] E.C.D.R. 424, App (Milano)

Carroll v. Bent see Carroll v. Fearon

Carroll v. Fearon; Barclay v. Dunlop Ltd; Carroll v. Bent [1999] E.C.C 73; [1998] P.I.Q.R. P416; *Times*, January 26, 1998, CA. . . . . *Digested*, 98/**3995**

Carroll v. Manek (2000) 79 P. & C.R. 173; *Times*, August 18, 1999, Ch D . . . . *Digested*, 99/**4349**

CARROLL PRODUCTS/ Display units (T883/97) [1999] E.P.O.R. 248, EPO (Technical Bd App)

Carrolls Transport Ltd v. Alderman (Unreported, March 7, 2000), CC (Brentford) [*Ex rel.* Tianne Bell, Barrister, Hardwicke Building, New Square, Lincoln's Inn, London] . *Digested*, 00/**331**

Carron v. Lion Plant Ltd (Unreported, November 18, 1997), CC (Liverpool) [*Ex rel.* Tim Grover, Barrister, Martins Building, 2nd Floor, 4 Water Street, Liverpool] . . . . . . *Digested*, 98/**1752**

Carrs Bury St Edmunds Ltd v. Barnes Group see Carrs Bury St Edmunds Ltd v. Whitworth Partnership

Carrs Bury St Edmunds Ltd v. Whitworth Partnership; Carrs Bury St Edmunds Ltd v. Barnes Group 84 B.L.R. 117; (1997) 13 Const. L.J. 199, QBD (OR) . . . . *Digested*, 97/**552**:
Considered, 99/372

Carslogie Steamship Co Ltd v. Royal Norwegian Government (The Carslogie) [1952] A.C. 292; [1952] 1 All E.R. 20; [1951] 2 Lloyd's Rep. 441; [1951] 2 T.L.R. 1099; 95 S.J. 801, HL; reversing [1951] P. 167; (1950) 84 Ll. L. Rep. 399; 66 T.L.R. (Pt. 2) 683; 94 S.J. 594, CA; reversing (1950) 84 Ll. L. Rep. 148; [1950] W.N. 388, PDAD . . . . *Digested*, 47-51/**10521**:
Considered, 61/2345, 94/1442, 98/3914: *Distinguished*, 58/882

Carstairs (Inspector of Taxes) v. Sykes [2000] S.T.C. 1103; 73 T.C. 225; [2000] S.T.I. 1544; *Times*, December 20, 2000, Ch D; reversing . . . . *Digested*, 01/**5266**

Carter v. Automobile Association (Unreported, January 20, 1998), CC (Leicester) [*Ex rel.* Edmund Young, Bolt Burdon Solicitors, 16 Theberton Street, Islington, London] . . . . *Digested*, 98/**1681**

Carter v. Eason (Unreported, February 18, 2000), CC (Liverpool) [*Ex rel.* Beachcroft Wansbroughs Solicitors, 13 Police Street, Manchester] . . . . *Digested*, 00/**2592**

Carter v. Eastbourne BC (2000) 164 J.P. 273; [2000] 2 P.L.R. 60; [2000] C.O.D. 263, QBD . . . . *Digested*, 00/**1079**

Carter v. Lotus Leisure Group Ltd [2001] EWCA Civ 1205; [2001] N.P.C. 123, CA

Carter v. Reiner Moritz Associates Ltd [1997] I.C.R. 881, EAT . . . . *Digested*, 98/**2223**

Carter (t/a New Chapel Developments) v. TG Baynes & Sons [1998] E.G.C.S. 109, Ch D

Carter (Leroy) v. Trinidad and Tobago see Charles v. Trinidad and Tobago

Carter (Steve) v. Trinidad and Tobago see Charles v. Trinidad and Tobago

Carter Commercial Developments v. Bedford BC [2001] EWHC Admin 669; [2001] 34 E.G.C.S. 99, QBD (Admin Ct)

Carter-Knight (A Bankrupt) v. Peat [2000] B.P.I.R. 968; (2000) 97(30) L.S.G. 40; *Times*, August 11, 2000, Ch D . . . . *Digested*, 00/**3457**

Cartonneries de Thulin SA v. CTP White Knight Ltd [2001] R.P.C. 6; (2000) 23(9) I.P.D. 23068, CA; reversing in part (1999) 22(2) I.P.D. 22013, Pat Ct. . . . . *Digested*, 00/**3664**

Cartonneries de Thulin SA v. CTP White Knight Ltd (Costs) [1999] F.S.R. 922, Pat Ct . . *Digested*, 00/**415**

Cartwright, Re; *sub nom* Avis v. Newman (1889) L.R. 41 Ch. D. 532, Ch D . . . . *Applied*, 00/**3939**

Cartwright v. Staffordshire and Moorlands DC [1998] B.P.I.R. 328, CA. . . . . *Digested*, 98/**3295**

Carus-Wilson and Greene's Arbitration, Re (1887) L.R. 18 Q.B.D. 7, CA. . . . . *Applied*, 59/438, 01/349

Caruso v. Poulson (Unreported, November 28, 1997), CC (Slough) [*Ex rel.* Mark Whalan, Barrister, 2 Gray's Inn Square, London] . . . . *Digested*, 98/**488**

Carvel v. Council of the European Union (T194/94); Guardian Newspapers Ltd v. Council of Ministers of the European Communities [1996] All E.R. (E.C.) 53; [1995] E.C.R. II-2765; [1995] 3 C.M.L.R. 359; [1996] C.E.C. 282; *Times,* November 2, 1995, CFI (2nd Chamber) . . . .
Digested, 95/**2234**: *Considered,* 98/2327

Carver v. Queens Square Petroleum Ltd (Unreported, June 15, 1998), CC (Kingston upon Hull) [*Ex rel.* Pitmans Solicitors, 47 Castle Street, Reading, Berkshire] . . . .
Digested, 99/**1512**

Carver v. Saudi Arabian Airlines [1999] 3 All E.R. 61; [1999] I.C.R. 991; [1999] I.R.L.R. 370; [1999] Disc. L.R. 216; (1999) 149 N.L.J. 521; *Times,* March 24, 1999; *Independent,* March 23, 1999, CA . . . .
Digested, 99/**2055**

Carvill v. Inland Revenue Commissioners (Remit Principles) [1996] S.T.C. 126; 70 T.C. 126; *Times,* January 24, 1996; *Independent,* February 19, 1996 (C.S.), Ch D . . . .
Digested, 96/**5628**

Carvill v. Inland Revenue Commissioners (Transfer Purpose) [2000] S.T.C. (S.C.D.) 143; [2000] S.T.I. 584, Sp Comm. . . . .
Digested, 00/**5021**

CAS (Nominees) Ltd v. Nottingham Forest Plc (Application for Disclosure); *sub nom* Nottingham Forest Plc, Re [2001] 1 All E.R. 954; (2000) 97(40) L.S.G. 42; (2000) 150 N.L.J. 1264; *Times,* September 5, 2000, Ch D . . . .
Digested, 00/**671**

Casado Coca v. Spain (A/285) (1994) 18 E.H.R.R. 1; *Times,* April 1, 1994, ECHR . . . . . .
Digested, 94/**2415**: *Applied,* 97/2811: *Considered,* 98/3092

Casani v. Mattei (1998-99) 1 I.T.E.L.R. 925, Trib (I)

Casaubon v. 21st Century Film France [1999] E.T.M.R. 787, C d'A (Paris)

Cascella v. Garella [2000] E.C.D.R. 172, Trib (Biella)

Casella London v. Banai [1990] I.C.R. 215; (1990) 87(4) L.S.G. 39, EAT . . . .
Digested, 90/**1891**: *Not followed,* 99/5265

Casey v. Hartley (Unreported, January 17, 2000), CC (Ashford) [*Ex rel.* Tim Kevan, Barrister, 1 Temple Gardens, Temple, London] . . . .
Digested, 00/**2567**: *Cited,* 00/2580

Casey v. Hugh James Jones & Jenkins [1999] Lloyd's Rep. P.N. 115, QBD. . . . .
Digested, 99/**4052**

Casey v. Morane Ltd [2001] I.C.R. 316; [2001] I.R.L.R. 166; (2000) 97(21) L.S.G. 38; *Times,* May 10, 2000, CA. . . . .
Digested, 00/**1486**

Casey v. Neal (Unreported, February 25, 1997), CC (Birkenhead) [*Ex rel.* Michael W Halsall, Solicitor] . . . .
Digested, 97/**505**: *Followed,* 97/1760

Cashman v. Westland Group Plc (Unreported, May 21, 1998), CC (Central London) [*Ex rel.* A.G. Ritchie, Barrister, 9 Gough Square, London, EC4A 3DE] . . . .
Digested, 98/**1585**

Casimir v. Alexander [2001] W.T.L.R. 939, Ch D . . . .
Digested, 01/**5152**

Casino Copenhagen K/S v. Ministry of Taxes (Court Settlement) (19 B-2006-99) 3 I.T.L. Rep. 447, OL (DK)

Casio Computer Co Ltd v. Sayo (No.3) [2001] EWCA Civ 661; [2001] I.L.Pr. 43, CA; affirming (2001) 98(6) L.S.G. 45; *Times,* February 6, 2001, Ch D . . . .
Digested, 01/**809**

Casio Computer Co Ltd's European Patent Application (No.93103140.5) see CASIO/Right to be heard (T951/97)

CASIO/Right to be heard (T951/97); *sub nom* Casio Computer Co Ltd's European Patent Application (No.93103140.5) [1999] E.P.O.R. 160; (1998) 21(5) I.P.D. 21055, EPO (Technical Bd App)

Caspian Basin Specialised Emergency Salvage Administration v. Bouygues Offshore SA (No.4) see Bouygues Offshore SA v. Caspian Shipping Co (No.4)

Caspian Basin Specialised Emergency Salvage Administration v. Bouygues Offshore SA (Nos.1, 3, 4 and 5) see Bouygues Offshore SA v. Caspian Shipping Co (Nos.1, 3, 4 and 5)

Cassell v. Crutchfield (Inspector of Taxes) (No.1) [1995] S.T.C. 663; 69 T.C. 253; *Times,* June 8, 1995; *Independent,* July 3, 1995 (C.S.), Ch D . . . .
Digested, 95/**5021**

Cassell v. Crutchfield (Inspector of Taxes) (No.2); *sub nom* Crutchfield (Inspector of Taxes) v. Cassell [1997] S.T.C. 423; 69 T.C. 259; [1997] B.T.C. 178, Ch D . . . . . .
Digested, 97/**4742**: *Applied,* 00/5263

Cassidy (Deceased), Re [1979] V.R. 369, Sup Ct (Vic) . . . .
Applied, 00/5263

Cassidy v. Hawcroft [2001] C.P. Rep. 49; [2000] C.P.L.R. 624, CA . . . .
Digested, 00/**345**

Cassin v. Bexley LBC; *sub nom* Bexley LBC v. Cassin (1999) 1 L.G.L.R. 810; [1999] B.L.G.R. 694; (1999) 11 Admin. L.R. 495; (1999) 163 J.P.N. 854; *Times,* February 15, 1999, CA. . . . .
Digested, 99/**2888**

Cassis de Dijon see Rewe-Zentral AG v. Bundesmonopolverwaltung fur Branntwein (C120/78)

Casson v. Ostley PJ Ltd [2001] EWCA Civ 1013; [2001] N.P.C. 105, CA; reversing [2001] B.L.R. 126, QBD. . . . .
Digested, 01/**952**

Cast v. Croydon College [1998] I.C.R. 500; [1998] I.R.L.R. 318; (1998) 95(16) L.S.G. 26; (1998) 142 S.J.L.B. 119; *Times,* March 26, 1998, CA; reversing [1998] I.C.R. 77; [1997] I.R.L.R. 14, EAT. . . . .
Digested, 98/**2200**: *Applied,* 01/2234: *Cited,* 00/2183

Castanho v. Brown & Root (UK) Ltd [1981] A.C. 557; [1980] 3 W.L.R. 991; [1981] 1 All E.R. 143; [1981] 1 Lloyd's Rep. 113; 124 S.J. 884, HL; affirming [1980] 1 W.L.R. 833; [1980] 3 All E.R. 72; [1980] 2 Lloyd's Rep. 423; 124 S.J. 375, CA; reversing [1980] 1 All E.R. 689, QBD . . . .
Digested, 81/**2200**: *Applied,* 77/2969, 83/2963, 84/2641, 86/2639, 94/3695, 98/616: *Considered,* 92/3516, 93/151, 93/1978, 94/3708: *Distinguished,* 87/3024: *Referred to,* 83/2970

Castellain *v.* Preston (1882-83) L.R. 11 Q.B.D. 380, CA; reversing (1881-82) L.R. 8
  Q.B.D. 613, QBD . . . . *Applied*, 57/1763,
               61/8360, 70/1370, 71/6016, 79/1509, 88/3235, 88/4568, 89/3392:
        Considered, 73/1046, 74/1885, 96/3605, 99/793: *Distinguished*, 93/2414:
                                      Followed, 97/3151
Castillo Algar *v.* Spain (28194/95) (2000) 30 E.H.R.R. 827; [1998] H.R.C.D. 961,
  ECHR . . . . *Digested*, 01/**3501**
Castle (CICB: Quantum: 1998), Re (Unreported, July 14, 1998), CICB (London) [*Ex rel.*
  Gerard Martin, Barrister, Exchange Chambers, Pearl Assurance House, Derby
  Square, Liverpool] . . . . *Digested*, 98/**1493**
Castle *v.* DPP, *Times*, April 3, 1998, QBD . . . . *Digested*, 98/**948**
Castle Cement *v.* Environment Agency; *sub nom* R. *v.* Environment Agency Ex p.
  Castle Cement Ltd; R. (on the application of Castle Cement Ltd) *v.* Environment
  Agency [2001] EWHC Admin 224; [2001] 2 C.M.L.R. 19; [2001] Env. L.R. 46;
  (2001) 98(14) L.S.G. 42; [2001] N.P.C. 64, QBD (Admin Ct)
Castle Point BC *v.* Platt (2000) 15 P.A.D. 189, Planning Inspector
Castle Point BC *v.* Post Office (2000) 15 P.A.D. 704, Planning Inspector
Castle Wharf Developments Ltd *v.* J Jarvis & Sons Ltd see J Jarvis & Sons Ltd *v.* Castle
  Wharf Developments Ltd
Castleford Homes *v.* Secretary of State for Environment, Transport and the Regions see
  Castleford Homes Ltd *v.* Secretary of State for the Environment, Transport and
  the Regions
Castleford Homes Ltd *v.* Secretary of State for the Environment, Transport and the
  Regions; *sub nom* Castleford Homes *v.* Secretary of State for Environment,
  Transport and the Regions [2001] EWHC Admin 77; [2001] P.L.C.R. 29; [2001]
  J.P.L. 1217 (Note); [2001] 7 E.G.C.S. 160; (2001) 98(7) L.S.G. 42; [2001]
  N.P.C. 25, QBD (Admin Ct)
Castleton Management Service Ltd *v.* Kirkwood (Inspector of Taxes) see Castleton
  Management Services Ltd *v.* Kirkwood (Inspector of Taxes)
Castleton Management Services Ltd *v.* Kirkwood (Inspector of Taxes); *sub nom*
  Castleton Management Service Ltd *v.* Kirkwood (Inspector of Taxes) [2001]
  S.T.C. (S.C.D.) 95; [2001] S.T.I. 782; (2001) 151 N.L.J. 1034, Sp Comm . . . . *Digested*, 01/**5218**
CASTLETON/Re-establishment of rights (J13/90) [1994] E.P.O.R. 76, EPO (Legal Bd
  App) . . . . *Applied*, 00/3654
Castro *v.* Internal Revenue Commissioner (2001-02) 4 I.T.E.L.R. 45, US Ct
Catania *v.* Giannattasio [1999] I.L.Pr. 630, CA (Ont) . . . . *Digested*, 00/**766**
Caterham Car Sales & Coachworks Ltd's Community Trade Mark Application (R63/1999-
  3) [2000] E.T.M.R. 14, OHIM (3rd Bd App) . . . . *Digested*, 00/**3736**
Cathiship SA *v.* Allanasons Ltd (The Catherine Helen) [1998] 3 All E.R. 714; [1998] 2
  Lloyd's Rep. 511; [1998] C.L.C. 1310; *Times*, July 25, 1998, QBD (Comm Ct) . . . *Digested*, 98/**252**
Catholic Care Consortium Ltd *v.* Customs and Excise Commissioners [2001] B.V.C.
  2381, V&DTr . . . . *Digested*, 01/**6922**
Catnic Components Ltd *v.* Hill & Smith Ltd (No.1); *sub nom* Catnic Components Ltd *v.*
  Hills & Rutter [1981] F.S.R. 60; [1982] R.P.C. 183, HL; reversing [1979] F.S.R.
  619, CA; reversing in part [1978] F.S.R. 405, Ch D . . . . *Digested*, 81/**2042**:
             Applied, 91/2699, 91/2700, 91/2708, 92/3291, 92/3302, 93/3028, 93/3041,
                95/3758, 95/3777, 00/3624: *Considered*, 91/2698, 95/3799, 99/3472:
              Followed, 84/2496, 98/3467: *Not followed*, 83/2772, 84/434, 94/3434,
            95/3757: *Referred to*, 84/2495, 93/3029, 94/3430, 99/3480, 00/3679
Catnic Components Ltd *v.* Hills & Rutter see Catnic Components Ltd *v.* Hill & Smith
  Ltd (No.1)
Caton's Administrators, Re see Couch (Inspector of Taxes) *v.* Administrators of the Estate
  of Caton
Caton's Administrators *v.* Couch (Inspector of Taxes) see Couch (Inspector of Taxes) *v.*
  Administrators of the Estate of Caton
Caton's Application, Re [1999] 4 P.L.R. 72; [1999] 3 E.G.L.R. 121; [1999] 38 E.G. 193, Lands
  Tr . . . . *Digested*, 99/**4261**
Catscratch Ltd *v.* Glasgow City Licensing Board (No.1); *sub nom* Catscratch Ltd,
  Petitioners 2001 S.C. 218; 2001 S.L.T. 344; 2001 S.C.L.R. 209; [2000] 17
  S.L.L.P. 7; 2000 G.W.D. 28-1098, OH . . . . *Digested*, 01/**6782**
Catscratch Ltd *v.* Glasgow City Licensing Board (No.2) 2001 S.C.L.R. 817; [2001]
  U.K.H.R.R. 1309; [2001] 20 S.L.L.P. 10; 2001 G.W.D. 19-748, OH
Catscratch Ltd, Petitioners see Catscratch Ltd *v.* Glasgow City Licensing Board (No.1)
Catt *v.* Church of Scientology Religious Education College Inc [2001] C.P. Rep. 41,
  QBD . . . . *Digested*, 01/**549**
Catt *v.* Tourle (1868-69) L.R. 4 Ch. App. 654, CA in Chancery . . . . *Considered*, 65/3878,
                                66/12029, 67/3906, 99/685
Caudle *v.* Sharp; Grove *v.* Sharp [1995] L.R.L.R. 433; [1995] 4 Re. L.R. 389; *Lloyd's*
  List, August 3, 1995 (I.D.), CA; reversing [1995] L.R.L.R. 80; *Times*, March 8,
  1994, QBD . . . . *Digested*, 95/**2923**
Cavalier *v.* Pope; *sub nom* Cavalier and Wife *v.* Pope [1906] A.C. 428, HL; affirming
  [1905] 2 K.B. 757, CA . . . . *Applied*, 47-51/6711,
               47-51/6727, 47-51/6929, 47-51/7886, 93/3796, 99/3735:
        Considered, 71/7843, 72/2352: *Distinguished*, 54/2232, 84/2300

Cavalier and Wife v. Pope see Cavalier v. Pope

Cave v. Crome (Unreported, February 3, 2000), CC (Chelmsford) [*Ex rel.* Neil Ashley, Barrister, 63 Wickham Road, Witham, Essex] . . . . *Digested,* 00/**1716**

Cave v. Robinson Jarvis & Rolf (A Firm); *sub nom* Robinson Jarvis & Rolf (A Firm) v. Cave; Cave v. Robinson Jarvis & Rolfe (A Firm); TNS, HL; reversing [2001] EWCA Civ 245; [2001] C.P. Rep. 66; 78 Con. L.R. 1; [2001] Lloyd's Rep. P.N. 290; [2001] P.N.L.R. 23; (2001) 17 Const. L.J. 262; [2001] 9 E.G.C.S. 229; [2001] N.P.C. 36; *Independent,* April 9, 2001 (C.S), CA . . . . *Digested,* 01/**630**

Cave v. Robinson Jarvis & Rolfe (A Firm) see Cave v. Robinson Jarvis & Rolf (A Firm)

Cavendish v. Relay Roads Ltd see Charlesworth v. Relay Roads Ltd (No.2)

Cavendish Funding Ltd v. Henry Spencer & Sons Ltd [1998] P.N.L.R. 122; [1998] 1 E.G.L.R. 104; [1998] 06 E.G. 146; [1997] E.G.C.S. 146; [1997] N.P.C. 150, CA; affirming in part [1996] P.N.L.R. 554; [1996] E.G.C.S. 60, Ch D . . . . *Digested,* 98/**4030**

Caviar Anzali SA v. L'Institut National de la Propriete Industrielle [2000] E.T.M.R. 513, C d'A (Paris)

Cavity Trays Ltd v. RMC Panel Products Ltd [1996] R.P.C. 361; *Times,* February 10, 1996, CA . . . . *Digested,* 96/**4559**: *Followed,* 97/3917, 98/3528

Cawley, Re see R. v. Oldham Justices Ex p. Cawley

Cawston v. Chartered Trust Plc (Unreported, February 29, 2000), CC (Colchester) [*Ex rel.* Andrew Granville Stafford, Barrister, 4 King's Bench Walk, 2nd Floor, Temple, London] . . . . *Digested,* 00/**2602**

Cawthorn v. DPP see Cawthorn v. Newcastle upon Tyne Crown Court

Cawthorn v. Newcastle upon Tyne Crown Court; *sub nom* Cawthorn v. DPP (2000) 164 J.P. 527; [2000] R.T.R. 45; *Times,* August 31, 1999, QBD . . . . *Digested,* 99/**957**

Cazenave de la Roche v. France (25549/94) (2001) 33 E.H.R.R. 7; [1998] H.R.C.D. 620, ECHR . . . . *Digested,* 01/**3505**

CB and JB (Minors) (Care Proceedings: Guidelines), Re see B (Minors) (Care Proceedings: Practice), Re

CBS Records Australia Ltd v. Telmak Teleproducts (Aust) Pty Ltd (1987) 9 I.P.R. 440. . . *Considered,* 98/3418

CBS Songs Ltd v. Amstrad Consumer Electronics Plc (No.1) [1988] A.C. 1013; [1988] 2 W.L.R. 1191; [1988] 2 All E.R. 484; [1988] 2 F.T.L.R. 168; [1988] R.P.C. 567; (1988) 132 S.J. 789; *Times,* May 13, 1988; *Independent,* May 17, 1988 (C.S.); *Financial Times,* May 18, 1988; *Guardian,* May 19, 1988, HL; affirming [1988] Ch. 61; [1987] 3 W.L.R. 144; [1987] 3 All E.R. 151; [1987] 1 F.T.L.R. 488; [1987] R.P.C. 429; (1987) 84 L.S.G. 1243, CA; reversing *Times,* May 9, 1986, Ch D . . . *Digested,* 88/**503**: *Considered,* 89/2805, 99/3462: *Followed,* 00/3576: *Referred to,* 93/3041, 00/3570

CCS (NI) Ltd (t/a Granville Cold Storage Co) v. Commissioner of Valuation for Northern Ireland [1999] R.A. 142, Lands Tr (NI). . . . . *Digested,* 99/**5469**

CD and MD (Care Proceedings: Practice), Re [1998] 1 F.L.R. 825; [1998] Fam. Law 317, Fam Div . . . . *Digested,* 98/**2404**

CD Rom Price Fixing, Re [1998] E.C.C. 215, BGH (Ger)

CE King Ltd (In Administration), Re; *sub nom* CE King Ltd v. Kodak [2000] 2 B.C.L.C. 297, Ch D (Companies Ct) . . . . *Digested,* 00/**3459**

CE King Ltd v. Kodak see CE King Ltd (In Administration), Re

CECA/Procedural timetable (T97/94) [1999] E.P.O.R. 65, EPO (Technical Bd App) . . . *Digested,* 00/**3651**

Cedac Ltd, Re see Secretary of State for Trade and Industry v. Langridge

Cedarwood Productions Ltd, Re; *sub nom* Secretary of State for Trade and Industry v. Rayna; Secretary of State for Trade and Industry v. Newstead; Inter City Print & Finishing Ltd, Re; Secretary of State for Trade and Industry v. Murfitt [2001] EWCA Civ 1083; (2001) 98(30) L.S.G. 37; *Times,* July 12, 2001, CA; affirming [2001] 2 B.C.L.C. 48; (2001) 98(20) L.S.G. 42; *Times,* April 3, 2001, Ch D . . . . *Digested,* 01/**709**

Cedeno v. Logan [2001] 1 W.L.R. 86; (2001) 145 S.J.L.B. 7, PC (Trin) . . . . *Digested,* 01/**50**

Celador Productions Ltd v. Danmarks Radio [2000] E.C.D.R. 158, OL (DK)

Celanese International Corp v. BP Chemicals Ltd [1999] R.P.C. 203; (1999) 22(1) I.P.D. 22002; *Times,* November 5, 1998, Pat Ct . . . . *Digested,* 98/**3469**

Celltech Chiroscience Ltd v. Medimmune Inc (2001) 24(11) I.P.D. 24074, Pat Ct

CELLTECH/Chrymosin (T690/91) [1998] E.P.O.R. 228, EPO (Technical Bd App)

Cellular Clothing Co Ltd v. Maxton & Murray [1899] A.C. 326, HL; affirming (1898) 25 R. 1098, 1 Div . . . . *Followed,* 01/**3877**

Celsteel Ltd v. Alton House Holdings Ltd (No.1) [1986] 1 W.L.R. 512; [1986] 1 All E.R. 608; (1986) 83 L.S.G. 700; (1986) 130 S.J. 204, CA; reversing [1985] 1 W.L.R. 204; [1982] 2 All E.R. 562; (1985) 49 P. & C.R. 165; (1985) 82 L.S.G. 1168; (1985) 129 S.J. 115, Ch D . . . . *Digested,* 86/**1114**: *Applied,* 00/4634

Celtec Ltd v. Astley [2001] I.R.L.R. 788; [2001] Emp. L.R. 1353, EAT

Celtic Extraction Ltd (In Liquidation), Re; *sub nom* Official Receiver (as Liquidator of Celtic Extraction Ltd and Bluestone Chemicals Ltd) *v.* Environment Agency; Bluestone Chemicals Ltd *v.* Environment Agency [2001] Ch. 475; [2000] 2 W.L.R. 991; [1999] 4 All E.R. 684; [2000] B.C.C. 487; [1999] 2 B.C.L.C. 555; [2000] Env. L.R. 86; [1999] B.P.I.R. 986; [1999] 3 E.G.L.R. 21; [1999] 46 E.G. 187; (1999) 96(32) L.S.G. 33; [1999] N.P.C. 92; *Times,* August 5, 1999 ; *Independent,* October 4, 1999, CA . . . . *Digested,* 99/**3308**:
Applied, 00/3864
Celtic Football and Athletic Co Ltd *v.* Customs and Excise Commissioners [1983] S.T.C. 470; 1983 S.L.T. 662, 1 Div . . . . *Digested,* 83/**5078**:
Considered, 98/4915
CELTRIX/Correction of errors (G11/91) [1993] E.P.O.R. 245, EPO (Enlarged Bd App) . . *Considered,* 01/3884
CELTRIX/Glu-Gln (T184/91) [2001] E.P.O.R. 28, EPO (Technical Bd App) . . . . *Digested,* 01/**3884**
CEM Connections Ltd, Re [2000] B.C.C. 917, Ch D (Companies Ct) *Digested,* 01/**706**
Cement Makers Federation Agreement (No.2), Re [1974] 2 All E.R. 219; [1974] I.C.R. 445, RPC . . . . *Digested,* 74/**3810**:
Applied, 97/862, 99/701: *Followed,* 98/732
Centaur Clothes Group Ltd *v.* Walker (Inspector of Taxes) see Walker (Inspector of Taxes) *v.* Centaur Clothes Group Ltd
Center Optical (Hong Kong) Ltd *v.* Jardine Transport Services (China) Ltd [2001] 2 Lloyd's Rep. 678, CFI (HK)
Centrafarm BV *v.* American Home Products Corp (C3/78) [1978] E.C.R. 1823; [1979] 1 C.M.L.R. 326; [1979] F.S.R. 189, ECJ [1978] 2 C.M.L.R. 63; [1978] F.S.R. 403, RB (Rotterdam) . . . . *Digested,* 79/**1258**:
Considered, 98/3514: *Distinguished,* 96/5713: *Referred to,* 93/3980
Central Bank of Yemen *v.* Cardinal Financial Investments Corp see Cardinal Financial Investment Corp *v.* Central Bank of Yemen (No.1)
Central Capital Corp, Re Unreported . . . . *Followed,* 00/3482
Central London Commercial Estates Ltd *v.* Kato Kagaku Ltd [1998] 4 All E.R. 948; [1998] 3 E.G.L.R. 55; [1998] 46 E.G. 185; [1998] E.G.C.S. 117; (1998) 95(29) L.S.G. 28; (1998) 95(37) L.S.G. 37; (1998) 142 S.J.L.B. 252; [1998] N.P.C. 125; *Times,* July 27, 1998, CA . . . . *Digested,* 98/**4339**
Central London Property Trust *v.* High Trees House [1947] K.B. 130; [1956] 1 All E.R. 256 (Note); 62 T.L.R. 557; [1947] L.J.R. 77; 175 L.T. 333, KBD . . . . *Digested,* 47-51/**5601**:
Applied, 47-51/1638, 47-51/1779, 47-51/5432, 47-51/5590, 47-51/7248, 64/2067, 69/479, 72/465, 74/357, 76/1868, 79/2635, 80/83, 81/2481:
Considered, 47-51/673, 47-51/1782, 47-51/1806, 64/1357, 67/1497, 68/1462, 68/3830, 72/493, 77/2032, 79/1598, 80/348, 82/1146, 83/1364, 93/2504, 94/2771, 95/2533, 96/3781: *Distinguished,* 47-51/1711, 47-51/3014, 47-51/3033, 52/3552.9, 55/979, 63/3006, 65/1486, 66/1739:
Followed, 47-51/5799, 47-51/5800, 98/3593
Centralcrest Engineering Ltd, Re; *sub nom* Inland Revenue Commissioners *v.* Nelmes [2000] B.C.C. 727, Ch D (Companies Ct) . . . . *Digested,* 00/**3480**
Centrax Ltd, Re see Centrax Ltd *v.* Customs and Excise Commissioners
Centrax Ltd *v.* Citibank NA [1999] 1 All E.R. (Comm) 557, CA . . . . *Digested,* 99/**737**
Centrax Ltd *v.* Customs and Excise Commissioners; *sub nom* Centrax Ltd, Re [1999] B.V.C. 2057; [1998] V. & D.R. 369, V&DTr . . . . *Digested,* 99/**5012**
Centremodel Projects Ltd *v.* Royal Bank of Scotland [2000] N.P.C. 76, CA
Centrepoint Community Growth Trust, Re (2000-01) 3 I.T.E.L.R. 269, HC (NZ) . . . . . . *Digested,* 01/**384**
Centro Latino Americano de Commercio Exterior SA *v.* Owners of the Kommunar (The Kommunar) (No.1); *sub nom* CLACE *v.* Owners of the Ship Kommunar [1997] 1 Lloyd's Rep. 1; [1996] C.L.C. 1919; *Times,* July 9, 1996, QBD (Adm Ct) . . . . *Digested,* 96/**5289**:
Applied, 00/4740
Centro Latino Americano de Commercio Exterior SA *v.* Owners of the Kommunar (The Kommunar) (No.3) [1997] 1 Lloyd's Rep. 22, QBD (Adm Ct) . . . . *Digested,* 97/**4489**:
Distinguished, 00/3472
Centro Servisi Spediporto Srl *v.* Spedisioni Marittima del Golfo Srl (C96/94) see Centro Servizi Spediporto Srl *v.* Spedizioni Marittima del Golfo Srl (C96/94)
Centro Servizi Spediporto Srl *v.* Spedizione Marittima del Golfo Srl (C96/94) see Centro Servizi Spediporto Srl *v.* Spedizioni Marittima del Golfo Srl (C96/94)
Centro Servizi Spediporto Srl *v.* Spedizioni Marittima del Golfo Srl (C96/94); *sub nom* Centro Servisi Spediporto Srl *v.* Spedisioni Marittima del Golfo Srl (C96/94); Centro Servizi Spediporto Srl *v.* Spedizione Marittima del Golfo Srl (C96/94) [1995] E.C.R. I-2883; [1996] 4 C.M.L.R. 613, ECJ (6th Chamber) . . . . *Applied,* 98/2325
Centros Ltd *v.* Erhvervs-og Selskabsstyrelsen (C212/97) [2000] Ch. 446; [2000] 2 W.L.R. 1048; [2000] All E.R. (EC) 481; [1999] E.C.R. I-1459; [1999] B.C.C. 983; [2000] 2 B.C.L.C. 68; [1999] 2 C.M.L.R. 551; [2000] C.E.C. 290, ECJ . . . *Digested,* 99/**2253**:
Applied, 01/2498
Centrosteel Srl *v.* Adipol GmbH (C456/98) [2000] E.C.R. I-6007; [2000] 3 C.M.L.R. 711; [2000] C.E.C. 527, ECJ (1st Chamber) . . . . *Digested,* 00/**116**
Century 21 Real Estate Corp's Application (R135/1998-2) [1999] E.T.M.R. 781, OHIM (2nd Bd App) . . . . *Digested,* 00/**3720**
Century Life Plc *v.* Customs and Excise Commissioners see Customs and Excise Commissioners *v.* Century Life Plc

Century National Merchant Bank & Trust Co Ltd *v.* Davies [1998] A.C. 628; [1998] 2
   W.L.R. 779; (1998) 142 S.J.L.B. 110, PC (Jam) . . . .   *Digested*, 98/**281**
Century Traders *v.* Roshan Lal Duggar & Co [1978] A.I.R. Delhi 250 . . . .   *Followed*, 98/3521
Cerberus Software Ltd *v.* Rowley; *sub nom* Rowley *v.* Cerberus Software Ltd [2001]
   EWCA Civ 78; [2001] I.C.R. 376; [2001] I.R.L.R. 160; *Times*, February 20, 2001;
   Independent, February 1, 2001, CA; reversing [2000] I.C.R. 35; [1999] I.R.L.R.
   690, EAT . . . .   *Digested*, 01/**2323**
Cerberus Software Ltd *v.* Rowley (Costs) [2001] EWCA Civ 497; [2001] C.P. Rep. 114,
   CA
Ceredigion CC *v.* Davies (2001) 16 P.A.D. 71, Planning Inspector
Ceredigion CC *v.* National Assembly for Wales [2001] EWHC Admin 694; [2001] 42
   E.G.C.S. 136; [2001] N.P.C. 140, QBD (Admin Ct)
Cero Navigation Corp *v.* Jean Lion & Cie (The Solon) [2000] 1 All E.R. (Comm) 214;
   [2000] 1 Lloyd's Rep. 292; [2000] C.L.C. 593, QBD (Comm Ct) . . . .   *Digested*, 00/**4698**
CERRUTI 1881 Trade Mark (1999) 22(5) I.P.D. 22048, TMR
Cert Plc *v.* George Hammond Plc [1999] 2 All E.R. (Comm) 976; [2000] C.L.C. 387,
   QBD (Comm Ct) . . . .   *Digested*, 00/**5160**
Cesana SpA's European Patent (No.0348653) see CESANA/Shower cubicle (T120/96)
CESANA/Shower cubicle (T120/96); *sub nom* Cesana SpA's European Patent
   (No.0348653) [2001] E.P.O.R. 13; (1998) 21 (10) I.P.D. 21107, EPO (Technical
   Bd App) . . . .   *Digested*, 01/**3915**
Cesky *v.* Czech Republic (33644/96) (2001) 33 E.H.R.R. 8, ECHR . . . .   *Digested*, 01/**3547**
Cevello *v.* Currys Group Plc [2000] B.P.I.R. 976, Ch D . . . .   *Digested*, 01/**3779**
Ceylan *v.* Turkey (23556/94) (2000) 30 E.H.R.R. 73, ECHR . . . .   *Digested*, 00/**3187**
Ceylon *v.* Chandris [1963] 2 Q.B. 327; [1963] 2 W.L.R. 1097; [1963] 2 All E.R. 1;
   [1963] 1 Lloyd's Rep. 214; 107 S.J. 316, QBD (Comm Ct) . . . .   *Digested*, 63/**136**:
                            Approved, 86/107, 87/124: *Considered*, 01/338
CF Leisure Mobility Ltd *v.* Customs and Excise Commissioners [2001] S.T.I. 30, V&DTr
CGI Pension Trust Ltd *v.* Customs and Excise Commissioners [1999] B.V.C. 2152, VAT Tr
CH, Re; *sub nom* Solicitors (Northern Ireland) Order 1976, Re [2000] N.I. 62, QBD
   (NI) . . . .   *Digested*, 00/**5618**
CH (A Child) (Family Proceedings: Court Bundles), Re; *sub nom* H (A Child) (Court
   Bundles: Disallowance of Fees), Re [2000] 2 F.C.R. 193; [2000] Fam. Law 516;
   [2000] Fam. Law 713; (2000) 97 (24) L.S.G. 41; *Times*, June 6, 2000, Fam Div .   *Digested*, 00/**2554**
CH (A Minor) (Care or Interim Care Order), Re [1998] 1 F.L.R. 402; [1998] 2 F.C.R. 347;
   [1998] Fam. Law 132, CA . . . .   *Digested*, 98/**2402**:
                                             Doubted, 01/2562
CH *v.* Austria (27629/95) (2000) 29 E.H.R.R. CD123, ECHR
CH Giles & Co Ltd *v.* Morris [1972] 1 W.L.R. 307; [1972] 1 All E.R. 960; (1971) 116 S.J.
   176, Ch D . . . .   *Digested*, 72/**520**:
                           Applied, 00/1851: *Considered*, 86/1841
Chaaban *v.* Bundesanstalt fur Arbeit (C96/99) see Khalil *v.* Bundesanstalt fur Arbeit
   (C95/99)
Chabba *v.* Turbogame Ltd [2001] EWCA Civ 1073; [2001] N.P.C. 110; (2001) 82 P. &
   C.R. D24, CA
Chadha & Osicom Technologies Inc *v.* Dow Jones & Co Inc [1999] I.L.Pr. 829; [1999]
   E.M.L.R. 724; (1999) 96(23) L.S.G. 34; *Times*, May 18, 1999, CA . . . .   *Digested*, 99/**750**
Chadwick *v.* Ismail-Zade (Unreported, November 20, 1998), CC (Central London) [*Ex
   rel.* James R Candlin, Barrister, 46 Essex Street, London] . . . .   *Digested*, 99/**1551**
Chaffe *v.* Kingsley (2000) 79 P. & C.R. 404; [2000] 1 E.G.L.R. 104; [2000] 10 E.G.
   173; (2000) 79 P. & C.R. D14, CA; affirming (1999) 77 P. & C.R. 281, Ch D   . . .   *Digested*, 00/**4640**
Chaggar *v.* Chaggar [1997] 1 All E.R. 104; [1997] 1 F.L.R. 566; [1997] 2 F.C.R. 486;
   [1997] Fam. Law 324; [1996] E.G.C.S. 116, CA; affirming [1995] 4 All E.R. 795;
   [1996] 1 F.L.R. 450; [1996] Fam. Law 281, Ch D . . . .   *Digested*, 97/**3342**:
                              Distinguished, 00/3958: *Followed*, 98/409
Chahal *v.* United Kingdom (22414/93) (1997) 23 E.H.R.R. 413; 1 B.H.R.C. 405; *Times*,
   November 28, 1996; *Independent*, November 20, 1996, ECHR . . . .   *Digested*, 96/**3130**:
                             Applied, 97/2764: *Followed*, 98/3069
Chailease Finance Corp *v.* Credit Agricole Indosuez see Credit Agricole Indosuez *v.*
   Chailease Finance Corp
Chalegrove Properties Ltd *v.* Customs and Excise Commissioners [2001] B.V.C. 2279;
   [2001] S.T.I. 1065, V&DTr
Chalk *v.* Devizes Reclamation Co Ltd (1999) 96(12) L.S.G. 34; *Times*, April 2, 1999,
   CA . . . .   *Digested*, 99/**4011**
Chalk *v.* Kahn see CIL Realisations Ltd (In Liquidation), Re
Chalmers *v.* Johns [1999] 1 F.L.R. 392; [1999] 2 F.C.R. 110; [1999] Fam. Law 16, CA . .   *Digested*, 99/**2439**
Chamberlain *v.* Boodle & King [1982] 1 W.L.R. 1443; [1982] 3 All E.R. 188; 125 S.J.
   257; *Times*, April 1, 1981, CA; affirming 124 S.J. 186 . . . .   *Digested*, 82/**3080**:
                                               Cited, 00/451
Chamberlain *v.* De La Mare (1983) 4 F.L.R. 434; (1983) 13 Fam. Law 15, CA . . . .   *Digested*, 83/**2447**:
           Applied, 87/2487, 96/543, 01/2595: *Considered*, 95/3482, 96/644:
                                   Followed, 87/2492, 88/2340
Chamberlain *v.* Edrich (Unreported, November 4, 1998), CC (Taunton) [*Ex rel.* Harris
   Fowler Solicitors, Powlett House, High Street, Taunton, Somerset] . . . .   *Digested*, 99/**325**

Chamberlain v. Lindon [1998] 1 W.L.R. 1252; [1998] 2 All E.R. 538; *Times*, April 6,
    1998, QBD . . . .   *Digested*, 98/**926**
Chambers (Deceased), Re see Watson v. National Children's Home
Chambers v. Cardiff Community Housing Association Ltd (Unreported, March 28,
    2000), CC (Cardiff) [*Ex rel.* Julian Reed, Barrister, 9 Park Place, Cardiff] . . . . . .   *Digested*, 00/**1686**
Chambers v. Flynn (Unreported, June 21, 2000), CC (Portsmouth) [*Ex rel.* Paul
    Hepher, Barrister, 2 Gray's Inn Square Chambers, 2 Gray's Inn, London] . . . . . .   *Digested*, 00/**1500**
Chambre Nationale des Commissaires Priseurs v. NART SAS [2001] E.C.C. 24, Trib Gde
    Inst (Paris)
Chambre Nationale des Commissaires-Priseurs v. Fabris [2000] E.C.C. 132, Cass (F)
Chambre Regionale des Commissaires Priseurs d'Anjou v. Tailleur [2001] E.C.C. 27, Cass
    (F)
Champion Stationery Mfg Co Ltd v. Council of the European Union (T147/97); Sun
    Kwong Metal Manufacturer Co Ltd v. Council of the European Union (T147/97);
    US Ring Binder Corp v. Council of the European Union (T147/97) [1998]
    E.C.R. II-4137; [1999] 1 C.M.L.R. 588, CFI (4th Chamber) . . . .   *Digested*, 00/**720**
Chan v. Hackney LBC [1997] I.C.R. 1014, EAT . . . .   *Digested*, 98/**2099**
Chan Kwok-kin v. Mok Kwan-hing [1991] 1 H.K.L.R. 631, CA (HK). . . . .   *Applied*, 98/2140
Chana (Gravinder) v. Chana (Harjit Kaur) [2001] W.T.L.R. 205, Ch D . . . .   *Digested*, 01/**5167**
Chandler v. Brown [2001] C.P. Rep. 103, Ch D . . . .   *Digested*, 01/**510**
Chandler v. Church (1987) 137 N.L.J. 451; *Independent*, April 30, 1987 . . . .   *Digested*, 87/**3059**:
                                                                                                        Applied, 99/3330
Chandler v. Halifax Plc see Halifax Plc v. Chandler
Chandlers Garage Holdings v. Customs and Excise Commissioners [2000] S.T.I. 1168,
    V&DTr
Chandree v. Trinidad and Tobago see Ajodha v. Trinidad and Tobago
Chandris v. Isbrandtsen Moller Co Inc [1951] 1 K.B. 240; [1950] 2 All E.R. 618; (1950)
    84 Ll. L. Rep. 347; 66 T.L.R. (Pt. 2) 358; 94 S.J. 534, CA; reversing in part
    [1950] 1 All E.R. 768; (1949-50) 83 Ll. L. Rep. 385; 66 T.L.R. (Pt. 1) 971; 94
    S.J. 303, KBD . . . .   *Digested*, 47-51/**9921**:
                    Applied, 47-51/123, 80/84: *Approved*, 84/123: *Considered*, 68/3634,
                                         '75/3042, 85/2850, 85/3189, 86/1760, 98/844
Chanel Ltd v. FW Woolworth & Co Ltd [1981] 1 W.L.R. 485; [1981] 1 All E.R. 745;
    [1981] F.S.R. 196; 125 S.J. 202; *Times*, November 14 1980, CA . . . . .   *Digested*, 81/**2126**:
                    Applied, 92/576, 93/587: *Considered*, 93/3211, 93/3235, 94/3675:
                    Distinguished, 87/3031, 97/2721: *Followed*, 97/3904: *Referred to*, 95/4240,
                                                                                                        99/435
Chanel Ste v. Citycom SA [2000] E.T.M.R. 1068, Trib Gde Inst (Paris)
Chanelle Veterinary Ltd v. Pfizer (Ireland) Ltd (t/a Pfizer Animal Health) (No.1) [1998]
    Eu. L.R. 278, HC (Irl)
Chanelle Veterinary Ltd v. Pfizer (Ireland) Ltd (t/a Pfizer Animal Health) (No.2) [1999]
    E.C.C. 340; [1999] Eu. L.R. 723, Sup Ct (Irl); affirming [1998] Eu. L.R. 296, HC
    (Irl) . . . .   *Digested*, 99/**671**
Channel 5 Broadcasting Ltd's Trade Mark Application (No.2122230) (1999) 22(9) I.P.D.
    22088, TMR
Channel Tunnel Group Ltd v. Balfour Beatty Construction Ltd; France Manche SA v.
    Balfour Beatty Construction Ltd [1993] A.C. 334; [1993] 2 W.L.R. 262; [1993]
    1 All E.R. 664; [1993] 1 Lloyd's Rep. 291; 61 B.L.R. 1; 32 Con. L.R. 1; [1993]
    I.L.Pr. 607; (1993) 137 S.J.L.B. 36; [1993] N.P.C. 8; *Times*, January 25, 1993,
    HL; affirming [1992] Q.B. 656; [1992] 2 W.L.R. 741; [1992] 2 All E.R. 609;
    [1992] 2 Lloyd's Rep. 7; 56 B.L.R. 23; (1992) 8 Const. L.J. 150; (1992) 136
    S.J.L.B. 54; [1992] N.P.C. 7; *Times*, January 23, 1992; *Financial Times*, January
    29, 1992, CA. . . . .   *Digested*, 93/**151**:
                    Applied, 94/374, 94/3734, 95/4180, 97/939: *Considered*, 94/478, 94/3673,
                                         95/4184, 97/271, 01/46: *Distinguished*, 99/1639
Channon v. Lindley Johnstone (A Firm) [2000] 2 F.L.R. 734; [2000] Fam. Law 712,
    QBD . . . .   *Digested*, 00/**597**
Chao v. British Traders & Shippers Ltd (No.1) see Kwei Tek Chao (t/a Zung Fu Co) v.
    British Traders & Shippers Ltd (No.1)
Chaplin v. Boys see Boys v. Chaplin
Chaplin Patents Holdings Co Inc v. Group Lotus Plc, *Times*, January 12, 1994;
    Independent, January 10, 1994 (C.S.), CA. . . . .   *Digested*, 94/**3452**:
                                                                                 Considered, 96/4543, 01/3882
Chapman, Re; *sub nom* National Trust for Places of Historic Interest or Natural Beauty
    v. Royal National Institute for the Blind; National Trust for Places of Historic
    Interest or Natural Beauty v. Imperial Cancer Research Fund; National Trust for
    Places of Historic Interest or Natural Beauty v. National Kidney Research Fund
    (1998-99) 1 I.T.E.L.R. 863, Ch D [*Ex rel.* Jeffrey Terry, Barrister, 8 King Street
    Chambers, 8 King Street, Manchester] . . . .   *Digested*, 99/**4647**
Chapman v. Barclays Bank Plc [1997] 6 Bank. L.R. 315; [1998] P.N.L.R. 14, CA . . . . . .   *Digested*, 97/**331**
Chapman v. Barking and Dagenham LBC QBENF 97/0816/1, CA; affirming [1997] 2
    E.G.L.R. 141; [1997] 48 E.G. 154; [1997] N.P.C. 82, QBD. . . . .   *Digested*, 98/**4053**
Chapman v. Bennett (Unreported, April 6, 1998), QBD [*Ex rel.* Morris Goddard &
    Ward Solicitors, 28 St John Street, Devizes, Wiltshire] . . . .   *Digested*, 98/**1567**

Chapman v. Ellesmere; *sub nom* Chapman v. Lord Ellesmere [1932] 2 K.B. 431, CA. . . .   *Considered*, 98/1771:
                                                Followed, 47-51/7, 47-51/1764, 47-51/5689
Chapman v. Lord Ellesmere see Chapman v. Ellesmere
Chapman v. Ross (Unreported, October 22, 1998), CC (Tunbridge Wells) [*Ex rel.* Peter
   Skelton, Barrister, 35 Essex Street, Temple, London] . . . .   *Digested*, 98/**404**
Chapman v. Simon [1994] I.R.L.R. 124, CA . . . .   *Digested*, 94/**1967**:
                      Applied, 98/2183: *Considered*, 01/2320: *Distinguished*, 00/2236
Chapman v. United Kingdom (27238/95) (2001) 33 E.H.R.R. 18; 10 B.H.R.C. 48;
   Times, January 30, 2001, ECHR . . . .   *Digested*, 01/**4744**
Chappel v. Hart [1999] Lloyd's Rep. Med. 223, HC (Aus). . . . .   *Digested*, 99/**3987**
Chappell v. DPP see DPP v. Billington
Chappell v. TDC Motor Factors (Unreported, November 1, 1999), QBD [*Ex rel.* Giles
   Colin, Barrister, Crown Office Row Chambers, Bleinhein House, 120 Church St,
   Brighton] . . . .   *Digested*, 00/**1586**
Chapple v. Charters (Unreported, November 13, 1998), CC (Carlisle) [*Ex rel.* Martin
   Spencer, Barrister, 4 Paper Buildings, Temple, London] . . . .   *Digested*, 99/**551**
Chapple v. Williams [1999] C.P.L.R. 731, CA . . . .   *Digested*, 00/**365**
Charai v. Sheraton Hotels (Heathrow) Ltd [2001] 1 Q.R. 13, CC (Central London) [*Ex*
   rel. Maurice Rifat, Barrister, Verulam Chambers, Verulam Street, London]. . . . . . .   *Digested*, 01/**1675**
Charalambous v. Poseidon Film Distributors Ltd see Christoffer v. Poseidon Film
   Distributors Ltd
Chard Bowling Club v. Customs and Excise Commissioners [1998] B.V.C. 2014; [1997]
   V. & D.R. 375, V&DTr . . . .   *Digested*, 00/**5320**
Charkham (Deceased) v. Inland Revenue Commissioners [2000] R.V.R. 7, Lands Tr . . . .   *Digested*, 00/**5026**
Charles v. Hugh James Jones & Jenkins [2000] 1 W.L.R. 1278; [2000] 1 All E.R. 289;
   [2001] P.I.Q.R. P1; [2000] Lloyd's Rep. P.N. 207; *Times*, December 22, 1999,
   CA . . . .   *Digested*, 00/**1468**
Charles v. Trinidad and Tobago; Carter (Steve) v. Trinidad and Tobago; Carter (Leroy) v.
   Trinidad and Tobago [2000] 1 W.L.R. 384; *Times*, May 27, 1999, PC (Trin) . . . . .   *Digested*, 99/**1037**:
                                                    Considered, 01/1094
Charles Church Development Ltd v. South Northamptonshire DC [1998] E.G.C.S. 87,
   QBD
Charles E Ford Ltd v. AFEC Inc [1986] 2 Lloyd's Rep. 307, QBD (Comm Ct) . . . .   *Digested*, 87/**3331**:
                     Applied, 00/892: *Distinguished*, 96/1247: *Referred to*, 94/4023
Charles M Willie & Co (Shipping) Ltd v. Ocean Laser Shipping Ltd (The Smaro); George
   Roussos Sons SA v. Charles M Willie & Co (Shipping) Ltd [1999] 1 Lloyd's
   Rep. 225; [1999] C.L.C. 301, QBD (Comm Ct) . . . .   *Digested*, 99/**4455**
Charles Robertson (Developments) Ltd v. Advertising Standards Authority see R. v.
   Advertising Standards Authority Ltd Ex p. Charles Robertson (Developments)
   Ltd
Charleston v. News Group Newspapers Ltd [1995] 2 A.C. 65; [1995] 2 W.L.R. 450;
   [1995] 2 All E.R. 313; [1995] E.M.L.R. 129; (1995) 145 N.L.J. 490; (1995) 139
   S.J.L.B. 100; *Times*, March 31, 1995; *Independent*, March 31, 1995, HL;
   affirming [1994] E.M.L.R. 186; *Times*, January 12, 1994; *Independent*, January
   14, 1994; *Guardian*, February 26, 1994, CA . . . .   *Digested*, 95/**3126**:
                                                Followed, 99/1634
Charlesworth v. Relay Roads Ltd (No.1) (1999) 22(6) I.P.D. 22052, Ch D
Charlesworth v. Relay Roads Ltd (No.2); *sub nom* Cavendish v. Relay Roads Ltd
   [2000] 1 W.L.R. 230; [1999] 4 All E.R. 397; [2000] C.P. Rep. 37; [2000]
   C.P.L.R. 109; [2000] R.P.C. 300; (1999) 22(11) I.P.D. 22104; (1999) 96(32)
   L.S.G. 33; (1999) 149 N.L.J. 1254; (1999) 143 S.J.L.B. 222; *Times*, August 31,
   1999; *Independent*, October 18, 1999 (C.S), Ch D . . . .   *Digested*, 99/**502**:
                                       Applied, 01/582: *Followed*, 99/453
Charley v. Secretary of State for the Environment, Transport and the Regions [2001]
   J.P.L. 112 (Note), QBD
Charlson v. Warner (Unreported, December 9, 1999), CC (West London) [*Ex rel.*
   Beachcroft Wansbroughs Solicitors, 100 Fetter Lane, London] . . . .   *Digested*, 00/**4043**
Charlton v. AAH Plc (Unreported, November 25, 1998), CC (Reading) [*Ex rel.* Wayne
   Beglan, Barrister, 2-3 Gray's Inn Square, London] . . . .   *Digested*, 99/**1559**
Charlton v. Fisher; *sub nom* Churchill Insurance v. Charlton [2001] EWCA Civ 112;
   [2001] 3 W.L.R. 1435; [2001] 1 All E.R. (Comm) 769; [2001] R.T.R. 33; [2001]
   Lloyd's Rep. I.R. 387; [2001] P.I.Q.R. P23; (2001) 98(10) L.S.G. 45; *Times*,
   February 21, 2001; *Independent*, March 12, 2001 (C.S); *Daily Telegraph*,
   February 20, 2001, CA . . . .   *Digested*, 01/**3843**
Charlwood Alliance Holdings Ltd v. CR Vending & Electronics Ltd (1999) 78 P. & C.R.
   D44, CA
Charnwood BC v. Cooper (2000) 15 P.A.D. 315, Planning Inspector
Charron v. United States [2000] 1 W.L.R. 1793, PC (Bah) . . . .   *Digested*, 00/**2423**
Chartered Institute of Bankers v. Customs and Excise Commissioners [1998] B.V.C.
   2344, V&DTr . . . .   *Digested*, 99/**5008**
Chartered Society of Physiotherapy v. Customs and Excise Commissioners [1998]
   B.V.C. 2003, V&DTr

Chartered Trust v. Pitcher [1988] R.T.R. 72; (1987) 84 L.S.G. 1147; (1987) 131 S.J. 503,
    CA . . . .   *Digested,* 88/**3166**:
                                                                                      Applied, 98/2500
Chartered Trust Plc v. Bamford (Unreported, April 22, 1999), CC (Gloucester) [*Ex rel.*
    Clarke Willmott & Clarke Solicitors, The Waterfront, Welsh Back, Bristol] . . . .   *Digested,* 99/**2512**:
                                                                                      Cited, 00/2602
Chartered Trust Plc v. Conlay (Unreported, May 22, 1998), CC (Romford) [*Ex rel.*
    Richard Hayes, Barrister, Lamb Chambers, Temple, London, EC4Y 7AS] . . . .   *Digested,* 98/**2516**
Chartered Trust Plc v. Davies (1998) 76 P. & C.R. 396; [1997] 2 E.G.L.R. 83; [1997] 49
    E.G. 135; [1997] N.P.C. 125, CA . . . .   *Digested,* 97/**3302**
Chartered Trust Plc v. Kervill (Unreported, November 10, 1997), CC (Winchester) [*Ex rel.*
    Phillip Rainey, Barrister, 2nd Floor, Francis Taylor Building, Temple, London,
    EC4Y 7BY] . . . .   *Digested,* 98/**2492**
Charterers Mutual Assurance Association Ltd v. British & Foreign [1998] I.L.Pr. 838,
    QBD (Comm Ct) . . . .   *Digested,* 98/**762**
Charterhouse Development (France) Ltd v. Financial Instututions Insurance Brokers Ltd
    see Charterhouse Development (France) Ltd v. Sharp
Charterhouse Development (France) Ltd v. Royal Bank Insurance Services Ltd see
    Charterhouse Development (France) Ltd v. Sharp
Charterhouse Development (France) Ltd v. Sharp; Charterhouse Development (France)
    Ltd v. Financial Instututions Insurance Brokers Ltd; Charterhouse Development
    (France) Ltd v. Royal Bank Insurance Services Ltd [1998] Lloyd's Rep. I.R. 266,
    QBD (Comm Ct) . . . .   *Digested,* 98/**3371**
Chartwell Land Development Ltd v. Secretary of State for the Environment, Transport
    and the Regions [1999] E.G.C.S. 57; [1999] 96(17) L.S.G. 26, QBD
Chase v. Kachia (Unreported, January 8, 2001), CC (Woolwich) [*Ex rel.* Christopher
    Camp, Barrister, Goldsmith Buildings, Temple, London] . . . .   *Digested,* 01/**453**
Chase v. Ram Technical Services Ltd [2000] 2 Lloyd's Rep. 418, QBD (Comm Ct) . . . .   *Digested,* 00/**748**
Chase Manhattan Bank v. HIH Casualty & General Insurance Ltd see HIH Casualty &
    General Insurance Ltd v. Chase Manhattan Bank
Chasemore v. Richards [1843-60] All E.R. Rep. 77; (1859) 7 H.L. Cas. 349, HL . . . . . .   *Applied,* 88/**2446**:
                                     Considered, 99/4366: *Followed,* 69/2408, 70/2444
Chasen Ryder & Co v. Hedges [1993] 08 E.G. 119; [1993] N.P.C. 6, CA . . . .   *Digested,* 93/**67**:
                                                                                      Considered, 01/111
Chassagnou v. France (25088/94, 28331/95, 28443/95) (2000) 29 E.H.R.R. 615; 7
    B.H.R.C. 151, ECHR . . . .   *Digested,* 00/**3204**
Chassot AG's Application (Opposition by Pfizer Inc) [1999] E.T.M.R. 295, OHIM
    (Opposition Div) . . . .   *Digested,* 00/**3784**
Chatterjee v. City and Hackney Community Services NHS Trust (1999) 49 B.M.L.R.
    55, Ch D . . . .   *Digested,* 00/**2715**:
                                     Disapproved, 01/2892: *Not followed,* 01/2928
Chatters v. Burke [1986] 1 W.L.R. 1321; [1986] 3 All E.R. 168; (1986) 8 Cr. App. R.
    (S.) 222; (1986) 150 J.P. 581; [1986] R.T.R. 396; (1986) 83 L.S.G. 3161; (1986)
    136 N.L.J. 777; (1986) 130 S.J. 666, QBD . . . .   *Digested,* 86/**2914**:
                                     Applied, 89/3278, 92/1262: *Considered,* 88/3127, 89/3277, 00/1203
Chatterton v. Terrell; *sub nom* Terrell v. Chatterton [1923] A.C. 578, HL; affirming
    [1922] 2 Ch. 647, CA . . . .   *Applied,* 01/**4195**
Chattey v. Farndale Holdings Inc (1998) 75 P. & C.R. 298; [1997] 1 E.G.L.R. 153;
    [1997] 06 E.G. 152; [1996] N.P.C. 136; *Times,* October 17, 1996, CA; reversing
    [1996] N.P.C. 92, Ch D . . . .   *Digested,* 96/**4945**
Chattopadhyay v. Headmaster of Holloway School [1982] I.C.R. 132; [1981] I.R.L.R.
    487, EAT. . . . .   *Digested,* 82/**1063**:
                         Approved, 00/5526: *Considered,* 87/1352, 88/1293, 88/1296, 89/1448:
                                                                            Referred to, 91/1670, 91/1948
Chatwani v. Bhimji see Bhimji v. Chatwani (No.2)
Chaudhary v. Chaudhary [1985] Fam. 19; [1985] 2 W.L.R. 350; [1984] 3 All E.R.
    1017; [1985] Fam. Law 26; (1984) 81 L.S.G. 2855; (1984) 128 S.J. 736, CA;
    affirming (1983) 13 Fam. Law 177; *Times,* May 18, 1983, Fam Div. . . . .   *Digested,* 85/**1080**:
                                     Distinguished, 93/4834: *Followed,* 00/2505: *Not followed,* 83/1126
Chauhan v. Paul CCRTF 97/0003/C, CA . . . .   *Digested,* 98/**3990**
Chaussures Bally SA v. Belgium (C18/92) [1997] S.T.C. 209; [1993] E.C.R. I-2871;
    Times, July 22, 1993; *Independent,* September 20, 1993 (C.S.), ECJ (6th
    Chamber) . . . .   *Digested,* 93/**4408**:
                                     Applied, 00/5364, 01/5555: *Distinguished,* 96/5891: *Followed,* 01/5614
Chavunduka v. Minister of Home Affairs 8 B.H.R.C. 390, Sup Ct (Zim)
Cheal v. Hale Allen 59 Con. L.R. 106, CA. . . . .   *Digested,* 98/**4028**
Cheapside Land Development Co v. Messels Service Co see United Scientific Holdings
    v. Burnley BC
Chechi v. Bashier [1999] 2 F.L.R. 489; [1999] 2 F.C.R. 241; [1999] Fam. Law 528;
    (1999) 143 S.J.L.B. 113; *Times,* March 25, 1999, CA . . . .   *Digested,* 99/**2438**

Cheese v. Thomas [1994] 1 W.L.R. 129; [1994] 1 All E.R. 35; [1994] 1 F.L.R. 118; [1995] 1 F.C.R. 162; (1994) 26 H.L.R. 427; (1995) 69 P. & C.R. 316; [1994] Fam. Law 80; [1993] E.G.C.S. 149; (1993) 143 N.L.J. 1368; *Times,* August 24, 1993; *Independent,* August 31, 1993, CA . . . . *Digested,* 95/**842**:
Applied, 00/4662: *Considered,* 94/3299, 95/2451
Cheeseman (t/a Well in Tune) v. Customs and Excise Commissioners; *sub nom* Cheesman (t/a Well in Tune) v. Customs and Excise Commissioners [2000] S.T.C. 1119; [2000] B.T.C. 5436; [2001] B.V.C. 39; [2000] S.T.I. 1545, Ch D; reversing [2000] B.V.C. 2218, V&DTr . . . . *Digested,* 01/**5547**
Cheesman v. Church Commissioners [2000] 1 A.C. 19; [1999] 3 W.L.R. 631; (1999) 143 S.J.L.B. 197; *Times,* March 18, 1999, PC (UK) . . . . *Digested,* 99/**1645**
Cheesman (t/a Well in Tune) v. Customs and Excise Commissioners see Cheeseman (t/a Well in Tune) v. Customs and Excise Commissioners
Cheesman v. R Brewer Contracts Ltd [2001] I.R.L.R. 144, EAT. . . . . *Digested,* 01/**2333**
Chelsea Cloisters (In Liquidation), Re (1981) 41 P. & C.R. 98, CA . . . . *Digested,* 82/**1757**:
Applied, 99/3304
CHELSEA MAN Trade Mark [1989] R.P.C. 111, Ch D . . . . *Digested,* 90/**4513**:
Considered, 98/3539
Chelsea Yacht & Boat Co Ltd v. Pope [2000] 1 W.L.R. 1941; [2001] 2 All E.R. 409; (2001) 33 H.L.R. 25; [2000] L. & T.R. 401; [2000] 2 E.G.L.R. 23; [2000] 22 E.G. 139; (2000) 80 P. & C.R. D36; *Times,* June 7, 2000, CA. . . . . *Digested,* 00/**3880**
Cheltenham & Gloucester Building Society v. Norgan [1996] 1 W.L.R. 343; [1996] 1 All E.R. 449; [1996] 2 F.L.R. 257; [1996] 3 F.C.R. 621; (1996) 28 H.L.R. 443; (1996) 72 P. & C.R. 46; [1996] Fam. Law 610; [1995] E.G.C.S. 198; (1996) 93(2) L.S.G. 29; (1995) 145 N.L.J. 1849; (1996) 140 S.J.L.B. 11; [1995] N.P.C. 192; *Times,* December 8, 1995; *Independent,* December 14, 1995, CA . . . . *Digested,* 96/**2913**:
Applied, 96/4979: *Followed,* 98/4357
Cheltenham & Gloucester Building Society v. Obi (1996) 28 H.L.R. 22, CA . . . . *Digested,* 96/**4977**:
Distinguished, 99/4382
Cheltenham and Gloucester College of Higher Education Students Union v. Customs and Excise Commissioners [1999] B.V.C. 2053, V&DTr . . . . *Digested,* 99/**4975**
Cheltenham & Gloucester Plc v. Moore Manton QBENF 98/0078/1, CA . . . . *Digested,* 98/**633**
Cheltenham BC v. JP Homes Ltd (1999) 14 P.A.D. 546, Planning Inspector
Cheltenham Laminating Co v. Polyfibre Ltd [2001] C.P. Rep. 4, CA . . . . *Digested,* 00/**613**
Chemfinder Cambridgesoft Corp's Community Trade Mark Application [2000] E.T.M.R. 250, OHIM (2nd Bd App) . . . . *Digested,* 00/**3725**
Chemidus Wavin Ltd v. Societe pour la Transformation et l'Exploitation des Resines Industrielles SA [1978] 3 C.M.L.R. 514; [1977] F.S.R. 181, CA; affirming [1976] 2 C.M.L.R. 387; [1977] F.S.R. 19, Ch D . . . . *Digested,* 79/**1126**:
Considered, 94/2765, 94/2766: *Followed,* 95/644, 98/718
Chemie Linz AG v. Commisision of the European Communities (T15/89) see Huls AG v. Commission of the European Communities (C199/92 P)
Chemische Afvalstoffen Dusseldorp BV v. Minister van Volkshuisvesting, Ruimtelijke Ordening en Milieubeheer (C203/96) [1999] All E.R. (EC) 25; [1998] E.C.R. I-4075; [1998] 3 C.M.L.R 873; [1999] Env. L.R. 360, ECJ (6th Chamber) . . . . . . *Digested,* 99/**2245**
Chemisphere UK Inc's Community Trade Mark Application [1999] E.T.M.R. 999, OHIM (3rd Bd App) . . . . *Digested,* 00/**3714**
Chen v. Immigration Officer (Heathrow) [1998] I.N.L.R. 642, IAT. . . . . *Digested,* 99/**3212**
Cheng v. Stephenson (Valuation Officer) [1999] R.V.R. 123, Lands Tr. . . . . *Digested,* 99/**4337**
Cheng I Food Co Ltd v. Theotoko Maritime Inc 1995 Folio No.1648, QBD (Comm Ct) . . *Digested,* 00/**615**
Cheng Yuen v. Royal Hong Kong Golf Club [1998] I.C.R. 131, PC (HK) . . . . *Digested,* 98/**2140**
Chequepoint (UK) Ltd v. Customs and Excise Commissioners [2000] S.T.I. 1689, V&DTr
Chequepoint Sarl v. Arden McClelland Maccorp Holdings Ltd see Chequepoint Sarl v. McClelland
Chequepoint Sarl v. McClelland; *sub nom* Chequepoint Sarl v. Arden McClelland Maccorp Holdings Ltd [1996] 1 W.L.R. 1431, HL; affirming [1997] Q.B. 51; [1996] 3 W.L.R. 341; [1997] 2 All E.R. 384; [1997] 1 B.C.L.C. 17; [1996] I.L.Pr. 602; (1996) 140 S.J.L.B. 166; *Times,* June 18, 1996, CA . . . . *Digested,* 96/**731**:
Considered, 99/401
Cherry Tree Investments v. Greater Manchester Rent Assessment Committee see Queensway Housing Association Ltd v. Chiltern, Thames and Eastern Rent Assessment Committee
Cherry Tree Machine Co Ltd v. Dawson see Shell Tankers UK Ltd v. Jeromson
Cherwell DC v. John Mowlem & Co Plc (1998) 13 P.A.D. 456, Planning Inspector
Cherwell DC v. Joyce (1998) 13 P.A.D. 118, Planning Inspector
Cherwell DC v. Transdevelopment International Ltd (1999) 14 P.A.D. 367, Planning Inspector
Cheshire CC v. Hull see Warrington BC v. Hull
Chessington World of Adventures Ltd v. Reed [1998] I.C.R. 97; [1997] I.R.L.R. 556, EAT . . . . *Digested,* 98/**2194**
Chessington World of Adventures Ltd v. Reed (Restricted Reporting Order) see A v. B Ex p. News Group Newspapers Ltd

Chester le Street DC *v.* Cooperative Wholesale Society Ltd see Cooperative Wholesale
    Society Ltd *v.* Chester le Street DC
Chesterfield *v.* Zahid [1989] 29 E.G. 75 . . . .   *Digested,* 89/**54**:
                                                                    Considered, 90/109.10, 93/67, 01/112
Chesterfield Properties Ltd *v.* BHP Petroleum Great Britain Ltd see BHP Petroleum
    Great Britain Ltd *v.* Chesterfield Properties Ltd
Chesterfield Properties Plc *v.* Secretary of State for the Environment, Transport and the
    Regions; Kwik Save Group Plc *v.* Secretary of State for the Environment,
    Transport and the Regions (1998) 76 P. & C.R. 117; [1998] J.P.L. 568; [1997]
    N.P.C. 122; *Times,* August 1, 1997, QBD . . . .   *Digested,* 97/**4042**:
                                                      Followed, 01/4677
Chestnutt *v.* Martin (Unreported, January 12, 1999), CC (Central London) [*Ex rel.* AE
    Wyeth & Co Solicitors, Bridge House, High Street, Dartford, Kent] . . . .   *Digested,* 00/**3061**
Cheston *v.* Letkey (1999) 99(4) Q.R. 4, CC (Kingston on Thames) . . . .   *Digested,* 99/**1493**
Cheung *v.* Minister of Employment and Immigration [1997] I.N.L.R. 80, CA (Can) . . . . .   *Digested,* 98/**3246**
Cheung *v.* Parry (1999) 99(4) Q.R. 7, CC (St Helens) [*Ex rel.* Forster Dean Solicitors,
    Westminster House, 32/34 Widnes Road, Widnes, Cheshire] . . . .   *Digested,* 99/**1587**
Chevassus-Marche *v.* Conseil Regionale de la Reunion (C212/96) [1998] E.C.R. I-743;
    [1998] 2 C.M.L.R. 330, ECJ
Cheverell Estates Ltd *v.* Harris [1998] 1 E.G.L.R. 27; [1998] 02 E.G. 127; [1997] N.P.C.
    126, QBD . . . .   *Digested,* 98/**3620**
Chez Nico (Restaurants), Re [1991] B.C.C. 736; [1992] B.C.L.C. 192 . . . .   *Digested,* 92/**402**:
                                                       Considered, 00/649
Chichester DC *v.* Searle see South Buckinghamshire DC *v.* Porter
Chichester DC *v.* Secretary of State for the Environment, Transport and the Regions
    [1998] E.G.C.S. 94, QBD . . . .   *Digested,* 98/**4233**
Chichester DC *v.* West Sussex Properties Ltd see West Sussex Properties Ltd *v.*
    Chichester DC
Chichester DC *v.* Zwinkels (for Madestein UK Ltd) (1998) 13 P.A.D. 681, Planning
    Inspector
Chiciak, Re (C129/97); *sub nom* Fromagerie Chiciak and Fol, Re (C129/97); Criminal
    Proceedings against Fol (C130/97) [1998] E.C.R. I-3315; [1998] E.T.M.R. 550,
    ECJ
Chief Adjudication Officer *v.* Askew, *Times,* March 19, 1998, CA . . . .   *Digested,* 98/**4547**
Chief Adjudication Officer *v.* Bath [2000] 1 F.L.R. 8; [2000] 1 F.C.R. 419; [2001]
    W.T.L.R. 55; [2000] Fam. Law 91; *Times,* October 28, 1999; *Independent,*
    November 9, 1999, CA. . . . .   *Digested,* 99/**4523**
Chief Adjudication Officer *v.* Creighton [2000] N.I. 222, CA (NI) . . . .   *Digested,* 00/**5689**
Chief Adjudication Officer *v.* Eggleton (Unreported, March 17, 1995), CA . . . .   *Distinguished,*
                                                       00/6687
Chief Adjudication Officer *v.* Faulds [2000] 1 W.L.R. 1035; [2000] 2 All E.R. 961; 2000
    S.C. (H.L.) 116; 2000 S.L.T. 712; 2000 S.C.L.R. 713; [2000] I.C.R. 1297;
    (2000) 97(22) L.S.G. 46; 2000 G.W.D. 17-703; *Times,* May 16, 2000;
    Independent, June 19, 2000, HL; affirming 1998 S.L.T. 1203; 1998 S.C.L.R. 719;
    1998 G.W.D. 22-1145, Ex Div . . . .   *Digested,* 00/**4846**:
                                                       Considered, 00/4845
Chief Adjudication Officer *v.* Gibbon see Chief Adjudication Officer *v.* Quinn
Chief Adjudication Officer *v.* Graham see Graham *v.* Secretary of State for Social
    Security (C92/94)
Chief Adjudication Officer *v.* Maguire [1999] 1 W.L.R. 1778; [1999] 2 All E.R. 859;
    (1999) 96(21) L.S.G. 40; (1999) 143 S.J.L.B. 122; *Times,* March 29, 1999, CA. .   *Digested,* 99/**4582**
Chief Adjudication Officer *v.* Quinn; Chief Adjudication Officer *v.* Gibbon [1996] 1
    W.L.R. 1184; [1996] 4 All E.R. 72; (1997-98) 1 C.C.L. Rep. 529; (1996) 93(37)
    L.S.G. 27; (1996) 146 N.L.J. 1150; (1996) 140 S.J.L.B. 207; *Times,* August 8,
    1996, HL. . . . .   *Digested,* 96/**5473**
Chief Adjudication Officer *v.* Rhodes [1999] I.C.R. 178; [1999] I.R.L.R. 103; (1998)
    95(36) L.S.G. 32; (1998) 142 S.J.L.B. 228; *Times,* August 25, 1998, CA . . . . . .   *Digested,* 98/**4542**
Chief Adjudication Officer *v.* Stafford see Stafford *v.* Chief Adjudication Officer
Chief Adjudication Officer *v.* Uprichard [1999] N.I. 331, CA (NI) . . . .   *Digested,* 00/**5733**
Chief Adjudication Officer *v.* Webber [1998] 1 W.L.R. 625; [1997] 4 All E.R. 274;
    [1997] E.L.R. 404; (1997) 94(28) L.S.G. 25; (1997) 147 N.L.J. 1274; (1997) 141
    S.J.L.B. 195; *Times,* July 11, 1997; *Independent,* July 4, 1997, CA . . . .   *Digested,* 97/**4664**:
                                                       Distinguished, 99/4578
Chief Adjudication Officer *v.* Wolke see Secretary of State for Social Security *v.* Remilien
Chief Adjudication Officer *v.* Woods SSTRF 96/1668/B, CA.   *Digested,* 98/**4511**
Chief Commissioner of Stamp Duties *v.* ISPT Pty Ltd (1999-2000) 2 I.T.E.L.R. 1, Sup Ct
    (NSW)
Chief Constable of Derbyshire *v.* Goodman; *sub nom* Goodman *v.* Chief Constable of
    Derbyshire; Chief Constable of Derbyshire *v.* Newton; CO 707-98, QBD;
    reversing (Unreported, January 16, 1998), Crown Ct (Derby) [*Ex rel.* Hill
    Dickinson Solicitors, 34 Cuppin Street, Chester] . . . .   *Digested,* 98/**945**:
                                                       Considered, 00/395
Chief Constable of Derbyshire *v.* Newton see Chief Constable of Derbyshire *v.*
    Goodman

Chief Constable of Greater Manchester v. Hope [1999] I.C.R. 338, EAT . . . .   *Digested*, 99/**2098**
Chief Constable of Gwent v. Dash [1986] R.T.R. 41; [1985] Crim. L.R. 674, QBD. . . . . .   *Digested*, 86/**2969**:
                                       Applied, 92/3789: *Followed*, 99/5870
Chief Constable of Humberside v. McQuade see McQuade v. Chief Constable of
    Humberside
Chief Constable of Kent v. Rixon see Rixon v. Chief Constable of Kent
Chief Constable of Lincolnshire v. Stubbs [1999] I.C.R. 547; [1999] I.R.L.R. 81, EAT. . .   *Digested*, 00/**2211**
Chief Constable of Merseyside v. Porter see Webb v. Chief Constable of Merseyside
Chief Constable of North Wales v. Evans see R. v. Chief Constable of North Wales Ex p.
    Evans
Chief Constable of North Yorkshire v. Audsley [2000] Lloyd's Rep. P.N. 675, QBD. . . . .   *Digested*, 00/**470**
Chief Constable of North Yorkshire v. Saddington see DPP v. Saddington
Chief Constable of Thames Valley v. Kellaway [2000] I.R.L.R. 170, EAT . . . .   *Digested*, 00/**2147**
Chief Constable of the Royal Ulster Constabulary v. A (Sergeant) [2000] N.I. 261, CA
    (NI) . . . .   *Digested*, 00/**5527**
Chief Constable of West Yorkshire v. A (No.1) [2001] I.C.R. 128; [2000] I.R.L.R. 465,
    EAT . . . .   *Digested*, 00/**2154**
Chief Constable of West Yorkshire v. A (No.2); Chief Constable of West Yorkshire v.
    Secretary of State for Education and Employment *Daily Telegraph*, October 9,
    2001, EAT
Chief Constable of West Yorkshire v. Khan; *sub nom* Khan v. Chief Constable of West
    Yorkshire [2001] UKHL 48; [2001] 1 W.L.R. 1947; [2001] 4 All E.R. 834; [2001]
    I.C.R. 1065; [2001] I.R.L.R. 830; [2001] Emp. L.R. 1399; (2001) 98(42) L.S.G.
    37; (2001) 145 S.J.L.B. 230; *Times*, October 16, 2001; *Daily Telegraph*, October
    16, 2001, HL; reversing [2000] I.C.R. 1169; [2000] I.R.L.R. 324; (2000) 150
    N.L.J. 308; *Times*, March 15, 2000; *Independent*, March 3, 2000, CA . . . .   *Digested*, 01/**2302**:
                                         Cited, 00/2186
Chief Constable of West Yorkshire v. S see S v. S (Chief Constable of West Yorkshire
    Intervening)
Chief Constable of West Yorkshire v. Schofield see Schofield v. Chief Constable of West
    Yorkshire
Chief Constable of West Yorkshire v. Secretary of State for Education and Employment
    see Chief Constable of West Yorkshire v. A (No.2)
Chief Constable of West Yorkshire v. Vento (No.1) [2001] I.R.L.R. 124, EAT . . . .   *Digested*, 01/**2320**
Chiemgauer Membran und Zeltbau GmbH (formerly Koch Hightex GmbH) v. New
    Millennium Experience Co Ltd (formerly Millennium Central Ltd) (No.2); *sub*
    nom Chiemgauer Membran und Zeltbau GmbH (formerly Koch Hightex GmbH)
    v. New Millennium Experience Co Ltd (formerly Millennium Central Ltd) (2001)
    98(5) L.S.G. 36; *Times*, January 16, 2001, Ch D . . . .   *Digested*, 01/**948**
Chiemgauer Membran und Zeltbau GmbH (formerly Koch Hightex GmbH) v. New
    Millennium Experience Co Ltd (formerly Millennium Central Ltd) see
    Chiemgauer Membran und Zeltbau GmbH (formerly Koch Hightex GmbH) v.
    New Millennium Experience Co Ltd (formerly Millennium Central Ltd) (No.2)
Chilean Nitrate Sales Corp v. Marine Transportation Co Ltd (The Hermosa); Marine
    Transportation Co Ltd v. Pansuiza Compania de Navegacion SA; Nitrate Corp of
    Chile Ltd v. Pansuiza Compania de Navegacion SA [1982] 1 Lloyd's Rep. 570;
    Times, March 4, 1982, CA; affirming [1980] 1 Lloyd's Rep. 638, QBD (Comm
    Ct) . . . .   *Digested*, 82/**2877**:
                                         Applied, 00/870
Chiltern DC v. Hodgetts see Hodgetts v. Chiltern DC
Chiltern DC v. Stewart-Liberty (2001) 16 P.A.D. 30, Planning Inspector
Chiltern DC v. Williams (2000) 15 P.A.D. 758, Planning Inspector
Chilton v. Surrey CC [1999] C.P.L.R. 525, CA . . . .   *Digested*, 00/**582**
China Agribusiness Development Corp v. Balli Trading [1998] 2 Lloyd's Rep. 76; [1997]
    C.L.C. 1437, QBD (Comm Ct) . . . .   *Digested*, 97/**269**
China and South Seas Bank Ltd v. Tan [1990] 1 A.C. 536; [1990] 2 W.L.R. 56; [1989] 3
    All E.R. 839; [1990] 1 Lloyd's Rep. 113; (1989) 86(46) L.S.G. 37; (1989) 139
    N.L.J. 1669; (1990) 134 S.J. 165; *Times*, November 14, 1989; *Independent*,
    January 2, 1990; *Daily Telegraph*, January 29, 1990, PC (HK) . . . .   *Digested*, 90/**2440**:
                       Applied, 90/3213, 93/2263: *Considered*, 92/3154, 93/2887, 01/3750:
                                      Followed, 95/3600, 96/4988
China Offshore Oil (Singapore) International Pte Ltd v. Giant Shipping Ltd [2001] 1 All
    E.R. (Comm) 429; [2001] 1 Lloyd's Rep. 697, QBD (Comm Ct). . . . .   *Digested*, 01/**4908**
China Shipbuilding Corp v. Nippon Yusen Kabukishi Kaisha (The Seta Maru, The Saikyo
    and The Suma) [2000] 1 Lloyd's Rep. 367; [2000] C.L.C. 566, QBD (Comm
    Ct) . . . .   *Digested*, 00/**4738**
China Shipping Development Co Ltd v. State Bank of Saurashtra [2001] 2 Lloyd's Rep.
    691, QBD (Comm Ct)
Chinamasa, Re 9 B.H.R.C. 519, Sup Ct (Zim). . . . .   *Digested*, 01/**834**
Chipperfield v. Streatfield (Unreported, July 29, 1997), CA. . . . .   *Applied*, 98/**494**:
                                         Considered, 99/418
Chipping Sodbury Town Trust v. Customs and Excise Commissioners [2000] B.V.C.
    2386; [2000] S.T.I. 1271, V&DTr
Chiron Corp v. Evans Medical Supplies Ltd see Evans Medical Ltd's Patent

Chiron Corp *v.* Murex Diagnostics Ltd (No.8) [1995] All E.R. (E.C.) 88; [1995] F.S.R. 309; *Times*, October 14, 1994; *Independent*, October 24, 1994 (C.S.), CA . . . . . .   *Digested*, 95/**4201**: *Referred to*, 01/4030

Chiron Corp *v.* Organon Teknika Ltd (Application for Expedited Appeal) see Unilever Plc *v.* Chefaro Proprietaries Ltd (Application for Expedited Appeal)

Chiron Corp *v.* OrganonTeknika Ltd (No.11) [1995] F.S.R. 589, CA . . . .   *Digested*, 95/**3751**: *Cited*, 99/3466

Chiron Corp *v.* Organon Teknika Ltd (No.7) [1994] F.S.R. 458; *Independent*, April 11, 1994 (C.S.), Pat Ct . . . .   *Digested*, 95/**3750**: *Applied*, 96/4568: *Considered*, 98/3460

Chiron Corp *v.* Sorin Biomedica SpA [2001] E.N.P.R. 6, Trib (Milano)

Chishty Coveney & Co *v.* Raja see Arbuthnot Latham Bank Ltd *v.* Trafalgar Holdings Ltd

Chissell *v.* Poole Hospital NHS Trust [1998] Lloyd's Rep. Med. 357, CC (Bournemouth) . . . .   *Digested*, 99/**3985**

Chiswell Shipping and Liberian JaguarTransports Inc *v.* National IranianTankers Co (The World Symphony and The World Renown) [1992] 2 Lloyd's Rep. 115, CA; affirming [1991] 2 Lloyd's Rep. 251, QBD (Comm Ct) . . . .   *Digested*, 92/**3941**: *Considered*, 01/4910

Chiswick PierTrust *v.* Hardwidge [1999] N.P.C. 69, Ch D

Chittock (Deceased), Re see Chittock *v.* Stevens

Chittock *v.* Stevens; *sub nom* Chittock (Deceased), Re [2000] W.T.L.R. 643; (2000) 97(16) L.S.G. 42; (2000) 144 S.J.L.B. 166; *Times*, April 5, 2000, Ch D . . . .   *Digested*, 00/**4909**

Chitty Wholesale Ltd *v.* Ministry of Agriculture, Fisheries and Food see Mayne *v.* Ministry of Agriculture, Fisheries and Food

Cho Yang Shipping Co Ltd *v.* Commission of the European Communities (Order I) (T191/98) (No.1) [1999] E.C.R. II-3909; [2001] 4 C.M.L.R. 30, CFI . . . .   *Digested*, 01/**2450**

Cho Yang Shipping Co Ltd *v.* Commission of the European Communities (Order I) (T191/98) (No.2) [2000] E.C.R. II-2551; [2001] 4 C.M.L.R. 31, CFI. . . . .   *Digested*, 01/**2451**

Cho Yang Shipping Co Ltd *v.* Commission of the European Communities (Order II) (C361/00 P(R)) [2001] 4 C.M.L.R. 32, ECJ . . . .   *Digested*, 01/**2453**

Choay SA *v.* Boehringer Ingelheim International GmbH [2001] E.T.M.R. 64, OHIM (1st Bd App) . . . .   *Digested*, 01/**3987**

Chocosuisse Union des Fabricants Suisses de Chocolat *v.* Cadbury Ltd [1999] E.T.M.R. 1020; [1999] R.P.C. 826; (1999) 22(8) I.P.D. 22079; *Times*, March 15, 1999, CA; affirming [1998] E.T.M.R. 205; [1998] R.P.C. 117; (1998) 21 (1) I.P.D. 21007; *Times*, November 25, 1997, Ch D . . . .   *Digested*, 99/**3562**

Chohan *v.* Times Newspapers Ltd (Limitation Periods) see Times Newspapers Ltd *v.* Chohan (Limitation Periods)

Chohan Clothing Co (Manchester) Ltd *v.* Fox Brooks Marshall, *Times*, December 9, 1997, CA. . . . .   *Digested*, 98/**589**

Chong Yeo & Partners *v.* Guan Ming Hardware and Engineering Pte Ltd Unreported, CA (Sing) . . . .   *Considered*, 00/4009

Choraria *v.* Sethia [1998] C.L.C. 625; (1998) 95(7) L.S.G. 31; (1998) 142 S.J.L.B. 53; *Times*, January 29, 1998, CA . . . .   *Digested*, 98/**611**: *Applied*, 99/555: *Considered*, 00/344: *Followed*, 99/548

Chorherr *v.* Austria (A/266-B) (1994) 17 E.H.R.R. 358, ECHR . . . .   *Digested*, 94/**2418**: *Considered*, 96/3123, 98/3090

Chorion Plc *v.* Lane (1999) 22(7) I.P.D. 22070; *Times*, April 7, 1999, Ch D . . . .   *Digested*, 99/**2062**

Choudhury *v.* Inland Revenue Commissioners [2000] B.C.C. 765; [2000] B.P.I.R. 246, CA . . . .   *Digested*, 00/**3455**

Chowdhury *v.* Entry Clearance Officer (Dhaka) (Unreported, December 30, 1994), IAT .   *Considered*, 01/3622

Christ Church, Alsager, Re [1999] Fam. 142; [1998] 3 W.L.R. 1394; [1999] 1 All E.R. 117; *Times*, October 22, 1998, Chancery Ct of York. . . . .   *Digested*, 98/**1786**: *Applied*, 01/1848, 01/3481: *Considered*, 00/1770

Christ Church, Waltham Cross, Re [2001] 3 W.L.R. 1481, Cons Ct (St Albans)

Christchurch BC *v.* Billington see Christchurch BC *v.* Secretary of State for the Environment, Transport and the Regions

Christchurch BC *v.* Secretary of State for the Environment, Transport and the Regions [2001] J.P.L. 606, QBD

Christchurch BC *v.* Secretary of State for the Environment, Transport and the Regions; Christchurch BC *v.* Billington [2001] J.P.L. 1265, QBD (Admin Ct)

Christensen *v.* Scott [1996] 1 N.Z.L.R. 273 . . . .   *Distinguished*, 99/4046

Christer (CICB: Quantum: 1998), Re (Unreported, March 12, 1998), CICB (Durham) [*Ex rel.* Nicholas Peacock, Barrister, Westgate Chambers, 67a Westgate Road, Newcastle uponTyne, NE1 1SG] . . . .   *Digested*, 98/**1554**

Christian Brothers of Ireland in Canada (In Liquidation) *v.* Rowland see Rowland *v.* Vancouver College Ltd

Christian Dior Couture *v.* FashionTV Paris [2001] E.T.M.R. 12, Trib Gde Inst (F)

Christian Dior Couture SA *v.* Liage International Inc [2000] E.T.M.R. 773, Arbitration . . .   *Digested*, 01/**3874**

Christian Education South Africa *v.* Minister of Education 9 B.H.R.C. 53, Const Ct (SA)   *Digested*, 01/**3482**

Christian Lawyers Association of South Africa *v.* Minister of Health (1999) 50 B.M.L.R. 241, Provincial Div (SA) . . . .   *Digested*, 00/**3161**

Christiansborg, The (1885) L.R. 10 P.D. 141, CA . . . . *Applied*, 47-51/7898.a,
55/2200, 60/2579, 00/4712: *Distinguished*, 68/3618, 69/2922:
Followed, 67/3239
Christie v. Hudson (Valuation Officer) [2000] R.V.R. 313, Lands Tr. . . . . *Digested*, 01/**4826**
Christie v. Leachinsky; *sub nom* Leachinsky v. Christie [1947] A.C. 573; [1947] 1 All
E.R. 567; 63 T.L.R. 231; (1947) 111 J.P. 224; [1947] L.J.R. 757; 176 L.T. 443, HL;
affirming [1946] K.B. 124, CA . . . . *Digested*, 47-51/**6152**:
Applied, 70/2512, 71/10199, 75/2960, 75/2964, 80/2304, 82/2715, 86/638:
Considered, 67/3994, 68/3982, 76/402, 80/2312, 81/2328, 98/4286:
Distinguished, 47-51/6153, 47-51/6154, 47-51/6159: *Followed*, 80/2074,
81/2090: *Referred to*, 93/4889
Christie v. Wilson; *sub nom* Wilson v. Christie [1998] 1 W.L.R. 1694; [1999] 1 All E.R.
545; [1998] P.N.L.R. 748; (1998) 95(30) L.S.G. 25; (1998) 142 S.J.L.B. 205;
Times, July 6, 1998; *Independent*, June 22, 1998 (C.S.), CA. . . . . *Digested*, 98/**3722**
Christien (t/a Rose's Lace Boutique) v. Parcles BVBA [2000] E.T.M.R. 1, CA (Bru)
Christmas v. Hampshire CC (Breach of Duty and Damage) [1998] E.L.R. 1, QBD . . . . . . *Digested*, 98/**3943**:
Previous proceedings, 94/1878, 95/1927, 95/3452
Christmas v. Hampshire CC (Duty of Care) see E (A Minor) v. Dorset CC
Christmas v. Hampshire CC (Duty of Care) see X (Minors) v. Bedfordshire CC
Christoffer v. Poseidon Film Distributors Ltd; Poseidon Film Distributors Ltd v. Paik;
Poseidon Film Distributors Ltd v. Christoffer; Charalambous v. Poseidon Film
Distributors Ltd [2000] E.C.D.R. 487, Ch D . . . . *Digested*, 01/**3853**
Christofi v. Barclays Bank Plc [2000] 1 W.L.R. 937; [1999] 4 All E.R. 437; [1999] 2
All E.R. (Comm) 417; [1999] Lloyd's Rep. Bank. 469; [2000] 1 F.L.R. 163;
[1999] B.P.I.R. 855; [2000] Fam. Law 161; (1999) 96(29) L.S.G. 29; *Times*, July
1, 1999, CA; affirming [1998] 1 W.L.R. 1245; [1998] 2 All E.R. 484; [1998]
Lloyd's Rep. Bank. 208; [1998] B.P.I.R. 452; *Times*, February 3, 1998, Ch D   . . . *Digested*, 99/**273**
Christopher Moran Holdings Ltd v. Bairstow see Park Air Services Plc, Re
Christopher Moran Holdings Ltd v. Carden & Godfrey (A Firm) 73 Con. L.R. 28, QBD
(T&CC) . . . . *Digested*, 01/**4510**
Christopher Tasker's Design Right References, Re [2001] R.P.C. 3, PO . . . . *Digested*, 01/**3863**
Chua v. Minister of National Revenue 2 I.T.L. Rep. 914, Fed Ct (Can)
Chua v. Minister of National Revenue (No.2) 3 I.T.L. Rep. 271, Fed Ct (Can)
Chubb Insurance Co of Europe SA v. Customs and Excise Commissioners Unreported,
V&DTr. . . . . *Not followed*, 00/5038
Chung Ja Huh v. R. 2 I.T.L. Rep. 902, Tax Ct (Can)
Chung Tak Lam v. Brennan (t/a Namesakes of Torbay); *sub nom* Lam v. Torbay BC; R. v.
Lam [1998] E.H.L.R. 111; [1997] P.I.Q.R. P488; [1997] 3 P.L.R. 22; [1998]
P.L.C.R. 30; [1997] N.P.C. 135, CA; affirming (Unreported, January 24, 1996)
[*Ex rel.* Veitch Penny, Solicitors] . . . . *Digested*, 97/**4087**:
Considered, 01/4495
Church v. West Lancashire NHS Trust (No.1) [1998] I.C.R. 423; [1998] I.R.L.R. 4, EAT. . *Digested*, 98/**2186**:
Applied, 99/2107
Church v. West Lancashire NHS Trust (No.2) [1999] I.C.R. 586; [1998] I.R.L.R. 492,
EAT . . . . *Digested*, 98/**2237**
Church Commissioners for England v. Baines see Wellcome Trust Ltd v. Hamad
Church Commissioners for England v. Ibrahim [1997] 1 E.G.L.R. 13; [1997] 03 E.G. 136;
[1996] E.G.C.S. 25, CA . . . . *Digested*, 97/**3248**:
Distinguished, 96/3714: *Followed*, 98/431
Church Commissioners for England v. Mummery (Valuation Officer) [1998] 3 E.G.L.R.
209; [1998] R.A. 327, Lands Tr. . . . . *Digested*, 99/**4319**
Church Commissioners for England v. Ve Ri Best Manufacturing Co Ltd [1957] 1 Q.B.
238; [1956] 3 W.L.R. 990; [1956] 3 All E.R. 777; 100 S.J. 875, QBD . . . . *Digested*, 56/**4745**:
Distinguished, 00/3911
Church Norton Churchyard, Re [1989] Fam. 37; [1989] 3 W.L.R. 272; (1989) 133 S.J. 917,
Cons Ct (Chichester). . . . . *Digested*, 89/**1301**:
Considered, 94/1786, 95/1863, 00/1770
Church of Jesus Christ of Latter Day Saints (Great Britain) v. West Yorkshire Fire and Civil
Defence Authority see Capital and Counties Plc v. Hampshire CC
Church of Spiritual Technology v. Dataweb [2000] E.C.D.R. 83, RB (Den Haag)
Church Schools Foundation Ltd v. Customs and Excise Commissioners; *sub nom*
Customs and Excise Commissioners v. Church Schools Foundation Ltd ;
Commissioners of Customs and Excise v. Church Schools Foundation Ltd
[2001] EWCA Civ 1745; [2001] S.T.C. 1661; [2001] S.T.I. 1519, CA; reversing
[2000] S.T.C. 651; [2000] B.T.C. 5326; [2000] B.V.C. 353; [2000] S.T.I. 1000;
[2000] E.G.C.S. 93; [2000] N.P.C. 81, Ch D [2000] B.V.C. 2213; [2000] S.T.I.
759, V&DTr . . . . *Digested*, 00/**5347**
Churchill v. A Yeates & Sons Ltd [1983] I.C.R. 380; [1983] I.R.L.R. 187, EAT. . . . . *Digested*, 83/**1310**:
Applied, 88/1355: *Considered*, 94/2032, 96/2666, 99/2146
Churchill Insurance v. Charlton see Charlton v. Fisher

Cia de Seguros Imperio v. Heath (REBX) Ltd (formerly CE Heath & Co (America) Ltd); *sub nom* Companhia de Seguros Imperio v. Heath (REBX) Ltd [2001] 1 W.L.R. 112; [2000] 2 All E.R. (Comm) 787; [2000] C.L.C. 1543; [2001] Lloyd's Rep. I.R. 109; [2000] Lloyd's Rep. P.N. 795; (2000-01) 3 I.T.E.L.R. 134; *Times,* September 26, 2000; *Independent,* October 23, 2000 (C.S), CA; affirming [1999] 1 All E.R. (Comm) 750; [1999] C.L.C. 997; [1999] Lloyd's Rep. I.R. 571; [1999] Lloyd's Rep. P.N. 571; *Independent,* May 3, 1999 (C.S.), QBD (Comm Ct) . . . . *Digested,* 00/**513**
CIA Security International SA v. Signalson SA (C194/94) [1996] All E.R. (EC) 557; [1996] E.C.R. I-2201; [1996] 2 C.M.L.R. 781, ECJ . . . . *Digested,* 96/**1065**:
Cited, 00/4458: *Distinguished,* 98/866
CIBA CORNING/Acridinium esters (T615/95) [1999] E.P.O.R. 546, EPO (Technical Bd App). . . . . *Digested,* 00/**3600**
Ciba Vision UK Ltd v. Coopervision Ltd see Wesley Jessen Corp v. Coopervision Ltd
CIBC Mortgages Plc v. Pitt [1994] 1 A.C. 200; [1993] 3 W.L.R. 802; [1993] 4 All E.R. 433; [1994] 1 F.L.R. 17; [1994] 1 F.C.R. 374; (1994) 26 H.L.R. 90; (1994) 13 Tr. L.R. 180; [1994] C.C.L.R. 68; [1993] Fam. Law 79; [1993] E.G.C.S. 174; (1993) 143 N.L.J. 1514; (1993) 137 S.J.L.B. 240; [1993] N.P.C. 136; *Times,* October 22, 1993; *Independent,* October 22, 1993, HL; affirming (1993) 25 H.L.R. 439; (1993) 66 P. & C.R. 179; [1993] E.G.C.S. 66; [1993] N.P.C. 61; *Times,* April 7, 1993, CA . . . . *Digested,* 94/**3293**:
Applied, 94/3299, 95/2451, 96/419, 97/4241: *Considered,* 95/2449, 95/4659, 96/4970, 97/4232, 00/4662: *Referred to,* 94/5914, 95/2448, 96/4971, 96/4973
Cibo Participations SA v. Directeur Regional des Impots du Nord Pas de Calais (C16/ 00) [2001] E.C.R. I-6663; [2001] S.T.I. 1377, ECJ (1st Chamber)
Cidrerie Ruwet SA v. Cidre Stassen SA (C3/99) [2000] E.C.R. I-8749; [2000] 3 C.M.L.R. 1390, ECJ (6th Chamber) . . . . *Digested,* 01/**2489**
Cie Maritime Belge Transports SA v. Commission of the European Communities (C395/ 96) see Compagnie Maritime Belge Transports SA v. Commission of the European Communities (C395/96)
Cigna Life Insurance Co of Europe SA NV v. Intercaser SA de Seguros y Reaseguros [2001] C.L.C. 1356; [2001] Lloyd's Rep. I.R. 821, QBD (Comm Ct) . . . . *Digested,* 01/**3836**
Cil v. First National Bank of Maryland (The Turiddu) see Cil v. Owners of the Turiddu (The Turiddu)
Cil v. Owners of the Turiddu (The Turiddu); *sub nom* Cil v. First National Bank of Maryland (The Turiddu) [1999] 2 All E.R. (Comm) 161; [1999] 2 Lloyd's Rep. 401; [1999] C.L.C. 1737; [2000] I.C.R. 354; *Times,* July 8, 1999, CA; affirming [1998] 2 Lloyd's Rep. 278; [1998] C.L.C. 1043, QBD (Adm Ct) . . . . *Digested,* 99/**4459**
CIL Realisations Ltd (In Liquidation), Re; *sub nom* Chalk v. Kahn [2001] B.C.C. 300; [2000] 2 B.C.L.C. 361, Ch D . . . . *Digested,* 00/**3483**
Ciliz v. Netherlands (29192/95) [2000] 2 F.L.R. 469; [2000] Fam. Law 799, ECHR . . . *Digested,* 01/**3553**
Cimenteries CBR SA v. Commission of the European Communities (T25/95) [2000] E.C.R. II-491; [2000] 5 C.M.L.R. 204, CFI (4th Chamber) . . . . *Digested,* 00/**710**
Cinpres Ltd, Re see Ladney and Hendry's International Application, Re
Cinque v. O'Donegan (Unreported, January 28, 1998), CC (Kingston on Thames) [*Ex rel.* LS Hughes-Preston, Amery-Parkes Solicitors, 12a London Street, Basingstoke]. . . . . *Digested,* 98/**1701**
Ciola v. Land Vorarlberg (C224/97) [1999] E.C.R. I-2517; [1999] 2 C.M.L.R. 1220, ECJ . . . . *Digested,* 99/**2252**
Cipeke - Comercio Industria de Papel Lda v. Commission of the European Communities (T84/96) [1997] E.C.R. II-2081, CFI . . . . *Considered,* 01/3886
Ciraklar v. Turkey (19061/92) (2001) 32 E.H.R.R. 23; [1998] H.R.C.D. 955, ECHR . . . . . *Followed,* 00/3193, 01/3477
Circle 33 v. Watt (Unreported, January 22, 1999), CC (Edmonton) [*Ex rel.* Dominic Preston, Barrister, and Marsons Solicitors, Arden Chambers, 27 John Street, London] . . . . *Digested,* 99/**3041**
Circuit Systems Ltd v. Zuken Redac (UK) Ltd [2001] EWCA Civ 481; [2001] B.L.R. 253, CA . . . . *Digested,* 01/**671**
Circuit Systems Ltd (In Liquidation) v. Zuken-Redac (UK) Ltd see Norglen Ltd (In Liquidation) v. Reeds Rains Prudential Ltd
Cirillo (A Bankrupt) Ex p. Official Trustee in Bankruptcy, Re see Bankrupt Estate of Cirillo Ex p. Official Trustee in Bankruptcy (No.1), Re
Citadel Management Inc v. Equal Ltd; *sub nom* Citadel Management Inc v. Thompson [1999] 1 F.L.R. 21; [1998] Fam. Law 738; (1998) 95(36) L.S.G. 32; (1998) 142 S.J.L.B. 253; *Times,* September 25, 1998, CA . . . . *Digested,* 98/**3727**
Citadel Management Inc v. Thompson see Citadel Management Inc v. Equal Ltd
Citibank International Plc v. Kessler [1999] Lloyd's Rep. Bank. 123; [1999] 2 C.M.L.R. 603; [1999] Eu. L.R. 733; [1999] E.G.C.S. 40; (1999) 96(15) L.S.G. 29; [1999] N.P.C. 32; (1999) 78 P. & C.R. D7; *Times,* March 24, 1999, CA . . . . *Digested,* 99/**4380**
Citibank International Plc v. Schleider, *Times,* March 26, 1999, Ch D . . . . *Digested,* 99/**2505**
Citibank Investments Ltd v. Griffin (Inspector of Taxes) see Griffin (Inspector of Taxes) v. Citibank Investments Ltd

Citibank NA v. Excess Insurance Co Ltd (t/a ITT London and Edinburgh) [1999] C.L.C.
120, QBD . . . .   *Digested*, 99/**3422**:
                                                                                                    Applied, 01/474
Citoma Trading Ltd v. Brazil see JH Rayner (Mincing Lane) Ltd v. Cafenorte SA
Importadora
Citro (Carmine) (A Bankrupt), Re see Citro (Domenico) (A Bankrupt), Re
Citro (Domenico) (A Bankrupt), Re; Citro (Carmine) (A Bankrupt), Re [1991] Ch. 142;
[1990] 3 W.L.R. 880; [1990] 3 All E.R. 952; [1991] 1 F.L.R. 71; (1990) 154
N.L.J. 1073; (1990) 134 S.J. 806, CA . . . .   *Digested*, 91/**261**:
                            Applied, 01/3723: *Considered*, 92/2131, 98/3291: *Distinguished*, 93/1846,
                                                        94/3303, 95/2214: *Followed*, 95/2365
Citrone v. Customs and Excise Commissioners [2000] S.T.I. 1381, V&DTr
City Alliance Ltd v. Oxford Forecasting Services Ltd [2001] 1 All E.R. (Comm) 233, CA   *Digested*, 01/**942**
City and Westminster Properties (1934) Ltd v. Mudd [1959] Ch. 129; [1958] 3 W.L.R.
312; [1958] 2 All E.R. 733; 102 S.J. 582, Ch D . . . .   *Digested*, 58/**1788**:
                                                                                                    Applied, 00/2587
City Axis Ltd v. Jackson 64 Con. L.R. 84, QBD (OR) . . . .   *Digested*, 99/**784**
City Logistics Ltd v. Northamptonshire County Fire Officer; *sub nom* County Fire
Officer v. City Logistics Ltd [2001] EWCA Civ 1216; [2001] 33 E.G.C.S. 86;
(2001) 98(35) L.S.G. 34; (2001) 98(31) L.S.G. 38; (2001) 145 S.J.L.B. 217;
[2001] N.P.C. 127; *Times*, September 4, 2001, CA; reversing [2001] EWHC
Admin 80; [2001] 33 E.G.C.S. 86; [2001] N.P.C. 127, QBD (Admin Ct) . . . .   *Digested*, 01/**873**
City Mortgage Corp Ltd v. Baptiste [1997] C.C.L.R. 64, CC (Bow). . . . .   *Digested*, 98/**572**
City of Boisbriand v. Commission des Droits de la Personne et des Droits de la
Jeunesse du Quebec see City of Montreal v. Commission des Droits de la
Personne et des Droits de la Jeunesse du Quebec
City of Bradford MBC v. Secretary of State for the Environment see R. v. Secretary of
State for the Environment Ex p. Nottinghamshire CC
City of Glasgow DC v. Zafar see Glasgow City Council v. Zafar
City of London v. Reeve & Co Ltd; G Lawrence Wholesale Meat Co Ltd v. Citigen
(London) Ltd [2000] C.P. Rep. 73; [2000] B.L.R. 211, QBD (T&CC). . . . .   *Digested*, 00/**878**
City of London Building Society v. Flegg [1988] A.C. 54; [1987] 2 W.L.R. 1266; [1987]
3 All E.R. 435; [1988] 1 F.L.R. 98; (1987) 19 H.L.R. 484; (1987) 54 P. & C.R.
337; [1988] Fam. Law 17; (1987) 84 L.S.G. 1966; (1987) 137 N.L.J. 475; (1987)
131 S.J. 806, HL; reversing [1986] Ch. 605; [1986] 2 W.L.R. 616; [1986] 1 All
E.R. 989; (1986) 52 P. & C.R. 193; (1986) 83 L.S.G. 1394; (1986) 136 N.L.J.
311; (1985) 130 S.J. 300, CA . . . .   *Digested*, 87/**2540**:
                                                Considered, 89/2342: *Distinguished*, 00/4658
City of London Corp v. Bovis Construction Ltd [1992] 3 All E.R. 697; 49 B.L.R. 1; 84
L.G.R. 660; (1988) 4 Const. L.J. 203; [1989] J.P.L. 263; (1989) 153 L.G. Rev.
166; *Times*, April 21, 1988, CA . . . .   *Digested*, 89/**3133**:
                        Applied, 89/2990, 90/3704, 90/4131, 91/3303, 93/3852: *Cited*, 01/4706:
                                    Considered, 92/4263: *Distinguished*, 94/4421, 95/4841, 95/4875
City of Montreal v. Commission des Droits de la Personne et des Droits de la Jeunesse
du Quebec; City of Boisbriand v. Commission des Droits de la Personne et des
Droits de la Jeunesse du Quebec 8 B.H.R.C. 476, Sup Ct (Can) . . . .   *Digested*, 00/**3177**
City of Westminster Assurance Co Ltd v. Registrar of Companies; City of Westminster
Assurance Co Ltd v. Thomas Jourdan Plc [1997] B.C.C. 960, CA. . . . .   *Digested*, 98/**656**:
                                                                                            Considered, 98/3620

City of Westminster Assurance Co Ltd v. Thomas Jourdan Plc see City of Westminster
Assurance Co Ltd v. Registrar of Companies
City Pram & Toy Co Ltd, Re; *sub nom* Secretary of State for Trade and Industry v. Phillips
[1998] B.C.C. 537, Ch D (Companies Ct). . . . .   *Digested*, 98/**667**
City Technology Ltd v. Alphasense Ltd A3/2000/3437, CA; affirming (2000) 23(12)
I.P.D. 23102, Ch D
City Trust Ltd v. Levy see United Bank of Kuwait v. Hammoud
Cityflyer Express Ltd v. Commission of the European Communities (T16/96) [1998]
E.C.R. II-757; [1998] 2 C.M.L.R. 537, CFI (5th Chamber) . . . .   *Followed*, 00/2366
Citymax Trading Information Systems Ltd (t/a EDS Citymax) v. Cristal Software Ltd
[1998] F.S.R. 196, Ch D . . . .   *Digested*, 98/**3441**
CityPark Properties Ltd v. Bolton MBC [2000] R.V.R. 343, Lands Tr . . . .   *Digested*, 01/**4765**
CIUFFO GATTO/Trade Mark (T480/98) [2000] E.P.O.R. 494, EPO (Technical Bd App)   *Digested*, 01/**3908**
Civet v. France (29340/95) (2001) 31 E.H.R.R. 38, ECHR . . . .   *Digested*, 01/**3497**
Civil Aviation Authority v. Jet Services Ltd see R. (on the application of Jet Services
Ltd) v. Civil Aviation Authority
CJ O'Shea Construction Ltd v. Bassi [1998] I.C.R. 1130, EAT . . . .   *Digested*, 99/**2092**
CJ Williams Funeral Service of Telford v. Customs and Excise Commissioners [2000]
B.V.C. 2111; [1999] V. & D.R. 318; [2000] S.T.I. 42, V&DTr . . . .   *Digested*, 00/**5304**
CJD Litigation (No.1), Re see Creutzfeldt-Jakob Disease Litigation (No.1), Re
CJD Litigation (No.2), Re see Newman v. Secretary of State for Health (No.1)
CJD Litigation (No.3), Re see Creutzfeldt-Jakob Disease Litigation (No.3), Re
CJD Litigation (No.4), Re see Newman v. Secretary of State for Health (No.1)
CJD Litigation (No.5), Re see Group B Plaintiffs v. Medical Research Council
CJD Litigation (No.6), Re see Newman v. Secretary of State for Health (No.2)

CJD Litigation (No.7), Re see Creutzfeldt-Jakob Disease Litigation (Group A and C Plaintiffs), Re
CJD Litigation (No.8), Re see Straddlers Groups A and C v. Secretary of State for Health
CJD Litigation (No.9), Re see Andrews v. Secretary of State for Health (Damages Assessments)
CL v. Sweden (22771/93) (2000) 29 E.H.R.R. CD125, ECHR
CLACE v. Owners of the Ship Kommunar see Centro Latino Americano de Commercio Exterior SA v. Owners of the Kommunar (The Kommunar) (No.1)
Clack v. Arthur's Engineering Ltd [1959] 2 Q.B. 211; [1959] 2 W.L.R. 916; [1959] 2 All E.R. 503; 103 S.J. 471, CA . . . . *Digested,* 59/**617**:
Not followed, 98/616

Claim against Croatian Branch of Slovenian Bank, Re [1998] I.L.Pr. 269, BGH (Ger)
Claim by a Polish Producer of Zinc and Copper Products, Re [1998] I.L.Pr. 727, OLG (Ger)
Claim for Remuneration Under a Building Contract (VII ZR 408/97), Re [2001] I.L.Pr. 26, BGH (Ger)
Clamp v. Customs and Excise Commissioners [1999] V. & D.R. 520; [2000] S.T.I. 649, V&DTr . . . . *Digested,* 00/**5371**
Clampin v. Palmer (Unreported, February 2, 2000), CC (Southend) [*Ex rel.* Browne Jacobson, Solicitors, Aldwych House, 81 Aldwych, London] . . . . *Digested,* 00/**3549**
Clancy v. Caird (No.1) 2000 S.C. 441; 2000 S.L.T. 546; 2000 S.C.L.R. 526; [2000] H.R.L.R. 557; [2000] U.K.H.R.R. 509; 2000 G.W.D. 13-455; *Times,* May 9, 2000, Ex Div 2000 G.W.D. 1-4, OH . . . . *Digested,* 00/**478**
Clancy v. Cannock Chase Technical College; Clancy v. Parker [2001] I.R.L.R. 331; [2001] Pens. L.R. 175, EAT . . . . *Digested,* 01/**2342**
Clancy v. Parker see Clancy v. Cannock Chase Technical College
Clapson v. British Airways Plc [2001] I.R.L.R. 184; *Times,* February 21, 2001, EAT . . . . . *Digested,* 01/**2276**
Clarapede & Co v. Commercial Union Association (1884) 32 W.R. 262 . . . . *Cited,* 99/499:
Considered, 87/2330
Clare Taverns (A Firm) (t/a Durty Nelly's) v. Gill (t/a Universal Business Systems) [2001] I.L.Pr. 20, HC (Irl) . . . . *Digested,* 01/**937**
Clarence Cafe Ltd v. Comchester Properties Ltd (t/a Comchester Finance) [1999] L. & T.R. 303, Ch D . . . . *Digested,* 99/**3264**
Clarina Live-in Care Services v. Customs and Excise Commissioners [2000] S.T.I. 650, V&DTr
Clarion Ltd v. National Provident Institution [2000] 1 W.L.R. 1888; [2000] 2 All E.R. 265, Ch D . . . . *Digested,* 00/**121**
Claritas (UK) Ltd v. Post Office [2001] U.K.C.L.R. 2; [2001] E.C.C. 12; [2001] E.T.M.R. 63, Ch D
Clark v. Allied Signal Ltd (Unreported, August 14, 1998), CC (Carlisle) [*Ex rel.* Hough, Halton & Soal Solicitors, 32 Abbey Street, Carlisle] . . . . *Digested,* 99/**1489**
Clark v. Ardington Electrical Services (No.1) [2001] EWCA Civ 585, CA [*Ex rel.* Morgan Cole, Solicitors, Apex Plaza Commercial Office, PO Box 2898, Reading]
Clark v. Associated Newspapers Ltd [1998] 1 W.L.R. 1558; [1998] 1 All E.R. 959; [1998] E.C.C. 185; [1998] R.P.C. 261; (1998) 21 (3) I.P.D. 21025; (1998) 95(7) L.S.G. 31; (1998) 148 N.L.J. 157; *Times,* January 28, 1998; *Independent,* January 23, 1998, Ch D . . . . *Digested,* 98/**3413**
Clark v. Brazier (No.1) (Unreported, July 31, 1997), CC (Birmingham) [*Ex rel.* Nicholas Xydias, Barrister, 5 Fountain Court, Steelhouse Lane, Birmingham] . . . . *Referred to,* 98/438
Clark v. Brazier (No.2) (Unreported, August 28, 1997), CC (Birmingham) [*Ex rel.* Sinclair Cramsie, Barrister, 13 King's Bench Walk, London, EC4] . . . . *Digested,* 98/**423**
Clark (Inspector of Taxes) v. British Telecom Pension Scheme Trustees see Clarke (Inspector of Taxes) v. BT Pension Scheme Trustees
Clark v. Bye (Inspector of Taxes) [1997] S.T.C. 311; 69 T.C. 305; [1997] B.T.C. 121, Ch D . . . . *Digested,* 97/**2947**
Clark v. Chief Constable of Cleveland [2000] C.P. Rep. 22; (1999) 96(21) L.S.G. 38; *Times,* May 13, 1999, CA . . . . *Digested,* 99/**1392**
Clark (George Nowell) v. Clark (Julia Oriska) [1999] 2 F.L.R. 498; [1999] 3 F.C.R. 49; [1999] Fam. Law 533; *Independent,* June 14, 1999 (C.S.), CA . . . . *Digested,* 99/**2429**
Clark v. Dix [2001] 1 Q.R. 15, CC (Ashford) [*Ex rel.* Hodgkinsons Solicitors, The Old Manse, 14 Lumley Avenue, Skegness, Lincolnshire] . . . . *Digested,* 01/**1686**
Clark v. Environment Agency see Rhondda Waste Disposal Ltd (In Administration), Re
Clark v. Nomura International Plc [2000] I.R.L.R. 766, QBD . . . . *Digested,* 00/**2098**
Clark v. Novacold Ltd see Clark v. TDG Ltd (t/a Novacold Ltd)
Clark v. Oxfordshire HA [1998] I.R.L.R. 125; (1998) 41 B.M.L.R. 18, CA . . . . *Digested,* 98/**2137**:
Considered, 97/2282: *Followed,* 99/2045
Clark v. Perks (Inspector of Taxes) see Clark (Inspector of Taxes) v. Perks
Clark (Inspector of Taxes) v. Perks; *sub nom* Clark v. Perks (Inspector of Taxes); Perks v. Clark (Inspector of Taxes); Macleod (Inspector of Taxes) v. Perks; Guild (Inspector of Taxes) v. Newrick [2001] EWCA Civ 1228; [2001] 2 Lloyd's Rep. 431; [2001] S.T.C. 1254; [2001] B.T.C. 336; [2001] S.T.I. 1086; (2001) 98(33) L.S.G. 32; (2001) 145 S.J.L.B. 214; *Times,* October 2, 2001, CA; reversing [2000] S.T.C. 428; [2000] B.T.C. 133; [2000] S.T.I. 667; (2000) 97(19) L.S.G. 44; *Times,* May 3, 2000, Ch D . . . . *Digested,* 01/**5269**

Clark (Inspector of Taxes) v. Perks (Permission to Appeal); *sub nom* Perks (Inspector of Taxes) v. Clark; McNicholas Construction Co Ltd v. Customs and Excise Commissioners; Jenkins v. BP Oil UK Ltd; Perks (Inspector of Taxes) v. Macleod; Guild v. Newrick [2001] 1 W.L.R. 17; [2000] 4 All E.R. 1; [2000] S.T.C. 1080; [2000] B.T.C. 282; [2000] B.V.C. 365; [2000] S.T.I. 1676; (2000) 150 N.L.J. 1376, CA. . . . .   *Previous proceedings,* 00/5007, 00/5348

Clark v. Singh (Unreported, May 18, 2001), CC (Peterborough) [*Ex rel.* Roy Roebuck, Barrister, Bell Yard Chambers, 116/118 Chancery Lane, London] . . . .   *Digested,* 01/**1780**

Clark v. TDG Ltd (t/a Novacold Ltd); *sub nom* Clark v. Novacold Ltd [1999] 2 All E.R. 977; [1999] I.C.R. 951; [1999] I.R.L.R. 318; [1999] Disc. L.R. 240; (1999) 48 B.M.L.R. 1; *Times,* April 1, 1999, CA; reversing [1998] I.C.R. 1044; [1998] I.R.L.R. 420; [1999] Disc. L.R. 22; (1998) 42 B.M.L.R. 101; *Times,* June 11, 1998, EAT . .   *Digested,* 99/**2022**:
Applied, 99/2024, 01/2239, 01/2240, 01/6461: *Followed,* 00/2127

Clark (Inspector of Taxes) v. Trustees of the British Telecom Pension Scheme see Clarke (Inspector of Taxes) v. BT Pension Scheme Trustees

Clark v. University of Lincolnshire and Humberside [2000] 1 W.L.R. 1988; [2000] 3 All E.R. 752; [2000] Ed. C.R. 553; [2000] E.L.R. 345; [2000] C.O.D. 293; (2000) 150 N.L.J. 616; (2000) 144 S.J.L.B. 220; *Times,* May 3, 2000; *Independent,* May 3, 2000, CA . . . .   *Digested,* 00/**2001**

Clark & Tokeley Ltd (t/a Spellbrook Ltd) v. Oakes [1998] 4 All E.R. 353; [1999] I.C.R. 276; [1998] I.R.L.R. 577; (1998) 95(37) L.S.G. 36; (1998) 142 S.J.L.B. 253; *Times,* September 10, 1998, CA; affirming [1997] I.R.L.R. 564, EAT. . . . .   *Digested,* 98/**2215**

Clark Boyce v. Mouat [1994] 1 A.C. 428; [1993] 3 W.L.R. 1021; [1993] 4 All E.R. 268; (1993) 143 N.L.J. 1440; (1993) 137 S.J.L.B. 231; [1993] N.P.C. 128; *Times,* October 7, 1993; *Independent,* October 12, 1993, PC (NZ). . . . .   *Digested,* 93/**3750**:
Applied, 00/4247: *Considered,* 99/4390: *Distinguished,* 00/4273

Clark Care Group Ltd v. Norman Hitchcox Partnership Ltd see Tesco Stores Ltd v. Norman Hitchcox Partnership Ltd

Clark Goldring & Page Ltd v. ANC Ltd (Costs) (2001) 98(20) L.S.G. 43; *Times,* March 27, 2001, Ch D . . . .   *Digested,* 01/**501**

Clark (Administrator of Cosslett (Contractors) Ltd) v. Mid Glamorgan CC see Cosslett (Contractors) Ltd, Re

Clark's Refrigerated Transport Pty Ltd, Re [1982] V.R. 989 . . . .   *Considered,* 98/2519

Clarke, Re (Unreported, November 26, 1997), CICB [*Ex rel.* Ashley Murray, Barrister, Oriel Chambers, 14 Water Street, Liverpool] . . . .   *Digested,* 98/**927**

Clarke (C) (Deceased) v. Customs and Excise Commissioners; Clarke (A) v. Customs and Excise Commissioners [1998] B.V.C. 2036, V&D Tr

Clarke (Inspector of Taxes) v. BT Pension Scheme Trustees; *sub nom* Clarke (Inspector of Taxes) v. Trustees of BT Pension Scheme; Trustees of BT Pension Scheme v. Clark (Inspector of Taxes); British Telecom Pension Scheme Trustees v. Clarke (Inspector of Taxes); Clark (Inspector of Taxes) v. British Telecom Pension Scheme Trustees; Clark (Inspector of Taxes) v. Trustees of the British Telecom Pension Scheme [2000] S.T.C. 222; [2000] O.P.L.R. 53; [2000] Pens. L.R. 157; 72 T.C. 472; [2000] B.T.C. 64; [2000] S.T.I. 217; (2000) 97(10) L.S.G. 37; (2000) 144 S.J.L.B. 119; *Times,* March 7, 2000, CA; reversing [1998] S.T.C. 1075; [1998] O.P.L.R. 243; [1998] B.T.C. 362; (1998) 142 S.J.L.B. 268; *Times,* October 16, 1998; *Independent,* October 26, 1998 (C.S.), Ch D [1997] O.P.L.R. 279, Sp Comm . . . .   *Digested,* 00/**5000**

Clarke v. Chief Constable of Northamptonshire; *sub nom* Clarke v. Crew (1999) 96(24) L.S.G. 38; (1999) 149 N.L.J. 899; *Times,* June 14, 1999, CA. . . . .   *Digested,* 99/**3971**

Clarke v. Chief Constable of West Midlands; *sub nom* Clarke v. Ryley [2001] EWCA Civ 1169; (2001) 98(30) L.S.G. 38; *Times,* September 4, 2001, CA . . . .   *Digested,* 01/**4785**

Clarke v. Crew see Clarke v. Chief Constable of Northamptonshire

Clarke (A) v. Customs and Excise Commissioners see Clarke (C) (Deceased) v. Customs and Excise Commissioners

Clarke v. Fogg (Unreported, February 23, 2000), CC (Birkenhead) [*Ex rel.* David Higginson, Solicitor, 8 Greenlea Close, Bebington, Merseyside] . . . .   *Digested,* 00/**393**

Clarke v. General Accident Fire & Life Assurance Corp Plc see Clarke v. Kato

Clarke v. Kato; *sub nom* Clarke v. General Accident Fire & Life Assurance Corp Plc; Cutter v. Eagle Star Insurance Co Ltd [1998] 1 W.L.R. 1647; [1998] 4 All E.R. 417; (1999) 163 J.P. 502; [1999] R.T.R. 153; [1999] P.I.Q.R. P1; (1998) 95(43) L.S.G. 31; (1998) 148 N.L.J. 1640; (1998) 142 S.J.L.B. 278; [1998] N.P.C. 142; *Times,* October 23, 1998; *Independent,* October 27, 1998, HL; reversing [1997] 1 W.L.R. 208; [1997] R.T.R. 264; [1997] P.I.Q.R. P27; *Times,* December 11, 1996, CA . . . .   *Digested,* 98/**3395**:
Applied, 01/4449: *Previous proceedings,* 97/3164

Clarke v. Marlborough Fine Art (London) Ltd (Constructive Trusts), *Times,* July 5, 2001, Ch D . . . .   *Digested,* 01/**5505**

Clarke v. Marlborough Fine Art (London) Ltd (Amendments) (2001) 145 S.J.L.B. 278; *Times,* December 4, 2001, Ch D

Clarke v. Mediguard Services Ltd [2000] N.I. 73, CA (NI) . . . .   *Digested,* 00/**5529**

Clarke v. Melton BC see Clarke v. Secretary of State for the Environment

Clarke v. Nationwide Anglia Building Society [1998] E.G.C.S. 47; (1998) 95(12) L.S.G. 29; [1998] N.P.C. 45; (1998) 76 P. & C.R. D5, CA .... *Digested*, 98/**4033**

Clarke v. Norton [1910] V.L.R. 494 .... *Applied*, 01/1822

Clarke v. O'Keefe (2000) 80 P. & C.R. 126; (1998) 75 P. & C.R. D18, CA .... *Digested*, 01/**4847**

Clarke v. Parkes, *Independent*, March 5, 2001 (C.S), EAT

Clarke v. Ryley see Clarke v. Chief Constable of West Midlands

Clarke v. Secretary of State for the Environment; Clarke v. Melton BC (1993) 65 P. & C.R. 85; [1992] 3 P.L.R. 146; [1992] 42 E.G. 100; [1993] J.P.L. 32; [1993] C.O.D. 80; (1996) 160 L.G. Rev. 50; [1992] E.G.C.S. 88; [1992] N.P.C. 82; *Times*, June 24, 1992, CA; reversing (1992) 63 P. & C.R. 429; [1992] 1 P.L.R. 22; [1991] E.G.C.S. 77; [1991] N.P.C. 87, QBD .... *Digested*, 93/**3813**: *Applied*, 99/4179: *Considered*, 96/4717, 96/4723: *Followed*, 95/4743

Clarke v. Secretary of State for the Environment, Transport and the Regions; *sub nom* R. (on the application of Clarke) v. Secretary of State for the Transport, Local Government and the Regions; C/2001/2506, CA [2001] EWHC Admin 800; [2001] N.P.C. 164; *Times*, November 9, 2001, QBD (Admin Ct) .... *Digested*, 01/**4745**

Clarke v. South Yorkshire Transport Ltd [1998] P.I.Q.R. Q104, CA .... *Digested*, 98/**1631**

Clarke (Inspector of Taxes) v. Trustees of BT Pension Scheme see Clarke (Inspector of Taxes) v. BT Pension Scheme Trustees

Clarke v. Vauxhall Motors Ltd (Unreported, January 19, 1999), CC (Wandsworth) [*Ex rel*. Rowley Ashworth Solicitors, 247 The Broadway, Wimbledon, London] ..... *Digested*, 99/**1532**

Clarke v. Vedel [1979] R.T.R. 26, CA. .... *Digested*, 79/**2346**: *Considered*, 98/506

Clarke v. Wilmot see Laverick v. DPP

Clarke Homes v. Secretary of State for the Environment (1993) 66 P. & C.R. 263; [1993] E.G.C.S. 29; [1993] N.P.C. 26, CA .... *Digested*, 93/**3925**: *Applied*, 99/4236

Clarkson v. Gilbert (Rights of Audience) [2000] C.P. Rep. 58; [2000] 2 F.L.R. 839; [2000] 3 F.C.R. 10; [2000] Fam. Law 808; *Times*, July 4, 2000; *Independent*, July 17, 2000 (C.S), CA. .... *Digested*, 00/**537**

Classic Catering Ltd v. Donington Park Leisure Ltd; *sub nom* Classic Catering Ltd v. Donnington Park Leisure Ltd [2001] 1 B.C.L.C. 537, Ch D .... *Digested*, 01/**509**

Classic Catering Ltd v. Donnington Park Leisure Ltd see Classic Catering Ltd v. Donington Park Leisure Ltd

Classic Furniture (Newport) Ltd v. Customs and Excise Commissioners [2001] S.T.I. 656, V&DTr

Classic Manufacturing (Aust) Pty Ltd's Trade Mark Application (No.2016809) (1998) 21 (6) I.P.D. 21067, TMR

Classick v. Blazenby; Bavin v. Ferguson; (Unreported, November 27, 2000), CC (Southend) [*Ex rel*. Richard Miles, Barrister, 2 King's Bench Walk Chambers, Temple, London] .... *Digested*, 01/**900**: *Followed*, 01/901

Claughton v. Charalambous [1999] 1 F.L.R. 740; [1998] B.P.I.R. 558; [1999] Fam. Law 205, Ch D .... *Digested*, 99/**3244**

Claughton v. Price; *sub nom* Trustee in Bankruptcy of Arthur Knapton v. Price (1998) 30 H.L.R. 396; [1997] E.G.C.S. 51; (1997) 74 P. & C.R. D15, CA .... *Digested*, 97/**4270**

Claughton (Liquidator of Hollicourt (Contracts) Ltd) v. Bank of Ireland see Hollicourt (Contracts) Ltd (In Liquidation) v. Bank of Ireland

Clay v. Boyd [2001] 5 Q.R. 11, CC (Lincoln) [*Ex rel*. Paul Rogers, Barrister, Crown Office Row Chambers, 120 Church Street, Brighton] .... *Digested*, 01/**1594**

Clay v. Clay [2001] W.T.L.R. 393; (2000-01) 3 I.T.E.L.R. 525, HC (Aus) .... *Digested*, 01/**5529**

Clayton v. Bank Cafe (Unreported, November 3, 1997), CC (Gwent) [*Ex rel*. Robert O'Leary, 33 Park Place, Cardiff] .... *Digested*, 98/**1582**

Cleadon Trust Ltd, Re [1939] Ch. 286, CA; affirming [1938] Ch. 660, Ch D .... *Applied*, 00/**272**

Clean Car Autoservice GmbH v. Landeshauptmann von Wien (C350/96) [1998] All E.R. (EC) 434; [1998] E.C.R. I-2521; [1998] 2 C.M.L.R. 637; *Times*, May 13, 1998, ECJ (6th Chamber) .... *Digested*, 98/**2154**

Clear v. Stephenson Unreported, CC (Peterborough) [*Ex rel*. Nicholas A Peacock, Barrister, Ground Floor, 6 Pump Court, Temple, London] .... *Digested*, 99/**1516**

Clear Focus Imaging Inc v. Contra Vision Ltd; *sub nom* Contra Vision Ltd's Application to Amend UK Patent (No.GB 2165292C); CH/2001/APP/010716, Pat Ct; affirming (2000) 23(6) I.P.D. 23048, PO

Cleaver v. Delta American Reinsurance Co (In Liquidation) [2001] UKPC 6; [2001] 2 A.C. 328; [2001] 2 W.L.R. 1202; [2001] 1 B.C.L.C. 482; [2001] B.P.I.R. 438; (2001) 145 S.J.L.B. 85, PC (CI) .... *Digested*, 01/**3772**

Cleaves v. Evans [2001] 1 Q.R. 8, CC (Canterbury) [*Ex rel*. Timothy Petts, Barrister, 12, Kings Bench Walk, London] .... *Digested*, 01/**1733**

Clees v. Hauptzollamt Wuppertal (C259/97) [1998] E.C.R. I-8127; *Times*, January 4, 1999, ECJ (4th Chamber) .... *Digested*, 99/**4661**

Clef Aquitaine Sarl v. Laporte Materials (Barrow) Ltd; *sub nom* Clef Aquitaine Sarl v. Sovereign Chemical Industries Ltd [2001] Q.B. 488; [2000] 3 W.L.R. 1760; [2000] 3 All E.R. 493, CA. .... *Digested*, 00/**1452**

Clef Aquitaine Sarl v. Sovereign Chemical Industries Ltd see Clef Aquitaine Sarl v. Laporte Materials (Barrow) Ltd

Clements v. Udal; *sub nom* Clements v. Udall [2001] B.C.C. 658; [2001] B.P.I.R. 454;
  (2000) 97(30) L.S.G. 39; *Times*, July 7, 2000, Ch D . . . .   *Digested*, 00/**3476**
Clements v. Udall see Clements v. Udal
Clerk of the Parliaments Reference Regarding Criminal Legal Aid Taxation [2000] 1 Costs
  L.R. 7
Cleveland Structural Engineering (Hong Kong) Ltd v. Advanced Specialist Treatment
  Engineering Ltd see Advanced Specialist Treatment Engineering Ltd v. Cleveland
  Structural Engineering (Hong Kong) Ltd
Clibbery v. Allan; *sub nom* Cliberry v. Allan; B1/01/1526, CA; affirming [2001] 2 F.L.R.
  819; [2001] 2 F.C.R. 577; [2001] Fam. Law 654; (2001) 98(27) L.S.G. 40;
  (2001) 151 N.L.J. 969; (2001) 145 S.J.L.B. 160; *Times*, July 2, 2001;
  Independent, July 30, 2001 (C.S), Fam Div . . . .   *Digested*, 01/**2622**
Cliberry v. Allan see Clibbery v. Allan
Clickex Ltd v. McCann (2000) 32 H.L.R. 324; [1999] 2 E.G.L.R. 63; [1999] 30 E.G.
  96; [1999] E.G.C.S. 73; (1999) 96(21) L.S.G. 41; *Times*, May 26, 1999, CA;
  reversing (Unreported, December 4, 1998), CC (Brentford) [*Ex rel.* Alastair
  Panton, Barrister, Fleet Chambers, 4th Floor, Mitre House, 44-46 Fleet Street,
  London] . . . .   *Digested*, 99/**3653**:
                                                                                             Considered, 00/3874
Cliffe v. Forrester, *Times*, September 10, 1998, CA. . . . .   *Digested*, 98/**385**
Clifford v. First American Corp see First American Corp v. Sheikh Zayed Al-Nahyan
Clift v. Welsh Office [1999] 1 W.L.R. 796; [1998] 4 All E.R. 852; (1999) 78 P. & C.R.
  32; [1998] R.V.R. 303; (1998) 95(36) L.S.G. 31; (1998) 76 P. & C.R. D46;
  Times, August 24, 1998; *Independent*, July 29, 1998, CA; affirming [1997] R.V.R.
  12, Lands Tr . . . .   *Digested*, 98/**4041**
Clifton v. Barclays Bank Plc [1998] B.P.I.R. 565, Ch D . . . .   *Digested*, 99/**3323**
Clingham v. Kensington and Chelsea RLBC; *sub nom* R. (on the application of
  Clingham) v. Marylebone Magistrates Court [2001] EWHC Admin 1; (2001) 165
  J.P. 322; (2001) 165 J.P.N. 306; *Times*, February 20, 2001, QBD (Admin Ct) . . .   *Digested*, 01/**396**
Clinique Laboratories Inc's Application [1999] E.T.M.R. 750, OHIM (2nd Bd App) . . . . .   *Digested*, 00/**3785**
Clinton v. Bradley [2000] N.I. 196, CA (NI) . . . .   *Digested*, 00/**5473**
Clinton (Chief Inspector of the Royal Ulster Constabulary) v. Cahill [1998] N.I. 200, CA
  (Crim Div) (NI) . . . .   *Digested*, 99/**5204**
Clinton v. Chief Constable of the Royal Ulster Constabulary; Donnelly v. Chief
  Constable of the Royal Ulster Constabulary [1999] N.I. 215, CA (NI). . . . .   *Digested*, 00/**5490**
Clinton v. News Group Newspapers Ltd; Barry v. News Group Newspapers Ltd 1999
  S.C. 367; 1999 S.L.T. 590; 1999 G.W.D. 2-66; *Times*, March 22, 1999, OH . . . . .   *Digested*, 99/**5657**
Clinton v. Windsor Life Assurance Co Ltd QBENF 96/0821/C, CA. . . . .   *Digested*, 98/**3382**
Clive Brooks & Co Ltd v. Baynard, *Times*, April 30, 1998, CA . . . .   *Digested*, 98/**451**
Clonard Developments Ltd v. Humberts (A Firm) [1999] E.G.C.S. 7; (1999) 96(4)
  L.S.G. 41, CA; affirming [1997] E.G.C.S. 124, QBD
Clore (Deceased) (No.1), Re [1982] Fam. 113; [1982] 2 W.L.R. 314; (1982) 12 Fam. Law 85;
  126 S.J. 85, Fam Div . . . .   *Applied*, 00/**4905**:
                                                                                             Subsequent proceedings, 82/264, 82/1347
Clore's Settlement Trusts, Re; *sub nom* Sainer v. Clore [1966] 1 W.L.R. 955; [1966] 2 All
  E.R. 272; 21 A.L.R.3d 795; (1966) 110 S.J. 252, Ch D . . . .   *Digested*, 66/**11045**:
                                                                                             Applied, 01/5507
Close Asset Finance v. Care Graphics Machinery Ltd [2000] C.C.L.R. 43; (2000)
  97(12) L.S.G. 42; (2000) 144 S.J.L.B. 134; *Times*, March 21, 2000, QBD . . . . . .   *Digested*, 00/**849**
Clough v. Tameside and Glossop HA [1998] 1 W.L.R. 1478; [1998] 2 All E.R. 971;
  [1998] 3 F.C.R. 133; [1998] P.I.Q.R. P219; [1998] Lloyd's Rep. Med. 69; (1998)
  42 B.M.L.R. 166, QBD . . . .   *Digested*, 98/**326**:
                                                                                             Doubted, 99/321
Cloutte v. Storey [1911] 1 Ch. 18, CA . . . .   *Considered*, 01/**5511**
Clowes Developments (UK) Ltd v. Mulchinock [1998] 1 W.L.R. 42; [1997] N.P.C. 47,
  Ch D . . . .   *Digested*, 98/**4372**
CLT-UFA SA v. This Domain Is For Sale [2001] E.T.M.R. 43, Arbitration . . . .   *Digested*, 01/**3871**
Club Europe Holidays Ltd v. British Airways Plc see CLUB EUROPE Trade Mark
CLUB EUROPE Trade Mark; *sub nom* Club Europe Holidays Ltd v. British Airways Plc
  [2000] R.P.C. 329; (1999) 22(10) I.P.D. 22101; (1999) 96(33) L.S.G. 32; *Times*,
  August 2, 1999, Ch D . . . .   *Digested*, 99/**3546**
Clube de Futebol Uniao de Coimbra v. Portugal [1998] H.R.C.D. 770; (2000) 29
  E.H.R.R. CD24, ECHR
Clunies-Ross, Re [2000] B.P.I.R. 714, Fed Ct (Aus) (Full Ct) . . . .   *Digested*, 01/**3713**
Clunis v. Camden and Islington HA [1998] Q.B. 978; [1998] 2 W.L.R. 902; [1998] 3
  All E.R. 180; (1997-98) 1 C.C.L. Rep. 215; (1998) 40 B.M.L.R. 181; [1998]
  P.N.L.R. 262; (1998) 95(2) L.S.G. 23; (1998) 142 S.J.L.B. 38; *Times*, December
  10, 1997; *Independent*, December 9, 1997, CA; reversing *Times*, December 27,
  1996, QBD . . . .   *Digested*, 98/**3937**:
                                                                                             Followed, 99/1413
Clutton v. Clutton [1991] 1 W.L.R. 359; [1991] 1 All E.R. 340; [1991] 1 F.L.R. 242;
  [1991] F.C.R. 265; [1991] Fam. Law 304; (1990) 134 S.J. 1682; *Independent*,
  October 30, 1990, CA . . . .   *Digested*, 91/**1804**:
                                                                                             Applied, 00/2520: *Followed*, 96/2884

Clwb Rygbi Nant Conwy v. Customs and Excise Commissioners [2000] B.V.C. 2168; [2000] S.T.I. 316,V&DTr
Clyde & Co v. Secretary of State for the Environment [1977] 1 W.L.R. 926; [1977] 3 All E.R. 1123; 75 L.G.R. 660; (1978) 35 P. & C.R. 410; (1977) 244 E.G. 1024; [1977] J.P.L. 521; 121 S.J. 512, CA; reversing [1977] 1 All E.R. 333; [1977] J.P.L. 31; *Times*, October 27, 1976, QBD . . . . *Digested*, 77/**2922**:
Applied, 81/2710, 82/3181: *Considered*, 90/4354, 94/4320, 95/4767, 00/5658
Clyde & Co v. Sovrybflot 1997-C-1142, QBD . . . . *Digested*, 98/**586**
Clydesdale Bank Plc v. Davidson 1998 S.C. (H.L.) 51; 1998 S.L.T. 522; 1998 S.C.L.R. 278; [1997] N.P.C. 182; 1998 G.W.D. 1-41; *Times*, December 20, 1997, HL; affirming 1996 S.L.T. 437, 2 Div; affirming 1994 S.C.L.R. 828, Sh Pr . . . . *Digested*, 98/**6031**
Clynes v. Bundy (Unreported, June 8, 2001), CC (Manchester) [*Ex rel.* John Cunningham & Associates, 44 New Court Way, Ormskirk] . . . . *Digested*, 01/**1510**
CMI Centers for Medical Innovation GmbH v. Phytopharm Plc [1999] F.S.R. 235; (1998) 21 (11) I.P.D. 21123, Ch D . . . . *Digested*, 99/**583**
CMS Dolphin Ltd v. Simonet [2001] 2 B.C.L.C. 704, Ch D
CNA International Reinsurance Co Ltd v. Companhia de Seguros Tranquilidade SA [1999] C.L.C. 140; [1999] Lloyd's Rep. I.R. 289, QBD . . . . *Digested*, 99/**3427**
Cnl-Sucal NV SA v. Hag GF AG (C10/89) [1990] E.C.R. I-3711; [1990] 3 C.M.L.R. 571; [1991] F.S.R. 99; *Times*, December 7, 1990; *Independent*, December 17, 1990 (C.S.), ECJ . . . . *Digested*, 92/**4427**:
Applied, 94/4876, 96/5709: *Considered*, 98/3514: *Referred to*, 93/3980
CNS Inc's Community Trade Mark Application [2000] E.T.M.R. 609, OHIM (1st Bd App) *Digested*, 00/**3715**
Coach Ferry Travel v. NST Travel Group PLC (Unreported, June 22, 2001), CC (Preston) [*Ex rel.* Mason Bond Solicitors, King Charles House, King Charles Court, Leeds] . . . . *Digested*, 01/**498**
Coady v. Hankins (Unreported, May 14, 1998), CC (Reading) [*Ex rel.* Piers Martin, Barrister, 2 Temple Gardens, London] . . . . *Digested*, 98/**489**
Coal Authority v. HJ Banks & Co Ltd; *sub nom* HJ Banks & Co Ltd v. Coal Authority; A3/1997/0408, CA; affirming [1997] Eu. L.R. 610, QBD (Comm Ct) . . . . *Digested*, 98/**366**
Coard v. National Westminster Bank Ltd see Salmon (Deceased), Re
Coard v. United States 9 B.H.R.C. 150, IA Comm HR . . . . *Digested*, 01/**3532**
Coastal (Bermuda) Ltd v. Esso Petroleum Co Ltd [1984] 1 Lloyd's Rep. 11; *Times*, October 21, 1983, CA . . . . *Digested*, 84/**3092**:
Applied, 00/892
Coath, Re [2000] B.P.I.R. 981, CC (Aylesbury) . . . . *Digested*, 01/**3792**
Cobbett v. Wood [1908] 2 K.B. 420, CA; reversing [1908] 1 K.B. 590, KBD . . . . *Applied*, 00/451
Cobham v. Frett [2001] 1 W.L.R. 1775; (2001) 145 S.J.L.B. 7; *Times*, January 24, 2001, PC (BVI) . . . . *Digested*, 01/**49**
Cobra Beer Ltd's Community Trade Mark Application [2000] E.T.M.R. 638, OHIM (Opposition Div) . . . . *Digested*, 00/**3742**
Cobra Golf Inc v. Rata (No.2) [1998] Ch. 109; [1997] 2 W.L.R. 629; [1997] 2 All E.R. 150; [1997] F.S.R. 317; (1997) 20(2) I.P.D. 20013; *Times*, October 11, 1996, Ch D
. . . . *Digested*, 96/**689**
Cobra Precision Engineering Ltd v. Customs and Excise Commissioners [2001] S.T.I. 179,V&DTr
Cobrecaf SA v. Commission of the European Communities (T514/93) [1995] E.C.R. II-621, CFI . . . . *Digested*, 95/**2387**:
Distinguished, 99/2240
Coca Cola Co v. British Telecommunications Plc [1999] I.T.C.L.R. 365; [1999] F.S.R. 518, Ch D . . . . *Digested*, 99/**319**
Coca-Cola Co v. Commission of the European Communities (T125/97); Coca-Cola Enterprises Inc v. Commission of the European Communities (T127/97) [2000] All E.R. (EC) 460; [2000] E.C.R. II-1733; [2000] 5 C.M.L.R. 467, CFI . . . . *Digested*, 00/**713**
Coca-Cola Enterprises Inc v. Commission of the European Communities (T127/97) see Coca-Cola Co v. Commission of the European Communities (T125/97)
Coca-Cola Financial Corp v. Finsat International Ltd (The Ira) [1998] Q.B. 43; [1996] 3 W.L.R. 849; [1996] 2 Lloyd's Rep. 274; [1996] 2 B.C.L.C. 626; [1996] C.L.C. 1564; *Times*, May 1, 1996; *Lloyd's List*, June 5, 1996, CA . . . . *Digested*, 96/**2782**
Cockbone v. Atkinson Dacre & Slack see Arthur JS Hall & Co v. Simons
Cockerill v. Tambrands Ltd; Jackson v. Pinchbeck; Prolaw Ltd v. Adams (t/a Nigel Adams & Co) [1998] 1 W.L.R. 1379; [1998] 3 All E.R. 97; (1998) 95(23) L.S.G. 27; (1998) 142 S.J.L.B. 172; [1998] N.P.C. 88; *Times*, June 4, 1998, CA . . . . *Digested*, 98/**395**:
Joined proceedings, 98/392, 98/397
Cocking v. Sandhurst (Stationers) [1974] I.C.R. 650; (1975) 10 I.T.R. 6, NIRC; reversing (1975) 10 I.T.R. 6 . . . . *Digested*, 75/**1119**:
Applied, 77/1165, 83/1240, 00/2151: *Considered*, 88/73, 89/78, 95/2114:
Distinguished, 93/1760
Cocks v. Thanet DC [1983] 2 A.C. 286; [1982] 3 W.L.R. 1121; [1982] 3 All E.R. 1135; 81 L.G.R. 81; [1984] R.V.R. 31; 126 S.J. 820, HL. . . . . *Digested*, 82/**1465**:
Applied, 95/2551, 96/3087: *Considered*, 83/2943, 83/3679, 84/1344, 87/2378, 87/3052, 88/24, 89/35, 90/2959, 90/3908, 96/5578, 97/2674, 98/98: *Distinguished*, 84/10, 85/9, 92/79, 92/2267: *Followed*, 96/3026

Cockshott v. Bennett (1788) 2 Term Rep. 763 . . . .   *Considered*, 65/217:
                                                                                                Distinguished, 00/121
Coco v. AN Clark (Engineers) Ltd [1968] F.S.R. 415; [1969] R.P.C. 41, Ch D . . . .   *Digested*, 68/**1458**:
                               Applied, 88/3403, 99/3437, 01/4415: *Considered*, 86/412, 87/1294:
                                                                                                Referred to, 73/2498
CODAS Trade Mark [2001] R.P.C. 14, TMR . . . .   *Digested*, 01/**4053**
COFFEEMIX Trade Mark [1998] R.P.C. 717, Appointed Person . . . .   *Digested*, 99/**3526**:
                                                                Considered, 00/3792: *Followed*, 99/3528
Coflexip SA v. Stolt Comex Seaway MS Ltd [2001] 1 All E.R. 952 (Note); [2001]
    R.P.C. 9; (2000) 23(10) I.P.D. 23081, CA; affirming [1999] 2 All E.R. 593;
    [1999] F.S.R. 473; (1999) 22(4) I.P.D. 22035; (1999) 22(4) I.P.D. 22036;
    (1999) 149 N.L.J. 196; *Times*, February 4, 1999; *Independent*, February 3, 1999,
    Pat Ct . . . .   *Digested*, 99/**3504**
Coflexip SA v. Stolt Comex Seaway MS Ltd (Interrogatories); *sub nom* Coflexip SA v.
    Stolt Comex Seaways MS Ltd (No.2) [1999] F.S.R. 911, Pat Ct . . . .   *Digested*, 00/**3681**
Coflexip SA v. Stolt Comex Seaways MS Ltd (No.2) see Coflexip SA v. Stolt Comex
    Seaway MS Ltd (Interrogatories)
Coggin v. Portaway Minerals (Elton) Ltd (1999) 99(4) Q.R. 6, CC (Buxton) [*Ex rel.*
    Prickett Partnership Solicitors, 12 Hardwick Street, Buxton, Derbyshire] . . . .   *Digested*, 99/**1520**
Coggins (t/a PC Transport) v. LKW Walter International Transportorganisation AG
    [1999] 1 Lloyd's Rep. 255, CC (Central London) . . . .   *Digested*, 99/**4944**
Coghlan v. Cumberland [1898] 1 Ch. 704, CA . . . .   *Considered*, 74/1069:
                                                                                                Followed, 98/323
Cogniaux v. Paillard [1998] E.C.C. 94, C d'A (Dijon)
Cohen v. Selby; *sub nom* Simmon Box (Diamonds) Ltd, Re [2001] 1 B.C.L.C. 176, CA;
    reversing [2000] B.C.C. 275, Ch D . . . .   *Digested*, 01/**3745**
Cohmor Holdings Plc v. Therma-Tru Corp see Therma-Tru Corp's Patent
Cohort Construction (UK) Ltd v. M Julius Melchior (A Firm) [2001] C.P. Rep. 23, CA . .   *Digested*, 01/**679**
Coin Controls Ltd v. Suzo International (UK) Ltd [1999] Ch. 33; [1998] 3 W.L.R. 420;
    [1997] 3 All E.R. 45; [1997] F.S.R. 660; (1997) 20(8) I.P.D. 20073, Ch D . . . . .   *Digested*, 97/**896**:
                                                                Approved, 98/3466: *Considered*, 98/3455
Coker v. Diocese of Southwark see Diocese of Southwark v. Coker
Coker v. Lord Chancellor; *sub nom* Lord Chancellor v. Coker; Osamor v. Lord
    Chancellor [2001] EWCA Civ 1756; (2001) 145 S.J.L.B. 268; *Times*, December
    3, 2001; *Independent*, November 28, 2001; *Daily Telegraph*, November 27, 2001,
    CA; affirming [2001] I.C.R. 507; [2001] I.R.L.R. 116; *Times*, January 23, 2001,
    EAT; reversing [1999] I.R.L.R. 396, ET . . . .   *Digested*, 01/**2311**:
                                                                                                Followed, 01/5771
Colaingrove v. Customs and Excise Commissioners [2000] B.V.C. 2054, V&DTr
Colaingrove v. Customs and Excise Commissioners [2001] S.T.I. 658, V&DTr
Colbeck v. Ellis (Unreported, February 22, 2001), CC (Wakefield) [*Ex rel.* Simon Plaut,
    Barrister, Park Lane Chambers, 19 Westgate, Leeds] . . . .   *Digested*, 01/**3841**
Colchester BC v. Orange PCS Ltd (1998) 13 P.A.D. 250, Planning Inspector
Colchester Estates (Cardiff) v. Carlton Industries Plc [1986] Ch. 80; [1984] 3 W.L.R.
    693; [1984] 2 All E.R. 601; (1984) 271 E.G. 778; (1984) 81 L.S.G. 2699, Ch D .   *Digested*, 84/**2588**:
                               Approved, 95/2983: *Considered*, 86/366, 88/2067, 92/2555:
                                                                Not followed, 97/3845, 98/4029
Colchester Sixth Form College v. Customs and Excise Commissioners [2000] B.V.C.
    2095, V&DTr
Coldbeck v. Mohamed (Unreported, January 13, 1999), CC (Nottingham) [*Ex rel.*
    Josephine Henderson, Barrister, Arden Chambers, 27 John Street, London] . . .   *Digested*, 99/**1399**
Cole (A Bankrupt), Re; *sub nom* Ex p. Trustee v. Cole [1964] Ch. 175; [1963] 3 W.L.R.
    621; [1963] 3 All E.R. 433; 107 S.J. 664, CA; reversing *Times*, March 23, 1963;
    Guardian, March 23, 1963 . . . .   *Digested*, 63/**1582**:
                                                                Applied, 64/1636, 01/3782: *Distinguished*, 66/5482
Cole v. British Telecommunications Plc [2000] 2 Costs L.R. 310; *Independent*, October
    2, 2000 (C.S), CA . . . .   *Digested*, 00/**390**
Cole v. Kelly [1920] 2 K.B. 106, CA . . . .   *Applied*, 59/1203,
                                                                59/1860: *Considered*, 79/1634: *Followed*, 98/3683
Cole v. Park see Park, Re
Coleman v. Customs and Excise Commissioners [2000] B.V.C. 2042; [1999] V. & D.R.
    133, V&DTr . . . .   *Digested*, 00/**5356**
Coleman v. Dunlop Ltd (No.1) [1998] P.I.Q.R. P398, CA . . . .   *Digested*, 99/**4008**
Coleman v. Myers [1977] 2 N.Z.L.R. 225, Sup Ct (NZ) . . . .   *Digested*, 78/**232**:
                                                                                                Considered, 00/649
Coleman v. Stubbs (Unreported, October 15, 1998), CC (Leicester) [*Ex rel.* Paul
    McGrath, Barrister, 1 Temple Gardens, Temple, London] . . . .   *Digested*, 98/**422**:
                                                                                                Distinguished, 01/3841
Coleman Taymar Ltd v. Oakes [2001] 2 B.C.L.C. 749; (2001) 98(35) L.S.G. 32; (2001)
    145 S.J.L.B. 209; *Times*, September 3, 2001, Ch D . . . .   *Digested*, 01/**723**
Coles v. Barnsley MBC see Leeds City Council v. Carr
Coles v. Camborne Justices see Coles v. East Penwith Justices
Coles v. DPP see Coles v. East Penwith Justices

Coles v. East Penwith Justices; *sub nom* Coles v. DPP; Coles v. Camborne Justices (1998) 162 J.P. 687; (1998) 162 J.P.N. 722; *Times,* July 27, 1998; *Independent,* June 22, 1998 (C.S.), QBD. . . . . *Digested,* 98/**1013**

Coles v. Lewis [2000] 4 Q.R. 7, CC (Swansea) [*Ex rel.* Leo Abse & Cohen Solicitors, 40 Churchill Way, Cardiff] . . . . *Digested,* 00/**1743**

Coles v. Thompson see Howard Holdings Inc, Re

Coles v. William Hill Organisation Ltd [1998] L. & T.R. 14; [1998] E.G.C.S. 40; (1998) 95(11) L.S.G. 37, Ch D . . . . *Digested,* 99/**3658**

Colgan, Re [1996] N.I. 24; [1997] 1 C.M.L.R. 53, QBD (NI)

Colim NV v. Bigg's Continent Noord NV (C33/97) [1999] E.C.R. I-3175; [2000] 2 C.M.L.R. 135, ECJ (5th Chamber) . . . . *Digested,* 00/**2385**

Colk v. Firth Brown Ltd (Unreported, October 22, 1998), CC (Sheffield) [*Ex rel.* Nelson & Co Solicitors, St Andrews House, St Andrews Street, Leeds] . . . . *Digested,* 99/**463**

Coll v. Tattum, *Times,* December 3, 2001, Ch D

Collard v. Wilmot (Unreported, March 5, 2001), CC (Weston Super Mare) [*Ex rel.* Graeme Wood, Barrister, Assize Court Chambers, 14 Small Street, Bristol] . . . . . *Digested,* 01/**896**

Collective Licensing of Fax Machines (I ZR 208/96), Re [2000] E.C.C. 345, BGH (Ger)

Collector Guns GmbH & Co KG v. Hauptzollamt Koblenz (C252/84) see Daiber v. Hauptzollamt Reutlingen (C200/84)

Collett v. Bean [2000] 1 Q.R. 8, CC (Wandsworth) [*Ex rel.* Andrew Ritchie, Barrister, 9 Gough Square, London] . . . . *Digested,* 99/**1497**

Collett (otherwise Sakazova) v. Collett [1968] P. 482; [1967] 3 W.L.R. 280; [1967] 2 All E.R. 426; 111 S.J. 294, PDAD. . . . . *Digested,* 67/**1876**:
Applied, 67/1332, 76/803: *Approved,* 99/4523: *Considered,* 67/200, 68/199, 87/2998

Colley v. Council for Licensed Conveyancers (Right of Appeal) [2001] EWCA Civ 1137; [2001] 4 All E.R. 998; [2001] 30 E.G.C.S. 115; (2001) 98(33) L.S.G. 31; (2001) 151 N.L.J. 1249; (2001) 145 S.J.L.B. 201; [2001] N.P.C. 116; *Times,* August 6, 2001, CA. . . . . *Digested,* 01/**426**

Colley v. Secretary of State for the Environment, Transport and the Regions (1999) 77 P. & C.R. 190; [1998] C.O.D. 491, CA . . . . *Digested,* 99/**4277**

Colley's Application, Re [1999] R.P.C. 97; (1999) 22(3) I.P.D. 22027, PO . . . . *Digested,* 99/**3467**

Collin v. Duke of Westminster [1985] Q.B. 581; [1985] 2 W.L.R. 553; [1985] 1 All E.R. 463; (1985) 17 H.L.R. 246; (1985) 50 P. & C.R. 380; [1985] 1 E.G.L.R. 109; (1985) 273 E.G. 881; [1985] R.V.R. 4; (1985) 82 L.S.G. 767; (1985) 129 S.J. 116, CA . . . . *Digested,* 85/**1891**:
Applied, 00/836: *Considered,* 94/3079, 00/4656

Collings v. Lee [2001] 2 All E.R. 332; (2001) 82 P. & C.R. 3; [2000] E.G.C.S. 115; (2000) 97(42) L.S.G. 37; (2000) 97(42) L.S.G. 45; [2000] N.P.C. 106; (2001) 81 P. & C.R. D12; *Times,* October 26, 2000; *Independent,* October 25, 2000, CA . . . . *Digested,* 00/**4620**

Collino v. Telecom Italia SpA (C343/98) [2001] All E.R. (EC) 405; [2000] E.C.R. I-6659; [2000] I.R.L.R. 788, ECJ (6th Chamber) . . . . *Digested,* 01/**2337**

Collins v. Brebner [2000] Lloyd's Rep. P.N. 587, CA. . . . . *Digested,* 00/**2332**

Collins v. Jones [2001] W.T.L.R. 1229; *Times,* February 3, 2000, Ch D . . . . *Digested,* 00/**2318**

Collins v. Vaughan [2001] 4 Q.R. 12, CC (Reading) [*Ex rel.* David Mc Hugh, Barrister, Bracton Chambers, London] . . . . *Digested,* 01/**1637**

Collins v. Whipp (Unreported, October 13, 1997), CC (Barnet) [*Ex rel.* Lisa A Sinclair, Barrister, 7 New Square, Lincoln's Inn, London] . . . . *Digested,* 98/**1586**

Collins (Pontefract) Ltd v. British Coal Corp (1998) 76 P. & C.R. 219, CA; affirming (1997) 73 P. & C.R. 102; [1996] R.V.R. 258, Lands Tr. *Digested,* 98/**3908**

Collinson v. Travel Promotions Ltd (t/a Voyages Jules Verne) (Unreported, September 30, 1997), CC (Kingston on Thames) [*Ex rel.* Marcus Grant, Barrister, 1 Temple Gardens, Temple, London] . . . . *Digested,* 98/**1429**

Collison (CICA: Quantum: 2001), Re [2001] 6 Q.R. 13, CICAP [*Ex rel.* Caspar Glyn, Barrister, Cloisters, 1 Pump Court, Temple, London] . . . . *Digested,* 01/**1644**

Collison v. BBC [1998] I.C.R. 669; [1998] I.R.L.R. 238; (1998) 95(27) L.S.G. 25, EAT . *Digested,* 98/**2104**

Colls v. Home & Colonial Stores Ltd; *sub nom* Home & Colonial Stores Ltd v. Colls [1904] A.C. 179, HL; reversing [1902] 1 Ch. 302, CA . . . . *Applied,* 64/1200, 70/825, 71/3750, 78/2205, 79/797, 84/1150, 85/1085: *Considered,* 00/4633

Colonial Bank v. European Grain & Shipping Ltd see Bank of Boston Connecticut (formerly Colonial Bank) v. European Grain & Shipping Ltd (The Dominique)

Colozza v. Italy (A/89) (1985) 7 E.H.R.R. 516, ECHR. . . . . *Applied,* 98/3113, 98/3143

Colt Group Ltd v. Couchman [2000] I.C.R. 327, EAT . . . . *Digested,* 00/**2122**

Coltman v. Bibby Tankers Ltd (The Derbyshire) [1988] A.C. 276; [1987] 3 W.L.R. 1181; [1987] 3 All E.R. 1068; [1988] 1 Lloyd's Rep. 109; [1988] I.C.R. 67; [1988] F.T.L.R. 217; (1988) 85(3) L.S.G. 36; (1987) 137 N.L.J. 1157; (1987) 131 S.J. 1658, HL; reversing [1987] 2 W.L.R. 1098; [1987] 1 All E.R. 932; [1987] 1 Lloyd's Rep. 411; [1987] I.C.R. 619; [1987] 1 F.T.L.R. 353; (1987) 84 L.S.G. 743; (1987) 131 S.J. 166, CA; reversing [1986] 1 W.L.R. 751; [1986] 2 All E.R. 65; [1986] 1 Lloyd's Rep. 418; (1986) 83 L.S.G. 1399; (1986) 130 S.J. 447, QBD (Adm Ct) . . . . *Digested,* 88/**1258**:
Applied, 93/2016: *Considered,* 92/4179, 98/2832

Columbia Tristar Home Video (International) Inc v. Polygram Film International BV
(formerly Manifesto Film Sales BV) [2000] 1 All E.R. (Comm) 385, CA . . . . . .   *Digested*, 00/**882**
Colwyn Bay Motorcycles v. Poole (Unreported, March 30, 2000), CC (Chester) [*Ex rel.*
Huw Roberts, Barrister, Sedan House, Stanley Place, Chester] . . . .   *Digested*, 00/**4675**
Colzani v. RUWA Polstereimaschinen GmbH (C24/76) see Estasis Salotti di Colzani
Aimo e Gianmario Colzani v. RUWA Polstereimaschinen GmbH (C24/76)
Comafrica SpA v. Commission of the European Communities (C73/97); France v.
Commission of the European Communities [1999] E.C.R. I-185; [1999] 2
C.M.L.R. 87, ECJ. . . . .   *Digested*, 99/**2260**
Comatra Ltd v. Lloyd's Underwriters see Comatra Ltd v. Various Underwriters (The Abt
Rasha)
Comatra Ltd v. Various Underwriters (The Abt Rasha); *sub nom* Comatra Ltd v. Lloyd's
Underwriters [2000] 2 All E.R. (Comm) 609; [2000] 2 Lloyd's Rep. 575;
[2001] C.L.C. 11, CA; reversing [1999] 2 All E.R. (Comm) 1002; [2000] 1
Lloyd's Rep. 8; [2000] C.L.C. 354, QBD (Comm Ct) . . . .   *Digested*, 00/**4726**
Comercial Iberica de Exclusivas Deportivas SA (CIDESPORT) v. Nike International Ltd
[2000] E.T.M.R. 189, Trib Sup (Sp)
Comet BV v. Produktschap voor Siergewassen (C45/76) see Rewe-Zentralfinanz eG v.
Landwirtschaftskammer fur das Saarland (C33/76)
Comet Products (UK) Ltd v. Hawkex Plastics Ltd [1971] 2 Q.B. 67; [1971] 2 W.L.R.
361; [1971] 1 All E.R. 1141; [1971] F.S.R. 7; [1972] R.P.C. 691; 114 S.J. 975; *Times*,
December 9, 1970, CA. . . . .   *Digested*, 71/**9083**:
                     Applied, 80/145, 88/2837: *Considered*, 84/2591, 86/1503, 92/2848,
                     93/2629: *Distinguished*, 95/587: *Followed*, 00/336
Comingersoll SA v. Portugal (2001) 31 E.H.R.R. 31, ECHR . . . .   *Digested*, 01/**3516**
Comitato Porturario d'Importazione die Carboni Fossili de Genova v. Instone & Co (Italy)
Ltd (1924) 18 Ll. L. Rep. 129, HL; reversing (1922) 12 Ll. L. Rep. 409; [1922]
W.N. 260, CA; affirming (1922) 11 Ll. L. Rep. 110, KBD . . . .   *Considered*, 99/396
Comite Central d'Entreprise de la Societe Generale des Grandes Sources v. Commission of
the European Communities (T96/92) [1995] E.C.R. II-1213; [1995] I.R.L.R.
381; *Financial Times*, May 2, 1995, CFI . . . .   *Digested*, 96/**1053**:
                     Applied, 98/2307
Comite International de la Rayonne et des Fibres Synthetiques (CIRFS) v. Commission of
the European Communities (C313/90) [1993] E.C.R. I-1125, ECJ (5th
Chamber) . . . .   *Digested*, 93/**4393**:
                     Applied, 98/2334
Comite Intersyndical du Livre Parisien, Re [2000] E.C.C. 303, C Concurrence (F)
Commercial Acceptances Ltd v. Townsend Investments Inc [2000] C.P.L.R. 421; *Times*,
April 26, 2000, CA . . . .   *Digested*, 00/**362**
Commercial Bank of Australia v. Amadio (1983) 46 A.L.R. 402 . . . .   *Cited*, 93/2496,
                     95/3016: *Considered*, 01/4564
Commercial Banking Co of Sydney v. Jalsard Pty [1973] A.C. 279; [1972] 3 W.L.R.
566; [1972] 2 Lloyd's Rep. 529; 116 S.J. 695, PC (Aus) . . . .   *Digested*, 72/**181**:
                     Applied, 00/280
Commercial Bridging Plc v. Nelsons Ch.1995-C-4130, Ch D . . . .   *Digested*, 98/**4018**
Commercial Farmers Union v. Minister of Lands, Agriculture and Resettlement 10
B.H.R.C. 1, Sup Ct (Zim) . . . .   *Digested*, 01/**3451**
Commercial Guarantee Ltd, Re see Company (No.005448 of 1996), Re
Commercial Union Assurance Co Plc v. NRG Victory Reinsurance Ltd; Skandia
International Insurance Corp v. NRG Victory Reinsurance Ltd [1998] 2 All E.R.
434; [1998] 2 Lloyd's Rep. 600; [1998] C.L.C. 920; [1998] Lloyd's Rep. I.R.
439; *Times*, March 19, 1998, CA; reversing [1998] 1 Lloyd's Rep. 80; [1997]
C.L.C. 1561, QBD (Comm Ct) . . . .   *Digested*, 98/**3409**
Commercial Union Assurance Co Plc v. Shaw (Inspector of Taxes) [1999] S.T.C. 109; 72
T.C. 101; [1999] B.T.C. 12; 1 I.T.L. Rep. 381; *Times*, January 20, 1999;
Independent, January 13, 1999, CA; affirming [1998] S.T.C. 386; [1998] B.T.C.
89, Ch D . . . .   *Digested*, 99/**4678**:
                     Referred to, 99/4674
Commercial Union Assurance Co Plc v. Simat Helliesen & Eichner Inc [2000] I.L.Pr.
239; [2001] Lloyd's Rep. I.R. 172, QBD (Comm Ct) . . . .   *Digested*, 00/**747**
Commercial Union Life Assurance Co Ltd v. Label Ink Ltd [2001] L. & T.R. 29, Ch D
Commercial Union Life Assurance Co Ltd v. Moustafa [1999] L. & T.R. 489; [1999] 2
E.G.L.R. 44; [1999] 24 E.G. 155, QBD . . . .   *Digested*, 99/**3667**
COMMISSARIAT A L'ENERGIE ATOMIQUE/Welding (T243/96) [2001] E.P.O.R. 53, EPO
(Technical Bd App) . . . .   *Digested*, 01/**3913**
Commission for the New Towns v. Cooper (Great Britain) Ltd (formerly Coopind UK);
sub nom Milton Keynes Development Corp v. Cooper (Great Britain) [1995] Ch.
259; [1995] 2 W.L.R. 677; [1995] 2 All E.R. 929; (1996) 72 P. & C.R. 270;
[1995] 2 E.G.L.R. 113; [1995] E.G.C.S. 30; (1995) 139 S.J.L.B. 87; [1995]
N.P.C. 34; *Times*, March 3, 1995; *Independent*, March 15, 1995, CA; affirming in
part [1993] E.G.C.S. 142; [1993] N.P.C. 115, Ch D . . . .   *Digested*, 95/**780**:
                   Applied, 96/3756, 99/3658
Commission for the New Towns v. Horsham DC (2000) 79 P. & C.R. 443; [2000]
P.L.C.R. 70; [1999] N.P.C. 95, CA [1999] P.L.C.R. 207, QBD . . . .   *Digested*, 00/**4475**

Commission for the New Towns v. Milton Keynes DC [1999] J.P.L. 1008, QBD . . . .   *Digested*, 00/**4438**
Commission of the European Communites v. Belgium (C133/94) [1996] E.C.R. I-2323,
ECJ . . . .   *Applied*, 97/2319:
                                                                                            Followed, 99/2161
Commission of the European Communities v. Anic Partecipazioni SpA (C49/92) [1999]
E.C.R. I-4125; [2001] 4 C.M.L.R. 17, ECJ (6th Chamber) . . . .   *Digested*, 01/**758**
Commission of the European Communities v. AssiDoman Kraft Products AB (C310/97
P) [1999] All E.R. (EC) 737; [1999] E.C.R. I-5363; [1999] 5 C.M.L.R. 1253;
Times, October 19, 1999, ECJ; reversing [1997] All E.R. (E.C.) 769; [1997]
E.C.R. II-1185; [1997] 5 C.M.L.R. 364; [1997] C.E.C. 1013, CFI (2nd Chamber) .   *Digested*, 99/**2223**
Commission of the European Communities v. Atlantic Container Line AB (C149/95)
[1995] E.C.R. I-2165; [1997] 5 C.M.L.R. 167, ECJ [1995] All E.R. (E.C.) 853;
[1995] E.C.R. I-2165, CFI . . . .   *Digested*, 96/**1064**:
                                                                                            Considered, 01/772
Commission of the European Communities v. Belgium (C11/95); *sub nom* Cable
Television Broadcasts, Re [1996] E.C.R. I-4115; [1996] E.C.R. I-4155; [1997] 2
C.M.L.R. 289; [1998] E.M.L.R. 71, ECJ . . . .   *Digested*, 98/**3856**:
                                                                                            Applied, 97/3569
Commission of the European Communities v. Belgium (C173/91); *sub nom* Redundant
Women Employees (C173/91), Re [1993] E.C.R. I-673; [1993] 2 C.M.L.R. 165;
[1993] I.R.L.R. 404; *Financial Times*, February 23, 1993, ECJ [1993] E.C.R. I-
673, AGO . . . .   *Digested*, 93/**4276**:
                                                                                            Followed, 00/2163
Commission of the European Communities v. Belgium (C176/97 & C177/97) [1998]
E.C.R. I-3557; [1999] 1 C.M.L.R. 1443, ECJ . . . .   *Digested*, 99/**2251**
Commission of the European Communities v. Belgium (C203/98) [1999] E.C.R. I-
4899; [2000] 1 C.M.L.R. 866, ECJ (4th Chamber) . . . .   *Digested*, 00/**2391**
Commission of the European Communities v. Belgium (C207/97) [1999] E.C.R. I-275;
[2001] 1 C.M.L.R. 23; [1999] Env. L.R. D22, ECJ (6th Chamber)
Commission of the European Communities v. Belgium (C217/99) [2000] E.C.R. I-10251;
[2001] 2 C.M.L.R. 17, ECJ (6th Chamber)
Commission of the European Communities v. Belgium (C300/90) see Bachmann v.
Belgium (C204/90) (No.1)
Commission of the European Communities v. Belgium (C307/98) [2000] E.C.R. I-
3933; [2001] Env. L.R. D5, ECJ
Commission of the European Communities v. Belgium (C355/98) [2000] E.C.R. I-1221;
[2000] 2 C.M.L.R. 357; [2000] C.E.C. 131, ECJ (5th Chamber) . . . .   *Digested*, 00/**2399**
Commission of the European Communities v. Belgium (C356/85) see VAT Rates on
Wine (C356/85), Re
Commission of the European Communities v. Belgium (C42/89); *sub nom* Drinking
Water (C42/89), Re [1990] E.C.R. I-2821; [1992] 1 C.M.L.R. 22; [1993] Env.
L.R. 1, ECJ . . . .   *Followed*, 00/2160
Commission of the European Communities v. Belgium (C478/98) [2000] S.T.C. 830;
[2000] E.C.R. I-7587; [2000] 3 C.M.L.R. 1111; [2000] B.T.C. 301; [2000] S.T.I.
1446, ECJ. . . . .   *Digested*, 01/**5312**
Commission of the European Communities v. Belgium (No.1) (C149/79); *sub nom*
Public Employees (No.1) (C149/79), Re [1980] E.C.R. 3881; [1981] 2 C.M.L.R.
413, ECJ . . . .   *Digested*, 81/**1049**:
                                                                                            Applied, 99/5272, 01/5769
Commission of the European Communities v. Brazzelli Lualdi (C136/92) [1994] E.C.R.
I-1981, ECJ [1994] E.C.R. I-1981, AGO. . . . .   *Followed*, 00/2363
Commission of the European Communities v. Council of Ministers of the European
Communities (C309/95) [1998] E.C.R. I-655; [1998] 2 C.M.L.R. 1265, ECJ
(6th Chamber)
Commission of the European Communities v. Council of the European Union (C170/96);
sub nom Joint Act on Air Transit, Re [1998] E.C.R. I-2763; [1998] 2 C.M.L.R.
1092; [1999] I.N.L.R. 1, ECJ . . . .   *Digested*, 99/**2229**
Commission of the European Communities v. Denmark (C143/83) see Equal Pay
Concepts (C143/83), Re
Commission of the European Communities v. France (C1/00), *Times*, December 19,
2001, ECJ
Commission of the European Communities v. France (C147/00) [2001] E.C.R. I-2387;
[2001] Env. L.R. D13, ECJ
Commission of the European Communities v. France (C159/94) see Commission of the
European Communities v. Netherlands (C157/94)
Commission of the European Communities v. France (C166/97) [1999] E.C.R. I-1719;
[1999] 2 C.M.L.R. 723; [1999] Env. L.R. 781, ECJ (5th Chamber) . . . .   *Digested*, 99/**2154**
Commission of the European Communities v. France (C18/84); *sub nom* Aid to French
Newspapers, Re (C18/84) [1985] E.C.R. 1339; [1986] 1 C.M.L.R. 605, ECJ . . .   *Digested*, 86/**1433**:
                                                                                            Applied, 98/4517
Commission of the European Communities v. France (C184/96) [1998] E.C.R. I-6197;
[2000] 3 C.M.L.R. 1308, ECJ (6th Chamber) . . . .   *Digested*, 01/**2508**
Commission of the European Communities v. France (C225/97) [1999] E.C.R. I-3011;
[2000] 2 C.M.L.R. 996, ECJ (6th Chamber) . . . .   *Digested*, 00/**2353**

Commission of the European Communities v. France (C23/99) [2000] E.C.R. I-7653; [2001] E.C.D.R. 2; [2001] F.S.R. 25, ECJ [2000] E.C.R. I-7653; [2000] E.C.D.R. 462, AGO . . . . *Digested,* 01/**2487**

Commission of the European Communities v. France (C230/99) [2001] E.C.R. I-1169; [2001] 3 C.M.L.R. 10, ECJ (6th Chamber) . . . . *Digested,* 01/**2475**

Commission of the European Communities v. France (C265/95) [1997] E.C.R. I-6959; *Times,* December 11, 1997, ECJ . . . . *Digested,* 98/**729**

Commission of the European Communities v. France (C266/99) [2001] E.C.R. I-1981; [2001] Env. L.R. D14, ECJ

Commission of the European Communities v. France (C345/99) [2001] E.C.R. I-4493; [2001] S.T.I. 939, ECJ

Commission of the European Communities v. France (C374/98) [2000] E.C.R. I-10799; [2001] Env. L.R. D9, ECJ

Commission of the European Communities v. France (C38/99) [2000] E.C.R. I-10941; [2001] Env. L.R. 43, ECJ (6th Chamber)

Commission of the European Communities v. France (C381/93); *sub nom* Port Dues (C381/93), Re [1994] E.C.R. I-5145; [1995] 2 C.M.L.R. 485, ECJ . . . . *Digested,* 95/**4973**:
Applied, 98/4517: *Distinguished,* 99/3191

Commission of the European Communities v. France (C40/00) [2001] E.C.R. I-4539; [2001] S.T.I. 939, ECJ

Commission of the European Communities v. France (C429/97) [2001] S.T.C. 156; [2001] E.C.R. I-637; [2001] 2 C.M.L.R. 20; [2001] B.T.C. 5051; [2001] B.V.C. 140; [2001] S.T.I. 103, ECJ (6th Chamber) . . . . *Digested,* 01/**5589**

Commission of the European Communities v. France (C43/96) [1998] All E.R. (EC) 951; [1998] S.T.C. 805; [1998] E.C.R. I-3903; [1999] R.T.R. 171; *Times,* July 2, 1998, ECJ (6th Chamber) . . . . *Digested,* 98/**4894**:
Considered, 98/72: *Followed,* 99/4992

Commission of the European Communities v. France (C481/98) [2001] S.T.C. 919; [2001] E.C.R. I-3369; [2001] B.T.C. 5227; [2001] B.V.C. 302; [2001] S.T.I. 781, ECJ (6th Chamber) . . . . *Digested,* 01/**5571**

Commission of the European Communities v. France (C60/96) [1999] S.T.C. 480; [1997] E.C.R. I-3827, ECJ (6th Chamber) . . . . *Digested,* 99/**4971**

Commission of the European Communities v. France (C68/92); *sub nom* VAT on Advertising, Re; Commission of the European Communities v. Luxembourg (C69/92); Commission of the European Communities v. Spain (C73/92) [1997] S.T.C. 684; [1993] E.C.R. I-5881; [1995] 2 C.M.L.R. 1; *Financial Times,* November 23, 1993, ECJ . . . . *Digested,* 97/**5015**:
Applied, 97/5019, 01/5558: *Considered,* 98/4962

Commission of the European Communities v. France (C76/99) [2001] E.C.R. I-249; [2001] 1 C.M.L.R. 48, ECJ (6th Chamber) . . . . *Digested,* 01/**5560**

Commission of the European Communities v. France (C96/98) [1999] E.C.R. I-8531; [2000] 2 C.M.L.R. 681; [2000] Env. L.R. D28, ECJ (5th Chamber) . . . . *Digested,* 00/**2258**

Commission of the European Communities v. Germany (C102/97) [1999] E.C.R. I-5051; [1999] 3 C.M.L.R. 631; [2000] Env. L.R. D8, ECJ (5th Chamber) . . . . *Digested,* 00/**2303**

Commission of the European Communities v. Germany (C107/84) see Value Added Tax on Postal Transport (C107/84), Re

Commission of the European Communities v. Germany (C178/84); *sub nom* Purity Requirements for Beer (C178/84), Re [1987] E.C.R. 1227; [1988] 1 C.M.L.R. 780; *Times,* March 23, 1987, ECJ . . . . *Digested,* 88/**1514**:
Followed, 01/2508

Commission of the European Communities v. Germany (C184/97) [1999] E.C.R. I-7837; [2000] Env. L.R. D29, ECJ

Commission of the European Communities v. Germany (C191/95) [1999] All E.R. (EC) 483; [1998] E.C.R. I-5449; [1999] 2 C.M.L.R. 1265; *Times,* October 10, 1998, ECJ . . . . *Digested,* 98/**2313**

Commission of the European Communities v. Germany (C198/97) [1999] E.C.R. I-3257; [2000] Env. L.R. D3, ECJ

Commission of the European Communities v. Germany (C217/97) [1999] E.C.R. I-5087; [1999] 3 C.M.L.R. 277; [2000] Env. L.R. 141, ECJ (6th Chamber) . . . . *Digested,* 00/**2394**

Commission of the European Communities v. Germany (C248/83) see Sex Discrimination Laws (C248/83), Re

Commission of the European Communities v. Germany (C301/95) [1998] E.C.R. I-6135, ECJ . . . . *Followed,* 99/2161

Commission of the European Communities v. Germany (C431/92); *sub nom* Grosskrotzenburg Power Station (C431/92), Re [1995] E.C.R. I-2189; [1996] 1 C.M.L.R. 196, ECJ . . . . *Digested,* 96/**2718**:
Followed, 00/4460

Commission of the European Communities v. Germany (C57/89) [1991] E.C.R. I-883; *Times,* March 20, 1991, ECJ . . . . *Digested,* 91/**3905**:
Considered, 00/5882

Commission of the European Communities v. Germany (C59/89) [1991] E.C.R. I-2607, ECJ . . . . *Followed,* 00/2353

Commission of the European Communities v. Germany (C61/94); *sub nom* International
Dairy Agreement (C61/94), Re [1996] E.C.R. I-3989; [1997] 1 C.M.L.R. 281,
ECJ . . . . *Applied*, 00/4960:
Referred to, 99/3555

Commission of the European Communities v. Germany (C62/90); *sub nom* Private
Imports of Medicines (C62/90), Re [1992] E.C.R. I-2575; [1992] 2 C.M.L.R.
549, ECJ . . . . *Digested,* 92/**4763**:
Applied, 98/4517

Commission of the European Communities v. Germany (C68/99) [2001] E.C.R. I-1865;
[2001] 2 C.M.L.R. 35, ECJ (6th Chamber) . . . . *Digested,* 01/**5129**

Commission of the European Communities v. Germany (C70/72) see Investment Grants
for Mining, Re

Commission of the European Communities v. Greece (C123/94) [1995] E.C.R. I-1457,
ECJ . . . . *Digested,* 95/**2006**:
Followed, 99/2161

Commission of the European Communities v. Greece (C185/96) [1998] E.C.R. I-6601;
[2001] 1 C.M.L.R. 28, ECJ (5th Chamber) . . . . *Digested,* 01/**2503**

Commission of the European Communities v. Greece (C187/96) [1998] E.C.R. I-1095;
[1998] I.C.R. 1249; *Times,* March 25, 1998, ECJ (5th Chamber) . . . . *Digested,* 98/**2152**

Commission of the European Communities v. Greece (C187/98) [1999] E.C.R. I-7713;
[2000] 1 C.M.L.R. 465; [2000] C.E.C. 41, ECJ (6th Chamber) . . . . *Digested,* 00/**2160**

Commission of the European Communities v. Greece (C259/94) [1995] E.C.R. I-1947,
ECJ . . . . *Digested,* 95/**2249**:
Applied, 99/2154

Commission of the European Communities v. Greece (C329/88) [1989] E.C.R. 4159,
ECJ . . . . *Applied,* 00/3583

Commission of the European Communities v. Greece (C375/95) [1997] E.C.R. I-5981;
[1998] C.E.C. 420, ECJ (5th Chamber) . . . . *Digested,* 98/**4663**:
Applied, 01/5190

Commission of the European Communities v. Greece (C387/97) [2000] E.C.R. I-5047;
[2001] Env. L.R. D2; *Times,* July 7, 2000, ECJ . . . . *Digested,* 00/**2301**

Commission of the European Communities v. Greece (C398/98) see Emergency Stocks
of Petroleum Products (C398/98), Re

Commission of the European Communities v. Greece (C401/98) [1999] E.C.R. I-5543,
ECJ (5th Chamber) . . . . *Applied,* 00/3583

Commission of the European Communities v. Greece (C68/88); *sub nom* Cargo of the
Alfonsina, Re (C68/88) [1989] E.C.R. 2965; [1991] 1 C.M.L.R. 31; *Times,*
October 28, 1989, ECJ . . . . *Digested,* 91/**3915**:
Considered, 99/2232

Commission of the European Communities v. ICI Plc (C286/95) [2001] All E.R. (EC)
439; [2000] E.C.R. I-2341; [2000] 5 C.M.L.R. 413, ECJ (5th Chamber) . . . . . . *Digested,* 00/**2369**:
Joined proceedings, 00/2370

Commission of the European Communities v. Ireland (C212/98) [1999] E.C.R. I-8571;
[2000] E.C.D.R. 201, ECJ (5th Chamber) . . . . *Digested,* 00/**3583**

Commission of the European Communities v. Ireland (C30/99) [2001] E.C.R. I-4619;
[2001] 3 C.M.L.R. 28; *Times,* September 3, 2001, ECJ (5th Chamber) . . . . *Digested,* 01/**2491**

Commission of the European Communities v. Ireland (C370/99) [2001] E.C.R. I-297;
[2001] E.C.D.R. 13, ECJ [2001] E.C.R. I-297; [2001] E.C.D.R. 9, AGO . . . . *Digested,* 01/**2461**

Commission of the European Communities v. Ireland (C392/96) [2000] Q.B. 636;
[2000] 2 W.L.R. 958; [1999] E.C.R. I-5901; [1999] 3 C.M.L.R. 727; [1999] 4
P.L.R. 107; [2000] Env. L.R. D15; *Times,* October 19, 1999, ECJ (5th Chamber) . *Digested,* 99/**2161**

Commission of the European Communities v. Italy (C112/97) [1999] E.C.R. I-1821;
[2001] 1 C.M.L.R. 18, ECJ (6th Chamber)

Commission of the European Communities v. Italy (C158/94) see Commission of the
European Communities v. Netherlands (C157/94)

Commission of the European Communities v. Italy (C184/85) [1987] E.C.R. 2013, ECJ   *Cited,* 00/2406

Commission of the European Communities v. Italy (C203/87); *sub nom* Zero-rating for
Earthquake Victims (C203/87), Re [1989] E.C.R. 371; [1989] 2 C.M.L.R. 461,
ECJ . . . . *Digested,* 90/**2235**:
Cited, 93/4403

Commission of the European Communities v. Italy (C225/96) [1997] E.C.R. I-6887;
[1998] Env. L.R. 370, ECJ (5th Chamber) . . . . *Digested,* 98/**2571**

Commission of the European Communities v. Italy (C35/96); *sub nom* Customs Agents,
Re (C35/96) [1998] E.C.R. I-3851; [1998] 5 C.M.L.R. 889, ECJ (5th
Chamber) . . . . *Followed,* 01/761

Commission of the European Communities v. Italy (C365/97) [1999] E.C.R. I-7773;
[2001] Env. L.R. D8, ECJ

Commission of the European Communities v. Italy (C45/95) [1997] S.T.C. 1062; [1997]
E.C.R. I-3605; [1997] C.E.C. 1009; [1997] B.T.C. 5422; [1997] B.V.C. 536, ECJ
(6th Chamber) [1997] E.C.R. I-3605; [1997] C.E.C. 1002, AGO . . . . *Digested,* 97/**4988**:
Considered, 00/5291

Commission of the European Communities v. Italy (C7/68) see Export Tax on Art
Treasures (C7/68), Re

Commission of the European Communities v. Lisrestal (C32/95P) [1996] E.C.R. I-5373; [1997] 2 C.M.L.R. 1, ECJ (6th Chamber) .... *Applied*, 99/2240
Commission of the European Communities v. Luxembourg (C111/91); *sub nom* Maternity Allowances (C111/91), Re [1993] E.C.R. I-817; [1994] 2 C.M.L.R. 781; *Financial Times*, March 16, 1993, ECJ .... *Digested*, 93/**4376**: *Applied*, 00/2389

Commission of the European Communities v. Luxembourg (C266/00) [2001] E.C.R. I-2073; [2001] Env. L.R. D15, ECJ
Commission of the European Communities v. Luxembourg (C348/99) [2000] E.C.R. I-2917; [2000] E.C.D.R. 437, ECJ [2000] E.C.R. I-2917; [2000] E.C.D.R. 246, AGO .... *Digested*, 01/**2460**
Commission of the European Communities v. Luxembourg (C473/93); *sub nom* Public Service Employment (C473/93), Re [1996] E.C.R. I-3207; [1996] 3 C.M.L.R. 981, ECJ .... *Applied*, 99/5272, 01/5769

Commission of the European Communities v. Luxembourg (C69/92) see Commission of the European Communities v. France (C68/92)
Commission of the European Communities v. Luxembourg (C69/92) [1997] S.T.C. 712; [1993] E.C.R. I-5907; *Financial Times*, November 23, 1993, ECJ .... *Digested*, 97/**5016**: *Applied*, 01/5558

Commission of the European Communities v. National Association of Licensed Opencast Operators (NALOO) (C180/01); *sub nom* National Association of Licensed Opencast Operators (NALOO) v. Commission of the European Communities (T89/98) [2001] E.C.R. II-515; [2001] 4 C.M.L.R. 34, CFI (2nd Chamber) .... *Digested*, 01/**2472**
Commission of the European Communities v. Netherlands (C157/94); Commission of the European Communities v. Italy (C158/94); Commission of the European Communities v. France (C159/94); Commission of the European Communities v. Spain (C160/94) [1997] E.C.R. I-5699; [1998] 2 C.M.L.R. 373, ECJ
Commission of the European Communities v. Netherlands (C3/96) [1998] E.C.R. I-3031; [1999] Env. L.R. 147, ECJ .... *Digested*, 99/**2155**
Commission of the European Communities v. Netherlands (C338/98) [2001] S.T.I. 1418; *Times*, December 10, 2001, ECJ (5th Chamber) AGO
Commission of the European Communities v. Netherlands (C339/87); *sub nom* Protection of Wild Birds (C339/87), Re [1990] E.C.R. I-851; [1993] 2 C.M.L.R. 360, ECJ .... *Followed*, 00/2303
Commission of the European Communities v. Netherlands (C68/89); *sub nom* Entry into Dutch Territory, Re (C68/89) [1991] E.C.R. I-2637; [1993] 2 C.M.L.R. 389, ECJ .... *Followed*, 99/3212
Commission of the European Communities v. Portugal (C150/97) [1999] E.C.R. I-259; [1999] Env. L.R. D20, ECJ (5th Chamber)
Commission of the European Communities v. Portugal (C276/98) [2001] E.C.R. I-1699; [2001] B.T.C. 5135; [2001] B.V.C. 209, ECJ (6th Chamber) .... *Digested*, 01/**5609**
Commission of the European Communities v. Spain (C114/97) [1998] E.C.R. I-6717; [1999] 2 C.M.L.R. 701, ECJ (5th Chamber) .... *Digested*, 99/**2254**
Commission of the European Communities v. Spain (C124/96) [1998] S.T.C. 1237; [1998] E.C.R. I-2501, ECJ (6th Chamber) .... *Digested*, 99/**4984**
Commission of the European Communities v. Spain (C160/94) see Commission of the European Communities v. Netherlands (C157/94)
Commission of the European Communities v. Spain (C214/96) [1998] E.C.R. I-7661, ECJ .... *Applied*, 99/2154
Commission of the European Communities v. Spain (C355/90) [1993] E.C.R. I-4221, ECJ .... *Digested*, 94/**4833**: *Applied*, 00/2258: *Considered*, 96/2698
Commission of the European Communities v. Spain (C414/97) [1999] E.C.R. I-5585; [2001] 2 C.M.L.R. 4, ECJ .... *Digested*, 01/**5568**
Commission of the European Communities v. Spain (C73/92) see Commission of the European Communities v. France (C68/92)
Commission of the European Communities v. United Kingdom (C340/96) [1999] E.C.R. I-2023; [2000] Env. L.R. D5; *Times*, April 30, 1999, ECJ (5th Chamber) . *Digested*, 99/**5047**
Commission of the European Communities v. United Kingdom (C353/85) [1988] 2 All E.R. 557; [1988] S.T.C. 251; [1988] E.C.R. 817, ECJ .... *Digested*, 88/**1574**: *Applied*, 93/4113, 97/4993, 01/5600: *Considered*, 97/5057, 98/4961: *Referred to*, 95/5093

Commission of the European Communities v. United Kingdom (C359/97) [2000] S.T.C. 777; [2000] E.C.R. I-6355; [2000] 3 C.M.L.R. 919; [2001] B.T.C. 5383; [2001] B.V.C. 458; [2000] S.T.I. 1396; *Times*, October 10, 2000, ECJ .... *Digested*, 00/**5352**
Commission of the European Communities v. United Kingdom (C416/85); *sub nom* Zero-rating (C416/85), Re [1990] 2 Q.B. 130; [1988] 3 W.L.R. 1261; [1989] 1 All E.R. 364; [1988] S.T.C. 456; [1988] E.C.R. 3127; [1988] 3 C.M.L.R. 169; (1988) 85(46) L.S.G. 43; (1988) 132 S.J. 1671; *Times*, June 22, 1988; *Independent*, June 28, 1988; *Financial Times*, June 29, 1988, ECJ .... *Digested*, 89/**1685**: *Considered*, 01/5559: *Followed*, 99/5031

Commission of the European Communities *v.* United Kingdom (C69/99) [2000] E.C.R.
I-10979; *Times,* December 19, 2000, ECJ . . . . *Digested,* 01/**2420**
Commissioner of Police *v.* Stunt see R. (on the application of Stunt) *v.* Mallett
Commissioner of Police of the Metropolis *v.* Harley [2001] I.C.R. 927; [2001] I.R.L.R.
263, EAT . . . . *Digested,* 01/**2234**
Commissioner of Police of the Metropolis *v.* Lowrey Nesbitt [1999] I.C.R. 401; *Times,*
July 29, 1998, EAT . . . . *Digested,* 98/**2141**:
Considered, 01/2346

Commissioner of Taxation *v.* Consolidated Press Holdings Ltd 3 I.T.L. Rep. 744, HC
(Aus) 2 I.T.L. Rep. 165, Fed Ct (Aus) (Full Ct)
Commissioner of Taxation *v.* Coombes (No.2) 1 I.T.L. Rep. 397, Fed Ct (Aus) (Sgl
judge)
Commissioners of Customs and Excise *v.* Church Schools Foundation Ltd see Church
Schools Foundation Ltd *v.* Customs and Excise Commissioners
Commonwealth Reserves *v.* Chodar (2000-01) 3 I.T.E.L.R. 549, HC (NZ)
Commune d'Almelo ea *v.* NV Energiebedrijf Ijsselmij (C393/92) see Gemeente Almelo *v.*
Energiebedrijf Ijsellmij NV (C393/92)
Community Concepts AG *v.* Office for Harmonisation in the Internal Market (Trade
Marks and Designs) (OHIM) (T360/99) [2000] E.C.R. II-3545; [2001] E.T.M.R.
17, CFI (4th Chamber) . . . . *Digested,* 01/**3997**
Comninos *v.* Prudential Assurance Co Ltd see National Justice Compania Naviera SA
v. Prudential Assurance Co Ltd (The Ikarian Reefer) (No.2)
Compagnie de Saint-Gobain, Zweigniederlassung Germany *v.* Finanzamt Aachen-
Innenstadt (C307/97) [2000] S.T.C. 854; [1999] E.C.R. I-6161; [2001] 3
C.M.L.R. 34, ECJ [1999] E.C.R. I-6161; 1 I.T.L. Rep. 789, AGO . . . . *Digested,* 01/**5212**
Compagnie des Courtiers Jures Piqueurs de Vins de Paris *v.* Societe DDB Needham
[2000] E.C.C. 128, Cass (F)
Compagnie Maritime Belge Transports SA *v.* Commission of the European Communities
(C395/96); *sub nom* Cie Maritime Belge Transports SA *v.* Commission of the
European Communities (C395/96); Dafra-Lines A/S *v.* Commission of the
European Communities (C396/96) [2000] All E.R. (EC) 385; [2000] E.C.R. I-
1365; [2000] 4 C.M.L.R. 1076, ECJ (5th Chamber) . . . . *Digested,* 00/**709**
Compagnie Nationale Air France *v.* Commission of the European Communities (T358/
94) [1996] E.C.R. II-2109; [1997] 1 C.M.L.R. 492, CFI (2nd Chamber) . . . . *Followed,* 00/2343
Compagnie Noga d'Importation et d'Exportation SA *v.* Abacha (No.2); Attorney General
of Nigeria *v.* Abacha [2001] 3 All E.R. 513; [2001] C.P. Rep. 93; (2001) 151
N.L.J. 693, QBD (Comm Ct) . . . . *Digested,* 01/**579**
Companhia de Mocambique *v.* British South Africa Co see British South Africa Co *v.*
Companhia de Mocambique
Companhia de Seguros Imperio *v.* Heath (REBX) Ltd see Cia de Seguros Imperio *v.*
Heath (REBX) Ltd (formerly CE Heath & Co (America) Ltd)
Companhia Europeia de Transportes Aeros SA *v.* British Aerospace Plc, *Times,* January
12, 1999, CA . . . . *Digested,* 99/**451**
Compania Maritima San Basilio SA *v.* Oceanus Mutual Underwriting Association
(Bermuda) Ltd [1977] Q.B. 49; [1976] 3 W.L.R. 265; [1976] 3 All E.R. 243;
[1976] 2 Lloyd's Rep. 171; 120 S.J. 486, CA . . . . *Digested,* 76/**2570**:
Considered, 96/5697, 00/4744

Compania Panamena Europea Navegacion Limitada *v.* Frederick Leyland & Co Ltd see
Panamena Europea Navegacion Compania Limitada *v.* Frederick Leyland & Co
Ltd
Compania Sudamericana de Fletes SA *v.* African Continental Bank Ltd (The Rosarino)
[1973] 1 Lloyd's Rep. 21, QBD (Comm Ct) . . . . *Digested,* 73/**3110**:
Not followed, 00/5438

Companies Act 1985, Re see Lo-Line Electric Motors, Re
Company (No.00996 of 1979), Re see Racal Communications Ltd, Re
Company (No.003729 of 1982), Re [1984] 1 W.L.R. 1090; [1984] 3 All E.R. 78; (1984) 81
L.S.G. 2693; (1984) 128 S.J. 580, Ch D . . . . *Digested,* 84/**329**:
Distinguished, 91/2163, 98/3328: *Followed,* 93/2361
Company (No.000596 of 1986), Re [1987] B.C.L.C. 133 . . . . *Digested,* 87/**351**:
Considered, 98/692

Company (No.002180 of 1986), Re see Alipour *v.* Ary
Company (No.00370 of 1987), Re, Ex p. Glossop see Company (No.00370 of 1987), Ex p.
Glossop, Re
Company (No.00370 of 1987), Ex p. Glossop, Re; *sub nom* Company (No.00370 of
1987), Re, Ex p. Glossop [1988] 1 W.L.R. 1068; (1988) 4 B.C.C. 506; [1988]
B.C.L.C. 570; [1988] P.C.C. 351; (1988) 85(41) L.S.G. 43; (1988) 132 S.J. 1388,
Ch D . . . . *Digested,* 88/**369**:
Considered, 90/4779, 98/694: *Not followed,* 90/568
Company (No.000359 of 1987), Re; *sub nom* International Westminster Bank *v.*
Okeanos Maritime Corp [1988] Ch. 210; [1987] 3 W.L.R. 339; [1987] 3 All E.R.
137; [1987] B.C.L.C. 450; [1988] P.C.C. 64; (1987) 84 L.S.G. 1811; (1987) 131
S.J. 938, Ch D . . . . *Digested,* 87/**375**:
Applied, 97/3090: *Considered,* 92/2579, 99/3350, 99/3351
Company (No.005009 of 1987) (No.1), Re see MC Bacon Ltd (No.1), Re

Company (No.005009 of 1987) (No.2), Re see MC Bacon Ltd (No.2), Re
Company (No.005685 of 1988), Re (1989) 5 B.C.C. 79; [1989] B.C.L.C. 424; [1989]
    P.C.C. 438 . . . .   *Digested*, 89/**356**:
                      Applied, 00/689: *Considered*, 91/435, 93/391
Company (No.005685 of 1988) (No.2), Re [1989] B.C.L.C. 427 . . . .   *Digested*, 90/**540**:
                                          Considered, 00/620
Company (No.003079 of 1990), Re [1991] B.C.C. 683; [1991] B.C.L.C. 235 . . . .   *Digested*, 92/**2590**:
                                        Considered, 99/3348
Company (No.004055 of 1991) Ex p. Record Tennis Centres, Re [1991] 1 W.L.R. 1003;
    [1991] B.C.C. 509; [1991] B.C.L.C. 865, Ch D . . . .   *Digested*, 92/**2570**:
                                  Distinguished, 00/3498
Company (No.000709 of 1992), Re see O'Neill v. Phillips
Company (No.001127 of 1992), Re [1992] B.C.L.C. 477 . . . .   *Disapproved*, 99/3354
Company (No.007816 of 1994), Re see Secretary of State for Trade and Industry v. Great
    Western Assurance Co SA
Company (No.007818 of 1994), Re see Secretary of State for Trade and Industry v. Great
    Western Assurance Co SA
Company (No.007819 of 1994), Re see Secretary of State for Trade and Industry v. Great
    Western Assurance Co SA
Company (No.007820 of 1994), Re see Secretary of State for Trade and Industry v. Great
    Western Assurance Co SA
Company (No.007821 of 1994), Re see Secretary of State for Trade and Industry v. Great
    Western Assurance Co SA
Company (No.007822 of 1994), Re see Secretary of State for Trade and Industry v. Great
    Western Assurance Co SA
Company (No.007923 of 1994), Re; Company (No.007924 of 1994), Re [1995] 1 W.L.R.
    953; [1995] B.C.C. 634; [1995] 1 B.C.L.C. 440; (1995) 92(8) L.S.G. 39; *Times*,
    February 2, 1995, CA. . . . .   *Digested*, 95/**2850**:
                                    Distinguished, 99/3354
Company (No.007924 of 1994), Re see Company (No.007923 of 1994), Re
Company (No.002613 of 1996), Re see Senator Hanseatische Verwaltungsgesellschaft
    mbH, Re
Company (No.005448 of 1996), Re; Company (No.005449 of 1996), Re; Commercial
    Guarantee Ltd, Re [1998] 1 B.C.L.C. 98, Ch D . . . .   *Digested*, 98/**502**
Company (No.005449 of 1996), Re see Company (No.005448 of 1996), Re
Company (No.007020 of 1996), Re; *sub nom* Shepherd Hill Civil Engineering Ltd v.
    Brophy Landscape [1998] 2 B.C.L.C. 54, Ch D . . . .   *Digested*, 97/**3084**
Company (No.003025 of 1997), Re see Galileo Group Ltd, Re
Company (No.004601 of 1997), Re [1998] 2 B.C.L.C. 111, Ch D (Companies Ct) . . . . .   *Digested*, 98/**3327**
Company (No.006140 of 1997), Re (Unreported, April 27, 1998), Ch D [*Ex rel.* Jeffrey
    Green Russell Solicitors, Apollo House, 56 New Bond Street, London] . . . .   *Digested*, 98/**3328**
Company (No.5669 of 1998), Re see Secretary of State for Trade and Industry v. Travel Time
    (UK) Ltd
Company (No.003689 of 1998), Re, *Times*, October 7, 1998, Ch D (Companies Ct)
Company (No.007130 of 1998), Re [2000] 1 B.C.L.C. 582, Ch D . . . .   *Digested*, 00/**3496**
Company (No.007356/98), Re [2000] B.C.C. 214, Ch D . . . .   *Digested*, 00/**3503**
Company (No.3461 of 1999), Re, *Independent*, July 3, 2000 (C.S), Ch D
Company (No.005174 of 1999), Re [2000] 1 W.L.R. 502; [2000] B.C.C. 698; [2000] 1
    B.C.L.C. 593; [2000] I.C.R. 263; *Times*, November 2, 1999, Ch D . . . .   *Digested*, 99/**3268**
Company Directors Disqualification Act 1986, Re see Britannia Homes Centres Ltd, Re
Compaq Computer Corp v. Internal Revenue Commissioner 2 I.T.L. Rep. 227; 4 I.T.L.
    Rep. 338, US Ct
Compaq Computer Corp v. Internal Revenue Commissioner 2 I.T.L. Rep. 323, US Ct
Compaq Computer Corp v. Internal Revenue Commissioner 2 I.T.L. Rep. 337, US Ct
Compaq Computer Ltd v. Hsi Kuang Ma (1998) 21(6) I.P.D. 21058, Pat Ct
Compassion in World Farming Ltd v. Customs and Excise Commissioners [1998] B.V.C.
    2041; [1997] V. & D.R. 281, V&DTr . . . .   *Digested*, 00/**5326**
COMPLETE Trade Mark see Procter & Gamble Co's Trade Mark Application (COMPLETE)
Compliance of the Death Penalty with the Constitution of the Republic of Lithuania, Re 6
    B.H.R.C. 283, Const Ct (LT)
Comptoir Commercial d' Orient SA v. Medtrafina SA [1999] I.L.Pr. 336, Cass (F) . . . . .   *Digested*, 99/**740**
Computer & Systems Engineering Plc v. John Lelliott (Ilford) 54 B.L.R. 1; *Times*,
    February 21, 1991, CA; affirming *Times*, May 23, 1989, QBD. . . . .   *Digested*, 93/**309**:
                                      Considered, 00/3519
Comunidad Autonoma de Cantabria v. Council of the European Union (T238/97)
    [1998] E.C.R. II-2271; [1999] 3 C.M.L.R. 656, CFI (1st Chamber) . . . .   *Digested*, 00/**2408**
Concord Petroleum Corp v. Gosford Marine Panama SA see Owners of Cargo Laden
    on Board the Albacruz v. Owners of the Albazero
Concorde Investments Ltd v. Borch [2000] C.P. Rep. 34, QBD (Comm Ct) . . . .   *Digested*, 00/**479**
Conde Nast Publication Ltd v. MGN Ltd [1998] F.S.R. 427, Ch D . . . .   *Digested*, 98/**3424**
Conder Structures v. Kvaerner Construction Ltd. . . . .   *Applied*, 00/228
Condon, Re v. Ex p. James see Condon Ex p. James, Re

Condon v. Basi [1985] 1 W.L.R. 866; [1985] 2 All E.R. 453; (1985) 135 N.L.J. 485; (1985) 129 S.J. 382, CA . . . .   *Digested*, 85/**2329**:
Followed, 01/4544

Condon Ex p. James, Re; *sub nom* Condon, Re v. Ex p. James (1873-74) L.R. 9 Ch. App. 609; [1874-80] All E.R. Rep. 388, CA in Chancery . . . .   *Applied*, 70/310,
72/189, 74/171, 74/357, 75/170: *Considered*, 99/3258: *Distinguished*, 72/197,
82/195, 87/3806, 88/3612: *Not applied*, 99/3230

Condron v. United Kingdom (35718/97) (No.1) [1999] Crim. L.R. 984, ECHR

Condron v. United Kingdom (35718/97) (No.2) (2001) 31 E.H.R.R. 1; 8 B.H.R.C. 290; [2000] Crim. L.R. 679; *Times*, May 9, 2000, ECHR . . . .   *Digested*, 00/**1075**:
Applied, 00/1076, 01/997: *Considered*, 00/1073

Coney (A Bankrupt), Re [1998] B.P.I.R. 333, Ch D   *Digested*, 98/**3286**

Congdon v. Saunders (Unreported, February 11, 1998), CC (Plymouth) [*Ex rel.* Veitch Penny Solicitors, 1 Manor Court, Dix's Field, Exeter, Devon] . . . .   *Digested*, 98/**432**

Congleton BC v. Bossons (1999) 14 P.A.D. 155, Planning Inspector

Conlan v. Chief Constable of Northumbria FC2+A 1999/7677/B1, CA.   *Digested*, 00/**623**

Conlon v. Allen (Unreported, April 3, 2000), CC (Chichester) [*Ex rel.* David McHugh, Barrister, Bracton Chambers, 2nd Floor, 95A Chancery Lane, London] . . . .   *Digested*, 00/**1462**

Connaught Laboratories Inc's Patent (Surrender) see SmithKline Beecham Biologicals SA v. Connaught Laboratories Inc (Surrender of Patent)

Connecticut Fire Insurance Co v. Kavanagh [1892] A.C. 473, PC (Can) . . . .   *Applied*, 63/32,
63/251: *Approved*, 66/1083: *Followed*, 00/581

Connelly v. DPP; *sub nom* R. v. Connelly (Charles) [1964] A.C. 1254; [1964] 2 W.L.R. 1145; [1964] 2 All E.R. 401; (1964) 48 Cr. App. R. 183; (1964) 128 J.P. 418; 108 S.J. 356, HL; affirming [1963] 3 W.L.R. 839; [1963] 3 All E.R. 510; 107 S.J. 793, CCA . . . .   *Digested*, 64/**768**:
Applied, 64/768.a, 65/732, 65/826, 70/941, 82/511, 84/513, 84/971,
85/1147, 86/1176, 86/2936, 89/597, 92/3814, 94/658, 00/5485:
Considered, 64/767, 65/2771, 66/11738, 69/1456, 69/2155, 70/458,
73/3278, 74/3452, 75/665, 84/578, 84/3351, 85/3360, 87/699, 97/1317:
Distinguished, 67/2830, 70/421, 77/633: *Explained*, 67/706:
Not applied, 74/687, 76/488

Connelly v. RTZ Corp Plc (No.2) [1998] A.C. 854; [1997] 3 W.L.R. 373; [1997] 4 All E.R. 335; [1997] C.L.C. 1357; [1997] I.L.Pr. 805; [1998] Env. L.R. 318; (1997) 94(32) L.S.G. 28; (1997) 147 N.L.J. 1346; (1997) 141 S.J.L.B. 199; *Times*, August 4, 1997, HL; affirming [1997] I.L.Pr. 643; *Times*, July 12, 1996, CA . . . . .   *Digested*, 97/**908**:
Considered, 98/3476, 99/718

Connelly v. RTZ Corp Plc (No.3) [1999] C.L.C. 533, QBD . . . .   *Digested*, 99/**474**

Connemara Machine Turf Co Ltd v. Coillte Teoranta (C306/97) [1999] 1 W.L.R. 62; [1999] All E.R. (EC) 62; [1998] E.C.R. I-8761; [1999] 2 C.M.L.R. 457, ECJ (5th Chamber) . . . .   *Digested*, 99/**2280**

Connex South Eastern Ltd v. National Union of Rail Maritime and Transport Workers [1999] I.R.L.R. 249, CA; affirming (Unreported, December 11, 1998), QBD . . . . .   *Digested*, 99/**2074**

Connolly v. Commission of the European Communities (C274/99); *sub nom* Connolly v. Commission of the European Communities (T34/96) [2001] E.C.R. I-1611; [2001] 3 C.M.L.R. 58, ECJ

Connolly v. Commission of the European Communities (T34/96) see Connolly v. Commission of the European Communities (C274/99)

Connolly v. Secretary of State for Northern Ireland [1994] N.I. 75, CA (NI) . . . .   *Digested*, 00/**5387**

Connolly v. Sellers Arenascene Ltd (No.2) see Sellers Arenascene Ltd v. Connolly (No.2)

Connolly v. Tasker see Heil v. Rankin

Connolly v. Tasker (Costs) see Heil v. Rankin (Costs)

Connolly v. Turner & Newall Ltd (Unreported, December 17, 1999), CC (Oldham) [*Ex rel.* John Pickering & Partners Solicitors, 9 Church Lane, Oldham] . . . .   *Digested*, 00/**512**

Connolly-Martin v. D see Connolly-Martin v. Davis

Connolly-Martin v. Davis; *sub nom* Connolly-Martin v. D [1999] Lloyd's Rep. P.N. 790; [1999] P.N.L.R. 826; (1999) 96(23) L.S.G. 35; *Times*, June 8, 1999; *Independent*, June 18, 1999, CA; reversing [1999] P.N.L.R. 350; *Times*, August 17, 1998, Ch D . . . .   *Digested*, 99/**3953**

Connor v. Secretary of State for Scotland 2000 Rep. L.R. 18; 2000 G.W.D. 1-29; *Times*, March 22, 2000, OH . . . .   *Digested*, 00/**6585**

Connors v. Reigate and Banstead BC [2000] J.P.L. 1178 (Note), CA. . . . .   *Digested*, 01/**4706**

Conoco Ltd v. Customs and Excise Commissioners (No.1) [1995] S.T.C. 1022, QBD; reversing [1995] V. & D.R. 48, VAT Tr (London) . . . .   *Digested*, 96/**5906**:
Followed, 98/4891

Conran v. Conran [1997] 2 F.L.R. 615; [1998] 1 F.C.R. 144; [1997] Fam. Law 724; *Times*, July 14, 1997, Fam Div . . . .   *Digested*, 97/**2482**

Conroy v. Kenny [1999] 1 W.L.R. 1340; [1999] Lloyd's Rep. Bank. 43; [1999] C.C.L.R. 35; (1999) 96(7) L.S.G. 36; *Times*, January 27, 1999, CA . . . .   *Digested*, 99/**2515**

Consafe Engineering (UK) Ltd v. Emtunga UK Ltd [1999] R.P.C. 154; (1998) 21 (11) I.P.D. 21121, Pat Ct. . . . .   *Digested*, 99/**3514**

Consiglio Nazionale Degli Spedizionieri Doganali (CNSD) *v.* Commission of the
  European Communities (T513/93) [2000] E.C.R. II-1807; [2000] 5 C.M.L.R.
  614, CFI (5th Chamber) . . . .   *Digested,* 01/**755**
Consolidated Foods Corp *v.* Brandon & Co [1965] A.I.R. Bom. 35. . . . .   *Applied,* 98/3521
Consorzio del Prosciutto di Parma *v.* Asda Food Stores Ltd; *sub nom* Consorzio del
  Prosciutto di Parma *v.* Asda Stores Ltd; Consorzio del Prosciutto di Parma *v.*
  Hygrade Foods Ltd [2001] UKHL 7; [2001] 1 C.M.L.R. 43; [2001] E.T.M.R. 53,
  HL; reversing [1999] 1 C.M.L.R. 696; [1999] Eu. L.R. 437; [1999] E.T.M.R. 319;
  [1999] F.S.R. 563; (1999) 17 Tr. L.R. 545; (1999) 22(2) I.P.D. 22015; (1999)
  96(2) L.S.G. 29; (1999) 143 S.J.L.B. 46; *Times,* December 4, 1998, CA;
  affirming [1998] 2 C.M.L.R. 215; [1998] Eu. L.R. 192; [1998] E.T.M.R. 481;
  [1998] F.S.R. 697; (1998) 17 Tr. L.R. 56; (1998) 21(8) I.P.D. 21090; *Times,*
  February 3, 1998, Ch D . . . .   *Digested,* 99/**2599**
Consorzio del Prosciutto di Parma *v.* Asda Stores Ltd see Consorzio del Prosciutto di
  Parma *v.* Asda Food Stores Ltd
Consorzio del Prosciutto di Parma *v.* Hygrade Foods Ltd see Consorzio del Prosciutto di
  Parma *v.* Asda Food Stores Ltd
Consorzio Gruppo di Azione Locale Murgia Messapica *v.* Commission of the European
  Communities (T465/93) [1994] E.C.R. II-361, CFI . . . .   *Applied,* 98/2311
Consorzio per la Tutela del Formaggio Gorgonzola *v.* Kaserei Champignon Hofmeister
  GmbH & Co KG (C87/97); *sub nom* GORGONZOLA/CAMBOZOLA [1999]
  E.C.R. I-1301; [1999] 1 C.M.L.R. 1203; [1999] E.T.M.R. 454, ECJ [1999] E.C.R.
  I-1301; [1999] E.T.M.R. 195, AGO [1999] E.T.M.R. 135, VGH (Frankfurt Am
  Main) . . . .   *Digested,* 99/**3570**
Constantine *v.* McGregor Cory Ltd [2000] I.C.R. 938, EAT . . . .   *Digested,* 00/**2190**
Constantinescu *v.* Romania (28871/95) (2001) 33 E.H.R.R. 33, ECHR
Constantinou *v.* Ozcan (Unreported, September 15, 1999), CC (Edmonton) [*Ex rel.*
  Andrew Petersen, Barrister, 9 Gough Square, London] . . . .   *Digested,* 99/**2479**
Consumer and Industrial Press (No.1), Re (1988) 4 B.C.C. 68; [1988] B.C.L.C. 177; [1988]
  P.C.C. 436, Ch D (Companies Ct) . . . .   *Digested,* 88/**290:**
                               Disapproved, 90/508: *Distinguished,* 90/503, 99/3275
Consumer Ombudsman *v.* Mattel Scandinavia A/S (E8/94 and E9/94);
  Forbrukerombudet *v.* Lego Norge A/S [1996] 1 C.M.L.R. 313, EFTA . . . .   *Applied,* 98/3855
Consumer Protection for Foreign Customers, Re [2000] E.C.C. 39, BGH (Ger)
Conteh *v.* Secretary of State for the Home Department [1992] Imm. A.R. 594, CA . . . .   *Digested,* 93/**2225:**
                               Considered, 00/3289
Conti *v.* AIP Private Bank Ltd (formerly Ueberseebank AG); *sub nom* Conti, Petitioner
  2000 S.C. 240; 2000 S.L.T. 1015; [2000] B.C.C. 172; 2000 G.W.D. 3-83; *Times,*
  March 15, 2000, Ex Div; reversing 1999 S.L.T. 580; *Times,* October 12, 1998,
  OH . . . .   *Digested,* 00/**5956**
Conti, Petitioner see Conti *v.* AIP Private Bank Ltd (formerly Ueberseebank AG)
Contigroup Companies Inc (formerly Continental Grain Co) *v.* China Petroleum
  Technology & Development Corp see LG Caltex Gas Co Ltd *v.* China National
  Petroleum Corp
Continental Assurance Co of London Plc (In Liquidation), Re see Singer *v.* Beckett
Continental Assurance Co of London Plc (In Liquidation) (No.1), Re; *sub nom* Secretary
  of State for Trade and Industry *v.* Burrows [1996] B.C.C. 888; [1997] 1 B.C.L.C.
  48; (1996) 93(28) L.S.G. 29; (1996) 140 S.J.L.B. 156; *Times,* July 2, 1996, Ch D
  (Companies Ct) . . . .   *Digested,* 96/**981**
Continental Assurance Co of London Plc (In Liquidation) (No.2), Re [1998] 1 B.C.L.C. 583,
  Ch D (Companies Ct) . . . .   *Digested,* 98/**3333**
Continental Assurance Co of London Plc (In Liquidation) (No.3), Re; *sub nom* Hughes *v.*
  Hogg Insurance Brokers Ltd [2000] B.C.C. 65; [1999] 1 B.C.L.C. 751; (1999)
  96(6) L.S.G. 32; *Times,* January 14, 1999, Ch D . . . .   *Digested,* 99/**3360**
Continental Bank NA *v.* Aeakos Compania Naviera SA [1994] 1 W.L.R. 588; [1994] 2
  All E.R. 540; [1994] 1 Lloyd's Rep. 505; [1994] I.L.Pr. 413; *Times,* November 26,
  1993, CA . . . .   *Digested,* 94/**3715:**
                       Applied, 00/750, 00/756, 01/808: *Considered,* 96/1219, 97/882:
                                        Followed, 96/1093
Continental Pacific Shipping Ltd *v.* Deemand Shipping Co Ltd (The Lendoudis
  Evangelos II) [1997] 1 Lloyd's Rep. 404; [1997] C.L.C. 432; *Independent,*
  December 16, 1996 (C.S.), QBD (Comm Ct) . . . .   *Digested,* 97/**4594:**
                                 Applied, 01/4917
Continuum (Europe) Ltd *v.* Customs and Excise Commissioners [1998] B.V.C. 2131;
  [1998] V. & D.R. 70, V&DTr . . . .   *Digested,* 98/**4900**
Contra Vision Ltd's Application to Amend UK Patent (No.GB 2165292C) see Clear Focus
  Imaging Inc *v.* Contra Vision Ltd
Contrada *v.* Italy [1998] H.R.C.D. 795, ECHR
Control Ltd *v.* Customs and Excise Commissioners [2001] S.T.I. 617, V&DTr
Convenience Co Ltd *v.* Noton see Convenience Co Ltd *v.* Roberts
Convenience Co Ltd *v.* Roberts; Convenience Co Ltd *v.* Noton [2001] F.S.R. 35, QBD .   *Digested,* 01/**960**
Conway (CICA: Quantum: 2001), Re [2001] 6 Q.R. 5, CICAP [*Ex rel.* Jonathan Clarke,
  Barrister, Old Square Chambers, Hanover House, 47 Corn Street, Bristol] . . . . .   *Digested,* 01/**1593**

Conway v. Lagou (Unreported, October 7, 1999), CC (West London) [*Ex rel.* Tim
Kevan, Barrister, 1 Temple Gardens, Temple, London] . . . . *Digested,* 00/**837**
Conway v. Rimmer [1968] A.C. 910; [1968] 2 W.L.R. 998; [1968] 1 All E.R. 874; 112
S.J. 191, HL; reversing [1967] 1 W.L.R. 1031; [1967] 2 All E.R. 1260; 111 S.J. 479,
CA . . . . *Digested,* 68/**3098**:
Applied, 71/4680, 71/9764, 72/2729, 72/2731, 73/2642, 75/2612, 77/2324,
79/2129, 81/2146, 85/1998, 93/1758, 93/3235, 94/1947, 94/3675:
Considered, 71/9186, 72/1610, 76/2138, 82/2471, 83/2936, 86/1519,
87/1688, 00/5392: *Subsequent proceedings,* 68/3099
Conwell v. Newham LBC; *sub nom* Newham LBC v. Conwell [2000] 1 W.L.R. 1;
[2000] 1 All E.R. 696; [2000] I.C.R. 42; [2000] 1 F.L.R. 595; [1999] 3 F.C.R.
625; (2000) 2 L.G.L.R. 901; [2000] B.L.G.R. 370; [2000] Fam. Law 241, EAT . *Digested,* 00/**3200**
Conwy CBC v. Wain Homes (Chester) Ltd (2001) 16 P.A.D. 24, Planning Inspector
Conwy CBC v. Windjen Power Ltd (2001) 16 P.A.D. 37, Planning Inspector
Cook, Re [1999] B.P.I.R. 881, Ch D . . . . *Digested,* 00/**3441**
Cook (A Minor) v. Burton (Unreported, October 21, 1997), CC (Kingston upon Hull)
[*Ex rel.* Paul Stott, Carrick, Carr & Wright Solicitors, Hull] . . . . *Digested,* 98/**594**
Cook (Inspector of Taxes) v. Billings [2001] S.T.C. 16; 73 T.C. 580; [2001] B.T.C. 3;
[2000] S.T.I. 1712; *Times,* January 16, 2001, CA; reversing [1999] S.T.C. 661;
[1999] B.T.C. 220; (1999) 96(23) L.S.G. 35; *Times,* June 8, 1999, Ch D . . . . . . *Digested,* 01/**5261**
Cook v. Financial Insurance Co Ltd [1998] 1 W.L.R. 1765; [1999] Lloyd's Rep. I.R. 1;
(1999) 46 B.M.L.R. 1; (1999) 96(3) L.S.G. 31; (1999) 143 S.J.L.B. 52; *Times,*
December 4, 1998, HL; reversing [1997] 6 Re. L.R. 300, CA. . . . . *Digested,* 99/**3387**
Cook v. HA Timm Motors (Unreported, August 25, 2000), CC (Birmingham) [*Ex rel.*
Levenes Solicitors, The McLaren Building, 35 Dale End, Birmingham] . . . . *Digested,* 01/**1760**
Cook (Inspector of Taxes) v. Medway Housing Society Ltd see Medway Housing
Society Ltd v. Cook (Inspector of Taxes)
Cook v. Ministry of Defence (Unreported, May 14, 1984) . . . . *Distinguished,* 00/2242
Cook v. R. 5 B.H.R.C. 163, Sup Ct (Can) . . . . *Digested,* 99/**3139**
Cook v. Thorne House Autistic Community [1999] Disc. L.R. 100, EAT . . . . *Digested,* 99/**2058**
Cooke v. Austria (25878/94) (2001) 31 E.H.R.R. 11, ECHR. . . . . *Digested,* 01/**3508**
Cooke v. National Westminster Bank Plc [1998] 2 F.L.R. 783; [1998] 3 F.C.R. 643;
[1998] Fam. Law 665; *Times,* July 27, 1998, CA. . . . . *Digested,* 98/**305**
Cooke v. Routledge [1998] N.I. 174, CA (NI) . . . . *Digested,* 99/**5404**
Cooke v. Whiteley (Unreported, October 27, 1999), CC (Doncaster) [*Ex rel.* Helen
Waddington, Barrister, Park Lane Chambers, 19 Westgate, Leeds] . . . . *Digested,* 00/**2569**:
Applied, 00/2587: *Followed,* 00/2577
Cool Carriers AB v. HSBC Bank USA [2001] 2 All E.R. (Comm) 177; [2001] 2 Lloyd's
Rep. 22; [2001] C.P. Rep. 82, QBD (Comm Ct) . . . . *Digested,* 01/**648**
Coombs v. Warren (Unreported, November 3, 1998), CC (Bridgwater) [*Ex rel.* Adam
Posta, Barrister, South Western Chambers, 12 Middle Street, Taunton,
Somerset] . . . . *Digested,* 99/**1558**
Cooper (CICB: Quantum: 1999), Re (1999) 99(6) Q.R. 5, CICB (Liverpool) [*Ex rel.*
Antonis Georges, Barrister, Martins Bank Buildings, 4 Water Street, Liverpool] . . *Digested,* 99/**1483**
Cooper v. Billingham (Inspector of Taxes); *sub nom* Edwards (Inspector of Taxes) v.
Fisher; Billingham (Inspector of Taxes) v. Cooper; Fisher v. Edwards (Inspector of
Taxes) [2001] EWCA Civ 1041; [2001] S.T.C. 1177; [2001] B.T.C. 282; [2001]
S.T.I. 1017; (2001) 98(31) L.S.G. 37; *Times,* July 16, 2001; *Independent,* July 13,
2001, CA; affirming [2000] S.T.C. 122; [2000] B.T.C. 28; [2000] S.T.I. 100;
(2000) 97(6) L.S.G. 36; (2000) 144 S.J.L.B. 85; *Times,* February 25, 2000,
Ch D . . . . *Digested,* 01/**5186**
Cooper (Inspector of Taxes) v. C&J Clark Ltd [1982] S.T.C. 335; 54 T.C. 670, Ch D . . . *Digested,* 84/**463**:
Followed, 00/5000
Cooper v. Hatton; *sub nom* Hatton v. Cooper [2001] EWCA Civ 623; [2001] R.T.R.
36, CA . . . . *Digested,* 01/**4465**
Cooper v. Kaur [2001] 1 F.C.R. 12; *Independent,* October 18, 2000, CA. . . . . *Digested,* 00/**2523**
Cooper v. Martin (1867-68) L.R. 3 Ch. App. 47, CA in Chancery . . . . *Applied,* 47-51/**7427**:
Considered, 01/5508
Cooper v. P&O Stena Line Ltd [1999] 1 Lloyd's Rep. 734; *Times,* February 8, 1999,
QBD (Adm Ct) . . . . *Digested,* 99/**504**
Cooper v. P&O Stena Line Ltd (Quantum) (Unreported, October 30, 1998), QBD
(Adm Ct) [*Ex rel.* Timothy Lord, Barrister, 2 Temple Gardens, London] . . . . *Digested,* 99/**1480**
Cooper v. Scammell (Unreported, July 6, 1998), CC (Staines) [*Ex rel.* Blandy &
Blandy Solicitors, 1 Friar Street, Reading, Berkshire] . . . . *Digested,* 98/**1455**
Cooper v. Smith Llewelyn Partnership [2000] C.P.L.R. 52, CA; affirming [1999]
P.N.L.R. 576, QBD. . . . . *Digested,* 99/**4032**
Cooper's Conveyance Trusts, Re; *sub nom* Crewdson v. Bagot [1956] 1 W.L.R. 1096;
[1956] 3 All E.R. 28; 100 S.J. 620, Ch D . . . . *Digested,* 56/**1008**:
Applied, 00/295
Cooperatieve Rabobank Vecht en Plassengebied BA v. Minderhoud (C104/96) [1998] 1
W.L.R. 1025; [1997] E.C.R. I-7211; [1998] 2 B.C.L.C. 507; [1998] 2 C.M.L.R.
270, ECJ (6th Chamber) . . . . *Digested,* 98/**660**

Cooperatieve Vereniging de Verenigde Bloemenveilingen Aalsmeer BA (VBA) *v.* Florimex
BV (C265/97 P); *sub nom* Florimex BV *v.* Commission of the European
Communities (T70/92) [2000] E.C.R. I-2061; [2001] 5 C.M.L.R. 37, ECJ (5th
Chamber) [1997] All E.R. (E.C.) 798; [1997] E.C.R. II-693; [1997] 5 C.M.L.R.
769, CFI (1st Chamber) . . . . *Digested,* 98/**2315**

Cooperative Insurance Society Ltd *v.* Argyll Stores (Holdings) Ltd [1998] A.C. 1; [1997]
2 W.L.R. 898; [1997] 3 All E.R. 297; [1997] C.L.C. 1114; [1997] 1 E.G.L.R. 52;
[1997] 23 E.G. 141; [1997] E.G.C.S. 81; (1997) 94(26) L.S.G. 30; (1997) 147
N.L.J. 845; (1997) 141 S.J.L.B. 131; [1997] N.P.C. 79; *Times,* May 26, 1997;
Independent, June 5, 1997, HL; reversing [1996] Ch. 286; [1996] 3 W.L.R. 27;
[1996] 3 All E.R. 934; (1996) 72 P. & C.R. 130; [1996] 1 E.G.L.R. 71; [1996] 09
E.G. 128; [1995] N.P.C. 199; *Times,* December 29, 1995; *Independent,* January
25, 1996, CA. . . . . *Digested,* 97/**3260**

Cooperative Retail Services Ltd *v.* Carillion Construction Ltd (formerly Tarmac
Construction (Contracts) Ltd) see Cooperative Retail Services Ltd *v.* Taylor
Young Partnership Ltd

Cooperative Retail Services Ltd *v.* East Midlands Electricity Electrical Installations
Services Ltd (t/a Hall Electrical) (In Liquidation) see Cooperative Retail Services
Ltd *v.* Taylor Young Partnership Ltd

Cooperative Retail Services Ltd *v.* Hoare Lea & Partners see Cooperative Retail
Services Ltd *v.* Taylor Young Partnership Ltd

Cooperative Retail Services Ltd *v.* Taylor Young Partnership Ltd; Cooperative Retail
Services Ltd *v.* Hoare Lea & Partners; Cooperative Retail Services Ltd *v.* Carillion
Construction Ltd (formerly Tarmac Construction (Contracts) Ltd); Cooperative
Retail Services Ltd *v.* East Midlands Electricity Electrical Installations Services
Ltd (t/a Hall Electrical) (In Liquidation); TNS, HL; affirming [2000] 2 All E.R.
865; [2000] B.L.R. 461; (2001) 3 T.C.L.R. 4; 74 Con. L.R. 12; [2001] Lloyd's
Rep. I.R. 122; (2000) 16 Const. L.J. 347; *Independent,* October 2, 2000 (C.S);
Independent, July 14, 2000, CA; affirming [2000] 1 All E.R. (Comm) 721;
(2000) 16 Const. L.J. 204; [2000] E.G.C.S. 6, QBD (T&CC) . . . . *Digested,* 00/**3535**

Cooperative Retail Services Ltd *v.* Tesco Stores Ltd (1998) 76 P. & C.R. 328; [1998]
E.G.C.S. 5; [1998] N.P.C. 5; (1998) 75 P. & C.R. D46, CA. . . . . *Digested,* 98/**4242**

Cooperative Wholesale Society Ltd (t/a CWS Engineering Group) *v.* Birse Construction
Ltd (formerly Peter Birse Ltd); *sub nom* Birse Construction (formerly Peter
Birse Ltd) *v.* Cooperative Wholesale Society Ltd (t/a CWS Engineering Group)
[1997] C.L.C. 1290; 84 B.L.R. 58; 57 Con. L.R. 98; (1997) 94(29) L.S.G. 29;
Times, August 13, 1997, QBD; affirming 46 Con. L.R. 110, QBD. . . . . *Digested,* 97/**924**

Cooperative Wholesale Society Ltd *v.* Chester le Street DC; *sub nom* Chester le Street
DC *v.* Cooperative Wholesale Society Ltd (1998) 10 Admin. L.R. 592; [1998] 3
E.G.L.R. 11; [1998] 38 E.G. 153; [1998] R.V.R. 202; [1998] E.G.C.S. 76; (1998)
95(19) L.S.G. 25, CA; affirming (1997) 73 P. & C.R. 111; [1996] 2 E.G.L.R. 143;
[1996] 46 E.G. 158; [1996] R.V.R. 185, Lands Tr . . . . *Digested,* 98/**4175**:
                                               Considered, 99/4186

Cooperative Wholesale Society Ltd *v.* Customs and Excise Commissioners [2000]
S.T.C. 727; [2000] B.T.C. 5315; [2000] B.V.C. 348; [2000] S.T.I. 1083; (2000)
97(39) L.S.G. 42; *Times,* August 31, 2000, CA; affirming [1999] S.T.C. 1096;
[1999] B.T.C. 5423; [2000] B.V.C. 13; *Independent,* January 31, 2000 (C.S),
QBD; affirming [1999] B.V.C. 2101, V&DTr. . . . . *Digested,* 00/**5344**:
         Applied, 01/5604: *Considered,* 00/5343: *Distinguished,* 00/5304

Coote *v.* Granada Hospitality Ltd [1999] 3 C.M.L.R. 334; [1999] I.C.R. 942; [1999]
I.R.L.R. 452; *Times,* June 3, 1999, EAT . . . . *Digested,* 99/**2112**:
                                       Previous proceedings, 98/2149

Coote *v.* Granada Hospitality Ltd (C185/97) [1998] All E.R. (EC) 865; [1998] E.C.R.
I-5199; [1998] 3 C.M.L.R. 958; [1999] C.E.C. 515; [1999] I.C.R. 100; [1998]
I.R.L.R. 656; *Times,* October 1, 1998, ECJ . . . . *Digested,* 98/**2149**:
               Distinguished, 01/2322: *Subsequent proceedings,* 99/2112

Coots *v.* Stead McAlpine & Co Ltd [2000] 3 Q.R. 7, CC (Carlisle) [*Ex rel.* Hough
Halton & Soal Solicitors, 32 Abbey Street, Carlisle] . . . . *Digested,* 00/**1593**

Cooze *v.* Secretary of State for Social Security (C328/91) see Secretary of State for
Social Security *v.* Thomas (C328/91)

Copas *v.* Windsor and Maidenhead RBC [2001] EWCA Civ 180; [2001] J.P.L. 1169;
[2001] 8 E.G.C.S. 166; [2001] N.P.C. 27, CA; reversing CO/3647/99, QBD

Copeland *v.* Houlton; *sub nom* 26 Clarendon Villas, Hove (Trusts Affecting), Re [1955]
1 W.L.R. 1072; [1955] 3 All E.R. 178; 99 S.J. 708, Ch D . . . . *Digested,* 55/**2154**:
                                     Considered, 98/452: *Followed,* 97/586

Copeland *v.* Smith; *sub nom* Copeland *v.* Smith & Goodwin [2000] 1 W.L.R. 1371;
[2000] 1 All E.R. 457; [2000] C.P. Rep. 14; (1999) 143 S.J.L.B. 276; *Times,*
October 20, 1999, CA . . . . *Digested,* 99/**457**

Copeland *v.* Smith & Goodwin see Copeland *v.* Smith

Copeland BC *v.* Hayton Builders Ltd (No.1) (1998) 14 Const. L.J. 412, QBD

Copeland BC *v.* Hayton Builders Ltd (No.2) (1999) 15 Const. L.J. 38; (1997) 13
Const. L.J. 253, QBD (OR) . . . . *Digested,* 97/**929**

Copeland BC *v.* Secretary of State for the Environment (1976) 31 P. & C.R. 403;
(1976) 239 E.G. 503; [1976] J.P.L. 304, QBD . . . . *Digested,* 76/**2697**:
Applied, 80/2673, 81/2684, 81/2714, 00/4452: *Considered,* 90/4363
Copeman (Inspector of Taxes) *v.* Coleman; *sub nom* Copeman (Inspector of Taxes) *v.*
Coleman Minors [1939] 2 K.B. 484, KBD . . . . *Applied,* 66/6173,
98/4683
Copeman (Inspector of Taxes) *v.* Coleman Minors see Copeman (Inspector of Taxes) *v.*
Coleman
Copenhagen Reinsurance Co (UK) Ltd *v.* Polygram Holdings Inc see Gerling Konzern
General Insurance Co *v.* Polygram Holdings Inc
Copoc *v.* Chief Constable of South Yorkshire see Alcock *v.* Chief Constable of South
Yorkshire
Coppen (Trustees of Thames Ditton Lawn Tennis Club) *v.* Bruce-Smith; *sub nom* Coppin
v. Bruce-Smith; Trustees of Thames Ditton Lawn Tennis Club *v.* Bruce-Smith
(1999) 77 P. & C.R. 239; [1998] J.P.L. 1077; [1998] E.G.C.S. 55; (1998) 76 P. &
C.R. D7, CA . . . . *Digested,* 98/**3609**
Copper Communications Sarl *v.* France Telecom SA [2001] E.C.C. 32, Cass (F)
Coppin *v.* Bruce-Smith see Coppen (Trustees of Thames Ditton Lawn Tennis Club) *v.*
Bruce-Smith
Copthorne Hotel (Newcastle) Ltd *v.* Arup Associates (Costs) 58 Con. L.R. 130, QBD
(OR). . . . . *Considered,* 00/458
Copthorne Hotel (Newcastle) Ltd *v.* Arup Associates (No.1) 58 Con. L.R. 105; (1996)
12 Const. L.J. 402, QBD (OR) . . . . *Digested,* 97/**3812**
Copthorne Hotel (Newcastle) Ltd *v.* Arup Associates (No.2) 85 B.L.R. 22, CA . . . . . . *Digested,* 98/**818**
Copyright in Newspaper Articles Offered, Re [1998] E.C.C. 238, OLG (Dusseldorf)
Copyright in the Translation of a Literary Work (I ZR 57/97), Re [2001] E.C.C. 33, BGH (Ger)
Copyright in Translated Legal Document, Re (4 Ob 2363/96w) [1999] E.C.C.131, OGH (A)
Coral Group Trading Plc *v.* Hilton Group Plc (formerly Ladbroke Group Plc) A3/2001/
0996, CA; reversing [2001] 2 Lloyd's Rep. 373, QBD (Comm Ct) . . . . *Digested,* 01/**739**
Corbenstoke (No.2), Re (1989) 5 B.C.C. 767; [1990] B.C.L.C. 60 . . . . *Digested,* 89/**343**:
Applied, 99/3314

Corbett *v.* Bond Pearce (A Firm) [2001] EWCA Civ 531; [2001] 3 All E.R. 769; [2001]
Lloyd's Rep. P.N. 501; [2001] P.N.L.R. 31; [2001] W.T.L.R. 419; (2001) 151
N.L.J. 609, CA; reversing [2000] Lloyd's Rep. P.N. 805; [2001] P.N.L.R. 24;
[2000] W.T.L.R. 655, QBD . . . . *Digested,* 01/**4537**
Corbett *v.* Corbett [1998] B.C.C. 93, Ch D . . . . *Digested,* 98/**688**
Corbett *v.* Corbett (otherwise Ashley) (No.1) [1971] P. 83; [1970] 2 W.L.R. 1306;
[1970] 2 All E.R. 33; (1969) 113 S.J. 982, PDAD . . . . *Digested,* 70/**808**:
Applied, 83/610, 00/2539: *Considered,* 87/2922: *Distinguished,* 00/2538:
Followed, 96/3172, 01/2652
Corbett *v.* Newey [1998] Ch. 57; [1996] 3 W.L.R. 729; [1996] 2 All E.R. 914; [1996]
2 F.L.R. 554; [1996] Fam. Law 724; (1996) 146 N.L.J. 333; (1996) 140 S.J.L.B.
65; *Times,* February 5, 1996; *Independent,* February 7, 1996, CA; reversing
[1994] Ch. 388; [1994] 3 W.L.R. 548; [1995] 1 All E.R. 570; (1994) 91(26)
L.S.G. 36; *Times,* May 12, 1994, Ch D . . . . *Digested,* 96/**5558**
Corbett *v.* Restormel BC see R. (on the application of Parkyn) *v.* Restormel BC
Corbin *v.* Penfold Metallising Co Ltd [2000] Lloyd's Rep. Med. 247; (2000) 97(17)
L.S.G. 35; (2000) 144 S.J.L.B. 203; *Times,* May 2, 2000, CA . . . . *Digested,* 00/**524**:
Considered, 01/601
Cordle *v.* Cordle [2001] EWCA Civ 1791; (2001) 145 S.J.L.B. 262; *Times,* December 7,
2001; *Independent,* November 22, 2001, CA . . . . *Digested,* 01/**2630**
Cordoba Shipping Co *v.* National State Bank, Elizabeth, New Jersey (The Albaforth)
[1984] 2 Lloyd's Rep. 91; (1984) 81 L.S.G. 1360, CA. . . . . *Digested,* 84/**2671**:
Considered, 00/769
Coreck Maritime GmbH *v.* Handelsveem BV (C387/98) see Handelsveem BV *v.* Coreck
Maritime GmbH (C387/98)
Corfe Joinery Ltd (In Liquidation), Re see Wills *v.* Corfe Joinery Ltd (In Liquidation)
CORGI Trade Mark [1999] R.P.C. 549, Appointed Person . . . . *Digested,* 99/**3562**
Cork *v.* Katz; *sub nom* Imagemaster Ltd, Re; (Unreported, October 15, 1996), Ch D . . . *Followed,* 98/3306
Cork *v.* Rawlins; *sub nom* Insolvency Act 1986, Re; Rawlins, Re [2001] EWCA Civ
202; [2001] Ch. 792; [2001] 3 W.L.R. 300; [2001] 4 All E.R. 50; [2001] B.P.I.R.
222; [2001] Lloyd's Rep. I.R. 587; (2001) 98(18) L.S.G. 44; *Times,* March 15,
2001; *Independent,* March 19, 2001 (C.S), CA; affirming [2000] B.P.I.R. 654;
(2000) 97(27) L.S.G. 38; *Times,* June 27, 2000, Ch D . . . . *Digested,* 01/**3732**
Cork *v.* Rolph (2001) 98(7) L.S.G. 40; *Times,* December 21, 2000, Ch D . . . . *Digested,* 01/**3767**
Cormack *v.* Excess Insurance Co Ltd see Cormack *v.* Washbourne (formerly t/a
Washbourne & Co)
Cormack *v.* Washbourne (formerly t/a Washbourne & Co); *sub nom* Cormack *v.* Excess
Insurance Co Ltd [2000] C.P.L.R. 358; [2000] C.L.C. 1039; [2000] Lloyd's
Rep. P.N. 459; (2000) 97(15) L.S.G. 39; *Times,* March 30, 2000; *Independent,*
March 31, 2000, CA; affirming [1999] Lloyd's Rep. P.N. 389, QBD (T&CC) . . . . *Digested,* 00/**413**
Cornelius *v.* De Taranto [2001] EWCA Civ 1511, CA; affirming [2001] E.M.L.R. 12,
QBD . . . . *Digested,* 01/**1828**
Cornelius *v.* Southwark LBC [1998] Ed. C.R. 165; [1998] E.L.R. 563, CA . . . . *Digested,* 98/**2242**

Cornelius v. Sweden CO/2205/97, CA . . . . *Digested*, 98/**2344**
Cornelius v. University College of Swansea [1987] I.R.L.R. 141; (1987) 84 L.S.G. 1141;
(1987) 131 S.J. 359, CA. . . . . *Digested*, 87/**1372**:
                                                                        Applied, 01/**2302**
Cornell v. Green QBENF 96/0838 CMSI, CA . . . . *Digested*, 98/**1485**
Corner v. Osment (Unreported, December 15, 1999), CC (Brentford) [*Ex rel.* Lawrence
Caun, Barrister, Lamb Chambers, Lamb Buildings, Temple, London] . . . . *Digested*, 00/**1565**
Cornick v. Cornick (No.3) [2001] 2 F.L.R. 1240; [2001] Fam. Law 871, Fam Div . . . . . . *Previous proceedings*,
                                                                        96/2872
CORNILLEAU/Table tennis table (T280/96) [1998] E.P.O.R. 129, EPO (Technical Bd App)
Corning Inc'sThree DimensionalTrade Mark Application [2001] E.T.M.R. 83, OHIM (2nd Bd
App). . . . . *Digested*, 01/**3999**
Cornwall County Care Ltd v. Brightman [1998] I.C.R. 529; [1998] I.R.L.R. 228; *Times*,
March 10, 1998, EAT . . . . *Digested*, 98/**2222**
Cornwall Gardens Pte Ltd v. RO Garrard & Co Ltd [2001] EWCA Civ 699; *Times*, June
19, 2001, CA. . . . . *Digested*, 01/**5354**
Cornwell v. United Kingdom (36578/97); Leary v. United Kingdom (38890/97)
(2001) 29 E.H.R.R. CD62; (2000) 29 E.H.R.R. CD30; *Times*, May 10, 2000,
ECHR . . . . *Digested*, 00/**4881**
Coronation Insurance Co v. Clearly Canadian Beverage Corp [1997] 6 Re. L.R. 344,
Sup Ct (BC) . . . . *Digested*, 98/**3364**
Corporacion Nacional del Cobre de Chile v. Metallgesellschaft AG Ltd; *sub nom*
Corporacion Nacional del Cobre de Chile v. Metallgesellschaft Ltd AG [1999]
C.P.L.R. 309; *Times*, January 6, 1999, Ch D . . . . *Digested*, 99/**447**
Corporacion Nacional del Cobre de Chile v. Metallgesellschaft Ltd AG see Corporacion
Nacional del Cobre de Chile v. Metallgesellschaft AG Ltd
Correction/Priority declaration (J09/91) [1998] E.P.O.R. 352, EPO (Legal Bd App)
Corsica Ferries France SA v. Gruppo Antichi Ormeggiatori del Porto di Genova Coop arl
(C266/96) [1998] E.C.R. I-3949; [1998] 5 C.M.L.R. 402; [1998] C.E.C. 697,
ECJ . . . . *Digested*, 98/**730**
Cortellessa v. Customs and Excise Commissioners [2000] B.V.C. 2158; [2000] S.T.I.
267, V&DTr
Cortese v. Nowsco Well Service Ltd [2001] I.L.Pr. 16, CA (Alta); affirming [1999]
I.L.Pr. 767, QB (Alta) . . . . *Digested*, 00/**772**
Corus UK Ltd v. Commission of the European Communities (T171/99) [2001] 5
C.M.L.R. 34; *Times*, November 15, 2001, CFI (1st Chamber) . . . . *Digested*, 01/**2483**
Cory v. Thames Ironworks & Shipbuilding Co Ltd (1867-68) L.R. 3 Q.B. 181, QB . . . . . *Applied*, 47-51/**1604**,
                     47-51/2562, 47-51/5222, 47-51/9482, 47-51/9490, 49/3656, 98/4384
Coryright v. East see DPP v. Billington
COSBY/Fluid circuit (T442/97) [1998] E.P.O.R. 212, EPO (Technical Bd App)
Cosgrove v. Caesar & Howie [2001] I.R.L.R. 653, EAT . . . . *Digested*, 01/**6461**
Cosgrove v. Pattison [2001] C.P. Rep. 68; [2001] C.P.L.R. 177; *Times*, February 13,
2001, Ch D. . . . . *Digested*, 01/**690**:
                                                                  Cited, 01/689
Cosmedent Inc's Application [1998] E.T.M.R. 658, OHIM (3rd Bd App)
Cosmopolitan Investments Ltd v. New Hearts Ltd see New Hearts Ltd v. Cosmopolitan
Investments Ltd
Cosmotron Manufacturing Co Ltd v. Inland Revenue Commissioner [1997] 1 W.L.R.
1288; [1997] S.T.C. 1134; 70 T.C. 292; [1997] B.T.C. 465; (1997) 141 S.J.L.B.
215, PC (HK) . . . . *Digested*, 97/**1064**
Cossey v. Lonnkvist; *sub nom* Peter Lingham & Co v. Lonnkvist [2000] Lloyd's Rep.
P.N. 885; [2000] N.P.C. 82, CA. . . . . *Digested*, 01/**938**
Cossey v. United Kingdom (A/184); *sub nom* C v. United Kingdom (A/184) [1991] 2
F.L.R. 492; [1993] 2 F.C.R. 97; (1991) 13 E.H.R.R. 622; [1991] Fam. Law 362;
Times, October 17, 1990, ECHR . . . . *Digested*, 92/**2371**:
                                               Referred to, 93/2156, 98/3163
Cosslett (Contractors) Ltd, Re; *sub nom* Clark (Administrator of Cosslett (Contractors)
Ltd) v. Mid Glamorgan CC [1998] Ch. 495; [1998] 2 W.L.R. 131; [1997] 4 All
E.R. 115; [1997] B.C.C. 724; [1999] 1 B.C.L.C. 205; 85 B.L.R. 1, CA; affirming
[1997] Ch. 23; [1996] 3 W.L.R. 299; [1996] 4 All E.R. 46; [1996] B.C.C. 515;
[1996] 1 B.C.L.C. 407; 78 B.L.R. 104; 49 Con. L.R. 56, Ch D . . . . *Digested*, 97/**3057**
Cosslett (Contractors) Ltd (In Administration) (No.2), Re see Smith (Administrator of
Cosslett (Contractors) Ltd) v. Bridgend CBC
Costa v. Georgiou (Unreported, May 2, 1984) . . . . *Applied*, 00/**4254**
Costain Building & Civil Engineering Ltd v. Scottish Rugby Union Plc 1993 S.C. 650;
1994 S.L.T. 573; 1994 S.C.L.R. 257, IH (Ct of 5 judges). . . . . *Digested*, 94/**6112**:
                                                 Distinguished, 95/6195, 00/5977
Costain Building & Civil Engineering Ltd v. Smith [2000] I.C.R. 215, EAT
Costain Civil Engineering Ltd v. Zanen Dredging and Contracting Co Ltd (No.1) 85
B.L.R. 77, QBD (OR) . . . . *Digested*, 98/**821**
Costain Civil Engineering Ltd v. Zanen Dredging and Contracting Co Ltd (No.2) (1998)
14 Const. L.J. 44, QBD (OR) . . . . *Digested*, 98/**234**
Costello v. Chief Constable of Derbyshire [2001] EWCA Civ 381; [2001] 1 W.L.R.
1437; [2001] 3 All E.R. 150; [2001] 2 Lloyd's Rep. 216, CA . . . . *Digested*, 01/**4789**

Costello v. Chief Constable of Northumbria [1999] 1 All E.R. 550; [1999] I.C.R. 752; (1999) 11 Admin. L.R. 81; (1999) 163 J.P.N. 634; (1998) 148 N.L.J. 1880; *Times*, December 15, 1998, CA . . . . *Digested*, 99/**3970**:
Followed, 01/4479
Costello v. Customs and Excise Commissioners [2000] S.T.I. 1408, V&DTr
Costello-Roberts v. United Kingdom (A/247-C) [1994] 1 F.C.R. 65; (1995) 19 E.H.R.R. 112; *Times*, March 26, 1993; *Independent*, March 26, 1993; *Guardian*, March 26, 1993, ECHR . . . . *Digested*, 93/**2118**:
Considered, 97/427, 98/3065, 01/1147
Costelloe v. Thomson Tour Operations Ltd (Unreported, October 6, 1999), CC (Exeter) [*Ex rel.* Alexander Pelling, Barrister, New Court Chambers, 5 Verulam Buildings, Gray's Inn, London] . . . . *Digested*, 00/**4046**
Costellow v. Somerset CC [1993] 1 W.L.R. 256; [1993] 1 All E.R. 952; [1993] P.I.Q.R. P147; *Times*, November 25, 1992; *Independent*, November 25, 1992, CA . . . . . . *Digested*, 93/**3338**:
Applied, 94/4559: *Considered*, 93/3204, 94/3904, 95/3932, 95/3933,
95/4241, 96/676, 97/69, 97/783, 97/784: *Distinguished*, 94/3635:
Followed, 97/753, 98/354, 98/384
Coster v. Chief Constable of Sussex (Unreported, December 22, 1998), CC (Lewes) [*Ex rel.* Alexander Uff, Pupil Barrister, 1 Serjeant's Inn, 5th Floor, Fleet Street, London] . . . . *Digested*, 99/**4279**
Coster v. United Kingdom (24876/94) (2001) 33 E.H.R.R. 20; *Times*, January 30, 2001, ECHR . . . . *Joined proceedings*,
01/4744
Costes v. Ministere Public [2000] E.C.C. 451, C d'A (Paris)
Cotter v. Minister for Social Welfare (C286/85) see McDermott v. Minister for Social Welfare (C286/85)
Cotterell v. Cotterell [1998] 3 F.C.R. 199, CA . . . . *Digested*, 98/**2448**
Cotterell v. Leeds Day see Cotterell v. Leeds Day
Cotterrell v. Leeds Day; *sub nom* Cotterell v. Leeds Day [2001] W.T.L.R. 435, CA; reversing 99/TLQ/1288, QBD
Cottingham v. Attey Bower & Jones [2000] Lloyd's Rep. P.N. 591; [2000] P.N.L.R. 557; [2000] E.G.C.S. 48; (2000) 97(19) L.S.G. 43; [2000] N.P.C. 37; *Times*, April 19, 2000, Ch D . . . . *Digested*, 00/**4267**
Cotton v. Derbyshire Dales DC, *Times*, June 20, 1994, CA. . . . . *Digested*, 94/**4286**:
Considered, 00/4240, 01/4496
Cotton v. Freddie Martin (Scaffolding) Ltd TNS, CA. . . . . *Digested*, 98/**1638**
Cotton v. Navarro (Unreported, July 6, 1998), CC (Romford) [*Ex rel.* Paul McGrath, Barrister, 1 Temple Gardens] . . . . *Digested*, 98/**1741**
Cottrell v. Redbridge Healthcare NHS Trust (2001) 61 B.M.L.R. 72, QBD
Couch (Inspector of Taxes) v. Administrators of the Estate of Caton; *sub nom* Administrators of the Estate of Caton v. Couch (Inspector of Taxes); Caton's Administrators, Re; Caton's Administrators v. Couch (Inspector of Taxes); Couch (Inspector of Taxes) v. Caton's Administrators [1997] S.T.C. 970; 70 T.C. 10; [1997] B.T.C. 360; (1997) 94(30) L.S.G. 29; *Times*, July 16, 1997; *Independent*, July 14, 1997 (C.S.), CA; affirming [1996] S.T.C. 201; *Times*, December 28, 1995; *Independent*, January 29, 1996 (C.S.), Ch D . . . . *Digested*, 97/**336**
Couch (Inspector of Taxes) v. Caton's Administrators see Couch (Inspector of Taxes) v. Administrators of the Estate of Caton
Couez v. France [1998] H.R.C.D. 810, ECHR
Coughlan v. Thomson Holidays Ltd (Unreported, March 20, 2001), CC (Romford) [*Ex rel.* Martina Murphy, Barrister, Tanfield Chambers, Francis Taylor Building, Temple, London] . . . . *Digested*, 01/**4276**
Couldry v. Hull Daily Mail Publications Ltd (Unreported, December 15, 1997), CC (Liverpool) [*Ex rel.* Dibb Lupton Alsop Solicitors, 101 Barbirolli Square, Manchester] . . . . *Digested*, 98/**597**
Coulter v. HM Advocate see Montgomery v. HM Advocate
Coulthard v. Disco Mix Club Ltd [2000] 1 W.L.R. 707; [1999] 2 All E.R. 457; [1999] E.M.L.R. 434; [1999] F.S.R. 900; *Times*, March 25, 1999; *Independent*, March 8, 1999 (C.S.), Ch D . . . . *Digested*, 99/**458**
Coulthard v. Neville Russell (A Firm) [1998] B.C.C. 359; [1998] 1 B.C.L.C. 143; [1998] P.N.L.R. 276; *Times*, December 18, 1997, CA. . . . . *Digested*, 98/**3926**
Council of Civil Service Unions v. Minister for the Civil Service [1985] A.C. 374; [1984] 1 W.L.R. 1174; [1984] 3 All E.R. 935; [1985] I.C.R. 14; [1985] I.R.L.R. 28; (1985) 82 L.S.G. 437; (1984) 128 S.J. 837, HL; reversing [1984] I.R.L.R. 353, CA; reversing [1984] I.R.L.R. 309, DC . . . . *Digested*, 85/**12**:
Applied, 86/2165, 86/3554, 87/1922, 87/2460, 88/50, 88/1843, 88/3553,
89/17, 89/4022, 93/24, 93/1758, 94/75, 94/1947, 94/2485, 95/5905,
97/2785, 00/4114: *Considered*, 85/656, 86/950, 86/2017, 86/2934, 87/10,
87/12, 87/20, 87/47, 87/3694, 88/6, 88/2713, 88/3510, 90/4, 91/43, 91/55,
91/76, 93/31, 93/2100, 94/8, 94/55, 94/1462, 94/3974, 94/4984, 95/20,
95/67, 95/88, 95/3252, 95/4255, 95/4413, 96/316, 97/6229, 00/4447:
Distinguished, 96/2520: *Followed*, 87/14, 93/5413, 96/1994:
Referred to, 92/5981, 93/5483, 94/2320, 95/2543, 95/4779, 95/4820

Council of Ministers of the European Communities (Germany, France and United Kingdom
    intervening) v. European Parliament (C34/86) see 1986 Budget (C34/86), Re
Council of State Case (2551/1997) 2 I.T.L. Rep. 517, Sym Ep (GR)
Council of State Case (5014/1996) 2 I.T.L. Rep. 513, Sym Ep (GR)
Council of the European Union v. Hautala (C353/99 P); *sub nom* Hautala v. Council of
    the European Union (T14/98) [1999] E.C.R. II-2489; [1999] 3 C.M.L.R. 528,
    CFI . . . .   *Digested*, 00/**2393**
Country Farm Inns Ltd, Re see Secretary of State for Trade and Industry v. Ivens
Countryside Residential (North Thames) Ltd v. T (A Child) (2001) 81 P. & C.R. 2;
    [2000] 3 P.L.R. 55; [2000] 2 E.G.L.R. 59; [2000] 34 E.G. 87; [2000] J.P.L.
    1251; (2000) 97(17) L.S.G. 34; (2000) 144 S.J.L.B. 198; [2000] Env. L.R. D31;
    Times, April 4, 2000, CA . . . .   *Digested*, 00/**4666**
Countrywide Banking Corp Ltd v. Dean (Liquidator of CB Sizzlers Ltd) [1998] A.C.
    338; [1998] 2 W.L.R. 441; [1998] B.C.C. 105; [1998] 1 B.C.L.C. 306; [1998]
    B.P.I.R. 676; (1998) 142 S.J.L.B. 53, PC (NZ) . . . .   *Digested*, 98/**3329**
Countrywide Communications Ltd v. ICL Pathway Ltd [2000] C.L.C. 324, QBD . . . . . .   *Digested*, 00/**2330**
County Fire Officer v. City Logistics Ltd see City Logistics Ltd v. Northamptonshire
    County Fire Officer
County Natwest Ltd v. Barton see Barton v. County Natwest Ltd
County of Gloucester Bank v. Rudry Merthyr Steam & House Coal Colliery Co [1895]
    1 Ch. 629, CA . . . .   *Followed*, 98/**3310**
County of Herefordshire DC (formerly Leominster DC) v. Grayburn (2000) 15 P.A.D.
    588, Planning Inspector
County Personnel (Employment Agency) Ltd v. Alan R Pulver & Co [1987] 1 W.L.R.
    916; [1987] 1 All E.R. 289; [1986] 2 E.G.L.R. 246; (1987) 84 L.S.G. 1409;
    (1986) 136 N.L.J. 1138; (1987) 131 S.J. 474; *Times*, October 29, 1986, CA . . . . .   *Digested*, 87/**3551**:
                            Applied, 91/1315, 91/1319, 93/2989, 00/1483: *Considered*, 88/1051, 89/1199,
                         90/1567, 92/1533, 94/1758, 96/4502, 99/4031: *Distinguished*, 98/4018:
                                           Followed, 98/3959, 98/4025
County Properties Ltd v. Scottish Ministers 2001 S.L.T. 1125; [2001] 4 P.L.R. 122; 2001
    G.W.D. 26-1068, Ex Div; reversing 2000 S.L.T. 965; [2000] H.R.L.R. 677;
    [2000] 4 P.L.R. 83; [2001] J.P.L. 170; 2000 G.W.D. 26-1007; *Times*, September
    19, 2000, OH . . . .   *Digested*, 01/**6853**
Couper v. Athawes [2001] 5 Q.R. 14, CC (Swindon) [*Ex rel.* Philip Kolvin, Barrister, 2-
    3 Grays Inn Square, London] . . . .   *Digested*, 01/**1639**
Courage & Co Ltd v. Carpenter [1910] 1 Ch. 262, Ch D . . . .   *Considered*, 99/685
Courage Group's Pension Schemes, Re; Ryan v. Imperial Brewing and Leisure [1987] 1
    W.L.R. 495; [1987] 1 All E.R. 528; [1987] 1 F.T.L.R. 210; (1987) 84 L.S.G.
    1573; (1987) 131 S.J. 507; *Times*, December 22, 1986; *Financial Times*,
    December 16, 1986, Ch D . . . .   *Digested*, 87/**2822**:
                            Applied, 00/6616: *Considered*, 91/2726: *Distinguished*, 01/4628
Courage Ltd v. Crehan (C453/99); *sub nom* Crehan v. Courage Ltd (C453/99) [2001]
    3 W.L.R. 1646; [2001] All E.R. (EC) 886; [2001] E.C.R. I-6297; [2001] 5
    C.M.L.R. 28; [2001] C.E.C. 297; *Times*, October 4, 2001; *Daily Telegraph*,
    September 25, 2001, ECJ . . . .   *Digested*, 01/**783**
Courage Ltd v. Crehan (No.1); *sub nom* Byrne v. Tibsco Ltd; Inntrepreneur Beer Supply
    Co Ltd v. Byrne; Inntrepreneur Beer Supply Co Ltd v. Langton; Greenalls
    Management Ltd v. Smith; Walker Cain Ltd v. McCaughey; Inntrepreneur Pub Co
    (CPC) Ltd v. Haigh [1999] U.K.C.L.R. 110; [1999] E.C.C. 455; [1999] Eu. L.R.
    834; [1999] 2 E.G.L.R. 145; [1999] E.G.C.S. 85; [1999] E.G.C.S. 86; (1999)
    96(25) L.S.G. 29; (1999) 143 S.J.L.B. 182; *Times*, June 14, 1999, CA; affirming
    [1999] Eu. L.R. 409; [1998] E.G.C.S. 171, Ch D . . . .   *Digested*, 99/**684**:
                                 Applied, 01/2519: *Subsequent proceedings*, 99/3665
Courage Ltd v. Crehan (No.2) [1999] U.K.C.L.R. 407, CA . . . .   *Digested*, 00/**707**:
                                       Subsequent proceedings, 01/783
Coursier v. Fortis Bank SA (C267/97) [1999] E.C.R. I-2543; [2000] I.L.Pr. 202, ECJ
    (5th Chamber) [1998] I.L.Pr. 674, CSJ (Lux) . . . .   *Digested*, 00/**3468**
Court Lodge Development Co, Re [1973] 1 W.L.R. 1097; [1973] 3 All E.R. 425; 117 S.J. 648,
    Ch D . . . .   *Digested*, 73/**339**:
                                              Cited, 99/603
Courtaulds Northern Spinning Ltd v. Moosa [1984] I.C.R. 218; [1984] I.R.L.R. 43;
    (1983) 80 L.S.G. 3158, EAT . . . .   *Digested*, 84/**1301**:
                         Applied, 95/2091: *Considered*, 97/2285, 98/2228: *Overruled in part*, 93/1811
Courtney Plc v. Murphy (Valuation Officer) (No.1) [1998] R.A. 77, Lands Tr . . . .   *Digested*, 98/**4310**
Courtney Plc v. Murphy (Valuation Officer) (No.2); *sub nom* Murphy (Valuation
    Officer) v. Courtney Plc (No.2) [1999] R.A. 1, Lands Tr . . . .   *Digested*, 99/**4328**
Coutts & Co v. Stock [2000] 1 W.L.R. 906; [2000] 2 All E.R. 56; [2000] Lloyd's Rep.
    Bank. 14; [2000] B.C.C. 247; [2000] 1 B.C.L.C. 183; [2000] B.P.I.R. 400;
    (1999) 96(48) L.S.G. 39; (2000) 144 S.J.L.B. 24; *Times*, November 30, 1999,
    Ch D . . . .   *Digested*, 00/**3465**
Couzens v. Couzens [2001] EWCA Civ 992; [2001] 2 F.L.R. 701; [2001] 3 F.C.R.
    289; [2001] Fam. Law 729, CA . . . .   *Digested*, 01/**451**
Coven SpA v. Hong Kong Chinese Insurance Co [1999] C.L.C. 223; [1999] Lloyd's
    Rep. I.R. 565, CA . . . .   *Digested*, 99/**3406**

Coventry & Solihull Waste Disposal Co Ltd *v.* Russell (Valuation Officer) [1999] 1 W.L.R. 2093; [2000] 1 All E.R. 97; [2000] R.A. 1; [1999] E.G.C.S. 141; (1999) 96(47) L.S.G. 32; (2000) 144 S.J.L.B. 10; [1999] N.P.C. 146; *Times,* November 30, 1999, HL; affirming [1998] R.A. 427; *Times,* June 11, 1998, CA; reversing [1997] R.A. 89, Lands Tr . . . . *Digested,* 00/**4609**
Coventry Building Society *v.* William Martin & Partners [1997] 2 E.G.L.R. 146; [1997] 48 E.G. 159; [1997] E.G.C.S. 106, QBD . . . . *Digested,* 98/**4031**
Coventry City Council *v.* Aldi Stores Ltd (1999) 14 P.A.D. 326, Planning Inspector
Coventry City Council *v.* Padgett Brothers (A to Z) Ltd see Padgett Brothers (A-Z) Ltd *v.* Coventry City Council
Coville *v.* Adeptus (2000) 80 P. & C.R. D14, CA
Covita AVE *v.* Greece (C370/96) [1998] E.C.R. I-7711, ECJ . . . . *Referred to,* 00/4954
Cowan *v.* Chief Constable of Avon and Somerset, *Times,* December 11, 2001; *Independent,* November 21, 2001, CA . . . . *Digested,* 01/**4479**
Cowan *v.* Commissioner of Police of the Metropolis see Cowan *v.* Condon
Cowan *v.* Condon; *sub nom* Cowan *v.* Commissioner of Police of the Metropolis [2000] 1 W.L.R. 254; [2000] 1 All E.R. 504; (1999) 96(33) L.S.G. 30; *Times,* August 31, 1999, CA . . . . *Digested,* 99/**899**
Cowan *v.* Cowan [2001] EWCA Civ 679; [2001] 3 W.L.R. 684; [2001] 2 F.L.R. 192; [2001] 2 F.C.R. 331; [2001] Fam. Law 498; *Times,* May 17, 2001, CA . . . . *Digested,* 01/**2633**
Cowan *v.* Department of Economic Development; *sub nom* Cowan *v.* Department of Enterprise, Trade and Investment [2000] N.I. 122, Ch D (NI) . . . . *Digested,* 00/**5656**
Cowan *v.* Department of Enterprise, Trade and Investment see Cowan *v.* Department of Economic Development
Cowan *v.* Tresor Public (C186/87) [1989] E.C.R. 195; [1990] 2 C.M.L.R. 613; *Times,* February 13, 1989, ECJ . . . . *Digested,* 91/**3984**: *Applied,* 98/2309
Cowen *v.* Haden Carrier Ltd see Haden Carrier Ltd *v.* Cowen
Cowen *v.* McElroy (Unreported, June 8, 2001), CC (Blackpool) [*Ex rel.* John G Baldwin, Barrister, Oriel Chambers, 14 Water Street, Liverpool] . . . . *Digested,* 01/**614**
Cowen *v.* Secretary of State for the Environment, Transport and the Regions (2000) 79 P. & C.R. 457; [1999] 3 P.L.R. 108; [2000] J.P.L. 171; (1999) 96(23) L.S.G. 36, CA . . . . *Digested,* 00/**4410**
Cowley *v.* Mersey Regional Ambulance Service NHS Trust [2001] 6 Q.R. 5, CC (Liverpool) [*Ex rel.* Tim Hirst, Barrister, Park Court Chambers, 16 Park Place, Leeds] . . . . *Digested,* 01/**1580**
Cowlin *v.* Elvin (Unreported, May 10, 1999), CC (Central London) [*Ex rel.* Jerome Mayhew, Barrister, Goldsmith Building, Temple, London] . . . . *Digested,* 99/**1409**
Cox *v.* Conway (Unreported, August 6, 1999), CC (Bath) [*Ex rel.* Lyons Davidson Solicitors, Bridge House, 48-52 Baldwin Street, Bristol] . . . . *Digested,* 99/**1581**
Cox *v.* Hockenhull [2000] 1 W.L.R. 750; [1999] 3 All E.R. 582; [1999] R.T.R. 399; [2000] P.I.Q.R. Q230; (1999) 96(26) L.S.G. 27; (1999) 143 S.J.L.B. 188; *Times,* June 17, 1999, CA . . . . *Digested,* 99/**1381**
Cox *v.* London South West Valuation and Community Charge Tribunal [1994] R.V.R. 171, QBD . . . . *Digested,* 95/**3207**: *Considered,* 98/4308
Cox *v.* Sun Alliance Life Ltd [2001] EWCA Civ 649; [2001] I.R.L.R. 448; [2001] Emp. L.R. 660, CA . . . . *Digested,* 01/**2254**
Cox *v.* Woodley (Unreported, October 7, 1998), CC (Altrincham) [*Ex rel.* Paul Cain, Principal Solicitor, Litigation Unit, Eagle Star Insurance Co Ltd, Regency Suite, India Buildings, Water Street, Liverpool] . . . . *Digested,* 98/**491**
Cox Homes Ltd *v.* Ideal Homes (Midlands) Ltd [1998] E.G.C.S. 20, CA
Cox (WE Toner International) Ltd *v.* Crook [1981] I.C.R. 823; [1981] I.R.L.R. 443, EAT . *Digested,* 82/**1097**: *Applied,* 01/2226
Coyle *v.* Reid [2000] N.I. 7, CA (NI) . . . . *Digested,* 00/**5672**
Coyne *v.* Home Office see Home Office *v.* Coyne
Cozens *v.* Customs and Excise Commissioners [2000] B.P.I.R. 252, CA . . . . *Digested,* 00/**3488**
CP Henderson & Co *v.* Comptoir d'Escompte de Paris (1873-74) L.R. 5 P.C. 253; (1874) 2 Asp. 98; (1874) 21 W.R. 873; (1874) 42 L.J. P.C. 60; (1874) 29 L.T. 192, PC (HK) . . . . *Applied,* 00/4683
CP Holdings *v.* Dugdale [1998] N.P.C. 97, Ch D
CPS *v.* K (Age of Consent: Reasonable Belief) see R. *v.* K (Age of Consent: Reasonable Belief)
CR Smith Glaziers (Dunfermline) Ltd *v.* Customs and Excise Commissioners; *sub nom* CR Smith Glaziers (Dunfermline) Ltd *v.* Edinburgh VAT and Duties Tribunal [2001] S.T.C. 770; 2001 S.C. 646; [2001] S.T.I. 830; 2001 G.W.D. 7-290, Ex Div; affirming [2000] B.V.C. 2146; [2000] S.T.I. 264, V&DTr . . . . *Digested,* 01/**6920**
CR Smith Glaziers (Dunfermline) Ltd *v.* Edinburgh VAT and Duties Tribunal see CR Smith Glaziers (Dunfermline) Ltd *v.* Customs and Excise Commissioners
Crabb *v.* Arun DC (No.1) [1976] Ch. 179; [1975] 3 W.L.R. 847; [1975] 3 All E.R. 865; (1976) 32 P. & C.R. 70; 119 S.J. 711, CA . . . . *Digested,* 75/**1191**: *Applied,* 76/1524, 77/2509, 78/2901, 79/1083, 79/1085, 79/2635, 79/2651, 81/2732, 82/1149: *Considered,* 80/1073, 85/3647, 86/1901, 86/3551, 93/1852, 94/2109, 95/4560, 96/4949, 98/123

Craddock *v.* Customs and Excise Commissioners; Walker *v.* Customs and Excise Commissioners [2000] S.T.I. 865, V&DTr

Craggs *v.* Rowan Hankinson Ltd (1998) 98(2) Q.R. 8; (1997) 97(5/6) Q.R. 10, CC (Newcastle) . . . . *Digested*, 98/**1668**

Crago *v.* Julian [1992] 1 W.L.R. 372; [1992] 1 All E.R. 744; [1992] 1 F.L.R. 478; [1992] 2 F.C.R. 387; (1992) 24 H.L.R. 306; (1992) 63 P. & C.R. 356; [1992] 1 E.G.L.R. 84; [1992] 17 E.G. 108; [1992] Fam. Law 294; [1991] E.G.C.S. 124; (1992) 89(3) L.S.G. 32; [1991] N.P.C. 124; *Times*, December 4, 1991; *Independent*, November 22, 1991, CA . . . . *Digested*, 92/**2708**: *Followed*, 98/3047

Craig (A Minor) *v.* Erdman Lewis Ltd (Unreported, June 29, 1998), CC (Nottingham) [*Ex rel.* Nelsons Solicitors, Pennine House, 8 Stanford Street, Nottingham] . . . . *Digested*, 98/**1755**

Craig *v.* Humberclyde Industrial Finance Group Ltd; *sub nom* Hinckley Island Hotel Ltd, Re [1999] 1 W.L.R. 129; [1999] B.C.C. 378; [1998] 2 B.C.L.C. 526; [1999] B.P.I.R. 53; *Times*, July 15, 1998, CA . . . . *Digested*, 98/**3302**

Craig *v.* Shropshire CC [2000] 2 F.C.R. 628; *Times*, March 22, 2000; *Independent*, April 3, 2000 (C.S.), QBD . . . . *Digested*, 00/**4898**

Craigdallie *v.* Aikman (1813) 1 Dow 1, HL . . . . *Considered*, 01/**5501**

Craiglaw Developments Ltd *v.* Gordon Wilson & Co 1997 S.C. 356; 1998 S.L.T. 1046; 1997 S.C.L.R. 1157; [1998] B.C.C. 530; 1997 G.W.D. 21-1050; *Times*, September 11, 1997, Ex Div . . . . *Digested*, 97/**6162**

Crake *v.* Supplementary Benefits Commission; Butterworth *v.* Supplementary Benefits Commission [1982] 1 All E.R. 498, QBD . . . . *Digested*, 82/**3035**: *Considered*, 83/3179, 90/2896, 91/2313: *Followed*, 00/2542

Crane *v.* Premier Prison Services Ltd (Unreported, January 26, 2001), QBD [*Ex rel.* Nicholas Yell, Barrister, No. 1 Serjeants' Inn, Fleet Street, London] . . . . *Digested*, 01/**3298**

Craneheath Securities Ltd *v.* York Montague Ltd [2001] Lloyd's Rep. P.N. 348; [1996] 1 E.G.L.R. 130; [1996] 07 E.G. 141; [1995] E.G.C.S. 113; [1995] N.P.C. 104, CA; affirming [1994] 21 E.G. 124; [1993] E.G.C.S. 213, Ch D . . . . *Digested*, 95/**3719**

Crank *v.* Her Majesty's Stationery Office [1985] I.C.R. 1, EAT . . . . *Digested*, 85/**1224**: *Followed*, 99/2124

Crantrave Ltd (In Liquidation) *v.* Lloyds Bank Plc [2000] Q.B. 917; [2000] 3 W.L.R. 877; [2000] 4 All E.R. 473; [2000] 2 All E.R. (Comm) 89; [2000] Lloyd's Rep. Bank. 181; [2000] C.L.C. 1194; [2001] B.P.I.R. 57; (2000) 97(20) L.S.G. 42; (2000) 144 S.J.L.B. 219; *Times*, April 24, 2000, CA . . . . *Digested*, 00/**272**

Crate *v.* Mathison [2001] 2 Q.R. 8, CC (Plymouth) [*Ex rel.* Michael Melville-Shreeve, Barrister, Walnut House, 63 St. David's Hill, Exeter] . . . . *Digested*, 01/**1582**

Craughwell *v.* Lambeth LBC (Unreported, June 18, 2001), CC (Lambeth) [*Ex rel.* William Latimer-Sayer, Barrister, Cloisters, 1 Pump Court, Temple, London] . . . . . *Digested*, 01/**584**

Craven *v.* Cammell Laird & Co Ltd (The Thetis) (Discovery) see Duncan *v.* Cammell Laird & Co Ltd (Discovery)

Craven *v.* Jervis (Unreported, February 28, 2000), CC (Edmonton) [*Ex rel.* Corries Solicitors, Rowntree Wharf, Navigation Road, York] . . . . *Digested*, 00/**463**

Craven (Inspector of Taxes) *v.* White (Brian) see Craven (Inspector of Taxes) *v.* White (Stephen)

Craven (Inspector of Taxes) *v.* White (Stephen); Baylis (Inspector of Taxes) *v.* Gregory; Inland Revenue Commissioners *v.* Bowater Property Developments Ltd; Craven (Inspector of Taxes) *v.* White (Brian) [1989] A.C. 398; [1988] 3 W.L.R. 423; [1988] 3 All E.R. 495; [1988] S.T.C. 476; (1988) 85(34) L.S.G. 49; (1988) 138 N.L.J. Rep. 219; (1988) 132 S.J. 1120, HL; affirming [1987] 3 W.L.R. 660; [1987] 3 All E.R. 27; [1987] S.T.C. 297; [1987] 1 F.T.L.R. 551; (1987) 84 L.S.G. 2362; (1987) 131 S.J. 1124; *Times*, April 2, 1987, CA; affirming [1985] 1 W.L.R. 1024; [1985] 3 All E.R. 125; [1985] S.T.C. 531; [1985] P.C.C. 385; (1985) 82 L.S.G. 3085; (1985) 129 S.J. 417, Ch D . . . . *Digested*, 88/**257**: *Applied*, 92/611, 92/2518, 92/2519, 93/337, 95/876, 00/5043: *Considered*, 90/2685, 96/428, 96/5891: *Followed*, 86/262: *Referred to*, 95/527

Craven (Builders) Ltd *v.* Secretary of State for Health [2000] 1 E.G.L.R. 128; [1999] E.G.C.S. 126, Ch D . . . . *Digested*, 00/**1449**

Craven Textile Engineers Ltd *v.* Batley Football Club Ltd [2001] B.C.C. 679, CA

Crawford *v.* Clark see Crawford *v.* Clarke (Extension of Time)

Crawford *v.* Clarke (Caution against Dealing) [1999] E.G.C.S. 113, CA

Crawford *v.* Clarke (Continuation of Stay) (1999) 78 P. & C.R. D35, CA

Crawford *v.* Clarke (Extension of Time); *sub nom* Crawford *v.* Clark [2000] E.G.C.S. 33; (2000) 97(12) L.S.G. 45; (2000) 80 P. & C.R. D5, CA

Crawford *v.* Dunlop (1900) 2 F. (Ct. of Sess.) 987, CS . . . . *Cited*, 99/1629

Crawford *v.* Sunderland HA CCRTI 97/0550/G, CA . . . . *Digested*, 98/**354**

Crawley BC *v.* B (2000) 32 H.L.R. 636; (2000) 97(10) L.S.G. 35; (2000) 144 S.J.L.B. 108; *Times*, March 28, 2000; *Independent*, March 2, 2000, CA . . . . *Digested*, 00/**3141**: *Distinguished*, 00/3148

Crawley BC *v.* Bass Taverns Ltd (1999) 14 P.A.D. 280, Planning Inspector

Crawley BC *v.* Harveys Furnishing Group (2001) 16 P.A.D. 96, Planning Inspector

Crawley BC *v.* Hickmet Ltd (1998) 75 P. & C.R. 500; [1998] J.P.L. 210; [1997] N.P.C. 95, CA . . . . *Digested*, 97/**4038**

Crawley BC v. Sawyer (1988) 20 H.L.R. 98; 86 L.G.R. 629, CA . . . .   *Digested*, 88/**2078**:
                                                     Applied, 01/4216: *Considered*, 96/3836
Crawley BC v. Ure [1996] Q.B. 13; [1995] 3 W.L.R. 95; [1996] 1 All E.R. 724; [1995]
    1 F.L.R. 806; [1996] 1 F.C.R. 6; (1995) 27 H.L.R. 524; 93 L.G.R. 307; (1996) 71
    P. & C.R. 12; [1995] Fam. Law 411; [1995] N.P.C. 24; *Times*, February 23, 1995;
    Independent, April 18, 1995 (C.S.), CA . . . .   *Digested*, 95/**2997**:
                                                                      Applied, 01/4172
Crawley Green Road Cemetery, Luton, Re [2001] Fam. 308; [2001] 2 W.L.R.1175; [2001]
    H.R.L.R. 21; [2001] W.T.L.R. 1269; *Independent*, October 29, 2001 (C.S), Cons
    Ct (St Albans) . . . .   *Digested*, 01/**3481**
Crawley MBC v. Bradford & Bingley Building Society (1999) 1 L.G.L.R. 84, CA . . . . . .   *Digested*, 99/**2514**
Crayford Tandoori v. Customs and Excise Commissioners [2000] S.T.I. 1667, V&DTr
Crean Davidson Investments Ltd v. Earl Cadogan [1998] 2 E.G.L.R. 96; [1998] 20 E.G.
    136, CC (Central London) . . . .   *Digested*, 98/**3637**
Creasey v. Breachwood Motors Ltd [1992] B.C.C. 638; [1993] B.C.L.C. 480; *Times*,
    July 29, 1992 . . . .   *Digested*, 93/**383**:
                                                                      Overruled, 98/377

Credit Agricole Indosuez v. Chailease Finance Corp; *sub nom* Chailease Finance Corp v.
    Credit Agricole Indosuez [2000] 1 All E.R. (Comm) 399; [2000] 1 Lloyd's Rep.
    348; [2000] Lloyd's Rep. Bank. 119; [2000] C.L.C. 754; [2000] I.L.Pr. 776;
    Independent, March 27, 2000 (C.S), CA . . . .   *Digested*, 00/**284**
Credit Agricole Indosuez (London) v. Credit Suisse First Boston (Zurich) [2001] 1 All
    E.R. (Comm) 1088; [2001] Lloyd's Rep. Bank. 218, QBD (Comm Ct) . . . .   *Digested*, 01/**380**
Credit Agricole Indosuez v. Generale Bank (No.1) [1999] 2 All E.R. (Comm) 1009, QBD
    (Comm Ct) . . . .   *Digested*, 00/**283**
Credit Agricole Indosuez v. Generale Bank (No.2) [1999] 2 All E.R. (Comm) 1016;
    [2000] 1 Lloyd's Rep. 123; [2000] C.L.C. 205, QBD (Comm Ct) . . . .   *Digested*, 00/**281**
Credit Agricole Indosuez v. Muslim Commercial Bank Ltd [2000] 1 All E.R. (Comm)
    172; [2000] 1 Lloyd's Rep. 275; [2000] Lloyd's Rep. Bank. 1; [2000] C.L.C. 437,
    CA . . . .   *Digested*, 00/**280**
Credit Lyonnais Bank Nederland NV v. Burch [1997] 1 All E.R. 144; [1996] 5 Bank. L.R.
    233; [1997] C.L.C. 95; [1997] 1 F.L.R. 11; [1997] 2 F.C.R. 1; (1997) 29 H.L.R.
    513; (1997) 74 P. & C.R. 384; [1997] Fam. Law 168; (1996) 93(32) L.S.G. 33;
    (1996) 146 N.L.J. 1421; (1996) 140 S.J.L.B. 158; [1996] N.P.C. 99; *Times*, July 1,
    1996; *Independent*, June 27, 1996, CA . . . .   *Digested*, 96/**2784**:
                                         Applied, 01/954, 01/4880: *Considered*, 97/4244, 01/4878:
                                                                     Distinguished, 00/2333
Credit Lyonnais Bank Nederland NV (now Generale Bank Nederland NV) v. Export Credits
    Guarantee Department; *sub nom* Generale Bank Nederland NV (formerly Credit
    Lyonnais Bank Nederland NV) v. Export Credits Guarantee Department [2000]
    1 A.C. 486; [1999] 2 W.L.R. 540; [1999] 1 All E.R. 929; [1999] 1 Lloyd's Rep.
    563; [1999] C.L.C. 823; (1999) 96(10) L.S.G. 30; (1999) 143 S.J.L.B. 89;
    Times, February 19, 1999; *Independent*, February 23, 1999, HL; affirming [1998]
    1 Lloyd's Rep. 19; [1997] 6 Bank. L.R. 355; (1997) 94(34) L.S.G. 29; (1997)
    141 S.J.L.B. 194; *Times*, August 4, 1997, CA; affirming [1996] 1 Lloyd's Rep. 200;
    [1996] C.L.C. 11, QBD (Comm Ct) . . . .   *Digested*, 99/**280**:
                                     Applied, 00/4316: *Distinguished*, 97/3137: *Referred to*, 99/3493
Credit Lyonnais Commercial Finance Ltd v. Singh and Kaur (t/a Mander Fashions)
    (Unreported, November 30, 1999), QBD [*Ex rel*. Sunil Iyer, Barrister, Bracton
    Chambers, 8 Bell Yard, London] . . . .   *Digested*, 00/**2596**
Credit Suisse v. Allerdale BC [1997] Q.B. 306; [1996] 3 W.L.R. 894; [1996] 4 All E.R.
    129; [1996] 2 Lloyd's Rep. 241; [1996] 5 Bank. L.R. 249; (1997) 161 J.P. Rep.
    88; *Times*, May 20, 1996; *Independent*, June 7, 1996, CA; affirming [1995] 1
    Lloyd's Rep. 315; (1995) 159 L.G. Rev. 549; *Independent*, June 17, 1994, QBD
    (Comm Ct) . . . .   *Digested*, 96/**4060**:
                                         Considered, 96/4026, 96/4059, 97/3307, 98/3769, 98/3845
Credit Suisse v. Beegas Nominees Ltd [1994] 4 All E.R. 803; (1995) 69 P. & C.R. 177;
    [1994] 12 E.G. 189; [1994] 11 E.G. 151; [1993] E.G.C.S. 157; [1993] N.P.C. 123;
    Independent, September 15, 1993, Ch D . . . .   *Digested*, 95/**2982**:
                                                       Applied, 99/3738: *Considered*, 99/3695
Credit Suisse Fides Trust SA v. Cuoghi [1998] Q.B. 818; [1997] 3 W.L.R. 871; [1997] 3
    All E.R. 724; [1997] C.L.C. 1187; [1998] I.L.Pr. 41; *Times*, July 3, 1997, CA . . . . .   *Digested*, 97/**893**:
                                                     Considered, 98/563, 00/490
Credit Suisse First Boston (Europe) Ltd v. Cracknell see Credit Suisse First Boston
    (Europe) Ltd v. Padiachy
Credit Suisse First Boston (Europe) Ltd v. Lister [1999] 1 C.M.L.R. 710; [1999] I.C.R.
    794; [1998] I.R.L.R. 700; (1998) 95(44) L.S.G. 35; (1998) 142 S.J.L.B. 269;
    Times, October 22, 1998; *Independent*, November 9, 1998 (C.S.), CA . . . .   *Digested*, 98/**2216**
Credit Suisse First Boston (Europe) Ltd v. MLC (Bermuda) Ltd [1999] 1 All E.R.
    (Comm.) 237; [1999] 1 Lloyd's Rep. 767; [1999] C.L.C. 579, QBD (Comm Ct). .   *Digested*, 99/**744**
Credit Suisse First Boston (Europe) Ltd v. Padiachy; Credit Suisse First Boston (Europe)
    Ltd v. Winram; Credit Suisse First Boston (Europe) Ltd v. Cracknell [1998] 2
    C.M.L.R. 1322; [1999] I.C.R. 569; [1998] I.R.L.R. 504; *Times*, July 16, 1998,
    QBD . . . .   *Digested*, 98/**2217**

Credit Suisse First Boston (Europe) Ltd *v.* Seagate Trading Co Ltd [1999] 1 All E.R.
(Comm.) 261; [1999] 1 Lloyd's Rep. 784; [1999] C.L.C. 600, QBD (Comm Ct) .   *Digested*, 99/**745**
Credit Suisse First Boston (Europe) Ltd *v.* Winram see Credit Suisse First Boston
(Europe) Ltd *v.* Padiachy
Creditnet Ltd, Re see Austintel Ltd, Re
Creek *v.* Petryszyn (Unreported, September 11, 1997), CC (Reading) [*Ex rel.* Elaine
Strachan, Barrister, 3 Paper Buildings, Temple] . . . .   *Digested*, 98/**1735**
Crees *v.* Royal London Mutual Insurance Society Ltd; *sub nom* Greaves *v.* Kwik Save
Stores Ltd; Kwik Save Stores Ltd *v.* Greaves [1998] I.C.R. 848; [1998] I.R.L.R.
245; (1998) 95(15) L.S.G. 33; (1998) 142 S.J.L.B. 94; *Times*, March 5, 1998;
Independent, March 5, 1998, CA; reversing [1997] I.R.L.R. 85, EAT . . . .   *Digested*, 98/**2172**:
Applied, 98/2168: *Considered*, 98/5825: *Distinguished*, 96/2628, 97/2237:
Followed, 99/2076: *Overruled*, 01/2318: *Previous proceedings*, 97/2236
Crehan *v.* Courage Ltd (C453/99) see Courage Ltd *v.* Crehan (C453/99)
CREOLA Trade Mark [1997] R.P.C. 507, QBD . . . .   *Digested*, 97/**4900**:
Considered, 00/3789
Crescent Oil & Shipping Services Ltd *v.* Importang UEE (No.1) [1998] 1 W.L.R. 919;
[1997] 3 All E.R. 428; [1997] C.L.C. 1198, QBD (Comm Ct) . . . .   *Digested*, 97/**717**
Creska Ltd *v.* Hammersmith and Fulham LBC [1998] L. & T.R. 207; [1998] 3 E.G.L.R.
35; [1998] 37 E.G. 165; [1998] E.G.C.S. 96; [1998] N.P.C. 101, CA . . . .   *Digested*, 98/**3627**
Creska Ltd *v.* Hammersmith and Fulham LBC (No.2); *sub nom* Hammersmith and
Fulham LBC *v.* Creska Ltd (No.2) [2000] L. & T.R. 288; (1999) 78 P. & C.R.
D46; *Independent*, July 19, 1999 (C.S.), Ch D   *Digested*, 99/**442**
Cressingham Properties Ltd, Re [1999] 2 E.G.L.R. 117; [1999] 27 E.G. 123, Lands Tr . . .   *Digested*, 99/**3683**
Cresswell *v.* Duke of Westminster [1985] 2 E.G.L.R. 151; (1985) 275 E.G. 461; [1985]
R.V.R. 144, CA . . . .   *Digested*, 85/**1889**:
Considered, 01/4182
Cresswell *v.* Pearson (1998) 75 P. & C.R. 404; [1997] J.P.L. 860; *Times*, April 8, 1997,
QBD . . . .   *Digested*, 97/**4066**
Cresswell *v.* Proctor; *sub nom* Cresswell (Trustees of the Cobbett Settlement) *v.*
Proctor (Trustees of the Convent of the Holy Family) [1968] 1 W.L.R. 906;
[1968] 2 All E.R. 682; 19 P. & C.R. 516; 112 S.J. 420, CA. . . . .   *Digested*, 68/**3333**:
Considered, 00/5613: *Distinguished*, 75/2798, 76/2300
Cresswell (Trustees of the Cobbett Settlement) *v.* Proctor (Trustees of the Convent of
the Holy Family) see Cresswell *v.* Proctor
Cresswell *v.* Sandwell MBC (Unreported, October 26, 2000), CC (Birmingham) [*Ex
rel.* C Rowlands, Barrister, Victoria Chambers, 177 Corporation Street,
Birmingham] . . . .   *Digested*, 01/**4211**
Cresswell *v.* Sirl [1948] 1 K.B. 241; [1947] 2 All E.R. 730; 63 T.L.R. 620; 112 J.P. 69;
46 L.G.R. 109; [1948] L.J.R. 654; 91 S.J. 653, CA . . . .   *Digested*, 47-51/**342**:
Applied, 47-51/343, 47-51/370, 47-51/371, 60/87, 62/76, 62/3197:
Followed, 61/248: *Referred to*, 00/186
Crest Homes (South West) Ltd *v.* Gloucestershire CC [1999] N.P.C. 77, CA
Crest Homes Plc *v.* Marks [1987] A.C. 829; [1987] 3 W.L.R. 293; [1987] 2 All E.R.
1074; [1988] R.P.C. 21; (1987) 84 L.S.G. 2362; (1987) 137 N.L.J. 662; (1987)
131 S.J. 1003, HL; affirming [1987] 3 W.L.R. 48; (1987] F.S.R. 305; (1987) 84
L.S.G. 2048; (1987) 137 N.L.J. 318, CA. . . . .   *Digested*, 87/**2885**:
Applied, 88/2837, 91/2858, 93/3212, 93/4265, 96/5659, 98/471, 01/554:
Considered, 88/2833, 92/3475, 93/3211, 96/762: *Distinguished*, 96/689,
00/309: *Followed*, 97/465, 99/321
Creutzfeldt-Jakob Disease Litigation (Group A and C Plaintiffs), Re; *sub nom* Creutzfeldt-
Jakob Disease Litigation (No.7), Re; CJD Litigation (No.7), Re (2000) 54
B.M.L.R. 100, QBD . . . .   *Digested*, 00/**4193**
Creutzfeldt-Jakob Disease Litigation (No.1), Re; *sub nom* CJD Litigation (No.1), Re
(2000) 54 B.M.L.R. 1, QBD . . . .   *Digested*, 00/**4194**
Creutzfeldt-Jakob Disease Litigation (No.2), Re see Newman *v.* Secretary of State for
Health (No.1)
Creutzfeldt-Jakob Disease Litigation (No.3), Re; *sub nom* CJD Litigation (No.3), Re
(2000) 54 B.M.L.R. 79, QBD. . . . .   *Digested*, 00/**4199**:
Subsequent proceedings, 98/3962
Creutzfeldt-Jakob Disease Litigation (No.4), Re see Newman *v.* Secretary of State for
Health (No.1)
Creutzfeldt-Jakob Disease Litigation (No.5), Re see Group B Plaintiffs *v.* Medical Research
Council
Creutzfeldt-Jakob Disease Litigation (No.6), Re see Newman *v.* Secretary of State for
Health (No.2)
Creutzfeldt-Jakob Disease Litigation (No.7), Re see Creutzfeldt-Jakob Disease Litigation
(Group A and C Plaintiffs), Re
Creutzfeldt-Jakob Disease Litigation (No.8), Re see Straddlers Groups A and C *v.*
Secretary of State for Health
Creutzfeldt-Jakob Disease Litigation (No.9), Re see Andrews *v.* Secretary of State for
Health (Damages Assessments)
Crew Members of the Ever Success *v.* Owners of the Ever Success see Ever Success,
The

Crewdson *v.* Bagot see Cooper's Conveyance Trusts, Re
Crewe and Nantwich BC *v.* Secretary of State for the Environment, Transport and the
　　Regions [2001] J.P.L. 377 (Note), QBD
Crewe Services & Investment Corp *v.* Silk (2000) 79 P. & C.R. 500; [1998] 2 E.G.L.R.
　　1; [1998] 35 E.G. 81; [1997] E.G.C.S. 170; [1997] N.P.C. 170; *Times*, January 2,
　　1998, CA . . . . 　*Digested*, 98/**122**:
　　　　　　　　　　　　　　　　　　　　　　　　　　　　　　　　　　Considered, 00/1449
Cricket Ltd *v.* Shaftesbury Plc [1999] 3 All E.R. 283; [2000] L. & T.R. 13; [1999] 2
　　E.G.L.R. 57; [1999] 28 E.G. 127, Ch D . . . . 　*Digested*, 99/**3669**
Criminal Cases Review Commission's Reference under s.14(3) of Criminal Appeal Act 1995
　　see R. *v.* Gordon (Iain Hay)
Criminal Proceedings against Ambry (C410/96) [1998] E.C.R. I-7875; [2001] 1 C.M.L.R.
　　24, ECJ
Criminal Proceedings against Arblade (C369/96); Criminal Proceedings against Leloup
　　(C376/96) [1999] E.C.R. I-8453; [2001] I.C.R. 434; *Times*, December 7, 1999,
　　ECJ . . . . 　*Digested*, 00/**2398**
Criminal Proceedings against Arcaro (C168/95) [1997] All E.R. (EC) 82; [1996] E.C.R. I-
　　4705; [1997] 1 C.M.L.R. 179; [1998] Env. L.R. 39, ECJ (4th Chamber) . . . . 　*Digested*, 97/**2383**:
　　　　　　　　　　　　　　　　　　　　　　　　　　　　　　　　Distinguished, 00/4458
Criminal Proceedings against Awoyemi (C230/97); *sub nom* Awoyemi (C230/97), Re
　　[1998] E.C.R. I-6781; [2001] 1 C.M.L.R. 15, ECJ (2nd Chamber)
Criminal Proceedings against Bashir (C291/96); *sub nom* Criminal Proceedings against
　　Grado (C291/96) [1997] E.C.R. I-5531; [1998] 1 C.M.L.R. 984, ECJ (2nd
　　Chamber)
Criminal Proceedings against Becu (C22/98), Re; *sub nom* Becu (C22/98), Re [1999]
　　E.C.R. I-5665; [2001] 4 C.M.L.R. 26, ECJ . . . . 　*Digested*, 01/**780**
Criminal Proceedings against Bernaldez (C129/94) [1996] All E.R. (E.C.) 741; [1996]
　　E.C.R. I-1829; [1996] 2 C.M.L.R. 889; *Times*, May 6, 1996, ECJ (5th Chamber) . 　*Digested*, 96/**3614**:
　　　　　　　　　　　　　　　　　　　　　　　　　　　　　　　　　　Followed, 00/3547
Criminal Proceedings against Bickel (C274/96); *sub nom* Bickel, Re (C274/96);
　　Criminal Proceedings against Franz, Re [1998] E.C.R. I-7637; [1999] 1 C.M.L.R.
　　348; [1999] C.E.C. 119; *Times*, December 1, 1998, ECJ . . . . 　*Digested*, 99/**1031**
Criminal Proceedings against Bluhme (C67/97) [1998] E.C.R. I-8033; [1999] 1 C.M.L.R.
　　612; [2000] Env. L.R. D1, ECJ (5th Chamber)
Criminal Proceedings against Calfa (C348/96); *sub nom* Calfa, Re (C348/96) [1999]
　　All E.R. (EC) 850; [1999] E.C.R. I-11; [1999] 2 C.M.L.R. 1138; [1999] C.E.C.
　　477; [1999] I.N.L.R. 333; (1999) 96(19) L.S.G. 30; *Times*, January 21, 1999,
　　ECJ . . . . 　*Digested*, 99/**1132**
Criminal Proceedings against Denuit (C14/96) [1997] E.C.R. I-2785; [1997] 3 C.M.L.R.
　　943; [1998] C.E.C. 3; [1998] E.M.L.R. 60; *Times*, June 23, 1997, ECJ (6th
　　Chamber) . . . . 　*Digested*, 97/**3569**
Criminal Proceedings against DJ Ferne see Criminal Proceedings against E Clarke & Sons
　　(Coaches) Ltd (C47/97)
Criminal Proceedings against E Clarke & Sons (Coaches) Ltd (C47/97); Criminal
　　Proceedings against DJ Ferne [1998] E.C.R. I-2147; [1998] R.T.R. 333; [1998] 2
　　C.M.L.R. 699; *Times*, May 1, 1998, ECJ (1st Chamber). . . . . 　*Digested*, 98/**4860**
Criminal Proceedings against Fol (C130/97) see Chiciak, Re (C129/97)
Criminal Proceedings against Fornasar (C318/98) see Fornasar (C318/98), Re
Criminal Proceedings against Forsakringsaktiebolaget Skandia (C241/97) [1999] E.C.R. I-
　　1879; [1999] 2 C.M.L.R. 933, ECJ. . . . . 　*Digested*, 99/**3377**
Criminal Proceedings against Franz, Re see Criminal Proceedings against Bickel (C274/96)
Criminal Proceedings against Franzen (C189/95) [1997] E.C.R. I-5909; [1998] 1 C.M.L.R.
　　1231, ECJ . . . . 　*Considered*, 99/2222:
　　　　　　　　　　　　　　　　　　　　　　　　　　　　　　　　　　Followed, 00/2400
Criminal Proceedings against Geffroy (C366/98); *sub nom* Geffroy and Casino France
　　SNC's Reference (C366/98) [2001] All E.R. (EC) 222; [2000] E.C.R. I-6579;
　　[2001] 2 C.M.L.R. 25; [2001] E.T.M.R. 1, ECJ. . . . . 　*Digested*, 01/**916**
Criminal Proceedings against Giovanni (C342/94) see Criminal Proceedings against
　　Tombesi (C304/94)
Criminal Proceedings against Goerres (C385/96) [1998] E.C.R. I-4431; *Times*, August
　　21, 1998, ECJ (5th Chamber). . . . . 　*Digested*, 98/**2591**
Criminal Proceedings against Goodwin (C3/97) see R. *v.* Goodwin (John Charles) (C3/
　　97)
Criminal Proceedings against Grado (C291/96) see Criminal Proceedings against Bashir
　　(C291/96)
Criminal Proceedings against Guimont (C448/98), Re see Guimont (C448/98), Re
Criminal Proceedings against Heinonen (C394/97) [1999] E.C.R. I-3599; [2000] 2
　　C.M.L.R. 1037, ECJ (5th Chamber) . . . . 　*Digested*, 00/**2400**
Criminal Proceedings against Hume (C193/99); *sub nom* Hume (C193/99), Re [2000]
　　All E.R. (EC) 852; [2000] E.C.R. I-7809; [2001] R.T.R. 10; [2001] 1 C.M.L.R. 1;
　　[2000] C.E.C. 722; [2001] I.R.L.R. 103; *Times*, October 5, 2000, ECJ (1st
　　Chamber). . . . . 　*Digested*, 00/**5168**:
　　　　　　　　　　　　　　　　　　　　　　　　　　　　　　　　　　Applied, 01/5441

Criminal Proceedings against Keck (C267/91); Criminal Proceedings against Mithouard
(C268/91) [1993] E.C.R. I-6097; [1995] 1 C.M.L.R. 101; *Times*, November 25,
1993; *Financial Times*, November 30, 1993, ECJ . . . . *Digested*, 94/**4885**:
             Considered, 94/4874, 96/2801, 01/2486: *Followed*, 98/3855, 00/4165
Criminal Proceedings against Kortas (C319/97) [1999] E.C.R. I-3143; [2000] 3 C.M.L.R.
962, ECJ . . . . *Digested*, 01/**2459**
Criminal Proceedings against Leloup (C376/96) see Criminal Proceedings against Arblade
(C369/96)
Criminal Proceedings against Lemmens (C226/97) [1998] All E.R. (EC) 604; [1998]
E.C.R. I-3711; [1998] 3 C.M.L.R. 261; *Times*, July 20, 1998, ECJ . . . . *Digested*, 98/**866**
Criminal Proceedings against Mithouard (C268/91) see Criminal Proceedings against
Keck (C267/91)
Criminal Proceedings against Nunes (C186/98); *sub nom* Nunes (C186/98), Re [1999]
E.C.R. I-4883; [1999] 2 C.M.L.R. 1403; [1999] C.E.C. 367; *Times*, August 5,
1999, ECJ (1st Chamber) . . . . *Digested*, 99/**2232**
Criminal Proceedings against Raso (C163/96) [1998] E.C.R. I-533; [1998] 4 C.M.L.R.
737; [1998] C.E.C. 528, ECJ (5th Chamber) . . . . *Digested*, 98/**722**
Criminal Proceedings against Romanelli (C366/97) [1999] All E.R. (EC) 473; [1999]
E.C.R. I-855, ECJ (6th Chamber) . . . . *Digested*, 99/**2528**
Criminal Proceedings against Santella (C330/94) see Criminal Proceedings against
Tombesi (C304/94)
Criminal Proceedings against Savini (C224/95) see Criminal Proceedings against Tombesi
(C304/94)
Criminal Proceedings against Sjoberg (C387/96) [1998] E.C.R. I-1225; [1998] 2 C.M.L.R.
1304; *Times*, March 23, 1998, ECJ (5th Chamber) . . . . *Digested*, 98/**4844**
Criminal Proceedings against Skills Motor Coaches Ltd (C297/99) see Skills Motor
Coaches Ltd v. Denman (C297/99)
Criminal Proceedings against Tombesi (C304/94); Criminal Proceedings against Giovanni
(C342/94); Criminal Proceedings against Savini (C224/95); Criminal Proceedings
against Santella (C330/94) [1997] All E.R. (E.C.) 639; [1997] E.C.R. I-3561; [1997]
3 C.M.L.R. 673; [1998] Env. L.R. 59; *Times*, August 1, 1997, ECJ (6th Chamber)   *Digested*, 97/**2360**:
                        Applied, 98/2308: *Followed*, 99/2207
Criminal Proceedings against Unterweger (318/85) [1986] E.C.R. 955, ECJ . . . . *Followed*, 00/2381
Criminal Proceedings against Van der Laan (C383/97); *sub nom* van de Laan (C383/
97), Re [1999] E.C.R. I-731; [2000] 1 C.M.L.R. 563, ECJ (1st Chamber) . . . . . . *Digested*, 00/**844**
Criminal Proceedings against Van Schaik (C55/93) [1994] E.C.R. I-4837, ECJ . . . . *Digested*, 95/**4905**:
                                        Followed, 01/2512
Criminal Proceedings against Webb (C279/80); *sub nom* Webb, Re [1981] E.C.R. 3305;
[1982] 1 C.M.L.R. 719, ECJ . . . . *Digested*, 82/**1215**:
                                         Applied, 98/4517
Criminal Proceedings against Wijsenbeek (C378/97) see Wijsenbeek (C378/97), Re
Cripps v. Heritage Distribution Corp; New England International Surety Inc v. Cripps
[1999] C.P.L.R. 858; (1999) 96(44) L.S.G. 39; (1999) 143 S.J.L.B. 263; *Times*,
November 10, 1999, CA . . . . *Digested*, 99/**402**
Crispoltoni v. Fattoria Autonoma Tabacchi (C133/93) [1994] E.C.R. I-4863, ECJ . . . . . *Digested*, 95/**286**:
                                         Followed, 00/2346
Crittenden v. Crittenden [1990] 2 F.L.R. 361; [1991] F.C.R. 70; *Times*, April 12, 1990,
CA . . . . *Digested*, 91/**1793**:
                                  Not followed, 94/2177
Crittenden (Warren Park) Ltd v. Elliott (1998) 75 P. & C.R. 20, CA . . . . *Digested*, 98/**3661**
Croft's Application, Re [1997] N.I. 457, CA (NI); affirming [1997] N.I. 1, QBD (NI) . . . . . *Digested*, 99/**5463**
Crofter Hand Woven Harris Tweed Co Ltd v. Veitch [1942] A.C. 435; [1942] 1 All E.R.
147; 1943 S.L.T. 2, HL; affirming 1940 S.L.T. 210, 2 Div . . . . *Applied*, 47-51/10047,
      52/3396, 52/3507, 57/3586, 58/3441, 80/279: *Considered*, 62/3063, 69/295,
                          81/2649, 98/4069: *Followed*, 67/3981
Crolla (CICB: Quantum: 1999), Re (Unreported, August 4, 1999), CICB (Manchester) [*Ex*
  rel. Rowlands Solicitors, 3 York Street, Manchester] . . . . *Digested*, 00/**1521**
Crompton v. Sevalco Ltd see Hall v. Sevalco Ltd
Cromwell Developments Ltd v. Godfrey; Cromwell Developments Ltd v. Wright (1999)
78 P. & C.R. 197; [1998] 2 E.G.L.R. 62; [1998] 33 E.G. 72; [1998] N.P.C. 67,
CA . . . . *Digested*, 98/**3606**
Cromwell Developments Ltd v. Wright see Cromwell Developments Ltd v. Godfrey
CROMWELLS MADHOUSE Trade Mark [1998] R.P.C. 511, TMR . . . . *Digested*, 98/**3533**
Crook, Ex p. see R. v. Central Criminal Court Ex p. Crook
Crooks v. Ebanks [1999] 1 W.L.R. 1287, PC (Jam) . . . . *Digested*, 99/**4009**
Crosby-Clarke v. Air Foyle Ltd see Rossiter v. Pendragon Plc
Crosdale v. Queen, The; *sub nom* Crosland v. Queen, The [1995] 1 W.L.R. 864; [1995]
2 All E.R. 500; [1995] Crim. L.R. 958; (1995) 92(24) L.S.G. 38; (1995) 145
N.L.J. 594; (1995) 139 S.J.L.B. 143, PC (Jam) . . . . *Digested*, 96/**1604**:
                                    Applied, 98/1050, 00/1111
Crosland v. Queen, The see Crosdale v. Queen, The
Cross, Re see National Assurance & Investment Association, Re
Cross v. Highland and Islands Enterprise see Cross v. Highlands and Islands Enterprise

Cross v. Highlands and Islands Enterprise; *sub nom* Cross v. Highland and Islands Enterprise; Macdonald v. Highlands and Islands Enterprise 2001 S.L.T. 1060; 2001 S.C.L.R. 547; [2001] Eu. L.R. 256; [2001] I.R.L.R. 336; 2001 Rep. L.R. 26; 2000 G.W.D. 40-1506, OH. . . . .   *Digested*, 01/**6665**
Cross v. Kirkby, *Times*, April 5, 2000, CA . . . .   *Digested*, 00/**5110**
Cross v. Kirklees MBC [1998] 1 All E.R. 564; *Times*, July 10, 1997, CA . . . .   *Digested*, 97/**3786**:
                                           Considered, 99/2887, 99/2890
Cross AM Lines see Union Transport v. Continental Lines SA
Cross (F) & Sons v. Spencer (Valuation Officer) see F Cross & Sons v. Spencer (Valuation Officer)
Cross Electrical & Building Services Ltd v. Customs and Excise Commissioners [2001] S.T.I. 576, V&DTr
Cross's Trade Mark (2000) 23(9) I.P.D. 23078, TMR
Crosse & Crosse v. Lloyds Bank Plc see Lloyds Bank Plc v. Crosse & Crosse
Crossland v. Crossland [1993] 1 F.L.R. 175; [1992] 2 F.C.R. 45; [1993] Fam. Law 186, DC . . . .   *Digested*, 93/**1917**:
                           Distinguished, 99/1032: *Followed*, 99/1157
Crossland v. United Kingdom (36120/97) (2001) 29 E.H.R.R. CD34, ECHR
Crossley v. North Western Road Car Co Ltd (Unreported, June 18, 1999), CC (Sheffield) [*Ex rel*. Sean D Yates, Barrister, 10 Park Square, Leeds]. . . . .   *Digested*, 99/**408**:
                                             Cited, 00/450
Crosville Wales Ltd v. Tracey see Tracey v. Crosville Wales Ltd
Crouchman v. Burke (1998) 40 B.M.L.R. 163, QBD . . . .   *Digested*, 98/**3985**
Croudace Construction Ltd v. Cawoods Concrete Products Ltd [1978] 2 Lloyd's Rep. 55; 8 B.L.R. 20, CA . . . .   *Digested*, 78/**313**:
                                  Applied, 99/796: *Cited*, 97/1751
Crowe v. Hutt (Unreported, June 12, 2000), CC (Central London) [*Ex rel*. Simon Brindle, Barrister, 199 Strand, London] . . . .   *Digested*, 00/**404**:
                                     Distinguished, 01/3841
Crown Estate Commissioners v. John Mowlem & Co Ltd 70 B.L.R. 1; 40 Con. L.R. 36; (1994) 10 Const. L.J. 311, CA . . . .   *Digested*, 95/**491**:
                           Applied, 01/876: *Distinguished*, 99/5784
Crown Forestry Rental Trust, Re see Latimer v. Inland Revenue Commissioner
Crown Prosecution Service v. Barnard see DPP v. Barnard
Crown Prosecution Service v. Green see DPP v. Green
Crown Prosecution Service v. Humphries; *sub nom* DPP v. Humphries [2000] 2 Cr. App. R. (S.) 1; (2000) 164 J.P. 502; [2000] R.T.R. 52; *Times*, December 3, 1999, QBD . . . .   *Digested*, 00/**1203**
Crown Prosecution Service v. Scarlett see DPP v. Scarlett
Crown Prosecution Service v. Speede see DPP v. Speede
Crown Prosecution Service v. Tweddell; *sub nom* DPP v. Tweddell [2001] EWHC Admin 188; [2001] A.C.D. 83, QBD (Admin Ct)
Crown Prosecution Service v. Weeks see DPP v. Weeks
Crown Trust Co v. Rosenberg (1986) 60 O.R. (2d) 87, HC (Ont) . . . .   *Followed*, 00/3482,
                                                     01/3776
Crowther v. Haigh (1999) 78 P. & C.R. D22, CA
Croydon Hotel & Leisure Co Ltd v. Customs and Excise Commissioners [1997] V. & D.R. 254, V&DTr . . . .   *Digested*, 98/**4956**
Croydon LBC v. KOP Pavement Shopping Ltd (1998) 13 P.A.D. 565, Planning Inspector
Croydon LBC v. Maxon Systems Incorporated (London) Ltd [1999] R.A. 286; [1999] E.G.C.S. 68, QBD . . . .   *Digested*, 99/**4326**
Croydon LBC v. Mills and Allen Ltd (1999) 14 P.A.D. 276, Planning Inspector
Croydon LBC v. Moody (1999) 31 H.L.R. 738; (1999) 2 C.C.L. Rep. 92, CA . . . .   *Digested*, 99/**3741**
Croydon LBC v. R; *sub nom* R (A Minor) (Child Case: Procedure), Re [1997] 2 F.L.R. 675; [1997] 3 F.C.R. 704; [1997] Fam. Law 653; (1997) 161 J.P.N. 724, Fam Div . . . .   *Digested*, 98/**2399**
Croydon LBC v. Secretary of State for the Environment, Transport and the Regions; *sub nom* R. v. Secretary of State for the Environment, Transport and the Regions Ex p. Croydon LBC [2000] P.L.C.R. 171, QBD . . . .   *Digested*, 00/**4485**
Croydon (Unique) Ltd v. Wright [2001] Ch. 318; [2000] 2 W.L.R. 683; [1999] 4 All E.R. 257; (2000) 32 H.L.R. 670; [2000] L. & T.R. 20; [1999] 3 E.G.L.R. 28; [1999] 40 E.G. 189; (1999) 96(33) L.S.G. 31; (1999) 149 N.L.J. 1473; [1999] N.P.C. 113; (1999) 78 P. & C.R. D40; *Times*, August 24, 1999, CA . . . .   *Digested*, 99/**3677**
Crozier v. Crozier [1994] Fam. 114; [1994] 2 W.L.R. 444; [1994] 2 All E.R. 362; [1994] 1 F.L.R. 126; [1994] 1 F.C.R. 781; [1994] Fam. Law 244; (1993) 143 N.L.J. 1784; *Times*, December 9, 1993; *Independent*, December 9, 1993, Fam Div . . . .   *Digested*, 94/**2175**:
                                     Considered, 98/2470
CRT France International SA v. Directuer Regional des Imports de Bourgogne (C109/98) [1999] E.C.R. I-2237; (1999) 96(31) L.S.G. 43, ECJ (1st Chamber)
Cruise v. Express Newspapers Plc [1999] Q.B. 931; [1999] 1 W.L.R. 327; [1998] E.M.L.R. 780; *Times*, September 1, 1998, CA. . . . .   *Digested*, 98/**1769**

Cruise v. Terrell [1922] 1 K.B. 664, CA . . . . *Considered*, 99/4386:
Distinguished, 53/1956
Crummock (Scotland) Ltd v. HM Advocate 2000 J.C. 408; 2000 S.L.T. 677; 2000
S.C.C.R. 453; 2000 GW.D. 12-420; *Times*, May 9, 2000, HCJ Appeal . . . . *Digested*, 00/**6087**
Crump v. Gilmore 68 L.G.R. 56; (1969) 113 S.J. 998; *Times*, November 5, 1969, DC . . . *Digested*, 69/**1189**:
Considered, 99/1832
Crump v. Inspiration East Ltd (Unreported, August 18, 1997), CC (Reigate) [*Ex rel*. SW
Morris, Solicitor, 3 Telford Close, Garston, Watford] . . . . *Digested*, 98/**1427**
Crutchfield (Inspector of Taxes) v. Cassell see Cassell v. Crutchfield (Inspector of Taxes)
(No.2)
Cryer v. Scott Bros (Sunbury) Ltd (1988) 55 P. & C.R. 183, CA . . . . *Digested*, 88/**3523**:
Applied, 00/4627
CSC Financial Services Ltd v. Customs and Excise Commissioners (C235/00) see
Customs and Excise Commissioners v. CSC Financial Services Ltd (C235/00)
CSCS v. Minister for Education see Campaign to Separate Church and State Ltd v.
Minister for Education
Cselko v. Camden Listing Officer [2001] R.V.R. 280, QBD
CT Cogstad & Co (The SS Lord) v. H Newsum Sons & Co Ltd; *sub nom* Arbitration
between Cogstad & Co and H Newsum Sons & Co Ltd, Re [1921] 2 A.C. 528;
(1921) 8 Ll. L. Rep. 399, HL; affirming [1921] 1 K.B. 87; (1920) 4 Ll. L. Rep.
376, CA; affirming [1920] 1 K.B. 846; (1920) 2 Ll. L. Rep. 276, KBD (Comm
Ct) . . . . *Distinguished*, 65/100:
Not followed, 98/4413
Cuckmere Brick Co v. Mutual Finance [1971] Ch. 949; [1971] 2 W.L.R. 1207; [1971] 2
All E.R. 633; (1971) 22 P. & C.R. 624; 115 S.J. 288, CA . . . . *Digested*, 71/**7479**:
Applied, 72/2205, 83/2484, 88/2388, 90/3213, 01/4873:
Considered, 82/339, 99/3286, 00/4657: *Distinguished*, 78/2024, 79/1355:
Followed, 84/2306
Cuflet Chartering v. Carousel Shipping Co Ltd [2001] 1 All E.R. (Comm) 398; [2001]
1 Lloyd's Rep. 707, QBD (Comm Ct) . . . . *Digested*, 01/**341**
Cuisine de la Mer Cuisimer SA v. Maumenee [2000] E.T.M.R. 880, Cass (F)
Cuke v. O'Callaghan (Unreported, June 2, 1998), CC (Central London) [*Ex rel*. Jerome
Mayhew, Barrister, Goldsmith Building, Temple] . . . . *Digested*, 98/**1722**
Cullen v. Chief Constable of the Royal Ulster Constabulary [1999] N.I. 237, CA (NI) . . . *Digested*, 00/**5662**
Cullen v. Customs and Excise Commissioners [2001] S.T.I. 1120, V&DTr
Culley v. Cue International Ltd [2001] 6 Q.R. 6, CC (Manchester) [*Ex rel*. Christopher
Taft, Barrister, St. James's Chambers, 68 Quay Street, Manchester] . . . . *Digested*, 01/**1606**
Cullin v. London Fire and Civil Defence Authority; *sub nom* White v. London Fire and
Civil Defence Authority; Sheehan v. London Fire and Civil Defence Authority
[1999] P.I.Q.R. P314, CA; affirming (Unreported, March 31, 1999), QBD [*Ex rel*.
Thompsons Solicitors, Congress House, Great Russell Street, London] . . . . *Digested*, 99/**3980**
Cullinane v. Inland Revenue Commissioners [2000] B.P.I.R. 996, Ch D . . . . *Digested*, 01/**592**
Culmer v. Queen, The [1997] 1 W.L.R. 1296; (1997) 141 S.J.L.B. 196, PC (Bah) . . . . *Digested*, 98/**1055**
Cumbernauld Development Corp v. Customs and Excise Commissioners TNS, 2 Div;
affirming [2001] S.T.I. 529, V&DTr
Cumbrian Industrials Ltd v. Parkman Consulting Engineers see Parkman Consulting
Engineers v. Cumbrian Industrials Ltd
Cumming v. Danson [1942] 2 All E.R. 653, CA . . . . *Applied*, 47-51/8597,
47-51/8598, 47-51/8678, 52/1958, 59/2824: *Cited*, 00/3157:
Considered, 83/2119, 97/2669, 97/2715, 01/4198
Cummings, Re see R. v. Secretary of State for the Home Department Ex p. Cummings
Cummings v. Claremont Petroleum NL [1998] B.P.I.R. 187, HC (Aus) . . . . *Digested*, 98/**3293**
Cummings v. DPP [1999] C.O.D. 288; (1999) 143 S.J.L.B. 112; [1999] E.H.L.R. Dig.
455; *Times*, March 26, 1999; *Independent*, March 8, 1999 (C.S.), QBD . . . . *Digested*, 99/**211**
Cumper v. Pothecary [1941] 2 K.B. 58; [1941] 2 All E.R. 516, CA . . . . *Applied*, 53/2874,
75/2670, 76/2182, 77/2382: *Considered*, 97/680: *Not applied*, 01/621
Cundy v. Lindsay; *sub nom* Lindsay v. Cundy (1877-78) L.R. 3 App. Cas. 459; [1874-
80] All E.R. Rep. 1149; (1878) 42 J.P. 483; (1878) 14 Cox C.C. 93; (1878) 26
W.R. 406; (1878) 47 L.J. Q.B. 481; (1878) 38 L.T. 573; 15 Sask. R. 233, HL;
affirming (1876-77) L.R. 2 Q.B.D. 96, CA; reversing (1875-76) L.R. 1 Q.B.D.
348, QBD . . . . *Applied*, 68/3545,
00/2600: *Considered*, 60/185, 60/550, 68/550: *Distinguished*, 90/262,
91/528: *Explained*, 69/526
Cunliffe v. Goodman [1950] 2 K.B. 237; [1950] 1 All E.R. 720; (1950) 66 T.L.R. (Pt.
2) 109; 94 S.J. 179, CA; reversing [1950] 1 K.B. 267; [1949] 2 All E.R. 946;
(1949) 65 T.L.R. 751, KBD . . . . *Digested*, 47-51/**5425**:
Applied, 56/1654, 56/4852, 56/4853, 56/4858, 61/7682, 62/1717, 75/510,
82/1722, 90/2766: *Considered*, 85/1856, 87/2129, 87/2132, 87/2229,
88/2007, 88/2014, 89/2192, 89/2194, 90/2772, 90/2777, 92/2667,
00/3904
Cunliffe v. Solihull MBC [1998] R.V.R. 64, Lands Tr . . . . *Digested*, 98/**4171**
Cunningham v. Birmingham City Council [1998] Env. L.R. 1; (1998) 30 H.L.R. 158;
[1998] J.P.L. 147; [1997] C.O.D. 448; *Times*, June 9, 1997; *Independent*, May 19,
1997 (C.S.), QBD . . . . *Digested*, 97/**2377**

Cunningham v. Cunningham 2001 Fam. L.R. 12; 2000 G.W.D. 36-1362, OH . . . .   *Digested*, 01/**6519**
Cunningham v. Customs and Excise Commissioners [2001] S.T.C. 736; [2001] S.T.I. 244, Ch D
Cunningham v. Damon (Unreported, December 1, 1999), CC (Medway) [*Ex rel.* Patrick McMorrow, Barrister, 169 Temple Chambers, Temple Avenue, London] . . . .   *Digested*, 00/**1460**:
                                             Followed, 01/3799
Cunningham v. Harrison [1973] Q.B. 942; [1973] 3 W.L.R. 97; [1973] 3 All E.R. 463; 117 S.J. 547, CA . . . .   *Digested*, 73/**740**:
                     Applied, 74/849: *Considered*, 75/795, 76/680, 99/1398:
             Distinguished, 82/801, 84/1013: *Followed*, 92/5649
Cunningham v. Kensington and Chelsea and Westminster AHA (1998) 98(6) Q.R. 3, QBD . . . .   *Digested*, 98/**1480**
Cunningham v. Tatlow [2001] 6 Q.R. 19, CC (Bury) [*Ex rel.* Christopher Taft, Barrister, St. James's Chambers, 68 Quay Street, Manchester] . . . .   *Digested*, 01/**1745**
Cuoghi, Re see R. v. Governor of Brixton Prison Ex p. Cuoghi
Curi v. Colina, *Times*, October 14, 1998, CA . . . .   *Digested*, 98/**1503**
Curing a Defective Service of Judgment, Re [1998] I.L.Pr. 819, OLG (Hamm)
Curl v. Angelo [1948] 2 All E.R. 189; [1948] L.J.R. 1756; 92 S.J. 513, CA . . . .   *Digested*, 47-51/**8532**:
                                Applied, 00/3878: *Followed*, 47-51/8496
Curley v. United Kingdom (32340/96) (2001) 31 E.H.R.R. 14; *Times*, April 5, 2000, ECHR . . . .   *Digested*, 00/**4323**
Curphey v. Ward (Unreported, July 31, 1997), CC (Kendal) [*Ex rel.* Beardsells Solicitors, Badger House, 43 Palmerston Street, Bollington, Macclesfield] . . . . .   *Digested*, 98/**1637**
Currencies Direct Ltd v. Ellis A2/2002/0199, CA; affirming *Times*, November 27, 2001, QBD . . . .   *Digested*, 01/**730**
Curri v. Westminster City Council [2000] E.H.L.R. 16; [1999] C.O.D. 395, QBD . . . .   *Digested*, 00/**2678**:
                                               Approved, 00/967
Currie (CICB: Quantum: 1999), Re (Unreported, September 21, 1999), CICB (Durham) [*Ex rel.* Simon E Wood, Barrister, Plowden Buildings, Temple, London] . . . .   *Digested*, 00/**1622**
Currie v. Magic Travel Group (Holidays) Ltd (Unreported, January 2, 2001), CC (Worcester) [*Ex rel.* James Morgan, Barrister, St. Philip's Chambers, Fountain Court, Steelhouse Lane, Birmingham] . . . .   *Digested*, 01/**4278**
Currie v. Misa see Misa v. Currie
Currys Group Plc v. Martin [1999] 3 E.G.L.R. 165; [1999] E.G.C.S. 115; (1999) 96(39) L.S.G. 40; [1999] N.P.C. 116, QBD . . . .   *Digested*, 00/**4277**
Curtis v. Betts [1990] 1 W.L.R. 459; [1990] 1 All E.R. 769; (1990) 87(9) L.S.G. 41; (1990) 134 S.J. 317, CA. . . . .   *Digested*, 90/**174**:
                   Considered, 98/3990, 00/205: *Followed*, 91/166, 95/320
Curtis v. Chairman of London Rent Assessment Committee see Curtis v. London Rent Assessment Committee
Curtis v. London Rent Assessment Committee see Spath Holme Ltd v. Greater Manchester and Lancashire Rent Assessment Committee (No.2)
Curtis v. London Rent Assessment Committee; *sub nom* Curtis v. Chairman of London Rent Assessment Committee [1999] Q.B. 92; [1998] 3 W.L.R. 1427; [1997] 4 All E.R. 842; (1998) 30 H.L.R. 733; [1998] 1 E.G.L.R. 79; [1998] 15 E.G. 120; [1997] E.G.C.S. 132; [1997] N.P.C. 140, CA . . . .   *Digested*, 98/**3670**:
                      Considered, 98/3671: *Followed*, 98/3669, 98/3672
Cushing (t/a Fakenham Steam Laundry) v. Webber (Valuation Officer) (No.2) see Almond (Valuation Officer) v. Heathfield Laundry (Birmingham) Ltd
Cussons (New Zealand) Pty Ltd v. Unilever Plc; *sub nom* Unilever Plc v. Cussons (New Zealand) Pty Ltd [1998] A.C. 328; [1998] 2 W.L.R. 95; [1998] R.P.C. 369; (1998) 21(2) I.P.D. 21012; (1997) 141 S.J.L.B. 239, PC (NZ) . . . .   *Digested*, 98/**3492**
Custins v. Peacock see Peacock v. Custins
Custom Made Commercial Ltd v. Stawa Metallbau GmbH (C288/92) [1994] E.C.R. I-2913; [1994] I.L.Pr. 516, ECJ [1993] I.L.Pr. 490, BGH (Ger) . . . .   *Digested*, 94/**4800**:
                               Applied, 00/764: *Considered*, 00/739
Customglass Boats Ltd v. Salthouse Bros Ltd [1976] R.P.C. 589, Sup Ct (NZ) . . . .   *Digested*, 76/**2784**:
                                                  Considered, 99/3524
Customs Agents, Re (C35/96) see Commission of the European Communities v. Italy (C35/96)
Customs and Excise Commissioners v. A&D Goddard (A Firm) [2001] S.T.C. 725; [2001] B.T.C. 5206; [2001] B.V.C. 295; [2001] S.T.I. 597; (2001) 98(20) L.S.G. 44; *Times*, March 27, 2001, Ch D . . . .   *Digested*, 01/**5612**
Customs and Excise Commissioners v. Anchor Foods Ltd (No.1) [1999] V. & D.R. 425; *Independent*, July 13, 1998 (C.S.), QBD; affirming [1998] V. & D.R. 32, V&DTr . .   *Digested*, 00/**4960**
Customs and Excise Commissioners v. Anchor Foods Ltd (No.2) [1999] 1 W.L.R. 1139; [1999] 3 All E.R. 268; [2000] C.P. Rep. 19; (1999) 96(12) L.S.G. 34; (1999) 143 S.J.L.B. 96; *Times*, April 1, 1999; *Independent*, March 8, 1999 (C.S.), Ch D .   *Digested*, 99/**489**
Customs and Excise Commissioners v. Anchor Foods Ltd (No.3), *Times*, September 28, 1999, Ch D . . . .   *Digested*, 99/**385**
Customs and Excise Commissioners v. Anchor Foods Ltd (No.4) HC 1999 00651, Ch D [1999] V. & D.R. 1, V&DTr
Customs and Excise Commissioners v. BAA Plc see BAA Plc v. Customs and Excise Commissioners

Customs and Excise Commissioners *v.* Barclays Bank Plc [2001] EWCA Civ 1513; [2001] S.T.C. 1558; [2001] B.T.C. 5531; [2001] B.V.C. 606; [2001] S.T.I. 1359; (2001) 98(44) L.S.G. 36, CA; reversing [2000] S.T.C. 665; [2000] B.T.C. 5320; [2000] B.V.C. 332; [2000] S.T.I. 998; (2000) 97(30) L.S.G. 41; (2000) 144 S.J.L.B. 221; *Times*, August 11, 2000, Ch D . . . . *Digested*, 01/**5615**

Customs and Excise Commissioners *v.* British Airways Plc; *sub nom* British Airways Plc *v.* Customs and Excise Commissioners [1990] S.T.C. 643, CA; affirming [1989] S.T.C. 182; [1989] C.O.D. 247; *Times*, August 8, 1988; *Independent*, August 8, 1988 (C.S.); *Daily Telegraph*, September 8, 1988, QBD; reversing [1987] V.A.T.T.R. 120, VAT Tr . . . . *Digested*, 91/**3671**:
Applied, 92/4561, 92/6530, 94/4575, 94/4608, 94/4611, 99/4993:
Distinguished, 94/4617, 97/4977: *Referred to*, 95/5090, 95/5098

Customs and Excise Commissioners *v.* British Field Sports Society [1998] 1 W.L.R. 962; [1998] 2 All E.R. 1003; [1998] S.T.C. 315; [1998] B.T.C. 5064; [1998] B.V.C. 82; *Times*, February 4, 1998; *Independent*, February 3, 1998, CA; affirming [1997] S.T.C. 746; [1997] B.T.C. 5213; [1997] B.V.C. 295; *Independent*, April 28, 1997 (C.S.), QBD . . . . *Digested*, 98/**4928**

Customs and Excise Commissioners *v.* British Telecommunications Plc (1997) [1999] 1 W.L.R. 1376; [1999] 3 All E.R. 961; [1999] S.T.C. 758; [1999] B.T.C. 5273; [1999] B.V.C. 306; (1999) 96(28) L.S.G. 27; *Times*, July 5, 1999 ; *Independent*, July 8, 1999, HL; reversing [1998] S.T.C. 544; [1998] B.T.C. 5155; [1998] B.V.C. 186; (1998) 95(17) L.S.G. 30; *Times*, March 24, 1998, CA; reversing [1997] S.T.C. 475; [1997] B.T.C. 5111; [1997] B.V.C. 222; *Independent*, March 17, 1997 (C.S.), QBD. . . . . *Digested*, 99/**4993**:
Distinguished, 98/835

Customs and Excise Commissioners *v.* British United Provident Association Ltd see Customs and Excise Commissioners *v.* Wellington Private Hospital Ltd

Customs and Excise Commissioners *v.* Broomco (1984) Ltd (formerly Anchor Foods Ltd) [2000] B.T.C. 8035; *Times*, August 17, 2000; *Independent*, October 19, 2000, CA; affirming 8219 of 1999, Ch D . . . . *Digested*, 00/**4956**

Customs and Excise Commissioners *v.* BRS Automotive Ltd [1998] S.T.C. 1210; [1998] B.T.C. 5459; [1998] B.V.C. 477; *Independent*, November 19, 1998, CA; reversing [1997] S.T.C. 336; [1997] B.T.C. 5072; [1997] B.V.C. 183, QBD . . . . . . *Digested*, 98/**4934**

Customs and Excise Commissioners *v.* Brunt (1999) 163 J.P. 161; *Times*, November 25, 1998; *Independent*, November 23, 1998 (C.S.), QBD. . . . . *Digested*, 98/**1026**

Customs and Excise Commissioners *v.* Bugeja (No.2) see Littlewoods Organisation Plc *v.* Customs and Excise Commissioners

Customs and Excise Commissioners *v.* Cantor Fitzgerald International (C108/99) see Customs and Excise Commissioners *v.* Mirror Group Plc (C409/98)

Customs and Excise Commissioners *v.* Cantor Fitzgerald International (C108/99); *sub nom* Cantor Fitzgerald International *v.* Customs and Excise Commissioners [2001] 3 C.M.L.R. 56; [2001] B.T.C. 5540; [2001] 46 E.G.C.S. 177; [2001] N.P.C. 144, ECJ (6th Chamber) [1998] S.T.C. 948; [1998] B.T.C. 5383; [1998] B.V.C. 384, QBD; reversing [1997] V. & D.R. 233, V&DTr . . . . *Digested*, 98/**4920**:
Joined proceedings, 01/5602

Customs and Excise Commissioners *v.* Century Life Plc; *sub nom* Century Life Plc *v.* Customs and Excise Commissioners [2001] S.T.C. 38; [2001] B.T.C. 5043; [2001] B.V.C. 116; [2001] S.T.I. 10, CA; affirming [2000] S.T.C. 276; [2000] B.T.C. 5112; [2000] B.V.C. 142; [2000] S.T.I. 249, QBD; reversing [1999] B.V.C. 2129, V&DTr . . . . *Digested*, 00/**5294**

Customs and Excise Commissioners *v.* Chinese Channel (HK) Ltd [1998] S.T.C. 347; [1998] B.T.C. 5073; [1998] B.V.C. 91, QBD . . . . *Digested*, 98/**4963**

Customs and Excise Commissioners *v.* Chitolie [2000] B.P.I.R. 275, CA . . . . *Digested*, 00/**418**

Customs and Excise Commissioners *v.* Church Schools Foundation Ltd see Church Schools Foundation Ltd *v.* Customs and Excise Commissioners

Customs and Excise Commissioners *v.* City of London Magistrates Court; *sub nom* R. *v.* Customs and Excise Commissioners Ex p. City of London Magistrates Court [2000] 1 W.L.R. 2020; [2000] 4 All E.R. 763; [2000] S.T.C. 447; [2000] 2 Cr. App. R. 348; [2000] B.T.C. 5194; [2000] B.V.C. 224; [2000] Crim. L.R. 841; [2000] S.T.I. 782; *Independent*, June 26, 2000 (C.S.), QBD. . . . . *Digested*, 00/**5288**

Customs and Excise Commissioners *v.* Civil Service Motoring Association Ltd [1998] S.T.C. 111; [1998] B.T.C. 5003; [1998] B.V.C. 21; *Times*, December 10, 1997, CA; affirming [1997] S.T.C. 344; [1997] B.T.C. 5092; [1997] B.V.C. 203, QBD; affirming [1996] V. & D.R. 340, VAT Tr (London) . . . . *Digested*, 98/**4899**:
Applied, 00/5304

Customs and Excise Commissioners *v.* Colour Offset Ltd [1995] S.T.C. 85; [1995] C.O.D. 229; *Independent*, February 13, 1995 (C.S.), QBD. . . . . *Digested*, 95/**5116**:
Considered, 98/4975

Customs and Excise Commissioners *v.* Cresta Holidays Ltd [2001] EWCA Civ 215; [2001] S.T.C. 386; [2001] S.T.I. 241, CA; reversing in part [2001] S.T.I. 152; (2001) 98(14) L.S.G. 40, Ch D . . . . *Digested*, 01/**5289**

Customs and Excise Commissioners *v.* CSC Financial Services Ltd (C235/00); *sub nom* CSC Financial Services Ltd *v.* Customs and Excise Commissioners (C235/00) [2001] S.T.I. 1775, ECJ (5th Chamber)

Customs and Excise Commissioners v. CSC Financial Services Ltd (formerly Continuum (Europe) Ltd) [2000] S.T.I. 1267, QBD

Customs and Excise Commissioners v. Darfish Ltd [2001] Env. L.R. 3; (2000) 97(15) L.S.G. 40; (2000) 144 S.J.L.B. 165; *Times*, March 28, 2000, QBD . . . .   *Digested*, 00/**5042**

Customs and Excise Commissioners v. DFDS A/S (C260/95) [1997] 1 W.L.R. 1037; [1997] All E.R. (E.C.) 342; [1997] S.T.C. 384; [1997] E.C.R. I-1005; [1997] B.T.C. 5167; [1997] B.V.C. 279; (1997) 94(27) L.S.G. 24; *Times*, February 24, 1997, ECJ (5th Chamber) . . . .   *Digested*, 97/**5021**: *Considered*, 98/4963

Customs and Excise Commissioners v. Direct Bargain Supplies Ltd see Customs and Excise Commissioners v. Invicta Poultry Ltd

Customs and Excise Commissioners v. Dougall; *sub nom* Debtor (No.5795 of 1998), Re; Dougall v. Customs and Excise Commissioners [2001] B.P.I.R. 269, Ch D . .   *Digested*, 01/**3725**

Customs and Excise Commissioners v. E Reece Ltd, *Times*, October 11, 2000, Ch D   . . .   *Digested*, 00/**4958**

Customs and Excise Commissioners v. Eastwood Care Homes (Ilkeston) Ltd see Eastwood Care Homes (Ilkeston) Ltd v. Customs and Excise Commissioners

Customs and Excise Commissioners v. Eastwood Care Homes (Ilkeston) Ltd [2001] C.P. Rep. 18; (2000) 97(7) L.S.G. 41; (2000) 144 S.J.L.B. 85; *Times*, March 7, 2000, QBD . . . .   *Digested*, 00/**5279**

Customs and Excise Commissioners v. Evans (t/a Grape Escape Wine Bar) [1982] S.T.C. 342, DC. . . . .   *Digested*, 82/**3338**: *Followed*, 98/4887

Customs and Excise Commissioners v. Eye-Tech Opticians see Customs and Excise Commissioners v. Leightons Ltd

Customs and Excise Commissioners v. FDR Ltd; *sub nom* FDR Ltd v. Customs and Excise Commissioners [2000] S.T.C. 672; [2000] B.T.C. 5277; [2000] B.V.C. 311; [2000] S.T.I. 999; *Independent*, October 9, 2000 (C.S), CA; affirming [1999] B.V.C. 2248; [1999] V. & D.R. 67, V&DTr . . . .   *Digested*, 00/**5289**

Customs and Excise Commissioners v. First Choice Holidays Plc [2000] S.T.C. 609; [2000] B.T.C. 5267; [2000] B.V.C. 301; [2000] S.T.I. 950; (2000) 97(29) L.S.G. 46; *Times*, July 25, 2000, Ch D; affirming [2000] B.V.C. 2175; [2000] S.T.I. 317, V&DTr . . . .   *Digested*, 00/**5316**

Customs and Excise Commissioners v. First National Bank of Chicago (C172/96) see First National Bank of Chicago v. Customs and Excise Commissioners (C172/96)

Customs and Excise Commissioners v. G see R. v. G (Conspiracy to Cheat)

Customs and Excise Commissioners v. General Instrument (UK) Ltd; *sub nom* General Instrument (UK) Ltd v. Customs and Excise Commissioners [2000] 1 C.M.L.R. 34; [1999] V. & D.R. 443, QBD . . . .   *Digested*, 00/**4950**

Customs and Excise Commissioners v. Gil Insurance Ltd; Customs and Excise Commissioners v. UK Consumer Electronics Ltd [2000] S.T.C. 204; [2000] B.T.C. 8009; [2000] S.T.I. 190, QBD . . . .   *Digested*, 00/**5039**

Customs and Excise Commissioners v. Glassborow (t/a Bertram & Co) [1975] Q.B. 465; [1974] 2 W.L.R. 851; [1974] 1 All E.R. 1041; [1974] S.T.C. 142; [1974] T.R. 161; 118 S.J. 170, QBD . . . .   *Digested*, 74/**3916**: *Applied*, 75/3494: *Considered*, 98/4939: *Followed*, 82/418

Customs and Excise Commissioners v. Granton Marketing Ltd; Customs and Excise Commissioners v. Wentwalk [1996] S.T.C. 1049, CA; affirming [1995] S.T.C. 510; *Times*, May 12, 1995; *Independent*, May 30, 1995 (C.S.), QBD . . . .   *Digested*, 95/**5092**: *Applied*, 01/5598: *Followed*, 00/5290

Customs and Excise Commissioners v. Grattan Plc see Customs and Excise Commissioners v. Next Plc

Customs and Excise Commissioners v. Guy Butler (International) Ltd (No.1); *sub nom* Guy Butler (International) Ltd v. Customs and Excise Commissioners (No.1) [1977] Q.B. 377; [1976] 3 W.L.R. 370; [1976] 2 All E.R. 700; [1976] S.T.C. 254; 120 S.J. 489, CA; affirming [1976] Q.B. 106; [1975] 2 W.L.R. 36; [1975] 2 All E.R. 245; [1975] S.T.C. 299; [1975] T.R. 239; 119 S.J. 424, QBD; reversing in part [1974] V.A.T.T.R. 19, VAT Tr . . . .   *Digested*, 76/**2833**: *Cited*, 00/5298

Customs and Excise Commissioners v. H&T Walker see Customs and Excise Commissioners v. Mitsui & Co UK Plc

Customs and Excise Commissioners v. Harris (1999) 163 J.P. 408; [1999] C.O.D. 300; *Times*, February 24, 1999; *Independent*, February 15, 1999 (C.S.), QBD . . . .   *Digested*, 99/**1010**

Customs and Excise Commissioners v. Help the Aged [1997] S.T.C. 406; [1998] R.T.R. 120; (1997) 37 B.M.L.R. 157; [1997] B.T.C. 5098; [1997] B.V.C. 209; (1997) 94(11) L.S.G. 36; (1997) 141 S.J.L.B. 73; *Times*, March 4, 1997; *Independent*, April 21, 1997 (C.S.), QBD; affirming [1996] V. & D.R. 258, VAT Tr (London)   . . .   *Digested*, 97/**5052**

Customs and Excise Commissioners v. Hodges [2000] S.T.C. 262; [2000] B.T.C. 5096; [2000] B.V.C. 126; [2000] S.T.I. 232, QBD

Customs and Excise Commissioners v. Hubbard Foundation Scotland [1981] S.T.C. 593; 1981 S.C. 244; 1982 S.L.T. 277, 1 Div . . . .   *Digested*, 82/**4440**: *Followed*, 98/4878

Customs and Excise Commissioners v. Invicta Poultry Ltd; *sub nom* Invicta Poultry Ltd
v. Customs and Excise Commissioners; Customs and Excise Commissioners v.
Direct Bargain Supplies Ltd; Fareway Trading Co Ltd v. Customs and Excise
Commissioners [1998] 3 C.M.L.R. 70; [1998] V. & D.R. 128 (Note); *Times*, June
1, 1998; *Independent*, June 8, 1998 (C.S.), CA; affirming [1997] V. & D.R. 56;
(1997) 94(28) L.S.G. 26; (1997) 141 S.J.L.B. 171; *Times*, July 29, 1997, QBD;
reversing [1996] V. & D.R. 291, VAT Tr (London) . . . .   *Digested*, 98/**4637**:
Applied, 00/4952

Customs and Excise Commissioners v. Jamieson see Jamieson v. Customs and Excise
Commissioners
Customs and Excise Commissioners v. JDL Ltd see JDL Ltd v. Customs and Excise
Commissioners
Customs and Excise Commissioners v. JH Corbitt (Numismatists) Ltd [1981] A.C. 22;
[1980] 2 W.L.R. 653; [1980] 2 All E.R. 72; [1980] S.T.C. 231; [1980] T.R. 165;
124 S.J. 292, HL; reversing [1979] 3 W.L.R. 300; [1979] S.T.C. 504; [1979] T.R.
295; 123 S.J. 306, CA; reversing [1979] 3 W.L.R. 291; [1978] S.T.C. 531;
[1978] T.R. 205; 122 S.J. 827, DC; reversing [1977] V.A.T.T.R. 194, VAT Tr
(Manchester) . . . .   *Digested*, 80/**2780**:
Applied, 89/3764, 94/650: *Considered*, 95/5012, 96/5842, 98/4954:
Referred to, 95/5011

Customs and Excise Commissioners v. Kilroy Television Co Ltd; *sub nom* R. v. Customs
and Excise Commissioners Ex p. Kilroy Television Co Ltd [1997] S.T.C. 901;
[1997] B.T.C. 5308; [1998] C.O.D. 78; *Times*, June 30, 1997; *Independent*, June
9, 1997 (C.S.), QBD . . . .   *Digested*, 97/**5004**
Customs and Excise Commissioners v. Kingscrest Associates Ltd see Kingscrest
Associates Ltd v. Customs and Excise Commissioners
Customs and Excise Commissioners v. Le Rififi Ltd [1995] S.T.C. 103; (1995) 92(7)
L.S.G. 39; (1995) 139 S.J.L.B. 56; *Times*, December 14, 1994; *Independent*,
February 13, 1995 (C.S.), CA . . . .   *Digested*, 95/**5027**:
Applied, 01/5547: *Considered*, 96/5843: *Followed*, 95/5023, 95/5026,
96/5845, 96/5846: *Referred to*, 95/5077

Customs and Excise Commissioners v. Leicester University Student Union see Customs
and Excise Commissioners v. Leicester University Students Union
Customs and Excise Commissioners v. Leicester University Students Union; *sub nom*
Customs and Excise Commissioners v. University of Leicester Students Union;
Customs and Excise Commissioners v. Leicester University Student Union
[2001] EWCA Civ 1972, CA; affirming [2001] S.T.C. 550; [2001] B.T.C. 5187;
[2001] B.V.C. 252; [2001] S.T.I. 599, Ch D; reversing [2001] B.V.C. 2102; [2001]
S.T.I. 53, V&D Tr . . . .   *Digested*, 01/**5562**
Customs and Excise Commissioners v. Leightons Ltd; *sub nom* Leightons Ltd v.
Customs and Excise Commissioners; Customs and Excise Commissioners v.
Eye-Tech Opticians [1995] S.T.C. 458; *Times*, April 13, 1995; *Independent*, May
30, 1995 (C.S.), QBD; affirming [1994] 2 C.M.L.R. 308; [1993] V.A.T.T.R. 1, VAT
Tr (London). . . . .   *Digested*, 95/**5093**:
Applied, 00/5346: *Considered*, 98/4961, 99/5007

Customs and Excise Commissioners v. Littlewoods Organisation Plc see Littlewoods
Organisation Plc v. Customs and Excise Commissioners
Customs and Excise Commissioners v. Liverpool Institute for Performing Arts; *sub nom*
Customs and Excise Commissioners v. Liverpool School of Performing Arts
[2001] UKHL 28; [2001] 1 W.L.R. 1187; [2001] S.T.C. 891; [2001] 3 C.M.L.R. 5;
[2001] B.T.C. 5258; [2001] B.V.C. 333; [2001] S.T.I. 848; (2001) 98(26)
L.S.G. 45; (2001) 145 S.J.L.B. 150; *Times*, June 1, 2001; *Independent*, June 14,
2001, HL; affirming [1999] S.T.C. 424; [1999] B.T.C. 5187; [1999] B.V.C. 199;
Times, April 1, 1999, CA; reversing [1998] S.T.C. 274; [1998] B.T.C. 5022;
[1998] B.V.C. 40; *Times*, February 10, 1998, QBD . . . .   *Digested*, 01/**5582**
Customs and Excise Commissioners v. Liverpool School of Performing Arts see
Customs and Excise Commissioners v. Liverpool Institute for Performing Arts
Customs and Excise Commissioners v. Lloyds TSB Group Ltd [1998] S.T.C. 528; [1998]
B.T.C. 5160; [1998] B.V.C. 173, QBD . . . .   *Digested*, 98/**4904**
Customs and Excise Commissioners v. Madgett (t/a Howden Court Hotel) (No.1)
(C308/96) see Madgett (t/a Howden Court Hotel) v. Customs and Excise
Commissioners (No.1) (C308/96)
Customs and Excise Commissioners v. McConnachie 1999 S.C.L.R. 762; [1999] V. &
D.R. 59; 1999 G.W.D. 13-616, 2 Div . . . .   *Digested*, 99/**6457**
Customs and Excise Commissioners v. McMaster Stores (Scotland) Ltd (In
Receivership) [1995] S.T.C. 846; 1996 S.L.T. 935, 1 Div. . . . .   *Digested*, 96/**7394**:
Distinguished, 00/5354

Customs and Excise Commissioners v. Midland Bank Plc (C98/98) see Midland Bank
Plc v. Customs and Excise Commissioners (C98/98)

Customs and Excise Commissioners v. Mirror Group Plc (C409/98); *sub nom* Mirror Group Plc v. Customs and Excise Commissioners (C409/98); Cantor Fitzgerald International v. Customs and Excise Commissioners (C108/99); Customs and Excise Commissioners v. Cantor Fitzgerald International (C108/99) [2001] S.T.C. 1453; [2001] 3 C.M.L.R. 55; [2001] B.T.C. 5547; [2001] S.T.I. 1344; [2001] N.P.C. 143; *Times*, November 7, 2001, ECJ (6th Chamber)AGO . . . .   *Digested*, 01/**5602**

Customs and Excise Commissioners v. Mitsui & Co UK Plc; Customs and Excise Commissioners v. H&T Walker [2000] 1 C.M.L.R. 85, QBD. . . . .   *Digested*, 00/**4955**

Customs and Excise Commissioners v. Morrish [1998] S.T.C. 954; [1998] 3 E.G.L.R. 117; [1998] 44 E.G. 214; [1998] B.T.C. 5388; [1998] B.V.C. 378; [1998] E.G.C.S. 111; [1998] N.P.C. 114; *Independent*, July 13, 1998 (C.S.), QBD. . . . .   *Digested*, 98/**4979**

Customs and Excise Commissioners v. Morrison's Academy Boarding Houses Association [1978] S.T.C. 1; 1977 S.C. 279; 1977 S.L.T. 197, 1 Div . . . .   *Digested*, 77/**3812**:
Applied, 79/2743, 95/5121: *Considered*, 01/5579: *Distinguished*, 98/6219

Customs and Excise Commissioners v. News International Newspapers Ltd; *sub nom* News International Newspapers Ltd v. Customs and Excise Commissioners [1998] V. & D.R. 267; (1998) 142 S.J.L.B. 130; *Times*, April 9, 1998; *Independent*, April 2, 1998, CA; affirming [1996] V. & D.R. 434; *Times*, October 9, 1996; *Independent*, October 21, 1996 (C.S.), QBD . . . .   *Digested*, 98/**4650**

Customs and Excise Commissioners v. Next Plc; *sub nom* Customs and Excise Commissioners v. Grattan Plc [1995] S.T.C. 651; *Independent*, March 6, 1995 (C.S.), QBD. . . . .   *Digested*, 95/**5083**:
Considered, 97/4982: *Followed*, 98/4949, 00/5314

Customs and Excise Commissioners v. Peachtree Enterprises Ltd [1994] S.T.C. 747, QBD. . . . .   *Digested*, 94/**4593**:
Applied, 00/5335

Customs and Excise Commissioners v. Pilgrims Language Courses Ltd see Pilgrims Language Courses Ltd v. Customs and Excise Commissioners

Customs and Excise Commissioners v. Ping (Europe) Ltd; *sub nom* Ping (Europe) Ltd v. Customs and Excise Commissioners [2001] S.T.C. 1144; [2001] B.T.C. 5320; [2001] B.V.C. 395; [2001] S.T.I. 992, Ch D; affirming [2000] V. & D.R. 405; [2001] S.T.I. 743, V&DTr . . . .   *Digested*, 01/**5597**

Customs and Excise Commissioners v. Plantiflor Ltd; *sub nom* Plantiflor Ltd v. Customs and Excise Commissioners [2000] S.T.C. 137; [2000] B.T.C. 5050; [2000] B.V.C. 103; [2000] S.T.I. 128; *Times*, February 10, 2000, CA; reversing [1999] S.T.C. 51; [1999] B.T.C. 5038; [1999] B.V.C. 37; *Times*, November 25, 1998; *Independent*, November 23, 1998 (C.S.), QBD; reversing [1997] B.V.C. 2380; [1997] V. & D.R. 301; [1997] S.T.I. 998, V&DTr . . . .   *Digested*, 00/**5286**:
Approved, 98/4916

Customs and Excise Commissioners v. Primback Ltd; *sub nom* Primback Ltd v. Customs and Excise Commissioners [1996] S.T.C. 757; [1996] 3 C.M.L.R. 589; [1996] C.C.L.R. 81; (1996) 140 S.J.L.B. 123; *Times*, April 30, 1996, CA; reversing [1994] S.T.C. 957; *Independent*, September 12, 1994 (C.S.), QBD . . . .   *Digested*, 96/**5891**:
Subsequent proceedings, 01/5555

Customs and Excise Commissioners v. Primback Ltd (C34/99); *sub nom* Primback Ltd v. Customs and Excise Commissioners (C34/99) [2001] 1 W.L.R. 1693; [2001] All E.R. (EC) 714; [2001] S.T.C. 803; [2001] E.C.R. I-3833; [2001] 2 C.M.L.R. 42; [2001] C.E.C. 132; [2001] B.T.C. 5240; [2001] B.V.C. 315; [2001] S.T.I. 835; *Times*, June 8, 2001, ECJ. . . . .   *Digested*, 01/**5555**:
Previous proceedings, 96/5891

Customs and Excise Commissioners v. Rannoch School Ltd 1994 S.L.T. 170; [1993] B.V.C. 118, 2 Div. . . . .   *Digested*, 93/**5952**:
Considered, 98/4978

Customs and Excise Commissioners v. Ray [2000] 3 C.M.L.R. 1095; (2000) 97(25) L.S.G. 38; *Times*, June 14, 2000, Ch D . . . .   *Digested*, 00/**2402**

Customs and Excise Commissioners v. Redrow Group Plc [1999] 1 W.L.R. 408; [1999] 2 All E.R. 1; [1999] S.T.C. 161; [1999] B.T.C. 5062; [1999] B.V.C. 96; [1999] E.G.C.S. 20; (1999) 96(9) L.S.G. 32; (1999) 143 S.J.L.B. 58; [1999] N.P.C. 18; *Times*, February 18, 1999; *Independent*, February 18, 1999, HL; reversing [1997] S.T.C. 1053; [1997] B.T.C. 5347; [1997] B.V.C. 461; [1997] E.G.C.S. 92; *Times*, July 3, 1997; *Independent*, July 14, 1997 (C.S.), CA; reversing [1996] S.T.C. 365; [1995] E.G.C.S. 202, QBD; affirming [1995] V. & D.R. 115, VAT Tr (Manchester) . . . .   *Digested*, 99/**4994**

Customs and Excise Commissioners v. Rosner [1994] S.T.C. 228; [1994] B.V.C. 31; *Times*, January 10, 1994; *Independent*, January 10, 1994, QBD. . . . .   *Digested*, 94/**4584**:
Applied, 98/4927: *Considered*, 98/4933

Customs and Excise Commissioners v. Schindler (C275/92) [1994] Q.B. 610; [1994] 3 W.L.R. 103; [1994] 2 All E.R. 193; [1994] E.C.R. I-1039; [1995] 1 C.M.L.R. 4; *Times*, March 30, 1994; *Financial Times*, March 29, 1994, ECJ . . . .   *Digested*, 94/**4907**:
Followed, 99/588, 99/2250, 00/2384, 00/2397

Customs and Excise Commissioners v. School of Finance and Management (London) Ltd see School of Finance and Management (London) Ltd v. Customs and Excise Commissioners

Customs and Excise Commissioners *v.* Scott [1978] S.T.C. 191, DC . . . .   *Digested,* 78/**3044**:
Applied, 79/2762, 79/2763, 00/5346: *Distinguished,* 93/4092

Customs and Excise Commissioners *v.* Shah (1999) 163 J.P. 759; (2000) 164 J.P.N. 66; (2000) 164 J.P.N. 224, QBD . . . .   *Digested,* 00/**1054**

Customs and Excise Commissioners *v.* Shaklee International; *sub nom* Shaklee International *v.* Customs and Excise Commissioners [1981] S.T.C. 776; [1981] T.R. 411; 124 S.J. 34; *Times,* October 28, 1981, CA; affirming [1980] S.T.C. 708; [1980] Com. L.R. 6; [1980] T.R. 317, QBD; reversing [1978] V.A.T.T.R. 267, VAT Tr (London). . . . .   *Digested,* 81/**2842**:
Applied, 94/4580: *Considered,* 98/4914, 98/4915

Customs and Excise Commissioners *v.* Simply Travel Ltd see Simply Travel Ltd *v.* Customs and Excise Commissioners

Customs and Excise Commissioners *v.* Sinclair Collis Ltd see Sinclair Collis Ltd *v.* Customs and Excise Commissioners

Customs and Excise Commissioners *v.* St Dunstan's Educational Foundation see Jubilee Hall Recreation Centre Ltd *v.* Customs and Excise Commissioners

Customs and Excise Commissioners *v.* St Martins Hospital see Customs and Excise Commissioners *v.* Wellington Private Hospital Ltd

Customs and Excise Commissioners *v.* Svenska International Plc see Svenska International Plc *v.* Customs and Excise Commissioners

Customs and Excise Commissioners *v.* T (1998) 162 J.P. 193, QBD. . . . .   *Digested,* 97/**1107**

Customs and Excise Commissioners *v.* Thorn Materials Supply Ltd; *sub nom* Thorn Materials Supply Ltd *v.* Customs and Excise Commissioners [1998] 1 W.L.R. 1106; [1998] 3 All E.R. 342; [1998] S.T.C. 725; [1998] B.T.C. 5252; [1998] B.V.C. 270; (1998) 95(28) L.S.G. 31; (1998) 142 S.J.L.B. 194; *Times,* June 25, 1998; *Independent,* June 23, 1998, HL; affirming [1996] S.T.C. 1490; [1997] B.V.C. 55, CA. . . . . .   *Digested,* 98/**4950**:
Followed, 00/5310

Customs and Excise Commissioners *v.* Top High Developments Ltd [1998] F.S.R. 464, MC. . . . . . .   *Digested,* 98/**3504**

Customs and Excise Commissioners *v.* Town & County Factors Ltd see Town & County Factors Ltd *v.* Customs and Excise Commissioners

Customs and Excise Commissioners *v.* UK Consumer Electronics Ltd see Customs and Excise Commissioners *v.* Gil Insurance Ltd

Customs and Excise Commissioners *v.* University of Leicester Students Union see Customs and Excise Commissioners *v.* Leicester University Students Union

Customs and Excise Commissioners *v.* Upton (t/a Fagomatic) CHRVF/2001/1104/A3, CA; affirming [2001] S.T.C. 912; [2001] S.T.I. 756, Ch D; reversing [2001] B.V.C. 2099; [2000] S.T.I. 1771, V&DTr . . . .   *Digested,* 01/**5575**

Customs and Excise Commissioners *v.* Wellington Private Hospital Ltd; Customs and Excise Commissioners *v.* British United Provident Association Ltd; Customs and Excise Commissioners *v.* St Martins Hospital [1997] S.T.C. 445; [1997] B.T.C. 5140; [1997] B.V.C. 251; *Times,* February 11, 1997, CA; reversing [1995] S.T.C. 628; *Independent,* May 30, 1995 (C.S.), QBD . . . .   *Digested,* 97/**5057**:
Applied, 01/5604: *Followed,* 99/4978

Customs and Excise Commissioners *v.* Wentwalk see Customs and Excise Commissioners *v.* Granton Marketing Ltd

Customs and Excise Commissioners *v.* West Herts College; *sub nom* West Herts College *v.* Customs and Excise Commissioners [2001] S.T.C. 1245; [2001] S.T.I. 1057, Ch D; affirming [2001] B.V.C. 2068; [2000] S.T.I. 1555, V&DTr . . . .   *Digested,* 01/**5576**

Customs and Excise Commissioners *v.* Westmorland Motorway Services Ltd [1998] S.T.C. 431; [1998] R.T.R. 440; [1998] B.T.C. 5136; [1998] B.V.C. 154; *Times,* February 5, 1998, CA; affirming [1997] S.T.C. 400; [1997] B.T.C. 5087; [1997] B.V.C. 198; (1997) 94(9) L.S.G. 32; (1997) 141 S.J.L.B. 72; *Times,* March 4, 1997, Ch D; reversing [1996] V. & D.R. 185, VAT Tr (Manchester) . . . .   *Digested,* 98/**4936**:
Considered, 01/5556

Customs and Excise Commissioners *v.* Wiggett Construction Ltd see Wiggett Construction Ltd *v.* Customs and Excise Commissioners

Customs and Excise Commissioners *v.* Yarburgh Children's Trust see Yarburgh Childrens Trust *v.* Customs and Excise Commissioners

Customs and Excise Commissioners *v.* Young [1993] S.T.C. 394; 1993 S.C. 339, 1 Div . .   *Digested,* 96/**7393**:
Applied, 94/4559, 01/5612

Customs and Excise Commissioners *v.* Zielinski Baker & Partners Ltd; *sub nom* Zielinski Baker & Partners Ltd *v.* Customs and Excise Commissioners; A3/2001/1003, CA; reversing [2001] S.T.C. 585; [2001] B.T.C. 5168; [2001] 13 E.G.C.S. 148; *Independent,* May 7, 2001 (C.S), Ch D; reversing [2001] B.V.C. 2059; [2000] S.T.I. 1502, V&DTr . . . .   *Digested,* 01/**5559**

Customs and Excise Commissioners *v.* Zoological Society of London; *sub nom* Zoological Society of London *v.* Customs and Excise Commissioners [1999] B.T.C. 5284; [1999] B.V.C. 317, QBD [1998] B.V.C. 2328, V&DTr . . . .   *Digested,* 99/**5000**

Cutler *v.* Egerton [2000] P.I.Q.R. Q84, CC (Portsmouth) . . . .   *Digested,* 00/**1472**

Cutter *v.* Eagle Star Insurance Co Ltd see Clarke *v.* Kato

Cutter v. Eagle Star Insurance Co Ltd [1997] 1 W.L.R. 1082; [1997] 2 All E.R. 311;
　　[1998] R.T.R. 309; *Times*, December 3, 1996; *Independent*, December 3, 1996,
　　CA . . . . *Digested*, 97/**3164**:
　　　　　　　　　　　　　　　　　　　　　　　Subsequent proceedings, 98/3395
Cutts v. Head [1984] Ch. 290; [1984] 2 W.L.R. 349; [1984] 1 All E.R. 597; (1984) 81
　　L.S.G. 509; (1984) 128 S.J. 117; *Times*, December 14, 1983, CA . . . . *Digested*, 84/**2608**:
　　　　　　　　　　　Applied, 86/1517, 92/3449, 99/349: *Considered*, 85/2702, 88/2956,
　　　　　　　　　　　　　　　　89/1701, 96/697, 96/1276: *Followed*, 94/3561, 00/319
CW Young (Builders Merchants) Ltd v. Secretary of State for the Environment, Transport
　　and the Regions see R. (on the application of CW Young Ltd) v. Secretary of
　　State for the Environment, Transport and the Regions
Cygnet Healthcare Plc v. Higgins City Ltd (2000) 16 Const. L.J. 394, QBD (T&CC)
Cyprus v. Turkey (25781/94) 11 B.H.R.C. 45, ECHR
Cyril Leonard & Co v. Simo Securities Trust Ltd [1972] 1 W.L.R. 80; [1971] 3 All E.R.
　　1318; (1971) 115 S.J. 911, CA; reversing [1971] 3 All E.R. 1313; 115 S.J. 811, Ch D
　　. . . . . *Digested*, 72/**2781**:
　　　　　　　　　　　　　　　　　　　　　　　　　Considered, 00/313
Czarnikow-Rionda Sugar Trading Inc v. Standard Bank London Ltd [1999] 1 All E.R.
　　(Comm) 890; [1999] 2 Lloyd's Rep. 187; [1999] Lloyd's Rep. Bank. 197; [1999]
　　C.L.C. 1148; *Independent*, June 14, 1999 (C.S.), QBD (Comm Ct) . . . . *Digested*, 99/**287**

D (A Child) (Care or Supervision Order), Re [2000] Fam. Law 600, Fam Div
D (A Child) (Evidence: Facilitated Communication), Re; *sub nom* D (A Child) (Wardship:
　　Evidence of Abuse), Re [2001] 1 F.L.R. 148; [2001] 1 F.C.R. 707; [2001] Fam.
　　Law 11; *Times*, July 26, 2000; *Independent*, October 9, 2000 (C.S), Fam Div . . . *Digested*, 00/**2558**
D (A Child) (Grant of Care Order: Refusal of Freeing Order), Re; *sub nom* Kent CC v. R;
　　Kent CC v. D [2001] 1 F.L.R. 862; [2001] 1 F.C.R. 501, CA . . . . *Digested*, 01/**2533**
D (A Child) (IVF Treatment), Re; *sub nom* D (A Child) (Parental Responsibility: IVF
　　Baby), Re [2001] EWCA Civ 230; [2001] 1 F.L.R. 972; [2001] 1 F.C.R. 481;
　　[2001] Fam. Law 504, CA. . . . . *Digested*, 01/**2591**
D (A Child) (Parental Responsibility: IVF Baby), Re see D (A Child) (IVF Treatment), Re
D (A Child) (Residence: Ability to Parent), Re [2001] EWCA Civ 742; [2001] 2 F.C.R. 751,
　　CA . . . . *Digested*, 01/**2670**
D (A Child) (Residence: Natural Parent), Re [1999] 2 F.L.R. 1023; [2000] 1 F.C.R. 97;
　　[1999] Fam. Law 755; *Times*, June 17, 1999, Fam Div . . . . *Digested*, 99/**2393**
D (A Child) (Threshold Criteria: Issue Estoppel), Re [2001] 1 F.L.R. 274; [2001] 1 F.C.R. 124;
　　[2000] Fam. Law 875; (2001) 165 J.P.N. 565; *Times*, October 13, 2000, CA . . . *Digested*, 00/**2468**
D (A Child) (Wardship: Evidence of Abuse), Re see D (A Child) (Evidence: Facilitated
　　Communication), Re
D (A Child) v. J Sainsbury Plc (Unreported, March 24, 2000), CC (Brighton) [*Ex rel.*
　　Donne Mileham & Haddock Solicitors, 100 Queens Road, Brighton, East
　　Sussex] . . . . *Digested*, 00/**1748**
D (A Child) v. Lynch (Unreported, April 19, 2001), CC (York) [*Ex rel.* Sam Healy,
　　Barrister, York Chambers, 14 Toft Green, York] . . . . *Digested*, 01/**1757**
D (A Child) v. Penning (Unreported, August 3, 2000), CC (Bury) [*Ex rel.* Fayaz
　　Hammond, Barrister, St James' Chambers, 68 Quay Street, Manchester] . . . . . . *Digested*, 01/**1785**
D (A Child) v. Sefton MBC (Unreported, January 20, 2000), CC (Liverpool) [*Ex rel.*
　　Tracey Bloom, Barrister, Doughty Street Chambers, 11 Doughty Street, London]. *Digested*, 00/**1747**
D (A Child) v. Walker; *sub nom* Walker v. D (A Child) [2000] 1 W.L.R. 1382; [2000]
　　C.P.L.R. 462; [2001] H.R.L.R. 1; [2000] U.K.H.R.R. 648; [2000] P.I.Q.R. P193;
　　(2000) 97(22) L.S.G. 44; *Times*, May 17, 2000; *Independent*, June 12, 2000
　　(C.S), CA . . . . *Digested*, 00/**321**:
　　　　　　　　　　　　　　　　Considered, 01/402: *Followed*, 01/690
D (A Child) v. Wells [2001] 5 Q.R. 12, CC (Nottingham) [*Ex rel.* Stephen Garner,
　　Barrister, 8 Fountain Court, Steelhouse Lane, Birmingham] . . . . *Digested*, 01/**1753**
D (A Minor) (Contact: Interim Order), Re; *sub nom* D v. R (Interim Contact Order)
　　[1995] 1 F.L.R. 495; [1995] 1 F.C.R. 501; [1995] Fam. Law 239; (1995) 159
　　J.P.N. 268; *Times*, February 1, 1995, Fam Div. . . . . *Digested*, 95/**3480**:
　　　　　　　　　　　　　　　　　　　　　　　　　Applied, 00/2499
D (A Minor) (Reporting Restrictions), Re see R. v. Manchester Crown Court Ex p. H (A
　　Juvenile)
D (A Minor) (Residence: Natural Parent), Re see D (Care: Natural Parent Presumption), Re
D (A Minor) v. Martin (Unreported, July 19, 1999), CC (Swindon) [*Ex rel.* David
　　McHugh, Barrister, Bracton Chambers, 95A Chancery Lane, London] . . . . *Digested*, 99/**1515**
D (A Minor) v. White (Unreported, April 27, 1999), CC (Sunderland) [*Ex rel.* Ben Hoare
　　Bell Solicitors, 47 John Street, Sunderland] . . . . *Digested*, 99/**1526**
D (Abduction: Acquiescence: Father's Removal from United States to England), Re [1999]
　　1 F.L.R. 36; [1998] Fam. Law 722, Fam Div . . . . *Digested*, 99/**2313**
D (Abduction: Acquiescence: Mother's Removal from Australia to Wales), Re [1998] 2
　　F.L.R. 335; [1999] 3 F.C.R. 468; [1999] 2 F.C.R. 84; [1998] Fam. Law 512, CA;
　　affirming [1998] 1 F.L.R. 686; [1998] Fam. Law 309, Fam Div . . . . *Digested*, 98/**2373**:
　　　　　　　　　　　　　　　　　　　　　　　　　Considered, 00/2440

D (Abduction: Custody Rights), Re [1999] 2 F.L.R. 626; [1999] 3 F.C.R. 686; [1999] Fam.
Law 609, Fam Div. . . . .   *Digested*, 99/**2325**
D (Abduction: Discretionary Return), Re [2000] 1 F.L.R. 24; [2000] 1 F.C.R. 208; [2000]
Fam. Law 8, Fam Div. . . . .   *Digested*, 00/**2442**
D (Adoption: Foreign Guardianship), Re [1999] 2 F.L.R. 865; [1999] 3 F.C.R. 418; [1999]
Fam. Law 685, Fam Div. . . . .   *Digested*, 00/**2435**:
                                                        Not followed, 00/2436
D (Adult: Medical Treatment), Re [1998] 1 F.L.R. 411; [1998] 1 F.C.R. 498; (1997) 38
B.M.L.R. 1; [1997] Fam. Law 787, Fam Div . . . .   *Digested*, 98/**2650**
D (Care: Natural Parent Presumption), Re; *sub nom* D (Minors) (Natural Parent
Presumption), Re; D (A Minor) (Residence: Natural Parent), Re [1999] 1 F.L.R.
134; [1999] 2 F.C.R. 118; [1999] Fam. Law 12; (2000) 164 J.P.N. 45, CA. . . . . .   *Digested*, 99/**2356**:
                                                        Followed, 99/2393
D (Care: Threshold Criteria: Significant Harm), Re [1998] Fam. Law 656, Fam Div
D (Children) (Adoption: Freeing Order), Re [2001] 1 F.L.R. 403; [2001] Fam. Law 91; *Times*,
July 18, 2000, Fam Div . . . .   *Digested*, 00/**2429**
D (Children) (Shared Residence Orders), Re; *sub nom* D v. D (Children) (Shared
Residence Orders), Re [2001] 1 F.L.R. 495; [2001] 1 F.C.R. 147; [2001] Fam.
Law 183; (2001) 165 J.P.N. 347; *Times*, January 5, 2001; *Daily Telegraph*,
December 19, 2000, CA . . . .   *Digested*, 01/**2666**
D (CICA: Quantum: 2000), Re (Unreported, May 4, 2000), CICA (Durham) [*Ex rel.* Roger
Cooper, Barrister, Plowden buildings, Temple, London] . . . .   *Digested*, 01/**1569**
D (CICB: Quantum: 1998), Re; *sub nom* D (Compensation: Psychiatric Disability after
Sexual Abuse), Re; (Unreported, February 16, 1998), CICB (Torquay) [*Ex rel.*
Miranda Robertshaw, Barrister, King's Bench Chambers, 115 North Hill,
Plymouth, Devon, PL4 8JY] . . . .   *Digested*, 98/**1513**
D (Compensation: Psychiatric Disability after Sexual Abuse), Re see D (CICB: Quantum:
1998), Re
D (Contact: Reasons for Refusal), Re [1997] 2 F.L.R. 48; [1998] 1 F.C.R. 321; [1997] Fam.
Law 471, CA . . . .   *Digested*, 97/**436**
D (Jurisdiction: Programme of Assessment or Therapy), Re; *sub nom* D (Residential
Assessment), Re [1999] 2 F.L.R. 632; [2000] 1 F.C.R. 436; [1999] Fam. Law
615; (2000) 164 J.P.N. 502, CA. . . . .   *Digested*, 99/**2361**
D (Medical Treatment: Consent), Re see D (Medical Treatment: Mentally Disabled Patient),
Re
D (Medical Treatment: Mentally Disabled Patient), Re; *sub nom* D (Medical Treatment:
Consent), Re [1998] 2 F.L.R. 22; [1998] 2 F.C.R. 178; (1998) 41 B.M.L.R. 81;
[1998] Fam. Law 324; (1997) 94(48) L.S.G. 30; (1998) 142 S.J.L.B. 30; *Times*,
January 14, 1998, Fam Div . . . .   *Digested*, 98/**2649**
D (Mental Patient: Habeas Corpus), Re; *sub nom* D v. Barnet Healthcare Trust [2000] 2
F.L.R. 848; [2001] 1 F.C.R. 218; [2000] Fam. Law 805; *Times*, May 19, 2000,
CA . . . .   *Digested*, 00/**4176**
D (Minors) (Adoption Reports: Confidentiality), Re [1996] A.C. 593; [1995] 3 W.L.R. 483;
[1995] 4 All E.R. 385; [1995] 2 F.L.R. 687; [1996] 1 F.C.R. 205; [1996] Fam. Law 8;
(1995) 145 N.L.J. 1612, HL; reversing [1995] 1 W.L.R. 356; [1995] 1 F.L.R. 631;
(1995) 139 S.J.L.B. 13; *Times*, December 8, 1994; *Independent*, December 6,
1994; *Guardian*, December 5, 1994, CA . . . .   *Digested*, 96/**474**:
                        Applied, 96/508, 97/356, 99/2360, 99/6065, 00/2534:
                                              Distinguished, 99/6064
D (Minors) (Child Abuse: Interviews), Re; *sub nom* D (Minors) (Sexual Abuse:
Evidence), Re [1998] 2 F.L.R. 10; [1998] 2 F.C.R. 419; (1998) 162 J.P.N. 702;
Times, March 11, 1998, CA . . . .   *Digested*, 98/**2388**
D (Minors) (Conciliation: Disclosure of Information), Re; *sub nom* D (Minors)
(Conciliation: Privilege), Re [1993] Fam. 231; [1993] 2 W.L.R. 721; [1993] 2 All
E.R. 693; [1993] 1 F.L.R. 932; [1993] 1 F.C.R. 877; [1993] Fam. Law 410;
(1993) 143 N.L.J. 438; *Times*, February 12, 1993, CA . . . .   *Digested*, 93/**2865**:
                                          Followed, 97/2497, 00/2552
D (Minors) (Conciliation: Privilege), Re see D (Minors) (Conciliation: Disclosure of
Information), Re
D (Minors) (Natural Parent Presumption), Re see D (Care: Natural Parent Presumption), Re
D (Minors) (Sexual Abuse: Evidence), Re see D (Minors) (Child Abuse: Interviews), Re
D (Protection of Party Anonymity), Re (1997-98) 1 C.C.L. Rep. 190; (1999) 45 B.M.L.R. 191,
QBD . . . .   *Digested*, 98/**75**
D (Residential Assessment), Re see D (Jurisdiction: Programme of Assessment or
Therapy), Re
D (Secure Accommodation Order), Re [1999] Fam. Law 311, CC (Watford)
D (Simultaneous Applications for Care Order and Freeing Order), Re [1999] 2 F.L.R. 49;
[1999] 3 F.C.R. 65; [1999] Fam. Law 441; (2000) 164 J.P.N. 127, CA . . . .   *Digested*, 99/**2357**
D v. A (Unreported, May 11, 2000), Fam Div [*Ex rel.* DA Pears, Barrister, Francis Taylor
Building, Temple, London] . . . .   *Digested*, 00/**2531**
D v. Barnet Healthcare Trust see D (Mental Patient: Habeas Corpus), Re
D v. Criminal Injuries Compensation Board see X v. Criminal Injuries Compensation
Board

D v. D (Children) (Shared Residence Orders), Re see D (Children) (Shared Residence Orders), Re

D v. D (Financial Provision: Lump Sum Order) [2001] 1 F.L.R. 633; [2001] 1 F.C.R. 561; [2001] Fam. Law 254, Fam Div . . . . *Digested,* 01/**2639**

D v. Donald [2001] P.I.Q.R. Q5; *Independent,* December 4, 2000 (C.S), QBD . . . . *Digested,* 01/**1513**

D v. DPP (1998) 142 S.J.L.B. 254; *Times,* August 7, 1998, QBD . . . . *Digested,* 98/**898**

D v. P (Forum Conveniens) [1998] 2 F.L.R. 25; [1998] 3 F.C.R. 403; [1998] Fam. Law 458, Fam Div . . . . *Digested,* 98/**2462**

D v. Queen's University of Belfast see Deman v. Queen's University of Belfast

D v. R (Interim Contact Order) see D (A Minor) (Contact: Interim Order), Re

D v. Registrar General; *sub nom* L (A Minor) (Adoption: Disclosure of Information), Re [1998] Fam. 19; [1997] 2 W.L.R. 739; [1997] 1 F.L.R. 715; [1997] 2 F.C.R. 240; [1997] Fam. Law 314; (1997) 94(4) L.S.G. 26; (1997) 141 S.J.L.B. 21; *Times,* January 9, 1997; *Independent,* February 10, 1997 (C.S.), CA; affirming [1996] 1 F.L.R. 707; [1996] 2 F.C.R. 248; [1996] Fam. Law 398, Fam Div . . . . *Digested,* 97/**347**

D v. S (Rights of Audience); *sub nom* S v. D (Rights of Audience) [1997] 1 F.L.R. 724; [1997] 2 F.C.R. 217; [1997] Fam. Law 403; (1997) 161 J.P.N. 532; *Times,* January 1, 1997, CA . . . . *Digested,* 97/**49**: *Applied,* 99/87, 01/637: *Considered,* 97/50, 00/537

D v. Scottish Ministers see A v. Scottish Ministers

D v. United Kingdom (1997) 24 E.H.R.R. 423; 2 B.H.R.C. 273; (1998) 42 B.M.L.R. 149; *Times,* May 12, 1997, ECHR . . . . *Digested,* 97/**2763**: *Considered,* 01/3611

D v. W (C384/98) [2000] E.C.R. I-6795; [2000] S.T.I. 1398; *Times,* October 24, 2000, ECJ (5th Chamber) . . . . *Digested,* 00/**5295**

D and D (Minors) (CICB: Quantum: 1998), Re (Unreported, December 17, 1997), CICB (London) [*Ex rel.* Laraine Roblin, Barrister, 2 King's Walk, Temple, London] . . . . . *Digested,* 98/**1512**

D and K (Children) (Care Plan: Concurrent Planning), Re see D and K (Children) (Care Plan: Twin Track Planning), Re

D and K (Children) (Care Plan: Twin Track Planning), Re; *sub nom* D and K (Children) (Care Plan: Concurrent Planning), Re [2000] 1 W.L.R. 642; [1999] 4 All E.R. 893; [1999] 2 F.L.R. 872; [1999] 3 F.C.R. 109; [1999] Fam. Law 750; (2000) 164 J.P.N. 244; (1999) 149 N.L.J. 1405; *Times,* July 29, 1999, Fam Div . . . . *Digested,* 99/**2359**: *Considered,* 00/2462

D and K (CICB: Quantum: 1998), Re (Unreported, February 23, 1998), CICB (London) [*Ex rel.* Baljinder Uppal, Barrister, College Chambers, 19 Carlton Crescent, Southampton] . . . . *Digested,* 98/**1518**

D Gokal & Co (HK) Ltd v. Rippleworth Ltd (Unreported, October 5, 1998), QBD (Comm Ct) [*Ex rel.* Jeffrey Terry, Barrister, 8 King Street Chambers, 8 King Street, Manchester] . . . . *Digested,* 98/**370**

D Hilton Ltd, Re see Denis Hilton Ltd, Re

D&F Estates Ltd v. Church Commissioners for England [1989] A.C. 177; [1988] 3 W.L.R. 368; [1988] 2 All E.R. 992; 41 B.L.R. 1; 15 Con. L.R. 35; [1988] 2 E.G.L.R. 213; (1988) 4 Const. L.J. 100; (1988) 85(33) L.S.G. 46; (1988) 138 N.L.J. Rep. 210; (1988) 132 S.J. 1092, HL; affirming 36 B.L.R. 72; 11 Con. L.R. 12; [1987] 1 F.T.L.R. 405; (1987) Const. L.J. 110, CA; affirming in part 7 Con. L.R. 40, OR . . . . *Digested,* 88/**3410**: *Applied,* 89/3516, 90/3289, 92/3197, 94/321: *Considered,* 89/2537, 90/3288, 90/3884, 90/5485, 90/5487, 91/2661, 92/3219, 93/2997: *Distinguished,* 96/4437: *Not followed,* 98/3924

D&L Underwriting Agencies Ltd see Secretary of State for Trade and Industry v. Great Western Assurance Co SA

D-R (Adult: Contact), Re; *sub nom* D-R v. D-R; D-R (Contact: Mentally Incapacitated Adult), Re [1999] 1 F.L.R. 1161; [1999] 2 F.C.R. 49; [1999] Fam. Law 299; *Times,* February 8, 1999, CA . . . . *Digested,* 99/**2380**

D-R (Contact: Mentally Incapacitated Adult), Re see D-R (Adult: Contact), Re

D-R v. D-R see D-R (Adult: Contact), Re

D'Abo v. Paget (No.1) [2001] W.T.L.R. 73; *Times,* August 10, 2000, Ch D . . . . *Digested,* 00/**5271**

D'Abo v. Paget (No.2) [2000] W.T.L.R. 863; (2000) 97(38) L.S.G. 43; *Times,* August 10, 2000, Ch D . . . . *Digested,* 01/**455**

D'Ambrmenil v. Customs and Excise Commissioners [1999] B.V.C. 2193, V&DTr

D'Eye v. Avery [2001] W.T.L.R. 227, QBD . . . . *Digested,* 01/**5165**

D'Souza, Re (Unreported, August 19, 1998), CICB (London) [*Ex rel.* Thompsons Solicitors, Congress House, Great Russell Street, London] . . . . *Digested,* 98/**929**

D'Souza v. Lambeth LBC (No.1) see Lambeth LBC v. D'Souza (No.1)

Dabbs (Lawrence Stanley) (Deceased), Re see Hart v. Dabbs

DACA/ Monitor screens (T141/92) [1999] E.P.O.R. 258, EPO (Technical Bd App) . . . . *Digested,* 00/**3632**

Dacorum BC v. Chipperfield Garage Ltd (1999) 14 P.A.D. 692, Planning Inspector

Dacorum BC v. G&M Wiedman (1999) 14 P.A.D. 1, Planning Inspector

Dacorum BC v. Horne see Horne (A Bankrupt), Re

Dacorum BC v. Secretary of State for the Environment, Transport and the Regions and Walsh [2001] J.P.L. 380 (Note); [2001] J.P.L. 420, QBD . . . . *Digested,* 01/**4734**

Dad v. General Dental Council [2000] 1 W.L.R. 1538; [2000] Lloyd's Rep. Med. 299; (2000) 56 B.M.L.R. 130; *Times,* April 19, 2000, PC (UK) . . . . *Digested,* 00/**38**

Dada v. Metal Box Co Ltd [1974] I.C.R. 559; [1974] I.R.L.R. 251; [1974] I.T.R. 390,
    NIRC. . . . .   *Digested,* 74/**1586**:
                                                                                            Considered, 99/2060
Daejan Properties Ltd v. Bloom [2000] E.G.C.S. 85; (2000) 97(28) L.S.G. 34; (2000)
    97(30) L.S.G. 42, CA
Daejan Properties Ltd v. London Leasehold Valuation Tribunal see R. (on the application
    of Daejan Properties Ltd) v. London Leasehold Valuation Tribunal
Daejan Properties Ltd v. Mahoney (1996) 28 H.L.R. 498; [1995] 2 E.G.L.R. 75; [1995]
    45 E.G. 128; [1995] E.G.C.S. 4; [1995] N.P.C. 7, CA . . . .   *Digested,* 95/**3077**:
                                                        Considered, 97/3274, 98/2988: *Followed,* 98/3054
Daejan Properties Ltd v. Weeks [1998] 3 E.G.L.R. 125; [1998] 36 E.G. 146, Lands Tr . . .   *Digested,* 98/**3643**
Dafra-Lines A/S v. Commission of the European Communities (C396/96) see
    Compagnie Maritime Belge Transports SA v. Commission of the European
    Communities (C395/96)
Dag v. Secretary of State for the Home Department [2001] Imm. A.R. 587, IAT
Dahmane v. Secretary of State for the Home Department Unreported, IAT . . . .   *Doubted,* 99/3175
Daiber v. Hauptzollamt Reutlingen (C200/84); Collector Guns GmbH & Co KG v.
    Hauptzollamt Koblenz (C252/84) [1985] E.C.R. 3363, ECJ . . . .   *Digested,* 85/**1418**:
                                                                                            Considered, 99/4661
Daido Kogyo KK's Patent [1984] R.P.C. 97, CA . . . .   *Distinguished,*
                                                                                            99/3469
Daihatsu Australia Pty Ltd v. Commissioner of Taxation (No.1) 3 I.T.L. Rep. 310, Fed Ct
    (Aus) (Sgl judge)
Daihatsu Australia Pty Ltd v. Commissioner of Taxation (No.2) 3 I.T.L. Rep. 723, Fed Ct
    (Aus) (Sgl judge)
Daihatsu Australia Pty Ltd v. Deputy Commissioner of Taxation 3 I.T.L. Rep. 276, Fed Ct
    (Aus) (Sgl judge)
Daimler Chrysler AG v. Alavi (t/a Merc); *sub nom* Daimlerchrysler AG v. Alavi [2001]
    E.T.M.R. 98; [2001] R.P.C. 42; (2001) 24(5) I.P.D. 24028; (2001) 98(13) L.S.G.
    41; *Times,* February 16, 2001, Ch D . . . .   *Digested,* 01/**4035**
Daimlerchrysler AG v. Alavi see Daimler Chrysler AG v. Alavi (t/a Merc)
Dairygold Cooperative Society Ltd's Trade Mark Application [2001] E.T.M.R. 110, PO (Irl)
Dakin v. Greater Manchester & Lancashire Rent Assessment Committee see Dakin v.
    Rent Assessment Committee
Dakin v. North Western Rent Assessment Committee see Queensway Housing
    Association Ltd v. Chiltern, Thames and Eastern Rent Assessment Committee
Dakin v. Rent Assessment Committee; *sub nom* Dakin v. Greater Manchester &
    Lancashire Rent Assessment Committee (1998) 75 P. & C.R. D48, QBD
Daktaras v. Lithuania (42095/98) (Admissibility of Application) (2000) 29 E.H.R.R.
    CD135, ECHR
Dalban v. Romania (28114/95) (2001) 31 E.H.R.R. 39; 8 B.H.R.C. 91, ECHR . . . .   *Digested,* 00/**3188**:
                                                                                            Considered, 00/3248
Dale v. British Coal Corp (No.2) (1992) 136 S.J.L.B. 199; *Times,* July 2, 1992, CA . . . . .   *Digested,* 92/**2832**:
                                                                                            Considered, 00/528
Dale v. de Soissons [1950] 2 All E.R. 460; 66 T.L.R. (Pt. 2) 223; 43 R. & I.T. 886; 32
    T.C. 118; [1950] T.R. 221; [1950] W.N. 354; 94 S.J. 455, CA; affirming [1950] 1
    All E.R. 912; 66 T.L.R. (Pt.1) 1099, Ch D . . . .   *Digested,* 47-51/**4784**:
                                                        Applied, 97/2974: *Considered,* 01/5274
Dale v. Smith [1967] 1 W.L.R. 700; [1967] 2 All E.R. 1133; (1967) 131 J.P. 378; 111 S.J.
    330, QBD . . . .   *Digested,* 67/**918**:
                                                        Applied, 94/1150: *Considered,* 99/2189
Dale Farm Dairy Group Ltd (t/a Northern Dairies) v. Akram [1998] I.C.R. 349, CA . . . . .   *Digested,* 97/**865**
Daley, Re see R. v. Islington North Juvenile Court Ex p. Daley
Daley v. Queen, The; Montique v. Queen, The [1998] 1 W.L.R. 494; (1998) 142
    S.J.L.B. 54, PC (Jam) . . . .   *Digested,* 98/**1054**:
                                                                                            Applied, 99/1023
Daley v. Rotherham MBC [2001] 3 Q.R. 16, CC (Rotherham) [*Ex rel.* Dermot Hughes,
    Barrister, Paradise Square Chambers, Sheffield] . . . .   *Digested,* 01/**1795**
Dalia v. France (26102/95) (2001) 33 E.H.R.R. 26; [1998] H.R.C.D. 258, ECHR
Dalimpex Ltd v. Janicki [2000] I.L.Pr. 180, CJ (Gen Div) (Ont) . . . .   *Digested,* 00/**241**
Dallas Application, Re [1996] N.I. 276, QBD (NI)
Dallison v. Caffery [1965] 1 Q.B. 348; [1964] 3 W.L.R. 385; [1964] 2 All E.R. 610;
    128 J.P. 379; 108 S.J. 560, CA; affirming *Times,* July 3, 1963 . . . .   *Digested,* 64/**2337**:
                                                Applied, 93/3077, 01/1143: *Considered,* 68/941, 76/402, 89/748, 90/1020,
                                                                            97/3417: *Followed,* 98/4257
Daly v. Newbold Domestic Appliances Ltd (Unreported, November 5, 1997), CC
    (Warrington) [*Ex rel.* Brian McCluggage, 9 St John Street, Manchester M3
    4DN] . . . .   *Digested,* 98/**1756**
Dalziel (CICA: Quantum: 2000), Re [2001] 2 Q.R. 9, CICA (Birmingham) [*Ex rel.* Pickering
    & Butters Solicitors, Market Square, Rugeley, Staffordshire] . . . .   *Digested,* 01/**1602**
Damage Caused by Kitchen Stove, Re [2000] E.C.C. 137, OGH (A)
Damberg v. Damberg (2001-02) 4 I.T.E.L.R. 65, CA (NSW)
Dampskibsselskabet AF 1912 A/S v. Motis Exports Ltd see Motis Exports Ltd v.
    Dampskibsselskabet AF 1912 A/S (No.1)

Dana (UK) Ltd, Re [1999] 2 B.C.L.C. 239, Ch D . . . . *Digested,* 99/**3266**
Danae Air Transport SA *v.* Air Canada [2000] 1 W.L.R. 395; [2000] 2 All E.R. 649;
[1999] 2 All E.R. (Comm) 943; [1999] 2 Lloyd's Rep. 547; [2000] C.P. Rep. 25;
[1999] C.L.C. 1859; (1999) 96(32) L.S.G. 31; [1999] N.P.C. 108; *Times,*
August 5, 1999, CA; reversing [1999] 1 All E.R. (Comm) 794; [1999] 2 Lloyd's
Rep. 105; (1999) 96(15) L.S.G. 29; *Times,* March 31, 1999, QBD (Comm Ct) . . . *Digested,* 99/**229**
Dance *v.* Harns (Unreported, April 22, 1998), CC (Reading) [*Ex rel.* Shoosmiths &
Harrison Solicitors, Russell House, Solent Business Park, Whiteley, Fareham] . . . *Digested,* 98/**417**
Dance *v.* Welwyn Hatfield DC [1990] 1 W.L.R. 1097; [1990] 3 All E.R. 572; (1990) 22
H.L.R. 339; (1991) 155 L.G. Rev. 189, CA. . . . . *Digested,* 90/**2519**:
Applied, 93/2106: *Considered,* 93/2105, 93/2111, 97/2718:
Followed, 97/2731, 98/3056: *Overruled,* 98/3055
Dangol (t/a Great Kathmandu Tandoori) *v.* Customs and Excise Commissioners see R. *v.*
Customs and Excise Commissioners Ex p. Dangol (t/a Great Kathmandu
Tandoori)
Danial and Roywest Trust Corp (Cayman) Ltd's Deed of Settlement, Re [2000] W.T.L.R.
713, Grand Court (CI) . . . . *Digested,* 01/**5522**
Danian *v.* Secretary of State for the Home Department [2000] Imm. A.R. 96; [1999]
I.N.L.R. 533; (1999) 96(43) L.S.G. 34; *Times,* November 9, 1999 ; *Independent,*
December 13, 1999 (C.S.), CA; reversing [1998] Imm. A.R. 462; [1998]
I.N.L.R. 375, IAT . . . . *Digested,* 99/**3179**:
Followed, 00/3313
Daniells *v.* Mendonca (1999) 78 P. & C.R. 401, CA . . . . *Digested,* 00/**5127**
Daniels *v.* Griffiths [1998] E.M.L.R. 489; (1997) 94(48) L.S.G. 29; (1997) 147 N.L.J.
1809; (1998) 142 S.J.L.B. 22; *Times,* December 2, 1997; *Independent,*
December 3, 1997, CA. . . . . *Digested,* 98/**1778**
Danish Satellite TV A/S (Eurotica Rendez Vous Television) *v.* Commission of the European
Communities (T69/99) [2001] All E.R. (EC) 577; [2000] E.C.R. II-4039, CFI
(2nd Chamber) . . . . *Digested,* 01/**4420**
Danka Rentals Ltd *v.* Xi Software Ltd (1998) 17 Tr. L.R. 74, QBD . . . . *Digested,* 98/**4380**
Danmarks Aktive Handelsrejsende *v.* Lonmodtagernes Garantifond (C117/96); *sub nom*
Danmarks Aktive Handelsrejsende (On behalf of Mosbaek) *v.* Lonmodtagernes
Garantifond (C117/96) [1998] 1 All E.R. (E.C.) 112; [1997] E.C.R. I-5017; [1998]
2 B.C.L.C. 395; [1998] 1 C.M.L.R. 366; [1998] I.C.R. 954; [1998] I.R.L.R. 150;
Times, November 20, 1997, ECJ (5th Chamber) . . . . *Digested,* 97/**2232**:
Distinguished, 00/2133
Danmarks Aktive Handelsrejsende (On behalf of Mosbaek) *v.* Lonmodtagernes
Garantifond (C117/96) see Danmarks Aktive Handelsrejsende *v.*
Lonmodtagernes Garantifond (C117/96)
Danns *v.* Department of Health [1998] P.I.Q.R. P226, CA; affirming [1996] P.I.Q.R.
P69, QBD . . . . *Digested,* 98/**3984**
Dansk Metalarbejderforbund *v.* Lonmodtagernes Garantifond (C250/97) [1998] E.C.R.
I-8737; [2001] 1 C.M.L.R. 39, ECJ. . . . . *Digested,* 01/**2304**
Dansk Skibsfinansiering A/S *v.* Brothers [2001] 2 B.C.L.C. 324, CFA (HK)
Dansommer A/S *v.* Gotz (C8/98) [2001] 1 W.L.R. 1069; [2000] E.C.R. I-393; [2001]
I.L.Pr. 28, ECJ . . . . *Digested,* 01/**824**
Dansommer AS *v.* Gotz [1998] I.L.Pr. 583, LG (Heilbronn)
Darbiye *v.* Entry Clearance Officer (Nairobi) [1998] Imm. A.R. 64, CA. . . . . *Digested,* 98/**3228**
Darby *v.* Josephs [1999] I.L.Pr. 339, Cass (F) . . . . *Digested,* 99/**730**
Darby *v.* Meehan, *Times,* November 25, 1998, Ch D . . . . *Digested,* 98/**4068**
Darby *v.* National Trust for Places of Historic Interest or Natural Beauty [2001] EWCA
Civ 189; (2001) 3 L.G.L.R. 29; [2001] P.I.Q.R. P27; *Times,* February 23, 2001,
CA . . . . *Digested,* 01/**4504**
Darby *v.* Sweden (A/187) (1991) 13 E.H.R.R. 774, ECHR . . . . *Applied,* 01/1844
Dareway Properties Ltd *v.* Glovers 1996-NJ-0537, QBD . . . . *Digested,* 98/**4025**
Darker *v.* Chief Constable of the West Midlands; *sub nom* Docker (Deceased) *v.* Chief
Constable of the West Midlands [2001] 1 A.C. 435; [2000] 3 W.L.R. 747;
[2000] 4 All E.R. 193; (2000) 97(32) L.S.G. 38; (2000) 150 N.L.J. 1421;
(2000) 144 S.J.L.B. 243; *Times,* August 1, 2000; *Independent,* November 6,
2000 (C.S.), HL; reversing (1998) 95(17) L.S.G. 31; (1998) 142 S.J.L.B. 134;
Times, April 29, 1998, CA. . . . . *Digested,* 00/**4543**:
Applied, 01/401
Darley's Application, Re [1997] N.I. 384, CA (NI) . . . . *Digested,* 99/**5265**
Darlington BC *v.* Sterling (1997) 29 H.L.R. 309, CA. . . . . *Digested,* 97/**2717**:
Applied, 97/2669: *Considered,* 01/4198
Darlington Building Society *v.* O'Rourke James Scourfield & McCarthy [1999] Lloyd's
Rep. P.N. 33; [1999] P.N.L.R. 365; *Times,* November 20, 1998, CA . . . . *Digested,* 98/**601**:
Considered, 01/626
Darmalingum *v.* Mauritius [2000] 1 W.L.R. 2303; [2000] 2 Cr. App. R. 445; 8
B.H.R.C. 662; *Times,* July 18, 2000; *Independent,* October 9, 2000 (C.S.), PC
(Mau) . . . . *Digested,* 00/**1104**:
Distinguished, 01/1152
Darmanin *v.* Vauxhall Motors Ltd (Unreported, January 12, 1999), CC (Luton) [*Ex rel.*
James Laughland, Barrister, 1 Temple Gardens, Temple, London] . . . . *Digested,* 99/**1612**

Darragh v. Chief Constable of Thames Valley (1998) 95(43) L.S.G. 32; *Times*, October 20, 1998, CA . . . . *Digested*, 98/**521**

Dart v. Addishire see Dart v. Ely

Dart v. Dart [1996] 2 F.L.R. 286; [1997] 1 F.C.R. 21; [1996] Fam. Law 607, CA . . . . . . *Digested*, 96/**2858**: *Considered*, 97/2482, 00/2530

Dart v. Ely; Dart v. Addishire [2000] N.P.C. 103, CA

Dartmoor National Park Authority v. RP&S Heywood (Haulage) Ltd Retirement Benefit Scheme (2001) 16 P.A.D. 11, Planning Inspector

Daryanani v. Gerrey see Daryanani v. Kumar & Co

Daryanani v. Kumar & Co; Daryanani v. Gerrey [2001] C.P. Rep. 27; [2001] C.P.L.R. 307, CA; affirming 1991 D No 2830, QBD . . . . *Digested*, 01/**673**

Das v. Ganju [1999] P.I.Q.R. P260; [1999] Lloyd's Rep. Med. 198; (1999) 96(19) L.S.G. 28; (1999) 143 S.J.L.B. 129; *Times*, May 4, 1999, CA; affirming (1998) 42 B.M.L.R. 28, QBD . . . . *Digested*, 99/**470**: *Considered*, 01/601

Dashiell v. Luttit; *sub nom* Dashiell v. Luttitt [2000] 3 Q.R. 4, QBD [*Ex rel.* Bruce Silvester, Barrister, Devereux Chambers, Devereux Court, London] . . . . *Digested*, 00/**1505**

Dashiell v. Luttitt see Dashiell v. Luttit

Dassanayake (CICA: Quantum: 2001), Re [2001] 5 Q.R. 10, CICA (London) [*Ex rel.* Laura Elfield, Barrister, 9 Gough Square, London] . . . . *Digested*, 01/**1578**

Dassonville v. Commission of the European Communities (C8/74) see Procureur du Roi v. Dassonville (C8/74)

Data Access Corp v. Powerflex Services Pty Ltd; *sub nom* Powerflex Services Pty v. Data Access Corp [1997-98] Info. T.L.R. 224; [1998-99] Info. T.L.R. 294, Fed Ct (Aus) (Full Ct). . . . . *Digested*, 01/**3858**

Data Professionals Srl v. Mercantile Sisitemi Srl [1998] E.T.M.R. 670, Trib (Napoli)

Datadeck Ltd, Re [1998] B.C.C. 694, Ch D (Companies Ct) . . . . *Digested*, 98/**3335**

Dataschool Ltd v. Sandhu; *sub nom* Sandhu v. Raymond Dyers Ltd; (Unreported, December 3, 1997), CC (Leicester) [*Ex rel.* Sunil Iyer, Barrister, Counsel's Chambers, 2 New Street, Leicester] . . . . *Digested*, 98/**408**

Dattani v. Trio Supermarkets Ltd [1998] I.C.R. 872; [1998] I.R.L.R. 240; (1998) 95(9) L.S.G. 29; (1998) 142 S.J.L.B. 77; *Times*, February 20, 1998, CA . . . . *Digested*, 98/**2190**

Daud v. Portugal (22600/93) (2000) 30 E.H.R.R. 400; 4 B.H.R.C. 522; [1998] H.R.C.D. 442, ECHR . . . . *Digested*, 98/**3114**

Davenport v. Hammersmith and Fulham LBC (1999) 78 P. & C.R. 421; [1999] 2 P.L.R. 96; [1999] J.P.L. 1122; (1999) 149 N.L.J. 521; *Times*, April 26, 1999, QBD . . . . . *Digested*, 99/**4240**

Daventry DC v. Haines (2001) 16 P.A.D. 61, Planning Inspector

Daventry DC v. Secretary of State for the Environment, Transport and the Regions (1998) 95(31) L.S.G. 37, QBD

Davey (Valuation Officer) v. O'Kelly [1999] R.A. 245, Lands Tr . . . . *Digested*, 99/**4323**

David & Snape v. Sampson [2000] I.L.Pr. 474, Sup Ct (NS) . . . . *Digested*, 00/**783**: *Cited*, 01/544

David Hallam Ltd v. Langford (Unreported, February 10, 2000), CC (Sheffield) [*Ex rel.* Graham Robinson, Barrister, Paradise Chambers, 26 Paradise Square, Sheffield] *Digested*, 00/**542**

David J Instance Ltd v. Denny Bros Printing Ltd (Patent Action) see Instance v. Denny Bros Printing Ltd (Patent Action)

David Wilson Homes Ltd v. Kirklees MBC [2000] P.L.C.R. 333; [2000] J.P.L. 1078 (Note); (2000) 97(8) L.S.G. 38, QBD . . . . *Digested*, 00/**4464**

David Wilson Homes Ltd v. Survey Services Ltd (In Liquidation) [2001] EWCA Civ 34; [2001] 1 All E.R. (Comm) 449; [2001] B.L.R. 267; (2001) 3 T.C.L.R. 13; 80 Con. L.R. 8, CA. . . . . *Digested*, 01/**349**

David Yablon Minton (A Firm) v. Kenburgh Investments (Northern) Ltd (In Liquidation) see Kenburgh Investments (Northern) Ltd (In Liquidation) v. David Yablon Minton (A Firm)

Davidson v. City Electrical Factors Ltd [1998] I.C.R. 443; [1998] I.R.L.R. 108, EAT . . . . *Digested*, 98/**5826**

Davidson v. Strong [1998] C.O.D. 3; *Times*, March 20, 1997; *Independent*, March 3, 1997 (C.S.), QBD. . . . . *Digested*, 97/**243**

Davies (Alfred James), Re [1998] C.O.D. 30, QBD . . . . *Digested*, 98/**2351**

Davies v. Andrews (Unreported, June 24, 1997), CC (Birkenhead) [*Ex rel.* Milners Solicitors, Crown House, 81-89 Great George Street, Leeds] . . . . *Digested*, 98/**599**

Davies v. Black Prince Holidays Ltd see Davies v. Secretary of State for the Environment

Davies v. Clarkson 1994 D 2958A, QBD . . . . *Digested*, 99/**1436**

Davies v. Customs and Excise Commissioners [1975] 1 W.L.R. 204; [1975] 1 All E.R. 309; [1975] S.T.C. 28; [1974] T.R. 317; (1974) 119 S.J. 100, DC . . . . *Digested*, 75/**3477**: *Applied*, 00/5364

Davies v. Davies [2000] 1 F.L.R. 39; [1999] 3 F.C.R. 745; [2000] Fam. Law 23, CA . . . *Digested*, 00/**2504**

Davies v. Edmonds (Unreported, January 12, 1999), CC (Cardiff) [*Ex rel.* Andrew Arentsen, Barrister, 33 Park Place, Cardiff] . . . . *Digested*, 99/**1556**

Davies (Joseph Owen) v. Eli Lilly & Co (No.1) [1987] 1 W.L.R. 1136; [1987] 3 All E.R. 94; [1987] 2 F.T.L.R. 154; (1987) 84 L.S.G. 2042; (1987) 137 N.L.J. 1183, CA; reversing [1987] 2 F.T.L.R. 143; (1987) 84 L.S.G. 1881; (1987) 131 S.J. 807, HC . *Digested*, 87/**2942**: *Considered*, 00/409

Davies v. Gravelle Plant Ltd (Unreported, July 1, 1999), CC (Swansea) [Ex rel. Bryan
Thomas, Barrister, 33 Park Place, Cardiff] . . . .   Digested, 00/**1623**
Davies v. Gwynedd Hospitals NHS Trust [2001] 1 Q.R. 10
Davies v. Hardwick (Unreported, March 19, 1999), Ch D [Ex rel. Stephen Beresford,
Barrister, 24 The Ropewalk, Nottingham] . . . .   Digested, 99/**4954**
Davies v. Hayter 00/TLQ/0268, QBD . . . .   Digested, 00/**1570**
Davies v. Hillier Nurseries Ltd; sub nom Davies v. Hillier Park Nurseries Ltd [2001]
EWHC Admin 28; [2001] Env. L.R. 42; Times, February 16, 2001; Independent,
March 12, 2001 (C.S), QBD . . . .   Digested, 01/**2412**
Davies v. Hillier Park Nurseries Ltd see Davies v. Hillier Nurseries Ltd
Davies v. Inman [1999] P.I.Q.R. Q26, CA. . . . .   Digested, 99/**1415**
Davies v. MJ Wyatt (Decorators) Ltd [2000] I.R.L.R. 759; Times, October 24, 2000,
EAT . . . .   Digested, 00/**2198**:
                                                                                                         Followed, 01/6471
Davies v. Neath Port Talbot CBC [1999] I.C.R. 1132; [1999] I.R.L.R. 769; Times,
October 26, 1999, EAT . . . .   Digested, 99/**2085**
Davies v. Newham LBC [1998] R.V.R. 11, Lands Tr   Digested, 98/**2985**
Davies v. Norwich Union Life Insurance Society (1999) 78 P. & C.R. 119; (1999) 77 P.
& C.R. D40, CA . . . .   Digested, 00/**4644**
Davies v. Presbyterian Church of Wales [1986] 1 W.L.R. 323; [1986] 1 All E.R. 705;
[1986] I.C.R. 280; [1986] I.R.L.R. 194; (1986) 83 L.S.G. 968; (1986) 130 S.J.
203, HL (Unreported, May 11, 1982), IT . . . .   Digested, 86/**1172**:
                                        Applied, 90/1863, 95/2078, 98/2137: Considered, 96/2652
Davies v. Secretary of State for the Environment; Davies v. Black Prince Holidays Ltd
[1999] N.P.C. 71, QBD
Davies v. Shropshire CC (Unreported, February 29, 2000), CC (Telford) [Ex rel.
Hodgkinsons Solicitors, The Old Manse, 14 Lumley Avenue, Skegness,
Lincolnshire] . . . .   Digested, 00/**1632**
Davies v. Sumner; sub nom Sumner v. Davies [1984] 1 W.L.R. 1301; [1984] 3 All E.R.
831; (1985) 149 J.P. 110; [1985] R.T.R. 95; 84 L.G.R. 123; (1985) 149 J.P.N. 11;
(1985) 82 L.S.G. 45; (1984) 128 S.J. 814; (1985) 4 Tr. L. 1, HL; affirming [1984]
1 W.L.R. 405; (1984) 81 L.S.G. 360; (1984) 128 S.J. 18; Times, August 11,
1983, QBD . . . .   Digested, 84/**3100**:
                                    Applied, 88/3168, 90/4039, 91/3183: Considered, 96/7320, 99/4406:
                                                                                                         Referred to, 00/3570
Davies v. Taylor (No.2) [1974] A.C. 225; [1973] 2 W.L.R. 610; [1973] 1 All E.R. 959;
117 S.J. 246, HL . . . .   Digested, 73/**2671**:
                                                    Applied, 83/590, 83/2548, 84/553: Considered, 99/3758
Davies v. Wyre Forest DC [1998] P.I.Q.R. P58, QBD . . . .   Digested, 98/**3993**
Davies Application, Re [2001] 03 E.G. 134; [2001] 01 E.G. 111, Lands Tr . . . .   Digested, 01/**4886**
Davies Middleton & Davies Ltd v. Toyo Engineering Corp 85 B.L.R. 59, CA. . . . .   Digested, 98/**241**
Davis v. AG Barr Plc (1999) 99(4) Q.R. 6, CC (Mansfield) [Ex rel. Flint Bishop &
Barnett Solicitors, Royal Oak House, Market Place, Derby] . . . .   Digested, 99/**1531**
Davis v. Customs and Excise Commissioners [2001] S.T.I. 1234, V&D Tr
Davis v. Izatt (Unreported, September 1, 1999), CC (Tunbridge Wells) [Ex rel. Paul
McGrath, Barrister, 1 Temple Gardens, Temple, London] . . . .   Digested, 99/**2478**
Davis v. Jacobs [1999] Lloyd's Rep. Med. 72; (2000) 51 B.M.L.R. 42, CA . . . .   Digested, 99/**469**
Davis v. Martin-Sklan see Hussein (Essengin), Re
Davis v. Secretary of State for Social Security; sub nom Secretary of State for Social
Security v. Davis [2001] EWCA Civ 105; Independent, February 12, 2001 (C.S),
CA
Davis v. Thomson Holidays Ltd (Unreported, February 18, 1999), CC (Welshpool) [Ex
rel. Richard Mullan, Barrister, Sedan House, Stanley Place, Chester] . . . .   Digested, 99/**3826**
Davis v. Trustee in Bankruptcy of the Estate of Davis [1998] B.P.I.R. 572, Ch D . . . .   Digested, 99/**3223**
Davis Contractors v. Fareham Urban DC [1956] A.C. 696; [1956] 3 W.L.R. 37; [1956]
2 All E.R. 145; 54 L.G.R. 289; 100 S.J. 378, HL; affirming [1955] 1 Q.B. 302;
[1955] 2 W.L.R. 388; [1955] 1 All E.R. 275; 99 S.J. 109, CA . . . .   Digested, 56/**874**:
                                        Applied, 59/540, 60/535, 63/3200, 64/3379, 68/320, 72/485, 72/1219,
                                        72/3202, 73/3109, 74/1159, 75/410, 75/1097, 76/336, 80/355, 80/1604,
                                        81/76, 81/1538, 83/466, 84/221, 86/1178, 98/2108: Considered, 70/1849,
                                        76/133, 89/3353, 90/4065, 91/1695, 92/518: Followed, 73/1118, 74/1250
Davison v. AR Allen (t/a Allen's Transport) (Unreported, September 24, 1997), CC
(Portsmouth) [Ex rel. Paul Fretwell, Blake Lapthorn Solicitors, Harbour Court,
Portsmouth] . . . .   Digested, 98/**2832**
Davison v. Customs and Excise Commissioners [2001] S.T.I. 1040, V&D Tr
Davison v. Interpan Services Ltd (1999) 99(2) Q.R. 8, CC (King's Lynn) [Ex rel. Ward
Gethin Solicitors, 8/12 Tuesday Market Place, King's Lynn, Norfolk] . . . .   Digested, 99/**1611**
Davy International Ltd v. Voest Alpine Industrieanlagenblau GmbH [1999] 1 All E.R. 103;
[2000] I.L.Pr. 148; Independent, July 28, 1998, CA. . . . .   Digested, 98/**760**
Dawes v. Hawkins 141 E.R. 1399; (1860) 8 C.B. N.S. 848 . . . .   Applied, 00/4641
Dawes & Henderson (Agencies) Ltd (In Liquidation) (No.2), Re; sub nom Shuttleworth v.
Secretary of State for Trade and Industry [2000] B.C.C. 204; [1999] 2 B.C.L.C.
317; (1999) 96(8) L.S.G. 29; Times, February 9, 1999, Ch D . . . .   Digested, 99/**617**:
                                                                                                         Considered, 01/716

Dawkins (Valuation Officer) v. Ash Bros & Heaton Ltd; *sub nom* Almond v. Ash Bros & Heaton [1969] 2 A.C. 366; [1969] 2 W.L.R. 1024; [1969] 2 All E.R. 246; (1969) 133 J.P. 319; 67 L.G.R. 499; 113 S.J. 345, HL; affirming [1968] 1 W.L.R. 133; [1967] 3 All E.R. 952; (1968) 132 J.P. 49; 66 L.G.R. 35; 13 R.R.C. 181; 111 S.J. 757, CA; affirming 1119 E.G. 275; [1966] R.A. 533; [1966] R.V.R. 624; 12 R.R.C. 268, LandsTr . . . . *Digested,* 69/**3019**: *Considered,* 70/1500, 87/3193, 00/4613

Dawkins v. Royal Leamington Spa BC; Dawkins v. Warwickshire CC [1961] R.V.R. 291; 8 R.R.C. 241; [1961] J.P.L. 264, LandsTr . . . . *Digested,* 61/**7423.25**: *Applied,* 79/2229.1, 00/6646: *Considered,* 87/3193: *Explained,* 85/2840

Dawkins v. Warwickshire CC see Dawkins v. Royal Leamington Spa BC

Dawnay Day & Co Ltd v. Cantor Fitzgerald International [2000] R.P.C. 669; (1999) 22(9) I.P.D. 22091; *Times,* July 14, 1999, CA; affirming *Times,* January 26, 1998, Ch D . . . . *Digested,* 99/**600**

Dawnay Day & Co Ltd v. de Braconier d'Alphen [1998] I.C.R. 1068; [1997] I.R.L.R. 442; (1997) 94(26) L.S.G. 30; (1997) 141 S.J.L.B. 129; *Times,* June 24, 1997, CA; affirming [1997] I.R.L.R. 285; *Times,* February 24, 1997, Ch D . . . . *Digested,* 97/**2257**: *Followed,* 00/2202

Dawodu v. American Express Bank [2001] B.P.I.R. 983, Ch D

Dawson v. Cherry Tree Machine Co Ltd see Shell Tankers UK Ltd v. Jeromson

Dawson v. Wearmouth [1999] 2 A.C. 308; [1999] 2 W.L.R. 960; [1999] 2 All E.R. 353; [1999] 1 F.L.R. 1167; [1999] 1 F.C.R. 625; [1999] Fam. Law 378; (1999) 96(17) L.S.G. 24; (1999) 143 S.J.L.B. 114; *Times,* March 26, 1999; *Independent,* May 10, 1999 (C.S.), HL; affirming [1998] Fam. 75; [1998] 2 W.L.R. 392; [1998] 1 All E.R. 271; [1997] 2 F.L.R. 629; [1998] 1 F.C.R. 31; [1998] Fam. Law 15; (1997) 94(35) L.S.G. 34; (1997) 141 S.J.L.B. 200; *Times,* August 22, 1997; *Independent,* October 9, 1997, CA . . . . *Digested,* 99/**2377**: *Applied,* 01/2609: *Considered,* 98/2431: *Followed,* 99/2375

Dawson (Bradford) Ltd v. Dove [1971] 1 Q.B. 330; [1971] 2 W.L.R. 1; [1971] 1 All E.R. 554; 114 S.J. 974, QBD . . . . *Digested,* 71/**9572**: *Considered,* 98/633

Dax Cosmetics Zaklady Kosmetyczno - Chemiczne Jacek Majdax I Wojciech Szulc SC's Trade Mark Application (1063/90) [2001] E.T.M.R. 47, Urzsd Patentowy (PL)

Day v. Bell (Unreported, June 19, 1999), CC (Norwich) [*Ex rel.* Ruth Blair, Barrister, 2 King's Bench Walk, Temple, London] . . . . *Digested,* 99/**1449**

Day v. CGU Life (Unreported, April 23, 2001), CC (Medway) [*Ex rel.* Alexander Booth, Pupil Barrister, 1 Temple Gardens, Temple, London] . . . . *Digested,* 01/**906**

Day v. Cook [2001] EWCA Civ 592; [2001] Lloyd's Rep. P.N. 551; [2001] P.N.L.R. 32, CA; reversing in part [2000] P.N.L.R. 178, QBD (Merc Ct) . . . . *Digested,* 01/**749**

Day v. McCrum [1996] N.I. 607, Ch D (NI)

Day v. RAC Motoring Services Ltd see Day v. Royal Automobile Club Motoring Services Ltd

Day v. Royal Automobile Club Motoring Services Ltd; *sub nom* Day v. RAC Motoring Services Ltd [1999] 1 W.L.R. 2150; [1999] 1 All E.R. 1007; *Times,* November 24, 1998; *Independent,* November 2, 1998 (C.S.), CA . . . . *Digested,* 98/**514**

Day v. T Pickles Farms Ltd [1999] I.R.L.R. 217, EAT . . . . *Digested,* 99/**2116**

Dayani v. Bromley LBC (No.1) [1999] 3 E.G.L.R. 144; [1999] E.G.C.S. 135; (1999) 96(45) L.S.G. 35, QBD (T&CC) . . . . *Digested,* 00/**3939**

Dayani v. Bromley LBC (No.2) [2001] B.L.R. 503, QBD (T&CC)

DB and YB (Children) (CICA: Quantum: 2000), Re (Unreported, November 3, 1999), CICA (Manchester) [*Ex rel.* Rowlands Solicitors, 3 York Street, Manchester] . . . . . . *Digested,* 00/**1532**

DB Ramsden & Co Ltd v. Nurdin & Peacock Plc see Nurdin & Peacock Plc v. DB Ramsden & Co Ltd (Rectification Claim)

DC v. United Kingdom [2000] B.C.C. 710, ECHR . . . . *Digested,* 00/**667**: *Applied,* 00/666

DDM Italia SpA v. Zippo Manufacturing Co see ZIPPO Trade Mark

De Beer v. Kanaar & Co (No.1) [2001] EWCA Civ 1318; [2001] C.P. Rep. 118, CA; reversing HC 97058094, Ch D

De Beers Consolidated Mines Ltd v. Howe (Surveyor of Taxes) [1906] A.C. 455, HL; affirming [1905] 2 K.B. 612, CA . . . . *Applied,* 99/5027, 01/798: *Explained,* 59/1519

De Bobadilla v. Museo Nacional del Prado (C234/97) [1999] E.C.R. I-4773; [1999] 3 C.M.L.R. 151, ECJ . . . . *Digested,* 00/**2176**

De Boer Stalinrichtingen BV's Application [2001] E.T.M.R. 79, OHIM (4th Bd App) . . . . *Digested,* 01/**3992**

De Brun's Application for Judicial Review, Re [2001] N.I. 442, CA (NI)

De Bussche v. Alt (1878) L.R. 8 Ch. D. 286, CA. . . . . *Applied,* 98/3387

De Cordova v. Vick Chemical Co (1951) 68 R.P.C. 103; [1951] W.N. 195; 95 S.J. 316, PC (Jam) . . . . *Digested,* 47-51/**10338**: *Applied,* 56/8806: *Considered,* 74/3829, 96/5712, 98/3530, 98/3537: *Distinguished,* 67/3947: *Referred to,* 99/3572

De Dampierre v. De Dampierre [1988] A.C. 92; [1987] 2 W.L.R. 1006; [1987] 2 All
  E.R. 1; [1987] 2 F.L.R. 300; [1987] Fam. Law 418; (1987) 84 L.S.G. 1493;
  (1987) 131 S.J. 471, HL; reversing [1987] 1 F.L.R. 511; [1986] Fam. Law 361,
  CA . . . . *Digested*, 87/**399**:
       Applied, 92/475, 95/2334, 99/2403: *Considered*, 92/3072, 94/3256,
                       97/2453: *Followed*, 92/5695: *Referred to*, 95/2303
De Falbe, Re see Leigh v. Taylor
De Four v. Trinidad and Tobago [1999] 1 W.L.R. 1731; (1999) 143 S.J.L.B. 215, PC
  (Trin) . . . . *Digested*, 00/**1111**
De Freitas v. Benny [1976] A.C. 239; [1975] 3 W.L.R. 388; [1976] Crim. L.R. 50; 119
  S.J. 610, PC (Trin) . . . . *Digested*, 75/**239**:
                       Followed, 96/1117: *Not followed*, 00/3201
De Freitas v. Permanent Secretary of Ministry of Agriculture, Fisheries, Lands and
  Housing [1999] 1 A.C. 69; [1998] 3 W.L.R. 675; 4 B.H.R.C. 563; (1998) 142
  S.J.L.B. 219, PC (Ant) . . . . *Digested*, 98/**3084**
De Haan v. Netherlands (1998) 26 E.H.R.R. 417, ECHR . . . . *Digested*, 98/**3127**:
                                   Applied, 98/3140, 00/3227
De Haan Beheer BV v. Inspecteur der Invoerrechten en Accijnzen te Rotterdam (C61/
  98) [1999] All E.R. (EC) 803; [1999] E.C.R. I-5003; [1999] 3 C.M.L.R. 211,
  ECJ (5th Chamber) . . . . *Digested*, 00/**2348**
De Haes v. Belgium (19983/92) (1998) 25 E.H.R.R. 1, ECHR . . . . *Digested*, 98/**3089**:
                       Applied, 98/3088: *Considered*, 98/3092
De Jong v. Netherlands (A/77) (1986) 8 E.H.R.R. 20, ECHR . . . . *Followed*, 98/3073
De Keyser Ltd v. Wilson; *sub nom* Wilson v. De Keyser Ltd [2001] I.R.L.R. 324, EAT . . . *Digested*, 01/**2271**
De Keyser's Royal Hotel Ltd, Re; *sub nom* De Keyser's Royal Hotel Ltd v. King, The
  [1920] A.C. 508, HL; affirming [1919] 2 Ch. 197, CA . . . . *Applied*, 54/479,
       54/480, 64/543, 72/1101, 79/321, 87/2868, 99/5188: *Considered*, 71/5455,
               76/31, 77/150, 82/369, 83/359: *Distinguished*, 84/21, 85/12:
                                            Followed, 67/128
De Keyser's Royal Hotel Ltd v. King, The see De Keyser's Royal Hotel Ltd, Re
De la Rue v. Hernu Peron & Stockwell Ltd [1936] 2 K.B. 164, CA . . . . *Applied*, 01/648:
                                         Considered, 00/738
De Lasala v. De Lasala [1980] A.C. 546; [1979] 3 W.L.R. 390; [1979] 2 All E.R. 1146;
  [1980] F.S.R. 443; (1979) 123 S.J. 301, PC (HK) . . . . *Digested*, 79/**2200**:
       Applied, 81/701, 82/952, 87/1745, 92/2115, 93/1905, 01/88:
       Considered, 82/907, 83/1097, 85/1051, 85/1053, 85/1675, 95/2324:
                                            Followed, 85/113
De Meyere v. Belgium (A/43) see Le Compte v. Belgium (A/43)
De Molestina v. Ponton (Application to Strike Out); *sub nom* Molestina v. Ponton
  [2001] C.L.C. 1412; *Independent*, July 16, 2001 (C.S), QBD (Comm Ct) . . . . . . *Digested*, 01/**669**
De Morgan v. Director General of Social Welfare; Sears v. Attorney General of New
  Zealand [1998] A.C. 275; [1998] 2 W.L.R. 427; (1997) 141 S.J.L.B. 217; *Times*,
  November 4, 1997, PC (NZ) . . . . *Digested*, 97/**918**
De Peijper (Managing Director of Centrafarm BV) (C104/75), Re see Officier van Justitie v.
  De Peijper (C104/75)
De Pfeiffer v. Papworth and Lovis (Nominated Underwriter of Syndicate No.37)
  (Unreported, March 31, 1998), CC (Cambridge) [*Ex rel*. Beardsells Solicitors,
  Vienna House, 281 Wellington Road South, Stockport, Cheshire] . . . . *Digested*, 98/**445**
De Rothschild v. Bell (A Bankrupt) see Rothschild v. Bell (A Bankrupt)
De Rothschild v. Secretary of State for Transport see R. v. Secretary of State for
  Transport Ex p. De Rothschild
De Serville v. Argee Ltd [2001] N.P.C. 82; (2001) 82 P. & C.R. D12, Ch D
De Smet v. Gold (1999) 99(1) Q.R. 5, CC (Brighton) . . . . *Digested*, 98/**1559**
De Sousa v. British South Africa Co see British South Africa Co v. Companhia de
  Mocambique
De Souza v. Automobile Association [1986] I.C.R. 514; [1986] I.R.L.R. 103; (1986) 83
  L.S.G. 288; (1986) 130 S.J. 110, CA; affirming [1985] I.R.L.R. 87; (1984) 81
  L.S.G. 3336, EAT . . . . *Digested*, 86/**1213**:
                       Applied, 01/2297: *Considered*, 98/2180
De Souza v. Automobile Association (Leave to Appeal) [1998] 2 C.M.L.R. 40, CA
De Vereeniging ter Bevordering van de Belangen des Boekhandels v. Eldi Records BV
  (106/79) [1980] E.C.R. 1137; [1980] 3 C.M.L.R. 719; [1981] F.S.R. 124, ECJ
  (2nd Chamber) [1980] 1 C.M.L.R. 584; [1980] F.S.R. 279, RB (Amsterdam) . . . *Digested*, 81/**1143**:
                                            Applied, 98/708
De Villalba v. Adex International Ltd (1999-2000) 2 I.T.E.L.R. 624, HC (BVI)
De Vitre v. Betts see Neilson v. Betts
De Weer v. Belgium see Deweer v. Belgium (A/35)
DE&ES Bauunternehmung GmbH v. Finanzamt Bergheim (C275/97) [1999] E.C.R. I-
  5331; [2000] B.C.C. 757; [2001] 1 C.M.L.R. 45, ECJ . . . . *Digested*, 00/**1**
Deadman v. Southwark LBC (2001) 33 H.L.R. 75; (2000) 97(40) L.S.G. 41; *Times*,
  August 31, 2000, CA; affirming (Unreported, October 22, 1998), CC (Lambeth)
  [*Ex rel*. Robert Bowker, Barrister, Taylor Building, Temple, London] . . . . *Digested*, 00/**3145**
Deaduck Ltd (In Liquidation), Re; *sub nom* Baker v. Secretary of State for Trade and
  Industry [2000] 1 B.C.L.C. 148, Ch D . . . . *Digested*, 00/**657**

Deakin v. Faulding (No.2); Specialist Group International Ltd v. Deakin (2001) 98(35) L.S.G. 32; *Times*, August 29, 2001, Ch D . . . . *Digested*, 01/**748**

Dealy v. Secretary of State for the Environment, Transport and the Regions [1999] J.P.L. 273, QBD . . . . *Digested*, 99/**4216**

Dean v. Allin & Watts [2001] EWCA Civ 758; [2001] 2 Lloyd's Rep. 249; [2001] Lloyd's Rep. P.N. 605; [2001] P.N.L.R. 39; (2001) 98(31) L.S.G. 36; (2001) 145 S.J.L.B. 157; *Times*, June 28, 2001, CA; reversing [2000] Lloyd's Rep. P.N. 469; [2000] P.N.L.R. 690; [2000] E.G.C.S. 5, Ch D . . . . *Digested*, 01/**4538**

Dean v. Dean (Appeal against Striking Out) (2000) 80 P. & C.R. 457; [2000] E.G.C.S. 76; (2000) 80 P. & C.R. D42, CA; reversing Ch. 1996-D-No.3694, Ch D . . . . *Digested*, 01/**4865**

Dean v. Griffin (Unreported, June 7, 2000), CC (Macclesfield) [*Ex rel.* Thorneycroft & Co Solicitors, Bridge Street Mills, Bridge Street, Macclesfield] . . . . *Digested*, 00/**443**

Dean v. Wundpets Ltd (Unreported, September 16, 1999), CC (Halifax) [*Ex rel.* Rhodes Thain & Collinson Solicitors, 27 Harrison Road, Halifax] . . . . *Digested*, 00/**1739**

Dean and Canons of Windsor v. Customs and Excise Commissioners [1999] B.V.C. 2010, V&DTr . . . . *Digested*, 99/**4974**: *Considered*, 01/5563

Dean & Dyball Construction Ltd v. Ministry of Defence see Scott Wilson Kirkpatrick & Partners v. Ministry of Defence

Dean's Rag Book Co Ltd v. Pomerantz & Sons (1930) 47 R.P.C. 485 . . . . *Applied*, 00/3696

Deanby Investment Co Ltd v. Brennan (Inspector of Taxes) see Brennan (Inspector of Taxes) v. Deanby Investment Co Ltd

Deanplan Ltd v. Mahmoud [1993] Ch. 151; [1992] 3 W.L.R. 467; [1992] 3 All E.R. 945; (1992) 64 P. & C.R. 409; [1992] 1 E.G.L.R. 79; [1992] 16 E.G. 100; [1992] E.G.C.S. 30; [1992] N.P.C. 31; *Times*, March 3, 1992, Ch D . . . . *Digested*, 92/**497**: *Considered*, 94/2795, 95/2844, 96/3515, 96/3518: *Doubted*, 00/3884

Dear v. Reeves [2001] EWCA Civ 277; [2001] 3 W.L.R. 662; [2001] 1 B.C.L.C. 643; [2001] B.P.I.R. 577; (2001) 98(18) L.S.G. 44; *Times*, March 22, 2001; *Independent*, April 9, 2001 (C.S), CA . . . . *Digested*, 01/**3735**

Dearman v. Simpletest Ltd, *Times*, February 14, 2000, CA . . . . *Digested*, 00/**497**

Debboub (alias Husseini Ali) v. France (37786/97) (2001) 33 E.H.R.R. 54, ECHR

Debenhams v. Westminster City Council [1987] A.C. 396; [1986] 3 W.L.R. 1063; [1987] 1 All E.R. 51; 85 L.G.R. 190; [1987] 1 E.G.L.R. 248; [1986] R.A. 249; (1987) 151 L.G. Rev. 188; (1987) 84 L.S.G. 341; (1986) 136 N.L.J. 1185; (1986) 130 S.J. 985, HL; reversing [1986] 1 E.G.L.R. 189; (1986) 278 E.G. 974; [1986] R.A. 114; [1986] J.P.L. 671; (1986) 83 L.S.G. 1479; (1986) 130 S.J. 483, CA; affirming [1985] 1 E.G.L.R. 159; (1985) 274 E.G. 826; [1985] R.A. 265, QBD . . . . *Digested*, 87/**3195**: *Applied*, 90/4416, 92/4288, 93/3900: *Considered*, 00/4473: *Followed*, 99/4327

Debrah v. Secretary of State for the Home Department [1998] Imm. A.R. 511; [1998] I.N.L.R. 383, IAT . . . . *Digested*, 99/**3175**

Debtor (No.20 of 1953), Re; *sub nom* Debtor, Ex p. v. Scott [1954] 1 W.L.R. 1190; [1954] 3 All E.R. 74; 98 S.J. 589, CA; reversing [1954] 1 W.L.R. 393; [1954] 1 All E.R. 454; 98 S.J. 127, Ch D . . . . *Digested*, 54/**222**

Debtor (No.644 of 1969), Re [2001] B.P.I.R. 901 (Note), CA

Debtor (No.59 of 1987), Re, *Independent*, February 1, 1988, Ch D . . . . *Considered*, 98/322

Debtor (No.2389 of 1989), Re [1991] Ch. 326; [1991] 2 W.L.R. 578; [1990] 3 All E.R. 984, Ch D . . . . *Digested*, 91/**262**: *Considered*, 94/2624, 95/424: *Disapproved*, 99/3247

Debtor (No.27 of 1990), Re see Brillouet v. Hachette Magazines Ltd

Debtor (No.222 of 1990), Ex p. Bank of Ireland, Re [1992] B.C.L.C. 137; *Times*, June 27, 1991 . . . . *Digested*, 92/**2565**: *Considered*, 00/3473

Debtor (No.259 of 1990), Re [1992] 1 W.L.R. 226; [1992] 1 All E.R. 641, Ch D . . . . . . *Digested*, 92/**234**: *Followed*, 98/3354

Debtor (No.340 of 1992), Re; *sub nom* Debtor v. First National Commercial Bank Plc [1996] 2 All E.R. 211; (1995) 92(15) L.S.G. 40; (1995) 139 S.J.L.B. 82; *Times*, March 6, 1995, CA; affirming [1994] 3 All E.R. 269; [1994] 2 B.C.L.C. 171; *Times*, July 19, 1993; *Independent*, September 13, 1993 (C.S.), Ch D . . . . *Digested*, 95/**420**: *Distinguished*, 01/3737

Debtor (No.367 of 1992), Re; *sub nom* Allen, Re [1998] B.P.I.R. 319, Ch D

Debtor (No.32 of 1993), Re [1994] 1 W.L.R. 899; [1994] B.C.C. 438; *Times*, March 1, 1994, Ch D . . . . *Digested*, 94/**284**: *Applied*, 00/3456, 01/3725

Debtor (No.162 of 1993) (No.2), Re see Doorbar v. Alltime Securities Ltd (No.2)

Debtor (No.6349 of 1994), Re; *sub nom* Inland Revenue Commissioners v. Debtor [1996] B.P.I.R. 271, Ch D . . . . *Applied*, 01/3725

Debtor (No.223 SD of 1995), Re see Laurier v. United Overseas Bank Ltd

Debtor (No.574 of 1995), Re; *sub nom* National Westminster Bank Plc v. Scher [1998] 2 B.C.L.C. 124; [1998] B.P.I.R. 224, Ch D . . . . *Digested*, 98/**3347**

Debtor (No.488-IO of 1996), Re; *sub nom* M (A Debtor), Re; J (A Debtor), Re; JP *v.* Debtor [1999] 2 B.C.L.C. 571; [1999] 1 F.L.R. 926; [1999] 2 F.C.R. 637; [1999] Fam. Law 293; *Times*, February 10, 1999, Ch D .... *Digested*, 99/**3242**: *Applied*, 00/3448

Debtor (No.90 of 1997), Re, *Times*, July 1, 1998, Ch D .... *Digested*, 98/**3343**

Debtor (No.169 of 1997), Re (Unreported, June 10, 1998), CC (Southend) [*Ex rel.* Richard Evans, Barrister, 5 Paper Buildings, Temple, London] .... *Digested*, 98/**3284**

Debtor (No.303 of 1997), Re see Hurst *v.* Bennett (No.1)

Debtor (No.325 of 1997), Re; *sub nom* Bhogal *v.* Cheema [1999] B.P.I.R. 13; [1999] L. & T.R. 59; [1998] 2 E.G.L.R. 50; [1998] 29 E.G. 117, Ch D .... *Digested*, 98/**3650**

Debtor (No.510 of 1997), Re see Oben *v.* Blackman

Debtor (No.620 of 1997), Re see Liveras *v.* Debtor (No.620 of 1997)

Debtor (No.17 of 1998), Re see Ashurst *v.* Coe

Debtor (No.46 of 1998), Re, *Times*, July 20, 1998, Ch D .... *Digested*, 98/**3271**

Debtor (No.5795 of 1998), Re see Customs and Excise Commissioners *v.* Dougall

Debtor (No.SD8/9 of 1998), Re see Salvidge *v.* Hussein

Debtor (No.87 of 1999), Re; *sub nom* Debtor *v.* Johnston [2000] B.P.I.R. 589; (2000) 97(7) L.S.G. 40; *Times*, February 14, 2000, Ch D .... *Digested*, 00/**3486**: *Considered*, 01/3780

Debtor (No.101 of 1999), Re (No.1) [2001] 1 B.C.L.C. 54; [2000] B.P.I.R. 998; (2000) 97(30) L.S.G. 40; *Times*, July 27, 2000, Ch D .... *Digested*, 00/**3473**

Debtor (No.101 of 1999), Re (No.2) [2001] B.P.I.R. 996, Ch D

Debtor (No.2672 of 2000), Re (2000) 97(42) L.S.G. 43; *Times*, December 5, 2000, Ch D .... *Digested*, 01/**596**

Debtor (No.50A-SD-1995), Re; *sub nom* Jelly *v.* All Type Roofing Co [1997] Ch. 310; [1997] 2 W.L.R. 57; [1997] 2 All E.R. 789; [1997] B.C.C. 465; [1997] 1 B.C.L.C. 280; [1996] B.P.I.R. 565, Ch D .... *Digested*, 97/**3021**: *Followed*, 00/3487

Debtor (No.638-IO-1994), Re (1999) 96(3) L.S.G. 31; *Times*, December 3, 1998, Ch D *Digested*, 99/**3346**

Debtor (No.647-SD-1999), Re see Bruton *v.* Inland Revenue Commissioners

Debtor (No.68-SD-1997), Re; *sub nom* Galloppa *v.* Galloppa [1998] 4 All E.R. 779; [1999] B.P.I.R. 352, Ch D .... *Digested*, 99/**3761**

Debtor (No.27/SD/1998), Re, *Independent*, March 15, 1999 (C.S.), Ch D

Debtor (No.544/SD/98), Re [2000] B.C.L.C. 103, CA; affirming *Independent*, July 5, 1999 (C.S.), Ch D .... *Digested*, 00/**3447**

Debtor *v.* First National Commercial Bank Plc see Debtor (No.340 of 1992), Re

Debtor *v.* Inland Revenue Commissioners see Wilkinson *v.* Inland Revenue Commissioners

Debtor *v.* Johnston see Debtor (No.87 of 1999), Re

Debtor Management Ltd, Re see Austintel Ltd, Re

Debtor, Ex p. *v.* Scott see Debtor (No.20 of 1953), Re

Debtors (Nos.4449 and 4450 of 1998), Re; *sub nom* McAllister *v.* Society of Lloyd's [1999] 1 All E.R. (Comm) 149; [1999] B.P.I.R. 548, Ch D .... *Digested*, 99/**3255**

Debtors (No.13-MISC-2000 and No.14-MISC-2000), Re (2000) 97(16) L.S.G. 40; (2000) 144 S.J.L.B. 174; *Times*, April 10, 2000; *Independent*, May 15, 2000 (C.S.), Ch D .... *Digested*, 00/**372**

Decal Co Ltd *v.* Customs and Excise Commissioners [2000] S.T.I. 75, V&DTr

Decker *v.* Caisse de Maladie des Employes Prives (C120/95); Kohll *v.* Union des Caisses de Maladie (C158/96) [1998] All E.R. (E.C.) 673; [1998] E.C.R. I-1831; [1998] 2 C.M.L.R. 879; (1999) 48 B.M.L.R. 32, ECJ .... *Digested*, 98/**4517**

Decon Laboratories Ltd *v.* Fred Baker Scientific Ltd [2001] E.T.M.R. 46; [2001] R.P.C. 17; (2001) 24(2) I.P.D. 24007; *Times*, February 28, 2001, Ch D .... *Digested*, 01/**4009**

Decorum Investments Ltd *v.* Atkin (The Elena G) [2001] 2 Lloyd's Rep. 378, QBD (Comm Ct) .... *Digested*, 01/**3826**

Dee *v.* Durham CC (Unreported, February 12, 2001), CC (Newcastle) [*Ex rel.* Dickinson Dees Solicitors, St Ann's Wharf, 112 Quayside, Newcastle upon Tyne] . *Digested*, 01/**4497**

Deemand Shipping Co Ltd *v.* Ministry of Food, Bangladesh (The Lendoudis Evangelos II); *sub nom* Demand Shipping Co Ltd *v.* Ministry of Food, Bangladesh (The Lendoudis Evangelos II) [2001] 2 Lloyd's Rep. 304; [2001] C.L.C. 1598, QBD (Comm Ct) .... *Digested*, 01/**4953**

Deen-Koroma *v.* Immigration Appeal Tribunal see R. *v.* Immigration Appeal Tribunal Ex p. Deen-Koroma

Deeny *v.* Gooda Walker Ltd (Agency Agreement: Construction) see Arbuthnott *v.* Fagan

Deeny *v.* Gooda Walker Ltd (Duty of Care) see Henderson *v.* Merrett Syndicates Ltd (No.1)

Deeny v. Gooda Walker Ltd (No.2); Albert v. Gooda Walker Ltd; Brownrigg v. Gooda Walker Ltd [1996] 1 W.L.R. 426; [1996] 1 All E.R. 933; [1996] L.R.L.R. 109; [1996] S.T.C. 299; [1996] 5 Re. L.R. 43; (1996) 93(15) L.S.G. 32; (1996) 146 N.L.J. 369; (1996) 140 S.J.L.B. 92; *Times*, March 8, 1996, HL; affirming [1996] S.T.C. 39; [1995] 4 Re. L.R. 361; 68 T.C. 481; (1995) 92(40) L.S.G. 22; (1995) 139 S.J.L.B. 214; *Times*, October 19, 1995; *Independent*, October 18, 1995, CA; affirming [1995] S.T.C. 439; 68 T.C. 458; [1995] S.T.I. 85; *Times*, January 26, 1995; *Independent*, February 27, 1995 (C.S.), QBD (Comm Ct) . . . .   *Digested*, 96/**3377**:   *Considered*, 98/4410, 99/3404: *Distinguished*, 96/3591

Deepak Fertilisers & Petrochemical Corp v. Davy McKee (London) Ltd; *sub nom* Deepak Fertilisers & Petrochemicals Corp v. ICI Chemicals & Polymers Ltd [1999] 1 All E.R. (Comm.) 69; [1999] 1 Lloyd's Rep. 387; [1999] B.L.R. 41; (1999) 1 T.C.L.R. 200; 62 Con. L.R. 86, CA; reversing in part [1998] 2 Lloyd's Rep. 139, QBD (Comm Ct) . . . .   *Digested*, 99/**796**:   *Applied*, 00/869

Deepak Fertilisers & Petrochemicals Corp v. ICI Chemicals & Polymers Ltd see Deepak Fertilisers & Petrochemical Corp v. Davy McKee (London) Ltd

Defective Horticultural Peat, Re [2000] E.C.C. 276, BGH (Ger)

Definitely Maybe (Touring) Ltd v. Marck Lieberberg Konzertagentur GmbH (No.1) see Definitely Maybe (Touring) Ltd v. Marek Lieberberg Konzertagentur GmbH (No.1)

Definitely Maybe (Touring) Ltd v. Marck Lieberberg Konzertagentur GmbH (No.2) see Definitely Maybe (Touring) Ltd v. Marek Lieberberg Konzertagentur GmbH (No.2)

Definitely Maybe (Touring) Ltd v. Marek Lieberberg Konzertagentur GmbH (No.1); *sub nom* Definitely Maybe (Touring) Ltd v. Marck Lieberberg Konzertagentur GmbH (No.1) [2001] I.L.Pr. 30, QBD . . . .   *Digested*, 01/**796**:   *Subsequent proceedings*, 01/797

Definitely Maybe (Touring) Ltd v. Marek Lieberberg Konzertagentur GmbH (No.2); *sub nom* Definitely Maybe (Touring) Ltd v. Marck Lieberberg Konzertagentur GmbH (No.2) [2001] 1 W.L.R. 1745; [2001] 4 All E.R. 283; [2001] 2 All E.R. (Comm) 1; [2001] 2 Lloyd's Rep. 455; *Daily Telegraph*, April 10, 2001, QBD (Comm Ct) . . . .   *Digested*, 01/**797**:   *Previous proceedings*, 01/796

Defrenne v. SA Belge d'Exploitation de la Navigation Aerienne (SABENA) (C43/75) see Defrenne v. SABENA (C43/75)

Defrenne v. SABENA (C166/99) [2000] E.C.R. I-6155; [2000] Pens. L.R. 261, ECJ (5th Chamber) . . . .   *Digested*, 00/**2163**

Defrenne v. SABENA (C43/75); *sub nom* Defrenne v. SA Belge d'Exploitation de la Navigation Aerienne (SABENA) (C43/75) [1981] 1 All E.R. 122; [1976] E.C.R. 455; [1976] 2 C.M.L.R. 98; [1976] I.C.R. 547, ECJ . . . .   *Digested*, 76/**1164**:   *Applied*, 81/1065, 87/1322, 90/1915, 98/4133, 00/2387:   *Considered*, 96/4609, 97/2214, 97/5378, 99/2226, 01/2279:   *Distinguished*, 00/2168: *Followed*, 96/2547, 96/2577

DEG-Deutsche Investitions und Entwicklungsgesellschaft mbH v. Koshy see Deutsche Investitions und Entwicklungsgesellschaft mbH (DEG) v. Koshy

DEG-Deutsche Investitions und Entwiclungsesellschaft mbH see DEG-Deutsche Investitions- und Entwicklungsgesellschaft mbH v. Koshy (Account of Profits: Limitations)

DEG-Deutsche Investitions- und Entwicklungsgesellschaft mbH v. Koshy (Account of Profits: Limitations); *sub nom* DEG-Deutsche Investitions und Entwiclungsesellschaft mbH; Gwembe Valley Development Co Ltd (In Receivership) v. Koshy *Times*, December 10, 2001, Ch D

DEG-Deutsche Investitions-Und Entwicklungsgesellschaft MbH v. Koshy see Gwembe Valley Development Co Ltd (In Receivership) v. Koshy (Costs)

Dehwari v. Netherlands (37014/97) (2001) 29 E.H.R.R. CD74, ECHR

Dekker v. Purvis (Unreported, January 4, 1999), CC (Portsmouth) [*Ex rel.* David Allan, Pupil Barrister, 9 Bedford Row, London] . . . .   *Digested*, 99/**534**

Del Commercial Properties Inc v. Commissioner of Internal Revenue Service 3 I.T.L. Rep. 860, US Ct

Del Commercial Properties Ltd v. Commissioner of Internal Revenue 2 I.T.L. Rep. 606, US Ct

Delaney v. RJ Staples (t/a De Montfort Recruitment) [1992] 1 A.C. 687; [1992] 2 W.L.R. 451; [1992] 1 All E.R. 944; [1992] I.C.R. 483; [1992] I.R.L.R. 191; (1992) 142 N.L.J. 384; *Times*, March 16, 1992; *Independent*, March 13, 1992, HL; affirming [1991] 2 Q.B. 47; [1991] 2 W.L.R. 627; [1991] 1 All E.R. 609; [1991] I.C.R. 331; [1991] I.R.L.R. 112; (1991) 141 N.L.J. 581, CA; reversing in part [1990] I.C.R. 364; [1990] I.R.L.R. 86; (1990) 87(10) L.S.G. 35, EAT . . . .   *Digested*, 92/**2028**:   *Applied*, 95/1981, 95/2040, 97/2294, 98/2208, 98/2245:   *Considered*, 00/2247, 01/5274: *Distinguished*, 96/2675, 98/5827:   *Followed*, 99/2017: *Not followed*, 90/1985, 91/1709

Delaney v. Secretary of State for the Environment, Transport and the Regions [2000] P.L.C.R. 40, CA . . . .   *Digested*, 00/**4440**

Delaware Mansions Ltd v. Westminster City Council; *sub nom* Flecksun Ltd v. Westminster City Council [2001] UKHL 55; [2001] 3 W.L.R. 1007; [2001] 4 All E.R. 737; 79 Con. L.R. 39; [2001] 44 E.G.C.S. 150; (2001) 98(45) L.S.G. 26; (2001) 151 N.L.J. 1611; (2001) 145 S.J.L.B. 259; [2001] N.P.C. 151; *Times*, October 26, 2001; *Independent*, December 17, 2001 (C.S), HL; affirming [2000] B.L.R. 1; 68 Con. L.R. 172; (2000) 32 H.L.R. 664; [1999] 3 E.G.L.R. 68; [1999] 46 E.G. 194; [1999] E.G.C.S. 110; [1999] N.P.C. 96; *Times*, August 25, 1999 ; *Independent*, October 18, 1999 (C.S.), CA; reversing 88 B.L.R. 99; 61 Con. L.R. 10; [1998] E.G.C.S. 48; [1998] N.P.C. 39; [1998] N.P.C. 43, QBD (OR). . . . . *Digested*, 01/**4548**
Delcourt v. Belgium (A/11) (1979-80) 1 E.H.R.R. 355, ECHR . . . . *Applied*, 98/3112,
                              98/3122, 98/3142, 98/3143: *Considered*, 00/6100
Delfin International (SA) Ltd (No.1), Re see Delfin Marketing (UK) Ltd, Re
Delfin International (SA) Ltd (No.2), Re see Secretary of State for Trade and Industry v. Delfin International (SA) Ltd
Delfin Marketing (UK) Ltd, Re; Delfin International (SA) Ltd (No.1), Re [2000] 1 B.C.L.C. 71, Ch D (Companies Ct) . . . . *Digested*, 99/**589**
Deliege v. Ligue Francophone de Judo et Disciplines Associees ASBL (C51/96) [2000] E.C.R. I-2549; *Times*, April 19, 2000, ECJ . . . . *Digested*, 00/**4049**
Delimitis v. Henninger Brau AG (C234/89) [1991] E.C.R. I-935; [1992] 5 C.M.L.R. 210; *Times*, March 18, 1991, ECJ . . . . *Digested*, 91/**3797**:
               Applied, 99/667, 99/688: *Considered*, 96/2806, 97/855, 97/861, 99/680,
                             99/686, 99/687, 00/707: *Followed*, 98/708
Dellow's Will Trusts, Re; *sub nom* Lloyds Bank v. Institute of Cancer Research [1964] 1 W.L.R. 451; [1964] 1 All E.R. 771; 108 S.J. 156, Ch D . . . . *Digested*, 64/**3808**:
                                             Considered, 01/2549
Deloitte & Touche AG v. Johnson [1999] 1 W.L.R. 1605; [1999] B.C.C. 992; [2000] 1 B.C.L.C. 485; (1998-99) 1 I.T.E.L.R. 771; *Times*, June 16, 1999, PC (CI) . . . . *Digested*, 99/**3314**:
                                             Considered, 01/3751
Delta Civil Engineering Co Ltd v. Dredging & Construction Co Ltd (No.1) see Dredging & Construction Co Ltd v. Delta Civil Engineering Co Ltd (No.1)
Delta Crompton Cables Ltd v. Copper Cable Co Ltd [1997] F.S.R. 850; (1997) 20(9) I.P.D. 20084, Pat Ct. . . . . *Digested*, 98/**440**
Delta Design and Engineering Ltd v. Secretary of State for the Environment, Transport and the Regions; Delta Design and Engineering Ltd v. South Cambridgeshire DC (2000) 80 P. & C.R. 76; [2000] 4 P.L.R. 1; [2000] J.P.L. 726, CA; reversing [1999] J.P.L. 612; [1998] E.G.C.S. 143, QBD . . . . *Digested*, 00/**4418**
Delta Design and Engineering Ltd v. South Cambridgeshire DC see Delta Design and Engineering Ltd v. Secretary of State for the Environment, Transport and the Regions
Delta Vale Properties Ltd v. Mills [1990] 1 W.L.R. 445; [1990] 2 All E.R. 176; (1990) 87(9) L.S.G. 44; (1990) 140 N.L.J. 290; (1990) 134 S.J. 316, CA . . . . *Digested*, 90/**685**:
                               Applied, 97/3256: *Considered*, 98/3598
Demaglass Holdings Ltd (Winding Up Petition: Application for Adjournment), Re [2001] 2 B.C.L.C. 633, Ch D
Deman v. Queen's University of Belfast; *sub nom* D v. Queen's University of Belfast [1996] N.I. 349; [1997] E.L.R. 431; *Times*, December 16, 1996, CA (NI)
Demand Shipping Co Ltd v. Ministry of Food, Bangladesh (The Lendoudis Evangelos II) see Deemand Shipping Co Ltd v. Ministry of Food, Bangladesh (The Lendoudis Evangelos II)
Demenagements-Manutention Transport SA (DMT) (C256/97), Re [1999] All E.R. (EC) 601; [1999] E.C.R. I-3913; [1999] 3 C.M.L.R. 1; [1999] C.E.C. 299, ECJ (6th Chamber) . . . . *Digested*, 99/**706**:
                                             Applied, 01/5346
Demetri v. Westminster City Council [2000] 1 W.L.R. 772; (2000) 32 H.L.R. 470; (1999) 96(45) L.S.G. 32; (1999) 143 S.J.L.B. 277; *Times*, November 11, 1999, CA . . . . *Digested*, 99/**3022**
Demetriou v. Panayi (Unreported, May 20, 1998), CC (Clerkenwell) [*Ex rel.* Andrzej Bojarski, Barrister, 36 Bedford Row, London, WC1R 4JH] . . . . *Digested*, 98/**3597**
Demir v. Turkey (21380/93) (2001) 33 E.H.R.R. 43; [1998] H.R.C.D. 860, ECHR
Demirel v. Stadt Schwabisch Gmund (C12/86) [1987] E.C.R. 3719; [1989] 1 C.M.L.R. 421, ECJ. . . . . *Digested*, 90/**2040**:
                Applied, 96/3277: *Considered*, 96/3292: *Followed*, 90/2151, 91/1996,
                                                 00/2380
Demirkaya v. Secretary of State for the Home Department [1999] Imm. A.R. 498; [1999] I.N.L.R. 441; *Times*, June 29, 1999, CA . . . . *Digested*, 99/**3173**
Demirtepe v. France (2001) 31 E.H.R.R. 28, ECHR. . . . . *Digested*, 01/**3583**
Demite Ltd v. Protec Health Ltd [1998] B.C.C. 638; *Times*, July 25, 1998, Ch D . . . . . . *Digested*, 98/**704**
DEMON ALE Trade Mark [2000] R.P.C. 345, Appointed Person. . . . . *Digested*, 00/**3713**:
                                             Applied, 01/4062
Den Danske Bank A/S v. Skipton Building Society [1998] 1 E.G.L.R. 140, QBD (Comm Ct) . . . . *Digested*, 98/**2490**

Den Norske Bank ASA v. Antonatos [1999] Q.B. 271; [1998] 3 W.L.R. 711; [1998] 3 All
E.R. 74; [1998] Lloyd's Rep. Bank. 253, CA . . . . *Digested,* 98/**325**:
                              Considered, 99/323: *Referred to,* 00/488
Denard v. Burton Retail Ltd see Surrey CC v. Burton Retail Ltd
Denbighshire CC v. Edwards (2000) 15 P.A.D. 139, Planning Inspector
Denby v. English & Scottish Maritime Insurance Co Ltd; *sub nom* Denby v. MJ
Marchant; Yasuda Fire & Marine Insurance Co of Europe Ltd v. Lloyd's
Underwriting Syndicate No.229 [1998] C.L.C. 870; [1998] Lloyd's Rep. I.R.
343; *Times,* March 16, 1998, CA; reversing [1996] L.R.L.R. 301, QBD (Comm
Ct) . . . . *Digested,* 98/**3403**
Denby v. MJ Marchant see Denby v. English & Scottish Maritime Insurance Co Ltd
Dench v. Flynn & Partners [1998] I.R.L.R. 653, CA . . . . *Digested,* 98/**2224**
Dendy v. Evans [1910] 1 K.B. 263, CA; affirming [1909] 2 K.B. 894, KBD . . . . *Applied,* 65/2230,
                                 80/1578: *Followed,* 98/3652
Denekamp v. Pearce (Inspector of Taxes) [1998] S.T.C. 1120; 71 T.C. 213; [1998] B.T.C.
413, Ch D . . . . *Digested,* 99/**4654**
Denham v. Nowman [2001] Lloyd's Rep. P.N. 623, Ch D
Denis Hilton Ltd, Re; *sub nom* Dennis Hilton Ltd, Re; D Hilton Ltd, Re *Times,* July 4,
2001, Ch D . . . . *Digested,* 01/**708**
Denkavit Nederland BV v. Commission of the European Communities (T20/99) [2000]
E.C.R. II-3011; [2000] 3 C.M.L.R. 1014, CFI (1st Chamber) . . . . *Digested,* 01/**2502**
Denley's Trust Deed, Re; *sub nom* Holman v. HH Martyn & Co [1969] 1 Ch. 373; [1968]
3 W.L.R. 457; [1968] 3 All E.R. 65; 112 S.J. 673, Ch D . . . . *Digested,* 68/**3586**:
                     Applied, 76/2499, 01/5501: *Considered,* 86/2804
Denman v. Brise [1949] 1 K.B. 22; [1948] 2 All E.R. 141; 64 T.L.R. 335; [1948] L.J.R.
1388; 92 S.J. 349, CA . . . . *Digested,* 47-51/**8852**:
                     Applied, 56/9081: *Distinguished,* 98/3663
Denman College v. Customs and Excise Commissioners [1998] B.V.C. 2259; [1998] V.
& D.R. 399, V&DTr. . . . . *Digested,* 98/**4943**
Denmark v. Commission of the European Communities (C289/96); Germany v.
Commission of the European Communities (C293/96); France v. Commission of
the European Communities (C299/96) [1999] E.C.R. I-1541; [2001] 1 C.M.L.R.
14; [1999] E.T.M.R. 478; (1999) 22(12) I.P.D. 22121; *Times,* April 17, 1999, ECJ . *Digested,* 99/**2575**
Denmark v. Commission of the European Communities (C348/85) [1987] E.C.R.
5225, ECJ . . . . *Followed,* 00/170
Denmark v. Turkey (34382/97) (2001) 29 E.H.R.R. CD35, ECHR
Denner AG v. Rivella AG [2001] E.T.M.R. CN10, BG (Swi)
Dennis (Deceased), Re; *sub nom* Dennis v. Lloyds Bank Plc [1981] 2 All E.R. 140; 124
S.J. 885; *Times,* November 14, 1980, Ch D . . . . *Digested,* 81/**2887**:
                                  Considered, 00/2528
Dennis v. Dennis [2000] Fam. 163; [2000] 3 W.L.R. 1443; [2000] 2 F.L.R. 231;
[2000] 2 F.C.R. 108; [2000] Fam. Law 605, Fam Div . . . . *Digested,* 00/**2500**
Dennis v. Lloyds Bank Plc see Dennis (Deceased), Re
Dennis Hilton Ltd, Re see Denis Hilton Ltd, Re
Dennison v. Krasner see Krasner v. Dennison
Denny v. Yeldon [1995] 3 All E.R. 624; [1995] 1 B.C.L.C. 560; [1995] P.L.R. 37, Ch D . *Digested,* 96/**4650**:
                                         Approved, 99/3274
Dent v. Davis Blank Furniss [2001] Lloyd's Rep. P.N. 534, Ch D . . . . *Digested,* 01/**4532**
Dent v. National Farmers Union, *Independent,* July 5, 1999 (C.S.), Ch D
Denton v. Chief Adjudication Officer [1999] E.L.R. 86, CA . . . . *Digested,* 99/**4577**
Denton v. Lambson Aviation Ltd (Unreported, July 17, 2000), CC (Central London)
[*Ex rel.* Robert Weir, Barrister, Devereux Chambers, Devereux Court, London] . . *Digested,* 00/**368**
Denty v. Hussein (1999) 96(24) L.S.G. 40, Ch D
Department of Health v. Pensions Ombudsman [2000] 1 W.L.R. 561; [1998] 4 All E.R.
508; [1998] O.P.L.R. 179; (1998) 95(37) L.S.G. 37; *Times,* August 25, 1998;
Independent, October 6, 1998, CA . . . . *Digested,* 98/**4130**
Department of Health and Social Services for Northern Ireland v. McMenamin see
Department of Health and Social Services for Northern Ireland v. Rodgers
Department of Health and Social Services for Northern Ireland v. Rodgers; Department of
Health and Social Services for Northern Ireland v. McMenamin [1997] N.I. 101,
CA (NI) . . . . *Digested,* 99/**5179**
Department of National Heritage v. Steensen Varming Mulcahy 60 Con. L.R. 33, QBD
(OR) . . . . *Digested,* 99/**804**
Department of the Environment v. Royal Insurance Plc (1987) 54 P. & C.R. 26; [1987]
1 E.G.L.R. 83; (1987) 282 E.G. 208, Ch D . . . . *Digested,* 87/**2134**:
                   Considered, 00/3886: *Disapproved,* 98/3603
Department of the Environment for Northern Ireland v. Bone (Unreported, September 15,
1993), CA (NI) . . . . *Considered,* 98/5133
Department of Trade and Industry v. Cedenio [2001] EWHC Admin 150; *Times,* March
22, 2001, QBD (Admin Ct) . . . . *Digested,* 01/**1008**
Department of Trade and Industry v. St Christopher Motorists Association Ltd [1974] 1
W.L.R. 99; [1974] 1 All E.R. 395; [1974] 1 Lloyd's Rep. 17; (1973) 117 S.J. 873,
Ch D . . . . *Digested,* 74/**1900**:
            Applied, 99/3411: *Cited,* 00/2567: *Considered,* 79/1505, 96/3571

Department of Transport v. Caird Environmental Services Ltd [1999] R.T.R. 137, QBD .. *Digested,* 98/**4710**
Department of Transport v. Chris Smaller (Transport) Ltd [1989] A.C. 1197; [1989] 2
   W.L.R. 578; [1989] 1 All E.R. 897; (1989) 139 N.L.J. 363; (1989) 133 S.J. 361,
   HL . . . . *Digested,* 89/**3071**:
                     Applied, 92/3605, 95/2963: *Considered,* 91/2841, 92/3456, 93/3334,
                                        93/3339, 94/3788, 94/3904, 98/619
Department of Transport v. Murfitts Transport Ltd see Murfitts Transport Ltd v.
   Department of Transport
Deposit Guarantee Directive (C233/94), Re see Germany v. European Parliament (C233/
   94)
Depot Corner Car Sales v. Customs and Excise Commissioners [2001] S.T.I. 339, V&DTr
Derby v. Scottish Equitable Plc see Scottish Equitable Plc v. Derby
Derby & Co Ltd v. Weldon (Documents: Disclosure), *Times,* October 20, 1988 ;
   Independent, November 2, 1988 ; *Independent,* October 31, 1988 (C.S.), Ch D . *Applied,* 99/339
Derby & Co Ltd v. Weldon (No.8) [1991] 1 W.L.R. 73; [1990] 3 All E.R. 762; (1991)
   88(2) L.S.G. 33; (1991) 135 S.J. 84; *Times,* August 29, 1990, CA . . . . *Digested,* 91/**2861**:
                                           Considered, 01/3851
Derby Daily Telegraph Ltd v. Pensions Ombudsman; Derby Daily Telegraph Ltd v.
   Thompson [1999] I.C.R. 1057; [1999] I.R.L.R. 476; [1999] O.P.L.R. 125; *Times,*
   May 12, 1999, Ch D . . . . *Digested,* 99/**4121**
Derby Daily Telegraph Ltd v. Thompson see Derby Daily Telegraph Ltd v. Pensions
   Ombudsman
Derby Resources AG v. Blue Corinth Marine Co Ltd (The Athenian Harmony) (No.1)
   [1998] 2 Lloyd's Rep. 410; [1998] C.L.C. 1159, QBD (Comm Ct) . . . . *Digested,* 98/**4774**
Derby Resources AG v. Blue Corinth Marine Co Ltd (The Athenian Harmony) (No.2)
   [1998] 2 Lloyd's Rep. 425, QBD (Comm Ct) . . . . *Digested,* 98/**1434**
Derby Specialist Fabrication Ltd v. Burton [2001] 2 All E.R. 840; [2001] I.C.R. 833;
   [2001] I.R.L.R. 69, EAT . . . . *Digested,* 01/**2295**
Derby YMCA v. Customs and Excise Commissioners [2001] S.T.I. 527, V&DTr
Derbyshire, The, *Times,* October 28, 1999, QBD (Adm Ct) . . . . *Digested,* 99/**4410**
Derbyshire v. Mackman see O'Reilly v. Mackman
Derbyshire CC v. Times Newspapers Ltd [1993] A.C. 534; [1993] 2 W.L.R. 449;
   [1993] 1 All E.R. 1011; 91 L.G.R. 179; (1993) 143 N.L.J. 283; (1993) 137 S.J.L.B.
   52; *Times,* February 19, 1993; *Independent,* February 19, 1993; *Guardian,*
   February 19, 1993, HL; affirming [1992] Q.B. 770; [1992] 3 W.L.R. 28; [1992] 3
   All E.R. 65; 90 L.G.R. 221; (1992) 4 Admin. L.R. 469; [1992] C.O.D. 305;
   (1992) 142 N.L.J. 276; *Times,* February 20, 1992; *Independent,* February 21,
   1992; *Guardian,* March 11, 1992, CA; reversing [1991] 4 All E.R. 795; *Times,* April
   8, 1991; *Independent,* March 21, 1991; *Guardian,* March 19, 1991; *Daily
   Telegraph,* April 15, 1991, QBD . . . . *Digested,* 93/**2581**:
                 Cited, 93/3803, 94/4290: *Considered,* 93/2579, 97/2035, 97/2036,
                                 98/1776: *Followed,* 97/2040, 01/1835
Derbyshire Dales DC v. Birch Plc (2000) 15 P.A.D. 739, Planning Inspector
Derouiche v. Secretary of State for the Home Department [1998] I.N.L.R. 286, IAT . . . . *Digested,* 98/**3165**
Derry v. Ministry of Defence (1999) 11 Admin. L.R. 758; [1999] P.I.Q.R. P204; (1999)
   49 B.M.L.R. 62; (1999) 96(16) L.S.G. 36; *Times,* March 30, 1999, CA; affirming
   (1999) 11 Admin. L.R. 1; *Times,* June 8, 1998, QBD . . . . *Digested,* 99/**261**
Derry v. Peek; *sub nom* Peek v. Derry (1889) L.R. 14 App. Cas. 337; (1889) 5 T.L.R.
   625, HL; reversing (1888) L.R. 37 Ch. D. 541, CA . . . . *Applied,* 47-51/86,
                     47-51/6584, 52/35, 58/771, 59/431, 75/641, 79/2432, 89/3077, 90/120,
             90/2829, 90/3805, 91/119, 97/4940, 01/3726: *Considered,* 69/882, 70/1881,
                      71/8000, 93/80, 93/1398: *Referred to,* 79/1884
Derwent DC v. Orange Personal Communications Services Ltd (1999) 14 P.A.D. 521,
   Planning Inspector
Desai v. Entry Clearance Officer; *sub nom* Desai v. Secretary of State for the Home
   Department [2000] I.N.L.R. 10, CA . . . . *Digested,* 00/**3359**
Desai v. Patel (Unreported, August 31, 2000), CC (Ilford) [*Ex rel.* Badhams Thompson
   Solicitors, 95 Aldwych, London] . . . . *Digested,* 00/**426**
Desai v. Secretary of State for the Home Department see Desai v. Entry Clearance
   Officer
Desborough v. Carlisle City Council (Unreported, January 22, 1990) [*Ex rel.* Brian
   Langstaff, Barrister] . . . . *Digested,* 90/**1634**:
                                       Considered, 00/1592
Deschamps v. Miller [1908] 1 Ch. 856, Ch D . . . . *Considered,* 98/768
Desert Sun Loan Corp v. Hill [1996] 2 All E.R. 847; [1996] 5 Bank. L.R. 98; [1996]
   C.L.C. 1132; [1996] I.L.Pr. 406; (1996) 140 S.J.L.B. 64; *Times,* February 21,
   1996, CA . . . . *Digested,* 96/**1102**:
                                       Considered, 00/785
Deshormes v. Commission of the European Communities (C17/78) [1979] E.C.R. 189,
   ECJ . . . . *Digested,* 80/**1188**:
                                     Distinguished, 00/713
Desi Ltd v. Spreckley see Worldpro Software Ltd v. Desi Ltd
Desi Ltd v. Worldpro Software Ltd see Worldpro Software Ltd v. Desi Ltd
Designation Fees, Re (G4/98) [2001] E.P.O.R. 42, EPO (Enlarged Bd App) . . . . *Digested,* 01/**3916**

Designers Guild Ltd v. Russell Williams (Textiles) Ltd (t/a Washington DC) (Cross
  Examination) [1998] F.S.R. 275, Ch D . . . .   *Digested*, 98/**3428**
Designers Guild Ltd v. Russell Williams (Textiles) Ltd (t/a Washington DC) [2000] 1
  W.L.R. 2416; [2001] 1 All E.R. 700; [2001] E.C.D.R. 10; [2001] F.S.R. 11; (2001)
  98(3) L.S.G. 42; (2000) 144 S.J.L.B. 290; *Times*, November 28, 2000, HL;
  reversing [2000] F.S.R. 121; (1999) 22(7) I.P.D. 22067, CA; reversing [1998]
  F.S.R. 803; (1998) 21(6) I.P.D. 21064, Ch D . . . .   *Digested*, 01/**3859**
Desouza v. Waterlow [1999] R.T.R. 71; [1998] P.I.Q.R. P87; *Independent*, October 27,
  1997 (C.S.), CA . . . .   *Digested*, 97/**3166**
Desquenne et Giral UK Ltd v. Richardson see Richardson v. Desquenne et Giral UK Ltd
Detente Ltd (Matter of Representation), Re see Smouha Family Trust, Re
Deumeland v. Germany (A/120) (1986) 8 E.H.R.R. 448, ECHR . . . .   *Applied*, 98/3135,
                                                                                                            98/3139
Deutsche Bahn AG v. Commission of the European Communities (C436/97 P); *sub
  nom* Deutsche Bahn AG v. Commission of the European Communities (T229/
  94) [1999] E.C.R. I-2387; [1999] 5 C.M.L.R. 776, ECJ (5th Chamber); affirming
  [1997] E.C.R. II-1689; [1998] 4 C.M.L.R. 220, CFI (1st Chamber) . . . .   *Digested*, 99/**658**
Deutsche Bahn AG v. Commission of the European Communities (T229/94) see
  Deutsche Bahn AG v. Commission of the European Communities (C436/97 P)
Deutsche Investitions und Entwicklungsgesellschaft mbH (DEG) v. Koshy; *sub nom*
  DEG-Deutsche Investitions und Entwicklungsgesellschaft mbH v. Koshy;
  Gwembe Valley Development Co Ltd v. Koshy [2001] EWCA Civ 79; [2001] 3
  All E.R. 878; [2001] C.P.L.R. 212; (2001) 151 N.L.J. 171; (2001) 145 S.J.L.B. 36;
  Times, February 20, 2001; *Independent*, February 6, 2001, CA; reversing
  (2000) 97(2) L.S.G. 29; (2000) 144 S.J.L.B. 42; *Times*, January 19, 2000, Ch D
  . . . .   *Digested*, 01/**4251**
Deutsche Krankenversicherung AG (DKV) v. Office for Harmonisation in the Internal
  Market (Trade Marks and Designs) (OHIM) (T359/99) [2001] E.C.R. II-1645;
  [2001] E.T.M.R. 81, CFI . . . .   *Digested*, 01/**4006**
Deutsche Milchkontor GmbH v. Germany (C205/82) [1983] E.C.R. 2633; [1984] 3
  C.M.L.R. 586, ECJ . . . .   *Digested*, 85/**1299**:
                                                                                      Applied, 88/1528, 96/5713, 99/2279
Deutsche Ost-Afrika Linie GmbH v. Legent Maritime Co Ltd [1998] 2 Lloyd's Rep. 71,
  QBD (Comm Ct) . . . .   *Digested*, 98/**4399**
Deutsche Post AG v. Citicorp Kartenservice GmbH (C148/97) see Deutsche Post AG v.
  Gesellschaft fur Zahlungssysteme mbH (C147/97)
Deutsche Post AG v. Gesellschaft fur Zahlungssysteme mbH (C147/97); Deutsche Post
  AG v. Citicorp Kartenservice GmbH (C148/97) [2000] E.C.R. I-825; [2000] 4
  C.M.L.R. 838; *Times*, March 15, 2000, ECJ . . . .   *Digested*, 00/**4556**
Deutsche Post AG v. International Express Carriers Conference (C428/98) [2000]
  E.C.R. I-3061; [2001] 4 C.M.L.R. 3, ECJ (4th Chamber) . . . .   *Digested*, 01/**4793**
Deutsche Post AG v. Sievers (C270/97) see Schroder v. Deutsche Telekom AG (C50/
  96)
Deutsche Renault AG v. Audi AG (C317/91) [1993] E.C.R. I-6227; [1995] 1 C.M.L.R.
  461; [1995] F.S.R. 738; *Financial Times*, December 7, 1993, ECJ . . . .   *Digested*, 96/**5709**:
                                                                                                            Referred to, 99/3572
Deutsche Ruckversicherung AG v. La Fondaria Assicurazioni SpA (formerly Societa
  Italia di Assicurazioni SpA) [2001] 2 Lloyd's Rep. 621, QBD (Comm Ct) . . . . . .   *Digested*, 01/**3807**
Deutsche Ruckversicherung AG v. Walbrook Insurance Co Ltd see Group Josi Re Co
  SA v. Walbrook Insurance Co Ltd
Deutsche Schachtbau- und Tiefbohrgesellschaft mbH v. Ras Al-Khaimah National Oil
  Co; *sub nom* DST v. Rakoil; Deutsche Schachtbau- und Tiefbohrgesellschaft
  mbH v. Ras Al-Khaimah National Oil Co (Garnishee Proceedings); Deutsche
  Schachtbau- und Tiefbohrgesellschaft mbH v. Shell International Petroleum Co
  Ltd (Nos.1 and 2) [1990] 1 A.C. 295; [1988] 3 W.L.R. 230; [1988] 2 All E.R.
  833; [1988] 2 Lloyd's Rep. 293; (1988) 85(28) L.S.G. 45; *Times*, June 25, 1988;
  Independent, June 24, 1988; *Financial Times*, June 28, 1988, HL; reversing
  [1987] 3 W.L.R. 1023; [1987] 2 All E.R. 769; [1987] 2 Lloyd's Rep. 246; [1987]
  1 F.T.L.R. 17; (1987) 131 S.J. 1486, CA. . . . .   *Digested*, 88/**2855**:
                                                                        Applied, 01/561; *Considered*, 98/523: *Previous proceedings*, 87/3013
Deutsche Schachtbau- und Tiefbohrgesellschaft mbH v. Shell International Petroleum Co
  Ltd (Nos.1 and 2) see Deutsche Schachtbau und Tiefbohrgesellschaft mbH v.
  Ras Al-Khaimah National Oil Co
Deutsche Telekom AG v. Schroder (C50/96) see Schroder v. Deutsche Telekom AG
  (C50/96)
Deutsche Telekom AG v. Vick (C234/96) see Schroder v. Deutsche Telekom AG (C50/
  96)
Deutsche Telekom AG's Trade Mark [2000] E.T.M.R. 939 (Note), OHIM (Cancellation Div)
Deutscher Teeverband EV's Application for Cancellation [2000] E.T.M.R. 546, OHIM
  (Cancellation Div) . . . .   *Digested*, 00/**3730**
Devanthery v. Jean-Pierre Niederhauser & Associates (BGE 125 III 328) [2001]
  E.C.D.R. CN2, BG (Swi)
Devine v. Designer Flowers Wholesale Florist Sundries [1993] I.R.L.R. 517, EAT . . . . . .   *Digested*, 94/**2011**:
                                                                                                            Cited, 00/6218

Devine v. Jefferys [2001] Lloyd's Rep. P.N. 301; [2001] P.N.L.R. 16, QBD (Merc Ct)
Devlin v. Baslington see Giles v. Thompson
Devlin v. United Kingdom (29545/95), *Times*, November 9, 2001, ECHR . . . .   *Digested*, 01/**5876**
Devon CC v. DB Cars Ltd [2001] EWHC Admin 521; (2001) 165 J.P.N. 945; *Daily
    Telegraph*, July 3, 2001, QBD (Admin Ct)
Devon CC v. George see R. v. Devon CC Ex p. George
Devonshire Reid Properties Ltd v. Trenaman [1997] 1 E.G.L.R. 45; [1997] 20 E.G. 148,
    Lands Tr . . . .   *Digested*, 97/**3271**:
                                                                                       Distinguished, 99/3697
Dew Group Ltd v. Costain Building & Civil Engineering Ltd 1997 S.L.T. 1020; 84 B.L.R.
    101; *Times*, December 20, 1996, OH . . . .   *Digested*, 97/**5724**
Dew Pitchmastic Plc v. Birse Construction Ltd 78 Con. L.R. 162, QBD (T&CC)
Dew Pitchmastic Plc v. Birse Construction Ltd (Compromise); *sub nom* Pitchmastic Plc
    v. Birse Construction Ltd (2000) 97(23) L.S.G. 41; *Times*, June 21, 2000, QBD .   *Digested*, 00/**540**
Deweer v. Belgium (A/35); *sub nom* De Weer v. Belgium [1980] E.C.C. 169; (1979-
    80) 2 E.H.R.R. 439, ECHR; affirming [1979] E.C.C. 83, Eur Comm HR . . . .   *Applied*, 98/3150,
                                                                                                    00/1104
DEWERT/Six-month period (G02/99) [2001] E.P.O.R. 34, EPO (Enlarged Bd App)
Dexter Ltd (In Administrative Receivership) v. Harley, *Times*, April 2, 2001, Ch D . . . . . .   *Digested*, 01/**810**
DFC Financial Services Ltd v. Samuel [1990] 3 N.Z.L.R. 156, CA (NZ)   *Followed*, 00/3481
DG Finance Ltd v. Scott and Eagle Star Insurance Co Ltd [1999] Lloyd's Rep. I.R. 387,
    CA . . . .   *Digested*, 00/**508**:
                                                                                       Considered, 97/4516
Dhak v. Insurance Co of North America (UK) Ltd [1996] 1 W.L.R. 936; [1996] 2 All
    E.R. 609; [1996] 1 Lloyd's Rep. 632; [1996] 5 Re. L.R. 83; [1997] P.I.Q.R. P101;
    (1996) 146 N.L.J. 247; *Times*, February 8, 1996; *Independent*, February 20,
    1996; *Lloyd's List*, May 9, 1996 (I.D.), CA . . . .   *Digested*, 96/**3542**:
                                                                        Applied, 97/6171: *Distinguished*, 99/5404
Dharamshi v. Dharamshi [2001] 1 F.L.R. 736; [2001] 1 F.C.R. 492; [2001] Fam. Law
    98, CA . . . .   *Digested*, 01/**2634**
Dhatt v. McDonald's Hamburgers [1991] 1 W.L.R. 527; [1991] 3 All E.R. 692; [1991]
    I.C.R. 226; [1991] I.R.L.R. 130; *Times*, November 13, 1990, CA; affirming [1988]
    I.C.R. 591; (1988) 85(20) L.S.G. 33, EAT . . . .   *Digested*, 92/**1955**:
                                                                                       Distinguished, 99/2098
Dhesi v. Chief Constable of the West Midlands, *Times*, May 9, 2000, CA . . . .   *Digested*, 00/**951**
Dhingra v. Dhingra (1999-2000) 2 I.T.E.L.R. 262, CA
Dhokia v. Secretary of State for the Environment, Transport and the Regions [2001]
    P.L.C.R. 9; [2001] J.P.L. 232 (Note), QBD . . . .   *Digested*, 01/**4747**
Dhutia v. Hazelhurst, CC (Maidstone) [*Ex rel.* Nigel Ffitch, Barrister, Phoenix
    Chambers, Gray's Inn chambers, Gray's Inn, London] . . . .   *Digested*, 01/**1622**
DI BV v. HS [2000] E.N.P.R. 194, OLG (Dusseldorf)
Di Luca v. Juraise (Springs) Ltd (2000) 79 P. & C.R. 193; [1998] 2 E.G.L.R. 125;
    [1998] 18 E.G. 131; (1998) 75 P. & C.R. D15, CA. . . . .   *Digested*, 98/**4371**
Diab v. Countrywide Rentals Plc, *Independent*, November 5, 2001 (C.S.), Ch D
Diageo Plc v. Zuccarini (t/a Cupcake Patrol) [2001] E.T.M.R. 45, Arbitration . . . .   *Digested*, 01/**3870**
Dialworth Ltd v. TG Organisation Europe Ltd (1998) 75 P. & C.R. 147, CA. . . . .   *Digested*, 98/**3654**
Diamalt AG v. Hauptzollamt Itzehoe (C16/77) see Firma Albert Ruckdeschel & Co v.
    Hauptzollamt Hamburg-St Annen (C117/76)
Diamant v. Morris Greenberg Ltd [2001] E.C.C. 54, Cass (F)
Diamantis v. Greece (C373/97) [2001] 3 C.M.L.R. 41, ECJ (6th Chamber)
Diamond v. Wylie [2000] 6 Q.R. 7, CC (Nuneaton) [*Ex rel.* JS Boora, Barrister, 24 The
    Ropewalk, Nottingham] . . . .   *Digested*, 00/**1560**
DIANA, PRINCESS OF WALES Trade Mark [2001] E.T.M.R. 25, TMR . . . .   *Digested*, 01/**4050**
Dianoor Jewels Ltd (Set Aside), Re [2001] 1 B.C.L.C. 450; [2001] B.P.I.R. 234, Ch D .   *Digested*, 01/**3707**:
                                                                                       Subsequent proceedings, 01/2637
Dibbs v. Campbell (1988) 20 H.L.R. 374; [1988] 2 E.G.L.R. 122; [1988] 30 E.G. 49,
    CA . . . .   *Digested*, 89/**2202**:
                                                                        Approved, 96/3837: *Considered*, 98/3682
Dible v. BBC see Attorney General v. BBC
Dibor v. Kentish Bus & Coach Co Ltd (Unreported, September 7, 1998), CC
    (Maidstone) [*Ex rel.* Tim Kevan, Barrister, 1 Temple Gardens, Temple, London] . . .   *Digested*, 98/**458**
Dicker v. Scammell see Scammell v. Dicker
Dickerson v. United States 8 B.H.R.C. 407, US Ct
Dickins v. Morgan (Unreported, January 10, 2000), CC (Shrewsbury) [*Ex rel.* Deni
    Matthews, Barrister, 8 Fountain Court, Steelhouse Lane, Birmingham] . . . .   *Digested*, 00/**4208**
Dickinson v. Hameed (Unreported, April 24, 2001), CC (Salford) [*Ex rel.* Peter Rickson
    & Partners, Solicitors, The Stock Exchange Building, 4 Norfolk Street,
    Manchester] . . . .   *Digested*, 01/**613**
Dicksmith (Manufacturing) Ltd (In Liquidation), Re [1999] 2 B.C.L.C. 686; *Times*, July 7,
    1999, Ch D . . . .   *Digested*, 99/**3313**
Dickson v. Atkins [1972] R.T.R. 209; [1972] Crim. L.R. 185, DC . . . .   *Digested*, 72/**3007**:
                                                                                       Considered, 98/1027

Dickson v. Bridge Hotel (1999) 99(6) Q.R. 7, CC (Whitehaven) [*Ex rel.* William Waldron, Barrister, Exchange Chambers, Pearl Assurance House, Derby Square, Liverpool] . . . . *Digested,* 99/**1564**
Dickson v. Pharmaceutical Society of Great Britain see Pharmaceutical Society of Great Britain v. Dickson
Didierlaurent v. Sanchez [2001] E.C.C. 44, Cass (F)
Diego Cali & Figli Srl v. Servizi Ecologici Porto di Genova SpA (SEPG) (C343/95) [1997] E.C.R. I-1547; [1997] 5 C.M.L.R. 484; [1997] C.E.C. 1183; [1998] Env. L.R. 31, ECJ . . . . *Digested,* 98/**717**
Diennet v. France (A/315-B) (1996) 21 E.H.R.R. 554, ECHR . . . . *Digested,* 96/**3151**:
Applied, 98/3131, 98/3149: *Distinguished,* 98/3127
Dietz v. Lennig Chemicals Ltd [1969] 1 A.C. 170; [1967] 3 W.L.R. 165; [1967] 2 All E.R. 282; (1967) 111 S.J. 354, HL; affirming [1966] 1 W.L.R. 1349; [1966] 2 All E.R. 962; 110 S.J. 448, CA. . . . . *Digested,* 67/**3106**:
Distinguished, 99/1422
Dietz v. Stichting Thuiszorg Rotterdam (C435/93) [1996] E.C.R. I-5223; [1997] 1 C.M.L.R. 199; [1996] I.R.L.R. 692; [1996] O.P.L.R. 385, ECJ (6th Chamber) . . *Digested,* 97/**2214**:
Followed, 98/4133

Diggen's Application, Re see Diggens Application, Re
Diggens Application, Re; *sub nom* Diggen's Application, Re [2000] 3 E.G.L.R. 87; [2000] 48 E.G. 121, LandsTr . . . . *Digested,* 01/**4885**
Digital Equipment Co Ltd v. Clements (No.1) [1996] I.C.R. 829; [1996] I.R.L.R. 513, EAT . . . . *Digested,* 96/**2664**
Digital Equipment Co Ltd v. Clements (No.2) [1998] I.C.R. 258; [1998] I.R.L.R. 134; (1998) 95(3) L.S.G. 24; *Times,* January 2, 1998, CA; reversing [1997] I.C.R. 237; [1997] I.R.L.R. 140; *Times,* December 11, 1996, EAT. . . . . *Digested,* 98/**2229**
Digital Equipment Co Ltd v. Hampshire CC see Capital and Counties Plc v. Hampshire CC
Digital Integration Ltd v. Software 2000 [1998] E.C.C. 289, CA
Dilexport Srl v. Amministrazione delle Finanze dello Stato (C343/96) [2000] All E.R. (EC) 600; [1999] E.C.R. I-579; [2000] 3 C.M.L.R. 791, ECJ (5th Chamber) . . . *Digested,* 00/**2406**
Dilieto v. Ealing LBC [2000] Q.B. 381; [1998] 3 W.L.R. 1403; [1998] 2 All E.R. 885; [1998] 2 P.L.R. 98; [1998] P.L.C.R. 212; *Times,* April 10, 1998, QBD . . . . *Digested,* 98/**4203**
Dillenkofer v. Germany (C178/94) [1997] Q.B. 259; [1997] 2 W.L.R. 253; [1996] All E.R. (E.C.) 917; [1996] E.C.R. I-4845; [1996] 3 C.M.L.R. 469; [1997] I.R.L.R. 60; *Times,* October 14, 1996, ECJ . . . . *Digested,* 96/**2802**:
Applied, 99/5274, 01/5581: *Followed,* 97/4672

Dillon v. Dillon (1998) 76 P. & C.R. D23, CA
Dillon v. ICI Plc (Unreported, July 27, 2001), QBD [*Ex rel.* Mark Beesley, Barrister, 7 Harrington Street, Liverpool] . . . . *Digested,* 01/**572**
Dimelow v. Gradwell (Unreported, June 21, 2000), CC (Bradford) [*Ex rel.* Dermot Hughes, Barrister, 26 Paradise Square, Sheffield] . . . . *Digested,* 00/**1687**
Dimond v. Lovell [2000] 2 W.L.R. 1121; [2000] 2 All E.R. 897; [2000] R.T.R. 243; [2000] C.C.L.R. 57; 2000 Rep. L.R. 62; (2000) 97(22) L.S.G. 47; (2000) 150 N.L.J. 740; *Times,* May 12, 2000; *Independent,* May 17, 2000, HL; affirming [2000] Q.B. 216; [1999] 3 W.L.R. 561; [1999] 3 All E.R. 1; [1999] R.T.R. 297; [1999] C.C.L.R. 46; (1999) 96(21) L.S.G. 40; (1999) 149 N.L.J. 681; (1999) 143 S.J.L.B. 181; *Times,* May 3, 1999, CA; reversing (Unreported, May 1, 1998), CC (Sheffield) . . . . *Digested,* 00/**2566**:
Applied, 99/2470, 99/2471, 99/2475, 99/2478, 99/2481, 00/2570, 00/2587, 01/881, 01/900, 01/1527: *Cited,* 99/2458, 99/2461, 99/2476, 99/2499, 00/425, 00/2574, 00/2580, 00/2592, 00/2593, 01/896, 01/899, 01/3830: *Considered,* 99/532, 99/2453, 99/2454, 99/2459, 99/2460, 99/2466, 99/2467, 99/2468, 99/2496, 00/311, 01/885, 01/888, 01/890, 01/898: *Distinguished,* 99/535, 99/2452, 99/2482, 99/2491, 99/2504, 00/2578, 00/2585, 00/2597, 01/893, 01/894: *Followed,* 99/2463, 99/2489, 00/2565, 00/2577, 00/2579, 01/657, 01/887, 01/901: *Referred to,* 99/2451, 99/2464, 99/2465, 99/2472, 99/2473, 99/2474, 99/2483, 99/2485, 99/2487, 99/2490, 00/2562, 00/2589, 01/1542

Dimskal Shipping Co SA v. International Transport Workers Federation (The Evia Luck) (No.2) [1992] 2 A.C. 152; [1991] 3 W.L.R. 875; [1991] 4 All E.R. 871; [1992] 1 Lloyd's Rep. 115; [1992] I.C.R. 37; [1992] I.R.L.R. 78; *Times,* November 8, 1991; *Independent,* January 15, 1992; *Financial Times,* November 12, 1991, HL; affirming [1990] 1 Lloyd's Rep. 319; [1990] I.C.R. 694; [1990] I.R.L.R. 102, CA; reversing [1989] 1 Lloyd's Rep. 166, QBD (Comm Ct) . . . . *Digested,* 92/**1916**:
Applied, 99/4477: *Considered,* 99/847
Din v. Carrington Viyella (Jersey Kapwood) [1982] I.C.R. 256; [1982] I.R.L.R. 281, EAT . . . . *Digested,* 82/**1055**:
Applied, 98/2122

Din (Taj) *v.* Wandsworth LBC [1983] 1 A.C. 657; [1981] 3 W.L.R. 918; [1981] 3 All
    E.R. 881; (1981-82) 1 H.L.R. 73; 78 L.G.R. 113; 125 S.J. 828; *Times,* November
    27, 1981, HL; reversing *Times,* June 30, 1981, CA. . . . .   *Digested,* 82/**1472**:
              Applied, 94/2345, 95/2580, 96/3049, 98/3000: *Approved,* 97/2666:
              Considered, 84/1638, 85/1615, 85/1621, 86/1621, 87/1878, 93/2064:
              Distinguished, 84/1641: *Followed,* 97/2665, 98/3011
Dinaro Ltd (t/a Fairway Lodge) *v.* Customs and Excise Commissioners [2001] S.T.I.
    1063, V&DTr
Dineley *v.* Kaye (Unreported, June 24, 1999), CC (Bury) [*Ex rel.* Marc Willems,
    Barrister, Cobden House Chambers, 19 Quay Street, Manchester] . . . .   *Digested,* 99/**2485**:
              Approved, 99/2472, 99/2490: *Followed,* 99/2459
Dingley *v.* Bromley LBC (Unreported, January 28, 2000), CC (Bromley) [*Ex rel.*
    Stephen Warner, Barrister, Hardwicke Building, Lincoln's Inn, London] . . . .   *Digested,* 00/**4244**
Dingley *v.* Bromley LBC (Quantum) [2000] 5 Q.R. 7, CC (Bromley) [*Ex rel.* Stephen
    Warner, Barrister, Hardwicke Building, Lincoln's Inn, London] . . . .   *Digested,* 00/**1631**
Dingley *v.* Chief Constable of Strathclyde (No.1) 2000 S.C. (H.L.) 77; 2000 S.C.L.R.
    309; (2000) 55 B.M.L.R. 1; 2000 G.W.D. 11-401, HL; affirming 1998 S.C. 548;
    1998 G.W.D. 13-677, 1 Div; reversing 1997 S.L.T. 880; 1997 Rep. L.R. (Quantum)
    1, OH . . . .   *Digested,* 00/**6579**
Dinkgreve *v.* Internationale Nederlanden Bank NV [1998] E.C.C. 178, HR (NL)
Dino Music Ltd, Re [2000] B.C.C. 696, Ch D . . . .   *Digested,* 00/**3431**
Dinter GmbH *v.* Hauptzollamt Bad Reichenhall (C81/92) [1993] E.C.R. I-4601, ECJ
    (4th Chamber) [1993] E.C.R. I-4601, AGO. . . . .   *Digested,* 94/**4758**:
              Followed, 00/2336
Diocese of Southwark *v.* Coker; *sub nom* Coker *v.* Diocese of Southwark [1998] I.C.R.
    140; (1997) 94(29) L.S.G. 29; (1997) 141 S.J.L.B. 169; *Times,* July 17, 1997,
    CA; affirming [1996] I.C.R. 896; *Times,* April 4, 1996, EAT; reversing [1995]
    I.C.R. 563; *Independent,* March 16, 1995, IT . . . .   *Digested,* 97/**2293**
DIP SpA *v.* Comune di Bassano del Grappa (C140/94); Lidl Italia Srl *v.* Comune di
    Chioggia (C141/94); Lingral Srl *v.* Comune di Chioggia (C142/94) [1995] E.C.R.
    I-3257; [1996] 4 C.M.L.R. 157, ECJ (2nd Chamber) . . . .   *Digested,* 96/**1045**:
              Applied, 98/2325
DIPL. ING/Storage Space for Liquids (T892/90) [2000] E.P.O.R. 331, EPO (Technical Bd
    App). . . . .   *Digested,* 00/**3642**
DIR International Film Srl *v.* Commission of the European Communities (C164/98 P)
    [2000] E.C.R. I-447; [2000] 1 C.M.L.R. 619, ECJ (6th Chamber) . . . .   *Digested,* 00/**2342**
Direccion General de Defensa de la Competencia *v.* Asociacion Espanola de Banca
    Privada (C67/91) [1992] E.C.R. I-4785; *Times,* November 26, 1992; *Financial
    Times,* July 28, 1992, ECJ . . . .   *Digested,* 92/**4706**:
              Followed, 01/768
Direccion General de Defensa de la Competencia (Spanish Competition Directorate) *v.*
    Ocaso SA [2001] E.C.C. 3, Trib Sup (Sp)
Direct Energy Marketing Ltd *v.* Hillson [2000] I.L.Pr. 102, QB (Alta) . . . .   *Digested,* 00/**742**
Direct Marketing Bureau *v.* Customs and Excise Commissioners [2000] S.T.I. 1454,
    V&DTr
Director General of Fair Trading *v.* First National Bank Plc [2001] UKHL 52; [2001] 3
    W.L.R. 1297; [2001] 2 All E.R. (Comm) 1000; (2001) 151 N.L.J. 1610; *Times,*
    November 1, 2001; *Daily Telegraph,* October 30, 2001, HL; reversing [2000] Q.B.
    672; [2000] 2 W.L.R. 1353; [2000] 2 All E.R. (Comm) 759; [2000] 1 All E.R. (Comm)
    371; [2000] Lloyd's Rep. Bank. 130; [2000] C.C.L.R. 31; (2000) 97(7) L.S.G.
    39; *Times,* March 14, 2000, CA; reversing [2000] 1 W.L.R. 98; [2000] 1 All E.R.
    240; [1999] Lloyd's Rep. Bank. 427; [2000] E.C.C. 169; (1999) 18 Tr. L.R.
    245; *Times,* September 21, 1999 ; *Independent,* November 8, 1999 (C.S.), Ch D .   *Digested,* 01/**910**:
              Applied, 01/3832
Director General of Fair Trading *v.* Pioneer Concrete (UK) Ltd; *sub nom* Supply of Ready
    Mixed Concrete (No.2), Re [1995] 1 A.C. 456; [1994] 3 W.L.R. 1249; [1995] 1
    All E.R. 135; [1995] I.C.R. 25; (1995) 92(1) L.S.G. 37; (1995) 145 N.L.J. 17;
    [1995] 139 S.J.L.B. 14; *Times,* November 25, 1994; *Independent,* November 30,
    1994, HL; reversing [1994] I.C.R. 57; [1994] I.R.L.R. 21; (1994) 13 Tr. L.R. 266;
    Times, July 8, 1993; *Independent,* July 14, 1993, CA . . . .   *Digested,* 95/**576**:
              Cited, 00/980: *Followed,* 99/3316
Director General of Fair Trading *v.* Proprietary Association of Great Britain; *sub nom*
    Medicaments and Related Classes of Goods (No.2), Re; Director General of Fair
    Trading *v.* Propriety Association of Great Britain [2001] 1 W.L.R. 700; [2001]
    U.K.C.L.R. 550; [2001] I.C.R. 564; [2001] H.R.L.R. 17; [2001] U.K.H.R.R. 429;
    (2001) 3 L.G.L.R. 32; (2001) 98(7) L.S.G. 40; (2001) 151 N.L.J. 17; (2001) 145
    S.J.L.B. 29; *Times,* February 2, 2001; *Independent,* January 12, 2001, CA
    (2001) 98(2) L.S.G. 41; (2000) 144 S.J.L.B. 289, RPC. . . . .   *Digested,* 01/**14**:
              Applied, 01/692, 01/856, 01/857
Director General of Fair Trading *v.* Proprietary Association of Great Britain (Costs); *sub
    nom* Medicaments and Related Classes of Goods (No.4), Re [2001] EWCA Civ
    1217; (2001) 98(34) L.S.G. 37; (2001) 151 N.L.J. 1372; (2001) 145 S.J.L.B.
    209; *Times,* August 7, 2001; *Daily Telegraph,* September 11, 2001, CA . . . .   *Digested,* 01/**84**

Director General of Fair Trading v. Propriety Association of Great Britain see Director
    General of Fair Trading v. Proprietary Association of Great Britain
Director of Buildings and Lands v. Shun Fung Ironworks Ltd [1995] 2 A.C. 111; [1995] 2
    W.L.R. 404; [1995] 1 All E.R. 846; [1995] 1 E.G.L.R. 19; [1995] 19 E.G. 147;
    [1995] R.V.R. 124; [1995] E.G.C.S. 36; (1995) 145 N.L.J. 379; (1995) 139
    S.J.L.B. 85; *Times*, February 27, 1995, PC (HK) . . . .   *Digested*, 95/**664**:
                                     Disapproved, 01/4662: *Followed*, 98/231
Discain Project Services Ltd v. Opecprime Development Ltd (Application for Summary
    Judgment) [2000] B.L.R. 402; (2001) 3 T.C.L.R. 16, QBD (T&CC) . . . .   *Digested*, 01/**861**
Discain Project Services Ltd v. Opecprime Development Ltd (Bias); *sub nom* Discain
    Project Services Ltd v. Opecprime Development Ltd (No.2) [2001] B.L.R. 285;
    (2001) 3 T.C.L.R. 17; 80 Con. L.R. 95, QBD (T&CC) . . . .   *Digested*, 01/**857**
Discain Project Services Ltd v. Opecprime Development Ltd (No.2) see Discain Project
    Services Ltd v. Opecprime Development Ltd (Bias)
Discontinued Models of White Goods, Re [2001] E.C.C. 41, BGH (Ger)
Discovery Communications Inc v. Discovery FM Ltd 2000 S.C. 69; 2000 S.L.T. 212;
    [2000] E.T.M.R. 516; 1999 G.W.D. 35-1722; *Times*, January 25, 2000, Ex Div;
    reversing 1999 G.W.D. 35-1723, OH . . . .   *Digested*, 00/**6521**
Discovision Associates v. Disctronics (UK) Ltd (Action for Infringement) (1998)
    21 (10) I.P.D. 21103, Pat Ct
Discovision Associates v. Disctronics (UK) Ltd (Application to Discontinue Claim)
    [1999] F.S.R. 196, Pat Ct . . . .   *Digested*, 99/**3499**
DISCOVISION Trade Mark [1977] R.P.C. 594, Ch D . . . .   *Digested*, 78/**2979**:
                                          Followed, 98/3498: *Referred to*, 94/4498
Disley v. Levine (t/a Airtrak Levine Paragliding) [2001] EWCA Civ 1087; [2001] C.L.C.
    1694; (2001) 98(33) L.S.G. 29; *Times*, August 29, 2001; *Independent*, October
    29, 2001 (C.S), CA; affirming [2001] P.I.Q.R. P10; *Daily Telegraph*, December
    12, 2000, QBD . . . .   *Digested*, 01/**5386**
Disney v. Plummer [1991] F.S.R. 165 (Note), CA . . . .   *Referred to*, 99/3497
Disparagement of Trade Marks (No.1) [1994] GRUR 808 . . . .   *Distinguished*,
                                                 99/3548
Disparagement of Trade Marks (No.2) [1995] GRUR 57 . . . .   *Distinguished*,
                                                 99/3548
Distribution of Newspapers, Re [1998] E.C.C. 12, BGH (Ger)
Ditta v. Duport Harper Foundries Ltd (Unreported, January 8, 1998), CC (Reading)
    [*Ex rel*. Edge & Ellison Solicitors, Rutland House, 148 Edmund Street,
    Birmingham] . . . .   *Digested*, 98/**336**
Divine-Bortey v. Brent LBC [1998] I.C.R. 886; [1998] I.R.L.R. 525; (1998) 95(22)
    L.S.G. 29; (1998) 142 S.J.L.B. 152; *Times*, May 20, 1998; *Independent*, May 20,
    1998, CA . . . .   *Digested*, 98/**2163**:
                                           Distinguished, 00/2236
Divisional Application (J08/98) [2000] E.P.O.R. 283, EPO (Legal Bd App) . . . .   *Digested*, 00/**3619**
Dixon v. Allgood (Leave to Appeal: Notices), *Times*, April 30, 1999; *Independent*, May
    4, 1999, CA . . . .   *Digested*, 99/**356**
Dixon v. Moon [2001] 6 Q.R. 12, CC (Weymouth) [*Ex rel*. Shoosmiths Solicitors] . . . . .   *Digested*, 01/**1654**
Dixon v. Stenor [1973] I.C.R. 157; [1973] I.R.L.R. 28; (1973) 8 I.T.R. 141, NIRC . . . .   *Digested*, 73/**1141**:
                                Considered, 88/1318, 89/1477: *Distinguished*, 01/2349
Dixon-Vincent, Re (Unreported, August 19, 1997), CC (Watford) [*Ex rel*. Joel CT Kendall,
    Barrister, 12 King's Bench Walk, Temple, London, EC4Y 7EL] . . . .   *Digested*, 97/**958**:
                                                 Followed, 98/1461
Dixons Group Plc v. Murray-Obodynski; *sub nom* Dixons Group Plc v. Murray-Oboynski
    86 B.L.R. 16, QBD (OR) . . . .   *Digested*, 98/**701**:
                                                 Applied, 00/815
Dixons Group Plc v. Murray-Oboynski (Breach of Warranties); *sub nom* Dixons Group
    Plc v. Murray-Oboynski (Breach of Warranties) [2000] 1 B.C.L.C. 1, CA . . . .   *Digested*, 00/**681**
Dixons Group Plc v. Murray-Obodynski see Dixons Group Plc v. Murray-Obodynski
Dixons Group Plc v. Murray-Oboynski (Breach of Warranties) see Dixons Group Plc v.
    Murray-Obodynski (Breach of Warranties)
Djengiz v. Thomson Holidays Ltd (Unreported, November 22, 1999), CC (Bedford)
    [*Ex rel*. Matthew Chapman, Barrister, Barnard's Inn Chambers, Halton House,
    20-23 Holborn, London] . . . .   *Digested*, 00/**4038**
DJH (CICB: Quantum: 1999), Re (1999) 99(3) Q.R. 5, CICB (Nottingham) [*Ex rel*. Stuart
    R Yeung, Barrister, 22 Albion Place, Northampton] . . . .   *Digested*, 99/**1448**
DKV Deutsche Krankenversicherung AG v. Office for Harmonisation in the Internal
    Market (Trade Marks and Designs) (OHIM) (T19/99) [2000] All E.R. (EC) 193;
    [2000] E.C.R. II-1; [2000] 1 C.M.L.R. 508; [2000] C.E.C. 102; [2000] E.T.M.R.
    271, CFI (4th Chamber) . . . .   *Digested*, 00/**3717**
DL Marketing (Direct Link) Ltd v. Customs and Excise Commissioners [2001] S.T.I. 744,
    V&DTr
DNB Mortgages Ltd v. Bullock & Lees [2000] Lloyd's Rep. P.N. 290; [2000] P.N.L.R.
    427; [2000] 1 E.G.L.R. 92; [2000] 17 E.G. 168; [2000] E.G.C.S. 16; *Times*,
    March 24, 2000; *Independent*, March 20, 2000 (C.S.), CA . . . .   *Digested*, 00/**581**
Dobbie v. Fife Council [1998] R.V.R. 119; 1998 Hous. L.R. 48, Lands Tr . . . .   *Digested*, 98/**5947**

Dobbie v. Medway HA [1994] 1 W.L.R. 1234; [1994] 4 All E.R. 450; [1994] P.I.Q.R.
P353; [1994] 5 Med. L.R. 160; (1994) 144 N.L.J. 828; *Times*, May 18, 1994;
Independent, June 6, 1994 (C.S.), CA; affirming [1992] 3 Med. L.R. 217, QBD . .   *Digested*, 95/**3171**:
    Applied, 00/525: *Distinguished*, 95/3169, 96/816

Dobell v. Thanet DC (Unreported, March 22, 1999), CC (Thanet) [*Ex rel*. AE Wyeth &
Co Solicitors, Bridge House, High Street, Dartford, Kent] . . . .   *Digested*, 00/**4240**

Dobson v. North Tyneside HA [1997] 1 W.L.R. 596; [1996] 4 All E.R. 474; [1997] 1
F.L.R. 598; [1997] 2 F.C.R. 651; [1997] 8 Med. L.R. 357; (1997) 33 B.M.L.R.
146; [1997] Fam. Law 326; (1996) 93(31) L.S.G. 29; (1996) 146 N.L.J. 1458;
(1996) 140 S.J.L.B. 165; *Times*, July 15, 1996; *Independent*, July 18, 1996, CA . .   *Digested*, 96/**5671**:
    Applied, 99/5196

Dobson v. Stanbra (Unreported, October 23, 2000), CC (Worksop) [*Ex rel*. Corries
Solicitors, Rowntree Wharf, Navigation Road, York] . . . .   *Digested*, 01/**513**:
    Considered, 01/521

Docker (Deceased) v. Chief Constable of the West Midlands see Darker v. Chief
Constable of the West Midlands

Dockerill v. Scanlon (Unreported, January 12, 1998), CC (Lambeth) [*Ex rel*. Tim Kevan,
Barrister, 1 Temple Gardens, Temple, London, EC4Y 9BB] . . . .   *Digested*, 98/**490**

Dodd v. Chief Constable of Cheshire, *Times*, December 2, 1998; *Independent*,
November 30, 1998 (C.S.), CA. . . . .   *Digested*, 99/**1394**

Dodd v. Stansted Airport Ltd (1998) 76 P. & C.R. 456; [1998] R.V.R. 107, Lands Tr . . . .   *Digested*, 98/**4170**

Dodd Properties (Kent) Ltd v. Canterbury City Council [1980] 1 W.L.R. 433; [1980] 1
All E.R. 928; 13 B.L.R. 45; (1979) 253 E.G. 1335; (1980) 124 S.J. 84, CA;
reversing [1979] 2 All E.R. 118; (1978) 248 E.G. 229, QBD . . . .   *Digested*, 80/**642**:
    Applied, 80/644, 83/2087, 84/214, 84/1892, 85/189, 86/3195, 87/3551,
    89/1185, 91/1303, 92/1515, 00/1474: *Considered*, 90/1567, 91/1315, 91/1319:
    Distinguished, 82/2164: *Followed*, 83/4462, 96/4514

Dodds v. Chief Constable of the Royal Ulster Constabulary [1998] N.I. 393, CA (NI) . .   *Digested*, 99/**5229**:
    Considered, 00/5490

Dodkins v. West Ham United Plc (Unreported, February 10, 2000), CC (Shoreditch)
[*Ex rel*. Robin Howard, Barrister, Trinity Chambers, 140 New London Road,
Chelmsford] . . . .   *Digested*, 00/**4226**

Dodson v. Peter H Dodson Insurance Services [2001] 1 W.L.R. 1012; [2001] 3 All E.R.
75; [2001] 1 All E.R. (Comm) 300; [2001] 1 Lloyd's Rep. 520; [2001] R.T.R.
13; [2001] Lloyd's Rep. I.R. 278; (2001) 98(4) L.S.G. 49; *Times*, January 24,
2001; *Independent*, January 26, 2001, CA . . . .   *Digested*, 01/**3829**

Dogan v. Securitised Endowment Brokers and Fairbarn (Unreported, March 11, 1998),
CC (Barnet) [*Ex rel*. Nigel Ffitch, Barrister, Trafalgar Chambers, 53 Fleet Street,
London, EC4Y 1BE] . . . .   *Digested*, 98/**2300**

Doherty v. Law (Unreported, July 6, 1998), CC (Barnsley) [*Ex rel*. Nicholas Hill,
Barrister, 6 Park Square, Leeds; Tim Hale, Ison Harrison & Co Solicitors, Leeds] .   *Digested*, 98/**1650**

Doherty v. Ministry of Defence [1991] N.I.J.B. 68 . . . .   *Considered*, 00/5392

Doherty's Application (No.2), Re; *sub nom* R. v. Doherty (Joseph) [1995] N.I. 144, CA
(NI)

Doldur v. Secretary of State for the Home Department see R. v. Secretary of State for
the Home Department Ex p. Doldur

Dole Dried Fruit & Nut Co v. Trustin Kerwood Ltd [1990] 2 Lloyd's Rep. 309; *Times*,
June 1, 1990; *Independent*, May 22, 1990; *Lloyd's List*, July 13, 1990, CA . . . . . .   *Digested*, 91/**2965**:
    Applied, 01/941: *Considered*, 99/410

Dolgellau Golf Club v. Hett (1998) 76 P. & C.R. 526; [1998] L. & T.R. 217; [1998] 2
E.G.L.R. 75; [1998] 34 E.G. 87; [1998] E.G.C.S. 59; [1998] N.P.C. 56; (1998)
76 P. & C.R. D24; *Times*, April 24, 1998, CA . . . .   *Digested*, 98/**3601**

Dollar Land (Cumbernauld) Ltd v. CIN Properties Ltd 1998 S.C. (H.L.) 90; 1998 S.L.T.
992; 1998 S.C.L.R. 929; [1998] 3 E.G.L.R. 79; [1998] 51 E.G. 83; 1998 G.W.D.
25-1268; *Times*, August 24, 1998, HL; affirming 1996 S.C. 331; 1997 S.L.T. 260;
1996 S.C.L.R. 697, Ex Div; affirming 1996 S.L.T. 186; *Times*, April 21, 1995, OH .   *Digested*, 98/**6034**:
    Followed, 00/6634

Dolling-Baker v. Merrett [1990] 1 W.L.R. 1205; [1991] 2 All E.R. 890; (1990) 134 S.J.
806, CA . . . .   *Digested*, 91/**2865**:
    Followed, 95/4122, 98/240

Dolonay v. Southwark LBC (Unreported, August 20, 1999), CC (Lambeth) [*Ex rel*.
Alexander Bastin, Barrister, Francis Taylor Building, Temple, London] . . . .   *Digested*, 99/**3712**

Dolphin Packaging Materials Ltd v. Pensions Ombudsman (1993) [1995] O.P.L.R. 331;
Times, December 2, 1993, QBD . . . .   *Digested*, 93/**3061**:
    Considered, 98/4146

Dolphin Showers Ltd v. Farmiloe; Brueton v. Farmiloe [1989] 1 F.S.R. 1, Pat Ct . . . .   *Digested*, 89/**2811**:
    Not followed, 98/3472

Dolton Bournes & Dolton Ltd v. Osmond (Valuation Officer) [1955] 1 W.L.R. 621;
[1955] 2 All E.R. 258; 119 J.P. 380; 53 L.G.R. 537; 48 R. & I.T. 295; 99 S.J. 352,
CA; reversing 164 E.G. 574; 47 R. & I.T. 679; [1954] J.P.L. 884, Lands Tr . . . . . .   *Digested*, 55/**2279**:
    Applied, 00/5678: *Followed*, 60/2687

Domansa v. Derin Shipping & Trading Co Inc (The Sletreal) [2001] 1 Lloyd's Rep. 362;
[2001] C.L.C. 211, QBD (Comm Ct) . . . .   *Digested*, 01/**798**

Dombo Beheer BV v. Netherlands (A/274-A) (1994) 18 E.H.R.R. 213, ECHR . . . .   *Digested,* 95/**2621**:
Applied, 97/2811, 98/3112

Domenichini v. Italy (15943/90) (2001) 32 E.H.R.R. 4, ECHR

Domicrest Ltd v. Swiss Bank Corp [1999] Q.B. 548; [1999] 2 W.L.R. 364; [1998] 3
All E.R. 577; [1999] 1 Lloyd's Rep. 80; [1998] C.L.C. 1451; [1999] I.L.Pr. 146;
Times, July 16, 1998; *Independent,* July 20, 1998 (C.S.), QBD . . . .   *Digested,* 98/**770**

Dominey v. Amenco (Poole) Ltd (1999) 99(4) Q.R. 3, QBD [*Ex rel.* Anthony Coleman,
Barrister, Winchester Chambers, 4 St Peter Steet, Winchester, Hampshire] . . . . .   *Digested,* 99/**1482**

Dominion Mosaics & Tile Co v. Trafalgar Trucking Co [1990] 2 All E.R. 246; 26 Con. L.R.
1; [1989] 16 E.G. 101; (1989) 139 N.L.J. 364; *Times,* March 31, 1989;
Independent, March 8, 1989, CA . . . .   *Digested,* 89/**1185**:
Considered, 94/3079, 98/4025

Don King Productions Inc v. Warren (No.1) [2000] Ch. 291; [1999] 3 W.L.R. 276;
[1999] 2 All E.R. 218; [1999] 1 Lloyd's Rep. 588; [2000] 1 B.C.L.C. 607; [1999]
E.M.L.R. 402; *Times,* February 9, 1999; *Independent,* January 25, 1999 (C.S.),
CA; affirming [1998] 2 All E.R. 608; [1998] 2 Lloyd's Rep. 176; [1998] 2
B.C.L.C. 132; [1998] R.P.C. 817; (1998) 95(21) L.S.G. 24; (1998) 142 S.J.L.B.
162; *Times,* April 13, 1998, Ch D . . . .   *Digested,* 99/**4092**:
Applied, 00/3864

Don King Productions Inc v. Warren (No.2), *Times,* June 18, 1998, Ch D . . . .   *Digested,* 98/**564**

Don King Productions Inc v. Warren (No.3) [1999] 2 Lloyd's Rep. 392; [2000] B.C.C.
263, Ch D . . . .   *Digested,* 00/**4318**

Donaldson v. Eastern Health and Social Services Board [1997] N.I. 232, QBD (NI) . . . .   *Digested,* 99/**5145**

Donaldson v. Hereford and Worcester CC (1998) 76 P. & C.R. 93; [1997] R.V.R. 242;
[1998] J.P.L. 496; (1997) 161 J.P.N. 1022, Lands Tr . . . .   *Digested,* 97/**4235**

Doncaster BC v. Hancock see Doncaster MBC v. Hancock

Doncaster BC v. Kelly see Doncaster MBC v. Kelly

Doncaster BC v. Stark see Doncaster MBC v. Stark

Doncaster MBC v. Hancock; *sub nom* Doncaster BC v. Hancock *Independent,* April 9,
2001 (C.S), QBD

Doncaster MBC v. Harrison Sales (1999) 14 P.A.D. 263, Planning Inspector

Doncaster MBC v. Kelly; *sub nom* Doncaster BC v. Kelly; (Unreported, April 26, 2001),
QBD [*Ex rel.* Adrian Jackson, Barrister, King Charles House, Standard Hill,
Nottingham] . . . .   *Digested,* 01/**441**

Doncaster MBC v. Stark; *sub nom* Doncaster BC v. Stark [1998] R.V.R. 80; [1998]
C.O.D. 230, QBD . . . .   *Digested,* 98/**4308**

Doneck v. First Choice Holidays & Flights Ltd (Unreported, February 4, 1999), CC
(Manchester) [*Ex rel.* Nicholls & Co Solicitors, 671 Manchester Road, Denton,
Manchester] . . . .   *Digested,* 99/**3823**

Donegan v. Dunnigan (Unreported, February 22, 2000), CC (Birkenhead) [*Ex rel.*
Michael W Halsall Solicitors, 2 The Parks, Newton-le-Willows] . . . .   *Digested,* 00/**1720**

Dong Wha Enterprise Co Ltd v. Crownson Shipping Ltd [1995] 1 Lloyd's Rep. 113, QBD
(Comm Ct) . . . .   *Digested,* 96/**884**:
Considered, 98/587

Dongre v. Whirlpool Corp, HC (Ind) . . . .   *Considered,* 00/3591

Donnelly v. Chief Constable of the Royal Ulster Constabulary see Clinton v. Chief
Constable of the Royal Ulster Constabulary

Donnelly v. Joyce [1974] Q.B. 454; [1973] 3 W.L.R. 514; [1973] 3 All E.R. 475;
[1973] 2 Lloyd's Rep. 130; 117 S.J. 488, CA . . . .   *Digested,* 73/**727**:
Applied, 74/849, 77/733, 82/206, 83/2516, 84/1822, 93/1418, 99/2455:
Considered, 76/680, 85/958, 86/989, 92/1539, 98/2505, 99/2456,
99/2462, 99/2498, 00/311: *Distinguished,* 99/1406: *Followed,* 78/721,
98/2502: *Not followed,* 98/1453

Donnelly v. Regency Hotel [1985] N.I. 144; [1985] 5 N.I.J.B. 27 . . . .   *Digested,* 86/**2370**:
Considered, 00/5658

Donoghue v. Doncaster Amalgamated Collieries Ltd see Nokes v. Doncaster
Amalgamated Collieries Ltd

Donoghue v. Poplar Housing & Regeneration Community Association Ltd see Poplar
Housing & Regeneration Community Association Ltd v. Donoghue

Donoghue v. Stevenson; *sub nom* McAlister v. Stevenson [1932] A.C. 562; 1932 S.C.
(H.L.) 31; 1932 S.L.T. 317; [1932] W.N. 139, HL . . . . *Applied*, 47-51/6681,
47-51/6693, 47-51/6761, 47-51/6789, 47-51/6881, 47-51/6897, 52/1563,
52/2362, 53/639, 53/2422, 56/904, 56/11829, 57/1415, 57/2371, 61/825,
62/2028, 62/2188, 63/2362, 64/1670, 65/416, 65/2669, 68/2673, 68/4511,
69/2403, 70/1493, 70/1850, 71/7843, 72/1104, 72/2350, 72/2352, 72/2408,
72/2409, 74/2579, 75/933, 75/3994, 77/2025, 77/2027, 78/1789, 78/2065,
78/3467, 78/3538, 81/1829, 81/1849, 82/2135, 85/2301, 87/2579, 88/3410,
89/1286, 01/4509: *Considered*, 47-51/351, 47-51/6734, 47-51/9683,
47-51/9691, 55/1839, 62/2083, 62/3080, 65/2663, 65/2671, 68/1314,
69/1157, 72/2528, 74/363, 75/2343, 76/228, 87/2580, 88/2418, 88/2433,
88/3376, 88/3409, 90/3288, 90/3315, 91/2657, 91/2661, 93/2983,
94/3352, 95/4519, 98/3995, 99/3960, 00/4227: *Distinguished*, 47-51/6584,
47-51/6705, 47-51/6711, 47-51/6727, 47-51/6929, 47-51/7886, 47-51/3988,
52/2392, 52/4290, 57/2366, 57/2639, 63/330, 63/2360, 64/2516,
66/6884, 72/2361, 83/2746: *Followed*, 76/3296, 84/4347, 85/4437
Donohue v. Armco Inc [2001] UKHL 64, HL; reversing [2000] 1 All E.R. (Comm) 641;
[2000] 1 Lloyd's Rep. 579; [2000] C.L.C. 1090; [2001] I.L.Pr. 48, CA; reversing
[2000] 1 All E.R. (Comm) 425; [1999] 2 Lloyd's Rep. 649; [1999] C.L.C.
1748; [2000] I.L.Pr. 321, QBD (Comm Ct) . . . . *Digested*, 00/**749**
Donovan v. Electricity Supply Board [1998] Eu. L.R. 212, Sup Ct (Irl); affirming [1995]
E.C.C. 34, HC (Irl) . . . . *Digested*, 98/**724**
Donovan v. Gwentoys Ltd [1990] 1 W.L.R. 472; [1990] 1 All E.R. 1018; (1990) 87(15)
L.S.G. 40; (1990) 134 S.J. 910; *Times*, March 23, 1990; *Independent*, March 23,
1990; *Guardian* March 28, 1990, HL; reversing *Times*, June 7, 1989, CA . . . . . . *Digested*, 90/**2960**:
Applied, 92/2811, 94/5183, 99/464: *Considered*, 96/830, 97/667, 99/476,
00/512, 01/601
Donovan v. Ministry of Defence (Unreported, June 15, 2001), HC [*Ex rel*. Robert Weir,
Barrister, Devereux Chambers, Devereux Court, London] . . . . *Digested*, 01/**3297**
Donovan Data Systems Europe v. Dragon Rouge Holding [2000] I.L.Pr. 21, Cass (F)
Doodeward v. Spence (1908) 6 C.L.R. 406. . . . . *Applied*, 98/979:
Considered, 96/5671
Doolan v. EP Cornall & Sons (Unreported, May 11, 2001), CC (Lincoln) [*Ex rel*.
Langleys, Solicitors, Newporte House, Doddington Road Business Park,
Lincoln] . . . . *Digested*, 01/**324**
Dooley v. Law Society (2001) 151 N.L.J. 1768; (2001) 145 S.J.L.B. 269, Ch D
Doonan (Superintendent of Police) v. Darcy [1995] N.I. 378, CA (NI)
Doone (Sylvia) (Deceased), Re (1999-2000) 2 I.T.E.L.R. 425, HC (BVI)
Doorbar v. Alltime Securities Ltd (No.2); *sub nom* Debtor (No.162 of 1993) (No.2), Re
[1995] B.C.C. 728; [1995] 2 B.C.L.C. 513; [1996] B.P.I.R. 128, Ch D . . . . *Digested*, 96/**3520**:
Considered, 96/3706: *Followed*, 98/3355: *Subsequent proceedings*, 96/3521
Doorbar v. Alltime Securities Ltd (Nos.1 and 2) [1996] 1 W.L.R. 456; [1996] 2 All E.R.
948; [1995] B.C.C. 1149; [1996] 1 B.C.L.C. 487; [1996] B.P.I.R. 582; [1996] 2
E.G.L.R. 33; [1996] 32 E.G. 70; (1996) 93(2) L.S.G. 28; *Times*, December 7,
1995, CA . . . . *Digested*, 96/**3521**:
Followed, 98/3354: *Previous proceedings*, 95/2842, 96/3520
Dopson v. Oscar Faber Group Ltd (Unreported, July 13, 1998), CC (Swindon) [*Ex rel*.
Helen Gower, Barrister, Old Square Chambers, Hanover House, 47 Corn Street,
Bristol] . . . . *Digested*, 98/**1737**
Dora v. Simper [2000] 2 B.C.L.C. 561, CA; affirming [1999] B.C.C. 836; *Times*, May
26, 1999, Ch D . . . . *Digested*, 01/**3754**
Dore v. Insall see Gleaves v. Insall
Dorman Long & Co Ltd, Re; South Durham Steel & Iron Co Ltd, Re [1934] Ch. 635, Ch D
Applied, 54/438:
Considered, 84/318, 85/317, 98/3340
Dorney v. Chippenham College (Unreported, May 12, 1997), EAT . . . . *Applied*, 98/2167,
00/2148
Dorney-Kingdom v. Dorney-Kingdom [2000] 2 F.L.R. 855; [2000] 3 F.C.R. 20;
[2000] Fam. Law 794; (2000) 97(30) L.S.G. 39; *Times*, July 25, 2000, CA . . . *Digested*, 00/**2520**
Dorricott v. Glennan; Gayler v. Better Tasting Products Ltd (1998) 21(6) I.P.D. 21068,
Pat Ct
Dorsch Consult Ingenieurgesellschaft mbH v. Bundesbaugesellschaft Berlin mbH (C54/
96) [1998] All E.R. (E.C.) 262; [1997] E.C.R. I-4961; [1998] 2 C.M.L.R. 237,
ECJ . . . . *Digested*, 98/**2320**
Dorsch Consult Ingenieurgesellschaft mbH v. Commission of the European
Communities see Dorsch Consult Ingenieurgesellschaft mbH v. Council of the
European Union (T184/95) (Application to intervene)
Dorsch Consult Ingenieurgesellschaft mbH v. Council of the European Union (C237/98
P); *sub nom* Dorsh Consult Ingenieurgesellschaft mbH v. Council of Ministers
of the European Communities (T184/95); Dorsch Consult Ingenieurgesellschaft
mbH v. Council of the European Union (T184/95) [2000] E.C.R. I-4549, ECJ
(5th Chamber); affirming [1998] E.C.R. II-667; [1998] 2 C.M.L.R. 758, CFI (2nd
Chamber)

Dorsch Consult Ingenieurgesellschaft mbH *v.* Council of the European Union (T184/95) see Dorsch Consult Ingenieurgesellschaft mbH *v.* Council of the European Union (C237/98 P)

Dorsch Consult Ingenieurgesellschaft mbH *v.* Council of the European Union (T184/95) (Application to Intervene); *sub nom* Dorsch Consult Ingenieurgesellschaft mbH *v.* Commission of the European Communities (T184/95) (Application to Intervene) [1997] E.C.R. II-351; [1998] 1 C.M.L.R. 135, CFI (2nd Chamber)

Dorset CC *v.* Rothchild Estates Ltd see Dorset CC *v.* Secretary of State for the Environment, Transport and the Regions

Dorset CC *v.* Secretary of State for the Environment, Transport and the Regions; Dorset CC *v.* Rothchild Estates Ltd [1999] J.P.L. 633, QBD [*Ex rel.* Mr A Winterton, 15 Roslin Road South, Talbot Woods, Bournemouth] . . . . *Digested*, 99/**4255**

Dorset CC *v.* Southern Felt Roofing Co 48 B.L.R. 96; (1990) 10 Tr. L.R. 96; (1990) 6 Const. L.J. 37, CA; affirming 26 Con. L.R. 128 . . . . *Digested*, 90/**636**:

Applied, 01/865: *Distinguished*, 01/952

Dorsett *v.* Grant (Unreported, July 7, 2000), CC (Bradford) [*Ex rel.* Sean D Yates, Barrister, 10 Park Square, Leeds] . . . . *Digested*, 00/**340**

Dorsett *v.* Grant (Quantum) (Unreported, July 7, 2000), CC (Bradford) [*Ex rel.* Sean D Yates, Barrister, 10 Park Square, Leeds] . . . . *Digested*, 00/**1577**

Dorsh Consult Ingenieurgesellschaft mbH *v.* Council of Ministers of the European Communities (T184/95) (Application to Intervene) see Dorsch Consult Ingenieurgesellschaft mbH *v.* Council of the European Union (T184/95) (Application to intervene)

Dorsh Consult Ingenieurgesellschaft mbH *v.* Council of Ministers of the European Communities (T184/95) see Dorsch Consult Ingenieurgesellschaft mbH *v.* Council of the European Union (C237/98 P)

Double S Printers Ltd (In Liquidation), Re [1999] B.C.C. 303; [1999] 1 B.C.L.C. 220; *Times*, June 2, 1998, DR (Leeds) . . . . *Digested*, 98/**3296**

Doublerange Ltd *v.* National Power Plc; Harris *v.* National Power Plc [1997] Eu. L.R. 589, QBD (Comm Ct) . . . . *Digested*, 98/**2304**

Dougall *v.* Customs and Excise Commissioners see Customs and Excise Commissioners *v.* Dougall

Dougan *v.* Mackman see O'Reilly *v.* Mackman

Douglas 1990 Settlement, Re (1999-2000) 2 I.T.E.L.R. 682, Royal Ct (Jer)

Douglas *v.* Fensome [2001] 3 Q.R. 14, CC (Basildon) [*Ex rel.* Andrew Granville Stafford, Barrister, 4 King's Bench Walk, Temple, London] . . . . *Digested*, 01/**1628**

Douglas *v.* Hello! Ltd [2001] Q.B. 967; [2001] 2 W.L.R. 992; [2001] 2 All E.R. 289; [2001] E.M.L.R. 9; [2001] 1 F.L.R. 982; [2001] H.R.L.R. 26; [2001] U.K.H.R.R. 223; 9 B.H.R.C. 543; [2001] F.S.R. 40; *Times*, January 16, 2001; *Daily Telegraph*, January 9, 2001, CA . . . . *Digested*, 01/**567**:

Applied, 01/2583: *Considered*, 01/1824

Douglas Narayan & Partners *v.* Khan see R. *v.* Basra (Wasted Costs Order)

Dougoz *v.* Greece (40907/98) 10 B.H.R.C. 306, ECHR . . . . *Digested*, 01/**3566**

Dougoz *v.* Greece (40907/98) (Admissibility of Application) (2000) 29 E.H.R.R. CD147, ECHR

Douiyeb *v.* Netherlands (2000) 30 E.H.R.R. 790, ECHR . . . . *Digested*, 01/**3561**

Doustaly *v.* France [1998] H.R.C.D. 466, ECHR

Dover DC *v.* Folkestone and Dover Water Services Ltd (2001) 16 P.A.D. 56, Planning Inspector

Dover DC *v.* George Wimpey Strategic Land Management (2001) 16 P.A.D. 78, Planning Inspector

Dover DC *v.* Ullman (1999) 14 P.A.D. 287, Planning Inspector

Dow *v.* Dow (Unreported, March 27, 1998), QBD [*Ex rel.* Anthony Gold, Lerman & Muirhead Solicitors, New London Bridge House, 25 London Bridge Street, London, SE1 9TW] . . . . *Digested*, 98/**1683**

Dow Chemical Corp *v.* Manfred S***** [2001] E.T.M.R. 84, OGH (A)

Dow Europe SA *v.* Novoklav Inc [1998] 1 Lloyd's Rep. 306, QBD (Comm Ct) . . . . *Digested*, 97/**4595**

DOW/Costs (T622/89) [1998] E.P.O.R. 463, EPO (Technical Bd App)

DOW/Mold-release (T206/93) [2001] E.P.O.R. 9, EPO (Technical Bd App) . . . . *Digested*, 01/**3949**

Dowall *v.* Johnson (Unreported, July 4, 2000), CC (Salisbury) [*Ex rel.* Scott Rees & Co Solicitors, Centaur House, Gardiners Place, Skelmersdale, Lancashire] . . . . . *Digested*, 00/**2576**

Dowdall *v.* Inner London Magistrates Court see R. (on the application of Dowdall) *v.* Inner London Magistrates Court South Western Division

Dowdie *v.* Camberwell HA [1997] 8 Med. L.R. 368, QBD . . . . *Digested*, 98/**3973**

Dowle *v.* Graham (Unreported, March 26, 1999), CC (Taunton) [*Ex rel.* Bond Pearce Solicitors, Darwin House, Southernhay Gardens, Exeter] . . . . *Digested*, 00/**1538**

Dowles Manor Properties Ltd *v.* Bank of Namibia [1999] C.P.L.R. 259; *Times*, March 18, 1999, CA . . . . *Digested*, 99/**564**

Dowling *v.* Wallis (2000) 80 P. & C.R. 362, Ch D . . . . *Digested*, 00/**4669**

Dowling & Rutter *v.* Abacus Frozen Foods Ltd (No.1) 2000 G.W.D. 12-412; *Times*, April 26, 2000, OH . . . . *Digested*, 00/**5986**

Downes *v.* Cottam see Beddoe, Re

Downes *v.* Hammond (Unreported, June 19, 2000), CC (Bow) [*Ex rel.* Katya Melluish, Barrister, 3 Paper Buildings, Temple, London] . . . . *Digested*, 00/**2574**

Downie v. Coe, *Times*, November 28, 1997, CA . . . . *Digested*, 98/**907**
Downie v. Williams (Unreported, August 16, 2000), CC (Birkenhead) [*Ex rel.* Richard
Menzies, Barrister, 8 Stone Buildings, Lincoln's Inn, London] . . . . *Digested*, 00/**1682**
Downsview Nominees Ltd v. First City Corp Ltd (No.1); *sub nom* First City Corp Ltd v.
Downsview Nominees Ltd (No.1) [1993] A.C. 295; [1993] 2 W.L.R. 86;
[1993] 3 All E.R. 626; [1993] B.C.C. 46; [1994] 2 B.C.L.C. 49; (1992) 89(45)
L.S.G. 26; (1992) 136 S.J.L.B. 324; *Times*, December 15, 1992; *Independent*,
December 14, 1992 (C.S.), PC (NZ); reversing in part [1990] 3 N.Z.L.R. 265, HC
(NZ) . . . . *Digested*, 93/**2881**:
Applied, 95/3600, 96/4988: *Considered*, 00/4657, 01/4541
Dowsett v. Clifford (Unreported, August 25, 2000) . . . . *Considered*, 01/**896**:
Followed, 00/2584
Doyle v. Leslie [1994] N.I. 270, Ch D (NI) . . . . *Digested*, 00/**5778**
Doyle v. Wallace [1998] P.I.Q.R. Q146; (1998) 95(30) L.S.G. 25; (1998) 142 S.J.L.B.
196; *Times*, July 22, 1998, CA . . . . *Digested*, 98/**1447**:
Considered, 01/1531: *Referred to*, 99/1575
DPP v. Alsford see DPP v. Nock
DPP v. Anderson [1998] C.O.D. 363, QBD
DPP v. Anderson (t/a Spotmix RMC) [1998] R.T.R. 16, QBD. . . . . *Not followed*, 98/4710
DPP v. Ara [2001] EWHC Admin 493; [2001] 4 All E.R. 559; (2001) 98(32) L.S.G.
36; *Times*, July 16, 2001, QBD (Admin Ct) . . . . *Digested*, 01/**1106**
DPP v. Armstrong (Andrew) [2000] Crim. L.R. 379; (1999) 96(45) L.S.G. 32; (1999)
143 S.J.L.B. 279; *Times*, December 10, 1999, QBD . . . . *Digested*, 00/**995**
DPP v. Armstrong-Braun see DPP v. Braun (Klaus Armstrong)
DPP v. Arnup see Gorman v. DPP
DPP v. Aston (John Allen) [1989] R.T.R. 198; [1989] 2 C.M.L.R. 297, QBD . . . . *Digested*, 89/**3313**:
Considered, 99/4946
DPP v. Atkins see Atkins v. DPP
DPP v. Avery [2001] EWHC Admin 748; (2001) 165 J.P. 789; (2001) 165 J.P.N. 1003;
Times, November 8, 2001; *Independent*, December 3, 2001, QBD (Admin Ct) . . *Digested*, 01/**4788**
DPP (Jamaica) v. Bailey [1995] 1 Cr. App. R. 257; [1995] Crim. L.R. 313, PC (Jam) . . . *Digested*, 96/**1648**:
Applied, 01/1056
DPP v. Baldwin (2000) 164 J.P. 606; [2000] R.T.R. 314; (2000) 97(19) L.S.G. 42;
Times, May 17, 2000, QBD. . . . . *Digested*, 00/**939**
DPP v. Barber (1999) 163 J.P. 457, QBD . . . . *Digested*, 99/**886**
DPP v. Barnard; *sub nom* Crown Prosecution Service v. Barnard [2000] Crim. L.R.
371; (1999) 96(42) L.S.G. 40; (1999) 143 S.J.L.B. 256; *Times*, November 9,
1999, QBD . . . . *Digested*, 99/**964**
DPP v. Bell (Derek) [1992] R.T.R. 335; [1992] Crim. L.R. 176; (1992) 156 J.P.N. 461;
Times, November, 21, 1991, DC. . . . . *Digested*, 93/**3507**:
Considered, 95/4430: *Distinguished*, 01/1032
DPP v. Bhagwan see R. v. Bhagwan (Dharam Singh)
DPP v. Bignall; *sub nom* DPP v. Bignell [1998] 1 Cr. App. R. 1; (1997) 161 J.P. 541;
[1997-98] Info. T.L.R. 168; [1998] I.T.C.L.R. 33; [1998] Masons C.L.R. Rep. 141;
[1998] Crim. L.R. 53; (1997) 161 J.P.N. 698; (1997) 161 J.P.N. 770; *Times*,
June 6, 1997; *Independent*, May 21, 1997, QBD . . . . *Digested*, 97/**1184**:
Overruled, 99/2288
DPP v. Bignell see DPP v. Bignall
DPP v. Billington; Chappell v. DPP; DPP v. Rumble; Coryright v. East [1988] 1 W.L.R.
535; [1988] 1 All E.R. 435; (1988) 87 Cr. App. R. 68; (1988) 152 J.P. 1; [1988]
R.T.R. 231; [1987] Crim. L.R. 772; (1987) 151 J.P.N. 860; (1988) 132 S.J. 498;
Independent, July 22, 1987, QBD . . . . *Digested*, 88/**3094**:
Considered, 91/3117, 91/3131, 92/3795, 93/3486, 94/3973, 97/1314, 00/960:
Followed, 91/3118
DPP v. Braun (Klaus Armstrong); *sub nom* DPP v. Armstrong-Braun (1999) 163 J.P.
271; [1999] Crim. L.R. 416; *Times*, October 26, 1998, QBD . . . . *Digested*, 98/**977**
DPP v. Bristow (1997) 161 J.P. 35; [1998] R.T.R. 100; (1997) 161 J.P.N. 110; *Times*,
October 28, 1996, QBD . . . . *Digested*, 97/**1684**:
Considered, 97/1685
DPP v. Brodzky [1997] R.T.R. 425, QBD . . . . *Digested*, 98/**896**
DPP v. Brown (Andrew Earle); DPP v. Teixeira (Jose) [2001] EWHC Admin 931; *Times*,
December 3, 2001, QBD (Admin Ct)
DPP v. Camplin see R. v. Camplin (Paul)
DPP v. Chalmers [2000] C.O.D. 2, QBD
DPP v. Charles; DPP v. Kukadia; Ruxton v. DPP; Reaveley v. DPP; Healy v. DPP;
McKean v. DPP; Edge v. DPP [1996] R.T.R. 247, QBD . . . . *Digested*, 96/**5057**:
Considered, 98/1029
DPP v. Coleman [1998] 1 W.L.R. 1708; [1998] 1 All E.R. 912; [1998] 2 Cr. App. R. 7;
(1997) 94(48) L.S.G. 30; *Times*, December 13, 1997; *Independent*, December 2,
1997, QBD . . . . *Digested*, 98/**1003**
DPP v. Cornell see DPP v. Skinner
DPP v. Cornhill see DPP v. Skinner
DPP v. Cornwell see DPP v. Skinner
DPP v. Cosier [2000] C.O.D. 284, QBD

DPP v. Crofton [1994] R.T.R. 279, DC . . . .   *Digested*, 94/**3982**:
                                                                                                              Applied, 98/896
DPP v. DA (A Child) [2001] Crim. L.R.140, QBD
DPP v. Darby (No.1) see R. v. Henn (Maurice Donald) (No.1)
DPP v. Donnelly (Ronald Francis) [1998] R.T.R. 188, QBD . . . .   *Digested*, 97/**1311**:
                                                                                                              Considered, 97/1308

DPP v. Doot; *sub nom* R. v. Doot (Robert Leroy); R. v. Shanahan (Thomas); R. v. Watts
      (James Wesley); R. v. Fay (Michael Augustus); R. v. Loving (Jeffrey Richard);
      R. v. Shannahan (Thomas); DPP v. Shanahan (Thomas); DPP v. Watts (James
      Wesley); DPP v. Fay (Michael Augustus); DPP v. Loving (Jeffrey Richard) [1973]
      A.C. 807; [1973] 2 W.L.R. 532; [1973] 1 All E.R. 940; (1973) 57 Cr. App. R.
      600; [1973] Crim. L.R. 292; 117 S.J. 266, HL; reversing [1973] 1 Q.B. 73; [1973]
      Q.B. 73; [1972] 3 W.L.R. 33; [1972] 2 All E.R. 1046; (1973) 57 Cr. App. R. 13;
      [1972] Crim. L.R. 500; 116 S.J. 445, CA (Crim Div) . . . .   *Digested*, 73/**493**:
                                            Applied, 83/613, 84/580, 89/854: *Considered*, 73/491, 82/686, 83/574,
                                                          83/607, 88/801, 91/914, 93/930: *Followed*, 96/1473, 00/6029
DPP v. Dunn [2001] 1 Cr. App. R. 22; (2001) 165 J.P. 130; [2001] Crim. L.R. 130;
      (2001) 165 J.P.N. 124; *Times*, November 1, 2000, QBD . . . .   *Digested*, 00/**976**
DPP v. Edgar (2000) 164 J.P. 471; (2000) 164 J.P.N. 665, QBD . . . .   *Digested*, 00/**1086**
DPP v. Falzarano; *sub nom* R. (on the application of Falzarano) v. Crown Prosecution
      Service (2001) 165 J.P. 201; [2001] R.T.R. 14; (2000) 97(44) L.S.G. 45; *Times*,
      November 24, 2000, QBD . . . .   *Digested*, 00/**959**
DPP v. Fay (Michael Augustus) see DPP v. Doot
DPP v. Fellowes; *sub nom* Fellowes v. DPP (1993) 157 J.P. 936; [1993] Crim. L.R.
      523; *Times*, February 1, 1993, DC . . . .   *Digested*, 94/**1095**:
                                                                                                              Followed, 00/198

DPP v. Fontenau see Fonteneau v. DPP
DPP v. Fonteneau see Fonteneau v. DPP
DPP v. Furby [2000] R.T.R. 181; (2000) 97(16) L.S.G. 42; (2000) 144 S.J.L.B. 156;
      Times, March 23, 2000, QBD . . . .   *Digested*, 00/**957**:
                                                                                                              Followed, 01/1130
DPP v. Gibbons (Stuart Michael) [2001] EWHC Admin 385; (2001) 165 J.P. 812,
      QBD (Admin Ct)
DPP v. Goddard [1998] R.T.R. 463, QBD . . . .   *Digested*, 99/**1122**
DPP v. Gomez (Edwin) [1993] A.C. 442; [1992] 3 W.L.R. 1067; [1993] 1 All E.R. 1;
      (1993) 96 Cr. App. R. 359; (1993) 157 J.P. 1; [1993] Crim. L.R. 304; (1993) 157
      J.P.N. 15; (1993) 137 S.J.L.B. 36; *Times*, December 8, 1992; *Independent*,
      December 4, 1992, HL; reversing [1991] 1 W.L.R. 1334; [1991] 3 All E.R. 394;
      (1991) 93 Cr. App. R. 156; (1991) 155 J.P.N. 474; (1991) 88(24) L.S.G. 40;
      (1991) 141 N.L.J. 599; *Times*, April 24, 1991; *Independent*, June 4, 1991;
      Independent, May 20, 1991 (C.S.); *Daily Telegraph*, May 3, 1991, CA (Crim Div) .   *Digested*, 93/**994**:
                                            Applied, 98/1065, 00/1012: *Considered*, 94/1152
DPP v. Goodfellow [1998] C.O.D. 94; *Times*, November 24, 1997; *Independent*,
      October 20, 1997 (C.S.), QBD . . . .   *Digested*, 97/**1106**
DPP v. Green; *sub nom* Green v. Lincolnshire Stipendiary Magistrate; Green v. DPP;
      Crown Prosecution Service v. Green [2001] 1 W.L.R. 505; (2000) 164 J.P. 477;
      [2001] Env. L.R. 15; *Times*, June 29, 2000; *Independent*, July 31, 2000 (C.S),
      QBD . . . .   *Digested*, 00/**192**
DPP v. Guy (David Andrew) (1997) 161 J.P. 727; [1998] R.T.R. 82; [1997] 3 C.M.L.R.
      1161; *Times*, July 3, 1997; *Independent*, July 7, 1997 (C.S.), QBD . . . .   *Digested*, 97/**4367**
DPP v. H see DPP v. Harper
DPP v. H see I v. DPP
DPP v. Harper; *sub nom* DPP v. H [1997] 1 W.L.R. 1406; (1997) 161 J.P. 697; [1998]
      R.T.R. 200; (1998) 39 B.M.L.R. 91; (1997) 94(18) L.S.G. 31; *Times*, May 2, 1997;
      Independent, April 28, 1997 (C.S.), QBD . . . .   *Digested*, 97/**1199**
DPP v. Harris (Nigel) [1995] 1 Cr. App. R. 170; (1994) 158 J.P. 896; [1995] R.T.R. 100;
      [1995] Crim. L.R. 73; [1994] C.O.D. 384; (1994) 158 J.P.N. 666; *Times*, March
      16, 1994, QBD . . . .   *Digested*, 95/**4407**:
                                                                                    Approved, 98/972: *Considered*, 97/3770
DPP v. Henn (No.1) see R. v. Henn (Maurice Donald) (No.1)
DPP v. Heywood [1998] R.T.R. 1, QBD . . . .   *Digested*, 97/**1316**
DPP v. Humphries see Crown Prosecution Service v. Humphries
DPP v. Humphrys (Bruce Edward); *sub nom* R. v. Humphrys (Bruce Edward) [1977]
      A.C. 1; [1976] 2 W.L.R. 857; [1976] 2 All E.R. 497; (1976) 63 Cr. App. R. 95;
      [1976] R.T.R. 339; [1977] Crim. L.R. 421; 120 S.J. 420, HL; reversing [1976]
      Q.B. 191; [1975] 3 W.L.R. 81; [1975] 2 All E.R. 1023; (1976) 62 Cr. App. R. 1;
      [1975] Crim. L.R. 708; 119 S.J. 473, CA (Crim Div) . . . .   *Digested*, 76/**488**:
                                            Applied, 82/511, 83/3098, 84/971, 85/2126, 00/5485: *Considered*, 78/464,
                                                          81/1682, 83/2309, 94/655: *Distinguished*, 77/633: *Followed*, 97/1107,
                                                          00/1106

DPP *v.* Hutchinson; *sub nom* R. *v.* Secretary of State for Defence Ex p. Parker; R. *v.* Secretary of State for Defence Ex p. Hayman; DPP *v.* Smith (Georgina) [1990] 2 A.C. 783; [1990] 3 W.L.R. 196; (1991) 155 J.P. 71; 89 L.G.R. 1; (1990) 2 Admin. L.R. 741; [1991] C.O.D. 4; (1990) 154 J.P.N. 674; (1990) 154 L.G. Rev. 872; (1990) 140 N.L.J. 1035; (1990) 134 S.J. 1041, HL; reversing [1989] Q.B. 583; [1989] 3 W.L.R. 281; [1989] 1 All E.R. 1060; (1989) 153 J.P. 453; 87 L.G.R. 347; [1989] Crim. L.R. 208; [1989] C.O.D. 251; (1989) 153 J.P.N. 631; (1989) 153 L.G. Rev. 609; (1989) 133 S.J. 946; *Times*, October 25, 1988; *Independent*, October 21, 1988, QBD . . . . *Digested*, 91/**87**:
Applied, 90/2645, 91/2084, 97/1, 97/4101, 99/4359: *Referred to*, 95/870
DPP *v.* Hyde [1999] 2 C.M.L.R. 1380, HC (Irl)
DPP *v.* Hynde [1998] 1 W.L.R. 1222; [1998] 1 All E.R. 649; [1998] 1 Cr. App. R. 288; (1997) 161 J.P. 671; [1998] Crim. L.R. 72; (1997) 161 J.P.N. 858; *Times*, July 18, 1997; *Independent*, July 9, 1997, QBD . . . . *Digested*, 97/**1235**
DPP *v.* I see I *v.* DPP
DPP *v.* Jackson see Hinds *v.* Queen, The
DPP *v.* Jackson (Failure to Provide Specimen); Stanley *v.* DPP [1999] 1 A.C. 406; [1998] 3 W.L.R. 514; [1998] 3 All E.R. 769; [1999] 1 Cr. App. R. 204; (1999) 163 J.P. 474; [1998] R.T.R. 397; (1999) 45 B.M.L.R. 53; [1998] Crim. L.R. 900; (1998) 95(33) L.S.G. 35; (1998) 148 N.L.J. 1180; *Times*, July 30, 1998, HL; reversing [1998] R.T.R. 141; [1998] C.O.D. 12, QBD . . . . *Digested*, 98/**1028**
DPP *v.* Jimale [2001] Crim. L.R. 138, QBD (Admin Ct)
DPP *v.* John; DPP *v.* Lee [1999] 1 W.L.R. 1883; [1999] Crim. L.R. 821; (1999) 96(7) L.S.G. 35; *Times*, January 28, 1999, QBD . . . . *Digested*, 99/**4354**
DPP *v.* Jones [1990] R.T.R. 33; (1990) 154 J.P.N. 597, DC . . . . *Digested*, 90/**3971**:
Applied, 01/1032: *Distinguished*, 91/930, 92/3783, 93/3507
DPP *v.* Jones (Christopher) see DPP *v.* McKeown (Sharon)
DPP *v.* Jones (Margaret) [1999] 2 A.C. 240; [1999] 2 W.L.R. 625; [1999] 2 All E.R. 257; [1999] 2 Cr. App. R. 348; (1999) 163 J.P. 285; 6 B.H.R.C. 513; [1999] Crim. L.R. 672; (1999) 163 J.P.N. 355; [1999] E.G.C.S. 36; (1999) 96(13) L.S.G. 31; (1999) 96(11) L.S.G. 71; (1999) 143 S.J.L.B. 98; [1999] N.P.C. 31; *Times*, March 5, 1999; *Independent*, March 9, 1999, HL; reversing [1998] Q.B. 563; [1997] 2 W.L.R. 578; [1997] 2 All E.R. 119; [1997] 2 Cr. App. R. 59; (1997) 161 J.P. 324; [1997] Crim. L.R. 599; (1997) 161 J.P.N. 434; (1997) 94(6) L.S.G. 27; (1997) 147 N.L.J. 162; *Times*, January 27, 1997; *Independent*, January 30, 1997, QBD . . . . *Digested*, 99/**965**
DPP *v.* Jowle (1999) 163 J.P. 85; *Times*, December 13, 1997, QBD . . . . *Digested*, 98/**1176**
DPP *v.* Kavaz [1999] R.T.R. 40, QBD . . . . *Digested*, 00/**929**
DPP *v.* Kay (1999) 163 J.P. 108; [1999] R.T.R. 109; *Times*, April 13, 1998, QBD . . . . *Digested*, 98/**895**
DPP *v.* Kitching (1990) 154 J.P. 293; [1990] Crim. L.R. 394; [1990] C.O.D. 149; (1990) 154 J.P.N. 172; *Times*, November 17, 1989; *Independent*, December 4, 1989 (C.S.), QBD . . . . *Digested*, 91/**893**:
Considered, 98/912
DPP *v.* Kukadia see DPP *v.* Charles
DPP *v.* L [1999] Crim. L.R. 752; *Times*, February 1, 1999, QBD . . . . *Digested*, 99/**907**
DPP *v.* Lawrence [1998] C.O.D. 361, QBD
DPP *v.* Lee see DPP *v.* John
DPP *v.* Lonsdale [2001] EWHC Admin 95; [2001] R.T.R. 29; [2001] Crim. L.R. 659; (2001) 98(10) L.S.G. 44; *Times*, February 16, 2001, QBD . . . . *Digested*, 01/**1130**
DPP *v.* Loving (Jeffrey Richard) see DPP *v.* Doot
DPP *v.* M see I *v.* DPP
DPP *v.* M [1998] Q.B. 913; [1998] 2 W.L.R. 604; [1997] 2 All E.R. 749; [1997] 2 Cr. App. R. 70; (1997) 161 J.P. 491; [1997] 2 F.L.R. 804; [1998] Fam. Law 11, QBD . . . . *Digested*, 97/**1131**
DPP *v.* Marshall; *sub nom* Mills *v.* Marshall [1998] I.C.R. 518; [1998] I.R.L.R. 494, EAT . *Digested*, 98/**2195**
DPP *v.* McCarthy (1999) 163 J.P. 585; [1999] R.T.R. 323; (1999) 96(5) L.S.G. 37; *Times*, January 8, 1999; *Independent*, December 21, 1998 (C.S.), QBD . . . . *Digested*, 99/**956**
DPP *v.* McDonald (Robert Alan Michael) see DPP *v.* Morgan (William Anthony)
DPP *v.* McKeown (Sharon); DPP *v.* Jones (Christopher) [1997] 1 W.L.R. 295; [1997] 1 All E.R. 737; [1997] 1 Cr. App. R. 155; (1997) 161 J.P. 356; [1997] R.T.R. 162; [1997] Crim. L.R. 522; (1997) 161 J.P.N. 482; (1997) 147 N.L.J. 289; *Times*, February 21, 1997; *Independent*, March 7, 1997, HL; reversing [1995] Crim. L.R. 69, QBD . . . . *Digested*, 97/**1093**:
Applied, 97/1147: *Considered*, 98/897, 00/914
DPP *v.* McLarty (Robert) see DPP *v.* Morgan (William Anthony)
DPP *v.* Mooney [1997] R.T.R. 434; [1997] Crim. L.R. 137, QBD . . . . *Digested*, 98/**900**
DPP *v.* Morgan (William Anthony); *sub nom* R. *v.* Morgan (William Anthony); DPP *v.* McDonald (Robert Alan Michael); DPP *v.* McLarty (Robert); DPP *v.* Parker (Michael Andrew) [1976] A.C. 182; [1975] 2 W.L.R. 913; [1975] 2 All E.R. 347; (1975) 61 Cr. App. R. 136; [1975] Crim. L.R. 717; 119 S.J. 319, HL; affirming in part [1975] 1 All E.R. 8, CA (Crim Div) . . . . *Digested*, 75/**682**:
Applied, 83/693, 84/502.3, 84/709, 87/825, 00/1002: *Considered*, 77/637, 81/1564, 86/702, 95/977

DPP v. Moseley (Joanna); DPP v. Selvanayagam (Valerie); DPP v. Woodling (Stephen)
   Times, June 23, 1999 ; *Independent*, June 21, 1999 (C.S.), QBD . . . .   *Digested*, 99/**940**
DPP v. Nock; *sub nom* R. v. Nock (David Michael); R. v. Alsford (Kevin Charles); DPP
   v. Alsford [1978] A.C. 979; [1978] 3 W.L.R. 57; [1978] 2 All E.R. 654; (1978) 67
   Cr. App. R. 116; [1978] Crim. L.R. 483; 122 S.J. 417, HL . . . .   *Digested*, 78/**430**:
               Applied, 78/422, 79/414: *Considered*, 00/995: *Distinguished*, 78/429, 79/419,
                                           79/420
DPP v. Noe [2000] R.T.R. 351; (2000) 97(20) L.S.G. 43; *Times*, April 19, 2000, QBD . .   *Digested*, 00/**960**
DPP v. Pal [2000] Crim. L.R. 756, QBD
DPP v. Parker (Michael Andrew) see DPP v. Morgan (William Anthony)
DPP v. Pearman (1993) 157 J.P. 883; [1992] R.T.R. 407; (1993) 157 J.P.N. 444; *Times*,
   March 27, 1992, DC . . . .   *Digested*, 93/**3500**:
                          Applied, 94/3982: *Considered*, 00/959
DPP v. Percy see Bugg v. DPP
DPP v. Potts [2000] R.T.R. 1, QBD. . . . .   *Digested*, 00/**1001**
DPP v. Ramos [2000] Crim. L.R. 768; [2000] C.O.D. 287, QBD
DPP v. Ramsdale [2001] EWHC Admin 106; *Independent*, March 19, 2001 (C.S), QBD
   (Admin Ct)
DPP v. Ray; *sub nom* Ray v. Sempers [1974] A.C. 370; [1973] 3 W.L.R. 359; [1973] 3
   All E.R. 131; (1974) 58 Cr. App. R. 130; [1974] Crim. L.R. 181; 117 S.J. 663, HL;
   reversing [1973] 1 W.L.R. 317; [1973] 1 All E.R. 860; (1973) 57 Cr. App. R. 324;
   [1973] Crim. L.R. 182, DC . . . .   *Digested*, 73/**578**:
                     Applied, 99/950: *Considered*, 93/991
DPP v. Rogers [1998] Crim. L.R. 202, QBD. . . . .   *Digested*, 98/**936**
DPP v. Rumble see DPP v. Billington
DPP v. Saddington; *sub nom* Chief Constable of North Yorkshire v. Saddington (2001)
   165 J.P. 122; [2001] R.T.R. 15; [2001] Crim. L.R. 41; *Times*, November 1, 2000;
   Independent, November 3, 2000, QBD. . . . .   *Digested*, 00/**1000**
DPP v. Scarlett; *sub nom* Crown Prosecution Service v. Scarlett [2000] 1 W.L.R. 515;
   Times, February 7, 2000 ; *Independent*, January 19, 2000, CA. . . . .   *Digested*, 00/**39**
DPP v. Selvanayagam (Valerie) see DPP v. Moseley (Joanna)
DPP v. Shanahan (Thomas) see DPP v. Doot
DPP v. Skinner; *sub nom* DPP v. Cornwell; DPP v. Cornhill; DPP v. Cornell [1990]
   R.T.R. 254, DC . . . .   *Digested*, 91/**3118**:
                      Considered, 91/3117, 00/960
DPP v. Smith (Georgina) see DPP v. Hutchinson
DPP v. Smith (Robert James) [2000] R.T.R. 341, QBD . . . .   *Digested*, 01/**1131**
DPP v. Speede; *sub nom* Crown Prosecution Service v. Speede; R. v. Liverpool
   Magistrates Court Ex p. Collins; R. v. Liverpool Magistrates Court Ex p. Santos
   [1998] 2 Cr. App. R. 108, QBD . . . .   *Digested*, 98/**1068**
DPP v. Spurrier see R. v. Crown Prosecution Service Ex p. Spurrier
DPP v. Swann (2000) 164 J.P. 365, QBD . . . .   *Digested*, 00/**997**
DPP v. Teixeira (Jose) see DPP v. Brown (Andrew Earle)
DPP v. Tilly; Tilly v. DPP [2001] EWHC Admin 821; *Times*, November 27, 2001;
   Independent, December 10, 2001 (C.S); *Daily Telegraph*, October 30, 2001, QBD
   (Admin Ct) . . . .   *Digested*, 01/**1063**
DPP v. Tokai; *sub nom* Attorney General of Trinidad and Tobago v. Tokai [1996] A.C.
   856; [1996] 3 W.L.R. 149; (1996) 140 S.J.L.B. 149, PC (Trin) . . . .   *Digested*, 96/**3167**:
                                  Considered, 99/1037
DPP v. Tomkinson [2001] EWHC Admin 182; [2001] R.T.R. 38, QBD . . . .   *Digested*, 01/**1032**
DPP v. Turner; *sub nom* R. v. Turner (John Eric) [1974] A.C. 357; [1973] 3 W.L.R. 352;
   [1973] 3 All E.R. 124; (1973) 57 Cr. App. R. 932; [1974] Crim. L.R. 186; 117 S.J.
   664, HL; reversing [1973] 1 W.L.R. 653; [1973] 2 All E.R. 828; (1973) 57 Cr.
   App. R. 650; [1973] Crim. L.R. 370; 117 S.J. 303, CA (Crim Div) . . . .   *Digested*, 73/**579**:
         Applied, 75/637, 76/532, 79/591, 80/591, 94/4570, 95/5051, 96/5854,
                                       99/1386
DPP v. Tweddell see Crown Prosecution Service v. Tweddell
DPP v. Varley (1999) 163 J.P. 443; [1999] Crim. L.R. 753, QBD . . . .   *Digested*, 99/**1009**
DPP v. Vivier [1991] 4 All E.R. 18; (1991) 155 J.P. 970; [1991] R.T.R. 205; [1991] Crim.
   L.R. 637; (1991) 155 L.G. Rev. 588, DC . . . .   *Digested*, 92/**3813**:
        Applied, 92/3858, 93/3509, 93/3512: *Considered*, 94/3991, 95/4431:
                                Distinguished, 01/1033
DPP v. Ward [1998] Masons C.L.R. 250, QBD. . . . .   *Digested*, 99/**885**
DPP v. Ward (Jack); *sub nom* R. v. DPP Ex p. Ward (Jack) [1999] R.T.R. 11; *Times*,
   March 24, 1997, QBD . . . .   *Digested*, 97/**1314**

DPP *v.* Warren [1993] A.C. 319; [1992] 3 W.L.R. 884; [1992] 4 All E.R. 865; (1993) 96 Cr. App. R. 312; (1993) 157 J.P. 297; [1993] R.T.R. 58; (1993) 157 J.P.N. 205; (1992) 142 N.L.J. 1684; (1992) 136 S.J.L.B. 316; *Times,* November 6, 1992; *Independent,* November 6, 1992, HL; reversing (1992) 156 J.P. 753; [1992] R.T.R. 129; [1992] Crim. L.R. 200; (1992) 156 J.P.N. 554; *Independent,* November 4, 1991 (C.S.), QBD . . . . *Digested,* 93/**3484**:
Applied, 93/3485, 93/3487, 93/3488, 94/3969, 94/3994, 98/1028:
Considered, 94/3970, 94/3973, 94/3974, 95/4411, 95/4413, 96/5056, 96/5065, 97/1308, 97/1313, 98/1029: *Distinguished,* 93/5767:
Followed, 93/5768: *Not followed,* 94/6229: *Referred to,* 97/1310, 97/1311
DPP *v.* Watts (James Wesley) see DPP *v.* Doot
DPP *v.* Weeks; *sub nom* Crown Prosecution Service *v.* Weeks *Independent,* July 17, 2000 (C.S), QBD
DPP *v.* West (2000) 150 N.L.J. 1591, QBD
DPP *v.* Williams (Michael) CO 2203/98, QBD . . . . *Digested,* 98/**954**
DPP *v.* Wilson [2001] EWHC Admin 198; (2001) 165 J.P. 715; (2001) 165 J.P.N. 845; (2001) 98(18) L.S.G. 45; *Times,* March 21, 2001, QBD (Adm Ct). . . . . *Digested,* 01/**972**
DPP *v.* Woodling (Stephen) see DPP *v.* Moseley (Joanna)
DPP for Northern Ireland *v.* Lynch [1975] A.C. 653; [1975] 2 W.L.R. 641; [1975] 1 All E.R. 913; (1975) 61 Cr. App. R. 6; [1975] Crim. L.R. 707; 119 S.J. 233, HL. . . . . . *Digested,* 75/**622**:
Applied, 86/649: *Considered,* 76/499, 95/1256, 99/1020:
Distinguished, 76/513: *Overruled,* 87/800
DPP for Northern Ireland's Application, Re [1999] N.I. 106, QBD (NI) . . . . *Digested,* 99/**5205**
DPP for Northern Ireland's Application for Judicial Review, Re see Ballyedmond Castle Farms Ltd's Application, Re
DPP for Northern Ireland's Application for Judicial Review, Re [2000] N.I. 49, QBD (NI) *Digested,* 00/**5469**
DPP for Northern Ireland's Application for Judicial Review, Re [2001] N.I. 60, QBD (NI) *Digested,* 01/**5736**
DQ Henriques Ltd *v.* Buchler see ASRS Establishment Ltd (In Administrative Receivership and Liquidation), Re
Dr Martens International Trading GmbH's Trade Mark Application [2000] E.T.M.R. 1151, OHIM (Opposition Div) . . . . *Digested,* 01/**3985**
Dr Robert Winzer Pharma GmbH's Application to Cancel a Trade Mark of Alcon Pharmaceuticals Ltd [2000] E.T.M.R. 217, OHIM (Cancellation Div). . . . . *Digested,* 00/**3727**
Drabble *v.* Demolition Services Ltd (Unreported, May 8, 2000), CC (Bradford) [*Ex rel.* Edward T Legard, Barrister, York Chambers, 14 Toft Green, York] . . . . *Digested,* 00/**1646**
Draehmpaehl *v.* Urania Immobilienservice ohG (C180/95) [1997] All E.R. (E.C.) 719; [1997] E.C.R. I-2195; [1997] 3 C.M.L.R. 1107; [1998] I.C.R. 164; [1997] I.R.L.R. 538; *Times,* May 2, 1997, ECJ. . . . . *Digested,* 97/**2218**:
Considered, 00/5529
Dragages et Travaux Publics (Hong Kong) Ltd *v.* Citystate Insurance Ltd (2001) 17 Const. L.J. 523, CA (HK)
Drage *v.* Governing Body of Greenford High School; *sub nom* Drage *v.* Governors of Greenford High School [2000] I.C.R. 899; [2000] I.R.L.R. 314; [2000] Ed. C.R. 382; (2000) 97(14) L.S.G. 42; (2000) 144 S.J.L.B. 165; *Times,* March 28, 2000, CA . . . . *Digested,* 00/**2242**
Drage *v.* Governors of Greenford High School see Drage *v.* Governing Body of Greenford High School
Drage *v.* Grassroots Ltd (Unreported, September 5, 2000), CC (Watford) [*Ex rel.* Andrew Ritchie, Barrister, 9 Gough Square, London] . . . . *Digested,* 00/**2967**
Drake *v.* Pontefract HA [1998] Lloyd's Rep. Med. 425, QBD. . . . . *Digested,* 99/**4001**
Drake & Scull Engineering Ltd *v.* J Jarvis & Sons Plc (Leave to Appeal) 58 Con. L.R. 39, CA
Drake Insurance Plc, Re [2001] Lloyd's Rep. I.R. 643, Ch D (Companies Ct). . . . . *Digested,* 01/**3808**
Drake Insurance Plc (Addendum Judgment), Re 2927 of 2000, Ch D (Companies Ct) . *Previous proceedings,*
01/3808
Dray *v.* Doherty (Unreported, November 3, 1998), CC (Clerkenwell) [*Ex rel.* Andrew Ritchie, Barrister, 9 Gough Square, London] . . . . *Digested,* 99/**525**
Dream Factory Ltd *v.* Crown Estate Commissioners [2000] 3 E.G.L.R. 107; [1998] E.G.C.S. 136; *Times,* October 22, 1998, Ch D . . . . *Digested,* 98/**3633**
Dreamgate Properties Ltd *v.* Arnot (1998) 76 P. & C.R. 25; [1997] E.G.C.S. 121, CA . . . *Digested,* 98/**3665**
Dredging & Construction Co Ltd *v.* Delta Civil Engineering Co Ltd (No.1); *sub nom* Delta Civil Engineering Co Ltd *v.* Dredging & Construction Co Ltd (No.1) [2000] C.L.C. 213; 68 Con. L.R. 87, QBD (T&CC) . . . . *Digested,* 00/**233**
Dredging & Construction Co Ltd *v.* Delta Civil Engineering Co Ltd (No.2) (2000) 2 T.C.L.R. 438; 72 Con. L.R. 99, QBD (Comm Ct)
Dresser UK *v.* Falcongate Freight Management (The Duke of Yare) [1992] Q.B. 502; [1992] 2 W.L.R. 319; [1992] 2 All E.R. 450; [1991] 2 Lloyd's Rep. 557; [1992] I.L.Pr. 164; (1991) 135 S.J.L.B. 126; *Times,* August 8, 1991; *Financial Times,* August 2, 1991, CA . . . . *Digested,* 92/**3534**:
Applied, 94/482, 94/487, 01/830: *Considered,* 96/920:
Distinguished, 92/3401, 93/3127
Dreverton *v.* Regal Garage Ltd (Unreported, October 9, 1997), CC (Wigan) [*Ex rel.* Bernard Lo, Barrister, 17 Bedford Row, London] . . . . *Digested,* 98/**4382**
Drew (A Bankrupt), Re [1929] I.R. 504. . . . . *Approved,* 00/3921

Drew-Morgan v. Hamid-Zadeh (2000) 32 H.L.R. 216; [1999] L. & T.R. 503; [1999] 2
    E.G.L.R. 13; [1999] 26 E.G. 156; [1999] E.G.C.S. 72, CA . . . .   *Digested,* 99/**3652**
Drexfine Holdings Ltd v. Cherwell DC [1998] J.P.L. 361, QBD . . . .   *Digested,* 98/**4205**
Drinking Water (C42/89), Re see Commission of the European Communities v. Belgium
    (C42/89)
Driscoll v. Church Commissioners for England; *sub nom* Driscoll's Application, Re
    [1957] 1 Q.B. 330; [1956] 3 W.L.R. 996; [1956] 3 All E.R. 802; (1957) 7 P. &
    C.R. 371; 100 S.J. 872, CA; affirming 167 E.G. 663; [1956] J.P.L. 535, Lands Tr .   *Digested,* 56/**7343**:
                    Applied, 65/2230, 81/1532: *Considered,* 89/3627: *Followed,* 98/3652
Driscoll's Application, Re see Driscoll v. Church Commissioners for England
Driskel v. Peninsula Business Services Ltd [2000] I.R.L.R. 151, EAT . . . .   *Digested,* 00/**2208**
Driver v. No. 1 Auto Salvage [2001] 2 Q.R. 12, CC (Rotherham) [*Ex rel.* Andrew Bailey,
    Barrister, Paradise Square Chambers, 26 Paradise Square, Sheffield] . . . .   *Digested,* 01/**1805**
Driver v. Purbeck DC (Unreported, May 17, 1999), CC (Bournemouth) [*Ex rel.* David
    Carter, Barrister, Arden Chambers, 27 John Street, London] . . . .   *Digested,* 99/**3066**
Drouot Assurances SA v. Consolidated Metallurgical Industries [2000] I.L.Pr. 421, Cass
    (F)
Drouot Assurances SA v. Consolidated Metallurgical Industries (CMI Industrial Sites)
    (C351/96) [1999] Q.B. 497; [1999] 2 W.L.R. 163; [1998] All E.R. (E.C.) 483;
    [1998] E.C.R. I-3075; [1998] C.L.C. 1270; [1998] I.L.Pr. 485; [1999] Lloyd's
    Rep. I.R. 338; *Times,* June 10, 1998, ECJ (5th Chamber) . . . .   *Digested,* 98/**745**
Drummie v. Society of Lloyd's see Morrison v. Society of Lloyd's
Drummond-Rees v. Dorset CC (Trading Standards Department) (1998) 162 J.P. 651;
    (1998) 162 J.P.N. 645, QBD . . . .   *Digested,* 97/**967**
Drury v. Camden LBC [1972] R.T.R. 391 . . . .   *Digested,* 72/**3082**:
                                   Considered, 99/4070
Drury v. Grimsby HA [1997] 8 Med. L.R. 38; (1998) 42 B.M.L.R. 208, QBD . . . .   *Digested,* 97/**662**
Dryhurst v. Dale (Unreported, January 8, 1998), CC (Manchester) [*Ex rel.* Pannone &
    Partners Solicitors, 123 Deansgate, Manchester]. . . . .   *Digested,* 99/**1499**
DS v. Gloucestershire CC see S v. Gloucestershire CC
DSG Retail Ltd v. Lexington Insurance Co see DSG Retail Ltd v. QBE International
    Insurance Ltd
DSG Retail Ltd v. Oxford CC see DSG Retail Ltd v. Oxfordshire CC
DSG Retail Ltd v. Oxfordshire CC; *sub nom* DSG Retail Ltd v. Oxford CC [2001] EWHC
    Admin 253; [2001] 1 W.L.R. 1765; (2001) 165 J.P. 409; [2001] B.L.G.R. 301;
    (2001) 165 J.P.N. 362; (2001) 98(19) L.S.G. 36; (2001) 145 S.J.L.B. 91; *Times,*
    March 23, 2001; *Daily Telegraph,* March 27, 2001, QBD . . . .   *Digested,* 01/**913**
DSG Retail Ltd v. PC World Ltd [1998] E.T.M.R. 321, HC (Irl)
DSG Retail Ltd v. QBE International Insurance Ltd; DSG Retail Ltd v. Royal London
    General Insurance Co Ltd; DSG Retail Ltd v. Reliance National Insurance Co;
    DSG Retail Ltd v. Lexington Insurance Co; DSG Retail Ltd v. Sirius (UK)
    Insurance Plc [1999] Lloyd's Rep. I.R. 283, QBD (Comm Ct) . . . .   *Digested,* 99/**3394**
DSG Retail Ltd v. Reliance National Insurance Co see DSG Retail Ltd v. QBE
    International Insurance Ltd
DSG Retail Ltd v. Royal London General Insurance Co Ltd see DSG Retail Ltd v. QBE
    International Insurance Ltd
DSG Retail Ltd v. Sirius (UK) Insurance Plc see DSG Retail Ltd v. QBE International
    Insurance Ltd
DSL Group Ltd v. Unisys International Services Ltd (No.1) 41 Con. L.R. 33, QBD (OR). .   *Applied,* 00/826:
                                    Considered, 99/789
DSM NV's Patent see Novo Nordisk A/S v. DSM NV
DSM/Astaxanthin (T737/96) [2000] E.P.O.R. 557, EPO (Technical Bd App) . . . .   *Digested,* 01/**3923**
DSND Subsea Ltd (formerly DSND Oceantech Ltd) v. Petroleum Geo Services ASA
    [2000] B.L.R. 530, QBD (T&CC) . . . .   *Applied,* 01/872
DSR Senator Lines GmbH v. Commission of the European Communities (C364/99);
    sub nom DSR-Senator Lines GmbH v. Commission of the European
    Communities (T191/98) [1999] E.C.R. I-8733; [2000] 5 C.M.L.R. 600, ECJ . . .   *Digested,* 01/**754**
DSR-Senator Lines GmbH v. Commission of the European Communities (T191/98) see
    DSR Senator Lines GmbH v. Commission of the European Communities
    (C364/99)
DST v. Rakoil see Deutsche Schachtbau und Tiefbohrgesellschaft mbH v. Ras Al-
    Khaimah National Oil Co
DSV Silo und Verwaltungsgesellschaft mbH v. Owners of the Sennar (The Sennar)
    (No.2) [1985] 1 W.L.R. 490; [1985] 2 All E.R. 104; [1985] 1 Lloyd's Rep. 521;
    (1985) 82 L.S.G. 1863; (1985) 135 N.L.J. 316; (1985) 129 S.J. 248, HL;
    affirming [1984] 2 Lloyd's Rep. 142, CA; reversing [1983] 2 Lloyd's Rep. 399,
    QBD (Adm Ct) . . . .   *Digested,* 85/**1291**:
           Applied, 90/2019, 95/3559: *Considered,* 86/3078, 00/785
DTC (CNC) Ltd v. Gary Sergeant & Co [1996] 1 W.L.R. 797; [1996] 2 All E.R. 369;
    [1996] B.C.C. 290; [1996] 1 B.C.L.C. 529; *Times,* January 25, 1996, Ch D . . . .   *Digested,* 96/**8**:
                                   Considered, 98/4
DTE Financial Services Ltd v. Inspector of Taxes see DTE Financial Services Ltd v.
    Wilson (Inspector of Taxes)

DTE Financial Services Ltd v. Wilson (Inspector of Taxes); *sub nom* DTE Financial
Services Ltd v. Inspector of Taxes [2001] EWCA Civ 455; [2001] S.T.C. 777;
[2001] B.T.C. 159; [2001] S.T.I. 670; (2001) 98(21) L.S.G. 40; *Times*, May 3,
2001; *Daily Telegraph*, April 10, 2001, CA; affirming [1999] S.T.C. 1061; [1999]
B.T.C. 415; (1999) 96(44) L.S.G. 41; (1999) 143 S.J.L.B. 270; *Times*, November
9, 1999, Ch D . . . . *Digested*, 01/**5237**
DTZ Debenham Thorpe Ltd v. Shropshire CC [1998] E.H.L.R. 93; [1997] N.P.C. 112,
QBD. . . . . *Digested*, 97/**2376**
Du Cross Application, Re see W&G du Cros Ltd's Application, Re
Du Pont de Nemours (EI) & Co v. AMA Antoon Michielsen Automobiles vof (t/a Protech
Nederland Teflon Lakbescherming) (KG C0000459/BR) [2001] E.T.M.R. 70,
Hof ('s-Hertogenbosch)
Du Pont Merck Pharmaceutical Co's European Patent (J42/92) (1998) 21 (8) I.P.D. 21088,
EPO (Legal Bd App)
DU PONT/Fibre filled elastomer (T345/96); *sub nom* El du Pont de Nemours European
Patent Application (No.90120556.7) [2001] E.P.O.R. 15; (1999) 22(10) I.P.D.
22095, EPO (Technical Bd App) . . . . *Digested*, 01/**3941**
DU PONT/Hybridoma (T906/91) [1999] E.P.O.R. 423, EPO (Technical Bd App). . . . . . *Digested*, 00/**3626**
DU PONT/Suspected partiality (T1028/96); *sub nom* El du Pont de Nemours and Co's
European Patent (No.0203469) [2001] E.P.O.R. 17; (2000) 23(3) I.P.D. 23018,
EPO (Technical Bd App) . . . . *Digested*, 01/**3885**
DU PONT/Tetrafluoroethylene (T619/88) [1998] E.P.O.R. 233, EPO (Technical Bd App)
Du Sautoy v. Symes [1967] Ch. 1146; [1967] 2 W.L.R. 342; [1967] 1 All E.R. 25; 111
S.J. 133, Ch D . . . . *Digested*, 67/**2202**:
Applied, 00/4651: *Followed*, 75/1830
Dualit Ltd v. Rowlett Catering Appliances Ltd 9901306, Ch D . . . . *Digested*, 00/**371**
Dualit Ltd v. Rowlett Catering Appliances Ltd (Fresh Evidence) [1999] F.S.R. 865,
Ch D . . . . *Digested*, 00/**3711**
Dualit Ltd's Trade Mark Application (No.2023846) [1999] R.P.C. 890; (1999) 22(11) I.P.D.
22107; *Times*, July 19, 1999, Ch D; affirming [1999] R.P.C. 304; (1999) 22(1)
I.P.D. 22010, TMR . . . . *Digested*, 99/**3583**:
Referred to, 01/4030
Duarte v. Mount Cook Land Ltd [2001] 33 E.G.C.S. 87, QBD
Dubai Aluminium Co Ltd v. Al-Alawi [1999] 1 W.L.R. 1964; [1999] 1 All E.R. 703;
[1999] 1 All E.R. (Comm.) 1; [1999] 1 Lloyd's Rep. 478; *Times*, January 6, 1999;
Independent, December 21, 1998 (C.S.), QBD (Comm Ct). . . . . *Digested*, 99/**338**:
Applied, 01/398
Dubai Aluminium Co Ltd v. Amhurst see Dubai Aluminium Co Ltd v. Salaam
Dubai Aluminium Co Ltd v. Amhurst Brown Martin & Nicholson see Dubai Aluminium
Co Ltd v. Salaam
Dubai Aluminium Co Ltd v. Salaam; Dubai Aluminium Co Ltd v. Amhurst; Dubai
Aluminium Co Ltd v. Amhurst Brown Martin & Nicholson [2001] Q.B. 113;
[2000] 3 W.L.R. 910; [2000] 2 Lloyd's Rep. 168; [2000] Lloyd's Rep. P.N. 497;
[2000] P.N.L.R. 578; *Times*, April 21, 2000, CA; reversing [1999] 1 Lloyd's
Rep. 415; (1998) 148 N.L.J. 1301; *Times*, September 4, 1998, QBD (Comm Ct). . *Digested*, 00/**4316**:
Applied, 01/4267
Dubai Bank Ltd v. Abbas [1998] Lloyd's Rep. Bank. 230; [1998] I.L.Pr. 391, QBD
(Comm Ct) . . . . *Digested*, 98/**754**
Dubai Bank Ltd v. Galadari (Mareva Injunction) [1990] 1 Lloyd's Rep. 120; [1990]
B.C.L.C. 90, CA. . . . . *Digested*, 91/**2916**:
Considered, 99/487, 01/764: *Followed*, 96/846
Dubai Bank Ltd v. Galadari (No.6), *Times*, October 14, 1992; *Independent*, November
24, 1992, CA; reversing *Times*, April 22, 1991; *Independent*, May 6, 1991 (C.S.),
Ch D . . . . *Digested*, 92/**3476**:
Considered, 99/3330
Dubai Bank Ltd v. Galadari (No.7) [1992] 1 W.L.R. 106; [1992] 1 All E.R. 658; (1992)
89(7) L.S.G. 31, Ch D . . . . *Digested*, 92/**3484**:
Disapproved, 01/553
Dubai Islamic Bank PJSC v. Paymentech Merchant Services Inc [2001] 1 All E.R.
(Comm) 514; [2001] 1 Lloyd's Rep. 65; [2001] C.L.C. 173; (2000) 97(47)
L.S.G. 39; *Times*, November 24, 2000, QBD (Comm Ct) . . . . *Digested*, 00/**239**
Dublin Well Woman Centre v. Ireland (A/246) see Open Door Counselling Ltd v. Ireland
(A/246)
DUCATI Trade Mark [1998] R.P.C. 227; (1998) 21 (3) I.P.D. 21032, TMR . . . . *Digested*, 98/**3536**:
Distinguished, 01/3982: *Not followed*, 01/4042
Ducker (CICB: Quantum: 1999), Re [2000] 1 Q.R. 5, CICB (London) [*Ex rel*. Paul Rogers,
Barrister, Crown Office Row Chambers, Blenheim House, 120 Church Street,
Brighton] . . . . *Digested*, 99/**1453**
Ducker's Trade Mark, Re [1929] 1 Ch. 113; (1928) 45 R.P.C. 397, CA . . . . *Referred to*, 98/3500
Duckett v. Ministry of Defence (Unreported, October 10, 1997), CC (Stoke on Trent)
[*Ex rel*. Chapman Everatt, Solicitors, Shaw Road, Wolverhampton] . . . . *Digested*, 98/**400**
Duckitt v. Farrand see Duckitt v. Pensions Ombudsman
Duckitt v. Pensions Ombudsman; *sub nom* Duckitt v. Farrand [2001] O.P.L.R. 113;
[2001] Pens. L.R. 155, CA; affirming [2000] O.P.L.R. 167, Ch D

Ducks Unlimited's Trade Mark Application (849/1999) [2000] E.T.M.R. 820, OHIM
(Opposition Div) . . . .   *Digested,* 01/**4011**

Duckwari Plc (No.2), Re; *sub nom* Duckwari Plc *v.* Offerventure Ltd (No.2) [1999] Ch.
253; [1998] 3 W.L.R. 913; [1999] B.C.C. 11; [1998] 2 B.C.L.C. 315; (1998)
95(22) L.S.G. 28; (1998) 95(20) L.S.G. 36; (1998) 142 S.J.L.B. 163; *Times,*
May 18, 1998, CA; reversing [1997] Ch. 201; [1997] 2 W.L.R. 48; [1997] B.C.C.
45; [1997] 2 B.C.L.C. 729; *Times,* July 23, 1996, Ch D . . . .   *Digested,* 98/**685**:
   Applied, 00/5955

Duckwari Plc (No.3), Re; *sub nom* Duckwari Plc *v.* Offerventure Ltd (No.3) [1999] Ch.
268; [1999] 2 W.L.R. 1059; [1999] 1 B.C.L.C. 168; (1999) 96(4) L.S.G. 37;
(1999) 143 S.J.L.B. 29; *Times,* January 11, 1999, CA . . . .   *Digested,* 99/**630**

Duckwari Plc *v.* Offerventure Ltd (No.2) see Duckwari Plc (No.2), Re

Duckwari Plc *v.* Offerventure Ltd (No.3) see Duckwari Plc (No.3), Re

Duclos *v.* France (20940/92) (2001) 32 E.H.R.R. 5, ECHR

Dudgeon *v.* United Kingdom (No.2) (A/45) (1982) 4 E.H.R.R. 149, ECHR . . . .   *Applied,* 98/3159:
   Considered, 98/3104

Dudley MBC *v.* Henley Foundries Ltd [1999] Env. L.R. 895; [1999] Crim. L.R. 976,
QBD . . . .   *Digested,* 99/**2189**

Dudney *v.* R. see R. *v.* Dudney

Duer *v.* Frazer [2001] 1 W.L.R. 919; [2001] 1 All E.R. 249, QBD . . . .   *Digested,* 01/**578**

Duffen *v.* FRA BO SpA (No.1) [1999] E.C.C 58; *Times,* June 15, 1998, CA. . . . .   *Digested,* 98/**111**

Duffen *v.* FRA BO SpA (No.2); *sub nom* Duffen *v.* Frabo SpA (No.2) [2000] 1 Lloyd's
Rep. 180; [2000] E.C.C. 61; [2000] Eu. L.R. 167; (1999) 18 Tr. L.R. 342, CC
(Central London) . . . .   *Digested,* 00/**119**

Duffen *v.* Frabo SpA (No.2) see Duffen *v.* FRA BO SpA (No.2)

Duffill *v.* South Somerset DC (Unreported, October 29, 1999), CC (Yeovil) [*Ex rel.*
Marsh, Warry & Arrow Solicitors, Market Square, South Petherton, Somerset] . .   *Digested,* 00/**4236**

Duffus *v.* Southgate (Unreported, December 2, 1999), CC (Edmonton) [*Ex rel.* Ian
Bridge, Barrister, Mitre Court Chambers, Temple, London] . . . .   *Digested,* 00/**2562**

Duffy *v.* Carnaby (Unreported, March 24, 2000), CC (Kingston upon Hull) [*Ex rel.*
Graham & Rosen Solicitors, 8 Parliament Street, Hull] . . . .   *Digested,* 00/**1737**

Duffy *v.* First Choice Holidays & Flights Ltd [2000] 4 Q.R. 8, CC (Guildford) [*Ex rel.*
Michael Chapman, Barrister, Barnard's Inn Chambers, Chancery Lane, London
DX 336 Chancery Llane] . . . .   *Digested,* 00/**1658**

Duffy *v.* Lamb (t/a Vic Lamb Developments) (1998) 75 P. & C.R. 364; [1997]
E.G.C.S. 50; [1997] N.P.C. 52, CA . . . .   *Digested,* 98/**4346**

Duffy *v.* Newcastle United Football Co Ltd, *Times,* July 7, 2000, CA . . . .   *Digested,* 00/**873**

Duguid *v.* Secretary of State for the Environment, Transport and the Regions (2001) 82
P. & C.R. 6; [2000] 4 P.L.R. 107; [2001] J.P.L. 323; [2000] N.P.C. 92, CA;
affirming (2000) 80 P. & C.R. 389; [2000] J.P.L. 704, QBD . . . .   *Digested,* 01/**4696**

Duijnstee (Liquidator) *v.* Lodewijk Goderbauer (C288/82) [1983] E.C.R. 3663; [1985]
1 C.M.L.R. 220; [1985] F.S.R. 221, ECJ (4th Chamber) . . . .   *Digested,* 85/**1454**:
   Considered, 98/3455

Duke, Re (Unreported, May 15, 1995), CICB (York) [*Ex rel.* Abdul S Iqbal, Barrister] . . .   *Digested,* 95/**1679**:
   Considered, 01/1585

Duke, Re; *sub nom* Hannah *v.* Duke (1880-81) L.R. 16 Ch. D. 112, CA. . . . .   *Cited,* 00/5264

Duke *v.* GEC Reliance Ltd; *sub nom* Duke *v.* Reliance Systems Ltd [1988] A.C. 618;
[1988] 2 W.L.R. 359; [1988] 1 All E.R. 626; [1988] 1 C.M.L.R. 719; [1988]
I.C.R. 339; [1988] I.R.L.R. 118; [1988] 1 F.T.L.R. 398; (1988) 85(11) L.S.G. 42;
(1988) 132 S.J. 226; *Times,* February 12, 1988; *Independent,* February 12, 1988;
Financial Times, February 17, 1988; *Guardian,* February 12, 1988; *Daily Telegraph,*
February 19, 1988, HL; affirming [1988] Q.B. 108; [1987] 2 W.L.R. 1225;
[1987] 2 All E.R. 858; [1987] 2 C.M.L.R. 24; [1987] I.C.R. 491; [1987] I.R.L.R.
139; (1987) 84 L.S.G. 981; (1987) 131 S.J. 624, CA . . . .   *Digested,* 88/**1325**:
   Applied, 91/2115, 92/2505: *Considered,* 96/2611: *Distinguished,* 98/2194:
   Followed, 94/1987, 95/4562: *Referred to,* 89/2649

Duke *v.* Reliance Systems Ltd see Duke *v.* GEC Reliance Ltd

Duke Group Ltd (In Liquidation), Re [2001] B.C.C. 144, Ch D

Duke Group Ltd *v.* Carver [2001] B.P.I.R. 459, Ch D . . . .   *Digested,* 01/**3749**

Duke of Norfolk's Settlement Trusts, Re; *sub nom* Earl of Perth *v.* Fitzalan-Howard [1982]
Ch. 61; [1981] 3 W.L.R. 455; [1981] 3 All E.R. 220; 125 S.J. 554, CA; reversing
[1979] Ch. 37; [1978] 3 W.L.R. 655; [1978] 3 All E.R. 907; 122 S.J. 595, Ch D
. . . .   *Digested,* 81/**2462**:
   Considered, 99/3274

Duke of Westminster *v.* Birrane [1995] Q.B. 262; [1995] 2 W.L.R. 270; [1995] 3 All
E.R. 416; (1995) 27 H.L.R. 321; [1995] 1 E.G.L.R. 89; [1995] 11 E.G. 141; [1994]
E.G.C.S. 178; (1995) 92(3) L.S.G. 37; (1995) 139 S.J.L.B. 17; [1994] N.P.C.
141; *Times,* November 17, 1994; *Independent,* December 19, 1994 (C.S.), CA. . . .   *Digested,* 95/**3022**:
   Applied, 01/4180

Duke of Westminster *v.* Guild [1985] Q.B. 688; [1984] 3 W.L.R. 630; [1984] 3 All E.R.
144; (1984) 48 P. & C.R. 42; (1983) 267 E.G. 763; (1984) 128 S.J. 581, CA . . .   *Digested,* 84/**1893**:
   Applied, 85/1896, 98/3683: *Approved,* 98/3622, 99/3672:
   Considered, 88/2082

Dukeminster (Ebbgate House One) Ltd v. Somerfield Property Co Ltd (formerly
Gateway Properties Ltd) (1998) 75 P. & C.R. 154; [1997] 2 E.G.L.R. 125; [1997]
40 E.G. 157; [1997] E.G.C.S. 126; [1997] N.P.C. 127; *Times,* August 13, 1997,
CA; reversing [1996] E.G.C.S. 56; [1996] N.P.C. 44, Ch D . . . . *Digested,* 97/**3323**
Dulaurans v. France (34553/97) (2001) 33 E.H.R.R. 45, ECHR
Dullaghan v. Customs and Excise Commissioners [2000] V. & D.R. 189, V&DTr
Dumfries and Galloway Acute & Maternity Hospitals NHS Trust v. Fraser, *Independent,*
June 11, 2001 (C.S), EAT
Dun & Bradstreet Software Services (England) Ltd v. Provident Mutual Life Assurance
Association [1998] 2 E.G.L.R. 175; [1997] E.G.C.S. 89; [1997] N.P.C. 91, CA;
affirming [1996] E.G.C.S. 62; [1996] N.P.C. 57, Ch D . . . . *Digested,* 99/**3659**
Dunbar v. Plant [1998] Ch. 412; [1997] 3 W.L.R. 1261; [1997] 4 All E.R. 289; [1998]
1 F.L.R. 157; [1997] 3 F.C.R. 669; [1998] Fam. Law 139; (1997) 94(36) L.S.G.
44; (1997) 141 S.J.L.B.191; *Times,* August 13, 1997, CA . . . . *Digested,* 97/**4729**
Dunbar Bank Plc v. Nadeem [1998] 3 All E.R. 876; [1998] 2 F.L.R. 457; [1998] 3
F.C.R. 629; (1999) 31 H.L.R. 402; [1998] Fam. Law 595; *Times,* July 1, 1998,
CA; affirming [1997] 2 All E.R. 253; [1997] 1 F.L.R. 318; [1997] 1 F.C.R. 197;
[1997] Fam. Law 247; (1997) 147 N.L.J. 217; [1996] N.P.C. 156; *Times,*
November 13, 1996, Ch D . . . . *Digested,* 98/**4362**
Duncan v. British Coal Corp see Frost v. Chief Constable of South Yorkshire
Duncan v. Cammell Laird & Co Ltd (Discovery); Craven v. Cammell Laird & Co Ltd
(The Thetis) (Discovery) [1942] A.C. 624; [1942] 1 All E.R. 587; (1942) 73 Ll. L.
Rep. 109; (1942) 86 S.J. 287, HL; affirming [1941] 1 K.B. 640; (1941) 69 Ll. L.
Rep. 84, CA . . . . *Applied,* 53/2794,
55/2114, 58/2661, 61/6962, 67/3142: *Considered,* 55/3496, 56/12134,
62/2417, 64/2937, 65/3136, 67/3141, 00/5392: *Disapproved,* 64/2936:
Distinguished, 53/2796, 55/2117: *Not followed,* 68/3098
Duncan Investments Ltd v. Underwoods [1998] P.N.L.R. 754; [1998] E.G.C.S. 98;
[1998] N.P.C.102, CA; reversing [1997] P.N.L.R. 521, Ch D . . . . *Digested,* 99/**4018**
Duncliffe v. Caerfelin Properties [1989] 27 E.G. 89 . . . . *Digested,* 89/**2118**:
Followed, 99/3729
Dunkeyson v. Kirklees MBC (1999) 99(2) Q.R. 6, CC (Huddersfield) [*Ex rel.* Ridley &
Hall Solicitors, Permanent House, 1 Dundas Street, Huddersfield] . . . . *Digested,* 99/**1519**
Dunkiert v. Taylor [2001] 2 Q.R. 11, CC (Doncaster) [*Ex rel.* Paul Kirtley, Barrister, 37
Park Square Chambers, 37 Park Square, Leeds] . . . . *Digested,* 01/**1694**
Dunkley v. Queen, The; Robinson v. Queen, The [1995] 1 A.C. 419; [1994] 3 W.L.R.
1124; [1995] 1 All E.R. 279; (1994) 91(41) L.S.G. 41; (1994) 138 S.J.L.B. 203;
Independent, November 1, 1994, PC (Jam) . . . . *Digested,* 95/**2634**:
Followed, 99/3136
Dunlop v. Customs and Excise Commissioners (1998) 95(17) L.S.G. 31; (1998) 142
S.J.L.B. 135; *Times,* March 17, 1998, CA . . . . *Digested,* 98/**4780**
Dunlop v. Lambert (1839) 6 Cl. & F. 600. . . . . *Applied,* 61/8210,
74/3564, 94/319, 95/487, 98/809: *Distinguished,* 76/2529
Dunlop International AG v. Pardoe (Inspector of Taxes) [1999] S.T.C. 909; 72 T.C. 71;
[1999] B.T.C. 392; *Times,* October 5, 1999, CA; affirming [1998] S.T.C. 459;
[1998] B.T.C.117; *Times,* March 16, 1998, Ch D . . . . *Digested,* 99/**4664**
Dunlop Pneumatic Tyre Co Ltd v. New Garage & Motor Co Ltd [1915] A.C. 79, HL . . . . *Applied,* 47-51/1721,
52/1550, 61/3908, 61/3909, 62/850, 62/1397, 62/2502, 62/2842, 63/1643,
72/501, 76/1618, 82/407, 98/111, 00/2115: *Considered,* 54/1463, 66/3146,
93/500, 95/493: *Followed,* 96/6701
Dunlop Tyres Ltd v. Blows [2001] EWCA Civ 1032; [2001] I.R.L.R. 629, CA;
reversing EAT/350/99, EAT . . . . *Digested,* 01/**2287**
Dunn v. British Coal Corp [1993] I.C.R. 591; [1993] I.R.L.R. 396; [1993] P.I.Q.R.
P275; (1993) 137 S.J.L.B. 81; *Times,* March 5, 1993; *Independent,* March 10,
1993, CA . . . . *Digested,* 93/**3223**:
Considered, 95/4119, 95/4120, 98/337, 99/325, 99/326
Dunn v. Lewisham LBC, MCLC [*Ex rel.* William Latimer-Sayer, Barrister, Cloisters, 1
Pump Court, Temple, London] . . . . *Digested,* 01/**418**
Dunn v. Queen, The [1896] 1 Q.B. 116, CA . . . . *Considered,* 53/2820,
87/10, 98/4785: *Followed,* 59/504
Dunn v. Riza (Unreported, June 22, 2001), CC (Birmingham) [*Ex rel.* Stephen Garner,
Barrister, 8 Fountain Court, Steelhouse Lane, Birmingham] . . . . *Digested,* 01/**1783**
Dunn International Ltd v. CDE 57 Con. L.R.11, QBD (OR) . . . . *Digested,* 98/**819**
Dunne v. Kier Group Plc (Unreported, April 7, 2000), CC (Plymouth) [*Ex rel.* Robert
Weir, Barrister, Devereux Chambers, Devereux Court, London] . . . . *Digested,* 00/**326**
Dunnetts (Birmingham) Ltd v. Gutt (Valuation Officer) [2000] R.V.R. 310, Lands Tr . . . . *Digested,* 01/**4818**
Dunsford v. Bankway Properties Ltd see Bankway Properties Ltd v. Dunsford
Dunthorne v. Bentley [1996] R.T.R. 428; [1996] P.I.Q.R. P323; *Times,* March 11, 1996,
CA . . . . *Digested,* 96/**5652**:
Distinguished, 99/4070
Duomatic Ltd, Re [1969] 2 Ch. 365; [1969] 2 W.L.R.114; [1969] 1 All E.R.161; 112 S.J. 922,
Ch D . . . . *Digested,* 69/**412**:
Applied, 73/324, 74/321, 80/268, 80/269, 99/607, 00/654, 01/748:
Considered, 98/704: *Distinguished,* 90/487

Duphar BV v. Netherlands (C238/82) [1984] E.C.R. 523; [1985] 1 C.M.L.R. 256, ECJ . *Digested, 85/***1473.4***:*
Applied, 98/4517: Followed, 99/2693
Dupovac v. Secretary of State for the Home Department [2000] Imm. A.R. 265;
Times, February 16, 2000; *Independent,* March 6, 2000 (C.S.), CA . . . . *Digested, 00/***3284**
Durand v. Molino [2000] E.C.D.R. 320, Ch D *Digested, 00/***3576**
Durant & Co v. Roberts see Keighley Maxsted & Co v. Durant (t/a Bryan Durant & Co)
Dureau v. Evans [1996] P.I.Q.R. Q18; (1996) 146 N.L.J. 1280, CA . . . . *Digested, 96/***2136**:
Followed, 98/1631

Durham CC v. Cooperative Wholesale Society Ltd see Holman v. Cooperative
Wholesale Society Ltd
Durham Trading Standards v. Kingsley Clothing Ltd (1990) 154 J.P. 124; [1989] R.P.C.
695; (1990) 9 Tr. L.R. 50; [1989] Crim. L.R. 911; (1990) 154 J.P.N. 74, DC. . . . . *Digested, 90/***4519**:
Considered, 98/3531

Durley House Ltd v. Cadogan [2000] 1 W.L.R. 246; [2000] L. & T.R. 255; [2000] 1
E.G.L.R. 60; [2000] 09 E.G. 183; [1999] E.G.C.S. 120; (1999) 96(43) L.S.G. 34;
(1999) 96(41) L.S.G. 37; *Times,* November 12, 1999, Ch D *Digested, 99/***3730**
Durnsford v. South Gloucestershire DC [1999] R.V.R. 70, Lands Tr . . . . *Digested, 99/***4184**
Durojaiye v. Secretary of State for the Home Department [1991] Imm. A.R. 307, CA . . . *Digested, 92/***2403**:
Cited, 94/2498: Followed, 98/3234
Durose v. Novaceta (Unreported, December 3, 1997), CC (Nottingham) [*Ex rel.*
Andrew J McGrath, Barrister, 5 Fountain Court, Steelhouse Lane, Birmingham] . *Digested, 98/***1531**
Durrant v. Branksome Urban DC [1897] 2 Ch. 291, CA . . . . *Distinguished,*
01/5632:
Followed, 99/5036

Durrington Cemetery, Re [2001] Fam. 33; [2000] 3 W.L.R. 1322; [2001] W.T.L.R. 83;
(2000) 97(28) L.S.G. 31; *Times,* July 5, 2000, Cons Ct (Chichester) . . . . *Digested, 00/***1770**:
Applied, 01/3481

Dutton v. Boydle (Unreported, May 17, 2000), CC (Truro) [*Ex rel.* A. Butler, Barrister,
2nd Floor, Francis Taylor Building, Temple, London] . . . . *Digested, 00/***570**
Dutton v. Dutton [2001] W.T.L.R. 553, Ch D *Digested, 01/***5164**
Duxbury v. Duxbury [1992] Fam. 62; [1991] 3 W.L.R. 639; [1990] 2 All E.R. 77, CA . . . *Considered, 00/1470*
DV GmbH v. A AG B (2 U 110/95, 4 O 10/95) [2000] E.N.P.R. 120, OLG (Dusseldorf)
DW Moore v. Ferrier [1988] 1 W.L.R. 267; [1988] 1 All E.R. 400; (1988) 132 S.J. 227,
CA . . . . *Digested, 88/***2154**:
Applied, 91/2343, 01/4526: Considered, 88/2160, 89/2585, 93/2997,
94/2912, 00/2621: Distinguished, 97/713
Dwek v. Associated Newspapers Ltd see Dwek v. Macmillan Publishers Ltd
Dwek v. Macmillan Publishers Ltd; Dwek v. Associated Newspapers Ltd [2000]
E.M.L.R. 284, CA . . . . *Digested, 99/***1628**
DWS (Deceased), Re; *sub nom* S (Deceased), Re; S (A Child) v. G; EHS (Deceased),
Re; TWGS (A Child) v. JMG [2001] Ch. 568; [2000] 3 W.L.R. 1910; [2001] 1 All
E.R. 97; [2001] 1 F.C.R. 339; [2001] W.T.L.R. 445; (2000) 97(46) L.S.G. 39;
(2000) 150 N.L.J. 1788; *Times,* November 22, 2000; *Daily Telegraph,* November
21, 2000, CA; affirming [2000] 2 All E.R. 83, Ch D . . . . *Digested, 00/***4908**
Dwyer v. SCA Packaging [2001] 6 Q.R. 10, CC (Cardiff) [*Ex rel.* Andrew Arentsen,
Barrister, Thirty Three Park Place, Cardiff] . . . . *Digested, 01/***1649**
Dyason v. Secretary of State for the Environment, Transport and the Regions (No.1)
(1998) 75 P. & C.R. 506; [1998] 2 P.L.R. 54; [1998] J.P.L. 778; [1998] E.G.C.S.
11; (1998) 142 S.J.L.B. 62; [1998] N.P.C. 9; *Independent,* January 30, 1998,
CA . . . . *Digested, 98/***4160**:
Distinguished, 00/4485

Dyer (A Minor) v. Lambeth, Southwark and Lewisham HA (Unreported, June 3, 1998),
QBD [*Ex rel.* Martin Spencer, Barrister, 4 Paper Buildings, Temple, London] . . . . *Digested, 98/***1478**
Dyer v. Burgess (1999) 99(3) Q.R. 6, CC (Norwich) [*Ex rel.* Anthony Bate, Barrister,
East Anglian Chambers, 57 London Street, Norwich] . . . . *Digested, 99/***1456**
Dyer v. Commissioner of Police of the Metropolis (Unreported, October 26, 1998),
QBD . . . . *Considered, 00/1501*
Dyer v. Customs and Excise Commissioners [2000] S.T.I. 270, V&DTr
Dyer v. Dorset CC [1989] Q.B. 346; [1988] 3 W.L.R. 213; (1988) 20 H.L.R. 490; 86
L.G.R. 686; [1989] R.V.R. 41; (1988) 152 L.G. Rev. 992; (1988) 85(25) L.S.G.
43; (1988) 132 S.J. 934, CA . . . . *Digested, 88/***1758**:
Applied, 94/4335: Considered, 92/2313, 94/4314, 95/4860, 00/4450,
00/4473
Dyli v. Secretary of State for the Home Department [2000] Imm. A.R. 652; [2000]
I.N.L.R. 372, IAT . . . . *Digested, 01/***3637**
Dymond v. Pearce [1972] 1 Q.B. 496; [1972] 2 W.L.R. 633; [1972] 1 All E.R. 1142;
[1972] R.T.R. 169; 116 S.J. 62, CA; affirming in part [1971] R.T.R. 417, Assizes
(Exeter) . . . . *Digested, 72/***3095**:
Applied, 72/3081, 72/3082, 75/2455: Considered, 99/4070:
Distinguished, 73/2979
Dyno Rod Plc v. Reeve [1999] F.S.R. 148, Ch D . . . . *Digested, 98/***727**:
Considered, 01/960
Dyrlund v. Appleton see Dyrlund Smith A/S v. Turberville Smith Ltd

Dyrlund Smith A/S v. Turberville Smith Ltd; Dyrlund v. Appleton [1998] F.S.R. 774; (1998) 21 (8) I.P.D. 21089; *Times*, June 4, 1998, CA; reversing [1998] F.S.R. 403; (1998) 21 (2) I.P.D. 21019, Ch D .... *Digested*, 98/**3445**
Dysan Magnetics Ltd v. Customs and Excise Commissioners; *sub nom* Hanny Magnetics (Europe) Ltd v. Customs and Excise Commissioners [2000] V. & D.R. 422, V&DTr
Dyson v. Leeds City Council (No.1) [2000] C.P. Rep. 42, CA .... *Digested*, 00/**51**
Dyson v. Leeds City Council (No.2) see Fairchild v. Glenhaven Funeral Services Ltd (t/a GH Dovener & Son)
Dyson Appliances Ltd v. Hoover Ltd (No.1) [2001] EWCA Civ 1440; (2001) 24 (12) I.P.D. 24077, CA; affirming [2001] R.P.C. 26; (2000) 23 (12) I.P.D. 23101, Pat Ct.. *Digested*, 01/**3960**
Dyson Appliances Ltd v. Hoover Ltd (No.2) [2001] R.P.C. 27; (2001) 24 (3) I.P.D. 24014; (2001) 98 (14) L.S.G. 41; *Times*, February 21, 2001, Pat Ct .... *Digested*, 01/**3961**

E (A Child) v. Anderson (Unreported, March 30, 2000), CC (Ashford) [*Ex rel.* Richard Menzies, Barrister, 8 Stone Buildings, Lincoln's Inn, London] .... *Digested*, 00/**1665**
E (A Child) v. Calderdale MBC [2000] 4 Q.R. 7, CC (Halifax) [*Ex rel.* Rhodes Thain & Collinson Solicitors, 27 Harrison Road, Halifax] .... *Digested*, 00/**1619**
E (A Child) v. North Middlesex Hospital NHS Trust (Unreported, December 13, 1999), QBD [*Ex rel.* Bolt Burdon Solicitors, 1 Providence Place, Islington, London] .... *Digested*, 00/**1751**
E (A Child) v. Souls Garages Ltd, *Times*, January 23, 2001, QBD .... *Digested*, 01/**4484**
E (A Donor), Re see E (Enduring Power of Attorney), Re
E (A Minor) v. Dorset CC see X (Minors) v. Bedfordshire CC
E (A Minor) v. Dorset CC; Christmas v. Hampshire CC (Duty of Care); Keating v. Bromley LBC (No.1) [1994] 3 W.L.R. 853; [1994] 4 All E.R. 640; [1995] 1 F.C.R. 1; 92 L.G.R. 484; (1994) 144 N.L.J. 755; *Times*, May 4, 1994; *Independent*, May 4, 1994, CA .... *Digested*, 95/**1927**:
Overruled in part, 95/3452: *Subsequent proceedings*, 98/3943
E (A Minor) v. Greaves (Unreported, June 16, 1998), CC (Pontefract) [*Ex rel.* Richard Copnall, Barrister, Park Lane Chambers, Third Floor, 19 Westgate, Leeds, West Yorkshire] .... *Digested*, 99/**1514**
E (A Minor) v. Hatton (1999) 99 (5) Q.R. 7, CC (Torquay & Ntn Abbott) [*Ex rel.* Steven Ball, Barrister, 11 Old Square, Lincoln's Inn, London] .... *Digested*, 99/**1523**
E (Abduction: Non Convention Country), Re see O v. E
E (Children) (Care Proceedings: Social Work Practice), Re [2000] 2 F.L.R. 254; [2000] 2 F.C.R. 297; [2000] Fam. Law 610; (2000) 164 J.P.N. 703; *Times*, May 10, 2000, Fam Div .... *Digested*, 00/**2458**
E (Children) (Residence Order), Re [2001] EWCA Civ 567; [2001] 2 F.C.R. 662, CA .. *Digested*, 01/**2668**
E (Enduring Power of Attorney), Re; *sub nom* E (A Donor), Re; X v. Y (Enduring Powers of Attorney) [2001] Ch. 364; [2000] 3 W.L.R. 1974; [2000] 3 All E.R. 1004; [2000] 1 F.L.R. 882; [2000] 3 F.C.R. 320; [2000] W.T.L.R. 383; [2000] Fam. Law 469, Ch D .... *Digested*, 00/**73**
E (Family Assistance Order), Re [1999] 2 F.L.R. 512; [1999] 3 F.C.R. 700; [1999] Fam. Law 529; (2000) 164 J.P.N. 762, Fam Div.............................. *Digested*, 99/**2379**
E (Minors) (Residence: Imposition of Conditions), Re; *sub nom* E (Minors) (Residence Orders), Re [1997] 2 F.L.R. 638; [1997] 3 F.C.R. 245; [1997] Fam. Law 606; (1997) 161 J.P.N. 937; *Times*, May 16, 1997, CA........................ *Digested*, 97/**444**:
Followed, 01/2667
E (Minors) (Residence Orders), Re see E (Minors) (Residence: Imposition of Conditions), Re
E v. E; *sub nom* A v. B [2001] 2 F.L.R. 1; [2001] Fam. Law 418, CA.............. *Digested*, 01/**1462**
E v. E (Child Abduction: Intolerable Situation) [1998] 2 F.L.R. 980; [1998] Fam. Law 722, Fam Div .... *Digested*, 99/**2331**
E v. Hampshire CC [2000] E.L.R. 651, CA.............................. *Digested*, 01/**2027**
E Alton & Co Ltd v. Orchard Development Holdings Ltd [1998] J.P.L. 1138, CA
E Hulton & Co v. Mountain (1921) 8 Ll. L. Rep. 249, CA; affirming (1921) 7 Ll. L. Rep. 31, KBD .... *Applied*, 01/**3806**
E-UK Controls Ltd's Licence of Right (Copyright) Application [1998] R.P.C. 833, PO .. *Digested*, 99/**3448**:
Considered, 01/3854: *Referred to*, 00/3579
EA Grimstead & Son Ltd v. McGarrigan [1998-99] Info. T.L.R. 384, CA .... *Digested*, 01/**966**:
Considered, 01/953
Eager v. British Actors Equity Association (Unreported, July 18, 2000), Certification Officer [*Ex rel.* Certification Office for Trade Unions and Employers Associations, Brandon House, 180 Brandon High Street, London] .... *Digested*, 01/**2329**
Eager v. Lawlor; *sub nom* Eagor v. Lawlor [2001] 5 Q.R. 14, CC (Nottingham) [*Ex rel.* Nelsons, Solicitors, Pennine House, 8 Stanford Street, Nottingham]. .... *Digested*, 01/**1641**
Eagerpath Ltd v. Edwards (Inspector of Taxes) [2001] S.T.C. 26; 73 T.C. 427; [2001] B.T.C. 12; [2000] S.T.I. 1737; (2001) 98 (5) L.S.G. 37; *Times*, January 23, 2001, CA; affirming [1999] S.T.C. 771; [1999] B.T.C. 253; *Times*, May 21, 1999, Ch D . *Digested*, 01/**5200**
Eagle Recovery Services v. Parr (Unreported, September 22, 1997), CC (St Helens) [*Ex rel.* David McHugh, Barrister, Bracton Chambers, 95A Chancery Lane] .... *Digested*, 98/**3379**

Eagle Star Insurance Co v. Yuval Insurance Co [1978] 1 Lloyd's Rep. 357, CA. . . . .   *Digested*, 78/**1710**:
                                                     Considered, 87/126, 01/345
Eagle Star Insurance Co Ltd v. Kausar see Kausar v. Eagle Star Insurance Co Ltd
Eagle Star Life Assurance Co Ltd v. Griggs [1998] 1 Lloyd's Rep. 256; *Independent*,
   October 20, 1997 (C.S.), CA. . . . .   *Digested*, 98/**3373**
Eagleview Ltd v. Worthgate Ltd [1998] E.G.C.S. 119; [1998] N.P.C. 26, Ch D
Eagor v. Lawlor see Eager v. Lawlor
Ealing Community Transport Ltd v. Ealing LBC [1999] C.O.D. 492, CA
Ealing LBC v. Anbush Ltd (2001) 16 P.A.D. 46, Planning Inspector
Ealing LBC v. Asra Greater London Housing Association (2000) 15 P.A.D. 604,
   Planning Inspector
Ealing LBC v. El Isaac [1980] 1 W.L.R. 932; [1980] 2 All E.R. 348; 78 L.G.R. 417;
   (1980) 40 P. & C.R. 423; 124 S.J. 344, CA. . . . .   *Digested*, 80/**410**:
                                                     Applied, 01/**5801**
Ealing LBC v. Garry; *sub nom* Garry v. Ealing LBC [2001] EWCA Civ 1282; [2001]
   I.R.L.R. 681; [2001] Emp. L.R. 1165, CA; reversing *Daily Telegraph*, November 7,
   2000, EAT . . . .   *Digested*, 01/**2297**
Ealing LBC v. Kashyap (2001) 16 P.A.D. 69, Planning Inspector
Ealing LBC v. Lipka (2000) 15 P.A.D. 799, Planning Inspector
Ealing LBC v. Metha (1998) 30 H.L.R. 793, CA
Ealing LBC v. Nijjar Property Ltd (2001) 16 P.A.D. 7, Planning Inspector
Ealing LBC v. Race Relations Board [1972] A.C. 342; [1972] 2 W.L.R. 71; [1972] 1 All
   E.R. 105; 70 L.G.R. 219; (1971) 116 S.J. 60; *Times*, December 17, 1971, HL;
   reversing [1971] 1 Q.B. 309; [1970] 3 W.L.R. 921; [1971] 1 All E.R. 424; 68
   L.G.R. 807; (1970) 114 S.J. 807, QBD. . . . .   *Digested*, 72/**28**:
       Applied, 76/939, 01/1065: *Considered*, 82/980, 98/5811: *Followed*, 87/3203
Ealing LBC v. Surdonja see Mohamed v. Hammersmith and Fulham LBC
Ealing LBC v. White see White v. Aldridge (President of the Special Educational Needs
   Tribunal)
Eardley v. North West Anglia Health Care NHS Trust (Unreported, June 27, 1997), QBD
   [*Ex rel.* Anthony Snelson, Barrister, Thomas More Chambers, 51-52 Carey
   Street, Lincoln's Inn, London] . . . .   *Digested*, 98/**1613**
Earl v. Wilhelm; Wilhelm v. Hickson [2001] W.T.L.R. 1275, CA (Sask)
Earl Cadogan v. Morris see Viscount Chelsea v. Morris
Earl of Perth v. Fitzalan-Howard see Duke of Norfolk's Settlement Trusts, Re
Earl of Radnor's Will Trusts, Re (1890) L.R. 45 Ch. D. 402, CA . . . .   *Considered*, 98/481
Earle v. East Riding of Yorkshire Council [1999] R.V.R. 200, Lands Tr   *Digested*, 99/**4356**
Earley v. Thomas Ware & Sons (Unreported, April 8, 1998), QBD [*Ex rel.* Christopher
   Taylor, Barrister, All Saints Chambers, 9/11 Broad Street, Bristol] . . . .   *Digested*, 98/**1614**
Earliba Finance Co Ltd, Re see Macro (Ipswich) Ltd, Re
Early v. Lewis (Unreported, May 9, 2001), CC (Clerkenwell) [*Ex rel.* Benjamin Williams,
   Barrister, 1 Temple Gardens, Temple, London] . . . .   *Digested*, 01/**894**
Earnshaw v. Hartley [2000] Ch. 155; [1999] 3 W.L.R. 709; [1999] 2 E.G.L.R. 100;
   [1999] 32 E.G. 89; [1999] E.G.C.S. 52; (1999) 96(19) L.S.G. 27; (1999) 96(16)
   L.S.G. 37; (1999) 143 S.J.L.B. 129; *Times*, April 29, 1999; *Independent*, May 10,
   1999 (C.S.), CA. . . . .   *Digested*, 99/**4641**
Easington DC v. Matthew Fox Developments Ltd (2000) 15 P.A.D. 350, Planning
   Inspector
Eason v. Brownrigg (Unreported, April 3, 1998), Ch D [*Ex rel.* Wolferstans Solicitors,
   Deptford Chambers, 60/64 North Hill, Plymouth, Devon] . . . .   *Digested*, 98/**3659**
East v. Maurer [1991] 1 W.L.R. 461; [1991] 2 All E.R. 733, CA. . . . .   *Digested*, 91/**1306**:
                                                Applied, 00/1452, 01/965
East Cambridgeshire DC v. Thompson (1999) 14 P.A.D. 388, Planning Inspector
East Coast Aggregates Ltd v. Para-Pagan see Ross v. Owners of the Bowbelle
East Devon DC v. Colyfield Ltd (2001) 16 P.A.D. 22, Planning Inspector
East Devon DC v. Dunkeswell Kart Racing Club Ltd (1998) 13 P.A.D. 747, Planning
   Inspector
East Devon DC v. Wills (1999) 14 P.A.D. 168, Planning Inspector
East Dorset DC v. Brayne (1999) 14 P.A.D. 767, Planning Inspector
East Dorset DC v. Verwood Sports and Social Club (1998) 13 P.A.D. 81, Planning
   Inspector
East Dunbartonshire Council v. Mactaggart & Mickel Ltd see East Dunbartonshire
   Council v. Secretary of State for Scotland
East Dunbartonshire Council v. Secretary of State for Scotland; *sub nom* East
   Dunbartonshire Council v. Mactaggart & Mickel Ltd 1999 S.L.T. 1088; 1999
   S.C.L.R. 396; [1999] 1 P.L.R. 53; 1998 G.W.D. 40-2079, Ex Div . . . .   *Digested*, 99/**6410**:
                                               Followed, 00/4499
East Hampshire DC v. Erskine-Tulloch (2000) 15 P.A.D. 407, Planning Inspector
East Hampshire DC v. Secretary of State for Health (2000) 15 P.A.D. 450, Planning
   Inspector
East Hertfordshire DC v. Isabel Hospice Trading Ltd; *sub nom* East Hertfordshire DC v.
   Isobel Hospice Trading Ltd [2001] J.P.L. 597, QBD
East Hertfordshire DC v. Isobel Hospice Trading Ltd see East Hertfordshire DC v. Isabel
   Hospice Trading Ltd

East Kent Medical Services Ltd v. Customs and Excise Commissioners [1999] B.V.C. 2299, V&DTr

East Lindsay DC v. Thompson see East Lindsey DC v. Thompson

East Lindsey DC v. Castle Square Developments Ltd (2000) 15 P.A.D. 367, Planning Inspector

East Lindsey DC v. Thompson; *sub nom* East Lindsay DC v. Thompson; East Lindsey DC v. Thomson [2001] EWHC Admin 81; [2001] 2 P.L.R. 26; [2001] J.P.L. 1382; [2001] 8 E.G.C.S. 165; *Independent*, March 19, 2001 (C.S), QBD (Admin Ct)

East Lindsey DC v. Thomson see East Lindsey DC v. Thompson

East London Bus & Coach Co Ltd v. Nijjar (Unreported, November 22, 2000), CC (Maidstone) [*Ex rel.* Paul Mitchell, Barrister, 4 Paper Buildings, Temple, London] . *Digested*, 01/**1535**

East Northamptonshire DC v. Measures Farms Ltd (1998) 13 P.A.D. 32, Planning Inspector

East Northants DC v. Stilp (2001) 16 P.A.D. 28, Planning Inspector

East Riding of Yorkshire CC v. Hewson (1999) 14 P.A.D. 319, Planning Inspector

East Riding of Yorkshire CC v. Shufflebottom (1999) 14 P.A.D. 298, Planning Inspector

East Riding of Yorkshire Council v. Yorkshire Water Services Ltd [2001] Env. L.R. 7; [2000] C.O.D. 446, QBD. . . . . *Digested*, 01/**2429**

East Riding of Yorkshire DC v. Gibson; *sub nom* Gibson v. East Riding of Yorkshire DC [2000] 3 C.M.L.R. 329; [2000] I.C.R. 890; [2000] I.R.L.R. 598; *Times*, July 6, 2000, CA; reversing [1999] 3 C.M.L.R. 190; [1999] I.C.R. 622; [1999] I.R.L.R. 358; *Times*, February 12, 1999, EAT . . . . *Digested*, 00/**2095**

East Staffordshire BC v. Barnes (2000) 15 P.A.D. 468, Planning Inspector

East Staffordshire BC v. Fairless [1999] Env. L.R. 525; [1999] E.H.L.R. 128; (1999) 31 H.L.R. 677; [1998] E.G.C.S. 140; (1998) 95(41) L.S.G. 46; *Times*, October 26, 1998; *Independent*, October 19, 1998 (C.S.), QBD. . . . . *Digested*, 98/**4049**:
Followed, 00/6602

East Sussex CC v. Reprotech (Pebsham) Ltd see R. (on the application of Reprotech (Pebsham) Ltd) v. East Sussex CC

East Sussex CC v. Southern Water Services (2001) 16 P.A.D. 83, Planning Inspector

East West Transport Ltd v. DPP [1996] R.T.R. 184; [1998] Masons C.L.R. Rep. 75; [1995] Crim. L.R. 642; [1995] C.O.D. 174, QBD . . . . *Digested*, 97/**1120**

Eastbourne BC v. Allen (Valuation Officer) [2001] R.A. 273, Lands Tr

Eastbourne BC v. Dawson (Unreported, May 21, 1999), MC [*Ex rel.* Christopher Balogh, Barrister, Arden Chambers, 27 John Street, London] . . . . *Digested*, 99/**2151**

Eastbourne BC v. Foster (No.1) [2001] EWCA Civ 1091; [2001] Emp. L.R. 1079; (2001) 3 L.G.L.R. 53; [2001] B.L.G.R. 529; (2001) 98(33) L.S.G. 30; *Times*, August 17, 2001; *Independent*, July 18, 2001, CA . . . . *Digested*, 01/**2230**

Eastbourne BC v. Stirling [2001] R.T.R. 7; [2001] Crim. L.R. 42; (2000) 97(47) L.S.G. 40; *Times*, November 16, 2000; *Independent*, December 11, 2000 (C.S), QBD (Admin Ct) . . . . *Digested*, 00/**5244**

Eastbourne Town Radio Cars Association v. Customs and Excise Commissioners [2001] UKHL 19; [2001] 1 W.L.R. 794; [2001] 2 All E.R. 597; [2001] S.T.C. 606; [2001] B.T.C. 5196; [2001] S.T.I. 671; (2001) 98(22) L.S.G. 36; (2001) 151 N.L.J. 571; (2001) 145 S.J.L.B. 118; *Times*, April 10, 2001; *Independent*, May 21, 2001 (C.S), HL; affirming [1998] S.T.C. 669; [1998] B.T.C. 5179; [1998] B.V.C. 197; (1998) 95(23) L.S.G. 26; (1998) 142 S.J.L.B. 163; *Times*, May 12, 1998; *Independent*, May 18, 1998 (C.S.), CA; reversing [1996] S.T.C. 1469; [1997] B.V.C. 44; *Independent*, October 28, 1996 (C.S.), QBD . . . . *Digested*, 01/**5607**

Easterbrook v. Green [2001] 6 Q.R. 20, CC (Cardiff) [*Ex rel.* Jane Foulser McFarlane, Barrister, Temple Chambers, 32 Park Place, Cardiff] . . . . *Digested*, 01/**1770**
Followed, 01/5385

Eastern Airlines Inc v. Floyd 499 U.S. 530, US Ct. . . . .

Eastern Power Ltd v. Azienda Comunale Energia e Ambiente [2001] I.L.Pr. 6, CA (Ont) . *Digested*, 01/**801**:
Applied, 01/803

Eastgate Group Ltd v. Lindsey Morden Group Inc [2001] EWCA Civ 1446; [2001] 2 All E.R. (Comm) 1050; [2001] C.P.L.R. 525; (2001) 98(43) L.S.G. 34; (2001) 145 S.J.L.B. 243, CA; reversing [2001] Lloyd's Rep. P.N. 511; [2001] P.N.L.R. 40; (2001) 151 N.L.J. 458, QBD (Comm Ct). . . . . *Digested*, 01/**609**

Eastleigh BC v. Railtrack Plc (2001) 16 P.A.D. 105, Planning Inspector

Easton v. Ellis (Unreported, January 16, 1998), CC (Pontypridd) [*Ex rel.* Neil Bidder, Barrister, 33 Park Place, Cardiff] . . . . *Digested*, 98/**1525**

Eastwood (Deceased), Re; *sub nom* Lloyds Bank Ltd v. Eastwood [1975] Ch. 112; [1974] 3 W.L.R. 454; [1974] 3 All E.R. 603; 118 S.J. 533, CA; reversing [1973] 3 W.L.R. 795; [1973] 3 All E.R. 1079; 117 S.J. 487, Ch D . . . . *Digested*, 74/**2927**:
Applied, 76/2129, 81/837, 94/2154, 94/4556, 95/4019, 99/393, 00/390:
Considered, 83/2915

Eastwood v. Kirby (Unreported, September 14, 1999), CC (Milton Keynes) [*Ex rel.* Andrew Petersen, Pupil Barrister, 9 Gough Square, London] . . . . *Digested*, 99/**2472**:
Referred to, 99/2490

Eastwood Care Homes (Burton) Ltd v. Customs and Excise Commissioners see Eastwood Care Homes (Ilkeston) Ltd v. Customs and Excise Commissioners

Eastwood Care Homes (Ilkeston) Ltd *v.* Customs and Excise Commissioners; *sub nom*
Customs and Excise Commissioners *v.* Eastwood Care Homes (Ilkeston) Ltd;
Eastwood Care Homes (Mansfield) Ltd *v.* Customs and Excise Commissioners;
Eastwood Care Homes (Nottingham) Ltd *v.* Customs and Excise
Commissioners; Eastwood Care Homes (Burton) Ltd *v.* Customs and Excise
Commissioners; Eastwood Care Homes (Walsall) Ltd *v.* Customs and Excise
Commissioners [2001] S.T.C. 1629; [2001] B.T.C. 5574; [2001] S.T.I. 1419, Ch D;
reversing [2000] B.V.C. 2082; [1999] V. & D.R. 369, V&DTr . . . . *Digested,* 00/**5330**
Eastwood Care Homes (Mansfield) Ltd *v.* Customs and Excise Commissioners see
Eastwood Care Homes (Ilkeston) Ltd *v.* Customs and Excise Commissioners
Eastwood Care Homes (Nottingham) Ltd *v.* Customs and Excise Commissioners see
Eastwood Care Homes (Ilkeston) Ltd *v.* Customs and Excise Commissioners
Eastwood Care Homes (Walsall) Ltd *v.* Customs and Excise Commissioners see
Eastwood Care Homes (Ilkeston) Ltd *v.* Customs and Excise Commissioners
Eastwood's Application, Re [1997] N.I. 73, QBD (NI). . . . . *Digested,* 99/**5422**
Easyjet Airline Co Ltd *v.* British Airways Ltd [1998] Eu. L.R. 350, QBD (Comm Ct). . . . *Digested,* 98/**716**
EasyJet Airline Co Ltd *v.* Dainty (t/a easyRealestate) [2001] E.B.L.R. 104; (2001) 24(7)
I.P.D. 24045, Ch D
Easyplan (R 109/1998-2), Re (Unreported, February 11, 1999). . . . . *Distinguished,* 01/4051
Eaton Ltd *v.* King see King *v.* Eaton Ltd (No.2)
Eaton Square Properties Ltd *v.* O'Higgins (2001) 33 H.L.R. 68; [2001] L. & T.R. 15;
[2000] E.G.C.S. 118; (2000) 97(44) L.S.G. 46, CA . . . . *Digested,* 01/**4196**
Eaton Square Properties Ltd *v.* Ogilvie [2000] 1 E.G.L.R. 73; [2000] 16 E.G. 143, Rent
Assessment Panel. . . . . *Digested,* 00/**3946**

eBay Inc *v.* Bidder's Edge Inc [2001] E.B.L.R. 61, US Ct
Ebert *v.* Birch; Ebert *v.* Venvil [2000] Ch. 484; [1999] 3 W.L.R. 670; [2000] B.P.I.R.
14; (1999) 96(19) L.S.G. 28; (1999) 149 N.L.J. 608; (1999) 143 S.J.L.B. 130;
[1999] N.P.C. 46; *Times,* April 28, 1999; *Independent,* April 28, 1999, CA. . . . . . . *Digested,* 99/**575**
Ebert *v.* Official Receiver (No.1); Ebert *v.* Venvil (Trustee in Bankruptcy) [2001] EWCA
Civ 209, CA . . . . *Previous proceedings,*
99/575:
Subsequent proceedings, 01/687
Ebert *v.* Official Receiver (No.2) [2001] EWCA Civ 340; [2001] 3 All E.R. 942;
[2001] A.C.D. 66; *Independent,* March 21, 2001, CA . . . . *Digested,* 01/**687**
Ebert *v.* Trustee of the Property of Wolff [1998] Lloyd's Rep. Bank. 280, CA . . . . *Digested,* 98/**3268**
Ebert *v.* Venvil see Ebert *v.* Birch
Ebert *v.* Venvil (Trustee in Bankruptcy) see Ebert *v.* Official Receiver (No.1)
Ebied *v.* Hopkins see Wellcome Trust Ltd *v.* Hamad
Ebn Al Waleed, The [2000] 1 Lloyd's Rep. 270, Fed Ct (Can) . . . . *Digested,* 00/**4682**
Ebrahimi *v.* Westbourne Galleries Ltd; *sub nom* Westbourne Galleries, Re [1973] A.C.
360; [1972] 2 W.L.R. 1289; [1972] 2 All E.R. 492; 116 S.J. 412, HL; reversing
[1971] Ch. 799; [1971] 2 W.L.R. 618; [1971] 1 All E.R. 561; 115 S.J. 74, CA;
reversing [1970] 1 W.L.R. 1378; [1970] 3 All E.R. 374; 114 S.J. 785, Ch D . . . . . *Digested,* 72/**393**:
Applied, 75/312, 76/267, 83/343, 87/350, 92/5295, 97/5711:
Considered, 83/330, 83/332, 84/312, 85/308, 89/321, 92/423, 98/694,
99/634, 99/646, 00/691: *Distinguished,* 75/315, 76/277: *Referred to,* 00/693
EC (A Minor) (Care Proceedings: Disclosure), Re see C (A Minor) (Care Proceedings:
Disclosure), Re
EC (Disclosure of Material), Re see C (A Minor) (Care Proceedings: Disclosure), Re
EC Gransden & Co Ltd *v.* Ballard (Kent) Ltd [2001] N.P.C. 80, QBD (T&CC)
Ecclestone *v.* National Union of Journalists [1999] I.R.L.R. 166, Ch D . . . . *Digested,* 99/**2126**
Ecco Sko A/S *v.* Nike Denmark ApS (FS 2632/1999) [2001] E.T.M.R. 34, Byret (DK)
Echaurren Faranda *v.* Italian Post Office [2001] E.C.D.R. 14, Trib (Rome)
Echirolles Distribution SA *v.* Association du Dauphine (C9/99) [2000] E.C.R. I-8207;
[2001] E.C.D.R. 3, ECJ (6th Chamber). . . . . *Digested,* 01/**778**
Eckersley *v.* Binnie 18 Con. L.R. 1; [1955-95] P.N.L.R. 348, CA. . . . . *Considered,* 96/3580
Eckle *v.* Germany (A/51) (1983) 5 E.H.R.R. 1, ECHR. . . . . *Applied,* 98/3132,
98/3150, 99/3130, 00/6074, 00/6090: *Considered,* 00/6083
ECM (Vehicle Delivery Services) Ltd *v.* Cox [1999] 4 All E.R. 669; [2000] 1 C.M.L.R.
224; [1999] I.C.R. 1162; [1999] I.R.L.R. 559, CA; affirming [1998] I.C.R. 631;
[1998] I.R.L.R. 416; *Times,* June 10, 1998, EAT . . . . *Digested,* 99/**2133**:
Applied, 01/2333: *Cited,* 01/2338: *Followed,* 00/2226
Eco Swiss China Time Ltd *v.* Benetton International NV (C126/97) [1999] 2 All E.R.
(Comm) 44; [1999] E.C.R. I-3055; [1999] U.K.C.L.R. 183; [2000] 5 C.M.L.R.
816, ECJ. . . . . *Digested,* 99/**238**
Ecolab Inc's European Patent Application (No.92901186.4) see ECOLAB/Conveyor
lubricant (T392/96)
ECOLAB/Conveyor lubricant (T392/96); *sub nom* Ecolab Inc's European Patent
Application (No.92901186.4) [2001] E.P.O.R. 16; (1999) 22(10) I.P.D. 22096,
EPO (Technical Bd App) . . . . *Digested,* 01/**3930**

Economides v. Commercial Union Assurance Co Plc [1998] Q.B. 587; [1997] 3
W.L.R. 1066; [1997] 3 All E.R. 636; [1997] C.L.C. 1169; [1998] Lloyd's Rep. I.R.
9; *Times,* June 27, 1997, CA . . . . *Digested,* 97/**3137**
Ecotrade Srl v. Altiforni e Ferriere di Servola SpA (AFS) (C200/97) [1998] E.C.R. I-
7907; [1999] 2 C.M.L.R. 804, ECJ . . . . *Digested,* 99/**707**
ED Srl v. Fenocchio (C412/97) [1999] E.C.R. I-3845; [2000] 3 C.M.L.R. 855, ECJ
(5th Chamber) . . . . *Digested,* 01/**2488**
ED&F Man (Sugar) Ltd v. Haryanto Yani (No.1) [1986] 2 Lloyd's Rep. 44, CA . . . . *Digested,* 86/**2999**
ED&F Man (Sugar) Ltd v. Haryanto Yani (No.2) [1991] 1 Lloyd's Rep. 429; [1991] I.L.Pr.
393; *Financial Times,* January 23, 1991, CA; affirming [1991] 1 Lloyd's Rep. 161;
Financial Times, June 6, 1990, QBD (Comm Ct) . . . . *Digested,* 92/**468**:
Considered, 98/244
ED&F Man (Sugar) Ltd v. Haryanto Yani (No.3), *Times,* August 9, 1996, CA; affirming
Times, November 24, 1995, QBD . . . . *Digested,* 96/**797**
EDC v. United Kingdom [1998] B.C.C. 370, Eur Comm HR. . . . . *Digested,* 98/**3134**
Edell v. Sitzer (2001-02) 4 I.T.E.L.R. 149, CJ (Gen Div) (Ont)
Edelman v. Harcott (Unreported, February 21, 2001), CC (Ilford) [*Ex rel.* Jamas
Hodivala, Barrister, Trinity Chambers, 140 New London Road, Chelmsford,
Essex] . . . . *Digested,* 01/**4545**
Eden v. Weardale Iron & Coal Co (No.2) (1887) L.R. 35 Ch. D. 287, CA . . . . *Considered,* 68/3200,
00/5439
Eden DC v. Braid [1999] R.T.R. 329; [1998] C.O.D. 259, QBD . . . . *Digested,* 98/**944**
Eden Restaurants (Holborn) Ltd *v.* Secretary of State for the Environment, Transport and
the Regions [2000] P.L.C.R. 188, QBD . . . . *Digested,* 00/**4506**
Edennote Ltd, Re; *sub nom* Tottenham Hotspur Plc *v.* Ryman [1996] B.C.C. 718; [1996]
2 B.C.L.C. 389; (1996) 93(25) L.S.G. 28; (1996) 140 S.J.L.B. 176; *Times,* June
3, 1996, CA; reversing in part [1995] B.C.C. 389; [1995] 2 B.C.L.C. 248, Ch D
. . . . *Digested,* 96/**3490**:
Applied, 01/3750: *Considered,* 01/3720
Edgar v. Edgar [1980] 1 W.L.R. 1410; [1980] 3 All E.R. 887; (1981) 2 F.L.R. 19; (1980)
11 Fam. Law 20; 124 S.J. 809; *Times,* July 24, 1980, CA. . . . . *Digested,* 80/**791**:
Applied, 91/1794, 95/2323, 95/2340, 95/2344, 96/2857:
Considered, 83/2622, 93/2824, 94/2166, 95/2336: *Distinguished,* 83/1100,
96/2875, 97/2477, 99/4635: *Followed,* 83/1104, 84/1118:
Referred to, 86/1098, 87/1750, 93/5228
Edgar v. Meteorological Office; *sub nom* Met Office *v.* Edgar; Meteorological Office *v.*
Edgar *Times,* August 15, 2001, EAT. . . . . *Digested,* 01/**2348**
Edgar v. Rayson (Unreported, October 23, 2000), CC (Altrincham) [*Ex rel.* NDH
Edwards, Barrister, 8, King Street, Manchester] . . . . *Digested,* 01/**5349**
Edgar Rice Burroughs Inc *v.* Beukenoord (No.492/00 KG) [2001] E.C.D.R. 15, Hof
(Amsterdam)
Edgar Rice Burroughs Inc *v.* Beukenoord BV (No.492/99 KG) [2001] E.T.M.R. CN21,
Hof (Amsterdam)
Edge v. DPP see DPP *v.* Charles
Edge v. Pensions Ombudsman [2000] Ch. 602; [2000] 3 W.L.R. 79; [1999] 4 All E.R.
546; [2000] I.C.R. 748; [1999] O.P.L.R. 179; [1999] Pens. L.R. 215; (1999)
96(35) L.S.G. 39; (1999) 149 N.L.J. 1442; *Times,* October 19, 1999, CA;
affirming [1998] Ch. 512; [1998] 3 W.L.R. 466; [1998] 2 All E.R. 547; [1998]
O.P.L.R. 51; [1999] Pens. L.R. 215; *Times,* December 13, 1997, Ch D . . . . *Digested,* 99/**4155**:
Applied, 99/3380: *Considered,* 00/4356: *Followed,* 01/4605
Edgeworth Construction Ltd *v.* ND Lea & Associates Ltd; Edgeworth Construction Ltd
v. Walji 66 B.L.R. 56, Sup Ct (Can); reversing in part 54 B.L.R. 11, CA (BC) . . . . . *Distinguished,* 01/4469
Edgeworth Construction Ltd *v.* Walji see Edgeworth Construction Ltd *v.* ND Lea &
Associates Ltd
Edicom Decision (C271/94), Re see European Parliament *v.* Council of the European
Union (C271/94)
Edificaciones March Gallego SA *v.* Spain (28028/95) (2001) 33 E.H.R.R. 46; [1998]
H.R.C.D. 287, ECHR
Edilizia Indistriale Siderurgica Srl (EDIS) *v.* Ministero delle Finanze (C231/96) [1998]
E.C.R. I-4951; [1999] 2 C.M.L.R. 995; [1999] C.E.C. 337, ECJ . . . . *Digested,* 99/**2276**
Edinburgh Castle, The [1999] 2 Lloyd's Rep. 362, QBD (Adm Ct). . . . . *Digested,* 00/**4740**
Edinburgh City Council *v.* Brown [1999] I.R.L.R. 208, EAT . . . . *Digested,* 99/**6027**
Edinburgh City Council *v.* Rapley 2000 S.C. 78; [2000] O.P.L.R. 67; 1999 G.W.D. 39-
1873, Ex Div . . . . *Digested,* 00/**5899**
Edinburgh City Council *v.* Secretary of State for Scotland; Revival Properties Ltd *v.*
Edinburgh City Council; Secretary of State for Scotland *v.* Revival Properties Ltd
[1997] 1 W.L.R. 1447; [1998] 1 All E.R. 174; 1998 S.C. (H.L.) 33; 1998 S.L.T.
120; 1997 S.C.L.R. 1112; [1997] 3 P.L.R. 71; [1998] J.P.L. 224; [1997] E.G.C.S.
140; (1997) 94(42) L.S.G. 31; (1997) 141 S.J.L.B. 228; [1997] N.P.C. 146; 1997
G.W.D. 33-1693; *Times,* October 31, 1997, HL; affirming in part 1996 S.C.L.R.
600, 2 Div. . . . . *Digested,* 97/**6350**:
Applied, 99/4178: *Considered,* 99/4218, 01/4743: *Followed,* 97/4116, 99/6411
Edinburgh Petroleum Services Ltd *v.* Customs and Excise Commissioners [2000] S.T.I.
758, V&DTr

Edison & Swan United Electric Light Co *v.* Holland (Third Party Injunction) (1889) L.R.
41 Ch. D. 28; (1889) 6 R.P.C. 243, CA . . . . *Considered*, 94/3440,
00/5439: *Disapproved*, 73/2531

Edison First Power Ltd *v.* Secretary of State for the Environment, Transport and the
Regions see R. (on the application of Edison First Power Ltd) *v.* Secretary of
State for the Environment, Transport and the Regions

Editor *v.* Inspector of Taxes [2000] S.T.C. (S.C.D.) 377; [2000] S.T.I. 1128, Sp Comm. . .   *Digested*, 00/**4919**

Edler *v.* Auerbach [1950] 1 K.B. 359; [1949] 2 All E.R. 692; 65 T.L.R. 645; 1 P. & C.R.
10; 93 S.J. 727, KBD . . . . *Digested*, 47-51/**5609**:
Applied, 63/1650: *Approved*, 65/2197, 99/849

Edmeades *v.* Thames Board Mills Ltd [1969] 2 Q.B. 67; [1969] 2 W.L.R. 668; [1969]
2 All E.R. 127; [1969] 1 Lloyd's Rep. 221; 113 S.J. 88, CA . . . . *Digested*, 69/**2923**:
Applied, 70/2346, 71/3216, 72/835, 76/2195, 77/2323: *Considered*, 92/3604,
99/1416: *Distinguished*, 71/9522

Edmonds *v.* Lawson; *sub nom* Edmunds *v.* Lawson [2000] Q.B. 501; [2000] 2 W.L.R.
1091; [2000] I.C.R. 567; [2000] I.R.L.R. 391; (2000) 97(14) L.S.G. 42;
(2000) 144 S.J.L.B. 151; *Times*, March 16, 2000; *Independent*, March 16, 2000,
CA; reversing [2000] I.R.L.R. 18; (1999) 96(39) L.S.G. 38; (1999) 143
S.J.L.B. 234; *Times*, October 11, 1999, QBD . . . . *Digested*, 00/**2097**

Edmunds *v.* Coleman (Inspector of Taxes) [1997] S.T.C. 1406; 70 T.C. 322; [1997]
B.T.C. 564; (1997) 94(44) L.S.G. 35; *Times*, November 25, 1997; *Independent*,
November 10, 1997 (C.S.), Ch D . . . . *Digested*, 97/**2956**

Edmunds *v.* Lawson see Edmonds *v.* Lawson

Edmunds *v.* Simmonds [2001] 1 W.L.R. 1003; [2001] R.T.R. 24; [2001] P.I.Q.R. P21;
Times, November 21, 2000; *Independent*, November 13, 2000 (C.S), QBD . . . . . *Digested*, 00/**1463**

Edward Hack's Application (1941) 58 R.P.C. 91 . . . . *Applied*, 97/4893:
Considered, 93/3991, 99/3537: *Followed*, 69/3568

Edward Owen Engineering Ltd *v.* Barclays Bank International Ltd [1978] Q.B. 159;
[1977] 3 W.L.R. 764; [1978] 1 All E.R. 976; [1978] 1 Lloyd's Rep. 166; 6 B.L.R. 1;
121 S.J. 617, CA . . . . *Digested*, 77/**162**:
Applied, 93/4734: *Considered*, 96/407, 00/819: *Distinguished*, 90/666,
91/510: *Followed*, 98/293: *Referred to*, 81/147, 81/2402, 95/2491

Edward Wong Finance Co Ltd *v.* Johnson Stokes & Master [1984] A.C. 296; [1984] 2
W.L.R. 1; (1983) 80 L.S.G. 3163; (1983) 127 S.J. 784, PC (HK) . . . . *Digested*, 84/**3624**:
Applied, 01/4263

Edwards (CICA: Quantum: 2001), Re [2001] 6 Q.R. 15, CICA (Manchester) [*Ex rel.*
Christopher Taft, Barrister, St. James's Chambers, 68 Quay Street, Manchester] .   *Digested*, 01/**1676**

Edwards (Inspector of Taxes) *v.* Bairstow; Edwards (Inspector of Taxes) *v.* Harrison
[1956] A.C. 14; [1955] 3 W.L.R. 410; [1955] 3 All E.R. 48; 48 R. & I.T. 534; 36
T.C. 207; (1955) 34 A.T.C. 198; [1955] T.R. 209; (1955) 99 S.J. 558, HL;
reversing (1954) 47 R. & I.T. 340; (1954) 33 A.T.C. 131; [1954] T.R. 155, CA;
affirming 46 R. & I.T. 177; (1954) 33 A.T.C. 58; [1954] T.R. 65, QBD . . . . *Digested*, 55/**1287**:
Applied, 56/4272, 59/1529, 62/1506, 66/6053, 67/1949, 71/999, 71/3949,
74/319, 76/250, 77/2446, 81/1419, 82/476, 82/1617, 82/1647, 83/1225,
83/1976, 84/460, 89/125, 89/3189, 90/754, 90/2675, 92/3364, 93/2274,
94/262, 95/391, 95/876, 98/2137, 98/2140, 98/4622, 99/3066, 99/6471:
Considered, 74/485, 74/1816, 74/1834, 74/1873, 74/2097, 81/2812, 81/3710,
82/3282, 83/3412, 84/3218, 84/3253, 87/3193, 90/1864, 91/2373, 92/164,
93/332, 93/3778, 94/7, 94/357, 94/639, 95/155, 95/896, 95/5020,
98/4604, 99/4660, 99/4663: *Distinguished*, 56/4853

Edwards *v.* British Athletic Federation; Edwards *v.* International Amateur Athletic
Federation [1998] 2 C.M.L.R. 363; (1997) 94(30) L.S.G. 29; (1997) 141
S.J.L.B. 154; *Times*, June 30, 1997; *Independent*, July 1, 1997, Ch D . . . .   *Digested*, 97/**3389**

Edwards *v.* Derby City Council [1999] I.C.R. 114, EAT . . . .   *Digested*, 99/**2079**

Edwards *v.* Devon and Cornwall Constabulary [2001] EWCA Civ 388; [2001] C.P.L.R.
323, CA

Edwards (Inspector of Taxes) *v.* Fisher see Cooper *v.* Billingham (Inspector of Taxes)

Edwards *v.* Governors of Hanson School [2001] I.R.L.R. 733, EAT . . . .   *Digested*, 01/**2345**

Edwards (Inspector of Taxes) *v.* Harrison see Edwards (Inspector of Taxes) *v.* Bairstow

Edwards *v.* International Amateur Athletic Federation see Edwards *v.* British Athletic
Federation

Edwards *v.* Mid Suffolk DC [2001] I.C.R. 616; [2001] I.R.L.R. 190, EAT . . . .   *Digested*, 01/**2237**

Edwards *v.* Motor Union Insurance Co Ltd (The White Rose) see John Edwards & Co
v. Motor Union Insurance Co Ltd

Edwards *v.* Owen (Unreported, June 17, 1998), CC (Medway) [*Ex rel.* Marcus Grant,
Barrister, 1 Temple Gardens, Temple, London] . . . .   *Digested*, 98/**1748**

Edwards *v.* Peter Black Healthcare (Southern) Ltd [2000] I.C.R. 120; *Times*, May 27,
1999, CA . . . .   *Digested*, 99/**311**

Edwards *v.* Pryce (Unreported, August 23, 1999), CC (Liverpool) [*Ex rel.* Stephen
Cottrell, Pupil Barrister, 3 Paper Buildings, Temple, London] . . . .   *Digested*, 00/**1713**

Edwards (PG) *v.* Secretary of State for the Environment see Secretary of State for the
Environment *v.* Edwards (PG)

Edwards *v.* Somerset CC (Unreported, January 31, 2000), ET [*Ex rel.* County Solicitor,
Somerset County Council, County Hall, Taunton] . . . .   *Digested*, 00/**2174**

Edwards v. Surrey CC [1999] R.V.R. 223, Lands Tr . . . .   *Digested,* 99/**4169**
Edwards v. Surrey Police [1999] I.R.L.R. 456, EAT [*Ex rel.* Gordon Menzies, Barrister,
    6 Pump Court, Temple, London] . . . .   *Digested,* 99/**2145**
Edwards v. Teams Roofing Ltd [2000] 1 Q.R. 6, HC
Edwards v. United Kingdom (A/247B) (1993) 15 E.H.R.R. 417; *Times,* January 21,
    1993, ECHR . . . .   *Digested,* 93/**2125**:
          Applied, 01/1097: *Distinguished,* 00/3219
Edwin Lord v. Pacific Steam Navigation Co see Oropesa, The
Edwin Shirley Productions Ltd v. Workspace Management Ltd [2001] 23 E.G. 158,
    Ch D . . . .   *Digested,* 01/**4868**
EE Caledonia Ltd v. London Bridge Engineering Ltd (No.1); *sub nom* Elf Enterprise
    Caledonia Ltd v. London Bridge Engineering Ltd (No.1) 1997 G.W.D. 33-1658;
    Times, November 28, 1997, OH . . . .   *Digested,* 98/**5708**

eFax.com Inc v. Oglesby [2000] Masons C.L.R. 28; (2000) 23(4) I.P.D. 29031; *Times,*
    March 16, 2000, Ch D . . . .   *Digested,* 00/**3589**
Effer SpA v. Kantner (C38/81) [1982] E.C.R. 825; [1984] 2 C.M.L.R. 667, ECJ (1st
    Chamber) . . . .   *Digested,* 83/**1437**:
          Considered, 89/3015, 99/715, 00/767
Effort Shipping Co Ltd v. Linden Management SA (The Giannis NK) [1998] A.C. 605;
    [1998] 2 W.L.R. 206; [1998] 1 All E.R. 495; [1998] 1 Lloyd's Rep. 337; [1998]
    C.L.C. 374; (1998) 95(7) L.S.G. 32; (1998) 148 N.L.J. 121; (1998) 142 S.J.L.B.
    54; *Times,* January 29, 1998; *Independent,* January 27, 1998, HL; affirming
    [1996] 1 Lloyd's Rep. 577; [1996] C.L.C. 943; *Times,* February 5, 1996;
    Independent, February 6, 1996, CA; affirming [1994] 2 Lloyd's Rep. 171; *Times,*
    May 5, 1994, QBD (Comm Ct) . . . .   *Digested,* 98/**4400**:
          Considered, 98/4395
EFKA Chemicals BV's European Patent Application (T0074/98) (2001) 24(4) I.P.D.
    24026, EPO (Technical Bd App)
EFTA Surveillance Authority v. Norway (E3/00) [2001] 2 C.M.L.R. 47, EFTA . . . .   *Digested,* 01/**2847**
Egan v. Canada [1995] 2 S.C.R. 513, Sup Ct (Can)   *Followed,* 98/3160
Egan Lawson Ltd v. Standard Life Assurance Co; *sub nom* Standard Life Assurance Co
    v. Egan Lawson Ltd [2001] 1 E.G.L.R. 27; [2001] 08 E.G. 168; [2000] N.P.C.
    128, CA . . . .   *Digested,* 01/**111**
Egbale v. Secretary of State for the Home Department [1997] I.N.L.R. 88, IAT . . . .   *Digested,* 98/**3214**
Egbert v. National Crown Bank [1918] A.C. 903, PC (Can)   *Applied,* 01/4877
Egmatra v. Marco Trading Corp [1999] 1 Lloyd's Rep. 862; [1998] C.L.C. 1552, QBD
    (Comm Ct) . . . .   *Digested,* 99/**225**:
          Applied, 01/347: *Considered,* 00/217
Egmont Film A/S v. Laserdisken see Foreningen af danske Videogramdistributorer v.
    Laserdisken (C61/97)
Egon Ronay Associates Ltd v. Leading Guides International Ltd see Leading Guides
    International Ltd (In Liquidation), Re
EHS (Deceased), Re see DWS (Deceased), Re
El Du Pont de Nemours & Co (Witsiepe's) Application [1982] F.S.R. 303, HL; affirming
    [1981] F.S.R. 377, CA . . . .   *Digested,* 82/**2284**:
          Referred to, 01/3965
El du Pont de Nemours European Patent Application (No.90120556.7) see DU PONT/Fibre
    filled elastomer (T345/96)
Eidarous, Re see R. (on the application of Al-Fawwaz) v. Governor of Brixton Prison
Eidarous v. Governor of Brixton Prison see R. (on the application of Al-Fawwaz) v.
    Governor of Brixton Prison
Eide UK Ltd v. Lowndes Lambert Group Ltd [1999] Q.B. 199; [1998] 3 W.L.R. 643;
    [1998] 1 All E.R. 946; [1998] 1 Lloyd's Rep. 389; [1998] C.L.C. 266; (1998)
    95(4) L.S.G. 34; (1998) 148 N.L.J. 86; *Times,* December 29, 1997, CA; affirming
    (1997) 94(33) L.S.G. 28; *Times,* October 23, 1997, QBD . . . .   *Digested,* 98/**3391**
Eiderous, Re see R. (on the application of Al-Fawwaz) v. Governor of Brixton Prison
Eila Orvokki Homer v. Homer's Bar Maunula OY [1998] E.T.M.R. 591, KKO (Fin)
Eilbeck (Inspector of Taxes) v. Rawling see WT Ramsay Ltd v. Inland Revenue
    Commissioners
EinStein Stadtcafe Verwaltungs- und Betriebsgesellschaft mbH's Trade Mark Application
    [2000] E.T.M.R. 952, OHIM (Opposition Div) . . . .   *Digested,* 01/**4022**
EISAI/ Medicament for Gastritis (T913/94) [2001] E.P.O.R. 46, EPO (Technical Bd App)
          Digested, 01/**3925**
EISAI/Antihistamines (T164/83) [1987] E.P.O.R. 205, EPO (Technical Bd App) . . . . . .   *Distinguished,*
          00/**3635**
EISAI/Benzodioxane derivatives (T334/92) [2000] E.P.O.R. 172, EPO (Technical Bd App)
          Digested, 00/**3635**
EISAI/Second medical indication (G05/83) [1979-85] E.P.O.R. B241; [1985] O.J. E.P.O.
    64, EPO (Enlarged Bd App) . . . .   *Applied,* 00/**3628**:
          Referred to, 97/3908, 01/3965
Ekinci v. Hackney LBC; *sub nom* Hackney LBC v. Ekinci [2001] EWCA Civ 776;
    (2001) 98(28) L.S.G. 43; *Times,* July 24, 2001; *Independent,* June 7, 2001, CA .   *Digested,* 01/**3427**

Ekpe v. Commissioner of Police of the Metropolis [2001] I.C.R. 1084; [2001] I.R.L.R. 605; [2001] Emp. L.R. 741, EAT . . . . *Digested*, 01/**2242**

EL v. Switzerland 3 B.H.R.C. 348; [2000] W.T.L.R. 873, ECHR . . . . *Digested*, 98/**3144**

El Ajou v. Dollar Land Holdings Plc (No.1) [1994] 2 All E.R. 685; [1994] B.C.C. 143; [1994] 1 B.C.L.C. 464; [1993] N.P.C. 165; *Times*, January 3, 1994, CA; reversing [1993] 3 All E.R. 717; [1993] B.C.C. 698; [1993] B.C.L.C. 735, Ch D . . . . *Digested*, 94/**416**:
Applied, 99/3288, 01/4529

El Boujaidi v. France (2000) 30 E.H.R.R. 223, ECHR . . . . *Digested*, 00/**3240**

EL CANAL DE LAS ESTRELLAS Trade Mark [2000] R.P.C. 291, Appointed Person . . . . *Digested*, 00/**3766**:
Followed, 01/4052

El du Pont de Nemours and Co's European Patent (No.0203469) see DU PONT/Suspected partiality (T1028/96)

El Fadl v. El Fadl [2000] 1 F.L.R. 175; [2000] 1 F.C.R. 685; [2000] Fam. Law 84, Fam Div . . . . *Digested*, 00/**2505**

El Jawhary v. Bank of Credit and Commerce International SA (No.1); Pharaon v. Bank of Credit and Commerce International SA; Adham v. Bank of Credit and Commerce International SA (No.1) [1993] B.C.L.C. 396, Ch D . . . . *Digested*, 93/**2376**:
Followed, 99/3952

El Naschie v. Pitt Place (Epsom) Ltd (1999) 31 H.L.R. 278; (1999) 78 P. & C.R. 44; [1998] N.P.C. 83; *Times*, May 27, 1998, CA. . . . . *Digested*, 98/**3642**

El-Kaisi (Deceased), Re see Midland Bank Trustee (Jersey) Ltd v. MacLeod

El-Yassini v. Secretary of State for the Home Department (C416/96) [1999] All E.R. (EC) 193; [1999] E.C.R. I-1209; [1999] 2 C.M.L.R. 32; [1999] I.N.L.R. 131; (1999) 96(31) L.S.G. 43; *Times*, March 11, 1999, ECJ . . . . *Digested*, 99/**3213**

Elanay Contracts Ltd v. Vestry [2001] B.L.R. 33; (2001) 3 T.C.L.R. 6, QBD (T&CC). . . . *Digested*, 01/**852**:
Considered, 01/855

Elanco Products Ltd v. Mandops (Agrochemical Specialists) Ltd [1979] F.S.R. 46; [1980] R.P.C. 213, CA . . . . *Digested*, 79/**347**:
Applied, 93/579: *Considered*, 83/492, 84/436, 98/3422

Elderbrant v. Cape Darlington Ltd (Unreported, March 13, 2000), CC (Newcastle) [*Ex rel.* Frank Burton Q.C., 12 King's Bench Walk, London] . . . . *Digested*, 00/**1652**

Elderslie Steamship Co Ltd v. Borthwick; *sub nom* Borthwick v. Elderslie Steamship Co Ltd (No.1) [1905] A.C. 93, HL; affirming [1904] 1 K.B. 319, CA . . . . *Considered*, 98/**4874**

Eldon Garages Ltd v. Kingston upon Hull CBC [1974] 1 W.L.R. 276; [1974] 1 All E.R. 358; 72 L.G.R. 456; (1973) 27 P. & C.R. 48; (1973) 117 S.J. 853, Ch D . . . . *Digested*, 74/**3740**:
Considered, 01/4690

Eldridge v. Attorney General of British Columbia 3 B.H.R.C. 137, Sup Ct (Can). . . . . *Digested*, 98/**3074**:
Applied, 98/3160

Electra Private Equity Partners v. KPMG Peat Marwick [2000] B.C.C. 368; [2001] 1 B.C.L.C. 589; [1999] Lloyd's Rep. P.N. 670; [2000] P.N.L.R. 247, CA; reversing [1998] P.N.L.R. 135, Ch D . . . . *Digested*, 99/**4014**:
Considered, 00/4205

Electricite de France, Re [1999] E.C.C. 9, C d'A (Paris)

Electricity Supply Nominees Ltd v. Farrell [1997] 1 W.L.R. 1149; [1997] 2 All E.R. 498; [1998] 1 Costs L.R. 49; *Times*, March 10, 1997; *Independent*, March 10, 1997 (C.S.), CA . . . . *Digested*, 97/**528**

Electricity Supply Nominees Ltd v. IAF Group Ltd [1993] 1 W.L.R. 1059; [1993] 3 All E.R. 372; (1994) 67 P. & C.R. 28; [1993] 2 E.G.L.R. 95; [1993] 37 E.G. 155; [1992] E.G.C.S. 145; *Times*, January 21, 1993, QBD . . . . *Digested*, 93/**2465**:
Applied, 98/3680: *Followed*, 98/3660, 99/3746

Electricity Supply Nominees Ltd v. National Magazine Co Ltd (2000) 2 T.C.L.R. 169; [1999] 1 E.G.L.R. 130; [1998] E.G.C.S. 162, QBD (T&CC). . . . . *Digested*, 99/**3663**

Electrix Ltd v. Electrolux Ltd; *sub nom* Electrix Ltd's Application, Re [1960] A.C. 722; [1959] 3 W.L.R. 503; [1959] 3 All E.R. 170; [1959] R.P.C. 283; 103 S.J. 755, HL; affirming [1958] R.P.C. 176, CA; affirming [1954] R.P.C. 369, TMR . . . . *Digested*, 59/**3350**:
Applied, 94/4497, 94/4498: *Considered*, 74/3833, 95/4943, 98/3541:
Previous proceedings, 54/3347

Electrix Ltd's Application, Re see Electrix Ltd v. Electrolux Ltd

Electro Cad Australia Pty Ltd v. Mejati RCS SDN BHD [1999] F.S.R. 291, HC (Mal) . . . *Digested*, 99/**584**

Electrolux Northern Ltd v. Black & Decker [1996] F.S.R. 595; *Times*, May 6, 1996, Pat Ct . . . . *Digested*, 96/**4545**:
Considered, 97/3912: *Referred to*, 99/3514

Electronic Techniques (Anglia) Ltd v. Critchley Components Ltd [1997] F.S.R. 401; (1997) 20(4) I.P.D. 20037, Ch D . . . . *Digested*, 97/**1030**:
Considered, 99/3462

Electrotec Services Ltd v. Issa Nicholas (Grenada) Ltd [1998] 1 W.L.R. 202, PC (Gren) . *Digested*, 98/**449**

Eleko v. Officer Administering Nigeria (No.2) [1931] A.C. 662, PC (Nig) . . . . *Applied*, 68/**959**,
69/822: *Considered*, 00/5113

Elf Enterprise Caledonia Ltd v. London Bridge Engineering Ltd (No.1) see EE Caledonia Ltd v. London Bridge Engineering Ltd (No.1)

Elgie v. Hodges (Unreported, May 5, 1999), CC (Lincoln) [*Ex rel.* Langleys Solicitors, 34 Silver Street, Lincoln] . . . . *Digested*, 99/**1429**

Elgindata (No.2), Re [1992] 1 W.L.R. 1207; [1993] 1 All E.R. 232; [1993] B.C.L.C. 119; (1992) 89(27) L.S.G. 33; (1992) 136 S.J.L.B. 190; *Times*, June 18, 1992, CA . . .   *Digested*, 93/**3144**: *Applied*, 97/550, 01/503: *Considered*, 95/4004, 96/3828, 99/3456, 00/386, 00/398, 00/457, 00/3673: *Distinguished*, 95/855: *Followed*, 98/1472, 00/396

Elguzouli-Daf *v.* Commissioner of Police of the Metropolis; McBrearty *v.* Ministry of Defence [1995] Q.B. 335; [1995] 2 W.L.R. 173; [1995] 1 All E.R. 833; (1995) 7 Admin. L.R. 421; (1995) 145 N.L.J. 151; *Times*, November 23, 1994, CA . . . .   *Digested*, 95/**3652**: *Applied*, 98/4778

Elhasoglu *v.* Secretary of State for the Home Department see R. *v.* Secretary of State for the Home Department Ex p. Elhasoglu

Eli Lilly & Co *v.* Clayton (2001) 24(12) I.P.D. 24081, Arbitration

Eli Lilly & Co *v.* Dowelhurst Ltd see Boehringer Ingelheim KG *v.* Swingward Ltd

Eli Lilly & Co *v.* Dowelhurst Ltd (Defence Amendments) see Glaxo Group Ltd *v.* Dowelhurst Ltd (Defence Amendments)

Eli Lilly & Co *v.* Dowelhurst Ltd (Infringement Action) see Glaxo Group Ltd *v.* Dowelhurst Ltd (Infringement Action)

Eli Lilly & Co *v.* Novo Nordisk A/S (No.1) [2001] C.L.C. 519; [2000] I.L.Pr. 73, CA . . . .   *Digested*, 00/**771**: *Applied*, 01/814

Eli Lilly & Co *v.* Novo Nordisk A/S (No.2) (1999) 22(8) I.P.D. 22075, Pat Ct

Eli Lilly's European Patent (No.063491) (T667/92) see ELI LILLY/Ruminant lactation improvement (T667/92)

ELI LILLY/Nizatidine (T55/99) [2000] E.P.O.R. 430, EPO (Technical Bd App) . . . .   *Digested*, 00/**3637**

ELI LILLY/Re-establishment of rights (T667/92) [2000] E.P.O.R.167; [1998] E.P.O.R. 250, EPO (Technical Bd App) . . . .   *Digested*, 00/**3660**

ELI LILLY/Ruminant lactation improvement (T667/92); *sub nom* Eli Lilly's European Patent (No.063491) (T667/92) [2001] E.P.O.R. 12; (1997) 20(6) I.P.D. 20055, EPO (Technical Bd App) . . . .   *Digested*, 01/**3950**

ELI LILLY/Serotonin receptor (T241/95) [2001] E.P.O.R. 38, EPO (Technical Bd App) . .   *Digested*, 01/**3936**

Elias Gale Racing *v.* Customs and Excise Commissioners [1999] S.T.C. 66; [1999] B.T.C. 5015; [1999] B.V.C. 68; (1999) 96(6) L.S.G. 31; (1998) 148 N.L.J. 1845; *Times*, December 28, 1998; *Independent*, December 14, 1998 (C.S.), QBD . . . . .   *Digested*, 99/**5026**

Elida Gibbs Ltd *v.* Colgate Palmolive Ltd [1983] F.S.R. 95, Ch D . . . .   *Digested*, 83/**2788**: *Followed*, 99/3524

Elida Gibbs Ltd *v.* Customs and Excise Commissioners (C317/94) [1996] S.T.C. 1387; [1996] E.C.R. I-5339; [1996] C.E.C. 1022; [1997] B.V.C. 80; *Times*, November 12, 1996, ECJ (6th Chamber). . . . .   *Digested*, 96/**5908**: *Considered*, 01/5556: *Distinguished*, 01/5614: *Joined proceedings*, 96/5909

Elitestone *v.* Secretary of State for Wales see R. *v.* Swansea City Council Ex p. Elitestone Ltd

Elitestone Ltd *v.* Davies see Elitestone Ltd *v.* Morris

Elitestone Ltd *v.* Morris; Elitestone Ltd *v.* Davies [1997] 1 W.L.R. 687; [1997] 2 All E.R. 513; (1998) 30 H.L.R. 266; [1997] 2 E.G.L.R. 115; [1997] 27 E.G. 116; [1997] E.G.C.S. 62; (1997) 94(19) L.S.G. 25; (1997) 147 N.L.J. 721; (1997) 141 S.J.L.B. 113; [1997] N.P.C. 66; *Times*, May 7, 1997, HL; reversing (1997) 73 P. & C.R. 259; [1995] N.P.C. 142, CA. . . . .   *Digested*, 97/**3304**: *Applied*, 00/3880: *Distinguished*, 00/6537

Elitestone's Application for Judicial Review, Re see R. *v.* Swansea City Council Ex p. Elitestone Ltd

ELLE Trade Marks (Opposition); *sub nom* Safeway Stores Plc *v.* Hachette Filipacchi Presse (Opposition) [2000] E.T.M.R. 311, Ch D . . . .   *Digested*, 00/**3770**

ELLE Trade Marks (Revocation); *sub nom* Safeway Stores Plc *v.* Hachette Filipacchi Presse (Revocation); Hachette Filipacchi Presse *v.* Safeway Stores Plc [1997] E.T.M.R. 552; [1997] F.S.R. 529, Ch D; affirming (1997) 20(2) I.P.D. 20018, TMR. . . . .   *Digested*, 97/**4903**: *Applied*, 00/3711, 01/4028: *Followed*, 00/3795

Ellen *v.* Linh Hoa Ly [2001] 6 Q.R. 10, CC (Bow) [*Ex rel.* James Candlin, Barrister, 46 Essex Street, London]. . . . .   *Digested*, 01/**1646**

Eller *v.* Grovecrest Investments Ltd [1995] Q.B. 272; [1995] 2 W.L.R. 278; [1994] 4 All E.R. 845; (1995) 70 P. & C.R. 350; [1994] 27 E.G. 139; [1994] E.G.C.S. 28; (1994) 144 N.L.J. 390; [1994] N.P.C. 21, CA . . . .   *Digested*, 95/**3052**: *Considered*, 01/4153

Ellerine Bros Pty Ltd *v.* Klinger [1982] 1 W.L.R. 1375; [1982] 2 All E.R. 737; (1982) 79 L.S.G. 987; 126 S.J. 592, CA . . . .   *Digested*, 82/**92**: *Applied*, 91/200, 92/3614, 97/4485: *Considered*, 00/222: *Followed*, 94/4053

Elles *v.* Hambros Bank Ltd see Galileo Group Ltd, Re

Ellinas (t/a Hunts Cross Supper Bar) *v.* Customs and Excise Commissioners; *sub nom* Ellis (t/a Hunts Cross Supper Bar) *v.* Customs and Excise Commissioners [1998] B.V.C. 2137, V&DTr . . . .   *Digested*, 98/**4879**

Elliot *v.* NE Railway Co (1863) 10 H.L. Cas. 333 . . . .   *Considered*, 99/4177

Elliott *v.* Agrevo UK Ltd [2001] Env. L.R. D7, QBD (T&CC)

Elliott *v.* Brown (Unreported, May 5, 1998), CC (Plymouth) [*Ex rel.* Lyons Davidson Solicitors, Endeavour House, Parkway Court, Marsh Mills, Plymouth] . . . .   *Digested*, 98/**419**

Elliott *v.* Elliott [2001] 1 F.C.R. 477, CA

Elliott v. Hill Samuel (Unreported, July 28, 1999), CC (Leicester) [*Ex rel.* Sunil Iyer, Barrister, Bracton Chambers, 95A Chancery Lane, London] . . . . *Digested*, 99/**3385**
Elliott v. Hollies Ltd [1998] 1 B.C.L.C. 627, Ch D (Companies Ct) . . . . *Digested*, 97/**840**
Elliott v. Loake [1983] Crim. L.R. 36, DC. . . . . *Digested*, 83/**634**:
Applied, 00/928: *Explained*, 94/910
Elliott v. Pensions Ombudsman [1998] O.P.L.R. 21; (1997) 94(45) L.S.G. 27; (1998) 142 S.J.L.B. 19; *Times*, November 20, 1997, Ch D . . . . *Digested*, 97/**518**:
Followed, 99/373
Elliott v. Planet Organic Ltd; *sub nom* Planet Organic Ltd, Re [2000] B.C.C. 610; [2000] 1 B.C.L.C. 366, Ch D . . . . *Digested*, 00/**693**:
Considered, 01/741
Elliott Turbomachinery v. Bates [1981] I.C.R. 218, EAT . . . . *Digested*, 81/**910**:
Not followed, 98/2186
Ellis, Re see R. v. Governor of Belmarsh Prison Ex p. Gilligan
Ellis v. Broadway (Valuation Officer) [1998] R.A. 1, Lands Tr . . . . *Digested*, 98/**4321**
Ellis v. Chief Adjudication Officer [1998] 1 F.L.R. 184; [1998] 2 F.C.R. 51; [1997] Fam. Law 794; *Times*, May 14, 1997; *Independent*, May 14, 1997, CA . . . . *Digested*, 97/**4660**
Ellis (t/a Hunts Cross Supper Bar) v. Customs and Excise Commissioners see Ellinas (t/a Hunts Cross Supper Bar) v. Customs and Excise Commissioners
Ellis v. Lambeth LBC (2000) 32 H.L.R. 596; (2000) 2 L.G.L.R. 353; [1999] E.G.C.S. 101; *Times*, September 28, 1999 ; *Independent*, October 11, 1999 (C.S.), CA . . . . *Digested*, 99/**4350**
Ellis v. Lawrence (Unreported, June 17, 1999), CC (Plymouth) [*Ex rel.* James Rees, Barrister, 2 King's Bench Walk, Temple, London] . . . . *Digested*, 99/**2496**
Ellis v. Liverpool City Council (Unreported, March 27, 1998), CC (Manchester) [*Ex rel.* J James Rowley, Barrister, 28 St John Street, Manchester, M3 4DJ] . . . . *Digested*, 98/**1658**
Ellis v. Rothen (Unreported, July 3, 1998), CC (Barnsley) [*Ex rel.* Andrew Lewis, Barrister, Sovereign Chambers, 25 Park Square, Leeds] . . . . *Digested*, 98/**1684**
Ellis Shipping Corp v. Voest Alpine Intertrading (The Lefthero) [1992] 2 Lloyd's Rep. 109; *Financial Times*, April 15, 1992, CA; affirming [1991] 2 Lloyd's Rep. 599, QBD (Comm Ct) . . . . *Digested*, 92/**3946**:
Applied, 00/4698
Ellis Tylin Ltd v. Cooperative Retail Services Ltd [1999] B.L.R. 205; 68 Con. L.R. 137, QBD . . . . *Digested*, 99/**844**
Ellis-Don Ltd v. Parking Authority of Toronto 28 B.L.R. 98, HC (Ont) . . . . *Digested*, 85/**198**:
Considered, 99/784
Ellora Industries v. Banarsi Dass & Ors; *sub nom* Banarsi Dass, Re . . . . *Considered*, 00/3591
Ellwand v. Fitzgerald (Unreported, January 13, 1999), QBD [*Ex rel.* Weightmans Solicitors, Richmond House, 1 Rumford Place, Liverpool] . . . . *Digested*, 99/**4070**
ELM/Forged evidence (T19/92) [1999] E.P.O.R. 396, EPO (Technical Bd App) . . . . . . *Digested*, 99/**3487**
Elmbridge BC v. Esher College & Meridian (Brighton) Ltd (1999) 14 P.A.D. 705, Planning Inspector
Elmbridge BC v. Octagon Developments Ltd (2001) 16 P.A.D. 62, Planning Inspector
Elmbridge BC v. Secretary of State for the Environment, Transport and the Regions see R. (on the application of Elmbridge BC) v. Secretary of State for the Environment, Transport and the Regions
Elmcroft Developments Ltd v. IAB see Elmcroft Developments Ltd v. Tankersley-Sawyer
Elmcroft Developments Ltd v. Rogers see Elmcroft Developments Ltd v. Tankersley-Sawyer
Elmcroft Developments Ltd v. Tankersley-Sawyer; Elmcroft Developments Ltd v. IAB; Elmcroft Developments Ltd v. Rogers (1984) 15 H.L.R. 63; (1984) 270 E.G. 140, CA . . . . *Digested*, 84/**1958**:
Applied, 98/3624, 00/3931: *Considered*, 87/2140, 89/2195:
Distinguished, 01/4160: *Explained*, 85/1610
Elmes v. Hygrade Food Products Plc [2001] EWCA Civ 121; [2001] C.P. Rep. 71, CA. . . *Digested*, 01/**644**:
Considered, 01/643, 01/645
Elmi v. Australia 6 B.H.R.C. 433; [1999] I.N.L.R. 341, UN CAT . . . . *Digested*, 99/**3088**
Elmi v. Harrods Ltd see Harrods Ltd v. Remick
ELO Entertainment Ltd v. Grand Metropolitan Retailing Ltd; Lyons v. Grand Metropolitan Retailing Ltd [1999] 1 All E.R. (Comm) 473, CA . . . . *Digested*, 99/**1388**
Elpis, The [1999] 1 Lloyd's Rep. 606, QBD (Adm Ct) . . . . *Digested*, 99/**4418**
Elsden v. Pick [1980] 1 W.L.R. 898; [1980] 3 All E.R. 235; (1980) 40 P. & C.R. 550; (1980) 254 E.G. 503; 124 S.J. 312, CA. . . . . *Digested*, 80/**30**:
Considered, 93/2084, 01/4189
Elsen v. Bundesversicherungsanstalt fur Angestellte (C135/99) [2000] E.C.R. I-10409; *Times*, February 14, 2001, ECJ . . . . *Digested*, 01/**5075**
Elshani v. Secretary of State for the Home Department see R. v. Secretary of State for the Home Department Ex p. Elshani
Elsholz v. Germany [2000] 2 F.L.R. 486; [2000] 3 F.C.R. 385; [2000] Fam. Law 800, ECHR . . . . *Digested*, 01/**3556**:
Followed, 01/6510
ELSWORTH/Modified yeast (T484/98) [2001] E.P.O.R. 27, EPO (Technical Bd App) . . *Digested*, 01/**3946**
Eltek (UK) Ltd v. Thomson [2000] I.C.R. 689, EAT . . . . *Digested*, 00/**2236**
Elve, The see Bernisse, The (No.1)

Elvee Ltd v. Taylor [2001] EWCA Civ 1943; *Times,* December 18, 2001, CA; affirmingHC0003913, Ch D
Elvis Presley Enterprises Inc, Re see ELVIS PRESLEY Trade Marks
Elvis Presley Enterprises Inc v. Sid Shaw Elvisly Yours see ELVIS PRESLEY Trade Marks
ELVIS PRESLEY Trade Marks; *sub nom* Elvis Presley Enterprises Inc, Re; Elvis Presley Enterprises Inc v. Sid Shaw Elvisly Yours [1999] R.P.C. 567; (1999) 22(5) I.P.D. 22050; *Times,* March 22, 1999, CA; affirming [1997] R.P.C. 543; (1997) 20(5) I.P.D. 20044; *Times,* March 25, 1997, Ch D . . . .   *Digested,* 99/**3574**:
           Considered, 98/3437, 99/3593: *Followed,* 01/4050: *Referred to,* 01/3983
Emaco Ltd v. Dyson Appliances Ltd [1999] E.T.M.R. 903; (1999) 22(6) I.P.D. 22056; (1999) 96(7) L.S.G. 36; *Times,* February 8, 1999, Ch D . . . .   *Digested,* 99/**3535**
Emaco Ltd v. Dyson Appliances Ltd (Remedies Hearing) (1999) 22(6) I.P.D. 22057, CA
EMAP Business Communications Ltd v. Planit Media AB [2000] E.C.D.R. 93, HR (Skane and Blekinge)
Emap National Publications Ltd v. Security Publications Ltd [1997] F.S.R. 891; (1997) 20(12) I.P.D. 20128, Ch D . . . .   *Digested,* 98/**3427**
Embassy Limousines & Services v. European Parliament (T203/96) [1998] E.C.R. II-4239; [1999] 1 C.M.L.R. 667, CFI (4th Chamber)
Emeh v. Kensington and Chelsea and Westminster AHA [1985] Q.B. 1012; [1985] 2 W.L.R. 233; [1984] 3 All E.R. 1044; (1984) 81 L.S.G. 2856; (1984) 128 S.J. 705, CA . . . .   *Digested,* 85/**2322**:
           Applied, 93/1416, 96/833, 00/1464: *Considered,* 86/422: *Followed,* 98/6116:
                                        Overruled, 00/4200
Emergency Stocks of Petroleum Products (C398/98), Re; *sub nom* Commission of the European Communities v. Greece (C398/98) [2001] E.C.R. I-7915; [2001] 3 C.M.L.R. 62, ECJ (5th Chamber) AGO
Emery v. UCB Corporate Services Ltd (formerly UCB Bank Plc) (No.1) [1999] B.P.I.R. 480, Ch D . . . .   *Digested,* 99/**3340**
Emesa Sugar (Free Zone) NV v. Aruba (C17/98) (No.1) [2000] E.C.R. I-665; *Times,* February 29, 2000, ECJ . . . .   *Digested,* 00/**2375**
Emesa Sugar (Free Zone) NV v. Aruba (C17/98) (No.2) [2000] E.C.R. I-675; *Times,* February 29, 2000, ECJ . . . .   *Digested,* 00/**2401**
EMI v. CBS Grammofon A/S (C86/75) see EMI Records Ltd v. CBS United Kingdom Ltd (C51/75)
EMI v. CBS Schallplatten GmbH (C96/75) see EMI Records Ltd v. CBS United Kingdom Ltd (C51/75)
EMI Group Electronics Ltd v. Coldicott (Inspector of Taxes); *sub nom* Thorn EMI Electronics Ltd v. Coldicott (Inspector of Taxes) [2000] 1 W.L.R. 540; [1999] S.T.C. 803; [1999] I.R.L.R. 630; 71 T.C. 455; [1999] B.T.C. 294; (1999) 96(32) L.S.G. 34; (1999) 143 S.J.L.B. 220; *Independent,* October 11, 1999 (C.S.), CA; affirming [1997] S.T.C. 1372; [1997] B.T.C. 532; (1997) 94(43) L.S.G. 29; (1997) 141 S.J.L.B. 222; *Times,* November 14, 1997; *Independent,* November 10, 1997 (C.S.), Ch D; affirming [1996] S.T.C. (S.C.D.) 455, Sp Comm . . . .   *Digested,* 99/**4729**:
                                        Considered, 01/5274
EMI Group Plc v. Cubic (UK) Ltd TNS, Ch D . . . .   *Digested,* 00/**493**
EMI Records Ltd v. CBS United Kingdom Ltd (C51/75); EMI v. CBS Grammofon A/S (C86/75); EMI v. CBS Schallplatten GmbH (C96/75) [1976] E.C.R. 871; [1976] E.C.R. 913; [1976] E.C.R. 811; [1976] 2 C.M.L.R. 235; [1976] F.S.R. 457, ECJ . .   *Digested,* 76/**1163**:
                                        Considered, 91/3578
EMITEC/Opposition Division (T476/95) [1999] E.P.O.R. 479, EPO (Technical Bd App)   *Digested,* 00/**3661**
EMM Capricorn Trustees Ltd v. Compass Trustees Ltd [2001] W.T.L.R. 997; (2001-02) 4 I.T.E.L.R. 34, Royal Ct (Jer)
Emma Hotels Ltd v. Secretary of State for the Environment (No.2) (1981) 41 P. & C.R. 255; (1980) 258 E.G. 64; [1981] J.P.L. 283, QBD. . . . .   *Digested,* 81/**2675**:
         Considered, 86/3347: *Distinguished,* 84/3492, 85/3404, 99/4220
Emmanuel v. DBS Management Plc [1999] Lloyd's Rep. P.N. 593, Ch D . . . .   *Digested,* 99/**112**
Emmanuel v. Locabail (UK) Ltd see Locabail (UK) Ltd v. Bayfield Properties Ltd (No.3)
Emmerson v. McClelland (Unreported, September 14, 1999), CC (Croydon) [*Ex rel.* Aryan Stedman, Barrister, and Corries Solicitors, Rowntrees Wharf, Navigation Road, York] . . . .   *Digested,* 00/**603**
Emmott v. Attorney General (C208/90) see Emmott v. Minister for Social Welfare (C208/90)
Emmott v. Minister for Social Welfare (C208/90); Emmott v. Attorney General (C208/90) [1991] E.C.R. I-4269; [1991] 3 C.M.L.R. 894; [1993] I.C.R. 8; [1991] I.R.L.R. 387, ECJ. . . . .   *Digested,* 92/**4840**:
      Considered, 95/1987, 95/2112, 96/2573, 96/2576: *Distinguished,* 95/4639,
                                97/3983, 99/5284: *Followed,* 92/1974
Empire Paper Ltd (In Liquidation), Re [1999] B.C.C. 406, Ch D (Companies Ct) . . . . . .   *Digested,* 99/**3353**
Empire Resolution Ltd v. MPW Insurance Brokers Ltd [1999] B.P.I.R. 486, QBD (T&CC) . . . .   *Digested,* 99/**3312**

Empire Stores Ltd *v.* Customs and Excise Commissioners (C33/93) [1994] 3 All E.R.
90; [1994] S.T.C. 623; [1994] E.C.R. I-2329; [1995] 1 C.M.L.R. 751; *Times,* July
8, 1994, ECJ (6th Chamber) [1992] 3 C.M.L.R. 639; [1994] V.A.T.T.R. 145, VAT
Tr (Manchester). . . . . *Digested,* 95/**5084**:
              Applied, 97/4976, 98/4936, 00/5319, 00/5339: *Considered,* 98/4945,
                                      01/5599: *Followed,* 97/4975
Employment Equality Bill 1996, Re 4 B.H.R.C. 91, Sup Ct (Irl)
Empress Car Co (Abertillery) Ltd *v.* National Rivers Authority see Environment Agency
(formerly National Rivers Authority) *v.* Empress Car Co (Abertillery) Ltd
Empress of India Restaurant *v.* Customs and Excise Commissioners [1997] V. & D.R.
242, V&DTr . . . . *Digested,* 98/**4881**
Encon Insulation (Nottingham) Ltd *v.* Nottingham City Council [1999] R.A. 382; (1999)
96(24) L.S.G. 40; *Independent,* June 28, 1999 (C.S.), QBD. . . . . *Digested,* 99/**4336**
Encyclopaedia Britannica Inc *v.* SS Hong Kong Producer [1969] 2 Lloyd's Rep. 536;
422 F.2d 7, US Ct . . . . *Digested,* 70/**2652**:
                Applied, 00/866, 00/4213: *Considered,* 74/3542:
                                  Previous proceedings, 69/3291
Endemol Entertainment Holding BV *v.* Commission of the European Communities
(T221/95) [1999] All E.R. (EC) 385; [1999] E.C.R. II-1299; [1999] 5 C.M.L.R.
611, CFI (4th Chamber) . . . . *Digested,* 99/**677**
Enderby *v.* Frenchay HA (No.2); *Evesham v.* North Hertfordshire HA; *Hughes v.* West
Berkshire HA [2000] I.C.R. 612; [2000] I.R.L.R. 257; *Times,* February 29, 2000,
CA; affirming [1999] I.R.L.R. 155, EAT . . . . *Digested,* 00/**2156**
Endersby *v.* Osborne (Unreported, March 14, 2001), CC (Penzance) [*Ex rel.* Ramsay
Quaife, Barrister, Godolphin Chambers, 23 Frances Street, Truro] . . . . *Digested,* 01/**899**
Enduring Powers of Attorney Act 1985, Re see C (Enduring Power of Attorney), Re
ENER-CAP Trade Mark [1999] R.P.C. 362, Appointed Person . . . . *Digested,* 99/**3540**
Energy Conversion Devices Inc's Applications [1982] Com. L.R. 219; [1982] F.S.R. 544;
[1983] R.P.C. 231; *Times,* July 2, 1982, HL . . . . *Digested,* 83/**2764**:
               Applied, 84/2489: *Explained,* 95/2749: *Followed,* 98/4670:
                                     Referred to, 84/2488
Enfield LBC *v.* B (A Minor); *sub nom* Enfield LBC *v.* DB (A Child) [2000] 1 W.L.R.
2259; [2000] 1 All E.R. 255; (2000) 32 H.L.R. 799; *Times,* September 7, 1999 ;
Independent, November 8, 1999 (C.S.), CA. . . . . *Digested,* 99/**3042**
Enfield LBC *v.* DB (A Child) see Enfield LBC *v.* B (A Minor)
Enfield LBC *v.* Final Developments Ltd (2001) 16 P.A.D. 91, Planning Inspector
Enfield LBC *v.* Gay see Gay *v.* Sheeran
Enfield LBC *v.* Mahoney [1983] 1 W.L.R. 749; [1983] 2 All E.R. 901; (1983) 127 S.J.
392, CA . . . . *Digested,* 83/**2901**:
                                       Followed, 98/945
Enfield LBC *v.* Servite Houses (1999) 14 P.A.D. 175, Planning Inspector
Enforcement of a French Interlocutory Order (9 W 69/97), Re [2001] I.L.Pr. 17, OLG
(Karlsruhe)
Enforcement of a Guarantee, Re (IX ZB 2/98) [2001] I.L.Pr. 29, BAG (Ger)
Enforcement of a Notarised Document, Re [2000] I.L.Pr. 249, OLG (Hamburg)
Enforcement of a US Judgment in Germany, Re [1998] I.L.Pr. 601, BGH (Ger)
Engel *v.* Netherlands (No.1) (A/22) (1979-80) 1 E.H.R.R. 647, ECHR . . . . *Applied,* 88/2973,
                              98/3119, 00/3235: *Considered,* 01/98
Engel *v.* Netherlands (No.2) (A/22) (1979-80) 1 E.H.R.R. 706, ECHR. . . . . *Applied,* 99/3126
Engineering Construction Pte Ltd *v.* Attorney General of Singapore (1998) 14 Const.
L.J. 120, HC (Sing) . . . . *Digested,* 98/**811**
Engineers and Managers Association *v.* Advisory, Conciliation and Arbitration Service
(ACAS) [1980] 1 W.L.R. 302; [1980] 1 All E.R. 896; [1980] I.C.R. 215; [1980]
I.R.L.R. 164; 124 S.J. 202, HL; reversing [1979] 1 W.L.R. 1113; [1979] 3 All E.R.
223; [1979] 3 All E.R. 227; [1979] I.C.R. 637; [1979] I.R.L.R. 246; 123 S.J. 353,
CA; reversing [1978] I.C.R. 875 . . . . *Digested,* 80/**2742**:
                Applied, 01/2890: *Considered,* 86/2693, 87/3190: *Followed,* 84/439
England *v.* England (1979) 10 Fam. Law 86. . . . . *Digested,* 80/**764**:
                                       Applied, 99/2401
England *v.* Guardian Insurance Ltd [1999] 2 All E.R. (Comm) 481; [2000] Lloyd's Rep.
I.R. 404, QBD (T&CC) . . . . *Digested,* 99/**3431**
England *v.* Magill see Porter *v.* Magill
England *v.* National Coal Board see National Coal Board *v.* England
England *v.* Purves see JN Taylor Finance Pty Ltd, Re
England *v.* Smith; *sub nom* Southern Equities Corp Ltd (In Liquidation), Re [2001] Ch.
419; [2000] 2 W.L.R. 1141; [2000] B.C.C. 123; [2000] 2 B.C.L.C. 21; [2000]
I.L.Pr. 730; [2000] B.P.I.R. 28; (1999) 96(47) L.S.G. 29; (2000) 144 S.J.L.B. 8;
Times, December 3, 1999 ; *Independent,* November 30, 1999, CA; reversing
[1999] B.P.I.R. 589, Ch D . . . . *Digested,* 00/**3463**:
                                      Considered, 01/3749
English *v.* North Lanarkshire Council 1999 S.C.L.R. 310; [1999] Eu. L.R. 701; 1999
Rep. L.R. 53; 1999 G.W.D. 7-351, OH . . . . *Digested,* 99/**6226**

English Property Corp Plc *v.* Kingston upon Thames RLBC (1999) 77 P. & C.R. 1;
[1999] R.V.R. 316; [1998] J.P.L. 1158; [1998] E.G.C.S. 35; [1998] N.P.C. 36,
CA; reversing in part [1997] R.V.R. 99, Lands Tr. . . . . *Digested,* 99/**4188**
Enichem Base *v.* Comune di Cinisello Balsamo (C380/87) [1989] E.C.R. 2491; [1991]
1 C.M.L.R. 313; *Times,* August 10, 1989, ECJ (5th Chamber) . . . . *Digested,* 91/**4058**:
Applied, 99/2016
Eno *v.* Dunn (1890) L.R. 15 App. Cas. 252; (1890) 7 R.P.C. 311, HL; reversing (1889)
L.R. 41 Ch. D. 439, CA. . . . . *Considered,* 77/3058:
Referred to, 99/3587
Enoch and Zaretsky Bock & Co's Arbitration, Re [1910] 1 K.B. 327, CA . . . . *Distinguished,*
60/2461,
77/319, 78/266, 01/2276: *Followed,* 76/1788
ENS Ltd (formerly Ebasco Ltd) *v.* Derwent Cogeneration Ltd 62 Con. L.R. 141, QBD
(T&CC) . . . . *Digested,* 99/**811**
Ente Partecipazioni e Finanziamento Industria Manifatturiera (EFIM) *v.* Commission of the
European Communities (T127/96) see Breda Fucine Meridionali SpA (BFM) *v.*
Commission of the European Communities (T126/96)
Enterprise Inns Plc *v.* Secretary of State for the Environment, Transport and the Regions
(2001) 81 P. & C.R. 18; [2000] 4 P.L.R. 52; [2000] J.P.L. 1256; [2000]
E.G.C.S. 58; (2000) 97(20) L.S.G. 47, QBD . . . . *Digested,* 01/**4676**
Enterprise Miniere et Chimique (EMC) *v.* Commission of the European Communities
(C30/95) see France *v.* Commission of the European Communities (C68/94)
Entertainment Group of Companies Ltd *v.* Customs and Excise Commissioners [2000]
B.V.C. 2369; [2000] V. & D.R. 447; [2000] S.T.I. 1452, V&DTr
Entick *v.* Carrington (1795) 19 St. Tr. 1029 . . . . *Considered,* 00/2212
Entidad de Gestion de Derechos de los Productores Audiovisuales (EGEDA) *v.* Hosteleria
Asturiana SA (HOASA) (C293/98) [2000] E.C.R. I-629; [2000] E.C.D.R. 231;
[2000] E.M.L.R. 523, ECJ (6th Chamber) . . . . *Digested,* 00/**3584**
Entreprenorforeningens Affalds/Miljosektion (FFAD) (acting for Sydenhavnens Sten &
Grus ApS) *v.* Kobenhavns Kommune (C209/98) see Entreprenorforeningens
Affalds/Miljosektion (FFAD) *v.* Kobenhavns Kommune (C209/98)
Entreprenorforeningens Affalds/Miljosektion (FFAD) *v.* Kobenhavns Kommune (C209/
98); *sub nom* FFAD (for Sydenhavnens Sten & Grus ApS) *v.* Kobenhavns
Kommune (C209/98); Entreprenorforeningens Affalds/Miljosektion
(FFAD) (acting for Sydenhavnens Sten & Grus ApS) *v.* Kobenhavns Kommune
(C209/98) [2000] E.C.R. I-3743; [2001] 2 C.M.L.R. 39; [2001] Env. L.R. D4,
ECJ . . . . *Digested,* 01/**793**
Entry into Dutch Territory, Re (C68/89) see Commission of the European Communities *v.*
Netherlands (C68/89)
Entwistle *v.* Furniss & White (Foundries) Ltd (1999) 99(4) Q.R. 7, CC (Reading) [*Ex
rel.* Pitmans Solicitors, 47 Castle Street, Reading, Berkshire] . . . . *Digested,* 99/**1606**
Environment Agency *v.* ABS Skip Hire (2001) 16 P.A.D. 12, Planning Inspector
Environment Agency *v.* Anglian Water Services Ltd see R. (on the application of
Anglian Water Services Ltd) *v.* Environment Agency
Environment Agency *v.* Brock Plc [1998] Env. L.R. 607; [1998] 4 P.L.R. 37; [1998]
J.P.L. 968; [1998] E.H.L.R. Dig. 277; *Times,* March 26, 1998, QBD . . . . *Digested,* 98/**2288**
Environment Agency *v.* Campbell see Holmes *v.* Campbell
Environment Agency *v.* Clark see Rhondda Waste Disposal Ltd (In Administration), Re
Environment Agency (formerly National Rivers Authority) *v.* Empress Car Co
(Abertillery) Ltd; *sub nom* Empress Car Co (Abertillery) Ltd *v.* National Rivers
Authority [1999] 2 A.C. 22; [1998] 2 W.L.R. 350; [1998] 1 All E.R. 481; [1998]
Env. L.R. 396; [1988] E.H.L.R. 3; [1998] E.G.C.S. 16; (1998) 95(8) L.S.G. 32;
(1998) 148 N.L.J. 206; (1998) 142 S.J.L.B. 69; [1998] N.P.C. 16; *Times,*
February 9, 1998, HL; affirming [1997] Env. L.R. 227; [1997] J.P.L. 908, QBD . . *Digested,* 98/**2291**:
Applied, 98/2288, 99/3987
Environment Agency *v.* Giles [1998] Env. L.R. D15, QBD
Environment Agency *v.* Maber (1999) 14 P.A.D. 513, Planning Inspector
Environment Agency *v.* Martin (2001) 16 P.A.D. 50, Planning Inspector
Environment Agency *v.* Milford Haven Port Authority (The Sea Empress); *sub nom* R.
v. Milford Haven Port Authority [2000] 2 Cr. App. R. (S.) 423; [2000] Env. L.R.
632; [2000] J.P.L. 943, CA (Crim Div); reversing in part [1999] 1 Lloyd's Rep.
673, Crown Ct (Cardiff). . . . . *Digested,* 00/**2291**
Environment Agency *v.* SBS Spares Ltd (1999) 14 P.A.D. 489, Planning Inspector
Environment Agency *v.* Short [1999] Env. L.R. 300; [1999] E.H.L.R. 3; [1999] J.P.L.
263; [1998] C.O.D. 462, QBD . . . . *Digested,* 99/**2202**
Environment Agency *v.* Singer [1998] Env. L.R. 380, QBD . . . . *Digested,* 98/**2284**
Environment Agency *v.* Stanford [1999] Env. L.R. 286; [1998] C.O.D. 373, QBD . . . . . *Digested,* 99/**2205**
Environment Agency *v.* Steve Parr Haulage & Plant Hire Ltd [2000] Env. L.R. 710;
[2000] 2 P.L.R. 45; *Independent,* November 15, 1999 (C.S.), QBD
Environment Agency *v.* Stout see Mineral Resources Ltd, Re
ENZO/Polynucleotides (T442/95) [2001] E.P.O.R. 24, EPO (Technical Bd App). . . . . . *Digested,* 01/**3934**
EP *v.* Italy (31127/96) (2001) 31 E.H.R.R. 17, ECHR . . . . *Digested,* 01/**3548**
Ephson and Ewell BC *v.* Lords (1998) 13 P.A.D. 380, Planning Inspector

Epon (C419/97), Re see ARCO Chemie Nederland Ltd v. Minister van Volkshuisvesting, Ruimtelijke Ordening en Milieubeheer (C418/97)

Eppe v. Commission of the European Communities (C354/92); *sub nom* Eppe v. Commission of the European Communities (T59/91); Eppe v. Commission of the European Communities (T79/91) [1993] E.C.R. I-7027, ECJ . . . . *Followed,* 00/**2363**

Eppe v. Commission of the European Communities (T59/91) see Eppe v. Commission of the European Communities (C354/92)

Eppe v. Commission of the European Communities (T79/91) see Eppe v. Commission of the European Communities (C354/92)

Epping Forest DC v. Marie Stopes International (2000) 15 P.A.D. 264, Planning Inspector

Epping Forest DC v. Philcox see R. (on the application of Philcox) v. Epping Forest DC

Epsom and Ewell BC v. St James Homes Ltd (2001) 16 P.A.D. 21, Planning Inspector

Epsom BC v. Nicholls (1999) 78 P. & C.R. 348, QBD . . . . *Digested,* 00/**4616**

Epsom Skip Hire Ltd v. Secretary of State for the Environment, Transport and the Regions [1998] E.G.C.S. 58; (1998) 95(14) L.S.G. 24, QBD

Equal Pay Concepts (C143/83), Re; *sub nom* Commission of the European Communities v. Denmark (C143/83) [1985] E.C.R. 427; [1986] 1 C.M.L.R. 44, ECJ . . . . *Digested,* 86/**1460**: *Followed,* 00/2160

Equitable Debenture Assets Corp v. Moss (William) Group Ltd 11 Con. L.R. 1; (1984) 1 Const. L.J. 131, QBD (OR) . . . . *Digested,* 85/**221**: *Applied,* 85/220: *Considered,* 99/804

Equitable Life Assurance Society v. Hyman [2000] 3 W.L.R. 529; [2000] 3 All E.R. 961; [2001] Lloyd's Rep. I.R. 99; [2000] O.P.L.R. 101; [2000] Pens. L.R. 249; (2000) 144 S.J.L.B. 239; *Times,* July 21, 2000; *Independent,* October 30, 2000 (C.S), HL; affirming [2000] 2 W.L.R. 798; [2000] 2 All E.R. 331; [2000] O.P.L.R. 71; [2000] Pens. L.R. 129; (2000) 97(5) L.S.G. 34; (2000) 144 S.J.L.B. 57; *Times,* January 26, 2000 ; *Independent,* January 28, 2000, CA; reversing [1999] O.P.L.R. 213; [1999] Pens. L.R. 297; *Times,* October 12, 1999, Ch D . . . . *Digested,* 00/**4395**

Equitas Ltd v. Trygg Hansa Insurance Co Ltd see Trygg Hansa Insurance Co Ltd v. Equitas Ltd

Equity & Law Home Loans Ltd v. Prestridge and Brown [1992] 1 W.L.R. 137; [1992] 1 All E.R. 909; [1992] 1 F.L.R. 485; [1992] 1 F.C.R. 353; (1992) 24 H.L.R. 76; (1992) 63 P. & C.R. 403; [1992] Fam. Law 288; (1992) 89(2) L.S.G. 31; [1991] N.P.C. 103; *Times,* October 9, 1991; *Independent,* October 10, 1991, CA . . . . *Digested,* 92/**3160**: *Followed,* 99/4392

Equity Nominees Ltd, Re [2000] B.C.C. 84; [1999] 2 B.C.L.C. 19, Ch D (Companies Ct) . . . . *Digested,* 99/**3301**: *Not followed,* 01/3767

ER Ives Investment Ltd v. High [1967] 2 Q.B. 379; [1967] 2 W.L.R. 789; [1967] 1 All E.R. 504; 110 S.J. 963, CA . . . . *Digested,* 67/**2196**: *Applied,* 75/1191: *Considered,* 68/2185, 84/1154, 85/1083: *Distinguished,* 68/1313, 00/4658

Erdagoz v. Turkey (21890/93) (2001) 32 E.H.R.R. 19; [1998] H.R.C.D. 30, ECHR

Erewash BC v. Friesland School (1998) 13 P.A.D. 503, Planning Inspector

Ergi v. Turkey (23818/94) (2001) 32 E.H.R.R. 18; [1998] H.R.C.D. 726, ECHR

Eridania SpA (formerly Cereol Italia Srl) v. Oetker (The Fjord Wind) [2000] 2 All E.R. (Comm) 108; [2000] 2 Lloyd's Rep. 191; [2000] C.L.C. 1376, CA; affirming [1999] 1 Lloyd's Rep. 307; [1998] C.L.C. 1186, QBD (Comm Ct) . . . . *Digested,* 00/**4704**

Eriksen v. Norway (2000) 29 E.H.R.R. 328, ECHR . . . . *Digested,* 00/**3176**

Erikson v. Italy (37900/97) (2000) 29 E.H.R.R. CD152, ECHR

Erkalo v. Netherlands (1999) 28 E.H.R.R. 509; [1998] H.R.C.D. 834, ECHR . . . . *Digested,* 00/**3171**

Ernesto Stoppani SPA v. Stoppani France [1999] I.L.Pr. 384, Cass (F)

Ernst & Young v. Customs and Excise Commissioners [1997] V. & D.R. 183, V&DTr . . . . *Digested,* 98/**4912**

Ernst & Young Inc v. Central Guaranty Trust Co (2000-01) 3 I.T.E.L.R. 605, QB (Alta)

Eron Park Ltd v. Secretary of State for the Environment, Transport and the Regions (No.1); *sub nom* Eronpark Ltd v. Secretary of State for Transport [2000] 2 E.G.L.R. 165, Lands Tr . . . . *Digested,* 01/**4661**

Eron Park Ltd v. Secretary of State for the Environment, Transport and the Regions (No.2) [2001] R.V.R. 5, Lands Tr . . . . *Digested,* 01/**4671**

Eronpark Ltd v. Secretary of State for Transport see Eron Park Ltd v. Secretary of State for the Environment, Transport and the Regions (No.1)

Erridge v. Coole & Haddock (2000) 97(27) L.S.G. 38, Ch D

Errington v. Errington and Woods [1952] 1 K.B. 290; [1952] 1 All E.R. 149; [1952] 1 T.L.R. 231; 96 S.J. 119, CA . . . . *Digested,* 52/**1973**: *Applied,* 52/257, 52/1596, 52/1969, 52/1972, 52/1974, 54/1512, 80/2408, 93/2073, 98/3599: *Approved,* 66/6674, 67/2196: *Considered,* 55/1519, 74/2103, 78/1794, 80/348, 96/4953: *Distinguished,* 66/5825: *Not followed,* 88/2042

ES, Petitioner (Adoption) see S v. M (Consent: Missing Parent)

Esal (Commodities) Ltd (1988), Re [1989] B.C.L.C. 59; [1988] P.C.C. 443, CA . . . . . . *Digested,* 89/**346**: *Applied,* 00/659

Esal Commodities Ltd, Re (No.2) [1990] B.C.C. 125 . . . .   *Digested*, 91/**2164**:
                                                    Applied, 94/2620, 99/3330
Esal (Commodities) Ltd v. Mahendra Pujara [1989] 2 Lloyd's Rep. 479, CA . . . .   *Digested*, 90/**3780.a**:
                                                    Applied, 00/768
Esanda Finance Corp Ltd v. Peat Marwick Hungerfords [2000] Lloyd's Rep. P.N. 684;
   (1997) 142 A.L.R. 750, HC (Aus). . . . .   *Digested*, 00/**4246**
Escoubet v. Belgium (26780/95) (2001) 31 E.H.R.R. 46, ECHR . . . .   *Digested*, 01/**3498**
Escritt v. Escritt (1982) 3 F.L.R. 280 . . . .   *Digested*, 83/**595.u**:
                                        Distinguished, 96/5548, 00/4909
Esdaile v. Payne see Lane v. Esdaile
Eshelby v. Federated European Bank Ltd [1932] 1 K.B. 423, CA; affirming [1932] 1
   K.B. 254, KBD. . . . .   *Distinguished*,
                                                   66/11104,
                     86/2680, 87/3082: *Followed*, 84/2689: *Not followed*, 98/401
Espinosa v. Bourke; Espinosa v. Isaacs; Espinosa v. Wilson [1999] 1 F.L.R. 747; [1999]
   3 F.C.R. 76; [1999] Fam. Law 210, CA . . . .   *Digested*, 99/**4639**:
                                                 Considered, 00/2528
Espinosa v. Isaacs see Espinosa v. Bourke
Espinosa v. Wilson see Espinosa v. Bourke
Esselte AB v. Pearl Assurance Plc [1997] 1 W.L.R. 891; [1997] 2 All E.R. 41; (1998) 75
   P. & C.R. 30; [1997] 1 E.G.L.R. 73; [1997] 02 E.G. 124; [1996] E.G.C.S. 178;
   (1996) 93(44) L.S.G. 29; (1996) 140 S.J.L.B. 259; [1996] N.P.C. 157; *Times,*
   November 14, 1996; *Independent*, December 9, 1996 (C.S.), CA; reversing
   (1996) 72 P. & C.R. 21; [1995] 2 E.G.L.R. 61; [1995] 37 E.G. 173; [1995]
   E.G.C.S. 81, Ch D . . . .   *Digested*, 96/**3716**:
                                                    Applied, 96/3709
Esselte Meto A/S v. Tryk & Tryk APS (H-0284-92) [2000] E.C.D.R. 506, SH (DK)
Essex Furniture Plc v. National Provident Institution [2001] L. & T.R. 3, Ch D . . . .   *Digested*, 01/**4154**
Esslemont v. Marshall (Inspector of Taxes) [1996] S.T.C. 1086; 68 T.C. 596, CA;
   affirming [1994] S.T.C. 813, Ch D . . . .   *Digested*, 98/**4670**
Esso Australia Resources Ltd v. Commissioner of Taxation 2 I.T.L. Rep. 429, HC (Aus)
Esso Petroleum Co Ltd v. Harper's Garage (Stourport) Ltd [1968] A.C. 269; [1967] 2
   W.L.R. 871; [1967] 1 All E.R. 699; 111 S.J. 174, HL; reversing in part [1966] 2
   Q.B. 514; [1966] 2 W.L.R. 1043; [1966] 1 All E.R. 725; 110 S.J. 265, CA;
   reversing [1965] 3 W.L.R. 469; [1965] 2 All E.R. 933; 109 S.J. 511, QBD . . . . . .   *Digested*, 67/**3906**:
                 Applied, 66/12023, 68/3886, 69/3523, 76/2770, 77/2487, 77/3027, 79/2139,
                            82/415, 83/453, 85/397, 91/444, 93/3979, 94/4506, 00/2114:
                 Considered, 71/11629, 74/1270, 77/397, 80/369, 84/405, 91/3301, 94/451,
                                      99/3703: *Disapproved*, 66/12029
Esso Petroleum Co Ltd v. Mardon [1976] Q.B. 801; [1976] 2 W.L.R. 583; [1976] 2 All
   E.R. 5; [1976] 2 Lloyd's Rep. 305; 2 B.L.R. 82; 120 S.J. 131, CA; reversing in part
   [1975] Q.B. 819; [1975] 2 W.L.R. 147; [1975] 1 All E.R. 203; (1974) 119 S.J.
   81; *Times*, August 2, 1974, QBD . . . .   *Digested*, 76/**341**:
                     Applied, 76/1868, 77/1804, 78/2822, 79/2562, 83/971, 84/396, 84/1580:
                 Considered, 77/2032, 78/2067, 89/429, 89/469, 93/2997, 95/770, 95/2462:
                            Distinguished, 00/4188: *Not followed*, 80/3525, 84/4180:
                                             Referred to, 81/1852
Esso Petroleum Co Ltd v. Milton [1997] 1 W.L.R. 938; [1997] 2 All E.R. 593; [1997]
   C.L.C. 634; (1997) 16 Tr. L.R. 250; *Times*, February 13, 1997; *Independent*,
   February 19, 1997, CA . . . .   *Digested*, 97/**799**:
                                        Applied, 00/499: *Considered*, 99/410
Estasis Salotti di Colzani Aimo e Gianmario Colzani v. RUWA Polstereimaschinen GmbH
   (C24/76); *sub nom* Colzani v. RUWA Polstereimaschinen GmbH (C24/76)
   [1976] E.C.R. 1831; [1977] 1 C.M.L.R. 345; *Times*, December 20, 1976, ECJ . . . .   *Digested*, 77/**1242**:
                          Applied, 85/1452, 89/4512, 01/800, 01/3838: *Considered*, 96/1097
Estee Lauder Cosmetics GmbH & Co OHG v. Lancaster Group GmbH (C220/98)
   [2000] All E.R. (EC) 122; [2000] E.C.R. I-117; [2000] 1 C.M.L.R. 515; [2000]
   C.E.C. 317, ECJ (5th Chamber) . . . .   *Digested*, 00/**2386**:
                                                   Followed, 01/2489
Estee Lauder Cosmetics Ltd v. Fragrance Counter Inc (315 0 25/99) [2000] E.T.M.R.
   843, LG (Hamburg)
Esteem Settlement, Re see Grupo Torras SA v. Al-Sabah (No.6)
Esterhuizen v. Allied Dunbar Assurance Plc [1998] 2 F.L.R. 668; [1998] Fam. Law
   527; *Times*, June 10, 1998, QBD . . . .   *Digested*, 98/**4593**
Estill v. Cowling Swift & Kitchin; Bean v. Cowling Swift & Kitchin [2000] Lloyd's Rep.
   P.N. 378; [2000] W.T.L.R. 417, Ch D . . . .   *Digested*, 00/**4255**
Estima Jorge v. Portugal [1998] H.R.C.D. 447, ECHR . . . .   *Considered*, 01/3516
ET v. Administrative Office Rheinfelden 2 I.T.L. Rep. 95, BG (Swi)
ETA (J03/95) [1998] E.P.O.R. 103, EPO (Legal Bd App)
ETA/Request with a view to revision (G01/97) [2001] E.P.O.R. 1, EPO (Enlarged Bd App)
                                                       Digested, 01/**3890**

Etablissement Commercial Kamira v. Schiazzano [1985] Q.B. 93; [1984] 3 W.L.R. 95; [1984] 2 All E.R. 465; (1984) 16 H.L.R. 1; (1984) 48 P. & C.R. 8; (1984) 271 E.G. 369; (1984) 81 L.S.G. 1684; (1984) 128 S.J. 432, CA . . . .   *Digested, 84/***1964**: *Applied,* 00/3916

Etablissements Consten Sarl v. Commission of the European Communities (C56/64) (Authority to Intervene) [1966] E.C.R. 299; [1966] E.C.R. 556, ECJ . . . .   *Applied,* 98/2306

Etablissements Delhaize Freres & Compagnie Le Lion SA v. Promalvin SA & AGE Bodegas Unidas SA (C47/90) [1992] E.C.R. I-3669; *Financial Times,* June 16, 1992, ECJ . . . .   *Digested, 92/***4764**: *Considered,* 01/2490

Etam Plc v. Baker Almond [2001] 8 E.G.C.S. 164, Ch D   *Digested, 99/***3981**

Etheridge v. K (A Minor) [1999] Ed. C.R. 550, QBD . . . .   *Digested, 99/***3981**

Etheridge v. Strathclyde RC [1992] I.C.R. 579; [1992] I.R.L.R. 392, EAT . . . .   *Digested, 92/***1933**: *Considered,* 00/2189

Ethicon Inc's European Patent (T514/92) (1998) 21 (9) I.P.D. 21101, EPO (Technical Bd App)

Etridge v. Gore [1998] N.P.C. 32, QBD

Etridge v. Pritchard Englefield [1999] Lloyd's Rep. P.N. 702; [1999] P.N.L.R. 839, CA . .   *Digested, 99/***4030**

ETS Vehicles Ltd v. Fargate Developments Ltd [1997] N.I. 25, CA (NI) . . . .   *Digested, 99/***5407**

Ettl v. Austria (A/117) (1988) 10 E.H.R.R. 255, ECHR . . . .   *Applied,* 98/3141

Euclid, Ohio v. Ambler Realty Co see Village of Euclid, Ohio v. Ambler Realty Co

Eugstar v. Edgcombe Tea and Coffee Co Ltd (Unreported, May 10, 1999), CC (Wandsworth) [*Ex rel.* Tim Petts, Barrister, 12 King's Bench Walk, London] . . . . .   *Digested, 99/***2471**

Eurest SA v. EIH Ltd see Radhakrishna Hospitality Service Private Ltd v. EIH Ltd

Eurim-Pharm Arzneimittel GmbH v. Beiersdorf AG (C71/94) see Bristol Myers Squibb v. Paranova (C427/93)

Euro Fire Ltd v. Davison (Inspector of Taxes); Hill v. Davison (Inspector of Taxes) [1999] S.T.C. 1050 (Note); 71 T.C. 535; [1999] B.T.C. 433, CA; affirming [1997] S.T.C. 538; [1997] B.T.C. 191, Ch D . . . .   *Digested, 00/***5033**

Eurobait Ltd v. Customs and Excise Commissioners [2001] S.T.I. 1275, V&DTr

Eurobell (Holdings) Plc v. Barker [1998] I.C.R. 299; *Times,* November 12, 1997, EAT . . .   *Digested, 97/***2226**

Eurocross Sales Ltd v. Cornhill Insurance Plc [1995] 1 W.L.R. 1517; [1995] 4 All E.R. 950; [1996] L.R.L.R. 1; [1995] B.C.C. 991; [1995] 2 B.C.L.C. 384; *Times,* September 5, 1995; *Lloyd's List,* November 15, 1995 (I.D.), CA . . . .   *Digested, 95/***4011**: *Considered,* 00/431: *Followed,* 96/682: *Not followed,* 96/3855

Eurofinance Group Ltd, Re see Parkinson v. Eurofinance Group Ltd

EUROLAMB Trade Mark [1997] R.P.C. 279, Appointed Person . . . .   *Digested, 97/***4891**: *Followed,* 99/3587

Euromarket Designs Inc v. Peters [2000] E.T.M.R. 1025; [2001] F.S.R. 20, Ch D . . . . . .   *Digested, 01/***3979**

Euromepa SA v. R Esmerian Inc [1999] I.L.Pr. 694, US Ct

Europaische Wirtschaftliche Interessenvereinigung see European Information Technology Observatory (C402/96), Re

Europe Mortgage Co Ltd v. GA Property Services Ltd [1999] Lloyd's Rep. P.N. 709; [1999] 3 E.G.L.R. 53; [1999] 50 E.G. 77, QBD . . . .   *Digested, 99/***4053**: *Considered,* 00/4279

European Coal and Steel Community v. Acciaierie e Ferriere Busseni SpA (In Liquidation) (C221/88) [1990] E.C.R. I-495, ECJ . . . .   *Applied,* 00/3582

European Economic Community v. Irish Sugar see Irish Sugar Plc v. Commission of the European Communities (C497/99 P)

European Economic Community v. Italy see Italian Ports Employment Policy, Re

European Economic Community v. Italy see Piloting Tariffs in the Port of Genoa, Re

European Gas Turbines Ltd (formerly Ruston Gas Turbines Ltd) v. MSAS Cargo International Inc [2001] C.L.C. 880, QBD . . . .   *Digested, 01/***4487**

European Information Technology Observatory (C402/96), Re; *sub nom* European Information Technology Observatory's Reference (C402/96); Europaische Wirtschaftliche Interessenvereinigung [1997] E.C.R. I-7515; [1998] 2 C.M.L.R. 156; [1998] E.T.M.R. 161, ECJ (5th Chamber)

European Information Technology Observatory's Reference (C402/96) see European Information Technology Observatory (C402/96), Re

European Ltd v. Economist Newspaper Ltd [1998] E.T.M.R. 307; [1998] E.M.L.R. 536; [1998] F.S.R. 283; (1998) 21 (3) I.P.D. 21022, CA; affirming [1996] E.M.L.R. 394; [1996] F.S.R. 431; (1996) 19(7) I.P.D. 19067, Ch D . . . .   *Digested, 98/***3509**: *Applied,* 01/4056

European Night Services Ltd (ENS) v. Commission of the European Communities (T374/94) [1998] E.C.R. II-3141; [1998] 5 C.M.L.R. 718; [1998] C.E.C. 955, CFI (2nd Chamber) . . . .   *Digested, 99/***694**

European Parliament v. Council of the European Union (C164/97) [1999] E.C.R. I-1139; [1999] Env. L.R. 604, ECJ (5th Chamber) . . . .   *Digested, 99/***2609**

European Parliament v. Council of the European Union (C22/96) [1998] E.C.R. I-3231; [1999] 1 C.M.L.R. 160, ECJ . . . .   *Digested, 99/***2228**: *Applied,* 00/2407

European Parliament v. Council of the European Union (C271/94); *sub nom* Edicom Decision (C271/94), Re [1996] E.C.R. I-1689; [1996] 2 C.M.L.R. 481, ECJ . . . .   *Applied,* 00/2407

European Parliament v. Council of the European Union (C42/97) [1999] E.C.R. I-869;
    [2000] 2 C.M.L.R. 73, ECJ . . . .   *Digested,* 00/**2407**
Europeenne Automobile Sarl v. Commission of the European Communities (T9/96)
    [1999] E.C.R. II-3639; [2001] 4 C.M.L.R. 9, CFI (1st Chamber). . . . .   *Digested,* 01/**2471**
Europhone International Ltd v. Frontel Communications Ltd see Europhone International
    Ltd v. Frontel Communications Ltd (t/a Frontier Communications International)
Europhone International Ltd v. Frontel Communications Ltd (t/a Frontier
    Communications International); *sub nom* Europhone International Ltd v. Frontier
    Communications International ; Europhone International Ltd v. Frontel
    Communications Ltd [2001] S.T.C. 1399; [2001] B.T.C. 5454; [2001] B.V.C. 516;
    [2001] S.T.I. 1250; (2001) 98(36) L.S.G. 37; *Times,* September 11, 2001, Ch D .   *Digested,* 01/**5572**
Europhone International Ltd v. Frontier Communications International see Europhone
    International Ltd v. Frontel Communications Ltd (t/a Frontier Communications
    International)
Europieces SA v. Sanders (C399/96) [1999] All E.R. (EC) 831; [1998] E.C.R. I-6965;
    [2001] 1 C.M.L.R. 25, ECJ (2nd Chamber). . . . .   *Digested,* 00/**2225**
Europs Ltd v. Sunshine Lifestyle Products Ltd NWL 211/98, Ch D . . . .   *Digested,* 98/**750**
Eurosteel Ltd v. Stinnes AG [2000] 1 All E.R. (Comm) 964; [2000] C.L.C. 470, QBD
    (Comm Ct) . . . .   *Digested,* 00/**736**
Eurostock Meat Marketing Ltd, Re [1999] N.I. 13, CA (NI) . . . .   *Digested,* 99/**5082**
Eurostock Meat Marketing Ltd v. Department of Agriculture for Northern Ireland (C477/
    98) [2000] E.C.R. I-10695; [2001] 1 C.M.L.R. 32, ECJ . . . .   *Digested,* 01/**5675**
Eurotunnel SA v. SeaFrance (C408/95) [1997] E.C.R. I-6315; [1998] 2 C.M.L.R. 293;
    [1998] C.E.C. 433; [1998] B.T.C. 5200; [1998] B.V.C. 221, ECJ. . . . .   *Digested,* 98/**4654**
Eurowings Luftverkehrs AG v. Finanzamt Dortmund Unna (C294/97) [1999] E.C.R. I-
    7447; [2001] 3 C.M.L.R. 64; 2 I.T.L. Rep. 570, ECJ
Evangelischer Krankenhausverein Wien v. Abgabenberufungskommission Wien (C437/
    97); Wein & Co Handelsges mbH v. Oberosterreichische Landesregierung
    (C437/97) [2001] All E.R. (EC) 735; [2000] E.C.R. I-1157; [2001] 3 C.M.L.R.
    38, ECJ (5th Chamber) . . . .   *Digested,* 01/**5276**
Evans (CICA: Quantum: 2001), Re (Unreported, September 12, 2001), CICA (Cardiff) [*Ex
    rel.* Robert O'Leary, Barrister, 33 Park Place, Cardiff] . . . .   *Digested,* 01/**38**
Evans (Deceased), Re see Evans v. Westcombe
Evans v. Absolute Clean Rooms Ltd [2001] 1 Q.R. 14, QBD
Evans v. Bartlam; *sub nom* Bartlam v. Evans [1937] A.C. 473; [1937] 2 All E.R. 646,
    HL; reversing [1936] 1 K.B. 202, CA. . . . .   *Applied,* 47-51/**1400,**
                             47-51/**3046,** 47-51/**3168,** 47-51/**5225,** 47/**5225,** 53/**709,** 60/**1034,** 65/**3066,**
                             65/**3242,** 69/**3679,** 76/**2107,** 77/**1683,** 82/**2400,** 83/**2864,** 86/**2667,** 00/**536:**
                          Considered, 64/**3039,** 73/**1153,** 73/**1154,** 82/**2066,** 83/**3045,** 84/**2745,**
                                   90/**1036,** 91/**2203,** 94/**2765,** 97/**583:** *Distinguished,* 52/**3665:**
                    Followed, 47-51/**2470,** 47-51/**2522,** 47-51/**2533,** 47-51/**2535,** 47/**2522,**
                                                  97/**4151**
Evans v. Berkeley Farm Dairy (Unreported, February 20, 2001), CC (Swindon) [*Ex rel.*
    Ford & Warren Solicitors, Westgate Point, Westgate, Leeds] . . . .   *Digested,* 01/**901**
Evans (Darren Michael) v. DPP [2001] EWHC Admin 369; *Times,* July 9, 2001, QBD
    (Admin Ct) . . . .   *Digested,* 01/**1189**
Evans v. Evans [1990] 1 W.L.R. 575; [1990] 2 All E.R. 147; [1990] 1 F.L.R. 319;
    [1990] F.C.R. 498; [1990] Fam. Law 215; (1990) 154 J.P.N. 424; (1990) 87(12)
    L.S.G. 40; (1990) 140 N.L.J. 291; (1990) 134 S.J. 785, Fam Div . . . .   *Digested,* 90/**2297:**
                                         Considered, 95/**4030,** 99/**2421**
Evans v. Governor of Brockhill Prison see R. v. Governor of Brockhill Prison Ex p.
    Evans (No.2)
Evans v. Guinness Mahon & Co Ltd see Ward v. Guinness Mahon & Co Ltd
Evans v. Hafeez (Unreported, January 20, 1998), MCLC [*Ex rel.* Simpson Millar
    Solicitors, 101 Borough High Street, London Bridge, London] . . . .   *Digested,* 98/**1678**
Evans v. Higgins (Unreported, August 25, 2001), CC (Woolwich) [*Ex rel.* Nigel Ffitch,
    Barrister, Phoenix Chambers, Gray's Inn, London] . . . .   *Digested,* 01/**1521**
Evans v. James (Administratrix of Hopkin's Estate) see James v. Evans
Evans v. Jibb (Unreported, October 16, 1995), CC (Bolton) [*Ex rel.* John Marsland,
    Solicitor] . . . .   *Digested,* 95/**1804:**
                                         Referred to, 00/**1723**
Evans v. Lewis (Unreported, May 12, 2000), CC (Merthyr Tydfil) [*Ex rel.* Matthew
    White, Barrister, St. John's Chambers, Small Street, Bristol] . . . .   *Digested,* 00/**1695**
Evans v. London Hospital Medical College (University of London) [1981] 1 W.L.R.
    184; [1981] 1 All E.R. 715; (1981) 125 S.J. 48, QBD.   *Digested,* 81/**2184:**
                   Considered, 98/**4784:** *Distinguished,* 83/**2531,** 90/**5493:** *Followed,* 98/**1768**
Evans v. Morton (1998) 98(3) Q.R. 7, CC (Oxford) . . . .   *Digested,* 98/**1702**
Evans v. Motor Insurers Bureau; Mighell v. Reading; White v. White [1999] 1 C.M.L.R.
    1251; [1999] Eu. L.R. 389; [1999] Lloyd's Rep. I.R. 30; [1999] P.I.Q.R. P101;
    Times, October 12, 1998, CA; affirming [1997] 3 C.M.L.R. 1218; *Times,*
    November 10, 1997, QBD (Comm Ct) . . . .   *Digested,* 98/**3396:**
                                       Subsequent proceedings, 01/**2479**
Evans v. Radford (Unreported, July 7, 1998), CC (Harrogate) [*Ex rel.* Rebecca
    Bensted, Barrister, Bracton Chambers, Chancery Lane, London] . . . .   *Digested,* 98/**1463**

Evans v. Secretary of State for the Environment, Transport and the Regions [2001]
EWCA Civ 32; [2001] 2 C.M.L.R. 10, CA; affirming [2001] P.I.Q.R. P3, QBD . . .   *Digested,* 01/**2479**:
Previous proceedings, 98/3396

Evans (John) v. Secretary of State for the Environment, Transport and the Regions see
Buckland v. Secretary of State for the Environment, Transport and the Regions

Evans v. Shah (Unreported, July 15, 1997), CC (Reigate) [*Ex rel.* Richard Parker,
Robert Gray & Co, 6 Linkfield Corner, Redhill, Surrey] . . . .   *Digested,* 98/**493**

Evans v. Silvery Lynx Products Ltd [2001] 4 Q.R. 11, CC (Preston) [*Ex rel.* Barrie
Searle, Barrister, St James' Chambers, 68 Quay street, Manchester] . . . .   *Digested,* 01/**1612**

Evans v. United Kingdom (8027/77) see McVeigh v. United Kingdom (8022/77)

Evans v. Westcombe; *sub nom* Evans (Deceased), Re [1999] 2 All E.R. 777; (1999)
96(10) L.S.G. 28; (1999) 143 S.J.L.B. 72; *Times,* March 10, 1999, Ch D . . . .   *Digested,* 99/**4634**

Evans Construction Co Ltd v. Bass Holdings Ltd see Evans Construction Co Ltd v.
Charrington & Co Ltd

Evans Construction Co Ltd v. Charrington & Co Ltd; Evans Construction Co Ltd v. Bass
Holdings Ltd [1983] Q.B. 810; [1983] 2 W.L.R. 117; [1983] 1 All E.R. 310;
(1982) 264 E.G. 347; (1982) 79 L.S.G. 1138, CA . . . .   *Digested,* 83/**3025**:
Applied, 90/480: *Considered,* 89/2104, 90/2770, 90/4055, 91/3204:
Followed, 98/374

Evans Medical Ltd v. Chiron Corp [2001] E.N.P.R. 9, Hof (Den Haag)

Evans Medical Ltd's Patent; *sub nom* Chiron Corp v. Evans Medical Supplies Ltd
[1998] R.P.C. 517; (1998) 43 B.M.L.R. 39; (1998) 21(4) I.P.D. 21035; *Times,*
January 20, 1998, Pat Ct . . . .   *Digested,* 98/**3474**:
Considered, 98/3470

EVANS/Antigenic preparations (T780/95) [2001] E.P.O.R. 56, EPO (Technical Bd App)   *Digested,* 01/**3910**

Evensis Ltd v. Customs and Excise Commissioners [2001] S.T.I. 1230, V&DTr

Ever Success, The; *sub nom* Crew Members of the Ever Success v. Owners of the Ever
Success [1999] 1 Lloyd's Rep. 824, QBD (Adm Ct) . . . .   *Digested,* 99/**4458**

Eveready Battery Co Inc (EP(UK) 0469776), Re see Eveready Battery Co Inc's Patent, Re

Eveready Battery Co Inc's Patent, Re; *sub nom* Patents Act 1977, Re; Eveready Battery
Co Inc (EP(UK) 0469776), Re [2000] R.P.C. 852; (2000) 23(7) I.P.D. 23054,
Pat Ct . . . .   *Digested,* 00/**3688**

Everest Trust, Re see Rosewood Trust Ltd v. Schmidt

Everett v. Secretary of State for the Environment, Transport and the Regions [2001]
EWHC Admin 701; (2001) 98(37) L.S.G. 40, QBD (Admin Ct)

Eversheds v. Osman [2000] 1 Costs L.R. 54, CA . . . .   *Digested,* 00/**4027**

Everson v. Flurry (Unreported, February 22, 1999), CC (Slough) [*Ex rel.* Silverbeck
Rymer Solicitors, Heywoods Building, 5 Brunswick Street, Liverpool] . . . .   *Digested,* 99/**3411**:
Cited, 01/3830: *Considered,* 01/897: *Distinguished,* 00/2583:
Followed, 99/2467, 00/3551, 00/3552: *Referred to,* 00/2580

Everson v. Secretary of State for Trade and Industry (C198/98) [2000] All E.R. (EC)
29; [1999] E.C.R. I-8903; [2000] 1 C.M.L.R. 489; [2000] C.E.C. 115; [2000]
I.C.R. 525; [2000] I.R.L.R. 202; *Times,* February 1, 2000, ECJ (5th Chamber) . .   *Digested,* 00/**2133**

Eves v. DPP (Unreported, March 2, 2000), Crown Ct (Chester) [*Ex rel.* Ben Collins,
Barrister, Sedan Houses, Stanley Place, Chester] . . . .   *Digested,* 00/**198**

Evesham v. North Hertfordshire HA see Enderby v. Frenchay HA (No.2)

Evgenia Papadopoulo NV (t/a Interexpress) v. GJ Van der Vaart Beheer BV (t/a All
Transport Rotterdam BV) [1998] I.L.Pr. 782, Hof (Den Haag)

Evpo Agnic, The [1988] 1 W.L.R. 1090; [1988] 3 All E.R. 810; [1988] 2 Lloyd's Rep. 411;
(1988) 85(32) L.S.G. 33; (1988) 132 S.J. 1299, CA . . . .   *Digested,* 89/**3340**:
Applied, 00/4743

Ewen Developments v. Secretary of State for the Environment [1980] J.P.L. 404, DC . .   *Digested,* 80/**2645**:
Distinguished, 01/4698

Ewing v. Bennett [2001] W.T.L.R. 249, CA . . . .   *Digested,* 01/**5166**

Ewing v. Buttercup Margarine Co Ltd [1917] 2 Ch. 1; (1917) 34 R.P.C. 232, CA . . . . . .   *Applied,* 74/3824,
98/3497: *Considered,* 95/4732, 98/3516

Ewing v. Orr Ewing (No.1) (1883-84) L.R. 9 App. Cas. 34, HL; affirming (1883) L.R.
22 Ch. D. 456, CA . . . .   *Applied,* 85/**3131**:
Considered, 98/768

Ewing v. Stockham Valve Ltd Staff Retirement Benefits Scheme Trustees [2000]
O.P.L.R. 257, CA (NI) . . . .   *Digested,* 01/**5915**

Ex p. Trustee v. Cole see Cole (A Bankrupt), Re

Ex p. Guardian Newspapers Ltd, Re [1999] 1 W.L.R. 2130; [1999] 1 All E.R. 65; [1999] 1 Cr.
App. R. 284; (1998) 95(39) L.S.G. 34; (1998) 148 N.L.J. 1514; (1998) 142 S.J.L.B.
255; *Times,* October 9, 1998; *Independent,* October 8, 1998, CA (Crim Div) . . . .   *Digested,* 98/**985**

Excalibur Airways Ltd (In Liquidation), Re [1998] 1 B.C.L.C. 436; [1998] B.P.I.R. 598, Ch D
(Companies Ct) . . . .   *Digested,* 98/**3344**:
Applied, 01/3788

Excelsior SNC di Pedrotti Bruna & C v. Ente Autonomo Fiera Internazionale di Milano
(C260/99) see Agora Srl v. Ente Autonomo Fiera Internazionale di Milano
(C223/99)

Excess Insurance Co Ltd v. Allendale Mutual Insurance Co [2001] Lloyd's Rep. I.R. 524,
CA . . . .   *Applied,* 00/762

Excess Insurance Co Ltd *v.* Astra SA Insurance & Reinsurance Co [1996] L.R.L.R. 380; [1997] C.L.C. 160; [1997] I.L.Pr. 252; [1996] 5 Re. L.R. 471, CA; affirming [1995] L.R.L.R. 464, QBD (Comm Ct) . . . . *Digested,* 97/**710**: *Not followed,* 98/583

Excess Insurance Co Ltd *v.* Mander [1997] 2 Lloyd's Rep. 119; [1995] L.R.L.R. 358; *Lloyd's List,* May 18, 1995 (I.D.), QBD (Comm Ct) . . . . *Digested,* 95/**2921**: *Followed,* 98/242

Exchange Travel (Holdings) Ltd (No.3), Re; *sub nom* Katz *v.* McNally (Liquidator's Indemnity for Costs) [1997] B.C.C. 784; [1997] 2 B.C.L.C. 579; [1998] B.P.I.R. 30, CA; reversing [1996] B.C.C. 933; [1996] 2 B.C.L.C. 524; [1997] B.P.I.R. 623, Ch D . . . . *Digested,* 97/**3103**

Exchange Travel (Holdings) Ltd (No.4), Re; *sub nom* Katz *v.* McNally (Recovery of Preferences) [1999] B.C.C. 291, CA . . . . *Digested,* 99/**3357**

Exchange Travel Agency Ltd *v.* Triton Property Trust [1991] B.C.L.C. 396, DC . . . . *Digested,* 92/**2530.a**: *Considered,* 93/516, 99/3272: *Distinguished,* 94/2738, 94/2739, 96/3519

Excomm Ltd *v.* Ahmed Abdul-Qawi Bamaodah (The St Raphael) [1985] 1 Lloyd's Rep. 403; (1985) 82 L.S.G. 761, CA. . . . . *Digested,* 85/**120**: *Applied,* 86/119, 87/155: *Considered,* 00/812

Exeter CC *v.* Weldon Leigh Ltd (1998) 13 P.A.D. 320, Planning Inspector

Exeter City Council *v.* Palmer (Unreported, April 6, 2000), CC (Exeter) [*Ex rel.* Crosse & Crosse Solicitors, 14 Southernhay West, Exeter] . . . . *Digested,* 00/**3927**

Expandable Grafts Partnership *v.* Boston Scientific BV see Palmaz *v.* Boston Scientific BV

Expandable Grafts Partnership *v.* Boston Scientific BV (Dutch Proceedings) see Palmaz *v.* Boston Scientific BV (Dutch Proceedings)

Expert Clothing Service & Sales Ltd *v.* Hillgate House Ltd [1987] 1 E.G.L.R. 65; (1987) 282 E.G. 715, HL; affirming in part [1986] Ch. 340; [1985] 3 W.L.R. 359; [1985] 2 All E.R. 998; (1985) 50 P. & C.R. 317; [1985] 2 E.G.L.R. 85; (1985) 275 E.G. 1011; (1985) 82 L.S.G. 2010; (1985) 129 S.J. 484, CA . . . . *Digested,* 87/**2146**: *Applied,* 99/5407: *Considered,* 85/1844, 87/2156, 91/2226, 92/2664, 94/2760, 96/3744, 01/4195: *Followed,* 00/3944

Expert Witness Institute *v.* Customs and Excise Commissioners [2001] EWCA Civ 1882; [2001] S.T.I. 1771; *Times,* December 21, 2001, CA; affirming [2001] 1 W.L.R. 1658; [2001] S.T.C. 679; [2001] B.T.C. 5499; [2001] B.V.C. 571; [2001] S.T.I. 731; *Times,* April 12, 2001, Ch D; reversing [2001] B.V.C. 2125; [2001] S.T.I. 226, V&DTr . . . . *Digested,* 01/**5566**: *Considered,* 01/507

Expo International Pty Ltd *v.* Chant [1978] 40 A.C.L.C. 452, Sup Ct (NSW)

Export Tax on Art Treasures (C7/68), Re; *sub nom* Commission of the European Communities *v.* Italy (C7/68) [1968] E.C.R. 617; [1969] C.M.L.R. 1, ECJ . . . . . . *Digested,* 69/**1396**: *Considered,* 00/2384

Exportslachterijen van Oordegem BVBA *v.* Belgische Dienst voor Bedrifsleven en Landbouw (C2/93) [1994] E.C.R. I-2283, ECJ (6th Chamber) [1994] E.C.R. I-2283, AGO . . . . *Digested,* 94/**4748**: *Followed,* 00/170, 00/2337

Express & Echo Publications Ltd *v.* Tanton [1999] I.C.R. 693; [1999] I.R.L.R. 367; (1999) 96(14) L.S.G. 31; *Times,* April 7, 1999; *Independent* April 19, 1999 (C.S.), CA . . . . *Digested,* 99/**2045**: *Distinguished,* 01/6468

Express Medicare Ltd *v.* Customs and Excise Commissioners [2001] B.V.C. 2152; [2000] V. & D.R. 377; [2001] S.T.I. 577, V&DTr

Express Newspapers Pensions Trustees Ltd *v.* Express Newspapers Plc [1998] O.P.L.R. 261; [1999] Pens. L.R. 9, Ch D . . . . *Digested,* 99/**4151**

Express Newspapers Plc *v.* News (UK) Ltd [1990] 1 W.L.R. 1320; [1990] 3 All E.R. 376; [1991] F.S.R. 36; [1990] F.S.R. 359; (1990) 87(35) L.S.G. 41; *Times,* February 13, 1990; *Independent,* February 14, 1990; *Guardian,* March 14, 1990, Ch D . . . . *Digested,* 91/**2978**: *Considered,* 98/3422

Extrudakerb (Maltby Engineering) Ltd *v.* Whitemountain Quarries Ltd [1996] N.I. 567; [1996] C.L.C. 1747; *Times,* July 10, 1996, QBD (NI) . . . . *Digested,* 96/**1137**

Exxon Corp *v.* Internal Revenue Commissioner 2 I.T.L. Rep. 279, US Ct

Eyckeler & Malt AG *v.* Commission of the European Communities (T42/96) [1998] E.C.R. II-401; [1998] 3 C.M.L.R. 1077, CFI . . . . *Applied,* 01/4121: *Distinguished,* 00/4953: *Followed,* 00/2350

Eyre *v.* McCracken (2001) 33 H.L.R. 16; (2000) 80 P. & C.R. 220; [2000] L. & T.R. 411, CA; reversing CC (Central London) . . . . *Digested,* 00/**3936**

Eyup *v.* Landesgeschaftsstelle des Arbeitsmarktservice Vorarlberg (C65/98) [2000] E.C.R. I-4747; [2000] 3 C.M.L.R. 1049, ECJ (6th Chamber) . . . . *Digested,* 01/**2458**

Ezekiel *v.* Lehrer A3/2001/0782 CHANI, CA; affirming [2001] Lloyd's Rep. P.N. 401; [2001] P.N.L.R. 33; (2001) 98(20) L.S.G. 42; (2001) 145 S.J.L.B. 109; *Times,* April 4, 2001, Ch D . . . . *Digested,* 01/**604**

Ezekiel *v.* Orakpo [1977] Q.B. 260; [1976] 3 W.L.R. 693; [1976] 3 All E.R. 659; 120 S.J. 504, CA . . . . *Digested,* 76/**154**: *Followed,* 97/3291, 99/3272

F, Re see K (Enduring Powers of Attorney), Re

F (A Child) (Care Order: Sexual Abuse), Re see F (A Child) (Mental Health Act: Guardianship), Re

F (A Child) (Contact Order), Re [2001] 1 F.C.R. 422; (2001) 165 J.P.N. 489, CA . . . . . *Digested*, 01/**2655**

F (A Child) (Mental Health Act: Guardianship), Re; *sub nom* F (A Child) (Care Order: Sexual Abuse), Re [2000] 1 F.L.R. 192; [2000] 1 F.C.R. 11; (1999) 2 C.C.L. Rep. 445; (2000) 51 B.M.L.R. 128; [2000] Fam. Law 18; (1999) 96(39) L.S.G. 38; *Times*, October 19, 1999; *Independent*, October 12, 1999, CA. . . . . *Digested*, 99/**3934**

F (A Child) v. Bedford BC (Unreported, March 17, 2000), CC (Northampton) [*Ex rel.* Jonathan Hand, Barrister, 35 Essex Street, Temple, London] . . . . *Digested*, 00/**1541**

F (A Child) v. Bronham (Unreported, April 26, 2001), CC (Cardiff) [*Ex rel.* Andrew Arentsen, Barrister, Thirty Three Park Place, Cardiff]. . . . . *Digested*, 01/**1755**

F (A Child) v. Budget Rent a Car International Inc [*Ex rel.* Amanda Millmore, Barrister, 4 King's Bench Walk, Temple, London] . . . . *Digested*, 01/**1773**

F (A Child) v. Merewood Group Ltd [2001] 5 Q.R. 17, CC (Carlisle) [*Ex rel.* Hough Halton & Soal, Solicitors, 32 Abbey Street, Carlisle CA3 8RJ]. . . . . *Digested*, 01/**1743**

F (A Minor) (Abduction: Custody Rights), Re; *sub nom* F (A Minor) (Abduction: Jurisdiction), Re [1991] Fam. 25; [1990] 3 W.L.R. 1272; [1990] 3 All E.R. 97; [1991] 1 F.L.R. 1; [1991] F.C.R. 227; [1990] Fam. Law 178; (1990) 140 N.L.J. 1193; *Independent*, August 9, 1990, CA . . . . *Digested*, 91/**2526**:
Applied, 95/3443, 95/3444, 95/3445: *Considered*, 96/529, 99/2332

F (A Minor) (Abduction: Jurisdiction), Re see F (A Minor) (Abduction: Custody Rights), Re

F (A Minor) (Contact: Child in Care), Re [1995] 1 F.L.R. 510; [1994] 2 F.C.R. 1354; [1995] Fam. Law 231; (1994) 158 J.P.N. 856, Fam Div . . . . *Digested*, 95/**3395**:
Applied, 95/3393, 95/3408, 99/2399

F (A Minor) (Contact: Enforcement: Representation of Child), Re [1998] 1 F.L.R. 691; [1998] 3 F.C.R. 216; [1998] Fam. Law 319, CA . . . . *Digested*, 98/**2420**

F (A Minor) v. Brent LBC; *sub nom* R. v. F (A Minor); R. v. Brent LBC Ex p. AF [2000] Ed. C.R. 425; [2000] E.L.R. 550, QBD. . . . . *Digested*, 00/**1941**

F (A Minor) v. Slater (Unreported, September 14, 1999), CC (Blackpool) [*Ex rel.* Blackburn & Co Solicitors, 7 Crescent East, Thornton Cleveleys, Lancashire] . . . *Digested*, 00/**1640**

F (A Minor) v. Willcocks (No.1) (Unreported, January 12, 1998), CC (Barnet) [*Ex rel.* Tim Kevan. Barrister, 1 Temple Gardens, Temple, London, EC4Y 9BB] . . . . *Digested*, 98/**465**:
Considered, 98/454

F (A Minor) v. Willcocks (No.2) (Unreported, May 14, 1998), CC (Barnet) [*Ex rel.* Louise Neilson, Barrister, 9 Gough Square, London] . . . . *Digested*, 99/**406**

F (Abduction: Child's Right to Family Life), Re [1999] Fam. Law 806, Fam Div

F (Adult: Court's Jurisdiction), Re; *sub nom* F (Adult Patient), Re [2001] Fam. 38; [2000] 3 W.L.R. 1740; [2000] 2 F.L.R. 512; [2000] 3 F.C.R. 30; [2000] U.K.H.R.R. 712; (2000) 3 C.C.L. Rep. 210; [2000] Lloyd's Rep. Med. 381; (2000) 55 B.M.L.R. 81; [2000] Fam. Law 709; (2000) 97(35) L.S.G. 37; (2000) 97(36) L.S.G. 41; *Times*, July 25, 2000; *Independent*, July 6, 2000, CA . *Digested*, 00/**4171**:
Applied, 01/2662

F (Adult Patient), Re see F (Adult: Court's Jurisdiction), Re

F (An Infant) v. Chief Constable of Kent [1982] Crim. L.R. 682, DC . . . . *Digested*, 82/**1949**:
Followed, 00/1080

F (Care: Party Status: Directions), Re [1999] Fam. Law 295, Fam Div

F (Children) (Adoption: Freeing Order), Re [2000] 2 F.L.R. 505; [2000] 3 F.C.R. 337; [2000] Fam. Law 788; (2000) 164 J.P.N. 981; *Times*, July 6, 2000, CA. . . . . . . *Digested*, 00/**2430**

F (Children) (Care Proceedings: Contact), Re see F (Children) (Care: Termination of Contact), Re

F (Children) (Care: Termination of Contact), Re; *sub nom* F (Children) (Care Proceedings: Contact), Re [2000] 2 F.C.R. 481; [2000] Fam. Law 708; (2000) 164 J.P.N. 703; *Times*, June 22, 2000, Fam Div. . . . . *Digested*, 00/**2474**

F (Children: Care Planning), Re see F v. Lambeth LBC

F (CICB: Quantum: 1998), Re (Unreported, June 16, 1998), CICB (London) [*Ex rel.* Tamala McGee, Barrister, 4 King's Bench Walk, Temple, London] . . . . *Digested*, 98/**1507**

F (CICB: Quantum: 2000), Re [2000] 4 Q.R. 4, CICB (London) [*Ex rel.* Bell Pope Solicitors, Ashley House, 5 Grosvenor Square, Southampton] . . . . *Digested*, 00/**1524**

F (In Utero), Re [1988] Fam. 122; [1988] 2 W.L.R. 1288; [1988] 2 All E.R. 193; [1988] 2 F.L.R. 307; [1988] F.C.R. 529; [1988] Fam. Law 337; (1988) 152 J.P.N. 538; (1988) 138 N.L.J. Rep. 37; (1989) 133 S.J. 1088; (1988) 132 S.J. 820, CA . . . . *Digested*, 88/**2397**:
Applied, 98/4783: *Considered*, 94/2345, 95/2580

F (Mental Patient: Sterilisation), Re see F v. West Berkshire HA

F (Time Limit for Appeals: Delay in Obtaining Legal Aid Certificate), Re [1999] Ed. C.R. 985; [1999] E.L.R. 251; [1999] C.O.D. 222, QBD . . . . *Digested*, 99/**359**

F v. Child Support Agency [1999] 2 F.L.R. 244; [1999] 2 F.C.R. 385; [1999] Fam. Law 540; (1999) 163 J.P.N. 795; (1999) 96(17) L.S.G. 25; *Times*, April 9, 1999, QBD . . . . *Digested*, 99/**2443**

F v. F (Ancillary Relief: Substantial Assets) [1995] 2 F.L.R. 45; [1996] 2 F.C.R. 397; [1995] Fam. Law 546, Fam Div . . . . *Digested*, 96/**2864**:
Considered, 96/2855: *Overruled*, 98/2467

F *v.* F (Contact: Committal) [1998] 2 F.L.R. 237; [1999] 2 F.C.R. 42; [1998] Fam.
Law 519, CA . . . . *Digested,* 98/**2417**
F *v.* Harrow LBC see B *v.* Harrow LBC (No.1)
F *v.* Inland Revenue Commissioners [2000] W.T.L.R. 505, Sp Comm . . . . *Digested,* 01/**5258**
F *v.* Lambeth LBC; *sub nom* F (Children: Care Planning), Re [2001] 3 F.C.R. 738, Fam
Div
F *v.* London Fire and Civil Defence Authority; *sub nom* London Fire and Civil Defence
Authority *v.* F; EAT/0042/00, EAT/0573/01, EAT; reversing (Unreported, May
22, 2001), ET [*Ex rel.* Mohinderpal Sethi, Barrister, No 1 Sergeants' Inn, Fleet
Street, London] . . . . *Digested,* 01/**1534**
F *v.* Pazuki (Unreported, June 7, 2000), CC (Barnet) [*Ex rel.* Andrew Slaughter,
Barrister, Bridewell Chambers, 2 Bridewell Place, London] . . . . *Digested,* 00/**3874**
F *v.* Richmond Twickenham and Roehampton HA see Farrell *v.* Merton Sutton and
Wandsworth HA
F *v.* Special Education Needs Tribunal see B *v.* Harrow LBC (No.1)
F *v.* West Berkshire HA; *sub nom* F (Mental Patient: Sterilisation), Re [1990] 2 A.C. 1;
[1989] 2 W.L.R. 1025; [1989] 2 All E.R. 545; [1989] 2 F.L.R. 376; (1989) 139
N.L.J. 789; (1989) 133 S.J. 785, HL; affirming (1989) 86(10) L.S.G. 42, CA . . . *Digested,* 89/**3044**:
Applied, 94/3850, 95/4266: *Considered,* 90/3139, 90/3679.a, 91/2462,
91/2463, 91/2548, 92/2981, 93/2712, 95/3578, 95/4102, 95/4104,
96/2846, 96/7002, 97/2597, 97/6266, 99/2380, 00/2780, 00/4247,
01/2662: *Referred to,* 91/5262
F Cross & Sons *v.* Spencer (Valuation Officer); *sub nom* Cross (F) & Sons *v.* Spencer
(Valuation Officer) [2000] R.A. 71, Lands Tr . . . . *Digested,* 00/**4588**
F Hoffmann La Roche & Co AG *v.* Centrafarm Vertriebsgesellschaft Pharmazeutischer
Erzeugnisse mbH (102/77) [1978] E.C.R. 1139; [1978] 3 C.M.L.R. 217; [1978]
F.S.R. 598, ECJ . . . . *Digested,* 78/**1406**:
Applied, 96/5713: *Considered,* 98/3514, 99/3560: *Followed,* 97/4879
F Hoffmann La Roche & Co AG *v.* Inter Continental Pharmaceuticals Ltd; JR Geigy SA *v.*
Inter Continental Pharmaceuticals [1965] Ch. 795; [1965] 2 W.L.R. 1045;
[1965] 2 All E.R. 15; [1965] R.P.C. 226; 109 S.J. 209, CA; reversing [1965]
R.P.C. 215, Ch D . . . . *Digested,* 65/**2957**:
Applied, 66/9072, 76/1735: *Considered,* 86/1775, 87/2050, 98/3445
F Hoffmann La Roche & Co AG *v.* Secretary of State for Trade and Industry [1975] A.C.
295; [1974] 3 W.L.R. 104; [1974] 2 All E.R. 1128; 118 S.J. 500, HL; affirming
[1973] 3 W.L.R. 805; [1973] 3 All E.R. 945; 117 S.J. 713, CA;
reversing (Unreported, July 13, 1973) . . . . *Digested,* 74/**3801**:
Applied, 85/324, 89/3658, 92/2904, 01/4425: *Considered,* 78/24, 87/1326,
88/1274, 90/3697, 90/3912, 91/4030, 91/4032, 92/394, 94/3740:
Distinguished, 88/2863, 89/2991, 89/3081: *Followed,* 95/6105
F&I Services Ltd *v.* Customs and Excise Commissioners; R. *v.* Customs and Excise
Commissioners Ex p. F&I Services Ltd [2001] EWCA Civ 762; [2001] S.T.C.
939; [2001] B.T.C. 5266; [2001] B.V.C. 347; [2001] S.T.I. 850, CA; affirming
[2000] S.T.C. 364; [2000] B.T.C. 5137; [2000] B.V.C. 177; [2000] S.T.I. 639;
(2000) 97(21) L.S.G. 41; *Times,* April 26, 2000, QBD; affirming [1999] B.V.C.
2161, VAT Tr . . . . *Digested,* 01/**5598**
F-B (Minors) (Leave to Appeal), Re; B (A Minor), Re [1999] 1 F.C.R. 713; (1999) 163 J.P.N.
971, CA . . . . *Digested,* 99/**2304**
FA Wellworth & Co Ltd *v.* Philip Russell Ltd (No.1) [1996] N.I. 558, QBD (NI)
FA Wellworth & Co Ltd *v.* Philip Russell Ltd (No.2) [1997] N.I. 175, QBD (NI) . . . . *Digested,* 99/**5428**
FA Wellworth & Co Ltd's Application, Re; Boots the Chemist Ltd, Re [1996] N.I. 509; *Times,*
December 16, 1996, CA (NI)
Faaborg-Gelting Linien A/S *v.* Finanzamt Flensburg (C231/94) [1996] All E.R. (E.C.)
656; [1996] S.T.C. 774; [1996] E.C.R. I-2395; [1996] 3 C.M.L.R. 535; [1996]
C.E.C. 587; *Times,* May 9, 1996, ECJ (6th Chamber) . . . . *Digested,* 96/**5902**:
Considered, 98/4904
FABIO PERINI/Automatic surface rewinder (T883/93) [2000] E.P.O.R. 100, EPO
(Technical Bd App) . . . . *Digested,* 00/**3685**
Fabris *v.* SA Nationale de Television France 2 [2000] E.C.C. 258, Trib Gde Inst (Paris)
Faccenda Chicken Ltd *v.* Fowler; Fowler *v.* Faccenda Chicken Ltd [1987] Ch. 117;
[1986] 3 W.L.R. 288; [1986] 1 All E.R. 617; [1986] I.C.R. 297; [1986] I.R.L.R.
69; [1986] F.S.R. 291; (1986) 83 L.S.G. 288; (1986) 136 N.L.J. 71; (1986) 130
S.J. 573; *Times,* December 11, 1985, CA; affirming [1985] 1 All E.R. 724;
[1984] I.C.R. 589; [1984] I.R.L.R. 61; [1985] F.S.R. 105; (1984) 134 N.L.J. 255;
Times, November 16, 1983, Ch D . . . . *Digested,* 86/**1167**:
Applied, 91/1611, 98/2109, 99/2004: *Considered,* 86/412, 87/1294, 92/1908:
Distinguished, 91/428.a, 96/2598: *Followed,* 89/4288, 92/5345, 97/3377,
01/4064
Facey *v.* Midas Retail Security (No.1) [2001] I.C.R. 287; [2000] I.R.L.R. 812, EAT. . . . . *Digested,* 01/**2268**
Facia Footwear Ltd (In Administration) *v.* Hinchcliffe [1998] 1 B.C.L.C. 218, Ch D . . . . *Digested,* 98/**3265**
Factortame Ltd *v.* Secretary of State for Transport (No.6) see R. *v.* Secretary of State
for Transport Ex p. Factortame Ltd (No.6)
Fadil *v.* Secretary of State for the Home Department see Fadli *v.* Secretary of State for
the Home Department

Fadli (Application for Judicial Review), Re see Fadli v. Secretary of State for the Home Department

Fadli v. Secretary of State for the Home Department; *sub nom* R. v. Secretary of State for the Home Department Ex p. Fadli; Fadli (Application for Judicial Review), Re; Fadil v. Secretary of State for the Home Department [2001] Imm. A.R. 392; [2001] I.N.L.R. 168; (2001) 98(2) L.S.G. 40; *Times*, December 12, 2000, CA; affirming CO 832/1999, QBD . . . . *Digested*, 01/**3636**

Fagtun EHF v. Byggingarnefnd Borgarholtsskola; Fagtun EHF v. Government of Iceland; Fagtun EHF v. City of Reykjavik and the Municipality of Mosfellbaer [1999] 2 C.M.L.R. 960, EFTA . . . . *Digested*, 99/**675**

Fagtun EHF v. City of Reykjavik and the Municipality of Mosfellbaer see Fagtun EHF v. Byggingarnefnd Borgarholtsskola

Fagtun EHF v. Government of Iceland see Fagtun EHF v. Byggingarnefnd Borgarholtsskola

Fahy's Will Trusts, Re [1962] 1 W.L.R. 17; [1962] 1 All E.R. 73; 106 S.J. 15, Ch D . . . . . . *Digested*, 62/**2391**:
Considered, 99/3676: *Not followed*, 80/2124, 81/2136

FAI General Insurance Co Ltd v. Godfrey Merrett Robertson Ltd [1999] C.L.C. 566, CA *Digested*, 99/**317**

FAI General Insurance Co Ltd v. Ocean Marine Mutual Protection and Indemnity Association (No.1) [1997] 6 Re. L.R. 316, HC (Aus) . . . . *Digested*, 98/**3400**

FAI General Insurance Co Ltd v. Ocean Marine Mutual Protection and Indemnity Association (No.2) [1998] Lloyd's Rep. I.R. 24, HC (Aus) . . . . *Digested*, 98/**3406**

Faircharm Investments Ltd v. Citibank International Plc [1998] Lloyd's Rep. Bank. 127; *Times*, February 20, 1998, CA . . . . *Digested*, 98/**4361**

Fairchild v. Glenhaven Funeral Services Ltd (t/a GH Dovener & Son); Babcock International Co Plc; Fox v. National Grid Co Plc; Fox v. Spousal (Midlands) Ltd; Matthews v. Associated Portland Cement Manufacturers (1978) Ltd; Dyson v. Leeds City Council (No.2); Pendleton v. Stone & Webster Engineering Ltd; Matthews v. British Uralite PlcHL; reversing [2001] EWCA Civ 1881; *Times*, December 13, 2001; *Independent*, December 21, 2001; *Daily Telegraph*, December 20, 2001, CA; affirming 00/TLQ/1284, QBD

Fairclough Homes Ltd v. Secretary of State for the Environment [1999] P.L.C.R. 94, QBD . . . . *Digested*, 99/**4253**

Fairey v. Southampton CC [1956] 2 Q.B. 439; [1956] 3 W.L.R. 354; [1956] 2 All E.R. 843; 120 J.P. 434; 54 L.G.R. 388; 100 S.J. 509, CA; affirming [1956] 2 W.L.R. 517; [1956] 1 All E.R. 419; 54 L.G.R. 135; 100 S.J. 133, QBD . . . . *Digested*, 56/**3869**:
Applied, 99/2886: *Considered*, 97/2338

Fairhurst v. St Helens and Knowsley HA [1995] P.I.Q.R. Q1; [1994] 5 Med. L.R. 422, HC . . . . *Not followed*, 99/1533

Fairley v. John Thompson (Design and Contracting Division) Ltd [1973] 2 Lloyd's Rep. 40, CA . . . . *Digested*, 73/**731**:
Considered, 98/1485: *Distinguished*, 77/798

Fairmile Portfolio Management Ltd v. Davies Arnold Cooper [1998] E.G.C.S. 149; (1998) 95(42) L.S.G. 34; *Times*, November 17, 1998, Ch D . . . . *Digested*, 98/**2520**

Fairport, The (No.5) [1967] 2 Lloyd's Rep. 162, PDAD . . . . *Digested*, 67/**3599**:
Applied, 00/4740

Fairview New Homes Plc v. Government Row Residents Association [1998] E.G.C.S. 92, Ch D

Fairweather v. Customs and Excise Commissioners [1998] V. & D.R. 65, V&DTr . . . . . . *Digested*, 00/**4987**

Fairweather v. Ghafoor (Unreported, September 14, 2000), CC (Rawtenstall) [*Ex rel.* James Fryer-Spedding, Barrister, St James's Chambers, 68 Quay Street, Manchester] . . . . *Digested*, 01/**4164**

Falco Finance Ltd v. Gough (1999) 17 Tr. L.R. 526; [1999] C.C.L.R. 16, CC (Macclesfield) . . . . *Digested*, 99/**2516**

Falkirk Council v. Whyte [1997] I.R.L.R. 560, EAT . . . . *Digested*, 98/**5819**

Fallon v. Bateman (Unreported, August 14, 2000), CC (Bournemouth) [*Ex rel.* Nigel S Brockley, Barrister, Bracton Chambers, Bell House, 8 Bell Yard, London] . . . . . . *Digested*, 00/**1576**

Fallon (Morgan's Executors) v. Fellows (Inspector of Taxes) [2001] S.T.C. 1409; [2001] B.T.C. 438; [2001] S.T.I. 1104, Ch D; reversing [2001] S.T.C. (S.C.D.) 45; [2001] S.T.I. 632, Sp Comm. . . . . *Digested*, 01/**5183**

Falmouth and Truro Port HA v. South West Water Ltd see R. v. Falmouth and Truro Port HA Ex p. South West Water Ltd

Family Housing Association v. Donellan see Family Housing Association v. Donnellan

Family Housing Association v. Donnellan; *sub nom* Family Housing Association v. Donellan [2001] 30 E.G.C.S. 114; [2001] N.P.C. 125, Ch D

Family Housing Association (Manchester) v. Michael Hyde & Partners [1993] 1 W.L.R. 354; [1993] 2 All E.R. 567; [1993] 2 E.G.L.R. 239; [1992] E.G.C.S. 150; *Times*, December 15, 1992, CA . . . . *Digested*, 93/**1858**:
Considered, 00/334

Fanning v. Waltham Forest Community Based Housing Association; *sub nom* Waltham Forest Community Based Housing Association v. Fanning [2001] L. & T.R. 41, QBD

Fantask A/S *v.* Industriministeriet (Erhvervsministeriet) (C188/95); *sub nom* Fantask A/
  S *v.* Ministry of Industry and Trade (C188/95) [1998] All E.R. (E.C.) 1; [1997]
  E.C.R. I-6783; [1998] 1 C.M.L.R. 473; [1998] C.E.C. 359, ECJ . . . .   *Digested*, 98/**655**:
                                                        Applied, 99/5284, 00/4462
Fantask A/S *v.* Ministry of Industry and Trade (C188/95) see Fantask A/S *v.*
  Industriministeriet (Erhvervsministeriet) (C188/95)
Fantoni *v.* Dunscombe (Unreported, September 11, 1998), CC (Clerkenwell) [*Ex rel.*
  Marcus Grant, Barrister, 1 Temple Gardens, Temple, London] . . . .   *Digested*, 98/**3721**
FANUC/Bubble memory system (T15/85) [1998] E.P.O.R. 185, EPO (Technical Bd App)
Far *v.* Far (C12/98) [2000] E.C.R. I-527; [2000] S.T.I. 127, ECJ (2nd Chamber)
Far Eastern Shipping Plc *v.* Scales Trading Ltd; *sub nom* Scales Trading Ltd *v.* Far Eastern
  Shipping Plc [2001] 1 All E.R. (Comm) 319; [2001] Lloyd's Rep. Bank. 29;
  [2001] C.L.C. 412, PC (NZ) . . . .   *Digested*, 01/**694**:
                                                        Applied, 01/4877
Faradene Ltd *v.* Secretary of State for the Environment, Transport and the Regions
  (1999) 96(33) L.S.G. 33, QBD . . . .   *Digested*, 00/**4442**
Farah *v.* British Airways, *Times*, January 26, 2000 ; *Independent*, January 18, 2000,
  CA . . . .   *Digested*, 00/**4219**
Farah *v.* Commissioner of Police of the Metropolis [1998] Q.B. 65; [1997] 2 W.L.R.
  824; [1997] 1 All E.R. 289; (1997) 9 Admin. L.R. 601; (1996) 93(41) L.S.G. 29;
  (1996) 140 S.J.L.B. 227; *Times*, October 10, 1996; *Independent*, October 17,
  1996, CA . . . .   *Digested*, 97/**4181**
Farah *v.* Moody [1998] E.G.C.S. 1; (1998) 95(3) L.S.G. 26, CA
Faraj *v.* Secretary of State for the Home Department [1999] I.N.L.R. 451; *Independent*,
  May 17, 1999 (C.S.), CA . . . .   *Digested*, 99/**3176**
Fareham BC *v.* Barton see Fareham BC *v.* Secretary of State for the Environment,
  Transport and the Regions
Fareham BC *v.* Hitchcock Management Services (Guernsey) Ltd (1998) 13 P.A.D. 164,
  Planning Inspector
Fareham BC *v.* Hordell (1998) 13 P.A.D. 291, Planning Inspector
Fareham BC *v.* Secretary of State for the Environment, Transport and the Regions; *sub*
  nom Fareham BC *v.* Barton [2001] EWHC Admin 462; (2001) 98(25) L.S.G. 48,
  QBD (Admin Ct)
Fareway Trading Co Ltd *v.* Customs and Excise Commissioners see Customs and Excise
  Commissioners *v.* Invicta Poultry Ltd
Farinelli *v.* Saatchi & Saatchi Advertising Srl [2000] E.C.D.R. 309, It Cass (I)
Farley *v.* Brown [2001] 5 Q.R. 16, CC (Lambeth) [*Ex rel.* Nigel S Brockley, Barrister,
  Bracton Chambers, 8 Bell Yard, London] . . . .   *Digested*, 01/**1730**
Farley *v.* Premium Life Assurance Co Ltd see Macaulay *v.* Premium Life Assurance Co
  Ltd
Farley *v.* Skinner (No.2); *sub nom* Skinner *v.* Farley [2001] UKHL 49; [2001] 3 W.L.R.
  899; [2001] 4 All E.R. 801; 79 Con. L.R. 1; [2001] 49 E.G. 120; [2001] 48 E.G.
  131; [2001] 42 E.G.C.S. 139; (2001) 98(40) L.S.G. 41; (2001) 145 S.J.L.B. 230;
  [2001] N.P.C. 146; *Times*, October 15, 2001; *Independent*, November 26, 2001
  (C.S.); *Daily Telegraph*, October 16, 2001, HL; reversing 73 Con. L.R. 70; [2000]
  Lloyd's Rep. P.N. 516; [2000] P.N.L.R. 441; [2000] 2 E.G.L.R. 125; [2000]
  E.G.C.S. 52; (2000) 97(15) L.S.G. 41; [2000] N.P.C. 40; *Times*, April 14, 2000,
  CA . . . .   *Digested*, 01/**4539**
Farmer *v.* Brewer see Farmer *v.* Moseley (Holdings) Ltd (t/a RTK Marine)
Farmer (Valuation Officer) *v.* Buxted Poultry Ltd; Hambleton DC *v.* Buxted Poultry Ltd
  [1993] A.C. 369; [1993] 2 W.L.R. 34; [1993] 1 All E.R. 117; 91 L.G.R. 121; [1993]
  R.A. 1; (1993) 157 L.G. Rev. 361; [1992] E.G.C.S. 163; (1993) 143 N.L.J. 51;
  [1992] N.P.C. 157; *Times*, December 18, 1992; *Independent*, January 27, 1993,
  HL; affirming [1992] 1 W.L.R. 330; [1992] 2 All E.R. 70; 90 L.G.R. 54; [1992] 1
  E.G.L.R. 179; [1992] 11 E.G. 118; [1991] R.A. 267; (1992) 156 L.G. Rev. 223;
  (1991) 135 S.J.L.B. 130; *Times*, August 8, 1991, CA; reversing [1990] R.A. 105;
  (1990) 154 L.G. Rev. 691, Lands Tr . . . .   *Digested*, 93/**3389**:
                                                        Considered, 99/4316
Farmer (Valuation Officer) *v.* Hambleton DC [1999] R.A. 61; [1999] E.G.C.S. 5; *Times*,
  January 21, 1999, CA; reversing [1997] R.A. 361, Lands Tr . . . .   *Digested*, 99/**4316**
Farmer *v.* Moseley (Holdings) Ltd (t/a RTK Marine); Farmer *v.* Brewer (2000) 23(6)
  I.P.D. 23047, Pat Ct
Farmer *v.* Moseley (Holdings) Ltd (Security for Costs) [2001] 2 B.C.L.C. 572, Ch D
Farmers Build Ltd (In Liquidation) *v.* Carier Bulk Materials Handling Ltd [2000] E.C.D.R.
  42; [1999] I.T.C.L.R. 297; [1999] R.P.C. 461; (1999) 22(3) I.P.D. 22031; *Times*,
  December 23, 1998, CA; reversing (1997) 20(7) I.P.D. 20069, Ch D . . . .   *Digested*, 99/**3463**:
                         Applied, 01/3861: *Considered*, 00/3586: *Followed*, 00/3569
Farmitalia Carlo Erba Srl's SPC Application (C392/97), Re [1999] E.C.R. I-5553; [2000] 2
  C.M.L.R. 253; [2000] R.P.C. 580, ECJ (5th Chamber) . . . .   *Digested*, 00/**3690**
Farmizer (Products) Ltd, Re; *sub nom* Moore *v.* Gadd [1997] B.C.C. 655; [1997] 1
  B.C.L.C. 589; (1997) 94(8) L.S.G. 27; (1997) 141 S.J.L.B. 45; *Times*, February
  17, 1997; *Independent*, March 10, 1997 (C.S.), CA; affirming [1995] B.C.C. 926;
  [1995] 2 B.C.L.C. 462; *Independent*, June 19, 1995 (C.S.), Ch D . . . .   *Digested*, 97/**3056**:
                                                       Distinguished, 01/3784

Faro Technologies Inc's Trade Mark Application (2000) 23(12) I.P.D. 23104, OHIM (1st Bd App)

Farrage v. North Wiltshire DC; *sub nom* Trustees of Chippenham Golf Club v. North Wiltshire DC (1992) 64 P. & C.R. 527; (1992) 156 L.G. Rev. 863; [1991] E.G.C.S. 135; [1991] N.P.C. 139; *Times*, December 31, 1991; *Independent*, January 13, 1992 (C.S.), CA; reversing 89 L.G.R. 785; (1991) 62 P. & C.R. 643, Ch D . . . .   *Digested*, 93/**551**:
                               Followed, 97/3307, 98/3769

Farrakhan v. Secretary of State for the Home Department see R. (on the application of Farrakhan) v. Secretary of State for the Home Department

Farrant v. Woodroffe School [1998] I.C.R. 184; [1998] I.R.L.R. 176, EAT . . . .   *Digested*, 98/**2239**

Farrell v. Avon HA [2001] Lloyd's Rep. Med. 458, QBD

Farrell v. First National Bank Plc see Farrell v. Sandwell MBC

Farrell v. Long (C295/95) [1997] Q.B. 842; [1997] 3 W.L.R. 613; [1997] All E.R. (E.C.) 449; [1997] E.C.R. I-1683; [1997] I.L.Pr. 343; [1998] 1 F.L.R. 559; [1997] 3 F.C.R. 460; [1998] Fam. Law 246; *Times*, April 8, 1997, ECJ (6th Chamber) . .   *Digested*, 97/**892**

Farrell v. Merton Sutton and Wandsworth HA; *sub nom* F v. Richmond Twickenham and Roehampton HA (2001) 57 B.M.L.R. 158, QBD . . . .   *Digested*, 01/**4455**

Farrell v. Northern Ireland Electricity Service [1977] N.I. 39, Assizes . . . .   *Digested*, 79/**1971**:
                               Overruled, 99/5435

Farrell v. Sandwell MBC; Farrell v. First National Bank Plc [2001] EWCA Civ 1107; (2001) 98(27) L.S.G. 41, CA; reversing [2000] R.V.R. 211, Lands Tr . . . .   *Digested*, 00/**4617**

Farrelly v. Courtaulds Chemicals (Unreported, August 11, 1999), CC (Nottingham) [*Ex rel.* Timothy Mayer, Barrister, 5 Fountain Court, Steelhouse Lane, Birmingham] . .   *Digested*, 00/**1678**

Farrer v. Copley Singletons [1998] P.N.L.R. 22; (1998) 76 P. & C.R. 169; [1997] N.P.C. 113, CA . . . .   *Digested*, 97/**3826**:
                           Distinguished, 97/3821

Farrington v. Rank Organisation (1999) 99(1) Q.R. 7, CC (Stoke on Trent)

Farrow's Bank Ltd, Re [1921] 2 Ch. 164, CA . . . .   *Applied*, 47-51/**5337**:
                           Distinguished, 00/114

Farrugia (T230/94) v. Commission of the European Communities (T230/94) [1996] E.C.R. II-195, CFI . . . . *Distinguished*, 99/2226

Farthing v. North East Essex HA [1998] Lloyd's Rep. Med. 37, CA . . . .   *Digested*, 98/**558**

Faryab (A Bankrupt) v. Philip Ross & Co see Faryab (A Bankrupt) v. Smith (Trustee in Bankruptcy)

Faryab (A Bankrupt) v. Smith (Trustee in Bankruptcy); Faryab (A Bankrupt) v. Philip Ross & Co [2001] B.P.I.R. 246, CA . . . .   *Digested*, 01/**3720**

Faryab v. Smyth (Stay of Appeal: Champerty) FC2 97/7761/3; FC2 98/5635/3, CA . .   *Digested*, 98/**411**:
                             Followed, 00/3472

Fashade v. North Middlesex Hospital NHS Trust [2001] 4 Q.R. 13, QBD [*Ex rel.* Richard Davison, Barrister, Thomas More Chambers, 51/52 Carey Street, Lincoln's Inn, London] . . . .   *Digested*, 01/**1712**

Fashion Brokers Ltd v. Clarke Hayes [2000] Lloyd's Rep. P.N. 398; [2000] P.N.L.R. 473, CA . . . .   *Digested*, 00/**4218**

Fassoulas v. Ramey 450 So.2d 822 (Fla 1984), US Ct . . . .   *Considered*, 01/1509

Fast Ferries One SA v. Ferries Australia Pty Ltd [2000] 1 Lloyd's Rep. 534, QBD (Comm Ct) . . . .   *Digested*, 00/**4739**

Fastrack Contractors Ltd v. Morrison Construction Ltd [2000] B.L.R. 168; 75 Con. L.R. 33; (2000) 16 Const. L.J. 273, QBD (T&CC) . . . .   *Digested*, 00/**227**:
                             Considered, 01/858

Fattell, Re (195664) 1 I.T.L. Rep. 252, CE (F)

Faulkner v. Chief Adjudication Officer [1994] P.I.Q.R. P244; *Times*, April 8, 1994, CA . .   *Digested*, 94/**4136**:
                             Applied, 98/4542
                             Applied, 98/513

Faulkner v. Dunne Unreported. . . . .

Faulkner v. Inland Revenue Commissioners [2001] S.T.C. (S.C.D.) 112; [2001] W.T.L.R. 1295; [2001] S.T.I. 943, Sp Comm . . . .   *Digested*, 01/**5287**

Faulkner v. Shamji (Unreported, February 11, 2000), CC (Milton Keynes) [*Ex rel.* Pannone & Partners Solicitors, 123 Deansgate, Manchester] . . . .   *Digested*, 00/**1703**

Faulkner v. United Kingdom, *Times*, January 11, 2000, ECHR . . . .   *Digested*, 00/**3224**

Faurisson v. France 2 B.H.R.C. 1, UN HRC . . . .   *Digested*, 97/**2779**:
                             Applied, 01/3484

Fawcett (Inspector of Taxes) v. Lancaster Farmers Auction Mart Co Ltd see Fawcett (Inspector of Taxes) v. Special Commissioners of Income Tax

Fawcett (Inspector of Taxes) v. Special Commissioners of Income Tax; *sub nom* Fawcett (Inspector of Taxes) v. Lancaster Farmers Auction Mart Co Ltd [1997] S.T.C. 171; 69 T.C. 279; [1997] B.T.C. 24; *Times*, December 27, 1996; *Independent*, February 24, 1997 (C.S.), CA; reversing [1995] S.T.C. 61; (1995) 92(9) L.S.G. 41; (1995) 139 S.J.L.B. 57; *Times*, December 31, 1994; *Independent*, February 13, 1995 (C.S.), Ch D . . . .   *Digested*, 97/**4766**

Fawcett Properties Ltd v. Buckingham CC [1961] A.C. 636; [1960] 3 W.L.R. 831;
[1960] 3 All E.R. 503; (1961) 125 J.P. 8; 59 L.G.R. 69; (1961) 12 P. & C.R. 1; 104
S.J. 912, HL; affirming [1959] Ch. 543; [1959] 2 W.L.R. 884; [1959] 2 All E.R.
321; (1959) 123 J.P. 322; 57 L.G.R. 285; (1959) 10 P. & C.R. 240; 103 S.J.
470, CA; reversing [1958] 1 W.L.R. 1161; [1958] 3 All E.R. 521; (1959) 123 J.P.
54; 56 L.G.R. 421; (1959) 10 P. & C.R. 16; 102 S.J. 859, Ch D . . . . *Digested*, 60/**3110**:
Applied, 63/3426, 64/3600, 70/2777, 72/3358, 77/2972, 80/963, 84/3489,
85/3475, 92/4341, 92/4371: *Considered*, 78/2888, 91/3520, 96/5688,
00/5507

Fay v. DPP [1988] C.O.D. 339, QBD
Fazenda Publica v. Camara Municipal do Porto (C446/98) [2001] S.T.C. 560; [2000]
E.C.R. I-11435; [2001] B.T.C. 5414; [2001] B.V.C. 493; [2000] S.T.I. 1736, ECJ
(5th Chamber) . . . . *Digested*, 01/**5561**

Fazenda Publica v. Fricarnes SA (C28/96) [1997] S.T.C. 1348; [1997] E.C.R. I-4939;
[1997] C.E.C. 1251, ECJ (5th Chamber) . . . . *Digested*, 98/**4969**

Fazenda Publica v. Solisnor-Estaleiros Navais SA (C130/96) [1998] S.T.C. 191; [1997]
E.C.R. I-5053; [1998] C.E.C. 599; [1998] B.T.C. 5371; [1998] B.V.C. 350, ECJ
(1st Chamber) . . . . *Digested*, 98/**4944**:
Applied, 01/5276

Fazenda Publica v. Uniao das Cooperativas Abastecedoras de Leite de Lisboa (UCAL)
(C347/95) [1997] S.T.C. 1333; [1997] E.C.R. I-4911, ECJ (5th Chamber) . . . . . *Digested*, 98/**4970**

FDR Ltd v. Customs and Excise Commissioners see Customs and Excise
Commissioners v. FDR Ltd

FE v. France (2000) 29 E.H.R.R. 591; [1998] H.R.C.D. 995, ECHR . . . . *Digested*, 00/**3212**

Feary v. Buckingham (Unreported, May 13, 1999), CC (Basingstoke) [*Ex rel*. Benjamin
Williams, Barrister, Oxford Chambers, 1 Alfred Street, Oxford] . . . . *Digested*, 99/**2452**:
Approved, 99/2466: *Referred to*, 99/2490

Featherstone v. Ideal Standard Ltd see Afzal v. Ford Motor Co Ltd

Fecht v. Deloitte & Touche [2000] I.L.Pr. 398, CJ (Gen Div) (Ont) . . . . *Digested*, 00/**330**

Federal Airports Corp v. Makucha Developments Pty Ltd (1993) 115 A.L.R. 697, Fed
Ct (Aus) (Sgl judge) . . . . *Approved*, 01/**5945**

Federal Bank of the Middle East v. Hadkinson (Security for Costs) (No.1) [2000] C.P.
Rep. 31, CA. . . . . *Digested*, 00/**436**

Federal Bank of the Middle East v. Hadkinson (Security for Costs) (No.2); Hadkinson v.
Saab (No.2) [2000] 1 Costs L.R. 94; (1999) 96(45) L.S.G. 31; *Times*,
December 7, 1999, CA. . . . . *Digested*, 00/**388**

Federal Bank of the Middle East v. Hadkinson (Stay of Action); Hadkinson v. Saab
(No.1) [2000] 1 W.L.R. 1695; [2000] 2 All E.R. 395; [2000] C.P.L.R. 295;
[2000] B.P.I.R. 597; (2000) 97(12) L.S.G. 42; (2000) 150 N.L.J. 393; (2000)
144 S.J.L.B. 128; *Times*, March 16, 2000; *Independent*, March 14, 2000, CA;
reversing [2000] B.P.I.R. 44; (1999) 96(24) L.S.G. 38; *Times*, May 28, 1999,
Ch D . . . . *Digested*, 00/**16**

Federal Bank of the Middle East Ltd v. Hadkinson (Lifting of Stay) HC 1999 03177, Ch D
. . . . *Digested*, 00/**592**

Federal Commerce & Navigation Co Ltd v. Molena Alpha Inc (The Nanfri); Federal
Commerce & Navigation Co Ltd v. Molena Beta Inc (The Benfri); Federal
Commerce & Navigation Co Ltd v. Molena Gamma Inc (The Lorfri) [1979] A.C.
757; [1978] 3 W.L.R. 991; [1979] 1 All E.R. 307; [1979] 1 Lloyd's Rep. 201; 122
S.J. 843, HL; affirming in part [1978] Q.B. 927; [1978] 3 W.L.R. 309; [1978] 3
All E.R. 1066; 1978] 2 Lloyd's Rep. 132; 122 S.J. 347, CA; reversing [1978] 1
Lloyd's Rep. 581, QBD (Comm Ct). . . . . *Digested*, 79/**2452**:
Applied, 79/342, 80/1627, 80/2457, 81/2484, 94/4062, 01/941:
Considered, 79/100, 79/156, 80/2460, 85/259, 85/2604, 85/3203, 93/2495,
94/2797, 97/3366: *Distinguished*, 80/2792, 82/2925, 83/3413:
Referred to, 80/99

Federal Commerce & Navigation Co Ltd v. Molena Beta Inc (The Benfri) see Federal
Commerce & Navigation Co Ltd v. Molena Alpha Inc (The Nanfri)

Federal Commerce & Navigation Co Ltd v. Molena Gamma Inc (The Lorfri) see Federal
Commerce & Navigation Co Ltd v. Molena Alpha Inc (The Nanfri)

Federal Commissioner of Taxation v. Century Yuasa Batteries Pty Ltd 1 I.T.L. Rep. 274,
Fed Ct (Aus) (Full Ct)

Federal Insurance Co v. Transamerica Occidental Life Insurance Co; Transamerica
Occidental Life Insurance Co v. Federal Insurance Co [1999] 2 All E.R. (Comm)
138; [1999] 2 Lloyd's Rep. 286; [1999] C.L.C. 1406; (1999) 149 N.L.J. 1037,
QBD (Comm Ct) . . . . *Digested*, 99/**222**

Federal Mogul Corp v. Secretary of State for the Environment, Transport and the
Regions CO/4486/1999, QBD (Admin Ct). . . . . *Previous proceedings*,
01/4757

Federal Mogul Corp v. Secretary of State for the Environment, Transport and the
Regions [2000] J.P.L. 1181 (Note), QBD . . . . *Digested*, 01/**4757**

Federal Steam Navigation Co Ltd *v.* Department of Trade and Industry (The Huntingdon); *sub nom* R. *v.* Federal Steam Navigation Co Ltd; R. *v.* Moran (Derek Ernest) [1974] 1 W.L.R. 505; [1974] 2 All E.R. 97; [1974] 1 Lloyd's Rep. 520; (1974) 59 Cr. App. R. 131; 118 S.J. 478, HL; affirming [1973] 1 W.L.R. 1373; [1973] 3 All E.R. 849; [1974] 1 Lloyd's Rep. 8; (1974) 58 Cr. App. R. 68; [1973] Crim. L.R. 575; 117 S.J. 712, CA (Crim Div) . . . . *Digested*, 74/**3626**:
Considered, 99/5209: *Distinguished*, 91/5046: *Followed*, 83/4180
Federal Trade Commission *v.* Affordable Media (1999-2000) 2 I.T.E.L.R. 73, US Ct
Federal Trust Co Ltd *v.* Macdonald-Smith (2001-02) 4 I.T.E.L.R. 211, Royal Ct (Gue)
Federatie van Nederlandse Kraanverhuurbedrijven (FNK) *v.* Commission of the European Communities (T18/96) see Stichting Certificatie Kraanverhuurbedrijf (SCK) *v.* Commission of the European Communities (T213/95)
Federation Belge des Chambres Syndicales de Medecins ASBL *v.* Belgium (C93/97) [1998] E.C.R. I-4837; (2001) 57 B.M.L.R. 126, ECJ (5th Chamber) . . . . *Digested*, 01/**2493**
Federation of Dutch Industries *v.* Inspector of Customs and Excise (C51/76) see Verbond Van Nederlandse Ondernemingen *v.* Inspecteur der Invoerrechten en Accijnzen (C51/76)
Federation of Icelandic Trade *v.* Iceland (E2/98) [1999] 1 C.M.L.R. 907, EFTA . . . . *Digested*, 99/**2700**
Federazione Nazionale del Commercio Oleano (FEDEROLIO) *v.* Commission of the European Communities (T122/96) [1997] All E.R. (E.C.) 929; [1997] E.C.R. II-1559; [1998] 1 C.M.L.R. 71, CFI (5th Chamber) . . . . *Digested*, 98/**2334**:
Followed, 00/2408
Fee *v.* Ashtead Group Plc (Unreported, June 28, 2001), CC (Whitehaven) [*Ex rel.* Ford & Warren Solicitors, Westgate Point, Westgate, Leeds] . . . . *Digested*, 01/**887**
Fees Charged by the Nice Bar, Re [2001] E.C.C. 29, C Concurrence (F)
Fehmi *v.* DPP see Harris *v.* DPP
Feldbrugge *v.* Netherlands (A/99) (1986) 8 E.H.R.R. 425, ECHR . . . . *Applied*, 98/**3139**:
Distinguished, 98/3127
Felgate (Valuation Officer) *v.* Lotus Leisure Enterprises Ltd [2000] R.A. 89, Lands Tr. . . *Digested*, 00/**4591**
Felix *v.* DPP [1998] Crim. L.R. 657; [1998] E.H.L.R. Dig. 278; *Times*, May 5, 1998, QBD . . . . *Digested*, 98/**2275**
FELIX THE CAT Productions Inc *v.* Polygram [1999] E.T.M.R. 370, Trib Gde Inst (Paris)
Fell *v.* Gould Grimwade Shirbon Partnership 36 Con. L.R. 62, QBD . . . . *Considered*, 99/372:
Followed, 97/552
Fellowes *v.* Clyde Helicopters Ltd; *sub nom* Herd *v.* Clyde Helicopters Ltd [1997] A.C. 534; [1997] 2 W.L.R. 380; [1997] 1 All E.R. 775; 1997 S.C. (H.L.) 86; 1997 S.L.T. 672; 1997 S.C.L.R. 308; (1997) 94(12) L.S.G. 22; (1997) 141 S.J.L.B. 64; 1997 G.W.D. 9-360; *Times*, March 7, 1997, HL; affirming 1996 S.L.T. 976, 2 Div . . . . . . *Digested*, 97/**5595**:
Applied, 01/5386
Fellowes *v.* DPP see DPP *v.* Fellowes
Fellows (t/a Spar) *v.* Moore (Valuation Officer) [1997] R.A. 427, Lands Tr . . . . *Digested*, 98/**4331**
Felstead *v.* King, The [1914] A.C. 534, HL . . . . *Considered*, 99/942
Feltrim Underwriting Agencies Ltd *v.* Arbuthnott see Henderson *v.* Merrett Syndicates Ltd (No.1)
Fenech *v.* East London and City HA [2000] Lloyd's Rep. Med. 35; [2000] P.N.L.R. 205, CA . . . . *Digested*, 00/**516**
Fenland DC *v.* Reuben Rose (Properties) Ltd see Fenland DC *v.* Rueben Rose (Properties) Ltd
Fenland DC *v.* Rueben Rose (Properties) Ltd; *sub nom* Fenland DC *v.* Reuben Rose (Properties) Ltd [2000] P.L.C.R. 376; [2000] E.G.C.S. 46; (2000) 97(14) L.S.G. 44; [2000] N.P.C. 34, CA . . . . *Digested*, 01/**4715**
Fenn *v.* Stewart (Unreported, October 9, 1996), CC (Basingstoke) [*Ex rel.* Marcus Grant, Barrister] . . . . *Digested*, 96/**2140**:
Considered, 98/337, 99/326
Fennelly *v.* Connex South Eastern Ltd [2001] I.R.L.R. 390; *Independent*, January 22, 2001 (C.S), CA
Fenney *v.* Horsfall (Unreported, November 21, 1997), CC (Bury) [*Ex rel.* David Johnson, Berrymans Lace Mawer, Solicitors, 42 King Street West, Manchester]. . *Digested*, 98/**446**
Fennon *v.* Anthony Hodari & Co [2001] Lloyd's Rep. P.N. 183, CA . . . . *Digested*, 01/**605**
Fennoscandia Ltd *v.* Clarke [1999] 1 All E.R. (Comm.) 365; [1999] Lloyd's Rep. Bank. 108, CA . . . . *Digested*, 99/**3952**
Fenton *v.* J Thorley & Co Ltd [1903] A.C. 443, HL . . . . *Applied*, 63/1818,
63/2564, 71/10224, 72/3015, 00/4845: *Considered*, 75/3205, 79/1498
Fenton *v.* Secretary of State for the Environment, Transport and the Regions [2000] J.P.L. 1179 (Note), QBD . . . . *Digested*, 01/**4739**
Fentum *v.* William Baird Plc (Unreported, June 8, 1999), CC (Exeter) [*Ex rel.* Thomas Bradnock, Barrister, Colleton Chambers, Exeter, Devon] . . . . *Digested*, 99/**1616**
Ferguson *v.* Inland Revenue Commissioners (Bonus Payments) [2001] S.T.C. (S.C.D.) 1; [2000] S.T.I. 1679, Sp Comm . . . . *Digested*, 01/**5262**
Ferguson *v.* Welsh [1987] 1 W.L.R. 1553; [1987] 3 All E.R. 777; [1988] I.R.L.R. 112; 86 L.G.R. 153; (1987) 137 N.L.J. 1037; (1987) 131 S.J. 1552, HL . . . . *Digested*, 87/**2612**:
Distinguished, 00/4206
Fernandez *v.* Singapore see R. *v.* Governor of Pentonville Prison Ex p. Fernandez

Fernando v. Sri Lanka Broadcasting Corp 1 B.H.R.C. 104, Sup Ct (SrL) . . . . *Digested*, 97/**2776**:
Applied, 01/838
Fernback v. Harrow LBC see R. (on the application of Fernback) v. Harrow LBC
Ferngold Plant Hire Ltd v. BW Contractors see Ferngold Plant Hire Ltd v. Wenham (t/a
BW Contractors)
Ferngold Plant Hire Ltd v. Crowe Underwriting Services (Unreported, January 23,
1998), CC (Central London) [*Ex rel.* David Platt, Barrister, 1 Paper Buildings,
Temple, London] . . . . *Digested*, 99/**3399**:
Applied, 99/1396
Ferngold Plant Hire Ltd v. Wenham (t/a BW Contractors); *sub nom* Ferngold Plant Hire
Ltd v. BW Contractors; CCRTF 1999/0293/B2, CA; affirming(Unreported,
December 17, 1998), CC (Canterbury) [*Ex rel.* David Platt, Barrister, 1 Paper
Buildings, Temple, London] . . . . *Digested*, 00/**1474**
Fernhill Mining Ltd v. Kier Construction Ltd [2000] C.P. Rep. 69; [2000] C.P.L.R. 23,
CA . . . . *Digested*, 00/**438**
Fernlee Estates Ltd v. Swansea City and County Council [2001] EWHC Admin 360;
[2001] 24 E.G.C.S. 161; (2001) 98(22) L.S.G. 37, QBD
Fernley v. NEI Control Systems Ltd (Unreported, March 19, 1998), CC (Manchester)
[*Ex rel.* T.H. Stead, Barrister, 6 Park Square, Leeds, LS1 2LX] . . . . *Digested*, 98/**1749**
Ferranti International Plc, Re see Powdrill v. Watson
Ferrarini SpA v. Magnol Shipping Co Ltd (The Sky One) [1988] 1 Lloyd's Rep. 238,
CA . . . . *Digested*, 88/**2967**:
Followed, 98/586
Ferrazzini v. Italy (44759/98) [2001] S.T.C. 1314; 3 I.T.L. Rep. 918; [2001] S.T.I. 1224,
ECHR . . . . *Digested*, 01/**5298**
Ferretti's Application for Revocation (No.9206), Re see Gracey's Registration
(No.1335163), Re
Ferrishurst Ltd v. Wallcite Ltd see Wallcite Ltd v. Ferrishurst Ltd
Ferrous Protection Ltd v. Health & Safety Executive [2000] C.O.D. 273, QBD
Fertin A/S's Community Trade Mark Application [2000] E.T.M.R. 652, OHIM (1st Bd App)
Digested, 00/**3731**
Fesentzou v. Lidiolo (Unreported, July 14, 1999), CC (Ilford) [*Ex rel.* James Browne,
Barrister, 96 Gray's Inn Road, London] . . . . *Digested*, 99/**2463**
Fessi v. Whitmore [1999] 1 F.L.R. 767; [1999] Fam. Law 221, Ch D . . . . *Digested*, 99/**4633**
Fetim BV v. Oceanspeed Shipping Ltd (The Flecha) [1999] 1 Lloyd's Rep. 612, QBD
(Adm Ct) . . . . *Digested*, 98/**4394**:
Considered, 01/4907: *Followed*, 98/582
Fey v. Austria (A/255-A) (1993) 16 E.H.R.R. 387, ECHR . . . . *Digested*, 94/**2400**:
Considered, 98/3090
Feyrer v. Landkreis Rottal-Inn (C374/97) [1999] E.C.R. I-5153; [2001] 1 C.M.L.R. 44,
ECJ (2nd Chamber) . . . . *Digested*, 01/**2484**
FFAD (for Sydenhavnens Sten & Grus ApS) v. Kobenhavns Kommune (C209/98) see
Entreprenorforeningens Affalds/Miljosektion (FFAD) v. Kobenhavns Kommune
(C209/98)
Fforestfach Medical Centre v. Customs and Excise Commissioners [2000] S.T.I. 1072,
V&DTr
FH Bertling Ltd v. Tube Developments Ltd [1999] 2 Lloyd's Rep. 55; 1998 G.W.D. 39-
1998, OH . . . . *Digested*, 99/**5630**
FHG Publications Ltd v. Tee-Hillman (Unreported, November 21, 2000), CC
(Southampton) [*Ex rel.* Brian D Cummins, Barrister, Bridewell Chambers, 2
Bridewell Place, London] . . . . *Digested*, 01/**662**
Fiat Auto (France) SA v. Sofisud SA [2001] E.C.C. 17, C d'A (Paris)
Fidan v. Turkey (24209/94) (2000) 29 E.H.R.R. CD162, ECHR
Field v. Leeds City Council [2001] C.P.L.R. 129; [1999] C.P.L.R. 833; (2000) 32
H.L.R. 618; [2000] 1 E.G.L.R. 54; [2000] 17 E.G. 165; *Times*, January 18, 2000;
Independent, December 16, 1999, CA. . . . . *Digested*, 00/**327**
Field v. United Amusement Corp [1971] C.S. 283, Sup Ct (Que) . . . . *Considered*, 99/3121
Field Place Caravan Park Ltd v. Harding (Valuation Officer); *sub nom* Harding (Valuation
Officer) v. Field Place Caravan Park Ltd [1966] 2 Q.B. 484; [1966] 3 W.L.R.
198; [1966] 3 All E.R. 247; (1966) 130 J.P. 397; 64 L.G.R. 399; 198 E.G. 785;
[1966] R.A. 393; [1966] R.V.R. 446; 13 R.R.C. 74; 110 S.J. 386, CA; affirming
196 E.G. 469; [1965] R.A. 521; 11 R.R.C. 273; [1966] J.P.L. 45, LandsTr . . . . . . *Digested*, 66/**10227**:
Applied, 01/4806: *Considered*, 92/3680, 97/3498
Fielder v. Trupia (Unreported, December 5, 2000), CC (Watford) [*Ex rel.* Benjamin
Williams, Barrister, 1 Temple Gardens, Temple, London] . . . . *Digested*, 01/**898**
Fielding & Platt Ltd v. Selim Najjar [1969] 1 W.L.R. 357; [1969] 2 All E.R. 150; 113 S.J.
160, CA . . . . *Digested*, 69/**173**:
Applied, 99/2059
Fieldman v. Markovic see Fieldman v. Markovitch
Fieldman v. Markovitch; *sub nom* Fieldman v. Markovic [2001] C.P. Rep. 119; *Times*,
July 31, 2001, Ch D . . . . *Digested*, 01/**423**
Fifield v. W&R Jack Ltd [2001] L. & T.R. 4, PC (NZ) . . . . *Digested*, 01/**350**

Figgett v. Davies; *sub nom* Figgett v. Davis [1998] 1 W.L.R. 1184; [1998] 2 All E.R. 356; [1998] P.I.Q.R. P149; (1998) 95(8) L.S.G. 33; (1998) 142 S.J.L.B. 69; *Times*, February 11, 1998, CA . . . .   *Digested*, 98/**396**: *Distinguished*, 99/551

Figgett v. Davis see Figgett v. Davies

Figot v. Leithauser GmbH & Co [2001] I.L.Pr. 2, Cass (F)

Figre Ltd v. Mander [1999] Lloyd's Rep. I.R. 193, QBD (Comm Ct) . . . .   *Digested*, 99/**3424**

Film Alterations for Television Screening, Re [2000] E.C.C. 266, OGH (A)

Filmlab Systems International Ltd v. Pennington [1995] 1 W.L.R. 673; [1994] 4 All E.R. 673; (1993) 143 N.L.J. 1405; *Times*, July 9, 1993, Ch D . . . .   *Digested*, 95/**4033**: *Considered*, 94/3623: *Distinguished*, 01/539

Filross Securities Ltd v. Midgeley (1999) 31 H.L.R. 465; [1998] 3 E.G.L.R. 43; [1998] 43 E.G. 134; [1998] E.G.C.S. 124; (1998) 95(30) L.S.G. 26, CA . . . .   *Digested*, 98/**2299**

Finagra (UK) Ltd v. OT Africa Line Ltd [1998] 2 Lloyd's Rep. 622; [1998] C.L.C. 1419, QBD (Comm Ct) . . . .   *Digested*, 99/**4411**

Finance for Mortgages Ltd v. Farley & Co [1998] P.N.L.R. 145; [1996] E.G.C.S. 35; [1996] N.P.C. 19, QBD . . . .   *Digested*, 96/**837**

Financial Services Authority v. Goodwill Merchant Financial Ltd see Goodwill Merchant Financial Services Ltd, Re

Financial Services Authority (FSA) v. Rourke (t/a JE Rourke & Co) (2001) 98(46) L.S.G. 36; *Times*, November 12, 2001, Ch D . . . .   *Digested*, 01/**543**

Financial Systems Software (UK) Ltd v. Financial Software Systems Inc; *sub nom* Financial Systems Software (UK) Ltd's Trade Mark Application [2001] EWCA Civ 386; [2001] R.P.C. 41, CA . . . .   *Digested*, 01/**4031**

Financial Systems Software (UK) Ltd's Trade Mark Application see Financial Systems Software (UK) Ltd v. Financial Software Systems Inc

Financings v. Stimson [1962] 1 W.L.R. 1184; [1962] 3 All E.R. 386, CA. . . . .   *Digested*, 62/**1407**: *Approved*, 66/3146: *Considered*, 01/880

Finanzamt Burgdorf v. Fischer (C322/99) see Fischer v. Finanzamt Burgdorf (C322/99)

Finanzamt Dusseldorf-Mettmann v. Brandenstein (C323/99) see Fischer v. Finanzamt Burgdorf (C322/99)

Finanzamt Goslar v. Breitsohl (C400/98) [2001] S.T.C. 355; [2000] E.C.R. I-4321; [2001] 1 C.M.L.R. 37; [2000] S.T.I. 1513, ECJ (6th Chamber) . . . .   *Digested*, 01/**5577**

Finanzamt Koln-Altstadt v. Schumacker (C279/93) [1996] Q.B. 28; [1995] 3 W.L.R. 498; [1995] All E.R. (E.C.) 319; [1995] S.T.C. 306; [1995] E.C.R. I-225; [1996] 2 C.M.L.R. 450; *Times*, February 24, 1995, ECJ . . . .   *Digested*, 95/**2773**: *Considered*, 96/3341: *Followed*, 95/2786, 01/5245

Finanzamt Osnabruck-Land v. Langhorst (C141/96) [1998] 1 W.L.R. 52; [1998] All E.R. (E.C.) 178; [1997] S.T.C. 1357; [1997] E.C.R. I-5073; [1998] 1 C.M.L.R. 673; [1997] C.E.C. 1236; [1997] B.T.C. 5463; [1998] B.V.C. 6; *Times*, November 20, 1997, ECJ . . . .   *Digested*, 97/**4981**

Finbow v. Air Ministry [1963] 1 W.L.R. 697; [1963] 2 All E.R. 647; 107 S.J. 535, QBD .   *Digested*, 63/**38**: *Applied*, 68/3341, 68/3342: *Considered*, 83/61: *Followed*, 98/939

Fincar SRL v. 109/113 Mount Street Management Co Ltd; *sub nom* Fincar SRL v. Mount Street Management Co Ltd [1999] L. & T.R. 161; [1998] E.G.C.S. 173; [1998] N.P.C. 155, CA

Fincar SRL v. Mount Street Management Co Ltd see Fincar SRL v. 109/113 Mount Street Management Co Ltd

Finchimica SpA's European Patent Application (No.0402887) (2000) 23(9) I.P.D. 23070, EPO (Technical Bd App)

Findlay, Re; *sub nom* Findlay v. Secretary of State for the Home Department [1985] A.C. 318; [1984] 3 W.L.R. 1159; [1984] 3 All E.R. 801; [1985] Crim. L.R. 154; (1985) 82 L.S.G. 38; (1984) 128 S.J. 816, HL; affirming *Times*, July 7, 1984, CA; affirming *Times*, May 23, 1984, DC . . . .   *Digested*, 84/**2756**: *Applied*, 94/4983, 99/5221, 00/4490: *Cited*, 94/2469: *Considered*, 87/20, 87/3617, 93/2556, 94/43, 95/3098, 95/3099, 95/3252, 99/2684: *Followed*, 97/3934

Findlay v. Secretary of State for the Home Department see Findlay, Re

Findlay v. United Kingdom (1997) 24 E.H.R.R. 221; *Times*, February 27, 1997; *Independent*, March 4, 1997, ECHR . . . .   *Digested*, 97/**2807**: *Applied*, 97/2808: *Considered*, 97/288, 00/3227, 01/366: *Distinguished*, 01/358: *Explained*, 98/256: *Followed*, 99/3090, 99/3091, 00/3215

Fine v. Secretary of State for Trade and Industry see Verby Print for Advertising Ltd, Re

Fine Cotton Spinners and Doublers Association Ltd v. Harwood Case & Co Ltd [1907] 2 Ch. 184, Ch D . . . .   *Considered*, 00/5608

Finegan v. Heywood 2000 J.C. 444; 2000 S.L.T. 905; 2000 S.C.C.R. 460; 2000 G.W.D. 15-633; *Times*, May 10, 2000, HCJ Appeal . . . .   *Digested*, 00/**6026**

Finley v. Connell Associates (Application to Strike Out) [1999] Lloyd's Rep. P.N. 895; (1999) 96(26) L.S.G. 27; *Times*, June 23, 1999, QBD . . . .   *Digested*, 99/**4400**

Finn v. Kerslake see Sedgwick v. Watney Combe Reid & Co Ltd

Finnegan *v.* Parkside HA [1998] 1 W.L.R. 411; [1998] 1 All E.R. 595; [1998] Lloyd's
    Rep. Med. 149; (1997) 94(47) L.S.G. 30; (1997) 147 N.L.J. 1724; (1997) 141
    S.J.L.B. 249; *Times*, December 16, 1997, CA . . . .   *Digested*, 98/**384**
Finnegan *v.* Wiltshire (Unreported, April 5, 2000), CC (Mansfield) [*Ex rel.* Richard
    Gregory, Barrister, 24 The Ropewalk, Nottingham] . . . .   *Digested*, 00/**1543**
Fiona Roberta Hankin Trade Mark Application (No.2123875) (1999) 22(11) I.P.D. 22109,
    TMR
Fir Mill *v.* Royton Urban DC (1960) 175 E.G. 1029; 7 R.R.C. 171; 53 R. & I.T. 389;
    [1960] J.P.L. 500; 110 L.J. 401, Lands Tr. . . . . *Digested*, 60/**2669.75**:
    Applied, 77/2452.1, 01/4833: *Considered*, 85/2932, 00/4590
Fire Brigades Union *v.* Fraser [1998] I.R.L.R. 697; 1998 G.W.D. 21-1086, Ex Div;
    reversing [1997] I.R.L.R. 671, EAT . . . .   *Digested*, 99/**6042**
Firle Investments Ltd *v.* Datapoint International Ltd [2001] EWCA Civ 1106; [2001] C.P.
    Rep. 101; [2001] N.P.C. 106, CA; reversing HT-99-119, QBD (T&CC) . . . .   *Digested*, 01/**502**
Firm of Solicitors (Wasted Costs Order) (No.2 of 1999), Re see Harry Jagdev & Co (Wasted
    Costs Order) (No.2 of 1999), Re
Firma Albert Ruckdeschel & Co *v.* Hauptzollamt Hamburg-St Annen (C117/76); Diamalt
    AG *v.* Hauptzollamt Itzehoe (C16/77); Moulins et Huileries de Pont-a-Mousson
    SA *v.* Office National Interprofessionnel des Cereales (C124/76); Societe
    Cooperative Providence Agricole de la Champagne *v.* Office National
    Interprofessionnel des Cereales (C20/77) [1977] E.C.R. 1795; [1977] E.C.R.
    1753; [1979] 2 C.M.L.R. 445, ECJ . . . .   *Digested*, 78/**1226**:
    Followed, 00/2640
Firma C-Trade SA *v.* Newcastle Protection and Indemnity Association (The Fanti);
    Socony Mobil Oil Co Inc *v.* West of England Shipowners Mutual Insurance
    Association (London) Ltd (The Padre Island) (No.2) [1991] 2 A.C. 1; [1990] 3
    W.L.R. 78; [1990] 2 All E.R. 705; [1990] 2 Lloyd's Rep. 191; [1990] B.C.L.C.
    625; (1990) 134 S.J. 833, HL; reversing [1989] 1 Lloyd's Rep. 239; *Times*,
    December 27, 1988, CA; reversing in part [1987] 2 Lloyd's Rep. 299, QBD
    (Comm Ct) . . . .   *Digested*, 90/**4098**:
    Applied, 92/3972, 93/3619, 97/4597, 00/3514: *Considered*, 95/2926,
    96/1136: *Distinguished*, 98/3354: *Followed*, 97/3139, 99/3227, 00/4693:
    Previous proceedings, 88/3239
Firma Industrie Tessili Italiana Como *v.* Firma Dunlop AG (C12/76) see Industrie Tessili
    Italiana Como *v.* Dunlop AG (C12/76)
Firma Rheinmuhlen-Dusseldorf *v.* Einfuhrund Vorratsstelle fur Getreide und Futtermittel
    (C166/73); *sub nom* Rheinmuhlen-Dusseldorf *v.* EVST (C166/73) [1974] E.C.R.
    33; [1974] 1 C.M.L.R. 523, ECJ . . . .   *Digested*, 74/**1497**:
    Applied, 82/560, 99/76
Firma Sloman Neptun Schiffahrts AG *v.* Seebetriebsrat Bodo Ziesemer (C72/91 and
    C73/91) [1993] E.C.R. I-887; [1995] 2 C.M.L.R. 97; *Times*, March 26, 1993;
    Financial Times, March 23, 1993, ECJ . . . .   *Digested*, 93/**4389**:
    Applied, 98/2130
Firma Sohl & Sohlke *v.* Hauptzollamt Bremen (C48/98) [1999] E.C.R. I-7877; [2000] 1
    C.M.L.R. 351, ECJ (6th Chamber) . . . .   *Digested*, 00/**2349**
Firma Steinike und Weinlig *v.* Bundesamt fur Ernahrung und Forstwirtschaft (C78/76)
    see Iannelli & Volpi SpA *v.* Ditta Paolo Meroni (C74/76)
First American Corp *v.* Al-Nahyan see First American Corp *v.* Sheikh Zayed Al-Nahyan
First American Corp *v.* Price Waterhouse LLP [1999] I.L.Pr. 745, US Ct. . . . .   *Digested*, 00/**317**
First American Corp *v.* Sheikh Zayed Al-Nahyan; *sub nom* First American Corp *v.* Al-
    Nahyan; Clifford *v.* First American Corp [1999] 1 W.L.R. 1154; [1998] 4 All E.R.
    439; [1998] Lloyd's Rep. Bank. 213; [1998] C.L.C. 1225; [1999] I.L.Pr. 179;
    Times, August 17, 1998, CA . . . .   *Digested*, 98/**350**:
    Applied, 01/406
First City Corp Ltd *v.* Downsview Nominees Ltd (No.1) see Downsview Nominees Ltd
    v. First City Corp Ltd (No.1)
First City Insurance Group Ltd *v.* Frizzell Group Ltd [1997] N.P.C. 163, CA; reversing
    [1996] N.P.C. 173, Ch D . . . .   *Digested*, 98/**3684**
First Corporate Shipping Ltd (t/a Bristol Port Co) *v.* North Somerset Council [2001]
    EWCA Civ 693; [2001] J.P.L. 1444 (Note); *Times*, June 15, 2001, CA; affirming
    [2001] EWHC Admin 19; [2001] J.P.L. 1209 (Note), QBD (Admin Ct) . . . .   *Digested*, 01/**4720**
First Fashions Pensions Scheme *v.* List (Valuation Officer) [1999] R.A. 93, Lands Tr . . .   *Digested*, 99/**4342**
First Interstate Bank of California *v.* Cohen Arnold & Co [1996] 5 Bank. L.R. 150;
    [1996] C.L.C. 174; [1996] P.N.L.R. 17; [1995] E.G.C.S. 188; (1996) 140 S.J.L.B.
    12; *Times*, December 11, 1995, CA. . . . .   *Digested*, 96/**4482**:
    Considered, 98/3604
First Island Financial Services Ltd *v.* Novastar Developments (Kelowna Orchard
    Gardens) Ltd (1998-99) 1 I.T.E.L.R. 877, Sup Ct (BC)
First Mortgage Securities (No.1) Plc *v.* Malhotra (1998) 76 P. & C.R. D22, CA (Crim
    Div)

First National Bank of Chicago v. Customs and Excise Commissioners (C172/96); *sub nom* Customs and Excise Commissioners v. First National Bank of Chicago (C172/96) [1999] Q.B. 570; [1999] 2 W.L.R. 230; [1998] All E.R. (E.C.) 744; [1998] S.T.C. 850; [1998] E.C.R. I-4387; [1998] 3 C.M.L.R. 353; [1998] C.E.C. 896; [1998] B.T.C. 5332; [1998] B.V.C. 389; *Times*, July 20, 1998, ECJ (5th Chamber) .... *Digested*, 98/**4948**
First National Bank Plc v. Ann & Ann [1998] C.C.L.R. 1, CC (Colchester) .... *Digested*, 97/**963**:
                 Considered, 97/961, 99/4387: *Followed*, 97/962, 98/2495, 99/2507
First National Bank Plc v. Peacock see Jarrett v. Barclays Bank Plc
First National Bank Plc v. Walker [2001] 1 F.L.R. 505; [2001] 1 F.C.R. 21; [2001] Fam. Law 182; *Times*, February 13, 2001, CA..................................... *Digested*, 01/**2653**
First Point International Ltd v. Department of Trade and Industry (2000) 164 J.P. 89; (1999) 163 J.P.N. 971; *Times*, August 24, 1999, QBD..................... *Digested*, 99/**2036**
First Realty Plc v. Norton Rose [1999] 2 B.C.L.C. 428; [1999] N.P.C. 53, CA .... *Digested*, 99/**852**
First Roodhill Leasing Ltd v. Gillingham Operating Co; *sub nom* Roodhill v. Medway General [2001] N.P.C. 109, Ch D
First Security Bank National Association v. Compagnie Nationale Air Gabon (No.1) [1999] I.L.Pr. 617, QBD (Comm Ct) .... *Digested*, 00/**737**
First Security Bank National Association v. Compagnie Nationale Air Gabon (No.2) [1999] 2 Lloyd's Rep. 450, QBD (Comm Ct) .... *Digested*, 00/**5146**
First Tokyo Index Trust Ltd v. Morgan Stanley Trust Co, *Times*, October 6, 1995, CA; affirming [1996] B.P.I.R. 406; *Times*, December 1, 1993, OH .... *Digested*, 96/**916**:
                                   Followed, 97/495, 99/357
Firth v. Geo Ackroyd Junior Ltd [2001] P.I.Q.R. Q4; [2000] Lloyd's Rep. Med. 312, QBD... *Digested*, 01/**1529**
Firth v. Mallender [2001] W.T.L.R. 1109, CA
Fisanotti v. Italy [1998] H.R.C.D. 463, ECHR
Fischer v. Austria (A/312) (1995) 20 E.H.R.R. 349, ECHR .... *Digested*, 96/**3152**:
                         Applied, 96/3119, 96/3120, 98/3120
Fischer v. Finanzamt Burgdorf (C322/99); *sub nom* Finanzamt Burgdorf v. Fischer (C322/99); Finanzamt Dusseldorf-Mettmann v. Brandenstein (C323/99); Brandenstein v. Finanzamt Dusseldorf-Mettmann (C323/99) [2001] S.T.C. 1356; [2001] E.C.R. I-4049; [2001] S.T.I. 1103, ECJ (5th Chamber)
Fischer v. Finanzamt Donaueschingen (C283/95) [1998] All E.R. (E.C.) 567; [1998] S.T.C. 708; [1998] E.C.R. I-3369; [1998] 3 C.M.L.R. 1055; [1998] C.E.C. 879; [1998] B.T.C. 5423; [1998] B.V.C. 431; *Times*, July 2, 1998, ECJ (6th Chamber) . *Digested*, 98/**4911**:
                 Considered, 98/4891: *Joined proceedings*, 98/4966
Fisher v. Adesanwo (Unreported, April 30, 1999), CC (Clerkenwell) [*Ex rel.* Marcus Baldwin, Barrister, 8 Stone Buildings, Lincoln's Inn, London] .... *Digested*, 99/**2467**
Fisher v. Cragg [2001] 5 Q.R. 13, CC (Cambridge) [*Ex rel.* Andrew Granville Stafford, Barrister, 4 King's Bench Walk, Temple, London] .... *Digested*, 01/**1633**
Fisher v. Dukes Transport (Craigavon) Ltd see Birkett v. Vehicle Inspectorate
Fisher v. Edwards (Inspector of Taxes) see Cooper v. Billingham (Inspector of Taxes)
Fisher v. Hughes [1999] Ed. C.R. 409; [1998] E.L.R. 475; [1998] C.O.D. 281, QBD.... *Digested*, 98/**1984**
Fisher v. Minister of Public Safety and Immigration (No.1) [1998] A.C. 673; [1998] 3 W.L.R. 201; 4 B.H.R.C. 191; (1998) 142 S.J.L.B. 36; *Times*, December 26, 1997, PC (Bah) .... *Digested*, 98/**780**
Fisher v. Minister of Public Safety and Immigration (No.2) [2000] 1 A.C. 434; [1999] 2 W.L.R. 349; 6 B.H.R.C. 244; (1998) 142 S.J.L.B. 261; *Times*, October 10, 1998, PC (Bah) .... *Digested*, 98/**3067**:
                                  Applied, 00/3172
Fisher v. Unione Italiana de Riassicurazione SPA [1998] C.L.C. 682, QBD .... *Digested*, 98/**3408**
Fisher v. Val de Travers Asphalte Co (No.2) (1875-76) L.R. 1 C.P.D. 511, CPD .... *Applied*, 47-51/**2491**:
                                   Considered, 99/244
Fisher v. Winch [1939] 1 K.B. 666; [1939] 2 All E.R. 144, CA .... *Applied*, 57/**241**,
               57/2578: *Considered*, 97/4224: *Distinguished*, 99/4352
Fisher v. Wychavon DC [2001] J.P.L. 694; [2000] E.G.C.S. 126; (2000) 97(46) L.S.G. 40; (2000) 97(45) L.S.G. 43; [2000] N.P.C. 118; *Times*, November 22, 2000, CA .... *Digested*, 00/**4494**
Fisher Reeves & Co Ltd v. Armour & Co Ltd [1920] 3 K.B. 614; (1920) 4 Ll. L. Rep. 268, CA; reversing [1920] 2 K.B. 329; (1920) 3 Ll. L. Rep. 245, KBD (Comm Ct) .... *Applied*, 00/**4673**
Fisscher v. Stichting Bedrijfspensioenfonds voor de Detailhandel (C128/93) see Vroege v. NCIV Instituut voor Volkshuisvesting BV (C57/93)
Fisscher v. Voorhuis Hengelo BV (C128/93) see Vroege v. NCIV Instituut voor Volkshuisvesting BV (C57/93)
Fitt v. United Kingdom see Rowe v. United Kingdom
Fitt v. United Kingdom (2000) 30 E.H.R.R. 480, ECHR .... *Digested*, 01/**3511**
Fitton v. Goss (Unreported, April 23, 1996) .... *Considered*, 00/**1447**
Fitzgerald v. Lloyd Williams see Fitzgerald v. Williams
Fitzgerald v. Smith (Unreported, March 10, 1999), CC (Tunbridge Wells) [*Ex rel.* James Browne, Barrister, 96 Gray's Inn Road, London] .... *Digested*, 99/**1553**

Fitzgerald v. Williams; *sub nom* Fitzgerald v. Lloyd Williams; O'Regan v. Williams [1996]
    Q.B. 657; [1996] 2 W.L.R. 447; [1996] 2 All E.R. 171; [1996] C.L.C. 646; [1996]
    I.L.Pr. 275; *Times*, January 3, 1996; *Independent*, February 12, 1996 (C.S.), CA. .   *Digested*, 96/**726**:
                                            Applied, 00/439: *Distinguished*, 99/5701: *Followed*, 96/731
Fitzgerald & Law v. Ralph [1998] B.P.I.R. 49, Ch D . . . .   *Digested*, 98/**3290**
Fitzpatrick v. Inland Revenue Commissioners (No.2) see Smith (Inspector of Taxes) v.
    Abbott
Fitzpatrick v. Osler (Unreported, August 12, 1999), CC (Birkenhead) [*Ex rel.* Scott
    Rees & Co Solicitors, Centaur House, Gardiners Place, Skelmersdale,
    Lancashire]. . . . .   *Digested*, 99/**2484**
Fitzpatrick v. Royal Taxis (Unreported, June 1, 2000), CC (Oldham) [*Ex rel.* Bruce
    Henry, Barrister, 15 Winckley Square, Preston] . . . .   *Digested*, 00/**1692**
Fitzpatrick v. Sterling Housing Association Ltd [2001] 1 A.C. 27; [1999] 3 W.L.R. 1113;
    [1999] 4 All E.R. 705; [2000] 1 F.L.R. 271; [1999] 2 F.L.R. 1027; [2000] 1
    F.C.R. 21; [2000] U.K.H.R.R. 25; 7 B.H.R.C. 200; (2000) 32 H.L.R. 178; [2000]
    L. & T.R. 44; [2000] Fam. Law 14; [1999] E.G.C.S. 125; (1999) 96(43) L.S.G.
    3; [1999] N.P.C. 127; (2000) 79 P. & C.R. D4; *Times*, November 2, 1999 ;
    Independent, November 2, 1999, HL; reversing [1998] Ch. 304; [1998] 2 W.L.R.
    225; [1997] 4 All E.R. 991; [1998] 1 F.L.R. 6; [1998] 1 F.C.R. 417; (1998) 30
    H.L.R. 576; [1997] Fam. Law 784; [1997] E.G.C.S. 122; (1997) 147 N.L.J. 1275;
    [1997] N.P.C. 118; *Times*, July 31, 1997; *Independent*, July 29, 1997, CA . . . . . .   *Digested*, 99/**3715**:
                                            Applied, 00/4147: *Considered*, 99/24
Fitzwilliam Executive Search Ltd (t/a Fitzwilliam Technical Services) v. Bestuur van het
    Landelijk Instituut Sociale Verzekeringen (C202/97) [2000] Q.B. 906; [2000] 3
    W.L.R. 1107 (Note); [2000] All E.R. (EC) 144; [2000] E.C.R. I-883; [2000] 1
    C.M.L.R. 708; [2000] C.E.C. 175; *Times*, March 15, 2000, ECJ . . . .   *Digested*, 00/**2099**:
                                            Applied, 00/4817, 01/5000
Fivecourts Ltd v. JR Leisure Development Co Ltd (2001) 81 P. & C.R. 22; [2001] L. &
    T.R. 5, QBD . . . .   *Digested*, 01/**4161**
Fixtures Marketing Ltd v. AB Svenska Spel [2001] E.C.D.R. 29, TR (Swe)
FJL Realisations Ltd, Re see Inland Revenue Commissioners v. Lawrence
Flack v. Hudson [2001] Q.B. 698; [2001] 2 W.L.R. 982; [2001] P.I.Q.R. P22; (2000)
    97(45) L.S.G. 40; (2000) 144 S.J.L.B. 281; *Times*, November 22, 2000, CA . . .   *Digested*, 00/**196**
Flaherty v. Coal Authority see Mason v. Coal Authority
Flairline Properties Ltd v. Hassan [1999] 1 E.G.L.R. 138; [1998] E.G.C.S. 169, QBD . . . .   *Digested*, 99/**3668**
Flanagan v. South Bucks DC see South Buckinghamshire DC v. Flanagan
Flannery v. Halifax Estate Agencies Ltd (t/a Colleys Professional Services) [2000] 1
    W.L.R. 377; [2000] 1 All E.R. 373; [2000] C.P. Rep. 18; [1999] B.L.R. 107;
    (1999) 11 Admin. L.R. 465; (1999) 15 Const. L.J. 313; (1999) 96(13) L.S.G. 32;
    (1999) 149 N.L.J. 284; [1999] N.P.C. 22; *Times*, March 4, 1999; *Independent*,
    February 26, 1999, CA. . . . .   *Digested*, 99/**37**:
                            Applied, 00/1476, 01/559: *Considered*, 01/50: *Referred to*, 00/3457
Flecksun Ltd v. Westminster City Council see Delaware Mansions Ltd v. Westminster
    City Council
Fleet Disposal Services Ltd, Re; *sub nom* Spratt v. AT&T Automotive Services Ltd
    [1995] B.C.C. 605; [1995] 1 B.C.L.C. 345, Ch D . . . .   *Digested*, 95/**2866**:
                                            Considered, 00/3433
Fleet Electrics v. Jacey Investments [1956] 1 W.L.R. 1027; [1956] 3 All E.R. 99; 100
    S.J. 586; 100 S.J. 628, CA. . . . .   *Digested*, 56/**4853**:
                                            Considered, 56/4854, 90/2777, 00/3904
Fleming (Inspector of Taxes) v. Associated Newspapers Ltd see Associated Newspapers
    Group v. Fleming (Inspector of Taxes)
Fleming v. Secretary of State for Trade and Industry; *sub nom* Fleming v. Xaniar Ltd (In
    Liquidation) 1998 S.C. 8; 1998 S.L.T. 703; [1997] I.R.L.R. 682; 1997 G.W.D. 31-
    1582, 1 Div . . . .   *Digested*, 98/**5812**:
                                            Followed, 98/2188
Fleming v. Xaniar Ltd (In Liquidation) see Fleming v. Secretary of State for Trade and
    Industry
Flender Werft AG v. Aegean Maritime Ltd [1990] 2 Lloyd's Rep. 27, QBD (Comm Ct) . .   *Digested*, 91/**2831**:
                                            Considered, 96/724, 99/401
Fletcher (CICB: Quantum: 2000), Re (Unreported, February 9, 2000), CICB (Nottingham)
    [*Ex rel.* Nick Blake, Barrister, 24 The Ropewalk, Nottingham]. . . . .   *Digested*, 00/**1600**
Fletcher v. Midland Bank Plc (No.1) (C78/98) see Preston v. Wolverhampton
    Healthcare NHS Trust (No.1) (C78/98)
Fletcher v. Midland Bank Plc (No.2) see Preston v. Wolverhampton Healthcare NHS
    Trust (No.2)
Fletcher v. RAC see Fletcher v. Royal Automobile Club Ltd
Fletcher v. Royal Automobile Club Ltd; *sub nom* Fletcher v. RAC; CHANF: 99/0550
    A3, CA; affirming [2000] 1 B.C.L.C. 331; (1999) 96(11) L.S.G. 69; (1999) 143
    S.J.L.B. 94; *Times*, March 3, 1999, Ch D . . . .   *Digested*, 00/**648**
Fletcher v. Sutton (Unreported, September 8, 1997), CC (Nottingham) [*Ex rel.* Colin J
    Furness, Barrister, Park Lane Chambers, Park Lane House, 19 Westgate, Leeds] .   *Digested*, 98/**1453**
Fletcher v. Thames Valley Police Commissioner [2001] 1 Q.R. 12, CC (Central London)
    [*Ex rel.* Andrew Ritchie, Barrister, 9, Gough Square, London] . . . .   *Digested*, 01/**1682**

Fletcher v. Trinidad and Tobago see Ajodha v. Trinidad and Tobago
Fletcher v. United Counties Omnibus Co Ltd [1998] P.I.Q.R. P154, CA . . . .   *Digested*, 98/**3992**:
                                                                                                    Followed, 00/4207
Fletcher v. Vooght [2000] B.P.I.R. 435; (2000) 97(12) L.S.G. 39; (2000) 144 S.J.L.B.
    135, Ch D
Fletcher & Son v. Jubb Booth & Helliwell [1920] 1 K.B. 275, CA. . . . .   *Applied*, 55/2631:
                                                                                                    Considered, 01/589
Fletcher Challenge Nominees Ltd v. Wrightson Ltd see Wrightson Ltd v. Fletcher
    Challenge Nominees Ltd
Fletcher Estates (Harlescott) Ltd v. Secretary of State for the Environment, Transport
    and the Regions; *sub nom* Secretary of State for the Environment, Transport and
    the Regions v. Fletcher Estates (Harlescott) Ltd; Secretary of State for the
    Environment, Transport and the Regions v. Newell; Newell v. Secretary of State
    for the Environment, Transport and the Regions [2000] 2 A.C. 307; [2000] 2
    W.L.R. 438; [2000] 1 All E.R. 929; [2000] B.L.G.R. 240; (2000) 80 P. & C.R.
    95; [2000] 1 P.L.R. 93; [2000] 1 E.G.L.R. 13; [2000] 11 E.G. 141; [2000] R.V.R.
    215; [2000] J.P.L. 923; [2000] E.G.C.S. 24; (2000) 97(9) L.S.G. 41; (2000)
    144 S.J.L.B. 110; [2000] N.P.C. 14; *Times*, February 23, 2000; *Independent*,
    February 24, 2000, HL; affirming [1999] Q.B. 1144; [1999] 2 W.L.R. 730;
    [1998] 4 All E.R. 838; (1998) 10 Admin. L.R. 545; (1998) 76 P. & C.R. 382;
    [1998] 3 P.L.R. 99; [1998] 3 E.G.L.R. 13; [1998] 38 E.G. 155; [1999] R.V.R. 35;
    [1998] J.P.L. 1169; [1998] C.O.D. 352; [1998] E.G.C.S. 91; (1998) 95(24)
    L.S.G. 35; (1998) 142 S.J.L.B. 197; [1998] N.P.C. 105; *Times*, July 1, 1998;
    Independent, June 19, 1998, CA; reversing (1998) 76 P. & C.R. 140; [1998] 2
    E.G.L.R. 7; [1998] 21 E.G. 162; [1998] R.V.R. 16; *Times*, July 11, 1997, QBD . . . . .   *Digested*, 00/**4427**
Fleurose v. Disciplinary Appeal Tribunal of the Securities & Futures Authority Ltd see R.
    (on the application of Fleurose) v. Securities and Futures Authority Ltd
Flinn v. Wills (Unreported, January 19, 2001), CC (Exeter) [*Ex rel.* Crosse & Crosse,
    Solicitors, 14 Southernhay West, Exeter] . . . .   *Digested*, 01/**412**
Flint v. Sowerby (Unreported, May 31, 2000), CC (Newcastle) [*Ex rel.* NDH Edwards,
    Barrister, 8 King Street Chambers, Manchester] . . . .   *Digested*, 00/**2582**
Flintshire CC v. Jones (2000) 15 P.A.D. 182, Planning Inspector
Flintshire CC v. K [2001] 2 F.L.R. 476; [2001] 2 F.C.R. 724; [2001] Fam. Law 578,
    Fam Div . . . .   *Digested*, 01/**2538**
Flintshire CC v. Trustees of the Pentrehobyn Settlement (2000) 15 P.A.D. 848,
    Planning Inspector
Floods of Queensferry Ltd v. Shand Construction Ltd (Costs), CA; reversing in part
    [2001] B.L.R. 446, QBD (T&CC)
Floods of Queensferry Ltd v. Shand Construction Ltd (No.2) [1999] B.L.R. 319, QBD
    (T&CC) . . . .   *Digested*, 99/**810**
Floods of Queensferry Ltd v. Shand Construction Ltd (No.3) [2000] B.L.R. 81, QBD
    (T&CC) . . . .   *Digested*, 00/**818**
Floor Fourteen Ltd, Re see Lewis v. Inland Revenue Commissioners
Florent v. Horez (1984) 12 H.L.R. 1; (1984) 48 P. & C.R. 166; (1983) 268 E.G. 807,
    CA . . . .   *Digested*, 83/**2150**:
                                                                                                    Applied, 00/3923
Floridienne SA v. Belgium (C142/99) [2001] All E.R. (EC) 37; [2000] S.T.C. 1044;
    [2000] E.C.R. I-9567; [2001] 1 C.M.L.R. 26; [2001] C.E.C. 11; [2001] B.T.C.
    5003; [2001] B.V.C. 76; [2000] S.T.I. 1633, ECJ . . . .   *Digested*, 01/**5578**
Florimex BV v. Commission of the European Communities (T70/92) see Cooperatieve
    Vereniging de Verenigde Bloemenveilingen Aalsmeer BA (VBA) v. Florimex BV
    (C265/97 P)
FLORIS Trade Mark [2001] R.P.C. 19, Appointed Person . . . .   *Digested*, 01/**4063**
Flowers v. Queen, The [2000] 1 W.L.R. 2396; (2000) 144 S.J.L.B. 267; *Times*,
    December 1, 2000, PC (Jam) . . . .   *Digested*, 01/**1152**:
                                                                        Applied, 01/1101: *Distinguished*, 01/1094
Floyd v. Crown Prosecution Service see Floyd v. DPP
Floyd v. DPP; *sub nom* Floyd v. Crown Prosecution Service [2000] Crim. L.R. 411,
    QBD
Floyd v. Matsushita Electric (UK) Ltd, CC (Cardiff) [*Ex rel.* Andrew Arentsen, Barrister
    33 Park Place, Cardiff] . . . .   *Digested*, 01/**1787**
Floyd's Application, Re [1997] N.I. 414, QBD (NI) . . . .   *Digested*, 99/**5459**
Floyer-Acland v. Osmond (2000) 80 P. & C.R. 229; [2000] 2 E.G.L.R. 1; [2000] 22
    E.G. 142; [2000] E.G.C.S. 53; [2000] N.P.C. 39, CA. . . . .   *Digested*, 00/**3868**
Fluff Ltd (t/a Mag-it) v. Customs and Excise Commissioners [2001] S.T.C. 674; [2001]
    B.T.C. 5477; [2001] B.V.C. 489; [2000] S.T.I. 752; *Independent*, June 19, 2000
    (C.S.), QBD; affirming [1999] B.V.C. 2121, V&DTr . . . .   *Digested*, 01/**5625**
Fluor Daniel Properties Ltd v. Shortlands Investments Ltd [2001] 4 E.G.C.S. 145;
    (2001) 98(14) L.S.G. 39; (2001) 98(4) L.S.G. 51; *Times*, February 21, 2001,
    Ch D . . . .   *Digested*, 01/**4210**
Flynn v. Robin Thompson & Partners; *sub nom* Flynn v. Robins Thompson & Partners
    (2000) 97(6) L.S.G. 36; (2000) 144 S.J.L.B. 102; *Times*, March 14, 2000;
    Independent, April 17, 2000 (C.S.), CA . . . .   *Digested*, 00/**578**
Flynn v. Robins Thompson & Partners see Flynn v. Robin Thompson & Partners

FNCB Ltd (formerly First National Commercial Bank Plc) v. Barnet Devanney (Harrow) Ltd (formerly Barnet Devanney & Co Ltd); *sub nom* FNCB Ltd v. Barnet Devanney & Co Ltd [1999] 2 All E.R. (Comm) 233; [1999] Lloyd's Rep. P.N. 908; [2000] P.N.L.R. 248; (1999) 96(28) L.S.G. 28; *Times*, September 28, 1999 ; *Independent*, July 19,1999 (C.S.), CA; reversing [1999] C.L.C. 11; [1999] Lloyd's Rep. I.R. 43, QBD . . . . *Digested*, 99/**4020**

FNCB Ltd v. Barnet Devanney & Co Ltd see FNCB Ltd (formerly First National Commercial Bank Plc) v. Barnet Devanney (Harrow) Ltd (formerly Barnet Devanney & Co Ltd)

Focsa Services (UK) Ltd v. Birkett [1996] I.R.L.R. 325, EAT . . . . *Digested*, 96/**2522**: *Applied*, 98/2098: *Distinguished*, 00/2131

Foenander v. Bond Lewis & Co [2001] EWCA Civ 759; [2001] 2 All E.R. 1019; [2001] C.P. Rep. 94; [2001] C.P.L.R. 333; (2001) 151 N.L.J. 890; *Times*, June 18, 2001; *Independent*, June 8, 2001, CA . . . . *Digested*, 01/**431**

Fogarty v. United Kingdom (No.1) (37112/97) (2000) 29 E.H.R.R. CD157, ECHR

Fogarty v. United Kingdom (No.2) (37112/97), *Times*, November 26, 2001, ECHR

Foglia (Pasquale) v. Novello (Mariella) (No.2) (C244/80) [1981] E.C.R. 3045; [1982] 1 C.M.L.R. 585, ECJ . . . . *Digested*, 82/**1224**: *Applied*, 98/2318

Foley v. Classique Coaches Ltd [1934] 2 K.B. 1, CA . . . . *Applied*, 58/868, 58/2069: *Considered*, 66/12029, 67/3906, 83/466, 84/1932, 88/442, 89/482, 00/4299: *Distinguished*, 69/2050, 71/9897: *Followed*, 80/1629, 81/1574, 81/1583

Foley v. Post Office; *sub nom* Post Office v. Foley; HSBC Bank Plc (formerly Midland Bank Plc) v. Madden [2001] 1 All E.R. 550; [2000] I.C.R. 1283; [2000] I.R.L.R. 827; *Times*, August 17, 2000; *Independent*, October 10, 2000, CA; reversing [2000] 2 All E.R. 741; [2000] I.R.L.R. 288, EAT . . . . *Digested*, 00/**2237**: *Applied*, 01/427, 01/2236

Foley v. Summerfield (Unreported, December 16, 1998), CC (Bromley) [*Ex rel.* Gary Blaker, Barrister, FrancisTaylor Building, Temple, London] . . . . *Digested*, 99/**1568**

Follen (Gary) v. HM Advocate [2001] UKPC D2; [2001] 1 W.L.R. 1668; 2001 S.C. (P.C.) 105; 2001 S.L.T. 774; 2001 S.C.C.R. 255; 2001 G.W.D. 12-409, PC (Sc) . . *Digested*, 01/**6352**

Follows v. Smith Cooper & Partners see Siddell v. Smith Cooper & Partners

Fone v. Caw Skip Hire Ltd (Unreported, January 15, 1998), CC (Barrow) [*Ex rel.* Ivan Bowley, Barrister, Lincoln House Chambers, 1 Brazennose Street, Manchester] . . . *Digested*, 98/**1676**

Fontaine SA v. Aqueducs Automobiles SARL (C128/95) [1997] E.C.R. I-967; [1997] 5 C.M.L.R. 39, ECJ (2nd Chamber) . . . . *Applied*, 98/743

Fonteneau v. DPP; *sub nom* DPP v. Fonteneau; DPP v. Fontenau [2001] 1 Cr. App. R. (S.) 15; [2000] Crim. L.R. 611, QBD . . . . *Digested*, 01/**1233**

Foot v. Kenny Transport Ltd (1999) 99(2) Q.R. 6, CC (Lincoln) [*Ex rel.* Peter Wright, Barrister, Queen Elizabeth Building, Temple, London] . . . . *Digested*, 99/**1513**

Foot & Bowden v. Anglo Europe Corp Ltd PTA+A1999/6718/B1, CA . . . . *Digested*, 00/**509**

Footwear Corp Ltd v. Amplight Properties Ltd [1999] 1 W.L.R. 551; [1998] 3 All E.R. 52; (1999) 77 P. & C.R. 418; [1998] L. & T.R. 30; [1998] 2 E.G.L.R. 38; [1998] 25 E.G. 171; [1998] E.G.C.S. 52; (1998) 95(13) L.S.G. 29; [1998] N.P.C. 53, Ch D . . . . *Digested*, 98/**3617**

FOR YOU Trade Mark Application (I ZB 47/96) [2001] E.T.M.R. 4, BGH (Ger)

Forall Metal Products Ltd v. Composite Gutters Ltd (1998) 21 (2) I.P.D. 21013, CA

Forbes v. Scott Ltd (Unreported, January 23, 1998), CC (Newcastle) [*Ex rel.* Thompsons Solicitors, Percy House, Percy Street, Newcastle uponTyne] . . . . . . *Digested*, 98/**1660**

Forbes v. Smith [1998] 1 All E.R. 973; [1998] 1 F.L.R. 835; [1998] 2 F.C.R. 342; [1998] F.S.R. 295; [1998] Fam. Law 256; *Times*, January 14, 1998, Ch D . . . . . *Digested*, 98/**49**

Forbes v. Wandsworth HA [1997] Q.B. 402; [1996] 3 W.L.R. 1108; [1996] 4 All E.R. 881; [1996] 7 Med. L.R. 175; (1997) 36 B.M.L.R. 1; (1996) 93(15) L.S.G. 32; (1996) 146 N.L.J. 477; (1996) 140 S.J.L.B. 85; *Times*, March 21, 1996, CA . . . . *Digested*, 96/**4466**: *Applied*, 00/517: *Considered*, 97/664: *Distinguished*, 97/650, 98/555: *Followed*, 97/666

Forbrukerombudet v. Lego Norge A/S see Consumer Ombudsman v. Mattel Scandinavia A/S (E8/94 and E9/94)

Ford v. Burnley BC; *sub nom* Ford v. Burnley Magistrates Court (1996) 160 J.P. 540; [1995] R.A. 205; (1996) 160 J.P.N. 731; (1995) 159 L.G. Rev. 669; *Times*, March 6, 1995, QBD . . . . *Digested*, 95/**4321**: *Followed*, 99/4326

Ford v. Burnley Magistrates Court see Ford v. Burnley BC

Ford v. GKR Construction Ltd [2000] 1 W.L.R. 1397; [2000] 1 All E.R. 802; [1999] C.P.L.R. 788; *Times*, November 4, 1999, CA . . . . *Digested*, 99/**379**: *Cited*, 01/620: *Considered*, 01/503

Ford v. Metropolitan and Metropolitan District Railway Cos (1886) L.R. 17 Q.B.D. 12, CA . . . . *Applied*, 00/4293: *Followed*, 72/824

Ford AG-Werke AG v. Transtec Automotive (Campsie) Ltd; *sub nom* TransTec Automotive (Campsie) Ltd, Re [2001] B.C.C. 403, Ch D (Companies Ct) . . . . . *Digested*, 01/**3709**

Ford Motor Co v. Office for Harmonisation in the Internal Market (Trade Marks and
    Designs) (OHIM) (T91/99) [2000] E.C.R. II-1925; [2000] 2 C.M.L.R. 276;
    [2000] C.E.C. 251; [2000] E.T.M.R. 554; (2000) 23(7) I.P.D. 23049, CFI (4th
    Chamber) . . . .   *Digested*, 00/**3723**
Ford Motor Co's CommunityTrade Mark Application [2000] E.T.M.R. 679, OHIM (1st Bd
    App). . . . .   *Digested*, 00/**3734**
Ford Motor Credit Co v. Harmack, *Times*, July 7, 1972, CA . . . .   *Digested*, 72/**1649**:
                                                                                            Followed, 99/2448
Fordgate Wandsworth Ltd v. Bernard Neville & Co [1999] E.G.C.S. 98, Ch D
Forebury Estates Ltd v. Chiltern Thames and Eastern Rent Assessment Committee see
    Forebury Estates Ltd v. ChilternThames and Eastern Rent Assessment Panel
Forebury Estates Ltd v. Chiltern Thames and Eastern Rent Assessment Panel; *sub nom*
    Forebury Estates Ltd v. Chiltern Thames and Eastern Rent Assessment
    Committee (2001) 33 H.L.R. 64; (2000) 97(27) L.S.G. 38; *Times*, July 11, 2000,
    QBD . . . .   *Digested*, 00/**3867**
Foreign Silent Partnership Participation, Re 2 I.T.L. Rep. 859, BFH (Ger)
Foreman v. O'Driscoll & Partners [2000] Lloyd's Rep. P.N. 720, QBD . . . .   *Digested*, 00/**4254**:
                                                        Distinguished, 01/4535: *Not followed*, 01/4520
Foreningen af Arbejdsledere i Danmark v. Daddy's Dance Hall A/S (C324/86) [1988]
    E.C.R. 739; [1989] 2 C.M.L.R. 517; [1988] I.R.L.R. 315, ECJ (3rd Chamber) . . .   *Digested*, 90/**2226.d**:
                                                        Applied, 98/2216, 98/2217: *Considered*, 96/2646, 01/2332
Foreningen af Arbejdsledere i Danmark v. Danmols Inventar A/S (In Liquidation) (C105/
    84) see Mikkelsen v. Danmols Inventar A/S (C105/84)
Foreningen af danske Videogramdistributorer v. Laserdisken (C61/97); *sub nom* Egmont
    Film A/S v. Laserdisken [1999] All E.R. (EC) 366; [1998] E.C.R. I-5171; [1999]
    1 C.M.L.R. 1297; [2000] E.C.D.R. 139; [1999] E.M.L.R. 681, ECJ . . . .   *Digested*, 99/**3452**
Forest Heath Council v. Jeremy Noseda Racing Ltd (2000) 15 P.A.D. 616, Planning
    Inspector
Forest Heath DC v. Smoke House Inns Ltd (2001) 16 P.A.D. 42, Planning Inspector
Forest of Dean DC v. Clapham (2001) 16 P.A.D. 49, Planning Inspector
Forever Living Products Ltd v. Customs and Excise Commissioners [2000] S.T.I. 43,
    V&DTr
Forexia (UK) Ltd v. Customs and Excise Commissioners [2001] E.B.L.R. 30; [1999]
    B.V.C. 2266, V&DTr . . . .   *Digested*, 01/**5626**
Forfeiture Act 1982 (Manslaughter: Forfeiture of Widow's Pension), Re [1999] Pens. L.R.1,
    SS Comm . . . .   *Digested*, 99/**4122**
Forkes v. Norwich CC (1998) 98(6) Q.R. 8, CC (Norwich) . . . .   *Digested*, 98/**1689**
Former King of Greece v. Greece (25701/94) (2001) 33 E.H.R.R. 21, ECHR
Formula One Autocentres Ltd v. Birmingham City Council (1999) 163 J.P. 234; [1999]
    R.T.R. 195; *Times*, December 29, 1998; *Independent*, December 7, 1998 (C.S.),
    QBD . . . .   *Digested*, 99/**826**
Fornasar (C318/98), Re; *sub nom* Criminal Proceedings against Fornasar (C318/98)
    [2000] E.C.R. I-4785; [2001] Env. L.R. D1, ECJ
Forrest v. Greenwich Overseers (1858) 8 El. & Bl. 890. . . . .   *Considered*, 00/3880
Forrest v. Reigate and Banstead BC see R. (on the application of McLellan) v.
    Bracknell Forest BC
Forrest v. Royal Trust Co see Barker, Re
Forrest v. Towry Law Financial Services Ltd (1999) 96(45) L.S.G. 32; (1999) 143
    S.J.L.B. 280; *Times*, December 3, 1999, Ch D . . . .   *Digested*, 00/**594**
Forrester v. UYCF Ltd see UYCF Ltd (formerly Night Trunkers (London) Ltd) v.
    Forrester
Forrester & Lamego Ltd, Re [1997] 2 B.C.L.C. 155, Ch D . . . .   *Digested*, 98/**3304**
Forsakringsaktiebolaget Skandia (C240/99), Re; *sub nom* Proceedings brought by
    Forsakringsaktiebolaget Skandia (C240/99) [2001] 1 W.L.R. 1617; [2001] All
    E.R. (EC) 822; [2001] S.T.C. 754; [2001] E.C.R. I-1951; [2001] 2 C.M.L.R. 34;
    [2001] B.T.C. 5213; [2001] B.V.C. 281; [2001] S.T.I. 501; *Times*, March 20, 2001,
    ECJ (1st Chamber) . . . .   *Digested*, 01/**5564**
Forsikringsaktieselskapet Vesta v. Butcher [1989] A.C. 852; [1989] 2 W.L.R. 290;
    [1989] 1 All E.R. 402; [1989] 1 Lloyd's Rep. 331; [1989] Fin. L.R. 223; (1989)
    133 S.J. 184, HL; affirming [1988] 3 W.L.R. 565; [1988] 2 All E.R. 43; [1988] 1
    Lloyd's Rep. 19; [1988] 1 F.T.L.R. 78; [1988] Fin. L.R. 67; (1988) 4 Const. L.J.
    75; (1988) 85(31) L.S.G. 33; (1988) 132 S.J. 1181, CA; affirming [1986] 2 All
    E.R. 488; [1986] 2 Lloyd's Rep. 179, QBD (Comm Ct) . . . .   *Digested*, 89/**386**:
                                    Applied, 95/2496, 96/2993, 98/2490: *Distinguished*, 88/2034:
                                                        Followed, 86/170, 99/3947, 00/3563: *Not followed*, 99/3984
Forster v. Friedland (Unreported, November 10, 1992), CA . . . .   *Followed*, 01/397
Forster v. Outred & Co [1982] 1 W.L.R. 86; [1982] 2 All E.R. 753; 125 S.J. 309, CA . . .   *Digested*, 82/**1849**:
                                    Applied, 81/1621, 83/1765, 84/3170, 85/2012, 89/2585, 91/2343, 01/4526,
                                    01/4527: *Considered*, 84/1579, 93/2997, 94/2912, 00/2621, 01/946:
                                                        Distinguished, 85/2291, 87/229, 88/2158: *Doubted*, 83/2215:
                                                                                            Followed, 88/2154
Forster v. Page see Page v. Scottish Insurance Corp Ltd

Fort Dodge Animal Health Ltd v. Akzo Nobel NV; *sub nom* Akzo Nobel NV's European Patent (No.189958) [1998] I.L.Pr. 732; [1998] F.S.R. 222; (1998) 21(1) I.P.D. 21003, CA; affirming (1997) 20(12) I.P.D. 20120; *Times,* October 24, 1997, Ch D
. . . . *Digested,* 98/**3466**

Fort Sterling Ltd v. South Atlantic Cargo Shipping NV (The Finnrose) [1994] 1 Lloyd's Rep. 559, QBD (Comm Ct) . . . . *Digested,* 95/**4504**:
Applied, 00/244: *Considered,* 00/569

Forte (UK) Ltd v. Restormel BC see Forte (UK) Ltd v. Secretary of State for the Environment, Transport and the Regions

Forte (UK) Ltd v. Secretary of State for the Environment, Transport and the Regions; *sub nom* R. v. Secretary of State for the Environment, Transport and the Regions Ex p. Forte (UK) Ltd; Forte (UK) Ltd v. Restormel BC [2000] J.P.L. 1303 (Note); (2000) 97(15) L.S.G. 41, QBD . . . . *Digested,* 01/**4760**

Forth Estuary Engineering v. Litster see Litster v. Forth Dry Dock and Engineering Co Ltd

Forthright Finance Ltd v. Carlyle Finance Ltd [1997] 4 All E.R. 90; [1997] C.C.L.R. 84, CA . . . . *Digested,* 97/**972**:
Distinguished, 00/849

Forum (Holdings) Ltd v. Brook Street Computers Ltd [1998] Masons C.L.R. 256, CA. . *Digested,* 99/**841**

Forward v. West Sussex CC [1995] 1 W.L.R. 1469; [1995] 4 All E.R. 207; *Times,* July 6, 1995; *Independent,* July 31, 1995 (C.S.), CA . . . . *Digested,* 96/**886**:
Applied, 96/885, 97/705: *Distinguished,* 00/306

Foskett v. Brown (Unreported, February 17, 1998), CC (Barnstaple) [*Ex rel.* Richard French, Barrister, Rougement Chambers, 15 Barnfield Road, Exeter, Devon] . . . . *Digested,* 98/**2497**

Foskett v. McKeown [2001] 1 A.C. 102; [2000] 2 W.L.R. 1299; [2000] 3 All E.R. 97; [2000] Lloyd's Rep. I.R. 627; [2000] W.T.L.R. 667; (1999-2000) 2 I.T.E.L.R. 711; (2000) 97(23) L.S.G. 44; *Times,* May 24, 2000; *Independent,* July 3, 2000 (C.S), HL; reversing [1998] Ch. 265; [1998] 2 W.L.R. 298; [1997] 3 All E.R. 392; [1997] N.P.C. 83; *Times,* June 27, 1997, CA . . . . *Digested,* 00/**2328**

Foster v. Biosil (2001) 59 B.M.L.R. 178, CC (Central London) . . . . *Digested,* 01/**918**

Foster v. British Gas Plc (C188/89) [1991] 1 Q.B. 405; [1991] 2 W.L.R. 258; [1990] 3 All E.R. 897; [1990] E.C.R. I-3313; [1990] 2 C.M.L.R. 833; [1991] I.C.R. 84; [1990] I.R.L.R. 353; *Times,* July 13, 1990, ECJCA . . . . *Digested,* 91/**1672.a:**
Applied, 92/1977, 94/2009, 95/2070, 95/5037, 98/2111: *Approved,* 91/1673:
Considered, 95/2031: *Followed,* 96/2625: *Referred to,* 97/2277

Foster v. Driscoll; Lindsay v. Attfield; Lindsay v. Driscoll [1929] 1 K.B. 470, CA . . . . . . *Applied,* 56/1512, 57/1262, 97/689: *Considered,* 98/271

Foster v. Hampshire Fire & Rescue Service [1999] Disc. L.R. 1; (1998) 43 B.M.L.R. 186, EAT. . . . . *Digested,* 99/**2023**

Foster v. Robinson [1951] 1 K.B. 149; [1950] 2 All E.R. 342; 66 T.L.R. (Pt. 2) 120; 94 S.J. 474, CA . . . . *Digested,* 47-51/**8895**:
Applied, 54/2840, 59/2840, 59/2841, 68/229, 98/3650:
Considered, 58/2929, 00/3894: *Doubted,* 52/624, 52/1973:
Explained, 53/1638, 53/3155: *Followed,* 81/1562

Foster v. Turnbull, *Times,* May 22, 1990, CA . . . . *Digested,* 90/**3787**:
Considered, 95/4211, 97/672: *Distinguished,* 98/633

Foster v. Tyne and Wear CC [1986] 1 All E.R. 567, CA. . . . . *Digested,* 86/**1067**:
Considered, 98/1485

Foucher v. France (1998) 25 E.H.R.R. 234, ECHR . . . . *Digested,* 98/**3123**:
Distinguished, 99/3131

Foulcer v. Bhatti [2001] C.P. Rep. 37, QBD . . . . *Digested,* 00/**324**

Foulkes v. Chief Constable of Merseyside [1998] 3 All E.R. 705; [1998] 2 F.L.R. 789; [1999] 1 F.C.R. 98; [1998] Fam. Law 661; *Times,* June 26, 1998; *Independent,* June 16, 1998, CA . . . . *Digested,* 98/**4258**:
Applied, 00/950

FOUNTAIN Trade Mark [1999] R.P.C. 490, Appointed Person . . . . *Digested,* 99/**3571**

Fournier v. Fournier [1998] 2 F.L.R. 990; [1999] 2 F.C.R. 20; [1998] Fam. Law 662, CA . . . . *Digested,* 99/**2525**

Fowler v. Faccenda Chicken Ltd see Faccenda Chicken Ltd v. Fowler

Fowler v. Fowler (1859) 4 De G. & J. 250. . . . . *Considered,* 98/3659

Fowler v. Secretary of State for the Environment and Berwick Trust [1992] 3 P.L.R. 140; [1993] J.P.L. 365, QBD . . . . *Digested,* 93/**3947**:
Applied, 01/4683

Fox v. Graham Group Ltd, *Times,* August 3, 2001, Ch D . . . . *Digested,* 01/**607**

Fox v. Henderson Investment Fund Ltd [1999] 2 Lloyd's Rep. 303, QBD (Comm Ct) . . *Digested,* 00/**780**

Fox v. Jolly; *sub nom* Jolly v. Brown [1916] 1 A.C. 1, HL; affirming [1914] 2 K.B. 109, CA. . . . . *Applied,* 91/2226, 98/3616: *Considered,* 85/1900, 90/2796, 91/2227, 94/2760:
Followed, 59/1802

Fox v. McKay (Inspector of Taxes) see Fox v. Uxbridge General Commissioners

Fox v. Murray (Unreported, September 6, 2000), CC (Newcastle) [*Ex rel.* Irwin Mitchell Solicitors, 146 West Street, Sheffield] . . . . *Digested,* 00/**448**

Fox v. Spousal (Midlands) Ltd see Fairchild v. Glenhaven Funeral Services Ltd (t/a GH Dovener & Son)

Fox *v.* Star Newspaper Co Ltd [1900] A.C. 19, HL; affirming [1898] 1 Q.B. 636, CA . . .   *Applied*, 98/**616**:
                                                        Referred to, 95/3764

Fox *v.* United Kingdom (A/182); Campbell *v.* United Kingdom; Hartley *v.* United
Kingdom (1991) 13 E.H.R.R. 157; *Times*, October 16, 1990; *Guardian*, October 4,
1990, ECHR . . . .   *Digested*, 90/**2526**:
             Applied, 98/3110: *Considered*, 98/3071: *Subsequent proceedings*, 92/2334
Fox *v.* Uxbridge General Commissioners; *sub nom* Fox *v.* McKay (Inspector of Taxes)
[2001] S.T.I. 1521, Ch D
Fox & Widley *v.* Guram [1998] 1 E.G.L.R. 91; [1998] 03 E.G. 142, QBD. . . . .   *Digested*, 98/**3676**
Foxley *v.* United Kingdom (2001) 31 E.H.R.R. 25; 8 B.H.R.C. 571; *Times*, July 4, 2000,
ECHR . . . .   *Digested*, 00/**3166**:
                                        Previous proceedings, 95/918

Foxlow Ltd *v.* Secretary of State for the Environment, Transport and the Regions
[2001] J.P.L. 1215 (Note); (2000) 97(48) L.S.G. 38, QBD (Admin Ct)
Foy *v.* Governor of Brixton Prison [2000] C.O.D. 308, QBD
Framework Case, Re (No.11206) (Unreported, November 20, 1990), It Cass (I) . . . . . .   *Considered*, 99/3388
Framlingham Tractors Ltd *v.* Secretary of State for the Environment, Transport and the
Regions; R.v Secretary of State for the Environment, Transport and the Regions
Ex p. Framlingham Tractors Ltd [2001] J.P.L. 727 (Note), QBD
France *v.* Commission of the European Communities see Comafrica SpA *v.*
Commission of the European Communities (C73/97)
France *v.* Commission of the European Communities (C235/97) [1998] E.C.R. I-7555,
ECJ . . . .   *Followed*, 00/2337
France *v.* Commission of the European Communities (C241/94); *sub nom* Kimberly
Clark (C241/94), Re [1996] E.C.R. I-4551; [1997] 1 C.M.L.R. 983; [1997]
I.R.L.R. 415, ECJ . . . .   *Digested*, 97/**2399**:
                                                 Followed, 00/2415

France *v.* Commission of the European Communities (C299/96) see Denmark *v.*
Commission of the European Communities (C289/96)
France *v.* Commission of the European Communities (C301/87) [1990] E.C.R. I-307,
ECJ . . . .   *Followed*, 99/705
France *v.* Commission of the European Communities (C68/94); Societe Commerciale
des Potasses et de l'Azote (SCPA) (C30/95); Enterprise Miniere et Chimique
(EMC) *v.* Commission of the European Communities (C30/95) [1998] E.C.R. I-
1375; [1998] 4 C.M.L.R. 829, ECJ. . . . .   *Applied*, 99/**692**:
                                                 Followed, 01/3886
France *v.* Ladbroke Racing Ltd (C83/98) [2000] E.C.R. I-3271; [2000] 3 C.M.L.R.
555, ECJ . . . .   *Digested*, 00/**2343**
France *v.* Ladbroke Racing Ltd (T67/94); *sub nom* Ladbroke Racing Ltd *v.*
Commission of the European Communities (T67/94) [1998] E.C.R. II-1; [2000]
3 C.M.L.R. 611; [1998] C.E.C. 172, CFI (2nd Chamber) . . . .   *Digested*, 98/**740**
France Aviation *v.* Commission of the European Communities (T346/94) [1996] All
E.R. (E.C.) 177; [1995] E.C.R. II-2841; [1996] 1 C.M.L.R. 875, CFI (1st
Chamber) . . . .   *Digested*, 96/**2791**:
                                                 Followed, 00/2350

France Manche SA *v.* Balfour Beatty Construction Ltd see Channel Tunnel Group Ltd *v.*
Balfour Beatty Construction Ltd
France Telecom and Transpac's Data Transmission Activities, Re [1999] E.C.C. 220, C d'A
(Paris). . . . .   *Digested*, 99/**670**
France Telecom SA *v.* MA Editions Sarl [2001] E.C.C. 4, Trib Comm (Paris)
France Telecom SA *v.* Numericable SNC [2001] E.C.C. 2, Cass (F)
Frances Holland School *v.* Wassef [2001] 29 E.G. 123, CC (Central London) . . . .   *Digested*, 01/**4881**
Francis *v.* Brown (1998) 30 H.L.R. 143, CA . . . .   *Digested*, 97/**3286**:
                                                 Followed, 01/4164
Francis *v.* Mutual Life Association of Australasia Ltd [2001] B.P.I.R. 480, Sup Ct (Qld) .   *Digested*, 01/**3721**
Francis Day & Hunter *v.* Bron [1963] Ch. 587; [1963] 2 W.L.R. 868; [1963] 2 All E.R.
16; 107 S.J. 193, CA. . . . .   *Digested*, 63/**566**:
                                                 Followed, 99/3446
Francisco *v.* Diedrick, *Times*, April 3, 1998, QBD . . . .   *Digested*, 98/**361**
Francisco Hernandez Vidal SA *v.* Perez (C127/96); Santner *v.* Hoechst AG (C229/96);
Montana *v.* Claro Sol SA (C74/97) [1998] E.C.R. I-8179; [1999] I.R.L.R. 132,
ECJ (5th Chamber). . . . .   *Digested*, 00/**2229**
Franco *v.* Queen, The (2001) 145 S.J.L.B. 216; *Times*, October 11, 2001, PC (Ant) . . . . .   *Digested*, 01/**1151**
Francom *v.* Williams (Unreported, October 30, 1998), CC (Birkenhead) [*Ex rel*. Tim
Kevan, Barrister, 1 Temple Gardens, Temple, London and Edward Lewis
Solicitors] . . . .   *Digested*, 99/**1416**
Francovich *v.* Italy (C6/90); Bonifacti *v.* Italy (C9/90) [1991] E.C.R. I-5357; [1993] 2
C.M.L.R. 66; [1995] I.C.R. 722; [1992] I.R.L.R. 84; *Times*, November 20, 1991,
ECJ . . . .   *Digested*, 92/**4815**:
        Applied, 98/2570, 98/3396, 99/3620: *Cited*, 00/2380: *Considered*, 92/2904,
            94/3046, 95/2015, 95/2031, 95/2052, 96/2566, 96/2597, 96/2629,
                  96/2792, 96/2803, 97/4627: *Followed*, 97/2265

Frank H Wright (Constructions), Ltd v. Frodoor Ltd [1967] 1 W.L.R. 506; [1967] 1 All
    E.R. 433; 111 S.J. 210, QBD . . . . *Digested,* 67/**2526**:
                              Applied, 73/2471, 74/2742, 99/4077: *Considered,* 71/1373
Frankland v. Inland Revenue Commissioners [1997] S.T.C. 1450; [1997] B.T.C. 8045;
    Times, December 2, 1997; *Independent,* December 8, 1997 (C.S.), CA; affirming
    [1996] S.T.C. 735, Ch D . . . . *Digested,* 98/**4687**
Franklin v. Assherton-Salton see Franklin v. Assheton-Salton
Franklin v. Assheton-Salton; *sub nom* Franklin v. Assherton-Salton (2000) 79 P. &
    C.R. D17, CA
Franklin v. Challis (Unreported, August 12, 1998), CC (Yeovil) [*Ex rel.* Ivor Collet,
    Barrister, 1 Serjeants' Inn, Fleet Street, London] . . . . *Digested,* 98/**1602**
Frankling v. BPS Public Sector Ltd [1999] I.C.R. 347; [1999] I.R.L.R. 212; [1999]
    O.P.L.R. 295, EAT . . . . *Digested,* 99/**2132**:
                                            Considered, 00/4404
Frankum & Kaye Ltd v. Reynolds (Unreported, November 4, 1997), CC (Central
    London) [*Ex rel.* Gordon Dawes, Barrister, Goldsmith Building, Temple] . . . . *Digested,* 98/**1450**
Frans Maas Logistics (UK) Ltd v. CDR Trucking BV [1999] 1 All E.R. (Comm) 737;
    [1999] 2 Lloyd's Rep. 179, QBD (Comm Ct) . . . . *Digested,* 99/**732**:
                                            Approved, 01/5419
Frans Maas (UK) Ltd v. Habib Bank AG Zurich [2001] Lloyd's Rep. Bank. 14; [2001]
    C.L.C. 89, QBD . . . . *Digested,* 01/**379**
Frantisek v. Secretary of State for the Home Department; *sub nom* Katrinak v.
    Secretary of State for the Home Department [2001] EWCA Civ 832; [2001] 3
    F.C.R. 367; [2001] I.N.L.R. 499; [2001] Fam. Law 726; *Times,* June 12, 2001,
    CA . . . . *Digested,* 01/**3627**
Fraser v. Barton see Taylor v. Rajan
Fraser v. Canterbury Diocesan Board of Finance [2001] Ch. 669; [2001] 2 W.L.R.
    1103; (2001) 82 P. & C.R. 13; [2000] E.G.C.S. 141; (2001) 98(4) L.S.G. 50;
    Times, January 10, 2001; *Independent,* December 1, 2000, CA; affirming [2000]
    N.P.C. 1; *Times,* February 22, 2000, Ch D . . . . *Digested,* 01/**5534**
Fraser v. Customs and Excise Commissioners [2000] S.T.I. 1721, V&DTr
Fraser v. Doncaster MBC (Unreported, May 12, 1998), CC (Doncaster) [*Ex rel.* Dermot
    Hughes, Barrister, 26 Paradise Square, Sheffield, S1 2DE] . . . . *Digested,* 98/**1656**
Fraser v. Greater Glasgow Health Board 1997 S.L.T. 554; 1996 S.C.L.R. 1108; 1996
    Rep. L.R. 58, OH . . . . *Digested,* 97/**5933**:
                                  Considered, 00/6424: *Not followed,* 99/3974
Fraser v. Lakeside Corp Ltd (Unreported, April 8, 1998), CC (Newcastle) [*Ex rel.*
    Jayne Atkinson, Barrister, New Court Chambers, 3 Broad Chare, Newcastle
    upon Tyne] . . . . *Digested,* 98/**1691**
Fraser v. State Hospitals Board for Scotland 2001 S.L.T. 1051; 2001 S.C.L.R. 357;
    2000 Rep. L.R. 94; 2000 G.W.D. 25-952; *Times,* September 12, 2000, OH . . . . *Digested,* 00/**6582**
Fraser v. Winchester HA (2000) 55 B.M.L.R. 122; *Times,* July 12, 1999, CA . . . . *Digested,* 99/**3962**
Fraser and Public Service Staff Relations Board, Re (1985) 23 D.L.R. (4th) 122, Sup Ct
    (Can) . . . . *Considered,* 98/3084
Fraser Homes Ltd v. Fraser Houses (NI) Ltd [1996] N.I. 481, CA (NI)
Fraser Homes Ltd v. Fraser Houses (NI) Ltd (Joint Tenancy: Right to Partition) [1998]
    N.I. 214, Ch D . . . . *Digested,* 99/**5410**
Fraser Park South Estates Ltd v. Lang Michener Lawrence & Shaw [2001] N.P.C. 30,
    CA (BC)
Fraser River Pile & Dredge Ltd v. Can-Dive Services Ltd [2000] 1 Lloyd's Rep. 199, Sup
    Ct (Can) . . . . *Digested,* 00/**3531**
Fratelli Costanzo SpA v. Comune di Milano (103/88) [1989] E.C.R. 1839; [1990] 3
    C.M.L.R. 239, ECJ . . . . *Digested,* 91/**4050**:
                                    Applied, 98/2111: *Cited,* 00/4458
Fratelli Graffione SNC v. Ditta Fransa (C313/94) see Fratelli Graffione SNC v. Fransa
    (C313/94)
Fratelli Graffione SNC v. Fransa (C313/94); *sub nom* Fratelli Graffione SNC v. Ditta
    Fransa (C313/94) [1996] E.C.R. I-6039; [1997] 1 C.M.L.R. 925; [1997]
    E.T.M.R. 71; [1997] F.S.R. 538, ECJ . . . . *Digested,* 97/**4876**:
                                   Followed, 01/2489: *Referred to,* 99/3572
Fratelli Rubino Industrie Olearie SpA v. Commission of the European Communities see
    Oleifici Italiani SpA v. Commission of the European Communities (T54/96)
Frawley v. Neill [2000] C.P. Rep. 20; (1999) 96(12) L.S.G. 33; (1999) 143 S.J.L.B.
    98; *Times,* April 5, 1999, CA . . . . *Digested,* 99/**4369**
Frayling Furniture Ltd v. Premier Upholstery Ltd (1999) 22(5) I.P.D. 22051, Ch D . . . . . *Digested,* 99/**3461**
Fred Drughorn Ltd v. Rederiaktiebolaget Transatlantic; *sub nom* Rederi Aktienbolaget
    Transatlantic v. Fred Drughorn Ltd [1919] A.C. 203, HL; affirming [1918] 1 K.B.
    394, CA . . . . *Applied,* 67/49,
                          00/3870: *Considered,* 79/1643, 94/120
Frederic J Whyte & Partners v. IAF Properties Ltd 59 Con. L.R. 93, CA . . . . *Digested,* 98/**532**
Frederick Leyland & Co Ltd v. Compania Panamena Europea Navegacion Limitada see
    Panamena Europea Navegacion Compania Limitada v. Frederick Leyland & Co
    Ltd
Free World Trust v. Electro Sante Inc [2001] F.S.R. 45, Sup Ct (Can)

Freeguard v. Rogers (No.1) [1999] 1 W.L.R. 375; [1998] E.G.C.S. 145; (1998) 95(45) L.S.G. 40; (1999) 143 S.J.L.B. 12; *Times*, October 22, 1998, CA . . . . *Digested*, 98/**4340**
Freeguard v. Royal Bank of Scotland Plc (2000) 79 P. & C.R. 81; (1998) 95(13) L.S.G. 29, CA . . . . *Digested*, 00/**4649**
Freeman v. Cox (1878) L.R. 8 Ch. D. 148, Ch D . . . . *Considered*, 99/4650
Freeman v. Jeffries (1868-69) L.R. 4 Ex. 189, Ex Ct . . . . *Applied*, 01/4153
Freeman v. Lomas (1851) 9 Hare 109 . . . . *Considered*, 01/3780
Freeman v. Sovereign Chicken [1991] I.C.R. 853; [1991] I.R.L.R. 408; *Times*, September 24, 1991, EAT . . . . *Digested*, 92/**93**:
Distinguished, 01/2347
Freeman & Lockyer v. Buckhurst Park Properties (Mangal) Ltd [1964] 2 Q.B. 480; [1964] 2 W.L.R. 618; [1964] 1 All E.R. 630; 108 S.J. 96, CA . . . . *Digested*, 64/**444**:
Applied, 72/525, 73/420, 74/30, 77/2890, 84/27, 85/21, 94/554, 95/775:
Considered, 67/33, 72/1649, 80/14, 83/202, 00/4024:
Distinguished, 94/362: *Followed*, 94/5374, 01/6105
Freemans Plc v. Customs and Excise Commissioners (C86/99); *sub nom* Freemans Plc v. Customs and Excise Commissioners (No.1) [2001] 1 W.L.R. 1713; [2001] S.T.C. 960; [2001] E.C.R. I-4167; [2001] 2 C.M.L.R. 46; [2001] C.E.C. 118; [2001] B.T.C. 5307; [2001] B.V.C. 365; [2001] S.T.I. 871; *Times*, June 18, 2001, ECJ (6th Chamber) [1998] B.V.C. 2354, V&DTr . . . . *Digested*, 01/**5587**
Freemans Plc v. Customs and Excise Commissioners (No.1) see Freemans Plc v. Customs and Excise Commissioners (C86/99)
Freemans Plc v. Customs and Excise Commissioners (No.2) [2001] S.T.I. 766, V&DTr
Freight Transport Association v. Customs and Excise Commissioners [1997] V. & D.R. 330, V&DTr . . . . *Digested*, 00/**4957**
Freistaat Sachsen v. Commission of the European Communities (T132/96); Volkswagen AG v. Commission of the European Communities (T143/96) [1999] E.C.R. II-3663; [2000] 3 C.M.L.R. 485, CFI (2nd Chamber)
Fremont Insurance Co Ltd v. Fremont Indemnity Co [1997] C.L.C. 1428, QBD (Comm Ct) . . . . *Digested*, 98/**585**:
Considered, 98/587
French v. Barclays Bank Plc [1998] I.R.L.R. 646, CA . . . . *Digested*, 98/**2106**
French v. Champkin [1920] 1 K.B. 76, KBD . . . . *Considered*, 98/4300
French v. Mason (No.1) No.003704 of 1995, Ch D . . . . *Digested*, 98/**694**
French v. Mason (No.2) [1999] F.S.R. 597; *Times*, November 13, 1998, Pat Ct . . . . *Digested*, 98/**3454**
French Connection Ltd v. Sutton (t/a Teleconexus Email) [2000] E.T.M.R. 341; [2000] I.T.C.L.R. 509; (2000) 23(2) I.P.D. 23013, Ch D . . . . *Digested*, 00/**3592**
French, French and French v. Barlow (Unreported, May 4, 1994), CC (Colchester) [*Ex rel.* Liddell Zurbrugg, Solicitors] . . . . *Digested*, 94/**3566**:
Considered, 97/567, 98/398
Frencon Builders v. Marashi (Unreported, June 14, 2000), CC (Brentford) [*Ex rel.* Nigel Ffitch, Barrister, Phoenix Chambers, Gray's Inn Chambers, Gray's Inn, London] . *Digested*, 00/**2577**
FRESH BANKING Trade Mark; *sub nom* Sainsbury's Bank Plc's Trade Mark Application [1998] R.P.C. 605, Appointed Person; affirming (1998) 21(1) I.P.D. 21009, TMR . . . . *Digested*, 98/**3543**
Fresh Breath Co Ltd's Trade Mark Application (No.2133080) [2000] E.T.M.R. 644; (2000) 23(3) I.P.D. 23025, TMR . . . . *Digested*, 00/**3787**
Fresh (Retail) Ltd v. Emsden (Unreported, January 18, 1999), CC (Ipswich) [*Ex rel.* Phillip Bliss Aliker, Barrister, 2 Pump Court, Temple, London] . . . . *Digested*, 99/**3693**
Fresh Marine Co AS v. Commission of the European Communities (T178/98) [2000] E.C.R. II-3331; [2001] 3 C.M.L.R. 35, CFI (3rd Chamber)
Fresh Mix Ltd v. Bilwinco A/S [1999] I.L.Pr. 775, CJ (Gen Div) (Ont) . . . . *Digested*, 00/**757**
Freshbright Cemeteries Ltd v. Edinburgh City Council [2001] R.V.R. 285, Lands Tr (Scot)
Fressoz v. France (29183/95) (2001) 31 E.H.R.R. 2; 5 B.H.R.C. 654, ECHR . . . . *Digested*, 99/**3105**
Frey v. Royal Bank of Scotland (Nassau) Ltd; *sub nom* Frey's Settlement, Re [2001] W.T.L.R. 1009; (2000-01) 3 I.T.E.L.R. 775, Sup Ct (Bah) . . . . *Digested*, 01/**5510**
Frey's Settlement, Re see Frey v. Royal Bank of Scotland (Nassau) Ltd
Friction Division Products Inc and El Du Pont de Nemours & Co Inc (No.2), Re (1986) 56 O.R. (2d) 722, HC (Ont) . . . . *Considered*, 00/330
Friedrich Binder GmbH & Co KG v. Hauptzollamt Bad Reichenhall (161/88) [1989] E.C.R. 2415, ECJ . . . . *Applied*, 00/4959
Friedrischfeld AG v. Acuna & Fombona SA [2001] E.C.C. 5, Trib Sup (Sp)
Friend v. Civil Aviation Authority (No.1) [1998] I.R.L.R. 253; *Times*, February 5, 1998, CA . . . . *Digested*, 98/**1771**
Friend v. Civil Aviation Authority (No.2) [2001] EWCA Civ 1204; [2001] 4 All E.R. 385; [2001] I.R.L.R. 819; [2001] Emp. L.R. 1141; *Independent*, November 26, 2001 (C.S), CA; reversing TNS, QBD . . . . *Digested*, 01/**675**
Friend v. Institution of Professional Managers and Specialists [1999] I.R.L.R. 173, QBD . *Digested*, 99/**4062**
Friend v. Young [1897] 2 Ch. 421, Ch D . . . . *Considered*, 00/513
Friends Provident Life Office, Re see Friends Provident Linked Life Assurance Ltd, Re

Friends Provident Life Office *v.* British Railways Board [1996] 1 All E.R. 336; (1997) 73
　　P. & C.R. 9; [1995] 2 E.G.L.R. 55; [1995] 48 E.G. 106; [1995] N.P.C. 143;
　　Times, July 31, 1995; *Independent,* September 14, 1995, CA . . . .　　*Digested,* 96/**3759**:
　　　　　　　　　　　　　　　　　　　　　　Considered, 97/3093: *Followed,* 98/3615
Friends Provident Life Office *v.* Hillier Parker May & Rowden [1997] Q.B. 85; [1996] 2
　　W.L.R. 123; [1995] 4 All E.R. 260; (1996) 71 P. & C.R. 286; [1995] E.G.C.S.
　　64; [1995] N.P.C. 63; *Times,* April 15, 1995, CA. . . . .　　*Digested,* 96/**2781**:
　　　　　　　　　　　　　　　　　　　　　　　　　　Distinguished, 00/1448
Friends Provident Life Office *v.* Secretary of State for the Environment, Transport and the
　　Regions see R. (on the application of Friends Provident Life Office) *v.* Secretary
　　of State for the Environment, Transport and the Regions
Friends Provident Linked Life Assurance Ltd, Re; *sub nom* Friends Provident Life Office,
　　Re [1999] 2 All E.R. (Comm) 437; [2000] 2 B.C.L.C. 203; *Times,* July 26,
　　1999, CA; reversing [1999] 1 All E.R. (Comm.) 28; [1999] 1 B.C.L.C. 192;
　　(1999) 96(4) L.S.G. 38; (1999) 143 S.J.L.B. 27; *Times,* January 4, 1999;
　　Independent, December 14, 1998 (C.S), Ch D (Companies Ct)　　　　　　　*Digested,* 99/**3429**
Froggatt *v.* Secretary of State for the Environment, Transport and the Regions see
　　Wilson *v.* Secretary of State for the Environment, Transport and the Regions
Frogmore Developments Ltd *v.* Shirayama Shokusan Co [2000] 1 E.G.L.R. 121; [1997]
　　N.P.C. 14, Ch D . . . .　　*Digested,* 00/**4633**
Fromagerie Chiciak and Fol, Re (C129/97) see Chiciak, Re (C129/97)
Fromex SA's Community Trade Mark Application [1999] E.T.M.R. 989, OHIM (Opposition
　　Div) . . . .　　*Digested,* 00/**3740**
Froom *v.* Butcher [1976] Q.B. 286; [1975] 3 W.L.R. 379; [1975] 3 All E.R. 520;
　　[1975] 2 Lloyd's Rep. 478; [1975] R.T.R. 518; 119 S.J. 613, CA; reversing [1974]
　　1 W.L.R. 1297; [1974] 3 All E.R. 517; [1974] 2 Lloyd's Rep. 541; [1974] R.T.R.
　　528; 118 S.J. 758, QBD . . . .　　*Digested,* 75/**2295**:
　　　　　　　　　Applied, 80/1875, 84/2292, 01/4447: *Considered,* 77/2013, 77/2643,
　　　　　　　　　77/3350, 78/738, 78/2611, 79/2965, 82/2157, 82/3700, 82/4059, 83/1055,
　　　　　　　　　89/2536, 89/2555, 93/2954, 94/3344: *Distinguished,* 79/2367:
　　　　　　　　　Followed, 74/2565, 75/2299: *Referred to,* 99/1378
FROOT LOOPS Trade Mark [1998] R.P.C. 240, Appointed Person . . . .　　*Digested,* 98/**3541**
Frost *v.* Chief Constable of South Yorkshire; White *v.* Chief Constable of South
　　Yorkshire; Duncan *v.* British Coal Corp [1999] 2 A.C. 455; [1998] 3 W.L.R.
　　1509; [1999] 1 All E.R. 1; [1999] I.C.R. 216; [1999] I.R.L.R. 110; (1999) 45
　　B.M.L.R. 1; (1999) 96(2) L.S.G. 28; (1998) 148 N.L.J. 1844; (1999) 143
　　S.J.L.B. 51; *Times,* December 4, 1998; *Independent,* December 9, 1998, HL;
　　reversing [1998] Q.B. 254; [1997] 3 W.L.R. 1194; [1997] 1 All E.R. 540; [1997]
　　I.R.L.R. 173; (1997) 33 B.M.L.R. 108; (1996) 146 N.L.J. 1651; *Times,* November
　　6, 1996; *Independent,* November 5, 1996, CA; reversing *Times,* July 3, 1995,
　　QBD . . . .　　*Digested,* 99/**4059**:
　　　　　　　　　Applied, 01/4462: *Considered,* 97/2615, 00/4213, 00/4220:
　　　　　　　　　Followed, 99/3980: *Referred to,* 00/6598
Frost *v.* Furness (Unreported, July 14, 1997), CC (Reading) [*Ex rel.* David McHugh,
　　Barrister, Bracton Chambers, Chancery Lane]. . . . .　　*Digested,* 97/**1886**:
　　　　　　　　　　　　　　　　　　　　　　　　　　Applied, 00/1580
Frost *v.* James Finlay Bank Ltd A3 2001 2367, CA; reversing [2001] Lloyd's Rep.
　　Bank. 302; [2001] Lloyd's Rep. P.N. 629; [2001] N.P.C. 101, Ch D . . . .　　*Digested,* 01/**4514**
Frost *v.* Unity Trust Bank Plc (No.1) [1998] B.P.I.R. 459, 1 Div . . . .　　*Digested,* 98/**6013**
Frota Oceanica Brasiliera SA *v.* Steamship Mutual Underwriting Association (Bermuda)
　　Ltd (The Frotanorte) [1996] 2 Lloyd's Rep. 461; [1997] C.L.C. 230; *Times,*
　　August 13, 1996, CA; affirming [1995] 2 Lloyd's Rep. 254; *Lloyd's List,* June 29,
　　1995 (I.D.), QBD (Comm Ct) . . . .　　*Digested,* 96/**5291**:
　　　　　　　　　　　　　　　　　　　　　　　　　　Followed, 00/222
Fruchthandelsgesellschaft mbH Chemnitz *v.* Commission of the European Communities
　　(T254/97) [1999] E.C.R. II-2743; [1999] 3 C.M.L.R. 508, CFI (5th Chamber). .　　*Digested,* 00/**2404**
Fry *v.* First National Leasing Ltd (Unreported, June 7, 2000), CC (Salisbury) [*Ex rel.*
　　Michael Morris, Barrister, 169 Temple Chambers, Temple Avenue, London] . . . . .　　*Digested,* 00/**838**
Fry *v.* Ford Motor Co Ltd Unreported . . . .　　*Referred to,* 00/1555
Frydenson *v.* Reid (Unreported, January 10, 2001), CC (Barnet) [*Ex rel.* Marcus Grant,
　　Barrister, 1 Temple Gardens, London] . . . .　　*Digested,* 01/**685**
Frydlender *v.* France (30979/96) (2001) 31 E.H.R.R. 52, ECHR . . . .　　*Digested,* 01/**3523**
Fryer *v.* Pearson, *Times,* April 4, 2000, CA . . . .　　*Digested,* 00/**4241**
Fryer *v.* Royal Institution of Chartered Surveyors; *sub nom* Royal Institution of
　　Chartered Surveyors *v.* Wiseman Marshall [2000] Lloyd's Rep. P.N. 534; [2000]
　　P.N.L.R. 649; *Times,* May 16, 2000, CA . . . .　　*Digested,* 00/**469**
Fryers *v.* Hirst (Unreported, August 4, 2000), CC (Bradford) [*Ex rel.* David S Dixon,
　　Barrister, Sovereign Chambers, 25 Park Square, Leeds] . . . .　　*Digested,* 00/**1568**
FSA Business Software Ltd, Re [1990] B.C.C. 465; [1990] B.C.L.C. 825 . . . .　　*Digested,* 90/**530**:
　　　　　　　　　　　　　　　　　　　　　　　　　　Not followed, 98/3324
FSS Trade Mark [2001] R.P.C. 40, Appointed Person. . . . .　　*Digested,* 01/**3981**
FSS Travel & Leisure Systems Ltd *v.* Johnson [1998] I.R.L.R. 382; [1999] I.T.C.L.R. 218;
　　[1999] F.S.R. 505, CA. . . . .　　*Digested,* 98/**2193**:
　　　　　　　　　　　　　　　　　　　　　　　　　　Followed, 00/2116

Fu v. Camden LBC [2001] I.R.L.R. 186, EAT . . . . *Digested*, 01/**2238**
Fuchs Lubricants Plc v. Staybrite Windows Ltd (Unreported, June 29, 1999), CC
    (Derby) [*Ex rel.* Gordon Hamilton Solicitors, St Francis House, Ipswich] . . . . . . *Digested*, 99/**2470**
Fuensanta v. Antena 3 TV SA [2001] E.C.D.R. 23, Aud (Sp)
Fuji Photo Film Co Ltd's Application [1998] E.T.M.R. 343, OHIM (2nd Bd App) . . . . . . *Distinguished*, 00/3756
Fuji Photo Film Co Ltd's Community Trade Mark Application (No.45518) (1998) 21 (7) I.P.D.
    21079
Fujitsu Ltd's European Patent Application (No.88307913.9) (2000) 23(9) I.P.D. 23073,
    EPO (Technical Bd App)
Fujitsu Ltd's Patent Application (No.9204959.2) [1997-98] Info.T.L.R.103; [1997] R.P.C.
    608; (1997) 16 Tr. L.R. 352; [1998] Masons C.L.R. Rep. 99; (1997) 20(7) I.P.D.
    20060; *Times*, March 14, 1997, CA; affirming [1997-98] Info. T.L.R. 101; [1996]
    R.P.C. 511; [1998] Masons C.L.R. Rep. 112; (1996) 19(9) I.P.D. 19078; *Times*,
    June 18, 1996, Pat Ct. . . . . *Digested*, 97/**3915**
FUJITSU/Removal of organic resist (T311/99) [2000] E.P.O.R. 488, EPO (Technical Bd
    App) . . . . *Digested*, 01/**3907**
FUJITSU/Semiconductor (T610/89) [1999] E.P.O.R. 36, EPO (Technical Bd App)
Full Cup International Trading Ltd, Re; *sub nom* Antoniades v. Wong [1998] B.C.C. 58;
    [1997] 2 B.C.L.C. 419, CA; affirming [1995] B.C.C. 682, Ch D . . . . *Digested*, 98/**693**
Fullard (Deceased), Re; *sub nom* Fuller (Deceased), Re [1982] Fam. 42; [1981] 3
    W.L.R. 743; [1981] 2 All E.R. 796; (1981) 11 Fam. Law 116; *Times*, February 3,
    1981, CA. . . . . *Digested*, 82/**3385**:
                                                            Applied, 01/5155: *Considered*, 87/1737
Fullarton Computer Industries Ltd v. Central Arbitration Committee [2001] I.R.L.R. 752;
    2001 G.W.D. 23-864, OH
Fuller (Deceased), Re see Fullard (Deceased), Re
Fuller v. Cyracuse Ltd [2001] B.C.C. 806; [2001] 1 B.C.L.C. 187, Ch D (Companies
    Ct)
Fuller v. Evans [2000] 1 All E.R. 636; [2000] 2 F.L.R. 13; [2000] 1 F.C.R. 494;
    [2000] W.T.L.R. 5; (1999-2000) 2 I.T.E.L.R. 392; [2000] Fam. Law 542; (1999)
    96(41) L.S.G. 36; (1999) 149 N.L.J. 1561; (1999) 143 S.J.L.B. 248; *Times*,
    November 10, 1999 ; *Independent*, October 19, 1999; *Independent*, November
    22, 1999 (C.S.), Ch D . . . . *Digested*, 99/**4952**
Fuller v. Happy Shopper Markets Ltd [2001] 1 W.L.R. 1681; [2001] 2 Lloyd's Rep. 49;
    [2001] L. & T.R. 16; [2001] 25 E.G. 159; [2001] 9 E.G.C.S. 226; (2001) 98(11)
    L.S.G. 43; (2001) 145 S.J.L.B. 62; [2001] N.P.C. 35; *Times*, March 6, 2001,
    Ch D . . . . *Digested*, 01/**4153**
Fuller v. Haymills (Contractors) Ltd (Unreported, September 26, 1997), CC
    (Peterborough) [*Ex rel.* Steven Weddle, Barrister, Hardwicke Building, New
    Square, Lincoln's Inn, London] . . . . *Digested*, 98/**1687**:
                                                                          Considered, 00/1501
Fuller v. Strum [2001] EWCA Civ 1879; (2001-02) 4 I.T.E.L.R. 454, CA; reversing
    [2001] W.T.L.R. 677; (2001) 98(6) L.S.G. 45; *Times*, February 14, 2001, Ch D . . *Digested*, 01/**403**
Fulton Motors Ltd v. Toyota (GB) Ltd [1998] Eu. L.R. 327, Ch D . . . . *Digested*, 99/**667**
Fulton Motors Ltd v. Toyota (GB) Ltd (Costs) [2000] C.P. Rep. 24, CA . . . . *Digested*, 00/**427**
Fulton's Application for Judicial Review, Re [2000] N.I. 447; [2001] H.R.L.R. 11, QBD (NI)
                                                                          Digested, 01/**5906**
Fulwell v. Mason [2001] 3 Q.R. 15, CC (Walsall) [*Ex rel.* Hunt & Coombs Solicitors,
    35 Thorpe Road, Peterborough] . . . . *Digested*, 01/**1659**
Funke v. France (A/256-A) [1993] 1 C.M.L.R. 897; (1993) 16 E.H.R.R. 297, ECHR . . . . *Digested*, 94/**2431**:
                                            Applied, 00/5031: *Considered*, 98/3150, 00/6043, 01/974
Funtime Ltd, Re; *sub nom* Secretary of State for Trade and Industry v. Doe [2000] 1
    B.C.L.C. 247, Ch D (Companies Ct) . . . . *Digested*, 00/**662**
Furbert v. Queen, The [2000] 1 W.L.R. 1716, PC (Ber)
Furniss (Inspector of Taxes) v. Dawson [1984] A.C. 474; [1984] 2 W.L.R. 226; [1984]
    1 All E.R. 530; [1984] S.T.C. 153; 55 T.C. 324; (1985) 82 L.S.G. 2782; (1984) 81
    L.S.G. 739; (1984) 134 N.L.J. 341; (1984) 128 S.J. 132, HL; reversing [1983] 3
    W.L.R. 635; [1983] S.T.C. 549; (1983) 127 S.J. 619, CA; affirming [1982]
    S.T.C. 267; 126 S.J. 83, Ch D . . . . *Digested*, 84/**270**:
                Applied, 85/243, 85/3364, 85/3407, 86/258, 86/2203, 86/3204, 90/2649,
                    95/876, 00/5043: *Cited*, 92/334, 93/336: *Considered*, 86/262, 88/66,
                                88/257, 90/2685, 96/4804, 97/2979, 00/4916, 01/5199:
                        Distinguished, 87/270, 87/282, 93/337, 95/2750: *Not applied*, 87/3848,
                                                            88/3639: *Referred to*, 85/456
FURUKAWA/Flexible composite pipe (T1002/95) [2000] E.P.O.R. 544, EPO (Technical
    Bd App) . . . . *Digested*, 01/**3924**
Fusetron Ltd v. Whitehouse (Valuation Officer); JGW Coatings Ltd v. Whitehouse
    (Valuation Officer) [1999] R.A. 295, Lands Tr . . . . *Digested*, 99/**4325**
Futures Transactions, Re [1998] I.L.Pr. 327, OLG (Dusseldorf)
FW Cook Ltd v. Shimizu (UK) Ltd [2000] B.L.R. 199, QBD (T&CC) . . . . *Digested*, 00/**805**
FW Farnsworth Ltd v. McCoid [1999] I.C.R. 1047; [1999] I.R.L.R. 626; (1999) 96(16)
    L.S.G. 35; (1999) 149 N.L.J. 522; *Times*, March 31, 1999, CA; affirming [1998]
    I.R.L.R. 362, EAT . . . . *Digested*, 99/**2122**

FWK Howells (t/a Buckingham Commercial Motor Co) *v.* Customs and Excise Commissioners [2000] S.T.I. 835,V&DTr

Fyffes Group Ltd *v.* Templeman [2000] 2 Lloyd's Rep. 643; (2000) 97(25) L.S.G. 40; *Times,* June 14, 2000, QBD (Comm Ct) . . . . *Digested,* 00/**5104**

Fylde BC *v.* Kensington Developments Ltd (2001) 16 P.A.D. 80, Planning Inspector

Fylde Microsystems Ltd *v.* Key Radio Systems Ltd [1997-98] Info. T.L.R. 374; [1998] I.T.C.L.R. 77; [1998] F.S.R. 449; [1998] Masons C.L.R. 190; (1998) 21 (5) I.P.D. 21045; *Times,* February 18, 1998, Ch D . . . . *Digested,* 98/**3442**:
Referred to, 99/3455

G (A Child), Re see Phelps *v.* Hillingdon LBC

G (A Child) (Adoption: Disclosure), Re see H (A Child) (Adoption: Consultation of Unmarried Fathers), Re

G (A Child) (Care Order: Threshold Criteria), Re; *sub nom* G (A Child) (Care Proceedings: Split Trials), Re [2001] 1 F.L.R. 872; [2001] 1 F.C.R. 165, CA . . . . . *Digested,* 01/**2566**

G (A Child) (Care Proceedings: Split Trials), Re see G (A Child) (Care Order: Threshold Criteria), Re

G (A Child) (Costs: Child Case), Re [1999] 2 F.L.R. 250; [1999] 3 F.C.R. 463; [1999] Fam. Law 381, CA. . . . . *Digested,* 99/**2410**

G (A Child) (Domestic Violence: Direct Contact), Re [2000] 2 F.L.R. 865; [2001] 2 F.C.R. 134; [2000] Fam. Law 789; (2001) 165 J.P.N. 526, Fam Div . . . . *Digested,* 01/**2564**

G (A Child) (Non Accidental Injury: Standard of Proof), Re [2001] 1 F.C.R. 97, CA . . . . *Digested,* 01/**2549**

G (A Child) (Secure Accommodation Order), Re [2000] 2 F.L.R. 259; [2000] 2 F.C.R. 385; [2000] Fam. Law 716, CA. . . . . *Digested,* 00/**2491**

G (A Child) (Secure Accommodation Order), Re [2001] 1 F.L.R. 884; [2001] 3 F.C.R. 47; [2001] Fam. Law 263, Fam Div . . . . *Digested,* 01/**2673**

G (A Child) *v.* Bennett [2001] 6 Q.R. 17, CC (Maidstone) [*Ex rel.* Christopher Bamford, Barrister, Tanfield Chambers, Francis Taylor Building, Temple, London] . . . . *Digested,* 01/**1707**

G (A Child) *v.* Bromley LBC see Phelps *v.* Hillingdon LBC

G (A Child) *v.* Bromley LBC (2000) 2 L.G.L.R. 237; [2000] Ed. C.R. 49; [1999] E.L.R. 356; *Times,* October 28, 1999, CA . . . . *Digested,* 99/**3967**:
Subsequent proceedings, 00/1947

G (A Child) *v.* Grindal [2000] 4 Q.R. 6, CC (Nuneaton) [*Ex rel.* L J Deegan, Barrister, Fenners Chambers, 3 Madingley Road, Cambridge] . . . . *Digested,* 00/**1542**

G (A Child) *v.* Kingsmill (No.1) [1998] P.I.Q.R. P24; [1998] P.N.L.R. 157, QBD . . . . *Digested,* 98/**4012**

G (A Child) *v.* Lancashire CC (Unreported, September 18, 2000), CC (Blackpool) [*Ex rel.* Karim Sabry, Barrister, 8, King Street, Manchester] . . . . *Digested,* 01/**1792**

G (A Child) *v.* Lancashire CC [2001] 3 Q.R. 12, CC (Burnley) [*Ex rel.* Blackhurst Swainson, Solicitors, 9 Cannon Street, Preston] . . . . *Digested,* 01/**1600**

G (A Child) *v.* Pitt (t/a KP Group) (Unreported, April 4, 2000), CC (Trowbridge) [*Ex rel.* Amanda Drane, Barrister, 4 King's Bench Walk, Temple, London] . . . . *Digested,* 00/**1740**

G (A Child) *v.* Punch Retail Ltd [2001] 3 Q.R. 20, CC (Portsmouth) [*Ex rel.* Dyer Burdett & Co, Solicitors, 64 West Street, Havant, Hampshire] . . . . *Digested,* 01/**1807**

G (A Child) *v.* South Gloucestershire Council [2000] Ed. C.R. 401; [2000] E.L.R. 136, QBD . . . . *Digested,* 00/**1950**

G (A Minor), Re see R. *v.* Governor of Glen Parva Young Offender Institution Ex p. G (A Minor)

G (A Minor) (Adoption Order), Re; *sub nom* J (A Minor) (Adoption Order), Re [1999] 1 F.L.R. 400; [1999] 1 F.C.R. 482; [1999] Fam. Law 9; (1999) 163 J.P.N. 414; *Times,* October 14, 1998, CA . . . . *Digested,* 98/**2370**

G (A Minor) (Care Orders: Threshold Conditions), Re; *sub nom* G (A Minor) (Care Proceedings), Re [1995] Fam. 16; [1994] 3 W.L.R. 1211; [1994] 2 F.L.R. 69; 93 L.G.R. 162; [1994] Fam. Law 485, Fam Div . . . . *Digested,* 95/**3401**:
Considered, 99/2358

G (A Minor) (Care Proceedings), Re see G (A Minor) (Care Orders: Threshold Conditions), Re

G (A Minor) (Care Proceedings: Disclosure), Re see G (A Minor) (Social Worker: Disclosure), Re

G (A Minor) (Child Protection: Investigations), Re see G (A Minor) (Social Worker: Disclosure), Re

G (A Minor) (Leave to Appeal: Jurisdiction), Re [1999] 1 F.L.R. 771; [1999] 3 F.C.R. 281; [1999] Fam. Law 292, CA. . . . . *Digested,* 99/**2391**

G (A Minor) (Social Worker: Disclosure), Re; *sub nom* G (A Minor) (Care Proceedings: Disclosure), Re; G (A Minor) (Child Protection: Investigations), Re [1996] 1 W.L.R. 1407; [1996] 2 All E.R. 65; [1996] 1 F.L.R. 276; [1996] 3 F.C.R. 77; (1996) 31 B.M.L.R. 175; [1996] Fam. Law 143; (1996) 146 N.L.J. 85; *Times,* November 14, 1995; *Independent,* December 8, 1995, CA . . . . *Digested,* 97/**378**:
Considered, 98/2389

G (A Minor) *v.* Calderdale MBC (1999) 99(2) Q.R. 7, CC (Bradford) [*Ex rel.* Rhodes Thain & Collinson Solicitors, 27 Harrison Road, Halifax] . . . . *Digested,* 99/**1603**

G (Care Proceedings: Threshold Conditions), Re see G (Children) (Care Order: Evidence), Re

G (Chambers Proceedings: McKenzie Friend), Re [1999] 1 W.L.R. 1828 (Note); [1999] 2
F.L.R. 59; [1999] Fam. Law 454, CA . . . . *Digested*, 99/**43**
G (Children) (Adoption Proceedings: Representation of Parents), Re [2001] 1 F.C.R. 353;
(2001) 165 J.P.N. 625, CA. . . . . *Digested*, 01/**2644**
G (Children) (Care Order: Evidence), Re; *sub nom* G (Children) (Care Order: Threshold
Criteria), Re; G (Care Proceedings: Threshold Conditions), Re [2001] EWCA
Civ 968; [2001] 1 W.L.R. 2100; [2001] 2 F.L.R. 1111; [2001] 2 F.C.R. 757;
[2001] Fam. Law 727; (2001) 98(29) L.S.G. 37; (2001) 145 S.J.L.B. 166; *Times*,
July 5, 2001; *Independent*, June 28, 2001, CA . . . . *Digested*, 01/**2569**
G (Children) (Care Order: Threshold Criteria), Re see G (Children) (Care Order: Evidence),
Re
G (Children) (Care Proceedings: Wasted Costs), Re; *sub nom* G, S and M (Children)
(Wasted Costs), Re; G, S and H (Care Proceedings: Wasted Costs), Re [2000]
Fam. 104; [2000] 2 W.L.R. 1007; [1999] 4 All E.R. 371; [2000] 1 F.L.R. 52;
[1999] 3 F.C.R. 303; [2000] Fam. Law 24, Fam Div . . . . *Digested*, 00/**2466**:
                                                   Considered, 00/2554
G (CICB: Quantum: 1998), Re (Unreported, March 24, 1998), CICB (London) [*Ex rel.*
Timothy Briden, Barrister, 8 Stone Buildings, Lincoln's Inn, London] . . . . *Digested*, 98/**1494**
G (Minors) (Celebrities: Publicity), Re [1999] 1 F.L.R. 409; [1999] 3 F.C.R. 181; [1999] Fam.
Law 141; *Times*, October 28, 1998, CA . . . . *Digested*, 98/**7**
G v. A Borough Council [2000] Fam. Law 11, CC (Llangefni)
G v. Aldridge (President of the Special Education Needs Tribunal) see G v. Barnet LBC
(No.2)
G v. Barnet LBC [1998] Ed. C.R. 30; [1998] E.L.R. 480, QBD . . . . *Digested*, 98/**1966**
G v. Barnet LBC (No.2); G v. Aldridge (President of the Special Education Needs
Tribunal) [1999] E.L.R. 161, QBD . . . . *Digested*, 99/**1880**:
                                           Distinguished, 01/2037
G v. C (Residence Order: Committal); *sub nom* C v. G [1998] 1 F.L.R. 43; [1998] 1
F.C.R. 592; [1997] Fam. Law 785; *Times*, October 14, 1996, CA. . . . . *Digested*, 96/**2833**
G v. DPP [1998] Q.B. 919; [1998] 2 W.L.R. 609; [1997] 2 All E.R. 755; [1997] 2 Cr.
App. R. 78; (1997) 161 J.P. 498; [1997] 2 F.L.R. 810; [1998] Fam. Law 12,
QBD . . . . *Digested*, 97/**1173**
G v. F (Contact and Shared Residence: Applications for Leave) see G v. F (Shared
Residence: Parental Responsibility)
G v. F (Contact: Allegations of Violence) [1999] Fam. Law 809, Fam Div
G v. F (Non Molestation Order: Jurisdiction); *sub nom* G v. G (Non Molestation Order:
Jurisdiction) [2000] Fam. 186; [2000] 3 W.L.R. 1202; [2000] 2 F.L.R. 533;
[2000] 2 F.C.R. 638; [2000] Fam. Law 519; [2000] Fam. Law 703; (2000)
97(25) L.S.G. 40; *Times*, May 24, 2000, Fam Div . . . . *Digested*, 00/**2542**
G v. F (Shared Residence: Parental Responsibility); *sub nom* G v. F (Contact and
Shared Residence: Applications for Leave) [1998] 2 F.L.R. 799; [1998] 3 F.C.R.
1; [1998] Fam. Law 587, Fam Div. . . . . *Digested*, 98/**2443**
G v. G (Financial Provision: Separation Agreement) [2000] 2 F.L.R. 18; [2000] Fam.
Law 472, Fam Div . . . . *Digested*, 00/**2532**
G v. G (Minors: Custody Appeal) [1985] 1 W.L.R. 647; [1985] 2 All E.R. 225; [1985]
F.L.R. 894; [1985] Fam. Law 321; (1985) 83 L.S.G. 2010; (1985) 82 L.S.G.
2010; (1985) 135 N.L.J. 439; (1985) 129 S.J. 315, HL . . . . *Digested*, 85/**2594**:
         Applied, 86/2145, 86/2189, 86/2196, 87/1773, 87/2489, 87/2490, 87/2527,
         91/2553, 92/3032, 94/2155, 94/3191, 94/3263, 95/3372, 95/3390,
         95/3468, 95/3469, 95/3474, 95/3486, 95/3489, 95/3493, 95/3503,
         95/3561, 95/3563, 96/563, 96/604, 96/607, 96/614, 96/6976:
         Approved, 98/2398: *Considered*, 86/2182, 87/3119, 88/2345, 88/2952,
         89/2410, 89/2459, 89/2466, 90/3125, 94/55, 95/67, 95/3386, 95/3498,
         95/3532, 96/608, 97/384, 00/2489: *Distinguished*, 88/2935:
         Explained, 87/2439: *Followed*, 86/1099, 86/2068, 86/2201, 96/560,
         96/609: *Referred to*, 86/3641, 94/3220
G v. G (Non Molestation Order: Jurisdiction) see G v. F (Non Molestation Order:
Jurisdiction)
G v. G (Occupation Order: Conduct) [2000] 2 F.L.R. 36; [2000] 3 F.C.R. 53; [2000]
Fam. Law 466, CA . . . . *Digested*, 00/**2548**
G v. G (Periodical Payments: Jurisdiction to Vary) [1998] Fam. 1; [1997] 2 W.L.R. 614;
[1997] 1 All E.R. 272; [1997] 1 F.L.R. 368; [1997] 1 F.C.R. 441; [1996] Fam. Law
722; (1997) 161 J.P.N. 86, CA . . . . *Digested*, 97/**2489**:
                                          Disapproved, 00/2533
G v. Germany (1989) 60 D. & R. 256, Eur Comm HR . . . . *Considered*, 98/3084
G v. Italy see S v. Italy
G v. Minister of Health and Community Services 7 B.H.R.C. 615, Sup Ct (Can) . . . . *Digested*, 00/**3226**
G v. Southampton and South West Hampshire HA [2001] EWCA Civ 855, CA;
affirming (2001) 57 B.M.L.R. 148, QBD . . . . *Digested*, 01/**4456**
G v. United Kingdom (Children: Right of Contact) (32346/96) [2001] 1 F.L.R. 153;
[2000] 3 F.C.R. 193; (2001) 33 E.H.R.R. 1; 2001 Fam. L.R. 103; [2000] Fam.
Law 880; *Times*, November 1, 2000, ECHR . . . . *Digested*, 00/**3232**
G v. Wakefield MDC see R. v. Wakefield MDC Ex p. G

G Lawrence Wholesale Meat Co Ltd *v.* Citigen (London) Ltd see City of London *v.* Reeve & Co Ltd

G Percy Trentham Ltd *v.* Archital Luxfer Ltd [1993] 1 Lloyd's Rep. 25; 63 B.L.R. 44, CA .   *Digested*, 93/**294**: *Considered*, 00/812

G Scammell and Nephew Ltd *v.* HC&JG Ouston [1941] A.C. 251, HL . . . .   *Applied*, 53/660, 68/35: *Considered*, 00/837: *Distinguished*, 53/661

G&C Kreglinger *v.* New Patagonia Meat & Cold Storage Co Ltd; *sub nom* Kreglinger *v.* New Patagonia Meat & Cold Storage Co Ltd [1914] A.C. 25, HL. . . . .   *Applied*, 65/2548, 69/2291, 78/2023, 01/4876: *Followed*, 60/2030, 67/2533

G&GB Hewitt Ltd *v.* SA Namur-Assurances du Credit [1999] 1 All E.R. (Comm.) 851; (1999) 96(10) L.S.G. 30; (1999) 143 S.J.L.B. 59; *Times*, March 8, 1999, CA . . .   *Digested*, 99/**3386**

G-A (A Child), Re see A (A Child) (Permission to Remove Child from Jurisdiction: Human Rights), Re

G's application, Re see R. *v.* Devon CC Ex p. George

G, S and H (Care Proceedings: Wasted Costs), Re see G (Children) (Care Proceedings: Wasted Costs), Re

G, S and M (Children) (Wasted Costs), Re see G (Children) (Care Proceedings: Wasted Costs), Re

GAB Robins Holdings Ltd *v.* Specialist Computer Centres [1999] 15 Const. L.J. 43, CA   *Digested*, 99/**543**

Gabalfrisa SL *v.* Agencia Estatal de Administracion Tributaria (AEAT) (C147/98) [2000] E.C.R. I-1577; [2000] S.T.I. 502, ECJ . . . .   *Applied*, 01/5577

Gabriel *v.* Schlank & Schick GmbH (5 Nd 522/99) [2000] I.L.Pr. 677, OGH (A)

Gaddafi *v.* Telegraph Group Ltd (No.1) [2000] E.M.L.R. 431, CA . . . .   *Digested*, 99/**1626**

Gaddie *v.* Mitie Group Plc (Unreported, January 13, 2000), CC (Cheltenham) [*Ex rel.* Archna Dawar, Barrister, Assize Court Chambers, 14 Small Street, Bristol] . . . . .   *Digested*, 00/**1701**

Gadget Shop Ltd *v.* Bug.Com Ltd [2001] C.P. Rep. 13; [2001] F.S.R. 26; (2001) 24(1) I.P.D. 24004; (2000) 97(27) L.S.G. 38; *Times*, June 28, 2000, Ch D . . . .   *Digested*, 00/**564**

Gaffoor (Abdul) Trustees *v.* Ceylon Commissioner of Income Tax see Caffoor (Trustees of the Abdul Gaffoor Trust) *v.* Income Tax Commissioner (Colombo)

Gafford *v.* Graham (1999) 77 P. & C.R. 73; [1999] 3 E.G.L.R. 75; [1999] 41 E.G. 159; (1999) 96(40) L.S.G. 44; (1998) 95(21) L.S.G. 36; (1998) 142 S.J.L.B. 155; [1998] N.P.C. 66; *Times*, May 1, 1998, CA . . . .   *Digested*, 98/**4341**

Gahan *v.* Mattison Scaffolding & Cradle Contractors see Gahan *v.* Szerelmey (UK) Ltd

Gahan *v.* Szerelmey (UK) Ltd; Gahan *v.* Mattison Scaffolding & Cradle Contractors [1996] 1 W.L.R. 439; [1996] 2 All E.R. 291; [1996] P.I.Q.R. P83; (1995) 92(43) L.S.G. 26; (1995) 139 S.J.L.B. 246; *Times*, November 16, 1995, CA . . . .   *Digested*, 95/**3891**: *Cited*, 99/548

Gaillard *v.* Chekili (C518/99) [2001] E.C.R. I-2771; [2001] I.L.Pr. 33, ECJ (6th Chamber) [2000] I.L.Pr. 695, App (Brussels) . . . .   *Digested*, 01/**823**

Gaiman *v.* National Association for Mental Health [1971] Ch. 317; [1970] 3 W.L.R. 42; [1970] 2 All E.R. 362; 114 S.J. 416, Ch D . . . .   *Digested*, 70/**280**: *Considered*, 94/432, 01/3460

Gairy *v.* Attorney General of Grenada [2001] UKPC 30; [2001] 3 W.L.R. 779; *Times*, June 25, 2001, PC (Gren) . . . .   *Digested*, 01/**849**

Gala Leisure Ltd *v.* Secretary of State for the Environment, Transport and the Regions (2001) 82 P. & C.R. 11; [2001] J.P.L. 844 (Note); [2000] E.G.C.S. 135, QBD (Admin Ct) . . . .   *Digested*, 01/**4677**

Galashiels Gas Co Ltd *v.* Millar; *sub nom* Millar *v.* Galashiels Gas Co Ltd [1949] A.C. 275; [1949] 1 All E.R. 319; 1949 S.C. 31; 1949 S.C. (H.L.) 31; 1949 S.L.T. 223; 65 T.L.R. 76; 47 L.G.R. 213; [1949] L.J.R. 540; 93 S.J. 71, HL; affirming 1948 S.C. 191; 1948 S.L.T. 282; 1948 S.L.T. (Notes) 15, 2 Div; affirming 1947 S.L.T. (Notes) 46, OH . . . .   *Digested*, 49/**1552**: *Applied*, 74/3240: *Considered*, 99/2880, 00/4228: *Distinguished*, 53/1441, 53/2513, 55/1078, 59/2062, 60/1994: *Followed*, 52/1386

Galaxy Electronics Pty Ltd *v.* Sega Enterprises [1997-98] Info. T.L.R. 203, Fed Ct (Aus) (Full Ct) . . . .   *Digested*, 98/**3444**

Galaxy Energy International Ltd *v.* Assuranceforeningen Skuld (Ejensidie) (The Oakwell) [1999] 1 Lloyd's Rep. 249; [1999] C.L.C. 216, QBD (Comm Ct) . . . .   *Digested*, 99/**4463**

Galaxy Energy International Ltd *v.* Bayoil SA (The Ama Ulgen) [2001] 1 All E.R. (Comm) 289; [2001] 1 Lloyd's Rep. 512, CA . . . .   *Digested*, 01/**4949**

Galaxy Energy International Ltd (BVI) *v.* Eurobunker SpA [2001] 2 All E.R. (Comm) 912; [2001] 2 Lloyd's Rep. 725; [2001] C.L.C. 1725, QBD (Comm Ct)

Galaxy Energy International Ltd *v.* Novorossiysk Shipping Co (The Petr Schmidt) [1998] 2 Lloyd's Rep. 1; [1998] C.L.C. 894; *Times*, March 26, 1998, CA; affirming [1997] 1 Lloyd's Rep. 284; [1997] C.L.C. 402; *Independent*, January 13, 1997 (C.S.), QBD (Comm Ct) . . . .   *Digested*, 98/**4415**

Galbraith *v.* Grimshaw [1910] A.C. 508, HL; affirming [1910] 1 K.B. 339, CA. . . . .   *Applied*, 01/3835: *Considered*, 78/2376, 97/3045

GALDERMA/Benzimidazole Derivatives (T1129/97) [2001] E.P.O.R. 59, EPO (Technical Bd App)

Gale v. Superdrug Stores Plc [1996] 1 W.L.R. 1089; [1996] 3 All E.R. 468; [1996] P.I.Q.R. P330; (1996) 93(19) L.S.G. 29; (1996) 140 S.J.L.B. 124; *Times*, May 2, 1996, CA .... *Digested*, 96/**759**:
Cited, 99/499, 01/412: *Considered*, 97/1047, 00/353, 00/355, 01/548: *Distinguished*, 00/354

Galeforce Pleating Co Ltd, Re [1999] 2 B.C.L.C. 704, Ch D (Companies Ct) .... *Digested*, 00/**656**

Galeries Segoura Sprl v. Firma Rahim Bonakdarian (C25/76) [1976] E.C.R. 1851; [1977] 1 C.M.L.R. 361, ECJ .... *Digested*, 77/**1243**:
Applied, 85/1452: *Considered*, 01/937: *Distinguished*, 01/800

Galgate Cricket Club v. Doyle (Valuation Officer) [2001] R.A. 21, Lands Tr .... *Digested*, 01/**4830**

Galileo Group Ltd, Re; *sub nom* Company (No.003025 of 1997), Re; Elles v. Hambros Bank Ltd [1999] Ch. 100; [1998] 2 W.L.R. 364; [1998] 1 All E.R. 545; [1998] B.C.C. 228; [1998] 1 B.C.L.C. 318; (1997) 94(46) L.S.G. 30; (1998) 142 S.J.L.B. 21; *Times*, December 10, 1997, Ch D .... *Digested*, 98/**306**

Gallagher v. Airtours Holidays Ltd (Unreported, October 23, 2000), CC (Preston) [*Ex rel*. Alan Saggerson, Barrister, No.1 Serjeants' Inn, London] .... *Digested*, 01/**4280**

Gallagher v. Bond Pearce [2001] 6 Q.R. 15, CC (Plymouth) [*Ex rel*. Gaurang Naik, Barrister, 9 Gough Square, London] .... *Digested*, 01/**1668**

Gallagher v. Castle Vale Action Trust Ltd [2001] EWCA Civ 944; (2001) 33 H.L.R. 72, CA

Gallagher v. Jones (Inspector of Taxes) see Threlfall v. Jones (Inspector of Taxes)

Gallaher Ltd v. Customs and Excise Commissioners [2000] B.V.C. 2189; [2000] S.T.I. 529, V&DTr

Galliard Homes Ltd v. J Jarvis & Sons Plc see Jarvis Interiors Ltd v. Galliard Homes Ltd

Gallie v. Lee see Saunders (Executrix of the Estate of Rose Maud Gallie) v. Anglia Building Society (formerly Northampton Town and County Building Society) (Costs)

Galloppa v. Galloppa see Debtor (No.68-SD-1997), Re

Galloway (CICB: Quantum: 1998), Re (Unreported, May 13, 1998), CICB (York) [*Ex rel*. Andrew McNamara, Barrister, 50 High Pavement, Nottingham, NG1 1HW] ..... *Digested*, 98/**1657**

Galloway v. Guardian Royal Exchange (UK) Ltd [1999] Lloyd's Rep. I.R. 209, CA ..... *Digested*, 99/**3391**

Galoo Ltd v. Bright Grahame Murray [1994] 1 W.L.R. 1360; [1994] 1 All E.R. 16; [1994] B.C.C. 319; *Times*, January 14, 1994, CA .... *Digested*, 95/**3691**:
Applied, 96/3588, 00/4186: *Considered*, 95/2562, 97/2661, 98/4002, 98/4989, 00/4249, 01/938, 01/5900: *Referred to*, 96/1272, 97/4871

Gambill (No.1), Re (Unreported, August 12, 1997), CICB (Liverpool) [*Ex rel*. Christopher J Buckley, Barrister, First National Chambers, 24 Fenwick Street, Liverpool] ..... *Digested*, 97/**1846**

Gambill (No.2) (CICB: Quantum: 1997), Re (Unreported, August 12, 1997), CICB (Liverpool) [*Ex rel*. Christopher J Buckley, Barrister First National Chambers, Second Floor, 24 Fenwick Street, Liverpool] .... *Digested*, 98/**1532**

Gamble v. Rowe (Inspector of Taxes) [1998] S.T.C. 1247; 71 T.C. 190; [1998] B.T.C. 456, Ch D .... *Digested*, 99/**4724**

Games Workshop Ltd v. Customs and Excise Commissioners [2001] S.T.I. 618, V&DTr

Gan v. Wood [1998] E.G.C.S. 77, CA

Gan Insurance Co Ltd v. Tai Ping Insurance Co Ltd (No.1); Royal Reinsurance Co Ltd v. Central Insurance Co Ltd [1999] 2 All E.R. (Comm) 54; [1999] C.L.C. 1270; [1999] I.L.Pr. 729; *Independent*, June 30, 1999, CA; affirming [1998] C.L.C. 1072; [1999] Lloyd's Rep. I.R. 229, QBD (Comm Ct) .... *Digested*, 99/**3426**

Gan Insurance Co Ltd v. Tai Ping Insurance Co Ltd (No.2) [2001] EWCA Civ 1047; [2001] 2 All E.R. (Comm) 299; [2001] C.L.C. 1103; [2001] Lloyd's Rep. I.R. 667, CA .... *Digested*, 01/**3839**

Gan Insurance Co Ltd v. Tai Ping Insurance Co Ltd (Preliminary Issues) [2001] C.L.C. 776; [2001] Lloyd's Rep. I.R. 291, QBD (Comm Ct) .... *Digested*, 01/**3834**

Gander Music Ltd's Trade Mark Application see MESSIAH FROM SCRATCH Trade Mark

Gangadeen v. Secretary of State for the Home Department see R. v. Secretary of State for the Home Department Ex p. Gangadeen

Gangway Ltd v. Caledonian Park Investments (Jersey) Ltd [2001] 2 Lloyd's Rep. 715, QBD (Comm Ct)

Gao Yao v. Council of the European Union (C75/92) [1994] E.C.R. I-3141, ECJ ...... *Distinguished*, 00/720

Gapper v. Chief Constable of Avon and Somerset [2000] Q.B. 29; [1999] 2 W.L.R. 928; [1998] 4 All E.R. 248, CA .... *Digested*, 98/**912**

Garage Molenheide BVBA v. Belgium (C286/94); Schepens v. Belgium (C340/95); Bureau Rik Decan-Business Research & Development NV (BRD) v. Belgium (C401/95); Sanders BVBA v. Belgium (C47/96) [1998] All E.R. (E.C.) 61; [1998] S.T.C. 126; [1997] E.C.R. I-7281; [1998] 1 C.M.L.R. 1186; [1998] C.E.C. 208; [1998] B.T.C. 5088; [1998] B.V.C. 106, ECJ (5th Chamber) .... *Digested*, 98/**4931**:
Applied, 00/5356

Garamella v. New York Medical College [1999] Lloyd's Rep. Med. 343, US Ct

Garces v. Secretary of State for the Home Department [1999] I.N.L.R. 460, IAT ...... *Digested*, 00/**3323**

Garcia Ruiz v. Spain (30544/96) (2001) 31 E.H.R.R. 22, ECHR .... *Digested*, 01/**3500**

Gardener v. Lewis [1998] 1 W.L.R. 1535; (1998) 142 S.J.L.B. 237; *Times*, July 25, 1998, PC (Jam) .... *Digested*, 98/**4376**

Gardiner v. South Essex HA (Unreported, December 10, 1998), QBD .... *Considered*, 99/1422

Gardiner Fire Ltd *v.* Jones (1998) 95(44) L.S.G. 35; (1998) 142 S.J.L.B. 271; *Times,*
    October 22, 1998; *Independent,* October 23, 1998, CA . . . .   *Digested,* 98/**51**:
    Applied, 01/49
Gardner, Re Unreported, CA . . . .   *Considered,* 99/2417
Gardner (A Minor) (CICB: Quantum: 1998), Re (Unreported, February 19, 1998), CICB
    (Durham) [*Ex rel.* Simon Wood, Barrister, Trinity Chambers, 9-12 Trinity Chare,
    Quayside, Newcastle upon Tyne] . . . .   *Digested,* 98/**1529**
Gardner (John Lewis) (CICB: Quantum: 1998), Re (1998) 98(3) Q.R. 5, CICB (Durham)
    Digested, 98/**1504**

Gardner (Michelle) (CICB: Quantum: 1998), Re (Unreported, February 19, 1998), CICB
    (Durham) [*Ex rel.* Simon Wood, Barrister, Trinity Chambers, 9-12 Trinity Chare,
    Quayside, Newcastle upon Tyne] . . . .   *Digested,* 98/**1541**
Gardner *v.* Davis [1999] E.H.L.R. 13; (1998) 95(29) L.S.G. 28; [1998] N.P.C. 123, CA. .   *Digested,* 99/**4071**
Gardner *v.* Marsh & Parsons [1997] 1 W.L.R. 489; [1997] 3 All E.R. 871; [1997]
    P.N.L.R. 362; (1998) 75 P. & C.R. 319; [1997] 1 E.G.L.R. 111; [1997] 15 E.G. 137;
    [1996] E.G.C.S. 186; (1996) 93(46) L.S.G. 28; (1996) 140 S.J.L.B. 262;
    [1996] N.P.C. 162; *Times,* December 2, 1996, CA . . . .   *Digested,* 97/**3843**
Gardner *v.* Moore [1984] A.C. 548; [1984] 2 W.L.R. 714; [1984] 1 All E.R. 1100;
    [1984] 2 Lloyd's Rep. 135; [1984] R.T.R. 209; (1984) 81 L.S.G. 1444; (1984)
    128 S.J. 282, HL . . . .   *Digested,* 84/**3050**:
    Applied, 01/3843

Gargano, Re (Unreported, July 22, 1998), CICB (London) [*Ex rel.* John Bassett, Barrister,
    5 Essex Court, Temple, London] . . . .   *Digested,* 99/**1521**
Gargaro (t/a Spex Opticians) *v.* Customs and Excise Commissioners [2000] S.T.I. 1167,
    V&DTr
Garland *v.* United Kingdom (28120/95) (2001) 29 E.H.R.R. CD81, ECHR
Garner *v.* Cleggs [1983] 1 W.L.R. 862; [1983] 2 All E.R. 398, CA . . . .   *Digested,* 83/**3023**:
    Applied, 00/425: *Considered,* 95/3997
Garner (Inspector of Taxes) *v.* Pounds see Garner (Inspector of Taxes) *v.* Pounds
    Shipowners & Shipbreakers Ltd
Garner (Inspector of Taxes) *v.* Pounds Shipowners & Shipbreakers Ltd; *sub nom*
    Pounds Shipowners & Shipbreakers Ltd *v.* Garner (Inspector of Taxes); Garner
    (Inspector of Taxes) *v.* Pounds [2000] 1 W.L.R. 1107; [2000] 3 All E.R. 218;
    [2000] S.T.C. 420; [2000] 2 E.G.L.R. 69; [2000] 34 E.G. 84; 72 T.C. 561;
    [2000] B.T.C. 190; [2000] S.T.I. 783; [2000] E.G.C.S. 62; (2000) 97(23) L.S.G.
    41; [2000] N.P.C. 58; *Times,* May 19, 2000; *Independent,* May 24, 2000, HL;
    affirming [1999] S.T.C. 19; [1998] B.T.C. 495; [1998] E.G.C.S. 172; *Times,*
    December 1, 1998, CA; reversing [1997] S.T.C. 551; [1997] B.T.C. 223; (1997)
    94(11) L.S.G. 35; (1997) 141 S.J.L.B. 71; *Times,* March 6, 1997; *Independent,*
    April 21, 1997 (C.S.), Ch D . . . .   *Digested,* 00/**4922**
Garner *v.* Secretary of State for the Environment (1998) 75 P. & C.R. 273, QBD . . . . . .   *Digested,* 97/**4063**
Garner *v.* Stonestreet, *Times,* May 28, 1999, CA . . . .   *Digested,* 99/**430**
Garofalo *v.* Ministero della Sanita (C69/96); Garofalo *v.* Unita Sanitaria Locale (USL)
    No.58 di Palermo (C69/96 to C79/96) [1997] E.C.R. I-5603; [1998] 1 C.M.L.R.
    1087, ECJ
Garofalo *v.* Unita Sanitaria Locale (USL) No.58 di Palermo (C69/96 to C79/96) see
    Garofalo *v.* Ministero della Sanita (C69/96)
Garrow *v.* Society of Lloyd's [2000] C.L.C. 241; [1999] B.P.I.R. 885; [2000] Lloyd's
    Rep. I.R. 38; (1999) 96(42) L.S.G. 40; *Times,* October 28, 1999, CA; affirming
    [1999] B.P.I.R. 668; *Times,* June 18, 1999, Ch D . . . .   *Digested,* 99/**3315**
Garry *v.* Ealing LBC see Ealing LBC *v.* Garry
Garside *v.* Bradford & Northern Housing Association Ltd (Unreported, July 17, 2001),
    CC (Blackpool) [*Ex rel.* Langleys Solicitors, Queens House, Micklegate, York] . .   *Digested,* 01/**4498**
Garston *v.* Scottish Widows Fund & Life Assurance Society [1998] 1 W.L.R. 1583;
    [1998] 3 All E.R. 596; [1998] L. & T.R. 230; [1998] 2 E.G.L.R. 73; [1998] 32
    E.G. 88; [1998] E.G.C.S. 101; (1998) 95(26) L.S.G. 32; (1998) 142 S.J.L.B. 199;
    [1998] N.P.C. 109; *Times,* July 14, 1998; *Independent,* July 7, 1998, CA;
    reversing [1996] 1 W.L.R. 834; [1996] 4 All E.R. 282; [1996] 1 E.G.L.R. 113;
    [1996] 23 E.G. 131; [1996] N.P.C. 49, Ch D . . . .   *Digested,* 98/**3614**
Garton (t/a The Dolly Tub) *v.* Customs and Excise Commissioners [2000] S.T.I. 41, V&DTr
Garvin *v.* City of London Police Authority [1944] K.B. 358, KBD . . . .   *Considered,* 55/351,
    55/2193, 94/2201, 95/1980, 96/4862: *Explained,* 99/4299:
    Followed, 47-51/7361, 47-51/7864, 47-51/7882
Garyfallou AEBE *v.* Greece (1999) 28 E.H.R.R. 344, ECHR . . . .   *Digested,* 99/**3129**
Gas Council *v.* Eldridge see Solihull Corp *v.* Gas Council
GASCO/Solid lipid microspheres (T79/99) [2000] E.P.O.R. 419, EPO (Technical Bd App)
    Digested, 00/**3670**
Gascoine *v.* Wharton (Inspector of Taxes) [1996] S.T.C. 1481; 69 T.C. 147; *Times,*
    October 25, 1996, Ch D . . . .   *Digested,* 96/**3399**
Gashi *v.* Secretary of State for the Home Department [1997] I.N.L.R. 96, IAT . . . .   *Digested,* 98/**3243**:
    Followed, 98/3206: *Referred to,* 98/3197
Gashi *v.* Secretary of State for the Home Department (Certified Case) see R. *v.*
    Secretary of State for the Home Department Ex p. Gashi (Besnik)

Gaskill & Chambers Ltd v. Measure Master Ltd [1993] R.P.C. 76, Pat Ct . . . .   *Digested*, 94/**3441**:
Considered, 00/3695

Gasson v. OCS Group Ltd (Unreported, February 16, 2000), QBD [*Ex rel.* Frank R
Moat, Barrister, 3 Pump Court, Temple, London] . . . .   *Digested*, 00/**1513**

Gast v. Germany (29357/95) (2001) 33 E.H.R.R. 37, ECHR

Gasus Dosier und Fordertechnik GmbH v. Netherlands (A/306-B) (1995) 20 E.H.R.R.
403, ECHR . . . .   *Digested*, 96/**3162**:
Applied, 98/3133, 01/3522

Gates v. McKenna [1998] Lloyd's Rep. Med. 405; (1999) 46 B.M.L.R. 9, QBD . . . .   *Digested*, 98/**3916**

Gates v. Owen (Unreported, November 5, 1997) [*Ex rel.* Michael Halsall, Solicitor, 2
The Parks, Newton le Willows, WA12 0NZ] . . . .   *Digested*, 98/**475**

Gates Estate Trust, Re (2000-01) 3 I.T.E.L.R. 113, Royal Ct (Jer)

Gateshead MBC v. B see Gateshead MBC v. L

Gateshead MBC v. Blaydon Rugby Football Club (2000) 15 P.A.D. 44, Planning
Inspector

Gateshead MBC v. L; *sub nom* Gateshead MBC v. B [1996] Fam. 55; [1996] 3 W.L.R.
427; [1996] 3 All E.R. 264; [1996] 2 F.L.R. 179; [1996] 3 F.C.R. 582; [1996]
Fam. Law 401; (1997) 161 J.P. Rep. 10; (1997) 161 J.P.N. 41; *Times*, March 19,
1996, Fam Div. . . . .   *Digested*, 96/**484**:
Applied, 97/366: *Considered*, 99/2312: *Followed*, 99/2352

Gateshead Metropolitan BC v. Fraser (1999) 14 P.A.D. 116, Planning Inspector

Gatewhite Ltd v. Iberia Lineas Aereas de Espana SA [1990] 1 Q.B. 326; [1989] 3
W.L.R. 1080; [1989] 1 All E.R. 944; [1989] 1 Lloyd's Rep. 160; (1989) 86(39)
L.S.G. 35; (1989) 133 S.J. 1337; *Times*, August 8, 1988, QBD (Comm Ct) . . . . .   *Digested*, 89/**252**:
Cited, 00/5164

Gatoil International Inc v. Arkwright-Boston Manufacturers Mutual Insurance Co (The
Sandrina) [1985] A.C. 255; [1985] 2 W.L.R. 74; [1985] 1 All E.R. 129; [1985] 1
Lloyd's Rep. 181; 1985 S.L.T. 68; (1985) 82 L.S.G. 524; (1984) 120 S.J. 870,
HL; reversing 1984 S.L.T. 462; [1985] E.C.C. 119, 2 Div . . . .   *Digested*, 85/**4803**:
Applied, 91/3259, 92/3908, 00/752: *Considered*, 85/555, 91/3205,
93/2556, 95/3098: *Followed*, 99/243

Gatoil International Inc v. Panatlantic Carriers Corp see Gatoil International Inc v. Tradax
Petroleum Ltd (The Rio Sun)

Gatoil International Inc v. Tradax Petroleum Ltd (The Rio Sun); Gatoil International Inc v.
Panatlantic Carriers Corp [1985] 1 Lloyd's Rep. 350, QBD (Comm Ct) . . . .   *Digested*, 85/**3152**:
Considered, 00/899

Gatwick Parking Service Ltd v. Sargent see Gatwick Parking Services Ltd v. Sargent

Gatwick Parking Services Ltd v. Sargent; *sub nom* Gatwick Parking Service Ltd v.
Sargent [2000] 3 P.L.R. 25; [2000] 2 E.G.L.R. 45; [2000] E.G.C.S. 11; (2000)
97(5) L.S.G. 36; (2000) 80 P. & C.R. D18, CA . . . .   *Digested*, 00/**3892**

Gaud v. Leeds HA (1999) 49 B.M.L.R. 105; *Times*, May 14, 1999, CA . . . .   *Digested*, 99/**3975**

Gaudiya Mission v. Brahmachary [1998] Ch. 341; [1998] 2 W.L.R. 175; [1997] 4 All
E.R. 957; *Times*, September 24, 1997, CA; reversing *Times*, April 1, 1997, Ch D . .   *Digested*, 97/**344**

Gautrin v. France (1999) 28 E.H.R.R. 196; [1998] H.R.C.D. 555, ECHR . . . .   *Digested*, 99/**3132**:
Applied, 98/3093

Gavira v. Secretary of State for the Home Department see R. (on the application of
Gavira) v. Secretary of State for the Home Department

Gay v. Sheeran (1998) 76 P. & C.R. D34, CA

Gay v. Sheeran; *sub nom* Enfield LBC v. Gay [2000] 1 W.L.R. 673; [1999] 3 All E.R.
795; [1999] 2 F.L.R. 519; [1999] 2 F.C.R. 705; (1999) 31 H.L.R. 1126; [1999]
Fam. Law 619; (1999) 96(30) L.S.G. 29; [1999] N.P.C. 70; *Times*, June 30,
1999, CA . . . .   *Digested*, 99/**3742**

Gayler v. Better Tasting Products Ltd see Dorricott v. Glennan

Gaynes Park Mansion, Epping, Essex, Re see Rainbow Estates Ltd v. Tokenhold Ltd

Gazzetta v. Instituto Nazionale della Prevedenza Sociale (INPS) (C373/95) see Maso
v. Instituto Nazionale della Prevedenza Sociale (INPS) (C373/95)

Gbaja-Biamila v. DHL International (UK) Ltd [2000] I.C.R. 730, EAT . . . .   *Digested*, 00/**2181**

Gbangbola v. Smith & Sherriff Ltd [1998] 3 All E.R. 730; (1999) 1 T.C.L.R. 136, QBD
(T&CC) . . . .   *Digested*, 98/**235**

GC v. JC see C v. C (Privilege: Criminal Communications)

GE Simplex (Holdings) v. Secretary of State for the Environment (1989) 57 P. & C.R.
306; [1988] 3 P.L.R. 25; [1988] J.P.L. 809; *Times*, June 2, 1988; *Daily Telegraph*,
May 13, 1988, CA . . . .   *Digested*, 89/**3578**:
Applied, 01/4728: *Considered*, 99/4230

GE Trade Mark see General Electric Co Ltd (USA) v. General Electric Co Ltd

GE Tunbridge Ltd, Re [1994] B.C.C. 563; [1995] 1 B.C.L.C. 34, Ch D . . . .   *Digested*, 95/**2818**:
Considered, 01/733

Geall v. Secretary of State for the Environment, Transport and the Regions (1999) 78 P.
& C.R. 264; [1999] 2 P.L.R. 1; [1999] J.P.L. 909; [1998] E.G.C.S. 183; (1999)
96(6) L.S.G. 31; [1998] N.P.C. 165, CA; affirming (1998) 95(41) L.S.G. 46,
Lands Tr . . . .   *Digested*, 99/**4231**:
Followed, 99/4167

Gee v. BBC, *Times*, November 26, 1984 . . . .   *Digested*, 84/**2016**:
Applied, 00/600

Geenty v. Channel Four Television Corp Ltd [1998] E.M.L.R. 524; *Times*, February 11, 1998, CA . . . . *Digested*, 98/**1767**
Geest Plc v. Fyffes Plc [1999] 1 All E.R. (Comm) 672, QBD (Comm Ct) . . . . *Digested*, 99/**857**
Gefco (UK) Ltd v. Mason (No.1) [1998] 2 Lloyd's Rep. 585; [1998] C.L.C. 1468; (1998) 95(31) L.S.G. 35; (1998) 142 S.J.L.B. 206; *Times*, August 24, 1998, CA . . . . *Digested*, 98/**4809**
Gefco (UK) Ltd v. Mason (No.2) [2000] 2 Lloyd's Rep. 555, QBD (Merc Ct) . . . . *Digested*, 01/**949**
Geffroy and Casino France SNC's Reference (C366/98) see Criminal Proceedings against Geffroy (C366/98)
Gehe AG v. NBTY Inc [1999] C.L.C. 1949, QBD (Comm Ct) . . . . *Digested*, 00/**871**
Gelder v. British Steel Plc (Unreported, January 20, 2000), CC (Bury) [*Ex rel.* Whitfield Hallam Goodall Solicitors, 23/25 Henrietta Street, Batley] . . . . *Digested*, 00/**523**
Gemeente Almelo v. Energiebedrijf Ijsellmij NV (C393/92); *sub nom* Municipality of Almelo v. NV Energibedrijf Ijsselmij (C393/92); Commune d'Almelo ea v. NV Energiebedrijf Ijsselmij (C393/92) [1994] E.C.R. I-1477; [1994] 2 C.E.C. 281; *Financial Times*, May 10, 1994, ECJ (5th Chamber) . . . . *Digested*, 94/**4781**:
Applied, 98/2325
Gemeente Arnhem v. BFI Holding BV (C360/96); *sub nom* BFI Holding BV v. Municipality of Arnhem (C360/96) [1999] All E.R. (EC) 709; [1998] E.C.R. I-6821; [2001] 1 C.M.L.R. 6; (2000) 2 L.G.L.R. 245, ECJ . . . . *Digested*, 99/**2274**:
Applied, 99/2280
Gencor ACP Ltd v. Dalby [2000] 2 B.C.L.C. 734; [2001] W.T.L.R. 825, Ch D . . . . *Digested*, 01/**722**:
Applied, 01/705
Gencor Ltd v. Commission of the European Communities (T102/96) (Applications to Intervene) [1997] E.C.R. II-879; [1998] 1 C.M.L.R. 142; [1997] 5 C.M.L.R. 290, CFI (5th Chamber) . . . . *Digested*, 99/**2231**
Gencor Ltd v. Commission of the European Communities (T102/96) [1999] All E.R. (EC) 289; [1999] E.C.R. II-753; [1999] B.C.C. 877; [1999] 4 C.M.L.R. 971; [1999] C.E.C. 395, CFI (5th Chamber) . . . . *Digested*, 99/**692**
GENENTECH I/Polypeptide expression (T292/85) [1989] E.P.O.R. 1, EPO (Technical Bd App) . . . . *Applied*, 00/3629
Genentech Inc v. Delta Biotechnology Ltd (T649/92) see GENENTECH/DNA for HSA (T649/92)
Genentech Inc's European Patent (No.0073646) (T649/92) see GENENTECH/DNA for HSA (T649/92)
GENENTECH/DNA for HSA (T649/92); *sub nom* Genentech Inc's European Patent (No.0073646) (T649/92); Genentech Inc v. Delta Biotechnology Ltd (T649/92) [1998] E.P.O.R. 317; (1997) 20(11) I.P.D. 20113, EPO (Technical Bd App) . . *Subsequent proceedings*, 00/3653
GENENTECH/Human Growth Hormone Production (T158/91) [2001] E.P.O.R. 60, EPO (Technical Bd App)
General Accident Plc v. Chief Constable of Gloucestershire (Unreported, December 31, 1997), CC (Gloucester) [*Ex rel.* Dolmans Solicitors, 17 Windsor Place, Cardiff] . . *Digested*, 98/**4260**
Applied, 00/866
General Electric Co v. MV Nedlloyd 817 F.2d 1022, US Ct. . . . .
General Electric Co Ltd (USA) v. General Electric Co Ltd; *sub nom* GE Trade Mark [1972] 1 W.L.R. 729; [1972] 2 All E.R. 507; [1972] F.S.R. 225; [1973] R.P.C. 297; 116 S.J. 412, HL; reversing [1970] F.S.R. 113; [1970] R.P.C. 339, CA; reversing [1969] F.S.R. 186; [1969] R.P.C. 418, Ch D . . . . *Digested*, 72/**3435**:
Applied, 74/3830, 77/3055: *Considered*, 93/3263, 95/4734, 95/4945, 98/3500: *Followed*, 96/5715, 98/3521
General Feeds Inc Panama v. Slobodna Plovidba Yugoslavia (The Krapan J) [1999] 1 Lloyd's Rep. 688, QBD (Comm Ct) . . . . *Digested*, 99/**244**
General Healthcare Group Ltd v. Customs and Excise Commissioners [2001] S.T.I. 1026, V&DTr
General Hospital Corp's European Patent (No.222886); *sub nom* Bracco SpA Petition for Revocation, Re [2000] F.S.R. 633; (2000) 23(3) I.P.D. 23017, CA; affirming (1999) 22(12) I.P.D. 22115, Pat Ct . . . . *Digested*, 00/**3669**
General Instrument (UK) Ltd v. Customs and Excise Commissioners see Customs and Excise Commissioners v. General Instrument (UK) Ltd
General Medical Council v. BBC [1998] 1 W.L.R. 1573; [1998] 3 All E.R. 426; [1998] E.M.L.R. 833; (1998) 43 B.M.L.R. 143; (1998) 95(25) L.S.G. 32; (1998) 148 N.L.J. 942; (1998) 142 S.J.L.B. 182; *Times*, June 11, 1998; *Independent*, June 17, 1998, CA . . . . *Digested*, 98/**16**
General Mediterranean Holdings SA v. Patel [2000] 1 W.L.R. 272; [1999] 3 All E.R. 673; [1999] C.P.L.R. 425; [1999] 2 Costs L.R. 10; [2000] H.R.L.R. 54; [2000] U.K.H.R.R. 273; [1999] Lloyd's Rep. P.N. 919; [1999] P.N.L.R. 852; (1999) 149 N.L.J. 1145; [1999] N.P.C. 98; *Times*, August 12, 1999, QBD (Comm Ct) . . . *Digested*, 99/**335**:
Applied, 01/552
General Motors Acceptance Corp (UK) Plc v. Customs and Excise Commissioners [1999] B.V.C. 2347; [1999] V. & D.R. 456, V&DTr . . . . *Digested*, 00/**5293**
General Motors Corp v. Yplon SA (C375/97) [1999] All E.R. (EC) 865; [1999] E.C.R. I-5421; [1999] 3 C.M.L.R. 427; [1999] C.E.C. 528; [1999] E.T.M.R. 950; [2000] R.P.C. 572; (1999) 22(11) I.P.D. 22112, ECJ [1999] E.C.R. I-5421; [1999] E.T.M.R. 122, AGO [1998] E.T.M.R. 576, Trib Comm (Tournai) . . . . *Digested*, 00/**3790**

GENERAL MOTORS/Refusal of reimbursement (J32/95) [2000] E.P.O.R. 289, EPO
(Legal Bd App) . . . .   *Digested,* 00/**3656**
General Nursing Council for England and Wales v. St Marylebone BC; *sub nom* General
Nursing Council for England and Wales v. St Marylebone Corp [1959] A.C.
540; [1959] 2 W.L.R. 308; [1959] 1 All E.R. 325; 123 J.P. 169; 57 L.G.R. 101; 4
R.R.C. 53; 52 R. & I.T. 119; 103 S.J. 154, HL; affirming [1958] Ch. 421; [1957] 3
W.L.R. 1039; [1957] 3 All E.R. 685; 122 J.P. 67; 56 L.G.R. 43; 2 R.R.C. 302;
50 R. & I.T. 818; 101 S.J. 973, CA; reversing [1957] 1 W.L.R. 941; [1957] 2 All
E.R. 791; 121 J.P. 497; 55 L.G.R. 450; 2 R.R.C. 80; 50 R. & I.T. 446; 101 S.J. 647,
Ch D . . . .   *Digested,* 59/**2766**:
                    Applied, 58/1387, 58/2846: *Considered,* 01/3849: *Distinguished,* 58/2842,
                                                            59/2771
General Nursing Council for England and Wales v. St Marylebone Corp see General
Nursing Council for England and Wales v. St Marylebone BC
General of Berne Insurance Co Ltd v. Jardine Reinsurance Management Ltd [1998] 1
W.L.R. 1231; [1998] 2 All E.R. 301; [1998] C.L.C. 768; [1998] 1 Costs L.R. 1;
[1998] Lloyd's Rep. I.R. 211; (1998) 95(11) L.S.G. 35; (1998) 142 S.J.L.B. 86;
Times, February 20, 1998, CA; reversing [1997] 2 Costs L.R. 66, QBD . . . .   *Digested,* 98/**469**:
                                                 Considered, 99/411: *Followed,* 00/452
General Tire & Rubber Co v. Firestone Tyre & Rubber Co Ltd (No.1) [1971] F.S.R. 417;
[1972] R.P.C. 457, CA; affirming [1970] F.S.R. 268; [1971] R.P.C. 173, Ch D . . .   *Digested,* 72/**2574**:
                  Applied, 86/972, 86/2496, 93/3041, 95/3756, 95/3778, 96/4557, 97/3902,
                  99/3518: *Considered,* 90/3474, 94/3437, 97/1032, 97/3906, 98/3453,
                  98/3470, 00/3677: *Distinguished,* 94/3433, 94/4489: *Followed,* 97/3901,
                                              98/3477: *Referred to,* 00/3679
General Tire & Rubber Co v. Firestone Tyre & Rubber Co Ltd (No.2) [1975] 1 W.L.R.
819; [1975] 2 All E.R. 173; [1975] F.S.R. 273; [1976] R.P.C. 197; 119 S.J. 389,
HL; reversing in part [1974] F.S.R. 122; [1975] R.P.C. 203, CA; affirming [1973]
F.S.R. 79, Ch D . . . .   *Digested,* 75/**2503**:
                      Applied, 75/2502, 00/3523: *Considered,* 97/1032: *Followed,* 73/2506,
                                          75/2501: *Referred to,* 98/3496
Generale Bank Nederland NV (formerly Credit Lyonnais Bank Nederland NV) v. Export
Credits Guarantee Department see Credit Lyonnais Bank Nederland NV (now
Generale Bank Nederland NV) v. Export Credits Guarantee Department
Generics BV v. Smith Kline & French Laboratories Ltd (C316/95) [1997] E.C.R. I-
3929; [1998] 1 C.M.L.R. 1; [1997] C.E.C. 1046; [1997] R.P.C. 801; (1998) 41
B.M.L.R. 116; (1997) 94(34) L.S.G. 30, ECJ [1997] C.E.C. 1029, HR (NL) . . . . .   *Digested,* 98/**728**:
                                                     Applied, 01/3961
Generics (UK) Ltd v. Smith Kline & French Laboratories Ltd (C191/90) [1992] E.C.R. I-
5335; [1993] 1 C.M.L.R. 89; [1993] F.S.R. 592; [1993] R.P.C. 333; *Times,*
December 8, 1992; *Financial Times,* November 3, 1992, ECJ [1990] 1 C.M.L.R.
416, CA . . . .   *Digested,* 93/**4362**:
                                                    Applied, 97/3892, 98/728
Genira Trade & Finance Inc v. Refco Capital Markets Ltd see Refco Capital Markets Ltd
v. Credit Suisse First Boston Ltd
Genius Holding BV v. Staatssecretaris van Financien (C342/87) [1991] S.T.C. 239;
[1989] E.C.R. 4227, ECJ . . . .   *Digested,* 91/**3648**:
                                                    Considered, 00/5311
GENIUS Trade Mark [1999] R.P.C. 741, TMR . . . .   *Digested,* 99/**3576**
GEOBANK Trade Mark [1999] R.P.C. 682, TMR . . . .   *Digested,* 99/**3528**
Geogas SA v. Trammo Gas Ltd (The Baleares) [1993] 1 Lloyd's Rep. 215; *Times,*
December 1, 1992; *Independent,* November 23, 1992, CA . . . .   *Digested,* 92/**3929**:
                                                    Considered, 99/227
George (CICA: Quantum: 2000), Re (Unreported, July 18, 2000), CICA (Cardiff) [*Ex rel.*
Joan Campbell, Barrister, Chambers of John Charles Rees Q.C., 33 Park Place,
Cardiff] . . . .   *Digested,* 01/**1665**
George v. Brauncewell Quarries Ltd (Unreported, September 7, 2000), CC (Lincoln)
[*Ex rel.* Langleys Solicitors, Newporte House, Doddington Road Business Park,
Lincoln] . . . .   *Digested,* 01/**597**
George (t/a Top Six Hairdressing) v. Customs and Excise Commissioners [2001] S.T.I.
578, V&DTr
George v. Ministry of Defence (Unreported, October 8, 1999), CC (Manchester) [*Ex
rel.* William Waldron, Barrister, Exchange Chambers, Pearl Assurance House,
Derby Square, Liverpool] . . . .   *Digested,* 00/**1636**
George Ballantine & Son Ltd v. FER Dixon & Son Ltd [1974] 1 W.L.R. 1125; [1974] 2 All
E.R. 503; [1974] F.S.R. 415; [1975] R.P.C. 111; 118 S.J. 566, Ch D . . . .   *Digested,* 74/**2940**:
                                                    Applied, 00/5516
George Barkes (London) Ltd v. LFC (1988) Ltd (t/a LFC Insurance Group) [2000]
P.N.L.R. 21, CC (Central London) . . . .   *Digested,* 00/**4251**
George Fischer Holdings Ltd v. Davis Langdon & Everest see George Fischer Holdings
Ltd v. Multi Design Consultants Ltd
George Fischer Holdings Ltd v. Multi Design Consultants Ltd; George Fischer Holdings
Ltd v. Davis Langdon & Everest 61 Con. L.R. 85; *Independent,* May 4, 1998
(C.S.), QBD (OR) . . . .   *Digested,* 98/**808**

George Hensher Ltd *v.* Restawile Upholstery (Lancs) Ltd [1976] A.C. 64; [1974] 2
W.L.R. 700; [1974] 2 All E.R. 420; [1974] F.S.R. 173; [1975] R.P.C. 31; 118 S.J.
329, HL; affirming [1973] 3 W.L.R. 453; [1973] 3 All E.R. 414; [1973] F.S.R.
477; 117 S.J. 615, CA; reversing [1973] 1 W.L.R. 144; [1973] 1 All E.R. 160;
[1972] F.S.R. 557; (1972) 117 S.J. 32, Ch D . . . . *Digested,* 74/**473**:
Applied, 84/426.7: *Considered,* 00/3572
George Mitchell (Chesterhall) Ltd *v.* Finney Lock Seeds Ltd [1983] 2 A.C. 803; [1983]
3 W.L.R. 163; [1983] 2 All E.R. 737; [1983] 2 Lloyd's Rep. 272; [1983] Com.
L.R. 209, HL; affirming [1983] Q.B. 284; [1982] 3 W.L.R. 1036; [1983] 1 All
E.R. 108; [1983] 1 Lloyd's Rep. 168; (1982) 79 L.S.G. 1444; 126 S.J. 689, CA;
affirming [1981] 1 Lloyd's Rep. 476, QBD (Comm Ct) . . . . *Digested,* 83/**3314**:
Applied, 85/385, 87/423, 88/2388, 94/548, 00/895: *Considered,* 92/1553:
Followed, 83/3329
George Roussos Sons SA *v.* Charles M Willie & Co (Shipping) Ltd see Charles M Willie
& Co (Shipping) Ltd *v.* Ocean Laser Shipping Ltd (The Smaro)
George Wimpey & Co *v.* Minister of Housing and Local Government see Jelson *v.*
Minister of Housing and Local Government
GEORGETOWN UNIVERSITY/Pericardial access (T35/99) [2001] E.P.O.R. 21, EPO
(Technical Bd App) . . . . *Digested,* 01/**3954**
Georgiadis *v.* Greece (21522/93) (1997) 24 E.H.R.R. 606, ECHR . . . . *Digested,* 98/**3118**:
Followed, 98/3121
Georgiadis *v.* Greece (41209/98) (2001) 33 E.H.R.R. 22, ECHR
Georgian Maritime Corp *v.* Sealand Industries (Bermuda) Ltd (The North Sea) [1999] 1
Lloyd's Rep. 21; [1998] C.L.C. 1395, CA; affirming [1997] 2 Lloyd's Rep. 324,
QBD (Comm Ct) . . . . *Digested,* 99/**4434**
Georgiou (t/a Marios Chippery) *v.* United Kingdom (40042/98) [2001] S.T.C. 80; 3
I.T.L. Rep. 145; [2001] S.T.I. 70, ECHR . . . . *Digested,* 01/**3522**:
Applied, 01/5291
Gephav SA *v.* Biotherm et Compagnie [1999] E.C.C. 264, Cass (F) . . . . *Digested,* 99/**703**
GEPPERT/ Tensioning Device (T315/87) [2001] E.P.O.R. 47, EPO (Technical Bd App) . *Digested,* 01/**3904**
Geraets-Smits *v.* Stichting Ziekenfonds VGZ (C157/99); Peerbooms *v.* Stichting CZ
Groep Zorgverzekeringen (C157/99) [2001] E.C.R. I-5473; (2001) 62 B.M.L.R.
101; *Times,* September 4, 2001, ECJ . . . . *Digested,* 01/**5133**
Geraghty & Co *v.* Awwad see Awwad *v.* Geraghty & Co
Gerald *v.* Commissioner of Police of the Metropolis, *Times,* June 26, 1998, CA . . . . *Digested,* 98/**1439**
Gerani Compania Naviera SA *v.* Alfred C Toepfer (The Demosthenes V) (No.2) [1982] 1
Lloyd's Rep. 282, QBD (Comm Ct) . . . . *Digested,* 82/**2871**:
Considered, 00/4711
Gerber Garment Technology Inc *v.* Lectra Systems Ltd [1997] R.P.C. 443; [1998]
Masons C.L.R. Rep. 135; (1997) 20(5) I.P.D. 20046; *Times,* January 17, 1997,
CA; reversing in part [1995] R.P.C. 383; [1998] Masons C.L.R. Rep. 64, Pat Ct . *Digested,* 97/**3903**:
Considered, 96/4555, 99/3448: *Distinguished,* 96/1272, 97/1032:
Followed, 98/3496
Gerling Konzern General Insurance Co *v.* Polygram Holdings Inc; Copenhagen
Reinsurance Co (UK) Ltd *v.* Polygram Holdings Inc [1998] 2 Lloyd's Rep. 544,
QBD (Comm Ct) . . . . *Digested,* 99/**3403**
Germany *v.* Commission of the European Communities (18/76) [1979] E.C.R. 343,
ECJ . . . . *Digested,* 80/**1081**:
Followed, 00/170
Germany *v.* Commission of the European Communities (C156/98) [2000] E.C.R. I-
6857; 3 I.T.L. Rep. 159, ECJ
Germany *v.* Commission of the European Communities (C240/90) [1992] E.C.R. I-
5383; *Financial Times,* November 3, 1992, ECJ . . . . *Digested,* 93/**4195**:
Followed, 00/2349
Germany *v.* Commission of the European Communities (C248/84); *sub nom* Regional
Aid Plans (C248/84), Re [1987] E.C.R. 4013; [1989] 1 C.M.L.R. 591, ECJ . . . . *Digested,* 90/**2216**:
Applied, 00/729
Germany *v.* Commission of the European Communities (C263/95) [1998] E.C.R. I-
441; [1998] 2 C.M.L.R. 1235, ECJ
Germany *v.* Commission of the European Communities (C293/96) see Denmark *v.*
Commission of the European Communities (C289/96)
Germany *v.* Commission of the European Communities (C329/93); Hanseatische
Industrie-Beteiligungen GmbH *v.* Commission of the European Communities
(C62/95); Bremer Vulkan Verbund AG *v.* Commission of the European
Communities (C63/95) [1996] E.C.R. I-5151; [1998] 1 C.M.L.R. 591, ECJ (6th
Chamber)
Germany *v.* Commission of the European Communities (C54/91) [1993] E.C.R. I-
3399, ECJ . . . . *Digested,* 93/**4207**:
Followed, 00/2337
Germany *v.* Commission of the European Communities (C54/95) [1999] E.C.R. I-35,
ECJ . . . . *Followed,* 00/2337
Germany *v.* Commission of the European Communities (C8/88); *sub nom* Suckler
Cows (C8/88), Re [1990] E.C.R. I-2321; [1992] 1 C.M.L.R. 409, ECJ . . . . *Followed,* 00/170

Germany *v.* Commission of the European Communities (European Parliament Intervening) (C281/85); *sub nom* Immigration of Non Community Workers (C281/85), Re [1987] E.C.R. 3203; [1988] 1 C.M.L.R. 11; *Times,* September 17, 1987, ECJ . . . . *Digested,* 88/**1498**:
Followed, 88/1879, 89/1984, 00/2415

Germany *v.* Council of the European Communities (C280/93) [1994] E.C.R. I-4973; *Financial Times,* October 11, 1994, ECJ (5th Chamber) . . . . *Digested,* 95/**208**:
Followed, 00/2403

Germany *v.* Council of the European Union (C122/95); *sub nom* Banana Framework Agreement (C122/95), Re [1998] E.C.R. I-973; [1998] 3 C.M.L.R. 570, ECJ

Germany *v.* European Parliament (C233/94); *sub nom* Deposit Guarantee Directive (C233/94), Re [1997] E.C.R. I-2405; [1997] 3 C.M.L.R. 1379, ECJ. . . . . *Followed,* 00/2382

Germany *v.* European Parliament (C376/98); R. *v.* Secretary of State for Health Ex p. Imperial Tobacco Ltd (C74/99) [2000] All E.R. (EC) 769; [2000] E.C.R. I-8419; [2000] 3 C.M.L.R. 1175; *Times,* October 10, 2000, ECJ . . . . *Digested,* 00/**2417**

Germany *v.* Kumar; *sub nom* Kumar, Re [2000] Crim. L.R. 504, QBD

Germany *v.* Sotheby's (No.2) see Gotha City *v.* Sotheby's (No.2)

Germax Securities Ltd *v.* Spiegal (1979) 37 P. & C.R. 204; (1978) 250 E.G. 449; 123 S.J.164, CA . . . . *Digested,* 79/**1586**:
Applied, 80/1584: *Considered,* 98/3598: *Followed,* 91/120

Gerster *v.* Freistaat Bayern (C1/95) [1997] E.C.R. I-5253; [1998] 1 C.M.L.R. 303; [1998] I.C.R. 327; [1997] I.R.L.R. 699; *Times,* November 24, 1997, ECJ (6th Chamber) . . . . *Digested,* 97/**2217**

Gertsch *v.* Aspasia (1999-2000) 2 I.T.E.L.R. 342, Sup Ct (NSW)

Gestevision Telecinco SA *v.* Commission of the European Communities (T95/96) [1998] All E.R. (E.C.) 918; [1998] E.C.R. II-3407; [1998] 3 C.M.L.R. 1112, CFI (3rd Chamber) . . . . *Digested,* 99/**2238**

GF Sharp & Co Ltd *v.* McMillan [1998] I.R.L.R. 632, EAT . . . . *Digested,* 98/**2108**

GH Marshall Ltd, Re see Brownlow *v.* GH Marshall Ltd

Ghazilian's Trade Mark Application; *sub nom* TINY PENIS Trade Mark [2001] R.P.C. 33; (2001) 24 (4) I.P.D. 24027, TMR . . . . *Digested,* 01/**3980**

Ghosh *v.* General Medical Council [2001] UKPC 29; [2001] 1 W.L.R. 1915; [2001] U.K.H.R.R. 987; [2001] Lloyd's Rep. Med. 433; *Times,* June 25, 2001, PC (UK) . . *Digested,* 01/**2894**

Giacomelli Sport SpA's Community Trade Mark Application [2000] E.T.M.R. 277; (2000) 23(12) I.P.D. 23103, OHIM (2nd Bd App) . . . . *Digested,* 00/**3739**

Giambrone *v.* Sunworld Holidays Ltd (Unreported, January 24, 2001), DR (Birmingham) [*Ex rel.* Irwin Mitchell, Solicitors, Imperial House, 31 Temple Street, Birmingham] . . . . *Digested,* 01/**485**

Gibbens *v.* Wood (Unreported, July 4, 2000), CC (Plymouth) [*Ex rel.* Clare Vines, Barrister, 35 Essex Street, London] . . . . *Digested,* 00/**1671**

Gibbons *v.* Gibbons (Unreported, May 11, 1998), CC (Plymouth) [*Ex rel.* Hugh Hamill, Barrister, 12 King's Bench Walk, London] . . . . *Digested,* 98/**2500**

Gibbons *v.* Nelsons (A Firm) [2000] Lloyd's Rep. P.N. 603; [2000] P.N.L.R. 734; [2000] W.T.L.R. 453; (2000) 97(19) L.S.G. 44; *Times,* April 21, 2000, Ch D . . . *Digested,* 00/**4225**

Gibbons *v.* South West Water Services Ltd see AB *v.* South West Water Services Ltd

Gibbs *v.* McDonnell see Hetherington (Deceased), Re

Gibbs *v.* Rea [1998] A.C. 786; [1998] 3 W.L.R. 72; (1998) 142 S.J.L.B. 98; *Times,* February 4, 1998, PC (CI) . . . . *Digested,* 98/**4777**

Gibbs Mew Plc *v.* Gemmell [1999] E.C.C. 97; [1998] Eu. L.R. 588; [1999] 1 E.G.L.R. 43; [1999] 01 E.G. 117; [1998] N.P.C. 124, CA . . . . *Digested,* 99/**688**:
Applied, 01/2519: *Considered,* 99/76, 99/684: *Followed,* 99/680

Giblett *v.* P & NE Murray Ltd (1999) 96(22) L.S.G. 34; *Times,* May 25, 1999, CA . . . . . *Digested,* 99/**3978**

Gibney, Re (1998) 98(1) Q.R. 4; (1997) 97(5/6) Q.R. 8, CICB (Birmingham) . . . . *Digested,* 98/**1527**

Gibson *v.* Chief Constable of Strathclyde see Gibson *v.* Orr

Gibson *v.* East Riding of Yorkshire DC see East Riding of Yorkshire DC *v.* Gibson

Gibson *v.* Orr; *sub nom* Gibson *v.* Chief Constable of Strathclyde 1999 S.C. 420; 1999 S.C.L.R. 661; 1999 Rep. L.R. 78; 1999 G.W.D. 11-520; *Times,* May 11, 1999, OH. . *Digested,* 99/**6370**

Gibson Lea Retail Interiors Ltd *v.* Makro Self Service Wholesalers Ltd [2001] B.L.R. 407, QBD (T&CC) . . . . *Digested,* 01/**854**

Gibson's Settlement Trusts, Re; *sub nom* Mellors *v.* Gibson [1981] Ch. 179; [1981] 2 W.L.R. 1; [1981] 1 All E.R. 233; 125 S.J. 48; *Times,* May 20, 1980, Ch D . . . . *Digested,* 81/**2136**:
Applied, 95/4030: *Considered,* 85/2636, 99/3676

GIE Group Concorde *v.* Master of the Vessel Suhadiwarno Panjan (C440/97) see GIE Groupe Concorde *v.* Master of the Vessel Suhadiwarno Panjan (C440/97)

GIE Groupe Concorde *v.* Master of the Vessel Suhadiwarno Panjan (C440/97); *sub nom* GIE Group Concorde *v.* Master of the Vessel Suhadiwarno Panjan (C440/97) [2000] All E.R. (EC) 865; [1999] 2 All E.R. (Comm) 700; [1999] E.C.R. I-6307; [1999] C.L.C. 1976; [2000] I.L.Pr. 626, ECJ [1999] I.L.Pr. 141, Cass (F) . *Digested,* 00/**764**

Gil Insurance Ltd *v.* Customs and Excise Commissioners [2001] Eu. L.R. 401, V&DTr

Gilbert *v.* Kembridge Fibres [1984] I.C.R. 188; [1984] I.R.L.R. 52; (1984) 134 N.L.J. 256, EAT . . . . *Digested,* 84/**1285**:
Distinguished, 01/2347

Gildert *v.* John Wilman Ltd (Unreported, May 4, 2000), CC (Manchester) [*Ex rel.* Thompsons Solicitors, 8, Exchange Street, Manchester] . . . . *Digested,* 01/**1691**

Gilding v. DPP (1998) 162 J.P.N. 523; *Times*, May 20, 1998, QBD . . . . *Digested*, 98/**1335**
Giles v. Goss (Unreported, March 24, 2000), CC (Newport, Gwent) [*Ex rel.* Andrew
  Arentsen, Barrister, 33 Park Place, Cardiff] . . . . *Digested*, 00/**1563**
Giles v. Rhind [2001] 2 B.C.L.C. 582; (2001) 98(34) L.S.G. 37; (2001) 145 S.J.L.B.
  209; *Times*, August 6, 2001, Ch D . . . . *Digested*, 01/**746**
Giles v. Thompson; Devlin v. Baslington; Sanders v. Templar [1994] 1 A.C. 142; [1993]
  2 W.L.R. 908; [1993] 3 All E.R. 321; [1993] R.T.R. 289; (1993) 143 N.L.J. 884;
  (1993) 137 S.J.L.B. 151; *Times*, June 1, 1993, HL; affirming (1993) 143 N.L.J.
  284; *Times*, January 13, 1993, CA . . . . *Digested*, 93/**3332**:
                                    Applied, 97/3159, 98/1453, 98/2497, 98/2505, 99/2454, 99/2455:
                              Cited, 99/2489: *Considered*, 96/2145, 97/960, 98/1454, 99/1406, 99/2462:
                                    Distinguished, 99/3411, 00/1460: *Followed*, 97/1803, 99/392:
                                                              Referred to, 97/1787, 00/464
Giles v. United Kingdom see McDaid v. United Kingdom
Giles v. Walker (1890) L.R. 24 Q.B.D. 656, QBD . . . . *Applied*, 47-51/4234:
                                    Doubted, 57/241, 57/2578: *Followed*, 98/3933: *Not followed*, 78/2201:
                                                              Overruled, 79/2004, 80/2006
Gilgham v. Immigration Appeal Tribunal; *sub nom* R. v. Immigration Appeal Tribunal Ex
  p. Gilgham [1995] Imm. A.R. 129, CA . . . . *Digested*, 95/**2689**
Gilham v. Browning [1998] 1 W.L.R. 682; [1998] 2 All E.R. 68; (1998) 142 S.J.L.B.
  99; *Times*, February 26, 1998, CA . . . . *Digested*, 98/**616**
Gilham v. Kent CC (No.2) [1985] I.C.R. 233; [1985] I.R.L.R. 18, CA . . . . *Digested*, 85/**1259**:
                                                    Applied, 86/1278, 00/2239, 00/2240
Gilje v. Charlegrove Securities Ltd; *sub nom* Gilje v. Charlgrove Securities Ltd [2001]
  EWCA Civ 1777, CA; affirming [2001] L. & T.R. 17; [2000] 3 E.G.L.R. 89;
  [2000] 44 E.G. 148, Lands Tr . . . . *Digested*, 01/**4194**
Gilje v. Charlgrove Securities Ltd see Gilje v. Charlegrove Securities Ltd
Gilkes v. Venizelos ANESA [2000] I.L.Pr. 487, QBD (Comm Ct) . . . . *Digested*, 00/**756**
Gill v. Cremadez (Unreported, May 22, 2000), CC (Brentford) [*Ex rel.* Alastair Panton,
  Barrister, 10 King's Bench Walk, Temple, London] . . . . *Digested*, 00/**3876**
Gill v. DPP [1998] R.T.R. 166, QBD
Gill v. Hughes (Unreported, March 13, 1998), CC (Chester) [*Ex rel.* Helen Waller, Pupil
  Barrister, Sedan House, Stanley Place, Chester] . . . . *Digested*, 98/**1575**
Gillan v. News Group Newspapers Ltd see Mapp v. News Group Newspapers Ltd
Gillatt v. Sky Television Ltd (formerly Sky Television Plc) [2000] 1 All E.R. (Comm) 461;
  [2000] 2 B.C.L.C. 103, CA . . . . *Digested*, 00/**901**
Gillen's Application, Re [1988] N.I. 40; [1988] 1 N.I.J.B. 47, DC . . . . *Digested*, 88/**2508**:
                                                              Disapproved, 00/5662
Gillenden Development Co Ltd v. Surrey CC (1997) 74 P. & C.R. 119; [1998] 1 P.L.R.
  25; [1997] J.P.L. 944; [1997] E.G.C.S. 4, CA . . . . *Digested*, 97/**4069**
Gillespie (t/a Gillespie Transport) v. Anglo Irish Beef Processors Ltd [1994] N.I. 65, QBD
  (NI) . . . . *Digested*, 00/**5439**
Gillespie v. Northern Health and Social Services Board (C342/93) [1996] All E.R.
  (E.C.) 284; [1996] E.C.R. I-475; [1996] 2 C.M.L.R. 969; [1996] I.C.R. 498;
  [1996] I.R.L.R. 214; (1996) 31 B.M.L.R. 65; *Times*, February 22, 1996, ECJ . . . . *Digested*, 96/**2570**:
                              Applied, 97/2239, 97/2241, 00/2161, 00/2164: *Considered*, 99/2079,
                                                    00/2204: *Followed*, 00/2165
Gillett v. Holt [2001] Ch. 210; [2000] 3 W.L.R. 815; [2000] 2 All E.R. 289; [2000] 2
  F.L.R. 266; [2000] 1 F.C.R. 705; [2000] W.T.L.R. 195; [2000] Fam. Law 714;
  (2000) 97(12) L.S.G. 40; [2000] 144 S.J.L.B. 141; [2000] N.P.C. 25; (2000) 80
  P. & C.R. D3; *Times*, March 17, 2000, CA; reversing [1998] 3 All E.R. 917;
  [1998] 2 F.L.R. 470; [1998] Fam. Law 596; (1998) 95(26) L.S.G. 31; *Times*,
  June 18, 1998, Ch D . . . . *Digested*, 00/**2321**:
                                                    Considered, 01/4859: *Followed*, 01/5158
GILLETTE/Public prior use (T17/91) [1998] E.P.O.R. 310, EPO (Technical Bd App)
Gillick v. West Norfolk and Wisbech AHA [1986] A.C. 112; [1985] 3 W.L.R. 830;
  [1985] 3 All E.R. 402; [1986] Crim. L.R. 113; (1985) 82 L.S.G. 3531; (1985) 135
  N.L.J. 1055; (1985) 129 S.J. 738, HL; reversing [1985] 2 W.L.R. 413; [1985] 1
  All E.R. 533; [1985] Fam. Law 165; (1985) 82 L.S.G. 762; (1985) 135 N.L.J. 81;
  (1985) 129 S.J. 42, CA; reversing [1984] Q.B. 581; [1983] 3 W.L.R. 859;
  [1984] 1 All E.R. 365; (1983) 147 J.P. 888; [1984] Fam. Law 207; (1983) 80
  L.S.G. 2678; (1983) 133 N.L.J. 888; (1983) 127 S.J. 696, QBD . . . . *Digested*, 85/**2230**:
                              Applied, 87/2483, 92/35, 93/2845: *Cited*, 92/2919: *Considered*, 86/19,
                                    90/1571, 91/2512, 93/2730, 94/3234, 95/4105, 99/2681:
                                                    Distinguished, 92/3135: *Referred to*, 94/3229
Gillies v. Craig (Unreported, September 13, 2000), CC (Manchester) [*Ex rel.* DLA &
  Partners, Solicitors, 101 Barbirolli Square, Manchester] . . . . *Digested*, 01/**658**
Gilligan (No.1), Re see R. v. Governor of Belmarsh Prison Ex p. Gilligan
Gillingham v. Gillingham [2001] EWCA Civ 906; [2001] C.P. Rep. 89; [2001] C.P.L.R.
  355, CA; reversing HC-99-02457, Ch D . . . . *Digested*, 01/**633**
Gillings v. Kirklees MBC [1999] Env. L.R. D2, CA
Gillmartin (A Bankrupt), Re [1989] 1 W.L.R. 513; [1989] 2 All E.R. 835; (1989) 86(23)
  L.S.G. 36; (1989) 133 S.J. 877; *Independent*, November 21, 1988 (C.S.), Ch D . *Digested*, 89/**167**:
                                                    Cited, 00/3488: *Considered*, 00/4562

Gilly v. Directeur des Services Fiscaux du Bas-Rhin (C336/96) [1998] All E.R. (E.C.) 826; [1998] S.T.C. 1014; [1998] E.C.R. I-2793; [1998] 3 C.M.L.R. 607; [1998] B.T.C. 335; 1 I.T.L. Rep. 29, ECJ . . . . *Digested*, 98/**4638**

Giloy (Bernd) v. Hauptzollamt Frankfurt am Main-Ost (C130/95) [1997] E.C.R. I-4291 . *Referred to*, 99/3555

Gimblett v. Swansea City Council [2000] 3 Q.R. 5, CC (Neath & Port Talbot) [*Ex rel.* Bryan Thomas, Barrister, 33 Park Place, Cardiff] . . . . *Digested*, 00/**1561**

Gina Shoes Ltd v. Davies (t/a Future) CCRTI 1998/1508/2, CA . . . . *Digested*, 99/**421**

Gina Shoes Ltd v. Medici Ltd (2001) 24(5) I.P.D. 24029, Ch D

Ging v. Ellward (Lancs) Ltd [1991] I.C.R. 222 (Note); (1978) 13 I.T.R. 265, EAT . . . . . . *Digested*, 79/**974**: *Considered*, 91/1653, 91/1683: *Distinguished*, 83/1308, 84/1301: *Followed*, 98/2228

Gio Personal Investment Services Ltd v. Liverpool and London Steamship Protection and Indemnity Association Ltd [1999] 1 W.L.R. 984; (1999) 96(6) L.S.G. 35; *Times*, January 13, 1999, CA. . . . . *Digested*, 99/**318**

Giraud UK Ltd v. Smith [2000] I.R.L.R. 763, EAT. . . . . *Digested*, 00/**2115**

Girl Power Toys Ltd (Registered Designs Nos.2068328, 2068329, 2068330, 2068331 and 2068332) see Spice Girls Ltd's Application for Cancellation of Registered Designs

Girobank Plc v. Clarke (Inspector of Taxes) [1998] 1 W.L.R. 942; [1998] 4 All E.R. 312; [1998] S.T.C. 182; 70 T.C. 387; [1998] B.T.C. 24; (1998) 95(6) L.S.G. 25; (1998)142 S.J.L.B. 43; *Times*, January 6, 1998; *Independent*, January 26, 1998 (C.S.), CA; affirming [1996] S.T.C. 540; 70 T.C. 387; [1996] E.G.C.S. 45; (1996) 93(16) L.S.G. 32; (1996) 140 S.J.L.B. 100; *Times*, March 21, 1996, Ch D . . . . . . *Digested*, 98/**4600**

Girvan v. Inverness Farmers Dairy (No.2) 1998 S.C. (H.L.) 1; 1998 S.L.T. 21; 1998 S.C.L.R. 72; 1997 G.W.D. 37-1883; *Times*, December 15, 1997, HL; affirming 1996 S.C. 134; 1996 S.L.T. 631, Ex Div . . . . *Digested*, 98/**5478**

Girvan (Inspector of Taxes) v. Orange Personal Communications Services Ltd [1998] S.T.C. 567; 70 T.C. 602; [1998] B.T.C. 181; (1998) 95(20) L.S.G. 34; (1998) 142 S.J.L.B. 149; *Times*, April 22, 1998, Ch D . . . . *Digested*, 98/**4627**

Gissing v. Gissing [1971] A.C. 886; [1970] 3 W.L.R. 255; [1970] 2 All E.R. 780; (1970) 21 P. & C.R. 702; 114 S.J. 550, HL; reversing [1969] 2 Ch. 85; [1969] 2 W.L.R. 525; [1969] 1 All E.R. 1043; (1969) 20 P. & C.R. 276; 113 S.J. 187, CA . . . . *Digested*, 70/**1243**: *Applied*, 70/1233, 70/1234, 70/1246, 71/5474, 71/5503, 72/1684, 72/2923, 77/2498, 83/1834, 83/1836, 84/1676, 90/1996, 91/1763, 95/2184, 95/2188, 96/2887, 96/5546, 01/5503: *Considered*, 71/5476, 74/1834, 75/3110, 79/2414, 83/1835, 84/1675, 84/1677, 85/2267, 85/2950, 85/3647, 86/1661, 86/1857, 86/3034, 86/3551, 87/1439, 92/2031: *Distinguished*, 85/3047: *Followed*, 85/1284, 86/3037, 96/4943

Gissing v. Walkers Smith Snack Foods Ltd (Unreported, July 12, 1999), CC (Lincoln) [*Ex rel.* Langleys Solicitors, Newporte House, Doddington Road Business Park, Lincoln] . . . . *Digested*, 99/**3983**

Gitonas v. Greece (1998) 26 E.H.R.R. 691, ECHR. . . . . *Digested*, 99/**3102**

Gittens v. Commissioners see Gittins v. Customs and Excise Commissioners

Gittins v. Customs and Excise Commissioners; *sub nom* Gittens v. Commissioners [1974] V.A.T.T.R. 109, VAT Tr . . . . *Digested*, 74/**3923.10**: *Followed*, 98/4878

Giuliani SpA v. Sofar SpA [2000] E.N.P.R. 217, App (Milano)

Givry Automobiles Sarl v. Sodirac SA [1999] E.C.C. 258, Cass (F) . . . . *Digested*, 99/**668**

Gizzonio v. Chief Constable of Derbyshire, *Times*, April 29, 1998, CA. . . . . *Digested*, 98/**4786**

GJ v. Luxembourg [2000] B.P.I.R. 1021, ECHR . . . . *Digested*, 01/**3518**

GKN Centrax Gears Ltd v. Matbro Ltd [1976] 2 Lloyd's Rep. 555; 120 S.J. 401, CA . . . . *Digested*, 76/**95**: *Applied*, 78/93, 79/98, 98/4384: *Distinguished*, 89/119

GKR Karate (UK) Ltd v. Yorkshire Post Newspapers Ltd (No.1) [2000] 1 W.L.R. 2571; [2000] 2 All E.R. 931; [2000] C.P. Rep. 47; [2000] E.M.L.R. 396; (2000) 97(4) L.S.G. 32; (2000) 144 S.J.L.B. 50; *Times*, February 9, 2000 ; *Independent*, February 21, 2000 (C.S.), CA . . . . *Digested*, 00/**1762**

GKR Karate (UK) Ltd v. Yorkshire Post Newspapers Ltd (No.2) [2000] E.M.L.R. 410, QBD . . . . *Digested*, 00/**1763**: *Applied*, 01/1823

Gladding v. Channel Four Television Corp [1999] E.M.L.R. 475; (1998) 95(35) L.S.G. 36; (1998) 142 S.J.L.B. 217; *Times*, October 10, 1998, CA . . . . *Digested*, 98/**380**

Glaister v. Greenwood [2001] Lloyd's Rep. P.N. 412; [2001] P.N.L.R. 25, Ch D . . . . *Digested*, 01/**4521**

Glamorgan CC v. Carter [1963] 1 W.L.R. 1; [1962] 3 All E.R. 866; 127 J.P. 28; 61 L.G.R. 50; (1963) 14 P. & C.R. 88; 106 S.J. 1069, QBD . . . . *Digested*, 62/**3002**: *Considered*, 01/4702: *Distinguished*, 93/5924: *Followed*, 93/1613, 93/1621, 95/1858

Glasgow City Council v. Al-Abassi 2001 Hous. L.R. 23; 2001 G.W.D. 8-298, Sh Ct (Glasgow) . . . . *Digested*, 01/**6696**

Glasgow City Council v. Customs and Excise Commissioners (No.1) [1998] B.V.C. 2239, V&DTr . . . . *Digested*, 98/**6219**

Glasgow City Council v. Customs and Excise Commissioners (No.2) [2000] B.V.C. 2363; [2000] S.T.I. 1216, V&DTr . . . . *Digested*, 01/**6921**

Glasgow City Council v. Marshall [2000] 1 W.L.R. 333; [2000] 1 All E.R. 641; 2000
S.C. (H.L.) 67; 2000 S.L.T. 429; 2000 S.C.L.R. 889; [2000] I.C.R. 196; [2000]
I.R.L.R. 272; (2000) 2 L.G.L.R. 679; [2000] B.L.G.R. 229; (2000) 97(7) L.S.G.
39; (2000) 144 S.J.L.B. 101; Times, February 8, 2000 ; Independent, March 27,
2000 (C.S.), HL; affirming 1998 S.C. 274; 1998 S.L.T. 799; 1998 S.C.L.R. 33;
1997 G.W.D. 40-2089, 1 Div. . . . .   *Digested,* 00/**6214**

Glasgow City Council v. Zafar; sub nom City of Glasgow DC v. Zafar; Strathclyde RC v.
Zafar; Zafar v. Glasgow City Council [1997] 1 W.L.R. 1659; [1998] 2 All E.R.
953; 1998 S.C. (H.L.) 27; 1998 S.L.T. 135; [1998] I.C.R. 120; [1998] I.R.L.R. 36;
(1997) 94(48) L.S.G. 29; (1998) 142 S.J.L.B. 30; Times, December 8, 1997,
HL; affirming 1996 S.C. 502; 1997 S.L.T. 281; 1996 S.C.L.R. 1084; [1997]
I.R.L.R. 229, 2 Div. . . . .   *Digested,* 98/**5810**:
                                           Cited, 00/2183: *Considered,* 01/2301, 01/2320

Glasgow Corp v. Taylor [1922] 1 A.C. 44; [1921] All E.R. Rep. 1; 29 A.L.R. 846, HL . . . .   *Applied,* 47-51/**6739**,
                     53/2452, 54/2226, 55/1830, 64/1670, 83/3640: *Considered,* 47-51/**6694**,
                         47-51/**6746**, 82/2147, 83/2545, 00/4240: *Explained,* 47-51/**6740**

Glasgow Harley (A Firm) v. McDonald see Harley v. McDonald

Glass v. McManus [1996] N.I. 401, QBD (NI)

Glastonbury Abbey v. Customs and Excise Commissioners [1996] V. & D.R. 307, VAT
Tr (London). . . . .   *Digested,* 97/**4984**:
                                                           Considered, 01/5563

Glaxo Group Ltd v. Dowelhurst Ltd see Boehringer Ingelheim KG v. Swingward Ltd

Glaxo Group Ltd v. Dowelhurst Ltd (Defence Amendments); Boehringer Ingelheim KG
v. Dowelhurst Ltd (Defence Amendments); SmithKline Beecham Plc v.
Dowelhurst Ltd (Defence Amendments); Eli Lilly & Co v. Dowelhurst Ltd
(Defence Amendments); Boehringer Ingelheim KG v. Swingward Ltd (Defence
Amendments); Glaxo Group Ltd v. Swingward Ltd (Defence Amendments)
[2000] U.K.C.L.R. 278; [2000] E.C.C. 193; [2000] Eu. L.R. 493; [2000]
E.T.M.R. 118; [2000] F.S.R. 371; (2000) 55 B.M.L.R. 137; (2000) 23(1) I.P.D.
23006, Pat Ct . . . .   *Digested,* 00/**3704**

Glaxo Group Ltd v. Dowelhurst Ltd (Infringement Action); Boehringer Ingelheim KG v.
Dowelhurst Ltd (Infringement Action); SmithKline Beecham Plc v. Dowelhurst
Ltd (Infringement Action); Eli Lilly & Co v. Dowelhurst Ltd (Infringement Action);
Boehringer Ingelheim KG v. Swingward Ltd (Infringement Action); Glaxo Group
Ltd v. Swingward Ltd (Infringement Action) [2000] 2 C.M.L.R. 571; [2000]
E.T.M.R. 415; [2000] F.S.R. 529; (2000) 55 B.M.L.R. 157; (2000) 23(6) I.P.D.
23046; Times, March 14, 2000, Pat Ct . . . .   *Digested,* 00/**3703**:
           Applied, 01/4034: *Considered,* 01/6728: *Subsequent proceedings,* 01/2480

Glaxo Group Ltd v. Inland Revenue Commissioners [1996] S.T.C. 191; 68 T.C. 166;
(1996) 140 S.J.L.B. 35; Times, December 26, 1995; Independent, January 8,
1996 (C.S.), CA; affirming [1995] S.T.C. 1075; Times, November 21, 1995;
Independent, December 11, 1995 (C.S.), Ch D . . . .   *Digested,* 96/**1313**:
                                                           Considered, 99/4682

Glaxo Group Ltd v. Knoll AG [1999] E.T.M.R. 358, SH (DK)

Glaxo Group Ltd v. Swingward Ltd see Boehringer Ingelheim KG v. Swingward Ltd

Glaxo Group Ltd v. Swingward Ltd (Defence Amendments) see Glaxo Group Ltd v.
Dowelhurst Ltd (Defence Amendments)

Glaxo Group Ltd v. Swingward Ltd (Infringement Action) see Glaxo Group Ltd v.
Dowelhurst Ltd (Infringement Action)

Glaxo Group Ltd's Trade Mark [2001] E.T.M.R. 9; (2000) 23(9) I.P.D. 23077, TMR . . . .   *Digested,* 01/**4012**

Gleaves v. Insall; Dore v. Insall; Bolton v. Insall [1999] 2 Cr. App. R. 466; [1999]
E.M.L.R. 779; [1999] C.O.D. 402; Times, March 24, 1999; Independent, April 19,
1999 (C.S.), QBD . . . .   *Digested,* 99/**998**

Gleeson v. J Wippell & Co Ltd [1977] 1 W.L.R. 510; [1977] 3 All E.R. 54; [1977]
F.S.R. 301; 121 S.J. 157, Ch D . . . .   *Digested,* 77/**1212**:
           Applied, 98/618, 98/3385: *Cited,* 00/346: *Considered,* 82/2514, 93/3153

Glegg v. Bromley [1912] 3 K.B. 474, CA . . . .   *Applied,* 64/**3384**,
                                 80/346: *Cited,* 00/859: *Considered,* 97/3369

Glen Express Ltd, Re [2000] B.P.I.R. 456, Ch D

Glencore Grain Ltd v. Agros Trading Co Ltd; sub nom Agros Trading Co Ltd v. Glencore
Grain Ltd [1999] 2 All E.R. (Comm) 288; [1999] 2 Lloyd's Rep. 410; [1999]
C.L.C. 1696; (1999) 96(31) L.S.G. 42; Times, July 12, 1999, CA. . . . .   *Digested,* 99/**2509**

Glencore Grain Ltd v. Commission of the European Communities (C404/96 P) [1998]
E.C.R. I-2435; [1999] 1 C.M.L.R. 538, ECJ

Glencore Grain Ltd v. Flacker Shipping Ltd (The Happy Day) [2001] 1 All E.R. (Comm)
659; [2001] 1 Lloyd's Rep. 754; [2001] C.L.C. 813; Times, February 22, 2001,
QBD (Comm Ct) . . . .   *Digested,* 01/**4912**

Glencore International AG v. Bank of China [1996] 1 Lloyd's Rep. 135; [1996] 5 Bank.
L.R. 1; [1996] C.L.C. 111; [1998] Masons C.L.R. Rep. 78; Times, November 27,
1995, CA; affirming [1996] C.L.C. 95, QBD (Comm Ct) . . . .   *Digested,* 96/**415**:
                                         Applied, 97/328: *Considered,* 99/286

Glencore International AG v. Metro Trading International Inc (formerly Metro Bunkering
& Trading Co) (No.2) see Glencore International AG v. Metro Trading
International Inc (No.2)

Glencore International AG *v.* Metro Trading International Inc (No.1); Metro Trading International Inc *v.* Itochu Petroleum Co (S) PTE Ltd (No.1) [1999] 2 All E.R. (Comm) 899; [1999] 2 Lloyd's Rep. 632; [2000] C.P. Rep. 26; [2000] C.L.C. 83; [2000] I.L.Pr. 358, QBD (Comm Ct) . . . . *Digested*, 00/**750**

Glencore International AG *v.* Metro Trading International Inc (No.2); *sub nom* Glencore International AG *v.* Metro Trading International Inc (formerly Metro Bunkering & Trading Co) (No.2) [2001] 1 All E.R. (Comm) 103; [2001] 1 Lloyd's Rep. 284; [2001] C.L.C. 1732, QBD (Comm Ct) . . . . *Digested*, 01/**813**

Glencore International AG *v.* Ryan (The Beursgracht) (No.1); Glencore International AG *v.* Ryan (The Beursgracht) (No.2) [2001] EWCA Civ 2051, CA; affirming [2001] 2 Lloyd's Rep. 602, CC (Central London)

Glencore International AG *v.* Ryan (The Beursgracht) (No.2) [2001] 2 Lloyd's Rep. 608, CC (Central London)

Glencore International AG *v.* Ryan (The Beursgracht) (No.2) (CA) see Glencore International AG *v.* Ryan (The Beursgracht) (No.1)

Glencore International AG *v.* Shell International Trading & Shipping Co Ltd [1999] 2 All E.R. (Comm) 922; [1999] 2 Lloyd's Rep. 692; [2000] C.L.C. 104, QBD (Comm Ct) . . . . *Digested*, 00/**738**

Glencot Development & Design Co Ltd *v.* Ben Barrett & Son (Contractors) Ltd [2001] B.L.R. 207; (2001) 3 T.C.L.R. 11; 80 Con. L.R. 14; (2001) 17 Const. L.J. 336, QBD (T&CC) . . . . *Digested*, 01/**856**: *Followed*, 01/857

Glenfall House Trust *v.* Customs and Excise Commissioners [2000] S.T.I. 1379, V&DTr

Glenister *v.* Rowe (Costs); *sub nom* Rowe *v.* Rowe [2000] Ch. 76; [1999] 3 W.L.R. 716; [1999] 3 All E.R. 452; [1999] B.P.I.R. 674; (1999) 96(20) L.S.G. 39; (1999) 149 N.L.J. 858; *Times*, April 28, 1999; *Independent*, June 14, 1999 (C.S.), CA . . . . *Digested*, 99/**3229**

Glenn Miller Productions Inc *v.* Stichting Bill Bakers Big Band Corp; Schmidt & Salden GmbH *v.* Stichting Bill Bakers Big Band Corp [1999] E.T.M.R. 247, RB (Den Haag)

Glennie *v.* Independent Magazines (UK) Ltd [1999] I.R.L.R. 719; *Times*, June 25, 1999 ; *Independent*, July 12, 1999 (C.S.), CA. . . . . *Digested*, 99/**2037**

Glinski *v.* McIver [1962] A.C. 726; [1962] 2 W.L.R. 832; [1962] 1 All E.R. 696; 106 S.J. 261, HL; affirming [1960] Crim. L.R. 428; *Times*, February 6, 1960, CA; reversing [1959] Crim. L.R. 56; *Times*, November 1, 1958, QBD . . . . *Digested*, 62/**1887**: *Applied*, 66/7586, 00/470: *Considered*, 64/2337

Global Asset Management Ltd's Application [2001] E.T.M.R. CN1, OHIM (2nd Bd App)

Global Container Lines Ltd *v.* Bonyad Shipping Co (No.1) [1998] 1 Lloyd's Rep. 528, QBD (Comm Ct) . . . . *Digested*, 98/**4442**

Global Container Lines Ltd *v.* Bonyad Shipping Co (No.2) [1999] 1 Lloyd's Rep. 287; [1998] C.L.C. 1324; *Times*, July 14, 1998, QBD (Comm Ct) . . . . *Digested*, 98/**376**

Global Container Lines Ltd *v.* State Black Sea Shipping Co [1999] 1 Lloyd's Rep. 127, CA . . . . *Digested*, 99/**4482**

Global Custodians Ltd *v.* Mesh (1999-2000) 2 I.T.E.L.R. 327, Sup Ct (NSW)

Global Financial Recoveries Ltd *v.* Jones [2000] B.P.I.R. 1029; (2000) 97(2) L.S.G. 30; (2000) 144 S.J.L.B. 32; *Times*, February 23, 2000, Ch D . . . . *Digested*, 00/**4656**

Global Info Ltd, Re; *sub nom* Secretary of State for Trade and Industry *v.* Wiper [1999] C.P.L.R. 76; [1999] 1 B.C.L.C. 74, Ch D . . . . *Digested*, 99/**316**

Global Marine Drilling Co *v.* Triton Holdings Ltd (The Sovereign Explorer) (No.2) [2001] 1 Lloyd's Rep. 60; 2000 G.W.D. 5-210, OH

Globe Equities Ltd *v.* Globe Legal Services Ltd; Globe Equities Ltd *v.* Kotrie; Kotrie *v.* Globe Equities Ltd [2000] C.P.L.R. 233; [1999] B.L.R. 232; *Times*, April 14, 1999; *Independent*, March 15, 1999 (C.S.), CA . . . . *Digested*, 99/**390**: *Applied*, 00/423

Globe Equities Ltd *v.* Kotrie see Globe Equities Ltd *v.* Globe Legal Services Ltd

Glolite Ltd *v.* Jasper Conran Ltd, *Times*, January 28, 1998, Ch D . . . . *Digested*, 98/**3510**

Glossop *v.* Copnall [2001] Pens. L.R. 263, Ch D

Gloster *v.* Chief Constable of Greater Manchester [2000] P.I.Q.R. P114, CA . . . . *Digested*, 00/**204**

Gloucester City Council *v.* Secretary of State for the Environment, Transport and the Regions [2001] J.P.L. 380 (Note), QBD

Gloucestershire CC *v.* P; *sub nom* P (A Minor) (Residence Orders), Re [2000] Fam. 1; [1999] 3 W.L.R. 685; [1999] 2 F.L.R. 61; [1999] 3 F.C.R. 114; [1999] Fam. Law 444; (1999) 96(20) L.S.G. 39; *Times*, April 30, 1999; *Independent*, May 20, 1999, CA . . . . *Digested*, 99/**2390**

Gloucestershire CC *v.* Tintern Estates Ltd (1998) 13 P.A.D. 221, Planning Inspector

Gloucestershire HA *v.* MA Torpy & Partners Ltd (t/a Torpy & Partners) (No.2) [1999] Lloyd's Rep. I.R. 203, QBD (OR) . . . . *Digested*, 99/**376**: *Distinguished*, 01/474

Gloucestershire HA *v.* MA Torpy & Partners Ltd (t/a Torpy & Partners) (No.1) 55 Con. L.R. 124, QBD (OR) . . . . *Digested*, 98/**4006**

Glouchkov *v.* Forbes Inc see Berezovsky *v.* Forbes Inc (No.1)

Glouchkov *v.* Michaels see Berezovsky *v.* Forbes Inc (No.1)

Glover *v.* Emerson Developments Ltd (Unreported, April 18, 2001), CC (Sheffield) [*Ex rel.* Ison Harrison & Co, Solicitors, Duke House, 54 Wellington Street, Leeds]. . . *Digested*, 01/**892**

Glover *v.* Secretary of State for the Environment [1981] J.P.L. 110 . . . . 　*Digested,* 81/**2724**:
　　　　　　　　　　　　　　　　　　　　　　　　　　　　　　　　　　　Applied, 00/4445
Glover *v.* Stuart (1999) 99(6) Q.R. 7, CC (Exeter) [*Ex rel.* Bond Pearce Solicitors,
　Darwin House, Southernhay Gardens, Exeter, Devon] . . . . 　*Digested,* 99/**1618**
Gloyne *v.* Richardson [2001] EWCA Civ 716; [2001] 2 B.C.L.C. 669, CA
Gloystarne & Co Ltd *v.* Martin [2001] I.R.L.R. 15, EAT . . . . 　*Digested,* 01/**2347**
Gluckspiel GmbH (ZI.97/17/0175-12), Re [2001] E.C.C. 18, VwGH (A)
Glynn *v.* MacKay (Unreported, April 7, 1998), CC (Central London) [*Ex rel.* Mark
　Loveday, Barrister, Francis Taylor Building, 3rd Floor, Temple, London] . . . . 　*Digested,* 98/**3649**
GMAC Commercial Credit Development Ltd *v.* Sandhu [2001] EWCA Civ 1209; [2001]
　2 All E.R. (Comm) 782, CA
GMB *v.* MAN Truck & Bus UK Ltd [2000] I.C.R. 1101; [2000] I.R.L.R. 636, EAT . . . . . . 　*Digested,* 00/**2188**
GMB Srl *v.* Amministrazione delle Finanze dello Stato (C281/96) see Ansaldo Energia
　SpA *v.* Amministrazione delle Finanze dello Stato (C279/96)
GMR *v.* United Kingdom see IJL *v.* United Kingdom
Gnali *v.* Immigration Appeal Tribunal see R. *v.* Immigration Appeal Tribunal Ex p. Gnali
Gnanam *v.* Secretary of State for the Home Department [1999] Imm. A.R. 436;
　[1999] I.N.L.R. 219, CA . . . . 　*Digested,* 99/**3178**
Gnanavarathan *v.* Special Adjudicator see R. *v.* Special Adjudicator Ex p.
　Gnanavarathan
GNER *v.* Avon Insurance Plc see Great North Eastern Railway Ltd *v.* Avon Insurance
　Plc
Gnitrow Ltd *v.* Cape Plc [2000] 1 W.L.R. 2327; [2000] 3 All E.R. 763; [2001] C.P.
　Rep. 21; (2000) 150 N.L.J. 1109; *Times,* July 18, 2000, CA . . . . 　*Digested,* 00/**312**:
　　　　　　　　　　　　　　　　　　　　　　　　　　　　　　　　　　　Cited, 01/620
Goacher *v.* Pearman (Unreported, May 13, 1998), CC (Swindon) [*Ex rel.* Irwin Mitchell
　Solicitors, Huttons Buildings, 146 West Street, Sheffield] . . . . 　*Digested,* 98/**1584**
Goberdhan *v.* Caribbean Insurance Co Ltd [1998] 2 Lloyd's Rep. 449; [1998] R.T.R.
　432; (1998) 142 S.J.L.B. 183, PC (Trin) . . . . 　*Digested,* 99/**3412**
Goble *v.* Airedale Hospitals NHS Trust (Unreported, July 27, 1998), QBD [*Ex rel.*
　Armstrongs, Solicitors, Kipling House, 24 Otley Street, Skipton, North
　Yorkshire] . . . . 　*Digested,* 99/**1433**
Godard *v.* Houdelinckx [2000] E.C.C. 134, Cass (F)
Godbout *v.* Longueuil (1997) 152 D.L.R. (4th) 577, Sup Ct (Can) . . . . 　*Applied,* 99/3121
Goddard *v.* Nationwide Building Society [1987] Q.B. 670; [1986] 3 W.L.R. 734;
　[1986] 3 All E.R. 264; (1986) 83 L.S.G. 3592; (1986) 137 N.L.J. 775; (1986)
　130 S.J. 803, CA. . . . . 　*Digested,* 86/**1516**:
　　　　　　　Applied, 87/3060, 87/3086, 88/1596, 01/3851: *Considered,* 88/1592,
　　　　　　　　　　　　　　　　　　　　　89/1698: *Referred to,* 93/3108
Godfrey *v.* Bernard Matthews Plc (Unreported, June 21, 1999), CC (Norwich) [*Ex rel.*
　Philip Kolvin, Barrister, 2-3 Gray's Inn Square, London] . . . . 　*Digested,* 99/**1498**
Godfrey *v.* Conwy CBC [2001] Env. L.R. 38; [2001] E.H.L.R. 10; [2001] J.P.L. 1162;
　[2000] E.G.C.S. 131, QBD . . . . 　*Digested,* 01/**4550**
Godfrey *v.* Demon Internet Ltd (Application to Strike Out) [2001] Q.B. 201; [2000] 3
　W.L.R. 1020; [1999] 4 All E.R. 342; [1999] E.M.L.R. 542; [1998-99] Info. T.L.R.
　252; [1999] I.T.C.L.R. 282; [1999] Masons C.L.R. 267; (1999) 149 N.L.J. 609;
　Times, April 20, 1999, QBD . . . . 　*Digested,* 99/**1636**:
　　　　　　　　　　　　　　　　　　　　Applied, 01/1825: *Cited,* 00/1758
Godfrey *v.* Gnitrow Ltd [2000] 1 Q.R. 8, CC (Oldham) [*Ex rel.* John Pickering and
　Partners Solicitors, 9 Church Lane, Oldham] . . . . 　*Digested,* 99/**1537**
Godfrey *v.* Simm (Valuation Officer) [2000] 3 E.G.L.R. 85; [2000] 47 E.G. 177;
　[2000] R.V.R. 247, Lands Tr . . . . 　*Digested,* 00/**4589**
Godwin *v.* Swindon BC [2001] EWCA Civ 1478; [2001] 4 All E.R. 641; *Independent,*
　October 19, 2001, CA . . . . 　*Digested,* 01/**653**
Goff (A Minor) *v.* Broadland Properties Ltd (1998) 98(3) Q.R. 8, CC (Portsmouth) . . . 　*Digested,* 98/**1654**
Gogay *v.* Hertfordshire CC [2000] I.R.L.R. 703; [2001] 1 F.L.R. 280; [2001] 1 F.C.R.
　455; (2001) 3 L.G.L.R. 14; [2000] Fam. Law 883; (2000) 97(37) L.S.G. 40;
　Times, October 3, 2000, CA. . . . . 　*Digested,* 00/**4890**
Gohar *v.* Entry Clearance Officer (Islamabad) [1998] I.N.L.R. 297, IAT . . . . 　*Digested,* 98/**3226**
Gojra *v.* Railtrack Plc see Railtrack Plc *v.* Gojra
Gold *v.* Essex CC [1942] 2 K.B. 293; [1942] 2 All E.R. 237; 40 L.G.R. 249, CA . . . . . . 　*Applied,* 47-51/**5751**,
　　　　47-51/6227, 47-51/6867, 47-51/6868, 47-51/6870, 47-51/10052, 52/3420,
　　　　　　　53/2519, 80/640, 93/180, 98/3978: *Considered,* 54/1886, 81/1845:
　　　　　　　　　　　　　　　　　　　　　Followed, 54/2291, 54/4047
Gold *v.* Hill; Hill *v.* Gold [1999] 1 F.L.R. 54; [1998] Fam. Law 664; (1998) 95(35)
　L.S.G. 37; (1998) 142 S.J.L.B. 226; *Times,* August 24, 1998, Ch D . . . . 　*Digested,* 98/**4589**
Gold *v.* Mincoff Science & Gold [2001] Lloyd's Rep. P.N. 423; (2001) 98(3) L.S.G.
　44; [2001] N.P.C. 6, Ch D . . . . 　*Digested,* 01/**4527**
Goldberg *v.* Hogger (1999) 99(4) Q.R. 7, CC (Reading) [*Ex rel.* Marcus Grant,
　Barrister, 1 Temple Gardens, London] . . . . 　*Digested,* 99/**2469**
Goldberg *v.* Hogger (Quantum) (Unreported, May 19, 1999), CC (Reading) [*Ex rel.*
　Marcus Grant, Barrister, 1 Temple Gardens, Temple, London] . . . . 　*Digested,* 99/**1590**

Goldcorp Exchange Ltd (In Receivership), Re; *sub nom* Kensington *v.* Unrepresented
    Non-Allocated Claimants; Goldcorp Finance Ltd, Re [1995] 1 A.C. 74; [1994] 3
    W.L.R. 199; [1994] 2 All E.R. 806; [1994] 2 B.C.L.C. 578; (1994) 13 Tr. L.R.
    434; (1994) 91 (24) L.S.G. 46; (1994) 144 N.L.J. 792; (1994) 138 S.J.L.B. 127;
    Times, June 2, 1994, PC (NZ) . . . . *Digested*, 94/**4034**:
                      Applied, 94/259, 95/2211: *Considered*, 01/2430
Goldcorp Finance Ltd, Re see Goldcorp Exchange Ltd (In Receivership), Re
Golden Bay Cement Co Ltd *v.* Inland Revenue Commissioners [1998] S.T.C. 1172;
    [1998] B.T.C. 448, PC (NZ) . . . . *Digested*, 99/**4669**
GOLDENBERG/Tumour localisation (T683/90) [1998] E.P.O.R. 278, EPO (Technical Bd
    App)
Golder *v.* United Kingdom (A/18) (1979-80) 1 E.H.R.R. 524, ECHR . . . . *Applied*, 97/2934:
                                              Considered, 01/1099
Goldfinch Transport Ltd *v.* Customs and Excise Commissioners [1996] V. & D.R. 484,
    VAT Tr (London) . . . . *Digested*, 98/**4895**
Golding *v.* Mason (Unreported, September 14, 1999), CC (Romford) [*Ex rel.* Richard
    Miles, Barrister, Fleet Chambers, 44-46 Fleet Street, London] . . . . *Digested*, 99/**2477**:
                                             Cited, 00/2580
Goldman *v.* Hargrave; *sub nom* Hargrave *v.* Goldman [1967] 1 A.C. 645; [1966] 3
    W.L.R. 513; [1966] 2 All E.R. 989; [1966] 2 Lloyd's Rep. 65; 110 S.J. 527;
    (1963) 37 A.L.J.R. 277, HC (Aus) . . . . *Digested*, 66/**8145**:
                Applied, 78/2201, 79/2004, 80/2006, 86/2249, 00/4292:
               Considered, 82/4057, 87/2597, 87/4737, 00/4287, 01/4548
Goldman *v.* Hesper [1988] 1 W.L.R. 1238; [1988] 3 All E.R. 97; [1997] Costs L.R.
    (Core Vol.) 99; [1989] 1 F.L.R. 195; [1989] Fam. Law 152; (1988) 138 N.L.J.
    Rep. 272, CA; affirming 1987 Fam. L.R. 352; [1987] Fam. Law 315, Fam Div . . . *Digested*, 89/**1697**:
               Distinguished, 90/5804: *Followed*, 89/2720, 98/471, 99/321
Goldman *v.* Thai Airways International [1983] 1 W.L.R. 1186; [1983] 3 All E.R. 693;
    (1983) 127 S.J. 441, CA; reversing 125 S.J. 413 . . . . *Digested*, 83/**2553**:
                                       Applied, 94/362, 00/5157
Goldsmith *v.* Bhoyrul [1998] Q.B. 459; [1998] 2 W.L.R. 435; [1997] 4 All E.R. 268;
    [1997] E.M.L.R. 407; (1997) 94(28) L.S.G. 26; (1997) 141 S.J.L.B. 151; *Times*,
    June 20, 1997, QBD . . . . *Digested*, 97/**2035**
Goldsmith *v.* Customs and Excise Commissioners [2001] EWHC Admin 285; [2001] 1
    W.L.R. 1673; (2001) 165 J.P. 517; (2001) 98(23) L.S.G. 41; (2001) 145
    S.J.L.B. 124; *Times*, June 12, 2001, QBD (Admin Ct) . . . . *Digested*, 01/**41**
Goldsmith Foundation for European Affairs *v.* Customs and Excise Commissioners
    [2000] B.V.C. 2273; [2000] S.T.I. 933, V&DTr
Goldsmith Plants Inc's Trade Mark Application (No.543/2000) [2000] E.T.M.R. 840
    (Note), OHIM (Opposition Div)
Goldsmiths Co *v.* West Metropolitan Railway Co [1904] 1 K.B. 1, CA . . . . *Applied*, 47-51/9032:
                Considered, 73/1147, 99/2465: *Distinguished*, 62/2947
Goldsmiths (Jewellers) Ltd *v.* Customs and Excise Commissioners [1997] V. & D.R.
    325, V&DTr . . . . *Digested*, 00/**5285**:
                                 Previous proceedings, 97/4974
Goldsmiths (Jewellers) Ltd *v.* Customs and Excise Commissioners (C330/95) [1997]
    S.T.C. 1073; [1997] E.C.R. I-3801; [1997] 3 C.M.L.R. 978; [1997] B.T.C. 5380;
    [1997] B.V.C. 494; *Times*, July 25, 1997, ECJ (6th Chamber) . . . . *Digested*, 97/**4974**:
                             Subsequent proceedings, 00/5285
Goldstein *v.* Conley [2001] EWCA Civ 637; [2001] L. & T.R. 30; (2001) 98(25)
    L.S.G. 46; *Independent*, June 11, 2001 (C.S), CA; affirming [1999] 1 E.G.L.R.
    95; [1999] 03 E.G. 137, Lands Tr . . . . *Digested*, 01/**4176**
Goldtech Investments Ltd *v.* Mainwaring see Mainwaring *v.* Goldtech Investments Ltd
    (No.2)
Gomez *v.* Secretary of State for the Home Department [2000] I.N.L.R. 549, IAT
Gomez Rivero *v.* Bundesanstalt fur Arbeit (C211/97); *sub nom* Rivero *v.* Bundesanstalt
    fur Arbeit (C211/97) [1999] E.C.R. I-3219; [1999] C.E.C. 259; [2000] I.C.R. 20,
    ECJ (5th Chamber) . . . . *Digested*, 99/**4503**
Gomilsek *v.* Haringey LBC see Nabadda *v.* Westminster City Council
Gomm *v.* Woolwich Plc see Woolwich Plc *v.* Gomm
Gondal *v.* Dillon Newsagents Ltd [1998] N.P.C. 127, CA. . . . . *Digested*, 98/**3604**
GONZALEZ GARCIA/Deemed Withdrawal (J29/94) [1998] E.P.O.R. 342, EPO (Legal Bd
    App)
Good, Re (Unreported, July 23, 1998), CICB (London) [*Ex rel.* Graham Crosthwaite,
    Barrister, 1 King's Bench Walk, Temple, London] . . . . *Digested*, 99/**1452**
Good *v.* Epping Forest DC [1994] 1 W.L.R. 376; [1994] 2 All E.R. 156; 92 L.G.R. 306;
    [1993] 3 P.L.R. 135; [1994] 27 E.G. 135; [1993] E.G.C.S. 188; (1993) 137
    S.J.L.B. 277; *Times*, November 11, 1993, CA; affirming [1992] 3 P.L.R. 103;
    [1993] J.P.L. 127; [1992] E.G.C.S. 64; [1992] N.P.C. 60 . . . . *Digested*, 94/**4435**:
                                   Considered, 93/3936, 94/4462
Gooda Walker Ltd *v.* Deeny see Henderson *v.* Merrett Syndicates Ltd (No.1)
Goodacre *v.* Bates [2000] I.L.Pr. 527, CA . . . . *Digested*, 00/**434**

Goodall (CICB: Quantum: 1999), Re (Unreported, May 13, 1999), CICB (London) [*Ex rel.* Paul Cairnes, Barrister, 3 Paper Buildings at Bournemouth, Lorne Park Road, Bournemouth] . . . . *Digested*, 00/**1583**

Goodaston Ltd *v.* FH Burgess Plc [1998] L. & T.R. 46, Ch D . . . . *Digested*, 99/**3696**

Goodbrand (Inspector of Taxes) *v.* Loffland Bros North Sea Inc; *sub nom* Loffland Brothers North Sea Inc *v.* Goodbrand (Inspector of Taxes); Poseidon Inc *v.* Inspector of Taxes [1998] S.T.C. 930; [1998] B.T.C. 297; *Times*, July 15, 1998; *Independent*, July 2, 1998, CA; affirming [1997] S.T.C. 102; [1997] B.T.C. 100; *Times*, January 24, 1997, Ch D; reversing [1996] S.T.C. (S.C.D.) 273, Sp Comm . *Digested*, 98/**4619**

Goodchild (Deceased), Re see Goodchild *v.* Goodchild

Goodchild *v.* Goodchild; *sub nom* Goodchild (Deceased), Re [1997] 1 W.L.R. 1216; [1997] 3 All E.R. 63; [1997] 2 F.L.R. 644; [1997] 3 F.C.R. 601; [1997] Fam. Law 660; (1997) 147 N.L.J. 759; *Times*, May 12, 1997; *Independent*, May 9, 1997, CA; affirming [1996] 1 W.L.R. 694; [1996] 1 All E.R. 670; [1996] 1 F.L.R. 591; [1997] 1 F.C.R. 45; [1996] Fam. Law 209; *Times*, December 22, 1995; *Independent*, January 8, 1996 (C.S.), Ch D . . . . *Digested*, 97/**4726**: *Applied*, 99/4639

Goode *v.* Martin [2001] EWCA Civ 1899, CA; reversing [2001] 3 All E.R. 562, QBD (Adm Ct) . . . . *Digested*, 01/**421**: *Distinguished*, 01/419

Gooden *v.* Northamptonshire CC [2001] EWCA Civ 1744; [2001] 49 E.G.C.S. 116; [2001] N.P.C. 167, CA; affirming [2000] N.P.C. 90, Ch D

Goodes *v.* East Sussex CC [2000] 1 W.L.R. 1356; [2000] 3 All E.R. 603; [2000] R.T.R. 366; (2001) 3 L.G.L.R. 6; [2000] B.L.G.R. 465; [2000] P.I.Q.R. P148; [2001] J.P.L. 70; [2000] E.G.C.S. 75; (2000) 97(26) L.S.G. 38; (2000) 150 N.L.J. 949; [2000] N.P.C. 65; *Times*, June 16, 2000; *Independent*, June 20, 2000, HL; reversing [1999] R.T.R. 210; (1999) 1 L.G.L.R. 364; (1999) 96(5) L.S.G. 36; (1999) 143 S.J.L.B. 38; *Times*, January 7, 1999, CA . . . . *Digested*, 00/**4237**: *Followed*, 01/4499

Goodeve-Docker *v.* Leonard Ross & Craig see Yudt *v.* Leonard Ross & Craig

Goodger *v.* Willis [1999] E.G.C.S. 32, Ch D

Goodland *v.* DPP see Atkins *v.* DPP

Goodman *v.* Chief Constable of Derbyshire see Chief Constable of Derbyshire *v.* Goodman

Goodman *v.* Darby (Unreported, July 27, 2000), CC (Bodmin) [*Ex rel.* James Hassall, Barrister, Guildhall Chambers, Broad Street, Bristol] . . . . *Digested*, 01/**1640**

Goodman *v.* Evely [2001] EWCA Civ 104; [2001] L. & T.R. 31; [2001] N.P.C. 43, CA

Goodridge *v.* Chief Constable of Hampshire [1999] 1 W.L.R. 1558; [1999] 1 All E.R. 896, QBD . . . . *Digested*, 99/**337**

Goodridge *v.* Ferguson (1997) 97(5/6) Q.R. 8, QBD . . . . *Digested*, 98/**1484**

Goodwill *v.* British Pregnancy Advisory Service [1996] 1 W.L.R. 1397; [1996] 2 All E.R. 161; [1996] 2 F.L.R. 55; [1996] 2 F.C.R. 680; [1996] P.I.Q.R. P197; [1996] 7 Med. L.R. 129; (1996) 31 B.M.L.R. 83; (1996) 93(5) L.S.G. 31; (1996) 146 N.L.J. 173; (1996) 140 S.J.L.B. 37; *Times*, January 29, 1996; *Independent*, January 19, 1996, CA. . . . . *Digested*, 96/**4470**: *Applied*, 98/697

Goodwill Merchant Financial Services Ltd, Re; *sub nom* Financial Services Authority *v.* Goodwill Merchant Financial Ltd [2001] 1 B.C.L.C. 259, Ch D (Companies Ct) . *Digested*, 01/**3759**

Goodwin *v.* Cabletel UK Ltd [1998] I.C.R. 112; [1997] I.R.L.R. 665, EAT . . . . *Digested*, 98/**2103**

Goodwin *v.* Curtis (Inspector of Taxes) [1998] S.T.C. 475; 70 T.C. 478; [1998] B.T.C. 176; (1998) 95(12) L.S.G. 27; (1998) 142 S.J.L.B. 91; *Times*, March 2, 1998; *Independent*, March 2, 1998 (C.S.), CA; affirming [1996] S.T.C. 1146; (1996) 140 S.J.L.B. 186; *Times*, August 14, 1996; *Independent*, October 14, 1996 (C.S.), Ch D . . . . *Digested*, 98/**4609**

Goodwin *v.* Fryer (Unreported, August 17, 1998), CC (Tunbridge Wells) [*Ex rel.* Cripps Harries Hall Solicitors, Seymour House, 11-13 Mount Ephraim Road, Tunbridge Wells, Kent] . . . . *Digested*, 98/**1500**

Goodwin *v.* GKN Sheepbridge Stokes Ltd (Unreported, January 10, 2000), CC (Chesterfield) [*Ex rel.* Craig Moore, Barrister, Park Lane Chambers, 19 Westgate, Leeds] . . . . *Digested*, 00/**1637**

Goodwin *v.* Patent Office [1999] I.C.R. 302; [1999] I.R.L.R. 4; [1999] Disc. L.R. 104; *Times*, November 11, 1998, EAT . . . . *Digested*, 98/**2114**: *Applied*, 00/2125, 01/2242

Goodwin *v.* United Kingdom (17488/90) (1996) 22 E.H.R.R. 123; 1 B.H.R.C. 81; *Times*, March 28, 1996, ECHR . . . . *Digested*, 96/**3145**: *Applied*, 98/3089, 98/3090; *Considered*, 97/2780, 98/3422

Goose *v.* Wilson Sandford & Co (No.1) (1998) 95(12) L.S.G. 27; (1998) 142 S.J.L.B. 92; *Times*, February 19, 1998, CA . . . . *Digested*, 98/**50**: *Applied*, 98/51, 01/49

Goose *v.* Wilson Sandford & Co (No.2) [2001] Lloyd's Rep. P.N. 189, CA . . . . *Digested*, 01/**5356**

Gopee *v.* Beat [2001] B.P.I.R. 258, Ch D . . . . *Digested*, 01/**3781**

Gordon, Re see Gordon *v.* Omgate Ltd

Gordon v. JB Wheatley & Co; *sub nom* Gordon v. Wheatley & Co [2000] Lloyd's Rep.
P.N. 605; [2000] P.N.L.R. 755; (2000) 97(24) L.S.G. 40; *Times*, June 6, 2000,
CA; reversing1998-G-No.513, QBD . . . .   *Digested,* 00/**4256**
Gordon v. Omgate Ltd; *sub nom* Gordon, Re [2001] B.P.I.R. 909, Ch D
Gordon v. Reith 1997 S.L.T. 62; [1998] E.H.L.R. Dig. 137, HCJ Appeal . . . .   *Digested,* 97/**5599**
Gordon v. United Kingdom see Moore v. United Kingdom
Gordon v. Wheatley & Co see Gordon v. JB Wheatley & Co
Gordon Coutts Thomson (A Firm) v. Council of the Law Society of Scotland (No.1)
1999 S.C.L.R. 823; 1999 G.W.D. 11-515; *Times*, May 13, 1999, Ex Div . . . .   *Digested,* 99/**6341**
Gore v. Jones, *Times*, February 21, 2001, Ch D   *Digested,* 01/**473**
GORGONZOLA/CAMBOZOLA see Consorzio per la Tutela del Formaggio Gorgonzola v.
Kaserei Champignon Hofmeister GmbH & Co KG (C87/97)
Gorham v. British Telecommunications Plc [2000] 1 W.L.R. 2129; [2000] 4 All E.R.
867; [2001] Lloyd's Rep. I.R. 531; [2000] Lloyd's Rep. P.N. 897; [2001] P.N.L.R.
2; [2000] Pens. L.R. 293; (2000) 97(38) L.S.G. 44; (2000) 144 S.J.L.B. 251;
Times, August 16, 2000, CA. . . . .   *Digested,* 00/**4253**
Goringe v. Twinsectra (Unreported, April 20, 1994), CC (Staines) [*Ex rel.* Karen
Walden-Smith, Barrister] . . . .   *Digested,* 94/**2723**:
   Approved, 98/3682
Gorman v. DPP; DPP v. Arnup [1997] R.T.R. 409, QBD. . . . .   *Digested,* 98/**1029**
Gormley v. EMI Records (Ireland) Ltd [2000] E.C.C. 370; [2000] E.C.D.R. 31, Sup Ct
(Irl) . . . .   *Digested,* 00/**3574**
Gornall v. Yandell (Unreported, May 10, 1999), CC (Hertford) [*Ex rel.* Andrew Granville
Stafford, Barrister, 4 King's Bench Walk, Temple, London] . . . .   *Digested,* 99/**1576**
Goscomb v. News Group Newspapers Ltd see Mapp v. News Group Newspapers Ltd
Gosling v. Burrard-Lucas (Unreported, November 4, 1998), CC (Tunbridge Wells) [*Ex
rel.* Simon Brindle, Barrister, 199 Strand, London] . . . .   *Digested,* 99/**1802**
Gosport BC v. Tutton (1999) 14 P.A.D. 551, Planning Inspector
Gotha City v. Sotheby's (No.1) [1998] 1 W.L.R. 114; (1997) 94(30) L.S.G. 28; (1997)
141 S.J.L.B. 152; *Times*, July 3, 1997, CA . . . .   *Digested,* 97/**470**:
   Approved, 98/330
Gotha City v. Sotheby's (No.2); Germany v. Sotheby's (No.2) *Times*, October 8, 1998,
QBD . . . .   *Digested,* 98/**775**
Gott v. McGrath (Unreported, July 14, 1999), CC (Southport) [*Ex rel.* Fletchers
Solicitors, 160/162 Lord Street, Southport] . . . .   *Digested,* 99/**1583**
Gottrup-Klim Grovvareforeninger v. Dansk Landsbrugs Grovvareselskab AMBA (C250/
92) [1994] E.C.R. I-5641; [1996] 4 C.M.L.R. 191, ECJ (5th Chamber) . . . .   *Digested,* 95/**617**:
   Considered, 97/855: *Referred to,* 99/3498
Goudie v. Night Freight (East) Ltd (Unreported, October 20, 1999), CC (Ipswich) [*Ex
rel.* Jackaman, Smith & Mulley Solicitors, 7 Northgate Street, Ipswich] . . . .   *Digested,* 00/**1572**
Gough v. Chief Constable of Derbyshire; *sub nom* Miller v. Leeds Magistrates Court;
Lilley v. DPP; R. (on the application of Miller) v. Leeds Magistrates Court; C/
2001/1698, CA; affirming [2001] EWHC Admin 554; [2001] 3 W.L.R. 1392;
[2001] 4 All E.R. 289; [2001] 3 C.M.L.R. 29; [2001] Eu. L.R. 701; (2001)
98(33) L.S.G. 30; *Times*, July 19, 2001; *Independent*, November 5, 2001 (C.S),
QBD (Admin Ct) . . . .   *Digested,* 01/**1062**
Gough v. Consolidated Beryllium Ceramics Ltd (Unreported, December 11, 1998),
QBD [*Ex rel.* Ann Broadhead, Pupil Barrister, 30 Park Place, Cardiff] . . . .   *Digested,* 99/**1533**
Gough v. Thorne [1966] 1 W.L.R. 1387; [1966] 3 All E.R. 398; 110 S.J. 529, CA . . . . .   *Digested,* 66/**8076**:
   Considered, 98/3994
Goulden v. Wilson Barca (A Firm); *sub nom* Wilson Barca (A Firm) v. Goulden [2000]
1 W.L.R. 167; (1999) 96(31) L.S.G. 35; (1999) 143 S.J.L.B. 212; *Times*, August
20, 1999 ; *Independent*, October 4, 1999, CA . . . .   *Digested,* 99/**3772**
Gourdain (Liquidator) v. Nadler (C133/78) [1979] E.C.R. 733; [1979] 3 C.M.L.R. 180,
ECJ . . . .   *Digested,* 79/**1168**:
   Applied, 00/765: *Distinguished,* 96/1111
Gouriet v. Union of Post Office Workers; *sub nom* Attorney General v. Gouriet [1978]
A.C. 435; [1977] 3 W.L.R. 300; [1977] 3 All E.R. 70; 121 S.J. 543, HL; reversing
[1977] Q.B. 729; [1977] 2 W.L.R. 310; [1977] 1 All E.R. 696; 121 S.J. 103, CA . .   *Digested,* 77/**690**:
   Applied, 78/2377, 80/1838, 85/3406, 86/3390.d, 88/2994, 89/3133:
   Considered, 77/2996, 78/2910, 85/2042, 86/3390.c, 87/2984, 89/2990,
   90/3704, 95/4102, 96/2846, 97/2185: *Distinguished,* 81/1433, 81/2720,
   84/3469: *Followed,* 84/1659, 85/2666: *Not followed,* 99/1043
Govell v. United Kingdom (Unreported, January 14, 1998), ECHR . . . .   *Applied,* 00/3249:
   Considered, 00/943
Governing Body of Clifton Middle School v. Askew; *sub nom* Askew v. Governing Body
of Clifton Middle School [2000] I.C.R. 286; [1999] I.R.L.R. 708; (2000) 2
L.G.L.R. 313; [2000] B.L.G.R. 97; [1999] Ed. C.R. 800; [1999] E.L.R. 425;
(1999) 96(33) L.S.G. 30; *Times*, August 2, 1999, CA; affirming [1997] I.C.R.
808, EAT . . . .   *Digested,* 99/**2007**
Governors of the Peabody Donation Fund v. Grant (1982) 264 E.G. 925, CA . . . .   *Digested,* 83/**2145**:
   Applied, 00/6462, 00/6463: *Considered,* 87/2240

Governors of the Peabody Donation Fund v. Higgins; *sub nom* Peabody Donation Fund v. Higgins [1983] 1 W.L.R. 1091; [1983] 3 All E.R. 122; (1982-83) 10 H.L.R. 85; (1983) 127 S.J. 596, CA .... *Digested,* 83/**2146**:
Applied, 98/**2984**

Govett American Endeavour Fund Ltd v. Trueger [1999] I.L.Pr. 639, US Ct

Gowa v. Attorney General [1985] 1 W.L.R. 1003; (1985) 82 L.S.G. 3170; (1985) 129 S.J. 541, HL; affirming (1985) 82 L.S.G. 681; (1985) 129 S.J. 131, CA .... *Digested,* 85/**1710**:
Applied, 92/2435, 93/2167: *Distinguished,* 00/3288

GP&P Ltd v. Bulcraig & Davis [1988] 12 E.G. 103, CA; reversing [1986] 2 E.G.L.R. 148; (1986) 280 E.G. 356, QBD .... *Digested,* 88/**1066**:
Followed, 98/**4025**

GPT Ltd's European Patent Application (No.95938496.7) see GPT/Procedural Request (T685/98)

GPT SA v. Ste Cartier France [1998] E.T.M.R. 382, Trib Gde Inst (Paris)

GPT/Procedural Request (T685/98); *sub nom* GPT Ltd's European Patent Application (No.95938496.7) [1999] E.P.O.R. 560; (1999) 22(1) I.P.D. 22008, EPO (Technical Bd App) .... *Digested,* 00/**3658**

GR Amylum NV v. Council of the European Communities (C116/77); Tunnel Refineries Ltd v. Council of the European Communities (124/77); Koninklijke Scholten Honig NV v. Council of the European Communities (C143/77) [1979] E.C.R. 3497; [1978] E.C.R. 893; [1982] 2 C.M.L.R. 590, ECJ .... *Digested,* 82/**1154**:
Followed, 98/**2306**

Grace v. Customs and Excise Commissioners [1998] V. & D.R. 86, V&DTr .... *Digested,* 00/**5300**

Grace v. Stagecoach Ltd (Unreported, June 23, 2000), CC (Exeter) [*Ex rel.* Crosse & Crosse Solicitors, 14 Southernhay West, Exeter] .... *Digested,* 00/**1624**

Grace Baptist Church v. Customs and Excise Commissioners [1999] B.V.C. 2294, V&DTr

Gracechurch International SA v. Tribhovan (2001) 33 H.L.R. 28, CA .... *Digested,* 01/**4147**

Gracey's Registration (No.1335163), Re; Ferretti's Application for Revocation (No.9206), Re (2000) 23(8) I.P.D. 23064, Appointed Person

Grady v. United Kingdom (No.1) see Smith v. United Kingdom (No.1)

Grady v. United Kingdom (No.2) see Smith v. United Kingdom (No.2)

Graf v. Filzmoser Maschinenbau GmbH (C190/98) [2000] All E.R. (EC) 170; [2000] E.C.R. I-493; [2000] 1 C.M.L.R. 741; [2000] C.E.C. 82, ECJ .... *Digested,* 00/**2175**

Graffin v. Famac Network Ltd (Unreported, January 24, 1997), CA (NI) .... *Considered,* 99/**5230**

Graham (t/a Excel Tutoring Services) v. Customs and Excise Commissioners [2001] S.T.I. 157, V&DTr

Graham v. Irving (Unreported, December 9, 1998), CC (Birkenhead) [*Ex rel.* Ivan Cartwright, Barrister, Derby Square Chambers, Merchant's Court, Derby Square, Liverpool] .... *Digested,* 99/**2456**

Graham v. Morini [2000] 5 Q.R. 8, CC (Blackpool) [*Ex rel.* John G Baldwin, Barrister, Oriel Chambers, 14 Water Street, Liverpool] .... *Digested,* 00/**1664**

Graham v. Potterton (Unreported, June 29, 2000), CC (Exeter) [*Ex rel.* Easthams Solicitors, 292/302 Church Street, Blackpool] .... *Digested,* 01/**1542**

Graham v. Quinn [1997] N.I. 338, CA (NI) .... *Digested,* 99/**5230**

Graham v. Secretary of State for Social Security (C92/94); *sub nom* Secretary of State for Social Security v. Graham; Chief Adjudication Officer v. Graham [1995] All E.R. (E.C.) 736; [1995] E.C.R. I-2521; [1995] 3 C.M.L.R. 169; [1996] I.C.R. 258; *Times,* September 25, 1995; *Independent,* October 9, 1995 (C.S.), ECJ (6th Chamber) .... *Digested,* 96/**5391**:
Considered, 98/**4547**

Graham v. Taylor [2001] 6 Q.R. 21, CC (Nottingham) [*Ex rel.* Jinder S Boora, Barrister, 24, The Ropewalk, Nottingham] .... *Digested,* 01/**1775**

Graham v. Teesdale 81 L.G.R. 117, DC .... *Digested,* 83/**2229**:
Considered, 86/2017, 87/3162: *Distinguished,* 00/4110

Grahame v. Bestuur van de Nieuwe Algemene Bedrijfsvereniging (C248/96) [1997] E.C.R. I-6407, ECJ [1997] E.C.R. I-6407, AGO .... *Distinguished,* 00/**4818**

Graigola Merthyr Co Ltd v. Mayor, Aldermen and Burgesses of Swansea see Graigola Merthyr Co Ltd v. Swansea Corp

Graigola Merthyr Co Ltd v. Swansea Corp; *sub nom* Graigola Merthyr Co Ltd v. Mayor, Aldermen and Burgesses of Swansea [1929] A.C. 344, HL; affirming [1928] Ch. 235, CA; affirming [1928] Ch. 31, Ch D .... *Applied,* 99/**5286**

Grainger Investment Property Ltd v. Southern and South Eastern Rent Assessment Commitee see Queensway Housing Association Ltd v. Chiltern, Thames and Eastern Rent Assessment Committee

Grammer v. Lane; Grammer v. Stone [2000] 2 All E.R. 245; [2000] L. & T.R. 264; [2000] 1 E.G.L.R. 1; [2000] 04 E.G. 135; (1999) 96(48) L.S.G. 39; (2000) 144 S.J.L.B. 17; [1999] N.P.C. 149; *Times,* December 2, 1999, CA .... *Digested,* 00/**3869**

Grammer v. Stone see Grammer v. Lane

Grampian RC v. Aberdeen DC see Grampian Regional Council v. City of Aberdeen DC

Grampian RC v. Secretary of State for Scotland see Grampian Regional Council v. City of Aberdeen DC

Grampian RC v. Secretary of State for Scotland [1983] 1 W.L.R. 1340; [1983] 3 All
E.R. 673; 1984 S.L.T. 212; (1984) 47 P. & C.R. 540; (1984) 271 E.G. 625; [1983]
R.V.R. 263; [1984] J.P.L. 416; (1984) 81 L.S.G. 43; (1984) 134 N.L.J. 36;
(1983) 127 S.J. 804; *Times*, November 16, 1983, HL . . . . *Digested*, 84/**3789**:
Applied, 91/455, 91/3426, 92/4178: *Considered*, 91/3523, 00/4427

Grampian Regional Council v. City of Aberdeen DC; *sub nom* Grampian RC v.
Aberdeen DC; Grampian RC v. Secretary of State for Scotland 1984 S.C. (H.L.)
58; 1984 S.L.T. 197; (1984) 47 P. & C.R. 633, HL . . . . *Digested*, 84/**4734**:
Considered, 91/3524, 99/4240: *Followed*, 96/7257: *Referred to*, 89/3636,
91/5757, 00/4509

Gran Gelato Ltd v. Richcliff (Group) Ltd [1992] Ch. 560; [1992] 2 W.L.R. 867; [1992]
1 All E.R. 865; [1992] 1 E.G.L.R. 297; [1991] E.G.C.S. 136; (1992) 142 N.L.J. 51;
Times, December 19, 1991; *Independent*, December 18, 1991, Ch D . . . . *Digested*, 92/**4085**:
Applied, 98/3939: *Considered*, 93/3789, 01/871

Granada Hospitality Ltd v. Secretary of State for the Environment, Transport and the
Regions (2001) 81 P. & C.R. 36; [2001] P.L.C.R. 5; [2001] J.P.L. 222 (Note),
QBD . . . . *Digested*, 01/**4709**

Granby Village (Manchester) Management Co Ltd v. Unchained Growth III Plc see
Unchained Growth III Plc v. Granby Village (Manchester) Management Co Ltd

Grand Garage Albigeois SA v. Garage Massol Sarl (C226/94); Nissan France SA v.
Dupasquier (C309/94) [1996] E.C.R. I-651; [1996] 4 C.M.L.R. 778; [1996]
C.E.C. 538, ECJ (2nd Chamber) . . . . *Digested*, 96/**1043**:
Applied, 98/743

Grange Oversands Golf Club v. Customs and Excise Commissioners see Keswick Golf
Club v. Customs and Excise Commissioners

Granger Builders v. Customs and Excise Commissioners [1996] V. & D.R. 438, VAT Tr
(Manchester) . . . . *Digested*, 98/**4976**

Graniti Fiandre v. La Societe Mothes [2001] I.L.Pr. 13, Cass (F)

Granovsky v. Minister of Employment and Immigration 10 B.H.R.C. 619, Sup Ct (Can) . . *Digested*, 01/**3454**

Grant v. Australian Knitting Mills Ltd; *sub nom* Australian Knitting Mills v. Grant Ltd
[1936] A.C. 85; (1934) 50 C.L.R. 387, HC (Aus); reversing (1933) 50 C.L.R.
387, Sup Ct (SAus) (Sgl judge) . . . . *Applied*, 54/2979,
58/3034, 60/2686, 67/3537, 72/2408: *Considered*, 65/3516, 68/3526,
74/3426, 79/2089, 90/3314, 91/2658, 98/399: *Disapproved*, 70/2605:
Distinguished, 72/2361, 94/3352, 95/4519

Grant v. Edwards [1986] Ch. 638; [1986] 3 W.L.R. 114; [1986] 2 All E.R. 426; [1987]
1 F.L.R. 87; [1986] Fam. Law 300; (1986) 83 L.S.G. 1996; (1986) 136 N.L.J.
439; (1986) 130 S.J. 408, CA . . . . *Digested*, 86/**3034**:
Applied, 88/491, 89/468, 92/2034, 92/3160, 95/2188, 96/2887, 01/5503:
Considered, 90/1251, 91/1090: *Distinguished*, 90/1989, 91/1716:
Followed, 96/4943: *Referred to*, 89/1516, 91/1721

Grant v. Gregory (1999) 99(5) Q.R. 7, CC (Birmingham) [*Ex rel.* Andrew Willets, Pupil
Barrister, Victoria Chambers, 177 Corporation Street, Birmingham] . . . . *Digested*, 99/**1594**
Considered, 01/2228

Grant v. John Grant & Sons Pty Ltd (1954) 91 C.L.R. 112, HC (Aus) . . . . *Cited*, 00/4679

Grant v. Norway (1851) 10 C.B. 665 . . . . *Digested*, 98/**2107**

Grant v. South West Trains Ltd [1998] I.R.L.R. 188, QBD . . . .

Grant v. South West Trains Ltd (C249/96) [1998] All E.R. (EC) 193; [1998] E.C.R. I-
621; [1998] 1 C.M.L.R. 993; [1998] C.E.C. 263; [1998] I.C.R. 449; [1998]
I.R.L.R. 206; [1998] 1 F.L.R. 839; [1998] 1 F.C.R. 377; 3 B.H.R.C. 578; [1999]
Pens. L.R. 69; [1998] Fam. Law 392; (1998) 162 J.P.N. 266; *Times*, February
23, 1998, ECJ . . . . *Digested*, 98/**2145**:
Applied, 98/262, 01/2285

Grant v. Sun Shipping Co Ltd [1948] A.C. 549; [1948] 2 All E.R. 238; (1947-48) 81
Ll. L. Rep. 383; 1948 S.C. (H.L.) 73; 1949 S.L.T. 25; 1949 S.L.T. (Notes) 66;
[1949] L.J.R. 727; 92 S.J. 513, HL; reversing (1947) 80 Ll. L. Rep. 45; 1948
S.L.T. (Notes) 85, 2 Div . . . . *Digested*, 47-51/**6706**:
Applied, 47-51/6624, 47-51/6637, 47-51/6675, 53/2287, 63/330, 00/4255:
Distinguished, 88/2034: *Followed*, 58/2241: *Not followed*, 59/2186

Grant v. Watton (Inspector of Taxes); *sub nom* Andrew Grant Services Ltd v. Watton
(Inspector of Taxes) [1999] S.T.C. 330; 71 T.C. 333; [1999] B.T.C. 85; *Times*,
March 31, 1999; *Independent*, March 1, 1999 (C.S.), Ch D . . . . *Digested*, 99/**4705**:
Followed, 99/2483

Grantham Cricket Club v. Customs and Excise Commissioners [1998] B.V.C. 2272,
V&DTr. . . . . *Digested*, 98/**4971**

Granton Marketing Ltd v. Customs and Excise Commissioners; Wentwalk Ltd v.
Customs and Excise Commissioners [1999] B.V.C. 2336; [1999] V. & D.R. 383,
V&DTr. . . . . *Digested*, 00/**5290**

Grape Bay Ltd v. Attorney General of Bermuda [2000] 1 W.L.R. 574, PC (Ber) . . . . *Digested*, 00/**4408**

GRASS AIR/Air drying apparatus (T92/86) [1999] E.P.O.R. 574, EPO (Technical Bd App)
Digested, 00/**3638**

Grattan v. McNaughton [2001] W.T.L.R. 1305, Ch D

Grave v. GA Bonus Plc [1999] 2 Lloyd's Rep. 716, DR (Preston) . . . . *Digested*, 00/**3517**

Graves v. Smith (Unreported, November 17, 1998), CC (Sheffield) [*Ex rel.* Nabarro
Nathanson Solicitors, 1 South Quay, Victoria Quays, Sheffield, South Yorkshire] . . *Digested*, 99/**413**

Gravesham BC *v.* Secretary of State for the Environment (1984) 47 P. & C.R. 142; [1983] J.P.L. 307, QBD . . . . *Digested,* 84/**3421**:
Approved, 98/4169: *Considered,* 85/3405, 01/4656
Gray *v.* Braer Corp [1999] 2 Lloyd's Rep. 541; 1999 S.L.T. 1410; 1999 S.C.L.R. 336; 1999 G.W.D. 5-279; *Times,* March 10, 1999, OH . . . . *Digested,* 99/**6421**
Gray *v.* Brown (1993) 25 H.L.R. 144; [1993] 07 E.G. 97; *Times,* November 3, 1992, CA . *Digested,* 93/**2541**:
Followed, 98/3632
Gray *v.* Buss Murton [1999] P.N.L.R. 882, QBD . . . . *Digested,* 00/**4224**
Gray (t/a William Gray & Sons) *v.* Customs and Excise Commissioners [2000] S.T.C. 880; [2000] B.T.C. 5373; [2000] B.V.C. 396; [2000] S.T.I. 1495; *Times,* November 7, 2000, Ch D . . . . *Digested,* 00/**5327**
Gray *v.* DPP (1999) 163 J.P. 710; [1999] R.T.R. 339, QBD . . . . *Digested,* 99/**960**
Gray *v.* Richards Butler (Recovery) [2001] W.T.L.R. 625; (1996) 93(29) L.S.G. 29; (1996) 140 S.J.L.B. 194; *Times,* July 23, 1996, Ch D . . . . *Digested,* 96/**5556**
Gray *v.* Richards Butler (Supervision of Execution) [2000] W.T.L.R. 143, Ch D . . . . *Digested,* 00/**4259**
Gray *v.* Smiths Shiprepairers (North Shields) Ltd see Thompson *v.* Smiths Shiprepairers (North Shields) Ltd
Gray *v.* Stead [1999] 2 Lloyd's Rep. 559, CA; reversing [1999] 1 Lloyd's Rep. 377; *Independent,* November 2, 1998 (C.S.), QBD (Comm Ct) . . . . *Digested,* 99/**2554**
Gray *v.* Taylor [1998] 1 W.L.R. 1093; [1998] 4 All E.R. 17; (1999) 31 H.L.R. 262; [1998] L. & T.R. 50; [1998] E.G.C.S. 62; (1998) 95(20) L.S.G. 34; (1998) 142 S.J.L.B. 141; [1998] N.P.C. 60; *Times,* April 24, 1998, CA . . . . *Digested,* 98/**3599**
Gray's Inn Construction Co Ltd, Re [1980] 1 W.L.R. 711; [1980] 1 All E.R. 814; 124 S.J. 463, CA . . . . *Digested,* 80/**290**:
Considered, 87/380, 92/2645: *Distinguished,* 00/3465
Grayan Building Services Ltd (In Liquidation), Re [1995] Ch. 241; [1995] 3 W.L.R.1; [1995] B.C.C. 554, CA . . . . *Digested,* 95/**582**:
Applied, 00/660: *Considered,* 96/985, 99/610: *Followed,* 97/824
Grayline Coaches *v.* Dickson (Unreported, May 22, 1997), CC (Reading) [*Ex rel.* Davies Arnold Cooper, Solicitors, 6-8 Bouverie Street, London] . . . . *Digested,* 97/**718**:
Followed, 99/537
Grayson-Crowe *v.* Ministry of Defence (Unreported, June 30, 1992), HC [*Ex rel.* Hodge Jones & Allen, Solicitors] . . . . *Digested,* 92/**1663**:
Considered, 98/1630
GREA Real Property Investments *v.* Williams (1979) 250 E.G. 651 . . . . *Digested,* 79/**1636**:
Considered, 79/1637, 99/4057
Greasley *v.* Cooke [1980] 1 W.L.R. 1306; [1980] 3 All E.R. 710; 124 S.J. 629, CA . . . . . *Digested,* 80/**1066**:
Considered, 83/3895, 86/1301, 86/3034, 87/1444, 90/2776:
Distinguished, 95/2339: *Referred to,* 94/2109, 00/2321
Great American Bagel Factory Ltd *v.* Customs and Excise Commissioners [2001] S.T.I. 746, V&DTr
Great Atlantic Insurance Co *v.* American Foreign Insurance Association see Great Atlantic Insurance Co *v.* Home Insurance Co
Great Atlantic Insurance Co *v.* CE Heath & Co (International) see Great Atlantic Insurance Co *v.* Home Insurance Co
Great Atlantic Insurance Co *v.* Frank Elger & Co see Great Atlantic Insurance Co *v.* Home Insurance Co
Great Atlantic Insurance Co *v.* Home Insurance Co; *sub nom* Great Atlantic Insurance Co *v.* American Foreign Insurance Association; Great Atlantic Insurance Co *v.* CE Heath & Co (International); Great Atlantic Insurance Co *v.* Frank Elger & Co [1981] 1 W.L.R. 529; [1981] 2 All E.R. 485; [1981] 2 Lloyd's Rep. 138; 125 S.J. 203, CA; affirming [1981] 2 Lloyd's Rep. 219, QBD (Comm Ct) . . . . *Digested,* 81/**2522**:
Applied, 83/2937, 84/1528, 85/2649, 86/2620, 95/4121:
Distinguished, 94/3670, 95/4125
Great China Metal Industries Co Ltd *v.* Malaysian International Shipping Corp Bhd (The Bunga Seroja) [1999] 1 Lloyd's Rep. 512; 1999 A.M.C. 427, HC (Aus); affirming [1994] 1 Lloyd's Rep. 455, Sup Ct (NSW) . . . . *Digested,* 99/**4420**
Great Eastern Railway Co *v.* Lord's Trustee; *sub nom* Trustee of the Property of Lord (A Bankrupt) *v.* Great Eastern Railway Co [1909] A.C. 109, HL; affirming in part [1908] 2 K.B. 54, CA; reversing [1908] 1 K.B. 195, KBD . . . . *Applied,* 00/**674**
Great Future International Ltd *v.* Sealand Housing Corp (Contempt of Court) see Great Future International Ltd *v.* Sealand Housing Corp (No.2)
Great Future International Ltd *v.* Sealand Housing Corp (No.2); *sub nom* Great Future International Ltd *v.* Sealand Housing Corp (Contempt of Court) [2001] C.P.L.R. 293, Ch D . . . . *Digested,* 01/**17**
Great North Eastern Railway Ltd *v.* Avon Insurance Plc; *sub nom* Great Northern Eastern Railway Ltd *v.* Avon Insurance Plc; GNER *v.* Avon Insurance Plc [2001] EWCA Civ 780; [2001] 2 All E.R. (Comm) 526; [2001] 2 Lloyd's Rep. 649; [2001] Lloyd's Rep. I.R. 793, CA99/1073, QBD . . . . *Digested,* 01/**3815**
Great Northern Eastern Railway Ltd *v.* Avon Insurance Plc see Great North Eastern Railway Ltd *v.* Avon Insurance Plc
Great Ormond Street Hospital NHS Trust *v.* Secretary of State for Health 56 Con. L.R. 1, QBD (OR) . . . . *Digested,* 98/**250**

Great Peace Shipping Ltd v. Tsavliris Salvage (International) Ltd (2001) 151 N.L.J. 1696, QBD (Comm Ct)

Great Portland Estates Plc v. Westminster City Council see Westminster City Council v. Great Portland Estates Plc

Great Yarmouth BC v. Alterman (Unreported, January 28, 1998), CC (Great Yarmouth) [*Ex rel.* Council Solicitor for Great Yarmouth, Town Hall, Hall Quay, Great Yarmouth, Norfolk] . . . . *Digested*, 98/**3353**

Great Yarmouth Corp v. Gibson [1956] 1 Q.B. 573; [1956] 2 W.L.R. 356; [1956] 1 All E.R. 113; 120 J.P. 94; 54 L.G.R. 186, CA; reversing (1955) 105 L.J. 684, CC . . . . *Digested*, 56/**7183**: *Applied*, 99/427

Greater Glasgow Health Board v. Hannah see Secretary of State for Scotland v. Wright

Greater Glasgow Health Board v. Wright see Secretary of State for Scotland v. Wright

Greater London Council v. Cleveland Bridge and Engineering Co Ltd 34 B.L.R. 50; 8 Con. L.R. 30, CA; affirming [1984] C.I.L.L. 106, HC . . . . *Digested*, 87/**245**: *Considered*, 00/826

Greatorex v. Greatorex [2000] 1 W.L.R. 1970; [2000] 4 All E.R. 769; [2001] R.T.R. 1; (2000) 97(24) L.S.G. 41; *Times*, June 6, 2000; *Independent*, July 3, 2000 (C.S), QBD . . . . *Digested*, 00/**4220**

Greaves v. Kwik Save Stores Ltd see Crees v. Royal London Mutual Insurance Society Ltd

Greek Taverna, Re [1999] B.C.C. 153, Ch D . . . . *Digested*, 99/**3317**

Green v. British Gas (North Eastern) Plc see Afzal v. Ford Motor Co Ltd

Green v. Cobham [2000] W.T.L.R. 1101, Ch D . . . . *Digested*, 01/**5515**: *Followed*, 01/5532

Green v. Collyer-Bristow [1999] Lloyd's Rep. P.N. 798; [1999] N.P.C. 56, QBD . . . . *Digested*, 99/**4034**

Green v. Doncaster MBC [2001] R.V.R. 117, Lands Tr . . . . *Digested*, 01/**4664**

Green v. DPP see DPP v. Green

Green v. Green (1993) [1993] 1 F.L.R. 326; [1993] Fam. Law 119, Fam Div . . . . *Digested*, 94/**2177**: *Overruled*, 98/2467

Green v. Hancocks (A Firm) [2001] Lloyd's Rep. P.N. 212, CA; affirming [2000] Lloyd's Rep. P.N. 813; [2001] P.N.L.R. 10; *Times*, August 15, 2000, Ch D . . . . . . *Digested*, 01/**4517**

Green v. Leicester CC [2000] 4 Q.R. 7, CC (Mansfield) [*Ex rel.* Richard Gregory, Barrister, 24 The Ropewalk, Nottingham] . . . . *Digested*, 00/**1732**

Green v. Lincolnshire Stipendiary Magistrate see DPP v. Green

Green v. Satsangi [1998] 1 B.C.L.C. 458; [1998] B.P.I.R. 55, Ch D . . . . *Digested*, 98/**3283**

Green v. Staples see R. v. City of London Magistrates Court Ex p. Green

Green v. Turner [1999] P.N.L.R. 28, Ch D . . . . *Digested*, 98/**3987**

Green v. Wheatley (1999) 99(22) L.S.G. 36, CA

Green Environmental Industries Ltd, Re see R. v. Hertfordshire CC Ex p. Green Environmental Industries Ltd

Green Environmental Industries Ltd v. Hertfordshire CC see R. v. Hertfordshire CC Ex p. Green Environmental Industries Ltd

Green Star Shipping Co Ltd v. London Assurance (No.1) [1933] 1 K.B. 378; (1931) 39 Ll. L. Rep. 213, KBD . . . . *Applied*, 00/**4725**

Green Street Action Group Ltd v. Newham LBC CO/1692/97, QBD . . . . *Digested*, 98/**2866**

Greenacre Publishing Group v. Manson Group see Greenacre Publishing Ltd, Re

Greenacre Publishing Ltd, Re; *sub nom* Greenacre Publishing Group v. Manson Group [2000] B.C.C. 11; *Times*, December 17, 1998, Ch D . . . . *Digested*, 99/**3348**

Greenalls Management Ltd v. Canavan (No.2) [1998] Eu. L.R. 507; [1997] N.P.C. 128; *Times*, August 20, 1997, CA . . . . *Digested*, 97/**3306**: *Applied*, 01/2519; *Followed*, 99/680, 99/688

Greenalls Management Ltd v. Philbin [1998] Eu. L.R. 540, QBD . . . . *Digested*, 99/**686**

Greenalls Management Ltd v. Smith see Courage Ltd v. Crehan (No.1)

Greenaway v. Newport BC (Unreported, January 12, 1999), CC [*Ex rel.* Beatrice Prevatt, Barrister, 2 Garden Court Chambers, 2 Garden Court, Middle Temple, London] . . . . *Digested*, 99/**3065**

Greenaway v. Rover Group Ltd (Unreported, February 16, 2000), CC (Dudley) [*Ex rel.* Taylor Joynson Garrett Solicitors, Carmelite, 50 Victoria Embankment, Blackfriars, London] . . . . *Digested*, 00/**400**

Greenbank v. Pickles [2001] 1 E.G.L.R. 1; [2001] 09 E.G. 230; [2000] N.P.C. 107; (2001) 81 P. & C.R. D13; *Times*, November 7, 2000, CA . . . . *Digested*, 00/**3873**

Greenfield v. Flather see Greenfield v. Irwin (A Firm)

Greenfield v. Irwin (A Firm); *sub nom* Greenfield v. Flather [2001] EWCA Civ 113; [2001] 1 W.L.R. 1279; [2001] 1 F.L.R. 899; [2001] P.I.Q.R. Q7; [2001] Lloyd's Rep. Med. 143; (2001) 59 B.M.L.R. 43; *Times*, February 6, 2001, CA . . . . *Digested*, 01/**4463**

Greenfield v. Secretary of State for the Home Department see R. (on the application of Greenfield) v. Secretary of State for the Home Department (No.1)

Greenhaven Motors Ltd (In Liquidation), Re [1999] B.C.C. 463; [1999] 1 B.C.L.C 635, CA; reversing [1997] B.C.C. 547; [1997] 1 B.C.L.C. 739, Ch D . . . . *Digested*, 99/**3352**

Greenhow v. Rilmac Ltd (1999) 99(4) Q.R. 4, CC (Kingston upon Hull) [*Ex rel.* Philip Hamer & Co Solicitors, 9/11 Scale Lane, Hull] . . . . *Digested*, 99/**1541**

Greening (t/a Automania) v. Williams [2000] C.P. Rep. 40; *Times*, December 10, 1999, CA . . . . *Digested*, 00/**546**

Greenock Corp v. Caledonian Railway Co; Greenock Corp v. Glasgow & South
Western Railway Co [1917] A.C. 556, HL . . . . *Considered*, 01/**4547**:
Distinguished, 67/**3315**
Greenock Corp v. Glasgow & South Western Railway Co see Greenock Corp v.
Caledonian Railway Co
Greenpeace Ltd v. Customs and Excise Commissioners [2000] S.T.I. 1424, V&DTr
Greensmith v. Chadwick (Unreported, November 27, 2000), CC (Bury) [*Ex rel.* Tarran
& Co Solicitors, 5th Floor, Old Bank Chambers, 2 Old Bank Street,
Manchester] . . . . *Digested*, 01/**884**
Greenwich Healthcare NHS Trust v. London & Quadrant Housing Trust [1998] 1 W.L.R.
1749; [1998] 3 All E.R. 437; (1999) 77 P. & C.R. 133; (1998) 95(22) L.S.G.
30; (1998) 142 S.J.L.B. 197; [1998] N.P.C. 90; *Times*, June 11, 1998, Ch D . . . . *Digested*, 98/**4369**
Greenwich LBC v. Bater see Bater v. Greenwich LBC
Greenwich LBC v. Coleman (Unreported, October 26, 2000), CC (Woolwich) [*Ex rel.*
Jon Holbrook, Barrister, 2 Garden Court, London] . . . . *Digested*, 01/**635**
Greenwich LBC v. Globetrotter Investment Corp (1999) 14 P.A.D. 165, Planning
Inspector
Greenwich LBC v. Grogan (2001) 33 H.L.R. 12; (2000) 97(9) L.S.G. 40; (2000) 80 P.
& C.R. D7; *Times*, March 28, 2000, CA. . . . . *Digested*, 00/**3926**
Greenwich LBC v. Powell [1989] A.C. 995; [1989] 2 W.L.R. 7; [1989] 1 All E.R. 65;
(1989) 21 H.L.R. 218; 87 L.G.R. 423; (1989) 57 P. & C.R. 249; [1989] 1 P.L.R.
108; [1989] J.P.L. 513; (1989) 153 L.G. Rev. 328; (1989) 86(3) L.S.G. 44;
(1989) 133 S.J. 46, HL; reversing (1988) 20 H.L.R. 411; (1989) 57 P. & C.R. 49;
(1988) 152 L.G. Rev. 911, CA . . . . *Digested*, 89/**2293**:
Applied, 92/4268: *Considered*, 01/**4691**
Greenwich LBC v. Turner (1999) 14 P.A.D. 210, Planning Inspector
Greenwich LBC v. Ziya (2000) 15 P.A.D. 652, Planning Inspector
Greenwich Ltd v. National Westminster Bank Plc [1999] 2 Lloyd's Rep. 308; [1999]
I.L.Pr. 599; (1999) 96(18) L.S.G. 34; *Times*, April 13, 1999; *Independent*, May 17,
1999 (C.S.), Ch D . . . . *Digested*, 99/**401**
Greenwich Property Ltd v. Customs and Excise Commissioners see R. (on the
application of Greenwich Property Ltd) v. Customs and Excise Commissioners
Greenwich Property Ltd v. Customs and Excise Commissioners (Right of Appeal)
[2000] V. & D.R. 167; [2000] S.T.I. 1556, V&DTr
Greenwood v. British Airways Plc [1999] I.C.R. 969; [1999] I.R.L.R. 600, EAT . . . . *Digested*, 99/**2028**
Greenwood v. Martins Bank Ltd [1933] A.C. 51, HL; affirming [1932] 1 K.B. 371, CA . . *Applied*, 52/**237**,
52/1347, 66/6906, 67/621: *Approved*, 85/150: *Distinguished*, 47-51/**3687**:
Followed, 01/369
Greenwood v. Newalls Insulation Co Ltd (Unreported, July 30, 1998), CC
(Sunderland) [*Ex rel.* Jeremy Freedman, Barrister, New Court Chambers, 3
Broad Chare, Newcastle upon Tyne] . . . . *Digested*, 99/**1538**
Greer v. Kettle [1938] A.C. 156, HL . . . . *Applied*, 69/1071,
01/**4872**
Greer v. Northern Ireland Housing Executive [1997] R.V.R. 262, Lands Tr. . . . . *Digested*, 98/**5244**
Gregg v. Customs and Excise Commissioners (C216/97) [1999] All E.R. (EC) 775;
[1999] S.T.C. 934; [1999] E.C.R. I-4947; [1999] 3 C.M.L.R. 343; [1999] C.E.C.
460; [1999] B.T.C. 5341; [1999] B.V.C. 395; *Times*, October 19, 1999, ECJ . . . . . *Digested*, 99/**4986**
Gregg v. Raytheon see Bremer Vulkan Schiffbau und Maschinenfabrik v. South India
Shipping Corp Ltd
Gregori Sud Est SA v. Ziliani (t/a Cave Ferruccio Ziliani) [2001] I.L.Pr. 45, Cass (F)
Gregory v. Bartlett (Deceased) (Unreported, May 3, 2000), CC (Winchester) [*Ex rel.*
Robert Weir, Barrister, Devereux Chambers, Devereux Court, London] . . . . *Digested*, 00/**1473**:
Applied, 01/418
Gregory v. Bartlett (Deceased) (Leg Injuries) [2001] 2 Q.R. 10, CC (Aldershot &
Farnham) [*Ex rel.* Ian Miller, Pupil Barrister, No.1 Serjeant's Inn, Fleet Street,
London] . . . . *Digested*, 01/**1685**
Gregory v. Portsmouth City Council [2000] 1 A.C. 419; [2000] 2 W.L.R. 306; [2000]
1 All E.R. 560; (2000) 2 L.G.L.R. 667; [2000] B.L.G.R. 203; (2000) 97(6)
L.S.G. 36; (2000) 150 N.L.J. 131; (2000) 144 S.J.L.B. 82; *Times*, February 2,
2000 ; *Independent*, February 1, 2000, HL; affirming (1998) 10 Admin. L.R.
505; (1997) 94(46) L.S.G. 29; *Times*, November 26, 1997, CA . . . . *Digested*, 00/**5117**
Gregory v. Secretary of State for the Environment; Rawlins v. Secretary of State for the
Environment (1990) 60 P. & C.R. 413; [1990] 1 P.L.R. 110; [1990] J.P.L. 326;
(1990) 154 L.G. Rev. 993, CA; affirming [1989] J.P.L. 439, DC . . . . *Digested*, 91/**3469**:
Considered, 93/3860: *Followed*, 98/4186
Gregory v. Shepherds (A Firm) [2000] Lloyd's Rep. P.N. 724; [2000] P.N.L.R. 769;
(2001) 81 P. & C.R. 10; [2000] 3 E.G.L.R. 49; [2000] 50 E.G. 100; [2000]
E.G.C.S. 78; (2000) 97(28) L.S.G. 32; (2000) 97(26) L.S.G. 39; [2000] N.P.C.
69; *Times*, June 28, 2000, CA; reversing [1999] Lloyd's Rep. P.N. 720; [2000]
P.N.L.R. 44; [2000] 50 E.G. 100; (1999) 96(8) L.S.G. 29; (1999) 96(7) L.S.G.
37; *Times*, February 18, 1999; *Independent*, February 22, 1999 (C.S.), Ch D . . . . *Digested*, 00/**4258**:
Followed, 01/4263
Gregory v. Sir John Barlow (A Firm) (Unreported, December 15, 2000), CC
(Manchester) [*Ex rel.* Weightmans, Solicitors, 41 Spring Gardens, Manchester] . . *Digested*, 01/**4475**

Gregory v. United Kingdom (22299/93) (1998) 25 E.H.R.R. 577; *Times*, February 27, 1997; *Independent*, March 5, 1997, ECHR . . . .
   Digested, 97/**2802**:
   Distinguished, 00/3231

Gregory v. Wallace [1998] I.R.L.R. 387, CA . . . .
   Digested, 98/**2205**

Gregson v. Channel Four Television Co Ltd see Gregson v. Channel Four Television Corp (Amendment of Party Name)

Gregson v. Channel Four Television Corp (Amendment of Party Name); *sub nom* Gregson v. Channel Four Television Co Ltd [2000] C.P. Rep. 60; *Times*, August 11, 2000; *Independent*, October 2, 2000 (C.S.), CA; affirming HQ990963, QBD .
   Digested, 00/**587**

Gregson v. Cyril Lord Ltd [1963] 1 W.L.R. 41; [1962] 3 All E.R. 907; [1962] R.V.R. 730; 106 S.J. 899, CA . . . .
   Digested, 62/**1717**:
   Applied, 83/2108: *Approved*, 84/1913: *Considered*, 87/2129, 90/2777, 93/2450, 96/3776: *Followed*, 98/3609

Greig v. South Wales Fire Service (Unreported, January 19, 2000), CC (Cardiff) [*Ex rel*. Andrew Arentsen, Barrister, 33 Park Place, Cardiff] . . . .
   Digested, 00/**1666**

Greig Middleton & Co Ltd v. Denderowicz (No.2); Olaleye-Oruene v. London Guildhall University [1998] 1 W.L.R. 1164; [1997] 4 All E.R. 181; (1997) 94(31) L.S.G. 36; (1997) 147 N.L.J. 1097; *Times*, July 28, 1997, CA . . . .
   Digested, 97/**738**

Grell-Taurel Ltd v. Caribbean Home Insurance Co Ltd [2000] Lloyd's Rep. I.R. 614, HC (Trin) . . . .
   Digested, 01/**3795**

Gremesty v. Secretary of State for the Home Department [2001] I.N.L.R. 132, IAT . . . . .
   Digested, 01/**3687**

Grey Marlin Ltd, Re [2000] 1 W.L.R. 370; [1999] 4 All E.R. 429; [2000] B.C.C. 410; [1999] 2 B.C.L.C. 658; *Times*, June 29, 1999, Ch D (Companies Ct) . . . .
   Digested, 99/**3358**

Greyhound Guaranty v. Caulfield (Unreported, April 9, 1981), CC (Leeds) . . . .
   Digested, 81/**1808**:
   Considered, 99/4385

Greystoke (A Bankrupt), Re; *sub nom* Supperstone v. Greystoke [1998] B.P.I.R. 77, Ch D . . . .
   Digested, 97/**3025**

Greyvest Leasing Ltd v. Merkur Unreported, CJ (Gen Div) (Ont) . . . .
   Followed, 00/**3482**

Gribler v. Harrow LBC [2000] E.H.L.R. 188, QBD . . . .
   Digested, 00/**2250**

Griffin (Inspector of Taxes) v. Citibank Investments Ltd; *sub nom* Citibank Investments Ltd v. Griffin (Inspector of Taxes) [2000] S.T.C. 1010; 73 T.C. 352; [2000] B.T.C. 324; [2000] S.T.I. 1546; (2000) 97(45) L.S.G. 42; (2000) 144 S.J.L.B. 266; *Times*, November 14, 2000, Ch D; affirming [2000] S.T.C. (S.C.D.) 92; [2000] S.T.I. 165, Sp Comm. . . . .
   Digested, 00/**4916**

Griffin v. Clwyd HA [2001] EWCA Civ 818; [2001] P.I.Q.R. P31, CA

Griffin v. Griffin [2000] C.P.L.R. 452; [2000] 2 F.L.R. 44; [2000] 2 F.C.R. 302; [2000] Fam. Law 531; (2000) 97(20) L.S.G. 42; (2000) 144 S.J.L.B. 213; *Times*, April 28, 2000, CA . . . .
   Digested, 00/**2506**

Griffin v. Mersey Regional Ambulance Service [1998] P.I.Q.R. P34, CA . . . .
   Digested, 97/**3770**

Griffin (t/a K&D Contractors) v. Midas Homes Ltd 78 Con. L.R. 152, QBD (T&CC)

Griffin v. Squires [1958] 1 W.L.R. 1106; [1958] 3 All E.R. 468; 123 J.P. 40; 56 L.G.R. 442; 103 S.J. 5; 102 S.J. 828, DC . . . .
   Digested, 58/**3016**:
   Applied, 91/3164: *Followed*, 00/988

Griffin v. Wakefield MDC [2000] R.V.R. 226, CA . . . .
   Digested, 00/**4562**

Griffin Credit Services Ltd v. ACE Conveyor Equipment Ltd (Unreported, December 11, 1998), QBD [*Ex rel*. Stephen Beresford, Barrister, 24 The Ropewalk, Nottingham] . . . .
   Digested, 99/**410**

Griffin Trading Co, Re [2000] B.P.I.R. 256, Ch D . . . .
   Digested, 00/**3461**

Griffiths v. Bean (1911) 27 T.L.R. 346, CA . . . .
   Applied, 00/591

Griffiths v. British Coal Corp [2001] EWCA Civ 336; [2001] 1 W.L.R. 1493; [2001] P.I.Q.R. Q11; (2001) 60 B.M.L.R. 188; *Times*, March 13, 2001, CA . . . .
   Digested, 01/**1548**

Griffiths v. Brown; Griffiths v. Lindsay [1999] P.I.Q.R. P131; *Times*, October 23, 1998, QBD . . . .
   Digested, 98/**3946**

Griffiths v. Flying Colours Holidays Ltd (t/a Sunset Holidays) (Unreported, January 7, 1999), CC (St Helens) [*Ex rel*. Mason Bond Solicitors, King Charles House, King Charles Croft, Leeds] . . . .
   Digested, 99/**3820**

Griffiths (Inspector of Taxes) v. Jackson [1983] S.T.C. 184; 56 T.C. 583, DC . . . .
   Digested, 83/**1978**:
   Applied, 00/4924

Griffiths v. Lex Transfleet Ltd (Unreported, October 20, 2000), CC (Great Grimsby) [*Ex rel*. Darren Finlay, Barrister, Sovereign Chambers, 25 Park Square, Leeds] . . . . .
   Digested, 01/**574**

Griffiths v. Lindsay see Griffiths v. Brown

Griffiths v. Pembrokeshire CC [2000] Env. L.R. 622; [2000] E.H.L.R. 359; (2000) 97(18) L.S.G. 36; (2000) 150 N.L.J. 512; [2000] N.P.C. 38; *Times*, April 19, 2000, QBD . . . .
   Digested, 00/**4296**

Griffiths v. Richard Medlins Contracts (Unreported, November 30, 1999), QBD [*Ex rel*. Veale Wasbroughs Solicitors, Orchard Court, Orchard Lane, Bristol] . . . .
   Digested, 00/**1585**

Griffiths v. Solutia UK Ltd; *sub nom* Solutia UK Ltd (formerly Monsanto Chemicals UK Ltd) v. Griffiths [2001] EWCA Civ 736; [2001] C.P. Rep. 92; [2001] C.P.L.R. 419; [2001] 2 Costs L.R. 247, CA; affirming [2001] 1 Costs L.R. 99, QBD . . . . .
   Digested, 01/**523**

Griffiths v. WE & DT Cave Ltd (1999) 78 P. & C.R. 8; (1998) 95(48) L.S.G. 32, CA . . . .
   Digested, 99/**4394**

Grigoriades v. Greece (24348/94) (1999) 27 E.H.R.R. 464; 4 B.H.R.C. 43; [1998] H.R.C.D. 103, ECHR . . . .
   Digested, 98/**3082**:
   Applied, 99/3111

Grimaldi Compagnia di Navigazione SpA v. Sekihyo Lines Ltd (The Seki Rolette) [1999]
    1 W.L.R. 708; [1998] 3 All E.R. 943; [1998] 2 Lloyd's Rep. 638; [1998] C.L.C.
    1403; *Times,* July 20, 1998, QBD (Comm Ct) . . . .   *Digested,* 98/**245**
Grimm v. Newman [2001] S.T.I. 1406; [2001] N.P.C. 155, Ch D
Grimwood-Taylor v. Inland Revenue Commissioners [2000] W.T.L.R. 321, Sp Comm. . .   *Digested,* 01/**5278**
Grindal v. Hooper [1999] E.G.C.S. 150; (2000) 97(3) L.S.G. 35; (1999) 96(48) L.S.G.
    41; (2000) 144 S.J.L.B. 33; *Times,* February 8, 2000, Ch D . . . .   *Digested,* 00/**4645**
Grinnell v. Deeley (2000) 80 P. & C.R. D15, CA
Grobbelaar v. News Group Newspapers Ltd [2001] EWCA Civ 33; [2001] 2 All E.R.
    437; [2001] E.M.L.R. 18; (2001) 151 N.L.J. 102; *Daily Telegraph,* January 30,
    2001, CA
Grobbelaar v. Sun Newspapers Ltd, *Times,* August 12, 1999, CA . . . .   *Digested,* 99/**312**
Gromax Plasticulture Ltd v. Don & Low Nonwovens Ltd [1999] R.P.C. 367; (1998)
    21 (9) I.P.D. 21098, Ch D . . . .   *Digested,* 99/**3592**:
                                Applied, 01/4062: *Followed,* 01/4047: *Referred to,* 01/4024
Groninger Vleeshandel BV v. Commission of the European Communities (T198/97) see
    Weyl Beef Products BV v. Commission of the European Communities (T197/
    97)
Groom v. Crocker [1939] 1 K.B. 194; (1938) 60 Ll. L. Rep. 393, CA; reversing (1937)
    58 Ll. L. Rep. 396, KBD. . . . .   *Applied,* 47-51/9802,
                                64/3468: *Considered,* 92/1537, 93/2997, 00/4023:
                                Distinguished, 47-51/9801: *Followed,* 66/9533, 67/3114:
                                                                Not followed, 83/3610
Groom v. RSM Fabrications Ltd (1999) 99(3) Q.R. 7, CC (Gloucester) [*Ex rel.* Davis
    Gregory Solicitors, 25 Rodney Road, Cheltenham, Gloucestershire] . . . .   *Digested,* 99/**1504**
Groom v. Selby [2001] EWCA Civ 1522, CA; affirming [2001] Lloyd's Rep. Med. 39,
    QBD . . . .   *Digested,* 01/**4462**
Gross, Re see R. v. Governor of Brixton Prison Ex p. Gross
Gross v. Governor of Brixton Prison see R. v. Governor of Brixton Prison Ex p. Gross
Gross v. Southwark Crown Court [1998] C.O.D. 445, QBD . . . .   *Digested,* 98/**1085**:
                                                                Not followed, 99/900
Grosskrotzenburg Power Station (C431/92), Re see Commission of the European
    Communities v. Germany (C431/92)
Grossman v. Hooper [2001] EWCA Civ 615; [2001] 3 F.C.R. 662; [2001] 27 E.G. 135,
    CA . . . .   *Digested,* 01/**4852**
GROTE & HARTMANN/Box Spring (T506/95) [2001] E.P.O.R. 62, EPO (Technical Bd
    App)
Groundpremium Property Management Ltd v. Longmint Ltd [1998] 1 E.G.L.R. 131;
    [1998] 11 E.G. 183, LVT . . . .   *Digested,* 98/**3668**
Groundshire v. VHE Construction [2001] B.L.R. 395, QBD (T&CC)
Group B Plaintiffs v. Medical Research Council; *sub nom* Creutzfeldt-Jakob Disease
    Litigation (No.5), Re; CJD Litigation (No.5), Re [2000] Lloyd's Rep. Med. 161;
    (2000) 54 B.M.L.R. 92; (1998) 41 B.M.L.R. 157, QBD. . . . .   *Digested,* 98/**3981**
Group Josi Re (formerly Group Josi Reassurance SA) v. Walbrook Insurance Co Ltd see
    Group Josi Re Co SA v. Walbrook Insurance Co Ltd
Group Josi Re Co SA v. Walbrook Insurance Co Ltd; *sub nom* Group Josi Re (formerly
    Group Josi Reassurance SA) v. Walbrook Insurance Co Ltd; Deutsche
    Ruckversichering AG v. Walbrook Insurance Co Ltd [1996] 1 All E.R. 791; [1996]
    1 Lloyd's Rep. 345; [1996] 5 Re. L.R. 91, CA; affirming [1995] 1 W.L.R. 1017;
    [1994] 4 All E.R. 181; [1995] 1 Lloyd's Rep. 153; (1994) 91(25) L.S.G. 30;
    (1994) 138 S.J.L.B. 111; *Times,* May 6, 1994, QBD (Comm Ct) . . . .   *Digested,* 96/**3568**:
                                                Considered, 01/743: *Followed,* 97/3137
Group Josi Reinsurance Co SA v. Compagnie d'Assurances Universal General Insurance
    Co (UGIC) (C412/98) see Universal General Insurance Co (UGIC) v. Group
    Josi Reinsurance Co SA (C412/98)
Group Josi Reinsurance Co SA v. Universal General Insurance Co (UGIC) see Universal
    General Insurance Co (UGIC) v. Group Josi Reinsurance Co SA (C412/98)
Groupama Navigation et Transports v. Catatumbo CA Seguros [2000] 2 All E.R.
    (Comm) 193; [2000] 2 Lloyd's Rep. 350; [2000] C.L.C. 1534; [2001] Lloyd's
    Rep. I.R. 141, CA; affirming [1999] 2 All E.R. (Comm) 970; [2000] 1 Lloyd's Rep.
    266; [2000] C.L.C. 381; [2000] Lloyd's Rep. I.R. 434, QBD (Comm Ct) . . . . . .   *Digested,* 00/**3563**
Groupe Progres SA v. Syndicat National des Journalistes [2001] E.C.C. 8, C d'A (Lyon)
Groupe Volkswagen France SA v. Euro Car SA [2001] E.C.C. 46, C d'A (Paris)
Groupement d'Achat des Centres Leclerc (SCA GALEC) v. Comite National Olympique et
    Sportif Francais (CNOSF) [2001] E.T.M.R. 33, Cass (F)
Groupement des Cartes Bancaires v. Messadek [2001] E.C.C. 38, C d'A (Paris)
Grove v. Advantage Healthcare (T10) Ltd; *sub nom* Advantage Healthcare (T10) Ltd,
    Re [2000] B.C.C. 985; [2000] 1 B.C.L.C. 661, Ch D . . . .   *Digested,* 00/**653**
Grove v. Lloyds British Testing Co Ltd see Sedgwick v. Watney Combe Reid & Co Ltd
Grove v. Sharp see Caudle v. Sharp
Grovedeck Ltd v. Capital Demolition Ltd [2000] B.L.R. 181; (2000) 2 T.C.L.R. 689;
    Independent, May 8, 2000 (C.S.), QBD (T&CC)
Groves v. Minor see Minor v. Groves

Groves v. Pretty (Unreported, May 19, 1999), CC (Clerkenwell) [*Ex rel*. Stuart Nicol, Barrister, 3 Temple Gardens, London] . . . . *Digested*, 99/**1592**
Grovewood Holdings Plc v. James Capel & Co Ltd [1995] Ch. 80; [1995] 2 W.L.R. 70; [1994] 4 All E.R. 417; [1995] B.C.C. 760; [1994] 2 B.C.L.C. 782; [1994] E.G.C.S. 136; (1994) 144 N.L.J. 1405; *Times*, August 15, 1994; *Independent*, September 20, 1994, Ch D . . . . *Digested*, 95/**2824**:
Considered, 96/3855, 98/411: *Followed*, 96/682
Grovewood (1998) Ltd v. Customs and Excise Commissioners [2001] B.V.C. 2258; [2001] S.T.I. 1024, V&DTr
Grovit v. Doctor [1997] 1 W.L.R. 640; [1997] 2 All E.R. 417; [1997] C.L.C. 1038; (1997) 94(20) L.S.G. 37; (1997) 147 N.L.J. 633; (1997) 141 S.J.L.B. 107; *Times*, April 25, 1997; *Independent*, May 1, 1997, HL; affirming *Independent*, December 13, 1993 (C.S.), CA . . . . *Digested*, 97/**489**:
Applied, 98/614: *Considered*, 98/611, 98/619, 00/348
Grubb v. Price Waterhouse Coopers see Grubb v. PricewaterhouseCoopers
Grubb v. PricewaterhouseCoopers; *sub nom* Grubb v. Price Waterhouse Coopers (2001) 3 L.G.L.R. 15; [2001] B.L.G.R. 32; *Times*, October 17, 2000, QBD . . . . . . *Digested*, 00/**4110**
Grundig Italiana SpA v. Ministero delle Finanze (C68/96) [1998] E.C.R. I-3775; [1999] 2 C.M.L.R. 62, ECJ (6th Chamber) . . . . *Digested*, 99/**4683**
Grundy v. Summit Group Holdings Ltd [1998] E.G.C.S. 45, Ch D
Grundy (Teddington) v. Willis [1976] I.C.R. 323; [1976] I.R.L.R. 118; [1976] I.T.R. 26 . . . *Digested*, 76/**1002**:
Applied, 00/2239
Gruner und Jahr Communication GmbH v. Editions Economica SA see Prisma Presse Ste v. Editions Economica SA
Grunshaw v. Gwynedd CC see Gwynedd CC v. Grunshaw
Grupo Grifols SA's Application (Opposition by Glaxo Group Ltd) [1999] E.T.M.R. 507, OHIM (Opposition Div) . . . . *Digested*, 00/**3753**
Grupo Mexicano de Desarollo SA v. Alliance Bond Fund Inc (1999-2000) 2 I.T.E.L.R. 117, US Ct
Grupo Torras SA v. Al-Sabah (No.1) [1996] 1 Lloyd's Rep. 7; [1995] I.L.Pr. 667; *Independent*, July 5, 1995, CA; affirming [1995] 1 Lloyd's Rep. 374, QBD (Comm Ct) . . . . *Digested*, 96/**1112**:
Followed, 98/583, 98/588
Grupo Torras SA v. Al-Sabah (No.3); Jaffar v. Grupo Torras SA [1997] C.L.C. 1553; [1998] Masons C.L.R. Rep. 90; (1997) 94(30) L.S.G. 28; (1997) 141 S.J.L.B. 169; *Times*, October 13, 1997, QBD . . . . *Digested*, 97/**476**
Grupo Torras SA v. Al-Sabah (No.4) [2000] C.P. Rep. 76; [1999] C.L.C. 885; *Times*, March 30, 1999; *Independent*, February 25, 1999, CA. . . . . *Digested*, 99/**342**
Grupo Torras SA v. Al-Sabah (No.5); *sub nom* Al-Sabah v. Grupo Torras SA; Bonafonte v. Grupo Torras SA [2001] Lloyd's Rep. Bank. 36; [2001] C.L.C. 221; [2001] Lloyd's Rep. P.N. 117, CA; reversing [1999] C.L.C. 1469, QBD (Comm Ct) . . . . . *Digested*, 01/**721**:
Applied, 01/809
Grupo Torras SA v. Al-Sabah (No.6); *sub nom* Esteem Settlement, Re; Abacus (CI) Ltd v. Al-Sabah (2001-02) 4 I.T.E.L.R. 555, CA (Jer); affirming [2001] W.T.L.R. 641; (2000-01) 3 I.T.E.L.R. 467, Royal Ct (Jer) . . . . *Digested*, 01/**5507**
Grupo Torras SA v. Bank of Butterfield International (Cayman) Ltd (2000-01) 3 I.T.E.L.R. 712, Grand Court (CI) . . . . *Digested*, 01/**554**
Gruzuka v. Andrews (Unreported, August 5, 1998), CC (Rawtenstall) [*Ex rel*. James Hurd, Barrister, St James's Chambers, 68 Quay Street, Manchester] . . . . *Digested*, 98/**455**
Grzelczyk v. Centre Public d'Aide Sociale d'Ottignies Louvain la Neuve (C184/99) [2001] E.C.R. I-6193; *Times*, November 16, 2001, ECJ . . . . *Digested*, 01/**2496**
GS v. Austria (26297/95) (2001) 31 E.H.R.R. 21, ECHR . . . . *Digested*, 01/**3513**
Gschwind v. Cessna Aircraft Co [1999] I.L.Pr. 703, US Ct
Gschwind v. Finanzamt Aachen-Aussenstadt (C391/97) [2001] S.T.C. 331; [1999] E.C.R. I-5451; [2001] 1 C.M.L.R. 3; [2000] B.T.C. 294; 2 I.T.L. Rep. 113, ECJ . . . *Digested*, 01/**5245**
GST Telecommunications v. Provenzano [2001] I.L.Pr. 32, Sup Ct (BC) . . . . *Digested*, 01/**4083**
GT Link A/S v. De Danske Statsbaner (DSB) (C242/95) [1997] E.C.R. I-4449; [1997] 5 C.M.L.R. 601; [1998] C.E.C. 19, ECJ (6th Chamber) . . . . *Digested*, 98/**720**
GTR Group's Application (Opposition of Jean Patou) [1999] E.T.M.R. 164, TMR . . . . . . *Digested*, 99/**3568**
Guaber Srl v. Greece [1999] E.T.M.R. 879, Protodikeio (Athens)
Guangdong Shantou Overseas Chinese Materials Marketing Co v. Tsavliris Salvage (International) Ltd see Tsavliris Salvage (International) Ltd v. Guangdong Shantou Overseas Chinese Materials Marketing Co (The Pa Mar)
Guaranty Trust Co of New York v. Hannay & Co [1915] 2 K.B. 536; 12 A.L.R. 1, CA; affirming [1915] W.N. 38, KBD. . . . . *Applied*, 53/576,
53/1084, 67/200, 68/199, 72/2778, 98/3528: *Considered*, 53/2055, 75/104, 87/2426, 88/2276, 95/4102, 96/2846: *Distinguished*, 54/3380, 66/1240, 67/412, 79/2098
Guardhouse v. Blackburn (1865-69) L.R. 1 P. & D. 109, Ct of Probate . . . . *Disapproved*, 01/**5167**:
Not followed, 69/3662, 70/2935
Guardian Newspapers Ltd v. Council of Ministers of the European Communities see Carvel v. Council of the European Union (T194/94)
Gubbins v. Bailie [2001] 5 Q.R. 8, CC (Bristol) [*Ex rel*. Colin Mendoza, Barrister, Devereux Chambers, Devereux Court, London] . . . . *Digested*, 01/**1564**

Gubisch Maschinenfabrik KG v. Palumbo (C144/86) [1987] E.C.R. 4861; [1989] E.C.C.
　　420; Times, January 12, 1988, ECJ (6th Chamber) . . . .　　　　*Digested*, 91/**3934**:
　　　　　　　　　　　　　　　　　　　Considered, 96/7098, 00/5442: *Distinguished*, 92/4436
Gudge v. Milroy [2000] 4 Q.R. 6, CC (Hitchin) [*Ex rel.* Kevin Haven, Barrister, 2 Gray's
　　Inn Square Chambers, Gray's Inn, London] . . . .　　　*Digested*, 00/**1567**
Guenoun, Re (184474) 2 I.T.L. Rep. 869, CE (F)
Guerdon Metier Marketry Ltd v. Oldaker (Unreported, November 10, 1998), CC
　　(Colchester) [*Ex rel.* Michael Lane, Barrister, East Anglian Chambers, 52 North
　　Hill, Colchester] . . . .　　　*Digested*, 99/**391**
Guerin v. France see Omar v. France
Guerin Automobiles v. Commission of the European Communities (C186/94) [1997]
　　E.C.R. I-1503; [1997] 5 C.M.L.R. 447, ECJ; affirming [1995] E.C.R. II-1753;
　　[1996] 4 C.M.L.R. 685, CFI (3rd Chamber) . . . .　　　　*Applied*, 99/695:
　　　　　　　　　　　　　　　　　　　　　　　　　　　　　　　　　　　Followed, 00/2367
Guerra v. Baptiste [1996] A.C. 397; [1995] 3 W.L.R. 891; [1995] 4 All E.R. 583;
　　[1996] 1 Cr. App. R. 533; (1995) 139 S.J.L.B. 244; Times, November 8, 1995;
　　Independent, November 15, 1995, PC (Trin) . . . .　　　*Digested*, 96/**3128**:
　　　　　　　　　　　　　　　　　　　　　　　　　　　　　　　　　Considered, 98/780
Guerra v. Italy (1998) 26 E.H.R.R. 357; 4 B.H.R.C. 63; [1998] H.R.C.D. 277, ECHR . . . .　*Digested*, 98/**3096**:
　　　　　　　　　　　　　　　　　　　Applied, 01/1544: *Considered*, 98/3154
Guest v. Chief Adjudication Officer SSTRF 97/1674/CMSI, CA . . . .　　*Digested*, 98/**4540**
Guidera's Estate, Re; *sub nom* Bingham v. Guidera [2001] N.I. 71; (2000-01) 3 I.T.E.L.R.
　　397, Ch D (NI) . . . .　　　*Digested*, 01/**6034**
Guidezone Ltd, Re; *sub nom* Kaneria v. Patel [2001] B.C.C. 692; [2000] 2 B.C.L.C.
　　321, Ch D (Companies Ct) . . . .　　　*Digested*, 00/**691**
Guild v. Eskandar Ltd (formerly Ambleville Ltd); *sub nom* Nabavi v. Guild; A3/2001/
　　0649, CA; reversing [2001] F.S.R. 38; (2001) 24(7) I.P.D. 24047, Ch D . . . . . .　　　*Digested*, 01/**3862**
Guild v. Newrick see Clark (Inspector of Taxes) v. Perks (Permission to Appeal)
Guild (Inspector of Taxes) v. Newrick see Clark (Inspector of Taxes) v. Perks
Guild (Claims) Ltd v. Eversheds [2000] Lloyd's Rep. P.N. 910; Times, August 16, 2000,
　　Ch D . . . .　　　*Digested*, 00/**4247**
Guildford BC v. Debenhams Plc (1998) 13 P.A.D. 543, Planning Inspector
Guildford BC v. Keen (1998) 13 P.A.D. 621, Planning Inspector
Guildford BC v. Whittle (2000) 15 P.A.D. 824, Planning Inspector
Guillemin v. France (1998) 25 E.H.R.R. 435; [1998] H.R.C.D. 849, ECHR . . . .　　*Digested*, 98/**3132**
Guimont (C448/98), Re; *sub nom* Criminal Proceedings against Guimont (C448/98),
　　Re [2000] E.C.R. I-10663; [2001] E.T.M.R. 14, ECJ . . . .　　　*Digested*, 01/**771**
Guinle v. Kirreh; Kinstreet Ltd v. Balmargo Corp Ltd; Interfisa Management Inc v.
　　Hamam [2000] C.P. Rep. 62, Ch D . . . .　　　*Digested*, 01/**434**
Guinness Ireland Group v. Kilkenny Brewing Co Ltd [1999] E.T.M.R. 807; [2000] F.S.R.
　　112, HC (Irl) . . . .　　　*Digested*, 00/**3593**
Guinness Mahon & Co Ltd v. Kensington and Chelsea RLBC [1999] Q.B. 215; [1998] 3
　　W.L.R. 829; [1998] 2 All E.R. 272; [1998] Lloyd's Rep. Bank. 109; [1998]
　　C.L.C. 662; (1998) 95(13) L.S.G. 28; (1998) 148 N.L.J. 366; (1998) 142
　　S.J.L.B. 92; Times, March 2, 1998, CA . . . .　　　*Digested*, 98/**304**
Guinness Peat Group Plc v. British Land Co Plc [1999] B.C.C. 536; [1999] 2 B.C.L.C.
　　243; [1998] N.P.C. 168, CA . . . .　　　*Digested*, 99/**651**
Guise v. Drew (2001) 82 P. & C.R. D25, Ch D
Gul v. Regierungsprasident Dusseldorf (131/85) [1986] E.C.R. 1573; [1987] 1
　　C.M.L.R. 501, ECJ (4th Chamber) . . . .　　　*Digested*, 87/**1629**:
　　　　　　　　　　　　　　　　　　　　　　　　　　　　　　　　　　Applied, 98/4517
Gula v. Sapa Ltd (Unreported, March 2, 1998), CC (Leeds) [*Ex rel.* Rowley Ashworth
　　Solicitors, Suite 1B, Josephs Well, Hanover Walk, Leeds] . . . .　　　*Digested*, 98/**441**
Gulati v. General Medical Council [2001] UKPC 22; (2001) 61 B.M.L.R. 146, PC (UK)
Gulec v. Turkey (1999) 28 E.H.R.R. 121; [1998] H.R.C.D. 721, ECHR . . . .　　*Digested*, 99/**3144**
Gulf Azov Shipping Co Ltd v. Chief Idisi (No.2); United Kingdom Mutual Steamship
　　Assurance Association (Bermuda) Ltd v. Lonestar Drilling Nigeria Ltd; Gulf Azov
　　Shipping Co Ltd v. Lonestar Drilling Nigeria Ltd; United Kingdom Mutual
　　Steamship Assurance Association (Bermuda) Ltd v. Lonestar Overseas Ltd
　　[2001] EWCA Civ 505; [2001] 2 All E.R. (Comm) 673; [2001] 1 Lloyd's Rep.
　　727, CA . . . .　　　*Digested*, 01/**4951**
Gulf Azov Shipping Co Ltd v. Lonestar Drilling Nigeria Ltd see Gulf Azov Shipping Co
　　Ltd v. Chief Idisi (No.2)
Gulf Interstate Oil Co v. ANT Trade & Transport Ltd of Malta (The Giovanna) [1999] 1
　　All E.R. (Comm.) 97; [1999] 1 Lloyd's Rep. 867; [1999] C.L.C. 554;
　　Independent, January 11, 1999 (C.S.), QBD (Comm Ct) . . . .　　　*Digested*, 99/**491**
Gulf Oil (GB) Ltd v. Phillis [1998] P.N.L.R. 166, Ch D . . . .　　*Digested*, 98/**542**
Gulf Trading and Management Ltd v. Customs and Excise Commissioners [2001] S.T.I.
　　252, V&DTr
Gulson v. Zurich Insurance Co [1998] I.R.L.R. 118, EAT . . . .　　*Digested*, 98/**2164**
Gummer v. Pitman, CC (Yeovil) [*Ex rel.* James Hassall, Barrister, Guildhall Chambers,
　　22-26 Broad Street, Bristol] . . . .　　　*Digested*, 01/**1523**
Gumpo v. Church of Scientology Religious Education College Inc [2000] C.P. Rep. 38,
　　QBD . . . .　　　*Digested*, 00/**320**

Gunaydin v. Freistaat Bayern (C36/96) [1997] E.C.R. I-5143; [1998] 1 C.M.L.R. 871, ECJ (6th Chamber)

Gundem v. Turkey (22275/93) (2001) 32 E.H.R.R. 17; [1998] H.R.C.D. 571, ECHR

Gundem (Ozgur) v. Turkey (23144/93) (2001) 31 E.H.R.R. 49, ECHR . . . . *Digested*, 01/**3467**

Gundry v. Sainsbury [1910] 1 K.B. 645; [1997] Costs L.R. (Core Vol.) 1, CA; affirming [1910] 1 K.B. 99, KBD . . . . *Applied*, 73/2634: *Followed*, 99/380

Gunn v. Wallsend Slipway and Engineering Co, *Times*, January 23, 1989, QBD . . . . *Digested*, 89/**2548**: *Considered*, 99/448

Gunn-Russo v. Nugent Care Society; *sub nom* R. (on the application of Gunn-Russo) v. Nugent Care Society [2001] EWHC Admin 566; [2001] U.K.H.R.R. 1320; [2001] A.C.D. 86; (2001) 151 N.L.J. 1250, QBD (Admin Ct)

Gunnell v. United Kingdom see Thynne v. United Kingdom (A/190)

Gunning v. Mirror Group Newspapers; *sub nom* Mirror Group Newspapers Ltd v. Gunning [1986] 1 W.L.R. 546; [1986] 1 All E.R. 385; [1986] I.C.R. 145; [1986] I.R.L.R. 27; (1986) 136 N.L.J. 967; (1985) 130 S.J. 242, CA; reversing [1985] 1 W.L.R. 394; [1984] I.C.R. 706; [1985] I.R.L.R. 60; (1984) 81 L.S.G. 2376; (1985) 129 S.J. 205; *Times*, July 24, 1984, EAT . . . . *Digested*, 86/**1237**: *Applied*, 98/5133, 99/2046

Guns v. Seagate Technology (Ireland) [2000] N.I. 83, CA (NI) . . . . *Digested*, 00/**5526**

Gunton v. Richmond upon Thames RLBC [1981] 1 W.L.R. 28, HL [1981] Ch. 448; [1980] 3 W.L.R. 714; [1980] 3 All E.R. 577; [1980] I.C.R. 755; [1980] I.R.L.R. 321; 79 L.G.R. 241; 124 S.J. 792, CA . . . . *Digested*, 80/**895**: *Applied*, 84/1202, 85/1181, 85/1272, 86/1279, 87/1419, 93/1734, 98/2098: *Considered*, 96/2522, 99/2013: *Followed*, 98/2242

Gupta (Prabha) v. General Medical Council; *sub nom* R. (on the application of Gupta) v. General Medical Council [2001] EWHC Admin 631; *Times*, October 16, 2001, QBD (Admin Ct) . . . . *Digested*, 01/**2898**

Gurney v. Spence (Inspector of Taxes) [2001] S.T.I. 1496, Ch D

Gurtner v. Beaton [1993] 2 Lloyd's Rep. 369; *Times*, March 26, 1992, CA . . . . *Digested*, 94/**362**: *Applied*, 00/5157

Gurtner v. Circuit [1968] 2 Q.B. 587; [1968] 2 W.L.R. 668; [1968] 1 All E.R. 328; [1968] 1 Lloyd's Rep. 171; 112 S.J. 63; 112 S.J. 73, CA . . . . *Digested*, 68/**3160**: *Applied*, 69/2895: *Considered*, 69/2846, 71/9385, 79/2346, 94/425, 98/506, 98/528, 98/591: *Distinguished*, 00/547

GUS Home Shopping Ltd v. Green [2001] I.R.L.R. 75, EAT . . . . *Digested*, 01/**2317**

Gussman v. Gratton Storey (1968) 112 S.J. 884, CA . . . . *Digested*, 68/**2676**: *Considered*, 98/3911

Gustafson (Rolf) v. Sweden (1998) 25 E.H.R.R. 623, ECHR . . . . *Digested*, 98/**3064**

Gustafsson v. Sweden (Revision) [1998] H.R.C.D. 763; (1998) 26 E.H.R.R. CD 13, ECHR

Gut Springenheide GmbH v. Oberkreisdirektor des Kreises Steinfurt - Amt fur Lebensmitteluberwachung (C210/96) [1998] E.C.R. I-4657; [1999] 1 C.M.L.R. 1383, ECJ (5th Chamber) . . . . *Digested*, 99/**814**: *Applied*, 00/2386

Guthrie v. Milton (Unreported, May 23, 1998), CC (Colchester) [*Ex rel.* Michael Horne, Barrister, 3 Serjeant's Inn, London] . . . . *Digested*, 98/**3976**

Guthrie v. Scottish Environmental Protection Agency [1998] Env. L.R. 128; 1997 G.W.D. 6-244, OH . . . . *Digested*, 97/**6022**

Guy Butler (International) Ltd v. Customs and Excise Commissioners (No.1) see Customs and Excise Commissioners v. Guy Butler (International) Ltd (No.1)

Guy's & St Thomas NHS Trust v. P&O Developments Ltd see P&O Developments Ltd v. Guy's & St Thomas NHS Trust

Guyer v. Walton (Inspector of Taxes) [2001] S.T.C. (S.C.D.) 75; [2001] S.T.I. 732, Sp Comm . . . . *Digested*, 01/**5320**

Guzzardi v. Italy (A/39) (1981) 3 E.H.R.R. 333, ECHR . . . . *Considered*, 97/2766: *Distinguished*, 98/3078

Gwembe Valley Development Co Ltd v. Koshy see Deutsche Investitions und Entwicklungsgesellschaft mbH (DEG) v. Koshy

Gwembe Valley Development Co Ltd v. Koshy [1998] 2 B.C.L.C. 613, Ch D . . . . *Digested*, 99/**627**

Gwembe Valley Development Co Ltd (In Receivership) v. Koshy see DEG-Deutsche Investitions- und Entwicklungsgesellschaft mbH v. Koshy (Account of Profits: Limitations)

Gwembe Valley Development Co Ltd (In Receivership) v. Koshy [2000] B.C.C. 1127; [2000] 2 B.C.L.C. 705; *Times*, February 8, 2000, Ch D . . . . *Digested*, 00/**3481**

Gwembe Valley Development Co Ltd (In Receivership) v. Koshy (Costs); DEG-Deutsche Investitions-Und Entwicklungsgesellschaft MbH v. Koshy; A3/2000/6504, CA; reversing (2000) 97(11) L.S.G. 38; *Times*, March 30, 2000, Ch D . . . . *Digested*, 00/**396**

Gwynedd CC v. Grunshaw; *sub nom* Grunshaw v. Gwynedd CC [2000] 1 W.L.R. 494; [1999] 4 All E.R. 304; (2000) 32 H.L.R. 610; (1999) 149 N.L.J. 1286; [1999] N.P.C. 101; *Times*, August 30, 1999 ; *Independent*, October 18, 1999 (C.S.), CA . . *Digested*, 99/**31**

Gwynedd Council v. Wright (2000) 15 P.A.D. 675, Planning Inspector

Gymboree Corp's Trade Mark Application (No.1577166) (1999) 22(6) I.P.D. 22055, Ch D . . . . *Digested*, 99/**3577**

Gyte *v.* Customs and Excise Commissioners [1999] V. & D.R. 241, V&DTr . . . .   *Digested,* 00/**5334**

H (A Child) (Abduction: Habitual Residence: Consent), Re; *sub nom* H (Child Abduction:
    Wrongful Retention), Re [2000] 2 F.L.R. 294; [2000] 3 F.C.R. 412; [2000]
    Fam. Law 590, Fam Div. . . . .   *Digested,* 00/**2439**
H (A Child) (Adoption: Consultation of Unmarried Fathers), Re; *sub nom* H (A Child)
    (Adoption: Disclosure), Re; G (A Child) (Adoption: Disclosure), Re [2001] 1
    F.L.R. 646; [2001] 1 F.C.R. 726; [2001] Fam. Law 175; *Times,* January 5, 2001,
    Fam Div . . . .   *Digested,* 01/**2541**
H (A Child) (Adoption: Disclosure), Re see H (A Child) (Adoption: Consultation of
    Unmarried Fathers), Re
H (A Child) (Care Proceedings: Intervener), Re [2000] 1 F.L.R. 775; [2000] 2 F.C.R. 53;
    [2000] Fam. Law 464; (2000) 164 J.P.N. 606; *Times,* March 22, 2000, CA . . .   *Digested,* 00/**2514**
H (A Child) (Contact: Mother's Opposition), Re; *sub nom* H (A Child) (Indirect Contact),
    Re [2001] 1 F.C.R. 59; (2001) 165 J.P.N. 168, CA . . . .   *Digested,* 01/**2656**
H (A Child) (Court Bundles: Disallowance of Fees), Re see CH (A Child) (Family
    Proceedings: Court Bundles), Re
H (A Child) (Indirect Contact), Re see H (A Child) (Contact: Mother's Opposition), Re
H (A Child) (Isle of Man: Adoption), Re see J (A Child) (Adoption Procedure: Isle of Man),
    Re
H (A Child) (Occupation Order: Power of Arrest), Re see H *v.* H (A Child) (Occupation
    Order: Power of Arrest)
H (A Child) (Removal from Jurisdiction), Re see H (A Minor) (Abduction: Rights of
    Custody), Re
H (A Child) *v.* Butlins Ltd [2001] 6 Q.R. 16, CC (Manchester) [*Ex rel.* Pannone &
    Partners, Solicitors, 123 Deansgate, Manchester] . . . .   *Digested,* 01/**1696**
H (A Child) *v.* Clark (Clavicle) (Unreported, January 17, 2001), CC (Colchester) [*Ex rel.*
    Richard Menzies, Barrister, 8 Stone Buildings, Lincoln's Inn, London] . . . .   *Digested,* 01/**1661**
H (A Child) *v.* Clark (Knee) (Unreported, January 17, 2001), CC (Colchester) [*Ex rel.*
    Richard Menzies, Barrister, 8 Stone Buildings, Lincoln's Inn, London] . . . .   *Digested,* 01/**1797**
H (A Child) *v.* Cooper (Unreported, February 16, 2000), CC (Neath & Port Talbot) [*Ex
    rel.* Gareth John Jones, Barrister, 33 Park Place, Cardiff] . . . .   *Digested,* 00/**1618**
H (A Child) *v.* Gray (Unreported, April 6, 2000), CC (Telford) [*Ex rel.* Hodgkinsons
    Solicitors, The Old Manse, 14 Lumley Avenue, Skegness, Lincolnshire] . . . .   *Digested,* 00/**1719**
H (A Child) *v.* H and CL Ltd (Unreported, November 30, 2000), QBD [*Ex rel.* Alicia
    Collinson, Barrister, 2 Harcourt Buildings, Temple, London] . . . .   *Digested,* 01/**1710**
H (A Child) *v.* Hillingdon HA [2000] 4 Q.R. 4, QBD [*Ex rel.* Harris & Cartwright
    Solicitors, Windsor Crown House, 7 Windsor Road, Slough, Berkshire] . . . .   *Digested,* 00/**1507**
H (A Child) *v.* Merck & Co Inc see Horne-Roberts *v.* Smithkline Beecham Plc
H (A Child) *v.* Merk & Co Inc see Horne-Roberts *v.* Smithkline Beecham Plc
H (A Child) *v.* Minister for Immigration and Multicultural Affairs [2000] I.N.L.R. 455,
    HC (Aus) . . . .   *Digested,* 01/**3628**
H (A Child) *v.* Parsons (Unreported, September 29, 1999), CC (Leicester) [*Ex rel.*
    Holyoak & Co Solicitors, 6 Peacock Lane, Leicester] . . . .   *Digested,* 00/**1655**
H (A Child) *v.* Reed (Unreported, February 16, 2000), CC (Swansea) [*Ex rel.* David
    Harris, Barrister, Iscoed Chambers, 86 St. Helens Road, Swansea] . . . .   *Digested,* 00/**1499**
H (A Child) *v.* Smithkline Beecham Plc see Horne-Roberts *v.* Smithkline Beecham Plc
H (A Debtor) (No.38-SD of 1997), Re see Regional Collection Services Ltd *v.* Heald
H (A Minor) (Abduction: Rights of Custody), Re; *sub nom* H (A Child) (Removal from
    Jurisdiction), Re [2000] 2 A.C. 291; [2000] 2 W.L.R. 337; [2000] 2 All E.R. 1;
    [2000] 1 F.L.R. 374; [2000] 1 F.C.R. 225; [2000] Fam. Law 310; (2000) 97(7)
    L.S.G. 40; (2000) 144 S.J.L.B. 101; *Times,* February 8, 2000 ; *Independent,*
    February 8, 2000, HL; affirming [2000] 1 F.L.R. 201; [2000] Fam. Law 80;
    (1999) 96(47) L.S.G. 30; (1999) 143 S.J.L.B. 283; *Times,* November 16, 1999 ;
    Independent, November 17, 1999, CA. . . . .   *Digested,* 00/**2447**
H (A Minor) (CICB: Quantum: 1998), Re (Unreported, September 3, 1998), CICB (London)
    [*Ex rel.* Jonathan Ashworth, Pupil Barrister, 6 King's Bench Walk, Temple,
    London] . . . .   *Digested,* 99/**1444**
H (A Minor) (CICB: Quantum: 1999), Re (Unreported, July 21, 1999), CICB (Plymouth) [*Ex
    rel.* David Cadin, Barrister, 115 North Hill, Plymouth, Devon] . . . .   *Digested,* 99/**1552**
H (A Minor) (Parental Responsibility), Re; *sub nom* RH (A Minor) (Parental
    Responsibility), Re [1998] 1 F.L.R. 855; [1998] 2 F.C.R. 89; [1998] Fam. Law
    325; *Independent,* February 12, 1998, CA. . . . .   *Digested,* 98/**2437**
H (A Minor) (Reporting Restrictions), Re see R. *v.* Manchester Crown Court Ex p. H (A
    Juvenile)
H (A Minor) (Shared Residence), Re [1994] 1 F.L.R. 717; [1993] Fam. Law 463, CA. . .   *Digested,* 95/**3560**:
                                           Considered, 94/3263, 95/3561: *Not followed,* 01/2666
H (A Minor) *v.* Bass Plc (1999) 99(6) Q.R. 7, CC (Eastbourne) [*Ex rel.* Stephen
    Rimmer & Co Solicitors, 28 Hyde Gardens, Eastbourne, East Sussex] . . . .   *Digested,* 99/**1608**
H (A Minor) *v.* Lincolnshire CC (Unreported, July 14, 1998), CC (Skegness) [*Ex rel.*
    Hodgkinsons Solicitors, The Old Manse, 14 Lumley Avenue, Skegness,
    Lincolnshire] . . . .   *Digested,* 99/**1459**

H (A Minor) *v.* MHT Services Ltd (1999) 99(4) Q.R. 6, CC (Nottingham) [*Ex rel.*
  Nelsons Solicitors, Pennine House, 8 Stanford Street, Nottingham] . . . .   *Digested,* 99/**1530**
H (A Patient), Re; *sub nom* H (Adult: Incompetent), Re [1998] 2 F.L.R. 36; [1998] 3
  F.C.R. 174; (1997) 38 B.M.L.R. 11; [1998] Fam. Law 460, Fam Div. . . . .   *Digested,* 98/**2651**
H (Abduction: Child of 16), Re; *sub nom* H (Child Abduction: Child of Sixteen), Re
  [2000] 2 F.L.R. 51; [2000] 3 F.C.R. 404; [2000] Fam. Law 530, Fam Div. . . . .   *Digested,* 00/**2441**
H (Adult: Incompetent), Re see H (A Patient), Re
H (Application to Remove from Jurisdiction), Re [1998] 1 F.L.R. 848; [1999] 2 F.C.R. 34;
  [1998] Fam. Law 390, CA. . . . .   *Digested,* 98/**2441**:
                                                    Applied, 00/2485

H (Child Abduction: Child of Sixteen), Re see H (Abduction: Child of 16), Re
H (Child Abduction: Whereabouts Order to Solicitors), Re [2000] 1 F.L.R. 766; [2000] 1
  F.C.R. 499; [2000] Fam. Law 392, Fam Div. . . . .   *Digested,* 00/**2450**
H (Child Abduction: Wrongful Retention), Re see H (A Child) (Abduction: Habitual
  Residence: Consent), Re
H (Children) (Residence Order: Condition), Re see H (Children: Residence Order:
  Relocation), Re
H (Children) (Adjournment: Refusal), Re see H (Children) (Care Proceedings: Sexual
  Abuse), Re
H (Children) (Care Proceedings: Sexual Abuse), Re; *sub nom* H (Children)
  (Adjournment: Refusal), Re [2000] 2 F.C.R. 499; (2000) 164 J.P.N. 839;
  (2000) 164 J.P.N. 879, CA
H (Children) (Contact: Domestic Violence), Re see L (A Child) (Contact: Domestic
  Violence), Re
H (Children) (Contact Order) (No.1), Re [2001] 1 F.C.R. 49, CA
H (Children) (Contact Order) (No.2), Re [2001] 3 F.C.R. 385; [2001] Fam. Law 795; *Times,*
  August 10, 2001, Fam Div . . . .   *Digested,* 01/**2585**
H (Children: Residence Order: Relocation), Re; *sub nom* H (Children) (Residence
  Order: Condition), Re [2001] EWCA Civ 1338; [2001] 2 F.L.R. 1277; [2001] 3
  F.C.R. 182; [2001] Fam. Law 870; *Times,* August 29, 2001, CA . . . .   *Digested,* 01/**2597**
H (CICA: Quantum: 2000: Knee), Re (Unreported, August 7, 2000), CICA (Birmingham)
  [*Ex rel.* Nicholas Tarbitt, Barrister, 6, Fountain Court, Steelhouse Lane,
  Birmingham] . . . .   *Digested,* 01/**1798**
H (CICB: Quantum: 1998), Re; *sub nom* H (Compensation: Sexual Abuse), Re;
  (Unreported, October 28, 1997), CICB [*Ex rel.* Holyoak & Co Solicitors, 6
  Peacock Lane, Leicester]. . . . .   *Digested,* 98/**1516**
H (CICB: Quantum: 1998) (HIV), Re (1999) 99(4) Q.R. 8, CICB (London) [*Ex rel.* D
  Samuels, Board's Advocate, Morley House, 26-30 Holborn Viaduct, London] . .   *Digested,* 99/**1547**
H (CICB: Quantum: 1999) (Sexual Abuse), Re (1999) 99(5) Q.R. 5, CICB (Birmingham)
  [*Ex rel.* David Maxwell, Barrister, Claremont Chambers, 26 Waterloo Road,
  Wolverhampton] . . . .   *Digested,* 99/**1446**
H (CICB: Quantum: 2000), Re [2000] 6 Q.R. 6, CICB (Bath) [*Ex rel.* James Hassall,
  Barrister, Guildhall Chambers, 23 Broad Street, Bristol] . . . .   *Digested,* 00/**1529**
H (Compensation: Sexual Abuse), Re see H (CICB: Quantum: 1998), Re
H (Contact: Domestic Violence), Re; *sub nom* M (Minors) (Contact), Re [1998] 2 F.L.R.
  42; [1998] 3 F.C.R. 385; [1998] Fam. Law 392; *Times,* February 13, 1998, CA . .   *Digested,* 98/**2423**
H (In Bankruptcy), Re see Regional Collection Services Ltd *v.* Heald
H (Minors) (Abduction: Acquiescence), Re see H *v.* H (Child Abduction: Acquiescence)
H (Minors) (Adoption: Putative Father's Rights) (No.3), Re see H (Minors) (Local
  Authority: Parental Rights) (No.3), Re
H (Minors) (Care: Change in Care Plan), Re [1998] 1 F.L.R. 193; [1998] 2 F.C.R. 657; [1998]
  Fam. Law 70, CA . . . .   *Digested,* 98/**2413**
H (Minors) (Child Abuse: Threshold Conditions), Re see H (Minors) (Sexual Abuse:
  Standard of Proof), Re
H (Minors) (Local Authority: Parental Rights) (No.3), Re; *sub nom* H (Minors)
  (Adoption: Putative Father's Rights) (No.3), Re [1991] Fam. 151; [1991] 2 W.L.R.
  763; [1991] 2 All E.R. 185; [1991] 1 F.L.R. 214; [1991] F.C.R. 361; 89 L.G.R.
  537; [1991] Fam. Law 306; (1991) 135 S.J. 16; *Times,* November 21, 1990, CA. .   *Digested,* 91/**2500**:
           Applied, 94/3194, 95/3531, 95/3533, 98/2437: *Considered,* 92/3112,
                   93/2832, 95/3532, 96/592, 96/594, 98/2425, 99/2382:
                                            Distinguished, 92/3113

H (Minors) (Sexual Abuse: Standard of Proof), Re; *sub nom* H (Minors) (Child Abuse:
  Threshold Conditions), Re; H and R (Child Sexual Abuse: Standard of Proof),
  Re [1996] A.C. 563; [1996] 2 W.L.R. 8; [1996] 1 All E.R. 1; [1996] 1 F.L.R. 80;
  [1996] 1 F.C.R. 509; [1996] Fam. Law 74; (1995) 145 N.L.J. 1887; (1996) 140
  S.J.L.B. 24; *Times,* December 15, 1995; *Independent,* January 17, 1996, HL;
  affirming [1995] 1 F.L.R. 643; [1995] 2 F.C.R. 384; [1995] Fam. Law 401;
  (1995) 159 J.P.N. 338, CA . . . .   *Digested,* 96/**632**:
                 Applied, 96/490, 96/496, 98/2401, 00/949, 01/1975, 01/2566:
                  Considered, 95/3509, 96/482, 96/610, 01/721, 01/2549:
                                             Distinguished, 01/2550

H (Residence: Grandparent), Re [2000] Fam. Law 715, Fam Div
H (Residence Order: Child's Application for Leave), Re [2000] 1 F.L.R. 780; [2000] Fam.
  Law 404, Fam Div. . . . .   *Digested,* 00/**2490**

H (Jangheer) see R. v. Khan (Nazaqat)
H (Kadeer) see R. v. Khan (Nazaqat)
H v. Barnet & Chase Farm Hospitals NHS Trust [*Ex rel*. Dowse & Co, Solicitors, 23/25
 Dalston Lane, London] . . . .   *Digested*, 01/**1722**
H v. DPP see I v. DPP
H v. Gloucestershire CC; *sub nom* R. v. Gloucestershire CC Ex p. H [2000] E.L.R. 357;
 Times, January 21, 2000, QBD . . . .   *Digested*, 00/**1962**
H v. H [2001] EWCA Civ 653; [2001] 3 F.C.R. 628, CA
H v. H (A Child) (Occupation Order: Power of Arrest); *sub nom* H (A Child)
 (Occupation Order: Power of Arrest), Re [2001] 1 F.L.R. 641; [2001] 1 F.C.R.
 370; [2001] Fam. Law 261; *Times*, January 10, 2001; *Independent*, January 15,
 2001 (C.S), CA. . . . .   *Digested*, 01/**2654**
H v. H (Child Abduction: Acquiescence); *sub nom* H (Minors) (Abduction:
 Acquiescence), Re [1998] A.C. 72; [1997] 2 W.L.R. 563; [1997] 2 All E.R. 225;
 [1997] 1 F.L.R. 872; [1997] 2 F.C.R. 257; [1997] Fam. Law 468; *Times*, April
 17, 1997; *Independent*, April 15, 1997, HL; reversing [1996] 2 F.L.R. 570; [1996]
 3 F.C.R. 425; [1996] Fam. Law 718; (1996) 93(35) L.S.G. 33; (1996) 140
 S.J.L.B. 207; *Times*, August 14, 1996, CA . . . .   *Digested*, 97/**387**:
                              Considered, 99/2315, 00/2441: *Followed*, 99/2317
H v. H (Financial Provision: Conduct) see H v. H (Financial Relief: Conduct)
H v. H (Financial Relief: Conduct); *sub nom* H v. H (Financial Provision: Conduct)
 [1998] 1 F.L.R. 971; [1999] 1 F.C.R. 225; [1999] Fam. Law 395, Fam Div . . . . .   *Digested*, 98/**2464**
H v. H (Financial Relief: Costs) [1997] 2 F.L.R. 57; [1998] 2 F.C.R. 27; [1997] Fam.
 Law 537, Fam Div . . . .   *Digested*, 97/**2475**
H v. Home Office (Unreported, November 23, 1998), CC (Bristol) [*Ex rel*. Gordon &
 Penney Solicitors, 48 Boulevard, Weston-super-Mare, Somerset]. . . . .   *Digested*, 99/**1443**
H v. Kent CC [2000] E.L.R. 660, QBD   *Digested*, 01/**2039**
H v. L [1998] 1 W.L.R. 854; *Times*, February 3, 1998; *Independent*, February 4, 1998,
 QBD . . . .   *Digested*, 98/**1078**
H v. Lambeth, Southwark and Lewisham HA [2001] EWCA Civ 1455; [2001] C.P.
 Rep. 117; *Times*, October 8, 2001, CA . . . .   *Digested*, 01/**558**
H v. Leicestershire CC; *sub nom* R. v. Leicestershire CC Ex p. H [2000] E.L.R. 471,
 QBD . . . .   *Digested*, 00/**1942**
H v. Ministry of Defence [1991] 2 Q.B. 103; [1991] 2 W.L.R. 1192; [1991] 2 All E.R.
 834; (1991) 141 N.L.J. 420; *Times*, April 1, 1991; *Independent*, March 22, 1991;
 Guardian, March 27, 1991; *Daily Telegraph*, April 1, 1991, CA . . . .   *Digested*, 91/**2936**:
                                                                             Considered, 98/75
H v. Norfolk CC [1997] 1 F.L.R. 384; [1997] 2 F.C.R. 334; [1997] Fam. Law 231, CA . .   *Digested*, 97/**424**:
                                                                             Overruled, 00/4212
H v. Northamptonshire CC [2000] Ed. C.R. 238, QBD . . . .   *Digested*, 00/**1958**
H v. Nottinghamshire CC (Unreported, January 5, 1998), CC (Nottingham) [*Ex rel*.
 Nelsons Solicitors, Pennine House, 8 Stanford Street, Nottingham, NG1 7BQ] . .   *Digested*, 98/**1520**
H v. West Sussex CC [1998] 1 F.L.R. 862; [1998] 3 F.C.R. 126; [1998] Fam. Law 317,
 Fam Div . . . .   *Digested*, 98/**2428**
H (A Barrister), Ex p. see Barrister (Wasted Costs Order) (No.1 of 1991), Re
H and M v. DPP [1998] Crim. L.R. 653, CA (Crim Div)
H and R (Child Sexual Abuse: Standard of Proof), Re see H (Minors) (Sexual Abuse:
 Standard of Proof), Re
H Laing Demolition Building Contractors Ltd, Re [1998] B.C.C. 561, Ch D
H Tempest (Cardiff) Ltd v. Customs and Excise Commissioners [1995] V.A.T.T.R. 482,
 VAT Tr (London) . . . .   *Distinguished*,
                                                                             98/4953
H&L TOOTH/EPO communications (J09/96) [1999] E.P.O.R. 198, EPO (Legal Bd App)
H&N Emanuel v. Greater London Council [1971] 2 All E.R. 835; [1971] 2 Lloyd's Rep.
 36; 69 L.G.R. 346; 115 S.J. 226, CA; affirming (1970) 114 S.J. 653; *Times*, July
 21, 1970, QBD . . . .   *Digested*, 71/**7847**:
                                          Applied, 00/4238: *Considered*, 75/2325
H&R Ecroyd Holdings Ltd v. Commission of the European Communities (T220/97)
 [1999] E.C.R. II-1677; [1999] 2 C.M.L.R. 1361, CFI (4th Chamber) . . . .   *Digested*, 00/**2373**
H(B) (An Infant), Re; *sub nom* W (Adoption: Parental Agreement), Re; W(N) (An
 Infant), Re; W (Minors) (Custody), Re (1983) 4 F.L.R. 614; (1983) 13 Fam. Law
 144; (1983) 133 N.L.J. 1099; (1983) 127 S.J. 86, CA . . . .   *Digested*, 83/**2424**:
                              Considered, 84/2200, 86/2208, 87/2490, 98/2365
H5 Air Service Norway AS v. Civil Aviation Authority [1998] 1 Lloyd's Rep. 364; [1998]
 C.L.C. 11, CA; affirming [1997] C.L.C. 1264, QBD . . . .   *Digested*, 98/**4793**
Haagman v. Sadeg (Unreported, October 20, 1999), CC (Uxbridge) [*Ex rel*. Nicholas
 Preston, Barrister, Bracton Chambers, 8 Bell Yard, London] . . . .   *Digested*, 00/**2571**
Haahr Petroleum Ltd v. Abenra Havn (C90/94) [1997] E.C.R. I-4085; [1998] 1
 C.M.L.R. 771; [1998] C.E.C. 68, ECJ (6th Chamber) . . . .   *Digested*, 98/**4634**:
                                                                             Applied, 00/2405
Haarhuis v. Kunnan Enterprises Ltd [2000] B.P.I.R. 734, US Ct
Haberman v. Jackel International Ltd [1999] F.S.R. 683; (1999) 22(3) I.P.D. 22024;
 Times, January 21, 1999, Pat Ct . . . .   *Digested*, 99/**3506**
Habermann v. Koehler (No.2) [2000] E.G.C.S. 125; *Times*, November 22, 2000, CA . . .   *Digested*, 00/**4660**

Habermehl v. Attorney General [1996] E.G.C.S. 148; [1996] N.P.C. 129, Ch D . . . .   *Applied*, 01/5534
Habib Bank Ltd v. Ahmed; *sub nom* Ahmed v. Habib Bank Ltd [2001] EWCA Civ 1270;
    [2001] C.P. Rep. 111, CA; reversing (2000) 97(43) L.S.G. 37; (2000) 144
    S.J.L.B. 275; *Times*, November 2, 2000, QBD . . . .   *Digested*, 01/**559**
Habib Bank Ltd v. Habib Bank AG [1981] 1 W.L.R. 1265; [1981] 2 All E.R. 650; [1982]
    R.P.C. 1; 125 S.J. 512, CA . . . .   *Digested*, 82/**3262**:
                                      Applied, 95/4938: *Considered*, 89/2104, 92/586, 99/4369:
                                 Disapproved, 99/4856: *Distinguished*, 93/3979: *Followed*, 84/440, 96/4953
Habib Bank Ltd v. Jaffer (Gulzar Haider); Habib Bank Ltd v. Jaffer (Haider Ladhu)
    [2000] C.P.L.R. 438; (2000) 97(17) L.S.G. 34; (2000) 144 S.J.L.B. 187; *Times*,
    April 5, 2000, CA . . . .   *Digested*, 00/**344**
Habib Bank Ltd v. Jaffer (Haider Ladhu) see Habib Bank Ltd v. Jaffer (Gulzar Haider)
Hachette Filipacchi Presse v. Safeway Stores Plc see ELLE Trade Marks (Revocation)
Hacker v. Euro-Relais GmbH (C280/90) [1992] E.C.R. I-1111; [1992] I.L.Pr. 515, ECJ . .   *Digested*, 92/**4829**:
                                                                                         Distinguished, 01/824
Hackett v. Advanced Medical Computer Systems Ltd [1999] C.L.C. 160, QBD . . . .   *Digested*, 99/**111**
Hackman v. Hounslow LBC (Unreported, December 1, 1999), CC (Portsmouth) [*Ex rel.*
    Steven Weddle, Barrister, Hardwicke Building, New Square, Lincoln's Inn,
    London] . . . .   *Digested*, 00/**354**
Hackney African Organisation v. Hackney LBC see Hackney LBC v. Hackney African
    Organisation
Hackney LBC v. Bard (1998) 13 P.A.D. 446, Planning Inspector
Hackney LBC v. Cedar Trading Ltd (1999) 163 J.P. 749; [1999] E.T.M.R. 801; *Times*,
    April 30, 1999, QBD . . . .   *Digested*, 99/**2603**
Hackney LBC v. Ekinci see Ekinci v. Hackney LBC
Hackney LBC v. Hackney African Association see Hackney LBC v. Hackney African
    Organisation
Hackney LBC v. Hackney African Organisation; *sub nom* Hackney LBC v. Hackney
    African Association; Hackney African Organisation v. Hackney LBC [1999] L. &
    T.R. 117; [1998] E.G.C.S. 139; (1999) 77 P. & C.R. D18, CA
Hackney LBC v. Olukotun (Unreported, October 25, 2000), CC (Shoreditch) [*Ex rel.*
    Simon Butler, Barrister, 10 King's Bench Walk, Temple, London] . . . .   *Digested*, 01/**470**
Hackney LBC v. Redford (Unreported, January 31, 2001), CC (Shoreditch) [*Ex rel.* Jon
    Holbrook, Barrister, 2 Garden Court, London] . . . .   *Digested*, 01/**4165**
Hackney LBC v. Silaydin see Hackney LBC v. Silyadin
Hackney LBC v. Silyadin; *sub nom* Hackney LBC v. Silaydin [1999] Ed. C.R. 479;
    [1998] E.L.R. 571; *Times*, September 17, 1998, QBD . . . .   *Digested*, 98/**1979**
Hackney LBC v. Snowden (2001) 33 H.L.R. 49; [2001] L. & T.R. 6, CA . . . .   *Digested*, 01/**4189**
Hackney LBC v. Thompson [2001] L. & T.R. 7, CA . . . .   *Digested*, 01/**958**
Hacksaw v. Hacksaw see Hackshaw v. Hackshaw
Hackshaw v. Hackshaw; *sub nom* Hacksaw v. Hacksaw [1999] 2 F.L.R. 876; [1999] 3
    F.C.R. 451; [1999] Fam. Law 697; (2000) 164 J.P.N. 326; *Times*, July 29, 1999,
    Fam Div . . . .   *Digested*, 99/**2418**
Haddad v. Secretary of State for the Home Department [2000] I.N.L.R. 117, IAT . . . . . .   *Digested*, 00/**3299**
Haddon v. Van Den Bergh Foods Ltd [1999] I.C.R. 1150; [1999] I.R.L.R. 672, EAT . . . .   *Digested*, 00/**2239**:
                                                                                   Overruled in part, 00/2237
Haddow v. Secretary of State for the Environment, Transport and the Regions [2000]
    Env. L.R. 212, CA; affirming (1998) 95(7) L.S.G. 33; [1998] N.P.C. 10, QBD . . .   *Digested*, 00/**4221**
Haden Carrier Ltd v. Cowen; *sub nom* Cowen v. Haden Carrier Ltd [1983] I.C.R. 1;
    [1982] I.R.L.R. 314; 126 S.J. 725; *Times*, July 15, 1982, CA; reversing [1982]
    I.R.L.R. 225; 126 S.J. 411; *Times*, May 8, 1982, EAT . . . .   *Digested*, 83/**1276**:
                                      Applied, 85/1198, 86/1265: *Considered*, 85/1175, 96/2593, 97/2249,
                                                                                                98/2186
Hadjipanayi v. Yeldon [2001] B.P.I.R. 487; [2000] E.G.C.S. 122, Ch D . . . .   *Digested*, 01/**4855**
Hadkinson v. Saab (No.1) see Federal Bank of the Middle East v. Hadkinson (Stay of
    Action)
Hadkinson v. Saab (No.2) see Federal Bank of the Middle East v. Hadkinson (Security
    for Costs) (No.2)
Hadley v. Baxendale (1854) 9 Ex. 341, Ex Ct . . . .   *Applied*, 47-51/5368,
            47-51/5562, 53/3775, 55/2559, 56/50, 62/829, 66/3146, 66/11174, 66/12340,
                 67/3623, 77/2881, 79/1391, 79/2391, 80/640, 81/138, 86/980, 90/2764,
                        91/1316, 93/517, 93/4846, 98/4384, 99/1379, 01/1507:
                Considered, 47-51/1604, 47-51/2562, 47-51/5222, 47-51/9482, 47-51/9490,
                      49/3656, 61/2343, 67/3605, 67/3615, 68/1013, 69/881, 73/3466, 86/2760,
                              87/2429, 90/670, 94/5413, 96/401, 96/1196, 97/989, 97/3839, 00/5981:
                      Distinguished, 47-51/2561, 47-51/2565, 47-51/2566, 47/2561, 85/1282,
                              99/3946: *Followed*, 67/3527, 69/3379, 88/1065, 98/1472:
                                                        Referred to, 83/1216, 83/4027
Hadley v. Kemp [1999] E.M.L.R. 589, Ch D . . . .   *Digested*, 99/**835**
Hadley Industries Plc v. Metal Sections Ltd (No.1); Hadley Industries Plc v. Metsec (UK)
    Ltd (1999) 22(1) I.P.D. 22004, Pat Ct
Hadley Industries Plc v. Metal Sections Ltd (No.2); Hadley Industries Plc v. Metsec
    (UK) Ltd (2000) 23(1) I.P.D. 23003; *Times*, October 28, 1999, Pat Ct . . . .   *Digested*, 99/**3466**

Hadley Industries Plc v. Metsec (UK) Ltd see Hadley Industries Plc v. Metal Sections Ltd (No.1)

Hadley Industries Plc v. Metsec (UK) Ltd see Hadley Industries Plc v. Metal Sections Ltd (No.2)

Hadmere Ltd v. Secretary of State for the Environment, Transport and the Regions see R. (on the application of Elmbridge BC) v. Secretary of State for the Environment, Transport and the Regions

Hadnum v. Smith (Unreported, May 24, 1999), CC (Altrincham) [*Ex rel.* Elliotts Solicitors, Centurion House, Deansgate, Manchester] . . . .   *Digested*, 99/**2487**

Hagee (London) Ltd v. AB Erikson and Larson [1976] Q.B. 209; [1975] 3 W.L.R. 272; [1975] 3 All E.R. 234; 29 P. & C.R. 512; 119 S.J. 354, CA . . . .   *Digested*, 75/**1884**:
       Applied, 86/1838, 99/689, 99/3669: *Considered*, 91/2218, 94/465, 94/2817

Haggart Construction Ltd v. Canadian Imperial Bank of Commerce [1998] Lloyd's Rep. Bank. 297, QB (Alta) . . . .   *Digested*, 99/**288**

Haghiran v. Allied Dunbar Insurance [2001] 1 All E.R. (Comm) 97, CA . . . .   *Digested*, 01/**3814**

Hagieni, The and Barbarossa, The [2000] 2 Lloyd's Rep. 292, QBD. . . . .   *Digested*, 00/**4705**

Hague v. Deputy Governor of Parkhurst Prison see R. v. Deputy Governor of Parkhurst Prison Ex p. Hague

Haibe v. Secretary of State for the Home Department [1997] I.N.L.R. 119, IAT . . . .   *Digested*, 98/**3239**:
       Distinguished, 00/3322

Haig v. Aitken [2001] Ch. 110; [2000] 3 W.L.R. 1117; [2000] 3 All E.R. 80; [2000] B.P.I.R. 462, Ch D . . . .   *Digested*, 00/**3442**:
       Considered, 01/3732

Haigh v. Customs and Excise Commissioners [1999] B.V.C. 2113, VAT Tr (Manchester)

Haigh v. Ousey (1857) 7 El. & Bl. 578, QBD. . . . .   *Approved*, 00/**4027**

Haile v. West [1940] 1 K.B. 250; [1939] 4 All E.R. 339, CA. . . . .   *Considered*, 94/3566,
       95/3973, 97/567: *Distinguished*, 98/398: *Followed*, 98/399

Hair v. Gillman (2000) 80 P. & C.R. 108; [2000] 3 E.G.L.R. 74; [2000] 48 E.G. 117, CA . . . .   *Digested*, 00/**4629**

Haiselden v. P&O Properties Ltd (1998) 95(21) L.S.G. 37; (1998) 142 S.J.L.B. 158; *Times*, July 16, 1998; *Independent*, June 8, 1998 (C.S.), CA . . . .   *Digested*, 98/**420**

Haji-Ioannou v. Frangos [1999] 2 All E.R. (Comm) 865; [1999] 2 Lloyd's Rep. 337; [1999] C.L.C. 1075, CA; affirming [1998] C.L.C. 61, Ch D . . . .   *Digested*, 99/**713**:
       Applied, 00/738

Hakansson v. Sweden (A/171); *sub nom* Sturesson v. Sweden (1991) 13 E.H.R.R. 1, ECHR . . . .   *Applied*, 98/3064,
       98/3145, 01/564: *Distinguished*, 98/3121

Halbauer v. Brighton Corp [1954] 1 W.L.R. 1161; [1954] 2 All E.R. 707; (1954) 118 J.P. 446; 98 S.J. 572, CA. . . . .   *Digested*, 54/**582**:
       Considered, 66/571, 86/151: *Followed*, 99/833

Halcro-Johnston v. Customs and Excise Commissioners [2001] S.T.I. 1042, V&DTr

Hale v. Bellway Homes Ltd [1998] E.G.C.S. 83, Ch D

Hale v. Guildarch [1999] P.N.L.R. 44, QBD . . . .   *Digested*, 99/**4019**

Hale v. Norfolk CC [2001] Ch. 717; [2001] 2 W.L.R. 1481; [2001] R.T.R. 26; [2001] J.P.L. 1093; [2000] E.G.C.S. 137; (2001) 98(2) L.S.G. 40; (2000) 144 S.J.L.B. 289; [2000] N.P.C. 122; *Times*, December 19, 2000; *Independent*, November 22, 2000, CA . . . .   *Digested*, 00/**4636**

Hale v. Tanner (Practice Note) [2000] 1 W.L.R. 2377; [2000] 2 F.L.R. 879; [2000] 3 F.C.R. 62; [2000] Fam. Law 876; (2001) 165 J.P.N. 184; (2000) 164 J.P.N. 861; *Times*, August 22, 2000, CA . . . .   *Digested*, 00/**2541**

Halewood International Ltd v. Addleshaw Booth & Co [2000] Lloyd's Rep. P.N. 298; [2000] P.N.L.R. 788, Ch D . . . .   *Digested*, 00/**4021**

Halford v. Brookes (No.1) [1991] 1 W.L.R. 428; [1991] 3 All E.R. 559; *Times*, November 28, 1990; *Independent*, November 27, 1990; *Guardian*, November 28, 1990, CA . . . .   *Digested*, 91/**2348**:
       Cited, 97/668: *Considered*, 96/836, 97/669, 99/470

Halford v. United Kingdom [1997] I.R.L.R. 471; (1997) 24 E.H.R.R. 523; 3 B.H.R.C. 31; [1998] Crim. L.R. 753; (1997) 94(27) L.S.G. 24; *Times*, July 3, 1997, ECHR . . . .   *Digested*, 97/**2795**:
       Applied, 98/3106, 00/3252: *Considered*, 00/3248, 01/3576

Halfpenny v. IGE Medical Systems Ltd [2001] I.C.R. 73; [2001] I.R.L.R. 96; (2001) 58 B.M.L.R. 1; (2001) 98(7) L.S.G. 39; *Times*, December 19, 2000; *Independent*, February 12, 2001 (C.S), HL; reversing [1999] I.C.R. 834; [1999] I.R.L.R. 177; [1999] Disc. L.R. 265; [1999] 1 F.L.R. 944; (2000) 52 B.M.L.R. 153; (1999) 96(5) L.S.G. 36; (1999) 143 S.J.L.B. 38; *Times*, January 4, 1999, CA; reversing [1997] I.C.R. 1007; [1998] I.R.L.R. 10, EAT . . . .   *Digested*, 01/**2318**:
       Considered, 98/5825

Halifax v. Blay (1999) 77 P. & C.R. D37, CA

Halifax Building Society v. Urquart-Dykes & Lord [1997] R.P.C. 55; [2000] Lloyd's Rep. P.N. 318, Ch D . . . .   *Digested*, 97/**4871**

Halifax Financial Services Ltd v. Intuitive Systems Ltd [1999] 1 All E.R. (Comm) 303; (2000) 2 T.C.L.R. 35, QBD . . . .   *Digested*, 99/**1639**

Halifax Mortgage Services Ltd v. Muirhead (1998) 76 P. & C.R. 418; [1997] N.P.C. 171, CA . . . .   *Digested*, 98/**4355**

Halifax Mortgage Services Ltd v. S & S (A Firm) [1998] P.N.L.R. 616, QBD . . . .   *Digested*, 98/**4026**

Halifax Mortgage Services Ltd *v.* Simpson 64 Con. L.R. 117, QBD. . . . .   *Digested,* 99/**4057**
Halifax Plc *v.* Alexander LTA 98/7696/2, CA . . . .   *Digested,* 99/**4378**
Halifax Plc *v.* Chandler; *sub nom* Chandler *v.* Halifax Plc [2001] EWCA Civ 1750;
   [2001] N.P.C. 189, CA
Halifax Plc *v.* Customs and Excise Commissioners (Input Tax on Building Works) TNS,
   Ch D; reversing in part [2001] B.V.C. 2240; [2001] S.T.I. 1022, V&DTr . . . .   *Digested,* 01/**5608**:
                                                                                            Applied, 01/5550
Halifax Plc *v.* Customs and Excise Commissioners (Taxation of Waste Paper) [2001]
   B.V.C. 2029; [2000] S.T.I. 1483, V&DTr
Halifax Plc *v.* Davidson (Inspector of Taxes) [2000] S.T.C. (S.C.D.) 251; [2000] S.T.I.
   1002, Sp Comm . . . .   *Digested,* 00/**4933**:
                                                 Followed, 00/4932, 00/4934, 00/4935
Halifax Plc *v.* Gould & Swayne [1999] P.N.L.R. 184; [1998] 3 E.G.L.R. 177; [1998]
   E.G.C.S. 127; [1998] N.P.C. 128, CA . . . .   *Digested,* 99/**4033**
Halifax Plc *v.* Purvis (1999) 77 P. & C.R. D29, CA
Halifax Plc *v.* Ringrose & Co [2000] Lloyd's Rep. P.N. 309; [2000] P.N.L.R. 483;
   (2000) 150 N.L.J. 58; [1999] N.P.C. 157, QBD . . . .   *Digested,* 00/**4268**:
                                                                                         Considered, 00/4254
Halifax Plc *v.* Taffs 99/PA/10093, CA. . . . .   *Digested,* 99/**4385**
Halil *v.* Lambeth LBC [2001] R.V.R. 181, Lands Tr . . . .   *Digested,* 01/**4672**
Halki Shipping Corp *v.* Sopex Oils Ltd (The Halki) [1998] 1 W.L.R. 726; [1998] 2 All
   E.R. 23; [1998] 1 Lloyd's Rep. 465; [1998] C.L.C. 583; (1998) 142 S.J.L.B. 44;
   [1998] N.P.C. 4; *Times,* January 19, 1998; *Independent,* January 12, 1998 (C.S.),
   CA; affirming [1997] 1 W.L.R. 1268; [1997] 3 All E.R. 833; [1998] 1 Lloyd's
   Rep. 49; (1997) 94(28) L.S.G. 26; (1997) 141 S.J.L.B. 172; *Times,* October 13,
   1997, QBD (Adm Ct) . . . .   *Digested,* 98/**246**:
                                                                                         Followed, 00/227
Hall *v.* Bank of England [2000] Lloyd's Rep. Bank. 186, CA; affirming [1999] Lloyd's
   Rep. Bank. 478, Ch D . . . .   *Digested,* 00/**286**
Hall *v.* Customs and Excise Commissioners [2001] S.T.I. 681, V&DTr
Hall *v.* Dart Valley Light Railway Plc (Unreported, August 5, 1997), CC (Torquay & Ntn
   Abbott) [*Ex rel.* Simon Osborne, Solicitor, Railtrack Plc, Railtrack House, Euston
   Square, London] . . . .   *Digested,* 98/**3933**
Hall *v.* Heward (1886) L.R. 32 Ch. D. 430, CA . . . .   *Followed,* 99/4349
Hall *v.* Kingston upon Hull City Council see R. *v.* Birmingham City Council Ex p. Ireland
Hall *v.* Queen, The (1977) 24 W.I.R. 547 . . . .   *Considered,* 01/1055
Hall *v.* Secretary of State for the Environment, Transport and the Regions [1998] J.P.L.
   1055, QBD . . . .   *Digested,* 98/**4217**
Hall *v.* Sevalco Ltd; Crompton *v.* Sevalco Ltd [1996] P.I.Q.R. P344; *Times,* March 27,
   1996, CA . . . .   *Digested,* 96/**795**:
                     Cited, 97/480: *Considered,* 96/792, 99/447: *Followed,* 97/3879
Hall *v.* Woolf (1908) 7 C.L.R. 207, HC (NZ) . . . .   *Applied,* 01/3715
Hall *v.* Woolston Hall Leisure Ltd [2001] 1 W.L.R. 225; [2000] 4 All E.R. 787; [2001]
   I.C.R. 99; [2000] I.R.L.R. 578; (2000) 97(24) L.S.G. 39; (2000) 150 N.L.J.
   833; *Times,* May 31, 2000; *Independent,* June 8, 2000, CA; reversing [1998]
   I.C.R. 651, EAT . . . .   *Digested,* 00/**2205**
Hall *v.* Yorkshire Bank Plc see Yorkshire Bank Plc *v.* Hall
Hall & Co Ltd *v.* Shoreham by Sea Urban DC [1964] 1 W.L.R. 240; [1964] 1 All E.R. 1;
   128 J.P. 120; 62 L.G.R. 206; (1964) 15 P. & C.R. 119; 107 S.J. 1001, CA;
   reversing 61 L.G.R. 508; (1963) 15 P. & C.R. 192, QBD . . . .   *Digested,* 64/**3600**:
                     Applied, 72/3358, 86/3325, 87/3676: *Considered,* 93/3936, 94/4462,
                                           95/4784, 99/2215: *Distinguished,* 68/3837
Hall & Tawse South Ltd *v.* Ivory Gate Ltd 62 Con. L.R. 117, QBD (OR) . . . .   *Digested,* 99/**803**
Hallam *v.* Avery; *sub nom* Hallam *v.* Cheltenham BC; Smith *v.* Cheltenham BC [2001]
   UKHL 15; [2001] 1 W.L.R. 655; [2001] I.C.R. 408; [2001] I.R.L.R. 312; [2001]
   B.L.G.R. 278; (2001) 98(21) L.S.G. 39; (2001) 145 S.J.L.B. 116; *Times,* March
   27, 2001, HL; affirming [2000] 1 W.L.R. 966; [2000] I.C.R. 583; [2000]
   B.L.G.R. 452; (2000) 97(1) L.S.G. 23; (2000) 144 S.J.L.B. 32; *Times,* February
   7, 2000 ; *Independent,* December 21, 1999, CA . . . .   *Digested,* 01/**3492**
Hallam *v.* Cheltenham BC see Hallam *v.* Avery
Hallam-Eames *v.* Merrett Syndicates Ltd see Henderson *v.* Merrett Syndicates Ltd
   (No.1)
Hallam-Eames *v.* Merrett Syndicates Ltd (No.1) [1996] 5 Re. L.R. 110; [1996] 7 Med.
   L.R. 122; [2001] Lloyd's Rep. P.N. 178; [1955-95] P.N.L.R. 672; *Times,* January
   25, 1995; *Independent,* January 25, 1995, CA; reversing *Times,* June 16, 1995,
   QBD . . . .   *Digested,* 95/**3166**:
                                         Applied, 97/650, 00/4197: *Followed,* 95/3169
Hallatt *v.* North West Anglia HA [1998] Lloyd's Rep. Med. 197, CA . . . .   *Digested,* 98/**3969**
Halle *v.* Trax BW Ltd [2000] B.C.C. 1020, Ch D . . . .   *Digested,* 01/**481**
HALLELUJAH Trade Mark [1976] R.P.C. 605, TMR . . . .   *Digested,* 76/**2798**:
                                                                                            Followed, 01/3980

Hallen Co v. Brabantia (UK) Ltd (No.1) [1991] R.P.C. 195; *Independent*, October 26, 1990; *Financial Times*, October 24, 1990, CA; affirming [1989] R.P.C. 307, Pat Ct . . . . *Digested*, 92/**3318**:
Applied, 98/3453: *Considered*, 95/3750, 95/3780: *Distinguished*, 95/3778: *Followed*, 01/3967: *Referred to*, 94/3438
Halliard Property Co Ltd v. Jack Segal Ltd [1978] 1 W.L.R. 377; [1978] 1 All E.R. 1219; (1978) 36 P. & C.R. 134; (1977) 245 E.G. 230; 122 S.J. 180, Ch D . . . . *Digested*, 78/**1787**:
Followed, 99/3750
Halliburton Co Germany GmbH v. Ministry of the Treasury 4 I.T.L. Rep. 19, OL (DK)
Halliday (Valuation Officer) v. Priory Hospital Group of the Nottingham Clinic [2001] R.A. 355, Lands Tr
Hallinan v. DPP (1999) 163 J.P. 651; [1998] Crim. L.R. 754; *Times*, May 7, 1998, QBD . . *Digested*, 98/**973**
Hallisey v. Petmoor Developments Ltd; *sub nom* Hallisey v. Petmoore Developments Ltd [2000] E.G.C.S. 124; [2000] N.P.C. 114; *Times*, November 7, 2000, Ch D . . *Digested*, 00/**3915**:
Applied, 01/4192
Hallisey v. Petmoore Developments Ltd see Hallisey v. Petmoor Developments Ltd
Halliwell v. Pizaz Direct Ltd CH-1997-H-4702, Ch D . . . . *Digested*, 98/**3517**
Hallmark Furniture Co Ltd v. Collins (t/a Furniture Direct) [1998] N.I. 4, CA (NI) . . . . . . *Digested*, 99/**5143**:
Considered, 99/5471
Halls v. David see Produce Marketing Consortium (In Liquidation) (No.1), Re
Halpern v. Somak Travel Ltd (Unreported, October 27, 1997), CC (Central London) [*Ex rel*. Daniel Barnett, Barrister, 2 Gray's Inn Square Chambers, London] . . . . *Digested*, 98/**1428**
Halsall v. Brizell [1957] Ch. 169; [1957] 2 W.L.R. 123; [1957] 1 All E.R. 371; 101 S.J. 88, Ch D . . . . *Digested*, 57/**3005**:
Applied, 66/6674, 67/2196, 77/2709, 78/787: *Considered*, 66/10313, 98/4345
Halsey v. Customs and Excise Commissioners [1996] V. & D.R. 508, VAT Tr (London) . *Digested*, 98/**4923**
Halson Packaging Ltd, Re [1997] B.C.C. 993; [1997] B.P.I.R. 194, Ch D . . . . *Digested*, 97/**3079**:
Considered, 98/3306: *Followed*, 01/3792
Halstead v. Manchester City Council; *sub nom* Manchester City Council v. Halstead [1998] 1 All E.R. 33; (1998) 76 P. & C.R. 8; [1998] 1 E.G.L.R. 1; [1998] 06 E.G. 143; [1997] R.V.R. 266; [1998] J.P.L. 771; (1997) 94(42) L.S.G. 31; [1997] N.P.C. 148; *Times*, November 14, 1997; *Independent*, November 17, 1997 (C.S.), CA . . . . *Digested*, 97/**4048**
Halstuk v. Venvil see Baron Investments (Holdings) Ltd, Re
Halton BC v. Wignall (1998) 13 P.A.D. 49, Planning Inspector
HAMAMATSU/Requests (T1105/96) [1998] E.P.O.R. 26, EPO (Technical Bd App)
Hambis v. Boon (Unreported, August 4, 1999), CC (Oxford) [*Ex rel*. Edward Hutchin, Barrister, Bracton Chambers, 8 Bell Yard, London] . . . . *Digested*, 99/**1580**
Hamble Fisheries Ltd v. L Gardner & Sons Ltd (The Rebecca Elaine) [1999] 2 Lloyd's Rep. 1; (1999) 15 Const. L.J. 152; (1999) 96(6) L.S.G. 34; *Times*, January 5, 1999, CA . . . . *Digested*, 99/**3960**
Hambleton DC v. Bird [1995] 3 P.L.R. 8; [1996] J.P.L. 675; [1995] E.G.C.S. 67; [1995] N.P.C. 58, CA . . . . *Digested*, 96/**4743**:
Applied, 01/4729
Hambleton DC v. Buxted Poultry Ltd see Farmer (Valuation Officer) v. Buxted Poultry Ltd
Hambleton DC v. Secretary of State for the Environment, Transport and the Regions (2000) 97(46) L.S.G. 41, QBD (Admin Ct)
Hamblin v. Field [2000] B.P.I.R. 621; (2000) 97(21) L.S.G. 41; *Times*, April 26, 2000, CA; affirming [2000] B.P.I.R. 270, Ch D . . . . *Digested*, 00/**605**
Hamilton v. Al-Fayed (Costs) A2/2001/1718, CA; affirming *Times*, July 25, 2001, QBD . *Digested*, 01/**1817**
Hamilton v. Al-Fayed (Joined Party) (2000) 97(41) L.S.G. 40; *Times*, October 13, 2000; *Independent*, October 27, 2000, CA . . . . *Digested*, 00/**547**
Hamilton v. Al-Fayed (No.1) [2001] 1 A.C. 395; [2000] 2 W.L.R. 609; [2000] 2 All E.R. 224; [2000] E.M.L.R. 531; (2000) 97(14) L.S.G. 43; (2000) 144 S.J.L.B. 157; *Times*, March 28, 2000; *Independent*, April 5, 2000, HL; affirming [1999] 1 W.L.R. 1569; [1999] 3 All E.R. 317; [1999] E.M.L.R. 501; (1999) 96(19) L.S.G. 28; (1999) 149 N.L.J. 560; (1999) 143 S.J.L.B. 134; *Times*, March 30, 1999; *Independent*, April 20, 1999, CA . . . . *Digested*, 00/**1767**
Hamilton v. Al-Fayed (No.2), *Times*, March 30, 1999, CA . . . . *Digested*, 99/**1632**
Hamilton v. Al-Fayed (No.4) [2001] E.M.L.R. 15; *Independent*, January 25, 2001; *Daily Telegraph*, January 16, 2001, CA. . . . . *Digested*, 01/**634**
Hamilton v. Law Debenture Trustees Ltd see Barings Plc (In Liquidation), Re
Hamilton v. Official Receiver [1998] B.P.I.R. 602, Ch D . . . . *Digested*, 99/**3278**
Hamilton v. Watson (1845) 12 Cl. & F. 109 . . . . *Considered*, 95/401, 01/4564
Hamilton-Johnson v. Royal Society for the Prevention of Cruelty to Animals see Hamilton-Johnson v. RSPCA
Hamilton-Johnson v. RSPCA; *sub nom* Hamilton-Johnson v. Royal Society for the Prevention of Cruelty to Animals [2000] 2 Cr. App. R. (S.) 390; (2000) 164 J.P. 345; (2000) 164 J.P.N. 484; (2000) 97(20) L.S.G. 42; *Times*, April 20, 2000, QBD . . . . *Digested*, 00/**1041**

Hamlet International Plc (In Administration), Re; *sub nom* Trident International Ltd *v.*
Barlow; Jeffrey Rogers (Imports) Ltd, Re [2000] B.C.C. 602; [1999] 2 B.C.L.C.
506, CA; affirming [1998] 2 B.C.L.C. 164; (1998) 95(16) L.S.G. 24; *Times,*
March 13, 1998, Ch D (Companies Ct) . . . .   *Digested,* 00/**674**

Hamlin *v.* Edwin Evans (A Firm) 80 B.L.R. 85; 52 Con. L.R. 106; (1997) 29 H.L.R. 414;
[1996] P.N.L.R. 398; [1996] 2 E.G.L.R. 106; [1996] 47 E.G. 141; [1996]
E.G.C.S. 120; (1996) 93(27) L.S.G. 29; (1996) 140 S.J.L.B. 167; [1996] N.P.C.
110; *Times,* July 15, 1996; *Independent,* July 24, 1996, CA . . . .   *Digested,* 96/**822**:
Considered, 99/481, 99/3944

Hamlyn *v.* John Houston & Co [1903] 1 K.B. 81, CA . . . .   *Applied,* 00/5105

Hammant *v.* Stockport MBC (Unreported, June 20, 2000), CC (Stoke on Trent) [*Ex
rel.* Glaisyers Solicitors, 6th Floor, Manchester House, 18-20 Bridge Street,
Manchester] . . . .   *Digested,* 00/**1609**

Hammersmith & Fulham LBC *v.* Brown (Unreported, November 2, 1999), CC
(Willesden) [*Ex rel.* Beatrice Prevatt, Barrister, 2 Garden Court, Middle Temple,
London] . . . .   *Digested,* 00/**3157**

Hammersmith and Fulham LBC *v.* Clarke (2001) 33 H.L.R. 77; (2001) 81 P. & C.R. D20,
CA

Hammersmith and Fulham LBC *v.* Creska Ltd (No.2) see Creska Ltd *v.* Hammersmith
and Fulham LBC (No.2)

Hammersmith and Fulham LBC *v.* Farnsworth [2000] I.R.L.R. 691, EAT . . . .   *Digested,* 00/**2127**

Hammersmith and Fulham LBC *v.* Hill (1995) 27 H.L.R. 368; 92 L.G.R. 665; [1994] 35
E.G. 124; (1994) 158 L.G. Rev. 781; [1994] E.G.C.S. 70; (1994) 91(22) L.S.G.
35; *Times,* April 25, 1994; *Independent,* May 2, 1994 (C.S.), CA . . . .   *Digested,* 95/**3042**:
Applied, 94/3297, 96/4977, 01/4168: *Considered,* 01/4166:
Distinguished, 99/4382

Hammersmith and Fulham LBC *v.* Jesuthasan; *sub nom* Jesuthasan *v.* Hammersmith
and Fulham LBC [1998] 2 C.M.L.R. 940; [1998] I.C.R. 640; [1998] I.R.L.R.
372; (1998) 95(15) L.S.G. 33; (1998) 142 S.J.L.B. 101; *Times,* March 5, 1998;
Independent, March 17, 1998, CA; reversing [1996] I.C.R. 991, EAT . . . .   *Digested,* 98/**2177**

Hammersmith and Fulham LBC *v.* Ladejobi [1999] I.C.R. 673, EAT . . . .   *Digested,* 99/**2039**

Hammersmith and Fulham LBC *v.* Lemeh (2001) 33 H.L.R. 23; [2000] L. & T.R. 423;
(2000) 80 P. & C.R. D25, CA . . . .   *Digested,* 01/**4169**:
Applied, 01/4166: *Considered,* 01/4168

Hammersmith and Fulham LBC *v.* Monk; Barnet LBC *v.* Smith [1992] 1 A.C. 478;
[1990] 3 W.L.R. 1144; [1992] 1 All E.R. 1; [1992] 1 F.L.R. 465; (1992) 24 H.L.R.
207; 90 L.G.R. 38; (1992) 63 P. & C.R. 373; [1992] 1 E.G.L.R. 65; [1992] 09
E.G. 135; [1992] Fam. Law 292; (1992) 156 L.G. Rev. 481; [1991] E.G.C.S. 130;
(1992) 89(3) L.S.G. 32; (1991) 141 N.L.J. 1697; (1992) 136 S.J.L.B. 10; [1991]
N.P.C. 132; *Times,* December 6, 1991; *Independent,* December 10, 1991, HL;
affirming (1991) 23 H.L.R. 114; 89 L.G.R. 357; (1991) 61 P. & C.R. 414; [1991] 1
E.G.L.R. 263; *Times,* November 5, 1990; *Independent,* November 23, 1990, CA .   *Digested,* 92/**2684**:
Applied, 95/2997, 01/4172: *Considered,* 93/2462, 93/2479, 97/89, 98/2473:
Followed, 95/2996, 96/3819, 97/2703: *Referred to,* 97/2490

Hammersmith and Fulham LBC *v.* Secretary of State for the Environment, Transport and
the Regions CO/2273/97, QBD . . . .   *Digested,* 98/**4181**

Hammersmith Hospitals NHS Trust *v.* Troup Bywaters & Anders [2001] EWCA Civ 793,
CA; affirming [2000] Env. L.R. 343, QBD (T&CC) . . . .   *Digested,* 00/**4250**

Hammond *v.* Bristow Helicopters Ltd see King *v.* Bristow Helicopters Ltd

Hammond *v.* West Lancashire HA [1998] Lloyd's Rep. Med. 146; (1998) 95(14) L.S.G.
23; *Times,* March 5, 1998, CA . . . .   *Digested,* 98/**2645**

Hammond *v.* Wilkinson (2001) 165 J.P. 786; [2001] Crim. L.R. 323; (2001) 165 J.P.N.
810, QBD

Hampden's Settlement Trusts, Re [1977] T.R. 177; [2001] W.T.L.R. 195, Ch D . . . .   *Digested,* 77/**243**

Hampshire CC *v.* J & W Ltd (1999) 14 P.A.D. 341, Planning Inspector

Hampshire CC *v.* Southcombe (2000) 15 P.A.D. 387, Planning Inspector

Hampshire Land Co (No.2), Re [1896] 2 Ch. 743, Ch D . . . .   *Applied,* 54/2971,
54/2972, 54/2991, 54/2993, 99/3382: *Considered,* 95/4535, 96/3568:
Distinguished, 00/5348

Hampson *v.* Department of Education and Science [1991] 1 A.C. 171; [1990] 3 W.L.R.
42; [1990] 2 All E.R. 513; [1990] I.C.R. 511; [1990] I.R.L.R. 302; (1990) 154
L.G. Rev. 811; (1990) 140 N.L.J. 853; (1990) 134 S.J. 1123, HL; reversing [1990]
2 All E.R. 25; [1989] I.C.R. 179; [1989] I.R.L.R. 69; (1989) 86(13) L.S.G. 43;
(1989) 133 S.J. 151, CA; affirming [1988] I.C.R. 278; [1988] I.R.L.R. 87, EAT . .   *Digested,* 90/**80**:
Applied, 91/452, 99/2029: *Considered,* 89/2124, 91/1672:
Referred to, 93/1774

Hampton *v.* Minns (2001) 98(20) L.S.G. 41; *Times,* March 27, 2001, Ch D . . . .   *Digested,* 01/**961**

Hamptons Residential Ltd *v.* Field [1998] 2 Lloyd's Rep. 248; (1998) 95(23) L.S.G. 28,
CA; reversing [1997] 1 Lloyd's Rep. 302; *Independent,* December 2, 1996
(C.S.), QBD (Comm Ct) . . . .   *Digested,* 98/**3398**

Han (t/a Murdishaw Supper Bar) v. Customs and Excise Commissioners; Martins v. Customs and Excise Commissioners; Morris v. Customs and Excise Commissioners; Yau v. Customs and Excise Commissioners [2001] EWCA Civ 1048; [2001] 1 W.L.R. 2253; [2001] 4 All E.R. 687; [2001] S.T.C. 1188; [2001] H.R.L.R. 54; [2001] U.K.H.R.R. 1341; [2001] B.V.C. 415; 3 I.T.L. Rep. 873; [2001] S.T.I. 1015; (2001) 98(32) L.S.G. 37; (2001) 151 N.L.J. 1033; (2001) 145 S.J.L.B. 174; Times, August 3, 2001; Independent, July 5, 2001, CA; affirming [2001] B.V.C. 2163; 3 I.T.L. Rep. 224; [2001] S.T.I. 87, V&DTr . . . .   Digested, 01/**5557**
Hanbury v. Bateman [1920] 1 Ch. 313, Ch D . . . .   Applied, 00/5778
Hanbury v. Hanbury [1999] 2 F.L.R. 255; [1999] 3 F.C.R. 217; [1999] Fam. Law 447, CC (Cambridge) . . . .   Digested, 99/**4640**
Hancock (CICB: Quantum: 1998), Re (Unreported, January 12, 1998), CICB (London) [Ex rel. Alastair Smail, Barrister, 4 Fountain Court, Steelhouse Lane, Birmingham] . .   Digested, 98/**1505**
Hancock (Deceased), Re; sub nom Snapes v. Aram [1998] 2 F.L.R. 346; [1999] 1 F.C.R. 500; [1998] Fam. Law 520; (1998) 95(20) L.S.G. 35; (1998) 142 S.J.L.B. 167; Times, May 8, 1998, CA . . . .   Digested, 98/**4586**
Hancock v. BW Brazier (Anerley) Ltd [1966] 1 W.L.R. 1317; [1966] 2 All E.R. 901, CA; affirming [1966] 2 All E.R. 1; 110 S.J. 368, QBD . . . .   Digested, 66/**12401**:
                Applied, 98/801: Considered, 94/2736: Distinguished, 74/265
Hancock v. Doncaster MBC (No.1) [1998] I.C.R. 900, EAT . . . .   Digested, 98/**2162**
Hancock v. Tucker [1999] Lloyd's Rep. P.N. 814, QBD . . . .   Digested, 99/**4017**
Hancock Family Memorial Foundation Ltd v. Belle Rosa Holdings Pty Ltd see Hancock Family Memorial Foundation Ltd v. Porteous
Hancock Family Memorial Foundation Ltd v. Porteous; Hancock Prospecting Pty Ltd v. Belle Rosa Holdings Pty Ltd; Hancock Prospecting Pty Ltd v. Porteous; Hancock Family Memorial Foundation Ltd v. Belle Rosa Holdings Pty Ltd; Hancock Memorial Foundation Ltd v. Johanna Lacson Nominees Pty Ltd [2000] W.T.L.R. 1113, Sup Ct (WA) (Sgl judge) . . . .   Digested, 01/**5504**
Hancock Memorial Foundation Ltd v. Johanna Lacson Nominees Pty Ltd see Hancock Family Memorial Foundation Ltd v. Porteous
Hancock Prospecting Pty Ltd v. Belle Rosa Holdings Pty Ltd see Hancock Family Memorial Foundation Ltd v. Porteous
Hancock Prospecting Pty Ltd v. Porteous see Hancock Family Memorial Foundation Ltd v. Porteous
Hand v. Multimotion Display Ltd (Unreported, August 31, 2000), CC (Croydon) [Ex rel. Scott Rees & Co, Solicitors, Centaur House, Gardiners Place, Skelmersdale, Lancashire] . . . .   Digested, 01/**885**
Handels- og Kontorfunktionaerernes Forbund i Danmark v. Junckers Industrier A/S see P Bork International A/S v. Foreningen af Arbejdsledere i Danmark (C101/87)
Handels-og Kontorfunktionaerernes Forbund i Danmark (Union of Clerical and Commercial Employees) (for Hertz) v. Dansk Arbejdsgiverforening (Danish Employers Association) (for Aldi Marked K/S) (C179/88) [1990] E.C.R. I-3979; [1992] I.C.R. 332; [1991] I.R.L.R. 31; Times, December 20, 1990, ECJ . . . .   Digested, 91/**4077**:
                Considered, 92/1970, 93/1789, 98/2147, 98/2148: Referred to, 96/2615
Handels-og Kontorfunktionaerernes Forbund i Danmark v. Dansk Handel & Service (C400/95); sub nom Handels-og Kontorfunktionaerernes Forbund i Danmark (for Larsson) v. Dansk Handel & Service (for Fotex Supermarked A/S) (C400/95) [1997] E.C.R. I-2757; [1997] 2 C.M.L.R. 915; [1997] I.R.L.R. 643, ECJ (6th Chamber) . . . .   Digested, 98/**2147**:
                Not followed, 98/2148
Handels-og Kontorfunktionaerernes Forbund i Danmark v. Dansk Handel & Service (C66/96) see Hoj Pederson v. Kvickly Skive (C66/96)
Handels-og Kontorfunktionaerernes Forbund i Danmark (for Larsson) v. Dansk Handel & Service (for Fotex Supermarked A/S) (C400/95) see Handels-og Kontorfunktionaerernes Forbund i Danmark v. Dansk Handel & Service (C400/95)
Handels-og Kontorfunktionaerernes Forbund i Danmark v. Dansk Tandlaegeforening (C66/96) see Hoj Pederson v. Kvickly Skive (C66/96)
Handels-og Kontorfunktionaerernes Forbund i Danmark v. Faellesforeningen for Danmarks Brugsforeninger (C66/96) see Hoj Pederson v. Kvickly Skive (C66/96)
Handelsveem BV v. Coreck Maritime GmbH (C387/98); sub nom Coreck Maritime GmbH v. Handelsveem BV (C387/98) [2000] E.C.R. I-9337; [2001] C.L.C. 550; [2001] I.L.Pr. 39; Times, December 1, 2000, ECJ (5th Chamber) [1999] I.L.Pr. 721, HR (NL) . . . .   Digested, 01/**795**
Handelswekerij GJ Bier BV and Stichting Reinwater (The Reinwater Foundation) v. Mines de Potasse D'Alsace SA (C21/76) [1978] Q.B. 708; [1977] 3 W.L.R. 479; [1976] E.C.R. 1735; [1977] 1 C.M.L.R. 284; 121 S.J. 677; Times, December 6, 1976, ECJ . . . .   Digested, 77/**1283**:
                Considered, 92/2790, 96/7098: Followed, 95/705, 98/770:
                Referred to, 97/895

Handoll v. Warner Goodman & Streat (A Firm) 93 L.G.R. 293; (1995) 70 P. & C.R.
627; [1995] 1 E.G.L.R. 173; [1995] 25 E.G. 157; [1994] N.P.C. 158; *Times*,
December 26, 1994, CA; reversing (1993) 66 P. & C.R. 78; [1993] 12 E.G. 131;
[1992] N.P.C. 132, Ch D .... *Digested*, 95/**4856**:
Applied, 00/4452

Handyside v. Durbridge see Leigh's Will Trusts, Re
Hanif v. Middleweeks (A Firm) [2000] Lloyd's Rep. P.N. 920, CA .... *Digested*, 01/**4536**
Hanina v. Morland (2000) 97(47) L.S.G. 41, CA
Hanley Smith v. Darlington [2001] 26 E.G.C.S. 160, QBD (T&CC)
Hanlon v. Law Society [1981] A.C. 124; [1980] 2 W.L.R. 756; [1980] 2 All E.R. 199;
124 S.J. 360, HL; affirming [1980] 1 All E.R. 763, CA .... *Digested*, 80/**1664**:
Applied, 83/2194, 84/1994, 85/1988: *Considered*, 81/1347, 81/1604,
83/1857, 84/2013, 91/2310: *Distinguished*, 83/2183, 87/2295, 88/2183:
Followed, 96/3894, 97/3362, 00/3996

Hanlon v. University of Huddersfield [1999] Disc. L.R. 82, EAT .... *Digested*, 99/**2027**
Hannah v. Duke see Duke, Re
Hannan v. TNT-IPEC (UK) Ltd [1986] I.R.L.R. 165, EAT .... *Digested*, 86/**1276**:
Considered, 98/2237

Hannaway's Application, Re [1995] N.I. 159, QBD (NI)
Hannigan v. Hannigan [2000] 2 F.C.R. 650; *Independent*, July 3, 2000 (C.S);
Independent, May 23, 2000, CA .... *Digested*, 00/**367**:
Applied, 01/415

Hannon v. 169 Queens Gate Ltd [2000] 1 E.G.L.R. 40; [2000] 09 E.G. 179; *Times*,
November 23, 1999, Ch D .... *Digested*, 99/**3697**
Hanny Magnetics (Europe) Ltd v. Customs and Excise Commissioners see Dysan
Magnetics Ltd v. Customs and Excise Commissioners
Hanover Insurance Brokers Ltd v. Schapiro [1994] I.R.L.R. 82; *Times*, November 17,
1993, CA .... *Digested*, 94/**1927**:
Followed, 00/2202: *Referred to*, 96/2602

Hanrahan v. Home Office [2000] 3 Q.R. 8, CC (Leeds) [*Ex rel*. Tim Capstick, Barrister,
6 Park Square, Leeds] .... *Digested*, 00/**1633**
Hans Place Ltd, Re [1992] B.C.C. 737; [1993] B.C.L.C. 768; [1992] 44 E.G. 143, Ch D
(Companies Ct) .... *Digested*, 93/**2384**:
Considered, 99/3278, 01/3750

Hanseatische Industrie-Beteiligungen GmbH v. Commission of the European
Communities (C62/95) see Germany v. Commission of the European
Communities (C329/93)
Hansen v. Junckers Industrier A/S see P Bork International A/S v. Foreningen af
Arbejdsledere i Danmark (C101/87)
Hansen-Tangen v. Sanko Steamship Co Ltd see Reardon Smith Line Ltd v. Hansen-
Tangen (The Diana Prosperity)
Hanson v. Moore (Unreported, October 27, 1998), CC (Ipswich) [*Ex rel*. Andrew
Granville Stafford, Barrister, 4 King's Bench Walk, Temple, London] .... *Digested*, 98/**1725**
Hanuman v. United Kingdom [2000] E.L.R. 685, ECHR .... *Digested*, 01/**3457**
Haq v. Singh [2001] EWCA Civ 957; [2001] 1 W.L.R. 1594; [2001] C.P. Rep. 95;
[2001] B.P.I.R. 1002; *Times*, July 10, 2001, CA .... *Digested*, 01/**414**
Haque v. Bevis Trustees Ltd [1996] O.P.L.R. 271, Ch D .... *Digested*, 98/**4114**
Haque v. Customs and Excise Commissioners [1999] B.V.C. 2272; [1999] V. & D.R.
219, V&DTr .... *Digested*, 00/**5355**
Harada Ltd (t/a Chequepoint UK Ltd) v. Turner [2001] EWCA Civ 599, CA; reversing
[2000] I.L.Pr. 574, EAT .... *Digested*, 00/**2109**
Harakal v. Secretary of State for the Home Department see Harakel v. Secretary of
State for the Home Department
Harakel v. Secretary of State for the Home Department; *sub nom* Harakal v. Secretary
of State for the Home Department [2001] EWCA Civ 884; (2001) 98(28)
L.S.G. 44, CA
Harbig Leasing Two Ltd v. Customs and Excise Commissioners [2001] B.V.C. 2134;
[2000] V. & D.R. 469; [2001] S.T.I. 228, V&DTr .... *Digested*, 01/**5594**
Harbige v. Earl (Unreported, January 27, 2000), CC (Reading) [*Ex rel*. Benjamin
Williams, Barrister, 1 Temple Gardens, Temple, London] .... *Digested*, 00/**1578**
Harbinger Corp v. Office for Harmonisation in the Internal Market (Trade Marks and
Designs) (OHIM) (T345/99) [2000] E.C.R. II-3525; [2001] E.T.M.R. 2, CFI (4th
Chamber) .... *Digested*, 01/**4019**
Harbinger UK Ltd v. GE Information Services Ltd [2000] 1 All E.R. (Comm) 166;
(2000) 2 T.C.L.R. 463; [2000] I.T.C.L.R. 501, CA; reversing [1999] Masons
C.L.R. 335, QBD (T&CC) .... *Digested*, 00/**872**
Harbor Insurance Co v. Continental Bank Corp 922 F.2d 357, US Ct .... *Considered*, 98/3364
Harborough DC v. C Walton Ltd (Grain Store) (1998) 13 P.A.D. 158, Planning
Inspector

Harbour and General Works Ltd v. Environment Agency [2000] 1 W.L.R. 950; [2000] 1
    All E.R. 50; [1999] 2 All E.R. (Comm) 686; [2000] 1 Lloyd's Rep. 65; [2001]
    C.L.C. 868; [1999] B.L.R. 409; (2000) 2 T.C.L.R. 811; 68 Con. L.R. 1; [2000] L.
    & T.R. 97; (1999) 96(43) L.S.G. 32; *Times*, October 22, 1999, CA; affirming
    [1999] 1 All E.R. (Comm) 953; [1999] C.L.C. 786; [1999] B.L.R. 143, QBD
    (Comm Ct) . . . . *Digested*, 99/**248**
Harbour Assurance Co (UK) Ltd v. Kansa General International Assurance Co Ltd
    [1993] Q.B. 701; [1993] 3 W.L.R. 42; [1993] 3 All E.R. 897; [1993] 1 Lloyd's
    Rep. 455; *Times*, March 1, 1993, CA; reversing [1992] 1 Lloyd's Rep. 81; *Financial
    Times*, October 15, 1991, QBD (Comm Ct) . . . . *Digested*, 93/**153**:
                            Applied, 99/3830: *Considered*, 96/1219, 98/244: *Distinguished*, 99/745
Harbour Park Ltd v. Arun DC [1998] E.G.C.S. 150, Ch D
Harbun v. Home Office [2001] 3 Q.R. 18, CC (Norwich) [*Ex rel*. Anthony Bate,
    Barrister, East Anglian Chambers, 15 The Close, Norwich, Norfolk] . . . . *Digested*, 01/**1809**
Harcourt Brace & Co's Community Trade Mark Application [2000] E.T.M.R. 382, OHIM (1st
    Bd App) . . . . *Digested*, 00/**3721**
Hardaker v. Newcastle HA [2001] Lloyd's Rep. Med. 512, QBD
Hardcastle v. Inland Revenue Commissioners [2000] S.T.C. (S.C.D.) 532; [2001]
    W.T.L.R. 91; [2000] S.T.I. 1520, Sp Comm . . . . *Digested*, 01/**5284**
Hardi International A/S's Community Trade Mark Application [2001] E.T.M.R. 21, OHIM
    (Opposition Div)
Hardie v. CD Northern Ltd [2000] I.C.R. 207; [2000] I.R.L.R. 87, EAT . . . . *Digested*, 00/**2123**:
                                                                                Applied, 00/2122
Hardie v. Edinburgh City Council 2000 S.L.T. 130; 1999 G.W.D. 37-1780; *Times*,
    February 16, 2000, OH . . . . *Digested*, 00/**6205**
Harding v. Basingstoke and Deane BC [2000] 3 Q.R. 7, CC (Salisbury) [*Ex rel*.
    Lawrence Marsh, Barrister, 4 Pump Court, Temple, London] . . . . *Digested*, 00/**1613**
Harding (Valuation Officer) v. Field Place Caravan Park Ltd see Field Place Caravan
    Park Ltd v. Harding (Valuation Officer)
Harding v. Joy Manufacturing Holdings Ltd; *sub nom* Joy Manufacturing Holdings Ltd
    and Pension & Life Assurance Scheme Trustees, Petitioners 2000 S.L.T. 843;
    [2001] O.P.L.R. 235; 1999 G.W.D. 7-353; *Independent*, April 21, 1999, 1 Div. . . . *Digested*, 99/**6396**
Harding (Owner of the Lutra II) v. Owners of the Ruta see Owners of the Carbonnade v.
    Owners of the Ruta
Harding Maughan Hambly Ltd v. Compagnie Europeenne de Courtage d'Assurances et
    de Reassurances SA [2000] 1 All E.R. (Comm) 225; [2000] 1 Lloyd's Rep. 316;
    [2000] C.L.C. 524; [2000] Lloyd's Rep. I.R. 293, QBD (Comm Ct) . . . . *Digested*, 00/**3520**
Harding-Price v. General Medical Council (No.1) [2001] EWHC Admin 299; (2001) 61
    B.M.L.R. 136, QBD
Hardisty v. Stamper [1999] R.V.R. 120, Lands Tr . . . . *Digested*, 99/**4341**
Hardman v. Amin [2000] Lloyd's Rep. Med. 498; (2001) 59 B.M.L.R. 58; [2001]
    P.N.L.R. 11, QBD . . . . *Digested*, 01/**4464**:
                                                                                Applied, 01/4462
Hardoon v. Belilios [1901] A.C. 118, PC (HK) . . . . *Followed*, 00/4367
Hardwick v. Hudson [1999] 1 W.L.R. 1770; [1999] 3 All E.R. 426; [1999] P.I.Q.R.
    Q202; [1999] Lloyd's Rep. Med. 208; (1999) 96(22) L.S.G. 34; (1999) 149
    N.L.J. 806; *Times*, May 20, 1999; *Independent*, May 27, 1999, CA . . . . *Digested*, 99/**1398**
Hare v. Gocher [1962] 2 Q.B. 641; [1962] 3 W.L.R. 339; [1962] 2 All E.R. 763; 126
    J.P. 395; 60 L.G.R. 278; 13 P. & C.R. 298; 106 S.J. 531, DC. . . . . *Digested*, 62/**2947**:
                    Applied, 99/2451: *Approved*, 67/3259: *Considered*, 73/1147, 99/2465:
                                                                                Followed, 79/2853
Hare Trust, Re see Ukert v. Interface Trustees Ltd
Hargrave v. Goldman see Goldman v. Hargrave
Hargrave v. Stroud DC see R. (on the application of Hargrave) v. Stroud DC
Haringey Healthcare NHS Trust v. Independent Insurance Ltd see Martin v. Lancashire
    CC
Haringey LBC v. Awaritefe (2000) 32 H.L.R. 517; *Times*, June 3, 1999, CA . . . . *Digested*, 99/**4555**
Haringey LBC v. Cotter (1997) 29 H.L.R. 682; *Times*, December 9, 1996; *Independent*,
    December 16, 1996 (C.S.), CA . . . . *Digested*, 97/**2692**:
                            Applied, 97/2691: *Distinguished*, 00/4828: *Followed*, 98/4528
Haringey LBC v. Jowett [1999] E.H.L.R. 410; (2000) 32 H.L.R. 308; [1999] B.L.G.R.
    667; [1999] E.G.C.S. 64; [1999] N.P.C. 52; (1999) 78 P. & C.R. D24; [2000]
    Env. L.R. D6; *Times*, May 20, 1999; *Independent*, June 14, 1999 (C.S.), QBD . . . . *Digested*, 99/**2213**
Harker v. Caledonian Insurance Co [1980] 1 Lloyd's Rep. 556; [1980] R.T.R. 241, HL;
    affirming [1979] 2 Lloyd's Rep. 193, CA; affirming [1977] 2 Lloyd's Rep. 556;
    [1978] R.T.R. 143, QBD (Comm Ct) . . . . *Digested*, 80/**1511**:
                                                        Applied, 89/2056: *Considered*, 99/3412
Harkins v. Tycon Plant Hire Ltd [2001] 6 Q.R. 19, CC (Swansea) [*Ex rel*. T Crowther,
    Barrister, Temple Chambers, 32 Park Place, Cardiff] . . . . *Digested*, 01/**1749**
Harksen v. Lane NO 3 B.H.R.C. 519, Const Ct (SA) . . . . *Digested*, 98/**3276**:
                                                                                Applied, 98/2124, 98/3109
Harley v. Glasgow Harley see Harley v. McDonald

Harley v. McDonald; *sub nom* Harley v. McDonald Glasgow Harley; Harley v. Glasgow
    Harley; Glasgow Harley (A Firm) v. McDonald [2001] UKPC 18; [2001] 2 A.C.
    678; [2001] 2 W.L.R. 1749; [2001] Lloyd's Rep. P.N. 584; *Times,* May 15, 2001,
    PC (NZ) . . . . *Digested,* 01/**4256**
Harley v. McDonald Glasgow Harley see Harley v. McDonald
Harlow v. National Westminster Bank Plc see Jennings (Deceased), Re
Harman Pictures, NV v. Osborne [1967] 1 W.L.R. 723; [1967] 2 All E.R. 324; 111 S.J.
    434, Ch D . . . . *Digested,* 67/**3169**:
                             Applied, 69/3032, 70/2436, 01/3853: *Not followed,* 71/1893, 72/533
Harmon CFEM Facades (UK) Ltd v. Corporate Officer of the House of Commons 67
    Con. L.R. 1; (2000) 2 L.G.L.R. 372, QBD (T&CC) . . . . *Digested,* 00/**824**
Harmon CFEM Facades (UK) Ltd v. Corporate Officer of the House of Commons
    (Interim Payment) [2001] C.P. Rep. 20; 72 Con. L.R. 21; (2001) 17 Const. L.J.
    401; (2000) 97(29) L.S.G. 46; *Times,* November 15, 2000, QBD (T&CC) . . . . . . *Digested,* 00/**1454**
Harmony Carpets v. Chaffin-Laird [2000] B.C.C. 893; [2000] B.P.I.R. 61; *Independent,*
    December 13, 1999 (C.S), Ch D . . . . *Digested,* 00/**3495**
Harmony Healthcare Plc v. Drewery, *Independent,* November 20, 2000 (C.S), EAT
Harold v. Lord Chancellor [1999] 1 Costs L.R. 14, QBD . . . . *Digested,* 00/**4010**:
                                        Not followed, 01/1115
Harper (A Bankrupt), Re see Harper v. O'Reilly
Harper v. O'Reilly; *sub nom* Harper (A Bankrupt), Re [1997] 2 F.L.R. 816; [1998] 3
    F.C.R. 475; [1997] B.P.I.R. 656; [1998] Fam. Law 18, Ch D . . . . *Digested,* 98/**3280**
Harper v. Wilson (t/a Royal Star Public House) (Quantum) (Unreported, October 26,
    1998), MCLC [*Ex rel.* Richard Menzies, Barrister, 8 Stone Buildings, Lincoln's Inn,
    London] . . . . *Digested,* 99/**1492**
Harper v. Wilson (t/a Royal Star Public House) [2000] C.P. Rep. 82, CA . . . . *Digested,* 99/**362**
Harpers Leisure International Ltd v. Secretary of State for the Environment, Transport
    and the Regions (2001) 82 P. & C.R. 7; [2001] J.P.L. 378 (Note), QBD . . . . *Digested,* 01/**4728**
Harries v. Collins (Unreported, March 12, 1998), CC (Cardiff) [*Ex rel.* Andrew Arentsen,
    Barrister, 33 Park Place, Cardiff, South Glamorgan] . . . . *Digested,* 98/**1608**
Harriet's House Ltd v. Customs and Excise Commissioners [2000] B.V.C. 2130; [2000]
    S.T.I. 138, V&DTr
Harrikissoon v. Attorney General of Trinidad and Tobago [1980] A.C. 265; [1979] 3
    W.L.R. 62; 123 S.J. 97, PC (Trin) . . . . *Digested,* 79/**19**:
                          Applied, 84/211: *Distinguished,* 99/3101
Harrild v. Ministry of Defence [2001] Lloyd's Rep. Med. 117, QBD . . . . *Digested,* 01/**4460**
Harrington v. Bennett; *sub nom* Bennett, Re [2000] B.P.I.R. 630; [2000] E.G.C.S. 41,
    Ch D . . . . *Digested,* 01/**3723**
Harrington v. Newham LBC (1998) 98(6) Q.R. 5, CC (Romford) . . . . *Digested,* 98/**1555**
Harris (Personal Representatives of Andrews (Deceased)) v. Lewisham and Guys
    Mental Health NHS Trust see Andrews (Deceased) v. Lewisham and Guys
    Mental Health NHS Trust
Harris v. Best, Riley & Co (1892) 68 L.T. 76 . . . . *Applied,* 47-51/**9492**:
                                        Considered, 00/4696
Harris v. Bolt Burdon [2000] C.P. Rep. 70; [2000] C.P.L.R. 9, CA . . . . *Digested,* 00/**625**
Harris v. Crosby (Unreported, February 14, 2001), CC (Manchester) [*Ex rel.* Silverbeck
    Rymer, Solicitors, County Square, 100 New London Road, Chelmsford] . . . . . . *Digested,* 01/**452**
Harris v. DPP; Fehmi v. DPP [1993] 1 W.L.R. 82; [1993] 1 All E.R. 562; (1993) 96 Cr.
    App. R. 235; (1992) 156 J.P.N. 716; (1992) 136 S.J.L.B. 228; *Times,* August 14,
    1992, QBD . . . . *Digested,* 93/**970**:
                                  Applied, 95/5789, 98/966
Harris v. Evans [1998] 1 W.L.R. 1285; [1998] 3 All E.R. 522; [1998] E.H.L.R. 142;
    Times, May 5, 1998, CA . . . . *Digested,* 98/**3935**
Harris v. Flower & Sons (1905) 74 L.J. Ch. 127; (1904) 91 L.T. 816, CA . . . . *Applied,* 00/**4635**:
             Considered, 87/1233: *Distinguished,* 79/796, 84/1153, 99/4367:
                                            Followed, 97/205
Harris v. Griffith see Anderson Berry, Re
Harris v. Gross [2001] B.P.I.R. 586, Ch D . . . . *Digested,* 01/**3731**
Harris v. Habanec (1998) 76 P. & C.R. D33, CA
Harris v. Harris [2001] 1 F.C.R. 68; *Independent,* January 15, 2001 (C.S); *Daily
    Telegraph,* December 19, 2000, CA
Harris v. Harris; *sub nom* Attorney General v. Harris [2001] 2 F.L.R. 895; [2001] 3
    F.C.R. 193; [2001] Fam. Law 651, Fam Div . . . . *Digested,* 01/**2583**
Harris v. Harris (Contempt of Court: Application to Purge) [2001] EWCA Civ 1645;
    [2001] 3 F.C.R. 640; (2001) 145 S.J.L.B. 270; *Times,* November 19, 2001;
    Independent, November 14, 2001, CA; reversing in part [2001] Fam. 502;
    [2001] 3 W.L.R. 765; [2001] 2 F.L.R. 955; [2001] Fam. Law 730; (2001)
    98(29) L.S.G. 39; (2001) 145 S.J.L.B. 163; *Times,* August 6, 2001, Fam Div . . . *Digested,* 01/**1112**
Harris v. Knight (1890) L.R. 15 P.D. 170, CA . . . . *Applied,* 61/**9156**:
                                Considered, 75/3576, 99/4647
Harris v. National Power Plc see Doublerange Ltd v. National Power Plc
Harris v. Pinnington see MH v. GP (Child: Emigration)
Harris v. Scholfield Roberts & Hall see Arthur JS Hall & Co v. Simons
Harris v. Scholfield Roberts & Hill see Arthur JS Hall & Co v. Simons

Harris *v.* Welsh Development Agency [1999] 3 E.G.L.R. 207; [2000] R.V.R. 49, Lands
Tr . . . . *Digested,* 00/**4430**
Harris *v.* Wyre Forest DC see Smith *v.* Eric S Bush (A Firm)
Harris Bus Co Ltd, Re [2000] B.C.C. 1151, Ch D
Harrison *v.* Akester Plc (Unreported, January 19, 1998), CC (Kingston upon Hull) [*Ex
rel.* Andrew M Jackson Solicitors, Essex House, Manor Street, Hull] . . . . *Digested,* 98/**595**
Harrison *v.* Bloom Camillin (Costs) [2000] Lloyd's Rep. P.N. 404, Ch D . . . . *Digested,* 00/**1480**
Harrison *v.* Bloom Camillin (No.1), *Independent,* June 28, 1999 (C.S.), Ch D
Harrison *v.* Bloom Camillin (No.2) [2000] Lloyd's Rep. P.N. 89; [2001] P.N.L.R. 7;
(1999) 96(45) L.S.G. 32; *Times,* November 12, 1999, Ch D . . . . *Digested,* 99/**1421**
Harrison *v.* Bloom Camillin (Preliminary Issues) [2000] C.P. Rep. 83, Ch D . . . . *Digested,* 00/**580**
Harrison *v.* Bowden (Unreported, November 20, 1998), CC (Birkenhead) [*Ex rel.*
Keogh Ritson Solicitors, Tarleton House, 112a/116 Chorley New Road, Bolton] . . *Digested,* 99/**1407**
Harrison *v.* Festus (Unreported, October 28, 1997), QBD [*Ex rel.* Mark Watson-Gandy,
Barrister, 3 Paper Buildings, Temple, London] . . . . *Digested,* 98/**4**
Harrison *v.* Harrison see Harrison's Settlement, Re
Harrison *v.* Matthew Brown Plc [1998] Eu. L.R. 493, CA; affirming CH.1996-H-3184,
Ch D . . . . *Digested,* 99/**687**
Harrison *v.* Ministry of Defence (Unreported, December 1, 1997), CC (Newport,
Gwent) [*Ex rel.* Mark Allen, Barrister, 30 Park Place, Cardiff] . . . . *Digested,* 98/**3929**
Harrison *v.* Mo (t/a White Rose Chinese Restaurant) (Unreported, June 24, 1999), CC
(Cheltenham) [*Ex rel.* Morris Orman Hearle Solicitors, Thornbury House, 18 High
Street, Cheltenham] . . . . *Digested,* 99/**1584**
Harrison *v.* Norwest Holst Group Administration Ltd see Norwest Holst Group
Administration Ltd *v.* Harrison
Harrison *v.* Sun Alliance and London Assurance Plc (Unreported, February 18, 1998),
CA [*Ex rel.* Shoosmiths & Harrison Solicitors, Russell House, Solent Business
Park, Whiteley, Fareham, Hampshire] . . . . *Digested,* 98/**517**
Harrison *v.* Tew [1990] 2 A.C. 523; [1990] 2 W.L.R. 210; [1990] 1 All E.R. 321; (1990)
87(8) L.S.G. 44; (1990) 134 S.J. 374, HL; affirming [1989] Q.B. 307; [1988] 2
W.L.R. 1; [1987] 3 All E.R. 865; (1987) 137 N.L.J. 711; (1987) 131 S.J. 1626,
CA . . . . *Digested,* 90/**3617**:
Applied, 99/416
Harrison *v.* Tex Industrial Plastics Ltd (Unreported, April 3, 2001), CC (Derby) [*Ex rel.*
Buller Jeffries, Solicitors, 36 Bennetts Hill, Birmingham] . . . . *Digested,* 01/**4494**
Harrison *v.* Thanet DC 1996-P-975, QBD . . . . *Digested,* 98/**3918**
Harrison *v.* Touche Ross, *Times,* February 14, 1995; *Independent,* April 18, 1995 (C.S.),
CA . . . . *Digested,* 95/**4247**:
Considered, 99/578
Harrison Bowden Ltd *v.* Bowden [1994] I.C.R. 186, EAT . . . . *Digested,* 94/**2003**:
Followed, 98/2214
Harrison Ex p. Jay, Re (1880) L.R. 14 Ch. D. 19, CA . . . . *Considered,* 01/3778
Harrison's Settlement, Re; *sub nom* Harrison *v.* Harrison; Ropner's Settlement, Re;
Ropner *v.* Ropner; Williams Will Trust, Re [1955] Ch. 260; [1955] 2 W.L.R. 256;
[1955] 1 All E.R. 185; 99 S.J. 74; *Times,* December 22, 1954, CA; affirming
[1954] 3 W.L.R. 156; [1954] 2 All E.R. 453; 98 S.J. 456, Ch D . . . . *Digested,* 55/**2140**:
Applied, 01/581
Harrods (Buenos Aires) Ltd (No.1), Re; *sub nom* Intercomfinanz SA *v.* Ladenimor SA
[1991] 4 All E.R. 334; [1991] B.C.C. 249; [1991] B.C.L.C. 666; [1991] I.L.Pr.
331; (1991) 135 S.J.L.B. 184; *Times,* January 11, 1991; *Financial Times,* January
25, 1991, CA; reversing [1990] B.C.C. 481; [1991] B.C.L.C. 69, Ch D . . . . *Digested,* 91/**476**:
Applied, 96/5344, 00/761, 00/762, 00/771: *Cited,* 93/3051:
Considered, 94/483
Harrods (Buenos Aires) Ltd (No.2), Re [1992] Ch. 72; [1991] 3 W.L.R. 397; [1991] 4 All E.R.
348; [1992] I.L.Pr. 453; *Times,* March 25, 1991; *Financial Times,* March 26, 1991,
CA . . . . *Digested,* 92/**475**:
Applied, 01/814: *Followed,* 00/763, 01/376
Harrods Ltd *v.* Harrods (Buenos Aires) Ltd (No.1) [1999] F.S.R. 187; (1998) 21(8)
I.P.D. 21091; *Times,* June 1, 1998, CA; affirming [1997] F.S.R. 420; (1997) 20(6)
I.P.D. 20058, Ch D . . . . *Digested,* 98/**3499**
Harrods Ltd *v.* Remick; Harrods Ltd *v.* Seely; Elmi *v.* Harrods Ltd [1998] 1 All E.R. 52;
[1998] I.C.R. 156; [1997] I.R.L.R. 583; *Times,* July 22, 1997; *Independent,* July
22, 1997, CA; affirming [1996] I.C.R. 846; [1997] I.R.L.R. 9; *Times,* May 28,
1996, EAT . . . . *Digested,* 97/**2243**:
Applied, 99/2092
Harrods Ltd *v.* Secretary of State for the Environment, Transport and the Regions C/
2001/1743, CA; affirming [2001] EWHC Admin 600; [2001] 31 E.G.C.S. 101;
Times, November 15, 2001, QBD (Admin Ct) . . . . *Digested,* 01/**4657**
Harrods Ltd *v.* Seely see Harrods Ltd *v.* Remick
Harrogate BC *v.* Secretary of State for the Environment, Transport and the Regions see
Macgay Ltd *v.* Secretary of State for the Environment, Transport and the
Regions
Harrogate DC *v.* AB Welfare & Wildlife Trust (1999) 14 P.A.D. 618, Planning Inspector

Harrold v. Wiltshire Healthcare NHS Trust [1999] Disc. L.R. 232, EAT . . . .   *Digested*, 00/**2184**:
       Not applied, 01/2295

Harron v. Commissioner of Valuation for Northern Ireland [1997] R.A. 271, Lands Tr
   (NI) . . . .   *Digested*, 97/**5405**:
       Applied, 00/5678

Harrow LBC v. Johnstone [1997] 1 W.L.R. 459; [1997] 1 All E.R. 929; [1997] 1 F.L.R.
   887; [1997] 2 F.C.R. 225; (1997) 29 H.L.R. 475; [1997] Fam. Law 478; (1997)
   161 J.P. Rep. 580; [1997] E.G.C.S. 41; (1997) 94(15) L.S.G. 26; (1997) 147
   N.L.J. 413; [1997] N.P.C. 40; *Times*, March 14, 1997, HL; reversing [1995] 2
   F.L.R. 191; [1995] 3 F.C.R. 132; 93 L.G.R. 435; [1995] Fam. Law 550; [1995]
   E.G.C.S. 53; [1995] N.P.C. 47; *Times*, March 31, 1995, CA . . . .   *Digested*, 97/**2703**:
       Considered, 00/2529

Harrow LBC v. Shah [2000] 1 W.L.R. 83; [1999] 3 All E.R. 302; [1999] 2 Cr. App. R.
   457; (1999) 163 J.P. 525; [2000] Crim. L.R. 692; *Independent*, May 17, 1999
   (C.S.), QBD . . . .   *Digested*, 99/**952**

Harrow LBC v. WH Smith Trading Ltd see Bilon v. WH Smith Trading Ltd

Harry Jagdev & Co, Re see Harry Jagdev & Co (Wasted Costs Order) (No.2 of 1999), Re

Harry Jagdev & Co (Wasted Costs Order) (No.2 of 1999), Re; *sub nom* Harry Jagdev &
   Co, Re; Firm of Solicitors (Wasted Costs Order) (No.2 of 1999), Re (1999)
   96(33) L.S.G. 32; *Times*, August 12, 1999 ; *Independent*, November 1, 1999
   (C.S.), CA (Crim Div) . . . .   *Digested*, 99/**987**

Harry Lester Ltd v. Southwark LBC [1999] 3 E.G.L.R. 179, Lands Tr . . . .   *Digested*, 00/**4429**

Harry Neal Ltd v. Clarke (1998) 75 P. & C.R. D47, CA

Hart v. Dabbs; *sub nom* Dabbs (Lawrence Stanley) (Deceased), Re [2001] W.T.L.R.
   527, Ch D . . . .   *Digested*, 01/**5169**

Hart v. Jayne (Unreported, February 14, 2000) . . . .   *Cited*, 00/311

Hart DC v. BCA Ltd (formerly ADT Auctions Ltd) (2000) 15 P.A.D. 143, Planning
   Inspector

Hart DC v. Plummer (1998) 13 P.A.D. 646, Planning Inspector

Hartford Fire Insurance Co v. Novocargo USA Inc (The Pacific Senator) (No.1) [2001] 2
   Lloyd's Rep. 674, US Ct

Hartle v. Laceys (A Firm) [1999] Lloyd's Rep. P.N. 315; (2000) 16 Const. L.J. 44, CA . .   *Digested*, 97/**3839**:
       Distinguished, 99/3946

Hartley v. Birmingham City Council [1992] 1 W.L.R. 968; [1992] 2 All E.R. 213;
   Independent, August 16, 1991, CA . . . .   *Digested*, 92/**2811**:
      Applied, 90/2960, 00/527: *Considered*, 96/830, 97/667, 99/476, 00/512

Hartley v. Magill see Porter v. Magill

Hartley v. Minister of Housing and Local Government [1970] 1 Q.B. 413; [1970] 2
   W.L.R. 1; [1969] 3 All E.R. 1658; (1970) 21 P. & C.R. 1; 113 S.J. 900, CA;
   affirming [1969] 2 Q.B. 46; [1969] 2 W.L.R. 137; [1969] 1 All E.R. 309; 133 J.P.
   147; 67 L.G.R. 332; (1969) 20 P. & C.R. 166; (1968) 113 S.J. 35; *Times*,
   December 12, 1968, QBD. . . . .   *Digested*, 70/**2764**:
     Applied, 76/2734, 81/2670, 82/3139, 82/3145, 83/3703, 89/3569, 92/4217:
       Followed, 00/4409

Hartley v. United Kingdom see Fox v. United Kingdom (A/182)

Hartley's Application for Judicial Review, Re [2000] N.I. 376, CA (NI) . . . .   *Digested*, 01/**5653**

Hartman v. P&O Cruises Ltd (Unreported, May 6, 1998), CC (Carmarthen) [*Ex rel.*
   Geraint Jones, Barrister, 9 Park Place, Cardiff] . . . .   *Digested*, 98/**3732**

Hartridge (t/a Hartridge Consultancy) v. Customs and Excise Commissioners [1998]
   B.V.C. 2281, V&DTr. . . . .   *Digested*, 98/**4927**

Hartshorn v. Secretary of State for the Home Department CCRTF 98/1030/2, CA. . . . .   *Digested*, 99/**4012**

Hartwell v. Grayson, Rollo and Clover Docks [1947] K.B. 901; (1947) 80 Ll. L. Rep.
   381; [1947] L.J.R. 1038, CA. . . . .   *Digested*, 47-51/**6704**:
      Applied, 55/1791, 65/2663: *Considered*, 56/5868, 56/6957, 66/8132,
       99/4003: *Distinguished*, 58/2243

Hartwell Plc v. Customs and Excise Commissioners [2001] S.T.I. 1772, Ch D; reversing
   [2001] B.V.C. 2217; [2001] S.T.I. 880, V&DTr

Harvard Securities Ltd (In Liquidation), Re; *sub nom* Holland v. Newbury [1998] B.C.C.
   567; [1997] 2 B.C.L.C. 369; *Times*, July 18, 1997, Ch D . . . .   *Digested*, 97/**3074**

Harvest Press Ltd v. McCaffrey [1999] I.R.L.R. 778, EAT . . . .   *Digested*, 00/**2241**

Harvest Town Circle Ltd v. Rutherford [2001] 3 C.M.L.R. 33; [2001] I.R.L.R. 599;
   Times, August 22, 2001, EAT. . . . .   *Digested*, 01/**2308**

Harvey v. Beck & Pollitzer (Unreported, February 17, 2000), CC (Bristol) [*Ex rel.* Veale
   Wasbrough Solicitors, Orchard Court, Orchard Lane, Bristol]. . . . .   *Digested*, 00/**1630**

Harvey v. Blount [2000] 5 Q.R. 6, CC (Luton) [*Ex rel.* Andrew Granville Stafford,
   Barrister, 4 King's Bench Walk, Temple, London] . . . .   *Digested*, 00/**1575**

Harvey v. Institute of the Motor Industry (No.2) see Institute of the Motor Industry v.
   Harvey (No.2)

Harvey v. Ipswich and Norwich Cooperative Society (Unreported, August 10, 1999),
   CC (Norwich) [*Ex rel.* Philip Kolvin, Barrister, 2-3 Gray's Inn Square, London] . .   *Digested*, 00/**4242**

Harvey v. Port of Tilbury (London) Ltd [1999] I.C.R. 1030; [1999] I.R.L.R. 693, EAT . . .   *Digested*, 00/**2151**

Harvey Jones Ltd v. Woolwich Plc see Smith v. Lloyds TSB Bank Plc

Harvey Nichols & Co Ltd v. Thames Water Utilities [1999] N.P.C. 139, QBD (T&CC)

Harwood v. Baker 13 E.R. 117; (1840) 3 Moo. P.C. 282, PC (UK) . . . . *Applied*, 47-51/10956, 47-51/10958, 01/5165
Harwood (t/a RSBS Group) v. Smith [1998] 1 E.G.L.R. 5; [1998] 11 E.G. 178; [1997] E.G.C.S. 160; [1997] N.P.C. 158; *Times*, December 8, 1997; *Independent*, November 20, 1997, CA . . . . *Digested*, 97/**85**
Harwood-Smart v. Caws [2000] O.P.L.R. 227; [2000] Pens. L.R. 101, Ch D . . . . *Digested*, 00/**4355**
Harz v. Deutsche Tradax GmbH (C79/83) see Von Colson v. Land Nordrhein-Westfahlen (C14/83)
Hasan v. Bulgaria (30985/96) 10 B.H.R.C. 646, ECHR . . . . *Digested*, 01/**3486**
Hasan v. Mayo [2001] 5 Q.R. 13, CC (Kingston on Thames) [*Ex rel.* Benjamin Williams, Barrister, 1 Temple Gardens, Temple, London] . . . . *Digested*, 01/**1624**
Hasbro Canada Inc v. R. 1 I.T.L. Rep. 341, Tax Ct (Can)
Hasbro UK Ltd's Application for Declaration of Trade Mark Invalidity (No. 2002288) (1998) 21 (6) I.P.D. 21066, TMR
Haseldine v. Hosken [1933] 1 K.B. 822; (1933) 45 Ll. L. Rep. 59, CA; reversing (1932) 44 Ll. L. Rep. 127, KBD . . . . *Applied*, 47-51/10073: *Considered*, 99/5404
Haseldine v. Smith (Unreported, November 16, 1999), CC (Croydon) [*Ex rel.* Paul McGrath, Barrister, 1 Temple Gardens, Temple, London] . . . . *Digested*, 00/**385**
Haseley v. Morrell [2001] 6 Q.R. 4, CC (Telford) [*Ex rel.* Shoosmiths Solicitors] . . . . . . *Digested*, 01/**1560**
Haseley v. Stadtwerke Altena GmbH (C258/96) see Kampelmann v. Landschaftsverband Westfalen-Lippe (C253/96)
Hasham v. Zenab (Executrix of Harji) [1960] A.C. 316; [1960] 2 W.L.R. 374; 104 S.J. 125, PC (EA) . . . . *Digested*, 60/**3282**: *Applied*, 01/3418
Hashman v. United Kingdom (2000) 30 E.H.R.R. 241; 8 B.H.R.C. 104; [2000] Crim. L.R. 185; *Times*, December 1, 1999, ECHR . . . . *Digested*, 00/**3185**
Hashwani v. Customs and Excise Commissioners see Hashwani v. Letherby
Hashwani v. Letherby; *sub nom* Hashwani v. Customs and Excise Commissioners (1998) 162 J.P. 153; (1998) 162 J.P.N. 266; *Independent*, November 3, 1997 (C.S.), QBD . . . . *Digested*, 97/**1740**
Haskins Garden Centres Ltd v. East Dorset DC [1998] E.G.C.S. 71; [1998] N.P.C. 75; *Times*, May 7, 1998; *Independent*, May 11, 1998 (C.S.), QBD . . . . *Digested*, 98/**836**
Hassall v. Secretary of State for Social Security [1995] 1 W.L.R. 812; [1995] 3 All E.R. 909; [1995] R.T.R. 316; [1995] P.I.Q.R. P292; (1995) 92(8) L.S.G. 41; (1995) 139 S.J.L.B. 57; *Times*, December 26, 1994; *Independent*, December 16, 1994, CA . . . . *Digested*, 95/**1645**: *Applied*, 96/2161: *Cited*, 97/1820: *Considered*, 01/1571: *Not followed*, 96/2113
Hassan (Hassan Najeeb) v. Immigration Appeal Tribunal [2001] Imm. A.R. 83, CA . . . . *Digested*, 01/**3625**
Hassan v. Odeon Cinemas Ltd [1998] I.C.R. 127, EAT . . . . *Digested*, 98/**2207**
Hassard v. McGrath [1996] N.I. 586, CA (NI)
Hassneh Insurance Co of Israel v. Stuart J Mew [1993] 2 Lloyd's Rep. 243, QBD (Comm Ct) . . . . *Digested*, 94/**3662**: *Applied*, 94/210, 96/3619: *Considered*, 98/240
Hastie & Jenkerson v. McMahon [1990] 1 W.L.R. 1575; [1991] 1 All E.R. 255; [1990] R.V.R. 172; (1990) 134 S.J. 725, CA . . . . *Digested*, 91/**2950**: *Followed*, 98/3193
Hastings v. Hastings (Unreported, May 9, 2000), CA [*Ex rel.* Nigel S Brockley, Barrister, Bracton Chambers, Bell House, 8 Bell Yard, London] . . . . *Digested*, 00/**12**
Hastings-Bass (Deceased), Re; *sub nom* Hastings-Bass Trustees v. Inland Revenue Commissioners; Hastings-Bass v. Inland Revenue Commissioners [1975] Ch. 25; [1974] 2 W.L.R. 904; [1974] 2 All E.R. 193; [1974] S.T.C. 211; [1974] T.R. 87; 118 S.J. 422, CA . . . . *Digested*, 74/**993**: *Applied*, 83/3364, 01/5515: *Considered*, 01/5508
Hastings-Bass v. Inland Revenue Commissioners see Hastings-Bass (Deceased), Re
Hastings-Bass Trustees v. Inland Revenue Commissioners see Hastings-Bass (Deceased), Re
Hatami v. Sweden [1998] H.R.C.D. 951, ECHR
Hatfield v. Hiscock [1998] C.C.L.R. 68, CC (Southampton) . . . . *Digested*, 98/**2501**: *Approved*, 01/898: *Considered*, 99/2454: *Distinguished*, 99/2500, 99/5789: *Not followed*, 00/2568
Hatt v. Newman (Inspector of Taxes) [2000] S.T.C. 113; 72 T.C. 462; [2000] B.T.C. 42; [2000] S.T.I. 85, Ch D . . . . *Digested*, 00/**4924**
Hatton v. Cooper see Cooper v. Hatton
Hatton v. Hall [1997] R.T.R. 212; [1999] Lloyd's Rep. I.R. 313; *Times*, May 15, 1996, CA . *Digested*, 96/**3615**
Hatton v. United Kingdom (36022/97) 11 B.H.R.C. 634; *Times*, October 8, 2001, ECHR . . . . *Digested*, 01/**5378**
Haug v. Borgersen [1998] I.L.Pr. 804, HR (N)
Haughey v. Prendiville [1996] N.I. 367, Ch D (NI)
Hauptzollamt Giessen v. Deutsche Fernsprecher Gmbh (C64/89) [1990] E.C.R. I-2535, ECJ . . . . *Followed*, 00/2349
Hauptzollamt Neubrandenburg v. Lensing & Brockhausen GmbH (C233/98) [1999] E.C.R. I-7349, ECJ . . . . *Applied*, 01/4120

Hauschildt *v.* Denmark (A/154) (1990) 12 E.H.R.R. 266, ECHR . . . .   *Applied,* 98/3093,
       00/6092: *Considered,* 96/3119, 96/3120, 01/635: *Distinguished,* 97/2811
Hautala *v.* Council of the European Union (T14/98) see Council of the European Union
    v. Hautala (C353/99 P)
Havair Ltd *v.* Vile (Unreported, January 31, 2000), CC (Basildon) [*Ex rel.* James
    Fieldsend, Barrister, Second Floor, Francis Taylor Building, Temple, London] . . . .   *Digested,* 00/**848**
Havant BC *v.* South Coast Shipping Ltd (No.1) (1998) 14 Const. L.J. 420, QBD
    (Comm Ct) . . . .   *Digested,* 99/**235**
Havant BC *v.* South Coast Shipping Ltd (No.2) (1998) 14 Const. L.J. 430, QBD (OR) .   *Digested,* 99/**231**
Havant International Holdings Ltd *v.* Lionsgate (H) Investment Ltd [2000] L. & T.R.
    297; [1999] E.G.C.S. 144; (1999) 96(47) L.S.G. 34, Ch D . . . .   *Digested,* 00/**3885**
Havenledge Ltd *v.* Graeme John & Partners [2001] Lloyd's Rep. P.N. 223; [2001]
    P.N.L.R. 17; [2001] N.P.C. 9, CA; reversing [2000] Lloyd's Rep. P.N. 614; [2000]
    P.N.L.R. 804, QBD . . . .   *Digested,* 01/**4526**
Havering LBC *v.* Network Sites Ltd [1998] 1 P.L.R. 103; [1998] J.P.L. 648; *Times,*
    January 2, 1998, QBD . . . .   *Digested,* 98/**4157**
Havering LBC *v.* Next Generation Clubs Ltd (1999) 14 P.A.D. 480, Planning Inspector
Havering LBC *v.* Turner (Preliminary Issue) (Unreported, November 23, 1998), EAT [*Ex
    rel.* David Giles, Barrister, Verulam Chambers, Peer House, 8-14 Verulam Street,
    London] . . . .   *Digested,* 99/**2144**
Haverson *v.* Maintenance Contract Management Ltd (Unreported, August 24, 1999),
    CC (Norwich) [*Ex rel.* Nicholas Yell, Barrister, No.1 Serjeants' Inn, Fleet Street,
    London] . . . .   *Digested,* 99/**360**
Havill *v.* Wilson (Unreported, December 15, 1999), CC (Bournemouth) [*Ex rel.* Paul
    Cairnes, Barrister, 3 Paper Buildings, 20 Lorne Park Rd, Bournemouth] . . . .   *Digested,* 00/**1608**
Hawa Bibi Uddin *v.* Immigration Appeal Tribunal; *sub nom* R. *v.* Immigration Appeal
    Tribunal Ex p. Uddin [1991] Imm. A.R. 134; [1991] C.O.D. 299, CA; affirming
    [1990] Imm. A.R. 309; [1990] C.O.D. 250, QBD . . . .   *Digested,* 92/**2427.a**:
                                         Followed, 98/3228
Hawe *v.* Northern Ireland Housing Executive R/19/1997, Lands Tr (NI) . . . .   *Explained,* 00/5655
Hawes *v.* Chief Constable of Avon and Somerset, *Times,* May 20, 1993, CA . . . .   *Digested,* 93/**3197**:
                                         Considered, 99/356
Hawk Insurance Co Ltd, Re [2001] EWCA Civ 241; [2001] 2 B.C.L.C. 480, CA; reversing
    [2001] B.C.C. 57, Ch D (Companies Ct) . . . .   *Digested,* 01/**3752**
Hawken *v.* Apex Bodyworks Ltd (Unreported, October 16, 1997), CC (Portsmouth)
    [*Ex rel.* Richard Egleton, Barrister, 18 Carlton Crescent, Southampton] . . . .   *Digested,* 98/**1639**
Hawker *v.* British Steel Corp (Unreported, November 2, 1999), CC (Cardiff) [*Ex rel.*
    Dolmans Solicitors, 17-20 Windsor Place, Cardiff] . . . .   *Digested,* 00/**417**
Hawkes *v.* Garside (Unreported, November 6, 1997), HC [*Ex rel.* Iain Wightwick,
    Assize Court Chambers, 14 Small Street, Bristol] . . . .   *Digested,* 98/**1674**
Hawkes *v.* Southwark LBC (Unreported, February 20, 1998), CA . . . .   *Applied,* 00/4233:
                                  Distinguished, 00/2981
Hawkey *v.* Secretary of State for the Environment (1971) 22 P. & C.R. 610, QBD . . . . . .   *Digested,* 71/**11427**:
                                         Applied, 00/4420
Hawkins *v.* Keppe Shaw Solicitors [2001] EWCA Civ 1160; (2001) 98(37) L.S.G. 39;
    Times, September 25, 2001, CA . . . .   *Digested,* 01/**433**
Hawkins *v.* Poole (Unreported, May 24, 2001), CC (Bath) [*Ex rel.* Sarah Boyd,
    Barrister, Assize Court Chambers, 14 Small Street, Bristol] . . . .   *Digested,* 01/**1800**
Hawkins *v.* Secretary of State for the Environment, Transport and the Regions (2000)
    97(21) L.S.G. 42, QBD
Hawkins and Cadwaladr *v.* Gator Tool Hire & Sales Ltd (Unreported, May 1, 1998), CC
    (Blackwood) [*Ex rel.* Mark Allen, Barrister, 30 Park Place, Cardiff, CF1 3BA] . . .   *Digested,* 98/**1697**
Hawkyard *v.* North Yorkshire CC (Unreported, June 11, 1998), CC (Leeds) [*Ex rel.* Burn
    & Co Solicitors, Kendal House, 11 Lendal, York] . . . .   *Digested,* 99/**2887**
Hawthorn *v.* Smallcorn [1998] S.T.C. 591; [1998] B.T.C. 5083; [1998] B.V.C. 101, Ch D
    . . . .   *Digested,* 98/**4939**
Hay *v.* George Hanson (Building Contractors) Ltd [1996] I.R.L.R. 427, EAT . . . .   *Digested,* 96/**6959**:
                                         Followed, 98/2187
Hay *v.* Hughes [1975] Q.B. 790; [1975] 2 W.L.R. 34; [1975] 1 All E.R. 257; [1975] 1
    Lloyd's Rep. 12; 118 S.J. 883, CA; affirming [1974] 1 Lloyd's Rep. 475; (1973) 117
    S.J. 915, Fam Div . . . .   *Digested,* 75/**772**:
            Considered, 74/836, 75/785, 78/708, 82/206, 88/1056, 00/1451:
                                         Referred to, 76/672
Hayden *v.* Hayden [1992] 1 W.L.R. 986; [1993] 2 F.L.R. 16; [1992] P.I.Q.R. Q111;
    [1993] Fam. Law 466; *Times,* April 8, 1992, CA . . . .   *Digested,* 93/**1395**:
                                         Distinguished, 98/931
Haydon *v.* Kent CC [1978] Q.B. 343; [1978] 2 W.L.R. 485; [1978] 2 All E.R. 97; 76
    L.G.R. 270; [1978] J.P.L. 174; 121 S.J. 894, CA . . . .   *Digested,* 78/**1547**:
           Considered, 94/4517, 95/4976, 97/3786, 99/2890: *Followed,* 98/2858
Hayes (Application for Habeas Corpus), Re, *Daily Telegraph,* October 31, 2000, QBD
Hayes *v.* Airtours Holidays Ltd (Unreported, September 26, 2000), CC (Norwich) [*Ex
    rel.* David Thomson, Barrister, No 1 Sergeants Inn, London, EC4Y 1LH] . . . .   *Digested,* 01/**4283**
Hayes *v.* Airtours Holidays Ltd (Costs) (Unreported, January 8, 2001), CC (Norwich)
    [*Ex rel.* David Thompson, Barrister, No.1 Serjeants' Inn, London] . . . .   *Digested,* 01/**512**

Hayes v. Humberside Valuation Tribunal [1998] R.A. 37, CA; affirming [1997] R.A. 236; [1997] E.G.C.S. 6; [1997] N.P.C. 4, QBD .... *Digested,* 98/**4299**
Hayes v. Security Facilities Division see Security and Facilities Division v. Hayes
Haynes v. British Railways Board (Unreported, September 8, 1997), MCLC [*Ex rel.* Sarah Paneth, Barrister, No.1 Serjeants' Inn, Fleet Street] .... *Digested,* 98/**1675**
Haystead v. Chief Constable of Derbyshire; *sub nom* Haystead v. DPP [2000] 3 All E.R. 890; [2000] 2 Cr. App. R. 339; (2000) 164 J.P. 396; [2000] Crim. L.R. 758; [2000] C.O.D. 288; (2000) 164 J.P.N. 569; *Times,* June 2, 2000, QBD ... *Digested,* 00/**1016**
Haystead v. DPP see Haystead v. Chief Constable of Derbyshire
Hayward (Deceased), Re [1997] Ch. 45; [1996] 3 W.L.R. 674; [1997] 1 All E.R. 32; [1997] B.P.I.R. 456, Ch D .... *Digested,* 96/**1111**:
　　　　　　　　　　　　　　　　　　　　　　　　　　　　　　　Distinguished, 01/3736
Hayward v. Norwich Union Insurance Ltd [2001] EWCA Civ 243; [2001] 1 All E.R. (Comm) 545; [2001] R.T.R. 35; [2001] Lloyd's Rep. I.R. 410; *Times,* March 8, 2001; *Independent,* March 2, 2001; *Daily Telegraph,* March 6, 2001, CA; reversing [2000] Lloyd's Rep. I.R. 382; *Independent,* December 20, 1999 (C.S.), QBD .... *Digested,* 01/**3810**
Hayward v. Sharrard (2000) 56 B.M.L.R. 155, CA .... *Digested,* 01/**4461**
Hayward Gill & Associates Ltd v. Customs and Excise Commissioners [1998] B.V.C. 2336; [1998] V. & D.R. 352, V&DTr .... *Digested,* 99/**5007**
Hazelacre Ltd v. Customs and Excise Commissioners [2000] V. & D.R. 185; [2000] S.T.I. 1724, V&DTr
Hazell v. Hammersmith and Fulham LBC [1992] 2 A.C. 1; [1991] 2 W.L.R. 372; [1991] 1 All E.R. 545; 89 L.G.R. 271; (1991) 3 Admin. L.R. 549; [1991] R.V.R. 28; (1991) 155 J.P.N. 527; (1991) 155 L.G. Rev. 527; (1991) 88(8) L.S.G. 36; (1991) 141 N.L.J. 127; *Times,* January 25, 1991; *Independent,* January 25, 1991; *Financial Times,* January 29, 1991; *Guardian,* January 25, 1991; *Daily Telegraph,* February 4, 1991, HL; reversing [1990] 2 W.L.R. 1038; [1990] 3 All E.R. 33; 88 L.G.R. 433; [1990] R.V.R. 140; (1990) 87(20) L.S.G. 36; (1990) 134 S.J. 637, CA; reversing in part [1990] 2 W.L.R. 17; [1989] R.V.R. 188; [1989] R.V.R. 188; [1990] C.O.D. 112; (1990) 87(2) L.S.G. 36; (1989) 134 S.J. 21, QBD .... *Digested,* 91/**2420**:
　　　　　　　　　　Applied, 92/4327.a, 95/6406: *Considered,* 91/537, 93/2662, 93/2668,
　　　　　　　　　　　　　　　　95/789, 96/1084, 96/3114, 96/4149, 96/4866, 98/2297:
　　　　　　　　　Distinguished, 94/2969, 95/3239: *Followed,* 00/4110: *Referred to,* 94/6018,
　　　　　　　　　　　　　　　　　　　　　　　　　　　　　　　　95/5586, 95/6118
Hazell v. Taylor (Unreported, February 11, 1998), CC (Milton Keynes) [*Ex rel.* Fennemores Solicitors, 196 Silbury Boulevard, Central Milton Keynes, MK9 1EL] .... *Digested,* 98/**1729**
Hazlett v. Sefton MBC [2000] 4 All E.R. 887; [2001] 1 Costs L.R. 89; [2000] Env. L.R. 416; (1999) 149 N.L.J. 1869; [1999] N.P.C. 152, QBD .... *Digested,* 00/**4295**:
　　　　　　　　　　　　　　　　　　　　　　　　　　　　　　　Considered, 01/1116
HB (Abduction: Children's Objections) (No.1), Re [1998] 1 F.L.R. 422; [1998] 1 F.C.R. 398; [1998] Fam. Law 128, CA; reversing [1997] 1 F.L.R. 392; [1997] 3 F.C.R. 235; [1997] Fam. Law 312, Fam Div .... *Digested,* 98/**2377**
HB (Abduction: Children's Objections) (No.2), Re [1998] 1 F.L.R. 564; [1999] 1 F.C.R. 331; [1998] Fam. Law 244, Fam Div .... *Digested,* 98/**2376**
HB Property Developments Ltd v. Secretary of State for the Environment, Transport and the Regions (1999) 78 P. & C.R. 108; [1998] L. & T.R. 238, CA .... *Digested,* 99/**3661**
Head v. RJB Mining (UK) Ltd [2001] 1 Q.R. 10, CC (Cardiff) [*Ex rel.* Leo Abse & Cohen Solicitors, 40 Churchill Way, Cardiff] .... *Digested,* 01/**1645**
Healds Foods Ltd v. Hyde Dairies Ltd (Unreported, December 1, 1994)............. *Applied,* 98/701
Healey v. Healey [1915] 1 K.B. 938, KBD .... *Distinguished,* 98/4775
Healing Herbs Ltd v. Bach Flower Remedies Ltd see BACH and BACH FLOWER REMEDIES Trade Marks
Health and Safety Executive v. Roberts Unreported, CC (Swansea) [*Ex rel.* Bryan Thomas, Barrister, Gower Chambers, 57 Walter Road, Swansea]............ *Digested,* 98/**2837**
Healy v. DPP see DPP v. Charles
Heaney v. Ireland (34720/97) (2001) 33 E.H.R.R. 12; [2001] Crim. L.R. 481, ECHR
Heaney v. Ireland (Admissibility) (34720/97) (2001) 29 E.H.R.R. CD166, ECHR
Heap v. Partridge (Unreported, March 19, 1998), CC (Tunbridge Wells) [*Ex rel.* Dawson Hart Solicitors, The Old Grammar School, Church Street, Uckfield, East Sussex] . *Digested,* 98/**1646**
Heard v. Heard [1995] 1 F.L.R. 970; [1996] 1 F.C.R. 33; [1995] Fam. Law 477, CA [*Ex rel.* Christopher Naish, Barrister] .... *Digested,* 96/**2888**:
　　　　　　　　　　　　　　　　　　　　　　　　　　　　　　　Considered, 99/3261
Hearne v. National Assembly for Wales; *sub nom* Hearne v. Secretary of State for Wales *Times,* November 10, 1999 ; *Independent,* November 11, 1999, CA; affirming [2000] J.P.L. 161, QBD .... *Digested,* 01/**4691**
Hearne v. Secretary of State for Wales see Hearne v. National Assembly for Wales
Hearts of Oak Assurance Co Ltd v. Attorney General [1932] A.C. 392, HL; reversing [1931] 2 Ch. 370, CA... *Applied,* 99/605
Heath v. Tang; Stevens v. Peacock [1993] 1 W.L.R. 1421; [1993] 4 All E.R. 694; *Times,* August 11, 1993; *Independent,* October 14, 1993, CA....................... *Digested,* 93/**222**:
　　　　　　　　　　Applied, 98/3293, 00/3442: *Considered,* 99/3261, 01/3732:
　　　　　　　　　　Followed, 95/419, 01/3718: *Referred to,* 94/3445, 95/861

Heathcote Ball & Co (Commercial Auctions) Ltd *v.* Barry see Barry *v.* Davies (t/a Heathcote Ball & Co)

Heather (Inspector of taxes) *v.* PE Consulting Group Ltd [1973] Ch. 189; [1972] 3 W.L.R. 833; [1973] 1 All E.R. 8; 48 T.C. 293; [1972] T.R. 237; 116 S.J. 824, CA; affirming [1972] 2 W.L.R. 918; [1972] 2 All E.R. 107; [1971] T.R. 465; (1971) 116 S.J. 125, Ch D . . . . *Digested,* 72/**1755**:
Applied, 00/4933: *Considered,* 74/482, 80/397: *Followed,* 85/462, 86/453

Heathrow Airport Ltd *v.* Baldwin (Unreported, October 5, 1998), QBD . . . . *Followed,* 99/441

Heathrow Airport Ltd *v.* Forte (UK) Ltd [1998] E.C.C. 357; [1998] Eu. L.R. 98; [1998] E.G.C.S. 13; (1998) 95(6) L.S.G. 26; [1998] N.P.C. 6, Ch D . . . . *Digested,* 98/**719**

Heathrow Airport Ltd *v.* Gross [1999] C.P.L.R. 247, QBD . . . . *Digested,* 99/**441**

Heaton *v.* Axa Equity & Law Life Assurance Society Plc TNS, HL; affirming [2001] Ch. 173; [2000] 3 W.L.R. 1341; [2000] 4 All E.R. 673; [2001] C.P. Rep. 10; [2000] C.P.L.R. 505; *Times,* June 7, 2000; *Independent,* July 3, 2000 (C.S), CA; reversing *Times,* July 19, 1999, Ch D . . . . *Digested,* 00/**377**

Heaton (t/a Freshmaid Sandwiches Take Away) *v.* Customs and Excise Commissioners [2000] S.T.I. 1380, V&DTr

Hector *v.* Lyons (1989) 58 P. & C.R. 156; *Times,* December 19, 1988, CA. . . . . *Digested,* 90/**659**:
Applied, 01/917: *Considered,* 97/3312

Hedley Byrne & Co Ltd *v.* Heller & Partners Ltd [1964] A.C. 465; [1963] 3 W.L.R. 101; [1963] 2 All E.R. 575; [1963] 1 Lloyd's Rep. 485; 107 S.J. 454, HL; affirming [1962] 1 Q.B. 396; [1961] 3 W.L.R. 1225; [1961] 3 All E.R. 891; 105 S.J. 910, CA; affirming *Times,* December 21, 1960, QBD . . . . *Digested,* 63/**2416**:
Applied, 63/330, 67/2677, 69/1998, 70/1493, 70/1880, 70/1881, 71/8000, 71/9949, 72/38, 72/2364, 73/325, 73/2307, 73/2309, 74/2597, 76/341, 76/1868, 77/1804, 77/2886, 78/1512, 78/1695, 78/2822, 79/213, 79/1859, 80/363, 81/1837, 81/1849, 81/1860, 81/2752, 83/2574, 85/2304, 85/2324, 88/2422, 88/2430, 89/56, 90/3266, 94/3362, 95/3701, 97/3787, 97/3818, 01/1508: *Considered,* 65/2671, 65/3076, 66/9394, 67/3099, 68/3054, 69/882, 69/2463, 70/1849, 72/2363, 74/3638, 75/2326, 76/1343, 77/157, 77/1452, 77/2009, 77/2032, 79/1864, 79/1884, 80/362, 80/1898, 83/1734, 83/2534, 86/215, 87/2579, 87/2580, 87/2591, 87/2619, 88/1710, 88/2433, 88/2444, 88/2456, 88/3409, 89/304, 89/469, 89/2543, 89/2566, 89/2585, 90/3288, 90/4312, 91/2661, 92/3192, 92/3213, 93/2983, 93/2997, 93/2999, 94/3383, 94/4234, 95/770, 95/3667, 95/3689, 95/4838, 96/4531, 98/3920, 00/4200, 00/4205: *Distinguished,* 64/3468, 67/2731, 71/7804, 71/7843, 71/10472, 71/11921, 72/2349, 72/2352, 73/2312, 86/2258, 87/2576, 98/3922: *Explained,* 72/107, 94/1918:
Followed, 60/2462, 64/2565, 65/2727, 74/453, 74/2576, 75/419, 92/6091, 96/1012, 96/4439, 96/4488, 98/3951, 98/3987: *Referred to,* 81/1852, 88/4958, 95/5841

Hedley Lomas (Ireland) Ltd *v.* Commission of the European Communities (T455/93) [1997] E.C.R. II-1095; [1998] 1 C.M.L.R. 572, CFI (4th Chamber)

Heer *v.* Tutton; Pickles *v.* Holdsworth; Lovell *v.* Porter [1995] 1 W.L.R. 1336; [1995] 4 All E.R. 547; *Times,* June 5, 1995; *Independent,* July 3, 1995 (C.S), CA . . . . *Digested,* 96/**903**:
Considered, 97/733, 98/528: *Distinguished,* 95/4092, 96/751:
Followed, 96/902

Heffer *v.* Tiffin Green, *Times,* December 28, 1998, CA . . . . *Digested,* 99/**456**

Hegan's Application for Judicial Review, Re [2000] N.I. 461, QBD (NI) . . . . *Digested,* 01/**5647**

Heger *v.* Pellegrini [2000] I.L.Pr. 515, Cass (F)

Heggie *v.* Uniroyal Englebert Tyres Ltd 2000 S.L.T. 227; [1999] I.R.L.R. 802; 1999 G.W.D. 30-1432, 2 Div; reversing [1998] I.R.L.R. 425, EAT . . . . *Digested,* 00/**6217**

Heginbotham's Petition, Re (1999-2000) 2 I.T.E.L.R. 95, HC (IoM)

Heil *v.* Rankin; Rees *v.* Mabco (102) Ltd (Non-Pecuniary Damages); Schofield *v.* Saunders & Taylor Ltd; Ramsay *v.* Rivers; Kent *v.* Griffiths (Non-Pecuniary Damages); W (A Child) *v.* Northern General Hospital NHS Trust; Annable *v.* Southern Derbyshire HA; Connolly *v.* Tasker [2001] Q.B. 272; [2000] 2 W.L.R. 1173; [2000] 3 All E.R. 138; [2000] I.R.L.R. 334; [2000] P.I.Q.R. Q187; [2000] Lloyd's Rep. Med. 203; (2000) 97(14) L.S.G. 41; (2000) 150 N.L.J. 464; (2000) 144 S.J.L.B. 157; *Times,* March 24, 2000; *Independent,* March 28, 2000, CA . . . . *Digested,* 00/**1478**:
Considered, 00/1529, 00/6165, 01/612, 01/1585, 01/6421:
Followed, 00/1495, 00/1500, 00/1511, 00/1644, 00/1733:
Previous proceedings, 99/1534, 00/4203: *Subsequent proceedings,* 00/1492

Heil *v.* Rankin (Appeal against Damages) [2001] P.I.Q.R. Q3; *Times,* June 20, 2000; *Independent,* June 16, 2000, CA . . . . *Digested,* 00/**1482**

Heil *v.* Rankin (Costs); Rees *v.* Mabco (102) Ltd (Costs); Schofield *v.* Saunders & Taylor Ltd (Costs); Ramsay *v.* Rivers (Costs); Kent *v.* Griffiths (Costs); W (A Child) *v.* Northern General Hospital NHS Trust (Costs); Annable *v.* Southern Derbyshire HA (Costs); Connolly *v.* Tasker (Costs) [2000] C.P. Rep. 55, CA. . . . *Digested,* 00/**397**

Heilbut Symons & Co *v.* Buckleton [1913] A.C. 30, HL. . . . . *Applied,* 47-51/1705, 47-51/4199, 47-51/4200, 57/3208, 61/7971, 66/10832: *Considered,* 65/3520, 70/358: *Followed,* 00/876

Heiluth (Valuation Officer), Re [1999] R.A. 109, Lands Tr . . . . *Digested,* 99/**4329**

Heinl v. Jyske Bank (Gibraltar) Ltd [1999] Lloyd's Rep. Bank. 511; (1999) 96(34)
L.S.G. 33; *Times*, September 28, 1999, CA . . . .   *Digested*, 99/**2217**:
                  Applied, 00/3566

Helberg-Hensen v. Mansfield (Unreported, October 8, 1999), CC (Wrexham) [*Ex rel.*
Clement Jones Solicitors, Hoywell House, Parkway Business Centre, Deeside
Park, Flintshire] . . . .   *Digested*, 00/**441**

Helby v. Matthews [1895] A.C. 471, HL; reversing [1894] 2 Q.B. 262, CA . . . .   *Applied*, 00/**849**:
                   Considered, 91/557: *Distinguished*, 64/3479: *Followed*, 97/972

Helene Plc (In Liquidation), Re see Secretary of State for Trade and Industry v. Forsyth

Helgadottir v. Hjaltason (E7/00) [2001] 3 C.M.L.R. 27, EFTA. . . . .   *Digested*, 01/**3831**

Helle v. Finland (1998) 26 E.H.R.R. 159; [1998] H.R.C.D. 186, ECHR . . . .   *Digested*, 98/**3140**

Hellenic & General Trust, Re [1976] 1 W.L.R. 123; [1975] 3 All E.R. 382; 119 S.J. 845, Ch D
                                         Digested, 75/**301**:
                                 Considered, 00/683

Hellesdon Developments Ltd v. Customs and Excise Commissioners [2001] S.T.I. 222,
V&DTr

Hellyer (A Bankrupt), Re [1998] B.P.I.R. 695, Ch D . . . .   *Digested*, 99/**3236**

Hellyer Brothers Ltd v. McLeod; Boston Deep Sea Fisheries v. Wilson [1987] 1 W.L.R.
728; [1987] I.C.R. 526; [1987] I.R.L.R. 232; (1987) 84 L.S.G. 1056; (1987) 131
S.J. 805, CA; affirming [1986] I.C.R. 122; (1986) 83 L.S.G. 44, EAT . . . .   *Digested*, 87/**1354**:
               Considered, 97/2195: *Distinguished*, 86/1234: *Followed*, 98/2137

Hely-Hutchinson v. Brayhead Ltd [1968] 1 Q.B. 549; [1967] 3 W.L.R. 1408; [1967] 3
All E.R. 98; 111 S.J. 830, CA; affirming [1967] 2 W.L.R. 1312; [1967] 2 All E.R.
14; 111 S.J. 329, QBD . . . .   *Digested*, 67/**33**:
         Applied, 72/1649, 74/30: *Considered*, 88/311: *Distinguished*, 98/3382

Hembach v. Quikpak Corp [2000] B.P.I.R. 744, US Ct

Henderson (Widow and Administratrix of the Estate of Henderson (George Arthur)) v.
Henry E Jenkins & Sons see Henderson v. Henry E Jenkins & Sons

Henderson v. Chief Constable of Cleveland [2001] EWCA Civ 335; [2001] 1 W.L.R.
1103; *Times*, March 16, 2001, CA . . . .   *Digested*, 01/**4790**

Henderson (t/a Tony's Fish & Chip Shop) v. Customs and Excise Commissioners [2001]
S.T.C. 47; [2001] B.T.C. 5369; [2001] B.V.C. 444; [2000] S.T.I. 951, Ch D . . . . .   *Digested*, 01/**5592**

Henderson v. Henderson [1843-60] All E.R. Rep. 378; (1843) 67 E.R. 313; (1843) 3
Hare 100, Ct of Chancery. . . . .   *Applied*, 65/100,
        67/1498, 91/1736, 97/461, 97/997, 98/80, 98/2162, 98/2163, 98/3454,
        99/3313, 99/4025, 00/5111, 01/4678: *Considered*, 75/2463, 84/2704,
        88/2920, 89/1534, 93/3308, 94/3285, 94/3746, 95/3894, 96/1105,
        98/244, 98/518, 98/618, 98/4067, 99/620, 00/604, 00/785, 01/410,
        01/6474: *Distinguished*, 47-51/3681, 99/549, 99/4384, 00/349, 00/2605:
        Followed, 99/3952, 00/2322: *Not applied*, 99/1376, 99/3732:
                                 Referred to, 99/4014

Henderson v. Henry E Jenkins & Sons; *sub nom* Henderson (Widow and
Administratrix of the Estate of Henderson (George Arthur)) v. Henry E Jenkins &
Sons [1970] A.C. 282; [1969] 3 W.L.R. 732; [1969] 3 All E.R. 756; [1969] 2
Lloyd's Rep 603; 113 S.J. 856, HL; reversing [1969] 2 Q.B. 188; [1969] 2 W.L.R.
147; [1969] 1 All E.R. 401; (1968) 112 S.J. 909, CA.   *Digested*, 69/**2422**:
                Applied, 69/2454, 88/1582, 89/2580, 96/7224, 00/4223:
                              Distinguished, 83/2537

Henderson v. Inland Revenue Commissioners [2000] S.T.C. (S.C.D.) 572; [2000] S.T.I.
1656, Sp Comm . . . .   *Digested*, 01/**5296**

Henderson v. Merrett Syndicates Ltd (Application for Expedited Appeal) see Unilever
Plc v. Chefaro Proprietaries Ltd (Application for Expedited Appeal)

Henderson v. Merrett Syndicates Ltd (No.1); *sub nom* McLarnon Deeney v. Gooda
Walker Ltd; Gooda Walker Ltd v. Deeny; Hallam-Eames v. Merrett Syndicates
Ltd; Hughes v. Merrett Syndicates Ltd; Feltrim Underwriting Agencies Ltd v.
Arbuthnott; Deeny v. Gooda Walker Ltd (Duty of Care) [1995] 2 A.C. 145;
[1994] 3 W.L.R. 761; [1994] 3 All E.R. 506; [1994] 2 Lloyd's Rep. 468; (1994)
144 N.L.J. 1204; *Times*, July 26, 1994; *Independent*, August 3, 1994, HL;
affirming [1994] E.C.C. 537; *Times*, December 30, 1993; *Independent*,
December 14, 1993, CA; affirming [1994] 2 Lloyd's Rep. 193; *Times*, October 20,
1993, QBD (Comm Ct) . . . .   *Digested*, 94/**3362**:
        Applied, 95/3667, 95/3701, 98/795, 01/1508, 01/4487, 01/4490:
        Cited, 00/4218: *Considered*, 94/3383, 95/2496, 95/4838, 96/2993,
        96/3580, 97/692, 98/3920: *Followed*, 96/1133, 99/3984:
                              Referred to, 99/4023

Henderson v. Secretary of State for Social Security see Secretary of State for Social
Security v. Henderson

Henderson v. Temple Pier Co Ltd [1998] 1 W.L.R. 1540; [1998] 3 All E.R. 324; [1999]
P.I.Q.R. P61; (1998) 95(20) L.S.G. 35; (1998) 142 S.J.L.B. 156; *Times*, May 2,
1998; *Independent*, April 29, 1998, CA. . . . .   *Digested*, 98/**543**:
                         Followed, 99/3959: *Referred to*, 99/457

Hendry v. Chartsearch Ltd [1998] C.L.C. 1382; (2000) 2 T.C.L.R. 115; *Times*,
September 16, 1998, CA . . . .   *Digested*, 98/**401**

Hendry v. World Professional Billiards & Snooker Association Ltd; *sub nom* Hendry v. WPBSA [2001] Eu. L.R. 770, Ch D

Hendry v. WPBSA see Hendry v. World Professional Billiards & Snooker Association Ltd

Henke v. Gemeinde Schierke (C298/94); *sub nom* Henke v. Verwaltungsgemeinschaft Brocken (C298/94) [1997] All E.R. (E.C.) 173; [1996] E.C.R. I-4989; [1997] 1 C.M.L.R. 373; [1997] I.C.R. 746; [1996] I.R.L.R. 701, ECJ . . . .   *Digested*, 97/**2273**:
                                                                                              Cited, 01/2336: *Distinguished*, 98/2221

Henke v. Verwaltungsgemeinschaft Brocken (C298/94) see Henke v. Gemeinde Schierke (C298/94)

Henkel Hellas ABEE v. Greece (C350/98) [2000] S.T.C. 399; [1999] E.C.R. I-8013; [2000] S.T.I. 781, ECJ (6th Chamber) . . . .   *Digested*, 00/**4962**

Henkel KGaA v. Office for Harmonisation in the Internal Market (Trade Marks and Designs) (OHIM) (T337/99) [2001] C.E.C. 266, CFI (2nd Chamber)

Henlow Grange Health Farm Ltd v. Bedfordshire CC see R. (on the application of Henlow Grange Health Farm Ltd) v. Bedfordshire CC

Henn v. DPP (No.1) see R. v. Henn (Maurice Donald) (No.1)

HENNAFLOR Trade Mark (7 A 93/96-29) [2001] E.T.M.R. CN3, VrS (Prague)

Henra v. France [1998] H.R.C.D. 484, ECHR

Henriques v. Stephens (Valuation Officer) [2001] R.A. 366, Lands Tr

Henry v. Environment Agency (No.1) see Wilmott Trading Ltd (No.1), Re

Henry v. Environment Agency (No.2) see Wilmott Trading Ltd (No.2), Re

Henry v. Lambeth LBC see Lambeth LBC v. Henry

Henry v. London General Transport Services Ltd; London General Transport Services Ltd v. Henry; A/2001/0146/A, CA; affirming [2001] I.R.L.R. 132, EAT . . . .   *Digested*, 01/**2226**

Henry Ansbacher & Co Ltd v. Binks Stern [1998] Lloyd's Rep. Bank. 1; [1998] P.N.L.R. 221; (1997) 94(27) L.S.G. 22; (1997) 141 S.J.L.B. 151; *Times*, June 26, 1997, CA . . . .   *Digested*, 97/**3372**

Henry Boot Construction v. Alston Combined Cycles see Henry Boot Construction Ltd v. Alstom Combined Cycles Ltd

Henry Boot Construction Ltd v. Alstom Combined Cycles Ltd; *sub nom* Henry Boot Construction v. Alston Combined Cycles; Henry Boot Construction Ltd v. GEC Alstom Combined Cycles Ltd [2000] C.L.C. 1147; [2000] B.L.R. 247; (2000) 2 T.C.L.R. 735; 69 Con. L.R. 27; (2000) 16 Const. L.J. 400; (2000) 97(17) L.S.G. 32; (2000) 144 S.J.L.B. 204; *Times*, April 11, 2000; *Independent*, May 22, 2000 (C.S.), CA; reversing [1999] B.L.R. 123; 64 Con. L.R. 32, QBD (T&CC) . .   *Digested*, 00/**816**

Henry Boot Construction Ltd v. GEC Alstom Combined Cycles Ltd see Henry Boot Construction Ltd v. Alstom Combined Cycles Ltd

Henry Boot Construction (UK) Ltd v. Malmaison Hotel (Manchester) Ltd (Leave to Appeal) [2001] Q.B. 388; [2000] 3 W.L.R. 1824; [2001] 1 All E.R. 257; [2000] 2 All E.R. (Comm) 960; [2000] 2 Lloyd's Rep. 625; [2000] C.L.C. 1689; [2000] B.L.R. 509; (2001) 3 T.C.L.R. 7; 72 Con. L.R. 1; (2000) 150 N.L.J. 867; *Times*, August 31, 2000; *Independent*, July 10, 2000 (C.S), CA . . . .   *Digested*, 00/**218**

Henry Boot Construction (UK) Ltd v. Malmaison Hotel (Manchester) Ltd 70 Con. L.R. 32, QBD (T&CC) . . . .   *Digested*, 00/**232**

Henry Boot Homes Ltd v. Secretary of State for the Environment, Transport and the Regions [2001] EWHC Admin 942; [2001] N.P.C. 172, QBD (Admin Ct)

Henry Brothers (Magherafelt) Ltd v. Ministry of Defence (Revocation of Patent) [1999] R.P.C. 442; (1999) 22(3) I.P.D. 22023, CA; affirming [1997] R.P.C. 693; (1997) 20(10) I.P.D. 20096, Pat Ct . . . .   *Digested*, 99/**3505**

Henry J Garratt & Co v. Ewing [1991] 1 W.L.R. 1356; [1991] 4 All E.R. 891; (1991) 135 S.J.L.B. 171; *Times*, October 17, 1991, CA . . . .   *Digested*, 92/**3389**:
                                                                                              Applied, 99/573

Henry Smith's Charity Trustees v. AWADA Trading & Promotion Services Ltd see Trustees of Henry Smith's Charity v. AWADA Trading & Promotion Services Ltd

Henshaw v. North East Lincolnshire BC (Unreported, February 9, 1999), CC (Great Grimsby) [*Ex rel.* Langleys Solicitors, Newporte House, Doddington Rd Business Park, Lincoln] . . . .   *Digested*, 99/**2892**

Henwood (Inspector of Taxes) v. Clarke [1997] S.T.C. 789; 69 T.C. 611; [1997] B.T.C. 278; (1997) 94(20) L.S.G. 37; (1997) 141 S.J.L.B. 113; *Times*, May 14, 1997; *Independent*, June 9, 1997 (C.S.), Ch D . . . .   *Digested*, 97/**2946**

Henwood v. Customs and Excise [1998] B.P.I.R. 339, CA

Hepatitis C Litigation, Re see A v. National Blood Authority (No.1)

Hepple v. Adjudication Officer (C196/98) [2000] All E.R. (EC) 513; [2000] E.C.R. I-3701; [2000] 3 C.M.L.R. 271; [2000] C.E.C. 351; *Times*, May 30, 2000, ECJ . . .   *Digested*, 00/**4775**

Hepworth v. Gotch (Unreported, August 5, 1998), CC (Worcester) [*Ex rel.* Stephen J Murray, Barrister, No 8 Chambers, Fountain Court, Steelhouse Lane, Birmingham] . . . .   *Digested*, 98/**1594**

Hepworth Building Products Ltd v. Coal Authority see Hepworth Building Projects Ltd (formerly Ellistown Pipes Ltd) v. Coal Authority (formerly British Coal)

Hepworth Building Projects Ltd (formerly Ellistown Pipes Ltd) v. Coal Authority (formerly British Coal); *sub nom* Hepworth Building Products Ltd v. Coal Authority [1999] 3 E.G.L.R. 99; [1999] 41 E.G. 157; (1999) 96(40) L.S.G. 44; *Times*, July 9, 1999, CA; reversing in part [1997] R.V.R. 207, Lands Tr. . . . .   *Digested*, 99/**4375**

Herbalife International Inc'sTrade MarkApplication [1999] E.T.M.R.882,OHIM (Opposition
Div) . . . . *Digested*, 00/**3743**
Herbert *v.*Vaughan [1972] 1 W.L.R. 1128; [1972] 3 All E.R. 122; 116 S.J. 415, Ch D . . . . *Digested*, 72/**2785**:
Considered, 00/579
Herbert Morris Ltd *v.* Saxelby [1916] 1 A.C. 688, HL; affirming [1915] 2 Ch. 57, CA. . . . *Applied*, 47-51/3628,
47-51/3630, 47-51/3632, 47-51/3633, 56/3180, 57/1285, 58/1217, 66/12025,
84/406.a, 91/1611, 99/2167: *Considered*, 69/1286, 70/924, 80/369, 84/405,
85/1134, 86/1167: *Distinguished*, 64/1307, 72/487: *Followed*, 96/1243,
97/3377
Herbert Smith (A Firm) *v.* Honour (Inspector of Taxes) [1999] S.T.C. 173; 72 T.C. 130;
[1999] B.T.C. 44; [1999] E.G.C.S. 23; (1999) 96(11) L.S.G. 70; (1999) 149
N.L.J. 250; (1999) 143 S.J.L.B. 72; [1999] N.P.C. 24; *Times,* March 4, 1999;
Independent, February 19, 1999, Ch D . . . . *Digested*, 99/**4722**
Hercules Chemicals NV *v.* Commission of the European Communities (C51/92 P); *sub
nom* Polypropylene Cartel (T7/89), Re; Hercules Chemicals NV *v.* Commission
of the European Communities (T7/89) [1999] E.C.R. I-4235; [1999] 5 C.M.L.R.
976, ECJ (6th Chamber); affirming [1991] E.C.R. II-1711; [1992] 4 C.M.L.R. 84,
CFI (1st Chamber) . . . . *Digested*, 00/**2377**
Hercules Chemicals NV *v.* Commission of the European Communities (T7/89) see
Hercules Chemicals NV *v.* Commission of the European Communities (C51/92
P)
Herczegfalvy *v.* Austria (A/242B) (1993) 15 E.H.R.R. 437, ECHR. . . . . *Digested*, 93/**2154**:
Considered, 01/4431: *Referred to*, 00/4322
Herd *v.* Clyde Helicopters Ltd see Fellowes *v.* Clyde Helicopters Ltd
Hereford and Worcester CC *v.* Lane see White *v.* Ealing LBC
Hereford and Worcester CC *v.* Newman; *sub nom* Worcestershire CC *v.* Newar [1975] 1
W.L.R. 901; [1975] 2 All E.R. 673; 73 L.G.R. 461; 30 P. & C.R. 381; 119 S.J.
354, CA; affirming in part [1974] 1 W.L.R. 938; [1974] 2 All E.R. 867; 72 L.G.R.
616; 118 S.J. 330, QBD . . . . *Digested*, 75/**1546**:
Considered, 78/1547, 98/2874
Hereford CC *v.* L CO 1348/97, QBD. . . . . *Digested*, 98/**1961**
Hereford City Council (Compulsory Purchase Order 1996) (1999) 14 P.A.D. 123, Planning
Inspector
Heritage Joinery *v.* Krasner [1999] B.P.I.R. 683; [1999] Lloyd's Rep. P.N. 825; [1999]
P.N.L.R. 906, Ch D . . . . *Digested*, 99/**3959**
Herkanaidu *v.* Lambeth LBC [1999] N.P.C. 159; *Times*, February 28, 2000, Ch D . . . . . *Digested*, 00/**4622**
Hermes International *v.* FHT Marketing Choice BV (C53/96) [1998] E.C.R. I-3603;
[1998] E.T.M.R. 425; [1998] I.L.Pr. 630; [1999] R.P.C. 107, ECJ . . . . *Digested*, 99/**3555**
HERMES Trade Mark [1982] Com. L.R. 98; [1982] R.P.C. 425, Ch D . . . . *Digested*, 82/**3265**:
Referred to, 01/4063
Heron *v.* First National Bank Plc (Unreported, February 23, 1998), CC (Caerphilly) [*Ex
rel.* Stephen J Neville, Barrister, Gough Square Chambers, 6-7 Gough Square,
London] . . . . *Digested*, 98/**2495**:
Considered, 99/4387: *Followed*, 99/2507
Heron International Ltd *v.* Lew Grade see Heron International Ltd *v.* Lord Grade
Heron International Ltd *v.* Lord Grade; *sub nom* Heron International Ltd *v.* Lew Grade
[1983] B.C.L.C. 244; [1982] Com. L.R. 108, CA. . . . . *Digested*, 82/**334**:
Considered, 86/317, 98/691
Heron Service Stations *v.* Coupe; *sub nom* Blakemore *v.* Heron Service Stations [1973]
1 W.L.R. 502; [1973] 2 All E.R. 110; 71 L.G.R. 313; (1973) 25 P. & C.R. 349; 117
S.J. 305, HL; affirming 69 L.G.R. 363; (1971) 22 P. & C.R. 601; 115 S.J. 248,
QBD . . . . *Digested*, 73/**3222**:
Followed, 98/3609
Herrington *v.* British Railways Board see British Railways Board *v.* Herrington
Herschel Engineering Ltd *v.* Breen Property Ltd [2000] B.L.R. 272; (2000) 2 T.C.L.R.
473; 70 Con. L.R. 1; (2000) 16 Const. L.J. 366; *Times*, May 10, 2000, QBD
(T&CC) . . . . *Digested*, 00/**809**
Hersey *v.* Queens Moat Houses Plc see Bairstow *v.* Queens Moat Houses Plc
Hersey *v.* Queens Moat Houses Plc (Assessment of Costs) see Bairstow *v.* Queens
Moat Houses Plc (Assessment of Costs)
Hersey *v.* Queens Moat Houses Plc (Costs) see Bairstow *v.* Queens Moat Houses Plc
(Costs)
Hersi *v.* Secretary of State for the Home Department; Uslusow *v.* Secretary of State
for the Home Department; Nur *v.* Secretary of State for the Home Department;
Warsame *v.* Secretary of State for the Home Department; Kahie *v.* Secretary of
State for the Home Department [1996] Imm. A.R. 569, CA. . . . . *Digested*, 97/**2912**:
Considered, 00/3364: *Referred to*, 98/3228
Hertel *v.* Switzerland (1999) 28 E.H.R.R. 534; 5 B.H.R.C. 260; [1998] H.R.C.D. 817,
ECHR . . . . *Digested*, 99/**3111**:
Referred to, 01/3533
Hertfordshire Investments Ltd *v.* Bubb [2000] 1 W.L.R. 2318; [2001] C.P. Rep. 38;
[2000] C.P.L.R. 588; *Times*, August 31, 2000, CA . . . . *Digested*, 00/**562**
Hertsmere BC *v.* Brent Walker Group [1994] 1 P.L.R. 1; [1994] E.G.C.S. 4, Ch D . . . . . . *Digested*, 95/**4869**:
Applied, 99/4359

Hertsmere BC v. Harty see South Buckinghamshire DC v. Porter
Hertsmere BC v. Harty (Application for Permission to Appeal) [2001] EWCA Civ 1238;
　　[2001] C.P. Rep. 115, CA
Hertsmere BC v. Reid Estates Ltd (2001) 81 P. & C.R. 16; [2001] J.P.L. 336; [2001]
　　A.C.D. 22; [2000] E.G.C.S. 74; (2000) 97(25) L.S.G. 42, QBD. . . . . 　*Digested*, 01/**4648**
Hertsmere BC v. Rexton House Nursery School (2001) 16 P.A.D. 52, Planning
　　Inspector
HESCO BASTION/Cage structure (T652/97) [2000] E.P.O.R. 371, EPO (Technical Bd
　　App). . . . . 　*Digested*, 00/**3615**
Hescorp Italia SpA v. Morrison Construction Ltd 75 Con. L.R. 51; (2000) 16 Const.
　　L.J. 413, QBD (T&CC)
Heselwood v. Collett [1999] P.I.Q.R. Q136; [1999] Lloyd's Rep. Med. 42, QBD . . . . . . 　*Digested*, 99/**1422**
Hesford v. General Council of the Bar, *Times*, August 20, 1999, Visitors (Inns of Ct) . . . . 　*Digested*, 99/**3792**
Heskell v. Continental Express Ltd [1950] 1 All E.R. 1033; (1949-50) 83 Ll. L. Rep.
　　438; [1950] W.N. 210; 94 S.J. 339, KBD . . . . 　*Digested*, 47/**1069**:
　　　　　　　　Applied, 47-51/6584, 00/4185: *Considered*, 92/3202: *Doubted*, 56/4423
Hesketh v. Birmingham Corp [1924] 1 K.B. 260, CA. . . . . 　*Applied*, 01/1544:
　　　　　　　　　　　　　　　　　　　　　　　　　　　　　　　　　　Considered, 53/3802
Heslop v. British Aluminium Plc [2001] 3 Q.R. 11, CC (Swansea) [*Ex rel.* Leo Abse &
　　Cohen, Solicitors, 40 Churchill Way, Cardiff] . . . . 　*Digested*, 01/**1607**
Hetherington (Deceased), Re; *sub nom* Gibbs v. McDonnell [1990] Ch. 1; [1989] 2
　　W.L.R. 1094; [1989] 2 All E.R. 129; (1989) 133 S.J. 457, Ch D . . . . 　*Digested*, 89/**262**:
　　　　　　　　　　　　　　　　　　　　　　　　　　　　　　　　　　Considered, 01/5021
Hever Golf Club Plc v. Secretary of State for the Environment, Transport and the
　　Regions; Hever Golf Club Plc v. Sevenoaks DC (1998) 95(4) L.S.G. 35, QBD
Hever Golf Club Plc v. Sevenoaks DC see Hever Golf Club Plc v. Secretary of State for
　　the Environment, Transport and the Regions
Hewett v. Chef & Brewer Ltd (Unreported, November 20, 1997), CC (Norwich) [*Ex
　　rel.* Marc Rivalland, Barrister, No.1 Serjeants' Inn, Fleet Street, London] . . . . 　*Digested*, 98/**1542**
Hewitson v. Hewitson [1999] 2 F.L.R. 74; [1999] Fam. Law 450, QBD. . . . . 　*Digested*, 99/**2404**
Hewitt v. P McCann Ltd [1998] F.S.R. 688; (1998) 21(6) I.P.D. 21056, Pat Ct . . . . . . 　*Digested*, 98/**3459**
Hewitt v. Rowlands [1924] All E.R. Rep. 344; (1924) 93 L.J. K.B. 1080; (1924) 131
　　L.T. 757, CA. . . . . 　*Applied*, 99/**3663**:
　　　　　　　　　　　　Considered, 89/2195: *Distinguished*, 83/2087, 84/1892
Hewitt v. Wirral and West Cheshire Community NHS Trust see Totty v. Snowden
Hewlett Packard GmbH v. Waters Corp; Waters Corp v. Hewlett Packard GmbH; A3/
　　2001/1133, A3/2001/1255, CA; reversing (2001) 24(11) I.P.D. 24071, Ch D
Hewlings v. McLean Homes East Anglia Ltd [2001] 2 All E.R. 281; [2001] Env. L.R.
　　17; [2001] E.H.L.R. 2; (2001) 33 H.L.R. 50; [2001] J.P.L. 226 (Note); [2001]
　　J.P.L. 425; [2000] E.G.C.S. 100; (2000) 97(39) L.S.G. 41; *Times*, August 31,
　　2000; *Independent*, October 30, 2000 (C.S.), QBD. 　*Digested*, 00/**2274**
Hextall's Application, Re (2000) 79 P. & C.R. 382, Lands Tr . . . . 　*Digested*, 00/**4626**
Heyes v. Pilkington Glass Ltd [1998] P.I.Q.R. P303, CA. . . . . 　*Digested*, 98/**2843**
Heyman v. Darwins Ltd [1942] A.C. 356; [1942] 1 All E.R. 337; (1942) 72 Ll. L. Rep.
　　65, HL . . . . 　*Applied*, 47-51/411,
　　　　　　47-51/413, 47-51/416, 47-51/417, 48/4042, 48/4043, 52/604, 53/147, 53/159,
　　　　　　53/631, 53/674, 53/1757, 56/1501, 58/126, 72/110, 78/304, 79/2777, 88/3202,
　　　　　　94/2705, 95/179: *Considered*, 61/360, 77/959, 78/317, 81/79, 93/491,
　　　　　　98/244: *Distinguished*, 47-51/4832, 79/121, 80/105: *Followed*, 84/221:
　　　　　　　　　　　　　　　　　　　　　　　　　　　　　　　　　　Not followed, 92/182
Heywood v. British Gas Plc (Unreported, January 4, 1999) . . . . 　*Considered*, 99/328
Heywood v. Wellers (A Firm) [1976] Q.B. 446; [1976] 2 W.L.R. 101; [1976] 1 All E.R.
　　300; [1976] 2 Lloyd's Rep. 88; (1975) 120 S.J. 9, CA . . . . 　*Digested*, 76/**2637**:
　　　　　　　　　　　Applied, 00/4266: *Distinguished*, 85/1145, 87/1303, 96/3911:
　　　　　　　　　　　　　　　　　　　　　　　　　　　　　　　　　　Followed, 77/3143
HF Pension Trustees Ltd v. Ellison [1999] Lloyd's Rep. P.N. 489; [1999] P.N.L.R. 894;
　　[1999] O.P.L.R. 67; (1999) 96(8) L.S.G. 30; *Times*, March 5, 1999, Ch D . . . . . 　*Digested*, 99/**472**
HFB Holding fur Fernwarmetechnik Beteiligungsgesellschaft mbH & Co KG v.
　　Commission of the European Communities (T9/99 R) [1999] E.C.R. II-2429;
　　[2001] 4 C.M.L.R. 29, CFI . . . . 　*Digested*, 01/**2452**
HFC Bank Plc v. Grossbard (Unreported, November 17, 2000), CC (Leeds) [*Ex rel.*
　　Darren Finlay, Barrister, Sovereign Chambers, 25 Park Square, Leeds] . . . . 　*Digested*, 01/**908**
HFC Bank Plc v. HSBC Bank Plc (formerly Midland Bank Plc) [2000] C.P.L.R. 197;
　　(2000) 97(19) L.S.G. 43; (2000) 144 S.J.L.B. 182; *Times*, April 26, 2000;
　　Independent, April 3, 2000 (C.S.), CA; affirming [2000] F.S.R. 176; (1999)
　　22(12) I.P.D. 22119; *Times*, September 28, 1999, Ch D . . . . 　*Digested*, 00/**574**
HFI GmbH v. McKechnie Plc (Unreported, October 31, 1998), QBD [*Ex rel.* Jeffrey
　　Terry, Barrister, 8 King Street Chambers, 8 King Street, Manchester] . . . . 　*Digested*, 99/**570**
Hi Fert Pty Ltd v. Kiukiang Maritime Carriers Inc [1999] 2 Lloyd's Rep. 782, Fed Ct
　　(Aus) (Full Ct). . . . . 　*Digested*, 00/**242**
Hi-Lift Elevator Services v. Temple (1995) 70 P. & C.R. 620, CA . . . . 　*Digested*, 96/**3816**:
　　　　　　　　　　　　　　　　　　　　　　　　　　　　　　　　　Distinguished, 99/3728
Hi-Tec Sports (UK) Ltd v. Customs and Excise Commissioners CO 2420/97, QBD . . . . 　*Digested*, 98/**2305**
Hi-Tek Bags Ltd v. Sun 99 Ltd (1998) 21(1) I.P.D. 21002, CA

Hiap Hong & Co Pte Ltd v. Hong Huat Development Co (Pte) Ltd (2001) 17 Const. L.J. 530, CA (Sing)

Hibbs v. Thomas Cook Group Ltd (Unreported, February 24, 1999), CC (Reigate) [*Ex rel.* Field Fisher Waterhouse Solicitors, 35 Vine Street, London] . . . .　　*Digested*, 99/**3829**

Hibernia Foods Plc v. McAuslin (The Joint Frost) [1998] 1 Lloyd's Rep. 310, QBD (Comm Ct) . . . .　　*Digested*, 98/**3388**

Hichens v. General Guarantee Corp Ltd see Hitchens v. General Guarantee Corp Ltd

Hickey v. Laggan (t/a The Fly Bar) Unreported . . . .　　*Applied*, 99/**5284**

Hickey v. Miller [2001] 6 Q.R. 3, QBD [*Ex rel.* Sarah Paneth, Barrister, No. 1 Serjeants' Inn, Fleet Street, London] . . . .　　*Digested*, 01/**1556**

Hicking v. Basford Group Ltd (In Receivership) see Levez v. TH Jennings (Harlow Pools) Ltd (No.2)

Hicking v. Customs and Excise Commissioners [2001] S.T.I. 1003, V&DTr

Hickinson (A Minor) v. Chesterfield Transport Ltd (Unreported, March 16, 1998), CC (Chesterfield) [*Ex rel.* Kelly & Anderson Solicitors, 71 Saltergate, Chesterfield, Derbyshire, S40 1JS] . . . .　　*Digested*, 98/**1655**

Hickman & Rose (Wasted Costs Order) (No.10 of 1999), Re see R. v. A (Wasted Costs Order)

Hicks v. Curryland (1999) 99(1) Q.R. 7, CC (Worthing)

Hicks v. Russell Jones & Walker [2001] C.P. Rep. 25, CA . . . .　　*Digested*, 01/**525**

Higgins v. France (1999) 27 E.H.R.R. 703; [1998] H.R.C.D. 253, ECHR . . . .　　*Digested*, 99/**3128**

Higgs v. Minister of National Security [2000] 2 A.C. 228; [2000] 2 W.L.R. 1368; 8 B.H.R.C. 201; (2000) 144 S.J.L.B. 34; *Times*, December 23, 1999, PC (Bah) . . .　　*Digested*, 00/**3172**

High Peak BC v. L&A Middleton Ltd (1998) 13 P.A.D. 405, Planning Inspector

High Table Ltd v. Horst [1998] I.C.R. 409; [1997] I.R.L.R. 513; (1997) 94(28) L.S.G. 25; (1997) 141 S.J.L.B. 161; *Times*, July 9, 1997; *Independent*, July 23, 1997, CA .　　*Digested*, 97/**2250**: *Applied*, 98/2186, 99/2107

Higham (A Bankrupt), Re; *sub nom* Beer v. Higham [1997] B.P.I.R. 349, Ch D . . . .　　*Digested*, 97/**3014**: *Distinguished*, 98/3280

Higher Education Statistics Agency Ltd v. Customs and Excise Commissioners [2000] S.T.C. 332; [2000] B.T.C. 5120; [2000] B.V.C. 150; [2000] S.T.I. 543; *Times*, April 19, 2000, QBD; affirming [1999] B.V.C. 2132, V&DTr . . . .　　*Digested*, 00/**5353**

Highland and Universal Properties Ltd v. Safeway Properties Ltd (No.2) 2000 S.C. 297; 2000 S.L.T. 414; [2000] 3 E.G.L.R. 110; 2000 G.W.D. 6-231; *Times*, March 22, 2000, 1 Div; reversing in part 1998 G.W.D. 3-136, OH . . . .　　*Digested*, 00/**6526**

HIH Casualty & General Insurance Ltd v. Chase Manhattan Bank; Chase Manhattan Bank v. HIH Casualty & General Insurance Ltd [2001] EWCA Civ 1250; [2001] 2 Lloyd's Rep. 483; [2001] C.L.C. 1853; [2001] Lloyd's Rep. I.R. 703, CA; reversing in part [2001] 1 All E.R. (Comm) 719; [2001] 1 Lloyd's Rep. 30; [2001] C.L.C. 48; [2001] Lloyd's Rep. I.R. 191; *Times*, September 19, 2000, QBD (Comm Ct) . . . .　　*Digested*, 01/**3805**: *Considered*, 01/3840

HIH Casualty & General Insurance Ltd v. New Hampshire Insurance Co [2001] EWCA Civ 735; [2001] 2 All E.R. (Comm) 39; [2001] 2 Lloyd's Rep. 161; [2001] C.L.C. 1480; [2001] Lloyd's Rep. I.R. 596, CA; affirming [2001] 1 Lloyd's Rep. 378; [2001] C.L.C. 481, QBD (Comm Ct) . . . .　　*Digested*, 01/**3840**

HIJ Mannenmode BV v. Nienhaus & Lotz GmbH [1999] E.T.M.R. 730, RB (Utrecht)

Hilal v. United Kingdom (45276/99); *sub nom* R. v. Secretary of State for the Home Department Ex p. Hilal (2001) 33 E.H.R.R. 2; 11 B.H.R.C. 354; [2001] I.N.L.R. 595, ECHR [1998] Imm. A.R. 507, QBD . . . .　　*Digested*, 01/**3618**

Hill v. Alex Lawrie Factors Ltd; *sub nom* Burfoot (A Bankrupt), Re [2000] B.P.I.R. 1038; *Times*, August 17, 2000, Ch D . . . .　　*Digested*, 00/**3437**

Hill v. Apcoa Parking Ltd [2001] 3 Q.R. 17, CC (Kingston upon Hull) [*Ex rel.* JS Boora, Barrister, 24 The Ropewalk, Nottingham] . . . .　　*Digested*, 01/**1699**

Hill v. ARC (South Wales) Ltd (Unreported, July 21, 1998), CC (Cardiff) [*Ex rel.* Loe Abse & Cohen Solicitors, 40 Churchill Way, Cardiff] . . . .　　*Digested*, 98/**1563**

Hill v. CA Parsons & Co [1972] Ch. 305; [1971] 3 W.L.R. 995; [1971] 3 All E.R. 1345; 115 S.J. 868, CA . . . .　　*Digested*, 72/**1192**: *Applied*, 72/1253, 73/2659, 84/1202, 85/1181: *Considered*, 98/5814, 01/2244: *Distinguished*, 74/1350, 75/1095

Hill v. Chief Constable of West Yorkshire [1989] A.C. 53; [1988] 2 W.L.R. 1049; [1988] 2 All E.R. 238; 152 L.G.R. 709; (1988) 152 L.G. Rev. 709; (1988) 85(20) L.S.G. 34; (1988) 138 N.L.J. Rep. 126; (1988) 132 S.J. 700, HL; affirming [1988] Q.B. 60; [1987] 2 W.L.R. 1126; [1987] 1 All E.R. 1173; 151 L.G.R. 729; (1987) 151 L.G. Rev. 729; (1987) 84 L.S.G. 982; (1987) 137 N.L.J. 222; (1987) 131 S.J. 626, CA; affirming (1986) 136 N.L.J. 239, QBD . . . .　　*Digested*, 88/**2435**: *Applied*, 90/3278, 92/3354, 94/3345, 94/3384, 95/3452, 95/3652, 99/3963: *Considered*, 87/2580, 90/5493, 94/3345, 94/4296, 95/3652, 96/4441, 99/3970, 99/4009: *Disapproved*, 98/3102: *Distinguished*, 95/3686, 99/3972, 99/5434, 00/4229: *Followed*, 01/4479

Hill v. Church of Scientology of Toronto [1995] 2 S.C.R. 1130 . . . .　　*Applied*, 99/**3106**

Hill v. Davison (Inspector of Taxes) see Euro Fire Ltd v. Davison (Inspector of Taxes)

Hill v. Debenham Tewson & Chinnocks [1955-95] P.N.L.R. 44, QBD (OR)

Hill v. General Accident Fire & Life Assurance Corp Plc (No.1) 1999 S.L.T. 1157; 1998
S.C.L.R. 1031; [1998] I.R.L.R. 641; 1998 G.W.D. 31-1622, OH . . . .   *Digested,* 98/**5813**:
                                                                                        Followed, 99/6029
Hill v. Gold see Gold v. Hill
Hill v. Griffin [1987] 1 E.G.L.R. 81; (1987) 282 E.G. 85, CA . . . .   *Digested,* 87/**2131**:
                                                                                        Applied, 98/3651
Hill v. Hill [1998] 1 F.L.R. 198; [1997] 3 F.C.R. 477; [1997] Fam. Law 657;
Independent, June 19, 1997, CA; reversing [1997] 1 F.L.R. 730; [1997] Fam. Law
394, Fam Div . . . .   *Digested,* 97/**2481**
Hill v. Holmes (Unreported, September 9, 1999), CC (Reading) [*Ex rel.* Elaine
Strachan, Barrister, 1 Alfred St, Oxford] . . . .   *Digested,* 00/**1690**
Hill v. Irish Revenue Commissioners (C243/95) see Hill v. Revenue Commissioners
(C243/95)
Hill v. Mullis & Peake [1999] B.C.C. 325; [1998] E.G.C.S. 79, CA . . . .   *Digested,* 99/**4048**
Hill v. Revenue Commissioners (C243/95); *sub nom* Hill v. Irish Revenue
Commissioners (C243/95) [1998] All E.R. (E.C.) 722; [1998] E.C.R. I-3739;
[1998] 3 C.M.L.R. 81; [1998] C.E.C. 655; [1999] I.C.R. 48; [1998] I.R.L.R. 466;
Times, July 2, 1998, ECJ (6th Chamber) . . . .   *Digested,* 98/**2144**
Hill v. Rollerson (Unreported, April 6, 1998), CC (Plymouth) [*Ex rel.* Nash & Co
Solicitors, Beaumont House, Beaumont Park, Plymouth, Devon] . . . .   *Digested,* 98/**485**
Hill v. UNISON (Unreported, August 31, 2000), Certification Officer [*Ex rel.*
Certification Office, 180 Borough High Street, London] . . . .   *Digested,* 00/**2221**
Hill v. Virgin Trains Ltd (Unreported, January 17, 2001), CC (Chester) [*Ex rel.* Katya
Melluish, Barrister, 3 Paper Buildings, Temple, London] . . . .   *Digested,* 01/**5475**
Hill Ash Developments v. Customs and Excise Commissioners [2001] B.V.C. 2075;
[2000] S.T.I. 1557, V&DTr
Hill Samuel Life Assurance Ltd, Re; Ambassador Life Co Ltd, Re [1998] 3 All E.R. 176, Ch D
(Companies Ct) . . . .   *Digested,* 98/**3370**
Hillingdon Borough Football Club's Application (1999) 14 P.A.D. 471, Planning Inspector
Hillingdon LBC v. ARC Ltd (No.1) [1999] Ch. 139; [1998] 3 W.L.R. 754; [1999]
B.L.G.R. 282; [1998] 3 E.G.L.R. 18; [1998] 39 E.G. 202; [1998] R.V.R. 242;
(1998) 95(15) L.S.G. 34; (1998) 142 S.J.L.B. 149; *Times,* May 4, 1998, CA;
affirming [1998] 1 W.L.R. 174; [1997] 3 All E.R. 506; (1998) 75 P. & C.R. 346;
[1997] 2 E.G.L.R. 21; [1997] 29 E.G. 125; [1997] R.V.R. 163; [1997] E.G.C.S. 95;
Times, June 25, 1997; *Independent,* June 30, 1997 (C.S.), Ch D . . . .   *Digested,* 98/**4179**:
                              Applied, 00/4433, 01/4851: *Considered,* 99/4186
Hillingdon LBC v. ARC Ltd (No.2) [2001] C.P. Rep. 33; [2000] 3 E.G.L.R. 97; [2000]
R.V.R. 283; (2000) 80 P. & C.R. D29; *Independent,* June 21, 2000, CA;
reversing [1999] 3 E.G.L.R. 125, Ch D . . . .   *Digested,* 00/**518**:
                                                                                        Considered, 01/598
Hillingdon LBC v. Guinea Enterprises Ltd (1998) 76 P. & C.R. 338, QBD . . . .   *Digested,* 98/**4194**
Hillingdon LBC v. Hodson Developments Ltd (1998) 13 P.A.D. 537, Planning Inspector
Hillingdon LBC v. Salson Investments and Developments Ltd (1998) 13 P.A.D. 462,
Planning Inspector
Hillingdon LBC v. Secretary of State for the Environment, Transport and the Regions
[2000] Env. L.R. D11, QBD
Hillingdon LBC v. WE Black Ltd (2001) 16 P.A.D. 63, Planning Inspector
Hillsbridge Investments Ltd v. Moresfield Ltd [2000] 2 B.C.L.C. 241, Ch D . . . .   *Digested,* 00/**2**
Hillsdown Holdings Plc v. Inland Revenue Commissioners; R. v. Inland Revenue
Commissioners Ex p. Hillsdown Holdings Plc [1999] S.T.C. 561; [1999] O.P.L.R.
79; [1999] Pens. L.R. 173; 71 T.C. 356; [1999] B.T.C. 194; *Times,* May 13, 1999;
Independent, March 22, 1999 (C.S.), Ch D . . . .   *Digested,* 99/**4679**:
                                                                                        Considered, 01/5263
Hillsdown Holdings Plc v. Pensions Ombudsman [1997] 1 All E.R. 862; [1996] O.P.L.R.
291, QBD . . . .   *Digested,* 97/**4009**:
                                                                                        Applied, 00/4393
Hilti AG v. Commission of the European Communities (C53/92P); *sub nom* Hilti AG v.
Commission of the European Communities (T30/89) [1994] E.C.R. I-667;
[1994] 4 C.M.L.R. 614; [1994] F.S.R. 760; *Financial Times,* March 8, 1994, ECJ;
affirming [1991] E.C.R. II-1439; [1992] 4 C.M.L.R. 16; [1992] F.S.R. 210;
[1994] E.C.R. I-667, AGO; affirming . . . .   *Digested,* 94/**4774**:
                                                                                        Followed, 01/761
Hilti AG v. Commission of the European Communities (T30/89) see Hilti AG v.
Commission of the European Communities (C53/92P)
Hilti AG v. Commission of the European Communities (T30/89 A) [1990] E.C.R. II-
163; [1990] 4 C.M.L.R. 602, CFI (2nd Chamber) . . . .   *Digested,* 91/**3924**:
                                                                                        Followed, 99/2231
Hilton v. Plustitle [1989] 1 W.L.R. 149; [1988] 3 All E.R. 1051; (1989) 21 H.L.R. 72;
(1989) 58 P. & C.R. 25; [1989] 05 E.G. 94; (1988) 85(32) L.S.G. 45; (1988)
138 N.L.J. Rep. 340; (1988) 132 S.J. 1638, CA . . . .   *Digested,* 89/**2113**:
                                                                                        Considered, 01/4196
Hilton v. Shiner Ltd [2001] I.R.L.R. 727, EAT . . . .   *Digested,* 01/**2341**
Hilton International Co v. Racelet SA [2001] E.T.M.R. CN15, Trib Gde Inst (Paris)

Hilton International Hotels (UK) Ltd *v.* Kaissi [1994] I.C.R. 578; [1994] I.R.L.R. 270;
Times, March 7, 1994, EAT . . . . *Applied,* 96/2526,
98/2168: *Considered,* 97/2238
Hilton International Hotels (UK) Ltd *v.* Protopapa [1990] I.R.L.R. 316, EAT . . . . *Digested,* 91/**1614**:
Applied, 00/2110
Hilton International Hotels (UK) Ltd *v.* Smith; *sub nom* Smith *v.* Bass Plc; Smith *v.* Hilton
International Hotels (UK) Ltd [2001] P.I.Q.R. P14, QBD [*Ex rel.* Jonathan
Clarke, Barrister, Old Square Chambers, Hanover House, 47 Corn Street,
Bristol] . . . . *Digested,* 01/**5060**
Hinchcliffe *v.* Secretary of State for Trade and Industry see Secretary of State for Trade
and Industry *v.* Hinchcliffe
Hinckley and Bosworth BC *v.* Bass Taverns Ltd (t/a Holiday Inn Express) (1999) 14
P.A.D. 91, Planning Inspector
Hinckley and Bosworth BC *v.* Coker see Hinckley and Bosworth BC *v.* Shaw
Hinckley and Bosworth BC *v.* Shaw; Hinckley and Bosworth BC *v.* Coker (1999) 1
L.G.L.R. 385; [2000] B.L.G.R. 9, QBD . . . . *Digested,* 99/**3902**
Hinckley BC *v.* Chambers (1999) 14 P.A.D. 302, Planning Inspector
Hinckley Island Hotel Ltd, Re see Craig *v.* Humberclyde Industrial Finance Group Ltd
Hinckley Singapore Trading Pte Ltd *v.* Sogo Department Stores (S) Pte Ltd (Under
Judicial Management) (2001-02) 4 I.T.E.L.R. 301, CA (Sing)
Hind *v.* Evergreen Travel Services Ltd (Unreported, July 14, 1998), CC (Worthing) [*Ex
rel.* Dominic Bayne, Barrister, Plowden Buildings, Temple, London] . . . . *Digested,* 98/**1430**
Hind *v.* York HA [1998] P.I.Q.R. P235; [1997] 8 Med. L.R. 377, QBD . . . . *Digested,* 97/**666**
Hindcastle Ltd *v.* Barbara Attenborough Associates Ltd [1997] A.C. 70; [1996] 2
W.L.R. 262; [1996] 1 All E.R. 737; [1996] B.C.C. 636; [1996] 2 B.C.L.C. 234;
[1996] B.P.I.R. 595; [1996] 1 E.G.L.R. 94; [1996] 15 E.G. 103; [1996] E.G.C.S.
32; (1996) 93(12) L.S.G. 29; (1996) 140 S.J.L.B. 84; [1996] N.P.C. 28; Times,
February 23, 1996, HL; affirming [1995] Q.B. 95; [1994] 3 W.L.R. 1100; [1994]
4 All E.R. 129; [1994] B.C.C. 705; [1994] 2 B.C.L.C. 728; [1994] 43 E.G. 154;
[1994] E.G.C.S. 109; [1994] N.P.C. 86; Times, July 6, 1994; Independent, July
18, 1994 (C.S.), CA . . . . *Digested,* 96/**3704**:
Applied, 98/3650, 98/3651: *Distinguished,* 98/3620
Hinde *v.* Cocksedge (Unreported, March 10, 2000), CC (Bury) [*Ex rel.* John Parr,
Barrister, 8 King Street, Manchester] . . . . *Digested,* 00/**1698**
Hinde *v.* Liddell (1874-75) L.R. 10 Q.B. 265, QBD . . . . *Followed,* 98/3732
Hinds *v.* Attorney General of Barbados [2001] UKPC 56; (2001) 145 S.J.L.B. 278, PC
(Bar)
Hinds *v.* Queen, The; DPP *v.* Jackson [1977] A.C. 195; [1976] 2 W.L.R. 366; [1976] 1
All E.R. 353; [1976] Crim. L.R. 124; (1975) 119 S.J. 864, PC (Jam) . . . . *Digested,* 76/**183**:
Applied, 85/174, 92/1223, 94/496: *Considered,* 99/781
Hinduja *v.* Asia TV Ltd; *sub nom* Hinduja *v.* Asian TV Ltd [1998] E.M.L.R. 516; Times,
December 12, 1997, CA . . . . *Digested,* 98/**1766**:
Distinguished, 98/1767
Hinduja *v.* Asian TV Ltd see Hinduja *v.* Asia TV Ltd
Hines *v.* Birkbeck College [1987] Ch. 457; [1987] 3 W.L.R. 133; [1987] 3 All E.R.
1040; (1987) 131 S.J. 1485, CA; affirming [1986] Ch. 524; [1986] 2 W.L.R. 97;
[1985] 3 All E.R. 156; (1986) 130 S.J. 71, Ch D . . . . *Digested,* 88/**1225**:
Applied, 87/1276, 00/2001: *Doubted,* 86/3466
Hines *v.* Eastern Counties Farmers Cooperative Association Ltd see Sedgwick *v.*
Watney Combe Reid & Co Ltd
Hipperson *v.* Electoral Registration Officer for the District of Newbury [1985] Q.B.
1060; [1985] 3 W.L.R. 61; [1985] 2 All E.R. 456; 83 L.G.R. 638; (1985) 82
L.S.G. 2247; (1985) 129 S.J. 432, CA . . . . *Digested,* 85/**1127**:
Applied, 86/1604, 87/805, 88/809, 98/3007
Hipwood *v.* Gloucester HA [1995] I.C.R. 999; [1995] P.I.Q.R. P447; [1995] 6 Med.
L.R. 187; (1995) 139 S.J.L.B. 67; Times, February 21, 1995, CA . . . . *Digested,* 95/**4120**:
Considered, 98/337, 99/325, 99/326: *Distinguished,* 96/2140
Hirachand Punamchand *v.* Temple [1911] 2 K.B. 330, CA . . . . *Considered,* 98/370:
Distinguished, 97/3032
Hiranand *v.* Harilela (2000-01) 3 I.T.E.L.R. 297, CA (Sing) . . . . *Digested,* 01/**5168**
Hird *v.* Milner (t/a Versatile Ceramics) QBENI 98/0153/1, CA . . . . *Digested,* 99/**555**
Hiro Balani *v.* Spain (A/303-B) (1995) 19 E.H.R.R. 566, ECHR . . . . *Applied,* 99/3128
Hirst (A Minor) *v.* Tameside and Glossop HA (Unreported, January 19, 1998) [*Ex rel.*
Jones Maidment Wilson Solicitors, 5-7 Byrom Street, Manchester] . . . . *Digested,* 98/**1758**
Hirst *v.* Attorney General see R. (on the application of Pearson) *v.* Secretary of State
for the Home Department
Hirst *v.* Etherington [1999] Lloyd's Rep. P.N. 938; (1999) 96(31) L.S.G. 42; (1999)
149 N.L.J. 1110; Times, July 21, 1999 ; Independent, October 4, 1999, CA;
reversing [1998] N.P.C. 35, QBD . . . . *Digested,* 99/**3814**:
Applied, 01/4267
Hirst *v.* Secretary of State for the Home Department see R. *v.* Secretary of State for
the Home Department Ex p. Hirst
Hirst *v.* United Kingdom (40787/98) [2001] Crim. L.R. 919; Times, August 3, 2001,
ECHR . . . . *Digested,* 01/**4573**

Hiscox v. Outhwaite (No.1) [1992] 1 A.C. 562; [1991] 3 W.L.R. 297; [1991] 3 All E.R. 641; [1991] 2 Lloyd's Rep. 435; *Times*, July 29, 1991; *Independent*, July 31, 1991; *Financial Times*, July 31, 1991, HL; affirming [1991] 2 W.L.R. 1321; [1991] 3 All E.R. 124; [1991] 2 Lloyd's Rep. 1; *Times*, March 19, 1991; *Independent*, March 12, 1991; *Financial Times*, March 15, 1991, CA; affirming *Times*, March 7, 1991, QBD . **Digested, 92/169:** *Followed*, 98/771

Hislop (CICA: Quantum: 2000), Re [2001] 4 Q.R. 10, CICA (Bristol) [*Ex rel*. Matthew White, Barrister, St. John's Chambers, Small Street, Bristol] . . . . **Digested, 01/1579**

Hit Bit Software GmbH v. AOL Bertelsmann Online GmbH & Co KG (7 0 3625/98) [2001] E.C.D.R. 27, OLG (Munchen); reversing in part [2001] E.C.D.R. 18, LG (Munchen)

HIT Finance Ltd v. Cohen Arnold & Co [2000] Lloyd's Rep. P.N. 125, CA; reversing [1998] 1 E.G.L.R. 140, QBD . . . . **Digested, 00/4202**

HITACHI MAXELL/Procedural violation (T647/93) [1995] E.P.O.R. 195, EPO (Technical Bd App) . . . . **Considered, 00/3658**

Hitch v. Stone (Inspector of Taxes); *sub nom* Stone (Inspector of Taxes) v. Hitch [2001] EWCA Civ 63; [2001] S.T.C. 214; 73 T.C. 600; [2001] B.T.C. 78; [2001] S.T.I. 104; [2001] N.P.C. 19; *Times*, February 21, 2001, CA; reversing [1999] S.T.C. 431; [1999] B.T.C. 103; [1999] E.G.C.S. 44; [1999] N.P.C. 40; *Times*, April 7, 1999, Ch D . . . . **Digested, 01/5319**

Hitchcock v. Wheeler (Unreported, January 7, 1998), CC (Leicester) [*Ex rel*. Lisa Clarke, Barrister, Clapham Chambers, 21-25 Bedford Road, Clapham, London] . **Digested, 98/1717**

Hitchens v. General Guarantee Corp Ltd; *sub nom* Hichens v. General Guarantee Corp Ltd [2001] EWCA Civ 359; *Times*, March 13, 2001, CA; affirming CO 1997 H160, QBD . . . . **Digested, 01/880**

Hitco 2000 Ltd, Re; *sub nom* Official Receiver v. Cowan [1995] B.C.C. 161; [1995] 2 B.C.L.C. 63, Ch D . . . . **Digested, 96/993:** *Applied*, 00/664

HIV Haemophiliac Litigation, Re [1996] P.I.Q.R. P220; (1998) 41 B.M.L.R. 171; [1996] P.N.L.R. 290; (1990) 140 N.L.J. 1349; *Independent*, October 2, 1990; *Guardian*, September 28, 1990; *Daily Telegraph*, October 11, 1990, CA . . . . **Digested, 90/3249**

Hivac Ltd v. Park Royal Scientific Instruments Ltd [1946] Ch. 169, CA . . . . **Applied, 67/1420,** 82/1091, 00/2132: *Considered*, 69/3573: *Distinguished*, 91/408: *Followed*, 86/1267

HJ Banks & Co Ltd v. British Coal Corp (C128/92) [1994] E.C.R. I-1209; [1994] 5 C.M.L.R. 30; *Times*, May 13, 1994; *Financial Times*, April 19, 1994, ECJ . . . . **Digested, 94/4779:** *Followed*, 01/2472

HJ Banks & Co Ltd v. Coal Authority see Coal Authority v. HJ Banks & Co Ltd

HJ Banks & Co Ltd v. Coal Authority (C390/98) [2001] E.C.R. I-6117; [2001] 3 C.M.L.R. 51, ECJ

HJ Glawe Spiel- und Unterhaltungsgerate Aufstellungsgesellschaft mbH & Co KG v. Finanzamt Hamburg-Barmbek-Uhlenhorst (C38/93) [1994] S.T.C. 543; [1994] E.C.R. I-1679; [1995] 1 C.M.L.R. 70; *Times*, May 26, 1994, ECJ (6th Chamber) . **Digested, 94/4960:** *Considered*, 97/4973, 97/4978, 98/4891

HJ Heinz Co Ltd v. Kenrick [2000] I.C.R. 491; [2000] I.R.L.R. 144, EAT . . . . **Digested, 00/2129:** *Followed*, 00/2127

HL Motorworks (Willesden) v. Alwahbi [1977] R.T.R. 276, CA . . . . **Digested, 77/2021:** *Applied*, 01/1519

HLR v. France (1998) 26 E.H.R.R. 29, ECHR . . . . **Digested, 98/3069**

HM Advocate v. McIntosh (Robert) (No.1); *sub nom* McIntosh, Petitioner; McIntosh (Robert) v. HM Advocate [2001] UKPC D1; [2001] 3 W.L.R. 107; [2001] 2 All E.R. 638; 2001 S.C. (P.C.) 89; 2001 S.L.T. 304; 2001 S.C.C.R. 191; [2001] 2 Cr. App. R. 27; [2001] H.R.L.R. 20; [2001] U.K.H.R.R. 463; (2001) 98(11) L.S.G. 43; (2001) 145 S.J.L.B. 83; 2001 G.W.D. 6-206; *Times*, February 8, 2001; *Independent*, February 16, 2001, PC (UK); reversing 2001 J.C. 78; 2000 S.L.T. 1280; 2000 S.C.C.R. 1017; [2000] U.K.H.R.R. 751; 2000 G.W.D. 33-1284; *Times*, October 31, 2000, HCJ Appeal; reversing 2000 S.L.T. 1233; 2000 G.W.D. 25-937, HCJ . . . . **Digested, 01/6327**

HM Advocate v. Montgomery (David Shields) see Montgomery v. HM Advocate

HM Coroner for Kent v. Terrill [2001] A.C.D. 5, QBD

HM Prison Service v. Johnson; Armitage v. Johnson; Marsden v. Johnson; Johnson v. HM Prison Service [1997] I.C.R. 275; [1997] I.R.L.R. 162; *Times*, December 31, 1996, EAT . . . . **Digested, 97/2242:** *Applied*, 99/2090: *Considered*, 00/2183: *Not followed*, 98/5150

HM Prison Service v. Salmon [2001] I.R.L.R. 425, EAT . . . . **Digested, 01/2312**

HM Stationery Office v. AA Ltd see HM Stationery Office v. Automobile Association Ltd

HM Stationery Office v. Automobile Association Ltd; *sub nom* HM Stationery Office v. AA Ltd [2001] E.C.C. 34; (2000) 23(12) I.P.D. 23100, Ch D . . . . **Digested, 01/3847**

Ho Kok Cheong Ex p. Paribas, Re [2001] B.P.I.R. 278, HC (Sing) . . . . **Digested, 01/3729**

Hoadley v. Edwards [2001] P.N.L.R. 41; [2001] 14 E.G.C.S. 148, Ch D

Hoang v. France (A/243) (1993) 16 E.H.R.R. 53, ECHR . . . . **Digested, 93/2133:** *Applied*, 01/1237

Hoare, Re [1997] B.P.I.R. 683, Ch D . . . . **Digested, 98/3348**

Hoare (Valuation Officer) *v.* National Trust for Places of Historic Interest or Natural Beauty; *sub nom* National Trust for Places of Historic Interest or Natural Beauty *v.* Hoare; National Trust for Places of Historic Interest or Natural Beauty *v.* Spratling (Valuation Officer) (1999) 77 P. & C.R. 366; [1999] 1 E.G.L.R. 155; [1998] R.A. 391; [1998] E.G.C.S. 141; [1998] N.P.C. 139; *Times*, October 16, 1998; *Independent*, October 19, 1998 (C.S.), CA; reversing [1997] 2 E.G.L.R. 229; [1997] R.A. 295, Lands Tr .... *Digested*, 98/**4335**
Hoath *v.* Cripps Harries Hall [1998] B.P.I.R. 342, CA
Hobbs *v.* Marlowe [1978] A.C. 16; [1977] 2 W.L.R. 777; [1977] 2 All E.R. 241; [1977] R.T.R. 253; 121 S.J. 272, HL; affirming (1976) 120 S.J. 838; *Times*, October 27, 1976, CA. .... *Digested*, 77/**433**:
              Considered, 87/2965, 99/533: *Followed*, 86/459: *Referred to*, 92/3419
Hobday *v.* Secretary of State for the Environment (1991) 61 P. & C.R. 225; [1990] J.P.L. 923, CA. .... *Digested*, 91/**3514**:
               Applied, 01/5630: *Considered*, 96/4851
Hobhouse *v.* Hobhouse [1999] 1 F.L.R. 961; [1999] Fam. Law 212, CA .... *Digested*, 99/**2424**
Hobin *v.* Douglas (No.1), *Independent*, October 26, 1998 (C.S.), CA .... *Digested*, 98/**1431**
Hobin *v.* Douglas (No.2) [2000] P.I.Q.R. Q1; (1999) 96(4) L.S.G. 37; (1999) 143 S.J.L.B. 21; *Times*, December 29, 1998; *Independent*, December 14, 1998 (C.S.), CA .... *Digested*, 99/**397**
Hobson *v.* NTL Teeside Ltd see Hobson *v.* NTL Teesside Ltd
Hobson *v.* NTL Teesside Ltd; *sub nom* Hobson *v.* NTL Teeside Ltd; (Unreported, August 16, 2000), CC (Newcastle) [*Ex rel.* David Mason, Barrister, Milburn House Chambers, Floor A, Milburn House, Dean Street, Newcastle-upon-Tyne]. *Digested*, 00/**1611**
Hochstrasser (Inspector of Taxes) *v.* Mayes see Jennings *v.* Kinder (Inspector of Taxes)
Hockenjos *v.* Secretary of State for Social Security [2001] EWCA Civ 624; [2001] 2 C.M.L.R. 51; [2001] I.C.R. 966, CA .... *Digested*, 01/**5054**
Hocsman *v.* Ministre de l'Emploi et de la Solidarite (C238/98) [2000] All E.R. (EC) 899; [2000] E.C.R. I-6623; [2000] 3 C.M.L.R. 1025; [2000] C.E.C. 668, ECJ (5th Chamber) .... *Digested*, 01/**2931**
Hoddle *v.* CCF Construction [1992] 2 All E.R. 550, QBD .... *Digested*, 92/**3415**:
       Applied, 94/2117: *Considered*, 94/3557: *Distinguished*, 99/410:
                               Followed, 00/429
Hodge *v.* Newport BC (2001) 33 H.L.R. 18; [2001] B.L.G.R. 20; [2000] N.P.C. 28, CA .... *Digested*, 01/**3401**
Hodgetts *v.* Chiltern DC; *sub nom* Chiltern DC *v.* Hodgetts [1983] 2 A.C. 120; [1983] 2 W.L.R. 577; [1983] 1 All E.R. 1057; (1983) 147 J.P. 372; (1983) 45 P. & C.R. 402; [1983] J.P.L. 377, HL. .... *Digested*, 83/**3655**:
    Applied, 84/2281, 85/908, 85/2084, 86/199, 86/952: *Considered*, 93/3859,
              00/5467: *Distinguished*, 93/3808, 94/4305
Hodgkinson & Corby Ltd *v.* Wards Mobility Services Ltd (No.1) [1994] 1 W.L.R. 1564; [1995] F.S.R. 169; (1995) 14 Tr. L.R. 79; *Times*, August 3, 1994; *Independent*, October 17, 1994 (C.S.), Ch D .... *Digested*, 95/**4739**:
               Considered, 96/5706: *Referred to*, 98/3516
Hodgkinson & Corby Ltd *v.* Wards Mobility Services Ltd (No.2) [1998] F.S.R. 530, CA; reversing [1997] F.S.R. 178, Ch D .... *Digested*, 98/**518**
Hodgson *v.* Imperial Tobacco Ltd (No.1) [1998] 1 W.L.R. 1056; [1998] 2 All E.R. 673; [1998] 1 Costs L.R. 14; [1999] P.I.Q.R. Q1; (1998) 41 B.M.L.R. 1; (1998) 95(15) L.S.G. 31; (1998) 148 N.L.J. 241; (1998) 142 S.J.L.B. 93; *Times*, February 13, 1998; *Independent*, February 17, 1998, CA .... *Digested*, 98/**415**
Hodgson *v.* Imperial Tobacco Ltd (No.2) [1998] 2 Costs L.R. 27, QBD .... *Digested*, 00/**394**
Hodgson *v.* Imperial Tobacco Ltd (No.3) S97/113-116, QBD .... *Digested*, 99/**459**
Hodgson *v.* Marks [1971] Ch. 892; [1971] 2 W.L.R. 1263; [1971] 2 All E.R. 684; 22 P. & C.R. 586; 115 S.J. 224, CA; reversing [1970] 3 W.L.R. 956; [1970] 3 All E.R. 513; (1970) 21 P. & C.R. 737; 114 S.J. 770, Ch D .... *Digested*, 71/**6487**:
               Applied, 80/1847: *Considered*, 79/1826, 99/4395
Hodgson *v.* Trapp [1989] A.C. 807; [1988] 3 W.L.R. 1281; [1988] 3 All E.R. 870; (1988) 138 N.L.J. Rep. 327; (1988) 132 S.J. 1672, HL; reversing [1988] 1 F.L.R. 69; [1988] Fam. Law 60, QBD. .... *Digested*, 89/**1285**:
   Applied, 91/1501, 00/1461, 00/1471: *Followed*, 90/1718, 90/1718.19, 97/1958,
                                  98/1631
Hoechst AG *v.* Commission of the European Communities (T10/89) see Huls AG *v.* Commission of the European Communities (C199/92 P)
Hoechst AG *v.* DGI 3 I.T.L. Rep. 1, Ct Sup (Arg)
Hoechst AG *v.* Inland Revenue Commissioners (C410/98) see Metallgesellschaft Ltd *v.* Inland Revenue Commissioners (C397/98)
Hoechst Celanese Corp *v.* BP Chemicals Ltd (No.1); Hoechst Celanese Corp *v.* Purolite International Ltd [1999] F.S.R. 319; (1998) 21(10) I.P.D. 21105; *Times*, July 27, 1998, CA; affirming [1997] F.S.R. 547; (1997) 20(5) I.P.D. 20045; *Times*, February 13, 1997, Pat Ct .... *Digested*, 98/**3479**:
                             Considered, 98/3469
Hoechst Celanese Corp *v.* BP Chemicals Ltd (No.2) [1998] F.S.R. 586; *Times*, April 2, 1998, Pat Ct .... *Digested*, 98/**3470**

Hoechst Celanese Corp v. Purolite International Ltd see Hoechst Celanese Corp v. BP
    Chemicals Ltd (No.1)
Hoechst Celanese Corp v BP Chemicals Ltd (Costs) (Unreported, April 21, 1998), Pat Ct
                                       Followed, 00/3673
HOECHST/p-tert.butylbenzaldehyde (T199/84) [2001] E.P.O.R. 4, EPO (Technical Bd
    App). . . . .   *Digested*, 01/**3929**
HOECHST/Pharmaceutical preparation (T01/85) [1999] E.P.O.R. 57, EPO (Technical Bd
    App)
Hoekstra v. HM Advocate (No.3); Van Rijs (Jan) v. HM Advocate (No.3); Van Rijs
    (Ronny) v. HM Advocate (No.3); Van Rijs (Hendrik) v. HM Advocate (No.3)
    2000 J.C. 391; 2000 S.L.T. 605; 2000 S.C.C.R. 367; [2000] H.R.L.R. 410;
    [2000] U.K.H.R.R. 578; 2000 G.W.D. 12-417; *Times*, April 14, 2000, HCJ
    Appeal . . . .   *Digested*, 00/**6092**:
                                             Followed, 01/6249
Hoekstra v. HM Advocate (No.5); Van Rijs (Jan) v. HM Advocate (No.5); Van Rijs
    (Ronny) v. HM Advocate (No.5); Van Rijs (Hendrik) v. HM Advocate (No.5)
    [2001] 1 A.C. 216; [2000] 3 W.L.R. 1817; 2001 S.C. (P.C.) 37; 2001 S.L.T. 28;
    2000 S.C.C.R. 1121; (2000) 144 S.J.L.B. 272; 2000 G.W.D. 40-1486; *Times*,
    October 31, 2000, PC (Sc)   *Digested*, 00/**6057**
Hoever v. Land Nordrhein-Westfalen (C245/94); Zachow v. Land Nordrhein-Westfalen
    (C312/94) [1996] E.C.R. I-4895; [1996] 3 C.M.L.R. 611, ECJ (5th Chamber) . .   *Applied*, 98/4518
Hoey v. Hoey [1984] 1 W.L.R. 464; [1984] 1 All E.R. 177; [1984] Fam. Law 208;
    (1984) 81 L.S.G. 591; (1984) 128 S.J. 132, CA . . . .   *Digested*, 84/**477**:
                                             Applied, 99/4008
Hofer v. Strawson [1999] 2 B.C.L.C. 336; [1999] B.P.I.R. 501; (1999) 96(13) L.S.G.
    31; (1999) 143 S.J.L.B. 95; *Times*, April 17, 1999, Ch D . . . .   *Digested*, 99/**3254**
Hoff v. Filtertechniek Nederland BV; *sub nom* Societe Filtertechniek Nederland BV v.
    Hoff [2001] I.L.Pr. 8, Cass (F); affirming [1998] I.L.Pr. 196, C d'A (Paris)
Hoffmann v. South African Airways 10 B.H.R.C. 571, Const Ct (SA) . . . .   *Digested*, 01/**3455**
Hogefeld v. Germany (35402/97) (2000) 29 E.H.R.R. CD173, ECHR
Hogg v. Maxwell see Maxwell v. Hogg
Hogg Robinson Financial Services Ltd v. Pensions Ombudsman [1998] O.P.L.R. 131,
    Ch D . . . .   *Digested*, 01/**4614**
Hoggett v. Hoggett (1980) 39 P. & C.R. 121, CA . . . .   *Digested*, 80/**1621**:
                             Considered, 87/1762: *Distinguished*, 99/3740
Hoggett v. Knox (Unreported, November 12, 1999), CC (Central London) [*Ex rel.*
    Christopher Heather, Barrister, Francis Taylor Building, Temple, London] . . . .   *Digested*, 00/**3908**
Hoicrest Ltd, Re; *sub nom* Keene v. Martin [2000] 1 W.L.R. 414; [2000] B.C.C. 904;
    [2000] 1 B.C.L.C. 194; (1999) 96(44) L.S.G. 39; (1999) 143 S.J.L.B. 263;
    Times, November 15, 1999 ; *Independent*, January 17, 2000 (C.S.), CA; affirming
    [1998] 2 B.C.L.C. 175, Ch D (Companies Ct) . . . .   *Digested*, 99/**649**
Hoicrest Ltd (Leave to Appeal), Re; *sub nom* Keene v. Martin (Leave to Appeal) [1999]
    2 B.C.L.C. 346, CA . . . .   *Digested*, 99/**601**:
                                  Subsequent proceedings, 99/649
Hoj Pedersen v. Faellesforeningen for Danmarks Brugs-foreninger (C66/96) see Hoj
    Pederson v. Kvickly Skive (C66/96)
Hoj Pederson v. Kvickly Skive (C66/96); *sub nom* Hoj Pedersen v. Faellesforeningen
    for Danmarks Brugs-foreninger (C66/96); Handels-og Kontorfunktionaerernes
    Forbund i Danmark v. Faellesforeningen for Danmarks Brugsforeninger (C66/
    96); Handels-og Kontorfunktionaerernes Forbund i Danmark v. Dansk
    Tandlaegeforening (C66/96); Handels-og Kontorfunktionaerernes Forbund i
    Danmark v. Dansk Handel & Service (C66/96) [1999] All E.R. (EC) 138; [1998]
    E.C.R. I-7327; [1999] 2 C.M.L.R. 326; [1999] C.E.C. 26; [1999] I.R.L.R. 55;
    Times, December 1, 1998, ECJ (6th Chamber) . . . .   *Digested*, 99/**2066**
Hokkanen v. Finland (A/299-A) [1996] 1 F.L.R. 289; [1995] 2 F.C.R. 320; (1995) 19
    E.H.R.R. 139; [1996] Fam. Law 22, ECHR . . . .   *Digested*, 95/**2660**:
                                         Applied, 00/3232
Holaw (470) Ltd v. Stockton Estates Ltd (2001) 81 P. & C.R. 29; [2000] E.G.C.S. 89,
    Ch D . . . .   *Digested*, 01/**4867**
Holbeck Hall Hotel Ltd v. Scarborough BC [2000] Q.B. 836; [2000] 2 W.L.R. 1396;
    [2000] 2 All E.R. 705; [2000] B.L.R. 109; (2000) 2 T.C.L.R. 865; 69 Con. L.R.
    1; [2000] B.L.G.R. 412; [2000] E.G.C.S. 29; (2000) 97(11) L.S.G. 36; (2000)
    97(9) L.S.G. 44; (2000) 150 N.L.J. 307; (2000) 144 S.J.L.B. 109; [2000]
    N.P.C. 17; *Times*, March 2, 2000, CA; reversing 57 Con. L.R. 113; [1997] 2
    E.G.L.R. 213; [1997] N.P.C. 141; *Times*, October 15, 1997; *Independent*, October
    13, 1997 (C.S.), QBD (OR) . . . .   *Digested*, 00/**5121**
Holden v. Lancaster Magistrates Court (1998) 162 J.P. 789; [1998] C.O.D. 429;
    (1998) 162 J.P.N. 883; *Times*, October 2, 1998, QBD . . . .   *Digested*, 98/**208**
Holdenhurst Securities Plc v. Cohen [2001] 1 B.C.L.C. 460, Ch D . . . .   *Digested*, 01/**3710**
Holder v. Seath (Unreported, May 10, 1999), CC (Bristol) [*Ex rel.* Gabriel Farmer,
    Barrister, Guildhall Chambers, 22-26 Broad Street, Bristol] . . . .   *Digested*, 99/**2464**
Holder v. Supperstone [2000] 1 All E.R. 473; [1999] E.G.C.S. 145; (1999) 96(47)
    L.S.G. 34; *Independent*, December 7, 1999, Ch D . . . .   *Digested*, 00/**3458**
Holding & Barnes Plc v. Hill House Hammond Ltd CH 1998 H 6870, Ch D . . . .   *Digested*, 01/**4160**

Holding & Barnes Plc v. Hill House Hammond Ltd (Preliminary Issue) [2001] EWCA Civ
1334, CA; affirming [2000] L. & T.R. 428, Ch D
Holding & Management Ltd v. Property Holding & Investment Trust Plc [1989] 1 W.L.R.
1313; [1990] 1 All E.R. 938; (1989) 21 H.L.R. 596; [1990] 05 E.G. 75; (1989)
86(43) L.S.G. 38; (1990) 134 S.J. 262, CA; affirming [1988] 1 W.L.R. 644;
[1988] 2 All E.R. 702; [1988] 50 E.G. 45; (1988) 85(11) L.S.G. 43, Ch D . . . . .   *Digested*, 90/**2823**:
                                 Considered, 93/2463, 94/2819, 95/3079: *Followed*, 00/3947
Holdingmaatschappij de Telegraaf NV v. Nederlandse Omroep Stichting see Nederlandse
Omroep Stichting v. Holdingmaatschappij de Telegraaf NV
Hole & Pugsley v. Sumption (2001) 151 N.L.J. 1851, Ch D
Holgate v. Lancashire Mental Hospitals Board [1937] 4 All E.R. 19, Assizes (Liverpool) .   *Referred to*, 99/3963
Holgate-Mohammed v. Duke; *sub nom* Mohammed-Holgate v. Duke [1984] A.C. 437;
[1984] 2 W.L.R. 660; [1984] 1 All E.R. 1054; (1984) 79 Cr. App. R. 120; [1984]
Crim. L.R. 418, HL; affirming [1984] Q.B. 209; [1983] 3 W.L.R. 598; [1983] 3
All E.R. 526; (1984) 78 Cr. App. R. 65; [1983] Crim. L.R. 734, CA . . . .   *Digested*, 84/**147**:
                               Considered, 89/800, 90/864, 92/682.a, 01/4790
Holiday Inns (UK) Ltd v. Customs and Excise Commissioners [1993] V.A.T.T.R. 321, VAT
Tr (Manchester) . . . .   *Digested*, 94/**4599**:
                                          Considered, 98/4956
Holland v. Glendale Industries Ltd [1998] I.C.R. 493; *Times*, May 28, 1998, EAT . . . . .   *Digested*, 98/**2102**:
                                     Distinguished, 99/2091
Holland v. Hoechst Trespaphan [2001] 6 Q.R. 6, CC (Bristol) [*Ex rel.* Jonathan Clarke,
Barrister, Old Square Chambers, 47 Corn Street, Bristol] . . . .   *Digested*, 01/**1609**
Holland v. Lampen-Wolfe [2000] 1 W.L.R. 1573; [2000] 3 All E.R. 833; [2001] I.L.Pr.
49; [2000] U.K.H.R.R. 734; (2000) 97(32) L.S.G. 37; (2000) 144 S.J.L.B. 223;
Times, July 27, 2000; *Independent*, October 23, 2000 (C.S), HL; affirming
[1999] 1 W.L.R. 188; (1998) 95(36) L.S.G. 32; (1998) 142 S.J.L.B. 227; *Times*,
August 29, 1998, CA . . . .   *Digested*, 00/**3819**
Holland v. Newbury see Harvard Securities Ltd (In Liquidation), Re
Holland v. Russell (1861) 1 B. & S. 424, Ex Ct . . . .   *Applied*, 98/2298
Holland v. Ski Llandudno Ltd (Unreported, January 16, 1998), CC (Crewe) [*Ex rel.*
Paul Dowle, Solicitor, Dibb Lupton Alsop] . . . .   *Digested*, 98/**596**
Holland Colombo Trading Society Ltd v. Alawdeen (Segu Mohamed Khaja) [1954] 2
Lloyd's Rep. 45, PC (Cey) . . . .   *Digested*, 54/**2974**:
                                    Applied, 58/548, 58/3038, 99/4411
Holland Dredging (UK) Ltd v. Dredging & Construction Co 37 B.L.R. 1; 14 Con. L.R. 30,
CA . . . .   *Digested*, 88/**217**:
                                         Considered, 99/235
Holleran v. Daniel Thwaites Plc [1989] 2 C.M.L.R. 917, Ch D . . . .   *Digested*, 91/**3796**:
                                         Followed, 99/3498
Holley v. Smyth [1998] Q.B. 726; [1998] 2 W.L.R. 742; [1998] 1 All E.R. 853; [1998]
E.M.L.R. 133; (1998) 95(2) L.S.G. 23; (1998) 142 S.J.L.B. 35; *Times*, December
20, 1997, CA . . . .   *Digested*, 98/**1773**
Hollicourt (Contracts) Ltd (In Liquidation) v. Bank of Ireland; *sub nom* Bank of Ireland v.
Hollicourt (Contracts) Ltd; Claughton (Liquidator of Hollicourt (Contracts) Ltd)
v. Bank of Ireland [2001] Ch. 555; [2001] 2 W.L.R. 290; [2001] 1 All E.R. 289;
[2001] 1 All E.R. (Comm) 357; [2001] Lloyd's Rep. Bank. 6; [2000] B.C.L.C.
1210; [2001] 1 B.C.L.C. 233; [2001] B.P.I.R. 47; (2000) 97(45) L.S.G. 41; *Times*,
November 1, 2000; *Independent*, October 24, 2000, CA; reversing [2000] 1
W.L.R. 895; [2000] 2 All E.R. 45; [2000] Lloyd's Rep. Bank. 21; [2000] B.C.C.
237; [2000] 1 B.C.L.C. 171; (1999) 96(48) L.S.G. 39; (2000) 144 S.J.L.B. 24;
Times, November 30, 1999 ; *Independent*, January 31, 2000 (C.S.), Ch D . . . . .   *Digested*, 00/**3464**:
                                      Distinguished, 00/3465
Holliday (A Bankrupt), Re [1981] Ch. 405; [1981] 2 W.L.R. 996; [1980] 3 All E.R. 385;
(1980) 77 L.S.G. 340; 125 S.J. 411, CA . . . .   *Digested*, 80/**1406**:
          Considered, 93/1846, 94/3303, 95/2214: *Distinguished*, 91/261, 98/3291:
                                       Followed, 84/1696
Hollins v. Verney (1883-84) L.R. 13 Q.B.D. 304; (1884) 48 J.P. 580; (1884) 53 L.J.
Q.B. 430; (1884) 51 L.T. 753, CA; affirming (1882-83) L.R. 11 Q.B.D. 715, QBD .   *Applied*, 68/1313:
                                         Considered, 00/4641
Hollis v. Dudley MBC see R. v. Dudley Magistrates Court Ex p. Hollis
Hollis & Co v. Stocks [2000] U.K.C.L.R. 658; [2000] I.R.L.R. 712, CA . . . .   *Digested*, 00/**2203**
Hollister v. National Farmers Union [1979] I.C.R. 542; [1979] I.R.L.R. 238, CA;
reversing [1978] I.C.R. 712; [1978] I.R.L.R. 161, EAT . . . .   *Digested*, 79/**1029**:
                    Applied, 80/972, 80/991, 80/1050, 83/1344: *Considered*, 85/1271, 91/1689,
                                          98/2239
Holloway (CICB: Quantum: 2000), Re [2000] 4 Q.R. 5, CICB (London) [*Ex rel.* Katharine
Hogg, Barrister, 1 Crown Office Row, Temple, London] . . . .   *Digested*, 00/**1553**
Holloway Tenant Cooperative Housing Association Ltd v. Islington LBC 57 Con. L.R. 160,
QBD (OR) . . . .   *Digested*, 98/**4052**
Holly v. Inspector of Taxes [2000] S.T.C. (S.C.D.) 50; [2000] S.T.I. 161, Sp Comm . . . . .   *Digested*, 00/**5051**
Holmaengen Trust, Re (1998-99) 1 I.T.E.L.R. 901, HC (IoM)

Holman *v.* Cooperative Wholesale Society Ltd; *sub nom* Durham CC *v.* Cooperative Wholesale Society Ltd (2000) 164 J.P. 699; (2000) 164 J.P.N. 958; *Independent*, July 10, 2000 (C.S), QBD

Holman *v.* HH Martyn & Co see Denley's Trust Deed, Re

Holmes, Re [2000] Pens. L.R. 203, Pensions Ombudsman . . . . *Digested*, 00/**4359**

Holmes (ClCB: Quantum: 1998), Re (1998) 98(6) Q.R. 4, ClCB (Nottingham) . . . . *Digested*, 98/**1552**

Holmes *v.* Bangladesh Biman Corp [1989] A.C. 1112; [1989] 2 W.L.R. 481; [1989] 1 All E.R. 852; [1989] 1 Lloyd's Rep. 444; (1989) 133 S.J. 291, HL; reversing [1988] 2 Lloyd's Rep. 120; [1988] 1 F.T.L.R. 534, CA; affirming [1987] 2 Lloyd's Rep. 192, QBD. . . . . *Digested*, 89/**253**: *Applied*, 01/5386

Holmes *v.* Barnes (Unreported, February 26, 2001), CC (Bristol) [*Ex rel.* James Hassall, Barrister, Guildhall Chambers, 22-26 Broad Street, Bristol] . . . . *Digested*, 01/**585**

Holmes *v.* Barnes (Default Judgment) (Unreported, May 4, 2001), CC (Bristol) [*Ex rel.* James Hassall, Barrister, Guildhall Chambers, 22-26 Broad Street, Bristol] . . . . . . *Digested*, 01/**546**

Holmes *v.* Campbell; *sub nom* Environment Agency *v.* Campbell (1998) 162 J.P. 655; (1998) 162 J.P.N. 523; (1998) 95(23) L.S.G. 26; (1998) 142 S.J.L.B. 171; [1999] Env. L.R. D4; *Times*, May 18, 1998, QBD . . . . *Digested*, 98/**1040**

Holmes (t/a The Chicken Shop) *v.* Customs and Excise Commissioners [2000] S.T.I. 44, V&DTr

Holmes *v.* McMullan; *sub nom* Ratcliffe (Deceased), Re [1999] S.T.C. 262; [1999] B.T.C. 8017; (1999) 96(11) L.S.G. 70; *Times*, March 19, 1999, Ch D . . . . *Digested*, 99/**4741**

Holmes (t/a BR&M Holmes) *v.* Ministry of Agriculture, Fisheries and Food [2000] E.H.L.R. 369, QBD . . . . *Digested*, 00/**2677**

Holmes-More *v.* Tenon Ltd [2001] 3 Q.R. 18, QBD [*Ex rel.* Christopher Russell, Barrister, 2 Temple Gardens, London] . . . . *Digested*, 01/**1717**

Holt *v.* Faulks [2001] B.C.C. 50; [2000] 2 B.C.L.C. 816, Ch D . . . . *Digested*, 01/**750**

Holt *v.* Payne Skillington 77 B.L.R. 51; 49 Con. L.R. 99; [1996] P.N.L.R. 179; [1995] E.G.C.S. 201; (1996) 93(2) L.S.G. 29; (1996) 140 S.J.L.B. 30; [1995] N.P.C. 202; *Times*, December 22, 1995, CA. . . . . *Digested*, 96/**4531**: *Considered*, 98/795

Holt *v.* Surrey Heath BC (Unreported, January 9, 2000), CC (Kingston on Thames) [*Ex rel.* David Platt, Barrister, Crown Office Chambers, 1 Paper Buildings, Temple, London] . . . . *Digested*, 01/**4499**

Holtby *v.* Brigham & Cowan (Hull) Ltd [2000] 3 All E.R. 421; [2000] I.C.R. 1086; [2000] P.I.Q.R. Q293; [2000] Lloyd's Rep. Med. 254; (2000) 97(19) L.S.G. 44; (2000) 150 N.L.J. 544; (2000) 144 S.J.L.B. 212; *Times*, April 12, 2000, CA. . . . . *Digested*, 00/**5114**: *Applied*, 01/4448

Holtom *v.* Barnet LBC [1999] Ed. C.R. 740; [1999] E.L.R. 255, CA. . . . . *Digested*, 99/**1765**

Holub *v.* Secretary of State for the Home Department see R. (on the application of Holub) *v.* Secretary of State for the Home Department

Holy Cross, Pershore, Re [2001] 3 W.L.R. 1521, Cons Ct (Worcester)

Holy Monasteries *v.* Greece (Art.50) (1998) 25 E.H.R.R. 640, ECHR . . . . *Digested*, 98/**3079**

Holywell Union *v.* Halkyn District Mines Drainage Co [1895] A.C. 117, HL. . . . . *Applied*, 61/7469:
Cited, 01/4821: *Considered*, 88/3011

Homburg Houtimport BV *v.* Agrosin Private Ltd (The Starsin); Owners of Cargo Lately Laden on Board the Starsin *v.* Owners of the Starsin; Hunter Timber Ltd *v.* Agrosin Private Ltd [2001] EWCA Civ 56; [2001] 1 All E.R. (Comm) 455; [2001] 1 Lloyd's Rep. 437; [2001] C.L.C. 696, CA; reversing in part [1999] 2 All E.R. (Comm) 591; [2000] 1 Lloyd's Rep. 85; [1999] C.L.C. 1769, QBD (Comm Ct) . . . . *Digested*, 01/**4907**: *Applied*, 00/4679

Home & Colonial Stores Ltd *v.* Colls see Colls *v.* Home & Colonial Stores Ltd

Home Brewery Co *v.* Davis (William) & Co (Loughborough) see Home Brewery Co *v.* William Davis & Co (Leicester)

Home Brewery Co *v.* William Davis & Co (Leicester); *sub nom* Home Brewery Co *v.* William Davis & Co (Loughborough); Home Brewery Plc *v.* William Davis & Co (Loughborough) Ltd; Home Brewery Co *v.* Davis (William) & Co (Loughborough) [1987] Q.B. 339; [1987] 2 W.L.R. 117; [1987] 1 All E.R. 637; (1987) 84 L.S.G. 657; (1987) 131 S.J. 102; *Times*, August 13, 1986, QBD . . . . . . *Digested*, 87/**2759**.**a**: *Approved*, 99/4366

Home Brewery Co *v.* William Davis & Co (Loughborough) see Home Brewery Co *v.* William Davis & Co (Leicester)

Home Brewery Plc *v.* William Davis & Co (Loughborough) Ltd see Home Brewery Co *v.* William Davis & Co (Leicester)

Home Office *v.* Coyne; *sub nom* Coyne *v.* Home Office [2000] I.C.R. 1443; [2000] I.R.L.R. 838, CA; reversing EAT/244/97, EAT . . . . *Digested*, 01/**2316**

Home Office v. Dorset Yacht Co Ltd [1970] A.C. 1004; [1970] 2 W.L.R. 1140; [1970] 2
All E.R. 294; [1970] 1 Lloyd's Rep. 453; 114 S.J. 375, HL; affirming [1969] 2
Q.B. 412; [1969] 2 W.L.R. 1008; [1969] 2 All E.R. 564; 113 S.J. 227, CA;
affirming 113 S.J. 57; *Times*, December 20, 1968, QBD . . . . *Digested*, 70/**1849**:
　　　　　　　　　　Applied, 71/7843, 72/1104, 72/2352, 72/2532, 77/2030, 78/2068, 78/3250,
　　　　　　　　　　78/3606, 79/1865, 81/1859, 81/3409, 82/4055, 83/2531, 84/2298,
　　　　　　　　　　95/3730: *Approved*, 73/2308: *Considered*, 79/1866, 82/2126, 82/4057,
　　　　　　　　　　83/2538, 85/3549, 86/4338, 87/2580, 87/2597, 87/4737, 88/2435,
　　　　　　　　　　89/1286, 95/3452, 95/3681: *Distinguished*, 83/2746, 87/2857, 93/2958,
　　　　　　　　　　94/3384, 98/3938: *Followed*, 00/6585: *Referred to*, 72/2528, 73/2306,
　　　　　　　　　　75/2324, 79/1884
Homebase Ltd v. Allied Dunbar Assurance Plc see Allied Dunbar Assurance Plc v.
　　Homebase Ltd
Homepower Stores Ltd, Re see Powerstore (Trading) Ltd, Re
Homer Burgess Ltd v. Chirex (Annan) Ltd 2000 S.L.T. 277; [2000] B.L.R. 124; 71 Con.
　　L.R. 245; 1999 G.W.D. 38-1843; 1999 G.W.D. 38-1844; *Times*, January 25,
　　2000, OH . . . . *Digested*, 00/**5979**:
　　　　　　　　　　　　　　　　　　　　　　　　　　　Followed, 01/859
Homes v. Smith [2000] Lloyd's Rep. Bank. 139, CA . . . . *Digested*, 00/**4621**
Homestead Finance Ltd v. Warriner (Unreported, July 21, 1997), CC (Dewsbury) [*Ex rel.*
　　Nicholas Hill, Barrister, 6 Park Square, Leeds] . . . . *Digested*, 97/**961**:
　　　　　　　　　　Considered, 99/4387: *Not applied*, 98/2495: *Not followed*, 99/2507
Hone (A Bankrupt), Re; *sub nom* Trustee Ex p. v. Kensington BC [1951] Ch. 85; [1950]
　　2 All E.R. 716; 66 T.L.R. (Pt. 2) 350; 114 J.P. 495; 43 R. & I.T. 608, Ch D . . . . . . *Digested*, 47-51/**706**:
　　　　　　　　　　　　　　　　　　　　　　Considered, 85/1775: *Doubted*, 00/4621
Hone v. Going Places Leisure Travel Ltd [2001] EWCA Civ 947; *Times*, August 6, 2001;
　　Daily Telegraph, June 19, 2001, CA; affirming MA993390, QBD . . . . *Digested*, 01/**4284**
Honeychurch v. McKenna (Inspector of Taxes) [1997] R.V.R. 270, Lands Tr . . . . *Digested*, 98/**4612**
Hong Kong and Shanghai Banking Corp v. Kloeckner & Co AG [1990] 2 Q.B. 514;
　　[1990] 3 W.L.R. 634; [1989] 3 All E.R. 513; [1989] 2 Lloyd's Rep 323, QBD
　　(Comm Ct) . . . . *Digested*, 91/**510**:
　　　　　　　　　　　　　　　　　　Applied, 98/3680: *Followed*, 96/2782
Hong Kong and Shanghai Banking Corp v. Simon [2000] B.P.I.R. 754, US Ct
Hong Kong and Shanghai Banking Corp Ltd v. GD Trade Co Ltd [1998] C.L.C. 238, CA　　*Digested*, 98/**287**:
　　　　　　　　　　　　　　　　　　　　　　　　　　Followed, 98/2488
Hong Kong Borneo Services Co v. Pilcher [1992] 2 Lloyd's Rep. 593, QBD (Comm Ct)　　*Digested*, 93/**3611**:
　　　　　　　　　　　　　　　　　　　　　　　　　　　Applied, 99/3426
Hong Kong Special Administrative Region v. Ng Kung Siu 8 B.H.R.C. 244, CFA (HK);
　　reversing 6 B.H.R.C. 591, CA (HK) . . . . *Digested*, 00/**3186**
Hongkong Bank of Canada v. Phillips [1998] Lloyd's Rep. Bank. 343, QB (Man) . . . . . . *Digested*, 99/**274**
Hongkong Fir Shipping Co Ltd v. Kawasaki Kisen Kaisha Ltd (The Hongkong Fir)
　　[1962] 2 Q.B. 26; [1962] 2 W.L.R. 474; [1962] 1 All E.R. 474; [1961] 2 Lloyd's
　　Rep. 478; (1961) 106 S.J. 35, CA; affirming [1961] 2 W.L.R. 716; [1961] 2 All
　　E.R. 257; [1961] 1 Lloyd's Rep. 159; 105 S.J. 347, QBD (Comm Ct) . . . . *Digested*, 62/**2838**:
　　　　　　　　　　Applied, 71/1838, 75/3041, 78/2636, 79/2387, 99/3700, 00/874, 00/899:
　　　　　　　　　　Considered, 67/1833, 68/1777, 69/490, 70/362, 74/3426, 80/2393, 99/838,
　　　　　　　　　　00/3532: *Distinguished*, 66/1818, 83/262: *Explained*, 81/2433
Honourable Society of the Middle Temple v. Lloyds Bank Plc [1999] 1 All E.R. (Comm.)
　　193; [1999] Lloyd's Rep. Bank. 50; [1999] C.L.C. 664; *Times*, February 8,
　　1999, QBD (Comm Ct) . . . . *Digested*, 99/**276**
Hood v. United Kingdom (2000) 29 E.H.R.R. 365; *Times*, March 11, 1999, ECHR . . . . . . *Digested*, 99/**3090**:
　　　　　　　　　　　　　　　　　　　　　　　　　　　Applied, 00/3214
Hood Sailmakers Ltd v. Berthom Boat Co Ltd, *Independent*, May 10, 1999 (C.S.), CA
Hood Sailmakers Ltd v. Berthon Boat Co Ltd (Permission to Appeal) (2001) 81 P. &
　　C.R. D7, CA
HOOGOVENS/Admissibility (T118/95) [1999] E.P.O.R. 467, EPO (Technical Bd App) . . 　*Digested*, 00/**3613**
Hook v. First Choice Holiday & Flights Ltd (Unreported, September 30, 1998), CC
　　(Harrogate) [*Ex rel.* Arun Katyr, Barrister, 2 Kings Bench Walk Chambers, Temple,
　　London] . . . . *Digested*, 98/**1426**
Hook v. Honeywell FM Ltd (Unreported, December 22, 2000), CC (Bristol) [*Ex rel.*
　　Marianna Patane, Barrister, Farrar's Building, Temple, London] . . . . *Digested*, 01/**1667**
Hooker v. WJ Adams Estates Pty (1977) 138 C.L.R. 52; (1977) 51 A.L.J.R. 413, HC
　　(Aus) . . . . *Digested*, 79/**32**:
　　　　　　　　　　　　　　　　　　　　　　　　　　　Applied, 00/3520
Hooper, Re see Banco de Portugal v. Waddell
Hooper (t/a Masterclass) v. Customs and Excise Commissioners [2000] S.T.I. 1724,
　　V&DTr
Hooper v. Fynmores (A Firm) [2001] W.T.L.R. 1019; (2001) 98(26) L.S.G. 45; (2001)
　　145 S.J.L.B. 156; *Times*, July 19, 2001, Ch D . . . . *Digested*, 01/**4524**
Hooper v. Gorvin [2001] W.T.L.R. 575; [2001] 3 E.G.C.S. 130; [2000] N.P.C. 140,
　　Ch D . . . . *Digested*, 01/**2435**
Hooper v. Swansea City and County Council [2001] R.V.R. 153, Lands Tr . . . . *Digested*, 01/**4674**
Hooper v. Young [1998] Lloyd's Rep. Med. 61, CA; reversing (Unreported, November
　　9, 1994), QBD . . . . *Digested*, 96/**4461**

Hoover Ltd v. Depeazer (Unreported, January 19, 1998), CC (Altrincham) [Ex rel. Colemans Solicitors, Elisabeth House, 16 St Peter's Square, Manchester] . . . . . . *Digested,* 99/**444**
Hope v. Premierpace (Europe) Ltd [1999] B.P.I.R. 695, Ch D . . . . *Digested,* 99/**3233**
Hopes (Heathrow) Ltd, Re; *sub nom* Secretary of State for Trade and Industry v. Dyer [2001] 1 B.C.L.C. 575, Ch D (Companies Ct) . . . . *Digested,* 01/**714**
Hopewell Project Management Ltd v. Ewbank Preece Ltd [1998] 1 Lloyd's Rep. 448, QBD . . . . *Digested,* 98/**3377**
Hopewell-Smith v. Customs and Excise Commissioners [2000] S.T.I. 1534, V&DTr
Hopkins v. Clarke (Unreported, July 7, 1999), CC (Trowbridge) [Ex rel. Scott Rees & Co Solicitors, Centaur House, Gardiners Place, Skelmersdale, Lancashire] . . . . . *Digested,* 99/**2458**
Hopkins v. Mackenzie [1995] P.I.Q.R. P43; [1995] 6 Med. L.R. 26; [2001] Lloyd's Rep. P.N. 600; (1994) 91(45) L.S.G. 38; (1994) 138 S.J.L.B. 222; *Times,* November 3, 1994; *Independent,* October 27, 1994, CA . . . . *Digested,* 94/**2912**: *Considered,* 98/4021
Hopkins v. National Power Plc (C18/94); *sub nom* Hopkins v. Powergen Plc (C18/94) [1996] E.C.R. I-2281; [1996] 4 C.M.L.R. 745; [1996] C.E.C. 939, ECJ (6th Chamber) [1994] 1 C.M.L.R. 147; [1995] E.C.C. 392, QBD . . . . *Followed,* 01/2472
Hopkins v. Powergen Plc (C18/94) see Hopkins v. National Power Plc (C18/94)
Hopkinson v. Tupper (Unreported, January 30, 1997), CA. . . . . *Distinguished,* 00/4656
Hopu v. France 3 B.H.R.C. 597, UN HRC . . . . *Digested,* 98/**3153**
Horizon Technologies International Ltd v. Lucky Wealth Consultants Ltd [1992] 1 W.L.R. 24; [1992] 1 All E.R. 469; (1992) 89(2) L.S.G. 32; (1991) 135 S.J.L.B. 204; *Times,* November 21, 1991, PC (HK) . . . . *Digested,* 92/**3622**: *Followed,* 98/419
HORIZON Trade Mark; *sub nom* British-American Tobacco (Holdings) Ltd v. Fabriques de Tabac Reunies [1999] E.T.M.R. 32, OHIM (Opposition Div) . . . . *Digested,* 99/**3575**
Horn v. Sunderland Corp [1941] 2 K.B. 26, CA. . . . . *Applied,* 57/487, 65/510, 85/3398, 86/350, 91/453: *Approved,* 67/521: *Considered,* 55/381, 69/433, 78/272, 82/355, 84/341.1, 88/2729, 90/582, 90/587, 99/4357: *Followed,* 57/476, 60/455
Hornal v. Neuberger Products [1957] 1 Q.B. 247; [1956] 3 W.L.R. 1034; [1956] 3 All E.R. 970; 100 S.J. 915, CA . . . . *Digested,* 56/**3686**: *Applied,* 64/3808, 66/3592, 67/3754, 68/1689, 90/674, 91/522, 92/3224: *Considered,* 69/3342, 86/2595, 87/2937, 87/3162, 92/1533, 93/708, 94/4299, 01/2549: *Referred to,* 99/583, 99/2109
Horne (A Bankrupt), Re; *sub nom* Dacorum BC v. Horne; Horne v. Dacorum BC [2000] 4 All E.R. 550; [2000] B.P.I.R. 1047; *Times,* June 14, 2000; *Independent,* June 7, 2000, CA; reversing [1999] B.P.I.R. 898, Ch D . . . . *Digested,* 00/**3449**
Horne v. Dacorum BC see Horne (A Bankrupt), Re
Horne v. Prescot (No.1) Ltd (1999) 99(2) Q.R. 6, MCLC [Ex rel. Berrymans Lace Mawer Solicitors, Salisbury House, London Wall, London] . . . . *Digested,* 99/**1540**
Horne v. Smith (Unreported, January 30, 2001), CC (Birmingham) [Ex rel. Matthew Brunning, Barrister, 5 Fountain Court, Steelhouse Lane, Birmingham] . . . . *Digested,* 01/**542**
Horne Engineering Co Ltd v. Reliance Water Controls Ltd [2000] F.S.R. 90; (1999) 22(9) I.P.D. 22081, Pat Ct . . . . *Digested,* 00/**3679**
Horne-Roberts v. Smithkline Beecham Plc; *sub nom* MMR/MR Vaccine Litigation; H (A Child) v. Merk & Co Inc; Smithkline Beecham Plc v. H (A Child); H (A Child) v. Merck & Co Inc; H (A Child) v. Smithkline Beecham Plc [2001] EWCA Civ 2006, CA; affirming [2001] C.P. Rep. 80, QBD . . . . *Digested,* 01/**595**
Hornsby v. Clark Kenneth Leventhal [1998] P.N.L.R. 635, CA . . . . *Digested,* 98/**3951**
Hornsby v. Clark Kenneth Leventhal (Taxation of Costs) [2000] 4 All E.R. 567; [2000] 2 Costs L.R. 295; (2000) 150 N.L.J. 1338, QBD. . . . . *Digested,* 01/**457**
Hornsby v. Greece (1997) 24 E.H.R.R. 250; [1998] E.L.R. 365, ECHR . . . . *Digested,* 97/**2810**
Horrill v. Cooper (2000) 80 P. & C.R. D16, CA; affirming (1999) 78 P. & C.R. 336; [1998] E.G.C.S. 151, Ch D . . . . *Digested,* 00/**4651**
Horrocks v. Broome; *sub nom* Broome (A Debtor), Re; Thompson v. Broome [2000] B.C.C. 257; [1999] 1 B.C.L.C. 356; [1999] B.P.I.R. 66, Ch D . . . . *Digested,* 99/**3343**
Horsfall v. Haywards; *sub nom* Horsfall v. Haywards [1999] 1 F.L.R. 1182; [1999] Lloyd's Rep. P.N. 332; [1999] P.N.L.R. 583; [2000] W.T.L.R. 29; [1999] Fam. Law 383; (1999) 96(10) L.S.G. 31; (1999) 143 S.J.L.B. 66; [1999] N.P.C. 25; *Times,* March 11, 1999, CA . . . . *Digested,* 99/**4045**
Horsfall v. Haywards see Horsefall v. Haywards
Horsham v. United Kingdom (23390/94) see Sheffield (Kristina) v. United Kingdom (22885/93)
Horsham DC v. Priest (2001) 16 P.A.D. 38, Planning Inspector
Horsham DC v. Secretary of State for the Environment and Margram Plc (1992) 63 P. & C.R. 219; [1992] 1 P.L.R. 81; [1992] J.P.L. 334; [1992] C.O.D. 84; [1991] E.G.C.S. 84, CA; reversing [1991] C.O.D. 343, QBD . . . . *Digested,* 92/**4397**: *Applied,* 92/4268: *Distinguished,* 91/3489: *Referred to,* 00/4520
Horsham DC v. St Mary's, Billingshurst (Vicar and Churchwardens) (2000) 15 P.A.D. 688, Planning Inspector

Horvath v. Secretary of State for the Home Department [2001] 1 A.C. 489; [2000] 3
    W.L.R. 379; [2000] 3 All E.R. 577; [2000] Imm. A.R. 552; [2000] I.N.L.R. 239;
    (2000) 150 N.L.J. 1075; *Times*, July 7, 2000; *Independent*, July 11, 2000, HL;
    affirming [2000] Imm. A.R. 205; [2000] I.N.L.R. 15; (2000) 97(1) L.S.G. 24;
    (2000) 144 S.J.L.B. 33; *Times*, December 8, 1999, CA; affirming [1999] Imm.
    A.R. 121; [1999] I.N.L.R. 7, IAT . . . . *Digested*, 00/**3319**:
                      Applied, 00/3316: *Considered*, 00/3306, 01/3642
Hospital Plan Insurance Services Ltd v. Persaud (Valuation Officer) [1998] 3 E.G.L.R.
    189; [1998] R.A. 230, LandsTr . . . . *Digested*, 98/**4317**
Hossack v. General Dental Council (1998) 40 B.M.L.R. 97; (1997) 141 S.J.L.B. 100;
    Times, April 22, 1997, PC (UK) . . . . *Digested*, 97/**3635**
Hostgilt Ltd v. Megahart Ltd [1999] S.T.C. 141; [1999] B.T.C. 5057; [1999] B.V.C. 78;
    (1999) 77 P. & C.R. D34; *Times*, January 5, 1999, Ch D . . . . *Digested*, 99/**4969**
Hotel Services Ltd v. Hilton International Hotels (UK) Ltd (Leave to Appeal) LTA 98/
    6757/1, CA . . . . *Digested*, 99/**850**
Hotel Services Ltd v. Hilton International Hotels (UK) Ltd [2000] 1 All E.R. (Comm)
    750; [2000] B.L.R. 235, CA . . . . *Digested*, 00/**884**
Hotson v. East Berkshire HA; *sub nom* Hotson v. Fitzgerald [1987] A.C. 750; [1987] 3
    W.L.R. 232; [1987] 2 All E.R. 909; [1955-95] P.N.L.R. 330; [1987] 84 L.S.G.
    2365; (1987) 131 S.J. 975, HL; reversing [1987] 2 W.L.R. 287; [1987] 1 All E.R.
    210; (1987) 84 L.S.G. 37; (1986) 136 N.L.J. 1163; (1986) 130 S.J. 925, CA;
    affirming [1985] 1 W.L.R. 1036; [1985] 3 All E.R. 167; (1985) 82 L.S.G. 2818;
    (1985) 129 S.J. 558, QBD . . . . *Digested*, 87/**2604**:
              Applied, 96/4457, 00/4192: *Considered*, 94/1491, 94/1535, 00/4264
Hotson v. Fitzgerald see Hotson v. East Berkshire HA
Hough v. Chief Constable of Staffordshire [2001] EWCA Civ 39; (2001) 98(14) L.S.G.
    41; *Times*, February 14, 2001, CA . . . . *Digested*, 01/**4780**
Hough v. P&O Containers Ltd [1999] Q.B. 834; [1998] 3 W.L.R. 851; [1998] 2 All
    E.R. 978; [1998] 2 Lloyd's Rep. 318; [1998] C.L.C. 947; [1998] I.L.Pr. 713;
    (1998) 95(17) L.S.G. 32; (1998) 142 S.J.L.B. 127; *Times*, April 6, 1998, QBD
    (Adm Ct) . . . . *Digested*, 98/**766**:
                                           Considered, 01/937
Houghton v. Fayers [2000] Lloyd's Rep. Bank. 145; [2000] 1 B.C.L.C. 511; (1999-
    2000) 2 I.T.E.L.R. 512; *Times*, February 9, 2000, CA . . . . *Digested*, 00/**2316**
Houghton v. Liverpool City Council [2000] Crim. L.R. 574; *Independent*, November
    22, 1999 (C.S.), QBD . . . . *Digested*, 99/**897**
Houghton v. Secretary of State for the Environment, Transport and the Regions [2001]
    J.P.L. 495 (Note), QBD
Houldsworth v. Yorkshire Woolcombers Association Ltd see Illingworth v. Houldsworth
Hounslow LBC v. McBride (1999) 31 H.L.R. 143, CA . . . . *Digested*, 99/**3706**
Hounslow LBC v. Redland Readymix Ltd (1998) 13 P.A.D. 722, Planning Inspector
Hounslow LBC v. Secretary of State for Environment, Transport and the Regions
    [1999] J.P.L. 364, QBD . . . . *Digested*, 99/**4178**
House Builders Federation Ltd v. Stockport MBC see Housebuilders Federation Ltd v.
    Stockport MBC
House of Spring Gardens Ltd v. Waite (No.1) [1985] F.S.R. 173; [1985] J.P.L. 173;
    (1985) 82 L.S.G. 443; (1985) 129 S.J. 64; *Times*, November 12, 1984, CA;
    reversing [1984] F.S.R. 277, Ch D . . . . *Digested*, 85/**2674**:
             Applied, 87/376, 88/2870: *Considered*, 01/17: *Distinguished*, 86/2658,
                                              88/2900
House of Spring Gardens Ltd v. Waite (No.2) [1991] 1 Q.B. 241; [1990] 3 W.L.R. 347;
    [1990] 2 All E.R. 990, CA . . . . *Digested*, 90/**3686**:
                      Applied, 95/688: *Distinguished*, 01/4882
House of Stitches Pty Ltd's CommunityTrade Mark Application [1999] E.T.M.R. 994, OHIM
    (Opposition Div) . . . . *Digested*, 00/**3744**
Housebuilders Federation Ltd v. Stockport MBC; *sub nom* House Builders Federation
    Ltd v. Stockport MBC [2000] J.P.L. 616, QBD . . . . *Digested*, 00/**4444**
Housecroft v. Burnett [1986] 1 All E.R. 332; (1985) 135 N.L.J. 728, CA . . . . *Digested*, 86/**989**:
             Applied, 90/1578, 94/1542, 00/1464, 01/4464: *Considered*, 88/1172,
                                            89/1202, 93/1438
Household Articles Ltd's Registered Design (No.2044802) [1998] F.S.R. 676; (1998)
    21 (4) I.P.D. 21044, Pat Ct . . . . *Digested*, 98/**3493**
Household Mortgage Corp Plc v. Pringle (1998) 30 H.L.R. 250, CA . . . . *Digested*, 98/**4357**
Housing Corp v. Bryant; *sub nom* Bryant v. Housing Corp [1999] I.C.R. 123; (1998)
    95(26) L.S.G. 31; (1998) 142 S.J.L.B. 181; *Times*, June 1, 1998, CA . . . . . . *Digested*, 98/**2244**
Housing Loan Corp Plc v. William H Brown Ltd [1999] Lloyd's Rep. P.N. 185, CA;
    affirming [1997] E.G.C.S. 72; [1997] N.P.C. 72, QBD . . . . *Digested*, 99/**4054**
Housing of the Working Classes Act 1890 Ex p. Stevenson, Re [1892] 1 Q.B. 609, CA;
    affirming [1892] 1 Q.B. 394, QBD . . . . *Applied*, 82/3000,
                               83/3482: *Explained*, 98/381
Hovenden v. Lord Annesley (1806) 2 Sch. & L. 607 . . . . *Considered*, 00/513
How Engineering Services Ltd v. Lindner Ceilings Floors Partitions Plc [1999] 2 All E.R.
    (Comm) 374; 64 Con. L.R. 67, QBD (T&CC) . . . . *Digested*, 99/**227**:
                                         Subsequent proceedings, 01/346

How Engineering Services Ltd v. Lindner Ceilings Floors Partitions Plc (Appeal Against
Costs) see Lindner Ceilings Floors Partitions Plc v. How Engineering Services
Ltd
Howard v. Brixington Infants School; Howard v. Devon CC [1999] I.C.R. 1096; [2000]
Ed. C.R. 93; [1999] E.L.R. 191, EAT . . . . *Digested,* 99/**2031**
Howard v. Devon CC see Howard v. Brixington Infants School
Howard v. Edwards [2001] 5 Q.R. 17, CC (Mold) [*Ex rel.* Huw E Roberts, Barrister,
Sedan House, Stanley Place, Chester] . . . . *Digested,* 01/**1789**
Howard v. Kinvena Homes Ltd (2000) 32 H.L.R. 541; (1999) 96(25) L.S.G. 30, CA . . . *Digested,* 00/**893**
Howard Florey Institute of Experimental Physiology & Medicine's European Patent
No.0112149 see HOWARD FLOREY INSTITUTE/Joint opposition (T272/95)
HOWARD FLOREY INSTITUTE/Joint opposition (T272/95); *sub nom* Howard Florey
Institute of Experimental Physiology & Medicine's European Patent No.0112149
[2000] E.P.O.R. 235; (2000) 23(1) I.P.D. 23004, EPO (Technical Bd App) . . . . *Digested,* 00/**3598**
Howard Holdings Inc, Re; *sub nom* Coles v. Thompson [1998] B.C.C. 549, Ch D . . . . . *Digested,* 97/**3090**
Howarth v. United Kingdom (38081/97) (2001) 31 E.H.R.R. 37; 9 B.H.R.C. 253;
[2001] Crim. L.R. 229; *Times,* October 10, 2000, ECHR . . . . *Digested,* 00/**3216**:
Distinguished, 00/1186: *Previous proceedings,* 97/1547:
Subsequent proceedings, 01/717
Howe v. David Brown Tractors (Retail) Ltd [1991] 4 All E.R. 30, CA . . . . *Digested,* 92/**2829**:
Considered, 98/541, 00/498
Howe v. DT Tarmacadam (1999) 99(1) Q.R. 8, CC (Bristol) . . . . *Digested,* 98/**1680**
Howe & McColough v. Lees (1910) 11 C.L.R. 361, HC (Aus) . . . . *Considered,* 98/1781
Howell v. J Lyons & Co (1998) 98(6) Q.R. 7, CC (Barnsley) . . . . *Digested,* 98/**1651**
Howells (Solicitors), Re see R. v. M (Wasted Costs Order)
Howes v. Customs and Excise Commissioners [2001] S.T.I. 1165, V&DTr
Howglen Ltd (Application for Disclosure), Re [2001] 1 All E.R. 376; [2001] B.C.C. 245;
[2001] 2 B.C.L.C. 695; *Times,* April 21, 2000, Ch D . . . . *Digested,* 00/**308**
Howkins v. Ross (Unreported, June 17, 1998), CC (Sheffield) [*Ex rel.* Irwin Mitchell
Solicitors, Huttons Buildings, 146 West Street, Sheffield, S1 1FW] . . . . *Digested,* 98/**368**
Howkins & Harrison v. Tyler [2001] Lloyd's Rep. P.N. 1; [2001] P.N.L.R. 27; [2000]
E.G.C.S. 91; *Times,* August 8, 2000, CA; affirming [2001] P.N.L.R. 26; [2000]
E.G.C.S. 30; (2000) 97(10) L.S.G. 38; [2000] N.P.C. 20, Ch D . . . . *Digested,* 00/**1448**:
Applied, 01/609
Howlett v. Mannion (Unreported, September 17, 1998), CC (Rawtenstall) [*Ex rel.*
Antony Hodari & Co Solicitors, 34 High Street, Manchester] . . . . *Digested,* 98/**424**
Howlett Marine Services Ltd v. Bowlam [2001] I.C.R. 595; [2001] I.R.L.R. 201, EAT . . *Digested,* 01/**2307**
Howlett-Davies v. Allpaints Ltd (Unreported, January 19, 2001), CC (Slough) [*Ex rel.*
Palser Grossman, Solicitors, Waterside House, Town Quay, Southampton] . . . . . *Digested,* 01/**517**
Howse v. Newbury DC (1999) 77 P. & C.R. 231, CA . . . . *Digested,* 98/**4368**
Hoya Corp's European Patent see HOYA/Intraocular Lens (T494/96)
HOYA/Intraocular Lens (T494/96); *sub nom* Hoya Corp's European Patent (2001)
24(6) I.P.D. 24040, EPO (Technical Bd App)
Hoye v. Bush (1840) 1 Man. & G. 775 . . . . *Applied,* 01/**5650**:
Distinguished, 01/4790: *Followed,* 00/5663
HOYLAND FOX/Umbrella frame (T63/97) [1998] E.P.O.R. 448, EPO (Technical Bd App)
Hozee v. Netherlands 1 I.T.L. Rep. 258; [1998] H.R.C.D. 568, ECHR
HQ Service Children's Education (MOD) v. Davitt [1999] I.C.R. 978, EAT . . . . *Digested,* 00/**2189**
HRH Prince Jefri Bolkiah v. KPMG see Bolkiah v. KPMG
HS (Minors) (Chambers Proceedings: Right of Audience), Re [1998] 1 F.L.R. 868; [1998] 3
F.C.R. 245; [1998] Fam. Law 328; *Times,* February 25, 1998, CA . . . . *Digested,* 98/**82**:
Followed, 01/29
HS AG v. SSA (X ZB 3/97) [2001] E.N.P.R. 4, BGH (Ger)
HS Smith & Sons, Re, *Times,* January 6, 1999, Ch D . . . . *Digested,* 99/**3273**
HSBC Bank Plc v. Liberty Mutual Insurance Co (UK) Ltd; Liberty Mutual Insurance Co
(UK) Ltd v. HSBC Bank Plc; A3/2001/0450, CA; affirming *Times,* June 11,
2001, Ch D . . . . *Digested,* 01/**375**:
Previous proceedings, 01/3842
HSBC Bank Plc (formerly Midland Bank Plc) v. Madden see Foley v. Post Office
HSBC Life (UK) Ltd v. Stubbs (Inspector of Taxes); Nationwide Life Ltd v. Crisp
(Inspector of Taxes); Abbey Life Assurance Co Ltd v. Colclough (Inspector of
Taxes); TSB Life Ltd v. Colclough (Inspector of Taxes); Lloyds TSB Life Assurance
Co Ltd v. Colclough (Inspector of Taxes) [2001] S.T.I. 1667, Sp Comm
HSBC (HK) Ltd v. Secretary of Justice (2000-01) 3 I.T.E.L.R. 763, CFI (HK) . . . . *Digested,* 01/**5525**
Hsu v. Commissioner of Police of the Metropolis see Thompson v. Commissioner of
Police of the Metropolis
Huber v. France (1998) 26 E.H.R.R. 457; [1998] H.R.C.D. 263, ECHR . . . . *Digested,* 98/**3129**:
Applied, 99/3137
Hubertus AG (178389), Re 2 I.T.L. Rep. 637, CE (F)
Huckfield, Re see R. v. Manchester Crown Court Ex p. DPP
Hudgell Yeates & Co v. Watson [1978] Q.B. 451; [1978] 1 W.L.R. 661; [1978] 2 All E.R.
363; 121 S.J. 831, CA. . . . . *Digested,* 78/**2827**:
Considered, 98/4017

Hudscott Estates (East) Ltd v. Secretary of State for the Environment, Transport and the
Regions (2001) 82 P. & C.R. 8; [2001] 2 P.L.R. 11; [2001] J.P.L. 973, QBD
(Admin Ct) . . . . *Digested,* 01/**4714**
Hudson v. Elmbridge BC [1991] 1 W.L.R. 880; [1991] 4 All E.R. 55; *Times,* November
29, 1990, CA. . . . . *Digested,* 92/**3564**:
                      Considered, 98/440: *Distinguished,* 92/3561: *Followed,* 97/557, 99/372
Hudson v. Shogun Finance Ltd see Shogun Finance Ltd v. Hudson
Huggett v. Secretary of State for the Environment see Wendy Fair Markets Ltd v.
Secretary of State for the Environment
Hughes (A Minor) v. Filipe (Unreported, June 26, 1997), CC (Birkenhead) [*Ex rel.*
Michael W Halsall Solicitors, 2 The Parks, Newton-le-Willows] . . . . *Digested,* 97/**721**:
                                           Followed, 98/455
Hughes (Deceased), Re, *Times,* January 8, 1999, Ch D . . . . *Digested,* 99/**4648**
Hughes v. Bloor (Unreported, December 14, 1999), CC (Birmingham) [*Ex rel.* James
Morgan, Barrister, St. Philip's Chambers, Fountain Court, Steelhouse Lane,
Birmingham] . . . . *Digested,* 00/**1707**
Hughes (t/a Pennine Boat Trips of Skipton) v. Customs and Excise Commissioners
[1999] B.V.C. 2003, V&DTr. . . . . *Digested,* 99/**5032**
Hughes v. Davies (Unreported, September 4, 2000), CC (Neath & Port Talbot) [*Ex rel.*
Andrew Arentsen, Barrister, 33 Park Place, Cardiff] . . . . *Digested,* 01/**1566**
Hughes v. Greenwich LBC [1994] 1 A.C. 170; [1993] 3 W.L.R. 821; [1993] 4 All E.R.
577; [1994] I.C.R. 48; (1994) 26 H.L.R. 99; 92 L.G.R. 61; (1995) 69 P. & C.R.
487; (1990) 60 P. & C.R. 487; [1993] E.G.C.S. 166; (1993) 90(46) L.S.G. 38;
(1993) 137 S.J.L.B. 244; [1993] N.P.C. 137; *Times,* October 26, 1993, HL;
affirming (1992) 24 H.L.R. 605; (1993) 157 L.G. Rev. 41; [1992] E.G.C.S. 76;
[1992] N.P.C. 73; *Times,* May 22, 1992; *Independent,* June 4, 1992, CA . . . . *Digested,* 94/**2367**:
                             Considered, 01/5572: *Referred to,* 95/6179
Hughes v. Hannover Ruckversicherungs AG [1997] B.C.C. 921; [1997] 1 B.C.L.C. 497;
[1999] B.P.I.R. 224; [1997] 6 Re. L.R. 96; *Times,* March 6, 1997, CA . . . . *Digested,* 97/**3045**
Hughes v. Hogg Insurance Brokers Ltd see Continental Assurance Co of London Plc
(In Liquidation) (No.3), Re
Hughes v. Hughes see Hyman v. Hyman
Hughes v. Hughes (Declaration) [1995] N.I. 119, Ch D (NI)
Hughes v. Hunt (Unreported, December 13, 1999), CC (Epsom) [*Ex rel.* Tim Petts,
Barrister, 12 King's Bench Walk, Temple, London] . . . . *Digested,* 00/**1723**
Hughes v. Kingston upon Hull City Council [1999] Q.B. 1193; [1999] 2 W.L.R. 1229;
[1999] 2 All E.R. 49; [1999] Env. L.R. 579; (1999) 31 H.L.R. 779; (1998) 95(44)
L.S.G. 36; (1999) 143 S.J.L.B. 54; *Times,* December 9, 1998; *Independent,*
November 16, 1998 (C.S.), QBD . . . . *Digested,* 98/**3715**
Hughes v. Lloyds Bank Plc (Administrators of the Estate of Mukherjee) [1998] P.I.Q.R.
P98, CA . . . . *Digested,* 98/**344**
Hughes (Russell McDonald) v. Lord Advocate [1963] A.C. 837; [1963] 2 W.L.R. 779;
[1963] 1 All E.R. 705; 1963 S.C. 31; 1963 S.C. (H.L.) 31; 1963 S.L.T. 150; (1963)
107 S.J. 232, HL; reversing 1961 S.C. 310; 1962 S.L.T. 90, 1 Div . . . . *Digested,* 63/**4056**:
        Applied, 64/2500, 66/8175, 66/8283, 67/1197, 67/2675, 70/744, 75/933,
                       75/2288, 80/1904, 83/3962, 87/2614, 98/3988, 98/6107:
        Considered, 69/2412, 90/3285, 96/4427, 00/4239: *Distinguished,* 64/2499:
                                    Followed, 84/4347, 85/4437
Hughes v. MacPherson (1999) 78 P. & C.R. D26, CA
Hughes v. Merrett Syndicates Ltd see Henderson v. Merrett Syndicates Ltd (No.1)
Hughes v. Secretary of State for the Environment, Transport and the Regions; *sub nom*
Secretary of State for the Environment, Transport and the Regions v. Hughes
(2000) 80 P. & C.R. 397; [2000] 1 P.L.R. 76; [2000] J.P.L. 826; [2000]
E.G.C.S. 9; (2000) 97(5) L.S.G. 35; (2000) 144 S.J.L.B. 59; *Times,* February 18,
2000; *Independent,* March 6, 2000 (C.S.), CA; reversing (1999) 78 P. & C.R.
309; [2000] J.P.L. 83; [1999] E.G.C.S. 55, QBD . . . . *Digested,* 00/**4409**
Hughes v. St Helens MBC (Unreported, April 22, 1999), CC (St Helens) [*Ex rel.* David
Knifton, Barrister, Corn Exchange Chambers, Fenwick Street, Liverpool] . . . . . . *Digested,* 99/**1607**
Hughes v. Tee (Unreported, November 5, 1998), CC (Liverpool) [*Ex rel.* Dibb Lupton
Alsop Solicitors, 101 Barbirolli Square, Manchester] . . . . *Digested,* 99/**537**
Hughes v. West Berkshire HA see Enderby v. Frenchay HA (No.2)
Hughes v. Wrexham Maelor Hospital NHS Trust (Unreported, April 7, 2000), CC
(Chester) [*Ex rel.* Christopher Limb, Barrister, Young Street Chambers, 38 Young
Street, Manchester] . . . . *Digested,* 00/**328**
HUGHES AIRCRAFT/Admissibility (T562/94) [1999] E.P.O.R. 472, EPO (Technical Bd
App) . . . . *Digested,* 00/**3617**:
                                             Considered, 00/3613
Hughes Application, Re (Gaming Licence) [1997] N.I. 133, CA (NI) . . . . *Digested,* 99/**5423**
HUGHES JVC/Colour projection apparatus (T31/98) [1999] E.P.O.R. 437, EPO (Technical
Bd App) . . . . *Digested,* 99/**3481**
Hugin Cash Registers v. Commission of the European Communities (C22/78) see
Hugin Kassaregister AB v. Commission of the European Communities (C22/
78)

Hugin Kassaregister AB v. Commission of the European Communities (C22/78); Hugin
Cash Registers v. Commission of the European Communities (C22/78) [1979]
E.C.R.1869; [1979] 3 C.M.L.R. 345, ECJ . . . . *Digested*, 79/**1205**:
Considered, 98/716, 98/719

Hugo Boss (Germany) Ste v. Les Editions des Dernieres Nouvelles D'Alsace [1998]
E.T.M.R. 197, Trib Gde Inst (Strasbourg)

Hulme (CICB: Quantum: 2000), Re [2000] 3 Q.R. 4, CICB (Manchester) [*Ex rel.* Rowlands
Solicitors, 3 York Street, Manchester] . . . . *Digested*, 00/**1537**

Huls AG v. Commission of the European Communities (C199/92 P); *sub nom* Huls AG
v. Commission of the European Communities (T9/89); Hoechst AG v.
Commission of the European Communities (T10/89); Shell International
Chemical Co Ltd v. Commission of the European Communities (T11/89); Solvay
et Cie SA v. Commission of the European Communities (T12/89); ICI Plc v.
Commission of the European Communities (T13/89); Montedipe SpA v.
Commission of the European Communities (T14/89); Chemie Linz AG v.
Commisision of the European Communities (T15/89) [1999] E.C.R. I-4287;
[1999] 5 C.M.L.R. 1016, ECJ (6th Chamber); affirming [1992] E.C.R. II-499, CFI
(1st Chamber) . . . . *Digested*, 00/**2376**

Huls AG v. Commission of the European Communities (T9/89) see Huls AG v.
Commission of the European Communities (C199/92 P)

Hulse v. Chambers [2001] 1 W.L.R. 2386; *Times*, July 13, 2001; *Independent*, June 25,
2001 (C.S), QBD . . . . *Digested*, 01/**4500**

Hulsta Furniture (UK) Ltd v. Customs and Excise Commissioners [2000] S.T.I. 77,
V&DTr

Humber Oil Terminal Trustee Ltd v. Owners of the Sivand [1998] 2 Lloyd's Rep. 97;
[1998] C.L.C. 751, CA . . . . *Digested*, 98/**3914**

Hume (C193/99), Re see Criminal Proceedings against Hume (C193/99)

Humen v. Poland (26614/95) (2001) 31 E.H.R.R. 53, ECHR . . . . *Digested*, 01/**3517**:
Referred to, 01/3513

Humic SA v. Sapec-Agro SA see HUMIC SA Trade mark

HUMIC SA Trade mark; *sub nom* Humic SA v. Sapec-Agro SA [1999] E.T.M.R. 26,
OHIM (Opposition Div) . . . . *Digested*, 99/**3579**

Humphreys v. Oxford University see Oxford University v. Humphreys

Humphreys-Jones (t/a Cathedral Frames) v. Welsby [2001] R.A. 67, Lands Tr . . . . *Digested*, 01/**4834**

Humphries v. HG Transport (Unreported, June 17, 1998), CC (Sheffield) [*Ex rel.*
Dermot Hughes, Barrister, Paradise Square Chambers, 26 Paradise Square,
Sheffield] . . . . *Digested*, 98/**1721**

Hung v. Miao [2001] B.P.I.R. 34, CFA (HK) . . . . *Digested*, 01/**819**

Hunt v. A Robinson & Co [2001] 3 Q.R. 18, CC (Basingstoke) [*Ex rel.* Lamport
Bassitt, Solicitors, 46 The Avenue, Southampton] . . . . *Digested*, 01/**1713**

Hunt v. Edge & Ellison Trustees Ltd; *sub nom* Torvale Group Ltd, Re [2000] B.C.C.
626; [1999] 2 B.C.L.C. 605, Ch D . . . . *Digested*, 00/**654**

Hunt v. Luck [1902] 1 Ch. 428, CA; affirming [1901] 1 Ch. 45, Ch D . . . . *Applied*, 56/8456,
60/1775, 69/2286, 88/1650, 89/1757: *Considered*, 66/9814, 66/9874, 70/1511,
95/2348, 98/4367

Hunt v. Peasegood [2001] B.P.I.R. 76, CA . . . . *Digested*, 01/**3718**:
Previous proceedings, 00/363

Hunt v. Peasegood (Set Aside), *Times*, October 20, 2000, CA . . . . *Digested*, 00/**363**:
Subsequent proceedings, 01/3718

Hunt v. Rigby LTA 98/6845/1, CA . . . . *Digested*, 99/**559**

Hunt v. RM Douglas (Roofing) Ltd [1990] 1 A.C. 398; [1988] 3 W.L.R. 975; [1988] 3
All E.R. 823; (1989) 86(1) L.S.G. 40; (1988) 138 N.L.J. Rep. 324; (1988) 132
S.J. 1592, HL; reversing (1988) 85(3) L.S.G. 33; (1987) 137 N.L.J. 1133; (1988)
132 S.J. 935, CA . . . . *Digested*, 89/**2935**:
Applied, 92/3447, 95/3987, 95/5010, 97/541, 97/5027:
Considered, 90/3760, 90/3811, 91/725, 97/528, 01/476:
Distinguished, 91/2827: *Referred to*, 89/2956

Hunt v. Severs; *sub nom* Severs v. Hunt [1994] 2 A.C. 350; [1994] 2 W.L.R. 602;
[1994] 2 All E.R. 385; [1994] 2 Lloyd's Rep. 129; [1994] P.I.Q.R. Q60; (1994)
144 N.L.J. 603; (1994) 138 S.J.L.B. 104; *Times*, May 2, 1994; *Independent*, May
5, 1994, HL; reversing [1993] Q.B. 815; [1993] 3 W.L.R. 558; [1994] P.I.Q.R.
Q6; (1993) 143 N.L.J. 1225; *Times*, May 13, 1993; *Independent*, May 13, 1993,
CA; reversing in part [1993] P.I.Q.R. Q43, QBD . . . . *Digested*, 94/**1530**:
Applied, 97/534, 97/1770, 98/1455, 98/2503, 99/1406, 00/1488, 00/2566,
01/1527: *Considered*, 97/1024, 98/2502, 98/2505, 99/1398, 99/2456,
99/2498, 00/311, 00/2592, 01/885: *Distinguished*, 99/2504:
Explained, 99/2462: *Followed*, 96/6905, 98/1453, 98/1576, 99/2457

Hunt-Wesson Inc, Re see SWISS MISS Trade Mark

Hunter v. British Coal Corp [1999] Q.B. 140; [1998] 3 W.L.R. 685; [1998] 2 All E.R.
97; [1999] I.C.R. 72; (1998) 42 B.M.L.R. 1; (1998) 95(12) L.S.G. 27; (1998) 142
S.J.L.B. 85; *Times*, February 27, 1998, CA; affirming (Unreported, April 24,
1997), CC (Sheffield) [*Ex rel.* Nabarro Nathanson, Solicitors, Sheffield] . . . . *Digested*, 98/**4035**

Hunter v. British Railways Board (Unreported, August 14, 2000), QBD [*Ex rel.*
Townsends Solicitors, 42 Cricklade Street, Swindon, Wiltshire] . . . . *Digested*, 01/**1714**

Hunter v. Butler [1996] R.T.R. 396; *Times*, December 28, 1995; *Independent*, January 2, 1996, CA. . . . . *Digested*, 96/**2123**: *Distinguished*, 99/1381

Hunter v. Canary Wharf Ltd; *sub nom* Hunter v. London Docklands Development Corp [1997] A.C. 655; [1997] 2 W.L.R. 684; [1997] 2 All E.R. 426; [1997] C.L.C. 1045; 84 B.L.R. 1; 54 Con. L.R. 12; [1997] Env. L.R. 488; [1997] 2 F.L.R. 342; (1998) 30 H.L.R. 409; [1997] Fam. Law 601; [1997] E.G.C.S. 59; (1997) 94(19) L.S.G. 25; (1997) 147 N.L.J. 634; (1997) 141 S.J.L.B. 108; [1997] N.P.C. 64; *Times*, April 25, 1997; *Independent*, May 2, 1997, HL; affirming [1996] 2 W.L.R. 348; [1996] 1 All E.R. 482; [1996] C.L.C. 197; 75 B.L.R. 27; 47 Con. L.R. 136; [1996] Env. L.R. 138; (1996) 28 H.L.R. 383; [1995] E.G.C.S. 153; (1995) 92(39) L.S.G. 28; (1995) 145 N.L.J. 1645; (1995) 139 S.J.L.B. 214; [1995] N.P.C. 155; *Times*, October 13, 1995; *Independent*, October 19, 1995, CA; affirming in part *Independent*, January 23, 1995 (C.S.); *Independent*, December 20, 1994, QBD . . . . *Digested*, 97/**3865**: *Applied*, 01/3800: *Considered*, 99/4067: *Distinguished*, 00/4297: *Followed*, 98/4040, 99/3681

Hunter v. Chief Constable of the West Midlands; McIlkenny v. Chief Constable of the West Midlands; Walker v. Chief Constable of the West Midlands; Power v. Chief Constable of Lancashire [1982] A.C. 529; [1981] 3 W.L.R. 906; [1981] 3 All E.R. 727; 125 S.J. 829; *Times*, November 26, 1981, HL; affirming [1980] Q.B. 283; [1980] 2 W.L.R. 689; [1980] 2 All E.R. 227; 124 S.J. 83, CA . . . . *Digested*, 82/**2382**: *Applied*, 80/798, 80/1411, 81/732, 81/1349, 83/1128, 90/3542, 93/623, 93/624, 94/663, 94/3517, 94/4572, 95/688, 95/2857, 95/3699, 96/4496, 00/2250, 00/4269: *Considered*, 88/2768, 89/3073, 90/2857, 90/3540, 91/1737, 93/2525, 96/853, 97/628, 00/597: *Distinguished*, 88/2610, 92/3351, 93/3084, 99/313: *Explained*, 99/485: *Followed*, 96/3912, 96/4490, 97/1107, 98/4865, 99/4021, 00/332: *Referred to*, 93/3243, 95/3882, 97/3355

Hunter (t/a Blues Hairshop) v. Customs and Excise Commissioners [2000] S.T.I. 936, V&DTr

Hunter v. Deuchart CO/5095/84, CC . . . . *Digested*, 98/**1502**
Hunter v. Earnshaw [2001] P.N.L.R. 42, QBD . . . . *Digested*, 01/**4530**
Hunter v. Gerald Duckworth & Co Ltd [2000] I.L.Pr. 229, HC (Irl) . . . . *Digested*, 00/**1759**
Hunter v. London Docklands Development Corp see Hunter v. Canary Wharf Ltd
Hunter v. Perth and Kinross Council 2001 S.C.L.R. 856; 2001 Rep. L.R. 95 (Note); 2001 G.W.D. 25-974, OH
Hunter v. Southam Inc [1984] 2 S.C.R. 145, Sup Ct (Can) . . . . *Considered*, 99/3120
Hunter Timber Ltd v. Agrosin Private Ltd see Homburg Houtimport BV v. Agrosin Private Ltd (The Starsin)
Huntingdon v. Armstrong (Unreported, June 17, 1998), CC (Sunderland) [*Ex rel.* Keith SH Miller, Barrister, Fountain Chambers, Cleveland Business Centre, 1 Watson Street, Middlesbrough] . . . . *Digested*, 98/**1618**
Huntingdon Life Sciences Ltd v. Curtin, *Times*, December 11, 1997, QBD . . . . *Digested*, 98/**953**
Huntingdon Life Sciences Ltd v. Curtin (Order for Substituted Service) [1998] Env. L.R. D9, CA
Huntingdonshire DC v. Denyaz Promotions (1998) 13 P.A.D. 558, Planning Inspector
Huntingdonshire DC v. Hopkin (1998) 13 P.A.D. 570, Planning Inspector
Huntington v. Secretary of State for the Environment, Transport and the Regions, *Times*, October 2, 1998, QBD . . . . *Digested*, 98/**570**
Hurley v. Hurley [1998] 1 F.L.R. 213; [1998] 2 F.C.R. 14; [1998] Fam. Law 16, CA . . . . . *Digested*, 98/**410**
Hurley v. Taylor (Inspector of Taxes) [1999] S.T.C. 1; 71 T.C. 268; [1998] B.T.C. 479; *Times*, November 23, 1998; *Independent*, November 2, 1998 (C.S.), CA; reversing [1998] S.T.C. 202; [1998] B.T.C. 32; *Times*, February 10, 1998; *Independent*, February 16, 1998 (C.S.), Ch D . . . . *Digested*, 98/**4668**
Hurlingham Estates Ltd v. Wilde & Partners [1997] 1 Lloyd's Rep. 525; [1997] S.T.C. 627; [1997] B.T.C. 240; (1997) 147 N.L.J. 453; *Times*, January 3, 1997; *Independent*, February 17, 1997 (C.S.), Ch D . . . . *Digested*, 97/**3842**: *Referred to*, 00/4255
Hurnam v. Paratian [1998] A.C. 707; [1998] 2 W.L.R. 790; (1998) 142 S.J.L.B. 100, PC (Mau) . . . . *Digested*, 98/**3115**
Hurst, Re see Hurst v. Bennett (Insolvency Act Application)
Hurst v. Bennett (Insolvency Act Application); *sub nom* Hurst, Re *Independent*, April 9, 2001 (C.S), Ch D
Hurst v. Bennett (No.1); *sub nom* Debtor (No.303 of 1997), Re [2001] EWCA Civ 182; [2001] 2 B.C.L.C. 290; [2001] B.P.I.R. 287; (2001) 98(17) L.S.G. 38; *Times*, March 15, 2001, CA; affirming [2001] B.P.I.R. 89; *Times*, October 3, 2000, Ch D

. . . . *Digested*, 01/**3780**
Hurst v. Bryk [2000] 2 W.L.R. 740; [2000] 2 All E.R. 193; [2000] 2 B.C.L.C. 117; [2000] E.G.C.S. 49; (2000) 97(17) L.S.G. 35; (2000) 150 N.L.J. 511; (2000) 144 S.J.L.B. 189; *Times*, April 4, 2000, HL; affirming [1999] Ch. 1; [1998] 2 W.L.R. 269; [1997] 2 All E.R. 283; *Times*, March 20, 1997; *Independent*, February 7, 1997, CA . . . . *Digested*, 00/**4317**: *Considered*, 00/4320

Hurst v. Hampshire CC [1997] 2 E.G.L.R. 164; [1997] 44 E.G. 206; (1998) 14 Const.
L.J. 204; (1997) 94(30) L.S.G. 30; (1997) 147 N.L.J. 1025; (1997) 141 S.J.L.B.
152; [1997] N.P.C. 99; *Times*, June 26, 1997, CA . . . .   *Digested*, 97/**4855**
Hurst v. Picture Theatres [1915] 1 K.B. 1, CA . . . .   *Applied*, 47-51/5148,
        70/2436: *Approved*, 47-51/5514, 47-51/5515: *Considered*, 99/698
Hurst v. Pigott (Unreported, November 9, 1989), CC (Ilford) . . . .   *Digested*, 89/**1258**:
                            Considered, 00/1501

Hurst v. Russell [2001] 6 Q.R. 16, CC (Blackburn) [*Ex rel.* Pannone & Partners,
Solicitors, 123 Deansgate, Manchester] . . . .   *Digested*, 01/**1692**
Hurst-Bannister v. New Cap Reinsurance Co Ltd [2000] Lloyd's Rep. I.R. 166, Ch D . .   *Digested*, 01/**3835**
Hurstanger Ltd v. Wood (Unreported, November 30, 1998), CC (Hitchin) [*Ex rel.* Marc
Beaumont, Harrow-on-the-Hill Chambers, 60 High Street, Harrow-on-the-Hill,
Middlesex] . . . .   *Digested*, 99/**2507**
Husain v. Bank of Credit and Commerce International SA see Bank of Credit and
Commerce International SA (In Liquidation) v. Ali (No.3)
Hussain v. Cuddy Woods & Cochrane [2001] Lloyd's Rep. P.N. 134, CA . . . .   *Digested*, 01/**4515**
Hussain v. Elonex Plc [1999] I.R.L.R. 420, CA . . . .   *Digested*, 99/**2138**
Hussain v. Fazil [*Ex rel.* Stephen Garner, Barrister, 8 Fountain Court, Steelhouse Lane,
Birmingham] . . . .   *Digested*, 01/**1664**
Hussain v. Heywood, CC (Sheffield) [*Ex rel.* Sheldon Davidson & Co, Solicitors, 223,
Bury New Road, Whitefield, Manchester] . . . .   *Digested*, 01/**616**
Hussain v. Lancaster City Council [2000] Q.B. 1; [1999] 2 W.L.R. 1142; [1999] 4 All
E.R. 125; [1998] E.H.L.R. 166; (1999) 31 H.L.R. 164; (1999) 1 L.G.L.R. 37;
(1999) 77 P. & C.R. 89; [1998] E.G.C.S. 86; (1998) 95(23) L.S.G. 27; (1998)
142 S.J.L.B. 173; [1998] N.P.C. 85; (1998) 76 P. & C.R. D31; *Times*, May 26,
1998; *Independent*, May 19, 1998, CA; reversing 1997 H No.469, QBD . . . .   *Digested*, 98/**4047**:
     Applied, 01/584, 01/4197: *Distinguished*, 99/4066: *Followed*, 99/3681
Hussain v. Nawaz, CC (Derby) [*Ex rel.* Richard Gregory, Barrister, 24 The Ropewalk,
Nottingham] . . . .   *Digested*, 00/**1546**
Hussain v. New Taplow Paper Mills Ltd [1988] A.C. 514; [1988] 2 W.L.R. 266; [1988]
1 All E.R. 541; [1988] I.C.R. 259; [1988] I.R.L.R. 167; (1988) 138 N.L.J. Rep. 45;
(1988) 132 S.J. 226, HL; affirming [1987] 1 W.L.R. 336; [1987] 1 All E.R. 417;
[1987] I.C.R. 28; (1987) 84 L.S.G. 1242; (1987) 131 S.J. 358, CA . . . .   *Digested*, 88/**1070**:
     Considered, 90/1716, 96/2133, 97/1024, 99/810: *Distinguished*, 90/1718,
                           90/1718.19, 99/793
Hussain v. United Kingdom; Singh v. United Kingdom (1996) 22 E.H.R.R. 1; 1 B.H.R.C.
119; *Times*, February 26, 1996, ECHR . . . .   *Digested*, 96/**3135**:
                Applied, 00/4323: *Considered*, 97/3924
Hussein (Essengin), Re; *sub nom* Davis v. Martin-Sklan [1995] B.C.C. 1122; [1995] 2
B.C.L.C. 483; [1996] B.P.I.R. 160, Ch D . . . .   *Digested*, 96/**3522**:
             Considered, 98/3306: *Followed*, 99/3338
Hussein v. Mehlman [1992] 2 E.G.L.R. 287; [1992] 32 E.G. 59 . . . .   *Digested*, 93/**2462**:
                    Followed, 97/3302, 99/3700
Hussey v. Eels [1990] 2 Q.B. 227; [1990] 2 W.L.R. 234; [1990] 1 All E.R. 449;
[1990] 19 E.G. 77; (1990) 140 N.L.J. 53, CA . . . .   *Digested*, 90/**1565**:
             Considered, 91/1503, 01/4152: *Followed*, 97/3843
Husseyin v. Crumplin [1997] P.I.Q.R. P481, CA . . . .   *Digested*, 98/**580**
Hussman (Europe) Ltd v. Al Ameen Development & Trade Co; *sub nom* Hussmann
(Europe) Ltd v. Al Ameen Development & Trade Co [2000] 2 Lloyd's Rep. 83;
[2000] C.L.C. 1243, QBD (Comm Ct) . . . .   *Digested*, 00/**228**
Hussman Manufacturing Ltd v. Weir [1998] I.R.L.R. 288; (1998) 95(31) L.S.G. 34, EAT   *Digested*, 98/**5827**
Hussmann (Europe) Ltd v. Al Ameen Development & Trade Co see Hussman (Europe)
Ltd v. Al Ameen Development & Trade Co
Huston v. Turner Entertainment [1992] E.C.C. 334, Cass (F) . . . .   *Considered*, 98/3423
Hutchings v. Coinseed Ltd [1998] I.R.L.R. 190, CA . . . .   *Digested*, 98/**2208**
Hutchings v. Islington LBC [1998] 1 W.L.R. 1629; [1998] 3 All E.R. 445; [1998] I.C.R.
1230; (1999) 1 L.G.L.R. 1; *Times*, May 6, 1998, CA. . . . .   *Digested*, 98/**4129**
Hutchinson v. Cunningham (Unreported, May 11, 2000), CC (Tameside) [*Ex rel.* BT
McCluggage, Barrister, 9 St John Street, Manchester] . . . .   *Digested*, 00/**1603**
Hutchinson v. DPP; *sub nom* Hutchinson v. Newbury Magistrates Court *Independent*,
November 20, 2000 (C.S), QBD
Hutchinson v. Jones [2001] 5 Q.R. 13, CC (Nottingham) [*Ex rel.* Jinder S Boora,
Barrister, Ropewalk Chambers, 24 The Ropewalk, Nottingham] . . . .   *Digested*, 01/**1750**
Hutchinson v. Newbury Magistrates Court see Hutchinson v. DPP
Hutchison v. Westward Television Ltd [1977] I.C.R. 279; [1977] I.R.L.R. 69; (1976) 12
I.T.R. 125; *Times*, December 18, 1976, EAT . . . .   *Digested*, 77/**1073**:
                Applied, 98/2194: *Considered*, 97/2264
Hutchison Personal Communications Ltd v. Hook Advertising Ltd (No.1) [1995] F.S.R.
365, Ch D . . . .   *Digested*, 95/**860**:
                   Followed, 98/1048, 98/3430
Hutton (CICB: Quantum: 1999), Re (1999) 99(5) Q.R. 5, CICB (Manchester) [*Ex rel.*
Stephensons Solicitors, 26 Union Street, Leigh] . . . .   *Digested*, 99/**1426**
Hutton v. East Dyfed HA [1998] Lloyd's Rep. Med. 335, QBD . . . .   *Digested*, 99/**3990**

Huxley *v.* Child Support Officer [2000] 1 F.L.R. 898; [2000] 1 F.C.R. 448; [2000] Fam. Law 465; *Independent*, February 14, 2000 (C.S.), CA . . . . *Digested*, 00/**2455**

Huxter *v.* Lock (1998) 98(6) Q.R. 8, CC (Weymouth) . . . . *Digested*, 98/**1690**

Huyton *v.* Mersey Docks & Harbour Co (Unreported, July 10, 1998), CC (Birkenhead) [*Ex rel.* Berrymans Lace Mawer Solicitors, 43 Castle Street, Liverpool] . . . . *Digested*, 98/**346**

Huyton SA *v.* Jakil SpA [1999] 2 Lloyd's Rep. 83; [1998] C.L.C. 937, CA . . . . *Digested*, 98/**227**

Huyton SA *v.* Peter Cremer GmbH & Co [1999] 1 Lloyd's Rep. 620; [1999] C.L.C. 230, QBD (Comm Ct) . . . . *Digested*, 99/**4477**

HW Nevill (Sunblest) Ltd *v.* Wilhaum Press & Sons see HW Nevill (Sunblest) Ltd *v.* William Press & Sons Ltd

HW Nevill (Sunblest) Ltd *v.* William Press & Sons Ltd; *sub nom* HW Nevill (Sunblest) Ltd *v.* Wilhaum Press & Sons 20 B.L.R. 78, QBD . . . . *Digested*, 83/**253**:
Applied, 98/801: *Considered*, 94/2736

HW Smith (Cabinets) Ltd *v.* Brindle; *sub nom* Brindle *v.* HW Smith (Cabinets) Ltd [1972] 1 W.L.R. 1653; [1973] 1 All E.R. 230; [1973] I.C.R. 12; [1972] I.R.L.R. 125; 13 K.I.R. 203; (1973) 8 I.T.R. 69; 116 S.J. 967, CA; reversing 13 K.I.R. 195; (1972) 7 I.T.R. 378, NIRC . . . . *Digested*, 73/**1032**:
Considered, 73/1026, 80/1022, 82/1101, 00/2131: *Distinguished*, 72/1155, 73/1033, 73/1151, 73/1152, 74/1322: *Followed*, 74/1347: *Referred to*, 73/1154

Hyams *v.* Plender; *sub nom* Plender *v.* Hyams [2001] 1 W.L.R. 32; [2001] 2 All E.R. 179; [2001] C.P. Rep. 40; [2001] 1 Costs L.R. 109, CA . . . . *Digested*, 01/**432**

Hyde *v.* Clive Warcup Transport Ltd (Unreported, June 17, 1999), CC (Preston) [*Ex rel.* Meloy Whittle Robinson Solicitors, 5,6 & 7 Cannon Street, Preston, PR1 3PY] . . *Digested*, 99/**1599**

Hyde HA *v.* Brown (Unreported, March 10, 1999), CC (Woolwich) [*Ex rel.* Christopher Heather, Barrister, Francis Taylor Buildings, Temple, London] . . . . *Digested*, 99/**3709**

Hyde Park Funding Ltd *v.* Ioannou (Unreported, November 19, 1998), CC (Barnet) [*Ex rel.* Miles Croally, Barrister, 17 Bedford Row, London] . . . . *Digested*, 99/**4382**

Hyde Park Residence Ltd *v.* Secretary of State for the Environment, Transport and the Regions; Hyde Park Residence Ltd *v.* Westminster City Council (2000) 80 P. & C.R. 419; [2000] 1 P.L.R. 85; [2000] J.P.L. 936; [2000] E.G.C.S. 14; [2000] N.P.C. 7; *Times*, March 14, 2000, CA; affirming [1999] 3 P.L.R. 1; [1999] J.P.L. 897, QBD . . . . *Digested*, 00/**4422**

Hyde Park Residence Ltd *v.* Westminster City Council see Hyde Park Residence Ltd *v.* Secretary of State for the Environment, Transport and the Regions

Hyde Park Residence Ltd *v.* Yelland [2001] Ch. 143; [2000] 3 W.L.R. 215; [2000] E.C.D.R. 275; [2000] E.M.L.R. 363; [2000] R.P.C. 604; (2000) 23(5) I.P.D. 23040; (2000) 97(8) L.S.G. 35; *Times*, February 16, 2000; *Independent*, February 18, 2000, CA; reversing [1999] E.M.L.R. 654; [1999] R.P.C. 655; (1999) 18 Tr. L.R. 217; (1999) 22(7) I.P.D. 22065; *Times*, March 24, 1999, Ch D . . . . *Digested*, 00/**3573**:
Considered, 01/3850: *Followed*, 99/3437, 01/570

Hydrema *v.* Kieffer [2001] I.L.Pr. 42, Cass (F)

Hydril UK Ltd *v.* Customs and Excise Commissioners [2000] S.T.I. 840, V&DTr

Hydro Agri Espana SA *v.* Charles M Willie & Co (Shipping) Ltd [1998] C.L.C. 511; *Times*, March 5, 1998, CA . . . . *Digested*, 98/**561**

Hylands *v.* McClintock [1999] N.I. 28, Ch D (NI) . . . . *Digested*, 99/**5403**

Hyman *v.* Hyman; Hughes *v.* Hughes [1929] A.C. 601, HL; affirming [1929] P. 1, CA . . . *Applied*, 47-51/1711, 47-51/2733, 47-51/3014, 47-51/3016, 47-51/3017, 47-51/3033, 52/1058, 55/855, 63/1087, 70/795, 79/141, 79/1410, 80/791, 84/1702: *Considered*, 47-51/3060, 67/1290, 74/1052, 87/1743: *Distinguished*, 56/2748, 99/4635

Hypo-Mortgage Services Ltd *v.* David Parry & Co see Birmingham Midshires Mortgage Services Ltd *v.* David Parry & Co

Hytec Information Systems Ltd *v.* Coventry City Council [1997] 1 W.L.R. 1666; (1997) 13 Const. L.J. 344; *Times*, December 31, 1996, CA . . . . *Digested*, 97/**768**:
Applied, 99/568, 99/569, 01/673: *Considered*, 99/559, 99/3790, 00/488: *Distinguished*, 99/565: *Followed*, 98/629, 99/446, 99/564, 00/630

Hyundai Heavy Industries Co Ltd *v.* Papadopoulos [1980] 1 W.L.R. 1129; [1980] 2 All E.R. 29; [1980] 2 Lloyd's Rep. 1; 124 S.J. 592, HL; affirming [1979] 1 Lloyd's Rep. 130, CA . . . . *Digested*, 80/**2504**:
Applied, 98/861: *Distinguished*, 96/5327: *Followed*, 91/497: *Referred to*, 95/772

Hyundai Merchant Marine Co Ltd *v.* Karander Maritime Inc (The Nizuru) [1996] 2 Lloyd's Rep. 66; [1996] C.L.C. 749, QBD (Comm Ct) . . . . *Digested*, 96/**5308**:
Distinguished, 01/4911

I (Abduction: Acquiescence), Re [1999] 1 F.L.R. 778; [1999] 2 F.C.R. 674; [1999] Fam. Law 204, Fam Div. . . . . *Digested*, 99/**2316**

I (Adoption Order: Nationality), Re [1998] 2 F.L.R. 997; [1999] 1 F.C.R. 759; [1998] Fam. Law 580, Fam Div. . . . . *Digested*, 99/**2306**

I v. DPP; *sub nom* R. v. West London Youth Court Ex p. M; DPP v. M; DPP v. H; DPP v.
    I; M v. DPP; H v. DPP [2001] UKHL 10; [2001] 2 W.L.R. 765; [2001] 2 All E.R.
    583; [2001] 2 Cr. App. R. 14; (2001) 165 J.P. 437; [2001] Crim. L.R. 491;
    (2001) 165 J.P.N. 506; (2001) 98(20) L.S.G. 40; (2001) 151 N.L.J. 385; (2001)
    145 S.J.L.B. 101; *Times*, March 9, 2001; *Independent*, March 13, 2001, HL;
    reversing [2000] 1 Cr. App. R. 251; [2000] Crim. L.R. 45; *Times*, July 7, 1999,
    QBD . . . .   *Digested*, 01/**1002**
I v. H (Contact Hearing: Procedure) see I and H (Minors) (Contact: Right to Give
    Evidence), Re
I v. Special Adjudicator see R. (on the application of I) v. Special Adjudicator
I and H (Minors) (Contact: Right to Give Evidence), Re; *sub nom* I v. H (Contact Hearing:
    Procedure) [1998] 1 F.L.R. 876; [1998] 2 F.C.R. 433; [1998] Fam. Law 327,
    CA . . . .   *Digested*, 98/**2416**
I CAN'T BELIEVE IT'S YOGURT Trade Mark [1992] R.P.C. 533, Secr of State for Trade . .   *Referred to*, 95/4945,
    98/3529, 99/3526
I'm Your Man Ltd v. Secretary of State for the Environment, Transport and the Regions
    (1999) 77 P. & C.R. 251; [1998] 4 P.L.R. 107; [1999] P.L.C.R. 109; [1998] N.P.C.
    131; *Times*, September 25, 1998, QBD . . . .   *Digested*, 98/**4215**
I, L and S (CICB: Quantum: 1998), Re (Unreported, July 15, 1998), CICB (York) [*Ex rel.*
    Stephen J Glover, Barrister, 37 Park Square, Leeds] . . . .   *Digested*, 98/**1764**
Ian Flockton Developments Ltd v. Customs and Excise Commissioners [1987] S.T.C.
    394, QBD . . . .   *Digested*, 87/**3815**:
    Applied, 91/3649, 96/5864: *Considered*, 98/4912, 98/4923
Iannelli & Volpi SpA v. Ditta Paolo Meroni (C74/76); *sub nom* Iannelli & Volpi SpA v.
    Meroni (C74/76); Firma Steinike und Weinlig v. Bundesamt fur Ernahrung und
    Forstwirtschaft (C78/76) [1977] E.C.R. 595; [1977] E.C.R. 557; [1977] 2
    C.M.L.R. 688, ECJ . . . .   *Digested*, 78/**1403**:
    Followed, 98/2332, 01/786
Iannelli & Volpi SpA v. Meroni (C74/76) see Iannelli & Volpi SpA v. Ditta Paolo Meroni
    (C74/76)
Iatridis v. Greece (2000) 30 E.H.R.R. 97, ECHR . . . .   *Digested*, 00/**3203**
Ibbotson v. Iqbal (Unreported, May 6, 1999), CC (Leeds) [*Ex rel.* Nelson & Co
    Solicitors, St Andrew's House, St Andrew's Street, Leeds] . . . .   *Digested*, 99/**532**
Ibbotson v. United Kingdom [1999] Crim. L.R. 153, ECHR
IBBOTT/ Ionizing Fluids (T157/97) [2001] E.P.O.R. 44, EPO (Technical Bd App) . . . . . .   *Digested*, 01/**3931**
IBC Vehicles Ltd v. Durr Ltd 1995-I-1167, QBD . . . .   *Digested*, 00/**584**
IBCOS Computers Ltd v. Barclays Mercantile Highland Finance Ltd [1994] F.S.R. 275;
    [1998] Masons C.L.R. Rep. 1, Ch D . . . .   *Digested*, 95/**854**:
    Applied, 99/3454: *Considered*, 98/3416: *Referred to*, 97/1055, 99/3455
Iberian UK Ltd v. BPB Industries Plc [1996] 2 C.M.L.R. 601; [1996] E.C.C. 467; [1997]
    Eu. L.R. 1; [1997] I.C.R. 164; *Times*, May 15, 1996, Ch D . . . .   *Digested*, 96/**2806**:
    Applied, 98/366
Ibex Trading Co Ltd v. Walton [1994] I.C.R. 907; [1994] I.R.L.R. 564; *Times*, July 29,
    1994, EAT . . . .   *Digested*, 94/**2018**:
    Followed, 95/5911: *Not followed*, 98/2214
IBM Corp v. Commission of the European Communities (C60/81); *sub nom*
    International Business Machines Corp v. Commission of the European
    Communities (C60/81) [1981] E.C.R. 2639; [1981] 3 C.M.L.R. 635, ECJ . . . . .   *Digested*, 81/**1266**:
    Followed, 00/2365
IBM Corp's Application see International Business Machine Corp's Application
IBM Corp's European Patent Application (No.91107112.4) (T1173/97) see IBM/Computer
    programs (T1173/97)
IBM Corp's European Patent Application (No.96305851.6) (T935/97) see IBM/Computer
    programs (T935/97)
IBM Corp's Patent Application (20 W (PAT) 8/99) [2000] E.N.P.R. 309, BPG (Ger)
IBM/Computer programs (T1173/97); *sub nom* IBM Corp's European Patent Application
    (No.91107112.4) (T1173/97) [2000] E.P.O.R. 219; (1999) 22(6) I.P.D. 22058,
    EPO (Technical Bd App) . . . .   *Digested*, 00/**3665**
IBM/Computer programs (T935/97); *sub nom* IBM Corp's European Patent Application
    (No.96305851.6) (T935/97) [1999] E.P.O.R. 301; [1998-99] Info. T.L.R. 135;
    [1999] R.P.C. 861; [1999] Masons C.L.R. 280; (1999) 22(6) I.P.D. 22059;
    Times, April 15, 1999, EPO (Technical Bd App) . . . .   *Digested*, 99/**3488**
IBM/Computer related claims (T410/96) [1999] E.P.O.R. 318, EPO (Technical Bd App)   *Digested*, 99/**3474**
IBM/External interface simulation (T833/91) [1998] E.P.O.R. 431, EPO (Technical Bd App)
Ibrahim v. Dovecorn Reversions Ltd [2001] 30 E.G. 116; [2001] 12 E.G.C.S. 165, Ch D
    . . . .   *Digested*, 01/**4192**
Ibrahim v. Secretary of State for the Home Department see R. (on the application of
    Ibrahim (Ayman)) v. Secretary of State for the Home Department
Ibrahim v. Secretary of State for the Home Department [1998] I.N.L.R. 511, IAT . . . .   *Digested*, 99/**3146**:
    Applied, 99/3147, 99/3150
Ibrahim Shanker Co v. Distos Compania Naviera SA see Owners of Cargo Lately Laden
    on Board the Siskina v. Distos Compania Naviera SA

Icart SA's CommunityTrade Mark Application [2000] E.T.M.R.180, OHIM (Opposition Div)
　　　　　　　　　　　　　　　　　　　　　　　　　　　　　Digested, 00/**3741**
ICCO International Corn Co NV *v.* Interbulk see Interbulk Ltd *v.* Aiden Shipping Co (The
　　Vimeira) (No.1)
Iceland Foodstores Ltd *v.* Customs and Excise Commissioners [1999] B.V.C. 2106,
　　V&DTr
Iceland Frozen Foods Ltd *v.* Jones [1983] I.C.R. 17; [1982] I.R.L.R. 439; (1982) 79
　　L.S.G. 1257; *Times*, August 5, 1982, EAT. . . . .　*Digested*, 83/**1325**:
　　　　　　　　　　Applied, 86/1278, 97/2288, 97/2289, 00/2240: *Considered*, 96/2651,
　　　　　　　　　　　　　　　　　　　　　　　00/**2239**: *Referred to*, 00/2237
ICFI Corporate Securities Fund Plc *v.* International Corp for Finance & Investments 1999
　　Folio No.386, QBD (Comm Ct) . . . .　*Digested*, 99/**490**
ICI AMERICAS/Leukotriene antagonist (T852/91) [1998] E.P.O.R. 31, EPO (Technical Bd
　　App)
ICI Chemicals & Polymers Ltd *v.* Customs and Excise Commissioners [1998] V. & D.R.
　　310, V&DTr . . . .　*Digested*, 00/**5040**
ICI Ltd *v.* Commission of the European Communities (C48/69) [1972] E.C.R. 619;
　　[1972] C.M.L.R. 557, ECJ . . . .　*Digested*, 72/**1312**:
　　　　　　　　　　　　　　　　　　　　　　　　　　　　Considered, 00/3704
ICI Plc *v.* Colmer (Inspector of Taxes) (No.2) [1999] 1 W.L.R. 2035; [2000] 1 All E.R.
　　129; [1999] S.T.C. 1089; [2000] 1 C.M.L.R. 142; 72 T.C. 1; [1999] B.T.C. 440;
　　(1999) 96(46) L.S.G. 40; (2000) 144 S.J.L.B. 7; *Times*, November 24, 1999, HL;
　　reversing [1993] 4 All E.R. 705; [1993] S.T.C. 710; [1993] S.T.I. 1077; (1993)
　　90(38) L.S.G. 44; *Times*, August 11, 1993; *Independent*, August 9, 1993 (C.S.),
　　CA; affirming [1992] S.T.C. 51; *Times*, December 20, 1991, Ch D . . . .　*Digested*, 99/**4667**
ICI Plc *v.* Colmer (Inspector of Taxes) (C264/96) [1999] 1 W.L.R. 108; [1998] All E.R.
　　(E.C.) 585; [1998] S.T.C. 874; [1998] E.C.R. I-4695; [1998] 3 C.M.L.R. 293;
　　[1998] C.E.C. 861; [1998] B.T.C. 304; *Times*, August 20, 1998, ECJ. . . . .　*Digested*, 98/**4620**:
　　　　　　　　Considered, 01/5212: *Followed*, 01/2499: *Previous proceedings*, 92/607,
　　　　　　　　　　　　　　　　　　　　　　　　　　　　93/608, 96/1303
ICI Plc *v.* Commission of the European Communities (C200/92) [1999] E.C.R. I-4399;
　　[1999] 5 C.M.L.R. 1110, ECJ (6th Chamber). . . . .　*Digested*, 00/**2379**
ICI Plc *v.* Commission of the European Communities (T13/89) see Huls AG *v.*
　　Commission of the European Communities (C199/92 P)
ICI Plc *v.* Commission of the European Communities (T36/91) see Solvay et Cie SA *v.*
　　Commission of the European Communities (C287/95)
Icon Health & Fitness Ltd *v.* Precise Exercise Equipment Inc (2001) 24(8) I.P.D. 24054,
　　Ch D
ICP Developments Ltd *v.* Secretary of State for the Environment [1997] J.P.L. 930;
　　[1997] E.G.C.S. 43; [1997] N.P.C. 45, QBD . . . .　*Digested*, 97/**4115**:
　　　　　　　　　　　　　　　　　　　　　　　　　　　　Considered, 99/4256
ICTS (UK) Ltd *v.* Tchoula see Tchoula *v.* ICTS (UK) Ltd
Ideal Tourisme SA *v.* Belgium (C36/99) [2001] S.T.C. 1386; [2000] E.C.R. I-6049;
　　[2001] 3 C.M.L.R. 45; [2000] S.T.I. 1001, ECJ (6th Chamber)
Idenburg *v.* General Medical Council (2000) 55 B.M.L.R. 101, PC (UK) . . . .　*Digested*, 00/**303**
IFPI Belgium *v.* Beckers [2000] E.C.D.R. 440, RB (Antwerp)
IFPI Belgium VZW *v.* Belgacom Skynet NV; *sub nom* Belgacom Skynet NV *v.* IFPI
　　Belgium VZW; IFPI VZW *v.* Belgacom Skynet NV [2000] E.C.D.R. 239, Trib
　　Comm (Brussels)
IFPI VZW *v.* Belgacom Skynet NV see IFPI Belgium VZW *v.* Belgacom Skynet NV
Igbo *v.* Johnson Matthey Chemicals [1986] I.C.R. 505; [1986] I.R.L.R. 215; (1986) 83
　　L.S.G. 2089; (1986) 130 S.J. 524, CA; reversing [1986] I.C.R. 82; [1985]
　　I.R.L.R. 189; (1985) 82 L.S.G. 1011, EAT . . . .　*Digested*, 86/**1263**:
　　　　　　　　　　　Applied, 97/5234: *Considered*, 87/1319: *Distinguished*, 99/2124
Ignaccolo-Zenide *v.* Romania (31679/96) (2001) 31 E.H.R.R. 7, ECHR . . . .　*Digested*, 01/**3550**
Igwemma *v.* Chief Constable of Greater Manchester [2001] EWCA Civ 953; [2001] 4
　　All E.R. 751; (2001) 98(33) L.S.G. 31; (2001) 145 S.J.L.B. 173; *Times*, July 20,
　　2001, CA . . . .　*Digested*, 01/**54**
IHT Internationale Heiztechnik GmbH *v.* Ideal Standard GmbH (C9/93) [1994] E.C.R. I-
　　2789; [1994] 3 C.M.L.R. 857; [1995] F.S.R. 59; *Times*, July 7, 1994; *Financial*
　　Times, June 28, 1994, ECJ. . . . .　*Digested*, 94/**4870**:
　　　　　　　　　　　Applied, 96/5713: *Followed*, 01/4029: *Referred to*, 98/3506, 99/3572
IJL *v.* United Kingdom; GMR *v.* United Kingdom; AKP *v.* United Kingdom (2001) 33
　　E.H.R.R. 11; 9 B.H.R.C. 222; [2001] Crim. L.R. 133; *Times*, October 13, 2000,
　　ECHR . . . .　*Digested*, 00/**3234**
IJS Contractors Ltd *v.* Dew Construction Ltd (2001) 17 Const. L.J. 274, CA
Ikimi *v.* Ikimi (Divorce: Habitual Residence) [2001] EWCA Civ 873; [2001] 3 W.L.R.
　　672; [2001] 2 F.L.R. 1288; [2001] 2 F.C.R. 385; [2001] Fam. Law 660; (2001)
　　98(27) L.S.G. 38; (2001) 145 S.J.L.B. 163; *Times*, July 18, 2001; *Independent*,
　　June 20, 2001, CA; affirming [2001] 1 F.L.R. 913, Fam Div . . . .　*Digested*, 01/**2617**
Ilion Group Plc *v.* Connor [1999] Disc. L.R. 200, EAT. . . . .　*Digested*, 00/**2141**

Illingworth *v.* Houldsworth; *sub nom* Houldsworth *v.* Yorkshire Woolcombers
    Association Ltd; Yorkshire Woolcombers Association Ltd, Re [1904] A.C. 355,
    HL; affirming [1903] 2 Ch. 284, CA . . . .   *Applied,* 79/2389,
                       88/306, 01/732: *Considered,* 59/2597, 95/567: *Followed,* 82/2177
IM Properties Plc *v.* Cape & Dalgleish [1999] Q.B. 297; [1998] 3 W.L.R. 457; [1998] 3
    All E.R. 203; (1998) 95(31) L.S.G. 34; (1998) 95(24) L.S.G. 34; (1998) 148
    N.L.J. 906; (1998) 142 S.J.L.B. 174; *Times,* May 28, 1998, CA . . . .   *Digested,* 98/**1433**
Imagemaster Ltd, Re see Cork *v.* Katz
Imbrioscia *v.* Switzerland (A/275) (1994) 17 E.H.R.R. 441, ECHR . . . .   *Digested,* 94/**2407**:
               Applied, 00/3223: *Considered,* 98/3146, 01/6760: *Followed,* 97/2817
Immigration Advisory Service *v.* Oommen [1997] I.C.R. 683, EAT . . . .   *Digested,* 97/**2227**:
             Applied, 99/2059: *Distinguished,* 00/2096: *Not followed,* 99/2039
Immigration & Naturalization Service *v.* Aguirre-Aguirre [2000] I.N.L.R. 60, US Ct
Immigration of Non Community Workers (C281/85), Re see Germany *v.* Commission of
    the European Communities (European Parliament Intervening) (C281/85)
Immobiliare Saffi *v.* Italy (2000) 30 E.H.R.R. 756; 7 B.H.R.C. 256, ECHR . . . .   *Digested,* 00/**3182**
IMMUNEX/Divisional application (J29/96) [1998] E.P.O.R. 358, EPO (Legal Bd App)
Immunity of Special Rapporteur, Re, *Times,* May 19, 1999, ICJ . . . .   *Digested,* 99/**3597**
Imperial Cancer Research Fund *v.* Bradley see Broadbent (Deceased), Re
Imperial Group Plc *v.* Philip Morris Ltd [1984] R.P.C. 293, Ch D . . . .   *Considered,* 99/3539:
                                         Followed, 00/3777
Imperial Square Developments (Hoxton) Ltd *v.* Aegon Insurance Co (UK) Ltd 62 Con.
    L.R. 59, QBD (OR) . . . .   *Digested,* 99/**562**
Imperial Tobacco Ltd *v.* Attorney General [1981] A.C. 718; [1980] 2 W.L.R. 466; [1980]
    1 All E.R. 866; 124 S.J. 271, HL; reversing [1979] Q.B. 555; [1979] 2 W.L.R.
    805; [1979] 2 All E.R. 592; 123 S.J. 283, CA; reversing [1979] Crim. L.R. 315;
    (1980) 130 N.L.J. 847, QBD . . . .   *Digested,* 80/**1317**:
          Applied, 85/423: *Considered,* 97/3098: *Distinguished,* 87/2426, 88/2276,
                      01/543: *Followed,* 94/615, 95/856, 99/589
Imperial Tobacco Ltd *v.* Secretary of State for Health see R. (on the application of
    Imperial Tobacco Ltd) *v.* Secretary of State for Health
IMPERIAL TOBACCO/Smoking article (T524/98) [2000] E.P.O.R. 412, EPO (Technical Bd
    App) . . . .   *Digested,* 00/**3629**
Implants International Ltd *v.* Stratec Medical [1999] 2 All E.R. (Comm) 933, QBD
    (Merc Ct) . . . .   *Digested,* 00/**754**
Implementation of the Open Network Provision Directive, Re [2000] E.C.C. 391, C
    Concurrence (F)
Impro Ltd *v.* Helping Hand Co (Ledbury) Ltd see Impro Ltd's Patent (No.2140773)
Impro Ltd's Patent (No.2140773); *sub nom* Impro Ltd *v.* Helping Hand Co (Ledbury)
    Ltd [1998] F.S.R. 299; (1997) 20(9) I.P.D. 20092, Pat Ct . . . .   *Digested,* 98/**3464**:
                                        Followed, 98/3463
Improver Corp *v.* Remington Consumer Products Ltd [1990] F.S.R. 181, Pat Ct . . . .   *Digested,* 91/**2698**:
        Applied, 95/3758, 96/4568, 99/3472: *Considered,* 00/3639:
        Followed, 95/3799, 97/3901, 98/3467: *Referred to,* 99/3480
Imutran Ltd *v.* Uncaged Campaigns Ltd [2001] 2 All E.R. 385; [2001] C.P. Rep. 28;
    [2001] E.C.D.R. 16; [2001] E.M.L.R. 21; [2001] H.R.L.R. 31; (2001) 24(5) I.P.D.
    24031; (2001) 98(14) L.S.G. 40; *Times,* January 30, 2001, Ch D   *Digested,* 01/**570**
Incal *v.* Turkey (2000) 29 E.H.R.R. 449; 4 B.H.R.C. 476; [1998] H.R.C.D. 650, ECHR . .   *Digested,* 98/**3093**:
                       Distinguished, 01/358: *Followed,* 00/3193, 01/3477
Inchcape Management Services Ltd *v.* Customs and Excise Commissioners [2000]
    B.V.C. 2104; [1999] V. & D.R. 397, V&DTr . . . .   *Digested,* 00/**5282**
Inco Europe Ltd *v.* First Choice Distribution [2000] 1 W.L.R. 586; [2000] 2 All E.R.
    109; [2000] 1 All E.R. (Comm) 674; [2000] 1 Lloyd's Rep. 467; [2000] C.L.C.
    1015; [2000] B.L.R. 259; (2000) 2 T.C.L.R. 487; 74 Con. L.R. 55; (2000)
    97(12) L.S.G. 39; (2000) 144 S.J.L.B. 134; [2000] N.P.C. 22; *Times,* March 10,
    2000; *Independent,* March 15, 2000, HL; affirming [1999] 1 W.L.R. 270; [1999]
    1 All E.R. 820; [1999] C.L.C. 165; (1999) 1 T.C.L.R. 169; (1998) 95(41) L.S.G.
    45; (1998) 142 S.J.L.B. 269; *Times,* October 22, 1998; *Independent,* October 12,
    1998 (C.S.), CA . . . .   *Digested,* 00/**220**
Incorporated Council of Law Reporting for England and Wales *v.* Attorney General [1972]
    Ch. 73; [1971] 3 W.L.R. 853; [1971] 3 All E.R. 1029; 115 S.J. 808, CA;
    affirming [1971] Ch. 626; [1971] 2 W.L.R. 550; [1971] 1 All E.R. 436; 47 T.C. 321;
    (1970) 115 S.J. 142; *Times,* December 4, 1970, Ch D . . . .   *Digested,* 71/**1125**:
          Applied, 81/220: *Considered,* 96/1299: *Distinguished,* 80/241, 81/226,
                                         00/5256
Incorporated National Association of British and Irish Millers Ltd's Scheme, Re; *sub nom*
    Medicaments Reference No.2, Re L.R.1 R.P. 267; [1960] 1 W.L.R. 63; [1959] 2
    All E.R. 780 (Note); 104 S.J. 90, RPC . . . .   *Digested,* 59/**3294**:
                                         Considered, 99/701
Ind *v.* Plant Hire Co (Stroud) Ltd [1999] Env. L.R. D15, QBD
Indata Equipment Supplies Ltd (t/a Autofleet) *v.* ACL Ltd [1998] 1 B.C.L.C. 412; [1998]
    F.S.R. 248; (1997) 141 S.J.L.B. 216; *Times,* August 14, 1997, CA; affirming in
    part [1996] C.L.C. 957, QBD . . . .   *Digested,* 97/**2526**

Independent Television Publications Ltd *v.* Commission of the European Communities
(C242/91) see Radio Telefis Eireann *v.* Commission of the European
Communities (C241/91)
Independent Trustee Services Ltd *v.* Rowe [1998] O.P.L.R. 77, Ch D . . . .   *Digested*, 00/**4367**
India *v.* India Steamship Co Ltd (The Indian Endurance and The Indian Grace) (No.2)
[1998] A.C. 878; [1997] 3 W.L.R. 818; [1997] 4 All E.R. 380; [1998] 1 Lloyd's
Rep. 1; [1997] C.L.C. 1581; [1998] I.L.Pr. 511; (1997) 94(43) L.S.G. 29; (1997)
147 N.L.J. 1581; (1997) 141 S.J.L.B. 230; *Times*, October 23, 1997, HL; affirming
[1997] 2 W.L.R. 538; [1996] 3 All E.R. 641; [1996] 2 Lloyd's Rep. 12; [1996]
C.L.C. 1548; *Times*, May 1, 1996, CA; reversing [1994] 2 Lloyd's Rep. 331; *Times*,
June 9, 1994, QBD (Adm Ct) . . . .   *Digested*, 97/**875**:
                                                                                                     Applied, 00/2320
INDUPACK, GENENTECH/Third party opposition (G03/97, G04/97) [2000] E.P.O.R. 81,
EPO (Enlarged Bd App) . . . .   *Digested*, 00/**3653**
INDUPACK/Straw man (T301/95) [1998] E.P.O.R. 142, EPO (Technical Bd App) . . . . .   *Subsequent proceed-*
                                                                                                     ings, 00/3653
Industria e Comercio de Cosmeticos Natura AS's Trade Mark Application [2001] E.T.M.R. 71,
Rel (Lisboa)
Industrial Diseases Compensation Ltd *v.* Marrons [2001] B.P.I.R. 600, Ch D . . . .   *Digested*, 01/**3728**
Industrie Aeronautiche e Meccaniche Rinaldo Piaggio SpA *v.* International Factors Italia
SpA (IFITALIA) (C295/97) [1999] E.C.R. I-3735; [2000] 3 C.M.L.R. 825, ECJ
(5th Chamber) . . . .   *Digested*, 01/**2517**
Industrie des Poudres Spheriques *v.* Council of the European Union (T5/97) [2000]
E.C.R. II-3755; [2001] 4 C.M.L.R. 28, CFI (5th Chamber) . . . .   *Digested*, 01/**766**
Industrie Tessili Italiana Como *v.* Dunlop AG (C12/76); *sub nom* Firma Industrie Tessili
Italiana Como *v.* Firma Dunlop AG (C12/76) [1976] E.C.R. 1473; [1977] 1
C.M.L.R. 26; *Times*, October 11, 1976, ECJ [1976] E.C.R. 1473, AGO . . . .   *Digested*, 77/**1281**:
                                                      Applied, 89/4503, 90/5353, 00/764
Infante *v.* Rai-Radiotelevisione Italiana SpA (1999) 96(11) L.S.G. 70; *Times*, March 11,
1999, CA . . . .   *Digested*, 99/**454**
Infantino *v.* MacLean [2001] 3 All E.R. 802; [2001] C.P. Rep. 99; *Times*, July 20,
2001; *Independent*, July 30, 2001 (C.S), QBD . . . .   *Digested*, 01/**645**:
                                                                                                     Followed, 01/643
Infocall Universal Ltd (t/a Psychic Centre) *v.* Customs and Excise Commissioners [2001]
S.T.I. 340, V&DTr
Informationsverein Lentia *v.* Austria (A/276) (1994) 17 E.H.R.R. 93, ECHR . . . .   *Digested*, 94/**2416**:
                                                                                                     Applied, 98/3095
Ing Lease (UK) Ltd *v.* Griswold [1998] B.C.C. 905, Ch D . . . .   *Digested*, 99/**3341**
Ingall *v.* Moran [1944] K.B. 160, CA . . . .   *Applied*, 47-51/8798,
                                            53/2907, 94/3826: *Considered*, 83/2948: *Disapproved*, 01/414
Ingelby *v.* Secretary of State for the Environment, Transport and the Regions [2001]
J.P.L. 615 (Note), QBD
Ingles *v.* Toronto City Corp (2001) 17 Const. L.J. 540, Sup Ct (Can)
Ingmar GB Ltd *v.* Eaton Leonard Inc (formerly Eaton Leonard Technologies Inc) (Post
European Reference) [2001] C.L.C. 1825; [2001] Eu. L.R. 755, QBD
Ingmar GB Ltd *v.* Eaton Leonard Technologies Inc (C381/98) [2001] All E.R. (EC) 57;
[2001] 1 All E.R. (Comm) 329; [2000] E.C.R. I-9305; [2001] 1 C.M.L.R. 9;
Times, November 16, 2000, ECJ (5th Chamber) [1999] E.C.C. 49; [1999] Eu.
L.R. 88; (1999) 18 Tr. L.R. 327, CA . . . .   *Digested*, 00/**115**
Ingosstrakh Ltd *v.* Latvian Shipping Co [2000] I.L.Pr. 164, CA . . . .   *Digested*, 00/**760**
Ingram *v.* Department of the Environment for Northern Ireland (Unreported,
September 6, 1993), CA (NI) . . . .   *Followed*, 01/**5901**
Ingram *v.* Foxon [1984] I.C.R. 685; [1985] I.R.L.R. 5; (1984) 81 L.S.G. 1678; (1984)
134 N.L.J. 473, EAT . . . .   *Digested*, 84/**1197**:
                                                                                                     Not followed, 98/2231
Ingram (Executors of the Estate of Lady Ingram) *v.* Inland Revenue Commissioners
[2000] 1 A.C. 293; [1999] 2 W.L.R. 90; [1999] 1 All E.R. 297; [1999] S.T.C. 37;
[1999] L. & T.R. 85; [1998] B.T.C. 8047; [1998] E.G.C.S. 181; (1999) 96(3)
L.S.G. 33; (1999) 143 S.J.L.B. 52; [1998] N.P.C. 160; *Times*, December 16,
1998; *Independent*, December 15, 1998, HL; reversing [1997] 4 All E.R. 395;
[1997] S.T.C. 1234; [1997] B.T.C. 8009; (1997) 94(34) L.S.G. 29; (1997) 141
S.J.L.B. 204; [1997] N.P.C. 129; *Times*, September 11, 1997, CA; reversing
[1995] 4 All E.R. 334; [1995] S.T.C. 564; (1995) 92(23) L.S.G. 33; (1995) 139
S.J.L.B. 128; [1995] N.P.C. 92; *Times*, May 23, 1995; *Independent*, June 5,
1995 (C.S.), Ch D . . . .   *Digested*, 99/**4740**
Ingram *v.* Little [1961] 1 Q.B. 31; [1960] 3 W.L.R. 504; [1960] 3 All E.R. 332; 104 S.J.
704, CA . . . .   *Digested*, 60/**550**:
                                                      Distinguished, 99/2512: *Doubted*, 71/1801
Ingram *v.* Sykes (1987) 137 N.L.J. 1135, CA . . . .   *Digested*, 87/**2956**:
                                                                                                     Considered, 00/391
Ingrasci *v.* Greatwood (Unreported, April 7, 1998), CC (Kingston on Thames) [*Ex rel.*
Taner Dedezade, Barrister, Tindal Chambers, 3-5 New Street, Chelmsford,
Essex] . . . .   *Digested*, 98/**1710**

Inhale Therapeutic Systems Inc v. Quadrant Healthcare Plc (2001) 24(11) I.P.D. 24075,
    Pat Ct

Inland Revenue Commissioner v. Agnew see Brumark Investments Ltd, Re

Inland Revenue Commissioner v. Auckland Harbour Board [2001] UKPC 1; [2001]
    B.T.C. 360; [2001] S.T.I. 150, PC (NZ) . . . . *Digested*, 01/**5275**

Inland Revenue Commissioner v. Colonial Mutual Life Assurance Society Ltd [2001]
    UKPC 54; [2001] S.T.I. 1770, PC (NZ)

Inland Revenue Commissioner v. Dick (2001-02) 4 I.T.E.L.R. 317, HC (NZ)

Inland Revenue Commissioner v. New Zealand Forest Research Institute Ltd [2000] 1
    W.L.R. 1755; [2000] S.T.C. 522; 72 T.C. 628; [2000] B.T.C. 245; [2000] S.T.I.
    885, PC (NZ) . . . . *Digested*, 00/**4928**

Inland Revenue Commissioner v. Secan Ltd 3 I.T.L. Rep. 496, CFA (HK)

Inland Revenue Commissioner v. Wattie [1999] 1 W.L.R. 873; [1998] S.T.C. 1160; 72
    T.C. 639; [1998] B.T.C. 438, PC (NZ) . . . . *Digested*, 99/**4719**

Inland Revenue Commissioner v. Yick Fung Estates Ltd 2 I.T.L. Rep. 489, CA (HK);
    affirming in part 1 I.T.L. Rep. 181, CFI (HK)

Inland Revenue Commissioners v. Aberdeen Milk Co Ltd [1999] S.T.C. 787; 2000
    S.C.L.R. 37; 73 T.C. 563; [1999] B.T.C. 378; 1999 G.W.D. 24-1127, Ex Div . . . . . *Digested*, 99/**6456**

Inland Revenue Commissioners v. Adam & Partners Ltd; *sub nom* Adam & Partners
    Ltd, Re [2001] 1 B.C.L.C. 222; [2000] B.P.I.R. 986; *Daily Telegraph*, October 31,
    2000, CA; affirming [2000] B.C.C. 513; [1999] 2 B.C.L.C. 730; [1999] B.P.I.R.
    868; *Times*, August 2, 1999 ; *Independent*, October 25, 1999 (C.S.), Ch D . . . . . *Digested*, 00/**3493**

Inland Revenue Commissioners v. Alexander Von Glehn & Co Ltd [1920] 2 K.B. 553;
    (1920) 2 Ll. L. Rep. 556, CA; affirming (1919) 1 Ll. L. Rep. 657, KBD (Comm
    Ct) . . . . *Considered*, 99/4701:
                                                  Distinguished, 52/1650

Inland Revenue Commissioners v. Amerada Hess Ltd see Amerada Hess Ltd v. Inland
    Revenue Commissioners

Inland Revenue Commissioners v. Ayrshire Employers Mutual Insurance Association
    Ltd; *sub nom* Ayrshire Employers Mutual Association Ltd v. Inland Revenue
    (1946) 79 Ll. L. Rep. 307; 1946 S.L.T. 235; 27 T.C. 331, HL; affirming 1945 S.L.T.
    102, 1 Div . . . . *Considered*, 00/4964

Inland Revenue Commissioners v. Bernstein [1961] Ch. 399; [1961] 2 W.L.R. 143;
    [1961] 1 All E.R. 320; 39 T.C. 391; (1960) 39 A.T.C. 415; [1960] T.R. 369; 105
    S.J. 128, CA; affirming [1960] Ch. 444; [1960] 2 W.L.R. 554; [1960] 1 All E.R.
    697; 53 R. & I.T. 301; (1960) 39 A.T.C. 117; [1960] T.R. 21; 104 S.J. 250, Ch D . . *Digested*, 61/**4269**:
                           Applied, 67/3072, 84/3131: *Considered*, 00/4628

Inland Revenue Commissioners v. Botnar [1999] S.T.C. 711; 72 T.C. 205; [1999] B.T.C.
    267; *Times*, July 6, 1999, CA; affirming [1998] S.T.C. 38; [1997] B.T.C. 613, Ch D
    . . . . *Digested*, 99/**4735**

Inland Revenue Commissioners v. Bowater Property Developments Ltd see Craven
    (Inspector of Taxes) v. White (Stephen)

Inland Revenue Commissioners v. Bullock [1976] 1 W.L.R. 1178; [1976] 3 All E.R. 353;
    [1976] S.T.C. 409; 51 T.C. 522; [1975] T.R. 179; 120 S.J. 591, CA; reversing
    [1975] 1 W.L.R. 1436; [1975] 3 All E.R. 541; [1975] S.T.C. 512; [1975] T.R. 179;
    119 S.J. 530, Ch D . . . . *Digested*, 76/**1414**:
                                 Applied, 81/2301: *Considered*, 99/4638

Inland Revenue Commissioners v. Challenge Corp [1987] A.C. 155; [1987] 2 W.L.R.
    24; [1986] S.T.C. 548; (1986) 83 L.S.G. 3598; (1987) 131 S.J. 46, PC (NZ) . . . *Digested*, 87/**2036**:
                                 Considered, 87/274, 01/5275

Inland Revenue Commissioners v. Debtor see Debtor (No.6349 of 1994), Re

Inland Revenue Commissioners v. Duce [1999] B.P.I.R. 189; *Times*, December 29, 1998,
    Ch D . . . . *Digested*, 99/**3347**

Inland Revenue Commissioners v. Duke of Westminster [1936] A.C. 1; 19 T.C. 490, HL . .   *Applied*, 47-51/2592,
             47-51/4819, 47-51/5229, 47-51/9946, 52/1642, 52/4132, 79/171, 00/4916:
             Considered, 57/3508, 81/1385, 85/3364, 86/3204, 87/274, 87/2036:
        Distinguished, 75/1676, 84/270: *Followed*, 59/1543: *Not followed*, 81/1608

Inland Revenue Commissioners v. Ernst & Young see R. v. Inland Revenue
    Commissioners Ex p. Bishopp

Inland Revenue Commissioners v. Fry [2001] S.T.C. 1715; [2001] S.T.I. 1665; (2001)
    151 N.L.J. 1820; (2001) 145 S.J.L.B. 279; *Times*, December 10, 2001, Ch D

Inland Revenue Commissioners v. Hashmi (2001) 98(41) L.S.G. 34; *Times*, November
    2, 2001, Ch D . . . . *Digested*, 01/**3783**

Inland Revenue Commissioners v. John Lewis Properties Ltd see John Lewis Properties
    Plc v. Inland Revenue Commissioners

Inland Revenue Commissioners v. Joiner; *sub nom* Joiner v. Inland Revenue
    Commissioners [1975] 1 W.L.R. 1701; [1975] 3 All E.R. 1050; [1975] S.T.C. 657;
    50 T.C. 449; [1975] T.R. 77; [1975] T.R. 257; 119 S.J. 827, HL; affirming [1975]
    1 W.L.R. 273; [1975] 1 All E.R. 755; [1975] S.T.C. 200; [1974] T.R. 383; 119
    S.J. 137; *Times*, December 13, 1974, CA; affirming [1973] 1 W.L.R. 690; [1973] 2
    All E.R. 379; [1973] S.T.C. 224; [1973] T.R. 23; 117 S.J. 323, Ch D . . . . *Digested*, 76/**1444**:
               Considered, 88/3026, 89/3186, 91/166, 95/320, 00/4943

Inland Revenue Commissioners v. Kahn see Toshoku Finance UK Plc (In Liquidation), Re

Inland Revenue Commissioners *v.* Laird Group Plc; *sub nom* Laird Group Plc *v.* Inland
Revenue Commissioners; A3/2001/1514, CA; reversing [2001] S.T.C. 689;
[2001] B.T.C. 137; [2001] S.T.I. 280; *Times*, March 13, 2001, Ch D; affirming
[2000] S.T.C. (S.C.D.) 75; [2000] S.T.I.104; (2001) 98(16) L.S.G. 35, ICTA Tr . .   *Digested,* 01/**5174**

Inland Revenue Commissioners *v.* Lawrence; *sub nom* FJL Realisations Ltd, Re [2001]
B.C.C. 663; [2001] 1 B.C.L.C. 204; [2001] I.C.R. 424; *Times*, August 2, 2000,
CA; affirming (2000) 97(9) L.S.G. 40; (2000) 144 S.J.L.B. 191; *Times*, March
21, 2000; *Independent*, April 3, 2000 (C.S.), Ch D . . . .   *Digested,* 00/**3429**

Inland Revenue Commissioners *v.* Lloyds Private Banking Ltd [1998] S.T.C. 559;
[1999] 1 F.L.R. 147; [1998] 2 F.C.R. 41; [1998] B.T.C. 8020; [1999] Fam. Law
309; (1998) 95(19) L.S.G. 23; (1998) 142 S.J.L.B. 164; *Times*, April 10, 1998,
Ch D . . . .   *Digested,* 98/**4689**:
    Considered, 01/5287

Inland Revenue Commissioners *v.* Lysaght; *sub nom* Lysaght *v.* Inland Revenue
Commissioners [1928] A.C. 234; [1928] All E.R. Rep. 575; 13 T.C. 511, HL;
reversing [1927] 2 K.B. 55, CA. . . . .   *Applied,* 54/997,
    82/974, 83/1157, 85/1771: *Cited,* 99/4564: *Considered,* 80/852, 91/2373,
    95/3207

Inland Revenue Commissioners *v.* Mallender see Mallender *v.* Inland Revenue
Commissioners

Inland Revenue Commissioners *v.* McGuckian; McGuckian *v.* Inland Revenue
Commissioners [1997] 1 W.L.R. 991; [1997] 3 All E.R. 817; [1997] S.T.C. 908;
[1997] N.I. 157; 69 T.C. 1; [1997] B.T.C. 346; (1997) 94(27) L.S.G. 23; (1997)
141 S.J.L.B. 153; *Times*, June 20, 1997; *Independent*, July 28, 1997 (C.S.), HL
(NI); reversing [1994] S.T.C. 888; [1994] N.I. 1, CA (NI) . . . .   *Digested,* 97/**2979**:
    Applied, 00/5043, 01/5205: *Considered,* 99/4709

Inland Revenue Commissioners *v.* McGuckian (Time Limits) see McGuckian, Re

Inland Revenue Commissioners *v.* Metrolands (Property Finance) Ltd [1982] 1 W.L.R.
341; [1982] 2 All E.R. 557; [1982] S.T.C. 259; 80 L.G.R. 553; 54 T.C. 679;
[1982] J.P.L. 570; 126 S.J. 188, HL; reversing [1981] 1 W.L.R. 637; [1981] 2 All
E.R.166; [1981] S.T.C. 193; 79 L.G.R. 358; [1980] T.R. 457; 125 S.J. 19, Ch D . .   *Digested,* 82/**3135**:
    Applied, 92/344: *Approved,* 99/4704: *Referred to,* 95/529

Inland Revenue Commissioners *v.* Muller & Co's Margarine Ltd; *sub nom* Muller & Co's
Margarine Ltd *v.* Inland Revenue Commissioners [1901] A.C. 217, HL; affirming
[1900] 1 Q.B. 310, CA . . . .   *Applied,* 92/4143:
    Considered, 98/3497: *Explained,* 74/3681

Inland Revenue Commissioners *v.* National Federation of Self Employed and Small
Businesses Ltd see R. *v.* Inland Revenue Commissioners Ex p. National
Federation of Self Employed and Small Businesses Ltd

Inland Revenue Commissioners *v.* Nelmes see Centralcrest Engineering Ltd, Re

Inland Revenue Commissioners *v.* Oce van der Grinten NV; *sub nom* Oce van der
Grinten NV *v.* Inland Revenue Commissioners [2000] S.T.C. 951; [2001] 2
C.M.L.R. 9; [2001] B.T.C. 22; 2 I.T.L. Rep. 948; [2000] S.T.I. 1547; *Times*,
November 21, 2000, Ch D; affirming [2000] S.T.C. (S.C.D.) 127; 2 I.T.L. Rep.
614; [2000] S.T.I. 251, Sp Comm . . . .   *Digested,* 00/**4968**

Inland Revenue Commissioners *v.* Oldham Training and Enterprise Council [1996] S.T.C.
1218; 69 T.C. 231; *Times*, October 11, 1996; *Independent*, October 21, 1996
(C.S.), Ch D . . . .   *Digested,* 96/**1299**

Inland Revenue Commissioners *v.* Paget; *sub nom* Paget *v.* Inland Revenue
Commissioners [1938] 2 K.B. 25; 21 T.C. 677, CA; affirming [1937] 2 K.B. 711,
KBD . . . .   *Applied,* 58/1552,
    01/5205

Inland Revenue Commissioners *v.* Pricewaterhouse Coopers see R. *v.* Inland Revenue
Commissioners Ex p. Bishopp

Inland Revenue Commissioners *v.* Regent Oil Co Ltd see Regent Oil Co Ltd *v.* Strick
(Inspector of Taxes)

Inland Revenue Commissioners *v.* Robinson [1999] B.P.I.R. 329, Ch D . . . .   *Digested,* 99/**3249**

Inland Revenue Commissioners *v.* Rossminster Ltd see R. *v.* Inland Revenue
Commissioners Ex p. Rossminster Ltd

Inland Revenue Commissioners *v.* Trustees of the Sema Group Pension Scheme see
Trustees of the Sema Group Pension Scheme *v.* Inland Revenue Commissioners

Inland Revenue Commissioners *v.* Universities Superannuation Scheme Ltd [1997]
S.T.C. 1; [1997] O.P.L.R. 15; 70 T.C. 193; [1997] B.T.C. 3; *Independent*, November
18, 1996 (C.S.), Ch D; reversing [1995] S.T.C. 21, Sp Comm . . . .   *Digested,* 97/**2980**

Inland Revenue Commissioners *v.* Willoughby [1997] 1 W.L.R. 1071; [1997] 4 All E.R.
65; [1997] S.T.C. 995; 70 T.C. 57; [1997] B.T.C. 393; (1997) 94(29) L.S.G. 28;
(1997) 147 N.L.J. 1062; (1997) 141 S.J.L.B. 176; *Times*, July 16, 1997, HL;
affirming [1995] S.T.C. 143; (1995) 92(10) L.S.G. 39; (1995) 139 S.J.L.B. 44;
Times, January 6, 1995; *Independent*, February 13, 1995 (C.S.), CA . . . .   *Digested,* 97/**2942**:
    Considered, 96/1301

INLAND STEEL/Retraction of withdrawal (J10/87) [1989] E.P.O.R. 437, EPO (Legal Bd
App) . . . .   *Distinguished,*
    99/3469

Inlima SL's Application for a Three Dimensional Trade Mark [2000] R.P.C. 661, Appointed
    Person; affirming [2000] E.T.M.R. 325, TMR . . . . *Digested,* 00/**3782**
Inman *v.* Kenny [2001] EWCA Civ 35; [2001] P.I.Q.R. P18, CA . . . . *Digested,* 01/**4449**
Inntrepreneur Beer Supply Co Ltd *v.* Byrne see Courage Ltd *v.* Crehan (No.1)
Inntrepreneur Beer Supply Co Ltd *v.* Langton see Courage Ltd *v.* Crehan (No.1)
Inntrepreneur Estates (CPC) Ltd *v.* Bayliss [1998] Eu. L.R. 483; [1994] N.P.C. 19, Ch D   *Digested,* 94/**2767**
Inntrepreneur Estates (GL) Ltd *v.* Boyes [1995] E.C.C. 16; (1994) 68 P. & C.R. 77;
    [1993] 47 E.G. 140, CA . . . . *Digested,* 94/**2766**:
                                                                        Followed, 99/680
Inntrepreneur Estates Ltd *v.* Hollard 00/0594/A2, CA; affirming [1999] N.P.C. 137,
    QBD
Inntrepreneur Estates Ltd *v.* Mason [1993] 2 C.M.L.R. 293; (1994) 68 P. & C.R. 53;
    [1993] 45 E.G. 130, QBD . . . . *Digested,* 94/**2765**:
                       Considered, 94/2766: *Followed,* 99/680
Inntrepreneur Pub Co (GL) *v.* East Crown Ltd see Inntrepreneur Pub Co Ltd *v.* East
    Crown Ltd
Inntrepreneur Pub Co (CPC) Ltd *v.* Deans [1999] B.P.I.R. 361, QBD . . . . *Digested,* 99/**3702**
Inntrepreneur Pub Co Ltd *v.* East Crown Ltd; *sub nom* Inntrepreneur Pub Co (GL) *v.*
    East Crown Ltd [2000] 2 Lloyd's Rep. 611; [2000] 3 E.G.L.R. 31; [2000] 41 E.G.
    209; [2000] N.P.C. 93; *Times,* September 5, 2000, Ch D . . . . *Digested,* 00/**869**
Inntrepreneur Pub Co (CPC) Ltd *v.* Haigh see Courage Ltd *v.* Crehan (No.1)
Inntrepreneur Pub Co (CPC) Ltd *v.* Langton; Langton *v.* Inntrepreneur Pub Co (CPC)
    Ltd [2000] 1 E.G.L.R. 34; [2000] 08 E.G. 169; [1999] E.G.C.S. 124; (1999)
    96(44) L.S.G. 39; (1999) 143 S.J.L.B. 268; (2000) 79 P. & C.R. D7; *Times,*
    November 10, 1999, Ch D . . . . *Digested,* 99/**3665**:
                                           Previous proceedings, 99/684
Inntrepreneur Pub Co (CPC) Ltd *v.* Price [1999] E.C.C. 185; [1998] E.G.C.S. 167;
    [1998] N.P.C. 153; *Times,* December 4, 1998, Ch D . . . . *Digested,* 99/**3703**
Inoco Plc *v.* Gulf USA Corp (No.1) see Rowland *v.* Gulfpac Ltd (No.1)
Inquiry into Mirror Group Newspapers Plc, Re see Thomas *v.* Maxwell
Inside Sport Ltd (In Liquidation), Re; *sub nom* Inside Sports Ltd, Re [2000] B.C.C. 40;
    [2000] 1 B.C.L.C. 302; *Times,* November 27, 1998; *Independent,* November 16,
    1998 (C.S.), Ch D (Companies Ct) . . . . *Digested,* 98/**3322**:
                                                 Considered, 00/3507
Inside Sports Ltd, Re see Inside Sport Ltd (In Liquidation), Re
Insiger Trust (Guernsey) Ltd, Re (1999-2000) 2 I.T.E.L.R. 154, CA (Gue)
Insitute of Professional Representatives before the European Patent Office (EPI) *v.*
    Commission of the European Communities (T144/99) [2001] E.C.R. II-1087;
    [2001] 5 C.M.L.R. 2, CFI (2nd Chamber) . . . . *Digested,* 01/**3886**
Insolvency Act 1986, Re see Licence Holder, Re
Insolvency Act 1986, Re see Mineral Resources Ltd, Re
Insolvency Act 1986, Re see Cork *v.* Rawlins
Inspirations East Ltd *v.* Dudley MBC (1998) 162 J.P. 800; (1998) 162 J.P.N. 865, QBD . *Digested,* 99/**3824**
Instance *v.* Denny Bros Printing Ltd (Form of Order) (2000) 23(11) I.P.D. 23091, Pat
    Ct
Instance *v.* Denny Bros Printing Ltd (Interim Injunction) [2000] F.S.R. 869; (2000)
    23(11) I.P.D. 23090; (2000) 97(5) L.S.G. 35; (2000) 144 S.J.L.B. 56; *Times,*
    February 28, 2000, Pat Ct . . . . *Digested,* 00/**337**
Instance *v.* Denny Bros Printing Ltd (Patent Action); *sub nom* David J Instance Ltd *v.*
    Denny Bros Printing Ltd (Patent Action) [2001] EWCA Civ 939; (2001) 24(10)
    I.P.D. 24063; *Times,* June 22, 2001, CA; affirming (2000) 23(7) I.P.D. 23053,
    Pat Ct . . . . *Digested,* 01/**3963**
Instance's European Patent Application (J07/96) see Suspension of Proceedings (J07/96)
Institut Pasteur's European Patent (No.0424518) (1998) 21 (1) I.P.D. 21006, PO
INSTITUT PASTEUR/Lymphadenopathy-associated virus (T824/94) [2000] E.P.O.R.
    436, EPO (Technical Bd App) . . . . *Digested,* 00/**3650**
Institute of Chartered Accountants in England and Wales *v.* Customs and Excise
    Commissioners [1999] 1 W.L.R. 701; [1999] 2 All E.R. 449; [1999] S.T.C. 398;
    [1999] 2 C.M.L.R. 1333; [1999] B.T.C. 5165; [1999] B.V.C. 215; (1999) 96(20)
    L.S.G. 40; (1999) 149 N.L.J. 559; (1999) 143 S.J.L.B. 131; *Times,* March 29,
    1999; *Independent,* April 14, 1999, HL; affirming [1998] 1 W.L.R. 315; [1998] 4
    All E.R. 115; [1997] S.T.C. 1155; [1997] B.T.C. 5355; [1997] B.V.C. 469; (1997)
    94(25) L.S.G. 34; (1997) 141 S.J.L.B. 128; *Times,* May 19, 1997; *Independent,*
    May 22, 1997, CA; affirming [1996] S.T.C. 799; *Times,* February 19, 1996, QBD;
    affirming [1995] V. & D.R. 87, VAT Tr (London) . . . . *Digested,* 99/**4990**
Institute of Chartered Foresters *v.* Customs and Excise Commissioners [2001] S.T.I.
    259, V&DTr
Institute of Independent Insurance Brokers *v.* Director General of Fair Trading;
    Association of British Travel Agents Ltd *v.* Director General of Fair Trading [2001]
    Comp. A.R. 62; *Daily Telegraph,* September 25, 2001, CCAT
Institute of the Motor Industry *v.* Customs and Excise Commissioners [2000] B.V.C.
    2307; [2000] S.T.I. 1056, V&DTr . . . . *Digested,* 01/**5570**

Institute of the Motor Industry *v.* Customs and Excise Commissioners (C149/97) [1998]
    S.T.C. 1219; [1998] E.C.R. I-7053; [1999] 1 C.M.L.R. 326; [1998] B.T.C. 5484;
    [1999] B.V.C. 21; *Times*, November 19, 1998, ECJ (6th Chamber) [1996] V. &
    D.R. 370, V&DTr . . . . *Digested*, 98/**4901**
Institute of the Motor Industry *v.* Harvey (No.2); *sub nom* Harvey *v.* Institute of the
    Motor Industry (No.2) [1996] I.C.R. 981; [1995] I.R.L.R. 416, EAT . . . . *Digested*, 95/**2038**:
                                     Applied, 98/2100: *Distinguished*, 97/2241
Instone (formerly Macaulay) *v.* A Schroeder Music Publishing Co Ltd see A Schroeder
    Music Publishing Co Ltd *v.* Instone (formerly Macaulay)
Insurance Co *v.* Lloyd's Syndicate [1995] 1 Lloyd's Rep. 272; [1994] C.L.C. 1303;
    [1995] 4 Re. L.R. 37; *Times*, November 11, 1994; *Independent*, November 8,
    1994; *Lloyd's List*, February 1, 1995, QBD (Comm Ct) . . . . *Digested*, 96/**3619**:
                                           Considered, 98/240
Insurance Co of North America *v.* Societe Intramar [1999] I.L.Pr. 315, Cass (F) . . . . . . *Digested*, 99/**743**
Insurance Corp of the Channel Islands *v.* Royal Hotel Ltd [1998] Lloyd's Rep. I.R. 151,
    QBD (Comm Ct) . . . . *Digested*, 98/**3359**:
                                         Considered, 98/3360
Insurance Corp of the Channel Islands Ltd *v.* McHugh [1997] L.R.L.R. 94, QBD (Comm
    Ct) . . . . *Digested*, 97/**3120**:
                                         Applied, 00/3525
Insurance Premiums, Re see Bachmann *v.* Belgium (C204/90) (No.1)
Intel Corp *v.* Distilleerderijen Erven Lucas Bols BV [2001] E.T.M.R. CN20, Pat Val Apel
    Pad (LA)
Intelsec Systems Ltd *v.* Grech Cini [2000] 1 W.L.R. 1190; [1999] 4 All E.R. 11; [1999]
    Masons C.L.R. 296, Ch D . . . . *Digested*, 99/**2004**
Inter City Print & Finishing Ltd, Re see Cedarwood Productions Ltd, Re
Inter-Environnement Wallonie Asbl *v.* Region Wallone (C129/96) see Inter-
    Environnement Wallonie Asbl *v.* Region Wallonie (C129/96)
Inter-Environnement Wallonie Asbl *v.* Region Wallonie (C129/96); *sub nom* Inter-
    Environnement Wallonie Asbl *v.* Region Wallonne (C129/96); Inter-
    Environnement Wallonie Asbl *v.* Region Wallone (C129/96) [1998] All E.R. (E.C.)
    155; [1997] E.C.R. I-7411; [1998] 1 C.M.L.R. 1057; [1998] Env. L.R. 623, ECJ . . *Digested*, 98/**2308**:
                                          Followed, 99/2207
Inter-Environnement Wallonie Asbl *v.* Region Wallonne (C129/96) see Inter-
    Environnement Wallonie Asbl *v.* Region Wallonie (C129/96)
Inter-Leisure Ltd *v.* Lamberts [1997] N.P.C. 49, QBD . . . . *Considered*, 01/4536
Interallianz Finanz AG *v.* Independent Insurance Co Ltd [1997] E.G.C.S. 91; [1997]
    N.P.C. 89, QBD (Comm Ct) . . . . *Digested*, 98/**4029**
Interbet Ltd *v.* Customs and Excise Commissioners [1999] V. & D.R. 151, V&DTr . . . . . . *Digested*, 00/**4971**
Interbrew SA *v.* Competition Commission [2001] EWHC Admin 367; [2001]
    U.K.C.L.R. 954; [2001] E.C.C. 40; *Daily Telegraph*, May 29, 2001, QBD (Admin
    Ct) . . . . *Digested*, 01/**753**
Interbulk Ltd *v.* Aiden Shipping Co (The Vimeira) (No.1); ICCO International Corn Co
    NV *v.* Interbulk [1984] 2 Lloyd's Rep. 66, CA; reversing [1983] 2 Lloyd's Rep.
    424; [1983] Com. L.R. 142; (1983) 133 N.L.J. 575, QBD (Comm Ct) . . . . *Digested*, 84/**114**:
                               Applied, 98/233, 00/225: *Considered*, 85/105
Interbulk Ltd *v.* Ponte Dei Sospiri Shipping Co (The Standard Ardour) [1988] 2 Lloyd's
    Rep. 159, QBD (Comm Ct) . . . . *Digested*, 89/**3400**:
                                      Applied, 97/4514, 01/4931
Intercomfinanz SA *v.* Ladenimor SA see Harrods (Buenos Aires) Ltd (No.1), Re
Intercommunale voor Zeewaterontzilting (In Liquidation) *v.* Belgium (C110/94); *sub nom*
    Inzo *v.* Belgium (C110/94) [1996] S.T.C. 569; [1996] E.C.R. I-857; [1996]
    C.E.C. 490, ECJ . . . . *Digested*, 96/**5873**:
                                          Considered, 98/4918
Interdigital Communications Corp's Application [1999] E.T.M.R. 758, OHIM (3rd Bd App)

                                          Digested, 00/**3761**
Interessen Gemeinschaft von Papiergrosshandlern GmbH & Co KG (IGEPA) *v.* Papelara
    Guipuzcoana de Zicunaga SA (2000) 23(11) I.P.D. 23096, OHIM (1st Bd App)
Interfisa Management Inc *v.* Hamam see Guinle *v.* Kirreh
Interfoto Picture Library Ltd *v.* Stiletto Visual Programmes Ltd [1989] Q.B. 433; [1988]
    2 W.L.R. 615; [1988] 1 All E.R. 348; (1988) 7 Tr. L.R. 187; (1988) 85(9) L.S.G.
    45; (1987) 137 N.L.J. 1159; (1988) 132 S.J. 460, CA . . . . *Digested*, 88/**430**:
             Applied, 00/5989, 01/955: *Considered*, 88/61, 95/4501, 99/1801, 00/876,
                                             00/4710
Intergraph Corp *v.* Solid Systems CAD Services Ltd (No.2) [1995] E.C.C. 53; [1998]
    Eu. L.R. 223; [1998] Masons C.L.R. Rep. 7, Ch D . . . . *Digested*, 99/**3443**
Interlego AG *v.* Tyco Industries Inc [1989] A.C. 217; [1988] 3 W.L.R. 678; [1988] 3 All
    E.R. 949; 1 B.L.R. 271; [1988] 2 F.T.L.R. 133; [1988] R.P.C. 343; (1988) 132 S.J.
    698; *Times*, May 6, 1988; *Financial Times*, May 11, 1988, PC (HK); affirming
    [1987] F.S.R. 409, CA (HK) . . . . *Digested*, 88/**502**:
            Applied, 95/852: *Considered*, 94/622, 96/1277, 98/3416, 00/3586:
         Distinguished, 97/1036, 00/3572: *Explained*, 92/577: *Followed*, 96/1283,
                                          99/3496

Interlego AG's Trade Mark Applications [1998] R.P.C. 69; (1997) 20(8) I.P.D. 20079, Ch D

Digested, 98/**3498**:
Applied, 00/3712

Interlink Express Parcels Ltd v. Night Trunkers Ltd [2001] EWCA Civ 360; [2001] R.T.R. 23; (2001) 98(20) L.S.G. 43; *Times*, March 22, 2001, CA; reversing (2001) 165 J.P. 166; [2000] R.T.R. 324; (2000) 97(12) L.S.G. 40; (2000) 144 S.J.L.B. 133; *Times*, March 15, 2000, Ch D . . . .   *Digested*, 01/**2267**

Intermetal Group Ltd v. Worslade Trading Ltd [1998] I.L.Pr. 765, Sup Ct (Irl); affirming [1998] I.L.Pr. 746, HC (Irl)

International Air and Sea Cargo GmbH v. Owners of the Chitral [2000] 1 All E.R. (Comm) 932; [2000] 1 Lloyd's Rep. 529; [2000] C.L.C. 1021, QBD (Comm Ct) . . . .   *Digested*, 00/**4683**

International Asset Control Ltd (t/a IAC Films) v. Films Sans Frontieres Sarl [1999] E.M.L.R. 268; *Times*, October 26, 1998, CA . . . .   *Digested*, 98/**624**

International Business Machine Corp's Application; *sub nom* IBM Corp's Application [1998] E.T.M.R. 642, OHIM (2nd Bd App)

International Business Machines Corp v. Commission of the European Communities (C60/81) see IBM Corp v. Commission of the European Communities (C60/81)

International Computers Ltd v. Customs and Excise Commissioners [1996] V. & D.R. 459, VAT Tr (London) . . . .   *Digested*, 98/**4633**

International Consulting Services (UK) Ltd v. Hart [2000] I.R.L.R. 227, QBD . . . .   *Digested*, 00/**2199**

International Credit and Investment Co (Overseas) Ltd v. Adham (Appointment of Receiver) [1998] B.C.C. 134, Ch D . . . .   *Digested*, 98/**3311**

International Credit and Investment Co (Overseas) Ltd v. Adham (Share Ownership) [1999] I.L.Pr. 302, CA. . . . .   *Digested*, 99/**720**

International Dairy Agreement (C61/94), Re see Commission of the European Communities v. Germany (C61/94)

International Distillers and Vinters Ltd (t/a Percy Fox & Co) v. JF Hillebrand (UK) Ltd, *Times*, January 25, 2000, QBD . . . .   *Digested*, 00/**550**

INTERNATIONAL DOME SYSTEMS/Building structure (T812/94) [2001] E.P.O.R. 31, EPO (Technical Bd App) . . . .   *Digested*, 01/**3905**

International Drilling Fluids Ltd v. Louisville Investments (Uxbridge) Ltd [1986] Ch. 513; [1986] 2 W.L.R. 581; [1986] 1 All E.R. 321; (1986) 51 P. & C.R. 187; [1986] 1 E.G.L.R. 39; (1985) 277 E.G. 62; (1986) 83 L.S.G. 436; *Times*, November 29, 1985, CA; affirming [1985] 2 E.G.L.R. 74; (1985) 275 E.G. 802; (1985) 129 S.J. 854, Ch D . . . .   *Digested*, 86/**1824**:
Applied, 88/2016, 89/2139, 93/2481, 94/2770, 95/338:
Considered, 86/1860, 87/2116, 89/2152, 89/2154, 90/2871, 91/2238, 91/2239, 97/3250, 99/3671

International Express Carriers Conference v. Commission of the European Communities (T133/95) [1998] E.C.R. II-3645; [1998] 5 C.M.L.R. 992; *Times*, October 1, 1998, CFI . . . .   *Digested*, 98/**4294**

International Express Carriers Conference (IECC) v. Commission of the European Communities (C449/98); *sub nom* International Express Carriers Conference (IECC) v. Commission of the European Communities (T110/95) [2001] E.C.R. I-3875; [2001] 5 C.M.L.R. 7, ECJ. . . . .   *Digested*, 01/**784**

International Express Carriers Conference (IECC) v. Commission of the European Communities (C450/98) [2001] E.C.R. I-3947; [2001] 5 C.M.L.R. 8, ECJ . . . .   *Digested*, 01/**785**

International Express Carriers Conference (IECC) v. Commission of the European Communities (T110/95) see International Express Carriers Conference (IECC) v. Commission of the European Communities (C449/98)

International Factors v. Rodriguez [1979] Q.B. 351; [1978] 3 W.L.R. 877; [1979] 1 All E.R. 17; 122 S.J. 680, CA . . . .   *Digested*, 79/**265**:
Not followed, 98/4775

International Fina Services AG v. Katrina Shipping and Tonen Tanker Kabushiki Kaisha (The Fina Samco) [1995] 2 Lloyd's Rep. 344, CA; affirming [1994] 1 Lloyd's Rep. 153, QBD (Comm Ct) . . . .   *Digested*, 94/**4063**:
Applied, 99/4431

International Finance Corp v. Utexafrica Sprl [2001] C.L.C. 1361, QBD (Comm Ct) . . . .   *Digested*, 01/**587**

International Fruit Co NV v. Produktschap voor Groenten en Fruit (No.3) (C21/72) [1972] E.C.R. 1219; [1975] 2 C.M.L.R. 1, ECJ . . . .   *Digested*, 75/**1267**:
Followed, 00/2366: *Referred to*, 97/1043

International Planned Parenthood Federation v. Customs and Excise Commissioners [2000] V. & D.R. 396; [2001] S.T.I. 530, V&DTr

International Power Plc (formerly National Power Plc) v. Healy see National Grid Co Plc v. Mayes

International Technologies Consultants Inc v. Euroglas SA [1998] I.L.Pr. 528, US Ct

International Time Recorder Co Ltd v. Lavie Computers Ltd [2001] I.L.Pr. 24, CJ (Gen Div) (Ont). . . . .   *Digested*, 01/**805**

International Tin Council, Re [1989] Ch. 309; [1988] 3 W.L.R.1159; [1988] 3 All E.R. 257; (1988) 4 B.C.C. 653; [1989] P.C.C. 90; (1988) 132 S.J. 1494; *Times*, April 29, 1988; *Independent*, May 5, 1988; *Financial Times*, May 5, 1988, CA; affirming [1987] Ch. 419; [1987] 2 W.L.R. 1229; [1987] 1 All E.R. 890; [1987] B.C.L.C. 272; [1987] P.C.C. 283; [1987] 1 F.T.L.R. 305; (1987) 84 L.S.G. 1732; (1987) 131 S.J. 690, Ch D . . . . *Digested*, 89/**274**:
Considered, 94/3626, 95/2939, 96/3659, 01/5005: *Referred to*, 87/2093
International Trade and Exhibitions J/V Ltd *v.* Customs and Excise Commissioners [1996] B.V.C. 2905; [1996] V. & D.R. 165, V&DTr . . . . *Digested*, 97/**5019**:
Distinguished, 98/4962
International Transport Roth GmbH *v.* Secretary of State for the Home Department see R. (on the application of International Transport Roth GmbH) *v.* Secretary of State for the Home Department
International Westminster Bank *v.* Okeanos Maritime Corp see Company (No.000359 of 1987), Re
Internet Domain Name, Re [2000] E.C.C. 226, OGH (A)
Internet Trading Clubs Ltd *v.* Freeserve (Investments) Ltd [2001] E.B.L.R. 142, QBD
Interoute Telecommunications (UK) Ltd *v.* Fashion Gossip Ltd, *Times*, November 10, 1999, Ch D . . . . *Digested*, 99/**576**
Interporc Im-und Export GmbH *v.* Commission of the European Communities (T124/96) [1998] E.C.R. II-231; [1998] 2 C.M.L.R. 82, CFI (3rd Chamber)
Interpub Ltd *v.* Secretary of State for the Environment, Transport and the Regions (1998) (95)44 L.S.G. 36, QBD
Intertronic F Cornelis GmbH *v.* Commission of the European Communities (T117/96) [1997] E.C.R. II-141; [1998] 4 C.M.L.R. 520, CFI (3rd Chamber)
Intervention Board for Agricultural Produce *v.* Leidig; *sub nom* Leidig *v.* Intervention Board for Agricultural Produce [2000] Lloyd's Rep. P.N. 144, CA . . . . *Digested*, 00/**4188**
Intra Group Licensing of Trademarks, Re (IR 12/99) 3 I.T.L. Rep. 619, BFH (Ger)
Introductory Offer for a New Television Guide, Re [1999] E.C.C. 42, OGH (A)
Inverdeck Ltd, Re [1998] B.C.C. 256; [1998] 2 B.C.L.C. 242, Ch D . . . . *Digested*, 98/**703**
INVERMONT Trade Mark [1997] R.P.C. 125, TMR. . . . . *Digested*, 97/**4892**:
Considered, 00/3793: *Not followed*, 99/3544: *Referred to*, 99/3557, 00/3795
Inverness Taxi Owners and Drivers Association *v.* Highland Council 1999 S.L.T. 1316; 1999 G.W.D. 10-445; *Times*, May 5, 1999, OH . . . . *Digested*, 99/**5626**
Investment AB Torman *v.* Alltrans Group of Canada Ltd (The TFL Prosperity) see Tor Line A/B *v.* Alltrans Group of Canada Ltd (The TFL Prosperity)
Investment Grants for Mining, Re; *sub nom* Commission of the European Communities *v.* Germany (C70/72) [1973] E.C.R. 813; [1973] C.M.L.R. 741, ECJ . . . . *Digested*, 73/**1273**:
Followed, 99/705
Investors Compensation Scheme Ltd *v.* Hopkin & Sons see Investors Compensation Scheme Ltd *v.* West Bromwich Building Society (No.1)
Investors Compensation Scheme Ltd *v.* West Bromwich Building Society (No.1); Investors Compensation Scheme Ltd *v.* Hopkin & Sons; Alford *v.* West Bromwich Building Society; Armitage *v.* West Bromwich Building Society [1998] 1 W.L.R. 896; [1998] 1 All E.R. 98; [1998] 1 B.C.L.C. 531; [1997] C.L.C. 1243; [1997] P.N.L.R. 541; (1997) 147 N.L.J. 989; *Times*, June 24, 1997, HL; reversing [1998] 1 B.C.L.C. 521; [1997] C.L.C. 363; [1997] P.N.L.R. 166; [1997] N.P.C. 104; *Times*, November 8, 1996, CA; affirming [1998] 1 B.C.L.C. 493; [1997] C.L.C. 348; *Times*, October 10, 1996, Ch D . . . . *Digested*, 97/**2537**:
Applied, 99/852, 99/3420, 99/5795, 00/900, 01/375, 01/959, 01/4272, 01/4950, 01/5508: *Cited*, 99/2489: *Considered*, 99/2480, 00/878, 00/3686, 00/5932, 01/2430: *Followed*, 98/807, 00/2173
Investors Compensation Scheme Ltd *v.* West Bromwich Building Society (No.2) [1999] Lloyd's Rep. P.N. 496, Ch D . . . . *Digested*, 99/**3964**
Invicta Poultry Ltd *v.* Customs and Excise Commissioners see Customs and Excise Commissioners *v.* Invicta Poultry Ltd
Inwards *v.* Baker [1965] 2 Q.B. 29; [1965] 2 W.L.R. 212; [1965] 1 All E.R. 446; 109 S.J. 75, CA . . . . *Digested*, 65/**1487**:
Applied, 66/6674, 67/2196, 72/3167, 73/235, 75/1191, 75/3365, 76/1524, 77/1214, 77/1738, 77/2509, 79/1083, 79/1085: *Considered*, 96/4949, 98/123: *Distinguished*, 66/6874, 69/3591, 77/1560: *Doubted*, 74/3144: *Followed*, 66/4174, 66/4176, 66/4521
Inze *v.* Austria (A/126) (1988) 10 E.H.R.R. 394; *Times*, November 13, 1987, ECHR . . . . . *Digested*, 87/**1915**:
Applied, 98/3132, 98/3154
Inzo *v.* Belgium (C110/94) see Intercommunale voor Zeewaterontzilting (In Liquidation) *v.* Belgium (C110/94)
Ioannou *v.* BBC see BBC *v.* Ioannou
Iomega Corp *v.* Mac & More Ltd (1998) 21 (9) I.P.D. 21096, HC
Iomega Corp *v.* Myrica (UK) Ltd (No.2); *sub nom* Iomega Corp, Petitioners 1998 S.C. 637; 1999 S.L.T. 796; 1998 S.C.L.R. 475; 1998 G.W.D. 16-774; *Times*, May 28, 1998, 1 Div . . . . *Digested*, 98/**5451**
Iomega Corp, Petitioners see Iomega Corp *v.* Myrica (UK) Ltd (No.2)
IP Metal Ltd *v.* Ruote Oz SpA [1993] 2 Lloyd's Rep. 60, QBD (Comm Ct) . . . . *Digested*, 93/**449**:
Applied, 00/754

IPC Magazines Ltd v. MGN Ltd [1998] F.S.R. 431, Ch D . . . . *Digested,* 98/**3426**
Ipk-Munchen GmbH v. Commission of the European Communities (C433/97); *sub nom* Ipk-Munchen GmbH v. Commission of the European Communities (T331/94) [2001] 3 C.M.L.R. 4, ECJ; reversing [1997] E.C.R. II-1665; [1998] 1 C.M.L.R. 1043, CFI (1st Chamber) . . . . *Digested,* 01/**2473**
Ipk-Munchen GmbH v. Commission of the European Communities (T331/94) see Ipk-Munchen GmbH v. Commission of the European Communities (C433/97)
Ipswich BC v. Duke see Ipswich BC v. Moore
Ipswich BC v. Moore; Ipswich BC v. Duke [2001] EWCA Civ 1273; *Times,* October 25, 2001, CA; affirming (2000) 97(27) L.S.G. 39; [2000] N.P.C. 72; *Times,* July 4, 2000, Ch D . . . . *Digested,* 01/**4888**
Iran Abad, The v. Merawi, The [1999] 1 Lloyd's Rep. 818, QBD (Adm Ct) . . . . *Digested,* 99/**4439**
Iran Nabuvat, The (1990) [1990] 1 W.L.R. 1115; [1990] 3 All E.R. 9; [1990] 2 Lloyd's Rep. 511, CA . . . . *Digested,* 90/**3735**:
Applied, 93/3111: *Considered,* 94/3529, 95/3926: *Followed,* 95/3925, 96/675, 96/916, 97/495, 00/363
Ireland v. Birmingham City Council see R. v. Birmingham City Council Ex p. Ireland
Ireland (Keegan) v. Stardust Compensation Tribunal [1986] I.R. 642, Sup Ct (Irl) . . . . . . *Digested,* 88/**6**:
Followed, 99/5078
Ireland v. United Kingdom (A/25) (1979-80) 2 E.H.R.R. 25, ECHR . . . . *Digested,* 79/**1175**:
Applied, 97/2764, 98/3162: *Considered,* 96/3138: *Followed,* 98/3069
Irina Zharkikh, The and Ksenia Zharkikh, The [2001] 2 Lloyd's Rep. 319, HC (NZ) . . . . . *Digested,* 01/**4905**
Irish Continental Group v. CCI Morlaix (IV/35.388) [1995] 5 C.M.L.R. 177, CEC . . . . *Applied,* 98/719
Irish Shipping Ltd v. Commercial Union Assurance Co Plc (The Irish Rowan) [1991] 2 Q.B. 206; [1990] 2 W.L.R. 117; [1989] 3 All E.R. 853; [1989] 2 Lloyd's Rep. 144; (1990) 87(5) L.S.G. 39; (1990) 134 S.J. 426; *Times,* May 5, 1989, CA. . . . . *Digested,* 90/**3768**:
Considered, 90/3744, 91/2921, 00/3516: *Distinguished,* 91/2188, 92/3976
Irish Sugar, Re see Irish Sugar Plc v. Commission of the European Communities (C497/99 P)
Irish Sugar Plc v. Commission of the European Communities (C497/99 P); *sub nom* European Economic Community v. Irish Sugar; Irish Sugar, Re; Irish Sugar Plc v. Commission of the European Communities (T228/97) [2001] E.C.R. I-5333; [2001] 5 C.M.L.R. 29, ECJ (5th Chamber); affirming [2000] All E.R. (EC) 198; [1999] E.C.R. II-2969; [1999] 5 C.M.L.R. 1300, CFI (3rd Chamber) [1997] 5 C.M.L.R. 666, CEC . . . . *Digested,* 00/**717**
Irish Sugar Plc v. Commission of the European Communities (T228/97) see Irish Sugar Plc v. Commission of the European Communities (C497/99 P)
IRSID/Opposition division (T251/88) [1990] E.P.O.R. 246, EPO (Technical Bd App). . . *Followed,* 00/3661
Irtelli v. Squatriti [1993] Q.B. 83; [1992] 3 W.L.R. 218; [1992] 3 All E.R. 294; (1992) 136 S.J.L.B. 100; *Times,* March 2, 1992, CA . . . . *Digested,* 92/**2059**:
Considered, 99/3153: *Not followed,* 99/3316
Irvani v. Irvani [2000] 1 Lloyd's Rep. 412; [2000] C.L.C. 477; *Times,* February 10, 2000, CA . . . . *Digested,* 00/**226**
Irvin v. Irvin [2001] 1 F.L.R. 178; [2001] Fam. Law 15, Fam Div . . . . *Digested,* 01/**2614**
Irvine v. Moran (1992) 24 H.L.R. 1; [1991] 1 E.G.L.R. 261 . . . . *Digested,* 92/**2670**:
Applied, 01/4192, 01/4211
Irving v. Associated Newspapers Ltd HQ-9900797, QBD. . . . . *Digested,* 99/**1625**
Irwin Toy Ltd v. Attorney General of Quebec [1989] 1 S.C.R. 927, Sup Ct (Can) . . . . . . *Applied,* 97/2777, 98/3085, 99/3106
Isaacs v. Robertson [1985] A.C. 97; [1984] 3 W.L.R. 705; [1984] 3 All E.R. 140; (1984) 81 L.S.G. 2769; (1984) 134 N.L.J. 745, PC (StV) . . . . *Digested,* 84/**2660**:
Applied, 87/2146: *Considered,* 84/2710, 85/2722: *Followed,* 98/3308
Isaacs v. Titus [1954] 1 W.L.R. 398; [1954] 1 All E.R. 470; 98 S.J. 143, CA . . . . *Digested,* 54/**2796**:
Considered, 98/3632: *Distinguished,* 55/2330
Iskcon v. United Kingdom . . . . *Applied,* 01/4761
Iske v. P&O European Ferries (Dover) Ltd [1997] I.R.L.R. 401, EAT . . . . *Digested,* 97/**2239**:
Considered, 01/2314
Islam (t/a Eurasia Property Services) v. Begum (Unreported, February 22, 2000), CC (Bow) [*Ex rel.* David Carter, Barrister, Arden Chambers, 27 John Street, London] . . . . *Digested,* 00/**3938**
Islam v. Secretary of State for the Home Department see R. v. Immigration Appeal Tribunal Ex p. Shah
Islamic Investment Co Isa v. Transorient Shipping Ltd (The Nour) [1999] 1 Lloyd's Rep. 1, CA . . . . *Digested,* 98/**4410**
Islamic Press Agency v. Al-Wazir see Al-Wazir v. Islamic Press Agency Inc (Interest)
Isle of Wight Council v. Davies (2000) 15 P.A.D. 176, Planning Inspector
Islington LBC v. Accor UK Economy Hotels Ltd (formerly Ibis (UK) Hotels Ltd) (2000) 15 P.A.D. 541, Planning Inspector
Islington LBC v. Clonis (2000) 80 P. & C.R. D24, QBD . . . . *Digested,* 00/**3902**
Islington LBC v. Demetriou (Unreported, February 28, 2001), CC (Clerkenwell) [*Ex rel.* Maurice Rifat, Barrister, Verulam Chambers, 8 - 14 Verulam Street, London] . . . . *Digested,* 01/**4216**
Islington LBC v. Islington and Shoreditch Housing Association (2001) 16 P.A.D. 45, Planning Inspector

Islington LBC v. Michaelides [2001] EWHC Admin 468; [2001] Crim. L.R. 843; (2001) 98(26) L.S.G. 46, QBD

Islington LBC v. Reeves (Unreported, November 19, 1996), CC (Clerkenwell) [Ex rel. Abimbola Badejo, Barrister] . . . . *Digested, 97/***2715**: *Cited, 00/3157*

Islington LBC v. Rogers; *sub nom* Rogers v. Islington LBC [2000] E.H.L.R. 3; (2000) 32 H.L.R. 138; [1999] 3 E.G.L.R. 17; [1999] 37 E.G. 178; (1999) 96(34) L.S.G. 33; [1999] N.P.C. 106; *Times*, August 30, 1999 ; *Independent*, October 8, 1999, CA . . . . *Digested, 99/***3704**

Ismail, Re [1999] 1 A.C. 320; [1998] 3 W.L.R. 495; [1998] 3 All E.R.1007; (1999) 163 J.P. 154; (1999) 11 Admin. L.R. 37; (1998) 95(35) L.S.G. 35; (1998) 148 N.L.J.1302; (1998) 142 S.J.L.B. 246; *Times*, August 20, 1998, HL; affirming CO/2905/96, QBD . . . . *Digested, 98/***2357**: *Applied, 01/5783*

Ispahani v. Bank Melli Iran [1998] Lloyd's Rep. Bank. 133; *Times*, December 29, 1997, CA . . . . *Digested, 98/***271**

Israel-British Bank Ltd (In Liquidation), Re; *sub nom* Wheatley v. Credit Suisse [2001] C.P. Rep. 91, Ch D (Companies Ct) . . . . *Digested, 01/***806**

ISS Machinery Services Ltd v. Aeolian Shipping SA (The Aeolian) see Aeolian Shipping SA v. ISS Machinery Services Ltd (The Aeolian)

Istanikzai v. Haque (Unreported, May 18, 2001), CC (Willesden) [Ex rel. Rachel Child, Pupil Barrister, 4 New Square, Lincoln's Inn, London] . . . . *Digested, 01/***533**

Isted v. Crown Prosecution Service; *sub nom* Isted v. DPP (1998) 162 J.P. 513; [1998] Crim. L.R. 194; [1998] C.O.D. 86; (1998) 162 J.P.N. 663; *Times*, December 11, 1997, QBD . . . . *Digested, 98/***221**

Isted v. DPP see Isted v. Crown Prosecution Service

Italian Leather SpA v. Weco Polstermobel GmbH & Co (IX ZB 31/99) [2000] I.L.Pr. 668, BGH (Ger)

Italian Ports Employment Policy, Re; *sub nom* European Economic Community v. Italy [1998] 4 C.M.L.R. 73, CEC

Italian Tax and Revenue Administration v. SA Simmenthal, Monza (Italy) (106/77) see Amministrazione delle Finanze dello Stato v. Simmenthal SpA (No.2) (106/77)

Italy v. Commission of the European Communities (C15/98); Sardegna Lines - Servizi Marittimi della Sardegna SpA v. Commission of the European Communities (C105/99) [2000] E.C.R. I-8855; [2001] 1 C.M.L.R. 10, ECJ (6th Chamber). . . *Digested, 01/***791**

Italy v. Commission of the European Communities (C47/91) [1994] E.C.R. I-4635, ECJ . . . . *Digested, 95/***4924**: *Followed, 99/2278*

Italy v. Commission of the European Communities (C6/97) [1999] E.C.R. I-2981; [2000] 2 C.M.L.R. 919, ECJ (6th Chamber). . . . . *Digested, 00/***5062**

Italy v. T [2001] E.C.D.R. 26, Trib (Turin)

ITM Corp Ltd (In Liquidation), Re; *sub nom* Stirling Estates v. Pickard UK Ltd; Sterling Estates v. Pickard UK Ltd [1997] B.C.C. 554; [1997] 2 B.C.L.C. 389; [1998] B.P.I.R. 402; [1997] 2 E.G.L.R. 33; [1997] 30 E.G. 124, Ch D . . . . *Digested, 97/***3094**

ITT Promedia NV v. Commission of the European Communities (T111/96) [1998] E.C.R. II-2937; [1998] 5 C.M.L.R. 491, CFI (4th Chamber)

ITT Schaub Lorenz Vertriebsgesellschaft mbH v. Birkart Johann Internationale Spedition GmbH & Co KG [1988] 1 Lloyd's Rep. 487; [1988] F.T.L.R. 463, CA . . . . *Digested, 88/***265**: *Applied, 99/4944*

Iurlaro v. Istituto Nazionale della Previdenza Sociale (INPS) (C322/95) [1998] All E.R. (E.C.) 366; [1997] E.C.R. I-4881, ECJ (5th Chamber). . . . . *Digested, 98/***4519**

Ivcher v. Peru 8 B.H.R.C. 522, IACHR

Iverans Rederei A/S v. MS Holstencruiser Seeschiffahrts GmbH & Co KG (The Holstencruiser) [1992] 2 Lloyd's Rep. 378, QBD (Comm Ct) . . . . *Digested, 93/***3591**: *Considered, 01/4906*

Ivey v. Secretary of State for Employment see Buchan v. Secretary of State for Employment

Ivory & Sime Trustlink Ltd v. Customs and Excise Commissioners [1998] S.T.C. 597; 1998 S.C. 774; 1998 S.C.L.R. 968; [1998] B.T.C. 5173; [1998] B.V.C. 191; 1998 G.W.D. 14-731, 1 Div. . . . . *Digested, 98/***6216**

Ivory Gate Ltd v. Spetale (1999) 77 P. & C.R. 141; [1998] L. & T.R. 58; [1998] 2 E.G.L.R. 43; [1998] 27 E.G. 139; [1998] E.G.C.S. 69; [1998] N.P.C. 72, CA; reversing in part [1996] N.P.C. 186, QBD . . . . *Digested, 98/***3652**: *Considered, 00/4623*

Ivresse v. Societe Tesserlana [1999] I.L.Pr. 332, C d'A (Paris) . . . . *Digested, 99/***452**

Izzard v. Field Palmer [2000] 1 E.G.L.R. 177, CA . . . . *Digested, 00/***1481**

Izzo v. Philip Ross & Co; *sub nom* Izzo v. Phillip Ross & Co (2001) 98(35) L.S.G. 37; (2001) 145 S.J.L.B. 216; *Times*, August 9, 2001, Ch D . . . . *Digested, 01/***608**

Izzo v. Phillip Ross & Co see Izzo v. Philip Ross & Co

J (A Child), Re see North Yorkshire CC v. Wiltshire CC

J (A Child) (Abduction: Declaration of Wrongful Removal), Re; *sub nom* J (A Child) (Abduction: Rights of Custody), Re [2000] 1 F.L.R. 78; [2000] 1 F.C.R. 160; [2000] Fam. Law 9, CA; affirming [1999] 2 F.L.R. 653; [1999] 3 F.C.R. 577; [1999] Fam. Law 611, Fam Div. . . . . *Digested*, 00/**2445**

J (A Child) (Abduction: Rights of Custody), Re see J (A Child) (Abduction: Declaration of Wrongful Removal), Re

J (A Child) (Adoption: Appointment of Guardian ad Litem), Re [1999] 2 F.L.R. 86; [1999] 3 F.C.R. 456; [1999] Fam. Law 375; *Times*, March 19, 1999, CA . . . . *Digested*, 99/**2305**

J (A Child) (Adoption Procedure: Isle of Man), Re; *sub nom* H (A Child) (Isle of Man: Adoption), Re [2000] 2 F.L.R. 633; [2000] 3 F.C.R. 97; [2000] Fam. Law 515; [2000] Fam. Law 597; (2000) 97(25) L.S.G. 40; *Times*, June 7, 2000, Fam Div . . . . *Digested*, 00/**2437**

J (A Child) (Adoption: Revocation of Freeing Order), Re see J (A Child) (Freeing for Adoption), Re

J (A Child) (Blood Tests), Re see O and J (Children) (Blood Tests: Constraint), Re

J (A Child) (Freeing for Adoption), Re; *sub nom* JS, Re; J (A Child) (Adoption: Revocation of Freeing Order), Re [2000] 2 F.L.R. 58; [2000] 2 F.C.R. 133; [2000] Fam. Law 598; (2000) 164 J.P.N. 606; (2000) 97(24) L.S.G. 39; *Times*, May 26, 2000; *Independent*, June 12, 2000 (C.S), Fam Div . . . . *Digested*, 00/**2432**

J (A Child) v. Jones (Unreported, November 23, 1999), CC (Uxbridge) [*Ex rel.* Paul Tropp, Barrister, Hardwicke Building, New Square, Lincoln's Inn, London] . . . . . *Digested*, 00/**1669**

J (A Child) v. North Lincolnshire CC [2000] B.L.G.R. 269; [2000] E.L.R. 245; [2000] P.I.Q.R. P84, CA . . . . *Digested*, 00/**4223**

J (A Child) v. Perrett (Unreported, April 9, 2001), CC (Hereford) [*Ex rel.* Archna Dewar, Barrister, Albion Chambers, Broad Street, Bristol] . . . . *Digested*, 01/**1736**

J (A Child) v. Reid (Unreported, May 9, 2001), CC (Brighton) [*Ex rel.* Anthony Hodari & Sons, Solicitors, 34 High Street, Manchester] . . . . *Digested*, 01/**1737**

J (A Child) v. Smith (Deceased) [2001] EWCA Civ 1264; [2001] C.P.L.R. 489, CA

J (A Child) v. Urdd Gobaith Cymru (Unreported, July 7, 2000), CC (Cardiff) [*Ex rel.* Jane HS Foulser McFarlane, Barrister, Temple Chambers, 32 Park Place, Cardiff] . . . . *Digested*, 00/**1741**

J (A Child) v. Wilkins [2001] R.T.R. 19; [2001] P.I.Q.R. P12; (2001) 98(7) L.S.G. 41; *Times*, February 6, 2001; *Daily Telegraph*, January 23, 2001, CA . . . . *Digested*, 01/**4447**: *Considered*, 01/4450

J (A Child) v. Wind (Unreported, March 7, 2000), CC (Liverpool) [*Ex rel.* Scott Rees & Co Solicitors, Centaur House, Gardiners Place, Skelmersdale, Lancs.] . . . . *Digested*, 00/**419**

J (A Debtor), Re see Debtor (No.488-IO of 1996), Re

J (A Minor) (Abduction: Custody Rights), Re see J (A Minor) (Abduction: Custody Rights), Re

J (A Minor) (Abduction: Custody Rights), Re; *sub nom* C v. S (Minors) (Abduction: Illegitimate Child); J (A Minor) (Abduction: Custody Rights), Re [1990] 2 A.C. 562; [1990] 3 W.L.R. 492; [1990] 2 All E.R. 961; [1990] 2 F.L.R. 442; [1991] F.C.R. 129; [1991] Fam. Law 57; (1990) 154 J.P.N. 674; (1990) 87(35) L.S.G. 39; (1990) 140 N.L.J. 1191; (1990) 134 S.J. 1039; *Times*, July 31, 1990; *Independent*, August 1, 1990; *Guardian*, July 27, 1990; *Daily Telegraph*, September 18, 1990, HL; affirming [1990] 2 All E.R. 449; (1990) 154 J.P.N. 563, CA . . . . *Digested*, 90/**3151**: *Applied*, 94/3155, 94/3156, 94/3158, 94/3280, 94/5446, 95/3438, 97/396: *Cited*, 99/4564: *Considered*, 95/3436, 95/3448, 96/530, 96/534, 96/643, 98/4536: *Followed*, 94/5440, 96/605

J (A Minor) (Adoption: Non-Patrial), Re [1998] 1 F.L.R. 225; [1998] 1 F.C.R. 125; [1998] I.N.L.R. 424; [1998] Fam. Law 130; *Independent*, October 30, 1997, CA . . . . . . *Digested*, 97/**349**

J (A Minor) (Adoption Order), Re see G (A Minor) (Adoption Order), Re

J (A Minor) (Expert Evidence: Hearsay), Re [1999] 2 F.L.R. 661; [1999] Fam. Law 614, Fam Div [*Ex rel.* JS Boora, Barrister, 24 The Ropewalk, Nottingham] . . . . *Digested*, 99/**2351**

J (A Minor) (Parental Responsibility), Re see M v. M (Parental Responsibility)

J (A Minor) (Prohibited Steps Order: Circumcision), Re; *sub nom* J (Childs Religious Upbringing and Circumcision), Re; J (A Minor) (Specific Issue Orders: Muslim Upbringing and Circumcision), Re; J (Specific Issue Orders: Child's Religious Upbringing and Circumcision), Re [2000] 1 F.L.R. 571; [2000] 1 F.C.R. 307; (2000) 52 B.M.L.R. 82; [2000] Fam. Law 246; (1999) 96(47) L.S.G. 30; *Times*, December 22, 1999, CA; affirming [1999] 2 F.L.R. 678; [1999] 2 F.C.R. 345; [1999] Fam. Law 543; *Times*, June 1, 1999; *Independent*, June 28, 1999 (C.S.), Fam Div . . . . *Digested*, 00/**2484**

J (A Minor) (Specific Issue Orders: Muslim Upbringing and Circumcision), Re see J (A Minor) (Prohibited Steps Order: Circumcision), Re

J (Care: Rehabilitation Plan), Re [1998] 2 F.L.R. 498; [1999] 1 F.C.R. 749; [1998] Fam. Law 516; (1999) 163 J.P.N. 872, CA . . . . *Digested*, 98/**2406** *Digested*, 01/**2669**

J (Children) (Residence: Expert Evidence), Re [2001] 2 F.C.R. 44, CA . . . .

J (Childs Religious Upbringing and Circumcision), Re see J (A Minor) (Prohibited Steps Order: Circumcision), Re

J (Christopher James) (A Juvenile) v. DPP [2000] Crim. L.R. 471, QBD

J (Minors) (Care: Care Plan), Re [1994] 1 F.L.R. 253, Fam Div. . . . . *Digested*, 95/**3389**: *Considered*, 01/2562: *Followed*, 97/364: *Referred to*, 99/2357

J (Minors) (Ex Parte Orders), Re [1997] 1 F.L.R. 606; [1997] 1 F.C.R. 325; [1997] Fam. Law
    317; (1997) 161 J.P.N. 111, Fam Div . . . . *Digested,* 97/**407**
J (Parental Responsibility), Re [1999] 1 F.L.R. 784; [1999] Fam. Law 216, Fam Div . . .   *Digested,* 98/**2425**
J (Specific Issue Orders: Child's Religious Upbringing and Circumcision), Re see J (A Minor)
    (Prohibited Steps Order: Circumcision), Re
J v. C (Child: Financial Provision) [1999] 1 F.L.R. 152; [1998] 3 F.C.R. 79; [1999]
    Fam. Law 78, Fam Div . . . .   *Digested,* 98/**2474**
J v. Grocott [2001] C.P. Rep. 15; [2000] P.I.Q.R. Q17, QBD . . . .   *Digested,* 00/**1479**
J v. Guy's & St Thomas NHS Hospital Trust [2001] 1 Q.R. 7
J (SR) v. J (DW); *sub nom* SRJ v. DWJ [1999] 2 F.L.R. 176; [1999] 3 F.C.R. 153;
    [1999] Fam. Law 448, CA. . . . .   *Digested,* 99/**2423**
J v. MerthyrTydfil BC [1997] Fam. Law 522   *Applied,* 99/2395
J v. Oyston [1999] 1 W.L.R. 694; (1999) 96(3) L.S.G. 31; (1999) 143 S.J.L.B. 47;
    Times, December 11, 1998, QBD . . . .   *Digested,* 99/**313**
J v. ST (formerly J) (Transsexual: Ancillary Relief); *sub nom* ST v. J (Transsexual: Void
    Marriage) [1998] Fam. 103; [1997] 3 W.L.R. 1287; [1998] 1 All E.R. 431; [1997]
    1 F.L.R. 402; [1997] 1 F.C.R. 349; [1997] Fam. Law 239; *Times,* November 25,
    1996; *Independent,* November 26, 1996, CA; affirming [1996] 2 F.C.R. 665,
    Fam Div . . . .   *Digested,* 96/**2896**:
                                                             Applied, 01/2544
J Alston & Sons Ltd v. Highways Agency [1999] R.V.R. 175, Lands Tr . . . .   *Digested,* 99/**4197**
J Crosby & Sons Ltd v. Portland Urban DC 5 B.L.R. 121, QBD . . . .   *Digested,* 80/**201**:
                                 Considered, 99/227: *Explained,* 92/3375
J Jarvis & Sons Ltd v. Castle Wharf Developments Ltd; J Jarvis & Sons Ltd v. Gleeds
    Management Services Ltd; J Jarvis & Sons Ltd v. Franklin Ellis Architects Ltd;
    Castle Wharf Developments Ltd v. J Jarvis & Sons Ltd [2001] EWCA Civ 19;
    [2001] Lloyd's Rep. P.N. 308; (2001) 17 Const. L.J. 430; [2001] N.P.C. 15;
    Times, February 28, 2001, CA . . . .   *Digested,* 01/**871**
J Jarvis & Sons Ltd v. Franklin Ellis Architects Ltd see J Jarvis & Sons Ltd v. Castle
    Wharf Developments Ltd
J Jarvis & Sons Ltd v. Gleeds Management Services Ltd see J Jarvis & Sons Ltd v.
    Castle Wharf Developments Ltd
J Paterson Brodie & Son v. Zirceram Ltd (In Liquidation) see Zirceram Ltd (In
    Liquidation), Re
J Rothschild Assurance Plc v. Collyear [1998] C.L.C. 1697; [1999] Lloyd's Rep. I.R. 6;
    [1999] Pens. L.R. 77; *Times,* October 15, 1998, QBD (Comm Ct) . . . .   *Digested,* 98/**3397**
J Sainsbury Ltd v. Savage; *sub nom* Savage v. J Sainsbury Ltd [1981] I.C.R. 1; [1980]
    I.R.L.R. 109, CA; affirming [1979] I.C.R. 96; [1978] I.R.L.R. 479, EAT . . . .   *Digested,* 81/**968**:
                  Applied, 79/1056, 98/2207: *Approved,* 86/1285: *Considered,* 95/2026:
                            Distinguished, 00/2242: *Followed,* 97/2245
J Sainsbury Plc v. Broadway Malyan 61 Con. L.R. 31; [1999] P.N.L.R. 286, QBD (OR) .   *Digested,* 99/**3949**
J Sainsbury Plc v. One in a Million Ltd see British Telecommunications Plc v. One in a
    Million Ltd
J Sainsbury Plc v. Secretary of State for the Environment [1993] E.G.C.S. 203; [1993]
    N.P.C. 164, CA; reversing [1993] 2 P.L.R. 32; [1993] J.P.L. 651, QBD . . . .   *Digested,* 94/**4344**:
                                                    Applied, 99/4268
J&F Stone Lighting & Radio Ltd v. Levitt [1947] A.C. 209; [1946] 2 All E.R. 653; 62
    T.L.R. 737; [1947] L.J.R. 65; 176 L.T. 1, HL; reversing [1945] 2 All E.R. 268;
    [1945] W.N. 154; 173 L.T. 174, CA. . . . .   *Digested,* 47-51/**8726**:
              Applied, 47-51/8558, 47-51/8587: *Considered,* 47-51/8723, 47-51/8724,
            95/3077, 98/2988: *Distinguished,* 47-51/8577, 47-51/8741, 57/3060
J&J Securities v. Khan (Unreported, March 1, 1999), CC (Bradford) [*Ex rel.* Wragge &
    Co Solicitors, 55 Colmore Row, Birmingham] . . . .   *Digested,* 99/**4387**
J&S Davis (Holdings) Ltd v. Wright Health Group Ltd [1988] R.P.C. 403, Ch D . . . . . .   *Digested,* 89/**495**:
                                                  Not followed, 98/3430
J&SA Wood (A Firm) v. Intervention Board for Agricultural Produce; *sub nom* Wood v.
    Intervention Board for Agricultural Produce [2001] EWCA Civ 1569, CA;
    affirming [2000] Eu. L.R. 672, QBD . . . .   *Digested,* 01/**304**
JA (A Minor) (Child Abduction: Non-Convention Country), Re; *sub nom* A (A Minor)
    (Abduction: Non-Convention Country), Re [1998] 1 F.L.R. 231; [1998] 2 F.C.R.
    159; [1997] Fam. Law 718; *Times,* July 3, 1997, CA . . . .   *Digested,* 98/**2381**
JA Chapman & Co Ltd (In Liquidation) v. Kadirga Denizcilik ve Ticaret AS [1998] C.L.C.
    860; [1998] Lloyd's Rep. I.R. 377; *Times,* March 19, 1998, CA . . . .   *Digested,* 98/**3393**
JA Mont (UK) Ltd v. Mills [1993] I.R.L.R. 172; [1993] F.S.R. 577; *Independent,* January
    7, 1993, CA . . . .   *Digested,* 93/**1732**:
                                                  Followed, 00/2200
JA Pye (Oxford) Ltd v. Graham [2001] EWCA Civ 117; [2001] Ch. 804; [2001] 2
    W.L.R. 1293; [2001] H.R.L.R. 27; (2001) 82 P. & C.R. 23; [2001] 18 E.G. 176;
    [2001] 7 E.G.C.S. 161; (2001) 98(8) L.S.G. 44; (2001) 145 S.J.L.B. 38; [2001]
    N.P.C. 29; (2001) 82 P. & C.R. D1; *Times,* February 13, 2001; *Independent,*
    February 13, 2001, CA; reversing [2000] Ch. 676; [2000] 3 W.L.R. 242; (2001)
    81 P. & C.R. 15; [2000] 2 E.G.L.R. 137; [2000] E.G.C.S. 21; (2000) 97(8)
    L.S.G. 36; (2000) 97(7) L.S.G. 42; (2000) 144 S.J.L.B. 107; [2000] N.P.C. 10;
    Times, March 14, 2000; *Independent,* March 27, 2000 (C.S.), Ch D . . . .   *Digested,* 01/**4840**

JA Pye (Oxford) Ltd *v.* Kingswood BC [1998] 2 E.G.L.R. 159; [2000] R.V.R. 40; (1998)
  95(15) L.S.G. 34; [1998] N.P.C. 65, CA . . . . *Digested,* 99/**4192**:
                                                                                                Considered, 00/4426

JA Pye (Oxford) Ltd *v.* South Gloucester DC see JA Pye (Oxford) Ltd *v.* South
  Gloucestershire DC (No.1)
JA Pye (Oxford) Ltd *v.* South Gloucestershire DC (Compulsory Purchase: Valuation)
  (2001) 81 P. & C.R. 31; [2000] N.P.C. 112, CA . . . . *Digested,* 01/**4678**
JA Pye (Oxford) Ltd *v.* South Gloucestershire DC (No.1); *sub nom* JA Pye (Oxford) Ltd
  v. South Gloucester DC [2001] EWCA Civ 450; [2001] 2 P.L.R. 66; [2001]
  J.P.L. 1425; [2001] 14 E.G.C.S. 149; (2001) 98(20) L.S.G. 41; (2001) 145
  S.J.L.B. 99; [2001] N.P.C. 66; *Times,* April 2, 2001; *Independent,* April 5, 2001,
  CA; affirming [2001] J.P.L. 713; [2000] E.G.C.S. 116; [2000] N.P.C. 105, Ch D . *Digested,* 01/**4682**
JA Pye (Oxford) Ltd *v.* South Gloucestershire DC (No.2) [2001] N.P.C. 187, Ch D
Jabari *v.* Turkey (40035/98) 9 B.H.R.C. 1; [2001] I.N.L.R. 136, ECHR . . . . *Digested,* 01/**3592**
Jabari *v.* Turkey (Admissibility) (40035/98) (2001) 29 E.H.R.R. CD178, ECHR
Jabs Construction Ltd *v.* R. 2 I.T.L. Rep. 552, Tax Ct (Can)
Jack Allen (Sales & Service) Ltd *v.* Smith 1999 S.L.T. 820; [1999] I.R.L.R. 19; 1998
  G.W.D. 38-1957, OH . . . . *Digested,* 99/**6031**
Jack L Israel Ltd *v.* Ocean Dynamic Lines SA and Ocean Victory Ltd (The Ocean
  Dynamic) [1982] 2 Lloyd's Rep. 88, QBD (Comm Ct) . . . . *Digested,* 82/**2792**:
                                                                                                Considered, 01/478

Jackson (CICB: Quantum: 1999), Re (Unreported, February 22, 1999), CICB (York) [*Ex rel.*
  Edward Legard, Barrister, York Chambers, 14 Toft Green, York] . . . . *Digested,* 00/**1540**
Jackson *v.* Bell [2001] EWCA Civ 387; [2001] B.P.I.R. 612; [2001] Fam. Law 879, CA . *Digested,* 01/**3727**
Jackson *v.* Department of Culture, Media and Sport (Unreported, March 16, 2001), CC
  (Brentford) [*Ex rel.* Benjamin Williams, Barrister, 1 Temple Gardens, Temple,
  London] . . . . *Digested,* 01/**612**
Jackson *v.* Greenfield [1998] B.P.I.R. 699, Ch D   *Digested,* 99/**3342**
Jackson *v.* Horizon Holidays Ltd [1975] 1 W.L.R. 1468; [1975] 3 All E.R. 92; 119 S.J.
  759, CA . . . . *Digested,* 75/**393**:
                    Applied, 75/2350, 76/2637, 96/711, 01/4275: *Considered,* 89/2952:
                                        Explained, 80/2792: *Followed,* 77/3143

Jackson *v.* Pinchbeck see Cockerill *v.* Tambrands Ltd
Jackson *v.* Pinchbeck (1998) 95(24) L.S.G. 34; (1998) 142 S.J.L.B. 174; *Times,* June
  4, 1998, CA. . . . . *Digested,* 98/**392**:
                                        Joined proceedings, 98/395, 98/397
Jackson *v.* Royal Bank of Scotland [2000] C.L.C. 1457, CA . . . . *Digested,* 01/**1507**
Jackson *v.* Secretary of State for the Environment, Transport and the Regions [1999]
  P.L.C.R. 86; [1998] E.G.C.S. 106, QBD. . . . . *Digested,* 99/**4252**
Jackson *v.* Tavern (Unreported, August 22, 2000), CC (Blackpool) [*Ex rel.* Paul Gillott,
  Barrister, 15 Winckley Square, Preston] . . . . *Digested,* 01/**464**
Jacobi *v.* Griffiths (1999) 174 D.L.R. (4th) 71   *Considered,* 01/5359
Jacobs (A Bankrupt), Re see Jacobs *v.* Official Receiver
Jacobs *v.* Barclays Bank Plc see Box *v.* Barclays Bank Plc
Jacobs *v.* Corniche Helicopters (1999) 99(3) Q.R. 7, QBD [*Ex rel.* Huw Davies,
  Barrister, Farrar's Building, Temple, London] . . . . *Digested,* 99/**1501**
Jacobs *v.* Coster (t/a Newington Commercials Service Station) [2000] Lloyd's Rep.
  I.R. 506, CA; reversing (Unreported, June 1, 1998), CC (Medway) [*Ex rel.*
  Andrew Burns, Barrister, Devereux Chambers, Devereux Court, London] . . . . . . *Digested,* 01/**3801**
Jacobs *v.* Moreton 72 B.L.R. 92, QBD . . . . *Digested,* 96/**4433**:
                                                                                                Considered, 99/4365

Jacobs *v.* Official Receiver; *sub nom* Jacobs (A Bankrupt), Re [1999] 1 W.L.R. 619;
  [1998] 3 All E.R. 250; [1998] B.P.I.R. 711; *Times,* June 16, 1998, Ch D . . . . *Digested,* 98/**3292**
Jacobs Engineering Group Inc *v.* United States of America 1 I.T.L. Rep. 645; 1 I.T.L. Rep.
  653, US Ct
Jacobsson *v.* Sweden (No.2) (16970/90) (2001) 32 E.H.R.R. 20; [1998] H.R.C.D.
  270, ECHR
Jacques *v.* Oxfordshire CC 66 L.G.R. 440, Assizes (Oxford). . . . . *Digested,* 68/**2727**:
                              Followed, 80/861: *Referred to,* 00/6588
Jacquet *v.* Land Nordrhein-Westfalen (C65/96) see Land Nordrhein-Westfalen *v.*
  Uecker (C64/96)
Jade Engineering (Coventry) Ltd *v.* Antiference Window Systems Ltd [1996] F.S.R. 461;
  (1996) 19(9) I.P.D. 19085, Ch D . . . . *Digested,* 96/**764**:
                                                                                                Considered, 99/3444
Jaeger AS *v.* Opel Norge AS (E3/97) [1999] 4 C.M.L.R. 147, EFTA . . . . *Digested,* 99/**697**
Jaffar *v.* Grupo Torras SA see Grupo Torras SA *v.* Al-Sabah (No.3)
Jagerskiold *v.* Gustafsson (C97/98) [1999] E.C.R. I-7319; [2000] 1 C.M.L.R. 235,
  ECJ (6th Chamber) . . . . *Digested,* 00/**2384**
Jaggard *v.* Sawyer [1995] 1 W.L.R. 269; [1995] 2 All E.R. 189; [1995] 1 E.G.L.R. 146;
  [1995] 13 E.G. 132; [1994] E.G.C.S. 139; [1994] N.P.C. 116; *Independent,*
  August 22, 1994 (C.S.), CA; affirming [1993] 1 E.G.L.R. 197, CC (Weymouth) . . *Digested,* 95/**4142**:
                              Cited, 01/1549: *Considered,* 98/4341, 00/5127
Jaggard *v.* United Kingdom see Laskey *v.* United Kingdom

Jaggers (t/a Shide Trees) v. Ellis (Inspector of Taxes) [1997] S.T.C. 1417; 71 T.C. 164; [1997] B.T.C. 571; (1997) 94(46) L.S.G. 29; *Times*, December 10, 1997, Ch D; affirming [1996] S.T.C. (S.C.D.) 440, Sp Comm . . . . *Digested*, 98/**4669**

Jain v. Secretary of State for the Home Department [2000] Imm. A.R. 76; [2000] I.N.L.R. 71, CA. . . . . *Digested*, 00/**3310**

Jaison Property Development Co Ltd v. Roux Restaurants Ltd see Roux Restaurants Ltd v. Jaison Property Development Co Ltd

Jaks (UK) Ltd v. Cera Investment Bank SA [1998] 2 Lloyd's Rep. 89, QBD (Comm Ct) . *Digested*, 98/**297**

JALON/Luminescent Security Fibres (T422/93) [1999] E.P.O.R. 486, EPO (Technical Bd App). . . . . *Digested*, 00/**3636**

Jamal v. Secretary of State for the Home Department . . . . *Distinguished*, 00/3278

James (A Minor) v. Robertson (Unreported, January 21, 1998), CC (Central London) [*Ex rel.* Gerard Boyle, Barrister, No.1 Serjeants' Inn, Fleet Street, London] . . . . . . *Digested*, 98/**1547**

James v. Belshaw [2001] 5 Q.R. 12, CC (Nottingham) [*Ex rel.* Jinder S Boora, Barrister, 24, The Ropewalk, Nottingham] . . . . *Digested*, 01/**1627**

James v. British General Insurance Co Ltd [1927] 2 K.B. 311; (1927) 27 Ll. L. Rep. 328, KBD . . . . *Applied*, 99/5404:
　　　　　　　　　　　Considered, 53/3273: *Distinguished*, 70/1368, 71/6012

James v. DPP (1999) 163 J.P. 89; [1997] Crim. L.R. 831, QBD . . . . *Digested*, 97/**1180**

James v. East Dorset HA (2001) 59 B.M.L.R. 196; *Times*, December 7, 1999, CA. . . . *Digested*, 00/**517**

James v. Eastleigh BC [1990] 2 A.C. 751; [1990] 3 W.L.R. 55; [1990] 2 All E.R. 607; [1990] I.C.R. 554; [1990] I.R.L.R. 288; (1991) 155 L.G. Rev. 205; (1990) 140 N.L.J. 926, HL; reversing [1990] 1 Q.B. 61; [1989] 3 W.L.R. 123; [1989] 2 All E.R. 914; [1989] I.C.R. 423; [1989] I.R.L.R. 318; 87 L.G.R. 651; (1989) 153 L.G. Rev. 848; (1989) 133 S.J. 850, CA . . . . *Digested*, 90/**2565**:
　　　Applied, 90/1937, 99/2098, 01/2316: *Considered*, 90/107, 92/1978, 93/1793, 94/1999, 95/1989, 95/2028, 95/2047, 00/2187: *Distinguished*, 92/1955, 92/1972, 00/5401: *Followed*, 99/2093, 99/2095

James v. Evans; *sub nom* Evans v. James (Administratrix of Hopkin's Estate) [2001] C.P. Rep. 36; [2000] 3 E.G.L.R. 1; [2000] 42 E.G. 173; [2000] E.G.C.S. 95; [2000] N.P.C. 85; (2000) 80 P. & C.R. D39; *Times*, August 2, 2000, CA . . . . *Digested*, 00/**4670**

James v. James [1964] P. 303; [1963] 3 W.L.R. 331; [1963] 2 All E.R. 465; 127 J.P. 352; 107 S.J. 116, DC . . . . *Digested*, 63/**200**:
　　　　　　　　　　　　　　　　　　　　　　　　　　Followed, 99/2433

James v. Johnson (Unreported, December 3, 1999), CC (Gloucester) [*Ex rel.* Archna Dawar, Barrister, Assize Court Chambers, 14 Small Street, Bristol] . . . . *Digested*, 00/**1718**

James v. London Electricity PLC (Unreported, July 3, 1998), CC (Central London) [*Ex rel.* Joel Donovan, Barrister, New Court Chambers, 5 Verulam Buildings, London] . . . . *Digested*, 98/**1528**

James v. Preseli Pembrokeshire DC [1993] P.I.Q.R. P114; *Independent*, November 16, 1992 (C.S.), CA. . . . . *Digested*, 93/**2966**:
　　　　　　　　　Applied, 00/4230, 01/4497: *Considered*, 97/3785: *Followed*, 99/2891

James v. Secretary of State for Wales (1998) 76 P. & C.R. 62, QBD . . . . *Digested*, 98/**4191**

James v. United Kingdom (A/44) see Young v. United Kingdom (A/44)

James v. United Kingdom (A/98) (1986) 8 E.H.R.R. 123; [1986] R.V.R. 139, ECHR . . . . *Digested*, 86/**1650**:
　　　　　　　　　　　　　　　Considered, 96/1118, 97/2796, 01/1844: *Followed*, 98/4201

James v. Van Leer Metallized Products, CC (Cardiff) [*Ex rel.* Andrew Arentsen, Barrister, 33 Park Place, Cardiff]. . . . . *Digested*, 01/**1802**

James v. Victoria Palace Theatre Ltd (1999) 99(4) Q.R. 4, CC (Wandsworth) [*Ex rel.* Keith Morton, Barrister, 1 Temple Gardens, Temple, London] . . . . *Digested*, 99/**1495**

James v. Williams [1973] J.P.L. 658, Lands Tr. . . . . *Digested*, 73/**2766.12**:
　　　　　　　　　　　　　　　　　　　　　　　　　　　Applied, 01/4809

James v. Williams [2000] Ch. 1; [1999] 3 W.L.R. 451; [1999] 3 All E.R. 309; [1999] 2 F.C.R. 498; (2000) 79 P. & C.R. 421; (1999) 96(15) L.S.G. 30; (1999) 78 P. & C.R. D17; *Times*, April 13, 1999; *Independent*, March 25, 1999, CA . . . . *Digested*, 99/**4956**:
　　　　　　　　　　　　　　　　　　　Subsequent proceedings, 01/655

James v. Williams (Application to Set Aside) [2001] C.P. Rep. 42, CA. . . . . *Digested*, 01/**655**:
　　　　　　　　　　　　　　　　　　　Previous proceedings, 99/4956

James Gilbert Ltd v. MGN Ltd [2000] E.M.L.R. 680, QBD . . . . *Digested*, 00/**1761**

James Howden & Co Ltd v. Taylor Woodrow Property Co Ltd 1998 S.C. 853; 1999 S.L.T. 841; 1998 S.C.L.R. 903; 1998 G.W.D. 27-1386, Ex Div; affirming 1997 G.W.D. 32-1637; *Times*, December 8, 1997, OH . . . . *Digested*, 98/**5550**

James Longley & Co Ltd v. Forest Giles Ltd [2001] EWCA Civ 1242, CA; affirming (2001) 17 Const. L.J. 424, QBD (T&CC)

James McNaughton Paper Group Ltd v. Hicks Anderson & Co [1991] 2 Q.B. 113; [1991] 2 W.L.R. 641; [1991] 1 All E.R. 134; [1990] B.C.C. 891; [1991] B.C.L.C. 235; [1991] E.C.C. 186; [1955-95] P.N.L.R. 574; (1990) 140 N.L.J. 1311; *Independent*, September 11, 1990, CA . . . . *Digested*, 91/**2652**:
　　　　　　　　　　　　　　　　　　　　　　　Considered, 98/3999

James Miller & Partners Ltd v. Whitworth Street Estates (Manchester) Ltd see Whitworth Street Estates (Manchester) Ltd v. James Miller & Partners Ltd

James Moore Earthmoving v. Miller Construction Ltd see Miller Construction Ltd v. James Moore Earthmoving

Jameson v. Central Electricity Generating Board (No.1) [2000] 1 A.C. 455; [1999] 2
W.L.R. 141; [1999] 1 All E.R. 193; [1999] 1 Lloyd's Rep. 573; [1999] P.I.Q.R. Q81;
(1999) 96(5) L.S.G. 37; (1999) 143 S.J.L.B. 29; *Times,* December 17, 1998,
HL; reversing [1998] Q.B. 323; [1997] 3 W.L.R. 151; [1997] 4 All E.R. 38;
[1997] P.I.Q.R. Q89; (1997) 141 S.J.L.B. 55; *Times,* February 25, 1997, CA . . . . .   *Digested,* 99/**1386**:
         Applied, 00/598: *Considered,* 00/377: *Distinguished,* 01/**656**:
         Followed, 99/1640: *Not applied,* 00/5122
Jameson v. Central Electricity Generating Board (No.2) [2000] C.P. Rep. 41, CA . . . . .   *Digested,* 00/**457**
Jamieson v. Customs and Excise Commissioners; *sub nom* Customs and Excise
Commissioners v. Jamieson [2001] S.T.I. 938, Ch D
Jamieson v. Watt's Trustee 1950 S.C. 265; 1950 S.L.T. 232, 2 Div . . . .   *Digested,* 50/**4764**:
         Applied, 52/375, 52/377, 54/3767, 54/4079: *Distinguished,* 00/5986:
         Followed, 47-51/3940
Jamil v. Customs and Excise Commissioners [2001] S.T.I. 54, V&DTr
Jamstalldhetsombudsmannen v. Orebro Lans Landsting (C236/98) [2000] E.C.R. I-
2189; [2000] 2 C.M.L.R. 708; [2000] C.E.C. 552; [2001] I.C.R. 249; [2000]
I.R.L.R. 421, ECJ (6th Chamber) . . . .   *Digested,* 00/**2159**
Jan De Nul (UK) Ltd v. Axa Royale Belge SA (formerly NV Royale Belge); *sub nom* Jan
De Nul (UK) Ltd v. Royale Belge SA; A3/2000/3228, CA; affirming [2000] 2
Lloyd's Rep. 700; [2001] Lloyd's Rep. I.R. 327, QBD (Comm Ct) . . . .   *Digested,* 01/**3800**
Jan De Nul (UK) Ltd v. Royale Belge SA see Jan De Nul (UK) Ltd v. Axa Royale Belge
SA (formerly NV Royale Belge)
JAN III SOBIESKI Trade Mark [1999] E.T.M.R. 874, Sad Najwyzszy (PL)
Jancey v. Higgins (Unreported, July 31, 1996), CC (Sheffield) [*Ex rel.* Irwin Mitchell,
Solicitors] . . . .   *Digested,* 97/**589**:
         Cited, 00/462
Janciuk v. Winerite [1998] I.R.L.R. 63, EAT . . . .   *Digested,* 98/**2098**
JANE AUSTEN Trade Mark [2000] R.P.C. 879, TMR . . . .   *Digested,* 01/**3983**
Janicki v. Secretary of State for Social Security; *sub nom* Janicki v. Secretary of State
for the Home Department [2001] I.C.R. 1220; *Times,* February 2, 2001, CA . . . .   *Digested,* 01/**5051**
Janicki v. Secretary of State for the Home Department see Janicki v. Secretary of State
for Social Security
Janowski v. Poland (2000) 29 E.H.R.R. 705; 5 B.H.R.C. 672, ECHR . . . .   *Digested,* 99/**3108**
Jansen Pharmaceutica NV v. Patent and Trade Marks Office [2001] E.T.M.R. 61, Rel
(Lisboa)
Jany v. Staatssecretaris van Justitie (C268/99), *Times,* December 11, 2001, ECJ
Japan Leasing (Europe) Plc, Re see Wallace v. Shoa Leasing (Singapore) PTE Ltd
Japan Line Ltd v. Aggeliki Charis Compania Maritima SA (The Angelic Grace); *sub nom*
Japan Line Ltd v. Davies and Potter [1980] 1 Lloyd's Rep. 288; 123 S.J. 487,
CA . . . .   *Digested,* 80/**80**:
         Applied, 81/84, 00/756
Japan Line Ltd v. Davies and Potter see Japan Line Ltd v. Aggeliki Charis Compania
Maritima SA (The Angelic Grace)
JAPAN SYNTHETIC RUBBER/Thermoplastic co-polymer (T737/92) [1998] E.P.O.R. 466,
EPO (Technical Bd App)
Japy Freres & Co v. RWJ Sutherland & Co; *sub nom* RJW Sutherland & Co v. Owners
of the SS Thoger (1921) 6 Ll. L. Rep. 381, CA; reversing (1920) 5 Ll. L. Rep.
122, KBD . . . .   *Applied,* 01/4917
Jarmain v. Secretary of State for the Environment, Transport and the Regions (No.1);
sub nom R. v. Secretary of State for the Environment, Transport and the Regions
Ex p. Jarmain [2000] 2 P.L.R. 126; [2000] J.P.L. 1063, CA; affirming [1999] 2
P.L.R. 89; [1999] J.P.L. 1106; [1999] E.G.C.S. 41; (1999) 96(15) L.S.G. 30;
(1999) 96(12) L.S.G. 35; *Times,* April 13, 1999; *Independent* April 19, 1999
(C.S), QBD . . . .   *Digested,* 00/**4454**
Jarmin (Inspector of Taxes) v. Rawlings [1994] S.T.C. 1005; 67 T.C. 130; [1994] S.T.I.
1373; [1994] E.G.C.S. 185; (1995) 92(2) L.S.G. 37; (1995) 139 S.J.L.B. 19;
Times, December 13, 1994; *Independent,* January 23, 1995, Ch D . . . .   *Digested,* 95/**532**:
         Considered, 95/533, 96/436, 00/4923
Jarrett v. Barclays Bank Plc; Jones v. First National Bank Plc; First National Bank Plc v.
Peacock [1999] Q.B. 1; [1997] 3 W.L.R. 654; [1997] 2 All E.R. 484; [1997] 6
Bank. L.R. 66; [1997] C.L.C. 391; [1997] I.L.Pr. 531; [1997] C.C.L.R. 32; (1997)
94(6) L.S.G. 27; (1996) 140 S.J.L.B. 252; [1996] N.P.C. 159; *Times,* November
18, 1996; *Independent,* November 6, 1996, CA . . . .   *Digested,* 96/**2912**
Jarrett v. Burford Estates & Property Co Ltd [1999] 1 E.G.L.R. 181, LandsTr . . . .   *Digested,* 99/**3687**
Jarvis (Isabella) v. DPP (2001) 165 J.P. 15; *Independent,* November 13, 2000 (C.S),
QBD . . . .   *Digested,* 01/**1265**
Jarvis v. Hampshire CC see Phelps v. Hillingdon LBC
Jarvis v. Hampshire CC [2000] 2 F.C.R. 310; (2000) 2 L.G.L.R. 636; [2000] Ed. C.R.
1; [2000] E.L.R. 36; *Times,* November 23, 1999, CA; reversing [1999] Ed. C.R.
785, QBD . . . .   *Digested,* 99/**3968**:
         Subsequent proceedings, 00/1947
Jarvis v. Ramsden, CC (Bridgend) [*Ex rel.* Andrew Arentsen, Barrister, 33 Park Place,
Cardiff] . . . .   *Digested,* 01/**1662**

Jarvis v. Swans Tours Ltd [1973] Q.B. 233; [1972] 3 W.L.R. 954; [1973] 1 All E.R. 71; 116 S.J. 822, CA . . . . *Digested*, 73/**723**:
    Applied, 75/1088, 75/2350, 76/875, 76/2637, 01/4275: *Considered*, 74/820, 74/821, 75/393, 85/952, 92/1514: *Distinguished*, 85/1145, 87/1303, 93/5148: *Followed*, 77/3143, 90/4310

Jarvis Interiors Ltd v. Galliard Homes Ltd; *sub nom* Galliard Homes Ltd v. J Jarvis & Sons Plc [2000] C.L.C. 411; [2000] B.L.R. 33; 71 Con. L.R. 219, CA . . . . *Digested*, 00/**812**

Jarvis Plc v. PricewaterhouseCoopers [2001] B.C.C. 670; [2000] 2 B.C.L.C. 368; (2000) 150 N.L.J. 1109; *Times*, October 10, 2000; *Independent*, October 9, 2000 (C.S), Ch D (Companies Ct) . . . . *Digested*, 00/**646**

Jasper v. United Kingdom see Rowe v. United Kingdom

Jasper v. United Kingdom (2000) 30 E.H.R.R. 441; [2000] Crim. L.R. 586, ECHR . . . . *Digested*, 01/**3512**:
    Considered, 01/989

Jassim v. Grand Metropolitan Information Services Ltd [2000] C.P. Rep. 78, CA . . . . . . *Digested*, 00/**611**

Jaundoo v. Attorney General of Guyana see Jaundoo (Olive Casey) v. Attorney General of Guyana

Jaundoo (Olive Casey) v. Attorney General of Guyana; *sub nom* Jaundoo v. Attorney General of Guyana [1971] A.C. 972; [1971] 3 W.L.R. 13; 115 S.J. 445, PC (Guy) . *Digested*, 71/**783**:
    Doubted, 01/849

Javad v. Aqil [1991] 1 W.L.R. 1007; [1991] 1 All E.R. 243; (1991) 61 P. & C.R. 164; [1990] 41 E.G. 61; (1990) 140 N.L.J. 1232, CA . . . . *Digested*, 91/**2218**:
    Applied, 00/4670: *Considered*, 91/122, 01/4162: *Not applied*, 98/3683

Javico International v. Yves Saint Laurent Parfums SA (C306/96) see Yves Saint Laurent Parfums SA v. Javico International (C306/96)

Jawando v. Sphinx Hairdressers (1998) 98(1) Q.R. 5, CC (Manchester) . . . . *Digested*, 98/**1558**

Jaworski v. Secretary of State for the Home Department Unreported, IAT . . . . *Approved*, 99/3175

Jay Benning Peltz (A Firm) v. Deutsch [2001] B.P.I.R. 510, Ch D . . . . *Digested*, 01/**663**

Jazayeri v. Secretary of State for the Home Department [2001] I.N.L.R. 489, IAT

JB v. Switzerland (31827/96) 3 I.T.L. Rep. 663; [2001] Crim. L.R. 748, ECHR

JC Penney Co Inc v. Penney's Ltd [1975] F.S.R. 367, CA . . . . *Digested*, 75/**3426**:
    Applied, 98/3497: *Followed*, 99/3524

JD Swain Ltd, Re [1965] 1 W.L.R. 909; [1965] 2 All E.R. 761; 109 S.J. 320, CA; affirming *Guardian*, January 19, 1965 . . . . *Digested*, 65/**487**:
    Applied, 83/342, 00/3507

JD Williams & Co Ltd v. Michael Hyde & Associates Ltd; *sub nom* Michael Hyde & Associates Ltd v. JD Williams & Co Ltd [2001] B.L.R. 99; (2001) 3 T.C.L.R. 1; [2000] Lloyd's Rep. P.N. 823; [2001] P.N.L.R. 8; [2000] N.P.C. 78; *Times*, August 4, 2000, CA . . . . *Digested*, 00/**4248**:
    Applied, 01/4513

JDE Plant Hire Ltd v. Barking and Dagenham LBC; *sub nom* R. v. Barking and Dagenham LBC Ex p. JDE Plant Hire Ltd [2000] R.A. 471, QBD . . . . *Digested*, 01/**4821**

JDL Ltd v. Customs and Excise Commissioners; *sub nom* Customs and Excise Commissioners v. JDL Ltd [2001] S.T.I. 1378, Ch D; affirming [2001] B.V.C. 2205; [2001] S.T.I. 877, V&DTr

JE Beale Plc [1999] B.V.C. 2144, V&DTr

Jean Lempereur SA v. Hifi Madison SA [1999] E.T.M.R. 1005, C d'A (Paris)

Jean Patou SA v. Ste Zag Zeitschriften Verlag AG [1999] E.T.M.R. 157, C d'A (Paris)

JEB Fasteners Ltd v. Marks Bloom & Co [1983] 1 All E.R. 583, CA; affirming [1981] 3 All E.R. 289; [1982] Com. L.R. 226, QBD . . . . *Digested*, 83/**2534**:
    Applied, 90/3322: *Considered*, 96/4517: *Distinguished*, 99/4054

Jebson v. Ministry of Defence [2000] 1 W.L.R. 2055; [2001] R.T.R. 2; [2000] I.C.R. 1220; [2000] P.I.Q.R. P201; (2000) 97(28) L.S.G. 32; *Times*, June 28, 2000; *Independent*, July 31, 2000 (C.S), CA . . . . *Digested*, 00/**4214**

Jefferies v. Byrne (1999) 99(3) Q.R. 6, CC (Basingstoke) [*Ex rel.* Elaine Strachan, Barrister, 3 Paper Buildings, Temple, London] . . . . *Digested*, 99/**1500**

Jefferies v. Home Office 1990-J.No.1626, QBD . . . . *Digested*, 99/**1414**

Jefferies v. Laws see National Grid Co Plc Group of the Electricity Supply Pension Scheme, Re

Jefferies v. Mayes see National Grid Co Plc v. Mayes

Jefferies v. Mayes (Pre-emptive Costs: Chancery) see National Grid Co Plc Group of the Electricity Supply Pension Scheme, Re

Jefferson v. Bhetcha [1979] 1 W.L.R. 898; [1979] 2 All E.R. 1108; 123 S.J. 389, CA . . . *Digested*, 79/**2184**:
    Applied, 86/3414, 88/2311, 98/681, 01/665: *Considered*, 01/718

Jefferson v. National Freight Carriers Plc [2001] EWCA Civ 2082; [2001] 2 Costs L.R. 313, CA

Jefford v. Gee [1970] 2 Q.B. 130; [1970] 2 W.L.R. 702; [1970] 1 All E.R. 1202; [1970] 1 Lloyd's Rep. 107; 114 S.J. 206, CA . . . . *Digested*, 70/**603**:
    Applied, 71/3203, 71/3237, 71/9424, 72/822, 72/837, 75/787, 76/2122, 77/385, 77/837, 77/2380, 83/986, 84/1044, 88/1056, 97/3171, 99/1415: *Considered*, 70/604, 70/2350, 71/9427, 73/862, 74/3009, 76/370, 77/2379, 78/713, 80/635, 85/477, 85/1037: *Distinguished*, 78/99: *Explained*, 76/760:
    Not followed, 77/735.a, 98/1431

Jeffrey v. Cape Insulation Ltd (1999) 99(2) Q.R. 5, QBD [*Ex rel.* Philip Hamer & Co Solicitors, 9/11 Scale Lane, Hull] . . . . *Digested*, 99/**1536**

Jeffrey v. CMB Speciality Packaging (UK) Ltd [2000] C.P. Rep. 1, CA. . . . .   *Digested*, 99/**461**
Jeffrey Rogers (Imports) Ltd, Re see Hamlet International Plc (In Administration), Re
Jeffries v. Fisher (Unreported, September 25, 2000), CC (Newport, Gwent) [*Ex rel.*
    Scott Rees & Co, Solicitors, Centaur House, Gardiners Place, Skelmersdale] . . .   *Digested*, 01/**618**
Jelle Zwemstra Ltd v. Walton and Claughton see Jelle Zwemstra Ltd v. Walton and
    Stuart
Jelle Zwemstra Ltd v. Walton and Stuart; *sub nom* Jelle Zwemstra Ltd v. Walton and
    Claughton; (Unreported, April 16, 1997), CC (Scarborough) [*Ex rel.* Sarah
    Clarke, Barrister, 10 Park Square, Leeds] . . . .   *Digested*, 97/**3002**:
                                                                   Distinguished, 99/3225
Jelley v. Iliffe [1981] Fam. 128; [1981] 2 W.L.R. 801; [1981] 2 All E.R. 29; 125 S.J.
    355, CA . . . .   *Digested*, 80/**2817**:
                   Considered, 82/3384, 82/3389, 83/3921, 84/3665, 00/4906
Jellinek's Application, Re (1946) 63 R.P.C. 59 . . . .   *Applied*, 93/3991,
                       97/4893: *Considered*, 96/5723: *Followed*, 98/3500
Jelly v. All Type Roofing Co see Debtor (No.50A-SD-1995), Re
Jelson v. Minister of Housing and Local Government; *sub nom* George Wimpey & Co
    v. Minister of Housing and Local Government [1970] 1 Q.B. 243; [1969] 3
    W.L.R. 282; [1969] 3 All E.R. 147; 133 J.P. 564; 67 L.G.R. 543; 20 P. & C.R.
    663; 113 S.J. 427, CA; affirming 67 L.G.R. 126; 19 P. & C.R. 746; 207 E.G. 437;
    [1968] R.V.R. 538; [1968] R.V.R. 521, QBD.   *Digested*, 69/**3480**:
            Considered, 91/455, 91/3426, 92/4178, 00/4427: *Distinguished*, 79/297:
                                        Followed, 97/4044, 98/4172
Jelson Ltd v. Derby City Council [1999] 4 P.L.R. 11; [1999] 3 E.G.L.R. 91; [1999] 39
    E.G. 149; [2000] J.P.L. 203; [1999] E.G.C.S. 88; (1999) 96(26) L.S.G. 30;
    [1999] N.P.C. 68; *Times*, September 22, 1999 ; *Independent*, July 5, 1999 (C.S.),
    Ch D . . . .   *Digested*, 99/**4359**
Jenkins v. BP Oil UK Ltd see Clark (Inspector of Taxes) v. Perks (Permission to Appeal)
Jenkins v. Essex CC [1999] 1 F.L.R. 420; [1999] 2 F.C.R. 743; [1999] Fam. Law 142;
    (2000) 164 J.P.N. 27; (1998) 95(45) L.S.G. 38; *Times*, October 15, 1998, Fam
    Div . . . .   *Digested*, 98/**2391**
Jenkins v. Holt [1999] R.T.R. 411; *Times*, May 27, 1999, CA . . . .   *Digested*, 99/**4060**
Jenkins v. Kingsgate (Clothing Productions) Ltd (C96/80) [1981] 1 W.L.R. 972;
    [1981] E.C.R. 911; [1981] 2 C.M.L.R. 24; [1981] I.C.R. 592; [1981] I.R.L.R. 228;
    125 S.J. 442, ECJ [1981] 1 W.L.R. 1485; [1980] 1 C.M.L.R. 81; [1981] I.C.R.
    715; [1980] I.R.L.R. 6; 125 S.J. 587; *Times*, November 15, 1979, EAT . . . .   *Digested*, 81/**1157**:
           Applied, 81/847, 82/1071, 86/1190, 87/1325, 91/1635, 94/5096, 98/2240:
           Considered, 83/2635, 84/1225, 86/1458, 87/1633, 87/4409, 95/2052,
                         96/2550, 96/2629: *Distinguished*, 98/5807
Jenkins v. Lumb (Unreported, July 24, 1998), CC (Leeds) [*Ex rel.* Irwin Mitchell
    Solicitors, Huttons Buildings, 146 West Street, Sheffield] . . . .   *Digested*, 98/**492**
Jenkins v. Stephens (Unreported, September 30, 1997), CC (Chichester) [*Ex rel.*
    Simon Kenny, Owen Kenny Partnership, Solicitors, Market Avenue, Chichester] .   *Digested*, 98/**429**
Jenkinson v. Docherty (Unreported, August 19, 1998), CC (Brighton) [*Ex rel.* Mark
    Harvey, 96 Station Road, Liss, Hampshire] . . . .   *Digested*, 99/**2454**
Jenks v. Dickinson (Inspector of Taxes) [1997] S.T.C. 853; 69 T.C. 458; [1997] B.T.C.
    286; *Times*, June 16, 1997, Ch D; affirming [1996] S.T.C. (S.C.D.) 299, Sp
    Comm . . . .   *Digested*, 97/**337**
Jenmain Builders Ltd v. Steed & Steed [2000] Lloyd's Rep. P.N. 549; [2000] P.N.L.R.
    616; (2000) 97(13) L.S.G. 45, CA
Jennings (Deceased), Re; *sub nom* Harlow v. National Westminster Bank Plc [1994]
    Ch. 286; [1994] 3 W.L.R. 67; [1994] 3 All E.R. 27; [1994] 1 F.L.R. 536; [1995]
    1 F.C.R. 257; [1994] Fam. Law 439; (1994) 91(7) L.S.G. 33; (1994) 138
    S.J.L.B. 31; *Times*, January 3, 1994, CA. . . . .   *Digested*, 95/**5147**:
                                               Distinguished, 98/4587
Jennings v. Kinder (Inspector of Taxes); *sub nom* Hochstrasser (Inspector of Taxes) v.
    Mayes [1960] A.C. 376; [1960] 2 W.L.R. 63; [1959] 3 All E.R. 817; 53 R. & I.T.
    12; 38 T.C. 673; (1959) 38 A.T.C. 360; [1959] T.R. 355, HL; affirming [1959]
    Ch. 22; [1958] 3 W.L.R. 215; [1958] 3 All E.R. 285; 51 R. & I.T. 767; (1958) 37
    A.T.C. 205; [1958] T.R. 237; 102 S.J. 546, CA; affirming [1958] 2 W.L.R. 982;
    [1958] 1 All E.R. 369; 51 R. & I.T. 321; (1957) 36 A.T.C. 356; [1957] T.R. 365;
    102 S.J. 419, Ch D . . . .   *Digested*, 59/**1543**:
       Applied, 64/1836, 76/1441, 78/1675, 82/1636, 89/2028, 90/2646, 91/2092,
          99/4729: *Considered*, 65/1946, 87/2034: *Distinguished*, 76/1438, 86/1762
Jennings v. Rice A3/2001/1013, CA; affirming [2001] W.T.L.R. 871, Ch D . . . .   *Digested*, 01/**5158**
Jensen v. Landbrugsministeriet, EF-Direktoratet (C132/95); Korn- Og
    Forderstofkompagniet A/S v. Landbrugsministeriet, EF-Direktoratet [1998] All
    E.R. (E.C.) 510; [1998] E.C.R. I-2975; [1998] 2 C.M.L.R. 1005, ECJ . . . .   *Digested*, 98/**2303**
Jephson Homes Housing Association Ltd v. Moisejevs; *sub nom* Moisjevs v. Jephson
    Homes Housing Association [2001] 2 All E.R. 901; (2001) 33 H.L.R. 54; [2001]
    L. & T.R. 18; [2000] E.G.C.S. 123; [2000] N.P.C. 115; *Times*, January 2, 2001,
    CA . . . .   *Digested*, 01/**4168**
Jerome v. Kelly (Inspector of Taxes) Ch/2001/App/010665, Ch D; reversing [2001]
    S.T.C. (S.C.D.) 170; [2001] S.T.I. 1145, Sp Comm

Jeromson v. Shell Tankers UK Ltd see Shell Tankers UK Ltd v. Jeromson
Jerrard v. Barclays Bank Plc CHANF 96/1720/3, CA . . . .   *Digested,* 98/**288**
Jerry Juhan Developments SA v. Avon Tyres Ltd; *sub nom* JJD v. Avon Tyres Ltd;
    QBENF 1999/0129/A2, CA; reversing [1999] C.L.C. 702; (1999) 22(4) I.P.D.
    22037; (1999) 96(6) L.S.G. 32; *Times,* January 25, 1999, QBD . . . .   *Digested,* 99/**834**
Jersey Society for the Prevention of Cruelty to Animals v. Rees (2001-02) 4 I.T.E.L.R.
    294, Royal Ct (Jer)
Jersild v. Denmark (A/298) (1995) 19 E.H.R.R. 1; *Times,* October 20, 1994, ECHR . . . . .   *Digested,* 95/**2645**:
                                        Applied, 98/3089, 01/3472, 01/3474
Jervis v. Kuoni Travel Ltd (Unreported, October 12, 1998), CC (Kingston on Thames)
    [*Ex rel.* Arun Katar, 2 Kings Bench Walk, Temple, London] . . . .   *Digested,* 98/**3733**
JERYL LYNN Trade Mark; *sub nom* Merck & Co Inc v. SmithKline Beecham Plc [2000]
    E.T.M.R. 75; [1999] F.S.R. 491; (1999) 49 B.M.L.R. 92; (1999) 22(2) I.P.D.
    22016; *Times,* December 18, 1998, Ch D . . . .   *Digested,* 99/**3545**
Jessamine Investment Co v. Schwartz [1978] Q.B. 264; [1977] 2 W.L.R. 145; [1976] 3
    All E.R. 521; (1977) 33 P. & C.R. 346; 120 S.J. 384, CA. . . . .   *Digested,* 76/**1559**:
                            Applied, 00/3916: *Considered,* 93/2485, 94/2758, 95/3009
Jesuthasan v. Hammersmith and Fulham LBC see Hammersmith and Fulham LBC v.
    Jesuthasan
Jevons v. Cosmosair Plc (1998) 162 J.P. 68; (1997) 161 J.P.N. 1173, QBD
Jewish Liturgical Association Cha'are Shalom Ve Tsedek v. France 9 B.H.R.C. 27, ECHR .   *Digested,* 01/**3483**
Jewo Ferrous BV v. Lewis Moore (A Firm) (Security for Costs) [2000] C.P. Rep. 57,
    CA . . . .   *Digested,* 00/**401**
Jewo Ferrous BV v. Lewis Moore (A Firm) [2001] Lloyd's Rep. P.N. 6; [2001] P.N.L.R.
    12; *Times,* November 30, 2000, CA . . . .   *Digested,* 01/**4261**
JF Finnegan Ltd v. Sheffield City Council 43 B.L.R. 124; (1989) Con. L.R. 54, QBD. . . .   *Digested,* 90/**646.a**:
                                                            Followed, 99/784
JFS (UK) Ltd (formerly Johnson Filtration Systems Ltd) v. South West Water Services
    Ltd; South West Water Services Ltd v. JFS (UK) Ltd (formerly Johnson Filtration
    Systems Ltd) 65 Con. L.R. 51, QBD (OR) . . . .   *Digested,* 00/**229**
JFS (UK) Ltd v. Dwr Cymru Cyf (No.1) [1999] 1 W.L.R. 231; [1999] B.L.R. 17; (1999)
    1 T.C.L.R. 187; (1998) 95(39) L.S.G. 40; (1998) 142 S.J.L.B. 256; *Times,*
    October 10, 1998, CA . . . .   *Digested,* 98/**538**
JFS (UK) Ltd v. Dwr Cymru Cyf (No.2) 65 Con. L.R. 92, QBD (T&CC) . . . .   *Digested,* 99/**5035**
JGW Coatings Ltd v. Whitehouse (Valuation Officer) see Fusetron Ltd v. Whitehouse
    (Valuation Officer)
JH v. United Kingdom (44787/98) see PG v. United Kingdom (44787/98)
JH Coles Proprietary Ltd (In Liquidation) v. Need [1934] A.C. 82, PC (Aus) . . . .   *Applied,* 99/**600**
JH Rayner (Mincing Lane) Ltd v. Brazil see JH Rayner (Mincing Lane) Ltd v. Cafenorte
    SA Importadora
JH Rayner (Mincing Lane) Ltd v. Cafenorte SA Importadora; *sub nom* JH Rayner
    (Mincing Lane) Ltd v. Brazil; Citoma Trading Ltd v. Brazil [1999] 2 All E.R.
    (Comm) 577; [1999] 2 Lloyd's Rep. 750; [1999] C.L.C. 1847, CA; affirming
    [1999] 1 All E.R. (Comm.) 120, QBD (Comm Ct) . . . .   *Digested,* 00/**502**
Jha v. American Life Insurance Co (Unreported, January 13, 2000), ET [*Ex rel.* Melvyn
    Harris, Barrister, 17 New Square, Lincoln's Inn, London] . . . .   *Digested,* 00/**2183**
Jhamat v. Inns of Court School of Law [1999] E.L.R. 450, Visitors (Inns of Ct) . . . .   *Digested,* 00/**1785**
Jhanjan v. Netherlands (C36/82) see Morson v. Netherlands (C35/82)
Jif Lemon case see Reckitt & Colman Products Ltd v. Borden Inc (No.3)
Jillas Application, Re [2000] 2 E.G.L.R. 99; [2000] 23 E.G. 147, Lands Tr . . . .   *Digested,* 00/**4627**
Jimaale v. London Buses Ltd (Unreported, February 28, 2000), CC (Uxbridge) [*Ex rel.*
    Tim Sheppard, Barrister, 8 Bell Yard, London] . . . .   *Digested,* 00/**599**
Jimmy Nicks Property Co Ltd's Application [1999] E.T.M.R. 445, Appointed Person . . .   *Digested,* 00/**6524**
Jippes v. Minister van Landbouw, Natuurbeheer en Visserij (C189/01) [2001] E.C.R. I-
    5689; *Times,* July 19, 2001, ECJ . . . .   *Digested,* 01/**176**
JJ v. Netherlands (1999) 28 E.H.R.R. 168; [1998] H.R.C.D. 370, ECHR . . . .   *Digested,* 99/**3127**
JJ Harrison (Properties) Ltd v. Harrison [2001] EWCA Civ 1467; [2001] W.T.L.R. 1327,
    CA; reversing in part [2001] 1 B.C.L.C. 158, Ch D
JJ Lloyd Instruments v. Northern Star Insurance Co (The Miss Jay Jay) [1987] 1 Lloyd's
    Rep. 32; [1987] F.T.L.R. 14; [1987] Fin. L.R. 120, CA; affirming [1985] 1 Lloyd's
    Rep. 264, QBD (Comm Ct) . . . .   *Digested,* 87/**3409**:
                                                            Applied, 00/3557
JJD v. Avon Tyres Ltd see Jerry Juhan Developments SA v. Avon Tyres Ltd
JL Harvey Ltd v. Schofield & Anderson Ltd BT/27/1998, Lands Tr . . . .   *Digested,* 99/**5411**
JN Nicholas (VIMTO) Ltd v. Rose & Thistle (1995) 20 I.P.L.R. 32, HC (Ind) . . . .   *Applied,* 98/3521
JN Taylor Finance Pty Ltd, Re; *sub nom* England v. Purves [1999] B.C.C. 197; [1999] 2
    B.C.L.C. 256; [1998] B.P.I.R. 347; *Times,* January 29, 1998, Ch D . . . .   *Digested,* 98/**3303**
Jo y Jo Ltd v. Matalan Retail Ltd [2000] E.C.D.R. 178; (1999) 22(6) I.P.D. 22060,
    Ch D . . . .   *Digested,* 00/**3569**
Joan Balcom Sales Inc v. Poirier 49 C.P.C. (2d) 180. . . . .   *Applied,* 01/801
Joanna Christina Gleeson and Gleeson Shirt Co v. HR Denne Ltd [1975] F.S.R. 250;
    [1975] R.P.C. 471, CA . . . .   *Digested,* 75/**441**:
                                                            Followed, 01/3852

Job Centre Coop arl, Re (C55/96) [1997] E.C.R. I-7119; [1998] 4 C.M.L.R. 708; [1998]
C.E.C. 507, ECJ (6th Chamber) . . . . *Digested,* 98/**742**
Job Centre Coop Arl (C111/94), Re [1995] E.C.R. I-3361, ECJ. . . . . *Digested,* 96/**2795**:
Followed, 00/2381

Jobling *v.* Associated Dairies [1982] A.C. 794; [1981] 3 W.L.R. 155; [1981] 2 All E.R.
752; 125 S.J. 481, HL; affirming [1981] Q.B. 389; [1980] 3 W.L.R. 704; [1980]
3 All E.R. 769; 124 S.J. 631, CA . . . . *Digested,* 81/**1835**:
Cited, 00/1482: *Considered,* 94/1442, 96/4424: *Distinguished,* 82/1082,
83/1306

Jobling *v.* Gala Leisure Ltd (Unreported, May 28, 1999), CC (Sunderland) [*Ex rel.* Sam
Faulks, Barrister, 33 Broad Chare Chambers, Broad Chare, Newcastle upon
Tyne] . . . . *Digested,* 99/**1572**
Jobserve Ltd *v.* Network Multimedia Television Ltd (Restored Injunction Hearing); *sub
nom* Network Multimedia Television Ltd (t/a Silicon.com) *v.* Jobserve Ltd
(Restored Injunction Hearing) [2001] EWCA Civ 2021, CA; affirming [2001]
U.K.C.L.R. 814; (2001) 24(6) I.P.D. 24039, Ch D . . . . *Digested,* 01/**764**
Jobsin Co UK Plc (t/a Internet Recruitment Solutions) *v.* Department of Health; *sub nom*
Jobsin.co.uk Plc *v.* Department of Health [2001] EWCA Civ 1241; [2001] Eu.
L.R. 685; (2001) 98(33) L.S.G. 29; *Times,* October 2, 2001, CA . . . . *Digested,* 01/**4406**
Jobsin.co.uk Plc *v.* Department of Health see Jobsin Co UK Plc (t/a Internet
Recruitment Solutions) *v.* Department of Health
Jobson *v.* Record (1998) 75 P. & C.R. 375; [1998] 1 E.G.L.R. 113; [1998] 09 E.G. 148;
[1997] N.P.C. 56, CA . . . . *Digested,* 97/**205**
Joe Cool (Manchester) Ltd's Trade Mark Application [2000] R.P.C. 926; (2000) 23(8)
I.P.D. 23065, TMR . . . . *Digested,* 01/**3982**
Jofar (CICA: Quantum: 2001), Re [2001] 6 Q.R. 6, CICAP [*Ex rel.* Woodbridge
Partnership, Solicitors, Windsor House, 42 Windsor Street, Uxbridge] . . . . *Digested,* 01/**1596**
Johal *v.* Johal CO/3322/98; CO/5157/98, QBD . . . . *Digested,* 99/**2432**
Johansen *v.* Norway (1997) 23 E.H.R.R. 33, ECHR . . . . *Digested,* 97/**2792**:
Applied, 98/3138: *Considered,* 98/3104: *Distinguished,* 99/2302

John (Julie), Re [1998] C.O.D. 306, QBD
John A Pike (Butchers) Ltd *v.* Independent Insurance Co Ltd [1998] Lloyd's Rep. I.R.
410, CA . . . . *Digested,* 99/**3393**
John *v.* Express Newspapers [2000] 1 W.L.R. 1931; [2000] 3 All E.R. 257; [2000]
E.M.L.R. 606; (2000) 97(21) L.S.G. 38; (2000) 150 N.L.J. 615; (2000) 144
S.J.L.B. 217; *Times,* April 26, 2000; *Independent,* May 2, 2000, CA; reversing
[2000] 1 W.L.R. 1931; (2000) 150 N.L.J. 342; *Independent,* March 7, 2000,
QBD . . . . *Digested,* 00/**14**
John *v.* Harris (1999) 78 P. & C.R. D4, CA
John *v.* Humphreys [1955] 1 W.L.R. 325; [1955] 1 All E.R. 793; 53 L.G.R. 321; 99 S.J.
222, DC . . . . *Digested,* 55/**2445**:
Applied, 68/3460, 73/2960, 73/3014, 75/2981, 87/3274: *Followed,* 00/929
John *v.* MGN Ltd [1997] Q.B. 586; [1996] 3 W.L.R. 593; [1996] 2 All E.R. 35; [1996]
E.M.L.R. 229; (1966) 146 N.L.J. 13; *Times,* December 14, 1995, CA . . . . *Digested,* 96/**5673**:
Applied, 97/1768: *Considered,* 96/2122, 96/5674, 00/1756
John *v.* PricewaterhouseCoopers (formerly Price Waterhouse) (Costs) (2001) 98(34)
L.S.G. 39; *Times,* August 22, 2001, Ch D . . . . *Digested,* 01/**490**
John Barker Construction Ltd *v.* London Portman Hotel Ltd 83 B.L.R. 31; 50 Con. L.R.
43; (1996) 12 Const. L.J. 277, QBD (OR) . . . . *Digested,* 96/**1157**:
Considered, 99/791

John D Wood & Co *v.* Dantata; Beauchamp Estates *v.* Dantata (1987) 283 E.G. 314,
CA; affirming [1985] 2 E.G.L.R. 44; (1985) 275 E.G. 1278 . . . . *Digested,* 87/**63**:
Applied, 89/54: *Considered,* 90/109.10, 92/89, 93/67, 01/112
John Dee Group Ltd *v.* WMH (21) Ltd (formerly Magnet Ltd) [1998] B.C.C. 972, CA;
affirming [1997] B.C.C. 518, Ch D . . . . *Digested,* 99/**858**
John Dee Ltd *v.* Customs and Excise Commissioners [1995] S.T.C. 941; *Times,* July 20,
1995, CA; affirming [1995] S.T.C. 265; *Times,* February 17, 1995, QBD;
reversing [1993] V.A.T.T.R. 196, VAT Tr (Manchester) . . . . *Digested,* 96/**5842**:
Considered, 00/5335

John Deere Ltd *v.* Commission of the European Communities (C7/95 P); New Ford
Holland *v.* Commission of the European Communities (C8/95 P) [1998] All E.R.
(E.C.) 481 (Note); [1998] E.C.R. I-3111; [1998] 5 C.M.L.R. 311; [1998] C.E.C.
611, ECJ (5th Chamber); affirming [1994] E.C.R. II-957, CFI . . . . *Digested,* 98/**2317**:
Followed, 00/2363

John Edwards & Co *v.* Motor Union Insurance Co Ltd; *sub nom* Edwards *v.* Motor
Union Insurance Co Ltd (The White Rose) [1922] 2 K.B. 249; (1922) 11 Ll. L.
Rep. 170, KBD . . . . *Considered,* 96/3555,
98/1461

John Harris Partnership *v.* Groveworld Ltd 75 Con. L.R. 7; [1999] P.N.L.R. 697, QBD
(T&CC) . . . . *Digested,* 99/**1417**
John Holland Construction & Engineering Ltd *v.* Majorca Products (2000) 16 Const.
L.J. 114, Sup Ct (Vic) . . . . *Digested,* 00/**811**
John Hudson & Co Ltd *v.* Kirkness (Inspector of Taxes) see Kirkness (Inspector of
Taxes) *v.* John Hudson & Co Ltd

John Laing & Son v. Kingswood Assessment Committee [1949] 1 K.B. 344; [1949] 1
　　All E.R. 224; 65 T.L.R. 80; 113 J.P. 111; 47 L.G.R. 64; 42 R. & I.T. 15; 93 S.J. 26,
　　CA; affirming [1948] 2 K.B. 116; [1948] 1 All E.R. 943; 64 T.L.R. 407, KBD .... *Digested*, 47-51/**8292**:
　　　　　　　　　　　　　Applied, 55/2275, 56/6585, 56/7264, 60/2685, 70/2414, 98/4319:
　　　　　　　　　　　　　Considered, 77/2453, 85/2924, 87/3181, 90/3917: *Distinguished*, 75/2776,
　　　　　　　　　　　　　　　　　　　　　　　　　99/4333: *Followed*, 99/4335, 01/4821
John Laing Construction v. Ince (Unreported, April 2, 2001), CC (Southend) [*Ex rel.*
　　Katya Melluish, Barrister, 3 Paper Buildings, Temple] . . . . *Digested*, 01/**4543**
John Lewis of Hungerford Ltd's Trade Mark Application [2001] E.T.M.R. 104; [2001] R.P.C.
　　28, Appointed Person; affirming [2001] E.T.M.R. 36, TMR . . . . *Digested*, 01/**4059**
John Lewis Plc v. Coyne [2001] I.R.L.R. 139; *Times*, January 5, 2001, EAT . . . . *Digested*, 01/**2343**
John Lewis Properties Plc v. Inland Revenue Commissioners; *sub nom* Inland Revenue
　　Commissioners v. John Lewis Properties Ltd [2001] S.T.C. 1118; [2001] B.T.C.
　　213; [2001] S.T.I. 937; (2001) 98(27) L.S.G. 40; (2001) 145 S.J.L.B. 164; *Times*,
　　June 22, 2001; *Independent*, July 30, 2001 (C.S), Ch D; affirming [2000]
　　S.T.C. (S.C.D.) 494; [2000] S.T.I. 1467, Sp Comm . . . . *Digested*, 01/**5205**
John Lyon's Free Grammar School v. Berman see John Lyon's Free Grammar School v.
　　Secchi
John Lyon's Free Grammar School v. Secchi; *sub nom* Keepers and Governors of the
　　Possessions, Revenues and Goods of the Free Grammar School of John Lyon v.
　　Secchi; Keepers and Governors of the Possessions, Revenues and Goods of
　　the Free Grammar School of John Lyon v. Berman; John Lyon's Free Grammar
　　School v. Berman (2000) 32 H.L.R. 820; [2000] L. & T.R. 308; [1999] 3
　　E.G.L.R. 49; [1999] 49 E.G. 100; [1999] E.G.C.S. 118; [1999] N.P.C. 121; (2000)
　　79 P. & C.R. D10, CA . . . . *Digested*, 00/**3910**
John Mowlem & Co Plc v. Hydra Tight & Co Plc see John Mowlem & Co Plc v. Hydra
　　Tight Ltd (t/a Hevilifts)
John Mowlem & Co Plc v. Hydra Tight Ltd (t/a Hevilifts); *sub nom* John Mowlem & Co
　　Plc v. Hydra Tight & Co Plc (2001) 17 Const. L.J. 358, QBD (T&CC)
John Munroe (Acrylics) Ltd v. London Fire and Civil Defence Authority see Capital and
　　Counties Plc v. Hampshire CC
John Reid Enterprises Ltd v. Pell [1999] E.M.L.R. 675, Ch D . . . . *Digested*, 99/**3929**
John Ridley Construction (Bucks) Ltd v. BP Collins & Co (Unreported, January 30,
　　1998), CA . . . . *Distinguished*, 98/451
John Village (Automotive) Ltd v. Customs and Excise Commissioners [1998] V. & D.R.
　　340, V&DTr . . . . *Digested*, 00/**5323**
John Wilson Cars Ltd v. Customs and Excise Commissioners [2000] S.T.I. 1350, V&DTr
John Wyeth & Bros Ltd v. Cigna Insurance Co of Europe SA NV (No.1) [2001] EWCA
　　Civ 175; [2001] C.L.C. 970; [2001] Lloyd's Rep. I.R. 420, CA; affirming 1997
　　Folio No 2248, QBD (Comm Ct) . . . . *Digested*, 01/**3812**
John Wyeth & Brother Ltd's Application; Schering AG's Application [1985] R.P.C. 545, Pat
　　Ct . . . . *Approved*, 00/3677
John-Davies v. Smith [2001] 6 Q.R. 8, CC (Cardiff) [*Ex rel.* Lisa Jane Thomas,
　　Barrister, 9 Park Place, Cardiff] . . . . *Digested*, 01/**1635**
Johns v. Deacon (Unreported, January 23, 1985), CA . . . . *Digested*, 85/**65.u**:
　　　　　　　　　　　　　　　　　　　　　　　　　　Considered, 98/4372
Johns v. Secretary of State for the Environment, Transport and the Regions [1998]
　　N.P.C. 41, QBD
Johnsey Estates (1990) Ltd v. Secretary of State for the Environment, Transport and the
　　Regions [2001] EWCA Civ 535; [2001] L. & T.R. 32; [2001] N.P.C. 79, CA . . . . *Followed*, 01/502
Johnson v. Bibi [2001] 5 Q.R. 13, CC (Northampton) [*Ex rel.* Nigel S Brockley,
　　Barrister, Bracton Chambers, 8 Bell Yard, London] . . . . *Digested*, 01/**1625**
Johnson v. Blackpool General Commissioners [1997] S.T.C. 1202; 70 T.C. 1; [1997]
　　B.T.C. 501; (1997) 94(34) L.S.G. 28; *Times*, July 11, 1997, CA; affirming [1996]
　　S.T.C. 277; *Times*, February 10, 1996, Ch D . . . . *Digested*, 97/**4743**:
　　　　　　　　　　　　　　　　　　　　　　　　　　Considered, 99/1535
Johnson v. British Midland Airways Ltd [1996] P.I.Q.R. Q8, QBD . . . . *Considered*, 99/1535
Johnson v. British Railways Board (Unreported, December 4, 1997), CC (Swindon)
　　[*Ex rel.* Townsends Solicitors, 42 Cricklade Street, Swindon, Wiltshire] . . . . *Digested*, 98/**1625**
Johnson v. Busfield (Deceased) (1997) 38 B.M.L.R. 29, QBD . . . . *Digested*, 98/**553**
Johnson v. Chief Adjudication Officer (No.2) (C410/92) [1995] All E.R. (E.C.) 258;
　　[1994] E.C.R. I-5483; [1995] 1 C.M.L.R. 725; [1995] I.C.R. 375; [1995] I.R.L.R.
　　157; *Times*, December 26, 1994; *Financial Times*, December 20, 1994, ECJ . . . . . *Digested*, 95/**4639**:
　　　　　　　　　　　Applied, 95/2112, 99/5284: *Considered*, 95/1987, 96/2576
Johnson v. Chief Constable of Surrey, *Times*, November 23, 1992, CA . . . . *Digested*, 92/**2817**:
　　　　　　　　　　　　　　　　　　　　　　　Applied, 01/4527: *Followed*, 96/5677
Johnson v. Davies [1999] Ch. 117; [1998] 3 W.L.R. 1299; [1998] 2 All E.R. 649;
　　[1999] B.C.C. 275; [1998] 2 B.C.L.C. 252; [1998] B.P.I.R. 607; (2000) 79 P. &
　　C.R. 14; [1998] L. & T.R. 69; [1998] 3 E.G.L.R. 72; [1998] 49 E.G. 153; (1998)
　　95(19) L.S.G. 23; (1998) 142 S.J.L.B. 141; [1998] N.P.C. 50; *Times*, March 31,
　　1998, CA; affirming [1997] 1 W.L.R. 1511; [1997] 1 All E.R. 921; [1997] 1
　　B.C.L.C. 580; [1997] B.P.I.R. 221; [1997] 1 E.G.L.R. 42; [1997] 19 E.G. 157;
　　(1996) 146 N.L.J. 1814, Ch D . . . . *Digested*, 98/**3351**:
　　　　　　　　　　　　　　　　　　　　　　　Considered, 99/3336, 00/3884

Johnson v. Deer (Unreported, June 21, 2000), CC (Liverpool) [*Ex rel.* Michael W
Halsall Solicitors, 2 The Parks, Newton-le-Willows] . . . .   *Digested*, 01/**619**
Johnson v. EBS Pension Trustees Ltd see Johnson v. EBS Pensioner Trustees Ltd
Johnson v. EBS Pensioner Trustees Ltd; *sub nom* Johnson v. EBS Pension Trustees Ltd;
A3/2001/0705, CA; affirming (2001) 98(19) L.S.G. 36; (2001) 145 S.J.L.B. 92;
(2001) 82 P. & C.R. D2, Ch D
Johnson v. Finbow [1983] 1 W.L.R. 879; (1983) 5 Cr. App. R. (S.) 95; (1983) 147 J.P.
563; [1983] R.T.R. 356; [1983] Crim. L.R. 480; (1983) 127 S.J. 411, DC . . . . . .   *Digested*, 83/**3289**:
                                          Applied, 00/5467: *Referred to*, 96/7302
Johnson v. Gore Wood & Co (No.1); *sub nom* Johnson v. Gore Woods & Co [2001] 2
W.L.R. 72; [2001] 1 All E.R. 481; [2001] C.P.L.R. 49; [2001] B.C.C. 820; [2001]
1 B.C.L.C. 313; [2001] P.N.L.R. 18; (2001) 98(1) L.S.G. 24; (2001) 98(8)
L.S.G. 46; (2000) 150 N.L.J. 1889; (2001) 145 S.J.L.B. 29; *Times*, December
22, 2000; *Independent*, February 7, 2001 (C.S), HL; reversing in part [1999]
C.P.L.R. 155; [1999] B.C.C. 474; [1999] Lloyd's Rep. P.N. 91; [1999] P.N.L.R.
426; [1998] N.P.C. 151, CA . . . .   *Digested*, 01/**410**:
           Applied, 99/3313, 01/746: *Considered*, 01/675, 01/708, 01/5710:
                                               Followed, 01/749
Johnson v. Gore Woods & Co see Johnson v. Gore Wood & Co (No.1)
Johnson v. Hill (Unreported, August 2, 1999), CC (Manchester) [*Ex rel.* Betesh Fox &
Co Solicitors, 16-17 Ralli Courts, West Riverside, Manchester] . . . .   *Digested*, 99/**1555**
Johnson v. HM Prison Service see HM Prison Service v. Johnson
Johnson v. John (1998) 148 N.L.J. 1229, CA
Johnson v. Khan (1998) 98(1) Q.R. 6, CC (Burnley) . . . .   *Digested*, 98/**1620**
Johnson v. Leicestershire Constabulary, *Times*, October 7, 1998, QBD. . . . .   *Digested*, 98/**1066**
Johnson v. McKean [2001] N.P.C. 179, QBD . . . .   *Previous proceedings*,
                                                 01/410
Johnson v. Pattenden (1998) 98(3) Q.R. 7, CC (Cheltenham) . . . .   *Digested*, 98/**1611**
Johnson (Inspector of Taxes) v. Prudential Assurance Co Ltd [1998] S.T.C. 439; 70 T.C.
445; [1998] B.T.C. 112; *Times*, February 24, 1998; *Independent*, February 23,
1998 (C.S.), CA; affirming [1996] S.T.C. 647; *Times*, July 5, 1996; *Independent*,
July 15, 1996 (C.S.), Ch D . . . .   *Digested*, 98/**4629**
Johnson v. Reed Corrugated Cases Ltd [1992] 1 All E.R. 169, QBD . . . .   *Digested*, 92/**3447**:
                   Applied, 98/474: *Considered*, 94/2154, 95/4019: *Followed*, 97/574
Johnson v. Rogers (Unreported, October 1, 1998), CC (Norwich) [*Ex rel.* Lawrence
Caun, Barrister, 2 Pump Court, Temple, London] . . . .   *Digested*, 99/**1470**
Johnson v. Ryan [2000] I.C.R. 236, EAT. . . . .   *Digested*, 00/**2112**
Johnson v. Secretary of State for Health [2001] Lloyd's Rep. Med. 385, CA
Johnson v. Shokat, CC (Nuneaton) [*Ex rel.* Stephen Garner, Barrister, No.8 Fountain
Court, Steelhouse Lane, Birmingham] . . . .   *Digested*, 01/**1768**
Johnson v. Silvers [2001] 6 Q.R. 22, CC (Birmingham) [*Ex rel.* Stephen Garner,
Barrister, 8 Fountain Court, Steelhouse Lane, Birmingham] . . . .   *Digested*, 01/**1799**
Johnson v. Taylor Bros & Co Ltd [1920] A.C. 144; (1919) 1 Ll. L. Rep. 183, HL. . . . .   *Applied*, 47-51/**7856**,
                             52/3210, 61/1426, 74/3035: *Referred to*, 00/5963
Johnson v. Trinidad and Tobago [1999] 1 W.L.R. 2000, PC (Trin). . . . .   *Digested*, 00/**984**
Johnson v. Unisys Ltd [2001] UKHL 13; [2001] 2 W.L.R. 1076; [2001] 2 All E.R. 801;
[2001] I.C.R. 480; [2001] I.R.L.R. 279; *Times*, March 23, 2001; *Independent*,
March 29, 2001, HL; affirming [1999] 1 All E.R. 854; [1999] I.C.R. 809; [1999]
I.R.L.R. 90, CA . . . .   *Digested*, 01/**2253**
Johnson v. United Kingdom (1999) 27 E.H.R.R. 296; (1998) 40 B.M.L.R. 1; [1998]
H.R.C.D. 41; *Times*, December 4, 1997, ECHR. . . . .   *Digested*, 98/**3898**:
                                               Applied, 00/3171
Johnson v. Valks (Permission to Appeal) [2000] 1 W.L.R. 1502; [2000] 1 All E.R. 450;
[2000] C.P. Rep. 36; (1999) 96(46) L.S.G. 40; (2000) 144 S.J.L.B. 10; *Times*,
November 23, 1999 ; *Independent*, January 31, 2000 (C.S.), CA . . . .   *Digested*, 99/**573**
Johnson v. Walden (Inspector of Taxes); King v. Walden (Inspector of Taxes) [1996]
S.T.C. 382; 68 T.C. 417, CA; affirming 68 T.C. 411, Ch D [1994] S.T.C. 124, Sp
Comm . . . .   *Digested*, 94/**2532**:
                                          Subsequent proceedings, 00/4989
Johnson v. Wilson (Unreported, June 29, 1998), CC (Keighley) [*Ex rel.* Simon
Anderson, Barrister, Broadway Chambers, 9 Bank Street, Bradford] . . . .   *Digested*, 98/**1457**
Johnson & Bloy (Holdings) Ltd v. Wolstenholme Rink Plc [1987] I.R.L.R. 499; [1987] 2
F.T.L.R. 502; [1989] 1 F.S.R. 135, CA . . . .   *Digested*, 89/**1408**:
                                               Referred to, 99/583
Johnson Underwood Ltd v. Montgomery see Montgomery v. Johnson Underwood Ltd
Johnsons News of London v. Ealing LBC (1990) 154 J.P. 33; [1990] C.O.D. 135;
(1989) 153 J.P.N. 756; (1989) 139 N.L.J. 1014; *Times*, July 26, 1989, QBD . . . .   *Digested*, 89/**3132**:
                               Disapproved, 99/4064: *Not followed*, 98/2248
Johnsons of London Ltd v. Protec Trust Management [2000] E.G.C.S. 114, Ch D
Johnston v. Chief Constable of the Royal Ulster Constabulary [1998] N.I. 188, CA
(NI) . . . .   *Digested*, 99/**5284**
Johnston v. Smiths Flour Mills Ltd [2001] 3 Q.R. 16, CC (Boston) [*Ex rel.* Richard
Gregory, Barrister, 24 The Ropewalk, Nottingham] . . . .   *Digested*, 01/**1677**

Johnston v. WH Brown Construction (Dundee) Ltd 2000 S.L.T. 791; 2000 S.C.L.R. 792; [2000] B.L.R. 243; 69 Con. L.R. 100; 2000 G.W.D. 14-521; *Times*, June 7, 2000, 1 Div; affirming 2000 S.L.T. 223; 1999 S.C.L.R. 1145; 68 Con. L.R. 70; 1999 G.W.D. 23-1088; *Times*, November 11, 1999, OH .... *Digested*, 00/**5981**

Joiner v. Inland Revenue Commissioners see Inland Revenue Commissioners v. Joiner

Joinglobal Ltd v. Secretary of State for the Environment, Transport and the Regions [2001] EWHC Admin 766; (2001) 98(39) L.S.G. 39, QBD

Joint Act on Air Transit, Re see Commission of the European Communities v. Council of the European Union (C170/96)

Jolley v. Carmel Ltd [2000] 3 E.G.L.R. 68; [2000] 43 E.G. 185, CA; affirming [2000] 2 E.G.L.R. 153; [2000] E.G.C.S. 72, Ch D .... *Digested*, 01/**4853**

Jolley v. DPP (2000) 97(18) L.S.G. 36, QBD

Jolley v. Sutton LBC [2000] 1 W.L.R. 1082; [2000] 3 All E.R. 409; [2000] 2 Lloyd's Rep. 65; [2000] 2 F.C.R. 392; (2001) 3 L.G.L.R. 2; [2000] B.L.G.R. 399; [2000] P.I.Q.R. P136; (2000) 97(23) L.S.G. 42; *Times*, May 24, 2000, HL; reversing [1998] 1 W.L.R. 1546; [1998] 3 All E.R. 559; [1998] 2 Lloyd's Rep. 240; [1998] 3 F.C.R. 443; [1998] P.I.Q.R. P377; (1998) 95(28) L.S.G. 31; (1998) 148 N.L.J. 1014; (1998) 142 S.J.L.B. 188; *Times*, June 23, 1998; *Independent*, June 25, 1998, CA; reversing [1998] 1 Lloyd's Rep. 433, QBD ... *Digested*, 00/**4239**: *Applied*, 00/4214

Jolliffe v. Exeter City Council see Jolliffe v. Exeter Corp

Jolliffe v. Exeter Corp; *sub nom* Jolliffe v. Exeter City Council [1967] 1 W.L.R. 993; [1967] 2 All E.R. 1099; 131 J.P. 421; 65 L.G.R. 401; 18 P. & C.R. 343; [1967] R.V.R. 413; 111 S.J. 414, CA; reversing [1967] 1 W.L.R. 350; [1967] 1 All E.R. 258; 131 J.P. 302; 65 L.G.R. 151; 18 P. & C.R. 264; [1966] R.V.R. 813; 110 S.J. 870, QBD .... *Digested*, 67/**535**: *Distinguished*, 99/4187

Jolly v. Brown see Fox v. Jolly

Jolly v. Circuit Judge of Staines see Jolly v. Hull

Jolly v. Hull; *sub nom* Jolly v. Circuit Judge of Staines; Jolly v. Jolly [2000] 2 F.L.R. 69; [2000] 2 F.C.R. 59; [2000] Fam. Law 399; *Times*, March 10, 2000, CA.... *Digested*, 00/**11**

Jolly v. Jolly see Jolly v. Hull

Jonathan Alexander Ltd v. Proctor [1996] 1 W.L.R. 518; [1996] 2 All E.R. 334; [1996] B.C.C. 598; [1996] 2 B.C.L.C. 91; *Times*, January 3, 1996; *Independent*, January 22, 1996 (C.S.), CA .... *Digested*, 96/**702**: *Applied*, 98/425

Jonathan Wren & Co Ltd v. Microdec Plc 65 Con. L.R. 157, QBD (T&CC)........... *Digested*, 00/**876**

Jones (A Minor) v. Wrexham CBC (Unreported, June 24, 1998), CC (Wrexham) [*Ex rel.* Stevens & Co Solicitors, Spring House, Holyhead Road, Chirk, Wrexham] ..... *Digested*, 98/**1669**

Jones (CICA: Quantum: 2000: Head Injuries), Re (Unreported, November 24, 1999), CICA (Liverpool) [*Ex rel.* Irwin Mitchell Solicitors, St Peter's House, Hartshead, Sheffield] .... *Digested*, 00/**1509**

Jones (CICA: Quantum: 2000: Multiple injuries), Re [2000] 6 Q.R. 5, CICA (London) [*Ex rel.* Andrew Ritchie, Barrister, 9 Gough Square, London] .... *Digested*, 00/**1495**

Jones (CICB: Quantum: 1999), Re (Unreported, August 12, 1999), CICB (London) [*Ex rel.* Simon Levene, Barrister, 199, Strand, London] .... *Digested*, 00/**1749**

Jones (Deceased), Re; *sub nom* Jones v. Midland Bank Trust Co Ltd [1998] 1 F.L.R. 246; [1997] 3 F.C.R. 697; [1997] Fam. Law 660; (1997) 94(18) L.S.G. 31; (1997) 141 S.J.L.B. 107; *Times*, April 29, 1997, CA .... *Digested*, 97/**4734**

Jones v. Adams (Unreported, April 7, 1998), CC (Birkenhead) [*Ex rel.* Kirwans Solicitors, 363 Woodchurch Road, Prenton, Birkenhead] .... *Digested*, 98/**1607**

Jones v. Aderogba (Unreported, February 27, 1998), CC (Maidstone) [*Ex rel.* David McIlroy, Barrister, 3 Paper Buildings, Temple, London] .... *Digested*, 98/**1705**

Jones v. Arthur (1840) 8 Dowl. Pr. Cas. 442 .... *Applied*, 00/4621

Jones v. Attorney General [1974] Ch. 148; [1973] 3 W.L.R. 608; [1973] 3 All E.R. 518; 117 S.J. 647, CA; reversing [1972] 1 W.L.R. 784; [1972] 2 All E.R. 637; 116 S.J. 392, Ch D .... *Digested*, 73/**312**: *Considered*, 81/882: *Followed*, 98/311

Jones v. Chief Constable of South Yorkshire see Alcock v. Chief Constable of South Yorkshire

Jones v. Chief Constable of West Mercia; *sub nom* Jones v. DPP (2001) 165 J.P. 6; [2001] R.T.R. 8; (2000) 97(42) L.S.G. 44; *Times*, October 20, 2000; *Independent*, November 20, 2000 (C.S), QBD .... *Digested*, 00/**1409**

Jones v. Customs and Excise Commissioners Unreported, V&DTr .... *Doubted*, 00/5301

Jones v. Department of Employment [1989] Q.B. 1; [1988] 2 W.L.R. 493; [1988] 1 All E.R. 725; (1988) 85(4) L.S.G. 35; (1987) 137 N.L.J. 1182; (1988) 132 S.J. 128, CA .... *Digested*, 88/**2438**: *Followed*, 89/259, 90/5493, 00/6686

Jones v. Dorset CC see Joyce v. Dorset DC

Jones v. DPP see Jones v. Chief Constable of West Mercia

Jones (James) v. DPP (1999) 163 J.P. 121; [1999] R.T.R. 1; *Times*, April 23, 1998, QBD . *Digested*, 98/**976**

Jones v. First National Bank Plc see Jarrett v. Barclays Bank Plc

Jones v. Forest Fencing Ltd [2001] EWCA Civ 1700; [2001] N.P.C. 165, CA

Jones v. Gerrard (Unreported, May 15, 2000), CC (Chester) [*Ex rel.* Michael Jones, Barrister, Cobden House Chambers, 19 Quay Street, Manchester] . . . .   *Digested,* 00/**2578**

Jones v. Gospel [1998] E.G.C.S. 108; [1998] N.P.C. 108; (1998) 76 P. & C.R. D43, CA

Jones v. Governing Body of Burdett Coutts School [1999] I.C.R. 38; [1998] I.R.L.R. 521; (1998) 95(18) L.S.G. 32; (1998) 142 S.J.L.B. 142; *Times,* April 22, 1998, CA; reversing [1997] I.C.R. 390, EAT . . . .   *Digested,* 98/**2128**

Jones v. Greater Manchester Passenger Transport Executive [1998] 3 E.G.L.R. 121; [1998] 36 E.G. 150, Lands Tr . . . .   *Digested,* 98/**4164**

Jones v. Greavison (Unreported, May 5, 1998), CC (Dudley) [*Ex rel.* Wansbroughs Willey Hargrave Solicitors, Somerset House, 37 Temple Street, Birmingham] . . .   *Digested,* 98/**327**

Jones v. Hall; *sub nom* Ron Jones (Burton on Trent) Ltd v. Hall (2000) 2 T.C.L.R. 195, QBD . . . .   *Digested,* 00/**2322**

Jones v. Hellard [1998] P.N.L.R. 484; (1998) 14 Const. L.J. 299; *Times,* March 23, 1998; *Independent,* March 19, 1998, QBD . . . .   *Digested,* 98/**796**

Jones v. Herxheimer [1950] 2 K.B. 106; [1950] 1 All E.R. 323; 66 T.L.R. (Pt. 1) 403; 94 S.J. 97, CA . . . .   *Digested,* 47-51/**5419**:
          Applied, 47-51/5426: *Considered,* 47-51/5420, 88/2007, 92/2667, 98/122

Jones v. Jones (Periodical Payments) [2001] Fam. 96; [2000] 3 W.L.R. 1505; [2000] 2 F.L.R. 307; [2000] 2 F.C.R. 201; [2000] Fam. Law 607; (2000) 97(17) L.S.G. 34; (2000) 144 S.J.L.B. 203; *Times,* April 11, 2000, CA . . . .   *Digested,* 00/**2533**

Jones (Agnes) v. Jones (William) [2001] N.I. 244, Ch D (NI) . . . .   *Digested,* 01/**5945**

Jones (Marilyn) v. Jones (Margaret), *Times,* November 11, 1999, CA . . . .   *Digested,* 99/**493**

Jones v. Kaiser (1999) 78 P. & C.R. D13, CA

Jones v. Lingfield Leisure Plc EATRF 1998/0801/3, CA . . . .   *Digested,* 99/**2134**

Jones v. Links Express Ltd (Unreported, September 8, 1998), CC (Birmingham) [*Ex rel.* Irwin Mitchell Solicitors, Huttons Buildings, 146 West Street, Sheffield] . . . .   *Digested,* 99/**433**

Jones v. Mahoney (Unreported, August 12, 1998), CC (Newport, Gwent) [*Ex rel.* Wansbroughs Willey Hargrave Solicitors, Drury House, Russell Street, London] .   *Digested,* 98/**503**

Jones v. Management Trustees of Pontesbury Public Hall (Unreported, January 25, 2000), CC (Telford) [*Ex rel.* Erica Power, Barrister, 1 Paper Buildings, Temple, London] . . . .   *Digested,* 00/**1638**

Jones v. May (Charging Orders) (Unreported, September 14, 2000), CC (Cardiff) [*Ex rel.* Everett & Tomlin, Solicitors, Clarence Chambers, Clarence Street, Pontypool] . . . .   *Digested,* 01/**444**

Jones v. Metcalfe [1967] 1 W.L.R. 1286; [1967] 3 All E.R. 205; 131 J.P. 494; 111 S.J. 563, QBD . . . .   *Digested,* 67/**751**:
        Applied, 67/752, 68/699: *Considered,* 97/1137: *Distinguished,* 80/2331:
                 Followed, 77/539, 78/2548, 99/873

Jones v. Mid Glamorgan CC (No.2) [1997] I.C.R. 815; [1997] I.R.L.R. 685, CA; reversing [1997] I.C.R. 417, EAT . . . .   *Digested,* 97/**2225**

Jones v. Midland Bank Trust Co Ltd see Jones (Deceased), Re

Jones v. Morgan [2001] EWCA Civ 995; [2001] Lloyd's Rep. Bank. 323; [2001] N.P.C. 104; *Times,* July 24, 2001, CA. . . . .   *Digested,* 01/**4876**

Jones v. Morgan (Injury to Spine) (Unreported, August 22, 2000), CC (Swansea) [*Ex rel.* Andrew Arentsen, Barrister, 33 Park Place, Cardiff] . . . .   *Digested,* 01/**1643**

Jones v. National Westminster Bank Plc see National Westminster Bank Plc v. Jones

Jones v. Nottingham HA (Unreported, June 14, 2000), CC (Nottingham) [*Ex rel.* Eversheds Solicitors, Fitzalan House, Fitzalan Road, Cardiff] . . . .   *Digested,* 00/**392**

Jones v. Patel see Patel v. Jones

Jones v. Post Office; *sub nom* Post Office v. Jones [2001] EWCA Civ 558; [2001] I.C.R. 805; [2001] I.R.L.R. 384; [2001] Emp. L.R. 527; *Times,* June 5, 2001; *Independent,* April 26, 2001, CA; affirming [2000] I.C.R. 388, EAT . . . .   *Digested,* 01/**2236**:
                 Applied, 01/6463

Jones v. Prothero [1952] 1 All E.R. 434; 116 J.P. 141, DC. . . . .   *Digested,* 52/**3070**:
                 Considered, 99/957

Jones v. Pugh see Jones v. Welsh Rugby Football Union

Jones v. Rhys-Jones (1975) 30 P. & C.R. 451; (1974) 234 E.G. 987; [1975] J.P.L. 349, CA . . . .   *Digested,* 75/**2798**:
                 Considered, 00/5613

Jones v. Secretary of State for the Environment [1998] 1 P.L.R. 33; [1997] E.G.C.S. 9, QBD . . . .   *Digested,* 98/**4199**

Jones v. Sherwood Computer Services Plc [1992] 1 W.L.R. 277; [1992] 2 All E.R. 170; *Times,* December 14, 1989, CA . . . .   *Digested,* 92/**419**:
        Applied, 92/2734, 92/2740, 99/4077: *Considered,* 96/690, 98/3677, 00/237:
            Distinguished, 93/2524: *Followed,* 96/1024, 98/701

Jones v. Skelton [1963] 1 W.L.R. 1362; [1963] 3 All E.R. 952; 107 S.J. 870, PC (Aus) . .   *Digested,* 63/**2002**:
         Applied, 68/2233, 69/2082, 99/1623: *Previous proceedings,* 62/2519

Jones v. Society of Lloyd's; Standen v. Society of Lloyd's *Times,* February 2, 2000, Ch D . . . .   *Digested,* 00/**3539**

Jones v. Stones [1999] 1 W.L.R. 1739; (1999) 78 P. & C.R. 293; [1999] 3 E.G.L.R. 81; [1999] 42 E.G. 135; (1999) 96(22) L.S.G. 34; *Times,* June 3, 1999, CA . . . . . .   *Digested,* 99/**4856**

Jones v. Stroud DC [1986] 1 W.L.R. 1141; [1988] 1 All E.R. 5; 34 B.L.R. 27; 8 Con.
  L.R. 23; 84 L.G.R. 886; [1986] 2 E.G.L.R. 133; (1986) 279 E.G. 213; (1986) 2
  Const. L.J.185; (1986) 130 S.J. 469, CA . . . .   *Digested*, 86/**1993**:
          Applied, 87/242, 01/885: *Cited*, 00/2592: *Doubted*, 01/1527:
          Followed, 99/2504: *Referred to*, 01/1542
Jones v. Swansea City Council (Unreported, March 3, 1998), CC (Swansea) [*Ex rel.*
  Robert O'Leary, Barrister, 33 Park Place, Cardiff] . . . .   *Digested*, 98/**1664**
Jones v. Swansea City Council [1990] 1 W.L.R. 1453; [1990] 3 All E.R. 737; 89 L.G.R.
  90; (1990) 134 S.J. 1437; *Independent*, November 16, 1990, HL; reversing
  [1990] 1 W.L.R. 54; [1989] 3 All E.R. 162; (1990) 87(7) L.S.G. 34; (1990) 134
  S.J. 341, CA . . . .   *Digested*, 91/**3411**:
          Applied, 95/4730: *Considered*, 99/4232
Jones v. Telford and Wrekin Council, *Times*, July 29, 1999, CA . . . .   *Digested*, 99/**530**
Jones v. Tower Boot Co Ltd see Tower Boot Co Ltd v. Jones
Jones v. Tower Hamlets LBC (No.2) [2001] R.P.C. 23; (2000) 97(41) L.S.G. 40;
  [2000] N.P.C. 102; *Times*, November 14, 2000, Ch D . . . .   *Digested*, 00/**3571**
Jones v. Twinsectra Ltd; Twinsectra Ltd v. Jones [1998] 2 E.G.L.R. 129; [1998] 23
  E.G. 134, Lands Tr. . . . .   *Digested*, 98/**3641**
Jones v. Welsh Rugby Football Union; Jones v. Pugh *Times*, January 6, 1998, CA;
  affirming *Times*, March 6, 1997, QBD . . . .   *Digested*, 98/**3740**
Jones v. Wentworth Securities see Jones v. Wrotham Park Settled Estates
Jones v. Whitbread Plc (Unreported, January 6, 1998), QBD [*Ex rel.* Veale Wasbrough
  Solicitors, Orchard Court, Orchard Lane, Bristol, BS1 5DS] . . . .   *Digested*, 98/**1615**
Jones v. Wright see Alcock v. Chief Constable of South Yorkshire
Jones v. Wrotham Park Settled Estates; *sub nom* Jones v. Wentworth Securities [1980]
  A.C. 74; [1979] 2 W.L.R. 132; [1979] 1 All E.R. 286; (1979) 38 P. & C.R. 77;
  123 S.J. 34, HL; reversing [1978] 3 W.L.R. 585; [1978] 3 All E.R. 527; (1979) 37
  P. & C.R. 289; (1978) 246 E.G. 223; 122 S.J. 557, CA; reversing (1977) 33 P.
  & C.R. 304; (1976) 240 E.G. 804; [1977] J.P.L. 36, Lands Tr . . . .   *Digested*, 79/**1610**:
          Considered, 99/5209
Jones & Son v. Whitehouse [1918] 2 K.B. 61, CA . . . .   *Considered*, 99/416
Joop! GmbH v. M&S Toiletries Ltd, *Times*, June 14, 2000, OH . . . .   *Digested*, 00/**6523**
Jordache Enterprises Inc v. Millennium Pte Ltd [1988] 2 M.L.J. 281 . . . .   *Applied*, 98/3497
Jordan, Re Unreported . . . .   *Followed*, 00/47
Jordan v. Bashford (Unreported, May 8, 2000), CC (Croydon) [*Ex rel.* Nigel Ffitch,
  Barrister, Phoenix Chambers, Gray's Inn, London] . . . .   *Digested*, 00/**2587**
Jordan v. Jordan [2000] 1 W.L.R. 210; [1999] 2 F.L.R. 1069; [1999] 3 F.C.R. 481;
  [1999] Fam. Law 695; (1999) 96(31) L.S.G. 39; (1999) 143 S.J.L.B. 211; *Times*,
  July 29, 1999, CA . . . .   *Digested*, 99/**2403**
Jordan v. Thomson Holidays Ltd (Unreported, May 27, 1999), CC (Bristol) [*Ex rel.*
  Dominic Bayne, Barrister, Plowden Buildings, Temple, London] . . . .   *Digested*, 99/**3828**
Jordan v. United Kingdom (24746/94) 11 B.H.R.C. 1; *Times*, May 18, 2001, ECHR . . . . .   *Digested*, 01/**3575**
Jordan v. United Kingdom (30280/96) (2001) 31 E.H.R.R. 6; *Times*, March 17, 2000,
  ECHR . . . .   *Digested*, 00/**3214**
Jordan Grand Prix Ltd v. Baltic Insurance Group; *sub nom* Baltic Insurance Group v.
  Jordan Grand Prix Ltd; Baltic Insurance Group v. Quay Financial Software
  [1999] 2 A.C. 127; [1999] 1 W.L.R. 134; [1999] 1 All E.R. 289; [1999] C.L.C.
  527; [1999] 1 Lloyd's Rep. I.R. 93; *Times*, December 17, 1998, HL; affirming
  [1998] 1 W.L.R. 1049; [1998] 3 All E.R. 418; [1998] Lloyd's Rep. I.R. 180;
  (1997) 94(43) L.S.G. 30; (1997) 141 S.J.L.B. 230; *Times*, November 14, 1997,
  CA . . . .   *Digested*, 99/**747**
Jorgensen v. Foreningen af Speciallaeger (C226/98) [2000] E.C.R. I-2447; [2000]
  I.R.L.R. 726, ECJ (6th Chamber) . . . .   *Digested*, 00/**2169**
Joscelyne v. Nissen [1970] 2 Q.B. 86; [1970] 2 W.L.R. 509; [1970] 1 All E.R. 1213;
  (1969) 114 S.J. 55, CA . . . .   *Digested*, 70/**379**:
          Applied, 71/11936, 73/3091, 83/3892: *Considered*, 73/1921, 75/3131,
          76/2508, 98/4875
Jose Aldao Ltd SA v. United Distillers, *Independent*, May 24, 1999 (C.S.), CA
Joseph v. Boyd & Hutchinson [1999] 1 Costs L.R. 74, Ch D
Joseph v. Joseph, *Independent*, December 14, 1998 (C.S.), Fam Div
Joseph Carter & Sons Ltd v. Baird (Inspector of Taxes); Wear Ironmongers Ltd v. Baird
  (Inspector of Taxes) [1999] S.T.C. 120; 72 T.C. 303, Ch D . . . .   *Digested*, 99/**4659**
Joseph Eagle 1989 Settlement, Re; *sub nom* Le Sueur & Raleigh Nominees Ltd (Matter
  of Representation), Re [2000] W.T.L.R. 137, Royal Ct (Jer) . . . .   *Digested*, 00/**5260**
Joseph Holt Plc, Re see Winpar Holdings Ltd v. Joseph Holt Group Plc
Joseph Hoyle & Son Ltd v. Ali EATRF 1997/1286/3, CA. . . . .   *Digested*, 99/**2052**
Josephs v. Sunworld Ltd (t/a Sunworld Holidays) (Unreported, April 7, 1998), CC
  (Bury) [*Ex rel.* Kippax Beaumont Lewis Solicitors, 28 Maudsley Street, Bolton,
  BL1 1LF] . . . .   *Digested*, 98/**3734**
Joshi (Mina) v. Ahmed (Male) (Unreported, October 17, 1997), CC (Birmingham) [*Ex
  rel.* Irwin Mitchell Solicitors, The Citadel, 190 Corporation Street, Birmingham] . .   *Digested*, 98/**487**
Joulesave Emes Ltd v. Customs and Excise Commissioners [2001] S.T.I. 1000, V&DTr

Jowett (Inspector of Taxes) v. O'Neill & Brennan Construction Ltd [1998] S.T.C. 482; 70
T.C. 566; [1998] B.T.C. 133; (1998) 95(16) L.S.G. 25; (1998) 142 S.J.L.B. 124;
Times, March 25, 1998; *Independent*, March 30, 1998 (C.S.), Ch D .... *Digested*, 98/**4622**
Jowitt v. McNeice (Unreported, June 6, 2000), CC (Southport) [*Ex rel.* Fiona
Ashworth, Barrister, 40 King Street, Manchester] .... *Digested*, 01/**1581**
Joy v. Newell (t/a Copper Room) [2000] N.I. 91, CA (NI) .... *Digested*, 00/**5626**
Joy Manufacturing Holdings Ltd and Pension & Life Assurance Scheme Trustees,
Petitioners see Harding v. Joy Manufacturing Holdings Ltd
Joyce v. Barlow (Unreported, November 17, 1998), CC (Poole) [*Ex rel.* Jeremy Burns,
Barrister, 17 Carlton Crescent, Southampton] .... *Digested*, 99/**2495**
Joyce v. Dorset DC; *sub nom* Jones v. Dorset CC [1997] E.L.R. 26, QBD .... *Digested*, 96/**2489**:
Applied, 98/1984
Joyce v. Ford Motor Co Ltd see Afzal v. Ford Motor Co Ltd
Joyce v. Lucey (Unreported, January 26, 1998), CC (Watford) [*Ex rel.* Douglas
Livingstone, New Court, Chambers of Christian Bevington, Temple, London] ... *Digested*, 98/**1727**
Joyce v. Morrissey [1999] E.M.L.R. 233; (1998) 95(47) L.S.G. 29; *Times*, November
16, 1998, CA .... *Digested*, 98/**4070**
Joyce v. Sengupta [1993] 1 W.L.R. 337; [1993] 1 All E.R. 897; (1992) 142 N.L.J.
1306; (1992) 136 S.J.L.B. 274; *Independent*, August 11, 1992; *Guardian*, August
12, 1992, CA . . . . *Digested*, 93/**3097**:
Applied, 94/3514: *Considered*, 93/3243, 95/3882, 96/682, 96/3855:
Followed, 00/5116
JP v. Debtor see Debtor (No.488-IO of 1996), Re
JP Morgan Securities Asia Private Ltd v. Malaysian Newsprint Industries Sdn Bhd
[2001] 2 Lloyd's Rep. 41, QBD (Comm Ct) . . . . *Digested*, 01/**647**
JP Morgan Trading & Finance v. Customs and Excise Commissioners [1998] B.V.C. 2147;
[1998] V. & D.R. 161, V&DTr . . . . *Digested*, 98/**4922**
JR Geigy SA v. Inter Continental Pharmaceuticals see F Hoffmann La Roche & Co AG
v. Inter Continental Pharmaceuticals Ltd
JR Reid Group Ltd's Registered Trade Mark (No.678189) (1998) 21 (10) I.P.D. 21114, TMR
JS, Re see J (A Child) (Freeing for Adoption), Re
JS (Private International Adoption), Re [2000] 2 F.L.R. 638; [2000] Fam. Law 787, Fam
Div . . . . *Digested*, 01/**2535**
JS Bloor (Measham) Ltd v. Calcott (No.1); *sub nom* Calcott v. JS Bloor (Measham) Ltd
[1998] 1 W.L.R. 1490; [1998] 3 E.G.L.R. 1; [1998] 40 E.G. 180; [1998]
E.G.C.S. 25; (1998) 95(8) L.S.G. 34; (1998) 142 S.J.L.B. 91; *Times*, March 5,
1998, CA . . . . *Digested*, 98/**121**
JS Bloor (Measham) Ltd v. Calcott (No.2), *Times*, December 12, 2001, Ch D
JS Bloor (Measham) Ltd v. Secretary of State for the Environment, Transport and the
Regions [2001] EWHC Admin 504; (2001) 98(28) L.S.G. 45, QBD (Admin
Ct)
JS Bloor Ltd v. Swindon BC; King v. Swindon BC [2001] EWHC Admin 966; [2001]
49 E.G.C.S. 118; [2001] N.P.C. 171; *Times*, December 4, 2001, QBD (Admin Ct)
JSF Finance & Currency Exchange Co Ltd v. Akma Solutions Inc [2001] 2 B.C.L.C. 307,
Ch D
JT (Adult: Refusal of Medical Treatment), Re [1998] 1 F.L.R. 48; [1998] 2 F.C.R. 662; [1998]
Fam. Law 23, Fam Div. . . . . *Digested*, 98/**3890**
JT v. United Kingdom [2000] 1 F.L.R. 909; [2000] Fam. Law 533; *Times*, April 5,
2000, ECHR . . . . *Digested*, 00/**4181**
JT's Corp Ltd v. Commission of the European Communities (T123/99) [2000] E.C.R.
II-3269; [2001] 1 C.M.L.R. 22; *Times*, October 18, 2000, CFI (4th Chamber) ... *Digested*, 00/**2372**
Jubilee Hall Recreation Centre Ltd v. Customs and Excise Commissioners; Customs and
Excise Commissioners v. St Dunstan's Educational Foundation [1999] S.T.C.
381; [1999] B.T.C. 5150; [1999] B.V.C. 184; [1998] E.G.C.S. 184; *Times*,
December 31, 1998, CA; reversing [1997] S.T.C. 414; [1997] B.T.C. 5132; [1997]
B.V.C. 243; [1997] E.G.C.S. 31; (1997) 94(13) L.S.G. 29; (1997) 141 S.J.L.B.
83; *Times*, March 28, 1997; *Independent*, April 14, 1997 (C.S.), QBD . . . . *Digested*, 99/**5031**
Judd v. Andrew White (Contracts) Ltd [2001] 5 Q.R. 15, QBD [*Ex rel.* Nicola Rushton,
Barrister, 5 Paper Buildings, Temple, London] . . . . *Digested*, 01/**1674**
Judd v. Brown; *sub nom* Bankrupts (Nos.9587 and 9588 of 1994), Re [1999] 1 F.L.R.
1191; [1999] B.P.I.R. 517; (2000) 79 P. & C.R. 491; [1999] Fam. Law 523, CA;
reversing [1998] 1 F.L.R. 360; [1997] B.P.I.R. 470; [1998] Fam. Law 514, Ch D
. . . . *Digested*, 99/**3250**:
Considered, 98/3291
Judd v. Official Assignee [2001] B.P.I.R. 468, CA (NZ) . . . . *Digested*, 01/**3786**
Judd v. Williams; *sub nom* Williams (A Bankrupt), Re [1998] B.P.I.R. 88; (1997)
94(25) L.S.G. 34; *Times*, July 16, 1997, Ch D . . . . *Digested*, 97/**2999**
Jules v. Wandsworth LBC [1998] E.L.R. 243, QBD . . . . *Digested*, 98/**1967**
Jules Dethier Equipement SA v. Dassy (C319/94); Jules Dethier Equipement SA v.
Sovam Sprl [1998] All E.R. (E.C.) 346; [1998] E.C.R. I-1061; [1998] 2 C.M.L.R.
611; [1998] C.E.C. 295; [1998] I.C.R. 541; [1998] I.R.L.R. 266; *Times*, March
18, 1998, ECJ (6th Chamber) . . . . *Digested*, 98/**2211**
Jules Dethier Equipement SA v. Sovam Sprl see Jules Dethier Equipement SA v. Dassy
(C319/94)

Julian v. Customs and Excise Commissioners [2000] B.V.C. 2251; [2000] S.T.I. 901, V&DTr

Julian Higgins Trade Mark Application; *sub nom* NASA v. Higgins [2000] R.P.C. 321; (1999) 22(9) I.P.D. 22085, Ch D .... *Digested*, 00/**3710**

Julian Hodge Bank Ltd v. Hall [1998] C.C.L.R. 14, CA .... *Digested*, 98/**2493**

Julius Fillibeck Sohne GmbH & Co KG v. Finanzamt Neustadt (C258/95) [1998] 1 W.L.R. 697; [1998] All E.R. (E.C.) 466; [1998] S.T.C. 513; [1997] E.C.R. I-5577; [1998] C.E.C. 459; [1998] B.T.C. 5226; [1998] B.V.C. 206; *Times*, November 27, 1997, ECJ (5th Chamber) .... *Digested*, 97/**4972**

Junior Books Ltd v. Veitchi Co Ltd [1983] 1 A.C. 520; [1982] 3 W.L.R. 477; [1982] 3 All E.R. 201; 1982 S.C. (H.L.) 244; 1982 S.L.T. 492; [1982] Com. L.R. 221; 21 B.L.R. 66; (1982) 79 L.S.G. 1413; 126 S.J. 538, HL; affirming 1982 S.L.T. 333, 2 Div .... *Digested*, 82/**4055**:
Applied, 83/2215, 83/2746, 88/2442, 88/3410: *Considered*, 83/52, 84/2333, 85/2311, 85/3170, 86/389, 86/2270, 87/2579, 87/2580, 87/3582, 88/2426, 88/2444, 89/218, 90/5485, 90/5487, 95/3689: *Distinguished*, 87/229, 88/2158, 88/3409: *Followed*, 98/3924: *Not followed*, 92/3219, 94/3348: *Referred to*, 83/2532

Jurisdiction Clause in an Auctioneer's Standard Contract, Re [1998] I.L.Pr. 243, BGH (Ger)

Jusline GmbH (formerly bOnline Software GmbH) v. O [1999] E.T.M.R. 173, OGH (A)

JUSTAMENTE/Waste compactor (T136/95) [1998] E.P.O.R. 301, EPO (Technical Bd App)

Juventus FC SpA v. Topps Italia Srl see Milan AC SpA v. Topps Italia Srl

JW Bollom & Co Ltd v. Byas Mosley & Co Ltd [2000] Lloyd's Rep. I.R. 136; [1999] Lloyd's Rep. P.N. 598, QBD (Comm Ct) .... *Digested*, 99/**3369**

Jyske Bank (Gibraltar) Ltd v. Spjeldnaes (No.1) (1998) 95(42) L.S.G. 33; (1998) 95(40) L.S.G. 37; (1998) 142 S.J.L.B. 262; *Times*, October 10, 1998, Ch D .... *Digested*, 98/**3316**

Jyske Bank (Gibraltar) Ltd v. Spjeldnaes (No.2) CHANF 1998/0315/3, 0317/3, 0318/3, 0319/3, 0320/3, 0322/3, 0323/3, CA; reversing in part [2000] B.C.C. 16; [1999] 2 B.C.L.C. 101; [1999] B.P.I.R. 525; (1998) 95(46) L.S.G. 35; (1998) 142 S.J.L.B. 287; *Times*, November 6, 1998, Ch D .... *Digested*, 00/**2324**

K (A Child), Re see K (A Child) v. BBC

K (A Child) (Secure Accommodation Order: Right to Liberty), Re; *sub nom* W BC v. DK; W BC v. AK [2001] Fam. 377; [2001] 2 W.L.R. 1141; [2001] 2 All E.R. 719; (2001) 165 J.P. 241; [2001] 1 F.L.R. 526; [2001] 1 F.C.R. 249; [2001] H.R.L.R. 13; (2001) 3 L.G.L.R. 39; [2001] A.C.D. 41; [2001] Fam. Law 99; (2001) 165 J.P.N. 585; (2000) 97(48) L.S.G. 36; (2000) 144 S.J.L.B. 291; *Times*, November 29, 2000; *Independent*, November 21, 2000, CA .... *Digested*, 00/**3245**:
Considered, 01/2599

K (A Child) v. BBC; *sub nom* K (A Child), Re; BBC v. K (A Child) [2001] Fam. 59; [2001] 2 W.L.R. 253; [2001] 1 All E.R. 323; [2001] 1 F.L.R. 197; [2000] 3 F.C.R. 509; [2000] Fam. Law 886; (2000) 97(39) L.S.G. 41; (2000) 150 N.L.J. 1538; (2000) 144 S.J.L.B. 250; *Times*, August 9, 2000; *Independent*, November 20, 2000 (C.S), Fam Div .... *Digested*, 00/**4162**

K (A Child) v. Gobbi (Unreported, March 6, 2000), CC (Southampton) [*Ex rel.* Amanda Gillett, Pupil Barrister, College Chambers, 19 Carlton Crescent, Southampton] .. *Digested*, 00/**1726**

K (A Child) v. Grocutt (Unreported, April 18, 2000), CC (Sheffield) [*Ex rel.* Irwin Mitchell Solicitors, Huttons Buildings, 146 West Street, Sheffield S1 1FW] ..... *Digested*, 01/**519**

K (A Child) v. Picken [2001] 6 Q.R. 22, CC (Telford) [*Ex rel.* Hodgkinsons, Solicitors, The Old Manse, 14 Lumley Avenue, Skegness] .... *Digested*, 01/**1796**

K (A Child) v. Portsmouth and South East Hampshire HA (Unreported, November 22, 1999), QBD [*Ex rel.* George Ide, Phillips Solicitors, 52 North Street, Chichester, West Sussex] .... *Digested*, 00/**1514**

K (A Child) v. Tesco Stores Ltd (Unreported, October 7, 1999), CC (Uxbridge) [*Ex rel.* The Woodbridge Partnership Solicitors, Windsor House, 42 Windsor Street, Uxbridge, Middlesex] .... *Digested*, 00/**1670**

K (A Minor) (Adoption Order: Nationality), Re [1995] Fam. 38; [1994] 3 W.L.R. 572; [1994] 3 All E.R. 553; [1994] 2 F.L.R. 577; [1994] 2 F.C.R. 617; [1994] Fam. Law 554; *Times*, April 26, 1994; *Independent*, May 27, 1994, CA .... *Digested*, 94/**3095**:
Considered, 96/466, 98/2362, 99/2299

K (A Minor) (Removal from Jurisdiction: Practice), Re [1999] 2 F.L.R. 1084; [1999] 3 F.C.R. 673; [1999] Fam. Law 754; (1999) 96(33) L.S.G. 29; *Times*, July 29, 1999, CA .. *Digested*, 99/**2384**

K (A Minor) (Residence Order: Securing Contact), Re [1999] 1 F.L.R. 583; [1999] 3 F.C.R. 365; [1999] Fam. Law 220; *Times*, January 8, 1999, CA .... *Digested*, 99/**2388**

K (Abduction: Consent), Re [1997] 2 F.L.R. 212; [1998] 1 F.C.R. 311; [1997] Fam. Law 532, Fam Div .... *Digested*, 97/**389**

K (Adoption: Disclosure of Information), Re [1997] 2 F.L.R. 74; [1998] 2 F.C.R. 388, Fam Div .... *Digested*, 97/**356**

K (Application to Remove Children from Jurisdiction), Re [1998] 2 F.L.R. 1006; [1999] 2 F.C.R. 410; [1998] Fam. Law 584, Fam Div .... *Digested*, 99/**2386**

K (Care Proceedings: Joinder of Father), Re; *sub nom* B (Care Proceedings: Notification of Father Without Parental Responsibility), Re [1999] 2 F.L.R. 408; [1999] 2 F.C.R. 391; [1999] Fam. Law 525; (1999) 163 J.P.N. 994, Fam Div .... *Digested*, 99/**2362**

K (Contact: Mother's Anxiety), Re [1999] 2 F.L.R. 703; [1999] Fam. Law 527, Fam Div   *Digested*, 99/**2378**

K (Enduring Powers of Attorney), Re; F, Re [1988] Ch. 310; [1988] 2 W.L.R. 781; [1988] 1 All E.R. 358; [1988] 2 F.L.R. 15; [1988] Fam. Law 203; (1987) 137 N.L.J.1039; (1987) 131 S.J. 1488, Ch D . . . .   *Digested*, 88/**59**:   *Considered*, 91/557, 01/5162

K (Infants), Re see Official Solicitor *v.* K

K (Minors) (Supervision Orders), Re [1999] 2 F.L.R. 303; [1999] 1 F.C.R. 337; [1999] Fam. Law 376; (1999) 163 J.P.N. 256; (1999) 163 J.P.N. 618, Fam Div . . . .   *Digested*, 99/**2341**

K (Replacement of Guardian Ad Litem), Re [2001] 1 F.L.R. 663; [2001] Fam. Law 256, Fam Div . . . .   *Digested*, 01/**2642**

K (Specific Issue Order), Re [1999] 2 F.L.R. 280; [1999] Fam. Law 455, Fam Div . . . .   *Digested*, 99/**2441**

K *v.* Craig; *sub nom* K, Petitioner 1999 S.C. (H.L.) 1; 1999 S.L.T. 219; 1999 S.C.L.R. 67; 1998 G.W.D. 40-2074; *Times*, December 7, 1998, HL; affirming 1997 S.C. 327; 1997 S.L.T. 748; 1997 S.C.L.R. 566; 1997 G.W.D. 11-482; *Times*, May 2, 1997, 1 Div; affirming 1997 S.C.L.R. 384, OH . . . .   *Digested*, 99/**6362**

K *v.* D [1998] 1 F.L.R. 700; [1998] 2 F.C.R. 436; [1998] Fam. Law 255, CC (Birmingham) . . . .   *Digested*, 98/**2460**

K *v.* Finland (25702/94) (No.1); T *v.* Finland (25702/94) (No.1) [2000] 2 F.L.R. 79; [2000] 3 F.C.R. 248; (2001) 31 E.H.R.R. 18; [2000] Fam. Law 534, ECHR . . . .   *Digested*, 00/**3241**

K *v.* Finland (25702/94) (No.2); *sub nom* T *v.* Finland (25702/94) (No.2) [2001] 2 F.L.R. 707; [2001] 2 F.C.R. 673; [2001] Fam. Law 733, ECHR . . . .   *Digested*, 01/**3551**

K *v.* Hickman (Unreported, October 18, 1999), QBD [*Ex rel.* Philip A Butler, Barrister, Deans Court Chambers, 24 St John Street, Manchester] . . . .   *Digested*, 00/**1516**

K *v.* K (Child Abduction) [1998] 3 F.C.R. 207, Fam Div. . . . .   *Digested*, 98/**2383**

K *v.* K (Enforcement) see Kimber *v.* Kimber

K *v.* M, M and L (Financial Relief: Foreign Orders) [1998] 2 F.L.R. 59; [1998] Fam. Law 396, Fam Div. . . . .   *Digested*, 98/**2471**

K *v.* Secretary of State for the Home Department [2001] Imm. A.R. 11, CA . . . .   *Digested*, 01/**3611**

K *v.* Secretary of State for the Home Office [2001] C.P. Rep. 39, QBD. . . . .   *Digested*, 01/**550**

K *v.* Southwark LBC see R. (on the application of K) *v.* Southwark LBC

K Lokumal & Sons (London) Ltd *v.* Lotte Shipping Co Pte Ltd (The August Leonhardt) [1985] 2 Lloyd's Rep. 28; *Financial Times*, April 23, 1985, CA; reversing [1984] 1 Lloyd's Rep. 322; (1984) 134 N.L.J. 125, QBD (Comm Ct) . . . .   *Digested*, 85/**2010**:   *Considered*, 94/3713, 95/689: *Followed*, 99/380

K-2 Trade Mark [2000] R.P.C. 413, TMR . . . .   *Digested*, 00/**3796**

K-F *v.* Germany (1998) 26 E.H.R.R. 390; [1998] H.R.C.D. 117, ECHR . . . .   *Digested*, 98/**3071**

K, Ex p. [2001] E.L.R. 311; *Daily Telegraph*, November 7, 2000, QBD (Admin Ct) . . . . .   *Digested*, 01/**1975**

K, Petitioner see K *v.* Craig

K/S Merc-Scandia XXXXII *v.* Lloyd's Underwriters (The Mercandian Continent); *sub nom* K/S Merc-Scandia XXXXII *v.* Underwriters of Lloyd's Policy 25T 105487 (The Mercandian Continent) [2001] EWCA Civ 1275; [2001] 2 Lloyd's Rep. 563; [2001] C.L.C. 1836; [2001] Lloyd's Rep. I.R. 802; *Times*, September 3, 2001, CA; affirming [2000] 2 All E.R. (Comm) 731; [2000] 2 Lloyd's Rep. 357; [2000] C.L.C. 1425; [2000] Lloyd's Rep. I.R. 694; (2000) 97(29) L.S.G. 45; *Times*, August 8, 2000, QBD (Comm Ct) . . . .   *Digested*, 01/**3827**

K/S Merc-Scandia XXXXII *v.* Underwriters of Lloyd's Policy 25T 105487 (The Mercandian Continent) see K/S Merc-Scandia XXXXII *v.* Lloyd's Underwriters (The Mercandian Continent)

KA & SBM Feakins Ltd *v.* Dover Harbour Board (1998) 10 Admin. L.R. 665; (1998) 95(36) L.S.G. 31; (1998) 142 S.J.L.B. 226; *Times*, September 9, 1998, QBD . . .   *Digested*, 98/**4434**

Kaasmakerij Passendale SA *v.* Cooperatives Reunies de l'Industrie du Lait Coberco [2000] E.T.M.R. 840 (Note), Trib Comm (Ypres)

Kaba *v.* Secretary of State for the Home Department (C356/98) [2000] All E.R. (EC) 537; [2000] E.C.R. I-2623; *Times*, April 19, 2000, ECJ . . . .   *Digested*, 00/**3354**

Kabba *v.* Secretary of State for the Home Department; *sub nom* R. *v.* Secretary of State for the Home Department Ex p. Kabba [1998] Imm. A.R. 532; [1998] I.N.L.R. 721, CA. . . . .   *Digested*, 99/**3159**

Kabushiki Kaisha Namco's Trade Mark Application see Namco Ltd's Trade Mark Application (No.2068253)

KABUSHIKI KAISHA TOSHIBA/Divisional application (T873/94) [1998] E.P.O.R. 71, EPO (Technical Bd App)

Kabushiki Kaisha Yakult Honsha's Trade Mark Application (Nos.1260017 and 1560018); *sub nom* Yakult Honsha KK's Trade Mark Application (Nos.1260017 and 1560018) [2001] R.P.C. 39; (2001) 24(4) I.P.D. 24022; *Daily Telegraph*, March 13, 2001, Ch D . . . .   *Digested*, 01/**4027**

KABUSHIKI/Vehicle testing bench (T06/98) [2001] E.P.O.R. 32, EPO (Technical Bd App) . . . .   *Digested*, 01/**3889**

Kacaj *v.* Secretary of State for the Home Department see Secretary of State for the Home Department *v.* Kacaj

Kacar *v.* Enfield LBC (2001) 33 H.L.R. 5, CA. . . . .   *Digested*, 01/**3424**

Kachelmann *v.* Bankhaus Hermann Lampe KG (C322/98) [2000] E.C.R. I-7505; [2001] I.R.L.R. 49, ECJ (5th Chamber) . . . .   *Digested*, 01/**2284**

Kadhim *v.* Brent LBC Housing Benefit Board see R. (on the application of Kadhim) *v.* Brent LBC Housing Benefit Review Board

Kadiman v. Freistaat Bayern (C351/95) [1997] E.C.R. I-2133, ECJ . . . . *Followed*, 01/**2458**
Kadubec v. Slovakia (27061/95) (2001) 33 E.H.R.R. 41; [1998] H.R.C.D. 844, ECHR
Kahie v. Secretary of State for the Home Department see Hersi v. Secretary of State
  for the Home Department
Kahn v. Inland Revenue Commissioners see Toshoku Finance UK Plc (In Liquidation),
  Re
KAIMANN Trade Mark see Wilhelm Kaimann's Trade Mark Application (No.20457617)
Kaiser Engineers and Constructors Inc v. Secretary of State for Tax Affairs 3 I.T.L. Rep.
  806, Sup Trib Admin (P)
Kaja v. Secretary of State for the Home Department see R. v. Secretary of State for the
  Home Department Ex p. Kaja
Kalac v. Turkey (20704/92) (1999) 27 E.H.R.R. 552, ECHR . . . . *Digested*, 99/**3126**
Kalam v. Khan (Unreported, February 4, 2000), CC (Nuneaton) [*Ex rel.* Benjamin
  Williams, Barrister, 1 Temple Gardens, Temple, London] . . . . *Digested*, 00/**2575**
Kalam v. Khan (Quantum) (Unreported, February 4, 2000), CC (Nuneaton) [*Ex rel.*
  Benjamin Williams, Barrister, 1 Temple Gardens, Temple, London] . . . . *Digested*, 00/**1721**
Kalanke v. Freie und Hansestadt Bremen (C450/93) [1996] All E.R. (E.C.) 66; [1995]
  E.C.R. I-3051; [1996] 1 C.M.L.R. 175; [1996] C.E.C. 208; [1996] I.C.R. 314;
  [1995] I.R.L.R. 660; *Times*, October 26, 1995, ECJ . . . . *Digested*, 96/**2624**:
    Considered, 00/2170: *Distinguished*, 98/2146
Kalfelis v. Bankhaus Schroder, Munchmeyer, Hengst & Co (t/a HEMA
  Beteiligungsgesellschaft mbH) (C189/87) [1988] E.C.R. 5565; [1989] E.C.C.
  407; *Times*, October 5, 1988, ECJ (5th Chamber) . . . . *Digested*, 91/**3936**:
    Applied, 91/5161, 94/5038, 96/5344, 97/898: *Considered*, 98/3466, 99/715:
      Distinguished, 96/7098: *Followed*, 94/5036, 96/1085: *Referred to*, 97/3890
Kalford Ltd v. Peterborough City Council [2001] 13 E.G.C.S. 150; [2001] N.P.C. 60, Ch
  D
Kall Kwik Printing (UK) Ltd v. Rush [1996] F.S.R. 114, Ch D . . . . *Digested*, 96/**1243**:
    Considered, 98/727
Kalmneft JSC v. Glencore International AG; *sub nom* AOOT Kalmneft v. Glencore
  International AG [2001] 2 All E.R. (Comm) 577; [2001] C.L.C. 1805; *Times*,
  November 20, 2001, QBD (Comm Ct) . . . . *Digested*, 01/**337**
Kalsep Ltd v. X-Flow BV (2001) 24(7) I.P.D. 24044; *Times*, May 3, 2001, Ch D . . . . . . *Digested*, 01/**954**
Kamal Trading Co v. Gillette (UK) Ltd (1988) 12 I.P.L.R. 135, HC (Ind) . . . . *Applied*, 98/**3521**
Kamania v. Metroline (Unreported, August 20, 1999), CC (York) [*Ex rel.* Berrymans
  Lace Mawer Solicitors, Castle Chambers, 43 Castle Street, Liverpool] . . . . *Digested*, 00/**449**
Kamasinski v. Austria (A/168) (1991) 13 E.H.R.R. 36; *Times*, January 1, 1990, ECHR . . . *Digested*, 90/**2540**:
    Applied, 98/3114: *Distinguished*, 98/3123
Kamenou v. Dodson see Kamenou (t/a Regency Developments) v. Pariser
Kamenou (t/a Regency Developments) v. Pariser; *sub nom* Kamenou v. Dodson [1999]
  2 All E.R. 764; [1999] B.L.R. 72; [1999] 2 Costs L.R. 117, QBD (T&CC) . . . . *Digested*, 99/**372**
Kaminski v. Somerville College 1997-K-466, QBD . . . . *Digested*, 00/**467**
Kammins Ballrooms Co Ltd v. Zenith Investments (Torquay) Ltd (No.1) [1971] A.C. 850;
  [1970] 3 W.L.R. 287; [1970] 2 All E.R. 871; (1971) 22 P. & C.R. 74; 114 S.J.
  590, HL; affirming [1970] 1 Q.B. 673; [1969] 3 W.L.R. 799; [1969] 3 All E.R.
  1268; (1969) 20 P. & C.R. 1087; 113 S.J. 640, CA . . . . *Digested*, 70/**1525**:
    Applied, 71/6578, 73/1020, 77/448, 78/382, 79/1594, 89/2104, 91/2215,
      92/2656, 92/2710, 96/3827, 96/4938: *Considered*, 71/6597, 71/6957,
      87/3126, 90/2775, 94/3146, 95/3430: *Distinguished*, 72/3333, 84/366,
        84/481, 85/1845: *Followed*, 96/5014, 98/4878
Kampelmann v. Landschaftsverband Westfalen-Lippe (C253/96); Stadtwerke Witten
  GmbH v. Schade (C257/96); Haseley v. Stadtwerke Altena GmbH (C258/96)
  [1997] E.C.R. I-6907; [1998] 2 C.M.L.R. 131; [1998] I.R.L.R. 333, ECJ (5th
  Chamber) . . . . *Digested*, 98/**2111**
Kane v. New Forest DC (No.1) [2001] EWCA Civ 878; [2001] 3 All E.R. 914; [2001]
  27 E.G.C.S. 132; [2001] N.P.C. 100; *Independent*, July 23, 2001 (C.S), CA . . . . . *Digested*, 01/**4495**
Kane v. Radley-Kane; *sub nom* Radley-Kane (Deceased), Re [1999] Ch. 274; [1998] 3
  W.L.R. 617; [1998] 3 All E.R. 753; [1998] 2 F.L.R. 585; [1998] 3 F.C.R. 502;
  [1998] Fam. Law 525; (1998) 95(24) L.S.G. 33; (1998) 142 S.J.L.B. 189; *Times*,
  June 1, 1998, Ch D . . . . *Digested*, 98/**4590**
Kane v. Secretary of State for the Home Department [2000] Imm. A.R. 250, IAT . . . . . . *Digested*, 00/**3346**
KANEGAFUCHI/Polymide film (T848/94) [1999] E.P.O.R. 270, EPO (Technical Bd App)
Kanematsu (Hong Kong) Ltd v. Eurasia Express Line LTA 97/6117/J, CA1996 Folio 1724,
  QBD (Comm Ct); affirming . . . . *Digested*, 98/**4404**
Kaneria v. Patel see Guidezone Ltd, Re
Kantor v. Leonard Ross & Craig see Yudt v. Leonard Ross & Craig
Kapadia v. Lambeth LBC [2000] I.R.L.R. 699; (2001) 57 B.M.L.R. 170; *Times*, July 4,
  2000; *Independent*, July 24, 2000 (C.S), CA; affirming [2000] I.R.L.R. 14, EAT. . . *Digested*, 00/**2124**
Kapela v. Secretary of State for the Home Department [1998] Imm. A.R. 294, IAT . . . . . *Digested*, 98/**3166**
Kapfunde v. Abbey National Plc [1998] E.C.C. 440; [1999] I.C.R. 1; [1998] I.R.L.R.
  583; [1999] Lloyd's Rep. Med. 48; (1999) 46 B.M.L.R. 176; *Times*, April 6, 1998;
  Independent, April 1, 1998, CA . . . . *Digested*, 98/**3931**
Kapitan Shvetsov, The [1998] 1 Lloyd's Rep. 199, CA (HK) . . . . *Digested*, 98/**774**

Kapniki Mikhailidis AE *v.* Idrima Kinonikon Asphaliseon (IKA) (C441/98); *sub nom*
　　Kapniki Mikhailidis AE *v.* Idryma Koinonikon Asfaliseon (IKA) [2000] E.C.R. I-
　　7145; [2001] 1 C.M.L.R. 13, ECJ (5th Chamber) . . . . 　*Digested,* 01/**5211**
Kapoor *v.* Bevington (Valuation Officer) [1997] R.A. 439, Lands Tr . . . . 　*Digested,* 98/**4332**
KappAhl Oy (C233/97), Re [1998] E.C.R. I-8069; [2001] 1 C.M.L.R. 30, ECJ (1st
　　Chamber) . . . . 　*Digested,* 01/**5210**
Kapur *v.* JW Francis & Co (No.1), *Times,* March 4, 1998, CA . . . . 　*Digested,* 98/**334**
Kapur *v.* JW Francis & Co (No.2) [2000] Lloyd's Rep. I.R. 361; [1999] Lloyd's Rep.
　　P.N. 834, CA . . . . 　*Digested,* 99/**3367**
Kapur *v.* Kapur [1985] Fam. Law 22; (1984) 81 L.S.G. 2543 . . . . 　*Digested,* 85/**1074**:
　　　　　　　　　　　　　　　　　　　　　　　　　　　　　　　　　　　　 Applied, 01/2612

Karaganda Ltd *v.* Midland Bank Plc; Kredietbank Antwerp *v.* Midland Bank Plc [1999]
　　1 All E.R. (Comm.) 801; [1999] Lloyd's Rep. Bank. 219; [1999] C.L.C. 1108;
　　Times, May 12, 1999; *Independent,* May 7, 1999, CA; affirming [1998] Lloyd's
　　Rep. Bank. 173; *Times,* October 31, 1997, QBD . . . . 　*Digested,* 99/**286**
Karakurt *v.* Austria (32441/96) (2001) 29 E.H.R.R. CD273, ECHR
Karakus *v.* Karakus (Unreported, June 6, 2000), CC (Bow) [*Ex rel.* Richard Colbey,
　　Barrister, Francis Taylor Building, Temple, London] . . . . 　*Digested,* 00/**53**
Karanakaran *v.* Secretary of State for the Home Department [2000] 3 All E.R. 449;
　　[2000] Imm. A.R. 271; [2000] I.N.L.R. 122; (2000) 97(5) L.S.G. 34; (2000)
　　97(10) L.S.G. 36; (2000) 144 S.J.L.B. 81; *Times,* February 16, 2000;
　　Independent, February 4, 2000, CA . . . . 　*Digested,* 00/**3307**
Karbachian *v.* Parvazian (Unreported, May 21, 1998), CA [*Ex rel.* Brian D Cummins,
　　Barrister, Bridewell Chambers, 2 Bridewell Place, London] . . . . 　*Digested,* 98/**612**
　　　　　　　　　　　　　　　　　　　　　　　　　　　　　　　　　　　　 Applied, 01/4643
Karger *v.* Paul [1984] V.R. 161 . . . . 　*Digested,* 99/**741**
Karlung *v.* Svensk Vagguide Comertex AB [1999] I.L.Pr. 298, HR (N)
KARO STEP Trade Mark [1977] R.P.C. 255, Ch D . . . . 　*Digested,* 77/**3061**:
　　　　　　　　　　Considered, 95/4948, 98/3426: *Followed,* 80/2724: *Not followed,* 95/4945
Kashmir Tandoori *v.* Customs and Excise Commissioners [1998] B.V.C. 2141; [1998] V.
　　& D.R. 104, V&DTr . . . . 　*Digested,* 98/**4880**
Kasir *v.* Darlington & Simpson Rolling Mills Ltd [2001] 2 Costs L.R. 228, QBD
Kasperbauer *v.* Griffith [2000] W.T.L.R. 333, CA . . . . 　*Digested,* 01/**5519**:
　　　　　　　　　　　　　　　　　　　　　　　　　　　　　　　　　　 Considered, 01/5518
Kassam *v.* Chartered Trust Plc [1998] R.T.R. 220; [1998] C.C.L.R. 54, CA . . . . 　*Digested,* 98/**2515**
Kasseer *v.* Freeman see Ravenseft Properties Ltd *v.* Hall
Kastner *v.* Rizla Ltd (No.1) [1995] R.P.C. 585; *Times,* June 23, 1995, CA . . . . 　*Followed,* 98/**3465**
Kataria *v.* Arpino (Unreported, December 8, 1997), CC (Watford) [*Ex rel.* Wayne
　　Beglan, Barrister, 2-3 Gray's Inn Square, London] . . . . 　*Digested,* 98/**1728**
Kataria *v.* Safeland Plc [1998] 1 E.G.L.R. 39; [1998] 05 E.G. 155; (1997) 94(45)
　　L.S.G. 27; (1997) 141 S.J.L.B. 246; (1998) 75 P. & C.R. D30; *Times,* December
　　3, 1997, CA . . . . 　*Digested,* 98/**3605**
Katchis (Contempt of Court), Re [2001] A.C.D. 70, QBD
Katherine Austin's Case 86 E.R. 124; (1672) 2 Vent. 183 . . . . 　*Applied,* 00/**4641**
Katikaridis *v.* Greece (19385/92) (2001) 32 E.H.R.R. 6, ECHR . . . . 　*Applied,* 01/**3541**
Katon *v.* O'Reilly (Unreported, September 13, 1999), CC (Yeovil) [*Ex rel.* Paul McGrath,
　　Barrister, 1 Temple Gardens, Temple, London] . . . . 　*Digested,* 00/**2590**
Katrinak *v.* Secretary of State for the Home Department see Frantisek *v.* Secretary of
　　State for the Home Department
Katsikas *v.* Konstantinidis (C132/91); Skreb *v.* PCO Stauereibetrieb Paetz & Co
　　Nachfolgar GmbH (C138/91); Schroll *v.* PCO Stauereibetrieb Paetz & Co
　　Nachfolgar GmbH (C139/91) [1992] E.C.R. I-6577; [1993] 1 C.M.L.R. 845;
　　[1993] I.R.L.R. 179, ECJ . . . . 　*Digested,* 93/**4280**:
　　　　　　　　　　　　　　　　　　　　　　　　　　　　　　　　　 Considered, 00/2228
Katte Klitsche de la Grange *v.* Italy (A/293-B) (1995) 19 E.H.R.R. 368, ECHR . . . . 　*Digested,* 95/**2652**:
　　　　　　　　　　　　　　　　　　　　　　　　　　　　　　　　　 Considered, 01/3522

Katz *v.* McNally (Liquidator's Indemnity for Costs) see Exchange Travel (Holdings) Ltd
　　(No.3), Re
Katz *v.* McNally (Recovery of Preferences) see Exchange Travel (Holdings) Ltd (No.4),
　　Re
Kaufring AG *v.* Commission of the European Communities (T186/97) [2001] E.C.R. II-
　　1337; [2001] 2 C.M.L.R. 43, CFI (3rd Chamber) . . . . 　*Digested,* 01/**2507**
Kaur (CICB: Quantum: 1999), Re (1999) 99(3) Q.R. 5, CICB (Nottingham) [*Ex rel.* Neil
　　Wylie, Barrister, King Charles House, Standard Hill, Nottingham] . . . . 　*Digested,* 99/**1425**
Kaur *v.* CTP Coil Ltd [2001] C.P. Rep. 34, CA . . . . 　*Digested,* 00/**535**:
　　　　　　　　　　　　　　　　　　　　　　　　　　 Applied, 01/645: *Considered,* 01/644
Kaur (t/a GK Trading) *v.* Customs and Excise Commissioners [1998] B.V.C. 2143, V&DTr 　*Digested,* 98/**4888**
Kaur *v.* DPP see R. *v.* Stipendiary Magistrate for Leicestershire Ex p. Kaur
Kaur (Sukhjinder) *v.* Secretary of State for the Home Department [1998] Imm. A.R. 1,
　　CA . . . . 　*Digested,* 98/**3234**
Kausar *v.* Eagle Star Insurance Co Ltd; *sub nom* Eagle Star Insurance Co Ltd *v.* Kausar
　　[1997] C.L.C. 129; [2000] Lloyd's Rep. I.R. 154; [1996] 5 Re. L.R. 191; (1996)
　　140 S.J.L.B. 150; *Times,* July 15, 1996, CA . . . . 　*Digested,* 96/**3574**:
　　　　　　　　　　　　　　　　　　　　　　　　　　　　　　　　　　　　 Followed, 98/3363
Kausar *v.* Entry Clearance Officer (Islamabad) [1998] I.N.L.R. 141, IAT . . . . 　*Digested,* 98/**3236**

Kavanagh v. Ideal Standard Ltd see Afzal v. Ford Motor Co Ltd
Kavanagh's Application, Re [1997] N.I. 368, CA (NI) . . . . *Digested*, 99/**5437**
Kawasaki Kisen Kaisha Ltd v. Tokai Shipping Co Ltd of Tokyo see Whistler International
    Ltd v. Kawasaki Kisen Kaisha Ltd (The Hill Harmony)
Kay v. Biggs, *Independent*, November 23, 1998 (C.S.), QBD . . . . *Digested*, 98/**2846**
Kay v. United Kingdom (1998) 40 B.M.L.R. 20, Eur Comm HR . . . . *Digested*, 98/**3889**:
                                      Previous proceedings, 89/2389, 90/3101
Kay Green v. Twinsectra Ltd (No.1) [1996] 1 W.L.R. 1587; [1996] 4 All E.R. 546;
    (1997) 29 H.L.R. 327; [1996] 2 E.G.L.R. 43; [1996] 38 E.G. 136; [1996] N.P.C.
    80; (1997) 73 P. & C.R. D13; *Times*, May 27, 1996; *Independent*, June 10, 1996
    (C.S.), CA . . . . *Digested*, 96/**3739**:
                            Applied, 97/3282: *Referred to*, 98/3641
Kaya v. Haringey LBC [2001] EWCA Civ 677; (2001) 98(25) L.S.G. 46; *Times*, June
    14, 2001, CA . . . . *Digested*, 01/**3421**
Kaya v. Turkey (1999) 28 E.H.R.R. 1; [1998] H.R.C.D. 291, ECHR . . . . *Digested*, 99/**3087**:
                                        Applied, 99/3144
Kaye v. Burrows see Sedgwick v. Watney Combe Reid & Co Ltd
Kaye v. Eyre Bros Ltd see Sedgwick v. Watney Combe Reid & Co Ltd
Kayford Ltd (In Liquidation), Re [1975] 1 W.L.R. 279; [1975] 1 All E.R. 604; (1974) 118 S.J.
    752, Ch D . . . . *Digested*, 75/**316**:
                       Applied, 99/3304: *Considered*, 93/1845
Kaysersberg v. Commission of the European Communities (T290/94) (No.1) [1995]
    E.C.R. II-2247, CFI. . . . . *Applied*, 99/**2231**
Kaysersberg SA v. Commission of the European Communities (T290/94) (No.2)
    [1997] E.C.R. II-2137; [1998] 4 C.M.L.R. 336, CFI (2nd Chamber)
Kaytech International Plc, Re; *sub nom* Secretary of State for Trade and Industry v.
    Kaczer; Potier v. Secretary of State for Trade and Industry; Secretary of State for
    Trade and Industry v. Potier; Secretary of State for Trade and Industry v. Solly
    [1999] B.C.C. 390; [1999] 2 B.C.L.C. 351; *Independent*, December 7, 1998
    (C.S.), CA . . . . *Digested*, 99/**622**:
                            Applied, 00/656: *Followed*, 00/658
Kayworth v. Highways Agency (1996) 72 P. & C.R. 433; [1998] R.V.R. 28, Lands Tr . . . *Digested*, 97/**4032**
Kazakstan Wool Processors (Europe) Ltd v. Nederlandsche Credietverzekering
    Maatschappij NV [2000] 1 All E.R. (Comm) 708; [2000] C.L.C. 822; [2000]
    Lloyd's Rep. I.R. 371, CA; affirming [1999] 2 All E.R. (Comm) 445; [1999]
    Lloyd's Rep. I.R. 596, QBD (Comm Ct) . . . . *Digested*, 00/**3529**
Kazantzis v. Chief Adjudication Officer (1999) 96(26) L.S.G. 28; *Times*, June 30,
    1999, CA . . . . *Digested*, 99/**4574**
KBC Bank v. Industrial Steels (UK) Ltd [2001] 1 All E.R. (Comm) 409; [2001] 1 Lloyd's
    Rep. 370, QBD (Comm Ct) . . . . *Digested*, 01/**5350**
KD (A Minor) (Ward: Termination of Access), Re [1988] A.C. 806; [1988] 2 W.L.R. 398;
    [1988] 1 All E.R. 577; [1988] 2 F.L.R. 139; [1988] F.C.R. 657; [1988] Fam. Law 288;
    (1988) 152 J.P.N. 558; (1988) 132 S.J. 301; *Times*, February 19, 1988;
    Independent, February 19, 1988, HL . . . . *Digested*, 88/**2294**:
            Applied, 90/3138, 01/2598: *Considered*, 90/1571, 91/2512, 95/3552,
                              95/4104: *Followed*, 93/2827, 95/3477
KDB v. Netherlands [1998] H.R.C.D. 374, ECHR
Keam v. Customs and Excise Commissioners [2000] S.T.I. 1435, V&DTr
Kearney v. Calsonic Llanelli Radiators Ltd (1999) 99(3) Q.R. 6, CC (Swansea) [*Ex rel.*
    Leo Abse & Cohen Solicitors, 40 Churchill Way, Cardiff] . . . . *Digested*, 99/**1466**
Kearney v. Northern Ireland Civil Service Commission [1996] N.I. 415, CA (NI)
Keary Developments Ltd v. Tarmac Construction Ltd [1995] 3 All E.R. 534; [1995] 2
    B.C.L.C. 395; 73 B.L.R. 115, CA . . . . *Digested*, 96/**724**:
                Applied, 96/692, 96/704, 98/450: *Followed*, 97/563
Keating v. Bromley LBC (No.1) see E (A Minor) v. Dorset CC
Keating v. Bromley LBC (No.2) see X (Minors) v. Bedfordshire CC
Kedem v. Leonard Ross & Craig see Yudt v. Leonard Ross & Craig
Kee v. Sharma (1999) 99(2) Q.R. 5, CC (Brighton) [*Ex rel.* Richard Case, Barrister, 3
    Paper Buildings, Temple, London] . . . . *Digested*, 99/**1586**
Keefe v. Arriva London South Ltd (Unreported, September 22, 1999), CC (Croydon)
    [*Ex rel.* Beth Coll, Barrister] . . . . *Digested*, 99/**2508**
Keegan v. Ireland (A/290) [1994] 3 F.C.R. 165; (1994) 18 E.H.R.R. 342, ECHR . . . . . . *Digested*, 95/**2659**:
                Applied, 97/2819, 01/2541: *Considered*, 96/3296
Keen v. Curwood [2001] 6 Q.R. 11, CC (Bury St Edmunds) [*Ex rel.* Alan Blake,
    Barrister, 4 King's Bench Walk, Temple, London] . . . . *Digested*, 01/**1652**
Keen v. Kennard (Unreported, August 27, 1999), CC (Plymouth) [*Ex rel.* Lyons
    Davidson Solicitors, No.1 Endeavour House, Parkway Court, Marsh Mills,
    Plymouth] . . . . *Digested*, 99/**383**
Keenan, Re [1998] B.P.I.R. 205, Ch D . . . . *Digested*, 98/**3277**
Keenan v. United Kingdom (27229/95) (2001) 33 E.H.R.R. 38; 10 B.H.R.C. 319;
    Times, April 18, 2001, ECHR . . . . *Digested*, 01/**3572**
Keene v. Martin see Hoicrest Ltd, Re
Keene v. Martin (Leave to Appeal) see Hoicrest Ltd (Leave to Appeal), Re

Keepers and Governors of the Possessions, Revenues and Goods of the Free Grammar
School of John Lyon v. Berman see John Lyon's Free Grammar School v. Secchi
Keepers and Governors of the Possessions, Revenues and Goods of the Free Grammar
School of John Lyon v. Secchi see John Lyon's Free Grammar School v. Secchi
Keeping Newcastle Warm v. Customs and Excise Commissioners [2000] S.T.C. 454;
[2000] B.T.C. 5108; [2000] B.V.C. 138; [2000] S.T.I. 215, QBD; affirming [1999]
B.V.C. 2126, VAT Tr (Manchester) . . . . *Digested*, 00/**5338**
Keesing (UK) Ltd v. Customs and Excise Commissioners [2001] S.T.I. 224, V&DTr
Kefalas v. Greece (C367/96) [1998] E.C.R. I-2843; [1999] 2 C.M.L.R. 144, ECJ . . . . . *Digested*, 99/**645**
Keighley Maxsted & Co v. Durant (t/a Bryan Durant & Co); *sub nom* Durant & Co v.
Roberts [1901] A.C. 240, HL; reversing [1900] 1 Q.B. 629, CA . . . . *Considered*, 00/2607:
                                                            Distinguished, 67/1501
Keith v. CPM Field Marketing Ltd [2001] C.P. Rep. 35; *Times*, August 29, 2000, CA . . . *Digested*, 00/**481**
Kellar v. Williams [2000] 2 B.C.L.C. 390, PC (TCI) . . . . *Digested*, 00/**694**
Kelley v. Corston [1998] Q.B. 686; [1998] 3 W.L.R. 246; [1997] 4 All E.R. 466;
[1998] E.C.C. 141; [1998] 1 F.L.R. 986; [1998] 1 F.C.R. 554; [1998] P.N.L.R. 37;
[1998] Fam. Law 399; (1997) 94(32) L.S.G. 28; (1997) 147 N.L.J. 1276;
(1997) 141 S.J.L.B. 206; [1997] N.P.C. 111; *Times*, August 20, 1997, CA . . . . *Digested*, 97/**3815**:
                                       Distinguished, 98/4012, 98/4013, 99/4021
Kellman v. Kellman [2000] 1 F.L.R. 785; [2000] Fam. Law 315, Fam Div . . . . *Digested*, 00/**2501**
Kelly v. Cooper [1993] A.C. 205; [1992] 3 W.L.R. 936; [1994] 1 B.C.L.C. 395; [1992]
E.G.C.S. 119; (1992) 136 S.J.L.B. 303; [1992] N.P.C. 134; *Times*, November 5,
1992, PC (Ber) . . . . *Digested*, 93/**72**:
                                                            Distinguished, 00/2132
Kelly v. Hemming (Unreported, April 22, 1999), CC (Slough) [*Ex rel.* Adrian Posta,
Barrister, South Western Chambers, 12 Middle Street, Taunton, Somerset] . . . . . *Digested*, 00/**1674**
Kelly v. Liverpool Maritime Terminals Ltd [1988] I.R.L.R. 310, CA . . . . *Digested*, 89/**1478**:
                Considered, 97/2238: *Distinguished*, 96/2628, 97/2237: *Followed*, 98/2168
Kelly v. Northern Ireland Housing Executive; Loughran v. Northern Ireland Housing
Executive [1999] 1 A.C. 428; [1998] 3 W.L.R. 735; [1998] N.I. 240; [1998]
I.C.R. 828; [1998] I.R.L.R. 593; (1998) 95(36) L.S.G. 31; (1998) 142 S.J.L.B.
254; *Times*, September 14, 1998, HL; reversing in part [1997] N.I. 125; [1998]
I.R.L.R. 70, CA (NI) . . . . *Digested*, 98/**5133**
Kelly v. Pilgrim (Unreported, May 3, 1998), CC (Leeds) [*Ex rel.* Louis Doyle, Barrister,
10 Park Square, Leeds] . . . . *Digested*, 98/**399**
Kelly v. Sherlock (1865-66) L.R. 1 Q.B. 686, QB . . . . *Considered*, 85/1994,
                                                     88/2123: *Distinguished*, 00/1758
Kelly (Deceased) v. Smith & Partners Ltd [2001] 3 Q.R. 19, QBD [*Ex rel.* David Platt,
Barrister, Crown Office Chambers, 1 Paper Buildings, Temple, London] . . . . *Digested*, 01/**1715**
Kelly v. Solari (1841) 9 M. & W. 54 . . . . *Applied*, 88/840,
                   89/900: *Considered*, 69/524, 83/447, 90/3914, 90/3918, 00/2331
Kelly v. South Manchester HA [1998] 1 W.L.R. 244; [1997] 3 All E.R. 274, QBD . . . . . . *Digested*, 97/**3343**
Kelly v. United Kingdom (30054/96), *Times*, May 18, 2001, ECHR . . . . *Joined proceedings*,
                                                                            01/3575
Kelly's Application for Judicial Review, Re [2000] N.I. 103, CA (NI) . . . . *Digested*, 00/**5619**
Kelsall (Inspector of Taxes) v. Investment Chartwork Ltd [1994] S.T.C. 33, Ch D . . . . . . *Digested*, 94/**650**:
                                                              Applied, 99/4660
Kemble v. Hicks (No.1) see Scientific Investment Pension Plan (No.2), Re
Kemble v. Hicks (No.2) see Scientific Investment Pension Plan (No.3), Re
Kemmings v. Sandwell MBC, *Independent*, February 8, 1999 (C.S.), CA
Kemp v. Burden (No.1) (Unreported, October 15, 1997), CC (Milton Keynes) [*Ex rel.*
Benjamin Williams, Barrister, 3 Paper Buildings, 1 Alfred Street, Oxford] . . . . *Digested*, 98/**1712**
Kemp v. Burden (No.2) (1998) 98(1) Q.R. 8, CC (Milton Keynes) . . . . *Digested*, 98/**1707**
Kemp v. Ling (Unreported, March 26, 1998), CC (Thanet) [*Ex rel.* Tim Kevan, Barrister,
1 Temple Gardens, Temple, London] . . . . *Digested*, 98/**2502**:
                                       Considered, 99/2454: *Followed*, 99/5789
Kemp v. R. (1951) 82 C.L.R. 341 . . . . *Considered*, 00/5485:
                                                          Not applied, 76/488
Kempe v. Ambassador Insurance Co (In Liquidation); *sub nom* Mentor Assurance Ltd,
Re [1998] 1 W.L.R. 271; [1998] B.C.C. 311; [1998] 1 B.C.L.C. 234; (1998) 142
S.J.L.B. 28; *Times*, January 3, 1998, PC (Ber); reversing (Unreported, March 14,
1996), CA (Ber); reversing [1995] 4 Re. L.R. 271, Sup Ct (Ber) . . . . *Digested*, 98/**3299**:
                                       Applied, 01/3748: *Considered*, 99/642
Kemper Reinsurance Co v. Minister of Finance (Bermuda) [2000] 1 A.C. 1; [1998] 3
W.L.R. 630; (1998) 142 S.J.L.B. 175; *Times*, May 18, 1998, PC (Ber) . . . . *Digested*, 98/**381**:
                                                            Distinguished, 00/360
Kempin (t/a British Bulldog Ice Cream) v. Brighton and Hove Council [2001] EWHC
Admin 140; [2001] E.H.L.R. 19; (2001) 98(13) L.S.G. 40; *Times*, March 13, 2001,
QBD . . . . *Digested*, 01/**4317**
Kempster v. Ashfield (Unreported, November 11, 1999), CC (Southampton) [*Ex rel.*
Kevin Haven, Barrister, 2 Gray's Inn Square Chambers, Gray's Inn, London] . . . . *Digested*, 00/**1574**
Kemra (Management) Ltd v. Lewis (Unreported, July 7, 1999), CC (Central London)
[*Ex rel.* Andrew Butler, Barrister, 2nd Floor, Francis Taylor Building, Temple,
London] . . . . *Digested*, 99/**3729**

Ken Randall Associates Ltd v. MMI Companies Inc [1997] L.R.L.R. 648; [1998] Lloyd's
Rep. I.R. 243, QBD (Comm Ct) . . . . *Digested*, 97/**3180**

Kena Kena Properties Ltd v. Attorney General of New Zealand [2001] UKPC 51; (2001)
145 S.J.L.B. 270, PC (NZ)

Kenburgh Investments (Northern) Ltd (In Liquidation) v. David Yablon Minton (A Firm);
sub nom David Yablon Minton (A Firm) v. Kenburgh Investments (Northern) Ltd
(In Liquidation) [2000] C.P.L.R. 551; [2001] B.C.C. 648; [2001] B.P.I.R. 64;
[2000] Lloyd's Rep. P.N. 736; (2000) 97(29) L.S.G. 46; *Times*, July 11, 2000,
CA . . . . *Digested*, 00/**5122**:
Distinguished, 01/656

Kenburn Waste Management Ltd v. Bergmann A3/2001/1161, CA; affirming *Times*, July
9, 2001, Ch D . . . . *Digested*, 01/**799**

Kenco Restaurants Inc v. Internal Revenue Commissioner 1 I.T.L. Rep. 323, US Ct

Kendall v. Cardiff CC [2001] 4 Q.R. 15, CC (Cardiff) [*Ex rel*. Andrew Arentsen,
Barrister, Chambers of John Charles Rees Q.C., 33 Park Place, Cardiff] . . . . *Digested*, 01/**1791**

Kenfield Motors Ltd v. Hayles & Rees (Unreported, October 8, 1997), CC (Uxbridge)
[*Ex rel*. Richard Case, Barrister, 3 Paper Buildings, Temple] . . . . *Digested*, 98/**3919**

Kennecott Utah Copper Corp v. Cornhill Insurance Plc (t/a Allianz Cornhill International)
[1999] 2 All E.R. (Comm) 801; [2000] C.L.C. 273; [2000] Lloyd's Rep. I.R.
179, QBD (Comm Ct) . . . . *Digested*, 00/**3524**

Kennedy v. Trinidad and Tobago 8 B.H.R.C. 230, UN HRC . . . . *Digested*, 00/**3173**

Kennedy and Kennedy v. Berry (Unreported, September 11, 1998), CC (Reading) [*Ex
rel*. Benjamin Williams, Barrister, Oxford Chambers, 1 Alfred Street, Oxford] . . . . *Digested*, 98/**1731**

Kennet DC v. Newby-Vincent (1998) 13 P.A.D. 597, Planning Inspector

Kennet DC v. Williamson-Carey (2000) 15 P.A.D. 247, Planning Inspector

Kennet DC v. Young (1999) 163 J.P. 622; (1999) 163 J.P. 854; [1999] R.T.R. 235;
Times, October 16, 1998, QBD . . . . *Digested*, 98/**975**

Kenny v. Hampshire Constabulary [1999] I.C.R. 27; [1999] I.R.L.R. 76; [1999] Disc.
L.R. 118; *Times*, October 22, 1998, EAT . . . . *Digested*, 98/**2119**

Kenny v. Hewdon Stuart Crane Hire Ltd (Unreported, September 25, 1998), CC
(Central London) [*Ex rel*. Andrew Ritchie, Barrister, 9 Gough Square, London] . *Digested*, 99/**1509**

Kenny & Good Pty Ltd v. MGICA (1992) Ltd [2000] Lloyd's Rep. P.N. 25, HC (Aus) . . *Digested*, 00/**4275**

Kensington v. Unrepresented Non-Allocated Claimants see Goldcorp Exchange Ltd (In
Receivership), Re

Kensington and Chelsea RLBC v. Alba Life and Atlantic Speciality Retail Ltd (2001) 16
P.A.D. 64, Planning Inspector

Kensington and Chelsea RLBC v. Harvey Nichols & Co Ltd [2001] EWCA Civ 702;
[2001] 3 P.L.R. 71; *Independent*, June 18, 2001 (C.S.), CA; affirming [2001] 15
E.G.C.S. 135; [2001] N.P.C. 70, QBD

Kensington and Chelsea RLBC v. Ropemaker Properties Ltd (2000) 15 P.A.D. 785,
Planning Inspector

Kensington and Chelsea RLBC v. Simmonds [1996] 3 F.C.R. 246; (1997) 29 H.L.R.
507; (1996) 160 J.P. Rep. 993; *Times*, July 15, 1996, CA . . . . *Digested*, 96/**3767**:
Followed, 99/3707, 00/3156

Kensington Housing Trust v. Oliver (1998) 30 H.L.R. 608; [1997] N.P.C. 119, CA . . . . . . *Digested*, 97/**2721**

Kent v. Griffiths (Costs) see Heil v. Rankin (Costs)

Kent v. Griffiths (No.1) [1999] Lloyd's Rep. Med. 424, QBD . . . . *Digested*, 00/**4203**:
Subsequent proceedings, 00/1478

Kent v. Griffiths (No.2); *sub nom* Kent v. London Ambulance Service (2000) 3 C.C.L.
Rep. 98; [1999] P.I.Q.R. P192; [1999] Lloyd's Rep. Med. 58; (1999) 47 B.M.L.R.
125; (1999) 96(4) L.S.G. 39; (1999) 143 S.J.L.B. 28; *Times*, December 23,
1998, CA . . . . *Digested*, 99/**3956**

Kent v. Griffiths (No.3) [2001] Q.B. 36; [2000] 2 W.L.R. 1158; [2000] 2 All E.R. 474;
[2000] P.I.Q.R. P57; [2000] Lloyd's Rep. Med. 109; (2000) 97(7) L.S.G. 41;
(2000) 150 N.L.J. 195; (2000) 144 S.J.L.B. 106; *Times*, February 10, 2000;
Independent, February 9, 2000, CA . . . . *Digested*, 00/**4204**

Kent v. Griffiths (Non-Pecuniary Damages) see Heil v. Rankin

Kent v. London Ambulance Service see Kent v. Griffiths (No.2)

Kent v. Manchester Ship Canal Co (Unreported, September 15, 2000), CC
(Manchester) [*Ex rel*. Pannone & Partners, Solicitors, 123 Deansgate,
Manchester] . . . . *Digested*, 01/**463**

Kent CC v. Ashford BC [1999] Ed. C.R. 942; [1999] R.A. 367; (1999) 96(34) L.S.G.
33; *Times*, September 7, 1999, CA; affirming [1998] Ed. C.R. 192; [1998] R.A.
217, QBD . . . . *Digested*, 99/**4335**

Kent CC v. Barclays Bank Plc see Barclays Bank Plc v. Kent CC

Kent CC v. C [1993] Fam. 57; [1992] 3 W.L.R. 808; [1993] 1 All E.R. 719; [1993] 1
F.L.R. 308; [1993] Fam. Law 133, Fam Div . . . . *Digested*, 93/**2782**:
Applied, 95/3391: *Overruled in part*, 00/2482

Kent CC v. Curtis [1998] E.G.C.S. 100; (1998) 95(25) L.S.G. 34; *Independent*, June
22, 1998 (C.S.), QBD . . . . *Digested*, 98/**995**

Kent CC v. D see D (A Child) (Grant of Care Order: Refusal of Freeing Order), Re

Kent CC *v.* Kingsway Investments (Kent) Ltd; Kenworthy *v.* Kent CC [1971] A.C. 72; [1970] 2 W.L.R. 397; [1970] 1 All E.R. 70; 68 L.G.R. 301; 21 P. & C.R. 58; 114 S.J. 73, HL; reversing [1969] 2 Q.B. 332; [1969] 2 W.L.R. 249; [1969] 1 All E.R. 601; 133 J.P. 206; 67 L.G.R. 247; 20 P. & C.R. 189; 112 S.J. 1008, CA; reversing in part [1968] 3 All E.R. 197, QBD . . . .   *Digested,* 70/**2777**:
                   Applied, 72/3358, 85/2766, 92/4346, 00/4494: *Followed,* 94/4458,
                                                       95/4866
Kent CC *v.* Mingo [2000] I.R.L.R. 90, EAT . . . .   *Digested,* 00/**2126**
Kent CC *v.* Multi Media Marketing (Canterbury) Ltd; *sub nom* Meechie *v.* Multi Media Marketing (Canterbury) Ltd 94 L.G.R. 474; [1998] Masons C.L.R. Rep. 88; *Times,* May 9, 1995, QBD. . . . .   *Digested,* 95/**1286**
Kent CC *v.* R see D (A Child) (Grant of Care Order: Refusal of Freeing Order), Re
Kent CC *v.* Secretary of State for the Environment (1998) 75 P. & C.R. 410; [1997] J.P.L. 1115; [1997] C.O.D. 481; [1997] E.G.C.S. 64; [1997] N.P.C. 71; *Independent,* May 19, 1997 (C.S.), CA . . . .   *Digested,* 97/**4145**
Kent CC *v.* Upchurch River Valley Golf Course Ltd (1998) 75 P. & C.R. D37, QBD . . . . .   *Digested,* 98/**2855**
Kent Valuation Committee *v.* Southern Railway Co Ltd see Westminster City Council *v.* Southern Railway Co Ltd
Kentish Homes Ltd, Re see Powdrill and Lyle (Joint Liquidators of Kentish Homes Ltd) *v.* Tower Hamlets LBC
Kenworthy *v.* Kent CC see Kent CC *v.* Kingsway Investments (Kent) Ltd
Kenyon-Brown *v.* Desmond Banks & Co (Undue Influence) (No.2) see Royal Bank of Scotland Plc *v.* Etridge (No.2)
Kenyon-Brown *v.* Desmond Banks & Co (Undue Influence) (No.1) [2000] Lloyd's Rep. Bank. 80; [2000] Lloyd's Rep. P.N. 338; [2000] P.N.L.R. 266; (1999) 149 N.L.J. 1832; [1999] N.P.C. 140, CA . . . .   *Digested,* 00/**4273**:
                                                        Overruled, 01/4880
Keogh *v.* Rush (2001-02) 4 I.T.E.L.R. 221, CA (NSW)
Keppel *v.* Wheeler [1927] 1 K.B. 577, CA . . . .   *Applied,* 59/13:
                                     Distinguished, 00/2132: *Followed,* 85/23
KERNFORSCHUNGSZENTRUM/Gas separation (T215/85) [1999] E.P.O.R. 356, EPO (Technical Bd App) . . . .   *Digested,* 99/**3483**
Kernkraftwerke Lippe-EMS GmbH *v.* Commission of the European Communities (T149/94) see Kernkraftwerke Lippe-Ems GmbH *v.* Commission of the European Community (C161/97 P)
Kernkraftwerke Lippe-EMS GmbH *v.* Commission of the European Communities (T181/94) see Kernkraftwerke Lippe-Ems GmbH *v.* Commission of the European Community (C161/97 P)
Kernkraftwerke Lippe-Ems GmbH *v.* Commission of the European Community (C161/97 P); *sub nom* Kernkraftwerke Lippe-EMS GmbH *v.* Commission of the European Communities (T149/94); Kernkraftwerke Lippe-EMS GmbH *v.* Commission of the European Communities (T181/94) [1999] E.C.R. I-2057; [2000] 2 C.M.L.R. 489, ECJ (1st Chamber); affirming [1997] E.C.R. II-161; [1997] 3 C.M.L.R. 136, CFI (1st Chamber) . . . .   *Digested,* 00/**2363**
Kerojarvi *v.* Finland (17506/90); *sub nom* Kerojarvi *v.* Finland (A/322) (2001) 32 E.H.R.R. 8, ECHR . . . .   *Applied,* 98/3118,
                                                     99/3119
Kerojarvi *v.* Finland (A/322) see Kerojarvi *v.* Finland (17506/90)
Kerr (David), Petitioner; *sub nom* Kerr (David) *v.* HM Advocate *Times,* July 4, 2000, HCJ Appeal . . . .   *Digested,* 00/**6065**
Kerr *v.* ABC Credit Union BT/30/1998, LandsTr (NI) . . . .   *Digested,* 00/**5612**
Kerr *v.* Aitken; *sub nom* Aitken's Trustee *v.* Aitken [2000] B.P.I.R. 278; 1999 G.W.D. 39-1898, OH . . . .   *Digested,* 00/**6506**
Kerr *v.* British Leyland (Staff) Trustees Ltd [2001] W.T.L.R. 1071, CA
Kerr (David) *v.* HM Advocate see Kerr (David), Petitioner
Kerr *v.* United Kingdom (40451/98) (2001) 29 E.H.R.R. CD184, ECHR
Kerr's Application, Re [1997] N.I. 225, QBD (NI) . . . .   *Digested,* 99/**5177**:
                                                     Considered, 99/5213
Kerrier DC *v.* Elliot (2000) 15 P.A.D. 196, Planning Inspector
Kerrouche *v.* Secretary of State for the Home Department (No.1) see R. *v.* Secretary of State for the Home Department Ex p. Kerrouche (No.1)
Kerry *v.* Carter [1969] 1 W.L.R. 1372; [1969] 3 All E.R. 723; 113 S.J. 704, CA . . . .   *Digested,* 69/**2392**:
                                                     Considered, 01/4450
Kerry Foods Ltd *v.* Creber [2000] I.C.R. 556; [2000] I.R.L.R. 10, EAT . . . .   *Digested,* 00/**2223**:
                                                     Considered, 01/6476
Kesko Oy *v.* Commission of the European Communities (T22/97) [1999] E.C.R. II-3775; [2000] 4 C.M.L.R. 335, CFI (2nd Chamber) . . . .   *Digested,* 00/**723**
Kesse *v.* Secretary of State for the Home Department [2001] EWCA Civ 177; [2001] Imm. A.R. 366; *Times,* March 21, 2001; *Independent,* February 15, 2001, CA . . .   *Digested,* 01/**3688**
Keswick Golf Club *v.* Customs and Excise Commissioners; Silloth on Solway Golf Club *v.* Customs and Excise Commissioners; Carlisle Golf Club *v.* Customs and Excise Commissioners; Grange Oversands Golf Club *v.* Customs and Excise Commissioners [1998] B.V.C. 2250; [1998] V. & D.R. 276, V&DTr . . . .   *Digested,* 98/**4903**
Ketheeswaran (14797), Re (Unreported, March 26, 1997), IAT . . . .   *Doubted,* 98/3195

Ketley v. Gilbert [2001] 1 W.L.R. 986; [2001] R.T.R. 22; *Times*, January 17, 2001;
  Independent, January 19, 2001, CA . . . . *Digested*, 01/**904**:
  Distinguished, 01/903: *Not followed*, 01/886
Ketteman v. Hansel Properties Ltd [1987] A.C. 189; [1987] 2 W.L.R. 312; [1988] 1 All
  E.R. 38; 36 B.L.R. 1; [1987] 1 F.T.L.R. 284; 85 L.G.R. 409; [1987] 1 E.G.L.R. 237;
  (1987) 84 L.S.G. 657; (1987) 137 N.L.J. 100; (1987) 131 S.J. 134, HL;
  affirming [1984] 1 W.L.R. 1274; [1985] 1 All E.R. 352; 27 B.L.R. 1; (1985) 49 P.
  & C.R. 257; (1984) 271 E.G. 1099; [1984] C.I.L.L. 109; (1984) 81 L.S.G. 3018;
  (1984) 128 S.J. 800, CA . . . . *Digested*, 87/**2330**:
  Applied, 86/1993, 89/3048, 00/473: *Considered*, 87/229, 88/2158, 89/2093,
  90/3623, 92/581, 92/3401, 92/3575, 92/3581, 93/3127, 93/3299, 94/3746:
  Distinguished, 93/1760: *Referred to*, 86/2283, 93/2613, 93/3613
Kettering BC v. Anglian Water Services Plc [2001] N.P.C. 24, Lands Tr
Kettering BC v. Perkins [1999] J.P.L. 166, Crown Ct (Birmingham) . . . . *Digested*, 99/**4177**
Kevi A/S v. Suspa-Verein (UK) [1982] R.P.C. 173, Pat Ct . . . . *Digested*, 82/**2311**:
  Applied, 95/857: *Followed*, 00/3694
Key v. Courtaulds Textiles Plc [1999] O.P.L.R. 27, Ch D . . . . *Digested*, 01/**4603**
Keymed (Medical & Industrial Equipment) Ltd v. Forest Healthcare NHS Trust [1998] Eu.
  L.R. 71, QBD . . . . *Digested*, 98/**860**
Keymer v. Dive-In Ltd (Unreported, October 22, 1999), CC (Manchester) [*Ex rel.* Dibb
  Lupton Alsop Solicitors, 101 Barbirolli Square, Manchester] . . . . *Digested*, 00/**4209**
Keyse v. Commissioner of Police of the Metropolis see S (A Child) v. Keyse
Khabibulin v. R. 2 I.T.L. Rep. 390, Tax Ct (Can)
Khalfaoui v. France (34791/97) (2001) 31 E.H.R.R. 42, ECHR . . . . *Digested*, 01/**3499**
Khalil v. Bundesanstalt fur Arbeit (C95/99); Chaaban v. Bundesanstalt fur Arbeit
  (C96/99); Osseili v. Bundesanstalt fur Arbeit (C97/99); Nasser v.
  Landeshauptstadt Stuttgart (C98/99); Addou v. Land Nordrhein Westfalen
  (C180/99) [2001] 3 C.M.L.R. 50, ECJ
Khalili v. Bennett; *sub nom* Khilili v. Bennett; Khalili v. Webb [2000] E.M.L.R. 996, CA . . *Digested*, 00/**600**
Khalili v. Webb see Khalili v. Bennett
Khamassi v. Racjip [2001] 4 Q.R. 12, CC (Uxbridge) [*Ex rel.* Andrew Granville
  Stafford, Barrister, 4 King's Bench Walk, Temple, London] . . . . *Digested*, 01/**1746**
Khan (Barkat A) (Deceased), Re; *sub nom* Khan (Mohammed Aslam) v. Internal
  Revenue Commissioner 1 I.T.L. Rep. 625, US Ct
Khan v. Ali see Burridge v. Stafford
Khan v. Bibb (Unreported, October 22, 1998), CC (Bury) [*Ex rel.* Carl Chapman & Co
  Solicitors, 20/22 Bowkers Row, Nelson Square, Bolton] . . . . *Digested*, 99/**1585**
Khan v. Chief Constable of West Yorkshire see Chief Constable of West Yorkshire v.
  Khan
Khan v. Evans (Unreported, December 13, 2000), CC (West London) [*Ex rel.* Benjamin
  Williams, Barrister, 1 Temple Gardens, London] . . . . *Digested*, 01/**888**
Khan v. Hughes; Khan v. Moran; (Unreported, November 3, 1998), CC (Preston) [*Ex
  rel.* Silverbeck Rymer Solicitors, Heywoods Building, 5 Brunswick Street,
  Liverpool] . . . . *Digested*, 99/**3795**
Khan (Asif Mahmood) v. Immigration Appeal Tribunal see R. v. Secretary of State for
  the Home Department Ex p. Khan (Asif Mahmood)
Khan v. Inland Revenue Commissioners see Toshoku Finance UK Plc (In Liquidation),
  Re
Khan (Mohammed Aslam) v. Internal Revenue Commissioner see Khan (Barkat A)
  (Deceased), Re
Khan v. Islington LBC (2000) 32 H.L.R. 534; [2000] B.L.G.R. 1; [2001] R.V.R. 62;
  [1999] E.G.C.S. 87; *Times*, July 6, 1999; *Independent*, July 12, 1999 (C.S.), CA . *Digested*, 99/**3723**
Khan v. Jones (1998) 98(2) Q.R. 4, CC (Bradford) . . . . *Digested*, 98/**1487**
Khan v. Miah; *sub nom* Miah v. Khan [2000] 1 W.L.R. 2123; [2001] 1 All E.R. 20;
  [2001] 1 All E.R. (Comm) 282; (2000) 97(45) L.S.G. 41; (2000) 150 N.L.J.
  1658; (2000) 144 S.J.L.B. 282; *Times*, November 7, 2000, HL; reversing [1998]
  1 W.L.R. 477; [1998] C.L.C. 210; *Times*, January 13, 1998; *Times*, December 31,
  1997, CA. . . . . *Digested*, 00/**4312**
Khan v. Moran see Khan v. Hughes
Khan v. Mortgage Express (No.2) [2000] B.P.I.R. 473; [2000] E.G.C.S. 8, Ch D . . . . . *Digested*, 00/**3474**
Khan v. Newport General Commissioners 70 T.C. 239, CA [1994] S.T.C. 972; [1994]
  S.T.I. 1317, Ch D . . . . *Digested*, 95/**2752**
Khan v. Oldham (Unreported, February 18, 1998), CC (Leeds) [*Ex rel.* Mark Henley,
  Barrister, 9 Woodhouse Square, Leeds, LS3 1AD] . . . . *Digested*, 98/**1730**
Khan v. Permayer [2001] B.P.I.R. 95, CA . . . . *Digested*, 01/**3793**
Khan (Khalid) v. Secretary of State for the Home Department see R. v. Secretary of
  State for the Home Department Ex p. Gangadeen
Khan v. Simpson (Unreported, January 18, 2000), CC (Bury) [*Ex rel.* David A Tubby &
  Co, Solicitors, Alexander House, 2a Aughton Street, Ormskirk, Lancs] . . . . *Digested*, 00/**501**
Khan v. United Kingdom (35394/97) (Admissibility of Application) [1999] Crim. L.R.
  666, ECHR
Khan v. United Kingdom (35394/97) (2001) 31 E.H.R.R. 45; 8 B.H.R.C. 310; [2000]
  Crim. L.R. 684; *Times*, May 23, 2000, ECHR . . . . *Digested*, 00/**3249**:
  Considered, 01/980, 01/3576: *Distinguished*, 00/921

Khan-Ghauri v. Dunbar Bank Plc [2001] B.P.I.R. 618, Ch D . . . .   *Digested*, 01/**3739**
Khar v. Delbounty Ltd (1998) 75 P. & C.R. 232; [1996] E.G.C.S. 183; [1996] N.P.C.
   163, CA   *Digested*, 97/**3293**
Khatib-Shahidi v. Immigration Appeal Tribunal see R. v. Immigration Appeal Tribunal Ex
   p. Khatib-Shahidi
Khazanchi v. Faircharm Investments Ltd see McLeod v. Butterwick
Khilili v. Bennett see Khalili v. Bennett
Khodaparast v. Shad [2000] 1 W.L.R. 618; [2000] 1 All E.R. 545; [2000] E.M.L.R.
   265; *Times*, December 1, 1999 ; *Independent*, February 28, 2000 (C.S.), CA . . . .   *Digested*, 00/**5116**:
   Applied, 01/2309
Khorasandjian v. Bush [1993] Q.B. 727; [1993] 3 W.L.R. 476; [1993] 3 All E.R. 669;
   [1993] 2 F.L.R. 66; (1993) 25 H.L.R. 392; [1993] Fam. Law 679; (1993) 137
   S.J.L.B. 88; *Times*, February 18, 1993; *Independent*, March 16, 1993, CA . . . . . .   *Digested*, 93/**3251**:
   Considered, 01/3823: *Overruled in part*, 97/3865
Khreino v. Khreino (No.1) [2000] C.P. Rep. 29; [2000] 1 F.L.R. 578; [2000] 1 F.C.R.
   75; [2000] Fam. Law 611, CA . . . .   *Digested*, 00/**356**
Khreino v. Khreino (No.2) [2000] 1 F.C.R. 80, CA . . . .   *Digested*, 00/**2529**
Khris v. L'Institut National de la Propriete Intellectualle Ex p. Louis Vuitton Malletier (A
   Firm) [2001] E.T.M.R. 20, C d'A (Paris)
Kibble v. Bond (Unreported, July 30, 1998), CC (Central London) [*Ex rel.* Benjamin
   Williams, Barrister, Oxford Chambers, 1 Alfred Street, Oxford] . . . .   *Digested*, 98/**1596**
Kibby v. Bourdon (1999) 99(4) Q.R. 3, CC (Boston) . . . .   *Digested*, 99/**1476**
Kibiti v. Secretary of State for the Home Department [2000] Imm. A.R. 594, CA
Kickers International SA v. Paul Kettle Agencies Ltd [1990] F.S.R. 436, Ch D . . . .   *Digested*, 91/**2813**:
   Applied, 98/3427
Kidd v. Axa Equity & Law Life Assurance Society Plc [2000] I.R.L.R. 301, QBD . . . . .   *Digested*, 00/**2195**:
   Applied, 01/2254
Kidd v. Plymouth HA [2001] Lloyd's Rep. Med. 165, QBD . . . .   *Digested*, 01/**581**
Kijowski v. New Capital Properties 15 Con. L.R. 1, QBD . . . .   *Digested*, 90/**398**:
   Considered, 01/2430
Kik v. Office for Harmonisation in the Internal Market (Trade Marks and Designs)
   (OHIM) (T120/99) [2001] E.C.R. II-2235; [2001] E.T.M.R. 93; (2001) 24(9)
   I.P.D. 24060, CFI
Kilic v. Turkey (22492/93) (2001) 33 E.H.R.R. 58, ECHR
Kill v. Sussex Coastline Buses Ltd (Unreported, January 28, 2000), CC
   (Southampton) [*Ex rel.* DLA & Partners, Solicitors, Fountain Precinct, Balm
   Green, Sheffield] . . . .   *Digested*, 00/**2969**
Killick (Deceased), Re see Killick v. Pountney
Killick v. Pountney; *sub nom* Killick (Deceased), Re [2000] W.T.L.R. 41; *Times*, April
   30, 1999; *Independent*, May 10, 1999 (C.S.), Ch D . . . .   *Digested*, 99/**4650**
Killick v. PricewaterhouseCoopers (No.1) [2001] 1 B.C.L.C. 65; [2001] Lloyd's Rep.
   P.N. 17; [2001] P.N.L.R. 1; [2001] W.T.L.R. 699, Ch D . . . .   *Digested*, 01/**4507**
Killick v. Rendall; Nugent v. Rendall [2000] 2 All E.R. (Comm) 57; [2000] C.L.C. 1217;
   [2000] Lloyd's Rep. I.R. 581; *Independent*, April 19, 2000, CA. . . . .   *Digested*, 00/**3522**
Killick v. Roberts [1991] 1 W.L.R. 1146; [1991] 4 All E.R. 289; (1991) 23 H.L.R. 564;
   [1991] 2 E.G.L.R. 100; [1991] 41 E.G. 133; [1991] E.G.C.S. 66; [1991] N.P.C. 74;
   Times, June 21, 1991, CA . . . .   *Digested*, 92/**2715**:
   Considered, 93/2462, 98/2984
Killick v. Second Covent Garden Property Co [1973] 1 W.L.R. 658; [1973] 2 All E.R.
   337; (1973) 25 P. & C.R. 332; 117 S.J. 417, CA . . . .   *Digested*, 73/**1890**:
   Applied, 86/1859: *Considered*, 89/2139: *Distinguished*, 87/2116, 91/2238:
   Overruled, 01/4185
Kilmarnock Equitable Cooperative Society Ltd v. Inland Revenue Commissioners 1966
   S.L.T. 224; 42 T.C. 675; (1966) 45 A.T.C. 205; [1966] T.R. 185, 1 Div . . . .   *Digested*, 66/**13654**:
   Considered, 96/5565: *Distinguished*, 98/4603: *Followed*, 81/333
Kilvert v. Flackett (A Bankrupt) [1998] 2 F.L.R. 806; [1998] B.P.I.R. 721; [1998]
   O.P.L.R. 237; [1998] Fam. Law 582; *Times*, August 3, 1998, Ch D . . . .   *Digested*, 98/**3281**
Kimber v. Kimber; *sub nom* K v. K (Enforcement) [2000] 1 F.L.R. 383; [2000] Fam.
   Law 317, Fam Div . . . .   *Digested*, 00/**2527**
Kimberley Clark Ltd v. Fort Sterling Ltd see Kimberly Clark Ltd v. Fort Sterling Ltd
Kimberly Clark (C241/94), Re see France v. Commission of the European Communities
   (C241/94)
Kimberly Clark Corp's Patent Application (No.0339461) (2000) 23(11) I.P.D. 23095, EPO
   (Technical Bd App)
Kimberly Clark Ltd v. Fort Sterling Ltd; *sub nom* Kimberley Clark Ltd v. Fort Sterling Ltd
   [1997] F.S.R. 877; (1997) 20(7) I.P.D. 20066, Ch D . . . .   *Digested*, 98/**3516**
Kimberly Clark Worldwide Inc v. Procter & Gamble Ltd (No.1) [2000] F.S.R. 235;
   [2000] R.P.C. 422; (1999) 96(47) L.S.G. 32; (2000) 144 S.J.L.B. 9; *Times*,
   December 1, 1999, CA; reversing (1999) 22(10) I.P.D. 22093, Pat Ct. . . . .   *Digested*, 00/**3604**:
   Applied, 00/3667, 01/3901: *Considered*, 01/3879
Kimberly Clark Worldwide Inc v. Procter & Gamble Ltd (No.2) [2001] F.S.R. 22; (2000)
   23(10) I.P.D. 23087; (2000) 97(37) L.S.G. 40; *Times*, September 6, 2000, Pat
   Ct. . . . .   *Digested*, 00/**3678**

Kincardine Fisheries Ltd *v.* Sunderland Marine Mutual Insurance Co Ltd QBCMI 97/
 1248/B, CA; reversing [1997] C.L.C. 739; *Times*, February 12, 1997, QBD . . . . .   *Digested,* 98/**3363**
Kinch *v.* Bullard [1999] 1 W.L.R. 423; [1998] 4 All E.R. 650; [1999] 1 F.L.R. 66;
 [1998] 3 E.G.L.R. 112; [1998] 47 E.G. 140; [1998] Fam. Law 738; [1998]
 E.G.C.S. 126; [1998] N.P.C. 137; *Times*, September 16, 1998; *Independent,*
 October 12, 1998 (C.S.), Ch D . . . .   *Digested,* 98/**4347**
Kind *v.* Newcastle upon Tyne City Council [2001] 36 E.G.C.S. 179; (2001) 98(32)
 L.S.G. 38, QBD
Kinetics Technology International SpA *v.* Cross Seas Shipping Corp (The Mosconici)
 [2001] 2 Lloyd's Rep. 313, QBD (Comm Ct) . . . .   *Digested,* 01/**4936**
King *v.* Achilleas see Townsend *v.* Achilleas
King *v.* Anthony [1998] 2 B.C.L.C. 517; [1999] B.P.I.R. 73, CA . . . .   *Digested,* 99/**3344**
King (Inspector of Taxes) *v.* Boddy [2000] R.V.R. 77, Lands Tr . . . .   *Digested,* 00/**4927**
King *v.* Bristow Helicopters Ltd; *sub nom* Hammond *v.* Bristow Helicopters Ltd; Morris
 v. KLM Royal Dutch Airlines; TNS, HL; reversing [2001] 1 Lloyd's Rep. 95; 2001
 S.C. 54; 2001 S.L.T. 126; 2001 S.C.L.R. 393; 2000 G.W.D. 25-923; *Times,*
 October 25, 2000, 1 Div; reversing 1999 S.L.T. 919; 1998 G.W.D. 40-2028, OH .   *Digested,* 00/**6704**:
 Not followed, 01/5385: *Previous proceedings,* 01/5385
King *v.* Britannia Hotels Ltd (Unreported, June 29, 2000), CC (Bury) [*Ex rel.* Russell &
 Russell Solicitors, Colmar House, Middleton Gardens, Middleton] . . . .   *Digested,* 00/**1548**
King *v.* Co-Steel Sheerness Plc (Unreported, July 9, 1998), CC (Clerkenwell) [*Ex rel.*
 John Tughan, Barrister, 9 Gough Square, London] . . . .   *Digested,* 98/**1686**:
 Considered, 00/1501
King *v.* Dorset CC [1997] 1 E.G.L.R. 245; [1998] R.V.R. 35, Lands Tr . . . .   *Digested,* 97/**4134**
King *v.* DPP [2001] A.C.D. 7; *Independent,* July 31, 2000 (C.S), QBD
King *v.* Eaton Ltd (No.1) 1996 S.C. 74; 1997 S.L.T. 654; 1996 S.C.L.R. 232; [1996]
 I.R.L.R. 199; *Times*, February 1, 1996, 2 Div; reversing [1995] I.R.L.R. 75, EAT . .   *Digested,* 96/**6956**:
 Considered, 95/2103
King *v.* Eaton Ltd (No.2); *sub nom* Eaton Ltd *v.* King 1999 S.L.T. 656; 1998 S.C.L.R.
 1017; [1998] I.R.L.R. 686; 1998 G.W.D. 27-1381, 2 Div . . . .   *Digested,* 99/**6048**
King *v.* Gower (Unreported, July 7, 1999), CC (Plymouth) [*Ex rel.* Bond Pearce
 Solicitors, Ballard House, West Hoe Road, Plymouth] . . . .   *Digested,* 99/**2460**
King *v.* Great Britain China Centre [1992] I.C.R. 516; [1991] I.R.L.R. 513; *Times,*
 October 30, 1991; *Independent,* October 22, 1991; *Guardian,* October 16, 1991,
 CA . . . .   *Digested,* 92/**1959**:
 Applied, 97/2239, 97/6011, 98/5810, 98/5817, 01/2296:
 Considered, 01/2298: *Followed,* 97/2247, 97/2248
King *v.* Hundred of Hoo Nursery [1998] I.C.R. 865; [1998] I.R.L.R. 564; *Times*, June
 10, 1998, EAT . . . .   *Digested,* 98/**2171**
King *v.* Jackson (t/a Jackson Flower Co) (1998) 30 H.L.R. 541; [1998] 1 E.G.L.R. 30;
 [1998] 03 E.G. 138; [1997] N.P.C. 116; (1997) 74 P. & C.R. D30, CA . . . .   *Digested,* 97/**3285**
King *v.* RCO Support Services Ltd; King *v.* Yorkshire Traction Co Ltd [2001] I.C.R. 608;
 [2001] P.I.Q.R. P15; *Times,* February 7, 2001, CA . . . .   *Digested,* 01/**3303**
King *v.* Read; *sub nom* Read *v.* King [1999] 1 F.L.R. 425; [1999] Fam. Law 90, CA . . . .   *Digested,* 97/**1262**
King *v.* Swindon BC see JS Bloor Ltd *v.* Swindon BC
King *v.* T Tunnock Ltd 2000 S.C. 424; 2000 S.L.T. 744; [2001] E.C.C. 6; [2000] Eu.
 L.R. 531; [2000] I.R.L.R. 569; 2000 G.W.D. 12-408; *Times*, May 12, 2000, Ex
 Div; reversing (Unreported, December 24, 1997), Sh Pr; affirming 1996 S.C.L.R.
 742, Sh Ct . . . .   *Digested,* 00/**5846**
King *v.* Thomas McKenna Ltd [1991] 2 Q.B. 480; [1991] 2 W.L.R. 1234; [1991] 1 All
 E.R. 653; 54 B.L.R. 48; *Times*, January 30, 1991, CA . . . .   *Digested,* 91/**199**:
 Applied, 97/267: *Considered,* 93/168, 94/214, 94/2802, 94/2807, 00/229:
 Followed, 00/230
King *v.* Victoria Insurance Co Ltd [1896] A.C. 250, PC (Aus) . . . .   *Applied,* 57/1763,
 64/3384: *Distinguished,* 00/1460
King *v.* Walden (Inspector of Taxes) see Johnson *v.* Walden (Inspector of Taxes)
King *v.* Walden (Inspector of Taxes) [2001] S.T.C. 822; [2001] B.P.I.R. 1012; [2001]
 B.T.C. 170; 3 I.T.L. Rep. 682; [2001] S.T.I. 837; *Times*, June 12, 2001, Ch D;
 affirming [2000] S.T.C. (S.C.D.) 179; [2000] S.T.I. 641, Sp Comm . . . .   *Digested,* 01/**5291**
King *v.* Yorkshire Traction Co Ltd see King *v.* RCO Support Services Ltd
King Features Syndicate Inc *v.* O&M Kleeman Ltd [1941] A.C. 417; [1941] 2 All E.R.
 403, HL; reversing [1940] Ch. 806; [1940] 3 All E.R. 484, CA; reversing [1940]
 Ch. 523; [1940] 2 All E.R. 355, Ch D . . . .   *Applied,* 71/**1885**:
 Considered, 96/3632, 98/3421
King's Norton Metal Co *v.* Edridge Merrett & Co (1897) 14 T.L.R. 98 . . . .   *Applied,* 00/**2600**:
 Distinguished, 60/550, 90/659
King's Trade Mark Application [2000] E.T.M.R. 22, TMR . . . .   *Digested,* 00/**3777**
Kingcastle Ltd *v.* Owen-Owen, *Times*, March 18, 1999, CA . . . .   *Digested,* 99/**24**
Kingfisher Plc *v.* Customs and Excise Commissioners [2000] S.T.C. 992; [2000] B.T.C.
 5420; [2001] B.V.C. 49; [2000] S.T.I. 1610, Ch D; affirming [2000] B.V.C. 2152;
 [1999] V. & D.R. 508; [2000] S.T.I. 266, V&D Tr . . . .   *Digested,* 01/**5614**:
 Distinguished, 01/5598

Kingori v. Secretary of State for the Home Department; *sub nom* R. v. Secretary of
State for the Home Department Ex p. Mpyanguli [1994] Imm. A.R. 539, CA . . .   *Digested*, 95/**2695**:
 Applied, 95/2696, 96/3200: *Considered*, 96/3197: *Followed*, 99/6287
Kings v. Cleghorn [1998] B.P.I.R. 463, Ch D . . . .   *Digested*, 99/**3338**
Kings Quality Homes Ltd v. AJ Paints Ltd [1998] 1 W.L.R. 124; [1997] 3 All E.R. 267;
 (1997) 94(18) L.S.G. 32; (1997) 141 S.J.L.B. 99; *Times*, April 24, 1997, CA . . . .   *Digested*, 97/**617**
Kingsalton Ltd v. Thames Water Developments Ltd; *sub nom* Thames Water
 Developments Ltd v. Kingsalton Ltd [2001] EWCA Civ 20; [2001] 5 E.G.C.S.
 169; (2001) 98(17) L.S.G. 37; [2001] N.P.C. 16; *Times*, February 27, 2001;
 Independent, February 26, 2001 (C.S), CA . . . .   *Digested*, 01/**4861**
Kingscrest Associates Ltd v. Customs and Excise Commissioners; *sub nom* Kingscrest
 Residential Care Homes v. Customs and Excise Commissioners; Customs and
 Excise Commissioners v. Kingscrest Associates Ltd; CH/2001/APP/010500, Ch
 D; affirming [2001] B.V.C. 2326; [2001] S.T.I. 1066, V&DTr . . . .   *Distinguished*, 01/6922
Kingscrest Residential Care Homes v. Customs and Excise Commissioners see
 Kingscrest Associates Ltd v. Customs and Excise Commissioners
Kingscroft Insurance Co Ltd v. Nissan Fire & Marine Insurance Co Ltd (No.1) [1999]
 Lloyd's Rep. I.R. 371, CA; affirming *Lloyd's List*, May 16, 1996 (I.D.), QBD
 (Comm Ct) . . . .   *Digested*, 00/**3510**:
 Followed, 99/3382
Kingscroft Insurance Co Ltd v. Nissan Fire & Marine Insurance Co Ltd (No.2) [2000] 1
 All E.R. (Comm) 272; [1999] C.L.C. 1875; [1999] Lloyd's Rep. I.R. 603, QBD
 (Comm Ct) . . . .   *Digested*, 00/**3560**
Kingsley v. Secretary of State for the Environment, Transport and the Regions (2001)
 82 P. & C.R. 9; (2000) 97(45) L.S.G. 43, QBD (Admin Ct) . . . .   *Digested*, 01/**4762**
Kingsley v. United Kingdom (35605/97) (2001) 33 E.H.R.R. 13; *Times*, January 9,
 2001, ECHR . . . .   *Digested*, 01/**96**:
 Applied, 01/84
Kingsley v. United Kingdom (35605/97) (Admissibility) (2001) 29 E.H.R.R. CD191,
 ECHR
Kingsmill v. Millard (1855) 11 Ex. 313. . . . .   *Applied*, 01/4844:
 Followed, 74/2089
Kingston v. Swirl Service Group Ltd [2001] 5 Q.R. 17, CC (Croydon) [*Ex rel.* David
 McHugh, Barrister, Bracton Chambers, 8 Bell Yard, London] . . . .   *Digested*, 01/**1762**
Kingston Upon Hull City Council v. Mountain [1999] I.C.R. 715, EAT . . . .   *Digested*, 99/**2011**
Kingston upon Thames RLBC v. National Solus Sites (1994) 158 J.P. 70; [1994] J.P.L.
 251; [1994] C.O.D. 78; (1993) 157 J.P.N. 801; (1994) 158 L.G. Rev. 85; *Times*,
 June 24, 1993, DC. . . . .   *Digested*, 94/**4305**:
 Considered, 98/4158
Kingston upon Thames RLBC v. Prince [1999] 1 F.L.R. 593; (1999) 31 H.L.R. 794;
 [1999] B.L.G.R. 333; [1999] L. & T.R. 175; [1999] Fam. Law 84; [1998]
 E.G.C.S. 179; (1999) 96(2) L.S.G. 28; (1999) 143 S.J.L.B. 45; [1998] N.P.C.
 158; *Times*, December 7, 1998; *Independent*, December 14, 1998 (C.S.), CA . . . .   *Digested*, 99/**3733**
Kingston Upon Thames RLBC v. Slug and Lettuce Group Plc (1999) 14 P.A.D. 584,
 Planning Inspector
Kinnersley Engineering Ltd v. Secretary of State for the Environment, Transport and the
 Regions [2001] J.P.L. 1082; [2000] E.G.C.S. 109, QBD (Admin Ct) . . . .   *Digested*, 01/**4658**
Kinsella v. Chief Constable of Nottinghamshire, *Times*, August 24, 1999, QBD . . . .   *Digested*, 99/**3982**
Kinstreet Ltd v. Balmargo Corp Ltd see Guinle v. Kirreh
Kinstreet Ltd v. Balmargo Corp Ltd (Discovery) 95 K 4271, Ch D . . . .   *Digested*, 99/**322**
Kirby v. Harrogate School Board [1896] 1 Ch. 437, CA.   *Applied*, 84/2955:
 Considered, 93/427: *Not applied*, 99/4363
Kirby v. Telegraph Group Plc [1999] E.M.L.R. 303, CA.   *Digested*, 99/**370**
Kirin Amgen Inc's European Patent (No.148605) (Relief Pending Appeal); *sub nom* Kirin-
 Amgen Inc v. Transkaryotic Therapies Inc (No.4) (2001) 24(12) I.P.D. 24080,
 Pat Ct
Kirin-Amgen Inc v. Roche Diagnostics GmbH (No.1) see Kirin-Amgen Inc's European
 Patents (Nos.148605 and 411678) (No.1)
Kirin-Amgen Inc v. Transkaryotic Therapies Inc (No.1) see Kirin-Amgen Inc's European
 Patents (Nos.148605 and 411678) (No.1)
Kirin-Amgen Inc v. Transkaryotic Therapies Inc (No.2) see Kirin-Amgen Inc's European
 Patents (Nos.148605 and 411678) (No.2)
Kirin-Amgen Inc v. Transkaryotic Therapies Inc (No.3) see Kirin-Amgen Inc's European
 Patent (No.148605) (Extra-territorial Injunction)
Kirin-Amgen Inc v. Transkaryotic Therapies Inc (No.4) see Kirin Amgen Inc's European
 Patent (No.148605) (Relief Pending Appeal)
Kirin-Amgen Inc's European Patent (No.148605) (Extra-territorial Injunction); *sub nom*
 Kirin-Amgen Inc v. Transkaryotic Therapies Inc (No.3) (2001) 24(10) I.P.D.
 24068, Pat Ct
Kirin-Amgen Inc's European Patents (Nos.148605 and 411678) (No.1); *sub nom* Kirin-
 Amgen Inc v. Transkaryotic Therapies Inc (No.1); Kirin-Amgen Inc v. Roche
 Diagnostics GmbH (No.1) (2001) 24(8) I.P.D. 24050, Pat Ct . . . .   *Subsequent proceed-
ings*, 01/575

Kirin-Amgen Inc's European Patents (Nos.148605 and 411678) (No.2); *sub nom* Kirin-Amgen Inc *v.* Transkaryotic Therapies Inc (No.2) (2001) 24(8) I.P.D. 24051; (2001) 98(24) L.S.G. 45; *Times*, June 1, 2001, Pat Ct .... *Digested*, 01/**575**

Kirin-Amgen Inc's European Patents (Nos.148605, 209539, 205564 and 411678) (Stay of Proceedings) (1998) 21 (4) I.P.D. 21036, Pat Ct

KIRIN-AMGEN/Erythropoietin II (T636/97) [2000] E.P.O.R.135, EPO (Technical Bd App)
                                                      Digested, 00/**3599**

Kirkaldy & Sons Ltd *v.* Walker [1999] 1 All E.R. (Comm.) 334; [1999] C.L.C. 722; [1999] Lloyd's Rep. I.R. 410, QBD (Comm Ct) .... *Digested*, 99/**3408**

Kirkbi AG's Trade Mark Applications [1999] R.P.C. 733, TMR .... *Digested*, 99/**3582**

Kirkham *v.* Anderton see Kirkham *v.* Chief Constable of Greater Manchester

Kirkham *v.* Chief Constable of Greater Manchester; *sub nom* Kirkham *v.* Anderton [1990] 2 Q.B. 283; [1990] 2 W.L.R. 987; [1990] 3 All E.R. 246; (1990) 140 N.L.J. 209; (1990) 134 S.J. 758; *Independent*, February 10, 1989, CA; affirming [1989] 3 All E.R. 882; (1990) 87(13) L.S.G. 47, QBD .... *Digested*, 90/**3277**:
               Applied, 93/2943: *Considered*, 98/3977: *Followed*, 97/3817

Kirklees MBC *v.* Elliot's Bricks Ltd (1999) 14 P.A.D. 348, Planning Inspector

Kirklees MBC *v.* Farrell [2000] I.C.R.1335, EAT .... *Digested*, 01/**2278**

Kirklees MBC *v.* Field (1998) 162 J.P. 88; [1998] Env. L.R. 337; (1998) 30 H.L.R. 869; (1998) 10 Admin. L.R. 49; (1998) 162 J.P.N. 48; [1997] E.G.C.S. 151; (1997) 94(45) L.S.G. 28; (1997) 141 S.J.L.B. 246; [1997] N.P.C. 152; *Times*, November 26, 1997, QBD... *Digested*, 97/**2374**:
               Distinguished, 99/2209: *Overruled*, 00/2304

Kirklees MBC *v.* Ramfield Plc (1998) 13 P.A.D. 182, Planning Inspector

Kirklees MBC *v.* Wood (1998) 13 P.A.D. 27, Planning Inspector

Kirkness (Inspector of Taxes) *v.* John Hudson & Co Ltd; *sub nom* John Hudson & Co Ltd *v.* Kirkness (Inspector of Taxes) [1955] A.C. 696; [1955] 2 W.L.R. 1135; [1955] 2 All E.R. 345; 48 R. & I.T. 352; 36 T.C. 28; (1955) 34 A.T.C. 142; [1955] T.R. 145; 99 S.J. 368, HL; affirming [1954] 1 W.L.R. 40; [1954] 1 All E.R. 29; 47 R. & I.T. 12; (1953) 32 A.T.C. 435; [1953] T.R. 409; 98 S.J. 10, CA; affirming [1953] 1 W.L.R. 749; [1953] 2 All E.R. 64; 46 R. & I.T. 401; (1953) 32 A.T.C. 190; [1953] T.R. 159; 97 S.J. 403, Ch D .... *Digested*, 55/**1257**:
         Considered, 57/280, 58/1567, 59/1549, 61/8522, 62/2916, 94/349, 95/525, 99/4669

Kirkpatrick *v.* Todd (Unreported, April 13, 2000), CC (Basingstoke) [*Ex rel.* Shoosmiths Solicitors, Quantum House, Basing View, Basingstoke, Hants] .... *Digested*, 00/**1604**

Kirsammer-Hack *v.* Sidal (C189/91) [1993] E.C.R. I-6185; [1994] I.R.L.R.185, ECJ ... *Digested*, 94/**4815**:
                                                   Applied, 98/2130

Kirschel *v.* Fladgate Fielder [2001] N.P.C. 4, Ch D

Kirton Healthcare Group Ltd *v.* Customs and Excise Commissioners [2001] S.T.I. 879, V&DTr

Kish Glass Co Ltd *v.* Commission of the European Communities (C241/00 P); *sub nom* Kish Glass Co Ltd *v.* Commission of the European Communities (T65/96) [2000] E.C.R. II-1885; [2000] 5 C.M.L.R. 229, CFI (4th Chamber).......... *Digested*, 00/**715**

Kish Glass Co Ltd *v.* Commission of the European Communities (T65/96) see Kish Glass Co Ltd *v.* Commission of the European Communities (C241/00 P)

KITABAYASHI/Spray head (T900/90) [2000] E.P.O.R. 500, EPO (Technical Bd App) . *Digested*, 01/**3943**

Kitchen *v.* HSBC Bank Plc [2000] 1 All E.R. (Comm) 787; [2000] Lloyd's Rep. Bank. 173, CA. .... *Digested*, 00/**2603**

Kitchen *v.* Royal Air Force Association [1958] 1 W.L.R. 563; [1958] 2 All E.R. 241; [1955-95] P.N.L.R. 18; 102 S.J. 363, CA .... *Digested*, 58/**3230**:
       Applied, 65/2280, 67/3978, 83/252, 98/4023: *Approved*, 71/6818:
         Considered, 67/4286, 68/3719, 85/160, 94/1491, 94/2905, 99/1421

Kitchen Design & Advice Ltd *v.* Lea Valley Water Co [1989] 2 Lloyd's Rep. 221; *Times*, March 14, 1989, QBD. .... *Digested*, 90/**2687**:
                                                   Applied, 00/621

Kitchin Ex p. Young, Re (1881) L.R. 17 Ch. D. 668, CA .... *Applied*, 00/**5438**

KL *v.* United Kingdom [2000] 2 F.C.R. 274, Eur Comm HR .... *Digested*, 00/**3169**

KLA (An Infant) (Adoption: Freeing Order), Re; *sub nom* South and East Belfast Health and Social Services Trust *v.* RA [2000] N.I. 234, Fam Div (NI) .... *Digested*, 00/**5533**

Klass *v.* Germany (A/28) (1979-80) 2 E.H.R.R. 214, ECHR .... *Digested*, 80/**1388**:
               Applied, 97/2787: *Considered*, 98/3104, 00/3248

Klattner *v.* Greece (C389/95) [1998] S.T.C. 90; [1997] E.C.R. I-2719; [1997] 3 C.M.L.R.1301, ECJ (5th Chamber) .... *Digested*, 98/**4664**

Klavdianos *v.* Greece (38841/97) (2001) 29 E.H.R.R. CD199, ECHR

Kleinwort Benson Ltd v. Barbrak Ltd (The Myrto); Kleinwort Benson Ltd v. Choithram & Sons (London); Kleinwort Benson Ltd v. Chemical Importation and Distribution State Enterprises; Kleinwort Benson Ltd v. Shell Markets [1987] A.C. 597; [1987] 2 W.L.R. 1053; [1987] 2 All E.R. 289; [1987] 2 Lloyd's Rep. 1; [1987] 1 F.T.L.R. 43; (1987) 84 L.S.G. 1651; (1987) 137 N.L.J. 388; (1987) 131 S.J. 594, HL; reversing (Unreported, December 13, 1985), CA; reversing [1985] 2 Lloyd's Rep. 567, QBD (Adm Ct) . . . . *Digested*, 87/**3125**: *Applied*, 87/3124, 88/2960, 89/3039, 93/3317, 93/3357, 94/4050, 95/4248, 98/632, 99/579, 01/4946: *Considered*, 88/2961, 93/3311, 94/3825, 96/879, 00/594: *Followed*, 96/881, 97/714, 98/561, 98/633, 99/531
Kleinwort Benson Ltd v. Birmingham City Council see Kleinwort Benson Ltd v. Lincoln City Council
Kleinwort Benson Ltd v. Birmingham City Council [1997] Q.B. 380; [1996] 3 W.L.R. 1139; [1996] 4 All E.R. 733; [1996] C.L.C. 1791; *Times*, May 20, 1996, CA . . . . . *Digested*, 96/**425**: *Subsequent proceedings*, 98/2297
Kleinwort Benson Ltd v. Chemical Importation and Distribution State Enterprises see Kleinwort Benson Ltd v. Barbrak Ltd (The Myrto)
Kleinwort Benson Ltd v. Choithram & Sons (London) see Kleinwort Benson Ltd v. Barbrak Ltd (The Myrto)
Kleinwort Benson Ltd v. Glasgow City Council (No.2) [1999] 1 A.C. 153; [1997] 3 W.L.R. 923; [1997] 4 All E.R. 641; [1998] Lloyd's Rep. Bank. 10; [1997] C.L.C. 1609; [1998] I.L.Pr. 350; (1997) 9 Admin. L.R. 721; (1997) 94(44) L.S.G. 36; (1997) 147 N.L.J. 1617; (1997) 141 S.J.L.B. 237; *Times*, October 31, 1997, HL; reversing [1996] Q.B. 678; [1996] 2 W.L.R. 655; [1996] 2 All E.R. 257; [1996] 5 Bank. L.R. 116; [1996] C.L.C. 759; [1996] I.L.Pr. 218; *Times*, February 1, 1996, CA . . . . *Digested*, 97/**904**: *Cited*, 96/6686: *Considered*, 99/427, 00/739, 00/767: *Followed*, 98/747
Kleinwort Benson Ltd v. Kensington and Chelsea RLBC see Kleinwort Benson Ltd v. Lincoln City Council
Kleinwort Benson Ltd v. Lincoln City Council; Kleinwort Benson Ltd v. Birmingham City Council; Kleinwort Benson Ltd v. Southwark LBC; Kleinwort Benson Ltd v. Kensington and Chelsea RLBC [1999] 2 A.C. 349; [1998] 3 W.L.R. 1095; [1998] 4 All E.R. 513; [1998] Lloyd's Rep. Bank. 387; [1999] C.L.C. 332; (1999) 1 L.G.L.R. 148; (1999) 11 Admin. L.R. 130; [1998] R.V.R. 315; (1998) 148 N.L.J. 1674; (1998) 142 S.J.L.B. 279; [1998] N.P.C. 145; *Times*, October 30, 1998; *Independent*, November 4, 1998, HL . . . . *Digested*, 98/**2297**: *Applied*, 99/2218: *Considered*, 99/532: *Previous proceedings*, 96/425
Kleinwort Benson Ltd v. Sandwell BC see Westdeutsche Landesbank Girozentrale v. Islington LBC
Kleinwort Benson Ltd v. Shell Markets see Kleinwort Benson Ltd v. Barbrak Ltd (The Myrto)
Kleinwort Benson Ltd v. Southwark LBC see Kleinwort Benson Ltd v. Lincoln City Council
Kler Knitwear Ltd v. Lombard General Insurance Co Ltd [2000] Lloyd's Rep. I.R. 47, QBD . . . . *Digested*, 00/**3534**
Kling v. Keston Properties Ltd (1985) 49 P. & C.R. 212; (1984) 81 L.S.G. 1683, Ch D . . *Digested*, 85/**3607**: *Applied*, 01/4858
Klinische Versuche (Clinical Trials) II (X ZR 68/94) [1998] R.P.C. 423, BGH (Ger)
KLM Royal Dutch Airlines v. Morris see Morris v. KLM Royal Dutch Airlines
KLM Royal Dutch Airlines NV v. Flughafen Frankfurt/Main AG (IV/34.801) [1998] 4 C.M.L.R. 779, CEC
KLW v. Winnipeg Child and Family Services 9 B.H.R.C. 370, Sup Ct (Can) . . . . *Digested*, 01/**3488**
Knapdale (Nominees) Ltd v. Donald 2001 S.L.T. 617; 2000 S.C.L.R. 1013; 2000 GW.D. 19-730; *Times*, August 22, 2000, OH . . . . *Digested*, 00/**5850**
Knapp v. Ecclesiastical Insurance Group Plc [1998] Lloyd's Rep. I.R. 390; [1998] P.N.L.R. 172; *Times*, November 17, 1997, CA. . . . . *Digested*, 97/**645**: *Applied*, 01/4526: *Cited*, 99/3365: *Considered*, 00/2621
Knauf UK GmbH v. British Gypsum Ltd (No.1) [2001] EWCA Civ 1570; [2001] 2 All E.R. (Comm) 960; (2001) 145 S.J.L.B. 259; *Times*, November 15, 2001; *Independent*, November 7, 2001, CA; reversing [2001] 2 All E.R. (Comm) 332; [2001] C.L.C. 1141, QBD (Comm Ct) . . . . *Digested*, 01/**828**
Knibb v. National Coal Board [1987] Q.B. 906; [1986] 3 W.L.R. 895; [1986] 3 All E.R. 644; (1986) 52 P. & C.R. 354; [1986] 2 E.G.L.R. 11; (1986) 280 E.G. 92; [1986] R.V.R. 123; (1986) 83 L.S.G. 3340; (1986) 130 S.J. 840, CA; affirming in part (1985) 49 P. & C.R. 426; [1985] 1 E.G.L.R. 182; (1985) 273 E.G. 307; [1984] R.V.R. 220; [1985] J.P.L. 263, Lands Tr . . . . *Digested*, 87/**2429**: *Considered*, 01/4660: *Distinguished*, 94/623
Knight (practising as Dibb & Clegg, Barnsley), Re see Manlon Trading Ltd (Directors: Disqualification), Re
Knight v. Attorney General [1979] I.C.R. 194; 123 S.J. 32, EAT . . . . *Digested*, 79/**943**: *Applied*, 99/2075: *Not followed*, 79/945
Knight v. Communication Workers Union (Unreported, August 1, 2000), Certification Officer [*Ex rel.* Certification Office for Trade Unions and Employers Associations, Brandon House, 180 Brandon High Street, London] . . . . *Digested*, 01/**2330**

Knight v. Frost [1999] B.C.C. 819; [1999] 1 B.C.L.C 364, Ch D . . . .   *Digested*, 99/**628**
Knight v. Hooper (Unreported, October 14, 1993), CC (Reading) [*Ex rel*. Amanda
    Buckley-Clarke, Barrister.]   *Digested*, 93/**1584**:
    Considered, 00/1723
Knight v.West Kent HA [1998] Lloyd's Rep. Med. 18; (1998) 40 B.M.L.R. 61, CA . . . . .   *Digested*, 98/**3965**
Knightley v. Johns [1982] 1 W.L.R. 349; [1982] 1 All E.R. 851; [1982] R.T.R. 182; 126
    S.J. 101, CA. . . . .   *Digested*, 82/**2126**:
    Considered, 92/3216, 93/5668: *Distinguished*, 92/3354: *Followed*, 98/3932
Knighton Estates Ltd v. Gallic Management Co Ltd (1999) 78 P. & C.R. 52; [1998]
    E.G.C.S. 14, CA . . . .   *Digested*, 99/**3694**
Knights v. Seymour Pierce Ellis Ltd (formerly Ellis & Partners Ltd); *sub nom* Taylor
    Sinclair (Capital) Ltd (In Liquidation), Re [2001] 2 B.C.L.C. 176, Ch D
    (Companies Ct)
Knights of St Columbanus v. Commissioner of Valuation for Northern Ireland; *sub nom*
    Order of the Knights of St Columbanus v. Commissioner of Valuation for
    Northern Ireland [1998] R.V.R. 224, LandsTr (NI) . . . .   *Digested*, 98/**5306**
Knise v. Johnson see Kruse v. Johnson
Knott v. Blackburn [1944] K.B. 77, KBD . . . .   *Applied*, 72/770,
    00/1014: *Considered*, 54/3426, 62/3097
Knott v. Bolton; *sub nom* Knutt v. Bolton 45 Con. L.R. 127; (1995) 11 Const. L.J. 375;
    [1995] E.G.C.S. 59; *Independent*, May 8, 1995 (C.S.), CA . . . .   *Digested*, 96/**1211**:
    Overruled, 01/4539
Knott v. Haden Maintenance Ltd (Unreported, June 16, 1998), QBD [*Ex rel*. Martin
    Seaward, Barrister, 4 Brick Court, MiddleTemple, London] . . . .   *Digested*, 98/**1521**
Knott v. Secretary of State for the Environment (1998) 75 P. & C.R. 65; [1997] J.P.L.
    713; [1996] E.G.C.S. 175, QBD. . . . .   *Digested*, 97/**4094**
Knowles v. Coutts & Co [1998] B.P.I.R. 96, Ch D . . . .   *Digested*, 98/**3350**
Knowles v. Liverpool City Council [1993] 1 W.L.R. 1428; [1993] 4 All E.R. 321; [1994]
    1 Lloyd's Rep. 11; [1994] I.C.R. 243; [1993] I.R.L.R. 588; 91 L.G.R. 629; [1994]
    P.I.Q.R. P8; (1993) 143 N.L.J. 1479; *Times*, October 15, 1993; *Independent*,
    November 15, 1993 (C.S.); *Guardian*, October 19, 1993; *Lloyd's List*, November 5,
    1993, HL; affirming [1993] I.C.R. 21; [1993] I.R.L.R. 6; 90 L.G.R. 594; [1992]
    P.I.Q.R. P425; (1993) 157 L.G. Rev. 424; (1992) 136 S.J.L.B. 220; *Times*, July 2,
    1992, CA . . . .   *Digested*, 93/**2016**:
    Considered, 98/2832
Knowles v. Secretary of State for the Environment, Transport and the Regions [1998]
    J.P.L. 593; [1997] E.G.C.S. 141, QBD . . . .   *Digested*, 98/**4244**
Knowsley MBC v. Williams see R. (on the application of Knowsley MBC) v. Knowsley
    Magistrates Court
Knox v. Gye (1871-72) L.R. 5 H.L. 656, HL . . . .   *Considered*, 55/2138,
    99/458, 00/513
Knox v. Till [2000] Lloyd's Rep. P.N. 49; [2000] P.N.L.R. 67, CA (NZ) . . . .   *Digested*, 00/**4260**
KNS Industrial Services (Birmingham) Ltd v. Sindall Ltd (2001) 3 T.C.L.R. 10; 75 Con.
    L.R. 71; (2001) 17 Const. L.J. 170, QBD (T&CC) . . . .   *Digested*, 01/**858**
Knutt v. Bolton see Knott v. Bolton
Kocak (t/a Mediterranean Fish Bar) v. Customs and Excise Commissioners (Costs)
    [2001] S.T.I. 1394, V&DTr
Kocak (t/a Mediterranean Fish Bar) v. Customs and Excise Commissioners (No.1)
    [2000] S.T.I. 743, V&DTr
Kocak (t/a Mediterranean Fish Bar) v. Customs and Excise Commissioners (No.2)
    [2000] S.T.I. 1485, V&DTr
Kodak AG v. Jumbo Markt AG [2001] E.N.P.R. 11, BG (Swi)
KODAK Trade Mark (No.2) [1990] F.S.R. 49, Ch D . . . .   *Digested*, 90/**4528**:
    Considered, 98/3531
Koeppler Will Trusts, Re; *sub nom* Barclays Bank Trust Co Ltd v. Slack [1986] Ch. 423;
    [1985] 3 W.L.R. 765; [1985] 2 All E.R. 869; (1985) 135 N.L.J. 531; (1985) 129
    S.J. 670, CA; reversing [1984] Ch. 243; [1984] 2 W.L.R. 973; [1984] 2 All
    E.R. 111; (1984) 81 L.S.G. 1843; (1984) 128 S.J. 398, Ch D . . . .   *Digested*, 85/**266**:
    Considered, 98/309
Kohll v. Union des Caisses de Maladie (C158/96) see Decker v. Caisse de Maladie des
    Employes Prives (C120/95)
Kohll v. Union des Caisses de Maladie (C158/96) [1998] E.C.R. I-1931; [1998] 2
    C.M.L.R. 928, ECJ . . . .   *Joined proceedings*,
    98/4517
Kok Hoong v. Leong Cheong Kweng Mines [1964] A.C. 993; [1964] 2 W.L.R. 150;
    [1964] 1 All E.R. 300, PC (FMS) . . . .   *Digested*, 64/**1367**:
    Applied, 01/2433: *Considered*, 98/244
Kokkinakis v. Greece (A/260-A) (1994) 17 E.H.R.R. 397; *Times*, June 11, 1993;
    Independent, June 16, 1993; *Guardian*, June 14, 1993, ECHR . . . .   *Digested*, 94/**2419**:
    Applied, 01/3481: *Followed*, 97/2787, 98/3097, 01/3479
KOMAG/Conflicting divisional claim (T587/98) [2001] E.P.O.R. 19, EPO (Technical Bd
    App). . . . .   *Digested*, 01/**3945**
KONE ELEVATOR/Elevator fire door (T230/98) [2000] E.P.O.R. 123, EPO (Technical Bd
    App). . . . .   *Digested*, 00/**3608**

Koniarska *v.* United Kingdom (Decision on Admissibility) (Unreported, October 12, 2000), ECHR. . . . . *Applied*, 00/3245
Konica Corp's European Patent Application (No.390391) (2000) 23(9) I.P.D. 23074, EPO (Technical Bd App)
Konig *v.* Germany (No.1) (A/27) (1979-80) 2 E.H.R.R. 170, ECHR . . . . *Digested*, 80/**1382**:
Applied, 98/3131: *Considered*, 97/2791
Koninklijke Philips Electronics NV's European Patent Application (T1194/97) see PHILIPS/ Record carrier (T1194/97)
Koninklijke Philips Electronics NV's European Patent Application (T206/98) (2000) 23(9) I.P.D. 23072, EPO (Technical Bd App)
Koninklijke Scholten Honig NV *v.* Council of the European Communities (C143/77) see GR Amylum NV *v.* Council of the European Communities (C116/77)
Koninklijke Scholten-Honig NV *v.* Hoofdproduktschap voor Akkerbouwprodukten (C125/77) see Royal Scholten-Honig (Holdings) Ltd *v.* Intervention Board for Agricultural Produce (C103/77)
Koninklijke Vereeniging ter Bevordering van der Belangen des Boekhandels (KVB) *v.* Free Record Shop BV (C39/96) [1997] E.C.R. I-2303; [1997] 5 C.M.L.R. 521; [1997] C.E.C. 1098, ECJ (5th Chamber). . . . . *Digested*, 98/**708**
Konle *v.* Austria (C302/97) [1999] E.C.R. I-3099; [2000] 2 C.M.L.R. 963, ECJ. . . . . . . *Digested*, 00/**2383**
Konsumentombudsmannen (KO) *v.* De Agostini (Svenska) Forlag AB (C34/95); *sub nom* Konsumentombudsmannen (KO) *v.* TV Shop i Sverige AB (C34/95) [1997] All E.R. (E.C.) 687; [1997] E.C.R. I-3843; [1998] 1 C.M.L.R. 32; [1998] E.T.M.R. 44; [1998] E.M.L.R. 43; [1997-98] Info. T.L.R. 264, ECJ [1997] E.C.R. I-3843; [1997] C.E.C. 1053, AGO . . . . *Digested*, 98/**3855**
Konsumentombudsmannen (KO) *v.* Gourmet International Products AB (C405/98) [2001] All E.R. (EC) 308; [2001] E.C.R. I-1795; [2001] 2 C.M.L.R. 31; [2001] C.E.C. 98, ECJ (6th Chamber) . . . . *Digested*, 01/**2486**
Konsumentombudsmannen (KO) *v.* TV Shop i Sverige AB (C34/95) see Konsumentombudsmannen (KO) *v.* De Agostini (Svenska) Forlag AB (C34/95)
Kooltrade Ltd *v.* XTS Ltd [2001] E.C.D.R. 11; [2001] F.S.R. 13; (2000) 23(11) I.P.D. 23088, Pat Ct . . . . *Digested*, 01/**3966**
Koonjul *v.* Thameslink Healthcare Services [2000] P.I.Q.R. P123; *Times*, May 19, 2000, CA . . . . *Digested*, 00/**2983**:
Applied, 00/2970: *Followed*, 01/3305
Kopp *v.* Switzerland (1999) 27 E.H.R.R. 91; 4 B.H.R.C. 277; [1998] H.R.C.D. 356, ECHR . . . . *Digested*, 98/**3106**
Koppel *v.* Guinness Mahon & Co Ltd see Ward *v.* Guinness Mahon & Co Ltd
Korda *v.* ITF Ltd (t/a International Tennis Federation), *Independent*, April 21, 1999, CA; reversing *Times*, February 4, 1999; *Independent*, February 8, 1999 (C.S.), Ch D . *Digested*, 99/**3830**
Kording *v.* Senator fur Finanzen (C100/95) [1997] E.C.R. I-5289; [1998] 1 C.M.L.R. 395; [1997] I.R.L.R. 710, ECJ (6th Chamber) . . . . *Digested*, 98/**2178**
Korf *v.* Health Professions Council of South Africa (2000) 55 B.M.L.R. 244, Provincial Div (SA)
Korn- Og Forderstofkompagniet A/S *v.* Landbrugsministeriet, EF-Direktoratet see Jensen *v.* Landbrugsministeriet, EF-Direktoratet (C132/95)
Kotia *v.* Dewhirst (Unreported, October 6, 1999), QBD [*Ex rel.* Jonathan Godfrey, Barrister, St Paul's Chambers, 23 Park Square South, Leeds] . . . . *Digested*, 00/**407**
Kotrie *v.* Globe Equities Ltd see Globe Equities Ltd *v.* Globe Legal Services Ltd
Kova Establishment *v.* Sasco Investments Ltd [1998] 2 B.C.L.C. 83; *Times*, January 20, 1998, Ch D . . . . *Digested*, 98/**2519**
Kowlessur *v.* Suffolk HA see R. *v.* Suffolk HA Ex p. Kowlessur
KPMG *v.* Customs and Excise Commissioners [1997] V. & D.R. 192, V&DTr . . . . *Digested*, 98/**4913**
KPMG Peat Marwick McLintock *v.* Customs and Excise Commissioners [1993] V.A.T.T.R. 118, VAT Tr (Manchester) . . . . *Digested*, 94/**4580**:
Not followed, 98/4913
KR (A Child) (Abduction: Forcible Removal by Parents), Re; *sub nom* KR (A Minor) (Abduction: Forcible Removal), Re [1999] 4 All E.R. 954; [1999] 2 F.L.R. 542; [1999] 2 F.C.R. 337; [1999] Fam. Law 545; *Times*, June 16, 1999, Fam Div . . . . *Digested*, 99/**2323**
KR (A Minor) (Abduction: Forcible Removal), Re see KR (A Child) (Abduction: Forcible Removal by Parents), Re
Krafft *v.* Camden LBC (2001) 3 L.G.L.R. 37; *Daily Telegraph*, November 21, 2000, CA . . *Digested*, 01/**684**
Kraft Jacobs Suchard Ltd's Trade Mark Application [2001] E.T.M.R. 54, TMR . . . . *Digested*, 01/**4062**
Krajina *v.* Tass Agency [1949] 2 All E.R. 274; [1949] W.N. 309; 93 S.J. 539, CA . . . . . *Digested*, 47-51/**7897**:
Applied, 98/2233: *Considered*, 77/346
Kramer *v.* South Bedfordshire Community Health Care Trust (No.1) [1995] I.C.R. 1066; (1996) 30 B.M.L.R. 34; *Times*, October 16, 1995, Ch D . . . . *Digested*, 95/**3312**:
Disapproved, 01/2892: *Not followed*, 01/2928
Kranidiotes *v.* Paschali [2001] EWCA Civ 357; [2001] C.P. Rep. 81, CA . . . . *Digested*, 01/**556**
Krasner *v.* Dennison; *sub nom* Lesser *v.* Lawrence; Dennison *v.* Krasner; Lawrence *v.* Lesser [2001] Ch. 76; [2000] 3 W.L.R. 720; [2000] 3 All E.R. 234; [2000] B.P.I.R. 410; [2000] O.P.L.R. 299; [2000] Pens. L.R. 213; (2000) 97(19) L.S.G. 42; (2000) 150 N.L.J. 543; (2000) 144 S.J.L.B. 205; *Times*, April 18, 2000, CA; affirming . . . . *Digested*, 00/**3444**
Krasniqi *v.* Chief Adjudication Officer [1999] C.O.D. 154, CA

Krcmar *v.* Czech Republic (35376/97) (2001) 31 E.H.R.R. 41, ECHR . . . . *Digested*, 01/**3531**
Kredietbank Antwerp *v.* Midland Bank Plc see Karaganda Ltd *v.* Midland Bank Plc
Kreglinger *v.* New Patagonia Meat & Cold Storage Co Ltd see G&C Kreglinger *v.* New
    Patagonia Meat & Cold Storage Co Ltd
Kreglinger *v.* S Samuel & Rosenfeld see Porter *v.* Freudenberg
Kreil *v.* Germany (C285/98) [2000] E.C.R. I-69; *Times*, February 22, 2000, ECJ . . . . . *Digested*, 00/**268**
Kremzow *v.* Austria (A/268-B) (1994) 17 E.H.R.R. 322, ECHR . . . . *Digested*, 94/**2408**:
                                                                             Distinguished, 98/3123
Krenge *v.* Krenge [1999] 1 F.L.R. 969; [1999] Fam. Law 304, Fam Div . . . . *Digested*, 99/**2402**
Krippendorf *v.* General Medical Council [2001] 1 W.L.R. 1054; [2001] Lloyd's Rep.
    Med. 9; (2001) 59 B.M.L.R. 81; (2001) 145 S.J.L.B. 5; *Times*, November 29,
    2000, PC (UK) . . . . *Digested*, 01/**2927**
Krohn GmbH *v.* Varna Shipyard (No.1) [1998] I.L.Pr. 607, Royal Ct (Jer)
Krohn GmbH *v.* Varna Shipyard (No.2) [1998] I.L.Pr. 614, Royal Ct (Jer)
Krombach *v.* Bamberski (C7/98) see Bamberski *v.* Krombach (C7/98)
Kroon *v.* Netherlands (A/297-C) [1995] 2 F.C.R. 28; (1995) 19 E.H.R.R. 263, ECHR. . . *Applied*, 01/2541
Kruger *v.* Kreiskrankenhaus Ebersberg (C281/97) [1999] E.C.R. I-5127; [2001] 1
    C.M.L.R. 41; [1999] I.R.L.R. 808, ECJ (6th Chamber) . . . . *Digested*, 00/**2204**
Kruger GmbH & Co KG *v.* Hauptzollamt Hamburg-Jonas (C334/95) [1997] E.C.R. I-
    4517; [1998] 1 C.M.L.R. 520, ECJ
Kruger Tissue (Industrial) Ltd (formerly Industrial Cleaning Papers Ltd) *v.* Frank Galliers
    Ltd 57 Con. L.R. 1; (1998) 14 Const. L.J. 437, QBD (OR) . . . . *Digested*, 98/**804**
Kruidvat BVBA *v.* Commission of the European Communities (C70/97 P) [1998]
    E.C.R. I-7183; [1999] 4 C.M.L.R. 68, ECJ . . . . *Digested*, 99/**2244**
Kruse *v.* Johnson; *sub nom* Knise *v.* Johnson [1898] 2 Q.B. 91, QBD . . . . *Applied*, 59/325,
    63/3376, 64/2662, 64/3601, 67/1675.a, 68/1633, 78/2206, 78/2602, 79/2010,
    79/2356, 97/1: *Considered*, 93/2208, 93/3891, 94/2504, 94/2513, 96/5688,
    99/3161: *Followed*, 83/255, 94/4395, 95/2157, 96/4740
Kruslin *v.* France (A176-B) (1990) 12 E.H.R.R. 547; *Times*, May 3, 1990, ECHR . . . . *Digested*, 90/**2558**:
                                                                       Applied, 98/3106, 00/3252
Krzysztofowicz (Deceased), Re see Stoker *v.* Rose
Kuddus *v.* Chief Constable of Leicestershire [2001] UKHL 29; [2001] 2 W.L.R. 1789;
    [2001] 3 All E.R. 193; (2001) 3 L.G.L.R. 45; (2001) 98(28) L.S.G. 43; (2001)
    151 N.L.J. 936; (2001) 145 S.J.L.B. 166; *Times*, June 13, 2001; *Independent*,
    June 12, 2001; *Daily Telegraph*, June 12, 2001, HL; reversing (2000) 2 L.G.L.R.
    822; *Times*, March 16, 2000; *Independent*, February 17, 2000, CA . . . . *Digested*, 01/**1512**
Kudla *v.* Poland (30210/96) 10 B.H.R.C. 269, ECHR . . . . *Digested*, 01/**3543**
Kudmany (t/a Kasbah) *v.* Customs and Excise Commissioners [2001] S.T.I. 1167, V&DTr
Kudos Glass Ltd (In Liquidation), Re; *sub nom* Rout *v.* Lewis [2001] 1 B.C.L.C. 390;
    [2001] B.P.I.R. 517; (2001) 98(3) L.S.G. 43; *Times*, November 30, 2000, Ch D
    (Companies Ct) . . . . *Digested*, 01/**3788**
Kuijer *v.* Council of the European Union (T188/98) [2000] E.C.R. II-1959; [2000] 2
    C.M.L.R. 400; *Times*, April 14, 2000, CFI (4th Chamber) . . . . *Digested*, 00/**2392**
Kumar, Re see Germany *v.* Kumar
Kumar *v.* AGF Insurance Ltd [1999] 1 W.L.R. 1747; [1998] 4 All E.R. 788; [1999]
    Lloyd's Rep. I.R. 147; [1999] P.N.L.R. 269, QBD (Comm Ct) . . . . *Digested*, 99/**3420**
Kumar *v.* Kumar QBENF 96/1479/C, CA . . . . *Digested*, 98/**1576**
Kumchyk *v.* Derby CC [1978] I.C.R. 1116, EAT . . . . *Digested*, 79/**865**:
                        Applied, 98/2122: *Approved*, 99/2037: *Considered*, 81/940, 91/1647,
                                                           92/1963
Kundry SA's Application: Opposition by the President and Fellows of Harvard College
    [1998] E.T.M.R. 178, TMR
Kuopila *v.* Finland (27752/95) (2001) 33 E.H.R.R. 25, ECHR
Kupka-Floridi *v.* Economic and Social Committee (C244/92) [1993] E.C.R. I-2041,
    ECJ . . . . *Followed*, 00/2363
Kurs *v.* Glennon (Unreported, August 5, 1998), CC (Birkenhead) [*Ex rel.* Michael W
    Halsall Solicitors, 2 The Parks, Newton-le-Willows] . . . . *Digested*, 98/**615**
Kurt *v.* Turkey (1999) 27 E.H.R.R. 373; 5 B.H.R.C. 1; [1998] H.R.C.D. 576, ECHR . . . . . . *Digested*, 99/**3115**:
                                                         Applied, 99/3117: *Distinguished*, 01/3569
Kuruma *v.* Queen, The; *sub nom* Kuruma, Son of Kaniu *v.* Queen, The [1955] A.C. 197;
    [1955] 2 W.L.R. 223; [1955] 1 All E.R. 236; (1955) 119 J.P. 157; [1955] Crim.
    L.R. 339; 99 S.J. 73, PC (EA) . . . . *Digested*, 55/**588**:
                    Applied, 63/684, 66/8447, 77/517, 78/492, 80/2630, 85/2986, 01/3299:
                          Considered, 65/780, 99/338: *Distinguished*, 70/438
Kuruma, Son of Kaniu *v.* Queen, The see Kuruma *v.* Queen, The
Kurz *v.* Stella Musical Veranstaltungs GmbH [1992] Ch. 196; [1991] 3 W.L.R. 1046;
    [1992] 1 All E.R. 630; [1992] I.L.Pr. 261; *Times*, October 4, 1991, Ch D . . . . *Digested*, 92/**482**:
                                                Followed, 94/482, 98/766
Kushoom Koly Ltd *v.* Customs and Excise Commissioners [1998] V. & D.R. 363, V&DTr   *Digested*, 00/**5335**
Kuttapan *v.* Croydon LBC see Kuttappan *v.* Croydon LBC (Strike Out Order)
Kuttappan *v.* Croydon LBC (Strike Out Order); *sub nom* Kuttapan *v.* Croydon LBC
    [1999] I.R.L.R. 349, EAT . . . . *Digested*, 99/**2059**:
                                                         Distinguished, 99/2029

Kuwait Airways Corp v. Iraq Airways Co (No.6) see Kuwait Airways Corp v. Iraqi
    Airways Co (No.6)
Kuwait Airways Corp v. Iraqi Airways (No.5) see Kuwait Airways Corp v. Iraqi Airways
    Co (No.6)
Kuwait Airways Corp v. Iraqi Airways Co (No.1) [1995] 1 W.L.R. 1147; [1995] 3 All E.R.
    694; [1995] 2 Lloyd's Rep. 317; [1996] I.L.Pr. 339; (1995) 92(28) L.S.G. 28;
    (1995) 139 S.J.L.B. 176; *Times*, July 25, 1995; *Independent*, August 15, 1995,
    HL; affirming in part [1995] 1 Lloyd's Rep. 25; [1994] 1 Lloyd's Rep. 276; [1994]
    I.L.Pr. 427; (1993) 90(45) L.S.G. 39; *Times*, October 27, 1993, CA; reversing
    Financial Times, July 17, 1992, QBD. . . . .   *Digested*, 95/**2944**:
                                                                                  Cited, 01/88
Kuwait Airways Corp v. Iraqi Airways Co (No.2) (Interest on Costs) [1994] 1 W.L.R.
    985; [1995] 1 All E.R. 790; [1994] 1 Lloyd's Rep. 284; (1994) 91(8) L.S.G. 38;
    (1994) 138 S.J.L.B. 39; *Times*, February 19, 1994, CA . . . .   *Overruled*, 98/1432
Kuwait Airways Corp v. Iraqi Airways Co (No.4) (Application for Re-Opening of Trial)
    1991 Folio No.69, QBD (Comm Ct) . . . .   *Digested*, 98/**628**
Kuwait Airways Corp v. Iraqi Airways Co (No.5) [1999] C.L.C. 31; *Times*, May 12, 1998,
    QBD (Comm Ct) . . . .   *Digested*, 99/**723**:
                                               Subsequent proceedings, 00/5107
Kuwait Airways Corp v. Iraqi Airways Co (No.6); *sub nom* Kuwait Airways Corp v. Iraq
    Airways Co (No.6); Kuwait Airways Corp v. Iraqi Airways (No.5); TNS, HL;
    affirming [2001] 3 W.L.R. 1117; [2001] 1 All E.R. (Comm) 557; [2001] 1 Lloyd's
    Rep. 161; [2001] C.L.C. 262; (2000) 97(48) L.S.G. 37; (2001) 145 S.J.L.B. 5;
    Times, November 21, 2000; *Daily Telegraph*, November 21, 2000, CA; reversing
    in part [2000] 2 All E.R. (Comm) 360; (2000) 97(23) L.S.G. 44; *Times*, May 31,
    2000, QBD (Comm Ct) . . . .   *Digested*, 00/**5107**:
                                          Previous proceedings, 98/3552, 99/723
Kuwait Airways Corp v. Iraqi Airways Co (No.8) (Petition for Variation of Order) [2001]
    1 W.L.R. 429; [2001] 1 Lloyd's Rep. 485; (2001) 98(11) L.S.G. 44; (2001) 145
    S.J.L.B. 84; *Times*, February 14, 2001; *Daily Telegraph*, February 20, 2001, HL . . .   *Digested*, 01/**88**
Kuwait Airways Corp v. Iraqi Airways Corp (No.9) (Statement of Claim) A3/2001/
    1218, CA; affirming *Independent*, July 9, 2001 (C.S), QBD (Comm Ct)
Kuwait Airways Corp v. Kuwait Insurance Co (No.3) [2000] 1 All E.R. (Comm) 972;
    [2001] C.P. Rep. 60; [2000] Lloyd's Rep. I.R. 678, QBD (Comm Ct) . . . .   *Digested*, 00/**3523**:
                                                    Applied, 01/4936
Kuwait Airways Corp v. Kuwait Insurance Co SAK (No.1) [1999] 1 All E.R. (Comm.)
    481; [1999] 1 Lloyd's Rep. 803; [1999] C.L.C. 934, HL; affirming in part [1997]
    2 Lloyd's Rep. 687, CA; affirming in part [1996] 1 Lloyd's Rep. 664, QBD
    (Comm Ct) . . . .   *Digested*, 99/**3364**:
                               Applied, 00/**3561**: *Considered*, 01/3837
Kuwait Airways Corp v. Kuwait Insurance Co SAK (No.2) [2000] 1 All E.R. (Comm)
    182; [2000] 1 Lloyd's Rep. 252; [2000] C.L.C. 498; [2000] Lloyd's Rep. I.R.
    439, QBD (Comm Ct) . . . .   *Digested*, 00/**3514**
Kuwait Oil Tanker Co SAK v. Al-Bader (No.3) [2000] 2 All E.R. (Comm) 271; (2000)
    97(23) L.S.G. 44; *Times*, May 30, 2000; *Independent*, June 26, 2000 (C.S), CA;
    affirming *Independent*, January 11, 1999 (C.S), QBD (Comm Ct) . . . .   *Digested*, 00/**5106**
Kuwait Oil Tanker Co SAK v. Qabazard; *sub nom* Kuwait Oil Tanker Co SAK v. UBS AG;
    2001 0814 A3, CA; reversing in part [2001] I.L.Pr. 46, QBD (Comm Ct) . . . . . .   *Digested*, 01/**820**
Kuwait Oil Tanker Co SAK v. UBS AG see Kuwait Oil Tanker Co SAK v. Qabazard
Kuwait Petroleum (GB) Ltd v. Customs and Excise Commissioners see Littlewoods
    Organisation Plc v. Customs and Excise Commissioners
Kuwait Petroleum (GB) Ltd v. Customs and Excise Commissioners [2001] S.T.C. 62;
    [2001] B.T.C. 5516; [2001] B.V.C. 556; [2001] S.T.I. 12, Ch D; affirming [2000]
    B.V.C. 2300; [2000] S.T.I. 1055, V&DTr . . . .   *Digested*, 01/**5554**:
                                               Subsequent proceedings, 01/5556
Kuwait Petroleum (GB) Ltd v. Customs and Excise Commissioners (C48/97) [1999] All
    E.R. (EC) 450; [1999] S.T.C. 488; [1999] E.C.R. I-2323; [1999] 2 C.M.L.R.
    651; [1999] C.E.C. 201; [1999] B.T.C. 5203; [1999] B.V.C. 250; *Times*, May 14,
    1999, ECJ . . . .   *Digested*, 99/**4967**
Kvaerner John Brown Ltd v. Midland Bank Plc [1998] C.L.C. 446, QBD . . . .   *Digested*, 98/**2518**
Kvaerner Plc v. Staatssecretaris van Financien (C191/99) [2001] 3 W.L.R. 1663;
    [2001] S.T.C. 1007; [2001] E.C.R. I-4447; [2001] 3 C.M.L.R. 2; [2001] C.E.C.
    157; [2001] B.T.C. 8018, ECJ . . . .   *Digested*, 01/**3816**
Kwan Kong Co Ltd v. Town Planning Board (1996) 6 H.K.L.R. 237, CA (HK) . . . . *Distinguished*, 98/3128
Kwei Tek Chao (t/a Zung Fu Co) v. British Traders & Shippers Ltd (No.1); *sub nom* Chao
    v. British Traders & Shippers Ltd (No.1) [1954] 2 Q.B. 459; [1954] 2 W.L.R.
    365; [1954] 1 All E.R. 779; [1954] 1 Lloyd's Rep. 16; 98 S.J. 163, QBD . . . .   *Digested*, 54/**2993**:
                         Applied, 91/1868: *Followed*, 67/3527: *Referred to*, 00/5963
Kwiatkowski v. Townend see Winn v. Townend
Kwik Save Group Plc v. Secretary of State for the Environment, Transport and the
    Regions see Chesterfield Properties Plc v. Secretary of State for the
    Environment, Transport and the Regions
Kwik Save Stores Ltd v. Greaves see Crees v. Royal London Mutual Insurance Society
    Ltd

Kwik Save Stores Ltd v. Greaves [1997] I.C.R. 629; [1997] I.R.L.R. 268, EAT . . . . *Digested*, 97/**2236**:
       Considered, 98/5825: *Followed*, 98/2168: *Subsequent proceedings*, 98/2172
Kwik Save Stores Ltd v. Swain [1997] I.C.R. 49, EAT . . . . *Digested*, 97/**2221**:
                         Considered, 99/2048
Kwik-Fit (GB) Ltd v. Customs and Excise Commissioners [1998] S.T.C. 159; 1998 S.C.
 139; 1999 S.L.T. 301; [1998] B.T.C. 5042; [1998] B.V.C. 48; 1997 G.W.D. 38-
 1977, Ex Div . . . . *Digested*, 98/**6217**
Kyrris (No.1), Re [1998] B.P.I.R. 103, Ch D . . . . *Digested*, 98/**3262**
Kyrris (No.2), Re; *sub nom* Oldham v. Kyrris [1998] B.P.I.R. 111, Ch D (Companies Ct) . . *Digested*, 98/**3261**
Kyzuna Investments Ltd v. Ocean Marine Mutual Insurance Association (Europe)
 [2000] 1 All E.R. (Comm) 557; [2000] 1 Lloyd's Rep. 505; [2000] C.L.C. 925;
 [2000] Lloyd's Rep. I.R. 513; (2000) 97(12) L.S.G. 44; (2000) 144 S.J.L.B. 142;
 Times, March 31, 2000, QBD (Comm Ct) . . . . *Digested*, 00/**3543**

L, Re see R. v. Bournewood Community and Mental Health NHS Trust Ex p. L
L, Re [1994] E.L.R. 16, CA . . . . *Applied*, 98/1971
L (A Bankrupt), Re see Landau (A Bankrupt), Re
L (A Child) (CICA: Quantum: 2000), Re [2001] 3 Q.R. 8, CICA (Birmingham) [*Ex rel*. Peter
 Brooks, Barrister 9 Park Place, Cardiff] . . . . *Digested*, 01/**1554**
L (A Child) (Contact: Domestic Violence), Re; V (A Child) (Contact: Domestic Violence), Re;
 M (A Child) (Contact: Domestic Violence), Re; H (Children) (Contact: Domestic
 Violence), Re [2001] Fam. 260; [2001] 2 W.L.R. 339; [2000] 4 All E.R. 609; [2000]
 2 F.L.R. 334; [2000] 2 F.C.R. 404; [2000] Fam. Law 603; (2000) 164 J.P.N. 918;
 (2000) 144 S.J.L.B. 222; *Times*, June 21, 2000; *Independent*, June 22, 2000,
 CA . . . . *Digested*, 00/**2475**:
                         Applied, 01/2564
L (A Child) v. Anderson [2000] 5 Q.R. 8, CC (Ashford) [*Ex rel*. Richard Menzies,
 Barrister, 8 Stone Buildings, Lincoln's Inn, London] . . . . *Digested*, 00/**1673**
L (A Child) v. Bacon (Unreported, May 3, 2000), CC (Doncaster) [*Ex rel*. Frank Allen
 Pennington Solicitors, Hill House Chambers, 6/7 Regent Terrace, South Parade,
 Doncaster] . . . . *Digested*, 00/**1625**
L (A Child) v. Berkshire HA [2000] 4 Q.R. 4, QBD [*Ex rel*. Harris & Cartwright
 Solicitors, Windsor Crown House, 7 Windsor Road, Slough, Berkshire] . . . . *Digested*, 00/**1502**
L (A Child) v. Lift & Shift Skip Hire Ltd [2001] 6 Q.R. 23, CC (Portsmouth) [*Ex rel*.
 Dyer Burdett & Co, Solicitors, 64 West Street, Havant] . . . . *Digested*, 01/**1806**
L (A Child) v. Reading BC [2001] EWCA Civ 346; [2001] 1 W.L.R. 1575; [2001] 2
 F.L.R. 50; [2001] 1 F.C.R. 673; [2001] P.I.Q.R. P29; [2001] Fam. Law 421;
 (2001) 98(18) L.S.G. 44; (2001) 145 S.J.L.B. 92, CA. . . . . *Digested*, 01/**4481**
L (A Child) v. United Kingdom (Disclosure of Expert Evidence) [2000] 2 F.L.R. 322;
 [2000] 2 F.C.R. 145; [2000] Fam. Law 708, ECHR. . . . . *Digested*, 00/**3167**
L (A Minor), Re see L (Medical Treatment: Gillick Competence), Re
L (A Minor) (Adoption: Disclosure of Information), Re see D v. Registrar General
L (A Minor) (Interim Care Order: Power of Court), Re [1996] 2 F.L.R. 742; [1996] 2 F.C.R.
 706; [1997] Fam. Law 85; (1996) 160 J.P. Rep. 937, CA . . . . *Digested*, 95/**3388**:
                         Referred to, 99/2357
L (A Minor) (Police Investigation: Privilege), Re; *sub nom* L (Minors) (Disclosure of
 Medical Reports), Re; L (Minors) (Police Investigation: Privilege), Re [1997]
 A.C. 16; [1996] 2 W.L.R. 395; [1996] 2 All E.R. 78; [1996] 1 F.L.R. 731; [1996] 2
 F.C.R. 145; (1996) 32 B.M.L.R. 160; [1996] Fam. Law 400; (1996) 160 L.G.
 Rev. 417; (1996) 93(15) L.S.G. 30; (1996) 146 N.L.J. 441; (1996) 140 S.J.L.B.
 116; *Times*, March 22, 1996, HL; affirming [1995] 1 F.L.R. 999; [1996] 1 F.C.R.
 419; [1995] Fam. Law 474; (1995) 159 J.P.N. 624; *Times*, April 25, 1995;
 Independent, March 29, 1995, CA . . . . *Digested*, 96/**502**:
                Applied, 97/456: *Distinguished*, 00/2465
L (A Minor) (Section 37 Direction), Re [1999] 1 F.L.R. 984; [1999] 3 F.C.R. 642; [1999]
 Fam. Law 307; (2000) 164 J.P.N. 546; (2000) 164 J.P.N. 781; *Times*, February 11,
 1999, CA . . . . *Digested*, 99/**2397**
L (A Minor) v. Hereford and Worcester CC; *sub nom* L v. Worcestershire CC [2000] Ed.
 C.R. 492; [2000] E.L.R. 674; *Independent*, May 15, 2000 (C.S.), CA; affirming
 [2000] E.L.R. 375; [2000] C.O.D. 117, QBD . . . . *Digested*, 00/**1948**
L (Abduction: European Convention: Access), Re [1999] 2 F.L.R. 1089; [1999] Fam. Law
 753, Fam Div . . . . *Digested*, 00/**2480**
L (Abduction: Pending Criminal Proceedings), Re [1999] 1 F.L.R. 433; [1999] 2 F.C.R. 604;
 [1999] Fam. Law 140, Fam Div . . . . *Digested*, 99/**2330**
L (Care: Confidentiality), Re [1999] 1 F.L.R. 165; [1999] Fam. Law 81, Fam Div . . . . . . *Digested*, 99/**2349**
L (Care Proceedings: Disclosure to Third Party), Re [2000] 1 F.L.R. 913; [2000] Fam. Law
 397, Fam Div. . . . . *Digested*, 00/**4170**
L (Children) (Abduction: Declaration), Re [2001] 2 F.C.R. 1, Fam Div . . . . *Digested*, 01/**2548**
L (Children) (Care Proceedings: Cohabiting Solicitors), Re [2001] 1 W.L.R. 100; [2000] 2
 F.L.R. 887; [2000] 3 F.C.R. 71; [2000] Fam. Law 810; (2000) 97(40) L.S.G. 42;
 (2000) 144 S.J.L.B. 238; *Times*, July 27, 2000, Fam Div . . . . *Digested*, 00/**4020**
L (CICB: Quantum: 1999), Re (Unreported, June 8, 1999), CICB (Bath) [*Ex rel*. Vershal
 Relan, Barrister, 3 Paper Buildings, Lorne Park Road, Bournemouth] . . . . *Digested*, 00/**1527**

L (CICB: Quantum: 2000), Re (Unreported, January 27, 2000), CICB [*Ex rel.* Hough
  Halton & Soal, Solicitors, 32 Abbey Street, Carlisle] . . . . *Digested*, 00/**1496**
L (Medical Treatment: Gillick Competence), Re; *sub nom* L (A Minor), Re [1998] 2 F.L.R.
  810; [1999] 2 F.C.R. 524; (2000) 51 B.M.L.R. 137; [1998] Fam. Law 591, Fam
  Div . . . . *Digested*, 99/**2681**
L (Minors) (Care Proceedings: Appeal), Re see L (Minors) (Sexual Abuse: Standard of
  Proof), Re
L (Minors) (Care Proceedings: Contact), Re see L *v.* Bromley LBC
L (Minors) (Disclosure of Medical Reports), Re see L (A Minor) (Police Investigation:
  Privilege), Re
L (Minors) (Police Investigation: Privilege), Re see L (A Minor) (Police Investigation:
  Privilege), Re
L (Minors) (Sexual Abuse: Disclosure), Re; *sub nom* V and W (Minors), Re; V (Minors)
  (Sexual Abuse: Disclosure), Re [1999] 1 W.L.R. 299; [1999] 1 F.L.R. 267;
  [1999] 1 F.C.R. 308; (1999) 1 L.G.L.R. 316; [1999] Fam. Law 14; (1998) 95(45)
  L.S.G. 37; (1998) 142 S.J.L.B. 270; *Times*, October 9, 1998, CA; reversing
  [1998] 1 F.C.R. 258; *Times*, October 9, 1997, Fam Div . . . . *Digested*, 98/**2386**:
                            Considered, 00/7: *Distinguished*, 01/5131
L (Minors) (Sexual Abuse: Standard of Proof), Re; *sub nom* L (Minors) (Care
  Proceedings: Appeal), Re [1996] 1 F.L.R. 116; [1996] 2 F.C.R. 352; [1996] Fam.
  Law 73; (1995) 159 J.P.N. 812; *Times*, July 3, 1995, CA. . . . . *Digested*, 96/**482**:
                            Doubted, 01/2562: *Followed*, 00/2482
L (Removal from Jurisdiction: Holiday), Re [2001] 1 F.L.R. 241; [2001] Fam. Law 9, Fam Div
                                      Digested, 01/**2594**
L *v.* Bromley LBC; *sub nom* L (Minors) (Care Proceedings: Contact), Re [1998] 1
  F.L.R. 709; [1998] 3 F.C.R. 339; [1998] Fam. Law 251; (1997) 161 J.P.N. 960,
  Fam Div . . . . *Digested*, 98/**2403**
L (A Patient) *v.* Chief Constable of Staffordshire [2000] P.I.Q.R. Q349; *Times*, July 25,
  2000, CA . . . . *Digested*, 00/**1489**
L *v.* Clarke [1998] E.L.R. 129, QBD . . . . *Digested*, 98/**1978**:
                                      Applied, 00/1961
L (Fraser Martin) *v.* DPP [1998] 2 Cr. App. R. 69; [1998] C.O.D. 96, QBD . . . . *Digested*, 98/**1097**
L *v.* Finland [2000] 2 F.L.R. 118; [2000] 3 F.C.R. 219; (2001) 31 E.H.R.R. 30; [2000]
  Fam. Law 536, ECHR . . . . *Digested*, 00/**3210**
L *v.* Hesley Hall Ltd [2001] UKHL 22; [2001] 2 W.L.R. 1311; [2001] 2 All E.R. 769;
  [2001] I.C.R. 665; [2001] I.R.L.R. 472; [2001] 2 F.L.R. 307; [2001] 2 F.C.R. 97;
  (2001) 3 L.G.L.R. 49; [2001] E.L.R. 422; [2001] Fam. Law 595; (2001)
  98(24) L.S.G. 45; (2001) 151 N.L.J. 728; (2001) 145 S.J.L.B. 126; [2001] N.P.C.
  89; *Times*, May 10, 2001; *Independent*, June 11, 2001 (C.S); *Daily Telegraph*,
  May 8, 2001, HL; reversing *Times*, October 13, 1999; *Independent*, November 22,
  1999 (C.S.), CA . . . . *Digested*, 01/**5359**
L *v.* Inland Revenue Commissioners [2000] S.T.C. (S.C.D.) 138; [2000] S.T.I. 582, Sp
  Comm . . . . *Digested*, 00/**5011**
L *v.* J see R. (on the application of L (A Child)) *v.* J School Governors
L *v.* Kensington and Chelsea RLBC see Lucy *v.* Kensington and Chelsea RLBC
L *v.* Kent CC [1998] E.L.R. 140, QBD . . . . *Digested*, 98/**1968**
L *v.* L (Minors) (Separate Representation) [1994] 1 F.L.R. 156; [1994] 1 F.C.R. 890;
  [1994] Fam. Law 432, CA. . . . . *Digested*, 95/**3550**:
                            Applied, 01/2598: *Considered*, 95/3431
L *v.* Salford City Council [1998] E.L.R. 28, QBD . . . . *Digested*, 98/**1974**
L *v.* Tower Hamlets LBC see S *v.* Gloucestershire CC
L *v.* Worcestershire CC see L (A Minor) *v.* Hereford and Worcester CC
L Schuler AG *v.* Wickman Machine Tool Sales Ltd; *sub nom* Wickman Machine Tool
  Sales Ltd *v.* L Schuler AG [1974] A.C. 235; [1973] 2 W.L.R. 683; [1973] 2 All
  E.R. 39; [1973] 2 Lloyd's Rep. 53; 117 S.J. 340, HL; affirming [1972] 1 W.L.R.
  840; [1972] 2 All E.R. 1173; 116 S.J. 352, CA . . . . *Digested*, 73/**396**:
          Considered, 74/2064, 75/3430, 78/2716, 85/1920, 91/2268, 94/3430,
              95/3756, 99/3670: *Distinguished*, 73/955: *Followed*, 94/5810
L&J Lewis *v.* Customs and Excise Commissioners [1996] V. & D.R. 541, V&DTr . . . . . . *Digested*, 98/**4937**
L'Office Cherifien des Phosphates Unitramp SA *v.* Yamashita-Shinnihon Steamship Co
  Ltd (The Boucraa) [1994] 1 A.C. 486; [1994] 2 W.L.R. 39; [1994] 1 All E.R. 20;
  [1994] 1 Lloyd's Rep. 251; (1994) 138 S.J.L.B. 19; *Times*, December 20, 1993;
  Independent, January 19, 1994, HL; reversing [1993] 3 W.L.R. 266; [1993] 3 All
  E.R. 686; [1993] 2 Lloyd's Rep. 149; [1993] N.P.C. 64; *Times*, April 16, 1993,
  CA . . . . *Digested*, 94/**221**:
          Applied, 95/2038, 96/3566: *Considered*, 93/1081, 94/1211, 97/82, 97/1075:
                                      Followed, 99/5471, 00/105
L'Office Universitaire de Presse (OFUP) *v.* France Abonnements SA [2000] E.C.C. 1,
  Cass (F)
L'Oreal (UK) Ltd *v.* Johnson & Johnson [2000] E.T.M.R. 691; [2000] F.S.R. 686;
  (2000) 23(6) I.P.D. 23045, Ch D . . . . *Digested*, 00/**3707**
L'Oreal NV *v.* De Nieuwe AMCK PVBA (C31/80) [1980] E.C.R. 3775; [1981] 2
  C.M.L.R. 235; [1981] F.S.R. 507, ECJ [1980] E.C.R. 3775, AGO . . . . *Digested*, 81/**1154**:
                                      Followed, 00/715, 00/2365

L'Oreals EuropeanTrade Mark Application [2000] E.T.M.R.10, KHO (Fin)
L/M International Construction Inc v. Circle Ltd Partnership 49 Con. L.R.12, CA . . . . . . *Applied,* 98/**795**
La Boulangerie Ltd v. Jacobs (Valuation Officer) [2001] R.V.R.167, LandsTr . . . . *Digested,* 01/**4832**
La Croix du Arib SA v. Kwikform (UK) Ltd; *sub nom* Lacroix Duarib SA v. Kwikform
   (UK) Ltd [1998] F.S.R. 493; (1998) 21 (3) I.P.D. 21029, Pat Ct . . . . *Digested,* 98/**3468**
LA Gear Inc v. Hi-Tec Sports Plc [1992] F.S.R. 121; *Times,* December 20, 1991, CA. . . . . *Digested,* 92/**577**:
                                     Applied, 95/860, 97/1048: *Considered,* 97/1036, 01/3861:
             Distinguished, 96/1283: *Followed,* 96/1277, 98/3508: *Referred to,* 95/858,
                                                           98/3430
La Pintada Compania Navegacion SA v. President of India (No.1) see President of India
   v. La Pintada Compania Navigacion SA (The La Pintada) (No.1)
La SocieteVoyageurs du Monde v. Debrant [1999] E.C.C. 449, C d'A (Paris)
Laara v. Kihlakunnansyyttaja (Jyvaskyla) (C124/97) [1999] E.C.R. I-6067; [2001] 2
   C.M.L.R.14; *Times,* October 20, 1999, ECJ . . . . *Digested,* 99/**2250**
Laboratoire Garnier & Cie v. Copar Ste see Societe Laboratoires Garnier et Cie SNC v.
   Societe Copar
Laboratoires de Therapeutique Moderne (LTM) v. Fonds d'Intervention et de
   Regularisation du Marche du Sucre (FIRS) (C201/96) [1997] E.C.R. I-6147,
   ECJ . . . . *Applied,* 98/**4613**
Laboratoires Pharmaceutiques Bergaderm SA v. Commission of the European
   Communities (C352/98); *sub nom* Laboratoires Pharmaceutiques Bergaderm
   SA v. Commission of the European Communities (T199/96) [2000] E.C.R. I-
   5291, ECJ [1998] E.C.R. II-2805; (2001) 62 B.M.L.R.179, CFI
Laboratoires Pharmaceutiques Bergaderm SA v. Commission of the European
   Communities (T199/96) see Laboratoires Pharmaceutiques Bergaderm SA v.
   Commission of the European Communities (C352/98)
Laboratoires Sarget SA v. Fonds d'Intervention et de Regularisation du Marche du
   Sucre (FIRS) (C270/96) [1998] E.C.R. I-1121; [1998] 2 C.M.L.R. 1285, ECJ
   (4th Chamber)
Laboratorios Menarini SA v. Takeda Chemical Industries Ltd [2001] E.T.M.R. 65, OHIM
   (2nd Bd App) . . . . *Digested,* 01/**4010**
Labour Party v. Customs and Excise Commissioners [2001] S.T.I. 806,V&DTr
Lacambre v. Smet Hallyday [1999] E.C.C. 444; [2000] E.C.D.R. 271, C d'A (Paris);
   reversing in part [1999] E.C.C. 439,Trib Gde Inst (Paris)
Lacey v. Commissioner of Police of the Metropolis [2000] Crim. L.R. 853;
   Independent, June 19, 2000, QBD
Lacey v. Silk (W) & Son; *sub nom* Lacey v. W Silk & Son [1951] 2 All E.R. 128; [1951]
   W.N. 366; 95 S.J. 516, KBD . . . . *Digested,* 47-51/**7766**:
                                                      Approved, 01/5653
Lacey v. W Silk & Son see Lacey v. Silk (W) & Son
Laceys (Wholesale) Footwear Ltd v. Bowler International Freight Ltd [1997] 2 Lloyd's
   Rep. 369; *Times,* May 12, 1997, CA . . . . *Digested,* 97/**4287**:
                                                      Applied, 98/4807
Lackey v. Wolfe (Unreported, July 30, 1998), CC (Basingstoke) [*Ex rel.* Amery-Parkes
   Solicitors, 12a London Street, Basingstoke, Hampshire]. . . . . *Digested,* 98/**348**
Lacoste (formerly Heineman) v. Multimania Production SA [2001] E.C.C. 22, Trib Gde
   Inst (Nanterre)
Lacroix Duarib SA v. Kwikform (UK) Ltd see La Croix du Arib SA v. Kwikform (UK) Ltd
Ladbroke Group Plc v. One in a Million Ltd see British Telecommunications Plc v. One in
   a Million Ltd
Ladbroke (Football) Ltd v. William Hill (Football) Ltd; *sub nom* William Hill (Football)
   Ltd v. Ladbroke (Football) Ltd [1964] 1 W.L.R. 273; [1964] 1 All E.R. 465; 108
   S.J.135, HL; affirming [1980] R.P.C. 539; 107 S.J. 34, CA; reversing *Times,* June
   27, 1962; *Guardian,* June 27, 1962, Ch D . . . . *Digested,* 64/**611**:
                      Applied, 67/657, 77/406, 83/492, 83/2772, 84/434, 84/436, 85/428,
             94/617, 97/1038: *Considered,* 88/502: *Followed,* 95/869, 99/3440, 99/3446
Ladbroke (Palace Gate) Property Services Ltd v. Customs and Excise Commissioners
   [2001] B.V.C. 2023,V&DTr
Ladbroke Racing Ltd v. Commission of the European Communities (T67/94) see
   France v. Ladbroke Racing Ltd (T67/94)
Ladd v. Marshall [1954] 1 W.L.R.1489; [1954] 3 All E.R. 745; 98 S.J. 870, CA . . . . . . *Digested,* 54/**2507**:
                        Applied, 61/6769, 66/9796, 67/3202, 68/1544, 68/1545, 69/572, 71/3489,
                        73/2097, 84/1737, 88/2128, 91/2927, 91/2928, 92/604,
                  92/3384.A, 93/1855, 95/504, 95/3922, 96/654, 96/656, 96/5321,
                  97/2869, 98/3200, 00/302, 01/632, 01/633: *Considered,* 63/1013, 67/1339,
                 81/2110, 82/2382, 83/2702, 83/3016, 84/1255, 85/1256, 86/1853, 86/2017,
                 87/2494, 89/2245, 90/1552, 91/471, 94/2623, 94/3746, 95/3442, 96/680,
                 96/2994, 96/3242, 96/5722, 97/2865, 97/4903, 98/322, 00/305, 00/306,
                 00/562, 00/3292, 01/634, 01/3621: *Distinguished,* 61/2556, 61/6677,
                 63/603, 90/3542, 92/2059, 96/756, 97/3366, 99/3546: *Followed,* 59/2147,
                 83/2860, 92/3290, 97/458: *Not applied,* 97/3000, 00/3710:
                              Referred to, 99/3153, 99/3256, 99/4014
Laddingford Enclosures Ltd v. Forsyth see Ruxley Electronics and Construction Ltd v.
   Forsyth

Ladies Hosiery & Underwear Ltd *v.* West Middlesex Assessment Committee [1932] 2 K.B. 679, CA . . . . *Explained*, 62/1677: *Followed*, 00/4600

Ladjadj *v.* Bank of Scotland see Bank of Scotland *v.* Ladjadj

Ladney and Hendry's International Application, Re; *sub nom* Ladney's Application, Re; Cinpres Ltd, Re; Tamworth Mouldings Ltd, Re [1998] R.P.C. 319; (1997) 20(12) I.P.D. 20119, CA; reversing (1997) 20(3) I.P.D. 20025, Pat Ct . . . . *Digested*, 98/**3450**

Ladney's Application, Re see Ladney and Hendry's International Application, Re

Ladsky *v.* TSB Bank Plc see TSB Bank Plc *v.* Ladsky (No.2)

Lady Anne Tennant *v.* Associated Newspapers Group Ltd [1979] F.S.R. 298, Ch D . . . . *Digested*, 79/**359**: *Applied*, 96/1287: *Considered*, 95/4230, 98/3424

Lady Elizabeth Anson (t/a Party Planners) *v.* Trump see Anson (t/a Party Planners) *v.* Trump

Lady Lisa Ltd *v.* British Bata Shoe Co Ltd (2000) 16 Const. L.J. 142, QBD (OR)

Lady Manor Ltd *v.* Fat Cat Cafe Bars (No.1) [2000] E.G.C.S. 121, CC (Central London)

Lady Manor Ltd *v.* Fat Cat Cafe Bars (No.2) [2001] 33 E.G. 88; [2001] 23 E.G.C.S. 156, CC (West London)

Lafarge Plasterboard Ltd *v.* Fritz Peters & Co KG [2000] 2 Lloyd's Rep. 689, QBD (T&CC) . . . . *Digested*, 01/**800**

Lafarge Redland Aggregates Ltd *v.* Scottish Ministers 2001 S.C. 298; 2000 S.L.T. 1361; [2001] Env. L.R. 27; [2000] 4 P.L.R. 151; [2000] N.P.C. 109; 2000 G.W.D. 34- 1322, OH . . . . *Digested*, 01/**6854**

Lafarge Redland Aggregates Ltd (formerly Redland Aggregates Ltd) *v.* Shephard Hill Civil Engineering Ltd; *sub nom* Lafarge Redlands Aggregates Ltd *v.* Shepherd Hill Civil Engineering Ltd [2000] 1 W.L.R. 1621; [2001] 1 All E.R. 34; [2000] C.L.C. 1669; [2000] B.L.R. 385; (2000) 2 T.C.L.R. 642; 71 Con. L.R. 86; (2000) 97(32) L.S.G. 37; (2000) 144 S.J.L.B. 247; *Times*, August 11, 2000; *Independent*, October 11, 2000, HL; affirming [1999] B.L.R. 252, CA . . . . *Digested*, 00/**236**

Lafarge Redlands Aggregates Ltd *v.* Shepherd Hill Civil Engineering Ltd see Lafarge Redland Aggregates Ltd (formerly Redland Aggregates Ltd) *v.* Shephard Hill Civil Engineering Ltd

Lafi Office & International Business SL *v.* Meriden Animal Health Ltd [2001] 1 All E.R. (Comm) 54; [2000] 2 Lloyd's Rep. 51; [2001] I.L.Pr. 19, QBD . . . . *Digested*, 00/**763**

Laimond Properties Ltd *v.* Al-Shakarchi (1998) 30 H.L.R. 1099; [1998] L. & T.R. 90; [1998] E.G.C.S. 21; (1998) 95(8) L.S.G. 34; [1998] N.P.C. 19; *Times*, February 23, 1998, CA; affirming (Unreported, November 27, 1996), CC (Central London) [*Ex rel.* Paul St J Letman, Barrister] . . . . *Digested*, 98/**3682**: *Applied*, 01/4199

Laine *v.* Cadwallader (2001) 33 H.L.R. 36; [2001] L. & T.R. 8; (2000) 80 P. & C.R. D44, CA

Laing Management Ltd (formerly Laing Management Contracting Ltd) *v.* Aegon Insurance Co (UK) Ltd 86 B.L.R. 70; 55 Con. L.R. 1, QBD (OR) . . . . *Digested*, 98/**820**

Lainton *v.* P&N Construction [2000] C.P. Rep. 2, CA. . . . . *Digested*, 99/**358**

Laira Properties Ltd *v.* Chiltern, Thames and Eastern Rent Assessment Committee see Queensway Housing Association Ltd *v.* Chiltern, Thames and Eastern Rent Assessment Committee

Laird *v.* AK Stoddart Ltd [2001] I.R.L.R. 591, EAT . . . . *Digested*, 01/**6471**

Laird *v.* Laird [1999] 1 F.L.R. 791; [1999] Fam. Law 217, CA. . . . . *Digested*, 99/**4376**

Laird Group Plc *v.* Inland Revenue Commissioners see Inland Revenue Commissioners *v.* Laird Group Plc

Lait (t/a Lait Dance Club) *v.* Customs and Excise Commissioners [2001] S.T.I. 809, V&DTr

Lake *v.* Lake [1955] P. 336; [1955] 3 W.L.R. 145; [1955] 2 All E.R. 538; 99 S.J. 432, CA . . . . *Digested*, 55/**773**: *Applied*, 01/686: *Considered*, 84/388: *Distinguished*, 98/3670

Lake District National Park Authority *v.* Ball (2001) 16 P.A.D. 84, Planning Inspector

Lake District National Park Authority *v.* Buildings Renaissance Trust (1999) 14 P.A.D. 645, Planning Inspector

Lake District National Park Authority *v.* JB & PA Wilson (1999) 14 P.A.D. 747, Planning Inspector

Lake District Special Planning Board *v.* Secretary of State for the Environment 236 E.G. 417; [1975] J.P.L. 220; 119 S.J. 187 . . . . *Digested*, 75/**20**: *Applied*, 79/307, 80/313, 00/1787: *Considered*, 76/2676, 86/3328, 87/3658

Laker Airways Inc *v.* FLS Aerospace Ltd [2000] 1 W.L.R. 113; [1999] 2 Lloyd's Rep. 45; [1999] C.L.C. 1124; *Times*, May 21, 1999; *Independent*, May 24, 1999 (C.S.), QBD (Comm Ct) . . . . *Digested*, 99/**228**

Lakey *v.* Merton Sutton and Wandsworth HA [1999] Lloyd's Rep. Med. 119; (1999) 48 B.M.L.R. 18; *Times*, March 11, 1999, CA . . . . *Digested*, 99/**3996**

Lakin Ltd *v.* Secretary of State for Scotland 1988 S.L.T. 780, 2 Div . . . . *Digested*, 88/**5014**: *Considered*, 97/6352: *Distinguished*, 98/6151, 99/4266: *Referred to*, 94/5934

Lala *v.* Netherlands (A/297-A) (1994) 18 E.H.R.R. 586, ECHR . . . . *Digested*, 95/**2635**: *Distinguished*, 01/1196

Lam *v.* Torbay BC see Chung Tak Lam *v.* Brennan (t/a Namesakes of Torbay)

Lam Chi-Ming v. Queen, The [1991] 2 A.C. 212; [1991] 2 W.L.R. 1082; [1991] 3 All
　　E.R. 172; (1991) 93 Cr. App. R. 358; [1991] Crim. L.R. 914; (1991) 135 S.J.L.B.
　　445; Daily Telegraph, April 18, 1991, PC (HK) . . . .　　　*Digested*, 91/**628**:
　　　　　　　　　　　　　　　　　　　　　　　　　　　　　　　　　　　　　　　Applied, 00/907

Lamb & Shirley Ltd v. Bliss (Valuation Officer) see Bliss (Valuation Officer) v. Lamb &
　　Shirley Ltd
Lamb Head Shipping Co Ltd v. Jennings (The Marel) [1994] 1 Lloyd's Rep. 624, CA;
　　affirming [1992] 1 Lloyd's Rep. 402, QBD (Comm Ct) . . . .　　　*Digested*, 95/**4534**:
　　　　　　　　　　　　　　　　　　　　　　　　　　　　　　　　　　　　　　　Applied, 00/4724

Lamba Trading Co Ltd v. Salford City Council [1999] 3 E.G.L.R. 186; [2000] R.V.R. 249,
　　Lands Tr . . . .　　　*Digested*, 00/**4428**
Lambert v. Croydon College [1999] I.C.R. 409; [1999] I.R.L.R. 346, EAT . . . .　　　*Digested*, 99/**2124**
Lambert v. Environment Agency [2000] R.V.R. 327, Lands Tr . . . .　　　*Digested*, 01/**1537**
Lambert v. France (2000) 30 E.H.R.R. 346; [1998] H.R.C.D. 806, ECHR . . . .　　　*Digested*, 01/**3586**
Lambert (t/a Lambert Commercials) v. Fry (Unreported, November 5, 1999), CC
　　(Canterbury) [Ex rel. E Edwards Son & Noice Solicitors, 9/15 York Road, Ilford,
　　Essex] . . . .　　　*Digested*, 00/**113**
Lambert (Administrators of CID Pension Fund) v. Glover (Inspector of Taxes) [2001]
　　S.T.C. (S.C.D.) 250; [2001] S.T.I. 1524, Sp Comm
Lambert (Rae) v. HTV Cymru (Wales) Ltd [1998] E.M.L.R. 629; [1998] F.S.R. 874;
　　(1998) 21 (8) I.P.D. 21086; (1998) 95 (15) L.S.G. 30; (1998) 142 S.J.L.B. 1184;
　　Times, March 17, 1998, CA . . . .　　　*Digested*, 98/**847**
Lambert v. Keymood Ltd [1999] Lloyd's Rep. I.R. 80; [1997] 2 E.G.L.R. 70; [1997] 43
　　E.G. 131; [1996] N.P.C. 58, QBD . . . .　　　*Digested*, 98/**3619**
Lambert v. West Devon BC (1998) 75 P. & C.R. 282; [1997] 1 P.L.R. 103; [1997]
　　J.P.L. 735; (1997) 94 (11) L.S.G. 35; (1997) 141 S.J.L.B. 66; Times, March 27,
　　1997, QBD . . . .　　　*Digested*, 97/**3787**
Lambeth LBC v. Archangel; sub nom Archangel v. Lambeth LBC (2001) 33 H.L.R. 44;
　　[2000] E.G.C.S. 148, CA . . . .　　　*Digested*, 01/**4845**
Lambeth LBC v. Bigden; sub nom Bigden v. Lambeth LBC (2001) 33 H.L.R. 43;
　　[2000] E.G.C.S. 147; [2000] N.P.C. 138; Independent, January 15, 2001 (C.S.),
　　CA
Lambeth LBC v. Blackburn [2001] EWCA Civ 912; (2001) 33 H.L.R. 74; (2001) 82 P.
　　& C.R. 39; (2001) 98 (26) L.S.G. 46, CA . . . .　　　*Digested*, 01/**4843**
Lambeth LBC v. D'Souza (No.1); sub nom D'Souza v. Lambeth LBC (No.1) [1999]
　　I.R.L.R. 240, CA; reversing [1997] I.R.L.R. 677, EAT . . . .　　　*Digested*, 99/**2142**
Lambeth LBC v. Henry; sub nom Henry v. Lambeth LBC (2000) 32 H.L.R. 874;
　　[2000] 1 E.G.L.R. 33; [2000] 06 E.G. 169; [1999] E.G.C.S. 142, CA . . . .　　　*Digested*, 00/**3924**
Lambeth LBC v. Howard [2001] EWCA Civ 468; (2001) 33 H.L.R. 58, CA . . . .　　　*Digested*, 01/**4200**
Lambeth LBC v. Hughes (2001) 33 H.L.R. 33, CA . . . .　　　*Digested*, 01/**4166**
Lambeth LBC v. Lexadon Ltd, Independent, July 17, 2000 (C.S.), CA
Lambeth LBC v. Rogers see Rogers v. Lambeth LBC
Lambeth LBC v. Thomas (1998) 30 H.L.R. 89; (1997) 74 P. & C.R. 189; Times, March
　　31, 1997; Independent, April 16, 1997, CA . . . .　　　*Digested*, 97/**2750**
Lambeth LBC v. Vincent [2000] 2 E.G.L.R. 73; [2000] 19 E.G. 145; (2000) 97 (11)
　　L.S.G. 38; (2000) 144 S.J.L.B. 132; Times, March 29, 2000, Ch D . . . .　　　*Digested*, 00/**4623**
Lambie v. Thanet DC [2001] Env. L.R. 21; [2001] E.H.L.R. 3; [2001] J.P.L. 376 (Note);
　　(2000) 97 (32) L.S.G. 39; [2000] N.P.C. 96, QBD . . . .　　　*Digested*, 01/**2424**
Lamdec Ltd v. Customs and Excise Commissioners [1991] V.A.T.T.R. 296, VAT Tr
　　(Manchester) . . . .　　　*Distinguished*,
　　　　　　　　　　　　　　　　　　　　　　　　　　　　　　　　　　　　　　　00/5354

Lamey v. Queen, The [1996] 1 W.L.R. 902; (1996) 140 S.J.L.B. 174; Times, May 22,
　　1996; Independent, June 17, 1996 (C.S.), PC (Jam) . . . .　　　*Digested*, 96/**1485**:
　　　　　　　　　　　　　　　　　　　　　　　　　　　　　　　　　　　　　　　Applied, 98/1054

Lampon v. Midland Registration Ltd (Unreported, May 31, 2000), CC (Bromley) [Ex
　　rel. Andrew J Tobin, Barrister, Chambers of Patrick Eccles Q.C., 2 Harcourt
　　Buildings, Temple, London] . . . .　　　*Digested*, 00/**442**
Lana v. Positive Action Training in Housing (London) Ltd [2001] I.R.L.R. 501;
　　Independent, July 16, 2001 (C.S.), EAT . . . .　　　*Digested*, 01/**2314**
Lancashire CC v. A (A Child) see Lancashire CC v. B (A Child) (Care Orders:
　　Significant Harm)
Lancashire CC v. B (A Child) (Care Orders: Significant Harm); sub nom Lancashire CC
　　v. W (A Child) (Care Orders: Significant Harm); Lancashire CC v. A (A Child); BW
　　(Care Orders), Re; B and W (Children) (Threshold Criteria), Re [2000] 2 A.C.
　　147; [2000] 2 W.L.R. 590; [2000] 2 All E.R. 97; [2000] 1 F.L.R. 583; [2000] 1
　　F.C.R. 509; [2000] B.L.G.R. 347; [2000] Fam. Law 394; (2000) 164 J.P.N.
　　426; (2000) 97 (13) L.S.G. 42; (2000) 150 N.L.J. 429; (2000) 144 S.J.L.B. 151;
　　Times, March 17, 2000; Independent, March 21, 2000, HL; affirming [2000] 2
　　W.L.R. 346; [1999] 2 F.L.R. 833; [1999] 3 F.C.R. 241; [1999] Fam. Law 686;
　　Times, September 21, 1999 ; Independent, October 6, 1999, CA . . . .　　　*Digested*, 00/**2463**
Lancashire CC v. Customs and Excise Commissioners [1996] V. & D.R. 550, V&D Tr . . .　　　*Digested*, 98/**4953**
Lancashire CC v. Mason [1998] I.C.R. 907, EAT . . . .　　　*Digested*, 98/**2123**
Lancashire CC v. W (A Child) (Care Orders: Significant Harm) see Lancashire CC v. B
　　(A Child) (Care Orders: Significant Harm)

Lancashire Fires Ltd v. SA Lyons & Co Ltd (No.2) [2000] C.P. Rep. 86; (1999) 96(30) L.S.G. 28; *Times*, July 24, 1999, CA . . . .   *Digested*, 99/**3783**
Lancashire Waste Services Ltd v. Customs and Excise Commissioners [1999] V. & D.R. 490, V&DTr . . . .   *Digested*, 00/**5041**
Lancaster v. Bird (2000) 2 T.C.L.R. 136; 73 Con. L.R. 22; *Times*, March 9, 1999, CA . . .   *Digested*, 99/**800**
Lancaster v. Birmingham City Council (1999) 99(6) Q.R. 4, CC (Birmingham) [*Ex rel.* Kevin O'Donovan, Barrister, 5 Fountain Court, Birmingham] . . . .   *Digested*, 99/**1438**
Lancaster v. Midland Bank Plc see Alexander v. Midland Bank Plc
Lancaster City Council v. Fats and Proteins (UK) Ltd (1999) 14 P.A.D. 422, Planning Inspector
Lancaster Factoring Co Ltd v. Mangone [1998] I.L.Pr. 200, US Ct
Lancome Parfums et Beaute & Cie's Community Trade Mark Application [2001] E.T.M.R. 89, OHIM (Cancellation Div) . . . .   *Digested*, 01/**4014**
Land (t/a Crown Optical Centre) v. Customs and Excise Commissioners [1998] B.V.C. 2277, V&DTr . . . .   *Digested*, 98/**4935**
Land v. Sykes [1992] 1 E.G.L.R. 1; [1992] 03 E.G. 115; [1991] E.G.C.S. 98, CA; affirming [1992] 1 E.G.L.R. 18; [1991] 16 E.G. 125 . . . .   *Digested*, 92/**110**:
   Considered, 01/4162
Land Nordrhein-Westfalen v. Uecker (C64/96); *sub nom* Uecker v. Land Nordrhein-Westfalen (C64/96); Jacquet v. Land Nordrhein-Westfalen (C65/96) [1997] E.C.R. I-3171; [1997] 3 C.M.L.R. 963; [1997] I.C.R. 1025; [1998] I.N.L.R. 300; *Times*, August 11, 1997, ECJ (3rd Chamber) . . . .   *Digested*, 97/**2219**
Landau (A Bankrupt), Re; *sub nom* Pointer v. Landau; L (A Bankrupt), Re [1998] Ch. 223; [1997] 3 W.L.R. 225; [1997] 3 All E.R. 322; [1997] 2 B.C.L.C. 515; [1997] 2 F.L.R. 660; [1997] B.P.I.R. 229; [1996] O.P.L.R. 371; [1998] Fam. Law 68; (1997) 94(4) L.S.G. 25; (1997) 141 S.J.L.B. 28; *Times*, January 1, 1997, Ch D . .   *Digested*, 97/**3018**:
   Cited, 99/3234: *Considered*, 01/4626
Landau & Cohen v. Lord Chancellor's Department [1999] 2 Costs L.R. 5, QBD. . . . . . .   *Digested*, 00/**3976**
Landboden-Agrardienste GmbH & Co KG v. Finanzamt Calau (C384/95) [1998] S.T.C. 171; [1997] E.C.R. I-7387; [1998] C.E.C. 79; [1998] B.T.C. 5052; [1998] B.V.C. 70, ECJ (5th Chamber) . . . .   *Digested*, 98/**4960**:
   Considered, 99/5015
Landbrugsministeriet-EF-Directoratet v. Steff-Houlberg Export I/S (C366/95) [1998] E.C.R. I-2661; [1999] 2 C.M.L.R. 250, ECJ (5th Chamber) . . . .   *Digested*, 99/**2246**:
   Applied, 99/2279
Landcatch Ltd v. Braer Corp see Landcatch Ltd v. International Oil Pollution Compensation Fund
Landcatch Ltd v. International Oil Pollution Compensation Fund; Landcatch Ltd v. Braer Corp [1999] 2 Lloyd's Rep. 316; 1999 S.L.T. 1208; 1999 S.C.L.R. 709; 1999 G.W.D. 20-962; *Times*, June 14, 1999, 2 Div; affirming [1998] 2 Lloyd's Rep. 552; [1998] E.C.C. 314; 1998 G.W.D. 12-614; *Times*, March 6, 1998, OH . . .   *Digested*, 99/**6445**:
   Followed, 99/6447
Lander v. Premier Pict Petroleum Ltd 1997 S.L.T. 1361; [1998] B.C.C. 248; 1997 G.W.D. 17-759, OH . . . .   *Digested*, 98/**5524**
Landhurst Leasing Plc, Re see Secretary of State for Trade and Industry v. Ball
Landhurst Leasing Plc v. Marcq [1998] I.L.Pr. 822, CA . . . .   *Digested*, 98/**522**
Landre GmbH v. International Paper Co [2001] E.T.M.R. 73, OHIM (1st Bd App) . . . . . .   *Digested*, 01/**3986**
Lane v. Esdaile; *sub nom* Esdaile v. Payne [1891] A.C. 210, HL; affirming (1889) L.R. 40 Ch. D. 520, CA. . . . .   *Applied*, 82/2530,
   83/2997, 86/91, 87/3051, 88/2894, 92/3505: *Distinguished*, 89/2893,
   90/3733: *Followed*, 60/1949, 00/360: *Not applied*, 98/381
Lane v. Holloway [1968] 1 Q.B. 379; [1967] 3 W.L.R. 1003; [1967] 3 All E.R. 129; 111 S.J. 655, CA . . . .   *Digested*, 67/**1047**:
   Considered, 87/3795, 01/6045: *Distinguished*, 76/2133
Lane v. Lucas & Avalon Surfacing (Unreported, October 9, 1997), CC (Cardiff) [*Ex rel.* Peter Brooks, Barrister, 9 Park Place, Cardiff] . . . .   *Digested*, 98/**1589**
Lane v. Shire Roofing Co (Oxford) Ltd [1995] I.R.L.R. 493; [1995] P.I.Q.R. P417; *Times*, February 22, 1995, CA . . . .   *Digested*, 95/**2502**:
   Followed, 99/2047
Lanera v. Regan (Unreported, October 17, 1997), CC (Halifax) [*Ex rel.* Aisha Jamil, Broadway House Chambers, Bradford] . . . .   *Digested*, 98/**1667**
LANG/Wallpaper remover (T957/92) [1999] E.P.O.R. 401, EPO (Technical Bd App) . . .   *Digested*, 99/**3490**
Langden-Jones v. Rossiter (Unreported, April 14, 1999), CC (Northampton) [*Ex rel.* Benjamin Williams, Barrister, Oxford Chambers, 1 Alfred Street, Oxford] . . . .   *Digested*, 99/**1591**
Lange v. Atkinson (No.1) 71 of 1998, PC (NZ); reversing 4 B.H.R.C. 573, CA (NZ) . . . . .   *Digested*, 98/**1781**
Lange v. Atkinson (No.2) 8 B.H.R.C. 500, CA (NZ)
Lange v. Georg Schunemann GmbH (C350/99) [2001] All E.R. (EC) 481; [2001] E.C.R. I-1061; [2001] I.R.L.R. 244, ECJ (5th Chamber) . . . .   *Digested*, 01/**2465**
Langevad v. Chiswick Quay Freeholds Ltd; McAully v. Chiswick Quay Freeholds Ltd (1999) 31 H.L.R. 1009; (2000) 80 P. & C.R. 26; [1999] 1 E.G.L.R. 61; [1999] 08 E.G. 173; [1998] E.G.C.S. 163; (1999) 77 P. & C.R. D39, CA . . . .   *Digested*, 99/**3685**
Langford (Valuation Officer) v. Dudley MBC [1999] R.A. 229, Lands Tr . . . .   *Digested*, 99/**4305**
Langford v. Hebran [2001] EWCA Civ 361; [2001] P.I.Q.R. Q13, CA. . . . .   *Digested*, 01/**1531**

Langley v. Dray; Langley v. MT Motor Polices at Lloyds [1998] P.I.Q.R. P314, CA;
  affirming [1997] P.I.Q.R. P508, QBD . . . .   *Digested,* 98/**3932**
Langley v. MT Motor Polices at Lloyds see Langley v. Dray
Langley v. North West Water Authority [1991] 1 W.L.R. 697; [1991] 3 All E.R. 610;
  Times, April 9, 1991; *Daily Telegraph,* April 18, 1991, CA . . . .   *Digested,* 92/**3456**:
                                                                                  Applied, 01/630
Langley Preparatory School v. Day (Unreported, August 17, 1999), CC (Norwich) [*Ex
  rel.* Rogers & Norton Solicitors, The Old Chapel, 5-7 Willow Lane, Norwich,
  Norfolk] . . . .   *Digested,* 99/**1800**
Langnese Iglo GmbH v. Commission of the European Communities (C279/95); *sub
  nom* Langnese Iglo GmbH v. Commission of the European Communities (T7/
  93); Scholler Lebensmittel GmbH & Co KG v. Commission of the European
  Communities (T9/93) [1999] All E.R. (EC) 616; [1998] E.C.R. I-5609; [1998] 5
  C.M.L.R. 933, ECJ (5th Chamber); affirming [1995] E.C.R. II-1533; [1995] 5
  C.M.L.R. 602, CFI (2nd Chamber) . . . .   *Digested,* 99/**660**
Langnese Iglo GmbH v. Commission of the European Communities (T7/93) see
  Langnese Iglo GmbH v. Commission of the European Communities (C279/95)
Langston v. Amalgamated Union of Engineering Workers (Engineering Section) and
  Chrysler (UK) see Langston v. Amalgamated Union of Engineering Workers
  (No.2)
Langston v. Amalgamated Union of Engineering Workers (No.2); *sub nom* Langston v.
  Amalgamated Union of Engineering Workers (Engineering Section) and Chrysler
  (UK) [1974] I.C.R. 510; [1974] I.R.L.R. 182; 17 K.I.R. 74; 118 S.J. 660, NIRC . . . .   *Digested,* 74/**3873**:
                                                                                  Followed, 98/2125
Langston v. Cranfield University [1998] I.R.L.R. 172, EAT . . . .   *Digested,* 98/**2238**
Langton v. Inntrepreneur Pub Co (CPC) Ltd see Inntrepreneur Pub Co (CPC) Ltd v.
  Langton
Lankesheer (Deceased), Re see Rees v. Newbery
Lansdowne Tutors Ltd v. Younger (2000) 97(4) L.S.G. 34; (2000) 79 P. & C.R. D36,
  CA . . . .   *Digested,* 00/**3894**
Lansing Linde Executive Pension Scheme, Re see Lansing Linde Ltd v. Alber
Lansing Linde Ltd v. Alber; *sub nom* Lansing Linde Pension Scheme, Re; Lansing
  Linde Executive Pension Scheme, Re; A3/00/0042-3, CA [2000] O.P.L.R. 1;
  [2000] Pens. L.R. 15, Ch D . . . .   *Digested,* 00/**4382**
Lansing Linde Ltd v. Kerr [1991] 1 W.L.R. 251; [1991] 1 All E.R. 418; [1991] I.C.R. 428;
  [1991] I.R.L.R. 80; (1990) 140 N.L.J. 1458; *Independent,* October 11, 1990, CA .   *Digested,* 91/**446**:
        Applied, 93/3799, 98/2193: *Considered,* 97/2256: *Followed,* 97/6002,
                                                          00/2116: *Referred to,* 99/2004
Lansing Linde Pension Scheme, Re see Lansing Linde Ltd v. Alber
Lapthorne v. Eurofi Ltd [2001] EWCA Civ 993; [2001] U.K.C.L.R. 996, CA . . . .   *Digested,* 01/**951**
Larbi-Odam v. Council for Education 3 B.H.R.C. 561, Const Ct (SA) . . . .   *Digested,* 98/**2124**
Larby v. Thurgood [1993] I.C.R. 66; [1993] P.I.Q.R. P218; (1992) 136 S.J.L.B. 275;
  Times, October 27, 1992, QBD . . . .   *Digested,* 93/**3293**:
        Considered, 99/1416: *Distinguished,* 96/2114, 99/333: *Followed,* 98/348
Larissis v. Greece (1999) 27 E.H.R.R. 329; 4 B.H.R.C. 370; [1998] H.R.C.D. 297,
  ECHR . . . .   *Digested,* 98/**3097**
Larke v. Nugus; *sub nom* Moss, In the Estate of [2000] W.T.L.R. 1033; (1979) 123 S.J.
  337, CA . . . .   *Digested,* 79/**2565**
Larkos v. Cyprus (2000) 30 E.H.R.R. 597; 7 B.H.R.C. 244, ECHR . . . .   *Digested,* 00/**3183**
Larksworth Investments Ltd v. Temple House Ltd (No.2) [1999] B.L.R. 297, CA . . . . . .   *Digested,* 99/**3673**
Larne Enterprise Development Co Ltd v. Commissioner of Valuation for Northern Ireland
  [1998] R.V.R. 221, Lands Tr (NI) . . . .   *Digested,* 98/**5305**
Larner v. Solihull MBC [2001] R.T.R. 32; (2001) 3 L.G.L.R. 31; [2001] B.L.G.R. 255;
  [2001] P.I.Q.R. P17; (2001) 98(8) L.S.G. 45; *Times,* February 6, 2001, CA . . . . .   *Digested,* 01/**4483**
LARSEN/Backing board (T574/99) [2001] E.P.O.R. 18, EPO (Technical Bd App) . . . . .   *Digested,* 01/**3883**
Larussa-Chigi v. CS First Boston Ltd [1998] C.L.C. 277, QBD (Comm Ct) . . . .   *Digested,* 98/**2537**
Laskey v. United Kingdom; Jaggard v. United Kingdom; Brown v. United Kingdom
  (1997) 24 E.H.R.R. 39; *Times,* February 20, 1997; *Independent,* February 25,
  1997, ECHR . . . .   *Digested,* 97/**2794**:
                                                        Cited, 00/3251: *Considered,* 01/1089
Lassman v. Secretary of State for Trade and Industry; *sub nom* Secretary of State for
  Trade and Industry v. Lassman [2000] I.C.R. 1109; [2000] I.R.L.R. 411; *Times,*
  May 5, 2000; *Independent,* May 4, 2000, CA; reversing [1999] I.C.R. 416;
  [1999] I.R.L.R. 413, EAT . . . .   *Digested,* 00/**2194**
Last Viceroy Restaurant v. Jackson (Inspector of Taxes) [2000] S.T.C. 1093; 73 T.C.
  322; [2000] S.T.I. 1651, Ch D . . . .   *Digested,* 01/**5179**
Latham v. Farmer (Unreported, May 3, 2001), CC (Canterbury) [*Ex rel.* Azeem Ali,
  Barrister, Clock Chambers, 78 Darlington Street, Wolverhampton] . . . .   *Digested,* 01/**3799**
Lathrope v. Kuoni Travel Ltd (Unreported, June 15, 1999), CC (High Wycombe) [*Ex rel.*
  Dominic Bayne, Barrister, Plowden Buildings, Temple, London] . . . .   *Digested,* 99/**1382**
Latimer v. Inland Revenue Commissioner; *sub nom* Crown Forestry Rental Trust, Re
  (2001-02) 4 I.T.E.L.R. 246, HC (NZ)
Latour Trust Co Ltd and Latour Trustees (Jersey) Ltds' Representation, Re see Rabaiotti 1989
  Settlement, Re

Latreefers Inc, Re see Stocznia Gdanska SA *v.* Latreefers Inc
Latreefers Inc (In Liquidation) *v.* Tangent Shipping Co Ltd [2000] 1 B.C.L.C. 805, QBD
   (Comm Ct) . . . . *Digested,* 00/**3479**
Lau *v.* DPP [2000] 1 F.L.R. 799; [2000] Crim. L.R. 580; [2000] Fam. Law 610; *Times,*
   March 29, 2000; *Independent,* April 10, 2000 (C.S.), QBD . . . . *Digested,* 00/**942**:
                                                Applied, 01/1050: *Considered,* 01/1048
Lauko *v.* Slovakia (26138/95) (2001) 33 E.H.R.R. 40; [1998] H.R.C.D. 838, ECHR
Launchbury *v.* Morgans; *sub nom* Morgans *v.* Launchbury [1973] A.C. 127; [1972] 2
   W.L.R. 1217; [1972] 2 All E.R. 606; [1972] 1 Lloyd's Rep. 483; [1972] R.T.R. 406;
   116 S.J. 396, HL; reversing [1971] 2 Q.B. 245; [1971] 2 W.L.R. 602; [1971] 1
   All E.R. 642; [1971] 1 Lloyd's Rep. 197; [1971] R.T.R. 97; 115 S.J. 96, CA . . . . *Digested,* 72/**2376**:
                  Considered, 74/2595, 83/2583: *Followed,* 81/1861: *Referred to,* 01/4543
Launchexcept Ltd, Re; *sub nom* Secretary of State For Trade and Industry *v.* Tillman
   [1999] B.C.C. 703; [2000] 1 B.C.L.C. 36, CA . . . . *Digested,* 99/**620**
Launder, Re see R. *v.* Secretary of State for the Home Department Ex p. Launder (No.1)
Launder *v.* Governor of Brixton Prison see R. *v.* Secretary of State for the Home
   Department Ex p. Launder (No.3)
Laurentian Management Services Ltd *v.* Customs and Excise Commissioners [2000]
   B.V.C. 2210; [2000] S.T.I. 709, V&DTr
Lauricourt *v.* Brake Bros (Unreported, August 18, 1999), CC (Wandsworth) [*Ex rel.*
   Andrew Peterson, Pupil Barrister, 9 Gough Square, London] . . . . *Digested,* 99/**2459**:
                                   Approved, 99/2472: *Referred to,* 99/2490
Laurie (t/a Peacock Montessori Nursery) *v.* Customs and Excise Commissioners [2001]
   B.V.C. 2317; [2001] S.T.I. 1231, V&DTr . . . . *Digested,* 01/**5550**
Laurier *v.* United Overseas Bank Ltd; *sub nom* Debtor (No.223 SD of 1995), Re
   [1996] B.P.I.R. 635, Ch D . . . . *Digested,* 97/**3000**:
                                                      Followed, 98/322
Lauritzen Reefers *v.* Ocean Reef Transport Ltd SA (The Bukhta Russkaya) [1997] 2
   Lloyd's Rep. 744, QBD (Comm Ct) . . . . *Digested,* 98/**4412**
Lavarack *v.* Woods of Colchester [1967] 1 Q.B. 278; [1966] 3 W.L.R. 706; [1966] 3
   All E.R. 683; 1 K.I.R. 312; 110 S.J. 770, CA . . . . *Digested,* 66/**4415**:
              Applied, 84/1014, 98/2098: *Distinguished,* 73/1140: *Followed,* 97/6006
Laverick *v.* DPP; *sub nom* Laverick *v.* Wilmot; Clarke *v.* Wilmot [1999] R.T.R. 417, QBD . .   *Digested,* 00/**5240**
Laverick *v.* Wilmot see Laverick *v.* DPP
Lavers *v.* Northern Upholstery Ltd (t/a DFS Ltd) (Unreported, July 20, 2001), CC
   (Plymouth) [*Ex rel.* Nash & Co, Solicitors, Beaumont House, Beaumont Park,
   Plymouth] . . . . *Digested,* 01/**467**
Lavery *v.* MacLeod (Inspector of Taxes) [2000] S.T.C. (S.C.D.) 118; [2000] S.T.I. 169,
   Sp Comm
Lavery *v.* Ministry of Defence [1984] N.I. 99; [1984] 7 N.I.J.B. . . . . *Digested,* 85/**2366**:
                                              Applied, 94/5067, 98/5150
Lavery's Application, Re [1994] N.I. 209, QBD (NI) . . . . *Digested,* 00/**5401**
Lavington International Ltd *v.* Bareboat Charterers of Nore Challenger and Nore
   Commander [2001] 2 All E.R. (Comm) 667; [2001] 2 Lloyd's Rep. 103; [2001]
   C.L.C. 1217, QBD (Adm Ct) . . . . *Digested,* 01/**4945**
Law Debenture Trust Corp Plc *v.* Hereward Philips (A Firm) [1999] P.N.L.R. 725, Ch D .   *Digested,* 99/**1418**
Law Debenture Trust Corp Plc *v.* Malley; *sub nom* Law Debenture Trust Group Plc *v.*
   Pensions Ombudsman [1999] O.P.L.R. 167; *Independent,* October 25, 1999
   (C.S.), Ch D . . . . *Digested,* 99/**4125**
Law Debenture Trust Corp Plc *v.* Malley (Striking Out of Appeal) [1999] O.P.L.R. 153;
   [1999] Pens. L.R. 367; *Independent,* June 21, 1999 (C.S.), Ch D . . . . *Digested,* 99/**4154**
Law Debenture Trust Corp Plc *v.* Pensions Ombudsman [1998] 1 W.L.R. 1329; [1997] 3
   All E.R. 233; [1997] O.P.L.R. 31, Ch D . . . . *Digested,* 97/**3959**
Law Debenture Trust Group Plc *v.* Pensions Ombudsman see Law Debenture Trust Corp
   Plc *v.* Malley
Law Hospital NHS Trust *v.* Lord Advocate 1996 S.C. 301; 1996 S.L.T. 848; [1996] 2
   F.L.R. 407; (1998) 39 B.M.L.R. 166; [1996] Fam. Law 670; *Times,* May 20,
   1996, IH (Ct of 5 judges) . . . . *Digested,* 97/**6070**
Law Hospital NHS Trust *v.* Rush [2001] I.R.L.R. 611; 2001 G.W.D. 21-810, Ex Div;
   affirming EAT/842/99, EAT
Law Society *v.* Gilbert; *sub nom* Solicitor (CO/2504/2000), Re *Times,* January 12,
   2001, QBD . . . . *Digested,* 01/**4264**
Law Society *v.* KPMG Peat Marwick; *sub nom* R. *v.* KPMG Peat Marwick McLintock
   [2000] 1 W.L.R. 1921; [2000] 4 All E.R. 540; [2000] Lloyd's Rep. P.N. 929;
   [2000] P.N.L.R. 831; (2000) 97(30) L.S.G. 40; (2000) 150 N.L.J. 1017; *Times,*
   July 6, 2000; *Independent,* July 5, 2000, CA; affirming [2000] 1 All E.R. 515;
   [2000] E.C.C. 456; [2000] Lloyd's Rep. P.N. 219; [2000] P.N.L.R. 364; (1999)
   96(44) L.S.G. 40; (1999) 149 N.L.J. 1698; (1999) 143 S.J.L.B. 269; *Times,*
   November 3, 1999; *Independent,* December 13, 1999 (C.S.), Ch D . . . . *Digested,* 00/**4201**
Law Society *v.* Southall [2001] EWCA Civ 2001, CA; reversing [2001] B.P.I.R. 303;
   [2001] W.T.L.R. 719; [2000] N.P.C. 145, Ch D . . . . *Digested,* 01/**3782**
Lawden *v.* Chief Constable (1999) 99(6) Q.R. 6, CC (Carlisle)
Lawes *v.* Moore [2001] 1 Q.R. 14, CC (Weston Super Mare) [*Ex rel.* Helen Gower,
   Barrister, Old Square Chambers, Hanover House, 97 Corn Street, Bristol] . . . . . *Digested,* 01/**1693**

Lawless *v.* Thomson Holidays Ltd (Unreported, August 3, 1999), CC (Weston Super
    Mare) [*Ex rel.* Nicholas Cooper, Pupil Barrister, Assize Court Chambers, 14 Small
    Street, Bristol] . . . .   *Digested,* 99/**1385**
Lawrence, Re see R. *v.* Metropolitan Police Force Disciplinary Committee Ex p.
    Lawrence
Lawrence (Stephan Jay) (A Debtor), Re (1999-2000) 2 I.T.E.L.R. 283, US Ct
Lawrence *v.* Buchler see ASRS Establishment Ltd (In Administrative Receivership and
    Liquidation), Re
Lawrence *v.* Buchler; Buchler *v.* Morphitis [1999] N.P.C. 135, Ch D
Lawrence *v.* Commissioner of Police of the Metropolis; *sub nom* R. *v.* Lawrence (Alan)
    [1972] A.C. 626; [1971] 3 W.L.R. 225; [1971] 2 All E.R. 1253; (1971) 55 Cr.
    App. R. 471; 115 S.J. 565, HL; affirming [1971] 1 Q.B. 373; [1970] 3 W.L.R. 1103;
    [1970] 3 All E.R. 933; (1971) 55 Cr. App. R. 73; 114 S.J. 864, CA (Crim Div) . . .   *Digested,* 71/**2814**:
                    Applied, 79/594, 93/994, 98/1065, 00/1012: *Considered,* 83/921, 89/896,
                                    90/1102, 90/1172, 91/983, 92/805, 94/1152, 96/1529, 99/5204
Lawrence *v.* Lesser see Krasner *v.* Dennison
Lawrence *v.* Regent Office Care Ltd [2000] I.R.L.R. 608, CA; reversing [1999] I.C.R.
    654; [1999] I.R.L.R. 148; *Times,* November 24, 1998, EAT . . . .   *Digested,* 00/**2157**
Lawrence *v.* Scott Ltd (Unreported, January 20, 1998), CC (Central London) [*Ex rel.*
    Richard Viney, Barrister, 12 King's Bench Walk, Temple, London] . . . .   *Digested,* 98/**1662**
Lawrence *v.* WW Martin (Thanet) Ltd (Unreported, August 13, 1997), CC (Canterbury)
    [*Ex rel.* Michael Batey, Barrister, Stour Chambers, Barton Mill House, Barton Mill
    Road, Canterbury] . . . .   *Digested,* 98/**1523**
Lawrence & Co (Solicitors), Re 96/6180/S2, CA (Crim Div) . . . .   *Digested,* 98/**1016**
Lawrie-Blum *v.* Land Baden-Wurttenberg (C66/85) [1986] E.C.R. 2121; [1987] 3
    C.M.L.R. 389; [1987] I.C.R. 483, ECJ . . . .   *Digested,* 87/**1569**:
                                                                Applied, 91/3958, 00/2389
Laws *v.* National Grid Co Plc see National Grid Co Plc *v.* Mayes
Laws *v.* National Grid Co Plc (Pre-Emptive Costs: Court of Appeal) see National Grid
    Co Plc *v.* Laws (Pre-Emptive Costs: Court of Appeal)
Lawson (CICB: Quantum: 1997), Re; *sub nom* Lawson (CICB: Quantum: Severe Brain
    Damage), Re; (Unreported, September 2, 1997), CICB (Durham) [*Ex rel.* Ben
    Hoare Bell Solicitors, 10 Martin Terrace, Pallion, Sunderland, SR4 6JD] . . . .   *Digested,* 98/**1486**
Lawson (CICB: Quantum: Severe Brain Damage), Re see Lawson (CICB: Quantum: 1997),
    Re
Lawson *v.* Midland Travellers Ltd [1993] 1 W.L.R. 735; [1993] 1 All E.R. 989, CA. . . . . .   *Digested,* 93/**3323**:
                                                                    Applied, 98/632
Lawson's Trustees *v.* British Linen Co (1874) 1 R. 1065 . . . .   *Applied,* 00/5930
Lawyer's Duty to Inform Clients (IX ZR 129/99), Re [2001] E.C.C. 53, BGH (Ger)
Lawyer's Electronic Diary, Re [1998] E.C.C. 255, BGH (Ger)
Lawyers Online Ltd *v.* Lawyeronline Ltd [2000] E.T.M.R. 1056 (Note), Ch D
Laycock *v.* Lagoe [1997] P.I.Q.R. P518; (1998) 40 B.M.L.R. 82, CA . . . .   *Digested,* 98/**530**:
                                                                Followed, 99/333
Layher Ltd *v.* Lowe 58 Con. L.R. 42; [2000] Lloyd's Rep. I.R. 510; (1997) 73 P. & C.R.
    D37; *Times,* January 8, 1997, CA . . . .   *Digested,* 97/**3124**:
                                Considered, 98/3374: *Followed,* 01/3801
Lazard Bros & Co *v.* Banque Industrielle de Moscou see Lazard Bros & Co *v.* Midland
    Bank Ltd
Lazard Bros & Co *v.* Banque Industrielle de Moscou (Midland Bank Ltd, Garnishees.)
    see Lazard Bros & Co *v.* Midland Bank Ltd
Lazard Bros & Co *v.* Midland Bank Ltd; *sub nom* Lazard Bros & Co *v.* Banque
    Industrielle de Moscou (Midland Bank Ltd, Garnishees.); Lazard Bros & Co *v.*
    Banque Industrielle de Moscou [1933] A.C. 289; (1932) 44 Ll. L. Rep. 159, HL;
    reversing [1932] 1 K.B. 617, CA; reversing. . . . .   *Applied,* 53/1042,
                    66/3878, 67/1279, 91/2200: *Considered,* 76/1485, 76/3220, 90/3758,
                                    98/633: *Distinguished,* 47-51/5045, 93/3321
Lazarevic *v.* Secretary of State for the Home Department see Adan (Hassan Hussein)
    v. Secretary of State for the Home Department
LCB *v.* United Kingdom (1999) 27 E.H.R.R. 212; 4 B.H.R.C. 447; [1998] H.R.C.D. 628;
    Times, June 15, 1998, ECHR . . . .   *Digested,* 98/**3101**
LCI International Telecom Corp's Application [1998] E.T.M.R. 647, OHIM (3rd Bd App)
Le Book Editions Sarl *v.* EPC Edition Presse Communication Ste [1999] E.T.M.R. 554,
    Trib Gde Inst (Paris)
Le Brasseur SA *v.* Societe Automobile des Garages Sorin [2001] E.C.C. 15, Cass (F)
Le Calvez *v.* France (25554/94) (2001) 32 E.H.R.R. 21; [1998] H.R.C.D. 740, ECHR
Le Compte *v.* Belgium (A/43); Van Leuven *v.* Belgium (A/43); De Meyere *v.* Belgium
    (A/43) [1982] E.C.C. 240; (1982) 4 E.H.R.R. 1, ECHR; reversing [1980] E.C.C.
    294, Eur Comm HR . . . .   *Applied,* 97/2811,
                                                    98/3120, 98/3156, 00/2212
Le Compte *v.* Belgium (A/58) see Albert *v.* Belgium (A/58)
Le Crespelle (C323/93) see Societe Civile Agricole Crespelle *v.* Cooperative d'Elevage du
    Departement de la Mayenne (C323/93)
Le Foe *v.* Le Foe; Woolwich Plc *v.* Le Foe [2001] EWCA Civ 1870, CA; affirming
    [2001] 2 F.L.R. 970; [2001] Fam. Law 739, Fam Div

Le Page v. Kingston and Richmond HA [1997] 8 Med. L.R. 229, QBD . . . .   *Digested*, 98/**3968**
Le Sueur & Raleigh Nominees Ltd (Matter of Representation), Re see Joseph Eagle 1989
     Settlement, Re
Lea v. British Aerospace Plc see Thomas v. Bunn
Leach, Re; *sub nom* Leach v. Commissioner for Local Administration; R. (on the
     application of Leach) v. Commissioner for Local Administration [2001] EWHC
     Admin 455; [2001] C.P. Rep. 97; [2001] 4 P.L.R. 28; *Times*, August 2, 2001,
     QBD (Admin Ct) . . . .   *Digested*, 01/**488**
Leach v. Chief Constable of Gloucestershire [1999] 1 W.L.R. 1421; [1999] 1 All E.R.
     215; (1999) 46 B.M.L.R. 77; (1998) 148 N.L.J. 1425; *Times*, September 4, 1998,
     CA . . . .   *Digested*, 98/**3947**
Leach v. Commissioner for Local Administration see Leach, Re
Leach v. Pro Delta Systems Ltd (Unreported, January 31, 2000), CC (Bury) [*Ex rel*.
     Tarran & Co, Solicitors, 5th Floor, Old Bank Chambers, 2 Old Bank Street,
     Manchester] . . . .   *Digested*, 00/**1571**
Leachinsky v. Christie see Christie v. Leachinsky
Leachman, Re [1998] C.O.D. 466, QBD
Leacock v. Ward (Unreported, April 2, 1998), CC (Central London) [*Ex rel*. David
     Levene & Co Solicitors, Ashley House, 235/239 High Road, Wood Green,
     London] . . . .   *Digested*, 98/**1593**
Leadbeater (A Minor) v. Allied Domecq Ltd (1998) 98(6) Q.R. 8; (1998) 98(3) Q.R. 8,
     CC (Halifax) . . . .   *Digested*, 98/**1751**
Leadenhall Residential 2 Ltd v. Stirling; *sub nom* Stirling v. Leadenhall Residential 2 Ltd
     [2001] EWCA Civ 1011; [2001] 3 All E.R. 645; (2001) 98(35) L.S.G. 35;
     (2001) 151 N.L.J. 1005; [2001] N.P.C. 112; *Times*, July 25, 2001, CA . . . .   *Digested*, 01/**4146**
Leading Guides International Ltd (In Liquidation), Re; *sub nom* Egon Ronay Associates
     Ltd v. Leading Guides International Ltd [1998] 1 B.C.L.C. 620, Ch D
     (Companies Ct) . . . .   *Digested*, 98/**3321**
League Against Racism and Anti Semitism v. Yahoo! Inc (USA); *sub nom* LICRA v.
     Yahoo! Inc (USA) [2001] E.B.L.R. 110, Trib Gde Inst (Paris)
Leake v. Ainsley (Unreported, November 9, 1998), CC (York) [*Ex rel*. Scott Rees & Co
     Solicitors, Centaur House, Gardiners Place, Skelmersdale, Lancashire] . . . .   *Digested*, 99/**332**
Leakey v. National Trust for Places of Historic Interest or Natural Beauty [1980] Q.B.
     485; [1980] 2 W.L.R. 65; [1980] 1 All E.R. 17; 78 L.G.R. 100; 123 S.J. 606, CA;
     affirming [1978] Q.B. 849; [1978] 2 W.L.R. 774; [1978] 3 All E.R. 234; 76
     L.G.R. 488; 122 S.J. 231, QBD . . . .   *Digested*, 80/**2006**:
                 Applied, 81/2005, 83/2739, 84/2472, 85/2499.a, 87/2752, 97/4863,
                     00/5121, 01/4482, 01/4547: *Considered*, 82/667, 83/2741, 92/3223,
                                      00/4287, 01/1544: *Followed*, 88/2034
Leamington Spa Building Society v. Verdi; Bradford & Bingley Building Society v. Verdi
     (1998) 75 P. & C.R. D16, CA
Leander v. Sweden (A/116) (1987) 9 E.H.R.R. 433; *Times*, April 25, 1987, ECHR . . . . . .   *Digested*, 87/**1919**:
                                          Applied, 98/3096: *Considered*, 00/3248
Learoyd v. Whiteley; *sub nom* Whiteley v. Learoyd; Whiteley, Re (1887) L.R. 12 App.
     Cas. 727, HL; affirming (1886) L.R. 33 Ch. D. 347, CA; affirming (1886) L.R. 32
     Ch. D. 196, Ch D . . . .   *Applied*, 01/**5531**:
                 Cited, 00/5270: *Considered*, 84/3136, 85/3605: *Referred to*, 84/3136,
                                                       85/3605

Leary v. United Kingdom (38890/97) see Cornwell v. United Kingdom (36578/97)
Lease Management Services v. Purnell Secretarial Services; *sub nom* Purnell Secretarial
     Services v. Lease Management Services [1994] C.C.L.R. 127; *Times*, April 1,
     1994, CA . . . .   *Digested*, 95/**775**:
                                                Applied, 98/852
Lease Plan Luxembourg SA v. Belgium (C390/96) [1998] S.T.C. 628; [1998] E.C.R. I-
     2553; [1998] 2 C.M.L.R. 583; [1999] C.E.C. 374; [1998] B.T.C. 5404; [1998]
     B.V.C. 412, ECJ (5th Chamber). . . . .   *Digested*, 98/**4951**
Leathertex Divisione Sintetici SpA v. Bodetex BVBA (C420/97) [1999] 2 All E.R.
     (Comm) 769; [1999] E.C.R. I-6747; [1999] C.L.C. 1983; [2000] I.L.Pr. 273;
     (1999) 18 Tr. L.R. 334; *Times*, October 26, 1999, ECJ [1998] I.L.Pr. 505, Cass
     (B) . . . .   *Digested*, 99/**735**
LEC (Liverpool) Ltd v. Glover (t/a Rainhill Forge) [2001] Lloyd's Rep. I.R. 315, CA
Leclere v. Caisse Nationale des Prestations Familiales (C43/99) [2001] E.C.R. I-4265;
     [2001] 2 C.M.L.R. 49, ECJ . . . .   *Digested*, 01/**5053**
Leco Instruments (UK) Ltd v. Land Pyrometers Ltd [1982] R.P.C. 133, CA; reversing
     [1981] F.S.R. 325, Ch D . . . .   *Digested*, 82/**453**:
                                          Distinguished, 98/3426
Ledbury Amateur Dramatic Society v. Customs and Excise Commissioners [2001] S.T.I.
     229, V&DTr
Ledernes Hovedorganisation v. Dansk Arbejdsgiverforening (C48/94) [1995] E.C.R. I-
     2745; [1996] 3 C.M.L.R. 45; [1996] C.E.C. 26; [1996] I.R.L.R. 51; *Times*,
     October 20, 1995, ECJ . . . .   *Digested*, 95/**2072**:
                                          Applied, 00/2229, 00/2231
Ledgar v. Kidd (Unreported, April 22, 1998), CC (Stoke on Trent) [*Ex rel*. Andrew J.
     McGrath, Barrister, 5 Fountain Court, Steelhouse Lane, Birmingham, B4 6DR] .   *Digested*, 98/**1603**

Ledger v. Graham [2001] 2 Q.R. 10, CC (Southampton) [*Ex rel.* Catherine Purdy, Barrister, 3 Paper Buildings, 4 St. Peter Street, Winchester, Hampshire] . . . . . . *Digested*, 01/**1623**
Ledingham v. D'Adamo [2001] 3 Q.R. 20, CC (Halifax) [*Ex rel.* Rhodes Thain & Collinson, Solicitors, 27 Harrison Road, Halifax] . . . . *Digested*, 01/**1812**
Ledwood Construction Ltd v. Kier Construction Ltd 68 Con. L.R. 96, QBD (OR) . . . . . *Digested*, 00/**230**
Lee (A Bankrupt), Re see Lee v. Lee
Lee (A Bankrupt), Re see Lee v. Lee (A Bankrupt)
Lee (Albert) (Deceased), Re; *sub nom* Musson v. Lee [2000] N.P.C. 142, Ch D
Lee v. Clark CCRTF 97/0758 CMS2, CA . . . . *Digested*, 98/**1501**
Lee v. Customs and Excise Commissioners [1998] B.V.C. 2051, V&DTr
Lee v. Customs and Excise Commissioners (Input Tax) [2000] S.T.I. 1668, V&DTr
Lee (t/a Regal Sporting Club) v. Customs and Excise Commissioners [1998] B.V.C. 2297, V&DTr . . . . *Digested*, 98/**4902**
Lee v. Herbert-Smith [2000] R.V.R. 227, Lands Tr. . . . . *Digested*, 00/**3895**
Lee v. Jewitt (Inspector of Taxes) [2000] S.T.C. (S.C.D.) 517; [2000] S.T.I. 1517, Sp Comm . . . . *Digested*, 01/**5182**
Lee v. Lee; *sub nom* Lee (A Bankrupt), Re [1999] B.C.C. 268; [1998] 2 B.C.L.C. 219; [1998] 1 F.L.R. 1018; [1998] B.P.I.R. 375; [1998] Fam. Law 312; (1998) 95(14) L.S.G. 22; [1998] N.P.C. 27; *Times*, February 24, 1998, Ch D . . . . *Digested*, 98/**3273**
Lee v. Lee (A Bankrupt); *sub nom* Lee (A Bankrupt), Re [2000] B.C.C. 500; [2000] 1 F.L.R. 92; [1999] B.P.I.R. 926; [1999] Fam. Law 808; *Times*, September 22, 1999, CA . . . . *Digested*, 99/**3260**
Lee v. Lee's Air Farming Ltd [1961] A.C. 12; [1960] 3 W.L.R. 758; [1960] 3 All E.R. 420; 104 S.J. 869, PC (NZ); reversing [1959] N.Z.L.R. 393, CA (NZ) . . . . *Digested*, 60/**3342**:
Applied, 69/3508: *Considered*, 98/2188: *Distinguished*, 97/2251
Lee v. Leeds City Council see Ratcliffe v. Sandwell MBC
Lee v. Taunton and Somerset NHS Trust [2001] 1 F.L.R. 419; [2001] Fam. Law 103, QBD . . . . *Digested*, 01/**1508**
Lee v. United Kingdom (25289/94) (2001) 33 E.H.R.R. 29; *Times*, January 30, 2001, ECHR . . . . *Joined proceedings*, 01/4744
Lee Behrens & Co Ltd, Re [1932] 2 Ch. 46, Ch D . . . . *Applied*, 66/1495, 67/515, 00/670: *Disapproved*, 85/306: *Distinguished*, 69/390: *Followed*, 61/1089, 62/358
Lee Chun-Kong v. Queen, The see Thongjai v. Queen, The
Lee Ting Sang v. Chung Chi-Keung [1990] 2 A.C. 374; [1990] 2 W.L.R. 1173; [1990] I.C.R. 409; [1990] I.R.L.R. 236; (1990) 87(13) L.S.G. 43; (1990) 134 S.J. 909, PC (HK) . . . . *Digested*, 90/**1864**:
Applied, 98/2140
Lee-Parker v. Izzet (No.1) [1971] 1 W.L.R. 1688; [1971] 3 All E.R. 1099; (1971) 22 P. & C.R. 1098; 115 S.J. 641, Ch D . . . . *Digested*, 71/**6656**:
Applied, 79/2166: *Considered*, 79/1633, 94/2797: *Followed*, 76/2851: *Referred to*, 99/3729
Leebody v. Ministry of Defence (Unreported, July 9, 2001), CC (Bristol) [*Ex rel.* Nash & Co, Solicitors, Beaumont House, Beaumont Park, Plymouth] . . . . *Digested*, 01/**4544**
Leece v. United Kingdom see McDaid v. United Kingdom
Leech v. Deputy Governor of Parkhurst Prison see R. v. Deputy Governor of Parkhurst Prison Ex p. Leech
Leeds v. Islington LBC [1998] Env. L.R. 655; [1999] E.H.L.R. 218; (1999) 31 H.L.R. 545; [1998] C.O.D. 293; [1998] E.G.C.S. 15; (1998) 95(7) L.S.G. 33, QBD . . . . *Digested*, 98/**4051**:
Applied, 98/2249: *Distinguished*, 99/2214
Leeds & Holbeck Building Society v. Alex Morison & Co (No.2) 2001 S.C.L.R. 41; [2001] P.N.L.R. 13; 2000 G.W.D. 30-1194, OH . . . . *Digested*, 01/**6822**
Leeds and Holbeck Building Society v. Arthur & Cole [2001] Lloyd's Rep. P.N. 649, QBD
Leeds City Council v. Carr; *sub nom* Carr v. Leeds City Council; Coles v. Barnsley MBC; Wells v. Barnsley MBC [2000] 1 Costs L.R. 144; [2000] Env. L.R. 522; (2000) 32 H.L.R. 753; [2000] C.O.D. 10; *Times*, November 12, 1999, QBD . . . . . *Digested*, 99/**3798**
Leeds City Council v. Harte (Unreported, December 11, 1998), CC (Leeds) [*Ex rel.* Josephine Henderson, Barrister, Arden Chambers, 27 John Street, London] . . . *Digested*, 99/**4069**
Leeds City Council v. James (Unreported, February 20, 2000), CC (Leeds) [*Ex rel.* Adam Fullwood, Barrister, 5 Cooper Street, Manchester] . . . . *Digested*, 00/**473**
Leeds City Council v. KW Linfoot Plc (2001) 16 P.A.D. 27, Planning Inspector
Leeds City Council v. Redrow Homes (Yorkshire) Ltd (2000) 15 P.A.D. 150, Planning Inspector
Leeds City Council v. Spencer [1999] E.H.L.R. 394; (1999) 1 L.G.L.R. 917; [2000] B.L.G.R. 68; (1999) 11 Admin. L.R. 773; [1999] E.G.C.S. 69; [1999] N.P.C. 55; *Times*, May 24, 1999; *Independent*, May 21, 1999, CA . . . . *Digested*, 99/**2215**
Leeds City Council v. West Yorkshire Metropolitan Police [1983] 1 A.C. 29; [1982] 2 W.L.R. 186; [1982] 1 All E.R. 274; (1982) 74 Cr. App. R. 336; 80 L.G.R. 401; [1982] Crim. L.R. 364; 126 S.J. 79, HL . . . . *Digested*, 82/**2050**:
Applied, 90/3108: *Considered*, 89/2428: *Followed*, 98/2430
Leeds MBC v. Oakapple Partnerships Ltd (2000) 15 P.A.D. 170, Planning Inspector

Leeds Permanent Building Society v. United Kingdom see National & Provincial Building
  Society v. United Kingdom
Leeman v. Mohammed [2001] EWCA Civ 198; (2001) 82 P. & C.R. 14; [2001] 5
  E.G.C.S. 168, CA . . . .   *Digested*, 01/**4866**
Lees v. Norway (2000) 97(42) L.S.G. 43; *Times*, November 1, 2000, QBD   *Digested*, 00/**2425**
Lees Import and Export (Pvt) Ltd v. Zimbabwe Banking Corp Ltd 7 B.H.R.C. 647, Sup
  Ct (Zim) . . . .   *Digested*, 00/**3225**
Leeson v. DPP; Leeson v. Haringey Justices [2000] R.T.R. 385, QBD . . . .   *Digested*, 01/**991**
Leeson v. Haringey Justices see Leeson v. DPP
Leetham v. DPP [1999] R.T.R. 29, QBD . . . .   *Digested*, 00/**940**
Leeves v. Chief Adjudication Officer [1999] E.L.R. 90, CA . . . .   *Digested*, 99/**4576**
LEFEBVRE/Sealing Complex (T77/94) [2001] E.P.O.R. 52, EPO (Technical Bd App) . .   *Digested*, 01/**3935**
Legal Aid Board v. Comptroller General of Patents, *Independent*, November 13, 2000
  (C.S), Ch D
Legal & General Assurance Society Ltd v. Pensions Ombudsman; R. v. Pensions
  Ombudsman Ex p. Legal & General Assurance Society Ltd [2000] 1 W.L.R.
  1524; [2000] 2 All E.R. 577; (1999) 96(46) L.S.G. 40; (1999) 149 N.L.J. 1733;
  (2000) 144 S.J.L.B. 8; *Times*, December 7, 1999 ; *Independent*, December 20,
  1999 (C.S.), Ch D . . . .   *Digested*, 00/**4396**
Legal & General Mortgage Services Ltd v. HPC Professional Services [1997] P.N.L.R.
  567, QBD . . . .   *Digested*, 98/**4032**
Legal Costs Negotiators Ltd, Re; *sub nom* Morris v. Hateley [1999] B.C.C. 547; [1999]
  2 B.C.L.C. 171; (1999) 96(13) L.S.G. 31; *Times*, March 10, 1999; *Independent*,
  March 1, 1999 (C.S.), CA; reversing *Times*, July 15, 1998; *Independent*, July 13,
  1998 (C.S.), Ch D . . . .   *Digested*, 99/**635**
Legal Protection of Biotechnological Inventions (C377/98), Re see Netherlands v.
  European Parliament (C377/98)
Leggatt v. National Westminster Bank Plc see National Westminster Bank Plc v.
  Leggatt
Lego v. Distributor of B***** Building Blocks (4 Ob 196/00B) [2001] E.T.M.R. 80,
  OGH (A)
Lego Systems A/S v. Lego M Lemelstrich Ltd [1983] F.S.R. 155, Ch D . . . .   *Digested*, 83/**3786**:
          Applied, 90/4320: *Considered*, 97/4884, 98/3501:
                    Referred to, 95/4732, 97/4897
Lego Systems A/S v. Tyco Industries Inc [1999] E.T.M.R. 250, It Cass (I)
Lehideux v. France (2000) 30 E.H.R.R. 665; 5 B.H.R.C. 540; [1998] H.R.C.D. 891,
  ECHR . . . .   *Digested*, 99/**3110**
Lehman Bros Inc v. Phillips see Mid East Trading Ltd, Re
Lehtinen v. Finland (39076/97) (2000) 29 E.H.R.R. CD204, ECHR
Lehtonen v. Federation Royale Belge des Societes de Basket-Ball ASBL (FRBSB)
  (C176/96) [2001] All E.R. (EC) 97; [2000] E.C.R. I-2681; [2000] 3 C.M.L.R.
  409; [2000] C.E.C. 498, ECJ (6th Chamber) . . . .   *Digested*, 00/**2388**
Leicester City Council v. Aldwinckle (1992) 24 H.L.R. 40; *Times*, April 5, 1991, CA . . . .   *Digested*, 92/**2705**:
          Applied, 94/2778, 95/3042, 01/4168: *Distinguished*, 98/3045, 99/4382
Leicester City Council v. Lewis (2001) 33 H.L.R. 37, CA . . . .   *Digested*, 01/**1248**
Leicester University v. A [1999] I.C.R. 701; [1999] I.R.L.R. 352; *Times*, March 23,
  1999, EAT . . . .   *Digested*, 99/**2061**
Leicestershire CC v. G [1994] 2 F.L.R. 329; [1995] 1 F.C.R. 205; [1994] Fam. Law
  486; (1995) 159 J.P.N. 80, Fam Div . . . .   *Digested*, 95/**3424**:
                            Distinguished, 99/2355
Leidig v. Intervention Board for Agricultural Produce see Intervention Board for
  Agricultural Produce v. Leidig
Leigh v. National Union of Railwaymen [1970] Ch. 326; [1970] 2 W.L.R. 60; [1969] 3
  All E.R. 1249; 8 K.I.R. 629; 113 S.J. 852, Ch D . . . .   *Digested*, 69/**3571**:
          Applied, 73/3370: *Considered*, 81/2812, 81/3710, 82/3282, 99/2126
Leigh v. Taylor; *sub nom* De Falbe, Re; Ward v. Taylor [1902] A.C. 157, HL; affirming
  [1901] 1 Ch. 523, CA . . . .   *Applied*, 96/**4748**,
                            01/1841: *Considered*, 86/1940
Leigh and Sillivan Ltd v. Aliakmon Shipping Co Ltd (The Aliakmon) [1986] A.C. 785;
  [1986] 2 W.L.R. 902; [1986] 2 All E.R. 145; [1986] 2 Lloyd's Rep. 1; (1986) 136
  N.L.J. 415; (1986) 130 S.J. 357, HL; affirming [1985] Q.B. 350; [1985] 2 All
  E.R. 44; [1985] 1 Lloyd's Rep. 199; (1985) 82 L.S.G. 203; (1985) 135 N.L.J.
  285; (1985) 129 S.J. 69, CA; reversing [1983] 1 Lloyd's Rep. 203, QBD (Comm
  Ct) . . . .   *Digested*, 86/**2252**:
               Applied, 87/290, 88/2752, 01/4903: *Approved*, 87/4767:
        Considered, 87/2580, 00/4688: *Distinguished*, 86/2251: *Followed*, 93/5553:
                            Referred to, 88/3408
Leigh's Will Trusts, Re; *sub nom* Handyside v. Durbridge [1970] Ch. 277; [1969] 3
  W.L.R. 649; [1969] 3 All E.R. 432; 113 S.J. 758, Ch D . . . .   *Digested*, 69/**3668**:
                              Followed, 99/4641
Leighton v. Charlambous see Leighton v. Michael
Leighton v. Michael; Leighton v. Charlambous [1995] I.C.R. 1091; [1996] I.R.L.R. 67;
  Times, October 26, 1995, EAT . . . .   *Digested*, 95/**2045**:
                    Applied, 98/2227: *Approved*, 00/2205

Leightons Ltd v. Customs and Excise Commissioners see Customs and Excise
   Commissioners v. Leightons Ltd
Leisure Great Britain Plc v. Isle of Wight CC see Leisure Great Britain Plc v. Isle of Wight
   Council
Leisure Great Britain Plc v. Isle of Wight Council; *sub nom* Leisure Great Britain Plc v.
   Isle of Wight CC (2000) 80 P. & C.R. 370; [2000] P.L.C.R. 88; [1999] N.P.C.
   80, QBD . . . . *Digested*, 00/**4500**
Leisure (GB) Plc v. Secretary of State for the Environment, Transport and the Regions
   [1998] E.G.C.S. 54, QBD
Leisure Study Group Ltd, Re [1994] 2 B.C.L.C. 65, Ch D . . . . *Digested*, 95/**2841**:
                                               Applied, 95/428: *Considered*, 98/3306
Leisure Two Partnership v. Customs and Excise Commissioners [2001] S.T.I. 255, V&DTr
Leitgens v. Austria (8803/79) see Lingens v. Austria (No.1) (8803/79)
Lemar (A Minor) v. Lloyds Chemists Plc (Unreported, October 27, 1997), CC
   (Basingstoke) [*Ex rel.* Richard Egleton, Barrister, 18 Carlton Crescent,
   Southampton] . . . . *Digested*, 98/**1696**
Lemmerbell Ltd v. Britannia LAS Direct Ltd [1999] L. & T.R. 102; [1998] 3 E.G.L.R.
   67; [1998] 48 E.G. 188; [1998] E.G.C.S. 138; [1998] N.P.C. 135, CA; reversing
   [1997] N.P.C. 80, Ch D . . . . *Digested*, 98/**3608**
Lemmerz-Werke GmbH v. High Authority (C111/63) [1965] E.C.R. 716; [1965] E.C.R.
   835; [1968] C.M.L.R. 280, ECJ. . . . . *Digested*, 69/**1384**:
                                                                 Followed, 98/2306
Leng v. Goldsmith [*Ex rel.* Jinder S Boora, Barrister, Ropewalk Chambers, 24 The
   Ropewalk, Nottingham] . . . . *Digested*, 01/**1771**
Lennon v. Birmingham City Council [2001] EWCA Civ 435; [2001] I.R.L.R. 826, CA
Lennon v. Sharpe (Unreported, July 14, 2000), CC (Bolton) [*Ex rel.* Ian Snipe & Co
   Solicitors, 30 Orchard Road, Lytham St Annes] . . . . *Digested*, 01/**458**:
                                                                 Considered, 01/521
Lennox Ex p. Lennox, Re (1885-86) L.R. 16 Q.B.D. 315, CA . . . . *Applied*, 98/3284
Leon v. York-o-Matic, Ltd [1966] 1 W.L.R. 1450; [1966] 3 All E.R. 277; 110 S.J. 685,
   Ch D . . . . *Digested*, 66/**1474**:
                                                                 Considered, 99/3352
Leonard v. Niagara Holdings Ltd (1998) 98(3) Q.R. 5, QBD. . . . . *Digested*, 98/**1492**
Leonard v. Southern Derbyshire Chamber of Commerce [2001] I.R.L.R. 19, EAT . . . . . . *Digested*, 01/**2235**:
                                                                 Applied, 01/2242
Leonard v. Strathclyde Buses Ltd 1999 S.C. 57; 1999 S.L.T. 734; [1998] I.R.L.R. 693;
   1998 G.W.D. 31-1621, 2 Div . . . . *Digested*, 99/**6045**:
                                                                 Followed, 00/6218
Leonard Cheshire Foundation v. Drake [2001] E.T.M.R. 90, Arbitration . . . . *Digested*, 01/**3867**
Leonard Ogilvy (Application to Discharge an Undertaking), Re [1999] C.O.D. 399, QBD
Leonidas v. Customs and Excise Commissioners [2000] B.V.C. 2316; [2000] S.T.I.
   1091, V&DTr . . . . *Digested*, 01/**5591**
Lep Air Services v. Rolloswin Investments see Moschi v. Lep Air Services Ltd
Lepley v. Essex CC [2001] R.V.R. 147, Lands Tr. . . . . *Digested*, 01/**4665**
Leppington v. Coal Authority [1998] E.G.C.S. 165; (1998) 95(45) L.S.G. 42, QBD
Lerose Ltd v. Hawick Jersey International Ltd [1973] C.M.L.R. 83; [1973] F.S.R. 15;
   [1974] R.P.C. 42, Ch D . . . . *Digested*, 73/**1331**:
                                                                 Applied, 00/3572
Leroy (Arlette) v. SmithKline Beecham SA [1999] E.C.C. 358, Trib Gde Inst (Nanterre)
Les Editions Vice Versa Inc v. Aubry 5 B.H.R.C. 437, Sup Ct (Can) . . . . *Digested*, 99/**3121**
Les Laboratoires de la Roche Posay SA v. Parasante SA [1999] E.C.C. 126, Cass (F)
Les Laboratoires Leo SA v. Scovazzo [1999] E.C.C. 365, Cass (F)
Les Verreries de Saint-Gobain SA v. Martinswerk GmbH [1999] I.L.Pr. 296, Cass (F). . . *Digested*, 99/**722**
Lesquende Ltd v. Planning and Environment Committee of the States of Jersey [1998]
   1 E.G.L.R. 137, PC (Jer) . . . . *Digested*, 98/**4178**
Lesser v. Lawrence (CA) see Krasner v. Dennison
Lesser v. Lawrence 412 of 1994, Ch D . . . . *Subsequent proceed-*
                                                                 ings, 00/3444
Letang v. Cooper [1965] 1 Q.B. 232; [1964] 3 W.L.R. 573; [1964] 2 All E.R. 929;
   [1964] 2 Lloyd's Rep. 339; 108 S.J. 519, CA; reversing [1964] 2 Q.B. 53; [1964]
   2 W.L.R. 642; [1964] 1 All E.R. 669; [1964] 1 Lloyd's Rep. 188; 108 S.J. 180,
   QBD. . . . . *Digested*, 64/**3499**:
                         Applied, 92/2830, 92/4436, 93/2608, 00/2130: *Considered*, 68/2253,
                                              86/3464, 97/3592, 99/3944, 01/5354
Letellier v. France (A/207) (1992) 14 E.H.R.R. 83, ECHR . . . . *Digested*, 92/**2336**:
                                                                 Applied, 98/3070
Leterme v. France [1998] H.R.C.D. 489, ECHR
Letheby & Christopher Ltd v. Bond [1988] I.C.R. 480, EAT . . . . *Digested*, 88/**1339**:
                                                                 Followed, 00/2111

LETTER K Trade Mark (I ZB 4/98) [2001] E.T.M.R. 102, BGH (Ger)

Leur-Bloem v. Inspecteur der Belastingdienst/Ondernemingen Amsterdam 2 (C28/95)
[1998] Q.B. 182; [1998] 2 W.L.R. 27; [1997] All E.R. (E.C.) 738; [1997] S.T.C.
1205; [1997] E.C.R. I-4161; [1998] 1 C.M.L.R. 157; [1997] C.E.C. 1155; [1997]
B.T.C. 504, ECJ . . . . *Digested*, 97/**1083**:
Referred to, 99/3555

Levene v. Inland Revenue Commissioners [1928] A.C. 217; [1928] All E.R. Rep. 746,
HL; affirming [1927] 2 K.B. 38, CA. . . . . *Applied*, 47-51/1573,
47-51/3010, 47-51/4850, 54/997, 82/974, 83/1157, 85/1771:
Considered, 80/852, 91/2373, 93/2095, 94/2365, 95/3207, 98/4609,
99/4564: *Explained*, 52/1019, 52/1078: *Followed*, 67/2036

Lever Bros Ltd v. Bell see Bell v. Lever Bros Ltd
Levett v. Biotrace International Plc [1999] I.C.R. 818; [1999] I.R.L.R. 375; *Times*, May
11, 1999, CA . . . . *Digested*, 99/**2121**
Levett-Scrivener v. Customs and Excise Commissioners [2000] S.T.I. 318, V&DTr
Levez v. TH Jennings (Harlow Pools) Ltd (No.2); Hicking v. Basford Group Ltd (In
Receivership) [1999] 3 C.M.L.R. 715; [2000] I.C.R. 58; [1999] I.R.L.R. 764;
Times, November 10, 1999, EAT . . . . *Digested*, 99/**2068**:
Applied, 01/1092: *Previous proceedings*, 99/2067
Levez v. TH Jennings (Harlow Pools) Ltd (C326/96) [1999] All E.R. (EC) 1; [1998]
E.C.R. I-7835; [1999] 2 C.M.L.R. 363; [1999] C.E.C. 3; [1999] I.C.R. 521;
[1999] I.R.L.R. 36; *Times*, December 10, 1998, ECJ (1st Chamber). . . . . *Digested*, 99/**2067**:
Applied, 00/2162
Levi Strauss & Co v. Costco Wholesale UK Ltd (C416/99) see Zino Davidoff SA v. A&G
Imports Ltd (C414/99)
Levi Strauss & Co v. Parkway Ltd [2000] E.T.M.R. 977, Trib Gde Inst (Paris)
Levi Strauss & Co v. Tesco Stores Ltd (C415/99) see Zino Davidoff SA v. A&G Imports
Ltd (C414/99)
Levin (Application for a Writ of Habeas Corpus), Re see R. v. Governor of Brixton Prison Ex
p. Levin
Levine v. Morris [1970] 1 W.L.R. 71; [1970] 1 All E.R. 144; [1970] 1 Lloyd's Rep. 7;
(1969) 113 S.J. 798; *Times*, October 10 1969, CA . . . . *Digested*, 70/**1867**:
Applied, 01/6817: *Distinguished*, 00/4232
Levy v. ABN AMRO Bank NV see Norglen Ltd (In Liquidation) v. Reeds Rains
Prudential Ltd
Levy v. Assicurazione Generali [1940] A.C. 791; (1940) 67 Ll. L. Rep. 174, PC (Pal). . . . *Applied*, 01/3795
Levy v. Legal Aid Board see Levy v. Legal Services Commission (formerly Legal Aid
Board)
Levy v. Legal Services Commission (formerly Legal Aid Board); *sub nom* Levy v.
Legal Aid Board [2001] 1 All E.R. 895; [2001] 1 F.L.R. 435; [2001] 1 F.C.R. 178;
[2000] B.P.I.R. 1065; [2001] Fam. Law 92; (2000) 97(46) L.S.G. 39; (2000)
150 N.L.J. 1754; *Times*, December 1, 2000; *Independent*, November 16, 2000,
CA; reversing [2000] 1 F.L.R. 922; [2000] 1 F.C.R. 642; [2000] Fam. Law 608;
(2000) 97(8) L.S.G. 35; (2000) 150 N.L.J. 196; *Times*, March 16, 2000;
Independent, March 20, 2000 (C.S.), Ch D . . . . *Digested*, 00/**3448**
Levy Estate Trust, Re (Unreported, January 17, 2000), Ch D [*Ex rel.* RD Oughton, Barrister,
Cobden House Chambers, 19 Quay Street, Manchester] . . . . *Digested*, 00/**5263**
Lewen v. Denda (C333/97) [2000] All E.R. (EC) 261; [1999] E.C.R. I-7243; [2000] 2
C.M.L.R. 38; [2000] C.E.C. 415; [2000] I.C.R. 648; [2000] I.R.L.R. 67; *Times*,
November 16, 1999, ECJ (6th Chamber) . . . . *Digested*, 99/**2065**
Lewes DC v. Brand (1999) 14 P.A.D. 159, Planning Inspector
Lewes DC v. Secretary of State for the Environment, Transport and the Regions [1998]
J.P.L. 1093; [1998] E.G.C.S. 63, QBD. . . . . *Digested*, 98/**4182**
Lewin v. Barratt Homes Ltd (2000) 164 J.P. 182; [2000] 1 E.G.L.R. 77; [2000] 03
E.G. 132; [2000] Crim. L.R. 323; (2000) 164 J.P.N. 283; [1999] E.G.C.S. 139;
(1999) 96(46) L.S.G. 41; (2000) 79 P. & C.R. D20, QBD . . . . *Digested*, 00/**4619**
Lewis v. Asda Stores Ltd [2001] 6 Q.R. 23, CC (Manchester) [*Ex rel.* Peasegoods,
Solicitors, Bank Chambers, 937-941 Rochdale Road, Manchester] . . . . *Digested*, 01/**1804**
Lewis v. Associated Newspapers Ltd see Rubber Improvement Ltd v. Daily Telegraph
Ltd
Lewis v. Attorney General of Jamaica; Taylor (Patrick) v. Attorney General of Jamaica;
McLeod (Anthony) v. Attorney General of Jamaica; Brown (Christopher) v.
Attorney General of Jamaica [2001] 2 A.C. 50; [2000] 3 W.L.R. 1785; 9
B.H.R.C. 121; (2000) 144 S.J.L.B. 257; *Times*, October 11, 2000, PC (Jam). . . . . *Digested*, 00/**3201**
Lewis v. Averay (No.1) [1972] 1 Q.B. 198; [1971] 3 W.L.R. 603; [1971] 3 All E.R. 907;
115 S.J. 755, CA . . . . *Digested*, 71/**1801**:
Distinguished, 00/2600
Lewis v. Averay (No.2) [1973] 1 W.L.R. 510; [1973] 2 All E.R. 229; 117 S.J. 188, CA . . .   *Digested*, 73/**2637**:
Applied, 83/590, 84/553: *Cited*, 00/2602: *Distinguished*, 99/2512
Lewis v. BTR Plc [2000] 1 Q.R. 7, CC (Merthyr Tydfil) [*Ex rel.* Andrew Arentsen,
Barrister, 33 Park Place, Cardiff]. . . . . *Digested*, 99/**1465**
Lewis v. Cotton [2001] W.T.L.R. 1117; (2000-01) 3 I.T.E.L.R. 447, CA (NZ)
Lewis v. Daily Telegraph Ltd see Rubber Improvement Ltd v. Daily Telegraph Ltd
Lewis v. DPP [1998] C.O.D. 98, QBD

Lewis v. Frank Love Ltd [1961] 1 W.L.R. 261; [1961] 1 All E.R. 446; 105 S.J. 155, Ch D
　　　　　　　　　　　　　　　　　　　　　　　　　　　　　　　　　　Digested, 61/**5596**:
　　　　　　　　　　　　　　　　　　　　Applied, 01/4876: *Distinguished*, 94/594
Lewis v. Harewood [1997] P.I.Q.R. P58; *Times*, March 11, 1996, CA . . . . *Digested*, 96/**879**:
　　　　　　　　　　　　Applied, 99/579: *Considered*, 97/672, 99/531: *Distinguished*, 96/881
Lewis v. Hyde [1998] 1 W.L.R. 94; [1997] B.C.C. 976; [1998] B.P.I.R. 726; *Times*,
　　October 22, 1997, PC (NZ) . . . . *Digested*, 97/**3104**
Lewis v. Inland Revenue Commissioners; *sub nom* Floor Fourteen Ltd, Re [2001] 3 All
　　E.R. 499; [2001] 2 B.C.L.C. 392; (2000) 97(46) L.S.G. 39; *Times*, November
　　15, 2000; *Independent*, December 18, 2000 (C.S), CA; reversing [2000] B.C.C.
　　416; [1999] 2 B.C.L.C. 666, Ch D . . . . *Digested*, 00/**3505**
Lewis v. Lewis [1956] 1 W.L.R. 200; [1956] 1 All E.R. 375; 100 S.J. 134, PDAD . . . . . . *Digested*, 56/**2695**:
　　　　　　　　　　　　　　　　Considered, 99/4564: *Distinguished*, 62/981, 62/3329, 67/3122
Lewis v. McGoff (Unreported, October 19, 2000), CC (Salford) [*Ex rel.* Rowe &
　　Cohen Solicitors, Quay House, Quay Street, Manchester] . . . . *Digested*, 01/**520**
Lewis v. Moss, *Times*, March 23, 1998, QBD . . . . *Digested*, 98/**4861**
Lewis v. Motorworld Garages [1986] I.C.R. 157; [1985] I.R.L.R. 465, CA . . . . *Digested*, 86/**1261**:
　　　　　　　　　　　　　　　　　　　　　　　　　　　　　　　　　　Applied, 00/2132
Lewis v. MTC Cars Ltd [1975] 1 W.L.R. 457; [1975] 1 All E.R. 874; (1975) 29 P. &
　　C.R. 495; 119 S.J. 203, CA; affirming [1974] 1 W.L.R. 1499; [1974] 3 All E.R.
　　423; (1974) 28 P. & C.R. 294; 118 S.J. 565, Ch D . . . . *Digested*, 75/**1880**:
　　　　　　　　　　Applied, 77/1716, 78/1769: *Considered*, 79/1582, 91/2218, 01/4156
Lewis v. North Devon DC see R. v. North Devon DC Ex p. Lewis
Lewis v. Secretary of State for Trade and Industry see Secretary of State for Trade and
　　Industry v. Lewis
Lewis v. Summers [2001] 6 Q.R. 20, CC (Swindon) [*Ex rel.* Amanda Millmore,
　　Barrister, 4 King's Bench Walk, Temple, London] . . . . *Digested*, 01/**1764**
Lewis v. Surrey CC [1988] A.C. 323; [1987] 3 W.L.R. 927; [1987] 3 All E.R. 641;
　　[1987] I.C.R. 982; [1987] I.R.L.R. 509; 86 L.G.R. 97; (1987) 131 S.J. 1454, HL;
　　reversing [1987] I.C.R. 232; [1986] I.R.L.R. 455; 85 L.G.R. 345; (1986) 83
　　L.S.G. 2919; (1986) 130 S.J. 785, CA; reversing [1986] I.C.R. 404; [1986]
　　I.R.L.R. 11, EAT . . . . *Digested*, 87/**1391**:
　　　　　　　　　　　　　　　　　　　　　　　　　　　　　Distinguished, 99/2140
Lewisham and Guys Mental Health NHS Trust v. Andrews (Deceased) see Andrews
　　(Deceased) v. Lewisham and Guys Mental Health NHS Trust
Lewisham LBC v. Adeyemi [1999] E.G.C.S. 74, CA
Lewisham LBC v. Akinsola (2000) 32 H.L.R. 414, CA . . . . *Digested*, 00/**3146**
Lewisham LBC v. Gopee (1999) 78 P. & C.R. D14, CA
Lewisham LBC v. Laing Hyder South East London Ltd (2000) 15 P.A.D. 805, Planning
　　Inspector
Lewisham LBC v. Masterson (2000) 80 P. & C.R. 117; [2000] 1 E.G.L.R. 134, CA . . . . . *Digested*, 00/**3952**
Lewisham LBC v. Ranaweera (Unreported, May 14, 1999), Crown Ct [*Ex rel.* Paul
　　Latto, Barrister, 8 Warwick Court, Gray's Inn, London] . . . . *Digested*, 00/**3904**
Lex Services v. Johns (1990) 59 P. & C.R. 427; [1990] 10 E.G. 67; [1990] R.V.R. 51,
　　CA . . . . *Digested*, 90/**2782**:
　　　　　　　　　　　　　　　　　　　　　　　　　　　　　Distinguished, 01/3737
Lex Services Plc v. Customs and Excise Commissioners see Littlewoods Organisation
　　Plc v. Customs and Excise Commissioners
Lex Services Plc v. Customs and Excise Commissioners; *sub nom* Lex Service Plc v.
　　Customs and Excise Commissioners [2000] S.T.C. 697; [2001] R.T.R. 9; [2000]
　　B.T.C. 5305; [2000] B.V.C. 338; [2000] S.T.I. 1061; *Times*, October 17, 2000;
　　Independent, October 30, 2000 (C.S), Ch D (Companies Ct); affirming [1999]
　　B.V.C. 2307; [1999] V. & D.R. 156, V&DTr . . . . *Digested*, 00/**5319**:
　　　　　　　　　　　　　　　　　　　　　　　　　Subsequent proceedings, 01/5556
Lex Vehicle Leasing Ltd v. Lee (Unreported, November 23, 1998), CC (Altrincham) [*Ex
　　rel.* Weightmans Solicitors, Richmond House, 1 Rumford Place, Liverpool] . . . . . *Digested*, 99/**1420**
Leyland (CICB: Quantum: 1997), Re (Unreported, March 27, 1997), CICB (London) [*Ex rel.*
　　Boyes, Turner & Burrows, Solicitors, 10 Duke Street, Reading] . . . . *Digested*, 98/**1482**
Leyland DAF Ltd, Re; *sub nom* Buchler v. Talbot; B2/2000/3615, CA; affirming [2001]
　　1 B.C.L.C. 419, Ch D (Companies Ct)
Leyland DAF Ltd (No.2), Re see Powdrill v. Watson
Leyvand v. Barasch (2000) 97(11) L.S.G. 37; (2000) 144 S.J.L.B. 126; *Times*, March
　　23, 2000; *Independent*, March 27, 2000 (C.S.), Ch D . . . . *Digested*, 00/**435**
LG Caltex Gas Co Ltd v. China National Petroleum Corp; Contigroup Companies Inc
　　(formerly Continental Grain Co) v. China Petroleum Technology & Development
　　Corp [2001] EWCA Civ 788; [2001] 1 W.L.R. 1892; [2001] 4 All E.R. 875;
　　[2001] 2 All E.R. (Comm) 97; [2001] C.L.C. 1392; [2001] B.L.R. 325; (2001) 3
　　T.C.L.R. 22; (2001) 98(25) L.S.G. 46; (2001) 145 S.J.L.B. 142; *Times*, June 6,
　　2001, CA; reversing [2001] B.L.R. 235; *Times*, February 23, 2001; *Independent*,
　　February 26, 2001 (C.S), QBD (Comm Ct) . . . . *Digested*, 01/**336**
LHS Holdings Ltd v. Laporte Plc [2001] EWCA Civ 278; [2001] 2 All E.R. (Comm)
　　563, CA; affirming HC 1999 No. 04375, Ch D . . . . *Digested*, 01/**742**
Liability for a Defective Imported Trampoline (2 Ob 114/97x), Re [1998] E.C.C. 512, OGH (A)
Liability for Incorrect Legal Advice (IX ZR 233/96), Re [1998] E.C.C. 518, BGH (Ger)

Liability for Investment in Futures Options (XI ZR 377/97), Re [1999] I.L.Pr. 758, BGH (Ger)
Liability for Tax Advice to Longstanding Client (IX ZR 62/97), Re [1999] E.C.C. 351, BGH (Ger)
Liangsiriprasert v. United States [1991] 1 A.C. 225; [1990] 3 W.L.R. 606; [1990] 2 All E.R. 866; (1991) 92 Cr. App. R. 77; (1990) 134 S.J. 1123, PC (HK) . . . .   *Digested,* 91/**1743**:
      Applied, 90/948, 91/820, 00/952: *Considered,* 97/2441:
      Distinguished, 91/4777: *Followed,* 00/6029
Libby v. Kennedy [1998] O.P.L.R. 213, Ch D . . . .   *Digested,* 01/**4601**
Liberty Mutual Insurance Co (UK) Ltd v. HSBC Bank Plc see HSBC Bank Plc v. Liberty Mutual Insurance Co (UK) Ltd
Liberty Mutual Insurance Co (UK) Ltd v. HSBC Bank Plc (Subrogation) [2001] Lloyd's Rep. Bank. 224, Ch D . . . .   *Digested,* 01/**3842**
Libman v. Attorney General of Quebec 3 B.H.R.C. 269, Sup Ct (Can) . . . .   *Digested,* 98/**3085**
Libman v. General Medical Council [1972] A.C. 217; [1972] 2 W.L.R. 272; [1972] 1 All E.R. 798; (1971) 116 S.J. 123, PC (UK) . . . .   *Digested,* 72/**2838**:
      Applied, 74/2317: *Disapproved,* 00/2718: *Doubted,* 01/2891:
      Followed, 97/3635
Libyan Arab Foreign Bank v. Bankers Trust Co [1989] Q.B. 728; [1989] 3 W.L.R. 314; [1989] 3 All E.R. 252; [1988] 1 Lloyd's Rep. 259; [1987] 2 F.T.L.R. 509; (1989) 133 S.J. 568, QBD (Comm Ct) . . . .   *Digested,* 89/**376**:
      Applied, 00/5289: *Considered,* 00/780: *Distinguished,* 88/410, 89/383:
      Referred to, 88/3408
Licata v. Economic and Social Committee (C270/84) [1986] E.C.R. 2305, ECJ . . . . . .   *Applied,* 00/3582
Licence Holder, Re; Insolvency Act 1986, Re; Actual Services Ltd, Re; Abbot (John), Re [1997] B.C.C. 666; [1998] B.P.I.R. 171; (1997) 94(10) L.S.G. 31; (1997) 141 S.J.L.B. 64; *Times,* March 3, 1997, Ch D . . . .   *Digested,* 97/**3061**
Licensing Authority South Eastern Traffic Area v. British Gas Plc (C116/91) [1992] E.C.R. I-4071; (1994) 158 J.P. 606; [1992] 3 C.M.L.R. 65; (1994) 158 J.P.N. 486; *Times,* August 31, 1992, ECJ (2nd Chamber) . . . .   *Digested,* 92/**4864**:
      Applied, 94/6233, 99/4947: *Cited,* 96/7309: *Considered,* 96/5776
Licensing of a Trade Mark in Yugoslavia (3 Ob 115/95), Re [2000] E.C.C. 25, OGH (A)
LICRA v. Yahoo! Inc (USA) see League Against Racism and Anti Semitism v. Yahoo! Inc (USA)
Lidas Inc v. United States 3 I.T.L. Rep. 330, US Ct
Liddell v. Inland Revenue Commissioners 72 T.C. 62; 1997 G.W.D. 26-1344, OH . . . . . .   *Digested,* 00/**6699**
Lidl Italia Srl v. Comune di Chioggia (C141/94) see DIP SpA v. Comune di Bassano del Grappa (C140/94)
Lidl Properties v. Clarke Bond Partnership [1998] Env. L.R. 662, QBD (OR) . . . .   *Digested,* 98/**3940**
Lidl Stiftung & Co KG v. Savoy Hotel Plc [2001] E.T.M.R. 111, OHIM (2nd Bd App)
Lie v. Norway (25130/94) (2000) 29 E.H.R.R. CD210, ECHR
Liesbosch, The; *sub nom* Owner of Dredger Liesbosch v. Owners of SS Edison; Liesbosch Dredger v. SS Edison [1933] A.C. 449; [1933] All E.R. Rep. 144; (1933) 45 Ll. L. Rep. 123, HL; affirming in part [1932] P. 52; (1932) 42 Ll. L. Rep. 23, CA; reversing [1931] P. 230; (1931) 40 Ll. L. Rep. 333, PDAD . . . .   *Applied,* 61/7971,
      64/489, 65/512, 65/993, 78/2076, 92/4401, 01/1538: *Considered,* 47-51/9462,
      47-51/9561, 70/603, 72/2363, 76/1858, 98/3914: *Distinguished,* 67/52,
      73/734, 80/188, 82/2164, 83/4462, 93/1407, 00/1467
Liesbosch Dredger v. SS Edison see Liesbosch, The
LIESENFIELD/Courtesy service (J01/89) [1992] E.P.O.R. 284, EPO (Legal Bd App) . . .   *Followed,* 00/3622
Liew v. R. 7 B.H.R.C. 708, Sup Ct (Can) . . . .   *Digested,* 00/**3233**
LIFESAVERS Trade Mark [1997] R.P.C. 563, TMR . . . .   *Digested,* 97/**4874**:
      Not followed, 99/3528
Lifesource International Inc's Community Trade Mark Application (No.405514) [2001] E.T.M.R. 106, OHIM (Opposition Div)
LIFESYSTEMS Trade Mark [1999] R.P.C. 851, TMR
Lifting a Stay of Proceedings (7W1461/98), Re [1999] I.L.Pr. 291, OLG (Munchen) . . .   *Digested,* 99/**755**
Lightfoot v. Lord Chancellor see R. v. Lord Chancellor Ex p. Lightfoot
LIGHTHOUSE Trade Mark see Carless, Capel & Leonard v. F Pilmore Bedford & Sons
Lighting Electronics Ltd v. Thorn Lighting Ltd (1999) 22(9) I.P.D. 22082, Ch D
Lightning v. Lightning Electrical Contractors Ltd [1998] N.P.C. 71, QBD . . . .   *Digested,* 98/**768**
Lightways (Contractors) Ltd v. Associated Holdings Ltd 2000 S.C. 262; 2000 S.L.T. 1093; [2000] I.R.L.R. 247; 2000 G.W.D. 5-199, 2 Div . . . .   *Digested,* 00/**6216**
Ligouri v. Salford City Council [1997] E.L.R. 455, QBD . . . .   *Digested,* 98/**1962**
Ligue Nationale de Football v. Competition Council see Ligue Nationale de Football v. Nike France SA
Ligue Nationale de Football v. Nike France SA; *sub nom* Ligue Nationale de Football v. Competition Council [1999] E.C.C. 34, Cass (F); reversing in part [1996] E.C.C. 205, C d'A (Paris)
Lilley v. American Express Europe Ltd [2000] B.P.I.R. 70, Ch D . . . .   *Digested,* 99/**3247**
Lilley v. DPP see Gough v. Chief Constable of Derbyshire
Lillis v. North West Water Ltd [1999] R.V.R. 12, Lands Tr . . . .   *Digested,* 99/**4186**
Lilly v. Davison [1999] B.P.I.R. 81, Ch D . . . .   *Digested,* 99/**3327**
Lilly France SA v. Conseil de la Concurrence [2000] E.C.C. 17, Cass (F)
Lilly ICOS Ltd v. Pfizer Ltd (Interim Application) (2000) 23(11) I.P.D. 23089, Ch D

Lilly ICOS Ltd *v.* Pfizer Ltd (No.1); *sub nom* Pfizer Ltd's European Patent (UK) (No.0702555); A3/2000/3811, CA; affirming in part [2001] F.S.R. 16; (2001) 59 B.M.L.R. 123; (2001) 24(1) I.P.D. 23006; *Daily Telegraph*, November 21, 2000, Pat Ct . . . . *Digested*, 01/**3902**

Lim Poh Choo *v.* Camden and Islington AHA [1980] A.C. 174; [1979] 3 W.L.R. 44; [1979] 2 All E.R. 910; 123 S.J. 457, HL; affirming in part [1979] Q.B. 196; [1978] 3 W.L.R. 895; [1979] 1 All E.R. 332; 122 S.J. 508, CA; affirming 122 S.J. 82, QBD . . . . *Digested*, 79/**663**:
Applied, 81/582, 84/1004, 84/1032, 84/1042, 85/940, 85/942, 00/1479:
Distinguished, 81/243: *Followed*, 96/2125

Limb *v.* Union Jack Removals Ltd (In Liquidation); McGivern *v.* Brown; Partington *v.* Turners Bakery; Pyne-Edwards *v.* Moore Large & Co Ltd; Smith *v.* Brothers of Charity Services Ltd; Tomkins *v.* Griffiths [1998] 1 W.L.R. 1354; [1998] 2 All E.R. 513; [1999] P.I.Q.R. P16; (1998) 95(10) L.S.G. 27; (1998) 148 N.L.J. 277; (1998) 142 S.J.L.B. 177; *Times*, February 17, 1998, CA . . . . *Digested*, 98/**608**:
Applied, 01/630

Limburgse Vinyl Maatschappij NV *v.* Commission of the European Communities (C238/99); *sub nom* PVC Cartel II (T305/94), Re; Limburgse Vinyl Maatschappij NV *v.* Commission of the European Communities (T305/94)) [1999] E.C.R. II-931; [1999] 5 C.M.L.R. 303, CFI (3rd Chamber) . . . . *Digested*, 99/**659**

Limburgse Vinyl Maatschappij NV *v.* Commission of the European Communities (T305/94)) see Limburgse Vinyl Maatschappij NV *v.* Commission of the European Communities (C238/99)

Lincoln City Council *v.* Dobson (1999) 14 P.A.D. 676, Planning Inspector

Lincolnshire CC *v.* Machin (1998) 13 P.A.D. 234, Planning Inspector

Lincolnshire CC *v.* R-J (X Intervening); *sub nom* RJ, Re [1998] 1 W.L.R. 1679; [1998] 2 F.L.R. 82; [1998] 2 F.C.R. 580; (1998) 10 Admin. L.R. 429; [1998] Fam. Law 385; (1998) 95(10) L.S.G. 27; (1998) 142 S.J.L.B. 117; *Times*, February 20, 1998, Fam Div. . . . . *Digested*, 98/**2477**

Lincolnshire CC *v.* Safeway Stores Plc [1999] E.H.L.R. Dig. 456, QBD

Linda Jackson Pty Ltd's Community Trade Mark Application (520/2000) [2001] E.T.M.R. 35, OHIM (Opposition Div) . . . . *Digested*, 01/**3989**

LINDAHL/Protein Rib (T227/97); *sub nom* Lindahl's European Patent Application (No.94911348.4) [1999] E.P.O.R. 568; (1999) 22(1) I.P.D. 22007, EPO (Technical Bd App) . . . . *Digested*, 00/**3671**

LINDBERG/Re-establishment of rights (T338/98) [2000] E.P.O.R. 505, EPO (Technical Bd App) . . . . *Digested*, 01/**3944**

Linden Gardens Trust Ltd *v.* Lenesta Sludge Disposals Ltd; St Martins Property Corp Ltd *v.* Sir Robert McAlpine & Sons [1994] 1 A.C. 85; [1993] 3 W.L.R. 408; [1993] 3 All E.R. 417; 63 B.L.R. 1; 36 Con. L.R. 1; [1993] E.G.C.S. 139; (1993) 143 N.L.J. 1152; (1993) 137 S.J.L.B. 183; *Times*, July 23, 1993; *Independent*, July 30, 1993, HL; reversing in part 57 B.L.R. 57; 30 Con. L.R. 1; (1992) 8 Const. L.J. 180; *Times*, February 27, 1992; *Independent*, March 6, 1992; *Financial Times*, February 20, 1992, CA; reversing 52 B.L.R. 93; 25 Con. L.R. 28; [1991] E.G.C.S. 11, QBD . . . . *Digested*, 93/**303**:
Applied, 94/319, 95/487, 95/3701, 98/809, 99/832; *Cited*, 99/1417:
Considered, 94/549, 95/771, 95/4162, 99/440, 00/864: *Followed*, 98/401,
00/859, 00/5980

Linden's Application for Judicial Review, Re; *sub nom* Linden's Application, Re [1998] N.I. 316, QBD (NI) . . . . *Digested*, 99/**5218**

Lindner Ceilings Floors Partitions Plc *v.* How Engineering Services Ltd; How Engineering Services Ltd *v.* Lindner Ceilings Floors Partitions Plc (Appeal Against Costs) [2001] B.L.R. 90; (2001) 3 T.C.L.R. 12, QBD (T&CC) . . . . *Digested*, 01/**346**:
Previous proceedings, 99/227

Lindop *v.* Stewart Noble & Sons Ltd; *sub nom* Lindop *v.* Stuart Noble & Sons Ltd 1999 S.C.L.R. 889; [2000] B.C.C. 747; 1999 G.W.D. 23-1112, 2 Div; affirming 1998 S.C.L.R. 648; [1999] B.C.C. 616; *Times*, June 25, 1998, OH . . . . *Digested*, 00/**6514**

Lindop *v.* Stuart Noble & Sons Ltd see Lindop *v.* Stewart Noble & Sons Ltd

Lindsay (10673) Unreported, IAT . . . . *Followed*, 98/3214

Lindsay *v.* Alliance & Leicester Plc [2000] I.C.R. 1234, EAT . . . . *Digested*, 01/**2301**

Lindsay *v.* Attfield see Foster *v.* Driscoll

Lindsay *v.* Cundy see Cundy *v.* Lindsay

Lindsay *v.* Driscoll see Foster *v.* Driscoll

Lindsay *v.* Taylor (Unreported, August 21, 2000), CC (Middlesbrough) [*Ex rel.* Marc Davies, Barrister, Durham Barristers Chambers, 27 Old Elvet, Durham] . . . . *Digested*, 00/**1642**

Lindsay Bowman Ltd, Re [1969] 1 W.L.R. 1443; [1969] 3 All E.R. 601; 113 S.J. 791, Ch D
Digested, 69/**396**:
Cited, 99/603: *Followed*, 86/298, 87/338

Lindt & Sprungli SA *v.* Chocometz Ste [1999] E.T.M.R. 315, Cass (F)

Linea Naviera Paramaconi SA *v.* Abnormal Load Engineering Ltd [2001] 1 All E.R. (Comm) 946; [2001] 1 Lloyd's Rep. 763, QBD (Comm Ct) . . . . *Digested*, 01/**4931**

Lineham *v.* DPP; *sub nom* Linehan *v.* DPP [2000] Crim. L.R. 861; *Independent*, November 22, 1999 (C.S), QBD . . . . *Digested*, 01/**4787**

Linehan *v.* DPP see Lineham *v.* DPP

Linfood Cash & Carry v. Thomson [1989] I.R.L.R. 235; *Daily Telegraph*, June 8, 1989, EAT . . . . *Digested*, 90/**1949.a**

Ling Ex p. Enrobook Pty Ltd, Re v. [1998] B.P.I.R. 116, Fed Ct (Aus) (Sgl judge) . . . . . . *Digested*, 98/**3266**

Lingens v. Austria (No.1) (8803/79); Leitgens v. Austria (8803/79) (1982) 4 E.H.R.R. 373, Eur Comm HR . . . . *Applied*, 00/1169

Lingens v. Austria (No.2) (A/103) (1986) 8 E.H.R.R. 407, ECHR . . . . *Applied*, 95/3959:
Considered, 97/2036, 98/3090: *Referred to*, 01/3467, 01/3469

Lingral Srl v. Comune di Chioggia (C142/94) see DIP SpA v. Comune di Bassano del Grappa (C140/94)

Link v. Secretary of State for Trade and Industry see Scanfuture UK Ltd v. Secretary of State for Trade and Industry

Link Organisation Plc v. North Derbyshire Tertiary College [1999] Ed. C.R. 967; [1999] E.L.R. 20, CA . . . . *Digested*, 98/**92**

Link Stores Ltd v. Harrow LBC [2001] 1 W.L.R. 1479; (2001) 165 J.P. 575; (2001) 98(12) L.S.G. 41; (2001) 145 S.J.L.B. 39; *Times*, February 13, 2001, QBD (Admin Ct) . . . . *Digested*, 01/**912**

Linkleter v. Linkleter [1988] 1 F.L.R. 360; [1988] Fam. Law 360, CA . . . . *Digested*, 88/**2776**:
Applied, 01/451: *Considered*, 92/3404, 93/730

Linkrealm Ltd, Re [1998] B.C.C. 478, Ch D . . . . *Digested*, 98/**3319**

Linstead v. East Sussex, Brighton and Hove HA [2001] P.I.Q.R. P25, QBD . . . . *Digested*, 01/**552**

Linton v. Lancaster (Unreported, February 14, 2001), CC (Doncaster) [*Ex rel.* Morgan Cole, Solicitors, Apex Plaza Commercial Office, Reading] . . . . *Digested*, 01/**3819**

Linton v. RD Williams Haulage Ltd (Unreported, February 13, 2001), CC (Northampton) [*Ex rel.* Rory Clarke, Barrister, 2-3 Gray's Inn Square, London] . . *Digested*, 01/**516**

Lion Laboratories Ltd v. Evans [1985] Q.B. 526; [1984] 3 W.L.R. 539; [1984] 2 All E.R. 417; (1984) 81 L.S.G. 1233; (1984) 81 L.S.G. 2000; (1984) 128 S.J. 533, CA . . . . *Digested*, 84/**1325**:
Considered, 86/2646, 88/2859, 00/3573, 01/3850

Lion Nathan Ltd v. CC Bottlers Ltd [1996] 1 W.L.R. 1438; [1996] 2 B.C.L.C. 371; (1996) 93(24) L.S.G. 26; (1996) 140 S.J.L.B. 174; *Times*, May 16, 1996, PC (NZ) . . . . *Digested*, 96/**1237**:
Considered, 98/1440, 98/4032

Lipcon (Irmgard) v. Underwriters at Lloyd's London [1999] I.L.Pr. 675, US Ct

Lipkin Gorman v. Karpnale Ltd [1991] 2 A.C. 548; [1991] 3 W.L.R. 10; [1992] 4 All E.R. 512; (1991) 88(26) L.S.G. 31; (1991) 141 N.L.J. 815; (1991) 135 S.J.L.B. 36; *Times*, June 7, 1991; *Independent*, June 18, 1991; *Financial Times*, June 11, 1991; *Guardian*, June 13, 1991, HL; reversing [1989] 1 W.L.R. 1340; [1992] 4 All E.R. 409; [1989] B.C.L.C. 756; [1989] Fin. L.R. 137; (1990) 87(4) L.S.G. 40; (1989) 139 N.L.J. 76; (1990) 134 S.J. 234; *Times*, November 19, 1988; *Independent*, October 17, 1988 (C.S.); *Financial Times*, October 19, 1988; *Daily Telegraph*, October 28, 1988, CA; reversing [1987] 1 W.L.R. 987; [1992] 4 All E.R. 331; [1987] B.C.L.C. 159; [1986] F.L.R. 271; (1986) 136 N.L.J. 659; (1987) 131 S.J. 940, QBD . . . . *Digested*, 91/**502**:
Applied, 94/3911, 95/855, 95/4336, 00/2320: *Considered*, 88/177, 00/2331, 01/2434: *Followed*, 96/3453, 98/1472: *Referred to*, 96/5556

Lippiatt v. South Gloucestershire Council [2000] Q.B. 51; [1999] 3 W.L.R. 137; [1999] 4 All E.R. 149; (1999) 31 H.L.R. 1114; (1999) 1 L.G.L.R. 865; [1999] B.L.G.R. 562; (1999) 96(15) L.S.G. 31; *Times*, April 9, 1999; *Independent*, April 30, 1999, CA . . . . *Digested*, 99/**4066**

LIQUID FORCE Trade Mark [1999] R.P.C. 429, Appointed Person . . . . *Digested*, 99/**3573**

Liskojarvi v. Oy Liikenne AB (C172/99) see Oy Liikenne AB v. Liskojarvi (C172/99)

Lismane v. Hammersmith and Fulham LBC (1999) 31 H.L.R. 427; (1998) 10 Admin. L.R. 586; (1998) 162 J.P.N. 926; (1998) 95(31) L.S.G. 36; (1998) 142 S.J.L.B. 219; *Times*, July 27, 1998, CA . . . . *Digested*, 98/**3002**

Listers Solicitors Ltd v. Lambert (Unreported, January 27, 2000), EAT [*Ex rel.* John Worrall, Barrister, 10 Park Square, Leeds] . . . . *Digested*, 00/**2155**

Lite Ltd v. Customs and Excise Commissioners [1998] B.V.C. 2055, V&DTr

Lithuanian Composer's Works (3 U 171/94), Re [1999] E.C.C. 143, OLG (Hamburg)

Litster v. Forth Dry Dock and Engineering Co Ltd; *sub nom* Forth Estuary Engineering v. Litster [1990] 1 A.C. 546; [1989] 2 W.L.R. 634; [1989] 1 All E.R. 1134; 1989 S.L.T. 540; [1989] 2 C.M.L.R. 194; [1989] I.C.R. 341; [1989] I.R.L.R. 161; (1989) 86(23) L.S.G. 18; (1989) 139 N.L.J. 400; (1989) 133 S.J. 455, HL; reversing 1988 S.C. 178; 1989 S.L.T. 153, 2 Div . . . . *Digested*, 89/**4304**:
Applied, 95/300, 96/334, 00/2223: *Considered*, 95/2075, 96/2594, 97/2281, 98/2213, 99/2128, 00/2228: *Followed*, 93/5274, 95/5911, 97/2269: *Referred to*, 94/2003

Little v. George Little Sebire & Co [2001] EWCA Civ 894; [2001] S.T.C. 1065; [2001] B.T.C. 292, CA; affirming1995 L No 1025, QBD . . . . *Digested*, 01/**4508**

Little v. George Little Sebire & Co (Enhanced Interest), *Times*, November 17, 1999, QBD . . . . *Digested*, 99/**443**:
Considered, 00/1453

Little v. VSEL Birkenhead Ltd (Unreported, February 24, 1998), CC (Manchester) [*Ex rel.* John Pickering & Partners Solicitors, Old England Buildings, St Ann's Passage, 29/31 King Street, Manchester] . . . . *Digested*, 98/**1627**

Little Sisters Book & Art Emporium v. Minister of Justice 9 B.H.R.C. 409, Sup Ct (Can).　　*Digested*, 01/**3468**
Littlejohn (Victoria Hilary) v. McLeod 1999 J.C. 333; [2000] E.H.L.R. Dig. 272; 1999 G.W.D. 30-1402, HCJ Appeal
Littler v. Barraclough (Unreported, April 12, 2000), QBD [*Ex rel.* Steven Turner, Barrister, Morrish & Co, Leeds]　　　　　　　　　　　　*Digested*, 00/**369**
Littlewoods Organisation Ltd v. Harris [1977] 1 W.L.R. 1472; [1978] 1 All E.R. 1026; 121 S.J. 727, CA . . . .　　*Digested*, 78/**2941**:
　　　　　　　　　Considered, 97/2256: *Distinguished*, 00/2200
Littlewoods Organisation Plc v. Customs and Excise Commissioners [1997] V. & D.R. 408, V&DTr . . . .　　*Digested*, 00/**5314**
Littlewoods Organisation Plc v. Customs and Excise Commissioners; *sub nom* Customs and Excise Commissioners v. Littlewoods Organisation Plc; Customs and Excise Commissioners v. Bugeja (No.2); Lex Services Plc v. Customs and Excise Commissioners; Bugeja v. Customs and Excise Commissioners (No.2); Kuwait Petroleum (GB) Ltd v. Customs and Excise Commissioners [2001] EWCA Civ 1542; [2001] S.T.C. 1568; [2001] B.T.C. 5608; [2001] S.T.I. 1381; (2001) 98(46) L.S.G. 36; (2001) 145 S.J.L.B. 254; (2001) 145 S.J.L.B. 255; *Times*, November 15, 2001; *Times*, November 7, 2001, CA; reversing [2000] S.T.C. 588; [2000] B.T.C. 5299; [2000] B.V.C. 284; [2000] S.T.I. 916; *Times*, July 6, 2000, Ch D; reversing [2000] B.V.C. 2136; [2000] S.T.I. 139, V&DTr . . . .　　*Digested*, 01/**5556**:
　　　　　　　Previous proceedings, 00/5319, 00/5339, 01/5554
Littrell v. United States (No.2) [1995] 1 W.L.R. 82; [1994] 4 All E.R. 203; [1994] P.I.Q.R. P141; (1993) 137 S.J.L.B. 278; *Times*, November 24, 1993; *Independent*, December 2, 1993, CA . . . .　　*Digested*, 95/**2940**:
　　　　　　　Applied, 96/2632, 98/1775: *Considered*, 00/3819
Litwa v. Poland (26629/95) (2001) 33 E.H.R.R. 53, ECHR
Liveras v. Debtor (No.620 of 1997); *sub nom* Debtor (No.620 of 1997), Re [1999] B.P.I.R. 89; *Times*, June 18, 1998, Ch D　　　　　　　　　　　　　*Digested*, 98/**3270**
Liverpool and District Hospital for Diseases of the Heart v. Attorney General [1981] Ch. 193; [1981] 2 W.L.R. 379; [1981] 1 All E.R. 994; 125 S.J. 79; *Times*, November 4, 1980, Ch D . . . .　　*Digested*, 81/**263**:
　　　　　　　　　　　　　　　　　　Considered, 01/387
Liverpool City Council v. Everton Football Club (2000) 15 P.A.D. 106, Planning Inspector
Liverpool City Council v. Rosemary Chavasse Ltd (1999) 96(36) L.S.G. 29; [1999] N.P.C. 115, CA; reversing CH.1999-02528, Ch D
Liverpool City Council v. Rosemary Chavasse Ltd (Costs) [2000] C.P. Rep. 8; [1999] C.P.L.R. 802, Ch D . . . .　　*Digested*, 00/**428**
Liverpool City Council v. Walton Group Plc [2001] N.P.C. 135, Ch D
Liverpool City Council v. Worthington, *Times*, June 16, 1998, QBD. . . . .　　*Digested*, 98/**6**
Liverpool Roman Catholic Archdiocesan Trustees Inc v. Goldberg (No.1) [2001] 1 All E.R. 182; [2000] Lloyd's Rep. P.N. 836; [2001] P.N.L.R. 19; *Times*, July 18, 2000, Ch D . . . .　　*Digested*, 00/**534**:
　　　　　　　Applied, 01/4520, 01/4535: *Followed*, 01/4527
Liverpool Roman Catholic Archdiocesan Trustees Inc v. Goldberg (No.2) [2001] Lloyd's Rep. P.N. 518; (2001) 98(17) L.S.G. 38; *Times*, March 9, 2001, Ch D . . . .　　*Digested*, 01/**395**
Liverpool Roman Catholic Archdiocesan Trustees Inc v. Goldberg (No.3); *sub nom* Liverpool Roman Catholic Archdiocesan Trust v. Goldberg (No.3); Liverpool Roman Catholic Archdiocese Trustees Inc v. Goldberg (No.3) [2001] 1 W.L.R. 2337; [2001] 4 All E.R. 950; [2001] B.L.R. 479; (2001) 98(32) L.S.G. 37; (2001) 151 N.L.J. 1093; *Times*, August 14, 2001; *Daily Telegraph*, July 17, 2001, Ch D . . . .　　*Digested*, 01/**393**
Livesey (A Minor) v. Hammersmith and Fulham LBC (1999) 99(1) Q.R. 6, CC (West London) . . . .　　*Digested*, 98/**1553**
Livesey v. Chief Constable of Lancashire (Unreported, November 10, 1994) . . . .　　*Considered*, 00/204
Living Waters Christian Centres Ltd v. Conwy CBC [1999] E.H.L.R. 31; (1999) 31 H.L.R. 371; (1999) 77 P. & C.R. 54, CA. . . . .　　*Digested*, 98/**3038**
Living Waters Christian Centres Ltd v. Fetherstonhaugh [1999] 2 E.G.L.R. 1; [1999] 28 E.G. 121, CA
Livingstone v. Rawyards Coal Co (1879-80) L.R. 5 App. Cas. 25, HL. . . . .　　*Applied*, 79/2776,
　　　　86/3195, 87/3551, 88/1051, 89/1199, 90/1522, 91/1322, 92/1533:
　　　　Cited, 01/4593: *Considered*, 90/1567, 93/2504, 94/2771, 96/4483:
　　　　　　　　　　　　　　　　　　Referred to, 94/3437
Livingstone Homes UK Ltd v. Customs and Excise Commissioners [2000] B.V.C. 2400; [2000] S.T.I. 1313, V&DTr
Liyanage (Don John Francis Douglas) v. Queen, The [1967] 1 A.C. 259; [1966] 2 W.L.R. 682; [1966] 1 All E.R. 650; [1966] Crim. L.R. 102; 110 S.J. 14, PC (Cey) .　　*Digested*, 66/**10026**:
　　　　　　　　　　　　　　　　　　Applied, 00/96
Llanelec Precision Engineering Co Ltd v. Neath Port Talbot CBC [2000] 3 E.G.L.R. 158, Lands Tr　　　　　　　　　　　　　　　　　　　　　　　　*Digested*, 01/**598**
Llanelly Railway & Dock Co v. LNW Railway see Llanelly Railway & Dock Co v. London and North Western Railway Co

Llanelly Railway & Dock Co v. London and North Western Railway Co; *sub nom* Llanelly
Railway & Dock Co v. LNW Railway (1874-75) L.R. 7 H.L. 550, HL; affirming
(1872-73) L.R. 8 Ch. App. 942, CA in Chancery . . . . *Considered,*
47-51/1759,

47-51/1760, 99/4883: *Disapproved,* 47-51/5514, 47-51/5515:
Distinguished, 55/468, 78/337

Llanfyllin Group Practice v. Customs and Excise Commissioners [2000] B.V.C. 2021,
V&DTr
Lloyd v. Dugdale [2001] EWCA Civ 1754; [2001] 48 E.G.C.S. 129; (2001) 98(47)
L.S.G. 28; [2001] N.P.C. 168, CA
Lloyd v. McMahon [1987] A.C. 625; [1987] 2 W.L.R. 821; [1987] 1 All E.R. 1118; 85
L.G.R. 545; [1987] R.V.R. 58; (1987) 84 L.S.G. 1240; (1987) 137 N.L.J. 265;
(1987) 131 S.J. 409, HL; affirming 85 L.G.R. 348; [1986] R.V.R. 188, CA . . . . . . *Digested,* 87/**3162**:
Applied, 94/66, 00/538: *Considered,* 93/1679, 93/3757, 94/44, 94/3835,
94/4226, 94/6012, 95/162, 95/3252, 95/4668, 00/6628
Lloyd v. Popely A3/1999/0888, CA; affirming [2000] B.C.C. 338; [2000] 1 B.C.L.C.
19, Ch D . . . . *Digested,* 01/**743**
Lloyd v. Symonds [1998] E.H.L.R. Dig. 278, CA
Lloyd v. Taylor Woodrow Construction [1999] I.R.L.R. 782, EAT . . . . *Digested,* 00/**2191**
Lloyd Schuhfabrik Meyer & Co GmbH v. Klijsen Handel BV (C342/97) [1999] All E.R.
(EC) 587; [1999] E.C.R. I-3819; [1999] 2 C.M.L.R. 1343; [1999] C.E.C. 285;
[1999] E.T.M.R. 690; [2000] F.S.R. 77; (1999) 22(11) I.P.D. 22111; *Times,* June
30, 1999, ECJ [1999] E.C.R. I-3819; [1999] E.T.M.R. 10; [1999] F.S.R. 627,
AGO . . . . *Digested,* 99/**3538**:
Applied, 01/4056, 01/5881: *Followed,* 00/3773
Lloyd-Davies v. Lyth (Unreported, February 9, 2000), CC (Chester) [*Ex rel.* Kevin
Haven, Barrister, 2 Gray's Inn Square Chambers, Gray's Inn, London] . . . . *Digested,* 00/**1592**
Lloyd's Litigation: Note see Lloyd's Litigation: Outstanding Cases (No.3)
Lloyd's Litigation: Outstanding Cases (No.3); *sub nom* Lloyd's Litigation: Note *Times,*
November 4, 1999, QBD (Comm Ct) . . . . *Referred to,* 00/3540
Lloyd's Litigation: Outstanding Cases (No.4), *Times,* February 11, 2000, QBD (Comm Ct)
Digested, 00/**3540**
Lloyd's of London v. Khan see Society of Lloyd's v. Khan
Lloyd's Society v. Clementson; Society of Lloyd's v. Mason [1995] L.R.L.R. 307;
[1995] C.L.C. 117; [1995] 1 C.M.L.R. 693; [1995] E.C.C. 390; (1995) 92(43)
L.S.G. 26; *Times,* November 16, 1994; *Independent,* November 11, 1994, CA;
reversing [1994] E.C.C. 481; *Times,* January 11, 1994, QBD (Comm Ct) . . . . *Digested,* 94/**2685**:
Considered, 01/3823, 01/5572: *Followed,* 00/721
Lloyde v. West Midlands Gas Board [1971] 1 W.L.R. 749; [1971] 2 All E.R. 1240; 115
S.J. 227, CA . . . . *Digested,* 71/**8011**:
Applied, 88/1582, 89/2580: *Considered,* 00/4241
Lloyds Bank v. Institute of Cancer Research see Dellow's Will Trusts, Re
Lloyds Bank v. Peake see Morris, Re
Lloyds Bank Ltd v. Dalton [1942] Ch. 466, Ch D . . . . *Followed,* 00/4632
Lloyds Bank Ltd v. Eastwood see Eastwood (Deceased), Re
Lloyds Bank Plc v. Bowker Orford [1992] 2 E.G.L.R. 44; [1992] 31 E.G. 68 . . . . *Digested,* 93/**2542**:
Applied, 01/4194
Lloyds Bank PLC v. Burd Pearse [2001] Lloyd's Rep. P.N. 452; [2001] 12 E.G.C.S. 167,
CA; reversing [2000] P.N.L.R. 71; [1999] E.G.C.S. 99, Ch D . . . . *Digested,* 01/**4529**
Lloyds Bank Plc v. Byrne & Byrne [1993] 1 F.L.R. 369; [1993] 2 F.C.R. 41; (1991) 23
H.L.R. 472; [1991] E.G.C.S. 57, CA . . . . *Digested,* 92/**2131**:
Applied, 98/4356: *Distinguished,* 93/1846, 94/3303, 95/2214:
Doubted, 00/4659: *Followed,* 95/2365
Lloyds Bank Plc v. Crosse & Crosse; *sub nom* Crosse & Crosse v. Lloyds Bank Plc
[2001] EWCA Civ 366; [2001] P.N.L.R. 34; [2001] N.P.C. 59, CA . . . . *Digested,* 01/**4528**
Lloyds Bank Plc v. Dix B3/2000/6433, B3/2000/6435, B3/2000/6435, CA . . . . *Considered,* 01/3439
Lloyds Bank Plc v. Hawkins [1998] Lloyd's Rep. Bank. 379; [1998] 3 E.G.L.R. 109;
[1998] 47 E.G. 137; (1999) 77 P. & C.R. D15; *Times,* October 9, 1998, CA . . . . . *Digested,* 98/**579**
Lloyds Bank Plc v. Independent Insurance Co Ltd [2000] Q.B. 110; [1999] 2 W.L.R.
986; [1999] 1 All E.R. (Comm.) 8; [1999] Lloyd's Rep. Bank. 1; [1999] C.L.C.
510; (1999) 96(3) L.S.G. 31; *Times,* December 3, 1998, CA . . . . *Digested,* 99/**292**
Lloyds Bank Plc v. Lampert [1999] 1 All E.R. (Comm.) 161; [1999] Lloyd's Rep. Bank.
138; [1999] B.C.C. 507, CA . . . . *Digested,* 99/**2511**
Lloyds Bank Plc v. Parker Bullen [2000] Lloyd's Rep. P.N. 51; [1999] E.G.C.S. 107;
[1999] N.P.C. 99, Ch D . . . . *Digested,* 00/**4263**
Lloyds Bank Plc v. Rogers (No.2) [1999] 3 E.G.L.R. 83; [1999] 38 E.G. 187; [1999]
E.G.C.S. 106; (1999) 96(30) L.S.G. 30, CA . . . . *Digested,* 99/**4383**

Lloyds Bank Plc *v.* Rosset [1991] 1 A.C. 107; [1990] 2 W.L.R. 867; [1990] 1 All E.R. 1111; [1990] 2 F.L.R. 155; (1990) 22 H.L.R. 349; (1990) 60 P. & C.R. 311; (1990) 140 N.L.J. 478, HL; reversing [1989] Ch. 350; [1988] 3 W.L.R. 1301; [1988] 3 All E.R. 915; [1989] 1 F.L.R. 51; [1988] Fam. Law 472; (1989) 86(1) L.S.G. 39; (1988) 138 N.L.J. Rep. 149; (1988) 132 S.J. 1698; *Times*, May 23, 1988; *Independent*, June 3, 1988; *Guardian*, June 9, 1988; *Daily Telegraph*, June 9, 1988, CA . . . . *Digested*, 90/**706**:
Applied, 92/2034, 96/4993, 01/5503: *Approved*, 90/707:
Considered, 89/467, 92/2031, 96/4950, 96/4952, 96/4995, 97/4937:
Followed, 93/572, 95/2187, 96/4943

Lloyds Bank Plc *v.* Voller; *sub nom* Voller *v.* Lloyds Bank Plc [2000] 2 All E.R. (Comm) 978; [2001] Lloyd's Rep. Bank. 67, CA

Lloyds Bank Plc *v.* Wojcik, *Independent*, January 19, 1998 (C.S.), CA . . . . *Digested*, 98/**537**

Lloyds Bowmaker Ltd *v.* Britannia Arrow Holdings [1988] 1 W.L.R. 1337; [1988] 3 All E.R. 178; (1989) 86(1) L.S.G. 40; (1988) 132 S.J. 1527; *Times*, March 19, 1987, CA . . . . *Digested*, 89/**3031**:
Applied, 91/2884, 92/574, 92/576, 01/591: *Referred to*, 94/3525

Lloyds TSB Bank Plc (formerly Lloyds Bank Plc) *v.* Rasheed Bank see Shanning International Ltd (In Liquidation) *v.* Lloyds TSB Bank Plc (formerly Lloyds Bank Plc)

Lloyds TSB Bank Plc *v.* Shorney [2001] EWCA Civ 1161; (2001) 98(37) L.S.G. 38; [2001] N.P.C. 121; *Times*, October 25, 2001, CA . . . . *Digested*, 01/**4877**

Lloyds TSB General Insurance Holdings Ltd *v.* Lloyds Bank Group Insurance Co Ltd; Abbey National Plc *v.* Lee [2001] EWCA Civ 1643; [2001] Pens. L.R. 325, CA; affirming [2001] 1 All E.R. (Comm) 13; [2001] Lloyd's Rep. I.R. 237; [2001] Lloyd's Rep. P.N. 28, QBD (Comm Ct) . . . . *Digested*, 01/**3811**

Lloyds TSB Life Assurance Co Ltd *v.* Colclough (Inspector of Taxes) see HSBC Life (UK) Ltd *v.* Stubbs (Inspector of Taxes)

Lloyds UDT Finance Ltd *v.* Chartered Finance Trust Holdings Plc; Britax International GmbH *v.* Inland Revenue Commissioners; A3 2001 2678, CA; affirming [2001] S.T.C. 1652; [2001] B.T.C. 487; [2001] S.T.I. 1521; *Times*, December 12, 2001, Ch D

LM *v.* Essex CC [1999] 1 F.L.R. 988; [1999] 1 F.C.R. 673; [1999] Fam. Law 312; (1999) 163 J.P.N. 835, Fam Div . . . . *Digested*, 99/**2394**

LM Plast SA *v.* Fahr Bucher France Sarl [2001] I.L.Pr. 3, Cass (F)

LM Tenancies 1 Plc *v.* Inland Revenue Commissioners [1998] 1 W.L.R. 1269; [1998] S.T.C. 326; [1998] B.T.C. 8012; [1998] E.G.C.S. 10; (1998) 95(6) L.S.G. 26; (1998) 142 S.J.L.B. 69; [1998] N.P.C. 13; *Times*, February 4, 1998, CA; affirming [1996] S.T.C. 880; [1996] 2 E.G.L.R. 119; [1996] 46 E.G. 155; [1996] E.G.C.S. 111; (1996) 140 S.J.L.B. 157; *Times*, July 11, 1996; *Independent*, July 29, 1996 (C.S.), Ch D . . . . *Digested*, 98/**4703**

Lo Sterzo (A Minor) *v.* Hopkins (1999) 99(1) Q.R. 7, CC (West London) . . . . *Digested*, 98/**1732**

Lo-Line Electric Motors, Re; *sub nom* Companies Act 1985, Re [1988] Ch. 477; [1988] 3 W.L.R. 26; [1988] 2 All E.R. 692; (1988) 4 B.C.C. 415; [1988] B.C.L.C. 698; [1988] P.C.C. 236; [1988] 2 F.T.L.R. 107; (1988) 138 N.L.J. Rep. 119; (1988) 132 S.J. 851; *Times*, April 7, 1988; *Independent*, April 20, 1988; *Financial Times*, April 27, 1988, Ch D . . . . *Digested*, 88/**316**:
Approved, 91/401: *Referred to*, 01/714

LOADED Trade Mark; *sub nom* Valucci Designs Ltd (t/a Hugo Hog's) Trade Mark Application (No.2061604) (2001) 24(2) I.P.D. 24012, Pat Ct

Loader *v.* Lucas (1999) 99(5) Q.R. 8, QBD . . . . *Digested*, 99/**1620**

Lobb Partnership Ltd *v.* Aintree Racecourse Co Ltd [2000] C.L.C. 431; [2000] B.L.R. 65; 69 Con. L.R. 79, QBD (Comm Ct) . . . . *Digested*, 00/**235**

Lobo Machado *v.* Portugal (1997) 23 E.H.R.R. 79, ECHR . . . . *Digested*, 97/**2803**:
Applied, 97/2811, 98/3125, 98/3126

Locabail (UK) Ltd *v.* Bayfield Properties Ltd (Leave to Appeal); Locabail (UK) Ltd *v.* Waldorf Investment Corp (Leave to Appeal); Timmins *v.* Gormley; Williams *v.* Inspector of Taxes; R. *v.* Bristol Betting and Gaming Licensing Committee Ex p. O'Callaghan [2000] Q.B. 451; [2000] 2 W.L.R. 870; [2000] 1 All E.R. 65; [2000] I.R.L.R. 96; [2000] H.R.L.R. 290; [2000] U.K.H.R.R. 300; 7 B.H.R.C. 583; (1999) 149 N.L.J. 1793; [1999] N.P.C. 143; *Times*, November 19, 1999 ; *Independent*, November 23, 1999, CA . . . . *Digested*, 99/**38**:
Applied, 00/52, 00/53, 01/13, 01/2268: *Considered*, 00/4140, 00/6092, 01/334

Locabail (UK) Ltd *v.* Bayfield Properties Ltd (No.1); Locabail (UK) Ltd *v.* Waldorf Investment Corp (No.1) *Times*, March 31, 1999; *Independent* April 19, 1999 (C.S.), Ch D . . . . *Digested*, 99/**4392**

Locabail (UK) Ltd *v.* Bayfield Properties Ltd (No.2); Locabail (UK) Ltd *v.* Waldorf Investment Corp (No.2) (1999) 96(20) L.S.G. 39; (1999) 143 S.J.L.B. 148; *Times*, May 18, 1999, Ch D . . . . *Digested*, 99/**3796**

Locabail (UK) Ltd *v.* Bayfield Properties Ltd (No.3); Locabail (UK) Ltd *v.* Waldorf Investment Corp (No.3); Emmanuel *v.* Locabail (UK) Ltd [2000] 2 Costs L.R. 169; *Times*, February 29, 2000, Ch D . . . . *Digested*, 00/**455**

Locabail (UK) Ltd v. Waldorf Investment Corp (Leave to Appeal) see Locabail (UK) Ltd
  v. Bayfield Properties Ltd (Leave to Appeal)
Locabail (UK) Ltd v. Waldorf Investment Corp (No.1) see Locabail (UK) Ltd v. Bayfield
  Properties Ltd (No.1)
Locabail (UK) Ltd v. Waldorf Investment Corp (No.2) see Locabail (UK) Ltd v. Bayfield
  Properties Ltd (No.2)
Locabail (UK) Ltd v. Waldorf Investment Corp (No.3) see Locabail (UK) Ltd v. Bayfield
  Properties Ltd (No.3)
Locabail (UK) Ltd v. Waldorf Investment Corp (No.4) [2000] H.R.L.R. 623; [2000]
  U.K.H.R.R. 592; (2000) 97(25) L.S.G. 41; [2000] N.P.C. 62; *Times*, June 13,
  2000, Ch D . . . . *Digested*, 00/**3236**
Local Ireland Ltd v. Local Ireland-Online Ltd [2001] E.T.M.R. 42, HC (Irl) . . . . *Digested*, 01/**3876**
Local Sunday Newspapers Ltd v. Johnston Press Plc (2001) 24(9) I.P.D. 24062, Ch D
Lock v. Cardiff Railway Co Ltd [1998] I.R.L.R. 358, EAT . . . . *Digested*, 98/**2235**:
                                                    Distinguished, 00/2240
Locke v. Camberwell HA [1991] 2 Med. L.R. 249; *Times*, June 27, 1991, CA; reversing
  (1990) 140 N.L.J. 205; *Times*, December 11, 1989; *Independent*, January 29,
  1990 (C.S.), QBD . . . . *Digested*, 92/**4086**:
                     Applied, 95/4030: *Considered*, 94/3623: *Followed*, 98/496
Locker v. Secretary of State for the Environment, Transport and the Regions; *sub nom*
  R. v. Secretary of State for the Environment, Transport and the Regions Ex p.
  Locker [2000] 1 P.L.R. 42, QBD
Lockley v. Lea (Unreported, March 2, 2001), CC (Crewe) [*Ex rel.* Ford & Warren,
  Solicitors, Westgate Point, Westgate, Leeds] . . . . *Digested*, 01/**518**
Lockley v. National Blood Transfusion Service [1992] 1 W.L.R. 492; [1992] 2 All E.R.
  589; [1992] 3 Med. L.R. 173; *Times*, November 11, 1991; *Independent*, November
  4, 1991, CA . . . . *Digested*, 92/**2773**:
                         Applied, 01/525: *Considered*, 95/3108
Lockwood (Deceased), Re; *sub nom* Atherton v. Brooke [1958] Ch. 231; [1957] 3
  W.L.R. 837; [1957] 3 All E.R. 520; 101 S.J. 886, Ch D . . . . *Digested*, 57/**1353**:
                                                      Distinguished, 00/4908
Lockwood v. Lowe [1954] 2 Q.B. 267; [1954] 2 W.L.R. 296; [1954] 1 All E.R. 472;
  98 S.J. 127, CA . . . . *Digested*, 54/**2795**:
                        Considered, 98/3632: *Followed*, 54/2793, 54/2796
Loder v. Gaden (1999) 78 P. & C.R. 223; [1999] N.P.C. 47; (1999) 78 P. & C.R. D10,
  CA . . . . *Digested*, 00/**4641**
Lodhi, Re see Lodhi v. Governor of Brixton Prison
Lodhi v. Governor of Brixton Prison; *sub nom* Lodhi, Re [2001] EWHC Admin 178;
  Independent, May 7, 2001 (C.S.), QBD (Admin Ct)
Loendersloot (t/a F Loendersloot Internationale Expeditie) v. George Ballantine & Son
  Ltd (C349/95) [1997] E.C.R. I-6227; [1998] 1 C.M.L.R. 1015; [1998] E.T.M.R.
  10; [1998] F.S.R. 544, ECJ [1997] E.C.R. I-6227; [1997] E.T.M.R. 306, AGO . . *Digested*, 98/**3514**:
                                                        Distinguished, 98/3426
Loescher v. Dean; *sub nom* Loescher v. Woodbridge & Sons [1950] Ch. 491; [1950] 2
  All E.R. 124; 66 T.L.R. (Pt.1) 1208, Ch D . . . . *Digested*, 47-51/**9797**:
                    Applied, 52/254, 52/255, 57/2820: *Considered*, 99/5421
Loescher v. Woodbridge & Sons see Loescher v. Dean
Loewe SA's European Trade Mark Application (B.37889) [2000] E.T.M.R. 40, OHIM
  (Opposition Div) . . . . *Digested*, 00/**3778**
Loffland Brothers North Sea Inc v. Goodbrand (Inspector of Taxes) see Goodbrand
  (Inspector of Taxes) v. Loffland Bros North Sea Inc
Logabox v. Titherley [1977] I.C.R. 369; [1977] I.R.L.R. 97; (1977) 12 I.T.R. 158, EAT . . . *Digested*, 77/**943**:
                     Applied, 78/904, 98/2102: *Explained*, 77/935, 78/901
Logan v. Cahoon [1996] N.I. 266, QBD (NI)
Logarajan (15282) (Unreported, July 16, 1997), IAT . . . . *Doubted*, 98/3195
Logical Computer Supplies Ltd v. Euro Car Parks Ltd HQ004891, QBD [*Ex rel.* Nicholas
  Hill, Barrister, 6 Park Square, Leeds] . . . . *Digested*, 01/**3701**
Logicrose Ltd v. Southend United Football Club Ltd (No.1) [1988] E.G.C.S. 114;
  (1988) 132 S.J. 1591; *Times*, March 5, 1988, Ch D . . . . *Digested*, 88/**2828**:
                                                      Applied, 00/601
Logue v. Flying Colours Ltd (Unreported, March 7, 2001), CC (Central London) [*Ex
  rel.* Alan Saggerson, Barrister, No.1 Serjeants Inn, Fleet Street, London] . . . . *Digested*, 01/**4281**
Lohia v. Lohia [2001] EWCA Civ 1691, CA; affirming [2001] W.T.L.R. 101; (2000-01)
  3 I.T.E.L.R. 117, Ch D . . . . *Digested*, 01/**4891**
Loizidou v. Turkey (1996) (1997) 23 E.H.R.R. 513, ECHR . . . . *Digested*, 97/**2799**:
                                                    Considered, 98/3151
Loizidou v. Turkey (Art.50) [1998] H.R.C.D. 732; (1998) 26 E.H.R.R. CD 5, ECHR
Lomas v. Secretary of State for the Environment, Transport and the Regions see Moase
  v. Secretary of State for the Environment, Transport and the Regions
Lomax v. Wood [2001] EWCA Civ 1099; (2001) 98(25) L.S.G. 48, CA
Lomax Leisure Ltd, Re [2000] Ch. 502; [1999] 3 W.L.R. 652; [1999] 3 All E.R. 22; [2000]
  B.C.C. 352; [1999] 2 B.C.L.C. 126; [1999] L. & T.R. 519; [1999] 2 E.G.L.R. 37;
  [1999] 23 E.G. 143; [1999] E.G.C.S. 61; (1999) 96(21) L.S.G. 38; *Times*, May 4,
  1999; *Independent*, June 21, 1999 (C.S.), Ch D (Companies Ct) . . . . *Digested*, 99/**3272**

Lombard Bank Ltd *v.* Rawcliffe (Unreported, February 10, 1999), CC (Birkenhead) [*Ex rel.* Nicholas Preston, Barrister, Bracton Chambers, Second Floor, 95A Chancery Lane, London] . . . . *Digested,* 99/**2518**
Lombard Natwest Factors Ltd *v.* Arbis; *sub nom* Natwest Lombard Factors Ltd *v.* Arbis [2000] B.P.I.R. 79; *Times,* December 10, 1999, Ch D . . . . *Digested,* 00/**306**
Lombard North Central Plc *v.* Asphaltic Roofing Supplies Ltd (Unreported, August 9, 1997), CC (Central London) [*Ex rel.* Nicholas Preston, Barrister, 3 Temple Gardens, Temple, London] . . . . *Digested,* 98/**478**
Lombard North Central Plc *v.* Brook [1999] B.P.I.R. 701, Ch D . . . . *Digested,* 99/**3334**
Lombard North Central Plc *v.* Gate [1998] C.C.L.R. 51, CC (Walsall). . . . . *Digested,* 98/**2491**
Lombard Risk Systems Ltd's Trade Mark Application [2000] E.T.M.R. 1055 (Note), OHIM (2nd Bd App)
Lombard Tricity Finance *v.* Paton [1989] 1 All E.R. 918; (1989) 8 Tr. L.R. 129; (1988) 138 N.L.J. Rep. 333; *Times,* October 31, 1988; *Independent,* November 8, 1988; *Financial Times,* November 4, 1988, CA. . . . . *Digested,* 89/**402**:
Not followed, 01/4874
Lombardo *v.* Italy (A/249-B) (1996) 21 E.H.R.R. 188, ECHR . . . . *Digested,* 96/**4600**:
Followed, 98/3145
Lomond Services Ltd *v.* Customs and Excise Commissioners Unreported, V&DTr . . . . . *Not followed,* 00/5335
London and Caledonian Marine Insurance Co, Re (1879) L.R. 11 Ch. D. 140, CA . . . . . . *Applied,* 67/519:
Approved, 99/3279
London and Exmoor Estates *v.* Customs and Excise Commissioners [2000] S.T.I. 1500, V&DTr
London & Global Ltd *v.* Sahara Petroleum Ltd, *Times,* December 3, 1998, CA . . . . *Digested,* 99/**3355**
London and Winchester Properties Appeal, Re (1983) 45 P. & C.R. 429; (1983) 267 E.G. 685; [1983] J.P.L. 318, Lands Tr. . . . . *Digested,* 83/**2104**:
Applied, 00/3909
London Baggage Co (Charing Cross) Ltd *v.* Railtrack Plc (No.1) [2000] L. & T.R. 439; [2000] E.G.C.S. 57; (2000) 80 P. & C.R. D38, Ch D . . . . *Digested,* 01/**4162**
London Baggage Co (Charing Cross) Ltd *v.* Railtrack Plc (No.2) [2001] L. & T.R. 19; [2001] 4 E.G.C.S. 143; (2001) 82 P. & C.R. D13, Ch D . . . . *Digested,* 01/**4151**
London CC *v.* Agricultural Food Products; London CC *v.* Vitamins [1955] 2 Q.B. 218; [1955] 2 W.L.R. 925; [1955] 2 All E.R. 229; 59 L.G.R. 350; 99 S.J. 305, CA. . . *Digested,* 55/**1529**:
Applied, 57/1961, 00/3449
London CC *v.* Monks [1959] Ch. 239; [1959] 2 W.L.R. 17; [1958] 3 All E.R. 670; 103 S.J. 34, Ch D . . . . *Digested,* 59/**2596**:
Distinguished, 00/437
London CC *v.* Vitamins see London CC *v.* Agricultural Food Products
London Clubs Management Ltd *v.* Hood [2001] I.R.L.R. 719, EAT . . . . *Digested,* 01/**2239**
London Corp, The [1935] P. 70; (1935) 51 Ll. L. Rep. 67, CA; affirming (1934) 50 Ll. L. Rep. 14, PDAD . . . . *Applied,* 67/1021:
Followed, 99/2504
London Drugs Ltd *v.* Kuehne & Nagle International Ltd [1992] 3 S.C.R. 299 . . . . *Applied,* 00/3531
London Federation of Clubs for Young People *v.* Customs and Excise Commissioners [2001] B.V.C. 2225; [2001] S.T.I. 950, V&DTr
London Federation of Clubs for Young People *v.* Customs and Excise Commissioners (Pre Trial Review) [2000] S.T.I. 760, V&DTr
London Fire and Civil Defence Authority *v.* Betty [1994] I.R.L.R. 384, EAT . . . . *Digested,* 95/**2090**:
Distinguished, 01/2345
London Fire and Civil Defence Authority *v.* F see F *v.* London Fire and Civil Defence Authority
London General Insurance Co Ltd *v.* Customs and Excise Commissioners [1998] V. & D.R. 177, V&DTr . . . . *Digested,* 00/**5038**
London General Transport Services Ltd *v.* Henry see Henry *v.* London General Transport Services Ltd
London Life Association, Re, *Independent,* February 27, 1989 (C.S.), Ch D . . . . *Followed,* 98/3370:
Referred to, 94/2675, 95/2924
London Metallurgical Co, Re [1895] 1 Ch. 758, Ch D . . . . *Considered,* 84/179,
85/158, 01/507: *Followed,* 90/517
London North Securities Ltd *v.* Salt (Unreported, November 11, 1998), CC (Oldham) [*Ex rel.* Monty Palfrey, Barrister, Hardwicke Building, New Square, Lincoln's Inn, London] . . . . *Digested,* 99/**2502**:
Considered, 99/4387: *Followed,* 00/514
London Residuary Body *v.* Lambeth LBC; *sub nom* London Residuary Body *v.* Secretary of State for the Environment [1990] 1 W.L.R. 744; [1990] 2 All E.R. 309; (1991) 61 P. & C.R. 65; [1991] 3 P.L.R. 1; (1990) 154 L.G. Rev. 791; *Times,* May 11, 1990; *Independent,* May 11, 1990; *Guardian,* May 11, 1990, HL; reversing (1989) 58 P. & C.R. 370; [1990] J.P.L. 200; [1990] C.O.D. 72; *Times,* August 18, 1989, CA; reversing (1989) 58 P. & C.R. 256; [1988] 2 P.L.R. 79; [1988] J.P.L. 637, QBD . . . . *Digested,* 90/**4421**:
Applied, 99/4214: *Followed,* 94/4339, 95/4782
London Residuary Body *v.* Secretary of State for the Environment see London Residuary Body *v.* Lambeth LBC

London School of Electronics Ltd, Re [1986] Ch. 211; [1985] 3 W.L.R. 474; [1985] P.C.C. 248; (1985) 129 S.J. 573, Ch D . . . . *Digested*, 85/**308**: *Applied*, 01/741

London Scottish Benefit Society *v.* Chester see London Scottish Benefit Society *v.* Chorley

London Scottish Benefit Society *v.* Chorley; London Scottish Benefit Society *v.* Crawford; London Scottish Benefit Society *v.* Chester (1883-84) L.R. 13 Q.B.D. 872, CA; affirming (1883-84) L.R. 12 Q.B.D. 452, QBD . . . . *Applied*, 69/2820, 87/3010, 01/527: *Distinguished*, 52/2668

London Scottish Benefit Society *v.* Crawford see London Scottish Benefit Society *v.* Chorley

London Transport Executive *v.* Clarke [1981] I.C.R. 355; [1981] I.R.L.R. 166; 125 S.J. 306, CA; reversing [1980] I.C.R. 532, EAT . . . . *Digested*, 81/**941**: *Applied*, 82/1105, 87/1419: *Considered*, 85/1144, 94/2014: *Followed*, 98/2207

London Underground Ltd *v.* Edwards (No.2) [1999] I.C.R. 494; [1998] I.R.L.R. 364; (1998) 95(26) L.S.G. 32; (1998) 148 N.L.J. 905; (1998) 142 S.J.L.B. 182; *Times*, June 1, 1998; *Independent*, June 5, 1998, CA; affirming [1997] I.R.L.R. 157, EAT . . . . *Digested*, 98/**2198**: *Applied*, 99/2029

London Underground Ltd *v.* Kenchington Ford Plc 63 Con. L.R. 1, QBD (T&CC) . . . . . . *Digested*, 99/**789**

London Underground Ltd *v.* National Union of Rail Maritime and Transport Workers; *sub nom* National Union of Railwaymen Maritime and Transport Staff *v.* London Underground Ltd [2001] EWCA Civ 211; [2001] I.C.R. 647; [2001] I.R.L.R. 228; *Times*, March 7, 2001; *Independent*, February 20, 2001, CA; affirming2001 1 No, QBD . . . . *Digested*, 01/**2326**: *Considered*, 01/2288

London Underground Ltd *v.* Noel; *sub nom* Noel *v.* London Underground Ltd [2000] I.C.R. 109; [1999] I.R.L.R. 621; (1999) 96(31) L.S.G. 38; *Times*, July 7, 1999, CA . . . . *Digested*, 99/**2146**: *Considered*, 00/2243

London Underground Ltd *v.* Shell International Petroleum Co Ltd [1998] E.G.C.S. 97, Ch D

Londonderry's Settlement, Re; *sub nom* Peat *v.* Walsh [1965] Ch. 918; [1965] 2 W.L.R. 229; [1964] 3 All E.R. 855; 108 S.J. 896, CA; reversing [1964] Ch. 594; [1964] 3 W.L.R. 246; [1964] 2 All E.R. 572; 108 S.J. 379, Ch D . . . . *Digested*, 65/**3564**: *Considered*, 01/5512

Long (CICB: Quantum: 1999), Re (Unreported, September 29, 1999), CICB (Nottingham) [*Ex rel.* Richard Gregory, Barrister, 24 The Ropewalk, Nottingham] . . . . *Digested*, 00/**1530**

Long *v.* Tolchard & Sons Ltd [2001] P.I.Q.R. P2; *Times*, January 5, 2000, CA . . . . *Digested*, 00/**526**

Long *v.* Tower Hamlets LBC [1998] Ch. 197; [1996] 3 W.L.R. 317; [1996] 2 All E.R. 683; [1997] 1 E.G.L.R. 78; [1997] 05 E.G. 157; [1996] N.P.C. 48; *Times*, March 29, 1996, Ch D . . . . *Digested*, 96/**3691**

Long John Silver's, Inc's Application [2001] E.T.M.R. 11, OHIM (Opposition Div) . . . . . . *Digested*, 01/**4021**

Longden *v.* British Coal Corp [1998] A.C. 653; [1997] 3 W.L.R. 1336; [1998] 1 All E.R. 289; [1998] I.C.R. 26; [1998] I.R.L.R. 29; [1998] P.I.Q.R. Q11; [1998] O.P.L.R. 223; (1998) 95(1) L.S.G. 25; (1997) 147 N.L.J. 1774; (1998) 142 S.J.L.B. 28; *Times*, November 28, 1997, HL; affirming in part [1995] I.C.R. 957; [1995] I.R.L.R. 642; [1995] P.I.Q.R. Q48; (1995) 92(15) L.S.G. 40; (1995) 139 S.J.L.B. 88; *Times*, April 14, 1995, CA . . . . *Digested*, 98/**1468**: *Applied*, 98/1692: *Followed*, 99/5973

Longlands Farm, Re; *sub nom* Alford *v.* Superior Developments Ltd [1968] 3 All E.R. 552; 20 P. & C.R. 25, Ch D . . . . *Digested*, 68/**3996**: *Cited*, 00/4668

Longrigg Burrough & Trounson *v.* Smith [1979] 2 E.G.L.R. 42; (1979) 251 E.G. 847, CA . . . . *Digested*, 79/**1582**: *Considered*, 91/122, 91/2218, 01/4162: *Not applied*, 98/3683

Longson *v.* Baker (Inspector of Taxes) [2001] S.T.C. 6; 73 T.C. 415; [2001] B.T.C. 356; [2001] S.T.I. 44; (2001) 98(3) L.S.G. 43; *Times*, December 5, 2000, Ch D; affirming [2000] S.T.C. (S.C.D.) 244; [2000] S.T.I. 785, Sp Comm. . . . . *Digested*, 01/**5187**

Longstaff *v.* Birtles [2001] EWCA Civ 1219; [2001] 34 E.G.C.S. 98; (2001) 98(34) L.S.G. 43; (2001) 145 S.J.L.B. 210; [2001] N.P.C. 128; *Times*, September 18, 2001, CA . . . . *Digested*, 01/**2437**

Longstone Ltd *v.* Customs and Excise Commissioners [2001] S.T.I. 1040, V&DTr

Lonrho Exports Ltd *v.* Export Credits Guarantee Department [1999] Ch. 158; [1998] 3 W.L.R. 394; [1996] 4 All E.R. 673; [1996] 2 Lloyd's Rep. 649; [1997] C.L.C. 259, Ch D . . . . *Digested*, 97/**3219**

Lonrho Ltd *v.* Shell Petroleum Co Ltd (No.2) [1982] A.C. 173; [1981] 3 W.L.R. 33; [1981] 2 All E.R. 456; 125 S.J. 429, HL; affirming [1981] Com. L.R. 74; 125 S.J. 255, CA; affirming [1981] Com. L.R. 6; *Times,* December 2, 1980, QBD (Comm Ct) . . . . *Digested,* 81/**2649**:
Applied, 82/436, 87/516, 89/3520, 89/3528, 91/2456, 92/1524, 93/1391, 94/2281, 95/2901, 00/5111: *Considered,* 85/2774, 87/1315, 88/1324, 88/2905, 92/2547, 92/3651, 92/4130, 93/363, 95/3452, 96/5690, 00/5106: *Distinguished,* 88/3404, 96/7366: *Followed,* 96/1085: *Referred to,* 85/3384

Lonrho Plc (Contempt Proceedings), Re; *sub nom* Lonrho Plc and Observer, Re [1990] 2 A.C. 154; [1989] 3 W.L.R. 535; [1989] 2 All E.R. 1100; (1989) 139 N.L.J. 1073; (1989) 133 S.J. 120, HL . . . . *Digested,* 90/**3588**:
Considered, 98/79

Lonrho Plc *v.* Al-Fayed (No.1) [1992] 1 A.C. 448; [1991] 3 W.L.R. 188; [1991] 3 All E.R. 303; [1991] B.C.C. 641; [1991] B.C.L.C. 779; (1991) 141 N.L.J. 927; (1991) 135 S.J.L.B. 68; *Times,* July 3, 1991; *Independent,* July 3, 1991; *Financial Times,* July 3, 1991; *Guardian,* June 28, 1991, HL; affirming [1990] 2 Q.B. 479; [1989] 3 W.L.R. 631; [1989] 2 All E.R. 65; [1989] B.C.L.C. 485; [1989] P.C.C. 215; (1989) 139 N.L.J. 539, CA; reversing [1990] 1 Q.B. 490; [1989] 2 W.L.R. 356; (1988) 4 B.C.C. 688; [1989] B.C.L.C. 75; [1989] P.C.C. 173; (1989) 86(10) L.S.G. 43; (1988) 138 N.L.J. Rep. 225; (1989) 133 S.J. 220; *Independent,* July 19, 1988, QBD . . . . *Digested,* 92/**4130**:
Applied, 92/2: *Considered,* 98/4069: *Followed,* 94/4040

Lonrho Plc *v.* Tebbit [1992] 4 All E.R. 280; [1992] B.C.C. 779; [1993] B.C.L.C. 96; *Times,* June 10, 1992; *Independent,* June 9, 1992; *Guardian,* June 24, 1992, CA; affirming [1991] 4 All E.R. 973; [1992] B.C.C. 45; [1992] B.C.L.C. 67; *Times,* September 24, 1991; *Independent,* September 26, 1991; *Financial Times,* August 13, 1991; *Guardian,* August 14, 1991, Ch D . . . . *Digested,* 92/**2**:
Applied, 99/5434

Lonrho Plc and Observer, Re see Lonrho Plc (Contempt Proceedings), Re

LONZA/L-carnitine (T80/96); *sub nom* Lonza AG's European Patent (No.0434088) [2000] E.P.O.R. 323; (2000) 23(5) I.P.D. 23041, EPO (Technical Bd App) . . . . *Digested,* 00/**3641**

Look Ahead Housing Association *v.* Customs and Excise Commissioners [2001] B.V.C. 2107; [2001] S.T.I. 158, V&DTr . . . . *Digested,* 01/**5619**

Loosemore *v.* Financial Concepts [2001] Lloyd's Rep. P.N. 235, QBD (Merc Ct) . . . . . . *Digested,* 01/**4520**

Lopex Export GmbH *v.* Hauptzollamt Hamburg-Jonas (C315/96) [1998] E.C.R. I-317; [1998] 2 C.M.L.R. 737, ECJ (5th Chamber)

Lopez Ostra *v.* Spain (A/303-C) (1995) 20 E.H.R.R. 277, ECHR . . . . *Digested,* 96/**3118**:
Applied, 98/3096: *Considered,* 98/3154, 01/5378

Lord *v.* Alco Waste Management (Unreported, January 28, 1998), CC (Carlisle) [*Ex rel.* Hough, Halton & Soal Solicitors, 32 Abbey Street, Carlisle] . . . . *Digested,* 99/**1484**

Lord *v.* Carnell Ltd (Unreported, September 9, 2000), CC (Peterborough) [*Ex rel.* Langleys Solicitors, Newporte House, Doddington Road Business Park, Lincoln] . . . . *Digested,* 01/**588**

Lord *v.* Cryers (1999) 99(5) Q.R. 6, CC (Bolton) [*Ex rel.* John F Harrison, Barrister, St Pauls Chambers, St Paul's House, 23 Park Square, Leeds] . . . . *Digested,* 99/**1477**

Lord *v.* Taymix Transport Ltd (Unreported, March 17, 2000), CC (Cardiff) [*Ex rel.* Andrew Arentsen, Barrister, 33 Park Place, Cardiff] . . . . *Digested,* 00/**1660**

Lord Advocate, Petitioner (Evidence: Foreign Proceedings) 1998 S.C. 87; 1998 S.L.T. 835; 1997 G.W.D. 37-1882; *Times,* May 28, 1998, Ex Div . . . . *Digested,* 98/**5531**

Lord Ashburton *v.* Pape [1913] 2 Ch. 469, CA . . . . *Applied,* 75/2616, 86/1516, 87/3060, 87/3086, 88/1596: *Considered,* 70/1039, 94/3526, 01/3851: *Distinguished,* 81/1183, 81/2089, 81/2147, 82/1335: *Followed,* 64/1353, 65/1483

Lord Chancellor *v.* Coker see Coker *v.* Lord Chancellor

Lord Chancellor *v.* Taylor [2000] 1 Costs L.R. 1, QBD . . . . *Digested,* 00/**1040**

Lord Gray's Motion, Re [2000] 2 W.L.R. 664; 2000 S.C. (H.L.) 46; 2000 S.L.T. 1337; *Times,* November 12, 1999, HL . . . . *Digested,* 99/**5768**

Lord Mayhew of Twysden's Motion, Re [2000] 2 W.L.R. 719; *Times,* November 12, 1999, HL . . . . *Digested,* 99/**768**

Lord Napier and Ettrick *v.* Hunter see Lord Napier and Ettrick *v.* RF Kershaw Ltd (No.1)

Lord Napier and Ettrick *v.* RF Kershaw Ltd (No.1); Lord Napier and Ettrick *v.* Hunter [1993] A.C. 713; [1993] 2 W.L.R. 42; [1993] 1 All E.R. 385; [1993] 1 Lloyd's Rep. 197; (1993) 137 S.J.L.B. 44; *Times,* December 16, 1992; *Independent,* December 11, 1992, HL; reversing [1993] 1 Lloyd's Rep. 10; *Times,* July 17, 1992; *Financial Times,* July 22, 1992, CA; reversing in part (Unreported, May 14, 1992), Ch D . . . . *Digested,* 93/**2422**:
Applied, 99/3431: *Cited,* 99/3404: *Followed,* 96/3592, 00/3514

Lord Napier and Ettrick *v.* RF Kershaw Ltd (No.2); *sub nom* Society of Lloyd's *v.* Robinson; Society of Lloyd's *v.* Woodard [1999] 1 W.L.R. 756; [1999] 1 All E.R. (Comm.) 545; [1999] C.L.C. 987; [1999] Lloyd's Rep. I.R. 329; (1999) 96(22) L.S.G. 34; (1999) 143 S.J.L.B. 150; *Times,* March 29, 1999, HL; affirming in part [1997] L.R.L.R. 1; [1996] C.L.C. 1875; *Times,* November 7, 1996, CA . . . . *Digested,* 99/**3404**:
Previous proceedings, 96/3592

Lorimer v. Solihull MBC [1999] R.V.R. 55; [1998] R.V.R. 100, LandsTr . . . .   *Digested*, 98/**2882**
Losinjska Plovidba Brodarstovo DD v. Valfracht Maritime Co Ltd (The Lipa) [2001] 2
    Lloyd's Rep. 17, QBD (Comm Ct) . . . .   *Digested*, 01/**4917**
Loteak, Re [1989] 7 A.C.L.C. 998, Sup Ct (Qld) . . . .   *Applied*, 00/3465
Lothian Borders and Angus Cooperative Society Ltd v. Scottish Borders Council [1999]
    2 P.L.R. 19; 1999 G.W.D. 6-316; *Times*, March 10, 1999, OH . . . .   *Digested*, 99/**6408**
Lotteryking Ltd v. Amec Properties Ltd [1995] 2 E.G.L.R. 13; [1995] 28 E.G. 100;
    [1995] N.P.C. 55, Ch D . . . .   *Not followed*, 99/3729
Lotus Cars Ltd v. Southampton Cargo Handling Plc (The Rigoletto); *sub nom*
    Southampton Cargo Handling Plc v. Lotus Cars Ltd (The Rigoletto);
    Southampton Cargo Handling Plc v. Associated British Ports [2000] 2 All E.R.
    (Comm) 705; [2000] 2 Lloyd's Rep. 532; [2001] C.L.C. 25, CA . . . .   *Digested*, 00/**4678**
Louca v. O'Neill (Unreported, June 1, 2000), CC (Bromley) [*Ex rel*. Nigel Ffitch,
    Barrister, Phoenix Chambers, Gray's Inn, London] . . . .   *Digested*, 00/**1447**
Loudonhill Contracts Ltd v. John Mowlem Construction Ltd; *sub nom* Loundonhill
    Contracts Ltd v. John Mowlem Construction Ltd 2000 S.C.L.R. 1111; (2001) 3
    T.C.L.R. 23; 80 Con. L.R. 1; 2000 G.W.D. 25-930, 1 Div . . . .   *Digested*, 01/**6292**
Lough Neagh Exploration Ltd v. Morrice [1999] N.I. 258, CA (NI) . . . .   *Digested*, 00/**5442**
Loughran v. London Buses (Unreported, March 11, 1993), CC (Clerkenwell) . . . .   *Digested*, 93/**1476**:
                                                                   Considered, 01/1595
Loughran v. Northern Ireland Housing Executive see Kelly v. Northern Ireland Housing
    Executive
Louies v. Coventry Hood & Seating Co [1990] I.C.R. 54; [1990] I.R.L.R. 324, EAT . . . .   *Digested*, 90/**1975**:
                                                   Considered, 93/1815, 99/2138
Louis v. DPP (1998) 162 J.P. 287; [1998] R.T.R. 354; *Times*, July 21, 1997, QBD . . . . . .   *Digested*, 97/**1145**
Louis v. Sadiq 59 Con. L.R. 127; (1997) 74 P. & C.R. 325; [1997] 1 E.G.L.R. 136;
    [1997] 16 E.G. 126; [1996] E.G.C.S. 180; (1996) 93(46) L.S.G. 29; (1997) 141
    S.J.L.B. 6; [1996] N.P.C. 164; *Times*, November 22, 1996, CA . . . .   *Digested*, 96/**4990**
Louis Konyn & Sons Ltd v. Customs and Excise Commissioners [1999] V. & D.R. 189,
    V&DTr. . . . .   *Digested*, 00/**4952**
Lounadi v. Secretary of State for the Home Department Unreported, IAT . . . .   *Doubted*, 99/3175
Loundonhill Contracts Ltd v. John Mowlem Construction Ltd see Loudonhill Contracts
    Ltd v. John Mowlem Construction Ltd
Loutchansky v. Times Newspapers Ltd (No.1) [2001] EWCA Civ 536; [2001] 3 W.L.R.
    404; [2001] 4 All E.R. 115; [2001] E.M.L.R. 26; (2001) 151 N.L.J. 643; *Times*,
    April 26, 2001; *Independent*, May 1, 2001, CA; affirming HQ9904240, QBD . . . .   *Digested*, 01/**1823**
Loutchansky v. Times Newspapers Ltd (No.2) [2001] EWCA Civ 1805; (2001) 145
    S.J.L.B. 277; *Times*, December 7, 2001; *Independent*, December 11, 2001, CA;
    affirming [2001] E.M.L.R. 36, QBD . . . .   *Digested*, 01/**1825**
Loutchansky v. Times Newspapers Ltd (No.3) [2001] E.M.L.R. 37, QBD . . . .   *Digested*, 01/**1831**
Loutchansky v. Times Newspapers Ltd (No.4) [2001] E.M.L.R. 38, QBD . . . .   *Digested*, 01/**1829**:
                                                   Considered, 01/1832
Loutchansky v. Times Newspapers Ltd (No.5) [2001] E.M.L.R. 39, QBD . . . .   *Digested*, 01/**1818**
Loutchansky v. Times Newspapers Ltd (Striking Out), *Independent*, December 4,
    2000 (C.S), QBD
Loveday v. Renton (No.1), *Times*, March 31, 1988; *Guardian*, April 2, 1988, QBD . . . . . .   *Digested*, 88/**1599**:
                            Applied, 01/4454: *Considered*, 90/2896, 91/2313
Loveday v. Renton (No.2) [1992] 3 All E.R. 184, QBD . . . .   *Digested*, 92/**3452**:
                   Applied, 93/3169, 01/457: *Considered*, 99/5412: *Followed*, 96/3872
Lovejoy v. Secretary of State for the Environment, Transport and the Regions (1999)
    78 P. & C.R. 1; [1999] J.P.L. 441, QBD . . . .   *Digested*, 99/**4179**
Loveless v. Earl [1999] E.M.L.R. 530; *Times*, November 11, 1998, CA . . . .   *Digested*, 98/**1774**
Lovell v. Porter see Heer v. Tutton
Lovell Partnerships (Northern) Ltd v. AW Construction Plc 81 B.L.R. 83, QBD (Comm
    Ct) . . . .   *Digested*, 97/**925**:
                                                                   Applied, 01/339
Lovence (CICB: Quantum: 1999), Re (1999) 99(4) Q.R. 6, CICB (London) [*Ex rel*.
    Jonathan Ashworth, Pupil Barrister, 6 King's Bench Walk, Temple, London] . . . .   *Digested*, 99/**1527**
Lovens Kemiske Fabrik Produktionsaktieselskab v. Paranova A/S (B-3218-95) [2001]
    E.T.M.R. 28, OL (DK)
Lovett v. Bussey; *sub nom* Lovett v. RSPCA; Lovett v. Royal Society for the
    Prevention of Cruelty to Animals (1998) 162 J.P. 423; [1998] C.O.D. 349;
    [1999] Env. L.R. D1; *Times*, April 24, 1998, QBD . . . .   *Digested*, 98/**205**
Lovett v. RSPCA see Lovett v. Bussey
Lovie Ltd v. Anderson [1999] I.R.L.R. 164, EAT . . . .   *Digested*, 99/**2139**
Lowe v. Havering Hospitals NHS Trust (2001) 62 B.M.L.R. 69, QBD
Lowe v. Lombank [1960] 1 W.L.R. 196; [1960] 1 All E.R. 611; 104 S.J. 210, CA . . . .   *Digested*, 60/**1403**:
                           Considered, 01/966: *Distinguished*, 61/3918, 94/503
Lowe v. Marr-Wain [2001] 6 Q.R. 8, CC (Sheffield) [*Ex rel*. Tom Nossiter, Barrister,
    Park Lane Chambers, 19 Westgate, Leeds] . . . .   *Digested*, 01/**1632**
Lowe v. Swack, CC (Bury) [*Ex rel*. Berrymans Lace Mawer Solicitors, King's House,
    42 King Street West, Manchester] . . . .   *Digested*, 01/**668**
Lowe & Watson v. South Somerset DC [1998] Env. L.R. 143; [1998] J.P.L. 458;
    [1997] E.G.C.S. 113; *Times*, November 18, 1997, QBD . . . .   *Digested*, 97/**2373**

Lower v. Hagland (1998) 98(1) Q.R. 4, CC (Cardiff) . . . . *Digested,* 98/**1526**
Lower Street Properties Ltd (formerly Mirod Estates) v. Jones (1996) 28 H.L.R. 877;
    [1996] 2 E.G.L.R. 67; [1996] 48 E.G. 154; [1996] E.G.C.S. 37; [1996] N.P.C. 29,
    CA; affirming (Unreported, March 6, 1995), CC (Worthing) [*Ex rel.* Mark James,
    Barrister] . . . . *Digested,* 96/**3696**
Lownes v. Babcock Power Ltd [1998] P.I.Q.R. P253; (1998) 95(14) L.S.G. 22;
    (1998) 142 S.J.L.B. 84; *Times,* February 19, 1998; *Independent,* February 13,
    1998, CA . . . . : . . . . *Digested,* 98/**630**:
                                                   Followed, 99/446: *Referred to,* 99/555
Lowsley v. Forbes (t/a LE Design Services) [1999] 1 A.C. 329; [1998] 3 W.L.R. 501;
    [1998] 3 All E.R. 897; [1998] 2 Lloyd's Rep. 577; (1998) 95(35) L.S.G. 37;
    (1998) 148 N.L.J. 1268; (1998) 142 S.J.L.B. 247; *Times,* August 24, 1998, HL;
    reversing in part [1996] C.L.C. 1370; *Times,* April 5, 1996, CA . . . . *Digested,* 98/**539**
Lowson v. Coombes [1999] Ch. 373; [1999] 2 W.L.R. 720; [1999] 1 F.L.R. 799;
    [1999] 2 F.C.R. 731; [1999] Fam. Law 91; (1999) 96(1) L.S.G. 23; (1999) 77 P.
    & C.R. D25; *Times,* December 2, 1998, CA . . . . *Digested,* 99/**4368**
Loyalty Bonus Scheme (4 Ob 90/99k), Re [2001] E.C.C. 19, OGH (A)
LR v. Witherspoon [2000] 1 F.L.R. 82; [1999] 3 F.C.R. 202; [1999] Lloyd's Rep. P.N.
    401; [1999] P.N.L.R. 776; [2000] Fam. Law 19, CA . . . . *Digested,* 99/**4027**
LRC PRODUCTS/Prophylactic sheath (T839/91) [1998] E.P.O.R. 370, EPO (Technical Bd
    App)
LTU v. Eurocontrol (C29/76) see Lufttransportunternehmen GmbH & Co KG v.
    Organisation Europeenne pour la Securite de la Navigation Aerienne
    (Eurocontrol) (C29/76)
Lubbe v. Cape Plc (No.1) [1998] C.L.C. 1559; [1999] I.L.Pr. 113, CA . . . . *Digested,* 98/**749**:
                                                        Not applied, 99/718
Lubbe v. Cape Plc (No.2); Afrika v. Cape Plc [2000] 1 W.L.R. 1545; [2000] 4 All E.R.
    268; [2000] 2 Lloyd's Rep. 383; [2001] I.L.Pr. 12; (2000) 144 S.J.L.B. 250;
    Times, July 27, 2000; *Independent,* July 26, 2000, HL; reversing [2000] 1
    Lloyd's Rep. 139; [2000] C.L.C. 45; [2000] I.L.Pr. 438; (1999) 96(48) L.S.G.
    39; (2000) 144 S.J.L.B. 25; *Times,* December 3, 1999, CA . . . . *Digested,* 00/**775**:
                                                   Considered, 00/1756
Lubbock Fine & Co v. Customs and Excise Commissioners (C63/92) [1994] Q.B. 571;
    [1994] 3 W.L.R. 261; [1994] 3 All E.R. 705; [1994] S.T.C. 101; [1993] E.C.R. I-
    6665; [1994] 2 C.M.L.R. 633; [1993] E.G.C.S. 219; *Times,* December 27, 1993,
    ECJ [1991] V.A.T.T.R. 480, VAT Tr (London) . . . . *Digested,* 94/**4961**:
                Considered, 98/4920: *Distinguished,* 01/5602: *Followed,* 98/4956
Lube A/S v. Dansk Droge A/S (II 134/1998) [2001] E.T.M.R. 31, HR (DK)
Luberti v. Italy (A/75) (1984) 6 E.H.R.R. 440, ECHR . . . . *Applied,* 01/3564
Lubrizol Corp v. Esso Petroleum Co Ltd (No.5) [1998] R.P.C. 727; (1998) 21(8) I.P.D.
    21081, CA; affirming [1997] R.P.C. 195, Pat Ct . . . . *Digested,* 99/**3507**
Lubrizol Corp v. Esso Petroleum Co Ltd (No.6) [1997] F.S.R. 844; (1997) 20(10) I.P.D.
    20097, Pat Ct . . . . *Digested,* 98/**476**
Lubrizol Corp v. Esso Petroleum Co Ltd (No.7) (1998) 21(10) I.P.D. 21104, CA
Luc Thiet Thuan v. Queen, The [1997] A.C. 131; [1996] 3 W.L.R. 45; [1996] 2 All E.R.
    1033; [1996] 2 Cr. App. R. 178; (1996) 32 B.M.L.R. 112; [1996] Crim. L.R. 820;
    (1996) 93(16) L.S.G. 30; (1996) 146 N.L.J. 513; (1996) 140 S.J.L.B. 107;
    Times, April 2, 1996, PC (HK) . . . . *Digested,* 96/**1456**:
                 Considered, 97/1127, 00/986: *Not followed,* 98/960
Luca v. Italy [2001] Crim. L.R. 747, ECHR
Lucas v. R. 5 B.H.R.C. 409, Sup Ct (Can) . . . . *Digested,* 99/**3106**
Lucas v. Sketchley Plc (Unreported, June 19, 1998), CC (Worcester) [*Ex rel.* Parkinson
    Wright Solicitors, Haswell House, St Nicholas Street, Worcester] . . . . *Digested,* 98/**1652**
Lucas-Box v. Associated Newspapers Group Plc see Lucas-Box v. News Group
    Newspapers Ltd
Lucas-Box v. News Group Newspapers Ltd; Lucas-Box v. Associated Newspapers
    Group Plc [1986] 1 W.L.R. 147; [1986] 1 All E.R. 177; (1986) 83 L.S.G. 441;
    (1986) 130 S.J. 111, CA . . . . *Digested,* 86/**1984**:
              Applied, 86/1988, 88/2160, 90/2912, 90/2914, 98/1774:
                Considered, 87/2302, 87/3119, 88/2126, 88/2952
Luchtmansingh v. Grostate (Unreported, May 5, 2000), CC (Edmonton) [*Ex rel.*
    Joanna Droop, Barrister, 12 King's Bench Walk, Temple, London] . . . . *Digested,* 00/**621**
Lucot, Re (97-20882) 3 I.T.L. Rep. 38, Cass (F)
Lucy v. Kensington and Chelsea RLBC; *sub nom* L v. Kensington and Chelsea RLBC
    [1997] E.L.R. 155; [1997] C.O.D. 191, QBD . . . . *Digested,* 97/**2128**:
                                                     Followed, 98/4184
Ludgate Insurance Co Ltd v. Citibank NA [1998] Lloyd's Rep. I.R. 221, CA; affirming
    [1996] L.R.L.R. 247; *Lloyd's List,* June 12, 1996 (I.D.), QBD (Comm Ct) . . . . . . *Digested,* 98/**3410**
Ludi v. Switzerland (A/238) (1993) 15 E.H.R.R. 173; *Times,* August 13, 1992; *Guardian,*
    July 15, 1992, ECHR. . . . . *Digested,* 93/**2139**:
            Applied, 01/6323: *Considered,* 97/2766: *Distinguished,* 98/3122
Ludlow Music Inc v. Williams (No.1) [2001] E.M.L.R. 7; [2001] F.S.R. 19; (2000)
    23(11) I.P.D. 23093, Ch D

Lufttransportunternehmen GmbH & Co KG v. Organisation Europeenne pour la Securite de la Navigation Aerienne (Eurocontrol) (C29/76); *sub nom* LTU v. Eurocontrol (C29/76) [1976] E.C.R. 1541; [1977] 1 C.M.L.R. 88; *Times*, October 18, 1976, ECJ . . . . *Digested*, 77/**1282**:
Applied, 91/0235, 92/0204: *Distinguished*, 00/790

Luijckx BV v. ECC [2000] E.T.M.R. 530, Hof ('s-Hertogenbosch)

Lukoil-Kalingradmorneft Plc v. Tata Ltd (No.2) [1999] 2 Lloyd's Rep. 129, CA; affirming
[1999] 1 Lloyd's Rep. 365, QBD (Comm Ct). . . . . *Digested*, 99/**4490**

Lukowiak v. Unidad Editorial SA (No.1) [2001] E.M.L.R. 46; *Times*, July 23, 2001,
QBD . . . . *Digested*, 01/**1834**

Luksch v. Hauptzollamt Weiden (C31/98) [1999] E.C.R. I-2423; [2000] 2 C.M.L.R.
472, ECJ (1st Chamber). . . . . *Digested*, 00/**2336**

Luminar Leisure Ltd v. Apostole [2001] 42 E.G. 140, Ch D

Lumley v. Gye (1853) 2 El. & Bl. 216. . . . . *Applied*, 52/3396,
52/3507, 64/3702, 68/3955, 69/3574: *Cited*, 99/280: *Considered*, 88/503

Lummus Agricultural Services Ltd, Re; *sub nom* Lummus Agriculture Services Ltd, Re
[1999] B.C.C. 953; [2001] 1 B.C.L.C. 137, Ch D . . . . *Digested*, 00/**3500**

Lund v. Internal Revenue Commissioner; Zero Gee Enterprises Trust v. Internal Revenue
Commissioner (2000-01) 3 I.T.E.L.R. 343, US Ct

LUNDIA/Diffusion device (T265/88) [1990] E.P.O.R. 399, EPO (Technical Bd App). . . *Considered*, 00/3603

Lunnun v. Singh (Bhadur) see Lunnun v. Singh (Hajar)

Lunnun v. Singh (Hajar); Lunnun v. Singh (Hari); Lunnun v. Singh (Bhadur); Lunnun v.
Singh (Sher) [1999] C.P.L.R. 587; (1999) 96(31) L.S.G. 36; [1999] N.P.C. 83;
Times, July 19, 1999 ; *Independent*, July 26, 1999, CA . . . . *Digested*, 99/**1395**:
Applied, 01/547

Lunnun v. Singh (Hari) see Lunnun v. Singh (Hajar)

Lunnun v. Singh (Sher) see Lunnun v. Singh (Hajar)

Lunt v. Liverpool Justices (Unreported, March 5, 1991) . . . . *Considered*, 97/4856,
01/1524

Lunt v. Merseyside TEC Ltd [1999] I.C.R. 17; [1999] I.R.L.R. 458, EAT . . . . *Digested*, 99/**2137**

Lustig-Prean v. United Kingdom (No.1); Beckett v. United Kingdom (2000) 29
E.H.R.R. 548; 7 B.H.R.C. 65, ECHR . . . . *Joined proceedings*,
99/3113

Lustig-Prean v. United Kingdom (No.2) (2001) 31 E.H.R.R. 23, ECHR . . . . *Digested*, 01/**3579**

Luton BC v. Ball, *Independent*, May 14, 2001 (C.S), QBD

Lutz Quasdorf v. Les Sirenes SA [1999] E.T.M.R. 152, OHIM (Opposition Div) . . . . . . *Digested*, 99/**3586**

Luxembourg v. Linster (C287/98) [2000] E.C.R. I-6917; [2001] Env. L.R. D3; *Times*,
October 5, 2000, ECJ . . . . *Digested*, 00/**2354**

Lybert v. Warrington HA [1996] P.I.Q.R. P45; [1996] 7 Med. L.R. 71; [1955-95]
P.N.L.R. 693; (1995) 92(20) L.S.G. 40; *Times*, May 17, 1995, CA . . . . *Digested*, 95/**3680**

Lydiashourne Ltd v. Customs and Excise Commissioners [2000] V. & D.R. 127, QBD

Lyell v. Kennedy (No.3) (1884) L.R. 27 Ch. D. 1, CA. . . . . *Applied*, 74/2941,
81/1191, 83/2937, 84/1528: *Considered*, 93/3219: *Distinguished*, 01/553

Lymer v. Henson (Unreported, December 16, 1996), CC (Stoke on Trent) [*Ex rel.*
Frederick H Brown, Barrister]. . . . . *Digested*, 97/**1863**:
Considered, 00/1501

Lymington Precision Engineers & Co Ltd v. New Forest DC see Lymington Precision
Engineers & Co Ltd v. Secretary of State for the Environment, Transport and the
Regions

Lymington Precision Engineers & Co Ltd v. Secretary of State for the Environment,
Transport and the Regions; Lymington Precision Engineers & Co Ltd v. New
Forest DC [1999] J.P.L. 553, QBD . . . . *Digested*, 99/**4211**

Lynall (Deceased), Re see Lynall v. Inland Revenue Commissioners

Lynall v. Inland Revenue Commissioners; *sub nom* Lynall (Deceased), Re [1972] A.C.
680; [1971] 3 W.L.R. 759; [1971] 3 All E.R. 914; 47 T.C. 375; [1971] T.R. 309;
115 S.J. 872, HL; reversing [1970] Ch. 138; [1969] 3 W.L.R. 711; [1969] 3 All
E.R. 984; [1969] T.R. 353; 113 S.J. 723, CA; reversing [1969] 1 Ch. 421; [1968]
3 W.L.R. 1056; [1968] 3 All E.R. 322; [1968] T.R. 283; 112 S.J. 765, Ch D . . . . *Digested*, 71/**3309**:
Considered, 85/1932, 87/2204, 88/2729, 00/5028: *Distinguished*, 89/2181:
Followed, 69/1689

Lynch v. Farrand see Seifert v. Pensions Ombudsman

Lynch v. Pensions Ombudsman see Seifert v. Pensions Ombudsman

Lynch v. Secretary of State for the Environment, Transport and the Regions [1999]
J.P.L. 354, QBD . . . . *Digested*, 99/**4176**

Lyne-Pirkis v. Jones [1969] 1 W.L.R. 1293; [1969] 3 All E.R. 738; 113 S.J. 568, CA . . . . *Digested*, 69/**3522**:
Distinguished, 91/2685: *Followed*, 98/4024

Lynn v. Rokeby School Board of Governors [2001] Pens. L.R. 273, EAT . . . . *Digested*, 01/**2280**

Lyon v. Rhums Martiniquais Saint James SA [1999] E.T.M.R. 188, C d'A (Paris)

Lyon & Co v. London City and Midland Bank [1903] 2 K.B. 135, KBD. . . . . *Considered*, 01/854

Lyons v. Grand Metropolitan Retailing Ltd see ELO Entertainment Ltd v. Grand
Metropolitan Retailing Ltd

Lyons v. Metcalf (Unreported, June 8, 1999), CC (Swindon) [*Ex rel.* Tim Petts,
Barrister, 12 King's Bench Walk, Temple, London]. . . . . *Digested*, 99/**2494**

Lysaght *v.* Inland Revenue Commissioners see Inland Revenue Commissioners *v.* Lysaght

M, Re (Unreported, April 21, 1997), CICB (Torquay) [*Ex rel.* Sally King, Solicitor, Rudlings & Wakelam, 1 Woolhall Street, Bury St Edmunds] . . . .   *Digested,* 97/**1851**: *Considered,* 01/1585

M (A Child) (Abduction: Intolerable Situation), Re [2000] 1 F.L.R. 930; [2000] Fam. Law 593, Fam Div . . . .   *Digested,* 00/**2444**

M (A Child) (CICB: Quantum: 1999), Re (Unreported, June 15, 1999), CICB (London) [*Ex rel.* Anthony Rimmer, Barrister, Francis Taylor Building, Temple, London] . . . .   *Digested,* 00/**1531**

M (A Child) (Contact: Domestic Violence), Re see L (A Child) (Contact: Domestic Violence), Re

M (A Child) (Contact: Parental Responsibility), Re [2001] 2 F.L.R. 342; [2001] 3 F.C.R. 454; [2001] Fam. Law 594, Fam Div . . . .   *Digested,* 01/**2660**

M (A Child) (Interim Contact: Domestic Violence), Re [2000] 2 F.L.R. 377; [2000] Fam. Law 604, CA . . . .   *Digested,* 00/**2499**

M (A Child) (Medical Treatment: Consent) see M (A Child) (Refusal of Medical Treatment), Re

M (A Child) (Refusal of Medical Treatment), Re; *sub nom* M (A Child) (Medical Treatment: Consent) [1999] 2 F.L.R. 1097; [1999] 2 F.C.R. 577; (2000) 52 B.M.L.R. 124; [1999] Fam. Law 753, Fam Div. . . . .   *Digested,* 99/**2373**

M (A Child) (Section 91 (14) Order), Re see M (Care Orders: Restricting Applications), Re

M (A Child) (Secure Accommodation Order), Re see C (A Child) (Secure Accommodation Order: Representation), Re

M (A Child) *v.* Bukhari (Unreported, February 16, 2000), CC (Barnet) [*Ex rel.* Anna Kotzeva, Barrister, 1 Temple Gardens, London] . . . .   *Digested,* 00/**1704**

M (A Child) *v.* Chief Adjudication Officer (1999) 96(44) L.S.G. 41; (1999) 143 S.J.L.B. 267; *Times,* November 11, 1999 ; *Independent,* November 4, 1999, CA . . . .   *Digested,* 99/**4546**

M (A Child) *v.* Ferris [2001] 5 Q.R. 16, CC (Halifax) [*Ex rel.* Rhodes Thain & Collinson, Solicitors, 27 Harrison Road, Halifax] . . . .   *Digested,* 01/**1741**

M (A Child) *v.* Khan (Unreported, March 8, 2000), CC (Slough) [*Ex rel.* Owen White Solicitors, Senate House, 62-70 Bath Road, Berkshire] . . . .   *Digested,* 00/**1742**

M (A Child) *v.* London and Quadrant Housing Trust [2001] 1 Q.R. 15, CC (Bow) [*Ex rel.* Rebecca Tuck, Barrister, Old Square Chambers, 1 Verulam Buildings, Gray's Inn, London] . . . .   *Digested,* 01/**1706**

M (A Child) *v.* North & Mid Hamptonshire HA (Unreported, October 11, 1999), QBD [*Ex rel.* Frank R Moat, Barrister, 3 Pump Court, Temple, London] . . . .   *Digested,* 00/**1556**

M (A Child) *v.* Oraha (Unreported, February 10, 2000), CC (Central London) [*Ex rel.* Kevin Haven, Barrister, 2 Gray's Inn Square Chambers, Gray's Inn, London] . . . .   *Digested,* 00/**1712**

M (A Child) *v.* Secretary of State for Social Security [2001] UKHL 35; [2001] 1 W.L.R. 1453; [2001] 4 All E.R. 41; (2001) 61 B.M.L.R. 1; (2001) 98(32) L.S.G. 37; *Times,* July 6, 2001, HL . . . .   *Digested,* 01/**5005**

M (A Debtor), Re see Debtor (No.488-IO of 1996), Re

M (A Minor) (Abduction: Habitual Residence), Re [1996] 1 F.L.R. 887; [1996] 2 F.C.R. 333; [1996] Fam. Law 402; *Times,* January 3, 1996; *Independent,* January 29, 1996 (C.S.), CA . . . .   *Digested,* 96/**643**: *Applied,* 98/2382

M (A Minor) (Abduction: Leave to Appeal), Re [1999] 2 F.L.R. 550; [1999] Fam. Law 521, CA . . . .   *Digested,* 99/**2324**

M (A Minor) (Adoption or Residence Order), Re [1998] 1 F.L.R. 570; [1998] 1 F.C.R. 165; [1998] Fam. Law 188, CA . . . .   *Digested,* 98/**2365**

M (A Minor) (Adoption: Parental Consent), Re CCFMF 97/1510/F, CA . . . .   *Digested,* 98/**2360**

M (A Minor) (Care Order: Significant Harm), Re see M (A Minor) (Care Order: Threshold Conditions), Re

M (A Minor) (Care Order: Threshold Conditions), Re; *sub nom* M (A Minor) (Care Order: Significant Harm), Re [1994] 2 A.C. 424; [1994] 3 W.L.R. 558; [1994] 3 All E.R. 298; [1994] 2 F.C.R. 871; 92 L.G.R. 701; [1994] Fam. Law 501; (1994) 158 J.P.N. 651; (1994) 91 (3) L.S.G. 50; (1994) 138 S.J.L.B. 168; *Times,* July 22, 1994; *Independent,* August 18, 1994, HL; reversing [1994] Fam. 95; [1994] 2 W.L.R. 200; [1994] 1 All E.R. 424; [1994] 1 F.L.R. 73; [1994] 1 F.C.R. 849; [1994] Fam. Law 75; (1993) 143 N.L.J. 1567; *Times,* October 20, 1993; *Independent,* November 8, 1993 (C.S.), CA; reversing (Unreported, February 12, 1993), Fam Div . . . .   *Digested,* 94/**3141**: *Applied,* 94/3119, 95/3403, 95/3405, 96/486, 98/2411: *Considered,* 94/3119, 95/3391, 95/3403, 95/3578, 96/495: *Distinguished,* 95/3565

M (A Minor) (Contact: Supervision), Re [1998] 1 F.L.R. 727; [1998] Fam. Law 70; *Times,* June 10, 1997, CA . . . .   *Digested,* 97/**418**

M (A Minor) (Contempt of Court: Committal of Court's Own Motion), Re see M (Minors) (Breach of Contact Order: Committal), Re

M (A Minor) (Disclosure), Re [1998] 1 F.L.R. 734; [1998] 3 F.C.R. 517; [1998] Fam. Law 189, CA . . . .   *Digested,* 98/**2387**

M (A Minor) (Leave to Remove From Jurisdiction), Re [1999] Fam. Law 376, Fam Div

M (A Minor) *v.* Brent and Harrow HA (Unreported, July 29, 1998), CC (Central
London) [*Ex rel.* Bolt Burden Solicitors, 1 Providence Place, Islington, London] . *Digested*, 99/**1544**
M (A Minor) *v.* Craigavon BC [1998] N.I. 103, QBD (NI) . . . . *Digested*, 99/**5435**
M (A Minor) *v.* De Koning (Unreported, November 16, 1999), CC (Halifax) [*Ex rel.*
Rhodes Thain & Collinson Solicitors, 27 Harrison Road, Halifax] . . . . *Digested*, 00/**1734**
M (A Minor) *v.* Debenhams Plc (Unreported, August 19, 1999), CC (Cheltenham) [*Ex
rel.* Davis Gregory Solicitors, 25 Rodney Road, Cheltenham, Gloucestershire] . . *Digested*, 00/**1675**
M (A Minor) *v.* Liverpool City Council (Unreported, May 10, 1994), CC (Liverpool) [*Ex
rel.* Gregory Abrams, Solicitors] . . . . *Digested*, 94/**3774**:
Cited, 97/721: *Followed*, 98/454, 98/455
M (A Minor) *v.* Midland Rednorth (Unreported, July 23, 1998), CC [*Ex rel.* Russell
Jones & Walker Solicitors, Scottish Equitable House, 43 Temple Row,
Birmingham] . . . . *Digested*, 98/**454**:
Referred to, 99/403
M (A Minor) *v.* Newham LBC see X (Minors) *v.* Bedfordshire CC
M (A Minor) *v.* Snakes and Ladders Adventure Centres Ltd (Unreported, September 8,
1998), CC (Shoreditch) [*Ex rel.* Dowse & Co Solicitors, 23/25 Dalston Lane,
London] . . . . *Digested*, 99/**1496**
M (A Minor) *v.* Sun World Ltd (Unreported, July 19, 1999), CC (Cheltenham) [*Ex rel.*
Davis Gregory Solicitors, 25 Rodney Road, Cheltenham, Gloucestershire] . . . . . *Digested*, 99/**1614**
M (Abduction: Conflict of Jurisdiction), Re [2000] 2 F.L.R. 372; [2001] 1 F.C.R. 81; [2000]
Fam. Law 592, Fam Div. . . . . *Digested*, 00/**2446**
M (Abduction: Consent: Acquiescence), Re [1999] 1 F.L.R. 171; [1999] 1 F.C.R. 5; [1999]
Fam. Law 8, Fam Div. . . . . *Digested*, 99/**2318**
M (Adoption: Rights of Natural Father), Re [2001] 1 F.L.R. 745; [2001] Fam. Law 252, Fam
Div
M (Care: Challenging Decisions by Local Authority), Re [2001] 2 F.L.R. 1300; [2001] Fam.
Law 868, Fam Div
M (Care Orders: Restricting Applications), Re; *sub nom* M (A Child) (Section 91(14)
Order), Re [1999] 3 F.C.R. 400; [1999] Fam. Law 530; (2000) 164 J.P.N. 302,
CA . . . . *Digested*, 00/**2481**
M (Care Proceedings: Disclosure: Human Rights), Re; *sub nom* M (Disclosure: Police
Investigation), Re [2001] 2 F.L.R. 1316; [2001] Fam. Law 799, Fam Div
M (CICA: Quantum: Head Injury), Re [2001] 3 Q.R. 9, CICAP [*Ex rel.* Anthony Gold
Solicitors, New London Bridge House, 25 London Bridge Street, London] . . . . *Digested*, 01/**1571**
M (CICB: Quantum: 2000), Re (Unreported, June 6, 2000), CICB (Bath) [*Ex rel.* Rebecca
Tuck, Barrister, Old Square Chambers, 1 Verulam Buildings, Gray's Inn, London] . *Digested*, 00/**1601**
M (Contact: Family Assistance: McKenzie Friend), Re; *sub nom* M (Contact: Parental
Responsiblity: McKenzie Friend), Re [1999] 1 F.L.R. 75; [1999] 1 F.C.R. 703;
[1998] Fam. Law 727; (1999) 163 J.P.N. 795, Fam Div. . . . . *Digested*, 99/**2367**
M (Contact: Parental Responsiblity: McKenzie Friend), Re see M (Contact: Family
Assistance: McKenzie Friend), Re
M (Disclosure), Re [1998] 2 F.L.R. 1028; [1999] 1 F.C.R. 492; [1998] Fam. Law 729, CA

Digested, 99/**2360**
M (Disclosure: Police Investigation), Re see M (Care Proceedings: Disclosure: Human
Rights), Re
M (Leave to Remove Child From Jurisdiction), Re [1999] 2 F.L.R. 334; [1999] 3 F.C.R. 708,
Fam Div . . . . *Digested*, 99/**2344**
M (Minors) (Abduction: Peremptory Return Order), Re [1996] 1 F.L.R. 478; [1996] 1 F.C.R.
557; *Times*, November 20, 1995, CA . . . . *Digested*, 95/**3446**:
Considered, 99/2332: *Not followed*, 97/406, 98/2381
M (Minors) (Abduction: Psychological Harm), Re [1997] 2 F.L.R. 690; [1998] 2 F.C.R. 488;
[1997] Fam. Law 780, CA . . . . *Digested*, 98/**2380**
M (Minors) (Breach of Contact Order: Committal), Re; *sub nom* M (A Minor) (Contempt
of Court: Committal of Court's Own Motion), Re [1999] Fam. 263; [1999] 2
W.L.R. 810; [1999] 2 All E.R. 56; [1999] 1 F.L.R. 810; [1999] 1 F.C.R. 683;
[1999] Fam. Law 208; (1999) 96(6) L.S.G. 33; (1999) 143 S.J.L.B. 36; *Times*,
December 31, 1998; *Independent*, January 14, 1999, CA . . . . *Digested*, 99/**2365**
M (Minors) (Children's Welfare: Contact), Re [1995] 1 F.L.R. 274; [1995] 1 F.C.R. 753;
[1995] Fam. Law 174; (1995) 159 J.P.N. 248; *Independent*, November 2, 1994,
CA . . . . *Digested*, 95/**3485**:
Considered, 98/2426
M (Minors) (Contact), Re see H (Contact: Domestic Violence), Re
M (Minors) (Contact: Evidence), Re see M (Minors) (Contact: Restrictive Order:
Supervision), Re
M (Minors) (Contact: Restrictive Order: Supervision), Re; *sub nom* M (Minors)
(Contact: Evidence), Re [1998] 1 F.L.R. 721; [1998] 2 F.C.R. 538; [1998] Fam.
Law 252, CA . . . . *Digested*, 98/**2427**
M (Minors) (Contact: Violent Parent), Re [1999] 2 F.L.R. 321; [1999] 2 F.C.R. 56; [1999]
Fam. Law 380; (1999) 163 J.P.N. 651; (1998) 95(45) L.S.G. 37; *Times*, November
24, 1998, Fam Div . . . . *Digested*, 98/**2421**:
Followed, 00/2477
M (Neil) (A Juvenile) *v.* DPP [2000] 2 Cr. App. R. (S.) 43; [2000] Crim. L.R. 316;
[2000] C.O.D. 103, QBD . . . . *Digested*, 00/**1408**

M (Official Solicitor's Role), Re [1998] 2 F.L.R. 815; [1998] 3 F.C.R. 315; [1998] Fam. Law
594; (1998) 95(27) L.S.G. 26; *Times*, July 23, 1998, CA . . . .   *Digested*, 98/**2456**
M (Prohibited Steps Order: Application for Leave), Re [1993] 1 F.L.R. 275; [1993] 1 F.C.R.
78; [1993] Fam. Law 76 . . . .   *Digested*, 93/**2859**:
   Followed, 99/2369
M (Residential Assessment Directions), Re [1998] 2 F.L.R. 371; [1998] Fam. Law 518, Fam
Div . . . .   *Digested*, 98/**2410**
M (Restraint Order: External Confiscation Order), Re see United States *v.* Montgomery
M (Sexual Abuse Allegations: Interviewing Techniques), Re FAFMI 1999/0777/B1, CA;
affirming [1999] 2 F.L.R. 92; [1999] Fam. Law 445, Fam Div . . . .   *Digested*, 00/**2476**
M (Terminating Appointment of Guardian Ad Litem), Re [1999] 2 F.L.R. 717; [1999] 2 F.C.R.
625; [1999] Fam. Law 541, Fam Div . . . .   *Digested*, 99/**2431**
M (Threshold Criteria: Parental Concessions), Re [1999] 2 F.L.R. 728; [1999] Fam. Law
524, CA . . . .   *Digested*, 99/**2346**
M *v.* B (Ancillary Proceedings: Lump Sum) see Marshall *v.* Beckett
M *v.* Calderdale and Kirklees HA (formerly West Yorkshire HA) [1998] Lloyd's Rep.
Med. 157, CC (Huddersfield) . . . .   *Digested*, 98/**3978**
M *v.* DPP see I *v.* DPP
M *v.* H (Costs: Residence Proceedings) [2000] 1 F.L.R. 394; [2000] Fam. Law 313,
Fam Div . . . .   *Digested*, 00/**2488**
M *v.* Islington LBC (2001) 151 N.L.J. 1665, Fam Div
M *v.* London Guildhall University [1998] E.L.R. 149, CA. . . . .   *Digested*, 98/**2006**
M *v.* M (Costs in Children Proceedings) [2000] Fam. Law 877, Fam Div
M *v.* M (Defined Contact Application) [1998] 2 F.L.R. 244; [1998] Fam. Law 456,
Fam Div . . . .   *Digested*, 98/**2419**
M *v.* M (Divorce: Jurisdiction: Validity of Marriage); *sub nom* A-M *v.* A-M (Divorce:
Jurisdiction: Validity of Marriage) [2001] 2 F.L.R. 6; [2001] Fam. Law 495, Fam
Div . . . .   *Digested*, 01/**2615**
M *v.* M (Parental Responsibility); *sub nom* J (A Minor) (Parental Responsibility), Re
[1999] 2 F.L.R. 737; [1999] Fam. Law 538; *Times*, May 25, 1999, Fam Div . . . .   *Digested*, 99/**2382**
M *v.* Poland (24557/94) (2001) 31 E.H.R.R. 29, ECHR . . . .   *Digested*, 01/**3564**
M *v.* R. 5 B.H.R.C. 474, Sup Ct (Can)   *Digested*, 99/**3120**
M *v.* S (Consent: Missing Parent) see S *v.* M (Consent: Missing Parent)
M *v.* Vincent [1998] I.C.R. 73, EAT . . . .   *Digested*, 98/**2166**:
   Considered, 99/2061
M *v.* W (Non Molestation Order: Duration) [2000] 1 F.L.R. 107; [2000] Fam. Law 13,
Fam Div . . . .   *Digested*, 00/**2545**:
   Overruled, 00/2544
M and A (Application to Withold Confidential Information Within Children Act
Proceedings), Re see M and A (Disclosure of Information), Re
M and A (Disclosure of Information), Re; *sub nom* M and A (Application to Withold
Confidential Information Within Children Act Proceedings), Re [1999] 1 F.L.R.
443; [1999] Fam. Law 81, CC (Welshpool) . . . .   *Digested*, 99/**2412**
M and B (Children) (Contact: Domestic Violence), Re [2001] 1 F.C.R. 116, CA . . . .   *Digested*, 01/**2584**
M and J (Children) (Abduction: International Judicial Collaboration), Re [2000] 1 F.L.R.
803; [1999] 3 F.C.R. 721; [2000] Fam. Law 81, Fam Div. . . . .   *Digested*, 00/**2451**
M and N (Minors), Re [1990] Fam. 211; [1989] 3 W.L.R. 1136; [1990] 1 All E.R. 205; [1990] 1
F.L.R. 149; [1990] F.C.R. 395; [1990] Fam. Law 22; (1990) 154 J.P.N. 345; (1990)
87(1) L.S.G. 32; (1989) 139 N.L.J. 1154; (1990) 164 S.J. 165; *Times*, July 14, 1989,
CA . . . .   *Digested*, 90/**3190**:
                       Applied, 94/3243, 95/3544: *Considered*, 00/2535
M and R (Minors) (Child Abuse: Expert Evidence), Re; *sub nom* M and R (Minors)
(Expert Opinion: Evidence), Re [1996] 4 All E.R. 239; [1996] 2 F.L.R. 195;
[1996] 2 F.C.R. 617; [1996] Fam. Law 541; *Times*, July 1, 1996, CA . . . .   *Digested*, 96/**490**:
   Considered, 99/3440
M&G Securities Ltd *v.* Inland Revenue Commissioners; Schroder Unit Trusts Ltd *v.*
Inland Revenue Commissioners [1999] S.T.C. 315; [1999] B.T.C. 8003; *Times*,
February 2, 1999; *Independent*, February 1, 1999 (C.S.), Ch D . . . .   *Digested*, 99/**4763**
M&H Plastics Ltd *v.* Pettyfer (2001) 24(4) I.P.D. 24024, Pat Ct
M&J Seafoods (Wholesale) Ltd *v.* Customs and Excise Commissioners [1999] V. &
D.R. 27, V&DTr. . . . .   *Digested*, 00/**4953**
M, T, P, K and B (Children) (Care: Change of Name), Re [2000] 2 F.L.R. 645; [2000] Fam.
Law 601, Fam Div . . . .   *Digested*, 01/**2572**
M/S Alghanim Industries Inc *v.* Skandia International Insurance Corp [2001] 2 All E.R.
(Comm) 30, QBD (Comm Ct) . . . .   *Digested*, 01/**338**
M/S Aswan Engineering Establishment Co *v.* Lupdine Ltd; *sub nom* Aswan Engineering
Establishment Co *v.* Lupdine Ltd [1987] 1 W.L.R. 1; [1987] 1 All E.R. 135;
[1986] 2 Lloyd's Rep. 347; (1987) 6 Tr. L.R. 1; (1986) 83 L.S.G. 2661; (1986)
130 S.J. 712, CA . . . .   *Digested*, 87/**3337**:
   Applied, 98/4384
Ma Wan Farming Ltd *v.* Chief Executive in Council 4 B.H.R.C. 295, CA (HK) . . . .   *Digested*, 98/**3128**
Maaouia *v.* France (39652/98) (2001) 33 E.H.R.R. 42; 9 B.H.R.C. 205, ECHR . . . .   *Digested*, 01/**3526**

Maasland NV's Application for a Three Dimensional Trade Mark; *sub nom* Maasland NV's
 Trade Mark Application (No.2000360), Re [2000] R.P.C. 893; (2000) 23(2)
 I.P.D. 23014, Appointed Person . . . . *Digested*, 01/**4030**
Maatschappij Drijvende Bokken BV *v.* Stichting Pensioenfonds voor de Verdoer- en
 Havenbedrijven (C219/97) [1999] E.C.R. I-6121; [2000] 4 C.M.L.R. 599, ECJ . *Digested*, 00/**2359**:
                 Joined proceedings, 00/2357, 00/2358
Mabanaft International Ltd *v.* Erg Petroli SpA (The Yellow Star) [2000] 2 Lloyd's Rep.
 637, CC (Central London) . . . . *Digested*, 01/**4916**
Mabey *v.* Secretary of State for the Environment, Transport and the Regions [2001]
 P.L.C.R. 26; [2001] J.P.L. 999 (Note); [2001] A.C.D. 49, QBD (Admin Ct) . . . . *Digested*, 01/**4693**
Mabey & Johnson Ltd *v.* Ecclesiastical Insurance Office Plc (Costs) [2000] C.L.C.
 1570; [2001] Lloyd's Rep. I.R. 369, QBD (Comm Ct) . . . . *Digested*, 01/**459**
Mac No.1 Ltd *v.* Leftleys see Maes Finance Ltd *v.* Leftleys
McAlister *v.* Stevenson see Donoghue *v.* Stevenson
McAll *v.* Brooks [1984] R.T.R. 99, CA . . . . *Digested*, 84/**1822**:
    Applied, 99/2455: *Considered*, 92/1539, 98/2502, 99/413, 99/2456,
      99/2462, 99/2498: *Disapproved*, 98/1455: *Followed*, 98/2505:
               Not followed, 98/1453, 99/2457
McAllister *v.* Society of Lloyd's see Debtors (Nos.4449 and 4450 of 1998), Re
McAreavey *v.* Coal Authority (2000) 80 P. & C.R. 41; [2001] R.V.R. 135; [1999]
 E.G.C.S. 105; [1999] N.P.C. 97; (2000) 79 P. & C.R. D3; *Times*, September 7,
 1999, CA . . . . *Digested*, 99/**3940**
McAteer *v.* Lismore (Trustee of the Estate of James Kevin McAteer) (No.1) [2000] N.I.
 471, Ch D (NI) . . . . *Digested*, 01/**5880**
McAteer *v.* Lismore (Trustee of the Estate of James Kevin McAteer) (No.2) [2000]
 N.I. 477, Ch D (NI) . . . . *Digested*, 01/**5711**
Macaulay *v.* Pensions Ombudsman [1998] O.P.L.R. 107, Ch D . . . . *Digested*, 00/**4391**
Macaulay *v.* Premium Life Assurance Co Ltd; Farley *v.* Premium Life Assurance Co Ltd
 [2000] W.T.L.R. 261, Ch D . . . . *Digested*, 01/**599**
McAully *v.* Chiswick Quay Freeholds Ltd see Langevad *v.* Chiswick Quay Freeholds
 Ltd
McBlain *v.* Dolan 1998 S.L.T. 512; [2001] Lloyd's Rep. I.R. 309, OH . . . . *Digested*, 98/**6019**:
                    Considered, 01/622
McBray (Application to be Registered as a Trade Mark Agent), Re (1998) 21 (5) I.P.D.
 21052, PO
McBrearty *v.* Ministry of Defence see Elguzouli-Daf *v.* Commissioner of Police of the
 Metropolis
McBride *v.* Basildon and Thurrock Hospital NHS Trust [2000] 3 Q.R. 8, CC
 (Southend) [*Ex rel.* Sebastian Reid, Barrister, Francis Taylor Building, Temple,
 London] . . . . *Digested*, 00/**1746**
McBride *v.* County Borough of Galway [1999] 1 C.M.L.R. 1229, Sup Ct (Irl) . . . . *Digested*, 99/**2166**
McBride's Application, Re [1997] N.I. 269, QBD (NI) . . . . *Digested*, 99/**5178**
McBride's Application for Judicial Review, Re [1999] N.I. 299, QBD (NI) . . . . *Digested*, 00/**5436**
McBroom (Deceased), Re [1992] 2 F.L.R. 49; [1992] Fam. Law 376 . . . . *Digested*, 93/**4139**:
                   Distinguished, 00/5779
McC (A Minor), Re; *sub nom* McC (a Minor) *v.* Mullan [1985] A.C. 528; [1984] 3
 W.L.R. 1227; [1984] 3 All E.R. 908; [1984] N.I. 186; (1985) 81 Cr. App. R. 54;
 (1985) 149 J.P. 225; [1985] Crim. L.R. 152; (1985) 82 L.S.G. 117; (1984) 128
 S.J. 837; *Times*, November 28, 1984, HL; affirming [1983] 15 N.I.J.B., CA;
 reversing [1983] 8 N.I.J.B. . . . . *Digested*, 86/**2389**:
          Considered, 99/5147: *Followed*, 86/2068
McC (a Minor) *v.* Mullan see McC (A Minor), Re
McCafferty *v.* Merton Sutton & Wandsworth HA [1997] 8 Med. L.R. 387, QBD . . . . . . *Digested*, 98/**3974**
McCafferty *v.* Receiver for the Metropolitan Police District [1977] 1 W.L.R. 1073;
 [1977] 2 All E.R. 756; [1977] I.C.R. 799; 121 S.J. 678, CA . . . . *Digested*, 77/**999**:
    Applied, 83/2218, 97/656: *Considered*, 86/3142: *Referred to*, 90/2961,
                  97/651, 00/528
McCaffery's Application for Judicial Review, Re [2001] N.I. 378, QBD (NI)
McCain International *v.* Country Fair Foods [1981] R.P.C. 69, CA . . . . *Digested*, 81/**2793**:
               Followed, 92/4143, 01/3877
McCall *v.* Ward [1999] O.P.L.R. 147, Ch D . . . . *Digested*, 99/**4126**
McCallion's Application for Judicial Review, Re [2001] N.I. 401, QBD (NI)
McCamley *v.* Cammell Laird Shipbuilders Ltd [1990] 1 W.L.R. 963; [1990] 1 All E.R.
 854, CA . . . . *Digested*, 90/**1718.19**:
                  Distinguished, 00/1488
McCandless *v.* General Medical Council [1996] 1 W.L.R. 167; [1996] 7 Med. L.R. 379;
 (1996) 30 B.M.L.R. 53; (1996) 93(5) L.S.G. 31; (1996) 140 S.J.L.B. 28; *Times*,
 December 12, 1995, PC (UK) . . . . *Digested*, 96/**4187**:
                  Followed, 00/6401
McCandless *v.* Lynch (2001) 82 P. & C.R. D14, Lands Tr (NI)
McCann *v.* United Kingdom (A/324) (1996) 21 E.H.R.R. 97; *Times*, October 9, 1995;
 Independent, October 6, 1995, ECHR . . . . *Digested*, 95/**2665**:
                 Applied, 98/3157, 99/3144

McCann Erickson Advertising Ltd's Trade Mark Application [2001] E.T.M.R. 52, OHIM
(Opposition Div) . . . . *Digested*, 01/**4055**
McCarey *v.* Associated Newspapers Ltd [1965] 2 Q.B. 86; [1965] 2 W.L.R. 45;
[1964] 3 All E.R. 947; 108 S.J. 916; *Times*, November 7, 1964, CA; reversing
[1964] 1 W.L.R. 855; [1964] 2 All E.R. 335; 108 S.J. 564, QBD . . . . *Digested*, 65/**2255**:
Applied, 65/2254, 65/2260, 67/2276, 98/5150: *Approved*, 72/2745:
Considered, 89/2245, 90/1552: *Followed*, 67/2275
McCartan *v.* Finnegan [1994] N.I. 132, CA (NI) . . . . *Digested*, 00/**5620**
McCartan Turkington & Breen *v.* Lord St Oswald [1996] N.I. 65, QBD (NI)
McCartan Turkington & Breen *v.* Telegraph Plc [1996] N.I. 75, QBD (NI)
McCartan Turkington Breen *v.* Times Newspapers Ltd; *sub nom* Turkington *v.* Times
Newspapers Ltd [2001] 2 A.C. 277; [2000] 3 W.L.R. 1670; [2000] 4 All E.R.
913; [2000] N.I. 410; [2001] E.M.L.R. 1; [2001] U.K.H.R.R. 184; 9 B.H.R.C. 497;
(2000) 97(47) L.S.G. 40; (2000) 150 N.L.J. 1657; (2000) 144 S.J.L.B. 287;
Times, November 3, 2000; *Independent*, November 7, 2000, HL (NI); reversing
[1998] N.I. 358; *Times*, November 4, 1998, CA (NI) . . . . *Digested*, 00/**5491**
McCarthy (CICA: Quantum: 2000), Re (Unreported, September 5, 2000), CICA (London)
[*Ex rel*. Prince Evans, Solicitors, 77 Uxbridge Road, London] . . . . *Digested*, 01/**1555**
McCarthy *v.* Abbott Insulation (Unreported, December 4, 1998), MCLC [*Ex rel*. Allan
Gore, Barrister, 12 King's Bench Walk, Temple, London] . . . . *Digested*, 99/**1539**
McCarthy (t/a Croft Homes) *v.* Customs and Excise Commissioners [2001] S.T.I. 29,
V&DTr
McCarthy *v.* Davis (Unreported, January 19, 2000), CC (Reading) [*Ex rel*. Alison
McCormick, Barrister, 35 Essex Street, Temple, London] . . . . *Digested*, 00/**1647**
McCarthy *v.* Goldthorpe (Unreported, October 5, 1999), CC (Gravesend) [*Ex rel*.
Andrew Petersen, Barrister, 9 Gough Square, London] . . . . *Digested*, 99/**2490**
McCarthy *v.* Recticel Ltd [2000] P.I.Q.R. Q74; (1999) 96(2) L.S.G. 29; (1999) 143
S.J.L.B. 46; *Times*, December 11, 1998, QBD . . . . *Digested*, 99/**554**
McCarthy *v.* Secretary of State for the Environment [1999] J.P.L. 993, QBD . . . . *Digested*, 00/**4420**
McCarthy & Stone (Developments) Ltd *v.* Secretary of State for the Environment,
Transport and the Regions [2001] J.P.L. 499 (Note), QBD
McCauley *v.* Hope; *sub nom* McCauley *v.* Vine [1999] 1 W.L.R. 1977; [2000] R.T.R.
70; [1999] P.I.Q.R. P185; *Independent*, December 21, 1998 (C.S.), CA . . . . *Digested*, 99/**314**
McCauley *v.* Lamb (Unreported, March 2, 2000), CC (Brentford) [*Ex rel*. Charles
Bagot, Barrister, Hardwicke Building, New Square, Lincoln's Inn, London] . . . . . *Digested*, 00/**403**
McCauley *v.* Vine see McCauley *v.* Hope
McClean *v.* Boult [2000] 4 Q.R. 8, CC (Lambeth) [*Ex rel*. Samuel Warijay, Barrister,
Arden Chambers, 27 John Street, London] . . . . *Digested*, 00/**1634**
McClean Homes (East Anglia) Ltd *v.* Secretary of State for the Environment, Transport
and the Regions; *sub nom* McLean Homes (East Anglia) Ltd *v.* Secretary of
State for the Environment, Transport and the Regions [1999] 2 P.L.R. 49; [1999]
P.L.C.R. 372; [1999] E.G.C.S. 3; [1999] N.P.C. 4; *Independent*, January 25,
1999 (C.S.), QBD . . . . *Digested*, 99/**4168**
McClenaghan *v.* First East Belfast Liverpool Supporters Club [2000] N.I. 158, CA
(Crim Div) (NI) . . . . *Digested*, 00/**5467**
McClenaghan (Chief Inspector of the Royal Ulster Constabulary) *v.* McKenna [2001] N.I.
327, CA (Crim Div)
McClymont *v.* Primecourt Property Management Ltd [2000] E.G.C.S. 139, Ch D
McColl *v.* Listing Officer [2001] EWHC Admin 712; [2001] R.A. 342, QBD (Admin
Ct)
McConnell (Deceased), Re; *sub nom* University of Victoria *v.* British Columbia (2000-
01) 3 I.T.E.L.R. 24, Sup Ct (BC) . . . . *Digested*, 01/**3480**
McConnell *v.* Chief Constable of Greater Manchester [1990] 1 W.L.R. 364; [1990] 1
All E.R. 423; (1990) 91 Cr. App. R. 88; (1990) 154 J.P.N. 62; (1990) 87(6)
L.S.G. 41; (1990) 134 S.J. 457, CA . . . . *Digested*, 90/**1073**:
Followed, 01/1007
McConnell *v.* Police Authority for Northern Ireland [1997] N.I. 244; [1997] I.R.L.R.
625, CA (NI) . . . . *Digested*, 98/**5150**:
Applied, 99/5282, 00/2182: *Considered*, 00/2181
McCool *v.* Rushcliffe BC [1998] 3 All E.R. 889; (1999) 163 J.P. 46; [1999] B.L.G.R.
365; (1998) 162 J.P.N. 883; *Independent*, July 6, 1998 (C.S.), QBD . . . . *Digested*, 98/**4868**
McCormack (A Minor) *v.* Martin (Unreported, June 24, 1998), CC (Brentford) [*Ex rel*.
Tim Petts, Barrister, 12 King's Bench Walk, Temple, London] . . . . *Digested*, 98/**443**
McCrory's Application for Judicial Review, Re [2000] N.I. 487, QBD (NI) . . . . *Digested*, 01/**5783**
McCue *v.* Hemingway (Unreported, September 18, 2000), CC (Central London) [*Ex
rel*. Samantha Broadfoot, Barrister, 2 Field Court, Gray's Inn, London] . . . . *Digested*, 00/**4290**
McCullough *v.* BBC [1996] N.I. 580, QBD (NI)
McCullough's Application, Re [1997] N.I. 423, QBD (NI) . . . . *Digested*, 99/**5182**

McCutcheon *v.* David MacBrayne Ltd [1964] 1 W.L.R. 125; [1964] 1 All E.R. 430; [1964] 1 Lloyd's Rep. 16; 1964 S.C. (H.L.) 28; 1964 S.L.T. 66; 108 S.J. 93, HL; reversing [1963] 1 Lloyd's Rep. 123; 1962 S.C. 506; 1963 S.L.T. 30; 1962 S.L.T. (Notes) 98, 2 Div; affirming [1962] 1 Lloyd's Rep. 303; 1962 S.L.T. 231, OH. . . . *Digested,* 64/**4455**: *Applied,* 68/3526, 69/510, 70/369, 71/1741, 73/404, 74/442, 01/4261: *Considered,* 78/340, 90/4800, 91/4514, 92/1553: *Disapproved,* 72/470: *Distinguished,* 79/2431, 87/430: *Doubted,* 65/3517, 66/10837: *Followed,* 00/5989

McDaid *v.* United Kingdom; Ward *v.* United Kingdom; Giles *v.* United Kingdom; Leece *v.* United Kingdom; Shorters *v.* United Kingdom; Thwaites *v.* United Kingdom *Times,* October 18, 2000, ECHR . . . . *Digested,* 00/**258**

McDermott *v.* Minister for Social Welfare (C286/85); Cotter *v.* Minister for Social Welfare (C286/85) [1987] E.C.R. 1453; [1987] 2 C.M.L.R. 607, ECJ . . . . *Digested,* 87/**1636**: *Applied,* 98/2155

McDevitt *v.* Rochford Mouldings Ltd (Unreported, October 19, 1998), CC (Southend) [*Ex rel.* Bruce R Silvester, Barrister, Lamb Chambers, Lamb Building, Temple, London] . . . . *Digested,* 98/**1688**

McDonagh *v.* Ali see Triesman *v.* Ali

McDonagh *v.* Salisbury DC see R. (on the application of McDonagh) *v.* Salisbury DC

McDonald *v.* Charly Holdings Inc see O'Donnell *v.* Charly Holdings Inc

McDonald *v.* Ealing LBC (2001) 58 B.M.L.R. 210; *Independent,* May 15, 2000 (C.S.), EAT

MacDonald *v.* Federation International de Football Association 1999 S.L.T. 1129; 1999 S.C.L.R. 59; 1999 G.W.D. 1-48; *Times,* January 7, 1999, OH . . . . *Digested,* 99/**6369**

McDonald *v.* Geddis R/35/1999, LandsTr (NI) . . . . *Digested,* 00/**5390**

Macdonald *v.* Highlands and Islands Enterprise see Cross *v.* Highlands and Islands Enterprise

McDonald *v.* Horn [1995] 1 All E.R. 961; [1995] I.C.R. 685; [1994] Pens. L.R. 155; (1994) 144 N.L.J. 1515; *Times,* August 10, 1994; *Independent,* August 8, 1994, CA; affirming *Times,* October 12, 1993, Ch D . . . . *Digested,* 95/**3836**: *Considered,* 98/481, 98/482, 01/506, 01/3803: *Followed,* 97/3952

MacDonald *v.* KLM Royal Dutch Airlines (Unreported, October 12, 1998), CC (Lewes) [*Ex rel.* Paul Hepher, Barrister, 2 Grays Inn Square Chambers, 2nd Floor, 2 Grays Inn Square, London] . . . . *Digested,* 99/**538**

MacDonald *v.* Ministry of Defence see Advocate General for Scotland *v.* MacDonald

MacDonald *v.* Myerson [2001] EWCA Civ 66; [2001] 6 E.G.C.S. 162; (2001) 98(6) L.S.G. 47; [2001] N.P.C. 20, CA

MacDonald *v.* Platt see Newland *v.* Boardwell

MacDonald *v.* Richmond Boat Project (Unreported, March 16, 2000), CC (Staines) [*Ex rel.* William Latimer-Sayer, Barrister, Cloisters, 7 Pump Court, Temple, London] . . . . *Digested,* 00/**545**

MacDonald *v.* Taree Holdings Ltd [2001] C.P.L.R. 439; [2001] 1 Costs L.R. 147; (2001) 98(6) L.S.G. 45; *Times,* December 28, 2000, Ch D . . . . *Digested,* 01/**529**

MacDonald *v.* Thorn Plc; *sub nom* Thorn Plc *v.* MacDonald [1999] C.P.L.R. 660; *Times,* October 15, 1999, CA . . . . *Digested,* 99/**432**

McDonald's Corp *v.* McDonald's Corp Ltd [1997] F.S.R. 200, Sup Ct (Jam) [1997] F.S.R. 760, CA (Jam); affirming . . . . *Digested,* 98/**3518**

McDonald's Corp *v.* Rahmer [2000] E.T.M.R. 91, BGH (Ger)

McDonald's Corp *v.* Steel (No.1) [1995] 3 All E.R. 615; [1995] E.M.L.R. 527; *Times,* April 14, 1994; *Independent,* April 22, 1994, CA . . . . *Digested,* 96/**5676**: *Applied,* 99/1624: *Distinguished,* 98/1777

McDonald's Corp *v.* Steel (No.4); *sub nom* Steel *v.* McDonald's Corp (Locus Standi) *Independent,* May 10, 1999 (C.S.), CA; reversing in part (Unreported, June 19, 1997), QBD. . . . . *Considered,* 01/**1835**

McDonald's Hamburgers Ltd *v.* Burgerking (UK) Ltd [1987] F.S.R. 112, CA; reversing [1986] F.S.R. 45; (1985) 4 Tr. L. 226, Ch D . . . . *Digested,* 87/**2944.5**: *Applied,* 97/3917: *Distinguished,* 98/3423, 98/3528

McDonald's Property Co Ltd *v.* HSBC Bank Plc [2001] 36 E.G. 181; [2001] 19 E.G.C.S. 139; [2001] N.P.C. 81, Ch D . . . . *Digested,* 01/**4208**

McDonnell *v.* Congregation of Christian Brothers Trustees (formerly Irish Christian Brothers) [2001] EWCA Civ 2095, CA; affirming [2001] P.I.Q.R. P28; *Daily Telegraph,* March 20, 2001, QBD . . . . *Digested,* 01/**606**

McDonnell *v.* Griffey [1998] E.G.C.S. 70; [1998] N.P.C. 76, Ch D

McDonnell Information Systems Ltd *v.* Swinbank see MDIS Ltd (formerly McDonnell Information Systems Ltd) *v.* Swinbank

Macdougall *v.* Boote Edgar Esterkin [2001] 1 Costs L.R. 118, CA . . . . *Digested,* 01/**528**

McDougalls Catering Foods Ltd *v.* BSE Trading Ltd (1998) 76 P. & C.R. 312; [1997] 2 E.G.L.R. 65; [1997] 42 E.G. 174; [1997] E.G.C.S. 70; [1997] N.P.C. 67, CA. . . . . *Digested,* 97/**3335**

McDowell *v.* Smith [1996] N.I. 491, QBD (NI)

McElduff *v.* United Kingdom see Tinnelly & Sons Ltd *v.* United Kingdom

McElhinney *v.* Ireland (No.1) (31253/96) (2001) 29 E.H.R.R. CD214, ECHR

McElhinney *v.* Ireland (No.2) (31253/96), *Times,* November 26, 2001, ECHR . . . . *Digested,* 01/**3546**

McEvoy *v.* AA Welding & Fabrication Ltd [1998] P.I.Q.R. P266, CA. . . . . *Digested,* 98/**545**: *Considered,* 99/475

McEwan *v.* Bingham (t/a Studland Watersports) (Unreported, July 28, 2000), CC
(Hove) [*Ex rel.* William Emerson, Barrister, 12 North Pallent, Chichester] . . . .   *Digested,* 00/**4691**
McFadyen *v.* Annan 1992 J.C. 53; 1992 S.L.T. 163; 1992 S.C.C.R. 186; *Times,* February
11, 1992, HCJ Appeal . . . .   *Digested,* 92/**5466**:
       Applied, 92/5467, 94/5574, 95/5666, 97/5826, 00/6086:
       Considered, 95/5680, 00/6089: *Referred to,* 94/5610
McFarland's Application for Judicial Review, Re [2000] N.I. 403, QBD (NI) . . . .   *Digested,* 01/**5735**
McFarlane *v.* Clifford Smith & Buchanan (Unreported, September 26, 1999), QBD [*Ex
rel.* Hough Halton & Soal, Solicitors, 32 Abbey Street, Carlisle] . . . .   *Digested,* 00/**1620**
McFarlane *v.* Coggins & Griffiths (Liverpool) Ltd see Mersey Docks and Harbour
Board *v.* Coggins & Griffith (Liverpool) Ltd
McFarlane *v.* EE Caledonia Ltd [1994] 2 All E.R. 1; [1994] 1 Lloyd's Rep. 16; [1994]
P.I.Q.R. P154; (1993) 143 N.L.J. 1367; *Times,* September 30, 1993; *Independent,*
September 10, 1993, CA; reversing [1993] P.I.Q.R. P241, QBD . . . .   *Digested,* 94/**3353**:
       Considered, 01/5352
MacFarlane *v.* Glasgow City Council [2001] I.R.L.R. 7, EAT . . . .   *Digested,* 01/**6468**
McFarlane *v.* Tayside Health Board; *sub nom* Macfarlane *v.* Tayside Health Board
[2000] 2 A.C. 59; [1999] 3 W.L.R. 1301; [1999] 4 All E.R. 961; 2000 S.C. (H.L.)
1; 2000 S.L.T. 154; 2000 S.C.L.R. 105; [2000] 1 F.C.R. 102; [2000] P.I.Q.R.
Q101; [2000] Lloyd's Rep. Med. 1; (2000) 52 B.M.L.R. 1; (1999) 149 N.L.J.
1868; 1999 G.W.D. 39-1888; *Times,* November 26, 1999 ; *Independent,*
December 3, 1999, HL; reversing in part 1998 S.C. 389; 1998 S.L.T. 307; 1998
S.C.L.R. 126; (1998) 44 B.M.L.R. 140; 1998 G.W.D. 4-180; *Times,* May 8, 1998, 2
Div; reversing 1997 S.L.T. 211; 1996 Rep. L.R. 159; *Times,* November 11, 1996,
OH . . . .   *Digested,* 00/**6162**:
       Applied, 01/4462, 01/6412: *Cited,* 00/2777: *Considered,* 00/4200, 01/4463:
       Distinguished, 01/1508, 01/4464: *Followed,* 01/1509: *Not followed,* 98/6115
McFeeley *v.* United Kingdom (8317/78) (1981) 3 E.H.R.R. 161, Eur Comm HR . . . . . .   *Applied,* 00/3202
Macgay Ltd *v.* Harrogate BC see Macgay Ltd *v.* Secretary of State for the Environment,
Transport and the Regions
Macgay Ltd *v.* Secretary of State for the Environment, Transport and the Regions; *sub
nom* Macgay Ltd *v.* Harrogate BC; Harrogate BC *v.* Secretary of State for the
Environment, Transport and the Regions [2001] P.L.C.R. 21; [2000] E.G.C.S.
145, CA; affirming CO/1562/99, QBD . . . .   *Digested,* 01/**4750**
McGeachy *v.* Normand 1994 S.L.T. 429; 1993 S.C.C.R. 951, HCJ Appeal . . . .   *Digested,* 94/**5392**:
       Considered, 00/198
McGeown *v.* Northern Ireland Housing Executive [1995] 1 A.C. 233; [1994] 3 W.L.R.
187; [1994] 3 All E.R. 53; 92 L.G.R. 629; (1994) 91 (30) L.S.G. 32; (1994) 144
N.L.J. 901; (1994) 138 S.J.L.B. 156; [1994] N.P.C. 95; *Times,* June 24, 1994;
Independent, June 28, 1994, HL (NI) . . . .   *Digested,* 94/**4285**:
       Followed, 01/4498
McGhan Medical UK Ltd *v.* Nagor Ltd (2001) 24(7) I.P.D. 24043, Pat Ct . . . .   *Digested,* 01/**3964**
McGhee *v.* National Coal Board [1973] 1 W.L.R. 1; [1972] 3 All E.R. 1008; 1973 S.C.
(H.L.) 37; 1973 S.L.T. 14; 13 K.I.R. 471; 116 S.J. 967, HL; reversing 1972 S.L.T.
(Notes) 61, 1 Div . . . .   *Digested,* 73/**3841**:
       Applied, 83/2548, 92/1552, 94/3399, 99/3987, 00/4187:
       Considered, 85/2319, 87/2604, 96/4426, 00/5114: *Distinguished,* 87/2564,
       87/4758, 88/2415, 90/5497, 98/1501
McGinlay *v.* British Railways Board see Titchener *v.* British Railways Board
McGinley *v.* United Kingdom (1999) 27 E.H.R.R. 1; 4 B.H.R.C. 421; (1998) 42
B.M.L.R. 123; [1998] H.R.C.D. 624; *Times,* June 15, 1998, ECHR . . . .   *Digested,* 98/**3124**
McGivern *v.* Brown see Limb *v.* Union Jack Removals Ltd (In Liquidation)
McGivney *v.* Golderslea Ltd (2001) 17 Const. L.J. 454, CA
McGladdery *v.* McGladdery [1999] 2 F.L.R. 1102; [2000] 1 F.C.R. 315; [2000] B.P.I.R.
1078; [2000] Fam. Law 160; (1999) 96(32) L.S.G. 32; *Times,* October 5, 1999,
CA . . . .   *Digested,* 99/**2426**
McGonnell *v.* United Kingdom (2000) 30 E.H.R.R. 289; 8 B.H.R.C. 56; [2000] 2
P.L.R. 69; *Times,* February 22, 2000, ECHR . . . .   *Digested,* 00/**3227**
McGovern *v.* Attorney General [1982] Ch. 321; [1982] 2 W.L.R. 222; [1981] 3 All E.R.
493; [1982] T.R. 157; 125 S.J. 255, Ch D . . . .   *Digested,* 81/**220**:
       Considered, 84/276, 97/3593, 98/309
McGrath *v.* Chief Constable of the Royal Ulster Constabulary [2001] UKHL 39;
[2001] 2 A.C. 731; [2001] 3 W.L.R. 312; [2001] 4 All E.R. 334; [2001] N.I. 303;
Times, July 13, 2001; *Independent,* October 29, 2001 (C.S), HL (NI); reversing
[2000] N.I. 56, CA (NI) . . . .   *Digested,* 01/**5650**
McGrath *v.* Secretary of State for Northern Ireland [1994] N.I. 98, CA (NI) . . . .   *Digested,* 00/**5386**
McGrath *v.* Shah (1989) 57 P. & C.R. 452; *Times,* October 22, 1987, Ch D . . . .   *Digested,* 90/**650**:
       Applied, 96/3756, 00/869: *Followed,* 89/477
McGreevy *v.* DPP [1973] 1 W.L.R. 276; [1973] 1 All E.R. 503; (1973) 57 Cr. App. R.
424; [1973] Crim. L.R. 232; 117 S.J. 164, HL . . . .   *Digested,* 73/**522**:
       Considered, 77/525: *Followed,* 99/1055: *Not followed,* 77/524
McGregor *v.* Prudential Insurance Co Ltd [1998] 1 Lloyd's Rep. 112, QBD . . . .   *Digested,* 98/**3358**
McGregor Clothing Co Ltd's Trade Mark [1979] R.P.C. 36, Ch D . . . .   *Digested,* 78/**2970**:
       Cited, 01/4038: *Considered,* 93/3987

McGuckian, Re; *sub nom* Inland Revenue Commissioners v. McGuckian (Time Limits); R. v. Dickinson (Inspector of Taxes) Ex p. McGuckian [2000] S.T.C. 65; [2000] N.I. 30; 72 T.C. 343; [2000] B.T.C. 14; [2000] S.T.I. 68; *Times*, February 23, 2000, CA (NI); affirming [1999] S.T.C. 578; [1999] B.T.C. 152; *Times*, May 12, 1999, QBD (NI). . . . . *Digested*, 00/**5780**

McGuckian v. Inland Revenue Commissioners see Inland Revenue Commissioners v. McGuckian

McGuigan v. Pollock [1955] N.I. 74 . . . . *Considered*, 00/5471
McGuigan's Application, Re [1994] N.I. 143, CA (NI) . . . . *Digested*, 00/**5402**
McGuinness's Application, Re [1997] N.I. 359, QBD (NI). . . . . *Digested*, 99/**5164**
McHale v. Watson (1966) 115 C.L.R. 199, HC (Aus) . . . . *Digested*, 65/**3987**:
Considered, 99/3981: *Followed*, 98/3994
McHugh v. Carlisle City Council [2000] 3 Q.R. 6, CC (Carlisle) [*Ex rel.* Hough Halton & Soal Solicitors, 32 Abbey Street, Carlisle] . . . . *Digested*, 00/**1590**
McIlgorm v. Bell Lamb & Joynson [2001] P.N.L.R. 28, QBD . . . . *Digested*, 01/**4516**
McIlkenny v. Chief Constable of the West Midlands see Hunter v. Chief Constable of the West Midlands
McIlwee (A Minor) v. Zanussi Ltd (1998) 98(3) Q.R. 7, CC (Newbury) . . . . *Digested*, 98/**1641**
McInerney v. Portland Port Ltd [2001] 1 P.L.R. 104; [2001] J.P.L. 1295; [2001] A.C.D. 55; *Independent*, January 29, 2001 (C.S.), QBD
McIntosh (Robert) v. HM Advocate see HM Advocate v. McIntosh (Robert) (No.1)
McIntosh, Petitioner see HM Advocate v. McIntosh (Robert) (No.1)
McKay v. Essex AHA [1982] Q.B. 1166; [1982] 2 W.L.R. 890; [1982] 2 All E.R. 771; 126 S.J. 261, CA . . . . *Digested*, 82/**3117**:
Considered, 98/549: *Disapproved*, 86/363
Mackay v. McSparran [1974] N.I. 136 . . . . *Digested*, 76/**1998**:
Followed, 01/5163
McKay v. Northen Ireland Public Service Alliance [1994] N.I. 103, CA (NI) . . . . *Digested*, 00/**5507**
McKay Securities Plc v. Surrey CC [1998] E.G.C.S. 180, Ch D
McKeag v. Northern Ireland Housing Executive R/36/1998, LandsTr (NI) . . . . *Digested*, 00/**5655**
McKean v. DPP see DPP v. Charles
McKenna v. Best Travel Ltd [1998] E.C.C. 436, Sup Ct (Irl)
McKenna's Application, Re [1998] N.I. 287, CA (NI) . . . . *Digested*, 99/**5219**:
Applied, 99/5218
McKenzie v. McKenzie [1971] P. 33; [1970] 3 W.L.R. 472; [1970] 3 All E.R. 1034; 114 S.J. 667, CA . . . . *Digested*, 70/**2325**:
Applied, 84/2755: *Considered*, 74/3003, 92/1007: *Followed*, 01/608
McKeown v. Cardinal Heenan High School see R. v. Cardinal Heenan High School Appeal Committee Ex p. McKeown
McKerchar v. Campbell (Unreported, April 6, 2000), CC (Rawtenstall) [*Ex rel.* Paul Clark, Barrister, Exchange Chambers, Pearl Assurance House, Derby Square, Liverpool] . . . . *Digested*, 00/**1591**
McKerr v. United Kingdom (28883/95), *Times*, May 18, 2001, ECHR . . . . *Joined proceedings*, 01/3575
McKerry v. DPP see McKerry v. Teesdale and Wear Valley Justices
McKerry v. Teesdale and Wear Valley Justices; *sub nom* McKerry v. DPP (2000) 164 J.P. 355; [2001] E.M.L.R. 5; [2000] Crim. L.R. 594; [2000] C.O.D. 199; (2000) 97(11) L.S.G. 36; (2000) 144 S.J.L.B. 126; *Times*, February 29, 2000; *Independent*, March 27, 2000 (C.S.), QBD . . . . *Digested*, 00/**1306**
McKinney (Inspector of Taxes) v. Hagans Caravans (Manufacturing) Ltd [1997] S.T.C. 1023; [1997] N.I. 111; 69 T.C. 526; [1997] B.T.C. 402, CA (NI) . . . . *Digested*, 97/**5161**
McKinney v. University of Guelph [1990] 3 S.C.R. 229, Sup Ct (Can) . . . . *Applied*, 98/3074
Mackinnon v. Donaldson Lufkin & Jenrette Securities Corp [1986] Ch. 482; [1986] 2 W.L.R. 453; [1986] 1 All E.R. 653; [1987] E.C.C. 139; [1986] Fin. L.R. 225; (1986) 83 L.S.G. 1226; (1985) 130 S.J. 224, Ch D . . . . *Digested*, 86/**1501**:
Applied, 87/209: *Considered*, 94/270: *Referred to*, 98/3308
McKnight v. Adlestones (Jewellers) Ltd [1984] I.R.L.R. 453, CA (NI) . . . . *Digested*, 85/**1142**:
Applied, 96/2526, 98/2168
McKnight (Inspector of Taxes) v. Sheppard; *sub nom* Sheppard v. McKnight (Inspector of Taxes) [1999] 1 W.L.R. 1333; [1999] 3 All E.R. 491; [1999] S.T.C. 669; 71 T.C. 419; [1999] B.T.C. 236; (1999) 96(27) L.S.G. 34; (1999) 149 N.L.J. 966; (1999) 143 S.J.L.B. 188; *Times*, June 18, 1999 ; *Independent*, June 23, 1999, HL; affirming [1997] S.T.C. 846; [1997] B.T.C. 328; (1997) 94(21) L.S.G. 32; (1997) 141 S.J.L.B. 115; *Times*, May 12, 1997; *Independent*, May 13, 1997, CA; reversing [1996] S.T.C. 627; (1996) 140 S.J.L.B. 140; *Times*, May 21, 1996; *Independent*, July 8, 1996 (C.S.), Ch D . . . . *Digested*, 99/**4701**
McLaren v. Mumford (Inspector of Taxes) [1996] S.T.C. 1134; 69 T.C. 173; [1996] E.G.C.S. 138; (1996) 93(38) L.S.G. 42; *Times*, August 2, 1996, Ch D . . . . *Digested*, 96/**3356**
McLarnon Deeney v. Gooda Walker Ltd see Henderson v. Merrett Syndicates Ltd (No.1)
McLaughlin & Harvey Plc (In Liquidation), Re; *sub nom* B Mullan & Sons Contractors Ltd v. Ross [1996] N.I. 618; 86 B.L.R. 1; 54 Con. L.R. 163, CA (NI) . . . . *Digested*, 97/**5287**
McLaughlin's Application, Re Unreported, CA (NI) . . . . *Distinguished*, 01/5653
McLaughlin's Application, Re [1990] 6 N.I.J.B. 41 . . . . *Applied*, 00/5401

McLean v. Buchanan; *sub nom* Buchanan v. McLean [2001] UKPC D3; [2001] 1
W.L.R. 2425; 2001 S.L.T. 780; 2001 S.C.C.R. 475; [2001] H.R.L.R. 51; [2001]
U.K.H.R.R. 793; (2001) 98(28) L.S.G. 44; (2001) 145 S.J.L.B. 158; 2001 G.W.D.
19-720; *Times*, June 4, 2001, PC (Sc); affirming 2000 J.C. 603; 2000 S.L.T.
928; 2000 S.C.C.R. 682; [2000] U.K.H.R.R. 598; 2000 G.W.D. 22-850; *Times*,
August 11, 2000, HCJ Appeal . . . .   *Digested*, 01/**6760**
McLean Homes (East Anglia) Ltd v. Secretary of State for the Environment, Transport
and the Regions see McClean Homes (East Anglia) Ltd v. Secretary of State for
the Environment, Transport and the Regions
McLellan v. Bracknell Forest BC see R. (on the application of McLellan) v. Bracknell
Forest BC
McLelland v. Greater Glasgow Health Board 2001 S.L.T. 446; 2001 G.W.D. 10-357, Ex
Div; affirming in part 1999 S.C. 305; 1999 S.L.T. 543; 1998 S.C.L.R. 1081; 1999
Rep. L.R. 1; 1998 G.W.D. 34-1754; *Times*, October 14, 1998, OH . . . .   *Digested*, 01/**6412**
McLeod v. Amiras [2001] I.L.Pr. 38, Sup Ct (BC)
McLeod (Anthony) v. Attorney General of Jamaica see Lewis v. Attorney General of
Jamaica
McLeod v. Butterwick; *sub nom* Khazanchi v. Faircharm Investments Ltd [1998] 1
W.L.R. 1603; [1998] 2 All E.R. 901; (1999) 77 P. & C.R. 29; [1998] 3 E.G.L.R.
147; [1999] R.V.R. 190; [1998] E.G.C.S. 46; (1998) 95(17) L.S.G. 31; (1998) 148
N.L.J. 479; (1998) 142 S.J.L.B. 142; [1998] N.P.C. 47; (1998) 76 P. & C.R. D8;
Times, March 25, 1998, CA; affirming [1996] 1 W.L.R. 995; [1996] 3 All E.R.
236; *Times*, March 12, 1996, Ch D . . . .   *Digested*, 98/**3630**
Macleod v. National Grid Co Plc [1998] 2 E.G.L.R. 217; [1999] R.V.R. 94, LandsTr . . . .   *Digested*, 99/**4357**
Macleod (Inspector of Taxes) v. Perks see Clark (Inspector of Taxes) v. Perks
McLeod v. United Kingdom [1998] 2 F.L.R. 1048; [1999] 1 F.C.R. 193; (1999) 27
E.H.R.R. 493; 5 B.H.R.C. 364; [1999] Crim. L.R. 155; [1998] H.R.C.D. 878;
[1998] Fam. Law 734; *Times*, October 1, 1998, ECHR . . . .   *Digested*, 98/**3103**
McLoughlin v. O'Brian [1983] 1 A.C. 410; [1982] 2 W.L.R. 982; [1982] 2 All E.R. 298;
[1982] R.T.R. 209; (1982) 79 L.S.G. 922; 126 S.J. 347, HL; reversing [1981]
Q.B. 599; [1981] 2 W.L.R. 1014; [1981] 1 All E.R. 809; 125 S.J. 169, CA . . . .   *Digested*, 82/**2153**:
Applied, 84/2330, 87/2857, 91/2670, 91/2671, 92/3250, 92/3251, 95/6157:
Considered, 83/2609, 84/2342, 85/2322, 85/2326, 86/1069, 87/2580,
87/2608, 88/6, 90/1571, 90/3727, 91/2512, 00/4213, 00/4220:
Distinguished, 98/5723
McLoughlin v. Queens University Belfast [1995] N.I. 82, CA (NI) . . . .   *Considered*, 98/5133
MacMahon v. Hamilton see MacMahon v. James Doran & Co
MacMahon v. James Doran & Co; *sub nom* MacMahon v. Hamilton [2001] P.N.L.R.
35, QBD (NI) . . . .   *Digested*, 01/**5900**
McManus v. Griffiths (Inspector of Taxes) [1997] S.T.C. 1089; 70 T.C. 218; [1997]
B.T.C. 412; (1997) 94(33) L.S.G. 27; *Times*, August 5, 1997; *Independent*,
October 13, 1997 (C.S.), Ch D . . . .   *Digested*, 97/**2955**
McMaster v. Manchester Airport Plc [1998] I.R.L.R. 112, EAT . . . .   *Digested*, 98/**2203**
McMaster v. Prince Recycling Ltd (Unreported, November 10, 1998), CC (Cambridge)
[*Ex rel.* Andrew Granville Stafford, Barrister, 4 King's Bench Walk, Temple,
London] . . . .   *Digested*, 99/**1461**
McMeechan v. Secretary of State for Employment [1997] I.C.R. 549; [1997] I.R.L.R.
353, CA; affirming [1995] I.C.R. 444; [1995] I.R.L.R. 461, EAT . . . .   *Digested*, 97/**2195**:
Considered, 98/2137, 01/2264
McMillan (CICB: Quantum: 1999), Re (Unreported, August 12, 1999), CICB (London) [*Ex
rel.* Simon Levene, Barrister, 199, Strand, London] . . . .   *Digested*, 00/**1750**
MacMillan v. Edinburgh Voluntary Organisations Council [1995] I.R.L.R. 536, EAT . . . .   *Digested*, 96/**2611**:
Distinguished, 98/2194
Macmillan Inc v. Bishopsgate Investment Trust Plc (No.3) [1996] 1 W.L.R. 387; [1996]
1 All E.R. 585; [1996] B.C.C. 453; (1995) 139 S.J.L.B. 225; *Times*, November 7,
1995; *Independent*, December 11, 1995 (C.S.), CA; affirming [1995] 1 W.L.R.
978; [1995] 3 All E.R. 747, Ch D . . . .   *Digested*, 95/**693**:
Applied, 00/777
Macmillan Inc v. Bishopsgate Investment Trust Plc (No.4); *sub nom* MCC Proceeds Inc
v. Bishopsgate Investment Trust Plc (No.4) [1999] C.L.C. 417; *Times*, December
7, 1998, CA . . . .   *Digested*, 99/**728**
MacMillan Magazines Ltd v. RCN Publishing Co Ltd [1998] F.S.R. 9; (1997) 20(9)
I.P.D. 20089, Ch D . . . .   *Digested*, 98/**3511**
McMorris v. Brown [1999] 1 A.C. 142; [1998] 3 W.L.R. 971; (1998) 142 S.J.L.B. 256;
Times, August 29, 1998, PC (Jam) . . . .   *Digested*, 98/**4344**
McMullan v. Chief Adjudication Officer SSTRF 97/0500 CMS1, CA . . . .   *Digested*, 98/**4512**
McMullan's Application for Judicial Review, Re [2000] N.I. 498, QBD (NI) . . . .   *Digested*, 01/**5940**
McNally v. McWilliams [2001] N.I. 106, QBD (NI) . . . .   *Digested*, 01/**5710**
McNally v. RG Manufacturing Ltd [2001] Lloyd's Rep. I.R. 379, CC (Northampton). . . .   *Digested*, 01/**3299**
McNally v. Secretary of State for Education see R. (on the application of McNally) v.
Secretary of State for Education and Employment
Macnamara v. Customs and Excise Commissioners [1999] V. & D.R. 171, V&DTr . . . . . .   *Digested*, 00/**5373**
MacNeill v. Sutherland 1998 S.C.C.R. 474; [1999] E.H.L.R. 44; 1998 G.W.D. 27-1383,
HCJ Appeal; reversing [1998] E.H.L.R. Dig. 279, Sh Ct . . . .   *Digested*, 98/**5878**

McNicholas Construction Co Ltd v. Customs and Excise Commissioners see Clark (Inspector of Taxes) v. Perks (Permission to Appeal)

McNicholas Construction Co Ltd v. Customs and Excise Commissioners [2000] S.T.C. 553; [2000] B.T.C. 5225; [2000] B.V.C. 255; [2000] S.T.I. 889; *Independent*, July 24, 2000 (C.S), QBD . . . .   *Digested*, 00/**5348**

McNicholas Construction Co Ltd v. Customs and Excise Commissioners (Private Hearing) [1998] V. & D.R. 220,V&DTr . . . .   *Digested*, 00/**5298**:
Previous proceedings, 97/5035

McNicol v. Balfour Beatty Rail Maintenance Ltd see Rugamer v. Sony Music Entertainment UK Ltd

Macniven (Inspector of Taxes) v. Westmoreland Investments Ltd; *sub nom* Westmoreland Investments Ltd v. MacNiven (Inspector of Taxes) [2001] UKHL 6; [2001] 2 W.L.R. 377; [2001] 1 All E.R. 865; [2001] S.T.C. 237; 73 T.C. 1; [2001] B.T.C. 44; 3 I.T.L. Rep. 342; [2001] S.T.I. 168; (2001) 98(11) L.S.G. 44; (2001) 151 N.L.J. 223; (2001) 145 S.J.L.B. 55; *Times*, February 14, 2001; *Independent*, March 19, 2001 (C.S), HL; affirming [1998] S.T.C. 1131; [1998] B.T.C. 422; 1 I.T.L. Rep. 208; (1998) 95(44) L.S.G. 35; (1998) 142 S.J.L.B. 262; *Times*, October 26, 1998; *Independent*, November 2, 1998 (C.S.), CA; reversing [1997] S.T.C. 1103; [1997] B.T.C. 424; *Times*, August 19, 1997, Ch D . . . .   *Digested*, 01/**5199**:
Applied, 01/5205

McNulty v. Marshalls Food Group Ltd 1999 S.C. 195; 1999 Rep. L.R. 17 (Note); 1998 G.W.D. 36-1875; *Times*, January 7, 1999, OH . . . .   *Digested*, 99/**5972**

MacPherson v. European Strategic Bureau Ltd [2000] 2 B.C.L.C. 683; (2000) 97(35) L.S.G. 36; *Times*, September 5, 2000, CA; reversing [1999] 2 B.C.L.C. 203; *Times*, March 1, 1999, Ch D . . . .   *Digested*, 00/**670**

MacPherson v. Secretary of State for Scotland 1985 S.L.T. 134; [1985] J.P.L. 788, 1 Div . . . .   *Digested*, 85/**4892**:
Considered, 00/4455

McPherson v. Shiasson (Unreported, December 9, 1999), CC (Wakefield) [*Ex rel.* Nigel S Brockley, Barrister, Bracton Chambers, Bell House, 8 Bell Yard, London] .   *Digested*, 00/**1588**

McPhilemy v. Times Newspapers Ltd [2000] 1 W.L.R. 1732; [2000] C.P. Rep. 53; [2000] C.P.L.R. 335; [2000] E.M.L.R. 575; *Times*, June 7, 2000, CA . . . .   *Digested*, 00/**329**

McPhilemy v. Times Newspapers Ltd (Abuse of Process) [2001] EWCA Civ 871; [2001] E.M.L.R. 34; *Times*, June 19, 2001; *Independent*, July 23, 2001 (C.S); *Daily Telegraph*, June 19, 2001, CA . . . .   *Digested*, 01/**1816**

McPhilemy v. Times Newspapers Ltd (Costs) [2001] EWCA Civ 933; [2001] 4 All E.R. 861; [2001] 2 Costs L.R. 295; [2001] E.M.L.R. 35; *Times*, July 3, 2001, CA . . . .   *Digested*, 01/**484**

McPhilemy v. Times Newspapers Ltd (Re-Amendment: Justification) [1999] 3 All E.R. 775; [1999] C.P.L.R. 533; [1999] E.M.L.R. 751; *Times*, May 26, 1999; *Independent*, June 9, 1999, CA . . . .   *Digested*, 99/**1635**:
Applied, 00/568, 00/605: *Considered*, 99/312: *Followed*, 00/1757

McQuade v. Chief Constable of Humberside; *sub nom* Chief Constable of Humberside v. McQuade [2001] EWCA Civ 1330; (2001) 165 J.P. 729; (2001) 98(35) L.S.G. 33; *Times*, September 3, 2001, CA . . . .   *Digested*, 01/**1007**

McQuade v. Donald Cameron Holdings Ltd (Unreported, June 25, 1999), CC (Central London) [*Ex rel.* Lucy McLynn, Barrister, Dr Johnson's Chambers, 2 Dr Johnson's Buildings, Temple, London]. . . . .   *Digested*, 99/**558**

McQuilliams v. Secured Funding Ltd (Unreported, April 30, 1999) . . . .   *Doubted*, 00/**514**

Macrae v. Macrae [1949] P. 397; [1949] 2 All E.R. 34; 65 T.L.R. 547; 113 J.P. 342; 47 L.G.R. 537; [1949] L.J.R. 1671; 93 S.J. 449, CA; affirming [1949] P. 272, DC . .   *Digested*, 47-51/**3083**:
Applied, 47-51/1573, 47-51/3010: *Considered*, 67/3122, 71/7093, 72/2106, 99/4564: *Explained*, 52/1019, 52/1078: *Followed*, 56/2695

McRae v. Thomson Holidays Ltd (Unreported, October 26, 2000), CC (Epsom) [*Ex rel.* Matthew Chapman, Barrister, No 1 Serjeants' Inn, Fleet Street, London] . . . .   *Digested*, 01/**4291**

McSharry v. Lloyds TSB Bank Plc (Unreported, October 5, 2000), CC (Chorley) [*Ex rel.* William McCarthy, Barrister, New Bailey Chambers, 10 Lawson Street, Preston, Lancashire] . . . .   *Digested*, 00/**4037**

McVeigh v. United Kingdom (8022/77); O'Neill v. United Kingdom (8025/77); Evans v. United Kingdom (8027/77) (1983) 5 E.H.R.R. 71, Eur Comm HR . . . .   *Considered*, 99/**5182**

Macari v. Celtic Football & Athletic Co Ltd 1999 S.C. 628; 2000 S.L.T. 80; 2000 S.C.L.R. 209; [1999] I.R.L.R. 787; 1999 G.W.D. 25-1208, 1 Div; affirming 1999 S.L.T. 138; 1998 G.W.D. 10-506, OH . . . .   *Digested*, 00/**6221**

Macclesfield BC v. Bolton Emery Partnership (1998) 13 P.A.D. 311, Planning Inspector
Macclesfield BC v. Henbury High School (1998) 13 P.A.D. 204, Planning Inspector
Macclesfield BC v. Seddon (1998) 13 P.A.D. 691, Planning Inspector

Mace v. Rutland House Textiles Ltd (1999) 96(46) L.S.G. 37; (2000) 144 S.J.L.B. 7; [1999] N.P.C. 141; *Times*, January 11, 2000, Ch D . . . .   *Digested*, 00/**3912**

Macey-Lillie v. Lanarkshire Health Board 2001 S.L.T. 215; 2000 Rep. L.R. 109; 2000 G.W.D. 19-761; *Times*, June 28, 2000, OH . . . .   *Digested*, 00/**6161**

Macharia v. Immigration Appeal Tribunal; *sub nom* Macharia v. Secretary of State for the Home Department [2000] Imm. A.R. 190; [2000] I.N.L.R. 267; (1999) 96(46) L.S.G. 38; *Times*, November 25, 1999, CA. . . . .   *Digested*, 99/**3209**

Macharia v. Secretary of State for the Home Department see Macharia v. Immigration
Appeal Tribunal
Machin v. Adams 84 B.L.R. 79; 59 Con. L.R. 14; [1998] E.C.C. 75; [1997] E.G.C.S. 74;
[1997] N.P.C. 73, CA . . . . *Digested*, 98/**3999**
Machin v. National Power Plc (Appropriate Forum) CH. 1997-M-5114, Ch D . . . . *Digested*, 98/**482**:
Subsequent proceedings, 98/481
Machin v. National Power Plc (Pre-Emptive Costs: Court of Appeal) see National Grid
Co Plc v. Laws (Pre-Emptive Costs: Court of Appeal)
Machine Tool Industry Research Association v. Simpson [1988] I.C.R. 558; [1988]
I.R.L.R. 212, CA . . . . *Digested*, 88/**1355**:
Considered, 94/2032, 96/2666, 00/2243: *Followed*, 99/2146
Machinery Market Ltd v. Sheen Publishing Ltd [1983] F.S.R. 431, Ch D . . . . *Digested*, 83/**479**:
Considered, 99/3436: *Doubted*, 00/3575
Macieo Shipping Ltd v. Clipper Shipping Lines Ltd (The Clipper Sao Luis) [2000] 1 All
E.R. (Comm) 920; [2000] 1 Lloyd's Rep. 645; [2001] C.L.C. 762, QBD
(Comm Ct) . . . . *Digested*, 00/**4696**
Mackie Designs Inc v. Behringer (Ulrich Bernhard) see Mackie Designs Inc v. Behringer
Specialised Studio Equipment (UK) Ltd
Mackie Designs Inc v. Behringer Specialised Studio Equipment (UK) Ltd; *sub nom*
Mackie Designs Inc v. Behringer Spezielle Studiotechnik GmbH; Mackie Designs
Inc v. Behringer (Ulrich Bernhard) [2000] E.C.D.R. 445; [1998-99] Info. T.L.R.
125; [1999] R.P.C. 717; (2000) 16 Const. L.J. 161; (1999) 22(7) I.P.D. 22069,
Ch D . . . . *Digested*, 99/**3442**
Mackie Designs Inc v. Behringer Spezielle Studiotechnik GmbH see Mackie Designs Inc
v. Behringer Specialised Studio Equipment (UK) Ltd
Macob Civil Engineering Ltd v. Morrison Construction Ltd [1999] C.L.C. 739; [1999]
B.L.R. 93; (1999) 1 T.C.L.R. 113; 64 Con. L.R. 1; [1999] 3 E.G.L.R. 7; [1999] 37
E.G. 173; (1999) 15 Const. L.J. 300; (1999) 96(10) L.S.G. 28; *Times*, March 11,
1999; *Independent*, March 1, 1999 (C.S.), QBD (T&CC) . . . . *Digested*, 99/**794**:
Approved, 00/806: *Distinguished*, 00/807: *Referred to*, 99/795
Macro (Ipswich) Ltd, Re; *sub nom* Earliba Finance Co Ltd, Re; Macro v. Macro
(Ipswich) Ltd [1996] 1 W.L.R. 145; [1996] 1 All E.R. 814; [1997] 1 Costs L.R.
128, Ch D . . . . *Digested*, 96/**736**:
Distinguished, 01/11
Macro v. Macro (Ipswich) Ltd see Macro (Ipswich) Ltd, Re
Madan v. General Medical Council (Interim Suspension Order) [2001] EWHC Admin
577; [2001] Lloyd's Rep. Med. 539, QBD (Admin Ct)
Madden v. Pattni (Unreported, August 4, 1999), CC (Central London) [*Ex rel.*
Fennemores Solicitors, 200 Silbury Boulevard, Central Milton Keynes] . . . . *Digested*, 99/**540**
Madden & Finucane v. Causeway Health and Social Services Trust [1997] N.I. 20, QBD
(NI) . . . . *Digested*, 99/**5369**
Maddox v. Storer [1963] 1 Q.B. 451; [1962] 2 W.L.R. 958; [1962] 1 All E.R. 831; 126
J.P. 263; 61 L.G.R. 41; 106 S.J. 372, DC . . . . *Digested*, 62/**2932**:
Considered, 90/1153, 91/971, 98/4299, 98/4300: *Followed*, 64/3248,
65/3494
Maden v. Customs and Excise Commissioners [1996] V. & D.R. 449, V&DTr . . . . *Digested*, 98/**4636**
Madgecourt Ltd's Trade Mark Application (No.2104616) (2000) 23(9) I.P.D. 23076,
Appointed Person; affirming [2000] E.T.M.R. 825, TMR . . . . *Digested*, 01/**4039**
Madgett (t/a Howden Court Hotel) v. Customs and Excise Commissioners (No.1)
(C308/96); *sub nom* Customs and Excise Commissioners v. Madgett (t/a
Howden Court Hotel) (No.1) (C308/96); Madgett (t/a Howden Court Hotel) v.
Customs and Excise Commissioners (No.2) (C94/97) [1998] S.T.C. 1189;
[1998] E.C.R. I-6229; [1999] 2 C.M.L.R. 392; [1998] C.E.C. 1004; [1998]
B.T.C. 5440; [1998] B.V.C. 458, ECJ (5th Chamber) . . . . *Digested*, 99/**5002**
Madgett (t/a Howden Court Hotel) v. Customs and Excise Commissioners (No.2)
(C94/97) see Madgett (t/a Howden Court Hotel) v. Customs and Excise
Commissioners (No.1) (C308/96)
Madhavji v. Consort (Unreported, August 24, 1999), CC (Birmingham) [*Ex rel.* Wragge
& Co Solicitors, 55 Colmore Row, Birmingham] . . . . *Digested*, 99/**1402**
Maes Finance Ltd v. AL Phillips & Co, *Times*, March 25, 1997, Ch D . . . . *Digested*, 97/**3773**:
Applied, 99/1395: *Considered*, 98/333
Maes Finance Ltd v. Leftleys; Mac No.1 Ltd v. Leftleys *Times*, November 13, 1998, CA;
affirming [1998] P.N.L.R. 193, Ch D . . . . *Digested*, 98/**47**
Maes Finance Ltd v. Sharp & Partners 69 Con. L.R. 46, QBD (T&CC) . . . . *Digested*, 00/**4271**
Maes Finance Ltd v. Shriskantharaja [1998] N.P.C. 54, CA
Maes Finance Ltd v. WG Edwards & Partners [2000] 2 Costs L.R. 198, QBD
Mag Instrument Inc, Re (2000) 23(7) I.P.D. 23052, OHIM (2nd Bd App)
Mag Instrument Inc v. California Trading Co Norway, Ulsteen (E2/97) [1998] 1
C.M.L.R. 331; [1998] E.T.M.R. 85, EFTA . . . . *Followed*, 01/**2500**
Magee v. Armstrong Engineering Services (London) Ltd; Magee v. Taymech Ltd
[1994] P.I.Q.R. P299; (1997) 13 Const. L.J. 355; *Times*, February 10, 1994, CA . *Digested*, 98/**507**
Magee v. Taymech Ltd see Magee v. Armstrong Engineering Services (London) Ltd
Magee v. United Kingdom (28135/95) (2001) 31 E.H.R.R. 35; 8 B.H.R.C. 646; [2000]
Crim. L.R. 681; *Times*, June 20, 2000, ECHR . . . . *Digested*, 00/**3223**

MAGIC BALL Trade Mark see Nestle UK Ltd v. Zeta Espacial SA
Magill v. Porter see Porter v. Magill
Magill v. Weeks see Porter v. Magill
Magill Case (C241/91), Re see Radio Telefis Eireann v. Commission of the European Communities (C241/91)
MAGNETTI MARELLI/Pressure sensor (T708/95) [2001] E.P.O.R. 14, EPO (Technical Bd App) . . . . *Digested,* 01/**3903**
Magnin v. Teledyne Continental Motors [1998] I.L.Pr. 274, US Ct
Magon v. Barking and Dagenham LBC [2000] R.A. 459, QBD . . . . *Digested,* 01/**4820**
Magorrian v. Eastern Health and Social Services Board (C246/96) [1998] All E.R. (E.C.) 38; [1997] E.C.R. I-7153; [1998] C.E.C. 241; [1998] I.C.R. 979; [1998] I.R.L.R. 86; [1997] O.P.L.R. 353; *Times,* December 22, 1997, ECJ (6th Chamber) . . . . *Digested,* 98/**4133**: *Considered,* 01/2279

Maguire v. Fermanagh DC [1996] N.I. 110, CA (NI)
Maguire v. Makaronis [1955-95] P.N.L.R. 933, HC (Aus)
Mahadervan v. Mahadervan; *sub nom* Mahadevan v. Mahadevan [1964] P. 233; [1963] 2 W.L.R. 271; [1962] 3 All E.R. 1108; 106 S.J. 533, PDAD . . . . *Digested,* 63/**1684**: *Applied,* 01/2611: *Considered,* 74/1069, 99/3734: *Distinguished,* 64/1732
Mahadevan v. Mahadevan see Mahadervan v. Mahadervan
Maharani Restaurants v. Customs and Excise Commissioners [1999] S.T.C. 295; [1999] B.T.C. 5145; [1999] B.V.C. 179; *Independent,* February 15, 1999 (C.S.), QBD; affirming [2000] B.V.C. 2262, V&DTr . . . . *Digested,* 99/**5023**
Maher v. Minister for Agriculture, Food and Rural Development [2001] 2 C.M.L.R. 48, Sup Ct (Irl) . . . . *Digested,* 01/**835**
Mahlburg v. Land Mecklenburg Vorpommern (C207/98) [2000] E.C.R. I-549; [2001] 3 C.M.L.R. 40; [2001] I.C.R. 1032; [2000] I.R.L.R. 276; *Times,* February 17, 2000, ECJ (6th Chamber) . . . . *Digested,* 00/**2172**
Mahmood, Re see R. (on the application of Mahmood) v. Royal Pharmaceutical Society of Great Britain
Mahmood v. Qhreshi (Unreported, February 26, 2001), CC (Bristol) [*Ex rel.* James Hassall, Barrister, Guildhall Chambers, 22-26 Broad Street, Bristol] . . . . *Digested,* 01/**480**
Mahmood (Amjad) v. Secretary of State for the Home Department see R. (on the application of Mahmood (Amjad)) v. Secretary of State for the Home Department
Mahmood v. Vehicle Inspectorate CO/2730/97, QBD . . . . *Digested,* 98/**974**
Mahmood v. Watson (Unreported, March 1, 2001), CC (Dewsbury) [*Ex rel.* Tom Nossiter, Barrister, Park Lane Chambers, 19 Westgate, Leeds] . . . . *Digested,* 01/**531**
Mahmoud and Ispahani, Re; *sub nom* Arbitration between Mahmoud and Ispahani, Re; Mahmoud v. Ispahani [1921] 2 K.B. 716; (1921) 6 Ll. L. Rep. 344, CA . . . . *Applied,* 47-51/**984**, 62/483, 86/1775, 87/2050: *Considered,* 99/849: *Distinguished,* 61/1433: *Referred to,* 94/5488

Mahmud v. Bank of Credit and Commerce International SA (In Liquidation) see Malik v. Bank of Credit and Commerce International SA (In Liquidation)
Mahomed v. Bank of Baroda see Bank of Baroda v. Mahomed
Mahomed v. Morris (No.1) (2000) 97(7) L.S.G. 41; *Times,* March 1, 2000, CA . . . . *Digested,* 00/**477**
Mahomed v. Morris (No.2) [2001] B.C.C. 233; [2000] 2 B.C.L.C. 536, CA . . . . *Digested,* 01/**3750**
Mahon v. Rahn (No.1) [1998] Q.B. 424; [1997] 3 W.L.R. 1230; [1997] 3 All E.R. 687; [1997] E.M.L.R. 558; *Times,* June 12, 1997, CA; reversing (Unreported, June 19, 1996), QBD . . . . *Digested,* 97/**475**: *Considered,* 98/1768, 00/2627: *Followed,* 97/3078
Mahon v. Rahn (No.2) [2000] 1 W.L.R. 2150; [2000] 4 All E.R. 41; [2000] 2 All E.R. (Comm) 1; [2000] E.M.L.R. 873; (2000) 97(26) L.S.G. 38; (2000) 150 N.L.J. 899; *Times,* June 14, 2000, CA; reversing [1999] 2 All E.R. (Comm) 789, QBD . *Digested,* 00/**2627**
Maidment v. Commission of the European Communities [1999] I.C.R. 577, EAT . . . . . . *Digested,* 99/**2057**
Maidstone BC v. Hickmott (1998) 13 P.A.D. 429, Planning Inspector
Maidstone Grove Ltd v. Norman Hitchcox Partnership Ltd see Tesco Stores Ltd v. Norman Hitchcox Partnership Ltd
Maidstone Justices v. Williams [2000] Crim. L.R. 689, QBD
Maile v. Manchester City Council [1998] C.O.D. 19; *Times,* November 26, 1997, CA; affirming (1997) 74 P. & C.R. 443, QBD . . . . *Digested,* 97/**3518**
Maile v. Wigan MBC [2001] Env. L.R. 11; [2001] J.P.L. 118 (Note); [2001] J.P.L. 193, QBD . . . . *Digested,* 01/**2358**
Maillard v. France (1999) 27 E.H.R.R. 232; [1998] H.R.C.D. 618, ECHR . . . . *Digested,* 99/**3137**
Maimann v. Maimann (Application for Freezing Order) [2001] I.L.Pr. 27, QBD . . . . *Digested,* 01/**821**
Main v. Secretary of State for the Environment, Transport and the Regions (1999) 77 P. & C.R. 300; [1999] J.P.L. 195; (1998) 95(22) L.S.G. 30, QBD . . . . *Digested,* 99/**4220**
Main v. Swansea City Council; *sub nom* R. v. Swansea City Council Ex p. Main (1985) 49 P. & C.R. 26; [1985] J.P.L. 558, CA; affirming *Times,* December 23, 1981, QBD . . . . *Digested,* 85/**3463**: *Considered,* 90/4367, 01/4688
Mainstream Ventures Ltd v. Woolway (Valuation Officer) [2000] R.A. 395, Lands Tr. . . . . *Digested,* 00/**4592**

Mainwaring *v.* Goldtech Investments Ltd (No.2); Goldtech Investments Ltd *v.* Mainwaring [1999] 1 W.L.R. 745; [1999] 1 All E.R. 456; [1999] 1 Costs L.R. 96; (1998) 95(45) L.S.G. 38; (1999) 143 S.J.L.B. 13; *Times*, November 16, 1998; *Independent*, November 16, 1998 (C.S.), CA; reversing [1997] 4 All E.R. 16, Ch D . . . . *Digested*, 98/**439**

Mainwaring *v.* Trustees of Henry Smith's Charity [1998] Q.B. 1; [1996] 3 W.L.R. 1033; [1996] 2 All E.R. 220; (1996) 28 H.L.R. 583; (1997) 73 P. & C.R. 395; [1996] 2 E.G.L.R. 25; [1996] 29 E.G. 110; [1996] E.G.C.S. 31; [1996] N.P.C. 21; *Times*, February 20, 1996, CA. . . . . *Digested*, 96/**3842**

Mair *v.* Rio Grande Rubber Estates Ltd [1913] A.C. 853; 1913 S.C. (H.L.) 74; (1913) 2 S.L.T.166, HL; reversing 1913 S.C. 183, 1 Div . . . . *Considered*, 01/3805:
Distinguished, 94/5914

Majeed *v.* Incentive Group (Unreported, June 15, 1999), CC (Wandsworth) [*Ex rel.* Tim Kevan, Barrister, 1 Temple Gardens, Temple, London] . . . . *Followed*, 00/2568:
Subsequent proceedings, 99/2465

Majeed *v.* Incentive Group (Unreported, August 27, 1999), CC (Central London) [*Ex rel.* Tim Kevan, Barrister, 1 Temple Gardens, Temple, London, Rollingsons Solicitors, Chancery Lane] . . . . *Digested*, 99/**2465**:
Considered, 01/888: *Referred to*, 99/2490

Majestic Recording Studios, Re (1988) 4 B.C.C. 519; [1989] B.C.L.C. 1, DC . . . . *Digested*, 88/**317**:
Considered, 98/670

Majid *v.* TMV Finance Ltd (Unreported, January 20, 1999), CC (Swindon) [*Ex rel.* Julian Winn Reed, Barrister, 9 Park Place, Cardiff] . . . . *Digested*, 99/**2448**

Majid & Partners *v.* Customs and Excise Commissioners [1999] S.T.C. 585; [1999] B.T.C. 5242; *Independent*, December 7, 1998 (C.S.), QBD . . . . *Digested*, 99/**5024**

Major (Inspector of Taxes) *v.* Brodie [1998] S.T.C. 491; 70 T.C. 576; [1998] B.T.C. 141; (1998) 95(16) L.S.G. 25; (1998) 142 S.J.L.B. 124; *Times*, March 18, 1998, Ch D . . . . *Digested*, 98/**4678**

Makepeace *v.* Evans Brothers (Reading) [2000] B.L.R. 287; [2001] I.C.R. 241; (2000) 97(23) L.S.G. 42; *Times*, June 13, 2000, CA . . . . *Digested*, 00/**4206**

Makozo *v.* Secretary of State for the Home Department (Unreported, February 12, 1999), IAT. . . . . *Considered*, 01/3622

Mal Bower's Macquarie Electrical Centre Pty Ltd (In Liquidation), Re [1974] 1 N.S.W.L.R. 254 . . . . *Applied*, 00/3465

Malaysian Industrial Development Authority *v.* Jeyasingham [1998] I.C.R. 307, EAT . . . *Digested*, 98/**2233**

Malcolm *v.* Commissioner of Police of the Metropolis (Unreported, February 24, 1999), QBD [*Ex rel.* David Williams, Barrister, 2 Dr Johnson's Buildings, Temple, London] . . . . *Digested*, 99/**2880**

Malcolm *v.* Commissioner of Police of the Metropolis (Quantum) (Unreported, February 24, 1999), QBD [*Ex rel.* David Williams, Barrister, 2 Dr Johnson's Buildings, Temple, London] . . . . *Digested*, 99/**1494**

Malcolm *v.* Official Receiver [1999] B.P.I.R. 97, Ch D . . . . *Digested*, 99/**3238**

Malekshad *v.* Howard de Walden Estates Ltd [2001] EWCA Civ 761; [2001] 3 W.L.R. 824; [2001] 38 E.G. 190; [2001] 23 E.G.C.S. 157; (2001) 98(24) L.S.G. 46; (2001) 145 S.J.L.B. 157; *Times*, July 9, 2001, CA; reversing [2000] E.G.C.S. 37, CC (London) . . . . *Digested*, 01/**4180**

Malgar Ltd *v.* RE Leach (Engineering) Ltd [2000] C.P. Rep. 39; [2000] F.S.R. 393; (2000) 23(1) I.P.D. 23007; *Times*, February 17, 2000, Ch D . . . . *Digested*, 00/**383**

Malhotra *v.* Ropi Industries (1976) 1 Ind. L.R. 278, HC (Ind) . . . . *Followed*, 98/3521

Malige *v.* France (1999) 28 E.H.R.R. 578; [1998] H.R.C.D. 897, ECHR . . . . *Digested*, 00/**3235**

Malik *v.* Bank of Credit and Commerce International SA (In Liquidation); *sub nom* Mahmud *v.* Bank of Credit and Commerce International SA (In Liquidation); BCCI SA, Re [1998] A.C. 20; [1997] 3 W.L.R. 95; [1997] 3 All E.R. 1; [1997] I.C.R. 606; [1997] I.R.L.R. 462; (1997) 94(25) L.S.G. 33; (1997) 147 N.L.J. 917; *Times*, June 13, 1997; *Independent*, June 20, 1997, HL; reversing [1995] 3 All E.R. 545; [1995] I.R.L.R. 375; (1995) 145 N.L.J. 593; *Times*, April 12, 1995; *Independent*, March 17, 1995, CA; affirming [1994] I.R.L.R. 282; *Times*, February 23, 1994; *Independent*, March 21, 1994 (C.S.), Ch D . . . . *Digested*, 97/**2192**:
Applied, 99/2010, 01/2305: *Considered*, 98/2106, 99/2030, 99/2149, 01/2253: *Explained*, 99/2111

Malik (t/a Hotline Foods) *v.* Customs and Excise Commissioners [1998] S.T.C. 537; [1998] B.T.C. 5168; [1998] B.V.C. 181; *Independent*, March 23, 1998 (C.S.), QBD . . . . *Digested*, 98/**4984**

Malik *v.* FM De Rooy (No.1) (Unreported, April 4, 2000), CC (Manchester) [*Ex rel.* Laura Elfield, Barrister, 5 Pump Court, Temple, London] . . . . *Digested*, 00/**1456**:
Cited, 00/541

Malik *v.* FM De Rooy (No.2) (Unreported, July 13, 2000), CC (Manchester) [*Ex rel.* Laura Elfield, Barrister, 5 Pump Court, Temple, London] . . . . *Digested*, 00/**541**

Mallalieu v. Drummond (Inspector of Taxes) [1983] 2 A.C. 861; [1983] 3 W.L.R. 409;
   [1983] 2 All E.R. 1095; [1983] S.T.C. 665; (1983) 80 L.S.G. 2368; (1983) 133
   N.L.J. 869; (1983) 127 S.J. 538, HL; reversing [1983] 1 W.L.R. 252; [1983] 1
   All E.R. 801; [1983] S.T.C. 124; (1983) 127 S.J. 37, CA; affirming [1981] 1 W.L.R.
   908; [1981] S.T.C. 391; [1981] T.R. 105; 125 S.J. 205, Ch D .... *Digested,* 83/**1983**:
                      Applied, 85/1784: *Considered,* 90/2667, 99/4701: *Distinguished,* 97/2945:
                                                                      Followed, 96/3356

Mallender v. Inland Revenue Commissioners; *sub nom* Inland Revenue Commissioners
   v. Mallender [2001] S.T.C. 514; [2001] B.T.C. 8013; [2001] W.T.L.R. 459; [2001]
   S.T.I. 548; [2001] N.P.C. 62; *Times,* March 30, 2001; *Independent,* May 14,
   2001 (C.S), Ch D; reversing [2000] S.T.C. (S.C.D.) 574; [2000] S.T.I. 1656, Sp
   Comm .... *Digested,* 01/**5285**

Mallett v. McMonagle [1970] A.C. 166; [1969] 2 W.L.R. 767; [1969] 2 All E.R. 178;
   [1969] 1 Lloyd's Rep. 127; 6 K.I.R. 322; 113 S.J. 207, HL .... *Digested,* 69/**898**:
                      Applied, 00/4187: *Approved,* 70/614: *Considered,* 71/3100, 86/2276, 94/1491,
                                   98/1489: *Followed,* 98/3966: *Not followed,* 78/709, 78/713

Mallett (Inspector of Taxes) v. Staveley Coal & Iron Co Ltd [1928] 2 K.B. 405; 13 T.C.
   772; [1928] W.N. 97, CA .... *Applied,* 59/1527,
                      59/1528, 59/3778, 01/5201: *Considered,* 61/4200: *Followed,* 47-51/4744

Mallick v. Liverpool City Council (2000) 79 P. & C.R. 1; [1999] 2 E.G.L.R. 7; [1999]
   33 E.G. 77; [2000] R.V.R. 315; [2000] J.P.L. 521; [1999] E.G.C.S. 104; [1999]
   N.P.C. 91; *Times,* July 24, 1999; *Independent,* October 11, 1999 (C.S.), CA .... *Digested,* 99/**4189**

Mallinckrodt Group Inc's European Patent (T161/96) see NOVO NORDISK/Underpayment
   of Opposition Fee (T161/96)

Mallinson v. Secretary of State for Social Security [1994] 1 W.L.R. 630; [1994] 2 All
   E.R. 295; (1994) 144 N.L.J. 604; (1994) 138 S.J.L.B. 112; *Times,* April 28, 1994;
   Independent, April 26, 1994; *Guardian,* April 25, 1994, HL; reversing *Times,*
   April 2, 1993, CA.. *Digested,* 94/**4121**:
                                                                      Followed, 98/4511

Malloch v. Aberdeen Corp (No.1) [1971] 1 W.L.R. 1578; [1971] 2 All E.R. 1278; 1971
   S.C. (H.L.) 85; 1971 S.L.T. 245; 115 S.J. 756, HL; reversing 1970 S.L.T. 369, 2
   Div; affirming 1970 S.L.T. (Notes) 21, OH .... *Digested,* 71/**12835**:
                      Applied, 83/15: *Considered,* 75/3760, 76/3084, 77/3072, 80/99, 87/3162,
                      92/5290, 94/5369, 95/5443: *Distinguished,* 84/14, 93/5405, 98/2242:
                                                                      Followed, 83/24, 96/3961

Maloco v. Littlewoods Organisation Ltd; Smith v. Littlewoods Organisation Ltd [1987]
   A.C. 241; [1987] 2 W.L.R. 480; [1987] 1 All E.R. 710; 1987 S.C. (H.L.) 37; 1987
   S.L.T. 425; 1987 S.C.L.R. 489; (1987) 84 L.S.G. 905; (1987) 137 N.L.J. 149;
   (1987) 131 S.J. 226, HL; affirming 1986 S.L.T. 272, 1 Div; reversing 1982 S.L.T.
   267, OH .... *Digested,* 87/**4737**:
                      Applied, 95/3668: *Considered,* 88/2019, 92/3201, 93/2934, 93/2953,
                      94/3365, 95/494, 96/1162, 98/4037: *Distinguished,* 90/250, 96/3699:
                                                                      Not followed, 84/4347, 85/4437

Malone v. Button (Unreported, July 17, 1998), CC (Lowestoft) [*Ex rel.* Jonathan
   Hough, Barrister, 1 Temple Gardens, Temple, London]..................... *Digested,* 98/**495**

Malone v. Quinn (Inspector of Taxes) [2001] S.T.C. (S.C.D.) 63; [2001] S.T.I. 673, Sp
   Comm .... *Digested,* 01/**5236**

Malone v. United Kingdom (A/82) (1985) 7 E.H.R.R. 14, ECHR; affirming (1983) 5
   E.H.R.R. 385, Eur Comm HR .... *Applied,* 98/3106,
                      00/3252: *Considered,* 00/921, 01/3576: *Distinguished,* 94/705, 95/941

Maltbridge Island Management Co v. Secretary of State for the Environment, Transport
   and the Regions [1998] E.G.C.S. 134, QBD........................... *Digested,* 98/**4370**

Maltez v. Lewis (2000) 16 Const. L.J. 65; (1999) 96(21) L.S.G. 39; *Times,* May 4,
   1999; *Independent,* June 21, 1999, Ch D .... *Digested,* 99/**44**

Malvern Fishing Co Ltd v. Ailsa Craig Fishing Co Ltd (The Strathallan) see Ailsa Craig
   Fishing Co Ltd v. Malvern Fishing Co Ltd (The Strathallan)

Mamczynski v. GM Buses (North) Ltd (Unreported, January 11, 2000), CC (Oldham)
   [*Ex rel.* Andrew Granville Stafford, Barrister, 4 King's Bench Walk, Temple,
   London] .... *Digested,* 00/**1557**

Mamidoil-Jetoil Greek Petroleum Co SA v. Okta Crude Oil Refinery (No.1) [2001] EWCA
   Civ 406; [2001] 2 All E.R. (Comm) 193; [2001] 2 Lloyd's Rep. 76, CA;
   reversing [2000] 1 Lloyd's Rep. 554, QBD (Comm Ct) .... *Digested,* 01/**956**

Mamidoil-Jetoil Greek Petroleum Co SA v. Okta Crude Oil Refinery (No.2) [2001] 1
   Lloyd's Rep. 591, QBD (Comm Ct)..................................... *Digested,* 01/**582**

Man v. Customs and Excise Commissioners [2000] S.T.I. 1093, V&DTr

Management Corp Strata Title Plan No. 1933 v. Liang Huat Aluminium Ltd (formerly
   Liang Huai Aluminium Pte Ltd) [2001] B.L.R. 351; (2001) 17 Const. L.J. 555,
   CA (Sing)

Manan (Abdul), Re [1971] 1 W.L.R. 859; [1971] 2 All E.R. 1016; 115 S.J. 289, CA ..... *Digested,* 71/**822**:
                                                                      Applied, 73/4, 82/1555, 98/3007

Manatee Towing Co Ltd v. McQuilling Brokerage Partners Inc see Manatee Towing Co
   Ltd v. Oceanbulk Maritime SA (The Bay Ridge)

Manatee Towing Co Ltd v. McQuilling Brokerage Partners Inc (Discovery) see Manatee
   Towing Co Ltd v. Oceanbulk Maritime SA (The Bay Ridge) (Discovery)

Manatee Towing Co Ltd *v.* Oceanbulk Maritime SA (The Bay Ridge) (Discovery); Oceanbulk Maritime SA *v.* Manatee Towing Co Ltd (Discovery); Manatee Towing Co Ltd *v.* McQuilling Brokerage Partners Inc (Discovery) [1999] 1 Lloyd's Rep. 876; [1999] C.L.C. 1197; (1999) 143 S.J.L.B. 111; *Times*, May 11, 1999; *Independent*, March 15, 1999 (C.S.), QBD (Comm Ct) . . . .   *Digested*, 99/**327**

Manatee Towing Co Ltd *v.* Oceanbulk Maritime SA (The Bay Ridge); Oceanbulk Maritime SA *v.* Manatee Towing Co Ltd; Manatee Towing Co Ltd *v.* McQuilling Brokerage Partners Inc [1999] 2 All E.R. (Comm) 306; [1999] 2 Lloyd's Rep. 227; [1999] C.L.C. 1204, QBD (Comm Ct) . . . .   *Digested*, 99/**4483**

Manchanda *v.* Manchanda [1995] 2 F.L.R. 590; [1996] 1 F.C.R. 733; [1995] Fam. Law 603; (1995) 92(23) L.S.G. 32; (1995) 139 S.J.L.B. 116; *Times*, May 29, 1995; *Independent*, June 12, 1995 (C.S.), CA . . . .   *Digested*, 95/**2307**:   *Applied*, 00/2500

Manchester Airport Plc *v.* Dutton [2000] Q.B. 133; [1999] 3 W.L.R. 524; [1999] 2 All E.R. 675; (2000) 79 P. & C.R. 541; [1999] 1 E.G.L.R. 147; [1999] E.G.C.S. 31; (1999) 96(9) L.S.G. 34; (1999) 96(11) L.S.G. 69; (1999) 149 N.L.J. 333; (1999) 143 S.J.L.B. 89; [1999] Env. L.R. D19; *Times*, March 5, 1999; *Independent*, March 2, 1999, CA . . . .   *Digested*, 99/**4401**:   *Applied*, 00/4666

Manchester and District Housing Association *v.* Fearnley Construction Ltd (In Liquidation) (2000) 97(32) L.S.G. 39; [2000] N.P.C. 94; (2001) 81 P. & C.R. D2, Ch D

Manchester and Salford Hospital Saturday Fund *v.* Customs and Excise Commissioners [1999] S.T.C. 649; [1999] B.T.C. 8033, QBD; affirming [1998] V. & D.R. 191, V&DTr. . . . .   *Digested*, 99/**4742**

Manchester City Council *v.* Cochrane [1999] 1 W.L.R. 809; (1999) 31 H.L.R. 810; [1999] B.L.G.R. 626; [1999] L. & T.R. 190; (1999) 96(5) L.S.G. 36; (1999) 143 S.J.L.B. 37; [1998] N.P.C. 170; *Times*, January 12, 1999; *Independent*, January 20, 1999, CA . . . .   *Digested*, 99/**3071**

Manchester City Council *v.* Halstead see Halstead *v.* Manchester City Council

Manchester City Council *v.* Lawler (1999) 31 H.L.R. 119, CA . . . .   *Digested*, 99/**3713**:   *Applied*, 99/3041

Manchester City Council *v.* McCann [1999] Q.B. 1214; [1999] 2 W.L.R. 590; (1999) 31 H.L.R. 770; (1998) 95(48) L.S.G. 31; *Times*, November 26, 1998; *Independent*, November 20, 1998, CA . . . .   *Digested*, 98/**15**

Manchester City Council *v.* McLoughlin, *Times*, April 5, 2000, CA. . . . .   *Digested*, 00/**8**

Manchester City Council *v.* Special Educational Needs Tribunal [2000] Ed. C.R. 80; [2000] E.L.R. 144, QBD . . . .   *Digested*, 00/**1956**

Manchester City Council *v.* Worthington [2000] 1 F.L.R. 411; [2000] Fam. Law 238, CA . . . .   *Digested*, 00/**1084**

Manchester United Plc *v.* Customs and Excise Commissioners [2001] S.T.I. 1233, V&DTr

Mandal *v.* Rotherham Hospital NHS Trust (2001) 58 B.M.L.R. 112, QBD . . . .   *Digested*, 01/**2243**

Mandarim Records Ltd *v.* Mechanical Copyright Protection Society (Ireland) Ltd [2000] E.C.D.R. 77, HC (Irl) . . . .   *Digested*, 00/**3580**

Mander *v.* Commercial Union Assurance Co Plc; Mander *v.* Prudential Assurance Co Ltd; Mander *v.* Gyngell Dobinson Gregory Co Ltd [1998] Lloyd's Rep. I.R. 93, QBD (Comm Ct) . . . .   *Digested*, 98/**3394**

Mander *v.* Equitas Ltd [2000] C.L.C. 901; [2000] Lloyd's Rep. I.R. 520, QBD (Comm Ct) . . . .   *Digested*, 00/**3562**

Mander *v.* Evans [2001] 1 W.L.R. 2378; [2001] 3 All E.R. 811; [2001] B.P.I.R. 902; (2001) 98(28) L.S.G. 42; (2001) 151 N.L.J. 818; (2001) 145 S.J.L.B. 158; *Times*, June 25, 2001; *Independent*, July 9, 2001 (C.S), Ch D . . . .   *Digested*, 01/**3726**

Mander *v.* Gyngell Dobinson Gregory Co Ltd see Mander *v.* Commercial Union Assurance Co Plc

Mander *v.* Prudential Assurance Co Ltd see Mander *v.* Commercial Union Assurance Co Plc

Manderson-Jones *v.* Societe Internationale de Telecommunications Aeronautiques [1998] 1 W.L.R. 1486; (1998) 142 S.J.L.B. 255, PC (Jam) . . . .   *Digested*, 98/**511**

Mandla (Sewa Singh) *v.* Dowell Lee [1983] 2 A.C. 548; [1983] 2 W.L.R. 620; [1983] 1 All E.R. 1062; [1983] I.C.R. 385; [1983] I.R.L.R. 209; (1983) 127 S.J. 242, HL; reversing [1983] Q.B. 1; [1982] 3 W.L.R. 932; [1982] 3 All E.R. 1108; [1983] I.R.L.R. 17; 126 S.J. 726, CA . . . .   *Digested*, 83/**1163**:   *Applied*, 86/1212, 87/1353, 88/275, 89/267, 98/5811, 01/1065:   *Considered*, 84/1669, 85/3550, 91/1656, 92/1958

Manel *v.* Memon (2001) 33 H.L.R. 24; [2000] 2 E.G.L.R. 40; [2000] 33 E.G. 74; (2000) 80 P. & C.R. D22; *Times*, April 20, 2000; *Independent*, May 22, 2000 (C.S.), CA . . . .   *Digested*, 00/**3875**

Mangan (CICA: Quantum: 2000), Re (Unreported, August 10, 2000), CICA (London) [*Ex rel*. Laura Begley, Barrister, 9 Gough Square, London] . . . .   *Digested*, 01/**1559**

Mangham *v.* Taylor [2001] 6 Q.R. 22, CC (Bradford) [*Ex rel*. Jinder S Boora, Barrister, 24 The Ropewalk, Nottingham] . . . .   *Digested*, 01/**1794**

Mangistaumunaigaz Oil Production Association *v.* United World Trading Inc [1995] 1 Lloyd's Rep. 617; *Times*, February 24, 1995, QBD (Comm Ct) . . . .   *Digested,* 96/**359**: *Applied,* 00/235

Manifest Shipping Co Ltd *v.* Uni-Polaris Insurance Co Ltd (The Star Sea); *sub nom* Manifest Shipping Co Ltd *v.* Uni-Polaris Shipping Co Ltd (The Star Sea) [2001] UKHL 1; [2001] 2 W.L.R. 170; [2001] 1 All E.R. 743; [2001] 1 All E.R. (Comm) 193; [2001] 1 Lloyd's Rep. 389; [2001] C.L.C. 608; [2001] Lloyd's Rep. I.R. 247; *Times*, January 23, 2001, HL; affirming [1997] 1 Lloyd's Rep. 360; [1997] C.L.C. 481; [1997] 6 Re. L.R. 175; *Times*, January 23, 1997, CA; affirming [1995] 1 Lloyd's Rep. 651, QBD (Comm Ct) . . . .   *Digested,* 01/**3825**: *Applied,* 00/4696, 00/4744: *Considered,* 01/3827

Manito *v.* Elliott (Unreported, June 13, 2000), CC (Salford) [*Ex rel.* J Keith Park & Co Solicitors, 23 Westway, Maghull, Liverpool] . . . .   *Digested,* 00/**2593**

Manley *v.* New Forest DC [2000] E.H.L.R. 113; [1999] 4 P.L.R. 36; (1999) 96(31) L.S.G. 44; [2000] Env. L.R. D11, QBD . . . .   *Digested,* 00/**2308**

Manlon Trading Ltd (Directors: Disqualification), Re; Knight (practising as Dibb & Clegg, Barnsley), Re [1996] Ch. 136; [1995] 3 W.L.R. 839; [1995] 4 All E.R. 14; [1995] B.C.C. 579; [1995] 1 B.C.L.C. 578; *Times*, June 22, 1995, CA; affirming [1995] 3 W.L.R. 271; [1995] 1 All E.R. 988; [1995] 1 B.C.L.C. 84; *Times*, August 15, 1994, Ch D . . . .   *Digested,* 95/**591**: *Followed,* 98/674

Mann *v.* Chetty & Patel [2001] C.P. Rep. 24; [2001] Lloyd's Rep. P.N. 38, CA . . . .   *Digested,* 01/**438**

Mann *v.* Lexington Insurance Co [2001] 1 All E.R. (Comm) 28; [2001] 1 Lloyd's Rep. 1; [2000] C.L.C. 1409; [2001] Lloyd's Rep. I.R. 179; *Times*, November 29, 2000; *Daily Telegraph*, October 24, 2000, CA; reversing [2000] 2 All E.R. (Comm) 163; [2000] 2 Lloyd's Rep. 250; *Independent*, July 24, 2000 (C.S), QBD (Comm Ct) . . . .   *Digested,* 01/**3837**

Mann *v.* Nijar see Nijar *v.* Mann

Mann *v.* O'Neill (1997) 71 A.L.J.R. 903 . . . .   *Considered,* 00/4543

Mann *v.* Powergen Plc (Unreported, February 9, 1999), CC (Plymouth) [*Ex rel.* David Cadin, Barrister, King's Bench Chambers, 115 North Hill, Plymouth] . . . .   *Digested,* 99/**415**: *Cited,* 00/403

Mann *v.* Secretary of State for Education and Employment; *sub nom* Secretary of State for Employment *v.* Mann; Potter *v.* Secretary of State for Employment [1999] Eu. L.R. 992; [1999] I.C.R. 898; [1999] I.R.L.R. 566; *Times*, July 19, 1999, HL; affirming [1998] Eu. L.R. 388; [1997] I.C.R. 209; [1997] I.R.L.R. 21, CA; affirming in part [1996] I.C.R. 197; [1996] I.R.L.R. 4, EAT . . . .   *Digested,* 99/**2101**

Mannai Investment Co Ltd *v.* Eagle Star Life Assurance Co Ltd [1997] A.C. 749; [1997] 2 W.L.R. 945; [1997] 3 All E.R. 352; [1997] C.L.C. 1124; [1997] 1 E.G.L.R. 57; [1997] 25 E.G. 138; [1997] 24 E.G. 122; (1997) 16 Tr. L.R. 432; [1997] E.G.C.S. 82; (1997) 94(30) L.S.G. 30; (1997) 147 N.L.J. 846; (1997) 141 S.J.L.B. 130; [1997] N.P.C. 81; *Times*, May 26, 1997, HL; reversing [1995] 1 W.L.R. 1508; [1996] 1 All E.R. 55; (1996) 71 P. & C.R. 129; [1996] 1 E.G.L.R. 69; [1996] 06 E.G. 140; [1995] E.G.C.S. 124; (1995) 139 S.J.L.B. 179; [1995] N.P.C. 117; *Times*, July 19, 1995, CA . . . .   *Digested,* 97/**3256**: *Applied,* 98/3598, 00/5612, 01/4156, 01/4182: *Distinguished,* 98/3033, 98/3608, 00/3910: *Followed,* 98/3614, 00/3885, 00/4421

Mannesmann AG *v.* Goldman Sachs International 1999 HC 04861, Ch D . . . .   *Digested,* 00/**495**

Mannesmann Anlagenbau Austria AG *v.* Strohal Rotationsdruck GmbH (C44/96) [1998] E.C.R. I-73; [1998] 2 C.M.L.R. 805, ECJ

Mannesmann Kienzle GmbH *v.* Microsystem Design Ltd [1992] R.P.C. 569, Pat Ct . . . .   *Considered,* 94/3450, 96/4553, 01/3882

Mannesmannrohren-Werke AG *v.* Commission of the European Communities (T112/98) [2001] E.C.R. II-729; [2001] 5 C.M.L.R. 1, CFI . . . .   *Digested,* 01/**768**

Manning *v.* Hope (t/a Priory), *Times*, February 18, 2000, CA . . . .   *Digested,* 00/**5119**

Manning *v.* Society of Lloyd's; *sub nom* Society of Lloyd's *v.* Colfox; Philips *v.* Society of Lloyd's [1997] C.L.C. 1411; [1998] Lloyd's Rep. I.R. 186, QBD (Comm Ct) . . .   *Digested,* 98/**3384**

Mannion (Inspector of Taxes) *v.* Johnston see Atkinson (Inspector of Taxes) *v.* Dancer

Manoharan *v.* Secretary of State for the Home Department [1998] Imm. A.R. 455; [1998] I.N.L.R. 519, IAT . . . .   *Digested,* 99/**3169**: *Not followed,* 99/3170

Manor Bakeries Ltd *v.* Nazir [1996] I.R.L.R. 604, EAT . . . .   *Digested,* 96/**2574**: *Not followed,* 99/2085

Manotta *v.* London United Busways Ltd (Unreported, February 22, 2000), CC (Uxbridge) [*Ex rel.* Joanne Wardale, Barrister, 3 Paper Buildings, Temple, London] . . . .   *Digested,* 00/**1457**

Manpower Sarl, Strasbourg Regional Office *v.* Caisse Primaire d'Assurance Maladie de Strasbourg (C35/70) [1970] E.C.R. 1251; [1971] C.M.L.R. 222, ECJ . . . .   *Digested,* 71/**4508**: *Applied,* 00/2099

Mansfield *v.* Weetabix Ltd [1998] 1 W.L.R. 1263; [1998] R.T.R. 390; [1997] P.I.Q.R. P526, CA . . . .   *Digested,* 97/**3765**

Mansfield DC *v.* Peveril Securities (2000) 15 P.A.D. 629, Planning Inspector

Mansi v. Elstree Rural DC 62 L.G.R. 172; (1965) 16 P. & C.R. 153; 189 E.G. 341; 108
S.J. 178, QBD . . . . *Digested,* 64/**3580**:
Applied, 80/2635, 92/4163, 93/3857, 94/4416, 95/4769, 01/4696:
Considered, 86/3269, 87/3615, 91/3468: *Distinguished,* 69/3450, 78/2874,
93/3820: *Not applied,* 84/3434
Manson v. Barclays Bank Plc see Manson v. Vooght (No.1)
Manson v. Barclays Bank Plc (Application for Leave To Appeal) [1999] C.P.L.R. 825,
CA . . . . *Digested,* 00/**364**
Manson v. Coopers & Lybrand see Manson v. Vooght (No.1)
Manson v. Smith (Liquidator of Thomas Christy Ltd) [1997] 2 B.C.L.C. 161, CA. . . . . . . *Digested,* 98/**3341**
Manson v. Vooght (No.1); *sub nom* Manson v. Barclays Bank Plc; Manson v. Coopers
& Lybrand [1999] C.P.L.R. 133; [1999] B.P.I.R. 376; *Times,* November 20, 1998,
CA . . . . *Digested,* 98/**367**:
Considered, 01/4264
Manson v. Vooght (No.2) [2000] B.C.C. 838, CA . . . . *Digested,* 00/**346**
Manton v. Van Day [2001] E.T.M.R. CN17, Ch D
Mantovanelli v. France (1997) 24 E.H.R.R. 370, ECHR . . . . *Digested,* 98/**3126**
Mantovani v. Carapelli SpA [1980] 1 Lloyd's Rep. 375; 123 S.J. 568, CA; affirming
[1978] 2 Lloyd's Rep. 63, QBD (Comm Ct). . . . . *Digested,* 80/**2378**:
Applied, 01/560: *Distinguished,* 99/241
Manufacturers Life Assurance Co Ltd v. Cummins (Inspector of Taxes) [2001] S.T.C.
316; 73 T.C. 306; [2001] B.T.C. 27; [2000] S.T.I. 1544; *Times,* November 22,
2000, Ch D; affirming [2000] S.T.C. (S.C.D.) 222; [2000] S.T.I. 644, Sp
Comm . . . . *Digested,* 00/**4937**
Manx Ices Ltd v. Department of Local Government and the Environment [2001] Eu.
L.R. 650, HC (IoM)
Manzanilla Ltd v. Corton Property & Investments Ltd (No.1) CHANI 95/1014/B, CA . . . *Digested,* 97/**1009**:
Followed, 98/498
Manzanilla Ltd v. Corton Property & Investments Ltd (No.2) [1997] 3 F.C.R. 389;
Times, August 4, 1997, CA . . . . *Digested,* 97/**608**:
Followed, 00/470
Manzeke v. Secretary of State for the Home Department [1997] Imm. A.R. 524, CA . . . *Digested,* 98/**3178**:
Applied, 99/3146: *Followed,* 98/3194
Manzoni v. Italy (Unreported, July 1, 1997), ECHR . . . . *Considered,* 98/3071
Maple Division Ltd v. Wilson [1999] B.P.I.R. 102, Ch D . . . . *Digested,* 99/**3248**
Maple Environmental Services Ltd, Re [2000] B.C.C. 93; [2001] B.P.I.R. 321, Ch D . . . *Digested,* 00/**3492**
Mapp v. News Group Newspapers Ltd; Gillan v. News Group Newspapers Ltd;
Goscomb v. News Group Newspapers Ltd; Watton v. News Group Newspapers
Ltd [1998] Q.B. 520; [1998] 2 W.L.R. 260; [1997] E.M.L.R. 397; (1997) 147
N.L.J. 562; *Times,* March 10, 1997, CA . . . . *Digested,* 97/**2038**
Marais v. Governor of Brixton Prison see R. (on the application of Marais) v. Governor
of Brixton Prison
Marandi v. Secretary of State for the Home Department [2000] Imm. A.R. 346, CA . . . *Digested,* 00/**3314**
Marangos Hotel Co Ltd v. Stone see Polly Peck International Plc (In Administration)
(No.5), Re
Marc Rich Agriculture Trading SA v. Agrimex Ltd [2000] 1 All E.R. (Comm) 951; [2001]
C.L.C. 756; (2000) 97(20) L.S.G. 42; *Times,* April 26, 2000, QBD (Comm Ct). . *Digested,* 00/**238**
Marc Rich & Co AG v. Bishop Rock Marine Co Ltd (The Nicholas H) [1996] A.C. 211;
[1995] 3 W.L.R. 227; [1995] 3 All E.R. 307; [1995] 2 Lloyd's Rep. 299; [1996]
E.C.C. 120; (1995) 145 N.L.J. 1033; (1995) 139 S.J.L.B. 165; *Times,* July 7,
1995; *Independent,* August 18, 1995; *Lloyd's List* July 19, 1995 (I.D.), HL;
affirming [1994] 1 W.L.R. 1071; [1994] 3 All E.R. 686; [1994] 1 Lloyd's Rep. 492;
Times, February 23, 1994; *Independent,* March 2, 1994, CA; reversing [1992] 2
Lloyd's Rep. 481; [1993] E.C.C. 121; *Financial Times,* July 15, 1992; *Lloyd's List,*
August 14, 1992, QBD (Comm Ct) . . . . *Digested,* 95/**4519**:
Applied, 96/4448, 99/3963: *Considered,* 95/3648, 97/3816, 97/4087,
98/3951: *Distinguished,* 97/3776, 98/3923
Marc Rich & Co AG v. Societa Italiana Impianti pA (The Atlantic Emperor) (No.2) [1992]
1 Lloyd's Rep. 624; [1992] I.L.Pr. 544; *Financial Times,* January 24, 1992, CA . . . *Digested,* 92/**3508**:
Considered, 99/754
Marc Rich & Co Holding GmbH v. Krasner CHANI 99/0009/3, CA. . . . . *Digested,* 99/**487**
Marc Rich & Co Ltd v. Tourloti Compania Naviera SA (The Kalliopi A) [1988] 2 Lloyd's
Rep. 101; [1988] 2 F.T.L.R. 73, CA; reversing [1987] 2 Lloyd's Rep. 263; [1987]
1 F.T.L.R. 399, QBD (Comm Ct) . . . . *Digested,* 89/**3406**:
Applied, 92/3934, 92/3946, 00/4698
Marca Mode CV v. Adidas AG [1999] E.T.M.R. 791, HR (NL) . . . . *Subsequent proceed-*
ings, 00/3701
Marca Mode CV v. Adidas AG (C425/98) [2000] All E.R. (EC) 694; [2000] E.C.R. I-
4861; [2000] 2 C.M.L.R. 1061; [2000] C.E.C. 395; [2000] E.T.M.R. 723, ECJ
(6th Chamber) [2000] E.C.R. I-4861; [2000] E.T.M.R. 561, AGO . . . . *Digested,* 00/**3701**

Marcel v. Commissioner of Police of the Metropolis; Anchor Brewhouse
Developments v. Jaggard [1992] Ch. 225; [1992] 2 W.L.R. 50; [1992] 1 All E.R.
72; (1992) 4 Admin. L.R. 309; (1991) 141 N.L.J. 1224; (1991) 135 S.J.L.B. 125;
Times, August 7, 1991; *Independent*, July 24, 1991; *Guardian*, August 28, 1991,
CA; reversing in part [1991] 2 W.L.R. 1118; [1991] 1 All E.R. 845; *Times*,
December 5, 1990, Ch D . . . . *Digested*, 92/**3581**:
Applied, 92/2580, 00/934: *Referred to*, 92/3494, 93/3108, 95/3069

March v. E&MH Stramare Pty (1991) 171 C.L.R. 506, HC (Aus) . . . . *Digested*, 91/**2636**:
Applied, 99/3987: *Considered*, 94/533, 95/3691

Marchant v. Brown (Unreported, August 2, 1999), CC (Canterbury) [*Ex rel.* Antony
Hodari & Co Solicitors, 34 High Street, Manchester] . . . . *Digested*, 99/**2491**:
Followed, 01/893

Marchant v. Marchant (Unreported, February 26, 1999), CC (Walsall) [*Ex rel.* Gillespies
Solicitors, Darwall Street, Walsall, West Midlands] . . . . *Digested*, 99/**2401**

Marchant v. Onslow [1995] Ch. 1; [1994] 3 W.L.R. 607; [1994] 2 All E.R. 707; [1994]
13 E.G. 114; *Times*, November 12, 1993, Ch D . . . . *Digested*, 94/**607**:
Overruled, 01/5534

Marchant & Eliot Underwriting Ltd v. Higgins [1996] 2 Lloyd's Rep. 31; [1996] C.L.C.
327; [1996] 3 C.M.L.R. 349; [1997] E.C.C. 47; [1996] 5 Re. L.R. 63; *Times*,
January 12, 1996, CA; affirming [1996] 1 Lloyd's Rep. 313; [1996] C.L.C. 301;
[1996] 3 C.M.L.R. 313; [1997] E.C.C. 11; *Lloyd's List*, January 10, 1996 (I.D.),
QBD (Comm Ct) . . . . *Digested*, 96/**3627**:
Distinguished, 99/3498

Marchday Group Plc, Re [1998] B.C.C. 800, Ch D (Companies Ct) . . . . *Digested*, 99/**3356**

Marchday Group Plc v. Cafe Rouge Ltd [1998] N.P.C. 61, Ch D

Marchiori v. Environment Agency see R. (on the application of Marchiori) v.
Environment Agency

Marcic v. Thames Water Utilities Ltd A1/2001/1771, A1/2001/1930, CA; affirming in
part [2001] 4 All E.R. 326; [2001] B.L.R. 366; (2001) 3 T.C.L.R. 29; 77 Con.
L.R. 42; [2001] H.R.L.R. 53; (2001) 151 N.L.J. 1180; [2001] N.P.C. 113;
Independent, October 22, 2001 (C.S); *Daily Telegraph*, July 17, 2001, QBD
(T&CC) . . . . *Digested*, 01/**1525**

Marcic v. Thames Water Utilities Ltd (Preliminary Issues) [2001] 3 All E.R. 698; (2001)
3 T.C.L.R. 28; 77 Con. L.R. 42; [2001] H.R.L.R. 52; [2001] N.P.C. 95; [2001]
E.H.L.R. Dig. 6; *Independent*, July 9, 2001 (C.S), QBD (T&CC) . . . . *Digested*, 01/**1544**

Marcus v. Queens Moat Houses Plc see Bairstow v. Queens Moat Houses Plc

Marcus v. Queens Moat Houses Plc (Assessment of Costs) see Bairstow v. Queens
Moat Houses Plc (Assessment of Costs)

Marcus v. Queens Moat Houses Plc (Costs) see Bairstow v. Queens Moat Houses Plc
(Costs)

Marcus Publishing Plc v. Hutton-Wild Communications Ltd [1990] R.P.C. 576; *Times*,
October 31, 1989, CA . . . . *Digested*, 91/**3416**:
Followed, 99/3529

Maredelanto Compania Naviera SA v. Bergbau-Handel GmbH (The Mihalis Angelos)
[1971] 1 Q.B. 164; [1970] 3 W.L.R. 601; [1970] 3 All E.R. 125; [1970] 2 Lloyd's
Rep. 43; 114 S.J. 548, CA; reversing [1970] 2 W.L.R. 907; [1970] 1 All E.R. 673;
[1970] 1 Lloyd's Rep. 118, QBD (Comm Ct) . . . . *Digested*, 70/**357**:
Considered, 76/2547: *Followed*, 98/811, 00/4702

Mareva Navigation Co v. Canaria Armadora SA (The Mareva AS) [1977] 1 Lloyd's Rep.
368, QBD (Comm Ct) . . . . *Digested*, 77/**2757**:
Applied, 98/4408, 00/4703: *Referred to*, 78/2705

Margate Pier and Harbour Proprietors v. Margate Town Council (1869) 20 L.T. 564 . . . . *Applied*, 78/2201,
00/4292: *Distinguished*, 47-51/6972

Margey v. Tesco Stores Ltd (Unreported, July 28, 1998), CC (High Wycombe) [*Ex rel.*
Reynolds Parry-Jones & Crawford Solicitors, 10 Easton Street, High Wycombe,
Bucks] . . . . *Digested*, 99/**398**

Margulies v. Margulies (1999-2000) 2 I.T.E.L.R. 641, CA; affirming (1999) 77 P. &
C.R. D21, Ch D . . . . *Digested*, 01/**5518**

Marimpex Mineraloel Handelsgesellschaft mbH & Co KB v. Compagnie de Gestion et
d'Exploitation Ltd (The Ambor and the Once) [2001] 1 All E.R. (Comm) 182;
[2001] C.L.C. 138, QBD (Comm Ct) . . . . *Digested*, 01/**4910**

Marine Contractors Inc v. Shell Petroleum Development Co of Nigeria Ltd [1984] 2
Lloyd's Rep. 77; 27 B.L.R. 127; (1984) 81 L.S.G. 1044, CA; affirming [1983]
Com. L.R. 251 . . . . *Digested*, 84/**105**:
Applied, 00/217

Marine Transportation Co Ltd v. Pansuiza Compania de Navegacion SA see Chilean
Nitrate Sales Corp v. Marine Transportation Co Ltd (The Hermosa)

Marine Workers Union v. Mauritius Marine Authority see Societe United Docks v.
Mauritius

Marinho v. Ferreira & Matos Ltd [2001] E.C.C. 25, Rel (P)

Mario (Michel Azar) v. Secretary of State for the Home Department [1998] Imm. A.R.
281; [1998] I.N.L.R. 306, IAT . . . . *Digested*, 98/**3184**:
Applied, 99/3169: *Followed*, 99/3152

Maritrop Trading Corp v. Guangzhou Ocean Shipping Co [1998] C.L.C. 224, QBD
(Comm Ct) . . . . *Digested*, 98/**582**
Mark One (Oxford Street) Plc, Re [1999] 1 W.L.R.1445; [1999] 1 All E.R. 608; [1998] B.C.C.
984; [2000] 1 B.C.L.C. 462, Ch D (Companies Ct). . . . . *Digested*, 99/**3349**:
Considered, 01/3708
Mark Rowlands Ltd v. Berni Inns Ltd [1986] Q.B. 211; [1985] 3 W.L.R. 964; [1985] 3
All E.R. 473; [1985] 2 Lloyd's Rep. 437; [1985] 2 E.G.L.R. 92; (1985) 276 E.G.
191, CA. . . . . *Digested*, 86/**1787**:
Considered, 94/120, 98/3619: *Distinguished*, 90/411, 94/4086, 96/3751:
Followed, 94/5930: *Referred to*, 89/2093
Mark Wilkinson Furniture Ltd v. Construction Industry Training Board, *Times*, October 10,
2000, QBD . . . . *Digested*, 00/**3396**
Mark Wilkinson Furniture Ltd v. Woodcraft Designs (Radcliffe) Ltd [1998] F.S.R. 63;
(1997) 20(12) I.P.D. 20126; *Times*, October 13, 1997, Ch D . . . . *Digested*, 97/**1034**:
Referred to, 01/3863
Market Investigations v. Minister of Social Security [1969] 2 Q.B. 173; [1969] 2 W.L.R.
1; [1968] 3 All E.R. 732; 112 S.J. 905, QBD. . . . . *Digested*, 69/**2337**:
Applied, 72/525, 73/420, 80/891, 81/932, 90/1864, 92/2498, 01/2263:
Approved, 76/871: *Considered*, 94/2546: *Followed*, 72/1758, 73/1680
Market Wizard Systems (UK) Ltd, Re [1998] 2 B.C.L.C. 282; [1998-99] Info T.L.R. 19;
[1998] I.T.C.L.R. 171; [1999] Masons C.L.R. 1; (1998) 95(33) L.S.G. 34; (1998)
142 S.J.L.B. 229; *Times*, July 31, 1998, Ch D (Companies Ct) . . . . *Digested*, 98/**2534**
Markfield Investments Ltd v. Evans [2001] 1 W.L.R. 1321; [2001] 2 All E.R. 238;
(2001) 81 P. & C.R. 33; [2000] E.G.C.S. 127; [2000] N.P.C. 121; (2001) 81 P. &
C.R. D15, CA. . . . . *Digested*, 01/**4842**
Markowski v. Elson (Unreported, November 3, 2000), CC (Weymouth) [*Ex rel.*
Lamport Bassitt Solicitors, 46 The Avenue, Southampton] . . . . *Digested*, 01/**4477**
Marks v. Beyfus (1890) L.R. 25 Q.B.D. 494, CA . . . . *Applied*, 77/2324,
86/591, 90/1014, 91/778: *Considered*, 89/560, 90/929, 97/494:
Followed, 00/944: *Referred to*, 86/1519, 87/1688
Marks v. Lilley [1959] 1 W.L.R. 749; [1959] 2 All E.R. 647; 103 S.J. 658, Ch D . . . . . . *Digested*, 59/**3409**:
Applied, 01/3418: *Considered*, 60/3282
Marks & Spencer Plc v. Broadway (Valuation Officer) [1998] R.A. 17, Lands Tr . . . . *Digested*, 98/**4333**
Marks & Spencer Plc v. Cottrell (2001) 24(7) I.P.D. 24046, Ch D
Marks & Spencer Plc v. Customs and Excise Commissioners (No.1) [2000] S.T.C. 16;
[2000] 1 C.M.L.R. 256; [2000] Eu. L.R. 293; [2000] B.T.C. 5003; [2000]
B.V.C. 35; [2000] S.T.I. 22; *Times*, January 19, 2000, CA; reversing in part [1999]
S.T.C. 205; [1999] 1 C.M.L.R. 1152; [1999] Eu. L.R. 450; [1999] B.T.C. 5073;
[1999] B.V.C. 107; *Times*, January 19, 1999, QBD; affirming [1997] V. & D.R. 85,
V&DTr. . . . . *Digested*, 00/**5317**:
Considered, 00/4462: *Distinguished*, 01/6921:
Previous proceedings, 98/4926, 00/5360
Marks & Spencer Plc v. Customs and Excise Commissioners (No.2) [1998] Eu. L.R.
153; [1998] B.V.C. 2096; [1997] V. & D.R. 344, V&DTr . . . . *Digested*, 98/**4972**
Marks & Spencer Plc v. Customs and Excise Commissioners (No.3) [1998] V. & D.R.
93, V&DTr . . . . *Digested*, 00/**5360**:
Subsequent proceedings, 99/5001
Marks & Spencer Plc v. Customs and Excise Commissioners (No.4) [1998] Eu. L.R.
163; [1998] B.V.C. 2209; [1998] V. & D.R. 235, V&DTr . . . . *Digested*, 98/**4926**:
Subsequent proceedings, 99/5001
Marks & Spencer Plc v. Fernley (Valuation Officer) (2000) 79 P. & C.R. 514; [1999]
R.A. 409, CA; affirming [1999] R.A. 125, Lands Tr. . . . . *Digested*, 00/**4574**
Marks & Spencer Plc v. Martins; *sub nom* Martins v. Marks & Spencer Plc [1998] I.C.R.
1005; [1998] I.R.L.R. 326; *Times*, January 15, 1998, CA . . . . *Digested*, 98/**2182**
Marks & Spencer Plc v. One in a Million Ltd see British Telecommunications Plc v. One
in a Million Ltd
Marks & Spencer Plc's European Trade Mark Application [2000] E.T.M.R. 168, OHIM (3rd
Bd App) . . . . *Digested*, 00/**3737**
Marleasing SA v. La Comercial Internacional de Alimentacion SA (C106/89) [1990]
E.C.R. I-4135; [1993] B.C.C. 421; [1992] 1 C.M.L.R. 305, ECJ (6th Chamber) . . *Applied*, 97/2383,
00/5520: *Distinguished*, 94/2098, 95/2938
Marley v. Mutual Security Merchant Bank & Trust Co Ltd [2001] W.T.L.R. 483, PC
(Jam) . . . . *Digested*, 01/**5530**
Marlow v. Secretary of State for the Environment, Transport and the Regions; *sub nom*
R. v. Secretary of State for the Environment, Transport and the Regions Ex p.
Marlow (1999) 96(46) L.S.G. 41, QBD . . . . *Digested*, 00/**4419**
Marlowe Child & Family Services Ltd v. DPP [1999] 1 W.L.R. 997; [1998] 2 Cr. App. R.
(S.) 438; [1999] 1 F.L.R. 997; [1998] Crim. L.R. 594, QBD . . . . *Digested*, 98/**2430**
Marlton v. Turner [1998] 3 E.G.L.R. 185, CC (Norwich) . . . . *Digested*, 97/**4233**
Maronek v. Slovakia (32686/96) 10 B.H.R.C. 558, ECHR . . . . *Digested*, 01/**3465**
Marquess of Bute v. Barclays Bank Ltd [1955] 1 Q.B. 202; [1954] 3 W.L.R. 741; [1954]
3 All E.R. 365; 98 S.J. 805, QBD . . . . *Digested*, 54/**3422**:
Applied, 01/377: *Approved*, 79/265: *Considered*, 89/152

Marreco v. Richardson [1908] 2 K.B. 584, CA . . . . *Applied*, 00/**4621**:
Distinguished, 47-51/**706**, 85/**1775**
Marriott v. Lane (Inspector of Taxes) [1996] 1 W.L.R. 1211; [1996] S.T.C. 704; 69 T.C.
157; (1996) 93(21) L.S.G. 27; (1996) 140 S.J.L.B. 117; *Times*, April 26, 1996,
Ch D . . . . *Digested*, 96/**440**
Marriott v. Secretary of State for the Environment, Transport and the Regions [2001]
J.P.L. 559, QBD (Admin Ct)
Marriott v. West Midlands RHA [1999] Lloyd's Rep. Med. 23, CA . . . . *Digested*, 99/**3994**
Mars BV v. Societe des Produits Nestle SA [1999] E.T.M.R. 862, RB (Den Haag)
Mars GB Ltd's Trade Mark Application [1999] E.T.M.R. 402, OHIM (Opposition Div)
Mars UK Ltd v. Teknowledge Ltd (No.1) [2000] E.C.D.R. 99; [1998-99] Info. T.L.R.
331; [1999] Masons C.L.R. 322; (1999) 22(8) I.P.D. 22076; *Times*, June 23,
1999 ; *Independent*, July 1, 1999, Ch D . . . . *Digested*, 99/**3437**
Mars UK Ltd v. Teknowledge Ltd (No.2) [1999] 2 Costs L.R. 44; [2000] F.S.R. 138;
(1999) 22(10) I.P.D. 22097; *Times*, July 8, 1999, Ch D . . . . *Digested*, 99/**384**:
Applied, 01/**485**: *Followed*, 01/**471**: *Referred to*, 00/**3672**
Marsal v. Apong [1998] 1 W.L.R. 674, PC (Bru) . . . . *Digested*, 98/**560**
Marschall v. Land Nordrhein-Westfalen (C409/95) [1997] All E.R. (E.C.) 865; [1997]
E.C.R. I-6363; [1998] 1 C.M.L.R. 547; [1998] C.E.C. 152; [2001] I.C.R. 45;
[1998] I.R.L.R. 39; *Times*, December 13, 1997, ECJ . . . . *Digested*, 98/**2146**:
Considered, 00/**2170**
Marsden v. Elston [2001] EWCA Civ 1746, CA; reversing (Unreported, October 3,
2000), CC (Norwich) [*Ex rel*. Nicholas Yell, Barrister, No. 1 Serjeants' Inn, Fleet
Street, London] . . . . *Digested*, 01/**2678**
Marsden v. Gustar (Inspector of Taxes) [2000] S.T.C. (S.C.D.) 371; [2000] S.T.I. 1127,
Sp Comm . . . . *Digested*, 00/**4917**
Marsden v. Johnson see HM Prison Service v. Johnson
Marsh (A Minor) v. Igoe (Unreported, March 5, 1998), CC (Birkenhead) [*Ex rel*. Brian
Camp & Co Solicitors, 1 Europa House, Conway Street, Merseyside] . . . . *Digested*, 98/**1713**
Marsh v. Frenchay Healthcare NHS Trust, *Times*, March 13, 2001; *Independent*, March
12, 2001 (C.S), QBD . . . . *Digested*, 01/**621**
Marsh v. Marsh [1993] 1 W.L.R. 744; [1993] 2 All E.R. 794; [1993] 1 F.L.R. 467;
[1993] Fam. Law 346; (1993) 143 N.L.J. 364; *Times*, February 16, 1993, CA . . . *Digested*, 93/**1899**:
Applied, 95/**2339**, 01/**2631**: *Followed*, 96/**2835**, 98/**2458**:
Not applied, 01/**2630**
Marsh v. Powys CC (1998) 75 P. & C.R. 538; [1997] 2 E.G.L.R. 177; [1997] 33 E.G.
100; [1997] R.V.R. 283; [1998] J.P.L. 496, Lands Tr . . . . *Digested*, 97/**4231**
Marsh v. Thomson Tour Operators (Unreported, January 10, 2000), CC (Colchester)
[*Ex rel*. Dominic Bayne, Barrister, Plowden Buildings, Temple, London] . . . . *Digested*, 00/**4044**
Marsh v. Von Sternberg [1986] 1 F.L.R. 526; [1986] Fam. Law 160 . . . . *Digested*, 86/**1857**:
Considered, 00/**3941**
Marsh & McLennan Companies UK Ltd v. Pensions Ombudsman; *sub nom* Williamson,
Re [2001] I.R.L.R. 505; [2001] Pens. L.R. 51, Ch D; reversing [2000] Pens.
L.R. 117, Pensions Ombudsman . . . . *Digested*, 01/**4605**
Marshall v. Beckett; *sub nom* M v. B (Ancillary Proceedings: Lump Sum) [1998] 1
F.L.R. 53; [1998] 1 F.C.R. 213; [1998] Fam. Law 75; *Times*, October 15, 1997,
CA . . . . *Digested*, 97/**2471**
Marshall v. Betts see Neilson v. Betts
Marshall v. Bradford MDC [2001] EWCA Civ 594; [2001] 19 E.G.C.S. 140; *Daily
Telegraph*, May 8, 2001, CA
Marshall v. Harland & Wolff (No.1) [1972] 1 W.L.R. 899; [1972] 2 All E.R. 715; [1972]
1 R.L.R. 90; [1972] I.C.R. 101; [1972] I.R.L.R. 90; (1972) 7 I.T.R. 150; 116 S.J.
484, NIRC . . . . *Digested*, 72/**1219**:
Applied, 73/**1118**, 74/**1159**, 74/**1250**, 75/**1097**, 95/**1979**, 98/**2108**:
Explained, 74/**1283**
Marshall (Inspector of Taxes) v. Kerr [1995] 1 A.C. 148; [1994] 3 W.L.R. 299; [1994] 3
All E.R. 106; [1994] S.T.C. 638; 67 T.C. 81; (1994) 91(30) L.S.G. 32; (1994)
138 S.J.L.B. 155; *Times*, July 5, 1994; *Independent*, July 18, 1994 (C.S.), HL;
reversing [1993] S.T.C. 360; 67 T.C. 73; [1993] S.T.I. 353; (1993) 90(14) L.S.G.
45; *Times*, March 8, 1993; *Independent*, April 26, 1993 (C.S.), CA; reversing
[1991] S.T.C. 686; 67 T.C. 56; (1992) 89(3) L.S.G. 33; *Times*, November 13,
1991; *Independent*, December 2, 1991 (C.S.), Ch D . . . . *Digested*, 94/**359**:
Considered, 96/**438**, 99/**4704**: *Referred to*, 95/**529**
Marshall v. Osmond [1983] Q.B. 1034; [1983] 3 W.L.R. 13; [1983] 2 All E.R. 225;
[1983] R.T.R. 475; (1983) 127 S.J. 301, CA; affirming [1982] Q.B. 857; [1982]
3 W.L.R. 120; [1982] 2 All E.R. 610; [1983] R.T.R. 111; [1982] Crim. L.R. 441; 126
S.J. 210, QBD . . . . *Digested*, 83/**2833**:
Considered, 87/**2857**: *Distinguished*, 00/**4217**
Marshall v. Ritchie see Millar v. Dickson

Marshall *v.* Southampton and South West Hampshire AHA (No.1) (C152/84) [1986] Q.B. 401; [1986] 2 W.L.R. 780; [1986] 2 All E.R. 584; [1986] E.C.R. 723; [1986] 1 C.M.L.R. 688; [1986] I.C.R. 335; [1986] I.R.L.R. 140; (1986) 83 L.S.G. 1720; (1986) 130 S.J. 340, ECJ [1986] E.C.R. 723, AGO . . . .   *Digested*, 86/**1456**:
             Applied, 00/4458: *Considered*, 87/1370, 87/3084, 88/1244, 88/2159, 90/3417: *Followed*, 88/1879, 89/1984, 90/3990, 96/2625: *Referred to*, 87/2623, 88/1325

Marshall *v.* Southampton and South West Hampshire AHA (No.2); *sub nom* Southampton and South West Hampshire AHA *v.* Marshall (No.2) [1994] 1 A.C. 530; [1994] 2 W.L.R. 392; [1994] 1 All E.R. 736; [1994] I.C.R. 242, HL; reversing [1990] 3 C.M.L.R. 425; [1991] I.C.R. 136; [1990] I.R.L.R. 481; (1990) 134 S.J. 1368; *Times*, September 4, 1990; *Independent*, August 14, 1990; *Guardian*, August 30, 1990, CA; reversing [1989] 3 C.M.L.R. 771; [1990] I.C.R. 6; [1989] I.R.L.R. 459; *Times*, October 6, 1989; *Independent*, October 17, 1989; *Daily Telegraph*, October 2, 1989, EAT; reversing [1988] 3 C.M.L.R. 389; [1988] I.R.L.R. 325, IT . . . .   *Digested*, 94/**1988**:
             Applied, 98/2100: *Considered*, 91/814, 95/2031, 96/2551, 96/2606, 96/2625, 97/4672: *Previous proceedings*, 93/4275, 94/4927: *Subsequent proceedings*, 93/4275, 94/4927

Marshalltown Trowel Co *v.* CeKa Works Ltd [2001] F.S.R. 36; (2001) 24(5) I.P.D. 24032, Pat Ct

Marston *v.* Knight see Boughton *v.* Knight

Marston Thompson & Evershed Plc *v.* Benn CH.1995-M-30078, Ch D . . . .   *Digested*, 98/**4875**

Martell *v.* Consett Iron Co Ltd [1955] Ch. 363; [1955] 2 W.L.R. 463; [1955] 1 All E.R. 481; 99 S.J. 148; 99 S.J. 211, CA; affirming [1954] 3 W.L.R. 648; [1954] 3 All E.R. 339; 98 S.J. 768, Ch D . . . .   *Digested*, 55/**2680**:
             Applied, 81/298: *Considered*, 69/3662, 70/2935, 98/411: *Followed*, 67/128, 67/3776

Marten *v.* Bell [2001] 4 Q.R. 13, CC (Brighton) [*Ex rel.* Jeremy Cave, Barrister, Crown Office Row, Blenheim House, 120 Church Street, Brighton] . . . .   *Digested*, 01/**1670**

Martin (CICB: Quantum: 2000), Re [2000] 4 Q.R. 5, CICB (Durham) [*Ex rel.* Joseph PAP O'Brien, Barrister, Broad Chare Chambers, 33 Broad Chare, Newcastle upon Tyne] . . . .   *Digested*, 00/**1544**

Martin *v.* Britannia Life Ltd [2000] Lloyd's Rep. P.N. 412, Ch D . . . .   *Digested*, 00/**2621**

Martin *v.* Carfour Nottingham Ltd (Unreported, July 16, 1998), CC (Sheffield) [*Ex rel.* Irwin Mitchell Solicitors, St Peter's House, Hartshead, Sheffield] . . . .   *Digested*, 99/**424**

Martin *v.* Crown Prosecution Service see Martin *v.* DPP

Martin *v.* DPP; *sub nom* Martin *v.* Crown Prosecution Service [2000] 2 Cr. App. R. (S.) 18; (2000) 164 J.P. 405; [2000] R.T.R. 188; [2000] Crim. L.R. 320; (1999) 96(47) L.S.G. 33; (2000) 144 S.J.L.B. 5; *Times*, November 30, 1999, QBD . . . .   *Digested*, 00/**1201**

Martin *v.* Grey (1999) 99(3) Q.R. 8, QBD [*Ex rel.* Taylor Vinters Solicitors, Merlin Place, Milton Road, Cambridge] . . . .   *Digested*, 98/**1763**

Martin *v.* Lancashire CC; Bernadone *v.* Pall Mall Services Group Ltd; Haringey Healthcare NHS Trust *v.* Independent Insurance Ltd [2000] 3 All E.R. 544; [2001] I.C.R. 197; [2000] I.R.L.R. 487; [2000] Lloyd's Rep. I.R. 665; (2000) 2 L.G.L.R. 1026; (2000) 97(24) L.S.G. 39; *Times*, May 26, 2000, CA . . . .   *Digested*, 00/**2234**

Martin *v.* Maryland Estates Ltd (Forfeiture) (1999) 31 H.L.R. 218; [1999] L. & T.R. 30; [1998] 2 E.G.L.R. 81; [1998] 25 E.G. 169, CA . . . .   *Digested*, 98/**3646**

Martin *v.* Maryland Estates Ltd (Service Charges); Seale *v.* Maryland Estates Ltd (2000) 32 H.L.R. 116; [1999] L. & T.R. 541; [1999] 2 E.G.L.R. 53; [1999] 26 E.G. 151; [1999] E.G.C.S. 63; (1999) 96(18) L.S.G. 35; (1999) 78 P. & C.R. D27, CA . . . .   *Digested*, 99/**3743**

Martin *v.* Streamline Holdings Ltd (Unreported, August 13, 1999), CC (Birkenhead) [*Ex rel.* Scott Rees & Co Solicitors, Centaur House, Gardiners Place, Skelmersdale, Lancashire] . . . .   *Digested*, 99/**2488**

Martin *v.* Thomson Tour Operations Ltd (Unreported, May 27, 1999), CC (Central London) [*Ex rel.* Matthew Chapman, Barrister, Barnard's Inn Chambers, Halton House, 20-23 Holburn, London] . . . .   *Digested*, 99/**3818**

Martin *v.* Travel Promotions Ltd (t/a Voyages Jules Verne) (Unreported, February 9, 1999), CC (York) [*Ex rel.* Matther Chapman, Barrister, Barnard's Inn Chambers, Halton House, 20-23 Holburn, London] . . . .   *Digested*, 99/**3821**

Martin *v.* Watson [1996] A.C. 74; [1995] 3 W.L.R. 318; [1995] 3 All E.R. 559; (1995) 145 N.L.J. 1093; (1995) 139 S.J.L.B. 190; *Times*, July 14, 1995; *Independent*, July 19, 1995, HL; reversing [1994] Q.B. 425; [1994] 2 W.L.R. 500; [1994] 2 All E.R. 606; (1994) 91(12) L.S.G. 39; (1994) 138 S.J.L.B. 55; *Times*, January 27, 1994; *Independent*, January 26, 1994; *Guardian*, January 31, 1994, CA . . . .   *Digested*, 96/**5685**:
             Applied, 00/5118: *Followed*, 96/5686

Martin Maritime Ltd *v.* Provident Capital Indemnity Fund Ltd (The Lydia Flag) [1998] 2 Lloyd's Rep. 652, QBD (Comm Ct) . . . .   *Digested*, 99/**3407**

Martin-Smith *v.* Williams [1999] E.M.L.R. 571, CA; affirming [1998] E.M.L.R. 334, Ch D . . . .   *Digested*, 99/**855**

Martindale *v.* Duncan [1973] 1 W.L.R. 574; [1973] 2 All E.R. 355; [1973] 1 Lloyd's Rep. 558; [1973] R.T.R. 532; 117 S.J. 168, CA . . . .   *Digested*, 73/**734**:
             Followed, 98/1467

Martinez v. Customs and Excise Commissioners [1999] V. & D.R. 267; [2000] S.T.I.
197, V&DTr . . . . *Digested*, 00/**5301**
Martinez v. Ellesse International SpA CHANI 98/0855/3, CA . . . . *Digested*, 99/**861**
Martini Investments v. McGinn see Martini Investments v. McGuin
Martini Investments v. McGuin; *sub nom* Martini Investments v. McGinn [2000] 2
Lloyd's Rep. 313; [2001] Lloyd's Rep. I.R. 374, QBD (Comm Ct) . . . . *Digested*, 00/**3557**
Martins v. Customs and Excise Commissioners see Han (t/a Murdishaw Supper Bar) v.
Customs and Excise Commissioners
Martins v. Liverpool City Magistrates Court [1998] C.O.D. 180, QBD
Martins v. Marks & Spencer Plc see Marks & Spencer Plc v. Martins
Martins Moreira v. Portugal (A/133) (1991) 13 E.H.R.R. 517, ECHR . . . . *Applied*, 98/3136
Marubeni Corp v. Alafouzos (Unreported, November 6, 1986), CA . . . . *Digested*, 88/**2841**:
                                                       Followed, 99/321
Mary Norton (Deceased), Re (1945) 161 A.L.R. 439 . . . . *Considered*, 00/4908
Maryland Estates Ltd v. 63 Perham Road Ltd [1997] 2 E.G.L.R. 198; [1997] 35 E.G.
94, Lands Tr. . . . . *Digested*, 97/**3283**:
                                                      Applied, 99/3688
Maryland Estates Ltd v. Abbathure Flat Management Co Ltd [1999] 1 E.G.L.R. 100;
[1999] 06 E.G. 177, Lands Tr. . . . . *Digested*, 99/**3688**
Maryland Estates Ltd v. Bar-Joseph see Maryland Estates Ltd v. Joseph
Maryland Estates Ltd v. Joseph; *sub nom* Maryland Estates Ltd v. Bar-Joseph [1999] 1
W.L.R. 83; [1998] 3 All E.R. 193; (1999) 31 H.L.R. 269; (1999) 77 P. & C.R.
150; [1998] L. & T.R. 105; [1998] 2 E.G.L.R. 47; [1998] 27 E.G. 142; [1998]
E.G.C.S. 66; (1998) 95(17) L.S.G. 33; (1998) 95(21) L.S.G. 36; (1998) 142
S.J.L.B. 157; [1998] N.P.C. 70; *Times*, May 6, 1998; *Independent*, May 1, 1998,
CA; affirming [1997] 2 E.G.L.R. 96; [1997] 46 E.G. 155; (1997) 147 N.L.J. 1386,
CC (Central London) . . . . *Digested*, 98/**3634**
Maryniak v. Thomas Cook Ltd (Unreported, October 26, 1998), CC (Northampton)
[*Ex rel.* Berryman Lace Mawyer Solicitors, Salisbury House, London Wall,
London] . . . . *Digested*, 99/**3976**
Marzetti (A Bankrupt), Re [1998] B.P.I.R. 732, Sup Ct (Can) . . . . *Digested*, 99/**3239**
Masiak v. City Restaurants (UK) Ltd [1999] I.R.L.R. 780, EAT . . . . *Digested*, 00/**2246**
Maskeli Balo (E. 1999/7019, K. 2000/616), Re [2001] E.C.D.R. 32, Yrg (TR)
Maskell v. Maskell [2001] EWCA Civ 858; [2001] 3 F.C.R. 296, CA
Maso v. Instituto Nazionale della Prevedenza Sociale (INPS) (C373/95); Gazzetta v.
Instituto Nazionale della Prevedenza Sociale (INPS) (C373/95) [1997] E.C.R. I-
4051; [1997] 3 C.M.L.R. 1244, ECJ (5th Chamber) . . . . *Followed*, 00/2380
Mason v. Coal Authority; Flaherty v. Coal Authority [2001] N.P.C. 58, QBD
Mason v. Provident Clothing & Supply Co Ltd see Provident Clothing & Supply Co
Ltd v. Mason
Masquerade Music Ltd v. Springsteen; *sub nom* Springsteen v. Masquerade Music Ltd;
Springsteen v. Flute International Ltd [2001] EWCA Civ 563; [2001] C.P. Rep.
85; [2001] C.P.L.R. 369; [2001] E.M.L.R. 25; *Independent*, April 24, 2001; *Daily
Telegraph*, April 17, 2001, CA; affirming [1999] E.M.L.R. 180, Ch D . . . . *Digested*, 01/**392**
Masri v. SCF Finance Co Ltd (No.1) see SCF Finance Co Ltd v. Masri (No.1)
Massa v. Italy (A/265-B) (1994) 18 E.H.R.R. 266, ECHR . . . . *Digested*, 95/**2629**:
                      Applied, 98/3135, 00/3220: *Considered*, 01/3514
Massaquoi v. Secretary of State for the Home Department [2001] Imm. A.R. 309, CA . *Digested*, 01/**3617**
Massey v. Midland Bank Plc [1995] 1 All E.R. 929; [1994] 2 F.L.R. 342; [1995] 1
F.C.R. 380; (1995) 27 H.L.R. 227; [1994] Fam. Law 562; [1994] N.P.C. 44;
Times, March 23, 1994, CA . . . . *Digested*, 95/**2446**:
                   Considered, 97/4243: *Followed*, 94/3291, 95/2443, 00/4273:
                                          Referred to, 95/5982, 96/6577
Masson v. Netherlands (A/327) (1996) 22 E.H.R.R. 491, ECHR . . . . *Digested*, 97/**2801**:
                   Applied, 98/3156: *Distinguished*, 98/3121: *Followed*, 97/2805
Master and Fellows of University College (Oxford) v. Durdy see University College
(Oxford) v. Durdy
Master and Wardens of the Mystery or Art of Brewers of the City of London v. Attorney
General; *sub nom* Trustee of Dame Alice Owen's Foundation v. Attorney General
[2000] E.L.R. 117, Ch D . . . . *Digested*, 00/**5257**
Master Foods Ltd's Trade Mark Application [2001] E.T.M.R. 62, PO (Irl)
Masterfoods Ltd (t/a Mars Ireland) v. HB Ice Cream Ltd [1992] 3 C.M.L.R. 830; [1994]
E.C.C. 1; [1994] F.S.R. 1, HC (Irl) . . . . *Subsequent proceed-*
                                                         ings, 01/762
Masterfoods Ltd (t/a Mars Ireland) v. HB Ice Cream Ltd (C344/98) [2001] All E.R.
(EC) 130; [2000] E.C.R. I-11369; [2001] 4 C.M.L.R. 14; *Times*, February 2, 2001,
ECJ . . . . *Digested*, 01/**762**
Masters v. Leaver [2000] I.L.Pr. 387; [2000] B.P.I.R. 284; (1999) 96(33) L.S.G. 29;
Times, August 5, 1999, CA . . . . *Digested*, 99/**3328**

Masters v. Secretary of State for the Environment, Transport and the Regions; *sub nom*
R. v. Secretary of State for the Environment, Transport and the Regions Ex p.
Masters [2001] Q.B. 151; [2000] 3 W.L.R. 1894; [2000] 4 All E.R. 458; [2000]
4 P.L.R. 134; [2001] J.P.L. 340; (2000) 97(35) L.S.G. 39; (2000) 150 N.L.J.
1422; [2000] N.P.C. 95; *Times*, September 12, 2000, CA; affirming [2000] 2 All
E.R. 788; (2000) 79 P. & C.R. 338; [2000] 2 P.L.R. 31; *Independent*,
November 15, 1999 (C.S.), QBD ....   *Digested*, 00/**2294**
Masterson v. Chemical Services, Fabrications & Erection Ltd (Unreported, March 20,
1998), CC (Bury) [*Ex rel.* Christopher Limb, Barrister, Young Street Chambers, 38
Young Street, Manchester] ......   *Digested*, 98/**1566**
Mastin v. Rotherham HA (Unreported, April 14, 1999), CC (Doncaster) [*Ex rel.* Iain
MacLauchlan, Barrister, 26 Paradise Square, Sheffield] ......   *Digested*, 99/**1604**
Matadeen v. Minister of Education and Science see Matadeen v. Pointu
Matadeen v. Pointu; Matadeen v. Minister of Education and Science [1999] 1 A.C. 98;
[1998] 3 W.L.R. 18; (1998) 142 S.J.L.B. 100, PC (Mau) ......   *Digested*, 98/**781**
Matalimex Foreign Trade Corp v. Eugenie Maritime Ltd [1962] 1 Lloyd's Rep. 378, QBD
(Comm Ct) ......   *Digested*, 62/**2829**:
    Considered, 65/369: *Followed*, 98/253
Maternity Allowances (C111/91), Re see Commission of the European Communities v.
Luxembourg (C111/91)
Mathanakumar (12817) Unreported, IAT ......   *Disapproved*, 98/**3198**
Matharu v. Matharu [1994] 2 F.L.R. 597; [1994] 3 F.C.R. 216; (1994) 68 P. & C.R. 93;
[1994] Fam. Law 624; [1994] E.G.C.S. 87; (1994) 91(25) L.S.G. 31; (1994)
138 S.J.L.B. 111; [1994] N.P.C. 63; *Times*, May 13, 1994; *Independent*, May 18,
1994, CA ......   *Digested*, 95/**2221**:
    Cited, 98/123
Mathew, Re [2001] B.P.I.R. 531, Ch D ......   *Digested*, 01/**686**
Mathew v. Attorney General [1999] C.O.D. 393, QBD
Mathew v. Maughold Life Assurance Co Ltd [1955-95] P.N.L.R. 309; *Times*, February
19, 1987, CA; reversing *Times*, January 25, 1985 ......   *Digested*, 87/**2563**:
    Considered, 89/2585
Mathieson v. Customs and Excise Commissioners [1999] S.T.C. 835; [1999] B.T.C.
5310; [1999] B.V.C. 343; 1999 G.W.D. 18-860; *Times*, June 17, 1999, OH ......   *Digested*, 99/**6471**
Mathieu-Mohin v. Belgium (A/113) (1988) 10 E.H.R.R. 1, ECHR ......   *Applied*, 01/**4582**:
    Considered, 99/3102
Matlock Green Garage Ltd v. Potter Brooke-Taylor & Wildgoose [2000] Lloyd's Rep.
P.N. 935, QBD ......   *Digested*, 01/**4531**
Matos E Silva Lda v. Portugal (1997) 24 E.H.R.R. 573, ECHR ......   *Digested*, 98/**3133**
Matra v. Commission of the European Communities (C225/91) [1993] E.C.R. I-3203;
Financial Times, June 22, 1993, ECJ ......   *Digested*, 93/**4388**:
    Applied, 98/735, 98/2311: *Followed*, 01/786
Matra Communications SA v. Home Office [1999] 1 W.L.R. 1646; [1999] 3 All E.R.
562; [1999] B.L.R. 112; [1999] 1 C.M.L.R. 1454; [1999] Eu. L.R. 635; (1999) 1
L.G.L.R. 877; (1999) 11 Admin. L.R. 478; (1999) 163 J.P.N. 854; (1999) 143
S.J.L.B. 104; *Times*, March 8, 1999, CA ......   *Digested*, 99/**482**
Matrix Securities Ltd v. Inland Revenue Commissioners see R. v. Inland Revenue
Commissioners Ex p. Matrix Securities Ltd
Matrix Securities Ltd v. Theodore Goddard [1998] S.T.C. 1; [1998] P.N.L.R. 290; [1997]
B.T.C. 578; (1997) 147 N.L.J. 1847, Ch D ......   *Digested*, 98/**4011**
MATSUSHITA ELECTRIC INDUSTRIAL/Magnetoresistive materials (T610/96) [2001]
E.P.O.R. 54, EPO (Technical Bd App) ......   *Digested*, 01/**3928**
Matsushita Electric Works Ltd's Trade Mark Application [2000] E.T.M.R. 962, OHIM (1st Bd
App) ......   *Digested*, 01/**4017**
Matter v. Slovakia (2001) 31 E.H.R.R. 32, ECHR ......   *Digested*, 01/**3525**
Mattey Securities Ltd v. Ervin; Mattey Securities Ltd v. Sutton; Mattey Securities Ltd v.
Mitchell (1999) 77 P. & C.R. 160; [1998] 2 E.G.L.R. 66; [1998] 34 E.G. 91;
[1998] E.G.C.S. 61; [1998] N.P.C. 64; (1998) 76 P. & C.R. D29, CA ......   *Digested*, 99/**3701**
Mattey Securities Ltd v. Mitchell see Mattey Securities Ltd v. Ervin
Mattey Securities Ltd v. Sutton see Mattey Securities Ltd v. Ervin
Matthew Brown Plc v. Campbell [1998] Eu. L.R. 530, QBD ......   *Digested*, 99/**689**:
    Applied, 99/110
Matthew Gloag & Son Ltd v. Welsh Distillers Ltd [1998] 2 C.M.L.R. 203; [1999] Eu.
L.R. 625; [1998] E.T.M.R. 504; [1998] F.S.R. 718; (1998) 21(6) I.P.D. 21063;
Times, February 27, 1998, Ch D ......   *Digested*, 98/**3523**
Matthew Hall Ortech Ltd v. Tarmac Roadstone Ltd 87 B.L.R. 96, QBD (OR) ......   *Digested*, 98/**807**
Matthews v. Associated Portland Cement Manufacturers (1978) Ltd see Fairchild v.
Glenhaven Funeral Services Ltd (t/a GH Dovener & Son)
Matthews v. British Uralite Plc see Fairchild v. Glenhaven Funeral Services Ltd (t/a GH
Dovener & Son)
Matthews v. Poundsrollahzadeh [1998] N.P.C. 48, CA
Matthews v. Tarmac Bricks & Tiles Ltd [1999] C.P.L.R. 463; (2000) 54 B.M.L.R. 139;
(1999) 96(28) L.S.G. 26; (1999) 143 S.J.L.B. 196; *Times*, July 1, 1999, CA ....   *Digested*, 99/**577**
Matthews v. United Kingdom (1999) 28 E.H.R.R. 361; 5 B.H.R.C. 686; *Times*, March
3, 1999, ECHR ......   *Digested*, 99/**3103**

Matthewson v. Scottish Ministers 2001 G.W.D. 23-875; *Times*, October 24, 2001, OH . .   *Digested*, 01/**6833**
Mattison v. Ellis (Unreported, June 3, 1998), CC (Wigan) [*Ex rel.* Ian Smith, Scott Rees & Co Solicitors, Centaur House, Gardiners Place, Skelmersdale, Lancashire] . . . .   *Digested*, 98/**565**
Maudslay v. Maudslay Sons & Field see Maudslay Sons & Field, Re
Maudslay Sons & Field, Re; *sub nom* Maudslay v. Maudslay Sons & Field [1900] 1 Ch. 602, Ch D . . . .   *Considered*, 74/403: *Disapproved*, 00/777
Mauer v. Austria (1998) 25 E.H.R.R. 91, ECHR. . . . .   *Digested*, 98/**3111**
Maughan's Application, Re [1998] N.I. 293, QBD (NI) . . . .   *Digested*, 99/**5211**
Maunsell v. Olins [1975] A.C. 373; [1974] 3 W.L.R. 835; [1975] 1 All E.R. 16; (1974) 30 P. & C.R. 1; 118 S.J. 882; *Times*, November 28, 1974, HL; affirming [1974] 1 W.L.R. 830; [1974] 2 All E.R. 250; 27 P. & C.R. 460; 118 S.J. 278, CA . . . .   *Digested*, 75/**2857**: *Applied*, 92/2755, 97/90, 98/3682, 01/4206: *Considered*, 92/102, 97/3332
Maurice v. Betterware UK Ltd [2001] I.C.R. 14, EAT
Mavers v. Redbridge Healthcare NHS Trust, CC (Central London) [*Ex rel.* Nicholas Yell, Barrister, No.1 Serjeants' Inn, Fleet Street, London] . . . .   *Digested*, 01/**1719**
Mavronichis v. Cyprus (2001) 31 E.H.R.R. 54; [1998] H.R.C.D. 480, ECHR . . . .   *Digested*, 01/**3521**
Mawby v. Jaton Distribution Ltd [2001] 6 Q.R. 20, CC (Luton) [*Ex rel.* Jinder S Boora, Barrister, Ropewalk Chambers, 24 The Ropewalk, Nottingham] . . . .   *Digested*, 01/**1765**
Mawson v. Harvey (1999) 99(1) Q.R. 7, CC (Leeds) . . . .   *Digested*, 98/**1617**
Maxim's Ltd v. Dye; *sub nom* Maxims Ltd v. Dye [1977] 1 W.L.R. 1155; [1978] 2 All E.R. 55; [1977] 2 C.M.L.R. 410; [1977] F.S.R. 364; 121 S.J. 727, Ch D . . . .   *Digested*, 77/**3050**: *Followed*, 98/3518
MAXTOR/Media storage system (J27/92) [1995] E.P.O.R. 688, EPO (Legal Bd App) .   *Followed*, 00/3654
Maxwell v. Hogg; Hogg v. Maxwell (1866-67) L.R. 2 Ch. App. 307, CA in Chancery . .   *Distinguished*, 98/3497
Maxwell v. Minister for Agriculture, Food and Forestry [1999] 2 C.M.L.R. 170, HC (Irl) .   *Digested*, 99/**144**
Maxwell Communication Corp Plc (In Administration) v. New Hampshire Insurance Co Ltd see New Hampshire Insurance Co Ltd v. MGN Ltd (1996)
Maxwell Communication Corp Plc (In Administration) v. Societe Generale Plc [2000] B.P.I.R. 764, US Ct
Maxwell Fleet and Facilities Management Ltd (In Administration) (No.1), Re [2001] 1 W.L.R. 323; [2000] 1 All E.R. 464; [1999] 2 B.C.L.C. 721; [2000] B.P.I.R. 294, Ch D (Companies Ct) . . . .   *Digested*, 00/**3430**
Maxwell Fleet and Facilities Management Ltd (In Administration) (No.2), Re [2000] 2 All E.R. 860; [2000] 2 B.C.L.C. 155; [2000] 2 C.M.L.R. 948; [2000] I.C.R. 717; [2000] I.R.L.R. 368; (2000) 97(6) L.S.G. 35; (2000) 144 S.J.L.B. 108; *Times*, February 23, 2000; *Independent*, March 6, 2000 (C.S.), Ch D (Companies Ct) . . . .   *Digested*, 00/**2224**
May v. DPP [2000] R.T.R. 7, QBD . . . .   *Digested*, 00/**961**
May v. Newport CBC [2001] 6 Q.R. 16, CC (Cardiff) [*Ex rel.* Andrew Arentsen, Barrister, Thirty Three Park Place, Cardiff] . . . .   *Digested*, 01/**1697**
May v. Woollcombe Beer & Watts [1999] P.N.L.R. 283; [1998] 3 E.G.L.R. 94; [1998] 51 E.G. 88, QBD (Merc Ct) . . . .   *Digested*, 99/**4051**
Maybey v. Bayley (Unreported, July 27, 1998), CC (Southampton) [*Ex rel.* Daniel Nother, Barrister, College Chambers, 19 Carlton Crescent, Southampton] . . . . .   *Digested*, 98/**1598**
Mayer Parry Recycling Ltd v. Environment Agency [1999] 1 C.M.L.R. 963; [1999] Env. L.R. 489; (1999) 96(6) L.S.G. 32; *Times*, December 3, 1998, Ch D . . . .   *Digested*, 99/**2207**: *Considered*, 01/573: *Not applied*, 01/2413
Mayes v. Gayton International (Unreported, November 3, 1993), DC [*Ex rel.* Bermans, Solicitors] . . . .   *Digested*, 94/**3760**: *Followed*, 99/571
Mayeur v. Association Promotion de l'Information Messine (APIM) (C175/99) [2000] E.C.R. I-7755; [2000] I.R.L.R. 783, ECJ . . . .   *Digested*, 01/**2336**
Mayfair Brassware Ltd v. Aqualine International Ltd (Costs Order) [1998] F.S.R. 135, CA; affirming (1997) 20(11) I.P.D. 20118, Ch D . . . .   *Digested*, 98/**436**
Mayfair Projects Ltd's Trade Mark Application (1999) 22(5) I.P.D. 22049, TMR
Mayfield Secondary School Governing Body v. Pearce see Pearce v. Mayfield Secondary School Governing Body
Mayhew-Lewis v. Westminster Scaffolding Group Plc see Norglen Ltd (In Liquidation) v. Reeds Rains Prudential Ltd
Maymac Environmental Services Ltd v. Faraday Building Services Ltd 75 Con. L.R. 101, QBD (T&CC) . . . .   *Digested*, 01/**945**
Maynard v. West Midlands RHA; *sub nom* Maynard v. West Midlands AHA [1984] 1 W.L.R. 634; [1985] 1 All E.R. 635; (1984) 81 L.S.G. 1926; (1983) 133 N.L.J. 641; (1984) 128 S.J. 317; *Times*, May 9, 1983, HL . . . .   *Digested*, 84/**2324**: *Applied*, 85/135, 90/3264, 99/3997: *Considered*, 84/2282, 88/2453, 89/2558: *Distinguished*, 96/4469: *Referred to*, 90/3319, 92/3247, 92/5658
Mayne v. Ministry of Agriculture, Fisheries and Food; Chitty Wholesale Ltd v. Ministry of Agriculture, Fisheries and Food [2001] E.H.L.R. 5; *Times*, October 12, 2000; *Independent*, October 9, 2000 (C.S), QBD . . . .   *Digested*, 00/**2338**
Mayr-melnhof Kartongesellschaft mbh v. Commission of the European Communities (T347/94) [1998] E.C.R. II-1751, CFI . . . .   *Followed*, 01/768
MB Building Contractors v. Ahmed, *Independent*, November 23, 1998 (C.S.), CA . . . . .   *Digested*, 98/**447**

MB Pyramid Sound NV v. Briese Schiffahrts GmbH & Co KG MS Sina (The Ines) (No.1)
[1993] 2 Lloyd's Rep. 492, QBD (Comm Ct) . . . . *Digested,* 94/**3764**:
Disapproved, 98/4394
MB Pyramid Sound NV v. Briese Schiffahrts GmbH & Co KG MS Sina (The Ines)
(No.2) [1995] 2 Lloyd's Rep. 144, QBD (Comm Ct) . . . . *Considered,* 98/582:
Followed, 97/4494
MB Wines HB v. Alcohol Inspectorate [1999] 2 C.M.L.R. 877, Lansratt (Stockholm) . . . *Digested,* 99/**2222**
Mbanza v. Secretary of State for the Home Department see R. v. Secretary of State for
the Home Department Ex p. Mbanza
MBM Fabri-Clad Ltd v. Eisen und Huttenwerke Thale AG [2000] C.L.C. 373; [2000]
I.L.Pr. 505, CA . . . . *Digested,* 00/**739**
MBNA America Bank NA v. Freeman [2001] E.B.L.R. 13, Ch D . . . . *Digested,* 01/**3868**
MC Bacon Ltd (No.1), Re; *sub nom* Company (No.005009 of 1987) (No.1), Re [1990]
B.C.C. 78; [1990] B.C.L.C. 324; *Times,* December 1, 1989, Ch D . . . . *Digested,* 90/**526**:
Considered, 94/2627, 95/2836, 98/3330, 01/3743
MC Bacon Ltd (No.2), Re; *sub nom* Company (No.005009 of 1987) (No.2), Re [1991]
Ch. 127; [1990] 3 W.L.R. 646; [1990] B.C.C. 430; [1990] B.C.L.C. 607; *Times,*
April 12, 1990; *Independent,* May 7, 1990 (C.S.), Ch D . . . . *Digested,* 91/**2157**:
Applied, 00/3505: *Approved,* 99/3310: *Considered,* 97/3066
MCA Records Inc v. Charly Records Ltd (No.3) (1998) 21 (3) I.P.D. 21026, CA
MCA Records Inc v. Charly Records Ltd (No.4); *sub nom* MCA Records Inc v. Night
and Day Distribution Ltd (1999) 22 (10) I.P.D. 22098, Ch D
MCA Records Inc v. Charly Records Ltd (No.5) [2001] EWCA Civ 1441; *Independent,*
November 26, 2001 (C.S), CA; affirming [2000] E.M.L.R. 743; (2000) 23 (7)
I.P.D. 23056, Ch D
MCA Records Inc v. Night and Day Distribution Ltd see MCA Records Inc v. Charly
Records Ltd (No.4)
MCC Proceeds Inc v. Bishopsgate Investment Trust Plc (No.4) see Macmillan Inc v.
Bishopsgate Investment Trust Plc (No.4)
MCC Proceeds Inc v. Lehman Brothers International (Europe) [1998] 4 All E.R. 675;
[1998] 2 B.C.L.C. 659; (1998) 95 (5) L.S.G. 28; (1998) 142 S.J.L.B. 40; *Times,*
January 14, 1998; *Independent,* January 19, 1998 (C.S.), CA . . . . *Digested,* 98/**4775**
MD and TD (Minors) (No.2), Re [1994] Fam. Law 489, Fam Div . . . . *Disapproved,* 99/2390
MD Foods Plc v. Customs and Excise Commissioners [2001] S.T.I. 951, V&DTr
MDIS Ltd (formerly McDonnell Information Systems Ltd) v. Swinbank; *sub nom*
McDonnell Information Systems Ltd v. Swinbank [1999] 2 All E.R. (Comm) 722;
[1999] C.L.C. 1800, CA; affirming [1999] 1 Lloyd's Rep. I.R. 98, QBD (Comm
Ct) . . . . *Digested,* 00/**3556**:
Applied, 01/3813
Meachen v. Harwich Dock Co Ltd [2000] 5 Q.R. 7, MCLC [*Ex rel.* Colin McCaul,
Barrister, 39 Essex Street, London] . . . . *Digested,* 00/**1653**
Meacock v. Secretary of State for the Environment, Transport and the Regions [1998]
E.G.C.S. 8, QBD
Mead v. Wessex Windows Systems Plc (Unreported, April 30, 1998), CC
(Southampton) [*Ex rel.* Ashley Ailes, Barrister, 18 Carlton Crescent,
Southampton, SO15 2XR] . . . . *Digested,* 98/**394**
Mead Corp v. Riverwood Multiple Packaging Division of Riverwood International Corp
[1997] F.S.R. 484; (1997) 20 (8) I.P.D. 20072; *Times,* March 28, 1997, Ch D . . . *Digested,* 97/**3899**:
Followed, 00/3682: *Referred to,* 99/3493
MEAD/Printing plate (T160/92) [1995] E.P.O.R. 424, EPO (Technical Bd App) . . . . *Followed,* 00/3622
Meade v. British Fuels Ltd see Wilson v. St Helens BC
Meade v. British Fuels Ltd; Baxendale v. British Fuels Ltd [1996] I.R.L.R. 541, EAT . . . . *Digested,* 96/**2594**:
Subsequent proceedings, 97/2279
Meade v. Haringey LBC [1979] 1 W.L.R. 637; [1979] 2 All E.R. 1016; [1979] I.C.R.
494; 77 L.G.R. 577; 123 S.J. 216, CA . . . . *Digested,* 79/**816**:
Considered, 85/1598, 86/3443, 87/3769, 93/2855, 93/3933, 98/1903:
Followed, 01/1946: *Referred to,* 95/148
Meadows v. Clerical Medical & General Life Assurance Society [1981] Ch. 70; [1980]
2 W.L.R. 639; [1980] 1 All E.R. 454; (1980) 40 P. & C.R. 238; (1979) 255 E.G.
883; 124 S.J. 257, Ch D . . . . *Digested,* 80/**1578**:
Considered, 84/1967, 86/1844: *Followed,* 98/3652
Meadows Indemnity Co Ltd v. Insurance Corp of Ireland Plc; *sub nom* Meadows
Indemnity Co Ltd v. International Commercial Bank Plc [1989] 2 Lloyd's Rep.
298; *Times,* May 23, 1989, CA; reversing [1989] 1 Lloyd's Rep. 181; *Times,* June
3, 1988; *Independent,* July 5, 1988, QBD (Comm Ct) . . . . *Digested,* 90/**3640**:
Applied, 96/1144: *Followed,* 98/92
Meadows Indemnity Co Ltd v. International Commercial Bank Plc see Meadows
Indemnity Co Ltd v. Insurance Corp of Ireland Plc
Meah v. McCreamer [1985] 1 All E.R. 367; (1985) 135 N.L.J. 80, QBD . . . . *Digested,* 85/**967**:
Cited, 00/1526
Mealey Horgan Plc v. Horgan, *Times,* July 6, 1999, QBD . . . . *Digested,* 99/**344**:
Considered, 00/407
Mealing McLeod v. Common Professional Examination Board (Assessment of Costs)
[2000] 2 Costs L.R. 223, QBD . . . . *Digested,* 01/**461**

Mean v. Thomas [1998] E.G.C.S. 2; (1998) 95(5) L.S.G. 30, QBD
Mean Machines Ltd v. Blackheath Leisure (Carousel) Ltd (1999) 78 P. & C.R. D36, CA
Measor v. Secretary of State for the Environment, Transport and the Regions [1998] 4 P.L.R. 93; [1999] J.P.L. 182, QBD . . . . *Digested,* 99/**4171**
Mecanarte-Metalurgica da Lagoa v. Alfandega do Oporto (C348/89) [1991] E.C.R. I-3277, ECJ . . . . *Applied,* 00/4959
Mecca Leisure Ltd v. Renown Investments (Holdings) Ltd (1985) 49 P. & C.R. 12; [1984] 2 E.G.L.R. 137; (1984) 271 E.G. 989, CA . . . . *Digested,* 85/**1935**:
Applied, 85/1927, 86/1913: *Considered,* 85/1918, 87/2200, 90/2855, 99/3726: *Disapproved,* 91/5178: *Followed,* 00/3914: *Overruled,* 01/4207: *Referred to,* 95/3068
Mecklermedia Corp v. Benelux Trade Mark Office [2001] E.T.M.R. 49, Hof (Den Haag)
Mecklermedia Corp v. DC Congress GmbH [1998] Ch. 40; [1997] 3 W.L.R. 479; [1998] 1 All E.R. 148; [1997] E.T.M.R. 265; [1997] I.L.Pr. 629; [1997-98] Info. T.L.R. 132; [1997] F.S.R. 627; [1998] Masons C.L.R. Rep. 151; (1997) 20(4) I.P.D. 20042; *Times,* March 27, 1997, Ch D . . . . *Digested,* 97/**902**
Medcalf v. Mardell (Wasted Costs Order) [2001] C.P.L.R. 140; [2001] Lloyd's Rep. P.N. 146; [2001] P.N.L.R. 14; (2001) 98(5) L.S.G. 36; *Times,* January 2, 2001, CA . . . . *Digested,* 01/**536**: *Applied,* 01/5354

Medforth v. Blake [2000] Ch. 86; [1999] 3 W.L.R. 922; [1999] 3 All E.R. 97; [1999] B.C.C. 771; [1999] 2 B.C.L.C. 221; [1999] B.P.I.R. 712; [1999] Lloyd's Rep. P.N. 844; [1999] P.N.L.R. 920; [1999] 2 E.G.L.R. 75; [1999] 29 E.G. 119; [1999] E.G.C.S. 81; (1999) 96(24) L.S.G. 39; (1999) 149 N.L.J. 929; *Times,* June 22, 1999 ; *Independent,* June 24, 1999, CA . . . . *Digested,* 99/**3286**:
Applied, 01/4855: *Followed,* 01/3709
MedGen Inc v. Passion for Life Products Ltd [2001] F.S.R. 30, Ch D . . . . *Digested,* 01/**3878**
Media 9 Sarl v. Regie Autonome des Transports Parisiens (RATP) [2000] E.C.C. 130, Cass (F)
Media Sarl v. Scher [1998] E.C.C. 101, C d'A (Paris)
Medical and Dental Staff Training Ltd v. Customs and Excise Commissioners [2001] S.T.I. 771, V&DTr
Medical Aviation Services Ltd v. Customs and Excise Commissioners [1998] B.V.C. 2103, V&DTr . . . . *Digested,* 98/**4977**
Medical Centre Developments Ltd v. Customs and Excise Commissioners [1998] B.V.C. 2310, V&DTr
Medical Defence Union Ltd v. Department of Trade [1980] Ch. 82; [1979] 2 W.L.R. 686; [1979] 2 All E.R. 421; [1979] 1 Lloyd's Rep. 499; [1979] E.C.C. 101; 123 S.J. 338, Ch D . . . . *Digested,* 79/**1505**: *Distinguished,* 99/3411

Medicaments and Related Classes of Goods (No.1), Re [2001] I.C.R. 306; *Times,* April 14, 1999; *Independent,* April 19, 1999 (C.S.), RPC . . . . *Digested,* 99/**701**: *Considered,* 01/366

Medicaments and Related Classes of Goods (No.2), Re see Director General of Fair Trading v. Proprietary Association of Great Britain
Medicaments and Related Classes of Goods (No.4), Re see Director General of Fair Trading v. Proprietary Association of Great Britain (Costs)
Medicaments Reference No.2, Re see Incorporated National Association of British and Irish Millers Ltd's Scheme, Re
Medici Grimm KG v. Council of the European Union (T7/99) [2000] E.C.R. II-2671; [2000] 3 C.M.L.R. 374, CFI (4th Chamber) . . . . *Digested,* 00/**2347**
Medicine Shoppe International's Community Trade Mark see Cahill May Roberts Ltd's Application for a Declaration of Invalidity
Mediguard Services Ltd v. Thame [1994] I.C.R. 751; [1994] I.R.L.R. 504; *Times,* August 5, 1994; *Independent,* September 12, 1994 (C.S.), EAT . . . . *Digested,* 95/**2095**:
Applied, 95/2108, 96/2575, 98/2240: *Considered,* 95/2052, 96/2629, 98/2236
Mediterranean Shipping Co SA v. Atlantic Container Line AB TNS, CA . . . . *Digested,* 99/**4441**
Medivac Healthcare Ltd v. Customs and Excise Commissioners [2001] S.T.I. 181, V&DTr
Medjdoub (A Minor) v. Ayub (Unreported, March 2, 1998), CC (Nottingham) [*Ex rel.* Nelsons Solicitors, Pennine House, 8 Stanford Street, Nottingham] . . . . *Digested,* 98/**1581**
MEDTRONIC/Administrative agreement (G05/88) [1991] E.P.O.R. 225, EPO (Enlarged Bd App) . . . . *Applied,* 01/3898
Medway v. Doublelock Ltd [1978] 1 W.L.R. 710; [1978] 1 All E.R. 1261; 122 S.J. 248, Ch D . . . . *Digested,* 78/**2353**: *Applied,* 01/551

Medway Council v. BBC [2001] Fam. Law 883, Fam Div
Medway Housing Society Ltd v. Cook (Inspector of Taxes); *sub nom* Cook (Inspector of Taxes) v. Medway Housing Society Ltd [1997] S.T.C. 90; 69 T.C. 319; [1997] B.T.C. 63; *Times,* January 1, 1997, Ch D; affirming [1996] S.T.C. (S.C.D.) 393, Sp Comm . . . . *Digested,* 97/**1081**
Meechie v. Multi Media Marketing (Canterbury) Ltd see Kent CC v. Multi Media Marketing (Canterbury) Ltd

Meek v. Swift (Unreported, August 12, 1998), CC (Rawtenstall) [Ex rel. James Chapman & Co Solicitors, 76 King Street, Manchester] . . . . *Digested*, 98/**453**
Meespierson (Bahamas) Ltd v. GrupoTorras SA (1999-2000) 2 I.T.E.L.R. 29, CA (Bah)
Meeusen v. Hoofddirectie van de Informatie Beheer Groep (C337/97) [1999] E.C.R. I-3289; [2000] 2 C.M.L.R. 659, ECJ (5th Chamber) . . . . *Digested*, 00/**2389**
Meflah v. Secretary of State for the Home Department [1997] Imm. A.R. 555; [1998] I.N.L.R. 150, IAT . . . . *Digested*, 98/**3168**
Meftah v. LloydsTSB Bank Ltd (No.1), *Independent*, April 10, 2000 (C.S.), Ch D
Meftah v. Lloyds TSB Bank Plc (No.2) [2001] 2 All E.R. (Comm) 741; [2001] 14 E.G.C.S. 146, Ch D . . . . *Digested*, 01/**4474**
Meggs v. Liverpool Corp [1968] 1 W.L.R. 689; [1968] 1 All E.R. 1137; 132 J.P. 207; 65 L.G.R. 479; (1967) 111 S.J. 742, CA . . . . *Digested*, 67/**1808**:
Applied, 68/1747, 92/1524, 93/1391: *Considered*, 74/2584, 78/2053, 96/5670: *Distinguished*, 78/2054: *Followed*, 71/5223, 99/2891
Megner v. Innungskrankenkasse Vorderpfalz (C444/93); Scheffel v. Innungskrankenkasse Vorderpfalz (C444/93) [1995] E.C.R. I-4741; [1996] C.E.C. 516; [1996] I.R.L.R. 236, ECJ . . . . *Digested*, 96/**5389**:
Applied, 98/2178
Mehanne v. Westminster Housing Benefit Review Board see R. (on the application of Mehanne) v. Westminster Housing Benefit Review Board
Mehemi v. France (2000) 30 E.H.R.R. 739, ECHR . . . . *Digested*, 01/**3552**
Mehibas Dordtselaan BV v. Commission of the European Communities (T290/97) [2000] E.C.R. II-15; [2000] 2 C.M.L.R. 375, CFI (5th Chamber) . . . . *Digested*, 00/**2350**
Mehta v. Royal Bank of Scotland Plc (2000) 32 H.L.R. 45; [1999] L. & T.R. 340; [1999] 3 E.G.L.R. 153; (1999) 78 P. & C.R. D11; *Times*, January 25, 1999, QBD . *Digested*, 99/**3699**
Mei v. San Pellegrino SpA [1999] E.C.C. 550, Trib (Rome)
MEIJI/Feeds (T438/91) [1999] E.P.O.R. 333, EPO (Technical Bd App) . . . . *Digested*, 99/**3489**
Meints v. Minister van Landbouw, Natuurbeheer en Visserij (C57/96) [1997] E.C.R. I-6689; [1998] 1 C.M.L.R. 1159, ECJ
Mekwin v. National Westminster Bank Plc see Tony Mekwin Mtv & Co v. National Westminster Bank Plc
Melbury Road Properties 1995 Ltd v. Kreidi [1999] 3 E.G.L.R. 108; [1999] 43 E.G. 157, CC (West London) . . . . *Digested*, 00/**3896**
Meldrum v. Netherlands (A/304) see Schouten v. Netherlands (A/304)
Melea Ltd v. Cinpres Ltd (1998) 21 (12) I.P.D. 21125, Pat Ct
Meletti v. Lane (Unreported, February 22, 1999), CC (Cardiff) [Ex rel. Andrew Arentsen, Barrister, 33 Park Place, Cardiff] . . . . *Digested*, 99/**1615**
Melgar v. Ayuntamiento de Los Barrios (C438/99) [2001] I.R.L.R. 848, ECJ (5th Chamber)
Melia v. Ford Motor Co Ltd see Boyle v. Ford Motor Co Ltd
Melim v. City of Westminster (Unreported, November 23, 2000), CC (Central London) [Ex rel. Jon Holbrook, Barrister, 2 Garden Court, MiddleTemple, London] . . . . . *Digested*, 01/**3425**
Melin v. France (A/261-A) (1994) 17 E.H.R.R. 1, ECHR. *Digested*, 94/**2384**:
Applied, 98/3145: *Distinguished*, 98/3143
Melinek (A Bankrupt), Re see Bristol and West Building Society v. Trustee of the Property of John Julius Back (A Bankrupt)
Melles & Co Ltd v. Holme [1918] 2 K.B. 100, KBD . . . . *Followed*, 98/3623
Mellors v. Gibson see Gibson's Settlement Trusts, Re
Mellowes Archital Ltd v. Bell Projects Ltd; *sub nom* Mellowes Archital Ltd v. Bell Products Ltd 87 B.L.R. 26; 58 Con. L.R. 22; (1998) 14 Const. L.J. 444, CA . . . *Digested*, 97/**950**
Mellstrom v. Secretary of State for the Environment, Transport and the Regions [2001] EWCA Civ 1146; [2001] 47 E.G.C.S. 147, QBD (Admin Ct)
Melton BC v. Brandons Poultry Ltd (1999) 14 P.A.D. 309, Planning Inspector
Melton BC v. Saunders (2001) 16 P.A.D. 102, Planning Inspector
Melville v. Inland Revenue Commissioners [2001] EWCA Civ 1247; [2001] S.T.C. 1271; [2001] B.T.C. 8039; [2001] W.T.L.R. 887; (2001-02) 4 I.T.E.L.R. 231; [2001] S.T.I. 1106; (2001) 98(37) L.S.G. 39; [2001] N.P.C. 132; *Times*, October 9, 2001, CA; affirming [2000] S.T.C. 628; [2000] B.T.C. 8025; [2000] W.T.L.R. 887; [2000] S.T.I. 917; (2000) 97(26) L.S.G. 38; [2000] N.P.C. 70; *Times*, June 27, 2000, Ch D . . . . *Digested*, 01/**5286**
Melvin International SA v. Poseidon Schiffahrt GmbH (The Kalma) [1999] 2 All E.R. (Comm) 761; [1999] 2 Lloyd's Rep. 374; [1999] C.L.C. 1398, QBD (Comm Ct) . *Digested*, 99/**4435**
Memec Plc v. Inland Revenue Commissioners [1998] S.T.C. 754; 71 T.C. 77; [1998] B.T.C. 251; 1 I.T.L. Rep. 3; *Times*, July 1, 1998; *Independent*, June 15, 1998 (C.S.), CA; affirming [1996] S.T.C. 1336; *Times*, November 7, 1996, Ch D . . . . *Digested*, 98/**4623**
Memery Crystal v. O'Higgins [1998] E.C.C. 299, QBD
Memminger-IRO GmbH v. Trip-Lite Ltd [1992] R.P.C. 210; *Independent*, November 25, 1991 (C.S.), CA; affirming [1991] F.S.R. 322, Pat Ct . . . . *Digested*, 93/**3039**:
Considered, 94/3450, 01/3882: *Referred to*, 94/3451
Memory Corp Plc v. Sidhu (No.1); *sub nom* Sidhu v. Memory Corp Plc (No.1) [2000] 1 W.L.R. 1443; [2000] C.P.L.R. 171; [2000] F.S.R. 921; *Times*, February 15, 2000, CA; affirming (1999) 96(24) L.S.G. 38; *Times*, May 31, 1999, Ch D . . . . *Digested*, 00/**488**:
Considered, 01/764

Memory Corp Plc *v.* Sidhu (No.2) [2000] Ch. 645; [2000] 2 W.L.R. 1106; [2000] 1 All E.R. 434; (2000) 97 (4) L.S.G. 33; (2000) 144 S.J.L.B. 51; *Times,* December 3, 1999, Ch D . . . . *Digested,* 00/**336**
MEMTEC/Membranes (J03/87) [1989] E.P.O.R. 175, EPO (Legal Bd App) . . . .   *Followed,* 00/3622
Mendelssohn *v.* Normand [1970] 1 Q.B. 177; [1969] 3 W.L.R. 139; [1969] 2 All E.R. 1215; (1969) 113 S.J. 263, CA . . . . *Digested,* 69/**510**:
                        Applied, 75/273, 75/394, 76/335: *Considered,* 00/5250: *Distinguished,* 74/29
Mendip DC *v.* Shaftesbury Housing Association (2001) 16 P.A.D. 54, Planning Inspector
Mendip DC *v.* Trowbridge (1998) 13 P.A.D. 625, Planning Inspector
Mensah *v.* East Hertfordshire NHS Trust [1998] I.R.L.R. 531; *Independent,* June 18, 1998, CA . . . . *Digested,* 98/**2165**
Mental Health Review Tribunal *v.* Hempstock (1998) 39 B.M.L.R. 123; [1997] C.O.D. 443, QBD . . . . *Digested,* 98/**3894**
Mentes *v.* Turkey (1998) 26 E.H.R.R. 595; [1998] H.R.C.D. 122, ECHR . . . . *Digested,* 99/**3086**:
                                                   Applied, 99/3085

Mentford Ltd *v.* Customs and Excise Commissioners [2000] S.T.I. 1533, V&DTr
Mentor Assurance Ltd, Re see Kempe *v.* Ambassador Insurance Co (In Liquidation)
Mentor Corp *v.* Hollister Inc (No.2) [1993] R.P.C. 7, CA; affirming [1991] F.S.R. 557, Pat Ct . . . . *Digested,* 94/**3440**:
                                            Followed, 95/3777, 00/3678
MEP Research Services Ltd *v.* Customs and Excise Commissioners [1999] B.V.C. 2268, V&DTr
MEPC Holdings Ltd *v.* Taylor (Inspector of Taxes) see Taylor (Inspector of Taxes) *v.* MEPC Holdings Ltd
Merani *v.* Inland Revenue Commissioners [2001] S.T.C. (S.C.D.) 178 (Note); [2001] S.T.I. 1361, Sp Comm
Merc Property Ltd, Re [1999] 2 B.C.L.C. 286; *Times,* May 19, 1999; *Independent,* May 3, 1999 (C.S.), Ch D . . . . *Digested,* 99/**423**
Mercantile Credit Co Ltd *v.* Cross [1965] 2 Q.B. 205; [1965] 2 W.L.R. 687; [1965] 1 All E.R. 577; 109 S.J. 47, CA . . . . *Digested,* 65/**3175**:
                               Applied, 98/2500: *Considered,* 87/3332, 88/3166
Mercantile Credit Co Ltd *v.* Fenwick; Mercantile Credit Co Ltd *v.* Speechly Bircham [1999] 2 F.L.R. 110; [1999] Lloyd's Rep. P.N. 408; [1999] Fam. Law 453; [1999] E.G.C.S. 22; (1999) 96 (10) L.S.G. 30; (1999) 143 S.J.L.B. 74; *Times,* February 23, 1999, CA; affirming [1997] N.P.C. 120, Ch D . . . . *Digested,* 99/**3813**
Mercantile Credit Co Ltd *v.* Lancaster see Alliance & Leicester Building Society *v.* Edgestop Ltd (Application for Leave)
Mercantile Credit Co Ltd *v.* Speechly Bircham see Mercantile Credit Co Ltd *v.* Fenwick
Mercantile Group (Europe) AG *v.* Aiyela [1994] Q.B. 366; [1993] 3 W.L.R. 1116; [1994] 1 All E.R. 110; *Times,* August 4, 1993; *Independent,* August 12, 1993, CA; affirming [1993] F.S.R. 745, QBD (Comm Ct) . . . . *Digested,* 94/**3738**:
                                                   Applied, 01/45

Mercantile International Group Plc *v.* Chuan Soon Huat Industrial Group Ltd; *sub nom* Mercantile International Group Plc *v.* Chuan Soon Hat Industrial Group Plc; A3/ 2001/0951, CA; affirming [2001] 2 All E.R. (Comm) 632; [2001] C.L.C. 1222; [2001] E.C.C. 42; [2001] Eu. L.R. 612, QBD (Comm Ct) . . . . *Digested,* 01/**930**
Mercedes-Benz AG *v.* Leiduck [1996] A.C. 284; [1995] 3 W.L.R. 718; [1995] 3 All E.R. 929; [1995] 2 Lloyd's Rep. 417; (1995) 92 (28) L.S.G. 28; (1995) 145 N.L.J. 1329; (1995) 139 S.J.L.B. 195; *Times,* August 11, 1995, PC (HK) . . . . *Digested,* 96/**847**:
                               Applied, 01/46, 01/648: *Distinguished,* 96/3483
Mercedes-Benz Finance Ltd *v.* Clydesdale Bank Plc 1997 S.L.T. 905; 1996 S.C.L.R. 1005; [1998] Lloyd's Rep. Bank. 249; [1997] C.L.C. 81; *Times,* September 16, 1996, OH . . . . *Digested,* 96/**6576**
Mercers Co *v.* New Hampshire Insurance Co Ltd see Wardens and Commonalty of the Mystery of Mercers of the City of London *v.* New Hampshire Insurance Co Ltd
Merchant Navy Ratings Pension Fund Trustees Ltd *v.* Chambers [2001] Pens. L.R. 137; (2001) 98 (13) L.S.G. 40; *Times,* April 2, 2001, Ch D . . . . *Digested,* 01/**4628**
Merchants Marine Insurance Co Ltd *v.* North of England Protecting and Indemnity Association (1926) 26 Ll. L. Rep. 201, CA; affirming (1926) 25 Ll. L. Rep. 446, KBD . . . . *Considered,* 00/5007
Merck & Co Inc *v.* Commission of the European Communities (T60/96) [1997] All E.R. (E.C.) 785; [1997] E.C.R. II-849, CFI . . . . *Digested,* 98/**2333**
Merck & Co Inc *v.* Exler (C187/80) see Merck & Co Inc *v.* Stephar BV (C187/80)
Merck & Co Inc *v.* SmithKline Beecham Plc see JERYL LYNN Trade Mark
Merck & Co Inc *v.* Stephar BV (C187/80); Merck & Co Inc *v.* Exler (C187/80) [1981] E.C.R. 2063; [1981] 3 C.M.L.R. 463; [1982] F.S.R. 57, ECJ . . . . *Digested,* 82/**2296**:
                               Applied, 97/3892, 98/728: *Considered,* 85/2510, 87/2791, 96/4566:
                                                         Referred to, 94/3435
Merck Sharp & Dohme GmbH *v.* Paranova Pharmazeutika Handels GmbH (C443/99), ECJ [2001] E.T.M.R. 99, AGO
Mercury Communications Ltd *v.* Communication Telesystems International [1999] 2 All E.R. (Comm) 33; [1999] Masons C.L.R. 358, QBD (Comm Ct) . . . . *Digested,* 99/**738**

Mercury Communications Ltd *v.* Director General of Telecommunications [1996] 1
W.L.R. 48; [1996] 1 All E.R. 575; [1998] Masons C.L.R. Rep. 39; *Times,*
February 10, 1995; *Independent,* February 16, 1995, HL; reversing [1995]
Masons C.L.R. Rep. 2; (1994) 91 (36) L.S.G. 36; (1994) 138 S.J.L.B. 183; *Times,*
August 3, 1994; *Independent,* August 19, 1994, CA . . . . *Digested,* 95/**3907**:
                                              Considered, 98/3677, 99/791, 00/44
Mercury Communications Ltd *v.* Mercury Interactive (UK) Ltd [1995] F.S.R. 850, Ch D   *Digested,* 96/**5710**:
                                              Followed, 00/3794

Mercury Personal Communications *v.* Secretary of State for Trade and Industry; *sub
nom* R. *v.* Secretary of State for Trade and Industry Ex p. Mercury Personal
Communications Ltd [2000] U.K.C.L.R. 143; (1999) 96(41) L.S.G. 36; (1999)
149 N.L.J. 1646; (1999) 143 S.J.L.B. 247; *Times,* October 20, 1999;
Independent, December 6, 1999 (C.S.), CA; reversing *Times,* September 14,
1999, QBD . . . . *Digested,* 99/**4843**
Meridian Global Funds Management Asia Ltd *v.* Securities Commission [1995] 2 A.C.
500; [1995] 3 W.L.R. 413; [1995] 3 All E.R. 918; [1995] B.C.C. 942; [1995] 2
B.C.L.C. 116; (1995) 92(28) L.S.G. 39; (1995) 139 S.J.L.B. 152; *Times,* June 29,
1995, PC (NZ) . . . . *Digested,* 96/**969**:
                                              Considered, 00/980

Merino Garcia *v.* Bundesanstalt fur Arbeit (C266/95) [1997] E.C.R. I-3279; [1998]
I.C.R. 715, ECJ . . . . *Digested,* 98/**4518**
Merit Shipping Co Inc *v.* TK Boesen A/S (The Goodpal) [2000] 1 Lloyd's Rep. 638;
[2000] C.L.C. 628, QBD (Comm Ct) . . . . *Digested,* 00/**4694**
Merivale Moore Plc *v.* Strutt & Parker [1999] Lloyd's Rep. P.N. 734; [2000] P.N.L.R.
498; [1999] 2 E.G.L.R. 171; [1999] E.G.C.S. 59; (1999) 96(19) L.S.G. 27;
[1999] N.P.C. 48; *Times,* May 5, 1999, CA; affirming [1998] 2 E.G.L.R. 195;
[1997] E.G.C.S. 142, QBD . . . . *Digested,* 99/**4056**:
                                             Applied, 00/4277
MERLIN Trade Mark [1997] R.P.C. 871, TMR . . . . *Digested,* 98/**3500**
Merlis Investments Ltd *v.* Minister of National Revenue 3 I.T.L. Rep. 259, Fed Ct (Can)
Merrell Dow Pharmaceuticals Inc *v.* HN Norton & Co Ltd; Merrell Dow Pharmaceuticals
Inc *v.* Penn Pharmaceuticals Ltd [1996] R.P.C. 76; (1997) 33 B.M.L.R. 201;
(1996) 19(1) I.P.D. 19004; (1995) 92(45) L.S.G. 31; (1995) 139 S.J.L.B. 245;
Times, October 27, 1995, HL; affirming [1995] R.P.C. 233; *Independent,*
February 28, 1994 (C.S.), CA; affirming [1994] R.P.C. 1, Pat Ct . . . . *Digested,* 96/**4562**:
                                 Applied, 99/3518: *Considered,* 00/3677
Merrell Dow Pharmaceuticals Inc *v.* Penn Pharmaceuticals Ltd see Merrell Dow
Pharmaceuticals Inc *v.* HN Norton & Co Ltd
Merrett *v.* Babb [2001] EWCA Civ 214; [2001] Q.B. 1174; [2001] 3 W.L.R. 1; [2001]
B.L.R. 483; (2001) 3 T.C.L.R. 15; 80 Con. L.R. 43; [2001] Lloyd's Rep. P.N. 468;
[2001] P.N.L.R. 29; [2001] 1 E.G.L.R. 145; [2001] 8 E.G.C.S. 167; (2001)
98(13) L.S.G. 41; (2001) 145 S.J.L.B. 75; *Times,* March 2, 2001; *Independent,*
February 23, 2001, CA . . . . *Digested,* 01/**4540**
Merrett Holdings Plc *v.* Pensions Ombudsman [1998] O.P.L.R. 161, Ch D . . . . *Digested,* 01/**4618**
Merrill Lynch, Pierce Fenner & Smith Inc *v.* Raffa [2001] C.P. Rep. 44; [2001] I.L.Pr. 31;
Times, June 14, 2000, QBD . . . . *Digested,* 00/**590**
Merritt *v.* Secretary of State for the Environment, Transport and the Regions [2000] 3
P.L.R. 125; [2000] J.P.L. 371, QBD. . . . . *Digested,* 00/**4509**
Merrygold *v.* Horton see Salters Hall School Ltd (In Liquidation), Re
Mersey Docks and Harbour Board *v.* Coggins & Griffith (Liverpool) Ltd; *sub nom*
McFarlane *v.* Coggins & Griffiths (Liverpool) Ltd [1947] A.C. 1; [1946] 2 All E.R.
345; (1946) 79 Ll. L. Rep. 569; 62 T.L.R. 533; 115 L.J. K.B. 465; 175 L.T. 270,
HL; affirming [1945] K.B. 301, CA . . . . *Digested,* 47-51/**3610**:
          Applied, 47-51/3611, 47-51/6611, 52/1255, 53/962.277, 53/2510, 55/1870,
                                   56/3165, 57/1277, 57/3371, 58/1209, 58/3760, 01/2267:
                Considered, 75/2342: *Distinguished,* 57/2429, 70/1877: *Followed,* 47-51/3612
Mersey Docks and Harbour Board Trustees *v.* Gibbs; Mersey Docks and Harbour Board
Trustees *v.* Penhallow (1866) L.R. 1 H.L. 93, HL. . . . . *Applied,* 01/**387**:
                                          Considered, 66/29, 67/21
Mersey Docks and Harbour Board Trustees *v.* Penhallow see Mersey Docks and Harbour
Board Trustees *v.* Gibbs
Merseyside Cablevision Ltd *v.* Customs and Excise Commissioners [1987] 3 C.M.L.R.
290; [1987] V.A.T.T.R. 134, VAT Tr (Manchester) . . . . *Digested,* 88/**1573**:
                                              Followed, 00/5330
Merten's Patents, Re see Porter *v.* Freudenberg
Merton LBC *v.* Lowe 18 B.L.R. 130, CA . . . . *Digested,* 82/**231**:
                                              Considered, 98/795

Merz & Krell GmbH & Co *v.* Deutsches Patent- und Markenamt (C517/99); *sub nom*
Merz & Krell GmbH & Co's Trade Mark Application (C517/99) [2001] E.C.R. I-
6959, ECJ [2001] E.T.M.R. 105, AGO
Merz & Krell GmbH & Co's Trade Mark Application (C517/99) see Merz & Krell GmbH & Co
v. Deutsches Patent- und Markenamt (C517/99)
Merzouk *v.* Secretary of State for the Home Department [1999] I.N.L.R. 468, IAT . . . . . *Digested,* 00/**3322**

Meschia's Frozen Foods v. Customs and Excise Commissioners [2001] S.T.C. 1; [2000] S.T.I. 1084, Ch D; affirming [2000] S.T.I. 824, V&DTr . . . .   *Digested*, 01/**5620**
Mesco Laboratories Ltd, Re see Mesco Properties Ltd, Re
Mesco Properties Ltd, Re; *sub nom* Mesco Laboratories Ltd, Re [1980] 1 W.L.R. 96; [1980] 1 All E.R. 117; [1979] S.T.C. 788; 54 T.C. 238; [1979] T.R. 265; 123 S.J. 824, CA; affirming [1979] 1 W.L.R. 558; [1979] 1 All E.R. 302; [1979] S.T.C. 11; [1978] T.R. 387; 123 S.J. 79, Ch D . . . .   *Digested*, 80/**391**:
Applied, 99/3358, 00/3467
Messe Munchen GmbH v. Office for Harmonisation in the Internal Market (Trade Marks and Designs) (OHIM) (T32/00) [2000] E.C.R. II-3829; [2001] C.E.C. 3; [2001] E.T.M.R. 13; (2001) 24(1) I.P.D. 24002, CFI (4th Chamber) . . . .   *Digested*, 01/**3993**
MESSIAH FROM SCRATCH Trade Mark; *sub nom* Gander Music Ltd's Trade Mark Application [2000] R.P.C. 44; (1999) 22(9) I.P.D. 22090, Appointed Person . .   *Digested*, 00/**3758**
Messier Dowty Ltd v. Sabena SA [2000] 1 W.L.R. 2040; [2001] 1 All E.R. 275; [2000] 1 All E.R. (Comm) 833; [2000] 1 Lloyd's Rep. 428; [2000] C.P. Rep. 72; [2000] C.L.C. 889; [2001] I.L.Pr. 5; (2000) 97(10) L.S.G. 36; (2000) 144 S.J.L.B. 124; *Times*, March 14, 2000; *Independent*, February 29, 2000, CA . . . . .   *Digested*, 00/**778**:
Followed, 01/543
Messier Dowty Ltd v. Sabena SA (Stay of Proceedings) [2000] 1 All E.R. (Comm) 101; [2000] C.L.C. 464, QBD . . . .   *Digested*, 00/**753**
Met Office v. Edgar see Edgar v. Meteorological Office
Metagama, The (Costs) (1928) 30 Ll. L. Rep. 132; 1928 S.C. 21, OH . . . .   *Considered*, 98/3914
METAL-FREN/Friction pad assembly (T582/91) [1995] E.P.O.R. 574, EPO (Technical Bd App) . . . .   *Applied*, 01/3918
Metalfer Corp v. Pan Ocean Shipping Co Ltd [1998] 2 Lloyd's Rep. 632; [1997] C.L.C. 1574, QBD (Comm Ct) . . . .   *Digested*, 98/**253**
Metall und Rohstoff AG v. Donaldson Lufkin & Jenrette Inc [1990] 1 Q.B. 391; [1989] 3 W.L.R. 563; [1989] 3 All E.R. 14; (1989) 133 S.J. 1200, CA; reversing in part [1988] 3 W.L.R. 548; [1988] 3 All E.R. 116; [1988] 2 F.T.L.R. 93, QBD (Comm Ct) . . . .   *Digested*, 89/**3528**:
Applied, 93/3315: *Considered*, 90/2291, 90/3175, 96/1219, 97/713:
Distinguished, 93/3788: *Followed*, 98/749: *Not followed*, 98/583:
Overruled, 92/4130
METALLBAU UND BRANDSCHUTZTECHNIK/Ventilating hatch (T678/90) [1998] E.P.O.R. 174, EPO (Technical Bd App)
Metallgeseeschaft AG v. Hodapp [1998] I.L.Pr. 466, US Ct
Metallgesellschaft Ltd v. Inland Revenue Commissioners (C397/98); Hoechst AG v. Inland Revenue Commissioners (C410/98) [2001] Ch. 620; [2001] 2 W.L.R. 1497; [2001] All E.R. (EC) 496; [2001] S.T.C. 452; [2001] E.C.R. I-1727; [2001] 2 C.M.L.R. 32; [2001] B.T.C. 99; 3 I.T.L. Rep. 385; [2001] S.T.I. 498; *Times*, March 20, 2001, ECJ (5th Chamber) . . . .   *Digested*, 01/**5173**
Metalloy Supplies Ltd (In Liquidation) v. MA (UK) Ltd [1997] 1 W.L.R. 1613; [1997] 1 All E.R. 418; [1997] B.C.C. 165; [1997] 1 B.C.L.C. 165; [1998] 1 Costs L.R. 85; *Times*, December 12, 1996; *Independent*, October 21, 1996 (C.S.), CA . . . .   *Digested*, 96/**3464**
Metalmeccanica Fracasso SpA v. Amt der Salzburger Landesregierung fur den Bundesminister fur Wirtschaftliche Angelegenheiten (C27/98) [1999] E.C.R. I-5697; [2000] 2 C.M.L.R. 1150, ECJ (4th Chamber) . . . .   *Digested*, 00/**2416**
Metalsac Ticdaret Ve Sanayi Ltd STI v. Taylor Steel Inc [2001] I.L.Pr. 44, CJ (Gen Div) (Ont)
Metcalf-Wood v. Bradford's Building Supplies Ltd (Unreported, May 20, 1999), CC (Exeter) [*Ex rel.* Steven Ball, Barrister, 11 Old Square, Lincoln's Inn, London] . . . .   *Digested*, 99/**1485**
Meteorological Office v. Edgar see Edgar v. Meteorological Office
Methuen-Campbell v. Walters [1979] Q.B. 525; [1979] 2 W.L.R. 113; [1979] 1 All E.R. 606; (1979) 38 P. & C.R. 693; (1978) 247 E.G. 899; 122 S.J. 610, CA . . . .   *Digested*, 79/**1607**:
Applied, 88/1758: *Considered*, 92/2313, 94/4314, 95/4860, 00/4473:
Distinguished, 96/3732
Metix (UK) Ltd v. GH Maughan (Plastics) Ltd [1997] F.S.R. 718, Pat Ct . . . .   *Digested*, 98/**3430**
Metro SB-Grossmarkte GmbH & Co KG v. Cartier SA (C376/92) [1994] E.C.R. I-15; [1994] 5 C.M.L.R. 331; *Financial Times*, January 18, 1994, ECJ (5th Chamber) [1993] E.C.C. 289, OLG (Dusseldorf) . . . .   *Digested*, 94/**4792**:
Applied, 98/743
Metro SB-Grossmarkte GmbH & Co KG v. Commission of the European Communities (C26/76); *sub nom* Verband des SB-Grosshandels eV v. Commission of the European Communities (C26/76) [1977] E.C.R. 1875; [1978] 2 C.M.L.R. 1; [1978] F.S.R. 400, ECJ . . . .   *Digested*, 79/**1203**:
Applied, 98/735
Metro Trading International Inc v. Itochu Petroleum Co (S) PTE Ltd (No.1) see Glencore International AG v. Metro Trading International Inc (No.1)
Metronome Musik GmbH v. Music Point Hokamp GmbH (C200/96) [1998] E.C.R. I-1953; [1998] 3 C.M.L.R. 919; [2000] E.C.D.R. 11; [1999] E.M.L.R. 93; [1999] F.S.R. 576, ECJ; reversing [1997] E.C.C. 325, LG (Koln) . . . .   *Digested*, 99/**3451**
Metropole Television (M6) v. Commission of the European Communities (T112/99) [2001] 5 C.M.L.R. 33, CFI (3rd Chamber)

Metropole Television SA *v.* Commission of the European Communities (T206/99)
    [2001] E.C.R. II-1057; [2001] 4 C.M.L.R. 39, CFI (4th Chamber) . . . .   *Digested,* 01/**781**
Metropole Television SA *v.* Commission of the European Communities (T528/93)
    [1996] E.C.R. II-649; [1996] 5 C.M.L.R. 386; [1996] C.E.C. 794; [1998]
    E.M.L.R. 99, CFI (1st Chamber) . . . .   *Digested,* 98/**735**
Metropolitan Housing Trust *v.* Molesey (Unreported, May 30, 2000), CC (Lambeth) [*Ex
    rel.* Joanne Oxlade, Barrister, 33 Bedford Row, London] . . . .   *Digested,* 00/**3922**
Metropolitan Police District Receiver *v.* Palacegate Properties Ltd [2001] Ch. 131;
    [2000] 3 W.L.R. 519; [2000] 3 All E.R. 663; (2000) 80 P. & C.R. 32; [2000] L.
    & T.R. 358; [2000] 1 E.G.L.R. 63; [2000] 13 E.G. 187; (2000) 97(9) L.S.G.
    42; (2000) 150 N.L.J. 226; [2000] N.P.C. 13; (2000) 79 P. & C.R. D34; *Times,*
    March 21, 2000; *Independent,* February 16, 2000, CA . . . .   *Digested,* 00/**3893**
Metropolitan Police Service *v.* Hoar [2000] O.P.L.R. 267, Ch D . . . .   *Digested,* 01/**4617**
Metropolitan Property Holdings Ltd *v.* Finegold [1975] 1 W.L.R. 349; [1975] 1 All E.R.
    389; (1974) 29 P. & C.R. 161; 119 S.J. 151, QBD. . . . .   *Digested,* 75/**2840**:
                      Considered, 86/1888, 87/2115, 92/2719, 98/3671, 99/3721
Mettoy Pension Trustees Ltd *v.* Evans [1990] 1 W.L.R. 1587; [1991] 2 All E.R. 513;
    Financial Times, February 9, 1990, Ch D . . . .   *Digested,* 91/**2726**:
                                          Considered, 01/4626

Meux's Brewery Co *v.* City of London Electric Lighting Co see Shelfer *v.* City of
    London Electric Lighting Co (No.1)
Meyer *v.* Aries [2000] E.C.D.R. 369, Cass (F)
MH (A Child) (Care Proceedings: Children's Guardian), Re; SB (A Child) (Care
    Proceedings: Children's Guardian), Re [2001] 2 F.L.R. 1334; [2001] Fam. Law
    869; *Times,* November 15, 2001, Fam Div . . . .   *Digested,* 01/**2674**
MH *v.* GP (Child: Emigration); *sub nom* Harris *v.* Pinnington [1995] 2 F.L.R. 106;
    [1995] 3 F.C.R. 35; [1995] Fam. Law 542, Fam Div . . . .   *Digested,* 96/**543**:
                                           Applied, 00/2489
MHC Consulting Services Ltd *v.* Tansell; *sub nom* Abbey Life Assurance Co Ltd *v.*
    Tansell [2000] I.C.R. 789; [2000] I.R.L.R. 387; (2000) 97(19) L.S.G. 43;
    (2000) 150 N.L.J. 651; (2000) 144 S.J.L.B. 205; *Times,* April 19, 2000;
    Independent, May 22, 2000 (C.S.), CA; affirming [1999] I.C.R. 1211; [1999]
    I.R.L.R. 677, EAT. . . . .   *Digested,* 00/**2119**
Miah *v.* Khan see Khan *v.* Miah
Miah *v.* Sewell, *Times,* February 6, 1996, CA. . . . .   *Digested,* 96/**753**:
                                          Referred to, 01/588
Michael Gerson (Leasing) Ltd *v.* Wilkinson [2001] Q.B. 514; [2000] 3 W.L.R. 1645;
    [2001] 1 All E.R. 148; [2000] 2 All E.R. (Comm) 890; [2000] C.L.C. 1720;
    (2000) 97(35) L.S.G. 37; *Times,* September 12, 2000, CA . . . .   *Digested,* 00/**4674**
Michael Hyde & Associates Ltd *v.* JD Williams & Co Ltd see JD Williams & Co Ltd *v.*
    Michael Hyde & Associates Ltd
Michael O'Mara Books Ltd *v.* Express Newspapers Plc [1998] E.M.L.R. 383; [1999]
    F.S.R. 49; (1998) 21 (7) I.P.D. 21070; *Times,* March 6, 1998, Ch D . . . .   *Digested,* 98/**18**
Michael Peters Ltd *v.* Farnfield [1995] I.R.L.R. 190 . . . .   *Considered,* 98/2212:
                                          Referred to, 96/2642
Michael Shanley Group Ltd *v.* Secretary of State for the Environment, Transport and the
    Regions [2000] P.L.C.R. 136; [1999] E.G.C.S. 108; [1999] N.P.C. 94, CA;
    reversing in part [1999] P.L.C.R. 188; [1998] E.G.C.S. 142; [1998] N.P.C. 140,
    QBD . . . .   *Digested,* 99/**4267**
Michaels *v.* Frogmore Estates Plc see Michaels *v.* Harley House (Marylebone) Ltd
Michaels *v.* Harley House (Marylebone) Ltd; *sub nom* Michaels *v.* Frogmore Estates
    Plc [2000] Ch. 104; [1999] 3 W.L.R. 229; [1999] 1 All E.R. 356; [1999] B.C.C.
    967; [1999] 1 B.C.L.C 670; (1999) 31 H.L.R. 990; [1999] L. & T.R. 374;
    [1998] E.G.C.S. 159; [1998] N.P.C. 150, CA; affirming [1997] 1 W.L.R. 967;
    [1997] 3 All E.R. 446; [1997] 2 B.C.L.C. 166; [1997] 2 E.G.L.R. 44; [1997] 37
    E.G. 161; [1997] E.G.C.S. 29; (1997) 94(13) L.S.G. 29; (1997) 141 S.J.L.B. 83;
    [1997] N.P.C. 33; *Times,* March 10, 1997, Ch D . . . .   *Digested,* 99/**3680**
Michaels *v.* Taylor Woodrow Developments Ltd [2001] Ch. 493; [2001] 2 W.L.R. 224;
    [2000] 4 All E.R. 645; (2001) 81 P. & C.R. 23; (2000) 97(20) L.S.G. 47;
    [2000] N.P.C. 53, Ch D . . . .   *Digested,* 00/**5111**
Michalski *v.* Martin Stabin (Unreported, January 18, 1993) . . . .   *Digested,* 93/**1429**:
                                          Referred to, 00/1584
Micheletti *v.* Delegacion del Gobierno en Cantabria (C369/90) [1992] E.C.R. I-4239,
    ECJ . . . .   *Digested,* 92/**4781**:
                               Applied, 98/2309: *Considered,* 01/2445
MICKEY DEES (NIGHTCLUB) Trade Mark [1998] R.P.C. 359, TMR . . . .   *Digested,* 98/**3532**
Micro Leader Business *v.* Commission of the European Communities (T198/98)
    [2000] All E.R. (EC) 361; [1999] E.C.R. II-3989; [2000] 4 C.M.L.R. 886;
    [2000] C.E.C. 540; [2000] E.C.D.R. 217, CFI (3rd Chamber) . . . .   *Digested,* 00/**702**
Micro Leisure Ltd *v.* County Properties & Developments Ltd (No.2) 1999 S.L.T. 1428;
    [2000] B.C.C. 872; 1999 G.W.D. 33-1570; *Times,* January 12, 2000, OH . . . . . .   *Digested,* 00/**5955**
Microsoft Corp *v.* Backslash Distribution Ltd (No.2) [1999] Masons C.L.R. 24, Ch D . .   *Digested,* 99/**15**
Microsoft Corp *v.* Backslash Distribution Ltd (No.3), *Times,* March 15, 1999, Ch D . . . .   *Digested,* 99/**3762**

Microsoft Corp *v.* Computer Future Distribution Ltd [1998] E.T.M.R. 597; [1998-99]
    Info. T.L.R. 1; [1998] I.T.C.L.R. 88; [1998] Masons C.L.R. 204, Ch D . . . .   *Digested,* 98/**3544**
Microsoft Corp *v.* Electro-Wide Ltd [1998] E.C.C. 53; [1997-98] Info. T.L.R. 147;
    [1998] I.T.C.L.R. 56; [1997] F.S.R. 580; (1997) 16 Tr. L.R. 318; (1997) 20(6)
    I.P.D. 20057; *Times,* April 22, 1997, Ch D . . . .   *Digested,* 97/**1054**
Microsoft Corp *v.* Plato Technology Ltd [1999] Masons C.L.R. 370; (1999) 22(11)
    I.P.D. 22108; *Times,* August 17, 1999, CA; affirming [1999] F.S.R. 834; [1999]
    Masons C.L.R. 87; (1999) 22(5) I.P.D. 22047; *Independent* April 19, 1999 (C.S.),
    Ch D . . . .   *Digested,* 99/**3536**:
        Considered, 00/496
Microsoft Corp's Applications [1997-98] Info. T.L.R. 361, PO . . . .   *Digested,* 99/**3591**
Microsoft Corp's Trade Mark Application; *sub nom* NETMEETING Trade Mark [1999]
    E.T.M.R. 386, OHIM (3rd Bd App)
Mid Bedfordshire DC *v.* Way (1998) 13 P.A.D. 258, Planning Inspector
Mid Bedfordshire DC *v.* Old Road Securities Plc (1999) 14 P.A.D. 541, Planning
    Inspector
Mid East Trading Ltd, Re; *sub nom* Lehman Bros Inc *v.* Phillips; Phillips *v.* Lehman
    Brothers [1998] 1 All E.R. 577; [1998] B.C.C. 726; [1998] 1 B.C.L.C. 240;
    (1998) 95(3) L.S.G. 24; (1998) 142 S.J.L.B. 45; *Times,* December 20, 1997, CA;
    affirming [1997] 3 All E.R. 481; [1997] 2 B.C.L.C. 230; *Times,* May 6, 1997;
    Independent, April 28, 1997 (C.S.), Ch D (Companies Ct) . . . .   *Digested,* 98/**3308**
Mid Glamorgan CC *v.* Land Authority for Wales 49 B.L.R. 61; 32 Con. L.R. 50, QBD . . .   *Digested,* 92/**177**:
        Considered, 99/235
Middlege *v.* Thomson Holidays [2000] 5 Q.R. 8, CC (Bristol) [*Ex rel.* Lyons Davidson
    Solicitors, Victoria House, 51 Victoria Street, Bristol] . . . .   *Digested,* 00/**1657**
Middlesbrough BC *v.* Safeer [2001] EWHC Admin 525; [2001] 4 All E.R. 630; [2001]
    Crim. L.R. 922; (2001) 98(30) L.S.G. 37; *Times,* August 16, 2001, QBD (Admin
    Ct) . . . .   *Digested,* 01/**1181**
Middleton *v.* Middleton [1998] 2 F.L.R. 821; [1999] 2 F.C.R. 681; [1998] Fam. Law
    589, CA . . . .   *Digested,* 99/**2420**
Middleton *v.* Steeds Hudson [1998] 1 F.L.R. 738; [1998] Fam. Law 322, QBD . . . .   *Digested,* 98/**4010**
Midland Bank Executor and Trustee Co *v.* Forbes see Moritz, Re
Midland Bank Ltd *v.* Seymour [1955] 2 Lloyd's Rep. 147, QBD . . . .   *Digested,* 55/**161**:
    Applied, 00/280: *Approved,* 72/181
Midland Bank Plc *v.* Bardgrove Property Services Ltd 60 B.L.R. 1; 37 Con. L.R. 49;
    (1993) 65 P. & C.R. 153; [1992] 37 E.G. 126; (1993) 9 Const. L.J. 49; [1992]
    E.G.C.S. 87; [1992] N.P.C. 83, CA; affirming 24 Con. L.R. 98; [1991] 2 E.G.L.R.
    283 . . . .   *Digested,* 92/**3267**:
        Followed, 98/3367
Midland Bank Plc *v.* Cameron Thom Peterkin & Duncans 1988 S.L.T. 611; 1988 S.C.L.R.
    209, OH . . . .   *Digested,* 88/**4958**:
        Applied, 98/4003
Midland Bank Plc *v.* Cox McQueen [1999] Lloyd's Rep. Bank. 78; [1999] 1 F.L.R.
    1002; [1999] Lloyd's Rep. P.N. 223; [1999] P.N.L.R. 593; [1999] Fam. Law 310;
    [1999] E.G.C.S. 12; (1999) 96(6) L.S.G. 36; (1999) 149 N.L.J. 164; [1999]
    N.P.C. 11; *Times,* February 2, 1999; *Independent,* January 29, 1999, CA . . . . . .   *Digested,* 99/**3807**:
        Applied, 00/4281
Midland Bank Plc *v.* Customs and Excise Commissioners (C98/98); *sub nom* Customs
    and Excise Commissioners *v.* Midland Bank Plc (C98/98) [2000] 1 W.L.R.
    2080; [2000] All E.R. (EC) 673; [2000] S.T.C. 501; [2000] E.C.R. I-4177;
    [2000] 3 C.M.L.R. 301; [2000] C.E.C. 441; [2000] B.T.C. 5199; [2000] B.V.C.
    229; [2000] S.T.I. 852; *Times,* June 16, 2000, ECJ (2nd Chamber) . . . .   *Digested,* 00/**5302**:
    Applied, 01/5586: *Considered,* 01/5585
Midland Bank Plc *v.* Lanham (Valuation Officer) (1977) 246 E.G. 1018; (1977) 246 E.G.
    1117; [1978] R.A. 1; [1978] J.P.L. 475, Lands Tr . . . .   *Digested,* 79/**2229.22**:
    Considered, 00/4590: *Not applied,* 01/4833: *Referred to,* 83/3138.1
Midland Bank Plc *v.* Wallace see Royal Bank of Scotland Plc *v.* Etridge (No.2)
Midland Bank Trust Co Ltd *v.* Hett Stubbs & Kemp [1979] Ch. 384; [1978] 3 W.L.R. 167;
    [1978] 3 All E.R. 571; [1955-95] P.N.L.R. 95; 121 S.J. 830; *Times,* December 2,
    1977, Ch D . . . .   *Digested,* 78/**2822**:
    Applied, 97/3809, 99/1889, 99/4034: *Approved,* 83/3610, 94/3362:
    Considered, 89/2585, 93/2997, 95/3689, 97/649, 97/3829:
    Distinguished, 91/2343: *Followed,* 92/3212, 93/2980, 96/4498, 97/3825:
    Referred to, 81/1852
Midland Bank Trustee (Jersey) Ltd *v.* MacLeod; *sub nom* El-Kaisi (Deceased), Re
    [2001] W.T.L.R. 817, Royal Ct (Jer) . . . .   *Digested,* 01/**5170**
Midland International Trade Services *v.* Sudairy, *Financial Times,* May 2, 1990 . . . .   *Digested,* 90/**3780**:
        Considered, 98/844
Midland Marts Ltd *v.* Hobday [1989] 1 W.L.R. 1143; [1989] 3 All E.R. 246; (1989)
    86(27) L.S.G. 41; (1989) 133 S.J. 1109; *Times,* April 25, 1989, Ch D . . . .   *Digested,* 89/**2927**:
        Considered, 00/494
Midland Wheel Supplies Ltd's Application for Revocation [2000] E.T.M.R. 256, TMR. . .   *Digested,* 00/**3791**
Midlands Cooperative Society Ltd *v.* Customs and Excise Commissioners [2001] S.T.I.
    1496, Ch D; affirming [2001] S.T.I. 841, V&DTr

Midlands Electricity Plc *v.* Data Protection Registrar [1998-99] Info. T.L.R. 217, Data
    Protection Tr . . . . *Digested,* 01/**3705**
Midway Manufacturing Co *v.* Artic International Inc 704 F.2d 1009, US Ct . . . . *Approved,* 98/3444
Mienes *v.* Stone (Unreported, April 30, 1985), DC . . . . *Not followed,* 98/2250
Mighell *v.* Reading see Evans *v.* Motor Insurers Bureau
Mignini SpA *v.* Azienda di Stato per Gli Interventi sul Mercato Agricolo (AIMA) (C256/
    90) [1992] E.C.R. I-2651, ECJ (5th Chamber) . . . . *Digested,* 92/**4672**:
                                                 Followed, 00/2640
Migration Services International Ltd, Re; *sub nom* Webster *v.* Official Receiver [2000]
    B.C.C. 1095; [2000] 1 B.C.L.C. 666; (1999) 96(47) L.S.G. 29; *Times,* December
    2, 1999 ; *Independent,* January 17, 2000 (C.S.), Ch D (Companies Ct) . . . . *Digested,* 00/**668**
Mikkelsen *v.* Danmols Inventar A/S (C105/84); *sub nom* Foreningen af Arbejdsledere i
    Danmark *v.* Danmols Inventar A/S (In Liquidation) (C105/84) [1985] E.C.R.
    2639; [1986] 1 C.M.L.R. 316; *Times,* July 29, 1985, ECJ (5th Chamber) . . . . . . *Digested,* 86/**1360**:
                                                 Applied, 01/2337
Miklaszewicz *v.* Stolt Offshore Ltd; *sub nom* Stolt Offshore Ltd *v.* Miklaszewicz;
    Miklasewicz *v.* Stolt Offshore Ltd; Stolt Offshore Ltd *v.* Miklaszewicz; TNS, Ex
    Div; affirming [2001] I.R.L.R. 656; *Independent,* July 9, 2001 (C.S), EAT . . . . . *Digested,* 01/**6477**:
                                                 Applied, 01/2348
Mikulski *v.* Poland (27914/95) (2001) 29 E.H.R.R. CD64, ECHR
Milan AC SpA *v.* Topps Italia Srl; Juventus FC SpA *v.* Topps Italia Srl [1999] E.T.M.R.
    182, App (Milano)
Miles *v.* McGregor (Unreported, January 23, 1998) . . . . *Distinguished,* 99/548
Miles *v.* Secretary of State for the Environment, Transport and the Regions [2000]
    J.P.L. 192, QBD . . . . *Digested,* 99/**4198**
Milford Haven *v.* Andrews; *sub nom* R. *v.* Milford Haven Port Authority (Severance); R.
    v. Andrews (Mark Clive) [2000] Env. L.R. D2, CA (Crim Div)
Milford Haven Conservancy Board *v.* Inland Revenue Commissioners [1976] 1 W.L.R.
    817; [1976] 3 All E.R. 263; 74 L.G.R. 449; 120 S.J. 368, CA; affirming 73 L.G.R.
    390; [1975] 239 E.G. 47, DC . . . . *Digested,* 76/**2273**:
                                        Applied, 01/4816, 01/4817
Miliangos *v.* George Frank (Textiles) Ltd (No.1) [1976] A.C. 443; [1975] 3 W.L.R. 758;
    [1975] 3 All E.R. 801; [1976] 1 Lloyd's Rep. 201; [1975] 2 C.M.L.R. 585; 119 S.J.
    774, HL; affirming [1975] Q.B. 487; [1975] 2 W.L.R. 555; [1975] 1 All E.R.
    1076; [1975] 1 Lloyd's Rep. 587; [1975] 1 C.M.L.R. 630; 119 S.J. 322, CA;
    reversing [1975] 1 Lloyd's Rep. 436; [1975] 1 C.M.L.R. 121; (1974) 119 S.J. 10;
    Times, December 5, 1974, QBD . . . . *Digested,* 75/**2657**:
                Applied, 77/194, 77/735, 78/710, 87/365: *Considered,* 76/327, 77/731,
                        77/1602, 77/2728, 77/3735, 79/155, 81/260, 84/323, 00/1467:
                Distinguished, 78/3691, 80/642: *Followed,* 73/3142, 76/675, 77/2334,
                              77/2354, 77/3625: *Not followed,* 76/273, 82/335
Milk Marketing Board *v.* Cricket St Thomas Estate [1991] 3 C.M.L.R. 123; *Financial
    Times,* March 22, 1991, QBD . . . . *Digested,* 91/**3733**:
                                                 Considered, 98/2569
Milk Marketing Board of England and Wales *v.* Tom Parker Farms and Dairies Ltd [1998]
    2 C.M.L.R. 721; [1999] Eu. L.R. 154, QBD (Comm Ct) . . . . *Digested,* 99/**369**
Mill's Application, Re [1985] R.P.C. 339, CA . . . . *Followed,* 98/3448
Millar *v.* Criminal Injuries Compensation Board see P's Curator Bonis *v.* Criminal Injuries
    Compensation Board
Millar *v.* Dickson; Stewart *v.* Heywood; Payne *v.* Heywood; Tracey *v.* Heywood;
    Marshall *v.* Ritchie [2001] UKPC D4; 2001 S.L.T. 988; 2001 S.C.C.R. 741; [2001]
    H.R.L.R. 59; [2001] U.K.H.R.R. 999; 2001 G.W.D. 26-1015; *Times,* July 27,
    2001, PC (Sc); reversing 2000 J.C. 648; 2000 S.L.T. 1111; 2000 S.C.C.R. 793;
    [2000] U.K.H.R.R. 776; 2000 G.W.D. 27-1040, HCJ Appeal . . . . *Digested,* 01/**6372**
Millar *v.* Galashiels Gas Co Ltd see Galashiels Gas Co Ltd *v.* Millar
Millar *v.* Hornsby (2000-01) 3 I.T.E.L.R. 81, Sup Ct (Vic) . . . . *Digested,* 01/**5509**
Millbanks *v.* Home Office see O'Reilly *v.* Mackman
Millbanks *v.* Secretary of State for the Home Department see O'Reilly *v.* Mackman
Miller *v.* Allied Sainif (UK) Ltd, *Times,* October 31, 2000, Ch D . . . . *Digested,* 00/**577**
Miller *v.* Cameron (1936) 54 C.L.R. 572 . . . . *Followed,* 01/5523
Miller *v.* Council of the Law Society of Scotland 2000 S.L.T. 513; 2000 S.C.L.R. 849;
    2000 G.W.D. 1-25; *Times,* March 22, 2000, OH . . . . *Digested,* 00/**6552**
Miller *v.* Elliott Fire Protection Services Ltd [2001] 5 Q.R. 8, CC (Croydon) [*Ex rel.*
    Thomson Snell & Passmore, Solicitors, 3 Lonsdale Gardens, Tunbridge Wells] . . . *Digested,* 01/**1575**
Miller *v.* Eyo (1999) 31 H.L.R. 306; [1998] N.P.C. 95, CA . . . . *Digested,* 98/**3632**
Miller *v.* Hamworthy Engineering [1986] I.C.R. 846; [1986] I.R.L.R. 461; (1986) 83
    L.S.G. 1901, CA . . . . *Digested,* 87/**1377**:
                                                  Considered, 01/2226
Miller *v.* Hulbert (Unreported, May 15, 2000), CC (Romford) [*Ex rel.* Victoria Ling,
    Barrister, 1 Temple Gardens, Temple, London] . . . . *Digested,* 00/**2565**
Miller *v.* Leeds Magistrates Court see Gough *v.* Chief Constable of Derbyshire
Miller *v.* Stapleton [1996] 2 All E.R. 449; [1996] O.P.L.R. 73, QBD . . . . *Digested,* 97/**4000**:
                                           Considered, 97/4009, 99/2012
Miller *v.* Stapleton (Leave to Appeal) [1996] O.P.L.R. 281, CA . . . . *Digested,* 98/**4146**

Miller v. Wycombe DC [1997] J.P.L. 951; [1997] E.G.C.S. 26; [1997] N.P.C. 36, CA. . . . *Digested,* 97/**4070**:
    Considered, 99/4226: *Followed,* 98/4190
Miller Construction Ltd v. James Moore Earthmoving; *sub nom* James Moore
    Earthmoving v. Miller Construction Ltd [2001] EWCA Civ 654; [2001] 2 All E.R.
    (Comm) 598; [2001] B.L.R. 322, CA; reversing [2001] B.L.R. 10, QBD
    (T&CC) *Digested,* 01/**339**
Miller Freeman World-wide Plc v. Customs and Excise Commissioners (No.1) [1998]
    B.V.C. 2180, V&DTr. *Digested,* 98/**4914**
Miller Freeman World-wide Plc v. Customs and Excise Commissioners (No.2) [1998]
    B.V.C. 2197, V&DTr. *Digested,* 98/**4962**
Miller Gardner v. Lord Chancellor [1997] 2 Costs L.R. 29, QBD *Digested,* 98/**3698**
Miller Steamship Co Pty Ltd v. Overseas Tankship (UK) Ltd see Overseas Tankship (UK)
    Ltd v. Miller Steamship Co Pty Ltd (The Wagon Mound)
Miller-Mead v. Minister of Housing and Local Government [1963] 2 Q.B. 196; [1963]
    2 W.L.R. 225; [1963] 1 All E.R. 459; (1963) 127 J.P. 122; 61 L.G.R. 152; (1963)
    14 P. & C.R. 266; [1963] J.P.L. 151; 106 S.J. 1052, CA; reversing in part [1962]
    2 Q.B. 555; [1962] 3 W.L.R. 654; [1962] 3 All E.R. 99; 126 J.P. 457; 60 L.G.R.
    340; (1962) 13 P. & C.R. 425; 106 S.J. 492, QBD *Digested,* 63/**3406**:
    Applied, 64/3580, 64/3584, 65/3809, 65/3828, 66/11738, 66/11846,
    68/3830, 71/11427, 74/3740, 76/2696, 76/2697, 77/2942, 78/2877,
    85/3421, 86/3266, 87/3604, 91/3470, 99/4249: *Considered,* 69/3453,
    69/3470, 70/2775, 79/2625, 86/3268, 90/4360, 90/4367, 91/3520,
    94/2219, 95/4863, 95/4867, 96/4798: *Distinguished,* 63/3358:
    Followed, 94/4439: *Not followed,* 98/4183
Miller-Mead v. Warwick Rural DC see Warwick Rural DC v. Miller-Mead
Milliken & Co's Trade Mark Application [1999] E.T.M.R. 575, OHIM (1st Bd App) *Digested,* 00/**3732**
Milliken Denmark A/S v. Walk Off Mats Ltd [1996] F.S.R. 292; (1996) 19(5) I.P.D.
    19040, Pat Ct *Digested,* 96/**4557**:
    Considered, 98/3462
Millington v. Commissioner of Police of the Metropolis, *Times,* May 28, 1983 *Digested,* 83/**1076**:
    Doubted, 01/4780
Millington v. Secretary of State for the Environment, Transport and the Regions [1999]
    3 P.L.R. 118; [2000] J.P.L. 297; [1999] E.G.C.S. 95; (1999) 96(27) L.S.G. 35;
    [1999] N.P.C. 75; *Times,* June 29, 1999, CA; reversing (1999) 78 P. & C.R. 373;
    [1999] 1 P.L.R. 36; [1999] J.P.L. 644; [1998] E.G.C.S. 154, QBD *Digested,* 99/**4172**:
    Applied, 01/4657, 01/4755
Mills (CICA: Quantum: 2000), Re [2001] 4 Q.R. 9, CICAP [*Ex rel.* Suzanne Palmer,
    Barrister, Field Court Chambers, 2nd Floor, 3 Field Court, Gray's Inn, London] *Digested,* 01/**1576**
Mills v. Barnsley MBC [1992] P.I.Q.R. P291; (1993) 157 J.P.N. 831, CA. *Digested,* 93/**2967**:
    Applied, 00/4230, 01/4497: *Cited,* 96/4480: *Followed,* 99/2891:
    Referred to, 96/5670
Mills v. Blackwell (1999) 96(30) L.S.G. 30; [1999] N.P.C. 88; (1999) 78 P. & C.R.
    D43, CA
Mills v. Edict Ltd see Shapland Inc, Re
Mills v. Haywood (1877) L.R. 6 Ch. D. 196, CA *Disapproved,* 99/**4369**:
    Distinguished, 56/9054
Mills v. Marshall see DPP v. Marshall
Mills v. Morris Motorcycles (Unreported, April 12, 1994), CC (Cardiff) [*Ex rel.* Martin S
    Khan, Robin Thompson & Partners, Solicitors] *Digested,* 95/**1723**:
    Considered, 98/1638
Mills v. News Group Newspapers Ltd [2001] E.M.L.R. 41, Ch D *Digested,* 01/**3577**
Mills v. Secretary of State for the Environment, Transport and the Regions [1998] 3
    P.L.R. 12; [1998] E.G.C.S. 4; (1998) 95(4) L.S.G. 35; [1998] Env. L.R. D17,
    QBD *Digested,* 99/**4276**
Mills & Allen Ltd v. Commissioners for New Towns [2001] R.V.R. 114; [2001] N.P.C. 17,
    Lands Tr *Digested,* 01/**4663**
Mills & Rockley (Electronics) Ltd v. Technograph Printed Circuits Ltd; *sub nom*
    Technograph Printed Circuits Ltd v. Mills & Rockley (Electronics) Ltd [1971]
    F.S.R. 188; [1972] R.P.C. 346, HL; affirming [1969] F.S.R. 239; [1969] R.P.C.
    395, CA; reversing [1968] F.S.R. 230; [1968] R.P.C. 331, Ch D *Digested,* 71/**8624**:
    Applied, 91/2708: *Considered,* 94/3439, 95/3758, 99/3495
Millwall Football Club & Athletic Co (1985) Plc (In Administration), Re [1999] B.C.C. 455;
    [1998] 2 B.C.L.C. 272, Ch D (Companies Ct) *Digested,* 99/**3335**
Milmo v. Carreras [1946] K.B. 306, CA *Applied,* 91/2256,
    92/2754, 99/3662: *Followed,* 97/3307, 98/3769
Milne v. Kennedy [2000] C.P. Rep. 80; *Times,* February 11, 1999, CA. *Digested,* 99/**87**
Milne v. Mateus (Unreported, May 10, 1999), CC (Barnet) [*Ex rel.* Daniel Barnett,
    Barrister, 2 Gray's Inn Square Chambers, Gray's Inn, London] *Digested,* 99/**1577**
Milne v. Telegraph Group Ltd (No.2) [2001] E.M.L.R. 30, QBD *Digested,* 01/**1830**
Milne Berry v. Tower Hamlets LBC (1998) 30 H.L.R. 229; [1997] E.G.C.S. 37, CA;
    affirming (1996) 28 H.L.R. 225; [1995] E.G.C.S. 86, QBD *Digested,* 98/**3054**
Milne-Williamson v. Thomson Holidays Ltd (Unreported, May 14, 1999), CC
    (Guildford) [*Ex rel.* Sarah Tozzi, Barrister, Plowden Buildings, Temple, London] *Digested,* 99/**3827**
Milner, Re (1884-85) L.R. 15 Q.B.D. 605, CA *Distinguished,* 00/121

Milner Neocal Ltd *v.* Milner (Executor) (2000) 23(1) I.P.D. 23009, Pat Ct
Milner's Patent Application (1998) 21(12) I.P.D. 21128, PO
Milroy *v.* Lord (1862) 4 De G.F. & J. 264 . . . .   *Applied,* 56/2395,
                                    56/3778, 74/3501: *Considered,* 47/2611, 01/5514: *Distinguished,* 47-51/10791,
                                    47-51/10887, 52/933: *Explained,* 84/2947, 85/1589: *Followed,* 00/3536
Milton Keynes Council *v.* Dovecote Coarse Fishery (1999) 14 P.A.D. 687, Planning
    Inspector
Milton Keynes Council *v.* Tesco Stores Ltd (1999) 14 P.A.D. 187, Planning Inspector
Milton Keynes Development Corp *v.* Cooper (Great Britain) see Commission for the
    New Towns *v.* Cooper (Great Britain) Ltd (formerly Coopind UK)
Mimtec Ltd *v.* Inland Revenue Commissioners [2001] S.T.C. (S.C.D.) 101; [2001] S.T.I.
    942, Sp Comm . . . .   *Digested,* 01/**5273**
Minchin *v.* Sheffield City Council, *Times,* April 26, 2000, CA . . . .   *Digested,* 00/**3142**
Mindbender Ltd *v.* Abbott [2000] C.P. Rep. 27, CA . . . .   *Digested,* 00/**440**
Minelone Ltd *v.* Customs and Excise Commissioners [2000] S.T.I. 60, V&DTr
Mineral Resources Ltd, Re; *sub nom* Insolvency Act 1986, Re; Environment Agency *v.*
    Stout [1999] 1 All E.R. 746; [1999] B.C.C. 422; [1999] 2 B.C.L.C. 516; [1999]
    Env. L.R. 407; [1998] B.P.I.R. 576; [1998] 4 P.L.R. 56; [1998] E.G.C.S. 78;
    [1998] N.P.C. 78, Ch D (Companies Ct) . . . .   *Digested,* 99/**3309**:
                                Applied, 99/3279: *Followed,* 99/3263: *Not followed,* 99/3308
MINERVA Trade Mark; *sub nom* Reed Consumer Books Ltd *v.* Pomaco Ltd; Pomaco
    Ltd's Trade Mark Application (No.1372819) [2001] E.T.M.R. 92; [2000] F.S.R.
    734; (2000) 23(10) I.P.D. 23085, Ch D . . . .   *Digested,* 00/**3794**:
                                                                                              Applied, 01/4009
Minister for Aboriginal Affairs *v.* Peko Wallsend Ltd (1986) 162 C.L.R. 24, HC (Aus) . . .   *Applied,* 98/3091
Minister for Immigration and Ethnic Affairs *v.* Teoh (1995) 183 C.L.R. 273, HC (Aus) . . .   *Applied,* 98/2201:
                                            Considered, 00/3301: *Distinguished,* 98/3203
Minister for Immigration and Ethnic Affairs *v.* Wu Shan Liang (1996) 185 C.L.R. 259, HC
    (Aus) . . . .   *Applied,* 98/3091
Minister for Immigration and Multicultural Affairs *v.* Ibrahim [2001] I.N.L.R. 228, HC
    (Aus) . . . .   *Digested,* 01/**3694**
Minister for Social Security *v.* Greenham Ready Mixed Concrete Ltd see Ready Mixed
    Concrete (South East) Ltd *v.* Minister of Pensions and National Insurance
Minister for Social Security *v.* Ready Mixed Concrete (South East) Ltd see Ready
    Mixed Concrete (South East) Ltd *v.* Minister of Pensions and National
    Insurance
Minister for the Economy *v.* France Telecom [2000] E.C.C. 420, C d'A (Paris)
Minister for Welfare and Population Development *v.* Fitzpatrick 9 B.H.R.C. 78, Const Ct
    (SA) . . . .   *Digested,* 01/**832**
Ministere Public *v.* Deserbais (C286/86) [1988] E.C.R. 4907; [1989] 1 C.M.L.R. 516;
    Times, September 24, 1988, ECJ . . . .   *Digested,* 90/**2188**:
                                                                                              Followed, 01/2508
Ministerio Publico *v.* Epson Europe BV (C375/98) [2000] E.C.R. I-4243; [2000] S.T.I.
    1512, ECJ (5th Chamber)
Ministerio Publico *v.* Fazenda Publica (C393/98); *sub nom* Valente *v.* Fazenda Publica
    (C393/98) [2001] E.C.R. I-1327; [2001] 2 C.M.L.R. 29; [2001] C.E.C. 179, ECJ
    (5th Chamber) . . . .   *Digested,* 01/**5190**
Ministero delle Finanze *v.* IN.CO.GE.'90 Srl (C10/97) [1998] E.C.R. I-6307; [2001] 1
    C.M.L.R. 31, ECJ . . . .   *Digested,* 01/**5198**
Ministero delle Finanze *v.* Spac SpA (C260/96) [1998] E.C.R. I-4997; [1999] C.E.C.
    490, ECJ . . . .   *Digested,* 00/**2405**
Ministre de l'Economie des Finances et de l'Industrie *v.* Societe Andritz Sprout Bauer 4
    I.T.L. Rep. 1, C Adm A (F)
Ministre du Budget *v.* Societe Monte Dei Paschi di Siena (C136/99) [2001] S.T.C.
    1029; [2000] E.C.R. I-6109; [2000] S.T.I. 1515, ECJ . . . .   *Digested,* 01/**5583**
Ministry of Agriculture, Fisheries and Food *v.* Webbs Country Foods Ltd [1998] Eu. L.R.
    359, QBD . . . .   *Digested,* 99/**2579**
Ministry of Defence *v.* Ashman (1993) 66 P. & C.R. 195; [1993] 40 E.G. 144; [1993]
    N.P.C. 70, CA . . . .   *Digested,* 94/**2771**:
                                        Applied, 94/2772, 00/3952: *Referred to,* 95/2968
Ministry of Defence *v.* Blue Circle Industries Plc see Blue Circle Industries Plc *v.* Ministry
    of Defence
Ministry of Defence *v.* Donald see Ministry of Defence *v.* Wheeler
Ministry of Defence *v.* George see Ministry of Defence *v.* Wheeler
Ministry of Defence *v.* Hunt see Ministry of Defence *v.* Wheeler
Ministry of Defence *v.* Joslyn see Ministry of Defence *v.* Wheeler
Ministry of Defence *v.* Nixon see Ministry of Defence *v.* Wheeler

Ministry of Defence v. Wheeler; Ministry of Defence v. Hunt; Ministry of Defence v. George; Anderson v. Ministry of Defence; Stuart v. Ministry of Defence; Ministry of Defence v. Donald; Ministry of Defence v. Nixon; Ministry of Defence v. Joslyn [1998] 1 W.L.R. 637; [1998] 1 All E.R. 790; [1998] I.C.R. 242; [1998] I.R.L.R. 23; (1997) 94(45) L.S.G. 27; (1998) 142 S.J.L.B. 13; *Times*, November 19, 1997, CA; affirming [1996] I.C.R. 554; [1996] I.R.L.R. 139; *Times*, December 22, 1995, EAT . . . . *Digested, 97/***309***:*
Distinguished, 98/2229
Ministry of Defence v. Wiltshire CC [1995] 4 All E.R. 931; [1995] N.P.C. 78, Ch D . . . . . *Digested, 96/***4935***:*
Considered, 00/4616
Ministry of Defence's Application, Re [1994] N.I. 279, CA (NI). . . . . *Digested, 00/***5392***
Minja Properties Ltd v. Cussins Property Group Plc [1998] 2 E.G.L.R. 52; [1998] 30 E.G. 114; [1998] E.G.C.S. 23, Ch D . . . . *Digested, 98/***3628***
Minmetals Germany GmbH v. Ferco Steel Ltd [1999] 1 All E.R. (Comm.) 315; [1999] C.L.C. 647; *Times*, March 1, 1999; *Independent*, February 2, 1999, QBD (Comm Ct) . . . . *Digested, 99/***237***
Minnesota v. Philip Morris Inc [1998] I.L.Pr. 170, CA; reversing [1998] I.L.Pr. 158, QBD . *Digested, 97/***471***
Minnesota Mining & Manufacturing Co v. ATI Atlas Ltd [2001] F.S.R. 31; (2001) 24(3) I.P.D. 24017; *Times*, November 15, 2000, Pat Ct. *Digested, 00/***3631***
Minnesota Mining & Manufacturing Co v. Plastus Kreativ AB; *sub nom* Plastus Kreativ AB v. Minnesota Mining & Manufacturing Co [1997] R.P.C. 737; (1997) 20(8) I.P.D. 20076, CA; affirming (1996) 19(3) I.P.D. 19019, Ch D . . . . *Digested, 98/***3465***
Minnesota Mining & Manufacturing Co v. Rennicks (UK) Ltd (No.4) [2000] F.S.R. 727; (2000) 23(4) I.P.D. 23029, Pat Ct . . . . *Digested, 00/***3668***
Minnesota Mining & Manufacturing Co's (Suspension Aerosol Formulation) Patent [1999] R.P.C. 135, Pat Ct . . . . *Digested, 99/***3518***:*
Distinguished, 99/3469
MINNESOTA MINING/Reformatio in peius (T315/97) [2000] E.P.O.R. 15, EPO (Technical Bd App) . . . . *Digested, 00/***3607***
Minor v. Groves; *sub nom* Groves v. Minor (2000) 80 P. & C.R. 136; *Times*, November 20, 1997, CA . . . . *Digested, 97/***4263***
Minotaur Data Systems Ltd, Re; *sub nom* Official Receiver v. Brunt [1999] 1 W.L.R. 1129; [1999] 3 All E.R. 122; [1999] B.C.C. 571; [1999] 2 B.C.L.C. 766; [1999] 2 Costs L.R. 97; [1999] B.P.I.R. 560; (1999) 96(12) L.S.G. 33; (1999) 149 N.L.J. 415; (1999) 143 S.J.L.B. 98; [1999] N.P.C. 27; *Times*, March 18, 1999; *Independent*, March 10, 1999, CA; reversing [1999] 1 W.L.R. 449; [1998] 4 All E.R. 500; [1998] 2 B.C.L.C. 306; [1998] 2 Costs L.R. 38; [1998] B.P.I.R. 756; *Times*, June 25, 1998, Ch D . . . . *Digested, 99/***393***
Minster Chalets Ltd v. Irwin Park Residents Association [2001] N.P.C. 86, Lands Tr
Minster Investments Ltd v. Hyundai Precision & Industry Co Ltd [1988] 2 Lloyd's Rep. 621; *Times*, January 26, 1988; *Independent*, February 23, 1988, QBD (Comm Ct) . . . . *Digested, 89/***3093***:*
Not followed, 98/770
Mintz (Wasted Costs Order), Re, *Times*, July 16, 1999, CA . . . . *Digested, 99/***986***
Mira Oil Resources of Tortola v. Bocimar NV [1999] 1 All E.R. (Comm) 732; [1999] 2 Lloyd's Rep. 101; [1999] C.L.C. 819, QBD (Comm Ct) . . . . *Digested, 99/***4429***:*
Applied, 01/4916
Miret v. Fondo de Garantia Salarial (C334/92) [1993] E.C.R. I-6911; [1995] 2 C.M.L.R. 49, ECJ (5th Chamber) . . . . *Digested, 94/***4816***:*
Applied, 98/3396
Mirfin v. Spence; Clark Metal Industries Plc (1998) 98(2) Q.R. 8, CC (Barnsley) . . . . . . *Digested, 98/***1659***
Miron v. Trudel [1995] 2 S.C.R. 418, Sup Ct (Can) . . . . *Applied, 98/3074*
Mirpuri v. Jass 56 Con. L.R. 31, QBD (OR) . . . . *Digested, 98/***232***
Mirror Group Newspapers Ltd v. Customs and Excise Commissioners see Trinity Mirror Plc (formerly Mirror Group Newspapers Ltd) v. Customs and Excise Commissioners
Mirror Group Newspapers Ltd v. Gunning see Gunning v. Mirror Group Newspapers
Mirror Group Newspapers Plc v. Maxwell (No.1) [1998] B.C.C. 324; [1993] 1 B.C.L.C. 638; *Times*, July 15, 1997, Ch D . . . . *Digested, 97/***3072***
Mirror Group Newspapers Plc v. Maxwell (No.2) [2001] B.C.C. 488; (2000) 97(23) L.S.G. 40; *Times*, May 30, 2000; *Independent*, July 10, 2000 (C.S), Ch D . . . . . *Digested, 00/***432***
Mirror Group Newspapers Plc v. Maxwell (Receivers' Costs) [1999] B.C.C. 684, Ch D . *Digested, 99/***3287***
Mirror Group Plc v. Customs and Excise Commissioners (C409/98) see Customs and Excise Commissioners v. Mirror Group Plc (C409/98)
Mirror Group Plc v. Customs and Excise Commissioners (No.1) [1998] B.V.C. 2180; [1998] V. & D.R. 206, V&D Tr . . . . *Digested, 98/***4919***
Mirror Group Plc v. Customs and Excise Commissioners (No.2) [1999] B.V.C. 2042, V&D Tr. . . . . *Digested, 99/***5015***
Mirtha v. Seriwala (Unreported, April 19, 2000), CC (Preston) [*Ex rel.* Robert McGinty, Barrister, New Bailey Chambers, 10 Lawson Street, Preston, Lancs.] . . . . *Digested, 00/***1662***
Mirvahedy v. Henley [2001] EWCA Civ 1749; *Times*, December 11, 2001; *Daily Telegraph*, November 27, 2001, CA
Mirza v. Bhandal, *Independent*, June 14, 1999 (C.S.), QBD

Misa *v.* Currie; *sub nom* Currie *v.* Misa (1875-76) L.R. 1 App. Cas. 554, HL; affirming
(1874-75) L.R. 10 Ex. 153, Ex Chamber . . . . *Applied*, 99/2059:
Considered, 47-51/767: *Followed*, 88/2038
Missouri Steamship Co, Re (1889) L.R. 42 Ch. D. 321, CA . . . . *Applied*, 53/3366,
54/3082: *Distinguished*, 98/771
MISTER DONUT Trade Mark [1983] R.P.C. 117, TMR . . . . *Digested*, 83/**3776**:
Referred to, 98/3529

MISTER LONG Trade Mark; *sub nom* Unilever Plc's Trade Mark Application (MISTER
LONG) [1999] E.T.M.R. 406; [1998] R.P.C. 401, Appointed Person . . . . *Digested*, 98/**3529**
Mistral Finance (In Liquidation), Re [2001] B.C.C. 27, Ch D (Companies Ct) . . . . *Digested*, 01/**3743**
Mistry *v.* Interim National Medical and Dental Council of South Africa (2000) 53
B.M.L.R. 190, Const Ct (SA)
Mistry *v.* NE Computing (Unreported, March 20, 1997), CC (Slough) [*Ex rel.* Lloyd
Sefton-Smith, Barrister, Bridewell Chambers, London] . . . . *Digested*, 97/**533**:
Approved, 99/405: *Considered*, 98/495: *Referred to*, 97/571
Mitchell *v.* Buckingham International Plc (In Liquidation) see Buckingham International
Plc (In Liquidation) (No.2), Re
Mitchell (Inspector of Taxes) *v.* BW Noble Ltd [1927] 1 K.B. 719, CA . . . . *Applied*, 53/1699,
54/1561, 74/1860: *Considered*, 65/1922: *Followed*, 00/4933
Mitchell *v.* Carter (No.2) see Buckingham International Plc (In Liquidation) (No.2), Re
Mitchell *v.* Durham (t/a Trade Direct) (Unreported, December 17, 1998), CC
(Loughborough) [*Ex rel.* Moss Solicitors, 80-81 Wood Gate, Loughborough,
Leicestershire] . . . . *Digested*, 99/**1375**
Mitchell *v.* Ealing LBC [1979] Q.B. 1; [1978] 2 W.L.R. 999; [1975] 2 All E.R. 779; 76
L.G.R. 703; 122 S.J. 213, QBD . . . . *Digested*, 78/**137**:
Distinguished, 99/834: *Followed*, 90/4310
Mitchell *v.* Faber & Faber Ltd [1998] E.M.L.R. 807, CA . . . . *Digested*, 99/**1623**
Mitchell *v.* Fearnley (Valuation Officer) [1997] R.V.R. 259, Lands Tr . . . . *Digested*, 98/**4328**
Mitchell *v.* Laing 1998 S.C. 342; 1998 S.L.T. 203; 1998 S.C.L.R. 266; 1997 G.W.D. 40-
2035; *Times*, January 28, 1998, 1 Div . . . . *Digested*, 98/**5703**
Mitchell *v.* Queen, The [1896] 1 Q.B. 121 (Note), CA . . . . *Considered*, 98/4785
Mitchell (David) *v.* Queen, The; *sub nom* R. *v.* Mitchell (David) [1998] A.C. 695;
[1998] 2 W.L.R. 839; [1998] 2 Cr. App. R. 35; [1998] Crim. L.R. 422; (1998)
142 S.J.L.B. 61; *Times*, January 24, 1998, PC (Bah) . . . . *Digested*, 98/**1100**
Mitchell (John) *v.* Queen, The [1999] 1 W.L.R. 1679, PC (Jam) . . . . *Digested*, 99/**3136**
Mitchell *v.* Quick Corp see Wakeman *v.* Quick Corp
Mitchell *v.* Rivett (1998) 98(2) Q.R. 6, CC (Southampton) . . . . *Digested*, 98/**1733**:
Referred to, 00/1723

Mitchell *v.* Steers (Unreported, August 4, 2000), CC (Leicester) [*Ex rel.* Amanda
Millmore, Barrister, 4 King's Bench Walk, 2nd Floor, Temple, London] . . . . *Digested*, 01/**1630**
Mitchell *v.* Vickers Armstrong Ltd see Thompson *v.* Smiths Shiprepairers (North
Shields) Ltd
Mitre Pensions Ltd *v.* Pensions Ombudsman [2000] O.P.L.R. 349; 2000 G.W.D. 22-
868, Ex Div
Mitsubishi Denki Kabushiki Kaisha's European Patent Application (T223/95) (1998) 21 (8)
I.P.D. 21087, EPO (Technical Bd App)
Mitsubishi HiTec Paper Bielefeld GmbH (formerly Stora Carbonless Paper GmbH) *v.* Office
for Harmonisation in the Internal Market (Trade Marks and Designs) (OHIM)
(T331/99) [2001] E.C.R. II-433; [2001] E.T.M.R. 57; (2001) 24(5) I.P.D. 24034,
CFI (4th Chamber) . . . . *Digested*, 01/**4004**
MITSUBISHI/Gas laser device (T926/93) [1998] E.P.O.R. 94, EPO (Technical Bd App)
MITSUBISHI/Wire electrode (T211/96) [2000] E.P.O.R. 126, EPO (Technical Bd App) . *Digested*, 00/**3663**
Mitsui Construction Co Ltd *v.* Attorney General of Hong Kong 33 B.L.R. 1; 10 Con. L.R.
1; [1987] H.K.L.R. 1076; (1986) 2 Const. L.J. 133, PC (HK); reversing 26 B.L.R.
113, CA (HK) . . . . *Digested*, 84/**236**:
Considered, 00/900
MITSUI/Rubber resin composition (T86/94) [2000] E.P.O.R. 200, EPO (Legal Bd App)
Digested, 00/**3605**
Mitutoyo Corp's Trade Mark Application; *sub nom* ABSOLUTE Trade Mark [1999]
E.T.M.R. 39, Pat App Tr . . . . *Digested*, 99/**3565**
Mizon *v.* Comcon International Ltd (Unreported, August 19, 1999), CC (Kingston upon
Hull) [*Ex rel.* Stephen J Glover, Barrister, 37 Park Square, Leeds] . . . . *Digested*, 00/**1641**
MJB Enterprises Ltd *v.* Defence Construction (1951) Ltd (2000) 2 T.C.L.R. 235;
(1999) 15 Const. L.J. 455, Sup Ct (Can) . . . . *Digested*, 00/**830**
MJT Securities Ltd *v.* Chelmsford BC see Secretary of State for the Environment,
Transport and the Regions *v.* MJT Securities Ltd
MJT Securities Ltd *v.* Secretary of State for the Environment, Transport and the Regions
see Secretary of State for the Environment, Transport and the Regions *v.* MJT
Securities Ltd
Mlambo, Re 1992 (4) S.A. 144 (Z), Sup Ct (Zim) . . . . *Applied*, 98/3116
MM (A Child) (Medical Treatment), Re [2000] 1 F.L.R. 224; [2000] Fam. Law 92, Fam Div
Digested, 00/**2496**
MMM AG *v.* F AG (X ZR 56/96) [2000] E.N.P.R. 287, BGH (Ger)
MMR/MR Vaccine Litigation see Horne-Roberts *v.* Smithkline Beecham Plc

MNM v. Secretary of State for the Home Department [2000] I.N.L.R. 576, IAT

Mo och Domsjo AB v. Commission of the European Communities (C283/98P); *sub nom* Mo och Domsjo AB v. Commission of the European Communities (T352/94) [2000] E.C.R. I-9855; [2001] 4 C.M.L.R. 11, ECJ (5th Chamber); affirming [1998] E.C.R. II-1989, CFI (3rd Chamber)

Mo och Domsjo AB v. Commission of the European Communities (T352/94) see Mo och Domsjo AB v. Commission of the European Communities (C283/98P)

Moase v. Secretary of State for the Environment, Transport and the Regions; Lomas v. Secretary of State for the Environment, Transport and the Regions [2001] Env. L.R. 13, CA; affirming [2000] Env. L.R. 266, QBD. . . . .   *Digested,* 01/**5630**

Mobil North Sea Ltd v. Compagnie Francaise d'Entreprises Metalliques [2000] I.L.Pr. 749, Cass (F)

Mobil North Sea Ltd v. PJ Pipe & Valve Co Ltd (t/a PJ Valves or PJ Valve Ltd) [2001] EWCA Civ 741; [2001] 2 All E.R. (Comm) 289, CA; affirming HT 99 248, QBD. .   *Digested,* 01/**943**

Mobil Oil Co Ltd v. Birmingham City Council [2001] EWCA Civ 1608, CA; reversing in part (2000) 97(18) L.S.G. 38, Ch D

MOBIL OIL/Opposition by Proprietor (G01/84) [1986] E.P.O.R. 39, EPO (Enlarged Bd App). . . . .   *Applied,* 00/3653

MOBIL/Friction reducing additive (G02/88) [1990] E.P.O.R. 73; [1990] O.J. E.P.O. 93, EPO (Enlarged Bd App). . . . .   *Applied,* 00/3611: *Distinguished,* 99/3513

Mock v. Inland Revenue Commissioners [1999] I.R.L.R. 785, EAT . . . .   *Digested,* 00/**2096**

Mock v. Pensions Ombudsman [2000] O.P.L.R. 331; *Times,* April 7, 2000, Ch D . . . . . .   *Digested,* 00/**4400**

Mod-Tap W Corp v. BI Communications Plc [1999] R.P.C. 333, Pat Ct . . . .   *Digested,* 99/**3465**

Modahl v. British Athletic Federation Ltd (No.1), *Times,* July 23, 1999 ; *Independent,* July 27, 1999, HL; affirming QBEN1 96/1040/E, CA. . . . .   *Digested,* 99/**541**

Modahl v. British Athletic Federation Ltd (No.2) [2001] EWCA Civ 1447; (2001) 98(43) L.S.G. 34; (2001) 145 S.J.L.B. 238, CA; affirming HQ 0000498, QBD

Mode Jeune Diffusion SA v. Maglificio il Falco di Tiziana Goti [1998] I.L.Pr. 812, Cass (F)

Modelo SGPS SA v. Director-Geral dos Registros e Notariado (C56/98); *sub nom* Modelo SGPS SA v. Director-General dos Registros e Notariado (C56/98) [2001] S.T.C. 1043; [1999] E.C.R. I-6427; [2000] S.T.I. 779, ECJ (6th Chamber). . . . .   *Digested,* 01/**5189**

Modern Building (Wales) Ltd v. Limmer & Trinidad Co Ltd [1975] 1 W.L.R. 1281; [1975] 2 All E.R. 549; [1975] 2 Lloyd's Rep. 318; 14 B.L.R. 101; 119 S.J. 641, CA . . . . . .   *Digested,* 75/**101**: *Followed,* 00/222

Modern Homes (Whitworth) Ltd v. Lancashire CC [1998] E.G.C.S. 73; *Times,* May 14, 1998, QBD. . . . .   *Digested,* 98/**4243**

Modesto v. Portugal (34422/97) (2001) 33 E.H.R.R. 28, ECHR

MODINE MANUFACTURING/Condenser (T669/93) [2000] E.P.O.R. 39, EPO (Technical Bd App). . . . .   *Digested,* 00/**3601**

Modinos v. Cyprus (A/259) (1993) 16 E.H.R.R. 485; *Times,* May 17, 1993, ECHR . . . . .   *Digested,* 93/**4360**: *Applied,* 98/3159: *Considered,* 01/3633

Mohamed v. Alaga & Co; *sub nom* Mohammed v. Alaga & Co [2000] 1 W.L.R. 1815; [1999] 3 All E.R. 699; [2000] C.P. Rep. 87; [1999] 2 Costs L.R. 169; *Times,* July 29, 1999 ; *Independent,* July 14, 1999, CA; reversing in part [1998] 2 All E.R. 720; (1998) 95(17) L.S.G. 29; (1998) 142 S.J.L.B. 142; *Times,* April 2, 1998; *Independent,* March 27, 1998, Ch D . . . .   *Digested,* 99/**3805**

Mohamed v. Fahiya see Barclays Bank Plc v. Weeks Legg & Dean

Mohamed v. Hammersmith and Fulham LBC; *sub nom* Mohammed v. Hammersmith and Fulham LBC; Surdonja v. Ealing LBC; Ealing LBC v. Surdonja [2001] UKHL 57; [2001] 3 W.L.R. 1339; (2001) 98(45) L.S.G. 26; (2001) 151 N.L.J. 1664; (2001) 145 S.J.L.B. 253; [2001] N.P.C. 154; *Times,* November 2, 2001; *Independent,* November 8, 2001; *Daily Telegraph,* November 6, 2001, HL; affirming [2001] Q.B. 97; [2000] 3 W.L.R. 481; [2000] 2 All E.R. 597; (2000) 32 H.L.R. 481; [2000] N.P.C. 5; *Times,* February 11, 2000, CA . . . .   *Digested,* 01/**3419** *Followed,* 99/3146

Mohamed v. Secretary of State for the Home Department Unreported, IAT . . . .

Mohamed Amin v. Bannerjee [1947] A.C. 322; 63 T.L.R. 433; [1947] L.J.R. 963; 177 L.T. 451, PC (Ind). . . . .   *Digested,* 47-51/**6157**: *Followed,* 97/4862, 98/4779

Mohammed v. Alaga & Co see Mohamed v. Alaga & Co

Mohammed v. Bank of Kuwait and the Middle East KSC [1996] 1 W.L.R. 1483; [1996] C.L.C. 1835; [1996] I.L.Pr. 632; (1996) 140 S.J.L.B. 173; *Times,* May 30, 1996, CA . . . .   *Digested,* 96/**1091**: *Explained,* 99/719

Mohammed v. Hammersmith and Fulham LBC see Mohamed v. Hammersmith and Fulham LBC

Mohammed v. Minister for Immigration and Multicultural Affairs Unreported, Fed Ct (Aus) (Sgl judge) . . . .   *Followed,* 99/3179

Mohammed (Allie) v. Trinidad and Tobago [1999] 2 A.C. 111; [1999] 2 W.L.R. 552; 6 B.H.R.C. 177; *Times,* December 10, 1998, PC (Trin). . . . .   *Digested,* 99/**869**

Mohammed-Holgate v. Duke see Holgate-Mohammed v. Duke

Mohr v. Finanzamt Bad Segeberg (C215/94) [1996] All E.R. (E.C.) 450; [1996] S.T.C. 328; [1996] E.C.R. I-959; [1996] C.E.C. 370; *Times*, March 8, 1996, ECJ . . . . . . *Digested*, 96/**5879**: *Considered*, 98/4960

Moir v. Wallersteiner (No.2) see Wallersteiner v. Moir (No.2)

Moisjevs v. Jephson Homes Housing Association see Jephson Homes Housing Association Ltd v. Moisejevs

Mol v. Inspecteur der Invoerrechten en Accijnzen (C269/86); Vereniging Happy Family Rustenburgerstraat v. Inspecteur der Omzetbelasting (C289/86) [1988] E.C.R. 3627; [1989] 3 C.M.L.R. 729; *Times*, September 6, 1988, ECJ (6th Chamber) . . *Digested*, 88/**1571**: *Considered*, 97/5039: *Distinguished*, 99/5014

Mole Valley DC v. Allied Domecq Leisure (1998) 13 P.A.D. 477, Planning Inspector

Mole Valley DC v. Castlemore Securities Ltd (1998) 13 P.A.D. 409, Planning Inspector

Mole Valley DC v. Regal Rabbits (Regal Group UK) (1998) 13 P.A.D. 687, Planning Inspector

Mole Valley DC v. Smith; Reigate and Banstead BC v. Brown (1992) 24 H.L.R. 442; 90 L.G.R. 557; (1992) 64 P. & C.R. 491; [1992] 3 P.L.R. 22; [1992] E.G.C.S. 26; [1992] N.P.C. 26; *Times*, March 3, 1992, CA . . . . *Digested*, 92/**4263**: *Considered*, 95/4823: *Not applied*, 01/4729

Moles, Re [1981] Crim. L.R. 170, QBD . . . . *Digested*, 81/**367**: *Considered*, 01/1103: *Referred to*, 85/2079

Molestina v. Ponton see De Molestina v. Ponton (Application to Strike Out)

Molesworth, Re (1907) 51 S.J. 653. . . . . *Applied*, 01/3780

Molins Plc v. GD SpA [2000] 1 W.L.R. 1741; [2000] 2 Lloyd's Rep. 234; [2000] C.P. Rep. 54; [2000] C.L.C. 1027; [2001] I.L.Pr. 14; [2000] F.S.R. 893; *Times*, March 29, 2000; *Independent*, March 23, 2000, CA; reversing [2001] I.L.Pr. 1; (2000) 23(4) I.P.D. 23027; (2000) 97(8) L.S.G. 35; *Times*, March 1, 2000, Pat Ct. . . . . *Digested*, 00/**567**

Mollo v. Diez see Mollo v. Mollo

Mollo v. Mollo; *sub nom* Mollo v. Diez [2000] W.T.L.R. 227; [1999] E.G.C.S. 117, Ch D . . . . *Digested*, 01/**5503**

Molloy's Application, Re [1998] N.I. 78, QBD (NI) . . . . *Digested*, 99/**5215**: *Considered*, 99/5205

Molnlycke AB v. Procter & Gamble Ltd (No.4) [1992] 1 W.L.R. 1112; [1992] 4 All E.R. 47; [1992] R.P.C. 21, CA . . . . *Digested*, 92/**3285**: *Applied*, 94/3563: *Considered*, 99/546: *Referred to*, 93/3220, 95/4130

Molnlycke AB v. Procter & Gamble Ltd (No.5) [1994] R.P.C. 49, CA; affirming [1992] F.S.R. 549, Pat Ct . . . . *Digested*, 95/**3778**: *Applied*, 96/4568, 99/3471: *Considered*, 99/3495: *Followed*, 95/3777, 97/3901

Molnlycke AB v. Procter & Gamble Ltd (No.6) [1993] F.S.R. 154, Pat Ct . . . . *Digested*, 93/**3172**: *Considered*, 99/421: *Distinguished*, 95/3790: *Followed*, 98/440

Molvaer v. Whirly Bird Services Ltd (Unreported, March 6, 2000), CC (Norwich) [*Ex rel*. Philip Kolvin, Barrister, 2-3 Gray's Inn Square, London] . . . . *Digested*, 00/**1605**

Monaco (Principality) v. Project Planning Associates (International) Ltd (1980) 32 O.R. (2d) 438, CJ (Ont) . . . . *Applied*, 00/781

Monarch Airlines Ltd v. London Luton Airport Ltd [1998] 1 Lloyd's Rep. 403; [1997] C.L.C. 698, QBD (Comm Ct) . . . . *Digested*, 97/**222**

Monarch Assurance Plc v. Inland Revenue Commissioners see R. (on the application of Monarch Assurance Plc) v. Inland Revenue Commissioners

Mond v. Hammond Suddards (No.2); *sub nom* RS&M Engineering Co Ltd, Re [2000] Ch. 40; [1999] 3 W.L.R. 697; [2000] B.C.C. 445; [1999] 2 B.C.L.C. 485; [1999] B.P.I.R. 975; *Times*, June 18, 1999, CA . . . . *Digested*, 99/**3310**: *Applied*, 00/3505

Mond v. Hyde [1999] Q.B. 1097; [1999] 2 W.L.R. 499; [1998] 3 All E.R. 833; [1998] 2 B.C.L.C. 340; [1999] B.P.I.R. 728; (1998) 95(31) L.S.G. 35; (1998) 142 S.J.L.B. 242; [1998] N.P.C. 119; *Times*, July 29, 1998; *Independent*, July 24, 1998, CA; affirming [1997] B.P.I.R. 250, Ch D . . . . *Digested*, 98/**3288**

Money Markets International Stockbrokers Ltd (In Liquidation) v. London Stock Exchange Ltd [2001] 4 All E.R. 223; [2001] 2 All E.R. (Comm) 344; [2001] 2 B.C.L.C. 347; [2001] B.P.I.R. 1044; *Times*, September 25, 2001, Ch D . . . . *Digested*, 01/**3778**

Mongiardi v. IBC Vehicles see Burrows v. Vauxhall Motors Ltd

Monk v. Hereford and Worcester CC CO/2970/97, QBD . . . . *Digested*, 98/**1960**

Monk v. Warbey [1935] 1 K.B. 75; (1934) 50 Ll. L. Rep. 33, CA; affirming (1934) 48 Ll. L. Rep. 157, KBD . . . . *Applied*, 47-51/9111: *Considered*, 69/1897, 70/206, 00/3544: *Distinguished*, 70/1198, 71/11235, 94/2281, 95/2901: *Followed*, 71/3138

Monkton Court Ltd (t/a CATS) v. Perry Prowse (Insurance Services) Ltd [2000] 1 All E.R. (Comm) 566, QBD (Merc Ct) . . . . *Digested*, 01/**474**

Monmouthshire CC v. Costelloe & Kemple Ltd; *sub nom* Monmouth CC v. Costelloe & Kemple Ltd 5 B.L.R. 83; 63 L.G.R. 429, CA; reversing 63 L.G.R. 131 . . . . *Digested*, 66/**1121**: *Considered*, 99/235: *Followed*, 00/227

Monnell v. United Kingdom (A/115); Morris v. United Kingdom (A/115) (1988) 10 E.H.R.R. 205; *Times*, March 3, 1987, ECHR . . . . *Digested*, 88/**1803**: *Applied*, 98/3143

Monolithic Building Co, Re; *sub nom* Tacon *v.* Monolithic Building Co [1915] 1 Ch. 643, CA . . . . *Considered,* 80/1565, 81/1487, 92/411, 00/3428: *Distinguished,* 73/328, 74/331: *Followed,* 90/4783
Monro (Deceased) *v.* Inland Revenue Commissioners [2000] R.V.R. 81, Lands Tr. . . . . . .   *Digested,* 00/**5028**
Monrose Investments Ltd *v.* Orion Nominees; *sub nom* Montrose Investments *v.* Orion Nominees; Monrose Investments Ltd *v.* Orion Nominees Frichmond Corporate Service Ltd [2001] C.P. Rep. 109; *Independent*, December 17, 2001 (C.S), Ch D
. . . .   *Digested,* 01/**593**
Monsanto *v.* Transport and General Workers Union [1987] 1 W.L.R. 617; [1987] 1 All E.R. 358; [1987] I.C.R. 269; [1986] I.R.L.R. 406; (1987) 84 L.S.G. 1572; (1986) 136 N.L.J. 917; (1987) 131 S.J. 690, CA . . . .   *Digested,* 87/**3770**:
Distinguished, 90/4541, 99/2074
Monsanto Co *v.* Merck & Co Inc (No.1) [2000] R.P.C. 77; (1999) 22(11) I.P.D. 22105, CA; reversing CH 1998 M No. 1421, Ch D . . . .   *Digested,* 00/**3675**
Monsanto Co *v.* Merck & Co Inc (No.2) [2000] R.P.C. 709; (2000) 23(5) I.P.D. 23036, Pat Ct . . . .   *Digested,* 00/**3624**
Monsanto Co *v.* Stauffer Chemical Co [1985] R.P.C. 515, CA; reversing [1985] F.S.R. 55; *Financial Times*, June 18, 1985, Pat Ct . . . .   *Digested,* 85/**2518**:
Followed, 99/3494
Monsanto Plc *v.* Farris (Valuation Officer) [1999] 1 E.G.L.R. 199; [1998] R.A. 107, Lands Tr . . . .   *Digested,* 98/**4314**
Monsanto Plc *v.* Tilly [2000] Env. L.R. 313; [1999] E.G.C.S. 143; (1999) 149 N.L.J. 1833; [1999] N.P.C. 147; *Times*, November 30, 1999, CA . . . .   *Digested,* 00/**186**
MONSANTO/Rheological testing (T71/93) [1998] E.P.O.R. 402, EPO (Technical Bd App)
Monsees *v.* Unabhangiger Verwaltungssenat fur Karnten (C350/97) [1999] E.C.R. I-2921; [2001] 1 C.M.L.R. 2, ECJ
MONSTER MUNCH Trade Mark [1997] R.P.C. 721, TMR . . . .   *Digested,* 98/**3448**
Mont Blanc Simplo GmbH *v.* Sepia Products Inc; *sub nom* Montblanc Simplo GmbH *v.* Sepia Products Inc (2000) 23(3) I.P.D. 23021; *Times*, February 2, 2000, Ch D .   *Digested,* 00/**3590**
Montagu *v.* Browning; *sub nom* Montague *v.* Browning [1954] 1 W.L.R. 1039; [1954] 2 All E.R. 601; 98 S.J. 492, CA. . . . .   *Digested,* 54/**2833**:
Considered, 98/4367: *Distinguished,* 70/2463
Montagu Evans (A Firm) *v.* Young 2000 S.L.T. 1083; 2000 G.W.D. 24-912; *Times*, September 19, 2000, OH . . . .   *Digested,* 00/**5927**
Montague *v.* Browning see Montagu *v.* Browning
Montana *v.* Claro Sol SA (C74/97) see Francisco Hernandez Vidal SA *v.* Perez (C127/96)
Montana *v.* Secretary of State for the Home Department see R. (on the application of Montana) *v.* Secretary of State for the Home Department
MONTAZS Trade Mark [2001] E.T.M.R. CN4, Legf Bir (H)
Montblanc Simplo GmbH *v.* Sepia Products Inc see Mont Blanc Simplo GmbH *v.* Sepia Products Inc
Montecatini SpA *v.* Commission of the European Communities (C235/92) [1999] E.C.R. I-4539; [2001] 4 C.M.L.R. 18, ECJ (6th Chamber) . . . .   *Digested,* 01/**2463**
Montedipe SpA *v.* Commission of the European Communities (T14/89) see Huls AG *v.* Commission of the European Communities (C199/92 P)
MONTEDISON/Hydraulic fluids (T207/91) [2000] E.P.O.R. 108, EPO (Technical Bd App)
    Digested, 00/**3657**
Monteith *v.* Clarke [1993] N.I. 376, QBD . . . .   *Followed,* 99/998
Montex Holdings Ltd *v.* Controller of Patents, Designs and Trade Marks [2000] E.T.M.R. 658, HC (Irl) . . . .   *Digested,* 00/**3781**
Montgomery *v.* HM Advocate; *sub nom* HM Advocate *v.* Montgomery (David Shields); Coulter *v.* HM Advocate [2001] 2 W.L.R. 779; 2001 S.C. (P.C.) 1; 2001 S.L.T. 37; 2000 S.C.C.R. 1044; [2001] U.K.H.R.R. 124; 9 B.H.R.C. 641; 2000 G.W.D. 40-1487; *Times*, December 6, 2000, PC (Sc) . . . .   *Digested,* 01/**6371**:
Previous proceedings, 00/6068
Montgomery *v.* Johnson Underwood Ltd; *sub nom* Johnson Underwood Ltd *v.* Montgomery [2001] EWCA Civ 318; [2001] I.C.R. 819; [2001] I.R.L.R. 269; (2001) 98(20) L.S.G. 40; *Times*, March 16, 2001; *Independent*, May 7, 2001 (C.S), CA; reversing EAT/509/98, EAT . . . .   *Digested,* 01/**2264**
Montgomery *v.* Sabella Ltd see Sabella Ltd *v.* Montgomery
Montin Ltd, Re [1999] 1 B.C.L.C 663, Ch D . . . .   *Digested,* 99/**3271**:
Applied, 99/3265
Montique *v.* Queen, The see Daley *v.* Queen, The
Montres Rolex SA *v.* Fogtmann [2001] E.T.M.R. 41, SH (DK)
Montrod Ltd *v.* Grundkotter Fleischvertriebs GmbH [2001] EWCA Civ 1954, CA; reversing in part [2001] 1 All E.R. (Comm) 368; [2001] C.L.C. 466, QBD (Comm Ct) . . . .   *Digested,* 01/**378**
Montrose Investments *v.* Orion Nominees see Monrose Investments Ltd *v.* Orion Nominees
Montupet (UK) Ltd *v.* Nolan [1997] N.I. 83, Ch D (NI) . . . .   *Digested,* 99/**5286**
Moody *v.* Tyler (Inspector of Taxes) [2000] S.T.C. 296; 72 T.C. 536; [2000] B.T.C. 128; [2000] S.T.I. 501, Ch D . . . .   *Digested,* 00/**5019**
Moody Jersey Settlement, Re . . . .   *Followed,* 00/5261

Mooney (A Minor) v. Sait (Unreported, November 26, 1997), CC (Torquay & Ntn Abbott) [*Ex rel.* Amanda Drane, Barrister, 4 King's Bench Walk, Temple, London] . . . . *Digested,* 98/**1551**
Mooney v. Cardiff Justices see Mooney v. Cardiff Magistrates Court
Mooney v. Cardiff Magistrates Court; *sub nom* Mooney v. Cardiff Justices (2000) 164 J.P. 220; (2000) 164 J.P.N. 283; (1999) 96(42) L.S.G. 40; *Times,* November 17, 1999 ; *Independent,* December 6, 1999 (C.S.), QBD . . . . *Digested,* 99/**984**
Moor v. Anglo Italian Bank (1878-79) L.R. 10 Ch. D. 681, Ch D . . . . *Applied,* 01/3772
Moorcock, The (1889) L.R. 14 P.D. 64; [1886-90] All E.R. Rep. 530, CA; affirming (1888) L.R. 13 P.D. 157, PDAD . . . . *Applied,* 83/2064,
93/2407: *Considered,* 76/1532, 86/421, 98/2492: *Distinguished,* 80/1643:
Doubted, 47-51/1756: *Referred to,* 84/1935, 85/1929
Moore (CICB: Quantum: 1998), Re (Unreported, August 4, 1998), CICB (London) [*Ex rel.* Christopher Hough, Barrister, 199 Strand, London] . . . . *Digested,* 98/**1562**
Moore v. Buchanan; *sub nom* Buchanan v. Moore-Pataleena [1968] 1 W.L.R. 103, HL; affirming [1967] 1 W.L.R. 1341; [1967] 3 All E.R. 273; (1967) 111 S.J. 772, CA; reversing *Times,* June 20, 1967 . . . . *Digested,* 68/**3122**:
Followed, 95/4068, 98/13
Moore v. Craven (1871-72) L.R. 7 Ch. App. 94 (Note), CA in Chancery . . . . *Considered,* 99/3444:
Followed, 96/764
Moore v. Gadd see Farmizer (Products) Ltd, Re
Moore v. Hopwood (Unreported, January 15, 1999), CC (Lincoln) [*Ex rel.* Paul G Kirtley, Barrister, 37 Park Square, Leeds] . . . . *Digested,* 99/**1472**
Moore v. James (Unreported, September 19, 2000), CC (Birkenhead) [*Ex rel.* Hill Dickinson, Solicitors, Pearl Assurance House, Derby Square, Liverpool] . . . . *Digested,* 01/**483**
Moore v. Piretta PTA Ltd [1999] 1 All E.R. 174; [1998] C.L.C. 992; [1998] E.C.C. 392; [1999] Eu. L.R. 32; (1998) 17 Tr. L.R. 161; *Times,* May 11, 1998, QBD . . . . *Digested,* 98/**113**:
Followed, 99/5629
Moore v. Secretary of State for the Environment, Transport and the Regions (1999) 77 P. & C.R. 114; [1998] 2 P.L.R. 65; [1998] J.P.L. 877; [1998] N.P.C. 20; *Times,* February 18, 1998, CA . . . . *Digested,* 98/**4169**:
Applied, 99/4241
Moore v. Thompson Holidays Ltd (Unreported, September 10, 1998), CC (Worcester) [*Ex rel.* Dominic Bayne, Barrister, Plowden Buildings, Temple, London] . . . . *Digested,* 98/**1425**
Moore v. United Kingdom; *sub nom* Gordon v. United Kingdom (2000) 29 E.H.R.R. 728, ECHR . . . . *Digested,* 00/**3215**
Moore v. Wm Morrison Supermarkets Plc, CC (Wakefield) [*Ex rel.* Tom Nossiter, Barrister, Park Lane Chambers, Leeds] . . . . *Digested,* 01/**1727**
Moore v. Zerfahs [1999] Lloyd's Rep. P.N. 144, CA . . . . *Digested,* 99/**3955**
Moores v. Bude-Stratton Town Council [2001] I.C.R. 271; [2000] I.R.L.R. 676; (2001) 3 L.G.L.R. 17; [2001] B.L.G.R. 129, EAT . . . . *Digested,* 00/**2110**
Moores v. Yakeley Associates Ltd BENF1998/1589/A2, CA; affirming (2000) 2 T.C.L.R. 146; 62 Con. L.R. 76, QBD (T&CC) . . . . *Digested,* 00/**810**
Moorgate Mercantile Co Ltd v. Twitchings [1977] A.C. 890; [1976] 3 W.L.R. 66; [1976] 2 All E.R. 641; [1976] R.T.R. 437; 120 S.J. 470, HL; reversing [1976] Q.B. 225; [1975] 3 W.L.R. 286; [1975] 3 All E.R. 314; [1975] R.T.R. 528; 119 S.J. 559, CA . . . . *Digested,* 76/**1343**:
Applied, 89/2554, 90/4026, 99/4203: *Considered,* 82/1145
Moran, Re see Attorney General's Reference (No.25 of 2001), Re
Moran v. Crown Prosecution Service (2000) 164 J.P. 562, QBD . . . . *Digested,* 00/**908**
Moran v. Lloyds [1983] Q.B. 542; [1983] 2 W.L.R. 672; [1983] 2 All E.R. 200; [1983] 1 Lloyd's Rep. 472; [1983] Com. L.R. 132, CA; affirming [1983] 1 Lloyd's Rep. 51; [1982] Com. L.R. 258, QBD (Comm Ct) . . . . *Digested,* 83/**147**:
Applied, 89/103, 98/234: *Considered,* 00/229
Morant v. Amtico Co Ltd (1998) 98(2) Q.R. 6, CC (Coventry) . . . . *Digested,* 98/**1634**
Morcom v. Campbell-Johnson [1956] 1 Q.B. 106; [1955] 3 W.L.R. 497; [1955] 3 All E.R. 264; 99 S.J. 745, CA . . . . *Digested,* 55/**2354**:
Applied, 67/4659, 68/3365, 75/1850, 98/3627
Morecambe and Heysham Corp v. Warwick 56 L.G.R. 283; 9 P. & C.R. 307, DC . . . . . . *Digested,* 58/**3330**:
Followed, 00/4497
Morel v. France (31430/96) (2001) 33 E.H.R.R. 47, ECHR
Morera-Loftus v. Wray Castle Ltd [1999] Lloyd's Rep. Med. 159, QBD . . . . *Digested,* 99/**3993**
Morfoot v. WF Smith & Co [2001] Lloyd's Rep. P.N. 658, Ch D
Morgan v. BBC (1998) 21 (2) I.P.D. 21020, HC
Morgan v. Brith Gof Cyf [2001] I.C.R. 978, EAT . . . . *Digested,* 01/**2270**
Morgan v. Croydon LBC see R. v. Croydon Magistrates Court Ex p. Morgan
Morgan v. Ford Motor Co Ltd (Unreported, June 6, 2000), CC (Bridgend) [*Ex rel.* Michael Brace, Barrister, 33 Park Place, Cardiff] . . . . *Digested,* 00/**1680**
Morgan v. Legal Aid Board [2000] 1 W.L.R. 1657; [2000] 3 All E.R. 974; [2001] 1 Costs L.R. 57; (2000) 97(21) L.S.G. 40; (2000) 150 N.L.J. 583; (2000) 144 S.J.L.B. 218; *Times,* April 24, 2000, Ch D . . . . *Digested,* 00/**3996**
Morgan v. Lloyds Bank Plc [1998] Lloyd's Rep. Bank. 73; [1998] N.P.C. 34, CA . . . . . . *Digested,* 98/**4354**
Morgan Grenfell & Co Ltd v. Istituto per i Servizi Assicurativi del Commercio Estero see Morgan Grenfell & Co Ltd v. SACE

Morgan Grenfell & Co Ltd v. SACE; sub nom Morgan Grenfell & Co Ltd v. Sezione
Speciale per l'Assicurazione del Credito all'Esportazione; Morgan Grenfell & Co
Ltd v. Istituto per i Servizi Assicurativi del Commercio Estero [2001] EWCA Civ
1932, CA; affirming in part1996 Folio Nos.786 & 787, QBD. . . . . *Digested*, 99/**3388**
Morgan Grenfell & Co Ltd v. Sezione Speciale per l'Assicurazione del Credito
all'Esportazione see Morgan Grenfell & Co Ltd v. SACE
Morgan Sindall Plc v. Sawston Farms (Cambs) Ltd [1999] 1 E.G.L.R. 90; [1999] 07
E.G. 135; [1998] E.G.C.S. 177; [1998] N.P.C. 159, CA; affirming [1997] E.G.C.S.
118, Ch D . . . . *Digested*, 99/**4403**
Morgan Stanley UK Group v. Puglisi Cosentino [1998] C.L.C. 481, QBD (Comm Ct) . . . *Digested*, 98/**2533**
Morgans v. DPP [2001] 1 A.C. 315; [2000] 2 W.L.R. 386; [2000] 2 All E.R. 522;
[2000] 2 Cr. App. R. 113; [1998-99] Info. T.L.R. 415; [2000] Crim. L.R. 576;
[2000] C.O.D. 98; (2000) 97(9) L.S.G. 39; *Times*, February 18, 2000, HL;
reversing in part [1999] 1 W.L.R. 968; [1999] 2 Cr. App. R. 99; (1999) 163 J.P.
543; [1998-99] Info. T.L.R. 93; [1999] Masons C.L.R. 102; [1999] Crim. L.R.
490; (1999) 163 J.P.N. 872; *Times*, December 29, 1998, QBD . . . . *Digested*, 00/**920**:
Distinguished, 01/980

Morgans v. Launchbury see Launchbury v. Morgans
Morgans v. Needham (1999) 96(44) L.S.G. 41; (1999) 143 S.J.L.B. 278; *Times*,
November 5, 1999, CA . . . . *Digested*, 99/**320**
Morguard Investments Ltd v. De Savoye [1990] 3 S.C.R. 1077 . . . . *Applied*, 00/783:
Followed, 01/803

Moriarty v. Fox [2001] 4 Q.R. 14, CC (Chichester) [*Ex rel.* Peter Collins, Barrister,
Solent Chambers, 1st Floor, Customs House, 9-10 Hampshire Terrace,
Portsmouth] . . . . *Digested*, 01/**1729**
Moritz, Re; sub nom Midland Bank Executor and Trustee Co v. Forbes [1960] Ch. 251;
[1959] 3 W.L.R. 939; [1959] 3 All E.R. 767; 103 S.J. 962, Ch D . . . . *Digested*, 59/**2591**:
Approved, 98/3302: *Considered*, 64/3019, 77/2496, 78/1415
Morland v. Secretary of State for the Environment, Transport and the Regions [1999]
J.P.L. 622, CA . . . . *Digested*, 99/**4271**
Morley v. Secretary of State for Social Security [2001] EWHC Admin 206;
Independent, April 9, 2001 (C.S), QBD (Admin Ct)
Morley v. Secretary of State for Social Security (C328/91) see Secretary of State for
Social Security v. Thomas (C328/91)
Morley v. Sussex Coastline Buses Ltd (Unreported, December 9, 1999), CC
(Southampton) [*Ex rel.* Nigel S Brockley, Barrister, Bracton Chambers, Bell
House, 8 Bell Yard, London] . . . . *Digested*, 00/**1580**
Morley Retreat & Conference House v. Customs and Excise Commissioners [2001] S.T.I.
1291, V&DTr
Morning Star Cooperative Society Ltd v. Express Newspapers Ltd [1979] F.S.R. 113,
Ch D . . . . *Digested*, 79/**2696**:
Applied, 98/3497
Morosi v. Broadcasting Station 2GB Pty Ltd [1980] 2 N.S.W.L.R. 418, CA (NSW) . . . . *Applied*, 99/1623
Morphites v. Bernasconi [2001] 2 B.C.L.C. 1, Ch D (Companies Ct) . . . . *Digested*, 01/**3744**
Morran v. Glasgow Council of Tenants Associations 1997 S.C. 279; 1997 S.L.T. 1133;
1997 S.C.L.R. 841; [1998] I.R.L.R. 67; 1997 G.W.D. 20-977, 1 Div . . . . *Digested*, 97/**6006**
Morrells of Oxford Ltd v. Oxford United Football Club Ltd [2001] Ch. 459; [2001] 2
W.L.R. 128; (2001) 81 P. & C.R. 13; [2001] 1 E.G.L.R. 76; [2001] 04 E.G. 147;
[2000] E.G.C.S. 96; (2000) 144 S.J.L.B. 248; [2000] N.P.C. 86; (2001) 81 P. &
C.R. D3; *Times*, August 15, 2000; *Independent*, October 5, 2000, CA; affirming
[2000] 3 E.G.L.R. 70; [2000] 45 E.G. 176; [2000] E.G.C.S. 73; (2000) 97(25)
L.S.G. 42, Ch D . . . . *Digested*, 00/**4628**
Morris, Re; sub nom Lloyds Bank v. Peake [1971] P. 62; [1970] 2 W.L.R. 865; [1970]
1 All E.R. 1057; (1969) 113 S.J. 923; *Times*, November 11, 1969, PDAD . . . . *Digested*, 70/**2935**:
Applied, 71/12165, 75/3573, 76/2896, 01/5167
Morris (Deceased), Re see Special Trustees for Great Ormond Street Hospital for Children v.
Rushin
Morris v. Agrichemicals Ltd see Bank of Credit and Commerce International SA (In
Liquidation) (No.8), Re
Morris v. Bank of America National Trust (Appeal against Striking Out) [2000] 1 All
E.R. 954; [2000] B.C.C. 1076; [2001] 1 B.C.L.C. 771; [2000] B.P.I.R. 83; (2000)
97(3) L.S.G. 37; (2000) 144 S.J.L.B. 48; *Times*, January 25, 2000, CA . . . . *Digested*, 00/**551**
Morris v. Banque Arabe et Internationale d'Investissement SA (No.1) [2000] C.P. Rep.
65; [2001] I.L.Pr. 37; (1999-2000) 2 I.T.E.L.R. 492; (2000) 97(1) L.S.G. 24;
Times, December 23, 1999, Ch D (Companies Ct) . . . . *Digested*, 00/**315**
Morris v. Banque Arabe Internationale d'Investissement SA (No.2); sub nom Bank of
Credit and Commerce International SA, Re; Banque Arabe Internationale
d'Investissement v. Morris; BCCI v. Morris [2001] 1 B.C.L.C. 263; (2000)
97(42) L.S.G. 43; *Times*, October 26, 2000, Ch D . . . . *Digested*, 00/**675**
Morris v. Coal Product Holdings Ltd (Unreported, November 24, 1999), CC (Barnsley)
[*Ex rel.* Richard Gregory, Barrister, 24 The Ropewalk, Nottingham] . . . . *Digested*, 00/**1661**
Morris v. Customs and Excise Commissioners see Han (t/a Murdishaw Supper Bar) v.
Customs and Excise Commissioners
Morris (t/a Reward) v. Customs and Excise Commissioners [2001] S.T.I. 230, V&DTr

Morris v. CW Martin & Sons Ltd; *sub nom* Morris v. Martin [1966] 1 Q.B. 716; [1965]
　3 W.L.R. 276; [1965] 2 All E.R. 725; [1965] 2 Lloyd's Rep. 63; 109 S.J. 451,
　CA . . . . *Digested*, 65/**178**:
　　　　　　　　　　　　　Applied, 66/11152, 67/169, 67/395, 70/119, 71/11071, 74/2582, 84/2320,
　　　　　　　　　　　　　01/5359: *Approved*, 78/136: *Considered*, 74/3548, 88/167, 90/4059,
　　　　　　　　　　　　　91/3213: *Distinguished*, 69/510
Morris v. European Islamic Ltd 002828 of 1999, Ch D (Companies Ct) . . . . *Digested*, 99/**3283**
Morris v. Grayson Automators [2001] 5 Q.R. 12, CC (Basingstoke) [*Ex rel.* Richard
　Case, Barrister, 3 Paper Buildings, Temple, London] . . . . *Digested*, 01/**1751**
Morris v. Harris [1927] A.C. 252, HL . . . . *Applied*, 47-51/1380,
　　　　　　　　　　54/477, 94/412: *Considered*, 97/652: *Distinguished*, 52/480, 86/298, 87/338,
　　　　　　　　　　98/376
Morris v. Hateley see Legal Costs Negotiators Ltd, Re
Morris v. John Grose Group Ltd [1998] I.C.R. 655; [1998] I.R.L.R. 499, EAT . . . . *Digested*, 98/**2214**
Morris v. KLM Royal Dutch Airlines; *sub nom* KLM Royal Dutch Airlines v. Morris
　[2001] EWCA Civ 790; [2001] 3 W.L.R. 351; [2001] 3 All E.R. 126; [2001] 2 All
　E.R. (Comm) 153; [2001] C.L.C. 1460; (2001) 98(26) L.S.G. 43; (2001) 151
　N.L.J. 851; (2001) 145 S.J.L.B. 142; *Times*, June 15, 2001; *Independent*, May 23,
　2001; *Daily Telegraph*, May 22, 2001, CA . . . . *Digested*, 01/**5385**:
　　　　　　　　　　　　　　　　　　　　　　　　　　　　　　　　　　Considered, 01/5386
Morris v. Knight (Unreported, October 22, 1998), CC (Bournemouth) [*Ex rel.* Jeremy
　Burns, Barrister, 17 Carlton Crescent, Southampton] . . . . *Digested*, 99/**3682**
Morris v. Lord Chancellor [2000] 1 Costs L.R. 88, QBD . . . . *Digested*, 00/**1037**
Morris v. Martin see Morris v. CW Martin & Sons Ltd
Morris v. Molesworth see Morris v. Wentworth-Stanley
Morris v. Morgan [1998] B.P.I.R. 764, CA . . . . *Digested*, 98/**3285**
Morris v. Patel [1987] 1 E.G.L.R. 75; (1987) 281 E.G. 419, CA . . . . *Digested*, 87/**2133**:
　　　　　　　　　　　　　　　　　　　Applied, 98/3613: *Considered*, 96/3827
Morris v. Rayners Enterprises Inc see Bank of Credit and Commerce International SA
　(In Liquidation) (No.8), Re
Morris v. Secretary of State for the Environment (1975) 31 P. & C.R. 216, DC . . . . *Digested*, 76/**2696**:
　　　　　　　　　　　　　　　　　　　　　　　　　　　　　　　　　Followed, 99/4202
Morris v. State Bank of India see Bank of Credit and Commerce International SA (In
　Liquidation) (No.13), Re
Morris v. United Kingdom (A/115) see Monnell v. United Kingdom (A/115)
Morris v. Walsh Western UK Ltd [1997] I.R.L.R. 562, EAT . . . . *Digested*, 98/**2231**
Morris v. Wentworth-Stanley; *sub nom* Morris v. Molesworth [1999] Q.B. 1004;
　[1999] 2 W.L.R. 470; [1999] 1 F.L.R. 83; (1998) 95(39) L.S.G. 34; (1998) 148
　N.L.J. 1551; (1998) 142 S.J.L.B. 258; *Times*, October 2, 1998, CA . . . . *Digested*, 98/**4067**
Morris v. West Hartlepool Steam Navigation Co Ltd [1956] A.C. 552; [1956] 1 W.L.R.
　177; [1956] 1 All E.R. 385; [1956] 1 Lloyd's Rep. 76; 100 S.J. 129, HL; reversing
　[1954] 2 Lloyd's Rep. 507; *Times*, December 10, 1954, CA . . . . *Digested*, 56/**5864**:
　　　　　　　　　　　Applied, 59/2244, 72/2340, 72/3938, 97/6295, 99/2554:
　　　　　　　　　　　Approved, 59/2251: *Considered*, 88/2462: *Followed*, 68/2701
Morris Holmes Ltd v. South Ribble BC see Morris Homes Ltd v. South Ribble BC
Morris Homes Ltd v. South Ribble BC; *sub nom* Morris Holmes Ltd v. South Ribble BC
　[2001] J.P.L. 614 (Note), QBD
Morris, In the estate of see Special Trustees for Great Ormond Street Hospital for Children v.
　Rushin
Morrisey v. Borderdown Communication Ltd (Unreported, August 25, 1999), CC
　(Northampton) [*Ex rel.* Jeffrey Deegan, Barrister, Northampton Chambers, 22
　Albion Place, Northampton] . . . . *Digested*, 99/**1522**
Morrisey v. R. 9 B.H.R.C. 179, Sup Ct (Can) . . . . *Digested*, 01/**3487**
Morrison v. Bewise Plc (Unreported, December 1, 1997), CC (Portsmouth) [*Ex rel.*
　Alan Collins, Solicitor, Dyer Burdett & Co, 64 West Street, Havant, Hampshire] . *Digested*, 98/**1550**
Morrison v. Society of Lloyd's; Drummie v. Society of Lloyd's [2000] I.L.Pr. 92, QB
　(NB) . . . . *Digested*, 00/**740**
Morrison Holdings Ltd v. Manders Property (Wolverhampton) Ltd [1976] 1 W.L.R. 533;
　[1976] 2 All E.R. 205; (1975) 32 P. & C.R. 218; (1975) 120 S.J. 63, CA . . . . *Digested*, 76/**1534**:
　　　　　　　　　　　Considered, 87/2134, 89/2106: *Distinguished*, 92/2654, 98/3663:
　　　　　　　　　　　Followed, 96/3705
Morrison's Application, Re [1998] N.I. 68, QBD (NI) . . . . *Digested*, 99/**5438**
Morrissey v. Home Office [2000] 6 Q.R. 8, CC (Liverpool) [*Ex rel.* Titus Gibson,
　Barrister, Oriel Chambers, 14 Water Street, Liverpool] . . . . *Digested*, 00/**1602**
Morrow v. Safeway Stores Plc [2001] Emp. L.R. 1303, EAT
Morrow's Application, Re [2001] N.I. 261, QBD (NI) . . . . *Digested*, 01/**5842**
Morse v. Wiltshire CC [1998] I.C.R. 1023; [1998] I.R.L.R. 352; [1999] Disc. L.R. 40;
　(1998) 44 B.M.L.R. 58; *Times*, May 11, 1998, EAT . . . . *Digested*, 98/**2121**:
　　　　　　　　　　　　　　　　　　　　　　　　　　　　　　　　　Applied, 01/2240
Morson v. Netherlands (C35/82); Jhanjan v. Netherlands (C36/82) [1982] E.C.R.
　3723; [1983] 2 C.M.L.R. 221, ECJ . . . . *Digested*, 83/**1501**:
　　　　　　　　　　　　　　　　　　　　　　　Applied, 99/5271: *Followed*, 99/2094
Mortgage Agency Services Ltd v. Bal (1998) 95(28) L.S.G. 31, CA
Mortgage Corp v. Alexander Johnson (A Firm), *Times*, September 22, 1999, Ch D . . . . . *Digested*, 99/**542**

Mortgage Corp v. Law Society see R. v. Law Society Ex p. Mortgage Corp
Mortgage Corp v. Lewis Silkin (A Firm) see Mortgage Corp v. Shaire
Mortgage Corp v. Shaire; Mortgage Corp v. Lewis Silkin (A Firm) [2001] Ch. 743;
    [2001] 3 W.L.R. 639; [2001] 4 All E.R. 364; [2000] 1 F.L.R. 973; [2000] 2
    F.C.R. 222; [2000] B.P.I.R. 483; [2000] 80 P. & C.R. 280; [2000] 3 E.G.L.R.
    131; [2000] W.T.L.R. 357; [2000] Fam. Law 402; [2000] E.G.C.S. 35; (2000)
    97(11) L.S.G. 37; Times, March 21, 2000, Ch D .... *Digested*, 00/**4659**
Mortgage Corp Plc v. Halifax (SW) Ltd (No.1), Times, July 15, 1998, QBD .... *Digested*, 98/**4348**
Mortgage Corp Plc v. Halifax (SW) Ltd (No.2) [1999] Lloyd's Rep. P.N. 159, QBD .... *Digested*, 99/**3946**
Mortgage Corp Plc v. Lambert & Co [2000] Lloyd's Rep. Bank. 207; [2000] B.L.R.
    265; [2000] Lloyd's Rep. P.N. 624; [2000] P.N.L.R. 820; Times, April 24, 2000,
    CA; affirming [1999] Lloyd's Rep. P.N. 947; [1999] 3 E.G.L.R. 59; [1999] 42
    E.G. 138; [1999] E.G.C.S. 109; Times, October 11, 1999, Ch D .... *Digested*, 00/**533**
Mortgage Corp Plc v. Rhys & Partners 1996-M-No.6538, Ch D .... *Digested*, 98/**333**
Mortgage Corp Plc v. Sandoes [1997] P.N.L.R. 263; (1997) 94(3) L.S.G. 28; (1997)
    141 S.J.L.B. 30; Times, December 27, 1996, CA....................... *Digested*, 97/**783**:
                        Applied, 97/625, 97/730: *Considered*, 97/462, 97/504, 99/432:
                            Distinguished, 97/272: *Followed*, 98/354, 98/384
Mortgage Corp Plc v. Solicitors Indemnity Fund Ltd [1998] P.N.L.R. 73, Ch D .... *Digested*, 98/**4022**
Mortgage Express v. McDonnell; sub nom Mortgage Express v. Robson [2001] EWCA
    Civ 887; [2001] 2 All E.R. (Comm) 886, CA
Mortgage Express v. Robson see Mortgage Express v. McDonnell
Mortgage Express Ltd v. Bowerman & Partners (No.1) [1996] 2 All E.R. 836; [1996]
    E.C.C. 228; [1996] P.N.L.R. 62; [1996] 1 E.G.L.R. 126; [1996] 04 E.G. 126;
    [1995] E.G.C.S. 129; [1995] N.P.C. 129; Times, August 1, 1995, CA; affirming
    [1994] 34 E.G. 116; [1994] E.G.C.S. 89; [1994] N.P.C. 68; Times, May 19, 1994;
    Independent, June 10, 1994, Ch D .... *Digested*, 96/**4497**:
                        Applied, 98/4027, 99/4379: *Considered*, 96/3916, 97/3373, 97/3829,
                                98/4020, 98/4026, 99/4037, 00/4271
Mortgage Express Ltd v. Bowerman & Partners (No.2) see Banque Bruxelles Lambert
    SA v. Eagle Star Insurance Co Ltd
Mortgage Express Ltd v. S Newman & Co (No.2) [2000] Lloyd's Rep. P.N. 745;
    [2001] P.N.L.R. 5, CA; reversing [2000] P.N.L.R. 298; [1999] E.G.C.S. 123,
    Ch D .... *Digested*, 00/**4031**
Mortgage Express Ltd v. S Newman & Co (No.3) [2001] Lloyd's Rep. P.N. 669, Ch D
Mortgage Funding Corp Plc v. Kashef-Hamadani (Unreported, April 23, 1993), CA .... *Applied*, 99/**409**
Mortgage Funding Corp Plc v. Tisdall Nelson Nari & Co [1998] P.N.L.R. 81, QBD (OR) . *Digested*, 98/**4015**
Mortimer v. Devon Valuation Tribunal [2000] R.V.R. 310, QBD................. *Digested*, 01/**430**
Mortimer v. Labour Party, Independent, February 28, 2000 (C.S.), Ch D
Morton (CICA: Quantum: 2000), Re (Unreported, July 13, 2000), CICA (York) [Ex rel.
    Jonathan Saul Godfrey, Barrister, St. Paul's Chambers, 23 Park Square South,
    Leeds] .... *Digested*, 00/**1626**
Morton v. South Ayrshire Council see South Ayrshire Council v. Morton
Morton-Norwich Products Inc v. Customs and Excise Commissioners see Norwich
    Pharmacal Co v. Customs and Excise Commissioners
Morts Dock & Engineering Co v. Overseas Tankship (UK) Ltd see Overseas Tankship
    (UK) Ltd v. Morts Dock & Engineering Co (The Wagon Mound)
Moschi, Re; sub nom B Ex p. Moschi v. Inland Revenue Commissioners 35 T.C. 92;
    (1953) 32 A.T.C. 495; [1954] T.R. 59.................................... *Digested*, 54/**229**:
                        Applied, 01/592: *Previous proceedings*, 52/1623
Moschi v. Lep Air Services Ltd; sub nom Moschi v. Rolloswin Investments Ltd; Lep
    Air Services v. Rolloswin Investments [1973] A.C. 331; [1972] 2 W.L.R. 1175;
    [1972] 2 All E.R. 393; 116 S.J. 372, HL; affirming [1971] 1 W.L.R. 934; [1971] 3
    All E.R. 45, CA .... *Digested*, 72/**1628**:
                        Applied, 80/1050, 90/4024, 01/961: *Considered*, 91/1870, 92/2204, 96/2905
Moschi v. Rolloswin Investments Ltd see Moschi v. Lep Air Services Ltd
Moseley v. London Underground Ltd 98/NJ/1250, QBD .... *Digested*, 99/**1467**
Moseneke v. Master of the High Court 10 B.H.R.C. 117, Const Ct (SA) .... *Digested*, 01/**5151**
Moser v. Land Baden-Wurttemberg (C180/83) [1984] E.C.R. 2539; [1984] 3
    C.M.L.R. 720, ECJ... *Digested*, 85/**1411**:
                                                                  Applied, 99/5271
Moses v. Trinidad and Tobago [1997] A.C. 53; [1996] 3 W.L.R. 534; (1996) 140
    S.J.L.B. 214, PC (Trin) .... *Digested*, 96/**1484**:
                        Applied, 00/984: *Followed*, 00/983: *Referred to*, 00/985
Moses & Cohen Ltd, Re [1957] 1 W.L.R. 1007; [1957] 3 All E.R. 232; 101 S.J. 780, Ch D
                                                                  Digested, 57/**445**:
                                                    Cited, 99/603: *Followed*, 73/339
Moskovsky Nauchno-Issledovatelsky Institut Mikrokhirurgii Glaza's Application
    Unreported.. *Followed*, 99/**3469**
Moss v. Elphick [1910] 1 K.B. 846, CA; affirming [1910] 1 K.B. 465, KBD .... *Applied*, 88/**2672**:
                                                                  Disapproved, 00/6604
Moss Bros Group Plc v. CSC Properties Ltd [1999] E.G.C.S. 47, Ch D
Moss, In the Estate of see Larke v. Nugus
Mother v. Inland Revenue Commissioners [1999] S.T.C. (S.C.D.) 278, Sp Comm...... *Applied*, 01/5314

MOTHERCARE Trade Mark [1996] I.R. 51
Mothew *v.* Bristol and West Building Society see Bristol and West Building Society *v.* Mothew (t/a Stapley & Co)
Motis Exports Ltd *v.* Dampskibsselskabet AF 1912 A/S (No.1); *sub nom* Dampskibsselskabet AF 1912 A/S *v.* Motis Exports Ltd [2000] 1 All E.R. (Comm) 91; [2000] 1 Lloyd's Rep. 211; [2000] C.L.C. 515; (2000) 97(3) L.S.G. 37; *Times,* January 26, 2000, CA; affirming [1999] 1 All E.R. (Comm) 571; [1999] 1 Lloyd's Rep. 837; [1999] C.L.C. 914; *Times,* March 31, 1999, QBD (Comm Ct) . . . . *Digested,* 00/**4680**
Motor Crown Petroleum Ltd *v.* SJ Berwin & Co; *sub nom* SJ Berwin & Co *v.* Motor Crown Petroleum Ltd [2000] Lloyd's Rep. P.N. 438; [2000] N.P.C. 26, CA; reversing in part1624, QBD . . . . *Digested,* 00/**4264**
MOTOR LODGE Trade Mark [1965] F.S.R. 41; [1965] R.P.C. 35 . . . . *Referred to,* 98/3540
Motor Vehicle Distribution System (I ZR 130/96), Re [2001] E.C.C.16, BGH (Ger)
Motorola Ltd *v.* Davidson [2001] I.R.L.R. 4, EAT . . . . *Digested,* 01/**6467**
Motorola New Zealand Superannuation Fund, Re (2000-01) 3 I.T.E.L.R. 578, HC (NZ)
MOTOROLA/Divisional application (T441/92) [1998] E.P.O.R. 218, EPO (Technical Bd App)
MOTOROLA/Isolated mistake-restitution (J02/86 and J03/86) [1987] E.P.O.R. 394, EPO (Legal Bd App) . . . . *Applied,* 00/3610:
                                       Followed, 00/3618
Mott *v.* Environment Agency, *Times,* January 25, 1999, CA . . . . *Digested,* 99/**2562**
Mouat *v.* DPP see R. (on the application of Ebrahim) *v.* Feltham Magistrates Court
Mouchell Superannuation Fund Trustees *v.* Oxfordshire CC [1992] 1 P.L.R. 97, CA . . . . . *Digested,* 92/**4344**:
                          Applied, 99/4240: *Referred to,* 95/4858
Moulins et Huileries de Pont-a-Mousson SA *v.* Office National Interprofessionnel des Cereales (C124/76) see Firma Albert Ruckdeschel & Co *v.* Hauptzollamt Hamburg-St Annen (C117/76)
Moulsdale *v.* Quinn [2001] 6 Q.R. 9, CC (Rhyl) [*Ex rel.* Paul Clark, Barrister, Exchange Chambers, Pearl Assurance House, Liverpool] . . . . *Digested,* 01/**1619**
Mount *v.* Barker Austin [1998] P.N.L.R. 493, CA . . . . *Digested,* 98/**4023**
Mount *v.* Oldham Corp [1973] Q.B. 309; [1973] 2 W.L.R. 22; [1973] 1 All E.R. 26; 71 L.G.R.105; 116 S.J. 944, CA . . . . *Digested,* 73/**402**:
                                     Considered, 99/1801
Mount Banking Corp Ltd *v.* Brian Cooper & Co [1992] 2 E.G.L.R. 142; [1992] 35 E.G. 123; [1992] N.P.C. 99 . . . . *Digested,* 93/**2999**:
                     Applied, 94/3387, 95/3716: *Followed,* 98/4032
Mount Carmel Investments Ltd *v.* Thurlow [1988] 1 W.L.R. 1078; [1988] 3 All E.R. 129; (1989) 57 P. & C.R. 396, CA . . . . *Digested,* 89/**2278**:
                                     Applied, 01/4842
Mount Cook Land Ltd *v.* Hartley [2000] E.G.C.S. 26, Ch D
Mount Cook Land Ltd *v.* Spring House (Freehold) Ltd see Spring House (Freehold) Ltd *v.* Mount Cook Land Ltd
Mount Credit Corp Ltd *v.* Abbey National Estate Agency Ltd (t/a J Trevor & Sons) (1998) 95(2) L.S.G. 24, QBD (OR)
Mount Eden Land Ltd *v.* Prudential Assurance Co Ltd; *sub nom* Prudential Assurance Co Ltd *v.* Mount Eden Land Ltd (1997) 74 P. & C.R. 377; [1997] 1 E.G.L.R. 37; [1997] 14 E.G. 130; [1996] E.G.C.S.179; [1996] N.P.C.165, CA . . . . *Digested,* 97/**3269**:
                                     Applied, 99/3670
Mount Eden Land Ltd *v.* Straudley Investments Ltd see Straudley Investments Ltd *v.* Mount Eden Land Ltd (No.1)
Mountain *v.* Tarmac Quarry Products Ltd (Unreported, August 17, 1998), CC (Lincoln) [*Ex rel.* Sean Yates, Barrister, 10 Park Square, Leeds] . . . . *Digested,* 98/**593**
Mousaka Inc *v.* Golden Seagull Maritime Inc [2001] 2 All E.R. (Comm) 794; [2001] 2 Lloyd's Rep. 657; [2001] C.L.C. 1716; (2001) 151 N.L.J. 1317; *Times,* October 3, 2001, QBD (Comm Ct) . . . . *Digested,* 01/**332**
Mouzouros (CICA: Quantum: 2000), Re [2001] 3 Q.R. 8, CICAP [*Ex rel.* Alaric Wilson, Barrister, 11 Stone Buildings, London] . . . . *Digested,* 01/**1558**
Movrin *v.* Landesversicherungsanstalt Westfalen (C73/99) [2000] E.C.R. I-5625; [2000] 3 C.M.L.R. 689; [2000] C.E.C. 481, ECJ (6th Chamber) . . . . *Digested,* 00/**4859**
Mowan *v.* Wandsworth LBC (2001) 33 H.L.R. 56; [2001] B.L.G.R. 228; [2001] 3 E.G.C.S.133; [2001] E.H.L.R. Dig. 5, CA . . . . *Digested,* 01/**4197**
Mowlem Northern Ltd *v.* Watson [1990] I.C.R. 751; [1990] I.R.L.R. 500, EAT . . . . *Digested,* 91/**1658**:
                                     Followed, 99/2124
MPA Pharma *v.* Rhone-Poulenc (C232/94) see Bristol Myers Squibb *v.* Paranova (C427/93)
Mphahlele *v.* First National Bank of South Africa Ltd 6 B.H.R.C. 481, Const Ct (SA) . . . *Digested,* 99/**770**
MS *v.* Sweden (1999) 28 E.H.R.R. 313; 3 B.H.R.C. 248; (1999) 45 B.M.L.R. 133, ECHR . . . . *Digested,* 98/**3105**
MS & DF Blake & Sons *v.* Secretary of State for the Environment [1998] Env. L.R. 309, QBD . . . . *Digested,* 98/**4228**
MSC Mediterranean Shipping Co SA *v.* Delumar BVBA (The MSC Rosa M) [2000] 2 All E.R. (Comm) 458; [2000] 2 Lloyd's Rep. 399; [2000] C.L.C. 1525, QBD (Adm Ct) . . . . *Digested,* 00/**4744**

MSC Mediterranean Shipping Co SA v. Owners of the Tychy see MSC Mediterranean
Shipping Co SA v. Polish Ocean Lines (The Tychy) (No.2)
MSC Mediterranean Shipping Co SA v. Polish Ocean Lines (The Tychy) (No.1) [1999] 1
All E.R. (Comm.) 819; [1999] 2 Lloyd's Rep. 11; [1999] C.L.C. 1046; (1999)
96(18) L.S.G. 33; *Times,* April 30, 1999, CA; affirming TNS, QBD (Adm Ct) ....   *Digested,* 99/**4425**
MSC Mediterranean Shipping Co SA v. Polish Ocean Lines (The Tychy) (No.2); *sub nom*
MSC Mediterranean Shipping Co SA v. Owners of the Tychy; Polish Ocean
Lines Joint Stock Co (formerly Polish Ocean Lines) v. MSC Mediterranean
Shipping Co SA [2001] EWCA Civ 1198; [2001] 2 Lloyd's Rep. 403, CA;
reversing [2001] 1 Lloyd's Rep. 10, QBD (Adm Ct) ....   *Digested,* 01/**4950**
MTI Holdings Ltd, Re see MTI Trading Systems Ltd (In Administration), Re
MTI Trading Systems Ltd (In Administration), Re; *sub nom* MTI Holdings Ltd, Re [1998]
B.C.C. 400, CA; affirming [1997] B.C.C. 703; [1998] 2 B.C.L.C. 246, Ch D   *Digested,* 98/**3260**
(Companies Ct) ....   *Digested,* 98/**3263**
MTI Trading Systems Ltd v. Winter [1998] B.C.C. 591, Ch D (Companies Ct) ....
MTM Construction Ltd v. William Reid Engineering Ltd 1998 S.L.T. 211; 1997 S.C.L.R.
778; 1997 Rep. L.R. 27; 1997 G.W.D. 7-260; *Times,* April 22, 1997, OH ....   *Digested,* 97/**6073**
MTV Europe v. BMG Records (UK) Ltd [1997] 1 C.M.L.R. 867; [1997] Eu. L.R. 100,
CA; affirming [1995] 1 C.M.L.R. 437; [1995] E.C.C. 216, Ch D ....   *Digested,* 97/**855**:
Considered, 96/2806, 97/861, 01/442

Mubarak v. Dianoor International Ltd see Mubarak v. Mubarak
Mubarak v. Dianoor Jewels Ltd see Mubarak v. Mubarak
Mubarak v. Mubarak; *sub nom* Mubarak v. Mubarik; Murbarak v. Murbarak; Mubarak v.
Wani; Mubarak v. Dianoor International Ltd; Mubarak v. Dianoor Jewels Ltd
[2001] 1 F.L.R. 698; [2001] 1 F.C.R. 193; [2001] Fam. Law 178; *Daily Telegraph,*
January 23, 2001, CA; reversing [2001] 1 F.L.R. 673; [2001] Fam. Law 177;
Times, November 30, 2000, Fam Div ....   *Digested,* 01/**2637**:
Previous proceedings, 01/3707

Mubarak v. Wani see Mubarak v. Mubarak
Mugford v. Midland Bank Plc [1997] I.C.R. 399; [1997] I.R.L.R. 208, EAT ....   *Digested,* 97/**2255**:
Applied, 98/2234, 98/2238
Mukheiber v. Raath (2000) 52 B.M.L.R. 49, Sup Ct (SA) ....   *Digested,* 00/**4191**
Mulcahy (Eleanor), Re see R. v. Managers of South Western Hospital Ex p. M
Mulder, Re [1943] 2 All E.R. 150, CA ....   *Distinguished,*
84/3661,
85/3640, 01/5164

Mulgate Investments Ltd v. Excel (London) Ltd (Unreported, November 16, 2000), CC
(Leeds) [*Ex rel.* Mark Henley, Barrister, 9 Woodhouse Square, Leeds] ....   *Digested,* 01/**471**
Mulholland v. Midland Bank Plc see Alexander v. Midland Bank Plc
Mulholland v. Mitchell (No.1) [1971] A.C. 666; [1971] 2 W.L.R. 93; [1971] 1 All E.R.
307; 115 S.J. 15, HL ....   *Digested,* 71/**3232**:
Applied, 73/716, 82/1511, 83/981, 83/1855, 89/2102: *Considered,* 82/369,
83/359, 86/1083, 00/305: *Followed,* 98/323
Mulkerrins v. PricewaterhouseCoopers; *sub nom* Mulkerrins v. Pricewaterhouse
Coopers [2001] B.P.I.R. 106; (2001) 98(5) L.S.G. 36; *Times,* January 12, 2001,
CA; reversing [2000] B.P.I.R. 506; (2000) 97(14) L.S.G. 42; (2000) 144
S.J.L.B. 158; *Times,* March 29, 2000, Ch D ....   *Digested,* 01/**3738**
Mullan v. Birmingham City Council [2000] C.P. Rep. 61; *Times,* July 29, 1999, QBD ....   *Digested,* 99/**361**:
Considered, 00/376

Mullaney v. Chief Constable of West Midlands [2001] EWCA Civ 700; *Independent,*
July 9, 2001 (C.S); *Daily Telegraph,* May 22, 2001, CA
Mullard v. Ben Line Steamers Ltd [1970] 1 W.L.R. 1414; [1971] 2 All E.R. 424; [1970]
2 Lloyd's Rep. 121; 9 K.I.R. 111; 114 S.J. 570, CA; reversing [1969] 2 Lloyd's Rep.
631, QBD ....   *Digested,* 70/**1843**:
Considered, 73/1449: *Followed,* 99/3962
Mullen v. Conoco Ltd [1998] Q.B. 382; [1997] 3 W.L.R. 1032; (1997) 94(17) L.S.G.
25; *Times,* April 30, 1997, CA ....   *Digested,* 97/**623**:
Applied, 01/547
Muller v. Linsley & Mortimer [1996] P.N.L.R. 74; (1995) 92(3) L.S.G. 38; (1995) 139
S.J.L.B. 43; *Times,* December 8, 1994, CA ....   *Digested,* 94/**3674**:
Applied, 99/349, 01/1536
Muller & Co's Margarine Ltd v. Inland Revenue Commissioners see Inland Revenue
Commissioners v. Muller & Co's Margarine Ltd
Mulligan v. Halton BC (Unreported, September 15, 1999), CC (St Helens) [*Ex rel.*
Adam Fullwood, Barrister, Chambers of Ian MacDonald Q.C., Waldorf House,
Cooper Street, Manchester] ....   *Digested,* 99/**3674**
Mulligan v. Lambeth LBC (Unreported, January 20, 2000), CC (Lambeth) [*Ex rel.*
David Giles, Barrister, Verulam Chambers, Peer House, 8-14 Verulam Street,
London] ....   *Digested,* 00/**503**
Mullin v. Richards [1998] 1 W.L.R. 1304; [1998] 1 All E.R. 920; [1998] P.I.Q.R. P276,
CA ....   *Digested,* 98/**3994**:
Applied, 99/3981
Mullinger v. Maybourn; *sub nom* Mullinger v. President of West Sussex Valuation
Tribunal [1997] R.V.R. 260, QBD ....   *Digested,* 98/**4336**

Mullinger v. President of West Sussex Valuation Tribunal see Mullinger v. Maybourn

Mullings v. Boahemaah [1998] 1 Costs L.R. 57, Ch D

Multi Guarantee Co, Re [1987] B.C.L.C. 257; *Financial Times*, June 24, 1986, CA . . . . .　*Digested*, 87/**1427**: *Distinguished*, 99/3304

Multicultural Media Centre for the Millennium Ltd, Re see Multicultural Media Centre for the Millennium Ltd v. Millennium Commission

Multicultural Media Centre for the Millennium Ltd v. Millennium Commission; *sub nom* Multicultural Media Centre for the Millennium Ltd, Re [2001] EWCA Civ 1687; *Times*, November 16, 2001, CA; reversing in partCH 000 3029, Ch D . . . .　*Digested*, 01/**636**

Multiform Printing Ltd v. Customs and Excise Commissioners [1996] V. & D.R. 580, V&DTr. . . . .　*Digested*, 98/**4975**

Multigroup Bulgaria Holding AD v. Oxford Analytica Ltd [2001] E.M.L.R. 28, QBD . . . .　*Digested*, 01/**1835**

Multiple Marketing Ltd's Trade Mark [2001] E.T.M.R. CN2, OHIM (Cancellation Div)

Muman v. Nagasena [2000] 1 W.L.R. 299; [1999] 4 All E.R. 178, CA . . . .　*Digested*, 00/**296**

Mumford v. Ashe see Ashe (Trustee in Bankruptcy of Henry Samuel Mumford) v. Mumford (No.2)

Mumford v. Bank of Scotland see Smith v. Bank of Scotland

Munden v. Rising Star Travel Ltd [2001] 5 Q.R. 18, CC (Sheffield) [*Ex rel*. Dermot Hughes, Barrister, Paradise Chambers, 26 Paradise Square, Sheffield] . . . .　*Digested*, 01/**1815**

Mundy v. Hook (1998) 30 H.L.R. 551; [1997] E.G.C.S. 119; [1997] N.P.C. 121; (1997) 74 P. & C.R. D45, CA; affirming (Unreported, December 9, 1996), CC (Bromley) [*Ex rel*. Adrian M Davis, Barrister] . . . .　*Digested*, 97/**3247**

Mungroo v. Vintners LTA 1998/7721/3, CA　*Digested*, 99/**522**

Municipal Gas Supplier (KVR 9/96), Re [1999] E.C.C. 23, BGH (Ger)

Municipal Mutual Insurance Ltd v. Harrop [1998] 2 B.C.L.C. 540; [1998] O.P.L.R. 199, Ch D . . . .　*Digested*, 99/**638**

Municipal Mutual Insurance Ltd v. Sea Insurance Co Ltd [1998] C.L.C. 957; [1998] Lloyd's Rep. I.R. 421, CA; reversing in part [1996] L.R.L.R. 265; [1996] C.L.C. 1515; *Lloyd's List*, June 11, 1996 (I.D.), QBD (Comm Ct) . . . .　*Digested*, 98/**3401**: *Applied*, 99/3426

Municipality of Almelo v. NV Energibedrijf Ijsselmij (C393/92) see Gemeente Almelo v. Energiebedrijf Ijsellmij NV (C393/92)

Munir v. Jang Publications [1989] I.C.R. 1; [1989] I.R.L.R. 224, CA; affirming [1988] I.C.R. 214; (1987) 84 L.S.G. 2450, EAT . . . .　*Digested*, 89/**1435**: *Considered*, 98/2162

Munkenbeck & Marshall v. Kensington Hotel (1999) 15 Const. L.J. 231, QBD . . . .　*Digested*, 99/**783**

Munkenbeck & Marshall v. Kensington Hotel Ltd (Counterclaim) 78 Con. L.R. 171, QBD (T&CC)

Munkenbeck & Marshall v. McAlpine 44 Con. L.R. 30; [1995] E.G.C.S. 24, CA . . . . . .　*Digested*, 96/**742**: *Considered*, 00/2148

Munkenbeck & Marshall v. Regent Health & Fitness Club Ltd (No.1) 59 Con. L.R. 139; [1996] E.G.C.S. 36, CA . . . .　*Digested*, 96/**1143**

Munkenbeck & Marshall v. Regent Health & Fitness Club Ltd (No.2) 59 Con. L.R. 145, QBD (OR) . . . .　*Digested*, 98/**799**

Munn v. North West Water Ltd [2001] C.P. Rep. 48, CA . . . .　*Digested*, 00/**507**

Munro v. Porthkerry Park Holiday Estates (1984) 81 L.S.G. 1368; *Times*, March 9, 1984 .　*Digested*, 84/**2305**: *Considered*, 00/5626

Munro v. Premier Associates Ltd (2000) 80 P. & C.R. 439; (2000) 97(11) L.S.G. 40; *Independent*, March 30, 2000, Ch D . . . .　*Digested*, 00/**4624**

Munting v. Hammersmith and Fulham LBC (Unreported, November 26, 1997), CC (West London) [*Ex rel*. Jon Holbrook, Barrister, Two Garden Court, Middle Temple, London] . . . .　*Digested*, 98/**3017**

Munton v. Greater London Council; *sub nom* Munton v. Newham LBC [1976] 1 W.L.R. 649; [1976] 2 All E.R. 815; 74 L.G.R. 416; (1976) 32 P. & C.R. 269; (1976) 239 E.G. 43; 120 S.J. 149, CA; affirming (1974) 29 P. & C.R. 278, Lands Tr . . . . .　*Digested*, 76/**2850**: *Applied*, 82/356, 01/598: *Previous proceedings*, 75/347.1

Munton v. Newham LBC see Munton v. Greater London Council

Murat v. Customs and Excise Commissioners [1998] S.T.C. 923; [1998] B.T.C. 5325; [1998] B.V.C. 343; *Independent*, July 20, 1998 (C.S.), QBD . . . .　*Digested*, 98/**4886**

Murbarak v. Murbarak see Mubarak v. Mubarak

Murdoch v. Glacier Metal Co Ltd [1998] Env. L.R. 732; [1998] E.H.L.R. 198; [1998] E.G.C.S. 6; (1998) 95(7) L.S.G. 31; *Times*, January 21, 1998, CA . . . .　*Digested*, 98/**4045**: *Applied*, 01/4550

Murdoch (t/a Nottingham Antiques) v. Secretary of State for the Environment, Transport and the Regions [2001] J.P.L. 841 (Note), QBD (Admin Ct)

Murfitts Transport Ltd v. Department of Transport; *sub nom* Department of Transport v. Murfitts Transport Ltd [1998] R.T.R. 229; [1998] C.O.D. 14, QBD . . . .　*Digested*, 97/**4363**

Murgitroyd & Co Ltd's Trade Mark Application (1999) 22(2) I.P.D. 22020, TMR

Murphy v. A Birrell & Sons Ltd [1978] I.R.L.R. 458, EAT . . . .　*Digested*, 78/**1008**: *Applied*, 98/2231: *Distinguished*, 84/1197

Murphy v. Automania Ltd [2001] 6 Q.R. 19, CC (Kingston on Thames) [*Ex rel*. Peter de Verneuil Smith, Barrister, 2 Temple Gardens, London] . . . .　*Digested*, 01/**1761**

Murphy v. Brentwood DC [1991] 1 A.C. 398; [1990] 3 W.L.R. 414; [1990] 2 All E.R.
908; [1990] 2 Lloyd's Rep. 467; 50 B.L.R. 1; 21 Con. L.R. 1; (1990) 22 H.L.R.
502; 89 L.G.R. 24; (1991) 3 Admin. L.R. 37; (1990) 6 Const. L.J. 304; (1990)
154 L.G. Rev. 1010; (1990) 87(30) L.S.G. 15; (1990) 134 S.J. 1076; *Times*, July
27, 1990; *Independent*, July 27, 1990, HL; reversing [1990] 2 W.L.R. 944;
[1990] 2 All E.R. 269; 88 L.G.R. 333; (1990) 87(5) L.S.G. 42; (1990) 134 S.J.
458; *Times*, December 27, 1989; *Independent*, January 26, 1990, CA; affirming
13 Con. L.R. 96, OR . . . . *Digested*, 91/**2661**:
Applied, 90/3290, 91/2660, 94/2881, 96/4433, 00/4227, 01/4509:
Considered, 92/3219, 93/2997, 94/3749, 94/4517, 95/2496, 95/3648,
95/3667, 95/4189, 96/2993, 96/4438, 96/4448, 96/7223, 97/3816:
Distinguished, 92/3199, 96/1156, 97/1752, 97/3776, 99/1409:
Followed, 98/3955: *Not followed*, 98/3924: *Referred to*, 94/6386
Murphy (Valuation Officer) v. Courtney Plc (No.2) see Courtney Plc v. Murphy
(Valuation Officer) (No.2)
Murphy v. Meywest Ltd see Murphy v. Moywest Ltd
Murphy v. Moywest Ltd; *sub nom* Murphy v. Meywest Ltd (1998) 98(1) Q.R. 7;
(1997) 97(5) Q.R. 10, CC (Liverpool) . . . . *Digested*, 98/**1661**
Murphy v. Murphy; *sub nom* Murphy's Settlements, Re [1999] 1 W.L.R. 282; [1998] 3
All E.R. 1; [1998] N.P.C. 62; *Times*, May 2, 1998; *Independent*, April 27, 1998
(C.S.), Ch D . . . . *Digested*, 98/**4872**
Murphy v. Rowlands (Unreported, September 25, 1998), CC (Pontypridd) [*Ex rel.*
Julian Winn Reed, Barrister, 9 Park Place, Cardiff] . . . . *Digested*, 98/**1706**
Murphy v. Secretary of State for Social Security (C328/91) see Secretary of State for
Social Security v. Thomas (C328/91)
Murphy v. Sun Alliance and London Insurance Plc see Murphy v. Young & Co's
Brewery Plc
Murphy v. Young & Co's Brewery Plc; Murphy v. Sun Alliance and London Insurance
Plc [1997] 1 W.L.R. 1591; [1997] 1 All E.R. 518; [1997] 1 Lloyd's Rep. 236;
[1997] C.L.C. 469; [1998] 1 Costs L.R. 94; [1997] 6 Re. L.R. 113; *Times*, January
8, 1997; *Independent*, December 6, 1996, CA; affirming [1996] L.R.L.R. 60;
Lloyd's List, August 16, 1995 (I.D.), QBD . . . . *Digested*, 97/**3113**:
Applied, 99/388, 99/3422, 00/413: *Considered*, 97/3159, 01/5712:
Distinguished, 99/405: *Followed*, 99/392

Murphy's Application for Judicial Review, Re [2001] N.I. 425, QBD (NI)
Murphy's Settlements, Re see Murphy v. Murphy
Murray (A Minor) v. Knowsley BC (Unreported, May 20, 1998), CC (Liverpool) [*Ex rel.*
Paul Simpson, Barrister, First National Chambers, 2nd Floor, First National Bank
Building, 24 Fenwick Street, Liverpool] . . . . *Digested*, 98/**1649**
Murray v. BBC [1999] I.L.Pr. 257, US Ct
Murray v. Derbyshire CC see R. (on the application of Murray) v. Derbyshire CC
Murray v. Foyle Meats Ltd [2000] 1 A.C. 51; [1999] 3 W.L.R. 356; [1999] 3 All E.R.
769; [1999] N.I. 291; [1999] I.C.R. 827; [1999] I.R.L.R. 562; (1999) 96(31)
L.S.G. 36; (1999) 143 S.J.L.B. 214; *Times*, July 9, 1999 ; *Independent*, October
11, 1999 (C.S.), HL (NI); affirming [1997] N.I. 429, CA (NI) . . . . *Digested*, 99/**5280**:
Considered, 01/2303
Murray v. Guinness [1998] N.P.C. 79, Ch D
Murray v. Newham Citizens Advice Bureau [2001] I.C.R. 708, EAT . . . . *Digested*, 01/**2233**
Murray v. United Kingdom (A/300-A) (1995) 19 E.H.R.R. 193; *Times*, November 1,
1994, ECHR . . . . *Digested*, 95/**2662**:
Considered, 98/3071, 99/5182: *Followed*, 98/3073
Murray v. United Kingdom (Right to Silence) (1996) 22 E.H.R.R. 29; *Times*, February
9, 1996; *Independent*, March 1, 1996, ECHR . . . . *Digested*, 96/**1516**:
Applied, 00/3228: *Considered*, 98/3150, 00/6043: *Distinguished*, 00/6070,
00/6071
Murray v. Yorkshire Fund Managers Ltd [1998] 1 W.L.R. 951; [1998] 2 All E.R. 1015;
[1998] F.S.R. 372; (1998) 95(3) L.S.G. 24; (1998) 95(4) L.S.G. 33; (1998) 142
S.J.L.B. 45; *Times*, December 18, 1997, CA . . . . *Digested*, 98/**3414**
Murray Vernon Ltd v. Customs and Excise Commissioners [1997] V. & D.R. 340, V&DTr   *Digested*, 00/**5067**
Murrell v. Customs and Excise Commissioners 2 I.T.L. Rep. 936; [2001] S.T.I. 256,
V&DTr
Murrell v. Healy [2001] EWCA Civ 486; [2001] 4 All E.R. 345; *Times*, May 1, 2001, CA . *Digested*, 01/**1536**
Murria v. Lord Chancellor [2000] 2 All E.R. 941; [2000] 1 Costs L.R. 81; (2000) 97(3)
L.S.G. 35; (2000) 150 N.L.J. 59; (2000) 144 S.J.L.B. 36; *Times*, January 11,
2000; *Independent*, February 7, 2000 (C.S.), QBD . . . . *Digested*, 00/**3973**
Murtagh (t/a Ruberry Rednal Cars) v. Bromsgrove DC, *Independent*, December 6, 1999
(C.S.); *Independent*, November 29, 1999 (C.S.), QBD
Murthy v. Sivajothi [1999] 1 W.L.R. 467; [1999] 1 All E.R. 721; [1999] I.L.Pr. 320;
Times, November 11, 1998; *Independent*, November 11, 1998, CA . . . . *Digested*, 98/**753**
Musah v. Secretary of State for the Home Department see R. v. Secretary of State for
the Home Department Ex p. Musah
Music Gallery Ltd v. Direct Line Insurance Plc [1998] E.M.L.R. 551, Ch D . . . . *Digested*, 98/**3433**
Musisi v. Secretary of State for the Home Department see Bugdaycay v. Secretary of
State for the Home Department

Musmar *v.* Kalala (Unreported, March 1, 1999), CC (Croydon) [*Ex rel.* Sadie Wright, Barrister, Goldsmith Building, Temple, London] . . . . *Digested,* 99/**1565**
Musselwhite *v.* CH Musselwhite & Son Ltd [1962] Ch. 964; [1962] 2 W.L.R. 374; [1962] 1 All E.R. 201; 106 S.J. 37, Ch D . . . . *Digested,* 62/**363**: *Considered,* 99/3680
Musson *v.* Lee see Lee (Albert) (Deceased), Re
Mustafa *v.* Ruddock (1998) 30 H.L.R. 495; [1997] E.G.C.S. 87, CA . . . . *Digested,* 98/**3595**
Mutch *v.* Allen [2001] EWCA Civ 76; [2001] C.P. Rep. 77; [2001] C.P.L.R. 200; [2001] P.I.Q.R. P26; *Independent,* March 5, 2001 (C.S), CA
Mutton *v.* Haydney (Unreported, February 14, 2001), CC (Truro) [*Ex rel.* Paul Mitchell, Barrister, 4 Paper Buildings, Temple, London] . . . . *Digested,* 01/**496**
Mutton *v.* Osarinwian (Unreported, May 25, 1999), CC (Bury) [*Ex rel.* Milners Solicitors, Crown House, 85-89 Great George Street, Leeds] . . . . *Digested,* 99/**492**: *Referred to,* 00/1456
Mutual Legal Assistance in Criminal Matters, Re [2001] I.L.Pr. 11, CA (Ont) . . . . *Digested,* 01/**986**
Mutual Shipping Corp of New York *v.* Bayshore Shipping Co of Monrovia (The Montan) [1985] 1 W.L.R. 625; [1985] 1 All E.R. 520; [1985] 1 Lloyd's Rep. 189; (1985) 82 L.S.G. 1329; (1985) 129 S.J. 219, CA; affirming [1984] 1 Lloyd's Rep. 389, QBD (Comm Ct) . . . . *Digested,* 85/**104**: *Applied,* 01/416: *Considered,* 85/105, 87/3093, 91/199
MV GmbH *v.* AG GmbH (2 U 101/95) [2001] E.N.P.R. 5, OLG (Dusseldorf)
MV Yorke Motors *v.* Edwards [1982] 1 W.L.R. 444; [1982] 1 All E.R. 1204; 126 S.J. 245, HL; affirming (1981) 125 S.J. 444, CA . . . . *Digested,* 82/**2398**: *Applied,* 96/811, 97/874, 00/316, 00/543: *Considered,* 96/724, 96/854, 97/1376, 97/4516, 00/509: *Explained,* 84/2723
MW Kellogg Ltd *v.* Tobin; *sub nom* MW Kellog Ltd *v.* Tobin [1999] L. & T.R. 513, QBD . . *Digested,* 00/**3889**
Mwanza *v.* Secretary of State for the Home Department [2001] Imm. A.R. 557; [2001] I.N.L.R. 616; *Independent,* November 9, 2000, CA . . . . *Digested,* 00/**3335**
MWB (Maidstone) Ltd *v.* City Centre Restaurants (UK) Ltd (1999) 78 P. & C.R. D4, Ch D
Myatt *v.* Dibb Lupton Alsop (Unreported, October 4, 1999), QBD [*Ex rel.* Kate Bentley, Pupil Barrister, 2 Crown Office Row, Second Floor, Temple, London] . . . . *Digested,* 00/**1491**
MYCOGEN/Modifying plant cells (T694/92) [1998] E.P.O.R. 114, EPO (Technical Bd App)
Myers *v.* Dortex International Ltd [2000] Lloyd's Rep. I.R. 529; *Times,* March 18, 1999, CA . . . . *Digested,* 99/**450**
Myers *v.* Elman; *sub nom* Myers *v.* Rothfield [1940] A.C. 282, HL; reversing [1939] 1 K.B. 109, CA . . . . *Applied,* 52/2729, 58/957, 62/979, 63/2755, 74/612, 87/3562, 01/4256: *Considered,* 65/3700, 83/2184, 84/1995, 85/2640, 86/2603, 89/631, 90/3615, 91/2823, 94/3623, 01/538: *Distinguished,* 72/2804: *Followed,* 93/3766, 94/4213
Myers *v.* Rothfield see Myers *v.* Elman

N (A Child) (Adoption: Foreign Guardianship), Re; *sub nom* AGN (Adoption: Foreign Adoption), Re [2000] 2 F.L.R. 431; [2000] 2 F.C.R. 512; [2000] Fam. Law 694; *Times,* June 27, 2000, Fam Div . . . . *Digested,* 00/**2434**
N (A Child) (Leave to Withdraw Care Proceedings), Re [2000] 1 F.L.R. 134; [2000] 1 F.C.R. 258; [2000] Fam. Law 12, Fam Div . . . . *Digested,* 00/**2459**
N (A Child) (Residence: Appointment of Solicitor: Placement with Extended Family), Re see N (A Child) (Residence Order) (Procedural Mismanagement), Re
N (A Child) (Residence Order: Procedural Mismanagement), Re; *sub nom* N (A Child) (Residence: Appointment of Solicitor: Placement with Extended Family), Re [2001] 1 F.L.R. 1028; [2001] Fam. Law 423, CA. . . . . *Digested,* 01/**2598**
N (A Child) *v.* Bird (Unreported, September 24, 2000), CC (Birkenhead) [*Ex rel.* Michael W Halsall Solicitors, 2 The Parks, Newton-le-Willows, Cheshire] . . . . . . *Digested,* 01/**468**
N (A Child) *v.* Entry Clearance Officer see N (A Child) *v.* Immigration Appeal Tribunal
N (A Child) *v.* Immigration Appeal Tribunal; *sub nom* N (A Child) *v.* Entry Clearance Officer; N (A Child) *v.* Immigration Officer [2001] I.N.L.R. 26; (2000) 97(36) L.S.G. 41; *Times,* September 6, 2000, CA . . . . *Digested,* 00/**3356**
N (A Child) *v.* Immigration Officer see N (A Child) *v.* Immigration Appeal Tribunal
N (A Child) *v.* Smith & Whiteinch Group (Unreported, March 20, 2000), CC (Croydon) [*Ex rel.* Amanda Drane, Barrister, 4 King's Bench Walk, 2nd Floor, Temple, London] . . . . *Digested,* 00/**1710**
N (A Minor), Re see A *v.* N (Committal: Refusal of Contact)
N (A Minor) *v.* Yorkshire Water Services Ltd (Unreported, March 22, 1999), CC (Halifax) [*Ex rel.* Rhodes Thain & Collinson Solicitors, 27 Harrison Road, Halifax]. . . . . *Digested,* 99/**1601**
N (Child Abduction: Habitual Residence), Re; *sub nom* N *v.* N (Child Abduction: Habitual Residence) [2000] 2 F.L.R. 899; [2000] 3 F.C.R. 84; [2000] Fam. Law 786, Fam Div. . . . . *Digested,* 00/**2449**
N (CICB: Quantum: 2000), Re (Unreported, January 26, 2000), CICB (Plymouth) [*Ex rel.* Carol Mashembo, Pupil Barrister, King's Bench Chambers, 115 North Hill, Plymouth] . . . . *Digested,* 00/**1526**
N (Forensic Examination: Negligence), Re see N *v.* Agrawal

N (Minors) (Child Abduction), Re [1991] 1 F.L.R. 413; [1991] F.C.R. 765; [1991] Fam. Law
    367, Fam Div. . . . . *Digested,* 91/**2530**:
                                         Applied, 96/536, 00/2441: *Referred to,* 94/5440
N *v.* Agrawal; *sub nom* N (Forensic Examination: Negligence), Re [1999] Lloyd's Rep.
    Med. 257; [1999] P.N.L.R. 939; *Times,* June 9, 1999, CA. . . . . *Digested,* 99/**3957**
N *v.* C (Property Adjustment Order: Surveyor's Negligence); *sub nom* N *v.* C (Property
    Valuation: Liability of Valuer) [1998] 1 F.L.R. 63; [1997] 2 F.C.R. 600; [1998]
    Fam. Law 19; *Independent,* April 28, 1997 (C.S.), CA. *Digested,* 97/**2485**
N *v.* C (Property Valuation: Liability of Valuer) see N *v.* C (Property Adjustment Order:
    Surveyor's Negligence)
N *v.* Governor of Dartmoor Prison see R. (on the application of N) *v.* Governor of
    Dartmoor Prison
N *v.* N (Child Abduction: Habitual Residence) see N (Child Abduction: Habitual
    Residence), Re
N *v.* N (Divorce: Antenuptial Agreement) see N *v.* N (Jurisdiction: Pre Nuptial
    Agreement)
N *v.* N (Divorce: Judaism) see N *v.* N (Jurisdiction: Pre Nuptial Agreement)
N *v.* N (Financial Provision: Sale of Company) [2001] 2 F.L.R. 69, Fam Div . . . . *Digested,* 01/**2635**
N *v.* N (Jurisdiction: Pre Nuptial Agreement); *sub nom* N *v.* N (Divorce: Judaism); N *v.*
    N (Divorce: Antenuptial Agreement) [1999] 2 F.L.R. 745; [1999] 2 F.C.R. 583;
    [1999] Fam. Law 691; (1999) 96(31) L.S.G. 39; (1999) 149 N.L.J. 1074; *Times,*
    July 12, 1999 ; *Independent,* July 9, 1999, Fam Div . . . . *Digested,* 99/**2407**:
                                                   Considered, 00/2502
N *v.* R (Non Molestation Order: Breach) (1998) 95(33) L.S.G. 33; (1998) 142
    S.J.L.B. 243; *Times,* September 1, 1998, CA . . . . *Digested,* 98/**12**
N AG *v.* Regional Tax Office for Upper Austria 2 I.T.L. Rep. 884, VwGH (A)
N Michalos & Sons Maritime SA *v.* Prudential Assurance Co (The Zinovia); Public Corp
    for Sugar Trade *v.* N Michalos & Sons Co [1984] 2 Lloyd's Rep. 264, QBD
    (Comm Ct) . . . . *Digested,* 84/**3175**:
                                                       Applied, 01/3824
N's 1989 Settlement, Re (1998-99) 1 I.T.E.L.R. 803, Royal Ct (Jer)
N's Application for Judicial Review, Re [2001] N.I. 115, QBD (NI) . . . . *Digested,* 01/**5745**
Na Na Trading Co Inc's Trade Mark Application (No. B1481619) (1999) 22(2) I.P.D. 22019,
    TMR
Nabadda *v.* Westminster City Council; Gomilsek *v.* Haringey LBC [2001] 3 C.M.L.R.
    39; [2000] I.C.R. 951; (2000) 2 L.G.L.R. 917; [2000] B.L.G.R. 360; [2000]
    E.L.R. 489; (2000) 97(8) L.S.G. 35; *Times,* March 15, 2000, CA . . . . *Digested,* 00/**1808**
Nabavi *v.* Guild see Guild *v.* Eskandar Ltd (formerly Ambleville Ltd)
Nacco Material Handling (NI) Ltd *v.* Customs and Excise Commissioners [1998] V. &
    D.R. 115, V&DTr . . . . *Digested,* 00/**4959**
Nadreph Ltd *v.* Willmett & Co; *sub nom* Nadreth *v.* Willmett & Co [1978] 1 W.L.R. 1537;
    [1978] 1 All E.R. 746; 122 S.J. 744, Ch D . . . . *Digested,* 78/**715**:
                                        Considered, 83/1071, 98/4025
Nadreth *v.* Willmett & Co see Nadreph Ltd *v.* Willmett & Co
Naeem *v.* Bank of Credit and Commerce International SA (2000) 97(21) L.S.G. 38;
    (2000) 150 N.L.J. 650, CA
Nagarajan *v.* Agnew; *sub nom* Swiggs *v.* Nagarajan (No.1); Nagarajan *v.* Swiggs (No.1)
    [1995] I.C.R. 520; [1994] I.R.L.R. 61, EAT . . . . *Digested,* 94/**1969**:
             Applied, 01/2313: *Considered,* 95/2026: *Followed,* 97/2245
Nagarajan *v.* London Regional Transport; *sub nom* Swiggs *v.* Nagarajan (No.2);
    Nagarajan *v.* Swiggs (No.2) [2000] 1 A.C. 501; [1999] 3 W.L.R. 425; [1999] 4
    All E.R. 65; [1999] I.C.R. 877; [1999] I.R.L.R. 572; (1999) 96(31) L.S.G. 36;
    (1999) 149 N.L.J. 1109; (1999) 143 S.J.L.B. 219; *Times,* July 19, 1999 ;
    Independent, October 11, 1999 (C.S.), HL; reversing [1998] I.R.L.R. 73, CA . . . . *Digested,* 99/**2093**:
                                                   Considered, 01/2301
Nagarajan *v.* Swiggs (No.1) see Nagarajan *v.* Agnew
Nagarajan *v.* Swiggs (No.2) see Nagarajan *v.* London Regional Transport
Nagle *v.* Fielden; *sub nom* Nagle *v.* Feilden [1966] 2 Q.B. 633; [1966] 2 W.L.R. 1027;
    [1966] 1 All E.R. 689; 110 S.J. 286, CA . . . . *Digested,* 66/**12099**:
         Considered, 73/3378, 74/3872, 78/24, 82/3286, 83/454, 91/43, 93/31:
                                   Distinguished, 00/2212: *Followed,* 78/21
Nagle *v.* Rottnest Island Authority (1992) 177 C.L.R. 423. . . . . *Considered,* 98/3918
Naheem *v.* National Westminster Bank Plc [1998] C.C.L.R. 10, CA . . . . *Digested,* 98/**2513**
Nahum *v.* Royal Holloway and Bedford New College [1999] E.M.L.R. 252; (1998)
    95(46) L.S.G. 33; (1998) 142 S.J.L.B. 286; *Times,* November 19, 1998, CA . . . . *Digested,* 98/**112**
Naidoo *v.* Naidu, *Times,* November 1, 2000, Ch D . . . . *Digested,* 00/**2334**
Naidu *v.* Yenula Properties Ltd see Yenula Properties Ltd *v.* Naidu
Nairne *v.* Camden LBC see Ali *v.* Westminster City Council
Naish *v.* Thorp Wright & Puxon 1993-N-No.907, QBD . . . . *Digested,* 98/**4024**
Najam, Re, *Independent,* October 19, 1998 (C.S.), QBD . . . . *Digested,* 98/**1081**
Nakajima All Precision Co Ltd *v.* Council of the European Communities (C69/89 R)
    [1991] E.C.R. I-2069; [1989] E.C.R. 1689, ECJ . . . . *Followed,* 00/2346,
                                                       00/2366

Nakos v. Stockholm Social Security Office [1999] 2 C.M.L.R. 1377, Lansratt (Stockholm)

Nalco Chemical Co's European Patent Application (J31/96) see NALCO/Correction of mistake (J31/96)

NALCO/Correction of mistake (J31/96); sub nom Nalco Chemical Co's European Patent Application (J31/96) [2000] E.P.O.R. 463; (1999) 22(1) I.P.D. 22006, EPO (Legal Bd App) . . . . Digested, 00/**3621**

Naletilic v. Croatia (51891/99) (2000) 29 E.H.R.R. CD219, ECHR

Namco Ltd's Trade Mark Application (No.2068253); sub nom Kabushiki Kaisha Namco's Trade Mark Application (1999) 22(10) I.P.D. 22103

Namusoke v. Northwick Park and St Mark's NHS Trust (No.1) [2000] C.P. Rep. 33, QBD . . . . Digested, 00/**506**

Nanglegan v. Royal Free Hampstead NHS Trust [2001] EWCA Civ 127; [2001] 3 All E.R. 793; [2001] C.P. Rep. 65; [2001] C.P.L.R. 225; Times, February 14, 2001, CA . . . . Digested, 01/**639**: Considered, 01/644

Nanthakumar v. Secretary of State for the Home Department [2000] I.N.L.R. 480, CA . Digested, 01/**3602**

Nanuwa v. Lufthansa German Airlines (Unreported, March 16, 1999), CC (Leicester) [Ex rel. The Simkins Partnership Solicitors, 45-51 Whitfield Street, London] . . . . Digested, 99/**4885**

Napier Brown Plc v. Commission of the European Communities (T207/98) see Tate & Lyle Plc v. Commission of the European Communities (T202/98)

Napp Pharmaceutical Group Ltd v. Asta Medica Ltd [1999] F.S.R. 370, Pat Ct . . . . . . Digested, 99/**3493**

Napp Pharmaceutical Holdings Ltd v. Director General of Fair Trading (No.1) [2001] Comp. A.R. 1, CCAT . . . . Digested, 01/**772**

Napp Pharmaceutical Holdings Ltd v. Director General of Fair Trading (No.2) [2001] Comp. A.R. 21, CCAT . . . . Digested, 01/**779**

Napp Pharmaceutical Holdings Ltd v. Director General of Fair Trading (No.3) [2001] Comp. A.R. 33, CCAT

Naraine v. Hoverspeed Ltd [2000] Eu. L.R. 321; Independent, November 18, 1999, CA . Digested, 99/**2273**

NASA v. Higgins see Julian Higgins Trade Mark Application

Nascimento v. Kerrigan, Times, June 23, 1999, CA . . . . Digested, 99/**511**

Nash v. Eli Lilly & Co [1993] 1 W.L.R. 782; [1993] 4 All E.R. 383; [1992] 3 Med. L.R. 353; Times, October 7, 1992, CA; affirming [1991] 2 Med. L.R. 169; Times, February 13, 1991, QBD . . . . Digested, 93/**2603**: Applied, 96/816, 96/827, 97/655: Cited, 97/668: Considered, 94/2908, 95/3171, 97/658, 97/663, 97/669: Followed, 96/835, 97/650, 97/664, 98/552

Nash v. Kingston and Richmond HA (1997) 36 B.M.L.R. 123, QBD . . . . Digested, 98/**3975**

Nash v. Mash/Roe Group Ltd [1998] I.R.L.R. 168, IT . . . . Digested, 98/**2240**

Nash v. Nash [1973] 2 All E.R. 704, CA . . . . Digested, 73/**887**: Applied, 01/2596: Considered, 83/2447, 95/3482

Nash v. Paragon Finance Plc see Paragon Finance Plc (formerly National Home Loans Corp) v. Nash

Nasri v. France (A/324) (1996) 21 E.H.R.R. 458, ECHR . . . . Digested, 96/**3129**: Applied, 98/3152

Nasser v. Landeshauptstadt Stuttgart (C98/99) see Khalil v. Bundesanstalt fur Arbeit (C95/99)

Nasser v. United Bank of Kuwait (Security for Costs) [2001] EWCA Civ 556; [2001] C.P. Rep. 105, CA

Nathu Ram Sohal's Trade Mark Application (No.B1528928) see OPEN COUNTRY Trade Mark

National Academy of Recording Arts & Sciences Inc v. International Federation of Phonographic Industry Danmark [2001] E.T.M.R. 23, HR (DK)

National & Provincial Building Society v. Lynd [1996] N.I. 47, Ch D (NI)

National & Provincial Building Society v. United Kingdom; Leeds Permanent Building Society v. United Kingdom; Yorkshire Building Society v. United Kingdom [1997] S.T.C. 1466; (1998) 25 E.H.R.R. 127; 69 T.C. 540; [1997] B.T.C. 624; [1998] H.R.C.D. 34; Times, November 6, 1997, ECHR . . . . Digested, 97/**2756**

National Association of Licensed Opencast Operators (NALOO) v. Commission of the European Communities (T89/98) see Commission of the European Communities v. National Association of Licensed Opencast Operators (NALOO) (C180/01)

National Assurance & Investment Association, Re; sub nom Cross, Re (1871-72) L.R. 7 Ch. App. 221, CA in Chancery . . . . Cited, 99/4154

National Bank v. Keegan [1931] I.R. 344, Sup Ct (Irl) . . . . Considered, 01/5945: Not followed, 99/5474

National Bank Ltd, Re [1966] 1 W.L.R. 819; [1966] 1 All E.R. 1006; 110 S.J. 226, Ch D . Digested, 66/**1305**: Applied, 00/683: Considered, 00/684

National Bank of Abu Dhabi v. Mohamed (1998) 30 H.L.R. 383; [1997] N.P.C. 62, CA . Digested, 97/**4243**

National Bank of Greece and Athens SA v. Metliss [1958] A.C. 509; [1957] 3 W.L.R.
1056; [1957] 3 All E.R. 608; 101 S.J. 972, HL; affirming [1957] 2 Q.B. 33;
[1957] 2 W.L.R. 570; [1957] 2 All E.R. 1; 101 S.J. 301, CA; affirming *Times*, July
13, 1956, QBD. . . . . *Digested*, 57/**505**:
Applied, 60/477, 92/3559, 00/736: *Considered*, 58/492, 59/476, 69/1733,
71/1572

National Bank of Greece SA v. Outhwaite; *sub nom* National Bank of Greece SA v. RM
Outhwaite 317 Syndicate at Lloyds [2001] C.P. Rep. 69; [2001] C.L.C. 591;
[2001] Lloyd's Rep. I.R. 652, QBD (Comm Ct) . . . . *Digested*, 01/**642**

National Bank of Greece SA v. Pinios Shipping Co No. 1; *sub nom* Pinios Shipping Co
No. 1 v. National Bank of Greece SA [1990] 1 A.C. 637; [1989] 3 W.L.R. 1330;
[1990] 1 All E.R. 78; [1990] 1 Lloyd's Rep. 225; [1988] 2 F.T.L.R. 9; [1988] Fin.
L.R. 249; [1990] C.C.L.R. 18; (1990) 87(4) L.S.G. 33; (1989) 139 N.L.J. 1711;
(1990) 134 S.J. 261; *Times*, December 1, 1989; *Independent*, December 6, 1989;
Financial Times, December 5, 1989, HL; reversing [1989] 3 W.L.R. 185; [1989]
1 All E.R. 213; [1988] 2 Lloyd's Rep. 126; (1989) 133 S.J. 817; *Times*, March 5,
1988; *Independent*, March 3, 1988; *Financial Times*, May 16, 1988, CA. . . . . *Digested*, 90/**267**:
Applied, 90/4101, 00/2603: *Distinguished*, 00/2624

National Bank of Greece SA v. RM Outhwaite 317 Syndicate at Lloyds see National
Bank of Greece SA v. Outhwaite

National Car Parks Ltd v. Trinity Development Co (Banbury) Ltd; *sub nom* R. (on the
application of National Car Parks Ltd) v. Trinity Development Co (Banbury) Ltd
[2001] EWCA Civ 1686, CA; affirming [2001] L. & T.R. 33; [2001] 28 E.G. 144;
[2000] E.G.C.S. 128; (2001) 81 P. & C.R. D21, Ch D . . . . *Digested*, 01/**4157**

National Coal Board v. England; *sub nom* England v. National Coal Board [1954] A.C.
403; [1954] 2 W.L.R. 400; [1954] 1 All E.R. 546; 98 S.J. 176, HL; reversing in
part [1953] 1 Q.B. 724; [1953] 2 W.L.R. 1059; [1953] 1 All E.R. 1194; 97 S.J.
352, CA . . . . *Digested*, 54/**2076**:
Applied, 54/2077: *Considered*, 69/2418, 87/1826, 01/4478

National Coal Board v. National Union of Mineworkers [1986] I.C.R. 736; [1986]
I.R.L.R. 439, Ch D . . . . *Digested*, 87/**3762**:
Applied, 97/2188, 01/2332: *Considered*, 91/1622

National Coal Board v. Ridgway and Fairbrother; *sub nom* Ridgway and Fairbrother v.
National Coal Board [1987] 3 All E.R. 582; [1987] I.C.R. 641; [1987] I.R.L.R. 80,
CA; reversing [1986] I.R.L.R. 379; (1986) 83 L.S.G. 2653; (1986) 130 S.J.
748, EAT. . . . . *Digested*, 87/**3766**:
Considered, 91/1703, 93/3933, 93/4001: *Distinguished*, 98/2209, 99/2122:
Overruled, 95/1990

National Coalition for Gay and Lesbian Equality v. Minister of Justice 6 B.H.R.C. 127,
Const Ct (SA). . . . . *Digested*, 99/**765**

National Commercial Banking Corp of Australia Ltd v. Batty (1986) 65 A.L.R. 385, HC
(Aus) . . . . *Considered*, 98/4069

National Deposit Friendly Society Trustees v. Skegness Urban DC [1959] A.C. 293;
[1958] 3 W.L.R. 172; [1958] 2 All E.R. 601; (1958) 122 J.P. 399; 56 L.G.R. 313;
3 R.R.C. 92; 51 R. & I.T. 474; 102 S.J. 526, HL; affirming [1957] 2 Q.B. 573;
[1957] 3 W.L.R. 550; [1957] 3 All E.R. 199; (1957) 121 J.P. 567; 55 L.G.R. 477;
2 R.R.C. 107; 50 R. & I.T. 574; 101 S.J. 664, CA; affirming [1957] 1 Q.B. 531;
[1957] 2 W.L.R. 322; [1957] 1 All E.R. 407; 121 J.P. 157; 55 L.G.R. 114; 1 R.R.C.
226; 50 R. & I.T. 75; 101 S.J. 173, QBD; affirming (1956) 49 R. & I.T. 795,
Quarter Sessions. . . . . *Digested*, 58/**2844**:
Applied, 57/2969, 57/2972, 58/1387, 58/2846, 58/2851, 59/2767, 59/2769,
59/2772, 89/1898, 90/2497: *Considered*, 59/2766, 89/3746, 90/4616,
01/3849: *Disapproved*, 60/2692: *Distinguished*, 57/2973, 58/2843

National Employers Mutual General Insurance Association v. Jones; *sub nom* NEMG
Insurance Association v. Jones [1990] 1 A.C. 24; [1988] 2 W.L.R. 952; [1988] 2
All E.R. 425; [1988] R.T.R. 289; (1989) 8 Tr. L.R. 43; (1988) 138 N.L.J. Rep.
118; (1988) 132 S.J. 658, HL; affirming [1987] 3 W.L.R. 901; [1987] 3 All E.R.
385; (1987) 84 L.S.G. 2458; (1987) 131 S.J. 1154, CA . . . . *Digested*, 88/**3177**:
Followed, 00/4675

National Enterprises Ltd v. Racal Communications Ltd; Racal Communications Ltd v.
National Enterprises Ltd [1975] Ch. 397; [1975] 2 W.L.R. 222; [1974] 3 All E.R.
1010; [1975] 1 Lloyd's Rep. 225; 118 S.J. 735, CA; affirming [1974] Ch. 251;
[1974] 2 W.L.R. 733; [1974] 1 All E.R. 1118; [1974] 2 Lloyd's Rep. 21; (1973) 118
S.J. 329, Ch D . . . . *Digested*, 75/**105**:
Applied, 81/1626: *Considered*, 01/5021

National Grid Co Plc v. Laws see National Grid Co Plc v. Mayes

National Grid Co Plc v. Laws (Pre-emptive Costs: Chancery) see National Grid Co Plc
Group of the Electricity Supply Pension Scheme, Re

National Grid Co Plc v. Laws (Pre-Emptive Costs: Court of Appeal); *sub nom* Laws v.
National Grid Co Plc (Pre-Emptive Costs: Court of Appeal); National Power Plc
v. Machin (Pre-Emptive Costs: Court of Appeal); Machin v. National Power Plc
(Pre-Emptive Costs: Court of Appeal) [1998] O.P.L.R. 187; [2001] W.T.L.R. 741,
Ch D . . . . *Digested*, 98/**481**:
Previous proceedings, 98/482: *Subsequent proceedings*, 99/4142

National Grid Co Plc *v.* Lewis see National Grid Co Plc *v.* Mayes

National Grid Co Plc *v.* M25 Group Ltd (No.1) [1999] 1 E.G.L.R. 65; [1999] 08 E.G. 169; [1999] E.G.C.S. 2, CA; reversing [1998] 2 E.G.L.R. 85; [1998] 32 E.G. 90; [1998] N.P.C. 172, Ch D . . . . *Digested,* 99/**3727**

National Grid Co Plc *v.* M25 Group Ltd (No.2) [1999] L. & T.R. 206, CA

National Grid Co Plc *v.* Mayes; *sub nom* National Grid Co Plc *v.* Laws; Jefferies *v.* Mayes; National Power Plc *v.* Feldon; Laws *v.* National Grid Co Plc; National Grid Co Plc *v.* Lewis; International Power Plc (formerly National Power Plc) *v.* Healy [2001] UKHL 20; [2001] 1 W.L.R. 864; [2001] 2 All E.R. 417; [2001] I.C.R. 544; [2001] I.R.L.R. 394; [2001] O.P.L.R. 15; [2001] Pens. L.R. 121; (2001) 98(23) L.S.G. 38; (2001) 151 N.L.J. 572; (2001) 145 S.J.L.B. 98; *Times,* April 10, 2001; *Independent,* April 11, 2001, HL; reversing [2000] I.C.R. 174; [1999] O.P.L.R. 95; [1999] Pens. L.R. 37; (1999) 96(9) L.S.G. 31; *Times,* February 25, 1999, CA; reversing [1997] O.P.L.R. 207; *Times,* June 30, 1997, Ch D; reversing [1997] O.P.L.R. 73, Pensions Ombudsman. . . . . *Digested,* 01/**4626**:
Considered, 01/**4631**: *Subsequent proceedings,* 97/3952, 98/481

National Grid Co Plc *v.* Mayes (Pre-emptive Costs: Chancery) see National Grid Co Plc Group of the Electricity Supply Pension Scheme, Re

National Grid Co Plc Group of the Electricity Supply Pension Scheme, Re; National Grid Co Plc *v.* Mayes (Pre-emptive Costs: Chancery); Jefferies *v.* Laws; National Grid Co Plc *v.* Laws (Pre-emptive Costs: Chancery); Jefferies *v.* Mayes (Pre-emptive Costs: Chancery) [1999] O.P.L.R. 161, Ch D . . . . *Digested,* 97/**3952**:
Subsequent proceedings, 97/3997

National Health Service Trust *v.* D [2000] 2 F.L.R. 677; [2000] 2 F.C.R. 577; [2000] Lloyd's Rep. Med. 411; (2000) 55 B.M.L.R. 19; [2000] Fam. Law 803; *Times,* July 19, 2000, Fam Div . . . . *Digested,* 00/**3247**

National Home Loans Corp Plc *v.* Giffen Couch & Archer [1998] 1 W.L.R. 207; [1997] 3 All E.R. 808; [1998] P.N.L.R. 111; [1997] N.P.C. 100; *Times,* October 9, 1997, CA; reversing (1997) 94(2) L.S.G. 24; (1997) 141 S.J.L.B. 29; *Times,* December 31, 1996; *Independent,* January 27, 1997 (C.S.), QBD . . . . *Digested,* 97/**3829**:
Applied, 00/2607: *Considered,* 98/4026, 00/4271: *Followed,* 97/3831

National Home Loans Corp Plc *v.* Kaufmann (Unreported, June 21, 1995), CA . . . . . . *Applied,* 01/4263

National Insurance & Guarantee Corp *v.* Imperio Reinsurance Co (UK) Ltd [1999] Lloyd's Rep. I.R. 249, QBD (Comm Ct). . . . . *Digested,* 99/**3425**

National Insurance Co of New Zealand *v.* Espagne (1961) 105 C.L.R. 569; (1961) 35 A.L.J.R. 4 . . . . *Digested,* 61/**2321**:
Applied, 71/3207, 72/836, 99/3987: *Considered,* 82/894, 90/1716

National Insurance Corp *v.* M/S Maritime Agencies Ltd (The Sinoda) see Trading Corp of Pakistan *v.* Inter Continental Oceanic Enterprises Corp (The Nitsa)

National Justice Compania Naviera SA *v.* Prudential Assurance Co Ltd (The Ikarian Reefer) (No.1) [1995] 1 Lloyd's Rep. 455, CA; reversing [1993] 2 Lloyd's Rep. 68; [1993] F.S.R. 563; [1993] 37 E.G. 158; *Times,* March 5, 1993, QBD (Comm Ct) . . . . *Digested,* 96/**3609**:
Considered, 94/3167, 95/3419, 99/343, 00/3517

National Justice Compania Naviera SA *v.* Prudential Assurance Co Ltd (The Ikarian Reefer) (No.2); *sub nom* Comninos *v.* Prudential Assurance Co Ltd [2000] 1 W.L.R. 603; [2000] 1 All E.R. 37; [1999] 2 All E.R. (Comm) 673; [2000] 1 Lloyd's Rep. 129; [2000] C.P. Rep. 13; [2000] C.L.C. 22; [2000] 1 Costs L.R. 37; [2000] I.L.Pr. 490; [2000] Lloyd's Rep. I.R. 230; (1999) 96(41) L.S.G. 35; (1999) 96(42) L.S.G. 40; (1999) 149 N.L.J. 1561; (1999) 143 S.J.L.B. 255; *Times,* October 15, 1999; *Independent,* October 20, 1999; *Independent,* November 22, 1999 (C.S.), CA; affirming [1999] 2 Lloyd's Rep. 621, QBD (Comm Ct) . . . . *Digested,* 99/**749**:
Considered, 00/455

National Power Plc, Re (C151/97P(I)); *sub nom* British Coal Corp *v.* Commission of the European Communities (T367/94); PowerGen Plc, Re (C157/97P(I)) [1997] All E.R. (E.C.) 673; [1997] E.C.R. I-3491; [1998] 4 C.M.L.R. 502, ECJ . . . . *Digested,* 98/**2306**:
Followed, 01/2472

National Power Plc *v.* Feldon see National Grid Co Plc *v.* Mayes

National Power Plc *v.* Machin (Pre-Emptive Costs: Court of Appeal) see National Grid Co Plc *v.* Laws (Pre-Emptive Costs: Court of Appeal)

National Power Plc *v.* Young see Young *v.* National Power Plc

National Provincial Bank Ltd *v.* Ainsworth; *sub nom* National Provincial Bank Ltd *v.* Hastings Car Mart Ltd (No.1); National Provincial Bank Ltd *v.* Hastings Car Mart Ltd (No.2) [1965] A.C. 1175; [1965] 3 W.L.R. 1; [1965] 2 All E.R. 472; 109 S.J. 415, HL; reversing [1964] Ch. 665; [1964] 2 W.L.R. 751; [1964] 1 All E.R. 688; 108 S.J. 115, CA; affirming [1964] Ch. 9; [1963] 2 W.L.R. 1015; [1963] 2 All E.R. 204; 107 S.J. 295, Ch D . . . . *Digested,* 65/**1850**:
Applied, 64/2067, 65/2179, 66/3975, 66/5819, 66/5825, 66/6733, 69/1645, 69/2286, 70/2414, 71/5455, 79/2733, 81/1494, 88/491, 89/468: *Considered,* 64/2064, 65/1849, 65/1853, 65/1862, 67/4094, 68/1819, 68/1824, 69/2051, 70/1240, 70/1511, 87/2247, 87/2540, 88/2061, 96/5031, 99/4395: *Distinguished,* 87/2178: *Subsequent proceedings,* 64/1741

National Provincial Bank Ltd v. Hastings Car Mart Ltd (No.1) see National Provincial
    Bank Ltd v. Ainsworth
National Provincial Bank Ltd v. Hastings Car Mart Ltd (No.2) see National Provincial
    Bank Ltd v. Ainsworth
National Provincial Bank of England Ltd v. Glanusk [1913] 3 K.B. 335, KBD . . . . *Considered*, 01/**4564**
National Trailer & Towing Association Ltd v. Chief Constable of Hampshire see National
    Trailer & Towing Association Ltd v. DPP
National Trailer & Towing Association Ltd v. DPP; *sub nom* National Trailer & Towing
    Association Ltd v. Chief Constable of Hampshire (1999) 163 J.P. 186; [1999]
    R.T.R. 89; *Times*, December 11, 1997, QBD. . . . . *Digested*, 98/**4864**
National Trust for Places of Historic Interest or Natural Beauty v. Attorney General see
    Verrall, Re
National Trust for Places of Historic Interest or Natural Beauty v. Hoare see Hoare
    (Valuation Officer) v. National Trust for Places of Historic Interest or Natural
    Beauty
National Trust for Places of Historic Interest or Natural Beauty v. Imperial Cancer Research
    Fund see Chapman, Re
National Trust for Places of Historic Interest or Natural Beauty v. Knipe [1998] 1 W.L.R.
    230; [1997] 4 All E.R. 627; (1998) 30 H.L.R. 449; [1997] 2 E.G.L.R. 9; [1997]
    40 E.G. 151; [1997] E.G.C.S. 73; (1997) 94(23) L.S.G. 27; (1997) 141 S.J.L.B.
    124; [1997] N.P.C. 745; *Times*, June 21, 1997, CA . . . . *Digested*, 97/**90**
National Trust for Places of Historic Interest or Natural Beauty v. National Kidney Research
    Fund see Chapman, Re
National Trust for Places of Historic Interest or Natural Beauty v. Royal National Institute
    for the Blind see Chapman, Re
National Trust for Places of Historic Interest or Natural Beauty v. Secretary of State for the
    Environment, Transport and the Regions [1999] J.P.L. 697; [1999] C.O.D. 235;
    [1998] N.P.C. 166, QBD. . . . . *Digested*, 99/**4398**
National Trust for Places of Historic Interest or Natural Beauty v. Spratling (Valuation
    Officer) see Hoare (Valuation Officer) v. National Trust for Places of Historic
    Interest or Natural Beauty
National Trustees Executors & Agency Co of Australia Ltd v. Tuck [1967] V.R. 847, Sup Ct
    (Vic). . . . . *Considered*, 00/**5263**
National Union of Rail Maritime and Transport Workers v. Midland Mainline Ltd [2001]
    EWCA Civ 1206; [2001] I.R.L.R. 813; [2001] Emp. L.R. 1097; (2001) 98(38)
    L.S.G. 37; *Times*, August 7, 2001, CA . . . . *Digested*, 01/**2327**
National Union of Railwaymen Maritime and Transport Staff v. London Underground Ltd
    see London Underground Ltd v. National Union of Rail Maritime and Transport
    Workers
National Westminster Bank Plc v. Kostopoulos [2000] 1 F.L.R. 815; [2000] Fam. Law
    403; *Times*, March 2, 2000, CA; affirming1998 CH 3353, Ch D . . . . *Digested*, 00/**4663**
National Westminster Bank Plc v. Amin TNS, HL; reversing (1999) 77 P. & C.R. D35,
    CA
National Westminster Bank Plc v. Beaton (1998) 30 H.L.R. 99; [1997] E.G.C.S. 53;
    [1997] N.P.C. 57; (1997) 74 P. & C.R. D19, CA . . . . *Digested*, 98/**4360**
National Westminster Bank Plc v. Breeds [2001] Lloyd's Rep. Bank. 98; (2001) 151
    N.L.J. 170; *Daily Telegraph*, February 20, 2001, Ch D . . . . *Digested*, 01/**4878**
National Westminster Bank Plc v. Caldeira (Unreported, October 12, 1998), CC
    (Kingston upon Hull) [*Ex rel.* Louis Doyle, Barrister, 10 Park Square, Leeds] . . . . *Digested*, 99/**3225**
National Westminster Bank Plc v. Customs and Excise Commissioners (V&DTr 15514)
    [1998] B.V.C. 2264; [1999] V. & D.R. 201, V&DTr . . . . *Digested*, 98/**4973**
National Westminster Bank Plc v. Customs and Excise Commissioners (V&DTr 17000)
    [2000] V. & D.R. 484; [2001] S.T.I. 714, V&DTr
National Westminster Bank Plc v. Daniel [1993] 1 W.L.R. 1453; [1994] 1 All E.R. 156,
    CA . . . . *Digested*, 94/**3799**:
                                                   Approved, 98/623: *Referred to*, 00/499
National Westminster Bank Plc v. Gill see Royal Bank of Scotland Plc v. Etridge (No.2)
National Westminster Bank Plc v. Jones; *sub nom* Jones v. National Westminster Bank
    Plc [2001] EWCA Civ 1541; (2001) 98(44) L.S.G. 35; (2001) 145 S.J.L.B. 246;
    Times, November 19, 2001; *Independent*, December 10, 2001 (C.S), CA;
    affirming [2001] 1 B.C.L.C. 98; [2000] B.P.I.R. 1092; [2000] E.G.C.S. 82;
    (2000) 97(28) L.S.G. 31; [2000] N.P.C. 73; *Times*, July 7, 2000, Ch D . . . . *Digested*, 01/**3785**:
                                                     Considered, 01/896
National Westminster Bank Plc v. Leggatt; *sub nom* Leggatt v. National Westminster
    Bank Plc [2001] 1 F.L.R. 563; [2001] 1 F.C.R. 523; (2001) 81 P. & C.R. 30;
    [2001] Fam. Law 106; (2000) 97(42) L.S.G. 44; (2001) 81 P. & C.R. D14; *Times*,
    November 16, 2000, CA . . . . *Digested*, 00/**4664**
National Westminster Bank Plc v. Pickering, CC (Chester) [*Ex rel.* John Baldwin,
    Barrister, Oriel Chambers, 14 Water Street, Liverpool] . . . . *Digested*, 01/**4872**
National Westminster Bank Plc v. Powney [1991] Ch. 339; [1990] 2 W.L.R. 1084;
    [1990] 2 All E.R. 416; (1990) 60 P. & C.R. 420; (1989) 86(46) L.S.G. 39;
    (1990) 134 S.J. 285; *Times*, October 11, 1989; *Independent*, October 30, 1989
    (C.S), CA . . . . *Digested*, 90/**2963**:
                                                 Applied, 01/578: *Followed*, 96/798

National Westminster Bank Plc v. Scher see Debtor (No.574 of 1995), Re
National Westminster Bank Plc v. Somer International (UK) Ltd [2001] EWCA Civ 970;
    [2001] Lloyd's Rep. Bank. 263; [2001] C.L.C. 1579; *Independent*, June 26,
    2001, CA . . . .   *Digested*, 01/**2434**
National Westminster Bank Plc v. Story [1999] Lloyd's Rep. Bank. 261; [1999] C.C.L.R.
    70; (1999) 96(20) L.S.G. 41; *Times*, May 14, 1999, CA. . . . .   *Digested*, 99/**2449**:
                                    Distinguished, 99/2485
National Westminster Bank Plc v. United States 1 I.T.L. Rep. 725, US Ct
National Westminster Bank Plc v. Utrecht-America Finance Co [2001] EWCA Civ 658;
    [2001] 3 All E.R. 733; [2001] 2 All E.R. (Comm) 7; [2001] Lloyd's Rep. Bank.
    285; [2001] C.L.C. 1372; (2001) 151 N.L.J. 784; *Independent*, May 17, 2001,
    CA; affirming [2001] C.L.C. 442, QBD (Comm Ct). . . . .   *Digested*, 01/**950**
National Wind Power Ltd v. Secretary of State for the Environment, Transport and the
    Regions [1999] N.P.C. 128, QBD
Nationsbanc Montgomery Securities LLC's Community Trade Mark Application [2000]
    E.T.M.R. 245, OHIM (2nd Bd App) . . . .   *Digested*, 00/**3726**
Nationwide Access Ltd v. Customs and Excise Commissioners, *Times*, March 22, 2000;
    Independent, April 3, 2000 (C.S.), QBD . . . .   *Digested*, 00/**4985**
Nationwide Anglia Building Society v. Lewis [1998] Ch. 482; [1998] 2 W.L.R. 915;
    [1998] 3 All E.R. 143; *Times*, March 6, 1998; *Independent*, March 9, 1998 (C.S.),
    CA; reversing [1997] 1 W.L.R. 1181; [1997] 3 All E.R. 498; *Times*, June 16,
    1997, Ch D . . . .   *Digested*, 98/**4017**
Nationwide Anglia Building Society v. Various Solicitors (No.1) [1999] P.N.L.R. 52;
    (1998) 95(6) L.S.G. 24; (1998) 148 N.L.J. 241; (1998) 142 S.J.L.B. 78; *Times*,
    February 5, 1998, Ch D . . . .   *Digested*, 98/**356**:
                                      Applied, 01/4268
Nationwide Anglia Building Society v. Various Solicitors (No.2), *Times*, May 1, 1998,
    Ch D . . . .   *Digested*, 98/**3713**
Nationwide Building Society v. Adams Delmar see Nationwide Building Society v.
    Various Solicitors (No.3)
Nationwide Building Society v. Archdeacons see Nationwide Building Society v. Various
    Solicitors (No.3)
Nationwide Building Society v. Archdeacons [1999] Lloyd's Rep. P.N. 549, Ch D . . . . .   *Digested*, 99/**4040**:
                               Joined proceedings, 99/1401
Nationwide Building Society v. ATM Abdullah & Co see Nationwide Building Society v.
    Various Solicitors (No.3)
Nationwide Building Society v. ATM Abdullah & Co [1999] Lloyd's Rep. P.N. 616, Ch D
    . . . .   *Digested*, 99/**4038**:
                                Joined proceedings, 99/1401
Nationwide Building Society v. Balmer Radmore see Nationwide Building Society v.
    Various Solicitors (No.3)
Nationwide Building Society v. Balmer Radmore [1999] Lloyd's Rep. P.N. 241; [1999]
    Lloyd's Rep. P.N. 558, Ch D . . . .   *Digested*, 99/**4037**:
                                Joined proceedings, 99/1401
Nationwide Building Society v. Borm Reid & Co see Nationwide Building Society v.
    Various Solicitors (No.3)
Nationwide Building Society v. Goodwin Harte see Nationwide Building Society v.
    Various Solicitors (No.3)
Nationwide Building Society v. Goodwin Harte [1999] Lloyd's Rep. P.N. 338, Ch D . . .   *Digested*, 99/**4043**:
                                Joined proceedings, 99/1401
Nationwide Building Society v. James Beauchamp (A Firm) [2001] EWCA Civ 275;
    [2001] 11 E.G.C.S. 172; (2001) 98(11) L.S.G. 45; [2001] N.P.C. 48, CA;
    reversing1994-N-864, Ch D
Nationwide Building Society v. JR Jones (A Firm) see Nationwide Building Society v.
    Various Solicitors (No.3)
Nationwide Building Society v. JR Jones (A Firm) [1999] Lloyd's Rep. P.N. 414, Ch D .   *Digested*, 99/**4039**:
                                Joined proceedings, 99/1401
Nationwide Building Society v. Littlestone & Cowan see Nationwide Building Society v.
    Various Solicitors (No.3)
Nationwide Building Society v. Littlestone & Cowan [1999] Lloyd's Rep. P.N. 625,
    Ch D . . . .   *Digested*, 99/**4042**:
                                Joined proceedings, 99/1401
Nationwide Building Society v. Purvis [1998] B.P.I.R. 625, CA . . . .   *Digested*, 99/**484**
Nationwide Building Society v. Richard Grosse & Co see Nationwide Building Society
    v. Various Solicitors (No.3)
Nationwide Building Society v. Richard Grosse & Co [1999] Lloyd's Rep. P.N. 348,
    Ch D . . . .   *Digested*, 99/**4044**:
                                Joined proceedings, 99/1401
Nationwide Building Society v. Singh & Garland Wells see Nationwide Building Society
    v. Various Solicitors (No.3)
Nationwide Building Society v. Thimbleby & Co [1999] Lloyd's Rep. P.N. 359; [1999]
    P.N.L.R. 733; [1999] E.G.C.S. 34; [1999] N.P.C. 29; *Independent*, March 15,
    1999 (C.S.), Ch D . . . .   *Digested*, 99/**4850**

Nationwide Building Society v. Thimbleby & Co (Case Management) CHANI 98/1143/
3, CA . . . . *Digested*, 99/**501**
Nationwide Building Society v. Vanderpump & Sykes see Nationwide Building Society
v. Various Solicitors (No.3)
Nationwide Building Society v. Vanderpump & Sykes [1999] Lloyd's Rep. P.N. 422,
Ch D . . . . *Digested*, 99/**4041**:
Joined proceedings, 99/1401
Nationwide Building Society v. Various Solicitors (No.3); Nationwide Building Society v.
Singh & Garland Wells; Nationwide Building Society v. Richard Grosse & Co;
Nationwide Building Society v. Archdeacons; Nationwide Building Society v.
Waters & Co; Nationwide Building Society v. JR Jones (A Firm); Nationwide
Building Society v. Borm Reid & Co; Nationwide Building Society v. Adams
Delmar; Nationwide Building Society v. Littlestone & Cowan; Nationwide
Building Society v. Goodwin Harte; Nationwide Building Society v. Vanderpump
& Sykes; Nationwide Building Society v. ATM Abdullah & Co; Nationwide
Building Society v. Balmer Radmore [1999] P.N.L.R. 606; [1999] E.G.C.S. 15;
(1999) 96(9) L.S.G. 31; (1999) 143 S.J.L.B. 58; [1999] N.P.C. 15; *Times*, March
1, 1999, Ch D . . . . *Digested*, 99/**1401**:
Joined proceedings, 99/4037, 99/4038, 99/4039, 99/4040, 99/4041,
99/4042, 99/4043, 99/4044
Nationwide Building Society v. Various Solicitors (No.4) [1999] C.P.L.R. 606; [2000]
Lloyd's Rep. P.N. 71; *Independent*, October 25, 1999 (C.S.), Ch D . . . . *Digested*, 99/**381**
Nationwide Building Society v. Waters & Co see Nationwide Building Society v. Various
Solicitors (No.3)
Nationwide Life Ltd v. Crisp (Inspector of Taxes) see HSBC Life (UK) Ltd v. Stubbs
(Inspector of Taxes)
Nationwide News Pty Ltd v. Copyright Agency Ltd (1996) 136 A.L.R. 273, Fed Ct
(Aus) (Full Ct) . . . . *Applied*, 00/3575
Nationwide News Pty Ltd v. Wills (1992) 177 C.L.R. 1, HC (Aus). . . . . *Applied*, 98/3091
Naturally Yours Cosmetics Ltd v. Customs and Excise Commissioners (C230/87)
[1988] S.T.C. 879; [1988] E.C.R. 6365; [1989] 1 C.M.L.R. 797; *Times*, November
29, 1988; *Daily Telegraph*, December 31, 1988, ECJ [1987] 2 C.M.L.R. 769;
[1987] V.A.T.T.R. 45, VAT Tr (London) . . . . *Digested*, 89/**1683**:
Applied, 90/4622, 91/3668, 94/4975, 97/4976, 98/4936, 00/5319, 01/5597:
Considered, 00/5347, 01/5556, 01/5598, 01/5599
NATURELLE Trade Mark [1999] R.P.C. 326, Appointed Person . . . . *Digested*, 99/**3542**
Natwest Lombard Factors Ltd v. Arbis see Lombard Natwest Factors Ltd v. Arbis
Navigas Ltd of Gibraltar v. Enron Liquid Fuels Inc [1997] 2 Lloyd's Rep. 759, QBD
(Comm Ct) . . . . *Digested*, 98/**4426**
Nawoor v. Barking Havering and Brentwood HA [1998] Lloyd's Rep. Med. 313, QBD . . *Digested*, 99/**3997**
Nawrot v. Chief Constable of Hampshire, *Independent*, January 7, 1992, CA . . . . *Digested*, 92/**3346**:
Followed, 99/313
Nayler v. Beard [2001] EWCA Civ 1201; [2001] C.P. Rep. 104; [2001] 2 F.L.R. 1346;
[2001] 3 F.C.R. 61; [2001] Fam. Law 801, CA . . . . *Digested*, 01/**551**
NBC Pension Trustees Ltd v. Paddock see Bus Employees Pension Trustees Ltd v. Harrod
NBPF Pension Trustees Ltd v. Paddock see Bus Employees Pension Trustees Ltd v.
Harrod
NCR International Inc's European Patent (No.0420643) see NCR/Late rectification (T939/
95)
NCR/Late rectification (T939/95); *sub nom* NCR International Inc's European Patent
(No.0420643) [1999] E.P.O.R. 167; (1998) 21 (5) I.P.D. 21054, EPO (Technical
Bd App)
Nea Agrex SA v. Baltic Shipping Co Ltd (The Agios Lazarus) [1976] Q.B. 933; [1976]
2 W.L.R. 925; [1976] 2 All E.R. 842; [1976] 2 Lloyd's Rep. 47; 120 S.J. 351,
CA . . . . *Digested*, 76/**2534**:
Applied, 77/119, 78/101, 82/105, 94/4057, 00/4728: *Considered*, 77/117:
Followed, 99/242, 99/4455, 99/4456: *Not followed*, 97/273
Nea Tyhi, The [1982] 1 Lloyd's Rep. 606; [1982] Com. L.R. 9, QBD (Adm Ct) . . . . *Digested*, 82/**2857**:
Applied, 00/4679: *Disapproved*, 86/2252
Neal v. Bingle [1998] Q.B. 466; [1998] 2 W.L.R. 57; [1998] 2 All E.R. 58; [1998]
P.I.Q.R. Q1; (1998) 40 B.M.L.R. 52; (1997) 94(34) L.S.G. 29; (1997) 141
S.J.L.B. 190; *Times*, July 24, 1997, CA. . . . . *Digested*, 97/**1820**
Neale v. Del Soto [1945] K.B. 144, CA. . . . . *Applied*, 47-51/8505,
47-51/8509, 47-51/8526, 47-51/8527, 55/2329, 58/2891, 91/2278, 01/5019:
Considered, 47-51/8513, 47-51/8528, 56/6962, 56/7441, 69/3065, 87/2240:
Distinguished, 47-51/7466, 47-51/7467, 47-51/8503, 47-51/8506,
47-51/8510, 47-51/8525, 52/2947
Neale v. RMJE (A Minor) (1985) 80 Cr. App. R. 20; [1984] Crim. L.R. 485, QBD . . . . . *Digested*, 85/**553**:
Applied, 01/1003: *Followed*, 84/583
Neary v. Dean of Westminster [1999] I.R.L.R. 288, Visitor (Westminster). . . . . *Digested*, 00/**2132**
Neasham v. John Thompson (t/a Thompson & Sons) LTA 1998/7547/1, CA . . . . *Digested*, 99/**1376**
NEC Information Systems Australia Pty Ltd v. Lockhart (1991) 2 N.S.W.L.R. 518, CA
(NSW) . . . . *Followed*, 00/3481

Necrews *v.* ARC Ltd (Unreported, March 10, 1997), CC (Cardiff) [*Ex rel.* Ivor Collett,
Barrister, No.1 Serjeant's Inn, Fleet Street, London, EC4Y 1LL] . . . . *Digested,* 97/**522**:
Considered, 98/453, 98/457: *Followed,* 98/424
Nederhoff *v.* Dijkgraaf en Hoogheemraden van het Hoogheemraadschap Rijnland
(C232/97) [1999] E.C.R. I-6385; [2000] 1 C.M.L.R. 681; [2000] Env. L.R. D17,
ECJ (6th Chamber) . . . . *Digested,* 00/**2305**:
Considered, 99/5044
Nederlandsche Banden Industrie Michelin NV *v.* Commission of the European
Communities (C322/81) [1983] E.C.R. 3461; [1985] 1 C.M.L.R. 282; [1985]
F.S.R. 250, ECJ. . . . . *Digested,* 85/**1319**:
Followed, 00/715
Nederlandse Omroep Stichting *v.* Holdingmaatschappij de Telegraaf NV; *sub nom*
Holdingmaatschappij de Telegraaf NV *v.* Nederlandse Omroep Stichting [2000]
E.C.D.R. 129, RB (Den Haag)
Nederlandse Reassurantie Groep Holding NV *v.* Bacon & Woodrow (No.3) [1997]
L.R.L.R. 678, QBD (Comm Ct) . . . . *Digested,* 98/**3998**
Nederlandse Reassurantie Groep Holding NV *v.* Bacon & Woodrow (No.4) [1998] 2
Costs L.R. 32, QBD. . . . . *Digested,* 00/**452**:
Considered, 99/411
Needler Financial Services *v.* Taber [2001] Pens. L.R. 253; (2001) 98(37) L.S.G. 39;
(2001) 151 N.L.J. 1283; (2001) 145 S.J.L.B. 219; *Times,* August 9, 2001, Ch D . *Digested,* 01/**4593**
Neigel *v.* France (2000) 30 E.H.R.R. 310, ECHR . . . . *Digested,* 01/**3529**:
Applied, 98/3119: *Considered,* 98/3129: *Referred to,* 01/3521
Neil *v.* Ryan [1998] 2 F.L.R. 1068; [1999] 1 F.C.R. 241; [1998] Fam. Law 728, Fam
Div. . . . . *Digested,* 99/**13**
Neil *v.* UEC Industries (Unreported, January 20, 2000), CC (Liverpool) [*Ex rel.* J Keith
Park & Co Solicitors, Claughton House, 39 Barrow Street, St. Helens,
Merseyside] . . . . *Digested,* 00/**1555**
Neill *v.* North Antrim Magistrates Court [1992] 1 W.L.R. 1220; [1992] 4 All E.R. 846;
(1993) 97 Cr. App. R. 121; (1993) 158 J.P. 197; (1994) 6 Admin. L.R. 85; [1993]
Crim. L.R. 945; (1993) 158 J.P.N. 380; *Times,* November 16, 1992, HL. . . . . *Digested,* 93/**680**:
Applied, 00/927: *Considered,* 96/1412, 98/884, 00/1084: *Followed,* 94/992,
95/983, 96/1558: *Subsequent proceedings,* 99/5147
Neill *v.* Wilson [1999] N.I. 1, QBD (NI) . . . . *Digested,* 99/**5147**
Neill Clerk (A Firm) *v.* Healey & Baker see Ball *v.* Banner
Neilson *v.* Betts; *sub nom* Betts *v.* Neilson; Betts *v.* De Vitre; De Vitre *v.* Betts; Tennent
v. Betts; Marshall *v.* Betts; Young *v.* Betts (1871-72) L.R. 5 H.L. 1, HL; affirming
(1867-68) L.R. 3 Ch. App. 429, Lord Chancellor . . . . *Applied,* 85/3384:
Followed, 98/3508
Neilson *v.* Young (Unreported, June 6, 2000), CC (Newcastle) [*Ex rel.* Joanna Droop,
Barrister, 12 King's Bench Walk, Temple, London] . . . . *Digested,* 00/**2584**
Nejad *v.* City Index Ltd [2000] C.C.L.R. 7, CA . . . . *Digested,* 00/**2597**
Nelder *v.* DPP, *Times,* June 11, 1998; *Independent,* June 8, 1998 (C.S.), QBD . . . . *Digested,* 98/**1039**
Nelidow Santis *v.* Secretary of State for the Home Department see Bugdaycay *v.*
Secretary of State for the Home Department
Nell Gwynn House Maintenance Fund Trustees *v.* Customs and Excise Commissioners;
sub nom Trustees of the Nell Gwynn House Maintenance Fund *v.* Customs and
Excise Commissioners [1999] 1 W.L.R. 174; [1999] 1 All E.R. 385; [1999] S.T.C.
79; (2000) 32 H.L.R. 13; [1999] B.T.C. 5025; [1999] B.V.C. 83; [1998]
E.G.C.S. 186; (1999) 143 S.J.L.B. 30; [1998] N.P.C. 163; *Times,* December 17,
1998, HL; reversing [1996] S.T.C. 310; (1996) 72 P. & C.R. 522, CA; reversing
[1994] S.T.C. 995; [1994] S.T.I. 1300; [1994] E.G.C.S. 163; *Times,* October 31,
1994; *Independent,* October 24, 1994, QBD . . . . *Digested,* 99/**5017**:
Considered, 97/4978, 97/4994, 98/4891: *Followed,* 96/5900, 97/4979
Nella *v.* Nella, *Independent,* November 1, 1999 (C.S.), Ch D
Nellins *v.* Chief Constable of the Royal Ulster Constabulary [1998] N.I. 1, QBD (NI). . . . *Digested,* 99/**5140**
Nelson *v.* Andrews (Unreported, October 10, 1997), CC (Bromley) [*Ex rel.* Richard
Case, Barrister, 3 Paper Buildings, Temple] . . . . *Digested,* 98/**428**
Nelson *v.* BBC (No.1) [1977] I.C.R. 649; [1977] I.R.L.R. 148; [1977] T.R. 273, CA . . . . . *Digested,* 77/**1123**:
Applied, 80/1041, 85/1198, 86/1265, 98/2237: *Considered,* 78/1157, 78/1173,
86/1276, 97/2249, 98/2186: *Distinguished,* 82/1067, 82/1120, 83/1276,
84/1262, 85/1203
Nelson *v.* BBC (No.2) [1980] I.C.R. 110; [1979] I.R.L.R. 346; 123 S.J. 552, CA . . . . *Digested,* 80/**1018**:
Applied, 83/1338, 85/1198, 86/1265: *Considered,* 91/1682, 96/2593,
97/2249, 98/2186: *Distinguished,* 82/1067, 82/1120, 83/1276
Nelson *v.* Chief Constable of Cumbria (Unreported, March 6, 2000), CC (Penrith) [*Ex*
rel. John G Baldwin, Barrister, Oriel Chambers, 14 Water Street, Liverpool] . . . . *Digested,* 00/**4217**
Nelson *v.* Greening & Sykes Builders Ltd (No.2) (1999) 77 P. & C.R. D23, CA
Nelson *v.* Kingston Cables Distributors Ltd, *Independent,* June 12, 2000 (C.S.), EAT
Nelson *v.* Nicholson, *Independent,* January 22, 2001 (C.S.), CA
Nelson *v.* Rye [1996] 1 W.L.R. 1378; [1996] 2 All E.R. 186; [1996] E.M.L.R. 37;
[1996] F.S.R. 313; *Times,* December 5, 1995, Ch D . . . . *Digested,* 96/**1236**:
Considered, 97/2378: *Not followed,* 99/458

Nembhard *v.* Hamilton (Unreported, December 13, 2000), CC (Sheffield) [*Ex rel.* Jinder S Boora, Barrister, 24 The Ropewalk, Nottingham] . . . . *Digested*, 01/**1774**
NEMG Insurance Association *v.* Jones see National Employers Mutual General Insurance Association *v.* Jones
Neo Investments Inc *v.* Cargill International SA [2001] 2 Lloyd's Rep. 33, QBD (Comm Ct) . . . . *Digested*, 01/**664**
Neocli *v.* Customs and Excise Commissioners [1999] B.V.C. 2088, V&DTr
NEOPOST/Thermal printing (T284/94) [2000] E.P.O.R. 24, EPO (Technical Bd App) . . *Digested*, 00/**3603**
Nesbit Evans Group Australia Pty Ltd *v.* Impro Ltd [1998] F.S.R. 306, Fed Ct (Aus) (Full Ct) . . . . *Digested*, 98/**3463**
Nessa *v.* Chief Adjudication Officer [1999] 1 W.L.R. 1937; [1999] 4 All E.R. 677; [1999] 2 F.L.R. 1116; [1999] 3 F.C.R. 538; [2000] Fam. Law 28; (1999) 96(42) L.S.G. 42; (1999) 149 N.L.J. 1619; (1999) 143 S.J.L.B. 250; *Times*, October 27, 1999; *Independent*, October 27, 1999, HL; affirming [1998] 2 All E.R. 728; [1998] 1 F.L.R. 879; [1998] 2 F.C.R. 461; [1998] Fam. Law 329; (1998) 142 S.J.L.B. 78; *Times*, February 11, 1998, CA . . . . *Digested*, 99/**4564**
Neste Chemicals SA *v.* DK Line SA (The Sargasso) [1994] 3 All E.R. 180; [1994] 2 Lloyd's Rep. 6; [1995] I.L.Pr. 553; *Times*, April 4, 1994, CA; affirming [1993] 1 Lloyd's Rep. 424, QBD (Adm Ct) . . . . *Digested*, 94/**487**: *Applied*, 01/830
Neste Markkinointi Oy *v.* Yotuuli Ky (C214/99) [2001] All E.R. (EC) 76; [2000] E.C.R. I-11121; [2001] 4 C.M.L.R. 27; [2001] C.E.C. 54, ECJ (6th Chamber) . . . . *Digested*, 01/**770**
Neste Oy *v.* Lloyds Bank Plc (The Tiiskeri, The Nestegas and The Enskeri) [1983] 2 Lloyd's Rep. 658; [1983] Com. L.R. 145; (1983) 133 N.L.J. 597, QBD (Comm Ct) . . . . *Digested*, 83/**201**:
Applied, 97/5578, 00/3433: *Considered*, 92/97, 92/489, 93/73
Nestle *v.* National Westminster Bank Plc [1993] 1 W.L.R. 1260; [1994] 1 All E.R. 118; [1992] N.P.C. 68; *Times*, May 11, 1992, CA; affirming [2000] W.T.L.R. 795; *Independent*, July 4, 1988 (C.S.), Ch D . . . . *Digested*, 01/**5531**
Nestle Holdings Inc *v.* Internal Revenue Commissioner 1 I.T.L. Rep. 613, US Ct
Nestle UK Ltd *v.* Zeta Espacial SA; *sub nom* MAGIC BALL Trade Mark [2000] E.T.M.R. 226; [2000] R.P.C. 439; (1999) 22(9) I.P.D. 22087, Ch D . . . . *Digested*, 00/**3793**
NESTLE/Legitimate expectation (T343/95) [2000] E.P.O.R. 452, EPO (Technical Bd App) . . . . *Digested*, 00/**3622**
Net Book Agreement 1957 (M and N), Re see Net Book Agreement 1957 (No.4), Re
Net Book Agreement 1957 (No.3), Re [1998] I.C.R. 741, RPC . . . . *Digested*, 98/**732**
Net Book Agreement 1957 (No.4), Re; *sub nom* Net Book Agreement 1957 (M and N), Re [1998] I.C.R. 753; [1997] E.M.L.R. 647; (1997) 94(16) L.S.G. 29; (1997) 141 S.J.L.B. 95; *Times*, March 20, 1997, RPC . . . . *Digested*, 97/**862**:
Applied, 99/701
Netherlands *v.* Commission of the European Communities (C11/76) [1979] E.C.R. 245, ECJ . . . . *Digested*, 80/**1082**:
Followed, 00/170
Netherlands *v.* Commission of the European Communities (C27/94) [1998] E.C.R. I-5581, ECJ . . . . *Followed*, 00/2337
Netherlands *v.* Commission of the European Communities (C28/94) [1999] E.C.R. I-1973; [2000] 2 C.M.L.R. 436, ECJ . . . . *Digested*, 00/**2337**
Netherlands *v.* Commission of the European Communities (C478/93) [1995] E.C.R. I-3081, ECJ . . . . *Digested*, 96/**2809**:
Followed, 00/2349
Netherlands *v.* Commission of the European Communities (C48/91) [1993] E.C.R. I-5611, ECJ . . . . *Digested*, 94/**4730**:
Followed, 00/170
Netherlands *v.* ECSC High Authority (C25/59) [1960] E.C.R. 386; [1960] E.C.R. 723, ECJ . . . . *Applied*, 98/2306
Netherlands *v.* European Parliament (C377/98); *sub nom* Legal Protection of Biotechnological Inventions (C377/98), Re [2001] E.C.R. I-7079; [2001] 3 C.M.L.R. 49, ECJ
Netherlands *v.* Fenby [1999] C.O.D. 468, QBD
Netherlands *v.* Goldnames Inc [2001] E.T.M.R. 97, Arbitration
Netherlands *v.* Hayward see Netherlands *v.* Youell
Netherlands *v.* Ruffer (C814/79) [1980] E.C.R. 3807; [1981] 3 C.M.L.R. 293, ECJ . . . . *Digested*, 81/**1037**:
Considered, 86/1512, 92/2790: *Distinguished*, 00/790
Netherlands *v.* Youell; Netherlands *v.* Hayward [1998] 1 Lloyd's Rep. 236; [1998] C.L.C. 44, CA; affirming [1997] 2 Lloyd's Rep. 440, QBD (Comm Ct) . . . . *Digested*, 98/**3392**
Netherlands BV, Re 1 I.T.L. Rep. 283, VwGH (A)
Nethermere (St Neots) Ltd *v.* Taverna [1984] I.C.R. 612; [1984] I.R.L.R. 240; (1984) 81 L.S.G. 2147; (1984) 134 N.L.J. 544, CA; reversing [1983] I.C.R. 319; [1983] I.R.L.R. 103, EAT . . . . *Digested*, 84/**1206**:
Considered, 98/2138, 01/2264: *Followed*, 97/2195, 98/2137
Netherton *v.* Netherton [2000] W.T.L.R. 1171; (1999-2000) 2 I.T.E.L.R. 241, Ch D . . . . *Digested*, 01/**5524**
NETMEETING Trade Mark see Microsoft Corp's Trade Mark Application
NetObjects Trade Mark Application; *sub nom* SITEPRODUCER Trade Mark [1998-99] Info. T.L.R. 265, OHIM (3rd Bd App) . . . . *Digested*, 01/**4002**

NETWORK 90 Trade Mark [1984] R.P.C. 549, Ch D . . . . *Followed*, 98/3498
Network Housing Association Ltd *v.* Westminster City Council [1995] Env. L.R. 176;
    (1995) 27 H.L.R. 189; 93 L.G.R. 280; [1994] E.G.C.S. 173; *Times*, November 8,
    1994; *Independent*, November 7, 1994 (C.S.), QBD . . . . *Digested*, 96/**2745**:
        Considered, 96/2744, 00/2304: *Distinguished*, 96/2746: *Followed*, 00/6602
Network Insurance Brokers Ltd *v.* Customs and Excise Commissioners [1998] S.T.C.
    742; [1998] B.T.C. 5241; [1998] B.V.C. 259; *Independent*, March 2, 1998 (C.S.),
    QBD . . . . *Digested*, 98/**4898**:
        Distinguished, 00/5304
Network Multimedia Television Ltd *v.* Jobserve Ltd (2001) 24(6) I.P.D. 24038; *Times*,
    January 25, 2001, Ch D . . . . *Digested*, 01/**566**
Network Multimedia Television Ltd (t/a Silicon.com) *v.* Jobserve Ltd (Restored Injunction
    Hearing) see Jobserve Ltd *v.* Network Multimedia Television Ltd (Restored
    Injunction Hearing)
Neudorf *v.* Nettwerk Productions Ltd [2000] R.P.C. 935, Sup Ct (BC) . . . . *Digested*, 01/**3856**
Neue Maxhutte Stahlwerke GmbH *v.* Commission of the European Communities (T129/
    95) [1999] E.C.R. II-17; [1999] 3 C.M.L.R. 366, CFI (5th Chamber) . . . . *Digested*, 00/**732**
Neurone Tech *v.* Neurones [1999] E.T.M.R. 611, Cass (F)
Neutral Red Trade Mark, Re [1998] E.T.M.R. 277, OLG (Karlsruhe)
Neutrogena Corp *v.* Golden Ltd (t/a Garnier) [1996] R.P.C. 473; (1996) 19(4) I.P.D.
    19028, CA; affirming Ch D . . . . *Digested*, 96/**5715**:
        Referred to, 98/3516
Neville Estates Ltd *v.* Madden [1962] Ch. 832; [1961] 3 W.L.R. 999; [1961] 3 All E.R.
    769; 105 S.J. 806, Ch D . . . . *Digested*, 61/**1002**:
        Applied, 71/12147: *Considered*, 68/365, 87/3759: *Followed*, 86/3434,
        86/3438, 99/3561
New Brunswick Railway Co Ltd *v.* British & French Trust Corp Ltd [1939] A.C. 1; [1938]
    4 All E.R. 747, HL. . . . . *Applied*, 55/1535,
        61/3265, 72/815, 78/536, 91/189, 99/3328: *Approved*, 68/1467:
        Considered, 96/497: *Distinguished*, 56/4946: *Followed*, 67/3134
New Bullas Trading Ltd, Re [1994] B.C.C. 36; [1994] 1 B.C.L.C. 485; *Times*, January 12,
    1994, CA; reversing [1993] B.C.C. 251; [1993] B.C.L.C. 1389, Ch D
    (Companies Ct) . . . . *Digested*, 94/**2601**:
        Considered, 95/567, 01/733: *Disapproved*, 01/732: *Distinguished*, 00/3483
New Century Cleaning Co *v.* Church [2000] I.R.L.R. 27; *Independent*, April 23, 1999,
    CA . . . . *Digested*, 99/**2148**
New England International Surety Inc *v.* Cripps see Cripps *v.* Heritage Distribution Corp
New Europe Consulting Ltd *v.* Commission of the European Communities (T231/97)
    [1999] E.C.R. II-2403; [1999] 2 C.M.L.R. 1452, CFI (4th Chamber) . . . . *Digested*, 99/**2240**
New Ford Holland *v.* Commission of the European Communities (C8/95 P) see John
    Deere Ltd *v.* Commission of the European Communities (C7/95 P)
New Forest DC *v.* Lascar Electronics Ltd (2001) 16 P.A.D. 59, Planning Inspector
New Forest DC *v.* New Forest Activities (1998) 13 P.A.D. 358, Planning Inspector
New Forest DC *v.* T Smith Mink Farms Ltd (2001) 16 P.A.D. 43, Planning Inspector
New Hampshire Insurance Co *v.* Rush & Tompkins Group Plc [1998] 2 B.C.L.C. 471, CA   *Digested*, 99/**3298**
New Hampshire Insurance Co Ltd *v.* Aerospace Finance Ltd [1998] 2 Lloyd's Rep. 539,
    QBD (Comm Ct) . . . . *Digested*, 99/**716**
New Hampshire Insurance Co Ltd *v.* MGN Ltd (1996); Maxwell Communication Corp
    Plc (In Administration) *v.* New Hampshire Insurance Co Ltd [1997] L.R.L.R. 24;
    [1996] C.L.C. 1728, CA; affirming [1996] C.L.C. 1692, QBD (Comm Ct) . . . . . . *Digested*, 96/**3572**:
        Applied, 99/3382, 99/4020: *Considered*, 01/3840
New Hampshire Insurance Co Ltd *v.* Philips Electronics North America Corp (No.1)
    [1998] C.L.C. 1062; [1998] I.L.Pr. 256; [1999] Lloyd's Rep. I.R. 58, CA . . . . . . *Digested*, 97/**890**:
        Considered, 98/777: *Followed*, 00/3516
New Hampshire Insurance Co Ltd *v.* Philips Electronics North America Corp (No.2)
    [1998] C.L.C. 1244; [1999] Lloyd's Rep. I.R. 66, QBD (Comm Ct) . . . . *Digested*, 99/**3395**
New Hearts Ltd *v.* Cosmopolitan Investments Ltd; *sub nom* Cosmopolitan Investments
    Ltd *v.* New Hearts Ltd [1997] 2 B.C.L.C. 249, OH . . . . *Digested*, 98/**5526**
New Islington and Hackney Housing Association Ltd *v.* Pollard Thomas and Edwards Ltd
    [2001] B.L.R. 74; (2001) 3 T.C.L.R. 25; [2001] Lloyd's Rep. P.N. 243; [2001]
    P.N.L.R. 20; (2001) 17 Const. L.J. 55, QBD (T&CC) . . . . *Digested*, 01/**4511**
New Jersey *v.* TLO 469 U.S. 325, US Ct . . . . *Considered*, 99/3120
New Technology Systems Ltd, Re; *sub nom* Official Receiver *v.* Prior [1997] B.C.C. 810,
    CA; affirming [1996] B.C.C. 694, Ch D . . . . *Digested*, 98/**675**
New Timbiqui Gold Mines Ltd, Re [1961] Ch. 319; [1961] 2 W.L.R. 344; [1961] 1 All E.R. 865;
    105 S.J. 206, Ch D . . . . *Digested*, 61/**1167**:
        Applied, 98/5521: *Considered*, 00/5956: *Followed*, 86/298, 87/338
New Windsor Corp *v.* Mellor [1975] Ch. 380; [1975] 3 W.L.R. 25; [1975] 3 All E.R. 44;
    73 L.G.R. 337; 30 P. & C.R. 429; 119 S.J. 440, CA; affirming [1974] 1 W.L.R.
    1504; [1974] 2 All E.R. 510; 72 L.G.R. 682; 118 S.J. 580, Ch D . . . . *Digested*, 75/**288**:
        Considered, 80/246.1, 94/380, 00/4616
New World Payphones Ltd *v.* Customs and Excise Commissioners [1999] B.V.C. 2188,
    V&DTr
New York Times Co Inc *v.* Tasini [2001] E.B.L.R. 90, US Ct

New Zealand Lotteries Commission's Trade Mark Application [1998] E.T.M.R. 569, OHIM
(3rd Bd App)

New Zealand Post Ltd v. Leng [1998-99] Info. T.L.R. 233, HC (NZ) . . . .   *Digested*, 01/**5357**

New Zealand Rail Ltd v. Accident Rehabilitation & Compensation Insurance Corp. . . . .   *Followed*, 00/4928

Newark and Sherwood DC v. Ballard Fort Ltd (2001) 16 P.A.D. 89, Planning Inspector

Newark and Sherwood DC v. Secretary of State for the Environment, Transport and the
Regions [1999] J.P.L. 447, QBD . . . .   *Digested*, 99/**4246**

Newbold v. Leicester City Council [1999] I.C.R. 1182; (2000) 2 L.G.L.R. 303; [2000]
B.L.G.R. 58; (1999) 96(31) L.S.G. 38; (1999) 143 S.J.L.B. 211; *Times*, August
20, 1999 ; *Independent*, July 23, 1999, CA . . . .   *Digested*, 99/**2014**

Newbury v. Bath DHA (1999) 47 B.M.L.R. 138, QBD. . . . .   *Digested*, 99/**3989**

Newbury v. Davis [1974] R.T.R. 367; [1974] Crim. L.R. 262; (1974) 118 S.J. 222, QBD .   *Digested*, 74/**3351**:
Approved, 95/6306: *Distinguished*, 75/2998, 76/2426: *Explained*, 92/3780:
Followed, 01/3832

Newbury DC v. Donfield Homes Ltd (1998) 13 P.A.D. 148, Planning Inspector

Newbury DC v. International Synthetic Rubber Co Ltd see Newbury DC v. Secretary of
State for the Environment

Newbury DC v. Secretary of State for the Environment; Newbury DC v. International
Synthetic Rubber Co Ltd [1981] A.C. 578; [1980] 2 W.L.R. 379; [1980] 1 All
E.R. 731; 78 L.G.R. 306; (1980) 40 P. & C.R. 148; [1980] J.P.L. 325; 124 S.J.
186, HL; reversing [1978] 1 W.L.R. 1241; [1979] 1 All E.R. 243; 77 L.G.R. 60;
(1979) 37 P. & C.R. 73; (1978) 248 E.G. 223; (1978) 248 E.G. 1017; [1979]
J.P.L. 26; 122 S.J. 524, CA; reversing 75 L.G.R. 608; (1978) 35 P. & C.R. 170;
(1977) 242 E.G. 377; [1977] J.P.L. 373; 121 S.J. 254, QBD . . . .   *Digested*, 80/**2667**:
Applied, 82/3185, 84/3413, 84/3465, 88/3530, 89/3541, 92/4363,
93/3936, 93/3948, 94/4435, 94/4462, 98/4212, 99/4221, 99/4243,
00/4418, 00/4479, 00/4511, 00/4515: *Considered*, 83/3719, 84/3478,
84/4734, 89/3643, 90/4452, 94/4331, 95/4784: *Distinguished*, 82/3169,
01/4699: *Referred to*, 83/3716, 90/4362, 91/3524, 91/5757

Newby v. Bird (Unreported, May 31, 2000), CC (Birkenhead) [*Ex rel.* Tim Grover,
Barrister, 7 Harrington Street, Liverpool]. . . . .   *Digested*, 00/**2564**

Newcastle Building Society v. Paterson Robertson & Graham 2001 S.C. 734; 2001
S.C.L.R. 737; [2001] P.N.L.R. 36; [2001] N.P.C. 63; 2001 G.W.D. 12-446, OH . .   *Digested*, 01/**6819**

Newcastle Protection and Indemnity Association Ltd v. Assurance Foreningen Gard
Gjensidig [1998] 2 Lloyd's Rep. 387, QBD (Comm Ct) . . . .   *Digested*, 98/**3390**

Newcastle upon Tyne City Council v. Morrison (2000) 32 H.L.R. 891; [2000] L. & T.R.
333, CA . . . .   *Digested*, 00/**3923**

Newell v. Secretary of State for the Environment, Transport and the Regions see
Fletcher Estates (Harlescott) Ltd v. Secretary of State for the Environment,
Transport and the Regions

Newham LBC v. Adan see Adan v. Newham LBC

Newham LBC v. Conwell see Conwell v. Newham LBC

Newham LBC v. Hills (1998) 76 P. & C.R. D24, CA

Newham LBC v. I [1997] 2 F.C.R. 629; (1997) 161 J.P.N. 676, Fam Div. . . . .   *Digested*, 97/**366**:
Not followed, 99/2352

Newham LBC v. Phillips [1998] 1 F.L.R. 613; (1998) 30 H.L.R. 859; (1998) 10 Admin.
L.R. 309; [1998] Fam. Law 140; [1997] E.G.C.S. 143; (1997) 94(45) L.S.G. 27;
(1997) 141 S.J.L.B. 251; [1997] N.P.C. 149; *Times*, November 12, 1997, CA . . . . .   *Digested*, 97/**2749**

Newland v. Boardwell; MacDonald v. Platt [1983] 1 W.L.R. 1453; [1983] 3 All E.R.
179; [1984] R.T.R. 189; (1983) 133 N.L.J. 847; (1983) 127 S.J. 580, CA . . . . . .   *Digested*, 84/**472**:
Distinguished, 92/3434: *Followed*, 98/368

Newlon Housing Trust v. Al-Sulaimen; *sub nom* Newlon Housing Trust v. Alsulaimen
[1999] 1 A.C. 313; [1998] 3 W.L.R. 451; [1998] 4 All E.R. 1; [1998] 2 F.L.R. 690;
[1998] 3 F.C.R. 183; (1998) 30 H.L.R. 1132; [1999] L. & T.R. 38; [1998] Fam.
Law 589; (1998) 95(35) L.S.G. 35; (1998) 148 N.L.J. 1303; (1998) 142
S.J.L.B. 247; *Times*, August 20, 1998, HL; reversing [1997] 1 F.L.R. 914; [1997]
2 F.C.R. 33; (1997) 29 H.L.R. 767; [1997] Fam. Law 397; (1997) 94(8) L.S.G.
27; (1997) 141 S.J.L.B. 36; *Times*, January 24, 1997, CA . . . .   *Digested*, 98/**2473**:
Followed, 99/2406

Newman v. Folkes B3/2001/1376, CAHQ9901169, QBD [*Ex rel.* Adam Walker,
Barrister, Lamb Chambers, Temple, London] . . . .   *Digested*, 01/**1511**

Newman (Inspector of Taxes) v. Hatt [2001] R.V.R. 307, Lands Tr

Newman (t/a Mantella Publishing) v. Modern Bookbinders Ltd [2000] 1 W.L.R. 2559;
[2000] 2 All E.R. 814; *Independent*, February 3, 2000, CA . . . .   *Digested*, 00/**17**

Newman v. Morgan (Inspector of Taxes) see Newman v. Pepper (Inspector of Taxes)

Newman v. Pepper (Inspector of Taxes); Newman v. Morgan (Inspector of Taxes)
[2000] S.T.C. (S.C.D.) 345; [2000] S.T.I. 1011, Sp Comm . . . .   *Digested*, 00/**4925**

Newman v. Secretary of State for Health (No.1); *sub nom* Creutzfeldt-Jakob Disease
Litigation (No.2), Re; CJD Litigation (No.2), Re; Creutzfeldt-Jakob Disease
Litigation (No.4), Re; CJD Litigation (No.4), Re; Newman v. United Kingdom
Medical Research Council (2000) 54 B.M.L.R. 85; *Times*, December 20, 1997,
CA; reversing [1996] 7 Med. L.R. 309; (2000) 54 B.M.L.R. 8, QBD . . . .   *Digested*, 98/**3962**:
Previous proceedings, 00/4199

Newman v. Secretary of State for Health (No.2); *sub nom* Creutzfeldt-Jakob Disease
  Litigation (No.6), Re; CJD Litigation (No.6), Re (2000) 54 B.M.L.R. 95, QBD . .   *Digested*, 00/**4195**
Newman v. United Kingdom Medical Research Council see Newman v. Secretary of
  State for Health (No.1)
Newpoint Plumbing Services v. Edmundson Electrical Ltd (Unreported, November 3,
  1999), CC (Central London) [*Ex rel.* Paul McGrath, Barrister, 1 Temple Gardens,
  Temple, London] . . . .   *Digested*, 00/**464**
Newport BC v. Secretary of State for Wales [1998] Env. L.R. 174; [1998] 1 P.L.R. 47;
  [1998] J.P.L. 377, CA . . . .   *Digested*, 98/**4214**
Newport CBC v. Powell (2000) 15 P.A.D. 485, Planning Inspector
Newry Building Supplies Ltd v. Commissioner of Valuation for Northern Ireland [1999]
  R.A. 420, Lands Tr (NI) . . . .   *Digested*, 00/**5678**
News Group Newspapers Ltd, Ex p. see R. v. News Group Newspapers Ltd
News International Newspapers Ltd v. Customs and Excise Commissioners see
  Customs and Excise Commissioners v. News International Newspapers Ltd
News International Plc v. Borgognon CHANI 97/1646 CMS3, CA; affirming CH.1997-N-
  2577, Ch D . . . .   *Digested*, 98/**583**
News Verlags GmbH & Co KG v. Austria (31457/97) (2001) 31 E.H.R.R. 8; 9 B.H.R.C.
  625, ECHR . . . .   *Digested*, 01/**3474**
Newspaper Discount Vouchers, Re [1998] E.C.C. 21, OGH (A)
Newspaper Licensing Agency Ltd v. Marks & Spencer Plc [2001] UKHL 38; [2001] 3
  W.L.R. 290; [2001] 3 All E.R. 977; [2001] E.C.C. 52; [2001] E.C.D.R. 28;
  [2001] E.M.L.R. 43; (2001) 24(9) I.P.D. 24055; (2001) 98(33) L.S.G. 32;
  Times, July 13, 2001; *Independent*, October 29, 2001 (C.S); *Daily Telegraph*, July
  17, 2001, HL; affirming [2001] Ch. 257; [2000] 3 W.L.R. 1256; [2000] 4 All
  E.R. 239; [2000] E.C.D.R. 381; [2000] E.M.L.R. 704; [2001] R.P.C. 5; (2000)
  23(8) I.P.D. 23059; (2000) 97(25) L.S.G. 38; (2000) 150 N.L.J. 900; *Times*,
  June 15, 2000; *Independent*, July 17, 2000 (C.S), CA; reversing [1999] E.C.C.
  425; [1999] E.M.L.R. 369; [1999] I.T.C.L.R. 350; [1999] R.P.C. 536; (1999)
  22(3) I.P.D. 22030; *Times*, January 26, 1999; *Independent*, January 28, 1999,
  Ch D . . . .   *Digested*, 01/**3857**
Newton (t/a RE Newton) v. Customs and Excise Commissioners [2001] S.T.I. 1231,
  V&DTr
Newton v. Whittaker (Unreported, January 7, 2000), CC (Sheffield) [*Ex rel.* Andrew
  Granville Stafford, Barrister, 4 King's Bench Walk, Temple, London] . . . .   *Digested*, 00/**1579**
Newton & Kluber Lubrications v. Prime Unreported [*Ex rel.* Richard Copnall, Barrister] .   *Digested*, 97/**567**:
                                                      Approved, 98/398
Newtons of Wembley Ltd v. Williams [1965] 1 Q.B. 560; [1964] 3 W.L.R. 888; [1964] 3
  All E.R. 532; 108 S.J. 619, CA; affirming [1964] 1 W.L.R. 1028; [1964] 2 All
  E.R. 135; 108 S.J. 621, QBD . . . .   *Digested*, 64/**3288**:
                      Distinguished, 87/**3345**, 97/2503, 00/4675
Next Generation Clubs Ltd v. Secretary of State for the Environment, Transport and the
  Regions; *sub nom* R. v. Secretary of State for the Environment, Transport and the
  Regions Ex p. Next Generation Ltd [2000] E.G.C.S. 109, CA; reversing (1999)
  96(45) L.S.G. 35, QBD
Next Plc v. National Farmers Union Mutual Insurance Co Ltd [1997] E.G.C.S. 181,
  Ch D . . . .   *Considered*, 98/3649
NEYNABER/Basic lead salts (T341/92) [1995] E.P.O.R. 563, EPO (Technical Bd App) .   *Considered*, 00/3611
NG (A Bankrupt), Re; *sub nom* Trustee of the Estate of NG v. NG [1997] B.C.C. 507;
  [1998] 2 F.L.R. 386; [1997] B.P.I.R. 267; [1998] Fam. Law 515, Ch D . . . .   *Digested*, 97/**3016**:
                     Applied, 97/3015: *Considered*, 99/3228
Ng Ka Ling v. Director of Immigration 6 B.H.R.C. 447, CFA (HK) . . . .   *Digested*, 99/**766**
Ngcobo v. Thor Chemicals Holdings Ltd, *Times*, November 10, 1995, CA . . . .   *Digested*, 96/**1076**:
                             Distinguished, 98/749
Ngee Hin Chong v. Commissioner of Taxation 2 I.T.L. Rep. 707, Fed Ct (Aus) (Full Ct);
  affirming 1 I.T.L. Rep. 75, AAT (Aus)
NGK INSULATORS/Zirconia ceramics (T155/88) [1998] E.P.O.R. 161, EPO (Technical Bd
  App)
NGK Spark Plug Co Ltd v. Biltema Sweden AB [2000] E.T.M.R. 507, HR (Swe)
Ngo v. Lewisham LBC (Unreported, February 2, 1999), CC (Bromley) [*Ex rel.* Jon
  Holbrook, Barrister, 2 Garden Court, Middle Temple, London] . . . .   *Digested*, 99/**1390**
Nguyen v. Immigration and Naturalization Service 10 B.H.R.C. 592, US Ct
Nguyen v. Searchnet Associates Ltd 2000 S.L.T. (Sh Ct) 83; 1999 S.C.L.R. 1075;
  [1999] 3 C.M.L.R. 413; 1999 G.W.D. 23-1106, Sh Pr . . . .   *Digested*, 99/**5680**
NHS Pensions Agency v. Pensions Ombudsman; *sub nom* Beechinor, Re [1997]
  O.P.L.R. 99, QBD . . . .   *Digested*, 98/**4136**
NHS Trust A v. H [2001] 2 F.L.R. 501; [2001] Fam. Law 664; *Times*, May 17, 2001, Fam
  Div . . . .   *Digested*, 01/**2935**
NHS Trust A v. M; NHS Trust B v. H [2001] Fam. 348; [2001] 2 W.L.R. 942; [2001] 1
  All E.R. 801; [2001] 2 F.L.R. 367; [2001] 1 F.C.R. 406; [2001] H.R.L.R. 12;
  [2001] Lloyd's Rep. Med. 28; (2001) 58 B.M.L.R. 87; [2001] Fam. Law 501;
  Times, November 29, 2000; *Daily Telegraph*, October 31, 2000, Fam Div . . . . . .   *Digested*, 01/**3571**
NHS Trust B v. H see NHS Trust A v. M

Niagara Mechanical Services International Ltd (In Administration), Re; *sub nom* Canary Wharf Contractors (DS6) Ltd *v.* Niagara Mechanical Services International Ltd (In Administration) [2001] B.C.C. 393; [2000] 2 B.C.L.C. 425, Ch D (Companies Ct) . . . . *Digested,* 00/**3460**
Niase, The; *sub nom* Shell Marketing (Oman) Ltd *v.* Owners of the Niase [2000] 1 Lloyd's Rep. 455; [2000] C.L.C. 768, QBD (Adm Ct) . . . . *Digested,* 00/**4708**
Nicholas *v.* Environment Agency [1999] Env. L.R. 276, QBD . . . . *Digested,* 98/**1012**
Nicholas *v.* Nicholas [1984] F.L.R. 285; [1984] Fam. Law 118, CA . . . . *Digested,* 84/**1121**:
                                                                                                                                 Followed, 01/3707
Nicholl *v.* Ryder [2000] E.M.L.R. 632; *Independent,* February 21, 2000 (C.S.), CA . . . . *Digested,* 00/**875**
Nicholls *v.* BBC [1999] E.M.L.R. 791, CA. . . . . *Digested,* 99/**3927**
Nicholls *v.* Highways Agency [2000] 2 E.G.L.R. 81; [2000] 24 E.G. 167; [2000] R.V.R. 230, Lands Tr. . . . . *Digested,* 00/**4432**
Nicholls *v.* Nicholls [1997] 1 W.L.R. 314; [1997] 2 All E.R. 97; [1997] 1 F.L.R. 649; [1997] 3 F.C.R. 14; [1997] Fam. Law 321; (1997) 147 N.L.J. 61; *Times,* January 21, 1997, CA . . . . *Digested,* 97/**2447**:
                                                                                                                                 Considered, 01/451
Nicholls (Everad) *v.* Queen, The, *Times,* January 30, 2001, PC (StV) . . . . *Digested,* 01/**1148**
Nicholls *v.* Yorkshire Water Services Ltd (Unreported, July 8, 1998), CC (Pontefract) [*Ex rel.* Stephen J Glover, Barrister, 37 Park Square, Leeds] . . . . *Digested,* 98/**1682**
Nichols Advanced Vehicle Systems Inc *v.* Rees (No.1) [1979] R.P.C. 127, Ch D . . . . *Digested,* 79/**354**:
                                                                                                                                 Considered, 98/3424
Nichols Advanced Vehicle Systems Inc *v.* Rees (No.2) [1985] R.P.C. 445; (1985) 82 L.S.G. 1715; (1985) 129 S.J. 401; *Times,* March 23, 1985, CA. . . . . *Digested,* 85/**2683**:
                                                                                                                                 Considered, 01/476
Nicholson *v.* Bath and North East Somerset Council (1998) 95(27) L.S.G. 26, QBD
Nicholson *v.* Halton General Hospital NHS Trust [1999] P.I.Q.R. P310; (2000) 56 B.M.L.R. 150, CA. . . . . *Digested,* 99/**572**
Nicholson *v.* Little [1956] 1 W.L.R. 829; [1956] 2 All E.R. 699; 100 S.J. 490, CA . . . . . *Digested,* 56/**1650**:
                                                                                                                                 Considered, 00/398
Nicholson *v.* Markham (1998) 75 P. & C.R. 428; [1997] N.P.C. 53, CA . . . . *Digested,* 97/**4255**
Nicholson *v.* Secretary of State for the Environment, Transport and the Regions (1998) 76 P. & C.R. 191; [1998] 2 P.L.R. 6; [1998] J.P.L. 553, QBD . . . . *Digested,* 98/**4207**
Nicholson *v.* Smiths Shiprepairers (North Shields) Ltd see Thompson *v.* Smiths Shiprepairers (North Shields) Ltd
Nickless *v.* Osborne (Unreported, October 1, 1999), CC (Torquay) [*Ex rel.* Adrian Posta, Barrister, South Western Chambers, 12 Middle Street, Taunton] . . . . *Digested,* 00/**1724**
Nicodemo *v.* Italy (Unreported, September 2, 1997), ECHR. *Considered,* 98/3129
Nicol *v.* DPP; Selvanayagam *v.* DPP (1996) 160 J.P. 155; [1996] Crim. L.R. 318; (1996) 160 J.P.N. 14; *Times,* November 22, 1995, QBD . . . . *Digested,* 95/**1240**:
                                                                                                                                 Approved, 00/950
Nicol & Andrew Ltd *v.* Brinkley [1996] O.P.L.R. 361, Ch D . . . . *Digested,* 98/**4135**
Niderost-Huber *v.* Switzerland (1998) 25 E.H.R.R. 709, ECHR . . . . *Digested,* 98/**3125**:
                                                                                                                                 Applied, 98/3126
Niedbala *v.* Poland (27915/95) (2001) 33 E.H.R.R. 48, ECHR
Nielsen *v.* Denmark (33488/96) (2001) 33 E.H.R.R. 9, ECHR . . . . *Digested,* 01/**3515**
Niemietz *v.* Germany (A/251B) (1993) 16 E.H.R.R. 97, ECHR. . . . . *Digested,* 93/**2157**:
                                                                     Applied, 98/3154: *Considered,* 00/3248
Niftylift Ltd *v.* Walker (Unreported, January 6, 1998), CC (Milton Keynes) [*Ex rel.* Robert Jan Temmink, 35 Essex Street, Temple, London] . . . . *Digested,* 98/**1743**
Nigerian National Shipping Lines Ltd (In Liquidation) *v.* Mutual Ltd (The Windfall) [1998] 2 Lloyd's Rep. 664, QBD (Comm Ct) . . . . *Digested,* 99/**4485**
Nightfreight Plc *v.* Customs and Excise Commissioners [1998] B.V.C. 2232, V&DTr . . . . *Digested,* 98/**4921**
Nightingale Holdings *v.* Customs and Excise Commissioners [2000] S.T.I. 1501, V&DTr
Nightingale Mayfair Ltd *v.* Mehta [2000] W.T.L.R. 901, Ch D . . . . *Digested,* 01/**5513**
Nijar *v.* Mann; *sub nom* Mann *v.* Nijar (2000) 32 H.L.R. 223; [1998] E.G.C.S. 188; (1999) 96(1) L.S.G. 25, CA . . . . *Digested,* 00/**3903**
Nijhuis *v.* Bestuur van het Landelijk Instituut Sociale Verzekeringen (C360/97) [1999] E.C.R. I-1919; [2000] 2 C.M.L.R. 801, ECJ. . . . . *Digested,* 00/**4818**
Nikitenko *v.* Leboeuf Lamb Greene & Macrae, *Times,* January 26, 1999, Ch D . . . . *Digested,* 99/**145**
Nikko Hotels (UK) Ltd *v.* MEPC Plc [1991] 2 E.G.L.R. 103; [1991] 28 E.G. 86, Ch D . . . *Digested,* 92/**2734**:
                                                                     Applied, 92/2740, 98/701, 00/3489: *Distinguished,* 93/2524
Nikolova *v.* Bulgaria (31195/96) (2001) 31 E.H.R.R. 3, ECHR . . . . *Digested,* 01/**3563**
Nilsen *v.* Norway (2000) 30 E.H.R.R. 878, ECHR. . . . . *Digested,* 01/**3464**
Ninian Spenceley Peckitt's Patent Application (No.2318058A), Re [1999] R.P.C. 337; (1999) 22(2) I.P.D. 22021, PO. . . . . *Digested,* 99/**3511**
Nippon Fire & Marine Insurance Co *v.* MV Tourcoing 167 F.3d 99, US Ct. . . . . *Considered,* 00/866
Nippon Yusen Kaisha Ltd *v.* Scindia Steam Navigation Co Ltd (The Jalagouri); *sub nom* Scindia Steamship Navigation Co Ltd Bombay *v.* Nippon Yusen Kaisha Ltd (The Jalagouri) [2000] 1 All E.R. (Comm) 700; [2000] 1 Lloyd's Rep. 515; [2000] C.L.C. 1051; *Independent,* April 7, 2000, CA; affirming [1999] 1 Lloyd's Rep. 903; [1998] C.L.C. 1054, QBD (Comm Ct) . . . . *Digested,* 00/**4703**
NIR Radiation II (W06/99), Re [2001] E.P.O.R. 57, EPO (Technical Bd App) . . . . *Digested,* 01/**3896**

Nissan France SA v. Dupasquier (C309/94) see Grand Garage Albigeois SA v. Garage
   Massol Sarl (C226/94)
Nissan France SA v. Dupasquier (C309/94) [1996] E.C.R. I-677; [1996] C.E.C. 503,
   ECJ . . . .   *Digested*, 96/**1044**:
                                                                                          Applied, 98/743
Nissan Motor Co Ltd's Patent Application (No.9027560.6) [1998] Masons C.L.R. Rep. 31,
   PO
NISSAN/Diesel engine (T775/96) [2000] E.P.O.R. 380, EPO (Technical Bd App) . . . .   *Digested*, 00/**3627**
NISSAN/N-alkylation (T713/97) [1998] E.P.O.R. 456, EPO (Technical Bd App)
Nitrate Corp of Chile Ltd v. Pansuiza Compania de Navegacion SA see Chilean Nitrate
   Sales Corp v. Marine Transportation Co Ltd (The Hermosa)
Nixon (CICB: Quantum: 1998), Re (Unreported, January 15, 1998), CICB (York) [*Ex rel.*
   Lester Morrill Solicitors, 59 St Paul's Street, Leeds, LS1 2TE] . . . .   *Digested*, 98/**1524**
Nixon v. FJ Morris Contracting Ltd, *Times*, February 6, 2001, QBD . . . .   *Digested*, 01/**4451**
NLA Group Ltd v. Bowers [1999] 1 Lloyd's Rep. 109, QBD (Comm Ct) . . . .   *Digested*, 99/**3392**
NMB Holdings Ltd v. Secretary of State for Social Security 73 T.C. 85; *Times*, October
   10, 2000, QBD . . . .   *Digested*, 00/**5043**
NN, Re (1998) 21 (1) I.P.D. 21011, EPO (Disciplinary Bd App)
NN/Association of representatives (J116/96) [1999] E.P.O.R. 202, EPO (Legal Bd App)
NN/Grounds of appeal (T167/97) [1999] E.P.O.R. 555, EPO (Technical Bd App) . . . . .   *Digested*, 00/**3612**
NN/Language (J18/96) [1999] E.P.O.R. 9, EPO (Legal Bd App)
NN/Percarbonate (W11/99) [2000] E.P.O.R. 515, EPO (Technical Bd App). . . . .   *Digested*, 01/**3962**
NOBEL/Hexanitrostilbene (T813/93) [1998] E.P.O.R. 151, EPO (Technical Bd App)
Noble v. Coutts & Co (Unreported, October 24, 2000), Ch D [*Ex rel.* Philip Rainey,
   Barrister, 2nd Floor, Francis Taylor Building, Temple, London] . . . .   *Digested*, 01/**4541**
Noble v. Harrison [1926] 2 K.B. 332, KBD . . . .   *Applied*, 47-51/4405,
                          47-51/6808, 47-51/6956, 47-51/10726, 00/4292: *Followed*, 97/3866
Noble v. Inner London Education Authority 83 L.G.R. 291; *Times*, December 2, 1983,
   CA; affirming (1983) 133 N.L.J. 1104 . . . .   *Digested*, 84/**1180**:
                                                                         Applied, 00/4087
Noble v. Leger Holidays Ltd (Unreported, January 27, 2000), CC (Leeds) [*Ex rel.*
   Mason Bond Solicitors, King Charles House, King Charles Croft, Leeds] . . . . . .   *Digested*, 00/**4039**
Noble Organisation v. Glasgow DC (No.3) 1991 S.L.T. 213; 1991 S.C.L.R. 380, 2 Div;
   affirming 1990 S.C.L.R. 64, Sh Ct. . . . .   *Digested*, 91/**5484**:
                                                                   Considered, 98/3746
Nodeco Ltd v. Texas Iron Works Inc see Texas Iron Works Inc's Patent Application
NODOZ Trade Mark [1962] R.P.C. 1 . . . .   *Digested*, 62/**3046**:
                                                  Applied, 77/3054: *Referred to*, 01/4063
Noel v. London Underground Ltd see London Underground Ltd v. Noel
Noel v. Poland [2001] 2 B.C.L.C. 645, QBD (Comm Ct)
Noge Sarl v. Gotz GmbH [1998] I.L. Pr. 189, Cass (F)
Nokes v. Doncaster Amalgamated Collieries Ltd; Donoghue v. Doncaster Amalgamated
   Collieries Ltd [1940] A.C. 1014, HL; reversing [1939] 2 K.B. 578, CA; affirming
   [1939] 1 K.B. 70; [1938] W.N. 327, KBD. . . . .   *Applied*, 58/411,
                        58/1291, 78/1638: *Considered*, 85/1220, 86/1237: *Distinguished*, 80/1447,
                                                  82/1574: *Explained*, 99/4092
Nokia Mobile Phones v. SA Bigg's [1998] E.C.C. 277, Trib Civil (Brussels)
Nolan v. Iceland Frozen Foods (Unreported, December 3, 1997), CC (Liverpool) [*Ex*
   rel. Soyab Patel, Solicitor, Fletchers Solicitors, Southport] . . . .   *Digested*, 98/**4037**
Nolan v. Secretary of State for the Environment, Transport and the Regions [1998]
   E.G.C.S. 7, QBD
Nolan's Trade Mark Application [2000] E.T.M.R. 208, PO (Irl) . . . .   *Digested*, 00/**3751**
NONOGRAM Trade Mark [2001] R.P.C. 21, TMR . . . .   *Digested*, 01/**4047**
Nooh v. Secretary of State for the Home Department see Adan (Hassan Hussein) v.
   Secretary of State for the Home Department
Noon v. Nixon (Unreported, June 24, 1999), CC (Huddersfield) [*Ex rel.* Tim Kevan,
   Barrister, 1 Temple Gardens, Temple, London] . . . .   *Digested*, 99/**2451**
Noon v. Princess Alice Hospice (1998) 98(6) Q.R. 7, CC (Epsom) . . . .   *Digested*, 98/**1636**
Noone v. North West Thames RHA (No.2); *sub nom* North West Thames RHA v. Noone
   (No.2) [1988] I.C.R. 813; [1988] I.R.L.R. 530; *Independent*, July 26, 1988, CA .   *Digested*, 89/**1452**:
                                           Applied, 91/1654: *Considered*, 97/308, 99/2090
Noorani v. Merseyside TEC Ltd [1999] I.R.L.R. 184, CA . . . .   *Digested*, 99/**2060**
Norbain SD Ltd v. Dedicated Micros Ltd [1998] E.C.C. 379; [1998] Eu. L.R. 266, QBD .   *Digested*, 99/**666**
Norbrook Laboratories (GB) Ltd v. Health and Safety Executive [1998] E.H.L.R. 207;
   Times, February 23, 1998, QBD . . . .   *Digested*, 98/**1045**
Norbrook Laboratories Ltd v. Ministry of Agriculture, Fisheries and Food (C127/95)
   [1998] E.C.R. I-1531; [1998] 3 C.M.L.R. 809, ECJ . . . .   *Considered*, 00/5317
Norbury Developments Ltd v. Customs and Excise Commissioners (C136/97) [1999]
   All E.R. (EC) 436; [1999] S.T.C. 511; [1999] E.C.R. I-2491; [1999] 2 C.M.L.R.
   633; [1999] C.E.C. 223; [1999] B.T.C. 5229; [1999] B.V.C. 270, ECJ (2nd
   Chamber) [1996] V. & D.R. 531, V&DTr . . . .   *Digested*, 99/**4985**
Nordbanken AB v. Ryden [2000] E.C.C. 93, HD (Swe)

Nordglimt, The [1988] Q.B. 183; [1988] 2 W.L.R. 338; [1988] 2 All E.R. 531; [1987] 2
Lloyd's Rep. 470; [1987] 2 F.T.L.R. 438; (1988) 132 S.J. 262; *Financial Times,*
August 11, 1987, QBD (Adm Ct) . . . . *Digested,* 88/**3219**:
                      Applied, 92/3927, 95/4504: *Considered,* 89/111, 90/195, 00/569
Nordic Holdings Ltd v. Mott Macdonald Ltd 77 Con. L.R. 88, QBD (T&CC)
Norditrack (UK) Ltd, Re [2000] 1 W.L.R. 343; [2000] 1 All E.R. 369; [2000] B.C.C. 441;
[2000] 1 B.C.L.C. 467; *Times,* November 11, 1999, Ch D (Companies Ct) . . . . . .   *Digested,* 99/**3361**
Nordstern Allgemeine Versicherungs AG v. Internav Ltd; Nordstern Allgemeine
Versicherungs AG v. Katsamas [1999] 2 Lloyd's Rep. 139; (1999) 96(23) L.S.G.
33; (1999) 143 S.J.L.B. 196; *Times,* June 8, 1999, CA . . . .   *Digested,* 99/**392**
Nordstern Allgemeine Versicherungs AG v. Katsamas see Nordstern Allgemeine
Versicherungs AG v. Internav Ltd
Noreiga v. Trinidad and Tobago see Ajodha v. Trinidad and Tobago
Norfolk CC's Application (1999) 14 P.A.D. 624, Planning Inspector
Norglen Ltd (In Liquidation) v. Reeds Rains Prudential Ltd; Mayhew-Lewis v.
Westminster Scaffolding Group Plc; Levy v. ABN AMRO Bank NV; Circuit
Systems Ltd (In Liquidation) v. Zuken-Redac (UK) Ltd [1999] 2 A.C. 1; [1997] 3
W.L.R. 1177; [1998] 1 All E.R. 218; [1998] B.C.C. 44; [1998] 1 B.C.L.C. 176; 87
B.L.R. 1; (1997) 94(48) L.S.G. 29; (1997) 147 N.L.J. 1773; (1998) 142 S.J.L.B.
26; (1998) 75 P. & C.R. D21; *Times,* December 1, 1997, HL; affirming [1996] 1
W.L.R. 864; [1996] 1 All E.R. 945; [1996] B.C.C. 532; [1996] 1 B.C.L.C. 690;
Times, December 6, 1995; *Independent,* January 12, 1996, CA; reversing [1994]
E.G.C.S. 21, Ch D . . . . *Digested,* 98/**375**:
                           Followed, 96/682, 98/401, 99/3312
Normaco Ltd v. Lundman [1999] C.P.L.R. 326; [1999] I.L.Pr. 381; (1999) 96(6) L.S.G.
32; *Times,* January 6, 1999, Ch D . . . . *Digested,* 99/**754**
Norman v. Ali (Limitation Period); Aziz v. Norman [2000] R.T.R. 107; [2000] Lloyd's
Rep. I.R. 395; [2000] P.I.Q.R. P72; (2000) 97(2) L.S.G. 30; (2000) 144
S.J.L.B. 18; *Times,* February 25, 2000; *Independent,* February 7, 2000 (C.S.),
CA . . . . *Digested,* 00/**3548**
Norman v. Aziz [2000] Lloyd's Rep. I.R. 52, QBD . . . . *Digested,* 00/**3544**
Norman v. Clarke [1997] O.P.L.R. 85, Ch D . . . . *Digested,* 98/**4143**
Norman v. Future Publishing Ltd [1999] E.M.L.R. 325, CA. *Digested,* 99/**1634**
Norman v. Secretary of State for the Home Department see Bugdaycay v. Secretary of
State for the Home Department
Norman v. Selvey (Unreported, May 18, 1999), CC (Bristol) [*Ex rel.* Tim Kevan,
Barrister, 1 Temple Gardens, Temple, London] . . . . *Digested,* 99/**2453**:
                        Referred to, 99/2490
Norminton v. Jowett (Unreported, February 24, 1999), CC (Manchester) [*Ex rel.* Ison
Harrison & Co Solicitors, Duke House, 54 Wellington Street, Leeds] . . . . *Digested,* 00/**445**
Norowzian v. Arks Ltd (No.1) [1999] E.M.L.R. 57; [1998] F.S.R. 394; (1998) 21(3)
I.P.D. 21027, Ch D . . . . *Digested,* 98/**3418**
Norowzian v. Arks Ltd (No.2) [2000] E.C.D.R. 205; [2000] E.M.L.R. 67; [2000]
F.S.R. 363; (2000) 23(3) I.P.D. 23026; (1999) 96(45) L.S.G. 31; (1999) 143
S.J.L.B. 279; *Times,* November 11, 1999 ; *Independent,* January 17, 2000 (C.S.),
CA; affirming [1999] E.M.L.R. 67; [1999] F.S.R. 79; (1998) 21(10) I.P.D. 21112;
(1998) 95(35) L.S.G. 37; (1998) 142 S.J.L.B. 227; *Times,* July 27, 1998, Ch D . *Digested,* 99/**3439**:
                         Applied, 01/3859
Norris (Clifford), Re [2001] UKHL 34; [2001] 1 W.L.R. 1388; [2001] 3 All E.R. 961; [2001] 3
F.C.R. 97; (2001) 98(30) L.S.G. 37; (2001) 151 N.L.J. 1094; *Times,* June 29, 2001;
Daily Telegraph, July 3, 2001, HL; reversing [2000] 1 W.L.R. 1094; (2000)
97(6) L.S.G. 34; (2000) 144 S.J.L.B. 84; [2000] N.P.C. 8; *Times,* February 25,
2000, CA . . . . *Digested,* 01/**5**
Norris v. Birmingham City Council [2001] R.V.R. 89, QBD . . . . *Digested,* 01/**4808**
Norris (Inspector of Taxes) v. Edgson [2000] S.T.C. 494; [2000] 2 F.L.R. 655; [2000]
2 F.C.R. 445; 72 T.C. 553; [2000] B.T.C. 197; [2000] Fam. Law 515; [2000]
Fam. Law 697; [2000] S.T.I. 751; (2000) 97(22) L.S.G. 46; *Times,* May 30,
2000, Ch D . . . . *Digested,* 00/**5008**
Norris v. Greatbatch (Unreported, June 17, 1998), CC (Portsmouth) [*Ex rel.* Alex
Glassbrook, Barrister, 1 Temple Gardens, Temple, London] . . . . *Digested,* 98/**1461**
Norris v. Ireland (A/142) (1991) 13 E.H.R.R. 186; *Times,* October 31, 1988, ECHR . . . . . *Digested,* 88/**1817**:
                        Applied, 98/3159
Norris v. Walls [1997] N.I. 45, Ch D (NI) . . . . *Digested,* 99/**5475**
North American Land & Timber Co Ltd v. Watkins [1904] 2 Ch. 233, CA; affirming
[1904] 1 Ch. 242, Ch D . . . . *Applied,* 00/513
North and West Belfast Health and Social Services Trust v. DH [2001] N.I. 351, Fam Div
(NI)
North Anderson Cars Ltd v. Customs and Excise Commissioners [1999] S.T.C. 902;
2000 S.C. 37; 2000 S.L.T. 619; 2000 S.C.L.R. 273; [1999] B.T.C. 5335; [1999]
B.V.C. 389; 1999 G.W.D. 30-1446, 2 Div; affirming [1998] B.V.C. 2174; [1998]
V. & D.R. 11, V&DTr. . . . . *Digested,* 99/**6472**
North Atlantic Insurance Co Ltd v. Bishopsgate Insurance Ltd [1998] 1 Lloyd's Rep.
459, QBD (Comm Ct) . . . . *Digested,* 98/**3404**

North British Housing Association Ltd v. Sheridan (2000) 32 H.L.R. 346; [2000] L. &
T.R. 115; [1999] 2 E.G.L.R. 138; (1999) 78 P. & C.R. D38, CA . . . . *Digested*, 00/**3883**
NORTH CAROLINA STATE UNIVERSITY/Plasmid pTR2030 (T576/91) [1998] E.P.O.R.
382, EPO (Technical Bd App)
North Devon DC v. Clark (1999) 14 P.A.D. 221, Planning Inspector
North Devon DC v. GA Estates (1999) 14 P.A.D. 578, Planning Inspector
North Devon DC v. Secretary of State for the Environment, Transport and the Regions
[1998] 4 P.L.R. 46; [1998] P.L.C.R. 356; [1998] E.G.C.S. 72; (1998) 95(21)
L.S.G. 38; (1998) 142 S.J.L.B. 165; [1998] N.P.C. 84; *Times*, May 12, 1998,
QBD . . . . *Digested*, 98/**4167**
North East Garages Ltd v. Customs and Excise Commissioners [1999] S.T.C. 1057;
[1999] B.T.C. 5410; [1999] B.V.C. 443; *Independent*, December 6, 1999 (C.S.),
QBD . . . . *Digested*, 00/**5357**
North East Lincolnshire CC v. Islamic Association of South Humberside (1998) 13
P.A.D. 769, Planning Inspector
North Ex p. Hasluck, Re [1895] 2 Q.B. 264, CA . . . . *Applied*, 47-51/**4688**,
52/1638: *Approved*, 67/1252, 68/1247: *Considered*, 68/1212, 68/4065,
95/2088, 99/2465
North Holdings Ltd v. Southern Tropics Ltd [1999] B.C.C. 746; [1999] 2 B.C.L.C. 625;
Independent, July 12, 1999 (C.S.), CA. . . . . *Digested*, 99/**629**:
Applied, 00/692
North Norfolk DC v. New Commons Trust (1999) 14 P.A.D. 758, Planning Inspector
North of England Zoological Society, Re; *sub nom* North of England Zoological Society
v. Chester Rural DC [1959] 1 W.L.R. 773; [1959] 3 All E.R. 116; 123 J.P. 469;
57 L.G.R. 252; 5 R.R.C. 49; 52 R. & I.T. 450; 103 S.J. 582, CA; affirming [1958]
1 W.L.R. 1258; [1958] 3 All E.R. 535; 123 J.P. 47; 57 L.G.R. 33; 51 R. & I.T.
762; 102 S.J. 915, Ch D . . . . *Digested*, 59/**2770**:
Considered, 99/4982
North of England Zoological Society v. Chester Rural DC see North of England
Zoological Society, Re
North of England Zoological Society v. Customs and Excise Commissioners [1999]
S.T.C. 1027; [1999] B.T.C. 5404; [1999] B.V.C. 437; (1999) 96(40) L.S.G. 42;
Times, November 2, 1999 ; *Independent*, November 15, 1999 (C.S.), QBD;
affirming [1999] B.V.C. 2015, V&DTr. . . . . *Digested*, 99/**4982**
North Sea Energy Holdings NV v. Petroleum Authority of Thailand [1999] 1 All E.R.
(Comm.) 173; [1999] 1 Lloyd's Rep. 483, CA; affirming [1997] 2 Lloyd's Rep.
418, QBD (Comm Ct) . . . . *Digested*, 99/**859**
North Somerset CC v. Lloyd (1999) 14 P.A.D. 73, Planning Inspector
North Somerset DC v. Kingsoak South West (2001) 16 P.A.D. 72, Planning Inspector
North Somerset DC v. Mead Realisations Ltd (1998) 13 P.A.D. 1, Planning Inspector
North Tyneside MBC v. Allsop [1992] I.C.R. 639; 90 L.G.R. 462; (1992) 4 Admin. L.R.
550; [1992] R.V.R. 104; [1992] C.O.D. 281; *Times*, March 12, 1992; *Independent*,
March 5, 1992, CA; affirming [1991] R.V.R. 209; (1992) 156 L.G. Rev. 1007;
Times, October 18, 1991; *Independent*, October 17, 1991, QBD . . . . *Digested*, 92/**2899**:
Cited, 99/3902: *Distinguished*, 99/2014
North Tyneside MBC v. Direct Developments Ltd (2001) 16 P.A.D. 79, Planning
Inspector
North Warwickshire BC v. Onyx Land Technologies Ltd (1998) 13 P.A.D. 772, Planning
Inspector
North West Holdings Plc (In Liquidation) (Costs), Re see Secretary of State for Trade and
Industry v. Backhouse
North West Lancashire HA v. A see R. v. North West Lancashire HA Ex p. A
North West Thames RHA v. Noone (No.2) see Noone v. North West Thames RHA (No.2)
North Western and North Wales Sea Fisheries Committee v. Davies [2000] C.O.D. 270,
DC
North Western Estates Development Ltd v. Merseyside and Cheshire Rent Assessment
Committee [1996] N.P.C. 174, QBD . . . . *Followed*, 98/3670
North Wiltshire DC v. Castle Combe Circuit Ltd (1999) 14 P.A.D. 570, Planning
Inspector
North Wiltshire DC v. Crest Homes (South West) Ltd (1998) 13 P.A.D. 654, Planning
Inspector
North Wiltshire DC v. Guide Dogs for the Blind Association (2000) 15 P.A.D. 305,
Planning Inspector
North Wiltshire DC v. Miller (2001) 16 P.A.D. 6, Planning Inspector
North Wiltshire DC v. Secretary of State for the Environment (1993) 65 P. & C.R. 137;
[1992] 3 P.L.R. 113; [1992] J.P.L. 955; [1992] E.G.C.S. 65; [1992] N.P.C. 57;
Times, April 21, 1992, CA; affirming [1991] 2 P.L.R. 67; [1991] E.G.C.S. 25. . . . . *Digested*, 93/**3930**:
Applied, 00/4519: *Considered*, 94/4421, 94/4464, 95/4841, 95/4875:
Distinguished, 96/4702
North York Moors v. Bradley (1998) 13 P.A.D. 638, Planning Inspector
North Yorkshire CC v. Wiltshire CC; *sub nom* J (A Child), Re; R (A Child), Re [1999]
Fam. 323; [1999] 3 W.L.R. 836; [1999] 4 All E.R. 291; [1999] 2 F.L.R. 560;
[1999] Fam. Law 620; (2000) 164 J.P.N. 244; (1999) 96(25) L.S.G. 29; *Times*,
June 1, 1999; *Independent*, June 21, 1999 (C.S.), Fam Div . . . . *Digested*, 99/**2352**

North's Application, Re (1998) 75 P. & C.R. 117, Lands Tr . . . .   *Digested*, 98/**4343**
Northampton BC *v.* Agrigen Ltd (1999) 14 P.A.D. 412, Planning Inspector
Northampton BC *v.* Guinness & Pittams (1998) 13 P.A.D. 423, Planning Inspector
Northampton BC *v.* Lovatt [1998] E.H.L.R. 59; [1998] 2 F.C.R. 182; (1998) 30 H.L.R.
    875; [1998] 1 E.G.L.R. 15; [1998] 07 E.G. 142; [1997] E.G.C.S. 156; (1998)
    95(10) L.S.G. 28; [1997] N.P.C. 159; *Times*, January 3, 1998; *Independent*,
    November 14, 1997, CA . . . .   *Digested*, 97/**2716**:
                                                                                                        Applied, 99/3041
Northampton CC *v.* Islington LBC see Northamptonshire CC *v.* Islington LBC
Northampton Coal Iron & Waggon Co *v.* Midland Waggon Co (1877-78) L.R. 7 Ch. D.
    500, CA . . . .   *Disapproved*, 73/2632:
                                                                                                        Followed, 01/508

Northamptonshire CC *v.* Islington LBC; *sub nom* Northampton CC *v.* Islington LBC
    [2001] Fam. 364; [2000] 2 W.L.R. 193; [1999] 2 F.L.R. 881; [1999] 3 F.C.R.
    385; [2000] B.L.G.R. 125; [1999] Fam. Law 687; (2000) 164 J.P.N. 166; *Times*,
    August 17, 1999, CA . . . .   *Digested*, 99/**2312**:
                                                                                                        Followed, 00/2461
Northern Bank Ltd *v.* Commissioner of Valuation for Northern Ireland [2001] R.A. 83,
    Lands Tr (NI) . . . .   *Digested*, 01/**5942**
Northern Bank Ltd *v.* Haggerty [1995] N.I. 211, Ch D (NI) . . . .   *Considered*, 99/5471
Northern Bank Ltd *v.* Jeffers [1996] N.I. 497, Ch D (NI)
Northern Bank Ltd *v.* Laverty [2001] N.I. 315, Ch D (NI)
Northern Bank Ltd *v.* Leyburn [1999] N.I. 62, Ch D (NI) . . . .   *Digested*, 99/**5412**
Northern Bank Ltd *v.* McKinstry [2001] N.I. 130, Ch D (NI) . . . .   *Digested*, 01/**5801**
Northern Contractors *v.* Hopwood (Unreported, March 24, 2000), CC (Reading) . . . . .   *Digested*, 00/**2572**:
                                                                                                        Followed, 00/2576
Northern Developments (Cumbria) Ltd *v.* J&J Nichol [2000] B.L.R. 158; (2000) 2
    T.C.L.R. 261, QBD (T&CC) . . . .   *Digested*, 00/**808**:
                                                                                                        Explained, 01/858
Northern Electric Plc *v.* Addison (1999) 77 P. & C.R. 168; [1997] 2 E.G.L.R. 111; [1997]
    39 E.G. 175; [1997] E.G.C.S. 98; (1997) 74 P. & C.R. D39, CA . . . .   *Digested*, 97/**3264**
Northern Electric Plc *v.* Stockton on Tees BC (Unreported, September 17, 1999), CC
    (Middlesbrough) [*Ex rel.* Hammond Suddards Solicitors, 2 Park Lane, Leeds] . .   *Digested*, 00/**561**
Northern Health and Social Services Board's Application, Re [1994] N.I. 165, QBD (NI)   *Digested*, 00/**5517**
Northern Ireland Electricity Plc's Application for Judicial Review, Re [1998] N.I. 300, CA
    (NI) . . . .   *Digested*, 99/**5248**
Northern Ireland Fish Producers Organisation Ltd (NIFPO) *v.* Department of Agriculture
    for Northern Ireland (C4/96); Northern Ireland Fishermen's Federation *v.*
    Department of Agriculture for Northern Ireland (C4/96) [1998] E.C.R. I-681;
    [1998] 1 C.M.L.R. 1288, ECJ
Northern Ireland Fishermen's Federation *v.* Department of Agriculture for Northern
    Ireland (C4/96) see Northern Ireland Fish Producers Organisation Ltd (NIFPO)
    v. Department of Agriculture for Northern Ireland (C4/96)
Northern Ireland Housing Executive *v.* Extravision BT/60/1999, Lands Tr (NI) . . . .   *Digested*, 00/**5610**
Northern Ireland Human Rights Commission's Application for Judicial Review, Re see R. (on
    the application of Northern Ireland Human Rights Commission) *v.* Greater Belfast
    Coroner
Northern Joint Police Board *v.* Power [1997] I.R.L.R. 610, EAT . . . .   *Digested*, 98/**5811**:
                                                                                                        Considered, 01/6473
Northern Leisure Plc *v.* Schofield [2001] 1 W.L.R. 1196; [2001] 1 All E.R. 660; (2000)
    164 J.P. 613; *Times*, August 3, 2000; *Independent*, October 2, 2000 (C.S.),
    QBD . . . .   *Digested*, 00/**4068**
Northern RHA *v.* Derek Crouch Construction Co Ltd [1984] Q.B. 644; [1984] 2
    W.L.R. 676; [1984] 2 All E.R. 175; 26 B.L.R. 1; [1986] C.I.L.L. 244; (1984) 128
    S.J. 279, CA; affirming 24 B.L.R. 60, OR . . . .   *Digested*, 84/**117**:
                                Considered, 84/2715, 85/207, 86/209, 86/225, 86/233, 97/945, 99/791:
                                Distinguished, 88/219, 97/930: *Followed*, 86/3589, 96/1157, 97/924,
                                                                                                        98/5055
Northern Rock Building Society *v.* Archer; Archer *v.* Hickmotts [1999] Lloyd's Rep.
    Bank. 32; (1999) 78 P. & C.R. 65; [1998] N.P.C. 132, CA . . . .   *Digested*, 99/**4390**
Northern Rock Plc *v.* Thorpe (Inspector of Taxes) [2000] S.T.C. (S.C.D.) 317; [2000]
    S.T.I. 1008, Sp Comm. . . . .   *Digested*, 00/**4934**
Northern Shipping Co *v.* Deutsche Seereederei GmbH (formerly Deutsche Seereederei
    Rostock GmbH) [2000] 2 Lloyd's Rep. 255; [2000] C.L.C. 933, CA. . . . .   *Digested*, 00/**4686**
Northfield *v.* DSM (Southern) Ltd (Unreported, May 12, 2000), CC (Basingstoke) [*Ex*
    rel. Stephen M Nichols & Co Solicitors, 27 Wote Street, Basingstoke, Hants.] . . .   *Digested*, 00/**461**
Northlands Cafe Inc, Re [1999] B.P.I.R. 747, QB (Alta). . . . .   *Digested*, 99/**3220**
Northumberland & Durham Property Trust Ltd *v.* London Rent Assessment Committee
    (57 Ifield Road, London) (1998) 30 H.L.R. 1091; [1998] 2 E.G.L.R. 99; [1998]
    24 E.G. 128; [1998] E.G.C.S. 22, QBD . . . .   *Digested*, 98/**3669**
Northumberland & Durham Property Trust Ltd *v.* London Rent Assessment Committee
    (72A Redcliffe Gardens, London) (1999) 31 H.L.R. 252; [1998] E.G.C.S. 56;
    (1998) 95(14) L.S.G. 24, QBD . . . .   *Digested*, 98/**3671**

Northumberland & Durham Property Trust Ltd *v.* London Rent Assessment Committee (Ealing Village, London) (1999) 31 H.L.R. 109; [1998] 3 E.G.L.R. 85; [1998] 43 E.G. 138; [1998] E.G.C.S. 42, QBD. . . . . *Digested*, 98/**3672**
Northwest Holdings Plc, Re [2000] B.C.C. 731, Ch D . . . . *Digested*, 00/**3498**
Norton Healthcare Ltd *v.* Minnesota Mining & Manufacturing Co (1998) 21(10) I.P.D. 21102, Pat Ct
Norton Healthcare Ltd *v.* Minnesota Mining & Manufacturing Co (Discovery) [1999] F.S.R. 636, Pat Ct . . . . *Digested*, 99/**3471**
Norton Tool Co Ltd *v.* Tewson [1973] 1 W.L.R. 45; [1973] 1 All E.R. 183; [1972] I.C.R. 501; [1972] I.R.L.R. 86; (1972) 13 K.I.R. 328; [1973] I.T.R. 23; 117 S.J. 33, NIRC. . . . . *Digested*, 73/**1136**:
Applied, 73/1132, 73/1137, 73/1186, 74/1294, 74/1305, 74/1312, 74/1346, 75/1145, 75/1165, 75/2702, 76/963, 76/965, 84/1289: *Considered*, 73/1143, 81/935, 97/2190, 98/2238: *Followed*, 74/1287, 74/1290, 76/960, 87/1388: *Referred to*, 88/1336
Nortrade Foods Ltd *v.* Customs and Excise Commissioners [1998] V. & D.R. 133, V&DTr. . . . . *Digested*, 00/**4954**
Norway *v.* Astra Norge A/S (E1/98) [1999] 1 C.M.L.R. 860; [2000] E.C.D.R. 20, EFTA . . . . *Digested*, 99/**3622**
Norway *v.* EFTA Surveillance Authority (E6/98) [1999] 2 C.M.L.R. 1033, EFTA . . . . . . *Digested*, 00/**729**
Norway *v.* EFTA Surveillance Authority (E6/98 R) [1999] 1 C.M.L.R. 851, EFTA . . . . . . *Digested*, 99/**3623**
Norway's Application, Re [1987] Q.B. 433; [1986] 3 W.L.R. 452; (1986) 83 L.S.G. 3248; (1986) 130 S.J. 730, CA . . . . *Digested*, 86/**1512**:
Considered, 96/1669: *Followed*, 98/350
Norwegian Bankers Association *v.* EFTA Surveillance Authority (E4/97) (No.1) [1998] 3 C.M.L.R. 281, EFTA
Norwegian Bankers' Association *v.* EFTA Surveillance Authority (E4/97) (No.2) [1999] 4 C.M.L.R. 1292, EFTA . . . . *Digested*, 99/**676**
Norwest Holst Group Administration Ltd *v.* Harrison; *sub nom* Harrison *v.* Norwest Holst Group Administration [1985] I.C.R. 668; [1985] I.R.L.R. 240; (1985) 82 L.S.G. 1410, CA; affirming [1984] I.R.L.R. 419, EAT . . . . *Digested*, 85/**1151**:
Considered, 98/2102: *Followed*, 97/2206
Norwich and Peterborough Building Society *v.* Steed (No.1) [1991] 1 W.L.R. 449; [1991] 2 All E.R. 880; (1993) 65 P. & C.R. 108; *Times*, March 14, 1991, CA . . . . . *Digested*, 91/**2778**:
Applied, 91/2779, 93/4045, 98/243: *Followed*, 97/2939
Norwich City Council *v.* Billings (1997) 29 H.L.R. 679, QBD. . . . . *Digested*, 98/**3039**
Norwich City Council *v.* Stringer (2001) 33 H.L.R. 15; (2000) 2 L.G.L.R. 1102; *Independent*, June 12, 2000 (C.S), CA . . . . *Digested*, 01/**5024**
Norwich Corp *v.* Sagnata Investments Ltd see Sagnata Investments Ltd *v.* Norwich Corp
Norwich Pharmacal Co *v.* Customs and Excise Commissioners; *sub nom* Morton-Norwich Products Inc *v.* Customs and Excise Commissioners [1974] A.C. 133; [1973] 3 W.L.R. 164; [1973] 2 All E.R. 943; [1973] F.S.R. 365; [1974] R.P.C. 101; 117 S.J. 567, HL; reversing [1972] 3 W.L.R. 870; [1972] 3 All E.R. 813; [1972] F.S.R. 405; [1972] R.P.C. 743; 116 S.J. 823, CA; reversing [1972] Ch. 566; [1972] 2 W.L.R. 864; [1972] 1 All E.R. 972; [1972] F.S.R. 1; (1971) 116 S.J. 315, Ch D . . . . *Digested*, 73/**2643**:
Applied, 74/2936, 80/2132, 80/2136, 90/3660, 93/3348, 98/3508, 98/4872: *Considered*, 81/2115, 84/2596, 84/2625, 85/155, 86/1501, 86/1503, 91/781, 93/3211, 93/3220, 95/3495, 95/4130, 95/4131, 96/553, 96/769, 97/2205, 98/332, 99/3444: *Distinguished*, 87/2992, 88/2832: *Followed*, 93/3280, 94/3738, 96/764, 00/5532: *Referred to*, 99/319, 01/4413
Norwich Union Life Insurance Co Ltd *v.* Qureshi see Aldrich *v.* Norwich Union Life Insurance Co Ltd (formerly Norwich Union Life Insurance Society)
Norwich Union Life Insurance Society *v.* P&O Property Holdings Ltd see P&O Property Holdings Ltd *v.* Norwich Union Life Insurance Society
Norwich Union Life Insurance Society *v.* Qureshi see Aldrich *v.* Norwich Union Life Insurance Co Ltd (formerly Norwich Union Life Insurance Society)
Norwich Union Life Insurance Society *v.* Shopmoor Ltd [1999] 1 W.L.R. 531; [1998] 3 All E.R. 32; [1998] 2 E.G.L.R. 167, Ch D . . . . *Digested*, 97/**3250**:
Applied, 98/3617
Notetry Ltd's Application [1999] E.T.M.R. 435, OHIM (1st Bd App) . . . . *Applied*, 00/3714
Nothman *v.* Barnet LBC (No.2); *sub nom* Barnet LBC *v.* Nothman (No.2) [1980] I.R.L.R. 65, CA . . . . *Digested*, 80/**1043**:
Considered, 01/2244
Nothman *v.* Cooper see Oppenheimer *v.* Cattermole (Inspector of Taxes)
Notting Hill Housing Trust *v.* Brackley [2001] EWCA Civ 601; [2001] L. & T.R. 34; [2001] 35 E.G. 106; [2001] W.T.L.R. 1353; [2001] 18 E.G.C.S. 175; (2001) 98(24) L.S.G. 44; (2001) 82 P. & C.R. D26; *Times*, June 15, 2001; *Daily Telegraph*, May 1, 2001, CA . . . . *Digested*, 01/**4172**
Notting Hill Housing Trust *v.* Rakey Jones [1999] L. & T.R. 397, CA. . . . . *Digested*, 99/**3731**
Nottingham Building Society *v.* Eurodynamics Systems Plc [1995] F.S.R. 605, CA; affirming [1993] F.S.R. 468, Ch D . . . . *Digested*, 95/**773**:
Followed, 98/525

Nottingham City Council *v.* Amin [2000] 1 W.L.R. 1071; [2000] 2 All E.R. 946; [2000] 1 Cr. App. R. 426; [2000] R.T.R. 122; [2000] H.R.L.R. 280; [2000] U.K.H.R.R. 134; [2000] Crim. L.R. 174; *Times*, December 2, 1999 ; *Independent*, January 24, 2000 (C.S.), QBD . . . .   *Digested*, 00/**919**: *Followed*, 01/992

Nottingham City Council *v.* Bellway Homes Ltd (East Midlands) (2001) 16 P.A.D. 53, Planning Inspector

Nottingham City Council *v.* Cutts (2001) 33 H.L.R. 7, CA. . . . .   *Digested*, 01/**16**

Nottingham City Council *v.* Farooq (Mohammed), *Times*, October 28, 1998, QBD . . . . .   *Digested*, 98/**4865**

Nottingham City Council *v.* October Films Ltd [1999] 2 F.L.R. 347; [1999] 2 F.C.R. 529; [1999] Fam. Law 536; (1999) 163 J.P.N. 929; (1999) 96(23) L.S.G. 33; *Times*, May 21, 1999, Fam Div . . . .   *Digested*, 99/**2340**

Nottingham City Council *v.* Z (A Child) [2001] EWCA Civ 1248; (2001) 98(39) L.S.G. 38; *Times*, August 29, 2001, CA. . . . .   *Digested*, 01/**4400**

Nottingham Community Housing Association Ltd *v.* Powerminster Ltd [2000] B.L.R. 309; (2000) 2 T.C.L.R. 678; 75 Con. L.R. 65; (2000) 16 Const. L.J. 449, QBD (T&CC) . . . .   *Digested*, 00/**820**

Nottingham Forest Plc, Re see CAS (Nominees) Ltd *v.* Nottingham Forest Plc (Application for Disclosure)

Nottinghamshire CC *v.* Secretary of State for the Environment see R. *v.* Secretary of State for the Environment Ex p. Nottinghamshire CC

Nottinghamshire CC *v.* Secretary of State for the Environment, Transport and the Regions [1999] P.L.C.R. 340; [1999] E.G.C.S. 35, QBD . . . .   *Digested*, 99/**4230**

Nottinghamshire CC *v.* Secretary of State for the Environment, Transport and the Regions [2001] EWHC Admin 293; [2001] 15 E.G.C.S. 134; [2001] N.P.C. 68, QBD (Admin Ct)

Noueiri *v.* Paragon Finance Plc (No.2); *sub nom* Paragon Finance Plc *v.* Noueiri (Practice Note) [2001] EWCA Civ 1402; [2001] 1 W.L.R. 2357; (2001) 98(40) L.S.G. 40; (2001) 145 S.J.L.B. 236; [2001] N.P.C. 138; *Times*, October 4, 2001; *Daily Telegraph*, October 2, 2001, CA . . . .   *Digested*, 01/**637**

Noune *v.* Secretary of State for the Home Department [2001] I.N.L.R. 526; (2001) 98(7) L.S.G. 40; *Times*, December 20, 2000, CA . . . .   *Digested*, 01/**3632**

Nourish *v.* Adamson [1998] 3 P.L.R. 21; [1998] J.P.L. 859, QBD . . . .   *Digested*, 98/**4212**

Nova (Jersey) Knit Ltd *v.* Kammgarn Spinnerei GmbH [1977] 1 W.L.R. 713; [1977] 2 All E.R. 463; [1977] 1 Lloyd's Rep. 463; 121 S.J. 170, HL; reversing [1976] 2 Lloyd's Rep. 155; 120 S.J. 351, CA . . . .   *Digested*, 77/**195**: *Considered*, 86/1594, 87/2911, 97/799, 98/246: *Distinguished*, 84/195, 86/2613

Novaknit Hellas SA *v.* Kumar Bros International Ltd [1998] Lloyd's Rep. Bank. 287; [1998] C.L.C. 971; *Independent*, May 4, 1998 (C.S.), CA. . . . .   *Digested*, 98/**2488**

Novartis AG's European Patent Application (No.91810144.5) see NOVARTIS/Transgenic plant (G01/98)

Novartis AG's European Patent Application (T990/96) see NOVARTIS/Erythro-compounds (T990/96)

NOVARTIS/Erythro-compounds (T990/96); *sub nom* Novartis AG's European Patent Application (T990/96) [1998] E.P.O.R. 441; (1998) 21(6) I.P.D. 21065, EPO (Technical Bd App)

NOVARTIS/Transgenic plant (G01/98); *sub nom* Novartis AG's European Patent Application (No.91810144.5); NOVARTIS/Transgenic plant (T1054/96) [2000] E.P.O.R. 303, EPO (Enlarged Bd App) [1999] E.P.O.R. 123; (1998) 21(11) I.P.D. 21116, EPO (Technical Bd App) . . . .   *Digested*, 00/**3655**

NOVARTIS/Transgenic plant (T1054/96) see NOVARTIS/Transgenic plant (G01/98)

Novell Inc's Community Trade Mark Application (No.228460) (2000) 23(10) I.P.D. 23083, OHIM (2nd Bd App)

Novo Nordisk A/S *v.* Banco Santander (Guernsey) Ltd (1999-2000) 2 I.T.E.L.R. 557, Royal Ct (Gue)

Novo Nordisk A/S *v.* DSM NV; *sub nom* DSM NV's Patent [2001] R.P.C. 35; (2001) 24(4) I.P.D. 24025, Pat Ct . . . .   *Digested*, 01/**3968**

NOVO NORDISK/Underpayment of Opposition Fee (T161/96); *sub nom* Mallinckrodt Group Inc's European Patent (T161/96) [1999] E.P.O.R. 492; (1998) 21(10) I.P.D. 21108, EPO (Technical Bd App). . . . .   *Digested*, 00/**3654**

NP Engineering & Security Products Ltd, Re; *sub nom* Official Receiver *v.* Pafundo [2000] B.C.C. 164; [1998] 1 B.C.L.C. 208, CA; reversing [1995] B.C.C. 1052; [1995] 2 B.C.L.C. 585, Ch D . . . .   *Digested*, 96/**842**

NRDC/Friction-reducing compositions (W34/89) [1998] E.P.O.R. 42, EPO (Technical Bd App)

Nsona *v.* Netherlands (23366/94) (2001) 32 E.H.R.R. 9, ECHR

Nsubuga *v.* Commercial Union Assurance Co Plc [1998] 2 Lloyd's Rep. 682, QBD (Comm Ct) . . . .   *Digested*, 98/**3366**

NT Gallagher & Son Ltd, Re see NT Gallagher & Sons Ltd *v.* Howard

NT Gallagher & Sons Ltd *v.* Howard; *sub nom* NT Gallagher & Son Ltd, Re; Shierson *v.* Tomlinson; CHBKI/2001/1557/A2, CA; reversing [2001] B.P.I.R. 1088; *Independent*, July 23, 2001 (C.S), Ch D (Companies Ct)

NUCLEUS Trade Mark [1998] R.P.C. 233, TMR . . . .   *Digested*, 98/**3539**

Nueva Esperanza Corp v. Tata Ltd (The Nea Elpis) see Nueva Fortuna Corp v. Tata Ltd (The NeaTyhi)

Nueva Fortuna Corp v. Tata Ltd (The NeaTyhi); Nueva Esperanza Corp v. Tata Ltd (The Nea Elpis) [1999] 2 Lloyd's Rep. 497; [1999] C.L.C. 1342, QBD (Comm Ct) ...   *Digested, 99/*__4436__

Nugent v. Benfield Greig Group Plc; *sub nom* Benfield Greig Group Plc, Re [2001] EWCA Civ 397, CA; reversing [2001] B.C.C. 92; [2000] 2 B.C.L.C. 488, Ch D (Companies Ct) ....   *Digested, 01/*__745__

Nugent v. Michael Goss Aviation Ltd [2000] 2 Lloyd's Rep. 222; [2000] C.L.C. 1228; [2000] P.I.Q.R. P175; *Times,* May 10, 2000, CA ....   *Digested, 00/*__5157__: *Considered, 00/4744*

Nugent v. Rendall see Killick v. Rendall

Nulyarimma v. Thompson; Buzzacott v. Hill 8 B.H.R.C. 135, Fed Ct (Aus) (Full Ct) .....   *Digested, 00/*__3812__

Nunes (C186/98), Re see Criminal Proceedings against Nunes (C186/98)

Nunnerley v. Warrington HA [2000] P.I.Q.R. Q69; [2000] Lloyd's Rep. Med. 170; (1999) 96(45) L.S.G. 32; *Times,* November 26, 1999, QBD ....   *Digested, 00/*__1450__

Nuova Safim SpA v. Sakura Bank Ltd [1999] 2 All E.R. (Comm) 526; [1999] C.L.C. 1830, CA; affirming [1998] Lloyd's Rep. Bank. 142; [1998] C.L.C. 306, QBD (Comm Ct) ....   *Digested, 99/*__293__

Nur v. Secretary of State for the Home Department see Hersi v. Secretary of State for the Home Department

Nurdin & Peacock Plc v. DB Ramsden & Co Ltd [1999] 1 W.L.R. 1249; [1999] 1 All E.R. 941; [1999] 1 E.G.L.R. 15; [1999] 10 E.G. 183; [1999] 09 E.G. 175; [1999] E.G.C.S. 19; (1999) 96(8) L.S.G. 29; (1999) 149 N.L.J. 251; [1999] N.P.C. 17; *Times,* February 18, 1999, Ch D ....   *Digested, 99/*__2218__

Nurdin & Peacock Plc v. DB Ramsden & Co Ltd (Rectification Claim); *sub nom* DB Ramsden & Co Ltd v. Nurdin & Peacock Plc [1999] 1 E.G.L.R. 119; [1998] E.G.C.S. 123; *Times,* September 14, 1998, Ch D ....   *Digested, 98/*__3658__

NutraSweet Co v. Council of the European Union (C77/98) see Ajinomoto Co Inc v. Council of the European Union (C76/98)

NutraSweet Co v. Council of the European Union (T160/94) see Ajinomoto Co Inc v. Council of the European Union (C76/98)

Nutrinova Nutrition Specialities & Food Ingredients GmbH v. Scanchem UK Ltd (Form of Order) [2001] F.S.R. 43, Pat Ct

Nutrinova Nutrition Specialities & Food Ingredients GmbH v. Scanchem UK Ltd (Infringement) [2001] F.S.R. 42; (2000) 23(7) I.P.D. 23055, Ch D

NUTRITIVE Trade Mark [1998] R.P.C. 621, TMR ....   *Digested, 98/*__3537__

Nutt v. Read (2000) 32 H.L.R. 761; (1999) 96(42) L.S.G. 44; *Times,* December 3, 1999, CA ....   *Digested, 00/*__3877__

Nuttall v. Vehicle Inspectorate see Vehicle Inspectorate v. Nuttall

NV Amsterdamsche Lucifersfabrieken v. H&H Trading Agencies Ltd [1940] 1 All E.R. 587, CA ....   *Applied, 54/*__2534__: *Considered, 56/1650, 00/398: Distinguished, 66/9547*

NV Immo-Part v. Belgium (199/FR/578) 1 I.T.L. Rep. 463, HvB (Brussels)

NV Konings Graanstokerij, Re see ST TRUDO Trade Mark

NV Koninklijke Rotterdamsche Lloyd v. Western Steamship Co Ltd (The Empire Jamaica); *sub nom* Western Steamship Co Ltd v. NV Koninklijke Rotterdamsche Lloyd (The Empire Jamaica) [1957] A.C. 386; [1956] 3 W.L.R. 598; [1956] 3 All E.R. 144; [1956] 2 Lloyd's Rep. 119; 100 S.J. 618, HL; affirming [1955] P. 259; [1955] 3 W.L.R. 385; [1955] 3 All E.R. 60; [1955] 2 Lloyd's Rep. 109; 99 S.J. 561, CA; affirming [1955] P. 52; [1955] 2 W.L.R. 435; [1955] 1 All E.R. 452; [1955] 1 Lloyd's Rep. 50; 99 S.J. 133, PDAD ....   *Digested, 56/*__8297__: *Applied, 00/4696*

Nwabueze v. General Medical Council [2000] 1 W.L.R. 1760; (2000) 56 B.M.L.R. 106; *Times,* April 11, 2000, PC (UK) ....   *Digested, 00/*__2719__

Nwogbe v. Nwogbe [2000] 2 F.L.R. 744; [2000] 3 F.C.R. 345; [2000] Fam. Law 797; *Times,* July 11, 2000, CA.....................   *Digested, 00/*__2546__ *Applied, 98/3084*

Nyambirai v. National Social Security Authority [1996] 1 L.R.C. 64, Sup Ct (Zim) .....

Nyckeln Finance Co Ltd (In Administration) v. Edward Symmons & Partners (No.1) [1996] P.N.L.R. 245, CA ....   *Digested, 96/*__770__: *Followed, 99/4057*

Nyckeln Finance Co Ltd (In Administration) v. Edward Symmons & Partners (No.2) [1999] Lloyd's Rep. P.N. 953, CA

NYCOMED/Contrast agent for NMR imaging (T655/92) [1998] E.P.O.R. 206, EPO (Technical Bd App)

Nykredit Mortgage Bank Plc v. Edward Erdman Group Ltd see Banque Bruxelles Lambert SA v. Eagle Star Insurance Co Ltd

Nykredit Mortgage Bank Plc v. Edward Erdman Group Ltd see South Australia Asset Management Corp v. York Montague Ltd

Nykredit Mortgage Bank Plc *v.* Edward Erdman Group Ltd (Interest on Damages)
[1997] 1 W.L.R. 1627; [1998] 1 All E.R. 305; [1998] Lloyd's Rep. Bank. 39;
[1998] C.L.C. 116; [1998] 1 Costs L.R. 108; [1998] P.N.L.R. 197; [1998] 1
E.G.L.R. 99; [1998] 05 E.G. 150; (1998) 95(1) L.S.G. 24; (1998) 142 S.J.L.B.
29; [1997] N.P.C. 165; (1998) 75 P. & C.R. D28; *Times*, December 3, 1997, HL. .   *Digested*, 98/**1432**:
           Applied, 99/4053, 01/4532: *Considered*, 98/3917, 99/477, 99/557, 01/946:
           Distinguished, 98/1472, 01/4527: *Followed*, 97/3845, 98/4021, 98/4029:
           Previous proceedings, 96/4519

Nynehead Developments Ltd *v.* RH Fibreboard Containers Ltd [1999] 1 E.G.L.R. 7;
[1999] 02 E.G. 139, Ch D . . . .   *Digested*, 99/**3700**

O (A Child) (Application for Judicial Review), Re see A (A Child) (Application for Judicial
Review), Re
O (A Child) (CICA: Quantum: 2000), Re [2001] 3 Q.R. 8, CICA (London) [*Ex rel.* Allan
Gore, Barrister, 12 King's Bench Walk, London EC4T 7EL] . . . .   *Digested*, 01/**1568**
O (A Child) (Interim Care: Removal to Foster Parents for Assessment), Re [2000] Fam. Law
461, Fam Div
O (A Child) (Supervision Order: Future Harm), Re [2001] EWCA Civ 16; [2001] 1 F.L.R. 923;
[2001] 1 F.C.R. 289; (2001) 165 J.P.N. 606; *Times*, February 20, 2001, CA . . . .   *Digested*, 01/**2675**
O (A Child) *v.* Singh [2001] 3 Q.R. 19, CC (Halifax) [*Ex rel.* Rhodes Thain & Collinson,
Solicitors, 27 Harrison Road, Halifax] . . . .   *Digested*, 01/**1734**
O (A Juvenile) *v.* DPP; *sub nom* O (Mustapha) (A Juvenile) *v.* Southwark Crown Court
(1999) 163 J.P. 725; [1999] C.O.D. 446; (1999) 163 J.P.N. 929; *Times*,
September 28, 1999 ; *Independent*, July 26, 1999 (C.S.), QBD . . . .   *Digested*, 99/**1053**
O (A Minor) (Adoption: Withholding Agreement), Re; *sub nom* O (A Minor) (Adoption:
Withholding Consent), Re [1999] 1 F.L.R. 451; [1999] 2 F.C.R. 262; [1999]
Fam. Law 76, CA . . . .   *Digested*, 99/**2300**
O (A Minor) (Costs: Liability of Legal Aid Board), Re; *sub nom* O (A Minor) (Legal Aid
Costs), Re [1997] 1 F.L.R. 465; [1997] Fam. Law 242; *Times*, November 25,
1996, CA . . . .   *Digested*, 96/**3870**:
           Applied, 01/491

O (A Minor) (Legal Aid Costs), Re see O (A Minor) (Costs: Liability of Legal Aid Board), Re
O (A Minor) *v.* Great Ormond Street Hospital for Children NHS Trust (1999) 99(3) Q.R.
7, CC (Central London) [*Ex rel.* Bolt Burden Solicitors, 1 Providence Place,
Islington, London] . . . .   *Digested*, 99/**1529**
O (A Minor) *v.* King's Healthcare NHS Trust (Unreported, June 21, 1999), QBD [*Ex rel.*
Alexander Johnson Solicitors, 10-11 Lanark Square, Glengall Bridge, London] . .   *Digested*, 00/**1506**
O (A Minor) *v.* Rowley (Unreported, March 25, 1999), CC (Willesden) [*Ex rel.* Rory
Clarke, Barrister, 2-3 Gray's Inn Square, London] . . . .   *Digested*, 99/**1562**
O (A Minor) *v.* Wilson (Unreported, February 19, 1999), CC (Burnley) [*Ex rel.* James
Chapman & Co Solicitors, 76 King Street, Manchester] . . . .   *Digested*, 99/**4004**:
           Cited, 00/4231

O (Abduction: Consent and Acquiescence), Re [1997] 1 F.L.R. 924; [1998] 2 F.C.R. 61;
[1997] Fam. Law 469, Fam Div . . . .   *Digested*, 97/**386**
O (Care: Discharge of Care Order), Re [1999] 2 F.L.R. 119; [1999] Fam. Law 442, Fam Div
           Digested, 99/**2350**

O (Child Abduction: Competing Orders), Re see O (Child Abduction: Re-Abduction), Re
O (Child Abduction: Re-Abduction), Re; *sub nom* O (Minors) (Abduction), Re; O (Child
Abduction: Competing Orders), Re [1997] 2 F.L.R. 712; [1998] 1 F.C.R. 107;
[1997] Fam. Law 719, Fam Div . . . .   *Digested*, 98/**2384**
O (Disclosure Order), Re; *sub nom* O (Restraint Order: Disclosure of Assets), Re [1991]
2 Q.B. 520; [1991] 2 W.L.R. 475; [1991] 1 All E.R. 330, CA. . . . .   *Digested*, 91/**871**:
           Applied, 92/973: *Considered*, 95/1196, 96/1666: *Followed*, 95/1197, 00/39
O (Family Appeals: Management), Re [1998] 1 F.L.R. 431; [1998] 3 F.C.R. 226; [1998] Fam.
Law 191, CA . . . .   *Digested*, 98/**2440**
O (Minors) (Abduction), Re see O (Child Abduction: Re-Abduction), Re
O (Mustapha) (A Juvenile) *v.* Southwark Crown Court see O (A Juvenile) *v.* DPP
O (Restraint Order: Disclosure of Assets), Re see O (Disclosure Order), Re
O *v.* Chief Constable of Wiltshire (Unreported, August 6, 1999), CC (Swindon) [*Ex rel.*
Lorna Skinner, Barrister, 1 Brick Court, Temple, London] . . . .   *Digested*, 00/**466**
O *v.* E; *sub nom* E (Abduction: Non Convention Country), Re [2000] Fam. 62;
[2000] 2 W.L.R. 1036; [1999] 2 F.L.R. 642; [1999] 3 F.C.R. 497; [1999] Fam.
Law 610; (1999) 96(30) L.S.G. 29; *Times*, July 7, 1999, CA . . . .   *Digested*, 99/**2332**
O *v.* Governor of Brixton Prison see O *v.* Governor of Holloway Prison
O *v.* Governor of Holloway Prison; *sub nom* O *v.* Governor of Brixton Prison [2000] 1
Cr. App. R. 195; [2000] 1 F.L.R. 147; [2000] Fam. Law 10; *Times*, August 2,
1999, QBD . . . .   *Digested*, 99/**2319**
O *v.* Harrow LBC [2001] EWCA Civ 2046, CA; reversing [2001] EWHC Admin 542;
(2001) 98(35) L.S.G. 33; *Times*, August 14, 2001, QBD (Admin Ct) . . . .   *Digested*, 01/**2037**
O *v.* O (Jurisdiction: Jewish Divorce) [2000] 2 F.L.R. 147; [2000] Fam. Law 532, CC
(Watford) . . . .   *Digested*, 00/**2502**
O *v.* Wandsworth LBC see R. *v.* Wandsworth LBC Ex p. O

O and J (Children) (Blood Tests: Constraint), Re; *sub nom* O and J (Children) (Paternity: Blood Tests), Re; J (A Child) (Blood Tests), Re [2000] Fam. 139; [2000] 2 W.L.R. 1284; [2000] 2 All E.R. 29; [2000] 1 F.L.R. 418; [2000] 1 F.C.R. 330; (2000) 55 B.M.L.R. 229; [2000] Fam. Law 324; (2000) 164 J.P.N. 839; (2000) 97(6) L.S.G. 35; (2000) 144 S.J.L.B. 85; *Times*, March 22, 2000; *Independent*, March 13, 2000 (C.S.), Fam Div . . . . *Digested*, 00/**2509**

O Co v. M Co [1996] 2 Lloyd's Rep. 347, QBD (Comm Ct) . . . . *Digested*, 96/**5330**: *Approved*, 97/464, 98/330

O Palomo SA v. Turner & Co see Turner & Co v. O Palomo SA

O&R Jewellers Ltd v. Terry [1999] Lloyd's Rep. I.R. 436, QBD . . . . *Digested*, 99/**3370**

O-Pro Ltd v. Customs and Excise Commissioners [2000] S.T.I. 1772, V&DTr

O'Boyle's Application for Judicial Review, Re; Plunkett's Application for Judicial Review, Re [1999] N.I. 126; [2000] Eu. L.R. 637, CA (NI); affirming [1998] N.I.J.B. 242, QBD (NI) . . . . *Digested*, 01/**5769**

O'Brien (A Minor) v. Worthing BC (Unreported, October 9, 1997), CC (Southampton) [*Ex rel.* Bell Pope, Solicitors, Ashley House, 5 Grosvenor Square, Southampton, Hampshire] . . . . *Digested*, 98/**1549**

O'Brien v. Croydon LBC (1999) 77 P. & C.R. 126; [1998] 4 P.L.R. 86; [1999] J.P.L. 47; [1998] E.G.C.S. 112; *Times*, July 27, 1998; *Independent*, July 13, 1998 (C.S.), QBD . . . . *Digested*, 98/**4158**

O'Brien v. Department of the Environment, Transport and the Regions [2001] J.P.L. 375 (Note), QBD (Admin Ct)

O'Brien v. Hale [2001] 6 Q.R. 9, CC (Watford) [*Ex rel.* Philip Goddard, Barrister, 4 King's Bench Walk, Temple, London] . . . . *Digested*, 01/**1629**

O'Brien v. Hertsmere BC (1998) 10 Admin. L.R. 445; (1998) 76 P. & C.R. 441; (1998) 162 J.P.N. 685, QBD . . . . *Digested*, 98/**4156**

O'Brien v. Home Office [2001] 5 Q.R. 11, CC (Dewsbury) [*Ex rel.* Simon Anderson, Barrister, Broadway House Chambers, 9 Bank Street, Bradford] . . . . *Digested*, 01/**1604**

O'Brien v. Inland Revenue Commissioners [2000] B.P.I.R. 306, Ch D . . . . *Digested*, 00/**3456**

O'Brien v. MGN Ltd [2001] EWCA Civ 1279; *Times*, August 8, 2001, CA . . . . *Digested*, 01/**955**

O'Brien v. Moyes QBENF 97/0474/CMSI, CA. . . . . *Digested*, 98/**1489**

O'Brien v. Rotherham Engineering Steels Ltd (Unreported, March 21, 1997), CC (Leeds) . . . . *Disapproved*, 99/1518

O'Brien v. Royal Society for Mentally Handicapped Children and Adults [2001] 1 Q.R. 9, CC (Clerkenwell) [*Ex rel.* David McHugh, Barrister, Bracton Chambers, 95A Chancery Lane, London] . . . . *Digested*, 01/**1642**

O'Brien v. Williams (Inspector of Taxes) [2000] S.T.C. (S.C.D.) 364; [2000] S.T.I. 1126, Sp Comm . . . . *Digested*, 00/**5010**

O'Byrne v. Secretary of State for the Environment, Transport and the Regions see R. (on the application of O'Byrne) v. Secretary of State for the Environment, Transport and the Regions

O'Callaghan v. Coral Racing Ltd, *Times*, November 26, 1998; *Independent*, November 26, 1998, CA. . . . . *Digested*, 98/**854**

O'Carroll v. O'Sullivan (Unreported, May 5, 1998) [*Ex rel.* Dermot Walker & Co Solicitors, 6 Queen Street, Derry, Northern Ireland, BT48 7EF] . . . . *Digested*, 98/**5251**

O'Connor v. BDB Kirby & Co; *sub nom* O'Connor v. DBD Kirby & Co [1972] 1 Q.B. 90; [1971] 2 W.L.R. 1233; [1971] 2 All E.R. 1415; [1971] 1 Lloyd's Rep. 454; [1971] R.T.R. 440; 115 S.J. 267, CA . . . . *Digested*, 71/**5993**: *Applied*, 99/3365: *Distinguished*, 76/1462: *Followed*, 99/3367

O'Connor v. Chief Adjudication Officer; O'Connor v. Secretary of State for Social Security [1999] 1 F.L.R. 1200; [1999] E.L.R. 209; (1999) 96(12) L.S.G. 34; (1999) 143 S.J.L.B. 96; *Times*, March 11, 1999, CA . . . . *Digested*, 99/**4578**

O'Connor v. DBD Kirby & Co see O'Connor v. BDB Kirby & Co

O'Connor v. Lynn, *Independent*, July 17, 2000 (C.S), QBD (Comm Ct)

O'Connor v. Secretary of State for Social Security see O'Connor v. Chief Adjudication Officer

O'Connor v. Secretary of State for the Environment, Transport and the Regions [2001] J.P.L. 840 (Note); (2000) 97(43) L.S.G. 39, QBD (Admin Ct)

O'Doherty v. Inns of Court School of Law [1999] E.L.R. 364, Visitors (Inns of Ct) . . . . . *Digested*, 00/**1786**

O'Donnell v. Charly Holdings Inc; *sub nom* McDonald v. Charly Holdings Inc; CCRTI 99/1216/B3, CA . . . . *Digested*, 00/**612**

O'Donnell v. Ford Rent A Car (Unreported, April 14, 1998), CC (Altrincham) [*Ex rel.* Badhams Thompson Solicitors, 8 Bedford Park, Croydon] . . . . *Digested*, 98/**459**

O'Donoghue v. Redcar and Cleveland BC [2001] EWCA Civ 701; [2001] I.R.L.R. 615; [2001] Emp. L.R. 711, CA; reversing EAT/647/97, EAT/1207/97, EAT/129/98, EAT/342/98, EAT/1132/98, EAT/106/99, EAT/1457/96, EAT . . . . *Digested*, 01/**2313**

O'Driscoll v. Dudley HA [1998] Lloyd's Rep. Med. 210, CA; reversing [1996] 7 Med. L.R. 408; (1997) 37 B.M.L.R. 146, QBD . . . . *Digested*, 98/**550**

O'Dwyer v. Chief Constable of the Royal Ulster Constabulary [1997] N.I. 403, CA (NI) . *Digested*, 99/**5434**: *Considered*, 99/5147

O'Flynn v. Adjudication Officer (C237/94) [1996] All E.R. (E.C.) 541; [1996] E.C.R. I-2617; [1996] 3 C.M.L.R. 103; [1998] I.C.R. 608; (1997) 33 B.M.L.R. 54; *Times*, June 7, 1996; *Independent*, July 8, 1996 (C.S.), ECJ (5th Chamber). . . . . *Digested*, 96/**5517**

O'Hara v. Central SMT Co Ltd 1941 S.C. 363; 1941 S.L.T. 202, 1 Div . . . . *Applied*, 52/**752**, 52/**754**, 52/**2798**, 71/**4587**: *Considered*, 00/**4217**: *Distinguished*, 48/**4584**, 57/**4189**, 98/**5564**: *Followed*, 47-51/**2502**, 47-51/**6908**, 47/**2502**, 50/**4686**, 50/**5313**, 66/**13332**

O'Hara v. Chief Constable of the Royal Ulster Constabulary [1997] A.C. 286; [1997] 2 W.L.R. 1; [1997] 1 All E.R. 129; [1996] N.I. 8; [1997] 1 Cr. App. R. 447; [1997] Crim. L.R. 432; (1997) 94(2) L.S.G. 26; (1996) 146 N.L.J. 1852; (1997) 141 S.J.L.B. 20; *Times*, December 13, 1996; *Independent*, December 18, 1996, HL. . . *Applied*, 01/**4780**: *Subsequent proceedings*, 01/**3560**

O'Hara v. Rye CCRTI 98/0862/2, CA . . . . *Digested*, 99/**565**
O'Hara v. United Kingdom (37555/97), *Times*, November 13, 2001, ECHR . . . . *Digested*, 01/**3560**
O'Keefe v. Harvey-Kemble (1999) 45 B.M.L.R. 74, CA . . . . *Digested*, 98/**1761**
O'Keefe v. Secretary of State for the Environment, Transport and the Regions; *sub nom* R. v. Secretary of State for the Environment, Transport and the Regions Ex p. O'Keefe (1998) 76 P. & C.R. 31; [1998] J.P.L. 468; [1997] N.P.C. 132; *Times*, August 5, 1997, CA; affirming [1996] J.P.L. 42, QBD . . . . *Digested*, 97/**2339**
O'Keeffe v. An Bord Pleanala [1993] 1 I.R. 39, Sup Ct (Irl) . . . . *Followed*, 99/**5078**
O'Leary v. Howlett (1998) 98(1) Q.R. 4, QBD . . . . *Digested*, 98/**1481**
O'Loughlin v. Cape Distribution Ltd; *sub nom* Cape Distribution Ltd v. O'Loughlin [2001] EWCA Civ 178; [2001] P.I.Q.R. Q8, CA; affirming 99 NJ 580/1997-0-1132, QBD . . . . *Digested*, 01/**1528**
O'Loughlin v. Chief Constable of Essex [1998] 1 W.L.R. 374; *Times*, December 12, 1997, CA . . . . *Digested*, 98/**4286**
O'Loughlin v. Fogarty (1842) 5 Ir. L.R. 54 . . . . *Applied*, 00/**5438**
O'Mahoney v. Joliffe; O'Mahoney v. Motor Insurers Bureau (1999) 163 J.P. 800; [1999] R.T.R. 245; [1999] Lloyd's Rep. I.R. 321; [1999] P.I.Q.R. P149; *Times*, February 24, 1999, CA . . . . *Digested*, 99/**3415**
O'Mahoney v. Motor Insurers Bureau see O'Mahoney v. Joliffe
O'Neil v. Inland Revenue Commissioner [2001] UKPC 17; [2001] 1 W.L.R. 1212; [2001] S.T.C. 742; [2001] S.T.I. 732, PC (NZ)
O'Neill v. Governors of St Thomas More Roman Catholic Voluntary Aided Upper School [1997] I.C.R. 33; [1996] I.R.L.R. 372; *Times*, June 7, 1996, EAT . . . . *Digested*, 96/**2621**: *Applied*, 99/**2113**, 99/**2115**

O'Neill v. Motor Insurers Bureau see O'Neill v. O'Brien
O'Neill v. O'Brien; O'Neill v. Motor Insurers Bureau [1997] P.I.Q.R. P223; *Times*, March 21, 1997, CA . . . . *Digested*, 97/**622**: *Applied*, 99/**431**: *Considered*, 98/**533**

O'Neill v. Phillips; *sub nom* Company (No.000709 of 1992), Re; Pectel Ltd, Re [1999] 1 W.L.R. 1092; [1999] 2 All E.R. 961; [1999] B.C.C. 600; [1999] 2 B.C.L.C. 1; (1999) 96(23) L.S.G. 33; (1999) 149 N.L.J. 805; *Times*, May 21, 1999, HL; affirming [1998] B.C.C. 417; [1997] 2 B.C.L.C. 739, CA . . . . *Digested*, 99/**634**: *Applied*, 00/**691**, 01/**747**

O'Neill v. Symm & Co Ltd [1998] I.C.R. 481; [1998] I.R.L.R. 233; [1999] Disc. L.R. 59; (1998) 95(27) L.S.G. 25; *Times*, March 12, 1998, EAT . . . . *Digested*, 98/**2116**: *Considered*, 98/**2120**, 00/**2129**: *Not followed*, 00/**2127**

O'Neill v. United Kingdom (8025/77) see McVeigh v. United Kingdom (8022/77)
O'Regan v. Bedford Hospital NHS Trust (Unreported, December 6, 1999), CC (Clerkenwell) [*Ex rel.* Richard Davison, Barrister, Thomas More Chambers, 51/52 Carey Street, Lincoln's Inn, London] . . . . *Digested*, 00/**1582**
O'Regan v. Williams see Fitzgerald v. Williams
O'Reilly v. Mackman; Millbanks v. Secretary of State for the Home Department; Derbyshire v. Mackman; Dougan v. Mackman; Millbanks v. Home Office [1983] 2 A.C. 237; [1982] 3 W.L.R. 1096; [1982] 3 All E.R. 1124; 126 S.J. 820, HL; affirming [1982] 3 W.L.R. 604; [1982] 3 All E.R. 680; (1982) 79 L.S.G. 1176; 126 S.J. 578, CA; reversing 126 S.J. 312, QBD . . . . *Digested*, 82/**2603**: *Applied*, 82/**1465**, 82/**2527**, 84/**14**, 84/**21**, 84/**447**, 85/**12**, 85/**316**, 85/**2230**, 86/**324**, 88/**2976**: *Considered*, 83/**2943**, 84/**1344**, 84/**1705**, 85/**1702**, 85/**2691**, 86/**2017**, 86/**2662**, 87/**12**, 87/**20**, 87/**2378**, 87/**3052**, 87/**3162**, 88/**1**, 88/**24**, 88/**2226**, 88/**3432**, 89/**35**, 90/**3908**, 94/**8**, 94/**43**, 95/**137**, 95/**835**, 95/**3252**, 95/**3907**, 97/**490**, 00/**44**, 01/**4715**: *Distinguished*, 83/**3679**, 84/**10**, 84/**2710**, 85/**9**, 85/**2722**, 92/**79**, 92/**2740**: *Doubted*, 00/**2001**: *Followed*, 83/**24**, 86/**2165**, 87/**2460**

O'Rourke (Deceased), Re see Cameron v. Treasury Solicitor
O'Rourke v. Camden LBC [1998] A.C. 188; [1997] 3 W.L.R. 86; [1997] 3 All E.R. 23; (1997) 29 H.L.R. 793; (1997) 9 Admin. L.R. 649; (1997) 161 J.P.N. 1038; (1997) 94(26) L.S.G. 30; (1997) 141 S.J.L.B. 139; [1997] N.P.C. 93; *Times*, June 21, 1997; *Independent*, June 17, 1997, HL; reversing (1996) 28 H.L.R. 600, CA . . . . *Digested*, 97/**2674**: *Applied*, 98/**98**

O'Shea (Robert) v. Kingston upon Thames RLBC [1995] P.I.Q.R. P208, CA . . . . *Considered*, 98/**3918**
O'Shea v. MGN Ltd [2001] E.M.L.R. 40; *Independent*, June 18, 2001 (C.S), QBD . . . . . *Digested*, 01/**1833**
O'Sullivan (Julie), Re [2001] B.P.I.R. 534, Ch D . . . . *Digested*, 01/**3790**
O'Sullivan v. Management Agency and Music Ltd [1985] Q.B. 428; [1984] 3 W.L.R. 448; [1985] 3 All E.R. 351, CA . . . . *Digested*, 84/**388**: *Considered*, 88/**311**, 94/**3299**, 95/**2451**, 01/**2436**: *Distinguished*, 86/**1738**

O'Toole (Deceased) *v.* Iarnod Eireann Irish Rail (Unreported, February 19, 1999), QBD
[*Ex rel.* Andrew Spink, Barrister, 35 Essex Street, Temple, London] . . . . *Digested*, 99/**3961**
O'Toole (Deceased) *v.* Iarnod Eireann Irish Rail (Quantum) (1999) 99(6) Q.R. 5, QBD
[*Ex rel.* Andrew Spink, Barrister, 35 Essex Street, Temple, London] . . . . *Digested*, 99/**1535**
O'Toole *v.* Knowsley MBC [1999] E.H.L.R. 420; (2000) 32 H.L.R. 420; (1999) 96(22)
L.S.G. 36; [1999] Env. L.R. D29; *Times*, May 21, 1999, QBD . . . . *Digested*, 99/**2210**
Oake *v.* Biddlecombe (Unreported, May 11, 1998), QBD [*Ex rel.* Annie Ward, Pupil
Barrister, 3 Pump Court, Upper Ground Floor, Temple, London, EC4Y 7A] . . . . . *Digested*, 98/**1632**
Oakes *v.* Commissioner of Stamp Duties of New South Wales [1954] A.C. 57; [1953]
3 W.L.R. 1127; [1953] 2 All E.R. 1563; 47 R. & I.T. 141; (1953) 32 A.T.C. 476;
[1953] T.R. 453; 97 S.J. 874, PC (Aus) . . . . *Digested*, 53/**978**:
Applied, 58/914: *Considered*, 58/913, 99/4952
Oakes (Inspector of Taxes) *v.* Equitable Life Assurance Society see Bibby (Inspector of
Taxes) *v.* Prudential Assurance Co Ltd
Oakes *v.* Hopcroft [2000] Lloyd's Rep. Med. 394; (2000) 56 B.M.L.R. 136; [2000]
Lloyd's Rep. P.N. 946; *Independent*, October 30, 2000 (C.S), CA . . . . *Digested*, 00/**4197**
Oaklee Housing Association Ltd's Application, Re [1994] N.I. 227, QBD (NI) . . . . *Digested*, 00/**5516**
Oakley (CICB: Quantum: 1998), Re (Unreported, February 13, 1998), CICB (London) [*Ex
rel.* Rachel Lawrence, Barrister, 1 Essex Court, First Floor, Temple, London] . . . . *Digested*, 98/**1759**
Oakley *v.* Birmingham City Council; *sub nom* Birmingham City Council *v.* Oakley
[2001] 1 A.C. 617; [2000] 3 W.L.R. 1936; [2001] 1 All E.R. 385; [2001] Env.
L.R. 37; [2001] E.H.L.R. 8; (2001) 33 H.L.R. 30; [2001] B.L.G.R. 110; [2000]
E.G.C.S. 144; (2000) 97(48) L.S.G. 38; (2000) 150 N.L.J. 1824; (2000) 144
S.J.L.B. 290; [2000] N.P.C. 136; *Times*, November 30, 2000, HL; reversing
[1999] E.H.L.R. 209; (1999) 31 H.L.R. 1070; [1999] Env. L.R. D17; *Times*,
January 8, 1999, QBD . . . . *Digested*, 01/**4551**
Oakley *v.* Rawlinson [1998] P.I.Q.R. P161, CA . . . . *Digested*, 98/**393**
Oasis Merchandising Services Ltd (In Liquidation), Re; *sub nom* Ward *v.* Aitken [1998]
Ch. 170; [1997] 2 W.L.R. 765; [1996] 1 All E.R. 1009; [1997] 1 B.C.L.C. 689;
(1996) 146 N.L.J. 1513; *Times*, October 14, 1996; *Independent*, November 11,
1996 (C.S.), CA; affirming [1995] B.C.C. 911; [1995] 2 B.C.L.C. 493; *Times*,
June 19, 1995, Ch D . . . . *Digested*, 96/**3489**:
Applied, 00/3505
Oasis Stores Ltd's Trade Mark Application [1999] E.T.M.R. 531; [1998] R.P.C. 631, TMR . *Digested*, 98/**3501**:
Referred to, 99/3562, 99/3587
Oastler *v.* Henderson (1876-77) L.R. 2 Q.B.D. 575, CA . . . . *Applied*, 73/1931,
81/2176: *Considered*, 00/3894
Oates *v.* Anthony Pittman & Co [1998] P.N.L.R. 683; (1998) 76 P. & C.R. 490;
[1998] E.G.C.S. 82, CA . . . . *Digested*, 98/**4008**:
Considered, 00/1483
Oates *v.* Harte Reade & Co [1999] 1 F.L.R. 1221; [1999] P.I.Q.R. P120; [1999] Lloyd's
Rep. P.N. 215; [1999] P.N.L.R. 763; [1999] Fam. Law 383, QBD . . . . *Digested*, 99/**480**
Obaray *v.* Gateway (London) Ltd [2001] L. & T.R. 20; [2000] E.G.C.S. 149; [2001]
N.P.C. 13, Ch D (Companies Ct) . . . . *Digested*, 01/**4175**
Oben *v.* Blackman; *sub nom* Debtor (No.510 of 1997), Re; Blackman (A Debtor), Re
[1999] B.C.C. 446; [2000] B.P.I.R. 302; *Times*, June 18, 1998, Ch D . . . . *Digested*, 99/**3325**
Oberschlick *v.* Austria (A/204) (1995) 19 E.H.R.R. 389; *Times*, August 20, 1991, ECHR . *Digested*, 95/**2646**:
Applied, 98/3127, 01/3501
Oberschlick *v.* Austria (No.2) (1998) 25 E.H.R.R. 357, ECHR . . . . *Digested*, 98/**3088**:
Followed, 01/3469
OBG Ltd *v.* Allan [2001] Lloyd's Rep. Bank. 365; [2001] B.P.I.R. 1111, Ch D
Oboh (CICB: Quantum: 1999), Re (Unreported, March 13, 1999), CICB (London) [*Ex rel.*
Carolyn D'Souza, Barrister, 12 King's Bench Walk, Temple, London] . . . . *Digested*, 99/**1528**
Observer and Guardian *v.* United Kingdom (A/216) (1992) 14 E.H.R.R. 153; *Times*,
November 27, 1991; *Independent*, November 27, 1991; *Guardian*, November 27,
1991, ECHR . . . . *Digested*, 92/**2359**:
Considered, 98/3422: *Distinguished*, 98/3096
Observer Publications Ltd *v.* Matthew [2001] UKPC 11; 10 B.H.R.C. 252, PC (Ant) . . . . *Digested*, 01/**837**
Occidental Petroleum Corp *v.* Buttes Gas and Oil Co (No.2) see Buttes Gas and Oil Co
v. Hammer (No.3)
Occo Ltd's Trade Mark (Application for Rectification) (1998) 21 (11) I.P.D. 21124, TMR
Oce van der Grinten NV *v.* Inland Revenue Commissioners see Inland Revenue
Commissioners *v.* Oce van der Grinten NV
Ocean Chemical Transport Inc *v.* Exnor Craggs Ltd [2000] 1 All E.R. (Comm) 519;
[2000] 1 Lloyd's Rep. 446, CA. . . . . *Digested*, 00/**4710**
Ocean Marine Mutual Protection and Indemnity Association *v.* FAI General Insurance Co
Ltd, *Independent*, October 5, 1998 (C.S.), QBD (Comm Ct)
Oceanbulk Maritime SA *v.* Manatee Towing Co Ltd see Manatee Towing Co Ltd *v.*
Oceanbulk Maritime SA (The Bay Ridge)
Oceanfocus Shipping Ltd *v.* Hyundai Merchant Marine Co Ltd (The Hawk) [1999] 1
Lloyd's Rep. 176, QBD (Comm Ct) . . . . *Digested*, 99/**4453**:
Applied, 01/4906
Oceanic Village Ltd *v.* Shirayama Shokusan Co Ltd; *sub nom* Oceanic Village Ltd *v.*
Shirayma Shokussan Co Ltd [2001] L. & T.R. 35; [2001] 7 E.G.C.S. 162, Ch D

Oceanic Village Ltd v. Shirayama Shokusan Co Ltd (Counterclaim for Rectification)
[1999] E.G.C.S. 83, Ch D
Oceanic Village Ltd v. United Attractions Ltd [2000] Ch. 234; [2000] 2 W.L.R. 476;
[2000] 1 All E.R. 975; [2000] 1 E.G.L.R. 148; [1999] E.G.C.S. 152; [1999]
N.P.C. 156; (2000) 79 P. & C.R. D42; *Times*, January 19, 2000, Ch D . . . .   *Digested*, 00/**3940**
Ochwat v. Watson Burton (Costs) [2000] C.P. Rep. 45, CA . . . .   *Digested*, 00/**409**
OCIC v. Croatia (46306/99) (2001) 29 E.H.R.R. CD220, ECHR
Ocular Sciences Ltd v. Aspect Vision Care Ltd (No.2) [1997] R.P.C. 289; (1997) 20(3)
I.P.D. 20022, Pat Ct. . . . .   *Digested*, 97/**3894**:
       Considered, 99/3462: *Followed*, 97/1035: *Referred to*, 01/3863
Ocwen Ltd v. Travis (Unreported, April 11, 2000), CC (Kingston upon Hull) [*Ex rel.*
Marc Beaumont, Barrister, Harrow-on-the-Hill Chambers, 60 High Street,
Harrow-on-the-Hill, Middlesex] . . . .   *Digested*, 00/**514**
Odebrecht Oil & Gas Services Ltd v. North Sea Production Co Ltd [1999] 2 All E.R.
(Comm) 405, QBD (T&CC). . . . .   *Digested*, 99/**837**
Odeon Associated Cinemas v. Jones see Odeon Associated Theatres Ltd v. Jones
Odeon Associated Theatres Ltd v. Jones; *sub nom* Odeon Associated Cinemas v. Jones
[1973] Ch. 288; [1972] 2 W.L.R. 331; [1972] 1 All E.R. 681; 48 T.C. 257; [1971]
T.R. 373; (1971) 115 S.J. 850, CA; affirming [1971] 1 W.L.R. 442; [1971] 2 All
E.R. 407; (1970) 49 A.T.C. 315; [1970] T.R. 299; 115 S.J. 224, Ch D . . . .   *Digested*, 72/**1751**:
       Applied, 75/2865, 94/639, 94/2522, 95/896, 00/4933: *Followed*, 71/5753
Odunsi v. Brent LBC (Unreported, February 25, 1999), CC (Willesden) [*Ex rel.* Paul
Stagg, Barrister, No. 1 Serjeant's Inn, Fleet Street, London] . . . .   *Digested*, 99/**3063**
Odyssey Re (London) Ltd (formerly Sphere Drake Insurance Plc) v. OIC Run Off Ltd
(formerly Orion Insurance Co Plc) (2000) 97(13) L.S.G. 42; (2000) 150 N.L.J.
430; (2000) 144 S.J.L.B. 142; *Times*, March 17, 2000; *Independent*, March 22,
2000, CA . . . .   *Digested*, 00/**332**
Oelmuhle Hamburg AG v. Bundesanstalt fur Landwirtschaft und Ernahrung (C298/96)
[1998] E.C.R. I-4767; [1999] 2 C.M.L.R. 492, ECJ. . . . .   *Digested*, 99/**2279**
Office des Produits Wallons ASBL v. Belgium (C184/00); *sub nom* Office des Produits
Walloons ASBL v. Belgium (C184/00) [2001] S.T.I. 1522, ECJ (3rd Chamber)
Office Overload Ltd v. Gunn [1977] F.S.R. 39; (1976) 120 S.J. 147, CA . . . .   *Digested*, 76/**2160**:
       Applied, 87/431: *Considered*, 98/727
Official Receiver v. Barnes see Structural Concrete Ltd, Re
Official Receiver v. Bond see SIG Security Services Ltd, Re
Official Receiver v. Brady [1999] B.C.C. 258, Ch D . . . .   *Digested*, 99/**608**
Official Receiver v. Brunt see Minotaur Data Systems Ltd, Re
Official Receiver v. Cooper [1999] B.C.C. 115, Ch D . . . .   *Digested*, 99/**624**
Official Receiver v. Cowan see Hitco 2000 Ltd, Re
Official Receiver v. Cummings-John [2000] B.P.I.R. 320, Ch D . . . .   *Digested*, 00/**15**
Official Receiver v. Davis [1998] B.P.I.R. 771, Ch D . . . .   *Digested*, 99/**3226**
Official Receiver v. Doshi [2001] 2 B.C.L.C. 235, Ch D
Official Receiver (as Liquidator of Celtic Extraction Ltd and Bluestone Chemicals Ltd) v.
Environment Agency see Celtic Extraction Ltd (In Liquidation), Re
Official Receiver v. Grant Thornton see Pantmaenog Timber Co Ltd, Re
Official Receiver v. Hannan; *sub nom* Cannonquest Ltd, Re [1997] B.C.C. 644; [1997]
2 B.C.L.C. 473; *Times*, March 20, 1997, CA . . . .   *Digested*, 97/**808**:
       Considered, 01/717
Official Receiver v. Hay see Pantmaenog Timber Co Ltd, Re
Official Receiver v. Ireland; *sub nom* Bradcrown Ltd, Re [2001] 1 B.C.L.C. 547, Ch D
(Companies Ct) . . . .   *Digested*, 01/**707**
Official Receiver v. Keam see Surrey Leisure Ltd, Re
Official Receiver v. McCahill see Britannia Homes Centres Ltd, Re
Official Receiver v. Meade-King (A Firm) see Pantmaenog Timber Co Ltd, Re
Official Receiver v. Milborn, *Independent*, July 26, 1999 (C.S.), Ch D
Official Receiver v. Pafundo see NP Engineering & Security Products Ltd, Re
Official Receiver v. Prior see New Technology Systems Ltd, Re
Official Receiver v. Stern (No.1) see Westminster Property Management Ltd (No.1), Re
Official Receiver v. Stern (No.2) see Westminster Property Management Ltd (No.2), Re
Official Receiver v. Turner [1998] B.P.I.R. 636, Ch D . . . .   *Digested*, 99/**3257**
Official Receiver v. Vass [1999] B.C.C. 516, Ch D . . . .   *Digested*, 99/**612**
Official Receiver v. Wadge Rapps & Hunt see Pantmaenog Timber Co Ltd, Re
Official Solicitor v. K; *sub nom* K (Infants), Re [1965] A.C. 201; [1963] 3 W.L.R. 408;
[1963] 3 All E.R. 191; 107 S.J. 616, HL; reversing [1963] Ch. 381; [1962] 3
W.L.R. 1517; [1962] 3 All E.R. 1000; 106 S.J. 900, CA; reversing [1962] 3
W.L.R. 752; [1962] 3 All E.R. 178; 106 S.J. 721, Ch D . . . .   *Digested*, 63/**1807**:
       Applied, 62/934, 63/1061, 63/1117, 63/2164, 64/2322, 72/2145, 94/3000,
       94/3219, 94/3244, 95/3622, 99/2412: *Approved*, 66/6287:
       Considered, 63/2164, 64/2322, 69/295, 93/3209, 96/474:
       Distinguished, 63/1768, 70/1359
Official Trustee in Bankruptcy v. Citibank Savings Ltd [1999] B.P.I.R. 754, Sup Ct
(NSW) . . . .   *Digested*, 99/**3299**

Officier van Justitie v. De Peijper (C104/75); *sub nom* De Peijper (Managing Director of
Centrafarm BV) (C104/75), Re [1976] E.C.R. 613; [1976] 2 C.M.L.R. 271, ECJ
[1976] 1 C.M.L.R. 19, Ktg (Rotterdam) . . . . *Digested*, 76/**1132**:
Applied, 97/4174, 99/214: *Considered*, 87/2412, 88/1530, 89/1635, 90/2191,
98/2660: *Followed*, 97/3616, 98/2659, 98/2661:
Subsequent proceedings, 77/1275
Oficemen v. Commission of the European Communities (T212/95) [1997] E.C.R. II-
1161; [1998] 1 C.M.L.R. 833, CFI (3rd Chamber)
Ogbulowelu v. United Kingdom Central Council for Nursing Midwifery and Health
Visiting [1999] C.O.D. 224, QBD
Ogefere v. Islington LBC (Unreported, April 22, 1999), CC (Clerkenwell) [*Ex rel.* Tracey
Bloom, Barrister, Doughty Street Chambers, 11 Doughty Street, London] . . . . . . *Digested*, 99/**1391**
Ogejebe v. East London Bus & Coach Co (Unreported, June 6, 2000) . . . . *Considered*, 00/404
Ogilvy Group (Holdings) Ltd v. Fondital Fonderie Italiane Nuova Valsabbia Ltd (1999)
143 S.J.L.B. 174; *Times*, May 21, 1999, QBD . . . . *Digested*, 99/**412**
Ogur v. Turkey (21594/93) (2001) 31 E.H.R.R. 40, ECHR . . . . *Digested*, 01/**3567**
Ogwo v. Taylor [1988] A.C. 431; [1987] 3 W.L.R. 1145; [1987] 3 All E.R. 961; (1988)
152 L.G. Rev. 589; (1988) 85(4) L.S.G. 35; (1987) 137 N.L.J. 110; (1987) 131
S.J. 1628, HL; affirming [1987] 2 W.L.R. 988; [1987] 1 All E.R. 668; (1987) 84
L.S.G.1882; (1987) 137 N.L.J. 99; (1987) 131 S.J. 506, CA . . . . *Digested*, 88/**2445**:
Followed, 98/3932
Ohio Art Co v. CreCon Spiel und Hobbyartikel GmbH [2000] E.T.M.R. 756, LG
(Munchen)
Oilgear Co's Application [1999] E.T.M.R. 291, OHIM (2nd Bd App) . . . . *Digested*, 00/**3765**
Ojjeh v. Galerie Moderne Ltd see Ojjeh v. Waller
Ojjeh v. Waller; Ojjeh v. Galerie Moderne Ltd (Unreported, December 14, 1998), QBD. . . *Digested*, 99/**4405**
Okcuoglu v. Turkey (24408/94) see Baskaya v. Turkey (23536/94)
Oke v. Rideout (Unreported, August 6, 1998), CC [*Ex rel.* Malcolm D Warner, Barrister,
Guildhall Chambers, 22-24 Broad Street, Bristol] . . . . *Digested*, 98/**4876**
Okereke v. Brent LBC [1967] 1 Q.B. 42; [1966] 2 W.L.R. 169; [1966] 1 All E.R. 150;
130 J.P. 126; 64 L.G.R. 72; 109 S.J. 956, CA . . . . *Digested*, 66/**5722**:
Considered, 93/3860, 98/3038: *Distinguished*, 66/5751, 67/1858
Okolo v. Secretary of State for the Environment; Omoregei v. Secretary of State for the
Environment [1997] 4 All E.R. 242; [1997] J.P.L. 1009; [1998] C.O.D. 8, CA;
reversing [1997] 2 All E.R. 911; [1997] 2 P.L.R. 91; [1997] J.P.L. 1005; [1997]
N.P.C. 9, QBD . . . . *Digested*, 97/**4045**
Oksuzoglu v. Kay [1998] 2 All E.R. 361; [1998] Lloyd's Rep. Med. 129; (1998) 42
B.M.L.R. 43; *Times*, February 26, 1998, CA. . . . . *Digested*, 98/**603**
Olakunori v. DPP [1998] C.O.D. 443, QBD
Olaleye-Oruene v. London Guildhall University see Greig Middleton & Co Ltd v.
Denderowicz (No.2)
Olawale v. Secretary of State for the Home Department [2001] Imm. A.R. 20, CA . . . . . *Digested*, 01/**3615**
Old & Campbell Ltd v. Liverpool Victoria Friendly Society see Taylor Fashions Ltd v.
Liverpool Victoria Trustees Co Ltd
Old England Properties Ltd v. Telford and Wrekin Council [2000] 3 E.G.L.R. 153; [2001]
R.V.R. 175, Lands Tr . . . . *Digested*, 01/**4651**
Old Grovebury Manor Farm Ltd v. W Seymour Plant Sales & Hire Ltd (No.2) [1979] 1
W.L.R. 1397; [1979] 3 All E.R. 504; (1980) 39 P. & C.R. 99; (1979) 252 E.G.
1103, CA; affirming (1979) 38 P. & C.R. 374, Ch D . . . . *Digested*, 79/**1622**:
Applied, 83/2146, 85/1914, 86/1852, 92/2682, 98/2984:
Referred to, 85/1906
Oldham v. Kyrris see Kyrris (No.2), Re
Oldham v. United Kingdom (36273/97) (2001) 31 E.H.R.R. 34; [2000] Crim. L.R.
1011; *Times*, October 24, 2000, ECHR . . . . *Digested*, 00/**4322**:
Considered, 01/4577
Oldham MBC v. D [2000] 2 F.L.R. 382; [2000] Fam. Law 599, Fam Div . . . . *Digested*, 00/**2431**
Oldham MBC v. Ruddy (2001) 16 P.A.D. 68, Planning Inspector
Oleifici Italiani SpA v. Commission of the European Communities (T267/94) [1997]
E.C.R. II-1239; [1998] 1 C.M.L.R. 692, CFI
Oleifici Italiani SpA v. Commission of the European Communities (T54/96); *sub nom*
Fratelli Rubino Industrie Olearie SpA v. Commission of the European
Communities [1998] E.C.R. II-3377; [1998] 3 C.M.L.R. 1181, CFI . . . . *Applied*, 99/2240
Oliveira v. Switzerland (1999) 28 E.H.R.R. 289; [1998] H.R.C.D. 755, ECHR. . . . . *Digested*, 99/**3125**
Oliver v. Burton (Unreported, December 13, 1999), CC (Newcastle) [*Ex rel.* Mark
Henley, Barrister, 9 Woodhouse Square, Leeds] . . . . *Digested*, 00/**1587**
Oliver v. Calderdale MBC, *Times*, July 7, 1999, CA. . . . . *Digested*, 99/**486**
Oliver v. Cox (t/a Focus Service Station) [1997] P.I.Q.R. Q133, CA. . . . . *Digested*, 98/**631**
Oliver v. Secretary of State for the Environment see Thrasyvoulou v. Secretary of State
for the Environment
Oliver Ashworth (Holdings) Ltd v. Ballard (Kent) Ltd see Ballard (Kent) Ltd v. Oliver
Ashworth (Holdings) Ltd
Olivers Wine Bar Ltd v. Newson-Smith (1999) 78 P. & C.R. D1, Ch D
Olivieri v. Customs and Excise Commissioners [2001] S.T.I. 682, V&DTr

Olivieri-Coenen *v.* Bestuur van de Nieuwe Algemene Bedrijfsvereniging (C227/94) [1995] E.C.R. I-3301; [1995] 3 C.M.L.R. 465, ECJ (1st Chamber) . . . . *Digested,* 96/**5440**: *Distinguished,* 00/4818

Olmedo Bustos *v.* Chile 10 B.H.R.C. 676, IACHR

Olsen *v.* Junckers Industrier A/S see P Bork International A/S *v.* Foreningen af Arbejdsledere i Danmark (C101/87)

Olsson *v.* Sweden (A/130) (1989) 11 E.H.R.R. 259; *Times,* March 28, 1988, ECHR . . . . *Digested,* 88/**1815**: *Applied,* 01/3548

Olympia & York Canary Wharf Ltd (No.1), Re; *sub nom* American Express Europe Ltd *v.* Adamson [1993] B.C.C. 154; [1993] B.C.L.C. 453, Ch D . . . . *Digested,* 93/**516**: *Applied,* 99/3264: *Considered,* 94/2788: *Distinguished,* 94/2738, 94/2739, 96/3519: *Followed,* 96/7084

Omar (A Bankrupt), Re; *sub nom* Trustee of the Estate of Omar (A Bankrupt) *v.* Omar (Diana Bridget) [2000] B.C.C. 434; [1999] B.P.I.R. 1001, Ch D . . . . *Digested,* 99/**3330**

Omar *v.* El-Wakil; *sub nom* Omar *v.* Wakil [2001] EWCA Civ 1090; (2001) 98(30) L.S.G. 40; [2001] N.P.C. 114; *Times,* November 2, 2001, CA. . . . . *Digested,* 01/**4854**

Omar *v.* France; Guerin *v.* France (2000) 29 E.H.R.R. 210; [1998] H.R.C.D. 734, ECHR . *Digested,* 00/**3209**: *Applied,* 01/3499: *Considered,* 01/1096

Omar (Mohamed) *v.* Omar (Chiiko Aikawa) [1995] 1 W.L.R. 1428; [1995] 3 All E.R. 571; [1996] Fam. Law 20; *Times,* December 27, 1994, Ch D . . . . *Digested,* 96/**769**: *Considered,* 98/362

Omar *v.* Wakil see Omar *v.* El-Wakil

Omar *v.* Worldwide News Inc (t/a United Press International) [1998] I.R.L.R. 291; (1998) 95(31) L.S.G. 34, EAT . . . . *Digested,* 98/**2167**: *Not followed,* 00/2148

Omega Trust Co Ltd *v.* Wright Son & Pepper (No.1) [1997] P.N.L.R. 424; (1998) 75 P. & C.R. 57; [1997] 1 E.G.L.R. 120; [1997] 18 E.G. 120; [1996] N.P.C. 189; (1997) 73 P. & C.R. D39, CA . . . . *Digested,* 97/**3851**

Omega Trust Co Ltd *v.* Wright Son & Pepper (No.2) [1998] P.N.L.R. 337, QBD . . . . *Digested,* 98/**4016**

Omnium de Traitement et de Valorisation SA *v.* Hilmarton Ltd [1999] 2 All E.R. (Comm) 146; [1999] 2 Lloyd's Rep. 222, QBD (Comm Ct) . . . . *Digested,* 99/**230**

Omoregei *v.* Secretary of State for the Environment see Okolo *v.* Secretary of State for the Environment

Omoruyi *v.* Secretary of State for the Home Department [2001] Imm. A.R. 175; [2001] I.N.L.R. 33; *Times,* November 3, 2000; *Independent,* December 4, 2000 (C.S), CA . . . . *Digested,* 00/**3311**

OMV Supply & Trading AG *v.* Clarke No.7346 of 1998, Ch D (Companies Ct) . . . . *Digested,* 99/**435**

On Demand Information Plc (In Administrative Receivership) *v.* Michael Gerson (Finance) Plc [2002] UKHL 13, HL; reversing [2001] 1 W.L.R. 155; [2000] 4 All E.R. 734; [2000] 2 All E.R. (Comm) 513; (2000) 150 N.L.J. 1300; *Times,* September 19, 2000, CA; affirming [1999] 2 All E.R. 811; [1999] 1 All E.R. (Comm.) 512; [2000] B.C.C. 289; *Times,* April 28, 1999, Ch D . . . . *Digested,* 00/**2326**

Oneac Corp *v.* Raychem Ltd [1998-99] Info. T.L.R. 57; (1998) 21(8) I.P.D. 21085, Pat Ct. . . . . *Digested,* 99/**3515**

Onslow-Edwards *v.* Cameron (1999) 96(5) L.S.G. 38; (1999) 77 P. & C.R. D38, CA

Oocl Bravery, The [2000] 1 Lloyd's Rep. 394, US Ct. *Digested,* 00/**866**

OPEN COUNTRY Trade Mark; *sub nom* Nathu Ram Sohal's Trade Mark Application (No.B1528928) [2000] E.T.M.R. 942 (Note); [2000] R.P.C. 477; (2000) 23(3) I.P.D. 23023, CA; reversing [1998] R.P.C. 408; (1998) 21(4) I.P.D. 21043, Ch D . . . . *Digested,* 00/**3774**

Open Door Counselling Ltd *v.* Ireland (A/7246); Dublin Well Woman Centre *v.* Ireland (A/246) (1993) 15 E.H.R.R. 244; *Times,* November 5, 1992; *Independent,* November 3, 1992; *Guardian,* November 3, 1992, ECHR . . . . *Digested,* 93/**2143**: *Applied,* 98/3080, 99/3110

Openbaar Ministerie *v.* Van Tiggele (C82/77) [1978] E.C.R. 25; [1978] 2 C.M.L.R. 528, ECJ . . . . *Digested,* 78/**1334**: *Applied,* 98/2130

Oppegard *v.* Norway (29327/95) (2000) 29 E.H.R.R. CD223, ECHR

Oppenheimer *v.* Cattermole (Inspector of Taxes); *sub nom* Nothman *v.* Cooper [1976] A.C. 249; [1975] 2 W.L.R. 347; [1975] 1 All E.R. 538; [1975] S.T.C. 91; 50 T.C. 159; [1975] T.R. 13; 119 S.J. 169, HL; affirming [1973] Ch. 264; [1972] 3 W.L.R. 815; [1972] 3 All E.R. 1106; 116 S.J. 802, CA; reversing [1972] Ch. 585; [1972] 2 W.L.R. 1045; [1972] 2 All E.R. 529; [1971] T.R. 507; (1971) 116 S.J. 256, Ch D . . . . *Digested,* 75/**1660**: *Considered,* 93/2168, 98/3552, 99/723, 00/5107: *Distinguished,* 88/1834

Optident Ltd *v.* Secretary of State for Health see Optident Ltd *v.* Secretary of State for Trade and Industry

Optident Ltd *v.* Secretary of State for Trade and Industry; Optident Ltd *v.* Secretary of State for Health [2001] UKHL 32; [2001] 3 C.M.L.R. 1; (2001) 61 B.M.L.R. 10; *Times,* July 2, 2001, HL; reversing [2000] 2 C.M.L.R. 283; (2000) 51 B.M.L.R. 74; (1999) 96(31) L.S.G. 39; *Times,* July 28, 1999 ; *Independent,* July 19, 1999 (C.S.), CA; reversing [1999] 1 C.M.L.R. 782; (1999) 46 B.M.L.R. 29; *Times,* October 8, 1998; *Independent,* October 12, 1998 (C.S.), QBD . . . . *Digested,* 01/**2515**

Optikinetics Ltd *v.* Whooley [1999] I.C.R. 984, EAT . . . . *Digested,* 00/**2238**

Optimum Personnel (Operations) Ltd *v.* Customs and Excise Commissioners
(Unreported, March 24, 1987), VAT Tr .... *Considered*, 99/5005
Optimum Solutions Ltd *v.* National Grid Co Plc (2001) 24(2) I.P.D. 24008, Ch D
Optos-Opus Sarl *v.* Haribo Ricqles Zan SA [1999] E.T.M.R. 362, Trib Gde Inst (Paris)
Oral-B Laboratories Trade Mark Application (No.1589316); Wisdom Toothbrushes Ltd's
Trade Mark Application (No.2008229) *Daily Telegraph*, December 5, 2000, CA;
affirming (1999) 22(10) I.P.D. 22099, Ch D
Orange *v.* Chief Constable of West Yorkshire [2001] EWCA Civ 611; [2001] 3 W.L.R.
736; (2001) 98(24) L.S.G. 44; (2001) 145 S.J.L.B. 125; *Times*, June 5, 2001;
Independent, May 9, 2001, CA. .... *Digested*, 01/**4480**
Orange Personal Communications Services Ltd *v.* Squires FC2 98/5196/1, CA .... *Digested*, 98/**623**
Orange Personal Communications Services Ltd's Community Trade Mark Application
(No.16139) [1998] E.T.M.R. 337; (1998) 21(7) I.P.D. 21078, OHIM (3rd Bd App)

Applied, 01/5881:
Considered, 99/3531, 00/3789
Orchard *v.* Phoenix Taxis (1999) 99(4) Q.R. 5, CC (Newcastle) [*Ex rel.* AM Ditchfield,
Barrister, Trinity Chambers, 9-12 Trinity Chare, Quayside, Newcastle upon Tyne] . *Digested*, 99/**1511**
Ord *v.* Belhaven Pubs Ltd [1998] B.C.C. 607; [1998] 2 B.C.L.C. 447; *Times*, April 7,
1998, CA .... *Digested*, 98/**377**:
Considered, 00/3485
Ord *v.* Upton [2000] Ch. 352; [2000] 2 W.L.R. 755; [2000] 1 All E.R. 193; [2000]
B.P.I.R. 104; [2000] P.I.Q.R. Q150; (2000) 97(1) L.S.G. 22; (1999) 149 N.L.J.
1904; (2000) 144 S.J.L.B. 35; *Independent*, January 11, 2000, CA; affirming
[1999] B.P.I.R. 775, Ch D .... *Digested*, 00/**3440**:
Applied, 01/3738: *Distinguished*, 00/3443
Order 17, Rule 11 of the County Court Rules, Re see Bannister *v.* SGB Plc
Order of the Knights of St Columbanus *v.* Commissioner of Valuation for Northern Ireland
see Knights of St Columbanus *v.* Commissioner of Valuation for Northern
Ireland
Ordre des Avocats a la Cour de Paris, Re [1999] E.C.C. 44, CE (F)
Ordre des Avocats au Barreau de Marseille *v.* Conseil de la Concurrence [2001] E.C.C.
47, Cass (F)
Oren *v.* Red Box Toy Factory Ltd; Tiny Love Ltd *v.* Martin Yaffe International Ltd; Tiny
Love Ltd *v.* Red Box Toy Factory Ltd; Tiny Love Ltd *v.* Red Box Toy (UK) Ltd; Tiny
Love Ltd *v.* Index Ltd [1999] F.S.R. 785; (1999) 22(4) I.P.D. 22038, Pat Ct .... *Digested*, 00/**3694**
Orfinger *v.* Belgium [2000] 1 C.M.L.R. 612, CE (B)
Organic Farmers & Growers (Marketing) Ltd *v.* Customs and Excise Commissioners
[1996] V. & D.R. 473, V&DTr .... *Digested*, 98/**4635**
Organisation International de Police Criminelle Interpol *v.* Setruck [1998] E.T.M.R. 664,
Trib Gde Inst (Paris)
Orgee *v.* Orgee [1997] E.G.C.S. 152; [1997] N.P.C. 156, CA .... *Digested*, 98/**123**
Oriental Diamond Inc *v.* Belgium (1989/FR/575) 2 I.T.L. Rep. 83, App (Brussels)
Oriental Gas Co Ltd, Re [1999] B.C.C. 237; [2000] 1 B.C.L.C. 209; (1998) 95(8) L.S.G. 33;
Times, February 27, 1998, Ch D (Companies Ct) .... *Digested*, 98/**697**
Origins Natural Resources Inc *v.* Origin Clothing Ltd [1995] F.S.R. 280, Ch D .... *Digested*, 95/**4940**:
Followed, 96/5716, 01/5881
Orinoco Navigation Ltd *v.* Ecotrade SpA (The Ikariada) [1999] 2 All E.R. (Comm) 257;
[1999] 2 Lloyd's Rep. 365; [1999] C.L.C. 1713, QBD (Comm Ct) .... *Digested*, 99/**4416**
Orion Finance Ltd *v.* Crown Financial Management Ltd (No.1) [1996] B.C.C. 621;
[1996] 2 B.C.L.C. 78, CA; affirming [1994] B.C.C. 897; [1994] 2 B.C.L.C. 607;
[1998] Masons C.L.R. Rep. 13, Ch D .... *Digested*, 96/**2910**:
Considered, 01/733: *Distinguished*, 97/983
Orion Finance Ltd *v.* Heritable Finance Ltd [1998] C.C.L.R. 25, CA; affirming
(Unreported, June 23, 1995), Ch D .... *Digested*, 97/**986**:
Distinguished, 97/983
Orion Finance Ltd *v.* JD Williams & Co Ltd [1998] C.C.L.R. 36, CA .... *Digested*, 97/**983**
Orion Insurance Co Plc *v.* Basler Versicherungs Gesellschaft see Sphere Drake Insurance
Plc *v.* Basler Versicherungs Gesellschaft
Orkem SA (formerly CdF Chimie SA) *v.* Commission of the European Communities
(C374/87); Solvay et Cie SA *v.* Commission of the European Communities
(C27/88) [1989] E.C.R. 3283; [1989] E.C.R. 3355; [1991] 4 C.M.L.R. 502;
Times, November 15, 1989; *Independent*, December 4, 1989 (C.S.), ECJ ...... *Digested*, 90/**2069**:
Considered, 00/2300: *Followed*, 01/768: *Referred to*, 00/2377
Orkney Islands Council *v.* Local Government Boundary Commission for Scotland see
Shetland Islands Council *v.* Local Government Boundary Commission for
Scotland
Orman (Bektas) *v.* Secretary of State for the Home Department [1998] Imm. A.R. 224;
[1998] I.N.L.R. 431, IAT. .... *Digested*, 98/**3198**
Ormrod *v.* Crosville Motor Services Ltd [1953] 1 W.L.R. 1120; [1953] 2 All E.R. 753;
97 S.J. 570, CA; affirming [1953] 1 W.L.R. 409; [1953] 1 All E.R. 711; 97 S.J.
154, Assizes (Chester). .... *Digested*, 53/**26**:
Applied, 68/2634, 71/7865: *Considered*, 70/628, 70/1366, 74/2595:
Distinguished, 61/63: *Followed*, 98/4038

ORO Amsterdam Beheer BV v. Inspecteur der Omzetbelasting Amsterdam (C165/88) [1991] S.T.C. 614; [1989] E.C.R. 4081; [1993] 2 C.M.L.R. 1015; *Times*, December 15, 1989, ECJ .... *Digested*, 90/**2240**: *Applied*, 99/4992

Oropesa, The; *sub nom* Edwin Lord v. Pacific Steam Navigation Co [1943] P. 32; [1943] 1 All E.R. 211; (1942) 74 Ll. L. Rep. 86, CA; affirming [1942] P. 140; (1942) 73 Ll. L. Rep. 148, PDAD .... *Applied*, 47-51/2545, 56/8249, 59/666, 82/2126, 88/3409: *Considered*, 98/3914

Orsank SA v. Spencer Associates (1998) 95(7) L.S.G. 31; (1998) 142 S.J.L.B. 79; *Times*, February 19, 1998, CA................................. *Digested*, 98/**606**

Ortho Pharmaceutical Corp's European Patent Application (T254/93) see ORTHO PHARMACEUTICAL/Prevention of skin atrophy (T254/93)

ORTHO PHARMACEUTICAL/Prevention of skin atrophy (T254/93); *sub nom* Ortho Pharmaceutical Corp's European Patent Application (T254/93) [1999] E.P.O.R. 1; (1997) 20(12) I.P.D. 20122, EPO (Technical Bd App) .... *Applied*, 00/3611

ORTHO/Monoclonal antibody (OKT11) (T498/94) [2001] E.P.O.R. 48, EPO (Technical Bd App).. *Digested*, 01/**3911**

ORTHO/Monoclonal antibody (OKT 5) (T510/94) [2001] E.P.O.R. 49, EPO (Technical Bd App).. *Digested*, 01/**3951**

ORTHO/Monoclonal antibody (T418/89) [1993] E.P.O.R. 338, EPO (Technical Bd App) .... *Considered*, 01/3911

ORTHO/Monoclonal antibody (T495/89) [1992] E.P.O.R. 48, EPO (Technical Bd App) *Considered*, 01/3911

Ortig v. W GmbH [2001] E.T.M.R. 94, OGH (A)

Ortiz v. Westminster City Council (1995) 27 H.L.R. 364, CA................. *Digested*, 95/**2576**: *Applied*, 97/2671: *Considered*, 96/3046, 96/3047, 99/3062: *Not followed*, 98/3018

Orwin v. Attorney General [1998] 2 B.C.L.C. 693; [1998] F.S.R. 415; (1998) 21(4) I.P.D. 21039, CA .... *Digested*, 98/**3438**

Osada v. Shepping see Shepping v. Osada

Osamor v. Lord Chancellor see Coker v. Lord Chancellor

Osborn v. Cole [1999] B.P.I.R. 251, Ch D .... *Digested*, 99/**382**

Oscar v. Chief Constable of the Royal Ulster Constabulary [1992] N.I. 290, CA (NI) ... *Not applied*, 99/5229

Oscar Bronner GmbH & Co KG v. Mediaprint Zeitungs und Zeitschriftenverlag GmbH & Co KG (C7/97) [1998] E.C.R. I-7791; [1999] 4 C.M.L.R. 112; [1999] C.E.C. 53, ECJ (6th Chamber) [1998] E.C.C. 1, OLG (Vienna) .... *Digested*, 99/**674**

Osei Bonsu v. Wandsworth LBC; *sub nom* Wandsworth LBC v. Osei Bonsu [1999] 1 W.L.R. 1011; [1999] 1 All E.R. 265; [1999] 1 F.L.R. 276; [1999] 3 F.C.R. 1; (1999) 31 H.L.R. 515; [1999] L. & T.R. 246; [1999] 1 E.G.L.R. 26; [1999] 11 E.G. 167; [1998] E.G.C.S. 148; (1998) 95(42) L.S.G. 34; (1998) 95(45) L.S.G. 40; (1998) 148 N.L.J. 1641; (1999) 143 S.J.L.B. 12; [1998] N.P.C. 141; *Times*, November 4, 1998, CA .... *Digested*, 98/**3631**

OSFC Holdings Ltd v. R. 4 I.T.L. Rep. 68, CA (Can); affirming 2 I.T.L. Rep. 522, Tax Ct (Can)

Osinuga v. DPP (1998) 162 J.P. 120; (1998) 30 H.L.R. 853; [1998] Crim. L.R. 216; (1998) 162 J.P.N. 88; *Times*, November 26, 1997, QBD

Osiris Insurance Ltd, Re [1999] 1 B.C.L.C. 182, Ch D (Companies Ct)........... *Digested*, 99/**632**

Osiris Trustees Ltd, Re [2000] W.T.L.R. 933; (1999-2000) 2 I.T.E.L.R. 404, HC (IoM) .. *Digested*, 01/**5511**

Osler v. Midland Bank Plc see Alexander v. Midland Bank Plc

Osman (No.1), Re see R. v. Governor of Pentonville Prison Ex p. Osman (No.1)

Osman v. Ferguson [1993] 4 All E.R. 344, CA.............................. *Considered*, 99/3972: *Distinguished*, 95/3686, 99/5434: *Subsequent proceedings*, 98/3102

Osman v. Kayum (Unreported, July 22, 1996), CC (Sheffield) [*Ex rel.* Irwin Mitchell, Solicitors] .... *Digested*, 97/**542**: *Not followed*, 98/485

Osman v. United Kingdom [1999] 1 F.L.R. 193; (2000) 29 E.H.R.R. 245; 5 B.H.R.C. 293; (1999) 1 L.G.L.R. 431; (1999) 11 Admin. L.R. 200; [1999] Crim. L.R. 82; [1998] H.R.C.D. 966; [1999] Fam. Law 86; (1999) 163 J.P.N. 297; *Times*, November 5, 1998, ECHR .... *Digested*, 98/**3102**: *Applied*, 01/3476, 01/3571: *Considered*, 99/3966, 99/3982, 00/3170, 00/3239, 01/3459: *Distinguished*, 01/82

Osmosis Group Ltd, Re [2000] B.C.C. 428; [1999] 2 B.C.L.C. 329, Ch D .... *Digested*, 99/**3265**

Osoba (Deceased), Re; *sub nom* Osoba v. Osoba [1979] 1 W.L.R. 247; [1979] 2 All E.R. 393; 123 S.J. 35, CA; reversing in part [1978] 1 W.L.R. 791; [1978] 2 All E.R. 1099; 122 S.J. 402, Ch D .... *Digested*, 79/**2804**: *Applied*, 99/4954: *Considered*, 80/2815

Osoba v. Osoba see Osoba (Deceased), Re

Osseili v. Bundesanstalt fur Arbeit (C97/99) see Khalil v. Bundesanstalt fur Arbeit (C95/99)

Osterreichische Unilever GmbH v. Smithkline Beecham Markenartikel GmbH (C77/97) [1999] E.C.R. I-431; [2001] 2 C.M.L.R. 50, ECJ (5th Chamber) .... *Digested*, 01/**2442**

Ostling v. Hastings (Unreported, November 14, 1997), CC (Guildford) [*Ex rel.* Stephen Reynolds, 29 Bedford Row, London, WC1R 4HE] .... *Digested*, 98/**1677**

Oswestry BC v. Cleaver (1998) 13 P.A.D. 529, Planning Inspector

OT Africa Line Ltd *v.* Hijazy (The Kribi) (No.1) [2001] 1 Lloyd's Rep. 76; [2001] C.L.C. 148; *Times,* November 28, 2000, QBD (Comm Ct) . . . . *Digested,* 01/**808**

OT Africa Line Ltd *v.* Vickers Plc [1996] 1 Lloyd's Rep. 700; [1996] C.L.C. 722, QBD (Comm Ct) . . . . *Digested,* 96/**1227**: *Considered,* 00/541

Otalor *v.* Chez Vicky Modern Hairdressing Salon (1998) 98(6) Q.R. 5, CC (Wandsworth) . . . . *Digested,* 98/**1557**

OTTO BOCK/Artificial knee joint (T190/83) [1998] E.P.O.R. 272, EPO (Technical Bd App)

Otto-Preminger Institute *v.* Austria (A/295-A) (1995) 19 E.H.R.R. 34, ECHR . . . . *Digested,* 95/**2648**: *Referred to,* 01/3467

Otway *v.* Gibbs [2001] W.T.L.R. 467, PC (Gren) . . . . *Digested,* 01/**2431**

Ouanes *v.* Secretary of State for the Home Department; *sub nom* Secretary of State for the Home Department *v.* Ouanes; R. *v.* Secretary of State for the Home Department Ex p. Ouanes [1998] 1 W.L.R. 218; [1998] Imm. A.R. 76; [1998] I.N.L.R. 230; (1997) 94(46) L.S.G. 30; (1997) 141 S.J.L.B. 249; *Times,* November 26, 1997; *Independent,* November 12, 1997, CA . . . . *Digested,* 97/**2872**

Outram *v.* Academy Plastics Ltd [2001] I.C.R. 367; [2000] I.R.L.R. 499; [2000] O.P.L.R. 321; [2000] Pens. L.R. 283; (2000) 97(20) L.S.G. 46; *Times,* April 26, 2000, CA . . . . *Digested,* 00/**4216**: *Followed,* 01/4613

Outwing Construction Ltd *v.* H Randell & Son Ltd [1999] B.L.R. 156; 64 Con. L.R. 59; (1999) 15 Const. L.J. 308, QBD (T&CC) . . . . *Digested,* 99/**795**: *Followed,* 01/863

Ouvaroff (A Bankrupt), Re [1997] B.P.I.R. 712, Ch D . . . . *Digested,* 98/**3274**

Oval (717) Ltd *v.* Aegon Insurance Co (UK) Ltd 85 B.L.R. 97; 54 Con. L.R. 74, QBD (OR) . . . . *Digested,* 97/**938**

Overcom Properties *v.* Stockleigh Hall Residents Management Ltd (1989) 58 P. & C.R. 1; [1989] 14 E.G. 78, Ch D . . . . *Digested,* 89/**2097**: *Applied,* 01/4857

Overland Shoes Ltd *v.* Schenkers International Deutschland GmbH see Overland Shoes Ltd *v.* Schenkers Ltd

Overland Shoes Ltd *v.* Schenkers Ltd; Overland Shoes Ltd *v.* Schenkers International Deutschland GmbH [1998] 1 Lloyd's Rep. 498; (1998) 95(11) L.S.G. 36; (1998) 142 S.J.L.B. 84; *Times,* February 26, 1998, CA . . . . *Digested,* 98/**3577**

Oversea Chinese Banking Corp Ltd's Trade Mark Application [1999] E.T.M.R. 887, OHIM (1st Bd App) . . . . *Digested,* 00/**3760**

Overseas Medical Supplies Ltd *v.* Orient Transport Services Ltd [1999] 1 All E.R. (Comm) 981; [1999] 2 Lloyd's Rep. 273; [1999] C.L.C. 1243, CA . . . . *Digested,* 99/**866**

Overseas Tankship (UK) Ltd *v.* Miller Steamship Co Pty Ltd (The Wagon Mound); *sub nom* Miller Steamship Co Pty Ltd *v.* Overseas Tankship (UK) Ltd; RW Miller & Co Pty Ltd *v.* Overseas Tankship (UK) Ltd [1967] 1 A.C. 617; [1966] 3 W.L.R. 498; [1966] 2 All E.R. 709; [1966] 1 Lloyd's Rep. 657; 110 S.J. 447, PC (Aus); reversing [1963] 1 Lloyd's Rep. 402, Sup Ct (NSW) . . . . *Digested,* 66/**3445**: *Applied,* 67/2676, 80/1904, 81/1855: *Considered,* 73/2318, 76/1858, 82/4057, 85/2496, 86/2481, 87/2597, 87/4737, 93/1828, 94/3410, 98/3914, 01/4548: *Distinguished,* 83/257: *Referred to,* 92/6076

Overseas Tankship (UK) Ltd *v.* Morts Dock & Engineering Co (The Wagon Mound); *sub nom* Morts Dock & Engineering Co *v.* Overseas Tankship (UK) Ltd [1961] A.C. 388; [1961] 2 W.L.R. 126; [1961] 1 All E.R. 404; [1961] 1 Lloyd's Rep. 1; 105 S.J. 85, PC (Aus); reversing [1959] 2 Lloyd's Rep. 697, CA (NSW); affirming [1958] 1 Lloyd's Rep. 575, Sup Ct (NSW). . . . . *Digested,* 61/**2343**: *Applied,* 64/2499, 66/8175, 67/1198, 67/2675, 67/2676, 68/2673, 68/4511, 73/2320, 80/1904, 81/1855, 83/2555: *Approved,* 66/8283, 67/1197: *Considered,* 63/969, 64/1004, 67/4282, 68/1201, 68/2640, 68/3227, 68/4233, 69/2412, 69/2435, 70/1849, 74/3704, 75/2343, 78/2074, 82/2126, 86/1069, 95/3682, 98/3914, 00/4239: *Distinguished,* 61/2348, 62/860, 62/862, 62/3311, 64/2500, 66/3445: *Followed,* 66/9533, 67/3114, 69/966, 69/1054

Overseas Transportation Co *v.* Mineralimportexport (The Sinoe) [1972] 1 Lloyd's Rep. 201; 116 S.J. 96, CA; affirming [1971] 1 Lloyd's Rep. 514, QBD (Comm Ct) . . . . . *Digested,* 72/**3199**: *Considered,* 77/118, 00/4696

Overseas Union Insurance Ltd *v.* New Hampshire Insurance Co (C351/89) [1992] Q.B. 434; [1992] 2 W.L.R. 586; [1992] 2 All E.R. 138; [1992] 1 Lloyd's Rep. 204; [1991] E.C.R. I-3317; [1991] I.L.Pr. 495; *Times,* August 20, 1991; *Financial Times,* July 19, 1991, ECJ (6th Chamber) . . . . *Digested,* 91/**3931**: *Applied,* 01/827

Owen (CICB: Quantum: 1999), Re (Unreported, April 23, 1999), CICB (Liverpool) [*Ex rel.* Graham Wood, Barrister, India Buildings, Water Street, Liverpool] . . . . *Digested,* 99/**1435**

Owen *v.* Burnham (Unreported, March 12, 2001), CC (Bradford) [*Ex rel.* Richard Paige, Barrister, New Bailey Chambers, 10 Lawson Street, Preston] . . . . *Digested,* 01/**534**

Owen *v.* Chief Adjudication Officer (No.2), *Independent,* May 11, 1999, CA . . . . *Digested,* 99/**4575**

Owen *v.* Fielding [1998] E.G.C.S. 110, Ch D

Owen v. Ministry of Agriculture, Fisheries and Food; sub nom Owen v. Ministry of Fisheries and Food [2001] E.H.L.R. 18, QBD . . . .   *Digested*, 01/**130**:
                                                   Previous proceedings, 01/153

Owens v. British Steel Plc (Unreported, November 14, 2000), CC (Cardiff) [*Ex rel.* David Regan, Barrister, St John's Chambers, Small Street, Bristol] . . . .   *Digested*, 01/**672**
Owens v. Redpath Offshore (South) Ltd FC3 98/6320/2, CA . . . .   *Digested*, 98/**323**
Owens Bank Ltd v. Bracco (C129/92) [1994] Q.B. 509; [1994] 2 W.L.R. 759; [1994] 1 All E.R. 336; [1994] E.C.R. I-117; [1994] 3 Bank. L.R. 93; [1994] I.L.Pr. 140; *Times*, February 3, 1994; *Financial Times*, January 25, 1994, ECJ (6th Chamber) . . . .   *Digested*, 94/**4801**:
                  Followed, 96/1093, 98/754: *Previous proceedings*, 92/464

Owner of Dredger Liesbosch v. Owners of SS Edison see Liesbosch, The
Owners and Charterers of the Navios Enterprise v. Owners of the Puritan [1998] 2 Lloyd's Rep. 16; [1998] C.L.C. 452, QBD (Adm Ct) . . . .   *Digested*, 98/**4416**
Owners and/or Demise Charterers of the Mineral Dampier v. Owners and/or Demise Charterers of the Hanjin Madras [2001] EWCA Civ 1278; [2001] 2 All E.R. (Comm) 805; [2001] 2 Lloyd's Rep. 419, CA; affirming [2000] 1 All E.R. (Comm) 870; [2000] 1 Lloyd's Rep. 282; [2000] C.L.C. 772, QBD (Adm Ct) . .   *Digested*, 00/**4709**
Owners of Cargo Laden on Board the Albacruz v. Owners of the Albazero; sub nom Concord Petroleum Corp v. Gosford Marine Panama SA [1977] A.C. 774; [1976] 3 W.L.R. 419; [1976] 3 All E.R. 129; [1976] 2 Lloyd's Rep. 467; 120 S.J. 570, HL; reversing [1975] 3 W.L.R. 491; [1975] 3 All E.R. 21; [1975] 2 Lloyd's Rep. 295; 119 S.J. 609, CA; affirming [1974] 2 All E.R. 906; [1974] 2 Lloyd's Rep. 38, QBD (Adm Ct) . . . .   *Digested*, 76/**2529**:
           Applied, 01/875: *Considered*, 00/864: *Distinguished*, 98/809
Owners of Cargo Lately Laden on Board the David Agmashenebeli v. Owners of the David Agmashenebeli [2001] C.L.C. 942, QBD (Adm Ct) . . . .   *Digested*, 01/**398**
Owners of Cargo Lately Laden on Board the Eleftheria v. Owners of the Eleftheria [1970] P. 94; [1969] 2 W.L.R. 1073; [1969] 2 All E.R. 641; [1969] 1 Lloyd's Rep. 237; 113 S.J. 407, PDAD . . . .   *Digested*, 69/**3293**:
        Applied, 81/2198, 01/4902: *Considered*, 79/308, 79/311, 80/317, 00/4685
Owners of Cargo Lately Laden on Board the KH Enterprise v. Owners of the Pioneer Container see Pioneer Container, The
Owners of Cargo Lately Laden on Board The Marble Islands v. Owners of The I Congreso del Partido see Owners of Cargo Lately Laden on Board the Playa Larga v. Owners of the I Congreso del Partido
Owners of Cargo Lately Laden on Board the MV Delos v. Delos Shipping Ltd [2001] 1 All E.R. (Comm) 763; [2001] 1 Lloyd's Rep. 703, QBD (Comm Ct) . . . .   *Digested*, 01/**344**
Owners of Cargo Lately Laden on Board the Playa Larga v. Owners of the I Congreso del Partido; sub nom Owners of Cargo Lately Laden on Board The Marble Islands v. Owners of The I Congreso del Partido [1983] 1 A.C. 244; [1981] 3 W.L.R. 328; [1981] 2 All E.R. 1064; [1981] 2 Lloyd's Rep. 367; [1981] Com. L.R. 190; 125 S.J. 528, HL; reversing [1981] 1 All E.R. 1092; [1980] 1 Lloyd's Rep. 23, CA; affirming [1978] Q.B. 500; [1977] 3 W.L.R. 778; [1978] 1 All E.R. 1169; [1977] 1 Lloyd's Rep. 536, QBD (Adm Ct) . . . .   *Digested*, 81/**285**:
        Applied, 82/1045, 83/1345, 94/3720, 95/2940, 01/376: *Considered*, 84/349,
                 94/3720, 95/2940, 95/2944: *Followed*, 80/328, 81/284
Owners of Cargo Lately Laden on Board the River Gurara v. Nigerian National Shipping Line Ltd [1998] Q.B. 610; [1997] 3 W.L.R. 1128; [1997] 4 All E.R. 498; [1998] 1 Lloyd's Rep. 225; [1997] C.L.C. 1322; (1997) 94(33) L.S.G. 27; (1997) 141 S.J.L.B. 175; *Times*, July 29, 1997, CA; affirming [1996] 2 Lloyd's Rep. 53; [1996] C.L.C. 927; *Times*, March 6, 1996, QBD (Adm Ct) . . . .   *Digested*, 98/**4405**
Owners of Cargo Lately Laden on Board the Siskina v. Distos Compania Naviera SA; Ibrahim Shanker Co v. Distos Compania Naviera SA [1979] A.C. 210; [1977] 3 W.L.R. 818; [1977] 3 All E.R. 803; [1978] 1 Lloyd's Rep 1; [1978] 1 C.M.L.R. 190, HL; reversing [1977] 3 W.L.R. 532; [1977] 2 Lloyd's Rep 230, CA; reversing [1977] 1 Lloyd's Rep 404; *Times*, December 23, 1976, QBD (Comm Ct) . . . . . .   *Digested*, 77/**2344**:
        Applied, 88/2922, 89/2989, 92/3539, 93/3284, 95/4179, 96/847, 01/726,
        01/735: *Considered*, 88/2909, 89/3040, 93/151, 94/3046, 95/4157,
                 96/2649: *Distinguished*, 96/3483: *Followed*, 99/3227
Owners of Cargo Lately Laden on Board the Starsin v. Owners of the Starsin see Homburg Houtimport BV v. Agrosin Private Ltd (The Starsin)
Owners of Cargo Lately Laden on Board the Tatry v. Owners of the Maciej Rataj (C406/92); sub nom Owners of Cargo Lately Laden on Board the Tatry v. Owners of the Tatry [1999] Q.B. 515; [1999] 2 W.L.R. 181; [1995] All E.R. (E.C.) 229; [1995] 1 Lloyd's Rep. 302; [1994] E.C.R. I-5439; [1995] I.L.Pr. 81; *Times*, December 28, 1994; *Financial Times*, December 13, 1994, ECJ [1992] 2 Lloyd's Rep. 552; [1995] I.L.Pr. 114; *Lloyd's List*, September 27, 1991, CA; affirming [1991] 2 Lloyd's Rep. 458, QBD (Adm Ct) . . . .   *Digested*, 95/**704**:
        Applied, 96/7098, 99/732, 00/738, 00/776: *Considered*, 97/900, 99/715,
                 00/5442: *Followed*, 96/1089
Owners of Cargo on Board the Visurgis v. Owners of the Visurgis [1999] 1 Lloyd's Rep. 218, QBD (Adm Ct) . . . .   *Digested*, 99/**4430**

Owners of the Annefield v. Owners of Cargo Lately Laden on Board the Annefield [1971] P. 168; [1971] 2 W.L.R. 320; [1971] 1 All E.R. 394; [1971] 1 Lloyd's Rep. 1, CA; affirming [1970] 2 Lloyd's Rep 252, PDAD . . . . *Digested,* 71/**10839**:
Considered, 83/3389, 84/3156, 84/3157: *Followed,* 00/222
Owners of the Carbonnade v. Owners of the Ruta; Harding (Owner of the Lutra II) v. Owners of the Ruta [2000] 1 W.L.R. 2068; [2001] 1 All E.R. 450; [2000] 1 All E.R. (Comm) 847; [2000] 1 Lloyd's Rep. 359; [2000] C.L.C. 784; [2000] I.C.R. 1024; (2000) 97(12) L.S.G. 39; (2000) 144 S.J.L.B. 135; *Times,* March 21, 2000, QBD (Adm Ct) . . . . *Digested,* 00/**4706**
Owners of the Enif v. Owners of the Alexia [1999] 1 Lloyd's Rep. 643, QBD (Adm Ct) . . *Digested,* 99/**4438**
Owners of the Hamtun v. Owners of the St John [1999] 1 All E.R. (Comm.) 587; [1999] 1 Lloyd's Rep. 883, QBD (Adm Ct) . . . . *Digested,* 99/**4472**
Owners of the Herceg Novi v. Owners of the Ming Galaxy [1998] 4 All E.R. 238; [1998] 2 Lloyd's Rep. 454; [1998] C.L.C. 1487; *Times,* July 30, 1998, CA; reversing [1998] 1 Lloyd's Rep. 167, QBD (Adm Ct) . . . . *Digested,* 98/**4422**
Owners of the Hontestroom v. Owners of the Durham Castle see Owners of the Hontestroom v. Owners of the Sogaporack
Owners of the Hontestroom v. Owners of the Sogaporack; Owners of the Hontestroom v. Owners of the Durham Castle [1927] A.C. 37; (1926) 25 Ll. L. Rep. 377, HL; reversing (1925) 22 Ll. L. Rep. 458, CA; reversing (1925) 21 Ll. L. Rep. 359, PDAD . . . . *Applied,* 47-51/2829,
47-51/2837, 47-51/5995, 47-51/7495, 47-51/9902, 59/431, 71/11754, 76/338,
80/1897, 81/1844, 01/4261: *Distinguished,* 56/8238
Owners of the Kumanovo v. Owners of the Massira [1998] 2 Lloyd's Rep. 301; *Times,* February 5, 1998, QBD (Adm Ct) . . . . *Digested,* 98/**4419**
Owners of the Pelopidas v. Owners of the TRSL Concord [1999] 2 All E.R. (Comm) 737; [1999] 2 Lloyd's Rep. 675, QBD (Adm Ct) . . . . *Digested,* 00/**4677**
Owners of the Selat Arjuna v. Owners of the Contship Success [2000] 1 All E.R. (Comm) 905; [2000] 1 Lloyd's Rep. 627; [2000] C.L.C. 1181, CA; affirming [1998] 2 Lloyd's Rep. 488; [1998] C.L.C. 1495, QBD (Adm Ct) . . . . *Digested,* 00/**4707**
Owners of the Sitarem v. Owners and/or Demise Charterers of the Spirit [2001] 2 All E.R. (Comm) 837; [2001] 2 Lloyd's Rep. 107; [2001] C.L.C. 1209, QBD (Adm Ct) . . . . *Digested,* 01/**4918**
Owners of The Spirit of Independence v. Wear Dockyard Ltd; *sub nom* Spirit of Independence, The (formerly known as Caribia Viva, The) [1999] 1 Lloyd's Rep. 43; [1999] C.L.C. 87, QBD (Adm Ct) . . . . *Digested,* 99/**4479**
Owners of the Thuroklint v. Owners of the Koningin Juliana [1975] 2 Lloyd's Rep. 111, HL; reversing [1974] 2 Lloyd's Rep. 353, CA; reversing [1973] 2 Lloyd's Rep. 308, QBD (Adm Ct) . . . . *Digested,* 75/**3186**:
Applied, 96/5321: *Considered,* 00/4705
Owusu v. London Fire and Civil Defence Authority [1995] I.R.L.R. 574, EAT. . . . . *Digested,* 96/**2583**:
Cited, 00/2183: *Considered,* 97/2264
Oxford v. Lowton [1978] R.T.R. 237; [1978] Crim. L.R. 295, DC. . . . . *Digested,* 78/**2557**:
Followed, 01/990
Oxford City Council v. Broadway (Valuation Officer) [1999] R.A. 169, Lands Tr . . . .
Oxford City Council v. Secretary of State for the Environment, Transport and the Regions [2001] J.P.L. 112 (Note), QBD
Oxford Diocesan Board of Finance v. West Oxfordshire DC [1998] P.L.C.R. 370, QBD. . *Digested,* 99/**4340**
Oxford Gene Technology Ltd v. Affymetrix Inc (Costs) (2001) 24(4) I.P.D. 24020, CA
Oxford Gene Technology Ltd v. Affymetrix Inc (No.1) [2001] F.S.R. 12, CA; reversing in part [2000] F.S.R. 741; (2000) 23(6) I.P.D. 23044, Pat Ct . . . . *Digested,* 99/**4226**
Oxford Gene Technology Ltd v. Affymetrix Inc (No.2) [2001] R.P.C. 18; *Times,* December 5, 2000, CA . . . . *Digested,* 00/**3686**
Oxford Gene Technology Ltd v. Affymetrix Inc (No.3) (2001) 24(3) I.P.D. 24015, Pat Ct *Digested,* 01/**3901**
Oxford Medical Ltd v. Magnex Scientific Ltd (1998) 21 (3) I.P.D. 21028, Ch D
Oxford Open Learning (Systems) Ltd v. Customs and Excise Commissioners [2000] B.V.C. 2026, V&DTr
Oxford Open Learning (Systems) Ltd v. Customs and Excise Commissioners [2001] S.T.I. 260, V&DTr
Oxford University v. Humphreys; *sub nom* Humphreys v. Oxford University [2000] 1 All E.R. 996; [2000] 1 C.M.L.R. 647; [2000] I.C.R. 405; [2000] I.R.L.R. 183; [2000] Ed. C.R. 246; *Times,* January 18, 2000; *Independent,* February 21, 2000 (C.S.), CA . . . . *Digested,* 00/**2228**
Oxford University Fixed Assets Ltd v. Architects Design Partnership [1999] C.L.C. 631; 64 Con. L.R. 12; [1999] Lloyd's Rep. P.N. 376; (1999) 15 Const. L.J. 470, QBD . *Digested,* 99/**790**
Oxfordshire CC v. Amor (Unreported, February 23, 2000), MC [*Ex rel.* A John Williams, Barrister, 13 King's Bench Walk, Temple, London] . . . . *Digested,* 00/**840**
Oxfordshire CC v. B; *sub nom* Oxfordshire CC v. GB; R. (on the application of GB) v. Oxfordshire CC [2001] EWCA Civ 1358, CA; reversing in part [2001] EWHC Admin 378; [2001] E.L.R. 797, QBD (Admin Ct)
Oxfordshire CC v. B (Care or Supervision Order) see Oxfordshire CC v. L (Care or Supervision Order)
Oxfordshire CC v. GB see Oxfordshire CC v. B

Oxfordshire CC *v.* L (Care or Supervision Order); *sub nom* Oxfordshire CC *v.* B (Care or Supervision Order) [1998] 1 F.L.R. 70; [1998] 3 F.C.R. 521; [1998] Fam. Law 22, Fam Div . . . . *Digested,* 98/**2412**
Oxfordshire CC *v.* R [1999] 1 F.C.R. 514, Fam Div . . . . *Digested,* 99/**2345**
Oxfordshire CC *v.* S (A Child) (Care Order) [2000] Fam. Law 20; *Times,* November 11, 1999, Fam. Div. . . . . *Digested,* 99/**2353**
Oxfordshire CC Trading Standards *v.* Singh (Unreported, February 29, 2000), MC [*Ex rel.* Guy Opperman, Barrister, 3 Paper Buildings, Temple, London] . . . . *Digested,* 00/**852**
Oxfordshire CC's Planning Application (1999) 14 P.A.D. 353, Planning Inspector
Oxley *v.* Coultous (Unreported, July 29, 1999), CC (Leeds) [*Ex rel.* Hamilton Ward & Co Solicitors, Century House, 107 Market Street, Hyde, Cheshire] . . . . *Digested,* 99/**2493**
Oxley *v.* Penwarden [2001] C.P.L.R. 1; [2001] Lloyd's Rep. Med. 347, CA. . . . . *Digested,* 01/**437**
Oxnard Financing SA *v.* Rahn (Legal Personality of Swiss Partnership) [1998] 1 W.L.R. 1465; [1998] 3 All E.R. 19; (1998) 95(19) L.S.G. 23; (1998) 142 S.J.L.B. 143; *Times,* April 22, 1998; *Independent,* April 27, 1998 (C.S.), CA . . . . *Digested,* 98/**373**
Oxted Financial Services Ltd *v.* Gordon [1998] B.P.I.R. 231, Ch D
OXY/Gel forming composition (T246/91) [2001] E.P.O.R. 22; [1995] E.P.O.R. 526, EPO (Technical Bd App) . . . . *Digested,* 01/**3955**
Oy Liikenne AB *v.* Liskojarvi (C172/99); *sub nom* Liskojarvi *v.* Oy Liikenne AB (C172/99) [2001] All E.R. (EC) 544; [2001] E.C.R. I-745; [2001] 3 C.M.L.R. 37; [2001] I.R.L.R. 171; *Times,* February 27, 2001, ECJ (6th Chamber) . . . . *Digested,* 01/**2335**
Oy Parlok AB *v.* Jonesco (Preston) Ltd (1998) 21 (5) I.P.D. 21049, Ch D . . . . *Digested,* 01/**3461**
Ozdep *v.* Turkey (2001) 31 E.H.R.R. 27, ECHR . . . . *Applied,* 98/3144,
Ozturk *v.* Germany (A/73) (1984) 6 E.H.R.R. 409, ECHR. . . . . 99/3141: *Considered,* 96/3123: *Followed,* 96/3119, 96/3120

P (A Child) (Care Orders: Injunctive Relief), Re [2000] 2 F.L.R. 385; [2000] 3 F.C.R. 426; [2000] Fam. Law 696, Fam Div. . . . . *Digested,* 00/**2457**
P (A Child) (Children Act 1989, ss.22 and 26: Local Authority Compliance), Re [2000] 2 F.L.R. 910; [2000] Fam. Law 792, Fam Div . . . . *Digested,* 01/**2563**
P (A Child) (Expert Evidence), Re [2001] EWCA Civ 154; [2001] 1 F.C.R. 751, CA
P (A Child) (Mirror Orders), Re; *sub nom* P (Jurisdiction: Mirror Orders), Re [2000] 1 F.L.R. 435; [2000] 1 F.C.R. 350; [2000] Fam. Law 240, Fam Div . . . . *Digested,* 00/**2473**
P (A Child) *v.* Hammersmith and Queen Charlotte's Special HA [2000] 3 Q.R. 3, QBD . *Digested,* 00/**1504**
P (A Child) *v.* Mid Kent Area Healthcare NHS Trust; *sub nom* P (A Child) *v.* Mid Kent Healthcare Trust (Practice Note); P (A Child) *v.* Mid Kent Healthcare NHS Trust [2001] EWCA Civ 1703; (2001) 98(48) L.S.G. 29; (2001) 145 S.J.L.B. 261; *Times,* November 19, 2001; *Daily Telegraph,* November 13, 2001, CA. . . . . *Digested,* 01/**405**
P (A Child) *v.* Slade [2001] 6 Q.R. 9, CC (York) [*Ex rel.* Sam Healy, Barrister, York Chambers, 14 Toft Green, York]. . . . . *Digested,* 01/**1756**
P (A Child) *v.* Whitbread Plc [2001] 3 Q.R. 20, CC (Birmingham) [*Ex rel.* Stephen Garner, Barrister, No 8 Chambers, Fountain Court, Steelhouse Lane, Birmingham] . . . . *Digested,* 01/**1766**
P (A Minor) (Abduction: Minor's Views), Re [1998] 2 F.L.R. 825; [1999] 1 F.C.R. 739; [1998] Fam. Law 580, CA. . . . . *Digested,* 99/**2328**
P (A Minor) (Care Order: Designated Local Authority), Re see P (Care Proceedings: Designated Authority), Re
P (A Minor) (Child Abduction: Declaration), Re [1995] 1 F.L.R. 831; [1995] Fam. Law 398; *Times,* February 16, 1995, CA. . . . . *Digested,* 95/**3437**: *Applied,* 01/2548
P (A Minor) (Parental Responsibility), Re [1998] 2 F.L.R. 96; [1998] 3 F.C.R. 98; [1998] Fam. Law 461, CA. . . . . *Digested,* 98/**2435**
P (A Minor) (Residence Order: Child's Welfare), Re; *sub nom* P (Section 91(14) Guidelines: Residence and Religious Heritage), Re [2000] Fam. 15; [1999] 3 W.L.R. 1164; [1999] 3 All E.R. 734; [1999] 2 F.L.R. 573; [1999] 3 F.C.R. 289; [1999] Fam. Law 531; (1999) 163 J.P.N. 712; (1999) 96(21) L.S.G. 38; (1999) 149 N.L.J. 719; (1999) 143 S.J.L.B. 141; *Times,* May 11, 1999, CA . . . . *Digested,* 99/**2389**
P (A Minor) (Residence Orders), Re see Gloucestershire CC *v.* P
P (A Minor) *v.* Hampshire CC (1999) 99(4) Q.R. 7, CC (Portsmouth) [*Ex rel.* Dyer Burdett & Co Solicitors, 64 West Street, Havant, Hampshire] . . . . *Digested,* 99/**1613**
P (A Minor) *v.* Humphreys (Unreported, November 13, 1998), CC (Bristol) [*Ex rel.* Davies & Partners Solicitors, 160 Aztec West, Almondsbury, Bristol] . . . . *Digested,* 99/**1460**
P (Barrister) (Wasted Costs Order), Re; *sub nom* R. *v.* P [2001] EWCA Crim 1728; [2001] Crim. L.R. 920; *Times,* July 31, 2001, CA (Crim Div). . . . . *Digested,* 01/**538**
P (Care Proceedings: Designated Authority), Re; *sub nom* P (A Minor) (Care Order: Designated Local Authority), Re [1998] 1 F.L.R. 80; [1998] 1 F.C.R. 653; [1998] Fam. Law 20; (1997) 161 J.P.N. 1138, Fam Div . . . . *Digested,* 98/**2407**
P (Care Proceedings: Father's Application to be Joined as Party), Re [2001] 1 F.L.R. 781; [2001] 3 F.C.R. 279, Fam Div
P (Change of Surname: Parent's Rights), Re see PC (Change of Surname), Re
P (Child Abduction: State Immunity), Re see P (Diplomatic Immunity: Jurisdiction), Re
P (CICA: Quantum: 2000), Re [2001] 3 Q.R. 9, CICA (Cardiff) [*Ex rel.* James Hassall, Barrister, Guildhall Chambers, Bristol]. . . . . *Digested,* 01/**1570**

P (Contact: Indirect Contact), Re [1999] 2 F.L.R. 893; [1999] Fam. Law 751, Fam Div . *Digested*, 00/**2478**
P (Diplomatic Immunity: Jurisdiction), Re; *sub nom* P (Child Abduction: State Immunity), Re; P *v.* P (Diplomatic Immunity: Jurisdiction) [1998] 1 F.L.R. 1026; [1998] Fam. Law 384; *Times,* March 25, 1998, CA; affirming [1998] 2 F.C.R. 525; [1998] Fam. Law 310; (1998) 95(15) L.S.G. 31; (1998) 142 S.J.L.B. 94; *Times,* March 2, 1998, Fam Div . . . . *Digested*, 98/**2374**
P (Jurisdiction: Mirror Orders), Re see P (A Child) (Mirror Orders), Re
P (Minors) (Children Act: Diplomatic Immunity), Re [1998] 1 F.L.R. 624; [1998] 2 F.C.R. 480; [1998] Fam. Law 12, Fam Div
P (Minors) (Contact: Discretion), Re [1998] 2 F.L.R. 696; [1999] 1 F.C.R. 566; [1998] Fam. Law 585; (1998) 95(34) L.S.G. 32; (1998) 142 S.J.L.B. 214; *Times,* July 30, 1998, Fam Div . . . . *Digested*, 98/**2424**
P (Restraint Order: Sale of Assets), Re [2000] 1 W.L.R. 473; [1999] 4 All E.R. 473; (1999) 96(31) L.S.G. 35; (1999) 143 S.J.L.B. 215; *Times,* August 2, 1999 ; *Independent,* November 1, 1999 (C.S.), CA . . . . *Digested*, 99/**927**
P (Section 91(14) Guidelines: Residence and Religious Heritage), Re see P (A Minor) (Residence Order: Child's Welfare), Re
P *v.* B (Paternity: Damages for Deceit) [2001] 1 F.L.R. 1041; [2001] Fam. Law 422, QBD . . . . *Digested*, 01/**5351**
P *v.* Harrow LBC [1993] 1 F.L.R. 723; [1993] 2 F.C.R. 341; [1992] P.I.Q.R. P296; [1993] Fam. Law 21; *Times,* April 22, 1992, QBD . . . . *Digested*, 94/**3365**:
Considered, 98/3944
P *v.* National Association of School Masters Union of Women Teachers (NASUWT); *sub nom* P *v.* National Association of Schoolmasters Union of Women Teachers (NASUWT) [2001] EWCA Civ 652; [2001] I.C.R. 1241; [2001] I.R.L.R. 532; [2001] E.L.R. 607; *Times,* May 25, 2001; *Independent,* May 16, 2001, CA; affirming *Times,* May 3, 2001; *Daily Telegraph,* April 17, 2001, QBD . . . . *Digested*, 01/**1945**
P *v.* P (Abduction: Acquiescence) [1998] 2 F.L.R. 835; [1998] 3 F.C.R. 550; [1998] Fam. Law 512, CA; affirming [1998] 1 F.L.R. 630; [1998] Fam. Law 245, Fam Div . . . . *Digested*, 99/**2317**:
Considered, 00/2441
P *v.* P (Contempt of Court: Mental Capacity) [1999] 2 F.L.R. 897; [1999] 3 F.C.R. 547; [1999] Fam. Law 690; *Times,* July 21, 1999, CA . . . . *Digested*, 99/**17**
P *v.* P (Diplomatic Immunity: Jurisdiction) see P (Diplomatic Immunity: Jurisdiction), Re
P *v.* P (Removal of Child to New Zealand) [2001] EWCA Civ 166; [2001] Fam. 473; [2001] 2 W.L.R. 1826; [2001] 1 F.L.R. 1052; [2001] 1 F.C.R. 425; [2001] H.R.L.R. 28; [2001] U.K.H.R.R. 484; (2001) 165 J.P.N. 466; (2001) 98(10) L.S.G. 41; (2001) 145 S.J.L.B. 61; *Times,* March 9, 2001; *Independent,* February 22, 2001; *Daily Telegraph,* February 27, 2001, CA . . . . *Digested*, 01/**2596**:
Applied, 01/2597
P *v.* S (Sex Discrimination) (C13/94) see P *v.* S and Cornwall CC (C13/94)
P *v.* S and Cornwall CC (C13/94); *sub nom* P *v.* S (Sex Discrimination) (C13/94) [1996] All E.R. (EC) 397; [1996] E.C.R. I-2143; [1996] 2 C.M.L.R. 247; [1996] C.E.C. 574; [1996] I.C.R. 795; [1996] I.R.L.R. 347; [1996] 2 F.L.R. 347; [1997] 2 F.C.R. 180; [1996] Fam. Law 609; *Times,* May 7, 1996, ECJ . . . . *Digested*, 96/**2536**:
Applied, 98/2194: *Considered*, 97/299, 99/2318: *Distinguished*, 98/2145, 00/2209: *Referred to*, 98/2195
P *v.* Swansea City and County Council, *Times,* December 1, 2000, QBD (Admin Ct) . . . *Digested*, 01/**2025**
P *v.* United Kingdom (35974/97) see B *v.* United Kingdom (36337/97)
P Bork International A/S *v.* Foreningen af Arbejdsledere i Danmark (C101/87); Olsen *v.* Junckers Industrier A/S; Hansen *v.* Junckers Industrier A/S; Handels- og Kontorfunktionaerernes Forbund i Danmark *v.* Junckers Industrier A/S [1988] E.C.R. 3057; [1990] 3 C.M.L.R. 701; [1989] I.R.L.R. 41, ECJ (3rd Chamber) . . . *Digested*, 91/**4133**:
Approved, 89/1508, 89/4304: *Considered*, 96/2594, 98/2211
P&B (Run-Off) Ltd *v.* Woolley A3/2001/0619, CA; affirming [2001] 1 All E.R. (Comm) 1120, QBD (Comm Ct) . . . . *Digested*, 01/**3822**
P&O Developments Ltd *v.* Guy's & St Thomas NHS Trust; Guy's & St Thomas NHS Trust *v.* P&O Developments Ltd [1999] B.L.R. 3; 62 Con. L.R. 38; (1999) 15 Const. L.J. 374, QBD (T&CC) . . . . *Digested*, 99/**1379**
P&O European Ferries (Dover) Ltd *v.* Iverson [1999] I.C.R. 1088, EAT . . . . *Digested*, 99/**2113**
P&O Property Holdings Ltd *v.* Glasgow City Council 2000 S.L.T. 444; 1999 S.C.L.R. 216; [2000] R.A. 447; 1998 G.W.D. 40-2080, OH . . . . *Digested*, 99/**6428**
P&O Property Holdings Ltd *v.* International Computers Ltd [2000] 2 All E.R. 1015; [1999] 2 E.G.L.R. 17; [1999] 18 E.G. 158, Ch D . . . . *Digested*, 00/**3945**
P&O Property Holdings Ltd *v.* Norwich Union Life Insurance Society; *sub nom* Norwich Union Life Insurance Society *v.* P&O Property Holdings Ltd (1994) 68 P. & C.R. 261, HL; affirming [1993] 1 E.G.L.R. 164; [1993] 13 E.G. 108; [1993] E.G.C.S. 69; [1993] N.P.C. 1, CA . . . . *Digested*, 95/**2967**:
Considered, 94/553, 99/791: *Distinguished*, 99/3727: *Followed*, 98/3677
P&O Scottish Ferries Ltd *v.* Braer Corp [1999] 2 Lloyd's Rep. 535; 1999 S.C.L.R. 540; 1999 G.W.D. 4-227; *Times,* March 10, 1999, OH. . . . . *Digested*, 99/**6446**

P&O Steam Navigation Co v. Customs and Excise Commissioners; *sub nom* Peninsular & Oriental Steam Navigation Co v. Customs and Excise Commissioners; Pacific & Oriental Steam Navigation Co Ltd v. Customs and Excise Commissioners [2000] S.T.C. 488; [2000] 3 C.M.L.R. 1104; [2000] B.T.C. 5163; [2000] B.V.C. 193; [2000] S.T.I. 753; (2000) 97(22) L.S.G. 46; *Times*, June 7, 2000; *Independent*, June 19, 2000, Ch D; affirming [2000] B.V.C. 2202; [1999] V. & D.R. 501; [2000] S.T.I. 648, V&DTr . . . . *Digested*, 00/**5324**

P-B (A Minor) (Child Cases: Hearings in Open Court), Re; *sub nom* PB (Hearings in Open Court), Re; PB (A Minor) (Hearing in Private), Re; P-B (Children Act: Open Court), Re [1997] 1 All E.R. 58; [1996] 2 F.L.R. 765; [1996] 3 F.C.R. 705; [1996] Fam. Law 606; (1996) 160 J.P.N. 1046; *Independent*, July 9, 1996, CA . *Digested*, 96/**612**: *Considered*, 00/3211

P-B (Children Act: Open Court), Re see P-B (A Minor) (Child Cases: Hearings in Open Court), Re

P-J (Minors) (Adoption Order: Practice on Appeal), Re see PJ (Adoption: Practice on Appeal), Re

P's Curator Bonis v. Criminal Injuries Compensation Board; *sub nom* A's Curator Bonis v. Criminal Injuries Compensation Board; Millar v. Criminal Injuries Compensation Board 1997 S.L.T. 1180; 1997 S.C.L.R. 69; (1998) 44 B.M.L.R. 70; 1997 Rep. L.R. 3; *Times*, January 24, 1997, OH . . . . *Digested*, 97/**5783**

PA Thomas & Co v. Mould [1968] 2 Q.B. 913; [1968] 2 W.L.R. 737; [1968] 1 All E.R. 963; (1967) 112 S.J. 216, QBD. . . . . *Digested*, 68/**3066**: *Referred to*, 99/583

Pacific & Oriental Steam Navigation Co Ltd v. Customs and Excise Commissioners see P&O Steam Navigation Co v. Customs and Excise Commissioners

Pacific Associates v. Baxter [1990] 1 Q.B. 993; [1989] 3 W.L.R. 1150; [1989] 2 All E.R. 159; 44 B.L.R. 33; 16 Con. L.R. 90; (1989) 139 N.L.J. 41; (1989) 133 S.J. 123; *Times*, December 28, 1988; *Independent*, January 6, 1989, CA; affirming 13 Con. L.R. 80, OR. . . . . *Digested*, 89/**2543**: *Applied*, 90/3263: *Considered*, 93/2997, 00/811: *Distinguished*, 01/871

Pacific Ocean Shipping Corp v. Sembawang Corp Ltd (No.1) [1999] C.L.C. 384, QBD . *Digested*, 99/**4475**

Pacitti v. Customs and Excise Commissioners [2000] S.T.I. 1692, V&DTr

Packard Bell NEC Inc's Trade Mark Application (R142/1998-3) [1999] E.T.M.R. 570, OHIM (3rd Bd App) . . . . *Digested*, 00/**3716**: *Followed*, 00/3788

Paco Holdings Ltd's Registered Trade Mark Application (Nos.2101219 and 2101220) see PACO/PACO LIFE IN COLOUR Trade Marks

PACO/PACO LIFE IN COLOUR Trade Marks; *sub nom* Paco Holdings Ltd's Registered Trade Mark Application (Nos.2101219 and 2101220) [2000] R.P.C. 451; (2000) 23(4) I.P.D. 23032, TMR . . . . *Digested*, 00/**3775**

Pacol Ltd v. Joint Stock Co Rossakhar [1999] 2 All E.R. (Comm) 778; [2000] 1 Lloyd's Rep. 109; [2000] C.L.C. 315, QBD (Comm Ct) . . . . *Digested*, 00/**225**

Paddington Churches Housing Association v. Sharif (1997) 29 H.L.R. 817, CA . . . . *Digested*, 98/**3679**

Paddington Churches Housing Association v. Technical and General Guarantee Co Ltd [1999] B.L.R. 244; 65 Con. L.R. 132; (2000) 16 Const. L.J. 216, QBD (T&CC) . *Digested*, 99/**802**

Paddock Cricket & Bowling Club v. Chilton-Merryweather (Valuation Officer) [1999] R.V.R. 91, Lands Tr . . . . *Digested*, 99/**4339**

Padgett Brothers (A-Z) Ltd v. Coventry City Council; *sub nom* Coventry City Council v. Padgett Brothers (A to Z) Ltd (1998) 162 J.P. 673; (1998) 162 J.P.N. 845; *Times*, February 24, 1998, QBD . . . . *Digested*, 98/**825**

Padhiar v. Patel [2001] Lloyd's Rep. P.N. 328, Ch D

Padmore v. Inland Revenue Commissioners [2001] S.T.C. 280; 73 T.C. 470; [2001] B.T.C. 36; 3 I.T.L. Rep. 315; [2001] S.T.I. 99; (2001) 98(6) L.S.G. 46; (2001) 145 S.J.L.B. 27; *Times*, February 21, 2001, Ch D; affirming [2000] S.T.C. (S.C.D.) 356; [2000] S.T.I. 1013, Sp Comm . . . . *Digested*, 01/**5265**: *Considered*, 00/3211

Padovani v. Italy (A/257 B) Unreported, ECHR

Padovano v. Societe Nationale de Television France 2 SA [2001] E.C.C. 23, Cass (F)

Padstow Total Loss and Collision Assurance Association, Re (1881-82) L.R. 20 Ch. D. 137, CA . . . . *Followed*, 98/3308

Paez v. Sweden [1998] H.R.C.D. 49, ECHR

Pafitis v. Greece (1999) 27 E.H.R.R. 566; [1998] H.R.C.D. 305, ECHR . . . . *Digested*, 99/**3084**

Pagarani, Re see T Choithram International SA v. Pagarani

Page v. Combined Shipping & Trading Co Ltd [1997] 3 All E.R. 656; [1996] C.L.C. 1952; [1999] Eu. L.R. 1; (1996) 15 Tr. L.R. 357, CA . . . . *Digested*, 97/**80**

Page (t/a Upledger Institute) v. Customs and Excise Commissioners [2000] S.T.I. 1349, V&DTr

Page v. Hull University Visitor see R. v. Lord President of the Privy Council Ex p. Page

Page v. Luckett (Unreported, September 10, 1998), CC (Milton Keynes) [*Ex rel.* Emma-Jane Hobbs, Barrister, 1 Temple Gardens, London] . . . . *Digested*, 98/**1609**

Page v. Scottish Insurance Corp Ltd; Forster v. Page (1929) 33 Ll. L. Rep. 134; (1929) 140 L.T.R. 571, CA; reversing (1928) 32 Ll. L. Rep. 147, KBD . . . . *Applied*, 00/3552: *Approved*, 01/3830: *Distinguished*, 00/3551: *Followed*, 00/3550, 01/3819

Page v. Sheerness Steel Co Plc see Wells v. Wells

Page v. Smith [1996] A.C. 155; [1995] 2 W.L.R. 644; [1995] 2 All E.R. 736; [1995] 2 Lloyd's Rep. 95; [1995] R.T.R. 210; [1995] P.I.Q.R. P329; (1995) 92(23) L.S.G. 33; (1995) 145 N.L.J. 723; (1995) 139 S.J.L.B. 173; *Times*, May 12, 1995; *Independent*, May 12, 1995; *Lloyd's List*, May 25, 1995 (I.D.), HL; reversing [1994] 4 All E.R. 522; [1994] R.T.R. 293; [1995] P.I.Q.R. P58; (1994) 144 N.L.J. 756; *Times*, May 4, 1994, CA; reversing [1993] P.I.Q.R. Q55, QBD . . . . . *Digested*, 95/**3682**:
Applied, 99/3978, 00/6582: *Considered*, 96/4426, 96/4478, 96/4862, 98/3954, 98/3981, 99/4059, 00/4220, 00/6598: *Followed*, 99/3980

Pagebar Properties Ltd v. Derby Investment Holdings Ltd [1972] 1 W.L.R. 1500; [1973] 1 All E.R. 65; 24 P. & C.R. 316; 116 S.J. 844, Ch D . . . . *Digested*, 72/**3519**:
Considered, 98/4372: *Distinguished*, 89/477

Pagemanor Ltd v. Ryan (No.1) (1998) 95(11) L.S.G. 37; [1998] N.P.C. 37, Ch D

Paget v. Inland Revenue Commissioners see Inland Revenue Commissioners v. Paget

Pailot v. France (2000) 30 E.H.R.R. 328; [1998] H.R.C.D. 451, ECHR. . . . . *Digested*, 01/**3519**

Paimano v. Raiss; *sub nom* Raiss v. Paimano; Palmano v. Raiss [2001] Lloyd's Rep. P.N. 341; [2001] P.N.L.R. 21; [2000] N.P.C. 101, QBD . . . . *Digested*, 01/**401**

Palacegate Properties Ltd v. Camden LBC (2001) 3 L.G.L.R. 18; (2001) 82 P. & C.R. 17; [2000] 4 P.L.R. 59; [2001] J.P.L. 373 (Note); [2001] A.C.D. 23, QBD . . . . . *Digested*, 01/**81**

Palaoro v. Austria (16718/90) (2001) 32 E.H.R.R. 10, ECHR

Palfrey v. Stagecoach Ltd (Unreported, May 18, 2000), CC (Exeter) [*Ex rel*. Crosse & Crosse Solicitors, 14 Southernhay West, Exeter EX1 1PL] . . . . *Digested*, 00/**1569**

Pallant, Re (1998) 98(2) Q.R. 4, CICB (Torquay) . . . . *Digested*, 98/**1522**

Pallant v. Morgan [1953] Ch. 43; [1952] 2 All E.R. 951; [1952] 2 T.L.R. 813, Ch D . . . . *Digested*, 52/**3571**:
Applied, 00/2317: *Approved*, 00/2327

Palmano v. Raiss see Paimano v. Raiss

Palmaz v. Boston Scientific BV; *sub nom* Palmaz's European Patents (UK), Re; Boston Scientific Ltd v. Palmaz; Expandable Grafts Partnership v. Boston Scientific BV [2000] R.P.C. 631; (2000) 23(6) I.P.D. 23043, CA; affirming [1999] R.P.C. 47; (1998) 21(9) I.P.D. 21093, Pat Ct . . . . *Digested*, 00/**3649**:
Referred to, 99/3466

Palmaz v. Boston Scientific BV (Dutch Proceedings); Expandable Grafts Partnership v. Boston Scientific BV (Dutch Proceedings) [1999] F.S.R. 352, Hof (Den Haag); reversing [1998] F.S.R. 199, RB (Den Haag) . . . . *Digested*, 99/**715**

Palmaz's European Patents (UK), Re see Palmaz v. Boston Scientific BV

Palmer v. Bowman [2000] 1 W.L.R. 842; [2000] 1 All E.R. 22; (1999) 96(41) L.S.G. 35; (1999) 96(41) L.S.G. 37; (1999) 143 S.J.L.B. 247; [1999] N.P.C. 122; (2000) 79 P. & C.R. D13; *Times*, November 10, 1999 ; *Independent*, November 29, 1999 (C.S.), CA . . . . *Digested*, 99/**4366**

Palmer v. Durnford Ford [1992] Q.B. 483; [1992] 2 W.L.R. 407; [1992] 2 All E.R. 122; (1991) 141 N.L.J. 591; *Times*, November 11, 1991, QBD. . . . . *Digested*, 92/**3499**:
Applied, 01/401: *Approved*, 94/4296: *Considered*, 93/3153:
Followed, 98/344

Palmer v. Maloney; *sub nom* Palmer v. Moloney [1999] S.T.C. 890; 71 T.C. 502; [1999] B.T.C. 357; (1999) 96(34) L.S.G. 34; (1999) 149 N.L.J. 1515; *Times*, September 22, 1999 ; *Independent*, November 1, 1999 (C.S.), CA; reversing [1998] S.T.C. 425; 71 T.C. 183; [1998] B.T.C. 106, Ch D . . . . *Digested*, 99/**4750**

Palmer v. Millwall, CC (Birkenhead) [*Ex rel*. Michael J Pickavance, Barrister, 7 Harrington Street, Liverpool] . . . . *Digested*, 01/**1563**

Palmer v. Moloney see Palmer v. Maloney

Palmer v. Southend on Sea BC [1984] 1 W.L.R. 1129; [1984] 1 All E.R. 945; [1984] I.C.R. 372; [1984] I.R.L.R. 119; (1984) 81 L.S.G. 893; (1984) 134 N.L.J. 148; (1984) 128 S.J. 262, CA . . . . *Digested*, 84/**1238**:
Considered, 96/2667, 99/2051, 99/2146: *Followed*, 89/4302

Palmer v. Tees HA (2000) 2 L.G.L.R. 69; [2000] P.I.Q.R. P1; [1999] Lloyd's Rep. Med. 351; [2000] P.N.L.R. 87; *Times*, July 6, 1999, CA; affirming [1998] Lloyd's Rep. Med. 447; (1999) 45 B.M.L.R. 88; *Times*, June 1, 1998, QBD . . . . *Digested*, 99/**3963**:
Considered, 01/550

Palmer Jeffery's Trade Mark Application (No. 2113079) (2000) 23(8) I.P.D. 23066, TMR

Palmers Ltd v. ABB Power Construction Ltd [1999] B.L.R. 426; (2000) 2 T.C.L.R. 322; 68 Con. L.R. 52; *Times*, October 6, 1999, QBD (T&CC) . . . . *Digested*, 99/**805**

Palmiero (Debtor No.3666 of 1999), Re; *sub nom* Bromley Park Garden Estates Ltd v. Palmeiro [1999] 3 E.G.L.R. 27; [1999] 38 E.G. 195, Ch D . . . . *Digested*, 99/**3679**

Palmisani v. Istituto Nazionale della Previdenza Sociale (INPS) (C261/95) [1997] E.C.R. I-4025; [1997] 3 C.M.L.R. 1356; (1997) 94(34) L.S.G. 30, ECJ (5th Chamber) . . . . *Followed*, 99/482

Pammel v. Germany (1998) 26 E.H.R.R. 100, ECHR . . . . *Digested*, 98/**3136**

Pamment v. Sutton, *Times*, December 15, 1998, Ch D . . . . *Digested*, 99/**582**

Pamplin v. Express Newspapers Ltd (No.2) [1988] 1 W.L.R. 116; [1988] 1 All E.R. 282; *Times*, March 18, 1985, CA; affirming Unreported, QBD . . . . *Digested*, 88/**2123**:
Applied, 97/1768: *Considered*, 88/1591, 89/1697, 00/1758:
Distinguished, 87/1710

Pamplin v. Gorman [1980] R.T.R. 54; [1980] Crim. L.R. 52, DC . . . . *Digested*, 80/**2332**:
Considered, 98/2295

Pan Atlantic Insurance Co Ltd v. Pine Top Insurance Co Ltd [1995] 1 A.C. 501; [1994] 3 W.L.R. 677; [1994] 3 All E.R. 581; [1994] 2 Lloyd's Rep. 427; (1994) 91 (36) L.S.G. 36; (1994) 144 N.L.J. 1203; (1994) 138 S.J.L.B. 182; *Times*, July 27, 1994; *Independent*, August 4, 1994, HL; affirming [1993] 1 Lloyd's Rep. 496; *Times*, March 8, 1993, CA; affirming [1992] 1 Lloyd's Rep. 101, QBD (Comm Ct) . . . .   *Digested*, 94/**2698**:
                   Applied, 94/2663, 97/3142: *Considered*, 95/2895, 01/3826:
                                  Distinguished, 97/3160

PANACHE PROMOTIONS/Wall mounted hair dryer (T729/91) [2000] E.P.O.R. 60, EPO (Technical Bd App) . . . .   *Digested*, 00/**3662**

Panamena Europea Navegacion Compania Limitada v. Frederick Leyland & Co Ltd; *sub nom* Compania Panamena Europea Navigacion Limitada v. Frederick Leyland & Co Ltd; Frederick Leyland & Co Ltd v. Compania Panamena Europea Navegacion Limitada [1947] A.C. 428; (1947) 80 Ll. L. Rep. 205; [1947] L.J.R 716; 176 L.T. 524, HL; affirming (1943) 76 Ll. L. Rep. 113, CA; affirming (1942) 74 Ll. L. Rep. 108, KBD . . . .   *Digested*, 47-51/**1008**:
                         Applied, 80/358: *Considered*, 99/791

Panatown Ltd v. Alfred McAlpine Construction Ltd see Alfred McAlpine Construction Ltd v. Panatown Ltd (No.1)

Panayi v. Hufran Estates Ltd CCRTI 99/0840/B1, CA.   *Digested*, 00/**607**

Panayi v. Roberts; Pyrkos v. Roberts (1993) 25 H.L.R. 421; [1993] 28 E.G. 125; [1993] N.P.C. 51; *Times*, April 2, 1993, CA. . . . .   *Digested*, 93/**2445**:
                             Considered, 98/3598

Pancenko v. Latvia (2000) 29 E.H.R.R. CD227, ECHR

Pancommerce SA v. Veecheema BV [1983] 2 Lloyd's Rep. 304; [1983] Com. L.R. 230, CA; reversing [1982] 1 Lloyd's Rep. 645, QBD (Comm Ct) . . . .   *Digested*, 83/**3343**:
                             Applied, 00/3848

Pancovics v. Daffy (Unreported, April 6, 1998), CC (Northampton) [*Ex rel.* Rupert Mayo, Barrister, 9 Bedford Row, London]. . . . .   *Digested*, 98/**1591**

Pangood Ltd v. Barclay Brown & Co Ltd [1999] 1 All E.R. (Comm.) 460; [1999] Lloyd's Rep. I.R. 405; [1999] Lloyd's Rep. P.N. 237; [1999] P.N.L.R. 678, CA. . .   *Digested*, 99/**3368**

Panini v. Autorita Garante della Concorrenza e del Mercato; Associazione Italiana Calciatori v. Autorita Garante della Concorrenza e del Mercato [1999] E.C.C. 245, TAR (Lazio) . . . .   *Digested*, 99/**696**

Panting v. Whitbread Plc (Unreported, November 24, 1998), CC (Gloucester) [*Ex rel.* Palser Grossman Solicitors, 1 Bridewell Street, Bristol]. . . . .   *Digested*, 99/**2009**

Pantmaenog Timber Co Ltd, Re; *sub nom* Official Receiver v. Hay; Pantmaenog Timber Co (In Liquidation), Re; Official Receiver v. Meade-King (A Firm); Official Receiver v. Wadge Rapps & Hunt; Official Receiver v. Grant Thornton [2001] EWCA Civ 1227; [2001] 4 All E.R. 588; [2001] 2 B.C.L.C. 555; (2001) 98(35) L.S.G. 32; (2001) 151 N.L.J. 1212; (2001) 145 S.J.L.B. 210; *Times*, August 8, 2001, CA; affirming [2001] 1 W.L.R. 730; (2000) 97(48) L.S.G. 36; *Times*, November 23, 2000, Ch D . . . .   *Digested*, 01/**3774**

Panton v. Secretary of State for the Environment, Transport and the Regions (1999) 78 P. & C.R. 186; [1999] 1 P.L.R. 92; [1999] J.P.L. 461; [1999] N.P.C. 3; *Times*, January 21, 1999; *Independent*, January 18, 1999 (C.S.), QBD . . . .   *Digested*, 99/**4219**:
            Considered, 01/4653: *Subsequent proceedings*, 00/4522

Panyda v. Marriot (Unreported, September 15, 2000), CC (Kingston on Thames) [*Ex rel.* Coleman Tilley Tarrant Sutton, Solicitors, 1-3 Union Street, Kingston-upon-Thames] . . . .   *Digested*, 01/**477**

Papachelas v. Greece (2000) 30 E.H.R.R. 923, ECHR . . . .   *Digested*, 01/**3541**

Papageorgiou v. Greece [1998] H.R.C.D. 24, ECHR

Papaloizou, Re [1999] B.P.I.R. 106, Ch D

Papamichalopoulos v. Greece (A/260-B) (1993) 16 E.H.R.R. 440, ECHR . . . .   *Distinguished*, 98/3133

Paperlight Ltd v. Swinton Group Ltd [1998] C.L.C. 1667, QBD . . . .   *Digested*, 98/**853**

Papeterie Hamelin SA v. Wiggins Teape Ltd [2000] E.T.M.R. 1047, C d'A (Paris)

Papon v. France [2001] Crim. L.R. 917, ECHR

Pappadakis v. Pappadakis [2000] W.T.L.R. 719; *Times*, January 19, 2000, Ch D . . . . .   *Digested*, 00/**3536**

Paradise Motor Co, Re [1968] 1 W.L.R. 1125; [1968] 2 All E.R. 625; 112 S.J. 271, CA . .   *Digested*, 68/**447**:
                     Considered, 94/435, 01/5153: *Followed*, 93/4821

Paradox Voyages SA v. Compagnie Air France [1998] E.C.C. 456, C d'A (Paris)

Paragon Finance Plc v. City of London Real Property Co Ltd (2001) 98(35) L.S.G. 37; *Times*, August 20, 2001, Ch D . . . .   *Digested*, 01/**4857**

Paragon Finance Plc v. Crangle & Co [1999] E.G.C.S. 25, Ch D

Paragon Finance Plc (formerly National Home Loans Corp Plc) v. Freshfields [1999] 1 W.L.R. 1183; [2000] C.P. Rep. 81; [1999] Lloyd's Rep. P.N. 446; (1999) 96(20) L.S.G. 40; (1999) 143 S.J.L.B. 136; [1999] N.P.C. 33; *Times*, March 22, 1999; *Independent*, March 16, 1999, CA. . . . .   *Digested*, 99/**4024**

Paragon Finance Plc (formerly National Home Loans Corp Plc) v. Gale [2000] C.P. Rep. 10, CA . . . .   *Digested*, 00/**305**

Paragon Finance Plc (formerly National Home Loans Corp Plc) v. Hare, *Times*, April 1, 1999, Ch D . . . .   *Digested*, 99/**503**

Paragon Finance Plc (formerly National Home Loans Corp) *v.* Nash; *sub nom* Nash *v.* Paragon Finance Plc; Staunton *v.* Paragon Finance Plc; Paragon Finance Plc *v.* Staunton [2001] EWCA Civ 1466; [2001] 2 All E.R. (Comm) 1025; (2001) 98(44) L.S.G. 36; (2001) 145 S.J.L.B. 244; *Times*, October 25, 2001, CA . . . . . *Digested*, 01/**4874**

Paragon Finance Plc *v.* Noueiri (Practice Note) see Noueiri *v.* Paragon Finance Plc (No.2)

Paragon Finance Plc *v.* Staunton see Paragon Finance Plc (formerly National Home Loans Corp) *v.* Nash

Paragon Finance Plc *v.* Thakerar & Co; Paragon Finance Plc *v.* Thimbleby & Co [1999] 1 All E.R. 400; (1998) 95(35) L.S.G. 36; (1998) 142 S.J.L.B. 243; *Times*, August 7, 1998, CA . . . . *Digested*, 98/**536**:
Applied, 00/513, 00/1452: *Considered*, 98/383, 99/501, 00/520, 01/626, 01/5505: *Followed*, 99/458

Paragon Finance Plc *v.* Thimbleby & Co see Paragon Finance Plc *v.* Thakerar & Co

Parallel Importer of Motor Vehicles (6 U 199/95), Re [1998] E.C.C. 207, OLG (Karlsruhe)

Paramananthan (Unreported, April 2, 1997), IAT . . . . *Doubted*, 98/3195

Paramanathan *v.* Minister for Immigration and Multicultural Affairs (1998) 160 A.L.R. 24, Fed Ct (Aus) (Full Ct) . . . . *Applied*, 01/3641

Paramount Airways Ltd (No.1), Re see Bristol Airport Plc *v.* Powdrill

Paramount Airways Ltd (No.2), Re; *sub nom* Powdrill *v.* Hambros Bank (Jersey) Ltd [1993] Ch. 223; [1992] 3 W.L.R. 690; [1992] 3 All E.R. 1; [1992] B.C.C. 416; [1992] B.C.L.C. 710; (1992) 89(14) L.S.G. 31; (1992) 136 S.J.L.B. 97; [1992] N.P.C. 27; *Times*, March 5, 1992; *Financial Times*, March 10, 1992, CA; reversing [1992] Ch. 160; [1991] 3 W.L.R. 318; [1991] 4 All E.R. 267; [1991] B.C.C. 559; [1991] B.C.L.C. 767; (1991) 135 S.J.L.B. 76; [1991] N.P.C. 75; *Times*, June 20, 1991, Ch D . . . . *Digested*, 92/**2528**:
Considered, 98/529

Paramount Airways Ltd (No.3), Re see Powdrill *v.* Watson

Parc (Battersea) Ltd (In Receivership) *v.* Hutchinson [1999] L. & T.R. 554; [1999] 2 E.G.L.R. 33; [1999] E.G.C.S. 45; (1999) 96(13) L.S.G. 33; (1999) 96(20) L.S.G. 39; (1999) 143 S.J.L.B. 142; *Times*, April 9, 1999; *Independent*, April 19, 1999 (C.S.), Ch D . . . . *Digested*, 99/**3662**

Pardeepan *v.* Secretary of State for the Home Department [2000] I.N.L.R. 447, IAT . . . *Digested*, 01/**3599**

Pardo *v.* France (Revision: Merits) (1998) 26 E.H.R.R. 302, ECHR . . . . *Digested*, 98/**1043**

Pardoe (Inspector of Taxes) *v.* Entergy Power Development Corp [2000] S.T.C. 286; 72 T.C. 617; [2000] B.T.C. 87; [2000] S.T.I. 216; (2000) 97(10) L.S.G. 37; *Times*, March 2, 2000, Ch D . . . . *Digested*, 00/**5053**

Pardoe *v.* Pennington; Vermuelen *v.* Pennington (1998) 75 P. & C.R. 264, CA . . . . *Digested*, 97/**4222**

Parents and Children Together (PACT) *v.* Customs and Excise Commissioners [2001] 3 C.M.L.R. 30; [2001] B.V.C. 2350; [2001] S.T.I. 1395, V&DTr . . . . *Digested*, 01/**5603**

Parfums Christian Dior SA *v.* Etos BV (98/550) [2000] E.T.M.R. 1057, Hof (Den Haag)

Parfums Christian Dior SA *v.* Evora BV (C337/95) [1997] E.C.R. I-6013; [1998] 1 C.M.L.R. 737; [1998] C.E.C. 91; [1998] E.T.M.R. 26; [1998] R.P.C. 166, ECJ [1997] E.C.R. I-6013; [1997] E.T.M.R. 323, AGO . . . . *Digested*, 98/**3505**:
Considered, 99/3560: *Distinguished*, 98/3426

Parfums Christian Dior SA *v.* Tuk Consultancy BV (C300/98); Assco Geruste GmbH *v.* Wilhelm Layher GmbH & Co KG (C392/98) [2000] E.C.R. I-11307; [2001] E.T.M.R. 26; [2001] E.C.D.R. 12, ECJ . . . . *Digested*, 01/**2478**

Parfums et Beaute Belgilux SA *v.* GB UNIC SA [1998] E.C.C. 259, Cass (B)

Parfums Marcel Rochas Vertriebs GmbH *v.* Bitsch (C1/70) [1970] E.C.R. 515; [1971] C.M.L.R. 104, ECJ . . . . *Digested*, 71/**4459**:
Applied, 98/708

Parinv (Hatfield) Ltd *v.* Inland Revenue Commissioners; *sub nom* Bishop Square Ltd (formerly Parinv (Hatfield) Ltd) *v.* Inland Revenue Commissioners [1998] S.T.C. 305; (1999) 78 P. & C.R. 169; [1998] B.T.C. 8003; [1997] N.P.C. 179; (1998) 75 P. & C.R. D35; *Times*, January 13, 1998; *Times*, December 31, 1997, CA; affirming [1996] S.T.C. 933, Ch D . . . . *Digested*, 98/**4702**

Paris Compact Disc Market (2000-D-70), Re [2001] E.C.C. 30, C Concurrence (F)

Parish *v.* DPP [2000] R.T.R. 143; (1999) 143 S.J.L.B. 280; *Times*, March 2, 2000, QBD . . . . *Digested*, 00/**937**

Parish *v.* Sharman [2001] W.T.L.R. 593, CA . . . . *Digested*, 01/**5157**

Park, Re; *sub nom* Cole *v.* Park (1889) L.R. 41 Ch. D. 326, CA . . . . *Considered*, 99/416

Park *v.* Chief Constable of Greater Manchester see Calveley *v.* Chief Constable of Merseyside

Park Air Services Plc, Re; *sub nom* Christopher Moran Holdings Ltd *v.* Bairstow [2000] 2 A.C. 172; [1999] 2 W.L.R. 396; [1999] 1 All E.R. 673; [1999] B.C.C. 135; [1999] 1 B.C.L.C. 155; [1999] B.P.I.R. 786; [1999] L. & T.R. 289; [1999] 1 E.G.L.R. 1; [1999] 14 E.G. 149; [1999] E.G.C.S. 17; (1999) 149 N.L.J. 195; [1999] N.P.C. 12; *Times*, February 5, 1999; *Independent*, February 12, 1999, HL; reversing [1997] 1 W.L.R. 1376; [1997] 3 All E.R. 193; [1997] B.C.C. 712; [1997] 2 B.C.L.C. 75; (1998) 75 P. & C.R. 161; [1997] 2 E.G.L.R. 36; [1997] 30 E.G. 127; [1997] E.G.C.S. 68; (1997) 94(19) L.S.G. 25; (1997) 141 S.J.L.B. 112; [1997] N.P.C. 68; *Times*, May 14, 1997, CA; reversing [1996] 1 W.L.R. 649; [1996] B.C.C. 556; [1996] 1 B.C.L.C. 547; [1996] B.P.I.R. 377; (1996) 72 P. & C.R. 174; [1996] 2 E.G.L.R. 49; [1996] 40 E.G. 136; [1995] N.P.C. 205, Ch D ..   *Digested*, 99/**3306**: *Followed*, 99/3272

Park Hotel *v.* Customs and Excise Commissioners [2001] S.T.I. 577, V&DTr

Park House Properties Ltd, Re; *sub nom* Secretary of State for Trade and Industry *v.* Carter [1998] B.C.C. 847; [1997] 2 B.C.L.C. 530; *Times*, August 14, 1997, Ch D
....   *Digested*, 98/**677**

Parker *v.* Connor (Unreported, April 7, 2000), CC (Peterborough) [*Ex rel.* Hunt & Coombs Solicitors, 35 Thorpe Road, Peterborough] ....   *Digested*, 00/**421**: *Doubted*, 01/617

Parker (t/a Sea Breeze Cafe) *v.* Customs and Excise Commissioners [2000] S.T.I. 269, V&DTr

Parker (Lee Christopher) *v.* DPP (2001) 165 J.P. 213; [2001] R.T.R. 16; *Times*, January 26, 2001; *Independent*, January 29, 2001 (C.S); *Daily Telegraph*, January 9, 2001, QBD ....   *Digested*, 01/**1067**

Parker *v.* Foster (Unreported, April 3, 2001), CC (Newcastle) [*Ex rel.* Keoghs, Solicitors, 2 The Parklands, Bolton] ....   *Digested*, 01/**657**

Parker *v.* Gibson; *sub nom* Parker's Estate, Re [1999] N.I. 315, Ch D (NI) ....   *Digested*, 00/**5779**

Parker *v.* Law Society (No.1) [1999] C.O.D. 183; (1999) 96(2) L.S.G. 29; (1999) 143 S.J.L.B. 45; *Times*, December 8, 1998; *Independent*, December 11, 1998, CA ...   *Digested*, 99/**7**: *Applied*, 01/92

Parker *v.* PFC Flooring Supplies Ltd [2001] EWCA Civ 1533, CA; affirming [2001] P.I.Q.R. P7, QBD ....   *Digested*, 01/**4491**

Parker (t/a NBC Services) *v.* Rasalingham (t/a MicroTec) HC 1999 04766, Ch D .....   *Subsequent proceedings*, 00/494

Parker (t/a NBC Services) *v.* Rasalingham (t/a MicroTec) (Inquiry into Damages), *Times*, July 25, 2000, Ch D ....   *Digested*, 00/**494**

Parker *v.* Schuller (1901) 17 T.L.R. 299 ....   *Applied*, 91/2959, 92/2814, 93/3314: *Considered*, 90/3782: *Not followed*, 98/583

Parker *v.* Taylor (Unreported, August 20, 1999), CC (Nottingham) [*Ex rel.* Dominic Bayne, Barrister, Plowden Buildings, Temple, London] ....   *Digested*, 99/**2473**

Parker Foundry Ltd *v.* Slack [1992] I.C.R. 302; [1991] I.R.L.R. 11; *Times*, October 30, 1991, CA; affirming [1989] I.C.R. 686, EAT ....   *Digested*, 92/**1989**: *Applied*, 95/2079, 00/2238

Parker Hale Ltd *v.* Customs and Excise Commissioners [2000] S.T.C. 388; [2000] B.T.C. 5153; [2000] B.V.C. 167; [2000] S.T.I. 579; *Times*, April 18, 2000; *Independent*, May 22, 2000 (C.S.), QBD; affirming [1999] B.V.C. 2208; [1999] V. & D.R. 258, V&DTr ....   *Digested*, 00/**5284**

Parker-Knoll Ltd *v.* Knoll International Ltd (No.2) [1962] R.P.C. 265, HL; affirming [1961] R.P.C. 346, CA; reversing [1961] R.P.C. 31 ....   *Digested*, 62/**3042**: *Considered*, 00/5608: *Referred to*, 93/3803, 94/4290

Parker-Tweedale *v.* Dunbar Bank (No.2) [1991] Ch. 26; [1990] 3 W.L.R. 780; [1990] 2 All E.R. 588; (1990) 87(29) L.S.G. 33; (1990) 134 S.J. 1040, CA ....   *Digested*, 90/**3212**: *Followed*, 00/3458

Parker's Estate, Re see Parker *v.* Gibson

Parkes *v.* Esso Petroleum Co Ltd see Parks *v.* Esso Petroleum Co Ltd

Parkes *v.* Parkes [1971] 1 W.L.R. 1481; [1971] 3 All E.R. 870; 115 S.J. 507, CA ....   *Digested*, 71/**3626**: *Considered*, 99/2401

Parkfield Group Plc (In Liquidation), Re; *sub nom* Bridisco Ltd *v.* Jordan [1997] B.C.C. 778; [1998] 1 B.C.L.C. 451, Ch D (Companies Ct) ....   *Digested*, 98/**3301**

Parkin *v.* Brew (Unreported, July 29, 1998), QBD [*Ex rel.* Peter Rickson & Partners Solicitors, 6 Winckley Square, Preston, Lancashire]...........................   *Digested*, 99/**446**

Parkin *v.* Westminster City Council (Appeal against Bankruptcy) see Parkins *v.* Westminster City Council (Appeal against Bankruptcy)

Parkins *v.* Westminster City Council (1998) 30 H.L.R. 894; [1998] 1 E.G.L.R. 22; [1998] 13 E.G. 145; (1998) 75 P. & C.R. D39, CA ....   *Digested*, 98/**3664**

Parkins *v.* Westminster City Council (Appeal against Bankruptcy); *sub nom* Parkin *v.* Westminster City Council (Appeal against Bankruptcy); Westminster City Council *v.* Parkin [2001] B.P.I.R. 1156, Ch D

Parkins *v.* Westminster City Council (Grepe v Loam Order) PTA 1998/6655/B1, PTA 1998/7808/B3, FC3 1999/5334/C, FC3 1999/5335/C, CCRTI 1998/1433/B1, CA ....   *Digested*, 00/**351**

Parkinson *v.* Customs and Excise Commissioners [2001] S.T.I. 1278, V&DTr

Parkinson *v.* Eurofinance Group Ltd; *sub nom* Eurofinance Group Ltd, Re [2001] 1 B.C.L.C. 720; (2000) 97(27) L.S.G. 37; *Times*, July 4, 2000, Ch D ....   *Digested*, 00/**688**

Parkinson v. Liverpool Corp [1950] 1 All E.R. 367; 66 T.L.R. (Pt. 1) 262; 114 J.P. 146; 48 L.G.R. 331; [1950] W.N. 43; 94 S.J. 161, CA . . . . *Digested*, 47-51/**6884**:
Applied, 76/2433: *Considered*, 47-51/6886, 98/3911

Parkinson v. March Consulting Ltd [1998] I.C.R. 276; [1997] I.R.L.R. 308; *Times*, January 9, 1997, CA. . . . . *Digested*, 97/**2290**:
Applied, 98/2232: *Followed*, 99/2104

Parkinson v. St James and Seacroft University Hospital NHS Trust [2001] EWCA Civ 530; [2001] 3 W.L.R. 376; [2001] 3 All E.R. 97; [2001] 2 F.L.R. 401; [2001] P.I.Q.R. Q12; [2001] Lloyd's Rep. Med. 309; (2001) 61 B.M.L.R. 100; [2001] P.N.L.R. 43; [2001] Fam. Law 592; (2001) 98(22) L.S.G. 35; (2001) 145 S.J.L.B. 118; *Times*, April 24, 2001; *Daily Telegraph*, April 17, 2001, CA. . . . . *Digested*, 01/**1509**

Parkman Consulting Engineers v. Cumbrian Industrials Ltd; *sub nom* BICC Ltd v. Parkman Consulting Engineers; Cumbrian Industrials Ltd v. Parkman Consulting Engineers [2001] EWCA Civ 1621; 79 Con. L.R. 112, CA; affirming 78 Con. L.R. 18, QBD (T&CC)

Parks v. Esso Petroleum Co Ltd; *sub nom* Parkes v. Esso Petroleum Co Ltd [2000] E.C.C. 45; [2000] Eu. L.R. 25; (1999) 18 Tr. L.R. 232, CA; affirming [1999] 1 C.M.L.R. 455; [1998] Eu. L.R. 550, Ch D . . . . *Digested*, 00/**120**

Parks v. Esso Petroleum Co Ltd (Permission to Appeal) (1999) 77 P. & C.R. D20, CA

Parlett v. Guppys (Bridport) Ltd (No.2) [1999] O.P.L.R. 309; [2000] Pens. L.R. 195, CA . . . . *Digested*, 00/**4385**

Parmar (t/a Ace Knitwear) v. Woods (Inspector of Taxes) [2001] S.T.C. (S.C.D.) 238; [2001] S.T.I. 1666, Sp Comm

Parr v. Smith [1995] 2 All E.R. 1031; [1996] 1 F.L.R. 490; [1996] Fam. Law 282; [1994] N.P.C. 5; *Independent*, March 7, 1994 (C.S.), CA . . . . *Digested*, 95/**3104**:
Considered, 00/3958

Parrington v. Marriott (Unreported, November 3, 1997), CC (Leicester) [*Ex rel.* David H Christie, Barrister, 9 Bedford Row, London] . . . . *Digested*, 98/**1509**

Parrott v. Jackson [1996] P.I.Q.R. P394; (1996) 93(22) L.S.G. 26; *Times*, February 14, 1996, CA . . . . *Digested*, 96/**904**:
Considered, 97/740: *Distinguished*, 97/633: *Followed*, 98/609

Parry v. Cleaver [1970] A.C. 1; [1969] 2 W.L.R. 821; [1969] 1 All E.R. 555; [1969] 1 Lloyd's Rep. 183; 6 K.I.R. 265; 113 S.J. 147, HL; reversing [1968] 1 Q.B. 195; [1967] 3 W.L.R. 739; [1967] 2 All E.R. 1168; 2 K.I.R. 844; 111 S.J. 415, CA. . . . . *Digested*, 69/**906**:
Applied, 69/917, 69/919, 71/3207, 72/836, 73/729, 73/740, 74/814, 75/3217, 76/677, 76/2517, 79/2472, 84/1004, 85/942, 85/3398, 86/350, 87/1220, 88/1069, 89/1285, 92/2029, 94/2039, 01/6413: *Considered*, 72/826, 72/834, 78/788, 80/630, 82/894, 83/1272, 86/981, 87/394, 87/1161, 88/1070, 88/1710, 96/1218, 96/4527, 96/6896, 98/2099, 99/810, 00/5816: *Disapproved*, 78/719: *Distinguished*, 95/1613, 96/3603, 99/3410: *Followed*, 77/773, 90/5070, 91/1327, 98/1468, 99/3411, 00/1488

Parry v. Edwards Geldard (No.1) (1999) 77 P. & C.R. 440, CA . . . . *Digested*, 99/**4047**

Parry v. Edwards Geldard (No.2) [2001] P.N.L.R. 44; [2001] N.P.C. 85, Ch D . . . . *Digested*, 01/**264**

Parry v. North West Surrey HA, *Times*, January 5, 2000, QBD . . . . *Digested*, 00/**1458**

Parry-Jones v. Law Society [1969] 1 Ch. 1; [1968] 2 W.L.R. 397; [1968] 1 All E.R. 177; 111 S.J. 910, CA; affirming [1968] Ch. 195; [1967] 3 W.L.R. 1305; [1967] 3 All E.R. 248; 111 S.J. 606, Ch D . . . . *Digested*, 68/**3703**:
Applied, 90/2642: *Considered*, 70/286, 01/5320

Parslow v. British Waterways Board (Unreported, July 7, 2000), CC (Scunthorpe) [*Ex rel.* Martin & Haigh Solicitors, 12-18 Frances Street, Scunthorpe, North Lincolnshire] . . . . *Digested*, 00/**1566**

Parsons v. Henry Smith's Charity see Parsons v. Viscount Gage (Trustees of Henry Smith's Charity)

Parsons v. Pitt [2001] 6 Q.R. 23, CC (Cardiff) [*Ex rel.* Andrew Arentsen, Barrister, 33 Park Place, Cardiff] . . . . *Digested*, 01/**1803**

Parsons v. Viscount Gage (Trustees of Henry Smith's Charity); *sub nom* Parsons v. Henry Smith's Charity [1974] 1 W.L.R. 435; [1974] 1 All E.R. 1162; (1974) 27 P. & C.R. 453; 118 S.J. 463, HL; affirming [1973] 1 W.L.R. 845; [1973] 3 All E.R. 23; (1973) 26 P. & C.R. 108; 117 S.J. 374, CA . . . . *Digested*, 74/**2099**:
Applied, 01/4180: *Considered*, 94/2768, 95/3022

Parsons Corp v. CV Scheepvaartonderneming Happy Ranger (The Happy Ranger) A3/2001/1695, CA; reversing [2001] 2 Lloyd's Rep. 530, QBD (Comm Ct)

Partenreederei MS Tilly Russ v. Haven & Vervoerbedrijf Nova (C71/83) [1985] Q.B. 931; [1985] 3 W.L.R. 179; [1984] E.C.R. 2417; [1984] 3 C.M.L.R. 499; (1985) 82 L.S.G. 2905; (1985) 129 S.J. 483, ECJ . . . . *Digested*, 85/**1452**:
Applied, 00/750

Partington v. Turners Bakery see Limb v. Union Jack Removals Ltd (In Liquidation)

Partition Acts 1868 and 1876, Re see Ulster Bank Ltd v. Carter

Partizan Ltd v. OJ Kilkenny & Co Ltd [1998] B.C.C. 912; [1998] 1 B.C.L.C. 157, Ch D (Companies Ct) . . . . *Digested*, 98/**371**

PARTNER WITH THE BEST Trade Mark [1998] E.T.M.R. 679, BGH (Ger)

Partridge v. Adjudication Officer (C297/96) [1998] E.C.R. I-3467; [1998] 3 C.M.L.R. 941; *Times*, July 2, 1998, ECJ (3rd Chamber) . . . . *Digested*, 98/**4490**

Partridge v. Black Country Development Corp [1999] R.V.R. 128, Lands Tr. . . . . *Digested*, 99/**4190**

Partridge *v.* Brian Perkins Ltd (Unreported, March 7, 2000), CC (Bristol) [*Ex rel.*
    Jeremy Ford, Barrister, 199 Strand, London] . . . . *Digested*, 00/**399**
Pasha *v.* Pasha [2001] EWCA Civ 466; [2001] 2 F.C.R. 185, CA. . . . . *Digested*, 01/**2631**
Passley *v.* Wandsworth LBC; Prince *v.* Wandsworth LBC (1998) 30 H.L.R. 165, CA . . . . *Digested*, 98/**3051**:
    Applied, 98/3623

Passmore *v.* Morland Plc [1999] 3 All E.R. 1005; [1999] 1 C.M.L.R. 1129; [1999]
    E.C.C. 367; [1999] Eu. L.R. 501; [1999] I.C.R. 913; [1999] 1 E.G.L.R. 51; [1999]
    15 E.G. 128; [1999] E.G.C.S. 14; *Times*, February 11, 1999;
    Independent, February 5, 1999, CA; affirming [1998] 4 All E.R. 468; [1998]
    E.C.C. 461; [1998] Eu. L.R. 580; [1998] E.G.C.S. 113; [1998] N.P.C. 117;
    Independent, July 20, 1998 (C.S.), Ch D . . . . *Digested*, 99/**683**:
    Considered, 99/3703: *Followed*, 99/682
Pasterfield (t/a Glider Advertising Design) *v.* Denham (t/a Denham Design) [1999]
    F.S.R. 168, CC (Plymouth) [*Ex rel.* Wolferstans Solicitors, Deptford Chambers,
    60-64 North Hill, Plymouth, Devon, PL4 8EP] . . . . *Digested*, 98/**3423**
Pate (t/a Yummies) *v.* Customs and Excise Commissioners [2001] S.T.I. 570, V&DTr
Patefield *v.* Belfast City Council [2000] I.R.L.R. 664, CA (NI) . . . . *Digested*, 00/**5528**
Patel *v.* Air India Ltd (Unreported, July 13, 1999), CC (Brentford) [*Ex rel.* Paul Hepher,
    Barrister, 2 Gray's Inn Square Chambers, 2 Gray's Inn Square, London] . . . . *Digested*, 99/**4904**
Patel *v.* Ali [1984] Ch. 283; [1984] 2 W.L.R. 960; [1984] 1 All E.R. 978; (1984) 48 P.
    & C.R. 118; (1984) 81 L.S.G. 1285; 128 S.J. 204, Ch D . . . . *Digested*, 84/**3630**:
    Cited, 00/3931
Patel *v.* Customs and Excise Commissioners (No.2) [1998] B.V.C. 2129, V&DTr . . . . . . *Digested*, 98/**4933**
Patel (Ajay Chandubhai) *v.* Customs and Excise Commissioners [2001] S.T.I. 1273,
    V&DTr
Patel *v.* Daybells [2001] EWCA Civ 1229; [2001] 32 E.G.C.S. 87; *Daily Telegraph*,
    September 11, 2001, CA; affirming [2000] Lloyd's Rep. P.N. 844; [2001]
    P.N.L.R. 3; [2000] E.G.C.S. 98, QBD . . . . *Digested*, 01/**4263**
Patel *v.* Hooper & Jackson [1999] 1 W.L.R. 1792; [1999] 1 All E.R. 992; [1999]
    Lloyd's Rep. P.N. 1; [1998] E.G.C.S. 160; (1998) N.L.J. 1751; [1998] N.P.C. 149;
    Times, December 3, 1998; *Independent*, November 18, 1998, CA . . . . *Digested*, 98/**3958**
Patel *v.* Jones; *sub nom* Jones *v.* Patel [2001] EWCA Civ 779; [2001] B.P.I.R. 919;
    (2001) 3 L.G.L.R. 44; [2001] Pens. L.R. 217; *Times*, May 29, 2001, CA; affirming
    [1999] B.P.I.R. 509; [1999] Pens. L.R. 203, Ch D . . . . *Digested*, 01/**3734**
Patel *v.* Mehtab (1982) 5 H.L.R. 78, QBD . . . . *Applied*, 99/4065
Patel *v.* Patel [1998] E.G.C.S. 144, CA
Patel (Jitendra) *v.* Patel (Dilesh) [2000] Q.B. 551; [1999] 3 W.L.R. 322; [1999] 1 All
    E.R. (Comm.) 923; [1999] B.L.R. 227; 65 Con. L.R. 140; (1999) 15 Const. L.J.
    484; (1999) 143 S.J.L.B. 134; *Times*, April 9, 1999, CA . . . . *Digested*, 99/**221**:
    Considered, 01/345
Patel *v.* RCMS Ltd [1999] I.R.L.R. 161, EAT . . . . *Digested*, 99/**2049**
Patel *v.* Shaylor Partners (Unreported, March 8, 2001), CC (Romford) [*Ex rel.* Royal &
    Sun Alliance UK, Legal Department, PO Box 8470, Birmingham] . . . . *Digested*, 01/**4476**
Patel *v.* Standard Chartered Bank [2001] Lloyd's Rep. Bank. 229, QBD (Comm Ct) . . . *Digested*, 01/**369**
Patents Act 1977, Re see Eveready Battery Co Inc's Patent, Re
Paterson *v.* Aggio (1987) 19 H.L.R. 551; (1987) 284 E.G. 508; (1987) 137 N.L.J. 809,
    CA . . . . *Digested*, 87/**2235**:
    Approved, 00/3921: *Followed*, 99/3750
Paterson *v.* Humberside CC (1996) 12 Const. L.J. 64; [1995] E.G.C.S. 39; [1995]
    N.P.C. 37; *Times*, April 19, 1995, QBD . . . . *Digested*, 95/**3661**:
    Applied, 98/4052
Pates *v.* Reid [2001] 6 Q.R. 12, CC (Croydon) [*Ex rel.* Amanda Millmore, Barrister, 4
    King's Bench Walk, Temple, London] . . . . *Digested*, 01/**1763**
Pathirana *v.* Pathirana [1967] 1 A.C. 233; [1966] 3 W.L.R. 666; 110 S.J. 547, PC (Cey) . *Digested*, 66/**8954**:
    Considered, 99/4092
Paton *v.* Fekade [2000] 5 Q.R. 7, CC (Central London) [*Ex rel.* Osbornes Solicitors,
    68 Parkway, Camden Town, London] . . . . *Digested*, 00/**1635**
Patrick *v.* De Zeeuw see Patrick's Estate, Re
Patrick and Lyon Ltd, Re [1933] Ch. 786, Ch D . . . . *Applied*, 85/295,
    90/496, 00/4186: *Considered*, 66/1457, 67/500
Patrick Stevedores Operations Pty Ltd *v.* International Transport Workers Federation
    [1998] 2 Lloyd's Rep. 523; [1998] C.L.C. 1022, QBD (Comm Ct) . . . . *Digested*, 98/**2158**
Patrick Stevedores (No.2) Pty Ltd *v.* Turakina (1998) 154 A.L.R. 666, Fed Ct (Aus) (Sgl
    judge) . . . . *Considered*, 00/4697
Patrick's Estate, Re; *sub nom* Patrick *v.* De Zeeuw [2000] N.I. 506, Ch D (NI) . . . . *Digested*, 01/**6033**
Patten *v.* Burke Publishing Co Ltd [1991] 1 W.L.R. 541; [1991] 2 All E.R. 821; [1991]
    F.S.R. 483, Ch D . . . . *Digested*, 91/**2853**:
    Considered, 91/2854: *Followed*, 01/543
Patten (t/a Anthony Patten & Co) *v.* Lord Chancellor [2001] 3 All E.R. 886; [2001] 2
    Costs L.R. 233; (2001) 151 N.L.J. 851, QBD . . . . *Digested*, 01/**1115**
Patterson *v.* Bassett, CC (Cardiff) [*Ex rel.* Andrew Arentsen, Barrister, 33 Park Place,
    Cardiff] . . . . *Digested*, 01/**1687**
Patterson *v.* Bunclark (Unreported, November 26, 1999), CC (Birkenhead) [*Ex rel.*
    David Knifton, Barrister, 7 Harrington Street, Liverpool] . . . . *Digested*, 00/**1501**

Patterson v. Midland Bank Plc (Unreported, January 31, 2000), CC (Pontefract) [*Ex rel.* Sean D Yates, Barrister, 10 Park Square, Leeds] . . . .   *Digested,* 00/**1628**
Patterson v. Vacation Brokers Inc [1998] I.L.Pr. 472, CA (Ont)
Pattison (CICB: Quantum: 1998), Re (Unreported, February 16, 1998), CICB (Durham) [*Ex rel.* Patterson, Glenton & Stracey Solicitors, Law Court Chambers, Waterloo Square, South Shields] . . . .   *Digested,* 99/**1432**
Pauger v. Austria (1998) 25 E.H.R.R. 105, ECHR . . . .   *Digested,* 98/**3145**:
                                                        Distinguished, 98/3121
Paul v. Glickman (Deceased) (Unreported, January 21, 1999), CC (Central London) [*Ex rel.* Charles Foster, Barrister, 6 Pump Court, Temple, London] . . . .   *Digested,* 99/**1542**
Paul v. Paul [1999] I.L.Pr. 839, CJ (Gen Div) (Ont) . . . .   *Digested,* 00/**745**
Paul v. Tuck (Unreported, May 11, 2001), CC (Chelmsford) [*Ex rel.* Lloyd Green & Co, Solicitors, Kensal House, 77 Springfield Road, Chelmsford, Essex] . . . .   *Digested,* 01/**515**
Paulsen-Medalen v. Sweden; Svensson v. Sweden (1998) 26 E.H.R.R. 260; [1998] H.R.C.D. 266, ECHR . . . .   *Digested,* 98/**3138**
Pavarotti v. Direct Tax Office (Modena) (985) 3 I.T.L. Rep. 60, Comm Tributaria SG (I); affirming 1 I.T.L. Rep. 869, Comm Tributaria PG (I)
Pavey v. Ministry of Defence [1999] P.I.Q.R. P67; [1999] Lloyd's Rep. Med. 9; *Times,* November 25, 1998; *Independent,* November 25, 1998, CA. . . . .   *Digested,* 98/**388**
Pavlov v. Stichting Pensioenfonds Medische Specialisten (C180/98) [2000] E.C.R. I-6451; [2001] 4 C.M.L.R. 1, ECJ . . . .   *Digested,* 01/**763**
Pawlowski (Collector of Taxes) v. Dunnington [1999] S.T.C. 550; (1999) 11 Admin. L.R. 565; [1999] B.T.C. 175; (1999) 96(21) L.S.G. 40; (1999) 149 N.L.J. 745; [1999] N.P.C. 57; *Times,* May 13, 1999, CA . . . .   *Digested,* 99/**4749**
Pawson v. Neil (Unreported, December 16, 1999), CC (Torquay) [*Ex rel.* Andrew Granville Stafford, Barrister, 4 King's Bench Walk, Temple, London] . . . .   *Digested,* 00/**1702**
Pawson v. Rowland (Valuation Officer) [1998] R.V.R. 314, Lands Tr . . . .   *Digested,* 99/**4324**
Payabi v. Armstel Shipping Corp (The Jay Bola); Baker Rasti Lari v. Armstel Shipping Corp (The Jay Bola) [1992] Q.B. 907; [1992] 2 W.L.R. 898; [1992] 3 All E.R. 329; [1992] 2 Lloyd's Rep. 62; (1992) 136 S.J.L.B. 52; *Times,* February 26, 1992, QBD (Comm Ct) . . . .   *Digested,* 92/**3628**:
               Applied, 92/3927, 96/5316: *Considered,* 98/587: *Followed,* 93/3324, 98/762
Payless Car Rental System Inc's Trade Mark Application [2000] E.T.M.R. 1136, OHIM (Opposition Div) . . . .   *Digested,* 01/**4013**
Payments to Combat Social Exclusion, Re see United Kingdom v. Commission of the European Communities (C106/96)
Payne v. Barnet LBC (1998) 30 H.L.R. 295; (1998) 10 Admin. L.R. 185; (1998) 76 P. & C.R. 293; *Times,* June 24, 1997, CA. . . . .   *Digested,* 97/**2732**
Payne v. Dean (Unreported, May 26, 2000), CC (Poole) [*Ex rel.* Lyons Davidson Solicitors, Victoria House, 51 Victoria Street, Bristol] . . . .   *Digested,* 00/**2573**
Payne v. Heywood see Millar v. Dickson
Payne v. Hunt, CC (Bristol) [*Ex rel.* Daniel Bennett, Pupil Barrister, Old Square Chambers, 47 Corn Street, Bristol]. . . . .   *Digested,* 01/**1530**
Payne v. John Setchell Ltd (2001) 3 T.C.L.R. 26, QBD (T&CC)
Payne's Patent Application [1985] R.P.C. 193, Pat Ct . . . .   *Followed,* 99/**3469**
Payton v. Brooks [1974] 1 Lloyd's Rep. 241; [1974] R.T.R. 169, CA . . . .   *Digested,* 74/**841**:
               Cited, 00/1484, 01/1543: *Considered,* 98/1450: *Followed,* 97/1815
Pazpena de Vire v. Pazpena de Vire [2001] 1 F.L.R. 460; [2001] Fam. Law 95, Fam Div .   *Digested,* 01/**2611**
PB (A Minor) (Hearing in Private), Re see P-B (A Minor) (Child Cases: Hearings in Open Court), Re
PB (Hearings in Open Court), Re see P-B (A Minor) (Child Cases: Hearings in Open Court), Re
PC (Change of Surname), Re; *sub nom* C (Minors) (Change of Surname), Re; P (Change of Surname: Parent's Rights), Re [1997] 2 F.L.R. 730; [1997] 3 F.C.R. 310; [1997] Fam. Law 722, Fam Div . . . .   *Digested,* 98/**2434**
PC Connection Inc's Community Trade Mark Application [2000] E.T.M.R. 362, OHIM (3rd Bd App) . . . .   *Digested,* 00/**3724**
PC Express AB v. Columbus IT Partner A/S [2001] I.L.Pr. 22, OL (DK)
PC Harrington Contractors Ltd v. Co Partnership Developments Ltd 88 B.L.R. 44; *Times,* April 30, 1998, CA. . . . .   *Digested,* 98/**805**
PCC of St Andrew's Church (Eakring) v. Customs and Excise Commissioners [1998] B.V.C. 2117, V&DTr . . . .   *Digested,* 98/**4980**
PCME Ltd v. Goyen Controls Co UK Ltd [1999] F.S.R. 801; (1999) 22(5) I.P.D. 22043, Pat Ct . . . .   *Digested,* 99/**3503**
PCR Ltd v. Dow Jones Telerate Ltd [1998] E.M.L.R. 407; [1998] F.S.R. 170; (1998) 21 (4) I.P.D. 21037, Ch D . . . .   *Digested,* 98/**3422**
PD Fuels Ltd, Re [1999] B.C.C. 450, Ch D (Companies Ct) . . . .   *Digested,* 99/**3275**
Peabody Donation Fund v. Higgins see Governors of the Peabody Donation Fund v. Higgins
Peace v. Edinburgh City Council 1999 S.L.T. 712; 1999 S.C.L.R. 593; [1999] I.R.L.R. 417; 1999 G.W.D. 8-394, OH . . . .   *Digested,* 99/**6033**
Peach (Clement Blair), Re see R. v. HM Coroner for Hammersmith Ex p. Peach
Peach v. Burton see R. v. HM Coroner for Hammersmith Ex p. Peach

Peach v. Tesco Stores Plc (Unreported, July 24, 1998), CC (Oxford) [*Ex rel.* LJ
    Deegan, Barrister, Northampton Chambers, 22 Albion Place, Northampton] . . .   *Digested,* 98/**1665**
Peach Publishing Ltd v. Slater & Co; Slater & Co v. Sheil Land Associates Ltd [1998]
    B.C.C. 139; [1998] P.N.L.R. 364, CA; reversing in part [1996] B.C.C. 751, Ch D
    . . . .   *Digested,* 97/**3**
Peacock v. Custin see Peacock v. Custins
Peacock v. Custins; *sub nom* Custins v. Peacock; Peacock v. Custin [2001] 2 All E.R.
    827; (2001) 81 P. & C.R. 34; [2001] 1 E.G.L.R. 87; [2001] 13 E.G. 152; [2000]
    E.G.C.S. 132; (2000) 97(48) L.S.G. 36; [2000] N.P.C. 124; *Times,* December 15,
    2000; *Independent,* November 24, 2000, CA . . . .   *Digested,* 00/**4635**
Pearce (Deceased), Re [1998] 2 F.L.R. 705; [1999] 2 F.C.R. 179; [1998] Fam. Law 588, CA
                                                                                              Digested, 98/**4587**
Pearce v. Duff (Unreported, June 4, 1999), CC (High Wycombe) [*Ex rel.* Benjamin
    Williams, Barrister, Oxford Chambers, 1 Alfred Street, Oxford] . . . .   *Digested,* 99/**2466**:
                                                                           Approved, 99/2472: *Referred to,* 99/2490
Pearce v. Humpit Removals Ltd (Unreported, October 13, 1999), CC (Reading) [*Ex rel.*
    Richard Menzies, Barrister, 8 Stone Buildings, Lincoln's Inn, London] . . . .   *Digested,* 00/**1685**
Pearce v. Mayfield Secondary School Governing Body; *sub nom* Mayfield Secondary
    School Governing Body v. Pearce; Pearce v. Mayfield School Governing Body;
    Peace v. Mayfield Secondary School Governing Body [2001] EWCA Civ 1347;
    [2001] I.R.L.R. 669; [2001] Emp. L.R. 1112; (2001) 98(37) L.S.G. 38; (2001)
    145 S.J.L.B. 218; *Times,* October 9, 2001, CA; affirming [2000] I.C.R. 920;
    [2000] I.R.L.R. 548; [2001] E.L.R. 1; *Times,* April 19, 2000, EAT . . . .   *Digested,* 01/**2315**
Pearce v. Ove Arup Partnership Ltd (Jurisdiction) [2000] Ch. 403; [2000] 3 W.L.R.
    332; [1999] 1 All E.R. 769; [1999] I.L.Pr. 442; [1999] F.S.R. 525; (1999) 22(4)
    I.P.D. 22041; (1999) 96(9) L.S.G. 31; [1999] N.P.C. 7; *Times,* February 10,
    1999, CA; reversing in part [1997] Ch. 293; [1997] 2 W.L.R. 779; [1997] 3 All
    E.R. 31; [1998] I.L.Pr. 10; [1997] F.S.R. 641; (1997) 20(8) I.P.D. 20081; (1997)
    94(15) L.S.G. 27; (1997) 141 S.J.L.B. 73; *Times,* March 17, 1997, Ch D . . . .   *Digested,* 99/**731**:
                                                                         Approved, 98/3466: *Followed,* 97/1046
Pearce v. Secretary of State for Defence [1988] A.C. 755; [1988] 2 W.L.R. 1027;
    [1988] 2 All E.R. 348; 132 S.J. 699; *Times,* April 29, 1988; *Independent,* April
    29, 1988, HL; affirming [1988] 2 W.L.R. 144; (1988) 85(7) L.S.G. 40; (1987)
    137 N.L.J. 933; 132 S.J. 127; *Times,* August 5, 1987, CA; affirming [1987] 2
    W.L.R. 782; (1987) 84 L.S.G. 1334; (1987) 137 N.L.J. 80; (1987) 131 S.J. 362,
    QBD . . . .   *Digested,* 88/**2417**:
                                                              Applied, 98/264, 99/261: *Considered,* 98/4785
Pearce v. United Bristol Healthcare NHS Trust [1999] E.C.C. 167; [1999] P.I.Q.R. P53;
    (1999) 48 B.M.L.R. 118, CA. . . . .   *Digested,* 98/**3986**
Pearce & High Ltd v. Baxter [1999] C.L.C. 749; [1999] B.L.R. 101; (1999) 1 T.C.L.R.
    157; 66 Con. L.R. 110; *Times,* March 24, 1999; *Independent,* March 4, 1999, CA .   *Digested,* 99/**792**
Pearl Assurance Plc v. Customs and Excise Commissioners [1999] B.V.C. 2176, V&DTr
Pearl Assurance Plc v. Kavanagh (Unreported, June 21, 2001), CC (Milton Keynes) [*Ex
    rel.* Laurence Jeffrey Deegan, Barrister, Fenners Chambers, 3 Madingley Road,
    Cambridge] . . . .   *Digested,* 01/**3832**
Pearl Maintenance Services Ltd, Re [1995] B.C.C. 657; [1995] 1 B.C.L.C. 449, Ch D . .   *Digested,* 95/**2817**:
                                                                                              Followed, 00/3483
Pearless de Rougemont & Co v. Pilbrow (No.2) [1999] 3 All E.R. 355; [1999] 2 Costs
    L.R. 109; [1999] 2 F.L.R. 139; (1999) 149 N.L.J. 441; (1999) 143 S.J.L.B. 114;
    Times, March 25, 1999; *Independent,* May 10, 1999 (C.S.), CA. . . . .   *Digested,* 99/**3806**
Pearman v. North Essex HA [2000] Lloyd's Rep. Med. 174, QBD . . . .   *Digested,* 00/**4190**
Pearn v. Mortgage Business Plc (1998) 95(5) L.S.G. 30, Ch D
Pearse v. Barnet HA [1998] P.I.Q.R. P39, QBD   *Digested,* 98/**556**
Pearshouse v. Birmingham City Council [1999] Env. L.R. 536; [1999] E.H.L.R. 140;
    (1999) 31 H.L.R. 756; [1999] B.L.G.R. 169; [1999] J.P.L. 725; [1999] C.O.D.
    132; *Independent,* November 16, 1998 (C.S.), QBD . . . .   *Digested,* 98/**2282**
Pearson v. British Midland Airways (Unreported, February 9, 1998), QBD [*Ex rel.*
    Pannone & Partners Solicitors, 123 Deansgate, Manchester] . . . .   *Digested,* 98/**1530**
Pearson v. Central Sheffield University Hospitals NHS Trust [2001] 1 Q.R. 8, CC
    (Sheffield) [*Ex rel.* Keeble Harrison Solicitors, St. James' Row, Sheffield] . . . . . .   *Digested,* 01/**1721**
Pearson v. Haringey LBC [1998] R.V.R. 252, QBD   *Digested,* 98/**4300**
Pearson v. Inland Revenue Commissioners; *sub nom* Pilkington Trustees v. Inland
    Revenue Commissioners [1981] A.C. 753; [1980] 2 W.L.R. 872; [1980] 2 All
    E.R. 479; [1980] S.T.C. 318; [1980] T.R. 177; 124 S.J. 377, HL; reversing [1980]
    Ch. 1; [1979] 3 W.L.R. 112; [1979] 3 All E.R. 7; [1979] S.T.C. 516; [1979] T.R.
    195; 123 S.J. 490, CA; affirming [1979] 2 W.L.R. 353; [1979] 1 All E.R. 273;
    [1978] S.T.C. 627; [1978] T.R. 349; 123 S.J. 185, Ch D . . . .   *Digested,* 80/**228**:
                                                                  Applied, 84/260, 01/5282: *Considered,* 81/1374
Pearson v. Lightning (1998) 95(20) L.S.G. 33; (1998) 142 S.J.L.B. 143; *Times,* April
    30, 1998, CA. . . . .   *Digested,* 98/**3953**
Pearson v. Sanders Witherspoon [2000] Lloyd's Rep. P.N. 151; [2000] P.N.L.R. 110;
    Independent, December 6, 1999 (C.S.), CA. . . . .   *Digested,* 00/**4009**:
                                                                                              Followed, 01/5900

Pearson v. Scott [2001] 3 Q.R. 13, CC (Boston) [*Ex rel.* Richard Gregory, Barrister, 24 The Ropewalk, Nottingham] . . . . *Digested,* 01/**1616**
Peasley v. Governors of Haileybury and Imperial Service College [2001] W.T.L.R. 1365, Ch D
Peat v. Walsh see Londonderry's Settlement, Re
Peaudouce SA v. Kimberly Clark Ltd [1996] F.S.R. 680; (1996) 19(7) I.P.D. 19057, Pat Ct. . . . . *Digested,* 96/**4555**:
Distinguished, 98/2661
Peci v. Governor of Brixton Prison, *Times,* January 12, 2000, QBD. . . . . *Digested,* 00/**2421**
Peck v. Chief Constable of Avon and Somerset (Unreported, May 18, 1999), CC (Bristol) [*Ex rel.* Russell Jones & Walker, Solicitors, 15 Clare Street, Bristol] . . . . *Digested,* 00/**2971**
Peckham v. Ellison (1999) 31 H.L.R. 1030; (2000) 79 P. & C.R. 276; [1998] E.G.C.S. 174; (1998) 95(47) L.S.G. 30; [1998] N.P.C. 154; (1999) 77 P. & C.R. D27; *Times,* December 4, 1998, CA . . . . *Digested,* 99/**4397**:
Considered, 00/4640
Pectel Ltd, Re see O'Neill v. Phillips
Peddubriwny v. Cambridge City Council [2001] EWHC Admin 200; [2001] R.T.R. 31; *Times,* March 27, 2001, QBD (Admin Ct) . . . . *Digested,* 01/**4312**
Pedelty v. Jarvis (Unreported, February 9, 1999), CC (Kingston upon Hull) [*Ex rel.* Ford & Warren Solicitors, Westgate Point, Westgate, Leeds] . . . . *Digested,* 99/**2500**
Pedro v. Immigration Appeal Tribunal see R. v. Immigration Appeal Tribunal Ex p. Pedro
Peek v. Derry see Derry v. Peek
Peel Investments (North) Ltd v. Bury MBC [1999] P.L.C.R. 307, CA; reversing [1999] J.P.L. 74; [1998] E.G.C.S. 67; [1998] N.P.C. 74, QBD . . . . *Digested,* 00/**4465**:
Distinguished, 00/4474
Peerbooms v. Stichting CZ Groep Zorgverzekeringen (C157/99) see Geraets-Smits v. Stichting Ziekenfonds VGZ (C157/99)
Peers v. Greece (28524/95) (2001) 33 E.H.R.R. 51; 10 B.H.R.C. 364, ECHR. . . . . *Digested,* 01/**3582**
Peeth v. Holstein (Unreported, October 2, 2000), CC (Manchester) [*Ex rel.* NDH Edwards, Barrister, 8 King Street Chambers, Manchester] . . . . *Digested,* 00/**549**
Pegasus Birds Ltd v. Customs and Excise Commissioners [2000] S.T.C. 91; [2000] B.T.C. 5036; [2000] B.V.C. 68; [2000] S.T.I. 82; *Times,* February 10, 2000, CA; affirming [1999] S.T.C. 95; [1999] B.T.C. 5003; [1999] B.V.C. 56; *Independent,* December 7, 1998 (C.S.), QBD. . . . . *Digested,* 00/**5351**
Pegler Ltd v. Wang (UK) Ltd (No.1) [2000] B.L.R. 218; 70 Con. L.R. 68; [2000] I.T.C.L.R. 617; [2000] Masons C.L.R. 19, QBD (T&CC) . . . . *Digested,* 00/**1465**
Pegramm v. Style Holidays Ltd (Unreported, January 18, 1999), CC (Bristol) [*Ex rel.* Archna Dawar, Barrister, Assize Court Chambers, 14 Small Street, Bristol] . . . . . *Digested,* 99/**1383**
Pehrsson v. Kinlan (Trustee in Bankruptcy) [2000] I.L.Pr. 685, Cass (F)
Pehrsson's Trustee, Re (1999-2000) 2 I.T.E.L.R. 230, PC (Gib)
Peirce v. City of Westminster (Unreported, January 18, 2001), CC (Willesden) [*Ex rel.* Jon Holbrook, Barrister, 2 Garden Court, London] . . . . *Digested,* 01/**4212**
Pelissier v. France (2000) 30 E.H.R.R. 715, ECHR . . . . *Digested,* 01/**3510**
Pell v. Walker (t/a The Media Group) (Unreported, December 3, 1997), CC (Bow) [*Ex rel.* Rachel Crasnow, Barrister, Cloisters, 1 Pump Court, Temple, London] . . . . . . *Digested,* 98/**4046**
Pellegrin v. France (2001) 31 E.H.R.R. 26, ECHR . . . . *Digested,* 01/**3514**:
Considered, 01/5876: *Followed,* 01/3523
Pellicano v. MEPC Plc [1994] 1 E.G.L.R. 104; [1994] 19 E.G. 138, Ch D . . . . *Applied,* 98/3651
Pelling v. Families Need Fathers Ltd [2001] EWCA Civ 1280; (2001) 151 N.L.J. 1284, CA
Pelling v. Pelling [1998] 1 F.L.R. 636; [1999] 2 F.C.R. 90; [1998] Fam. Law 253, CA . . *Digested,* 98/**479**
Pelzl v. Steiermarkische Landesregierung (C338/97); Wiener Stadtische Allgemeine Versicherungs AG v. Tiroler Landesregierung (C344/97); Stuag Bauaktiengesellschaft v. Karntner Landesregierung (C390/97) [1999] E.C.R. I-3319; [2000] 3 C.M.L.R. 889, ECJ (5th Chamber) [1999] E.C.R. I-3319, AGO . *Digested,* 01/**5574**
Pemberton v. Bright [1960] 1 W.L.R. 436; [1960] 1 All E.R. 792; 124 J.P. 265; 58 L.G.R. 183; 104 S.J. 349, CA . . . . *Digested,* 60/**2297**:
Distinguished, 00/4287
Pemberton v. Southwark LBC [2000] 1 W.L.R. 1672; [2000] 3 All E.R. 924; [2001] Env. L.R. 6; (2000) 32 H.L.R. 784; [2000] 2 E.G.L.R. 33; [2000] 21 E.G. 135; [2000] E.G.C.S. 56; *Times,* April 26, 2000, CA. . . . . *Digested,* 00/**4297**
Pembrokeshire Coast National Park v. European Crushed Concrete Services Ltd (2000) 15 P.A.D. 280, Planning Inspector
Pembrokeshire Coast National Park Authority v. Wrench (2001) 16 P.A.D. 41, Planning Inspector
Pendennis Shipyard Ltd v. Magrathea (Pendennis) Ltd; *sub nom* Pendennis Shipyard Ltd v. Margrathea (Pendennis) Ltd (In Liquidation) [1998] 1 Lloyd's Rep. 315; (1997) 94(35) L.S.G. 35; (1997) 141 S.J.L.B. 185; *Times,* August 27, 1997, QBD (Merc Ct) . . . . *Digested,* 97/**3112**
Pendle BC v. Lancaster (2000) 15 P.A.D. 819, Planning Inspector
Pendleton v. Stone & Webster Engineering Ltd see Fairchild v. Glenhaven Funeral Services Ltd (t/a GH Dovener & Son)

Pendragon Plc v. Jackson [1998] I.C.R. 215; [1998] I.R.L.R. 17; *Times*, November 19, 1997, EAT . . . . *Digested*, 97/**2210**: *Considered*, 98/2129

Penfold v. Da Silva (Unreported, November 1, 1999), CC (Bournemouth) [*Ex rel*. The Andrew Isaacs Practice, Solicitors, Wessex Chambers, 21 Lansdowne Road, Bournemouth] . . . . *Digested*, 00/**1550**

Peninsula Securities Ltd, Re [1998] Eu. L.R. 699, QBD . . . . *Digested*, 99/**2284**

Peninsular & Oriental Steam Navigation Co v. Customs and Excise Commissioners see P&O Steam Navigation Co v. Customs and Excise Commissioners

Penk v. Wright see Alcock v. Chief Constable of South Yorkshire

Penkethman v. Yates [2001] 3 Q.R. 13, CC (Stockport) [*Ex rel*. Karim Sabry, Barrister, 8 King Street Chambers, Manchester] . . . . *Digested*, 01/**1613**

Penman v. Upavon Enterprises Ltd [2001] EWCA Civ 956; [2001] 25 E.G.C.S. 158, CA

Penn v. Bristol and West Building Society; *sub nom* Brill & Co v. Penn [1997] 1 W.L.R. 1356; [1997] 3 All E.R. 470; [1997] 3 F.C.R. 789; [1997] P.N.L.R. 607; (1997) 74 P. & C.R. 210; [1997] E.G.C.S. 54; (1997) 94(18) L.S.G. 32; (1997) 141 S.J.L.B. 105; [1997] N.P.C. 58; *Times*, April 24, 1997, CA; affirming [1995] 2 F.L.R. 938; [1996] 2 F.C.R. 729; [1996] Fam. Law 28; (1995) 92(27) L.S.G. 31; (1995) 139 S.J.L.B. 164; *Times*, June 19, 1995, Ch D . . . . *Digested*, 97/**1023**: *Applied*, 98/4027, 99/4379: *Followed*, 99/4036

Penn v. Pierson see Brian D Pierson (Contractors) Ltd, Re

Penna v. Law Society (Application to Set Aside Notice of Intervention); *sub nom* Solicitor, Re (1999) 96(28) L.S.G. 25; *Times*, June 24, 1999; *Independent*, July 19, 1999 (C.S.), Ch D . . . . *Digested*, 99/**3812**

Pennant v. Sparks (Unreported, October 8, 1998), CC (Dartford) [*Ex rel*. Tim Petts, Barrister, 12 King's Bench Walk, Temple, London] . . . . *Digested*, 99/**405**

Pennell v. Payne [1995] Q.B. 192; [1995] 2 W.L.R. 261; [1995] 2 All E.R. 592; [1995] 1 E.G.L.R. 6; [1995] 06 E.G. 152; [1994] E.G.C.S. 196; (1995) 139 S.J.L.B. 17; [1994] N.P.C. 151; *Times*, December 13, 1994; *Independent*, January 23, 1995, CA . . . . *Digested*, 95/**189**: *Applied*, 97/92: *Approved*, 00/3871: *Followed*, 97/3332

Penney v. East Kent HA [2000] Lloyd's Rep. Med. 41; (2000) 55 B.M.L.R. 63; [2000] P.N.L.R. 323; (1999) 96(47) L.S.G. 32; (1999) 143 S.J.L.B. 269; *Times*, November 25, 1999 ; *Independent*, November 24, 1999, CA; affirming [1999] Lloyd's Rep. Med. 123, QBD. . . . . *Digested*, 99/**3995**

Penny Makinson's (PI Associates) Trade Mark Application [1999] E.T.M.R. 234, OHIM (3rd Bd App) . . . . *Digested*, 99/**3532**

Pensher Security Door Co Ltd v. Sunderland City Council [2000] R.P.C. 249; (1999) 22(8) I.P.D. 22077, CA; reversing in part (1998) 21 (2) I.P.D. 21021, Ch D . . . . . *Digested*, 00/**3570**

Pensionskasse fur die Angestellten der Barmer Ersatzkasse VVAG v. Menauer (C379/99) [2001] Pens. L.R. 297, ECJ

Pepin v. Watts [2001] C.P.L.R. 9; *Independent*, November 6, 2000 (C.S), CA . . . . *Digested*, 01/**424**

Pepper (Inspector of Taxes) v. Hart [1993] A.C. 593; [1992] 3 W.L.R. 1032; [1993] 1 All E.R. 42; [1992] S.T.C. 898; [1993] I.C.R. 291; [1993] I.R.L.R. 33; [1993] R.V.R. 127; (1993) 143 N.L.J. 17; [1992] N.P.C. 154; *Times*, November 30, 1992; *Independent*, November 26, 1992, HL; reversing [1991] Ch. 203; [1991] 2 W.L.R. 483; [1990] S.T.C. 786; [1991] I.C.R. 681; [1991] I.R.L.R. 125; (1990) 134 S.J. 1478; *Times*, November 15, 1990; *Financial Times*, November 16, 1990; *Guardian*, November 21, 1990; *Daily Telegraph*, November 19, 1990, CA; affirming [1990] 1 W.L.R. 204; [1990] S.T.C. 6; (1989) 86(46) L.S.G. 41, Ch D . . . . *Digested*, 93/**459**: *Applied*, 93/3714, 94/2514, 98/321, 98/966, 01/4489: *Cited*, 00/5239: *Considered*, 93/426, 93/1866, 93/2260, 93/3860, 94/968, 94/3900, 95/881, 96/1297, 96/1606, 96/3928, 01/5174: *Distinguished*, 94/125, 95/181, 95/2520, 97/4657, 00/2122, 01/4284: *Followed*, 96/4190: *Not applied*, 01/4206: *Referred to*, 93/486, 94/353, 94/2723, 94/2729, 94/3445, 94/5459, 94/5899, 95/522, 95/861

Pepperall v. Memory Lane Cakes Ltd (Unreported, November 19, 1999), CC (Cardiff) [*Ex rel*. Andrew Arentsen, Barrister, 33 Park Place, Cardiff] . . . . *Digested*, 00/**1735**

Peppermint Park Ltd, Re [1998] B.C.C. 23, Ch D (Companies Ct) . . . . *Digested*, 98/**666**

Pepsico Inc v. Flodor SA (1998) 21 (3) I.P.D. 21024, Ch D

Pera Tourism Inc v. Savile Row Tours & Travel Ltd [1998] I.L.Pr. 407, CC (Central London)

Perar BV v. General Surety & Guarantee Co Ltd 66 B.L.R. 72, CA . . . . *Considered*, 99/802

Perceval-Price v. Department of Economic Development [2000] N.I. 141; [2000] I.R.L.R. 380; *Times*, April 28, 2000, CA (NI) . . . . *Digested*, 00/**5520**

Percival v. Wright [1902] 2 Ch. 421, Ch D . . . . *Considered*, 00/649, 01/724

Percy v. DPP [1995] 1 W.L.R. 1382; [1995] 3 All E.R. 124; (1995) 159 J.P. 337; [1995] Crim. L.R. 714; (1995) 159 J.P.N. 228; (1995) 92(9) L.S.G. 38; (1995) 139 S.J.L.B. 34; *Times*, December 13, 1994, QBD . . . . *Digested*, 95/**1239**: *Distinguished*, 01/87

Peregrine Fixed Income Ltd (In Liquidation) v. Robinson Department Store Plc [2000] Lloyd's Rep. Bank. 304; [2000] C.L.C. 1328, QBD (Comm Ct) . . . . *Digested*, 00/**2612**

Perehenic v. Deboa Structuring (Unreported, July 7, 1998), CC (Banbury) [*Ex rel.* Benjamin Williams, Barrister, Oxford Chambers, 1 Alfred Street, Oxford] . . . . *Digested*, 98/**1467**
Perera v. Perera [1901] A.C. 354, PC (Cey) . . . . *Applied*, 52/**3662**:
Considered, 01/5167: *Distinguished*, 47-51/10956, 47-51/10958
Perez de Rada Cavanilles v. Spain (2000) 29 E.H.R.R. 109; [1998] H.R.C.D. 981, ECHR *Digested*, 00/**3237**
Perfector Skincare Ltd v. Customs and Excise Commissioners [2001] E.T.M.R. CN8, V&DTr
Perfetti SpA v. Warner Lambert Co; *sub nom* Perfetti SpA's Trade Mark Application (No.1478638); CHANF 1998/0452/3, CA; reversing (1998) 21 (6) I.P.D. 21059, Ch D . . . . *Digested*, 99/**3537**
Perfetti SpA's Trade Mark Application (No.1478638) see Perfetti SpA v. Warner Lambert Co
Performance Rights in La Boheme, Re [1998] E.C.C. 264, OLG (Frankfurt Am Main)
Performing Right Society Ltd v. Boizot [1999] E.M.L.R. 359; (1999) 22(5) I.P.D. 22045; *Times*, February 10, 1999, CA . . . . *Digested*, 99/**3450**
Performing Right Society Ltd v. British Entertainment and Dancing Association Ltd [1993] E.M.L.R. 325, Ch D . . . . *Digested*, 94/**613**
Performing Right Society Ltd v. London Theatre of Varieties Ltd [1924] A.C. 1, HL; affirming [1922] 2 K.B. 433, CA; reversing [1922] 1 K.B. 539, KBD . . . . *Applied*, 71/**1885**,
96/1287: *Considered*, 98/3451: *Followed*, 59/119, 59/3356
Performing Right Society Ltd v. Rowland; Rowland v. Turp [1997] 3 All E.R. 336; [1998] B.P.I.R. 128, Ch D . . . . *Digested*, 97/**3008**
Periera v. Merton LBC (Unreported, June 26, 2000), MCLC [*Ex rel.* Wayne Beglan, Barrister, 2-3 Gray's Inn Square, London] . . . . *Digested*, 00/**3144**
Perkins (CICB: Quantum: 1999), Re (Unreported, August 11, 1999), CICB (York) [*Ex rel.* Jonathan Godfrey, Barrister, St. Paul's Chambers, 23 Park Square South, Leeds] . . . . *Digested*, 00/**1536**
Perkins v. Wakelin [2000] 6 Q.R. 8, CC (Milton Keynes) [*Ex rel.* Giffen Couch & Archer Solicitors, Bridge House, Bridge Street, Leighton Buzzard, Bedfordshire] *Digested*, 00/**1677**
Perks v. Clark (Inspector of Taxes) see Clark (Inspector of Taxes) v. Perks
Perks (Inspector of Taxes) v. Clark see Clark (Inspector of Taxes) v. Perks (Permission to Appeal)
Perks (Inspector of Taxes) v. Macleod see Clark (Inspector of Taxes) v. Perks (Permission to Appeal)
Perks v. United Kingdom (2000) 30 E.H.R.R. 33; [2000] R.A. 487, ECHR . . . . *Digested*, 00/**3221**
Perotti v. Watson (Funds for Legal Representation) A3/2000/5456, CA. . . . . *Digested*, 00/**378**
Perotti v. Watson (Variation of Perfected Order) [2001] C.P. Rep. 5, CA. . . . . *Digested*, 00/**359**
Perrett v. Collins [1998] 2 Lloyd's Rep. 255; [1999] P.N.L.R. 77; *Times*, June 23, 1998, CA . . . . *Digested*, 98/**3923**
Perrin v. Drennan [1991] F.S.R. 81, Ch D . . . . *Digested*, 92/**3599**:
Considered, 98/3428
Perro v. Mansworth (Inspector of Taxes) [2001] S.T.C. (S.C.D.) 179; 4 I.T.L. Rep. 276; [2001] S.T.I. 1361, Sp Comm
Perry v. Adjudication Officer (Incapacity for Work: Prosthesis) [1999] N.I. 338, CA (NI) . . . . *Digested*, 00/**5741**
Perry v. Butlins Holiday World (t/a Butlins Ltd) [1998] Ed. C.R. 39; [1997] E.G.C.S. 171, CA. . . . . *Digested*, 98/**3991**
Perry v. Chief Adjudication Officer [1999] 2 C.M.L.R. 439; *Times*, October 20, 1998; *Independent*, October 21, 1998, CA . . . . *Digested*, 98/**4541**
Perry v. Chief Adjudication Officer (Application for Leave to Appeal) [1998] 2 C.M.L.R. 18, CA
Perry v. Kendricks Transport [1956] 1 W.L.R. 85; [1956] 1 All E.R. 154; 100 S.J. 52, CA . *Digested*, 56/**6024**:
Applied, 70/2745, 00/4238
Perry v. Moysey [1998] P.N.L.R. 657, QBD . . . . *Digested*, 98/**540**
Perry v. Sidney Phillips & Son [1982] 1 W.L.R. 1297; [1982] 3 All E.R. 705; 22 B.L.R. 120; (1982) 263 E.G. 888; (1982) 79 L.S.G. 1175; 126 S.J. 626, CA; reversing [1982] 1 All E.R. 1005; (1981) 260 E.G. 389, QBD . . . . *Digested*, 82/**2164**:
Applied, 83/990, 84/242, 85/2328, 88/1044, 89/2569, 90/1524, 90/1566, 92/1547, 01/3447: *Considered*, 89/1185, 89/2195, 90/1567, 90/3305, 90/3315, 91/1319, 91/2657, 97/6307: *Distinguished*, 89/1197, 90/1565, 90/1568: *Followed*, 92/1548, 97/3843: *Referred to*, 85/952, 85/2332, 88/2455
Perry v. Smith (Unreported, March 16, 2001), CC (Luton) [*Ex rel.* David McHugh, Barrister, Bracton Chambers, Bell House, 8 Bell Yard, London] . . . . *Digested*, 01/**689**
Perry's Application, Re [1997] N.I. 282, CA (NI) . . . . *Digested*, 99/**5290**
Persimmon Homes (Thames Valley) Ltd v. North Hertfordshire DC see R. (on the application of Persimmon Homes (Thames Valley) Ltd) v. North Hertfordshire DC
Persimmon Homes (North West) Ltd v. Secretary of State for the Environment, Transport and the Regions [2001] J.P.L. 999 (Note), QBD (Admin Ct)
PERSTORP/Appeal inadmissible (T1007/95) [2000] E.P.O.R. 255, EPO (Technical Bd App). . . . . *Digested*, 00/**3606**

Pertemps Group Ltd *v.* Crosher & James (Unreported, May 14, 1999), CC (Birmingham) [*Ex rel.* Claire Cunningham, Barrister, St Philip's Chambers, Fountain Court, Birmingham] . . . . *Digested,* 99/**3676**

Peskin *v.* Anderson [2001] B.C.C. 874; [2001] 1 B.C.L.C. 372, CA; affirming [2000] B.C.C. 1110; [2000] 2 B.C.L.C. 1, Ch D . . . . *Digested,* 01/**724**

Pesti *v.* Austria (27618/95) (2000) 29 E.H.R.R. CD229, ECHR

Pete Waterman Ltd *v.* CBS United Kingdom Ltd [1993] E.M.L.R. 27, Ch D . . . . *Digested,* 93/**3802**:
Considered, 97/4905: *Followed,* 98/3518

Peter Acatos No. 2 Settlement, Re see Stuart-Hutcheson *v.* Spread Trustee Co Ltd

Peter Buchanan Ltd *v.* McVey [1955] A.C. 516 (Note), Sup Ct (Irl) . . . . *Digested,* 56/**1380**:
Applied, 62/416: *Followed,* 99/729

Peter Carter-Ruck & Partners *v.* Holmes [2001] EWCA Civ 285; [2001] C.P. Rep. 79, CA . . . . *Digested,* 01/**631**

Peter Hulmes Patent (No.2185221) (1999) 22(7) I.P.D. 22064, Pat Ct

Peter Hynd (H) Settlement, Re [2001] W.T.L.R. 1027; (2000-01) 3 I.T.E.L.R. 701, Royal Ct (Jer)

Peter Lingham & Co *v.* Lonnkvist see Cossey *v.* Lonnkvist

Peter Yates & Co *v.* Bullock [1990] 2 E.G.L.R. 24; [1990] 37 E.G. 75, CA . . . . *Digested,* 90/**109.10**:
Applied, 01/111

Peterborough City Council *v.* H&H Holman Properties (1998) 13 P.A.D. 192, Planning Inspector

Peterborough City Council *v.* HM Prison Service (1999) 14 P.A.D. 526, Planning Inspector

Peterborough City Council *v.* Teesfield Developments Ltd (1998) 13 P.A.D. 52, Planning Inspector

Peters (Edgar), Re [1988] Q.B. 871; [1988] 3 W.L.R. 182; [1988] 3 All E.R. 46; [1989] C.O.D. 180, CA . . . . *Digested,* 88/**635**:
Distinguished, 99/2419

Peters *v.* Davison 2 I.T.L. Rep. 829, HC (NZ)

Petersson *v.* Pitt Place (Epsom) Ltd [2001] EWCA Civ 86; (2001) 82 P. & C.R. 21; [2001] L. & T.R. 21; [2001] 6 E.G.C.S. 160, CA . . . . *Digested,* 01/**4190**

Petitioning Creditor *v.* Awan (A Bankrupt) see Awan, Re

Petone, The [1917] P. 198, PDAD . . . . *Applied,* 01/4935

Petra *v.* Romania (2001) 33 E.H.R.R. 5; 5 B.H.R.C. 497; [1998] H.R.C.D. 886, ECHR . . *Digested,* 99/**3117**

Petra Fischer *v.* Comptroller of Patents see Petra Fischer's Patent Application

Petra Fischer's Patent Application; *sub nom* Petra Fischer *v.* Comptroller of Patents [1997] R.P.C. 899; (1997) 20(6) I.P.D. 20053, Pat Ct . . . . *Digested,* 98/**3473**

Petra Investments Ltd *v.* Jeffrey Rogers Plc (2001) 81 P. & C.R. 21; [2000] L. & T.R. 451; [2000] 3 E.G.L.R. 120; [2000] E.G.C.S. 66; [2000] N.P.C. 61, Ch D . . . . . *Digested,* 00/**3888**

Petrauskas *v.* West Yorkshire Police (Unreported, July 6, 2000), CC (Wakefield) [*Ex rel.* Iyr Tasaddat Hussain, Barrister, Broadway House Chambers, 9 Bank Street, Bradford] . . . . *Digested,* 00/**4549**

Petrie *v.* Bettoni (C90/96) see Petrie *v.* Universita degli Studi di Verona (C90/96)

Petrie *v.* Universita degli Studi di Verona (C90/96); Petrie *v.* Bettoni (C90/96) [1997] E.C.R. I-6527; [1998] 1 C.M.L.R. 711; [1998] C.E.C. 117, ECJ (5th Chamber) . . . *Digested,* 98/**2153**

Petrograde Inc *v.* Smith see Petrotrade Inc *v.* Smith (Jurisdiction)

Petroleo Brasiliero SA *v.* Mellitus Shipping Inc (The Baltic Flame) [2001] EWCA Civ 418; [2001] 1 All E.R. (Comm) 993; [2001] 2 Lloyd's Rep. 203; [2001] C.L.C. 1151; *Times,* April 5, 2001, CA . . . . *Digested,* 01/**610**

Petroleos de Portugal SA *v.* BP Oil International Ltd [1999] 1 Lloyd's Rep. 854, QBD (Comm Ct) . . . . *Digested,* 99/**220**

Petrolite Holdings Inc *v.* Dyno Oil Field Chemicals UK Ltd (No.1) [1998] F.S.R. 190; (1998) 21(2) I.P.D. 21014, Ch D . . . . *Digested,* 98/**3461**

Petrolite Holdings Inc *v.* Dyno Oil Field Chemicals UK Ltd (No.2) [1998] F.S.R. 646; (1998) 21(5) I.P.D. 21051, Pat Ct . . . . *Digested,* 98/**3460**

Petroships Pte Ltd of Singapore *v.* Petec Trading & Investment Corp of Vietnam (The Petro Ranger) [2001] 2 Lloyd's Rep. 348, QBD (Comm Ct) . . . . *Digested,* 01/**340**

Petrotrade Inc *v.* Smith (Jurisdiction); *sub nom* Petrograde Inc *v.* Smith [1999] 1 W.L.R. 457; [1998] 2 All E.R. 346; [1998] C.L.C. 298; *Times,* December 8, 1998, QBD (Comm Ct) . . . . *Digested,* 99/**526**

Petrotrade Inc *v.* Smith (Vicarious Liability) [2000] 1 Lloyd's Rep. 486; [2000] C.L.C. 916, QBD (Comm Ct) . . . . *Digested,* 00/**5105**

Petrotrade Inc *v.* Texaco Ltd [2001] 4 All E.R. 853; [2001] C.P. Rep. 29; [2000] C.L.C. 1341; *Times,* June 14, 2000; *Independent,* July 10, 2000 (C.S), CA; affirming 1998 Folio 1348, QBD (Comm Ct) . . . . *Digested,* 00/**539**:
Applied, 01/484

Petrou *v.* Kuti (Unreported, April 8, 1997), CC (Central London) [*Ex rel.* Lana Wood, Barrister, 3 Paper Buildings, Temple] . . . . *Digested,* 97/**1803**:
Disapproved, 98/2503

Petrovic *v.* Austria (20458/92) (2001) 33 E.H.R.R. 14; 4 B.H.R.C. 232; [1998] H.R.C.D. 366, ECHR . . . . *Digested,* 98/**3155**

Pettengell *v.* Edwards (Unreported, April 3, 1998), CC (Bromley) [*Ex rel.* Nigel Ffitch, Barrister, Trafalgar Chambers, 53 Fleet Street, London] . . . . *Digested,* 98/**460**:
Considered, 98/453, 98/457

Petter *v.* Secretary of State for the Environment, Transport and the Regions (2000) 79
P. & C.R. 214; [1999] P.L.C.R. 322; [1999] E.G.C.S. 42, CA; reversing [1998]
E.G.C.S. 88, QBD . . . . *Digested,* 00/**4491**
Pettifor's Will Trusts, Re; *sub nom* Roberts *v.* Roberts [1966] Ch. 257; [1966] 2 W.L.R.
778; [1966] 1 All E.R. 913; 110 S.J. 191, Ch D . . . . *Digested,* 66/**11074**:
Followed, 00/5263
Pettit *v.* SEP Industrial Holdings (Unreported, February 5, 2001), CC (Warrington) [*Ex*
rel. Haroon Rashid, Barrister, 12 Parnham Close, Radcliffe, Manchester] . . . . *Digested,* 01/**897**
Peugeot Motor Co Plc *v.* Customs and Excise Commissioners [1999] B.V.C. 2314,
V&DTr
Peugeot Motor Co Plc *v.* Customs and Excise Commissioners (Employee Incentive
Scheme) [2000] S.T.I. 1554, V&DTr
Peugeot Motor Co Plc *v.* Customs and Excise Commissioners (Second Hand Cars)
[1998] B.V.C. 2111; [1998] V. & D.R. 1, V&DTr . . . . *Digested,* 98/**4983**
Pexton *v.* Wellcome Trust Ltd (2001) 82 P. & C.R. 4, CA . . . . *Digested,* 01/**4883**
PF Ahern (London) Ltd *v.* Secretary of State for the Environment see R. *v.* Secretary of
State for the Environment Ex p. PF Ahern (London) Ltd
Pfarrmeier *v.* Austria (A/329C) (1996) 22 E.H.R.R. 175, ECHR . . . . *Digested,* 96/**3120**:
Followed, 98/3111
Pfeiffer Grosshandel GmbH *v.* Lowa Warenhandel GmbH (C255/97) [1999] E.C.R. I-
2835; [2001] 1 C.M.L.R. 7; [1999] E.T.M.R. 603, ECJ . . . . *Digested,* 00/**3799**
PFG Srl *v.* PR Inc (2 U 78/97) [2000] E.N.P.R. 263, OLG (Dusseldorf)
Pfizer Corp *v.* Ministry of Health [1965] A.C. 512; [1965] 2 W.L.R. 387; [1965] 1 All
E.R. 450; [1965] R.P.C. 261; 109 S.J. 149, HL; affirming [1964] Ch. 614; [1963]
3 W.L.R. 999; [1963] 3 All E.R. 779; 107 S.J. 828, CA; reversing [1963] 2
W.L.R. 286; [1963] 1 All E.R. 590; [1963] R.P.C. 173; (1962) 107 S.J. 56, Ch D
. . . . *Digested,* 65/**2940**:
Applied, 70/2828, 85/1855, 86/1837, 00/2777: *Considered,* 68/2473,
74/2786, 89/2507
Pfizer Inc *v.* Eurim-Pharm GmbH (C1/81) [1981] E.C.R. 2913; [1982] 1 C.M.L.R. 406;
[1982] F.S.R. 269, ECJ (1st Chamber) . . . . *Digested,* 83/**1651**:
Applied, 96/5713: *Considered,* 98/3514: *Followed,* 97/4879
Pfizer Inc *v.* Lestre Nederlandse Reformadviegbureau ENRA BV [2001] E.T.M.R. 15, RB
(Utrecht)
Pfizer Inc *v.* Monaco Telematique en Abrege MC Tel [2001] E.T.M.R. 16, Trib Prem Inst
(MC)
Pfizer Ltd *v.* Eurofood Link (UK) Ltd (Injunction) (1999) 22(4) I.P.D. 22039, Ch D
Pfizer Ltd *v.* Eurofood Link (UK) Ltd [2000] E.T.M.R. 896; [2001] F.S.R. 3, Ch D . . . . . *Digested,* 01/**4036**
Pfizer Ltd's European Patent (UK) (No.0702555) see Lilly ICOS Ltd *v.* Pfizer Ltd (No.1)
PFIZER/Quinuclidines (T50/97) [2000] E.P.O.R. 533, EPO (Technical Bd App) . . . . . . *Digested,* 01/**3906**
PFIZER/Sertraline (T158/96) [1999] E.P.O.R. 285, EPO (Technical Bd App)
PG *v.* United Kingdom (44787/98); JH *v.* United Kingdom (44787/98) *Times,* October
19, 2001, ECHR . . . . *Digested,* 01/**3576**
PG Vallance Ltd *v.* Secretary of State for the Environment [1993] 1 P.L.R. 74; [1994]
J.P.L. 50; *Independent,* November 19, 1992, QBD . . . . *Digested,* 93/**3924**:
Distinguished, 99/4203
Pharaon *v.* Bank of Credit and Commerce International SA see El Jawhary *v.* Bank of
Credit and Commerce International SA (No.1)
Pharaon *v.* Bank of Credit and Commerce International SA (In Liquidation); Price
Waterhouse *v.* Bank of Credit and Commerce International SA (In Liquidation)
[1998] 4 All E.R. 455; (1998) 142 S.J.L.B. 251; *Times,* August 17, 1998, Ch D . . *Digested,* 98/**278**
PHARLYSE/Mucolytic salts (T440/91) [1999] E.P.O.R. 408, EPO (Technical Bd App) . *Digested,* 99/**3485**
Pharmaceutical Management Agency Ltd *v.* Commissioner of Patents [2000] R.P.C.
857, CA (NZ); affirming [1999] R.P.C. 752, HC (NZ) . . . . *Digested,* 01/**3965**
Pharmaceutical Society of Great Britain *v.* Dickson; *sub nom* Dickson *v.* Pharmaceutical
Society of Great Britain [1970] A.C. 403; [1968] 3 W.L.R. 286; [1968] 2 All
E.R. 686; (1968) 112 S.J. 601, HL; affirming [1967] Ch. 708; [1967] 2 W.L.R.
718; [1967] 2 All E.R. 558; 111 S.J. 116, CA; affirming [1966] 1 W.L.R. 1539;
[1966] 3 All E.R. 404; 110 S.J. 685, Ch D . . . . *Digested,* 68/**3880**:
Applied, 00/2906: *Considered,* 78/24, 90/3072
Pharmacia & Upjohn SA (formerly Upjohn SA) *v.* Paranova A/S (C379/97); *sub nom*
Upjohn SA, Danmark *v.* Paranova A/S (C379/97) [2000] Ch. 571; [2000] 3
W.L.R. 303; [1999] All E.R. (EC) 880; [1999] E.C.R. I-6927; [2000] 1 C.M.L.R.
51; [1999] C.E.C. 630; [1999] E.T.M.R. 937; [2000] F.S.R. 621; (2001) 62
B.M.L.R. 150; (2000) 18 Tr. L.R. 457, ECJ [1999] E.C.R. I-6927; [1999] E.T.M.R.
97, AGO . . . . *Digested,* 00/**3709**
Pharmedica GmbH's International Trade Mark Application (No.649380) [2000] R.P.C.
536; (2000) 23(3) I.P.D. 23024; *Independent,* March 6, 2000 (C.S.), Ch D . . . *Digested,* 00/**3697**
Phato *v.* Attorney General of the Eastern Cape 1994 (2) S.A.C.R. 734, Sup Ct (SA) . . . *Applied,* 98/3116

Phelps *v.* Hillingdon LBC; *sub nom* G (A Child), Re; Anderton *v.* Clwyd CC; G (A Child) *v.* Bromley LBC; Jarvis *v.* Hampshire CC [2001] 2 A.C. 619; [2000] 3 W.L.R. 776; [2000] 4 All E.R. 504; [2000] 3 F.C.R. 102; (2001) 3 L.G.L.R. 5; [2000] B.L.G.R. 651; [2000] Ed. C.R. 700; [2000] E.L.R. 499; (2000) 3 C.C.L. Rep. 156; (2000) 56 B.M.L.R. 1; (2000) 150 N.L.J. 1198; (2000) 144 S.J.L.B. 241; *Times,* July 28, 2000; *Independent,* November 13, 2000 (C.S), HL; reversing [1999] 1 W.L.R. 500; [1999] 1 All E.R. 421; [1999] 1 F.C.R. 440; (1999) 1 L.G.L.R. 246; [1999] B.L.G.R. 103; [1999] Ed. C.R. 368; [1998] E.L.R. 587; (1999) 46 B.M.L.R. 100; (1998) 95(45) L.S.G. 41; (1998) 148 N.L.J. 1710; (1999) 143 S.J.L.B. 11; *Times,* November 9, 1998, CA; reversing [1997] 3 F.C.R. 621; (1997) 9 Admin. L.R. 657; [1998] Ed. C.R. 47; [1998] E.L.R. 38; (1998) 39 B.M.L.R. 51; (1997) 94(39) L.S.G. 39; (1997) 147 N.L.J. 1421; (1997) 141 S.J.L.B. 214; *Times,* October 10, 1997, QBD . . . .   *Digested,* 00/**1947**:
Applied, 99/1889, 99/4010, 01/4540: *Considered,* 99/3966, 99/3968: *Distinguished,* 99/3967: *Previous proceedings,* 99/1889, 99/3967, 99/4010

Phelps *v.* Spon Smith & Co (Amendment of Writ) (1999) 96(46) L.S.G. 38; (2000) 144 S.J.L.B. 6; *Times,* November 26, 1999, Ch D . . . .   *Digested,* 00/**586**:
Subsequent proceedings, 01/2430

Phelps *v.* Spon Smith & Co (Preliminary Issues) [2001] B.P.I.R. 326, Ch D . . . .   *Digested,* 01/**2430**:
Previous proceedings, 00/586

Phibro Energy AG *v.* Nissho Iwai Corp (The Honam Jade) [1991] 1 Lloyd's Rep. 38, CA .   *Digested,* 91/**508**:
Applied, 00/4684

Philex Plc *v.* Golban see Ridehalgh *v.* Horsefield

Philip Alexander Securities & Futures Ltd, Re [1998] B.C.C. 819; [1999] 1 B.C.L.C. 124, Ch D (Companies Ct) . . . .   *Digested,* 98/**3346**

Philip Alexander Securities & Futures Ltd (Lodging of Proxy Votes), Re [1998] B.P.I.R. 383, Ch D (Companies Ct) . . . .   *Digested,* 98/**3340**

Philip Collins Ltd *v.* Davis [2000] 3 All E.R. 808; [2001] E.C.D.R. 17; [2000] E.M.L.R. 815, Ch D . . . .   *Digested,* 00/**2320**

Philip Morris Inc, Re 1 I.T.L. Rep. 122, Trib (Milano)

Philip Morris Products Inc *v.* Rothmans International Enterprises Ltd [2001] EWCA Civ 1043; [2001] E.T.M.R. 108; (2001) 98(34) L.S.G. 37; *Times,* August 17, 2001, CA; affirming [2000] U.K.C.L.R. 912; (2000) 97(36) L.S.G. 41; *Times,* August 10, 2000, Ch D . . . .   *Digested,* 01/**731**

Philip Powis Ltd, Re [1998] B.C.C. 756; [1998] 1 B.C.L.C. 440; (1998) 95(11) L.S.G. 36; *Times,* March 6, 1998, CA; reversing [1997] 2 B.C.L.C. 481; *Times,* April 30, 1997; *Independent,* May 12, 1997 (C.S.), Ch D (Companies Ct) . . . .   *Digested,* 98/**686**:
Distinguished, 97/652

Philips *v.* Society of Lloyd's see Manning *v.* Society of Lloyd's

Philips *v.* Ward [1956] 1 W.L.R. 471; [1956] 1 All E.R. 874; 100 S.J. 317, CA . . . .   *Digested,* 56/**936**:
Applied, 67/381, 69/3380, 73/2311, 73/2330, 74/2591, 83/1074, 85/228, 85/2328, 87/2321, 89/2585, 92/1548, 98/3958: *Considered,* 61/889, 85/2332, 90/755, 90/1566, 91/1319: *Distinguished,* 70/2710, 82/2164, 89/1197, 90/1522: *Explained,* 64/3470: *Followed,* 71/11161, 78/2071, 78/3274, 96/4514, 97/3843, 97/3847

Philips Electronics NV *v.* Ingman Ltd [1998] 2 C.M.L.R. 839; [1998] Eu. L.R. 666; [1999] F.S.R. 112; (1998) 21(8) I.P.D. 21084, Pat Ct . . . .   *Digested,* 99/**3498**

Philips Electronics NV *v.* Remington Consumer Products Ltd (C299/99) [2001] E.T.M.R. 48; [2001] R.P.C. 38, AGO . . . .   *Digested,* 01/**4049**

Philips Electronics NV *v.* Remington Consumer Products Ltd (No.1) [1999] E.T.M.R. 816; [1999] R.P.C. 809; (1999) 22(9) I.P.D. 22084, CA [1998] E.T.M.R. 124; [1998] R.P.C. 283; (1998) 21(3) I.P.D. 21023; *Times,* February 2, 1998, Pat Ct .   *Digested,* 99/**3564**:
Applied, 99/3583, 00/3793: *Considered,* 99/3567, 01/4041: *Followed,* 00/3758: *Referred to,* 99/3593, 01/4026, 01/4030

Philips Electronics NV *v.* Remington Consumer Products Ltd (No.2) [1999] E.T.M.R. 835; (1999) 22(6) I.P.D. 22054, Ch D . . . .   *Digested,* 00/**3772**

Philips Electronique Grand Public SA *v.* British Sky Broadcasting Ltd [1995] E.M.L.R. 472; *Independent,* October 31, 1994 (C.S.), CA . . . .   *Digested,* 97/**4845**:
Considered, 00/4640

PHILIPS/ Image Projection Apparatus (T870/96) [2001] E.P.O.R. 43, EPO (Technical Bd App) . . . .   *Digested,* 01/**3940**

PHILIPS/Picture signal (T349/97) [1999] E.P.O.R. 52, EPO (Technical Bd App)

PHILIPS/Record carrier (T1194/97); *sub nom* Koninklijke Philips Electronics NV's European Patent Application (T1194/97) [2001] E.P.O.R. 25; (2001) 24(3) I.P.D. 24019, EPO (Technical Bd App) . . . .   *Digested,* 01/**3953**

Philis *v.* Greece (No.2) (1998) 25 E.H.R.R. 417, ECHR . . . .   *Digested,* 98/**3131**

Phillips *v.* Bacon (1808) 9 East 298, KBD . . . .   *Applied,* 00/**5438**

Phillips *v.* Brewin Dolphin Bell Lawrie Ltd see Phillips (Liquidator of AJ Bekhor & Co) *v.* Brewin Dolphin Bell Lawrie Ltd (formerly Brewin Dolphin & Co Ltd)

Phillips (Liquidator of AJ Bekhor & Co) v. Brewin Dolphin Bell Lawrie Ltd (formerly Brewin Dolphin & Co Ltd); *sub nom* Phillips v. Brewin Dolphin Bell Lawrie Ltd [2001] UKHL 2; [2001] 1 W.L.R. 143; [2001] 1 All E.R. 673; [2001] B.C.C. 864; [2001] 1 B.C.L.C. 145; [2001] B.P.I.R. 119; (2001) 98(12) L.S.G. 43; (2001) 145 S.J.L.B. 32; *Times*, January 23, 2001, HL; affirming [1999] 1 W.L.R. 2052; [1999] 2 All E.R. 844; [1999] B.C.C. 557; [1999] 1 B.C.L.C 714; [1999] B.P.I.R. 797; *Times*, March 30, 1999, CA; affirming [1998] 1 B.C.L.C. 700, Ch D . . . . . . *Digested*, 01/**3753**
Phillips v. Burrows (Inspector of Taxes) (Costs); Phillips (Deceased) v. Burrows (Inspector of Taxes) [2000] S.T.C. (S.C.D.) 107 (Note); [2000] S.T.I. 167, Sp Comm
Phillips v. Burrows (Inspector of Taxes) (Set Aside) [2000] S.T.C. (S.C.D.) 112; [2000] S.T.I. 168, Sp Comm. . . . . *Digested*, 00/**4988**
Phillips v. Cameron see Cameron (Deceased), Re
Phillips v. Derbyshire CC [1997] E.L.R. 461; [1997] C.O.D. 130, QBD . . . . *Digested*, 97/**2137**:
Distinguished, 98/1983: *Followed*, 99/359
Phillips v. Eyre (1870-71) L.R. 6 Q.B. 1, Ex Chamber; affirming (1868-69) L.R. 4 Q.B. 225, QB . . . . *Applied*, 67/547,
68/496, 69/469, 00/5663, 01/4903: *Considered*, 68/495, 89/3528, 94/4282, 95/4724, 95/4736: *Not applied*, 99/731
Phillips v. Lehman Brothers see Mid East Trading Ltd, Re
Phillips v. Magill see Porter v. Magill
Phillips v. Radnor DC; *sub nom* Phillips v. Radnorshire DC [1998] E.G.C.S. 30, CA
Phillips v. Symes (Stay of Proceedings) [2001] C.L.C. 1673; (2001) 98(34) L.S.G. 41; *Times*, October 2, 2001; *Independent*, October 22, 2001 (C.S), Ch D . . . . *Digested*, 01/**827**
Phillips v. Taunton and Somerset NHS Trust [1997] 8 Med. L.R. 348; (1997) 33 B.M.L.R. 154; *Times*, August 15, 1996, CA. . . . . *Digested*, 96/**877**:
Followed, 98/354
Phillips v. United Kingdom (41087/98) 11 B.H.R.C. 280; [2001] Crim. L.R. 817; *Times*, August 13, 2001, ECHR . . . . *Digested*, 01/**3537**
Phillips Application, Re [1995] N.I. 322, QBD (NI). . . . . *Considered*, 00/5436
Phillips-Turner v. Reading Transport Ltd (Unreported, January 26, 2000), CC (Guildford) [*Ex rel.* Ensor Byfield Solicitors, Equity Court, 73-75 Millbrook Road East, Southampton] . . . . *Digested*, 00/**4207**
Phillis Trading Ltd v. 86 Lordship Road Ltd; *sub nom* Phyllis Trading Ltd v. 86 Lordship Road Ltd [2001] EWCA Civ 350; [2001] 28 E.G. 147; (2001) 82 P. & C.R. D8; *Times*, March 16, 2001, CA. . . . . *Digested*, 01/**4179**
Phipps v. Boardman see Boardman v. Phipps
Phipps v. Pears [1965] 1 Q.B. 76; [1964] 2 W.L.R. 996; [1964] 2 All E.R. 35; 108 S.J. 236, CA . . . . *Digested*, 64/**1199**:
Applied, 70/824, 82/956: *Distinguished*, 01/4482
Phipps v. Royal Australasian College of Surgeons (2000) 56 B.M.L.R. 169, PC (NZ)
Phipps-Faire Ltd v. Malbern Construction [1987] 1 E.G.L.R. 129; (1987) 282 E.G. 460, Ch D . . . . *Digested*, 87/**2200**:
Considered, 99/3726: *Disapproved*, 91/5178
Phocas v. France (17869/91) (2001) 32 E.H.R.R. 11, ECHR
Phoenix General Insurance Co of Greece SA v. Administratia Asigurarilor de Stat; Phoenix General Insurance Co of Greece SA v. Halvanon Insurance [1988] Q.B. 216; [1987] 2 W.L.R. 512; [1987] 2 All E.R. 152; [1986] 2 Lloyd's Rep. 552; [1987] Fin. L.R. 48; (1987) 84 L.S.G. 1055; (1987) 131 S.J. 257; *Financial Times*, October 15, 1986, CA; reversing [1986] 1 All E.R. 908; [1985] 2 Lloyd's Rep. 599; [1985] Fin. L.R. 368; (1985) 135 N.L.J. 1081, QBD (Comm Ct) . . . . *Digested*, 87/**2050**:
Applied, 96/3566: *Considered*, 92/182, 99/110: *Followed*, 93/2415
Phoenix General Insurance Co of Greece SA v. Halvanon Insurance see Phoenix General Insurance Co of Greece SA v. Administratia Asigurarilor de Stat
Phoenix International Life Sciences Inc v. Rilett [2001] B.C.C. 115, Ch D . . . . *Digested*, 01/**962**
Phoenix Marine Inc v. China Ocean Shipping Co [1999] 1 All E.R. (Comm.) 138; [1999] 1 Lloyd's Rep. 682; [1999] C.L.C. 478, QBD (Comm Ct) . . . . *Digested*, 99/**753**
Phonographic Performance Ltd v. AEI Rediffusion Music Ltd see AEI Rediffusion Music Ltd v. Phonographic Performance Ltd (No.1)
Phonographic Performance Ltd v. AEI Rediffusion Music Ltd (Costs) see AEI Rediffusion Music Ltd v. Phonographic Performance Ltd (Costs)
Phonographic Performance Ltd v. Candy Rock Recording Ltd; *sub nom* Candy Rock Recording Ltd v. Phonographic Performance Ltd [2000] E.C.D.R. 526; [2000] E.M.L.R. 618; *Independent*, April 6, 2000, CA; affirming [1999] E.M.L.R. 806, Ch D; reversing in part [1999] E.M.L.R. 155; (1998) 21(12) I.P.D. 21129, Copyright Tr. . . . . *Digested*, 00/**3578**
Phonographic Performance Ltd v. Maitra; *sub nom* Phonographic Performance Ltd v. Saibal Maitra; Phonographic Performance Ltd v. Underworld (Bradford) Ltd [1998] 1 W.L.R. 870; [1998] 2 All E.R. 638; [1998] E.M.L.R. 370; [1998] F.S.R. 749; (1998) 21(5) I.P.D. 21048; (1998) 142 S.J.L.B. 75; *Times*, February 10, 1998; *Independent*, February 5, 1998, CA; reversing [1997] 3 All E.R. 673; *Times*, July 14, 1997, Ch D . . . . *Digested*, 98/**3425**
Phonographic Performance Ltd v. Saibal Maitra see Phonographic Performance Ltd v. Maitra

Phonographic Performance Ltd *v.* South Tyneside MBC [2001] 1 W.L.R. 400; [2001]
    E.M.L.R. 17; [2001] R.P.C. 29; [2001] B.L.G.R. 176; (2001) 98(3) L.S.G. 42;
    (2001) 145 S.J.L.B. 6; *Times*, December 19, 2000, Ch D . . . .   *Digested*, 01/**3849**
Phonographic Performance Ltd *v.* Underworld (Bradford) Ltd see Phonographic
    Performance Ltd *v.* Maitra
Phonographic Performance Ltd *v.* Virgin Retail Ltd see Virgin Retail Ltd *v.* Phonographic
    Performance Ltd
Phull *v.* Secretary of State for the Home Department see R. *v.* Secretary of State for
    the Home Department Ex p. Phull
Phyllis Trading Ltd *v.* 86 Lordship Road Ltd see Phillis Trading Ltd *v.* 86 Lordship Road
    Ltd
Phytheron International SA *v.* Jean Bourdon SA (C352/95) [1997] E.C.R. I-1729;
    [1997] 3 C.M.L.R. 199; [1997] E.T.M.R. 211; [1997] F.S.R. 936, ECJ (5th
    Chamber) . . . .   *Digested*, 98/**3506**
Pialopoulos *v.* Greece (37095/97) (2001) 33 E.H.R.R. 39, ECHR
Pianotist Co's Application, Re (1906) 23 R.P.C. 774 . . . .   *Applied*, 93/3991,
                96/5721: *Considered*, 68/3936, 96/5723, 98/3537: *Followed*, 95/4946
Piccadilly Property Management Ltd, Re [2000] B.C.C. 44; [1999] 2 B.C.L.C.145; [1999]
    B.P.I.R. 260; *Independent*, November 30, 1998 (C.S.), Ch D . . . .   *Digested*, 99/**3277**
Picker International Inc's European Patent Application (No.91302528.4) (2000) 23(3)
    I.P.D. 23020, EPO (Technical Bd App)
Pickering *v.* Secretary of State for the Environment Unreported, QBD . . . .   *Considered*, 99/4177
Pickering *v.* Teagles (Unreported, July 14, 1999), CC (Stourbridge) [*Ex rel.* A Young,
    Barrister, St Philip's Chambers, Fountain Court, Steelhouse Lane, Birmingham] .   *Digested*, 99/**404**
Pickford *v.* ICI Plc [1998] 1 W.L.R. 1189; [1998] 3 All E.R. 462; [1998] I.C.R. 673;
    [1998] I.R.L.R. 435; (1998) 43 B.M.L.R. 1; (1998) 95(31) L.S.G. 36; (1998) 148
    N.L.J. 978; (1998) 142 S.J.L.B. 198; *Times*, June 30, 1998; *Independent*, July 1,
    1998, HL; reversing [1997] I.C.R. 566; [1996] I.R.L.R. 622; [1998] I.T.C.L.R.
    196; [1997] 8 Med. L.R. 270; (1996) 93(39) L.S.G. 26; (1996) 140 S.J.L.B.
    202; *Times*, August 31, 1996, CA . . . .   *Digested*, 98/**2834**
Pickin *v.* Quinn [2001] 6 Q.R. 9, CC (Rhyl) [*Ex rel.* Paul Clark, Barrister, Exchange
    Chambers, Pearl Assurance House, Liverpool] . . . .   *Digested*, 01/**1618**
Pickles *v.* Holdsworth see Heer *v.* Tutton
Pickstone *v.* Freemans Plc [1989] A.C. 66; [1988] 3 W.L.R. 265; [1988] 2 All E.R.
    803; [1988] 3 C.M.L.R. 221; [1988] I.C.R. 697; [1988] I.R.L.R. 357; (1988) 138
    N.L.J. Rep. 193; *Times*, July 1, 1988; *Independent*, July 1, 1988; *Financial Times*,
    July 5, 1988; *Guardian*, July 1, 1988, HL; affirming [1987] 3 W.L.R. 811; [1987] 3
    All E.R. 756; [1987] 2 C.M.L.R. 572; [1987] I.C.R. 867; [1987] I.R.L.R. 218,
    CA; reversing [1986] I.C.R. 886, EAT . . . .   *Digested*, 88/**1268**:
                        Applied, 89/1508, 89/4304: *Followed*, 98/321
Picnic at Ascot *v.* Kalus Derigs [2001] F.S.R. 2, Ch D . . . .   *Digested*, 01/**486**
Picquet *v.* Sacinter SA [2000] I.L.Pr. 49, Cass (F)
Pierce *v.* Promco SA [1998-99] Info. T.L.R. 273; [1999] I.T.C.L.R. 233; [1999] Masons
    C.L.R. 116, Ch D . . . .   *Digested*, 99/**3455**
Piermay Shipping Co SA *v.* Chester (Preliminary Issue: Witness Statement) [1978] 1
    W.L.R. 411; [1978] 1 All E.R. 1233; [1979] 1 Lloyd's Rep. 17; 121 S.J. 795, CA . . .   *Digested*, 78/**1428**:
                                                                                              Followed, 98/819
Piermay Shipping Co SA *v.* Chester (The Michael) [1979] 2 Lloyd's Rep. 1, CA;
    affirming [1979] 1 Lloyd's Rep. 55, QBD (Comm Ct) . . . .   *Digested*, 79/**2471**:
                                                                                              Applied, 01/3825
Pierre Fabre Dermo Cosmetiques SA *v.* Breckler [2000] E.C.C. 296, C d'A (Versailles);
    reversing [2000] E.C.C. 291, Trib Comm (F)
Pierre-Bloch *v.* France (1998) 26 E.H.R.R. 202; [1998] H.R.C.D. 14, ECHR . . . .   *Digested*, 98/**3119**:
                                                                                              Applied, 01/3498
Piersack *v.* Belgium (A/53) (1983) 5 E.H.R.R. 169, ECHR . . . .   *Applied*, 00/**6092**:
                                                                                              Considered, 98/3090
Pierson *v.* Secretary of State for the Home Department see R. *v.* Secretary of State for
    the Home Department Ex p. Pierson
Pifco Ltd *v.* Phillips Domestic Appliances and Personal Care BV (1999) 22(3) I.P.D.
    22026; *Independent*, January 18, 1999 (C.S.), Ch D . . . .   *Digested*, 99/**3501**:
                                                                                              Applied, 00/415
Piglowska *v.* Piglowski [1999] 1 W.L.R. 1360; [1999] 3 All E.R. 632; [1999] 2 F.L.R.
    763; [1999] 2 F.C.R. 481; [1999] Fam. Law 617; (1999) 96(27) L.S.G. 34;
    (1999) 143 S.J.L.B. 190; *Times*, June 25, 1999, HL . . . .   *Digested*, 99/**2421**:
                                                Considered, 00/2489, 01/2632, 01/4450
Pigots's Case (1614) 11 Co. Rep. 266 . . . .   *Considered*, 91/**1868**:
                                                                                              Distinguished, 00/278
Pigott Foundations Ltd *v.* Shepherd Construction Ltd 67 B.L.R. 48; 42 Con. L.R. 98,
    QBD (OR) . . . .   *Considered*, 00/**826**
Pike *v.* BWOC Ltd (Unreported, August 4, 1998), CC (Bridgwater) [*Ex rel.* Jonathan
    Hand, Barrister, 35 Essex Street, London] . . . .   *Digested*, 98/**1592**
Pike *v.* Sefton MBC [2000] Env. L.R. D31; [2000] E.H.L.R. Dig. 272, QBD
Pilcher *v.* Bates (Unreported, September 27, 2000), CC (Chester) [*Ex rel.* Irwin
    Mitchell, Solicitors, 31 Temple Street, Birmingham] . . . .   *Digested*, 01/**532**

Pilgrims Language Courses Ltd *v.* Customs and Excise Commissioners; *sub nom* Customs and Excise Commissioners *v.* Pilgrims Language Courses Ltd [1999] S.T.C. 874; [2000] E.L.R. 18; [1999] B.T.C. 5295; [1999] B.V.C. 328; (1999) 96(32) L.S.G. 34; *Times,* September 22, 1999, CA; reversing [1998] S.T.C. 784; [1998] B.T.C. 5267; [1998] B.V.C. 285; *Independent,* July 27, 1998 (C.S.), QBD .   *Digested,* 99/**4983**

Pilkington *v.* Inland Revenue Commissioners; *sub nom* Pilkington's Will Trusts, Re; Pilkington *v.* Pilkington [1964] A.C. 612; [1962] 3 W.L.R. 1051; [1962] 3 All E.R. 622; 40 T.C. 416; (1962) 41 A.T.C. 285; [1962] T.R. 265; 106 S.J. 834, HL; reversing [1961] Ch. 466; [1961] 2 W.L.R. 776; [1961] 2 All E.R. 330; 105 S.J. 422, CA; reversing [1959] Ch. 699; [1959] 3 W.L.R. 116; [1959] 2 All E.R. 623; 103 S.J. 528, Ch D . . . . *Digested,* 62/**2800**:
                     Applied, 66/11045, 83/3364: *Considered,* 70/2628, 74/993, 88/3683,
                              01/5507: *Distinguished,* 67/4075

Pilkington *v.* Pilkington see Pilkington *v.* Inland Revenue Commissioners
Pilkington *v.* Wood [1953] Ch. 770; [1953] 3 W.L.R. 522; [1953] 2 All E.R. 810; 97 S.J. 572, Ch D . . . . *Digested,* 53/**3775**:
             Applied, 83/1074: *Considered,* 79/658: *Distinguished,* 99/4033:
                    Explained, 64/3470: *Followed,* 69/3372, 69/3378

Pilkington Plc's Trade Mark Application (K GLASS) [2000] E.T.M.R. 1130, OHIM (3rd Bd App) . . . . *Digested,* 01/**4015**

Pilkington Trustees *v.* Inland Revenue Commissioners see Pearson *v.* Inland Revenue Commissioners
Pilkington's Will Trusts, Re see Pilkington *v.* Inland Revenue Commissioners
Pilmer *v.* Duke Group Ltd (In Liquidation) [2001] 2 B.C.L.C. 773, HC (Aus)
Piloting Tariffs in the Port of Genoa, Re; *sub nom* European Economic Community *v.* Italy [1998] 4 C.M.L.R. 91, CEC
Pilsen Urquell *v.* Industrie Poretti [1998] E.T.M.R. 168, It Cass (I)
Pinder *v.* Martin (Unreported, June 22, 1998), CC (Salford) [*Ex rel.* Lisa O Burdett Solicitors, Wigham House, Wakering Road, Barking, Essex] . . . . *Digested,* 98/**1458**
Pine Top Insurance Co *v.* Unione Italiana Anglo Saxon Reinsurance Co [1987] 1 Lloyd's Rep. 476, QBD (Comm Ct) . . . . *Digested,* 87/**2074**:
                                 Applied, 99/3426

Pine Valley Developments *v.* Ireland (A/222) (1992) 14 E.H.R.R. 319; *Times,* December 11, 1991, ECHR . . . . *Digested,* 92/**2363**:
                                 Followed, 98/4201

Ping (Europe) Ltd *v.* Customs and Excise Commissioners see Customs and Excise Commissioners *v.* Ping (Europe) Ltd
Pinios Shipping Co No. 1 *v.* National Bank of Greece SA see National Bank of Greece SA *v.* Pinios Shipping Co No. 1
Pinna *v.* Caisse d'Allocations Familiales de la Savoie (C41/84) [1986] E.C.R. 1; [1988] 1 C.M.L.R. 350, ECJ . . . . *Digested,* 88/**1551**:
                                 Applied, 98/4518

Pinner *v.* Everett [1969] 1 W.L.R. 1266; [1969] 3 All E.R. 257; (1977) 64 Cr. App. R. 160; 133 J.P. 653; [1970] R.T.R. 3; 113 S.J. 674, HL; reversing [1969] Crim. L.R. 378, DC . . . . *Digested,* 69/**3144**:
      Applied, 69/3146, 69/3154, 70/2516, 70/2518, 71/14159, 72/3019, 73/2903,
           73/2926, 73/3955, 77/2590: *Considered,* 69/3152, 70/2517, 70/2538,
           72/3010, 72/3043, 73/2924, 73/2929, 73/2932, 74/3325, 99/957:
               Distinguished, 71/14160: *Followed,* 70/2519, 73/2930

Pinochet Ugarte (Habeas Corpus), Re (2000) 97(1) L.S.G. 24; (2000) 144 S.J.L.B. 26; *Times,* February 16, 2000 . . . . *Digested,* 00/**45**
Pinochet Ugarte (No.1), Re see R. *v.* Bow Street Metropolitan Stipendiary Magistrate Ex p. Pinochet Ugarte (No.1)
Pinochet Ugarte (No.2), Re see R. *v.* Bow Street Metropolitan Stipendiary Magistrate Ex p. Pinochet Ugarte (No.2)
Pioneer Aggregates (UK) Ltd *v.* Secretary of State for the Environment [1985] A.C. 132; [1984] 3 W.L.R. 32; [1984] 2 All E.R. 358; 82 L.G.R. 488; (1984) 48 P. & C.R. 95; (1984) 272 E.G. 425; [1984] J.P.L. 651; (1984) 81 L.S.G. 2148; (1984) 128 S.J. 416, HL; affirming 82 L.G.R. 112; (1983) 267 E.G. 941; [1983] J.P.L. 733, CA; affirming (1983) 46 P. & C.R. 113; [1982] J.P.L. 371, QBD . . . . *Digested,* 84/**3465**:
            Applied, 85/3476, 86/3348, 92/4357, 00/4515: *Approved,* 99/4255:
           Considered, 89/3569, 90/3917, 90/4435, 91/3457, 92/4272, 92/4373,
             93/3956, 95/4770, 98/6136: *Distinguished,* 86/3337, 87/3710:
                           Followed, 88/3517, 89/3553

Pioneer Container, The; *sub nom* Owners of Cargo Lately Laden on Board the KH Enterprise *v.* Owners of the Pioneer Container [1994] 2 A.C. 324; [1994] 3 W.L.R. 1; [1994] 2 All E.R. 250; [1994] 1 Lloyd's Rep. 593; (1994) 91(18) L.S.G. 37; (1994) 138 S.J.L.B. 85; *Times,* March 29, 1994, PC (HK) . . . . *Digested,* 94/**255**:
                          Distinguished, 96/5298, 00/4678

Pioneer Hi-Bred Corn Co *v.* Hy-Line Chicks Pty Ltd [1979] R.P.C. 410, CA (NZ); affirming [1976] R.P.C. 294; [1975] 2 N.Z.L.R. 422, Sup Ct (NZ) . . . . *Digested,* 79/**2685**:
                                 Applied, 98/3521

Pioneer Oil Tools Ltd's Licence of Right (Copyright) Application [1997] R.P.C. 573, PO .   *Digested,* 98/**3496**:
                          Considered, 01/3854: *Followed,* 99/3448

Pioneer Seafood Ltd *v.* Braer Corp 1999 S.C.L.R. 1126; [2000] B.C.C. 680; 1999
   G.W.D. 20-956, OH . . . .   *Digested*, 00/**5916**
Pipeline Case, The (II R 12/92); *sub nom* Bundesfinanzhof (II R 12/92) 1 I.T.L. Rep. 163,
   BFH (Ger)
Piper *v.* Davies (Unreported, August 3, 1999), CC (Croydon) [*Ex rel.* George Davies,
   Pupil Barrister, 1 Temple Gardens, Temple, London] . . . .   *Digested*, 99/**2474**
Pirelli Cables Ltd *v.* United Thai Shipping Corp Ltd [2000] 1 Lloyd's Rep. 663; [2001]
   C.P. Rep. 7; (2000) 97(20) L.S.G. 46; *Times*, May 12, 2000, QBD . . . .   *Digested*, 00/**633**
Pirelli General Cable Works Ltd *v.* Oscar Faber & Partners [1983] 2 A.C. 1; [1983] 2
   W.L.R. 6; [1983] 1 All E.R. 65; (1983) 265 E.G. 979; *Times*, December 11, 1982,
   HL; reversing (1982) 262 E.G. 879, CA . . . .   *Digested*, 83/**2216**:
                  Applied, 83/2215, 84/212, 84/2284, 84/2675, 85/208, 85/212, 87/229,
                  87/2330, 88/2158, 96/1156, 01/4511, 01/4907: *Considered*, 84/214, 85/189,
                  89/2585, 89/3516, 90/3290, 91/2660, 93/2997: *Disapproved*, 96/4438:
                  Distinguished, 85/228, 86/1993, 87/2321, 92/3219: *Followed*, 88/2154,
                  94/6161: *Not followed*, 85/2303: *Referred to*, 84/240
Pirie's Application, Re; *sub nom* Alex Pirie and Son's Application, Re (1933) 50 R.P.C.
   147 . . . .   *Applied*, 78/2983,
                  91/3585: *Considered*, 98/3539: *Referred to*, 98/3500
Pistre (C321/94), Re; *sub nom* Pistre *v.* France (C321/94) [1997] E.C.R. I-2343;
   [1997] 2 C.M.L.R. 565; [1997] E.T.M.R. 457, ECJ (5th Chamber) . . . .   *Followed*, 01/2508
Pistre *v.* France (C321/94) see Pistre (C321/94), Re
Pitchers Ltd *v.* Plaza (Queensbury) Ltd [1940] 1 All E.R. 151, CA . . . .   *Applied*, 85/118:
                                        Considered, 01/345

Pitchmastic Plc *v.* Birse Construction Ltd see Dew Pitchmastic Plc *v.* Birse
   Construction Ltd (Compromise)
Pitman Training Ltd *v.* Nominet UK [1997-98] Info. T.L.R. 177; [1998] I.T.C.L.R. 17;
   [1997] F.S.R. 797; (1998) 17 Tr. L.R. 173; [1998] Masons C.L.R. 125; (1997)
   20(8) I.P.D. 20080, Ch D . . . .   *Digested*, 97/**4875**
Pitt *v.* Mond [2001] B.P.I.R. 624, Ch D . . . .   *Digested*, 01/**3789**
Pittham *v.* North Glamorgan NHS Trust (Unreported, March 22, 1998), CC (Cardiff)
   [*Ex rel.* Andrew Arentsen, Barrister, 33 Park Place, Cardiff] . . . .   *Digested*, 99/**1571**
PJ (Adoption: Practice on Appeal), Re; *sub nom* P-J (Minors) (Adoption Order: Practice
   on Appeal), Re [1998] 2 F.L.R. 252; [1998] Fam. Law 453; *Times*, June 4,
   1998, CA . . . .   *Digested*, 98/**2359**
PL *v.* France (1998) 25 E.H.R.R. 481, ECHR. . . . .   *Digested*, 98/**3072**
Planet Organic Ltd, Re see Elliott *v.* Planet Organic Ltd
Plant *v.* Plant [1998] 1 B.C.L.C. 38; [1998] B.P.I.R. 243, Ch D . . . .   *Digested*, 97/**3078**
Plant Construction Ltd *v.* JMH Construction Services Ltd see Plant Construction Plc *v.*
   Clive Adams Associates (No.2)
Plant Construction Plc *v.* Clive Adams Associates (No.1) 86 B.L.R. 119; 55 Con. L.R. 41,
   QBD (OR). . . . .   *Digested*, 98/**3934**
Plant Construction Plc *v.* Clive Adams Associates (No.2); *sub nom* Plant Construction
   Ltd *v.* JMH Construction Services Ltd [2000] B.L.R. 137; (2000) 2 T.C.L.R. 513;
   69 Con. L.R. 106; *Times*, March 1, 2000, CA; reversing in part 58 Con. L.R. 1,
   QBD (OR). . . . .   *Digested*, 00/**829**
Plant Construction Plc *v.* Clive Adams Associates (No.3) [2000] B.L.R. 205, QBD
   (T&CC) . . . .   *Digested*, 00/**4185**
Plantiflor Ltd *v.* Customs and Excise Commissioners see Customs and Excise
   Commissioners *v.* Plantiflor Ltd
Planton *v.* DPP see R. (on the application of Planton) *v.* DPP
Plastus Kreativ AB *v.* Minnesota Mining & Manufacturing Co see Minnesota Mining &
   Manufacturing Co *v.* Plastus Kreativ AB
Platform Home Loans Ltd *v.* Oyston Shipways Ltd [2000] 2 A.C. 190; [1999] 2 W.L.R.
   518; [1999] 1 All E.R. 833; [1999] C.L.C. 867; (1999) 1 T.C.L.R. 18; [1999]
   P.N.L.R. 469; [1999] 1 E.G.L.R. 77; [1999] 13 E.G. 119; [1999] E.G.C.S. 26;
   (1999) 96(10) L.S.G. 31; (1999) 149 N.L.J. 283; (1999) 143 S.J.L.B. 65; [1999]
   N.P.C. 21; *Times*, February 19, 1999; *Independent*, March 5, 1999, HL; reversing
   [1998] Ch. 466; [1998] 3 W.L.R. 94; [1998] 4 All E.R. 252; [1998] P.N.L.R.
   512; [1998] 1 E.G.L.R. 108; [1998] 13 E.G. 148; [1997] E.G.C.S. 184; (1998)
   95(1) L.S.G. 26; (1998) 142 S.J.L.B. 46; [1997] N.P.C. 185; *Times*, January 15,
   1998, CA; reversing in part [1996] 2 E.G.L.R. 110; [1996] 49 E.G. 112; [1996]
   E.G.C.S. 146, Ch D . . . .   *Digested*, 99/**1389**:
                      Considered, 97/3846: *Followed*, 98/4005
Plato Films Ltd *v.* Speidel; *sub nom* Speidel *v.* Plato Films Ltd; Speidel *v.* Unity Theatre
   Society [1961] A.C. 1090; [1961] 2 W.L.R. 470; [1961] 1 All E.R. 876; 105 S.J.
   230, HL; affirming [1960] 3 W.L.R. 391; [1960] 2 All E.R. 521; 104 S.J. 602,
   CA . . . .   *Digested*, 61/**4974**:
          Applied, 61/4995: *Considered*, 62/1741, 72/2029, 01/1820:
                                 Distinguished, 66/7003
Platt *v.* London Underground Ltd [2001] 20 E.G.C.S. 227; (2001) 98(17) L.S.G. 37;
   Times, March 13, 2001; *Independent*, April 2, 2001 (C.S), Ch D . . . .   *Digested*, 01/**4152**

Platt v. Platt [2001] 1 B.C.L.C. 698, CA; reversing in part [1999] 2 B.C.L.C. 745, Ch D
.... *Digested,* 01/**1526**:
Considered, 00/649

Platts v. Trustee Savings Bank Plc see TSB Bank Plc v. Platts (No.2)
Plaumann & Co v. Commission of the European Communities (C25/62) [1963] E.C.R.
95; [1963] E.C.R. 199; [1964] C.M.L.R. 29, ECJ................................ *Digested,* 64/**1440**:
Applied, 65/1518, 98/735, 98/2311

Playhut Inc v. Spring Form Inc; Spring Form Inc v. Playhut Inc [2000] F.S.R. 327;
(1999) 22(12) I.P.D. 22117; *Independent,* November 22, 1999 (C.S), Pat Ct.... *Digested,* 99/**3491**
Pledger v. Martin [2000] P.I.Q.R. P31, QBD .... *Digested,* 00/**579**
Plender v. Hyams see Hyams v. Plender
Plews v. British Railways Board (No.2) (Unreported, January 28, 1999), CC (York) [*Ex*
rel. Kama Melly, Barrister, 37 Park Square, Leeds] .... *Digested,* 99/**1411**
Plough Investments v. Eclipse Radio & Television Services see Plough Investments v.
Manchester City Council
Plough Investments v. Manchester City Council; Plough Investments v. Eclipse Radio &
Television Services [1989] 1 E.G.L.R. 244.............................. *Considered,* 01/4210
Plum v. Allgemeine Ortskrankenkasse Rheinland (Regionaldirektion Koln) (C404/98)
[2001] All E.R. (EC) 240; [2000] E.C.R. I-9379; [2001] 2 C.M.L.R. 7, ECJ (6th
Chamber)... *Digested,* 01/**5000**
Plumb v. Ayres, *Times,* May 11, 1999, CA .... *Digested,* 99/**355**
Plumbly (Personal Representatives of the Estate of Harbour) v. Spencer (Inspector of
Taxes) [1999] 2 E.G.L.R. 191; 71 T.C. 399; [1999] B.T.C. 246; (1999) 96(26)
L.S.G. 30, CA; reversing [1997] S.T.C. 301; [1997] B.T.C. 147; (1997) 94(9)
L.S.G. 32; (1997) 141 S.J.L.B. 46; *Times,* March 4, 1997; *Independent,* March 17,
1997 (C.S), Ch D; affirming [1996] S.T.C. (S.C.D.) 295, Sp Comm .... *Digested,* 99/**4657**
Plume v. Mason Bros (Butchers) Ltd [2000] 4 Q.R. 6, CC (Burton on Trent) [*Ex rel.*
Richard Gregory, Barrister, 24 The Ropewalk, Nottingham] .... *Digested,* 00/**1607**
Plummer v. Customs and Excise Commissioners [2001] S.T.I. 653, V&DTr
Plummer v. Tibsco Ltd (Preliminary Issue) [2000] I.C.R. 509; [1999] E.G.C.S. 140;
(1999) 96(47) L.S.G. 32; *Times,* December 1, 1999, Ch D .... *Digested,* 00/**3913**
Plunkett's Application for Judicial Review, Re see O'Boyle's Application for Judicial Review,
Re
Plymouth City Airport Ltd v. Secretary of State for the Environment, Transport and the
Regions see R. (on the application of Plymouth City Airport Ltd) v. Secretary of
State for the Environment, Transport and the Regions
Plymouth City Council v. C see C (A Child) v. Plymouth City Council
Plymouth City Council v. Gigg (1998) 30 H.L.R. 284, CA .... *Digested,* 97/**2691**
Plymouth City Council v. SBC Properties (1999) 14 P.A.D. 34, Planning Inspector
Podbielski v. Poland [1998] H.R.C.D. 1006, ECHR
Podd v. Internal Revenue Commissioner 1 I.T.L. Rep. 485, US Ct
Podd v. Internal Revenue Commissioner (Further Hearings) 1 I.T.L. Rep. 539, US Ct
Poel v. Poel [1970] 1 W.L.R. 1469; 114 S.J. 720, CA .... *Digested,* 70/**777**:
Applied, 87/2487, 94/3210, 94/3281, 95/3971, 96/543, 01/2596:
Considered, 80/1836, 83/2447, 93/2824, 94/2166, 95/3482, 95/3483,
96/644, 01/2588: *Followed,* 87/2492, 88/2340

Poeton Industries Ltd v. Horton see AT Poeton (Gloucester Plating) Ltd v. Horton
Poh, Re [1983] 1 W.L.R. 2; [1983] 1 All E.R. 2; (1983) 127 S.J. 16, HL .... *Digested,* 83/**2997**:
Applied, 92/3505: *Distinguished,* 98/381

Pointe Gourde Quarrying & Transport Co v. Sub-Intendent of Crown Lands [1947] A.C.
565; 63 T.L.R. 486, PC (Trin) .... *Digested,* 47-51/**1435**:
Applied, 67/3806, 70/321, 71/8934, 71/8984, 77/3265, 78/269, 89/361,
00/4426, 01/4666: *Considered,* 55/382, 64/485, 72/49, 74/371, 76/297,
77/323, 78/272, 79/306.1, 87/394, 90/582, 94/439, 94/459, 95/666,
95/3917: *Distinguished,* 69/429, 69/436, 69/3481, 70/320, 71/1493, 77/326:
Followed, 66/1529: *Referred to,* 80/2907

Pointer v. Landau see Landau (A Bankrupt), Re
Pointing v. Customs and Excise Commissioners [1999] F.S.R. 394, Ch D .... *Digested,* 99/**3459**
Poitrimol v. France (A/277-A) (1994) 18 E.H.R.R. 130, ECHR.................... *Digested,* 94/**2404**:
Followed, 00/3209
POLACLIP Trade Mark [1999] R.P.C. 282, TMR .... *Digested,* 99/**3539**:
Considered, 99/3541

Poladon Ltd v. Customs and Excise Commissioners [2001] S.T.I. 180, V&DTr
Pole v. Peake [1998] E.G.C.S. 125; [1998] N.P.C. 121; *Times,* July 22, 1998, CA....... *Digested,* 98/**4373**
Poleon v. Ramdhanie (Unreported, July 22, 1998), CC (Birmingham) [*Ex rel.* Timothy
Mayer, Pupil Barrister, 5 Fountain Court, Steelhouse Lane, Birmingham] ...... *Digested,* 98/**1740**
Polglass v. Oliver (1831) 2 Cr. & J. 15. .... *Applied,* 00/4621
Polhill Garden Centre Ltd v. Secretary of State for the Environment, Transport and the
Regions [1998] J.P.L. 1070, QBD... *Digested,* 98/**4224**
Police v. Beggs 8 B.H.R.C. 116, HC (NZ) .... *Digested,* 00/**3261**
Polinere v. Felicien [2000] 1 W.L.R. 890, PC (StL).............................. *Digested,* 00/**4642**
Polish Ocean Lines Joint Stock Co (formerly Polish Ocean Lines) v. MSC Mediterranean
Shipping Co SA see MSC Mediterranean Shipping Co SA v. Polish Ocean Lines
(The Tychy) (No.2)

Polish Steamship Co v. Atlantic Maritime Co (The Garden City) (No.2) [1985] Q.B. 41; [1984] 3 W.L.R. 300; [1984] 3 All E.R. 59; [1984] 2 Lloyd's Rep. 37; (1984) 81 L.S.G. 1367; (1984) 128 S.J. 469, CA; reversing [1983] Q.B. 687; [1983] 2 W.L.R. 798; [1983] 2 All E.R. 532; [1983] 1 Lloyd's Rep. 485; (1983) 127 S.J. 304, QBD (Adm Ct) .... *Digested*, 84/**3187**: *Distinguished*, 98/4411

Polkey v. AE Dayton Services Ltd; *sub nom* Polkey v. Edmund Walker (Holdings) Ltd [1988] A.C. 344; [1987] 3 W.L.R. 1153; [1987] 3 All E.R. 974; [1988] I.C.R. 142; [1987] I.R.L.R. 503; (1987) 137 N.L.J. 1109; (1988) 138 N.L.J. Rep. 33; (1987) 131 S.J. 1624, HL; reversing [1987] 1 W.L.R. 1147; [1987] 1 All E.R. 984; [1987] I.C.R. 301; [1987] I.R.L.R. 13; (1987) 84 L.S.G. 2690; (1987) 131 S.J. 1062, CA .... *Digested*, 88/**1353**: *Applied*, 89/1500, 90/1927, 92/1985, 96/2655, 98/2238, 99/2115, 99/2135, 00/2190: *Considered*, 86/1266, 89/1440, 90/1895, 92/1946, 92/1988, 94/2022, 94/2025, 94/2026, 95/2079, 95/2098, 96/2664, 97/2283, 01/2313: *Explained*, 99/6048: *Referred to*, 91/1704

Polkey v. Edmund Walker (Holdings) Ltd see Polkey v. AE Dayton Services Ltd

Poll v. Mohammed (Unreported, September 29, 1998), CC (Redditch) [*Ex rel*. Mark Whitcombe, Barrister, Hanover House, 47 Corn Street, Bristol] .... *Digested*, 99/**1518**

Pollard v. Ashurst see Ashurst v. Pollard

Pollard v. Chief Constable of West Yorkshire [1999] P.I.Q.R. P219, CA .... *Digested*, 98/**4257**

Pollitt Ex p. Minor, Re [1893] 1 Q.B. 455, CA; affirming [1893] 1 Q.B. 175, QBD ...... *Applied*, 00/3460: *Distinguished*, 72/193

Polly Peck International Plc (In Administration) (No.1), Re [1991] B.C.C. 503, Ch D ... *Digested*, 92/**2526**

Polly Peck International Plc (In Administration) (No.2), Re [1992] B.C.L.C. 1025; *Independent*, May 18, 1992 (C.S.), Ch D .... *Digested*, 93/**2318**

Polly Peck International Plc (In Administration) (No.3), Re; *sub nom* Secretary of State for Trade and Industry v. Ellis (No.2) [1993] B.C.C. 890; [1994] 1 B.C.L.C. 574, Ch D .... *Digested*, 94/**399**: *Considered*, 95/582

Polly Peck International Plc (In Administration) (No.4), Re; *sub nom* Barlow v. Polly Peck International Finance Ltd [1996] 2 All E.R. 433; [1996] B.C.C. 486; [1996] 1 B.C.L.C. 428, Ch D .... *Digested*, 96/**1032**

Polly Peck International Plc (In Administration) (No.5), Re; Marangos Hotel Co Ltd v. Stone [1998] 3 All E.R. 812; [1998] 2 B.C.L.C. 185; *Times*, May 18, 1998; *Independent*, May 13, 1998, CA; reversing [1997] 2 B.C.L.C. 630; (1997) 94(1) L.S.G. 23; (1997) 141 S.J.L.B. 21; [1996] N.P.C. 176; *Times*, December 27, 1996, Ch D .... *Digested*, 98/**3264**

Polly Peck International Plc (In Administration) v. Henry [1999] 1 B.C.L.C 407; [1998] O.P.L.R. 323; *Times*, December 16, 1998, Ch D .... *Digested*, 99/**3274**

Polly Peck (Holdings) Plc v. Trelford [1986] Q.B. 1000; [1986] 2 W.L.R. 845; [1986] 2 All E.R. 84, CA .... *Digested*, 86/**1988**: *Applied*, 86/1990, 90/2910: *Followed*, 99/1626

Polo Lauren Co's Trade Mark Application; *sub nom* 10 ROYAL BERKSHIRE POLO CLUB Trade Mark [2001] R.P.C. 32; [2001] E.T.M.R. CN11, TMR .... *Digested*, 01/**4056**

Polo/Lauren Co LP v. PT Dwidua Langgeng Pratama International Freight Forwarders (C383/98) [2000] E.C.R. I-2519; [2000] E.T.M.R. 535; *Times*, April 14, 2000, ECJ (1st Chamber) .... *Digested*, 00/**2341**

Polonski v. Lloyds Bank Mortgages Ltd [1998] 1 F.L.R. 896; [1998] 1 F.C.R. 282; (1999) 31 H.L.R. 721; [1998] Fam. Law 327; (1997) 141 S.J.L.B. 114; *Times*, May 6, 1997, Ch D .... *Digested*, 97/**4249**

Polpen Shipping Co Ltd v. Commercial Union Assurance Co Ltd [1943] K.B. 161; (1942) 74 Ll. L. Rep. 157, KBD .... *Not followed*, 01/5269

POLY COLOR Trade Mark (Unreported, September 21, 1999) .... *Applied*, 01/4015

Polychronakis v. Richards & Jerrom Ltd [1998] Env. L.R. 346; [1998] J.P.L. 588; *Times*, November 19, 1997; *Independent*, October 22, 1997, QBD .... *Digested*, 97/**2370**

Polymasc Pharmaceutical Plc v. Charles [1999] F.S.R. 711, Pat Ct .... *Digested*, 99/**2109**

Polypropylene Cartel (T7/89), Re see Hercules Chemicals NV v. Commission of the European Communities (C51/92 P)

Polysar Investments Netherlands BV v. Inspecteur der Invoerrechten en Accijnzen Arnhem (C60/90) [1993] S.T.C. 222; [1991] E.C.R. I-311; [1991] E.C.R. I-3111; *Times*, October 3, 1991, ECJ .... *Digested*, 91/**4146**: *Applied*, 94/4607, 99/4990: *Considered*, 96/5893, 97/4968

Pomaco Ltd's Trade Mark Application (No.1372819) see MINERVA Trade Mark

Pompes Funebres des Alpes Maritimes Sarl's Application, Re [1998] E.C.C. 6, CE (F)

Pontiac Marina Pte Ltd v. CDL Hotels International Ltd [1998] F.S.R. 839, CA (Sing); reversing [1997] F.S.R. 725, HC (Sing). .... *Digested*, 99/**3524**

Poole v. Lockwood [1981] R.T.R. 285; [1980] Crim. L.R. 730, DC .... *Digested*, 81/**2332**: *Applied*, 00/939

Poole BC v. Poole Football Supporters Club (2000) 15 P.A.D. 570, Planning Inspector

Poole Harbour Yacht Club Marina Ltd v. Excess Marine Insurance Ltd [2001] Lloyd's Rep. I.R. 580, QBD (Comm Ct) .... *Digested*, 01/**3806**

Poole Shopmobility v. Customs and Excise Commissioners [2000] S.T.I. 110, V&DTr

Pope (A Bankrupt), Re; *sub nom* Trustee of the Property of Pope *v.* Birmingham
　　Midshires Building Society [1998] B.P.I.R. 143; *Times*, March 24, 1997, Ch D . . .　　*Digested*, 97/**3012**
Popely *v.* Scott (2001) 165 J.P. 742; [2001] Crim. L.R. 417; (2001) 165 J.P.N. 907,
　　QBD . . . .　　*Digested*, 01/**720**
Poplar Housing & Regeneration Community Association Ltd *v.* Donoghue; *sub nom*
　　Donoghue *v.* Poplar Housing & Regeneration Community Association Ltd;
　　Poplar Housing & Regeneration Community Association Ltd *v.* Donaghue
　　[2001] EWCA Civ 595; [2001] 3 W.L.R. 183; [2001] 4 All E.R. 604; [2001] 2
　　F.L.R. 284; [2001] 3 F.C.R. 74; [2001] U.K.H.R.R. 693; (2001) 33 H.L.R. 73;
　　(2001) 3 L.G.L.R. 41; [2001] B.L.G.R. 489; [2001] A.C.D. 76; [2001] Fam. Law
　　588; [2001] 19 E.G.C.S. 141; (2001) 98(19) L.S.G. 38; (2001) 98(23) L.S.G.
　　38; (2001) 145 S.J.L.B. 122; [2001] N.P.C. 84; *Times*, June 21, 2001;
　　Independent, May 2, 2001; *Daily Telegraph*, May 8, 2001, CA　　　　　　　　*Digested*, 01/**4145**
Porcelli *v.* Strathclyde RC [1986] I.C.R. 564, 1 Div; affirming [1985] I.C.R. 177; [1984]
　　I.R.L.R. 467, EAT . . . .　　*Digested*, 86/**1243**:
　　　　　　　　　　　Considered, 86/1213, 93/1788, 94/1992: *Followed*, 98/2202
Porczynska Marzena Gappol Przedsiebiorstwo Prywntne's Trade Mark [2001] E.T.M.R. 96,
　　Urzsd Patentowy (PL)
Pordea *v.* Times Newspapers Ltd [2000] I.L.Pr. 763, Cass (F) . . . .　　*Digested*, 01/**818**
Porrini *v.* European Atomic Energy Community (C65/74); Bellintani *v.* European
　　Atomic Energy Community (C65/74) [1975] E.C.R. 319, ECJ . . . .　　*Digested*, 76/**1072**:
　　　　　　　　　　　　　　　　　　　　　　　　　　　　　Followed, 99/2057
Port Dues (C381/93), Re see Commission of the European Communities *v.* France (C381/
　　93)
Port of Melbourne Authority *v.* Anshun Pty (1981) 147 C.L.R. 589, HC (Aus) . . . .　　*Digested*, 84/**2704**:
　　　　　　　　　　　　　　　　　　　　　　　　　　　　　Considered, 99/5146
Portable Concrete Buildings *v.* Bathcrete [1962] R.P.C. 49 . . . .　　*Digested*, 62/**2256**:
　　　　　　　　　　　　　　　　　　　　　　　　　　　Distinguished, 00/3694
Portapath Ltd's Application (No.2019640) (1998) 21 (3) I.P.D. 21030, TMR
Portedge Ltd, Re see RWH Enterprises Ltd *v.* Portedge Ltd
Porter *v.* Chief Constable of Merseyside see Webb *v.* Chief Constable of Merseyside
Porter *v.* Ford Motor Co Ltd see Boyle *v.* Ford Motor Co Ltd
Porter *v.* Freudenberg; *sub nom* Merten's Patents, Re; Kreglinger *v.* S Samuel &
　　Rosenfeld [1915] 1 K.B. 857, CA . . . .　　*Applied*, 54/462,
　　　　　　　　　　79/2346: *Considered*, 80/128, 99/529: *Followed*, 79/2180:
　　　　　　　　　　　　　　　　　　　　　　　　　　　　　Not followed, 60/2573
Porter *v.* Magill; *sub nom* Magill *v.* Porter; Magill *v.* Weeks; Weeks *v.* Magill; Hartley *v.*
　　Magill; England *v.* Magill; Phillips *v.* Magill [2001] UKHL 67; (2001) 151 N.L.J.
　　1886; [2001] N.P.C. 184; *Times*, December 14, 2001; *Daily Telegraph*, December
　　20, 2001, HL; reversing [2000] 2 W.L.R. 1420; (1999) 31 H.L.R. 823; (1999) 1
　　L.G.L.R. 523; [1999] B.L.G.R. 375; (1999) 11 Admin. L.R. 661; (1999) 163
　　J.P.N. 1025; (1999) 96(21) L.S.G. 39; (1999) 143 S.J.L.B. 147; *Times*, May 6,
　　1999, CA; reversing (1998) 30 H.L.R. 997, QBD . . . .　　*Digested*, 99/**3871**
Porter *v.* Queens Moat Houses Plc see Bairstow *v.* Queens Moat Houses Plc
Porter *v.* Reader (Unreported, January 21, 2000), CC (Lowestoft) [*Ex rel.* Nigel
　　Waddington, Barrister, 8 Stone Buildings, Lincoln's Inn, London] . . . .　　*Digested*, 00/**444**
Porter *v.* United Parcels Services Ltd (Unreported, March 18, 1998), CC (Carlisle) [*Ex
　　rel.* Hough, Halton & Soal Solicitors, 32 Abbey Street, Carlisle] . . . .　　*Digested*, 98/**1580**
Porter *v.* Wilton Contracts Ltd (1999) 99(4) Q.R. 5, CC (Woolwich) [*Ex rel.* Robert
　　Weir, Barrister, Devereux Chambers, Devereux Court, London] . . . .　　*Digested*, 99/**1505**
Portington *v.* Greece [1998] H.R.C.D. 856, ECHR
Portman *v.* Latter [1942] W.N. 97 . . . .　　*Applied*, 00/1449:
　　　　　　　　　　　　　　　　　　　　　　　　　　　Distinguished, 47-51/5419
Portman Building Society *v.* Bevan Ashford [2000] Lloyd's Rep. Bank. 96; [2000]
　　Lloyd's Rep. P.N. 354; [2000] P.N.L.R. 344; (2000) 80 P. & C.R. 239; [2000] 1
　　E.G.L.R. 81; [2000] 07 E.G. 131; [2000] E.G.C.S. 2; (2000) 79 P. & C.R. D25,
　　CA
Portman Building Society *v.* Bond, *Independent*, May 4, 1998 (C.S.), Ch D . . . .　　*Digested*, 98/**320**
Portman Building Society *v.* Dusangh [2000] 2 All E.R. (Comm) 221; [2000] Lloyd's
　　Rep. Bank. 197; [2001] W.T.L.R. 117; [2000] N.P.C. 51; (2000) 80 P. & C.R. D20,
　　CA . . . .　　*Digested*, 00/**2333**
Portman Building Society *v.* Hamlyn Taylor Neck [1998] 4 All E.R. 202; [1998] P.N.L.R.
　　664; (1999) 77 P. & C.R. 66; [1998] 2 E.G.L.R. 113; [1998] 31 E.G. 102, CA;
　　affirming [1997] N.P.C. 35, Ch D . . . .　　*Digested*, 98/**2298**:
　　　　　　　　　　　　　　　　　　　　　　　　　　　　Considered, 99/3233
Portman Building Society *v.* Royal Insurance Plc (t/a Fox & Sons) [1998] P.N.L.R. 672,
　　CA . . . .　　*Digested*, 98/**330**
Portman Mortgage Services Ltd *v.* Bishop (1998) 30 H.L.R. 684, CA. . . . .　　*Digested*, 97/**4239**
Portman Provincial Cinemas, Re (1964) 108 S.J. 581, CA . . . .　　*Digested*, 64/**483**:
　　　　　　　　　Applied, 69/408: *Considered*, 98/3324: *Distinguished*, 90/530
Portsmouth City Council *v.* Bryant see Bryant *v.* Portsmouth City Council
Portsmouth City Council *v.* Memocourt Ltd (1998) 13 P.A.D. 553, Planning Inspector
Portugal *v.* Commission of the European Communities (C159/96) [1998] E.C.R. I-
　　7379; [2001] 1 C.M.L.R. 33, ECJ (6th Chamber) . . . .　　*Digested*, 01/**2467**

Portuguese Consolidated Copper Mines Ltd Ex p. Badman, Re; *sub nom* Portuguese Consolidated Copper Mines Ltd Ex p. Bosanquet, Re (1890) L.R. 45 Ch. D. 16, CA

Portuguese Consolidated Copper Mines Ltd Ex p. Bosanquet, Re see Portuguese Consolidated Copper Mines Ltd Ex p. Badman, Re

Poseidon Film Distributors Ltd *v.* Christoffer see Christoffer *v.* Poseidon Film Distributors Ltd

Poseidon Film Distributors Ltd *v.* Paik see Christoffer *v.* Poseidon Film Distributors Ltd

Poseidon Inc *v.* Inspector of Taxes see Goodbrand (Inspector of Taxes) *v.* Loffland Bros North Sea Inc

Poseidon Schiffahrt GmbH *v.* Nomadic Navigation Co Ltd (The Trade Nomad) [1999] 1 All E.R. (Comm.) 454; [1999] 1 Lloyd's Rep. 723; [1999] C.L.C. 755, CA; affirming [1998] 1 Lloyd's Rep. 57; [1997] C.L.C. 1542; *Times,* October 9, 1997, QBD (Comm Ct) . . . . *Digested,* 99/**4431**

Post Office *v.* Adekeye see Adekeye *v.* Post Office (No.2)

Post Office *v.* Aquarius Properties Ltd [1987] 1 All E.R. 1055; (1987) 54 P. & C.R. 61; [1987] 1 E.G.L.R. 40; (1987) 281 E.G. 798; (1987) 84 L.S.G. 820, CA; affirming [1985] 2 E.G.L.R. 105; (1985) 276 E.G. 923 . . . . *Digested,* 87/**2141**:
Considered, 86/1854, 87/2140, 93/2463, 95/3062: *Distinguished,* 98/3628

Post Office *v.* British World Airlines Ltd [2000] 1 All E.R. (Comm) 532; [2000] 1 Lloyd's Rep. 378; [2000] C.L.C. 581, QBD (Comm Ct) . . . . *Digested,* 00/**4555**

Post Office *v.* Foley see Foley *v.* Post Office

Post Office *v.* Footitt [2000] I.R.L.R. 243, QBD. . . . . *Digested,* 00/**2979**

Post Office *v.* Howell [2000] I.C.R. 913; [2000] I.R.L.R. 224; *Times,* November 11, 1999, EAT. . . . . *Digested,* 99/**2050**:
Applied, 01/2270

Post Office *v.* Jones see Jones *v.* Post Office

Post Office *v.* Sanhotra [2000] I.C.R. 866, EAT . . . . *Digested,* 00/**2243**

Postbank NV *v.* Commission of the European Communities (T353/94) [1996] All E.R. (E.C.) 817; [1996] E.C.R. II-921; [1997] 4 C.M.L.R. 33, CFI (1st Chamber) . . . . . *Digested,* 97/**2389**:
Distinguished, 00/713

Postcards of Film Posters (99-D-34), Re [2000] E.C.C. 187, C Concurrence (F)

Postermobile Plc *v.* Brent LBC, *Times,* December 8, 1997, QBD . . . . *Digested,* 98/**4159**

Postermobile Plc *v.* Kensington and Chelsea RLBC (2000) 80 P. & C.R. 524; [2001] J.P.L. 196; [2000] C.O.D. 500; [2000] E.G.C.S. 68; (2000) 97(23) L.S.G. 46, QBD. . . . . *Digested,* 01/**4727**

Postle *v.* Norfolk and Norwich NHS Healthcare Trust (Unreported, September 19, 2000), CC (Norwich) [*Ex rel.* Nicholas Yell, Barrister, No. 1 Sergeants' Inn, Fleet Street, London]. . . . . *Digested,* 00/**2970**

Postle *v.* Norfolk and Norwich NHS Healthcare Trust (Damages) [2001] 1 Q.R. 10, CC (Norwich) [*Ex rel.* Nicholas Yell, Barrister, No. 1 Serjeants' Inn, Fleet Street, London] . . . . *Digested,* 01/**1648**

Postlethwaite, Re see Belgium *v.* Postlethwaite

POSTPERFECT Trade Mark [1998] R.P.C. 255, Appointed Person . . . . *Digested,* 98/**3524**

Potato Marketing Board *v.* Hampden-Smith [1997] Eu. L.R. 435, CA . . . . *Digested,* 98/**723**

Potier *v.* Secretary of State for Trade and Industry see Kaytech International Plc, Re

Potter *v.* Arafa [1995] I.R.L.R. 316; [1994] P.I.Q.R. Q73, CA . . . . *Digested,* 95/**1615**:
Considered, 98/1444

Potter *v.* Pinches & Son Ltd (Unreported, July 26, 2000), CC (Worcester) [*Ex rel.* Paul Considine, Barrister, 1 Fountain Court, Steelhouse Lane, Birmingham] . . . . *Digested,* 00/**3550**:
Applied, 01/905

Potter *v.* Secretary of State for Employment see Mann *v.* Secretary of State for Education and Employment

Pottinger (A Minor) *v.* Bendigo Construction Co Ltd (Unreported, April 7, 1998), CC (Nottingham) [*Ex rel.* Nelsons Solicitors, Pennine House, 8 Stanford Street, Nottingham] . . . . *Digested,* 98/**1693**

Potton Developments Ltd *v.* Thompson [1998] N.P.C. 49, Ch D

Potton Ltd *v.* Yorkclose Ltd [1990] F.S.R. 11; *Times,* April 4, 1989, Ch D . . . . *Digested,* 89/**492**:
Applied, 98/3496

Pounds Shipowners & Shipbreakers Ltd *v.* Garner (Inspector of Taxes) see Garner (Inspector of Taxes) *v.* Pounds Shipowners & Shipbreakers Ltd

Poundstretcher *v.* Secretary of State for the Environment [1988] 3 P.L.R. 69; [1989] J.P.L. 90 . . . . *Digested,* 89/**3560**:
Considered, 00/4506, 01/4736: *Referred to,* 96/4819

Powdrill *v.* Hambros Bank (Jersey) Ltd see Paramount Airways Ltd (No.2), Re

Powdrill *v.* Watson; *sub nom* Paramount Airways Ltd (No.3), Re; Talbot *v.* Cadge;
Talbot *v.* Grundy; Leyland DAF Ltd (No.2), Re; Ferranti International Plc, Re
[1995] 2 A.C. 394; [1995] 2 W.L.R. 312; [1995] 2 All E.R. 65; [1995] B.C.C.
319; [1994] 1 B.C.L.C. 386; [1995] I.C.R. 1100; [1995] I.R.L.R. 269; (1995)
92(17) L.S.G. 47; (1995) 145 N.L.J. 449; (1995) 139 S.J.L.B. 110; *Times,* March
23, 1995; *Independent,* March 23, 1995, HL; affirming [1994] 2 All E.R. 513;
[1994] B.C.C. 172; [1994] 2 B.C.L.C. 118; [1994] I.C.R. 395; [1994] I.R.L.R.
295; (1994) 91(22) L.S.G. 32; (1994) 91(15) L.S.G. 35; (1994) 144 N.L.J. 389;
(1994) 138 S.J.L.B. 76; *Times,* March 1, 1994; *Independent,* March 22, 1994,
CA; affirming [1993] B.C.C. 662; *Times,* September 14, 1993, Ch D (Companies
Ct) . . . . *Digested,* 95/**2816**:
Considered, 00/3430, 01/420: *Not followed,* 97/6158:
Previous proceedings, 94/2593, 95/1540
Powdrill and Lyle (Joint Liquidators of Kentish Homes Ltd) *v.* Tower Hamlets LBC; *sub
nom* Kentish Homes Ltd, Re [1993] B.C.C. 212; [1993] B.C.L.C. 1375; [1993]
R.A. 39; (1993) 137 S.J.L.B. 45; [1992] N.P.C. 12; *Times,* February 11, 1993 . . . . *Digested,* 93/**2626**:
Disapproved, 00/3467
Powell *v.* Boladz; *sub nom* Powell *v.* Boldaz [1998] Lloyd's Rep. Med. 116; (1998) 39
B.M.L.R. 35, CA
Powell *v.* Cheltenham BC [2001] R.V.R. 144, Lands Tr . . . . *Digested,* 01/**4850**
Powell *v.* Chief Constable of North Wales, *Times,* February 11, 2000, CA . . . . *Digested,* 00/**944**
Powell *v.* McFarlane (1979) 38 P. & C.R. 452, Ch D . . . . *Digested,* 79/**2248**:
Applied, 88/470, 89/449, 94/567, 94/568, 01/4843: *Considered,* 88/2155,
89/448, 89/3547, 91/546, 92/534, 99/4348: *Distinguished,* 92/568,
93/556: *Followed,* 01/4844: *Referred to,* 93/524, 95/843
Power *v.* Chief Constable of Lancashire see Hunter *v.* Chief Constable of the West
Midlands
Power *v.* Customs and Excise Commissioners [2001] B.V.C. 2082; [2000] V. & D.R.
175; [2000] S.T.I. 1622, V&DTr
Power *v.* Provincial Insurance Plc (1997) 161 J.P. 556; [1998] R.T.R. 60; (1997) 94(11)
L.S.G. 35; (1997) 141 S.J.L.B. 71; *Times,* February 27, 1997, CA . . . . *Digested,* 97/**3165**
Powerflex Services Pty *v.* Data Access Corp see Data Access Corp *v.* Powerflex
Services Pty Ltd
PowerGen Plc, Re (C157/97P(I)) see National Power Plc, Re (C151/97P(I))
Powergen UK Plc *v.* Leicester City Council; *sub nom* R. *v.* Leicester City Council Ex p.
Powergen UK Plc (2001) 81 P. & C.R. 5; [2000] J.P.L. 1037; [2000] E.G.C.S.
64; [2000] N.P.C. 57; *Independent,* July 3, 2000 (C.S), CA; affirming (2000)
80 P. & C.R. 176; [1999] 4 P.L.R. 91; [2000] J.P.L. 629; [2000] C.O.D. 85;
[1999] E.G.C.S. 130; (1999) 96(44) L.S.G. 42, QBD . . . . *Digested,* 01/**4756**:
Cited, 01/4738
Powerstore (Trading) Ltd, Re; Homepower Stores Ltd, Re [1997] 1 W.L.R. 1280; [1998] 1 All
E.R. 121; [1998] B.C.C. 305; [1998] 1 B.C.L.C. 90; (1997) 94(24) L.S.G. 31; (1997)
141 S.J.L.B. 137; *Times,* May 19, 1997, Ch D (Companies Ct) . . . . *Digested,* 97/**3051**:
Considered, 98/3346, 99/3361, 01/3708: *Not followed,* 99/3349
Powys CC *v.* Edwards (1998) 13 P.A.D. 433, Planning Inspector
Powys CC *v.* National Assembly for Wales [2000] P.L.C.R. 385; [2000] J.P.L. 1180
(Note); [2000] N.P.C. 35, QBD . . . . *Digested,* 01/**4743**
Poynter *v.* Hillingdon HA (1997) 37 B.M.L.R. 192, QBD . . . . *Digested,* 98/**3983**
Poyser *v.* Minors (1880-81) L.R. 7 Q.B.D. 329, CA . . . . *Applied,* 00/**5517**:
Considered, 64/320, 90/749
Pozzolanic Lytag Ltd *v.* Bryan Hobson Associates [1999] B.L.R. 267; (1999) 1 T.C.L.R.
233; 63 Con. L.R. 81; [1999] Lloyd's Rep. P.N. 125; (1999) 15 Const. L.J. 135;
(1999) 143 S.J.L.B. 30; *Times,* December 3, 1998, QBD (T&CC) . . . . *Digested,* 99/**3973**
PPG/Coating (T823/96) [1999] E.P.O.R. 417, EPO (Technical Bd App) . . . . *Digested,* 99/**3473**
PPG/Epoxide compositions (T579/94) [2000] E.P.O.R. 584, EPO (Technical Bd App) . *Digested,* 01/**3920**
PPG/Ungelled polyesters (T222/85) [1987] E.P.O.R. 99, EPO (Technical Bd App) . . . . *Followed,* 00/3612
Practice Direction (CA: Citation of Authorities) [2001] 1 W.L.R. 1001; [2001] 2 All E.R. 510;
[2001] 1 Lloyd's Rep. 725; [2001] C.P.L.R. 301; [2001] 1 F.C.R. 764; (2001) 145
S.J.L.B. 132; *Times,* May 1, 2001, CA. . . . . *Digested,* 01/**623**
Practice Direction (CA: Consolidation: Notice of Consolidation) [1999] 1 W.L.R. 1027;
[1999] 2 All E.R. 490; *Times,* April 26, 1999, CA . . . . *Digested,* 99/**507**:
Followed, 99/362, 99/2421, 01/80: *Referred to,* 00/477
Practice Direction (CA (Crim Div): Costs in Criminal Proceedings); *sub nom* Practice
Direction (Sup Ct: Crime: Costs) [1991] 1 W.L.R. 498; [1991] 2 All E.R. 924;
(1991) 93 Cr. App. R. 89; *Times,* May 20, 1991, CA (Crim Div) . . . . *Digested,* 91/**722**:
Considered, 94/3620, 98/1012: *Followed,* 99/984: *Referred to,* 99/1040
Practice Direction (CA (Crim Div): Crime: Antecedents) [1997] 1 W.L.R. 1482; [1997] 4 All
E.R. 350; [1998] 1 Cr. App. R. 213; *Times,* October 15, 1997, CA (Crim Div) . . . . *Digested,* 97/**1365**:
Referred to, 00/4001
Practice Direction (CA (Crim Div): Crime: Voluntary Bills) [1990] 1 W.L.R. 1633; [1991] 1 All
E.R. 288; (1991) 92 Cr. App. R. 146; [1991] Crim. L.R. 470; *Times,* December 13,
1990 ; *Independent,* December 14, 1990, CA (Crim Div) . . . . *Digested,* 91/**890**:
Superseded, 99/1042

Practice Direction (CA (Crim Div): Criminal Appeal Office Summaries) (No.1) [1992] 1
W.L.R. 938; [1992] 4 All E.R. 408; (1992) 95 Cr. App. R. 455; *Times*, October 7,
1992; *Independent*, October 14, 1992, CA (Crim Div) . . . .   *Digested*, 92/**681**:
                                      Cited, 00/1088

Practice Direction (CA (Crim Div): Criminal Appeal Office Summaries) (No.2) [2000] 1
W.L.R. 1177; [2000] 2 Cr. App. R. 178; (2000) 144 S.J.L.B. 164; *Times*, May 24,
2000, CA (Crim Div) . . . .   *Digested*, 00/**1088**

Practice Direction (CA (Crim Div): Criminal Appeals: Skeleton Arguments); *sub nom*
Practice Note (CA (Crim Div): Practice: Skeleton Arguments) [1999] 1 W.L.R.
146; [1999] 1 All E.R. 669; [1999] 1 Cr. App. R. 335; *Times*, December 31, 1998,
CA (Crim Div) . . . .   *Digested*, 99/**1041**

Practice Direction (CA (Crim Div): Custodial Sentences: Explanations); *sub nom* Practice
Direction (Sup Ct: Custodial Sentences) [1998] 1 W.L.R. 278; [1998] 1 All E.R.
733; [1998] 1 Cr. App. R. 397; (1998) 148 N.L.J. 158; (1998) 142 S.J.L.B. 52;
Times, January 24, 1998, CA (Crim Div) . . . .   *Digested*, 98/**1333**

Practice Direction (CA (Crim Div) (NI): Notice of Appeal Against Conviction or Sentence)
[1994] N.I. 73, CA (Crim Div) (NI) . . . .   *Digested*, 00/**5483**

Practice Direction (CA (Crim Div): Victim Personal Statements) [2001] 1 W.L.R. 2038;
[2001] 4 All E.R. 640; (2001) 165 J.P. 759; (2001) 145 S.J.L.B. 229; *Times*,
November 6, 2001, CA (Crim Div) . . . .   *Digested*, 01/**1180**

Practice Direction (CA: Hear-by Dates) [1998] 1 W.L.R. 1699; [1999] 1 All E.R. 287; *Times*,
November 16, 1998, CA . . . .   *Digested*, 98/**576**

Practice Direction (CA: Judges: Modes of Address) [1982] 1 W.L.R. 101; [1982] 1 All E.R.
320; (1982) 74 Cr. App. R. 193, CA . . . .   *Digested*, 82/**2516**:
                                   Superseded, 99/515

Practice Direction (CA: Jurisdiction: Consolidated Practice: Civil Appeals: Litigants in
Person) [1999] C.P.L.R. 330, CA. . . . .   *Digested*, 99/**510**

Practice Direction (CA: Leave to Appeal and Skeleton Arguments) [1999] 1 W.L.R. 2;
[1999] 1 All E.R. 186; *Times*, November 23, 1998, CA . . . .   *Digested*, 98/**575**:
              Applied, 99/511: *Explained*, 99/355

Practice Direction (CA: Procedural Changes) see Practice Direction (CA: Procedure)

Practice Direction (CA: Procedure); *sub nom* Practice Note (CA: Procedure); Practice
Direction (CA: Procedural Changes) [1995] 1 W.L.R. 1191; [1995] 3 All E.R.
850; [1995] 4 Re. L.R. 279, CA . . . .   *Digested*, 96/**865**:
        Considered, 98/379: *Superseded in part*, 97/696, 98/575

Practice Direction (CA: Revised Procedure); *sub nom* Practice Note (CA: Procedural
Changes) [1997] 1 W.L.R. 1013; [1997] 2 All E.R. 927; *Times*, May 14, 1997, CA .   *Digested*, 97/**697**:
                                   Superseded, 98/576

Practice Direction (CA: Skeleton Arguments and Case Management) [1997] 1 W.L.R.
1535; [1997] 4 All E.R. 830; [1998] 1 F.C.R. 45; *Times*, November 7, 1997, CA .   *Digested*, 97/**696**

Practice Direction (Ch D: Applications Made under Companies Act 1985 and Insurance Act
1982) [1999] B.C.C. 741, Ch D . . . .   *Digested*, 99/**639**

Practice Direction (Ch D: Bankruptcy: Substituted Service) [1987] 1 W.L.R. 82; [1987] 1 All
E.R. 604; (1987) 131 S.J. 1024, Ch D . . . .   *Digested*, 86/**2576**:
                                   Referred to, 00/3484

Practice Direction (Ch D: Companies Court: Directors Disqualification) (No.2 of 1995)
[1996] 1 W.L.R. 170; [1996] 1 All E.R. 442; [1996] B.C.C. 11, Ch D . . . .   *Digested*, 96/**1015**:
                                   Applied, 98/681

Practice Direction (Ch D: Estates of Deceased Lloyd's Names) [1998] 1 Lloyd's Rep. 223,
Ch D . . . .   *Digested*, 98/**573**:
                                   Superseded, 01/625

Practice Direction (Ch D: Insolvency Proceedings) (No.1) [1999] B.C.C. 727; [1999]
B.P.I.R. 441, Ch D . . . .   *Digested*, 99/**3318**:
                                   Cited, 01/3775

Practice Direction (Ch D: Insolvency Proceedings) (No.2) [2000] B.C.C. 927; [2000]
B.P.I.R. 647, Ch D . . . .   *Digested*, 01/**3775**

Practice Direction (Ch D: Interim Applications to Chancery Division); *sub nom* Practice
Note (Ch D: Civil Procedure Rules) [1999] B.C.C. 846; *Times*, May 4, 1999,
Ch D . . . .   *Digested*, 99/**506**

Practice Direction (Ch D: Trust Proceedings: Prospective Costs Orders) see Practice
Statement (Ch D: Trust Proceedings: Prospective Costs Orders)

Practice Direction (Coal Mining Vibration White Finger Actions) see Practice Direction
(QBD: Vibration White Finger Actions) (No.3)

Practice Direction (Committal Applications) (Unreported, May 28, 1999) . . . .   *Applied*, 01/2637

Practice Direction (Companies: Directors Disqualification Proceedings) [1999] B.C.C. 717
                                     Digested, 99/**640**

Practice Direction (CP: Court of Protection: Solicitors Fixed Costs) (2001) 145 S.J.L.B. 4,
CP

Practice Direction (CP: Solicitors Agreed Costs) (2000) 144 S.J.L.B. 265, CP

Practice Direction (Creutzfeldt-Jakob Disease Litigation: Damages) see Practice Direction
(Sup Ct: Creutzfeldt-Jakob Disease Litigation: Damages)

Practice Direction (Crown Ct: Abuse of Process Applications) [2000] 1 W.L.R. 1322;
[2000] 3 All E.R. 384; [2000] 2 Cr. App. R. 179; (2000) 144 S.J.L.B. 164;
Times, May 30, 2000, CA (Crim Div) . . . .   *Digested*, 00/**1094**

Practice Direction (Crown Ct: Allocation of Business) (No.1) [1995] 1 W.L.R.1083; [1995]
2 All E.R. 900; [1995] 2 Cr. App. R. 235, CA (Crim Div) . . . .   *Superseded in part,*
01/1178

Practice Direction (Crown Ct: Allocation of Business) (No.2); *sub nom* Practice Note
(Crown Ct: Allocation of Business) (No.2) [1998] 1 W.L.R. 1244; [1998] 3 All
E.R. 384; [1998] 2 Cr. App. R. 446, CA (Crim Div) . . . .   *Digested,* 98/**1076**:
Superseded in part, 00/1091, 01/1178

Practice Direction (Crown Ct: Allocation of Business) (No.3) [2000] 1 W.L.R. 203; [2000]
1 All E.R. 380; [2000] 1 Cr. App. R. 345; *Times,* January 18, 2000, Sup Ct . . . . .   *Digested,* 00/**1091**:
Superseded in part, 01/1178

Practice Direction (Crown Ct: Allocation of Business) (No.4) [2001] 1 W.L.R. 399; [2001]
2 All E.R. 703; [2001] 1 Cr. App. R. 30; (2001) 145 S.J.L.B. 51; *Times,* February 22,
2001, Sup Ct. . . . .   *Digested,* 01/**1178**

Practice Direction (Crown Ct: Business) [2001] 1 W.L.R. 1996; [2001] 4 All E.R. 635;
(2001) 145 S.J.L.B. 227, CA (Crim Div)

Practice Direction (Crown Ct: Fraud Trials) (No.3) [1993] 1 W.L.R.158; [1993] 1 All E.R. 41,
Sup Ct . . . .   *Superseded,* 98/1077

Practice Direction (Crown Ct: Fraud Trials) (No.4); *sub nom* Practice Direction (Sup Ct:
Criminal Justice Act 1987: Crown Court Centres); Practice Note (CA (Crim
Div): Crown Court: Distribution of Court Business) [1998] 1 W.L.R. 1692;
[1998] 4 All E.R. 1023; [1999] 1 Cr. App. R. 142; *Times,* November 13, 1998, Sup
Ct. . . . .   *Digested,* 98/**1077**

Practice Direction (Crown Ct: Plea and Directions Hearings) [1995] 1 W.L.R.1318; [1995] 4
All E.R. 379; [1995] 2 Cr. App. R. 600, Sup Ct . . . .   *Digested,* 96/**1658**:
Referred to, 00/3978

Practice Direction (Crown Ct: Trial of Children and Young Persons); *sub nom* Practice Note
(QBD: Crown Ct: Trial of Children and Young Persons) [2000] 1 W.L.R. 659;
[2000] 2 All E.R. 285; [2000] 1 Cr. App. R. 483; (2000) 144 S.J.L.B. 46; *Times,*
February 17, 2000, Sup Ct . . . .   *Digested,* 00/**1090**

Practice Direction (EAT: Procedure) [1996] I.C.R. 422; [1996] I.R.L.R. 430, EAT . . . . .   *Digested,* 96/**2579**:
Cited, 01/2268

Practice Direction (ECJ & CFI: Codified Version of the Rules of Procedure) [2001] All E.R.
(EC) 671, ECJ

Practice Direction (ECJ: References to the ECJ by CA and HC under Art.177) see Practice
Direction (Sup Ct: References to the Court of Justice of the European Communities)

Practice Direction (EFTA: Guidance of Counsel in Written and Oral Proceedings) [1999] All
E.R. (EC) 545; [1999] 2 C.M.L.R. 883, EFTA . . . .   *Digested,* 99/**3624**

Practice Direction (EFTA: Guidance on Requests by National Courts for Advisory Opinions)
[1999] 3 C.M.L.R. 525, EFTA . . . .   *Digested,* 00/**2362**

Practice Direction (Fam Div: Ancillary Relief Procedure) [2000] 1 W.L.R.1480; [2000] 3 All
E.R. 379; [2000] 1 F.L.R. 997; [2000] 2 F.C.R. 216; *Times,* July 4, 2000, Fam Div
Digested, 00/**2552**

Practice Direction (Fam Div: Arresting Officer: Attendance); *sub nom* President's
Direction (Family Law Act 1996: Attendance of Arresting Officer) [2000] 1
W.L.R. 83; [2000] 1 All E.R. 544; [2000] 1 F.L.R. 270; [2000] 1 F.C.R. 86;
Times, January 19, 2000, Fam Div . . . .   *Digested,* 00/**2549**

Practice Direction (Fam Div: Children Act 1989: Exclusion Requirement) see Practice
Direction (Fam Div: Exclusion Requirement: Procedure on Arrest)

Practice Direction (Fam Div: Civil Procedure Rules 1998: Allocation of Cases: Costs) see
Practice Direction (Fam Div: Family Proceedings: Allocation of Costs)

Practice Direction (Fam Div: Contempt of Court: Committal) see Practice Direction (Fam
Div: Domestic Violence: Procedure on Arrest) (No.2)

Practice Direction (Fam Div: Costs: Civil Procedure Rules 1998); *sub nom* Practice
Direction (Fam Div: Proceedings: Costs) [2000] 1 W.L.R. 1781; [2000] 4 All
E.R. 1072; [2000] 2 F.L.R. 428; [2000] 2 F.C.R. 767; *Times,* October 24, 2000,
Fam Div . . . .   *Digested,* 00/**2551**

Practice Direction (Fam Div: Deaths in USA on 11 September 2001) (2001) 145 S.J.L.B.
235, Fam Div

Practice Direction (Fam Div: Domestic Violence: Procedure on Arrest) (No.2); *sub nom*
Practice Direction (Fam Div: Family Law Act 1996 Part IV); Practice Direction
(Fam Div: Contempt of Court: Committal) [1998] 1 W.L.R. 476; [1998] 2 All
E.R. 927; [1998] 1 F.L.R. 496; [1998] 1 F.C.R. 337, Fam Div . . . .   *Digested,* 98/**2482**

Practice Direction (Fam Div: Exclusion Requirement: Procedure on Arrest); *sub nom*
Practice Direction (Fam Div: Children Act 1989: Exclusion Requirement) [1998]
1 W.L.R. 475; [1998] 2 All E.R. 928; [1998] 1 F.L.R. 495; [1998] 1 F.C.R. 338,
Fam Div . . . .   *Digested,* 98/**2481**

Practice Direction (Fam Div: Family Law Act 1996 Part IV) see Practice Direction (Fam Div:
Domestic Violence: Procedure on Arrest) (No.2)

Practice Direction (Fam Div: Family Proceedings: Allocation of Costs); *sub nom* Practice
Direction (Fam Div: Civil Procedure Rules 1998: Allocation of Cases: Costs);
Practice Direction (Fam Div: Family Proceedings: Costs) [1999] 1 W.L.R. 1128;
[1999] 3 All E.R. 192; [1999] 1 F.L.R. 1295; [1999] 2 F.C.R. 1; *Times,* May 4,
1999, Fam Div. . . . .   *Digested,* 99/**512**

Practice Direction (Fam Div: Family Proceedings: Allocation to Judiciary 1991) [1991] 1
    W.L.R. 1178; [1991] 4 All E.R. 764; [1991] 2 F.L.R. 463, Fam Div . . . .   *Digested*, 92/**2109**:
                                                  Referred to, 98/2483
Practice Direction (Fam Div: Family Proceedings: Allocation to Judiciary 1993)
    Unreported, Fam Div . . . .   *Superseded*, 98/2483
Practice Direction (Fam Div: Family Proceedings: Allocation to Judiciary 1997) [1997] 2
    F.L.R. 780; [1998] 1 F.C.R. 133, Fam Div. . . . .   *Digested*, 98/**2483**
Practice Direction (Fam Div: Family Proceedings: Allocation to Judiciary 1999) [1999] 2
    F.L.R. 799, Fam Div
Practice Direction (Fam Div: Family Proceedings: Case Management) [1995] 1 W.L.R. 332;
    [1995] 1 All E.R. 586; [1995] 1 F.L.R. 456; *Independent*, March 13, 1995, Fam Div

                                                  Digested, 95/**2296**:
               Considered, 96/489, 96/511: *Referred to*, 00/2550
Practice Direction (Fam Div: Family Proceedings: Committal) [2001] 1 W.L.R. 1253;
    [2001] 2 All E.R. 704; [2001] 1 F.C.R. 767, Fam Div . . . .   *Digested*, 01/**2661**
Practice Direction (Fam Div: Family Proceedings: Costs) see Practice Direction (Fam Div:
    Family Proceedings: Allocation of Costs)
Practice Direction (Fam Div: Family Proceedings: Court Bundles) [2000] 1 W.L.R. 737;
    [2000] 2 All E.R. 287; [2000] 1 F.L.R. 537; [2000] 1 F.C.R. 521; (2000) 144 S.J.L.B.
    74; *Times*, March 22, 2000, Fam Div. . . . .   *Digested*, 00/**2550**:
                                            Cited, 00/2553, 00/2554
Practice Direction (Fam Div: Family Proceedings: Financial Dispute Resolution) [1997] 1
    W.L.R. 1069; [1997] 3 All E.R. 768; [1997] 2 F.L.R. 304; [1997] 3 F.C.R. 476; *Times*,
    July 15, 1997, Fam Div . . . .   *Digested*, 97/**2497**:
                                                  Cited, 00/2552
Practice Direction (Fam Div: Human Rights Act 1998: Citation of Authorities); *sub nom*
    Practice Direction (Fam Div: Proceedings: Human Rights) [2000] 1 W.L.R.
    1782; [2000] 4 All E.R. 288; [2000] 2 F.L.R. 429; [2000] 2 F.C.R. 768; *Times*,
    October 12, 2000, Fam Div . . . .   *Digested*, 00/**2553**
Practice Direction (Fam Div: Injunctions: Undertakings as to Damages) [1974] 1 W.L.R.
    576; [1974] 2 All E.R. 400, Fam Div . . . .   *Digested*, 74/**1022**:
                                                  Applied, 01/2623
Practice Direction (Fam Div: Long Vacation 1998) [1998] 1 F.L.R. 1106; [1998] 2 F.C.R. 177,
    Fam Div . . . .   *Digested*, 98/**2484**
Practice Direction (Fam Div: Long Vacation 1999) [1999] 2 F.L.R. 397; [1999] 2 F.C.R. 433;
    Times, July 9, 1999, Fam Div . . . .   *Digested*, 99/**75**
Practice Direction (Fam Div: Long Vacation 2000) [2000] 2 F.L.R. 427; [2000] 2 F.C.R.
    661; (2000) 144 S.J.L.B. 173, Fam Div . . . .   *Digested*, 01/**2665**
Practice Direction (Fam Div: Names of Deceased: Death Certificates) see Practice
    Direction (Fam Div: Probate: Deceased's Names)
Practice Direction (Fam Div: Probate: Deceased's Names); *sub nom* Practice Direction
    (Fam Div: Names of Deceased: Death Certificates) [1999] 1 W.L.R. 259; [1999]
    1 All E.R. 832; [1999] 1 F.L.R. 503; [1999] 1 F.C.R. 481; *Times*, January 26,
    1999, Fam Div. . . . .   *Digested*, 99/**4644**
Practice Direction (Fam Div: Probate Records: Grants of Representation) (No.1) [1998] 1
    W.L.R. 1699; [1999] 1 All E.R. 384; [1998] 3 F.C.R. 531, Fam Div . . . .   *Digested*, 99/**4643**
Practice Direction (Fam Div: Proceedings: Costs) see Practice Direction (Fam Div: Costs:
    Civil Procedure Rules 1998)
Practice Direction (Fam Div: Proceedings: Human Rights) see Practice Direction (Fam Div:
    Human Rights Act 1998: Citation of Authorities)
Practice Direction (HC: Civil Litigation: Case Management); *sub nom* Practice Note (HC:
    Civil Litigation: Case Management); Practice Direction (QBD: Pre-trial
    Checklist: Civil Litigation); Practice Direction (QBD and Ch D: Case
    Management) [1995] 1 W.L.R. 262; [1995] 1 All E.R. 385; [1995] P.I.Q.R. P221;
    Times, January 25, 1995, QBD . . . .   *Digested*, 95/**3942**:
                         Followed, 97/484, 99/499: *Referred to*, 95/3940
Practice Direction (HC: Mareva Injunctions and Anton Piller Orders: Forms); *sub nom*
    Practice Direction (HC: Ex Parte Mareva Injunctions and Anton Piller Orders)
    [1996] 1 W.L.R. 1552; [1997] 1 All E.R. 288; [1997] 1 F.L.R. 138; [1997] 1 F.C.R.
    131; *Times*, October 31, 1996; *Independent*, November 4, 1996 (C.S.), HC . . . . . .   *Digested*, 96/**869**:
                                                  Referred to, 00/488
Practice Direction (HL: Civil Appeals) (2001) 145 S.J.L.B. 131, HL
Practice Direction (HL: Civil Procedure Amendments) [1999] 1 W.L.R. 1833, HL. . . . . .   *Digested*, 00/**557**
Practice Direction (HL: Criminal Appeals) (2001) 145 S.J.L.B. 130, HL
Practice Direction (HL: Criminal Procedure Amendments) [1999] 1 W.L.R. 1830; [2000] 1
    Cr. App. R. 73, HL . . . .   *Digested*, 00/**1092**
Practice Direction (HL: Taxation Procedure Amendment) [1999] 1 W.L.R. 1860; (1999) 143
    S.J.L.B. 234, HL . . . .   *Digested*, 00/**3995**
Practice Direction (IAT) (2000/1) see Practice Direction (IAT: Service of Documents:
    Interpreters)
Practice Direction (IAT) (2000/2) see Practice Direction (IAT: Applications for
    Adjournments: Asylum Appeals)
Practice Direction (IAT) (2000/3) see Practice Direction (IAT: Service of Notices)

Practice Direction (IAT) (2000/4) see Practice Direction (IAT: Immigration and Asylum Appeals (Procedure) Rules 2000)

Practice Direction (IAT) (2001/1) see Practice Direction (IAT: Allocation of Applications and Appeals Pursuant to the Immigration and Asylum Act 1999)

Practice Direction (IAT: Allocation of Applications and Appeals Pursuant to the Immigration and Asylum Act 1999); *sub nom* Practice Direction (IAT) (2001/1) [2001] Imm. A.R. 359; [2001] I.N.L.R. 477, IAT . . . . *Digested*, 01/**3693**

Practice Direction (IAT: Applications for Adjournments: Asylum Appeals); *sub nom* Practice Direction (IAT) (2000/2) [2000] Imm. A.R. 435; [2000] I.N.L.R. 238, IAT . . . . *Digested*, 00/**3388**

Practice Direction (IAT: Immigration and Asylum Appeals (Procedure) Rules 2000); *sub nom* Practice Direction (IAT) (2000/4) [2001] Imm. A.R. 172; [2001] I.N.L.R. 216, IAT . . . . *Digested*, 01/**3691**

Practice Direction (IAT: Service of Documents: Interpreters); *sub nom* Practice Direction (IAT) (2000/1) [2000] Imm. A.R. 407; [2000] I.N.L.R. 235, IAT . . . . *Digested*, 00/**3389**

Practice Direction (IAT: Service of Notices); *sub nom* Practice Direction (IAT) (2000/3) [2000] Imm. A.R. 551; [2000] I.N.L.R. 686, IAT. . . . . *Digested*, 01/**3692**

Practice Direction (Lands Tr: Appeals: Applications) (No.3 of 2000) [2000] R.V.R. 223, Lands Tr . . . . *Digested*, 00/**552**

Practice Direction (Lands Tr: Appeals: Applications) (No.1 of 1999) [1999] R.V.R. 2, Lands Tr

Superseded, 00/552

Practice Direction (LCD: Duties and Functions of Official Solicitor) [1991] 2 F.L.R. 471, LCD

Digested, 92/**3107**:
Approved, 98/2456: *Considered*, 99/2444

Practice Direction (Merc Ct: Bristol) (No.1) [1993] 1 W.L.R. 1522; [1993] 4 All E.R. 1023; *Times*, November 26, 1993, QBD (Merc Ct) . . . . *Digested*, 93/**3288**:
Superseded in part, 99/68

Practice Direction (Merc Ct: Bristol) (No.2); *sub nom* Practice Note (Merc Ct: Bristol) [1999] 1 W.L.R. 1278; [1999] 2 All E.R. 1024; *Times*, June 30, 1999, QBD (Merc Ct) . . . . *Digested*, 99/**68**

Practice Direction (Merc Ct: Wales and Chester) [2000] 1 W.L.R. 208; [2000] 2 All E.R. 448; [2000] 1 All E.R. (Comm) 384; *Times*, February 1, 2000, QBD (Merc Ct) . . *Digested*, 00/**558**

Practice Direction (Pat Ct: Consolidated Explanation: 1997); *sub nom* Practice Explanation (Pat Ct: Consolidated Practice Explanation) [1998] 1 W.L.R. 32; [1998] 1 All E.R. 279; [1998] F.S.R. 79; [1998] R.P.C. 18, Pat Ct . . . . *Digested*, 98/**3491**:
Considered, 98/3459

Practice Direction (Pat Ct: Consolidated Explanation: 1998) see Practice Direction (Pat Ct: Revised Procedure)

Practice Direction (Pat Ct: Revised Procedure); *sub nom* Practice Direction (Pat Ct: Consolidated Explanation: 1998) [1998] 1 W.L.R. 1414; [1998] 3 All E.R. 372; [1998] F.S.R. 571; [1998] R.P.C. 653, Pat Ct . . . . *Digested*, 98/**3490**

Practice Direction (PO: Claims to Programs for Computers); *sub nom* Practice Notice (PO: Claims to Programs for Computers) [1999] R.P.C. 563; (1999) 22(6) I.P.D. 22061, PO . . . . *Digested*, 99/**3523**

Practice Direction (PO: Hearsay Evidence) (No.2) [1999] R.P.C. 294, PO . . . . *Digested*, 99/**3522**

Practice Direction (QBD: Admin Ct: Establishment); *sub nom* Practice Direction (QBD: Admin Ct: Review of Crown Office List) [2000] 1 W.L.R. 1654; [2000] 4 All E.R. 1071; [2000] 2 Lloyd's Rep. 445; [2000] 2 Cr. App. R. 455; [2000] C.O.D. 290; *Times*, July 27, 2000, QBD . . . . *Digested*, 01/**1179**

Practice Direction (QBD: Admin Ct: Review of Crown Office List) see Practice Direction (QBD: Admin Ct: Establishment)

Practice Direction (QBD: Admiralty and Commercial Registry: Practice); *sub nom* Practice Direction (QBD: Comm Ct and Adm Ct: Setting Down and Skeleton Arguments) [1998] 1 W.L.R. 668; [1999] 1 Lloyd's Rep. 114; *Times*, March 24, 1998, QBD (Comm Ct) . . . . *Digested*, 98/**574**

Practice Direction (QBD and Ch D: Case Management) see Practice Direction (HC: Civil Litigation: Case Management)

Practice Direction (QBD: Comm Ct and Adm Ct: Setting Down and Skeleton Arguments) see Practice Direction (QBD: Admiralty and Commercial Registry: Practice)

Practice Direction (QBD: Comm Ct): Time Estimates for Commercial Summonses) [2000] 1 Lloyd's Rep. 626, QBD (Comm Ct) . . . . *Digested*, 00/**554**

Practice Direction (QBD: County Court Order: Enforcement) (No.1) [1991] 1 W.L.R. 695; [1991] 3 All E.R. 438, QBD . . . . *Digested*, 91/**2840**:
Superseded, 99/509

Practice Direction (QBD: County Court Order: Enforcement) (No.2) [1998] 1 W.L.R. 1557, QBD . . . . *Digested*, 99/**509**

Practice Direction (QBD: Crown Office List: Preparation for Hearings) [2000] 2 All E.R. 896; [2000] 2 Cr. App. R. 93; *Times*, March 24, 2000, QBD . . . . *Digested*, 00/**76**

Practice Direction (QBD: Crown Office List: Time Estimates, Skeleton Arguments and Paginated Bundles); *sub nom* Practice Note (QBD: Crown Office List: Penalties for Late Papers) [1994] 1 W.L.R. 1551; [1994] 4 All E.R. 671; *Times*, October 27, 1994; *Independent*, November 2, 1994, QBD. . . . . *Digested*, 94/**3654**:
Referred to, 00/76

Practice Direction (QBD: Justices: Clerk to Court) [2000] 1 W.L.R.1886; [2000] 4 All E.R.
    895; [2001] 1 Cr. App. R. 9; (2000) 164 J.P. 726; *Times,* October 11, 2000, QBD   *Digested,* 00/**1093**
Practice Direction (QBD: Kilrie Children's Home Litigation), *Times,* February 1, 2000, QBD

                                                                Digested, 00/**553**
Practice Direction (QBD: Magistrates Courts: Contempt) [2001] 1 W.L.R.1254; [2001] 3
    All E.R. 94; [2001] 2 Cr. App. R.17; (2001) 165 J.P. 462; *Times,* June 11, 2001, QBD

                                                                 Digested, 01/**1177**
Practice Direction (QBD: Organophosphate Litigation), *Times,* December 31, 1998, QBD   *Digested,* 99/**72**
Practice Direction (QBD: Peremptory Order); *sub nom* Practice Note (QBD: Unless
    Orders and other Peremptory Orders) [1986] 1 W.L.R. 948; [1986] 2 All E.R.
    576, QBD . . . .   *Digested,* 86/**2720**:
                                                                 Applied, 99/570
Practice Direction (QBD: Post Traumatic Stress Disorder Litigation against Ministry of
    Defence: Group Actions) (1999) 143 S.J.L.B. 262; *Times,* November 26, 1999,
    Sup Ct . . . .   *Digested,* 00/**556**
Practice Direction (QBD: Pre-trial Checklist: Civil Litigation) see Practice Direction (HC:
    Civil Litigation: Case Management)
Practice Direction (QBD: Vibration White Finger Actions) (No.3); *sub nom* Practice
    Direction (Coal Mining Vibration White Finger Actions) ; Practice Note (Vibration
    White Finger Actions) (No.3) *Times,* August 5, 1999, QBD . . . .   *Digested,* 99/**2874**
Practice Direction (Royal Courts of Justice: Reading List: Time Estimates) [2000] 1 W.L.R.
    208; [2000] 1 All E.R. 640; *Times,* February 1, 2000, Ch D . . . .   *Digested,* 00/**559**
Practice Direction (SENT: Postal Delays) [2000] E.L.R. 637, SENT . . . .   *Digested,* 01/**2041**
Practice Direction (SENT: Translations of Decisions) [2000] E.L.R. 469, SENT . . . . . .   *Digested,* 00/**1895**
Practice Direction (Sp Comm: Human Rights: Citation of Authorities) [2000] S.T.C.
    (S.C.D.) 465, Sp Comm. . . . .   *Digested,* 01/**628**
Practice Direction (Special Adjudicators: CA2 of 2000) [2000] Imm. A.R. 394 . . . . . .   *Digested,* 00/**3387**:
                                                                  Cited, 00/3386
Practice Direction (Special Adjudicators: CA3 of 2000) [2000] Imm. A.R. 395 . . . . . .   *Digested,* 00/**3386**
Practice Direction (Special Adjudicators: CA4 of 2000) [2000] I.N.L.R. 687
Practice Direction (Sup Ct: Civil Litigation: Procedure); *sub nom* Practice Directions
    (Civil Procedure Rules) [1999] 1 W.L.R. 1124; [1999] 3 All E.R. 380; *Times,* April
    26, 1999, Sup Ct . . . .   *Digested,* 99/**513**:
                        Applied, 99/512, 99/1410, 00/349, 00/424: *Cited,* 99/408, 00/239, 00/240,
              00/314, 00/340, 00/358, 00/369, 00/370, 00/393, 00/400, 00/419,
              00/449, 00/450, 00/470, 00/492, 00/545, 00/564, 00/2551, 00/3915,
              01/423, 01/441, 01/515, 01/521, 01/524, 01/529, 01/535, 01/558, 01/563,
              01/564, 01/572, 01/620, 01/624, 01/653, 01/662, 01/667, 01/672, 01/4890:
              Considered, 99/561, 99/640, 00/324, 01/426, 01/664: *Explained,* 99/505,
                        99/1419: *Referred to,* 99/343, 99/357, 00/392, 00/567
Practice Direction (Sup Ct: Costs: Summary Assessment); *sub nom* Practice Note (QBD
    and Ch D: Costs: Summary Assessment) [1999] 1 W.L.R. 420; [1999] 1 All
    E.R. 670; *Times,* February 3, 1999, QBD . . . .   *Digested,* 99/**514**
Practice Direction (Sup Ct: Court Dress) (No.1) [1994] 1 W.L.R. 1056; *Times,* July 20,
    1994, Sup Ct. . . . .   *Digested,* 94/**3522**:
                                  Approved, 95/3913: *Superseded in part,* 99/74
Practice Direction (Sup Ct: Court Dress) (No.3) [1998] 1 W.L.R.1764; [1999] 1 Cr. App. R.
    336; *Times,* December 3, 1998, Sup Ct . . . .   *Digested,* 99/**74**
Practice Direction (Sup Ct: Creutzfeldt-Jakob Disease Litigation: Damages); *sub nom*
    Practice Direction (Creutzfeldt-Jakob Disease Litigation: Damages) (2000) 54
    B.M.L.R. 174, Sup Ct . . . .   *Digested,* 00/**555**
Practice Direction (Sup Ct: Crime: Costs in Criminal Proceedings); *sub nom* Practice Note
    (Sup Ct: Criminal Law: Costs); Practice Direction (Sup Ct: Crime: Defence
    Costs) [1999] 1 W.L.R. 1832; [1999] 4 All E.R. 436; [2000] 1 Cr. App. R. 60;
    [2000] 1 Cr. App. R. 76; *Times,* October 6, 1999, Sup Ct . . . .   *Digested,* 99/**1040**
Practice Direction (Sup Ct: Crime: Costs) see Practice Direction (CA (Crim Div): Costs in
    Criminal Proceedings)
Practice Direction (Sup Ct: Crime: Defence Costs) see Practice Direction (Sup Ct: Crime:
    Costs in Criminal Proceedings)
Practice Direction (Sup Ct: Crime: Voluntary Bills) (No.2) [1999] 1 W.L.R.1613; [1999] 4 All
    E.R. 62; [1999] 2 Cr. App. R. 442; *Times,* August 5, 1999, Sup Ct . . . .   *Digested,* 99/**1042**
Practice Direction (Sup Ct: Criminal Justice Act 1987: Crown Court Centres) see Practice
    Direction (Crown Ct: Fraud Trials) (No.4)
Practice Direction (Sup Ct: Crown Court: Welsh Language) [1998] 1 W.L.R.1677; [1999] 1
    All E.R. 575; [1999] 2 Cr. App. R. 32; *Times,* October 29, 1998, Sup Ct . . . .   *Digested,* 98/**70**
Practice Direction (Sup Ct: Custodial Sentences) see Practice Direction (CA (Crim Div):
    Custodial Sentences: Explanations)
Practice Direction (Sup Ct: Devolution) [1999] 1 W.L.R. 1592; [1999] 3 All E.R. 466;
    [2000] 1 Cr. App. R.101; [1999] 2 Cr. App. R. 486; *Times,* July 5, 1999, Sup Ct .   *Digested,* 99/**779**
Practice Direction (Sup Ct: Form of Judgments, Paragraph Marking and Neutral Citation)
    see Practice Direction (Sup Ct: Judgments: Form and Citation)
Practice Direction (Sup Ct: Judges: Recorder of Cardiff) [1999] 1 W.L.R. 597; [1999] 2 All
    E.R. 352; [1999] 2 Cr. App. R. 187, Sup Ct . . . .   *Digested,* 99/**515**

Practice Direction (Sup Ct: Judgments: Form and Citation); *sub nom* Practice Direction
(Sup Ct: Form of Judgments, Paragraph Marking and Neutral Citation);
Practice Note (Sup Ct: Judgments: Neutral Citation) [2001] 1 W.L.R. 194;
[2001] 1 All E.R. 193; [2001] S.T.C. 78; [2001] 1 Cr. App. R. 29; [2001] 1 F.C.R.
286; [2001] B.V.C. 156; *Times*, January 16, 2001, Sup Ct . . . .   *Digested*, 01/**80**
Practice Direction (Sup Ct: References to the Court of Justice of the European
Communities); *sub nom* Practice Direction (ECJ: References to the ECJ by CA
and HC under Art.177) [1999] 1 W.L.R. 260; [1999] 1 Cr. App. R. 452; [1999] 2
C.M.L.R. 799; *Times*, January 19, 1999, Sup Ct . . . .   *Digested*, 99/**517**
Practice Direction (Sup Ct Taxing Office: Taxation: Practice) (No.2 of 1992) [1993] 1 W.L.R.
12; [1993] 1 All E.R. 263, Sup Ct Taxing Office . . . .   *Superseded in part*,
    98/577,
    99/411

Practice Direction (Sup Ct Taxing Office: Taxation: Wasted Costs) (No.1 of 1998) [1998] 1
W.L.R. 473; [1998] 1 All E.R. 383, Sup Ct Taxing Office. . . . .   *Digested*, 98/**577**
Practice Direction (Sup Ct: Vibration White Finger Actions) (No.1); *sub nom* Practice Note
(Vibration White Finger Actions) (No.1) *Times*, January 13, 1994, Sup Ct. . . . . . .   *Digested*, 94/**3744**:
    Superseded in part, 99/71, 99/2874

Practice Direction (Sup Ct: Vibration White Finger Actions) (No.2); *sub nom* Practice Note
(Vibration White Finger Actions) (No.2) *Times*, December 1, 1998, Sup Ct . . . .   *Digested*, 99/**71**
Practice Direction (TMR: Change of Practice on Retail Services) [2001] R.P.C. 2, TMR .   *Digested*, 01/**3972**
Practice Directions (Civil Procedure Rules) see Practice Direction (Sup Ct: Civil Litigation:
Procedure)
Practice Explanation (Pat Ct: Consolidated Practice Explanation) see Practice Direction
(Pat Ct: Consolidated Explanation: 1997)
Practice Note (CA: Assessment of Costs) [1999] 1 W.L.R. 871; [1999] 2 All E.R. 638; *Times*,
April 26, 1999, CA. . . . .   *Digested*, 99/**508**
Practice Note (CA: Civil Division: Hear by Dates and Listing Windows); *sub nom* Practice
Note (CA: Listing Windows) [2001] 1 W.L.R. 1517; [2001] 3 All E.R. 479;
Times, July 25, 2001, CA . . . .   *Digested*, 01/**422**
Practice Note (CA: Civil Division: Listing) see Practice Note (CA: Civil Division: Short
Warned List and Special Fixtures List)
Practice Note (CA: Civil Division: Short Warned List and Special Fixtures List); *sub nom*
Practice Note (CA: Civil Division: Listing) [2001] 1 W.L.R. 479; [2001] 2 All
E.R. 701; (2001) 145 S.J.L.B. 50; *Times*, February 27, 2001, CA. . . . .   *Digested*, 01/**624**
Practice Note (CA (Crim Div): Crown Court: Distribution of Court Business) see Practice
Direction (Crown Ct: Fraud Trials) (No.4)
Practice Note (CA (Crim Div): Practice: Skeleton Arguments) see Practice Direction (CA
(Crim Div): Criminal Appeals: Skeleton Arguments)
Practice Note (CA: Disposal of Bundles) [1999] 1 W.L.R. 1464; [1999] 3 All E.R. 384;
Times, June 30, 1999, CA . . . .   *Digested*, 99/**518**
Practice Note (CA: Listing Windows) see Practice Note (CA: Civil Division: Hear by Dates
and Listing Windows)
Practice Note (CA: Money Laundering: Discovery of Documents) see C *v.* S (Money
Laundering: Discovery of Documents) (Practice Note)
Practice Note (CA: Procedural Changes) see Practice Direction (CA: Revised Procedure)
Practice Note (CA: Procedure) see Practice Direction (CA: Procedure)
Practice Note (CAEW: Child Abduction and Custody Act 1985: Hague Convention:
Applications for Return Orders by Unmarried Fathers) see Practice Note (CAEW:
Hague Convention: Applications by Fathers without Parental Responsibility)
Practice Note (CAEW: Hague Convention: Applications by Fathers without Parental
Responsibility); *sub nom* Practice Note (CAEW: Child Abduction and Custody
Act 1985: Hague Convention: Applications for Return Orders by Unmarried
Fathers) [1998] 1 F.L.R. 491; [1998] 1 F.C.R. 253; (1998) 148 N.L.J. 179; (1998)
142 S.J.L.B. 114, CAEW. . . . .   *Digested*, 98/**2379**:
    Not followed, 00/2452
Practice Note (CFI: Constitution) [2000] All E.R. (EC) 1, CFI . . . .   *Digested*, 00/**2344**
Practice Note (CFI: Guidance in Written and Oral Proceedings) [1999] All E.R. (EC) 641, CFI
    Digested, 99/**2230**
Practice Note (Ch D: Civil Procedure Rules) see Practice Direction (Ch D: Interim
Applications to Chancery Division)
Practice Note (Ch D (Companies Ct): Skeleton Arguments: Time Limits); *sub nom* Practice
Statement (Ch D (Companies Ct)) [1999] B.C.C. 942; *Times*, June 25, 1999,
Ch D (Companies Ct) . . . .   *Digested*, 99/**519**
Practice Note (Crown Ct: Allocation of Business) (No.2) see Practice Direction (Crown Ct:
Allocation of Business) (No.2)
Practice Note (ECJ: Treaty Citation) (No.1) [1999] All E.R. (EC) 481, ECJ . . . .   *Digested*, 99/**2224**
Practice Note (ECJ: Treaty Citation) (No.2) [1999] All E.R. (EC) 646, ECJ . . . .   *Digested*, 99/**2225**
Practice Note (Fam Div: Official Solicitor: Appointment in Family Proceedings) [1995] 2
F.L.R. 479; [1996] 1 F.C.R. 78, Fam Div . . . .   *Followed*, 97/433,
    98/2420
Practice Note (HC: Civil Litigation: Case Management) see Practice Direction (HC: Civil
Litigation: Case Management)

Practice Note (Inter-Country Adoptions) see R (A Minor) (Inter-Country Adoptions: Practice) (No.2), Re

Practice Note (Merc Ct: Bristol) see Practice Direction (Merc Ct: Bristol) (No.2)

Practice Note (Officers of CAFCASS Legal Services and Special Casework: Appointment in Family Proceedings) [2001] 2 F.L.R. 151; [2001] 2 F.C.R. 562 . . . .   *Digested,* 01/**2663**

Practice Note (Official Solicitor: Appointment in Family Proceedings) [1999] 1 F.L.R. 310; [1999] 1 F.C.R. 1, Fam Div . . . .   *Digested,* 99/**2444**:
Superseded, 01/2663, 01/2664

Practice Note (Official Solicitor: Appointment in Family Proceedings) [2001] 2 F.L.R.155; [2001] 2 F.C.R. 566 . . . .   *Digested,* 01/**2664**

Practice Note (Official Solicitor: Declaratory Proceedings: Medical and Welfare Proceedings for Adults Who Lack Capacity) [2001] 2 F.L.R. 158; [2001] 2 F.C.R. 569 . . . .   *Digested,* 01/**2662**

Practice Note (Official Solicitor: Sterilisation) [1996] 2 F.L.R. 111; [1996] 3 F.C.R. 94; [1996] Fam. Law 439, Fam Div . . . .   *Digested,* 96/**599**:
Superseded, 01/2662

Practice Note (Official Solicitor: Vegetative State) [1996] 4 All E.R. 766; [1996] 2 F.L.R. 375; [1996] 3 F.C.R. 606; (1997) 34 B.M.L.R. 20; [1996] Fam. Law 579; (1996) 146 N.L.J. 1585, Sup Ct. . . . .   *Digested,* 96/**4216**:
Superseded, 01/2662

Practice Note (QBD and Ch D: Costs: Summary Assessment) see Practice Direction (Sup Ct: Costs: Summary Assessment)

Practice Note (QBD: Crown Ct: Trial of Children and Young Persons) see Practice Direction (Crown Ct: Trial of Children and Young Persons)

Practice Note (QBD: Crown Office List: Penalties for Late Papers) see Practice Direction (QBD: Crown Office List: Time Estimates, Skeleton Arguments and Paginated Bundles)

Practice Note (QBD: Mode of Trial: Guidelines) [1990] 1 W.L.R. 1439; [1991] 3 All E.R. 979; (1991) 92 Cr. App. R. 142, QBD . . . .   *Considered,* 94/999,
95/1176: *Referred to,* 99/1370

Practice Note (QBD: Unless Orders and other Peremptory Orders) see Practice Direction (QBD: Peremptory Order)

Practice Note (Sup Ct: Criminal Law: Costs) see Practice Direction (Sup Ct: Crime: Costs in Criminal Proceedings)

Practice Note (Sup Ct: Judgments: Neutral Citation) see Practice Direction (Sup Ct: Judgments: Form and Citation)

Practice Note (Sup Ct Taxing Office: Taxation: Indemnity Principle) (No.2 of 1998) [1998] 1 W.L.R. 1674; [1999] 1 All E.R. 128, Sup Ct Taxing Office . . . .   *Digested,* 99/**411**

Practice Note (Vibration White Finger Actions) (No.1) see Practice Direction (Sup Ct: Vibration White Finger Actions) (No.1)

Practice Note (Vibration White Finger Actions) (No.2) see Practice Direction (Sup Ct: Vibration White Finger Actions) (No.2)

Practice Note (Vibration White Finger Actions) (No.3) see Practice Direction (QBD: Vibration White Finger Actions) (No.3)

Practice Notice (PO: Proceedings before the Comptroller) (TPN 1/2000) [2000] R.P.C. 587, PO . . . .   *Digested,* 00/**3693**

Practice Notice (PO: Costs in Proceedings before the Comptroller) (TPN 2/2000) [2000] R.P.C. 598, PO . . . .   *Digested,* 00/**3692**

Practice Notice (PO: Claims to Programs for Computers) see Practice Direction (PO: Claims to Programs for Computers)

Practice Statement (CA (Crim Div): Juveniles: Murder Tariff) [2000] 1 W.L.R.1655; [2000] 4 All E.R. 831; [2000] 2 Cr. App. R. 457; *Times,* August 9, 2000, CA (Crim Div) .   *Digested,* 00/**1095**:
Cited, 00/1331

Practice Statement (Ch D: Applications to the Court in Relation to the Administration of a Trust: Prospective Costs Orders) see Practice Statement (Ch D: Trust Proceedings: Prospective Costs Orders)

Practice Statement (Ch D (Companies Ct)) see Practice Note (Ch D (Companies Ct): Skeleton Arguments: Time Limits)

Practice Statement (Ch D: Estates of Deceased Lloyd's Names) [2001] 3 All E.R. 765; (2001) 145 S.J.L.B. 133, Ch D . . . .   *Digested,* 01/**625**

Practice Statement (Ch D: Trust Proceedings: Prospective Costs Orders); *sub nom* Practice Statement (Ch D: Applications to the Court in Relation to the Administration of a Trust: Prospective Costs Orders); Practice Direction (Ch D: Trust Proceedings: Prospective Costs Orders) [2001] 1 W.L.R. 1082; [2001] 3 All E.R. 574; [2001] W.T.L.R. 949, Ch D . . . .   *Digested,* 01/**627**

Practice Statement (Comm Ct: Commercial Court Guide) [1999] 4 All E.R. 471; [1999] 2 All E.R. (Comm) 575, QBD (Comm Ct) . . . .   *Digested,* 99/**368**

Practice Statement (Companies Ct: Applications); *sub nom* Practice Statement (Companies Ct: Hearings) [2000] 1 W.L.R. 209; [2000] 1 All E.R. 928; [2000] B.C.C. 256; *Times,* January 19, 2000, Ch D . . . .   *Digested,* 00/**560**

Practice Statement (Companies Ct: Hearings) see Practice Statement (Companies Ct: Applications)

Practice Statement (EAT: Jurisdiction), *Times,* December 3, 1997, EAT . . . .   *Digested,* 98/**2129**

Practice Statement (HC: Bankruptcy: Contested Chambers Hearings) [1998] B.P.I.R. 426,
    Ch D . . . .   *Digested*, 98/**3339**
Practice Statement (Sup Ct: Judgments) (No.1) [1998] 1 W.L.R. 825; [1998] 2 All E.R. 667;
    [1998] 2 Cr. App. R. 144; [1998] 1 F.L.R. 1102; [1998] 2 F.C.R. 1; (1998) 148 N.L.J.
    631; *Times*, April 23, 1998, Sup Ct . . . .   *Digested*, 98/**71**:
                                    Cited, 00/504: *Superseded in part*, 99/73
Practice Statement (Sup Ct: Judgments) (No.2) [1999] 1 W.L.R. 1; [1999] 1 All E.R. 125;
    [1999] 1 Cr. App. R. 333; [1999] 1 F.L.R. 314; [1998] 3 F.C.R. 627; [1999] Fam. Law
    7; *Times*, December 2, 1998, Sup Ct . . . .   *Digested*, 99/**73**
Prager and Oberschlick v. Austria (A/313) (1996) 21 E.H.R.R. 1, ECHR . . . .   *Digested*, 96/**3144**:
                                    Applied, 98/3089: *Followed*, 01/3472
Prashar v. Secretary of State for the Environment, Transport and the Regions [2001]
    EWCA Civ 1231; [2001] 3 P.L.R. 116, CA
Prater v. Clarke (Unreported, February 27, 2001), CC (Bristol) [*Ex rel.* Benjamin
    Williams, Barrister, 1 Temple Gardens, London] . . . .   *Digested*, 01/**889**
Pratt v. Attorney General of Jamaica [1994] 2 A.C. 1; [1993] 3 W.L.R. 995; [1993] 4
    All E.R. 769; (1994) 91(3) L.S.G. 45; (1993) 143 N.L.J. 1639; (1993) 137
    S.J.L.B. 250; *Times*, November 4, 1993; *Independent*, November 3, 1993;
    Guardian, November 11, 1993, PC (Jam) . . . .   *Digested*, 94/**491**:
            Applied, 99/758: *Considered*, 96/3126, 96/3127, 98/780, 00/3201:
                                    Followed, 95/958, 95/1313, 96/3128
Pratt v. DPP [2001] EWHC Admin 483; (2001) 165 J.P. 800; (2001) 165 J.P.N. 750;
    Times, August 22, 2001, QBD (Admin Ct) . . . .   *Digested*, 01/**1048**
Pratt v. Kier Regional Ltd (Unreported, July 26, 1999), CC (Plymouth) [*Ex rel.* Irwin
    Mitchell Solicitors, Huttons Buildings, 146 West Street, Sheffield] . . . .   *Digested*, 00/**465**
Pre-School Learning Alliance v. Customs and Excise Commissioners [2001] S.T.I. 531,
    V&DTr
Prebble and Robinson's Arbitration, Re [1892] 2 Q.B. 602, QBD . . . .   *Considered*, 01/338
Precision Dippings Ltd v. Precision Dippings Marketing Ltd [1986] Ch. 447; [1985] 3
    W.L.R. 812; [1986] P.C.C. 105; (1985) 129 S.J. 683, CA . . . .   *Digested*, 85/**279**:
                                    Applied, 91/425: *Considered*, 01/729
Preiss v. General Dental Council; *sub nom* Preiss v. General Medical Council [2001]
    UKPC 36; [2001] 1 W.L.R. 1926; [2001] I.R.L.R. 696; [2001] H.R.L.R. 56;
    [2001] Lloyd's Rep. Med. 491; (2001) 98(33) L.S.G. 31; *Times*, August 14, 2001,
    PC (UK) . . . .   *Digested*, 01/**2891**
Preiss v. General Medical Council see Preiss v. General Dental Council
Premier Brands UK Ltd v. Typhoon Europe Ltd [2000] E.T.M.R. 1071; [2000] F.S.R. 767;
    (2000) 23(5) I.P.D. 23038; (2000) 97(5) L.S.G. 35; *Times*, February 22,
    2000, Ch D . . . .   *Digested*, 00/**3700**:
                        Not applied, 01/4009: *Not followed*, 00/3794
Premier Electronics (GB) Ltd, Re, *Times*, February 27, 2001, Ch D . . . .   *Digested*, 01/**726**
Premier Luggage & Bags Ltd v. Premier Co (UK) Ltd [2000]/2770, CA; reversing [2001]
    E.T.M.R. 6; [2001] F.S.R. 29; *Times*, October 18, 2000, Ch D . . . .   *Digested*, 00/**3705**
Premier Warehousing & Distribution Co Ltd v. Leicester City Council [2000] R.V.R. 351,
    Lands Tr . . . .   *Digested*, 01/**4673**
Prendergast's Patent Applications [2000] R.P.C. 446; (1999) 22(10) I.P.D. 22094, Pat Ct
                                                        Digested, 00/**3689**
Prenn v. Simmonds [1971] 1 W.L.R. 1381; [1971] 3 All E.R. 237; 115 S.J. 654, HL . . . . . .   *Digested*, 71/**1711**:
            Applied, 92/311, 01/3835: *Considered*, 86/9: *Referred to*, 94/3430
Prentice v. Hereward Housing Association [2001] EWCA Civ 437; [2001] 2 All E.R.
    (Comm) 900; *Times*, March 30, 2001, CA; reversing 98/NJ/1149, QBD . . . .   *Digested*, 01/**632**
Prentis Donegan & Partners Ltd v. Leeds & Leeds Co Inc [1998] 2 Lloyd's Rep. 326;
    [1998] C.L.C. 1132, QBD (Comm Ct) . . . .   *Digested*, 98/**3361**
PREPARE Trade Mark [1997] R.P.C. 884, Appointed Person . . . .   *Digested*, 98/**3545**
Prescott v. Hamnett (Unreported, September 30, 1998), CC (Altrincham) [*Ex rel.* Gepp
    & Sons Solicitors, 58 New London Road, Chelmsford] . . . .   *Digested*, 98/**1459**
Presentaciones Musicales SA v. Secunda [1994] Ch. 271; [1994] 2 W.L.R. 660; [1994]
    2 All E.R. 737; (1994) 138 S.J.L.B. 4; *Times*, November 29, 1993, CA; affirming
    [1995] E.M.L.R. 118, Ch D . . . .   *Digested*, 94/**107**:
                                    Applied, 97/325: *Considered*, 99/753
President of India v. Jadranska Slobodna Plovidba [1992] 2 Lloyd's Rep. 274; *Times*,
    March 30, 1992; *Financial Times*, April 3, 1992, QBD (Comm Ct) . . . .   *Digested*, 93/**163**
President of India v. La Pintada Compania Navigacion SA (The La Pintada) (No.1); *sub
    nom* La Pintada Compania Navegacion SA v. President of India (No.1) [1985]
    A.C. 104; [1984] 3 W.L.R. 10; [1984] 2 All E.R. 773; [1984] 2 Lloyd's Rep. 9;
    [1984] C.I.L.L. 110; (1984) 81 L.S.G. 1999; (1984) 128 S.J. 414, HL; reversing
    [1983] 1 Lloyd's Rep. 37; [1982] Com. L.R. 250; *Times*, November 1, 1982, QBD
    (Comm Ct) . . . .   *Digested*, 84/**123**:
            Applied, 84/120, 85/3160: *Cited*, 00/1453: *Considered*, 84/2346, 86/2760,
                        87/2429, 97/3839, 98/1433: *Followed*, 98/231
President of South Africa v. Hugo, Const Ct (SA) . . . .   *Applied*, 98/3276
President's Direction (Adopted Children Register: Restriction on Disclosure) [1999] 1
    F.L.R. 315; [1999] 1 F.C.R. 97, Fam Div. . . . .   *Digested*, 99/**2295**

President's Direction (Family Law Act 1996: Attendance of Arresting Officer) see Practice
   Direction (Fam Div: Arresting Officer: Attendance)
Prest v. Secretary of State for Wales 81 L.G.R. 193; (1983) 266 E.G. 527; [1983] R.V.R.
   11; 126 S.J. 708; *Times*, September 29, 1982, CA . . . .   *Digested*, 83/**359**:
                    Considered, 87/390, 88/385, 89/363, 90/588, 91/94, 92/452, 93/440,
                                        97/4347, 99/4248: *Followed*, 95/4845
Preston v. Preston [1982] Fam. 17; [1981] 3 W.L.R. 619; [1982] 1 All E.R. 41; 125 S.J.
   496, CA . . . .   *Digested*, 81/**714**:
                  Considered, 82/1493, 82/2917, 87/1755, 96/2855, 96/2858, 96/2889:
                              Followed, 00/2525: *Referred to*, 94/2179
Preston v. Secretary of State for Health (No.1) (C78/98) see Preston v.
   Wolverhampton Healthcare NHS Trust (No.1) (C78/98)
Preston v. Singleton (2000) 15 P.A.D. 13, Planning Inspector
Preston v. Torfaen BC 65 B.L.R. 1; 36 Con. L.R. 48; [1955-95] P.N.L.R. 625; [1993]
   E.G.C.S. 137; [1993] N.P.C. 111; *Times*, July 21, 1993; *Independent*, September
   24, 1993, CA; affirming (1991) 7 Const. L.J. 345, QBD (OR) . . . .   *Digested*, 94/**3398**
Preston v. Wolverhampton Healthcare NHS Trust (No.1) (C78/98); *sub nom* Preston v.
   Wolverhampton Health Care NHS Trust (No.1) (C78/98); Preston v. Secretary of
   State for Health (No.1) (C78/98); Fletcher v. Midland Bank Plc (No.1) (C78/
   98) [2001] 2 A.C. 415; [2001] 2 W.L.R. 408; [2000] All E.R. 714; [2000]
   E.C.R. I-3201; [2000] 2 C.M.L.R. 837; [2000] C.E.C. 587; [2000] I.C.R. 961;
   [2000] I.R.L.R. 506; [2000] O.P.L.R. 115; [2000] Pens. L.R. 171; *Times*, May 19,
   2000, ECJ [1998] 1 W.L.R. 280; [1998] 1 All E.R. 528; [1998] Eu. L.R. 631;
   [1998] I.C.R. 227; [1998] I.R.L.R. 197; [1998] O.P.L.R. 271; (1998) 95(8) L.S.G.
   33; (1998) 142 S.J.L.B. 82; *Times*, February 9, 1998, HL [1997] 2 C.M.L.R.
   754; [1997] Eu. L.R. 386; [1997] I.C.R. 899; [1997] I.R.L.R. 233; [1997]
   O.P.L.R. 335; *Independent*, March 13, 1997, CA; affirming [1996] I.R.L.R. 484;
   [1997] O.P.L.R. 307; *Times*, July 2, 1996, EAT; affirming in part [1995] O.P.L.R.
   205, IT . . . .   *Digested*, 00/**2162**:
                                   Subsequent proceedings, 01/2279
Preston v. Wolverhampton Healthcare NHS Trust (No.2); Fletcher v. Midland Bank Plc
   (No.2) [2001] UKHL 5; [2001] 2 A.C. 455; [2001] 2 W.L.R. 448; [2001] 3 All
   E.R. 947; [2001] 1 C.M.L.R. 46; [2001] I.C.R. 217; [2001] I.R.L.R. 237; [2001]
   O.P.L.R. 1; [2001] Pens. L.R. 39; (2001) 98(10) L.S.G. 41; (2001) 145 S.J.L.B.
   55; *Times*, February 9, 2001, HL . . . .   *Digested*, 01/**2279**
Preston BC v. McGrath, *Times*, May 19, 2000; *Independent*, May 19, 2000, CA;
   affirming (1999) 96(8) L.S.G. 30; *Times*, February 18, 1999, Ch D . . . .   *Digested*, 00/**934**
Preston BC v. Pillar Property Investments Plc (1998) 13 P.A.D. 698, Planning Inspector
Preston BC v. Riley [1995] B.C.C. 700; [1999] B.P.I.R. 284; [1995] R.A. 227; *Times*,
   April 19, 1995; *Independent*, May 30, 1995 (C.S.), CA . . . .   *Digested*, 95/**417**
Prestwich v. Royal Bank of Canada Trust Co (Jersey) Ltd 1 I.T.L. Rep. 565, Ch D
Pretoria City Council v. Walker 4 B.H.R.C. 324, Const Ct (SA)   *Digested*, 98/**3109**
Preussen Elektra AG v. Schleswag AG (C379/98) [2001] All E.R. (EC) 330; [2001]
   E.C.R. I-2099; [2001] 2 C.M.L.R. 36; [2001] C.E.C. 217, ECJ . . . .   *Digested*, 01/**2492**
Price (Graham) v. British Steel Plc (Unreported, December 6, 1996), CC
   (Middlesbrough) [*Ex rel.* JF Seager, Solicitor, Jacksons, 1-15 Queens Square,
   Middlesbrough] . . . .   *Digested*, 98/**416**
Price v. Dennis [1999] Ed. C.R. 747, CA
Price v. Rhondda Cynon Taff CBC (Unreported, August 20, 1999), CC (Cardiff) [*Ex rel.*
   Catherine Brown, Barrister, 12 King's Bench Walk, Temple, London] . . . .   *Digested*, 00/**4232**
Price v. Society of Lloyd's [2000] Lloyd's Rep. I.R. 453, QBD (Comm Ct) . . . .   *Digested*, 01/**3823**
Price v. United Engineering Steels Ltd [1998] P.I.Q.R. P407, CA . . . .   *Digested*, 99/**464**:
                                   Applied, 90/2960: *Followed*, 00/523
Price v. United Kingdom (33394/96) 11 B.H.R.C. 401; [2001] Crim. L.R. 916; *Times*,
   August 13, 2001, ECHR . . . .   *Digested*, 01/**3453**
Price Meats Ltd v. Barclays Bank Plc [2000] 2 All E.R. (Comm) 346; *Times*, January
   19, 2000, Ch D . . . .   *Digested*, 00/**277**:
                                   Applied, 01/369
Price Waterhouse v. Bank of Credit and Commerce International SA (In Liquidation)
   see Pharaon v. Bank of Credit and Commerce International SA (In Liquidation)
Price Waterhouse v. Kwan (1999-2000) 2 I.T.E.L.R. 611, CA (NZ)
Price's Application, Re [1997] N.I. 33, CA (NI) . . . .   *Digested*, 99/**5227**
Pride of Derby and Derbyshire Angling Association Ltd v. British Celanese Ltd [1953] Ch.
   149; [1953] 2 W.L.R. 58; [1953] 1 All E.R. 179; 117 J.P. 52; 51 L.G.R. 121; 97
   S.J. 28, CA; affirming [1952] 1 All E.R. 1326; [1952] 1 T.L.R. 1013; 50 L.G.R.
   488; [1952] W.N. 227; 96 S.J. 263, Ch D . . . .   *Digested*, 53/**3802**:
            Applied, 94/3405, 01/1544: *Considered*, 54/2700, 54/3264, 54/3265
Pride Valley Foods Ltd v. Hall & Partners (Contract Management) Ltd (No.1) [2001]
   EWCA Civ 1001; 76 Con. L.R. 1; [2001] N.P.C. 103, CA; reversing in part (2000)
   16 Const. L.J. 424; [2000] N.P.C. 55, QBD (T&CC) . . . .   *Digested*, 01/**4450**
Pride Valley Foods Ltd v. Independent Insurance Co Ltd [1999] 1 Lloyd's Rep. I.R. 120,
   CA . . . .   *Digested*, 99/**3381**
Pridean Ltd v. Forest Taverns Ltd (1998) 75 P. & C.R. 447, CA . . . .   *Digested*, 98/**3666**

Priestley v. Weyman (Unreported, June 22, 1995), CC (Barnet) [*Ex rel*. Jl Farquharson, Barrister] . . . . *Digested*, 95/**4074**:
Cited, 99/552

Primaplus Ltd v. Hall Aggregates Ltd [2001] N.P.C. 11, Ch D
Primark Stores Ltd v. Lollypop Clothing Ltd [2001] E.T.M.R. 30; [2001] F.S.R. 37, Ch D
. . . . *Digested*, 01/**4034**
Primback Ltd v. Customs and Excise Commissioners see Customs and Excise Commissioners v. Primback Ltd
Primback Ltd v. Customs and Excise Commissioners (C34/99) see Customs and Excise Commissioners v. Primback Ltd (C34/99)
Primecrown Ltd v. Medicines Control Agency see R. v. Medicines Control Agency Ex p. Smith & Nephew Pharmaceuticals Ltd (C201/94)
Primex Produkte Import-Export GmbH & Co KG v. Commission of the European Communities (T50/96) [1998] E.C.R. II-3773; [1999] 1 C.M.L.R. 99, CFI . . . . . *Digested*, 99/**2261**:
Followed, 00/2350

PRIMUS Trade Mark [1999] 3 C.M.L.R. 201, OGH (A)
Prince v. DPP [1996] Crim. L.R. 343, QBD . . . . *Applied*, 00/938
Prince v. Robinson (1999) 31 H.L.R. 89; (1998) 76 P. & C.R. D2, CA . . . . *Digested*, 98/**3663**
Prince v. Wandsworth LBC see Passley v. Wandsworth LBC
Prince Blucher Ex p. Debtor, Re [1931] 2 Ch. 70, CA . . . . *Distinguished*,
54/3172,
54/3173, 57/1961: *Followed*, 98/4528
Prince Plc v. Prince Sports Group Inc [1997-98] Info. T.L.R. 329; [1998] F.S.R. 21; [1998] Masons C.L.R. 139, Ch D . . . . *Digested*, 98/**3528**
Principles Retail Ltd's Community Trade Mark Application [2000] E.T.M.R. 240, OHIM (Opposition Div) . . . . *Digested*, 00/**3748**
Prinsloo v. Van der Linde 2 B.H.R.C. 334, Const Ct (SA) . . . . *Digested*, 97/**2793**:
Applied, 98/3109, 98/3276

Print v. Showmen's Guild of Great Britain [1999] N.P.C. 125, QBD
Print Concept GmbH v. GEW (EC) Ltd [2001] EWCA Civ 352; [2001] E.C.C. 36, CA . . *Digested*, 01/**826**
Printed Forms Equipments Ltd v. Societe Materiel Auxiliaire d'Informatique [2000] I.L.Pr. 597, C d'A (Paris)
Printers & Finishers Ltd v. Holloway (No.2) [1965] 1 W.L.R. 1; [1964] 3 All E.R. 731; [1965] R.P.C. 239; 109 S.J. 47, Ch D . . . . *Digested*, 64/**1284**:
Applied, 96/2598, 98/2193: *Considered*, 77/2162, 85/1134, 86/1167
Printpak v. AGF Insurance Ltd [1999] 1 All E.R. (Comm.) 466; *Times*, February 3, 1999, CA . . . . *Digested*, 99/**3390**
Prinz v. Austria (23867/94) (2001) 31 E.H.R.R. 12, ECHR. . . . . *Digested*, 01/**3507**
Priority Stainless (UK) Ltd, Re see Secretary of State for Trade and Industry v. Crane (No.2)
Priory Garage (Walthamstow) Ltd, Re [2001] B.P.I.R. 144, Ch D (Companies Ct) . . . . . *Digested*, 01/**3784**
Prisma Presse SNC v. Europe 1 Telecompagnie [1998] E.T.M.R. 515, Trib Gde Inst (Paris)
Prisma Presse Ste v. Editions Economica SA; Gruner und Jahr Communication GmbH v. Editions Economica SA [1999] E.T.M.R. 549, Trib Gde Inst (Paris)
Pritchard v. Briggs [1980] Ch. 338; [1979] 3 W.L.R. 868; [1980] 1 All E.R. 294; (1980) 40 P. & C.R. 1; (1979) 123 S.J. 705, CA; reversing [1978] 2 W.L.R. 317; [1978] 1 All E.R. 886; (1978) 35 P. & C.R. 266; (1977) 244 E.G. 211, Ch D . . . *Digested*, 80/**1563**:
Applied, 80/1846, 84/2952, 85/3607, 01/4858: *Considered*, 85/1143, 93/1617: *Distinguished*, 79/153, 01/3735
Pritchard v. Ford Motor Co Ltd; Riccio v. Ford Motor Co Ltd [1997] 1 Costs L.R. 39, QBD . . . . *Digested*, 98/**474**
Pritchard v. Gregory (Valuation Officer) [1999] R.V.R. 23, Lands Tr . . . . *Digested*, 99/**4330**
Pritchard v. Halifax Plc (Unreported, July 9, 1999), CC (Monmouth) [*Ex rel*. Brian Watson, Barrister, Guildhall Chambers, 23 Broad Street, Bristol] . . . . *Digested*, 99/**4061**
Private Imports of Medicines (C62/90), Re see Commission of the European Communities v. Germany (C62/90)
Privet v. Inland Revenue Commissioners [2001] S.T.C. (S.C.D.) 119, Sp Comm
Prize Competitions in German Magazine Sold in Austria, Re [2000] E.C.C. 215, OGH (A)
Prize Competitions in Periodicals, Re [2000] E.C.C. 118, OGH (A)
Pro Sieben Media AG v. Carlton UK Television Ltd [1999] 1 W.L.R. 605; [2000] E.C.D.R. 110; [1999] E.M.L.R. 109; [1999] I.T.C.L.R. 332; [1999] F.S.R. 610; (1999) 22(3) I.P.D. 22029; (1999) 96(5) L.S.G. 35; (1999) 143 S.J.L.B. 37; *Times*, January 7, 1999; *Independent*, January 22, 1999, CA; reversing [1998] E.C.C. 112; [1997] E.M.L.R. 509; [1998] F.S.R. 43; (1997) 20(10) I.P.D. 20101; *Times*, September 24, 1997, Ch D . . . . *Digested*, 99/**3438**:
Applied, 01/3851

Probert v. Dudley MBC see R. v. Dudley Magistrates Court Ex p. Hollis
Proceedings brought by Forsakringsaktiebolaget Skandia (C240/99) see Forsakringsaktiebolaget Skandia (C240/99), Re
Processed Vegetable Growers Association v. Customs and Excise Commissioners [1974] 1 C.M.L.R. 113; [1973] V.A.T.T.R. 87, VAT Tr . . . . *Digested*, 74/**3923.11**:
Considered, 76/2846.11, 01/5289
Procter & Gamble v. Controller of Patents, Designs and Trade Marks [2001] E.T.M.R. 112, HC (Irl)

Procter & Gamble Co v. Office for Harmonisation in the Internal Market (Trade Marks and Designs) (OHIM) (T163/98) see Procter & Gamble Co v. Office for Harmonisation in the Internal Market (Trade Marks and Designs) (OHIM) (C383/99 P)

Procter & Gamble Co v. Office for Harmonisation in the Internal Market (Trade Marks and Designs) (OHIM) (T122/99); *sub nom* Procter & Gamble Co's Community Trade Mark Application (Shaped Soap) [2000] E.C.R. II-265; [2000] 2 C.M.L.R. 303; [2000] C.E.C. 107; [2000] E.T.M.R. 580; (2000) 23(6) I.P.D. 23042, CFI (2nd Chamber); reversing in part [1999] E.T.M.R. 776, OHIM (3rd Bd App) . . . .   *Digested,* 00/**3788**:
Applied, 01/4004

Procter & Gamble Co v. Office for Harmonisation in the Internal Market (Trade Marks and Designs) (OHIM) (C383/99 P); *sub nom* Procter & Gamble Co v. Office for Harmonisation in the Internal Market (Trade Marks and Designs) (OHIM) (T163/98) [2001] E.C.R. I-6251; [2001] C.E.C. 325; (2001) 24(12) I.P.D. 24076; *Times,* October 3, 2001, ECJ [2000] 1 W.L.R. 91; [1999] All E.R. (EC) 648; [1999] E.C.R. II-2383; [1999] 2 C.M.L.R. 1442; [1999] C.E.C. 329; [1999] E.T.M.R. 767; [2001] E.C.R. I-6251; [2001] E.T.M.R. 75; *Times,* July 29, 1999, AGO; reversing [1999] E.T.M.R. 240, OHIM (1st Bd App) . . . .   *Digested,* 01/**4003**:
Applied, 01/4004, 01/4016: *Followed,* 00/3715: *Referred to,* 00/3717, 01/3994

Procter & Gamble Co v. Office for Harmonisation in the Internal Market (Trade Marks and Designs) (OHIM) (T129/00) [2001] C.E.C. 313, CFI (2nd Chamber)

Procter & Gamble Co v. Office for Harmonisation in the Internal Market (Trade Marks and Designs) (OHIM) (T121/00); *sub nom* Procter & Gamble France's Community Trade Mark Application (R 529/1999-1) CFI; affirming [2001] E.T.M.R. 22; (2000) 23(7) I.P.D. 23051, OHIM (1st Bd App) . . . .   *Digested,* 01/**4001**

Procter & Gamble Co v. Peaudouce (UK) Ltd [1989] 1 F.S.R. 180, CA. . . . .   *Digested,* 89/**2806**:
Considered, 98/3462

Procter & Gamble Co's Community Trade Mark Application (PERFECT BROW) [2000] E.T.M.R. 174, OHIM (3rd Bd App) . . . .   *Digested,* 00/**3779**

Procter & Gamble Co's Community Trade Mark Application (Shaped Soap) see Procter & Gamble Co v. Office for Harmonisation in the Internal Market (Trade Marks and Designs) (OHIM) (T122/99)

Procter & Gamble Co's European Patent (No.0181773) (T450/97) see PROCTER & GAMBLE/Shampoo composition (T450/97)

Procter & Gamble Co's Irish Trade Mark Application (Shaped Soap) [2000] E.T.M.R. 703, PO (Irl) . . . .   *Digested,* 00/**3764**

Procter & Gamble Co's Trade Mark Application (BOUNTY 3-D) [1998] E.T.M.R. 438, OHIM (1st Bd App)

Procter & Gamble Co's Trade Mark Application (COMPLETE); *sub nom* COMPLETE Trade Mark [1999] E.T.M.R. 664, OHIM (3rd Bd App) . . . .   *Digested,* 00/**3735**

Procter & Gamble Co's Trade Mark Application (Shaped Soap) [1998] R.P.C. 710, TMR .   *Digested,* 99/**3585**

Procter & Gamble Co's Trade Mark Application (SWEDISH FORMULA) [1999] E.T.M.R. 559, OHIM (2nd Bd App) . . . .   *Digested,* 00/**3757**

Procter & Gamble France's Community Trade Mark Application (R 529/1999-1) see Procter & Gamble Co v. Office for Harmonisation in the Internal Market (Trade Marks and Designs) (OHIM) (T121/00)

Procter & Gamble Ltd v. Registrar of Trade Marks see Procter & Gamble Ltd's Trade Mark Applications (Detergent Bottles)

Procter & Gamble Ltd's Trade Mark Applications (Detergent Bottles); *sub nom* Procter & Gamble Ltd v. Registrar of Trade Marks [1999] E.T.M.R. 375; [1999] R.P.C. 673; (1999) 22(4) I.P.D. 22040; (1999) 96(9) L.S.G. 32; *Times,* February 17, 1999, CA; affirming (1997) 20(12) I.P.D. 20123, Ch D . . . .   *Digested,* 99/**3567**:
Applied, 99/3583: *Referred to,* 01/4030

Procter & Gamble's Trade Mark Application (ULTRA MOIST) see ULTRA MOIST Trade Mark

PROCTER & GAMBLE/Gastrointestinal compositions (T317/95) [1999] E.P.O.R. 528, EPO (Technical Bd App) . . . .   *Digested,* 00/**3630**

PROCTER & GAMBLE/Shampoo composition (T450/97); *sub nom* Procter & Gamble Co's European Patent (No.0181773) (T450/97) [1999] E.P.O.R. 324; (1998) 21(11) I.P.D. 21119, EPO (Technical Bd App) . . . .   *Digested,* 99/**3476**

Proctor v. THK Refractories Ltd and Eagle Star Insurance Co (Unreported, October 6, 1997), CC (Middlesbrough) [*Ex rel.* Jacksons Solicitors, 1-15 Queens Square, Middlesbrough] . . . .   *Digested,* 98/**363**

Procureur du Roi v. Dassonville (C8/74); *sub nom* Dassonville v. Commission of the European Communities (C8/74); Procureur du Roi v. SA ETS Fourcroy; Procureur du Roi v. SA Breuval et Cie [1974] E.C.R. 837; [1974] 2 C.M.L.R. 436; [1975] F.S.R. 191, ECJ . . . .   *Digested,* 75/**1285**:
Applied, 98/728: *Considered,* 94/4885: *Followed,* 80/1160, 80/1193.a, 95/9, 96/4865, 01/2489, 01/2508

Procureur du Roi v. SA Breuval et Cie see Procureur du Roi v. Dassonville (C8/74)
Procureur du Roi v. SA ETS Fourcroy see Procureur du Roi v. Dassonville (C8/74)

Produce Marketing Consortium (In Liquidation)(No.1), Re; *sub nom* Halls v. David
[1989] 1 W.L.R. 745; [1989] 3 All E.R. 1; (1989) 5 B.C.C. 399; [1989] B.C.L.C.
513; [1989] P.C.C. 290; 133 S.J. 945; *Times*, February 18, 1989, Ch D . . . .   *Digested*, 89/**312**:
        Applied, 99/3294

Profer AG v. Owners of the Ship Tjaskemolen (Now Named Visvliet) see Tjaskemolen
(Now Named Visvliet), The (No.1)
Professional Contractors Group Ltd v. Inland Revenue Commissioners see R. (on the
application of Professional Contractors Group Ltd) v. Inland Revenue
Commissioners (Human Rights)
Professional Representation (J27/95), Re (1998) 21 (7) I.P.D. 21075, EPO (Legal Bd App)
Profilati Italia Srl v. Painewebber Inc [2001] 1 All E.R. (Comm) 1065; [2001] 1 Lloyd's
Rep. 715; [2001] C.L.C. 672, QBD (Comm Ct) . . . .   *Digested*, 01/**347**
Profinance Trust SA v. Gladstone [2001] EWCA Civ 1031; (2001) 98(30) L.S.G. 37;
Times, August 7, 2001; *Independent*, July 11, 2001, CA; reversing [2000] 2
B.C.L.C. 516, Ch D (Companies Ct) . . . .   *Digested*, 01/**741**
PROFITMAKER Trade Mark [1994] R.P.C. 613, Secr of State for Trade . . . .   *Digested*, 95/**4949**:
        Considered, 99/3526

Project Consultancy Group v. Trustees of the Gray Trust [1999] B.L.R. 377; (2000) 2
T.C.L.R. 72; 65 Con. L.R. 146, QBD (T&CC) . . . .   *Digested*, 00/**807**:
        Applied, 00/5979

Prolaw Ltd v. Adams (t/a Nigel Adams & Co) see Cockerill v. Tambrands Ltd
Prolaw Ltd v. Adams (t/a Nigel Adams & Co) (1998) 95(23) L.S.G. 27; (1998) 142
S.J.L.B. 175; *Times*, June 4, 1998, CA . . . .   *Digested*, 98/**397**:
        Joined proceedings, 98/392, 98/395

Promega Corp's European Patent Application (W01/97) see PROMEGA/Tandem repeat
loci (W01/97)
PROMEGA/Tandem repeat loci (W01/97); *sub nom* Promega Corp's European Patent
Application (W01/97) [2000] E.P.O.R. 128; (1998) 21(11) I.P.D. 21117, EPO
(Technical Bd App) . . . .   *Digested*, 00/**3597**
Promotion of a New Car Sales Business, Re [2000] E.C.C. 8, OGH (A)
Prontaprint Plc v. Landon Litho Ltd [1987] F.S.R. 315, Ch D . . . .   *Digested*, 87/**3737**:
     Considered, 98/727, 01/960: *Followed*, 96/1243
Property & Land Contractors Ltd v. Alfred McAlpine Homes (North) Ltd 76 B.L.R. 59;
47 Con. L.R. 74, QBD . . . .   *Digested*, 96/**1141**:
        Considered, 99/227, 99/784
Prosho v. Royal Devon & Exeter Healthcare Trust (Unreported, April 20, 2001), QBD
[*Ex rel.* Bevan Ashford, Solicitors, 35 Colston Avenue, Bristol] . . . .   *Digested*, 01/**4472**
Prospects Care Services Ltd v. Customs and Excise Commissioners [1997] V. & D.R.
209, V&DTr . . . .   *Digested*, 98/**4905**
Prosser v. Inland Revenue Commissioners [2001] R.V.R. 170, Lands Tr . . . .   *Digested*, 01/**5280**
Proszak v. Poland [1998] H.R.C.D. 162, ECHR . . . .   *Referred to*, 01/3521
Protection of Wild Birds (C339/87), Re see Commission of the European Communities v.
Netherlands (C339/87)
Protsch v. Austria (15508/89) (2001) 32 E.H.R.R. 12, ECHR
Prottey (t/a Lord Nelson) v. Customs and Excise Commissioners [2000] S.T.I. 1554,
V&DTr
Proudfoot v. Cheam High School (Unreported, February 8, 2001), CC (Epsom) [*Ex rel.*
James Leabeater, Barrister, 4 Pump Court, Temple, London] . . . .   *Digested*, 01/**902**
Proudfoot v. Hart (1890) L.R. 25 Q.B.D. 42, CA . . . .   *Applied*, 60/1727,
     64/2094, 98/3628, 99/3738: *Considered*, 93/2544: *Distinguished*, 87/2141
Proulx v. Governor of Brixton Prison; R. v. Bow Street Magistrates Court Ex p. Proulx
[2001] 1 All E.R. 57; [2000] Crim. L.R. 997; [2000] C.O.D. 454, QBD
Providence Capitol Trustees Ltd v. Ayres [1996] 4 All E.R. 760; [1996] O.P.L.R. 215,
Ch D . . . .   *Digested*, 97/**517**:
        Approved, 98/4146: *Cited*, 99/4154
Provident Clothing & Supply Co Ltd v. Mason; *sub nom* Mason v. Provident Clothing &
Supply Co Ltd [1913] A.C. 724, HL; reversing [1913] 1 K.B. 65, CA . . . .   *Applied*, 56/3180,
     76/2160, 98/2192: *Considered*, 94/2765, 97/2256: *Distinguished*, 65/1468:
        Explained, 72/515
Provincia Autonoma di Trento v. Dega di Depretto Gino Snc (C83/96); Provincia
Autonoma di Trento v. Ufficio del Medico Provinciale di Trento [1998] All E.R.
(E.C.) 252; [1997] E.C.R. I-5001; [1998] 1 C.M.L.R. 353, ECJ (1st Chamber) . .   *Digested*, 98/**2573**
Provincia Autonoma di Trento v. Ufficio del Medico Provinciale di Trento see Provincia
Autonoma di Trento v. Dega di Depretto Gino Snc (C83/96)
Provincial North West Plc v. Bennett; Provincial North West Plc v. Williams *Times*,
February 11, 1999, CA . . . .   *Digested*, 99/**289**
Provincial North West Plc v. Williams see Provincial North West Plc v. Bennett
Prudential Assurance Co Ltd v. Bibby (Inspector of Taxes) [1999] S.T.C. 952; 73 T.C.
142; [1999] B.T.C. 323; *Times*, July 24, 1999, Ch D . . . .   *Digested*, 99/**4674**
Prudential Assurance Co Ltd v. Customs and Excise Commissioners [2001] B.V.C. 2201;
[2001] S.T.I. 769, V&DTr
Prudential Assurance Co Ltd v. Eden Restaurants (Holborn) Ltd [2000] L. & T.R. 480,
CA . . . .   *Digested*, 01/**4155**

Prudential Assurance Co Ltd v. Fountain Page Ltd [1991] 1 W.L.R. 756; [1991] 3 All
E.R. 878, QBD. . . . . *Digested,* 91/**2870**:
                         Applied, 97/3887, 00/345: *Referred to,* 97/3888
Prudential Assurance Co Ltd v. McBains Cooper [2000] 1 W.L.R. 2000; [2001] 3 All
E.R. 1014; [2001] C.P. Rep. 19; [2000] C.P.L.R. 475; (2000) 97(24) L.S.G. 40;
(2000) 150 N.L.J. 832; *Times,* June 2, 2000, CA   *Digested,* 00/**504**
Prudential Assurance Co Ltd v. Mount Eden Land Ltd see Mount Eden Land Ltd v.
Prudential Assurance Co Ltd
Prudential Assurance Co Ltd v. Newman Industries Ltd (No.2) [1982] Ch. 204; [1982]
2 W.L.R. 31; [1982] 1 All E.R. 354, CA; reversing in part [1981] Ch. 257;
[1980] 3 W.L.R. 543; [1980] 2 All E.R. 841, Ch D . . . . *Digested,* 82/**331**:
             Applied, 98/691, 99/4025, 00/4257, 01/964: *Cited,* 00/5268:
             Considered, 81/251, 82/330, 96/1213, 00/371: *Followed,* 96/**682**:
                                   Referred to, 95/3755
Prudential Assurance Co Ltd v. Waterloo Real Estate Inc [1999] 2 E.G.L.R. 85; [1999]
17 E.G. 131; [1999] E.G.C.S. 10; [1999] N.P.C. 8; *Times,* February 8, 1999, CA;
affirming [1998] E.G.C.S. 51; [1998] N.P.C. 55; *Times,* May 13, 1998, Ch D . . . . *Digested,* 99/**4348**
Prudential Insurance Co v. Inland Revenue Commissioners [1904] 2 K.B. 658, KBD . . . *Applied,* 73/1704,
            74/1900, 99/3411: *Considered,* 79/1505, 94/2683, 95/2902, 96/3571
PSL Freight Ltd v. Customs and Excise Commissioners [2001] B.T.C. 5437; [2001]
B.V.C. 539, Ch D . . . . *Digested,* 01/**4120**
PTT Telecom BV Swiss PTT and Telia AB's Agreements see Unisource (IV/35.830), Re
Public Committee Against Torture in Israel v. Israel 7 B.H.R.C. 31, Sup Ct (Isr)
Public Corp for Sugar Trade v. N Michalos & Sons Co see N Michalos & Sons Maritime
SA v. Prudential Assurance Co (The Zinovia)
Public Employees (No.1) (C149/79), Re see Commission of the European Communities v.
Belgium (No.1) (C149/79)
Public Prosecution v. A (2000/1219) 3 I.T.L. Rep. 510, HR (N)
Public Prosecutor v. Olsson [2001] E.C.D.R. 22, HD (Swe)
Public Service Employment (C473/93), Re see Commission of the European Communities
v. Luxembourg (C473/93)
Public Trustee v. Cooper [2001] W.T.L.R. 901, Ch D . . . . *Digested,* 01/**5527**
Publication of Lawyers Pleadings (3 U 34/99), Re [2001] E.C.C. 31, OLG (Hamburg)
Pugh v. Arton (1869) L.R. 8 Eq. 626, Ct of Chancery . . . . *Followed,* 99/3679
Pugh v. Cantor Fitzgerald International [2001] EWCA Civ 307; [2001] C.P. Rep. 74;
[2001] C.P.L.R. 271; (2001) 98(18) L.S.G. 44; (2001) 145 S.J.L.B. 83; *Times,*
March 20, 2001, CA . . . . *Digested,* 01/**547**
Pugh v. Customs and Excise Commissioners [2001] S.T.I. 746, V&DTr
Pullar v. Aldi Stores Ltd 98/NJ/1827, QBD . . . . *Digested,* 99/**1502**
Pullman Garage v. Dodia, CC (Bow) [*Ex rel.* Robert Kay, Barrister, Mitre Court
Chambers, 199 Strand, London] . . . . *Digested,* 01/**511**
Pullum v. Crown Prosecution Service [2000] C.O.D. 206, QBD
Punford v. Gilberts Accountants [1999] E.C.C. 91; [1998] P.N.L.R. 763, CA . . . . *Digested,* 99/**4016**
Punjab National Bank v. De Boinville [1992] 1 W.L.R. 1138; [1992] 3 All E.R. 104;
[1992] 1 Lloyd's Rep. 7; [1992] E.C.C. 348; (1991) 141 N.L.J. 85; *Times,* June 4,
1991; *Financial Times,* June 5, 1991, CA; affirming *Financial Times,* February 1,
1991 . . . . *Digested,* 92/**2605**:
                     Applied, 97/3818: *Considered,* 93/2997, 94/115, 01/3840
Punzelt v. Czech Republic (31315/96) (2001) 33 E.H.R.R. 49, ECHR
Purba v. Purba [2000] 1 F.L.R. 444; [2000] 1 F.C.R. 652; [2000] Fam. Law 86, CA . . . *Digested,* 00/**2526**
Purdy v. Cambran [2000] C.P. Rep. 67; [1999] C.P.L.R. 843, CA . . . . *Digested,* 00/**609**
Pure Spirit Co v. Fowler (1890) L.R. 25 Q.B.D. 235, QBD . . . . *Disapproved,* 73/2632:
                                         Followed, 01/508
Purefuture Ltd v. Simmons & Simmons [2001] C.P. Rep. 30, CA . . . . *Digested,* 00/**617**
Purity Requirements for Beer (C178/84), Re see Commission of the European Communities
v. Germany (C178/84)
Purnell v. Chorlton [2000] B.C.C. 876, Ch D . . . . *Digested,* 00/**3506**
Purnell Secretarial Services v. Lease Management Services see Lease Management
Services v. Purnell Secretarial Services
Purves (Inspector of Taxes) v. Harrison [2001] S.T.C. 267; 73 T.C. 390; [2001] B.T.C. 69;
[2000] S.T.I. 1607; (2000) 97(46) L.S.G. 40; *Times,* November 23, 2000, Ch D
. . . . *Digested,* 00/**4923**
Purvis (CICB: Quantum: 1998), Re (Unreported, January 21, 1998), CICB (Durham) [*Ex rel.*
Roger B Cooper, Barrister, Trinity Chambers, 9-12 Trinity Chare, Quayside,
Newcastle Upon Tyne] . . . . *Digested,* 98/**1565**
Purvis (Withdrawal of Bankruptcy Petitions), Re [1997] 3 All E.R. 663; [1998] B.P.I.R. 153,
Ch D . . . . *Digested,* 97/**3019**
Purvis v. Buckinghamshire CC [1999] Ed. C.R. 542; [1999] E.L.R. 231, QBD . . . . *Digested,* 99/**3974**
Purvis v. Customs and Excise Commissioners [1999] B.P.I.R. 396, Ch D . . . . *Digested,* 99/**3256**
Purvis v. O'Brien (Unreported, August 17, 1998), CC (St Albans) [*Ex rel.* Benedict
Leech, Barrister, 3 Paper Buildings, Temple, London] . . . . *Digested,* 98/**464**
Pushpanathan v. Canada 6 B.H.R.C. 387; [1999] I.N.L.R. 36, Sup Ct (Can) . . . . *Digested,* 99/**3167**
Puttock v. Kodak Ltd (Unreported, March 31, 2000), CC (Guildford) [*Ex rel.* Richard
Davison, Barrister, Thomas More Chambers, Lincoln's Inn, London] . . . . *Digested,* 00/**1645**

Putz v. Austria (18892/91) (2001) 32 E.H.R.R. 13, ECHR . . . . *Applied*, 98/3119
PVC Cartel II (T305/94), Re see Limburgse Vinyl Maatschappij NV v. Commission of the
    European Communities (C238/99)
Pye v. Secretary of State for the Environment, Transport and the Regions and North
    Cornwall DC [1998] 3 P.L.R. 72; [1999] P.L.C.R. 28; [1998] E.G.C.S. 80;
    (1998) 95(19) L.S.G. 25, QBD. . . . . *Digested*, 98/**4209**:
                    Followed, 00/4502
Pye, Ex p. (1811) 18 Ves. Jr. 140 . . . . *Considered*, 99/4646
Pyne v. Brown [2001] 5 Q.R. 16, CC (Stoke on Trent) [*Ex rel.* Michael Halsall
    Solicitors, 2 The Parks, Newton-le-Willows, WA12 ONZ] . . . . *Digested*, 01/**1726**
Pyne-Edwards v. Moore Large & Co Ltd see Limb v. Union Jack Removals Ltd (In
    Liquidation)
Pyrkos v. Roberts see Panayi v. Roberts
Python (Monty) Pictures Ltd v. Paragon Entertainment Corp [1998] E.M.L.R. 640;
    Times, July 31, 1998, Ch D . . . . *Digested*, 98/**3415**
Pyx Granite Co Ltd v. Ministry of Housing and Local Government [1960] A.C. 260;
    [1959] 3 W.L.R. 346; [1959] 3 All E.R. 1; 123 J.P. 429; 58 L.G.R. 1; 10 P. & C.R.
    319; 103 S.J. 633, HL; reversing [1958] 1 Q.B. 554; [1958] 2 W.L.R. 371;
    [1958] 1 All E.R. 625; 122 J.P. 182; 56 L.G.R. 171; (1958) 9 P. & C.R. 204; 102
    S.J. 175, CA . . . . *Digested*, 59/**3260**:
                    Applied, 59/3229, 60/3110, 63/2259, 63/3426, 64/3556, 64/3600,
               64/3601, 69/1168, 70/11, 70/836, 71/5152, 71/6934, 72/3358, 73/2055,
               76/2727, 77/2973, 77/2976, 78/2889, 79/2634, 80/308, 82/2396, 83/2108,
               84/10, 85/9, 98/281: *Considered*, 63/3429, 63/8429, 68/3837, 69/2896,
               70/1757, 80/2667, 82/2489, 87/3097, 90/120, 90/2829, 90/3908, 91/119:
               Distinguished, 64/2433, 70/2778, 82/1264, 82/2928: *Not applied*, 75/2865

Q's Estate, Re [1999] 1 All E.R. (Comm.) 499; [1999] 1 Lloyd's Rep. 931; (1999) 149 N.L.J.
    442; *Independent*, March 19, 1999, QBD (Comm Ct) . . . . *Digested*, 99/**241**
Qatar v. Sheikh Khalifa (1999-2000) 2 I.T.E.L.R. 143, Royal Ct (Jer)
Qazi v. Waltham Forest LBC (2000) 32 H.L.R. 689, QBD . . . . *Digested*, 00/**4109**
QBE Insurance (UK) Ltd v. Mediterranean Insurance and Reinsurance Co Ltd [1992] 1
    W.L.R. 573; [1992] 1 All E.R. 12; [1992] 1 Lloyd's Rep. 435, QBD (Comm Ct) . . *Digested*, 92/**3561**:
                    Considered, 99/372: *Followed*, 97/552
QPS Consultants Ltd v. Kruger Tissue (Manufacturing) Ltd [1999] C.P.L.R. 710; [1999]
    B.L.R. 366, CA . . . . *Digested*, 00/**630**
QRS 1 ApS v. Frandsen [1999] 1 W.L.R. 2169; [1999] 3 All E.R. 289; [1999] S.T.C.
    616; [2000] I.L.Pr. 8; 71 T.C. 515; [1999] B.T.C. 8203; 1 I.T.L. Rep. 687; (1999)
    96(24) L.S.G. 39; *Times*, May 27, 1999, CA; affirming [1999] I.L.Pr. 432; 1 I.T.L.
    Rep. 673, QBD . . . . *Digested*, 99/**729**
QS BY S OLIVER Trade Mark [1999] R.P.C. 520, TMR . . . . *Digested*, 99/**3569**
Quadmost Ltd (In Liquidation) v. Reprotech (Pebsham) Ltd [2001] B.P.I.R. 349, QBD . *Digested*, 01/**964**
Quadrant Holdings Cambridge Ltd v. Quadrant Research Foundation (1999) 22(3)
    I.P.D. 22025, Pat Ct
Quadrant Holdings Cambridge Ltd v. Quadrant Research Foundation (Costs) [1999]
    F.S.R. 918, Pat Ct . . . . *Digested*, 00/**416**
Quantum Claims Compensation Specialists Ltd v. Powell 1998 S.C. 316; 1998 S.L.T.
    228; 1998 S.C.C.R. 173; 1998 G.W.D. 3-137; *Times*, February 26, 1998, Ex Div;
    affirming 1997 S.C.L.R. 242, Sh Pr . . . . *Digested*, 98/**5548**
Quantum Corp Ltd v. Plane Trucking Ltd; *sub nom* Quantum Corp Inc v. Plane Trucking
    Ltd; A3/2001/0985, CA; reversing [2001] 1 All E.R. (Comm) 916; [2001] 2
    Lloyd's Rep. 133; [2001] C.L.C. 1192, QBD (Comm Ct) . . . . *Digested*, 01/**5391**
Quaquah v. Group 4 Securities Ltd (No.2); *sub nom* Quaquah v. Group Four (Total
    Security) Ltd (No.2) *Times*, June 27, 2001, QBD. . . . . *Digested*, 01/**5358**
Quarcoopome v. Sock Shop Holdings Ltd [1995] I.R.L.R. 353, EAT . . . . *Digested*, 95/**2025**:
                    Considered, 00/2207
Quartz Hill Consolidated Gold Mining Co v. Eyre (1882-83) L.R. 11 Q.B.D. 674, CA. . . . *Applied*, 60/1953:
              Distinguished, 61/3318, 61/5397: *Followed*, 97/4862, 98/4779
Quaysiders Club Ltd v. Customs and Excise Commissioners [2001] S.T.I. 1169, V&DTr
Queens University of Belfast v. Commissioner of Valuation [2001] R.V.R. 112, Lands Tr
    (NI) . . . . *Digested*, 01/**5941**
Queensland v. Pioneer Concrete (Qld) Ltd Unreported, Fed Ct (Aus) (Sgl judge) . . . . . *Applied*, 00/5106
Queensland Mines Ltd v. Hudson (1978) 18 A.L.R. 1; (1978) 52 A.L.J.R. 399, PC (Aus) *Applied*, 01/5525
Queensway Housing Association Ltd v. Chiltern, Thames and Eastern Rent Assessment
    Committee; Laira Properties Ltd v. Chiltern, Thames and Eastern Rent
    Assessment Committee; Cherry Tree Investments v. Greater Manchester Rent
    Assessment Committee; Dakin v. North Western Rent Assessment Committee;
    Whinmoor Estates Ltd v. Merseyside and Cheshire Rent Assessment Committee;
    Grainger Investment Property Ltd v. Southern and South Eastern Rent
    Assessment Commitee (1999) 31 H.L.R. 945; (1999) 96(5) L.S.G. 36; (1999)
    143 S.J.L.B. 35; *Times*, December 11, 1998, QBD. . . . . *Digested*, 99/**3721**
Quelle Schickedanz AG und Co v. Oberfinanzdirektion Frankfurt am Main (C80/96)
    [1998] E.C.R. I-123; [1998] 1 C.M.L.R. 968, ECJ (1st Chamber)

Queneau v. Boue [2000] E.C.D.R. 343, Trib Gde Inst (F)
Queneau v. L (Christian) [1998] E.C.C. 47; [1997-98] Info. T.L.R. 257, Trib Gde Inst
  (Paris). . . . . *Digested,* 98/**3432**
Quentin v. Governor of Brixton Prison [1998] C.O.D. 193, QBD . . . . *Digested,* 98/**2349**
Questore di Verona v. Zenatti (C67/98) [1999] E.C.R. I-7289; [2000] 1 C.M.L.R. 201,
  ECJ [1999] E.C.R. I-7289, AGO. . . . . *Digested,* 00/**2397**
Quick v. Taff Ely BC [1986] Q.B. 809; [1985] 3 W.L.R. 981; [1985] 3 All E.R. 321;
  (1986) 18 H.L.R. 66; [1985] 2 E.G.L.R. 50; (1985) 276 E.G. 452, CA . . . . *Digested,* 85/**1610**:
              Applied, 87/2141, 98/2987: *Considered,* 90/2792, 91/2228, 93/2462,
          95/3062: *Distinguished,* 98/3628: *Followed,* 01/4203: *Referred to,* 87/2140
Quicks Plc v. Customs and Excise Commissioners [1999] B.V.C. 2117, V&DTr
Quigley v. Liverpool Housing Trust [2000] E.H.L.R. 130; [1999] E.G.C.S. 94; [2000]
  Env. L.R. D9, QBD. . . . . *Digested,* 99/**4073**
Quigley's Application, Re [1997] N.I. 202, QBD (NI) . . . . *Digested,* 99/**5212**
Quijano v. Secretary of State for the Home Department [1997] Imm. A.R. 227, CA . . . . *Digested,* 97/**2856**:
                                            Applied, 00/3318
Quillan v. West Lancashire DC [2001] 4 Q.R. 10, CC (Wigan) [*Ex rel.* Canter Levin&
  Berg, Solicitors, Whelmar House, Southway, Skelmersdale]. . . . . *Digested,* 01/**1742**
Quilter v. Attorney General of New Zealand 3 B.H.R.C. 461, CA (NZ) . . . . *Digested,* 98/**2478**
Quinlan v. Amann (1999) 78 P. & C.R. D30, CA
Quinlan v. B&Q Plc [1999] Disc. L.R. 76, EAT . . . . *Digested,* 99/**2025**
Quinn (Inspector of Taxes) v. Cooper [1998] S.T.C. 772; [1998] B.T.C. 266; (1998)
  95(31) L.S.G. 35; *Times,* July 20, 1998, Ch D . . . . *Digested,* 98/**4606**
Quinn v. Ireland (36887/97) (2000) 29 E.H.R.R. CD234, ECHR
Quinn v. Ministry of Defence [1998] P.I.Q.R. P387, CA . . . . *Digested,* 98/**4785**
Quinn v. Schwarzkopf Ltd [2001] I.R.L.R. 67, EAT. . . . . *Digested,* 01/**6462**:
                                       Not followed, 01/6463
Quinnen v. Hovells [1984] I.C.R. 525; [1984] I.R.L.R. 227; (1984) 81 L.S.G. 1438;
  (1984) 134 N.L.J. 360; (1984) 128 S.J. 431, EAT . . . . *Digested,* 84/**1272**:
                                         Applied, 98/5133
Quinta Communications SA v. Warrington [1999] 2 All E.R. (Comm) 123; [2000]
  Lloyd's Rep. I.R. 81, CA . . . . *Digested,* 99/**3398**
Quirk v. Burton Hospitals NHS Trust; *sub nom* Quirk v. Burton Hospital NHS Trust; A1/
  2001/0224, CA; affirming [2001] 2 C.M.L.R. 15; [2001] I.C.R. 415; [2001]
  I.R.L.R. 198, EAT . . . . *Digested,* 01/**2281**
Quistclose Investments Ltd v. Rolls Razor Ltd (In Voluntary Liquidation) see Barclays
  Bank Ltd v. Quistclose Investments Ltd
Qureshi v. Victoria University of Manchester [2001] I.C.R. 863 (Note), EAT. . . . . *Digested,* 01/**2296**:
                                         Approved, 01/2298

R (A Child), Re see North Yorkshire CC v. Wiltshire CC
R (A Child) (Adoption: Disclosure), Re see R (A Child) (Adoption: Duty to Investigate), Re
R (A Child) (Adoption: Duty to Investigate), Re; *sub nom* Z CC v. R; R (A Child)
  (Adoption: Disclosure), Re [2001] 1 F.L.R. 365; [2001] 1 F.C.R. 238; [2001]
  Fam. Law 8; *Times,* February 13, 2001, Fam Div. . . . . *Digested,* 01/**2534**
R (A Child) (Adoption: Father's Involvement), Re; *sub nom* S (A Child) (Adoption
  Proceedings: Joinder of Father), Re [2001] 1 F.L.R. 302; [2001] 1 F.C.R. 158;
  [2001] Fam. Law 91, CA . . . . *Digested,* 01/**2532**
R (A Child) (Care Proceedings: Disclosure), Re [2000] 2 F.L.R. 751; [2000] Fam. Law 793;
  (2001) 165 J.P.N. 104; (2000) 97(30) L.S.G. 39; *Times,* July 18, 2000, CA . . . . *Digested,* 00/**2516**
R (A Child) (Care Proceedings: Teenage Pregnancy), Re; *sub nom* R (A Child) (Care
  Proceedings: Teenage Mother), Re [2000] 2 F.L.R. 660; [2000] 2 F.C.R. 556;
  [2000] Fam. Law 791; *Times,* July 19, 2000, Fam Div . . . . *Digested,* 00/**2462**
R (A Child) (Contact: Human Fertilisation and Embryology Act 1990), Re [2001] 1 F.L.R.
  247; [2001] Fam. Law 10, Fam Div. . . . . *Digested,* 01/**2657**
R (A Child) (Surname: Using Both Parents), Re [2001] EWCA Civ 1344; [2001] 2 F.L.R.
  1358, CA
R (A Child) v. DPP [2001] EWHC Admin 17; (2001) 165 J.P. 349; [2001] Crim. L.R.
  396; (2001) 165 J.P.N. 267; *Times,* February 20, 2001; *Independent,* March 5,
  2001 (C.S), QBD (Admin Ct). . . . . *Digested,* 01/**1049**
R (A Child) v. Iberotravel Ltd (t/a Sunworld Ltd) (Unreported, March 9, 2000), QBD
  [*Ex rel.* Pannone & Partners, Solicitors, 123 Deansgate, Manchester] . . . . *Digested,* 01/**4453**
R (A Child) v. Palmer [2001] 6 Q.R. 19, CC (Merthyr Tydfil) [*Ex rel.* Andrew Arentsen,
  Barrister, 33 Park Place, Cardiff]. . . . . *Digested,* 01/**1744**
R (A Child) v. Taylor (Unreported, June 22, 2000), CC (Norwich) [*Ex rel.* Michael
  Morris, Barrister, 169 Temple Chambers, Temple Avenue, London] . . . . *Digested,* 00/**1728**
R (A Minor) (Blood Tests: Constraint), Re [1998] Fam. 66; [1998] 2 W.L.R. 796; [1998] 1
  F.L.R. 745; [1998] 1 F.C.R. 41; [1998] Fam. Law 256, Fam Div . . . . *Digested,* 98/**2480**
R (A Minor) (Child Case: Procedure), Re see Croydon LBC v. R
R (A Minor) (Court of Appeal: Order against Identification), Re [1999] 2 F.L.R. 145; [1999] 3
  F.C.R. 213; [1999] Fam. Law 446; *Times,* December 9, 1998, CA. . . . . *Digested,* 99/**9**
R (A Minor) (Inter-Country Adoptions: Practice) (No.1), Re [1999] 1 F.L.R. 1014; [1999] 1
  F.C.R. 385; [1999] Fam. Law 289, Fam Div . . . . *Digested,* 99/**2307**

R (A Minor) (Inter-Country Adoptions: Practice) (No.2), Re; *sub nom* Practice Note
(Inter-Country Adoptions) [1999] 1 W.L.R. 1324; [1999] 4 All E.R. 1015; [1999]
1 F.L.R. 1042; [1999] 1 F.C.R. 418; [1999] I.N.L.R. 568; [1999] Fam. Law 289;
(1999) 96(6) L.S.G. 34; *Times*, January 20, 1999, Fam Div . . . .   *Digested*, 99/**2308**

R (A Minor) (Leave to Make Applications), Re see R (A Minor) (Residence: Contact:
Restricting Applications), Re

R (A Minor) (Legal Aid: Costs), Re; *sub nom* R *v.* R (Children Cases: Costs) [1997] 2
F.L.R. 95; [1997] 1 F.C.R. 613; [1997] Fam. Law 391; (1997) 94(6) L.S.G. 27;   *Digested*, 97/**530**:
Times, January 9, 1997, CA . . . .   *Considered*, 99/2410

R (A Minor) (Residence: Contact: Restricting Applications), Re; *sub nom* R (A Minor)
(Leave to Make Applications), Re [1998] 1 F.L.R. 749; [1998] 2 F.C.R. 129;   *Digested*, 98/**2438**
[1998] Fam. Law 247, CA . . . .

R (A Minor) *v.* Calderdale MBC (1999) 99(6) Q.R. 7, CC (Halifax) [*Ex rel.* Rhodes
Thain & Collinson Solicitors, 27 Harrison Road, Halifax] . . . .   *Digested*, 99/**1600**

R (A Minor) *v.* Mohammed (Unreported, July 21, 1999), CC (Slough) [*Ex rel.* Daniel
Jones, Barrister, Phoenix Chambers, Gray's Inn, London] . . . .   *Digested*, 99/**1554**

R (Abduction: Consent), Re; *sub nom* R (Minors) (Abduction: Acquiescence), Re
[1999] 1 F.L.R. 828; [1999] 1 F.C.R. 87; [1999] Fam. Law 288, Fam Div . . . . . .   *Digested*, 99/**2321**

R (Adoption: Protection from Offenders Regulations), Re [1999] 1 F.L.R. 472; [1999] 2
F.C.R. 616; [1999] Fam. Law 10; (2000) 164 J.P.N. 84; (1999) 163 J.P.N. 1009, Fam
Div . . . .   *Digested*, 99/**2298**

R (Care Proceedings: Adjournment), Re [1998] 2 F.L.R. 390; [1998] 3 F.C.R. 654; [1998]
Fam. Law 454; (1999) 163 J.P.N. 94, CA . . . .   *Digested*, 98/**2405**:
     Referred to, 99/2357

R (Children) (Sexual Abuse: Standard of Proof), Re [2001] 1 F.C.R. 86; (2001) 165 J.P.N.
448, CA

R (CICB: Child Abuse: Quantum: 1998), Re (Unreported, March 26, 1998), CICB (Torquay)
[*Ex rel.* Jonathan Dingle, Barrister, South Western Chambers, 12 Middle Street,
Taunton, TA1 1SH] . . . .   *Digested*, 98/**1511**

R (CICB: Quantum: 1999), Re (Unreported, May 6, 1999) [*Ex rel.* Jonathan Ashworth,
Barrister, 6 King's Bench Walk, Temple, London] . . . .   *Digested*, 99/**1455**

R (CICB: Sexual Assault: Quantum: 1998), Re (Unreported, January 27, 1998), CICB
(London) [*Ex rel.* Rebecca Trowler, Barrister, 4 Brick Court, Temple, London] . . .   *Digested*, 98/**1519**

R (Disclosure), Re [1998] 1 F.L.R. 433; [1998] 3 F.C.R. 416; [1998] Fam. Law 134, Fam Div
   Digested, 98/**2486**

R (Minors) (Abduction: Acquiescence), Re see R (Abduction: Consent), Re

R (Minors) (Adoption: Disclosure), Re [1999] 2 F.L.R. 1123; [1999] 3 F.C.R. 334; [1999]
Fam. Law 806; *Times*, July 29, 1999, Fam Div . . . .   *Digested*, 99/**2296**

R (Minors) *v.* Putt (Unreported, May 18, 1999), CC (Weymouth) [*Ex rel.* Archna
Dawar, Barrister, Assize Court Chambers, 14 Small Street, Bristol] . . . .   *Digested*, 99/**1561**

R (Recovery Orders), Re [1998] 2 F.L.R. 401; [1998] 3 F.C.R. 321; [1998] Fam. Law 401,
Fam Div . . . .   *Digested*, 98/**2409**

R *v.* Central Independent Television Plc [1994] Fam. 192; [1994] 3 W.L.R. 20; [1994]
3 All E.R. 641; [1994] 2 F.L.R. 151; [1995] 1 F.C.R. 521; [1994] Fam. Law 500;
Times, February 19, 1994; *Independent*, February 17, 1994, CA . . . .   *Digested*, 95/**3544**:
     Applied, 01/2583: *Considered*, 94/3245, 95/3546

R *v.* Congdon [2001] 6 Q.R. 24, QBD [*Ex rel.* Richard Colbey, Barrister, Tanfield
Chambers, Francis Taylor Building, Temple, London] . . . .   *Digested*, 01/**1811**:
     Joined proceedings, 01/1813, 01/1814

R *v.* Croydon HA [1998] P.I.Q.R. Q26; [1998] Lloyd's Rep. Med. 44; (1998) 40
B.M.L.R. 40; *Times*, December 13, 1997; *Independent*, December 4, 1997, CA;
reversing [1997] P.I.Q.R. P444, QBD . . . .   *Digested*, 98/**1476**

R *v.* Gardner (Unreported, September 9, 1999), MCLC [*Ex rel.* Anthony Gold Lerman
& Muirhead Solicitors, New London Bridge House, 25 London Bridge Street,
London] . . . .   *Digested*, 00/**1656**

R (Norman Charles) *v.* HM Advocate 2000 J.C. 368; 2000 S.L.T. 1315; 2000 S.C.C.R.
354; [2000] H.R.L.R. 389; 2000 G.W.D. 8-276; *Times*, April 14, 2000, HCJ
Appeal . . . .   *Digested*, 00/**6122**

R *v.* Liverpool City Council (Unreported, November 23, 1988) [*Ex rel.* Brian Thompson
& Partners, Solicitors] . . . .   *Digested*, 89/**1255**:
     Considered, 98/1531

R *v.* R (Children Cases: Costs) see R (A Minor) (Legal Aid: Costs), Re

R *v.* R (Disclosure to Revenue); *sub nom* R *v.* R (Inland Revenue: Tax Evasion) [1998]
S.T.C. 237; [1998] 1 F.L.R. 922; [1998] 1 F.C.R. 597; 70 T.C. 119; [1998] B.T.C.
53; [1998] Fam. Law 321, Fam Div . . . .   *Digested*, 98/**4707**

R *v.* R (Inland Revenue: Tax Evasion) see R *v.* R (Disclosure to Revenue)

R *v.* R (Interim Declaration: Adult's Residence) [2000] 1 F.L.R. 451; [2001] 1 F.C.R.
94; [2000] Fam. Law 314, Fam Div . . . .   *Digested*, 00/**2487**

R *v.* Scottish Ministers see A *v.* Scottish Ministers

R v. Secretary of State for Scotland [1999] 2 A.C. 512; [1999] 2 W.L.R. 28; [1999] 1
All E.R. 481; 1999 S.C. (H.L.) 17; 1999 S.L.T. 279; 1999 S.C.L.R. 74; (1999)
96(4) L.S.G. 37; 1998 G.W.D. 40-2075; *Times*, December 7, 1998; *Independent*,
December 8, 1998, HL; reversing 1998 S.C. 49; 1998 S.L.T. 162; 1997 S.C.L.R.
1056; 1997 G.W.D. 35-1793, 2 Div; reversing 1997 S.L.T. 555, OH . . . . *Digested*, 99/**6363**:
                Applied, 00/4174: *Considered*, 99/6361, 00/6472
R (Robert) v. Ski Llandudno Ltd [2001] P.I.Q.R. P5, CA . . . . *Digested*, 01/**1551**
R v. Tilsley (2001) 60 B.M.L.R. 202, QBD . . . . *Digested*, 01/**4459**
R and S (CICB: Quantum: 1998), Re (Unreported, February 9, 1998), CICB [*Ex rel.* Mary
Ruck, Barrister, 10 King's Bench Walk, 1st Floor, Temple, London] . . . . *Digested*, 98/**1535**
R Durtnell & Sons Ltd v. Secretary of State for Trade and Industry [2001] 1 All E.R.
(Comm) 41; [2001] 1 Lloyd's Rep. 275; [2000] C.L.C. 1365; [2000] B.L.R. 321;
74 Con. L.R. 87; [2000] N.P.C. 64; *Times*, July 21, 2000, QBD (T&CC) . . . . *Digested*, 00/**221**
R Pagnan & Fratelli v. Corbisa Industrial Agropacuaria Ltd [1970] 1 W.L.R. 1306; [1970]
1 All E.R. 165; [1970] 2 Lloyd's Rep. 14; 114 S.J. 568, CA; affirming [1969] 2
Lloyd's Rep. 129, QBD (Comm Ct) . . . . *Digested*, 70/**748**:
                Considered, 90/1565: *Distinguished*, 01/943
R Taylor v. Secretary of State for the Environment, Transport and the Regions [1998]
E.G.C.S. 152, QBD
R Walia Opticians Ltd v. Customs and Excise Commissioners [1997] V. & D.R. 368,
V&DTr. . . . . *Digested*, 00/**5321**
R&B Customs Brokers Co Ltd v. United Dominions Trust Ltd [1988] 1 W.L.R. 321;
[1988] 1 All E.R. 847; [1988] R.T.R. 134; (1988) 85(11) L.S.G. 42; (1988) 132
S.J. 300, CA . . . . *Digested*, 88/**3168**:
        Applied, 90/4039, 91/3183, 93/504: *Considered*, 99/4406:
            Distinguished, 94/554, 95/775: *Referred to*, 00/3570
R&M International Engineering Ltd v. Customs and Excise Commissioners [2001] S.T.I.
1393, V&DTr
R&T Thew Ltd v. Reeves (No.1) [1982] Q.B. 172; [1981] 3 W.L.R. 190; [1981] 2 All
E.R. 964; 125 S.J. 358, CA . . . . *Digested*, 81/**1604**:
        Applied, 82/3088: *Approved*, 01/5653: *Considered*, 86/1973, 94/2849,
                96/3857: *Distinguished*, 00/3955
R&T Thew Ltd v. Reeves (No.2) [1982] Q.B. 1283; [1982] 3 W.L.R. 869; [1982] 3 All
E.R. 1086; 126 S.J. 674, CA . . . . *Digested*, 82/**3088**:
        Applied, 87/3562: *Considered*, 83/2184, 84/1995, 84/2747, 89/631, 01/538
R&V Haegeman Sprl v. Belgium (C181/73) [1974] E.C.R. 449; [1975] 1 C.M.L.R. 515,
ECJ . . . . *Digested*, 75/**1278**:
                Followed, 00/2380
R-B (A Patient) v. Official Solicitor see A (Mental Patient: Sterilisation), Re
R-J (Minors) (Fostering: Person Disqualified), Re see RJ (Foster Placement), Re
R. v. A (A Juvenile: Discharge of Jury Member) [1998] Crim. L.R. 134, CA (Crim Div)
R. v. A (Amos) see Attorney General's Reference (No.23 of 1997), Re
R. v. A (Barrie Owen); R. v. W (John Robert) [2001] EWCA Crim 296; [2001] 2 Cr.
App. R. 18; [2001] 2 Cr. App. R. (S.) 89; [2001] H.R.L.R. 32; [2001] Crim. L.R.
414; *Times*, February 27, 2001; *Independent*, March 26, 2001 (C.S), CA (Crim
Div) . . . . *Digested*, 01/**1217**
R. v. A (Brian Dennis) [1999] 2 Cr. App. R. (S.) 92, CA (Crim Div) . . . . *Digested*, 99/**1252**
R. v. A (Child Abduction) [2000] 1 W.L.R. 1879; [2000] 2 All E.R. 177; [2000] 1 Cr.
App. R. 418; [2000] Crim. L.R. 169; (1999) 96(40) L.S.G. 42; *Times*, October
15, 1999, CA (Crim Div) . . . . *Digested*, 99/**908**
R. v. A (Complainant's Sexual History); *sub nom* R. v. Y (Sexual Offence:
Complainant's Sexual History); R. v. A (No.2) [2001] UKHL 25; [2001] 2 W.L.R.
1546; [2001] 3 All E.R. 1; [2001] 2 Cr. App. R. 21; (2001) 165 J.P. 609; [2001]
H.R.L.R. 48; [2001] U.K.H.R.R. 825; 11 B.H.R.C. 225; [2001] Crim. L.R. 908;
(2001) 165 J.P.N. 750; *Times*, May 24, 2001; *Independent*, May 22, 2001; *Daily
Telegraph*, May 29, 2001, HL; affirming [2001] EWCA Crim 4; [2001] Crim.
L.R. 389; (2001) 145 S.J.L.B. 43; *Times*, February 13, 2001, CA (Crim Div) . . . . *Digested*, 01/**977**
R. v. A (David Roy) (A Juvenile); R. v. L (Robert) (A Juvenile) (1999) 163 J.P. 841;
(2000) 164 J.P.N. 102, CA (Crim Div) . . . . *Digested*, 00/**1113**
R. v. A (DJ) [2000] 1 Cr. App. R. (S.) 563, CA (Crim Div) . . . . *Digested*, 00/**1302**
R. v. A (Harold) [1999] Crim. L.R. 420; *Times*, April 13, 1998, CA (Crim Div) . . . . *Digested*, 98/**1042**
R. v. A (Informer: Reduction of Sentence); R. v. B (Informer: Reduction of Sentence)
[1999] 1 Cr. App. R. (S.) 52; [1998] Crim. L.R. 757; *Times*, May 1, 1998, CA
(Crim Div) . . . . *Digested*, 98/**1267**
R. v. A (James William) [1997] Crim. L.R. 883, CA (Crim Div) . . . . *Considered*, 98/906
R. v. A (John Hamblin) [1999] 1 Cr. App. R. (S.) 273, CA (Crim Div). . . . . *Digested*, 99/**1300**
R. v. A (Joinder of Appropriate Minister) [2001] 1 W.L.R. 789; *Times*, March 21, 2001;
Independent, March 27, 2001, HL . . . . *Digested*, 01/**3535**:
         Followed, 01/6228: *Subsequent proceedings*, 01/977
R. v. A (Lavinia); R. v. S (John William) [1999] 1 Cr. App. R. (S.) 240, CA (Crim Div) . . . *Digested*, 99/**1096**
R. v. A (No.2) see R. v. A (Complainant's Sexual History)
R. v. A (Patrick) [2000] 2 All E.R. 185, CA (Crim Div) . . . . *Digested*, 00/**1063**
R. v. A (Paul Eric) see Attorney General's Reference (No.8 of 1999), Re
R. v. A (Timothy) see Attorney General's Reference (No.54 of 1997), Re

R. v. A (Victor) (A Juvenile) [1999] 2 Cr. App. R. (S.) 74, CA (Crim Div) . . . .   *Digested*, 99/**1229**

R. v. A (Wasted Costs Order); *sub nom* R. v. Hickman & Rose; Hickman & Rose (Wasted Costs Order) (No.10 of 1999), Re [2000] P.N.L.R. 628; *Times*, May 3, 2000, CA (Crim Div) . . . .   *Digested*, 00/**1043**

R. v. A (Witness Reprisals) see R. v. H (Witness Reprisals)

R. v. A School Governors Ex p. T; *sub nom* R. v. A&S School Governors Ex p. T; R. v. Chair of Governors and Headteacher of A School Ex p. T [2000] Ed. C.R. 223; [2000] E.L.R. 274; [2000] C.O.D. 17, QBD . . . .   *Digested*, 00/**1923**

R. v. A&S School Governors Ex p. T see R. v. A School Governors Ex p. T

R. v. A-H (A Juvenile) [2000] 2 Cr. App. R. (S.) 158, CA (Crim Div) . . . .   *Digested*, 00/**1330**

R. v. AA (A Juvenile) see Attorney General's Reference (Nos.35 and 37 of 1997), Re

R. v. Abdie (Gary) see R. v. T (Craig Daniel)

R. v. Abdul (Naeem); R. v. Marsh (Barry Charles) [2001] 1 Cr. App. R. (S.) 4, CA (Crim Div) . . . .   *Digested*, 01/**1132**

R. v. Abdul-Hussain (Mustafa Shakir); R. v. Aboud (Saheb Sherif); R. v. Hasan (Hasan Saheb Abdul); R. v. Naji (Maged Mehdy); R. v. Muhssin (Mohammed Chamekh); R. v. Hoshan (Adnan) *Times*, January 26, 1999, CA (Crim Div) . . . .   *Digested*, 99/**922**: *Followed*, 01/1057

R. v. Abdulkarim (Khalid Ibrahim) [2000] 2 Cr. App. R. (S.) 16, CA (Crim Div) . . . .   *Digested*, 00/**1127**

R. v. ABE see R. v. E

R. v. Abiodun (Danny) see R. v. Odeyemi (Olujimi)

R. v. Aboud (Saheb Sherif) see R. v. Abdul-Hussain (Mustafa Shakir)

R. v. Abrar (Munawar Habib), *Times*, May 26, 2000, CA (Crim Div) . . . .   *Digested*, 00/**1060**

R. v. Accrington Youth Court Ex p. F [1998] 1 W.L.R. 156; [1998] 2 All E.R. 313; (1998) 10 Admin. L.R. 17; [1998] C.O.D. 75; (1997) 94(37) L.S.G. 41; (1997) 147 N.L.J. 1493; (1997) 141 S.J.L.B. 195; *Times*, October 10, 1997; *Independent*, October 2, 1997, QBD . . . .   *Digested*, 97/**3920**

R. v. Aceblade Ltd (t/a Rand & Asquith Ltd) [2001] 1 Cr. App. R. (S.) 105, CA (Crim Div) . . . .   *Digested*, 01/**1347**

R. (on the application of Crown Prosecution Service) v. Acton Youth Court see R. (on the application of DPP) v. Acton Youth Court

R. (on the application of DPP) v. Acton Youth Court; *sub nom* R. (on the application of Crown Prosecution Service) v. Acton Youth Court; R. v. Acton Youth Court Ex p. CPS [2001] EWHC Admin 402; [2001] 1 W.L.R. 1828; (2001) 165 J.P.N. 606; (2001) 98(26) L.S.G. 43; (2001) 145 S.J.L.B. 155; *Times*, June 21, 2001, QBD (Admin Ct) . . . .   *Digested*, 01/**1198**

R. v. Acton Youth Court Ex p. CPS see R. (on the application of DPP) v. Acton Youth Court

R. v. AD (A Juvenile) [2001] 1 Cr. App. R. (S.) 59; [2000] Crim. L.R. 867, CA (Crim Div) . . . .   *Digested*, 01/**1380**

R. v. Adam (Rafiq Ahmed) [1998] 2 Cr. App. R. (S.) 403, CA (Crim Div) . . . .   *Digested*, 99/**1276**: *Considered*, 01/1250

R. v. Adams [1996] Crim. L.R. 593, CA (Crim Div) . . . .   *Digested*, 97/**2928**: *Approved*, 00/978

R. v. Adams (David Anthony); R. v. Harding (William Henry) [2000] 2 Cr. App. R. (S.) 274, CA (Crim Div) . . . .   *Digested*, 00/**1352**

R. v. Adams (Denis John) (No.2) [1998] 1 Cr. App. R. 377; *Times*, November 3, 1997, CA (Crim Div) . . . .   *Digested*, 97/**1141**

R. v. Adamson (Michael Joseph) see R. v. Nazari (Fazlollah)

R. v. Addison (Robert) [1998] 1 Cr. App. R. (S.) 119, CA (Crim Div) . . . .   *Digested*, 98/**1223**

R. v. Adebayo (Prince Olubode) [1998] 1 Cr. App. R. (S.) 15, CA (Crim Div) . . . .   *Digested*, 98/**1318**

R. v. Adjei (Anthony Asafu) see R. v. Radak (Jason Dragon)

R. v. Adjudication Officer Ex p. Velasquez (1999) 96(17) L.S.G. 25; *Times*, April 30, 1999, CA . . . .   *Digested*, 99/**4525**

R. v. Admiralty Board of the Defence Council Ex p. Beckett see R. v. Ministry of Defence Ex p. Smith

R. v. Admiralty Board of the Defence Council Ex p. Lustig-Prean see R. v. Ministry of Defence Ex p. Smith

R. v. Adomako (John Asare); R. v. Sullman (Barry); R. v. Prentice (Michael Charles); R. v. Holloway (Stephen John) [1995] 1 A.C. 171; [1994] 3 W.L.R. 288; [1994] 3 All E.R. 79; (1994) 99 Cr. App. R. 362; (1994) 158 J.P. 653; [1994] 5 Med. L.R. 277; [1994] Crim. L.R. 757; (1994) 158 J.P.N. 507; (1994) 144 N.L.J. 936; *Times*, July 4, 1994; *Independent*, July 1, 1994, HL; affirming [1994] Q.B. 302; [1993] 3 W.L.R. 927; [1993] 4 All E.R. 935; (1994) 98 Cr. App. R. 262; *Times*, May 21, 1993; *Independent*, May 21, 1993, CA (Crim Div) . . . .   *Digested*, 94/**1124**: *Applied*, 95/875: *Considered*, 94/637, 96/47: *Distinguished*, 95/923: *Followed*, 01/1052

R. (on the application of SmithKline Beecham Plc) v. Advertising Standards Authority; *sub nom* SmithKline Beecham Plc v. Advertising Standards Authority [2001] EWHC Admin 6; [2001] E.M.L.R. 23; *Daily Telegraph*, February 7, 2001, QBD (Admin Ct) . . . .   *Digested*, 01/**692**

R. v. Advertising Standards Authority Ex p. Insurance Services (1990) 2 Admin. L.R. 77; (1990) 9 Tr. L.R. 169; [1990] C.O.D. 42; (1989) 133 S.J. 1545, QBD . . . . . .   *Digested*, 91/**8**: *Considered*, 01/5140

R. (on the application of Matthias Rath BV) *v.* Advertising Standards Authority Ltd; *sub nom* R. *v.* Advertising Standards Authority Ltd Ex p. Matthias Rath BV [2001] E.M.L.R. 22; [2001] H.R.L.R. 22; *Times*, January 10, 2001, QBD (Admin Ct) . . .   *Digested,* 01/**4409**

R. *v.* Advertising Standards Authority Ltd Ex p. Charles Robertson (Developments) Ltd; *sub nom* Charles Robertson (Developments) Ltd *v.* Advertising Standards Authority [2000] E.M.L.R. 463; *Times*, November 26, 1999, QBD . . . .   *Digested,* 00/**4146**

R. *v.* Advertising Standards Authority Ltd Ex p. Direct Line Financial Services Ltd [1998] C.O.D. 20, QBD

R. *v.* Advertising Standards Authority Ltd Ex p. Matthias Rath BV see R. (on the application of Matthias Rath BV) *v.* Advertising Standards Authority Ltd

R. *v.* Agius (Jean) see R. *v.* Farrugia (Francis)

R. *v.* AH (A Juvenile) [2000] 2 Cr. App. R. (S.) 280, CA (Crim Div) . . . .   *Digested,* 00/**1315**

R. *v.* Ahmadi (Nasser) (1994) 15 Cr. App. R. (S.) 254, CA (Crim Div) . . . .   *Considered,* 99/1276

R. *v.* Ahmed (Nabil) (1985) 80 Cr. App. R. 295; (1984) 6 Cr. App. R. (S.) 391; [1985] Crim. L.R. 250, CA (Crim Div) . . . .   *Digested,* 85/**828**:
                   Considered, 87/940, 88/911, 92/1266, 93/1148, 00/1215

R. *v.* Ahmed (Naveed) see Attorney General's Reference (Nos.26 and 27 of 1996), Re

R. *v.* Ahmetaj (Esad) [2000] 1 Cr. App. R. (S.) 66, CA (Crim Div) . . . .   *Digested,* 00/**1276**

R. *v.* Ahrens (Wayne Michael) (1995) 16 Cr. App. R. (S.) 7, CA (Crim Div) . . . .   *Digested,* 96/**2063**:
                   Considered, 98/1328, 00/1417, 01/1474

R. *v.* Airport Coordination Ltd Ex p. Aravco Ltd [1999] Eu. L.R. 939, CA . . . .   *Digested,* 00/**5135**

R. *v.* Airport Coordination Ltd Ex p. States of Guernsey Transport Board [1999] Eu. L.R. 745, QBD . . . .   *Digested,* 99/**4858**

R. *v.* Aitken (Thomas Adam); R. *v.* Bennett (Simon Christopher); R. *v.* Barson (Alan Robert) [1992] 1 W.L.R. 1006; [1992] 4 All E.R. 541; (1992) 95 Cr. App. R. 304; (1992) 136 S.J.L.B. 183; *Times*, June 10, 1992, CMAC . . . .   *Digested,* 93/**755**:
                   Applied, 99/946

R. *v.* Ajaib (Yasar) [2001] 1 Cr. App. R. (S.) 31; [2000] Crim. L.R. 770, CA (Crim Div) . .   *Digested,* 01/**1359**

R. *v.* Akhbar (Showkat) see R. *v.* Miah (Badrul)

R. *v.* Akhter (Janade) [2001] 1 Cr. App. R. (S.) 3, CA (Crim Div) . . . .   *Digested,* 01/**1212**

R. *v.* Aksar (Mohammed) see R. *v.* Kolton (Grzegorz)

R. *v.* Aksu (Ali) see R. *v.* Kaynak (Hussein)

R. *v.* Al-Banna (Marwan) (1984) 6 Cr. App. R. (S.) 426, CA (Crim Div) . . . .   *Digested,* 85/**760**:
              Cited, 92/1210: *Considered,* 00/1369

R. *v.* Al-Zubeidi (Nagi) [1999] Crim. L.R. 906, CA (Crim Div)

R. *v.* Alami (Samar) see R. *v.* Botmeh (Jawad)

R. *v.* Alford (James) see R. *v.* JF Alford Transport Ltd

R. *v.* Alford (John James) see R. *v.* Shannon (John James)

R. *v.* Ali; R. *v.* Rasool (1992) 89(12) L.S.G. 36, PC (Mau) . . . .   *Digested,* 92/**809**:
                   Considered, 99/1309

R. *v.* Ali (Asgar); R. *v.* Ali (Iqbal Begum) [1999] Crim. L.R. 663; *Independent*, December 7, 1998 (C.S.), CA (Crim Div) . . . .   *Digested,* 99/**875**

R. *v.* Ali (Askir) (1988) 10 Cr. App. R. (S.) 59, CA (Crim Div) . . . .   *Digested,* 90/**1362**:
                   Considered, 99/1263

R. *v.* Ali (Idris) [1998] 2 Cr. App. R. (S.) 123, CA (Crim Div) . . . .   *Digested,* 98/**1237**

R. *v.* Ali (Iqbal Begum) see R. *v.* Ali (Asgar)

R. *v.* Ali (Mudassir Mohammed) 199905370/Z4, CA (Crim Div) . . . .   *Subsequent proceedings,* 00/3229

R. *v.* Ali (Mudassir Mohammed) see R. *v.* Lambert (Steven)

R. *v.* Ali (Portab) see R. *v.* Banu (Amina)

R. *v.* Ali (Sajid Pasha) see R. *v.* Graham (Hemamali Krishna)

R. *v.* Allam (Peter John) see R. *v.* Cooney (Stephen)

R. *v.* Allan (John Paul); *sub nom* R. *v.* Allen (John Paul); R. *v.* Bunting (Michael); R. *v.* Boodhoo (Mohammed Noor) [2001] EWCA Crim 1027; [2001] Crim. L.R. 739, CA (Crim Div)

R. *v.* Allcock (Michael Clayton) [1999] 1 Cr. App. R. 227; [1999] Crim. L.R. 599, CA (Crim Div) . . . .   *Digested,* 99/**1013**

R. *v.* Allen (Brian Roger) see R. *v.* Dimsey (Dermot Jeremy)

R. *v.* Allen (Brian Roger) (Appeals against Sentence) see R. *v.* Dimsey (Dermot Jeremy) (Appeals against Sentence)

R. *v.* Allen (Brian Roger) [2001] UKHL 45; [2001] 3 W.L.R. 843; [2001] 4 All E.R. 768; [2001] S.T.C. 1537; [2001] B.T.C. 421; 4 I.T.L. Rep. 140; [2001] S.T.I. 1348; *Independent*, October 26, 2001, HL . . . .   *Digested,* 01/**5271**:
                 Previous proceedings, 99/4704

R. *v.* Allen (John Paul) see R. *v.* Allan (John Paul)

R. *v.* Allen (William) [2001] EWCA Crim 302; [2001] 2 Cr. App. R. (S.) 76, CA (Crim Div) . . . .   *Digested,* 01/**1305**

R. *v.* Allerdale DC Housing Benefit Review Board Ex p. Doughty [2000] C.O.D. 462, QBD

R. *v.* Alleyne (Emmanuel) (1995) 16 Cr. App. R. (S.) 506, CA (Crim Div) . . . .   *Considered,* 01/1500

R. *v.* Allsopp (Michael) see R. *v.* Simpson (David)

R. *v.* Alnwick DC Ex p. Robson [1998] C.O.D. 241; [1997] E.G.C.S. 144, QBD

R. *v.* Alowi (Zia) (Unreported, March 8, 1999), CA (Crim Div) . . . .   *Applied,* 00/1108:
                   Considered, 01/54

R. (on the application of B (A Child)) *v.* Alperton Community School Head Teacher and
Governing Body; *sub nom* R. *v.* Secretary of State for Education and
Employment Ex p. B; R. (on the application of T (A Child)) *v.* Wembley High
School Head Teacher; R. (on the application of C (A Child)) *v.* Cardinal Newman
Roman Catholic School Governing Body [2001] EWHC Admin 229; [2001]
E.L.R. 359; *Times*, June 8, 2001; *Independent*, May 14, 2001 (C.S), QBD (Admin
Ct) . . . .   *Digested*, 01/**1899**
R. *v.* Alsford (Kevin Charles) see DPP *v.* Nock
R. *v.* Altaf (Mohammed) [1999] 1 Cr. App. R. (S.) 429; [1999] E.H.L.R. Dig. 204, CA
(Crim Div) . . . .   *Digested*, 98/**1209**
R. *v.* Altun (Ibrahim) [1998] 2 Cr. App. R. (S.) 171, CA (Crim Div) . . . .   *Digested*, 98/**1191**
R. *v.* Alwan (Hisham) [2000] 2 Costs L.R. 326, Sup Ct Costs Office . . . .   *Digested*, 01/**1114**
R. *v.* Amersham Juvenile Court Ex p. W see R. *v.* Amersham Juvenile Court Ex p.
Wilson
R. *v.* Amersham Juvenile Court Ex p. Wilson; *sub nom* R. *v.* Amersham Juvenile Court
Ex p. W [1981] Q.B. 969; [1981] 2 W.L.R. 887; [1981] 2 All E.R. 315; (1981) 72
Cr. App. R. 365; [1981] Crim. L.R. 420; 125 S.J. 287, QBD . . . .   *Digested*, 81/**554**:
Disapproved, 82/742: *Followed*, 98/1102
R. *v.* Amin (Saidul Tuhin) [1998] 1 Cr. App. R. (S.) 63, CA (Crim Div) . . . .   *Digested*, 98/**1255**
R. *v.* Amlani (Chanudula); R. *v.* Smith (John) (1995) 16 Cr. App. R. (S.) 339, CA (Crim
Div) . . . .   *Considered*, 00/1180:
Referred to, 97/1577
R. *v.* AN see Attorney General's Reference (No.71 of 1999), Re
R. *v.* Anastasiou (Michael) [1998] Crim. L.R. 67, CA (Crim Div)
R. *v.* Anderson (Daniel Blake) (1992) 13 Cr. App. R. (S.) 325; [1992] Crim. L.R. 131;
Times, October 3, 1991, CA (Crim Div) . . . .   *Digested*, 93/**1202**:
Applied, 97/1589: *Considered*, 94/1405, 94/1409, 99/1218:
Referred to, 95/1503
R. *v.* Anderson (Lascelles Fitzalbert); R. *v.* Morris (Emmanuel) [1966] 2 Q.B. 110;
[1966] 2 W.L.R. 1195; [1966] 2 All E.R. 644; (1966) 50 Cr. App. R. 216; (1966)
130 J.P. 318; 110 S.J. 369, CCA . . . .   *Digested*, 66/**2603**:
Applied, 69/804, 81/1879, 84/667, 87/801, 88/698, 89/846, 00/5468:
Considered, 77/485, 94/1120, 95/1067, 95/1271, 95/1272:
Distinguished, 77/591, 94/665, 95/2634
R. *v.* Anderson (Lee) see R. *v.* McFeeley (Jason)
R. *v.* Anderson (Marcus), *Independent*, July 13, 1998 (C.S.), CA (Crim Div) . . . .   *Digested*, 98/**1099**
R. *v.* Anderson (Paul) see Attorney General's Reference (No.71 of 1998), Re
R. *v.* Anderson (Steven John) see Attorney General's Reference (No.52 of 1996), Re
R. *v.* Andre (Lyla) see R. *v.* Burton (Evelyn)
R. *v.* Andrews (Mark Clive) see Milford Haven *v.* Andrews
R. *v.* Andrews (Paul) (1986) 82 Cr. App. R. 148; [1986] Crim. L.R. 124; (1985) 135
N.L.J. 1163; (1985) 129 S.J. 869, CA (Crim Div) . . . .   *Digested*, 86/**943**:
Applied, 01/1144: *Considered*, 96/2076
R. *v.* Andrews (Russell) see R. *v.* Ward (Michael)
R. *v.* Andrews (Tracey) [1999] Crim. L.R. 156; (1998) 95(43) L.S.G. 32; (1998) 142
S.J.L.B. 268; *Times*, October 15, 1998; *Independent*, November 9, 1998 (C.S.),
CA (Crim Div) . . . .   *Digested*, 98/**1047**
R. *v.* Andrews Weatherfoil Ltd; R. *v.* Sporle (Sidney Frederick); R. *v.* Day (Peter
George) [1972] 1 W.L.R. 118; [1972] 1 All E.R. 65; (1972) 56 Cr. App. R. 31;
(1971) 115 S.J. 888, CA (Crim Div) . . . .   *Digested*, 72/**594**:
Applied, 84/977: *Considered*, 95/1222: *Followed*, 00/332
R. *v.* Angel (Anthoni Pillai) [1998] 1 Cr. App. R. (S.) 347, CA (Crim Div) . . . .   *Digested*, 98/**1243**
R. *v.* Anglia and Oxfordshire Mental Health Review Tribunal Ex p. Hagan [2000]
Lloyd's Rep. Med. 119; (2000) 53 B.M.L.R. 9; [2000] C.O.D. 352; *Times*,
January 21, 2000; *Independent*, January 11, 2000, CA; reversing [1999] C.O.D.
151, QBD . . . .   *Digested*, 00/**4175**
R. *v.* Anglian Water Services Ex p. Three Valleys Water Plc (2000) 97(3) L.S.G. 38,
QBD
R. *v.* Anglo-Spanish Fisheries Ltd [2001] 1 Cr. App. R. (S.) 73, CA (Crim Div) . . . .   *Digested*, 01/**2807**
R. *v.* Angus (Jamie John) see Attorney General's Reference (Nos.37 and 38 of 1997),
Re
R. *v.* Anomo (Taiye Olokun) [1998] 2 Cr. App. R. (S.) 269; [1998] Crim. L.R. 356;
Times, February 26, 1998; *Independent*, February 18, 1998, CA (Crim Div) . . . . .   *Digested*, 98/**1158**
R. *v.* Ansari (Mohammed); R. *v.* Horner (David); R. *v.* Ling (Peter); R. *v.* Ansari (Sayed)
[2000] 1 Cr. App. R. (S.) 94, CA (Crim Div) . . . .   *Digested*, 00/**1182**
R. *v.* Ansari (Sayed) see R. *v.* Ansari (Mohammed)
R. *v.* Anson (Warwick Jason Mark) [1999] 1 Cr. App. R. (S.) 331, CA (Crim Div) . . . . . .   *Digested*, 99/**1088**
R. *v.* Antoine (Pierre Harrison) [2001] 1 A.C. 340; [2000] 2 W.L.R. 703; [2000] 2 All
E.R. 208; [2000] 2 Cr. App. R. 94; (2000) 54 B.M.L.R. 147; [2000] Crim. L.R.
621; (2000) 97(18) L.S.G. 36; (2000) 144 S.J.L.B. 212; *Times*, April 4, 2000;
Independent, April 4, 2000, HL; affirming [1999] 3 W.L.R. 1204; [1999] 2 Cr.
App. R. 225; (1999) 96(21) L.S.G. 37; (1999) 143 S.J.L.B. 142; *Times*, May 10,
1999; *Independent*, May 12, 1999, CA (Crim Div) . . . .   *Digested*, 00/**982**
R. *v.* Anyanwu (Ebenezer Chukwuma) see R. *v.* Nazari (Fazlollah)

R. *v.* AO [2000] Crim. L.R. 617, CA (Crim Div)
R. *v.* Aplin (Malcolm) [2000] 2 Cr. App. R. (S.) 89, CA (Crim Div) . . . .   *Digested,* 00/**1250**
R. *v.* Appeal Committee of Brighouse School Ex p. G and B [1997] E.L.R. 39; [1996]
      C.O.D. 125, QBD . . . .   *Digested,* 97/**2108**:
                                                                                                                                                                      Considered, 00/1913
R. *v.* Appleton (Alvin Alphonse) [1999] 2 Cr. App. R. (S.) 289, CA (Crim Div) . . . .   *Digested,* 99/**1136**
R. *v.* Aramah (John Uzu) (1983) 76 Cr. App. R. 190; (1982) 4 Cr. App. R. (S.) 407;
      [1983] Crim. L.R. 271, CA (Crim Div). . . . .   *Digested,* 83/**764.19**:
                        Applied, 84/868, 85/703, 86/812, 86/834, 87/954, 87/1076, 88/871,
                        88/1007, 89/839, 89/939, 90/1185, 90/1284, 90/1285, 91/1097, 92/1227,
                        93/1108, 00/5487: *Considered,* 84/852, 86/719, 86/823, 86/845, 87/897,
                        87/898, 87/926, 87/940, 87/942, 87/952, 87/953, 88/872, 88/911, 88/922,
                        88/929, 88/930, 89/938, 89/949, 89/1011, 89/1028, 90/1290, 90/1291,
                        90/1297, 91/1103, 92/1247, 92/1248, 93/1328, 97/1510, 97/1517, 97/1518,
                        97/1522, 98/1177, 98/1180, 98/1181, 98/1183, 98/1195, 98/1197, 99/1127,
                        99/1129, 99/1134, 99/1140, 99/1145, 99/1148, 00/1206, 00/1207, 00/1211,
                        00/1218, 00/1233, 01/1282: *Distinguished,* 83/764.25: *Doubted,* 99/5226:
                        Explained, 85/727, 86/833: *Followed,* 84/904, 96/1857, 96/1863, 96/1873,
                        97/1512: *Not followed,* 87/1022, 88/969, 89/991, 89/1030, 90/1289:
                        Referred to, 83/820, 84/853, 86/757, 87/1054, 88/907, 89/993, 89/1027,
                        89/1033, 90/1268, 90/1292, 90/1301, 91/1046, 91/1092, 91/1093, 91/1112,
                        92/1242, 92/1245, 92/1257, 93/1123, 93/1127, 93/1130, 93/1131, 93/1137,
                        93/1139, 94/1403, 95/1360, 95/1367
R. *v.* Aranguren (Jose de Jesus); R. *v.* Aroyewumi (Bisi); R. *v.* Bioshogun (Nimota); R.
      v. Littlefield (John); R. *v.* Gould (Robert Sidney) (1994) 99 Cr. App. R. 347;
      (1995) 16 Cr. App. R. (S.) 211; [1994] Crim. L.R. 695; (1994) 144 N.L.J. 864;
      Times, June 23, 1994; *Independent,* June 30, 1994, CA (Crim Div)   *Digested,* 95/**1364**:
                        Considered, 96/1872, 96/1875, 96/1879, 98/1191, 99/1124, 99/1129, 00/1211,
                        00/1233: *Distinguished,* 96/1873: *Followed,* 97/1522
R. *v.* Archer (Patrick John); R. *v.* Purnell (Danny Lee); R. *v.* Eaton (Craig Keith) [1998]
      2 Cr. App. R. (S.) 76, CA (Crim Div) . . . .   *Digested,* 98/**1304**
R. *v.* Argent (Brian) [1997] 2 Cr. App. R. 27; (1997) 161 J.P. 190; [1997] Crim. L.R.
      346; (1997) 161 J.P.N. 260; *Times,* December 19, 1996, CA (Crim Div). . . . .   *Digested,* 97/**1163**:
                                                                                                                                                                      Applied, 00/1076
R. *v.* Arif (Mustafa) (1994) 15 Cr. App. R. (S.) 895, CA (Crim Div) . . . .   *Digested,* 95/**1366**:
                                                                                                      Considered, 96/1856, 98/1190, 98/1191, 99/1145
R. *v.* Arman (Yusuf) see R. *v.* Malik (Aleem Mushtaq)
R. *v.* Armsaramah (Robert) [2001] 1 Cr. App. R. (S.) 133; (2000) 164 J.P. 709;
      [2000] Crim. L.R. 1033; *Times,* October 25, 2000, CA (Crim Div) . . . .   *Digested,* 00/**1187**
R. *v.* Armston (Cedric Malcolm) (1981) 3 Cr. App. R. (S.) 320; [1982] Crim. L.R. 188,
      CA (Crim Div). . . . .   *Digested,* 82/**684.10**:
                        Applied, 86/786: *Considered,* 84/736, 86/783, 86/785, 89/934, 90/1218,
                                                                                                                                                                      99/1084
R. *v.* Arnold (Michael John) [1996] 1 Cr. App. R. (S.) 115, CA (Crim Div). . . . .   *Considered,* 98/1110,
                                                                                                                                                                      99/1065, 00/1122
R. *v.* Arnold (Michael Neil) [1998] 1 Cr. App. R. (S.) 416, CA (Crim Div) . . . .   *Digested,* 98/**1344**
R. *v.* Arnold (Neil Terry) see Attorney General's Reference (No.19 of 1994), Re
R. *v.* Arnold (Stephen) see R. *v.* Fellows (Alban)
R. *v.* Aroride (Tobare) [1999] 2 Cr. App. R. (S.) 406, CA (Crim Div) . . . .   *Digested,* 00/**1380**
R. *v.* Aroyewumi (Bisi) see R. *v.* Aranguren (Jose de Jesus)
R. *v.* Arthur (John Leighton) [2001] EWCA Crim 174; [2001] 2 Cr. App. R. (S.) 67, CA
      (Crim Div) . . . .   *Digested,* 01/**1257**
R. *v.* Arts Council of England Ex p. Women's Playhouse Trust [1998] C.O.D. 175; *Times,*
      August 20, 1997, QBD . . . .   *Digested,* 97/**481**
R. *v.* Arun DC Ex p. Fowler [1998] J.P.L. 674; [1997] E.G.C.S. 139, QBD. . . . .   *Digested,* 98/**4225**
R. *v.* AS [2000] 1 Cr. App. R. (S.) 491, CA (Crim Div) . . . .   *Digested,* 00/**1239**
R. *v.* Ash (Ian John) [1999] R.T.R. 347, CA (Crim Div) . . . .   *Digested,* 99/**882**
R. *v.* Ashby (Edward Moses) [1998] 2 Cr. App. R. (S.) 37, CA (Crim Div) . . . .   *Digested,* 98/**1122**
R. *v.* Ashby (Mark William) see R. *v.* Williams (David Omar)
R. *v.* Ashby (Nicholas Alexander) see R. *v.* Howells (Craig)
R. *v.* Ashford (David Leonard) [2000] 1 Cr. App. R. (S.) 389, CA (Crim Div). . . . .   *Digested,* 00/**1213**
R. *v.* Ashford BC Ex p. Shepway DC [1999] P.L.C.R. 12, QBD. . . . .   *Digested,* 99/**4249**:
                                                                                                                                                                      Followed, 98/4224
R. *v.* Ashley (Jennifer Anne) (1993) 14 Cr. App. R. (S.) 581, CA . . . .   *Digested,* 94/**1403**:
                                                                                                                                                                      Considered, 98/1184
R. *v.* Ashman (Mark Anthony) [1997] 1 Cr. App. R. (S.) 241; [1996] Crim. L.R. 755;
      Times, August 9, 1996, CA (Crim Div) . . . .   *Digested,* 96/**1892**:
                                                                      Considered, 98/1217, 98/1219, 98/1221, 99/1158, 99/1161
R. *v.* Ashton (Steven); *sub nom* R. *v.* Aston (Steven); R. *v.* N'Wandou (Simeon
      N'Wadiche) [1998] Crim.L.R. 498, CA (Crim Div)
R. (on the application of N) *v.* Ashworth Special Hospital Authority; *sub nom* R. *v.*
      Ashworth Special Hospital Authority Ex p. N [2001] EWHC Admin 339; [2001]
      H.R.L.R. 46; *Times,* June 26, 2001, QBD (Admin Ct) . . . .   *Digested,* 01/**4433**
R. *v.* Aspinall (John) see R. *v.* Smyth (Paul)

R. *v.* Aspinall (Paul James) [1999] 2 Cr. App. R. 115; (1999) 49 B.M.L.R. 82; [1999]
     Crim. L.R. 741; (1999) 96(7) L.S.G. 35; *Times,* February 4, 1999, CA (Crim Div) .   *Digested,* 99/**874**
R. *v.* Aspinall (Thomas) see R. *v.* Smyth (Paul)
R. *v.* Asquith (Martyn Arthur) (1995) 16 Cr. App. R. (S.) 453, CA (Crim Div) . . . .   *Approved,* 96/1859:
                                                              Considered, 98/1283: *Followed,* 97/1524
R. *v.* Asquith (Neil Henry) see Attorney General's Reference (No.8 of 1994), Re
R. *v.* Associated British Ports Ex p. Plymouth City Council see R. *v.* Coventry City
     Council Ex p. Phoenix Aviation
R. *v.* Associated Octel Co Ltd [1996] 1 W.L.R. 1543; [1996] 4 All E.R. 846; [1996]
     I.C.R. 972; [1997] I.R.L.R. 123; [1997] Crim. L.R. 355; (1996) 146 N.L.J. 1685;
     Times, November 15, 1996; *Independent,* November 21, 1996, HL; affirming
     [1994] 4 All E.R. 1051; [1995] I.C.R. 281; [1994] I.R.L.R. 540; (1994) 91(36)
     L.S.G. 37; (1994) 144 N.L.J. 1312; (1994) 138 S.J.L.B. 194; *Times,* August 3,
     1994; *Independent,* August 29, 1994 (C.S.), CA (Crim Div) . . . .   *Digested,* 96/**3019**:
                                    Applied, 95/2500, 96/3020: *Cited,* 00/980: *Considered,* 97/2611
R. (on the application of Sunspell Ltd (t/a Superlative Travel)) *v.* Association of British
     Travel Agents; *sub nom* R. *v.* Association of British Travel Agents Ex p. Sunspell
     Ltd (t/a Superlative Travel) [2001] A.C.D. 16; *Independent,* November 27, 2000
     (C.S), QBD (Admin Ct)
R. *v.* Aston (Steven) see R. *v.* Ashton (Steven)
R. (on the application of Husain) *v.* Asylum Support Adjudicator [2001] EWHC Admin
     852; *Times,* November 15, 2001, QBD (Admin Ct) . . . .   *Digested,* 01/**3610**
R. *v.* Atherley (Andrew) see R. *v.* MacDonald (Brian Anthony)
R. *v.* Atkins (David John) (1990) 12 Cr. App. R. (S.) 335, CA (Crim Div) . . . .   *Digested,* 92/**1371**:
                                                                          Considered, 99/1311
R. *v.* Attorney General Ex p. Rockall [2000] 1 W.L.R. 882; [1999] 4 All E.R. 312;
     [1999] Crim. L.R. 972; *Times,* July 19, 1999 ; *Independent,* July 26, 1999, QBD .   *Digested,* 99/**912**
R. *v.* Attorney General for Northern Ireland Ex p. Burns; *sub nom* Burns Application for
     Judicial Review, Re [1999] N.I. 175; [1999] I.R.L.R. 315, QBD (NI) . . . .   *Digested,* 99/**5274**
R. *v.* Audit (Richard Sylvian) (1994) 15 Cr. App. R. (S.) 36, CA. . . . .   *Considered,* 98/1106
R. *v.* Aujla (Ajit Singh); R. *v.* Aujla (Harbans Kaur); R. *v.* Aujla (Inderpal Singh) [1998]
     2 Cr. App. R. 16; *Times,* November 24, 1997, CA (Crim Div) . . . .   *Digested,* 97/**1130**:
                                                                           Followed, 00/921
R. *v.* Aujla (Harbans Kaur) see R. *v.* Aujla (Ajit Singh)
R. *v.* Aujla (Inderpal Singh) see R. *v.* Aujla (Ajit Singh)
R. *v.* Austen (Anthony) see R. *v.* Preston (Stephen)
R. *v.* Avbunudje (Tobora) [1999] 2 Cr. App. R. (S.) 189; [1999] Crim. L.R. 336, CA
     (Crim Div) . . . .   *Digested,* 99/**1317**
R. *v.* Avis (Edward) see R. *v.* Ellis (Paul Edward)
R. *v.* Avis (Tony); R. *v.* Barton (Richard); R. *v.* Thomas (Gerald John); R. *v.* Torrington
     (Richard Edward); R. *v.* Marquez (Shaun); R. *v.* Goldsmith (Harold Egan) [1998]
     1 Cr. App. R. 420; [1998] 2 Cr. App. R. (S.) 178; [1998] Crim. L.R. 428; *Times,*
     December 19, 1997, CA (Crim Div) . . . .   *Digested,* 98/**1214**:
                        Applied, 01/1299, 01/1308: *Considered,* 99/1158, 99/1160, 99/1161, 99/1162,
                        99/1164, 99/1165, 00/1242, 00/1244, 00/1245, 00/1247, 00/1250, 00/1252,
                        00/1253, 01/1298, 01/1304, 01/1312, 01/1313: *Followed,* 99/1168:
                                                                          Referred to, 99/1110
R. *v.* Avon CC Ex p. M [1994] 2 F.L.R. 1006; [1994] 2 F.C.R. 259; (1999) 2 C.C.L.
     Rep. 185; [1995] Fam. Law 66, QBD . . . .   *Digested,* 95/**3202**:
                                                                          Followed, 99/4622
R. *v.* Aylesbury Crown Court Ex p. Lait [1998] Masons C.L.R. 264, QBD . . . .   *Digested,* 99/**990**
R. *v.* Aylesbury Vale DC Ex p. Chaplin (1998) 76 P. & C.R. 207; [1997] 3 P.L.R. 55;
     [1998] J.P.L. 49; *Times,* August 19, 1997; *Independent,* October 6, 1997 (C.S.),
     CA; affirming [1996] E.G.C.S. 126; *Times,* July 23, 1996, QBD . . . .   *Digested,* 97/**4107**
R. *v.* Aylesbury Vale DC Ex p. Clare [2000] P.L.C.R. 29, QBD . . . . *Digested,* 00/**4495**
R. *v.* Aylott (Daniel Henry) [1996] 2 Cr. App. R. 169; [1996] Crim. L.R. 429, CA (Crim
     Div) . . . .   *Digested,* 96/**1624**:
                                                                          Considered, 01/54
R. *v.* Aylott (Walter Axel) (1988) 10 Cr. App. R. (S.) 111, CA (Crim Div) . . . .   *Digested,* 90/**1277**:
                                                              Cited, 90/1260: *Considered,* 99/1356
R. *v.* Ayodeji (Julian) [2001] 1 Cr. App. R. (S.) 106; *Times,* October 20, 2000, CA
     (Crim Div) . . . .   *Digested,* 00/**1128**
R. *v.* Azad (Afran) see Attorney General's Reference (No.19 of 1998), Re
R. *v.* Aziz (Abdul) [1996] 1 Cr. App. R. (S.) 265, CA (Crim Div) . . . .   *Digested,* 96/**2080**:
                                                              Considered, 98/1389, 00/1433
R. *v.* Aziz (Kazim); R. *v.* Tosun (Ali Yener); R. *v.* Yorganci (Metin) [1996] A.C. 41; [1995]
     3 W.L.R. 53; [1995] 3 All E.R. 149; [1995] 2 Cr. App. R. 478; (1995) 159 J.P.
     669; [1995] Crim. L.R. 897; (1995) 159 J.P.N. 756; (1995) 92(28) L.S.G. 41;
     (1995) 145 N.L.J. 921; [1995] 139 S.J.L.B. 158; *Times,* June 16, 1995;
     Independent, June 16, 1995, HL. . . . .   *Digested,* 95/**1044**:
                                                                          Considered, 98/1050
R. *v.* B see Attorney General's Reference (No.7 of 1998), Re
R. *v.* B see Attorney General's Reference (No.3 of 1999), Re
R. *v.* B see R. *v.* TM

R. v. B [1999] Crim. L.R. 594, CA (Crim Div)
R. v. B (A Juvenile) see Attorney General's Reference (Nos.52, 53, 54 and 55 of 1999), Re
R. v. B (A Juvenile) (Sentence: Jurisdiction); *sub nom* R. v. B (Candi) [1999] 1 W.L.R. 61; [1999] 1 Cr. App. R. (S.) 132; [1998] Crim. L.R. 588; (1998) 95(25) L.S.G. 33; (1998) 142 S.J.L.B. 180; *Times*, May 14, 1998; *Independent*, May 21, 1998, CA (Crim Div) . . . . *Digested*, 98/**1282**
R. v. B (A Juvenile) [2000] 1 Cr. App. R. (S.) 177, CA (Crim Div) . . . . *Digested*, 00/**1326**
R. v. B (A Juvenile) (Mode of Trial for Indecency) (2001) 98(6) L.S.G. 45; *Times*, February 27, 2001, CA (Crim Div) . . . . *Digested*, 01/**1162**
R. v. B (A Juvenile) (Contradictory Evidence); *sub nom* R. v. DLB [2001] EWCA Crim 194; [2001] 3 F.C.R. 341, CA (Crim Div). . . . . *Digested*, 01/**1157**
R. v. B (Andi) (A Juvenile) [2001] EWCA Crim 765; [2001] 2 Cr. App. R. (S.) 104; (2001) 165 J.P. 707; (2001) 165 J.P.N. 785, CA (Crim Div) . . . . *Digested*, 01/**1406**
R. v. B (Anthony James) (A Juvenile) [2001] 2 Cr. App. R. (S.) 13, CA (Crim Div) . . . . . *Digested*, 01/**1398**
R. v. B (Anthony Philip) (A Juvenile) [2000] Crim. L.R. 48, CA (Crim Div)
R. v. B (Anthony Richard) [2000] 1 Cr. App. R. (S.) 412, CA (Crim Div) . . . . *Digested*, 00/**1383**
R. v. B (Brian Phillip) see Attorney General's Reference (No.22 of 1999), Re
R. v. B (Candi) see R. v. B (A Juvenile) (Sentence: Jurisdiction)
R. v. B (Carl) (1993) 14 Cr. App. R. (S.) 774, CA . . . . *Digested*, 94/**1281**:
                                                 Considered, 98/1250
R. v. B (Caroline) [2001] 1 Cr. App. R. (S.) 74; *Times*, July 4, 2000, CA (Crim Div) . . . . . *Digested*, 00/**1285**
R. v. B (Christian Darren) (A Juvenile) see Attorney General's Reference (No.24 of 1997), Re
R. v. B (Christopher John) (A Juvenile) see R. v. F (Mark Frank)
R. v. B (Dale John) (A Juvenile) [2000] 2 Cr. App. R. (S.) 376, CA (Crim Div) . . . . *Digested*, 00/**1313**
R. v. B (David) (A Juvenile); R. v. D (Robert) (A Juvenile) [1999] 2 Cr. App. R. (S.) 331; [1999] Crim. L.R. 508, CA (Crim Div) . . . . *Digested*, 99/**1241**
R. v. B (David John) [2000] Crim. L.R. 50, CA (Crim Div)
R. v. B (David Wayne) [2000] 1 Cr. App. R. (S.) 3, CA (Crim Div) . . . . *Digested*, 00/**1389**
R. v. B (Derek Anthony) [2001] Crim. L.R. 471, CA (Crim Div)
R. v. B (Dexter) (A Juvenile) [2001] 1 Cr. App. R. (S.) 113; [2001] Crim. L.R. 50, CA (Crim Div). . . . . *Digested*, 01/**1377**
R. v. B (Douglas) see Attorney General's Reference (No.29 of 1998), Re
R. v. B (Extradition: Abuse of Process), *Times*, October 18, 2000; *Independent*, November 27, 2000 (C.S), CA (Crim Div) . . . . *Digested*, 00/**2420**
R. v. B (Informer: Reduction of Sentence) see R. v. A (Informer: Reduction of Sentence)
R. v. B (James David) see R. v. B (Longer Term Sentences)
R. v. B (Jason) [2001] 2 Cr. App. R. (S.) 14, CA (Crim Div) . . . . *Digested*, 01/**1323**
R. v. B (Joseph James) (A Juvenile) [2001] 1 Cr. App. R. (S.) 56, CA (Crim Div). . . . . . *Digested*, 01/**1386**
R. v. B (Kyle Mark) (A Juvenile) see R. v. KB (A Juvenile)
R. v. B (Lee James) (A Juvenile) [2001] 1 Cr. App. R. (S.) 89; [2000] Crim. L.R. 870, CA (Crim Div) . . . . *Digested*, 01/**1475**
R. v. B (Longer Term Sentences); *sub nom* R. v. B (James David) (1999) 96(5) L.S.G. 35; *Times*, December 31, 1998; *Independent*, December 21, 1998 (C.S.), CA (Crim Div). . . . . *Digested*, 99/**1344**
R. v. B (Lorraine Shirley) [1998] 2 Cr. App. R. (S.) 407, CA (Crim Div) . . . . *Digested*, 99/**1097**
R. v. B (Malcolm Kevin) see Attorney General's Reference (No.26a of 2001), Re
R. v. B (Nicholas) [2001] 1 Cr. App. R. (S.) 130, CA (Crim Div). . . . . *Digested*, 01/**1320**
R. v. B (Rape) [1999] 1 Cr. App. R. (S.) 232, CA (Crim Div) . . . . *Digested*, 99/**1297**
R. v. B (Raymond Christopher) (A Juvenile); R. v. Hall (John Anthony) [2001] EWCA Crim 224; [2001] 2 Cr. App. R. 16; [2001] Crim. L.R. 754, CA (Crim Div). . . . . . *Digested*, 01/**997**
R. v. B (Sharon Kristine) (1994) 15 Cr. App. R. (S.) 815, CA (Crim Div) . . . . *Digested*, 95/**1405**:
                                                 Considered, 00/1278
R. v. B (Stephen) [1999] 2 Cr. App. R. (S.) 97; [1999] Crim. L.R. 234, CA (Crim Div) . . *Digested*, 99/**1087**
R. v. B (T Danielle) (A Juvenile) see R. v. Reid (Sonni Lee)
R. v. B (Trevor Paul) [1999] 1 Cr. App. R. (S.) 174, CA (Crim Div) . . . . *Digested*, 99/**1192**
R. v. B (Victor) [1999] 2 Cr. App. R. (S.) 253, CA (Crim Div) . . . . *Digested*, 99/**1198**
R. v. B (Wayne) see R. v. Basnett (Wayne)
R. v. B (Wayne) (A Juvenile) see Attorney General's Reference (No.61 of 1999), Re
R. (on the application of C (A Child)) v. B School Governors see R. (on the application of W (A Child)) v. B School Governors
R. (on the application of W (A Child)) v. B School Governors see R. (on the application of L (A Child)) v. J School Governors
R. (on the application of W (A Child)) v. B School Governors; *sub nom* R. (on the application of C (A Child)) v. B School Governors; R. v. B School Governors Ex p. W (A Child) [2001] E.L.R. 285; (2000) 97(45) L.S.G. 40; *Times*, November 14, 2000, QBD (Admin Ct) . . . . *Digested*, 00/**1929**:
                                          Subsequent proceedings, 01/1979
R. v. B School Governors Ex p. W see R. (on the application of L (A Child)) v. J School Governors

R. *v.* Backshall (David Anthony) [1998] 1 W.L.R. 1506; [1999] 1 Cr. App. R. 35; [1998] R.T.R. 423; [1999] Crim. L.R. 662; (1998) 95(17) L.S.G. 30; (1998) 142 S.J.L.B. 126; *Times*, April 10, 1998, CA (Crim Div) . . . .   *Digested*, 98/**972**

R. *v.* Bacon's City Technology College Governors Ex p. W [1998] Ed. C.R. 236; [1998] E.L.R. 488, QBD . . . .   *Digested*, 98/**1902**

R. *v.* Bacon's School Governors Ex p. Inner London Education Authority [1990] C.O.D. 414, QBD . . . .   *Digested*, 91/**1559**:
Applied, 99/1887: *Considered*, 98/3025

R. *v.* Baer (Ronald) [1999] 1 Cr. App. R. (S.) 441, CA (Crim Div) . . . .   *Digested*, 99/**1163**

R. *v.* Bagga (Unreported, May 21, 1986), CA (Crim Div) . . . .   *Considered*, 98/871

R. *v.* Bahashwan (Anis Said) see Attorney General's Reference (Nos.53, 54, 55, 56 and 57 of 2001), Re

R. *v.* Bailey (Ivan) (1988) 10 Cr. App. R. (S.) 231; [1988] Crim. L.R. 628, CA . . . .   *Digested*, 89/**1091**:
Considered, 98/1137

R. *v.* Bailey (Paul John) [1996] 1 Cr. App. R. (S.) 129, CA.   *Considered*, 97/1676,
98/1279

R. *v.* Bailey (Simon Paul) see R. *v.* Earley (Simon)

R. *v.* Baines [1909] 1 K.B. 258, KBD . . . .   *Applied*, 98/364

R. *v.* Baker (Adrian Richard) [1998] Crim. L.R. 351, CA (Crim Div)

R. *v.* Baker (Graham David) (1989) 11 Cr. App. R. (S.) 513, CA (Crim Div) . . . .   *Digested*, 91/**1197**:
Considered, 97/1444, 99/1306, 99/1313

R. *v.* Baker (Henry) [1962] 2 Q.B. 530; [1961] 3 W.L.R. 1205; [1961] 3 All E.R. 703; (1962) 46 Cr. App. R. 47; 125 J.P. 650; [1962] Crim. L.R. 41, CCA. . . . .   *Digested*, 61/**3568**:
Disapproved, 00/966

R. *v.* Baker (James) [1998] N.I. 130, CA (Crim Div) (NI) . . . .   *Digested*, 99/**5217**

R. *v.* Baker (Janet); R. *v.* Wilkins (Carl) [1997] Crim. L.R. 497; *Times*, November 26, 1996, CA (Crim Div) . . . .   *Digested*, 97/**1188**:
Applied, 98/936

R. *v.* Baker (Tony) (No.1); R. *v.* Ward (Alan) [1999] 2 Cr. App. R. 335; *Times*, April 28, 1999, CA (Crim Div) . . . .   *Digested*, 99/**1020**:
Cited, 99/931

R. *v.* Baker (Wendy Ann) [2001] 1 Cr. App. R. (S.) 55; [2000] Crim. L.R. 700, CA (Crim Div). . . . .   *Digested*, 01/**1269**

R. *v.* Baldwin (Keith Alan) [2000] 1 Cr. App. R. (S.) 81, CA (Crim Div) . . . .   *Digested*, 00/**1375**

R. *v.* Balham Youth Court Ex p. K, *Independent*, December 20, 1999 (C.S), QBD

R. *v.* Ball (Alexander); R. *v.* Rugg (Colin Stuart) *Times*, February 17, 1998, CMAC. . . . . .   *Digested*, 98/**258**

R. *v.* Ball (Alfred) see R. *v.* Ball (Naylor)

R. *v.* Ball (Lisa Jane); R. *v.* Bateman (Darren) *Times*, December 1, 1997, CA (Crim Div) . .   *Digested*, 98/**1206**:
Considered, 98/1207

R. *v.* Ball (Naylor); R. *v.* Ball (Alfred) [2001] 1 Cr. App. R. (S.) 49, CA (Crim Div) . . . . . .   *Digested*, 01/**1447**

R. *v.* Balmer [1996] N.I. 171, CA (Crim Div) (NI)

R. *v.* Bamborough (David) (1995) 16 Cr. App. R. (S.) 602, CA (Crim Div) . . . .   *Considered*, 00/1366

R. *v.* Bamforth (Jason) [1999] 1 Cr. App. R. (S.) 123, CA (Crim Div) . . . .   *Digested*, 99/**1314**:
Cited, 00/1398

R. *v.* Banks [1916] 2 K.B. 621, CCA. . . . .   *Applied*, 79/2318,
98/3116: *Distinguished*, 88/3073

R. *v.* Banks (David Malcolm) [1997] 2 Cr. App. R. (S.) 110; [1997] Crim. L.R. 235, CA (Crim Div). . . . .   *Digested*, 97/**1471**:
Applied, 98/1150

R. *v.* Banks (Glen) [1999] 2 Cr. App. R. (S.) 231, CA (Crim Div) . . . .   *Digested*, 99/**1092**

R. *v.* Banks (Stephen John) [2001] 1 Cr. App. R. (S.) 12, CA (Crim Div) . . . .   *Digested*, 01/**1298**

R. *v.* Bansal (Sundeep Singh) [1999] Crim. L.R. 484; *Times*, December 29, 1998, CA (Crim Div). . . . .   *Digested*, 99/**975**

R. *v.* Banu (Amina); R. *v.* Ali (Portab) (1995) 16 Cr. App. R. (S.) 656, CA (Crim Div) . . .   *Digested*, 96/**1792**:
Considered, 98/1142

R. *v.* Barak (Alexander) (1985) 7 Cr. App. R. (S.) 404, CA (Crim Div) . . . .   *Digested*, 86/**841**:
Considered, 98/1300

R. *v.* Barber (John Richard) [2001] EWCA Crim 2267; (2001) 165 J.P.N. 987; *Times*, November 20, 2001; *Independent*, November 6, 2001, CA (Crim Div) . . . .   *Digested*, 01/**1449**

R. *v.* Barczi (Richard); R. *v.* Williams (Peter) [2001] EWCA Crim 528; [2001] 2 Cr. App. R. (S.) 90, CA (Crim Div) . . . .   *Digested*, 01/**1219**

R. *v.* Barker (Nicholas) [1999] 1 Cr. App. R. (S.) 71, CA (Crim Div) . . . .   *Digested*, 99/**1327**

R. *v.* Barker (Peter Andrew) [2001] 1 Cr. App. R. (S.) 142; [2001] Crim. L.R. 147; (2000) 97(44) L.S.G. 44; (2000) 144 S.J.L.B. 275; *Times*, November 8, 2000; *Independent*, December 11, 2000 (C.S), CA (Crim Div) . . . .   *Digested*, 00/**1173**

R. (on the application of L) *v.* Barking and Dagenham LBC; *sub nom* R. *v.* L; R. *v.* Barking and Dagenham LBC Ex p. L [2001] EWCA Civ 533; [2001] 2 F.L.R. 763; [2001] B.L.G.R. 421; [2001] Fam. Law 662; *Times*, June 11, 2001, CA; affirming [2001] B.L.G.R. 86, QBD . . . .   *Digested*, 01/**5099**

R. *v.* Barking and Dagenham LBC Ex p. JDE Plant Hire Ltd see JDE Plant Hire Ltd *v.* Barking and Dagenham LBC

R. *v.* Barking and Dagenham LBC Ex p. L see R. (on the application of L) *v.* Barking and Dagenham LBC

R. *v.* Barnard (Philip Charles) (1980) 70 Cr. App. R. 28; [1980] Crim. L.R. 235; 132
　S.J. 803, CA (Crim Div) . . . . *Digested*, 80/**446**:
　　　　　　　　　　　　　　　　　　　　　　　　　　　　　Distinguished, 01/5726
R. *v.* Barnes (Stephen) (1993) 14 Cr. App. R. (S.) 547, CA (Crim Div) . . . . *Digested*, 94/**1173**:
　　　　　　　　　　　　　　　　　　　　　　　　　　　　　Considered, 00/1123
R. (on the application of G) *v.* Barnet LBC [2001] EWCA Civ 540; [2001] 2 F.L.R. 877;
　[2001] 2 F.C.R. 193; (2001) 33 H.L.R. 59; [2001] Fam. Law 662; (2001)
　98(24) L.S.G. 43; *Times*, June 5, 2001; *Independent*, April 25, 2001, CA;
　reversing [2001] EWHC Admin 5; [2001] 1 F.C.R. 743; [2001] A.C.D. 59, QBD
　(Admin Ct) . . . . *Digested*, 01/**4378**
R. *v.* Barnet LBC Ex p. B [1994] 1 F.L.R. 592; [1994] 2 F.C.R. 781; [1994] Fam. Law
　185; *Independent*, November 17, 1993, QBD . . . . *Digested*, 95/**3252**
R. *v.* Barnet LBC Ex p. Foran (1999) 31 H.L.R. 708; (1999) 2 C.C.L. Rep. 329, CA. . . . . *Digested*, 99/**3046**
R. *v.* Barnet LBC Ex p. G [1998] Ed. C.R. 252, CA; affirming [1998] E.L.R. 281, QBD . . *Digested*, 98/**1973**
R. *v.* Barnet LBC Ex p. Pardes House School [1989] C.O.D. 512; *Independent*, May 4,
　1989, QBD . . . . *Digested*, 90/**1783**:
　　　　　　　　　　　　　　　　　　　　　　　　　　　　Distinguished, 00/4114
R. *v.* Barnet LBC Ex p. Shah (Nilish); Akbarali *v.* Brent LBC; Abdullah *v.* Shropshire CC;
　Shabpar *v.* Barnet LBC; Shah (Jitendra) *v.* Barnet LBC; Ablack *v.* Inner London
　Education Authority; R. *v.* Shropshire CC Ex p. Abdullah [1983] 2 A.C. 309;
　[1983] 2 W.L.R. 16; [1983] 1 All E.R. 226; 81 L.G.R. 305; (1983) 133 N.L.J. 61;
　(1983) 127 S.J. 36, HL; reversing [1982] Q.B. 688; [1982] 2 W.L.R. 474;
　[1982] 1 All E.R. 698; 80 L.G.R. 571; *Times*, November 12, 1981, CA; affirming
　[1981] 2 W.L.R. 86; [1980] 3 All E.R. 679; 79 L.G.R. 210; 125 S.J. 64, QBD. . . . *Digested*, 83/**1157**:
　　　　Applied, 80/853, 84/1138, 84/3033, 85/1074, 85/1732, 86/703, 86/1692,
　　　　87/3489, 98/3007, 01/2612, 01/2617: *Considered*, 82/973, 83/1815, 84/1173,
　　　　84/1645, 85/1107, 85/1108, 85/1127, 85/2165, 86/1136, 90/11, 91/2371,
　　　　91/2372, 95/3206, 99/4564, 00/2778: *Distinguished*, 83/1800:
　　　　Followed, 85/1735, 87/1928: *Referred to*, 91/2373
R. *v.* Barnet Magistrates Court Ex p. Cantor [1999] 1 W.L.R. 334; [1998] 2 All E.R.
　333; (1998) 162 J.P. 137; (1998) 162 J.P.N. 145; *Times*, January 20, 1998;
　Independent, January 21, 1998, QBD . . . . *Digested*, 98/**1007**
R. *v.* Barnett (Christopher George) see R. *v.* Chambers (Mark Howard)
R. *v.* Barnsby (Rupert Gerard) [1998] 2 Cr. App. R. (S.) 222, CA (Crim Div) . . . . *Digested*, 98/**1207**
R. *v.* Barr (Raymond) [1996] 2 Cr. App. R. (S.) 294, CA (Crim Div) . . . . *Digested*, 97/**1564**:
　　　　　　　　　　　　　　　　　　　　　　　　　Considered, 99/1178, 99/1184
R. *v.* Barraclough (Kevin David) [2000] Crim. L.R. 324, CA (Crim Div)
R. *v.* Barratt (Paul Albert) [2000] Crim. L.R. 847, CA (Crim Div)
R. *v.* Barrick (John) (1985) 81 Cr. App. R. 78; (1985) 7 Cr. App. R. (S.) 142; (1985)
　149 J.P. 705; (1985) 129 S.J. 416, CA (Crim Div) . . . . *Digested*, 85/**765**:
　　　　　Applied, 86/884, 86/885, 86/889: *Cited*, 88/999, 88/1001, 89/1123,
　　　　　　　　　　90/1429, 91/1228, 91/1230, 92/1442, 93/1294, 94/1366:
　　　　　Considered, 86/759, 87/457, 87/1013, 87/1015, 87/1056, 87/1057, 87/1061,
　　　　　87/1063, 87/1828, 88/925, 88/934, 88/1002, 88/1713, 89/1046, 89/1121,
　　　　　91/1173, 91/1225, 92/1167, 95/1385, 96/1752, 97/1549, 98/1316, 98/1391,
　　　　　　　　　　98/1392, 99/1174, 99/1277, 99/1359, 99/1362, 00/1436:
　　　　　Distinguished, 86/760, 87/1058: *Referred to*, 86/711, 87/1055, 87/1064
R. *v.* Barros (Joso Manuel) [2000] 2 Cr. App. R. (S.) 327; [2000] Crim. L.R. 601, CA
　(Crim Div) . . . . *Digested*, 00/**1295**
R. *v.* Barry (Christopher) [1975] 1 W.L.R. 1190; [1975] 2 All E.R. 760; (1975) 61 Cr.
　App. R. 172; [1975] Crim. L.R. 473; 119 S.J. 337, CA (Crim Div) . . . . *Digested*, 75/**1820**:
　　　　　　　　　Applied, 81/1484, 82/1708, 92/914: *Distinguished*, 99/1061
R. *v.* Barry Magistrates Court Ex p. Malpas [1998] C.O.D. 90, QBD . . . . *Followed*, 98/1087
R. *v.* Barson (Alan Robert) see R. *v.* Aitken (Thomas Adam)
R. *v.* Barthelmy (Robert) see Attorney General's Reference (Nos.44 and 46 of 1995),
　Re
R. *v.* Bartle Ex p. Pinochet Ugarte (No.1) see R. *v.* Bow Street Metropolitan Stipendiary
　Magistrate Ex p. Pinochet Ugarte (No.1)
R. *v.* Bartle Ex p. Pinochet Ugarte (No.2) see R. *v.* Bow Street Metropolitan
　Stipendiary Magistrate Ex p. Pinochet Ugarte (No.2)
R. *v.* Bartley (Roger Anthony) see Attorney General's Reference (No.10 of 1993), Re
R. *v.* Barton (Richard) see R. *v.* Avis (Tony)
R. *v.* Barwick (Robert Ernest); *sub nom* R. *v.* Barwick (Robert Earnest) [2001] 1 Cr.
　App. R. (S.) 129; [2001] Crim. L.R. 52; *Times*, November 10, 2000, CA (Crim
　Div) . . . . *Digested*, 00/**1172**
R. *v.* Bashir (Mohammed) see R. *v.* Khan (Sakina Bibi)
R. *v.* Bashir (Mohammed) (1983) 77 Cr. App. R. 59; [1982] Crim. L.R. 687, CA (Crim
　Div) . . . . *Digested*, 82/**679**:
　　　　　　　　　　　　　　Considered, 84/709, 85/681: *Not followed*, 01/1153
R. *v.* Basnett (Wayne); *sub nom* R. *v.* B (Wayne) [1996] 2 Cr. App. R. (S.) 305, CA
　(Crim Div) . . . . *Digested*, 96/**1945**:
　　　　　　　　　　　　　　　　　　　　　　　　　　　　Considered, 00/1293
R. *v.* Basra (Wasted Costs Order); *sub nom* Douglas Narayan & Partners *v.* Khan
　[1998] P.N.L.R. 535, CA (Crim Div) . . . . *Digested*, 98/**1017**

R. *v.* Bassetlaw DC Ex p. Oxby [1998] P.L.C.R. 283; [1997] N.P.C. 178; *Times,*
December 18, 1997; *Independent*, December 16, 1997, CA; reversing [1997]
J.P.L. 576, QBD . . . . *Digested*, 98/**4210**
R. *v.* Bateman (Darren) see R. *v.* Ball (Lisa Jane)
R. *v.* Bates (Jason Alan) see R. *v.* Greatrex (David Anthony)
R. *v.* Bath and North East Somerset Council Ex p. Master, Co-Brethren and Sisters of
the Hospital of St John the Baptist [1999] N.P.C. 89, QBD
R. *v.* Bath and North Somerset DC see R. *v.* Secretary of State for the Environment,
Transport and the Regions Ex p. Bath and North East Somerset DC
R. *v.* Bath Mental Healthcare NHS Trust Ex p. Beck (2000) 3 C.C.L. Rep. 5, QBD . . . . . *Digested*, 00/**2843**
R. *v.* Batt (Jeanne) [1999] 2 Cr. App. R. (S.) 223, CA (Crim Div) . . . . *Digested*, 99/**1141**:
Considered, 00/1223
R. *v.* Batt (Peter James) [1996] Crim. L.R. 910; *Times*, May 30, 1996; *Independent*,
July 1, 1996 (C.S.), CA (Crim Div) . . . . *Digested*, 96/**1555**:
Considered, 00/4020
R. *v.* BBC Ex p. Lavelle [1983] 1 W.L.R. 23; [1983] 1 All E.R. 241; [1983] I.C.R. 99;
[1982] I.R.L.R. 404; (1983) 133 N.L.J. 133; (1982) 126 S.J.L.B. 836, QBD . . . . *Digested*, 83/**15**:
Approved, 83/2943: *Considered*, 85/2672, 87/6, 89/12:
Not applied, 00/5836: *Referred to*, 85/1147, 86/1176
R. *v.* BBC Ex p. Quintavelle (1998) 10 Admin. L.R. 425, QBD . . . . *Digested*, 98/**93**
R. *v.* Beard (Jason Robert) [1998] Crim. L.R. 585, CA (Crim Div)
R. *v.* Beatrix Potter School Ex p. K [1997] E.L.R. 468, QBD . . . . *Digested*, 98/**1921**
R. *v.* Beaumont (Steven) (1992) 13 Cr. App. R. (S.) 270, CA (Crim Div) . . . . *Digested*, 93/**1013**:
Cited, 94/1313, 98/1309: *Considered*, 96/2021, 98/1308, 01/1437
R. *v.* Beck Ex p. Daily Telegraph Plc [1993] 2 All E.R. 177; (1992) 94 Cr. App. R. 376,
CA (Crim Div) . . . . *Digested*, 93/**735**:
Applied, 93/738: *Distinguished*, 01/1182
R. *v.* Beckford (Ian Anthony) [1996] 1 Cr. App. R. 94; (1995) 159 J.P. 305; [1995]
R.T.R. 253; [1995] Crim. L.R. 712; *Times*, January 27, 1995, CA (Crim Div) . . . . . *Digested*, 95/**1109**:
Considered, 97/1172, 97/1256, 98/1079
R. *v.* Beckham (Leigh Spencer) see Attorney General's Reference (No.43 of 1997), Re
R. *v.* Beckles (Keith Anderson); R. *v.* Montague (Rudolph Leopold) [1999] Crim. L.R.
148, CA (Crim Div)
R. *v.* Bedford (Roy John) (1993) 14 Cr. App. R. (S.) 336, CA (Crim Div) . . . . *Digested*, 94/**1314**:
Considered, 96/1993, 96/2021, 99/1076, 00/1267
R. (on the application of Aircraft Research Association Ltd) *v.* Bedford BC [2001] Env.
L.R. 40; [2001] E.H.L.R. 17, QBD (Admin Ct) . . . . *Digested*, 01/**2425**
R. (on the application of Henlow Grange Health Farm Ltd) *v.* Bedfordshire CC; *sub nom* R.
v. Bedfordshire CC Ex p. Henlow Grange Health Farm Ltd; Henlow Grange
Health Farm Ltd *v.* Bedfordshire CC [2001] EWHC Admin 179; [2001] J.P.L.
1435 (Note); [2001] 12 E.G.C.S. 166; (2001) 98(12) L.S.G. 45; [2001] N.P.C.
57, QBD (Admin Ct)
R. (on the application of W (A Child)) *v.* Bedfordshire CC [2001] EWHC Admin 47;
[2001] E.L.R. 645, QBD (Admin Ct)
R. *v.* Bedfordshire CC Ex p. Henlow Grange Health Farm Ltd see R. (on the application
of Henlow Grange Health Farm Ltd) *v.* Bedfordshire CC
R. *v.* Bedfordshire CC Ex p. Mason [1999] N.P.C. 93, QBD . . . . *Digested*, 99/**4263**
R. *v.* Bedfordshire Coroner Ex p. Local Sunday Newspapers Ltd (2000) 164 J.P. 283;
(2000) 164 J.P.N. 370, QBD . . . . *Digested*, 00/**47**
R. *v.* Bediako (Michael); R. *v.* Martin (Andrew) [2001] EWCA Crim 1967; *Times*,
October 16, 2001, CA (Crim Div) . . . . *Digested*, 01/**1424**
R. *v.* Bedlington Magistrates Court Ex p. Wilkinson (2000) 164 J.P. 156; (2000) 164
J.P.N. 264; *Times*, November 30, 1999, QBD . . . . *Digested*, 00/**1036**
R. *v.* Bedwellty Justices Ex p. Williams; *sub nom* Williams *v.* Bedwellty Justices [1997]
A.C. 225; [1996] 3 W.L.R. 361; [1996] 3 All E.R. 737; [1996] 2 Cr. App. R. 594;
(1996) 160 J.P. 549; (1996) 8 Admin. L.R. 643; [1996] Crim. L.R. 906;
[1997] C.O.D. 54; (1996) 160 J.P.N. 696; (1996) 93(34) L.S.G. 34; (1996) 146
N.L.J. 1149; (1996) 140 S.J.L.B. 192; *Times*, August 6, 1996, HL . . . . *Digested*, 96/**1558**:
Applied, 98/873: *Considered*, 98/884: *Followed*, 97/1117
R. *v.* Beedie (Thomas Sim) [1998] Q.B. 356; [1997] 3 W.L.R. 758; [1997] 2 Cr. App.
R. 167; (1997) 161 J.P. 313; [1997] Crim. L.R. 747; (1997) 161 J.P.N. 531; (1997)
94(15) L.S.G. 26; (1997) 141 S.J.L.B. 83; *Times*, March 14, 1997; *Independent*,
April 21, 1997 (C.S.), CA (Crim Div) . . . . *Digested*, 97/**1317**
R. *v.* Beeley (Geoffrey Terence) see R. *v.* Warren (John Barry)
R. *v.* Beer (Carmel Anne) [1998] 2 Cr. App. R. (S.) 248, CA (Crim Div) . . . . *Digested*, 98/**1113**:
Considered, 00/1127
R. *v.* Beevor (Julian Scott) [2001] EWCA Crim 620; [2001] 2 Cr. App. R. (S.) 77, CA
(Crim Div) . . . . *Digested*, 01/**1279**
R. *v.* Bell (Aaron James) [2001] 1 Cr. App. R. (S.) 108, CA (Crim Div) . . . . *Digested*, 01/**1453**
R. *v.* Bell (Roderick Garfield) [1998] Crim. L.R. 879, CA (Crim Div)
R. *v.* Bellamy (David John) [2001] 1 Cr. App. R. (S.) 34; [2000] Crim. L.R. 771, CA
(Crim Div) . . . . *Digested*, 01/**1353**
R. *v.* Bellikli (Dilaver) [1998] 1 Cr. App. R. (S.) 135; [1997] Crim. L.R. 612, CA (Crim
Div) . . . . *Digested*, 98/**1244**

R. _v._ Belmarsh Magistrates Court Ex p. Gilligan [1998] 1 Cr. App. R. 14; [1997] C.O.D.
     342, QBD . . . . _Digested,_ 98/**884**
R. _v._ Belmarsh Magistrates Court Ex p. Watts [1999] 2 Cr. App. R. 188, QBD . . . . _Digested,_ 99/**485**
R. _v._ Bendris (Faouzi) [2000] 2 Cr. App. R. (S.) 183, CA (Crim Div) . . . . _Digested,_ 00/**1370**
R. _v._ Benefits Agency Ex p. Zaheer see R. _v._ Secretary of State for Social Security Ex
     p. Vijeikis
R. _v._ Benjafield (Karl Robert) see R. _v._ Leal (Manoj)
R. _v._ Benjafield (Karl Robert) (Confiscation Order); R. _v._ Leal (Manoj) (Confiscation
     Order); R. _v._ Milford (David John); R. _v._ Rezvi (Syed); TNS, HL; affirming [2001]
     3 W.L.R. 75; [2001] 2 All E.R. 609; [2001] 2 Cr. App. R. 7; [2001] 2 Cr. App.
     R. (S.) 47; [2001] H.R.L.R. 25; 10 B.H.R.C. 19; [2001] Crim. L.R. 245; (2001)
     98(12) L.S.G. 41; _Times,_ December 28, 2000; _Independent,_ January 31, 2001,
     CA (Crim Div) . . . . _Digested,_ 01/**1237**:
                                                           Considered, 01/6327
R. _v._ Bennett (Jason David) (1994) 15 Cr. App. R. (S.) 213, CA (Crim Div) . . . . _Distinguished,_ 98/1336
R. _v._ Bennett (John) [1998] 1 Cr. App. R. (S.) 429, CA (Crim Div) . . . . _Digested,_ 98/**1193**:
                                                           Considered, 00/1205
R. _v._ Bennett (Simon Christopher) see R. _v._ Aitken (Thomas Adam)
R. _v._ Bentley (Derek) [2001] 1 Cr. App. R. 21; [1999] Crim. L.R. 330; _Times,_ July 31,
     1998, CA (Crim Div) . . . . _Digested,_ 98/**1051**:
                              Applied, 00/1023, 00/5999: _Referred to,_ 01/79
R. _v._ Beresford (Amanda Elizabeth) see Attorney General's Reference (Nos. 62, 63, 64
     and 65 of 1996), Re
R. _v._ Berkshire CC Ex p. P; _sub nom_ R. _v._ Royal County of Berkshire Ex p. P (1997-98)
     1 C.C.L. Rep. 141; (1997) 33 B.M.L.R. 71; [1997] C.O.D. 64; _Times,_ August 15,
     1996, QBD . . . . _Digested,_ 96/**5524**
R. _v._ Bernard (Basil Mortimer) [1997] 1 Cr. App. R. (S.) 135; (1997) 33 B.M.L.R. 23;
     [1996] Crim. L.R. 673; (1996) 140 S.J.L.B. 148; _Times,_ July 2, 1996, CA (Crim
     Div) . . . . _Digested,_ 96/**1877**:
                                       Approved, 97/1657: _Considered,_ 98/1322
R. _v._ Bernard (Stanley) see Attorney General's Reference (Nos. 72 and 73 of 1995), Re
R. _v._ Berry [1998] Crim. L.R. 487, CA (Crim Div) . . . . _Considered,_ 99/969
R. _v._ Berry (Arthur John) (1988) 10 Cr. App. R. (S.) 13; [1988] Crim. L.R. 325, CA
     (Crim Div) . . . . _Digested,_ 90/**1394**:
             Cited, 91/1194, 92/1377: _Considered,_ 93/1268, 94/1337, 99/1309, 00/1402:
                                                          Referred to, 95/1457
R. _v._ Berry (Charles Raymond) (1984) 6 Cr. App. R. (S.) 350; [1985] Crim. L.R. 327,
     CA (Crim Div) . . . . _Digested,_ 85/**811**:
                                         Considered, 96/1982, 98/1300, 98/1301
R. _v._ Berry (Paul Douglas) [2000] 1 Cr. App. R. (S.) 352; [1999] Crim. L.R. 855;
     (1999) 96(32) L.S.G. 31; _Times,_ October 20, 1999, CA (Crim Div) . . . . _Digested,_ 99/**1107**
R. _v._ Beswick (Darren Anthony) [1996] 1 Cr. App. R. 427; [1996] 1 Cr. App. R. (S.)
     343; (1996) 160 J.P. 33; (1995) 159 J.P.N. 826; _Times,_ October 10, 1995;
     Independent, October 23, 1995 (C.S.), CA (Crim Div) . . . . _Digested,_ 96/**1914**:
                                           Considered, 98/1135, 99/1144
R. _v._ Betrus (Unreported, July 10, 1998), MC [_Ex rel._ Paul McGrath, Barrister, 1 Temple
     Gardens, Temple, London] . . . . _Digested,_ 98/**1079**
R. _v._ Bett (Robert Adrian) [1999] 1 W.L.R. 2109; [1999] 1 All E.R. 600; [1999] 1 Cr.
     App. R. 361; (1999) 163 J.P. 65; [1999] Crim. L.R. 219; (1999) 163 J.P.N. 72;
     (1998) 95(45) L.S.G. 38; _Times,_ November 4, 1998; _Independent,_ October 28,
     1998, CA (Crim Div) . . . . _Digested,_ 98/**943**
R. _v._ Betts (Joseph) (1990) 12 Cr. App. R. (S.) 547, CA (Crim Div) . . . . _Digested,_ 92/**1171**:
                                                           Considered, 99/1091
R. _v._ Betty (Carol) (1964) 48 Cr. App. R. 6, CCA . . . . _Digested,_ 64/**802**:
                                    Applied, 95/1272: _Distinguished,_ 66/2603, 00/5468
R. _v._ Bevan (Paul Martin) [1996] 1 Cr. App. R. (S.) 14, CA (Crim Div) . . . . _Considered,_ 97/1676,
                                                  98/1279, 98/1364, 00/1195
R. _v._ Beveridge (Susan) see Attorney General's Reference (Nos. 57, 58 and 59 of
     1997), Re
R. _v._ Bevis (Robin) [2001] EWCA Crim 9; [2001] 2 Cr. App. R. (S.) 49; _Times,_
     February 8, 2001, CA (Crim Div) . . . . _Digested,_ 01/**1271**
R. _v._ Bexley LBC Ex p. B (Care Hours Provision) (2000) 3 C.C.L. Rep. 15, QBD . . . . _Digested,_ 95/**3225**
R. _v._ Bhad (Adam Ahmed) [1999] 2 Cr. App. R. (S.) 139, CA (Crim Div) . . . . _Digested,_ 99/**1118**
R. _v._ Bhagwan (Dharam Singh); _sub nom_ DPP _v._ Bhagwan [1972] A.C. 60; [1970] 3
     W.L.R. 501; [1970] 3 All E.R. 97; (1970) 54 Cr. App. R. 460; 114 S.J. 683, HL;
     affirming [1970] 2 W.L.R. 837; [1970] 1 All E.R. 1129; 114 S.J. 166, CA (Crim
     Div) . . . . _Digested,_ 70/**187**:
                       Considered, 72/591: _Distinguished,_ 92/2419: _Referred to,_ 99/2000
R. _v._ Bhatti (Mohammed Siddique) see R. _v._ Raja (Abdul Qayyum)
R. _v._ BHB Community Healthcare NHS Trust Ex p. B; _sub nom_ B, Re [1999] 1 F.L.R.
     106; (1999) 2 C.C.L. Rep. 5; [1999] Lloyd's Rep. Med. 101; (1999) 47 B.M.L.R.
     112; _Times,_ October 14, 1998, CA . . . . _Digested,_ 98/**3897**:
                                                            Applied, 00/3371
R. _v._ Bibby (Darren Robert) see R. _v._ Tantram (Peter John)

R. *v.* Bibby (John) see R. *v.* Gee (Arthur)
R. (on the application of L (A Child)) *v.* BicesterYouth Court see R. (on the application of
    DPP) *v.* RedbridgeYouth Court
R. *v.* Big M Drug Mart (1985) 18 D.L.R. (4th) 321, Sup Ct (Can) . . . .   *Followed,* 98/3108
R. *v.* Bigby (Wayne Edward) see Attorney General's Reference (No.12 of 1993), Re
R. *v.* Bigwood (Unreported, July 24, 2000), Crown Ct (Taunton) [*Ex rel.* Edward
    Counsell, Barrister, 12 Middle Street,Taunton] . . . .   *Digested,* 01/**1093**:
                                                                                                         Not applied, 01/1089
R. *v.* Bilinski (Edward) (1988) 86 Cr. App. R. 146; (1988) 9 Cr. App. R. (S.) 360;
    [1987] Crim. L.R. 782, CA (Crim Div). . . . .   *Digested,* 88/**930**:
                                       Applied, 88/993, 90/1300, 91/1094: *Approved,* 89/991, 90/1289:
                                     Cited, 88/871, 90/1284, 90/1288, 92/1245, 93/1123, 93/1127, 93/1128,
                                          93/1131, 94/1403: *Considered,* 88/912, 89/948, 89/949, 89/1027, 90/1268,
                                          90/1290, 90/1291, 90/1292, 90/1310, 91/1093, 91/1098, 92/1247, 00/1223:
                                                   Distinguished, 89/939, 90/1285: *Referred to,* 95/1367
R. *v.* Billam (Keith) [1986] 1 W.L.R. 349; [1986] 1 All E.R. 985; (1986) 82 Cr. App. R.
    347; (1986) 8 Cr. App. R. (S.) 48; [1986] Crim. L.R. 347, CA (Crim Div) . . . . . .   *Digested,* 86/**868**:
                                        Applied, 91/1192, 92/1374, 92/1376, 92/1379, 93/1265, 94/3837, 95/1411,
                                         96/1976, 96/1992, 96/2052, 99/1314, 00/1333: *Considered,* 87/1032,
                                          87/1033, 87/1036, 87/1076, 88/867, 88/868, 88/975, 88/976, 88/978,
                                           88/980, 88/1007, 90/1395, 90/1398, 96/1939, 96/2039, 96/2044,
                                          96/2045, 96/2047, 96/2048, 96/2051, 97/1432, 97/1452, 97/1454, 98/1143,
                                          98/1286, 98/1292, 98/1339, 98/1343, 98/1346, 98/1347, 98/1349, 98/1351,
                                           98/1352, 98/1354, 99/869, 99/1298, 99/1304, 99/1306, 99/1311, 00/1311,
                                          00/1392, 00/1395, 00/1401, 00/1402, 01/1455, 01/1463: *Followed,* 97/1645,
                                           99/1297, 99/1312: *Referred to,* 89/1105, 89/1213, 90/1220, 90/1392,
                                          90/1487, 91/1194, 91/1196, 92/1154, 92/1163, 92/1375, 92/1377, 93/1014,
                                            93/1214, 93/1257, 93/1260, 93/1261, 93/1264, 94/1307, 97/1646, 97/1648
R. *v.* Billericay Justices Ex p. Johnson [1979] Crim. L.R. 315, DC . . . .   *Digested,* 79/**609**:
                                                                                                         Not followed, 98/1102
R. *v.* Bingham (Graham Carlo); R. *v.* Cooke (Samuel David) [1999] 1 W.L.R. 598;
    [1999] N.I. 118; (1999) 96(15) L.S.G. 29; *Times,* March 15, 1999, HL (NI). . . . . .   *Digested,* 99/**5176**
R. *v.* Bioshogun (Nimota) see R. *v.* Aranguren (Jose de Jesus)
R. *v.* Birch (Christopher Louis) see Attorney General's Reference (No.67 of 1997), Re
R. *v.* Birch (David Brian) see R. *v.* Cole (Philip Francis)
R. *v.* Birchall (Keith) [1999] Crim. L.R. 311; *Times,* February 10, 1998, CA (Crim Div) . . .   *Digested,* 98/**1059**
R. *v.* Bird (Simon Lee) (1993) 14 Cr. App. R. (S.) 343; (1993) 157 J.P. 488; [1993]
    R.T.R. 1; [1993] Crim. L.R. 85; (1993) 157 J.P.N. 122; *Times,* October 22, 1992,
    CA . . . .   *Digested,* 93/**1313**:
                                                                                 Considered, 96/1716, 98/1357
R. *v.* Birkenhead Magistrates Court Ex p. Lewis, *Independent,* July 13, 1998 (C.S.),
    QBD . . . .   *Digested,* 98/**1094**
R. *v.* Birmingham CC Ex p. Killigrew see R. *v.* Birmingham City Council Ex p. Killigrew
R. (on the application of Y (A Child)) *v.* Birmingham City Council; *sub nom* R. *v.*
    Birmingham City Council Ex p. Y (A Child) [2001] EWCA Civ 287, CA; affirming
    [2001] B.L.G.R. 218; *Times,* January 10, 2001, QBD (Admin Ct) . . . .   *Digested,* 01/**1898**
R. *v.* Birmingham City Council Ex p. A (A Minor) [1997] 2 F.L.R. 841; [1997] 2 F.C.R.
    357; [1998] Fam. Law 23; *Times,* February 19, 1997, Fam Div . . . .   *Digested,* 97/**423**
R. *v.* Birmingham City Council Ex p. B; *sub nom* R. *v.* Birmingham City Council Ex p.
    M [1999] Ed. C.R. 573; [1999] E.L.R. 305; *Times,* October 13, 1998, QBD . . . . .   *Digested,* 98/**1915**
R. *v.* Birmingham City Council Ex p. Equal Opportunities Commission (No.1); *sub nom*
    Birmingham City Council *v.* Equal Opportunities Commission (No.1) [1989] A.C.
    1155; [1989] 2 W.L.R. 520; [1989] 1 All E.R. 769; [1989] I.R.L.R. 173; 87
    L.G.R. 557; (1989) 86(15) L.S.G. 36; (1989) 139 N.L.J. 292; (1989) 133 S.J.
    322; *Times,* February 24, 1989; *Independent,* February 24, 1989; *Guardian,*
    February 24, 1989, HL; affirming [1988] 3 W.L.R. 837; [1988] I.R.L.R. 430; 86
    L.G.R. 741; (1988) 152 L.G. Rev. 1039; *Times,* May 17, 1988; *Independent,* May
    18, 1988; *Guardian,* May 17, 1988; *Daily Telegraph,* May 20, 1988, CA; reversing
    [1988] I.R.L.R. 96; (1988) 152 L.G. Rev. 1035; *Times,* October 15, 1987, QBD . .   *Digested,* 89/**1371**:
                                          Considered, 89/2342, 95/2028, 00/2187: *Followed,* 99/2093:
                                                                                                         Referred to, 89/1923
R. *v.* Birmingham City Council Ex p. Ireland; *sub nom* Hall *v.* Kingston upon Hull City
    Council; Ireland *v.* Birmingham City Council; Baker *v.* Birmingham City Council;
    R. *v.* Kingston City Council Ex p. Hall; R. *v.* Kingston City Council Ex p. Baker
    [1999] 2 All E.R. 609; (2000) 164 J.P. 9; [1999] E.H.L.R. 243; (1999) 31 H.L.R.
    1079; [1999] B.L.G.R. 184; (1999) 163 J.P.N. 894; [1999] E.G.C.S. 4; (1999)
    149 N.L.J. 122; [1999] N.P.C. 5; [1999] Env. L.R. D19; *Times,* February 9, 1999,
    QBD . . . .   *Digested,* 99/**2214**:
                                                                            Applied, 00/2274: *Followed,* 00/6602
R. *v.* Birmingham City Council Ex p. Kett (2001) 33 H.L.R. 62, QBD
R. *v.* Birmingham City Council Ex p. Killigrew; *sub nom* R. *v.* Birmingham CC Ex p.
    Killigrew (2000) 3 C.C.L. Rep. 109, QBD . . . .   *Digested,* 01/**5098**
R. *v.* Birmingham City Council Ex p. L (A Child) [2000] Ed. C.R. 484; [2000] E.L.R.
    543, QBD . . . .   *Digested,* 00/**1915**

R. *v.* Birmingham City Council Ex p. M see R. *v.* Birmingham City Council Ex p. B
R. *v.* Birmingham City Council Ex p. Mohammed [1999] 1 W.L.R. 33; [1998] 3 All E.R.
   788; (1999) 31 H.L.R. 392; (1997-98) 1 C.C.L. Rep. 441; [1998] C.O.D. 404;
   Times, July 14, 1998, QBD . . . .   *Digested*, 98/**2990**
R. *v.* Birmingham City Council Ex p. Reece [1999] E.L.R. 373, QBD . . . .   *Digested*, 00/**1833**
R. *v.* Birmingham City Council Ex p. Y (A Child) see R. (on the application of Y (A
   Child)) *v.* Birmingham City Council
R. *v.* Birmingham Crown Court Ex p. Ali (Rashid); R. *v.* Bristol Magistrates Court Ex p.
   Davies; R. *v.* Immigration Appellate Authority Ex p. Davies (1999) 163 J.P. 145;
   [1999] Crim. L.R. 504; (1999) 163 J.P.N. 533; *Times*, October 16, 1998;
   Independent, October 19, 1998 (C.S.), QBD . . . .   *Digested*, 98/**87**:
                                 Considered, 99/81
R. *v.* Birmingham Justices Ex p. F (A Juvenile); *sub nom* R. *v.* Birmingham Youth Court
   Ex p. F (A Child) (2000) 164 J.P. 523; [2000] Crim. L.R. 588; (2000) 164
   J.P.N. 726; *Independent*, November 15, 1999 (C.S.), QBD . . . .   *Digested*, 00/**1114**
R. *v.* Birmingham Youth Court Ex p. F (A Child) see R. *v.* Birmingham Justices Ex p. F
   (A Juvenile)
R. *v.* Bishop (Alan) [2000] 1 Cr. App. R. (S.) 432; [2000] Crim. L.R. 60, CA (Crim
   Div) . . . .   *Digested*, 00/**1118**:
                                           Applied, 01/1176
R. *v.* Bishop (Harry) [2000] 1 Cr. App. R. (S.) 89, CA (Crim Div) . . . .   *Digested*, 00/**1412**
R. *v.* Bishop (Nicole) [2000] 2 Cr. App. R. (S.) 416, CA (Crim Div) . . . .   *Digested*, 01/**1329**
R. *v.* Bishop of Stafford Ex p. Owen [2001] A.C.D. 14, CA
R. *v.* Bisset (Ronald); R. *v.* Wray (Andrew Simon) [2000] 2 Cr. App. R. (S.) 397, CA
   (Crim Div) . . . .   *Digested*, 01/**1274**
R. *v.* BJ (A Juvenile) [2001] EWCA Crim 304; [2001] 2 Cr. App. R. (S.) 88, CA (Crim
   Div) . . . .   *Digested*, 01/**1397**
R. *v.* Black (Craig Adam) [2000] 2 Cr. App. R. (S.) 41; [2000] Crim. L.R. 317, CA
   (Crim Div) . . . .   *Digested*, 00/**1220**
R. *v.* Black (Jason George) (1992) 13 Cr. App. R. (S.) 262, CA (Crim Div) . . . .   *Digested*, 93/**1328**:
                                          Followed, 98/1198
R. *v.* Black (John William) see Attorney General's Reference (No.46 of 2001), Re
R. *v.* Blackburn Justices Ex p. Holmes (2000) 164 J.P. 163; [2000] Crim. L.R. 300;
   (2000) 164 J.P.N. 184; *Independent*, November 29, 1999 (C.S.), QBD . . . .   *Digested*, 00/**1045**
R. *v.* Blackfriars Crown Court Ex p. Sunworld Ltd see Sunworld Ltd *v.* Hammersmith
   and Fulham LBC
R. *v.* Blackham (Brian Francis) [1997] 2 Cr. App. R. (S.) 275, CA (Crim Div) . . . .   *Digested*, 97/**1505**:
                          Considered, 98/1193, 00/1212
R. *v.* Blackman (James Edward) [2001] EWCA Crim 150; [2001] 2 Cr. App. R. (S.)
   53, CA (Crim Div) . . . .   *Digested*, 01/**1260**
R. *v.* Blackman (Leigh Andrew) [1998] 2 Cr. App. R. (S.) 280, CA (Crim Div) . . . .   *Digested*, 98/**1251**
R. *v.* Blackpool BC Education Committee Ex p. Taylor [1999] E.L.R. 237, QBD . . . .   *Digested*, 99/**1837**
R. *v.* Blackwell (Warren Anthony) see Attorney General's Reference (No.83 of 1999),
   Re
R. *v.* Blades (Selhurst) [2000] 1 Cr. App. R. (S.) 463; [2000] Crim. L.R. 62; *Times*,
   October 13, 1999, CA (Crim Div) . . . .   *Digested*, 99/**1280**:
                                           Followed, 00/1414
R. *v.* Blanchard (Wayne) see R. *v.* Brewster (Alex Edward)
R. *v.* Blight (Tony); R. *v.* Cowlard (Gary Michael); R. *v.* Brereton (Scott Galvin); R. *v.*
   Collins (Jason Albert) [1999] 2 Cr. App. R. (S.) 196; [1999] Crim. L.R. 426, CA
   (Crim Div) . . . .   *Digested*, 99/**1293**
R. *v.* Bloody Sunday Inquiry Ex p. B see R. *v.* Lord Saville of Newdigate Ex p. B (No.1)
R. *v.* Bloomfield (Mark Andrew) [1997] 1 Cr. App. R. 135, CA (Crim Div) . . . .   *Digested*, 97/**1255**:
                                   Distinguished, 00/1046
R. *v.* Bloxham (Albert John) [1983] 1 A.C. 109; [1982] 2 W.L.R. 392; [1982] 1 All E.R.
   582; (1982) 74 Cr. App. R. 279; [1982] R.T.R. 129; [1982] Crim. L.R. 436, HL;
   reversing [1981] 1 W.L.R. 859; [1981] 2 All E.R. 647; (1981) 72 Cr. App. R. 323;
   [1981] R.T.R. 376; [1981] Crim. L.R. 337, CA (Crim Div) . . . .   *Digested*, 82/**621**:
                         Applied, 91/965, 99/941
R. *v.* Blundell (Jacqueline Louise) (Unduly Lenient Sentence) see Attorney General's
   Reference (No.4 of 1999), Re
R. *v.* Blundell (Raymond John) [1999] 2 Cr. App. R. (S.) 415, CA (Crim Div) . . . .   *Digested*, 00/**1433**
R. *v.* Boakye (Unreported, March 12, 1992) . . . .   *Considered*, 01/52
R. *v.* Boam (Gary) [1998] Crim. L.R. 205, CA (Crim Div)
R. *v.* Board of Visitors of Hull Prison Ex p. St Germain (No.2) [1979] 1 W.L.R. 1401;
   [1979] 3 All E.R. 545; [1979] Crim. L.R. 726; 123 S.J. 768, QBD . . . .   *Digested*, 79/**2196**:
            Considered, 87/3162, 98/1899: *Distinguished*, 80/10: *Followed*, 98/4076
R. *v.* Boffey (Kevin Paul) see Attorney General's Reference (No.14 of 2000), Re
R. *v.* Boid (Andrew) see R. *v.* Tantram (Peter John)
R. *v.* Boid (Clive Alan) see R. *v.* Tantram (Peter John)
R. *v.* Bolam Ex p. Haigh (1949) 93 S.J. 220, DC. . . . .   *Digested*, 47-51/**7554**:
                                           Considered, 98/79
R. *v.* Bolden (Robert Allen) see R. *v.* Dean (Jeanette)

R. v. Bolingbroke (Leslie John) [2001] 1 Cr. App. R. (S.) 80; *Times*, August 16, 2000;
Independent, October 2, 2000 (C.S), CA (Crim Div) . . . .   *Digested*, 00/**1382**:
                                                                                                  Considered, 00/1381
R. (on the application of Pepper) v. Bolsover DC; *sub nom* R. v. Bolsover DC Ex p.
Pepper (2001) 3 L.G.L.R. 20; [2001] B.L.G.R. 43; [2001] J.P.L. 804; [2000]
E.G.C.S. 107; *Times*, November 15, 2000; *Independent*, November 13, 2000
(C.S), QBD (Admin Ct) . . . .   *Digested*, 00/**4114**
R. v. Bolsover DC Ex p. Paterson [2001] J.P.L. 211; [2000] E.G.C.S. 83; (2000)
97(27) L.S.G. 40; [2000] N.P.C. 75, QBD . . . .   *Digested*, 01/**4717**
R. v. Bolsover DC Ex p. Pepper see R. (on the application of Pepper) v. Bolsover DC
R. v. Bolt (Thomas William) [1999] 2 Cr. App. R. (S.) 202, CA (Crim Div) . . . .   *Digested*, 99/**1361**
R. v. Bolton Justices Ex p. Merna; R. v. Richmond Justices Ex p. Haines (1991) 155
J.P. 612; [1991] Crim. L.R. 848; (1991) 155 J.P.N. 409; *Times*, April 26, 1991,
DC . . . .   *Digested*, 92/**946**:
                                                            Considered, 01/720: *Followed*, 95/993
R. v. Bolton Magistrates Court Ex p. Khan [1999] Crim. L.R. 912, QBD
R. v. Bolton MBC Ex p. Kirkman [1998] Env. L.R. 719; [1998] J.P.L. 787; [1998]
N.P.C. 80, CA; affirming [1998] Env. L.R. 560; (1998) 76 P. & C.R. 548; [1998]
C.O.D. 290; [1997] N.P.C. 188, QBD . . . .   *Digested*, 98/**4236**:
                                                                                                  Considered, 00/2278
R. v. Bolton Supplementary Benefits Appeal Tribunal Ex p. Fordham [1981] 1 W.L.R.
28; [1981] 1 All E.R. 50; 124 S.J. 593; *Times*, July 2 1980, CA; reversing 122 S.J.
844, QBD . . . .   *Digested*, 81/**2599**:
                                                                                                Distinguished, 99/4576
R. v. Bond (Duncan); R. v. Chapman (Mark Edward) (1994) 15 Cr. App. R. (S.) 196;
Times, June 29, 1993, CA (Crim Div) . . . .   *Digested*, 93/**999**:
                                                                                                  Considered, 98/1298
R. v. Bonehill (Mark Anthony) [1998] 2 Cr. App. R. (S.) 90, CA (Crim Div) . . . .   *Digested*, 98/**1323**
R. v. Boodhoo (Mohammed Noor) see R. v. Allan (John Paul)
R. v. Booker (Gary Andrew) (1982) 4 Cr. App. R. (S.) 53; [1982] Crim. L.R. 378, CA
(Crim Div) . . . .   *Digested*, 83/**765**:
                                                            Considered, 89/925, 90/1446, 98/1118
R. v. Bool (Christopher William); R. v. White (Jamie Anthony) [1998] 1 Cr. App. R. (S.)
32, CA (Crim Div) . . . .   *Digested*, 98/**1271**
R. v. Booth (Barry) [1998] 1 Cr. App. R. (S.) 132; [1997] Crim. L.R. 612, CA (Crim
Div) . . . .   *Digested*, 97/**1463**
R. v. Booth (Malcolm Alfred) [1997] 1 Cr. App. R. (S.) 103, CA (Crim Div) . . . .   *Digested*, 97/**1496**:
                                                                                                  Considered, 99/1276
R. v. Booth (Stephen); R. v. Molland (Noel Ray); R. v. Wood (Saxon Swayne) [1999]
1 Cr. App. R. 457; [1999] Crim. L.R. 413; (1999) 96(4) L.S.G. 37; (1999) 143
S.J.L.B. 53; *Times*, November 26, 1998, CA (Crim Div) . . . .   *Digested*, 98/**996**
R. v. Booth (Stephen) (Arson or Criminal Damage) [1999] Crim. L.R. 144, CA (Crim
Div)
R. v. Boothe (Gary) [1999] 1 Cr. App. R. (S.) 98, CA (Crim Div) . . . .   *Digested*, 99/**1273**:
                                                                                                Distinguished, 01/1315
R. v. Boreman (Victor); R. v. Byrne (Malcolm Matthew); R. v. Byrne (Michael John)
[2000] 1 All E.R. 307; [2000] 2 Cr. App. R. 17; [2000] Crim. L.R. 409, CA (Crim
Div) . . . .   *Digested*, 00/**1062**
R. v. Borg (Charles) see R. v. Farrugia (Francis)
R. v. Borthwick (Kevan) [1998] Crim. L.R. 274, CA (Crim Div)
R. v. Bosanko (Stephen) [2000] 2 Cr. App. R. (S.) 108, CA (Crim Div) . . . .   *Digested*, 00/**1366**
R. v. Boswell (James Thomas); R. v. Elliott (Jeffrey Terence); R. v. Daley (Frederick); R.
v. Rafferty (Robert Andrew) [1984] 1 W.L.R. 1047; [1984] 3 All E.R. 353;
(1984) 79 Cr. App. R. 277; (1984) 6 Cr. App. R. (S.) 257; [1984] R.T.R. 315;
[1984] Crim. L.R. 502; (1984) 81 L.S.G. 2618; (1984) 128 S.J. 566, CA (Crim
Div) . . . .   *Digested*, 85/**770**:
                    Applied, 85/704, 85/705, 86/792, 86/793, 86/795, 86/796, 89/943,
                    90/959, 90/1224, 90/1226, 91/800, 91/1033, 92/1178, 92/1182, 92/1187,
                    93/1047, 93/1053, 93/1158: *Cited*, 99/1329: *Considered*, 86/797, 87/876,
                    87/877, 88/873, 95/1343, 96/1758, 96/1762, 96/1821, 96/1822, 96/1823,
                    96/1824, 96/1826, 96/1830, 96/1831, 96/1833, 96/1834, 96/1835,
                    96/1837, 97/1660, 97/1668, 97/1669, 97/1671, 97/1673, 97/1675, 97/1676,
                    99/1234, 99/1326, 00/1195: *Disapproved*, 99/1318: *Distinguished*, 96/1836:
                    Followed, 97/1659, 97/1678: *Referred to*, 90/1251, 90/1361, 91/1031,
                    91/1036, 91/1090, 92/1176, 92/1179, 92/1180, 93/1043, 93/1048, 93/1050,
                    93/1052, 93/1320, 94/1197, 94/1198, 94/1341, 94/1401, 95/1317, 97/1661,
                                                                                                            97/1667
R. v. Bosworth (Gary) [1998] 1 Cr. App. R. (S.) 356, CA (Crim Div) . . . .   *Digested*, 98/**1211**
R. v. Botmeh (Jawad); R. v. Alami (Samar) [2001] EWCA Crim 2226; (2001) 98(46)
L.S.G. 35; (2001) 145 S.J.L.B. 255; *Times*, November 8, 2001, CA (Crim Div) . .   *Digested*, 01/**989**

R. v. Bouchereau (Pierre Roger) (C30/77) [1978] Q.B. 732; [1978] 2 W.L.R. 251;
[1981] 2 All E.R. 924; [1978] E.C.R. 1999; (1978) 66 Cr. App. R. 202; [1977] 2
C.M.L.R. 800; 122 S.J. 79, ECJ . . . .   *Digested,* 78/**629**:
Applied, 87/1938, 88/982, 89/1108, 00/3345: *Considered,* 83/1895,
93/5141, 97/2902: *Referred to,* 83/806, 89/977, 90/1405, 92/1227, 93/1108

R. v. Boulkhrif (Driss) [1999] Crim. L.R. 73, CA (Crim Div)

R. v. Boumphrey (William John) (1994) 15 Cr. App. R. (S.) 733, CA (Crim Div) . . . .   *Digested,* 95/**1395**:
Considered, 99/1180

R. v. Bournewood Community and Mental Health NHS Trust Ex p. L; *sub nom* L, Re
[1999] 1 A.C. 458; [1998] 3 W.L.R. 107; [1998] 3 All E.R. 289; [1998] 2 F.L.R.
550; [1998] 2 F.C.R. 501; (1997-98) 1 C.C.L. Rep. 390; (1998) 44 B.M.L.R. 1;
[1998] C.O.D. 312; [1998] Fam. Law 592; (1998) 95(29) L.S.G. 27; (1998) 148
N.L.J. 1014; (1998) 142 S.J.L.B. 195; *Times,* June 30, 1998; *Independent,* June
30, 1998, HL; reversing [1998] 2 W.L.R. 764; [1998] 1 All E.R. 634; (1997-98) 1
C.C.L. Rep. 201; [1998] C.O.D. 35; (1998) 95(1) L.S.G. 24; (1998) 142
S.J.L.B. 39; *Times,* December 8, 1997; *Independent,* December 5, 1997, CA;
reversing *Independent,* November 3, 1997 (C.S.), QBD . . . .   *Digested,* 98/**3896**

R. (on the application of Pelling) v. Bow County Court (No.2); *sub nom* R. v. Bow
County Court Ex p. Pelling (No.2) [2001] U.K.H.R.R. 165; [2001] A.C.D. 1; *Daily
Telegraph,* November 14, 2000, QBD (Admin Ct) . . . .   *Digested,* 01/**564**

R. v. Bow County Court Ex p. Pelling (No.1) [1999] 1 W.L.R. 1807; [1999] 4 All E.R.
751; [1999] 2 F.L.R. 1126; [1999] 3 F.C.R. 97; [1999] Fam. Law 698; (1999)
96(32) L.S.G. 33; (1999) 149 N.L.J. 1369; *Times,* August 18, 1999 ;
Independent, October 1, 1999, CA; affirming [1999] 2 All E.R. 582; [1999] 2
F.L.R. 149; [1999] 2 F.C.R. 97; [1999] C.O.D. 277; [1999] Fam. Law 384; *Times,*
March 8, 1999; *Independent,* March 11, 1999, QBD . . . .   *Digested,* 99/**46**

R. v. Bow County Court Ex p. Pelling (No.2) see R. (on the application of Pelling) v.
Bow County Court (No.2)

R. (on the application of Kashamu) v. Bow Street Magistrates Court see R. (on the
application of Kashamu) v. Governor of Brixton Prison (No.2)

R. (on the application of Makhlulif) v. Bow Street Magistrates Court see R. (on the
application of Kashamu) v. Governor of Brixton Prison (No.2)

R. v. Bow Street Magistrates Court Ex p. Allison (No.1) see R. v. Bow Street
Metropolitan Stipendiary Magistrate Ex p. United States (No.1)

R. v. Bow Street Magistrates Court Ex p. Allison (No.2) see R. v. Bow Street
Metropolitan Stipendiary Magistrate Ex p. United States (No.2)

R. v. Bow Street Magistrates Court Ex p. Germany [1998] Q.B. 556; [1998] 2 W.L.R.
498; [1998] C.O.D. 191, QBD . . . .   *Digested,* 98/**2343**

R. v. Bow Street Magistrates Court Ex p. McDonald (No.2) [1998] E.H.L.R. 216;
Times, July 11, 1997, CA . . . .   *Digested,* 97/**3417**

R. v. Bow Street Magistrates Court Ex p. Mitchell [2001] F.S.R. 18; [2000] C.O.D.
282, QBD

R. v. Bow Street Magistrates Court Ex p. Proulx see Proulx v. Governor of Brixton
Prison

R. v. Bow Street Magistrates Court Ex p. Redfearn see R. v. Leeds Crown Court Ex p.
Redfearn

R. v. Bow Street Magistrates Court Ex p. Screen Multimedia Ltd see R. v. Bow Street
Metropolitan Stipendiary Magistrate Ex p. Screen Multimedia Ltd

R. v. Bow Street Magistrates Court Ex p. Shayler [1999] 1 All E.R. 98; [1999] 1 Cr.
App. R. 355; *Times,* October 12, 1998; *Independent,* October 12, 1998 (C.S.),
QBD . . . .   *Digested,* 98/**3707**

R. v. Bow Street Metropolitan Stipendiary Magistrate Ex p. Pinochet Ugarte (No.1);
sub nom R. v. Evans Ex p. Pinochet Ugarte (No.1); Pinochet Ugarte (No.1), Re; R.
v. Bartle Ex p. Pinochet Ugarte (No.1) [2000] 1 A.C. 61; [1998] 3 W.L.R. 1456;
[1998] 4 All E.R. 897; 5 B.H.R.C. 209; (1998) 94(48) L.S.G. 31; (1998) 148
N.L.J. 1808; *Times,* November 26, 1998; *Independent,* December 1, 1998, HL;
reversing *Times,* November 3, 1998; *Independent,* October 30, 1998, QBD . . . . .   *Digested,* 98/**2354**

R. v. Bow Street Metropolitan Stipendiary Magistrate Ex p. Pinochet Ugarte (No.2);
sub nom Pinochet Ugarte (No.2), Re; R. v. Evans Ex p. Pinochet Ugarte (No.2);
R. v. Bartle Ex p. Pinochet Ugarte (No.2) [2000] 1 A.C. 119; [1999] 2 W.L.R.
272; [1999] 1 All E.R. 577; 6 B.H.R.C. 1; (1999) 11 Admin. L.R. 57; (1999) 96(6)
L.S.G. 33; (1999) 149 N.L.J. 88; *Times,* January 18, 1999; *Independent,*
January 19, 1999, HL . . . .   *Digested,* 99/**39**:
Applied, 99/38: *Considered,* 00/4140, 00/6092, 01/6705

R. v. Bow Street Metropolitan Stipendiary Magistrate Ex p. Pinochet Ugarte (No.3)
[2000] 1 A.C. 147; [1999] 2 W.L.R. 827; [1999] 2 All E.R. 97; 6 B.H.R.C. 24;
(1999) 96(17) L.S.G. 24; (1999) 149 N.L.J. 497; *Times,* March 25, 1999, HL . . .   *Digested,* 99/**2292**

R. v. Bow Street Metropolitan Stipendiary Magistrate Ex p. Screen Multimedia Ltd;
sub nom R. v. Bow Street Magistrates Court Ex p. Screen Multimedia Ltd; R. v.
Southwark Crown Court Ex p. Screen Multimedia Ltd (1998) 21(5) I.P.D.
21046; *Times,* January 28, 1998; *Independent,* February 16, 1998 (C.S.), QBD . .   *Digested,* 98/**3429**

R. v. Bow Street Metropolitan Stipendiary Magistrate Ex p. United States (No.1); *sub nom* R. v. United States Ex p. Allison; R. v. Bow Street Magistrates Court Ex p. Allison (No.1) [1997] C.O.D. 366; *Times*, June 5, 1997; *Independent*, June 9, 1997 (C.S.), QBD. . . . . *Digested*, 97/**2444**

R. v. Bow Street Metropolitan Stipendiary Magistrate Ex p. United States (No.2); *sub nom* R. v. Bow Street Magistrates Court Ex p. Allison (No.2); Allison, Re; R. v. Governor of Brixton Prison Ex p. Allison [2000] 2 A.C. 216; [1999] 3 W.L.R. 620; [1999] 4 All E.R. 1; [2000] 1 Cr. App. R. 61; [1999] I.T.C.L.R. 426; [1999] Masons C.L.R. 380; [1999] Crim. L.R. 970; (1999) 149 N.L.J. 1406; *Times*, September 7, 1999, HL; reversing in part [1999] Q.B. 847; [1998] 3 W.L.R. 1156; [1998] I.T.C.L.R. 133; [1998] Masons C.L.R. 234; *Times*, June 2, 1998; *Independent*, May 15, 1998, QBD . . . . *Digested*, 99/**2288**

R. v. Bowden (Brian Thomas) [1999] 1 W.L.R. 823; [1999] 4 All E.R. 43; [1999] 2 Cr. App. R. 176; (1999) 163 J.P. 337; (1999) 163 J.P.N. 387; (1999) 96(10) L.S.G. 28; (1999) 143 S.J.L.B. 73; *Times*, February 25, 1999, CA (Crim Div) . . . . *Digested*, 99/**896**

R. v. Bowden (Catherine) [1998] 2 Cr. App. R. (S.) 7, CA (Crim Div) . . . . *Digested*, 98/**1393**

R. v. Bowden (David Charles) (1986) 8 Cr. App. R. (S.) 155; [1986] Crim. L.R. 699, CA (Crim Div) . . . . *Digested*, 87/**1067**:
　　　　　　　　　　　　　　　Considered, 96/2024, 97/1718, 97/1719, 99/1365

R. v. Bowden (Jonathan) [2001] Q.B. 88; [2000] 2 W.L.R. 1083; [2000] 2 All E.R. 418; [2000] 1 Cr. App. R. 438; [2000] 2 Cr. App. R. (S.) 26; [2000] Crim. L.R. 381; (1999) 96(47) L.S.G. 29; (2000) 144 S.J.L.B. 5; *Times*, November 19, 1999 ; *Independent*, November 26, 1999, CA (Crim Div) . . . . *Digested*, 99/**947**:
　　　　　　　　　　　　Applied, 00/993, 01/1450: *Followed*, 00/6039

R. v. Bowen (Warren Anthony) [2001] 1 Cr. App. R. (S.) 82, CA (Crim Div) . . . . *Digested*, 01/**1430**

R. v. Bowers (Victor John); R. v. Taylor (David Patrick); R. v. Millan (John David) (1999) 163 J.P. 33; [1998] Crim. L.R. 817; (1998) 162 J.P.N. 1006; *Independent*, March 24, 1998, CA (Crim Div) . . . . *Digested*, 98/**1057**

R. v. Bowler (Kevin) (1994) 15 Cr. App. R. (S.) 78; [1993] Crim. L.R. 799, CA (Crim Div) . . . . *Cited*, 95/1419:
　　　　　　　　Considered, 94/1276, 94/1377, 96/1698, 96/1795, 99/1206, 00/1304:
　　　　　　　　　　　　　　　　　　　Referred to, 94/1299, 95/1417

R. v. Boyd (David Morton) see R. v. Spear (John)

R. v. Bozat (Hikmet); R. v. Ozen (Zervet); R. v. Kovaycin (Cafer) [1997] 1 Cr. App. R. (S.) 270; (1997) 9 Admin. L.R. 125; [1996] Crim. L.R. 840; (1996) 93(37) L.S.G. 26; (1996) 140 S.J.L.B. 201; *Times*, August 15, 1996, CA (Crim Div) . . . . *Digested*, 96/**1844**:
　　　　　　　　　　　　　　　　　　　Applied, 99/1244

R. (on the application of McLellan) v. Bracknell Forest BC; *sub nom* Forrest v. Reigate and Banstead BC; McLellan v. Bracknell Forest BC; R. (on the application of Johns) v. Bracknell Forest DC; Reigate and Banstead BC v. Benfield [2001] EWCA Civ 1510; (2001) 33 H.L.R. 86; (2001) 98(46) L.S.G. 35; (2001) 145 S.J.L.B. 258; [2001] N.P.C. 149; *Times*, December 3, 2001; *Independent*, October 24, 2001, CA; affirming (2001) 33 H.L.R. 45; (2001) 3 L.G.L.R. 22; *Daily Telegraph*, February 13, 2001, QBD (Admin Ct) . . . . *Digested*, 01/**4170**:
　　　　　　　　　　　　　　　　　　　Applied, 01/4171

R. (on the application of Johns) v. Bracknell Forest DC see R. (on the application of McLellan) v. Bracknell Forest BC

R. v. Bradbourn (Kathryn Ann) (1985) 7 Cr. App. R. (S.) 180; [1985] Crim. L.R. 682, CA (Crim Div) . . . . *Digested*, 86/**897**:
　　　　　　Applied, 93/1103: *Cited*, 88/1019, 94/1411: *Considered*, 98/1168:
　　　　　　　　　　　　　　　　　　　Referred to, 87/1050

R. v. Bradbury (Alan Henry); R. v. Edlin (Charles Ernest) [1921] 1 K.B. 562, CCA; affirming [1956] 2 Q.B. 262 (Note), Assizes (Winchester) . . . . *Approved*, 56/**1885**:
　　　　　　　　　　　　　　　　　　　Considered, 00/1098

R. v. Bradford City Council Ex p. Ali (Sikander) (1994) 6 Admin. L.R. 589; (1995) 159 L.G. Rev. 81; (1993) 90(40) L.S.G. 42; (1993) 137 S.J.L.B. 232; *Times*, October 21, 1993; *Independent*, November 22, 1993 (C.S.); *Guardian*, September 13, 1993, QBD . . . . *Digested*, 95/**1910**:
　　　　　　　　　　　　　　　　　　　Considered, 00/1913

R. v. Bradford Crown Court Ex p. Crossling; R. v. Teesside Crown Court Ex p. Crown Prosecution Service [2000] 1 Cr. App. R. 463; (1999) 163 J.P. 821; [2000] Crim. L.R. 171; [2000] C.O.D. 107; *Times*, September 21, 1999 ; *Independent*, October 25, 1999 (C.S.), QBD . . . . *Digested*, 99/**1015**

R. v. Bradford Justices Ex p. Sykes; *sub nom* R. v. Clerk to Bradford Justices Ex p. Sykes (1999) 163 J.P. 224; [1999] Crim. L.R. 748; (1999) 163 J.P.N. 212; (1999) 96(6) L.S.G. 34; *Times*, January 28, 1999; *Independent*, February 1, 1999 (C.S.), QBD . . . . *Digested*, 99/**1056**

R. v. Bradford Magistrates Court Ex p. Grant (1999) 163 J.P. 717; [1999] Crim. L.R. 324; (1999) 163 J.P.N. 570, QBD . . . . *Digested*, 00/**1082**

R. v. Bradford MBC Ex p. Pickering (2001) 33 H.L.R. 38, QBD . . . . *Digested*, 01/**3418**

R. v. Bradley (Andrew) [1997] 1 Cr. App. R. (S.) 59, CA (Crim Div). . . . . *Digested*, 97/**1506**:
　　　　　　　　　　　　　　　　　　　Considered, 01/1278

R. v. Bradley (John William) (1980) 2 Cr. App. R. (S.) 12, CA (Crim Div) . . . . *Digested*, 81/**525.8**:
　　　　　　　　　　　　　　　　　　　Applied, 99/5220

R. *v.* Bradley (Paul Richard) [1998] 1 Cr. App. R. (S.) 432, CA (Crim Div) . . . .   *Digested*, 98/**1125**:
         Considered, 00/1145

R. *v.* Bradshaw (Neil) [1997] 2 Cr. App. R. (S.) 128; [1997] Crim. L.R. 239, CA (Crim
   Div) . . . .   *Digested*, 97/**1493**:
         Disapproved, 97/1492: *Not applied*, 98/1387

R. *v.* Bradshaw (Wayne Martin); R. *v.* Waters (Paul Anthony) [2001] R.T.R. 4; *Times*,
   December 31, 1994, CA (Crim Div) . . . .   *Digested*, 95/**1304**:
         Followed, 00/1126

R. *v.* Brady (Derek) [2000] 1 Cr. App. R. (S.) 410, CA (Crim Div) . . . .   *Digested*, 00/**1149**

R. *v.* Braintree DC Ex p. Freeport Leisure Ltd [1999] P.L.C.R. 218, QBD . . . .   *Digested*, 99/**4260**

R. *v.* Braintree DC Ex p. Halls (2000) 32 H.L.R. 770; (2001) 3 L.G.L.R. 10; (2000) 80
   P. & C.R. 266; [2000] 3 E.G.L.R. 19; [2000] 36 E.G. 164; [2000] E.G.C.S. 32;
   Times, March 15, 2000; *Independent*, April 14, 2000, CA; reversing (2000) 80 P.
   & C.R. 145; [1999] E.G.C.S. 96; *Times*, July 21, 1999, QBD . . . .   *Digested*, 00/**3943**

R. *v.* Braithwaite see R. *v.* Silcott (Winston)

R. *v.* Bramble (Keith) see R. *v.* Gabbidon (Anthony Bernard)

R. *v.* Bramich (David) see R. *v.* Graham (Hemamali Krishna)

R. *v.* Bramich (David Jason) see R. *v.* Hewitson (James Robert)

R. *v.* Branch (David) see Attorney General's Reference (No.79 of 1999), Re

R. *v.* Brandy (Paul) [1997] 1 Cr. App. R. (S.) 38, CA (Crim Div) . . . .   *Digested*, 97/**1642**:
         Considered, 98/1344

R. *v.* Brandy (Terence) see R. *v.* Edwards (Anthony Paul)

R. *v.* Brannan (Glen Marvin) (1995) 16 Cr. App. R. (S.) 766, CA (Crim Div) . . . .   *Digested*, 96/**2019**:
         Considered, 97/1609, 99/1263

R. *v.* Breaks (Peter); R. *v.* Huggan (John Charles) [1998] Crim. L.R. 349, CA (Crim
   Div)

R. *v.* Breckland DC Ex p. Budgens Stores Ltd [1999] J.P.L. 85; (1998) 95(16) L.S.G.
   27, QBD . . . .   *Digested*, 99/**4251**

R. *v.* Breddick (Christopher); *sub nom* R. *v.* Briddick (Christopher) [2001] EWCA Crim
   984; *Independent*, May 21, 2001 (C.S), CA (Crim Div)

R. *v.* Brent LBC Ex p. AF see F (A Minor) *v.* Brent LBC

R. *v.* Brent LBC Ex p. Awua; *sub nom* Awua *v.* Brent LBC [1996] A.C. 55; [1995] 3
   W.L.R. 215; [1995] 3 All E.R. 493; [1995] 2 F.L.R. 819; [1995] 3 F.C.R. 278;
   (1995) 27 H.L.R. 453; [1996] Fam. Law 20; (1996) 160 L.G. Rev. 21; (1995)
   145 N.L.J. 1031; (1995) 139 S.J.L.B. 189; [1995] N.P.C. 119; *Times*, July 7, 1995;
   Independent, July 25, 1995, HL; affirming [1994] C.O.D. 490; (1995) 159 L.G.
   Rev. 1; *Times*, April 26, 1994; *Independent*, March 31, 1994, CA; reversing [1994]
   3 F.C.R. 53; (1993) 25 H.L.R. 626; [1994] C.O.D. 131; *Times*, July 1, 1993, QBD .   *Digested*, 95/**2569**:
     Applied, 97/2675, 98/3000: *Approved*, 97/2666: *Considered*, 96/3059,
     97/2654, 97/2661, 98/3004, 98/3026: *Followed*, 97/2653, 98/3011:
     Not followed, 98/2997

R. *v.* Brent LBC Ex p. Bariise (1999) 31 H.L.R. 50, CA; reversing (1998) 30 H.L.R.
   518, QBD . . . .   *Digested*, 98/**3010**

R. *v.* Brent LBC Ex p. Baruwa [1997] 3 F.C.R. 97; (1997) 29 H.L.R. 915; [1997] C.O.D.
   450; *Independent*, February 27, 1997, CA; reversing (1996) 28 H.L.R. 361,
   QBD . . . .   *Digested*, 97/**2662**:
         Followed, 98/3010

R. *v.* Brent LBC Ex p. D (1999) 31 H.L.R. 10; (1997-98) 1 C.C.L. Rep. 234, QBD . . . . . .   *Digested*, 98/**3007**:
         Considered, 99/3023: *Overruled*, 00/4895

R. *v.* Brent LBC Ex p. F [1999] E.L.R. 32; [1999] C.O.D. 38, QBD . . . .   *Digested*, 99/**1887**

R. *v.* Brent LBC Ex p. Morris (1998) 30 H.L.R. 324; (1997) 74 P. & C.R. D29, CA;
   affirming (1996) 28 H.L.R. 852; [1996] E.G.C.S. 20, QBD . . . .   *Digested*, 98/**3060**

R. *v.* Brent LBC Ex p. O'Connor; *sub nom* R. *v.* Brent LBC Ex p. O'Conner (1999) 31
   H.L.R. 923, QBD . . . .   *Digested*, 00/**3133**

R. *v.* Brent LBC Ex p. O'Malley; R. *v.* Secretary of State for the Environment Ex p.
   Walters (1998) 30 H.L.R. 328; (1998) 10 Admin. L.R. 265; [1998] C.O.D. 121;
   Times, September 2, 1997, CA . . . .   *Digested*, 97/**2700**:
         Applied, 98/3000: *Considered*, 98/3025

R. *v.* Brent LBC Ex p. Sadiq; *sub nom* Brent LBC *v.* Sadiq (2001) 33 H.L.R. 47; (2000)
   97(29) L.S.G. 45; *Times*, July 27, 2000, QBD . . . .   *Digested*, 00/**3148**

R. (on the application of Kadhim) *v.* Brent LBC Housing Benefit Review Board; *sub nom*
   Kadhim *v.* Brent LBC Housing Benefit Board; R. *v.* Brent LBC Housing Benefit
   Review Board Ex p. Khadim; R. (on the application of Khadim) *v.* Brent LBC
   Housing Benefit Review Board [2001] Q.B. 955; [2001] 2 W.L.R. 1674; (2001)
   33 H.L.R. 79; [2001] A.C.D. 35; (2001) 98(14) L.S.G. 40; [2001] N.P.C. 7;
   Times, March 27, 2001, CA; reversing [2000] C.O.D. 472, QBD . . . .   *Digested*, 01/**5021**

R. *v.* Brent Youth Court Ex p. A (A Juvenile) see R. *v.* Norwich Magistrates Court Ex p.
   Elliott

R. *v.* Brentford Justices Ex p. Wong [1981] Q.B. 445; [1981] 2 W.L.R. 203; [1981] 1
   All E.R. 884; (1981) 73 Cr. App. R. 67; [1981] R.T.R. 206; [1981] Crim. L.R. 336,
   QBD . . . .   *Digested*, 81/**1694**:
     Applied, 90/767: *Considered*, 82/1979, 85/1525, 85/2126, 86/1521:
     Distinguished, 82/2462, 99/5215

R. v. Brentwood BC Ex p. Peck [1998] E.M.L.R. 697, CA; affirming *Times*, December 18, 1997, QBD . . . .   *Digested*, 98/**3774**

R. v. Brentwood Justices Ex p. Nicholls [1992] 1 A.C. 1; [1991] 3 W.L.R. 201; [1991] 3 All E.R. 359; (1991) 93 Cr. App. R. 400; (1991) 155 J.P. 753; [1992] Crim. L.R. 52; (1991) 155 J.P.N. 572; (1991) 141 N.L.J. 964; (1991) 135 S.J. 70; *Times*, July 5, 1991; *Independent*, July 5, 1991; *Guardian*, July 5, 1991, HL; reversing [1990] 2 Q.B. 598; [1990] 3 W.L.R. 534; [1990] 3 All E.R. 516; (1990) 154 J.P. 487; [1990] Crim. L.R. 736; [1990] C.O.D. 452; (1990) 154 J.P.N. 442, QBD . .   *Digested*, 92/**942**:
                             Applied, 94/997: *Considered*, 94/750: *Followed*, 00/1082

R. v. Brereton (Scott Galvin) see R. v. Blight (Tony)

R. v. Bretscher (Gordon Maxwell) see R. v. Townsend (Philip Henry)

R. v. Brewster (Alex Edward); R. v. Thorpe (Terence George); R. v. Ishmael (Mark); R. v. Blanchard (Wayne); R. v. Woodhouse (Michael Charles); R. v. RH (A Juvenile) [1998] 1 Cr. App. R. 220; [1998] 1 Cr. App. R. (S.) 181; [1997] Crim. L.R. 690; (1997) 94(27) L.S.G. 22; (1997) 141 S.J.L.B. 161; *Times*, July 4, 1997, CA (Crim Div) . . . .   *Digested*, 97/**1423**:
               Considered, 98/1137, 98/1138, 98/1274, 98/1275, 98/1375, 99/1091, 99/1093, 00/1150, 00/1151

R. v. Brewster (David Edward) (1980) 71 Cr. App. R. 375; (1980) 2 Cr. App. R. (S.) 191; [1980] Crim. L.R. 736, CA (Crim Div) . . . .   *Digested*, 81/**525.18**:
                               Considered, 98/1137, 00/1151

R. v. Briddick (Christopher) see R. v. Breddick (Christopher)

R. v. Bridgend CBC Ex p. Jones (t/a Shamrock Coaches); *sub nom* Bridgend CBC v. Jones (t/a Shamrock Coaches) (2000) 2 L.G.L.R. 361; *Independent*, November 15, 1999 (C.S.), QBD

R. v. Bridgnorth DC Ex p. Prime Time Promotions Ltd [1999] C.O.D. 265; [1999] E.H.L.R. Dig. 455, QBD

R. v. Brierley (Anthony Michael) [2000] 2 Cr. App. R. (S.) 278, CA (Crim Div) . . . .   *Digested*, 00/**1144**

R. v. Brighton and Hove BC Ex p. Marmont (1998) 30 H.L.R. 1046; [1998] 2 P.L.R. 48; [1998] J.P.L. 670; *Times*, January 15, 1998, QBD . . . .   *Digested*, 98/**4366**

R. v. Brighton and Hove BC Ex p. Nacion (1999) 31 H.L.R. 1095; (1999) 11 Admin. L.R. 472; (1999) 163 J.P.N. 513; (1999) 96(11) L.S.G. 69; *Times*, February 3, 1999; *Independent*, February 4, 1999, CA. . . . .   *Digested*, 99/**3043**:
                               Considered, 00/3149

R. v. Brighton BC Ex p. Harvey (1998) 30 H.L.R. 670, QBD . . . .   *Digested*, 98/**3011**

R. v. Brignull (Sean) see Attorney General's Reference (Nos.36, 37, 38 and 39 of 1999), Re

R. v. Brindle (Lee Anthony) see R. v. Redfern (Andrew James)

R. v. Brindley (Trevor Charles) [1997] 2 Cr. App. R. (S.) 353, CA (Crim Div) . . . .   *Digested*, 98/**1229**

R. v. Bristol (Keith Anthony) see R. v. MacDonald (Brian Anthony)

R. v. Bristol (Kenturah Ann) [1998] 1 Cr. App. R. (S.) 47, CA (Crim Div) . . . .   *Digested*, 98/**1184**

R. v. Bristol Betting and Gaming Licensing Committee Ex p. O'Callaghan see Locabail (UK) Ltd v. Bayfield Properties Ltd (Leave to Appeal)

R. v. Bristol City Council Ex p. Anderson (2000) 79 P. & C.R. 358; [2000] P.L.C.R. 104; [1999] C.O.D. 532; (1999) 96(25) L.S.G. 30; *Times*, July 5, 1999, CA; reversing [1998] P.L.C.R. 314; [1998] E.G.C.S. 44, QBD. . . . .   *Digested*, 99/**4243**

R. v. Bristol City Council Ex p. DL Barrett & Sons (2001) 3 L.G.L.R. 11, QBD . . . .   *Digested*, 01/**4405**

R. v. Bristol City Council Ex p. Everett [1999] 1 W.L.R. 1170; [1999] 2 All E.R. 193; [1999] Env. L.R. 587; [1999] E.H.L.R. 265; (1999) 31 H.L.R. 1102; [1999] B.L.G.R. 513; [1999] 3 P.L.R. 14; [1999] E.G.C.S. 33; (1999) 96(13) L.S.G. 31; (1999) 96(10) L.S.G. 32; (1999) 149 N.L.J. 370; (1999) 143 S.J.L.B. 104; [1999] N.P.C. 28; *Times*, March 9, 1999, CA; affirming [1999] 1 W.L.R. 92; [1998] 3 All E.R. 603; [1999] Env. L.R. 256; [1999] E.H.L.R. 59; (1999) 31 H.L.R. 292; (1999) 77 P. & C.R. 216; [1998] 3 E.G.L.R. 25; [1998] 42 E.G. 166; (1998) 95(23) L.S.G. 26; (1998) 148 N.L.J. 836; (1998) 142 S.J.L.B. 173; [1998] N.P.C. 86; *Times*, May 27, 1998, QBD . . . .   *Digested*, 99/**4074**

R. v. Bristol City Council Ex p. Jacobs (2000) 32 H.L.R. 841; [2001] R.V.R. 109; *Times*, November 16, 1999, QBD. . . . .   *Digested*, 99/**4557**

R. v. Bristol City Council Ex p. Penfold (1997-98) 1 C.C.L. Rep. 315; [1998] C.O.D. 210, QBD . . . .   *Digested*, 98/**4573**

R. v. Bristol Magistrates Court Ex p. Davies see R. v. Birmingham Crown Court Ex p. Ali (Rashid)

R. v. Bristol Magistrates Court Ex p. E [1999] 1 W.L.R. 390; [1998] 3 All E.R. 798; [1999] 1 Cr. App. R. 144; (1999) 163 J.P. 56; [1999] Crim. L.R. 161; [1999] C.O.D. 16; (1998) 162 J.P.N. 806; *Independent*, June 29, 1998 (C.S.), QBD . . . .   *Digested*, 98/**925**

R. v. Bristow (Robert Stephen) (1991) 12 Cr. App. R. (S.) 632, CA (Crim Div) . . . .   *Digested*, 92/**1480**:
                               Considered, 98/927

R. v. British Coal Corp Ex p. Ibstock Building Products Ltd [1995] Env. L.R. 277; [1994] N.P.C. 133, QBD. . . . .   *Digested*, 95/**132**:
                               Applied, 99/2167

R. (on the application of Oxford Study Centre Ltd) v. British Council [2001] EWHC Admin 207; [2001] E.L.R. 803, QBD (Admin Ct)

R. v. British Standards Institution Ex p. Dorgard Ltd [2001] A.C.D. 15, QBD

R. *v.* British Steel Plc [1995] 1 W.L.R. 1356; [1995] I.C.R. 586; [1995] I.R.L.R. 310; [1995] Crim. L.R. 654; *Times,* December 31, 1994, CA (Crim Div) . . . .   *Digested,* 96/**3020**:
                                                                                                                                                               Cited, 00/980
R. *v.* Brizzi (Raphello) [2000] 1 Cr. App. R. (S.) 126, CA (Crim Div) . . . .   *Digested,* 00/**1254**
R. *v.* Broad DC Ex p. Lashley see R. (on the application of Lashley) *v.* Broadland DC
R. *v.* Broadbridge (Stephen) (1983) 5 Cr. App. R. (S.) 269, CA (Crim Div) . . . .   *Digested,* 84/**811**:
                                                                                                                                                               Considered, 98/1172
R. *v.* Broadcasting Standards Commission Ex p. BBC [2001] Q.B. 885; [2000] 3 W.L.R. 1327; [2000] 3 All E.R. 989; [2001] B.C.C. 432; [2001] 1 B.C.L.C. 244; [2000] E.M.L.R. 587; [2000] H.R.L.R. 374; [2000] U.K.H.R.R. 624; [2000] C.O.D. 322; (2000) 97(17) L.S.G. 32; (2000) 144 S.J.L.B. 204; *Times,* April 12, 2000; *Independent,* April 12, 2000, CA; reversing [1999] E.M.L.R. 858; [2000] H.R.L.R. 15; [2000] U.K.H.R.R. 158; [1999] C.O.D. 472; *Times,* September 14, 1999, QBD . . . .   *Digested,* 00/**4163**
R. (on the application of Lashley) *v.* Broadland DC; *sub nom* R. *v.* Broad DC Ex p. Lashley; R. *v.* Broadland DC Ex p. Lashley [2001] EWCA Civ 179; (2001) 3 L.G.L.R. 25; [2001] B.L.G.R. 264; *Times,* March 20, 2001; *Independent,* March 19, 2001 (C.S), CA; affirming (2000) 2 L.G.L.R. 933, QBD . . . .   *Digested,* 01/**4333**
R. *v.* Broadland DC Ex p. Dove [1998] P.L.C.R. 119; [1998] N.P.C. 7; *Independent,* March 2, 1998 (C.S.), QBD . . . .   *Digested,* 98/**4168**
R. *v.* Broadland DC Ex p. Lashley see R. (on the application of Lashley) *v.* Broadland DC
R. *v.* Broadley (Wayne) see R. *v.* Ward (Michael)
R. (on the application of Wilkinson) *v.* Broadmoor Hospital; *sub nom* R. (on the application of Wilkinson) *v.* Broadmoor Special Hospital Authority; R. (on the application of Wilkinson) *v.* Responsible Medical Officer Broadmoor Hospital [2001] EWCA Civ 1545; (2001) 98(44) L.S.G. 36; (2001) 145 S.J.L.B. 247; *Times,* November 2, 2001; *Independent,* December 10, 2001 (C.S); *Daily Telegraph,* October 30, 2001, CA . . . .   *Digested,* 01/**4431**
R. *v.* Broadmoor Special Hospital Authority Ex p. S [1998] C.O.D. 199; (1998) 95(8) L.S.G. 32; (1998) 142 S.J.L.B. 76; *Times,* February 17, 1998, CA; affirming *Times,* November 5, 1997, QBD . . . .   *Digested,* 98/**3899**
R. *v.* Brock (John Terrence); R. *v.* Wyner (Ruth Avril) [2001] 1 W.L.R. 1159; [2001] 2 Cr. App. R. 3; [2001] 2 Cr. App. R. (S.) 48; (2001) 165 J.P. 331; [2001] Crim. L.R. 320; (2001) 165 J.P.N. 225; (2001) 98(8) L.S.G. 43; (2001) 145 S.J.L.B. 44; *Times,* December 28, 2000, CA (Crim Div) . . . .   *Digested,* 01/**1159**
R. *v.* Brocklesby (David); R. *v.* Brocklesby (Peter) [1999] 1 Cr. App. R. (S.) 80, CA (Crim Div) . . . .   *Digested,* 99/**1147**
R. *v.* Brocklesby (Peter) see R. *v.* Brocklesby (David)
R. *v.* Brodie (Caine); R. *v.* Young (Michelle); R. *v.* Mould (Darren) [2000] Crim. L.R. 775, CA (Crim Div)
R. (on the application of Barker) *v.* Bromley LBC; *sub nom* R. *v.* Bromley LBC Ex p. Barker; R. *v.* Bromley LBC Ex p. Baker [2001] EWCA Civ 1766; [2001] 49 E.G.C.S. 117; [2001] N.P.C. 170; *Independent,* December 5, 2001, CA; affirming [2001] Env. L.R. 1; [2000] P.L.C.R. 399; [2000] J.P.L. 1302 (Note); [2000] E.G.C.S. 51, QBD . . . .   *Digested,* 01/**4701**
R. *v.* Bromley LBC Ex p. Baker see R. (on the application of Barker) *v.* Bromley LBC
R. *v.* Bromley LBC Ex p. Barker see R. (on the application of Barker) *v.* Bromley LBC
R. *v.* Bromsgrove DC Ex p. Kings see R. *v.* Bromsgrove DC Ex p. Norton
R. *v.* Bromsgrove DC Ex p. Norton; R. *v.* Bromsgrove DC Ex p. Kings [1998] J.P.L. 664, QBD . . . .   *Digested,* 98/**4162**
R. *v.* Brookes [1995] Crim. L.R. 630, CA (Crim Div) . . . .   *Followed,* 97/1259:
                                                                                                                                                               Overruled, 01/1061
R. *v.* Brookes (Barry) see Attorney General's Reference (No.73 of 2000), Re
R. *v.* Broom (Andrew William) (1993) 14 Cr. App. R. (S.) 677, CA (Crim Div) . . . .   *Digested,* 94/**1246**:
                                                                                                                                                               Considered, 98/1203
R. *v.* Brophy (Michael Andrew) (1995) 16 Cr. App. R. (S.) 652, CA (Crim Div) . . . .   *Digested,* 96/**2010**:
                                                                                                                                                               Considered, 99/1230
R. *v.* Broughton (Dennis) see R. *v.* O'Callaghan (Daniel Francis)
R. *v.* Brown [1991] Crim. L.R. 368, CA (Crim Div) . . . .   *Digested,* 91/**652**:
                                                                                                                                                               Followed, 99/893
R. *v.* Brown (Alva Lorenzo) [2000] 1 Cr. App. R. (S.) 300; [1999] Crim. L.R. 850, CA (Crim Div) . . . .   *Digested,* 00/**1210**
R. *v.* Brown (Anthony Azuris) [1999] 1 Cr. App. R. (S.) 47, CA (Crim Div) . . . .   *Digested,* 99/**1108**:
                                                                                                                                                               Referred to, 00/1148

R. *v.* Brown (Anthony Joseph); R. *v.* Laskey (Colin); R. *v.* Jaggard (Roland Leonard); R. *v.* Lucas (Saxon); R. *v.* Carter (Christopher Robert); R. *v.* Cadman (Graham William) [1994] 1 A.C. 212; [1993] 2 W.L.R. 556; [1993] 2 All E.R. 75; (1993) 97 Cr. App. R. 44; (1993) 157 J.P. 337; (1993) 157 J.P.N. 233; (1993) 143 N.L.J. 399; *Times,* March 12, 1993; *Independent,* March 12, 1993, HL; affirming [1992] Q.B. 491; [1992] 2 W.L.R. 441; [1992] 2 All E.R. 552; (1992) 94 Cr. App. R. 302; (1992) 156 J.P.N. 396; (1992) 142 N.L.J. 275; (1992) 136 S.J.L.B. 90; *Times,* February 21, 1992; *Independent,* February 20, 1992; *Guardian,* March 4, 1992, CA (Crim Div) . . . .   *Digested,* 93/**920**:
             Applied, 00/28: *Considered,* 91/1239, 92/1485, 99/961:
                                   Distinguished, 96/1436

R. *v.* Brown (Damien); R. *v.* Stratton (Simon) [1998] Crim. L.R. 485; [1998] Crim. L.R. 505, CA (Crim Div)

R. *v.* Brown (Davina) [2001] EWCA Crim 961; [2001] Crim. L.R. 675; *Times,* May 1, 2001, CA (Crim Div) . . . .   *Digested,* 01/**52**

R. *v.* Brown (Gary) see R. *v.* Richardson (Robin)

R. *v.* Brown (Gregory Michael) [1996] A.C. 543; [1996] 2 W.L.R. 203; [1996] 1 All E.R. 545; [1996] 2 Cr. App. R. 72; [1997] E.C.C. 105; [1998] Masons C.L.R. Rep. 108; [1996] Crim. L.R. 408; (1996) 93(10) L.S.G. 21; (1996) 146 N.L.J. 209; (1996) 140 S.J.L.B. 66; *Times,* February 9, 1996; *Independent,* February 13, 1996, HL; affirming [1994] Q.B. 547; [1994] 2 W.L.R. 673; (1994) 99 Cr. App. R. 69; (1993) 137 S.J.L.B. 151; *Times,* June 14, 1993, CA (Crim Div) . . . .   *Digested,* 96/**3423**

R. *v.* Brown (Jamie) [1998] Crim. L.R. 196; *Times,* December 13, 1997, CA (Crim Div) . .   *Digested,* 98/**1044**:
                                     Considered, 01/52

R. *v.* Brown (Kevin) (1984) 79 Cr. App. R. 115; [1984] Crim. L.R. 167, CA (Crim Div) . . .   *Digested,* 84/**624**:
     Applied, 95/1091, 97/1179, 01/1149: *Considered,* 86/667, 87/725, 87/777,
             87/864, 88/659, 88/786, 88/864, 92/785, 93/777, 93/778, 94/814,
             94/830, 94/1040, 94/1137, 95/1063, 96/1633, 96/1674, 97/1187:
                               Distinguished, 86/606, 99/1059

R. *v.* Brown (Mark Anthony) [1998] 2 Cr. App. R. (S.) 257, CA (Crim Div) . . . .   *Digested,* 98/**1380**

R. *v.* Brown (Milton) [1998] 2 Cr. App. R. 364; *Times,* May 7, 1998; *Independent,* May 8, 1998, CA (Crim Div) . . . .   *Digested,* 98/**887**

R. *v.* Brown (Nicholas Alexander) [1997] 1 Cr. App. R. (S.) 112, CA (Crim Div) . . . .   *Digested,* 97/**1579**:
                                     Considered, 00/1275

R. *v.* Brown (Raymond John); R. *v.* King (Martin John); R. *v.* Mahoney (Mark) [1999] 2 Cr. App. R. (S.) 284; *Times,* March 5, 1999; *Independent,* March 15, 1999 (C.S.); *Independent,* March 8, 1999 (C.S.), CA (Crim Div) . . . .   *Digested,* 99/**1285**

R. *v.* Brown (Sebert) [2000] 2 Cr. App. R. (S.) 435; [2000] Crim. L.R. 496, CA (Crim Div) . . . .   *Digested,* 01/**1289**

R. *v.* Brown (Winston) [1998] A.C. 367; [1997] 3 W.L.R. 447; [1997] 3 All E.R. 769; [1998] 1 Cr. App. R. 66; (1997) 161 J.P. 625; [1998] Crim. L.R. 60; (1997) 161 J.P.N. 838; (1997) 94(33) L.S.G. 28; (1997) 147 N.L.J. 1149; (1997) 141 S.J.L.B. 198; *Times,* July 25, 1997; *Independent,* October 15, 1997, HL; affirming [1994] 1 W.L.R. 1599; [1995] 1 Cr. App. R. 191; (1994) 91(31) L.S.G. 36; (1994) 138 S.J.L.B. 146; *Times,* June 20, 1994; *Independent,* June 22, 1994, CA (Crim Div) . . . .   *Digested,* 97/**1138**

R. *v.* Browne (Nicole Natalie) (1998) 10 Admin. L.R. 418; (1998) 162 J.P.N. 544; *Times,* August 23, 1997, CA (Crim Div) . . . .   *Digested,* 97/**1323**

R. *v.* Browne (Sandra) see R. *v.* Zafar (Mohammed)

R. *v.* Brownsword (Graham James) (1986) 8 Cr. App. R. (S.) 139; [1986] Crim. L.R. 638, CA (Crim Div) . . . .   *Digested,* 87/**869**:
                                     Considered, 98/1118

R. *v.* Broxtowe BC Ex p. B see R. *v.* Broxtowe BC Ex p. Bradford

R. *v.* Broxtowe BC Ex p. Bradford; *sub nom* R. *v.* Broxtowe BC Ex p. B [2000] I.R.L.R. 329; [2000] B.L.G.R. 386, CA; reversing CO/3229/97, QBD. . . . .   *Digested,* 99/**97**

R. *v.* Broyles [1991] 3 S.C.R. 595, Sup Ct (Can)   *Applied,* 99/3120

R. *v.* Bryan (Lloyd) [1998] 2 Cr. App. R. (S.) 109, CA (Crim Div) . . . .   *Digested,* 98/**1163**

R. *v.* Bryant (Christopher Paul) (1993) 14 Cr. App. R. (S.) 621, CA (Crim Div) . . . .   *Digested,* 94/**1306**:
                             Considered, 99/1261, 99/1266

R. *v.* Bryant (Geoffrey Delroy) (1993) 14 Cr. App. R. (S.) 707, CA (Crim Div) . . . .   *Digested,* 94/**1243**:
                                     Considered, 98/1203

R. *v.* Bryn Elian High School Board of Governors Ex p. W [1999] E.L.R. 380, QBD . . . .   *Digested,* 00/**1926**

R. *v.* Buck (Cameron) [2000] 1 Cr. App. R. (S.) 42, CA (Crim Div) . . . .   *Digested,* 00/**1415**

R. *v.* Buckfield (Derek) [1998] Crim. L.R. 673, CA (Crim Div)

R. *v.* Buckingham (Colin) [2001] 1 Cr. App. R. (S.) 62, CA (Crim Div) . . . .   *Digested,* 01/**1256**

R. *v.* Buckinghamshire CC Ex p. Sharma; R. *v.* Wiltshire CC Ex p. Kaur (Lakhbir) [1998] C.O.D. 182, QBD

R. *v.* Buckland (Andrew) [2000] 1 W.L.R. 1262; [2000] 1 All E.R. 907; [2000] 1 Cr. App. R. 471; [2000] 2 Cr. App. R. (S.) 217; [2000] Crim. L.R. 307; (2000) 97(6) L.S.G. 34; (2000) 144 S.J.L.B. 80; *Times,* February 3, 2000 ; *Independent,* January 27, 2000, CA (Crim Div) . . . .   *Digested,* 00/**1359**:
                            Considered, 00/1347, 01/1470

R. *v.* Buckley (Robert John) (1999) 163 J.P. 561; (1999) 163 J.P.N. 672; (1999) 96(23) L.S.G. 34; *Times,* May 12, 1999, CA (Crim Div) . . . .   *Digested,* 99/**871**

R. v. Buddo (Stephen John) (1982) 4 Cr. App. R. (S.) 268; [1982] Crim. L.R. 837, CA
    (Crim Div) . . . . *Digested,* 83/**809**:
                                               Cited, 91/1126: *Considered,* 99/1103
R. v. Buffrey (Paul Edward) (1993) 14 Cr. App. R. (S.) 511; [1993] Crim. L.R. 319, CA
    (Crim Div) . . . . *Digested,* 94/**1267**:
                               Considered, 97/1483, 99/1326, 00/1256: *Referred to,* 95/1485
R. v. Bulford District Court Martial Ex p. Bowyer CO 4111/98, QBD . . . . *Digested,* 99/**253**
R. v. Bull (Jamie) [2000] 2 Cr. App. R. (S.) 195, CA (Crim Div) . . . . *Digested,* 00/**1214**
R. v. Bull (Wilfred George) see R. v. Eley (David Colin)
R. v. Bullen (Ian John) see R. v. Hart (Simon)
R. v. Bullock (Christopher) (Unreported, July 15, 1998), CA (Crim Div) . . . . *Applied,* 99/991
R. v. Bullock (Richard) see Attorney General's Reference (No.23 of 2000), Re
R. v. Bunce (Mark Wayne) see Attorney General's Reference (No.53 of 1997), Re
R. v. Bunter (Kevin Leslie) see Attorney General's Reference (No.44 of 1997), Re
R. v. Bunting (Michael) see R. v. Allan (John Paul)
R. v. Burgess (Sean Maurice) [2001] 2 Cr. App. R. (S.) 2; *Times,* November 28, 2000,
    CA (Crim Div) . . . . *Digested,* 01/**1270**
R. v. Burke (Anthony) see R. v. McFarlane (Cyril)
R. v. Burke (Leslie Robert) [2000] Crim. L.R. 413, CA (Crim Div)
R. v. Burley (Unreported, March 15, 1995), CA (Crim Div) . . . . *Considered,* 98/871
R. v. Burley (Donald) [2000] Crim. L.R. 843, CA (Crim Div)
R. v. Burman (Rakesh) [2000] 2 Cr. App. R. (S.) 3, CA (Crim Div) . . . . *Digested,* 00/**1407**
R. v. Burnett (Edward Peter) see Attorney General's Reference (No.11 of 1991), Re
R. v. Burnley Crown Court Ex p. Lancashire CC see R. v. Preston Crown Court Ex p.
    Lancashire CC
R. v. Burns (Michael) (1995) 16 Cr. App. R. (S.) 821, CA (Crim Div) . . . . *Digested,* 96/**1822**:
                                               Considered, 98/1360: *Referred to,* 97/1665
R. v. Burns (Michael) [2001] 1 Cr. App. R. (S.) 63; [2001] F.S.R. 27, CA (Crim Div). . . . *Digested,* 01/**1250**
R. v. Burns (Paul Rudi) [2000] 2 Cr. App. R. (S.) 198, CA (Crim Div) . . . . *Digested,* 00/**1152**
R. v. Burstow (Anthony Christopher) see R. v. Ireland (Robert Matthew)
R. v. Burstow (Anthony Christopher) [1997] 1 Cr. App. R. 144; (1996) 160 J.P. 794;
    [1997] Crim. L.R. 452; (1996) 160 J.P.N. 1156; (1996) 93(35) L.S.G. 32; (1996)
    140 S.J.L.B. 194; *Times,* July 30, 1996, CA (Crim Div); affirming [1996] Crim.
    L.R. 331, Crown Ct . . . . *Digested,* 97/**1183**:
                                 Considered, 98/1239, 00/1272: *Distinguished,* 97/1578:
                                                          Subsequent proceedings, 97/1182
R. v. Burt (Sean David) (1997) 161 J.P. 77; [1996] Crim. L.R. 660; (1996) 160 J.P.N.
    1156, CA (Crim Div) . . . . *Disapproved,* 00/1049
R. v. Burt & Adams Ltd [1999] 1 A.C. 247; [1998] 2 W.L.R. 725; [1998] 2 All E.R.
    417; (1998) 162 J.P. 263; (1998) 162 J.P.N. 365; (1998) 95(18) L.S.G. 33;
    (1998) 148 N.L.J. 515; (1998) 142 S.J.L.B. 127; *Times,* April 3, 1998, HL;
    affirming (1996) 160 J.P. 669; [1996] Crim. L.R. 425; (1996) 160 J.P.N. 811;
    Times, November 22, 1995, CA (Crim Div) . . . . *Digested,* 98/**3754**:
                                                                       Applied, 96/1497
R. v. Burton (Evelyn); R. v. Andre (Lyla) [2001] EWCA Crim 1206; [2001] Crim. L.R.
    660, CA (Crim Div)
R. v. Burton (Lawrence John) (1990) 12 Cr. App. R. (S.) 559, CA (Crim Div) . . . . *Digested,* 92/**1150**:
                                               Considered, 96/1993, 00/1267, 00/1369
R. v. Burton (Thomas Terry) see R. v. Weaver (Tanya)
R. v. Burton on Trent Justices Ex p. Nicholson [1998] C.O.D. 262, QBD . . . . *Considered,* 01/1091
R. v. Burton on Trent Justices Ex p. Smith [1998] 1 Cr. App. R. (S.) 223; (1997) 161
    J.P. 741; [1997] Crim. L.R. 685; (1997) 161 J.P.N. 918; *Times,* July 15, 1997,
    QBD . . . . *Digested,* 97/**1634**
R. v. Burton on Trent Justices Ex p. Woolley (1995) 159 J.P. 165; [1995] R.T.R. 139;
    [1996] Crim. L.R. 340; *Times,* November 17, 1994; *Independent,* January 27,
    1995; *Independent,* December 29, 1994, QBD . . . . *Digested,* 95/**4413**:
                                               Considered, 95/4411: *Distinguished,* 01/990
R. v. Busby (Nicky Mark) [2000] 1 Cr. App. R. (S.) 279, CA (Crim Div) . . . . *Digested,* 00/**1207**
R. v. Butcher (Norman Mark) (1989) 11 Cr. App. R. (S.) 104, CA (Crim Div) . . . . *Digested,* 90/**1280**:
                                                                    Considered, 98/1172
R. v. Butler (Diana Helen) [1999] Crim. L.R. 835, CA (Crim Div)
R. v. Butler (Ian James) [1999] 2 Cr. App. R. (S.) 339, CA (Crim Div) . . . . *Digested,* 99/**1265**
R. v. Butler (Michael) [1999] Crim. L.R. 595, CA (Crim Div)
R. v. Butler-Rees (John Llewelyn) see R. v. Radak (Jason Dragon)
R. v. Butt (Imran Khurshid) [1999] Crim. L.R. 414, CA (Crim Div)
R. v. BW see Attorney General's Reference (No.66 of 1999), Re
R. v. Byfield (Barrington) (1994) 15 Cr. App. R. (S.) 674, CA (Crim Div) . . . . *Digested,* 95/**1471**:
                                                          Considered, 97/1693, 98/1381
R. v. Byrne (Alan) see Attorney General's Reference (Nos.19, 20 and 21 of 2001), Re
R. v. Byrne (Edward Joseph); R. v. Coughlan (Martin); R. v. Gillespie (Ann Bernadette);
    R. v. Gillespie (Eileen Theresa) (1976) 62 Cr. App. R. 159; [1976] Crim. L.R.
    142, CA (Crim Div) . . . . *Digested,* 76/**574**:
                                               Considered, 96/1718, 96/2083, 98/1213
R. v. Byrne (Francis Terrence) [1998] 1 Cr. App. R. (S.) 105, CA (Crim Div) . . . . *Digested,* 98/**1402**

R. v. Byrne (James) (1994) 15 Cr. App. R. (S.) 34, CA (Crim Div) . . . .   *Considered*, 00/1180:
                                     Referred to, 97/1577
R. v. Byrne (Joseph) [2000] 1 Cr. App. R. (S.) 282, CA (Crim Div) . . . .   *Digested*, 00/**1121**
R. v. Byrne (Kevin) (1995) 16 Cr. App. R. (S.) 140, CA (Crim Div) . . . .   *Digested*, 96/**2038**:
                                       Considered, 98/1130

R. v. Byrne (Malcolm Matthew) see R. v. Boreman (Victor)
R. v. Byrne (Michael John) see R. v. Boreman (Victor)
R. v. Byrne (Thomas Ross) [1996] 2 Cr. App. R. (S.) 34, CA (Crim Div) . . . .   *Digested*, 96/**1849**:
                 Considered, 97/1509, 99/1144, 00/1208, 00/1215
R. v. Byron (Darren), *Times*, March 10, 1999, CA (Crim Div) . . . .   *Digested*, 99/**889**
R. v. C [1999] Crim. L.R. 664, CA (Crim Div)
R. v. C (A Juvenile) see R. v. Chesterton (Simon)
R. v. C (A Juvenile), *Times*, July 5, 2000, CA (Crim Div) . . . .   *Digested*, 00/**1078**
R. v. C (A Juvenile) (Persistent Offender); *sub nom* R. v. C (Thomas Sean) (A
    Juvenile); R. v. C (Young Person: Persistent Offender) [2001] 1 Cr. App. R. (S.)
    120; (2000) 164 J.P. 685; *Times*, October 11, 2000; *Independent*, November 13,
    2000 (C.S), CA (Crim Div) . . . .   *Digested*, 00/**1318**
R. v. C (Alan Charles) [1997] 2 Cr. App. R. (S.) 85, CA (Crim Div) . . . .   *Digested*, 97/**1443**:
                                       Considered, 99/1193
R. v. C (Anthony) (A Juvenile) [2000] 1 Cr. App. R. (S.) 115, CA (Crim Div) . . . .   *Digested*, 00/**1314**
R. v. C (Brian Arthur) [1998] 2 Cr. App. R. (S.) 303, CA (Crim Div) . . . .   *Digested*, 98/**1143**
R. v. C (Clifford Paul) [2000] 1 Cr. App. R. (S.) 533, CA (Crim Div) . . . .   *Digested*, 00/**1293**
R. v. C (Craig) (A Juvenile) see Attorney General's Reference (Nos.19, 20 and 21 of
    2001), Re
R. v. C (Danny Gerald) (A Juvenile) see Attorney General's Reference (No.30 of 1997),
    Re
R. v. C (David) (A Juvenile) [1999] 2 Cr. App. R. (S.) 64, CA (Crim Div) . . . .   *Digested*, 99/**1223**
R. v. C (David Anthony) (A Juvenile), *Times*, October 13, 2000, CA (Crim Div) . . . .   *Digested*, 00/**1317**
R. v. C (Gary Justin) (A Juvenile) see Attorney General's Reference (Nos.30 and 31 of
    1998), Re
R. v. C (Hugh John) [1998] 1 Cr. App. R. (S.) 434; [1998] Crim. L.R. 141, CA (Crim
    Div) . . . .   *Digested*, 98/**1250**
R. v. C (John Francis) (1993) 14 Cr. App. R. (S.) 562, CA (Crim Div) . . . .   *Digested*, 94/**1255**:
                       Considered, 97/1452, 98/1349, 00/1396
R. v. C (Keith John) (A Juvenile) see Attorney General's Reference (Nos.30 and 31 of
    1998), Re
R. v. C (Leanne) (A Juvenile) see R. v. M (Jodie) (A Juvenile)
R. v. C (Liam James) [1998] 2 Cr. App. R. (S.) 349, CA (Crim Div) . . . .   *Digested*, 98/**1277**
R. v. C (Mark) see Attorney General's Reference (No.73 of 1999), Re
R. v. C (Michael) [1998] 2 Cr. App. R. (S.) 20, CA (Crim Div) . . . .   *Digested*, 98/**1275**
R. v. C (Neil David); R. v. J (Mark William) [2000] 1 Cr. App. R. (S.) 359; [2000]
    Crim. L.R. 61, CA (Crim Div) . . . .   *Digested*, 00/**1284**
R. v. C (Paul John); R. v. S (Jacqueline Rosemary) [2000] 2 Cr. App. R. (S.) 329, CA
    (Crim Div) . . . .   *Digested*, 00/**1274**
R. v. C (Richard Stephen) (1990) 12 Cr. App. R. (S.) 292, CA (Crim Div) . . . .   *Digested*, 92/**1376**:
                                         Considered, 98/1347
R. v. C (Robert) (1994) 15 Cr. App. R. (S.) 757, CA (Crim Div) . . . .   *Digested*, 95/**1457**:
                                         Considered, 00/1402
R. v. C (Sean Peter) [2001] EWCA Crim 1251; [2001] 2 F.L.R. 757; [2001] 3 F.C.R.
    409; [2001] Crim. L.R. 845; [2001] Fam. Law 732; (2001) 165 J.P.N. 1019;
    Times, June 14, 2001, CA (Crim Div) . . . .   *Digested*, 01/**1051**
R. v. C (Shaun Lee) (A Juvenile) see R. v. Reid (Sonni Lee)
R. v. C (Stephen) [1999] 2 Cr. App. R. (S.) 154, CA (Crim Div) . . . .   *Digested*, 99/**1269**
R. v. C (Terence) see Attorney General's Reference (No.5 of 2001), Re
R. v. C (Thomas Sean) (A Juvenile) see R. v. C (A Juvenile) (Persistent Offender)
R. v. C (Toby) (A Juvenile) (2000) 97(17) L.S.G. 35; (2000) 144 S.J.L.B. 190; *Times*,
    April 5, 2000, CA (Crim Div) . . . .   *Digested*, 00/**1321**
R. v. C (Trevor Anthony) 99/0642/W5, CA (Crim Div) . . . .   *Considered*, 99/877
R. v. C (Young Person: Persistent Offender) see R. v. C (A Juvenile) (Persistent
    Offender)
R. v. C-T (Ronnie) see Attorney General's Reference (No.43 of 2001), Re
R. v. C-T (Sarah) (A Juvenile) [2000] 2 Cr. App. R. (S.) 335; [2000] Crim. L.R. 401,
    CA (Crim Div) . . . .   *Digested*, 00/**1332**:
                                         Distinguished, 01/1233
R. v. Cadman (Graham William) see R. v. Brown (Anthony Joseph)
R. v. Cadman-Smith (David) (Leave to Appeal) see R. v. Smith (David Cadman)
    (Leave to Appeal)
R. v. Caernarfon Justices Ex p. Allen see R. v. Norwich Stipendiary Magistrate Ex p.
    Keable
R. v. Caerphilly CBC Housing Benefit Review Board Ex p. Jones (2000) 32 H.L.R. 82,
    QBD . . . .   *Digested*, 01/**5023**
R. v. Cairns (John) [1999] 2 Cr. App. R. 137; [2000] R.T.R. 15; [1999] Crim. L.R. 826;
    (1999) 96(11) L.S.G. 69; (1999) 143 S.J.L.B. 94; *Times*, April 5, 1999, CA (Crim
    Div) . . . .   *Digested*, 99/**1021**

R. *v.* Cairns (Leslie) (1988) 87 Cr. App. R. 287, CA (Crim Div) . . . .   *Digested,* 89/**675**:
                                                 Considered, 91/797: *Distinguished,* 98/1034
R. *v.* Cairns (Robert Emmett) (No.1) [2000] Crim. L.R. 473; *Times,* March 8, 2000, CA
    (Crim Div). . . . .   *Digested,* 00/**903**:
                                                      Followed, 00/905
R. *v.* Calder [1996] 1 S.C.R. 660, Sup Ct (Can) . . . .   *Applied,* 99/3139
R. (on the application of Donahue) *v.* Calderdale Magistrates Court; *sub nom* R. *v.*
    Calderdale Magistrates Court Ex p. Donahue [2001] Crim. L.R. 141, QBD (Admin
    Ct)
R. *v.* Calderdale MBC Ex p. Houghton (2000) 3 C.C.L. Rep. 228, QBD . . . .   *Digested,* 01/**5100**
R. *v.* Callaghan (David Michael) [2001] EWCA Crim 198; [2001] 2 Cr. App. R. (S.) 72,
    CA (Crim Div) . . . .   *Digested,* 01/**1234**
R. *v.* Callender (David Peter) [1998] Crim. L.R. 337, CA (Crim Div)
R. *v.* Camberwell Green Stipendiary Magistrate Ex p. Martin [2001] A.C.D. 8, QBD
R. *v.* Cambridge CC Ex p. Leach [1998] C.O.D. 101, QBD
R. *v.* Cambridge City Council Ex p. Lane [1999] R.T.R. 182; [1999] E.H.L.R. 156;
    (1998) 95(33) L.S.G. 3; *Times,* October 13, 1998, CA; affirming [1999] E.H.L.R.
    79; [1998] C.O.D. 424, QBD . . . .   *Digested,* 98/**4846**
R. *v.* Cambridge City Council Ex p. Warner Village Cinemas Ltd (Permission to Move
    for Judicial Review) [2001] 1 P.L.R. 7; [2001] P.L.C.R. 14; [2001] J.P.L. 119
    (Note), QBD . . . .   *Digested,* 01/**4746**
R. (on the application of Sier) *v.* Cambridge City Council Housing Benefit Review Board
    [2001] EWCA Civ 1523, CA; affirming [2001] EWHC Admin 160, QBD (Admin
    Ct) . . . .   *Previous proceedings,*
                                                      00/4824
R. *v.* Cambridge Crown Court Ex p. Buckland (1998) 95(32) L.S.G. 29; (1998) 142
    S.J.L.B. 206; *Times,* September 17, 1998, QBD . . . .   *Digested,* 98/**946**
R. *v.* Cambridge DHA Ex p. B (No.1) [1995] 1 W.L.R. 898; [1995] 2 All E.R. 129;
    [1995] 1 F.L.R. 1056; [1995] 2 F.C.R. 485; [1995] 6 Med. L.R. 250; [1995]
    C.O.D. 407; [1995] Fam. Law 480; (1995) 145 N.L.J. 415; *Times,* March 15,
    1995; *Independent,* March 14, 1995, CA; reversing *Times,* March 15, 1995;
    Independent, March 14, 1995, QBD . . . .   *Digested,* 95/**3620**:
                                                      Considered, 98/2653
R. *v.* Cambridge University Ex p. Beg (1999) 11 Admin. L.R. 505; [1999] E.L.R. 404;
    (1999) 163 J.P.N. 755, QBD . . . .   *Digested,* 99/**1929**
R. (on the application of K) *v.* Camden and Islington HA; *sub nom* R. *v.* Camden and
    Islington HA Ex p. K [2001] EWCA Civ 240; [2001] 3 W.L.R. 553; [2001]
    U.K.H.R.R. 1378; [2001] Lloyd's Rep. Med. 152; (2001) 61 B.M.L.R. 173; (2001)
    98(16) L.S.G. 34; (2001) 145 S.J.L.B. 69; *Times,* March 15, 2001; *Independent,*
    February 28, 2001, CA; affirming (2000) 3 C.C.L. Rep. 256; [2000] C.O.D.
    483, QBD . . . .   *Digested,* 01/**4430**
R. *v.* Camden LBC Ex p. Aranda (1998) 30 H.L.R. 76; [1997] C.O.D. 280, CA;
    affirming (1996) 28 H.L.R. 672, QBD . . . .   *Digested,* 98/**3015**
R. *v.* Camden LBC Ex p. Cosmo (1998) 30 H.L.R. 817, QBD . . . .   *Digested,* 98/**3013**
R. *v.* Camden LBC Ex p. H (A Minor) [1996] E.L.R. 360; *Times,* August 15, 1996, CA. . .   *Digested,* 96/**2448**:
                                                      Followed, 98/1899
R. *v.* Camden LBC Ex p. Hersi (2001) 33 H.L.R. 52; *Times,* October 11, 2000, CA . . . . .   *Digested,* 00/**3130**
R. *v.* Camden LBC Ex p. Hughes [1994] C.O.D. 253, QBD . . . .   *Digested,* 95/**3226**:
                                                      Applied, 00/4114
R. *v.* Camden LBC Ex p. Jibril (1997) 29 H.L.R. 785, QBD . . . .   *Digested,* 98/**3024**:
                                                      Considered, 98/2997
R. *v.* Camden LBC Ex p. Mohammed (1998) 30 H.L.R. 315; (1997) 9 Admin. L.R.
    639; (1997) 161 J.P.N. 1038; (1997) 94(35) L.S.G. 34; *Times,* June 20, 1997;
    Independent, June 12, 1997, QBD. . . . .   *Digested,* 97/**2676**:
                                                      Applied, 98/3019
R. *v.* Camden LBC Ex p. Pereira (No.2) (1999) 31 H.L.R. 317; [1998] N.P.C. 94, CA;
    reversing [1998] C.O.D. 318, QBD . . . .   *Digested,* 99/**3062**
R. *v.* Camden LBC Ex p. Williams [2000] 2 P.L.R. 93; [2000] J.P.L. 1147; *Times,* June
    6, 2000, QBD . . . .   *Digested,* 00/**4518**
R. *v.* Camden LBC Housing Benefit Review Board Ex p. Hassani-Kazhadeh [2000]
    N.P.C. 88, QBD
R. *v.* Camden LBC Housing Benefit Review Board Ex p. W (2000) 32 H.L.R. 879, CA . .   *Digested,* 01/**5022**
R. *v.* Cameron (Clarence Raymond) see Attorney General's Reference (Nos.62, 63 and
    64 of 1995), Re
R. *v.* Cameron (John McDougal) (1993) 14 Cr. App. R. (S.) 801, CA (Crim Div) . . . . . .   *Digested,* 94/**1358**:
                                   Applied, 01/1300: *Considered,* 97/1442
R. *v.* Cameron (Leon) [2001] EWCA Crim 562; [2001] Crim. L.R. 587; *Times,* May 3,
    2001, CA (Crim Div) . . . .   *Digested,* 01/**1197**
R. *v.* Campbell (Dale) [2000] 1 Cr. App. R. (S.) 291, CA (Crim Div) . . . .   *Digested,* 00/**1246**
R. *v.* Campbell (Maurice Wayne) [1998] 1 Cr. App. R. (S.) 264, CA (Crim Div). . . . .   *Digested,* 98/**1215**
R. *v.* Campbell (Patrick) [2001] EWCA Crim 262; [2001] 2 Cr. App. R. (S.) 79, CA
    (Crim Div). . . . .   *Digested,* 01/**1276**
R. *v.* Campbell (Raymond Charles) (1995) 16 Cr. App. R. (S.) 20, CA (Crim Div) . . . . . .   *Digested,* 96/**1842**:
                                                      Considered, 98/1317

R. *v.* Camplin (Paul); *sub nom* DPP *v.* Camplin [1978] A.C. 705; [1978] 2 W.L.R. 679;
　　[1978] 2 All E.R. 168; (1978) 67 Cr. App. R. 14; [1978] Crim. L.R. 432; 122 S.J.
　　280; *Times*, April 11, 1978, HL; affirming [1978] Q.B. 254; [1977] 3 W.L.R. 929;
　　[1978] 1 All E.R. 1236; (1978) 66 Cr. App. R. 37; [1977] Crim. L.R. 748; 121 S.J.
　　676, CA (Crim Div) . . . . *Digested*, 78/**558**:
　　　　　　　　　　　Applied, 82/676, 87/799, 89/859, 90/850: *Considered*, 87/803, 90/920,
　　　　　　　　　　　93/968, 94/681, 94/1127, 95/1280, 95/1281, 98/960, 00/986:
　　　　　　　　　　　Distinguished, 84/501, 85/503, 90/1132: *Referred to*, 00/1017
R. *v.* Canavan (Darren Anthony) see R. *v.* Kidd (Philip Richard)
R. *v.* Cannan (Adam John) [1998] Crim. L.R. 284, CA (Crim Div)
R. *v.* Cannon (Phillip) [2001] 1 Cr. App. R. (S.) 83, CA (Crim Div) . . . .　*Digested*, 01/**1427**
R. *v.* Canons Park Mental Health Review Tribunal Ex p. A [1995] Q.B. 60; [1994] 3
　　W.L.R. 630; [1994] 2 All E.R. 659; [1994] C.O.D. 480; (1994) 91 (22) L.S.G.
　　33; (1994) 138 S.J.L.B. 75; *Times*, March 2, 1994, CA; reversing [1994] 1 All
　　E.R. 481; [1994] C.O.D. 125; *Times*, August 24, 1993; *Independent*, September 1,
　　1993, QBD . . . . *Digested*, 94/**3066**:
　　　　　　　　　　　Disapproved, 00/4174: *Distinguished*, 98/6097: *Followed*, 97/6265
R. (on the application of Howson-Ball) *v.* Canterbury Crown Court [2001] Env. L.R. 36;
　　[2001] E.H.L.R. Dig. 2, QBD (Admin Ct)
R. (on the application of Regentford Ltd) *v.* Canterbury Crown Court; *sub nom* R. *v.*
　　Canterbury Crown Court Ex p. Regentford Ltd [2001] H.R.L.R. 18; [2001]
　　A.C.D. 40; *Times*, February 6, 2001, QBD (Admin Ct) . . . .　*Digested*, 01/**3539**
R. *v.* Canterbury Crown Court Ex p. Regentford Ltd see R. (on the application of
　　Regentford Ltd) *v.* Canterbury Crown Court
R. *v.* Canterbury Crown Court Ex p. Wagstaff see R. *v.* Customs and Excise
　　Commissioners Ex p. Wagstaff
R. *v.* Cappagh Public Works Ltd [1999] 2 Cr. App. R. (S.) 301, CA (Crim Div) . . . .　*Digested*, 99/**2858**
R. *v.* Caradon DC Ex p. Knott (2000) 80 P. & C.R. 154; [2000] 3 P.L.R. 1; *Times*,
　　March 3, 2000, QBD . . . .　*Digested*, 00/**4453**
R. *v.* Caradon DC Ex p. Lovejoy (1999) 78 P. & C.R. 243; [2000] J.P.L. 186, QBD. . . . .　*Digested*, 00/**4476**
R. *v.* Carawana (Unreported, May 23, 1997), CA (Crim Div) . . . .　*Considered*, 00/1151
R. *v.* Cardiff CC Ex p. Sears Group Properties Ltd [1998] 3 P.L.R. 55; [1998] P.L.C.R.
　　262; (1998) 95(17) L.S.G. 29; [1998] N.P.C. 46; *Times*, April 29, 1998, QBD . . .　*Digested*, 98/**4202**
R. *v.* Cardiff City Transport Services [2001] 1 Cr. App. R. (S.) 41, CA (Crim Div) . . . .　*Digested*, 01/**1349**
R. *v.* Cardiff Crown Court Ex p. M (A Minor) see R. *v.* Harrow Crown Court Ex p.
　　Perkins
R. *v.* Cardiff Magistrates Court Ex p. Czech [1999] 1 F.L.R. 95; [1999] 1 F.C.R. 721;
　　[1998] C.O.D. 392; [1998] Fam. Law 658; (1999) 163 J.P.N. 555, Fam Div. . . .　*Digested*, 99/**2433**
R. *v.* Cardinal Heenan High School Appeal Committee Ex p. McKeown; *sub nom*
　　McKeown *v.* Cardinal Heenan High School [1999] Ed. C.R. 340; [1998] E.L.R.
　　578, QBD . . . .　*Digested*, 99/**1833**
R. (on the application of C (A Child)) *v.* Cardinal Newman Roman Catholic School
　　Governing Body see R. (on the application of B (A Child)) *v.* Alperton
　　Community School Head Teacher and Governing Body
R. *v.* Carey (Harold Christopher) [1999] 1 Cr. App. R. (S.) 322, CA (Crim Div). . . . .　*Digested*, 99/**1173**:
　　　　　　　　　　　Considered, 00/1257, 01/1236
R. *v.* Carey (Stephen) [2000] 1 Cr. App. R. (S.) 179, CA (Crim Div) . . . .　*Digested*, 00/**1245**
R. *v.* Cargill (Warren) [1999] 2 Cr. App. R. (S.) 72, CA (Crim Div) . . . .　*Digested*, 99/**1142**
R. *v.* Carmarthenshire CC Ex p. W (A Child) [2001] E.L.R. 172, QBD . . . .　*Digested*, 01/**1985**
R. (on the application of Painter) *v.* Carmarthenshire CC Housing Benefit Review Board;
　　R. (on the application of Murphy) *v.* Westminster City Council [2001] EWHC
　　Admin 308; *Times*, May 16, 2001; *Independent*, June 18, 2001 (C.S), QBD
　　(Admin Ct) . . . .　*Digested*, 01/**5019**
R. *v.* Carpenter (Amber Louise) see Attorney General's Reference (No.67 of 2001), Re
R. *v.* Carpenter (John) see R. *v.* Jones (John McKinsie)
R. *v.* Carr (Leslie Joseph) [2000] 2 Cr. App. R. 149; [2000] Crim. L.R. 193, CA (Crim
　　Div) . . . .　*Digested*, 01/**1149**
R. *v.* Carrick DC Ex p. Prankerd (The Winnie Rigg) [1999] Q.B. 1119; [1999] 2 W.L.R.
　　489; [1998] 2 Lloyd's Rep. 675; (1998) 95(33) L.S.G. 34; (1998) 142 S.J.L.B.
　　228; *Times*, September 1, 1998; *Independent*, October 5, 1998 (C.S.), QBD. . . . .　*Digested*, 98/**4428**
R. *v.* Carrington (Lorton Vinston) [1999] 2 Cr. App. R. (S.) 206, CA (Crim Div) . . . .　*Digested*, 99/**1182**
R. *v.* Carroll (Stephen) (1995) 16 Cr. App. R. (S.) 488; [1995] Crim. L.R. 92, CA
　　(Crim Div). . . . .　*Considered*, 98/1357
R. *v.* Carter (Christopher Robert) see R. *v.* Brown (Anthony Joseph)
R. *v.* Carter (Jahroy) [1997] 1 Cr. App. R. (S.) 434, CA (Crim Div) . . . .　*Digested*, 97/**1459**:
　　　　　　　　　　　Considered, 00/1429, 00/1430
R. *v.* Case (Danny David) see Attorney General's Reference (Nos.62 and 63 of 1997),
　　Re
R. *v.* Casey (Brian Michael) [2000] 1 Cr. App. R. (S.) 221, CA (Crim Div) . . . .　*Digested*, 00/**1117**
R. *v.* Cassar (David) see R. *v.* McDonnell (James)
R. *v.* Casseeram (Ramjutee) (1992) 13 Cr. App. R. (S.) 384, CA (Crim Div) . . . .　*Digested*, 93/**1012**:
　　　　　　　　　　　Considered, 94/1314, 96/2021, 99/1076
R. *v.* Caswell (Mark Kevin) [1999] 1 Cr. App. R. (S.) 467, CA (Crim Div) . . . .　*Digested*, 99/**1257**

R. v. Cattell (Unreported, December 22, 2000), Crown Ct [*Ex rel*. David Lamming, Barrister, 2-3 Gray's Inn Square, London] . . . . *Digested*, 01/**1053**

R. v. Catterall (Darren Joseph) (1993) 14 Cr. App. R. (S.) 724; *Times*, March 29, 1993, CA (Crim Div) . . . . *Digested*, 94/**1311**: *Considered*, 99/1222: *Referred to*, 97/1527

R. v. Causley (Russell) [1999] Crim. L.R. 572, CA (Crim Div)

R. v. Cavanagh (James Michael); R. v. Shaw (William Anthony) [1972] 1 W.L.R. 676; [1972] 2 All E.R. 704; (1972) 56 Cr. App. R. 407; [1972] Crim. L.R. 389; 116 S.J. 372, CA (Crim Div) . . . . *Digested*, 72/**645**: *Considered*, 94/926: *Referred to*, 00/945

R. v. Cawley (William Boy) (1994) 15 Cr. App. R. (S.) 209, CA (Crim Div) . . . . *Approved*, 97/**1464**: *Considered*, 98/1337: *Distinguished*, 96/1741, 98/1148

R. v. Cawthorn (Robert) [2001] 1 Cr. App. R. (S.) 136; [2001] Crim. L.R. 51; *Times*, October 27, 2000, CA (Crim Div) . . . . *Digested*, 00/**1178**

R. v. CB see Attorney General's Reference (No.32 of 2000), Re

R. v. CC (A Juvenile) see R. v. Reid (Sonni Lee)

R. (on the application of Bright) v. Central Criminal Court see R. v. Central Criminal Court Ex p. Bright

R. v. Central Criminal Court Ex p. Abu-Wardeh [1998] 1 W.L.R. 1083; [1997] 1 All E.R. 159; [1999] 1 Cr. App. R. 43; (1997) 161 J.P. 142; (1996) 160 J.P.N. 1129; *Times*, July 30, 1996; *Independent*, June 18, 1996, QBD . . . . *Digested*, 96/**1585**: *Considered*, 97/1301, 01/1129

R. v. Central Criminal Court Ex p. Alton see R. v. Central Criminal Court Ex p. Bright

R. v. Central Criminal Court Ex p. Behbehani [1994] Crim. L.R. 352, QBD . . . . *Digested*, 94/**807**: *Considered*, 98/1082

R. v. Central Criminal Court Ex p. Bennett, *Times*, January 25, 1999, QBD . . . . *Digested*, 99/**1005**

R. v. Central Criminal Court Ex p. Boulding [1984] Q.B. 813; [1984] 2 W.L.R. 321; [1984] 1 All E.R. 766; (1984) 79 Cr. App. R. 100; (1983) 5 Cr. App. R. (S.) 433; (1984) 148 J.P. 174, QBD. . . . . *Digested*, 84/**2091**: *Applied*, 85/2083, 86/2071, 88/588, 89/699, 89/932, 91/1021: *Considered*, 98/1002

R. v. Central Criminal Court Ex p. Bright; *sub nom* R. v. Central Criminal Court Ex p. Observer; R. v. Central Criminal Court Ex p. Guardian; R. (on the application of Bright) v. Central Criminal Court; R. v. Central Criminal Court Ex p. Alton; R. v. Central Criminal Court Ex p. Rusbridger [2001] 1 W.L.R. 662; [2001] 2 All E.R. 244; [2001] E.M.L.R. 4; [2000] U.K.H.R.R. 796; (2000) 97(38) L.S.G. 43; *Times*, July 26, 2000, QBD . . . . *Digested*, 00/**1057**: *Applied*, 01/3421

R. v. Central Criminal Court Ex p. Crook (1985) 82 L.S.G. 1408; *Times*, November 8, 1984, DC . . . . *Digested*, 84/**975**: *Considered*, 99/84

R. v. Central Criminal Court Ex p. Crook; *sub nom* Crook, Ex p.; R. v. Central Criminal Court Ex p. Godwin [1995] 1 W.L.R. 139; [1995] 1 All E.R. 537; [1995] 2 Cr. App. R. 212; (1995) 159 J.P. 295; [1995] 1 F.L.R. 132; [1995] 2 F.C.R. 153; [1995] Crim. L.R. 509; [1995] Fam. Law 73; (1995) 159 J.P.N. 249; (1994) 91(39) L.S.G. 39; (1994) 138 S.J.L.B. 199; *Times*, August 16, 1994; *Independent*, September 5, 1994 (C.S.), CA (Crim Div) . . . . *Digested*, 95/**3546**: *Applied*, 01/83

R. v. Central Criminal Court Ex p. Fraser [1998] C.O.D. 415, QBD

R. v. Central Criminal Court Ex p. Godwin see R. v. Central Criminal Court Ex p. Crook

R. v. Central Criminal Court Ex p. Guardian see R. v. Central Criminal Court Ex p. Bright

R. v. Central Criminal Court Ex p. Johnson [1999] 2 Cr. App. R. 51; *Independent*, January 25, 1999 (C.S.), QBD . . . . *Digested*, 99/**1006**

R. v. Central Criminal Court Ex p. Marotta [1999] C.O.D. 13, QBD

R. v. Central Criminal Court Ex p. Observer see R. v. Central Criminal Court Ex p. Bright

R. v. Central Criminal Court Ex p. P see R. v. Central Criminal Court Ex p. S

R. v. Central Criminal Court Ex p. Propend Finance Property Ltd; *sub nom* R. v. Secretary of State for the Home Department Ex p. Propend Finance Pty Ltd [1996] 2 Cr. App. R. 26; [1994] C.O.D. 386; *Times*, April 5, 1994; *Independent*, March 29, 1994, QBD . . . . *Digested*, 95/**1200**: *Disapproved*, 98/1085

R. v. Central Criminal Court Ex p. Rusbridger see R. v. Central Criminal Court Ex p. Bright

R. v. Central Criminal Court Ex p. S; R. v. Central Criminal Court Ex p. P (1999) 163 J.P. 776; [1999] 1 F.L.R. 480; [1999] Crim. L.R. 159; [1999] Fam. Law 93; *Times*, October 26, 1998; *Independent*, October 26, 1998 (C.S.), QBD . . . . *Digested*, 98/**76**

R. v. Central Criminal Court Ex p. W [2001] 1 Cr. App. R. 2; [2000] C.O.D. 442, QBD

R. v. Central London County Court Ex p. London [1999] Q.B. 1260; [1999] 3 W.L.R. 1; [1999] 3 All E.R. 991; [2000] C.P. Rep. 75; [1999] 2 F.L.R. 161; (1999) 2 C.C.L. Rep. 256; [1999] C.O.D. 196; [1999] Fam. Law 452; (1999) 96(15) L.S.G. 30; *Times*, March 23, 1999; *Independent*, March 18, 1999, CA . . . . *Digested*, 99/**3937**

R. (on the application of Edison First Power Ltd) *v.* Central Valuation Officer see R. (on the application of Edison First Power Ltd) *v.* Secretary of State for the Environment, Transport and the Regions

R. *v.* Ceredigion CC Ex p. McKeown [1998] 2 P.L.R. 1; [1998] P.L.C.R. 90; [1997] C.O.D. 463, QBD . . . . *Digested, 98/535:*
Considered, 99/4260, 00/4518

R. *v.* Cevik (Bozkurt Bulent) (No.2) [1998] 2 Costs L.R. 1 . . . . *Digested, 00/3974*

R. *v.* Chadwick (Barry John) see Attorney General's Reference (No.7 of 1994), Re

R. *v.* Chahal (Ranjit Singh) [1998] 2 Cr. App. R. (S.) 93, CA (Crim Div). . . . . *Digested, 98/1279*

R. *v.* Chair of Governors and Headteacher of A School Ex p. T see R. *v.* A School Governors Ex p. T

R. *v.* Chairman of Stephen Lawrence Inquiry Ex p. A'Court, *Times*, July 25, 1998, QBD . . *Digested, 98/74*

R. *v.* Chalkley (Tony Michael); R. *v.* Jeffries (Tony Brisbane McEwan) [1998] Q.B. 848; [1998] 3 W.L.R. 146; [1998] 2 All E.R. 155; [1998] 2 Cr. App. R. 79; [1999] Crim. L.R. 214; (1998) 95(5) L.S.G. 29; (1998) 142 S.J.L.B. 40; *Times*, January 19, 1998; *Independent*, January 14, 1998, CA (Crim Div) . . . . *Digested, 98/1073:*
Applied, 99/974, 00/1025: Not followed, 00/1026

R. *v.* Challis (Barry) [1996] 2 Cr. App. R. (S.) 425, CA (Crim Div) . . . . *Digested, 97/1512:*
Considered, 98/1196

R. *v.* Chalmers (Andrew Robert) (Unreported, December 15, 1999), Crown Ct (Maidstone) [*Ex rel.* Trobridges Solicitors, 1 Ford Park Road, Mutley Plain, Plymouth] . . . . *Digested, 00/945*

R. *v.* Chamberlain (Gary Allen) [1998] 1 Cr. App. R. (S.) 49, CA (Crim Div) . . . . *Digested, 98/1194*

R. *v.* Chamberlain (Patrick Arthur) see Attorney General's Reference (Nos.17 and 18 of 1994), Re

R. *v.* Chamberlain (Raymond James) (1995) 16 Cr. App. R. (S.) 473; [1995] Crim. L.R. 85, CA (Crim Div) . . . . *Followed, 01/1441*

R. *v.* Chamberlain (Toby) see Attorney General's Reference (Nos.17 and 18 of 1994), Re

R. *v.* Chambers (Mark Howard); R. *v.* Barnett (Christopher George) [1999] 1 Cr. App. R. (S.) 262, CA (Crim Div) . . . . *Digested, 99/1143*

R. *v.* Chambers (Richard) [1994] N.I. 170, CA (Crim Div) (NI). . . . . *Digested, 00/5472:*
Followed, 00/5471

R. *v.* Chambers (Stephen Francis) (1983) 5 Cr. App. R. (S.) 190; [1983] Crim. L.R. 688, CA (Crim Div) . . . . *Digested, 84/887:*
Cited, 90/1357: Considered, 96/2000, 98/1305: Distinguished, 96/1998:
Followed, 96/2002

R. *v.* Chance Ex p. Coopers & Lybrand see R. *v.* Chance Ex p. Smith

R. *v.* Chance Ex p. Smith; R. *v.* Chance Ex p. Coopers & Lybrand [1995] B.C.C. 1095; (1995) 7 Admin. L.R. 821; *Times*, January 28, 1995, QBD . . . . *Digested, 95/147:*
Considered, 98/681

R. *v.* Chandler (Adrian Anthony) see Attorney General's Reference (No.39 of 1997), Re

R. *v.* Chapman (Jamie Lee) [2000] 1 Cr. App. R. 77; [2000] 1 Cr. App. R. (S.) 377; [1999] Crim. L.R. 852; *Times*, August 2, 1999, CA (Crim Div) . . . . *Digested, 99/1250:*
Considered, 00/1346, 01/1203, 01/1269

R. *v.* Chapman (Kraige Andrew) [1999] 2 Cr. App. R. (S.) 374, CA (Crim Div) . . . . *Digested, 00/1368*

R. *v.* Chapman (Lorraine) see R. *v.* Keyes (Anthony Matthew)

R. *v.* Chapman (Mark Edward) see R. *v.* Bond (Duncan)

R. *v.* Charity Commissioners for England and Wales Ex p. Baldwin (2001) 33 H.L.R. 48; [2001] W.T.L.R. 137, QBD . . . . *Digested, 01/386*

R. *v.* Charles (Jerome) (Leave to Appeal); R. *v.* Tucker (Lee Nigel) [2001] EWCA Crim 129; [2001] 2 Cr. App. R. 15; [2001] Crim. L.R. 732; *Times*, February 20, 2001; *Daily Telegraph*, February 7, 2001, CA (Crim Div) . . . . *Digested, 01/1096*

R. *v.* Charlton (Mark Robert); R. *v.* Mealing (David) [2000] 2 Cr. App. R. (S.) 102, CA (Crim Div). . . . . *Digested, 00/1379*

R. *v.* Chatfield (Philip Norman); R. *v.* Pender (Robert John) (1983) 5 Cr. App. R. (S.) 289; (1984) 148 J.P.N. 15, CA (Crim Div) . . . . *Digested, 84/852:*
Considered, 98/1177

R. *v.* Chauhan (Rashmikant Bhikhubhai); R. *v.* Holroyd (John Malcolm) [2000] 2 Cr. App. R. (S.) 230, CA (Crim Div) . . . . *Digested, 00/1256*

R. *v.* Chee Kew Ong [2001] 1 Cr. App. R. (S.) 117, CA (Crim Div) . . . . *Digested, 01/1246*

R. *v.* Cheeseborough (Colin Ian) (1982) 4 Cr. App. R. (S.) 394, CA (Crim Div) . . . . *Digested, 83/768:*
Considered, 99/1076, 00/1130, 00/1132, 00/1133, 00/1134

R. *v.* Chelmsford Crown Court Ex p. Farrer [2000] 1 W.L.R. 1468; (2000) 97(14) L.S.G. 42; (2000) 144 S.J.L.B. 158; *Times*, March 29, 2000, CA; reversing (1999) 96(41) L.S.G. 35; *Times*, November 5, 1999 ; *Independent*, November 15, 1999 (C.S.), QBD . . . . *Digested, 00/4065*

R. *v.* Chelmsford Crown Court Ex p. Mills (2000) 164 J.P. 1; (1999) 163 J.P.N. 915; *Times*, May 31, 1999, QBD . . . . *Digested, 99/1049*

R. (on the application of Lloyd) *v.* Chelmsford Justices; *sub nom* R. *v.* North Essex Justices Ex p. Lloyd; R. (on the application of Lloyd) *v.* North East Essex Justices; R. *v.* Chelmsford Justices Ex p. Lloyd [2001] 2 Cr. App. R. (S.) 15; (2001) 165 J.P. 117; [2001] Crim. L.R. 145; (2001) 165 J.P.N. 665; (2000) 97(47) L.S.G. 40; (2000) 144 S.J.L.B. 274; *Times*, December 5, 2000; *Daily Telegraph*, December 12, 2000, QBD (Admin Ct) . . . . *Digested, 01/1108*

R. (on the application of Nash) *v.* Chelsea College of Art and Design [2001] EWHC
     Admin 538; *Times*, July 25, 2001, QBD (Admin Ct) . . . .   *Digested*, 01/**95**
R. *v.* Chelsea College of Art and Design Ex p. Nash (Application for Judicial Review)
     [2000] Ed. C.R. 571; [2000] E.L.R. 686, QBD . . . .   *Digested*, 00/**1787**
R. *v.* Chen (Jia) see R. *v.* SBC (A Juvenile)
R. *v.* Chen (Ling) see R. *v.* SBC (A Juvenile)
R. *v.* Chen (Wen Ping) see R. *v.* SBC (A Juvenile)
R. *v.* Chen Cheng see R. *v.* Wang Lin Hal
R. *v.* Cheshire CC Ex p. C [1998] E.L.R. 66; *Times*, August 8, 1996, QBD. . . . .   *Digested*, 96/**2490**:
                                                                                                    Considered, 97/2128

R. *v.* Chester and North Wales Legal Aid Area Office (No.12) Ex p. Floods of
     Queensferry Ltd [1998] 1 W.L.R. 1496; [1998] B.C.C. 685; [1998] 2 B.C.L.C.
     436; (1998) 95(4) L.S.G. 34; (1998) 142 S.J.L.B. 43; *Times*, December 26,
     1997, CA; affirming [1998] C.O.D. 222; *Times*, November 7, 1997; *Independent*,
     November 3, 1997 (C.S.), QBD. . . . .   *Digested*, 98/**3690**:
                                                                                                    Applied, 99/832
R. *v.* Chester Magistrates Court Ex p. Ball (1999) 163 J.P. 757; (1999) 163 J.P.N. 813,
     QBD. . . . .   *Digested*, 00/**3980**
R. *v.* Chesterfield Justices Ex p. Bramley [2000] Q.B. 576; [2000] 2 W.L.R. 409;
     [2000] 1 All E.R. 411; [2000] 1 Cr. App. R. 486; [2000] Crim. L.R. 385; (1999)
     96(45) L.S.G. 34; (1999) 143 S.J.L.B. 282; *Times*, November 10, 1999, QBD . . .   *Digested*, 99/**900**
R. *v.* Chesterton (Simon); *sub nom* R. *v.* C (A Juvenile) [1997] 2 Cr. App. R. (S.) 297,
     CA (Crim Div) . . . .   *Digested*, 98/**1283**
R. *v.* Chevelleau (David) see Attorney General's Reference (No.49 of 1998), Re
R. *v.* Chichester and District Justices Ex p. Crowther [1999] C.O.D. 34; *Independent*,
     October 26, 1998 (C.S.), QBD . . . .   *Digested*, 98/**9**
R. *v.* Chichester DC Ex p. Kirdford Conservation Society [1999] J.P.L. 374, QBD. . . . . .   *Digested*, 99/**4227**
R. *v.* Chief Adjudication Officer Ex p. B [1999] 1 W.L.R. 1695; (1999) 96(4) L.S.G. 40;
     (1999) 143 S.J.L.B. 22; *Times*, December 23, 1998, CA; reversing *Times*, July
     27, 1998; *Independent*, July 6, 1998 (C.S.), QBD . . . .   *Digested*, 99/**4544**:
                                                                                                    Applied, 01/5005
R. *v.* Chief Adjudication Officer Ex p. Remelien see Secretary of State for Social
     Security *v.* Remilien
R. (on the application of Gashi) *v.* Chief Adjudicator (Need for Competent Interpreter)
     [2001] EWHC Admin 916; (2001) 98(39) L.S.G. 38; *Times*, November 12, 2001,
     QBD (Admin Ct) . . . .   *Digested*, 01/**3643**
R. *v.* Chief Constable of Avon and Somerset Ex p. Robinson [1989] 1 W.L.R. 793;
     [1989] 2 All E.R. 15; (1990) 90 Cr. App. R. 27; [1989] Crim. L.R. 440; [1989]
     C.O.D. 410; (1988) 138 N.L.J. 186; (1989) 133 S.J. 264, QBD. . . . .   *Digested*, 89/**764**:
                                                                                                    Applied, 01/4784
R. (on the application of A) *v.* Chief Constable of C; *sub nom* R. *v.* Chief Constables of C
     and D Ex p. A [2001] 1 W.L.R. 461; [2001] 2 F.C.R. 431; [2001] A.C.D. 43;
     Times, November 7, 2000; *Independent*, December 4, 2000 (C.S), QBD (Admin
     Ct) . . . .   *Digested*, 00/**107**
R. *v.* Chief Constable of Devon and Cornwall Ex p. Cornish (1999) 77 P. & C.R. D12,
     CA
R. (on the application of Fuller) *v.* Chief Constable of Dorset [2001] EWHC Admin 1057;
     [2001] N.P.C. 186, QBD (Admin Ct)
R. *v.* Chief Constable of Greater Manchester Ex p. Lainton [2000] I.C.R. 1324; (2000)
     97(16) L.S.G. 40; (2000) 144 S.J.L.B. 203; *Times*, April 4, 2000, CA; reversing
     Times, July 13, 1999 ; *Independent*, June 28, 1999 (C.S.), QBD . . . .   *Digested*, 00/**4545**
R. (on the application of R Cruickshank Ltd) *v.* Chief Constable of Kent [2001] EWHC
     Admin 123; *Independent*, April 2, 2001 (C.S), QBD (Admin Ct)
R. *v.* Chief Constable of Kent Ex p. Kent Police Federation Joint Branch Board [2000]
     2 Cr. App. R. 196; [2000] Crim. L.R. 857; [2000] C.O.D. 169; *Times*, December 1,
     1999, QBD . . . .   *Digested*, 00/**4547**
R. *v.* Chief Constable of Lancashire Ex p. Atkinson (1998) 162 J.P. 275; *Times*, March
     4, 1998, QBD . . . .   *Digested*, 98/**1004**
R. (on the application of Bennion) *v.* Chief Constable of Merseyside; *sub nom* R. *v.* Chief
     Constable of Merseyside Ex p. Bennion [2001] EWCA Civ 638; [2001] I.R.L.R.
     442; [2001] A.C.D. 93; (2001) 98(25) L.S.G. 47; *Times*, June 12, 2001;
     Independent, May 15, 2001, CA; reversing [2000] I.R.L.R. 821; [2001] A.C.D.
     19; (2000) 97(30) L.S.G. 40; (2000) 144 S.J.L.B. 221; *Times*, July 18, 2000,
     QBD . . . .   *Digested*, 01/**2247**
R. *v.* Chief Constable of North Wales Ex p. AB; *sub nom* R. *v.* Chief Constable of North
     Wales Ex p. Thorpe [1999] Q.B. 396; [1998] 3 W.L.R. 57; [1998] 3 All E.R.
     310; [1998] 2 F.L.R. 571; [1998] 3 F.C.R. 371; [1998] Fam. Law 529; (1998)
     95(17) L.S.G. 29; *Times*, March 23, 1998; *Independent*, March 26, 1998, CA;
     affirming [1997] 3 W.L.R. 724; [1997] 4 All E.R. 691; (2000) 3 C.C.L. Rep. 25;
     [1997] C.O.D. 395; (1997) 147 N.L.J. 1061; *Times*, July 14, 1997; *Independent*,
     July 16, 1997, QBD . . . .   *Digested*, 98/**4290**:
                          Applied, 00/7, 00/3250: *Considered*, 97/379: *Followed*, 00/107

R. v. Chief Constable of North Wales Ex p. Evans; *sub nom* Chief Constable of North
Wales v. Evans [1982] 1 W.L.R. 1155; [1982] 3 All E.R. 141; (1983) 147 J.P. 6;
(1982) 79 L.S.G. 1257; 126 S.J. 549, HL . . . .   *Digested*, 82/**1106**:
                     Considered, 83/3321, 00/4545: *Followed*, 85/2576
R. v. Chief Constable of North Wales Ex p. Thorpe see R. v. Chief Constable of North
Wales Ex p. AB
R. (on the application of Thompson) v. Chief Constable of Northumbria; *sub nom* R. v.
Chief Constable of Northumbria Ex p. Thompson [2001] EWCA Civ 321; [2001]
1 W.L.R. 1342; [2001] 4 All E.R. 354; (2001) 98(16) L.S.G. 34; (2001) 151
N.L.J. 417; *Times*, March 20, 2001; *Independent*, March 22, 2001, CA;
reversing CO 5018/99, QBD . . . .   *Digested*, 01/**4784**
R. v. Chief Constable of Northumbria Ex p. Charlton (1994) 158 L.G. Rev. 901; *Times*,
May 6, 1994, QBD . . . .   *Digested*, 94/**3506**:
                     Not followed, 98/4283
R. v. Chief Constable of Northumbria Ex p. Thompson see R. (on the application of
Thompson) v. Chief Constable of Northumbria
R. v. Chief Constable of Nottinghamshire Ex p. Sunderland see R. v. Chief Constable of
the West Midlands Ex p. Wiley
R. v. Chief Constable of Sussex Ex p. International Trader's Ferry Ltd [1999] 2 A.C.
418; [1998] 3 W.L.R. 1260; [1999] 1 All E.R. 129; [1999] 1 C.M.L.R. 1320;
(1999) 11 Admin. L.R. 97; (1998) 95(47) L.S.G. 29; (1998) N.L.J. 1750; (1998)
142 S.J.L.B. 286; *Times*, November 16, 1998, HL; affirming [1998] Q.B. 477;
[1997] 3 W.L.R. 132; [1997] 2 All E.R. 65; [1997] 2 C.M.L.R. 164; [1997] C.O.D.
311; *Times*, February 12, 1997; *Independent*, January 31, 1997, CA; reversing
[1996] Q.B. 197; [1995] 3 W.L.R. 802; [1995] 4 All E.R. 364; [1995] 3 C.M.L.R.
485; [1995] C.O.D. 401; (1995) 145 N.L.J. 1401; *Times*, July 31, 1995;
Independent, July 28, 1995, QBD . . . .   *Digested*, 98/**4259**
R. v. Chief Constable of Thames Valley Ex p. Cotton; *sub nom* R. v. Deputy Chief
Constable of Thames Valley Ex p. Cotton [1990] I.R.L.R. 344; *Times*, December
28, 1989; *Independent*, December 22, 1989, CA; affirming [1989] C.O.D. 318,
QBD . . . .   *Digested*, 91/**95**:
                     Considered, 92/955, 94/43, 98/3025: *Followed*, 99/97
R. v. Chief Constable of the British Transport Police Ex p. Farmer [1999] C.O.D. 518,
CA; reversing [1998] C.O.D. 484; (1998) 95(36) L.S.G. 31; *Times*, September 4,
1998, QBD . . . .   *Digested*, 98/**4282**
R. v. Chief Constable of the Ministry of Defence Ex p. Sweeney [1999] C.O.D. 122,
CA [1999] C.O.D. 97, QBD
R. v. Chief Constable of the Royal Ulster Constabulary Ex p. McKenna [1992] N.I. 116,
QBD (NI) . . . .   *Disapproved*, 00/5472
R. v. Chief Constable of the West Midlands Ex p. Wiley; R. v. Chief Constable of
Nottinghamshire Ex p. Sunderland [1995] 1 A.C. 274; [1994] 3 W.L.R. 433;
[1994] 3 All E.R. 420; [1995] 1 Cr. App. R. 342; [1994] C.O.D. 520; (1994)
91(40) L.S.G. 35; (1994) 144 N.L.J. 1008; (1994) 138 S.J.L.B. 156; *Times*, July
15, 1994; *Independent*, July 15, 1994, HL; reversing [1994] 1 W.L.R. 114;
[1994] 1 All E.R. 702; [1994] P.I.Q.R. P23; [1993] C.O.D. 431; (1993) 143 N.L.J.
1403; *Times*, September 30, 1993; *Independent*, October 8, 1993, CA; affirming
(1993) 5 Admin. L.R. 507; (1993) 157 L.G. Rev. 587; (1993) 137 S.J.L.B. 38,
QBD . . . .   *Digested*, 96/**876**:
                     Applied, 00/5464: *Considered*, 95/4123, 95/4124
R. v. Chief Constable of Warwickshire Ex p. F [1999] 1 W.L.R. 564; [1998] 1 All E.R.
65; [1998] Crim. L.R. 290; *Times*, November 26, 1997; *Independent*, October 13,
1997 (C.S.), QBD . . . .   *Digested*, 99/**901**
R. v. Chief Constables of C and D Ex p. A see R. (on the application of A) v. Chief
Constable of C
R. v. Chief Immigration Officer Ex p. Mapere see R. v. Secretary of State for the Home
Department Ex p. Mapere
R. v. Chief Immigration Officer Ex p. Quaquah; *sub nom* R. v. Secretary of State for the
Home Department Ex p. Quaquah [2000] H.R.L.R. 325; [2000] U.K.H.R.R.
375; [2000] I.N.L.R. 196; (2000) 97(3) L.S.G. 36; (2000) 144 S.J.L.B. 36;
Times, January 21, 2000 ; *Independent*, February 14, 2000 (C.S.), QBD . . . .   *Digested*, 00/**3290**
R. v. Chief National Insurance Commissioner Ex p. Connor [1981] Q.B. 758; [1981] 2
W.L.R. 412; [1981] 1 All E.R. 769; [1980] Crim. L.R. 579; 124 S.J. 478, QBD . . .   *Digested*, 81/**2619**:
                Applied, 90/96, 91/2484: *Considered*, 95/2327, 96/2852, 01/4702:
                     Followed, 80/55
R. v. Chief Probation Officer for the West Midlands Ex p. Ludhera [1999] C.O.D. 101,
QBD
R. v. Chief Rabbi of the United Hebrew Congregations of Great Britain and the
Commonwealth Ex p. Wachmann; *sub nom* R. v. Jacobovits Ex p. Wachmann
[1992] 1 W.L.R. 1036; [1993] 2 All E.R. 249; (1991) 3 Admin. L.R. 721; [1991]
C.O.D. 309; *Times*, February 7, 1991, QBD . . . .   *Digested*, 92/**12**:
            Applied, 92/38: *Considered*, 93/28, 95/47: *Followed*, 98/101
R. (on the application of Wirral MBC) v. Chief Schools Adjudicator [2001] E.L.R. 574,
QBD (Admin Ct) . . . .   *Digested*, 01/**1971**
R. v. Child Support Agency Ex p. Gibbons CO/3894/96, QBD . . . .   *Digested*, 99/**4532**

R. (on the application of National Association of Guardians ad Litem and Reporting Officers) *v.* Children and Family Court Advisory and Support Service [2001] EWHC Admin 693; [2001] Fam. Law 877, QBD (Admin Ct)

R. *v.* Chippendale (Martin Christopher) [1998] 1 Cr. App. R. (S.) 192, CA (Crim Div) . . . *Digested,* 98/**1174**

R. *v.* Chisholm (John); R. *v.* Flynn (Michael Patrick); R. *v.* Waters (Carl); R. *v.* Kilty (Stephen); R. *v.* Wright (Frederick Martin); R. *v.* Tobin (Alan) [1999] 2 Cr. App. R. (S.) 443, CA (Crim Div). . . . . *Digested,* 00/**1206**

R. *v.* Chong (Kwai Man) see R. *v.* SBC (A Juvenile)

R. *v.* Choudhury (Mifta) see R. *v.* Janjua (Nadeem Ahmed)

R. *v.* Choudhury (Zaheer Akbar) [1997] 2 Cr. App. R. (S.) 300, CA (Crim Div) . . . . *Digested,* 98/**1396**

R. *v.* Chowdury (Aminur Rahman) [1999] 2 Cr. App. R. (S.) 269, CA (Crim Div) . . . . . . *Digested,* 99/**1312**

R. *v.* Chuni (Narinder) [2000] 2 Cr. App. R. (S.) 64, CA (Crim Div). . . . . *Digested,* 00/**1191**

R. *v.* Church (John) see R. *v.* Wijs (Eric Jan)

R. *v.* Citrone (Carlo); R. *v.* Citrone (John) [1999] S.T.C. 29; [1999] B.T.C. 5050; [1999] B.V.C. 49; [1999] Crim. L.R. 327, CA (Crim Div) . . . . *Digested,* 99/**5018**

R. *v.* Citrone (John) see R. *v.* Citrone (Carlo)

R. *v.* City of Bath College Corp Ex p. Bashforth [1999] E.L.R. 459, QBD. . . . . *Digested,* 00/**1810**

R. *v.* City of London Justices Ex p. Chapman (1998) 162 J.P. 359; (1998) 95(16) L.S.G. 23; (1998) 142 S.J.L.B. 123; *Times,* March 17, 1998; *Independent,* March 16, 1998 (C.S.), QBD . . . . *Digested,* 98/**1151**

R. *v.* City of London Magistrates Court Ex p. Green; *sub nom* Green *v.* Staples [1997] 3 All E.R. 551; [1998] I.T.C.L.R. 42; [1998] Crim. L.R. 54; *Times,* March 13, 1997, QBD. . . . . *Digested,* 97/**1379**

R. (on the application of Jet Services Ltd) *v.* Civil Aviation Authority; *sub nom* R. *v.* Civil Aviation Authority Ex p. Jet Services Ltd; Civil Aviation Authority *v.* Jet Services Ltd [2001] EWCA Civ 610; [2001] 2 All E.R. (Comm) 769; (2001) 98(24) L.S.G. 44; (2001) 145 S.J.L.B. 127; *Independent,* May 10, 2001, CA; affirming CO/1905/00, QBD (Admin Ct). . . . . *Digested,* 01/**5403**

R. *v.* Clarence (Charles James) (1889) L.R. 22 Q.B.D. 23, Crown Cases Reserved . . . . *Applied,* 54/**786**: *Considered,* 94/1147, 95/1290: *Distinguished,* 00/1003: *Followed,* 83/685

R. *v.* Clark (Andrew Lee) [2001] 1 Cr. App. R. (S.) 57, CA (Crim Div) . . . . *Digested,* 01/**1218**

R. *v.* Clark (Brian James Hemmings) [2001] EWCA Crim 884; [2001] Crim. L.R. 572, CA (Crim Div)

R. *v.* Clark (Christopher David) (1992) 13 Cr. App. R. (S.) 124; [1991] Crim. L.R. 724, CA (Crim Div). . . . . *Digested,* 93/**1066**: *Considered,* 99/1102, 99/1103

R. *v.* Clark (Henry George) see Attorney General's Reference (Nos.73 and 74 of 1998), Re

R. *v.* Clark (Jeremy Patrick), *Times,* December 19, 2000, CA (Crim Div) . . . . *Digested,* 01/**1342**

R. *v.* Clark (Joan), *Times,* January 27, 1999, CA (Crim Div) . . . . *Digested,* 99/**1153**

R. *v.* Clark (Michael) [1999] Crim. L.R. 573, CA (Crim Div)

R. *v.* Clark (Raymond Dennis) [1996] 2 Cr. App. R. 282; [1996] 2 Cr. App. R. (S.) 351; [1996] Crim. L.R. 448; *Times,* April 10, 1996, CA (Crim Div) . . . . *Digested,* 96/**1944**: *Applied,* 98/1123, 98/1387: *Approved,* 97/1492: *Considered,* 99/1351: *Disapproved,* 97/1103: *Distinguished,* 97/1493: *Followed,* 99/1352

R. *v.* Clark (Robert) see R. *v.* Drury (Christopher)

R. *v.* Clark (Simon Jeffrey) (1995) 16 Cr. App. R. (S.) 546, CA (Crim Div). . . . . *Considered,* 98/**1132**, 99/1214

R. *v.* Clark (Trevor) [1998] 2 Cr. App. R. 137; [1998] 2 Cr. App. R. (S.) 95; [1998] Crim. L.R. 227; (1998) 95(2) L.S.G. 22; (1998) 142 S.J.L.B. 27; *Times,* December 4, 1997, CA (Crim Div) . . . . *Digested,* 98/**1392**: *Applied,* 00/1237, 01/1491: *Considered,* 98/1316, 98/1394, 99/1121, 99/1174, 99/1277, 99/1359, 99/1362, 99/1364, 00/1436

R. *v.* Clark Ex p. JD, *Times,* May 26, 2000, QBD . . . . *Digested,* 00/**1922**

R. *v.* Clarke (Anthony John); R. *v.* Purvis (James) (1992) 13 Cr. App. R. (S.) 552; *Times,* February 3, 1992, CA (Crim Div) . . . . *Digested,* 93/**1223**: *Cited,* 95/1358, 95/1371: *Considered,* 99/1146, 00/1213

R. *v.* Clarke (Christopher) [2000] 1 Cr. App. R. (S.) 224, CA (Crim Div) . . . . *Digested,* 00/**1138**

R. *v.* Clarke (Jonathan) [1999] 2 Cr. App. R. (S.) 400, CA (Crim Div) . . . . *Digested,* 00/**1270**

R. *v.* Clarke (Malcolm David) [1997] 2 Cr. App. R. (S.) 53, CA (Crim Div) . . . . *Digested,* 97/**1451**: *Considered,* 01/1371

R. *v.* Clarke (Michael Carson) see R. *v.* Rose (Newton Samuel)

R. *v.* Clarke (Nicholas Henry) see R. *v.* Preston (Stephen)

R. *v.* Clarke (Simon) (1992) 13 Cr. App. R. (S.) 640, CA (Crim Div) . . . . *Digested,* 93/**1011**: *Considered,* 96/1902: *Distinguished,* 00/1388

R. *v.* Clarke (Terence) [1997] 1 Cr. App. R. (S.) 323; *Times,* November 4, 1996, CA (Crim Div). . . . . *Digested,* 96/**1891**: *Considered,* 98/1219, 99/1161

R. *v.* Clarke (Vincent) see Attorney General's Reference (Nos.19 and 20 of 1990), Re

R. *v.* Clarkson (Lee Martin) see R. *v.* Williams (David Omar)

R. *v.* Clarkson (Michael) (1990) 12 Cr. App. R. (S.) 119, CA (Crim Div) . . . . *Considered,* 98/**1379**: *Referred to,* 97/1704, 99/1248

R. *v.* Clearbrook Group Plc; *sub nom* R. *v.* Havering LBC [2001] EWCA Crim 1654; [2001] 4 P.L.R. 78, CA (Crim Div)

R. *v.* Clegg (Lee William) (Double Jeopardy) [2000] N.I. 305, CA (Crim Div) (NI) . . . . . *Digested,* 00/**5485**
R. *v.* Clement (Ceri Carter) [2000] 2 Cr. App. R. (S.) 153, CA (Crim Div) . . . . *Digested,* 00/**1430**
R. *v.* Clerk to Bradford Justices Ex p. Sykes see R. *v.* Bradford Justices Ex p. Sykes
R. *v.* Clerk to Liverpool Justices Ex p. Larkin see R. (on the application of McCormick)
  v. Liverpool City Magistrates Court
R. *v.* Clerk to Liverpool Magistrates Court Ex p. Larkin see R. (on the application of
  McCormick) *v.* Liverpool City Magistrates Court
R. *v.* Clerk to Liverpool Magistrates Court Ex p. McCormick see R. (on the application
  of McCormick) *v.* Liverpool City Magistrates Court
R. *v.* Clerkenwell Justices Ex p. Hooper see R. *v.* Clerkenwell Metropolitan Stipendiary
  Magistrate Ex p. Hooper
R. *v.* Clerkenwell Metropolitan Stipendiary Magistrate Ex p. Hooper; *sub nom* R. *v.*
  Clerkenwell Justices Ex p. Hooper [1998] 1 W.L.R. 800; [1998] 4 All E.R. 193;
  [1999] 1 Cr. App. R. 345; (1998) 162 J.P. 215; (1998) 162 J.P.N. 243; (1998)
  142 S.J.L.B. 62; *Times,* January 28, 1998; *Independent,* February 16, 1998 (C.S.),
  QBD . . . . *Digested,* 98/**1002**
R. *v.* Cleveland Police Authority Ex p. Rodger CO/1870/97, QBD . . . . *Digested,* 98/**4283**
R. *v.* Clews (Stuart Dean) (1987) 9 Cr. App. R. (S.) 194; [1987] Crim. L.R. 586, CA
  (Crim Div) . . . . *Digested,* 89/**1063**:
                                                                                    Considered, 98/1271
R. *v.* Clift (Sean Kenneth) (1995) 16 Cr. App. R. (S.) 1022, CA (Crim Div) . . . . *Digested,* 96/**1725**:
                                                                        Considered, 98/1306, 00/1369
R. *v.* Clinton (Dean) [1993] 1 W.L.R. 1181; [1993] 2 All E.R. 998; (1993) 97 Cr. App.
  R. 320; (1993) 143 N.L.J. 471; *Times,* March 11, 1993; *Independent,* March 18,
  1993, CA (Crim Div) . . . . *Digested,* 93/**751**:
          Applied, 97/1223: *Considered,* 99/978: *Referred to,* 95/884, 95/1211
R. *v.* Clinton (James Patrick) [2001] N.I. 207, CA (Crim Div) (NI) . . . . *Digested,* 01/**5728**
R. *v.* Close (Craig) [2001] EWCA Crim 1066; [2001] Crim. L.R. 586, CA (Crim Div)
R. *v.* Cloud (Luke John) [2001] EWCA Crim 510; [2001] 2 Cr. App. R. (S.) 97, CA
  (Crim Div) . . . . *Digested,* 01/**1328**
R. *v.* Clowes (Peter) (No.1) [1992] 3 All E.R. 440; [1992] B.C.L.C. 1158; (1992) 95 Cr.
  App. R. 440, CCC . . . . *Digested,* 92/**819**:
          Approved, 99/873: *Considered,* 93/3207, 95/1264: *Distinguished,* 97/1143
R. *v.* Cobb (Kevin Nash) [2001] EWCA Crim 1228; [2001] Crim. L.R. 924, CA (Crim
  Div)
R. *v.* Cobbey (Andrew Stuart) (1993) 14 Cr. App. R. (S.) 82, CA (Crim Div) . . . . *Digested,* 93/**1159**:
                                                                            Distinguished, 98/1231
R. *v.* Cobham Hall School Ex p. G [1998] Ed. C.R. 79; [1998] E.L.R. 389; *Times,*
  December 13, 1997, QBD . . . . *Digested,* 98/**1870**
R. *v.* Cochrane [1993] Crim. L.R. 48, CA (Crim Div) . . . . *Digested,* 93/**633**:
                                                                            Distinguished, 00/996
R. *v.* Cochrane (Robert Brian) (1994) 15 Cr. App. R. (S.) 708; [1994] Crim. L.R. 382,
  CA (Crim Div) . . . . *Digested,* 95/**1425**:
                                            Applied, 99/1027: *Considered,* 97/1428, 01/1269
R. *v.* Cockeram (Kevin James) [1999] 2 Cr. App. R. (S.) 120, CA (Crim Div) . . . . *Digested,* 99/**1154**
R. *v.* Cockley (Wayne Edward) (1984) 79 Cr. App. R. 181; (1984) 148 J.P. 666; [1984]
  Crim. L.R. 429; (1984) 148 J.P.N. 667; (1984) 81 L.S.G. 1437, CA (Crim Div) . . *Digested,* 85/**492**:
                                                                            Considered, 99/969
R. *v.* Coid (Douglas Ian) [1998] Crim. L.R. 199, CA (Crim Div)
R. *v.* Colchester Justices Ex p. Abbott see R. (on the application of Abbott) *v.*
  Colchester Magistrates Court
R. (on the application of Abbott) *v.* Colchester Magistrates Court; *sub nom* R. *v.*
  Colchester Justices Ex p. Abbott [2001] EWHC Admin 136; (2001) 165 J.P.
  386; [2001] Crim. L.R. 564; (2001) 165 J.P.N. 869; (2001) 98(15) L.S.G. 32;
  Times, March 13, 2001; *Independent,* April 2, 2001 (C.S), QBD (Admin Ct) . . . . *Digested,* 01/**1168**
R. *v.* Cole (Andrew Stanley), *Independent,* April 30, 1998, CA (Crim Div) . . . . *Digested,* 98/**1011**:
                                              Considered, 00/1163, 00/1170: *Referred to,* 00/1171
R. *v.* Cole (John) see Attorney General's Reference (No.13 of 2001), Re
R. *v.* Cole (Philip Francis); R. *v.* Lees (Francis Gerard); R. *v.* Birch (David Brian) [1998]
  B.C.C. 87; [1998] 2 B.C.L.C. 234; (1997) 94(28) L.S.G. 25; (1997) 141 S.J.L.B.
  160; *Times,* July 17, 1997, CA (Crim Div) . . . . *Digested,* 97/**3043**:
                                                                            Considered, 01/717
R. *v.* Coleman (Anthony Neville) (1992) 95 Cr. App. R. 159; (1992) 13 Cr. App. R. (S.)
  508; [1992] Crim. L.R. 315; *Times,* December 10, 1991, CA (Crim Div) . . . . *Digested,* 93/**1224**:
          Cited, 01/1427: *Considered,* 97/1554, 99/1261, 00/1362: *Referred to,* 94/1306,
                                                                            95/1434, 97/1620
R. *v.* Coles (Barrie) [1997] 2 Cr. App. R. (S.) 95, CA (Crim Div) . . . . *Digested,* 97/**1559**:
                                                    Considered, 01/1336: *Distinguished,* 00/1265
R. *v.* Coles (Stuart) [1999] 1 Cr. App. R. (S.) 372, CA (Crim Div) . . . . *Digested,* 99/**1197**
R. *v.* Collier (Dean Russell) (1992) 13 Cr. App. R. (S.) 33, CA (Crim Div) . . . . *Digested,* 92/**1378**:
                                                            Considered, 99/1309: *Referred to,* 96/2043
R. *v.* Collin (Peter John) see R. *v.* Kaul (Natasha)
R. *v.* Collins [1987] 1 S.C.R. 265, Sup Ct (Can) . . . . *Applied,* 99/3139

R. *v.* Collins (Daniel) (1995) 16 Cr. App. R. (S.) 156; [1994] Crim. L.R. 872, CA (Crim Div) . . . . *Digested*, 96/**1963**:
Followed, 99/1219: *Overruled*, 00/1345

R. *v.* Collins (Jason Albert) see R. *v.* Blight (Tony)

R. *v.* Collins (Lezlie) [1997] 2 Cr. App. R. (S.) 302; [1997] R.T.R. 439; [1997] Crim. L.R. 578, CA (Crim Div) . . . . *Digested*, 98/**1365**

R. *v.* Collins (Terrence Francis) [2001] EWCA Crim 586; [2001] 2 Cr. App. R. (S.) 96, CA (Crim Div) . . . . *Digested*, 01/**1473**

R. *v.* Collins Ex p. Brady [2000] Lloyd's Rep. Med. 355; (2001) 58 B.M.L.R. 173, QBD . *Digested*, 00/**4172**:
Considered, 01/4431

R. *v.* Collins Ex p. MS see S (Application for Judicial Review), Re

R. *v.* Collins Ex p. S see S (Application for Judicial Review), Re

R. *v.* Collins Ex p. S (No.1) see St George's Healthcare NHS Trust *v.* S

R. *v.* Collins Ex p. S (No.2) see St George's Healthcare NHS Trust *v.* S (Guidelines)

R. *v.* Collis (George Edward) (Unreported, January 18, 1996), CA (Crim Div) . . . . *Considered*, 98/1207

R. *v.* Comerford (Thomas Anthony) [1998] 1 W.L.R. 191; [1998] 1 All E.R. 823; [1998] 1 Cr. App. R. 235; [1998] Crim. L.R. 285; (1997) 94(45) L.S.G. 28; (1997) 141 S.J.L.B. 251; *Times*, November 3, 1997; *Independent*, October 31, 1997, CA (Crim Div) . . . . *Digested*, 97/**1332**

R. *v.* Commissioner Cripps QC Ex p. Muldoon see R. *v.* Cripps Ex p. Muldoon

R. (on the application of Leach) *v.* Commissioner for Local Administration see Leach, Re

R. (on the application of Turpin) *v.* Commissioner for Local Administration [2001] EWHC Admin 503; [2001] A.C.D. 90, QBD (Admin Ct)

R. *v.* Commissioner for Local Administration Ex p. Croydon LBC [1989] 1 All E.R. 1033; 87 L.G.R. 221; [1989] C.O.D. 226; (1989) 153 L.G. Rev. 131; *Times*, June 9, 1988; *Independent*, June 9, 1988; *Guardian*, June 17, 1988, QBD . . . . *Digested*, 89/**2328**:
Applied, 94/1866, 95/1911: *Considered*, 92/1858, 97/2108, 98/1915, 00/1921: *Referred to*, 90/42, 92/1852

R. *v.* Commissioner for Local Administration Ex p. Field [2000] C.O.D. 58, QBD

R. *v.* Commissioner for Local Administration Ex p. H (A Minor) [1999] E.L.R. 314, CA; affirming (1999) 1 L.G.L.R. 932; [1999] C.O.D. 382; (1999) 96(5) L.S.G. 37; (1999) 143 S.J.L.B. 39; *Times*, January 8, 1999; *Independent*, January 11, 1999 (C.S.), QBD . . . . *Digested*, 99/**96**

R. *v.* Commissioner for Local Administration Ex p. S; *sub nom* R. *v.* Commissioner for Local Government Ex p. S (1999) 1 L.G.L.R. 633; [2000] Ed. C.R. 123; [1999] E.L.R. 102; [1999] C.O.D. 126, QBD . . . . *Digested*, 99/**1888**

R. *v.* Commissioner for Local Administration Ex p. Turpin see R. *v.* Local Government Ombudsman Ex p. Turpin (Application for Judicial Review)

R. *v.* Commissioner for Local Government Ex p. S see R. *v.* Commissioner for Local Administration Ex p. S

R. (on the application of La Rose) *v.* Commissioner of Police of the Metropolis see R. (on the application of M (A Child)) *v.* Commissioner of Police of the Metropolis

R. (on the application of M (A Child)) *v.* Commissioner of Police of the Metropolis; R. (on the application of La Rose) *v.* Commissioner of Police of the Metropolis [2001] EWHC Admin 553; [2001] A.C.D. 91; (2001) 98(34) L.S.G. 40; (2001) 151 N.L.J. 1213; (2001) 145 S.J.L.B. 215; *Times*, August 17, 2001, QBD (Admin Ct) . . . . *Digested*, 01/**3534**

R. (on the application of Rottman) *v.* Commissioner of Police of the Metropolis TNS, HL; reversing [2001] EWHC Admin 576; *Times*, October 26, 2001, QBD (Admin Ct) . . . . *Digested*, 01/**1069**

R. *v.* Commissioner of Police of the Metropolis Ex p. Blackburn (No.1) [1968] 2 Q.B. 118; [1968] 2 W.L.R. 893; [1968] 1 All E.R. 763; (1968) 112 S.J. 112, CA . . . . . . *Digested*, 68/**1703**:
Applied, 73/2580, 90/68: *Considered*, 87/2857, 90/28, 91/15, 92/1028:
Followed, 01/1072

R. *v.* Commissioner of Police of the Metropolis Ex p. Thompson [1997] 1 W.L.R. 1519; [1997] 2 Cr. App. R. 49; [1997] C.O.D. 313, QBD . . . . *Digested*, 97/**1274**:
Considered, 98/1004

R. *v.* Committee of the Judicial Committee of the Privy Council acting for the Visitor of the University of London Ex p. Vijayatunga see R. *v.* HM Queen in Council Ex p. Vijayatunga

R. *v.* Common Professional Examination Board Ex p. Mealing-McCleod, *Times*, May 2, 2000, CA . . . . *Digested*, 00/**437**

R. *v.* Condron (Karen); R. *v.* Condron (William) [1997] 1 W.L.R. 827; [1997] 1 Cr. App. R. 185; (1997) 161 J.P. 1; [1997] Crim. L.R. 215; (1997) 161 J.P.N. 40; *Times*, November 4, 1996, CA (Crim Div) . . . . *Digested*, 96/**1514**:
Followed, 98/1061

R. *v.* Condron (William) see R. *v.* Condron (Karen)

R. *v.* Coney (1881-82) L.R. 8 Q.B.D. 534, QBD . . . . *Applied*, 47-51/283,
63/621, 71/2031, 92/1038, 93/920, 00/28: *Considered*, 54/956, 70/1480, 78/636, 81/362, 94/815

R. *v.* Conlon (Patrick Joseph) (Deceased) see R. *v.* Maguire (Anne Rita)

R. *v.* Connelly (Charles) see Connelly *v.* DPP

R. *v.* Connor (Vincent) (1981) 3 Cr. App. R. (S.) 225; [1981] Crim. L.R. 791, CA (Crim
    Div) . . . . *Digested,* 82/**684.39**:
                       Considered, 00/1180

R. *v.* Cook (Leonard); R. *v.* Williamson (Roger) (1988) 10 Cr. App. R. (S.) 42; [1988]
    Crim. L.R. 329; *Times,* January 27, 1988, CA (Crim Div) . . . . *Digested,* 90/**1344**:
               Cited, 93/1193: *Considered,* 89/1130, 90/1437, 98/1254, 99/1198

R. *v.* Cook (Michael Barry) (1995) 16 Cr. App. R. (S.) 917, CA (Crim Div) . . . . *Considered,* 98/1230:
                       Distinguished, 98/1231

R. *v.* Cook Ex p. DPP [2001] Crim. L.R. 321, QBD

R. *v.* Cooke (Samuel David) see R. *v.* Bingham (Graham Carlo)

R. *v.* Cooks (David) [1998] Crim. L.R. 742, CA (Crim Div)

R. *v.* Coombes (Robert Peter) see R. *v.* Marshall (Adrian John)

R. *v.* Cooney (Nicholas) see R. *v.* El-Hinnachi (Samir)

R. *v.* Cooney (Stephen); R. *v.* Allam (Peter John); R. *v.* Wood (Colin John) [1999] 3 All
    E.R. 173; [1999] 2 Cr. App. R. 428; *Times,* April 17, 1999, CMAC. . . . .   *Digested,* 99/**1112**

R. *v.* Corah (Lisa Mary) see R. *v.* Lockley (Adrian Neil)

R. *v.* Corby Justices Ex p. Mort (1998) 162 J.P. 310; [1998] R.V.R. 283; (1998) 162
    J.P.N. 321; *Times,* March 13, 1998, QBD . . . .   *Digested,* 98/**65**

R. *v.* Corcoran (Terence) [1996] 1 Cr. App. R. (S.) 416, CA (Crim Div). . . . .   *Digested,* 96/**1768**:
                       Considered, 97/1656, 99/1321, 00/1155

R. *v.* Corelli (Ernesto) [2001] EWCA Crim 974; [2001] Crim. L.R. 913, CA (Crim Div)

R. *v.* Cornwall CC Ex p. E [1999] 1 F.L.R. 1055; [1999] 2 F.C.R. 685; [1999] Fam.
    Law 291; (2000) 164 J.P.N. 405, CA . . . .   *Digested,* 99/**2303**

R. *v.* Cornwall CC Ex p. H see R. *v.* Cornwall CC Ex p. LH

R. *v.* Cornwall CC Ex p. Hardy [2001] Env. L.R. 25; [2001] J.P.L. 786, QBD . . . .   *Digested,* 01/**2390**

R. *v.* Cornwall CC Ex p. Huntington; R. *v.* Devon CC Ex p. Isaac [1994] 1 All E.R. 694,
    CA; affirming [1992] 3 All E.R. 566; [1992] C.O.D. 223; (1992) 142 N.L.J. 348;
    Times, March 5, 1992, QBD . . . .   *Digested,* 94/**65**:
                  Applied, 96/4839, 97/4132, 99/4227, 01/4676

R. *v.* Cornwall CC Ex p. L see R. *v.* Cornwall CC Ex p. LH

R. *v.* Cornwall CC Ex p. LH; *sub nom* R. *v.* Cornwall CC Ex p. L; R. *v.* Cornwall CC Ex
    p. H [2000] 1 F.L.R. 236; [2000] 1 F.C.R. 460; [2000] B.L.G.R. 180; (2000) 3
    C.C.L. Rep. 362; [2000] C.O.D. 26; [2000] Fam. Law 89; (1999) 96(45)
    L.S.G. 31; (1999) 143 S.J.L.B. 282; *Times,* November 25, 1999, QBD . . . .   *Digested,* 99/**2339**

R. *v.* Coroner of the Queens Household Ex p. Al-Fayed (Interested Person) (2001) 58
    B.M.L.R. 205, QBD . . . .   *Digested,* 01/**454**

R. *v.* Corrish (Michael) [2001] 1 Cr. App. R. (S.) 126, CA (Crim Div) . . . .   *Digested,* 01/**1302**

R. *v.* Corry (Raymond Ronald) [2000] 1 Cr. App. R. (S.) 47, CA (Crim Div) . . . .   *Digested,* 00/**1247**

R. *v.* Cosgrove (Edward Philip) (1995) 16 Cr. App. R. (S.) 76, CA (Crim Div) . . . .   *Digested,* 96/**1972**:
                       Considered, 98/1403

R. *v.* Cosgrove (Kevin); R. *v.* Morgan (James) [1994] N.I. 182, CA (Crim Div) (NI);
    affirming (Unreported, March 18, 1993), Crown Ct (NI) . . . .   *Digested,* 00/**5471**:
                      Disapproved, 00/5472

R. *v.* Costen (Sharon Elizabeth) (1989) 11 Cr. App. R. (S.) 182; [1989] Crim. L.R. 601,
    CA (Crim Div) . . . .   *Digested,* 91/**1134**:
              Considered, 96/1717, 99/1168, 01/1468: *Referred to,* 92/1293, 93/1048

R. *v.* Costley (Peter John) (1989) 11 Cr. App. R. (S.) 357; [1989] Crim. L.R. 913, CA
    (Crim Div) . . . .   *Digested,* 90/**1307.a**:
                       Considered, 98/1135

R. *v.* Cotswold DC Ex p. Barrington Parish Council (1998) 75 P. & C.R. 515; [1997]
    E.G.C.S. 66; [1997] N.P.C. 70, QBD . . . .   *Digested,* 97/**4103**

R. *v.* Coughlan (Martin) see R. *v.* Byrne (Edward Joseph)

R. *v.* Coulson (Martin) [2001] 1 Cr. App. R. (S.) 121, CA (Crim Div) . . . .   *Digested,* 01/**1286**

R. *v.* Council for Licensed Conveyancers Ex p. Bradford & Bingley Building Society
    [1999] C.O.D. 5, QBD

R. *v.* Council for Licensed Conveyancers Ex p. Watson, *Times,* June 16, 2000, QBD . . . .   *Digested,* 00/**4015**

R. *v.* Council for Licensed Conveyancers Ex p. West [2000] E.G.C.S. 71; (2000)
    97(24) L.S.G. 42, QBD

R. *v.* Court Martial Administration Officer Ex p. Jordan [2000] C.O.D. 106, QBD

R. *v.* Cousin (David Peter) (1994) 15 Cr. App. R. (S.) 516; [1994] Crim. L.R. 300, CA
    (Crim Div) . . . .   *Digested,* 95/**1453**:
                       Distinguished, 98/1336

R. *v.* Coventry Airport Ex p. Phoenix Aviation see R. *v.* Coventry City Council Ex p.
    Phoenix Aviation

R. (on the application of Carton) *v.* Coventry City Council see R. (on the application of
    Morgan) *v.* Coventry City Council

R. (on the application of Larrad) *v.* Coventry City Council see R. (on the application of
    Morgan) *v.* Coventry City Council

R. (on the application of Morgan) *v.* Coventry City Council; R. (on the application of
    Larrad) *v.* Coventry City Council; R. (on the application of Carton) *v.* Coventry
    City Council [2001] A.C.D. 80; *Independent,* January 15, 2001 (C.S), QBD
    (Admin Ct)

R. *v.* Coventry City Council Ex p. Arrowcroft Group Plc [2001] P.L.C.R. 7, QBD . . . . . .   *Digested,* 01/**4738**

R. v. Coventry City Council Ex p. Coventry Heads of Independent Care Establishments
(CHOICE) (1997-98) 1 C.C.L. Rep. 379, QBD . . . . *Digested,* 98/**4580**
R. v. Coventry City Council Ex p. Phoenix Aviation; *sub nom* R. v. Coventry Airport Ex
p. Phoenix Aviation; R. v. Dover Harbour Board Ex p. Peter Gilder & Sons; R. v.
Associated British Ports Ex p. Plymouth City Council [1995] 3 All E.R. 37;
(1995) 7 Admin. L.R. 597; [1995] C.O.D. 300; (1995) 145 N.L.J. 559; *Times,*
April 17, 1995; *Independent,* April 13, 1995, QBD . . . . *Digested,* 95/**148**:
      Considered, 98/1903, 98/4434: *Followed,* 95/9, 96/4865
R. v. Coventry DC Housing Benefit Review Board Ex p. Bodden see R. v. Sheffield
Housing Benefit Review Board Ex p. Smith
R. (on the application of Mitchell) v. Coventry University [2001] EWHC Admin 167;
[2001] E.L.R. 594, QBD (Admin Ct) . . . . *Digested,* 01/**1897**
R. v. Cowan (Donald); R. v. Gayle (Ricky); R. v. Ricciardi (Carmine) [1996] Q.B. 373;
[1995] 3 W.L.R. 818; [1995] 4 All E.R. 939; [1996] 1 Cr. App. R. 1; (1996) 160
J.P. 165; [1996] Crim. L.R. 409; (1996) 160 J.P.N. 14; (1995) 92(38) L.S.G.
26; (1995) 145 N.L.J. 1611; (1995) 139 S.J.L.B. 215; *Times,* October 13, 1995;
Independent, October 25, 1995, CA (Crim Div). . . . . *Digested,* 96/**1511**:
      Applied, 98/1059, 00/1076: *Considered,* 97/1320, 97/4364:
      Followed, 00/1074
R. v. Cowap (Tracey) [2000] 1 Cr. App. R. (S.) 284, CA (Crim Div). . . . . *Digested,* 00/**1222**
R. v. Cowlard (Gary Michael) see R. v. Blight (Tony)
R. v. Cox; R. v. Railton (1884-85) L.R. 14 Q.B.D. 153; (1881-85) All E.R. Rep. 68,
Crown Cases Reserved . . . . *Applied,* 72/2732:
      Considered, 70/1039, 87/3059, 89/694, 91/781, 91/2859, 01/399:
      Explained, 88/845, 89/898, 90/1175: *Followed,* 80/2138
R. v. Cox (Allan) [2000] 2 Cr. App. R. (S.) 57; [2000] Crim. L.R. 319, CA (Crim Div) . . *Digested,* 00/**1192**
R. v. Cox (David Geoffrey) [1993] 1 W.L.R. 188; [1993] 2 All E.R. 19; (1993) 96 Cr.
App. R. 452; (1993) 14 Cr. App. R. (S.) 479; (1993) 157 J.P. 114; [1993] R.T.R.
185; [1993] Crim. L.R. 152; [1993] C.O.D. 382; (1993) 157 J.P.N. 92, CA (Crim
Div) . . . . *Digested,* 93/**1103**:
      Considered, 94/1318: *Referred to,* 94/1418, 98/1168
R. v. Cox (Francis Gerard); R. v. Thomas (Matthew) [1999] 2 Cr. App. R. 6; *Times,*
February 4, 1999, CA (Crim Div) . . . . *Digested,* 99/**991**
R. v. Cox (Paul Andrew) [1998] Crim. L.R. 810, CA (Crim Div)
R. v. Cox (Peter Stanley) [1968] 1 W.L.R. 88; [1968] 1 All E.R. 410; (1968) 52 Cr.
App. R. 106; 132 J.P. 162; (1967) 111 S.J. 966, CA (Crim Div) . . . . *Digested,* 68/**652**:
      Applied, 69/1453: *Considered,* 00/952
R. v. Cox (Shaun Carl) 96/7674/X3, CA (Crim Div) . . . . *Digested,* 97/**1509**:
      Considered, 98/1188
R. v. Coyne (David); R. v. Philpot (Julia Lesley); R. v. Ryan (Christopher Kersley);
(Unreported, December 19, 1997), CA (Crim Div) . . . . *Considered,* 98/1207
R. v. Cozens (Alan William) [1996] 2 Cr. App. R. (S.) 321; [1996] Crim. L.R. 522, CA
(Crim Div). . . . . *Digested,* 97/**1475**:
      Referred to, 00/1148
R. v. Cranfield University Senate Ex p. Bashir [1999] Ed. C.R. 772; [1999] E.L.R. 317,
CA . . . . *Digested,* 99/**1934**
R. v. Craven (Adrian) see R. v. Meredith (Christopher)
R. v. Craven (Stephen) [2001] 2 Cr. App. R. 12; [2001] Crim. L.R. 464; (2001) 98(15)
L.S.G. 32; (2001) 145 S.J.L.B. 76; *Times,* February 2, 2001, CA (Crim Div) . . . . *Digested,* 01/**1097**
R. v. Crawford (Charisse) [1997] 1 W.L.R. 1329; [1998] 1 Cr. App. R. 338; (1997) 161
J.P. 681; [1997] Crim. L.R. 749; (1997) 161 J.P.N. 899; (1997) 94(30) L.S.G. 27;
(1997) 141 S.J.L.B. 129; *Times,* June 10, 1997, CA (Crim Div) . . . . *Digested,* 97/**1099**
R. v. Crawford (John Joseph) [2001] 1 Cr. App. R. (S.) 35, CA (Crim Div) . . . . *Digested,* 01/**1301**
R. (on the application of Davies) v. Crawley BC [2001] EWHC Admin 854; [2001] 46
E.G.C.S. 178; (2001) 98(44) L.S.G. 37, QBD (Admin Ct)
R. v. Cridge (Rodger Paul) [2000] 2 Cr. App. R. (S.) 477; [2000] Crim. L.R. 603, CA
(Crim Div). . . . . *Digested,* 01/**1245**
R. (on the application of Hunt) v. Criminal Cases Review Commission; *sub nom* R. v.
Criminal Cases Review Commission Ex p. Hunt [2001] Q.B. 1108; [2001] 2
W.L.R. 319; [2000] S.T.C. 1110; [2001] 2 Cr. App. R. 6; 73 T.C. 406; [2001]
Crim. L.R. 324; [2000] S.T.I. 1608; *Times,* November 24, 2000, QBD (Admin
Ct) . . . . *Digested,* 00/**1098**
R. v. Criminal Cases Review Commission Ex p. Pearson [1999] 3 All E.R. 498; [2000]
1 Cr. App. R. 141; [1999] Crim. L.R. 732; [1999] C.O.D. 202, QBD . . . . *Digested,* 99/**976**:
      Applied, 01/1154: *Considered,* 01/1113
R. (on the application of A (A Child)) v. Criminal Injuries Compensation Appeals Panel;
sub nom R. v. Criminal Injuries Compensation Appeals Panel Ex p. A (A Child);
R. v. Criminal Injuries Compensation Appeals Panel Ex p. B (A Child); R. (on the
application of B (A Child)) v. Criminal Injuries Compensation Appeals Panel
[2001] Q.B. 774; [2001] 2 W.L.R. 1452; [2001] 2 All E.R. 874; *Times,* January 4,
2001, CA; affirming CO/456/99, QBD . . . . *Digested,* 01/**1022**:
      Previous proceedings, 00/28

R. (on the application of B (A Child)) v. Criminal Injuries Compensation Appeals Panel
see R. (on the application of A (A Child)) v. Criminal Injuries Compensation
Appeals Panel

R. v. Criminal Injuries Compensation Appeals Panel Ex p. B (2000) 97(30) L.S.G. 39;
Times, August 1, 2000, QBD . . . .　　　Digested, 00/**28**:
　　　　　　　　　　　　　　　　　　　　　　　　　　Subsequent proceedings, 01/1022

R. v. Criminal Injuries Compensation Appeals Panel Ex p. B (A Child) see R. (on the
application of A (A Child)) v. Criminal Injuries Compensation Appeals Panel

R. v. Criminal Injuries Compensation Appeals Panel Ex p. Bennett; sub nom R. v.
Criminal Injuries Compensation Authority Ex p. Bennet Independent, October 2,
2000 (C.S), QBD

R. v. Criminal Injuries Compensation Appeals Panel Ex p. Embling; sub nom R. v.
Criminal Injuries Compensation Authority Ex p. Embling [2000] P.I.Q.R. Q361;
Times, August 15, 2000, QBD . . . .　　　Digested, 00/**29**

R. v. Criminal Injuries Compensation Authority Ex p. Bennet see R. v. Criminal Injuries
Compensation Appeals Panel Ex p. Bennett

R. v. Criminal Injuries Compensation Authority Ex p. Embling see R. v. Criminal Injuries
Compensation Appeals Panel Ex p. Embling

R. v. Criminal Injuries Compensation Authority Ex p. Leatherland; R. v. Criminal Injuries
Compensation Board Ex p. Bramall; R. v. Criminal Injuries Compensation Panel
Ex p. Kay [2001] A.C.D. 13; Times, October 12, 2000, QBD . . . .　　　Digested, 00/**30**

R. (on the application of Mair) v. Criminal Injuries Compensation Board [2001] EWHC
Admin 412; Independent, July 16, 2001 (C.S), QBD (Admin Ct) . . . .　　　Digested, 01/**97**

R. (on the application of T) v. Criminal Injuries Compensation Board; sub nom R. v.
Criminal Injuries Compensation Board Ex p. T [2001] P.I.Q.R. Q2, QBD (Admin
Ct) . . . .　　　Digested, 01/**1023**

R. v. Criminal Injuries Compensation Board Ex p. A [1999] 2 A.C. 330; [1999] 2
W.L.R. 974; [1999] C.O.D. 244; (1999) 96(17) L.S.G. 25; (1999) 149 N.L.J.
522; (1999) 143 S.J.L.B. 120; Times, March 26, 1999; Independent, April 15,
1999, HL; reversing [1998] Q.B. 659; [1997] 3 W.L.R. 776; [1997] 3 All E.R.
745; [1997] C.O.D. 465; (1997) 94(24) L.S.G. 33; (1997) 141 S.J.L.B. 123;
Times, June 6, 1997; Independent, June 11, 1997, CA; affirming [1996] P.I.Q.R.
P403; [1996] C.O.D. 246, QBD . . . .　　　Digested, 99/**918**:
　　　　　　　　　　　　　　　　　　　　　　　　　　Applied, 98/860, 98/4210

R. v. Criminal Injuries Compensation Board Ex p. Bramall see R. v. Criminal Injuries
Compensation Authority Ex p. Leatherland

R. v. Criminal Injuries Compensation Board Ex p. Cowan CO/1389/97, QBD . . . .　　　Digested, 98/**928**

R. v. Criminal Injuries Compensation Board Ex p. K; R. v. Criminal Injuries
Compensation Board Ex p. M [1998] 1 W.L.R. 1458; [1998] P.I.Q.R. Q98;
[1998] C.O.D. 332; [1998] C.O.D. 417, QBD . . . .　　　Digested, 98/**930**

R. v. Criminal Injuries Compensation Board Ex p. K (Children) [1999] Q.B. 1131;
[1999] 2 W.L.R. 948; [1998] 2 F.L.R. 1071; [2000] P.I.Q.R. Q32; [1998] Fam.
Law 728; (1998) 95(35) L.S.G. 35; Times, August 25, 1998, QBD. . . . .　　　Digested, 98/**931**

R. v. Criminal Injuries Compensation Board Ex p. Keane see R. v. Criminal Injuries
Compensation Board Ex p. M (A Minor)

R. v. Criminal Injuries Compensation Board Ex p. Lain [1967] 2 Q.B. 864; [1967] 3
W.L.R. 348; [1967] 2 All E.R. 770; 111 S.J. 331, QBD. . . . .　　　Digested, 67/**724**:
　　Applied, 83/15, 84/21, 85/12, 87/21: Considered, 75/538, 83/2943, 91/43,
　　　　　　　93/31, 93/33, 98/932: Distinguished, 87/672: Followed, 76/425

R. v. Criminal Injuries Compensation Board Ex p. M see R. v. Criminal Injuries
Compensation Board Ex p. K

R. v. Criminal Injuries Compensation Board Ex p. M (A Minor); R. v. Criminal Injuries
Compensation Board Ex p. Keane [2000] R.T.R. 21; [1999] P.I.Q.R. Q195, CA;
affirming [1998] P.I.Q.R. P107; [1998] C.O.D. 128, QBD . . . .　　　Digested, 00/**31**

R. v. Criminal Injuries Compensation Board Ex p. Moore [1999] C.O.D. 241; Times,
May 14, 1999, CA; affirming [1999] 2 All E.R. 90, QBD . . . .　　　Digested, 99/**917**

R. v. Criminal Injuries Compensation Board Ex p. Parsons, Times, November 25, 1982,
CA; affirming Times, May 22, 1982 . . . .　　　Digested, 82/**535**:
　　　　　　　　　　　　　　　　　　　　　　　　　　Considered, 98/930

R. v. Criminal Injuries Compensation Board Ex p. T see R. (on the application of T) v.
Criminal Injuries Compensation Board

R. v. Criminal Injuries Compensation Board Ex p. Thomas (James Edward) [1995]
P.I.Q.R. P99; [1995] C.O.D. 210, QBD . . . .　　　Followed, 99/917

R. v. Criminal Injuries Compensation Board Ex p. Warner; R. v. Criminal Injuries
Compensation Board Ex p. Webb [1987] Q.B. 74; [1986] 3 W.L.R. 251; [1986] 2
All E.R. 478; (1986) 136 N.L.J. 536; (1986) 130 S.J. 468, CA; affirming
[1986] Q.B. 184; [1985] 3 W.L.R. 618; [1985] 2 All E.R. 1069; (1985) 81 Cr.
App. R. 335; (1985) 81 Cr. App. R. 355; (1985) 135 N.L.J. 412; (1985) 129 S.J.
432, QBD . . . .　　　Digested, 86/**535**:
　　　Applied, 01/1022: Considered, 00/28: Followed, 92/5537, 93/5068, 98/927

R. v. Criminal Injuries Compensation Board Ex p. Webb see R. v. Criminal Injuries
Compensation Board Ex p. Warner

R. v. Criminal Injuries Compensation Board Ex p. Williams [2000] P.I.Q.R. Q339, CA;
affirming CO/209/1999, QBD . . . .　　　Digested, 00/**27**

R. v. Criminal Injuries Compensation Panel Ex p. Kay see R. v. Criminal Injuries
    Compensation Authority Ex p. Leatherland
R. v. Crimp (Justin James) (1995) 16 Cr. App. R. (S.) 346, CA (Crim Div) . . . .   *Cited*, 01/**1427**
R. v. Cripps Ex p. Muldoon; *sub nom* R. v. Commissioner Cripps QC Ex p. Muldoon
    [1984] Q.B. 686; [1984] 3 W.L.R. 53; [1984] 2 All E.R. 705; 82 L.G.R. 439,
    CA; affirming [1984] Q.B. 68; [1983] 3 W.L.R. 465; [1983] 3 All E.R. 72, QBD .   *Digested*, 84/**2606**:
                                      Applied, 85/104: *Considered*, 87/3093, 89/2201, 01/4042
R. v. Crocker [2001] 1 Costs L.R. 25, Sup Ct Costs Office . . . .   *Digested*, 01/**1117**
R. v. Croft (Terence George), *Times*, July 6, 2000, CA (Crim Div) . . . .   *Digested*, 00/**1168**
R. v. Cronin-Simpson (June) [2000] 1 Cr. App. R. (S.) 54, CA (Crim Div) . . . .   *Digested*, 00/**1373**
R. v. Crook (Anthony Michael) see Attorney General's Reference (No.2 of 1994), Re
R. v. Crooks (James) [1999] N.I. 226, CA (Crim Div) (NI) . . . .   *Digested*, 00/**5468**
R. v. Crosbie (Derek Sinclair) (1991) 155 J.P. 171; (1991) 155 J.P.N. 27; *Times*, October
    12, 1990, CA (Crim Div). . . . .   *Digested*, 90/**1239**:
                           Cited, 92/1199: *Considered*, 92/1202, 93/1066, 99/1103
R. v. Crothers (Frederick Irvine) [2001] N.I. 55, CA (Crim Div) (NI). . . . .   *Digested*, 01/**5726**
R. v. Crow (William John); R. v. Pennington (Derek) (1995) 16 Cr. App. R. (S.) 409;
    [1994] Crim. L.R. 958, CA (Crim Div) . . . .   *Considered*, 94/1300,
                          96/1698, 96/1905, 98/1248, 99/1335, 00/1284
R. (on the application of Falzarano) v. Crown Prosecution Service see DPP v. Falzarano
R. v. Crown Prosecution Service Ex p. J see R. v. DPP Ex p. J
R. v. Crown Prosecution Service Ex p. Sorani see R. v. Uxbridge Magistrates Court Ex
    p. Adimi
R. v. Crown Prosecution Service Ex p. Spurrier; *sub nom* DPP v. Spurrier (2000) 164
    J.P. 369; [2000] R.T.R. 60; *Times*, August 12, 1999, QBD   *Digested*, 99/**883**
R. (on the application of Tompsett) v. Croydon Crown Court; *sub nom* R. v. Croydon
    Crown Court Ex p. Tompsett (2001) 165 J.P.N. 387, QBD (Admin Ct)
R. v. Croydon Crown Court Ex p. Britton (2000) 164 J.P. 729; *Times*, October 10,
    2000, QBD . . . .   *Digested*, 00/**1103**
R. v. Croydon Crown Court Ex p. Tompsett see R. (on the application of Tompsett) v.
    Croydon Crown Court
R. (on the application of WH Smith Ltd) v. Croydon Justices see R. v. Croydon Justices
    Ex p. WH Smith Ltd
R. v. Croydon Justices Ex p. Dean [1993] Q.B. 769; [1993] 3 W.L.R. 198; [1993] 3 All
    E.R. 129; (1994) 98 Cr. App. R. 76; (1993) 157 J.P. 975; [1993] Crim. L.R.
    759; [1993] C.O.D. 290; (1993) 157 J.P.N. 457; (1993) 143 N.L.J. 508; *Times*,
    March 15, 1993; *Independent*, March 9, 1993; *Guardian*, March 5, 1993, QBD . . .   *Digested*, 94/**663**:
                          Applied, 97/1255: *Considered*, 96/1655, 98/1079
R. v. Croydon Justices Ex p. WH Smith Ltd; *sub nom* R. (on the application of WH
    Smith Ltd) v. Croydon Justices [2001] E.H.L.R. 12; (2000) 97(46) L.S.G. 39;
    Times, November 22, 2000, QBD. . . . .   *Digested*, 00/**100**
R. v. Croydon LBC Ex p. Toth (1988) 20 H.L.R. 576 . . . .   *Digested*, 89/**1883**:
                                             Distinguished, 98/3061
R. (on the application of DPP) v. Croydon Magistrates Court [2001] EWHC Admin 552;
    Independent, October 22, 2001 (C.S), QBD (Admin Ct)
R. v. Croydon Magistrates Court Ex p. Morgan; *sub nom* Morgan v. Croydon LBC
    (1998) 162 J.P. 521; [1998] Crim. L.R. 219; (1998) 162 J.P.N. 585; *Independent*,
    June 30, 1997 (C.S.), QBD . . . .   *Digested*, 97/**1355**
R. (on the application of DPP) v. Croydon Youth Court (2001) 165 J.P. 181; (2001) 165
    J.P.N. 143, QBD (Admin Ct) . . . .   *Digested*, 01/**1160**
R. v. Croydon Youth Court Ex p. C (A Child) see C (A Child), Re
R. v. Croydon Youth Court Ex p. DPP [1997] 2 Cr. App. R. 411; [1997] C.O.D. 419,
    QBD . . . .   *Digested*, 98/**1069**
R. v. Crug Glas School Governors Ex p. D (A Child) see R. v. Head Teacher of Crug
    Glas School Ex p. D (A Child)
R. v. Cruickshank (Gary Edmund); *sub nom* R. v. Cruikshank (Gary Edmund) [2001]
    EWCA Crim 98; [2001] 2 Cr. App. R. (S.) 57; [2001] E.H.L.R. Dig. 7, CA (Crim
    Div) . . . .   *Digested*, 01/**1247**
R. v. Cubitt (Robert Michael) (1989) 11 Cr. App. R. (S.) 380, CA (Crim Div) . . . .   *Considered*, 98/1254,
                                       99/1198: *Distinguished*, 97/1581
R. v. Cuddington (Nigel Mark) (1995) 16 Cr. App. R. (S.) 246; [1994] Crim. L.R. 698,
    CA (Crim Div) . . . .   *Digested*, 95/**1404**:
                  Considered, 94/1393, 96/1941, 99/1299: *Followed*, 99/1087
R. v. Cumber (Frederick) (1989) 11 Cr. App. R. (S.) 470, CA (Crim Div). . . . .   *Digested*, 91/**1179**:
                                            Considered, 98/1325
R. v. Cumbria CC Ex p. Cumbria Professional Care Ltd (2000) 3 C.C.L. Rep. 79, QBD . .   *Digested*, 96/**5527**
R. v. Cunnington (Richard James) [1999] 2 Cr. App. R. (S.) 261, CA (Crim Div) . . . . . .   *Digested*, 99/**1140**
R. v. Curr (Patrick Vincent) [1968] 2 Q.B. 944; [1967] 2 W.L.R. 595; [1967] 1 All E.R.
    478; (1967) 51 Cr. App. R. 113; (1967) 131 J.P. 245; 111 S.J. 152, CA (Crim Div) .   *Digested*, 67/**1656**:
                                             Considered, 00/995
R. v. Currie (James) (1988) 10 Cr. App. R. (S.) 85, CA (Crim Div). . . . .   *Digested*, 90/**1334**:
                         Cited, 93/1192: *Considered*, 97/1586, 98/1264, 00/1300
R. v. Curry (Brian William), *Times*, March 23, 1998, CA (Crim Div) . . . .   *Digested*, 98/**1088**
R. v. Curry (David Francis) [1998] 2 Cr. App. R. (S.) 410, CA (Crim Div) . . . .   *Digested*, 99/**1184**

R. v. Curry (David Paul); R. v. Taylor (Kieron Thomas) [1997] 1 Cr. App. R. (S.) 417; [1997] Crim. L.R. 65, CA (Crim Div) . . . . *Digested, 97/**1703**: Considered, 98/1307*

R. v. Curt (Anthony) see R. v. Eastap (Robert Leslie)

R. v. Curtin (Joseph) [1996] Crim. L.R. 831, CA (Crim Div) . . . . *Followed, 98/1089*

R. v. Curtis (Anthony John) see Attorney General's Reference (Nos.33 and 34 of 2001), Re

R. v. Curtis (David Carwyn) (Unreported, July 31, 1997), CA (Crim Div) . . . . *Considered, 98/1307*

R. v. Cusick (Colin) [2000] 1 Cr. App. R. (S.) 444, CA (Crim Div) . . . . *Digested, 00/**1195***

R. (on the application of Building Societies Ombudsman Co Ltd) v. Customs and Excise Commissioners; *sub nom* R. v. Customs and Excise Commissioners Ex p. Building Societies Ombudsman Co Ltd [2000] S.T.C. 892; [2000] B.T.C. 5384; [2001] B.V.C. 3; [2000] S.T.I. 1516; *Times*, November 8, 2000, CA; reversing [1999] S.T.C. 974; [1999] B.T.C. 5356; [1999] B.V.C. 368; [1999] N.P.C. 90, QBD . . . . *Digested, 00/**5318***

R. (on the application of Greenwich Property Ltd) v. Customs and Excise Commissioners; *sub nom* Greenwich Property Ltd v. Customs and Excise Commissioners [2001] EWHC Admin 230; [2001] S.T.C. 618; [2001] B.T.C. 5158; [2001] S.T.I. 631; [2001] N.P.C. 67, QBD (Admin Ct) . . . . *Digested, 01/**5618***

R. v. Customs and Excise Commissioners Ex p. Allied Domecq Plc see R. v. Customs and Excise Commissioners Ex p. Kay & Co Ltd

R. v. Customs and Excise Commissioners Ex p. Association of Optometrists see R. v. Customs and Excise Commissioners Ex p. Kay & Co Ltd

R. v. Customs and Excise Commissioners Ex p. Bosworth Beverages Ltd, *Times*, April 24, 2000, QBD . . . . *Digested, 00/**4948***

R. v. Customs and Excise Commissioners Ex p. British Sky Broadcasting Group see British Sky Broadcasting Group Plc v. Customs and Excise Commissioners

R. v. Customs and Excise Commissioners Ex p. Building Societies Ombudsman Co Ltd see R. (on the application of Building Societies Ombudsman Co Ltd) v. Customs and Excise Commissioners

R. v. Customs and Excise Commissioners Ex p. City of London Magistrates Court see Customs and Excise Commissioners v. City of London Magistrates Court

R. v. Customs and Excise Commissioners Ex p. Colaingrove Ltd see R. v. Customs and Excise Commissioners Ex p. Kay & Co Ltd

R. v. Customs and Excise Commissioners Ex p. Daily Mail see R. v. HM Treasury Ex p. Daily Mail (C81/87)

R. v. Customs and Excise Commissioners Ex p. Dangol (t/a Great Kathmandu Tandoori); *sub nom* Dangol (t/a Great Kathmandu Tandoori) v. Customs and Excise Commissioners [2000] S.T.C. 107; [2000] B.T.C. 5067; [2000] B.V.C. 76; *Independent*, December 13, 1999 (C.S.), QBD . . . . *Digested, 00/**5358***

R. v. Customs and Excise Commissioners Ex p. EMU Tabac Sarl (C296/95) [1998] Q.B. 791; [1998] 3 W.L.R. 298; [1998] All E.R. (E.C.) 402; [1998] E.C.R. I-1605; [1998] 2 C.M.L.R. 1205; [1998] C.E.C. 558; *Times*, April 9, 1998, ECJ . . . . *Digested, 98/**4643**: Followed, 00/2349*

R. v. Customs and Excise Commissioners Ex p. F&I Services Ltd see F&I Services Ltd v. Customs and Excise Commissioners

R. v. Customs and Excise Commissioners Ex p. Faroe Seafood Co Ltd (C153/94); R. v. Customs and Excise Commissioners Ex p. Smith (t/a Arthur Smith) (C204/94) [1996] All E.R. (E.C.) 606; [1996] E.C.R. I-2465; [1996] 2 C.M.L.R. 821, ECJ (5th Chamber) . . . . *Digested, 96/**5576**: Followed, 00/4953*

R. v. Customs and Excise Commissioners Ex p. Faroe Seafood Co Ltd (No.2) [1998] C.O.D. 296, QBD

R. v. Customs and Excise Commissioners Ex p. Greater Manchester Police Authority [2001] EWCA Civ 213; [2001] S.T.C. 406; [2001] B.T.C. 5111; [2001] B.V.C. 186; [2001] S.T.I. 243; *Times*, March 13, 2001, CA; affirming [2000] S.T.C. 620; [2000] B.T.C. 5219; [2000] B.V.C. 249; [2000] S.T.I. 819; *Times*, June 28, 2000, QBD . . . . *Digested, 01/**5580***

R. v. Customs and Excise Commissioners Ex p. Greenlee Group Plc see R. v. Customs and Excise Commissioners Ex p. Kay & Co Ltd

R. v. Customs and Excise Commissioners Ex p. Kay & Co Ltd; R. v. Customs and Excise Commissioners Ex p. Rayner and Keeler; R. v. Customs and Excise Commissioners Ex p. Allied Domecq Plc; R. v. Customs and Excise Commissioners Ex p. Wardens and Commonality of the Mystery of Mercers of the City of London; R. v. Customs and Excise Commissioners Ex p. Colaingrove Ltd; R. v. Customs and Excise Commissioners Ex p. Greenlee Group Plc; R. v. Customs and Excise Commissioners Ex p. National Provident Institution; R. v. Customs and Excise Commissioners Ex p. Association of Optometrists [1996] S.T.C. 1500; [1997] B.T.C. 5010; [1997] B.V.C. 128; *Times*, December 10, 1996; *Independent*, January 13, 1997 (C.S.), QBD . . . . *Digested, 97/**5028**: Followed, 00/5310*

R. v. Customs and Excise Commissioners Ex p. Kilroy Television Co Ltd see Customs and Excise Commissioners v. Kilroy Television Co Ltd

R. *v.* Customs and Excise Commissioners Ex p. Littlewoods Home Shopping Group
Ltd [1998] S.T.C. 445; [1998] 2 C.M.L.R. 44; [1998] B.T.C. 5143; [1998] B.V.C.
161; *Times*, March 3, 1998; *Independent*, March 9, 1998 (C.S.), CA; reversing
[1997] S.T.C. 317; [1997] B.T.C. 5064; [1997] B.V.C. 175; *Independent*, March 17,
1997 (C.S.), QBD. . . . .   *Digested*, 98/**4949**

R. *v.* Customs and Excise Commissioners Ex p. Lunn Poly Ltd [1999] S.T.C. 350;
[1999] 1 C.M.L.R. 1357; [1999] Eu. L.R. 653; (1999) 96(13) L.S.G. 32; (1999)
143 S.J.L.B. 104; *Times*, March 11, 1999, CA; affirming [1998] S.T.C. 649; [1998]
2 C.M.L.R. 560; [1998] Eu. L.R. 438; *Times*, April 8, 1998, QBD . . . .   *Digested*, 99/**4743**:
                                 Applied, 01/5316, 01/5346: *Followed*, 01/118

R. *v.* Customs and Excise Commissioners Ex p. McNicholas Construction Ltd C0/
3406/96, QBD . . . .   *Digested*, 97/**5035**:
                                    Subsequent proceedings, 00/5298

R. *v.* Customs and Excise Commissioners Ex p. Mortimer [1999] 1 W.L.R. 17; [1998] 3
All E.R. 229; [1999] 1 Cr. App. R. 81; (1998) 162 J.P. 663; (1998) 95(17) L.S.G.
31; (1998) 142 S.J.L.B. 130; *Times*, March 12, 1998, QBD . . . .   *Digested*, 98/**4648**

R. *v.* Customs and Excise Commissioners Ex p. National Provident Institution see R. *v.*
Customs and Excise Commissioners Ex p. Kay & Co Ltd

R. *v.* Customs and Excise Commissioners Ex p. Popely; *sub nom* R. *v.* HM Customs
and Excise Ex p. Popely [1999] S.T.C. 1016; [1999] B.T.C. 5395; [1999] B.V.C.
410; [2000] Crim. L.R. 388; (1999) 149 N.L.J. 1516; *Independent*, October 22,
1999, QBD . . . .   *Digested*, 99/**920**

R. *v.* Customs and Excise Commissioners Ex p. Rayner and Keeler see R. *v.* Customs
and Excise Commissioners Ex p. Kay & Co Ltd

R. *v.* Customs and Excise Commissioners Ex p. Service Authority National Crime
Squad see R. *v.* HM Treasury Ex p. Service Authority for the National Crime
Squad

R. *v.* Customs and Excise Commissioners Ex p. Shepherd Neame Ltd; *sub nom* R. *v.*
HM Treasury Ex p. Shepherd Neame Ltd [1999] 1 C.M.L.R. 1274; [1999] Eu. L.R.
522; (1999) 11 Admin. L.R. 517; *Times*, February 17, 1999, CA; affirming [1998]
1 C.M.L.R. 1139; [1998] C.O.D. 237; *Times*, February 2, 1998; *Independent*,
January 29, 1998, QBD . . . .   *Digested*, 99/**4684**

R. *v.* Customs and Excise Commissioners Ex p. Smith (t/a Arthur Smith) (C204/94)
see R. *v.* Customs and Excise Commissioners Ex p. Faroe Seafood Co Ltd
(C153/94)

R. *v.* Customs and Excise Commissioners Ex p. Wagstaff; *sub nom* R. *v.* Canterbury
Crown Court Ex p. Wagstaff (1998) 162 J.P. 186; [1998] Crim. L.R. 287;
Independent, December 1, 1997 (C.S.), QBD . . . .   *Digested*, 98/**4644**

R. *v.* Customs and Excise Commissioners Ex p. Wardens and Commonality of the
Mystery of Mercers of the City of London see R. *v.* Customs and Excise
Commissioners Ex p. Kay & Co Ltd

R. *v.* Cutlan (Margaret Irene) [1998] 1 Cr. App. R. (S.) 1, CA (Crim Div). . . . .   *Digested*, 98/**1305**:
                                    Considered, 99/1262

R. *v.* Cutler (Saul Roland) see Attorney General's Reference (No.18 of 1997), Re

R. *v.* D [2001] 1 Cr. App. R. 13; [2001] Crim. L.R. 160, CA (Crim Div)

R. *v.* D (Andrew) (A Juvenile) see R. *v.* Webbe (Bernard)

R. *v.* D (Andrew) (A Juvenile) [1998] 1 Cr. App. R. (S.) 291, CA (Crim Div) . . . .   *Digested*, 98/**1296**

R. *v.* D (Anthony John) [2000] 1 Cr. App. R. (S.) 120, CA (Crim Div) . . . .   *Digested*, 00/**1279**:
                                    Considered, 00/1141

R. *v.* D (Brett) [1996] 1 Cr. App. R. (S.) 196, CA (Crim Div) . . . .   *Digested*, 96/**1793**:
                                    Considered, 99/1301

R. *v.* D (Carl) see Attorney General's Reference (No.5 of 1996), Re

R. *v.* D (Carl) (A Juvenile), *Times*, December 20, 2000, CA (Crim Div) . . . .   *Digested*, 01/**1383**

R. *v.* D (Craig George William) [1998] 2 Cr. App. R. (S.) 292, CA (Crim Div) . . . .   *Digested*, 98/**1287**

R. *v.* D (David John) (1993) 14 Cr. App. R. (S.) 639, CA (Crim Div) . . . .   *Digested*, 94/**1330**:
                          Considered, 97/1452, 98/1341, 00/1394

R. *v.* D (George Ernest) (1993) 14 Cr. App. R. (S.) 776, CA (Crim Div) . . . .   *Digested*, 94/**1180**:
                                    Considered, 00/1141

R. *v.* D (Ilhan) (A Juvenile) [2000] Crim. L.R. 178; (1999) 96(47) L.S.G. 29; (2000)
144 S.J.L.B. 5; *Times*, December 7, 1999, CA (Crim Div) . . . .   *Digested*, 00/**1074**

R. *v.* D (Jamie) (A Juvenile) (2001) 165 J.P. 1; *Independent*, December 4, 2000 (C.S.),
CA (Crim Div) . . . .   *Digested*, 01/**1394**

R. *v.* D (John) [1998] 1 Cr. App. R. (S.) 110, CA (Crim Div) . . . .   *Digested*, 98/**1311**:
                                    Considered, 00/1267

R. *v.* D (John) [2001] EWCA Crim 563; [2001] 2 Cr. App. R. (S.) 75, CA (Crim Div) . . .   *Digested*, 01/**1458**

R. *v.* D (Mathew David) (A Juvenile) see Attorney General's Reference (No.13 of
1998), Re

R. *v.* D (Miles) (A Juvenile) see R. *v.* Kelly (Lewis)

R. *v.* D (Peter) [1999] 2 Cr. App. R. (S.) 272, CA (Crim Div) . . . .   *Digested*, 99/**1268**

R. *v.* D (Robert) (A Juvenile) see R. *v.* B (David) (A Juvenile)

R. *v.* D (Sarah Louise) (A Juvenile) (2000) 164 J.P. 721; [2001] Crim. L.R. 126; *Times*,
November 2, 2000, CA (Crim Div) . . . .   *Digested*, 00/**911**

R. *v.* D (Simon Timothy) [1998] 1 Cr. App. R. (S.) 285, CA (Crim Div). . . . .   *Digested*, 98/**1345**

R. *v.* Dabhade (Nitin Jayat) [1993] Q.B. 329; [1993] 2 W.L.R. 129; [1992] 4 All E.R.
796; (1993) 96 Cr. App. R. 146; (1993) 157 J.P. 234; [1993] Crim. L.R. 67;
(1992) 156 J.P.N. 732; (1992) 142 N.L.J. 1195; *Times,* August 14, 1992;
Independent, August 28, 1992, CA (Crim Div) . . . . *Digested,* 93/**700**:
Considered, 94/887, 98/1040

R. *v.* Dacres (Robert Clive) see Attorney General's Reference (No.3 of 1994) (Unduly
Lenient Sentence), Re

R. *v.* Dadson (Peter Ernest) (1983) 77 Cr. App. R. 91; [1983] Crim. L.R. 540, CA
(Crim Div). . . . . *Digested,* 83/**630**:
Considered, 91/878, 92/981, 00/308

R. *v.* Dainty (Paul) see Attorney General's Reference (No.55 of 1997), Re

R. *v.* Daley (Frederick) see R. *v.* Boswell (James Thomas)

R. *v.* Dalton (Richard Charles) [2000] 2 Cr. App. R. (S.) 87, CA (Crim Div) . . . . *Digested,* 00/**1143**

R. *v.* Daly (Charles) (1981) 3 Cr. App. R. (S.) 340, CA (Crim Div) . . . . *Considered,* 98/1379:
Referred to, 97/1704, 99/1248

R. *v.* Daly (Sean) [1999] Crim. L.R. 88, CA (Crim Div)

R. *v.* Dame Alice Owens School Governors Ex p. S [1998] Ed. C.R. 101; [1998] C.O.D.
108, QBD . . . . *Digested,* 98/**1916**

R. *v.* Danga (Harbeer Singh) [1992] Q.B. 476; [1992] 2 W.L.R. 277; [1992] 1 All E.R.
624; (1992) 94 Cr. App. R. 252; (1992) 13 Cr. App. R. (S.) 408; (1992) 156 J.P.
382; [1992] Crim. L.R. 219; (1992) 156 J.P.N. 382; *Times,* November 1, 1991,
CA (Crim Div). . . . . *Digested,* 92/**1450**:
Applied, 94/1393, 96/1941, 00/1317: *Cited,* 95/1501

R. *v.* Daniel (Anthony Junior) [1998] 2 Cr. App. R. 373; (1998) 162 J.P. 578; [1998]
Crim. L.R. 818; (1998) 162 J.P.N. 663; *Times,* April 10, 1998, CA (Crim Div) . . . . *Digested,* 98/**1061**

R. *v.* Daniel (Craig) [2000] 2 Cr. App. R. (S.) 184, CA (Crim Div) . . . . *Digested,* 00/**1146**

R. *v.* Daniels (Antonio Eval) see R. *v.* Powell (Anthony Glassford)

R. *v.* Daniels (Brian Keith) (1986) 8 Cr. App. R. (S.) 257; [1986] Crim. L.R. 824, CA
(Crim Div). . . . . *Digested,* 87/**883**:
Followed, 98/1147

R. *v.* Dann (Anthony Ian) [1997] Crim. L.R. 46, CA (Crim Div) . . . . *Distinguished,* 00/2469

R. *v.* Danter (Jason Conrad) see Attorney General's Reference (Nos.58 and 59 of
2001), Re

R. *v.* Darah (Salam Ali) see Attorney General's Reference (No.20 of 1993), Re

R. *v.* Darby (John Frederick) (No.1) see R. *v.* Henn (Maurice Donald) (No.1)

R. *v.* Darke (Anthony) [2000] 1 Cr. App. R. (S.) 123; [1999] Crim. L.R. 754, CA (Crim
Div) . . . . *Digested,* 00/**1360**:
Considered, 00/1352

R. *v.* Darrach 11 B.H.R.C. 157, Sup Ct (Can)

R. *v.* Dashwood (Roger De Courcey) (1995) 16 Cr. App. R. (S.) 733; [1995] Crim.
L.R. 340; *Times,* December 12, 1994; *Independent,* January 30, 1995 (C.S.), CA
(Crim Div). . . . . *Digested,* 96/**1941**:
Considered, 99/1299

R. *v.* Dat (Sunil) [1998] Crim. L.R. 488, CA (Crim Div)

R. *v.* Datson (James) [1999] 1 Cr. App. R. (S.) 84, CA (Crim Div) . . . . *Digested,* 99/**1278**

R. *v.* Daubney (Garrick James) (2000) 164 J.P. 519; (2001) 165 J.P.N. 685, CA (Crim
Div) . . . . *Digested,* 00/**1072**

R. *v.* Davegun (Surbjeet Singh) (1985) 7 Cr. App. R. (S.) 110; [1985] Crim. L.R. 608,
CA (Crim Div) . . . . *Digested,* 86/**822**:
Considered, 99/1358

R. (on the application of Thornby Farms Ltd) *v.* Daventry DC; *sub nom* Thornby Farms Ltd
v. Daventry DC; R. *v.* Daventry DC Ex p. Thornby Farms; R. (on the application
of Murray) *v.* Derbyshire DC; R. (on the application of Murray) *v.* Derbyshire CC;
C/2000/3180, C2000/3300, CA; affirming [2001] Env. L.R. 20; [2001]
E.H.L.R. 6; [2001] J.P.L. 228 (Note); (2000) 97(35) L.S.G. 39; [2000] N.P.C.
91; *Times,* October 5, 2000, QBD . . . . *Digested,* 00/**2277**:
Previous proceedings, 00/4505

R. (on the application of Chief Constable of Northamptonshire) *v.* Daventry Justices; *sub
nom* R. *v.* Daventry Justices Ex p. Chief Constable of Northamptonshire [2001]
EWHC Admin 446; [2001] A.C.D. 92, QBD (Admin Ct)

R. *v.* Davies (Anthony Gerald) [1998] 2 Cr. App. R. (S.) 193, CA (Crim Div) . . . . *Digested,* 98/**1238**

R. *v.* Davies (Ceri) [1999] 2 Cr. App. R. (S.) 356, CA (Crim Div). . . . . *Digested,* 00/**1236**

R. *v.* Davies (David Patrick) [1996] 1 Cr. App. R. (S.) 28, CA (Crim Div) . . . . *Considered,* 96/2017,
97/1622, 99/1267

R. *v.* Davies (Grace); R. *v.* Poolton (Janet Marie) [2000] Crim. L.R. 297, CA (Crim
Div)

R. *v.* Davies (Gwyn George) [1998] 1 Cr. App. R. (S.) 252; [1997] Crim. L.R. 764, CA
(Crim Div). . . . . *Digested,* 97/**1478**:
Considered, 00/1176

R. *v.* Davies (Hilton) see Attorney General's Reference (Nos.37 and 38 of 1997), Re

R. *v.* Davies (Paul Stewart) see Attorney General's Reference (No.5 of 1998), Re

R. *v.* Davies (Robert Paul) (1990) 12 Cr. App. R. (S.) 308; [1991] Crim. L.R. 70, CA
(Crim Div). . . . . *Digested,* 92/**1145**:
Considered, 00/1269

R. *v.* Davies (Tarian John) [1998] 1 Cr. App. R. (S.) 380; [1998] Crim. L.R. 75; *Times,*
    October 22, 1997, CA (Crim Div) . . . . *Digested,* 97/**1413**:
                                                                Considered, 00/1142, 00/1144, 00/1279
R. *v.* Davis (Desmond John) [1998] Crim. L.R. 659, CA (Crim Div)
R. *v.* Davis (Frank O'Neill) see R. *v.* Williams (Barry Anthony)
R. *v.* Davis (Jennifer Anne) (1983) 5 Cr. App. R. (S.) 425; [1984] Crim. L.R. 245, CA
    (Crim Div) . . . . *Digested,* 84/**888**:
                                                                Considered, 98/1305, 00/1363
R. *v.* Davis (Michael George) (No.1); R. *v.* Rowe (Raphael George) (No.1); R. *v.*
    Johnson (Randolph Egbert) (No.1) [1993] 1 W.L.R. 613; [1993] 2 All E.R. 643;
    (1993) 97 Cr. App. R. 110; (1993) 137 S.J.L.B. 19; *Times,* January 19, 1993;
    Independent, January 22, 1993, CA (Crim Div) . . . . *Digested,* 94/**878**:
                                Applied, 94/876, 97/1342, 00/5464: *Considered,* 94/874
R. *v.* Davis (Michael George) (No.2); R. *v.* Rowe (Raphael George) (No.2); R. *v.*
    Johnson (Randolph Egbert) (No.2) *Times,* April 24, 2000, CA (Crim Div) . . . . .   *Digested,* 00/**1059**
R. *v.* Davis (Michael George) (No.3); R. *v.* Rowe (Raphael George) (No.3); R. *v.*
    Johnson (Randolph Egbert) (No.3) [2001] 1 Cr. App. R. 8; [2000] H.R.L.R.
    527; [2000] U.K.H.R.R. 683; [2000] Crim. L.R. 1012; *Times,* July 25, 2000;
    Independent, July 20, 2000, CA (Crim Div) . . . . *Digested,* 00/**1056**:
                                                                Applied, 01/1154: *Followed,* 01/5877
R. *v.* Davis (Reginald) [1998] Crim. L.R. 564, CA (Crim Div)
R. *v.* Davis (Stanley Eustace) [2001] 1 Cr. App. R. (S.) 53, CA (Crim Div) . . . .   *Digested,* 01/**1325**
R. *v.* Dawson (Neil Andrew) see Attorney General's Reference (No.36 of 1995), Re
R. *v.* Dawson (Stuart Ian) [1999] 1 Costs L.R. 4, Sup Ct Taxing Office. . . . .   *Digested,* 00/**3978**:
                                                                Distinguished, 00/1040
R. *v.* Day (Carl John) [1997] 2 Cr. App. R. (S.) 328; [1997] Crim. L.R. 529, CA (Crim
    Div) . . . . *Digested,* 98/**1148**
R. *v.* Day (Mario) [2000] 2 Cr. App. R. (S.) 312, CA (Crim Div) . . . .   *Digested,* 00/**1227**
R. *v.* Day (Mark Alan) see R. *v.* Exley (Warren)
R. *v.* Day (Mark Allen) see Attorney General's Reference (Nos.48 and 49 of 1997), Re
R. *v.* Day (Peter George) see R. *v.* Andrews Weatherfoil Ltd
R. *v.* De Brito (Max Domingos) [2000] 2 Cr. App. R. (S.) 255, CA (Crim Div) . . . .   *Digested,* 00/**1233**
R. *v.* De Silva (Dean) [2000] 2 Cr. App. R. (S.) 408; [2000] Crim. L.R. 502, CA
    (Crim Div) . . . .   *Digested,* 01/**1368**
R. *v.* De Simone (Gianni) [2000] 2 Cr. App. R. (S.) 332; [2000] Crim. L.R. 498, CA
    (Crim Div) . . . .   *Digested,* 00/**1189**
R. *v.* De St Aubin (Anthony) see Attorney General's Reference (No.86 of 1998), Re
R. *v.* Dean (Anthony Roger) see R. *v.* Richardson (Edward George)
R. *v.* Dean (Jeanette); R. *v.* Bolden (Robert Allen) [1998] 2 Cr. App. R. 171, CA (Crim
    Div) . . . .   *Digested,* 98/**984**
R. *v.* Dean (Paul Ashley) [2000] 2 Cr. App. R. (S.) 253, CA (Crim Div). . . . .   *Digested,* 00/**1156**
R. *v.* Dearn (Franklyn) (1990) 12 Cr. App. R. (S.) 526, CA (Crim Div) . . . .   *Digested,* 92/**1149**:
                                Cited, 93/1012, 95/1512: *Considered,* 96/2021, 00/1267
R. *v.* Dearnley (Roger); R. *v.* Threapleton (Michael) [2001] 2 Cr. App. R. (S.) 42, CA
    (Crim Div). . . . . *Digested,* 01/**1249**
R. *v.* Dearsley (Simon Robert) see R. *v.* Townsend (Philip Henry)
R. *v.* Deegan (Desmond Garcia) [1998] 2 Cr. App. R. 121; [1998] Crim. L.R. 562;
    (1998) 95(8) L.S.G. 32; (1998) 142 S.J.L.B. 77; *Times,* February 17, 1998;
    Independent, February 6, 1998, CA (Crim Div) . . . .   *Digested,* 98/**966**
R. *v.* Deeley (Andrew) [1998] 1 Cr. App. R. (S.) 113, CA (Crim Div) . . . .   *Digested,* 98/**1120**
R. *v.* Delaney (Richard Anthony); R. *v.* Hamill (Francis Martin); R. *v.* Murphy (Robert)
    [1998] 1 Cr. App. R. (S.) 325, CA (Crim Div) . . . . *Digested,* 98/**1375**
R. *v.* Dellaway (Phillip Charles) (Appeal against Confiscation Order) [2001] 1 Cr. App.
    R. (S.) 77; [2000] Crim. L.R. 1031, CA (Crim Div) . . . . *Digested,* 01/**1283**
R. *v.* Demel (Gem Delantha) [1997] 2 Cr. App. R. (S.) 5, CA (Crim Div) . . . . *Digested,* 97/**1445**:
                                Considered, 98/1249, 98/1257, 99/1203, 00/1288, 01/1354:
                                                                Disapproved, 99/1196
R. *v.* Dempster (Robert Dougan) [2001] EWCA Crim 571; [2001] Crim. L.R. 567, CA
    (Crim Div)
R. *v.* Dennard (William); R. *v.* Draper (John) [2000] 1 Cr. App. R. (S.) 232, CA (Crim
    Div) . . . .   *Digested,* 00/**1179**
R. *v.* Denslow (Paul) [1998] Crim. L.R. 566, CA (Crim Div) . . . .   *Considered,* 00/**1207**:
                                                                Referred to, 00/1209
R. *v.* Densu (Felix) [1998] 1 Cr. App. R. 400; (1998) 162 J.P. 55; [1998] Crim. L.R.
    345; (1998) 162 J.P.N. 305; (1998) 95(2) L.S.G. 22; (1997) 141 S.J.L.B. 250;
    Times, December 10, 1997, CA (Crim Div) . . . . *Digested,* 98/**965**
R. (on the application of Zietsman) *v.* Dental Practice Board; *sub nom* R. *v.* Dental
    Practice Board Ex p. Z [2001] Lloyd's Rep. Med. 124; *Times,* March 6, 2001;
    Independent, January 29, 2001 (C.S), QBD (Admin Ct) . . . . *Digested,* 01/**2890**
R. *v.* Dental Practice Board Ex p. Z see R. (on the application of Zietsman) *v.* Dental
    Practice Board
R. *v.* Denton (Clive) [2001] 1 Cr. App. R. 16; [2001] Crim. L.R. 225; *Times,* November
    22, 2000, CA (Crim Div) . . . .   *Digested,* 00/**926**

R. *v.* Department of Education and Employment Ex p. Amraf Training Plc see R. (on the application of Amraf Training Plc) *v.* Secretary of State for Education and Employment

R. *v.* Department of Education and Employment Ex p. B (A Minor) see R. *v.* Secretary of State for Education and Employment Ex p. B (A Minor)

R. *v.* Department of Health Ex p. Bhaugeerutty, *Times*, May 1, 1998, QBD . . . .   *Digested*, 98/**4582**

R. *v.* Department of Health Ex p. Source Informatics Ltd (No.1) [2001] Q.B. 424; [2000] 2 W.L.R. 940; [2000] 1 All E.R. 786; [2000] Eu. L.R. 397; [2001] F.S.R. 8; [2000] Lloyd's Rep. Med. 76; (2000) 52 B.M.L.R. 65; [2000] C.O.D. 76; *Times*, January 18, 2000 ; *Independent*, February 21, 2000 (C.S.), CA; reversing [1999] 4 All E.R. 185; [1999] I.T.C.L.R. 374; [1999] Lloyd's Rep. Med. 264; (1999) 49 B.M.L.R. 41; [1999] C.O.D. 413; *Times*, June 14, 1999, QBD . . . .   *Digested*, 00/**2909**

R. *v.* Department of Health Ex p. Source Informatics Ltd (No.2) [2000] C.O.D. 114, CA

R. *v.* Department of Social Security Ex p. Okito see R. *v.* Secretary of State for Social Security Ex p. Vijeikis

R. *v.* Department of Social Security Ex p. Scullion [1999] 3 C.M.L.R. 798; [2000] Eu. L.R. 429, QBD . . . .   *Digested*, 00/**4819**

R. *v.* Department of the Environment for Northern Ireland Ex p. Ava Leisure Ltd; *sub nom* Ava Leisure Ltd's Application for Judicial Review, Re [1999] N.I. 203, CA (NI) . . . .   *Digested*, 00/**5658**

R. *v.* Department of the Environment for Northern Ireland Ex p. UK Waste Management Ltd; *sub nom* UK Waste Management Ltd's Application for Judicial Review, Re [1999] N.I. 183, CA (NI) . . . .   *Digested*, 00/**5659**

R. (on the application of Alba Radio Ltd) *v.* Department of Trade and Industry; *sub nom* R. *v.* Department of Trade and Industry Ex p. Alba Radio Ltd *Daily Telegraph*, December 19, 2000, QBD (Admin Ct)

R. *v.* Deputy Chief Constable of Thames Valley Ex p. Cotton see R. *v.* Chief Constable of Thames Valley Ex p. Cotton

R. *v.* Deputy Controller of Buckley Hall Prison Ex p. Thomas [2000] C.O.D. 491, QBD

R. *v.* Deputy Governor of Long Lartin Prison Ex p. Prevot see R. *v.* Deputy Governor of Parkhurst Prison Ex p. Leech

R. *v.* Deputy Governor of Parkhurst Prison Ex p. Hague; *sub nom* Hague *v.* Deputy Governor of Parkhurst Prison; Weldon *v.* Home Office [1992] 1 A.C. 58; [1991] 3 W.L.R. 340; [1991] 3 All E.R. 733; (1993) 5 Admin. L.R. 425; [1992] C.O.D. 69; (1991) 135 S.J.L.B. 102; *Times*, July 25, 1991; *Independent*, September 4, 1991; *Guardian*, July 31, 1991, HL; affirming [1990] 3 W.L.R. 1210; [1990] 3 All E.R. 687; (1991) 3 Admin. L.R. 581; [1990] C.O.D. 459; (1990) 140 N.L.J. 1036; *Times*, June 22, 1990; *Independent*, June 15, 1990; *Guardian*, June 5, 1990, CA; reversing in part [1990] C.O.D. 67, QBD. . . . .   *Digested*, 92/**3651**:
    Applied, 93/2983, 00/5662: *Distinguished*, 94/4284: *Followed*, 92/3210,
    92/3657: *Previous proceedings*, 90/4313

R. *v.* Deputy Governor of Parkhurst Prison Ex p. Leech; *sub nom* Leech *v.* Deputy Governor of Parkhurst Prison; R. *v.* Deputy Governor of Long Lartin Prison Ex p. Prevot [1988] A.C. 533; [1988] 2 W.L.R. 290; [1988] 1 All E.R. 485; (1988) 85(11) L.S.G. 42; (1988) 138 N.L.J. Rep. 38; (1988) 132 S.J. 191, HL . . . .   *Digested*, 88/**2976**:
    Applied, 94/3850, 95/4266: *Considered*, 91/17, 92/12, 95/3538, 99/4106:
    Distinguished, 94/5246

R. *v.* Derby City Council Ex p. Third Wave Housing Ltd (2001) 33 H.L.R. 61, QBD

R. *v.* Derby Crown Court Ex p. Brooks (1985) 80 Cr. App. R. 164; [1985] Crim. L.R. 754; (1984) 148 J.P.N. 573, QBD. . . . .   *Digested*, 85/**2126**:
    Applied, 85/1525, 86/1521, 87/591, 89/539, 89/596, 89/650, 90/770,
    91/606, 91/610, 91/612, 92/616, 92/630, 99/2151, 99/5205:
    Considered, 90/2267, 91/605, 91/609, 91/849, 92/933, 92/3373, 93/620,
    96/1599, 97/1375, 99/5215: *Distinguished*, 94/939: *Followed*, 97/1258

R. (on the application of Hussain) *v.* Derby Magistrates Court [2001] EWHC Admin 507; [2001] 1 W.L.R. 2454; (2001) 145 S.J.L.B. 168, QBD (Admin Ct)

R. *v.* Derby Magistrates Court Ex p. B [1996] A.C. 487; [1995] 3 W.L.R. 681; [1995] 4 All E.R. 526; [1996] 1 Cr. App. R. 385; (1995) 159 J.P. 785; [1996] 1 F.L.R. 513; [1996] Fam. Law 210; (1995) 159 J.P.N. 778; (1995) 145 N.L.J. 1575; [1995] 139 S.J.L.B. 219; *Times*, October 25, 1995; *Independent*, October 27, 1995, HL; reversing *Times*, October 31, 1994, QBD . . . .   *Digested*, 96/**1402**:
    Applied, 97/1143: *Considered*, 99/335: *Followed*, 00/2465

R. *v.* Derby Magistrates Court Ex p. DPP, *Times*, August 17, 1999, QBD . . . .   *Digested*, 99/**1370**

R. (on the application of Murray) *v.* Derbyshire CC see R. (on the application of Thornby Farms Ltd) *v.* Daventry DC

R. (on the application of Murray) *v.* Derbyshire CC; *sub nom* R. *v.* Derbyshire CC Ex p. Murray; Murray *v.* Derbyshire CC [2001] Env. L.R. 26; [2001] 2 P.L.R. 1; [2001] J.P.L. 730 (Note); [2000] E.G.C.S. 110; (2000) 97(40) L.S.G. 44; [2000] N.P.C. 100; *Times*, November 8, 2000, QBD (Admin Ct) . . . .   *Digested*, 00/**4505**

R. *v.* Derbyshire CC Ex p. Poole [2001] P.L.C.R. 3; [2001] J.P.L. 221 (Note), QBD . . . .   *Digested*, 01/**4688**

R. *v.* Derbyshire CC Ex p. Woods [1998] Env. L.R. 277; [1997] J.P.L. 958, CA. . . . .   *Digested*, 97/**4106**:
    Applied, 99/4256, 00/4504, 01/4763: *Considered*, 00/4491:
    Referred to, 00/4520

R. (on the application of Murray) *v.* Derbyshire DC see R. (on the application of Thornby
    Farms Ltd) *v.* Daventry DC
R. *v.* Derodra (Kishor) [2000] 1 Cr. App. R. 41; [1999] Crim. L.R. 978; *Independent*,
    June 10, 1999, CA (Crim Div) . . . .   *Digested*, 99/**873**:
                                                 Distinguished, 00/927
R. *v.* Derwentside Magistrates Court Ex p. Heaviside (1996) 160 J.P. 317; [1996]
    R.T.R. 384; [1995] R.L.R. 557; (1995) 159 J.P.N. 703, QBD . . . .   *Considered*, 96/5053,
                                                  96/5068, 98/899, 98/900
R. *v.* Desmond (Patrick Michael) [1999] Crim. L.R. 313, CA (Crim Div)
R. *v.* Devichand [1991] Crim. L.R. 446; *Daily Telegraph*, November 29, 1990, CA (Crim
    Div) . . . .   *Digested*, 92/**908**:
                                                  Distinguished, 00/1060
R. *v.* Devine (Andrew Maley) [1999] 2 Cr. App. R. (S.) 409, CA (Crim Div) . . . .   *Digested*, 00/**1365**
R. *v.* Devizes Justices Ex p. Lee see R. *v.* Reading Crown Court Ex p. Hutchinson
R. *v.* Devizes Youth Court Ex p. A (2000) 164 J.P. 330, QBD . . . .   *Digested*, 00/**1112**
R. *v.* Devon CC Ex p. Baker; R. *v.* Durham CC Ex p. Curtis ; R. *v.* Devon CC Ex p.
    Ruxton [1995] 1 All E.R. 73; 91 L.G.R. 479; (1994) 6 Admin. L.R. 113; [1993]
    C.O.D. 253; *Times*, January 21, 1993; *Independent*, February 22, 1993 (C.S.),
    CA; affirming [1993] C.O.D. 138; *Times*, October 20, 1992, QBD . . . .   *Digested*, 95/**88**:
            Applied, 95/3252, 95/3272, 96/5526: *Considered*, 95/68, 95/2546,
                         01/6790: *Followed*, 97/4713: *Referred to*, 98/3001
R. *v.* Devon CC Ex p. George; *sub nom* Devon CC *v.* George; G's application, Re
    [1989] A.C. 573; [1988] 3 W.L.R. 1386; [1988] 3 All E.R. 1002; (1989) 153 J.P.
    375; [1989] 1 F.L.R. 146; 87 L.G.R. 413; [1989] Fam. Law 149; (1989) 153
    J.P.N. 434; (1989) 153 L.G. Rev. 428; (1988) 138 N.L.J. Rep. 349; (1988) 132
    S.J. 1730, HL; reversing [1988] 3 W.L.R. 49; (1988) 152 J.P. 586; [1988] 2
    F.L.R. 411; [1988] F.C.R. 185; 86 L.G.R. 647; [1988] Fam. Law 478; (1988) 152
    L.G. Rev. 873, CA; reversing *Independent*, April 29, 1987, QBD . . . .   *Digested*, 90/**1755**:
               Applied, 93/1707, 93/1708, 94/1871, 95/1909, 95/1928, 99/1882
R. *v.* Devon CC Ex p. Isaac see R. *v.* Cornwall CC Ex p. Huntington
R. *v.* Devon CC Ex p. L [1991] 2 F.L.R. 541; [1991] F.C.R. 784; (1992) 4 Admin. L.R.
    99; [1991] C.O.D. 205; [1991] Fam. Law 369; (1991) 155 L.G. Rev. 784 . . . . . .   *Digested*, 92/**3058**:
                                                    Considered, 01/5131
R. *v.* Devon CC Ex p. Ruxton see R. *v.* Devon CC Ex p. Baker
R. *v.* Dewberry (Rodney Brian); R. *v.* Stone (Gavin John) (1985) 7 Cr. App. R. (S.)
    202; [1985] Crim. L.R. 804, CA (Crim Div) . . . .   *Digested*, 86/**772**:
                 Applied, 87/984: *Considered*, 96/1958: *Referred to*, 00/1307
R. *v.* DH see Attorney General's Reference (No.51 of 1999), Re
R. *v.* Dhillon (Karamjit Singh) [2000] Crim. L.R. 760; *Times*, April 5, 2000, CA (Crim
    Div) . . . .   *Digested*, 00/**963**
R. *v.* Dhillon (Rajpaul Singh) see R. *v.* Preddy (John Crawford)
R. *v.* Dibden (Lawrence) [2000] 1 Cr. App. R. (S.) 64, CA (Crim Div) . . . .   *Digested*, 00/**1212**
R. *v.* Dickerson (Nigel Roy) see Attorney General's Reference (No.56 of 2000), Re
R. *v.* Dickinson (Anthony) [1998] R.T.R. 469; *Times*, March 13, 1997, CA (Crim Div) . . .   *Digested*, 97/**1663**
R. *v.* Dickinson (Inspector of Taxes) Ex p. McGuckian see McGuckian, Re
R. *v.* Dickson (William Ewing); R. *v.* Wright (Raymond Eric) [1991] B.C.C. 719; (1992)
    94 Cr. App. R. 7; [1991] Crim. L.R. 854, CA (Crim Div) . . . .   *Digested*, 92/**998**:
                                                     Applied, 99/3280
R. *v.* Dimond (Peter Charles) [2000] 1 Cr. App. R. 21; [1999] Crim. L.R. 584, CA
    (Crim Div) . . . .   *Digested*, 00/**992**
R. *v.* Dimsey (Dermot Jeremy) (Appeals against Sentence); R. *v.* Allen (Brian Roger)
    (Appeals against Sentence) [2000] 2 All E.R. 142; [2000] 1 Cr. App. R. (S.)
    497; [2000] Crim. L.R. 199; *Times*, October 13, 1999, CA (Crim Div) . . . .   *Digested*, 99/**910**:
                          Considered, 01/1111: *Distinguished*, 00/1162
R. *v.* Dimsey (Dermot Jeremy); R. *v.* Allen (Brian Roger) [2001] UKHL 46; [2001] 3
    W.L.R. 843; [2001] 4 All E.R. 786; [2001] S.T.C. 1520; [2001] B.T.C. 408; 4 I.T.L.
    Rep. 168; [2001] S.T.I. 1349; *Independent*, October 25, 2001, HL; affirming
    [2000] Q.B. 744; [2000] 3 W.L.R. 273; [1999] S.T.C. 846; [2000] 1 Cr. App. R.
    203; [1999] B.T.C. 335; 2 I.T.L. Rep. 32; (1999) 96(30) L.S.G. 28; *Times*, July
    14, 1999, CA (Crim Div) . . . .   *Digested*, 01/**5318**:
                                            Subsequent proceedings, 01/5271
R. *v.* Director General of Electricity Supply Ex p. London Electricity Plc, *Times*, June 13,
    2000, QBD . . . .   *Digested*, 00/**2090**
R. *v.* Director General of Fair Trading Ex p. Benhams Ltd [2001] 1 E.G.L.R. 21; [2001]
    02 E.G. 146, QBD . . . .   *Digested*, 01/**113**
R. *v.* Director General of Telecommunications Ex p. Cellcom Ltd [1999] E.C.C. 314;
    [1999] Masons C.L.R. 41; [1999] C.O.D. 105; (1999) 96(6) L.S.G. 31; *Times*,
    December 7, 1998; *Independent*, December 3, 1998, QBD . . . .   *Digested*, 99/**4840**
R. *v.* Director General of Water Services Ex p. Birmingham City Council see R. *v.*
    Director General of Water Services Ex p. Lancashire CC

R. v. Director General of Water Services Ex p. Lancashire CC; R. v. Director General of Water Services Ex p. Liverpool City Council; R. v. Director General of Water Services Ex p. Manchester City Council; R. v. Director General of Water Services Ex p. Tameside MBC; R. v. Director General of Water Services Ex p. Oldham MBC; R. v. Director General of Water Services Ex p. Birmingham City Council [1999] Env. L.R. 114; [1998] E.H.L.R. 226; (1999) 31 H.L.R. 224; *Times*, March 6, 1998, QBD . . . .   *Digested*, 98/**4994**

R. v. Director General of Water Services Ex p. Liverpool City Council see R. v. Director General of Water Services Ex p. Lancashire CC

R. v. Director General of Water Services Ex p. Manchester City Council see R. v. Director General of Water Services Ex p. Lancashire CC

R. v. Director General of Water Services Ex p. Oldham MBC see R. v. Director General of Water Services Ex p. Lancashire CC

R. v. Director General of Water Services Ex p. Tameside MBC see R. v. Director General of Water Services Ex p. Lancashire CC

R. v. Director of Gas Supply Ex p. Smith (Unreported, July 31, 1989), QBD . . . .   *Applied*, 98/2083

R. v. Director of the Serious Fraud Office Ex p. Smith; *sub nom* Smith v. Director of the Serious Fraud Office [1993] A.C. 1; [1992] 3 W.L.R. 66; [1992] 3 All E.R. 456; [1992] B.C.L.C. 879; (1992) 95 Cr. App. R. 191; [1992] Crim. L.R. 504; [1992] C.O.D. 270; (1992) 89(27) L.S.G. 34; (1992) 142 N.L.J. 895; (1992) 136 S.J.L.B. 182; *Times*, June 16, 1992; *Independent*, June 12, 1992; *Financial Times*, June 17, 1992; *Guardian*, July 1, 1992, HL; reversing [1992] 1 All E.R. 730; [1992] C.O.D. 188; (1992) 89(10) L.S.G. 33; (1991) 135 S.J.L.B. 214; *Times*, November 13, 1991; *Independent*, November 8, 1991; *Guardian*, November 13, 1991, QBD . . . .   *Digested*, 92/**980**:
      Considered, 92/2556, 93/2383, 94/968, 96/1606: *Followed*, 93/4890, 00/1057

R. v. Disciplinary Committee of the Jockey Club Ex p. The Aga Khan [1993] 1 W.L.R. 909; [1993] 2 All E.R. 853; [1993] C.O.D. 234; (1993) 143 N.L.J. 163; *Times*, December 9, 1992; *Independent*, December 22, 1992, CA; affirming [1992] C.O.D. 51; *Independent*, July 29, 1991 (C.S.), QBD . . . .   *Digested*, 93/**33**:
      Applied, 01/5140: *Considered*, 94/2677, 95/55: *Followed*, 95/760, 98/101

R. v. Dissanayake (Rohan Shivantha) see R. v. Nazari (Fazlollah)

R. v. District Auditor No.3 Audit District of West Yorkshire Metropolitan CC Ex p. West Yorkshire Metropolitan CC [1986] R.V.R. 24; [2001] W.T.L.R. 785, QBD . . . .   *Digested*, 86/**2804**

R. v. Divers (Saul Andrew) [1999] 2 Cr. App. R. (S.) 421; [1999] Crim. L.R. 843, CA (Crim Div) . . . .   *Digested*, 00/**1190**

R. v. Dix (Peter Anthony) (1994) 15 Cr. App. R. (S.) 397, CA (Crim Div) . . . .   *Considered*, 01/1231

R. v. Dixon (Gary) see R. v. Simpson (David)

R. v. Dixon (Leon) [2000] 1 W.L.R. 782; [1999] 3 All E.R. 889; [2000] 1 Cr. App. R. 173; (1999) 96(24) L.S.G. 39; *Times*, May 19, 1999; *Independent*, May 26, 1999, CA (Crim Div) . . . .   *Digested*, 99/**992**

R. v. Dixon (Stuart Andrew) [2000] 2 Cr. App. R. (S.) 7; [2000] O.P.L.R. 47; *Times*, November 24, 1999, CA (Crim Div) . . . .   *Digested*, 99/**4130**

R. v. Djahit (Turkesh) [1999] 2 Cr. App. R. (S.) 142, CA (Crim Div) . . . .   *Digested*, 99/**1137**:
      Applied, 01/1282: *Considered*, 00/1225

R. v. DLB see R. v. B (A Juvenile) (Contradictory Evidence)

R. v. Doak (Desmond Samuel) [1998] N.I. 169, CA (Crim Div) (NI) . . . .   *Digested*, 99/**5222**

R. v. Doak (John) (1993) 14 Cr. App. R. (S.) 128, CA (Crim Div) . . . .   *Digested*, 93/**1306**:
      Considered, 98/1399, 98/1402, 00/1136

R. v. Docherty (Michael) [1999] 1 Cr. App. R. 274, CA (Crim Div) . . . .   *Digested*, 99/**1016**

R. v. Docklands Estates Ltd [2001] 1 Cr. App. R. (S.) 78; (2000) 164 J.P. 505; [2000] 3 E.G.L.R. 17; [2000] 45 E.G. 175; (2000) 164 J.P.N. 726; *Times*, September 22, 2000; *Independent*, October 2, 2000 (C.S.), CA (Crim Div) . . . .   *Digested*, 00/**1241**

R. v. Dodds (Andrew Alistair) see R. v. Williams (David Omar)

R. v. Dodgson (Andrew) [2001] 1 Cr. App. R. (S.) 85, CA (Crim Div) . . . .   *Digested*, 01/**1201**

R. v. Dodman (Darryl Philip) [1998] 2 Cr. App. R. 338; *Times*, April 9, 1998, CMAC . . . .   *Digested*, 98/**263**

R. v. Doe (Clayton Christopher) (1995) 16 Cr. App. R. (S.) 718, CA (Crim Div) . . . .   *Digested*, 96/**2051**:
      Cited, 00/1398

R. v. Doherty (Joseph) see Doherty's Application (No.2), Re

R. v. Doherty (Stephen John) (1986) 8 Cr. App. R. (S.) 493; [1987] Crim. L.R. 284, CA (Crim Div) . . . .   *Digested*, 88/**986**:
      Cited, 90/1408, 94/1294: *Considered*, 96/1692, 98/1375

R. v. Dolgin (Perry Lloyd) (1988) 10 Cr. App. R. (S.) 447; [1989] Crim. L.R. 307, CA (Crim Div) . . . .   *Digested*, 91/**1094**:
      Cited, 95/1361: *Considered*, 00/1233

R. v. Dolphy (Richard Alexander) [1999] 1 Cr. App. R. (S.) 73, CA (Crim Div) . . . .   *Digested*, 99/**1360**

R. v. Donaldson (Andrew) see R. v. Wijs (Eric Jan)

R. v. Doncaster Justices Ex p. Christison (No.1) see R. v. Doncaster Justices Ex p. Jack (No.1)

R. v. Doncaster Justices Ex p. Christison (No.2) see R. v. Doncaster Justices Ex p. Jack (No.2)

R. *v.* Doncaster Justices Ex p. Hannan; *sub nom* R. *v.* Doncaster Magistrates Court Ex
   p. Hannan (1999) 163 J.P. 182; [1998] R.V.R. 254; (1999) 163 J.P.N. 234;
   (1998) 95(32) L.S.G. 30; (1998) 142 S.J.L.B. 218; *Times,* October 12, 1998,
   QBD . . . .   *Digested,* 98/**1008**
R. *v.* Doncaster Justices Ex p. Jack (No.1); R. *v.* Doncaster Justices Ex p. Christison
   (No.1) (2000) 164 J.P. 52; (1999) 163 J.P.N. 1026; *Times,* May 26, 1999, QBD .   *Digested,* 99/**11**:
                                                       Applied, 00/9
R. *v.* Doncaster Justices Ex p. Jack (No.2); R. *v.* Doncaster Justices Ex p. Christison
   (No.2) [1999] R.V.R. 308; [2000] C.O.D. 5, QBD . . . .   *Digested,* 00/**18**
R. *v.* Doncaster Magistrates Court Ex p. Hannan see R. *v.* Doncaster Justices Ex p.
   Hannan
R. (on the application of Heath) *v.* Doncaster MBC; *sub nom* R. *v.* Doncaster MBC Ex p.
   Heath [2001] A.C.D. 48, QBD (Admin Ct)
R. *v.* Doncaster MDC Ex p. British Railways Board [1987] J.P.L. 444 . . . .   *Digested,* 87/**3700**:
                                            Considered, 01/4688
R. *v.* Donnelly [1986] 3 N.I.J.B. 48 . . . .   *Digested,* 86/**2321**:
                                     Distinguished, 00/5473
R. *v.* Donnelly (Francis Gray) (1983) 5 Cr. App. R. (S.) 70, CA (Crim Div) . . . .   *Digested,* 84/**821**:
        Cited, 98/1309: *Considered,* 88/865, 88/866, 92/1149, 95/1262, 97/1625,
                                                   00/1369
R. *v.* Donnelly (Ian David) [1984] 1 W.L.R. 1017; (1984) 79 Cr. App. R. 76; [1984]
   Crim. L.R. 490; (1984) 81 L.S.G. 1994; (1984) 128 S.J. 514, CA (Crim Div) . . . .   *Digested,* 84/**623**:
                                     Followed, 01/1046
R. *v.* Donnelly (John Francis); R. *v.* Donnelly (Margaret) [1998] Crim. L.R. 131, CA
   (Crim Div)
R. *v.* Donnelly (Margaret) see R. *v.* Donnelly (John Francis)
R. *v.* Dooley (Lee Peter) [1999] 2 Cr. App. R. (S.) 364, CA (Crim Div) . . . .   *Digested,* 00/**1442**
R. *v.* Dooley (Stephen) see R. *v.* Knight (Peter)
R. *v.* Doot (Robert Leroy) see DPP *v.* Doot
R. *v.* Dootson (Robert) (1995) 16 Cr. App. R. (S.) 223; [1994] Crim. L.R. 702, CA
   (Crim Div) . . . .   *Digested,* 95/**1416**:
                            Considered, 99/1245, 00/1156
R. *v.* Doran (Brian Peter) (Appeal against Conviction) see R. *v.* Togher (Kenneth)
   (Appeal against Conviction)
R. *v.* Dorosz (Daniel) [2001] EWCA Crim 769; [2001] 2 Cr. App. R. (S.) 107, CA
   (Crim Div) . . . .   *Digested,* 01/**1285**
R. *v.* Dorrain (Graham Francis) see R. *v.* Dorrian (Graham Francis)
R. *v.* Dorrian (Graham Francis); *sub nom* R. *v.* Dorrain (Graham Francis) [2001] 1 Cr.
   App. R. (S.) 135; [2001] Crim. L.R. 56, CA (Crim Div) . . . .   *Digested,* 01/**1239**
R. (on the application of Beeson) *v.* Dorset CC [2001] EWHC Admin 986; [2001] N.P.C.
   175; *Times,* December 21, 2001; *Daily Telegraph,* December 13, 2001, QBD
   (Admin Ct)
R. *v.* Dorton (William John) (1987) 9 Cr. App. R. (S.) 514; (1988) 152 J.P. 197; [1988]
   Crim. L.R. 254, CA (Crim Div) . . . .   *Digested,* 90/**1246**:
                                      Considered, 99/1103
R. *v.* Dosanjh (Barjinder) [1998] 3 All E.R. 618; [1999] 1 Cr. App. R. 371; [1999] 1 Cr.
   App. R. (S.) 107; [1998] Crim. L.R. 593; (1998) 95(22) L.S.G. 28; (1998) 142
   S.J.L.B. 163; *Times,* May 7, 1998; *Independent,* May 5, 1998, CA (Crim Div) . . . .   *Digested,* 98/**1390**:
                      Considered, 99/1356, 99/1357, 00/1432
R. *v.* Dossetter (Anthony William) [1999] 2 Cr. App. R. (S.) 248; *Times,* February 5,
   1999, CA (Crim Div) . . . .   *Digested,* 99/**3800**
R. *v.* Doubtfire (Robert Henry) (No.1) see R. *v.* Van Tattenhove (Frans Willem)
R. *v.* Doubtfire (Robert Henry) (No.2) [2001] 2 Cr. App. R. 13; [2001] Crim. L.R. 813;
   (2001) 98(16) L.S.G. 32; (2001) 145 S.J.L.B. 77; *Times,* December 28, 2000,
   CA (Crim Div) . . . .   *Digested,* 01/**1100**
R. *v.* Dougan Unreported, CA (Crim Div) (NI) . . . .   *Considered,* 99/5459
R. *v.* Doughty (Barry Michael) see Attorney General's Reference (Nos.36, 37, 38 and
   39 of 1999), Re
R. *v.* Douglas (David) see Attorney General's Reference (Nos.35 and 36 of 2000), Re
R. *v.* Dover Harbour Board Ex p. Peter Gilder & Sons see R. *v.* Coventry City Council
   Ex p. Phoenix Aviation
R. *v.* Dover Magistrates Court Ex p. Webb (1998) 162 J.P. 295; [1998] C.O.D. 274,
   QBD . . . .   *Digested,* 98/**939**
R. *v.* Dover Youth Court Ex p. K; *sub nom* R. *v.* Kent Youth Court Ex p. K [1999] 1
   W.L.R. 27; [1998] 4 All E.R. 24; [1999] 1 Cr. App. R. (S.) 263; [1999] Crim. L.R.
   168; (1998) 95(30) L.S.G. 25; (1998) 142 S.J.L.B. 205; *Times,* July 22, 1998;
   Independent, June 29, 1998 (C.S.), QBD . . . .   *Digested,* 98/**1290**:
                                      Considered, 00/1319
R. *v.* Dowd (Jeffrey); R. *v.* Huskins (Malcom) [2000] 1 Cr. App. R. (S.) 349, CA (Crim
   Div) . . . .   *Digested,* 00/**1378**
R. (on the application of the Association of Pharmaceutical Importers) *v.* Dowelhurst Ltd
   see R. (on the application of the Association of Pharmaceutical Importers) *v.*
   Secretary of State for Health

R. *v.* Dowling (Stephen) (1989) 88 Cr. App. R. 88; *Times*, June 22, 1988, CA (Crim Div) .... *Digested, 89/***1132**:
Considered, 00/1176
R. *v.* Downes Ex p. Wandsworth LBC [2000] E.L.R. 425, QBD. .... *Digested, 00/***1911**
R. *v.* Downey (Conor Edward) see Attorney General's Reference (No.19 of 1993), Re
R. *v.* Downey (Thomas) see Attorney General's Reference (No.16 of 2000), Re
R. *v.* Downing (Justine) [1996] 1 Cr. App. R. (S.) 419, CA (Crim Div) .... *Digested, 96/***1769**:
Considered, 98/1370
R. *v.* Doyle (David Martin); R. *v.* Nicholaou (Nicolas Michael); R. *v.* Irving (Paul) [1996] 1 Cr. App. R. (S.) 341, CA (Crim Div) .... *Digested, 96/***1708**:
Considered, 00/1154
R. *v.* Doyle (Julie Marie) [1998] 1 Cr. App. R. (S.) 79, CA (Crim Div)............. *Digested, 98/***1186**:
Considered, 99/1135, 00/1210
R. *v.* Doyle (Sandra Esther) [2001] 2 Cr. App. R. (S.) 3, CA (Crim Div) .... *Digested, 01/***1306**
R. *v.* Doyle (Stephen) [1996] 1 Cr. App. R. (S.) 239, CA (Crim Div) .... *Digested, 96/***1727**:
Considered, 98/1306, 98/1307, 00/1369
R. *v.* Doyle (Steven Philip) [1999] 1 Cr. App. R. (S.) 383, CA (Crim Div) .... *Digested, 99/***1065**
R. *v.* Doyle (Thomas) (1988) 10 Cr. App. R. (S.) 5, CA (Crim Div)................ *Digested, 90/***1297**:
Considered, 99/1148
R. *v.* DPG Ex p. TDT [2001] A.C.D. 42, QBD (Admin Ct)
R. (on the application of C (A Child)) *v.* DPP; *sub nom* R. *v.* DPP Ex p. C (A Child) (2001) 165 J.P. 102; *Independent*, November 27, 2000 (C.S), QBD (Admin Ct) . *Digested, 01/***1186**
R. (on the application of Grant) *v.* DPP see R. *v.* Grant (Heather)
R. (on the application of Joseph) *v.* DPP [2001] Crim. L.R. 489, QBD (Admin Ct)
R. (on the application of Planton) *v.* DPP; *sub nom* Planton *v.* DPP [2001] EWHC Admin 450; (2001) 98(27) L.S.G. 40; *Times*, August 17, 2001, QBD (Admin Ct)...... *Digested, 01/***1033**
R. (on the application of Pretty) *v.* DPP [2001] UKHL 61; [2001] 3 W.L.R. 1598; 11 B.H.R.C. 589; (2001) 151 N.L.J. 1819; *Times*, December 5, 2001; *Daily Telegraph*, December 6, 2001, HL; affirming [2001] EWHC Admin 788; (2001) 98(45) L.S.G. 25; (2001) 151 N.L.J. 1572; (2001) 145 S.J.L.B. 252; *Times*, October 23, 2001; *Daily Telegraph*, October 23, 2001, QBD (Admin Ct) .... *Digested, 01/***1072**
R. *v.* DPP Ex p. Boukemiche (Ferine) see R. *v.* DPP Ex p. Kebilene
R. *v.* DPP Ex p. Branagan see Branagan *v.* DPP
R. *v.* DPP Ex p. Bull see R. *v.* Lord Chancellor Ex p. Child Poverty Action Group
R. *v.* DPP Ex p. C see R. *v.* DPP Ex p. Chaudhary
R. *v.* DPP Ex p. C (A Child) see R. (on the application of C (A Child)) *v.* DPP
R. *v.* DPP Ex p. Camelot Group Plc (1998) 10 Admin. L.R. 93; [1998] C.O.D. 54; (1998) 162 J.P.N. 67; *Independent*, April 22, 1997, QBD .... *Applied, 97/3616*
R. *v.* DPP Ex p. Chaudhary; *sub nom* R. *v.* DPP Ex p. C [1995] 1 Cr. App. R. 136; (1995) 159 J.P. 227; (1995) 7 Admin. L.R. 385; [1994] C.O.D. 375; (1995) 159 J.P.N. 214; *Times*, March 7, 1994, QBD .... *Digested, 95/***29**:
Considered, 95/122, 97/1372: Followed, 01/1072
R. *v.* DPP Ex p. Duckenfield; R. *v.* South Yorkshire Police Authority Ex p. Chief Constable of South Yorkshire [2000] 1 W.L.R. 55; [1999] 2 All E.R. 873; (2000) 2 L.G.L.R. 278; (1999) 11 Admin. L.R. 611; [1999] C.O.D. 216; *Times*, April 21, 1999, QBD .... *Digested, 99/***1043**:
Distinguished, 00/4540
R. *v.* DPP Ex p. J; *sub nom* R. *v.* X Justices Ex p. J; R. *v.* Crown Prosecution Service Ex p. J [2000] 1 W.L.R. 1215; [2000] 1 All E.R. 183; *Times*, July 8, 1999 ; *Independent*, July 5, 1999 (C.S), QBD .... *Digested, 99/***881**
R. *v.* DPP Ex p. Jones (Timothy) [2000] I.R.L.R. 373; [2000] Crim. L.R. 858, QBD. .... *Digested, 01/***1052**
R. *v.* DPP Ex p. Kebilene; *sub nom* R. *v.* DPP Ex p. Kebelene; R. *v.* DPP Ex p. Boukemiche (Ferine); R. *v.* DPP Ex p. Souidi (Sofiane); R. *v.* DPP Ex p. Rechachi [2000] 2 A.C. 326; [1999] 3 W.L.R. 972; [1999] 4 All E.R. 801; [2000] 1 Cr. App. R. 275; [2000] H.R.L.R. 93; [2000] U.K.H.R.R. 176; (2000) 2 L.G.L.R. 697; (1999) 11 Admin. L.R. 1026; [2000] Crim. L.R. 486; (1999) 96(43) L.S.G. 32; *Times*, November 2, 1999, HL; reversing [1999] 3 W.L.R. 175; (1999) 11 Admin. L.R. 785; [1999] Crim. L.R. 994; [1999] C.O.D. 207; *Times*, March 31, 1999, QBD .... *Digested, 99/***1045**:
Applied, 00/921, 00/5473, 01/564, 01/5291, 01/5879: Cited, 00/3230:
Considered, 99/881
R. *v.* DPP Ex p. Lee [1999] 1 W.L.R. 1950; [1999] 2 All E.R. 737; [1999] 2 Cr. App. R. 304; (1999) 163 J.P. 569; (1999) 163 J.P.N. 651; (1999) 143 S.J.L.B. 174; *Times*, April 26, 1999, QBD .... *Digested, 99/***880**
R. *v.* DPP Ex p. Manning [2001] Q.B. 330; [2000] 3 W.L.R. 463; [2001] H.R.L.R. 3; *Times*, May 19, 2000; *Independent*, June 6, 2000, QBD .... *Digested, 00/***1096**
R. *v.* DPP Ex p. McGeary see R. *v.* Gloucester Crown Court Ex p. McGeary
R. *v.* DPP Ex p. Merton LBC (No.1) [1999] C.O.D. 161, QBD
R. *v.* DPP Ex p. Merton LBC (No.2) [1999] C.O.D. 358, QBD
R. *v.* DPP Ex p. Rechachi see R. *v.* DPP Ex p. Kebilene
R. *v.* DPP Ex p. Souidi (Sofiane) see R. *v.* DPP Ex p. Kebilene
R. *v.* DPP Ex p. Taussik [2001] A.C.D. 10, QBD
R. *v.* DPP Ex p. Treadaway, *Times*, October 31, 1997, QBD .... *Digested, 97/***1371**:
Approved, 01/5878

R. *v.* DPP Ex p. Ward (Jack) see DPP *v.* Ward (Jack)
R. *v.* DR (Appeal against Sentence: Appellants Age) [2000] 2 Cr. App. R. (S.) 314,
   CA (Crim Div) . . . .   *Digested,* 00/**1141**
R. *v.* DR (Appeal against Sentence: Guilty Plea) [2000] 2 Cr. App. R. (S.) 239, CA
   (Crim Div) . . . .   *Digested,* 00/**1394**
R. *v.* Drabble (Stephen Jeffrey) [1996] 2 Cr. App. R. (S.) 322, CA (Crim Div) . . . .   *Digested,* 96/**2040**:
                                                       Considered, 00/1390
R. *v.* Drady (Elliott John) see Attorney General's Reference (Nos.48 and 49 of 1997),
   Re
R. *v.* Draper (John) see R. *v.* Dennard (William)
R. *v.* Drew (Alan Clive) [1998] 1 Cr. App. R. (S.) 75, CA (Crim Div) . . . .   *Digested,* 98/**1221**
R. *v.* Drew (Martin Ralph) [2000] 1 Cr. App. R. 91; [1999] Crim. L.R. 581;
   Independent, March 1, 1999 (C.S.), CA (Crim Div). . . . .   *Digested,* 99/**924**:
                                                       Followed, 99/925
R. *v.* Drury (Christopher); R. *v.* Clark (Robert); R. *v.* Reynolds (Thomas); R. *v.* O'Connell
   (Terance); R. *v.* Kingston (Thomas) [2001] EWCA Crim 975; [2001] Crim. L.R.
   847, CA (Crim Div)
R. *v.* Dryden (Sandra Lee) see R. *v.* Williams (Derek Anthony)
R. *v.* Drysdale (Andrew McDonald) (1993) 14 Cr. App. R. (S.) 15, CA (Crim Div) . . . . .   *Digested,* 93/**1190**:
                                                       Considered, 00/1277
R. *v.* DS see Attorney General's Reference (No.60 of 2000), Re
R. *v.* DS [1999] Crim. L.R. 911, CA (Crim Div)
R. *v.* Dudeye (Said) [1998] 2 Cr. App. R. (S.) 430, CA (Crim Div) . . . .   *Digested,* 99/**1244**
R. *v.* Dudley (Thomas); R. *v.* Stephens (Edward) (1884-85) L.R. 14 Q.B.D. 273, QBD . .   *Applied,* 86/649,
               87/800: *Considered,* 71/9950, 00/3246: *Distinguished,* 75/622
R. *v.* Dudley Magistrates Court Ex p. Hollis; Hollis *v.* Dudley MBC; Probert *v.* Dudley
   MBC [1999] 1 W.L.R. 642; [1998] 1 All E.R. 759; [1998] Env. L.R. 354; [1998]
   E.H.L.R. 42; (1998) 30 H.L.R. 902; [1998] 2 E.G.L.R. 19; [1998] 18 E.G. 133;
   [1998] J.P.L. 652; [1998] C.O.D. 186; [1997] N.P.C. 169; *Times,* December 12,
   1997, QBD . . . .   *Digested,* 98/**4048**
R. *v.* Dudley Magistrates Court Ex p. Power City Stores Ltd (1990) 154 J.P. 654;
   (1990) 154 J.P.N. 490; (1990) 140 N.L.J. 361, QBD. . . . .   *Digested,* 90/**892**:
                Considered, 92/747, 97/540: *Followed,* 98/468: *Referred to,* 96/1571
R. *v.* Dudney; *sub nom* Dudney *v.* R. 2 I.T.L. Rep. 627, CA (Can); affirming 1 I.T.L. Rep.
   371, Tax Ct (Can)
R. *v.* Duffy (Paula) (No.1) [1999] Q.B. 919; [1998] 3 W.L.R. 1060; [1999] 1 Cr. App.
   R. 307; [1998] Crim. L.R. 650; (1998) 95(20) L.S.G. 33; (1998) 142 S.J.L.B.
   149; *Times,* May 2, 1998, CA (Crim Div) . . . .   *Digested,* 98/**883**
R. *v.* Duggan (John William Thomas) [1999] 2 Cr. App. R. (S.) 65, CA (Crim Div) . . . . .   *Digested,* 99/**1121**
R. *v.* Duhaney (Michael) see R. *v.* Stoddart (John)
R. *v.* DuKett (Ian) [1998] 2 Cr. App. R. (S.) 59, CA (Crim Div) . . . .   *Digested,* 98/**1165**
R. *v.* Dunlop (William Vincent) [2001] 2 Cr. App. R. (S.) 27, CA (Crim Div) . . . .   *Digested,* 01/**1448**
R. *v.* Dunne (William Gerard) (1998) 162 J.P. 399; *Times,* March 16, 1998;
   Independent, March 20, 1998, CA (Crim Div) . . . .   *Digested,* 98/**961**
R. *v.* Dunraven School Governors Ex p. B (A Child) [2000] B.L.G.R. 494; [2000] Ed.
   C.R. 291; [2000] E.L.R. 156; (2000) 97(4) L.S.G. 32; (2000) 144 S.J.L.B. 51;
   Times, February 3, 2000, CA; reversing *Times,* November 10, 1999, QBD . . . . . .   *Digested,* 00/**1925**:
                                                       Applied, 01/1975
R. *v.* Dunscombe (James) see R. *v.* Gee (Arthur)
R. (on the application of Lowther) *v.* Durham CC; *sub nom* R. *v.* Durham CC Ex p.
   Lowther [2001] EWCA Civ 781; [2001] 3 P.L.R. 83; [2001] 22 E.G.C.S. 154;
   (2001) 98(23) L.S.G. 42; *Times,* June 22, 2001, CA; affirming [2001] Env. L.R.
   18; (2001) 81 P. & C.R. 4; [2001] J.P.L. 354, QBD . . . .   *Digested,* 01/**4659**
R. *v.* Durham CC Ex p. Curtis see R. *v.* Devon CC Ex p. Baker
R. *v.* Durham CC Ex p. Huddleston; *sub nom* R. *v.* Durham CC Ex p. Huddlestone
   [2000] 1 W.L.R. 1484; [2000] 2 C.M.L.R. 313; [2000] Eu. L.R. 514; [2000]
   Env. L.R. 488; [2000] 1 P.L.R. 122; [2000] J.P.L. 1125; [2000] E.G.C.S. 39;
   (2000) 97(13) L.S.G. 43; (2000) 144 S.J.L.B. 149; [2000] N.P.C. 24; [2000]
   Env. L.R. D20; *Times,* March 15, 2000, CA; reversing [2000] 2 C.M.L.R. 229;
   [2000] Env. L.R. 463; (2000) 80 P. & C.R. 481; *Times,* January 28, 2000,
   QBD . . . .   *Digested,* 00/**4458**
R. *v.* Durham CC Ex p. Huddleston (Leave to Appeal); *sub nom* R. *v.* Durham CC Ex p.
   Huddlestone (Leave to Appeal) [2000] J.P.L. 409; [2000] Env. L.R. D20,
   QBD . . . .   *Digested,* 00/**2267**
R. *v.* Durham CC Ex p. Huddlestone see R. *v.* Durham CC Ex p. Huddleston
R. *v.* Durham CC Ex p. Huddlestone (Leave to Appeal) see R. *v.* Durham CC Ex p.
   Huddleston (Leave to Appeal)
R. *v.* Durham CC Ex p. Lowther see R. (on the application of Lowther) *v.* Durham CC
R. *v.* Durham CC Ex p. Page [1998] N.P.C. 77, QBD
R. *v.* Duzgun (Selim) [2000] 2 Costs L.R. 316, Sup Ct Costs Office . . . .   *Digested,* 01/**4231**
R. *v.* Dyfed CC Ex p. S (Minors) [1995] 1 F.C.R. 113; (1994) 138 S.J.L.B. 194; *Times,*
   July 25, 1994; *Independent,* August 12, 1994, CA; affirming *Independent,*
   December 21, 1993, QBD. . . . .   *Digested,* 95/**1909**:
                                                       Followed, 98/1913

R. v. Dyke (Phillip) see Attorney General's Reference (No.12 of 1994), Re

R. v. Dyson (Gerald Frank) see Attorney General's Reference (No.46 of 2000), Re

R. v. E; *sub nom* R. v. ABE [2000] 1 Cr. App. R. (S.) 78, CA (Crim Div) . . . .   *Digested,* 00/**1355**:
Considered, 00/1352

R. v. E (Andrew Paul James) [1999] 1 Cr. App. R. (S.) 301, CA (Crim Div). . . . .   *Digested,* 99/**1094**

R. v. E (Jamie) (A Juvenile) [2001] EWCA Crim 582; [2001] 2 Cr. App. R. (S.) 93, CA
(Crim Div). . . . .   *Digested,* 01/**1379**

R. v. E (Nicholas) (A Juvenile) see Attorney General's Reference (No.33 of 2000), Re

R. v. E (Paul Martin) (A Juvenile), *Times,* December 3, 1999, CA (Crim Div). . . . .   *Digested,* 00/**1309**

R. v. E (Terry James) (A Juvenile) [2001] EWCA Crim 943; [2001] 2 Cr. App. R. (S.)
103; *Independent,* May 7, 2001 (C.S), CA (Crim Div)

R. v. E (Wendy Jacqueline) [1999] 2 Cr. App. R. (S.) 243; *Times,* March 22, 1999, CA
(Crim Div). . . . .   *Digested,* 99/**1149**

R. v. Eaglen (Timothy John) see Attorney General's Reference (No.13 of 1995), Re

R. v. Ealing DHA Ex p. Fox [1993] 1 W.L.R. 373; [1993] 3 All E.R. 170; (1993) 5
Admin. L.R. 596; [1993] 4 Med. L.R. 101; [1993] C.O.D. 478; (1992) 136
S.J.L.B. 220; *Times,* June 24, 1992, QBD . . . .   *Digested,* 93/**2740**:
Applied, 00/4178

R. v. Ealing Justices Ex p. Avondale see R. v. Ealing Magistrates Court Ex p. Avondale

R. v. Ealing Justices Ex p. Dixon [1990] 2 Q.B. 91; [1989] 3 W.L.R. 1098; [1989] 2 All
E.R. 1050; [1989] Crim. L.R. 656; [1989] Crim. L.R. 835; [1989] C.O.D. 504;
(1989) 153 J.P.N. 564, QBD . . . .   *Digested,* 90/**1023**:
Distinguished, 90/1019, 94/1006: *Not followed,* 90/1018, 91/864, 00/1098

R. v. Ealing Justices Ex p. Saleem see R. v. St Helens Justices Ex p. Jones

R. v. Ealing LBC Ex p. C (A Minor) (2000) 3 C.C.L. Rep. 122, CA . . . .   *Digested,* 00/**3115**

R. v. Ealing LBC Ex p. Fox (1998) 95(11) L.S.G. 35; *Times,* March 9, 1998, QBD . . . . . .   *Digested,* 98/**3016**

R. v. Ealing LBC Ex p. Jehan see R. v. Hackney LBC Ex p. Adebiri

R. v. Ealing LBC Ex p. Surdonja [1999] 1 All E.R. 566; [1999] 1 F.L.R. 650; (1999) 31
H.L.R. 686; [1999] C.O.D. 85; [1999] Fam. Law 85; (1998) 95(43) L.S.G. 32;
(1998) 142 S.J.L.B. 284; *Times,* October 29, 1998, QBD . . . .   *Digested,* 98/**3027**

R. v. Ealing Magistrates Court Ex p. Avondale; *sub nom* R. v. Ealing Justices Ex p.
Avondale [1999] Crim. L.R. 840; [1999] C.O.D. 291, QBD

R. v. Ealing Magistrates Court Ex p. Burgess (2001) 165 J.P. 82; [2000] Crim. L.R.
855; (2001) 165 J.P.N. 125; *Independent,* January 24, 2000 (C.S), QBD

R. v. Ealing Magistrates Court Ex p. Sahota (1998) 162 J.P. 73; [1998] C.O.D. 167;
(1998) 162 J.P.N. 105; (1997) 141 S.J.L.B. 251; *Times,* December 9, 1997, QBD .   *Digested,* 98/**1070**

R. v. Earley (Simon); R. v. Bailey (Simon Paul) [1998] 2 Cr. App. R. (S.) 158, CA
(Crim Div). . . . .   *Digested,* 98/**1109**

R. v. Easington DC Ex p. Seaham Harbour Dock Co Ltd (1999) 1 L.G.L.R. 327; [1999]
P.L.C.R. 225, QBD . . . .   *Digested,* 99/**4199**

R. v. East Devon DC Ex p. Robb (1998) 30 H.L.R. 922, QBD . . . .   *Digested,* 98/**3006**

R. v. East Devon DC Housing Benefit Review Board Ex p. P (1999) 31 H.L.R. 936,
QBD . . . .   *Digested,* 00/**4820**

R. v. East Gwent Licensing Justices Ex p. Chief Constable of Gwent (2000) 164 J.P.
339; (2000) 164 J.P.N. 464, QBD

R. v. East Hertfordshire DC Ex p. Beckman (1998) 76 P. & C.R. 333; [1998] J.P.L. 55;
[1997] E.G.C.S. 104; (1997) 147 N.L.J. 1185, QBD . . . .   *Digested,* 98/**4161**:
Considered, 00/4508

R. v. East Lancashire HA Ex p. B [1997] C.O.D. 267, QBD

R. (on the application of B) v. East London and the City Mental Health NHS Trust; *sub
nom* R. v. Tower Hamlets Healthcare NHS Trust Ex p. V; R. v. Tower Hamlets
Healthcare NHS Trust Ex p. B; R. v. East London and the City Mental Health NHS
Trust Ex p. B [2001] EWCA Civ 239; [2001] 3 W.L.R. 588; (2001) 61 B.M.L.R.
206; (2001) 98(15) L.S.G. 33; (2001) 145 S.J.L.B. 107; *Times,* February 28,
2001; *Independent,* March 1, 2001, CA; affirming in part (2000) 3 C.C.L. Rep.
189; *Independent,* October 2, 2000 (C.S), QBD . . . .   *Digested,* 01/**4429**

R. v. East Lothian Council Ex p. Scottish Coal Co Ltd see Scottish Coal Co Ltd v. East
Lothian Council

R. v. East Sussex CC Ex p. ARC Ltd; R. v. East Sussex CC Ex p. Ross Douglas; R. v.
East Sussex CC Ex p. Simpson (Rye Harbour) Ltd [1999] N.P.C. 111; [2000] Env.
L.R. D8; *Times,* October 13, 1999, QBD . . . .   *Digested,* 99/**4245**

R. v. East Sussex CC Ex p. Bird CO 1109 96, QBD . . . .   *Digested,* 98/**1975**

R. v. East Sussex CC Ex p. Reprotech (Pebsham) Ltd see R. (on the application of
Reprotech (Pebsham) Ltd) v. East Sussex CC

R. v. East Sussex CC Ex p. Ross Douglas see R. v. East Sussex CC Ex p. ARC Ltd

R. v. East Sussex CC Ex p. Simpson (Rye Harbour) Ltd see R. v. East Sussex CC Ex p.
ARC Ltd

R. v. East Sussex CC Ex p. Tandy; *sub nom* T (A Minor), Re [1998] A.C. 714; [1998] 2
W.L.R. 884; [1998] 2 All E.R. 769; [1998] 2 F.C.R. 221; (1998) 10 Admin. L.R.
453; [1998] Ed. C.R. 206; [1998] E.L.R. 251; (1997-98) 1 C.C.L. Rep. 352;
(1998) 42 B.M.L.R. 173; (1998) 95(24) L.S.G. 33; (1998) 148 N.L.J. 781;
(1998) 142 S.J.L.B. 179; *Times*, May 21, 1998; *Independent*, May 22, 1998, HL;
reversing [1997] 3 W.L.R. 884; [1997] 3 F.C.R. 542; (1997) Admin. L.R. 689;
[1998] E.L.R. 80; [1998] C.O.D. 23; (1997) 161 J.P.N. 1058; (1997) 94(34)
L.S.G. 27; (1997) 141 S.J.L.B. 207; *Times*, October 2, 1997; *Independent*,
October 8, 1997, CA; reversing [1997] 3 F.C.R. 525; (1997) 9 Admin. L.R. 573;
[1997] E.L.R. 311; *Times*, April 29, 1997; *Independent*, April 28, 1997 (C.S.),
QBD . . . . *Digested*, 98/**1871**:
Applied, 01/1960: *Considered*, 98/2997, 99/1899

R. v. East Sussex CC Ex p. W (A Minor) [1998] 2 F.L.R. 1082; [1999] 1 F.C.R. 536;
[1999] C.O.D. 55; [1998] Fam. Law 736; (1999) 163 J.P.N. 495, QBD . . . . *Digested*, 99/**2347**

R. v. East Sussex CC Ex p. Ward (2000) 3 C.C.L. Rep. 132, QBD . . . . *Digested*, 00/**4899**

R. v. Eastap (Robert Leslie); R. v. Curt (Anthony); R. v. Thompson (John William)
[1997] 2 Cr. App. R. (S.) 55; [1997] Crim. L.R. 241, CA (Crim Div) . . . . *Digested*, 97/**1415**:
Considered, 98/1132

R. v. Eastleigh Magistrates Court Ex p. Sansome; *sub nom* R. v. Southampton
Magistrates Court Ex p. Sansome [1999] 1 Cr. App. R. (S.) 112; [1998] Crim.
L.R. 595; [1998] C.O.D. 264; *Times*, May 14, 1998, QBD . . . . *Digested*, 98/**1010**

R. v. Easton (Christopher John) see R. v. Makanjuola (Oluwanfunso)

R. v. Eaton (Craig Keith) see R. v. Archer (Patrick John)

R. v. Eaton (Michael James), *Times*, December 29, 1997, CA (Crim Div) . . . . *Digested*, 98/**1201**

R. v. Eaton (Spencer William) (1989) 11 Cr. App. R. (S.) 475; *Times*, October 14, 1989,
CA (Crim Div) . . . . *Digested*, 91/**1166**:
Cited, 93/1204, 95/1433: *Considered*, 92/1338, 93/1224, 97/1591, 00/1366,
01/1423, 01/1434

R. v. Ebanks (Michael Anthony) [1998] 2 Cr. App. R. (S.) 339, CA (Crim Div) . . . . *Digested*, 98/**1379**

R. v. Ecclestone (Paul) (1995) 16 Cr. App. R. (S.) 9, CA (Crim Div) . . . . *Digested*, 96/**1894**:
Considered, 96/1891, 97/1538, 97/1539, 98/1219

R. v. Economic Secretary to the Treasury Ex p. Smedley see R. v. HM Treasury Ex p.
Smedley

R. v. Edgehill (Frank Lloyd) [1963] 1 Q.B. 593; [1963] 2 W.L.R. 170; [1963] 1 All E.R.
181; (1963) 47 Cr. App. R. 41; 106 S.J. 1054, CCA . . . . *Digested*, 63/**666.a**:
Applied, 00/5481: *Considered*, 63/666: *Explained*, 63/668

R. v. Edjedewe (Thomas) see R. v. Keyes (Anthony Matthew)

R. v. Edlin (Charles Ernest) see R. v. Bradbury (Alan Henry)

R. v. Edmonds (Ross Alexander) [1999] 1 Cr. App. R. (S.) 475, CA (Crim Div) . . . . *Digested*, 99/**1289**

R. v. Edmunds (Damien Joseph) [2000] 2 Cr. App. R. (S.) 62, CA (Crim Div) . . . . *Digested*, 00/**1410**

R. v. Edwards [1996] 132 D.L.R. (4th) 31, Sup Ct (Can) . . . . *Considered*, 99/3120

R. v. Edwards; R. v. Lake (Deceased) [1998] Crim. L.R. 756, CA (Crim Div)

R. v. Edwards (Angela) (1992) 13 Cr. App. R. (S.) 662, CA (Crim Div) . . . . *Digested*, 93/**1152**:
Considered, 98/1314

R. v. Edwards (Anthony Glen) [1998] 2 Cr. App. R. (S.) 213; [1998] Crim. L.R. 298,
CA (Crim Div) . . . . *Digested*, 98/**665**:
Followed, 99/1156

R. v. Edwards (Anthony Paul); R. v. Brandy (Terence) (1996) 93(22) L.S.G. 26;
(1996) 140 S.J.L.B. 135; *Times*, July 1, 1996; *Independent*, July 1, 1996 (C.S.),
CA (Crim Div) . . . . *Digested*, 96/**1750**:
Considered, 97/1417, 98/1138

R. v. Edwards (Brynley Maldwin) [2001] EWCA Crim 862; [2001] 2 Cr. App. R. (S.)
125, CA (Crim Div) . . . . *Digested*, 01/**1425**

R. v. Edwards (Duncan) [2000] 1 Cr. App. R. (S.) 98, CA (Crim Div) . . . . *Digested*, 00/**1170**

R. v. Edwards (Elroy Everton) [1998] Crim. L.R. 207, CA (Crim Div)

R. v. Edwards (Gareth Stephen) see Attorney General's Reference (No.18 of 2001), Re

R. v. Edwards (John) [1991] 1 W.L.R. 207; [1991] 2 All E.R. 266; (1991) 93 Cr. App.
R. 48; [1991] Crim. L.R. 372; (1991) 141 N.L.J. 91; *Times*, January 17, 1991;
Independent, January 17, 1991; *Daily Telegraph*, January 24, 1991, CA (Crim
Div) . . . . *Digested*, 91/**732**:
Applied, 97/2033, 00/932: *Considered*, 93/837, 94/798, 96/1410:
Followed, 96/1329

R. v. Edwards (Martin John) (1990) 12 Cr. App. R. (S.) 199, CA (Crim Div) . . . . *Digested*, 91/**1163**:
Considered, 97/1564, 99/1261

R. v. Edwards (Sean Karl) (1992) 13 Cr. App. R. (S.) 356, CA (Crim Div) . . . . *Digested*, 93/**1139**:
Considered, 97/1520, 00/1226: *Distinguished*, 97/1521

R. v. Edwards (Thomas) see Attorney General's Reference (Nos.24 and 25 of 2000),
Re

R. v. Edwards (Vincent) see Attorney General's Reference (Nos.41 and 42 of 1995), Re

R. *v.* Effik (Godwin Eno); R. *v.* Mitchell (Graham Martin) [1995] 1 A.C. 309; [1994] 3
W.L.R. 583; [1994] 3 All E.R. 458; (1994) 99 Cr. App. R. 312; [1994] Crim. L.R.
832; (1994) 158 J.P.N. 552; (1994) 91 (39) L.S.G. 39; (1994) 138 S.J.L.B. 167;
Times, July 22, 1994; *Independent,* July 29, 1994, HL; affirming (1992) 95 Cr.
App. R. 427; (1992) 156 J.P. 830; [1992] Crim. L.R. 580; (1992) 156 J.P.N. 476;
(1992) 142 N.L.J. 492; *Times,* March 23, 1992; *Independent,* March 31, 1992;
Guardian, April 29, 1992, CA (Crim Div) . . . .   *Digested,* 94/**685**:
            Applied, 93/664, 99/981: *Considered,* 95/2285, 97/1129: *Overruled,* 94/864,
                                                00/920

R. *v.* Egan (Michael) [1998] 1 Cr. App. R. 121; (1997) 35 B.M.L.R. 103; [1997] Crim.
L.R. 225; *Times,* October 14, 1996, CA (Crim Div) . . . .   *Digested,* 96/**3885**:
                 Disapproved, 00/982: *Distinguished,* 99/942: *Doubted,* 99/933

R. *v.* El-Hinnachi (Samir); R. *v.* Cooney (Nicholas); R. *v.* Ward (Francis); R. *v.* Tanswell
(Warren) [1998] 2 Cr. App. R. 226; [1998] Crim. L.R. 881, CA (Crim Div) . . . . .   *Digested,* 98/**901**

R. *v.* El-Kurd (Ussama Sammy) [2001] Crim. L.R. 234; *Independent,* October 26,
2000, CA (Crim Div) . . . .   *Digested,* 00/**1083**

R. *v.* Elahee [1999] Crim. L.R. 399, CA (Crim Div)

R. *v.* Elcock (David Haughton); R. *v.* Manton (Desmond) [1998] 2 Cr. App. R. (S.)
126, CA (Crim Div) . . . .   *Digested,* 98/**1231**

R. *v.* Eldridge [1999] Crim. L.R. 166, CA (Crim Div)

R. (on the application of Robertson) *v.* Electoral Registration Officer see R. (on the
application of Robertson) *v.* Wakefield MDC

R. *v.* Eley (David Colin); R. *v.* Bull (Wilfred George) [1999] 1 Cr. App. R. (S.) 252;
[1999] Env. L.R. D3, CA (Crim Div) . . . .   *Digested,* 99/**1150**

R. *v.* Eliot (Giles) (1988) 10 Cr. App. R. (S.) 454; [1989] Crim. L.R. 306, CA (Crim
Div) . . . .   *Digested,* 91/**1105**:
                     Considered, 99/1148: *Not followed,* 96/1852

R. *v.* Elliott (Denrick) [2000] Crim. L.R. 51, CA (Crim Div)

R. *v.* Elliott (Jeffrey Terence) see R. *v.* Boswell (James Thomas)

R. *v.* Elliott (Stephen James) [2000] 1 Cr. App. R. (S.) 264, CA (Crim Div) . . . .   *Digested,* 00/**1120**

R. *v.* Ellis (Norman) [1998] Crim. L.R. 660, CA (Crim Div)

R. *v.* Ellis (Paul Edward); R. *v.* Avis (Edward) [2000] 1 Cr. App. R. (S.) 38, CA (Crim
Div) . . . .   *Digested,* 00/**1229**

R. *v.* Ellis (Peter) (1995) 16 Cr. App. R. (S.) 773, CA (Crim Div) . . . .   *Digested,* 96/**2021**:
                                             Considered, 98/1307

R. *v.* Ellis (Reginald) (Leave to Appeal against Conviction) see R. *v.* Panayis
(Charalambos)

R. *v.* Ellis (Reginald) (Appeal against Sentence) [1999] 1 Cr. App. R. (S.) 374, CA
(Crim Div) . . . .   *Digested,* 99/**1172**

R. *v.* Ellis (Stephen) [1999] 1 Cr. App. R. (S.) 245, CA (Crim Div) . . . .   *Digested,* 99/**1253**:
                                             Considered, 99/1251

R. *v.* Ellis (Stephen John) [2001] 1 Cr. App. R. (S.) 43; [2000] Crim. L.R. 703, CA
(Crim Div) . . . .   *Digested,* 01/**1493**

R. *v.* Ellison (John James) [1998] 2 Cr. App. R. (S.) 382, CA (Crim Div) . . . .   *Digested,* 99/**1274**:
                                             Considered, 00/1370

R. *v.* Elmbridge BC Ex p. Active Office Ltd (1998) 10 Admin. L.R. 561; (1998) 162
J.P.N. 828; (1998) 95(1) L.S.G. 24; *Times,* December 29, 1997, QBD . . . .   *Digested,* 98/**4196**

R. *v.* Elton (Andrew) [1999] 2 Cr. App. R. (S.) 58, CA (Crim Div) . . . .   *Digested,* 99/**1260**:
                                             Considered, 00/1364

R. *v.* Elul (Gil) [2001] EWCA Crim 177; [2001] 2 Cr. App. R. (S.) 68, CA (Crim Div). . . .   *Digested,* 01/**1451**

R. *v.* Emery-Barker (Henry Keith) (1990) 12 Cr. App. R. (S.) 78, CA (Crim Div) . . . .   *Considered,* 95/1410,
                                             97/1586, 98/1258

R. *v.* Emmanuel (Dada) [1998] Crim. L.R. 347, CA (Crim Div)

R. *v.* Emmett (Brian); R. *v.* Emmett (Michael) [1998] A.C. 773; [1997] 3 W.L.R. 1119;
[1997] 4 All E.R. 737; [1998] 1 Cr. App. R. 247; [1998] Crim. L.R. 413; (1997)
94(46) L.S.G. 29; (1997) 147 N.L.J. 1690; (1997) 141 S.J.L.B. 247; *Times,*
November 17, 1997; *Independent,* November 18, 1997, HL . . . .   *Digested,* 97/**1470**:
                                             Followed, 00/1169

R. *v.* Emmett (Michael) see R. *v.* Emmett (Brian)

R. *v.* Emmett (Stephen Roy), *Times,* October 15, 1999; *Independent,* July 19, 1999
(C.S.), CA (Crim Div) . . . .   *Digested,* 99/**961**

R. *v.* Emmin (Suleyman) (1995) 16 Cr. App. R. (S.) 63, CA (Crim Div) . . . .   *Digested,* 96/**1691**:
                                             Considered, 98/1110

R. *v.* EMW see Attorney General's Reference (No.77 of 2000), Re

R. *v.* Enfield LBC Ex p. TF Unwin (Roydon) 46 B.L.R. 1; (1989) 1 Admin. L.R. 51;
[1989] C.O.D. 466; (1989) 153 L.G. Rev. 890, DC . . . .   *Digested,* 90/**59**:
                                   Considered, 94/43: *Followed,* 01/4405

R. *v.* English (Paul Anthony) see R. *v.* Williams (David Omar)

R. *v.* English (Philip) see R. *v.* Powell (Anthony Glassford)

R. *v.* Enkel (Andrew) see R. *v.* O'Brien (Paul)

R. *v.* Entry Clearance Officer Ex p. Aidoo [1999] Imm. A.R. 221, QBD . . . .   *Digested,* 99/**3203**

R. (on the application of Anglian Water Services Ltd) *v.* Environment Agency; *sub nom* R. *v.* Environment Agency Ex p. Anglian Water Services Ltd; Environment Agency *v.* Anglian Water Services Ltd; C/2000/3450, CA; affirming [2001] E.H.L.R. 22; [2000] N.P.C. 113, QBD (Admin Ct) . . . .   *Digested,* 01/**5631**

R. (on the application of Beevers) *v.* Environment Agency [2001] J.P.L. 845 (Note), QBD (Admin Ct)

R. (on the application of Castle Cement Ltd) *v.* Environment Agency see Castle Cement *v.* Environment Agency

R. (on the application of Lomas) *v.* Environment Agency see R. (on the application of Moase) *v.* Environment Agency

R. (on the application of Marchiori) *v.* Environment Agency; *sub nom* R. *v.* Environment Agency Ex p. Marchiori; Marchiori *v.* Environment Agency; C/2001/0828, CA; affirming [2001] EWHC Admin 267; [2001] Env. L.R. 47; [2001] J.P.L. 1438 (Note); (2001) 98(15) L.S.G. 34; *Times,* May 1, 2001; *Independent,* May 21, 2001 (C.S); *Daily Telegraph,* April 3, 2001, QBD (Admin Ct) . . . .   *Digested,* 01/**2395**

R. (on the application of Mayer Parry Recycling Ltd) *v.* Environment Agency (No.1); *sub nom* R. *v.* Environment Agency Ex p. Mayer Parry Recycling Ltd (No.1) [2001] Env. L.R. 31, QBD . . . .   *Previous proceedings,* 99/2207

R. (on the application of Mayer Parry Recycling Ltd) *v.* Environment Agency (No.2); *sub nom* R. *v.* Environment Agency Ex p. Mayer Parry Recycling Ltd (No.2) [2001] C.P. Rep. 63; [2001] Env. L.R. 35, QBD (Admin Ct) . . . .   *Digested,* 01/**573**

R. (on the application of Moase) *v.* Environment Agency; R. (on the application of Lomas) *v.* Environment Agency [2001] Env. L.R. D12, QBD . . . .   *Previous proceedings,* 01/5630

R. *v.* Environment Agency Ex p. Anglian Water Services Ltd see R. (on the application of Anglian Water Services Ltd) *v.* Environment Agency

R. *v.* Environment Agency Ex p. Castle Cement Ltd see Castle Cement *v.* Environment Agency

R. *v.* Environment Agency Ex p. Dockgrange Ltd [1998] Eu. L.R. 407; [1997] Env. L.R. 575; [1997] N.P.C. 86; *Times,* June 21, 1997, QBD . . . .   *Digested,* 97/**2351**

R. *v.* Environment Agency Ex p. Gibson (No.2); R. *v.* Environment Agency Ex p. Leam (No.2); R. *v.* Environment Agency Ex p. Sellers (No.2) [1999] Env. L.R. 73, QBD . . . .   *Digested,* 99/**2190**

R. *v.* Environment Agency Ex p. Leam (No.2) see R. *v.* Environment Agency Ex p. Gibson (No.2)

R. *v.* Environment Agency Ex p. Marchiori see R. (on the application of Marchiori) *v.* Environment Agency

R. *v.* Environment Agency Ex p. Mayer Parry Recycling Ltd (No.1) see R. (on the application of Mayer Parry Recycling Ltd) *v.* Environment Agency (No.1)

R. *v.* Environment Agency Ex p. Mayer Parry Recycling Ltd (No.2) see R. (on the application of Mayer Parry Recycling Ltd) *v.* Environment Agency (No.2)

R. *v.* Environment Agency Ex p. Petrus Oils Ltd [1999] Env. L.R. 732; [1999] J.P.L. 839, QBD . . . .   *Digested,* 99/**2206**

R. *v.* Environment Agency Ex p. Sellers (No.2) see R. *v.* Environment Agency Ex p. Gibson (No.2)

R. *v.* Environment Agency Ex p. Turnbull [2000] Env. L.R. 715, QBD . . . .   *Digested,* 01/**2416**

R. (on the application of Philcox) *v.* Epping Forest DC; *sub nom* R. *v.* Epping Forest DC Ex p. Philcox (Certificate: Unlawful Granting); Epping Forest DC *v.* Philcox [2000] N.P.C. 146, CA; affirming [2000] Env. L.R. 745; (2001) 81 P. & C.R. 26; [2000] 4 P.L.R. 47; [2000] J.P.L. 1262, QBD . . . .   *Digested,* 01/**4702**

R. *v.* Epping Forest DC Ex p. Philcox (Certificate: Unlawful Granting) see R. (on the application of Philcox) *v.* Epping Forest DC

R. *v.* Epping Forest DC Ex p. Philcox (Misstatement: Ownership) [2000] P.L.C.R. 57, QBD . . . .   *Digested,* 00/**4463**

R. *v.* Epping Justices Ex p. Quy [1998] R.T.R. 158 (Note); [1993] Crim. L.R. 970, QBD .   *Digested,* 94/**3973**

R. *v.* Erdman (Anthony) see R. *v.* McFeeley (Jason)

R. *v.* Eren (Birol) see R. *v.* Marshall (Adrian John)

R. *v.* Errington (Keith Jay) [1999] 1 Cr. App. R. (S.) 403; [1999] Crim. L.R. 91, CA (Crim Div) . . . .   *Digested,* 99/**1248**

R. *v.* Eskdale (Stuart Anthony) [2001] EWCA Crim 1159; *Times,* June 21, 2001, CA (Crim Div) . . . .   *Digested,* 01/**1487**

R. *v.* Essex CC Ex p. DL (Unreported, November 3, 1998), QBD [*Ex rel.* Bruce R Silvester, Barrister, Lamb Chambers, Lamb Building, Temple, London] . . . .   *Digested,* 99/**1030**

R. *v.* Essex CC Ex p. Tarmac Roadstone Holdings Ltd [1998] 1 P.L.R. 79; [1998] P.L.C.R. 56; [1997] E.G.C.S. 128; [1997] N.P.C. 134, QBD . . . .   *Digested,* 98/**4221**

R. *v.* ET (Child Pornography) see R. *v.* T (Child Pornography)

R. *v.* Eubank (Winston) [2001] EWCA Crim 891; [2001] Crim. L.R. 495; *Times,* May 3, 2001, CA (Crim Div) . . . .   *Digested,* 01/**1140**

R. *v.* Evans (Andrew) [2000] B.C.C. 901; *Times,* November 16, 1999, CA (Crim Div) . . .   *Digested,* 99/**623**: *Applied,* 01/709

R. *v.* Evans (Cheryl Eleanor) [2000] 1 Cr. App. R. (S.) 144; [1999] Crim. L.R. 758; *Times,* June 8, 1999 ; *Independent,* June 25, 1999, CA (Crim Div) . . . .   *Digested,* 99/**1353**: *Considered,* 00/1210

R. v. Evans (Daniel John) [1998] 2 Cr. App. R. (S.) 72, CA (Crim Div) . . . .   *Digested*, 98/**1325**
R. v. Evans (David James) [2001] 1 Cr. App. R. (S.) 128, CA (Crim Div) . . . .   *Digested*, 01/**1228**
R. v. Evans (Gareth) see R. v. Gray (Darren John)
R. v. Evans (Glenn Clifford) [2000] 1 Cr. App. R. (S.) 454, CA (Crim Div) . . . .   *Digested*, 00/**1424**
R. v. Evans (Kelvin) (1992) 13 Cr. App. R. (S.) 377; *Times*, October 18, 1991, CA (Crim
    Div) . . . .   *Digested*, 93/**1002**:
    Considered, 99/1343
R. v. Evans (Maurice Edward) (1988) 10 Cr. App. R. (S.) 308, CA (Crim Div) . . . .   *Considered*, 98/1254,
    99/1210, 99/1306
R. v. Evans (Raymond Frederick) [1959] 1 W.L.R. 26; [1958] 3 All E.R. 673; (1959)
    43 Cr. App. R. 66; 123 J.P. 128; 103 S.J. 17, CCA . . . .   *Digested*, 59/**2013**:
    Applied, 68/859, 69/753, 00/1332: *Cited*, 91/1188: *Considered*, 89/1098,
    90/1389: *Distinguished*, 90/1231, 91/1047, 92/1197
R. v. Evans (Roger Paul) [2000] 1 Cr. App. R. (S.) 107, CA (Crim Div) . . . .   *Digested*, 00/**1205**
R. v. Evans Ex p. Pinochet Ugarte (No.1) see R. v. Bow Street Metropolitan Stipendiary
    Magistrate Ex p. Pinochet Ugarte (No.1)
R. v. Evans Ex p. Pinochet Ugarte (No.2) see R. v. Bow Street Metropolitan
    Stipendiary Magistrate Ex p. Pinochet Ugarte (No.2)
R. v. Evans-Southall [1998] 1 Costs L.R. 68 . . . .   *Digested*, 00/**3981**
R. v. Everleigh (Martyn Latham) [2001] EWCA Crim 1276; [2001] Crim. L.R. 662;
    Times, May 16, 2001, CA (Crim Div) . . . .   *Digested*, 01/**1243**
R. v. Exley (Warren); R. v. Day (Mark Alan) [2000] 2 Cr. App. R. (S.) 189, CA (Crim
    Div) . . . .   *Digested*, 00/**1183**
R. v. Eyck (Dennis Jerrel); R. v. Hadakoglu (Yakup) [2000] 1 W.L.R. 1389; [2000] 3
    All E.R. 569; [2000] 2 Cr. App. R. 50; [2000] I.N.L.R. 277; [2000] Crim. L.R.
    299; (2000) 97(5) L.S.G. 34; (2000) 144 S.J.L.B. 59; *Times*, February 8, 2000,
    CA (Crim Div) . . . .   *Digested*, 00/**978**
R. v. F (A Minor) see F (A Minor) v. Brent LBC
R. v. F (Anthony) (1992) 13 Cr. App. R. (S.) 420, CA (Crim Div) . . . .   *Digested*, 93/**1193**:
    Considered, 98/1254, 99/1198
R. v. F (Anthony Robin) [1999] Crim. L.R. 306; *Times*, October 20, 1998;
    Independent, November 9, 1998 (C.S.), CA (Crim Div) . . . .   *Digested*, 98/**988**
R. v. F (Fabian) (A Juvenile) [1999] 1 Cr. App. R. (S.) 411, CA (Crim Div) . . . .   *Digested*, 99/**1158**
R. v. F (Frederick Joseph) see Attorney General's Reference (No.13 of 2000), Re
R. v. F (Mark Anthony) [2001] 1 Cr. App. R. (S.) 100, CA (Crim Div) . . . .   · *Digested*, 01/**1485**
R. v. F (Mark Frank); R. v. L (Claire Louise); R. v. ML (A Juvenile); R. v. B (Christopher
    John) (A Juvenile); R. v. H (Ann Nolene) (A Juvenile) [2001] 1 Cr. App. R. 17;
    [2000] Crim. L.R. 1018; *Times*, October 24, 2000, CA (Crim Div) . . . .   *Digested*, 00/**1073**
R. v. F (Nicholas) (A Juvenile) see Attorney General's Reference (Nos.11 and 12 of
    2000), Re
R. v. F (Paul) (A Juvenile); R. v. S (Matthew John) (A Juvenile) [2000] 1 W.L.R. 266;
    [2000] 1 Cr. App. R. (S.) 519; [2000] Crim. L.R. 113; *Times*, October 29, 1999,
    CA (Crim Div) . . . .   *Digested*, 99/**1232**
R. v. F (Paul) (A Juvenile); R. v. W (Dale) (A Juvenile) [2001] 1 Cr. App. R. (S.) 104;
    (2001) 165 J.P. 77; [2000] Crim. L.R. 1020, CA (Crim Div) . . . .   *Digested*, 01/**1224**
R. v. F (Richard John) see Attorney General's Reference (No.2 of 2001) (Unduly
    Lenient Sentence), Re
R. v. F (Suzzane) (A Juvenile) see R. v. T (Anita Grant) (A Juvenile)
R. v. F (Timothy Patrick) (A Juvenile) [1998] 1 Cr. App. R. (S.) 167, CA (Crim Div) . . . .   *Digested*, 98/**1295**
R. v. F (Toby) see Attorney General's Reference (No.24 of 1999), Re
R. v. F Howe & Son (Engineers) Ltd [1999] 2 All E.R. 249; [1999] 2 Cr. App. R. (S.)
    37; (1999) 163 J.P. 359; [1999] I.R.L.R. 434; [1999] Crim. L.R. 238; (1999)
    163 J.P.N. 693; (1998) 95(46) L.S.G. 34; *Times*, November 27, 1998;
    Independent, November 13, 1998, CA (Crim Div) . . . .   *Digested*, 98/**2839**:
    Applied, 99/2860, 01/3296: *Considered*, 00/2968, 01/1348, 01/1350:
    Followed, 99/2858
R. v. Faal (Adbou) [1999] Crim. L.R. 833, CA (Crim Div)
R. v. Fadden (Anthony) see R. v. Simpson (David)
R. v. Fairburn (David Charles); R. v. McCarthy (Keith Anthony) [1998] 2 Cr. App. R.
    (S.) 4, CA (Crim Div) . . . .   *Digested*, 98/**1187**
R. v. Fairfax (Kenneth) (No.2) see Attorney General's Reference (No.16 of 1994), Re
R. v. Fairfax (Kenneth) (No.1) [1995] Crim. L.R. 949, CA (Crim Div) . . . .   *Digested*, 96/**1412**:
    Considered, 98/884
R. v. Fairhurst (Brett) [2000] 1 Costs L.R. 34 [*Ex rel.* Vine Pemberton Joss, Practice
    Manager, St. Paul's Chambers, 23 Park Square, Leeds] . . . .   *Digested*, 00/**3971**

R. *v.* Fairhurst (Jonathan) [1986] 1 W.L.R. 1374; [1987] 1 All E.R. 46; (1987) 84 Cr.
App. R. 19; (1986) 8 Cr. App. R. (S.) 346; (1987) 151 J.P. 840; [1987] Crim. L.R.
60; (1987) 151 J.P.N. 684; (1986) 83 L.S.G. 2755; (1986) 130 S.J. 766, CA
(Crim Div) . . . .   *Digested,* 87/**1079**:
Applied, 87/965, 87/978, 88/941, 88/942, 88/943, 89/1058, 89/1059,
90/1481: *Cited,* 87/975, 88/912, 89/1060, 89/1063, 90/1310, 93/1337:
Considered, 88/812, 88/945, 88/946, 89/794, 89/1061, 90/1054,
90/1478.a, 90/1482, 91/1243, 96/1962, 96/1963, 96/1980,
97/1531, 98/1072, 98/1271, 98/1274, 98/1276, 98/1281, 98/1286, 98/1294,
98/1299, 00/1328: *Followed,* 95/1510, 96/1959, 97/1603:
Referred to, 95/1505, 95/1506
R. *v.* Fairoaks Airport Ltd Ex p. Roads (1999) 1 L.G.L.R. 511; [1999] C.O.D. 168;
[1999] Env. L.R. D14, QBD . . . .   *Digested,* 99/**92**
R. *v.* Falls (Raymond Carberry), *Times,* January 15, 1998, CMAC . . . .   *Digested,* 98/**1090**
R. *v.* Falmouth and Truro Port HA Ex p. South West Water Ltd; *sub nom* Falmouth and
Truro Port HA *v.* South West Water Ltd [2001] Q.B. 445; [2000] 3 W.L.R. 1464;
[2000] 3 All E.R. 306; [2000] Env. L.R. 658; [2000] E.H.L.R. 306; (2000) 2
L.G.L.R. 1061; [2000] J.P.L. 1174 (Note); [2000] E.G.C.S. 50; (2000) 97(23)
L.S.G. 41; [2000] N.P.C. 36; *Times,* April 24, 2000, CA; affirming (1999) 163
J.P. 589; [1999] Env. L.R. 833; [1999] E.H.L.R. 358; (1999) 1 L.G.L.R. 941;
[1999] C.O.D. 305; (1999) 163 J.P.N. 1025; [1999] E.G.C.S. 62; (1999) 96(18)
L.S.G. 35; [1999] N.P.C. 49; *Times,* May 6, 1999, QBD . . . .   *Digested,* 00/**2304**:
Applied, 01/4550: *Considered,* 01/2423, 01/2426
R. *v.* Falshaw (Michael) (1993) 14 Cr. App. R. (S.) 749, CA (Crim Div) . . . .   *Digested,* 94/**1247**:
Considered, 98/1181
R. *v.* Family Health Services Appeal Authority Ex p. Boots the Chemist Ltd (1997) 33
B.M.L.R. 1; *Times,* June 28, 1996, QBD . . . .   *Digested,* 96/**4419**:
Considered, 99/2846
R. *v.* Family Health Services Appeal Authority Ex p. E Moss Ltd (1999) 48 B.M.L.R.
204; [1999] C.O.D. 496, CA . . . .   *Digested,* 99/**2846**:
Applied, 99/2847
R. *v.* Family Health Services Appeal Authority Ex p. Elmfield Drugs Ltd; R. *v.* Family
Health Services Appeal Authority Ex p. Selles Dispensing Chemists Ltd
(Beverley); R. *v.* Family Health Services Appeal Authority Ex p. Selles Dispensing
Chemists Ltd (Caistor) (1999) 46 B.M.L.R. 191; [1998] C.O.D. 468; (1998)
95(35) L.S.G. 37; *Times,* September 16, 1998; *Independent,* October 5, 1998
(C.S.), CA; affirming [1998] C.O.D. 33; *Independent,* October 20, 1997 (C.S.),
QBD . . . .   *Digested,* 98/**2668**
R. *v.* Family Health Services Appeal Authority Ex p. Muralidhar [1999] C.O.D. 80, QBD .   *Digested,* 99/**2683**
R. *v.* Family Health Services Appeal Authority Ex p. Safeway Stores Plc [1999] J.P.L.
1133, QBD . . . .   *Digested,* 00/**2907**
R. *v.* Family Health Services Appeal Authority Ex p. Selles Dispensing Chemists Ltd
(Beverley) see R. *v.* Family Health Services Appeal Authority Ex p. Elmfield
Drugs Ltd
R. *v.* Family Health Services Appeal Authority Ex p. Selles Dispensing Chemists Ltd
(Caistor) see R. *v.* Family Health Services Appeal Authority Ex p. Elmfield Drugs
Ltd
R. *v.* Family Health Services Appeal Authority Ex p. Tesco Stores Ltd (No.2) (1999) 11
Admin. L.R. 1007; [1999] Lloyd's Rep. Med. 377; (2000) 53 B.M.L.R. 130;
[1999] C.O.D. 503; *Times,* August 25, 1999, QBD . . . .   *Digested,* 99/**2847**
R. *v.* Fanson (Christopher Edward) (1992) 13 Cr. App. R. (S.) 78, CA (Crim Div) . . . . . .   *Digested,* 92/**1146**:
Considered, 98/1106
R. *v.* Fantom (Mark Edward) [1999] 2 Cr. App. R. (S.) 275, CA (Crim Div) . . . .   *Digested,* 99/**1133**
R. *v.* Farah (Safia) [1997] 2 Cr. App. R. (S.) 333, CA (Crim Div) . . . .   *Digested,* 98/**1246**
R. *v.* Fareham Youth Court Ex p. Crown Prosecution Service; *sub nom* R. *v.* Fareham
Youth Court Ex p. DPP; R. *v.* Fareham Youth Court Ex p. M (1999) 163 J.P. 812;
[1999] Crim. L.R. 325; (2000) 164 J.P.N. 66, QBD . . . .   *Digested,* 00/**1333**
R. *v.* Fareham Youth Court Ex p. DPP see R. *v.* Fareham Youth Court Ex p. Crown
Prosecution Service
R. *v.* Fareham Youth Court Ex p. M see R. *v.* Fareham Youth Court Ex p. Crown
Prosecution Service
R. *v.* Farooqi (Numan) [1999] 1 Cr. App. R. (S.) 379, CA (Crim Div) . . . .   *Digested,* 99/**1135**
R. *v.* Farr (Roger John) (1999) 163 J.P. 193; [1999] Crim. L.R. 506; (1999) 163 J.P.N.
172; *Times,* December 10, 1998; *Independent,* December 10, 1998, CA (Crim
Div) . . . .   *Digested,* 99/**1055**
R. *v.* Farrow (Neil Jack) see Attorney General's Reference (No.89 of 1999), Re
R. *v.* Farrugia (Francis); R. *v.* Agius (Jean); R. *v.* Borg (Charles); R. *v.* Gauchi (Ronnie)
(1979) 69 Cr. App. R. 108; [1979] Crim. L.R. 672, CA (Crim Div) . . . .   *Digested,* 79/**540**:
Approved, 86/743, 87/994: *Considered,* 87/997, 92/1367, 96/1889, 96/2036,
98/1338, 00/1385: *Referred to,* 84/885, 89/1072
R. *v.* Faryab (Frank) [1999] B.P.I.R. 569; [2000] Crim. L.R. 180, CA (Crim Div) . . . . . .   *Digested,* 99/**868**
R. *v.* Faulkner [1998] 1 Costs L.R. 66

R. *v.* Fawcett (Kenneth John) (1983) 5 Cr. App. R. (S.) 158, CA (Crim Div) . . . .   *Digested,* 84/**836**:
          Applied, 00/1335: *Cited,* 93/1025, 96/1866: *Considered,* 96/1926, 97/1511,
                                        98/1172: *Followed,* 01/1385
R. *v.* Fay (Michael Augustus) see DPP *v.* Doot
R. *v.* Fazal (Naeem) [1999] 1 Cr. App. R. (S.) 152, CA (Crim Div) . . . .   *Digested,* 99/**1070**
R. *v.* Feakes (Stephen) [1998] 2 Cr. App. R. (S.) 295, CA (Crim Div) . . . .   *Digested,* 98/**1394**
R. *v.* Fearon (Paul) [1996] 2 Cr. App. R. (S.) 25; (1996) 160 J.P. 341, CA (Crim Div) . . .   *Digested,* 96/**1745**:
                                          Distinguished, 00/1118: *Followed,* 00/1380
R. *v.* Fearon (Robert) see Attorney General's Reference (No.7 of 1997), Re
R. *v.* Featherstone Prison Ex p. Bowen; R. *v.* Governor of Blundeston Prison Ex p.
    Bowen; R. *v.* Stafford Prison Ex p. Bowen; CO/1238/97, CO/3497/96, CO/
    4220/97, QBD . . . .   *Digested,* 99/**4106**
R. *v.* Federal Steam Navigation Co Ltd see Federal Steam Navigation Co Ltd *v.*
    Department of Trade and Industry (The Huntingdon)
R. *v.* Feld (Robert Philip) [1999] 1 Cr. App. R. (S.) 1, CA (Crim Div) . . . .   *Digested,* 99/**1170**
R. *v.* Fell (Tara Mary) [2000] 2 Cr. App. R. (S.) 464, CA (Crim Div) . . . .   *Digested,* 01/**1418**
R. *v.* Fellows (Alan) [2001] 1 Cr. App. R. (S.) 115, CA (Crim Div) . . . .   *Digested,* 01/**1497**
R. *v.* Fellows (Alban); R. *v.* Arnold (Stephen) [1997] 2 All E.R. 548; [1997] 1 Cr. App.
    R. 244; [1998] Masons C.L.R. Rep. 121; [1997] Crim. L.R. 524; *Times,* October
    3, 1996; *Independent,* October 28, 1996 (C.S.), CA (Crim Div) . . . .   *Digested,* 96/**1496**
R. (on the application of Rees) *v.* Feltham Justices; *sub nom* R. *v.* Feltham Justices Ex p.
    Rees [2001] 2 Cr. App. R. (S.) 1; [2001] Crim. L.R. 47, QBD . . . .   *Digested,* 01/**1107**
R. *v.* Feltham Justices Ex p. Rees see R. (on the application of Rees) *v.* Feltham
    Justices
R. (on the application of Ebrahim) *v.* Feltham Magistrates Court; *sub nom* R. *v.* Feltham
    Magistrates Court Ex p. Ebrahim; Mouat *v.* DPP; R. *v.* Feltham Magistrates
    Court Ex p. DPP [2001] EWHC Admin 130; [2001] 1 W.L.R. 1293; [2001] 1 All
    E.R. 831; [2001] 2 Cr. App. R. 23; [2001] Crim. L.R. 741; (2001) 151 N.L.J. 304;
    Times, February 27, 2001; *Independent,* February 27, 2001, QBD (Admin Ct) . . .   *Digested,* 01/**1190**
R. *v.* Feltham Magistrates Court Ex p. DPP see R. (on the application of Ebrahim) *v.*
    Feltham Magistrates Court
R. *v.* Feltham Magistrates Court Ex p. Ebrahim see R. (on the application of Ebrahim) *v.*
    Feltham Magistrates Court
R. *v.* Feltham Magistrates Court Ex p. Haid [1998] C.O.D. 440, QBD . . . .   *Digested,* 98/**1145**
R. *v.* Fenlon (Michael William); R. *v.* Jarpur (Keith John) (1985) 7 Cr. App. R. (S.) 175,
    CA (Crim Div) . . . .   *Digested,* 86/**769**:
                                     Considered, 98/1374: *Referred to,* 90/1408
R. *v.* Fennell (Peter) [2000] 1 W.L.R. 2011; [2000] 2 Cr. App. R. 318; (2000) 164 J.P.
    386; [2000] Crim. L.R. 677; (2000) 164 J.P.N. 528; (2000) 97(22) L.S.G. 43;
    Times, May 17, 2000, CA (Crim Div) . . . .   *Digested,* 00/**1049**
R. *v.* Fenny Stratford Justices Ex p. Watney Mann (Midlands) Ltd [1976] 1 W.L.R. 1101;
    [1976] 2 All E.R. 888; 120 S.J. 201, QBD . . . .   *Digested,* 76/**2004**:
                                                     Applied, 01/2423
R. *v.* Fenton (William Denis) [2001] N.I. 65, CA (Crim Div) (NI) . . . .   *Digested,* 01/**5725**
R. *v.* Ferguson (Roger Neil) [2001] 1 Cr. App. R. (S.) 91, CA (Crim Div) . . . .   *Digested,* 01/**1292**
R. *v.* Fernandes (Roland Anthony) [1996] 1 Cr. App. R. 175; *Times,* April 22, 1995;
    Independent, May 22, 1995 (C.S.), CA (Crim Div) . . . .   *Digested,* 95/**1299**:
                                                  Considered, 98/981
R. *v.* Fernandez (Joseph) see R. *v.* Nazari (Fazlollah)
R. *v.* Fernhill Manor School Ex p. A; R. *v.* Fernhill Manor School Ex p. Brown; R. *v.*
    Fernhill Manor School Ex p. B [1993] 1 F.L.R. 620; [1994] 1 F.C.R. 146; (1993) 5
    Admin. L.R. 159; [1992] C.O.D. 446, QBD . . . .   *Digested,* 93/**1683**:
                                                     Applied, 00/1851
R. *v.* Fernhill Manor School Ex p. B see R. *v.* Fernhill Manor School Ex p. A
R. *v.* Fernhill Manor School Ex p. Brown see R. *v.* Fernhill Manor School Ex p. A
R. *v.* Ferrett (Patrick) [1998] 2 Cr. App. R. (S.) 384, CA (Crim Div) . . . .   *Digested,* 99/**1222**
R. *v.* FG (Autrefois Acquit) [2001] EWCA Crim 1215; [2001] 1 W.L.R. 1727; [2001] 2
    Cr. App. R. 31; [2001] 165 J.P. 513; [2001] Crim. L.R. 898; (2001) 165 J.P.N.
    585; (2001) 98(24) L.S.G. 43; (2001) 145 S.J.L.B. 126; *Times,* May 25, 2001,
    CA (Crim Div) . . . .   *Digested,* 01/**1061**
R. *v.* Field (Jason) see Attorney General's Reference (Nos.19, 20 and 21 of 2001), Re
R. *v.* Fielder (Paul Martin) see Attorney General's Reference (No.23 of 2001), Re
R. *v.* Fielding (Craig) (1993) 14 Cr. App. R. (S.) 494; [1993] Crim. L.R. 229, CA (Crim
    Div) . . . .   *Digested,* 94/**1201**:
                                 Applied, 00/1158: *Distinguished,* 98/1146
R. *v.* Filonov (1993) 82 C.C.C. (3d) 516, CJ (Gen Div) (Ont) . . . .   *Approved,* 99/3123
R. (on the application of Fleurose) *v.* Financial Services Authority see R. (on the
    application of Fleurose) *v.* Securities and Futures Authority Ltd
R. (on the application of Wirral HA) *v.* Finnegan see R. (on the application of Wirral HA)
    v. Mental Health Review Tribunal
R. (on the application of Wirral HA) *v.* Finnegan (Permission to Appeal) see R. (on the
    application of Wirral HA) *v.* Mental Health Review Tribunal (Permission to
    Appeal)
R. *v.* Finney (John Paul) [1998] 2 Cr. App. R. (S.) 239, CA (Crim Div) . . . .   *Digested,* 98/**1136**

R. *v.* Firmston (John David) (1984) 6 Cr. App. R. (S.) 189; [1984] Crim. L.R. 575, CA (Crim Div). . . . . *Digested,* 85/**693**: *Considered,* 99/985

R. *v.* Firth Vickers Centrispinning Ltd [1998] 1 Cr. App. R. (S.) 293, CA (Crim Div). . . . .   *Digested,* 98/**2838**

R. *v.* Fisher (Malcolm) see Attorney General's Reference (Nos.37 and 38 of 2000), Re

R. *v.* Fisher (Robert Butler) (1987) 9 Cr. App. R. (S.) 462, CA (Crim Div) . . . .   *Digested,* 90/**1216**: *Considered,* 00/1141

R. *v.* Fitzpatrick (Gerald) [1999] Crim. L.R. 832; *Times,* February 19, 1999, CA (Crim Div). . . . .   *Digested,* 99/**895**

R. *v.* Fitzpatrick (Ian Michael) [2001] 1 Cr. App. R. (S.) 6, CA (Crim Div) . . . .   *Digested,* 01/**1278**

R. *v.* Fitzsimmons (Paul) see R. *v.* Wood (William Douglas)

R. *v.* Flaherty (Mark Gordon); R. *v.* McManus (Michael Francis) [2000] 1 Cr. App. R. (S.) 250, CA (Crim Div). . . . .   *Digested,* 00/**1432**

R. *v.* Flanagan (Sean Patrick) (1994) 15 Cr. App. R. (S.) 300, CA (Crim Div). . . . .   *Considered,* 00/1136

R. *v.* Flanagan (Susan) [1999] 1 Cr. App. R. (S.) 100, CA (Crim Div). . . . .   *Digested,* 99/**1077**

R. *v.* Flannagan (Gerard) see R. *v.* Thomas (Christopher Antonio)

R. *v.* Fleet (John Charles) (1985) 7 Cr. App. R. (S.) 245, CA (Crim Div) . . . .   *Digested,* 87/**1000**: *Considered,* 98/1400

R. *v.* Fletcher (Francis Royston) see R. *v.* Smith (Ruben)

R. *v.* Fletcher (James Lee) see R. *v.* Hooley (Gareth Mark)

R. *v.* Fletcher (Stephen Augustus) [1998] 1 Cr. App. R. (S.) 7, CA (Crim Div) . . . .   *Digested,* 98/**1107**: *Considered,* 00/1120

R. (on the application of Armstrong-Braun) *v.* Flintshire CC; *sub nom* R. *v.* Flintshire CC Ex p. Armstrong-Braun [2001] EWCA Civ 345; (2001) 3 L.G.L.R. 34; [2001] B.L.G.R. 344; (2001) 98(13) L.S.G. 40; *Times,* March 8, 2001, CA; reversing (2001) 3 L.G.L.R. 1; *Independent,* October 30, 2000 (C.S.), QBD. . . . .   *Digested,* 01/**4334**

R. *v.* Flintshire CC Ex p. Armstrong-Braun see R. (on the application of Armstrong-Braun) *v.* Flintshire CC

R. *v.* Flintshire CC Ex p. Somerfield Stores Ltd [1998] P.L.C.R. 336; [1998] E.G.C.S. 53, QBD . . . .   *Digested,* 99/**4259**

R. *v.* Flitter (Julian) [2001] Crim. L.R. 328; *Times,* February 13, 2001, CA (Crim Div) . . .   *Digested,* 01/**1153**

R. *v.* Flower (Eric) see R. *v.* Flower (Richard Arthur)

R. *v.* Flower (Richard Arthur); R. *v.* Siggins (Frederick George); R. *v.* Flower (Eric) [1966] 1 Q.B. 146; [1965] 3 W.L.R. 1202; [1965] 3 All E.R. 669; (1966) 50 Cr. App. R. 22; 129 J.P. 597; 109 S.J. 829, CCA . . . .   *Digested,* 65/**728**: *Applied,* 88/673, 90/853: *Considered,* 98/987: *Followed,* 93/690, 94/731

R. *v.* Flynn (Errol) [1998] 2 Cr. App. R. (S.) 413, CA (Crim Div) . . . .   *Digested,* 99/**1275**

R. *v.* Flynn (Michael Patrick) see R. *v.* Chisholm (John)

R. *v.* Foley (Michael John) see Attorney General's Reference (Nos.90 and 91 of 1998), Re

R. *v.* Forbes (Anthony Leroy) [2001] 1 A.C. 473; [2001] 2 W.L.R. 1; [2001] 1 All E.R. 686; [2001] 1 Cr. App. R. 31; (2001) 165 J.P. 61; [2001] Crim. L.R. 649; (2001) 165 J.P.N. 664; (2001) 98(8) L.S.G. 43; (2001) 145 S.J.L.B. 44; *Times,* December 19, 2000; *Independent,* December 21, 2000, HL; affirming [1999] 2 Cr. App. R. 501; (1999) 163 J.P. 629; (1999) 163 J.P.N. 735; (1999) 96(21) L.S.G. 37; *Times,* May 5, 1999; *Independent,* May 14, 1999, CA (Crim Div) . . . . .   *Digested,* 01/**994**: *Distinguished,* 99/894: *Doubted,* 99/890, 99/892

R. *v.* Forbes (Giles) [2001] UKHL 40; [2001] 3 W.L.R. 428; [2001] 4 All E.R. 97; [2001] Crim. L.R. 906; (2001) 98(34) L.S.G. 40; (2001) 145 S.J.L.B. 202; *Times,* July 20, 2001; *Independent,* July 25, 2001; *Daily Telegraph,* July 31, 2001, HL; affirming (2000) 97(18) L.S.G. 36; (2000) 144 S.J.L.B. 189; *Times,* April 4, 2000, CA (Crim Div) . . . .   *Digested,* 01/**1060**

R. *v.* Ford (Kevin Dexter) [1998] 2 Cr. App. R. (S.) 74, CA (Crim Div) . . . .   *Digested,* 98/**1351**: *Cited,* 00/1398

R. *v.* Forde [1923] 2 K.B. 400; [1923] All E.R. Rep. 479, CCA.   *Applied,* 64/758, 82/559: *Considered,* 84/976, 00/1004, 00/1025: *Distinguished,* 47-51/6010, 47-51/9852: *Not followed,* 85/608

R. *v.* Formosa (John); R. *v.* Upton (Anthony William) [1991] 2 Q.B. 1; [1990] 3 W.L.R. 1179; [1991] 1 All E.R. 131; (1991) 92 Cr. App. R. 11; (1991) 155 J.P. 97; [1990] Crim. L.R. 868; (1990) 154 J.P.N. 609; (1990) 87(41) L.S.G. 35; (1990) 134 S.J. 11; (1990) 134 S.J. 1191; *Times,* July 23, 1990; *Independent,* August 6, 1990; *Daily Telegraph,* August 6, 1990, CA (Crim Div). . . . .   *Digested,* 91/**971**: *Considered,* 98/4299

R. *v.* Foster (John) see R. *v.* Gordon (Neil)

R. *v.* Foster (Michael) [2001] 1 Cr. App. R. (S.) 111; [2000] Crim. L.R. 1030, CA (Crim Div) . . . .   *Digested,* 01/**1235**

R. *v.* Fowley (Garry), *Independent,* April 10, 2000 (C.S.), CA (Crim Div)

R. *v.* Fox (Michael) (1995) 16 Cr. App. R. (S.) 688; [1995] Crim. L.R. 259; *Times,* November 24, 1994; *Independent,* January 9, 1995 (C.S.), CA (Crim Div) . . . . . .   *Digested,* 94/**3838**: *Considered,* 98/1344

R. *v.* Fox (Shaun) [1999] 1 Cr. App. R. (S.) 332, CA (Crim Div) . . . .   *Digested,* 99/**1068**

R. *v.* Foxford [1974] N.I. 181 . . . .   *Digested,* 77/**2071**: *Approved,* 92/621: *Considered,* 87/2648: *Not followed,* 00/5464

R. *v.* Foxley (Gordon) [1995] 2 Cr. App. R. 523; (1995) 16 Cr. App. R. (S.) 879;
  [1995] Crim. L.R. 636; *Times,* February 9, 1995; *Independent,* April 3, 1995
  (C.S.), CA (Crim Div) . . . .   *Digested,* 95/**918**:
                                                                  Subsequent proceedings, 00/3166
R. *v.* France (James) [1999] 1 Cr. App. R. (S.) 85, CA (Crim Div) . . . .   *Digested,* 99/**1105**
R. *v.* Francis (Andrew Donald) (1995) 16 Cr. App. R. (S.) 95, CA (Crim Div) . . . .   *Digested,* 96/**1893**:
                                                                                Considered, 00/1242

R. *v.* Francis (Ollrick Mark) see Attorney General's Reference (No.84 of 2000), Re
R. *v.* Francis (Peter Robert) [1990] 1 W.L.R. 1264; [1991] 1 All E.R. 225; (1990) 91 Cr.
  App. R. 271; (1990) 154 J.P. 358; [1990] Crim. L.R. 431; (1990) 154 J.P.N. 265;
  (1990) 134 S.J. 860, CA (Crim Div) . . . .   *Digested,* 91/**634**:
                        Applied, 93/770, 93/907, 94/820, 97/1101: *Considered,* 93/898:
                                                                                Followed, 99/990
R. *v.* Frazer (Edgar Fitzroy) [1998] 1 Cr. App. R. (S.) 287, CA (Crim Div) . . . .   *Digested,* 98/**1180**
R. *v.* Freeder (David) [2000] 1 Cr. App. R. (S.) 25, CA (Crim Div) . . . .   *Digested,* 00/**1218**
R. *v.* French (Edward Charles) (1982) 75 Cr. App. R. 1; (1982) 4 Cr. App. R. (S.) 57;
  [1982] Crim. L.R. 380, CA (Crim Div) . . . .   *Digested,* 83/**757**:
                                                                             Applied, 86/877, 01/1140

R. *v.* French (Stephen Robert) see R. *v.* McCredie (Graeme George)
R. *v.* Fricker (Clive Frederick) (1999) 96(30) L.S.G. 29; *Times,* July 13, 1999, CA (Crim
  Div) . . . .   *Digested,* 99/**1018**
R. *v.* Friday (Ross) [1998] 1 Cr. App. R. (S.) 143, CA (Crim Div) . . . .   *Digested,* 98/**1216**:
                                                                                Considered, 99/1164
R. *v.* Friemel (Peter Godfrey) (1987) 9 Cr. App. R. (S.) 99, CA (Crim Div) . . . .   *Digested,* 89/**930**:
                        Cited, 92/1150, 96/1727: *Considered,* 96/1993, 00/1267
R. *v.* Friend (Alan Walter) [1998] 1 Cr. App. R. (S.) 163, CA (Crim Div) . . . .   *Digested,* 98/**1371**
R. *v.* Friend (Billy-Joe) [1997] 1 W.L.R. 1433; [1997] 2 All E.R. 1012; [1997] 2 Cr. App.
  R. 231; [1997] Crim. L.R. 817, CA (Crim Div) . . . .   *Digested,* 97/**1162**:
                                                                                Considered, 98/906
R. *v.* Friskies Petcare (UK) Ltd [2000] 2 Cr. App. R. (S.) 401, CA (Crim Div) . . . .   *Digested,* 01/**3296**
R. *v.* Frixou (Franos) [1998] Crim. L.R. 352, CA (Crim Div)
R. *v.* Frost (Paul William) [2001] 2 Cr. App. R. (S.) 26; [2001] Crim. L.R. 143; *Times,*
  January 5, 2001, CA (Crim Div) . . . .   *Digested,* 01/**1412**
R. *v.* Frostick (Jessie Albert) [1998] 1 Cr. App. R. (S.) 257, CA (Crim Div) . . . .   *Digested,* 98/**1357**
R. *v.* Fulham, Hammersmith and Kensington Rent Tribunal Ex p. Zerek [1951] 2 K.B. 1;
  [1951] 1 All E.R. 482; [1951] 1 T.L.R. 423; 115 J.P. 132; 49 L.G.R. 275; 95 S.J.
  237, KBD . . . .   *Digested,* 47-51/**8752**:
            Applied, 53/143, 75/297, 76/1573, 76/2645, 77/1764: *Considered,* 00/3869
R. *v.* Fuller (David) [1998] Crim. L.R. 61, CA (Crim Div)
R. *v.* Funderburk (Roy) [1990] 1 W.L.R. 587; [1990] 2 All E.R. 482; (1990) 90 Cr.
  App. R. 466; [1990] Crim. L.R. 405; (1990) 87(17) L.S.G. 31; (1990) 134 S.J.
  578, CA (Crim Div) . . . .   *Digested,* 90/**794**:
                        Applied, 91/732, 94/770: *Considered,* 92/651, 96/1583, 97/1098:
                                                                                Followed, 98/875
R. *v.* Funding Agency for Schools Ex p. Essex CC [1998] Ed. C.R. 219, QBD . . . .   *Digested,* 98/**1852**
R. *v.* Fyffe (John) (1994) 15 Cr. App. R. (S.) 13, CA (Crim Div) . . . .   *Considered,* 98/1177:
                                                                                Distinguished, 99/5226

R. *v.* G (Alan Robert) see Attorney General's Reference (No.28 of 1999), Re
R. *v.* G (B) 7 B.H.R.C. 97, Sup Ct (Can) . . . .   *Digested,* 00/**3162**
R. *v.* G (Carl Jason) [1998] 2 Cr. App. R. (S.) 61; [1998] Crim. L.R. 139, CA (Crim
  Div) . . . .   *Digested,* 98/**1253**
R. *v.* G (Christopher Ian) see Attorney General's Reference (No.64 of 1998), Re
R. *v.* G (Conspiracy to Cheat); *sub nom* Customs and Excise Commissioners *v.* G
  [2001] EWCA Crim 851; (2001) 98(20) L.S.G. 40; (2001) 145 S.J.L.B. 108;
  Times, March 30, 2001, CA (Crim Div) . . . .   *Digested,* 01/**1105**
R. *v.* G (Daniel) (A Juvenile) see R. *v.* J-R (Scott) (A Juvenile)
R. *v.* G (Entrapment) see Attorney General's Reference (No.3 of 2000), Re
R. *v.* G (Frederick) [1999] 1 Cr. App. R. (S.) 443, CA (Crim Div) . . . .   *Digested,* 99/**1270**
R. *v.* G (James Archibald) [2000] N.I. 118, CA (Crim Div) (NI) . . . .   *Digested,* 00/**5465**
R. *v.* G (Jamie Andrew) (A Juvenile) see Attorney General's Reference (No.63 of
  2001), Re
R. *v.* G (Jayne Elizabeth) see Attorney General's Reference (No.87 of 1998), Re
R. *v.* G (Joanne Rainey) (A Juvenile) see Attorney General's Reference (Nos.57 and
  58 of 1999), Re
R. *v.* G (John Thomas) (A Minor) see R. *v.* Gaskin (John Thomas)
R. *v.* G (Lee Eugene) (A Juvenile) see Attorney General's Reference (No.51 of 1996),
  Re
R. *v.* G (M) [1999] Crim. L.R. 763, CA (Crim Div)
R. *v.* G (Mark John); *sub nom* R. *v.* MG (Offences against Children); R. *v.* G (Offences
  against Children) [2001] EWCA Crim 2308; *Times,* November 12, 2001, CA
  (Crim Div) . . . .   *Digested,* 01/**1358**
R. *v.* G (Offences against Children) see R. *v.* G (Mark John)
R. *v.* G (Paul) (A Juvenile) [1999] Crim. L.R. 669, CA (Crim Div)
R. *v.* G (Richard) see Attorney General's Reference (No.15 of 2000), Re

R. *v.* G (Roy) see Attorney General's Reference (No.32 of 1998), Re
R. *v.* G (Sex Offence: Registration) see Attorney General's Reference (No.72 of 1999), Re
R. *v.* G (Stephen) (A Juvenile) [2001] 1 Cr. App. R. (S.) 17; *Times*, June 7, 2000; *Independent*, May 9, 2000, CA (Crim Div) . . . . *Digested*, 00/**1319**: *Considered*, 01/1475
R. *v.* G (Steven) [1998] Crim. L.R. 483, CA (Crim Div)
R. *v.* G (W) see R. *v.* WG
R. *v.* G (Wesley Stuart) (A Juvenile) see Attorney General's Reference (No.75 of 1999), Re
R. *v.* Gabbidon (Anthony Bernard); R. *v.* Bramble (Keith) [1997] 2 Cr. App. R. (S.) 19; [1997] Crim. L.R. 137, CA (Crim Div) . . . . *Digested*, 97/**1700**: *Considered*, 99/1335, 01/1473
R. *v.* Gadsby (Martin Geoffrey) [2001] EWCA Crim 1824; [2001] Crim. L.R. 828, CA (Crim Div)
R. *v.* Gal (Imrich) [2001] 1 Cr. App. R. (S.) 64, CA (Crim Div) . . . . *Digested*, 01/**1310**
R. *v.* Galbraith (George Charles) [1981] 1 W.L.R. 1039; [1981] 2 All E.R. 1060; (1981) 73 Cr. App. R. 124; [1981] Crim. L.R. 648; 125 S.J. 442, CA (Crim Div) . . . . *Digested*, 81/**513**: *Applied*, 88/845, 89/849, 89/898, 90/1175, 93/725, 93/1869, 96/1420, 97/1339: *Cited*, 00/1022: *Considered*, 86/926, 88/651, 89/769, 90/1043, 93/903, 95/1060, 95/1128, 96/1635: *Followed*, 96/1393, 97/1164, 01/1821
R. *v.* Gale (Stephen Allen) see Attorney General's Reference (No.47 of 1998), Re
R. *v.* Gall (Gerald) (1990) 90 Cr. App. R. 64; [1989] Crim. L.R. 745; *Times*, May 2, 1989, CA (Crim Div) . . . . *Digested*, 90/**811**: *Considered*, 00/5485
R. *v.* Gaming Board for Great Britain Ex p. Kingsley (No.2) [1996] C.O.D. 241, QBD . . . *Subsequent proceedings*, 01/96
R. *v.* Gani (Farouk) see Attorney General's Reference (Nos.51 and 52 of 1998), Re
R. *v.* Gani (Saleem Ibrahim) see Attorney General's Reference (Nos.51 and 52 of 1998), Re
R. *v.* Gannon (Christopher) (1990) 12 Cr. App. R. (S.) 545, CA (Crim Div) . . . . *Digested*, 92/**1139**: *Considered*, 97/1399, 97/1401, 99/1081, 00/1129
R. *v.* Garcia (Emilio) (1988) 87 Cr. App. R. 175; [1988] Crim. L.R. 115, CA (Crim Div). . . *Digested*, 89/**832**: *Considered*, 98/952
R. *v.* Gardner (Janet Susan) (1993) 14 Cr. App. R. (S.) 364, CA (Crim Div) . . . . *Digested*, 94/**1309**: *Considered*, 97/1619, 01/1433: *Followed*, 96/2018
R. *v.* Gardner Ex p. L see R. *v.* Hallstrom Ex p. W (No.2)
R. *v.* Garrett (Terence William) [1997] 1 Cr. App. R. (S.) 109, CA (Crim Div) . . . . *Digested*, 97/**2354**: *Considered*, 99/1151: *Distinguished*, 00/1440
R. *v.* Garrod (Keith Desmond) [1999] 1 Cr. App. R. (S.) 172, CA (Crim Div). . . . . *Digested*, 99/**1233**
R. *v.* Gaskin (John Thomas); *sub nom* R. *v.* G (John Thomas) (A Minor) (1985) 7 Cr. App. R. (S.) 28; [1985] Crim. L.R. 455, CA (Crim Div) . . . . *Digested*, 86/**904**: *Applied*, 01/1209: *Considered*, 98/1276: *Followed*, 86/764, 87/966: *Referred to*, 86/737, 87/974
R. *v.* Gass (Anthony) [2000] 1 Cr. App. R. (S.) 475, CA (Crim Div). . . . . *Digested*, 00/**1215**
R. *v.* Gastinger (Neale Arthur) see Attorney General's Reference (No.26 of 1999), Re
R. *v.* Gatehouse (Andrew Donald) [2001] EWCA Crim 459; [2001] 2 Cr. App. R. (S.) 94; [2001] Crim. L.R. 416, CA (Crim Div) . . . . *Digested*, 01/**1499**
R. *v.* Gateshead MBC Ex p. Nichol 87 L.G.R. 435; *Times*, June 2, 1988; *Independent*, June 2, 1988, CA . . . . *Digested*, 89/**1351**: *Considered*, 01/1959
R. *v.* Gateshead MBC Ex p. Smith (1999) 31 H.L.R. 97, QBD. . . . . *Digested*, 99/**3068**
R. *v.* Gateway Foodmarkets Ltd [1997] 3 All E.R. 78; [1997] 2 Cr. App. R. 40; [1997] I.C.R. 382; [1997] I.R.L.R. 189; [1997] Crim. L.R. 512; (1997) 94(3) L.S.G. 28; (1997) 141 S.J.L.B. 28; *Times*, January 2, 1997; *Independent*, February 10, 1997 (C.S.), CA (Crim Div) . . . . *Digested*, 97/**2611**: *Cited*, 00/980
R. *v.* Gateway Primary School Governors Ex p. X (A Child) [2001] E.L.R. 321, QBD . . . *Digested*, 01/**2007**
R. *v.* Gauchi (Ronnie) see R. *v.* Farrugia (Francis)
R. *v.* Gault (Michael Paul) (1995) 16 Cr. App. R. (S.) 1013; [1996] R.T.R. 348; [1995] Crim. L.R. 581, CA (Crim Div) . . . . *Considered*, 00/1364
R. *v.* Gayle (Michael) [1999] Crim. L.R. 502, CA (Crim Div)
R. *v.* Gayle (Nicholas Nehemiah) [1999] 2 Cr. App. R. 130, CA (Crim Div) . . . . *Digested*, 99/**891**
R. *v.* Gayle (Ricky) see R. *v.* Cowan (Donald)
R. *v.* Gaynor (Charles John) [2001] N.I. 418, CA (NI)
R. *v.* Gaynor (Lee) [2000] 2 Cr. App. R. (S.) 163; [2000] Crim. L.R. 397, CA (Crim Div) . . . . *Digested*, 00/**1372**
R. *v.* GBL see R. *v.* L (Glen Bernard)
R. *v.* GC see Attorney General's Reference (No.4 of 2000), Re
R. *v.* GE see R. *v.* H (Grant) (A Juvenile)
R. *v.* Geary (Mark) [1998] 2 Cr. App. R. (S.) 434, CA (Crim Div) . . . . *Digested*, 99/**1313**
R. *v.* Gee (Arthur); R. *v.* Bibby (John); R. *v.* Dunscombe (James) [1936] 2 K.B. 442, KBD . . . . *Applied*, 00/927: *Considered*, 96/1566: *Distinguished*, 47-51/2122

R. *v.* Gee (Stephen James) [1999] Crim. L.R. 397, CA (Crim Div)
R. *v.* General Commissioners of Income Tax for Tavistock Ex p. Worth; *sub nom* R. *v.*
     Tavistock General Commissioners Ex p. Worth [1985] S.T.C. 564; 59 T.C. 116;
     (1985) 82 L.S.G. 2501; *Times*, May 23, 1985, QBD . . . . *Digested*, 88/**11**:
                        Disapproved, 97/61: *Overruled*, 99/918
R. *v.* General Court Martial Sitting at RAF Uxbridge Ex p. Wright (1999) 11 Admin. L.R.
     747; *Times*, July 1, 1999, QBD . . . . *Digested*, 99/**263**
R. (on the application of Gupta) *v.* General Medical Council see Gupta (Prabha) *v.*
     General Medical Council
R. (on the application of Holmes) *v.* General Medical Council [2001] EWHC Admin 321;
     [2001] Lloyd's Rep. Med. 366, QBD (Admin Ct) . . . . *Digested*, 01/**2897**
R. (on the application of Nicolaides) *v.* General Medical Council [2001] EWHC Admin
     625; [2001] Lloyd's Rep. Med. 525, QBD (Admin Ct)
R. (on the application of Richards) *v.* General Medical Council [2001] Lloyd's Rep. Med.
     47; *Times*, January 24, 2001, QBD (Admin Ct) . . . . *Digested*, 01/**2896**:
                                         Applied, 01/2897
R. (on the application of X) *v.* General Medical Council; *sub nom* X *v.* General Medical
     Council [2001] EWHC Admin 447; *Independent*, July 16, 2001 (C.S), QBD
R. *v.* General Medical Council Ex p. Salvi see R. *v.* Professional Conduct Committee of
     the General Medical Council Ex p. Salvi
R. *v.* General Medical Council Ex p. Toth [2000] 1 W.L.R. 2209; [2000] Lloyd's Rep.
     Med. 368; (2001) 61 B.M.L.R. 149; (2000) 97(27) L.S.G. 39; *Times*, June 29,
     2000, QBD . . . . *Digested*, 00/**2717**:
                  Applied, 01/2897: *Considered*, 01/2896
R. *v.* General Officer Commanding, Second Division, the Army Ex p. Buchanan; R. *v.*
     General Officer Commanding, Second Division, the Army Ex p. Falls *Times*,
     October 20, 1998, QBD . . . . *Digested*, 98/**259**
R. *v.* General Officer Commanding, Second Division, the Army Ex p. Falls see R. *v.*
     General Officer Commanding, Second Division, the Army Ex p. Buchanan
R. *v.* Genese; R. *v.* Kaye [1998] Crim. L.R. 679, CA (Crim Div)
R. *v.* Gerald (Clovis Lloyd) [1999] Crim. L.R. 315, CA (Crim Div) . . . . *Considered*, 00/1023
R. *v.* GF (A Juvenile) [2000] 2 Cr. App. R. (S.) 364; [2000] Crim. L.R. 608, CA (Crim
     Div) . . . . *Digested*, 00/**1334**
R. *v.* GGM see Attorney General's Reference (No.43 of 1999), Re
R. *v.* Ghadami (Mohammed Reza) [1998] 1 Cr. App. R. (S.) 42; [1997] Crim. L.R.
     606; *Times*, May 21, 1997, CA (Crim Div) . . . . *Digested*, 97/**1467**
R. *v.* Ghosh (Deb Baran) [1982] Q.B. 1053; [1982] 3 W.L.R. 110; [1982] 2 All E.R.
     689; (1982) 75 Cr. App. R. 154; [1982] Crim. L.R. 608; 126 S.J. 429, CA (Crim
     Div) . . . . *Digested*, 82/**659**:
           Applied, 83/727, 84/677, 88/841, 90/910, 90/1140: *Cited*, 93/771, 94/838:
           Considered, 86/608, 86/611, 87/783, 90/909, 90/911, 91/604, 91/756,
           91/761.a, 92/652, 92/789, 97/3828, 01/2343: *Distinguished*, 92/806:
                                           Followed, 96/1512
R. *v.* Ghosh (Deb Baron) [1999] 1 Cr. App. R. (S.) 225, CA (Crim Div) . . . . *Digested*, 99/**1202**:
                                    Considered, 00/1290, 00/1294
R. *v.* Gibbons (Gary John) (1987) 9 Cr. App. R. (S.) 391; [1988] Crim. L.R. 129, CA
     (Crim Div). . . . . *Digested*, 89/**1052**:
                       Considered, 94/1279: *Not followed*, 98/1257
R. *v.* Gibbs (Barry Edward) [2000] 1 Cr. App. R. (S.) 261, CA (Crim Div) . . . . *Digested*, 00/**1151**
R. *v.* Gibbs (Maria) see R. *v.* Warneford (Timothy)
R. *v.* Gibbs (Robert John) see R. *v.* Hafeez (Fashwar Qullah)
R. *v.* Gibson (Barry) (1987) 9 Cr. App. R. (S.) 30; [1987] Crim. L.R. 346, CA (Crim
     Div) . . . . *Digested*, 88/**979**:
                                        Considered, 99/1311
R. *v.* Gibson (Christopher Howard) [1997] 2 Cr. App. R. (S.) 292, CA (Crim Div) . . . . . *Digested*, 98/**1309**
R. *v.* Gibson (Ivano) [1983] 1 W.L.R. 1038; [1983] 3 All E.R. 263; (1983) 77 Cr. App.
     R. 151; (1983) 147 J.P. 683; [1983] Crim. L.R. 679; (1983) 80 L.S.G. 2133;
     (1983) 127 S.J. 509, CA (Crim Div). . . . . *Digested*, 83/**2197**:
                       Considered, 84/2004: *Not followed*, 00/3961
R. *v.* Gibson (Leonard) [2000] Crim. L.R. 479; (2000) 97(10) L.S.G. 35; (2000) 144
     S.J.L.B. 124; *Times*, March 3, 2000, CA (Crim Div) . . . . *Digested*, 00/**981**
R. *v.* Gibson (Terence Michael) [1999] 2 Cr. App. R. (S.) 52, CA (Crim Div) . . . . *Digested*, 99/**1174**:
                                           Followed, 01/1318
R. *v.* Gidney (Rebecca Jane) [1999] 1 Cr. App. R. (S.) 138, CA (Crim Div). . . . . *Digested*, 99/**1365**:
                                    Considered, 00/1438
R. *v.* Gigaseri (Mohammed Hussan) see R. *v.* Panayis (Charalambos)
R. *v.* Gilbert (Jeremy Charles) [2001] EWCA Crim 615; [2001] 2 Cr. App. R. (S.) 100,
     CA (Crim Div) . . . . *Digested*, 01/**1332**
R. *v.* Gilfoyle (Norman Edward) (Appeal against Conviction) [2001] 2 Cr. App. R. 5;
     [2001] Crim. L.R. 312; *Times*, February 13, 2001, CA (Crim Div) . . . . *Digested*, 01/**975**
R. *v.* Gill (Christopher Martin) (1992) 13 Cr. App. R. (S.) 36, CA (Crim Div). . . . . *Digested*, 92/**1199**:
                                        Considered, 99/1103
R. *v.* Gill (Stephen Ian) [2001] 1 Cr. App. R. 11; [2000] Crim. L.R. 922; *Times*, August
     17, 2000, CA (Crim Div) . . . . *Digested*, 00/**1076**

R. *v.* Gill (Susan) see R. *v.* Smurthwaite (Keith)
R. *v.* Gillam (Leslie George); *sub nom* R. *v.* Gillan (1980) 2 Cr. App. R. (S.) 267; [1981]
    Crim. L.R. 55, CA (Crim Div) . . . . *Digested,* 81/**525.41**:
                              Applied, 87/855, 87/856, 88/859, 89/913: *Cited,* 89/912, 90/1187, 91/991:
                     Considered, 83/764.2, 84/874, 89/914, 94/1226, 96/1805, 00/1029:
                 Distinguished, 84/723, 86/703: *Followed,* 83/761, 87/1037, 88/860, 01/1441
R. *v.* Gillan see R. *v.* Gillam (Leslie George)
R. *v.* Gillespie (Ann Bernadette) see R. *v.* Byrne (Edward Joseph)
R. *v.* Gillespie (EileenTheresa) see R. *v.* Byrne (Edward Joseph)
R. *v.* Gillespie (Kevin) see R. *v.* Graham (Andrew Harvey)
R. *v.* Gillette (Arthur Stanley),*Times,* December 3, 1999, CA (Crim Div) . . . . *Digested,* 00/**1188**:
                                                 Distinguished, 00/1187
R. *v.* Gilmartin (Daniel John) [2001] 2 Cr. App. R. (S.) 45, CA (Crim Div) . . . . *Digested,* 01/**1258**
R. *v.* Gilmore,*Times,* May 21, 1986, CA (Crim Div) . . . . *Digested,* 86/**823**:
                       Applied, 99/5226: *Cited,* 88/871, 88/929, 89/938, 90/1284:
             Considered, 87/1022, 88/969, 90/1290, 90/1292, 90/1297, 91/1093
R. *v.* Gilmour (Thomas Robert) [2000] N.I. 367; [2000] 2 Cr. App. R. 407; [2000]
    Crim. L.R. 763; *Times,* June 21, 2000, CA (Crim Div) (NI) . . . . *Digested,* 00/**5466**
R. *v.* Gingell (Stuart Matthew) [2000] 1 Cr. App. R. 88; (1999) 163 J.P. 648; (1999)
    163 J.P.N. 915; (1999) 96(19) L.S.G. 27; *Times,* May 21, 1999, CA (Crim Div) . . *Digested,* 99/**941**
R. *v.* Giunta (Santo) [2000] 1 Cr. App. R. (S.) 365, CA (Crim Div) . . . . *Digested,* 00/**1219**
R. *v.* Gleeson (John Vincent) [2001] EWCA Crim 2023; *Times,* October 30, 2001;
    Independent, October 5, 2001, CA (Crim Div) . . . . *Digested,* 01/**1498**
R. *v.* Glennie (Alastair Kincaid) see R. *v.* Miller (Raymond Karl)
R. *v.* Glidewell (Raymond) (1999) 163 J.P. 557; (1999) 163 J.P.N. 915; *Times,* May 14,
    1999, CA (Crim Div) . . . . *Digested,* 99/**953**
R. *v.* Gloucester Crown Court Ex p. Betteridge (1997) 161 J.P. 721; [1998] Crim. L.R.
    218; [1997] C.O.D. 424; (1997) 161 J.P.N. 899; *Times,* August 4, 1997, QBD. . . . *Digested,* 97/**1396**
R. *v.* Gloucester Crown Court Ex p. Chester [1998] C.O.D. 365; *Independent,* July 6,
    1998 (C.S.), QBD . . . . *Digested,* 98/**989**
R. *v.* Gloucester Crown Court Ex p. McGeary; *sub nom* R. *v.* DPP Ex p. McGeary
    [1999] 2 Cr. App. R. (S.) 263; [1999] Crim. L.R. 430; *Independent,* February 22,
    1999 (C.S.), QBD . . . . *Digested,* 99/**1341**:
                                                   Followed, 01/1385
R. *v.* Gloucester Licensing Justices Ex p.Warner [1999] C.O.D. 90, QBD
R. *v.* Gloucestershire CC Ex p. Barry; *sub nom* R. *v.* Gloucestershire CC Ex p. Mahfood;
    R. *v.* Lancashire CC Ex p. Royal Association for Disability and Rehabilitation; R.
    v. Islington LBC Ex p. McMillan; R. *v.* Gloucestershire CC Ex p. Grinham; R. *v.*
    Gloucestershire CC Ex p. Dartnell [1997] A.C. 584; [1997] 2 W.L.R. 459; [1997]
    2 All E.R. 1; (1997) 9 Admin. L.R. 209; (1997-98) 1 C.C.L. Rep. 40; (1997) 36
    B.M.L.R. 92; [1997] C.O.D. 304; (1997) 94(14) L.S.G. 25; (1997) 147 N.L.J.
    453; (1997) 141 S.J.L.B. 91; *Times,* March 21, 1997; *Independent,* April 9, 1997,
    HL; reversing [1996] 4 All E.R. 421; (1997) 9 Admin. L.R. 69; (1997-98) 1 C.C.L.
    Rep. 19; (1997) 36 B.M.L.R. 69; [1996] C.O.D. 387; (1996) 93(33) L.S.G. 25;
    (1996) 140 S.J.L.B. 177; *Times,* July 12, 1996; *Independent,* July 10, 1996, CA;
    reversing (1996) 8 Admin. L.R. 181; (1997-98) 1 C.C.L. Rep. 7; (1996) 30
    B.M.L.R. 20; [1996] C.O.D. 67; (1996) 160 L.G. Rev. 321; *Times,* June 21, 1995;
    Independent, June 20, 1995, QBD . . . . *Digested,* 97/**4714**:
                     Applied, 97/2089, 97/4721, 98/2853: *Considered,* 96/5528, 99/3052,
                       99/4623: Followed, 95/3225, 96/3029, 96/5530, 97/4711, 98/1674
R. *v.* Gloucestershire CC Ex p. Dartnell see R. *v.* Gloucestershire CC Ex p. Barry
R. *v.* Gloucestershire CC Ex p. Grinham see R. *v.* Gloucestershire CC Ex p. Barry
R. *v.* Gloucestershire CC Ex p. H see H *v.* Gloucestershire CC
R. *v.* Gloucestershire CC Ex p. Mahfood see R. *v.* Gloucestershire CC Ex p. Barry
R. *v.* Gloucestershire CC Ex p. RADAR (1997-98) 1 C.C.L. Rep. 476; [1996] C.O.D.
    253, QBD . . . . *Digested,* 99/**4623**
R. *v.* Gloucestershire Justices Ex p. Daldry [2001] R.V.R. 242, QBD
R. *v.* Glowacki (Dariusz) see R. *v.* Howells (Craig)
R. *v.* Godber (Nicholas Lee) (1986) 8 Cr. App. R. (S.) 460; [1987] Crim. L.R. 278, CA
    (Crim Div). . . . . *Digested,* 88/**1017**:
                Applied, 92/1443, 93/1312: *Considered,* 98/1297: *Referred to,* 92/1452,
                                                93/1335
R. *v.* Godden-Wood (Peter David) [2001] EWCA Crim 1586; [2001] Crim. L.R. 810;
    Times, June 27, 2001, CA (Crim Div) . . . . *Digested,* 01/**1012**
R. *v.* Godfrey (David Simon) see R. *v.* T (Craig Daniel)
R. *v.* Godward (Cheryl Alison) [1998] 1 Cr. App. R. (S.) 385, CA (Crim Div) . . . . *Digested,* 98/**1111**
R. *v.* Gogana (Sanjeev), *Times,* July 12, 1999 ; *Independent,* July 12, 1999 (C.S.), CA
    (Crim Div) . . . . *Digested,* 99/**903**
R. *v.* Golder (Richard Anthony) [2000] 1 Cr. App. R. (S.) 59, CA (Crim Div) . . . . *Digested,* 00/**1232**
R. *v.* Goldman (Terence) [2001] EWCA Crim 1684; [2001] Crim. L.R. 822, CA (Crim
    Div)
R. *v.* Goldsmith (Harold Egan) see R. *v.* Avis (Tony)
R. *v.* Goldsmith (Simon) see Attorney General's Reference (No.6 of 2000), Re

R. *v.* Gooch (Malcolm George) (No.1) [1998] 1 W.L.R. 1100; [1998] 4 All E.R. 402; [1998] 2 Cr. App. R. 130; (1998) 95(7) L.S.G. 32; (1998) 142 S.J.L.B. 61; *Times,* January 29, 1998; *Independent,* January 22, 1998, CA (Crim Div) . . . .   *Digested,* 98/**987**:
Applied, 01/1096

R. *v.* Gooch (Malcolm George) (No.2) [1999] 1 Cr. App. R. (S.) 283; (1998) 142 S.J.L.B. 238; *Times,* July 15, 1998; *Independent,* July 3, 1998, CA (Crim Div) . . .   *Digested,* 98/**1178**
R. *v.* Goodman (Donald Walter) see R. *v.* Taylor (Nicholas James)
R. *v.* Goodman (Ivor Michael) [1993] 2 All E.R. 789; [1992] B.C.C. 625; [1994] 1 B.C.L.C. 349; (1993) 97 Cr. App. R. 210; (1993) 14 Cr. App. R. (S.) 147; [1992] Crim. L.R. 676, CA (Crim Div) . . . .   *Digested,* 93/**366**:
Considered, 01/717
R. *v.* Goodwin (Unreported, August 4, 1995), CA (Crim Div) . . . .   *Referred to,* 00/1281
R. *v.* Goodwin (Frankie) see Attorney General's Reference (Nos.59, 60 and 63 of 1998), Re
R. *v.* Goodwin (John Charles); R. *v.* Unstead (Edward Thomas) [1997] S.T.C. 22; [1997] B.T.C. 5226; [1997] B.V.C. 307, CA (Crim Div) . . . .   *Digested,* 97/**5039**:
Subsequent proceedings, 98/4966
R. *v.* Goodwin (John Charles) (C3/97); *sub nom* Criminal Proceedings against Goodwin (C3/97); R. *v.* Unstead (Edward Thomas) (C3/97) [1998] Q.B. 883; [1998] 3 W.L.R. 565; [1998] All E.R. (E.C.) 500; [1998] S.T.C. 699; [1998] E.C.R. I-3257; [1998] 3 C.M.L.R. 861; [1998] C.E.C. 646; [1998] B.T.C. 5316; [1998] B.V.C. 314; *Times,* June 10, 1998, ECJ (1st Chamber) . . . .   *Digested,* 98/**4966**:
Considered, 99/5014: *Followed,* 99/5018: *Joined proceedings,* 98/4911:
Previous proceedings, 97/5039
R. *v.* Goodwin (Reginald Barry) (1995) 16 Cr. App. R. (S.) 885, CA (Crim Div) . . . .   *Considered,* 00/1269
R. *v.* Goodwin (Sarah Jane) (1989) 11 Cr. App. R. (S.) 194; *Times,* April 27, 1989, CA (Crim Div). . . . .   *Digested,* 91/**1018.9**:
Cited, 93/1242: *Considered,* 98/1325: *Distinguished,* 92/1156
R. *v.* Gordon (Iain Hay); *sub nom* Criminal Cases Review Commission's Reference under s.14(3) of Criminal Appeal Act 1995 [1998] N.I. 275, CA (Crim Div) (NI) .   *Digested,* 99/**5209**
R. *v.* Gordon (Neil); R. *v.* Foster (John) [2001] 1 Cr. App. R. (S.) 58, CA (Crim Div) . . . .   *Digested,* 01/**1207**:
Considered, 01/1477
R. *v.* Gordon (Rohan) see R. *v.* Powell (Shaka)
R. *v.* Gore (Alan Robert) [1998] 1 Cr. App. R. (S.) 413, CA (Crim Div) . . . .   *Digested,* 98/**1261**
R. *v.* Goring (Jonathan) [1999] Crim. L.R. 670, CA (Crim Div)
R. *v.* Gorman (Vincent Dominic) [1987] 1 W.L.R. 545; [1987] 2 All E.R. 435; (1987) 85 Cr. App. R. 121; [1987] Crim. L.R. 624; (1987) 84 L.S.G. 1238, CA (Crim Div) . . . .   *Digested,* 87/**2099**:
Applied, 99/1017, 01/1144: *Considered,* 95/1302
R. *v.* Goscombe (John Lee) see Attorney General's Reference (No.14 of 1999), Re
R. *v.* Gosling (Kevin David) see R. *v.* Silver (Gavin Anthony)
R. *v.* Gough (Robert) [1993] A.C. 646; [1993] 2 W.L.R. 883; [1993] 2 All E.R. 724; (1993) 97 Cr. App. R. 188; (1993) 157 J.P. 612; [1993] Crim. L.R. 886; (1993) 157 J.P.N. 394; (1993) 143 N.L.J. 775; (1993) 137 S.J.L.B. 168; *Times,* May 24, 1993; *Independent,* May 26, 1993; *Guardian,* May 22, 1993, HL; affirming [1992] 4 All E.R. 481; (1992) 95 Cr. App. R. 433; (1993) 157 J.P. 612; [1992] Crim. L.R. 895; (1993) 157 J.P.N. 249; (1992) 142 N.L.J. 787; (1992) 136 S.J.L.B. 197; *Times,* June 3, 1992; *Independent,* June 3, 1992; *Guardian,* May 27, 1992, CA (Crim Div) . . . .   *Digested,* 93/**849**:
Applied, 93/853, 94/972, 96/11, 96/12, 96/2497, 97/1326, 98/1066,
99/1016, 99/2663, 99/4171, 99/4233, 99/5025, 01/334: *Cited,* 00/223:
Considered, 94/632, 94/743, 95/2952, 96/1003, 96/4678, 99/228,
99/3872, 99/4107, 00/2109, 00/4140, 01/692: *Followed,* 95/1227, 95/2950,
96/1584, 96/1662, 96/4679, 97/1328, 97/1341, 97/1342, 98/3179, 99/38
R. *v.* Gough (Steven Robert) [2001] EWCA Crim 2545; *Times,* November 19, 2001, CA (Crim Div) . . . .   *Digested,* 01/**1146**
R. *v.* Gould (Anthony Lawrence) (1983) 5 Cr. App. R. (S.) 72, CA (Crim Div) . . . .   *Digested,* 84/**790**:
Cited, 92/1394, 93/1277: *Considered,* 84/914, 00/1421: *Followed,* 90/1406,
91/1208
R. *v.* Gould (Robert Sidney) see R. *v.* Aranguren (Jose de Jesus)
R. *v.* Gould (Steven Lewis) [2000] 2 Cr. App. R. (S.) 173; [2000] Crim. L.R. 311, CA (Crim Div). . . . .   *Digested,* 00/**1263**
R. *v.* Goult (Raymond Arthur) (1983) 76 Cr. App. R. 140; (1982) 4 Cr. App. R. (S.) 355; [1983] Crim. L.R. 103, CA (Crim Div) . . . .   *Digested,* 83/**582**:
Considered, 83/764.13, 84/844, 98/1162
R. *v.* Gourley (Robert James) [1999] 2 Cr. App. R. (S.) 148, CA (Crim Div) . . . .   *Digested,* 99/**1165**
R. (on the application of St John) *v.* Governer of Brixton Prison see St John *v.* United States
R. *v.* Governor of Ashford Remand Centre Ex p. Bouzagou; *sub nom* Bouzagou, Re [1983] Imm. A.R. 69; (1984) 134 N.L.J. 407; (1983) 127 S.J. 596, CA . . . .   *Digested,* 84/**1765**:
Applied, 94/2494, 01/3681: *Considered,* 86/1696, 88/1837, 88/1838,
91/2006
R. *v.* Governor of Ashford Remand Centre Ex p. Postlethwaite see Belgium *v.* Postlethwaite

R. v. Governor of Belmarsh Prison Ex p. Gilligan; *sub nom* R. v. Woolwich Crown Court Ex p. Gilligan; Gilligan (No.1), Re; R. v. Secretary of State for the Home Department Ex p. Gilligan; Ellis, Re; R. v. Governor of Exeter Prison Ex p. Ellis [2001] 1 A.C. 84; [1999] 3 W.L.R. 1244; [2000] 1 All E.R. 113; (1999) 96(46) L.S.G. 37; (1999) 143 S.J.L.B. 281; *Times*, November 24, 1999, HL; affirming [1998] 2 All E.R. 1; [1998] C.O.D. 195; *Times*, January 20, 1998; *Independent*, January 28, 1998, QBD . . . .   *Digested*, 99/**2294**

R. v. Governor of Blundeston Prison Ex p. Bowen see R. v. Featherstone Prison Ex p. Bowen

R. (on the application of Abdel Bary) v. Governor of Brixton Prison see R. (on the application of Al-Fawwaz) v. Governor of Brixton Prison

R. (on the application of Al-Fawwaz) v. Governor of Brixton Prison; *sub nom* Al-Fawwaz v. Governor of Brixton Prison; Al-Fawwaz, Re; Abdel Bary v. Governor of Brixton Prison; Eidarous v. Governor of Brixton Prison; Abdel Bary, Re; Eidarous, Re; Eiderous, Re; R. (on the application of Abdel Bary) v. Governor of Brixton Prison; R. (on the application of Eidarous) v. Governor of Brixton Prison [2001] UKHL 69; *Times*, December 18, 2001, HL; affirming [2001] 1 W.L.R. 1234; (2001) 98(7) L.S.G. 40; *Times*, December 22, 2000, QBD (Admin Ct) . . . .   *Digested*, 01/**2524**

R. (on the application of Eidarous) v. Governor of Brixton Prison see R. (on the application of Al-Fawwaz) v. Governor of Brixton Prison

R. (on the application of Kashamu) v. Governor of Brixton Prison (No.2); *sub nom* R. (on the application of Maklulif) v. Bow Street Magistrates Court; R. (on the application of Makhlulif) v. Bow Street Magistrates Court; R. (on the application of Kashamu) v. Bow Street Magistrates Court [2001] EWHC Admin 980; (2001) 145 S.J.L.B. 277; *Times*, December 12, 2001, QBD (Admin Ct)

R. (on the application of Marais) v. Governor of Brixton Prison; *sub nom* Marais v. Governor of Brixton Prison [2001] EWHC Admin 1051; *Times*, December 18, 2001, QBD (Admin Ct)

R. (on the application of Saifi) v. Governor of Brixton Prison; *sub nom* Saifi v. Governor of Brixton Prison; R. v. Governor of Brixton Prison Ex p. Saifi [2001] 1 W.L.R. 1134; [2001] 4 All E.R. 168; [2001] Crim. L.R. 653; *Times*, January 24, 2001, QBD (Admin Ct) . . . .   *Digested*, 01/**2525**

R. v. Governor of Brixton Prison Ex p. Allison see R. v. Bow Street Metropolitan Stipendiary Magistrate Ex p. United States (No.2)

R. v. Governor of Brixton Prison Ex p. Burke see Burke, Re

R. v. Governor of Brixton Prison Ex p. Cuoghi; *sub nom* Cuoghi, Re [1998] 1 W.L.R. 1513; [1999] 1 All E.R. 466; (1998) 95(22) L.S.G. 28; (1998) 142 S.J.L.B. 152; *Times*, May 12, 1998, QBD . . . .   *Digested*, 98/**2350**

R. v. Governor of Brixton Prison Ex p. Debs, *Independent*, January 31, 2000 (C.S.), QBD

R. v. Governor of Brixton Prison Ex p. Gross; *sub nom* Gross v. Governor of Brixton Prison; Gross, Re [1999] Q.B. 538; [1998] 3 W.L.R. 1420; [1998] 3 All E.R. 624; *Times*, June 25, 1998; *Independent*, June 22, 1998 (C.S.), QBD . . . .   *Digested*, 98/**2346**

R. v. Governor of Brixton Prison Ex p. Levin; *sub nom* Levin (Application for a Writ of Habeas Corpus), Re [1997] A.C. 741; [1997] 3 W.L.R. 117; [1997] 3 All E.R. 289; [1998] 1 Cr. App. R. 22; [1997] Crim. L.R. 891; (1997) 94(30) L.S.G. 28; (1997) 147 N.L.J. 990; (1997) 141 S.J.L.B. 148; *Times*, June 21, 1997; *Independent*, July 2, 1997, HL; affirming [1997] Q.B. 65; [1996] 3 W.L.R. 657; [1996] 4 All E.R. 350; [1997] 1 Cr. App. R. 335; (1996) 140 S.J.L.B. 94; *Times*, March 11, 1996, QBD . . . .   *Digested*, 97/**2418**

R. v. Governor of Brixton Prison Ex p. Saifi see R. (on the application of Saifi) v. Governor of Brixton Prison

R. v. Governor of Brixton Prison Ex p. Soblen (No.2) [1963] 2 Q.B. 243, CA; affirming [1962] 3 W.L.R. 1154; [1962] 3 All E.R. 641; 106 S.J. 736, QBD . . . .   *Digested*, 62/**55**:
Applied, 65/1: *Considered*, 85/1521, 98/2353

R. v. Governor of Brockhill Prison Ex p. Evans (No.2); *sub nom* Evans v. Governor of Brockhill Prison [2001] 2 A.C. 19; [2000] 3 W.L.R. 843; [2000] 4 All E.R. 15; [2000] U.K.H.R.R. 836; (2000) 97(32) L.S.G. 38; (2000) 144 S.J.L.B. 241; *Times*, August 2, 2000; *Independent*, November 6, 2000 (C.S), HL; affirming [1999] Q.B. 1043; [1999] 1 W.L.R. 103; [1998] 4 All E.R. 993; (1999) 11 Admin. L.R. 6; [1998] C.O.D. 378; (1999) 163 J.P.N. 51; (1998) 95(33) L.S.G. 35; (1998) 142 S.J.L.B. 196; *Times*, July 6, 1998; *Independent*, June 24, 1998, CA; reversing CO 2955-96, QBD . . . .   *Digested*, 00/**5113**:
Applied, 01/1091: *Considered*, 01/1524

R. (on the application of N) v. Governor of Dartmoor Prison; *sub nom* N v. Governor of Dartmoor Prison; R. v. Governor of Dartmoor Prison Ex p. N [2001] EWHC Admin 93; *Times*, March 20, 2001; *Independent*, April 2, 2001 (C.S), QBD (Admin Ct) . . . .   *Digested*, 01/**4581**

R. v. Governor of Dartmoor Prison Ex p. N see R. (on the application of N) v. Governor of Dartmoor Prison

R. v. Governor of Durham Prison Ex p. Singh (Hardial); *sub nom* R. v. Secretary of State for the Home Department Ex p. Hardial Singh [1984] 1 W.L.R. 704; [1984] 1 All E.R. 983; [1983] Imm. A.R. 983; (1984) 128 S.J. 349, QBD . . . .   *Digested*, 84/**1726**:
Considered, 95/2726, 96/3278: *Distinguished*, 00/3347

R. v. Governor of Elmley Prison Ex p. Moorton [1999] 2 Cr. App. R. (S.) 165; [1999]
   Crim. L.R. 333, QBD . . . .   *Digested*, 99/**1348**
R. v. Governor of Exeter Prison Ex p. Ellis see R. v. Governor of Belmarsh Prison Ex p.
   Gilligan
R. v. Governor of Frankland Prison Ex p. Russell (Right to Meals) [2000] 1 W.L.R.
   2027; [2000] H.R.L.R. 512; [2001] A.C.D. 20; (2000) 144 S.J.L.B. 222; *Times*,
   August 1, 2000; *Independent*, July 21, 2000, QBD . . . .   *Digested*, 00/**3202**
R. v. Governor of Glen Parva Young Offender Institution Ex p. G (A Minor); *sub nom* G
   (A Minor), Re; R. v. HM Young Offenders Institution Glen Parva Ex p. G [1998]
   Q.B. 877; [1998] 3 W.L.R. 13; [1998] 2 All E.R. 295; [1998] 2 Cr. App. R. 349;
   (1998) 162 J.P. 225; (1998) 162 J.P.N. 220; (1998) 95(5) L.S.G. 29; (1998)
   142 S.J.L.B. 55; *Times*, January 24, 1998; *Independent*, February 16, 1998 (C.S.),
   QBD . . . .   *Digested*, 98/**1001**
                                          Applied, 00/1028
R. v. Governor of Kirkham Prison Ex p. Burke (Unreported, March 18, 1994), QBD . . . . .
R. v. Governor of Maidstone Prison Ex p. Peries; *sub nom* R. v. Secretary of State for
   the Home Department Ex p. Peries [1998] C.O.D. 150; *Times*, July 30, 1997,
   QBD . . . .   *Digested*, 97/**3927**
R. (on the application of Akhtar) v. Governor of Newhall Prison; *sub nom* R. v. Newhall
   Prison Ex p. Akhtar [2001] EWHC Admin 175; [2001] A.C.D. 69; *Independent*,
   April 30, 2001 (C.S), QBD (Admin Ct) . . . .   *Digested*, 01/**1267**
R. v. Governor of Pentonville Prison Ex p. Fernandez; *sub nom* Fernandez v. Singapore
   [1971] 1 W.L.R. 987; [1971] 2 All E.R. 691; 115 S.J. 469, HL . . . .   *Digested*, 71/**4784**:
                               Applied, 01/82: *Referred to*, 85/1728
R. v. Governor of Pentonville Prison Ex p. Osman (No.1); *sub nom* Osman (No.1), Re
   [1990] 1 W.L.R. 277; [1989] 3 All E.R. 701; (1990) 90 Cr. App. R. 281; [1988]
   Crim. L.R. 611; (1990) 87(7) L.S.G. 32; (1990) 134 S.J. 458; *Times*, April 13,
   1988, QBD . . . .   *Digested*, 90/**1175**:
                 Applied, 99/3441, 01/392: *Disapproved*, 01/1069
R. v. Governor of Risley Prison Ex p. Healey see R. v. Oldham Justices Ex p. Cawley
R. v. Governor of Risley Prison Ex p. Ryan see R. v. Oldham Justices Ex p. Cawley
R. v. Governor of Swaledale Prison Ex p. Francois see R. v. Secretary of State for the
   Home Department Ex p. Francois
R. v. Governor of Swaleside Prison Ex p. Wynter (1998) 10 Admin. L.R. 597; *Times*,
   June 2, 1998, QBD . . . .   *Digested*, 98/**4076**
R. v. Governor of Wandsworth Prison Ex p. Sorhaindo; *sub nom* R. v. Governor of
   Wandsworth Prison Ex p. Sorhaino (1999) 96(4) L.S.G. 38; (1999) 143 S.J.L.B.
   23; *Times*, January 5, 1999; *Independent*, December 21, 1998 (C.S.), QBD . . . . .   *Digested*, 99/**1316**
R. v. Governor of Wandsworth Prison Ex p. Sorhaino see R. v. Governor of
   Wandsworth Prison Ex p. Sorhaindo
R. (on the application of Ponting) v. Governor of Whitemoor Prison C/01/0830, CA;
   affirming [2001] EWHC Admin 241; *Independent*, May 14, 2001 (C.S), QBD
   (Admin Ct)
R. v. Governor of Whitemoor Prison Ex p. Main see R. v. Secretary of State for the
   Home Department Ex p. Simms
R. v. Governor of Winson Green Prison Ex p. Trotter (1992) 94 Cr. App. R. 29; (1991)
   155 J.P. 671; [1991] C.O.D. 462; (1991) 155 J.P.N. 458; (1991) 135 S.J. 30;
   Times, May 30, 1991, QBD . . . .   *Digested*, 91/**737**:
                                   Approved, 99/1051
R. v. Gowland-Wynn (Geoffrey) [2001] EWCA Crim 2715; *Times*, December 7, 2001,
   CA (Crim Div)
R. v. Goy (Anthony Charles) [2001] 1 Cr. App. R. (S.) 13, CA (Crim Div) . . . .   *Digested*, 01/**1486**
R. v. GR see R. v. H (Grant) (A Juvenile)
R. v. Grady (Eric Ernest) [2000] 2 Cr. App. R. (S.) 468, CA (Crim Div) . . . .   *Digested*, 01/**1481**
R. v. Graham [1996] N.I. 157, CA (NI)
R. v. Graham (Andrew Harvey); R. v. Gillespie (Kevin) *Independent*, November 23,
   1998 (C.S.), CA (Crim Div) . . . .   *Digested*, 98/**256**
R. v. Graham (Edward John) [1999] 2 Cr. App. R. (S.) 312; [1999] Crim. L.R. 677;
   (1999) 96(14) L.S.G. 31; *Times*, February 23, 1999, CA (Crim Div) . . . .   *Digested*, 99/**1342**
R. v. Graham (Garry Allan) see R. v. Graham (Hemamali Krishna)
R. v. Graham (Hemamali Krishna); R. v. Kansal (Rupe Lal); R. v. Ali (Sajid Pasha); R. v.
   Marsh (Terence Colin); R. v. Graham (Garry Allan); R. v. Price (Paul Graham); R. v.
   Bramich (David) [1997] 1 Cr. App. R. 302; [1997] Crim. L.R. 340; (1996)
   93(44) L.S.G. 29; (1996) 140 S.J.L.B. 253; *Times*, October 28, 1996;
   Independent, October 30, 1996, CA (Crim Div). . . . .   *Digested*, 96/**1532**:
             Applied, 97/1228, 98/892: *Approved*, 00/5480: *Considered*, 97/1224,
              97/1227, 97/1249: *Followed*, 97/1126: *Referred to*, 97/1225, 97/1229, 97/1230,
                                          97/1231, 97/1304
R. v. Graham (Robert) [1997] 2 Cr. App. R. (S.) 264, CA (Crim Div) . . . .   *Digested*, 97/**1442**:
                                   Applied, 01/1300
R. v. Graham (Steven Anthony); R. v. Howe (Stevey) [2001] EWCA Crim 768; [2001]
   2 Cr. App. R. (S.) 108, CA (Crim Div) . . . .   *Digested*, 01/**1472**
R. v. Graham-Campbell Ex p. Herbert [1935] 1 K.B. 594, KBD . . . .   *Considered*, 99/5164

R. *v.* Graham-Kerr (John) [1988] 1 W.L.R. 1098; (1989) 88 Cr. App. R. 302; (1989) 153 J.P. 171; (1989) 153 J.P.N. 170; (1988) 132 S.J. 1299, CA (Crim Div) . . . . . .   *Digested*, 89/**836**: *Applied*, 99/5835, 01/1058

R. *v.* Grainger (Terence) see Attorney General's Reference (No.59 of 1996), Re

R. *v.* Grant (Heather); *sub nom* R. (on the application of Grant) *v.* DPP [2001] EWCA Crim 2611; (2001) 145 S.J.L.B. 269; *Times*, December 10, 2001, CA (Crim Div)

R. *v.* Grant (Langford) (1986) 8 Cr. App. R. (S.) 4, CA (Crim Div) . . . .   *Digested*, 87/**875**: *Considered*, 01/1327

R. *v.* Grant (Martin Charles) (1992) 13 Cr. App. R. (S.) 54, CA (Crim Div) . . . .   *Digested*, 92/**1151**: *Considered*, 96/1993, 96/2021, 00/1369

R. *v.* Grant (Stephen) see R. *v.* Simpson (David)

R. *v.* Grantham (Paul Reginald) [1984] Q.B. 675; [1984] 2 W.L.R. 815; [1984] 3 All E.R. 166; (1984) 79 Cr. App. R. 86; [1984] Crim. L.R. 492, CA (Crim Div) . . . . .   *Digested*, 84/**627**: *Considered*, 86/608, 91/417, 92/783, 93/957: *Distinguished*, 00/675

R. *v.* Gratton (Paul) [2001] 2 Cr. App. R. (S.) 36, CA (Crim Div) . . . .   *Digested*, 01/**1417**

R. *v.* Gravesend Magistrates Court Ex p. Baker see R. *v.* Gravesham Magistrates Court Ex p. Baker

R. *v.* Gravesham Magistrates Court Ex p. Baker; *sub nom* R. *v.* Gravesend Magistrates Court Ex p. Baker (1997) 161 J.P. 765; [1998] R.T.R. 451; *Times*, April 30, 1997, QBD

R. *v.* Gray (Carlton) [2001] 1 Cr. App. R. (S.) 28, CA (Crim Div) . . . .   *Digested*, 01/**1275**

R. *v.* Gray (Darren John); R. *v.* Evans (Gareth) [1998] Crim. L.R. 570; *Times*, March 9, 1998; *Independent*, February 27, 1998, CA (Crim Div) . . . .   *Digested*, 98/**878**

R. *v.* Gray (Robin Peter) [1999] 1 Cr. App. R. (S.) 50, CA (Crim Div) . . . .   *Digested*, 99/**1189**

R. *v.* Gray (Shane) see R. *v.* Killgallon (Leonard Arthur)

R. *v.* Great Western Trains Co Ltd Ex p. Frederick [1998] C.O.D. 239, QBD

R. (on the application of Northern Ireland Human Rights Commission) *v.* Greater Belfast Coroner; *sub nom* Northern Ireland Human Rights Commission's Application for Judicial Review, Re [2001] N.I. 271; *Times*, May 11, 2001, CA (NI) . . . .   *Digested*, 01/**5642**

R. *v.* Greater Manchester Police Ex p. R (A Juvenile), *Independent*, October 23, 2000 (C.S), QBD

R. *v.* Greater Manchester Valuation Panel Ex p. Shell Chemicals UK Ltd [1982] Q.B. 255; [1981] 3 W.L.R. 752; 125 S.J. 588; *Times*, June 16, 1981, QBD . . . .   *Digested*, 81/**2274**: *Distinguished*, 98/4582

R. *v.* Greatrex (David Anthony); R. *v.* Bates (Jason Alan) [1999] 1 Cr. App. R. 126; [1998] Crim. L.R. 733; *Times*, April 2, 1998, CA (Crim Div) . . . .   *Digested*, 98/**1035**

R. *v.* Greaves (Anderson) [1999] 1 Cr. App. R. (S.) 319, CA (Crim Div) . . . .   *Digested*, 99/**1307**

R. *v.* Greaves (Brian Edwin) see R. *v.* Tan (Moira)

R. *v.* Greaves (Gloria Gina) see R. *v.* Tan (Moira)

R. *v.* Green (James William) see R. *v.* Zafar (Mohammed)

R. *v.* Green (Wayne); R. *v.* Withers (Simon) [1998] 1 Cr. App. R. (S.) 437, CA (Crim Div) . . . .   *Digested*, 98/**1195**

R. *v.* Greenwich Justices Ex p. Davidson see R. *v.* St Helens Justices Ex p. Jones

R. *v.* Greenwich Justices Ex p. Wright see R. *v.* St Helens Justices Ex p. Jones

R. *v.* Greenwich LBC Ex p. Dhadly (2000) 32 H.L.R. 829, QBD . . . .   *Digested*, 01/**5009**

R. *v.* Greenwich LBC Ex p. Dhadly (Leave Application) (1999) 31 H.L.R. 446, QBD . . . .   *Digested*, 99/**4556**

R. *v.* Greenwich LBC Ex p. Glen International Ltd [2000] E.H.L.R. 382; (2001) 33 H.L.R. 87; (2000) 97(17) L.S.G. 34; [2000] N.P.C. 29; *Times*, March 29, 2000, CA; affirming (2001) 33 H.L.R. 21; [1998] C.O.D. 475; [1998] E.G.C.S. 102; [1998] N.P.C. 107; *Times*, July 25, 1998; *Independent*, July 6, 1998 (C.S), QBD .   *Digested*, 00/**3125**

R. *v.* Greenwich LBC Ex p. John Ball Primary School Governors see R. *v.* Greenwich LBC Shadow Education Committee Ex p. John Ball Primary School Governors

R. *v.* Greenwich LBC Shadow Education Committee Ex p. John Ball Primary School Governors; *sub nom* R. *v.* Greenwich LBC Ex p. John Ball Primary School Governors 88 L.G.R. 589; (1990) 154 L.G. Rev. 678; *Times*, December 27, 1989; *Independent*, December 22, 1989; *Daily Telegraph*, January 26, 1990, CA; reversing [1990] C.O.D. 103; *Times*, November 17, 1989; *Independent*, November 23, 1989; *Guardian*, November 21, 1989, QBD . . . .   *Digested*, 90/**1772**: *Applied*, 93/1707: *Considered*, 93/1688, 95/1910, 00/1924: *Distinguished*, 94/1866, 95/1911: *Followed*, 91/1539, 92/1856, 92/1857: *Referred to*, 93/1687, 96/2381, 97/2107

R. *v.* Greenwich Magistrates Court Ex p. Deleon [1999] C.O.D. 116, QBD

R. *v.* Greenwood (Paul) see R. *v.* Tunnicliffe (Marcus)

R. *v.* Greer (James) [1998] Crim. L.R. 572, CA (Crim Div)

R. *v.* Gregory see R. *v.* Singfield

R. *v.* Gregson (Kathleen Mary) (1993) 14 Cr. App. R. (S.) 85, CA (Crim Div) . . . .   *Digested*, 93/**1242**: *Cited*, 94/1324: *Considered*, 94/1322, 98/1325

R. *v.* Grey (Anthony John) (1992) 13 Cr. App. R. (S.) 522, CA (Crim Div) . . . .   *Digested*, 93/**1210**: *Considered*, 00/1417, 01/1474

R. *v.* Grey (Donald) see R. *v.* Panae (George)

R. *v.* Grey (Kenneth) see Attorney General's Reference (No.39 of 1995), Re

R. *v.* Griffin (Daniel Joseph) [1998] Crim. L.R. 418, CA (Crim Div)

R. *v.* Griffin (Mark) [1999] 1 Cr. App. R. (S.) 213, CA (Crim Div) . . . .   *Digested*, 99/**1076**

R. *v.* Griffiths [1998] Crim. L.R. 567, CA (Crim Div)

R. *v.* Griffiths (Anthony James) [1998] Crim. L.R. 348, CA (Crim Div)
R. *v.* Griffiths (Colin Barry) [2000] 2 Cr. App. R. (S.) 224, CA (Crim Div) . . . .　　*Digested,* 00/**1153**
R. *v.* Griffiths (James Mervin); R. *v.* Griffiths (Susan Lindsey) [2001] EWCA Crim
　　2093; *Times,* October 17, 2001, CA (Crim Div) . . . .　　*Digested,* 01/**1109**
R. *v.* Griffiths (Peter Wyn) [2000] 1 Cr. App. R. (S.) 240, CA (Crim Div) . . . .　　*Digested,* 00/**1237**
R. *v.* Griffiths (Susan Lindsey) see R. *v.* Griffiths (James Mervin)
R. *v.* Groom (John Walter) [1977] Q.B. 6; [1976] 2 W.L.R. 618; [1976] 2 All E.R. 321;
　　(1976) 62 Cr. App. R. 242; [1976] Crim. L.R. 382; 120 S.J. 198, CA (Crim Div) .　　*Digested,* 76/**484**:
　　　　　　　　　　　　　　　　　　　　　　Applied, 98/1034: *Considered,* 89/677
R. *v.* Gross (Neville Emmanuel) [1996] 2 Cr. App. R. (S.) 189, CA (Crim Div) . . . .　　*Digested,* 96/**2100**:
　　　　　　　　　　　　　　　　　　　　　　Considered, 97/1053, 99/1173
R. *v.* Groves (Martin) [1998] Crim. L.R. 200, CA (Crim Div)
R. *v.* Groves (Scott Paul) (1995) 16 Cr. App. R. (S.) 768, CA (Crim Div) . . . .　　*Digested,* 96/**1834**:
　　　　　　　　　　　　　　　　　　　　　　Considered, 98/1360
R. *v.* Grzybowski (Stephen) [1998] 1 Cr. App. R. (S.) 4, CA (Crim Div) . . . .　　*Digested,* 98/**1116**
R. *v.* Guigno (Roger) [1998] 2 Cr. App. R. (S.) 217, CA (Crim Div) . . . .　　*Digested,* 98/**1138**
R. *v.* Guildford Crown Court Ex p. DPP see R. *v.* Southwark Crown Court Ex p.
　　Bowles
R. *v.* Guiver (Stuart Harold) (1987) 9 Cr. App. R. (S.) 407, CA (Crim Div) . . . .　　*Digested,* 90/**1491**:
　　　　　　　　　　　　　　　　　　　　　　Considered, 00/1329
R. *v.* Gummerson (James Wesley); R. *v.* Steadman [1999] Crim. L.R. 680, CA (Crim
　　Div)
R. *v.* Guney (Erkin Ramadan) [1998] 2 Cr. App. R. 242; [1999] Crim. L.R. 485;
　　(1998) 95(15) L.S.G. 30; (1998) 142 S.J.L.B. 99; *Times,* March 9, 1998;
　　Independent, March 6, 1998, CA (Crim Div) . . . .　　*Digested,* 98/**890**
R. *v.* Guy (Paul Richard) [1999] 2 Cr. App. R. (S.) 24, CA (Crim Div) . . . .　　*Digested,* 99/**1126**
R. *v.* Gwent CC Ex p. Bryant [1988] C.O.D. 19; *Times,* April 18, 1988; *Independent,*
　　April 19, 1988, QBD . . . .　　*Digested,* 88/**1191**:
　　　　　　　　　　　　　　　　　　　　　　Applied, 91/69: *Considered,* 95/30, 98/94
R. (on the application of Stokes) *v.* Gwent Magistrates Court [2001] EWHC Admin 569;
　　(2001) 165 J.P. 766; (2001) 165 J.P.N. 766, QBD (Admin Ct)
R. *v.* GY see R. *v.* Y (G)
R. *v.* H (Ann Nolene) (A Juvenile) see R. *v.* F (Mark Frank)
R. *v.* H (Arthur Henry); *sub nom* R. *v.* H (Sexual Assault); R. *v.* H (Henry) [1998] 2 Cr.
　　App. R. 161; [1998] Crim. L.R. 409; *Times,* December 4, 1997, CA (Crim Div) . . .　　*Digested,* 98/**1063**:
　　　　　　　　　　　　　　　　　　　　　　Considered, 99/1044
R. *v.* H (Assault of Child: Reasonable Chastisement) [2001] EWCA Crim 1024; [2001]
　　2 F.L.R. 431; [2001] 3 F.C.R. 144; *Times,* May 17, 2001, CA (Crim Div) . . . .　　*Digested,* 01/**1147**
R. *v.* H (Barry James) [2000] 1 Cr. App. R. (S.) 82, CA (Crim Div) . . . .　　*Digested,* 00/**1429**
R. *v.* H (Bilal) (A Juvenile) see Attorney General's Reference (No.69 of 1999), Re
R. *v.* H (Bruce William) see Attorney General's Reference (No.77 of 2001), Re
R. *v.* H (Choudhry Fiaz) (A Juvenile) [2000] 1 Cr. App. R. (S.) 181; [1999] Crim. L.R.
　　1004, CA (Crim Div) . . . .　　*Digested,* 00/**1176**
R. *v.* H (Colin) (A Juvenile) (1999) 96(11) L.S.G. 70; (1999) 143 S.J.L.B. 89; *Times,*
　　April 5, 1999, CA (Crim Div) . . . .　　*Digested,* 99/**1237**
R. *v.* H (Cyril Arthur) see Attorney General's Reference (No.3 of 1995), Re
R. *v.* H (Daniel) (A Juvenile) [1999] 1 Cr. App. R. (S.) 386, CA (Crim Div) . . . .　　*Digested,* 99/**1239**
R. *v.* H (David John) see Attorney General's Reference (No.41 of 2000), Re
R. *v.* H (David Lee) (A Juvenile) see Attorney General's Reference (No.25 of 1998), Re
R. *v.* H (David Leslie) (A Juvenile) see R. *v.* Howells (Craig)
R. *v.* H (Dean Anthony) (A Juvenile) [2001] EWCA Crim 239; [2001] 2 Cr. App. R.
　　(S.) 51, CA (Crim Div) . . . .　　*Digested,* 01/**1389**
R. *v.* H (Fitness to Plead) see R. *v.* M (Fitness to Plead)
R. *v.* H (Gavin Spencer) [2001] 1 F.L.R. 580; [2001] 1 F.C.R. 569; [2001] Crim. L.R.
　　318; [2001] Fam. Law 185; *Times,* December 20, 2000, CA (Crim Div) . . . .　　*Digested,* 01/**1050**:
　　　　　　　　　　　　　　　　　　　　　　Considered, 01/1048
R. *v.* H (Geoff) see R. *v.* H (Grant) (A Juvenile)
R. *v.* H (Grace M) (A Juvenile) see Attorney General's Reference (Nos.68 and 69 of
　　1996), Re
R. *v.* H (Grant) (A Juvenile); *sub nom* R. *v.* GR; R. *v.* GE; R. *v.* H (Geoff) [2001] 2 Cr.
　　App. R. (S.) 31; (2001) 165 J.P. 190; [2001] Crim. L.R. 236; (2001) 98(4) L.S.G.
　　49; (2001) 145 S.J.L.B. 22; *Times,* January 9, 2001, CA (Crim Div) . . . .　　*Digested,* 01/**1209**:
　　　　　　　　　　　　　　　　　　　　　　Considered, 01/1401
R. *v.* H (Harry) (A Juvenile) [2001] Crim. L.R. 227; *Times,* May 5, 2000, CA (Crim
　　Div) . . . .　　*Digested,* 00/**910**
R. *v.* H (Henry) see R. *v.* H (Arthur Henry)
R. *v.* H (Indecent Assault), *Times,* March 18, 1999, CA (Crim Div) . . . .　　*Digested,* 99/**1209**
R. *v.* H (Kevin Errol) (A Juvenile) see Attorney General's Reference (No.44 of 1997),
　　Re
R. *v.* H (Luke Clifford) (A Juvenile) see R. *v.* LH (A Juvenile) (Indecent Assault:
　　Sentencing)
R. *v.* H (Luke James) (A Juvenile) [1999] 1 Cr. App. R. (S.) 187, CA (Crim Div) . . . .　　*Digested,* 99/**1230**
R. *v.* H (Mahzer) see Attorney General's Reference (No.27 of 1998), Re
R. *v.* H (Marital Rape) [1999] 1 Cr. App. R. (S.) 470, CA (Crim Div) . . . .　　*Digested,* 99/**1296**

R. v. H (Martin Stanley) [1998] 2 Cr. App. R. (S.) 226, CA (Crim Div). . . . .   *Digested*, 98/**1298**
R. v. H (Martin Thomas) [2000] Crim. L.R. 189, CA (Crim Div)
R. v. H (Michael) [1997] 2 Cr. App. R. (S.) 339, CA (Crim Div). . . . .   *Digested*, 98/**1353**
R. v. H (Paul Raymond) (1994) 15 Cr. App. R. (S.) 373, CA (Crim Div) . . . .   *Considered*, 00/1402
R. v. H (Paula) (A Juvenile) [1998] 2 Cr. App. R. (S.) 396, CA (Crim Div). . . . .   *Digested*, 99/**1234**
R. v. H (Peter Charles) [1998] Crim. L.R. 877, CA (Crim Div)
R. v. H (Robert James) (A Juvenile) see Attorney General's Reference (Nos.53, 54, 55,
     56 and 57 of 2001), Re
R. v. H (Sexual Assault) see R. v. H (Arthur Henry)
R. v. H (Stephen James) (A Juvenile) [1999] Crim. L.R. 750, CA (Crim Div)
R. v. H (Steven) (Remand: Violent Offences) (Unreported, June 9, 1999), Crown Ct
     [*Ex rel*. David Allan, Barrister, 9 Bedford Row, London] . . . .   *Digested*, 99/**1027**
R. v. H (Steven Donald) see Attorney General's Reference (No.61 of 2001), Re
R. v. H (Tahir) see R. v. Khan (Nazaqat)
R. v. H (Terence) see Attorney General's Reference (No.35 of 1994), Re
R. v. H (Witness Reprisals); *sub nom* R. v. A (Witness Reprisals); R. v. W (Witness
     Reprisals); R. v. M (Witness Reprisals) [2001] Crim. L.R. 815; *Times*, July 6,
     2001, CA (Crim Div) . . . .   *Digested*, 01/**984**
R. v. H Sherman Ltd; *sub nom* R. v. Wolverhampton Deputy Recorder Ex p. DPP.
     [1949] 2 K.B. 674; [1949] 2 All E.R. 207; 65 T.L.R. 449; (1949) 33 Cr. App. R.
     151; 113 J.P. 412; 47 L.G.R. 669; 93 S.J. 526, CCA . . . .   *Digested*, 47-51/**9859**:
                              Distinguished, 81/1683, 82/1934, 82/1936, 98/2831
R. v. Hackett (Kavin Peter) (1988) 10 Cr. App. R. (S.) 388; [1989] Crim. L.R. 230, CA
     (Crim Div). . . . .   *Digested*, 90/**1242**:
                           Applied, 90/1244: *Considered*, 98/1153
R. (on the application of Lemon Land Ltd) v. Hackney LBC [2001] EWHC Admin 336;
     (2001) 3 L.G.L.R. 42; [2001] B.L.G.R. 555; [2001] 21 E.G.C.S. 165; (2001)
     98(21) L.S.G. 41; [2001] N.P.C. 91; *Independent*, July 2, 2001 (C.S); *Daily*
     Telegraph, May 22, 2001, QBD (Admin Ct)
R. (on the application of Structadene Ltd) v. Hackney LBC; *sub nom* R. v. Hackney LBC
     Ex p. Structadene Ltd; Structadene v. Hackney LBC [2001] 2 All E.R. 225;
     (2001) 3 L.G.L.R. 19; [2001] B.L.G.R. 204; (2001) 82 P. & C.R. 25; [2001] 1
     E.G.L.R. 15; [2001] 12 E.G. 168; [2000] E.G.C.S. 130; (2001) 98(1) L.S.G. 23;
     [2000] N.P.C. 119; *Times*, November 28, 2000, QBD (Admin Ct) . . . .   *Digested*, 01/**4375**
R. v. Hackney LBC Ex p. Adebiri; R. v. Merton LBC Ex p. Inparaja; R. v. Merton LBC Ex
     p. Parupathpilli; R. v. Ealing LBC Ex p. Jehan [1999] R.V.R. 24; *Times*,
     November 5, 1997, QBD . . . .   *Digested*, 97/**3499**
R. v. Hackney LBC Ex p. Ajayi (1998) 30 H.L.R. 473; [1997] C.O.D. 371, QBD . . . . . .   *Digested*, 97/**2666**
R. v. Hackney LBC Ex p. K (1998) 30 H.L.R. 760; (1998) 10 Admin. L.R. 464; (1997)
     94(43) L.S.G. 31; (1997) 141 S.J.L.B. 223; *Times*, November 17, 1997, CA . . . . .   *Digested*, 97/**2655**
R. v. Hackney LBC Ex p. Structadene Ltd see R. (on the application of Structadene
     Ltd) v. Hackney LBC
R. v. Hackney LBC Ex p. Tonnicodi (1998) 30 H.L.R. 916, QBD. . . . .   *Digested*, 98/**2998**
R. v. Hadakoglu (Yakup) see R. v. Eyck (Dennis Jerrel)
R. v. Hadjou (George) (1989) 11 Cr. App. R. (S.) 29; [1989] Crim. L.R. 390, CA (Crim
     Div) . . . .   *Digested*, 90/**1209**:
                 Cited, 91/1022: *Considered*, 96/1733, 00/1139
R. v. Hadzic (Kemil); *sub nom* R. v. Hodzic; (Unreported, June 17, 1997), CA (Crim
     Div) . . . .   *Considered*, 98/1321,
                                             99/1284
R. v. Hafeez (Fashwar Qullah); R. v. Gibbs (Robert John) [1998] 1 Cr. App. R. (S.)
     276, CA (Crim Div) . . . .   *Digested*, 98/**1319**
R. v. Hair (Lorraine) [2000] 1 Cr. App. R. (S.) 118, CA (Crim Div) . . . .   *Digested*, 00/**1252**
R. v. Hales (Robert) [1999] 2 Cr. App. R. (S.) 113, CA (Crim Div) . . . .   *Digested*, 99/**1078**:
                                           Considered, 00/1346
R. v. Halil (Gursel) see R. v. Zelzele (Behcet)
R. v. Hall (Christopher James) see Attorney General's Reference (No.36 of 2001), Re
R. v. Hall (Darren Dennis) see R. v. O'Brien (Michael Alan)
R. v. Hall (Ian John); R. v. Morgan (John Martin) (1995) 16 Cr. App. R. (S.) 921, CA
     (Crim Div). . . . .   *Digested*, 96/**1982**:
                                           Considered, 98/1301
R. v. Hall (Jennifer) see R. v. Hill (Valerie Mary)
R. v. Hall (John Anthony) see R. v. B (Raymond Christopher) (A Juvenile)
R. v. Hall (Michael) [1968] 2 Q.B. 788; [1968] 3 W.L.R. 359; [1968] 2 All E.R. 1009;
     (1968) 52 Cr. App. R. 528; (1968) 132 J.P. 417; [1968] Crim. L.R. 403; 112 S.J.
     621, CA (Crim Div) . . . .   *Digested*, 68/**755**:
                                           Applied, 99/1013
R. v. Hall & Co Ltd [1999] 1 Cr. App. R. (S.) 306, CA (Crim Div) . . . .   *Digested*, 99/**2859**:
                                           Considered, 01/1348
R. v. Hallam [1995] Crim. L.R. 323; *Times*, May 27, 1994; *Independent*, June 13, 1994
     (C.S.), CA (Crim Div). . . . .   *Considered*, 98/1063,
                                           00/1013
R. v. Haller (Pierre Egbert) see R. v. Wijs (Eric Jan)

R. v. Hallstrom Ex p. W (No.2); R. v. Gardner Ex p. L [1986] Q.B. 1090; [1986] 2
    W.L.R. 883; [1986] 2 All E.R. 306; (1986) 83 L.S.G. 786; (1985) 130 S.J. 204,
    QBD . . . .   *Digested*, 86/**2132**:
                             Applied, 94/3066: *Disapproved*, 98/3897
R. v. Halpin [1996] Crim. L.R. 112, CA (Crim Div) . . . .   *Considered*, 96/1370,
                                        98/890
R. v. Hambery (Cyril) [1977] Q.B. 924; [1977] 2 W.L.R. 999; [1977] 3 All E.R. 561;
    (1977) 65 Cr. App. R. 233; 121 S.J. 270, CA (Crim Div) . . . .   *Digested*, 77/**1683**:
                                       Considered, 98/380
R. v. Hambleton DC Ex p. Somerfield Stores Ltd (1999) 77 P. & C.R. 475; [1999] 1
    P.L.R. 66; [1999] P.L.C.R. 236; [1998] E.G.C.S. 155; (1998) 95(43) L.S.G. 33;
    [1998] N.P.C. 148, QBD . . . .   *Digested*, 99/**4265**
R. v. Hameed (Costs) [2001] 2 Costs L.R. 343, MC
R. v. Hamill (Francis Martin) see R. v. Delaney (Richard Anthony)
R. v. Hamilton (Erroll) (1998) 95(30) L.S.G. 25; (1998) 142 S.J.L.B. 214; *Times*, July
    25, 1998; *Independent*, July 6, 1998 (C.S.), CA (Crim Div) . . . .   *Digested*, 98/**874**
R. v. Hamilton (Linda Kelly) [2000] 1 Cr. App. R. (S.) 91, CA (Crim Div) . . . .   *Digested*, 00/**1221**
R. (on the application of Burkett) v. Hammersmith and Fulham LBC; *sub nom* R. v.
    Hammersmith and Fulham LBC Ex p. Burkett; Burkett, Re; TNS, HL; reversing
    [2001] Env. L.R. 39; [2001] 3 P.L.R. 1; [2001] J.P.L. 775; [2001] A.C.D. 50,
    CA . . . .   *Digested*, 01/**53**
R. v. Hammersmith and Fulham LBC Ex p. Avdic (1998) 30 H.L.R. 1; [1997] C.O.D.
    122, CA; affirming (1996) 28 H.L.R. 897; *Times*, June 11, 1996, QBD . . . .   *Digested*, 96/**3060**
R. v. Hammersmith and Fulham LBC Ex p. Burkett see R. (on the application of
    Burkett) v. Hammersmith and Fulham LBC
R. v. Hammersmith and Fulham LBC Ex p. Council for the Protection of Rural England
    (No.1) see R. v. Hammersmith and Fulham LBC Ex p. CPRE London Branch
    (Leave to Appeal) (No.1)
R. v. Hammersmith and Fulham LBC Ex p. Council for the Protection of Rural England
    (No.2) see R. v. Hammersmith and Fulham LBC Ex p. CPRE London Branch
    (Costs Order)
R. v. Hammersmith and Fulham LBC Ex p. Council for the Protection of Rural England
    (No.3) see R. v. Hammersmith and Fulham LBC Ex p. CPRE London Branch
    (Leave to Appeal) (No.2)
R. v. Hammersmith and Fulham LBC Ex p. CPRE London Branch (Costs Order); *sub
    nom* R. v. Hammersmith and Fulham LBC Ex p. Council for the Protection of
    Rural England (No.2) [2000] Env. L.R. 544; [2000] Env. L.R. D25, QBD . . . . .   *Digested*, 00/**430**:
                                         Followed, 01/4701
R. v. Hammersmith and Fulham LBC Ex p. CPRE London Branch (Leave to Appeal)
    (No.1); *sub nom* R. v. Hammersmith and Fulham LBC Ex p. Council for the
    Protection of Rural England (No.1) [2000] Env. L.R. 549; (2001) 81 P. & C.R. 7,
    CA; affirming [2000] Env. L.R. 532, QBD . . . .   *Digested*, 00/**4516**
R. v. Hammersmith and Fulham LBC Ex p. CPRE London Branch (Leave to Appeal)
    (No.2); *sub nom* R. v. Hammersmith and Fulham LBC Ex p. Council for the
    Protection of Rural England (No.3) [2000] C.P. Rep. 46; [2000] 2 C.M.L.R.
    1021; [2000] Env. L.R. 565; (2001) 81 P. & C.R. 6; [2000] C.O.D. 362; (2000)
    97(2) L.S.G. 32, QBD . . . .   *Digested*, 00/**4462**
R. v. Hammersmith and Fulham LBC Ex p. D [1999] 1 F.L.R. 642; [1999] 2 F.C.R. 401;
    (1999) 31 H.L.R. 786; [1999] B.L.G.R. 575; (1999) 2 C.C.L. Rep. 18; [1999]
    Fam. Law 213; (1999) 96(2) L.S.G. 28; *Times*, December 31, 1998, QBD . . . . . .   *Digested*, 99/**2398**:
                                         Applied, 01/2645
R. v. Hammersmith and Fulham LBC Ex p. Fleck (1998) 30 H.L.R. 679; [1998] C.O.D.
    43, QBD . . . .   *Digested*, 98/**3019**
R. v. Hammersmith and Fulham LBC Ex p. M; R. v. Lambeth LBC Ex p. P; R. v.
    Westminster City Council Ex p. A; R. v. Lambeth LBC Ex p. X (1998) 30 H.L.R.
    10; (1997) 9 Admin. L.R. 504; (1997-98) 1 C.C.L. Rep. 85; *Times*, February 19,
    1997; *Independent*, February 27, 1997, CA; affirming (1997-98) 1 C.C.L. Rep.
    69; [1997] C.O.D. 140; (1996) 93(42) L.S.G. 28; (1996) 140 S.J.L.B. 222;
    Times, October 10, 1996; *Independent*, October 16, 1996, QBD . . . .   *Digested*, 97/**2885**:
                 Applied, 98/3007, 00/4147: *Considered*, 97/4720, 99/4621:
                          Followed, 97/3429: *Referred to*, 97/2884, 98/4571
R. v. Hammersmith and Fulham LBC Ex p. People Before Profit Ltd 80 L.G.R. 322;
    (1983) 45 P. & C.R. 364; [1981] J.P.L. 869, QBD . . . .   *Digested*, 82/**3165**:
                           Considered, 94/80, 95/143, 00/2278
R. v. Hammersmith and Fulham LBC Ex p. Quigley (2000) 32 H.L.R. 379;
    Independent, May 24, 1999 (C.S.), QBD
R. v. Hammersmith Coroner Ex p. Peach see R. v. HM Coroner for Hammersmith Ex p.
    Peach
R. v. Hammersmith Hospitals NHS Trust Ex p. Reffell C/2000/0025, CA; affirming
    (2000) 3 C.C.L. Rep. 371; [2000] Lloyd's Rep. Med. 350; (2000) 55 B.M.L.R.
    130; (2000) 97(36) L.S.G. 42; *Times*, July 27, 2000; *Independent*, July 13,
    2000, QBD . . . .   *Digested*, 00/**2778**

R. *v.* Hammon (Terry Mark) [1998] 2 Cr. App. R. (S.) 202; [1998] Crim. L.R. 293, CA (Crim Div)... *Digested*, 98/**1146**: *Applied*, 00/1158

R. *v.* Hampshire CC Ex p. H [1999] 2 W.L.R. 359; [1999] 3 F.C.R. 129; [1999] Fam. Law 537; (2000) 164 J.P.N. 405; (1998) 95(29) L.S.G. 27; (1998) 142 S.J.L.B. 188; *Times*, June 22, 1998, CA.. *Digested*, 98/**2392**

R. *v.* Hampson (David Adrian) [2001] 1 Cr. App. R. (S.) 84, CA (Crim Div)......... *Digested*, 01/**1432**

R. *v.* Hann (Phillip) [1996] 1 Cr. App. R. (S.) 267; [1995] Crim. L.R. 907, CA (Crim Div).. *Digested*, 96/**2042**: *Considered*, 98/1343

R. *v.* Hanney (Darren Andrew), *Independent*, December 18, 2000 (C.S), CA (Crim Div)

R. *v.* Hanrahan (Thomas Martin) [1999] 1 Cr. App. R. (S.) 308, CA (Crim Div)....... *Digested*, 99/**1215**

R. *v.* Hanratty (James) (Order Granting Exhumation), *Times*, October 26, 2000, CA (Crim Div)... *Digested*, 00/**1110**

R. *v.* Harden (Alan Goldstone) [1963] 1 Q.B. 8; [1962] 2 W.L.R. 553; [1962] 1 All E.R. 286; (1962) 46 Cr. App. R. 90; 126 J.P. 130; 106 S.J. 264, CCA............. *Digested*, 62/**655**: *Applied*, 74/676, 81/1204: *Considered*, 66/5076, 69/1453, 86/1535, 87/807, 90/2274, 95/1332: *Followed*, 98/957

R. *v.* Harding (Ivor William) [2000] 1 Cr. App. R. (S.) 327, CA (Crim Div)......... *Digested*, 00/**1129**

R. *v.* Harding (William Henry) see R. *v.* Adams (David Anthony)

R. *v.* Hardwick (Gary Kevin) [2001] EWCA Crim 369; *Times*, February 28, 2001, CA (Crim Div).. *Digested*, 01/**998**

R. *v.* Hardwicke (Joseph Philip); R. *v.* Thwaites (Stefan Peter) [2001] Crim. L.R. 220; *Times*, November 16, 2000, CA (Crim Div)................................ *Digested*, 00/**917**

R. *v.* Hardy (Richard Nicholas) see Attorney General's Reference (No.70 of 2001), Re

R. *v.* Harfield (Gordon) [1993] 2 P.L.R. 23; [1993] J.P.L. 914, CA (Crim Div)....... *Digested*, 94/**4364**: *Applied*, 01/4696

R. *v.* Haringey Justices Ex p. Branco, *Independent*, December 1, 1997 (C.S.), QBD..... *Digested*, 98/**53**

R. *v.* Haringey Justices Ex p. Fawzy see R. *v.* Tottenham Youth Court Ex p. Fawzy

R. (on the application of Ben-Abdelaziz) *v.* Haringey LBC [2001] EWCA Civ 803; [2001] 1 W.L.R. 1485; [2001] A.C.D. 88; (2001) 98(26) L.S.G. 44; (2001) 145 S.J.L.B. 150; *Times*, June 19, 2001, CA; affirming [2001] A.C.D. 37, QBD (Admin Ct)... *Digested*, 01/**100**

R. (on the application of Haringey Consortium of Disabled People and Carers Association) *v.* Haringey LBC; *sub nom* R. *v.* Haringey LBC Ex p. Haringey Consortium of Disabled People and Carers Association (2001) 58 B.M.L.R. 160, QBD (Admin Ct)... *Digested*, 01/**4335**

R. (on the application of Hibbert) *v.* Haringey LBC; *sub nom* R. *v.* Haringey LBC Ex p. Hibbert [2001] Env. L.R. 29; [2001] E.H.L.R. Dig. 1, QBD (Admin Ct)........ *Digested*, 01/**2422**

R. *v.* Haringey LBC Ex p. Ayub (1993) 25 H.L.R. 566, QBD....................... *Digested*, 94/**2356**: *Considered*, 99/3709: *Followed*, 97/2692

R. *v.* Haringey LBC Ex p. Haringey Consortium of Disabled People and Carers Association see R. (on the application of Haringey Consortium of Disabled People and Carers Association) *v.* Haringey LBC

R. *v.* Haringey LBC Ex p. Hibbert see R. (on the application of Hibbert) *v.* Haringey LBC

R. *v.* Haringey LBC Ex p. Karaman (1997) 29 H.L.R. 366, QBD.................... *Considered*, 98/2997

R. *v.* Haringey LBC Ex p. Norton (No.1) (1997-98) 1 C.C.L. Rep. 168, QBD.......... *Digested*, 97/**4710**

R. *v.* Haringey LBC Ex p. Norton (No.2) [1999] C.O.D. 92, QBD

R. *v.* Haringey LBC Ex p. Sampaio (1999) 31 H.L.R. 1, QBD...................... *Digested*, 99/**3044**

R. *v.* Haringey Youth Court Ex p. A (A Juvenile), *Times*, May 30, 2000; *Independent*, June 12, 2000 (C.S), QBD... *Digested*, 00/**1316**

R. *v.* Harling (Andrew Bentley) see Attorney General's Reference (Nos.11 and 12 of 1995), Re

R. *v.* Harlow Justices Ex p. Gumble (Unreported, October 21, 1997), QBD [*Ex rel.* Bruce R Silvester, Barrister, Lamb Chambers, Temple]..................... *Digested*, 98/**3689**

R. *v.* Harlow Magistrates Court Ex p. O'Farrell [2000] Crim. L.R. 589, QBD

R. *v.* Harper [1990] N.I. 28... *Applied*, 00/5471

R. *v.* Harper (Christopher Randolph); R. *v.* Sabin (Steven Paul) *Times*, October 12, 1998, CA (Crim Div)... *Digested*, 98/**1404**

R. *v.* Harper (John Thomas) [1994] N.I. 199, Crown Ct (Belfast)................. *Digested*, 00/**5464**

R. *v.* Harrer [1995] 3 S.C.R. 562, Sup Ct (Can)........................ *Distinguished*, 99/3139

R. *v.* Harrington-Fry (Martin) (1995) 16 Cr. App. R. (S.) 893, CA (Crim Div)........ *Considered*, 99/1245

R. *v.* Harris (Andrew William) [2001] Env. L.R. 9; [2001] J.P.L. 206; [2000] J.P.L. 1307 (Note); *Times*, May 2, 2000, CA (Crim Div).................... *Digested*, 00/**2302**

R. *v.* Harris (Michael William) [1998] 1 Cr. App. R. (S.) 38; [1997] Crim. L.R. 526, CA (Crim Div)... *Digested*, 98/**1190**: *Considered*, 99/1145

R. *v.* Harris (Timothy John) see Attorney General's Reference (No.16 of 1999), Re

R. *v.* Harrison (J) see R. *v.* Taylor (Shaun Keith)

R. *v.* Harrison (Mark Philip) [1998] 2 Cr. App. R. (S.) 174; [1998] Crim. L.R. 295, CA (Crim Div)... *Digested*, 98/**1156**

R. *v.* Harrison (Michael John); R. *v.* Singleton (David) (1993) 14 Cr. App. R. (S.) 339,
CA (Crim Div) . . . .   *Digested,* 94/**1262**:
         Considered, 98/1298

R. *v.* Harrison (Robert) [1996] 2 Cr. App. R. (S.) 250, CA (Crim Div) . . . .   *Digested,* 96/**2007**:
         Cited, 01/1427: *Considered,* 99/1266

R. *v.* Harrow Crown Court Ex p. Dave [1994] 1 W.L.R. 98; [1994] 1 All E.R. 315;
(1994) 99 Cr. App. R. 114; (1994) 158 J.P. 250; [1994] Crim. L.R. 346; (1993)
143 N.L.J. 1676; *Times,* October 20, 1993, QBD . . . .   *Digested,* 94/**1064**:
         Applied, 00/1077

R. *v.* Harrow Crown Court Ex p. Lingard [1998] C.O.D. 254, QBD
R. *v.* Harrow Crown Court Ex p. Perkins; R. *v.* Cardiff Crown Court Ex p. M (A Minor)
(1998) 162 J.P. 527; (1998) 162 J.P.N. 483; *Times,* April 28, 1998, QBD . . . . . .   *Digested,* 98/**96**:
         Not followed, 99/84

R. *v.* Harrow Crown Court Ex p. UNIC Centre Sarl; *sub nom* UNIC Centre Sarl *v.*
Harrow Crown Court; UNIC Centre Sarl *v.* Brent and Harrow LBC Trading
Standards Service [2000] 1 W.L.R. 2112; [2000] 2 All E.R. 449; [2000] C.P.
Rep. 66; [2000] E.T.M.R. 595; [2000] I.L.Pr. 462; [2000] F.S.R. 667; [2000]
C.O.D. 194; *Independent,* February 14, 2000 (C.S.), QBD . . . .   *Digested,* 00/**790**

R. *v.* Harrow Justices Ex p. DPP [1991] 1 W.L.R. 395; [1991] 3 All E.R. 873; (1991) 93
Cr. App. R. 388; (1992) 156 J.P. 979; [1991] C.O.D. 413; (1991) 155 J.P.N. 378;
(1991) 135 S.J.L.B. 4; *Times,* April 1, 1991; *Independent,* April 9, 1991; *Daily
Telegraph,* April 15, 1991, QBD . . . .   *Digested,* 91/**1088**:
         Considered, 98/1152

R. *v.* Harrow Justices Ex p. Jordan [1997] 1 W.L.R. 84; [1997] 2 All E.R. 344; [1997]
1 Cr. App. R. (S.) 410; (1996) 160 J.P. 789; [1997] Crim. L.R. 60; [1997] C.O.D.
87; (1997) 161 J.P.N. 19; *Times,* November 1, 1996; *Independent,* November 18,
1996 (C.S.), QBD . . . .   *Digested,* 97/**1635**:
         Considered, 99/1281: *Followed,* 97/1634

R. (on the application of Carlton-Conway) *v.* Harrow LBC, CA; reversing [2001] EWHC
Admin 873; [2001] 46 E.G.C.S. 179; [2001] N.P.C. 157, QBD (Admin Ct)
R. (on the application of Fernback) *v.* Harrow LBC; *sub nom* Fernback *v.* Harrow LBC
[2001] EWHC Admin 278; [2001] 18 E.G.C.S. 173; (2001) 98(23) L.S.G. 39,
QBD (Admin Ct)
R. *v.* Harrow LBC Ex p. B [1999] E.L.R. 495, QBD . . . .   *Digested,* 00/**1939**
R. *v.* Harrow LBC Ex p. C see R. *v.* Richmond LBC Ex p. W
R. *v.* Harrow LBC Ex p. Fahia [1998] 1 W.L.R. 1396; [1998] 4 All E.R. 137; [1998] 3
F.C.R. 363; (1998) 30 H.L.R. 1124; (1998) 95(35) L.S.G. 38; (1998) 148 N.L.J.
1354; (1998) 142 S.J.L.B. 226; [1998] N.P.C. 122; *Times,* July 24, 1998, HL;
affirming (1997) 29 H.L.R. 974, CA; affirming (1997) 29 H.L.R. 94, QBD . . . . . .   *Digested,* 98/**3014**:
         Considered, 97/2666: *Followed,* 98/3011

R. *v.* Harrow Youth Court Ex p. Prussia see R. *v.* Hereford Magistrates Court Ex p.
Rowlands
R. *v.* Hart (Alan Leonard) (1986) 8 Cr. App. R. (S.) 337, CA (Crim Div) . . . .   *Digested,* 88/**924**:
         Cited, 90/1260, 92/1400: *Considered,* 99/1356: *Referred to,* 89/916

R. *v.* Hart (Michael John); R. *v.* McLean (Norman); (Unreported, April 23, 1998), CA
(Crim Div) [*Ex rel.* Rawdon Crozier, Barrister, 2 King's Bench Chambers,
Temple] . . . .   *Digested,* 98/**1056**
R. *v.* Hart (Paul Douglas) [1998] Crim. L.R. 417, CA (Crim Div)
R. *v.* Hart (Simon); R. *v.* Bullen (Ian John) [1999] 2 Cr. App. R. (S.) 233, CA (Crim
Div) . . . .   *Digested,* 99/**1083**
R. *v.* Hart (Stanley) see R. *v.* Jackson (Dennis James)
R. *v.* Harter (Anthony Roger) [1998] Crim. L.R. 336; [1998] E.H.L.R. Dig. 280, CA
(Crim Div)
R. *v.* Hartington Middle Quarter (Inhabitants) (1855) 4 El. & Bl. 780 . . . .   *Applied,* 83/3098:
         Considered, 99/5146: *Distinguished,* 47-51/3681

R. *v.* Hartwell (Nigel) see Attorney General's Reference (No.21 of 2000), Re
R. *v.* Harvey (Calvin David) see Attorney General's Reference (No.47 of 2000), Re
R. *v.* Harvey (Edward Charles) (1984) 6 Cr. App. R. (S.) 184; [1984] Crim. L.R. 572,
CA (Crim Div) . . . .   *Digested,* 85/**767**:
         Considered, 99/1084
R. *v.* Harvey (Ian) (No.1) [1999] Crim. L.R. 70, CA (Crim Div) . . . .   *Applied,* 01/1012
R. *v.* Harvey (Ian) (No.2) [1999] 1 All E.R. 710; [1999] 1 Cr. App. R. (S.) 354; (1998)
95(36) L.S.G. 32; *Times,* October 14, 1998, CA (Crim Div) . . . .   *Digested,* 98/**1154**
R. *v.* Harvey (Michael) see Attorney General's Reference (No.38 of 1995), Re
R. *v.* Harvey (Stephen Adrian) [1997] 2 Cr. App. R. (S.) 306, CA . . . .   *Digested,* 98/**1189**
R. *v.* Harvey (Vernon) see Attorney General's Reference (Nos.72 and 73 of 1995), Re
R. *v.* Harvey (Winston George) [2000] 1 Cr. App. R. (S.) 368; [1999] Crim. L.R. 849,
CA (Crim Div) . . . .   *Digested,* 00/**1228**
R. *v.* Harwood (Gerard) (1985) 7 Cr. App. R. (S.) 362; [1986] Crim. L.R. 264, CA
(Crim Div) . . . .   *Digested,* 87/**1002**:
         Considered, 96/2010, 99/1230, 99/1262

R. *v.* Hasan (Hasan Saheb Abdul) see R. *v.* Abdul-Hussain (Mustafa Shakir)
R. *v.* Hasguler (Gursel) [2001] 1 Cr. App. R. (S.) 36, CA (Crim Div) . . . .   *Digested,* 01/**1208**
R. *v.* Haslam (Simon Bernard) see R. *v.* Reddy (Gary Peter)

R. *v.* Hassall (Andrew Geoffrey) [1999] 2 Cr. App. R. (S.) 277; [1999] Crim. L.R. 676,
    CA (Crim Div) . . . . *Digested,* 99/**1079**
R. *v.* Hassall (Richard David) [2000] 1 Cr. App. R. (S.) 67, CA (Crim Div) . . . . *Digested,* 00/**1184**
R. *v.* Hassan (Ozdai); R. *v.* Schuller (Albert) (1989) 11 Cr. App. R. (S.) 8; [1989] R.T.R.
    129, CA (Crim Div) . . . . *Digested,* 89/**927**:
                  Considered, 91/1005, 97/1403, 98/1110: *Referred to,* 96/1691
R. *v.* Hastie (Philip) see R. *v.* Spear (John)
R. *v.* Hastings and Rother Magistrates Court Ex p. Anscombe (1998) 162 J.P. 340;
    [1998] Crim. L.R. 812; (1998) 162 J.P.N. 387, QBD . . . . *Digested,* 98/**1149**
R. *v.* Hastings Justices Ex p. McSpirit (1998) 162 J.P. 44; (1997) 161 J.P.N. 1118;
    Times, June 23, 1994, QBD . . . . *Digested,* 94/**2898**
R. *v.* Havering LBC see R. *v.* Clearbrook Group Plc
R. *v.* Havering LBC Ex p. K [1998] 1 F.C.R. 641; [1998] E.L.R. 402; *Times,* November
    18, 1997, QBD . . . . *Digested,* 97/**2144**
R. (on the application of DPP) *v.* Havering Magistrates Court; *sub nom* R. *v.* Havering
    Magistrates Court Ex p. DPP; R. *v.* Wirral Borough Magistrates Court Ex p.
    McKeown; R. (on the application of McKeown) *v.* Wirral Borough Magistrates
    Court [2001] 1 W.L.R. 805; [2001] 3 All E.R. 997; [2001] 2 Cr. App. R. 2;
    (2001) 165 J.P. 391; [2001] H.R.L.R. 23; [2001] Crim. L.R. 902; (2001) 165
    J.P.N. 665; *Times,* February 7, 2001; *Independent,* February 12, 2001 (C.S), QBD
    (Admin Ct) . . . . *Digested,* 01/**1103**:
                                                       Cited, 01/1128
R. *v.* Havering Magistrates Court Ex p. DPP see R. (on the application of DPP) *v.*
    Havering Magistrates Court
R. *v.* Hawkins (Christopher Joseph) see R. *v.* Pain (Roy)
R. *v.* Hawkins (Mark) (Unreported, January 15, 1999), CA (Crim Div) . . . . *Considered,* 00/1151
R. *v.* Hawkins (Paul Nigel) [1997] 1 Cr. App. R. 234; [1997] Crim. L.R. 134; (1996)
    93(36) L.S.G. 35; (1996) 140 S.J.L.B. 214; *Times,* August 6, 1996, CA (Crim
    Div) . . . . *Digested,* 96/**1548**:
                           Considered, 01/1113: *Followed,* 97/1260
R. *v.* Hayden (Joseph Anthony) [1975] 1 W.L.R. 852; [1975] 2 All E.R. 558; (1974)
    60 Cr. App. R. 304; [1975] Crim. L.R. 350; 119 S.J. 390, CA (Crim Div) . . . . *Digested,* 75/**723**:
                 Applied, 75/1803: *Cited,* 92/1209: *Considered,* 99/985
R. *v.* Hayes (Andrew Michael) see R. *v.* Liddle (Mark) (Appeal against Sentence)
R. *v.* Hayes (Darren) see Attorney General's Reference (No.29 of 1997), Re
R. *v.* Hayes (George Markie) (1992) 13 Cr. App. R. (S.) 626, CA (Crim Div) . . . . *Digested,* 93/**1027**:
                                    Considered, 98/1252, 00/1141
R. *v.* Hayles (George) see Attorney General's Reference (No.3 of 2000) (Unduly
    Lenient Sentence), Re
R. *v.* Hayward (John Victor) (Absence of Defendant at Trial) see R. *v.* Jones (Anthony
    William) (Absence of Defendant at Trial)
R. *v.* Hayward (John Victor) (Post Judgment Discussion) see R. *v.* Jones (Anthony
    William) (Post Judgment Discussion)
R. *v.* Hayward (John Victor) [1999] Crim. L.R. 71; (1998) 95(25) L.S.G. 33; (1998)
    142 S.J.L.B. 187; *Times,* July 13, 1998; *Independent,* June 10, 1998, CA (Crim
    Div) . . . . *Digested,* 98/**4653**
R. *v.* Haywards Heath Justices Ex p. White (2000) 164 J.P. 629; (2000) 164 J.P.N.
    685; (2000) 164 J.P.N. 743, QBD . . . . *Digested,* 00/**1108**
R. *v.* Haywood (Alan John) (1992) 13 Cr. App. R. (S.) 175, CA (Crim Div) . . . . *Digested,* 93/**1266**:
                                       Considered, 00/1402
R. *v.* Haywood (Andrew Philip) [1998] 1 Cr. App. R. (S.) 358, CA (Crim Div) . . . . *Digested,* 98/**1239**
R. *v.* Haywood (Craig Callan) [2000] 2 Cr. App. R. (S.) 418; [2000] Crim. L.R. 490,
    CA (Crim Div) . . . . *Digested,* 01/**1415**
R. *v.* Haywood (James) see Attorney General's Reference (No.44 of 1998), Re
R. *v.* Haywood (John Victor) (Absence of Defendant at Trial) see R. *v.* Jones (Anthony
    William) (Absence of Defendant at Trial)
R. *v.* Haywood (John Victor) (Post Judgment discussion) see R. *v.* Jones (Anthony
    William) (Post Judgment Discussion)
R. *v.* Hazeltine (Clifford) [1967] 2 Q.B. 857; [1967] 3 W.L.R. 209; [1967] 2 All E.R.
    671; (1967) 51 Cr. App. R. 351; 131 J.P. 401; 111 S.J. 351, CA (Crim Div) . . . . . . *Digested,* 67/**855**:
                                Applied, 80/550, 86/656, 00/1109
R. *v.* Head Teacher and Governing Body of Crug Glas School Ex p. W (A Minor)
    [1999] E.L.R. 484, QBD . . . . *Digested,* 00/**1959**
R. *v.* Head Teacher of Crug Glas School Ex p. D (A Child); *sub nom* R. *v.* Crug Glas
    School Governors Ex p. D (A Child); R. *v.* Swansea City Council Ex p. D (A
    Child) [2000] E.L.R. 69, QBD . . . . *Digested,* 00/**1963**
R. *v.* Head Teacher of Fairfield Primary School Ex p. W [1998] C.O.D. 106, QBD
R. *v.* Healy (John) [1998] 1 Cr. App. R. (S.) 107, CA (Crim Div) . . . . *Digested,* 97/**1719**:
                                   Considered, 99/**1367**:
R. *v.* Hearne (Simon John) [1999] 1 Cr. App. R. (S.) 333, CA (Crim Div) . . . . *Digested,* 99/**1337**:
                                   Considered, 00/**1434**
R. *v.* Heath (Patrick Nicholas) [2000] Crim. L.R. 109; *Times,* October 15, 1999, CA
    (Crim Div) . . . . *Digested,* 99/**931**
R. *v.* Hedges (Phillip Anthony) [1998] 1 Cr. App. R. (S.) 35, CA (Crim Div) . . . . *Digested,* 98/**1222**

R. *v.* Hedworth (Peter John) [1997] 1 Cr. App. R. 421, CA (Crim Div) . . . .   *Digested*, 96/**1611**:
                                              Applied, 98/990

R. *v.* Heighton (Mark Kristian) see Attorney General's Reference (No.88 of 2000), Re

R. *v.* Hemingway (Percy Walker) (1994) 15 Cr. App. R. (S.) 67, CA (Crim Div) . . . .   *Considered*, 98/**1316**,
                                                  98/**1391**

R. *v.* Hemmings (Raymond George); R. *v.* Miller (Michael Alan); R. *v.* Hoines (Patrick
     Michael) [2000] 1 W.L.R. 661; [2000] 2 All E.R. 155; [2000] 1 Cr. App. R. 360;
     [2000] Crim. L.R. 56; (1999) 96(40) L.S.G. 42; *Times*, October 15, 1999, CA
     (Crim Div) . . . .   *Digested*, 99/**1011**

R. *v.* Henderson (Ian) (1990) 12 Cr. App. R. (S.) 589, CA (Crim Div) . . . .   *Digested*, 92/**1315**:
                        Cited, 94/1273: *Considered*, 96/1939, 98/1251

R. *v.* Hendon Justices Ex p. DPP [1994] Q.B. 167; [1993] 2 W.L.R. 862; [1993] 1 All
     E.R. 411; (1993) 96 Cr. App. R. 227; (1993) 157 J.P. 181; [1993] Crim. L.R. 215;
     [1993] C.O.D. 61; (1992) 156 J.P.N. 746; (1992) 142 N.L.J. 1303; *Times*, July
     15, 1992; *Independent*, July 9, 1992; *Guardian*, July 15, 1992, QBD . . . .   *Digested*, 93/**865**:
                                                 Applied, 99/4244

R. *v.* Hendry (George) see Attorney General's Reference (Nos.14, 15 and 16 of 1995),
     Re

R. *v.* Henley (Clifford James) (Appeal against Conviction) [2000] Crim. L.R. 582, CA
     (Crim Div)

R. *v.* Henn (Maurice Donald) (No.1); *sub nom* Henn *v.* DPP (No.1); DPP *v.* Henn (No.1);
     DPP *v.* Darby (No.1); R. *v.* Darby (John Frederick) (No.1) [1979] 2 C.M.L.R.
     495, HL [1978] 1 W.L.R. 1031; [1978] 3 All E.R. 1190; (1979) 69 Cr. App. R. 137;
     [1978] 2 C.M.L.R. 688; [1979] Crim. L.R. 113; 122 S.J. 555, CA (Crim Div);
     affirming [1977] Crim. L.R. 743, Crown Ct (Ipswich) . . . .   *Digested*, 79/**1180**:
                        Applied, 86/1420: *Considered*, 82/560

R. *v.* Hennessey (Kevin Robert) [2000] 2 Cr. App. R. (S.) 480; [2000] Crim. L.R.
     602, CA (Crim Div) . . . .   *Digested*, 01/**1326**

R. *v.* Hennessy (Steven Martin) [1996] 2 Cr. App. R. (S.) 1, CA (Crim Div) . . . .   *Digested*, 96/**1895**:
                                     Considered, 98/1219, 98/1221

R. *v.* Henry (Christopher George) [1999] 2 Cr. App. R. (S.) 412, CA (Crim Div) . . . . . .   *Digested*, 00/**1362**:
                                                 Cited, 01/1427

R. *v.* Henry (Christopher Stephen) [1998] 1 Cr. App. R. (S.) 289, CA (Crim Div) . . . . . .   *Digested*, 98/**1131**:
                                  Considered, 00/1150, 00/1151

R. *v.* Henry (David James) see Attorney General's Reference (No.1 of 1995), Re

R. *v.* Henry (Errol George) (1988) 10 Cr. App. R. (S.) 327; [1989] Crim. L.R. 78, CA
     (Crim Div) . . . .   *Digested*, 89/**1070**:
                         Cited, 94/1297: *Considered*, 98/1343

R. *v.* Henry (Ian) see R. *v.* Rose (Newton Samuel)

R. *v.* Henry (Thomas Lashlie) see Attorney General's Reference (Nos.35 and 36 of
     2000), Re

R. *v.* Henworth (Frank) [2001] EWCA Crim 120; [2001] 2 Cr. App. R. 4; [2001] Crim.
     L.R. 505; *Times*, January 30, 2001, CA (Crim Div) . . . .   *Digested*, 01/**1094**

R. *v.* Herbert (Edward) [2001] 1 Cr. App. R. (S.) 21, CA (Crim Div) . . . .   *Digested*, 01/**1313**

R. *v.* Herbert (Stevie Jefferey) see R. *v.* Wright (Richard Arthur)

R. *v.* Hereford and Worcester CC Ex p. Smith (Tommy) [1994] C.O.D. 129, CA . . . .   *Digested*, 95/**73**:
                                                 Followed, 98/2854

R. *v.* Hereford Magistrates Court Ex p. Ingram see R. *v.* Hereford Magistrates Court Ex
     p. Rowlands

R. *v.* Hereford Magistrates Court Ex p. MacRae (1999) 163 J.P. 433; (1999) 96(4)
     L.S.G. 39; (1999) 143 S.J.L.B. 27; *Times*, December 31, 1998, QBD . . . .   *Digested*, 99/**1157**:
                                     Distinguished, 99/1032

R. *v.* Hereford Magistrates Court Ex p. Rowlands; R. *v.* Hereford Magistrates Court Ex
     p. Ingram; R. *v.* Harrow Youth Court Ex p. Prussia [1998] Q.B. 110; [1997] 2
     W.L.R. 854; [1997] 2 Cr. App. R. 340; (1997) 161 J.P. 258; (1997) 9 Admin.
     L.R. 186; [1997] C.O.D. 236; (1997) 161 J.P. Rep. 308; *Times*, February 17, 1997,
     QBD . . . .   *Digested*, 97/**63**

R. *v.* Herefordshire Youth Court Ex p. J (1998) 95(20) L.S.G. 34; (1998) 142 S.J.L.B.
     150; *Times*, May 4, 1998, QBD . . . .   *Digested*, 98/**1104**

R. *v.* Hersey (Ian) [1998] Crim. L.R. 281, CA (Crim Div)

R. *v.* Hertford College Oxford (1877-78) L.R. 3 Q.B.D. 693, CA; reversing (1876-77)
     L.R. 2 Q.B.D. 590, QBD . . . .   *Applied*, 47-51/**10532**:
                                  Distinguished, 99/5290: *Followed*, 78/3026

R. (on the application of A) *v.* Hertfordshire CC; *sub nom* R. *v.* Hertfordshire CC Ex p. A
     [2001] EWHC Admin 211; [2001] B.L.G.R. 435; [2001] E.L.R. 666; [2001]
     A.C.D. 85, CA; affirming [2001] E.L.R. 239, QBD (Admin Ct) . . . .   *Digested*, 01/**5131**

R. *v.* Hertfordshire CC Ex p. A see R. (on the application of A) *v.* Hertfordshire CC

R. v. Hertfordshire CC Ex p. Green Environmental Industries Ltd; *sub nom* Green Environmental Industries Ltd, Re; Green Environmental Industries Ltd v. Hertfordshire CC [2000] 2 A.C. 412; [2000] 2 W.L.R. 373; [2000] 1 All E.R. 773; [2000] Eu. L.R. 414; [2000] Env. L.R. 426; [2000] E.H.L.R. 199; [2000] H.R.L.R. 359; [2000] U.K.H.R.R. 361; (2000) 2 L.G.L.R. 754; [2000] B.L.G.R. 215; [2000] 1 P.L.R. 108; [2000] C.O.D. 223; [2000] E.G.C.S. 27; (2000) 97(9) L.S.G. 42; (2000) 150 N.L.J. 277; [2000] N.P.C. 15; *Times*, February 22, 2000; *Independent*, February 22, 2000, HL; affirming [1998] Env. L.R. 153; [1998] J.P.L. 481; *Times*, October 9, 1997, CA; affirming [1997] Env. L.R. 114; [1996] N.P.C. 119, QBD . . . . *Digested*, 00/**2300**: *Followed*, 00/1057

R. v. Hetherington (Peter) see Attorney General's Reference (No.4 of 1997), Re
R. v. Hewitson (James Robert); R. v. Bramich (David Jason); R. v. Vincent (Dean) [1999] Crim. L.R. 307, CA (Crim Div)
R. v. Hewitt (Gary) [1999] 1 Cr. App. R. (S.) 256, CA (Crim Div) . . . . *Digested*, 99/**1161**: *Considered*, 01/1312

R. v. Hewitt (Raymond Frederick) (1990) 12 Cr. App. R. (S.) 466; (1991) 155 J.P. 243; (1991) 155 J.P.N. 9; *Times*, October 23, 1990, CA (Crim Div) . . . . *Digested*, 92/**1201**: *Considered*, 97/1466, 00/1424

R. v. Hewitt (Shaun Anthony) see Attorney General's Reference (No.15 of 1998), Re
R. v. Hibbard (Terence) see Attorney General's Reference (Nos.64 and 65 of 1997), Re
R. v. Hickman (Philip) [2000] 2 Cr. App. R. (S.) 171, CA (Crim Div) . . . . *Digested*, 00/**1422**
R. v. Hickman & Rose see R. v. A (Wasted Costs Order)
R. v. Hicks (Ian John) [1999] 1 Cr. App. R. (S.) 228, CA (Crim Div). . . . . *Digested*, 99/**1328**
R. v. Hickson (William John) see R. v. Woodruff (John William)
R. v. Hier (Lynda Jean) [1998] 2 Cr. App. R. (S.) 306, CA (Crim Div) . . . . *Digested*, 98/**1411**
R. v. Higgins (John Francis) [1998] 1 Cr. App. R. (S.) 333, CA (Crim Div) . . . . *Digested*, 98/**1217**
R. v. Higgs (Christopher David) see Attorney General's Reference (No.27 of 1999), Re
R. v. Highbury Corner Magistrates Court Ex p. DJ Sonn & Co [1995] 1 W.L.R. 1365; [1995] 4 All E.R. 57; (1995) 159 J.P. 605; (1995) 159 J.P.N. 576; *Times*, May 23, 1995, QBD . . . . *Digested*, 96/**3881**: *Considered*, 98/3706

R. v. Higher Education Funding Council Ex p. Institute of Dental Surgery [1994] 1 W.L.R. 242; [1994] 1 All E.R. 651; [1994] C.O.D. 147; *Independent*, September 28, 1993, QBD . . . . *Digested*, 95/**162**: *Considered*, 94/49, 95/2534, 96/3207, 96/4799, 97/4107: *Followed*, 98/2008

R. v. Highfield (Kim) see Attorney General's Reference (No.95 of 1998), Re
R. v. Hill (Catherine Louise) see Attorney General's Reference (No.50 of 2001), Re
R. v. Hill (Graham) [1997] 2 Cr. App. R. (S.) 243; [1997] Crim. L.R. 459, CA (Crim Div) . . . . *Digested*, 97/**1458**: *Considered*, 00/1429

R. v. Hill (Jason Lee) [2000] 1 Cr. App. R. (S.) 8, CA (Crim Div) . . . . *Digested*, 00/**1271**
R. v. Hill (Norman David) [1999] 2 Cr. App. R. (S.) 388; (1999) 96(16) L.S.G. 35; (1999) 143 S.J.L.B. 111; *Times*, April 13, 1999, CA (Crim Div) . . . . *Digested*, 99/**1160**: *Considered*, 00/1254

R. v. Hill (Stephen) (1988) 10 Cr. App. R. (S.) 150, CA (Crim Div) . . . . *Digested*, 90/**1298**: *Cited*, 91/1092, 91/1100: *Considered*, 99/1133

R. v. Hill (Valerie Mary); R. v. Hall (Jennifer) (1989) 89 Cr. App. R. 74; [1989] Crim. L.R. 136; *Times*, October 6, 1988, CA (Crim Div) . . . . *Digested*, 90/**1086**: *Considered*, 95/1243: *Distinguished*, 98/926

R. v. Hillingdon BC Ex p. Streeting (No.2) [1980] 1 W.L.R. 1425; [1980] 3 All E.R. 413; 79 L.G.R. 167; (1980) 10 Fam. Law 249; 124 S.J. 514, CA; affirming 124 S.J. 274, QBD . . . . *Digested*, 80/**1359**: *Applied*, 98/3007: *Followed*, 98/3008

R. (on the application of Ward) v. Hillingdon LBC; *sub nom* Ward v. Hillingdon LBC; R. v. Hillingdon LBC Ex p. Ward [2001] EWHC Admin 91; [2001] H.R.L.R. 40; [2001] B.L.G.R. 457; *Independent*, March 26, 2001 (C.S), QBD (Admin Ct)
R. v. Hillingdon LBC Ex p. London Regional Transport [1999] B.L.G.R. 543; [1999] N.P.C. 112; *Times*, August 31, 1999, CA; reversing *Times*, January 20, 1999, QBD . . . . *Digested*, 99/**4883**

R. v. Hillingdon LBC Ex p. McDonagh [1999] E.H.L.R. 169; (1999) 31 H.L.R. 531; (1999) 1 L.G.L.R. 232; [1999] B.L.G.R. 459; [1999] 1 P.L.R. 22; [1999] C.O.D. 93; (1998) 95(46) L.S.G. 35; *Times*, November 9, 1998, QBD . . . . *Digested*, 98/**3832**
R. v. Hillingdon LBC Ex p. Royco Homes Ltd [1974] Q.B. 720; [1974] 2 W.L.R. 805; [1974] 2 All E.R. 643; 72 L.G.R. 516; 28 P. & C.R. 251; 118 S.J. 389, QBD . . . . . *Digested*, 74/**3763**: *Considered*, 83/3738, 85/11, 86/1203, 86/2542, 86/2542.3, 87/3697, 99/2215

R. v. Hillingdon LBC Ex p. Ward see R. (on the application of Ward) v. Hillingdon LBC
R. v. Hills (Gary William) see Attorney General's Reference (No.36 of 1992), Re
R. v. Hills (Ian Leslie) [1999] 2 Cr. App. R. (S.) 157, CA (Crim Div) . . . . *Digested*, 99/**1264**
R. v. Hinchliffe (Allen Patrick) see Attorney General's Reference (No.49 of 1999), Re
R. v. Hinds (Michael Joshua) see Attorney General's Reference (No.2 of 2000) (Unduly Lenient Sentence), Re

R. v. Hines (Malcolm) see Attorney General's Reference (No.84 of 1998), Re
R. v. Hinks (Karen Maria) [2001] 2 A.C. 241; [2000] 3 W.L.R. 1590; [2000] 4 All E.R.
   833; [2001] 1 Cr. App. R. 18; (2001) 165 J.P. 21; [2001] Crim. L.R. 162; (2000)
   97(43) L.S.G. 37; (2000) 144 S.J.L.B. 265; *Times*, October 27, 2000;
   Independent, November 2, 2000, HL; affirming [2000] 1 Cr. App. R. 1; [1998]
   Crim. L.R. 904, CA (Crim Div) .... *Digested*, 00/**1012**
R. v. Hinton (Roy) (1995) 16 Cr. App. R. (S.) 523, CA (Crim Div) .... *Considered*, 97/1449:
                                                               Followed, 98/1262
R. v. Hird (Justin) [1998] 2 Cr. App. R. (S.) 241; [1998] Crim. L.R. 296, CA (Crim
   Div) .... *Digested*, 98/**1278**
R. v. Hirst (Lewis) [2001] 1 Cr. App. R. (S.) 44, CA (Crim Div) .... *Digested*, 01/**1442**
R. v. Hiscock (John Andrew) (1992) 13 Cr. App. R. (S.) 24, CA (Crim Div) .... *Digested*, 92/**1305**:
                                 Cited, 94/1287: *Considered*, 96/1939, 00/1300, 00/1328
R. v. Hiscock (Nicholas Stephen) (1994) 15 Cr. App. R. (S.) 287, CA (Crim Div) ...... *Considered*, 00/1338
R. (on the application of Bentley) v. HM Coroner for Avon; *sub nom* R. (on the
   application of Bentley) v. HM Coroner for the District of Avon [2001] EWHC
   Admin 170; *Times*, March 23, 2001, QBD (Admin Ct) .... *Digested*, 01/**25**
R. v. HM Coroner for Avon Ex p. Smith (1998) 162 J.P. 403; [1998] C.O.D. 251, QBD .. *Digested*, 98/**40**
R. v. HM Coroner for Birmingham and Solihull Ex p. Benton (1998) 162 J.P. 807;
   [1997] 8 Med. L.R. 362, QBD .... *Digested*, 98/**43**
R. v. HM Coroner for Coventry Ex p. Chief Constable of Staffordshire (2000) 164 J.P.
   665; [2001] A.C.D. 6, QBD .... *Digested*, 01/**4782**:
                                                                    Applied, 01/26
R. v. HM Coroner for Derby and South Derbyshire Ex p. Hart (2000) 164 J.P. 429;
   [2000] C.O.D. 216; (2000) 164 J.P.N. 685, QBD .... *Digested*, 00/**50**
R. v. HM Coroner for Devon (Plymouth District) Ex p. Hay (1998) 162 J.P. 96, CA .... *Digested*, 98/**39**
R. (on the application of Dawson) v. HM Coroner for East Riding and Kingston upon Hull
   [2001] EWHC Admin 352; [2001] A.C.D. 68, QBD (Admin Ct)
R. v. HM Coroner for Greater Manchester Ex p. Tal [1985] Q.B. 67; [1984] 3 W.L.R.
   643; [1984] 3 All E.R. 240; [1984] Crim. L.R. 557; (1984) 128 S.J. 500, QBD .. *Digested*, 84/**447**:
            Considered, 86/678, 89/525, 90/50, 91/52, 91/2311, 92/2775, 93/32, 99/36:
                                        Disapproved, 98/1085: *Followed*, 95/4562
R. v. HM Coroner for Hammersmith Ex p. Peach; *sub nom* R. v. Hammersmith Coroner
   Ex p. Peach; Peach v. Burton; Peach (Clement Blair), Re [1980] Q.B. 211; [1980]
   2 W.L.R. 496; [1980] 2 All E.R. 7; 124 S.J. 17, CA; reversing [1980] Crim. L.R.
   168; 123 S.J. 861, QBD .... *Digested*, 80/**385**:
                                  Considered, 86/448, 94/637, 01/25
R. v. HM Coroner for Inner London North District Ex p. Thomas; *sub nom* R. v. HM
   Coroner for Poplar Ex p. Thomas [1993] Q.B. 610; [1993] 2 W.L.R. 547; [1993]
   2 All E.R. 381; (1993) 157 J.P. 506; [1993] C.O.D. 178; (1993) 157 J.P.N. 349;
   Times, December 23, 1992; *Independent*, January 20, 1992, CA; reversing
   [1992] 3 W.L.R. 485; [1992] C.O.D. 344; (1992) 156 J.P.N. 698; (1992) 136
   S.J.L.B. 140; *Times*, April 22, 1992; *Independent*, April 14, 1992; *Guardian*, April
   22, 1992, QBD .... *Digested*, 93/**593**:
        Applied, 00/48: *Considered*, 94/633, 95/874, 01/27: *Distinguished*, 98/40
R. v. HM Coroner for Inner London North Ex p. Touche see R. (on the application of
   Touche) v. HM Coroner for Inner North London District
R. v. HM Coroner for Inner London South District Ex p. Douglas-Williams [1999] 1 All
   E.R. 344; (1998) 162 J.P. 751; [1998] C.O.D. 358; *Times*, September 4, 1998,
   CA .... *Digested*, 98/**42**:
                                               Applied, 01/25
R. v. HM Coroner for Inner London South District Ex p. Kendall see R. v. HM Coroner
   for Southwark Ex p. Kendall
R. v. HM Coroner for Inner London West District Ex p. Dallaglio; R. v. HM Coroner for
   Inner London West District Ex p. Lockwood-Croft [1994] 4 All E.R. 139; (1995)
   159 J.P. 133; (1995) 7 Admin. L.R. 256; [1995] C.O.D. 20; *Times*, June 16,
   1994; *Independent*, June 17, 1994, CA; reversing [1994] C.O.D. 9, QBD .... *Digested*, 95/**872**:
             Applied, 99/4171: *Considered*, 00/2109: *Followed*, 97/1341
R. v. HM Coroner for Inner London West District Ex p. Lockwood-Croft see R. v. HM
   Coroner for Inner London West District Ex p. Dallaglio
R. (on the application of Touche) v. HM Coroner for Inner North London District; *sub
   nom* R. v. HM Coroners Court of St Pancras Ex p. Touche; R. v. HM Coroner for
   Inner London North Ex p. Touche; R. v. HM Coroner for Inner North London
   District Ex p. Touche; R. (on the application of Touche) v. Inner London North
   Coroner [2001] EWCA Civ 383; [2001] Q.B. 1206; [2001] 3 W.L.R. 148; [2001]
   2 All E.R. 752; (2001) 165 J.P. 526; [2001] Lloyd's Rep. 60
   B.M.L.R. 170; (2001) 165 J.P.N. 648; (2001) 98(20) L.S.G. 40; (2001) 145
   S.J.L.B. 109; *Times*, March 30, 2001; *Daily Telegraph*, March 27, 2001, CA;
   affirming (2000) 164 J.P. 509; [2001] Lloyd's Rep. Med. 67; [2000] C.O.D.
   439, QBD .... *Digested*, 01/**27**
R. v. HM Coroner for Inner North London District Ex p. Touche see R. (on the
   application of Touche) v. HM Coroner for Inner North London District

R. v. HM Coroner for Lincoln Ex p. Hay; *sub nom* R. v. HM Coroner for Lincolnshire Ex p. Hay (1999) 163 J.P. 666; [2000] Lloyd's Rep. Med. 264; [1999] C.O.D. 192; *Times,* March 30, 1999, QBD . . . . *Digested,* 99/**36**:
Disapproved, 01/27

R. v. HM Coroner for Lincolnshire Ex p. Hay see R. v. HM Coroner for Lincoln Ex p. Hay

R. v. HM Coroner for Newcastle upon Tyne Ex p. A (1998) 162 J.P. 387; [1998] C.O.D.163; *Times,* January 19,1998, QBD. . . . . *Digested,* 98/**45**

R. v. HM Coroner for North Humberside and Scunthorpe Ex p. Jamieson [1995] Q.B. 1; [1994] 3 W.L.R. 82; [1994] 3 All E.R. 972; (1994) 158 J.P. 1011; [1994] 5 Med. L.R. 217; [1994] C.O.D. 455; *Times,* April 28, 1994; *Independent,* April 27, 1994, CA; affirming [1994] C.O.D. 173; *Times,* July 23, 1993; *Independent,* October 18, 1993 (C.S.); *Independent,* October 4, 1993 (C.S.); *Guardian,* July 12, 1993, QBD . . . . *Digested,* 94/**631**:
Applied, 00/50, 01/26: *Cited,* 00/49: *Considered,* 94/629, 94/630, 95/872, 95/873, 96/42, 96/44, 96/49, 97/39, 01/27

R. v. HM Coroner for Northumberland Ex p. Jacobs (2000) 53 B.M.L.R. 21, CA . . . . . . *Digested,* 00/**102**

R. v. HM Coroner for Poplar Ex p. Thomas see R. v. HM Coroner for Inner London North District Ex p. Thomas

R. v. HM Coroner for Southwark Ex p. Fields (1998) 162 J.P. 411, QBD . . . . *Digested,* 98/**41**

R. v. HM Coroner for Southwark Ex p. Kendall; *sub nom* R. v. HM Coroner for Inner London South District Ex p. Kendall [1988] 1 W.L.R. 1186; [1989] 1 All E.R. 72; (1989) 153 J.P. 117; (1988) 152 J.P.N. 754; (1988) 132 S.J. 1460; *Times,* June 8, 1988; *Independent,* June 7, 1988 (C.S.); *Guardian,* June 2, 1988; *Daily Telegraph,* June 10, 1988, QBD . . . . *Digested,* 89/**523**:
Applied, 01/4484: *Considered,* 94/630, 94/632, 95/873

R. v. HM Coroner for Swansea and Gower Ex p. Chief Constable of Wales see R. v. HM Coroner for Swansea and Gower Ex p. Tristram

R. v. HM Coroner for Swansea and Gower Ex p. Tristram; *sub nom* R. v. HM Coroner for Swansea and Gower Ex p. Chief Constable of Wales (2000) 164 J.P. 191, QBD . . . . *Digested,* 00/**49**

R. (on the application of Bentley) v. HM Coroner for the District of Avon see R. (on the application of Bentley) v. HM Coroner for Avon

R. v. HM Coroners Court of St Pancras Ex p. Touche see R. (on the application of Touche) v. HM Coroner for Inner North London District

R. v. HM Customs and Excise Ex p. Popely see R. v. Customs and Excise Commissioners Ex p. Popely

R. v. HM Queen in Council Ex p. Vijayatunga; *sub nom* R. v. University of London Ex p. Vijayatunga; R. v. Committee of the Judicial Committee of the Privy Council acting for the Visitor of the University of London Ex p. Vijayatunga [1990] 2 Q.B. 444; [1989] 3 W.L.R. 13; [1989] 2 All E.R. 843; [1989] C.O.D. 440; (1989) 133 S.J. 818; *Times,* March 30, 1989; *Independent,* March 16, 1989; *Guardian,* April 4, 1989; *Daily Telegraph,* April 13, 1989, CA; affirming [1988] Q.B. 322; [1988] 2 W.L.R.106; [1987] 3 All E.R. 204; (1988) 132 S.J. 52, QBD . . . . *Digested,* 89/**1383**:
Applied, 99/1934: *Considered,* 97/3365

R. (on the application of University of Cambridge) v. HM Treasury (C380/98); *sub nom* R. v. HM Treasury Ex p. University of Cambridge (C380/98) [2000] 1 W.L.R. 2514; [2000] All E.R. (EC) 920; [2000] E.C.R. I-8035; [2000] 3 C.M.L.R. 1359; [2001] C.E.C. 30; (2001) 3 L.G.L.R. 13; *Times,* October 17, 2000, ECJ (5th Chamber) . . . . *Digested,* 00/**2002**

R. v. HM Treasury Ex p. British Telecommunications Plc [1994] 1 C.M.L.R. 621; [1995] C.O.D. 56; *Times,* December 2, 1993, CA . . . . *Digested,* 93/**3262**:
Considered, 97/4627, 99/5082

R. v. HM Treasury Ex p. Daily Mail (C81/87); R. v. Customs and Excise Commissioners Ex p. Daily Mail [1989] Q.B. 446; [1989] 2 W.L.R. 908; [1989] 1 All E.R. 328; [1988] S.T.C. 787; [1988] E.C.R. 5483; [1989] B.C.L.C. 206; [1988] 3 C.M.L.R. 713; (1989) 133 S.J. 693; *Times,* September 29, 1988, ECJ . . . . *Digested,* 89/**1556**:
Followed, 01/2499

R. v. HM Treasury Ex p. Service Authority for the National Crime Squad; *sub nom* R. v. Customs and Excise Commissioners Ex p. Service Authority National Crime Squad [2000] S.T.C. 638; [2000] B.T.C. 5255; [2000] B.V.C. 290; [2000] S.T.I. 918; *Times,* July 18, 2000, QBD . . . . *Digested,* 00/**5325**

R. v. HM Treasury Ex p. Shepherd Neame Ltd see R. v. Customs and Excise Commissioners Ex p. Shepherd Neame Ltd

R. v. HM Treasury Ex p. Smedley; *sub nom* R. v. Economic Secretary to the Treasury Ex p. Smedley [1985] Q.B. 657; [1985] 2 W.L.R. 576; [1985] 1 All E.R. 589; [1985] 1 C.M.L.R. 665; [1985] F.L.R. 180; (1985) 82 L.S.G. 761; (1985) 129 S.J. 48; *Times,* December 8, 1984, CA . . . . *Digested,* 85/**2502**:
Considered, 99/94

R. v. HM Treasury Ex p. University of Cambridge (C380/98) see R. (on the application of University of Cambridge) v. HM Treasury (C380/98)

R. v. HM Young Offenders Institution Glen Parva Ex p. G see R. v. Governor of Glen Parva Young Offender Institution Ex p. G (A Minor)

R. (on the application of Macneil) *v.* HMP Discretionary Lifer Panel see R. (on the application of Macneil) *v.* HMP Lifer Panel

R. (on the application of Macneil) *v.* HMP Lifer Panel; *sub nom* R. *v.* HMP Lifer Panel Ex p. Macneil; R. (on the application of Macneil) *v.* HMP Discretionary Lifer Panel; R. *v.* Parole Board Ex p. MacNeil [2001] EWCA Civ 448; (2001) 98(20) L.S.G. 43; *Times*, April 18, 2001, CA; affirming CO/1902/2000, QBD (Admin Ct) . . . . .   *Digested*, 01/**4577**

R. *v.* HMP Lifer Panel Ex p. Macneil see R. (on the application of Macneil) *v.* HMP Lifer Panel

R. *v.* Hobbs (Daniel) see Attorney General's Reference (Nos.44 and 46 of 1995), Re

R. *v.* Hobday (David Thomas) see Attorney General's Reference (No.37 of 1996), Re

R. *v.* Hobson (Kathleen) [1998] 1 Cr. App. R. 31; (1998) 43 B.M.L.R. 181; [1997] Crim. L.R. 759; *Times*, June 25, 1997; *Independent*, June 6, 1997, CA (Crim Div) . . . . .   *Digested*, 97/**1090**

R. *v.* Hobstaff (Anthony) (1993) 14 Cr. App. R. (S.) 605; [1993] Crim. L.R. 318; *Times*, February 8, 1993, CA (Crim Div) . . . .   *Digested*, 94/**1275**: *Considered*, 01/1208

R. *v.* Hochard (David Gaston) see Attorney General's Reference (No.75 of 2001), Re

R. *v.* Hockings (David Andrew) see R. *v.* Saunders (Kevin John)

R. *v.* Hodder (Unreported, November 18, 1997), CA (Crim Div) . . . .   *Considered*, 00/1197

R. *v.* Hodgetts (Valuation Officer) Ex p. Nationwide Building Society see R. *v.* Huelin (Valuation Officer) Ex p. Murphy Ltd

R. *v.* Hodgkinson (Walter Sidney) [1997] 1 Cr. App. R. (S.) 146, CA (Crim Div) . . . .   *Digested*, 97/**1616**: *Distinguished*, 99/5220

R. *v.* Hodgson (Rowland Jack) (1968) 52 Cr. App. R. 113; [1968] Crim. L.R. 46, CA (Crim Div) . . . .   *Digested*, 68/**848**: *Applied*, 87/1035, 88/977, 96/1987, 96/2049, 97/1645, 00/1346: *Approved*, 90/1350, 99/1250: *Considered*, 84/777, 85/813, 86/838, 88/950, 90/1351, 91/1161, 92/1329, 92/1486, 93/1211, 96/1912, 96/1985, 96/1986, 96/1989, 98/1233, 98/1346, 99/1251: *Followed*, 96/2050

R. *v.* Hodzic see R. *v.* Hadzic (Kemil)

R. *v.* Hoffman (Neville Anthony) see Attorney General's Reference (No.2 of 1997), Re

R. *v.* Hogg (Thomas Martin) [1994] N.I. 258, CA (Crim Div) (NI) . . . .   *Digested*, 00/**5487**

R. *v.* Hoines (Patrick Michael) see R. *v.* Hemmings (Raymond George)

R. *v.* Holah (Steven Richard) (1989) 11 Cr. App. R. (S.) 282; [1989] Crim. L.R. 751, CA (Crim Div) . . . .   *Digested*, 90/**1244**: *Considered*, 98/1153

R. *v.* Holderness BC Ex p. James Robert Developments Ltd (1993) 5 Admin. L.R. 470; (1993) 66 P. & C.R. 46; [1993] 1 P.L.R. 108; [1993] J.P.L. 659; (1993) 157 L.G. Rev. 643; [1992] N.P.C. 156; *Times*, December 22, 1992; *Independent*, December 21, 1992 (C.S.), CA; affirming (1992) 64 P. & C.R. 100; [1991] E.G.C.S. 128; [1991] N.P.C. 128, QBD . . . .   *Digested*, 93/**3933**: *Cited*, 95/3219: *Considered*, 94/2934: *Followed*, 01/4740

R. *v.* Holland (James Edward) [1998] 2 Cr. App. R. (S.) 265, CA (Crim Div) . . . .   *Digested*, 98/**1384**

R. *v.* Hollis (Barry Spencer) [1998] 2 Cr. App. R. (S.) 359, CA (Crim Div) . . . .   *Digested*, 99/**1091**

R. *v.* Holloway (Christopher George) (1982) 4 Cr. App. R. (S.) 128; [1982] Crim. L.R. 467; 126 S.J. 359; *Times*, March 17, 1982, CA (Crim Div) . . . .   *Digested*, 82/**700**: *Applied*, 85/821, 99/1271: *Cited*, 93/1152, 93/1235: *Considered*, 85/733, 85/734, 86/854, 86/855, 92/1359, 98/1314, 99/1272: *Distinguished*, 97/1638: *Followed*, 83/838: *Referred to*, 85/820, 85/823

R. *v.* Holloway (Stephen John) see R. *v.* Adomako (John Asare)

R. *v.* Holmes (Andrew); R. *v.* Holmes (Geoffrey) [1999] 2 Cr. App. R. (S.) 100, CA (Crim Div) . . . .   *Digested*, 99/**1117**

R. *v.* Holmes (Anthony) [1999] 2 Cr. App. R. (S.) 383, CA (Crim Div) . . . .   *Digested*, 00/**1251**

R. *v.* Holmes (Geoffrey) see R. *v.* Holmes (Andrew)

R. *v.* Holroyd (John Malcolm) see R. *v.* Chauhan (Rashmikant Bhikhubhai)

R. *v.* Home Office Ex p. A (A Juvenile) see R. *v.* Secretary of State for the Home Department Ex p. A (A Juvenile)

R. (on the application of McCollum) *v.* Home Secretary see R. (on the application of McCollum) *v.* Secretary of State for the Home Department

R. *v.* Honeyghon (Jason Norman) [1999] Crim. L.R. 221, CA (Crim Div)

R. *v.* Hong (Chong Kiong); R. *v.* Thien (Vui Kiun); R. *v.* Thien (Vui Tahung) [2001] EWCA Crim 785; [2001] 2 Cr. App. R. (S.) 116, CA (Crim Div) . . . .   *Digested*, 01/**1296**

R. *v.* Honz (Tomas) see R. *v.* Kaynak (Hussein)

R. *v.* Hooley (Gareth Mark); R. *v.* Ramsden (Stephen); R. *v.* Fletcher (James Lee) [2001] 2 Cr. App. R. (S.) 20, CA (Crim Div) . . . .   *Digested*, 01/**1480**

R. *v.* Hooper (Jonathan Andrew) see Attorney General's Reference (No.61 of 2000), Re

R. *v.* Hope (Marc John) see Attorney General's Reference (Nos.65 and 66 of 2001), Re

R. *v.* Hopkins (Kevin Alan) see R. *v.* Innes (Philip Gordon)

R. *v.* Hopkins (Richard Mark) see R. *v.* Kendrick (Kathleen)

R. *v.* Hopkins (Stephen) [1996] 1 Cr. App. R. (S.) 18, CA (Crim Div) . . . .   *Considered*, 00/1376

R. *v.* Hopkinson (Frank) [2001] EWCA Crim 84; [2001] 2 Cr. App. R. (S.) 54, CA (Crim Div) . . . .   *Digested*, 01/**1444**

R. *v.* Horley [1999] Crim. L.R. 488, CA (Crim Div)

R. *v.* Horn (Michael) [1997] 2 Cr. App. R. (S.) 172, CA (Crim Div) . . . .   *Digested,* 97/**1535**:
                                            Considered, 98/1217, 98/1220, 99/1163

R. *v.* Horner (David) see R. *v.* Ansari (Mohammed)
R. *v.* Horrex (Robert) [1999] Crim. L.R. 500, CA (Crim Div)
R. *v.* Horseferry Road Magistrates Court Ex p. DPP [1999] C.O.D. 441, QBD
R. *v.* Horseferry Road Magistrates Court Ex p. Hillier (1998) 162 J.P. 783; (1998) 162
     J.P.N. 983, QBD . . . .   *Digested,* 99/**1007**
R. *v.* Horseferry Road Magistrates Court Ex p. Rezouali see Westminster City Council
     v. Mendoza
R. *v.* Horseferry Road Magistrates Court Ex p. Rugless [2000] 1 Cr. App. R. (S.) 484;
     (2000) 164 J.P. 311; [2000] Crim. L.R. 119; (2001) 165 J.P.N. 85, QBD . . . .   *Digested,* 00/**1030**
R. *v.* Horsford (Harland) see R. *v.* Powell (Mark)
R. *v.* Horsham DC Ex p. Bayley [2001] P.L.C.R. 11; [2001] J.P.L. 224 (Note), QBD . . . . .   *Digested,* 01/**4740**
R. *v.* Horsham DC Ex p. Wenman [1995] 1 W.L.R. 680; [1994] 4 All E.R. 681; (1992)
     24 H.L.R. 669; (1995) 7 Admin. L.R. 73; [1992] C.O.D. 427; (1995) 159 L.G.
     Rev. 365; (1993) 143 N.L.J. 1477; [1993] N.P.C. 129; *Times,* October 21, 1993;
     Independent, October 7, 1993, QBD . . . .   *Digested,* 95/**135**:
                            Applied, 01/591: *Considered,* 95/3252: *Followed,* 98/1087
R. *v.* Horsham Justices Ex p. Reeves (1982) 75 Cr. App. R. 236; [1981] Crim. L.R.
     566, QBD . . . .   *Digested,* 83/**2309**:
                            Applied, 94/939: *Considered,* 85/2126, 99/5215
R. *v.* Horsman (Richard David) [1998] Q.B. 531; [1998] 2 W.L.R. 468; [1997] 3 All
     E.R. 385; [1997] 2 Cr. App. R. 418; (1997) 161 J.P. 757; [1998] Crim. L.R. 128;
     (1997) 161 J.P.N. 794; (1997) 94(30) L.S.G. 27; (1997) 147 N.L.J. 1026; (1997)
     141 S.J.L.B. 137; *Times,* July 3, 1997; *Independent,* June 26, 1997, CA (Crim
     Div) . . . .   *Digested,* 97/**1230**:
                                                           Applied, 01/1113
R. *v.* Horton (Richard David) see Attorney General's Reference (Nos.41 and 42 of
     1995), Re
R. *v.* Hoshan (Adnan) see R. *v.* Abdul-Hussain (Mustafa Shakir)
R. *v.* Hough (Julian) [2001] 1 Cr. App. R. (S.) 75, CA (Crim Div) . . . .   *Digested,* 01/**1438**
R. *v.* Houghton (Terence Paul) see R. *v.* Maisey (David William)
R. (on the application of Cal Brown Ltd (t/a CB Advertising Ltd)) *v.* Hounslow LBC [2001]
     EWHC Admin 864; [2001] 44 E.G.C.S. 149, QBD (Admin Ct)
R. *v.* Hounslow LBC Ex p. Dooley (2000) 80 P. & C.R. 405, QBD . . . .   *Digested,* 00/**4497**
R. *v.* Housing Benefit Review Board for Swale BC Ex p. Marchant see R. *v.* Swale BC
     Ex p. Marchant
R. *v.* Howard (Barrington) [1996] 2 Cr. App. R. (S.) 273, CA (Crim Div) . . . .   *Digested,* 97/**1520**:
                          Applied, 00/1227: *Considered,* 99/1142, 00/1226
R. *v.* Howard (Curtis) [1996] 2 Cr. App. R. (S.) 419; [1996] Crim. L.R. 756; *Times,*
     April 15, 1996, CA (Crim Div) . . . .   *Digested,* 96/**1988**:
                                                Referred to, 00/1189
R. *v.* Howard (Robert Lesarian) [1966] 1 W.L.R. 13; [1965] 3 All E.R. 684; (1966) 50
     Cr. App. R. 56; (1966) 130 J.P. 61; (1965) 109 S.J. 920, CCA . . . .   *Digested,* 65/**916**:
                                                Not followed, 98/971
R. *v.* Howarth (Jeremy John) see Attorney General's Reference (Nos.14, 15 and 16 of
     1995), Re
R. *v.* Howarth (Jeremy John) (Disqualification of Company Directors) see R. *v.* Ward
     (Michael Grainger) (Disqualification of Company Directors)
R. *v.* Howe (Stevey) see R. *v.* Graham (Steven Anthony)
R. *v.* Howell [1987] 5 N.I.J.B. 10 . . . .   *Digested,* 88/**2527**:
                                             Distinguished, 00/5472
R. *v.* Howell (Errol) [1982] Q.B. 416; [1981] 3 W.L.R. 501; [1981] 3 All E.R. 383;
     (1981) 73 Cr. App. R. 31; [1981] Crim. L.R. 697; 125 S.J. 462, CA (Crim Div) . . .   *Digested,* 82/**151**:
                     Applied, 94/989, 95/1239, 01/1007: *Considered,* 86/688:
                               Distinguished, 84/521: *Followed,* 96/1508
R. *v.* Howell (Mark) [1999] 1 Cr. App. R. (S.) 449, CA (Crim Div) . . . .   *Digested,* 99/**1326**
R. *v.* Howell (Patricia Ann) [1998] 1 Cr. App. R. (S.) 229, CA (Crim Div) . . . .   *Digested,* 97/**1618**
R. *v.* Howells (Craig); R. *v.* Ashby (Nicholas Alexander); R. *v.* Glowacki (Dariusz); R. *v.*
     R (Kevin Wayne) (A Juvenile); R. *v.* Jarvis (Martin); R. *v.* M (Stuart James) (A
     Juvenile); R. *v.* Shanoor (Mohammed); R. *v.* H (David Leslie) (A Juvenile)
     [1999] 1 W.L.R. 307; [1999] 1 All E.R. 50; [1999] 1 Cr. App. R. 98; [1999] 1 Cr.
     App. R. (S.) 335; (1998) 162 J.P. 731; [1998] Crim. L.R. 836; (1998) 162
     J.P.N. 761; *Times,* August 21, 1998; *Independent,* October 1, 1998, CA (Crim
     Div) . . . .   *Digested,* 98/**1168**:
                    Applied, 98/1209: *Considered,* 99/1288, 99/1363, 01/1842:
                                                Followed, 99/1271
R. *v.* Howes (Robert Charles) see Attorney General's Reference (No.11 of 1992), Re
R. *v.* Howson (Peter Alan) (1982) 74 Cr. App. R. 172; [1981] Crim. L.R. 720, CA (Crim
     Div) . . . .   *Digested,* 82/**733**:
                                                Considered, 98/1093
R. *v.* Hoyle (Damien James) see Attorney General's Reference (No.35 of 1996), Re
R. *v.* HS (A Juvenile) [2001] EWCA Crim 740; [2001] 2 Cr. App. R. (S.) 110, CA
     (Crim Div) . . . .   *Digested,* 01/**1393**

R. *v.* Huchet (Paul Francis) [1999] 1 Cr. App. R. (S.) 189, CA (Crim Div) . . . .   *Digested,* 99/**1186**
R. *v.* Huddart (Gavin) [1999] E.H.L.R. 281; [1999] Crim. L.R. 568, CA (Crim Div) . . . . .   *Digested,* 99/**921**
R. *v.* Hudson (Alan Harry) [1956] 2 Q.B. 252; [1956] 2 W.L.R. 914; [1956] 1 All E.R.
    814; (1956) 40 Cr. App. R. 55; 120 J.P. 216; 36 T.C. 561; (1956) 35 A.T.C. 63;
    [1956] T.R. 93; 100 S.J. 284, CCA . . . .   *Digested,* 56/**1885**:
        Applied, 86/3512, 87/764: *Considered,* 00/1098: *Followed,* 90/1077
R. *v.* Hudson (Graham Jeffrey) [1998] 1 Cr. App. R. (S.) 124, CA (Crim Div) . . . .   *Digested,* 98/**1219**:
        Considered, 99/1165
R. *v.* Hudson (Linda); R. *v.* Taylor (Elaine) [1971] 2 Q.B. 202; [1971] 2 W.L.R. 1047;
    [1971] 2 All E.R. 244; (1972) 56 Cr. App. R. 1; 115 S.J. 303, CA (Crim Div) . . . . .   *Digested,* 71/**2528**:
        Considered, 92/735, 93/732, 95/1256, 98/944
R. *v.* Huelin (Valuation Officer) Ex p. Murphy Ltd; R. *v.* Hodgetts (Valuation Officer) Ex
    p. Nationwide Building Society [2000] 1 E.G.L.R. 97; [2000] 05 E.G. 141;
    [2001] R.A. 30; [1999] E.G.C.S. 131; *Independent,* December 20, 1999 (C.S.),
    CA; affirming [1999] R.V.R. 153, QBD . . . .   *Digested,* 00/**4606**
R. *v.* Huggan (John Charles) see R. *v.* Breaks (Peter)
R. *v.* Hughes (Christopher Shane) (1988) 10 Cr. App. R. (S.) 169; [1988] Crim. L.R.
    545, CA (Crim Div) . . . .   *Digested,* 89/**1073**:
        Considered, 97/1564, 99/1261
R. *v.* Hughes (Colin David) [2000] 2 Cr. App. R. (S.) 399, CA (Crim Div) . . . .   *Digested,* 01/**1492**
R. *v.* Hughes (Gary) [1999] 2 Cr. App. R. (S.) 329, CA (Crim Div) . . . .   *Digested,* 99/**1134**
R. *v.* Hull University Visitor Ex p. Page see R. *v.* Lord President of the Privy Council Ex
    p. Page
R. *v.* Human Fertilisation and Embryology Authority Ex p. Blood; *sub nom* R. *v.* Human
    Fertilisation and Embryology Authority Ex p. DB [1999] Fam. 151; [1997] 2
    W.L.R. 807; [1997] 2 All E.R. 687; [1997] 2 C.M.L.R. 591; [1997] Eu. L.R. 370;
    [1997] 2 F.L.R. 742; [1997] 2 F.C.R. 501; (1997) 35 B.M.L.R. 1; [1997] C.O.D.
    261; [1997] Fam. Law 401; (1997) 147 N.L.J. 253; *Times,* February 7, 1997;
    Independent, February 11, 1997, CA; reversing [1996] 3 W.L.R. 1176; [1996] 3
    C.M.L.R. 921; [1997] 1 F.C.R. 170; (1996) 93(40) L.S.G. 25; (1996) 146 N.L.J.
    1542; (1996) 140 S.J.L.B. 227; *Times,* October 18, 1996; *Independent,* October
    23, 1996, QBD . . . .   *Digested,* 97/**3599**:
        Considered, 97/2446
R. *v.* Human Fertilisation and Embryology Authority Ex p. DB see R. *v.* Human
    Fertilisation and Embryology Authority Ex p. Blood
R. *v.* Humberstone (Alan) see Attorney General's Reference (No.40 of 1995), Re
R. *v.* Humphrey (Warren Martin) see Attorney General's Reference (No.30 of 2001), Re
R. *v.* Humphrys (Bruce Edward) see DPP *v.* Humphrys (Bruce Edward)
R. *v.* Hunt (Dennis) [1998] Crim. L.R. 343, CA (Crim Div)
R. *v.* Hunt (James) see Attorney General's Reference (Nos.36, 37, 38 and 39 of 1999),
    Re
R. *v.* Hunt (Nigel John) [1997] 1 Cr. App. R. (S.) 414, CA (Crim Div) . . . .   *Digested,* 97/**1403**:
        Considered, 00/1136
R. *v.* Hunter (Glen Ronald), *Times,* February 26, 1998, CA (Crim Div) . . . .   *Digested,* 98/**1114**:
        Considered, 00/1127
R. *v.* Hurley (Joseph Robert) [1998] 1 Cr. App. R. (S.) 299; [1997] Crim. L.R. 840;
    Times, October 3, 1997; *Times,* August 5, 1997, CA (Crim Div) . . . .   *Digested,* 97/**1508**
R. *v.* Husbands (Marva Sherrina) [1998] 2 Cr. App. R. (S.) 428, CA (Crim Div) . . . .   *Digested,* 99/**1277**
R. *v.* Huskins (Malcom) see R. *v.* Dowd (Jeffrey)
R. *v.* Hussain [1998] Crim. L.R. 820, CA (Crim Div)
R. *v.* Hussain (Mohammed Blayat) [1969] 2 Q.B. 567; [1969] 3 W.L.R. 134; [1969] 2
    All E.R. 1117; (1969) 53 Cr. App. R. 448; (1969) 113 S.J. 424, CA (Crim Div) . . .   *Digested,* 69/**854**:
        Applied, 86/617, 87/1113, 01/1060: *Approved,* 86/482: *Considered,* 76/506,
        83/612: *Followed,* 00/994
R. *v.* Hussein (Mohammed) see Attorney General's Reference (Nos.53, 54, 55, 56 and
    57 of 2001), Re
R. *v.* Hutchinson (James Kevin) (1994) 15 Cr. App. R. (S.) 134, CA (Crim Div) . . . .   *Considered,* 98/1353
R. *v.* Hutchinson (Jonathan) see Attorney General's Reference (No.90 of 1999), Re
R. *v.* Hutton (Michael Anthony) [1999] Crim. L.R. 74, CA (Crim Div)
R. *v.* I (Matthew Joseph) [1998] 2 Cr. App. R. (S.) 63; [1998] Crim. L.R. 140, CA
    (Crim Div) . . . .   *Digested,* 98/**1262**:
        Applied, 00/1281
R. *v.* I (Michael) [2000] 2 Cr. App. R. (S.) 167, CA (Crim Div) . . . .   *Digested,* 00/**1142**
R. *v.* Ibrahim (Turan) [1998] 1 Cr. App. R. (S.) 157, CA (Crim Div) . . . .   *Digested,* 98/**1313**:
        Considered, 99/1272
R. *v.* IM (A Juvenile) [2001] EWCA Crim 1891; [2001] Crim. L.R. 839, CA (Crim Div)
R. *v.* Immigration Appeal Ex p. Akhtar (Tahzeem) see Akhtar (Tahzeem) *v.* Immigration
    Appeal Tribunal
R. (on the application of Atputharajah) *v.* Immigration Appeal Tribunal; *sub nom* R. (on
    the application of Atputharajah) *v.* Secretary of State for the Home Department
    [2001] EWHC Admin 156; [2001] Imm. A.R. 566, QBD (Admin Ct)
R. (on the application of Ganidagli) *v.* Immigration Appeal Tribunal [2001] EWHC Admin
    70; [2001] I.N.L.R. 479, QBD (Admin Ct)

R. (on the application of Milisavljevic) *v.* Immigration Appeal Tribunal; *sub nom* R. (on the application of Milisavljevic) *v.* Secretary of State for the Home Department [2001] EWHC Admin 203; [2001] Imm. A.R. 580; *Independent*, May 7, 2001 (C.S), QBD (Admin Ct)

R. (on the application of Sarkisian) *v.* Immigration Appeal Tribunal [2001] EWHC Admin 486; [2001] Imm. A.R. 676, QBD (Admin Ct)

R. (on the application of Sivakumar) *v.* Immigration Appeal Tribunal; *sub nom* Sivakumar *v.* Secretary of State for the Home Department; R. (on the application of Sivakumar) *v.* Secretary of State for the Home Department [2001] EWCA Civ 1196; (2001) 98(35) L.S.G. 34; *Times*, November 7, 2001, CA; reversing [2001] EWHC Admin 109, QBD (Admin Ct) . . . .   *Digested*, 01/**3641**

R. (on the application of the Secretary of State for the Home Department) *v.* Immigration Appeal Tribunal [2001] EWHC Admin 261; [2001] Q.B. 1224; [2001] 3 W.L.R. 164; [2001] 4 All E.R. 430; [2001] I.N.L.R. 625; *Times*, June 12, 2001, QBD (Admin Ct) . . . .   *Digested*, 01/**3600**

R. *v.* Immigration Appeal Tribunal Ex p. Agbenyenu [1999] Imm. A.R. 460, IAT . . . .   *Digested*, 00/**3303**

R. *v.* Immigration Appeal Tribunal Ex p. Ahmed [1999] I.N.L.R. 473, QBD . . . .   *Digested*, 00/**3316**:
                                  Considered, 01/3629: *Distinguished*, 00/3309

R. *v.* Immigration Appeal Tribunal Ex p. Akpre; *sub nom* Akpre *v.* Immigration Appeal Tribunal [1998] Imm. A.R. 493, CA; affirming [1998] Imm. A.R. 205, QBD . . . .   *Digested*, 99/**3151**

R. *v.* Immigration Appeal Tribunal Ex p. Alexander; *sub nom* Alexander *v.* Immigration Appeal Tribunal [1982] 1 W.L.R. 1076; [1982] 2 All E.R. 766; [1982] Imm. A.R. 50; (1982) 79 L.S.G. 1175, HL; reversing [1982] 1 W.L.R. 430; [1982] 1 All E.R. 763; [1981] Imm. A.R. 175; 125 S.J. 120, CA . . . .   *Digested*, 84/**1762**:
                                       Considered, 00/3363

R. *v.* Immigration Appeal Tribunal Ex p. Alghali (Dhanniah Hahiru); R. *v.* Secretary of State for the Home Department Ex p. Alghali (Dhanniah Hahiru) [1986] Imm. A.R. 376, QBD . . . .   *Digested*, 87/**1947**:
                                         Applied, 00/3392

R. *v.* Immigration Appeal Tribunal Ex p. Ali [2001] Imm. A.R. 67, QBD . . . .   *Digested*, 01/**3597**

R. *v.* Immigration Appeal Tribunal Ex p. Ali (Mohammed Sarif) [1999] Imm. A.R. 48; [1998] I.N.L.R. 526; [1999] C.O.D. 64; *Times*, September 25, 1998, QBD . . . . .   *Digested*, 98/**3185**:
                                         Applied, 99/3150

R. *v.* Immigration Appeal Tribunal Ex p. Amin (Mohd) [1992] Imm. A.R. 367, QBD . . . . .   *Digested*, 93/**2218**:
                                         Applied, 00/3316

R. *v.* Immigration Appeal Tribunal Ex p. Anderson see R. *v.* Immigration Appeal Tribunal Ex p. Khatib-Shahidi

R. *v.* Immigration Appeal Tribunal Ex p. Antonissen (C292/89) [1991] E.C.R. I-745; [1991] 2 C.M.L.R. 373; (1991) 135 S.J. 6; *Times*, February 27, 1991; *Guardian*, March 7, 1991, ECJ . . . .   *Digested*, 91/**4007**:
                         Applied, 96/3164: *Considered*, 95/52, 98/4539

R. *v.* Immigration Appeal Tribunal Ex p. Arslan [1997] Imm. A.R. 63; [1997] C.O.D. 127, QBD . . . .   *Digested*, 97/**2840**:
                                         Followed, 00/3292

R. *v.* Immigration Appeal Tribunal Ex p. Aziz [1999] Imm. A.R. 476; [1999] I.N.L.R. 355, QBD . . . .   *Digested*, 00/**3292**

R. *v.* Immigration Appeal Tribunal Ex p. B [1989] Imm. A.R. 166, CA; affirming [1989] C.O.D. 270; *Times*, December 16, 1988; *Independent*, November 3, 1988, QBD . .   *Digested*, 91/**1967**:
                           Cited, 95/2689: *Not followed*, 99/3179

R. *v.* Immigration Appeal Tribunal Ex p. Balendran; R. *v.* Immigration Appeal Tribunal Ex p. Katheeskumaran [1998] Imm. A.R. 162; [1998] I.N.L.R. 158, QBD . . . .   *Digested*, 98/**3195**

R. *v.* Immigration Appeal Tribunal Ex p. Banu [1999] Imm. A.R. 161; [1999] I.N.L.R. 226, QBD . . . .   *Digested*, 99/**3202**

R. *v.* Immigration Appeal Tribunal Ex p. Bellache (No.2); *sub nom* R. *v.* Immigration Appellate Authority Ex p. Bellache (No.2); R. *v.* Secretary of State for the Home Department Ex p. Bellache; (Unreported, April 24, 1997), CA; reversing [1997] Imm. A.R. 486, QBD . . . .   *Digested*, 97/**2845**:
                                         Considered, 99/3161

R. *v.* Immigration Appeal Tribunal Ex p. Bogou [2000] Imm. A.R. 494, QBD . . . .   *Digested*, 01/**3595**

R. *v.* Immigration Appeal Tribunal Ex p. Bolanos [1999] Imm. A.R. 350, QBD. . . . .   *Digested*, 00/**3318**

R. *v.* Immigration Appeal Tribunal Ex p. Brylewicz (Unreported, March 26, 2000) . . . . .   *Applied*, 01/**3640**

R. *v.* Immigration Appeal Tribunal Ex p. Chavrimootoo (Prakashwatee) (No.2) [1995] Imm. A.R. 267, QBD . . . .   *Digested*, 96/**3269**:
                                         Followed, 00/3390

R. *v.* Immigration Appeal Tribunal Ex p. Deen-Koroma; *sub nom* Deen-Koroma *v.* Immigration Appeal Tribunal [1997] Imm. A.R. 242, CA. . . . .   *Digested*, 97/**2829**:
                                         Considered, 00/**6495**

R. *v.* Immigration Appeal Tribunal Ex p. Ez-Eldin [2001] Imm. A.R. 98, QBD. . . . .   *Digested*, 01/**3624**

R. *v.* Immigration Appeal Tribunal Ex p. Farooq (Mohamed) see R. *v.* Immigration Appeal Tribunal Ex p. Hassanin

R. *v.* Immigration Appeal Tribunal Ex p. Gedrimas [1999] Imm. A.R. 486, QBD. . . . .   *Digested*, 00/**3315**

R. *v.* Immigration Appeal Tribunal Ex p. Gilgham see Gilgham *v.* Immigration Appeal Tribunal

R. *v.* Immigration Appeal Tribunal Ex p. Gnali; *sub nom* Gnali *v.* Immigration Appeal
Tribunal [1998] Imm. A.R. 331, CA . . . .   *Digested,* 98/**3194**
R. *v.* Immigration Appeal Tribunal Ex p. Guang [2000] Imm. A.R. 59; [2000] I.N.L.R.
80, QBD . . . .   *Digested,* 00/**3274**
R. *v.* Immigration Appeal Tribunal Ex p. Hassanin; R. *v.* Immigration Appeal Tribunal Ex
p. Kandemir; R. *v.* Immigration Appeal Tribunal Ex p. Farooq (Mohamed) [1986]
1 W.L.R. 1448; [1987] 1 All E.R. 74; [1986] Imm. A.R. 502; (1986) 83 L.S.G.
3597; (1986) 130 S.J. 861; *Times,* October 18, 1986, CA; affirming in part [1985]
Imm. A.R. 206. . . . .   *Digested,* 87/**1937**:
Distinguished, 98/3221: *Followed,* 91/1961, 91/2029
R. *v.* Immigration Appeal Tribunal Ex p. Jeyeanthan see R. *v.* Secretary of State for the
Home Department Ex p. Jeyeanthan
R. *v.* Immigration Appeal Tribunal Ex p. Kandemir see R. *v.* Immigration Appeal Tribunal
Ex p. Hassanin
R. *v.* Immigration Appeal Tribunal Ex p. Katheeskumaran see R. *v.* Immigration Appeal
Tribunal Ex p. Balendran
R. *v.* Immigration Appeal Tribunal Ex p. Khan (Mahmud) [1983] Q.B. 790; [1983] 2
W.L.R. 759; [1983] 2 All E.R. 420; [1982] Imm. A.R. 134, CA . . . .   *Digested,* 83/**1919**:
Applied, 91/2030, 99/1882: *Considered,* 91/1995, 01/50:
Distinguished, 87/1985, 90/2592, 91/2032: *Followed,* 95/4845
R. *v.* Immigration Appeal Tribunal Ex p. Khatib-Shahidi; *sub nom* Khatib-Shahidi *v.*
Immigration Appeal Tribunal; R. *v.* Immigration Appeal Tribunal Ex p. Anderson
[2001] Imm. A.R. 124; [2000] I.N.L.R. 491; *Times,* August 3, 2000, CA;
affirming *Times,* March 22, 2000, QBD . . . .   *Digested,* 00/**3390**
R. *v.* Immigration Appeal Tribunal Ex p. Kilinc [1999] Imm. A.R. 588, CA . . . .   *Digested,* 00/**3294**
R. *v.* Immigration Appeal Tribunal Ex p. Kotecha [1983] 1 W.L.R. 487; [1983] 2 All E.R.
289; [1982] Imm. A.R. 88, CA; affirming *Times,* February 9, 1982, QBD . . . .   *Digested,* 83/**1927**:
Applied, 89/1946, 94/2502: *Considered,* 82/1536, 91/1961, 93/2182:
Distinguished, 86/1677, 87/1937, 89/1945, 90/2607, 91/2018.a, 95/2686,
96/3216: *Followed,* 99/3202
R. *v.* Immigration Appeal Tribunal Ex p. Lila, *Times,* October 29, 1977, QBD . . . .   *Digested,* 77/**5**:
Followed, 00/3390
R. *v.* Immigration Appeal Tribunal Ex p. Mubassir [1998] Imm. A.R. 304; [1998]
I.N.L.R. 446, QBD . . . .   *Digested,* 98/**3189**
R. *v.* Immigration Appeal Tribunal Ex p. Nelson [2001] Imm. A.R. 76, QBD . . . .   *Digested,* 01/**3663**
R. *v.* Immigration Appeal Tribunal Ex p. Nichalapillai [1998] Imm. A.R. 232, QBD . . . . . .   *Digested,* 98/**3193**:
Distinguished, 99/3162
R. *v.* Immigration Appeal Tribunal Ex p. Patel (Anilkumar Rabindrabhai) [1988] A.C.
910; [1988] 2 W.L.R. 1165; [1988] 2 All E.R. 378; [1988] Imm. A.R. 434; (1988)
132 S.J. 698; *Times,* May 6, 1988; *Independent,* May 9, 1988; *Guardian,* May
12, 1988; *Daily Telegraph,* May 13, 1988, HL; reversing [1988] 1 W.L.R. 375;
[1988] Imm. A.R. 35; (1988) 132 S.J. 335; *Times,* September 5, 1987;
Independent, August 21, 1987, CA; affirming [1987] Imm. A.R. 164, IAT . . . .   *Digested,* 88/**1882**:
Applied, 91/2037, 92/2400, 94/2507: *Followed,* 00/3288
R. *v.* Immigration Appeal Tribunal Ex p. Pedro; *sub nom* Pedro *v.* Immigration Appeal
Tribunal [2000] Imm. A.R. 489, CA . . . .   *Digested,* 01/**3638**
R. *v.* Immigration Appeal Tribunal Ex p. Rajendrakumar see R. *v.* Secretary of State for
the Home Department Ex p. Ravichandran (No.1)
R. *v.* Immigration Appeal Tribunal Ex p. S [1998] Imm. A.R. 252; [1998] I.N.L.R. 168;
[1998] C.O.D. 321; *Times,* February 25, 1998, QBD . . . .   *Digested,* 98/**3183**
R. *v.* Immigration Appeal Tribunal Ex p. Sahota [1995] Imm. A.R. 500, CA. . . . .   *Followed,* 99/3163
R. *v.* Immigration Appeal Tribunal Ex p. Saleem see R. *v.* Secretary of State for the
Home Department Ex p. Saleem
R. *v.* Immigration Appeal Tribunal Ex p. Sandralingam (No.1) see R. *v.* Secretary of
State for the Home Department Ex p. Ravichandran (No.1)
R. *v.* Immigration Appeal Tribunal Ex p. Secretary of State for the Home Department;
sub nom R. *v.* Vladic Ex p. Secretary of State for the Home Department; R. *v.*
Secretary of State for the Home Department Ex p. Vladic; Vladic *v.* Secretary of
State for the Home Department [1998] Imm. A.R. 542; [1998] I.N.L.R. 612;
Times, August 21, 1998, CA; affirming [1997] Imm. A.R. 619, QBD . . . .   *Digested,* 98/**3221**:
Considered, 99/3193
R. *v.* Immigration Appeal Tribunal Ex p. Secretary of State for the Home Department
(C370/90) [1992] 3 All E.R. 798; [1992] E.C.R. I-4265; [1992] 3 C.M.L.R. 358;
[1993] 1 F.L.R. 798; [1992] Imm. A.R. 565; [1993] Fam. Law 294; *Times,*
August 31, 1992; *Independent,* July 17, 1992; *Guardian,* July 15, 1992, ECJ . . . . .   *Digested,* 92/**4802**:
Applied, 95/2715: *Considered,* 97/2919, 98/3250
R. *v.* Immigration Appeal Tribunal Ex p. Senait [1999] Imm. A.R. 323; [1999] I.N.L.R.
580, QBD . . . .   *Digested,* 00/**3278**
R. *v.* Immigration Appeal Tribunal Ex p. Senga (Unreported, March 9, 1994) . . . .   *Applied,* 96/3211:
Considered, 95/2675, 98/3194, 00/3303: *Referred to,* 98/3178
R. *v.* Immigration Appeal Tribunal Ex p. Shaban [2000] Imm. A.R. 408, QBD . . . .   *Digested,* 00/**3293**

R. v. Immigration Appeal Tribunal Ex p. Shah; *sub nom* Secretary of State for the Home Department Ex p. Shah; Islam v. Secretary of State for the Home Department [1999] 2 A.C. 629; [1999] 2 W.L.R. 1015; [1999] 2 All E.R. 545; 6 B.H.R.C. 356; [1999] Imm. A.R. 283; [1999] I.N.L.R. 144; (1999) 96(17) L.S.G. 24; (1999) 143 S.J.L.B. 115; *Times*, March 26, 1999, HL; reversing [1998] 1 W.L.R. 74; [1998] 4 All E.R. 30; 2 B.H.R.C. 590; [1997] Imm. A.R. 584; [1998] I.N.L.R. 97; (1997) 94(36) L.S.G. 43; *Times*, October 13, 1997, CA; reversing [1997] Imm. A.R. 145; *Times*, November 12, 1996; *Independent*, December 2, 1996 (C.S.), QBD . . . .   *Digested*, 99/**3172**:
               Cited, 97/2856: *Considered*, 00/3311, 01/3642, 01/3651:
               Distinguished, 00/3293, 00/3315: *Followed*, 01/3638
R. v. Immigration Appeal Tribunal Ex p. Shandar [2000] Imm. A.R. 181, QBD . . . .   *Digested*, 00/**3381**
R. v. Immigration Appeal Tribunal Ex p. Shen [2000] I.N.L.R. 389, QBD . . . .   *Digested*, 01/**3631**
R. v. Immigration Appeal Tribunal Ex p. Shokar; R. v. Special Adjudicator Ex p. Shokar; R. v. Secretary of State for the Home Department Ex p. Shokar [1998] Imm. A.R. 447, QBD . . . .   *Digested*, 99/**3174**
R. v. Immigration Appeal Tribunal Ex p. Shokrollahy see R. v. Immigration Appellate Authority Ex p. Shockrollahy
R. v. Immigration Appeal Tribunal Ex p. Singh (Bakhtaur) [1986] 1 W.L.R. 910; [1986] 2 All E.R. 721; [1986] Imm. A.R. 352; (1986) 83 L.S.G. 2488; (1986) 130 S.J. 525, HL; reversing [1984] Imm. A.R. 217, CA . . . .   *Digested*, 86/**1684**:
         Applied, 88/1824: *Considered*, 87/1988, 00/3363: *Distinguished*, 93/2211:
                            Referred to, 87/1946, 87/1956
R. v. Immigration Appeal Tribunal Ex p. Singh (Makhan) [1999] Imm. A.R. 92, QBD . . . .   *Digested*, 99/**3163**
R. v. Immigration Appeal Tribunal Ex p. Singh (Tarlok); *sub nom* R. v. Secretary of State for the Home Department Ex p. Singh (Tarlok) [2000] Imm. A.R. 508, QBD. . . .   *Digested*, 01/**3661**
R. v. Immigration Appeal Tribunal Ex p. Sivanentheran; *sub nom* Sivanentheran v. Immigration Appeal Tribunal [1997] Imm. A.R. 504, CA . . . .   *Digested*, 98/**3176**
R. v. Immigration Appeal Tribunal Ex p. Subramaniam [2000] Imm. A.R. 173, CA; affirming [1999] Imm. A.R. 359, QBD . . . .   *Digested*, 00/**3317**
R. v. Immigration Appeal Tribunal Ex p. Subramaniam (Security against Deportation) [1977] Q.B. 190; [1976] 3 W.L.R. 630; [1976] 3 All E.R. 604; 120 S.J. 436, CA; affirming [1976] 1 All E.R. 915; 120 S.J. 302, QBD . . . .   *Digested*, 76/**13**:
          Approved, 76/12: *Considered*, 87/1946, 87/1956:
              Distinguished, 98/3221: *Followed*, 91/2071, 93/2212
R. v. Immigration Appeal Tribunal Ex p. Sui Rong Suen [1997] Imm. A.R. 355, QBD. . . .   *Digested*, 97/**2832**:
                                    Followed, 99/3148
R. v. Immigration Appeal Tribunal Ex p. Susikanth see Susikanth v. Secretary of State for the Home Department
R. v. Immigration Appeal Tribunal Ex p. Tharumakulasingham [1997] Imm. A.R. 550, QBD . . . .   *Digested*, 98/**3174**
R. v. Immigration Appeal Tribunal Ex p. Uddin see Hawa Bibi Uddin v. Immigration Appeal Tribunal
R. v. Immigration Appeal Tribunal Ex p. Vickneswaran; *sub nom* Vickneswaran v. Immigration Appeal Tribunal [1997] Imm. A.R. 477, CA . . . .   *Digested*, 98/**3175**
R. v. Immigration Appeal Tribunal Ex p. Vincent [2000] Imm. A.R. 547, QBD
R. v. Immigration Appeal Tribunal Ex p. Wanyoike [2000] Imm. A.R. 389; [2000] I.N.L.R. 286; (2000) 97(10) L.S.G. 36; (2000) 144 S.J.L.B. 125; *Times*, March 10, 2000, QBD . . . .   *Digested*, 00/**3382**
R. (on the application of Kolcak) v. Immigration Appellate Authority; *sub nom* R. (on the application of Kolcak) v. Secretary of State for the Home Department [2001] EWHC Admin 532; [2001] Imm. A.R. 666, QBD (Admin Ct)
R. v. Immigration Appellate Authority Ex p. Bellache (No.2) see R. v. Immigration Appeal Tribunal Ex p. Bellache (No.2)
R. v. Immigration Appellate Authority Ex p. Davies see R. v. Birmingham Crown Court Ex p. Ali (Rashid)
R. v. Immigration Appellate Authority Ex p. Mohammed (Mukhtar Shala); *sub nom* R. v. Special Adjudicator Ex p. Mohammed (Mukhtar Shala) [2001] Imm. A.R. 162, QBD . . . .   *Digested*, 01/**3622**
R. v. Immigration Appellate Authority Ex p. Secretary of State for the Home Department see R. v. Special Adjudicator Ex p. Secretary of State for the Home Department
R. v. Immigration Appellate Authority Ex p. Shockrollahy; *sub nom* R. v. Immigration Appeal Tribunal Ex p. Shokrollahy [2000] Imm. A.R. 580, QBD . . . .   *Digested*, 01/**3629**
R. (on the application of Uluyol) v. Immigration Officer [2001] I.N.L.R. 194, QBD (Admin Ct) . . . .   *Digested*, 01/**3681**
R. v. Immigration Officer Ex p. Bensaid; *sub nom* Bensaid v. Secretary of State for the Home Department [1998] Imm. A.R. 525, CA . . . .   *Digested*, 99/**3204**
R. v. Immigration Officer Ex p. X see R. (on the application of X) v. Secretary of State for the Home Department
R. v. Incorporated Froebel Educational Institute Ex p. L [1999] E.L.R. 488, QBD . . . . . .   *Digested*, 00/**1851**
R. v. Independent Appeal Panel of Sheffield City Council Ex p. N [2000] E.L.R. 700, QBD . . . .   *Digested*, 01/**1978**

R. v. Independent Appeals Tribunal of the Local Education Authority of Hillingdon LBC
Ex p. Governors of Mellow Lane School [2001] E.L.R. 200, QBD . . . .　　*Digested*, 01/**1976**

R. (on the application of TVDanmark 1 Ltd) v. Independent Television Commission; *sub nom* R.v Independent Television Commission Ex p. TVDanmark 1 Ltd; R. (on the application of TV Danmark 1 Ltd) v. Independent Television Commission; TVDanmark 1 Ltd v. Independent Television Commission [2001] UKHL 42; [2001] 1 W.L.R. 1604; [2001] 3 C.M.L.R. 26; [2001] Eu. L.R. 741; [2001] E.M.L.R. 42; (2001) 98(34) L.S.G. 43; *Times*, July 27, 2001; *Daily Telegraph*, July 31, 2001, HL; reversing [2001] 1 W.L.R. 74; [2001] E.C.C. 11; [2001] E.M.L.R. 2; (2000) 97(41) L.S.G. 40; *Times*, October 25, 2000; *Independent*, November 20, 2000 (C.S); *Daily Telegraph*, October 24, 2000, CA; reversing CO 3036/2000, QBD . . . .　*Digested*, 01/**4412**

R. v. Independent Television Commission Ex p. Flextech Plc [1999] E.M.L.R. 880; [1999] C.O.D. 108; *Times*, November 27, 1998, QBD . . . .　*Digested*, 99/**3928**

R. (on the application of Monarch Assurance Plc) v. Inland Revenue Commissioners; *sub nom* Monarch Assurance Plc v. Inland Revenue Commissioners [2001] EWCA Civ 1681; [2001] S.T.C. 1639; [2001] B.T.C. 467; [2001] S.T.I. 1421; *Times*, November 26, 2001; *Independent*, November 15, 2001, CA; affirming [2001] S.T.C. 92; [2001] S.T.I. 73, QBD (Admin Ct) . . . .　*Digested*, 01/**5317**

R. (on the application of Newfields Developments Ltd) v. Inland Revenue Commissioners; *sub nom* R. v. Inland Revenue Commissioners Ex p. Newfields Development Ltd; R. v. Inland Revenue Commissioners Ex p. Newfields Developments Ltd [2001] UKHL 27; [2001] 1 W.L.R. 1111; [2001] 4 All E.R. 400; [2001] S.T.C. 901; 73 T.C. 532; [2001] B.T.C. 196; [2001] S.T.I. 851; (2001) 98(26) L.S.G. 45; *Times*, June 8, 2001, HL; reversing [2000] S.T.C. 52; [2000] B.T.C. 3; [2000] S.T.I. 26; *Times*, February 15, 2000, CA; reversing [1999] S.T.C. 373; [1999] B.T.C. 145; *Times*, March 9, 1999, QBD . . . .　*Digested*, 01/**5206**

R. (on the application of Professional Contractors Group Ltd) v. Inland Revenue Commissioners (Human Rights); *sub nom* R. v. Inland Revenue Commissioners Ex p. Professional Contractors Group Ltd (Human Rights); Professional Contractors Group Ltd v. Inland Revenue Commissioners [2001] EWCA Civ 1945; 4 I.T.L. Rep. 483, CA; affirming [2001] EWHC Admin 236; [2001] S.T.C. 629; [2001] Eu. L.R. 514; [2001] H.R.L.R. 42; 3 I.T.L. Rep. 556; [2001] S.T.I. 669; (2001) 98(20) L.S.G. 44; (2001) 151 N.L.J. 535; *Times*, April 5, 2001, QBD (Admin Ct) . . . .　*Digested*, 01/**5316**

R. (on the application of Professional Contractors Group Ltd) v. Inland Revenue Commissioners (Taxation); *sub nom* R. v. Inland Revenue Commissioners Ex p. Professional Contractors Group Ltd (Taxation) [2001] Eu. L.R. 1, QBD

R. v. Inland Revenue Commissioners Ex p. Allan see R. v. Inland Revenue Commissioners Ex p. Bishopp

R. v. Inland Revenue Commissioners Ex p. Allen [1997] S.T.C. 1141; 69 T.C. 442; [1997] B.T.C. 487, QBD . . . .　*Digested*, 97/**4765**

R. v. Inland Revenue Commissioners Ex p. Archon Shipping Corp [1998] S.T.C. 1151; 71 T.C. 203; [1998] B.T.C. 405, QBD . . . .　*Digested*, 99/**4765**

R. v. Inland Revenue Commissioners Ex p. Banque Internationale a Luxembourg SA [2000] S.T.C. 708; 72 T.C. 597; [2000] B.T.C. 228; [2001] A.C.D. 21; [2000] S.T.I. 919; (2000) 97(27) L.S.G. 37; *Times*, July 27, 2000, QBD . . . .　*Digested*, 00/**5031**

R. v. Inland Revenue Commissioners Ex p. Bishopp; *sub nom* Inland Revenue Commissioners v. Pricewaterhouse Coopers; Inland Revenue Commissioners v. Ernst & Young; R. v. Inland Revenue Commissioners Ex p. Allan [1999] S.T.C. 531; (1999) 11 Admin. L.R. 575; 72 T.C. 322; [1999] B.T.C. 158; [1999] C.O.D. 354; (1999) 149 N.L.J. 682; [1999] N.P.C. 50; *Times*, May 18, 1999, QBD . . . . .　*Digested*, 99/**4682**

R. v. Inland Revenue Commissioners Ex p. Davis Frankel & Mead [2000] S.T.C. 595; 73 T.C. 185; [2000] B.T.C. 203; [2000] S.T.I. 887; *Times*, July 11, 2000; *Independent*, July 24, 2000 (C.S), QBD . . . .　*Digested*, 00/**5032**

R. v. Inland Revenue Commissioners Ex p. Hillsdown Holdings Plc see Hillsdown Holdings Plc v. Inland Revenue Commissioners　　　　　　　　　　　　　*Digested*, 96/**67**

R. v. Inland Revenue Commissioners Ex p. Lorimer [2000] S.T.C. 751; 73 T.C. 276; [2000] B.T.C. 257; [2000] S.T.I. 1125, QBD . . . .　*Digested*, 00/**4914**:
　　　　　　　　　　　　　　　　　　　　　　　　　　　　　　　　　　　Considered, 01/5320

R. v. Inland Revenue Commissioners Ex p. Matrix Securities Ltd; *sub nom* Matrix Securities Ltd v. Inland Revenue Commissioners [1994] 1 W.L.R. 334; [1994] 1 All E.R. 769; [1994] S.T.C. 272; 66 T.C. 629; *Times*, February 19, 1994; *Independent*, March 14, 1994 (C.S.), HL; affirming [1993] S.T.C. 773; 66 T.C. 606; [1993] E.G.C.S. 187; (1994) 91(4) L.S.G. 47; (1993) 137 S.J.L.B. 255; *Times*, November 10, 1993, CA; affirming 66 T.C. 587; *Times*, October 22, 1993, QBD . . . .　*Digested*, 94/**2569**:
Applied, 95/895: *Considered*, 00/5365: *Referred to*, 98/4011

R. v. Inland Revenue Commissioners Ex p. Matteson's Walls Ltd see R. v. Inland Revenue Commissioners Ex p. Unilever Plc

R. v. Inland Revenue Commissioners Ex p. MFK Underwriting Agencies see R. v. Inland Revenue Commissioners Ex p. MFK Underwriting Agents Ltd

R. *v.* Inland Revenue Commissioners Ex p. MFK Underwriting Agents Ltd; *sub nom* R. *v.* Inland Revenue Commissioners Ex p. MFK Underwriting Agencies [1990] 1 W.L.R. 1545; [1990] 1 All E.R. 91; [1990] S.T.C. 873; 62 T.C. 607; [1990] C.O.D. 143; (1989) 139 N.L.J. 1343; *Times,* July 17, 1989; *Independent,* August 7, 1989 (C.S.); *Independent,* August 4, 1989; *Financial Times,* July 19, 1989; *Guardian,* July 20, 1989, QBD . . . . *Digested,* 90/**2651**:
Applied, 90/50, 91/52, 93/32, 94/651, 96/249: *Considered,* 93/2254, 94/2569, 96/4799, 97/4107, 00/5365

R. *v.* Inland Revenue Commissioners Ex p. Mohammed [1999] S.T.C. 129; 73 T.C. 128; [1999] B.T.C. 20, QBD . . . . *Digested,* 99/**4768**

R. *v.* Inland Revenue Commissioners Ex p. Morgan Grenfell & Co Ltd see R. (on the application of Morgan Grenfell & Co Ltd) *v.* Special Commissioner of Income Tax

R. *v.* Inland Revenue Commissioners Ex p. National Federation of Self Employed and Small Businesses Ltd; *sub nom* Inland Revenue Commissioners *v.* National Federation of Self Employed and Small Businesses Ltd [1982] A.C. 617; [1981] 2 W.L.R. 722; [1981] 2 All E.R. 93; [1981] S.T.C. 260; 55 T.C. 133; 125 S.J. 325, HL; reversing [1980] Q.B. 407; [1980] 2 W.L.R. 579; [1980] 2 All E.R. 378; [1980] S.T.C. 261; [1980] T.R. 49; 124 S.J. 189, CA . . . . *Digested,* 81/**1433**:
Applied, 83/1981, 85/1782, 87/679, 90/2635, 91/3641: *Considered,* 85/316, 85/1479, 86/13, 86/324, 87/28, 87/274, 89/12, 90/10, 91/53, 94/80, 94/4367, 95/139, 95/140, 95/142, 95/143, 97/2785, 00/5436:
Distinguished, 87/5156

R. *v.* Inland Revenue Commissioners Ex p. Newfields Development Ltd see R. (on the application of Newfields Developments Ltd) *v.* Inland Revenue Commissioners

R. *v.* Inland Revenue Commissioners Ex p. Professional Contractors Group Ltd (Human Rights) see R. (on the application of Professional Contractors Group Ltd) *v.* Inland Revenue Commissioners (Human Rights)

R. *v.* Inland Revenue Commissioners Ex p. Professional Contractors Group Ltd (Taxation) see R. (on the application of Professional Contractors Group Ltd) *v.* Inland Revenue Commissioners (Taxation)

R. *v.* Inland Revenue Commissioners Ex p. Rossminster Ltd; *sub nom* Inland Revenue Commissioners *v.* Rossminster Ltd; Rossminster and Tucker, Re [1980] A.C. 952; [1980] 2 W.L.R. 1; [1980] 1 All E.R. 80; [1980] S.T.C. 42; (1980) 70 Cr. App. R. 157; [1979] T.R. 427, HL; reversing [1979] 3 All E.R. 385; [1979] S.T.C. 688; 52 T.C. 160; [1979] T.R. 312; [1980] Crim. L.R. 111; 123 S.J. 586, CA; reversing [1979] S.T.C. 677; [1979] T.R. 287; 123 S.J. 554, QBD . . . . *Digested,* 80/**2278**:
Applied, 91/2104, 97/1362, 99/4767: *Considered,* 88/3627, 89/667, 97/5033, 00/1098: *Not applied,* 89/3081

R. *v.* Inland Revenue Commissioners Ex p. Roux Waterside Inn Ltd [1997] S.T.C. 781; [1999] O.P.L.R. 239; 70 T.C. 545; [1997] B.T.C. 270; (1997) 94(16) L.S.G. 29; *Times,* April 23, 1997, QBD. . . . . *Digested,* 97/**2975**

R. *v.* Inland Revenue Commissioners Ex p. Tamosius & Partners see R. *v.* Middlesex Guildhall Crown Court Ex p. Tamosius & Partners

R. *v.* Inland Revenue Commissioners Ex p. Taylor (No.2) [1990] 2 All E.R. 409; [1990] S.T.C. 379; 62 T.C. 578, CA; affirming [1989] 3 All E.R. 353; [1989] S.T.C. 600, QBD . . . . *Digested,* 90/**2642**:
Applied, 01/5314: *Followed,* 00/4914

R. *v.* Inland Revenue Commissioners Ex p. TC Coombs & Co; *sub nom* TC Coombs & Co *v.* Inland Revenue Commissioners [1991] 2 A.C. 283; [1991] 2 W.L.R. 682; [1991] 3 All E.R. 623; [1991] S.T.C. 97; (1991) 3 Admin. L.R. 501; 64 T.C. 124; [1991] C.O.D. 338; *Times,* February 15, 1991; *Independent,* February 21, 1991; *Financial Times,* February 20, 1991; *Guardian,* February 19, 1991, HL; reversing [1989] S.T.C. 520; (1990) 2 Admin. L.R. 1; *Times,* June 1, 1989; *Independent,* June 26, 1989 (C.S.); *Financial Times,* June 20, 1989, CA; reversing [1989] S.T.C. 104; [1989] C.O.D. 394, QBD . . . . *Digested,* 91/**2104**:
Applied, 93/2285, 00/4914: *Considered,* 96/5580, 99/4765: *Distinguished,* 90/2642, 00/5780

R. *v.* Inland Revenue Commissioners Ex p. Ulster Bank Ltd see R. *v.* Special Commissioners of Income Tax Ex p. Inland Revenue Commissioners

R. *v.* Inland Revenue Commissioners Ex p. Ulster Bank Ltd [1997] S.T.C. 832; 69 T.C. 211; [1997] B.T.C. 314; *Times,* May 15, 1997; *Independent,* May 5, 1997 (C.S.), CA; affirming [1997] S.T.C. 636; [1997] B.T.C. 235, QBD . . . . *Digested,* 97/**4756**

R. *v.* Inland Revenue Commissioners Ex p. Unilever Plc; R. *v.* Inland Revenue Commissioners Ex p. Matteson's Walls Ltd [1996] S.T.C. 681; 68 T.C. 205; [1996] C.O.D. 421, CA; affirming [1994] S.T.C. 841; [1994] S.T.I. 1023; *Independent,* September 12, 1994 (C.S.), QBD . . . . *Digested,* 95/**895**:
Applied, 00/4072: *Considered,* 01/5605

R. *v.* Inner London Crown Court Ex p. I (A Juvenile) (2000) 97(22) L.S.G. 46; *Times,* May 12, 2000, QBD. . . . . *Digested,* 00/**1320**:
Considered, 01/1475

R. *v.* Inner London Crown Court Ex p. Lambeth LBC [2000] Crim. L.R. 303, QBD

R. *v.* Inner London Crown Court Ex p. Mentesh [2001] 1 Cr. App. R. (S.) 94, QBD . . . . *Digested,* 01/**1441**

R. v. Inner London Crown Court Ex p. N [2001] 1 Cr. App. R. (S.) 99; [2000] Crim. L.R. 871, QBD . . . . *Digested*, 01/**1385**

R. v. Inner London Crown Court Ex p. Provis [2000] C.O.D. 481; *Times*, July 11, 2000, QBD . . . . *Digested*, 00/**4067**

R. v. Inner London Education Authority Ex p. Ali (1990) 2 Admin. L.R. 822; [1990] C.O.D. 317; (1990) 154 L.G. Rev. 852, QBD . . . . *Digested*, 91/**1541**:
         Applied, 99/1887: *Considered*, 94/35, 94/55, 95/67, 95/3252

R. v. Inner London Education Authority Ex p. F see R. v. Inner London Education Authority Ex p. Futerfas

R. v. Inner London Education Authority Ex p. Futerfas; *sub nom* R. v. Inner London Education Authority Ex p. F *Times*, June 16, 1988, QBD . . . . *Digested*, 88/**1201**:
         Considered, 98/1966

R. (on the application of Dowdall) v. Inner London Magistrates Court South Western Division; *sub nom* Dowdall v. Inner London Magistrates Court [2001] Crim. L.R. 137, QBD (Admin Ct)

R. (on the application of Touche) v. Inner London North Coroner see R. (on the application of Touche) v. HM Coroner for Inner North London District

R. v. Inner London Youth Court Ex p. DPP (1997) 161 J.P. 178; [1996] Crim. L.R. 834; (1997) 161 J.P.N. 168; *Times*, April 4, 1996, QBD . . . . *Digested*, 96/**1639**:
         Considered, 98/1104

R. (on the application of Scott) v. Inner West London Coroner; *sub nom* R. v. Inner West London Coroner Ex p. Scott [2001] EWHC Admin 105; (2001) 165 J.P. 417; (2001) 61 B.M.L.R. 222; (2001) 165 J.P.N. 544, QBD (Admin Ct) . . . . *Digested*, 01/**26**

R. v. Inner West London Coroner Ex p. Scott see R. (on the application of Scott) v. Inner West London Coroner

R. v. Innes (Philip Gordon); R. v. Hopkins (Kevin Alan) (1985) 7 Cr. App. R. (S.) 52, CA (Crim Div) . . . . *Digested*, 86/**902.1**:
         Considered, 96/1958, 00/1310: *Referred to*, 00/1307

R. v. Inspector of Taxes Ex p. Bass Holdings Ltd; *sub nom* Richart (Inspector of Taxes) v. Bass Holdings Ltd [1993] S.T.C. 122, QBD . . . . *Digested*, 93/**601**:
         Considered, 98/4605

R. (on the application of Eliades) v. Institute of Chartered Accountants [2001] B.P.I.R. 363, QBD (Admin Ct) . . . . *Digested*, 01/**2**

R. v. Institute of Chartered Accountants in England and Wales Ex p. Brindle [1994] B.C.C. 297; *Times*, January 12, 1994, CA. . . . . *Digested*, 95/**54**:
         Applied, 98/681

R. (on the application of Gorlov) v. Institute of Chartered Accountants of England and Wales [2001] EWHC Admin 220; [2001] A.C.D. 73, QBD (Admin Ct)

R. v. International Stock Exchange of the United Kingdom and the Republic of Ireland Ltd Ex p. Else (1982) Ltd; R. v. International Stock Exchange of the United Kingdom and the Republic of Ireland Ltd Ex p. Thomas [1993] Q.B. 534; [1993] 2 W.L.R. 70; [1993] 1 All E.R. 420; [1993] B.C.C. 11; [1993] B.C.L.C. 834; [1993] 2 C.M.L.R. 677; (1994) 6 Admin. L.R. 67; [1993] C.O.D. 236; *Times*, November 2, 1992; *Independent*, November 24, 1992, CA; reversing [1993] C.O.D. 141, QBD . . . . *Digested*, 95/**614**:
         Applied, 01/2332: *Considered*, 94/4, 96/5906, 00/4404

R. v. International Stock Exchange of the United Kingdom and the Republic of Ireland Ltd Ex p. Thomas see R. v. International Stock Exchange of the United Kingdom and the Republic of Ireland Ltd Ex p. Else (1982) Ltd

R. v. Intervention Board for Agricultural Produce Ex p. First City Trading Ltd (C263/97) [1998] E.C.R. I-5537; [1999] 1 C.M.L.R. 727; [1998] 3 C.M.L.R. 993, ECJ (1st Chamber)

R. v. Investors Compensation Scheme Ltd Ex p. Taylor; *sub nom* Taylor v. Investors Compensation Scheme [1998] Q.B. 963; [1998] 3 W.L.R. 36; [1998] 1 All E.R. 711; (1998) 95(2) L.S.G. 23; (1998) 142 S.J.L.B. 36; *Times*, December 13, 1997, CA; reversing [1997] C.O.D. 162; *Times*, December 27, 1996, QBD . . . . . . *Digested*, 98/**2546**

R. v. Ioannou [1999] Crim. L.R. 586, CA (Crim Div)

R. v. Iqbal (Asif Ashraf), *Times*, September 5, 1995, CA (Crim Div) . . . . *Digested*, 95/**1510**:
         Considered, 98/1276

R. v. Iqbal (Khalid) (1985) 81 Cr. App. R. 145; (1985) 7 Cr. App. R. (S.) 35; [1985] Crim. L.R. 456, CA (Crim Div) . . . . *Digested*, 85/**860.1**:
         Considered, 99/1220

R. v. Iqbal (Zahir) [2000] 2 Cr. App. R. (S.) 119, CA (Crim Div). . . . . *Digested*, 00/**1226**

R. v. Ireland (Robert Matthew); R. v. Burstow (Anthony Christopher) [1998] A.C. 147; [1997] 3 W.L.R. 534; [1997] 4 All E.R. 225; [1998] 1 Cr. App. R. 177; (1997) 161 J.P. 569; [1998] 1 F.L.R. 105; [1997] Crim. L.R. 810; [1998] Fam. Law 137; (1997) 161 J.P.N. 816; (1997) 147 N.L.J. 1273; (1997) 141 S.J.L.B. 205; *Times*, July 25, 1997; *Independent*, July 30, 1997, HL; affirming [1997] Q.B. 114; [1996] 3 W.L.R. 650; [1997] 1 All E.R. 112; [1996] 2 Cr. App. R. 426; (1996) 160 J.P. 597; [1997] 1 F.L.R. 687; [1997] Crim. L.R. 434; [1997] Fam. Law 323; (1996) 160 J.P.N. 448; (1996) 93(23) L.S.G. 35; (1996) 140 S.J.L.B. 148; *Times*, May 22, 1996; *Independent*, July 15, 1996 (C.S.), CA (Crim Div) . . . . *Digested*, 97/**1182**:
         Applied, 00/4147: *Considered*, 98/927, 98/1182:
         Previous proceedings, 96/1438, 97/1183

R. v. Irving (David Stuart) [1998] 2 Cr. App. R. (S.) 162, CA (Crim Div) . . . .   *Digested,* 98/**1117**
R. v. Irving (Paul) see R. v. Doyle (David Martin)
R. v. Isaac (Inez) [1998] 1 Cr. App. R. (S.) 266, CA (Crim Div) . . . .   *Digested,* 98/**1141**
R. v. Iseton (Mark Andrew) see Attorney General's Reference (Nos.17 and 18 of 1996), Re
R. v. Ishmael (Mark) see R. v. Brewster (Alex Edward)
R. v. Islam (Abdul Khair) [1999] 1 Cr. App. R. 22; (1998) 162 J.P. 391; [1998] Crim.
    L.R. 575; (1998) 162 J.P.N. 445; (1998) 95(17) L.S.G. 29; (1998) 142 S.J.L.B.
    123; *Times,* March 18, 1998, CA (Crim Div) . . . .   *Digested,* 98/**1064**:
                                                        Applied, 01/1158
R. v. Isle of Anglesey CC District Auditor Ex p. Jones (1999) 1 L.G.L.R. 626, QBD . . . . .   *Digested,* 99/**3885**
R. (on the application of Reddy) v. Isle of Wight Healthcare NHS Trust; *sub nom* R. v. Isle
    of Wight Healthcare NHS Trust Ex p. Reddy [2001] Lloyd's Rep. Med. 137;
    [2001] A.C.D. 30, QBD (Admin Ct) . . . .   *Digested,* 01/**2246**
R. v. Isle of Wight Healthcare NHS Trust Ex p. Reddy see R. (on the application of
    Reddy) v. Isle of Wight Healthcare NHS Trust
R. (on the application of King) v. Isleworth Crown Court; *sub nom* R. v. Isleworth Crown
    Court Ex p. King (Murray) [2001] E.H.L.R. 14; [2001] A.C.D. 51; *Daily*
    Telegraph, February 13, 2001, QBD . . . .   *Digested,* 01/**3528**
R. v. Isleworth Crown Court Ex p. Buda [2000] 1 Cr. App. R. (S.) 538; [2000] Crim.
    L.R. 111, QBD . . . .   *Digested,* 00/**1032**
R. v. Isleworth Crown Court Ex p. Clarke [1998] 1 Cr. App. R. 257, QBD . . . .   *Digested,* 98/**999**
R. v. Isleworth Crown Court Ex p. King (Murray) see R. (on the application of King) v.
    Isleworth Crown Court
R. v. Isleworth Crown Court Ex p. Marland; Bryan v. Customs and Excise (1998) 162
    J.P. 251, QBD . . . .   *Digested,* 98/**880**
R. (on the application of Batantu) v. Islington LBC; *sub nom* R. v. Islington LBC Ex p.
    Batantu (2001) 33 H.L.R. 76, QBD (Admin Ct)
R. v. Islington LBC Ex p. A (A Child), *Times,* October 20, 2000, QBD . . . .   *Digested,* 00/**1943**
R. v. Islington LBC Ex p. B (1998) 30 H.L.R. 706; [1998] C.O.D. 44, QBD . . . .   *Digested,* 98/**3000**
R. v. Islington LBC Ex p. Batantu see R. (on the application of Batantu) v. Islington
    LBC
R. v. Islington LBC Ex p. Blissett (1998) 75 P. & C.R. D4, QBD
R. v. Islington LBC Ex p. Degnan (1998) 30 H.L.R. 723; [1998] C.O.D. 46; (1998) 75
    P. & C.R. D13, CA . . . .   *Digested,* 98/**3025**
R. v. Islington LBC Ex p. McMillan see R. v. Gloucestershire CC Ex p. Barry
R. v. Islington LBC Ex p. Okocha (1998) 30 H.L.R. 191, QBD . . . .   *Digested,* 97/**2672**
R. v. Islington LBC Ex p. Reilly (1999) 31 H.L.R. 651, QBD . . . .   *Digested,* 98/**3032**:
                                                        Applied, 00/3152
R. v. Islington LBC Ex p. Rixon [1997] E.L.R. 66; (1997-98) 1 C.C.L. Rep. 119; (1996)
    32 B.M.L.R. 136; *Times,* April 17, 1996, QBD . . . .   *Digested,* 96/**5530**:
                               Applied, 01/2025: *Followed,* 97/4713
R. v. Islington LBC Ex p. Thomas (1998) 30 H.L.R. 111, QBD . . . .   *Digested,* 98/**3020**
R. v. Islington North Juvenile Court Ex p. Daley; *sub nom* Daley, Re [1983] 1 A.C. 347;
    [1982] 3 W.L.R. 344; [1982] 2 All E.R. 974; (1982) 75 Cr. App. R. 280;
    [1982] Crim. L.R. 760; (1982) 79 L.S.G. 1412; 126 S.J. 524, HL. . . . .   *Digested,* 82/**742**:
                   Applied, 84/665, 86/628, 92/921: *Referred to,* 01/1170
R. v. Ismail (Ibrahim) (1992) 13 Cr. App. R. (S.) 395; [1992] Crim. L.R. 829, CA (Crim
    Div) . . . .   *Digested,* 93/**1184**:
                      Cited, 95/1395: *Considered,* 99/1180, 99/1181, 00/1261
R. v. Ivey (Keith Frederick) (1981) 3 Cr. App. R. (S.) 185; [1981] Crim. L.R. 722, DC . . .   *Digested,* 81/**525.102**:
                   Considered, 97/1561, 97/1571, 98/1235, 98/1236: *Referred to,* 97/1560
R. v. IWAT (No.1) [2000] 2 Cr. App. R. 189; [2000] Crim. L.R. 618, CA (Crim Div) . . . .   *Digested,* 00/**1102**
R. v. Iwuji (Alfred) [2001] 1 Cr. App. R. (S.) 131, CA (Crim Div) . . . .   *Digested,* 01/**1315**
R. v. J (A Juvenile) see Attorney General's Reference (Nos.52, 53, 54 and 55 of
    1999), Re
R. v. J (Andrew) see Attorney General's Reference (No.29 of 1999), Re
R. v. J (Andrew Paul) (A Juvenile) [1999] 2 Cr. App. R. (S.) 257, CA (Crim Div) . . . . . .   *Digested,* 99/**1228**
R. v. J (Christopher Kenneth) (A Juvenile) [2000] 2 Cr. App. R. (S.) 235, CA (Crim
    Div) . . . .   *Digested,* 00/**1308**
R. v. J (Colin) [2001] EWCA Crim 60; [2001] 2 Cr. App. R. (S.) 50, CA (Crim Div) . . . .   *Digested,* 01/**1351**
R. v. J (David Graham) see Attorney General's Reference (No.15 of 2001), Re
R. v. J (Drug Trafficking: Sentencing) [2001] 1 Cr. App. R. (S.) 79, CA (Crim Div) . . . . .   *Digested,* 01/**1290**
R. v. J (Gavin Donald) (A Juvenile) [2001] EWCA Crim 242; [2001] 2 Cr. App. R. (S.)
    52, CA (Crim Div) . . . .   *Digested,* 01/**1382**
R. v. J (Karen) (A Juvenile) [2001] 1 Cr. App. R. (S.) 7, CA (Crim Div) . . . .   *Digested,* 01/**1396**
R. v. J (Mark William) see R. v. C (Neil David)
R. v. J (Sarah Jane) (A Juvenile) [2001] 1 Cr. App. R. (S.) 81, CA (Crim Div) . . . .   *Digested,* 01/**1388**
R. v. J (Scott) (A Juvenile) see R. v. J-R (Scott) (A Juvenile)
R. v. J (Unreasonable Delay) see Attorney General's Reference (No.2 of 2001), Re
R. v. J (Vivian Sidney) see Attorney General's Reference (No.35 of 1998), Re

R. (on the application of L (A Child)) *v.* J School Governors; *sub nom* L *v.* J; W *v.* B; R. *v.*
    B School Governors Ex p. W; R. *v.* J School Governors Ex p. L; R. (on the
    application of W (A Child)) *v.* B School Governors [2001] EWCA Civ 1199;
    [2001] B.L.G.R. 561; *Times,* August 20, 2001; *Independent,* July 26, 2001, CA;
    affirming [2001] EWHC Admin 318; [2001] E.L.R. 411, QBD (Admin Ct) . . . . . .   *Digested,* 01/**1979**:
                                                         Previous proceedings, 00/1929
R. *v.* J-R (Scott) (A Juvenile); *sub nom* R. *v.* J (Scott) (A Juvenile); R. *v.* G (Daniel)
    (A Juvenile) [2001] 1 Cr. App. R. (S.) 109; (2001) 165 J.P. 140; [2000] Crim.
    L.R. 1022, CA (Crim Div) . . . .   *Digested,* 01/**1403**
R. *v.* Jabble (Pardeep Singh) [1999] 1 Cr. App. R. (S.) 298, CA (Crim Div) . . . .   *Digested,* 99/**1255**
R. *v.* Jackson (Christopher) [2000] 1 Cr. App. R. (S.) 405, CA (Crim Div) . . . .   *Digested,* 00/**1158**
R. *v.* Jackson (Christopher Anthony) [1998] 1 Cr. App. R. (S.) 259, CA (Crim Div) . . . .   *Digested,* 98/**1376**:
                                                        Considered, 00/1417, 01/1474
R. *v.* Jackson (Dennis James); R. *v.* Hart (Stanley) [1970] 1 Q.B. 647; [1969] 2 W.L.R.
    1339; [1969] 2 All E.R. 453; (1969) 53 Cr. App. R. 341; 133 J.P. 358; [1970]
    R.T.R. 165; 113 S.J. 310, CA (Crim Div) . . . .   *Digested,* 69/**3177**:
                          Considered, 70/1099, 01/1265: *Referred to,* 88/4841
R. *v.* Jackson (John Thomas) [2000] 1 Cr. App. R. 97 (Note); (1999) 96(20) L.S.G.
    39; *Times,* May 13, 1999, CA (Crim Div) . . . .   *Digested,* 99/**925**
R. *v.* Jackson (Leslie Joseph) [1999] 2 Cr. App. R. (S.) 77, CA (Crim Div) . . . .   *Digested,* 99/**1110**
R. *v.* Jackson (Stephen Shaun) [1999] 1 All E.R. 572; [1998] Crim. L.R. 835; *Times,*
    May 20, 1998; *Independent,* May 18, 1998 (C.S.), CA (Crim Div) . . . .   *Digested,* 98/**997**:
                                                         Applied, 99/991
R. *v.* Jackson (Steven Allan) [2000] Crim. L.R. 377; *Times,* January 05,2000;
    Independent, January 17, 2000 (C.S.), CA (Crim Div) . . . .   *Digested,* 00/**1058**
R. *v.* Jacobovits Ex p. Wachmann see R. *v.* Chief Rabbi of the United Hebrew
    Congregations of Great Britain and the Commonwealth Ex p. Wachmann
R. *v.* Jacobs (Emma Lisa) [2001] 2 Cr. App. R. (S.) 38; *Times,* December 28, 2000,
    CA (Crim Div) . . . .   *Digested,* 01/**1454**
R. *v.* Jacobs (Paul) see Attorney General's Reference (No.81 of 2000), Re
R. *v.* Jacques (Mark John) see Attorney General's Reference (Nos.22 and 23 of 1991),
    Re
R. *v.* Jacques (Richard Charles) see Attorney General's Reference (Nos.22 and 23 of
    1991), Re
R. *v.* Jaggard (Roland Leonard) see R. *v.* Brown (Anthony Joseph)
R. *v.* Jama (Hussein); R. *v.* Oliver (Austen Michael) [2000] 2 Cr. App. R. (S.) 98, CA
    (Crim Div) . . . .   *Digested,* 00/**1265**
R. *v.* James (Jim Isaac) [2001] 2 Cr. App. R. (S.) 32, CA (Crim Div) . . . .   *Digested,* 01/**1254**
R. *v.* James (Kenelm) [2000] 2 Cr. App. R. (S.) 258, CA (Crim Div) . . . .   *Digested,* 00/**1384**
R. *v.* James (Lance Norman) [1997] 2 Cr. App. R. (S.) 294, CA (Crim Div) . . . .   *Digested,* 98/**1388**
R. *v.* James (Maria) [2000] 1 Cr. App. R. (S.) 285, CA (Crim Div) . . . .   *Digested,* 00/**1436**
R. *v.* James (Martin Sylvester) see R. *v.* Williams (Derek Anthony)
R. *v.* James (Walter Joseph) [2000] Crim. L.R. 571; *Times,* May 9, 2000; *Independent,*
    May 11, 2000, CA (Crim Div) . . . .   *Digested,* 00/**904**
R. *v.* Jamil (Mohammed Ali) [2001] EWCA Crim 1687; *Times,* October 25, 2001, CA
    (Crim Div) . . . .   *Digested,* 01/**987**
R. *v.* Jane (Douglas Graham) [1998] 2 Cr. App. R. (S.) 363, CA (Crim Div) . . . .   *Digested,* 99/**1178**
R. *v.* Janjua (Nadeem Ahmed); R. *v.* Choudhury (Mifta) [1999] 1 Cr. App. R. 91;
    [1998] Crim. L.R. 675; *Times,* May 8, 1998, CA (Crim Div) . . . .   *Digested,* 98/**1053**
R. *v.* Jarpur (Keith John) see R. *v.* Fenlon (Michael William)
R. *v.* Jarrett (John Gordon) [2000] 2 Cr. App. R. (S.) 166, CA (Crim Div) . . . .   *Digested,* 00/**1437**
R. *v.* Jarvis (Martin) see R. *v.* Howells (Craig)
R. *v.* Jauncey (Jeffrey James) (1986) 8 Cr. App. R. (S.) 401; [1987] Crim. L.R. 215,
    CA (Crim Div) . . . .   *Digested,* 88/**901**:
                                                     Considered, 00/1184
R. *v.* Jefferson (Peter John) see R. *v.* Wild (Michael Keith) (No.2)
R. *v.* Jefferson (Peter John) [2001] EWCA Crim 1278, CA (Crim Div)
R. *v.* Jeffries (Tony Brisbane McEwan) see R. *v.* Chalkley (Tony Michael)
R. *v.* Jenkins (Ian) see Attorney General's Reference (No.92 of 2000), Re
R. *v.* Jenkins (Norman) [1998] Crim. L.R. 411, CA (Crim Div)
R. *v.* Jennison (Colin Albert) see Attorney General's Reference (No.84 of 1999), Re
R. *v.* Jepson (Lawrence) see Attorney General's Reference (No.8 of 1991), Re
R. *v.* Jeraj [1994] Crim. L.R. 595, CA (Crim Div) . . . .   *Digested,* 95/**1262**:
                                                     Followed, 01/1046
R. *v.* Jerome (Eccles) [2001] 1 Cr. App. R. (S.) 92, CA (Crim Div) . . . .   *Digested,* 01/**1341**
R. *v.* Jesson (Gary Martin) [2000] 2 Cr. App. R. (S.) 200, CA (Crim Div) . . . .   *Digested,* 00/**1386**
R. *v.* Jewitt (Andrew Mark) see Attorney General's Reference (Nos.8 and 9 of 1997),
    Re
R. *v.* Jewitt (Nicholas Ian) see Attorney General's Reference (Nos.8 and 9 of 1997), Re
R. *v.* Jewsbury (Barry) (1983) 3 Cr. App. R. (S.) 1, CA (Crim Div) . . . .   *Considered,*
                                                        83/764.35,
                                                        84/887, 00/1363

R. *v.* JF Alford Transport Ltd; R. *v.* Alford (James); R. *v.* Payne (Alex Peter) [1997] 2
    Cr. App. R. 326; [1999] R.T.R. 51; [1997] Crim. L.R. 745; (1997) 94(15) L.S.G.
    26; (1997) 141 S.J.L.B. 73; *Times*, March 31, 1997, CA (Crim Div) . . . .   *Digested,* 97/**4364**
R. *v.* JH [2000] 1 Cr. App. R. (S.) 551, CA (Crim Div) . . . .   *Digested,* 00/**1260**
R. *v.* JK [1999] Crim. L.R. 740, CA (Crim Div)
R. *v.* JMG [1986] 33 D.L.R. (4th) 277, CA (Ont) . . . .   *Followed,* 99/3120
R. *v.* JN see Attorney General's Reference (No.75 of 1998), Re
R. *v.* JO'B (A Juvenile) see Attorney General's Reference (Nos.59, 60 and 63 of 1998),
    Re
R. *v.* Johnson (Adrian) [1998] 1 Cr. App. R. (S.) 126; [1997] Crim. L.R. 609, CA (Crim
    Div) . . . .   *Digested,* 98/**1159**:
                         Cited, 00/1264: *Considered,* 00/1284, 00/1304: *Doubted,* 01/1243
R. *v.* Johnson (Andrew Phillip) [1998] 1 Cr. App. R. (S.) 169, CA (Crim Div) . . . .   *Digested,* 98/**1324**
R. *v.* Johnson (Brett Daniel) [1998] 2 Cr. App. R. (S.) 453, CA (Crim Div) . . . .   *Digested,* 99/**1319**
R. *v.* Johnson (Brian) see R. *v.* Sinclair (James)
R. *v.* Johnson (David Angus) (1994) 15 Cr. App. R. (S.) 827; [1994] Crim. L.R. 537,
    CA (Crim Div) . . . .   *Digested,* 95/**1469**:
                                             Considered, 98/1135
R. *v.* Johnson (Harold Robert) [2001] 1 Cr. App. R. 26; [2001] Crim. L.R. 125; *Times,*
    November 21, 2000; *Independent,* December 7, 2000, CA (Crim Div) . . . .   *Digested,* 00/**1023**
R. *v.* Johnson (Henry) see R. *v.* Smith (Patrick Joseph)
R. *v.* Johnson (Jason Leon) see Attorney General's Reference (No.36 of 1996), Re
R. *v.* Johnson (Mark Anthony) [1996] 2 Cr. App. R. (S.) 228, CA (Crim Div) . . . .   *Digested,* 96/**1901**:
                                    Distinguished, 98/1231
R. *v.* Johnson (Martin Clive) see Attorney General's Reference (No.48 of 2000), Re
R. *v.* Johnson (Orville Alexander) see R. *v.* Rose (Newton Samuel)
R. *v.* Johnson (Peter Lloyd) (1993) 14 Cr. App. R. (S.) 661, CA (Crim Div) . . . .   *Digested,* 94/**1313**:
                                      Considered, 01/1437
R. *v.* Johnson (Randolph Egbert) (No.1) see R. *v.* Davis (Michael George) (No.1)
R. *v.* Johnson (Randolph Egbert) (No.2) see R. *v.* Davis (Michael George) (No.2)
R. *v.* Johnson (Randolph Egbert) (No.3) see R. *v.* Davis (Michael George) (No.3)
R. *v.* Johnson (Ronald William) see R. *v.* Main (Ronald Alan)
R. (on the application of East Riding of Yorkshire Council) *v.* Joint Committee for the
    Purpose of Making Appointments to the Humberside Police Authority; *sub nom*
    R. *v.* Joint Committee for the Purpose of Making Appointments to the
    Humberside Police Authority Ex p. East Riding of Yorkshire Council (2001) 3
    L.G.L.R. 46; [2001] B.L.G.R. 292; [2001] A.C.D. 44, QBD (Admin Ct) . . . .   *Digested,* 01/**4786**
R. *v.* Joint Committee for the Purpose of Making Appointments to the Humberside
    Police Authority Ex p. East Riding of Yorkshire Council see R. (on the application
    of East Riding of Yorkshire Council) *v.* Joint Committee for the Purpose of
    Making Appointments to the Humberside Police Authority
R. *v.* Jones (Anthony Russell) see Attorney General's Reference (No.91 of 2001), Re
R. *v.* Jones (Anthony William) (Post Judgment Discussion); *sub nom* R. *v.* Haywood
    (John Victor) (Post Judgment discussion); R. *v.* Purvis (Paul Nigel) (Post
    Judgment Discussion); R. *v.* Hayward (John Victor) (Post Judgment
    Discussion); 200000830/X3, 199906468/X4, 200002586/Y3, CA (Crim Div)   *Digested,* 01/**1194**
R. *v.* Jones (Anthony William) (Absence of Defendant at Trial); *sub nom* R. *v.* Haywood
    (John Victor) (Absence of Defendant at Trial); R. *v.* Hayward (John Victor)
    (Absence of Defendant at Trial); R. *v.* Purvis (Paul Nigel) (Absence of Defendant
    at Trial); TNS, HL; affirming [2001] EWCA Crim 168; [2001] Q.B. 862; [2001] 3
    W.L.R. 125; [2001] 2 Cr. App. R. 11; (2001) 165 J.P. 281; [2001] Crim. L.R.
    502; (2001) 165 J.P.N. 665; (2001) 98(9) L.S.G. 38; (2001) 145 S.J.L.B. 53;
    Times, February 14, 2001; *Independent,* February 8, 2001, CA (Crim Div) . . . . . .   *Digested,* 01/**1196**
R. *v.* Jones (Beatrice) [1999] Crim. L.R. 820, CA (Crim Div)
R. *v.* Jones (Christopher Glen) [1999] 1 Cr. App. R. (S.) 427, CA (Crim Div) . . . .   *Digested,* 99/**1066**
R. *v.* Jones (Derek); R. *v.* Nelson (Gary) (1999) 96(18) L.S.G. 33; (1999) 143 S.J.L.B.
    122; *Times,* April 21, 1999, CA (Crim Div) . . . .   *Digested,* 99/**872**
R. *v.* Jones (Douglas Leary), *Times,* February 17, 1999, CA (Crim Div) . . . .   *Digested,* 99/**1059**
R. *v.* Jones (Fiona); R. *v.* Whicher (Desmond) [1999] 2 Cr. App. R. 253; (2000) 2
    L.G.L.R. 157, CA (Crim Div) . . . .   *Digested,* 99/**1939**
R. *v.* Jones (Jason) see Attorney General's Reference (No.78 of 2000), Re
R. *v.* Jones (Jason Robert) see Attorney General's Reference (Nos.62, 63, 64 and 65
    of 1996), Re
R. *v.* Jones (John McKinsie); R. *v.* Tomlinson (Eric); R. *v.* Warren (Dennis Michael); R. *v.*
    O'Shea (Kenneth Desmond); R. *v.* Carpenter (John); R. *v.* Llywarch (John
    Elfyn) (1974) 59 Cr. App. R. 120; [1974] I.C.R. 310; [1974] I.R.L.R. 117; [1974]
    Crim. L.R. 663; 118 S.J. 277, CA (Crim Div) . . . .   *Digested,* 74/**670**:
                      Applied, 79/592, 83/2333, 84/2110: *Considered,* 98/1032
R. *v.* Jones (Jonathan Huw) [1998] 2 Cr. App. R. 53, CA (Crim Div) . . . .   *Digested,* 98/**992**
R. *v.* Jones (Karl David) see Attorney General's Reference (No.58 of 1996), Re
R. *v.* Jones (Keith) (1997) 161 J.P. 597; [1998] Crim. L.R. 56; (1997) 161 J.P.N. 838;
    Times, April 24, 1997; *Independent,* April 28, 1997 (C.S.), CA
R. *v.* Jones (Kerry Mervin) [1998] Crim. L.R. 579, CA (Crim Div)
R. *v.* Jones (Lesley) see Attorney General's Reference (Nos.57, 58 and 59 of 1997), Re

R. *v.* Jones (Neil Andrew) see Attorney General's Reference (No.89 of 2000), Re
R. *v.* Jones (Robert Edward) (No.1) [1971] 2 Q.B. 456; [1971] 2 W.L.R. 1485; [1971] 2
    All E.R. 731; (1971) 55 Cr. App. R. 321; 115 S.J. 286, CA (Crim Div) . . . .   *Digested,* 71/**9003**:
                                                 Not applied, 01/1096
R. *v.* Jones (Ronald Gordon) (1990) 12 Cr. App. R. (S.) 233, CA (Crim Div) . . . .   *Digested,* 92/**1135**:
                                     Considered, 95/1320, 00/1136
R. *v.* Jones (Russell Thomas) [1999] 1 Cr. App. R. (S.) 473, CA (Crim Div) . . . .   *Digested,* 99/**1180**:
                                         Considered, 00/1261
R. *v.* Jones (Stephen David), *Times,* May 20, 1999, CA (Crim Div) . . . .   *Digested,* 99/**977**
R. *v.* Jones (Stephen John) see Attorney General's Reference (No.17 of 1990), Re
R. *v.* Jones (Stephen Michael) see Attorney General's Reference (No.48 of 1998), Re
R. *v.* Jones (Steven Martin) [1997] 1 Cr. App. R. 86; (1997) 33 B.M.L.R. 80; *Times,*
    July 23, 1996, CA (Crim Div) . . . .   *Digested,* 96/**1371**:
                                          Considered, 00/903
R. *v.* Jones (William) see R. *v.* L (Deferred Sentence)
R. *v.* Jordan (River) see R. *v.* Jordon (River)
R. *v.* Jordan (Shirley) see R. *v.* Lambert (Steven)
R. *v.* Jordon (River); *sub nom* R. *v.* Jordan (River) [1998] 2 Cr. App. R. (S.) 83;
    [1998] Crim. L.R. 353, CA (Crim Div) . . . .   *Digested,* 98/**1147**:
                                          Applied, 01/1488
R. *v.* Jorge (Manuel) [1999] 2 Cr. App. R. (S.) 1, CA (Crim Div) . . . .   *Digested,* 99/**1102**
R. *v.* Jory (Stephen) see R. *v.* Pain (Roy)
R. *v.* JP [1999] Crim. L.R. 401, CA (Crim Div)
R. *v.* JT (False Instruments) see Attorney General's Reference (No.1 of 2000), Re
R. *v.* JT (Indecent Assault: Sentencing) [2001] 1 Cr. App. R. (S.) 60; [2000] Crim.
    L.R. 866, CA (Crim Div) . . . .   *Digested,* 01/**1363**
R. *v.* JW [2000] 1 Cr. App. R. (S.) 234, CA (Crim Div) . . . .   *Digested,* 00/**1283**:
                                          Considered, 01/1371
R. *v.* K (Age of Consent: Reasonable Belief); *sub nom* CPS *v.* K (Age of Consent:
    Reasonable Belief) [2001] UKHL 41; [2001] 3 W.L.R. 471; [2001] 3 All E.R. 897;
    [2001] 3 F.C.R. 115; (2001) 98(34) L.S.G. 39; (2001) 145 S.J.L.B. 202; *Times,*
    July 26, 2001; *Independent,* July 27, 2001; *Daily Telegraph,* July 31, 2001, HL;
    reversing [2001] 1 Cr. App. R. 35; [2001] Crim. L.R. 134; (2000) 97(44) L.S.G.
    44; (2000) 144 S.J.L.B. 272; *Times,* November 7, 2000; *Independent,*
    November 8, 2000, CA (Crim Div) . . . .   *Digested,* 01/**1070**
R. *v.* K (Anthony) (A Juvenile) see R. *v.* T (Jean Pierre) (A Juvenile)
R. *v.* K (Corroboration) [1999] Crim. L.R. 980; *Times,* July 16, 1999, CA (Crim Div) . . . .   *Digested,* 99/**876**
R. *v.* K (Gary Francis) (A Juvenile) [2001] EWCA Crim 1030; [2001] Crim. L.R. 583,
    CA (Crim Div)
R. *v.* K (Imran) (A Juvenile) see Attorney General's Reference (Nos.7, 8, 9 and 10 of
    2000), Re
R. *v.* K (Michael John) (1995) 16 Cr. App. R. (S.) 966, CA (Crim Div) . . . .   *Considered,* 99/1301
R. *v.* K (Vincent James) [1998] 2 Cr. App. R. (S.) 368, CA (Crim Div) . . . .   *Digested,* 99/**1100**
R. *v.* Kallaway (Ronald) [1998] 2 Cr. App. R. (S.) 228, CA (Crim Div) . . . .   *Digested,* 98/**1367**:
                                           Considered, 99/1322
R. *v.* Kamar (Mete), *Times,* May 14, 1999, CA (Crim Div) . . . .   *Digested,* 99/**1022**:
                                          Applied, 00/5480
R. *v.* Kandola (Sundar Singh) (1987) 9 Cr. App. R. (S.) 162, CA (Crim Div) . . . .   *Digested,* 89/**1125**:
                                          Considered, 00/1438
R. *v.* Kanesarajah (Rajaratnam) see R. *v.* Naillie (Yabu Hurerali)
R. *v.* Kansal (Rupe Lal) see R. *v.* Graham (Hemamali Krishna)
R. *v.* Kansal (Yash Pal) (No.2) see R. *v.* Kansal (Yash Pal) (Change of Law)
R. *v.* Kansal (Yash Pal) [1993] Q.B. 244; [1992] 3 W.L.R. 494; [1992] 3 All E.R. 844;
    [1992] B.C.C. 615; [1992] B.C.L.C. 1009; (1992) 95 Cr. App. R. 348; (1992)
    89(27) L.S.G. 35; (1992) 142 N.L.J. 715; (1992) 136 S.J.L.B. 146; *Times,* May
    15, 1992; *Independent,* May 14, 1992; *Financial Times,* June 5, 1992; *Guardian,*
    June 3, 1992, CA (Crim Div) . . . .   *Digested,* 92/**979**:
                                      Subsequent proceedings, 01/1113
R. *v.* Kansal (Yash Pal) (Change of Law); *sub nom* R. *v.* Kansal (Yash Pal) (No.2)
    [2001] UKHL 62; [2001] 3 W.L.R. 1562; (2001) 145 S.J.L.B. 275; *Times,*
    December 4, 2001; *Independent,* December 4, 2001; *Daily Telegraph,* December
    6, 2001, HL; reversing [2001] EWCA Crim 1260; [2001] 3 W.L.R. 751; [2001] 2
    Cr. App. R. 30; (2001) 98(28) L.S.G. 43; (2001) 145 S.J.L.B. 157; *Times,* June
    11, 2001; *Independent,* June 6, 2001, CA (Crim Div) . . . .   *Digested,* 01/**1113**:
                                      Previous proceedings, 92/979
R. *v.* Karunaratne (Susantha Frederick); R. *v.* Whitnall (Steven John) (1983) 5 Cr. App.
    R. (S.) 2; [1983] Crim. L.R. 338, CA (Crim Div) . . . .   *Digested,* 84/**774**:
                       Cited, 94/1292: *Considered,* 86/840, 92/1324, 98/1300
R. *v.* Kashioulis (Adonis) [2001] EWCA Crim 235; [2001] E.H.L.R. 20, CA (Crim Div) . .   *Digested,* 01/**2834**
R. *v.* Kaul (Natasha); R. *v.* Collin (Peter John) [1998] Crim. L.R. 135; *Times,* November
    10, 1997, CA (Crim Div) . . . .   *Digested,* 97/**1169**
R. *v.* Kavanagh (John William) [1998] 1 Cr. App. R. (S.) 241, CA (Crim Div) . . . .   *Digested,* 98/**1166**:
                                            Considered, 00/1374
R. *v.* Kavanagh (Peter Dennis) see Attorney General's Reference (No.18 of 1993), Re

R. *v.* Kay (Joseph Brian) (1980) 2 Cr. App. R. (S.) 284, CA (Crim Div) . . . .   *Followed,* 98/1322:
            Referred to, 96/2064
R. *v.* Kayani (Abdul Hamid) [1997] 2 Cr. App. R. (S.) 313, CA (Crim Div) . . . .   *Digested,* 98/**1312**
R. *v.* Kayar (Sakir) [1998] 2 Cr. App. R. (S.) 355, CA (Crim Div) . . . .   *Digested,* 99/**1129**
R. *v.* Kaye see R. *v.* Genese
R. *v.* Kaynak (Hussein); R. *v.* Honz (Tomas); R. *v.* Simsek (Muslum); R. *v.* Aksu (Ali)
    [1998] 2 Cr. App. R. (S.) 283, CA (Crim Div) . . . .   *Digested,* 98/**1185**
R. *v.* KB see Attorney General's Reference (No.47 of 1999), Re
R. *v.* KB (A Juvenile); *sub nom* R. *v.* B (Kyle Mark) (A Juvenile) [2001] 1 Cr. App. R.
    (S.) 125; (2000) 164 J.P. 714; (2000) 164 J.P.N. 958, CA (Crim Div) . . . .   *Digested,* 01/**1460**
R. *v.* Keach (Walter Stacy); R. *v.* Steele (Deborah) (1984) 6 Cr. App. R. (S.) 402;
    [1985] Crim. L.R. 329, CA (Crim Div) . . . .   *Digested,* 85/**803**:
            Considered, 00/1233
R. *v.* Keane (Simon Wallace) [2001] F.S.R. 7, CA (Crim Div) . . . .   *Digested,* 01/**1014**
R. *v.* Keane (Stephen John) [1994] 1 W.L.R. 746; [1994] 2 All E.R. 478; (1994) 99 Cr.
    App. R. 1; [1995] Crim. L.R. 225; (1994) 144 N.L.J. 391; (1994) 138 S.J.L.B. 75;
    Times, March 15, 1994; *Independent,* March 16, 1994, CA (Crim Div) . . . .   *Digested,* 94/**876**:
         Applied, 94/872, 94/873, 95/1097, 95/1102, 96/1359, 97/1342, 00/5464:
            Considered, 94/881, 95/1106, 95/1168: *Disapproved,* 00/1059
R. *v.* Keaney (Leo Simon) [2001] 1 Cr. App. R. (S.) 37, CA (Crim Div) . . . .   *Digested,* 01/**1422**
R. *v.* Keast (Nigel Anthony) [1998] Crim. L.R. 748, CA (Crim Div)
R. *v.* Keegan (Anthony) see Attorney General's Reference (No.80 of 2000), Re
R. *v.* Keegstra [1990] 3 S.C.R. 697, Sup Ct (Can)   *Applied,* 99/3106
R. *v.* Keenan (Graham) [1990] 2 Q.B. 54; [1989] 3 W.L.R. 1193; [1989] 3 All E.R.
    598; (1990) 90 Cr. App. R. 1; (1990) 154 J.P. 67; [1989] Crim. L.R. 720; (1989)
    153 J.P.N. 802; (1990) 87(1) L.S.G. 30; (1990) 134 S.J. 114; *Times,* May 1,
    1989; *Independent,* May 15, 1989 (C.S.); *Daily Telegraph,* May 5, 1989, CA (Crim
    Div) . . . .   *Digested,* 90/**813**:
         Applied, 89/684, 90/817: *Considered,* 91/663, 92/978: *Distinguished,* 00/923
R. *v.* Kellam Ex p. South Wales Police Authority [2000] I.C.R. 632; *Times,* August 24,
    1999 ; *Independent,* July 26, 1999 (C.S.), QBD . . . .   *Digested,* 99/**4299**:
            Followed, 01/4778
R. *v.* Kelly (Anthony Noel); R. *v.* Lindsay (Neil) [1999] Q.B. 621; [1999] 2 W.L.R. 384;
    [1998] 3 All E.R. 741; (2000) 51 B.M.L.R. 142; *Times,* May 21, 1998;
    Independent, June 4, 1998, CA (Crim Div) . . . .   *Digested,* 98/**979**
R. *v.* Kelly (Edward) (No.1) see Attorney General's Reference (No.53 of 1998), Re
R. *v.* Kelly (Edward) (No.2) [2001] EWCA Crim 1751; [2001] Crim. L.R. 836, CA
    (Crim Div) . . . .   *Previous proceedings,*
            99/1249
R. *v.* Kelly (Lewis); R. *v.* D (Miles) (A Juvenile) [2001] EWCA Crim 170; [2001] 2 Cr.
    App. R. (S.) 73; [2001] Crim. L.R. 411, CA (Crim Div) . . . .   *Digested,* 01/**1191**
R. *v.* Kelly (Liam Paul) (1998) 162 J.P. 231; (1998) 162 J.P.N. 243; *Times,* February
    23, 1998, CA (Crim Div) . . . .   *Digested,* 98/**903**:
            Applied, 99/889
R. *v.* Kelly (Martin Patrick) (Forfeiture) 99/5255/Y3, CA (Crim Div) . . . .   *Previous proceedings,*
            00/1171
R. *v.* Kelly (Martin Patrick) (Confiscation Order) [2000] 2 Cr. App. R. (S.) 129; [2000]
    Crim. L.R. 392, CA (Crim Div) . . . .   *Digested,* 00/**1171**
R. *v.* Kelly (Michael) [1996] 1 Cr. App. R. (S.) 61, CA (Crim Div) . . . .   *Considered,* 99/1276
R. *v.* Kelly (Robert Joseph) [2001] R.T.R. 5, CA (Crim Div) . . . .   *Digested,* 01/**1488**
R. *v.* Keltbray Ltd [2001] 1 Cr. App. R. (S.) 39, CA (Crim Div) . . . .   *Digested,* 01/**1350**
R. *v.* Kendrick (Kathleen); R. *v.* Hopkins (Richard Mark) [1997] 2 Cr. App. R. 524;
    [1997] Crim. L.R. 359, CA (Crim Div) . . . .   *Digested,* 98/**1065**
R. *v.* Kennedy (Michael David Philip) [1999] 1 Cr. App. R. 54; [1998] Crim. L.R. 739,
    CA (Crim Div) . . . .   *Digested,* 99/**974**
R. *v.* Kennedy (Simon) [1999] Crim. L.R. 65, CA (Crim Div)
R. *v.* Kennet DC Ex p. Somerfield Property Co Ltd [1999] J.P.L. 361; [1999] Env. L.R.
    D13, QBD . . . .   *Digested,* 99/**4242**
R. *v.* Kennion (Patricia) [1997] R.T.R. 421, CA (Crim Div) . . . .   *Digested,* 98/**1358**
R. *v.* Kenny (Peter Dean) [1996] 1 Cr. App. R. (S.) 397; [1995] Crim. L.R. 964, CA
    (Crim Div) . . . .   *Digested,* 96/**1741**:
            Considered, 98/1148
R. *v.* Kensington and Chelsea RLBC Ex p. Bayani (1990) 22 H.L.R. 406; *Times,* June 1,
    1990; *Guardian,* June 7, 1990, CA; reversing (1989) 21 H.L.R. 580, QBD . . . . . .   *Digested,* 91/**1897**:
         Applied, 92/2247, 00/3144: *Considered,* 95/2556: *Followed,* 96/3068
R. *v.* Kensington and Chelsea RLBC Ex p. Byfield; R. *v.* Kensington and Chelsea RLBC
    Ex p. Rouass (1999) 31 H.L.R. 913, QBD . . . .   *Digested,* 00/**3128**:
            Overruled, 01/3436
R. *v.* Kensington and Chelsea RLBC Ex p. Eminian, *Times,* August 17, 2000;
    Independent, October 23, 2000 (C.S), QBD . . . .   *Digested,* 00/**3006**

R. v. Kensington and Chelsea RLBC Ex p. Kujtim [1999] 4 All E.R. 161; (2000) 32 H.L.R. 579; [1999] B.L.G.R. 761; (1999) 2 C.C.L. Rep. 340; (1999) 96(31) L.S.G. 41; *Times*, August 5, 1999 ; *Independent*, October 4, 1999, CA; affirming *Times*, April 20, 1999, QBD . . . . *Digested*, 99/**3052**:

Applied, 01/5132

R. v. Kensington and Chelsea RLBC Ex p. Lawrie Plantation Services Ltd [1999] 1 W.L.R. 1415; [1999] 3 All E.R. 929; (2000) 79 P. & C.R. 467; [1999] 3 P.L.R. 138; [2000] J.P.L. 181; [1999] E.G.C.S. 100; [1999] N.P.C. 86; *Times*, July 12, 1999 ; *Independent*, July 13, 1999, HL; reversing [1998] 1 P.L.R. 109; [1998] E.G.C.S. 3; [1998] N.P.C. 2; *Times*, January 21, 1998, CA; affirming (1997) 74 P. & C.R. 270; [1997] J.P.L. 997; [1997] N.P.C. 30, QBD . . . . *Digested*, 99/**4180**

R. v. Kensington and Chelsea RLBC Ex p. Rouass see R. v. Kensington and Chelsea RLBC Ex p. Byfield

R. v. Kensington and Chelsea RLBC Ex p. Silchenstedt (1997) 29 H.L.R. 728, QBD . . . . *Digested*, 98/**3022**

R. v. Kensington and Chelsea RLBC Ex p. Waddell; *sub nom* Waddell v. Kensington and Chelsea RLBC (2000) 2 L.G.L.R. 105; (2000) 79 P. & C.R. 567; (1999) 96(15) L.S.G. 31; *Times*, April 30, 1999, QBD . . . . *Digested*, 99/**2928**

R. (on the application of Hartley) v. Kensington and Chelsea RLBC Rent Officer [2001] EWHC Admin 291; (2001) 98(12) L.S.G. 45, QBD (Admin Ct)

R. v. Kensington Income Tax Commissioners Ex p. Princess Edmond de Polignac [1917] 1 K.B. 486, CA . . . . *Applied*, 56/2160,

81/1183, 81/2089, 81/2147, 82/1335, 94/3526: *Distinguished*, 00/5780:

Followed, 87/3021, 89/3030

R. v. Kent (Anthony) [1996] 2 Cr. App. R. (S.) 381, CA (Crim Div) . . . . *Digested*, 97/**1538**:

Considered, 99/1162

R. v. Kent CC Ex p. AMS (A Minor) [2000] Ed. C.R. 68; [2000] E.L.R. 209, QBD . . . . . *Digested*, 00/**1940**

R. v. Kent CC Ex p. C [1998] E.L.R. 108, QBD . . . . *Digested*, 98/**1913**

R. v. Kent CC Ex p. Pierre see R. v. Kent CC Ex p. S

R. v. Kent CC Ex p. S; R. v. Kent CC Ex p. Pierre [2000] 1 F.L.R. 155; [1999] 3 F.C.R. 193; (2000) 3 C.C.L. Rep. 38; [2000] Fam. Law 15, QBD . . . . *Digested*, 99/**4629**:

Followed, 01/4374

R. v. Kent Youth Court Ex p. K see R. v. Dover Youth Court Ex p. K

R. v. Kerr (Fitness to Plead) see R. v. M (Fitness to Plead)

R. v. Kerr (Trevor John) [1998] 2 Cr. App. R. (S.) 316, CA (Crim Div) . . . . *Digested*, 98/**1320**

R. v. Kerswell (John William) see Attorney General's Reference (No.57 of 1998), Re

R. v. Kesler (Justin) [2001] EWCA Crim 825; [2001] 2 Cr. App. R. (S.) 126; [2001] Crim. L.R. 582, CA (Crim Div) . . . . *Digested*, 01/**1287**

R. v. Kettering Justices Ex p. MRB Insurance Brokers Ltd see R. v. Kettering Magistrates Court Ex p. MRB Insurance Brokers Ltd

R. v. Kettering Magistrates Court Ex p. MRB Insurance Brokers Ltd; *sub nom* R. v. Kettering Justices Ex p. MRB Insurance Brokers Ltd [2000] 2 All E.R. (Comm) 353; (2000) 164 J.P. 585; [2000] C.C.L.R. 51; (2000) 164 J.P.N. 762; (2000) 97(20) L.S.G. 43; *Times*, May 12, 2000; *Independent*, May 15, 2000 (C.S.), QBD

R. v. Kewell (David Edward) [2000] 2 Cr. App. R. (S.) 38, CA (Crim Div) . . . . *Digested*, 00/**1139**

R. v. Keyes (Anthony Matthew); R. v. Edjedewe (Thomas); R. v. Chapman (Lorraine) [2000] 2 Cr. App. R. 181; [2000] Crim. L.R. 571; (2000) 97(14) L.S.G. 41; (2000) 144 S.J.L.B. 187; *Times*, April 5, 2000, CA (Crim Div) . . . . *Digested*, 00/**1097**

R. v. Keyte (David Andrew) [1998] 2 Cr. App. R. (S.) 165, CA (Crim Div) . . . . *Digested*, 98/**1332**

R. v. KH (A Juvenile) [2001] EWCA Crim 246; [2001] 2 Cr. App. R. (S.) 55, CA (Crim Div) . . . . *Digested*, 01/**1404**

R. v. Khan (Amjad Ahmed); R. v. Khan (Iftikhar Ahmed) [2000] E.H.L.R. Dig. 396, CA (Crim Div)

R. v. Khan (Iftikhar Ahmed) see R. v. Khan (Amjad Ahmed)

R. v. Khan (Jahan Zeb) see Attorney General's Reference (No.7 of 1992), Re

R. v. Khan (Jahinger) [2001] EWCA Crim 912; [2001] 2 Cr. App. R. (S.) 129; (2001) 82 P. & C.R. D15, CA (Crim Div) . . . . *Digested*, 01/**1293**

R. v. Khan (Khalid Mahmood) [2000] 2 Cr. App. R. (S.) 76; [2000] Crim. L.R. 202, CA (Crim Div) . . . . *Digested*, 00/**1163**

R. v. Khan (Nashad) (1990) 12 Cr. App. R. (S.) 352, CA (Crim Div) . . . . *Digested*, 92/**1383**:

Cited, 96/1840: *Considered*, 98/1371

R. v. Khan (Nazaqat); R. v. H (Tahir); H (Jangheer); H (Kadeer) [2001] EWCA Crim 104; [2001] 2 Cr. App. R. (S.) 59, CA (Crim Div) . . . . *Digested*, 01/**1457**

R. v. Khan (Rungzabe); R. v. Khan (Tahir) [1998] Crim. L.R. 830; *Times*, April 7, 1998; *Independent*, March 25, 1998, CA (Crim Div) . . . . *Digested*, 98/**958**

R. v. Khan (Sakina Bibi); R. v. Bashir (Mohammed) [1999] 1 Cr. App. R. (S.) 329, CA (Crim Div) . . . . *Digested*, 99/**1247**

R. v. Khan (Shakeel) [2001] EWCA Crim 486; [2001] Crim. L.R. 673, CA (Crim Div)

R. v. Khan (Sultan) [1997] A.C. 558; [1996] 3 W.L.R. 162; [1996] 3 All E.R. 289;
    [1996] 2 Cr. App. R. 440; [1996] Crim. L.R. 733; (1996) 93(28) L.S.G. 29;
    (1996) 146 N.L.J. 1024; (1996) 140 S.J.L.B. 166; *Times*, July 5, 1996;
    Independent, July 11, 1996, HL; affirming [1995] Q.B. 27; [1994] 3 W.L.R. 899;
    [1994] 4 All E.R. 426; [1995] 1 Cr. App. R. 242; [1994] Crim. L.R. 830;
    (1994) 91(27) L.S.G. 37; (1994) 144 N.L.J. 863; (1994) 138 S.J.L.B. 128; *Times*,
    June 1, 1994; *Independent*, June 14, 1994, CA (Crim Div) . . . . *Digested*, 96/**1321**:
              Applied, 01/3299: *Considered*, 00/921: *Followed*, 00/303
R. v. Khan (Tahir) see R. v. Khan (Rungzabe)
R. v. Khan (Touriq) (1995) 16 Cr. App. R. (S.) 180; [1994] Crim. L.R. 862, CA (Crim
    Div) . . . . *Digested*, 96/**2066**:
              Applied, 96/2072: *Considered*, 01/1269
R. v. Kidd (Philip Richard); R. v. Canavan (Darren Anthony); R. v. Shaw (Dennis)
    [1998] 1 W.L.R. 604; [1998] 1 All E.R. 42; [1998] 1 Cr. App. R. 79; [1998] 1 Cr.
    App. R. (S.) 243; (1997) 161 J.P. 709; [1997] Crim. L.R. 766; (1997) 161 J.P.N.
    838; (1997) 94(35) L.S.G. 33; (1997) 147 N.L.J. 1457; (1997) 141 S.J.L.B. 169;
    Times, July 21, 1997, CA (Crim Div) . . . . *Digested*, 97/**1492**:
              Considered, 98/1387, 99/1351, 99/1352
R. v. Killgallon (Leonard Arthur); R. v. Gray (Shane) [1998] 1 Cr. App. R. (S.) 279, CA
    (Crim Div) . . . . *Digested*, 98/**1123**
R. v. Kilty (Stephen) see R. v. Chisholm (John)
R. v. Kimber (David Patrick) (No.2) [2001] Crim. L.R. 897, CA (Crim Div)
R. v. Kime (Darren John) [1999] 2 Cr. App. R. (S.) 3, CA (Crim Div) . . . . *Digested*, 99/**1261**
R. v. King [1997] Crim. L.R. 298, CA (Crim Div) . . . . *Considered*, 99/1299
R. v. King (Ashley) [2000] 2 Cr. App. R. 391; [2000] Crim. L.R. 835, CA (Crim Div) . . . *Digested*, 01/**1171**
R. v. King (Brian) see R. v. Mitchell (Frank)
R. v. King (Dianne Susan) (1990) 12 Cr. App. R. (S.) 76, CA (Crim Div) . . . . *Considered*, 96/1708,
              00/1154
R. v. King (James George) [2000] 1 Cr. App. R. (S.) 105, CA (Crim Div) . . . . *Digested*, 00/**1174**
R. v. King (Mark Barrie) [2001] EWCA Crim 709; [2001] 2 Cr. App. R. (S.) 114;
    [2001] Crim. L.R. 493, CA (Crim Div) . . . . *Digested*, 01/**1225**
R. v. King (Martin John) see R. v. Brown (Raymond John)
R. v. King (Michael) see Attorney General's Reference (No.90 of 2000), Re
R. v. King (Michael John) [1999] 2 Cr. App. R. (S.) 376, CA (Crim Div) . . . . *Digested*, 00/**1396**
R. v. King (Michael Shaun) (1986) 82 Cr. App. R. 120; (1985) 7 Cr. App. R. (S.) 227;
    [1985] Crim. L.R. 748, CA (Crim Div) . . . . *Digested*, 86/**861**:
        Applied, 99/1126: *Considered*, 88/987, 98/1205: *Followed*, 97/1587:
              Referred to, 90/1408
R. v. King (Richard) (1987) 9 Cr. App. R. (S.) 173, CA (Crim Div) . . . . *Digested*, 89/**938**:
              Considered, 98/1180
R. v. King (Samuel Nathaniel) (1995) 16 Cr. App. R. (S.) 987; [1995] Crim. L.R. 580,
    CA (Crim Div) . . . . *Digested*, 96/**2065**:
         Cited, 00/1264: *Considered*, 97/1585, 00/1284, 01/1453:
              Distinguished, 98/1159
R. v. Kingham (Lee Robert) (1995) 16 Cr. App. R. (S.) 399, CA (Crim Div) . . . . *Considered*, 98/1203
R. v. Kingsnorth (Glyn Kevin) see R. v. Sparks (Seth Joseph)
R. v. Kingston (Thomas) see R. v. Drury (Christopher)
R. v. Kingston City Council Ex p. Baker see R. v. Birmingham City Council Ex p. Ireland
R. v. Kingston City Council Ex p. Hall see R. v. Birmingham City Council Ex p. Ireland
R. (on the application of Inland Revenue Commissioners) v. Kingston Crown Court
    [2001] EWHC Admin 581; [2001] 4 All E.R. 721; [2001] S.T.C. 1615; [2001]
    B.T.C. 322; [2001] S.T.I. 1240, QBD (Admin Ct) . . . . *Digested*, 01/**734**
R. v. Kingston Crown Court Ex p. B (A Juvenile) (2000) 164 J.P. 633; (2000) 164
    J.P.N. 901, QBD . . . . *Digested*, 00/**1077**
R. v. Kingston Crown Court Ex p. Mason CO 4566/97, QBD . . . . *Digested*, 98/**1356**
R. (on the application of Rhodes) v. Kingston upon Hull City Council [2001] E.L.R. 230,
    QBD . . . . *Digested*, 01/**1960**
R. v. Kingston upon Hull Justices Ex p. McCann (1991) 155 J.P. 569; (1991) 155
    J.P.N. 394, QBD . . . . *Applied*, 99/3131
R. v. Kingston upon Thames Justices Ex p. Martin [1994] Imm. A.R. 172; *Times*,
    December 10, 1993, QBD . . . . *Digested*, 94/**3519**:
          Applied, 96/3184, 01/3597: *Considered*, 96/670
R. v. Kirby (William) (1979) 1 Cr. App. R. (S.) 214, CA (Crim Div) . . . . *Digested*, 81/**525.192**:
          Followed, 98/1322: *Referred to*, 96/2064
R. v. Kirk (Alfred Alexander) [2000] 1 W.L.R. 567; [1999] 4 All E.R. 698; [2000] 1 Cr.
    App. R. 400, CA (Crim Div) . . . . *Digested*, 00/**922**
R. v. Kirkham (Gary) see Attorney General's Reference (No.76 of 1998), Re
R. v. Kirklees MBC Ex p. A (A Child) see A v. Kirklees MBC
R. v. Kirklees MBC Ex p. Beaumont; *sub nom* R. v. Kirklees MBC Ex p. Birkdale HS
    (2001) 3 L.G.L.R. 12; [2001] B.L.G.R. 187; [2001] E.L.R. 204; *Times*, November
    22, 2000; *Daily Telegraph*, October 24, 2000, QBD . . . . *Digested*, 00/**4087**
R. v. Kirklees MBC Ex p. Birkdale HS see R. v. Kirklees MBC Ex p. Beaumont
R. v. Kirklees MBC Ex p. Daykin (1997-98) 1 C.C.L. Rep. 512, QBD . . . . *Digested*, 97/**4711**
R. v. Kirklees MBC Ex p. Good (1997-98) 1 C.C.L. Rep. 506, QBD . . . . *Digested*, 96/**3029**

R. *v.* Kirkpatrick (Richard Dansby) [1998] Crim. L.R. 63, CA (Crim Div)
R. *v.* Kitchener (Marvine Wayne) see Attorney General's Reference (No.19 of 1999), Re
R. *v.* Kitching (Steven) [2000] 2 Cr. App. R. (S.) 194, CA (Crim Div) . . . .   *Digested,* 00/**1224**
R. *v.* Klair (Jaspal) (1995) 16 Cr. App. R. (S.) 660, CA (Crim Div) . . . .   *Digested,* 96/**1996**:
                                                         Considered, 99/1110
R. *v.* Klass (Kennedy Francis) [1998] 1 Cr. App. R. 453; (1998) 162 J.P. 105; (1998)
     162 J.P.N. 187; (1998) 95(1) L.S.G. 23; (1998) 142 S.J.L.B. 34; *Times,*
     December 17, 1997; *Independent,* December 17, 1997, CA (Crim Div) . . . .   *Digested,* 98/**915**
R. *v.* Klineberg (Jonathan Simon); R. *v.* Marsden (David) [1999] 1 Cr. App. R. 427;
     [1999] Crim. L.R. 417; (1998) 95(46) L.S.G. 34; *Times,* November 19, 1998;
     Independent, November 17, 1998, CA (Crim Div) . . . .   *Digested,* 98/**980**
R. *v.* Knibbs (Gordon Ralph) (1991) 12 Cr. App. R. (S.) 655, CA (Crim Div) . . . .   *Digested,* 92/**1317**:
                                 Considered, 95/1410, 97/1586, 98/1264, 00/1297
R. *v.* Knight (Derek) (1990) 12 Cr. App. R. (S.) 319, CA (Crim Div) . . . .   *Digested,* 92/**1359**:
                             Cited, 93/1234, 93/1235: *Considered,* 99/1272
R. *v.* Knight (Peter); R. *v.* Dooley (Stephen) [1998] 2 Cr. App. R. (S.) 23, CA (Crim
     Div) . . . .   *Digested,* 98/**1196**
R. *v.* Knightsbridge Crown Court Ex p. Abdillahi [1999] Env. L.R. D1, QBD
R. *v.* Knightsbridge Crown Court Ex p. Cataldi see SFI Group Plc (formerly Surrey Free
     Inns Plc) *v.* Gosport BC
R. *v.* Knightsbridge Crown Court Ex p. Cataldi [1999] Env. L.R. 62; [1999] E.H.L.R.
     426; [1999] E.H.L.R. Dig. 105, QBD . . . .   *Subsequent proceed-*
                                           ings, 99/4064
R. *v.* Knightsbridge Crown Court Ex p. Foot [1999] R.T.R. 21; [1998] C.O.D. 165;
     Times, February 18, 1998, QBD . . . .   *Digested,* 98/**916**
R. *v.* Knightsbridge Crown Court Ex p. International Sporting Club (London) [1982]
     Q.B. 304; [1981] 3 W.L.R. 640; [1981] 3 All E.R. 417; 125 S.J. 589, QBD . . . . . .   *Digested,* 81/**2168**:
                 Applied, 83/1743.a, 83/1747, 99/4008: *Considered,* 92/679:
                                           Referred to, 82/3295.7
R. (on the application of Knowsley MBC) *v.* Knowsley Magistrates Court; *sub nom* R.
     (on the application of Williams) *v.* Knowsley MBC; Knowsley MBC *v.* Williams; R.
     (on the application of Williams) *v.* Knowsley Magistrates Court [2001] Env. L.R.
     28; [2001] E.H.L.R. Dig. 3, QBD (Admin Ct) . . . .   *Digested,* 01/**2427**
R. (on the application of Williams) *v.* Knowsley Magistrates Court see R. (on the
     application of Knowsley MBC) *v.* Knowsley Magistrates Court
R. (on the application of Williams) *v.* Knowsley MBC see R. (on the application of
     Knowsley MBC) *v.* Knowsley Magistrates Court
R. *v.* Knutsford Crown Court Ex p. Jones (1985) 7 Cr. App. R. (S.) 448, QBD . . . .   *Digested,* 87/**863**:
                                         Considered, 00/1332
R. *v.* Kohn (1864) 4 F. & F. 68 . . . .   *Considered,* 56/1951,
               57/696, 57/697, 00/952: *Distinguished,* 56/1764, 56/1882, 68/652
R. *v.* Kohn (David James) (1979) 69 Cr. App. R. 395; [1979] Crim. L.R. 675, CA (Crim
     Div) . . . .   *Digested,* 80/**591**:
       Applied, 84/957, 88/839: *Considered,* 85/889, 86/929, 88/845, 89/898,
                          90/1175, 97/1249, 00/1013: *Referred to,* 84/965
R. *v.* Kolton (Grzegorz); R. *v.* Unlu (Emin); R. *v.* Aksar (Mohammed) [2000] Crim. L.R.
     761, CA (Crim Div)
R. *v.* Konscol [1993] Crim. L.R. 950, CA (Crim Div) . . . .   *Digested,* 94/**953**:
                                          Approved, 01/5724
R. *v.* Korkolis (Constantine) see R. *v.* Mereu (Jean-Marc)
R. *v.* Kosola (Jyri Jaakko) [2000] 1 Cr. App. R. (S.) 205, CA (Crim Div) . . . .   *Digested,* 00/**1196**
R. *v.* Kousourous (Adam) see Attorney General's Reference (No.6 of 1996), Re
R. *v.* Kovaycin (Cafer) see R. *v.* Bozat (Hikmet)
R. *v.* Kowalski (Roy) (1988) 86 Cr. App. R. 339; (1987) 9 Cr. App. R. (S.) 375;
     [1988] 1 F.L.R. 447; [1988] Crim. L.R. 124; [1988] Fam. Law 259, CA (Crim
     Div) . . . .   *Digested,* 88/**1654**:
                       Considered, 00/1293: *Referred to,* 94/1287, 96/1945
R. *v.* KPMG Peat Marwick McLintock see Law Society *v.* KPMG Peat Marwick
R. *v.* Krawec (Ihor) (1984) 6 Cr. App. R. (S.) 367; (1985) 149 J.P. 709; [1985] R.T.R.
     1; [1985] Crim. L.R. 108; (1985) 82 L.S.G. 202, CA (Crim Div) . . . .   *Digested,* 85/**3001**:
       Applied, 96/1772: *Considered,* 87/918, 89/983, 91/1081, 96/1771, 98/1370,
                                        99/1319: *Disapproved,* 99/1318
R. *v.* Kweller (Alan) (1981) 3 Cr. App. R. (S.) 9, CA (Crim Div) . . . .   *Considered,* 01/1442
R. *v.* Kyriakou (Georgina) (1990) 12 Cr. App. R. (S.) 603, CA . . . .   *Digested,* 92/**1156**:
                                   Cited, 93/1242: *Considered,* 98/1325
R. *v.* L see R. (on the application of L) *v.* Barking and Dagenham LBC
R. *v.* L (A Juvenile) see Attorney General's Reference (Nos.52, 53, 54 and 55 of
     1999), Re
R. *v.* L (Albert David) see Attorney General's Reference (No.64 of 1999), Re
R. *v.* L (Catherine Fiona) (A Juvenile) see Attorney General's Reference (Nos.57 and
     58 of 1999), Re
R. *v.* L (Claire Louise) see R. *v.* F (Mark Frank)
R. *v.* L (Darren Lee) [1998] 1 Cr. App. R. (S.) 217, CA (Crim Div) . . . .   *Digested,* 98/**1248**

R. *v.* L (Darren Mark) (A Juvenile); R. *v.* W (Nathan James) [1999] 1 Cr. App. R. (S.)
248, CA (Crim Div) . . . .   *Digested*, 99/**1240**
R. *v.* L (David) (A Juvenile) [2000] 1 Cr. App. R. (S.) 185, CA (Crim Div) . . . .   *Digested*, 00/**1307**
R. *v.* L (David Robert) [1999] 1 Cr. App. R. (S.) 415, CA (Crim Div) . . . .   *Digested*, 99/**1349**:
    Considered, 01/1367

R. *v.* L (Deferred Sentence); *sub nom* Attorney General's Reference (Nos.36 and 38 of
1998); R. *v.* Jones (William) [1999] 1 W.L.R. 479; [1999] 2 Cr. App. R. (S.) 7;
(1999) 163 J.P. 97; [1999] Crim. L.R. 236; (1999) 163 J.P.N. 33; (1998) 95(46)
L.S.G. 33; (1998) 142 S.J.L.B. 285; *Times*, November 17, 1998, CA (Crim Div) . .   *Digested*, 98/**1171**
R. *v.* L (Dennis John) [1999] 1 Cr. App. R. (S.) 57, CA (Crim Div) . . . .   *Digested*, 99/**1085**
R. *v.* L (Gareth Paul) [1998] 2 Cr. App. R. (S.) 230, CA (Crim Div) . . . .   *Digested*, 98/**1294**
R. *v.* L (Gemma Gail) (A Juvenile) see Attorney General's Reference (Nos.68 and 69
of 1996), Re
R. *v.* L (Glen Bernard); *sub nom* R. *v.* GBL *Times*, February 9, 2001; *Times*, January 12,
2001, CA (Crim Div) . . . .   *Digested*, 01/**1158**
R. *v.* L (Indecent Assault: Sentencing) [1999] 1 Cr. App. R. 117; [1999] 1 Cr. App. R.
(S.) 19; (1998) 95(26) L.S.G. 31; (1998) 142 S.J.L.B. 156; *Times*, April 28, 1998;
Independent, April 28, 1998, CA (Crim Div) . . . .   *Digested*, 98/**1257**:
    Applied, 99/1196: *Considered*, 99/1194, 99/1199, 99/1203, 99/1302,
    00/1288, 01/1354: *Followed*, 99/1207, 01/1484
R. *v.* L (Kenneth Peter) [1999] 1 Cr. App. R. (S.) 347, CA (Crim Div) . . . .   *Digested*, 99/**1203**:
    Considered, 00/1288
R. *v.* L (Michael John) [2000] 2 Cr. App. R. (S.) 177, CA (Crim Div) . . . .   *Digested*, 00/**1397**
R. *v.* L (Robert) (A Juvenile) see R. *v.* A (David Roy) (A Juvenile)
R. *v.* L (Stephen Howard) (A Juvenile) [2001] 2 Cr. App. R. (S.) 39, CA (Crim Div) . . .   *Digested*, 01/**1401**
R. *v.* L (Stephen Peter) see Attorney General's Reference (No.44 of 1999), Re
R. *v.* L (Wayne) (A Juvenile) see R. *v.* M (Jodie) (A Juvenile)
R. *v.* L (Young Offender: Time in Custody on Remand) see R. *v.* M (Young Offender:
Time in Custody on Remand)
R. *v.* Lacey (Steven Lloyd) see Attorney General's Reference (No.9 of 1989), Re
R. *v.* Lake (Deceased) see R. *v.* Edwards
R. *v.* Lalani (Rozamin) [1999] 1 Cr. App. R. 481; [1999] Crim. L.R. 992; (1999) 96(7)
L.S.G. 35; *Times*, January 28, 1999, CA (Crim Div) . . . .   *Digested*, 99/**954**
R. *v.* Lam see Chung Tak Lam *v.* Brennan (t/a Namesakes of Torbay)
R. *v.* Lamb (John) [1998] 1 Cr. App. R. (S.) 77, CA (Crim Div) . . . .   *Digested*, 98/**1315**
R. *v.* Lambert (Steven); R. *v.* Ali (Mudassir Mohammed); R. *v.* Jordan (Shirley) [2001]
UKHL 37; [2001] 3 W.L.R. 206; [2001] 3 All E.R. 577; [2001] 2 Cr. App. R. 28;
[2001] H.R.L.R. 55; [2001] U.K.H.R.R. 1074; [2001] Crim. L.R. 806; (2001)
98(33) L.S.G. 29; (2001) 145 S.J.L.B. 174; *Times*, July 6, 2001; *Independent*,
July 19, 2001; *Daily Telegraph*, July 17, 2001, HL; affirming [2001] 2 W.L.R. 211;
[2001] 1 All E.R. 1014; [2001] 1 Cr. App. R. 14; [2001] H.R.L.R. 4; [2000]
U.K.H.R.R. 864; (2000) 97(35) L.S.G. 36; *Times*, September 5, 2000, CA (Crim
Div) . . . .   *Digested*, 01/**3504**:
    Applied, 01/2315: *Followed*, 01/1193, 01/5271
R. (on the application of A) *v.* Lambeth LBC; *sub nom* A *v.* Lambeth LBC; R. *v.* Lambeth
LBC Ex p. A [2001] EWCA Civ 1624; [2001] 3 F.C.R. 673; [2001] N.P.C. 158;
Times, November 20, 2001; *Independent*, November 9, 2001, CA; affirming
[2001] EWHC Admin 376; [2001] 2 F.L.R. 1201; (2001) 33 H.L.R. 60; [2001]
B.L.G.R. 513; [2001] Fam. Law 876; *Times*, July 3, 2001, QBD (Admin Ct) . . . .   *Digested*, 01/**3434**
R. (on the application of L) *v.* Lambeth LBC [2001] EWHC Admin 900; [2001] N.P.C.
159, QBD (Admin Ct)
R. *v.* Lambeth LBC Ex p. A see R. (on the application of A) *v.* Lambeth LBC
R. *v.* Lambeth LBC Ex p. A; *sub nom* R. *v.* Lambeth LBC Ex p. A1; R. *v.* Lambeth LBC
Ex p. A2 (1998) 30 H.L.R. 933; (1998) 10 Admin. L.R. 209; (1997-98) 1 C.C.L.
Rep. 336; [1998] C.O.D. 213, CA . . . .   *Digested*, 98/**3049**
R. *v.* Lambeth LBC Ex p. A1 see R. *v.* Lambeth LBC Ex p. A
R. *v.* Lambeth LBC Ex p. A2 see R. *v.* Lambeth LBC Ex p. A
R. *v.* Lambeth LBC Ex p. Ashley (1997) 29 H.L.R. 385; [1996] C.O.D. 474, QBD . . . . . .   *Digested*, 97/**2698**:
    Applied, 00/3152: *Distinguished*, 98/3032
R. *v.* Lambeth LBC Ex p. C see R. *v.* Lambeth LBC Ex p. Caddell
R. *v.* Lambeth LBC Ex p. Caddell; *sub nom* R. *v.* Lambeth LBC Ex p. C [1998] 1 F.L.R.
253; [1998] 2 F.C.R. 6; [1998] Fam. Law 20; (1997) 94(30) L.S.G. 30; (1997)
141 S.J.L.B. 147; *Times*, June 30, 1997; *Independent*, July 7, 1997 (C.S.), QBD . .   *Digested*, 97/**361**:
    Followed, 99/4629, 01/4374
R. *v.* Lambeth LBC Ex p. Carroll (1988) 20 H.L.R. 142; (1988) 152 L.G. Rev. 227 . . . . .   *Digested*, 88/**1771**:
    Applied, 98/3018
R. *v.* Lambeth LBC Ex p. Crookes (1998) (1999) 31 H.L.R. 59, QBD . . . .   *Digested*, 98/**4528**
R. *v.* Lambeth LBC Ex p. Ekpo-Wedderman [1998] 3 F.C.R. 532; (1999) 31 H.L.R.
498, QBD . . . .   *Digested*, 98/**2997**
R. *v.* Lambeth LBC Ex p. K (A Child) (2000) 3 C.C.L. Rep. 141, QBD . . . .   *Digested*, 00/**4113**
R. *v.* Lambeth LBC Ex p. Ly (1987) 19 H.L.R. 51 . . . .   *Digested*, 87/**1875**:
    Distinguished, 98/2998
R. *v.* Lambeth LBC Ex p. Miah (1995) 27 H.L.R. 21; [1994] C.O.D. 408, QBD . . . .   *Digested*, 96/**3075**:
    Approved, 00/3148: *Followed*, 95/75

R. v. Lambeth LBC Ex p. P see R. v. Hammersmith and Fulham LBC Ex p. M
R. v. Lambeth LBC Ex p. Sarhangi (1999) 31 H.L.R. 1022; (1999) 1 L.G.L.R. 493;
　　[1999] B.L.G.R. 641; (1999) 2 C.C.L. Rep. 145; (1999) 143 S.J.L.B. 30; *Times*,
　　December 9, 1998, QBD . . . . 　*Digested*, 99/**3023**
R. v. Lambeth LBC Ex p. Shakes see R. v. Lambeth LBC Ex p. Touhey
R. v. Lambeth LBC Ex p. Touhey; *sub nom* R. v. Lambeth LBC Ex p. Shakes (2000) 32
　　H.L.R. 707, QBD . . . . 　*Digested*, 00/**3131**
R. v. Lambeth LBC Ex p. Trabi (1998) 30 H.L.R. 975, QBD . . . . 　*Digested*, 98/**2989**
R. v. Lambeth LBC Ex p. Wilson [1997] 3 F.C.R. 437; (1998) 30 H.L.R. 64; (1997)
　　94 (14) L.S.G. 25; (1997) 141 S.J.L.B. 91; *Times*, March 25, 1997, CA; reversing
　　[1996] 3 F.C.R. 146; (1997) 29 H.L.R. 104; (1996) 8 Admin. L.R. 376; [1996]
　　C.O.D. 281; (1996) 160 L.G. Rev. 484; *Times*, March 21, 1996, QBD . . . . 　*Digested*, 97/**607**
R. v. Lambeth LBC Ex p. Woodburne (1997) 29 H.L.R. 836, QBD . . . . 　*Digested*, 98/**3048**
R. v. Lambeth LBC Ex p. X see R. v. Hammersmith and Fulham LBC Ex p. M
R. v. Lamoon (Johnathon Joe) see Attorney General's Reference (No.52 of 2001), Re
R. v. Lancashire (Darrell Andrew) see R. v. Wakefield (Russell Eric)
R. v. Lancashire CC Ex p. CM (A Minor) [1989] 2 F.L.R. 279; [1989] Fam. Law 395;
　　(1990) 154 L.G. Rev. 112; (1989) 86 (17) L.S.G. 37; (1989) 133 S.J. 484, CA . . . 　*Digested*, 90/**1797**:
　　　　　　　　　　　　　　　　　　　　　　　　Applied, 99/1898: *Followed*, 96/2474
R. v. Lancashire CC Ex p. M see R. v. Lancashire CC Ex p. Maycock
R. v. Lancashire CC Ex p. Maycock; *sub nom* R. v. Lancashire CC Ex p. M [1994]
　　E.L.R. 478; (1995) 159 L.G. Rev. 201, QBD . . . . 　*Digested*, 96/**2383**:
　　　　　　　　　　　　　　　　　　　　　　　　　　　Distinguished, 99/1838
R. v. Lancashire CC Ex p. Royal Association for Disability and Rehabilitation see R. v.
　　Gloucestershire CC Ex p. Barry
R. v. Lancashire CC Ex p. Smith [2000] J.P.L. 1305 (Note), QBD . . . . 　*Digested*, 01/**4685**
R. v. Land (Michael) [1999] Q.B. 65; [1998] 3 W.L.R. 322; [1998] 1 All E.R. 403;
　　[1998] 1 Cr. App. R. 301; (1998) 162 J.P. 29; [1998] 1 F.L.R. 438; [1998] Crim.
　　L.R. 70; [1998] Fam. Law 133; (1997) 161 J.P.N. 1173; (1997) 94 (42) L.S.G.
　　32; *Times*, November 4, 1997; *Independent*, October 16, 1997, CA (Crim Div) . . . 　*Digested*, 97/**1160**
R. v. Lands Tribunal Ex p. Jafton Properties Ltd [2001] R.V.R. 87, QBD . . . . 　*Digested*, 01/**462**
R. v. Lang (Christopher Michael) (1976) 62 Cr. App. R. 50, CA (Crim Div) . . . . 　*Digested*, 76/**559**:
　　　　　　　　　　　　　　　　　　　　　　　　　　　Not followed, 98/971
R. v. Langley (Dean Ronald) [2001] EWCA Crim 732; [2001] Crim. L.R. 651, CA
　　(Crim Div)
R. v. Langstone (Gary) [2001] EWCA Crim 443; [2001] 2 Cr. App. R. (S.) 98; [2001]
　　Crim. L.R. 409; *Times*, March 14, 2001, CA (Crim Div) . . . . 　*Digested*, 01/**1409**
R. v. Lard (Gurdial Singh) [1998] 1 Cr. App. R. (S.) 40; *Independent*, May 19, 1997
　　(C.S.), CA (Crim Div) . . . . 　*Digested*, 97/**1536**
R. v. Laskey (Colin) see R. v. Brown (Anthony Joseph)
R. v. Latham (Daniel George) see Attorney General's Reference (No.33 of 1996), Re
R. v. Latif (Khalid); R. v. Shahzad (Mohammed Khalid) [1996] 1 W.L.R. 104; [1996] 1
　　All E.R. 353; [1996] 2 Cr. App. R. 92; [1996] Crim. L.R. 414; (1996) 93 (5)
　　L.S.G. 30; (1996) 146 N.L.J. 121; (1996) 140 S.J.L.B. 39; *Times*, January 23,
　　1996; *Independent*, January 23, 1996, HL; affirming [1995] 1 Cr. App. R. 270;
　　(1994) 15 Cr. App. R. (S.) 864; [1994] Crim. L.R. 750; (1994) 91 (18) L.S.G. 37;
　　(1994) 138 S.J.L.B. 85; *Times*, March 17, 1994, CA (Crim Div) . . . . 　*Digested*, 96/**1432**:
　　　　　　　　　Considered, 96/1599, 97/1503, 99/1129: *Distinguished*, 00/917:
　　　　　　　　　　　　　　　　　　　　　　　　　Followed, 00/1086, 01/992
R. v. Latif (Mahomed Arif); R. v. Latif (Naushad Sattar) [1999] 1 Cr. App. R. (S.) 191,
　　CA (Crim Div) . . . . 　*Digested*, 99/**1356**
R. v. Latif (Naushad Sattar) see R. v. Latif (Mahomed Arif)
R. v. Latimer (Neil Frazer) [1992] N.I. 45, CA (NI) . . . . 　*Not followed*, 00/5464
R. v. Lauder (Marcel O'Neill) (1999) 163 J.P. 721; (1999) 163 J.P.N. 813; (1998)
　　95 (45) L.S.G. 38; *Times*, November 5, 1998, CA (Crim Div) . . . . 　*Digested*, 98/**1368**
R. v. Laurent (Kenny Paul) [2001] 1 Cr. App. R. (S.) 65; [2000] Crim. L.R. 868, CA
　　(Crim Div) . . . . 　*Digested*, 01/**1244**
R. v. LAUTRO Ex p. Ross see R. v. Life Assurance Unit Trust Regulatory Organisation
　　Ex p. Ross
R. v. Lavin (Kevin) see R. v. Lavin (Thomas)
R. v. Lavin (Thomas); R. v. Lavin (Kevin); R. v. Wheeler (Stephen) [2000] 1 Cr. App. R.
　　(S.) 227, CA (Crim Div) . . . . 　*Digested*, 00/**1242**
R. v. Law (Jason) [1998] 2 Cr. App. R. (S.) 365, CA (Crim Div) . . . . 　*Digested*, 99/**1333**:
　　　　　　　　　　　　　　　　　　　　　　　　　　　Considered, 01/1479
R. v. Law (Richard) see Attorney General's Reference (No.30 of 1995), Re
R. v. Law (Richard Andrew) [1999] Crim. L.R. 837; *Times*, February 4, 1999;
　　Independent, February 15, 1999 (C.S.), CA (Crim Div) . . . . 　*Digested*, 99/**932**
R. (on the application of Pamplin) v. Law Society [2001] EWHC Admin 300;
　　Independent, July 9, 2001 (C.S.), QBD (Admin Ct)
R. v. Law Society Ex p. Alliance & Leicester Building Society see R. v. Law Society Ex
　　p. Mortgage Express Ltd
R. v. Law Society Ex p. Birkett (1999) 149 N.L.J. 1255, QBD

R. v. Law Society Ex p. Ingman Foods [1997] 2 All E.R. 666; [1997] P.N.L.R. 454; [1997] C.O.D. 234; (1997) 147 N.L.J. 254, QBD. . . . .   *Digested,* 97/**3374**: *Considered,* 99/3804

R. v. Law Society Ex p. Mortgage Corp; *sub nom* Mortgage Corp v. Law Society (2000) 97(46) L.S.G. 41, QBD (Admin Ct)

R. v. Law Society Ex p. Mortgage Express Ltd; R. v. Law Society Ex p. Alliance & Leicester Building Society [1997] 2 All E.R. 348; [1997] P.N.L.R. 469; *Independent,* January 23, 1997, CA; reversing [1997] P.N.L.R. 82; [1997] C.O.D. 7; [1996] N.P.C. 120, QBD . . . .   *Digested,* 97/**3373**: *Considered,* 97/3374, 97/3376, 99/3804

R. v. Law Society Ex p. Nielsen, *Times,* January 13, 1999, QBD . . . .   *Digested,* 99/**3804**

R. v. Lawless (Frank) [1998] 2 Cr. App. R. (S.) 176, CA (Crim Div) . . . .   *Digested,* 98/**1327**: *Applied,* 00/1422

R. v. Lawrence [2000] 2 Costs L.R. 334, Sup Ct Costs Office . . . .   *Digested,* 01/**4230**

R. v. Lawrence (Alan) see Lawrence v. Commissioner of Police of the Metropolis

R. v. Lawrence (Martin Lee) (1983) 5 Cr. App. R. (S.) 220; (1983) 147 J.P. 635, CA (Crim Div). . . . .   *Digested,* 84/**907**: *Considered,* 99/1330

R. v. Lawson (Raymond) [1998] Crim. L.R. 883, CA (Crim Div)

R. v. Laycock (Christopher Martin) see Attorney General's Reference (Nos.40 to 42 of 1997), Re

R. v. Le (Van Binh); R. v. Stark (Rudi) [1999] 1 Cr. App. R. (S.) 422; [1998] I.N.L.R. 677; [1999] Crim. L.R. 96; *Times,* October 15, 1998, CA (Crim Div) . . . .   *Digested,* 98/**1245**: *Considered,* 00/1275

R. v. Le Mouel (Andre Marcel) [1996] 1 Cr. App. R. (S.) 42, CA (Crim Div) . . . .   *Digested,* 96/**1831**: *Considered,* 97/1675, 98/1363, 98/1364, 00/1195, 00/1196: *Distinguished,* 97/1671

R. v. Leal (Manoj) (Confiscation Order) see R. v. Benjafield (Karl Robert) (Confiscation Order)

R. v. Leal (Manoj); R. v. Benjafield (Karl Robert) [2001] EWCA Crim 576, CA (Crim Div) . . . .   *Previous proceedings,* 01/1237

R. v. Leask (Stephen) see R. v. Lowe (Trevor)

R. v. Lee (Anthony William) (A Minor) [1993] 1 W.L.R. 103; [1993] 2 All E.R. 170; (1993) 96 Cr. App. R. 188; (1993) 157 J.P. 533; [1993] Crim. L.R. 65; (1992) 156 J.P.N. 746; *Times,* July 21, 1992, CA (Crim Div). . . . .   *Digested,* 93/**737**: *Followed,* 98/76, 99/85

R. v. Lee (Charles Sonny) see R. v. Loveridge (William) (Appeal against Conviction)

R. v. Lee (Christopher) see Attorney General's Reference (No.6 of 1994), Re

R. v. Lee (David) (1995) 16 Cr. App. R. (S.) 60, CA (Crim Div) . . . .   *Digested,* 96/**1743**: *Considered,* 00/1151, 00/1434

R. v. Lee (Dennis Percival) (Conviction) [2001] 1 Cr. App. R. 19; (2001) 165 J.P. 344; [2000] Crim. L.R. 991; (2001) 165 J.P.N. 250; (2000) 97(40) L.S.G. 41; (2000) 150 N.L.J. 1491; *Times,* October 24, 2000; *Independent,* October 20, 2000, CA (Crim Div) . . . .   *Digested,* 00/**1015**

R. v. Lee (John) (Unreported, April 17, 1998), Crown Ct (Harrow) [*Ex rel.* Sarah Clarke, Barrister, Ground Floor, Temple, London] . . . .   *Digested,* 98/**906**

R. v. Lee (Neville) [1998] 2 Cr. App. R. (S.) 272, CA (Crim Div) . . . .   *Digested,* 98/**1252**

R. v. Lee (Peter) [2001] 1 Cr. App. R. (S.) 1, CA (Crim Div). . . . .   *Digested,* 01/**1336**

R. v. Lee (Raymond) [1996] 1 Cr. App. R. (S.) 135; [1995] Crim. L.R. 960, CA (Crim Div) . . . .   *Considered,* 98/1153

R. v. Leeds City Council Ex p. Maloney (No.1) (1999) 31 H.L.R. 552, QBD . . . .   *Digested,* 99/**3040**

R. v. Leeds City Council Ex p. N [1999] Ed. C.R. 949; [1999] E.L.R. 324, CA; affirming [1999] Ed. C.R. 735, QBD . . . .   *Digested,* 99/**1763**

R. v. Leeds Combined Court Centre Ex p. Scarth, *Times,* July 8, 1999, CA . . . .   *Digested,* 99/**33**

R. (on the application of Wardle) v. Leeds Crown Court; *sub nom* R. v. Leeds Crown Court Ex p. Stubley; R. v. Leeds Crown Court Ex p. Wardle; R. v. Stubley [2001] UKHL 12; [2001] 2 W.L.R. 865; [2001] 2 All E.R. 1; [2001] 2 Cr. App. R. 20; (2001) 165 J.P. 465; [2001] H.R.L.R. 29; [2001] Crim. L.R. 468; [2001] A.C.D. 82; (2001) 165 J.P.N. 327; (2001) 98(21) L.S.G. 39; (2001) 151 N.L.J. 386; (2001) 145 S.J.L.B. 117; *Times,* March 13, 2001; *Independent,* April 30, 2001 (C.S), HL; affirming [1999] Crim. L.R. 822, QBD . . . .   *Digested,* 01/**1091**

R. v. Leeds Crown Court Ex p. Bagoutie; R. v. Leeds Crown Court Ex p. Quereshi; R. v. Leeds Crown Court Ex p. Callaghan *Times,* May 31, 1999, QBD . . . .   *Digested,* 99/**1050**

R. v. Leeds Crown Court Ex p. Briggs (No.1) [1998] 2 Cr. App. R. 413; [1998] Crim. L.R. 744; *Times,* February 19, 1998, QBD. . . . .   *Digested,* 98/**1083**

R. v. Leeds Crown Court Ex p. Briggs (No.2) [1998] 2 Cr. App. R. 424; (1998) 162 J.P. 623; [1998] Crim. L.R. 746; (1998) 162 J.P.N. 606; (1998) 95(14) L.S.G. 23; (1998) 142 S.J.L.B. 109; *Times,* March 10, 1998, QBD . . . .   *Digested,* 98/**1082**: *Followed,* 98/1084

R. v. Leeds Crown Court Ex p. Callaghan see R. v. Leeds Crown Court Ex p. Bagoutie

R. v. Leeds Crown Court Ex p. Hunt see R. v. Manchester Crown Court Ex p. McDonald

R. v. Leeds Crown Court Ex p. Quereshi see R. v. Leeds Crown Court Ex p. Bagoutie

R. *v.* Leeds Crown Court Ex p. Redfearn; *sub nom* R. *v.* Bow Street Magistrates Court Ex p. Redfearn [1998] C.O.D. 437, QBD

R. *v.* Leeds Crown Court Ex p. Stubley see R. (on the application of Wardle) *v.* Leeds Crown Court

R. *v.* Leeds Crown Court Ex p. Wardle see R. (on the application of Wardle) *v.* Leeds Crown Court

R. *v.* Leeds Crown Court Ex p. Whitehead, *Times,* September 16, 1998, QBD . . . .   *Digested,* 98/**1084**

R. *v.* Leeds Crown Court Ex p. Whitehead (No.2); *sub nom* Whitehead, Re (2000) 164 J.P. 102; (1999) 163 J.P.N. 813; (1999) 96(26) L.S.G. 27; (1999) 143 S.J.L.B. 205; *Times,* July 5, 1999 ; *Independent,* July 12, 1999 (C.S.), QBD . . . .   *Digested,* 99/**1051**

R. *v.* Leeds Crown Court Ex p. Wilson [1999] Crim. L.R. 738, QBD

R. *v.* Leeds Crown Court Ex p. Wilson (Leave Application) see R. *v.* Manchester Crown Court Ex p. McDonald

R. (on the application of Miller) *v.* Leeds Magistrates Court see Gough *v.* Chief Constable of Derbyshire

R. *v.* Leeds Metropolitan University Ex p. Manders [1998] E.L.R. 502, QBD . . . .   *Digested,* 98/**2007**

R. (on the application of AP) *v.* Leeds Youth Court; R. (on the application of MD) *v.* Leeds Youth Court; R. (on the application of JS) *v.* Leeds Youth Court [2001] EWHC Admin 215; (2001) 165 J.P. 684, QBD (Admin Ct). . . . .   *Digested,* 01/**1199**

R. (on the application of JS) *v.* Leeds Youth Court see R. (on the application of AP) *v.* Leeds Youth Court

R. (on the application of K (A Child)) *v.* Leeds Youth Court [2001] EWHC Admin 177; (2001) 165 J.P. 694, QBD (Admin Ct) . . . .   *Digested,* 01/**1169**

R. (on the application of MD) *v.* Leeds Youth Court see R. (on the application of AP) *v.* Leeds Youth Court

R. *v.* Lees (Francis Gerard) see R. *v.* Cole (Philip Francis)

R. *v.* Lees (Tracey) [1999] 1 Cr. App. R. (S.) 194, CA (Crim Div) . . . .   *Digested,* 99/**1343**

R. *v.* Lees (William John); *sub nom* BBC's Application, Re [2001] N.I. 233, CA (Crim Div) (NI) . . . .   *Digested,* 01/**5648**

R. *v.* Leese (Henry) see R. *v.* Williams (David Omar)

R. *v.* Leeson (John Anthony) [2000] 1 Cr. App. R. 233; (2000) 164 J.P. 224; [2000] Crim. L.R. 195; (2001) 165 J.P.N. 706; *Times,* November 2, 1999, CA (Crim Div) . . . .   *Digested,* 99/**926**

R. *v.* Legal Aid Area Committee Ex p. Parsons see R. *v.* Legal Aid Board Ex p. Parsons

R. *v.* Legal Aid Area No.1 (London) Appeal Committee Ex p. McCormick; *sub nom* R. *v.* Legal Aid Board Ex p. McCormick [2000] 1 W.L.R. 1804; [2000] C.O.D. 332; (2000) 97(25) L.S.G. 41; (2000) 150 N.L.J. 868; *Times,* June 13, 2000; *Independent,* June 14, 2000, QBD . . . .   *Digested,* 00/**3957**

R. *v.* Legal Aid Board (Merseyside) Area Office Ex p. Eccleston see R. *v.* Legal Aid Board No.15 Area Office (Liverpool) Ex p. Eccleston

R. *v.* Legal Aid Board Ex p. Burrows see R. (on the application of Burrows (t/a David Burrows (A Firm))) *v.* Legal Services Commission (formerly Legal Aid Board)

R. *v.* Legal Aid Board Ex p. Duncan [2000] C.O.D. 159; (2000) 150 N.L.J. 276; *Independent,* February 23, 2000, QBD. . . . .   *Digested,* 00/**3984**

R. *v.* Legal Aid Board Ex p. Edwin Coe (A Firm) [2000] 1 W.L.R. 1909; [2000] 3 All E.R. 193; (2000) 97(25) L.S.G. 41; *Times,* May 26, 2000; *Independent,* June 26, 2000 (C.S), CA. . . . .   *Digested,* 00/**3955**

R. *v.* Legal Aid Board Ex p. Kaim Todner; *sub nom* R. *v.* Legal Aid Board Ex p. T (A Firm of Solicitors) [1999] Q.B. 966; [1998] 3 W.L.R. 925; [1998] 3 All E.R. 541; (1998) 95(26) L.S.G. 31; (1998) 148 N.L.J. 941; (1998) 142 S.J.L.B. 189; *Times,* June 15, 1998; *Independent,* June 12, 1998, CA; affirming CO-330-97, QBD . . . .   *Digested,* 98/**83**

R. *v.* Legal Aid Board Ex p. McCormick see R. *v.* Legal Aid Area No.1 (London) Appeal Committee Ex p. McCormick

R. *v.* Legal Aid Board Ex p. Owners Abroad (Tour Operator) [1998] P.I.Q.R. P116; [1998] C.O.D. 224, QBD . . . .   *Digested,* 98/**3704**

R. *v.* Legal Aid Board Ex p. Parsons; *sub nom* R. *v.* Legal Aid Area Committee Ex p. Parsons [1999] 3 All E.R. 347; [1999] C.O.D. 363; *Times,* April 1, 1999; *Independent,* April 16, 1999, CA . . . .   *Digested,* 99/**3789**

R. *v.* Legal Aid Board Ex p. Rafina (1998) 148 N.L.J. 278; *Times,* February 19, 1998; *Independent,* March 3, 1998, QBD . . . .   *Digested,* 98/**3708**

R. *v.* Legal Aid Board Ex p. Reseigh [1999] C.O.D. 259; *Independent,* February 22, 1999 (C.S.), QBD . . . .   *Digested,* 99/**3782**

R. *v.* Legal Aid Board Ex p. T (A Firm of Solicitors) see R. *v.* Legal Aid Board Ex p. Kaim Todner

R. *v.* Legal Aid Board Ex p. W (Children); *sub nom* W (Children) *v.* Legal Services Commission [2000] 1 W.L.R. 2502; [2000] 2 F.L.R. 821; [2000] 3 F.C.R. 352; [2000] Fam. Law 802; (2000) 97(38) L.S.G. 44; (2000) 150 N.L.J. 1453; (2000) 144 S.J.L.B. 252; *Times,* September 19, 2000, CA; affirming [2000] 2 F.L.R. 154; [2000] 1 F.C.R. 165; [2000] Fam. Law 541; *Times,* November 25, 1999 ; *Independent,* January 17, 2000 (C.S.), QBD . . . .   *Digested,* 00/**3982**

R. *v.* Legal Aid Board No.15 Area Office (Liverpool) Ex p. Eccleston; *sub nom* R. *v.* Legal Aid Board (Merseyside) Area Office Ex p. Eccleston [1998] 1 W.L.R. 1279; [1999] P.I.Q.R. P38; [1998] C.O.D. 482; (1998) 95(20) L.S.G. 35; (1998) 142 S.J.L.B. 155; *Times*, May 6, 1998; *Independent*, May 4, 1998 (C.S), QBD . . . . . .   *Digested*, 98/**3705**

R. (on the application of Wulfsohn) *v.* Legal Service Commission C/2001/1317, CA; reversing [2001] EWHC Admin 409; *Independent*, July 30, 2001 (C.S), QBD (Admin Ct)

R. (on the application of Burrows (t/a David Burrows (A Firm))) *v.* Legal Services Commission (formerly Legal Aid Board); *sub nom* R. *v.* Legal Aid Board Ex p. Burrows; R. *v.* Legal Services Commission (formerly Legal Aid Board) Ex p. Burrows (t/a David Burrows (A Firm)) [2001] EWCA Civ 205; [2001] 2 F.L.R. 998; [2001] 2 F.C.R. 324; [2001] Fam. Law 503; (2001) 98(10) L.S.G. 43; (2001) 145 S.J.L.B. 52; *Times*, March 16, 2001, CA; affirming (2000) 150 N.L.J. 1263, QBD . . . .   *Digested*, 01/**4219**

R. (on the application of Jarrett) *v.* Legal Services Commission [2001] EWHC Admin 389; *Independent*, July 23, 2001 (C.S); *Daily Telegraph*, June 19, 2001, QBD (Admin Ct)

R. *v.* Leicester City Council Ex p. Bhikha see R. *v.* Wandsworth LBC Ex p. O

R. *v.* Leicester City Council Ex p. Blackfordby and Boothcorpe Action Group Ltd see R. *v.* Leicestershire CC Ex p. Blackfordby and Boothorpe Action Group Ltd

R. *v.* Leicester City Council Ex p. Powergen UK Plc see Powergen UK Plc *v.* Leicester City Council

R. *v.* Leicester City Council Ex p. Safeway Stores Plc; R. *v.* Wm Morrison Supermarkets Plc Ex p. Safeway Stores; R. *v.* Powergen (UK) Plc Ex p. Safeway Stores [1999] J.P.L. 691, QBD . . . .   *Digested*, 99/**98**

R. *v.* Leicester City Justices Ex p. Barrow [1991] 2 Q.B. 260; [1991] 3 W.L.R. 368; [1991] 3 All E.R. 935; (1991) 155 J.P. 901; [1991] R.A. 205; [1991] Crim. L.R. 556; (1991) 155 J.P.N. 736; (1991) 141 N.L.J. 1145; *Times*, August 5, 1991; *Independent*, August 7, 1991; *Guardian*, August 14, 1991, CA; reversing [1991] 2 W.L.R. 974; [1991] 2 All E.R. 437; (1991) 155 J.P. 533; [1991] R.A. 23; [1991] C.O.D. 240; (1991) 155 J.P.N. 171; (1991) 141 N.L.J. 93; *Times*, January 9, 1991; *Independent*, January 18, 1991; *Guardian*, January 16, 1991; *Daily Telegraph*, January 31, 1991, QBD . . . .   *Digested*, 92/**1007**:
Applied, 99/1007: *Considered*, 92/944, 92/2058, 92/2848, 92/2851, 92/2854, 93/2628, 93/2629

R. (on the application of Customs and Excise Commissioners) *v.* Leicester Crown Court; *sub nom* R. *v.* Leicester Crown Court Ex p. Customs and Excise Commissioners [2001] EWHC Admin 33; *Times*, February 23, 2001; *Independent*, March 5, 2001 (C.S), QBD . . . .   *Digested*, 01/**1118**

R. *v.* Leicester Crown Court Ex p. Customs and Excise Commissioners see R. (on the application of Customs and Excise Commissioners) *v.* Leicester Crown Court

R. *v.* Leicester Crown Court Ex p. S (A Minor) [1993] 1 W.L.R. 111; [1992] 2 All E.R. 659; (1992) 94 Cr. App. R. 153; [1991] Crim. L.R. 365; [1991] C.O.D. 231; (1991) 155 J.P.N. 139; *Times*, December 19, 1990; *Independent*, December 12, 1990; *Guardian*, December 13, 1990; *Daily Telegraph*, December 10, 1990, QBD .   *Digested*, 93/**736**:
Not followed, 98/76

R. *v.* Leicestershire CC Ex p. Blackfordby and Boothcorpe Action Group Ltd see R. *v.* Leicestershire CC Ex p. Blackfordby and Boothorpe Action Group Ltd

R. *v.* Leicestershire CC Ex p. Blackfordby and Boothorpe Action Group Ltd; *sub nom* R. *v.* Leicester City Council Ex p. Blackfordby and Boothcorpe Action Group Ltd; R. *v.* Leicestershire CC Ex p. Blackfordby and Boothorpe Action Group Ltd [2001] Env. L.R. 2; [2000] E.H.L.R. 215; [2000] J.P.L. 1266, QBD . . . .   *Digested*, 00/**2278**

R. *v.* Leicestershire CC Ex p. H see H *v.* Leicestershire CC

R. *v.* Leicestershire CC Ex p. Thompson (2000) 3 C.C.L. Rep. 45, QBD . . . .   *Digested*, 00/**4900**

R. *v.* Leighton Buzzard Justices Ex p. DPP (1990) 154 J.P. 41; [1989] Crim. L.R. 728; (1989) 153 J.P.N. 835, DC . . . .   *Digested*, 90/**995**:
Applied, 00/5469

R. *v.* Lemathy (Patrick Francis); R. *v.* Lemathy (Richard) (1991) 12 Cr. App. R. (S.) 636, CA (Crim Div) . . . .   *Digested*, 92/**1137**:
Considered, 96/1692, 99/1214

R. *v.* Lemathy (Richard) see R. *v.* Lemathy (Patrick Francis)

R. *v.* Lennard (Michael) [1973] 1 W.L.R. 483; [1973] 2 All E.R. 831; (1973) 57 Cr. App. R. 542; [1973] R.T.R. 252; [1973] Crim. L.R. 312; 117 S.J. 284, CA (Crim Div) . . . .   *Digested*, 73/**2896**:
Applied, 79/2309, 79/2323, 80/2299, 83/3220, 83/3225, 84/2996, 85/2990, 87/3236, 88/3082, 88/3091, 89/3220, 89/3224, 90/3979, 91/3116, 91/3117, 91/3123, 92/3793, 93/3493, 93/3501, 93/3503: *Approved*, 76/2393: *Considered*, 80/3544, 81/404, 83/3221, 86/2882, 86/2884, 87/3246, 00/959: *Explained*, 74/3286: *Followed*, 73/2903

R. *v.* Leominster DC Ex p. Pothecary (1998) 10 Admin. L.R. 484; (1998) 76 P. & C.R. 346; [1997] 3 P.L.R. 91; [1998] J.P.L. 335; (1997) 94(45) L.S.G. 28; [1997] N.P.C. 151; *Times*, November 18, 1997, CA; reversing [1997] J.P.L. 835; [1997] E.G.C.S. 2, QBD . . . .   *Digested*, 97/**4116**

R. (on the application of Heather) *v.* Leonard Cheshire Foundation; R. (on the application of Ward) *v.* Leonard Cheshire Foundation; C/2001/1813/A, CA; affirming [2001] EWHC Admin 429; [2001] A.C.D. 75; *Daily Telegraph*, June 26, 2001, QBD (Admin Ct)

R. (on the application of Ward) *v.* Leonard Cheshire Foundation see R. (on the application of Heather) *v.* Leonard Cheshire Foundation

R. *v.* Levantiz (Mark) [1999] 1 Cr. App. R. 465; (1999) 163 J.P. 129; [1999] Crim. L.R. 493; (1999) 163 J.P.N. 152; [1998] 95(46) L.S.G. 34; (1998) 142 S.J.L.B. 285; *Times*, November 17, 1998, CA (Crim Div) . . . .   *Digested*, 98/**1032**

R. *v.* Levitt (Darren Paul) see Attorney General's Reference (No.74 of 1999), Re

R. *v.* Lewes and Crowborough Magistrates Court Ex p. Mackelden (Unreported, June 30, 1998), QBD [*Ex rel.* Bruce Silvester, Barrister, Lamb Chambers, 2nd Floor, Lamb Building, Temple, London] . . . .   *Digested*, 98/**4296**

R. *v.* Lewes Justices Ex p. Gaming Board for Great Britain see Rogers *v.* Secretary of State for the Home Department

R. *v.* Lewes Justices Ex p. Secretary of State for the Home Department see Rogers *v.* Secretary of State for the Home Department

R. *v.* Lewes Juvenile Court Ex p. T (1985) 149 J.P. 186, DC. . . . .   *Digested*, 84/**2116**:
                                                 Applied, 92/921, 01/1170

R. *v.* Lewis, *Times*, November 4, 1999, CA (Crim Div) . . . .   *Digested*, 99/**1111**

R. *v.* Lewis (Christopher) [1997] 1 Cr. App. R. (S.) 208, CA (Crim Div) . . . .   *Digested*, 97/**1052**:
                                                 Considered, 98/1165, 99/1173

R. *v.* Lewis (Dilys Maria) [1998] 1 Cr. App. R. (S.) 13, CA (Crim Div). . . . .   *Digested*, 98/**1228**

R. *v.* Lewis (Martin) (1986) (1986) 8 Cr. App. R. (S.) 314, CA (Crim Div) . . . .   *Digested*, 88/**966**:
                                                 Considered, 96/1893, 00/1242

R. *v.* Lewis (Patrick Arthur) [2001] EWCA Crim 749; *Times*, April 26, 2001, CA (Crim Div) . . . .   *Digested*, 01/**1145**

R. *v.* Lewisham LBC Ex p. Patino (1999) 2 C.C.L. Rep. 152, QBD . . . .   *Digested*, 99/**3069**

R. *v.* LH (A Juvenile) (Indecent Assault: Sentencing); *sub nom* R. *v.* H (Luke Clifford) (A Juvenile) [1997] 2 Cr. App. R. (S.) 319, CA (Crim Div) . . . .   *Digested*, 98/**1286**

R. *v.* LH (A Juvenile) (Manslaughter: Sentencing) [2001] EWCA Crim 114; [2001] 2 Cr. App. R. (S.) 61, CA (Crim Div). . . . .   *Digested*, 01/**1391**

R. *v.* Li Ling Bin see R. *v.* Wang Lin Hal

R. *v.* Licensing Authority Established by the Medicines Act 1968 (represented by Medicines Control Agency) Ex p. Rhone Poulenc Rorer Ltd (C94/98) see R. *v.* Medicines Control Agency Ex p. Rhone Poulenc Rorer Ltd (C94/98)

R. *v.* Licensing Authority Ex p. ER Squibb & Sons see R. *v.* Licensing Authority Ex p. Generics (UK) Ltd

R. *v.* Licensing Authority Ex p. Generics (UK) Ltd; *sub nom* R. *v.* Secretary of State for Health Ex p. Generics (UK) Ltd (Interim Relief); R. *v.* Secretary of State for Health Ex p. ER Squibb & Sons Ltd; R. *v.* Licensing Authority Ex p. ER Squibb & Sons [1998] Eu. L.R. 146; (1998) 10 Admin. L.R. 145; (1998) 40 B.M.L.R. 90; [1997] C.O.D. 294; *Times*, February 25, 1997, CA; affirming [1997] 2 C.M.L.R. 201, QBD . . . .   *Digested*, 97/**631**

R. *v.* Licensing Authority Ex p. Generics (UK) Ltd (C368/96); R. *v.* Licensing Authority Ex p. Wellcome Foundation Ltd (C368/96); R. *v.* Licensing Authority Ex p. Glaxo Operations UK Ltd (C368/96) [1998] E.C.R. I-7967; [1999] 2 C.M.L.R. 181; (1999) 48 B.M.L.R. 161; *Times*, January 4, 1999, ECJ (5th Chamber) . . . .   *Digested*, 99/**2695**

R. *v.* Licensing Authority Ex p. Glaxo Operations UK Ltd (C368/96) see R. *v.* Licensing Authority Ex p. Generics (UK) Ltd (C368/96)

R. *v.* Licensing Authority Ex p. Novartis Pharmaceuticals UK Ltd (Application for Leave to Appeal) [2000] C.O.D. 232, QBD

R. *v.* Licensing Authority Ex p. Rhone Poulenc Rorer Ltd [1998] Eu. L.R. 127, QBD . . . .   *Digested*, 98/**2661**

R. *v.* Licensing Authority Ex p. Wellcome Foundation Ltd (C368/96) see R. *v.* Licensing Authority Ex p. Generics (UK) Ltd (C368/96)

R. (on the application of Lichfield Securities Ltd) *v.* Lichfield DC; *sub nom* R. *v.* Lichfield DC Ex p. Lichfield Securities Ltd [2001] EWCA Civ 304; (2001) 3 L.G.L.R. 35; [2001] 3 P.L.R. 33; [2001] P.L.C.R. 32; [2001] J.P.L. 1434 (Note); [2001] 11 E.G.C.S. 171; (2001) 98(17) L.S.G. 37; (2001) 145 S.J.L.B. 78; *Times*, March 30, 2001, CA; reversing (2001) 81 P. & C.R. 17; [2000] P.L.C.R. 458; [2001] J.P.L. 113 (Note); [2000] C.O.D. 258; [2000] E.G.C.S. 61; [2000] N.P.C. 56, QBD . . .   *Digested*, 01/**590**

R. *v.* Lichfield DC Ex p. Lichfield Securities Ltd see R. (on the application of Lichfield Securities Ltd) *v.* Lichfield DC

R. *v.* Lichniak see R. (on the application of Lichniak) *v.* Secretary of State for the Home Department

R. *v.* Liddey (Ian William) [1999] 2 Cr. App. R. (S.) 122; [1999] Crim. L.R. 340, CA (Crim Div). . . . .   *Digested*, 99/**1358**

R. *v.* Liddle (Frederick); R. *v.* Van Ackeren (Michael Staneley); R. *v.* Singh (Bhupinder) [2000] 2 Cr. App. R. (S.) 282, CA (Crim Div) . . . .   *Digested*, 00/**1275**

R. *v.* Liddle (Mark) (Appeal against Sentence); R. *v.* Hayes (Andrew Michael) [1999] 3
    All E.R. 816; [2000] 1 Cr. App. R. (S.) 131; [1999] Crim. L.R. 847; (1999)
    96(23) L.S.G. 34; *Times*, May 26, 1999; *Independent*, June 16, 1999, CA (Crim
    Div) . . . .   *Digested*, 99/**1188**:
                                             Applied, 01/1344: *Considered*, 01/1346
R. *v.* Life Assurance Unit Trust Regulatory Organisation Ex p. Ross; *sub nom* R. *v.*
    LAUTRO Ex p. Ross [1993] Q.B. 17; [1992] 3 W.L.R. 549; [1993] 1 All E.R. 545;
    [1993] B.C.L.C. 509; (1993) 5 Admin. L.R. 573; [1992] C.O.D. 455; *Times*,
    June 17, 1992; *Independent*, July 16, 1992; *Financial Times*, June 25, 1992, CA;
    affirming [1992] 1 All E.R. 422; [1992] B.C.L.C. 34; [1991] C.O.D. 503; (1991)
    141 N.L.J. 1001; *Times*, July 22, 1991; *Independent*, July 11, 1991; *Financial Times*,
    July 17, 1991, DC . . . .   *Digested*, 93/**43**:
                                               Considered, 94/43, 00/6502
R. *v.* Lightfoot (Robert Edwin) [1999] 2 Cr. App. R. (S.) 55, CA (Crim Div) . . . .   *Digested*, 99/**1322**
R. *v.* Liles (Anthony) [2000] 1 Cr. App. R. (S.) 31, CA (Crim Div) . . . .   *Digested*, 00/**1124**
R. *v.* Lillie (Lawrence) see R. *v.* Simpson (David)
R. *v.* Lincoln (Peter Alan) (1990) 12 Cr. App. R. (S.) 250, CA (Crim Div) . . . .   *Digested*, 92/**1144**:
                                               Considered, 00/1269
R. *v.* Lincoln Crown Court Ex p. Jude [1998] 1 W.L.R. 24; [1997] 3 All E.R. 737;
    [1998] 1 Cr. App. R. 130; (1997) 161 J.P. 589; (1997) 161 J.P.N. 838; (1997) 141
    S.J.L.B. 138; *Times*, April 30, 1997, QBD . . . .   *Digested*, 97/**1273**
R. *v.* Lincoln Justices Ex p. Count; *sub nom* R. *v.* Lincoln Magistrates Court Ex p.
    Count (1996) 8 Admin. L.R. 233; [1995] R.V.R. 195; [1995] C.O.D. 351;
    Independent, August 2, 1995, QBD . . . .   *Digested*, 95/**129**:
                                               Applied, 00/1957
R. *v.* Lincoln Magistrates Court Ex p. Count see R. *v.* Lincoln Justices Ex p. Count
R. *v.* Lincolnshire CC Ex p. Atkinson; R. *v.* Wealden DC Ex p. Wales; R. *v.* Wealden DC
    Ex p. Stratford (1996) 8 Admin. L.R. 529; [1997] J.P.L. 65; (1996) 160 L.G.
    Rev. 580; [1995] E.G.C.S. 145; [1995] N.P.C. 145; *Times*, September 22, 1995;
    Independent, October 3, 1995, QBD. . . . .   *Digested*, 96/**4152**:
                                               Considered, 98/3832, 99/4248
R. *v.* Lindsay (Ian Robert) [1998] 1 Cr. App. R. (S.) 324, CA (Crim Div) . . . .   *Digested*, 98/**1220**:
                                               Considered, 99/1163
R. *v.* Lindsay (Neil) see R. *v.* Kelly (Anthony Noel)
R. *v.* Linekar (Gareth) [1995] Q.B. 250; [1995] 2 W.L.R. 237; [1995] 3 All E.R. 69;
    [1995] 2 Cr. App. R. 49; [1995] Crim. L.R. 320; (1995) 92(2) L.S.G. 35; (1994)
    138 S.J.L.B. 227; *Times*, October 26, 1994; *Independent*, December 19, 1994
    (C.S.), CA (Crim Div) . . . .   *Digested*, 95/**1290**:
                                               Distinguished, 00/1003
R. *v.* Ling (Peter) see R. *v.* Ansari (Mohammed)
R. *v.* Lingham (Gary) [2001] 1 Cr. App. R. (S.) 46; [2000] Crim. L.R. 696; *Times*, June
    2, 2000, CA (Crim Div) . . . .   *Digested*, 00/**1159**
R. *v.* Litanzios (Phillip) [1999] Crim. L.R. 667, CA (Crim Div)
R. *v.* Litchfield [1998] Crim. L.R. 507, CA (Crim Div)
R. *v.* Little (David) see Attorney General's Reference (No.64 of 2001), Re
R. *v.* Littlefield (John) see R. *v.* Aranguren (Jose de Jesus)
R. *v.* Litwin (Jeffrey Simon) see R. *v.* Piggott (Luke Anthony)
R. *v.* Liverpool CC Ex p. Baby Products Association see R. *v.* Liverpool City Council Ex
    p. Baby Products Association
R. (on the application of Barry) *v.* Liverpool City Council; *sub nom* R. *v.* Liverpool City
    Council Ex p. Barry [2001] EWCA Civ 384; (2001) 3 L.G.L.R. 40; [2001]
    B.L.G.R. 361; *Times*, March 27, 2001; *Independent*, April 4, 2001, CA . . . .   *Digested*, 01/**4313**
R. *v.* Liverpool City Council Ex p. Arboine (1998) 75 P. & C.R. D49, QBD
R. *v.* Liverpool City Council Ex p. Baby Products Association; *sub nom* R. *v.* Liverpool
    CC Ex p. Baby Products Association (2000) 2 L.G.L.R. 689; [2000] B.L.G.R.
    171; [2000] C.O.D. 91; *Times*, December 1, 1999, QBD . . . .   *Digested*, 00/**853**
R. *v.* Liverpool City Council Ex p. Barry see R. (on the application of Barry) *v.*
    Liverpool City Council
R. *v.* Liverpool City Council Ex p. Filla [1996] C.O.D. 24, QBD . . . .   *Considered*, 01/591
R. (on the application of Larkin) *v.* Liverpool City Justices see R. (on the application of
    McCormick) *v.* Liverpool City Magistrates Court
R. (on the application of McCormack) *v.* Liverpool City Justices see R. (on the
    application of McCormick) *v.* Liverpool City Magistrates Court
R. (on the application of Larkin) *v.* Liverpool City Magistrates Court see R. (on the
    application of McCormick) *v.* Liverpool City Magistrates Court
R. (on the application of McCormick) *v.* Liverpool City Magistrates Court; *sub nom* R. *v.*
    Clerk to Liverpool Justices Ex p. Larkin; R. *v.* Clerk to Liverpool Magistrates
    Court Ex p. McCormick; R. (on the application of McCormack) *v.* Liverpool City
    Justices; R. *v.* Clerk to Liverpool Magistrates Court Ex p. Larkin; R. (on the
    application of Larkin) *v.* Liverpool City Magistrates Court; R. (on the application
    of Larkin) *v.* Liverpool City Justices [2001] 2 All E.R. 705; (2001) 165 J.P.
    362; (2001) 165 J.P.N. 204; *Times*, January 12, 2001; *Independent*, December
    18, 2000 (C.S), QBD (Admin Ct) . . . .   *Digested*, 01/**1116**
R. (on the application of H) *v.* Liverpool City Youth Court [2001] Crim. L.R. 487, QBD

R. (on the application of Shields) *v.* Liverpool Crown Court [2001] EWHC Admin 90; [2001] U.K.H.R.R. 610; [2001] A.C.D. 60; *Independent*, March 12, 2001 (C.S); *Daily Telegraph*, February 13, 2001, QBD (Admin Ct)

R. *v.* Liverpool Crown Court Ex p. Lord Chancellor (1994) 158 J.P. 821; (1994) 158 J.P.N. 587; *Times*, April 22, 1993; *Independent*, October 18, 1993 (C.S.); *Independent*, May 10, 1993 (C.S.), QBD . . . .   *Digested,* 93/**2568**: *Considered,* 98/3706

R. *v.* Liverpool Crown Court Ex p. Luxury Leisure Ltd (1999) 1 L.G.L.R. 222; [1999] B.L.G.R. 345; *Times*, October 26, 1998, CA. . . . .   *Digested,* 98/**3746**

R. *v.* Liverpool John Moores University Ex p. Hayes [1998] E.L.R. 261, QBD. . . . .   *Digested,* 98/**2005**

R. *v.* Liverpool Justices Ex p. Crown Prosecution Service (1990) 90 Cr. App. R. 261; (1990) 154 J.P. 1; [1990] R.T.R. 349; [1989] Crim. L.R. 655; (1989) 153 J.P.N. 593, QBD . . . .   *Digested,* 90/**999**: *Applied,* 00/1333

R. *v.* Liverpool Justices Ex p. DPP [1993] Q.B. 233; [1992] 3 W.L.R. 20; [1992] 3 All E.R. 249; (1992) 95 Cr. App. R. 222; (1992) 156 J.P. 634; [1992] Crim. L.R. 294; [1992] C.O.D. 180; (1992) 156 J.P.N. 235; *Times*, December 10, 1991, QBD . . . .   *Digested,* 92/**689**: *Applied,* 01/1103

R. *v.* Liverpool Justices Ex p. Nicholas [1998] C.O.D. 99, QBD

R. *v.* Liverpool Justices Ex p. P (1998) 162 J.P. 766; [1998] C.O.D. 453; (1998) 162 J.P.N. 962, QBD . . . .   *Digested,* 98/**1087**

R. *v.* Liverpool Magistrates Court Ex p. Abiaka (1999) 163 J.P. 497; (1999) 163 J.P.N. 555; (1999) 96(14) L.S.G. 32; (1999) 143 S.J.L.B. 135; *Times*, May 6, 1999; *Independent*, March 22, 1999 (C.S.), QBD . . . .   *Digested,* 99/**982**

R. *v.* Liverpool Magistrates Court Ex p. Ansen; *sub nom* Ansen, Re [1998] 1 All E.R. 692, QBD . . . .   *Digested,* 98/**1152**

R. *v.* Liverpool Magistrates Court Ex p. Banwell [1998] C.O.D. 144, QBD

R. *v.* Liverpool Magistrates Court Ex p. Collins see DPP *v.* Speede

R. *v.* Liverpool Magistrates Court Ex p. Quantrell [1999] 2 Cr. App. R. 24; (1999) 163 J.P. 420; [1999] Crim. L.R. 734; (1999) 163 J.P.N. 594; *Times*, February 2, 1999; *Independent*, February 8, 1999 (C.S.), QBD . . . .   *Digested,* 99/**980**

R. *v.* Liverpool Magistrates Court Ex p. Santos see DPP *v.* Speede

R. *v.* Liverpool Magistrates Court Ex p. Slade see R. *v.* Liverpool Stipendiary Magistrate Ex p. Slade

R. *v.* Liverpool Stipendiary Magistrate Ex p. Slade; *sub nom* R. *v.* Liverpool Magistrates Court Ex p. Slade [1998] 1 W.L.R. 531; [1998] 1 All E.R. 60; [1998] 1 Cr. App. R. 147; [1998] E.H.L.R. 103; [1997] C.O.D. 414; *Independent*, June 13, 1997, QBD . . . .   *Digested,* 97/**249**

R. *v.* Liverpool Youth Court Ex p. C CO/474/98, QBD. . . . .   *Digested,* 98/**1072**

R. *v.* LJL [1999] Crim. L.R. 489, CA (Crim Div)

R. *v.* Lloyd (David) [2000] 2 Cr. App. R. 355; [2001] Crim. L.R. 250, CA (Crim Div) . .   *Digested,* 00/**1067**

R. *v.* Lloyd (David Russell) see Attorney General's Reference (No.66 of 1995), Re

R. *v.* Lloyd (Grant Oaten) [1997] 2 Cr. App. R. (S.) 151, CA (Crim Div) . . . .   *Digested,* 97/**1053**: *Considered,* 98/1165

R. *v.* Lloyd (Leigh Cedric) see R. *v.* McCarthy (Colin Paul)

R. *v.* Lloyd (Paul Gabriel); R. *v.* Smith (Cyril) (1990) 12 Cr. App. R. (S.) 354, CA (Crim Div) . . . .   *Digested,* 92/**1287**: *Considered,* 00/1267

R. *v.* Lloyd (Robert) [2001] EWCA Crim 600; [2001] 2 Cr. App. R. (S.) 111, CA (Crim Div) . . . .   *Digested,* 01/**1294**

R. *v.* Lloyd (Stuart) (1987) 9 Cr. App. R. (S.) 254, CA (Crim Div) . . . .   *Digested,* 89/**1053**: *Considered,* 91/1140, 92/1310, 96/1942, 99/1210

R. *v.* Llywarch (John Elfyn) see R. *v.* Jones (John McKinsie)

R. *v.* Local Authority in the Midlands Ex p. LM [2000] 1 F.L.R. 612; [2000] 1 F.C.R. 736; [2000] U.K.H.R.R. 143; (2000) 2 L.G.L.R. 1043; [2000] C.O.D. 41; [2000] Fam. Law 83, QBD . . . .   *Digested,* 00/**7**

R. *v.* Local Commissioner for Administration for the North and East Area of England Ex p. Bradford City Council [1979] Q.B. 287; [1979] 2 W.L.R. 1; [1979] 2 All E.R. 881; 77 L.G.R. 305; [1978] J.P.L. 767; 122 S.J. 573, CA; affirming [1978] J.P.L. 706 . . . .   *Digested,* 79/**1693**: *Applied,* 01/4617

R. *v.* Local Commissioner for Administration in North and North East England Ex p. Liverpool City Council; *sub nom* R. *v.* Local Commissioner for Local Government for North and North East England Ex p. Liverpool City Council [2001] 1 All E.R. 462; (2000) 2 L.G.L.R. 603; [2000] B.L.G.R. 571; [2000] N.P.C. 18; *Times*, March 3, 2000, CA; affirming [1999] 3 All E.R. 85; (1999) 1 L.G.L.R. 614; (2000) 79 P. & C.R. 473; [1999] J.P.L. 844; [1999] C.O.D. 384, QBD . . . .   *Digested,* 00/**4140**

R. *v.* Local Commissioner for Local Government for North and North East England Ex p. Liverpool City Council see R. *v.* Local Commissioner for Administration in North and North East England Ex p. Liverpool City Council

R. (on the application of Hughes) *v.* Local Government Ombudsman [2001] EWHC
Admin 349; (2001) 3 L.G.L.R. 50; [2001] A.C.D. 89; (2001) 98(20) L.S.G. 45,
QBD (Admin Ct)
R. *v.* Local Government Ombudsman Ex p. Abernethy [2000] C.O.D. 56, QBD
R. *v.* Local Government Ombudsman Ex p. Turpin (Application for Judicial Review);
sub nom R. *v.* Commissioner for Local Administration Ex p. Turpin [1998]
E.G.C.S. 18, QBD
R. *v.* Lockley (Adrian Neil); R. *v.* Corah (Lisa Mary) [1995] 2 Cr. App. R. 554; *Times,*
June 27, 1995; *Independent,* June 15, 1995, CA (Crim Div) . . . . *Distinguished,* 96/1413:
Followed, 99/873

R. *v.* Lodde (Ann Elizabeth) see R. *v.* Lodde (David Anthony)
R. *v.* Lodde (David Anthony); R. *v.* Lodde (Ann Elizabeth) *Times,* March 8, 2000, CA
(Crim Div). . . . . *Digested,* 00/**1185**
R. *v.* Loke (Kwong Fatt) [1999] N.I. 165, CA (Crim Div) (NI) . . . . *Digested,* 00/**5481**
R. *v.* London (North) Industrial Tribunal Ex p. Associated Newspapers Ltd; *sub nom*
Associated Newspapers Ltd *v.* London (North) Industrial Tribunal [1998] I.C.R.
1212; [1998] I.R.L.R. 569; (1999) 1 L.G.L.R. 20; *Times,* May 13, 1998, QBD . . . . *Digested,* 98/**77**:
Considered, 99/2061
R. *v.* London Beth Din Ex p. Bloom [1998] C.O.D. 131, QBD. . . . . *Digested,* 98/**101**
R. *v.* London City Justices Ex p. Cropper see R. *v.* Uxbridge Magistrates Court Ex p.
Patel
R. *v.* London County Quarter Sessions Appeals Committee Ex p. Rossi; *sub nom*
Rossi, Re [1956] 1 Q.B. 682; [1956] 2 W.L.R. 800; [1956] 1 All E.R. 670; 120
J.P. 239; 100 S.J. 225, CA. . . . . *Digested,* 56/**5423**:
Applied, 74/2128, 89/2125, 90/4586, 94/501, 96/1174: *Considered,* 58/2025,
58/2976, 68/618, 70/2570, 72/2830, 72/3086, 81/2354, 87/1363, 88/1858,
90/2782: *Distinguished,* 59/2887, 66/11845, 68/617, 69/576, 97/2227,
99/3667: *Followed,* 72/3365
R. *v.* London Docklands Development Corp Ex p. Frost (1997) 73 P. & C.R. 199, QBD. . *Digested,* 97/**4095**:
Approved, 98/4209: *Followed,* 00/4502

R. (on the application of Daejan Properties Ltd) *v.* London Leasehold Valuation Tribunal;
sub nom Daejan Properties Ltd *v.* London Leasehold Valuation Tribunal; R. *v.*
London Leasehold Valuation Tribunal Ex p. Daejan Properties Ltd [2001] EWCA
Civ 1095; [2001] 43 E.G. 187; (2001) 98(35) L.S.G. 35; [2001] N.P.C. 117;
Times, August 10, 2001; *Independent,* July 17, 2001, CA; reversing [2001] L. &
T.R. 9; [2000] 3 E.G.L.R. 44; [2000] 49 E.G. 121; [2000] E.G.C.S. 108; (2000)
97(39) L.S.G. 43; *Times,* October 20, 2000; *Independent,* November 6, 2000
(C.S), QBD (Admin Ct) . . . . *Digested,* 01/**4217**
R. *v.* London Leasehold Valuation Tribunal Ex p. Daejan Properties Ltd see R. (on the
application of Daejan Properties Ltd) *v.* London Leasehold Valuation Tribunal
R. *v.* London Magistrates Court Ex p. Cropper see R. *v.* Uxbridge Magistrates Court Ex
p. Patel
R. (on the application of H) *v.* London North and East Region Mental Health Review
Tribunal see R. (on the application of H) *v.* Mental Health Review Tribunal for
North and East London Region
R. (on the application of Morris) *v.* London Rent Assessment Committee C/2001/1103
QBACF, CA; affirming [2001] EWHC Admin 309; [2001] L. & T.R. 36; [2001]
31 E.G. 104; [2001] N.P.C. 87; *Independent,* June 11, 2001 (C.S), QBD (Admin
Ct) . . . . *Digested,* 01/**4214**
R. *v.* London Rent Assessment Panel Ex p. Cadogan Estates Ltd [1998] Q.B. 398;
[1997] 3 W.L.R. 833; (1998) 30 H.L.R. 487; (1998) 76 P. & C.R. 410; [1997] 2
E.G.L.R. 134; [1997] 34 E.G. 88; [1997] C.O.D. 372; [1997] E.G.C.S. 88;
[1997] N.P.C. 88; *Times,* July 10, 1997, QBD . . . . *Digested,* 97/**3253**:
Applied, 01/4214

R. (on the application of C) *v.* London South and South West Region Mental Health
Review Tribunal see R. (on the application of C) *v.* Mental Health Review
Tribunal
R. *v.* London South and South West Region Mental Health Review Tribunal Ex p. M
[2000] Lloyd's Rep. Med. 143; *Times,* February 10, 2000, QBD . . . . *Digested,* 00/**4174**
R. *v.* London South East Valuation Tribunal Ex p. Moore [2001] R.V.R. 92, CA . . . . *Digested,* 01/**4809**
R. *v.* London South West Valuation Tribunal Ex p. De Melo [2000] R.V.R. 73, CA . . . . . . *Digested,* 00/**4570**
R. (on the application of Transport for London) *v.* London Underground Ltd [2001]
EWHC Admin 637; *Times,* August 2, 2001; *Daily Telegraph,* September 18, 2001,
QBD (Admin Ct) . . . . *Digested,* 01/**5448**
R. *v.* Long (Leonard) [1998] 2 Cr. App. R. 326; (1997) 161 J.P. 769; (1997) 161 J.P.N.
1080; *Times,* October 24, 1997, CA (Crim Div) . . . . *Digested,* 97/**1269**
R. *v.* Looseley (Grant Spencer) (No.2) see Attorney General's Reference (No.3 of
2000), Re
R. *v.* Looseley (Grant Spencer) (No.1); *sub nom* R. *v.* Loosely (No.1); 200000730 Y5,
CA (Crim Div). . . . . *Subsequent proceed-*
ings, 01/992

R. *v.* Loosely (Grant Spencer) see Attorney General's Reference (No.3 of 2000), Re
R. *v.* Loosely (No.1) see R. *v.* Looseley (Grant Spencer) (No.1)

R. v. Loosley (Grant Spencer) (No.2) see Attorney General's Reference (No.3 of 2000), Re

R. v. Lord Chancellor Ex p. Child Poverty Action Group; R. v. DPP Ex p. Bull [1999] 1 W.L.R. 347; [1998] 2 All E.R. 755; [1998] C.O.D. 267; (1998) 148 N.L.J. 20; *Times,* February 27,1998; *Independent,* February 11, 1998, QBD . . . . *Digested,* 98/**412**: *Applied,* 00/430

R. v. Lord Chancellor Ex p. Lightfoot; *sub nom* Lightfoot v. Lord Chancellor [2000] Q.B. 597; [2000] 2 W.L.R. 318; [1999] 4 All E.R. 583; [2000] B.C.C. 537; [2000] H.R.L.R. 33; [2000] B.P.I.R. 120; (1999) 96(31) L.S.G. 35; (1999) 149 N.L.J.1285; *Times,* August 18,1999 ; *Independent,* November 1,1999 (C.S.), CA; affirming [1999] 2 W.L.R. 1126; [1998] 4 All E.R. 764; [1999] B.P.I.R. 118; [1999] C.O.D. 87; (1998) 148 N.L.J. 1230; [1998] N.P.C. 134, QBD. . . . . *Digested,* 99/**3246**

R. v. Lord Chancellor Ex p. Witham [1998] Q.B. 575; [1998] 2 W.L.R. 849; [1997] 2 All E.R. 779; [1997] C.O.D. 291; (1997) 147 N.L.J. 378; (1997) 141 S.J.L.B. 82; *Times,* March 13,1997; *Independent,* March 21,1997, QBD . . . . *Digested,* 97/**11**: *Considered,* 97/698, 00/96, 01/5711: *Distinguished,* 99/3246: *Followed,* 99/540, 99/4107

R. v. Lord Chancellor's Department Ex p. Nangle [1992] 1 All E.R. 897; [1991] I.C.R. 743; [1991] I.R.L.R. 343; [1991] C.O.D. 484, QBD . . . . *Digested,* 91/**1624**: *Distinguished,* 98/4785

R. v. Lord Chancellor's Department Ex p. O' Toole [1998] C.O.D. 269, QBD

R. (on the application of Bulger) v. Lord Chief Justice see R. (on the application of Bulger) v. Secretary of State for the Home Department

R. v. Lord President of the Privy Council Ex p. Page; *sub nom* Page v. Hull University Visitor; R. v. Hull University Visitor Ex p. Page [1993] A.C. 682; [1993] 3 W.L.R. 1112; [1993] 1 All E.R. 97; [1993] I.C.R. 114; (1993) 143 N.L.J. 15; (1993) 137 S.J.L.B. 45; *Times,* December 15, 1992; *Independent,* December 9, 1992, HL; affirming [1991] 1 W.L.R. 1277; [1991] 4 All E.R. 747; [1991] I.C.R. 67; [1992] C.O.D. 34, CA; reversing [1991] C.O.D. 486, QBD . . . . *Digested,* 93/**61**: *Applied,* 93/62, 01/386

R. (on the application of A) v. Lord Saville of Newdigate (Bloody Sunday Inquiry); *sub nom* R. (on the application of Widgery Soldiers) v. Lord Saville of Newdigate [2001] EWCA Civ 2048; *Times,* December 21, 2001, CA; affirming [2001] EWHC Admin 888; (2001) 98(48) L.S.G. 29; (2001) 145 S.J.L.B. 262; *Times,* November 21, 2001; *Daily Telegraph,* November 20, 2001, QBD (Admin Ct) . . . . *Digested,* 01/**82**

R. (on the application of Widgery Soldiers) v. Lord Saville of Newdigate see R. (on the application of A) v. Lord Saville of Newdigate (Bloody Sunday Inquiry)

R. v. Lord Saville of Newdigate Ex p. A see R. v. Lord Saville of Newdigate Ex p. B (No.2)

R. v. Lord Saville of Newdigate Ex p. B (No.1); *sub nom* R. v. Bloody Sunday Inquiry Ex p. B *Times,* April 15,1999; *Independent,* April 27,1999, CA . . . . *Digested,* 99/**79**

R. v. Lord Saville of Newdigate Ex p. B (No.2); *sub nom* R. v. Lord Saville of Newdigate Ex p. A [2000] 1 W.L.R. 1855; [1999] 4 All E.R. 860; [1999] C.O.D. 436; (1999) 149 N.L.J. 1201; *Times,* July 29, 1999, CA; affirming (1999) 149 N.L.J. 965; *Times,* June 22,1999 ; *Independent,* June 22,1999, QBD . . . . *Digested,* 99/**80**: *Applied,* 01/82: *Considered,* 01/3684: *Followed,* 00/47

R. v. Loughlin (Matthew) [1997] 1 Cr. App. R. (S.) 277, CA (Crim Div) . . . . *Digested,* 97/**1704**: *Considered,* 98/1379: *Referred to,* 99/1248

R. v. Loughran [1999] Crim. L.R. 404, CA (Crim Div)

R. v. Louis (Terry) see Attorney General's Reference (No.49 of 2000), Re

R. v. Love (Colin Gilbert) [1998] 1 Cr. App. R. 458; *Times,* December 3, 1997; *Independent,* November 25,1997, CMAC . . . . *Digested,* 97/**293**

R. v. Love (Compensation Orders) [1999] 1 Cr. App. R. (S.) 484, CA (Crim Div) . . . . . . *Digested,* 99/**1103**

R. v. Love (James Thomas); R. v. Tomkins (Guy Michael); R. v. Shields (Michael) [1999] 1 Cr. App. R. (S.) 75, CA (Crim Div) . . . . *Digested,* 99/**1187**

R. v. Love (Mark Ryan) see R. v. T (Craig Daniel)

R. v. Loveridge (Christine) see R. v. Loveridge (William) (Appeal against Conviction)

R. v. Loveridge (William) (Appeal against Conviction); R. v. Lee (Charles Sonny); R. v. Loveridge (Christine) [2001] EWCA Crim 973; [2001] 2 Cr. App. R. 29; (2001) 98(23) L.S.G. 36; (2001) 145 S.J.L.B. 120; *Times,* May 3, 2001, CA (Crim Div) . *Digested,* 01/**983**

R. v. Loving (Jeffrey Richard) see DPP v. Doot

R. v. Low (Roy) [1998] 1 Cr. App. R. (S.) 68; [1997] Crim. L.R. 692, CA (Crim Div) . . . *Digested,* 98/**1342**

R. v. Lowe (Kenneth) [1997] 2 Cr. App. R. (S.) 324, CA (Crim Div) . . . . *Digested,* 98/**1366**: *Considered,* 01/1259

R. v. Lowe (Trevor); R. v. Leask (Stephen) [2000] 1 W.L.R. 153; [1999] 3 All E.R. 762; [1999] 2 Cr. App. R. (S.) 316; [1999] Crim. L.R. 423; *Times,* February 18,1999; *Independent,* March 1,1999 (C.S.), CA (Crim Div). . . . . *Digested,* 99/**1109**: *Considered,* 01/1244

R. v. Lowestoft Justices Ex p. DPP see R. v. Warley Magistrates Court Ex p. DPP

R. v. Lowry (Thomas Gordon) [1996] 2 Cr. App. R. (S.) 416, CA (Crim Div) . . . . *Digested,* 97/**1676**: *Considered,* 98/1364, 01/1263

R. v. Lubega (Thomas) (1999) 163 J.P. 221; (1999) 163 J.P.N. 331; *Times,* February 10, 1999; *Independent,* February 8, 1999 (C.S.), CA (Crim Div) . . . . *Digested,* 99/**911**

R. v. Lucas (Andrew) [1999] 1 Cr. App. R. (S.) 78, CA (Crim Div) . . . . *Digested,* 99/**1146**:
Considered, 00/1213
R. v. Lucas (Lawrence Owen) [2000] 1 Cr. App. R. (S.) 5, CA (Crim Div) . . . . *Digested,* 00/**1240**
R. v. Lucas (Richard Jon) [1998] 1 Cr. App. R. (S.) 195, CA (Crim Div) . . . . *Digested,* 98/**1361**
R. v. Lucas (Saxon) see R. v. Brown (Anthony Joseph)
R. v. Luke (Kwame) [1999] 1 Cr. App. R. (S.) 389, CA (Crim Div) . . . . *Digested,* 99/**1139**
R. v. Lumley (David) [2001] 2 Cr. App. R. (S.) 21, CA (Crim Div) . . . . *Digested,* 01/**1343**
R. v. Lundt-Smith [1964] 2 Q.B. 167; [1964] 2 W.L.R. 1063; [1964] 3 All E.R. 225
(Note); 128 J.P. 534; 62 L.G.R. 376; 108 S.J. 425, Assizes . . . . *Digested,* 64/**3194**:
Approved, 71/10171: *Considered,* 69/3177, 98/1365
R. v. Lunney (Daniel) [1999] N.I. 158, CA (Crim Div) (NI) . . . . *Digested,* 99/**5223**
R. v. Lunt (Kevin Anthony) [1998] 2 Cr. App. R. (S.) 348, CA (Crim Div) . . . . *Digested,* 98/**1362**
R. v. Luton Family Proceedings Court Justices Ex p. R FC3 97/6459/D; QBCOF 97/
0112/D, CA . . . . *Digested,* 98/**496**:
Followed, 98/499
R. v. Luton Justices Ex p. Abecasis (2000) 164 J.P. 265; (2000) 164 J.P.N. 344;
(2000) 97(13) L.S.G. 43; *Times,* March 30, 2000, CA; affirming (1999) 163 J.P.
828, QBD . . . . *Digested,* 00/**1055**
R. v. Luty (Philip Andrew) [1999] 2 Cr. App. R. (S.) 81, CA (Crim Div) . . . . *Digested,* 99/**1159**
R. v. Lyall (Javinder Singh) (1995) 16 Cr. App. R. (S.) 600, CA (Crim Div) . . . . *Considered,* 97/1514,
97/1515, 98/1195, 98/1196
R. v. Lynn (James) see Attorney General's Reference (No.3 of 1999) (Unduly Lenient
Sentence), Re
R. v. M (Aaron Shaun) [1998] 1 W.L.R. 363; [1998] 1 All E.R. 874; [1998] 2 Cr. App.
R. 57; [1998] 2 Cr. App. R. (S.) 128; [1998] 1 F.L.R. 900; [1998] Fam. Law 314;
Times, December 11, 1997, CA (Crim Div) . . . . *Digested,* 98/**1281**:
Considered, 99/1243, 00/1112, 00/1319, 00/1328: *Distinguished,* 99/1220
R. v. M (Abdul) (A Juvenile) [2000] 1 Cr. App. R. (S.) 27; [1999] Crim. L.R. 593, CA
(Crim Div) . . . . *Digested,* 00/**1312**
R. v. M (Admissibility: Background Evidence) see R. v. TM
R. v. M (Adrian Alexander) [1996] 2 Cr. App. R. (S.) 286, CA (Crim Div) . . . . *Digested,* 97/**1452**:
Considered, 98/1341, 00/1394, 00/1396
R. v. M (Alan) [2000] Lloyd's Rep. Med. 304, CA (Crim Div) . . . . *Digested,* 01/**979**
R. v. M (Albert) see Attorney General's Reference (No.46 of 1999), Re
R. v. M (Alexander) [1999] Crim. L.R. 857, CA (Crim Div)
R. v. M (Alfred John) (1993) 14 Cr. App. R. (S.) 286, CA (Crim Div) . . . . *Digested,* 94/**1272**:
Considered, 97/1443, 99/1193
R. v. M (Andrew) see Attorney General's Reference (No.12 of 1998), Re
R. v. M (Andrew Ian) (A Juvenile) [2001] EWCA Crim 79; [2001] 2 Cr. App. R. (S.)
56, CA (Crim Div) . . . . *Digested,* 01/**1387**
R. v. M (Andrew James) see Attorney General's Reference (No.18 of 1999), Re
R. v. M (Arthur John) see Attorney General's Reference (No.1 of 2001), Re
R. v. M (Bernard) (A Juvenile) see R. v. M (Patrick) (A Juvenile)
R. v. M (Brian) [2000] 1 Cr. App. R. 49; [1999] Crim. L.R. 922; (1999) 96(28) L.S.G.
25; *Times,* July 9, 1999 ; *Independent,* July 16, 1999, CA (Crim Div) . . . . *Digested,* 99/**1044**
R. v. M (David Paul) (A Juvenile) see R. v. R (Wesley) (A Juvenile)
R. v. M (Discretionary Life Sentence) see R. v. M (Young Offender: Time in Custody
on Remand)
R. v. M (Douglas James) (A Juvenile) see Attorney General's Reference (No.79 of
2001), Re
R. v. M (Evelyn) see R. v. M (George)
R. v. M (Fitness to Plead); R. v. Kerr (Fitness to Plead); R. v. H (Fitness to Plead)
[2001] EWCA Crim 2024; (2001) 98(41) L.S.G. 34; (2001) 145 S.J.L.B. 236;
Times, November 1, 2001, CA (Crim Div) . . . . *Digested,* 01/**1137**
R. v. M (George); *sub nom* R. v. M (Evelyn) [2000] 1 Cr. App. R. (S.) 296, CA (Crim
Div) . . . . *Digested,* 00/**1426**
R. v. M (George William) (A Juvenile) [2001] 2 Cr. App. R. (S.) 5, CA (Crim Div) . . . . . *Digested,* 01/**1428**
R. v. M (Grayham David) (A Juvenile) [1998] 1 Cr. App. R. (S.) 306, CA (Crim Div) . . . *Digested,* 98/**1284**
R. v. M (Incest: Sentencing) see Attorney General's Reference (No.56 of 1998), Re
R. v. M (Jodie) (A Juvenile); R. v. L (Wayne) (A Juvenile); R. v. C (Leanne) (A
Juvenile); R. v. M (Stuart) (A Juvenile) [2000] 1 Cr. App. R. (S.) 17; [1999]
Crim. L.R. 755, CA (Crim Div) . . . . *Digested,* 00/**1344**
Considered, 99/1192
R. v. M (John) (1981) 3 Cr. App. R. (S.) 285, CA (Crim Div) . . . . *Digested,* 98/**1140**
R. v. M (John Paul) [1998] 2 Cr. App. R. (S.) 208, CA (Crim Div) . . . . *Digested,* 98/**1140**
R. v. M (Junior) (A Juvenile) [2001] 1 Cr. App. R. (S.) 29, CA (Crim Div) . . . . *Digested,* 01/**1405**
R. v. M (Lee) (A Juvenile) see R. v. S (Paul) (A Juvenile)
R. v. M (Mark) [2000] 1 Cr. App. R. (S.) 457, CA (Crim Div) . . . . *Digested,* 00/**1398**
R. v. M (Michael Neil) [2000] 1 Cr. App. R. (S.) 416; [1999] Crim. L.R. 1003, CA
(Crim Div) . . . . *Digested,* 00/**1281**
R. v. M (Patrick) (A Juvenile); R. v. M (Bernard) (A Juvenile) [2000] 1 Cr. App. R. (S.)
6, CA (Crim Div) . . . . *Digested,* 00/**1343**
R. v. M (Paul Richard) (1995) 16 Cr. App. R. (S.) 770; [1995] Crim. L.R. 344, CA
(Crim Div) . . . . *Considered,* 98/1353,
98/1354, 99/1309, 00/1402

R. *v.* M (Paul Simon) (A Juvenile) [1998] 2 Cr. App. R. (S.) 398, CA (Crim Div) . . . . . . *Digested,* 99/**1213**
R. *v.* M (Peter Kenneth) [2000] 1 Cr. App. R. (S.) 419, CA (Crim Div) . . . . *Digested,* 00/**1391**
R. *v.* M (Rape: Specimen Charges) [1999] N.I. 45, CA (Crim Div) (NI) . . . . *Digested,* 99/**5195**
R. *v.* M (Richard) (A Juvenile) [2000] Crim. L.R. 372; *Times,* December 3, 1999, CA
    (Crim Div) . . . . *Digested,* 00/**1017**
R. *v.* M (Sarah Ruth) (A Juvenile) see Attorney General's Reference (Nos.78, 79 and
    85 of 1998), Re
R. *v.* M (Stuart) (A Juvenile) see R. *v.* M (Jodie) (A Juvenile)
R. *v.* M (Stuart James) (A Juvenile) see R. *v.* Howells (Craig)
R. *v.* M (Wasted Costs Order) [1996] 1 F.L.R. 750; [1997] 1 F.C.R. 42; [1996] Fam.
    Law 350; (1997) 161 J.P.N. 40, QBD . . . . *Digested,* 96/**935**:
                                                Followed, 99/989
R. *v.* M (Wasted Costs Order); *sub nom* Howells (Solicitors), Re [2000] P.N.L.R. 214,
    CA (Crim Div) . . . . *Digested,* 00/**1042**
R. *v.* M (William Andrew) (A Juvenile) see R. *v.* Webbe (Bernard)
R. *v.* M (Witness Reprisals) see R. *v.* H (Witness Reprisals)
R. *v.* M (Young Offender: Time in Custody on Remand); *sub nom* R. *v.* M
    (Discretionary Life Sentence); R. *v.* L (Young Offender: Time in Custody on
    Remand) [1999] 1 W.L.R. 485; [1998] 2 All E.R. 939; [1999] 1 Cr. App. R. (S.)
    6; [1998] Crim. L.R. 512; *Times,* April 7, 1998, CA (Crim Div) . . . . *Digested,* 98/**1269**:
                Applied, 99/5949, 00/1356, 01/1353, 01/1439: *Considered,* 99/1079,
            99/1248, 99/1255, 99/1268, 00/1351, 00/1352, 00/1354, 00/1355, 00/1360,
                       01/1298: *Followed,* 99/1241, 99/1252, 99/1257
R. *v.* Maben (Matthew) [1997] 2 Cr. App. R. (S.) 341, CA (Crim Div) . . . . *Digested,* 98/**1110**:
                            Considered, 99/1065, 00/1122
R. *v.* MacCaig (Duncan James) (1986) 8 Cr. App. R. (S.) 77, CA . . . . *Digested,* 87/**918**:
                            Considered, 98/1370
R. (on the application of Hadfield) *v.* Macclesfield BC (2001) 81 P. & C.R. D16, CA
R. *v.* MacDonald (Brian Anthony); R. *v.* Atherley (Andrew); R. *v.* Bristol (Keith
    Anthony) [1998] Crim. L.R. 808, CA (Crim Div)
R. *v.* Macdonald (Inspector of Taxes) Ex p. Hutchinson & Co Ltd [1998] S.T.C. 680;
    [1998] B.T.C. 217; *Times,* July 6, 1998, QBD . . . . *Digested,* 98/**4692**
R. *v.* MacDonald (Ronald John) (1983) 5 Cr. App. R. (S.) 22, CA (Crim Div) . . . . *Digested,* 84/**762**:
                       Considered, 92/1248, 95/1369, 99/1133
R. *v.* Mace (Steven Terence) see R. *v.* Xenofhontos (Xenophon Peter)
R. *v.* MacKenzie (AM) (Unreported, February 24, 1998), MC [*Ex rel.* Trobridges
    Solicitors, 1 Ford Park Road, Mutley, Plymouth] . . . . *Digested,* 98/**1027**
R. *v.* Mackie (Robert) (1973) 57 Cr. App. R. 453; [1973] Crim. L.R. 438; (1973) 137
    J.P.N. 203, CA (Crim Div) . . . . *Digested,* 73/**564**:
                          Applied, 79/508, 00/1017
R. *v.* MacLeod (Calum Iain) [2001] Crim. L.R. 589; *Times,* December 20, 2000, CA
    (Crim Div) . . . . *Digested,* 01/**1010**
R. *v.* MacMaster (Iain) [1999] 1 Cr. App. R. 402; [1999] Crim. L.R. 310; (1998)
    95(42) L.S.G. 33; *Times,* October 28, 1998; *Independent,* October 19, 1998
    (C.S.), CA (Crim Div) . . . . *Digested,* 98/**937**
R. *v.* Madan (Kanhya Lal) [1961] 2 Q.B. 1; [1961] 2 W.L.R. 231; [1961] 1 All E.R. 588;
    (1961) 45 Cr. App. R. 80; 125 J.P. 246; 105 S.J. 160, CCA . . . . *Digested,* 61/**4486**:
                       Applied, 65/2052, 98/2233
R. *v.* Madarbakus (Afzal Mohammed) (1992) 13 Cr. App. R. (S.) 542, CA (Crim Div) . . *Digested,* 93/**1299**:
                          Considered, 01/1293
R. *v.* Maddix (Claudette); *sub nom* R. *v.* Madix [2001] EWCA Crim 1179; *Independent,*
    June 18, 2001 (C.S), CA (Crim Div)
R. *v.* Madix see R. *v.* Maddix (Claudette)
R. *v.* MAFF Ex p. Lay (C165/95) [1997] E.C.R. I-5543; [1998] 1 C.M.L.R. 847, ECJ
    (6th Chamber)
R. *v.* Magee (Michael Gerard) [2001] N.I. 217, CA (Crim Div) (NI) . . . . *Digested,* 01/**5877**
R. *v.* Maginnis (Patrick Terrance) [1987] A.C. 303; [1987] 2 W.L.R. 765; [1987] 1 All
    E.R. 907; (1987) 85 Cr. App. R. 127; (1987) 151 J.P. 537; [1987] Crim. L.R. 564;
    (1987) 151 J.P.N. 286; (1987) 84 L.S.G. 1141; (1987) 131 S.J. 357, HL;
    reversing [1986] Q.B. 618; [1986] 2 W.L.R. 767; [1986] 2 All E.R. 110; (1986)
    82 Cr. App. R. 351; [1986] Crim. L.R. 237; (1986) 83 L.S.G. 436; (1986) 130
    S.J. 128, CA (Crim Div) . . . . *Digested,* 87/**797**:
                     Considered, 95/1254: *Followed,* 01/1073
R. *v.* Maguire (Anne Rita); R. *v.* Smyth (William John); R. *v.* Maguire (Vincent John); R.
    v. Maguire (Patrick Joseph); R. *v.* O'Neill (Patrick Joseph); R. *v.* Conlon (Patrick
    Joseph) (Deceased); R. *v.* Maguire (Patrick Joseph Paul) [1992] Q.B. 936;
    [1992] 2 W.L.R. 767; [1992] 2 All E.R. 433; (1992) 94 Cr. App. R. 133; *Times,*
    June 28, 1991; *Independent,* June 27, 1991; *Guardian,* June 27, 1991, CA (Crim
    Div) . . . . *Digested,* 92/**812**:
              Applied, 92/621, 00/2756: *Considered,* 96/1593
R. *v.* Maguire (Brian Michael) [1997] 1 Cr. App. R. (S.) 130; [1996] Crim. L.R. 838,
    CA (Crim Div) . . . . *Digested,* 97/**1504**:
                           Considered, 98/1180
R. *v.* Maguire (Patrick Joseph) see R. *v.* Maguire (Anne Rita)

R. *v.* Maguire (Vincent John) see R. *v.* Maguire (Anne Rita)
R. *v.* Mahmood (Fadel Fanta) see R. *v.* Moshaid (Abdul)
R. *v.* Mahon (Patrick) [1999] 2 Costs L.R. 151 . . . .   *Digested,* 00/**1035**
R. *v.* Mahoney (Mark) see R. *v.* Brown (Raymond John)
R. *v.* Mahood (Stephen Charles) (1986) 8 Cr. App. R. (S.) 188, CA (Crim Div) . . . .   *Digested,* 87/**868**:
                                               Considered, 00/1132
R. *v.* Maidstone BC Ex p. Tait [2001] J.P.L. 704, QBD (Admin Ct) . . . .   *Digested,* 01/**4683**
R. *v.* Maidstone Crown Court Ex p. Harrow LBC [2000] Q.B. 719; [2000] 2 W.L.R.
     237; [1999] 3 All E.R. 542; [2000] 1 Cr. App. R. 117; (2000) 53 B.M.L.R. 27;
     [1999] Crim. L.R. 838; (1999) 96(21) L.S.G. 38; *Times,* May 14, 1999, QBD   . . .   *Digested,* 99/**99**:
                                            Distinguished, 01/1118
R. *v.* Main (Ronald Alan); R. *v.* Johnson (Ronald William) [1997] 2 Cr. App. R. (S.) 63,
     CA (Crim Div) . . . .   *Digested,* 97/**1502**:
                                               Considered, 00/1229
R. *v.* Maisey (David William); R. *v.* Houghton (Terence Paul) [2001] 1 Cr. App. R. (S.)
     98; [2000] Crim. L.R. 1024, CA (Crim Div) . . . .   *Digested,* 01/**1314**
R. *v.* Major (Darren Mark) see Attorney General's Reference (No.2 of 1989), Re
R. *v.* Makanjuola (Oluwanfunso); R. *v.* Easton (Christopher John) [1995] 1 W.L.R.
     1348; [1995] 3 All E.R. 730; [1995] 2 Cr. App. R. 469; (1995) 159 J.P. 701;
     (1995) 92(22) L.S.G. 40; (1995) 139 S.J.L.B. 179; *Times,* May 17, 1995;
     Independent, June 6, 1995, CA (Crim Div) . . . .   *Digested,* 96/**1353**:
                                               Considered, 98/1064
R. *v.* Makeham (John Stephen) [2001] 2 Cr. App. R. (S.) 41, CA (Crim Div) . . . .   *Digested,* 01/**1446**
R. *v.* Maldon DC Ex p. Pattani (1999) 47 B.M.L.R. 54; [1999] 1 P.L.R. 13; [1999]
     P.L.C.R. 1; [1998] E.G.C.S. 135, CA; affirming [1998] 1 P.L.R. 91; [1998] P.L.C.R.
     132; [1997] E.G.C.S. 136; *Times,* November 7, 1997; *Independent,* November 17,
     1997 (C.S.), QBD. . . . .   *Digested,* 98/**4234**
R. *v.* Malik (Adam) [1998] 1 Cr. App. R. (S.) 115, CA (Crim Div) . . . .   *Digested,* 98/**1338**
R. *v.* Malik (Aleem Mushtaq); R. *v.* Arman (Yusuf) *Times,* May 30, 2000, CA (Crim
     Div) . . . .   *Digested,* 00/**1169**
R. *v.* Malik (Waseem) (Appeal against Conviction) [2000] 2 Cr. App. R. 8; [2000]
     Crim. L.R. 197, CA (Crim Div) . . . .   *Digested,* 00/**932**
R. (on the application of Stunt) *v.* Mallett; *sub nom* Commissioner of Police *v.* Stunt; R.
     v. Metropolitan Police Service Ex p. Stunt; R. *v.* Mallett Ex p. Stunt [2001]
     EWCA Civ 265; [2001] I.C.R. 989; (2001) 98(16) L.S.G. 34; (2001) 145
     S.J.L.B. 76; *Times,* March 20, 2001; *Independent,* March 6, 2001, CA; reversing
     Independent, June 12, 2000 (C.S), QBD. . . . .   *Digested,* 01/**4778**
R. *v.* Mallett Ex p. Stunt see R. (on the application of Stunt) *v.* Mallett
R. *v.* Mallone (Patrick) [1996] 1 Cr. App. R. (S.) 221, CA (Crim Div) . . . .   *Considered,* 97/1673,
                                                        01/1264
R. *v.* Malone (Christopher Alexander) [2001] 2 Cr. App. R. (S.) 43, CA (Crim Div). . . . .   *Digested,* 01/**1445**
R. *v.* Malone (Thomas Patrick) [1998] 2 Cr. App. R. 447; [1998] Crim. L.R. 834;
     Independent, May 7, 1998, CA (Crim Div) . . . .   *Digested,* 98/**971**
R. *v.* Maloney (Peter James) [1996] 2 Cr. App. R. 303; (1996) 140 S.J.L.B. 85; *Times,*
     March 25, 1996, CA (Crim Div) . . . .   *Digested,* 96/**1625**:
                      Considered, 01/54: *Distinguished,* 99/1061
R. *v.* Managers of South Western Hospital Ex p. M; *sub nom* R. *v.* South Western
     Hospital Managers Ex p. M; Mulcahy (Eleanor), Re [1993] Q.B. 683; [1993] 3
     W.L.R. 376; [1994] 1 All E.R. 161; (1994) 6 Admin. L.R. 229; *Times,* January 27,
     1993, QBD . . . .   *Digested,* 94/**3062**:
                 Disapproved, 97/3653: *Followed,* 99/3936, 01/4429
R. *v.* Managers of Warley Hospital Ex p. Barker see R. *v.* Warley Hospital Ex p. Barker
R. (on the application of L (A Child)) *v.* Manchester City Council; R. (on the application
     of R (A Child)) *v.* Manchester City Council [2001] EWHC Admin 707; *Times,*
     December 10, 2001, QBD (Admin Ct)
R. (on the application of R (A Child)) *v.* Manchester City Council see R. (on the
     application of L (A Child)) *v.* Manchester City Council
R. *v.* Manchester City Council Ex p. S see R. *v.* Richmond LBC Ex p. W
R. *v.* Manchester City Council Ex p. S (A Child) [1999] E.L.R. 414, QBD . . . .   *Digested,* 00/**1949**
R. *v.* Manchester City Justices Ex p. Lee see R. *v.* St Helens Justices Ex p. Jones
R. (on the application of M (A Child)) *v.* Manchester Crown Court; *sub nom* R. *v.*
     Manchester Crown Court Ex p. M (A Child) [2001] EWCA Civ 281; [2001] 1
     W.L.R. 1084; [2001] 4 All E.R. 264; (2001) 165 J.P. 545; [2001] H.R.L.R. 37;
     Times, March 9, 2001; *Independent,* March 20, 2001, CA; affirming [2001] 1
     W.L.R. 358; (2001) 165 J.P. 225; (2001) 165 J.P.N. 204; (2001) 98(2) L.S.G.
     40; (2000) 144 S.J.L.B. 287; *Times,* December 22, 2000; *Daily Telegraph,*
     December 12, 2000, QBD (Admin Ct) . . . .   *Digested,* 01/**10**:
                                               Applied, 01/41
R. (on the application of Manchester City Council) *v.* Manchester Crown Court; *sub nom*
     R. *v.* Manchester Crown Court Ex p. Manchester City Council [2001] A.C.D.
     53; *Daily Telegraph,* November 7, 2000, QBD
R. *v.* Manchester Crown Court Ex p. DPP see Ashton, Re

R. v. Manchester Crown Court Ex p. DPP; *sub nom* Huckfield, Re [1993] 1 W.L.R.
1524; [1993] 4 All E.R. 928; (1994) 98 Cr. App. R. 461; [1994] 1 C.M.L.R. 457;
(1993) 143 N.L.J. 1711; *Times*, November 26, 1993; *Independent*, December 7,
1993, HL; reversing [1993] 1 W.L.R. 693; [1993] 1 All E.R. 801; (1993) 96 Cr.
App. R. 210; [1992] 3 C.M.L.R. 329; [1993] Crim. L.R. 377; [1993] C.O.D. 123;
(1992) 136 S.J.L.B. 235; *Times*, July 29, 1992; *Independent*, July 3, 1992, QBD . 　　*Digested*, 94/**19**:
　　　　　　　　　　　　　　　　　　　Considered, 94/35, 95/969: *Followed*, 96/1550, 98/96
R. v. Manchester Crown Court Ex p. H (A Juvenile); *sub nom* D (A Minor) (Reporting
Restrictions), Re; H (A Minor) (Reporting Restrictions), Re [2000] 1 W.L.R. 760;
[2000] 2 All E.R. 166; [2000] 1 Cr. App. R. 262; *Times*, August 13, 1999, QBD . . 　　*Digested*, 99/**85**
R. v. Manchester Crown Court Ex p. M (A Child) see R. (on the application of M (A
Child)) v. Manchester Crown Court
R. v. Manchester Crown Court Ex p. Manchester City Council see R. (on the
application of Manchester City Council) v. Manchester Crown Court
R. v. Manchester Crown Court Ex p. McDonald; R. v. Leeds Crown Court Ex p. Hunt;
R. v. Winchester Crown Court Ex p. Forbes; R. v. Leeds Crown Court Ex p.
Wilson (Leave Application) [1999] 1 W.L.R. 841; [1999] 1 All E.R. 805; [1999] 1
Cr. App. R. 409; (1999) 163 J.P. 253; [1999] Crim. L.R. 736; (1999) 163
J.P.N. 134; (1999) 96(4) L.S.G. 38; (1999) 143 S.J.L.B. 55; *Times*, November 19,
1998, QBD . . . . 　　*Digested*, 98/**1025**:
　　　　　　　　　　　　　　　Applied, 00/1052: *Considered*, 99/1050
R. v. Manchester Crown Court Ex p. R (Legal Professional Privilege) [1999] 1 W.L.R.
832; [1999] 4 All E.R. 35; [1999] 2 Cr. App. R. 267; [1999] Crim. L.R. 743;
(1999) 96(10) L.S.G. 31; *Times*, February 15, 1999; *Independent*, February 15,
1999 (C.S.), QBD . . . . 　　*Digested*, 99/**879**:
　　　　　　　　　　　　　　　　　　　　　　　　Applied, 00/3371
R. v. Manchester Magistrates Court Ex p. Szakal; *sub nom* Szakal, Re [2000] 1 Cr.
App. R. 248; [2000] Crim. L.R. 47; *Independent*, October 18, 1999 (C.S.), QBD . 　　*Digested*, 99/**1048**
R. v. Manchester Stipendiary Magistrate Ex p. Granada Television Ltd [2001] 1 A.C.
300; [2000] 2 W.L.R. 1; [2000] 1 All E.R. 135; (2000) 97(2) L.S.G. 29; (2000)
144 S.J.L.B. 33; *Times*, December 22, 1999, HL; reversing [1999] Q.B. 1202;
[1999] 2 W.L.R. 460; [1999] Crim. L.R. 162; (1998) 95(46) L.S.G. 35; (1998)
148 N.L.J. 1603; (1999) 143 S.J.L.B. 14; *Times*, October 22, 1998, QBD . . . . 　　*Digested*, 00/**6126**
R. v. Mangan (Matthew) see R. v. Sang (Leonard Anthony)
R. v. Mangham (Fiona Pauline) [1998] 2 Cr. App. R. (S.) 344, CA (Crim Div) . . . . 　　*Digested*, 98/**1316**
R. v. Mann (Amrao Singh) [1998] 2 Cr. App. R. (S.) 275, CA (Crim Div) . . . . 　　*Digested*, 98/**1389**
R. v. Mann (Andrew) (2000) 97(14) L.S.G. 41; (2000) 144 S.J.L.B. 150; *Times*, April
11, 2000, CA (Crim Div) . . . . 　　*Digested*, 00/**977**
R. v. Mann (Andrew Stewart) [2001] EWCA Crim 646; [2001] 2 Cr. App. R. (S.) 115,
CA (Crim Div) . . . . 　　*Digested*, 01/**1252**
R. v. Manning (Cally) [1998] Crim. L.R. 198, CA (Crim Div)
R. v. Manning (John Laurence) [1999] Q.B. 980; [1999] 2 W.L.R. 430; [1998] 4 All
E.R. 876; [1998] 2 Cr. App. R. 461; [1999] Crim. L.R. 151; *Times*, July 23, 1998;
Independent, June 26, 1998, CA (Crim Div) . . . . 　　*Digested*, 98/**957**:
　　　　　　　　　　　　　　　　　　　　　　　　Applied, 00/952
R. v. Mannion (John Joseph) [1999] 2 Cr. App. R. (S.) 240, CA (Crim Div) . . . . 　　*Digested*, 99/**1176**
R. v. Mansell (Craig John); *sub nom* R. v. Manzell (Craig John) (1994) 15 Cr. App. R.
(S.) 771; *Times*, February 22, 1994; *Independent*, March 14, 1994 (C.S.), CA
(Crim Div) . . . . 　　*Digested*, 95/**1417**:
　　　　　　　Applied, 97/1700: *Considered*, 96/1947, 99/1335: *Referred to*, 95/1414
R. v. Mansfield DC Ex p. Ashfield Nominees Ltd [1999] E.H.L.R. 290; (1999) 31
H.L.R. 805, QBD . . . . 　　*Digested*, 99/**3073**
R. v. Mansfield Justices Ex p. Sharkey [1985] Q.B. 613; [1984] 3 W.L.R. 1328; [1985]
1 All E.R. 193; (1985) 149 J.P. 129; [1984] I.R.L.R. 496; [1985] Crim. L.R. 148;
(1985) 82 L.S.G. 599; (1984) 128 S.J. 872, QBD . . . . 　　*Digested*, 85/**2079**:
　　　　　　　　　　　　　　　　　　　Applied, 96/1439: *Considered*, 01/1103
R. v. Manton (Desmond) see R. v. Elcock (David Haughton)
R. v. Manzell (Craig John) see R. v. Mansell (Craig John)
R. v. Marcolino (Ana) [1999] Masons C.L.R. 392, CA (Crim Div) . . . . 　　*Digested*, 00/**914**
R. v. Marks (Errington Lloyd) [1998] Crim. L.R. 676, CA (Crim Div)
R. v. Marlow (Michael David) [1998] 1 Cr. App. R. (S.) 273; [1997] Crim. L.R. 897,
CA (Crim Div) . . . . 　　*Digested*, 97/**1201**
R. v. Marlow (Philip John) see R. v. Meah (Brian)
R. v. Marples (Christopher) [1998] 1 Cr. App. R. (S.) 335, CA (Crim Div) . . . . 　　*Digested*, 98/**1106**
R. v. Marquez (Shaun) see R. v. Avis (Tony)
R. v. Marriott (Francis Anthony); R. v. Shepherd (Brendan Sean) (1995) 16 Cr. App. R.
(S.) 428; [1995] Crim. L.R. 83, CA (Crim Div) . . . . 　　*Considered*, 97/1596,
　　　　　　　　　　　　　　　　　　　　　　　99/1239, 00/1334
R. v. Marsden (David) see R. v. Klineberg (Jonathan Simon)
R. v. Marsden (Matthew) (1994) 15 Cr. App. R. (S.) 177, CA (Crim Div) . . . . 　　*Considered*, 98/1402
R. v. Marsh (Barry Charles) see R. v. Abdul (Naeem)
R. v. Marsh (Peter James) see R. v. Williams (David Omar)
R. v. Marsh (Peter Michael) see Attorney General's Reference (No.16 of 1999), Re

R. *v.* Marsh (Stephen Leslie) (1986) 83 Cr. App. R. 165; [1986] Crim. L.R. 120, CA
(Crim Div) . . . . *Digested*, 86/**624**:
                                                                                      Followed, 98/875
R. *v.* Marsh (Terence Colin) see R. *v.* Graham (Hemamali Krishna)
R. *v.* Marshall (Adrian John); R. *v.* Coombes (Robert Peter); R. *v.* Eren (Birol) [1998] 2
Cr. App. R. 282; (1998) 162 J.P. 489; [1999] Crim. L.R. 317; (1998) 162 J.P.N.
504; (1998) 95(16) L.S.G. 24; (1998) 142 S.J.L.B. 111; *Times*, March 10, 1998;
Independent, March 11, 1998, CA (Crim Div). . . . . *Digested*, 98/**981**
R. *v.* Marshall (Raymond Martin) see Attorney General's Reference (Nos.19, 20, 21 and
22 of 1997), Re
R. *v.* Marshalleck (Clifton) see R. *v.* Menga (Luigi)
R. *v.* Marsland (Anthony John) (1994) 15 Cr. App. R. (S.) 665, CA (Crim Div) . . . . *Digested*, 95/**1359**:
                                      Considered, 99/1138, 00/1205: *Distinguished*, 97/1505
R. *v.* Martello (Andrew James) 9907052 X4, CA (Crim Div) . . . . *Applied*, 01/1053
R. *v.* Martens (Gerhard Werner) see R. *v.* Tuegel (Peter Johannes)
R. *v.* Martin (Alan) [1998] A.C. 917; [1998] 2 W.L.R. 1; [1998] 1 All E.R. 193; [1998] 1
Cr. App. R. 347; (1998) 95(3) L.S.G. 24; (1998) 148 N.L.J. 50; (1998) 142
S.J.L.B. 44; *Times*, December 17, 1997, HL . . . . *Digested*, 98/**260**
R. *v.* Martin (Andrew) see R. *v.* Bediako (Michael)
R. *v.* Martin (Anthony Edward) [2001] EWCA Crim 2245; (2001) 98(46) L.S.G. 35;
(2001) 145 S.J.L.B. 253; *Times*, November 1, 2001, CA (Crim Div) . . . . *Digested*, 01/**1054**
R. *v.* Martin (Caroline Ann) (1993) 14 Cr. App. R. (S.) 645, CA (Crim Div) . . . . *Digested*, 94/**1372**:
                                                                      Considered, 99/1365, 00/1438
R. *v.* Martin (Colin) [1989] 1 All E.R. 652; (1989) 88 Cr. App. R. 343; (1989) 153 J.P.
231; [1989] R.T.R. 63; [1989] Crim. L.R. 284, CA (Crim Div) . . . . *Digested*, 89/**860**:
                                      Considered, 94/1129, 94/3841, 95/1256, 95/4407, 99/922, 99/1021
R. *v.* Martin (David Paul) [2000] 2 Cr. App. R. 42; (2000) 164 J.P. 174; [2000] Crim.
L.R. 615; (2001) 165 J.P.N. 85; (2000) 97(4) L.S.G. 32; (2000) 144 S.J.L.B. 51;
Times, January 5, 2000, CA (Crim Div) . . . . *Digested*, 00/**1068**
R. *v.* Martin (Ellis Anthony); R. *v.* White (James Robert) [1998] 2 Cr. App. R. 385;
Times, March 17, 1998; *Independent*, February 24, 1998, CA (Crim Div) . . . . *Digested*, 98/**1021**:
                                                                                      Cited, 00/1210
R. *v.* Martin (John Patrick) see Attorney General's Reference (No.78 of 2001), Re
R. *v.* Martin (Kim Linda) (1989) 11 Cr. App. R. (S.) 424; [1990] Crim. L.R. 132, CA
(Crim Div) . . . . *Digested*, 91/**1263**:
                                                                                      Considered, 99/1103
R. *v.* Martin (Mark Anthony) see Attorney General's Reference (Nos.32 and 33 of
1995), Re
R. *v.* Martin (Patrick Hugh Sean) [1999] 1 Cr. App. R. (S.) 477; [1999] Crim. L.R. 97;
Times, November 5, 1998; *Independent*, November 6, 1998, CA (Crim Div) . . . . *Digested*, 98/**1213**
R. *v.* Martin (Vanessa Jane) (1992) 13 Cr. App. R. (S.) 392, CA (Crim Div) . . . . *Digested*, 93/**1310**:
                                                                                      Considered, 98/1410
R. *v.* Martin (William Henry) [1962] 1 Q.B. 221; [1961] 3 W.L.R. 17; [1961] 2 All E.R.
747; (1961) 45 Cr. App. R. 199; 125 J.P. 480; 112 L.J. 283; 105 S.J. 469, CCA . . *Digested*, 61/**1827**:
                                      Applied, 62/644, 62/655, 68/755, 99/1013: *Considered*, 72/659:
                                                                      Followed, 73/554, 74/641
R. (on the application of Clingham) *v.* Marylebone Magistrates Court see Clingham *v.*
Kensington and Chelsea RLBC
R. *v.* Marylebone Magistrates Court Ex p. Amdrell Ltd (t/a Get Stuffed Ltd) (1998)
162 J.P. 719; (1998) 162 J.P.N. 1020; (1998) 148 N.L.J. 1230; (1998) 142
S.J.L.B. 261; [1999] Env. L.R. D11; *Times*, September 17, 1998, QBD . . . . *Digested*, 98/**4289**
R. *v.* Marylebone Magistrates Court Ex p. Westminster City Council (2000) 32 H.L.R.
266, QBD . . . . *Digested*, 00/**3950**
R. *v.* Mashaollahi (Behrooz); *sub nom* R. *v.* Mashaolli [2001] 1 Cr. App. R. 6; [2001] 1
Cr. App. R. (S.) 96; [2000] Crim. L.R. 1029; (2000) 97(37) L.S.G. 39; *Times*,
August 4, 2000; *Independent*, October 12, 2000, CA (Crim Div) . . . . *Digested*, 00/**1216**
R. *v.* Mashaolli see R. *v.* Mashaollahi (Behrooz)
R. *v.* Masih (Patris) (Unreported, July 17, 1995), CA (Crim Div) . . . . *Considered*, 98/1224
R. *v.* Maskell (David John) (1991) 12 Cr. App. R. (S.) 638, CA (Crim Div) . . . . *Digested*, 92/**1377**:
                                      Considered, 98/1353, 00/1402: *Referred to*, 96/2043
R. *v.* Mason (Colin Arthur) (1986) 8 Cr. App. R. (S.) 226, CA (Crim Div) . . . . *Digested*, 87/**1062**:
                                                                                      Considered, 98/1316
R. *v.* Mason (John Leslie) (1995) 16 Cr. App. R. (S.) 968, CA (Crim Div) . . . . *Considered*, 00/1139
R. *v.* Massey (James) [2001] EWCA Crim 531; [2001] 2 Cr. App. R. (S.) 80, CA (Crim
Div) . . . . *Digested*, 01/**1220**
R. *v.* Massey (Lawrence Christian) [1998] 1 Cr. App. R. (S.) 206, CA (Crim Div) . . . . . . *Digested*, 98/**1224**:
                                                                                      Considered, 99/1164
R. *v.* Masters (Veronica Michelle) see Attorney General's Reference (Nos.73 and 74 of
1998), Re
R. *v.* Mather (Alistair) [1998] Crim. L.R. 821, CA (Crim Div)
R. *v.* Mati (Brinesh Charan) [1999] 2 Cr. App. R. (S.) 238, CA (Crim Div) . . . . *Digested*, 99/**1369**
R. *v.* Mattan (Mahmoud Hussein), *Times*, March 5, 1998; *Independent*, March 4, 1998,
CA (Crim Div) . . . . *Digested*, 98/**891**
R. *v.* Matthews (Lawrence Anthony) [2001] 2 Cr. App. R. (S.) 22, CA (Crim Div) . . . . . *Digested*, 01/**1216**

R. *v.* Matthews (Paul) [1998] 1 Cr. App. R. (S.) 220, CA (Crim Div) . . . . *Digested,* 98/**1339**
R. *v.* Matthews (Stanley Richard) [1999] 1 Cr. App. R. (S.) 309, CA (Crim Div) . . . . *Digested,* 99/**1299**
R. *v.* Matthews (Terence Roy) (1986) 8 Cr. App. R. (S.) 204, CA (Crim Div) . . . . *Digested,* 87/**1063**:
        Considered, 98/1316
R. *v.* Maughan (Reginald) (1934) 24 Cr. App. R. 130, CCA . . . . *Considered,* 00/1004
R. *v.* Mawdsley (Roy Wilfred) [2001] 1 Cr. App. R. (S.) 101, CA (Crim Div) . . . . *Digested,* 01/**1230**
R. *v.* Mawson (Gary) (1992) 13 Cr. App. R. (S.) 218; [1991] R.T.R. 418; [1992] Crim.
    L.R. 68; *Times,* July 23, 1991, CA (Crim Div) . . . . *Digested,* 92/**1175**:
              Cited, 94/1401: *Considered,* 99/1322
R. *v.* Maxwell-King (Paul John) [2001] 2 Cr. App. R. (S.) 28; (2001) 98(4) L.S.G. 49;
    (2001) 145 S.J.L.B. 21; *Times,* January 2, 2001, CA (Crim Div) . . . . *Digested,* 01/**1236**
R. *v.* Mayeri (Simon) [1999] 1 Cr. App. R. (S.) 304, CA (Crim Div) . . . . *Digested,* 99/**1130**
R. *v.* Mayhall (David John) see Attorney General's Reference (Nos.58 and 59 of 2001),
    Re
R. *v.* Mazo (Ellen) [1997] 2 Cr. App. R. 518; [1996] Crim. L.R. 435, CA (Crim Div) . . . . *Digested,* 96/**1529**:
        Distinguished, 98/1065
R. *v.* MB (Appeal Against Conviction) [2000] Crim. L.R. 181, CA (Crim Div)
R. *v.* MC see Attorney General's Reference (No.51 of 2001), Re
R. *v.* McAndrew-Bingham (Victor John) [1999] 1 W.L.R. 1897; [1999] 2 Cr. App. R.
    293; [1999] Crim. L.R. 830; (1999) 96(5) L.S.G. 35; (1999) 143 S.J.L.B. 38;
    Times, December 28, 1998, CA (Crim Div) . . . . *Digested,* 99/**902**:
        Applied, 01/985
R. *v.* McArdle (James) [2000] N.I. 390, CA (Crim Div) (NI) . . . . *Digested,* 01/**5733**
R. *v.* McArthur (Henry Charles) (1993) 14 Cr. App. R. (S.) 659, CA (Crim Div) . . . . *Digested,* 94/**1338**:
        Considered, 98/1347
R. *v.* McCabe (James) (1989) 11 Cr. App. R. (S.) 154, CA (Crim Div) . . . . *Digested,* 91/**1224**:
        Considered, 00/1411
R. *v.* McCamon (Andrew) [1998] 2 Cr. App. R. (S.) 81, CA (Crim Div) . . . . *Digested,* 98/**1134**:
        Considered, 00/1150
R. *v.* McCandless (Trevor) [2001] N.I. 86, CA (Crim Div) (NI) . . . . *Digested,* 01/**5729**
R. *v.* McCann (Robert Andrew) (1994) 15 Cr. App. R. (S.) 10, CA (Crim Div) . . . . *Considered,* 99/1081
R. *v.* McCann (Sean) [2000] 1 Cr. App. R. (S.) 495, CA (Crim Div) . . . . *Digested,* 00/**1374**
R. *v.* McCarthey (Stephen Michael) (1988) 10 Cr. App. R. (S.) 443, CA . . . . *Digested,* 91/**1017**:
        Considered, 00/1395
R. *v.* McCarthy (Colin Paul); R. *v.* Warren (Mark Stephen); R. *v.* Lloyd (Leigh Cedric);
    R. *v.* Warren (Robert John) [1998] R.T.R. 374, CA (Crim Div) . . . . *Digested,* 98/**867**
R. *v.* McCarthy (Keith Anthony) see R. *v.* Fairburn (David Charles)
R. *v.* McCarthy & Stone (Developments) Ltd (Unreported, March 12, 1998), Crown Ct
    (Newport, Gwent) [*Ex rel.* T Davey, Barrister, 2-3 Gray's Inn Square, London] . . *Digested,* 98/**4198**
R. *v.* McCay [1975] N.I. 5, CCA (NI) . . . . *Digested,* 77/**2073**:
        Followed, 00/5487
R. *v.* McComish [1996] N.I. 466, Crown Ct
R. *v.* McCormac (Conor Patrick) [2000] N.I. 189, CA (Crim Div) (NI) . . . . *Digested,* 00/**5480**
R. *v.* McCredie (Graeme George); R. *v.* French (Stephen Robert) [2000] B.C.C. 617;
    [2000] 2 B.C.L.C. 438; [2000] B.P.I.R. 1129; *Times,* October 5, 1999, CA (Crim
    Div) . . . . *Digested,* 99/**3282**
R. *v.* McCue (Gerald Samuel) (1987) 9 Cr. App. R. (S.) 17; [1987] Crim. L.R. 345, CA
    (Crim Div) . . . . *Digested,* 88/**975**:
            Cited, 00/1398: *Considered,* 93/1189, 95/1459
R. *v.* McCullough (James Daniel) [1999] N.I. 39, CA (Crim Div) (NI) . . . . *Digested,* 99/**5220**
R. *v.* McDonagh (Danny James) [1998] 2 Cr. App. R. (S.) 195, CA (Crim Div) . . . . *Digested,* 98/**1406**
R. *v.* McDonald (Colin Victor) [1999] N.I. 150, Crown Ct (NI) . . . . *Digested,* 99/**5185**
R. *v.* McDonald (David Wallis) [2001] EWCA Crim 860; [2001] 2 Cr. App. R. (S.) 127;
    [2001] Crim. L.R. 497, CA (Crim Div) . . . . *Digested,* 01/**1309**
R. *v.* McDonald (Joseph Ronald) (1989) 11 Cr. App. R. (S.) 468, CA (Crim Div) . . . . . . *Digested,* 91/**1140**:
        Considered, 99/1210
R. *v.* McDonnell (Amanda) see Attorney General's Reference (Nos.57, 58 and 59 of
    1997), Re
R. *v.* McDonnell (James); R. *v.* Cassar (David) (1990) 12 Cr. App. R. (S.) 600, CA
    (Crim Div) . . . . *Digested,* 92/**1166**:
        Considered, 99/1088
R. *v.* McDonnell (John Paul) [2000] N.I. 168, CA (Crim Div) (NI) . . . . *Digested,* 00/**5489**
R. *v.* McEnhill (Patrick), *Times,* February 4, 1999, CMAC . . . . *Digested,* 99/**254**
R. *v.* McFarlane (Cyril); R. *v.* Burke (Anthony) (1988) 10 Cr. App. R. (S.) 10; [1988]
    Crim. L.R. 394, CA (Crim Div) . . . . *Digested,* 90/**1478**:
          Cited, 90/1478.b: *Considered,* 00/1328
R. *v.* McFarlane (Sidney Lee), *Times,* March 24, 1999, CA (Crim Div) . . . . *Digested,* 99/**1008**
R. *v.* McFeeley (Jason); R. *v.* Anderson (Lee); R. *v.* Taberer (Lee Kenneth); R. *v.*
    Erdman (Anthony); R. *v.* Neale (Matthew) [1998] 2 Cr. App. R. (S.) 26; *Times,*
    December 10, 1997, CA (Crim Div) . . . . *Digested,* 98/**1329**

R. v. McGarry (Patrick John) [1999] 1 W.L.R. 1500; [1998] 3 All E.R. 805; [1999] 1
Cr. App. R. 377; [1999] Crim. L.R. 316; (1998) 95(35) L.S.G. 36; (1998) 142
S.J.L.B. 239; Times, August 7, 1998; Independent, July 23, 1998, CA (Crim
Div) . . . .   Digested, 98/**1062**:
Cited, 00/1073

R. v. McGilliard (Peter Wilson) see R. v. Offen (Matthew Barry) (No.2)
R. v. McGillivray (Charles) (1993) 97 Cr. App. R. 232; (1993) 157 J.P. 943; (1993)
157 J.P.N. 394; Times, January 3, 1993, CA (Crim Div) . . . .   Digested, 94/**711**:
Considered, 96/1412: Followed, 99/873

R. v. McGinn (Philip Lee) see Attorney General's Reference (No.33 of 1997), Re
R. v. McGinty (John James) see R. v. Tantram (Peter John)
R. v. McGowan (Barry Temple) [1998] 2 Cr. App. R. (S.) 219, CA (Crim Div) . . . .   Digested, 98/**1359**
R. v. McGrath (James Andrew) [2000] 1 Cr. App. R. (S.) 479, CA (Crim Div) . . . .   Digested, 00/**1131**:
Considered, 01/1214

R. v. McGrath (Paul William) (1992) 13 Cr. App. R. (S.) 83, CA (Crim Div). . . . .   Digested, 92/**1427**:
Considered, 01/1337

R. v. McGregor (Lee James) see Attorney General's Reference (No.14 of 1998), Re
R. v. McGregor (Thomas Hunter) see Attorney General's Reference (No.61 of 1996),
Re
R. v. McGregor-Read (Juan) [1999] Crim. L.R. 860, CA (Crim Div)
R. v. McGuinness (Cyril) [1999] Crim. L.R. 318, CA (Crim Div)
R. v. McHale (Michael James) [2001] EWCA Crim 529; [2001] 2 Cr. App. R. (S.) 92,
CA (Crim Div) . . . .   Digested, 01/**1205**
R. v. McIlwaine (David) [1998] N.I. 136, CA (Crim Div) (NI). . . . .   Digested, 99/**5226**
R. v. McIntosh (Stuart Robert) see Attorney General's Reference (No.33 of 1994), Re
R. v. McKendry (Mark Allan) [2001] EWCA Crim 578; Times, March 16, 2001, CMAC . .   Digested, 01/**359**
R. v. McKeown (Darren) see R. v. Offen (Matthew Barry) (No.2)
R. v. McKnight (Sonia), Times, May 5, 2000, CA (Crim Div) . . . .   Digested, 00/**1070**
R. v. McLaughlan (Frederick William) (1987) 9 Cr. App. R. (S.) 388, CA (Crim Div) . . . .   Digested, 89/**1019**:
Cited, 92/1400: Considered, 99/1356

R. v. McLaughlin (Lee Conrad) (1995) 16 Cr. App. R. (S.) 357, CA (Crim Div) . . . .   Considered, 98/1189,
98/1190

R. v. McLean (Julia Lila) see R. v. Parry (Jonathan Anthony)
R. v. McLean (Lancelot) (1994) 15 Cr. App. R. (S.) 706, CA (Crim Div) . . . .   Digested, 95/**1361**:
Considered, 00/1233

R. v. McLean (Martin) [1998] 2 Cr. App. R. (S.) 250, CA (Crim Div) . . . .   Digested, 98/**1289**
R. v. McLean (Norman) see R. v. Hart (Michael John)
R. v. McLoughlin (Anthony John) (1985) 7 Cr. App. R. (S.) 67, CA. . . . .   Digested, 86/**890**:
Considered, 91/1234, 98/1399: Referred to, 91/1154, 92/1285, 93/1056,
93/1057

R. v. McLoughlin (George Gerrard) see Attorney General's Reference (Nos.19 and 20
of 1990), Re
R. v. McLoughlin (John Joseph) 199903412/Y4, CA (Crim Div) . . . .   Doubted, 00/905
R. v. McManus (Michael Francis) see R. v. Flaherty (Mark Gordon)
R. v. McManus (Samuel Keith) see R. v. Robinson (Ben)
R. v. McMaster (Shane Anthony) see Attorney General's Reference (Nos.62 and 63 of
1997), Re
R. v. McMorrow (Francis Christopher) see Attorney General's Reference (No.19 of
1992), Re
R. v. McNally (John Stephen) [2000] 1 Cr. App. R. (S.) 535; Times, December 1, 1999,
CA (Crim Div) . . . .   Digested, 00/**1119**
R. v. McNamara (James) (1988) 87 Cr. App. R. 246; (1988) 152 J.P. 390; [1988]
Crim. L.R. 440; (1988) 152 J.P.N. 350; (1988) 132 S.J. 300; Times, February 16,
1988, CA (Crim Div) . . . .   Digested, 89/**823**:
Considered, 97/1223, 99/5832: Distinguished, 90/2339: Followed, 99/926

R. v. McNamara (Naomi); R. v. McNamara (Terence) [1998] Crim. L.R. 278, CA (Crim
Div)
R. v. McNamara (Terence) see R. v. McNamara (Naomi)
R. v. McNeil (Mark) [1997] 1 Cr. App. R. (S.) 266, CA (Crim Div) . . . .   Digested, 97/**1592**:
Considered, 98/1288

R. v. McNeill (Stephen Victor) [1993] N.I. 46, CA (NI) . . . .   Doubted, 01/5735
R. v. McNellis (Anthony) [2000] 1 Cr. App. R. (S.) 481, CA (Crim Div) . . . .   Digested, 00/**1439**
R. v. McPhail (Daniel) [1997] 1 Cr. App. R. (S.) 321, CA (Crim Div) . . . .   Digested, 96/**1858**:
Considered, 00/1211

R. v. McPhee (William Lawrence) [1998] 1 Cr. App. R. (S.) 201, CA (Crim Div) . . . .   Digested, 98/**1233**:
Considered, 01/1213

R. v. McQuiston (James Wallace) [1998] 1 Cr. App. R. 139; [1998] Crim. L.R. 69;
(1997) 161 J.P.N. 1173; Times, October 10, 1997; Independent, October 6, 1997
(C.S.), CA (Crim Div) . . . .   Digested, 97/**1174**
R. v. McWilliams [1996] N.I. 545, CA (NI)
R. v. MD [2000] 1 Cr. App. R. (S.) 426, CA (Crim Div). . . . .   Digested, 00/**1289**
R. v. Meah (Brian); R. v. Marlow (Philip John) (1991) 92 Cr. App. R. 254; (1990) 12
Cr. App. R. (S.) 461; Times, October 31, 1990, CA (Crim Div) . . . .   Digested, 91/**1117**:
Cited, 95/1361: Considered, 00/1233

R. v. Mealing (David) see R. v. Charlton (Mark Robert)
R. v. Medicines Control Agency Ex p. Pharma Nord (UK) Ltd [1998] 3 C.M.L.R. 109;
    [1999] Eu. L.R. 8; (1998) 10 Admin. L.R. 646; (1998) 44 B.M.L.R. 41; [1998]
    C.O.D. 315; *Times*, June 10, 1998, CA; affirming [1997] C.O.D. 439; *Times*, July
    29, 1997, QBD. . . . . *Digested*, 98/**2655**
R. v. Medicines Control Agency Ex p. Rhone Poulenc Rorer Ltd (C94/98); *sub nom* R.
    v. Licensing Authority Established by the Medicines Act 1968 (represented by
    Medicines Control Agency) Ex p. Rhone Poulenc Rorer Ltd (C94/98) [2000]
    All E.R. (EC) 46; [1999] E.C.R. I-8789; [2000] 1 C.M.L.R. 409; [2000] C.E.C.
    145; (2000) 56 B.M.L.R. 71, ECJ. . . . . *Digested*, 00/**2908**:
                                    Previous proceedings, 98/2659
R. v. Medicines Control Agency Ex p. Rhone Poulenc Rorer Ltd (No.1) CO-506-97,
    CO-1942-97, QBD. . . . . *Digested*, 98/**2659**
R. v. Medicines Control Agency Ex p. Rhone Poulenc Rorer Ltd (No.2) [1999] Eu.
    L.R. 181; (1999) 46 B.M.L.R. 199; [1998] C.O.D. 470, QBD. . . . . *Digested*, 98/**2660**
R. v. Medicines Control Agency Ex p. Smith & Nephew Pharmaceuticals Ltd [1999]
    R.P.C. 705; (1999) 49 B.M.L.R. 112, Ch D . . . . *Digested*, 99/**440**
R. v. Medicines Control Agency Ex p. Smith & Nephew Pharmaceuticals Ltd (C201/
    94); Primecrown Ltd v. Medicines Control Agency [1996] E.C.R. I-5819; [1997]
    1 C.M.L.R. 812; (1997) 34 B.M.L.R. 141, ECJ . . . . *Digested*, 97/**3621**:
                Applied, 98/2659, 99/181: *Considered*, 98/2660, 98/2661
R. v. Medland (Eric William) (1990) 12 Cr. App. R. (S.) 557, CA (Crim Div) . . . . *Digested*, 92/**1288**:
                                          Considered, 00/1268
R. v. Medway (Damian Paul) [2000] Crim. L.R. 415, CA (Crim Div)
R. v. Medway Justices Ex p. Bellinger [2000] R.V.R. 75, QBD. *Digested*, 00/**9**
R. v. Medway Youth Court Ex p. A (A Juvenile) [2000] 1 Cr. App. R. (S.) 191; (2000)
    164 J.P. 111; [1999] Crim. L.R. 915; (2000) 164 J.P.N. 102; *Times*, June 30, 1999
    ; *Independent*, July 19, 1999 (C.S.), QBD . . . . *Digested*, 99/**1242**
R. v. Meek (Brian Glen) see R. v. Meek (John George)
R. v. Meek (John George); R. v. Meek (Brian Glen) [2001] 2 Cr. App. R. (S.) 4, CA
    (Crim Div). . . . . *Digested*, 01/**1295**
R. v. Meghjee (Muntazir) see R. v. Radak (Jason Dragon)
R. v. Mehboob (Chand) [2000] 2 Cr. App. R. (S.) 343, CA (Crim Div) . . . . *Digested*, 00/**1258**
R. v. Mellor (Paul James) see Attorney General's Reference (No.23 of 1990), Re
R. v. Mendip DC Ex p. Fabre (2000) 80 P. & C.R. 500; [2000] J.P.L. 810; [2000]
    C.O.D. 372, QBD. . . . . *Digested*, 00/**4508**
R. v. Mendy [1992] Crim. L.R. 313, CA (Crim Div) . . . . *Digested*, 92/**914**:
                               Distinguished, 99/1061
R. v. Menga (Luigi); R. v. Marshalleck (Clifton) [1998] Crim. L.R. 58, CA (Crim Div)
R. v. Mental Health Act Commission Ex p. Smith (1997-98) 1 C.C.L. Rep. 451; (1998)
    43 B.M.L.R. 174; (1998) 142 S.J.L.B. 182; *Times*, May 18, 1998, QBD. . . . . *Digested*, 98/**3891**
R. (on the application of C) v. Mental Health Review Tribunal; *sub nom* R. (on the
    application of C) v. London South and South West Region Mental Health
    Review Tribunal [2001] EWCA Civ 1110; [2001] Lloyd's Rep. Med. 450; (2001)
    98(29) L.S.G. 39; (2001) 145 S.J.L.B. 167; *Times*, July 11, 2001; *Independent*,
    July 10, 2001, CA; reversing [2001] A.C.D. 63, QBD (Admin Ct). . . . . *Digested*, 01/**4424**
R. (on the application of Secretary of State for the Home Department) v. Mental Health
    Review Tribunal; *sub nom* R. v. Mental Health Review Tribunal for North East
    Thames Region Ex p. Secretary of State for the Home Department [2001]
    A.C.D. 62; *Times*, February 20, 2001, QBD (Admin Ct) . . . . *Digested*, 01/**4423**
R. (on the application of Wirral HA) v. Mental Health Review Tribunal; R. (on the
    application of Wirral HA) v. Finnegan [2001] EWCA Civ 1901; (2001) 145
    S.J.L.B. 270; *Times*, November 26, 2001, CA; affirming [2001] EWHC Admin
    312, QBD (Admin Ct) . . . . *Digested*, 01/**4425**
R. (on the application of Wirral HA) v. Mental Health Review Tribunal (Permission to
    Appeal); *sub nom* R. (on the application of Wirral HA) v. Finnegan (Permission to
    Appeal) [2001] EWCA Civ 1572, CA . . . . *Subsequent proceed-*
                                         ings, 01/4425
R. v. Mental Health Review Tribunal Ex p. Booth [1998] C.O.D. 203, QBD
R. v. Mental Health Review Tribunal Ex p. H [2000] 1 W.L.R. 1323; [1999] 4 All E.R.
    883; (1999) 2 C.C.L. Rep. 383; [1999] Lloyd's Rep. Med. 417; (2000) 51
    B.M.L.R. 117; [1999] C.O.D. 429; (1999) 96(33) L.S.G. 31; (1999) 149 N.L.J.
    1368; *Times*, October 5, 1999, CA; reversing [1999] 3 All E.R. 132; (1999) 2
    C.C.L. Rep. 361; [1999] Lloyd's Rep. Med. 274; [1999] C.O.D. 372; (1999) 149
    N.L.J. 638; *Times*, May 20, 1999, QBD . . . . *Digested*, 99/**3935**
R. v. Mental Health Review Tribunal Ex p. MacDonald [1998] C.O.D. 205, QBD
R. (on the application of H) v. Mental Health Review Tribunal for North and East London
    Region; *sub nom* R. (on the application of H) v. North and East London
    Regional Mental Health Review Tribunal; R. (on the application of H) v. London
    North and East Region Mental Health Review Tribunal [2001] EWCA Civ 415;
    [2001] 3 W.L.R. 512; [2001] H.R.L.R. 36; [2001] U.K.H.R.R. 717; [2001] Lloyd's
    Rep. Med. 302; (2001) 61 B.M.L.R. 163; [2001] A.C.D. 78; [2001] 98(21)
    L.S.G. 40; (2001) 145 S.J.L.B. 108; *Times*, April 2, 2001; *Independent*, April 3,
    2001, CA; reversing CO 2120/2000, QBD (Admin Ct). . . . . *Digested*, 01/**4432**

R. *v.* Mental Health Review Tribunal for North East Thames Region Ex p. Secretary of
State for the Home Department see R. (on the application of Secretary of State
for the Home Department) *v.* Mental Health Review Tribunal

R. *v.* Mental Health Review Tribunal for South Thames Region Ex p. Smith (1999) 47
B.M.L.R. 104; [1999] C.O.D. 148; *Times*, December 9, 1998, QBD . . . .   *Digested*, 99/**3938**

R. *v.* Mercredi (Barbara) [1997] 2 Cr. App. R. (S.) 204, CA (Crim Div) . . . .   *Digested*, 97/**1541**:
                                          Considered, 00/1244

R. *v.* Meredith (Christopher); R. *v.* Craven (Adrian) [2000] 1 Cr. App. R. (S.) 508, CA
(Crim Div) . . . .   *Digested*, 00/**1267**

R. *v.* Mereu (Jean-Marc); R. *v.* Korkolis (Constantine); R. *v.* Zografos (Thanassis); R. *v.*
Moussaoui (Djemel) [1998] 2 Cr. App. R. (S.) 351, CA (Crim Div). . . . .   *Digested*, 98/**1300**

R. *v.* Mernin (Simon Paul) [2001] 2 Cr. App. R. (S.) 6, CA (Crim Div) . . . .   *Digested*, 01/**1307**

R. *v.* Merry (Kathleen Anne) see R. *v.* Strudwick (Kevin Vincent)

R. *v.* Merryweather (Brian Paul) [2000] R.T.R. 150; *Times*, September 7, 1999, CA
(Crim Div). . . . .   *Digested*, 99/**1329**

R. *v.* Merseyside Mental Health Review Tribunal Ex p. K [1990] 1 All E.R. 694;
Independent, June 8, 1989, CA . . . .   *Digested*, 90/**3101**:
                                Subsequent proceedings, 98/3889

R. *v.* Merseyside Mental Health Review Tribunal Ex p. Kelly (1998) 39 B.M.L.R. 114,
QBD. . . . .   *Digested*, 97/**3649**

R. *v.* Merthyr Tydfil Crown Court Ex p. Chief Constable of Dyfed Powys (1998)
95(46) L.S.G. 35; (1998) 142 S.J.L.B. 284; *Times*, December 17, 1998, QBD . . .   *Digested*, 99/**399**:
                                          Cited, 00/395

R. *v.* Merton LBC Ex p. Barker [1998] J.P.L. 440; [1997] E.G.C.S. 77, QBD . . . .   *Digested*, 98/**4229**

R. *v.* Merton LBC Ex p. Inparaja see R. *v.* Hackney LBC Ex p. Adebiri

R. *v.* Merton LBC Ex p. Parupathpilli see R. *v.* Hackney LBC Ex p. Adebiri

R. *v.* Merton LBC Ex p. Sembi (2000) 32 H.L.R. 439; *Times*, June 9, 1999, QBD . . . . . .   *Digested*, 99/**3021**

R. *v.* Merton Sutton and Wandsworth HA Ex p. P (2000) 3 C.C.L. Rep. 378; [2001]
Lloyd's Rep. Med. 73; [2001] A.C.D. 9, QBD. . . . .   *Digested*, 01/**3289**

R. *v.* Messenger (Scott) [2001] 2 Cr. App. R. (S.) 24, CA (Crim Div) . . . .   *Digested*, 01/**1251**

R. *v.* Messom (Samuel Andrew) (1973) 57 Cr. App. R. 481; [1973] R.T.R. 140; [1973]
Crim. L.R. 252, CA (Crim Div) . . . .   *Digested*, 73/**2918**:
                                           Cited, 01/1265

R. *v.* Metropolitan Police Force Disciplinary Committee Ex p. Lawrence; *sub nom*
Lawrence, Re *Times*, July 13, 1999, QBD. . . . .   *Digested*, 99/**4282**

R. *v.* Metropolitan Police Service Ex p. Stunt see R. (on the application of Stunt) *v.*
Mallett

R. *v.* Metropolitan Stipendiary Magistrate Ex p. J see R. *v.* West London Youth Court
Ex p. J

R. *v.* Metropolitan Stipendiary Magistrate Ex p. London Waste Regulation Authority;
Berkshire CC *v.* Scott [1993] 3 All E.R. 113; [1993] Env. L.R. 417; *Times*, January
14, 1993, QBD. . . . .   *Digested*, 93/**3832**:
                                       Considered, 99/2198

R. *v.* MG (Offences against Children) see R. *v.* G (Mark John)

R. *v.* MG (Sex Offence: Registration) see Attorney General's Reference (No.72 of
1999), Re

R. *v.* MH [2001] EWCA Crim 761; [2001] 2 Cr. App. R. (S.) 101, CA (Crim Div). . . . . .   *Digested*, 01/**1352**

R. *v.* Miah (Badrul); R. *v.* Akhbar (Showkat) [1997] 2 Cr. App. R. 12; [1997] Crim. L.R.
351; *Times*, December 18, 1996, CA (Crim Div) . . . .   *Digested*, 97/**1327**:
                                          Followed, 01/1142

R. *v.* Miah (Mohbub) [2000] 2 Cr. App. R. (S.) 439; *Independent*, May 8, 2000
(C.S.), CA (Crim Div). . . . .   *Digested*, 01/**1346**

R. *v.* Mid Bedfordshire DC Ex p. Grimes (2000) 80 P. & C.R. 311, QBD . . . .   *Digested*, 00/**4423**

R. *v.* Midda (Julian Ellery) (Unduly Lenient Sentence) see Attorney General's
Reference (No.6 of 1999), Re

R. *v.* Middelkoop (Martin); R. *v.* Telli (David) [1997] 1 Cr. App. R. (S.) 423, CA (Crim
Div) . . . .   *Digested*, 97/**1503**:
                                  Considered, 98/1185, 99/1129

R. *v.* Middlemiss (Gary Anthony) [1999] 1 Cr. App. R. (S.) 62, CA (Crim Div) . . . .   *Digested*, 99/**1093**

R. *v.* Middlesbrough BC Ex p. Frostree Ltd (Unreported, December 16, 1988), QBD. . .   *Followed*, 00/4111

R. *v.* Middlesex Guildhall Crown Court Ex p. Okoli [2001] 1 Cr. App. R. 1; (2001) 165
J.P. 144; [2000] Crim. L.R. 921; (2000) 164 J.P.N. 901; (2000) 97(30) L.S.G.
39; *Times*, August 2, 2000; *Independent*, October 2, 2000 (C.S), QBD . . . .   *Digested*, 00/**1027**

R. *v.* Middlesex Guildhall Crown Court Ex p. Tamosius & Partners; *sub nom* R. *v.* Inland
Revenue Commissioners Ex p. Tamosius & Partners [2000] 1 W.L.R. 453;
[1999] S.T.C. 1077; [1999] B.T.C. 404; [2000] Crim. L.R. 390; (1999) 96(45)
L.S.G. 34; (1999) 143 S.J.L.B. 279; *Times*, November 10, 1999 ; *Independent*,
November 12, 1999, QBD. . . . .   *Digested*, 99/**4767**

R. *v.* Middlesex Justices Ex p. DPP see R. *v.* Middlesex Quarter Sessions Ex p. DPP

R. *v.* Middlesex Quarter Sessions Ex p. DPP; *sub nom* R. *v.* Middlesex Justices Ex p.
DPP [1952] 2 Q.B. 758; [1952] 2 All E.R. 312; [1952] 2 T.L.R. 135; (1952) 36
Cr. App. R. 114; 116 J.P. 457; 96 S.J. 482, QBD . . . .   *Digested*, 52/**1868**:
    Applied, 83/535, 00/1106: *Distinguished*, 84/497, 84/2112: *Followed*, 63/632

R. *v.* Middleton (Ernest) (1988) 10 Cr. App. R. (S.) 8; [1988] Crim. L.R. 327, CA
(Crim Div)... *Digested*, 90/**1343**:
Considered, 98/1247: *Referred to*, 90/1341
R. *v.* Middleton (Ronald) [2001] Crim. L.R. 251; *Times*, April 12, 2000, CA (Crim Div) .. *Digested*, 00/**1071**
R. *v.* Middleton (Steven Peter) see Attorney General's Reference (No.44 of 1994), Re
R. *v.* Midya (Tara Senkar) (1986) 8 Cr. App. R. (S.) 264, CA (Crim Div)............ *Digested*, 87/**1030**:
Considered, 99/1282
R. *v.* Mighty (Daniel Ivor) see Attorney General's Reference (No.29 of 1995), Re
R. *v.* Mildenhall Magistrates Court Ex p. Forest Heath DC see R. *v.* North West Suffolk
(Mildenhall) Magistrates Court Ex p. Forest Heath DC
R. *v.* Milford (David John) see R. *v.* Benjafield (Karl Robert) (Confiscation Order)
R. *v.* Milford (David John) [2001] Crim. L.R. 330, CA (Crim Div)
R. *v.* Milford Haven Port Authority see Environment Agency *v.* Milford Haven Port
Authority (The Sea Empress)
R. *v.* Milford Haven Port Authority (Severance) see Milford Haven *v.* Andrews
R. *v.* Mill (Garry Mcintosh) [1999] 2 Cr. App. R. (S.) 28, CA (Crim Div) .... *Digested*, 99/**1367**
R. *v.* Millan (John David) see R. *v.* Bowers (Victor John)
R. *v.* Millard (Andrew Derek) see Attorney General's Reference (No.39 of 1994), Re
R. *v.* Millard (Ray) (1994) 15 Cr. App. R. (S.) 445; [1994] Crim. L.R. 146, CA (Crim
Div)... *Considered*, 98/665
R. *v.* Miller (Keith Glenn) [1998] Crim. L.R. 209, CA (Crim Div)
R. *v.* Miller (Michael Alan) see R. *v.* Hemmings (Raymond George)
R. *v.* Miller (Raymond Karl); R. *v.* Glennie (Alastair Kincaid) [1983] 1 W.L.R. 1056;
[1983] 3 All E.R. 186; (1984) 78 Cr. App. R. 71; [1983] Crim. L.R. 615; (1983)
133 N.L.J. 745; (1983) 127 S.J. 580, QBD .... *Digested*, 84/**553**:
Applied, 00/4295: *Considered*, 01/1116: *Followed*, 99/3757
R. *v.* Miller (Simon) [1977] 1 W.L.R. 1129; [1977] 3 All E.R. 986; (1977) 65 Cr. App. R.
79; [1977] Crim. L.R. 562; 121 S.J. 423, CA (Crim Div) .... *Digested*, 77/**616**:
Considered, 99/2457
R. *v.* Miller (Stephen) [1999] 2 Cr. App. R. (S.) 392; [1999] Crim. L.R. 590, CA (Crim
Div) .... *Digested*, 00/**1387**
R. *v.* Mills (Brian John) [1998] 2 Cr. App. R. (S.) 252, CA (Crim Div) .... *Digested*, 98/**1340**
R. *v.* Mills (Gary); R. *v.* Poole (Anthony Keith) [1998] A.C. 382; [1997] 3 W.L.R. 458;
[1997] 3 All E.R. 780; [1998] 1 Cr. App. R. 43; (1997) 161 J.P. 601; [1998] Crim.
L.R. 64; (1997) 161 J.P.N. 858; (1997) 94(39) L.S.G. 39; (1997) 141 S.J.L.B.
211; *Times*, July 30, 1997, HL .... *Digested*, 97/**1140**
R. *v.* Mills (Jill Maureen) see R. *v.* Scammell (Philip David)
R. *v.* Mills (Peter Mark) [1998] 2 Cr. App. R. (S.) 198, CA (Crim Div) .... *Digested*, 98/**1108**
R. *v.* Millward (David Samuel) [1999] 1 Cr. App. R. 61; [1999] Crim. L.R. 164, CA
(Crim Div)... *Digested*, 99/**1061**:
Followed, 01/1145
R. (on the application of Saxby) *v.* Milton Keynes Housing Benefit Review Board; *sub
nom* R. *v.* Milton Keynes Housing Benefit Review Board Ex p. Saxby [2001]
EWCA Civ 456; (2001) 33 H.L.R. 82; [2001] B.L.G.R. 482; (2001) 98(23)
L.S.G. 41; [2001] N.P.C. 72; *Times*, June 7, 2001, CA; affirming CO/1620/99,
QBD... *Digested*, 01/**5028**
R. *v.* Milton Keynes Housing Benefit Review Board Ex p. Saxby see R. (on the
application of Saxby) *v.* Milton Keynes Housing Benefit Review Board
R. *v.* Milton Keynes Magistrates Court Ex p. Long see R. *v.* Norwich Magistrates Court
Ex p. Elliott
R. *v.* Minister of Energy Ex p. Guildford; *sub nom* R. *v.* Seeboard Plc Ex p. Guildford
Times, March 6, 1998, QBD .... *Digested*, 98/**2083**
R. *v.* Ministry of Agriculture Fisheries and Food Ex p. Lay [1998] C.O.D. 387, QBD
R. (on the application of Monsanto Plc) *v.* Ministry of Agriculture, Fisheries and Food
(C306/98) see R. *v.* Ministry of Agriculture, Fisheries and Food Ex p. Monsanto
Plc (C306/98)
R. (on the application of Mott) *v.* Ministry of Agriculture, Fisheries and Food; *sub nom* R.
v. Ministry of Agriculture, Fisheries and Food Ex p. Mott [2001] A.C.D. 52;
Independent, February 7, 2001 (C.S), CA; affirming [2000] C.O.D.183, QBD
R. *v.* Ministry of Agriculture, Fisheries and Food Ex p. Astonquest Ltd [2000] Eu. L.R.
371, CA; affirming [1999] Eu. L.R. 141, QBD .... *Digested*, 00/**2640**
R. *v.* Ministry of Agriculture, Fisheries and Food Ex p. Bray [1999] C.O.D. 187; (1999)
96(16) L.S.G. 36; *Times*, April 13, 1999, QBD .... *Digested*, 99/**2568**
R. *v.* Ministry of Agriculture, Fisheries and Food Ex p. British Agrochemicals
Association Ltd see Secretary of State for the Environment, Food and Rural
Affairs *v.* Crop Protection Association UK Ltd
R. *v.* Ministry of Agriculture, Fisheries and Food Ex p. British Agrochemicals
Association Ltd (C100/96) [1999] E.C.R. I-1499; [1999] 2 C.M.L.R. 1; *Times*,
March 30, 1999, ECJ (6th Chamber) .... *Digested*, 99/**181**:
Subsequent proceedings, 99/180
R. *v.* Ministry of Agriculture, Fisheries and Food Ex p. British Pig Industry Support
Group [2000] Eu. L.R. 724; [2001] A.C.D. 3, QBD .... *Digested*, 01/**118**
R. *v.* Ministry of Agriculture, Fisheries and Food Ex p. Callaghan (2000) 32 H.L.R. 8,
QBD.. *Digested*, 00/**4643**

R. *v.* Ministry of Agriculture, Fisheries and Food Ex p. Compassion in World Farming Ltd (C1/96) [1998] All E.R. (E.C.) 302; [1998] E.C.R. I-1251; [1998] 2 C.M.L.R. 661; *Times*, April 2, 1998, ECJ . . . .   *Digested*, 98/**219**

R. *v.* Ministry of Agriculture, Fisheries and Food Ex p. Cresswell [1999] N.P.C. 155, QBD

R. *v.* Ministry of Agriculture, Fisheries and Food Ex p. Cypruvex (UK) Ltd (C432/92) see R. *v.* Ministry of Agriculture, Fisheries and Food Ex p. SP Anastasiou (Pissouri) Ltd (C432/92)

R. *v.* Ministry of Agriculture, Fisheries and Food Ex p. Dairy Trade Federation Ltd [1998] Eu. L.R. 253; [1995] C.O.D. 3; [1995] C.O.D. 237, QBD

R. *v.* Ministry of Agriculture, Fisheries and Food Ex p. Federation Europeene de la Sante Animale (FEDESA) (C331/88) [1990] E.C.R. I-4023; [1991] 1 C.M.L.R. 507, ECJ (5th Chamber) . . . .   *Digested*, 91/**3765**:
                                            Followed, 00/2374

R. *v.* Ministry of Agriculture, Fisheries and Food Ex p. First City Trading Ltd (1996) [1997] 1 C.M.L.R. 250; [1997] Eu. L.R. 195; *Times*, December 20, 1996; *Independent*, February 3, 1997 (C.S.), QBD . . . .   *Digested*, 97/**2384**:
                     Considered, 98/2569: *Followed*, 00/2640, 01/118

R. *v.* Ministry of Agriculture, Fisheries and Food Ex p. Fisher (t/a TR&P Fisher) (C369/98) [2000] E.C.R. I-6751; *Times*, October 10, 2000, ECJ (4th Chamber) . . . . . .   *Digested*, 00/**125**

R. *v.* Ministry of Agriculture, Fisheries and Food Ex p. Geiden [2000] 1 C.M.L.R. 289; *Independent*, October 15, 1999, QBD . . . .   *Digested*, 99/**214**

R. *v.* Ministry of Agriculture, Fisheries and Food Ex p. H&R Ecroyd Holdings Ltd (C127/94) [1996] E.C.R. I-2731; [1996] 3 C.M.L.R. 214, ECJ (5th Chamber) . .   *Followed*, 00/2373

R. *v.* Ministry of Agriculture, Fisheries and Food Ex p. JH Cooke & Sons (C372/98) [2000] E.C.R. I-8683; *Times*, October 18, 2000, ECJ (6th Chamber) . . . .   *Digested*, 00/**124**

R. *v.* Ministry of Agriculture, Fisheries and Food Ex p. Lower Burytown Farms Ltd; R. *v.* Ministry of Agriculture, Fisheries and Food Ex p. National Farmers Union [1999] Eu. L.R. 129, QBD . . . .   *Digested*, 99/**2220**

R. *v.* Ministry of Agriculture, Fisheries and Food Ex p. Monsanto Plc (C306/98); *sub nom* R. (on the application of Monsanto Plc) *v.* Ministry of Agriculture, Fisheries and Food (C306/98) [2001] E.C.R. I-3279, ECJ (6th Chamber) . . . .   *Digested*, 01/**2362**

R. *v.* Ministry of Agriculture, Fisheries and Food Ex p. Monsanto Plc (No.1) C0/380/97, QBD . . . .   *Digested*, 97/**3911**

R. *v.* Ministry of Agriculture, Fisheries and Food Ex p. Monsanto Plc (No.2) [1999] Q.B. 1161; [1999] 2 W.L.R. 599; [1998] 4 All E.R. 321; [1999] F.S.R. 223; *Times*, October 10, 1998; *Independent*, October 7, 1998, QBD . . . .   *Digested*, 98/**3471**

R. *v.* Ministry of Agriculture, Fisheries and Food Ex p. Mott see R. (on the application of Mott) *v.* Ministry of Agriculture, Fisheries and Food

R. *v.* Ministry of Agriculture, Fisheries and Food Ex p. National Farmers Union see R. *v.* Ministry of Agriculture, Fisheries and Food Ex p. Lower Burytown Farms Ltd

R. *v.* Ministry of Agriculture, Fisheries and Food Ex p. National Farmers Union (C157/96); United Kingdom *v.* Commission of the European Communities (C180/96) [1998] E.C.R. I-2265; [1998] 2 C.M.L.R. 1125; (1998) 17 Tr. L.R. 243; *Times*, May 6, 1998, ECJ . . . .   *Digested*, 98/**148**

R. *v.* Ministry of Agriculture, Fisheries and Food Ex p. National Farmers' Union (C354/95) [1997] E.C.R. I-4559; [1998] 1 C.M.L.R. 195, ECJ (6th Chamber)

R. *v.* Ministry of Agriculture, Fisheries and Food Ex p. National Federation of Fishermen's Organisations (C44/94) [1995] E.C.R. I-3115, ECJ . . . .   *Digested*, 96/**234**:
                                              Applied, 99/3451

R. *v.* Ministry of Agriculture, Fisheries and Food Ex p. Owen [2001] E.H.L.R. 11, QBD . .   *Digested*, 01/**153**:
                                       Subsequent proceedings, 01/130

R. *v.* Ministry of Agriculture, Fisheries and Food Ex p. SP Anastasiou (Pissouri) Ltd (C432/92); R. *v.* Ministry of Agriculture, Fisheries and Food Ex p. Cypruvex (UK) Ltd (C432/92) [1994] E.C.R. I-3087; [1995] 1 C.M.L.R. 569; *Times*, July 13, 1994; *Financial Times*, July 12, 1994, ECJ. . . . .   *Digested*, 94/**4721**:
                                             Considered, 99/2262

R. *v.* Ministry of Agriculture, Fisheries and Food Ex p. SP Anastasiou (Pissouri) Ltd (No.3) [1999] 3 C.M.L.R. 469; [1999] Eu. L.R. 168, HL . . . .   *Digested*, 99/**2262**:
                                       Subsequent proceedings, 00/164

R. *v.* Ministry of Agriculture, Fisheries and Food Ex p. SP Anastasiou (Pissouri) Ltd (C219/98) [2000] E.C.R. I-5241; [2000] 3 C.M.L.R. 339; *Times*, July 18, 2000, ECJ . . . .   *Digested*, 00/**164**:
                                       Previous proceedings, 99/2262

R. *v.* Ministry of Agriculture, Fisheries and Food Ex p. Tracy [1998] Env. L.R. D18, QBD

R. *v.* Ministry of Defence Ex p. Grady see R. *v.* Ministry of Defence Ex p. Smith

R. *v.* Ministry of Defence Ex p. Murray [1998] C.O.D. 134; *Times*, December 17, 1997; *Independent*, December 18, 1997, QBD. . . . .   *Digested*, 98/**257**

R. *v.* Ministry of Defence Ex p. Smith; R. *v.* Admiralty Board of the Defence Council Ex
p. Lustig-Prean; R. *v.* Admiralty Board of the Defence Council Ex p. Beckett; R.
v. Ministry of Defence Ex p. Grady [1996] Q.B. 517; [1996] 2 W.L.R. 305;
[1996] 1 All E.R. 257; [1996] I.C.R. 740; [1996] I.R.L.R. 100; (1996) 8 Admin.
L.R. 29; [1996] C.O.D. 237; (1995) 145 N.L.J. 1689; *Times*, November 6, 1995;
Independent, November 7, 1995, CA; affirming [1995] 4 All E.R. 427; [1995]
I.R.L.R. 585; [1995] C.O.D. 423; (1995) 145 N.L.J. 887; *Times*, June 13, 1995;
Independent, June 8, 1995, QBD . . . . *Digested, 96/***383***:*
Applied, 97/4111, 00/7, 00/4172, 00/5325, 01/5879: Considered, 96/2535,
97/299, 97/3559, 99/3181, 99/3715, 01/3661, 01/3684: Followed, 96/249,
96/3256
R. *v.* Ministry of Defence Ex p. Walker [2000] 1 W.L.R. 806; [2000] 2 All E.R. 917;
[2000] C.O.D. 153; (2000) 97(19) L.S.G. 43; (2000) 144 S.J.L.B. 198; *Times*,
April 7, 2000; *Independent*, April 11, 2000, HL; affirming [1999] 1 W.L.R. 1209;
[1999] 3 All E.R. 935; [1999] P.I.Q.R. Q168; [1999] C.O.D. 252; *Times*, February
11, 1999; *Independent*, February 11, 1999, CA; affirming [1998] C.O.D. 334;
Independent, February 19, 1998, QBD . . . . *Digested, 00/***260**
R. *v.* Miranda (Juan Carlos); R. *v.* Shayler (James Arthur) [2000] 2 Cr. App. R. 164;
[2000] 2 Cr. App. R. (S.) 347; [2000] Crim. L.R. 393; (2000) 97(9) L.S.G. 40;
(2000) 144 S.J.L.B. 111; *Times*, March 8, 2000, CA (Crim Div) . . . . *Digested, 00/***1160***:*
Applied, 01/1242
R. *v.* Mitchell (Alvin Lorenzo) [1977] 1 W.L.R. 753; [1977] 2 All E.R. 168; (1977) 65
Cr. App. R. 185; [1977] Crim. L.R. 626; 121 S.J. 252, CA (Crim Div) . . . . *Digested, 77/***643.49***:*
Considered, 96/1548, 01/1113: Distinguished, 78/545
R. *v.* Mitchell (Clive); R. *v.* Mitchell (Jennifer) [2001] 2 Cr. App. R. (S.) 29; [2001]
Crim. L.R. 239; *Times*, January 9, 2001, CA (Crim Div) . . . . *Digested, 01/***1238**
R. *v.* Mitchell (David) see Mitchell (David) *v.* Queen, The
R. *v.* Mitchell (Emmerson) (1994) 26 H.L.R. 394; [1994] Crim. L.R. 66; *Independent*,
June 2, 1993, CA (Crim Div) . . . . *Digested, 95/***1063***:*
Applied, 01/1149
R. *v.* Mitchell (Frank); R. *v.* King (Brian) (1999) 163 J.P. 75; [1999] Crim. L.R. 496;
(1998) 162 J.P.N. 926; (1998) 95(35) L.S.G. 36; (1998) 142 S.J.L.B. 221;
Times, October 7, 1998, CA (Crim Div) . . . . *Digested, 98/***956**
R. *v.* Mitchell (Graham Martin) see R. *v.* Effik (Godwin Eno)
R. *v.* Mitchell (Jennifer) see R. *v.* Mitchell (Clive)
R. *v.* Mitchell (Nicholas Charles), *Times*, September 4, 1998, CA (Crim Div) . . . . *Digested, 98/***1119***:*
Considered, 00/1132
R. *v.* Mitchell (Robert Leslie) [1996] 2 Cr. App. R. (S.) 299, CA (Crim Div) . . . . *Digested, 96/***2086***:*
Considered, 98/1317
R. *v.* Mitchell-Crinkley (William) [1998] 1 Cr. App. R. (S.) 368, CA (Crim Div) . . . . *Digested, 98/***1162**
R. *v.* Mitchinson (Daniel Steven) see Attorney General's Reference (Nos.11 and 12 of
1995), Re
R. *v.* Mitty (Lee) (1991) 12 Cr. App. R. (S.) 619, CA (Crim Div) . . . . *Digested, 92/***1390***:*
Considered, 98/1379: Referred to, 97/1704
R. *v.* ML (A Juvenile) see R. *v.* F (Mark Frank)
R. *v.* MO'N see R. *v.* PJO'N
R. *v.* Mokrecovas (Andrius) [2001] EWCA Crim 1644; [2001] Crim. L.R. 911, CA
(Crim Div)
R. (on the application of Khan) *v.* Mold Crown Court [2001] 2 Costs L.R. 336
R. *v.* Molland (Noel Ray) see R. *v.* Booth (Stephen)
R. *v.* Monney (Isaac) 6 B.H.R.C. 336, Sup Ct (Can) . . . . *Digested, 99/***3095**
R. *v.* Monopolies and Mergers Commission Ex p. Milk Marque Ltd [2000] C.O.D. 329,
QBD
R. *v.* Montague (Rudolph Leopold) see R. *v.* Beckles (Keith Anderson)
R. *v.* Montgomery (Stephen) [1996] Crim. L.R. 507, CA (Crim Div) . . . . *Applied, 99/894*
R. *v.* Moore (Eugene William) (1992) 13 Cr. App. R. (S.) 130, CA (Crim Div) . . . . *Digested, 93/***1176***:*
Considered, 99/1184
R. *v.* Moore (George Alan) see R. *v.* Sheehan (Michael)
R. *v.* Moore (John Michael) see Attorney General's Reference (No.10 of 1996), Re
R. *v.* Moore (Robert John) see R. *v.* Webbe (Bernard)
R. *v.* Moran (Derek Ernest) see Federal Steam Navigation Co Ltd *v.* Department of
Trade and Industry (The Huntingdon)
R. *v.* Moran (Frank Adam) see Attorney General's Reference (No.25 of 2001), Re
R. *v.* More (Jonathan) see R. *v.* T (Craig Daniel)
R. *v.* More (Kevin Vincent) [1987] 1 W.L.R. 1578; [1987] 3 All E.R. 825; (1988) 86 Cr.
App. R. 234; [1988] Crim. L.R. 176, HL . . . . *Digested, 88/***786***:*
Considered, 90/950, 91/805, 92/785, 92/1265, 93/777, 93/1149, 94/830,
95/1063, 95/1262: Followed, 01/1046
R. *v.* Moreby (John Peter) (1994) 15 Cr. App. R. (S.) 53, CA (Crim Div) . . . . *Considered, 99/1266*
R. *v.* Morgan [1977] Crim. L.R. 488, CA (Crim Div) . . . . *Digested, 77/***643.25***:*
Applied, 85/721, 87/945, 87/946, 01/5725: Cited, 87/892, 88/886:
Considered, 87/947, 89/978, 95/1174
R. *v.* Morgan (James) see R. *v.* Cosgrove (Kevin)
R. *v.* Morgan (John Martin) see R. *v.* Hall (Ian John)

R. *v.* Morgan (Matthew) (1993) 14 Cr. App. R. (S.) 734, CA (Crim Div) . . . .   *Digested,* 94/**1305**:
Considered, 99/1265: *Distinguished,* 97/1158
R. *v.* Morgan (Raymond Nigel) (1982) 4 Cr. App. R. (S.) 358, CA (Crim Div) . . . .   *Digested,* 83/**567**:
Considered, 99/1103
R. *v.* Morgan (Reginald Edward); R. *v.* Morgan (Richard Pugh) [2000] 2 Cr. App. R.
(S.) 455; [2000] Crim. L.R. 865, CA (Crim Div) . . . .   *Digested,* 01/**1173**
R. *v.* Morgan (Richard Pugh) see R. *v.* Morgan (Reginald Edward)
R. *v.* Morgan (William Anthony) see DPP *v.* Morgan (William Anthony)
R. *v.* Morland [1998] Crim. L.R. 143, CA (Crim Div)
R. *v.* Morling (John Brian) [1998] 1 Cr. App. R. (S.) 421, CA (Crim Div)   *Digested,* 98/**1370**
R. *v.* Morris [1998] Crim. L.R. 416, CA (Crim Div)
R. *v.* Morris (Clarence Barrington) [1998] 1 Cr. App. R. 386; (1997) 94(43) L.S.G. 29;
(1997) 141 S.J.L.B. 231; *Times,* November 13, 1997; *Independent,* October 24,
1997, CA (Crim Div) . . . .   *Digested,* 97/**1149**
R. *v.* Morris (Emmanuel) see R. *v.* Anderson (Lascelles Fitzalbert)
R. *v.* Morris (Harold Linden) [2001] 1 Cr. App. R. 4; [2001] 1 Cr. App. R. (S.) 87;
[2000] Crim. L.R. 1027; *Times,* August 4, 2000; *Independent,* July 18, 2000, CA
(Crim Div). . . . .   *Digested,* 00/**1211**
R. *v.* Morris (Karl Clifford) [1999] 2 Cr. App. R. (S.) 146, CA (Crim Div) . . . .   *Digested,* 99/**1166**
R. *v.* Morris (Timothy Andrew) [1997] 2 Cr. App. R. (S.) 258, CA (Crim Div). . . . .   *Digested,* 97/**1668**:
Considered, 98/1360
R. *v.* Morrison (James Watson) see R. *v.* Whitehouse (Stuart John)
R. *v.* Morrison (Jamie Joe) [2001] 1 Cr. App. R. (S.) 5; [2000] Crim. L.R. 605, CA
(Crim Div). . . . .   *Digested,* 01/**1221**
R. *v.* Mortiboys (Derrick Godfrey) [1997] 1 Cr. App. R. (S.) 141, CA (Crim Div) . . . .   *Digested,* 97/**1625**:
Considered, 00/1369
R. *v.* Morton (Stephen Richard) see Attorney General's Reference (No.48 of 1999), Re
R. *v.* Moseley (Christopher) [1999] 1 Cr. App. R. (S.) 452, CA (Crim Div) . . . .   *Digested,* 99/**1183**
R. *v.* Moshaid (Abdul); R. *v.* Mahmood (Fadel Fanta) [1998] Crim. L.R. 420, CA (Crim
Div)
R. *v.* Moss (Mark David) [2000] 1 Cr. App. R. (S.) 307, CA (Crim Div) . . . .   *Digested,* 00/**1269**
R. *v.* Mould (Darren) see R. *v.* Brodie (Caine)
R. *v.* Mould (David Frederick) see R. *v.* Toomer (Martin Charles)
R. *v.* Mountaine (Dennis Andrew) [1998] 2 Cr. App. R. (S.) 66, CA (Crim Div) . . . .   *Digested,* 98/**1348**
R. *v.* Moussaoui (Djemel) see R. *v.* Mereu (Jean-Marc)
R. *v.* Moynihan (John) [1999] 1 Cr. App. R. (S.) 294; [1999] Env. L.R. D26, CA (Crim
Div) . . . .   *Digested,* 99/**1151**
R. *v.* Mruk (Stefan Paul) see R. *v.* Wood (Thomas James)
R. *v.* MS [2000] 2 Cr. App. R. (S.) 388, CA (Crim Div) . . . .   *Digested,* 01/**1450**
R. *v.* MS (A Juvenile) (Offence: Robbery) [2000] 1 Cr. App. R. (S.) 386; [2000]
Crim. L.R. 57, CA (Crim Div) . . . .   *Digested,* 00/**1335**
R. *v.* Muhssin (Mohammed Chamekh) see R. *v.* Abdul-Hussain (Mustafa Shakir)
R. *v.* Mulkerrins [1981] Crim. L.R. 512, CA (Crim Div). . . . .   *Digested,* 81/**525.71**:
Considered, 98/1185
R. *v.* Mullahy (James) [1997] 2 Cr. App. R. (S.) 343, CA (Crim Div) . . . .   *Digested,* 98/**1115**
R. *v.* Mullan [1998] N.I.J.B. 93, CA (Crim Div) (NI) . . . .   *Applied,* 99/5225
R. *v.* Mullen (Nicholas Robert) (No.2) [2000] Q.B. 520; [1999] 3 W.L.R. 777; [1999]
2 Cr. App. R. 143; [1999] Crim. L.R. 561; *Times,* February 15, 1999, CA (Crim
Div) . . . .   *Digested,* 99/**972**:
Applied, 00/1026, 00/1056, 01/5733: *Considered,* 00/1025
R. *v.* Mullen (Thomas); R. *v.* Mustapha (Turhan) [2000] Crim. L.R. 873, CA (Crim Div)
R. *v.* Mullings (Richard Wilbert) see Attorney General's Reference (Nos.24 and 25 of
2000), Re
R. *v.* Mullins (Christopher) [2000] 2 Cr. App. R. (S.) 372, CA (Crim Div) . . . .   *Digested,* 00/**1435**
R. *v.* Muncaster (Warwick) [1999] Crim. L.R. 409, CA (Crim Div)
R. *v.* Mungroo (Ivan Kimble) [1998] B.P.I.R. 784; (1997) 94(25) L.S.G. 33; (1997)
141 S.J.L.B. 129; *Times,* July 3, 1997, CA . . . .   *Digested,* 97/**1405**
R. *v.* Munnery (Vincent) (1992) 94 Cr. App. R. 164; [1992] Crim. L.R. 215, CA (Crim
Div) . . . .   *Digested,* 93/**898**:
Applied, 97/1101: *Followed,* 99/990
R. *v.* Munro (Tracey) [2001] 1 Cr. App. R. (S.) 14, CA (Crim Div). . . . .   *Digested,* 01/**1465**
R. *v.* Munson (Unreported, November 23, 1998), CA (Crim Div). . . . .   *Considered,* 00/1228
R. *v.* Muntham House School Ex p. C see R. *v.* Muntham House School Ex p. R
R. *v.* Muntham House School Ex p. R; *sub nom* R. *v.* Muntham House School Ex p. C
[2000] B.L.G.R. 255; [2000] Ed. C.R. 452; [2000] E.L.R. 287; *Times,* January
26, 2000, QBD . . . .   *Digested,* 00/**1964**
R. *v.* Murphy (Audie James) [2001] EWCA Crim 288; [2001] 2 Cr. App. R. (S.) 84,
CA (Crim Div). . . . .   *Digested,* 01/**1431**
R. *v.* Murphy (David Eric) see Attorney General's Reference (No.25 of 1999), Re
R. *v.* Murphy (Karen Amanda) see Attorney General's Reference (Nos.62, 63, 64 and
65 of 1996), Re
R. *v.* Murphy (Robert) see R. *v.* Delaney (Richard Anthony)

R. *v.* Murphy (Vincent Thomas) (1988) 10 Cr. App. R. (S.) 468, CA (Crim Div) . . . .   *Digested,* 91/**1209**:
               Considered, 92/1396, 93/1281, 98/1372, 98/1376, 00/1417, 01/1474:
                         Referred to, 92/1456, 93/1280
R. *v.* Murray (Leroy Xaviour) [1998] 1 Cr. App. R. (S.) 395, CA (Crim Div) . . . .   *Digested,* 98/**1385**
R. *v.* Murray (Michael) (1994) 15 Cr. App. R. (S.) 567; [1994] Crim. L.R. 383, CA
    (Crim Div) . . . .   *Digested,* 95/**1427**:
                                          Considered, 01/1481
R. *v.* Mustapha (Turhan) see R. *v.* Mullen (Thomas)
R. *v.* Myers (Melanie) [1998] A.C. 124; [1997] 3 W.L.R. 552; [1997] 4 All E.R. 314;
    [1998] 1 Cr. App. R. 153; (1997) 161 J.P. 645; [1997] Crim. L.R. 888; (1997) 161
    J.P.N. 858; (1997) 94(35) L.S.G. 33; (1997) 147 N.L.J. 1237; (1997) 141
    S.J.L.B. 211; *Times,* July 31, 1997, HL; affirming [1996] 2 Cr. App. R. 335; [1996]
    Crim. L.R. 735; (1996) 146 N.L.J. 751; (1996) 140 S.J.L.B. 109; *Times,* April 23,
    1996, CA (Crim Div) . . . .   *Digested,* 97/**1113**
R. *v.* Mynors (Kenneth) [1998] 2 Cr. App. R. (S.) 279, CA (Crim Div) . . . .   *Digested,* 98/**1170**
R. *v.* N (A Juvenile) [2001] EWCA Crim 805; [2001] Crim. L.R. 498, CA (Crim Div)
R. *v.* N (Andrew Robert) [2000] 1 Cr. App. R. 182; (2000) 164 J.P. 29; (2001) 165
    J.P.N. 706; (1999) 96(34) L.S.G. 33; *Times,* September 7, 1999 ; *Independent,*
    November 8, 1999 (C.S), CA (Crim Div) . . . .   *Digested,* 99/**894**
R. *v.* N (Anthony Norris); R. *v.* W (Travis) [1998] 1 Cr. App. R. (S.) 66, CA (Crim Div) . . .   *Digested,* 98/**1268**
R. *v.* N (Child Witnesses: Unsworn Evidence) [1998] N.I. 261, CA (Crim Div) (NI)   . . . .   *Digested,* 99/**5183**
R. *v.* N (Duane) (A Juvenile) [2000] 2 Cr. App. R. (S.) 105, CA (Crim Div) . . . .   *Digested,* 00/**1325**
R. *v.* N (George Michael) (A Juvenile) [2001] 1 Cr. App. R. (S.) 116; (2000) 164 J.P.
    689; [2001] Crim. L.R. 48; *Independent,* November 6, 2000 (C.S), CA (Crim
    Div) . . . .   *Digested,* 01/**1268**
R. *v.* N (Handling of Evidence) [1998] Crim. L.R. 886; *Times,* July 15, 1998, CA (Crim
    Div) . . . .   *Digested,* 98/**1049**
R. *v.* N (John Robert) (1989) 11 Cr. App. R. (S.) 437, CA (Crim Div) . . . .   *Digested,* 91/**1191**:
                                          Considered, 00/1311
R. *v.* N (Right to Silence), *Times,* February 13, 1998, CA (Crim Div) . . . .   *Digested,* 98/**1060**
R. *v.* N (Robert William) see Attorney General's Reference (No.32 of 1992), Re
R. *v.* N (Stephen James) (A Juvenile) see Attorney General's Reference (No.21 of
    1999), Re
R. *v.* N (Steven John) [1998] Crim. L.R. 737, CA (Crim Div)
R. *v.* N'Wandou (Simeon N'Wadiche) see R. *v.* Ashton (Steven)
R. *v.* Nabina (Fizeal) [2000] Crim. L.R. 481, CA (Crim Div)
R. *v.* Nagrecha (Chandu) [1997] 2 Cr. App. R. 401; [1998] Crim. L.R. 65, CA (Crim
    Div) . . . .   *Digested,* 98/**875**
R. *v.* Naillie (Yabu Hurerali); R. *v.* Kanesarajah (Rajaratnam) [1993] A.C. 674; [1993] 2
    W.L.R. 927; [1993] 2 All E.R. 782; (1993) 97 Cr. App. R. 388; (1993) 143 N.L.J.
    848; *Times,* May 27, 1993; *Independent,* June 1, 1993; *Guardian,* May 31, 1993,
    HL; affirming [1992] 1 W.L.R. 1099; [1992] 1 All E.R. 75; (1993) 96 Cr. App. R.
    161; [1992] Imm. A.R. 395; *Times,* April 20, 1992; *Independent,* May 8, 1992;
    Guardian, May 6, 1992, CA (Crim Div) . . . .   *Digested,* 93/**2196**:
                     Considered, 97/2928: *Distinguished,* 00/978
R. *v.* Naini (Jamshid Hashemi) [1999] 2 Cr. App. R. 398, CA (Crim Div) . . . .   *Digested,* 00/**952**
R. *v.* Naji (Maged Mehdy) see R. *v.* Abdul-Hussain (Mustafa Shakir)
R. *v.* Nall-Cain (Charles) [1998] 2 Cr. App. R. (S.) 145; [1998] Crim. L.R. 297, CA
    (Crim Div) . . . .   *Digested,* 98/**1322**
R. *v.* Nangle (Brendan Francis) [2001] Crim. L.R. 506; (2000) 97(45) L.S.G. 40;
    (2000) 144 S.J.L.B. 281; *Times,* January 9, 2001; *Independent,* December 18,
    2000 (C.S), CA (Crim Div) . . . .   *Digested,* 01/**1095**
R. *v.* Nasar (Azram) [2000] 1 Cr. App. R. (S.) 333, CA (Crim Div) . . . .   *Digested,* 00/**1125**
R. *v.* Nash (Denis Arthur) [1999] Crim. L.R. 308, CA (Crim Div)
R. *v.* Nasser (Prince Minaz), *Times,* February 19, 1998, CA (Crim Div) . . . .   *Digested,* 98/**994**
R. *v.* National Assembly for Wales Ex p. Robinson (2000) 80 P. & C.R. 348, QBD . . . . .   *Digested,* 00/**4639**
R. (on the application of Westminster City Council) *v.* National Asylum Support Services;
    sub nom Westminster City Council *v.* National Asylum Support Service; R. (on
    the application of Westminster City Council) *v.* Secretary of State for the Home
    Department [2001] EWCA Civ 512; (2001) 33 H.L.R. 83, CA; affirming [2001]
    EWHC Admin 138, QBD (Admin Ct)
R. *v.* National Lottery Commission Ex p. Camelot Group Plc [2001] E.M.L.R. 3; *Times,*
    October 12, 2000, QBD . . . .   *Digested,* 00/**4072**
R. *v.* National Trust for Places of Historic Interest or Natural Beauty Ex p. Scott see
    Scott *v.* National Trust for Places of Historic Interest or Natural Beauty
R. *v.* Nawaz (Mohammed); R. *v.* Swanton (Alan); R. *v.* Sharif (Haroon) *Times,* June 8,
    1999; *Independent,* May 19, 1999, CA (Crim Div) . . . .   *Digested,* 99/**1019**
R. *v.* Nawrot (Michael James) (1988) 10 Cr. App. R. (S.) 239, CA (Crim Div) . . . .   *Considered,* 00/1136
R. *v.* Naylor (George Stewart) [1998] Crim. L.R. 662, CA (Crim Div)
R. *v.* Naylor (George Stuart) (1987) 9 Cr. App. R. (S.) 302; [1988] Crim. L.R. 63, CA
    (Crim Div) . . . .   *Digested,* 89/**1071**:
                  Considered, 91/1159, 95/1435, 97/1618, 01/1433

R. v. Nazari (Fazlollah); R. v. Fernandez (Joseph); R. v. Dissanayake (Rohan Shivantha); R. v. Anyanwu (Ebenezer Chukwuma); R. v. Adamson (Michael Joseph) [1980] 1 W.L.R. 1366; [1980] 3 All E.R. 880; (1980) 71 Cr. App. R. 87; (1980) 2 Cr. App. R. (S.) 84; [1980] Crim. L.R. 447, CA (Crim Div) . . . . *Digested,* 80/**581**:
Cited, 88/982, 89/977, 89/1108, 90/1405, 92/1224, 92/1225, 92/1226, 92/1227, 93/1105, 93/1106, 93/1108, 93/1109: *Considered,* 80/1422, 84/1755, 87/1996, 97/2907, 99/1129: *Referred to,* 85/1714

R. v. Nazeer (Mohammed Azad) [1998] Crim. L.R. 750, CA (Crim Div)
R. v. Nazir (Jangeer) see Attorney General's Reference (Nos.26 and 27 of 1996), Re
R. v. Ndlovu (Russell) [2001] 1 Cr. App. R. (S.) 47, CA (Crim Div) . . . . *Digested,* 01/**1467**
R. v. Neal (John Frederick) (Sentencing) [1999] 2 Cr. App. R. (S.) 352; [1999] Crim. L.R. 509, CA (Crim Div) . . . . *Digested,* 00/**1161**:
Considered, 00/1170

R. v. Neale (Matthew) see R. v. McFeeley (Jason)
R. v. Neary (Anthony) [1999] 1 Cr. App. R. (S.) 431, CA (Crim Div) . . . . *Digested,* 99/**1364**
R. v. Neath and Port Talbot Justices Ex p. DPP see R. v. Neath and Port Talbot Magistrates Court Ex p. DPP
R. v. Neath and Port Talbot Magistrates Court Ex p. DPP; *sub nom* R. v. Neath and Port Talbot Justices Ex p. DPP [2000] 1 W.L.R. 1376; (2000) 164 J.P. 323; [2000] Crim. L.R. 674; (2001) 165 J.P.N. 706; (2000) 97(9) L.S.G. 41; *Times,* March 15, 2000, QBD . . . . *Digested,* 00/**1024**:
Applied, 01/1160

R. v. Neaven (David John) [2000] 1 Cr. App. R. (S.) 391, CA (Crim Div) . . . . *Digested,* 00/**1199**
R. v. Nedrick (Ransford Delroy) [1986] 1 W.L.R. 1025; [1986] 3 All E.R. 1; (1986) 83 Cr. App. R. 267; (1986) 8 Cr. App. R. (S.) 179; (1986) 150 J.P. 589; [1986] Crim. L.R. 792; (1986) 150 J.P.N. 637, CA (Crim Div) . . . . *Digested,* 86/**651**:
Applied, 90/1116, 90/1121: *Approved,* 98/1052: *Considered,* 90/1122, 91/953, 94/811, 95/1064, 00/1069

R. v. Neem (Zohair) (1993) 14 Cr. App. R. (S.) 18; *Times,* April 16, 1992, CA (Crim Div) . *Digested,* 93/**1195**:
Considered, 96/1943, 00/1289

R. v. Neil [1994] Crim. L.R. 441, CA . . . . *Digested,* 95/**1144**:
Considered, 98/869

R. v. Nelmes (Kevin), *Times,* February 6, 2001, CA (Crim Div) . . . . *Digested,* 01/**1231**
R. v. Nelson (Damien) see R. v. Nelson (Mark Jones)
R. v. Nelson (Garfield Alexander) [1997] Crim. L.R. 234, CA (Crim Div) . . . . *Considered,* 00/**1100**
R. v. Nelson (Gary) see R. v. Jones (Derek)
R. v. Nelson (Mark Jones); *sub nom* R. v. Nelson (Damien); R. v. Sutherland (Jason) [2001] Q.B. 55; [2000] 3 W.L.R. 300; [2000] 2 Cr. App. R. 160; (2000) 164 J.P. 293; [2000] Crim. L.R. 591; (2000) 164 J.P.N. 383; (2000) 97(9) L.S.G. 39; *Times,* March 7, 2000, CA (Crim Div) . . . . *Digested,* 00/**966**
R. v. Nelson (Patrick Alan) [2001] EWCA Crim 2264; *Times,* December 10, 2001; *Independent,* October 30, 2001, CA (Crim Div) . . . . *Digested,* 01/**1369**
R. v. Nelson (Sonia Eloise); R. v. Rose (Cynthia Delores) [1998] 2 Cr. App. R. 399; [1998] Crim. L.R. 814, CA (Crim Div) . . . . *Digested,* 98/**869**
R. v. Nelson Group Services (Maintenance) Ltd [1999] 1 W.L.R. 1526; [1998] 4 All E.R. 331; [1999] I.C.R. 1004; [1999] I.R.L.R. 646; *Times,* September 17, 1998, CA (Crim Div) . . . . *Digested,* 98/**2831**
R. v. Nethercott (Lee) [2001] EWCA Crim 2535; *Times,* December 12, 2001, CA (Crim Div)
R. v. Netts (Alan Frank) [1997] 2 Cr. App. R. (S.) 117, CA (Crim Div) . . . . *Digested,* 97/**1510**:
Considered, 98/1177, 98/1187, 99/1203, 00/1218

R. v. Neve (Leonard Henry) (1986) 8 Cr. App. R. (S.) 270, CA (Crim Div) . . . . *Digested,* 87/**899**:
Considered, 98/1120

R. v. Neville (Darren Jason) (1993) 14 Cr. App. R. (S.) 768; [1993] Crim. L.R. 463, CA (Crim Div) . . . . *Digested,* 94/**1394**:
Considered, 99/1293

R. v. Newberry (Colin Stewart) see Attorney General's Reference (No.1 of 1999) (Unduly Lenient Sentence), Re
R. v. Newbury (Stephen David) see Attorney General's Reference (No.68 of 2001), Re
R. v. Newbury DC Ex p. Blackwell [1998] J.P.L. 680; [1998] C.O.D. 155, QBD . . . . *Digested,* 98/**4192**
R. v. Newbury DC Ex p. Chieveley Parish Council (1998) 10 Admin. L.R. 676; [1999] P.L.C.R. 51; [1998] E.G.C.S. 131; (1998) 95(33) L.S.G. 33; (1998) 142 S.J.L.B. 222; *Times,* September 10, 1998; *Independent,* October 5, 1998 (C.S.), CA; affirming in part [1997] J.P.L. 1137; [1997] E.G.C.S. 105; [1997] N.P.C. 106; *Times,* July 22, 1997, QBD . . . . *Digested,* 98/**4226**:
Considered, 99/4259: *Followed,* 00/4516

R. v. Newcastle Upon Tyne City Council Ex p. Christian Institute [2001] B.L.G.R. 165, QBD . . . . *Digested,* 01/**4315**
R. v. Newcastle upon Tyne Justices Ex p. Devine (1998) 162 J.P. 602; [1998] R.A. 97; [1998] C.O.D. 420; (1998) 162 J.P.N. 483; (1998) 95(20) L.S.G. 33; (1998) 142 S.J.L.B. 155; *Times,* May 7, 1998, QBD . . . . *Digested,* 98/**4295**
R. v. Newcastle upon Tyne Magistrates Court Ex p. Poundstretcher Ltd [1998] C.O.D. 256, QBD . . . . *Digested,* 98/**1037**

R. *v.* Newhall Prison Ex p. Akhtar see R. (on the application of Akhtar) *v.* Governor of Newhall Prison

R. (on the application of Al-Nashed) *v.* Newham LBC see R. (on the application of Bibi) *v.* Newham LBC

R. (on the application of Bibi) *v.* Newham LBC; *sub nom* R. *v.* Newham LBC Ex p. Bibi; R. *v.* Newham LBC Ex p. Al-Nashed; R. (on the application of Al-Nashed) *v.* Newham LBC [2001] EWCA Civ 607; (2001) 33 H.L.R. 84; (2001) 98(23) L.S.G. 38; [2001] N.P.C. 83; *Times,* May 10, 2001, CA; reversing in partCO/1748/0159/99, QBD . . . . *Digested,* 01/**3426**

R. (on the application of J) *v.* Newham LBC [2001] EWHC Admin 992; *Independent,* December 10, 2001 (C.S.), QBD (Admin Ct)

R. (on the application of Sacupima) *v.* Newham LBC; *sub nom* R. *v.* Newham LBC Ex p. Sacupima [2001] 1 W.L.R. 563; (2001) 33 H.L.R. 2; [2000] N.P.C. 127; *Times,* December 1, 2000; *Independent,* November 28, 2000, CA; reversing in part (2001) 33 H.L.R. 1; [2000] C.O.D. 133; *Times,* January 12, 2000 ; *Independent,* December 2, 1999, QBD . . . . *Digested,* 01/**3428**:
Disapproved, 00/3147

R. (on the application of Tshikangu) *v.* Newham LBC; *sub nom* Tshikangu *v.* Newham LBC [2001] EWHC Admin 92; [2001] N.P.C. 33; *Times,* April 27, 2001, QBD (Admin Ct) . . . . *Digested,* 01/**591**

R. *v.* Newham LBC Ex p. Al-Nashed see R. (on the application of Bibi) *v.* Newham LBC

R. *v.* Newham LBC Ex p. Begum (Mashuda) [2000] 2 All E.R. 72; (2000) 32 H.L.R. 808; *Times,* October 11, 1999, QBD. . . . . *Digested,* 99/**3053**

R. *v.* Newham LBC Ex p. Bibi see R. (on the application of Bibi) *v.* Newham LBC

R. *v.* Newham LBC Ex p. C (1999) 31 H.L.R. 567, QBD. *Digested,* 99/**4627**

R. *v.* Newham LBC Ex p. Chowdhury (1999) 31 H.L.R. 383, QBD. . . . . *Digested,* 98/**3021**

R. *v.* Newham LBC Ex p. Dada [1996] Q.B. 507; [1995] 3 W.L.R. 540; [1995] 2 All E.R. 522; [1995] 1 F.L.R. 842; [1995] 2 F.C.R. 441; (1995) 27 H.L.R. 502; 93 L.G.R. 459; (1996) 29 B.M.L.R. 79; [1995] Fam. Law 410; (1996) 160 L.G. Rev. 341; (1995) 145 N.L.J. 490; *Times,* February 3, 1995, CA; reversing [1994] 2 F.L.R. 1027; [1995] 1 F.C.R. 248; [1995] Fam. Law 71; (1995) 159 J.P.N. 28; *Times,* July 29, 1994; *Independent,* September 16, 1994, QBD . . . . *Digested,* 95/**2580**:
Applied, 98/2999: *Followed,* 97/2678

R. *v.* Newham LBC Ex p. Gentle (1994) 26 H.L.R. 466, QBD . . . . *Digested,* 95/**2582**:
Considered, 94/2345, 95/2580, 98/373, 98/2999: *Followed,* 97/2678:
Referred to, 94/2320, 95/2543

R. *v.* Newham LBC Ex p. Gorenkin (1998) 30 H.L.R. 278; (1997-98) 1 C.C.L. Rep. 309; [1997] C.O.D. 391; (1997) 94(23) L.S.G. 27; (1997) 141 S.J.L.B. 138; *Times,* June 9, 1997; *Independent,* June 9, 1997 (C.S.), QBD . . . . *Digested,* 97/**3429**

R. *v.* Newham LBC Ex p. Hassan (1997) 29 H.L.R. 378, QBD . . . . *Digested,* 97/**2675**:
Considered, 98/3004: *Distinguished,* 98/2997, 98/3026

R. *v.* Newham LBC Ex p. Kaur (1997) 29 H.L.R. 776, QBD . . . . *Digested,* 98/**4527**

R. *v.* Newham LBC Ex p. Khan (2001) 33 H.L.R. 29; *Times,* May 9, 2000, QBD . . . . *Digested,* 00/**3147**

R. *v.* Newham LBC Ex p. Laronde (1995) 27 H.L.R. 215; [1994] C.O.D. 409; *Times,* March 11, 1994, QBD. . . . . *Digested,* 95/**2543**:
Considered, 94/2345, 95/2580, 98/2999

R. *v.* Newham LBC Ex p. Larwood (1998) 30 H.L.R. 716, CA; reversing (1997) 29 H.L.R. 670, QBD . . . . *Digested,* 98/**2999**

R. *v.* Newham LBC Ex p. Lumley (2001) 33 H.L.R. 11; [2000] C.O.D. 315, QBD

R. *v.* Newham LBC Ex p. Medical Foundation for the Care of Victims of Torture (1998) 30 H.L.R. 955; (1997-98) 1 C.C.L. Rep. 227; *Times,* December 26, 1997, QBD . . *Digested,* 98/**4572**:
Followed, 99/4627

R. *v.* Newham LBC Ex p. Miah (1995) see R. *v.* Newham LBC Ex p. Miah (Deferring Accommodation: Rent Arrears)

R. *v.* Newham LBC Ex p. Miah (Deferring Accommodation: Rent Arrears); *sub nom* R. *v.* Newham LBC Ex p. Miah (1995) (1996) 28 H.L.R. 279, QBD. . . . . *Digested,* 96/**3073**:
Considered, 96/3095, 97/2696, 98/3004

R. *v.* Newham LBC Ex p. Miah (Suitable Accommodation) (1998) 30 H.L.R. 691, QBD . *Digested,* 98/**3026**:
Considered, 98/3004

R. *v.* Newham LBC Ex p. Ojuri (No.1) CO/3427/97, QBD . . . . *Digested,* 98/**3004**

R. *v.* Newham LBC Ex p. Ojuri (No.2) (1999) 31 H.L.R. 452; *Times,* August 29, 1998, QBD. . . . . *Digested,* 98/**3023**:
Considered, 98/3027

R. *v.* Newham LBC Ex p. Ojuri (No.3) (1999) 31 H.L.R. 631, QBD . . . . *Digested,* 99/**3060**

R. *v.* Newham LBC Ex p. Plastin (1998) 30 H.L.R. 261; (1997-98) 1 C.C.L. Rep. 304, QBD . . . . *Digested,* 97/**4720**

R. *v.* Newham LBC Ex p. R [1994] C.O.D. 472, QBD . . . . *Digested,* 96/**2478**:
Considered, 99/1887

R. *v.* Newham LBC Ex p. Sacupima see R. (on the application of Sacupima) *v.* Newham LBC

R. *v.* Newham LBC Ex p. Trendgrove Properties Ltd (2000) 32 H.L.R. 424; (1999) 96(22) L.S.G. 36, QBD . . . . *Digested,* 00/**3127**

R. *v.* Newham LBC Ex p. Watts (2000) 32 H.L.R. 255, QBD . . . . *Digested,* 00/**3124**

R. v. Newman (Dean David) [2000] 2 Cr. App. R. (S.) 227; (2001) 57 B.M.L.R. 123; [2000] Crim. L.R. 309; (2000) 97(6) L.S.G. 34; (2000) 144 S.J.L.B. 80; *Times*, February 3, 2000, CA (Crim Div) . . . .   *Digested*, 00/**1353**

R. v. Newport (Stephen Roy) [1998] Crim. L.R. 581, CA (Crim Div)

R. v. Newport CBC Ex p. Avery (1999) 1 L.G.L.R. 205; [1999] J.P.L. 452, QBD . . . . . .   *Digested*, 99/**4233**

R. v. News Group Newspapers Ltd; *sub nom* News Group Newspapers Ltd, Ex p. *Times*, May 21, 1999, CA (Crim Div) . . . .   *Digested*, 99/**82**

R. v. Newsome (Peter Alan) [1997] 2 Cr. App. R. (S.) 69; [1997] Crim. L.R. 237, CA (Crim Div) . . . .   *Digested*, 97/**1428**:   *Applied*, 01/1231

R. v. Newton (Geoffrey Harold) [1999] 2 Cr. App. R. (S.) 172; [1999] Crim. L.R. 338, CA (Crim Div) . . . .   *Digested*, 99/**1294**

R. v. Newton (Paul Joseph) [1999] 1 Cr. App. R. (S.) 438, CA (Crim Div) . . . .   *Digested*, 99/**1181**:   *Considered*, 00/1261

R. v. Newton (Robert John) (1983) 77 Cr. App. R. 13; (1982) 4 Cr. App. R. (S.) 388; [1983] Crim. L.R. 198, CA (Crim Div) . . . .   *Digested*, 83/**815**:   *Applied*, 86/597, 87/693, 89/708, 89/3222, 90/1281: *Cited*, 90/1313, 93/827, 93/1145, 93/1146: *Considered*, 84/856, 85/723, 85/828, 86/598, 86/728, 87/937, 87/938, 87/940, 88/911, 88/912, 88/913, 89/1004, 89/1005, 90/1310, 95/1380, 99/5220: *Distinguished*, 86/729, 87/872, 88/915, 89/1008: *Followed*, 83/813: *Referred to*, 84/727, 84/851, 87/934, 89/1007, 90/1308

R. v. Ngan (Sui Soi) [1998] 1 Cr. App. R. 331; (1997) 94(33) L.S.G. 27; *Times*, July 24, 1997, CA (Crim Div) . . . .   *Digested*, 97/**1250**

R. v. NHS Executive Ex p. Ingoldby [1999] C.O.D. 167, QBD

R. v. Nicholaou (Nicolas Michael) see R. v. Doyle (David Martin)

R. v. Nicholls (Martin Richard) [1998] 2 Cr. App. R. (S.) 296, CA (Crim Div) . . . .   *Digested*, 98/**1173**

R. v. Nicholson (George) [1998] 1 Cr. App. R. (S.) 370, CA (Crim Div) . . . .   *Digested*, 98/**1247**

R. v. Nicholson (John) see R. v. Smith (Patrick Joseph)

R. v. Nicklin (David John) [1977] 1 W.L.R. 403; [1977] 2 All E.R. 444; (1977) 64 Cr. App. R. 205; [1977] Crim. L.R. 221; 121 S.J. 286; *Times*, November 16, 1976, CA (Crim Div) . . . .   *Digested*, 77/**568**:   *Applied*, 99/941

R. v. Nickolson [1999] Crim. L.R. 61, CA (Crim Div)

R. v. Nightingale (Sheila) see R. v. Walsh (John)

R. v. Nijjer (Satvinder Singh) [1999] 2 Cr. App. R. (S.) 385, CA (Crim Div) . . . .   *Digested*, 00/**1193**

R. v. Nixon (Gordon Leslie) (1994) 15 Cr. App. R. (S.) 492, CA (Crim Div) . . . .   *Digested*, 95/**1446**:   *Considered*, 99/1268

R. v. Nixon (John William) see Attorney General's Reference (Nos.19, 20, 21 and 22 of 1997), Re

R. v. Nixon (Thomas Agnew) see Attorney General's Reference (Nos.19, 20, 21 and 22 of 1997), Re

R. v. Nock (David Michael) see DPP v. Nock

R. v. Nodjoumi (Benham) (1985) 7 Cr. App. R. (S.) 183, CA (Crim Div) . . . .   *Digested*, 86/**864**:   *Cited*, 90/1259: *Considered*, 99/1343

R. v. Nolan (Leroy) (1992) 13 Cr. App. R. (S.) 144, CA (Crim Div) . . . .   *Digested*, 93/**1138**:   *Considered*, 00/1224

R. v. Norfolk CC Ex p. Thorpe [1998] C.O.D. 208; [1998] N.P.C. 11; *Times*, February 9, 1998, QBD . . . .   *Digested*, 98/**2853**

R. v. Normanton (Lee) [1998] Crim. L.R. 220, CA (Crim Div) . . . .   *Digested*, 97/**1178**

R. v. Norris-Copson (Brian) see Attorney General's Reference (Nos.36, 37, 38 and 39 of 1999), Re

R. v. North (Christopher) [2001] EWCA Crim 544; [2001] Crim. L.R. 746; *Daily Telegraph*, March 20, 2001, CA (Crim Div) . . . .   *Digested*, 01/**1044**

R. v. North (Sydney) [2001] 1 Cr. App. R. (S.) 32, CA (Crim Div) . . . .   *Digested*, 01/**1354**

R. (on the application of Bowhay) v. North and East Devon HA (2001) 60 B.M.L.R. 228; [2001] A.C.D. 25, QBD (Admin Ct) . . . .   *Digested*, 01/**472**

R. v. North and East Devon HA Ex p. Coughlan [2001] Q.B. 213; [2000] 2 W.L.R. 622; [2000] 3 All E.R. 850; (2000) 2 L.G.L.R. 1; [1999] B.L.G.R. 703; (1999) 2 C.C.L. Rep. 285; [1999] Lloyd's Rep. Med. 306; (2000) 51 B.M.L.R. 1; [1999] C.O.D. 340; (1999) 96(31) L.S.G. 39; (1999) 143 S.J.L.B. 213; *Times*, July 20, 1999 ; *Independent*, July 20, 1999, CA; affirming (1999) 2 C.C.L. Rep. 27; (1999) 47 B.M.L.R. 27; [1999] C.O.D. 174; *Times*, December 29, 1998, QBD . . .   *Digested*, 99/**2643**:   *Applied*, 00/4526, 01/5879: *Followed*, 99/3931, 00/1915

R. v. North and East Devon HA Ex p. Metcalfe see R. v. North and East Devon HA Ex p. Pow

R. v. North and East Devon HA Ex p. Pow; R. v. North and East Devon HA Ex p. Metcalfe (1997-98) 1 C.C.L. Rep. 280; (1998) 39 B.M.L.R. 77, QBD . . . .   *Digested*, 97/**3671**

R. (on the application of H) v. North and East London Regional Mental Health Review Tribunal see R. (on the application of H) v. Mental Health Review Tribunal for North and East London Region

R. v. North and East London Regional Mental Health Review Tribunal Ex p. T (Unreported, February 24, 2000), QBD [*Ex rel.* Mark Mullins, Barrister, Coram Chambers, 4 Brick Court, Temple, London] . . . .   *Digested*, 00/**4173**

R. v. North Derbyshire HA Ex p. Fisher (1998) 10 Admin. L.R. 27; (1997-98) 1 C.C.L.
Rep. 150; [1997] 8 Med. L.R. 327; (1997) 38 B.M.L.R. 76; *Times*, September 2,
1997, QBD .... *Digested*, 97/**3683**

R. v. North Devon DC Ex p. Lewis; *sub nom* Lewis v. North Devon DC [1981] 1
W.L.R. 328; [1981] 1 All E.R. 27; 79 L.G.R. 289; 124 S.J. 742, QBD .... *Digested*, 81/**1302**:
Considered, 81/1297, 82/1473: *Distinguished*, 00/3130: *Referred to*, 88/1770,
89/1876

R. (on the application of Lloyd) v. North East Essex Justices see R. (on the application
of Lloyd) v. Chelmsford Justices

R. v. North East Suffolk Magistrates Court Ex p. DPP see R. v. Warley Magistrates
Court Ex p. DPP

R. v. North Essex Justices Ex p. Lloyd see R. (on the application of Lloyd) v.
Chelmsford Justices

R. v. North Hampshire Youth Court Ex p. DPP (2000) 164 J.P. 377; (2000) 164 J.P.N.
583, QBD .... *Digested*, 00/**1115**

R. v. North Hertfordshire DC Ex p. Sullivan [1981] J.P.L. 752 .... *Digested*, 81/**2698**:
Applied, 01/1845: *Disapproved*, 97/4077

R. v. North Lincolnshire Council Ex p. Horticultural and Garden Products Sales
(Humberside) Ltd [1998] Env. L.R. 295; (1998) 76 P. & C.R. 363; [1998] 3
P.L.R. 1, QBD .... *Digested*, 98/**4201**

R. v. North London General Commissioners Ex p. Nii-Amaa [1999] S.T.C. 644; 72 T.C.
634; [1999] B.T.C. 242, QBD .... *Digested*, 99/**4652**

R. (on the application of Cadbury Garden Centre Ltd) v. North Somerset DC; *sub nom* R.
v. North Somerset DC Ex p. Cadbury Garden Centre Ltd [2001] J.P.L. 1070;
[2000] E.G.C.S. 120; *Times*, November 22, 2000, CA; reversing (1999) 96(43)
L.S.G. 35, QBD .... *Digested*, 00/**4501**

R. v. North Somerset DC Ex p. Cadbury Garden Centre Ltd see R. (on the application
of Cadbury Garden Centre Ltd) v. North Somerset DC

R. v. North Somerset DC Ex p. Garnett [1998] Env. L.R. 91; [1997] J.P.L. 1015, QBD ... *Digested*, 98/**100**

R. (on the application of J (A Child)) v. North Warwickshire BC; *sub nom* R. v. North
Warwickshire BC Ex p. J (A Child) [2001] EWCA Civ 315; [2001] 2 P.L.R. 59;
[2001] P.L.C.R. 31; [2001] J.P.L. 1434 (Note); [2001] N.P.C. 52; *Times*, March
30, 2001, CA; reversing [2001] J.P.L. 617 (Note), QBD .... *Digested*, 01/**4752**

R. v. North West Lancashire HA Ex p. A; *sub nom* North West Lancashire HA v. A; R.
v. North West Lancashire HA Ex p. D; R. v. North West Lancashire HA Ex p. G
[2000] 1 W.L.R. 977; [2000] 2 F.C.R. 525; (1999) 2 C.C.L. Rep. 419; [1999]
Lloyd's Rep. Med. 399; (2000) 53 B.M.L.R. 148; *Times*, August 24, 1999 ;
Independent, October 5, 1999, CA; affirming (Unreported, December 21, 1998),
QBD .... *Digested*, 99/**2684**

R. v. North West Lancashire HA Ex p. D see R. v. North West Lancashire HA Ex p. A

R. v. North West Lancashire HA Ex p. G see R. v. North West Lancashire HA Ex p. A

R. v. North West Leicestershire DC Ex p. Moses (No.1) [2000] J.P.L. 733; (1999)
96(37) L.S.G. 33, QBD .... *Digested*, 00/**4507**

R. v. North West Leicestershire DC Ex p. Moses (No.2) [2000] Env. L.R. 443; [2000]
J.P.L. 1287; [2000] E.G.C.S. 55; (2000) 97(17) L.S.G. 36, CA .... *Digested*, 00/**4461**

R. v. North West London Mental Health NHS Trust Ex p. S [1998] Q.B. 628; [1998] 2
W.L.R. 189; (1997) 4 All E.R. 871; (1998) 39 B.M.L.R. 105; *Times*, August 27,
1997, CA; affirming (1997) 36 B.M.L.R. 151; [1997] C.O.D. 42; *Times*, August 15,
1996, QBD .... *Digested*, 97/**3646**

R. v. North West Suffolk (Mildenhall) Magistrates Court Ex p. Forest Heath DC; *sub*
nom R. v. Mildenhall Magistrates Court Ex p. Forest Heath DC (1997) 161 J.P.
401; [1998] Env. L.R. 9; [1997] C.O.D. 352; (1997) 161 J.P.N. 602; *Times*, May
16, 1997, CA .... *Digested*, 97/**510**

R. v. North Yorkshire CC Ex p. Brown; R. v. North Yorkshire CC Ex p. Cartwright
[2000] 1 A.C. 397; [1999] 2 W.L.R. 452; [1999] 1 All E.R. 969; [1999] Env. L.R.
623; [1999] J.P.L. 116; [1999] J.P.L. 616; [1999] C.O.D. 273; (1999) 143
S.J.L.B. 150; *Times*, February 12, 1999; *Independent*, February 16, 1999, HL;
affirming [1998] 2 C.M.L.R. 166; [1998] Env. L.R. 385; (1998) 76 P. & C.R. 433;
[1998] 4 P.L.R. 29; [1998] J.P.L. 764; [1998] N.P.C. 8; *Times*, February 9,
1998, CA; reversing [1997] Env. L.R. 391; [1996] N.P.C. 160, QBD .... *Digested*, 99/**4270**:
Cited, 99/4244: *Considered*, 00/4510

R. v. North Yorkshire CC Ex p. Cartwright see R. v. North Yorkshire CC Ex p. Brown

R. v. North Yorkshire CC Ex p. Hargreaves (1997-98) 1 C.C.L. Rep. 331; [1997] C.O.D.
390; *Times*, June 12, 1997; *Independent*, May 20, 1997, QBD .... *Digested*, 97/**4717**

R. v. North Yorkshire CC Ex p. Scarborough BC [1999] Env. L.R. 768; [1999] J.P.L.
1087; *Independent*, February 22, 1999 (C.S.), QBD .... *Digested*, 99/**2199**

R. v. Northallerton Magistrates Court Ex p. Dove [2000] 1 Cr. App. R. (S.) 136; (1999)
163 J.P. 657; [1999] Crim. L.R. 760; [1999] C.O.D. 598; (1999) 163 J.P.N.
894; *Times*, June 17, 1999, QBD .... *Digested*, 99/**985**:
Cited, 00/4296

R. v. Northampton BC Ex p. Northampton Rapid Transit System [2000] N.P.C. 80,
QBD

R. v. Northampton BC Ex p. Rice & Co (Northampton) Ltd [1998] E.G.C.S. 84;
(1998) 95(20) L.S.G. 36; [1998] N.P.C. 82; [1999] Env. L.R. D9, QBD

R. *v.* Northampton Magistrates Court Ex p. Newell (1993) 157 J.P. 869; [1992] R.A.
283; (1993) 157 J.P.N. 490; (1993) 157 L.G. Rev. 801; *Times*, September 18,
1992; *Independent*, September 4, 1992, CA; affirming [1992] R.A. 190; *Times*,
April 20, 1992, QBD . . . . *Digested*, 93/**2627**:
                            Considered, 93/2632, 94/2935, 97/3435: *Followed*, 95/995, 00/18
R. *v.* Northamptonshire CC Ex p. Addison (1998) 75 P. & C.R. D49, QBD
R. *v.* Northamptonshire CC Ex p. D; *sub nom* R. *v.* Northamptonshire CC Ex p. W
[1998] Ed. C.R. 14; [1998] E.L.R. 291; [1998] C.O.D. 110, QBD . . . .   *Digested*, 98/**1898**:
                                                                                             Considered, 01/95
R. *v.* Northamptonshire CC Ex p. Marshall [1998] Ed. C.R. 262; [1998] C.O.D. 457,
QBD . . . .   *Digested*, 99/**1900**
R. *v.* Northamptonshire CC Ex p. W see R. *v.* Northamptonshire CC Ex p. D
R. *v.* Northumberland National Park Authority Ex p. Secretary of State for Defence
(1999) 77 P. & C.R. 120; [1998] C.O.D. 493; [1998] E.G.C.S. 120, QBD. . . . . . .   *Digested*, 99/**4229**
R. *v.* Northumbrian Water Ltd Ex p. Newcastle and North Tyneside HA [1999] Env.
L.R. 715; [1999] E.H.L.R. 296; [1999] J.P.L. 704; *Independent*, January 18,
1999 (C.S.), QBD . . . .   *Digested*, 99/**5048**
R. *v.* Norwich City Council see Secretary of State for the Environment, Transport and
the Regions *v.* Redland Aggregates Ltd
R. *v.* Norwich Crown Court Ex p. Parker (1993) 96 Cr. App. R. 68; (1992) 156 J.P.
818; [1992] Crim. L.R. 500; (1992) 156 J.P.N. 348; *Times*, February 20, 1992,
QBD . . . .   *Digested*, 93/**767**:
                            Considered, 95/1035, 98/1082: *Referred to*, 94/806
R. *v.* Norwich Magistrates Court Ex p. Elliott; R. *v.* South East Northumberland
Magistrates Court Ex p. Knox; R. *v.* Milton Keynes Magistrates Court Ex p. Long;
R. *v.* Brent Youth Court Ex p. A (A Juvenile) [2000] 1 Cr. App. R. (S.) 152,
QBD . . . .   *Digested*, 00/**1029**:
                                                        Applied, 00/1031, 01/1107
R. *v.* Norwich Stipendiary Magistrate Ex p. Benjafield see R. *v.* Norwich Stipendiary
Magistrate Ex p. Keable
R. *v.* Norwich Stipendiary Magistrate Ex p. Buttle see R. *v.* Norwich Stipendiary
Magistrate Ex p. Keable
R. *v.* Norwich Stipendiary Magistrate Ex p. Cossey see R. *v.* Norwich Stipendiary
Magistrate Ex p. Keable
R. *v.* Norwich Stipendiary Magistrate Ex p. Keable; R. *v.* Norwich Stipendiary
Magistrate Ex p. Benjafield; R. *v.* Norwich Stipendiary Magistrate Ex p. Cossey;
R. *v.* Norwich Stipendiary Magistrate Ex p. Buttle; R. *v.* Caernarfon Justices Ex p.
Allen [1998] Crim. L.R. 510; [1998] C.O.D. 169; *Times*, February 5, 1998, QBD .   *Digested*, 98/**964**:
                                                                                             Not followed, 00/1033
R. *v.* Norwood (James Alexander) (1989) 11 Cr. App. R. (S.) 479, CA (Crim Div) . . . . .   *Digested*, 91/**1234**:
                                                                                             Considered, 98/1402
R. *v.* Notice (Jeffrey) [2000] 1 Cr. App. R. (S.) 75, CA (Crim Div) . . . .   *Digested*, 00/**1272**
R. (on the application of AB) *v.* Nottingham City Council [2001] EWHC Admin 235;
[2001] 3 F.C.R. 350, QBD (Admin Ct) . . . .   *Digested*, 01/**5097**
R. *v.* Nottingham City Council Ex p. Edwards (1999) 31 H.L.R. 33, QBD . . . .   *Digested*, 99/**3057**
R. *v.* Nottingham City Council Ex p. Howitt [1999] C.O.D. 530, QBD
R. *v.* Nottingham Justices Ex p. Fohmann (1987) 84 Cr. App. R. 316; (1987) 151 J.P.
49; (1986) 150 J.P.N. 819, QBD. . . . .   *Digested*, 87/**627**:
                                                                                             Considered, 99/985
R. *v.* Nottingham Justices Ex p. Taylor [1992] Q.B. 557; [1991] 3 W.L.R. 694; [1991] 4
All E.R. 860; (1991) 93 Cr. App. R. 365; (1991) 155 J.P. 623; [1991] C.O.D. 350;
(1991) 155 J.P.N. 426; (1991) 135 S.J. 444; *Times*, March 26, 1991;
Independent, March 13, 1991; *Daily Telegraph*, March 21, 1991, QBD . . . .   *Digested*, 92/**921**:
                                                                                             Applied, 01/1170
R. (on the application of SR) *v.* Nottingham Magistrates Court [2001] EWHC Admin
802; *Independent*, December 17, 2001 (C.S), QBD (Admin Ct)
R. *v.* Nottingham Magistrates Court Ex p. Davidson [2000] 1 Cr. App. R. (S.) 167;
[2000] Crim. L.R. 118; [1999] C.O.D. 405; *Independent*, June 21, 1999 (C.S.),
QBD . . . .   *Digested*, 99/**1291**
R. *v.* Nottingham Mental Health Review Tribunal Ex p. Secretary of State for the Home
Department; R. *v.* Trent Mental Health Review Tribunal Ex p. Secretary of State
for the Home Department [1989] C.O.D. 221; *Times*, October 12, 1988;
Independent, October 10, 1988 (C.S.); *Guardian*, October 29, 1988, CA; affirming
Times, March 25, 1987, QBD . . . .   *Digested*, 88/**2270**:
                                                                                             Applied, 01/4423
R. *v.* Nottinghamshire CC Ex p. East Midland Development Ltd (2001) 81 P. & C.R. 19,
QBD . . . .   *Digested*, 01/**3326**:
R. *v.* Nova Scotia Pharmaceutical Society [1992] 2 S.C.R. 606, Sup Ct (Can). . . . .   *Applied*, 99/3106
R. (on the application of Gunn-Russo) *v.* Nugent Care Society see Gunn-Russo *v.*
Nugent Care Society
R. *v.* Nunn (Adam John) [1996] 2 Cr. App. R. (S.) 136, CA (Crim Div) . . . .   *Digested*, 96/**1836**:
                            Considered, 99/1321, 00/1155: *Followed*, 01/1466: *Not applied*, 99/1320
R. *v.* Nuttall (Marcus Joel) see Attorney General's Reference (Nos. 21 and 22 of 1990),
Re

R. *v.* Nuttall (Nathan Matthew) see Attorney General's Reference (Nos.21 and 22 of 1990), Re

R. *v.* O (David) [1999] 2 Cr. App. R. (S.) 280, CA (Crim Div) . . . . *Digested,* 99/**1099**

R. *v.* O (Gordon Edward) [1999] 1 Cr. App. R. (S.) 327, CA (Crim Div) . . . . *Digested,* 99/**1350**:
Considered, 00/1429, 01/1367

R. *v.* O (Jason Patrick) (A Juvenile) see Attorney General's Reference (Nos.78, 79 and 85 of 1998), Re

R. *v.* O (Liam Stuart) (A Juvenile) [1999] 1 Cr. App. R. (S.) 35, CA (Crim Div) . . . . *Digested,* 99/**1220**

R. *v.* O (PN) (A Juvenile) [2000] 1 Cr. App. R. (S.) 112, CA (Crim Div)

R. *v.* O (Stephen Mark) (A Juvenile) [2000] 1 Cr. App. R. (S.) 73, CA (Crim Div) . . . . . *Digested,* 00/**1329**

R. *v.* O'Boyle (Michael James) see Attorney General's Reference (No.41 of 1994), Re

R. *v.* O'Brien (James Arthur) [2001] 1 Cr. App. R. (S.) 22, CA (Crim Div) . . . . *Digested,* 01/**1466**

R. *v.* O'Brien (Michael) [1995] 2 Cr. App. R. 649; [1995] Crim. L.R. 734; (1995) 139 S.J.L.B. 130; *Times,* April 14, 1995, CA (Crim Div) . . . . *Digested,* 95/**1238**:
Applied, 00/5481

R. *v.* O'Brien (Michael Alan); R. *v.* Hall (Darren Dennis); R. *v.* Sherwood (Ellis) [2000] Crim. L.R. 676; *Times,* February 16, 2000; *Independent,* March 27, 2000 (C.S.), CA (Crim Div) . . . . *Digested,* 00/**906**

R. *v.* O'Brien (Paul); R. *v.* Enkel (Andrew) [2000] 2 Cr. App. R. (S.) 358; [2000] Env. L.R. 653; [2000] E.H.L.R. Dig. 273; *Times,* April 19, 2000, CA (Crim Div) . . . . . *Digested,* 00/**1440**

R. *v.* O'Brien (Robert Francis) [2000] Crim. L.R. 863; *Times,* March 23, 2000, CA (Crim Div). . . . . *Digested,* 00/**1005**

R. *v.* O'Brien (Shaun Patrick) (1994) 15 Cr. App. R. (S.) 556, CA (Crim Div) . . . . *Digested,* 95/**1371**:
Considered, 99/1146

R. *v.* O'Callaghan (Daniel Francis); R. *v.* Broughton (Dennis) (1987) 9 Cr. App. R. (S.) 58, CA (Crim Div) . . . . *Digested,* 88/**985**:
Cited, 94/1186: *Considered,* 92/1137, 98/1375

R. *v.* O'Connell (Terance) see R. *v.* Drury (Christopher)

R. *v.* O'Connor (Michael Joseph) (1994) 15 Cr. App. R. (S.) 473; [1994] Crim. L.R. 227, CA (Crim Div) . . . . *Considered,* 96/1989,
96/2003, 98/1342: *Followed,* 96/2004, 96/2005

R. *v.* O'Driscoll (James) (1986) 8 Cr. App. R. (S.) 121; [1986] Crim. L.R. 701, CA (Crim Div) . . . . *Digested,* 87/**1042**:
Applied, 97/1415: *Cited,* 90/1408: *Considered,* 87/860, 87/1040, 88/984, 88/1012, 92/1137, 97/1700, 98/1132, 99/1214, 01/1222

R. *v.* O'Dwyer (Timothy Augustine) (1988) 86 Cr. App. R. 313, CA (Crim Div) . . . . *Digested,* 88/**948**:
Applied, 87/991, 88/949, 89/1068: *Cited,* 91/1150: *Considered,* 86/719, 87/897, 87/1035, 88/977, 99/1251

R. *v.* O'Gorman (John) see Attorney General's Reference (Nos.64 and 65 of 1997), Re

R. *v.* O'Halloran (Paul Gerrard) see Attorney General's Reference (Nos.62, 63 and 64 of 1995), Re

R. *v.* O'Kane Ex p. Northern Bank Ltd [1996] S.T.C. 1249; 69 T.C. 187; *Times,* October 3, 1996; *Independent,* November 4, 1996 (C.S.), QBD . . . . *Digested,* 96/**5611**:
Disapproved, 97/4756

R. *v.* O'N see R. *v.* PJO'N

R. *v.* O'Neill [1998] N.I.J.B. 1, Crown Ct (Belfast) . . . . *Applied,* 01/5725

R. *v.* O'Neill (Patrick Joseph) see R. *v.* Maguire (Anne Rita)

R. *v.* O'Prey (John Warren) [1999] 2 Cr. App. R. (S.) 83; [1999] Crim. L.R. 233, CA (Crim Div) . . . . *Digested,* 99/**1330**

R. *v.* O'Rourke (Peter Kevin) see Attorney General's Reference (No.51 of 1997), Re

R. *v.* O'S (Peter) (1993) 14 Cr. App. R. (S.) 632; [1993] Crim. L.R. 405, CA (Crim Div) . . . . *Digested,* 94/**1271**:
Considered, 99/1193

R. *v.* O'Shea (Kenneth Desmond) see R. *v.* Jones (John McKinsie)

R. *v.* O'Shea (Michael John) [2000] 2 Cr. App. R. (S.) 412, CA (Crim Div) . . . . *Digested,* 01/**1308**

R. *v.* O'Toole (Robert John) (1971) 55 Cr. App. R. 206; [1974] R.T.R. 88, CA (Crim Div) . . . . *Digested,* 71/**10171**:
Considered, 98/1365: *Followed,* 96/1771

R. *v.* Oakes [1986] 1 S.C.R. 103, Sup Ct (Can) . . . . *Applied,* 98/3160

R. *v.* Oakley (Michael William) [1998] 1 Cr. App. R. (S.) 100, CA (Crim Div) . . . . *Digested,* 98/**1135**

R. *v.* Obermeier (Manfred) [1997] 2 Cr. App. R. (S.) 346, CA (Crim Div) . . . . *Digested,* 98/**1363**:
Considered, 00/1196

R. *v.* Ocego (Stephen Mark) [1998] 1 Cr. App. R. (S.) 408, CA (Crim Div) . . . . *Digested,* 98/**1175**:
Considered, 00/1378

R. *v.* Odey (Lee) [2001] EWCA Crim 465; [2001] 2 Cr. App. R. (S.) 85, CA (Crim Div) . . . . *Digested,* 01/**1489**

R. *v.* Odeyemi (Olujimi); R. *v.* Abiodun (Danny) [1999] Crim. L.R. 828, CA (Crim Div)

R. *v.* Offen (Matthew Barry) (No.1) [2000] 1 Cr. App. R. (S.) 565; [2000] Crim. L.R. 306, CA (Crim Div) . . . . *Digested,* 00/**1358**

R. v. Offen (Matthew Barry) (No.2); R. v. McGilliard (Peter Wilson); R. v. McKeown (Darren); R. v. Okwuegbunam (Kristova); R. v. S (Stephen) [2001] 1 W.L.R. 253; [2001] 2 All E.R. 154; [2001] 1 Cr. App. R. 24; [2001] 2 Cr. App. R. (S.) 10; [2001] Crim. L.R. 63; (2001) 98(1) L.S.G. 23; (2000) 144 S.J.L.B. 288; *Times,* November 10, 2000; *Independent,* November 17, 2000, CA (Crim Div) . . . . *Digested,* 00/**1347**: *Applied,* 01/1413, 01/1414: *Not followed,* 01/1412

R. v. Ofori (Noble Julius); R. v. Tackie (Nazar) (1994) 99 Cr. App. R. 223, CA (Crim Div) . . . . *Digested,* 95/**1216**: *Followed,* 00/941

R. v. Okanta (Kwasi) [1997] Crim. L.R. 451, CA (Crim Div) . . . . *Digested,* 97/**1226**: *Applied,* 98/892

R. v. Okee (Robert); R. v. West (Marcus) [1998] 2 Cr. App. R. (S.) 199, CA (Crim Div) . . *Digested,* 98/**1328**

R. v. Okolie (Frank), *Times,* June 16, 2000, CA (Crim Div) . . . . *Digested,* 00/**941**

R. v. Okwuegbunam (Kristova) see R. v. Offen (Matthew Barry) (No.2)

R. v. Oldham Justices Ex p. Cawley; *sub nom* Cawley, Re; R. v. Governor of Risley Prison Ex p. Ryan; R. v. Governor of Risley Prison Ex p. Healey; R. v. Stoke on Trent Justices Ex p. Cawley [1997] Q.B. 1; [1996] 2 W.L.R. 681; [1996] 1 All E.R. 464; (1996) 160 J.P. 133; [1996] C.O.D. 292; (1996) 160 J.P.N. 48; (1996) 146 N.L.J. 49; *Times,* December 7, 1995, QBD . . . . *Digested,* 96/**104**: *Considered,* 98/1145

R. v. Oldham MBC Ex p. Foster [2000] Env. L.R. 395; [2000] J.P.L. 711, QBD . . . . *Digested,* 00/**4510**

R. v. Oldsworth (Kenneth Anthony) see Attorney General's Reference (No.47 of 1997), Re

R. v. Oliver (Austen Michael) see R. v. Jama (Hussein)

R. v. Oliver (Laurence Charles) [1999] 1 Cr. App. R. (S.) 394; (1998) 95(43) L.S.G. 32; (1998) 95(40) L.S.G. 37; (1998) 142 S.J.L.B. 262; *Times,* October 13, 1998, CA (Crim Div) . . . . *Digested,* 98/**1112**

R. v. Oliver (Michael Roger) see Attorney General's Reference (No.86 of 2000), Re

R. v. Ollerenshaw (Paul Michael) [1999] 1 Cr. App. R. (S.) 65; [1998] Crim. L.R. 515; *Times,* May 6, 1998, CA (Crim Div) . . . . *Digested,* 98/**1169**: *Considered,* 99/1363, 00/1119, 00/1207, 00/1269: *Followed,* 99/1271

R. v. Olliver (Michael) see R. v. Olliver (Richard)

R. v. Olliver (Richard); R. v. Olliver (Michael) (1989) 11 Cr. App. R. (S.) 10; (1989) 153 J.P. 369; [1989] Crim. L.R. 387; (1989) 153 J.P.N. 390; *Times,* January 20, 1989; *Independent,* January 30, 1989 (C.S.); *Daily Telegraph,* January 27, 1989, CA (Crim Div) . . . . *Digested,* 90/**1317**: *Applied,* 89/1113, 90/1315, 96/1772, 97/1465, 99/2860: *Considered,* 97/1466

R. v. Olorunnibe (Henry Olusola) [1998] 2 Cr. App. R. (S.) 260, CA (Crim Div) . . . . *Digested,* 98/**1226**

R. v. Onabanjo (David Oluseun) [2001] 2 Cr. App. R. (S.) 7, CA (Crim Div) . . . . *Digested,* 01/**1345**

R. v. Ondhia (Chandraicant Vallabhji) [1998] 2 Cr. App. R. 150; [1998] Crim. L.R. 339, CA (Crim Div) . . . . *Digested,* 98/**952**

R. v. Onubogu (Godwin) see Attorney General's Reference (No.62 of 1998), Re

R. v. Onyon (Mark Richard) (1994) 15 Cr. App. R. (S.) 663, CA (Crim Div) . . . . *Digested,* 95/**1487**: *Referred to,* 99/1366

R. v. Ord (Daniel William); R. v. Ord (Stephen Frederick) (1990) 12 Cr. App. R. (S.) 12, CA (Crim Div) . . . . *Digested,* 91/**1008**: *Considered,* 97/1403, 98/1110

R. v. Ord (Stephen Frederick) see R. v. Ord (Daniel William)

R. v. Ormonde (Dean Andrew) see R. v. Redfern (Andrew James)

R. v. Orwin (Timothy) [1999] 1 Cr. App. R. (S.) 103, CA (Crim Div) . . . . *Digested,* 99/**1368**

R. v. Osborne-Odelli (Michael) [1998] Crim. L.R. 902; *Times,* June 22, 1998, CA (Crim Div) . . . . *Digested,* 98/**1098**

R. v. Osman (Ali) [1999] 1 Cr. App. R. (S.) 230, CA (Crim Div) . . . . *Digested,* 99/**1284**: *Followed,* 98/1227

R. v. Osman (Yacoub) [2000] 2 Cr. App. R. (S.) 112, CA (Crim Div) . . . . *Digested,* 00/**1299**

R. v. Owen (Darren Lee); R. v. Stephen (Kevin Kimberley) [1999] 1 W.L.R. 949; [1999] 2 Cr. App. R. 59; [1999] Crim. L.R. 406; (1998) 95(47) L.S.G. 29; (1998) 142 S.J.L.B. 285; *Times,* November 11, 1998, CA (Crim Div) . . . . *Digested,* 98/**872**

R. v. Owen (Henry Geoffrey) see Board of Trade v. Owen

R. v. Owen (Michael Cyrill) [1998] 1 Cr. App. R. (S.) 52, CA (Crim Div) . . . . *Digested,* 98/**1373**

R. v. Owen (Norman) [1976] 1 W.L.R. 840; [1976] 3 All E.R. 239; (1976) 63 Cr. App. R. 199; [1976] Crim. L.R. 753; 120 S.J. 470, CA (Crim Div) . . . . *Digested,* 76/**436**: *Considered,* 94/1218, 95/3961, 98/1162

R. v. Oxford CC Ex p. Doyle (1998) 30 H.L.R. 506, QBD . . . . *Digested,* 97/**2670**

R. v. Oxford CC Ex p. Wyatt Bros (Oxfordshire) Ltd [1998] Env. L.R. D10, QBD

R. v. Oxford City Council Ex p. Crowder (1999) 31 H.L.R. 485, QBD . . . . *Digested,* 99/**3045**

R. v. Oxford Crown Court Ex p. Monaghan, *Independent,* July 12, 1999 (C.S.), QBD

R. v. Oxford Regional Mental Health Tribunal Ex p. Secretary of State for the Home
Department; *sub nom* Campbell v. Secretary of State for the Home Department;
Secretary of State for the Home Department v. Oxford Regional Mental Health
Review Tribunal; R. v. Yorkshire Mental Health Review Tribunal Ex p. Secretary of
State for the Home Department [1988] A.C. 120; [1987] 3 W.L.R. 522; [1987]
3 All E.R. 8; (1987) 84 L.S.G. 2690; (1987) 137 N.L.J. 735; (1987) 131 S.J.
1086, HL; affirming [1986] 1 W.L.R. 1180; [1986] 3 All E.R. 239; (1986) 83
L.S.G. 1559; (1986) 130 S.J. 505, CA . . . . *Digested, 87/***2425**:
Applied, 88/2270, 93/2740, 01/4423
R. (on the application of GB) v. Oxfordshire CC see Oxfordshire CC v. B
R. (on the application of P (A Child)) v. Oxfordshire CC Exclusions Appeals Panel [2001]
EWHC Admin 301; [2001] E.L.R. 631, QBD (Admin Ct)
R. v. Oxfordshire CC Ex p. Lane CO/147/98, QBD . . . . *Digested,* 98/**2854**
R. v. Oxfordshire CC Ex p. Stokes; *sub nom* R. v. Oxfordshire Crown Court Ex p.
Stokes [1999] E.H.L.R. Dig. 205, QBD
R. v. Oxfordshire CC Ex p. Sunningwell Parish Council [2000] 1 A.C. 335; [1999] 3
W.L.R. 160; [1999] 3 All E.R. 385; [1999] B.L.G.R. 651; (2000) 79 P. & C.R.
199; [1999] 2 E.G.L.R. 94; [1999] 31 E.G. 85; [2000] J.P.L. 384; [1999]
E.G.C.S. 91; (1999) 96(29) L.S.G. 29; (1999) 149 N.L.J. 1038; (1999) 143
S.J.L.B. 205; [1999] N.P.C. 74; *Times,* June 25, 1999 ; *Independent,* June 29,
1999, HL; reversing CO 2744-96, QBD . . . . *Digested,* 99/**4393**
R. v. Oxfordshire Crown Court Ex p. Stokes see R. v. Oxfordshire CC Ex p. Stokes
R. v. Oyediran (Oyetokunbo) [1997] 2 Cr. App. R. (S.) 277, CA (Crim Div) . . . . *Digested,* 97/**1530**:
Followed, 99/1351
R. v. Ozakan (Mustafa) see R. v. Sehitoglu (Dervis)
R. v. Ozen (Zervet) see R. v. Bozat (Hikmet)
R. v. P see P (Barrister) (Wasted Costs Order), Re
R. v. P (A Bankrupt) [2000] 1 W.L.R. 1568; [2000] B.P.I.R. 1138; (2000) 97(16)
L.S.G. 40; (2000) 144 S.J.L.B. 156; *Times,* March 29, 2000; *Independent,* May
15, 2000 (C.S.), CA (Crim Div) . . . . *Digested,* 00/**3439**
R. v. P (A Juvenile), *Independent,* July 23, 2001 (C.S), CA (Crim Div)
R. v. P (Daniel Lee) (A Juvenile) see R. v. W (Sven Matthew) (A Juvenile)
R. v. P (Gareth) (A Juvenile) see Attorney General's Reference (Nos.7, 8, 9 and 10 of
2000), Re
R. v. P (Gary) see Attorney General's Reference (No.20 of 1998), Re
R. v. P (Indecent Assault) (Unreported, June 1, 1998), Crown Ct (Guildford) [*Ex rel.*
John M Burton, Barrister, Mitre Court Chambers, Temple, London] . . . . *Digested,* 98/**882**
R. v. P (Leroy Philip) [1998] Crim. L.R. 663, CA (Crim Div)
R. v. P (Louise) [2001] EWCA Crim 2664; *Times,* December 11, 2001, CA (Crim Div)
R. v. P (Paul Andrew) [2000] 1 Cr. App. R. (S.) 428; [1999] Crim. L.R. 918, CA (Crim
Div) . . . . *Digested,* 00/**1304**
R. v. P (Sentencing: Associated Offences) (2001) 165 J.P. 237; (2001) 165 J.P.N.
225, CA (Crim Div)
R. v. P (Telephone Intercepts: Admissibility of Evidence); *sub nom* R. v. X (Telephone
Intercepts: Admissibility of Evidence); R. v. Y (Telephone Intercepts: Admissibility
of Evidence); R. v. Z (Telephone Intercepts: Admissibility of Evidence) [2001] 2
W.L.R. 463; [2001] 2 All E.R. 58; [2001] 2 Cr. App. R. 8; (2001) 98(8) L.S.G.
43; (2001) 145 S.J.L.B. 28; *Times,* December 19, 2000; *Independent,* December
20, 2000, HL; affirming *Times,* May 23, 2000; *Independent,* June 19, 2000, CA
(Crim Div) . . . . *Digested,* 01/**980**:
Applied, 01/718
R. v. P Borough Council Ex p. S [1999] Fam. 188; [1999] 2 W.L.R. 777; [1999]
B.L.G.R. 203, Fam Div . . . . *Digested,* 99/**2343**
R. v. Pace (Paul) [1998] 1 Cr. App. R. (S.) 121, CA (Crim Div) . . . . *Digested,* 98/**1314**
R. v. Pacheco-Nunez (Jose Manuel) see R. v. Scamaronie (Carlos Alberto)
R. v. Pacholok (Paul Stefan) see Attorney General's Reference (No.43 of 2000), Re
R. v. Padley (Ian) [2000] 2 Cr. App. R. (S.) 201, CA (Crim Div) . . . . *Digested,* 00/**1197**
R. v. Page (Elliott) (1987) 9 Cr. App. R. (S.) 348, CA (Crim Div) . . . . *Digested,* 89/**994**:
Considered, 98/1210
R. v. Paget (Terence John) [1998] 1 Cr. App. R. (S.) 80, CA (Crim Div) . . . . *Digested,* 98/**1139**:
Distinguished, 99/1252
R. v. Pain (Roy); R. v. Jory (Stephen); R. v. Hawkins (Christopher Joseph) (1986) 82
Cr. App. R. 141; (1986) 150 J.P. 65; [1986] Crim. L.R. 168; (1986) 150 J.P.N. 95;
(1985) 82 L.S.G. 3696, CA (Crim Div) . . . . *Digested,* 86/**622**:
Distinguished, 98/1037
R. v. Paine (Nicholas) [1998] 1 Cr. App. R. 36; *Times,* June 21, 1997; *Independent,*
June 23, 1997 (C.S.), CMAC . . . . *Digested,* 97/**277**
R. v. Palin (Gareth Wayne) (1995) 16 Cr. App. R. (S.) 888; [1995] Crim. L.R. 435, CA
(Crim Div) . . . . *Digested,* 96/**2072**:
Considered, 01/1269
R. v. Palmer (Dale Stephen) (1995) 16 Cr. App. R. (S.) 642, CA (Crim Div) . . . . *Digested,* 96/**1950**:
Considered, 00/1142
R. v. PAM see R. v. TM

R. v. Panae (George); R. v. Grey (Donald) (1984) 6 Cr. App. R. (S.) 410; [1985] Crim. L.R. 327, DC . . . . *Digested*, 86/**840**: *Considered*, 98/1300

R. v. Panayioutou (Andronikus) (1989) 11 Cr. App. R. (S.) 535; [1990] Crim. L.R. 349, CA (Crim Div) . . . . *Digested*, 91/**1052**: *Considered*, 99/1102, 99/1103

R. v. Panayis (Charalambos); R. v. Ellis (Reginald) (Leave to Appeal against Conviction); R. v. Gigaseri (Mohammed Hussan); R. v. Panayis (Costas) [1999] Crim. L.R. 84, CA (Crim Div)

R. v. Panayis (Costas) see R. v. Panayis (Charalambos)

R. v. Panel of the Federation of Communication Services Ltd Ex p. Kubis (1999) 11 Admin. L.R. 43; [1998] C.O.D. 5, QBD . . . . *Digested*, 97/**4851**

R. v. Panel on Take-overs and Mergers Ex p. Datafin Plc [1987] Q.B. 815; [1987] 2 W.L.R. 699; [1987] 1 All E.R. 564; [1987] B.C.L.C. 104; [1987] 1 F.T.L.R. 181; (1987) 131 S.J. 23, CA . . . . *Digested*, 87/**21**: *Applied*, 91/83, 92/13, 01/5140: *Considered*, 90/50, 90/3912, 91/17, 91/43, 91/52, 91/76, 92/12, 93/28, 93/31, 93/32, 93/33, 94/2677, 95/47, 95/55

R. v. Panel on Take-overs and Mergers Ex p. Guinness [1990] 1 Q.B. 146; [1989] 2 W.L.R. 863; [1989] 1 All E.R. 509; (1988) 4 B.C.C. 714; [1989] B.C.L.C. 255; (1988) 138 N.L.J. Rep. 244; (1989) 133 S.J. 660, CA; affirming (1988) 4 B.C.C. 325; [1988] 2 F.T.L.R. 50, QBD . . . . *Digested*, 89/**3671**: *Applied*, 00/4485: *Followed*, 96/1056, 99/92

R. v. Panton (Andrew Anthony) [2001] EWCA Crim 611; (2001) 98(19) L.S.G. 36; (2001) 145 S.J.L.B. 90; *Times*, March 27, 2001, CA (Crim Div) . . . . *Digested*, 01/**1073**

R. v. Parke (Karl Brendon) [1999] Crim. L.R. 492, CA (Crim Div)

R. v. Parker (Andrew David) [1996] 2 Cr. App. R. (S.) 275; [1996] Crim. L.R. 445, CA (Crim Div) . . . . *Digested*, 96/**2064**: *Followed*, 98/1322

R. v. Parker (Carol Margaret) [1997] 1 Cr. App. R. (S.) 259, CA (Crim Div) . . . . *Digested*, 97/**1400**: *Considered*, 99/1077

R. v. Parker (David Andrew) [2000] 2 Cr. App. R. (S.) 294; [2000] Crim. L.R. 494, CA (Crim Div) . . . . *Digested*, 00/**1148**

R. v. Parker (Leslie Charles) (1986) 82 Cr. App. R. 69; [1985] Crim. L.R. 589, CA (Crim Div) . . . . *Digested*, 86/**524**: *Applied*, 01/1012

R. v. Parker (Robbie) (1995) 16 Cr. App. R. (S.) 525, CA (Crim Div) . . . . *Considered*, 00/1438

R. v. Parker (Timothy) [2000] 2 Cr. App. R. (S.) 60, CA (Crim Div) . . . . *Digested*, 00/**1268**

R. v. Parkhouse (Geoffrey) [1999] 2 Cr. App. R. (S.) 208, CA (Crim Div) . . . . *Digested*, 99/**1080**

R. v. Parking Adjudicator Ex p. Bexley LBC (1998) 162 J.P. 611; [1998] R.T.R. 128; [1998] C.O.D. 116; *Times*, October 22, 1997, QBD . . . . *Digested*, 97/**4338**

R. v. Parking Adjudicator Ex p. Wandsworth LBC [1998] R.T.R. 51; [1997] C.O.D. 155; (1996) 93(44) L.S.G. 29; (1996) 140 S.J.L.B. 261; *Times*, November 26, 1996; *Independent*, November 7, 1996, CA; reversing *Times*, July 22, 1996, QBD . . . . . *Digested*, 97/**4337**

R. v. Parlby (1889) L.R. 22 Q.B.D. 520, QBD . . . . *Applied*, 47-51/8153, 47-51/8154, 01/2429

R. v. Parliamentary Commissioner for Administration Ex p. Balchin (No.1) [1998] 1 P.L.R. 1; [1997] J.P.L. 917; [1997] C.O.D. 146; [1996] E.G.C.S. 166; [1996] N.P.C. 147, QBD . . . . *Digested*, 97/**4031**

R. v. Parliamentary Commissioner for Administration Ex p. Balchin (No.2) (2000) 2 L.G.L.R. 87; (2000) 79 P. & C.R. 157; [2000] R.V.R. 303; [2000] J.P.L. 267; [1999] E.G.C.S. 78, QBD . . . . *Digested*, 99/**4236**

R. v. Parliamentary Commissioner for Standards Ex p. Al-Fayed [1998] 1 W.L.R. 669; [1998] 1 All E.R. 93; (1998) 10 Admin. L.R. 69; [1998] C.O.D. 139; (1997) 94(42) L.S.G. 31; (1997) 147 N.L.J. 1689; *Times*, November 13, 1997; *Independent*, October 29, 1997, CA; affirming [1997] C.O.D. 376, QBD . . . . *Digested*, 97/**916**

R. (on the application of Giles) v. Parole Board [2001] EWHC Admin 834; *Independent*, December 17, 2001 (C.S), QBD (Admin Ct)

R. (on the application of Gordon) v. Parole Board; *sub nom* R. v. Parole Board Ex p. Gordon [2001] A.C.D. 47, QBD (Admin Ct)

R. v. Parole Board Ex p. Gordon see R. (on the application of Gordon) v. Parole Board

R. v. Parole Board Ex p. Harris [1998] C.O.D. 233, QBD

R. v. Parole Board Ex p. MacNeil see R. (on the application of Macneil) v. HMP Lifer Panel

R. v. Parole Board Ex p. Robinson, *Independent*, November 8, 1999 (C.S.), QBD

R. v. Parole Board Ex p. Watson [1996] 1 W.L.R. 906; [1996] 2 All E.R. 641; (1996) 8 Admin. L.R. 460; [1997] C.O.D. 72; *Times*, March 11, 1996, CA; affirming *Independent*, November 22, 1995, QBD . . . . *Digested*, 96/**4576**: *Applied*, 01/4570

R. v. Parry (Jonathan Anthony); R. v. McLean (Julia Lila) (1986) 8 Cr. App. R. (S.) 470, CA (Crim Div) . . . . *Digested*, 88/**890**: *Considered*, 96/1708, 98/1111, 00/1154

R. v. Parsons (Robert) (Appeal against Conviction) see R. v. Togher (Kenneth) (Appeal against Conviction)

R. *v.* Pashby (Richard Neil) (1982) 4 Cr. App. R. (S.) 382, CA (Crim Div) . . . . *Digested*, 83/**791**:
Considered, 89/965, 90/1243, 91/1056, 98/1134
R. *v.* Patchett Engineering Ltd [2001] 1 Cr. App. R. (S.) 40, CA (Crim Div) . . . . *Digested*, 01/**1348**
R. *v.* Patel (Assesh) [2000] 2 Cr. App. R. (S.) 10; [2000] Crim. L.R. 201, CA (Crim
Div) . . . . *Digested*, 00/**1165**
R. *v.* Patel (Moussa Mohammed) (1984) 6 Cr. App. R. (S.) 191, CA (Crim Div) . . . . *Digested*, 86/**831**:
Considered, 88/925, 99/1187, 00/1180: *Referred to*, 95/1400, 97/1577
R. *v.* Patel (Sima) [1998] 1 Cr. App. R. (S.) 170, CA (Crim Div) . . . . *Digested*, 98/**1202**
R. *v.* Patent Office Registrar Ex p. SAW Co Ltd see R. *v.* Registrar of Trade Marks Ex p.
SAW Co Ltd
R. *v.* Pathfinder NHS Trust Ex p. W (2000) 3 C.C.L. Rep. 271; [2000] C.O.D. 72, QBD . . *Digested*, 01/**4428**
R. *v.* Pattni [2001] Crim. L.R. 570, Crown Ct (Southwark)
R. *v.* Patwal (General) (1993) 14 Cr. App. R. (S.) 156, CA (Crim Div) . . . . *Digested*, 93/**1280**:
Considered, 98/1328, 98/1372
R. *v.* Paul (Benjamin) [1999] Crim. L.R. 79; (1998) 95(32) L.S.G. 30; (1998) 142
S.J.L.B. 243; *Times*, September 17, 1998, CA (Crim Div) . . . . *Digested*, 98/**949**
R. *v.* Paul (Ranjit Singh) see R. *v.* Shergill (Sukdev Singh)
R. *v.* Paul Wurth SA [2000] I.C.R. 860; *Times*, March 29, 2000, CA (Crim Div) . . . . *Digested*, 00/**2966**
R. *v.* Payne (Alex Peter) see R. *v.* JF Alford Transport Ltd
R. *v.* Peacock (Raymond) [1998] Crim. L.R. 681, CA (Crim Div)
R. *v.* Peak District National Park Authority Ex p. Bleaklow Industries Ltd (2000) 2
L.G.L.R. 171; [2000] J.P.L. 290; [1999] E.G.C.S. 58; [1999] Env. L.R. D28,
QBD. . . . . *Digested*, 99/**4244**
R. *v.* Pearce (Edgar) [2000] 2 Cr. App. R. (S.) 32, CA (Crim Div) . . . . *Digested*, 00/**1243**
R. *v.* Pearce (John) (1988) 10 Cr. App. R. (S.) 331, CA (Crim Div) . . . . *Considered*, 97/1435,
98/1139
R. *v.* Pearce (Stephen John) (1981) 72 Cr. App. R. 295; [1981] Crim. L.R. 639, CA
(Crim Div). . . . . *Digested*, 81/**462**:
Distinguished, 00/1097
R. *v.* Pearsall (Benjamin Paul) see R. *v.* Saphier (Paul Anthony)
R. *v.* Pearson (Colin), *Independent*, February 25, 1998, CA (Crim Div) . . . . *Digested*, 98/**1093**
R. *v.* Pearson (Geoffrey) see Attorney General's Reference (No.26 of 2000), Re
R. *v.* Pearson (Kirk Paul) [1996] 1 Cr. App. R. (S.) 309, CA (Crim Div) . . . . *Digested*, 96/**2053**:
Considered, 98/1354, 00/1402
R. *v.* Pearson (Richard) see R. *v.* Pollinger (Kevin)
R. *v.* Pedder (Timothy) [2000] 2 Cr. App. R. (S.) 36, CA (Crim Div) . . . . *Digested*, 00/**1154**
R. *v.* Pegg (Shane Robin) see Attorney General's Reference (Nos.32 and 33 of 1995),
Re
R. *v.* Pembrokeshire CC Ex p. Coker [1999] 4 All E.R. 1007; (2000) 2 L.G.L.R. 625;
[1999] N.P.C. 87, QBD . . . . *Digested*, 00/**4111**
R. *v.* Pender (Robert John) see R. *v.* Chatfield (Philip Norman)
R. *v.* Pendleton (Donald) [2001] UKHL 66; *Times*, December 17, 2001; *Independent*,
December 19, 2001; *Daily Telegraph*, December 20, 2001, HL; reversing 99/
0783/S1, CA (Crim Div)
R. *v.* Pennington (Derek) see R. *v.* Crow (William John)
R. *v.* Penny (Steven) [1998] 1 Cr. App. R. (S.) 389, CA (Crim Div) . . . . *Digested*, 98/**1397**
R. *v.* Pensions Ombudsman Ex p. Legal & General Assurance Society Ltd see Legal &
General Assurance Society Ltd *v.* Pensions Ombudsman
R. *v.* Percival (Brian) (1998) 95(27) L.S.G. 25; (1998) 142 S.J.L.B. 190; *Times*, July
20, 1998; *Independent*, July 8, 1998, CA (Crim Div) . . . . *Digested*, 98/**1096**:
Distinguished, 99/1025: *Doubted*, 99/1044
R. *v.* Percy (John Anthony) (1993) 14 Cr. App. R. (S.) 10, CA (Crim Div) . . . . *Digested*, 93/**1037**:
Considered, 95/1312, 98/1130
R. *v.* Perez (C167/97) see R. *v.* Secretary of State for Employment Ex p. Seymour-
Smith (C167/97)
R. *v.* Perez-Pinto (Stephen) [1996] 1 Cr. App. R. (S.) 22, CA (Crim Div) . . . . *Considered*, 97/1693,
00/1415, 01/1472
R. *v.* Perks (James Benjamin) [2001] 1 Cr. App. R. (S.) 19; [2000] Crim. L.R. 606;
Times, May 5, 2000, CA (Crim Div) . . . . *Considered*, 01/1208
R. *v.* Perry (Ronald Alan) (1986) 8 Cr. App. R. (S.) 132, CA (Crim Div) . . . . *Digested*, 87/**1068**:
Cited, 93/1297: *Considered*, 89/1125, 97/1719, 99/1365
R. *v.* Perry (Stephen Arthur), *Times*, April 28, 2000, CA (Crim Div) . . . . *Digested*, 00/**943**
R. *v.* Personal Investment Authority Ombudsman Ex p. Burns-Anderson Independent
Network Plc (1998) 10 Admin. L.R. 57; [1997] C.O.D. 379, CA . . . . *Digested*, 97/**2535**
R. *v.* Peterborough Crown Court Ex p. L [2000] Crim. L.R. 470; [2000] C.O.D. 214;
(2000) 97(1) L.S.G. 22; (2000) 144 S.J.L.B. 27; *Times*, December 7, 1999,
QBD. . . . . *Digested*, 00/**1052**
R. *v.* Peters (Duncan Robert) [1999] 2 Cr. App. R. (S.) 334, CA (Crim Div). . . . . *Digested*, 99/**1138**
R. *v.* Pettet (Stephen Mark) [1998] 1 Cr. App. R. (S.) 399, CA (Crim Div) . . . . *Digested*, 98/**1188**
R. *v.* Pettman (Unreported, May 2, 1985), CA (Crim Div) . . . . *Applied*, 99/870
R. *v.* Peverett (Robin) see Attorney General's Reference (No.44 of 2000), Re
R. *v.* PH [2001] 1 Cr. App. R. (S.) 52, CA (Crim Div) . . . . *Digested*, 01/**1464**
R. *v.* Philips (1844) 1 Cox C.C. 17. . . . . *Not followed*, 98/3115

R. v. Phillips (Keith) (1985) 7 Cr. App. R. (S.) 235; [1985] Crim. L.R. 802, CA (Crim Div) . . . . *Digested,* 87/**1005**:
Applied, 93/1225: *Cited,* 91/1162, 93/1220: *Considered,* 87/870, 88/952, 90/1323, 91/644, 91/1163, 91/1166, 92/1338, 93/1224, 99/1261
R. v. Philpot (Julia Lesley) see R. v. Coyne (David)
R. v. Piggott (Luke Anthony); R. v. Litwin (Jeffrey Simon) [1999] 2 Cr. App. R. 320; (1999) 149 N.L.J. 521; *Independent,* April 13, 1999, CA (Crim Div) . . . . *Digested,* 99/**970**
R. v. Pigott (Peter James Paul) [1999] 1 Cr. App. R. (S.) 392, CA (Crim Div) . . . . *Digested,* 99/**1263**
R. v. Pike (Colin) [1996] 1 Cr. App. R. (S.) 4, CA (Crim Div) . . . . *Approved,* 97/1581:
Considered, 00/1290, 00/1294
R. v. Pikesley (Michael Robert) [1996] 1 Cr. App. R. (S.) 198, CA (Crim Div) . . . . *Digested,* 96/**1915**
R. v. Pilgrim (Dennis Decosta) (1993) 14 Cr. App. R. (S.) 432, CA (Crim Div) . . . . *Digested,* 94/**1287**:
Considered, 96/1939, 98/1258, 00/1328
R. v. Pinchess (Daniel John) [2001] EWCA Crim 323; [2001] 2 Cr. App. R. (S.) 86, CA (Crim Div) . . . . *Digested,* 01/**1227**
R. v. Pinkney (Dale) see Attorney General's Reference (No.42 of 2000), Re
R. v. Pinkney (Stephen Robert) [1998] 1 Cr. App. R. (S.) 57; [1997] Crim. L.R. 527, CA (Crim Div) . . . . *Digested,* 98/**1297**
R. v. Pither (Stephen George) (1979) 1 Cr. App. R. (S.) 209, CA (Crim Div) . . . . *Considered,* 88/895, 91/1285, 92/1486, 93/1211, 99/1251, 00/1309: *Referred to,* 84/880, 86/722, 87/1099
R. v. Pitt (Anthony John) [1998] 1 Cr. App. R. (S.) 58; *Times,* May 6, 1997; *Independent,* May 19, 1997 (C.S.), CA (Crim Div) . . . . *Digested,* 97/**1623**
R. v. Pitt (Michael Andrew) [1998] 2 Cr. App. R. (S.) 52; [1998] Crim. L.R. 137, CA (Crim Div) . . . . *Digested,* 98/**1387**:
Considered, 99/1351
R. v. PJO'N; *sub nom* R. v. O'N; R. v. MO'N [2001] N.I. 136, Crown Ct (Belfast) . . . . *Digested,* 01/**5734**
R. v. Planning Inspectorate Cardiff Ex p. Howell [2000] N.P.C. 68, QBD
R. v. Platts (Ian) [1998] 2 Cr. App. R. (S.) 34, CA (Crim Div) . . . . *Digested,* 98/**1336**
R. v. Plymouth City Airport Ltd see R. (on the application of Plymouth City Airport Ltd) v. Secretary of State for the Environment, Transport and the Regions
R. v. Poggiani (Steven) [2001] EWCA Crim 78; [2001] 2 Cr. App. R. (S.) 64, CA (Crim Div) . . . . *Digested,* 01/**1303**
R. v. Pollin (Steven Lee) [1997] 2 Cr. App. R. (S.) 356, CA (Crim Div) . . . . *Digested,* 98/**1403**:
Considered, 98/1407, 00/1267
R. v. Pollinger (Kevin); R. v. Pearson (Richard) [1999] 1 Cr. App. R. (S.) 128, CA (Crim Div) . . . . *Digested,* 99/**1069**
R. v. Pollitt (Stephen) see R. v. Royle (Gary)
R. v. Pommell (Fitzroy Derek) [1995] 2 Cr. App. R. 607; (1995) 92(27) L.S.G. 32; (1995) 139 S.J.L.B. 178; *Times,* May 22, 1995; *Independent,* June 5, 1995 (C.S.), CA (Crim Div) . . . . *Digested,* 95/**1258**:
Considered, 99/922: *Distinguished,* 96/1444, 97/1188: *Followed,* 01/5728: *Referred to,* 01/1057
R. v. Poole (Anthony Keith) see R. v. Mills (Gary)
R. v. Poolton (Janet Marie) see R. v. Davies (Grace)
R. v. Popat (Chetan) (No.1) [1998] 2 Cr. App. R. 208; (1998) 162 J.P. 369; [1998] Crim. L.R. 825; (1998) 162 J.P.N. 423; *Times,* April 10, 1998, CA (Crim Div) . . . . *Digested,* 98/**904**:
Applied, 98/901: *Considered,* 99/891: *Disapproved,* 01/994: *Followed,* 99/890, 99/892: *Not applied,* 99/893
R. v. Popat (Chetan) (No.2) [2000] 1 Cr. App. R. 387; (2000) 164 J.P. 65; [2000] Crim. L.R. 54; *Times,* September 7, 1999, CA (Crim Div) . . . . *Digested,* 99/**892**
R. v. Pope (Alan) [2001] EWCA Crim 972; [2001] Crim. L.R. 499, CA (Crim Div)
R. v. Pope (Michael Dean) see Attorney General's Reference (No.24 of 1998), Re
R. v. Port Talbot BC Ex p. Jones [1988] 2 All E.R. 207; (1988) 20 H.L.R. 265, QBD . . . . *Digested,* 88/**36**:
Considered, 98/4210
R. v. Porter (Casey) [2001] 1 Cr. App. R. (S.) 70, CA (Crim Div) . . . . *Digested,* 01/**1311**
R. v. Porter (Eddie) [2001] EWCA Crim 222; [2001] 2 Cr. App. R. (S.) 78, CA (Crim Div) . . . . *Digested,* 01/**1226**
R. v. Porter (Michael) [1999] 2 Cr. App. R. (S.) 205, CA (Crim Div) . . . . *Digested,* 99/**1123**
R. v. Portsmouth City Council Ex p. Coles; R. v. Portsmouth City Council Ex p. George Austin (Builders) Ltd [1997] C.L.C. 407; 81 B.L.R. 1; 59 Con. L.R. 114; [1997] 1 C.M.L.R. 1135; (1997) 9 Admin. L.R. 535; (1997) 16 Tr. L.R. 83; (1997) 161 J.P. Rep. 312; *Times,* November 13, 1996, CA . . . . *Digested,* 96/**4081**:
Considered, 99/3863: *Followed,* 99/839
R. v. Portsmouth City Council Ex p. Faludy [1999] E.L.R. 115, CA [1998] 3 F.C.R. 271; [1999] Ed. C.R. 467; [1998] E.L.R. 619; *Times,* September 17, 1998, QBD . . . . *Digested,* 99/**1885**
R. v. Portsmouth City Council Ex p. George Austin (Builders) Ltd see R. v. Portsmouth City Council Ex p. Coles
R. v. Portsmouth Hospitals NHS Trust Ex p. G [1999] 2 F.L.R. 905; [1999] 3 F.C.R. 145; (1999) 11 Admin. L.R. 991; [1999] Lloyd's Rep. Med. 367; (1999) 50 B.M.L.R. 269; [2000] C.O.D. 54; [1999] Fam. Law 696; (1999) 96(32) L.S.G. 31; (1999) 143 S.J.L.B. 220; *Times,* July 26, 1999, CA . . . . *Digested,* 99/**2680**
R. v. Potter (David) [1999] 2 Cr. App. R. (S.) 448, CA (Crim Div) . . . . *Digested,* 00/**1411**:
Considered, 01/1469

R. *v.* Povey (John Stanley) [1999] 2 Cr. App. R. (S.) 323, CA (Crim Div) . . . .   *Digested,* 99/**1347**

R. *v.* Powell (Anthony Glassford); R. *v.* Daniels (Antonio Eval); R. *v.* English (Philip) [1999] 1 A.C. 1; [1997] 3 W.L.R. 959; [1997] 4 All E.R. 545; [1998] 1 Cr. App. R. 261; (1998) 162 J.P. 1; [1998] Crim. L.R. 48; (1998) 162 J.P.N. 26; (1997) 161 J.P.N. 1100; (1997) 147 N.L.J. 1654; *Times,* October 31, 1997; *Independent,* November 11, 1997, HL; affirming [1996] 1 Cr. App. R. 14; *Times,* June 2, 1995; *Independent,* June 26, 1995 (C.S.), CA (Crim Div) . . . .   *Digested,* 97/**1220**:
                      Applied, 00/5468, 00/5481: *Considered,* 97/1327, 98/959:
                                         Followed, 98/1035

R. *v.* Powell (Ashna George) [2001] 1 Cr. App. R. (S.) 76; *Times,* August 15, 2000, CA (Crim Div). . . . .   *Digested,* 00/**1385**

R. *v.* Powell (Mark); R. *v.* Horsford (Harland) [2001] EWCA Crim 1362; [2001] Crim. L.R. 925, CA (Crim Div)

R. *v.* Powell (Matthew Tristan), *Times,* October 5, 2000, CA (Crim Div) . . . .   *Digested,* 00/**1231**

R. *v.* Powell (Michael Edmund) see R. *v.* Toomer (Martin Charles)

R. *v.* Powell (Shaka); R. *v.* Gordon (Rohan) [1998] 1 Cr. App. R. (S.) 84, CA (Crim Div) . . . .   *Digested,* 98/**1306**:
                                       Considered, 00/1369

R. *v.* Powergen (UK) Plc Ex p. Safeway Stores see R. *v.* Leicester City Council Ex p. Safeway Stores Plc

R. *v.* Powys CC Ex p. Hambidge (No.1) [1998] 3 F.C.R. 190; (1997-98) 1 C.C.L. Rep. 458; (1999) 45 B.M.L.R. 203; (1998) 95(32) L.S.G. 30; (1998) 142 S.J.L.B. 232; (1998) 142 S.J.L.B. 238; *Times,* July 20, 1998; *Independent,* July 10, 1998, CA; affirming [1998] 1 F.L.R. 643; (1997-98) 1 C.C.L. Rep. 182; (1998) 40 B.M.L.R. 73; [1998] C.O.D. 73; [1998] Fam. Law 136; *Times,* November 5, 1997, QBD . . . .   *Digested,* 98/**4575**

R. *v.* Powys CC Ex p. Hambidge (No.2); *sub nom* R. *v.* Powys CC Ex p. Hambidge (No.2) [2000] 2 F.C.R. 69; (2000) 2 L.G.L.R. 926; [2000] B.L.G.R. 564; (2000) 3 C.C.L. Rep. 231; (2000) 54 B.M.L.R. 133; *Times,* March 16, 2000, CA; affirming (1999) 2 C.C.L. Rep. 460, QBD . . . .   *Digested,* 00/**4894**

R. *v.* Powys CC Ex p. Hambidge (No.2) see R. *v.* Powys CC Ex p. Hambidge (No.2)

R. *v.* PR see Attorney General's Reference (No.23 of 1999), Re

R. *v.* Pratt (Stuart Terence) [1997] 1 Cr. App. R. (S.) 419, CA (Crim Div) . . . .   *Digested,* 97/**1675**:
                                       Considered, 01/1263

R. *v.* Preddy (John Crawford); R. *v.* Slade (Mark); R. *v.* Dhillon (Rajpaul Singh) [1996] A.C. 815; [1996] 3 W.L.R. 255; [1996] 3 All E.R. 481; [1996] 2 Cr. App. R. 524; (1996) 160 J.P. 677; [1996] Crim. L.R. 726; (1996) 160 J.P.N. 936; (1996) 93(31) L.S.G. 29; (1996) 146 N.L.J. 1057; (1996) 140 S.J.L.B. 184; *Times,* July 11, 1996; *Independent,* July 17, 1996, HL; reversing [1995] Crim. L.R. 564, CA (Crim Div). . . . .   *Digested,* 96/**1530**:
       Applied, 97/1227: *Considered,* 96/1532, 96/1548, 97/1228, 97/1249, 97/1260,
                        97/1264, 97/2429, 98/980, 98/981, 99/973: *Distinguished,* 00/1013:
         Followed, 97/1226, 97/1229, 97/1230, 97/1231: *Referred to,* 97/1224, 97/1225,
                                         97/1304

R. *v.* Prentice (Michael Charles) see R. *v.* Adomako (John Asare)

R. (on the application of Ford) *v.* Press Complaints Commission [2001] EWHC Admin 683; *Daily Telegraph,* September 4, 2001, QBD (Admin Ct)

R. *v.* Preston (Stephen); R. *v.* Clarke (Nicholas Henry); R. *v.* Austen (Anthony); R. *v.* Salter (Jeremy); R. *v.* Preston (Zena) [1994] 2 A.C. 130; [1993] 3 W.L.R. 891; [1993] 4 All E.R. 638; (1994) 98 Cr. App. R. 405; [1994] Crim. L.R. 676; (1993) 137 S.J.L.B. 256; *Times,* November 8, 1993; *Independent,* November 9, 1993, HL; affirming (1992) 95 Cr. App. R. 355; [1992] Crim. L.R. 805; (1992) 136 S.J.L.B. 156; *Times,* May 13, 1992, CA (Crim Div) . . . .   *Digested,* 94/**864**:
       Applied, 00/920: *Cited,* 97/1129: *Considered,* 00/921: *Distinguished,* 01/980

R. *v.* Preston (Zena) see R. *v.* Preston (Stephen)

R. *v.* Preston Crown Court Ex p. Barraclough [1999] Crim. L.R. 973, QBD

R. *v.* Preston Crown Court Ex p. Campbell [1999] C.O.D. 407, QBD

R. *v.* Preston Crown Court Ex p. Chief Constable of Lancashire [1998] C.O.D. 272, QBD

R. *v.* Preston Crown Court Ex p. Lancashire CC; *sub nom* R. *v.* Burnley Crown Court Ex p. Lancashire CC [1999] 1 W.L.R. 142; [1998] 3 All E.R. 765; [1999] 1 Costs L.R. 58; [1998] C.O.D. 176, QBD . . . .   *Digested,* 98/**1014**

R. *v.* Preston Magistrates Court Ex p. North West Water Ltd [2000] E.H.L.R. 390, QBD . . . .   *Digested,* 00/**538**

R. *v.* Pretty (Martin Alan) (1992) 13 Cr. App. R. (S.) 280; [1992] Crim. L.R. 68, CA (Crim Div). . . . .   *Digested,* 93/**1339**:
                                        Considered, 99/1240

R. *v.* Price (Paul Graham) see R. *v.* Graham (Hemamali Krishna)

R. *v.* Price (Stephen John) [2001] 2 Cr. App. R. (S.) 23, CA (Crim Div). . . . .   *Digested,* 01/**1259**

R. *v.* Prince (Carlton) [1999] 2 Cr. App. R. (S.) 419, CA (Crim Div) . . . .   *Digested,* 00/**1217**:
                                    Not followed, 01/1277

R. *v.* Prince (Henry) (1872-75) L.R. 2 C.C.R. 154, Crown Cases Reserved . . . .   *Considered,* 63/635:
                                      Disapproved, 00/1002

R. *v.* Prince (James Peter) [1996] 1 Cr. App. R. (S.) 335, CA (Crim Div) . . . . *Digested,* 96/**1853**:
          Considered, 99/1136, 99/1141, 00/1221

R. *v.* Probert (Anthony David) see Attorney General's Reference (No.34 of 1999), Re

R. *v.* Probert (John Michael) (1994) 15 Cr. App. R. (S.) 891, CA (Crim Div) . . . .   *Digested,* 95/**1505**:
          Considered, 98/1271, 01/1379

R. *v.* Proctor (Jonathon Mark) [2000] 1 Cr. App. R. (S.) 295, CA (Crim Div) . . . .   *Digested,* 00/**1376**

R. *v.* Professional Conduct Committee of the General Medical Council Ex p. Salvi; *sub nom* R. *v.* General Medical Council Ex p. Salvi (1999) 46 B.M.L.R. 167; *Times,* February 24, 1998, QBD . . . .   *Digested,* 98/**2637**

R. *v.* Prokop (Xavier Alexander) (1995) 16 Cr. App. R. (S.) 598, CA (Crim Div) . . . .   *Considered,* 00/1290,
          00/1294: *Distinguished,* 97/1581

R. (on the application of L) *v.* Prosthetists and Orthotists Board [2001] EWCA Civ 837; (2001) 61 B.M.L.R. 128; [2001] A.C.D. 72; *Daily Telegraph,* June 19, 2001, CA; affirming [2001] A.C.D. 57; *Daily Telegraph,* January 30, 2001, QBD (Admin Ct) . . . .   *Digested,* 01/**3288**

R. *v.* Provincial Court of the Church in Wales Ex p. Williams [1999] C.O.D. 163, QBD

R. *v.* Pullen (Stuart) [2000] 2 Cr. App. R. (S.) 114, CA (Crim Div) . . . .   *Digested,* 00/**1354**

R. *v.* Purcell (Unreported, December 6, 1993) . . . .   *Considered,* 98/1403

R. *v.* Purcell (Colin) [1996] 1 Cr. App. R. (S.) 190, CA. . . . .   *Considered,* 98/1181

R. *v.* Purewal (Kulwinder Singh) see R. *v.* Shergill (Sukdev Singh)

R. *v.* Purnell (Danny Lee) see R. *v.* Archer (Patrick John)

R. *v.* Purvis (James) see R. *v.* Clarke (Anthony John)

R. *v.* Purvis (Paul Nigel) (Absence of Defendant at Trial) see R. *v.* Jones (Anthony William) (Absence of Defendant at Trial)

R. *v.* Purvis (Paul Nigel) (Post Judgment Discussion) see R. *v.* Jones (Anthony William) (Post Judgment Discussion)

R. *v.* Pydar Justices Ex p. Foster (1996) 160 J.P. 87; *Times,* May 23, 1995; *Independent,* June 12, 1995 (C.S.), QBD . . . .   *Digested,* 95/**1169**:
          Considered, 01/991

R. *v.* Pype (Michael James) see Attorney General's Reference (Nos.40 to 42 of 1997), Re

R. *v.* Pyrah see R. (on the application of Lichniak) *v.* Secretary of State for the Home Department

R. *v.* Qadi [2000] P.N.L.R. 137, CA (Crim Div) . . . .   *Digested,* 00/**472**

R. *v.* Qadir (Umran Wali) [1998] Crim. L.R. 828, CA (Crim Div)

R. *v.* Queen (John) (1984) 6 Cr. App. R. (S.) 178; [1984] Crim. L.R. 572, CA (Crim Div) . . . .   *Digested,* 86/**783**:
          Cited, 93/1027: *Considered,* 99/1084

R. *v.* Quinn [1990] Crim. L.R. 581, CA (Crim Div) . . . .   *Digested,* 90/**809**:
          Approved, 01/5724

R. *v.* Qureshi (Sajid) [2001] EWCA Crim 1807; *Times,* September 11, 2001, CA (Crim Div) . . . .   *Digested,* 01/**1142**

R. *v.* R (A Husband) see R. *v.* R (Rape: Marital Exemption)

R. *v.* R (Admissibility of Evidence), *Independent,* April 10, 2000 (C.S.), CA (Crim Div)

R. *v.* R (Colin Oliver) (A Juvenile) [2000] 1 Cr. App. R. (S.) 244, CA (Crim Div) . . . . . .   *Digested,* 00/**1327**

R. *v.* R (Daniel F), *Times,* November 1, 2000, CA (Crim Div) . . . .   *Digested,* 00/**1406**

R. *v.* R (Darren) see Attorney General's Reference (No.34 of 2000), Re

R. *v.* R (David) [1999] Crim. L.R. 909, CA (Crim Div)

R. *v.* R (David Anthony) [2000] Crim. L.R. 183; *Times,* September 14, 1999, CA (Crim Div) . . . .   *Digested,* 99/**888**

R. *v.* R (Dicky) see R. *v.* RD

R. *v.* R (Hugo Maurice), *Times,* August 17, 1999, CA (Crim Div) . . . .   *Digested,* 99/**1026**

R. *v.* R (Kevin Wayne) (A Juvenile) see R. *v.* Howells (Craig)

R. *v.* R (Michael) (A Juvenile) [1999] 2 Cr. App. R. (S.) 194, CA (Crim Div) . . . .   *Digested,* 99/**1236**

R. *v.* R (Paul Brian) (1993) 14 Cr. App. R. (S.) 772; [1993] Crim. L.R. 541, CA (Crim Div) . . . .   *Digested,* 94/**1282**:
          Considered, 98/1250

R. *v.* R (Peter) (Jurisdiction) [2001] 1 W.L.R. 1314; [2001] Crim. L.R. 314; (2001) 98(17) L.S.G. 37; (2001) 145 S.J.L.B. 78; *Times,* February 2, 2001, CA (Crim Div) . . . .   *Digested,* 01/**978**

R. *v.* R (Peter) (Abuse of Process) [2001] EWCA Crim 2844, CA (Crim Div) . . . .   *Previous proceedings,*
          01/978

R. *v.* R (Peter John) (1993) 14 Cr. App. R. (S.) 328, CA (Crim Div) . . . .   *Digested,* 94/**1334**:
          Considered, 97/1452, 00/1394, 00/1396

R. *v.* R (Rape: Marital Exemption); *sub nom* R. *v.* R (A Husband) [1992] 1 A.C. 599; [1991] 3 W.L.R. 767; [1991] 4 All E.R. 481; (1992) 94 Cr. App. R. 216; (1991) 155 J.P. 989; [1992] 1 F.L.R. 217; [1992] Crim. L.R. 207; [1992] Fam. Law 108; (1991) 155 J.P.N. 752; (1991) 141 N.L.J. 1481; (1991) 135 S.J.L.B. 181; *Times*, October 24, 1991; *Independent*, October 24, 1991; *Guardian*, October 30, 1991, HL; affirming [1991] 2 W.L.R. 1065; [1991] 2 All E.R. 257; (1991) 93 Cr. App. R. 1; (1991) 155 J.P. 373; [1991] Crim. L.R. 475; (1991) 155 J.P.N. 236; (1991) 141 N.L.J. 383; (1991) 135 S.J. 384; *Times*, March 15, 1991; *Independent*, March 15, 1991; *Guardian*, March 15, 1991, CA (Crim Div); affirming [1991] 1 All E.R. 747, Crown Ct (Leicester) . . . . *Digested*, 92/**1040**:
Considered, 93/1268, 94/1337, 01/1147
R. *v.* R (Stuart) (A Juvenile) [1999] 2 Cr. App. R. (S.) 170, CA (Crim Div) . . . . *Digested*, 99/**1235**
R. *v.* R (Thomas David John) (A Juvenile) [1999] 1 Cr. App. R. (S.) 456; [1999] Crim. L.R. 169, CA (Crim Div) . . . . *Digested*, 99/**1218**
R. *v.* R (Wesley) (A Juvenile); R. *v.* M (David Paul) (A Juvenile) [1999] 2 Cr. App. R. (S.) 245, CA (Crim Div) . . . . *Digested*, 99/**1212**
R. *v.* Radak (Jason Dragon); R. *v.* Adjei (Anthony Asafu); R. *v.* Butler-Rees (John Llewelyn); R. *v.* Meghjee (Muntazir) [1999] 1 Cr. App. R. 187; [1999] Crim. L.R. 223; *Times*, October 7, 1998, CA (Crim Div) . . . . *Digested*, 98/**885**:
Referred to, 00/945
R. *v.* Radio Authority Ex p. Bull [1998] Q.B. 294; [1997] 3 W.L.R. 1094; [1997] 2 All E.R. 561; [1997] E.M.L.R. 201; [1997] C.O.D. 382; (1997) 147 N.L.J. 489; *Times*, January 21, 1997; *Independent*, December 20, 1996, CA; affirming [1996] Q.B. 169; [1995] 3 W.L.R. 572; [1995] 4 All E.R. 481; [1996] E.M.L.R. 68; (1995) 145 N.L.J. 1297; *Times*, July 20, 1995; *Independent*, August 1, 1995, QBD . . . . . *Digested*, 97/**3594**
R. *v.* Radio Authority Ex p. Wildman [1999] C.O.D. 255, CA
R. *v.* Rae (Darryn) see R. *v.* Wijs (Eric Jan)
R. *v.* Rafferty (Daniel Lee) [1999] 1 Cr. App. R. 235; [1998] 2 Cr. App. R. (S.) 449; (1998) 162 J.P. 353; [1998] Crim. L.R. 433; (1998) 162 J.P.N. 387; *Times*, April 9, 1998, CA (Crim Div) . . . . *Digested*, 98/**1330**
R. *v.* Rafferty (Robert Andrew) see R. *v.* Boswell (James Thomas)
R. *v.* Raghip see R. *v.* Silcott (Winston)
R. *v.* Ragusa (Joseph Paul) (1993) 14 Cr. App. R. (S.) 118, CA (Crim Div) . . . . *Digested*, 93/**1187**:
Considered, 99/1251
R. *v.* Rahman (Abdul) [1998] 1 Cr. App. R. (S.) 391, CA (Crim Div) . . . . *Digested*, 98/**1310**
R. *v.* Rai (Krishan Raja); R. *v.* Robinson (Earl) [2000] 2 Cr. App. R. (S.) 120, CA (Crim Div) . . . . *Digested*, 00/**1261**
R. *v.* Rai (Thomas) [2000] 1 Cr. App. R. 242; (2000) 164 J.P. 121; [2000] Crim. L.R. 192; (2000) 164 J.P.N. 326; (1999) 96(44) L.S.G. 39; (1999) 143 S.J.L.B. 268; *Times*, November 10, 1999, CA (Crim Div) . . . . *Digested*, 99/**950**
R. *v.* Railton see R. *v.* Cox
R. *v.* Raja (Abdul Qayyum); R. *v.* Bhatti (Mohammed Siddique) (1985) 7 Cr. App. R. (S.) 424, CA (Crim Div) . . . . *Digested*, 86/**844**:
Cited, 92/1210: *Considered*, 98/1300
R. *v.* Rajcoomar (Jogendranath) [1999] Crim. L.R. 728, CA (Crim Div)
R. (on the application of Kenneally) *v.* Rampton Hospital Authority see R. (on the application of Kenneally) *v.* Snaresbrook Crown Court
R. *v.* Ramsden (Stephen) see R. *v.* Hooley (Gareth Mark)
R. *v.* Ramzan (Mohammed) [1998] 2 Cr. App. R. 328; *Times*, March 19, 1998, CA (Crim Div) . . . . *Digested*, 98/**1091**
R. *v.* Rana (Rajeev Paul) [1998] 2 Cr. App. R. (S.) 288, CA (Crim Div) . . . . *Digested*, 98/**1225**
R. *v.* Ranasinghe (Rohana) [1999] 2 Cr. App. R. (S.) 366, CA (Crim Div) . . . . *Digested*, 00/**1305**
R. *v.* Rance (Ian James) [1996] 1 Cr. App. R. (S.) 301, CA (Crim Div) . . . . *Digested*, 96/**1939**:
Considered, 00/1300, 01/1373
R. *v.* Rance (Richard) see Attorney General's Reference (No.70 of 1999), Re
R. *v.* Randhawa (Narinder) [1999] 2 Cr. App. R. (S.) 209, CA (Crim Div) . . . . *Digested*, 99/**1359**
R. *v.* Rasool see R. *v.* Ali
R. *v.* Rasool (Ghulam) (1991) 12 Cr. App. R. (S.) 771, CA (Crim Div) . . . . *Digested*, 92/**1325**:
Considered, 99/1309
R. *v.* Raven (Cyril William) (1988) 10 Cr. App. R. (S.) 354, CA (Crim Div) . . . . *Digested*, 90/**1356**:
Applied, 01/1469: *Considered*, 00/1411
R. *v.* Ravenscroft (Carl Wayne) [1996] 1 Cr. App. R. (S.) 71, CA (Crim Div) . . . . *Considered*, 98/1328,
98/1376, 98/1377
R. *v.* Rawlinson (Daniel Kevin), *Times*, October 27, 1999; *Independent*, November 29, 1999 (C.S.), CA (Crim Div) . . . . *Digested*, 99/**1054**
R. *v.* Rayner (Simon Nicholas) see Attorney General's Reference (Nos.24 and 45 of 1994), Re
R. *v.* Raynor (Stephen) (2001) 165 J.P. 149; (2001) 165 J.P.N. 664; *Times*, September 19, 2000, CA (Crim Div) . . . . *Digested*, 00/**927**
R. *v.* Rayson (David Ralph) [2000] 2 Cr. App. R. (S.) 317, CA (Crim Div) . . . . *Digested*, 00/**1123**
R. *v.* Razzaque (David Milne) [1997] 1 Cr. App. R. (S.) 154, CA (Crim Div) . . . . *Digested*, 97/**1643**:
Considered, 98/1344
R. *v.* RD; *sub nom* R. *v.* R (Dicky) [2001] EWCA Crim 248; [2001] 2 Cr. App. R. (S.) 58, CA (Crim Div) . . . . *Digested*, 01/**1356**

R. v. Reader (Spencer James) [2000] 2 Cr. App. R. (S.) 442, CA (Crim Div) . . . .   *Digested*, 01/**1333**
R. v. Reading and West Berkshire Stipendiary Magistrates Ex p. Dyas (2000) 164 J.P.
    117, QBD. . . . .   *Digested*, 00/**1105**
R. (on the application of Eliot) v. Reading Crown Court [2001] EWHC Admin 464;
    [2001] 4 All E.R. 625; [2001] Crim. L.R. 811; *Independent*, July 30, 2001 (C.S),
    QBD (Admin Ct) . . . .   *Digested*, 01/**1129**
R. v. Reading Crown Court Ex p. DPP see R. v. Reading Crown Court Ex p.
    Hutchinson
R. v. Reading Crown Court Ex p. Hutchinson; R. v. Devizes Justices Ex p. Lee; R. v.
    Reading Crown Court Ex p. DPP [1988] Q.B. 384; [1987] 3 W.L.R. 1062;
    [1988] 1 All E.R. 333; (1988) 87 Cr. App. R. 36; (1988) 152 J.P. 47; 86 L.G.R.
    71; [1987] Crim. L.R. 827; (1987) 151 J.P.N. 825; (1988) 152 L.G. Rev. 50;
    (1987) 131 S.J. 1987, QBD . . . .   *Digested*, 88/**593**:
                                             Applied, 00/1453
R. v. Reardon (Sara) (Unreported, April 2, 2001), Crown Ct (Newport, Gwent) [*Ex rel.*
    Martyn Kelly, Barrister, 9 Park Place, Cardiff] . . . .   *Digested*, 01/**1089**
R. v. Reardon (Sean) [1999] Crim. L.R. 392, CA (Crim Div)
R. v. Reay (Raymond) (1992) 13 Cr. App. R. (S.) 533; [1993] R.T.R. 189, CA (Crim
    Div) . . . .   *Digested*, 93/**1327**:
                             Cited, 93/1048: *Considered*, 01/1468
R. v. Rectory School Governors Ex p.WK (A Minor) [1997] E.L.R. 484, QBD . . . .   *Digested*, 98/**1900**
R. v. Redbridge LBC Ex p. B [1999] Ed. C.R. 959, QBD . . . .   *Digested*, 00/**1913**
R. (on the application of DPP) v. Redbridge Youth Court; R. (on the application of L (A
    Child)) v. Bicester Youth Court [2001] EWHC Admin 209; [2001] 1 W.L.R.
    2403; [2001] 4 All E.R. 411; [2001] 2 Cr. App. R. 25; [2001] 3 F.C.R. 615;
    [2001] Crim. L.R. 473; [2001] A.C.D. 81, QBD (Admin Ct) . . . .   *Digested*, 01/**985**
R. v. Redcar and Cleveland BC Ex p. A see R. v. Richmond LBC Ex p.W
R. v. Reddy (Gary Peter); R. v. Haslam (Simon Bernard) [2001] 2 Cr. App. R. (S.) 46,
    CA (Crim Div) . . . .   *Digested*, 01/**1206**
R. v. Redfern (Andrew James); R. v. Brindle (Lee Anthony); R. v. Ormonde (Dean
    Andrew) [2001] 2 Cr. App. R. (S.) 33, CA (Crim Div) . . . .   *Digested*, 01/**1423**
R. v. Reed (John) (1988) 10 Cr. App. R. (S.) 243, CA . . . .   *Considered*, 98/1374
R. v. Reed (Peter David) see Attorney General's Reference (No.34 of 1997), Re
R. v. Rees (Unreported, July 19, 1990) . . . .   *Considered*, 00/1172
R. v. Reeves (Royston Cedric) [2001] EWCA Crim 1053; [2001] Crim. L.R. 584, CA
    (Crim Div)
R. v. Reeves (Steven) see Attorney General's Reference (Nos.19, 20, 21 and 22 of
    1997), Re
R. v. Regional Director of Public Health (Trent) Ex p. X [2001] Lloyd's Rep. Med. 338,
    QBD . . . .   *Digested*, 01/**2899**
R. v. Registrar of Trade Marks Ex p. Interturbine Germany GmbH (Unreported,
    February 22, 1999), Ch D . . . .   *Applied*, 00/**3712**
R. v. Registrar of Trade Marks Ex p. SAW Co Ltd; *sub nom* R. v. Patent Office Registrar
    Ex p. SAW Co Ltd [1996] R.P.C. 507; (1996) 19(10) I.P.D. 19092, QBD . . . .   *Digested*, 97/**4896**:
                              Applied, 99/3576: *Referred to*, 99/3525
R. v. Reid (James Logan) [1998] 2 Cr. App. R. (S.) 10, CA (Crim Div) . . . .   *Digested*, 98/**1293**
R. v. Reid (Neil Anthony) [1998] 2 Cr. App. R. (S.) 40, CA (Crim Div) . . . .   *Digested*, 98/**1337**
R. v. Reid (Sonni Lee); R. v. Riches (John); R. v. W (Alan B) (A Juvenile); R. v. CC (A
    Juvenile); R. v. C (Shaun Lee) (A Juvenile); R. v. B (T Danielle) (A Juvenile)
    [2001] EWCA Crim 1806; *Times*, November 12, 2001, CA (Crim Div) . . . .   *Digested*, 01/**1183**
R. v. Reid (Stephen Anthony) (1992) 13 Cr. App. R. (S.) 513, CA (Crim Div) . . . .   *Digested*, 93/**1241**:
                          Considered, 98/1324, 99/1288, 00/1379
R. (on the application of Dinsdale) v. Rent Service; R. (on the application of Wilson) v.
    Rent Service; R. (on the application of Shaw) v. Rent Service; R. (on the
    application of Saadat) v. Rent Service [2001] EWCA Civ 1559; (2001) 98(44)
    L.S.G. 36; *Times*, November 6, 2001, CA; reversing [2001] EWHC Admin 65,
    QBD (Admin Ct) . . . .   *Digested*, 01/**5029**
R. (on the application of Saadat) v. Rent Service see R. (on the application of Dinsdale)
    v. Rent Service
R. (on the application of Shaw) v. Rent Service see R. (on the application of Dinsdale) v.
    Rent Service
R. (on the application of Wilson) v. Rent Service see R. (on the application of Dinsdale)
    v. Rent Service
R. (on the application of Wilkinson) v. Responsible Medical Officer Broadmoor Hospital
    see R. (on the application of Wilkinson) v. Broadmoor Hospital
R. (on the application of Corbett) v. Restormel BC see R. (on the application of Parkyn)
    v. Restormel BC
R. (on the application of Parkyn) v. Restormel BC; *sub nom* R. v. Restormel BC Ex p.
    Corbett; Corbett v. Restormel BC; R. v. Restormel BC Ex p. Parkyn; R. (on the
    application of Corbett) v. Restormel BC [2001] EWCA Civ 330; [2001] 1 P.L.R.
    108; [2001] J.P.L. 1415; [2001] 11 E.G.C.S. 173; [2001] N.P.C. 49, CA;
    affirming (2001) 82 P. & C.R. 18; [2001] J.P.L. 107 (Note); [2001] J.P.L. 445;
    [2000] E.G.C.S. 105, QBD. . . . .   *Digested*, 01/**4726**
R. v. Restormel BC Ex p. Corbett see R. (on the application of Parkyn) v. Restormel BC

R. *v.* Restormel BC Ex p. Parkyn see R. (on the application of Parkyn) *v.* Restormel BC
R. *v.* Revenue Adjudicator's Office Ex p. Drummond [1996] S.T.C. 1312; 70 T.C. 235;
    Independent, November 11, 1996 (C.S.), QBD . . . .   *Digested,* 96/**5610**
R. *v.* Reynolds (Lee) (1985) 7 Cr. App. R. (S.) 335; [1986] Crim. L.R. 125, CA (Crim
    Div) . . . .   *Digested,* 87/**1097**:
                      Cited, 92/1452, 93/1324, 93/1335: *Considered,* 87/1086, 88/1017, 98/1297
R. *v.* Reynolds (Mark) [1999] 2 Cr. App. R. (S.) 5, CA (Crim Div) . . . .   *Digested,* 99/**1082**
R. *v.* Reynolds (Thomas) see R. *v.* Drury (Christopher)
R. *v.* Rezvi (Syed) see R. *v.* Benjafield (Karl Robert) (Confiscation Order)
R. *v.* RH (A Juvenile) see R. *v.* Brewster (Alex Edward)
R. *v.* Rhodes (Michael Frank) (1985) 7 Cr. App. R. (S.) 341, CA (Crim Div) . . . .   *Digested,* 87/**957**:
                                                      Considered, 99/1200
R. (on the application of Kathro) *v.* Rhondda Cynon Taff CBC [2001] EWHC Admin 527;
    [2001] 4 P.L.R. 83, QBD (Admin Ct)
R. *v.* Ricciardi (Carmine) see R. *v.* Cowan (Donald)
R. *v.* Richards (David Michael) see R. *v.* Thomas (Heath)
R. *v.* Richards (Jake) [1998] 1 Cr. App. R. (S.) 87, CA (Crim Div) . . . .   *Digested,* 98/**1236**
R. *v.* Richards (Lee) [1998] 2 Cr. App. R. (S.) 346, CA (Crim Div) . . . .   *Digested,* 98/**1364**
R. *v.* Richards (Neil David) [1999] Crim. L.R. 598, CA (Crim Div)
R. *v.* Richards (Randall) (1999) 163 J.P. 246; [1999] Crim. L.R. 764, CA (Crim Div) . . .   *Digested,* 99/**3133**
R. *v.* Richardson (Anthony) [1999] Crim. L.R. 563, CA (Crim Div)
R. *v.* Richardson (Diane) [1999] Q.B. 444; [1998] 3 W.L.R. 1292; [1998] 2 Cr. App.
    R. 200; (1998) 43 B.M.L.R. 21; [1999] Crim. L.R. 62; (1998) 95(17) L.S.G. 30;
    (1998) 142 S.J.L.B. 131; *Times*, April 6, 1998; *Independent*, April 3, 1998, CA
    (Crim Div) . . . .   *Digested,* 98/**913**
R. *v.* Richardson (Edward George); R. *v.* Teixeira (Antotia de Abreu); R. *v.* Dean
    (Anthony Roger); R. *v.* Tredwin (Donald Roy) (1994) 15 Cr. App. R. (S.) 876;
    Times, March 18, 1994; *Independent*, April 4, 1994 (C.S.), CA (Crim Div) . . . . . .   *Digested,* 95/**1363**:
                    Considered, 96/1875, 97/1499, 97/1503, 98/1185, 99/1129:
                                        Followed, 95/950, 96/1871
R. *v.* Richardson (Mark Ian) [2000] 2 Cr. App. R. (S.) 373, CA (Crim Div) . . . .   *Digested,* 00/**1434**
R. *v.* Richardson (Nigel John) [1999] 1 Cr. App. R. 392; [1999] Crim. L.R. 494, CA
    (Crim Div) . . . .   *Digested,* 99/**946**
R. *v.* Richardson (Robin); R. *v.* Brown (Gary) [1998] 2 Cr. App. R. (S.) 87, CA (Crim
    Div) . . . .   *Digested,* 98/**1130**
R. *v.* Richart (Nicholas Eugene) (1995) 16 Cr. App. R. (S.) 977; [1995] Crim. L.R. 574;
    (1995) 139 S.J.L.B. 120; *Times*, April 14, 1995; *Independent*, May 8, 1995 (C.S.),
    CA (Crim Div) . . . .   *Digested,* 95/**1430**:
                                                    Considered, 98/1398
R. *v.* Riches (John) see R. *v.* Reid (Sonni Lee)
R. *v.* Richmond Justices Ex p. Haines see R. *v.* Bolton Justices Ex p. Merna
R. *v.* Richmond LBC Appeal Committee Ex p. JC (A Child); *sub nom* R. *v.* Richmond
    LBC Ex p. C (A Child); R. *v.* Richmond LBC Ex p. JC (A Child) [2001] B.L.G.R.
    146; [2001] E.L.R. 21; *Times*, August 10, 2000, CA; affirming [2000] Ed. C.R.
    587; [2000] E.L.R. 565; *Times*, April 26, 2000, QBD . . . .   *Digested,* 00/**1918**
R. *v.* Richmond LBC Ex p. C (A Child) see R. *v.* Richmond LBC Appeal Committee Ex
    p. JC (A Child)
R. *v.* Richmond LBC Ex p. JC (A Child) see R. *v.* Richmond LBC Appeal Committee Ex
    p. JC (A Child)
R. *v.* Richmond LBC Ex p. W; R. *v.* Redcar and Cleveland BC Ex p. A; R. *v.* Manchester
    City Council Ex p. S; R. *v.* Harrow LBC Ex p. C [2001] Q.B. 370; [2000] 3
    W.L.R. 1127; [2001] 1 All E.R. 436; [2000] B.L.G.R. 691; (2000) 3 C.C.L. Rep.
    276; (2001) 58 B.M.L.R. 219; (2000) 97(37) L.S.G. 40; *Times*, August 17, 2000;
    Independent, October 6, 2000, CA; affirming [2000] B.L.G.R. 318; (1999) 2
    C.C.L. Rep. 402; [2000] C.O.D. 63; *Times*, October 15, 1999, QBD . . . .   *Digested,* 00/**4179**
R. (on the application of T) *v.* Richmond upon Thames LBC; *sub nom* R. *v.* Richmond
    upon Thames LBC Ex p. T (2001) 33 H.L.R. 65, QBD (Admin Ct)
R. (on the application of Wainwright) *v.* Richmond upon Thames LBC [2001] EWCA Civ
    2062, CA; reversing [2001] EWHC Admin 310; [2001] 18 E.G.C.S. 174, QBD
    (Admin Ct)
R. *v.* Richmond upon Thames LBC Ex p. T see R. (on the application of T) *v.* Richmond
    upon Thames LBC
R. *v.* Rimac Ltd [2000] 1 Cr. App. R. (S.) 468, CA (Crim Div) . . . .   *Digested,* 00/**2968**
R. *v.* Rimmer (Martin) [1999] 1 Cr. App. R. (S.) 234, CA (Crim Div) . . . .   *Digested,* 99/**1125**
R. *v.* Ripley (Samuel) [1997] 1 Cr. App. R. (S.) 19, CA (Crim Div) . . . .   *Considered,* 00/**1364**
R. *v.* Risdale-Tomblin (Bernard), *Independent*, October 16, 2001, CA (Crim Div) . . . . . .   *Digested,* 01/**1110**
R. *v.* Riverside Mental Health Trust Ex p. Huzzey (1998) 43 B.M.L.R. 167; *Times*, May
    18, 1998, QBD . . . .   *Digested,* 98/**3900**
R. *v.* RLW see Attorney General's Reference (No.61 of 1998), Re
R. *v.* Robb (John George) [1997] 1 Cr. App. R. (S.) 212; [1996] Crim. L.R. 755, CA
    (Crim Div) . . . .   *Digested,* 97/**1539**:
                             Considered, 98/1217, 98/1221, 99/1161
R. *v.* Roberts (Unreported, July 9, 1993), CA (Crim Div) . . . .   *Applied,* 99/941
R. *v.* Roberts (Unreported, March 19, 1998) . . . .   *Followed,* 00/906

R. v. Roberts (Anthony Charles) see Attorney General's Reference (No.66 of 1997), Re
R. v. Roberts (Benjamin) [1998] 1 Cr. App. R. (S.) 155, CA (Crim Div) . . . . *Digested,* 98/**1198**:
Considered, 99/1139
R. v. Roberts (David Eric) see R. v. Taylor (Derek Roy)
R. v. Roberts (Dean) (Unreported, December 17, 1996), CA (Crim Div) . . . . *Considered,* 99/1244
R. v. Roberts (Gary Wayne) (1989) 11 Cr. App. R. (S.) 34, CA (Crim Div) . . . . *Digested,* 90/**1480**:
Cited, 92/1432: *Considered,* 96/1959, 98/1294
R. v. Roberts (Hugh Arfon); R. v. Roberts (Thomas Gwynedd) [1982] 1 W.L.R. 133;
[1982] 1 All E.R. 609; (1982) 74 Cr. App. R. 242; (1982) 4 Cr. App. R. (S.) 8;
[1982] Crim. L.R. 320, CA (Crim Div) . . . . *Digested,* 82/**703**:
Considered, 84/909, 85/833, 94/1333, 97/1432: *Distinguished,* 83/814,
83/881, 98/1351: *Referred to,* 87/1094, 89/937
R. v. Roberts (Jason) see R. v. Roberts (Michael)
R. v. Roberts (Karl Eric) [2000] 1 Cr. App. R. (S.) 569, CA (Crim Div) . . . . *Digested,* 00/**1235**
R. v. Roberts (Kenneth Joseph) (1972) 56 Cr. App. R. 95; [1972] Crim. L.R. 27; (1971)
115 S.J. 809, CA (Crim Div) . . . . *Digested,* 72/**576**:
Applied, 00/1017: *Approved,* 91/896, 92/1131: *Considered,* 95/1236
R. v. Roberts (Martin Stanley); *sub nom* R. v. Roberts (Michael Stanley) [1998] 1 Cr.
App. R. 441; (1998) 162 J.P. 169; [1998] Crim. L.R. 334; (1998) 162 J.P.N. 165;
(1998) 95(1) L.S.G. 23; (1998) 142 S.J.L.B. 29; *Times,* December 16, 1997, CA
(Crim Div) . . . . *Digested,* 98/**1031**
R. v. Roberts (Michael); R. v. Roberts (Jason) (1998) 162 J.P. 691; [1998] Crim. L.R.
682; (1998) 162 J.P.N. 544; *Times,* May 2, 1998, CA (Crim Div) . . . . *Digested,* 98/**909**
R. v. Roberts (Michael Stanley) see R. v. Roberts (Martin Stanley)
R. v. Roberts (Terry) [1998] 2 Cr. App. R. (S.) 455, CA (Crim Div) . . . . *Digested,* 99/**1152**
R. v. Roberts (Thomas Gwynedd) see R. v. Roberts (Hugh Arfon)
R. v. Roberts (William Clive) [1999] 1 Cr. App. R. (S.) 381, CA (Crim Div) . . . . *Digested,* 99/**1363**
R. v. Robertson (Malcolm) [1998] 1 Cr. App. R. (S.) 21, CA (Crim Div) . . . . *Digested,* 98/**1399**:
Considered, 00/1136
R. v. Robertson (Timothy) [2000] 1 Cr. App. R. (S.) 514, CA (Crim Div) . . . . *Digested,* 00/**1208**
R. v. Robinson (Ben); R. v. McManus (Samuel Keith) [1998] 1 Cr. App. R. (S.) 72, CA
(Crim Div) . . . . *Digested,* 98/**1285**
R. v. Robinson (Darren Lee) (1992) 13 Cr. App. R. (S.) 104, CA (Crim Div) . . . . *Digested,* 92/**1455**:
Considered, 00/1338
R. v. Robinson (Earl) see R. v. Rai (Krishan Raja)
R. v. Robinson (Kristian Paul); R. v. Scurry (Lee Patrick) (1994) 15 Cr. App. R. (S.)
452, CA (Crim Div) . . . . *Considered,* 98/1357
R. v. Robinson (Mark Leslie) see Attorney General's Reference (No.40 of 1996), Re
R. v. Robinson (Michael) [2001] EWCA Crim 214; [2001] Crim. L.R. 478, CA (Crim
Div)
R. v. Robotham (Jeffrey Paul) [2001] EWCA Crim 580; [2001] 2 Cr. App. R. (S.) 69,
CA (Crim Div) . . . . *Digested,* 01/**1280**
R. v. Rochdale MBC Ex p. B [2000] Ed. C.R. 117, QBD . . . . *Digested,* 00/**1914**
R. v. Rochdale MBC Ex p. Brown [1997] Env. L.R. 100; [1997] J.P.L. 337; [1997]
C.O.D. 74, QBD . . . . *Digested,* 97/**4128**:
Distinguished, 99/4258
R. v. Rochdale MBC Ex p. Deanbank Investments Ltd see R. v. Secretary of State for
the Environment, Transport and the Regions Ex p. Deanbank Investments Ltd
R. v. Rochdale MBC Ex p. Milne (No.1); R. v. Rochdale MBC Ex p. Tew [2000] Env.
L.R. 1; [1999] 3 P.L.R. 74; [2000] J.P.L. 54; [1999] E.G.C.S. 70; (1999) 96(20)
L.S.G. 41, QBD . . . . *Digested,* 00/**4479**
R. v. Rochdale MBC Ex p. Milne (No.2) [2001] Env. L.R. 22; (2001) 81 P. & C.R. 27;
[2001] J.P.L. 229 (Note); [2001] J.P.L. 470; [2000] E.G.C.S. 103, QBD . . . . . . *Digested,* 01/**4680**
R. v. Rochdale MBC Ex p. Tew see R. v. Rochdale MBC Ex p. Milne (No.1)
R. v. Roche (Gerard Martin) [1999] 2 Cr. App. R. (S.) 105; [1999] Crim. L.R. 339, CA
(Crim Div) . . . . *Digested,* 99/**1320**:
Followed, 01/1466
R. v. Rodenhurst (Steven) [2001] EWCA Crim 1508; *Independent,* July 23, 2001
(C.S), CA (Crim Div)
R. v. Rodger (Andrew); R. v. Rose (Keith John) [1998] 1 Cr. App. R. 143; *Times,* July
30, 1997, CA (Crim Div) . . . . *Digested,* 97/**1195**
R. v. Rodgers (Andrew Campbell) see Attorney General's Reference (Nos.80 and 81 of
1999), Re
R. v. Rodney (Radcliff) [1996] 2 Cr. App. R. (S.) 230; [1998] I.N.L.R. 118; [1996]
Crim. L.R. 357, CA (Crim Div) . . . . *Digested,* 97/**2907**:
Applied, 99/1244: *Considered,* 96/1844: *Followed,* 96/1845
R. v. Rodwell (Dylan) [1998] 2 Cr. App. R. (S.) 1, CA (Crim Div) . . . . *Digested,* 98/**1343**
R. v. Rogan (Gerard James) see Attorney General of Northern Ireland's Reference
(No.3 of 2000), Re
R. v. Rogers (Edward Richard) (1992) 13 Cr. App. R. (S.) 80, CA (Crim Div) . . . . *Digested,* 92/**1293**:
Considered, 01/1468
R. v. Rogers (Henry Norman) (1995) 16 Cr. App. R. (S.) 720, CA (Crim Div) . . . . *Digested,* 96/**2079**:
Referred to, 98/1388

R. v. Rogers (Hone) [1979] 1 All E.R. 693; (1979) 69 Cr. App. R. 96, Sup Ct Taxing
   Office . . . .   *Digested,* 79/**2127**:
                                               Considered, 84/2004, 98/3706
R. v. Rogers (Martin John) (1994) 15 Cr. App. R. (S.) 393, CA (Crim Div) . . . .   *Considered,* 99/1223,
                                                       00/1269
R. v. Rogers (Richard Craig) [1998] 1 Cr. App. R. (S.) 402, CA (Crim Div) . . . .   *Digested,* 98/**1132**
R. v. Roker (Stuart Caleb) [1998] 2 Cr. App. R. (S.) 254, CA (Crim Div) . . . .   *Digested,* 98/**1218**:
                                              Considered, 00/1244, 01/1312
R. v. Rollco Screw & Rivet Co Ltd [1999] 2 Cr. App. R. (S.) 436; [1999] I.R.L.R. 439;
   Times, April 29, 1999, CA (Crim Div) . . . .   *Digested,* 99/**2860**
R. v. Roman Catholic Schools Ex p. S [1998] Ed. C.R. 277; [1998] E.L.R. 304; [1998]
   C.O.D. 283; *Times,* December 26, 1997, QBD . . . .   *Digested,* 98/**1899**
R. (in Right of Ontario) v. Ron Engineering & Construction (Eastern) Ltd Unreported . .   *Not followed,* 00/830
R. v. Ronaldson (Douglas) (1990) 12 Cr. App. R. (S.) 91, CA (Crim Div) . . . .   *Considered,* 98/1407,
                                            98/1410: *Referred to,* 93/1311
R. v. Ronchetti (Jonathan) [1998] 2 Cr. App. R. (S.) 100; [1998] Crim. L.R. 227;
   (1998) 95(2) L.S.G. 22; (1998) 142 S.J.L.B. 30; *Times,* December 9, 1997, CA
   (Crim Div) . . . .   *Digested,* 98/**1183**:
                           Considered, 99/1127, 00/1206, 00/1218, 01/1274: *Followed,* 00/1232
R. v. Roncoli (Anthony Charles) [1998] Crim. L.R. 584, CA (Crim Div)
R. v. Rook (Philip) see Attorney General's Reference (No.28 of 1995), Re
R. v. Rose (Cynthia Delores) see R. v. Nelson (Sonia Eloise)
R. v. Rose (Keith John) see R. v. Rodger (Andrew)
R. v. Rose (Newton Samuel); R. v. Henry (Ian); R. v. Johnson (Orville Alexander); R. v.
   Clarke (Michael Carson) [1982] A.C. 822; [1982] 3 W.L.R. 192; [1982] 2 All
   E.R. 731; (1982) 75 Cr. App. R. 322; [1982] Crim. L.R. 696; 126 S.J. 479, HL;
   affirming [1982] 1 W.L.R. 614; [1982] 2 All E.R. 536; [1982] Crim. L.R. 520; 126
   S.J. 187, CA (Crim Div) . . . .   *Digested,* 82/**740**:
               Applied, 88/657, 88/780, 89/822: *Followed,* 98/996: *Referred to,* 83/827,
                                                         83/886
R. v. Rosenburg (David) [1999] 1 Cr. App. R. (S.) 365; [1999] Crim. L.R. 94, CA
   (Crim Div) . . . .   *Digested,* 99/**1351**
R. v. Ross (Keith) [2001] EWCA Crim 560; [2001] 2 Cr. App. R. (S.) 109; [2001]
   Crim. L.R. 405; *Times,* April 3, 2001, CA (Crim Div) . . . .   *Digested,* 01/**1241**
R. v. Ross-Duff (Alan William) see Attorney General's Reference (No.60 of 2001), Re
R. v. Ross-Goulding (Viola) [1997] 2 Cr. App. R. (S.) 348, CA (Crim Div) . . . .   *Digested,* 98/**1391**
R. v. Rotherham MBC Ex p. Clark [1998] 1 F.C.R. 509; (1998) 10 Admin. L.R. 153;
   [1998] Ed. C.R. 113; [1998] E.L.R. 152; (1998) 162 J.P.N. 165; *Times,* December
   4, 1997; *Independent,* November 26, 1997, CA; affirming *Times,* November 20,
   1997, QBD . . . .   *Digested,* 97/**2105**:
                                               Applied, 99/1838
R. v. Rotherham MBC Ex p. LT see R. v. Rotherham MBC Ex p. T
R. v. Rotherham MBC Ex p. T; *sub nom* R. v. Rotherham MBC Ex p. LT [2000]
   B.L.G.R. 338; [2000] Ed. C.R. 39; [2000] E.L.R. 76; *Times,* December 3, 1999,
   CA; affirming [1999] E.L.R. 500, QBD . . . .   *Digested,* 00/**1924**
R. v. Rout (Christopher) (1993) 14 Cr. App. R. (S.) 584, CA (Crim Div) . . . .   *Digested,* 94/**1263**:
                                              Considered, 00/1254
R. v. Routledge (Wayne Christopher) see Attorney General's Reference (Nos.40 to 42
   of 1997), Re
R. v. Rowde Parish Council Ex p. Ibbetson [1999] E.G.C.S. 76, QBD
R. v. Rowe (Raphael George) (No.1) see R. v. Davis (Michael George) (No.1)
R. v. Rowe (Raphael George) (No.2) see R. v. Davis (Michael George) (No.2)
R. v. Rowe (Raphael George) (No.3) see R. v. Davis (Michael George) (No.3)
R. v. Royal County of Berkshire Ex p. P see R. v. Berkshire CC Ex p. P
R. (on the application of Mahmood) v. Royal Pharmaceutical Society of Great Britain;
   sub nom Mahmood, Re; R. v. Royal Pharmaceutical Society of Great Britain Ex
   p. Mahmood [2001] EWCA Civ 1245; (2001) 98(37) L.S.G. 39; (2001) 145
   S.J.L.B. 217; *Times,* August 9, 2001, CA; affirming in part [2001] U.K.C.L.R. 148;
   [2000] C.O.D. 487; *Times,* October 18, 2000, QBD . . . .   *Digested,* 01/**3105**
R. v. Royal Pharmaceutical Society of Great Britain Ex p. Mahmood see R. (on the
   application of Mahmood) v. Royal Pharmaceutical Society of Great Britain
R. v. Royle (Gary); R. v. Pollitt (Stephen) [1997] 1 Cr. App. R. (S.) 184, CA (Crim Div) . .   *Digested,* 97/**1499**:
                                               Considered, 01/1274
R. v. Ruby (Kenneth) (1988) 86 Cr. App. R. 186; (1987) 9 Cr. App. R. (S.) 305;
   [1987] Crim. L.R. 785, CA (Crim Div) . . . .   *Digested,* 88/**952**:
                       Considered, 92/1338, 93/1224, 97/1564, 99/1261, 99/1266:
                           Referred to, 93/1219, 93/1220, 95/1434, 97/1620
R. v. Rugby BC Housing Benefit Review Board Ex p. Harrison see R. v. Sheffield
   Housing Benefit Review Board Ex p. Smith
R. v. Rugg (Colin Stuart) see R. v. Ball (Alexander)
R. v. Rugg (Vincent) [1997] 2 Cr. App. R. (S.) 350; [1997] Crim. L.R. 528, CA (Crim
   Div) . . . .   *Digested,* 98/**1172**
R. v. Rumbol (Charles) [2001] EWCA Crim 238; [2001] 2 Cr. App. R. (S.) 62, CA
   (Crim Div) . . . .   *Digested,* 01/**1420**

R. *v.* Russell (John Paul) [1998] 2 Cr. App. R. (S.) 375; [1998] Crim. L.R. 429, CA
 (Crim Div) . . . .   *Digested,* 99/**1231**:
                              Referred to, 00/1190
R. *v.* Russell (Robert John) see Attorney General's Reference (Nos.78, 79 and 85 of
 1998), Re
R. *v.* Rutherford (Wayne) [1998] Crim. L.R. 490, CA (Crim Div)
R. *v.* Ryan (Christopher Kersley) see R. *v.* Coyne (David)
R. *v.* Ryan (Deborah Marie) (1999) 163 J.P. 849; (1999) 163 J.P.N. 953; *Times,* April
 30, 1999, CA (Crim Div) . . . .   *Digested,* 99/**1290**
R. *v.* Ryan (James) [2001] EWCA Crim 824; [2001] 2 Cr. App. R. (S.) 128, CA (Crim
 Div) . . . .   *Digested,* 01/**1210**
R. *v.* Ryan (Malcolm Joseph), *Times,* October 13, 1999, CA (Crim Div) . . . .   *Digested,* 99/**890**
R. *v.* S (A Juvenile) (Service of Evidence: Delay), MC [*Ex rel.* Robert Kay, Barrister,
 Mitre Court Chambers, 199 Strand, London] . . . .   *Digested,* 01/**1161**
R. *v.* S (Abdul) [2000] 1 Cr. App. R. (S.) 40, CA (Crim Div) . . . .   *Digested,* 00/**1296**
R. *v.* S (Andrew Benjamin) (A Juvenile) [2001] 1 Cr. App. R. (S.) 18; (2000) 164 J.P.
 681; [2000] Crim. L.R. 613, CA (Crim Div) . . . .   *Digested,* 01/**1384**
R. *v.* S (Christopher Michael) see R. *v.* W (Jonathan Craig)
R. *v.* S (Dale James) (A Juvenile) [1999] 1 Cr. App. R. (S.) 417, CA (Crim Div) . . . .   *Digested,* 99/**1073**
R. *v.* S (Daniel Edward) (A Juvenile) see Attorney General's Reference (No.62 of
 2000), Re
R. *v.* S (David) (A Juvenile) [1998] 1 Cr. App. R. (S.) 145, CA (Crim Div) . . . .   *Digested,* 98/**1272**
R. *v.* S (David Gealy) see Attorney General's Reference (No.77 of 1999), Re
R. *v.* S (David John) see Attorney General's Reference (No.35 of 1999), Re
R. *v.* S (David William) see Attorney General's Reference (No.2 of 1995) (Unduly
 Lenient Sentence), Re
R. *v.* S (Densley) [1998] 2 Cr. App. R. (S.) 17, CA (Crim Div) . . . .   *Digested,* 98/**1254**
R. *v.* S (Graham) [2001] 1 Cr. App. R. 7; [2001] 1 Cr. App. R. (S.) 97; (2000) 97(36)
 L.S.G. 41; *Times,* August 29, 2000, CA (Crim Div) . . . .   *Digested,* 00/**1301**
R. *v.* S (Harold Nicholas) [1998] 1 Cr. App. R. (S.) 261, CA (Crim Div) . . . .   *Digested,* 98/**1350**
R. *v.* S (Jacqueline Rosemary) see R. *v.* C (Paul John)
R. *v.* S (Jason Lee) [1999] 2 Cr. App. R. (S.) 126, CA (Crim Div) . . . .   *Digested,* 99/**1067**:
                             Considered, 00/1123
R. *v.* S (Jayne Louise) (A Juvenile) [1999] 2 Cr. App. R. (S.) 211, CA (Crim Div) . . . . . .   *Digested,* 99/**1216**
R. *v.* S (Joe) (A Juvenile) see Attorney General's Reference (Nos.7, 8, 9 and 10 of
 2000), Re
R. *v.* S (John Alan) (A Juvenile) [2001] EWCA Crim 541; [2001] 2 Cr. App. R. (S.)
 102, CA (Crim Div) . . . .   *Digested,* 01/**1390**
R. *v.* S (John Ivor) see Attorney General's Reference (No.28 of 2000), Re
R. *v.* S (John William) see R. *v.* A (Lavinia)
R. *v.* S (Kenneth Mervyn) [2000] 2 Cr. App. R. (S.) 187, CA (Crim Div) . . . .   *Digested,* 00/**1356**
R. *v.* S (Kewal) see R. *v.* S (Satnam)
R. *v.* S (L Gavin) (A Juvenile) see Attorney General's Reference (No.10 of 1997), Re
R. *v.* S (Mark) (A Juvenile) [2000] 2 Cr. App. R. 431; [2000] Crim. L.R. 849; *Times,*
 June 14, 2000, CA (Crim Div) . . . .   *Digested,* 00/**905**
R. *v.* S (Matthew John) (A Juvenile) see R. *v.* F (Paul) (A Juvenile)
R. *v.* S (Matthew John) [1999] 1 Cr. App. R. (S.) 67, CA (Crim Div) . . . .   *Digested,* 99/**1095**
R. *v.* S (Nicole Dove) (A Juvenile) [1999] 2 Cr. App. R. (S.) 31, CA (Crim Div) . . . .   *Digested,* 99/**1227**
R. *v.* S (Paul) (A Juvenile); R. *v.* M (Lee) (A Juvenile); R. *v.* W (Michael) (A Juvenile);
 R. *v.* W (Paul) (A Juvenile) [2001] EWCA Crim 467; [2001] 2 Cr. App. R. (S.)
 82, CA (Crim Div) . . . .   *Digested,* 01/**1374**
R. *v.* S (Paul Albert) [2001] EWCA Crim 1017; [2001] 2 Cr. App. R. (S.) 119, CA (Crim
 Div) . . . .   *Digested,* 01/**1355**
R. *v.* S (Paul John) [1999] 1 Cr. App. R. 1; (1998) 162 J.P. 495; [1998] Crim. L.R. 576;
 Times, March 18, 1998; *Independent,* March 12, 1998, CA (Crim Div) . . . .   *Digested,* 98/**1033**
R. *v.* S (Paul William) see Attorney General's Reference (No.89 of 1998), Re
R. *v.* S (Ryan) (A Juvenile) [2001] 2 Cr. App. R. (S.) 37, CA (Crim Div) . . . .   *Digested,* 01/**1376**
R. *v.* S (Satnam); R. *v.* S (Kewal) (1984) 78 Cr. App. R. 149; [1985] Crim. L.R. 236,
 CA (Crim Div) . . . .   *Digested,* 84/**709**:
         Applied, 84/536: *Approved,* 95/977: *Considered,* 85/681, 99/5195
R. *v.* S (Stephen) see R. *v.* Offen (Matthew Barry) (No.2)
R. *v.* S (Thomas Henry) [1999] 1 Cr. App. R. (S.) 89, CA (Crim Div) . . . .   *Digested,* 99/**1086**
R. *v.* S (Wayne) [2000] 1 Cr. App. R. (S.) 62, CA (Crim Div) . . . .   *Digested,* 00/**1292**
R. *v.* SA [2000] 1 Cr. App. R. (S.) 36, CA (Crim Div) . . . .   *Digested,* 00/**1145**
R. *v.* Sabeddu (Simone) [2001] 1 Cr. App. R. (S.) 138; *Times,* November 30, 2000, CA
 (Crim Div) . . . .   *Digested,* 01/**1436**
R. *v.* Sabharwal (Tarsemwal Lal) [2001] EWCA Crim 392; [2001] 2 Cr. App. R. (S.)
 81, CA (Crim Div) . . . .   *Digested,* 01/**1291**
R. *v.* Sabin (Steven Paul) see R. *v.* Harper (Christopher Randolph)
R. *v.* Sadiq (Shahswar Akther) [1999] 2 Cr. App. R. (S.) 325, CA (Crim Div) . . . .   *Digested,* 99/**1286**
R. *v.* Sagoo (Harmeet) see Attorney General's Reference (No.93 of 1998), Re
R. *v.* Sagoo (Permjit) see Attorney General's Reference (No.93 of 1998), Re
R. *v.* Sagu (Delveear) see R. *v.* Shergill (Sukdev Singh)
R. *v.* Saia (Sebastiano Claudio) see R. *v.* Tuegel (Peter Johannes)

R. *v.* Salathiel (Emily) [1998] 1 Cr. App. R. (S.) 338, CA (Crim Div) . . . .　*Digested,* 98/**1317**

R. (on the application of McDonagh) *v.* Salisbury DC; *sub nom* McDonagh *v.* Salisbury
　DC [2001] EWHC Admin 567; *Times,* August 15, 2001, QBD (Admin Ct) . . . . . .　*Digested,* 01/**4171**

R. *v.* Salisbury Magistrates Court Ex p. G [2000] 1 Cr. App. R. (S.) 267; (1999) 163
　J.P. 732; (2000) 164 J.P.N. 84; *Times,* July 21, 1999, QBD . . . .　*Digested,* 99/**1292**

R. *v.* Salisbury, Tisbury and Mere Combined Juvenile Court Ex p. Ball (1985) 149 J.P.
　346; [1986] 1 F.L.R. 1; [1985] Fam. Law 313, QBD . . . .　*Digested,* 86/**2174**:
　　　　　　　　　　　　　　　　　　　　　　　　　　　　　　　　　Distinguished, 99/2432

R. *v.* Salter (Jeremy) see R. *v.* Preston (Stephen)

R. *v.* Samuel (Cornelius Joseph) [1988] Q.B. 615; [1988] 2 W.L.R. 920; [1988] 2 All
　E.R. 135; (1988) 87 Cr. App. R. 232; [1988] Crim. L.R. 299; (1988) 152 J.P.N.
　238, CA (Crim Div) . . . .　*Digested,* 88/**536**:
　　　　　　　Applied, 88/569, 88/630, 89/548, 89/550, 89/574, 91/718, 92/3790,
　　　　　　　92/3791: *Considered,* 90/775, 91/624: *Not followed,* 00/5471

R. *v.* Samuel (Michael Andrew) see Attorney General's Reference (Nos.62, 63, 64 and
　65 of 1996), Re

R. *v.* Samuel Smith Old Brewery see R. *v.* Selby DC Ex p. Samuel Smith Old Brewery
　Ltd (Permission to Move for Judicial Review)

R. *v.* Sanders (Robert Daniel) (1987) 9 Cr. App. R. (S.) 390, CA (Crim Div) . . . .　*Digested,* 89/**986**:
　　　　　　　　　　　　　　　　　　　　　　　　　　　　　　　　　Considered, 98/1370

R. *v.* Sandford (Terence) see Attorney General's Reference (No.53 of 1998), Re

R. *v.* Sandhu (Major) [1998] 1 P.L.R. 17; [1997] J.P.L. 853; [1997] Crim. L.R. 288;
　[1996] N.P.C. 179; *Times,* January 2, 1997, CA (Crim Div) . . . .　*Digested,* 97/**4078**

R. *v.* Sandwell MBC Ex p. Wilkinson (1999) 31 H.L.R. 22; [1998] C.O.D. 477, QBD . . . .　*Digested,* 99/**4551**

R. *v.* Sang (Leonard Anthony); R. *v.* Mangan (Matthew) [1980] A.C. 402; [1979] 3
　W.L.R. 263; [1979] 2 All E.R. 1222; (1979) 69 Cr. App. R. 282; [1979] Crim. L.R.
　655, HL; affirming [1979] 2 W.L.R. 439; [1979] 2 All E.R. 46; (1979) 68 Cr.
　App. R. 240; [1979] Crim. L.R. 389; 123 S.J. 232, CA (Crim Div) . . . .　*Digested,* 79/**448**:
　　　　　　　Applied, 80/2095, 80/2297, 80/2630, 83/655, 86/578, 89/658, 91/628,
　　　　　　　91/1745, 91/3119, 92/978, 92/2073: *Approved,* 89/579: *Cited,* 88/907,
　　　　　　　89/993: *Considered,* 80/2306, 80/2310, 85/898, 85/2126, 86/589, 89/580,
　　　　　　　90/801, 91/687, 92/20, 94/669, 95/921, 95/2282, 00/995:
　　　　　　　Followed, 85/561, 94/992, 95/983, 96/1321

R. *v.* Sanghera (Rashpal) [2001] 1 Cr. App. R. 20; [2001] Crim. L.R. 480; *Times,*
　October 26, 2000, CA (Crim Div) . . . .　*Digested,* 00/**923**

R. *v.* Sansom (Alec James); R. *v.* Williams (Thomas Richard); R. *v.* Smith (Nicholas
　James); R. *v.* Wilkins (Joseph Herbert) [1991] 2 Q.B. 130; [1991] 2 W.L.R. 366;
　[1991] 2 All E.R. 145; (1991) 92 Cr. App. R. 115; [1991] Crim. L.R. 126; (1990)
　134 S.J. 1300, CA (Crim Div) . . . .　*Digested,* 91/**820**:
　　　　　　　　　　　　　　　　　　　　　　　　Considered, 92/812, 00/952

R. *v.* Sant (Vicky) (1989) 11 Cr. App. R. (S.) 441, CA (Crim Div) . . . .　*Digested,* 91/**1141**:
　　　　　　　　　　　　　　　　　　　　　　　　　　　　　　　　　Considered, 00/1278

R. *v.* Saphier (Paul Anthony); R. *v.* Pearsall (Benjamin Paul) [1997] 1 Cr. App. R. (S.)
　235, CA (Crim Div) . . . .　*Digested,* 97/**1464**:
　　　　　　　　　　　　　　　　　　　　　　　　　　　　　　　　　Considered, 98/1337

R. *v.* Sargent (Ian Michael) [2001] UKHL 54; [2001] 3 W.L.R. 992; (2001) 98(44)
　L.S.G. 35; (2001) 145 S.J.L.B. 245; *Times,* October 30, 2001; *Independent,*
　October 31, 2001; *Daily Telegraph,* November 6, 2001, HL; reversing CA (Crim
　Div) . . . .　*Digested,* 01/**981**

R. *v.* Saunby (David) see R. *v.* Williams (David Omar)

R. *v.* Saunders (Joseph Brian) [2000] 1 Cr. App. R. 458; [2000] 2 Cr. App. R. (S.) 71;
　[2000] Crim. L.R. 314; (1999) 96(47) L.S.G. 30; (2000) 144 S.J.L.B. 10; *Times,*
　January 28, 2000; *Independent,* December 17, 1999, CA (Crim Div) . . . .　*Digested,* 00/**1388**:
　　　　　　　　　　　　　　　　　　　　　　　　　　　　　　　　　Considered, 01/1221

R. *v.* Saunders (Kevin John); R. *v.* Hockings (David Andrew); R. *v.* Williams (Paul)
　[2001] EWCA Crim 93; [2001] 2 Cr. App. R. (S.) 63; *Times,* February 20, 2001,
　CA (Crim Div) . . . .　*Digested,* 01/**1469**

R. *v.* Savage (Unreported, March 11, 1998), Crown Ct . . . .　*Not followed,* 99/932

R. *v.* Savage (Jefferson Scott) (1993) 14 Cr. App. R. (S.) 409; *Times,* November 6,
　1992, CA (Crim Div) . . . .　*Digested,* 94/**1250**:
　　　　　　　Considered, 97/1518, 97/1519, 99/1135, 00/1223: *Followed,* 98/1186

R. *v.* Sawoniuk (Anthony) [2000] 2 Cr. App. R. 220; [2000] Crim. L.R. 506, CA
　(Crim Div) . . . .　*Digested,* 00/**925**

R. *v.* Sawtell (Norman Michael) [2001] B.P.I.R. 381, CA (Crim Div) . . . .　*Digested,* 01/**1139**

R. *v.* Saxena (Ram Pratap) (No.2) 99/2782/Z2, CA (Crim Div) . . . .　*Previous proceedings,*
　　　　　　　　　　　　　　　　　　　　　　　　　　　　　　　　　99/1287

R. *v.* Saxena (Ram Pratap) (No.1) [1999] 1 Cr. App. R. (S.) 170, CA (Crim Div) . . . .　*Digested,* 99/**1287**:
　　　　　　　　　　　　　　　　　　　　　　　　　　　　　　　　　Considered, 01/1293

R. *v.* Saxon (Lee Roy) [1999] 1 Cr. App. R. (S.) 385, CA (Crim Div) . . . .　*Digested,* 99/**1288**

R. *v.* SBC (A Juvenile); R. *v.* Chong (Kwai Man); R. *v.* Chen (Ling); R. *v.* Chen (Wen
　Ping); R. *v.* Chen (Jia) [2001] EWCA Crim 885; *Times,* April 17, 2001, CA (Crim
　Div) . . . .　*Digested,* 01/**993**

R. *v.* Scamaronie (Carlos Alberto); R. *v.* Pacheco-Nunez (Jose Manuel) (1992) 13 Cr.
   App. R. (S.) 702, CA (Crim Div) . . . . *Digested,* 93/**1129**:
                                        Considered, 98/1185, 99/1129
R. *v.* Scammell (Philip David); R. *v.* Mills (Jill Maureen) [1998] 1 Cr. App. R. (S.) 321,
   CA (Crim Div) . . . . *Digested,* 98/**1144**
R. *v.* Scarley (Robert) [2001] 1 Cr. App. R. (S.) 24, CA (Crim Div) . . . . *Digested,* 01/**1468**
R. *v.* Schofield (Barry John) see R. *v.* Stewart (Heather)
R. *v.* Schofield (John) see R. *v.* Williams (David Omar)
R. (on the application of M (A Child)) *v.* School Organisation Committee [2001] EWHC
   Admin 245; [2001] A.C.D. 77, QBD (Admin Ct)
R. *v.* Schools Adjudicator Ex p. Wirral MBC [2000] Ed. C.R. 355; [2000] E.L.R. 620,
   QBD . . . . *Digested,* 00/**1919**
R. *v.* Schools Appeals Tribunal of the Wakefield Diocesan Board of Education Ex p. J
   (1999) 1 L.G.L.R. 216; [1999] Ed. C.R. 566, QBD . . . . *Digested,* 99/**1871**:
                                          Followed, 00/1787
R. *v.* Schuller (Albert) see R. *v.* Hassan (Ozdai)
R. *v.* Schultz (Karl) [1996] 1 Cr. App. R. (S.) 451, CA (Crim Div) . . . . *Digested,* 96/**2059**:
                           Applied, 00/1352: *Considered,* 97/1700
R. *v.* Scollan (Fergal Patrick) [1999] Crim. L.R. 566, CA (Crim Div)
R. *v.* Scott (Glenys Ruth) [1998] B.P.I.R. 471, Sup Ct (SA) . . . . *Digested,* 99/**3259**
R. *v.* Scott (Leigh Peter) [2001] EWCA Crim 8, CA (Crim Div) . . . . *Digested,* 01/**1223**
R. *v.* Scott (Paul James) (1995) 16 Cr. App. R. (S.) 451, CA (Crim Div) . . . . *Referred to,* 00/1260
R. *v.* Scott (Tracey) (1990) 12 Cr. App. R. (S.) 23; [1990] Crim. L.R. 440, CA (Crim
   Div) . . . . *Digested,* 91/**1274**:
              Cited, 92/1455: *Considered,* 92/1444, 93/1328, 93/1330, 98/1347
R. *v.* Scunthorpe Justices Ex p. M (1998) 162 J.P. 635; *Times,* March 10, 1998, QBD . . . *Digested,* 98/**1038**:
                          Applied, 00/1047: *Followed,* 98/1037, 00/1048
R. *v.* Scunthorpe Justices Ex p. S, *Times,* March 5, 1998, QBD . . . . *Digested,* 98/**3699**
R. *v.* Scurry (Lee Patrick) see R. *v.* Robinson (Kristian Paul)
R. *v.* Seaman (Barry Patrick) (1982) 4 Cr. App. R. (S.) 108, CA (Crim Div) . . . . *Digested,* 83/**837**:
                                          Considered, 99/1200
R. *v.* Searle (Wayne Thomas) see Attorney General's Reference (No.39 of 1996), Re
R. *v.* Searson (Raymond Martin) see Attorney General's Reference (No.88 of 1998), Re
R. *v.* Secretary of Satte for the Home Department Ex p. Aitsegeur see R. (on the
   application of Adan (Lul Omar)) *v.* Secretary of State for the Home Department
R. *v.* Secretary of State for Culture, Media and Sport Ex p. Danish Satellite Television
   [1999] 3 C.M.L.R. 919, CA; affirming CO-3153-98, QBD . . . . *Digested,* 00/**4149**
R. *v.* Secretary of State for Defence Ex p. Hayman see DPP *v.* Hutchinson
R. *v.* Secretary of State for Defence Ex p. Parker see DPP *v.* Hutchinson
R. *v.* Secretary of State for Defence Ex p. Perkins (No.1) [1997] 3 C.M.L.R. 310;
   [1997] I.R.L.R. 297; (1997) 94(14) L.S.G. 25; (1997) 141 S.J.L.B. 84; *Times,*
   April 8, 1997, QBD . . . . *Digested,* 97/**299**
R. *v.* Secretary of State for Defence Ex p. Perkins (No.2) [1998] 2 C.M.L.R. 1116;
   [1998] I.R.L.R. 508; [1999] 1 F.L.R. 491; [1999] C.O.D. 41; [1998] Fam. Law
   730; (1998) 95(33) L.S.G. 34; (1998) 142 S.J.L.B. 222; *Times,* July 16, 1998,
   QBD . . . . *Digested,* 98/**262**
R. *v.* Secretary of State for Defence Ex p. Wilkins [2000] 3 E.G.L.R. 11; [2000] 40 E.G.
   180; (2000) 97(28) L.S.G. 31; *Times,* July 26, 2000, QBD . . . . *Digested,* 00/**4618**
R. (on the application of Amraf Training Plc) *v.* Secretary of State for Education and
   Employment; *sub nom* R. *v.* Secretary of State for Education and Employment Ex
   p. Amraf Training Plc; R. *v.* Department of Education and Employment Ex p.
   Amraf Training Plc [2001] EWCA Civ 914; *Times,* June 28, 2001, CA; affirming
   [2001] E.L.R. 125; *Times,* October 18, 2000, QBD . . . . *Digested,* 01/**428**
R. (on the application of Buildstone Ltd) *v.* Secretary of State for Education and
   Employment, *Independent,* January 15, 2001 (C.S), QBD (Admin Ct)
R. (on the application of Liverpool Hope University College) *v.* Secretary of State for
   Education and Employment; *sub nom* R. *v.* Secretary of State for Education and
   Employment Ex p. Liverpool Hope University College [2001] EWCA Civ 362;
   [2001] E.L.R. 552, CA; affirming [2000] Ed. C.R. 330; [2000] E.L.R. 579,
   QBD . . . . *Digested,* 01/**1894**
R. (on the application of McNally) *v.* Secretary of State for Education and Employment;
   sub nom McNally *v.* Secretary of State for Education; R. *v.* Secretary of State
   for Education and Employment Ex p. McNally [2001] EWCA Civ 332; [2001] 2
   F.C.R. 11; (2001) 3 L.G.L.R. 47; [2001] E.L.R. 773; (2001) 98(19) L.S.G. 36;
   (2001) 145 S.J.L.B. 91; *Times,* March 23, 2001, CA; reversing [2001] E.L.R.
   348, QBD . . . . *Digested,* 01/**2248**
R. (on the application of Williamson) *v.* Secretary of State for Education and
   Employment; *sub nom* Williamson *v.* Secretary of State for Education and
   Employment [2001] EWHC Admin 960; *Times,* December 12, 2001, QBD (Admin Ct)
R. *v.* Secretary of State for Education and Employment Ex p. Amraf Training Plc see R.
   (on the application of Amraf Training Plc) *v.* Secretary of State for Education and
   Employment

R. v. Secretary of State for Education and Employment Ex p. B see R. (on the application of B (A Child)) v. Alperton Community School Head Teacher and Governing Body

R. v. Secretary of State for Education and Employment Ex p. B (A Minor); *sub nom* R. v. Department of Education and Employment Ex p. B (A Minor) [2000] 1 W.L.R. 1115; [2000] Ed. C.R. 140; [2000] E.L.R. 445; (1999) 96(35) L.S.G. 39; *Times*, September 14, 1999, CA; affirming [1999] E.L.R. 471, QBD . . . .   *Digested*, 99/**1704**:
       Applied, 01/3426

R. v. Secretary of State for Education and Employment Ex p. E [1996] E.L.R. 312; [1996] C.O.D. 30, QBD . . . .   *Digested*, 96/**2484**:
       Distinguished, 98/1966

R. v. Secretary of State for Education and Employment Ex p. Liverpool Hope University College see R. (on the application of Liverpool Hope University College) v. Secretary of State for Education and Employment

R. v. Secretary of State for Education and Employment Ex p. McNally see R. (on the application of McNally) v. Secretary of State for Education and Employment

R. v. Secretary of State for Education and Employment Ex p. National Union of Teachers [2000] Ed. C.R. 603; *Times*, August 8, 2000, QBD . . . .   *Digested*, 00/**2216**

R. v. Secretary of State for Education and Employment Ex p. P [2000] Ed. C.R. 669; [2000] E.L.R. 300, QBD . . . .   *Digested*, 00/**1944**

R. v. Secretary of State for Education and Employment Ex p. Portsmouth Football Club Ltd [1998] C.O.D. 142, QBD

R. v. Secretary of State for Education and Employment Ex p. RCO (A Child) [2000] Ed. C.R. 441; [2000] E.L.R. 307, QBD . . . .   *Digested*, 00/**1938**

R. v. Secretary of State for Education and Employment Ex p. Rochdale MBC [2001] EWCA Civ 248, CA; affirming [2000] Ed. C.R. 415; [2000] E.L.R. 709, QBD . . .   *Digested*, 00/**2006**

R. v. Secretary of State for Education and Employment Ex p. Shu Sang Li [1999] Imm. A.R. 367, QBD . . . .   *Digested*, 00/**3394**

R. v. Secretary of State for Education and Employment Ex p. T [2000] Ed. C.R. 652, QBD . . . .   *Digested*, 01/**2026**

R. v. Secretary of State for Education and Employment Ex p. W [1998] Ed. C.R. 135; [1998] E.L.R. 413; [1998] C.O.D. 112, QBD. . . . .   *Digested*, 98/**1917**

R. v. Secretary of State for Education and Science Ex p. Chance (Unreported, July 26, 1982), QBD. . . . .   *Applied*, 99/1887

R. v. Secretary of State for Education and Science Ex p. Davis [1989] 2 F.L.R. 190; [1989] Fam. Law 319; *Times*, January 6, 1989; *Independent*, November 24, 1988; *Guardian*, December 13, 1988, QBD . . . .   *Digested*, 90/**1796**:
       Followed, 98/1965, 98/1973

R. v. Secretary of State for Education and Science Ex p. E [1992] 1 F.L.R. 377; [1993] 2 F.C.R. 753; [1992] Fam. Law 189; (1992) 156 L.G. Rev. 167; *Times*, May 9, 1991; *Independent*, May 9, 1991; *Guardian*, May 10, 1991, CA; affirming [1991] C.O.D. 278; (1991) 155 L.G. Rev. 723; *Times*, January 17, 1991; *Independent*, January 24, 1991; *Daily Telegraph*, January 21, 1991, QBD . . . .   *Digested*, 92/**1877**:
       Applied, 95/1926, 00/1961: *Considered*, 96/2489

R. v. Secretary of State for Education and Science Ex p. J [1993] C.O.D. 146. . . . .   *Digested*, 93/**3214**:
       Applied, 01/5652

R. v. Secretary of State for Education and Science Ex p. Threapleton, *Times*, June 2, 1988; *Independent*, June 2, 1988, QBD . . . .   *Digested*, 88/**1217**:
       Considered, 90/1782, 01/1959

R. v. Secretary of State for Education Ex p. B (A Child) [2001] E.L.R. 333, QBD . . . . . .   *Digested*, 01/**1959**

R. v. Secretary of State for Education Ex p. W (Unreported, May 27, 1994) . . . .   *Applied*, 00/1961

R. v. Secretary of State for Employment Ex p. Equal Opportunities Commission [1995] 1 A.C. 1; [1994] 2 W.L.R. 409; [1994] 1 All E.R. 910; [1995] 1 C.M.L.R. 391; [1994] I.C.R. 317; [1994] I.R.L.R. 176; 92 L.G.R. 360; [1994] C.O.D. 301; (1994) 91(18) L.S.G. 43; (1994) 144 N.L.J. 358; (1994) 138 S.J.L.B. 84; *Times*, March 4, 1994; *Independent*, March 9, 1994; *Guardian*, March 7, 1994, HL; affirming [1993] 1 W.L.R. 872; [1993] 1 All E.R. 1022; [1993] 1 C.M.L.R. 915; [1993] I.C.R. 251; [1993] I.R.L.R. 10; *Times*, November 12, 1992; *Independent*, November 10, 1992; *Guardian*, November 10, 1992, CA; affirming [1992] 1 All E.R. 545; [1992] I.C.R. 341; [1991] I.R.L.R. 493; [1992] C.O.D. 112; (1991) 141 N.L.J. 1409; (1991) 135 S.J.L.B. 188; *Times*, October 11, 1991; *Independent*, October 11, 1991; *Guardian*, October 16, 1991, QBD . . . .   *Digested*, 94/**1981**:
       Applied, 95/2052, 96/2629, 96/6957, 97/2265, 98/2177, 98/2240, 00/2004: *Cited*, 94/2013, 95/2094, 95/2095: *Considered*, 95/1987, 95/2084, 95/2108, 96/2575, 96/2576, 96/2577, 96/2578, 96/2626, 01/2319: *Distinguished*, 98/4972: *Followed*, 95/2107, 95/2112

R. v. Secretary of State for Employment Ex p. Seymour-Smith (C167/97); *sub nom* R. v. Seymour-Smith (C167/97); R. v. Perez (C167/97) [1999] 2 A.C. 554; [1999] 3 W.L.R. 460; [1999] All E.R. (E.C.) 97; [1999] E.C.R. I-623; [1999] 2 C.M.L.R. 273; [1999] C.E.C. 79; [1999] I.C.R. 447; [1999] I.R.L.R. 253; *Times*, February 25, 1999, ECJ . . . .   *Digested*, 99/**2141**:
       Considered, 01/2319: *Followed*, 00/2160

R. *v.* Secretary of State for Employment Ex p. Seymour-Smith (No.1) [1997] 1 W.L.R.
473; [1997] 2 All E.R. 273; [1997] 2 C.M.L.R. 904; [1997] I.C.R. 371; [1997]
I.R.L.R. 315; (1997) 147 N.L.J. 414; *Times*, March 14, 1997, HL; reversing [1996]
All E.R. (E.C.) 1; [1995] I.C.R. 889; [1995] I.R.L.R. 464; *Times*, August 3, 1995;
Independent, August 8, 1995, CA; reversing [1994] I.R.L.R. 448; [1994] C.O.D.
474, QBD . . . . *Digested*, 97/**2265**:
Applied, 97/2262, 98/2240: *Considered*, 96/2540, 98/2236:
Referred to, 97/5233, 98/5826

R. *v.* Secretary of State for Employment Ex p. Seymour-Smith (No.2) [2000] 1 W.L.R.
435; [2000] 1 All E.R. 857; [2000] 1 C.M.L.R. 770; [2000] I.C.R. 244; [2000]
I.R.L.R. 263; (2000) 97(9) L.S.G. 40; *Times*, February 18, 2000, HL . . . .   *Digested*, 00/**2210**

R. (on the application of Bancoult) *v.* Secretary of State for Foreign and Commonwealth
Affairs see R. (on the application of Bancoult) *v.* Secretary of State for the
Foreign and Commonwealth Office

R. *v.* Secretary of State for Foreign and Commonwealth Affairs Ex p. British Council of
Turkish Cypriot Associations [1998] C.O.D. 336, QBD

R. *v.* Secretary of State for Foreign and Commonwealth Affairs Ex p. Butt (Ferhut)
[1999] C.O.D. 470, CA

R. *v.* Secretary of State for Foreign and Commonwealth Affairs Ex p. Ramanathan see
Ramanathan *v.* Secretary of State for Foreign and Commonwealth Affairs

R. *v.* Secretary of State for Foreign and Commonwealth Affairs Ex p. World
Development Movement Ltd [1995] 1 W.L.R. 386; [1995] 1 All E.R. 611; [1995]
C.O.D. 211; (1995) 145 N.L.J. 51; *Times*, December 27, 1994; *Independent*,
January 11, 1995, QBD . . . . *Digested*, 95/**140**:
Considered, 97/4101, 00/5436

R. (on the application of API) *v.* Secretary of State for Health see R. (on the application
of the Association of Pharmaceutical Importers) *v.* Secretary of State for Health

R. (on the application of Associated Newspapers Ltd) *v.* Secretary of State for Health see
R. *v.* Secretary of State for Health Ex p. Wagstaff

R. (on the application of Imperial Tobacco Ltd) *v.* Secretary of State for Health; *sub nom*
Imperial Tobacco Ltd *v.* Secretary of State for Health; R. *v.* Secretary of State
for Health Ex p. Imperial Tobacco Ltd [2001] 1 W.L.R. 127; [2001] 1 All E.R. 850;
[2001] 1 C.M.L.R. 34; [2001] Eu. L.R. 191; [2001] A.C.D. 32; *Times*, December
20, 2000, HL; reversing [2000] 2 W.L.R. 834; [2000] 1 All E.R. 572; [2000] 1
C.M.L.R. 307; [2000] Eu. L.R. 70; (2000) 52 B.M.L.R. 89; [2000] C.O.D. 20;
(2000) 97(2) L.S.G. 29; (2000) 144 S.J.L.B. 31; *Times*, December 17, 1999;
Independent, January 14, 2000, CA; reversing *Times*, November 16, 1999, QBD .   *Digested*, 01/**2462**

R. (on the application of L) *v.* Secretary of State for Health; *sub nom* R. *v.* Secretary of
State for Health Ex p. L (M) [2001] 1 F.L.R. 406; [2001] 1 F.C.R. 326; (2001)
58 B.M.L.R. 101; [2001] Fam. Law 101; *Times*, October 26, 2000; *Independent*,
November 20, 2000 (C.S); *Daily Telegraph*, October 24, 2000, QBD (Admin
Ct) . . . .   *Digested*, 00/**3242**

R. (on the application of Quintavalle) *v.* Secretary of State for Health c/2001/2624, CA;
reversing [2001] EWHC Admin 918; [2001] 4 All E.R. 1013; (2001) 151 N.L.J.
1732; *Times*, December 5, 2001, QBD (Admin Ct)

R. (on the application of the Association of Pharmaceutical Importers) *v.* Secretary of
State for Health; *sub nom* R. (on the application of API) *v.* Secretary of State for
Health; R. *v.* Secretary of State for Health Ex p. British Association of European
Pharmaceutical Distributors; R. (on the application of the Association of
Pharmaceutical Importers) *v.* Dowelhurst Ltd [2001] EWCA Civ 1896, CA;
affirming [2001] EWHC Admin 183; [2001] Eu. L.R. 464, QBD (Admin Ct) . . . .   *Digested*, 01/**777**

R. (on the application of Wagstaff) *v.* Secretary of State for Health see R. *v.* Secretary of
State for Health Ex p. Wagstaff

R. *v.* Secretary of State for Health and Social Security Ex p. Lai [2001] Lloyd's Rep.
Med. 417, QBD (Adm Ct)

R. *v.* Secretary of State for Health Ex p. Associated Newspapers Ltd see R. *v.*
Secretary of State for Health Ex p. Wagstaff

R. *v.* Secretary of State for Health Ex p. B; *sub nom* R. *v.* Secretary of State for Health
Ex p. C (Minors); R. *v.* Secretary of State for Health Ex p. CB [1999] 1 F.L.R.
656; [1999] 3 F.C.R. 162; (1999) 1 L.G.L.R. 477; [1999] Fam. Law 77; (1998)
95(45) L.S.G. 37; (1999) 143 S.J.L.B. 13; *Times*, November 11, 1998;
Independent, October 29, 1998, QBD . . . .   *Digested*, 98/**2475**

R. *v.* Secretary of State for Health Ex p. British Association of European
Pharmaceutical Distributors see R. (on the application of the Association of
Pharmaceutical Importers) *v.* Secretary of State for Health

R. *v.* Secretary of State for Health Ex p. C [2000] 1 F.L.R. 627; [2000] 1 F.C.R. 471;
[2000] H.R.L.R. 400; [2000] U.K.H.R.R. 639; (2000) 3 C.C.L. Rep. 412;
[2000] Fam. Law 311; (2000) 97(10) L.S.G. 35; (2000) 144 S.J.L.B. 118; *Times*,
March 1, 2000; *Independent*, March 1, 2000, CA; affirming [1999] 1 F.L.R.
1073; (1999) 2 C.C.L. Rep. 172; [1999] Fam. Law 295; (1999) 96(6) L.S.G. 31;
Times, January 18, 1999; *Independent*, January 18, 1999 (C.S.), QBD . . . .   *Digested*, 00/**2212**:
Applied, 00/3250

R. *v.* Secretary of State for Health Ex p. C (Minors) see R. *v.* Secretary of State for
Health Ex p. B

R. *v.* Secretary of State for Health Ex p. CB see R. *v.* Secretary of State for Health Ex
p. B

R. *v.* Secretary of State for Health Ex p. Eastside Cheese Co [1999] 3 C.M.L.R. 123;
[1999] Eu. L.R. 968; [2000] E.H.L.R. 52; (2000) 2 L.G.L.R. 41; (2000) 55
B.M.L.R. 38; [1999] C.O.D. 321, CA; reversing [1999] E.H.L.R. 313; (1999) 1
L.G.L.R. 335; (1999) 11 Admin. L.R. 254; (1999) 47 B.M.L.R. 1; (1999) 163
J.P.N. 453; *Times*, December 1, 1998; *Independent*, November 30, 1998 (C.S.),
QBD . . . .   *Digested*, 99/**2590**

R. *v.* Secretary of State for Health Ex p. ER Squibb & Sons Ltd see R. *v.* Licensing
Authority Ex p. Generics (UK) Ltd

R. *v.* Secretary of State for Health Ex p. Generics (UK) Ltd (Interim Relief) see R. *v.*
Licensing Authority Ex p. Generics (UK) Ltd

R. *v.* Secretary of State for Health Ex p. Imperial Tobacco Ltd see R. (on the
application of Imperial Tobacco Ltd) *v.* Secretary of State for Health

R. *v.* Secretary of State for Health Ex p. Imperial Tobacco Ltd (C74/99) see Germany
v. European Parliament (C376/98)

R. *v.* Secretary of State for Health Ex p. Imperial Tobacco Ltd (Leave Application)
[1999] Eu. L.R. 582; [1999] C.O.D. 138, QBD . . . .   *Digested*, 99/**94**

R. *v.* Secretary of State for Health Ex p. L (M) see R. (on the application of L) *v.*
Secretary of State for Health

R. *v.* Secretary of State for Health Ex p. M; *sub nom* R. *v.* Secretary of State for Health
Ex p.Hammersmith and Fulham LBC (1999) 31 H.L.R. 475; [1999] B.L.G.R. 354;
(1997-98) 1 C.C.L. Rep. 495; (1999) 49 B.M.L.R. 201; *Times*, September 9,
1998, CA; affirming (1998) 30 H.L.R. 525; (1997-98) 1 C.C.L. Rep. 96; *Times*,
July 31, 1997; *Independent*, July 15, 1997, QBD . . . .   *Digested*, 98/**4571**

R. *v.* Secretary of State for Health Ex p. Pfizer Ltd [1999] 3 C.M.L.R. 875; (1999) 2
C.C.L. Rep. 270; [1999] Lloyd's Rep. Med. 289; (2000) 51 B.M.L.R. 189; *Times*,
June 17, 1999, QBD . . . .   *Digested*, 99/**2693**

R. *v.* Secretary of State for Health Ex p. RP Scherer Ltd [1998] Eu. L.R. 1; (1996) 32
B.M.L.R. 12, QBD . . . .   *Digested*, 96/**4190**

R. *v.* Secretary of State for Health Ex p. Wagstaff; *sub nom* R. (on the application of
Wagstaff) *v.* Secretary of State for Health; R. (on the application of Associated
Newspapers Ltd) *v.* Secretary of State for Health; R. *v.* Secretary of State for
Health Ex p. Associated Newspapers Ltd [2001] 1 W.L.R. 292; [2000] H.R.L.R.
646; [2000] U.K.H.R.R. 875; (2000) 56 B.M.L.R. 199; [2001] A.C.D. 24;
(2000) 97(37) L.S.G. 39; (2000) 144 S.J.L.B. 249; *Times*, August 31, 2000;
Independent, October 30, 2000 (C.S), QBD . . . .   *Digested*, 00/**108**

R. *v.* Secretary of State for Health Ex p.Hammersmith and Fulham LBC see R. *v.*
Secretary of State for Health Ex p. M

R. *v.* Secretary of State for Home Department and Merseyside Police Authority Ex p.
Jones [1999] C.O.D. 98, QBD

R. *v.* Secretary of State for National Heritage Ex p. Continental Television BV [1993] 3
C.M.L.R. 387; [1993] E.M.L.R. 389; [1994] C.O.D. 121; *Guardian*, May 14, 1993,
CA; affirming [1993] 2 C.M.L.R. 333; [1993] C.O.D. 421, QBD . . . .   *Digested*, 94/**4**:
   Considered, 99/3916

R. *v.* Secretary of State for National Heritage Ex p. J Paul Getty Trust [1997] Eu. L.R.
407; *Independent*, November 7, 1994 (C.S.), CA . . . .   *Considered*, 01/5346

R. (on the application of Tucker) *v.* Secretary of State for Social Security; *sub nom* Tucker
v. Secretary of State for Social Security [2001] EWCA Civ 1646; [2001] N.P.C.
160; *Daily Telegraph*, November 13, 2001, CA; affirming [2001] EWHC Admin
260; [2001] A.C.D. 74, QBD (Admin Ct)

R. *v.* Secretary of State for Social Security Ex p. B see R. *v.* Secretary of State for
Social Security Ex p. Joint Council for the Welfare of Immigrants

R. *v.* Secretary of State for Social Security Ex p. Harris [1999] 1 F.L.R. 837; [1999]
Fam. Law 296, QBD . . . .   *Digested*, 99/**2342**

R. *v.* Secretary of State for Social Security Ex p. Joint Council for the Welfare of
Immigrants; R. *v.* Secretary of State for Social Security Ex p. B [1997] 1 W.L.R.
275; [1996] 4 All E.R. 385; (1997) 29 H.L.R. 129; (1997) 9 Admin. L.R. 1;
(1996) 146 N.L.J. 985; *Times*, June 27, 1996; *Independent*, June 26, 1996, CA .   *Digested*, 96/**3219**:
   Applied, 00/4422: *Followed*, 97/4657

R. *v.* Secretary of State for Social Security Ex p. Perry FC3 98/5130/4; FC3 98/5131/
4, CA . . . .   *Digested*, 98/**4513**

R. *v.* Secretary of State for Social Security Ex p. Remelien see Secretary of State for
Social Security *v.* Remilien

R. *v.* Secretary of State for Social Security Ex p. Singh (Newmarch) [2000] 2 F.L.R.
664; [2000] Fam. Law 698, QBD . . . .   *Digested*, 01/**2554**

R. *v.* Secretary of State for Social Security Ex p. Sutton (C66/95) [1997] All E.R.
(E.C.) 497; [1997] E.C.R. I-2163; [1997] 2 C.M.L.R. 382; [1997] C.E.C. 1110;
[1997] I.C.R. 961; [1997] I.R.L.R. 524; *Times*, April 25, 1997, ECJ . . . .   *Digested*, 97/**4672**:
   Followed, 00/4819

R. *v.* Secretary of State for Social Security Ex p. Taylor (C382/98) [2000] All E.R.
(EC) 80; [1999] E.C.R. I-8955; [2000] 1 C.M.L.R. 873; [2000] C.E.C. 3;
[2000] I.C.R. 843; *Times*, January 25, 2000, ECJ (6th Chamber) . . . .   *Digested*, 00/**4815**

R. *v.* Secretary of State for Social Security Ex p. Vijeikis; R. *v.* Department of Social
Security Ex p. Okito; R. *v.* Benefits Agency Ex p. Zaheer [1998] C.O.D. 49,
QBD . . . . *Digested,* 97/**4658**

R. *v.* Secretary of State for Social Security Ex p. W [1999] 1 F.L.R. 1233; [1999] 3
F.C.R. 574; [1999] Fam. Law 297; *Times,* November 26, 1998, CA [1999] 2
F.L.R. 604; [1999] Fam. Law 526; (2000) 164 J.P.N. 824; *Times,* May 19, 1999,
Fam Div . . . . *Digested,* 99/**2442**

R. *v.* Secretary of State for Social Security Ex p. Wolke see Secretary of State for
Social Security *v.* Remilien

R. *v.* Secretary of State for Social Services Ex p. Association of Metropolitan
Authorities [1986] 1 W.L.R. 1; [1986] 1 All E.R. 164; (1985) 17 H.L.R. 487; 83
L.G.R. 796; (1986) 130 S.J. 35, QBD . . . . *Digested,* 86/**1635**:
Applied, 93/5430, 97/4067: *Considered,* 96/2487, 98/94:
Distinguished, 97/2644

R. *v.* Secretary of State for Social Services Ex p. Gordon [2001] Lloyd's Rep. Med.
422, QBD

R. *v.* Secretary of State for Social Services Ex p. Hincks (1979) 123 S.J. 436 . . . . *Digested,* 79/**1839**:
Considered, 00/2843

R. *v.* Secretary of State for Social Services Ex p. Khan [1973] 1 W.L.R. 187; [1973] 2
All E.R. 104; (1972) 117 S.J. 55, CA . . . . *Digested,* 73/**2220**:
Applied, 98/4142

R. *v.* Secretary of State for the Environment Ex p. Bolton MDC see Bolton MBC *v.*
Secretary of State for the Environment

R. *v.* Secretary of State for the Environment Ex p. British Telecommunications Plc; *sub
nom* British Telecommunications Plc *v.* Secretary of State for the Environment
[1991] R.A. 307; [1991] N.P.C. 93; *Independent,* September 5, 1991, QBD . . . . . *Digested,* 92/**3679**:
Applied, 01/4817

R. *v.* Secretary of State for the Environment Ex p. Davies (1991) 61 P. & C.R. 487;
[1991] 1 P.L.R. 78; [1991] J.P.L. 540; [1991] C.O.D. 160; *Times,* November 5,
1990; *Independent,* October 31, 1990, CA; affirming (1990) 59 P. & C.R. 306;
[1989] 3 P.L.R. 73; [1989] C.O.D. 569; *Times,* May 15, 1989, QBD . . . . *Digested,* 91/**546**:
Considered, 01/4843

R. *v.* Secretary of State for the Environment Ex p. Enfield LBC 86 L.G.R. 549; *Times,*
April 5, 1988, QBD . . . . *Digested,* 89/**1909**:
Applied, 00/3942

R. *v.* Secretary of State for the Environment Ex p. Hammersmith and Fulham LBC
[1991] 1 A.C. 521; [1990] 3 W.L.R. 898; [1990] 3 All E.R. 589; 89 L.G.R. 129;
[1990] R.V.R. 188; (1991) 155 L.G. Rev. 48; (1990) 140 N.L.J. 1422; (1990) 134
S.J. 1226; *Times,* October 5, 1990; *Independent,* October 5, 1990; *Guardian,*
October 10, 1990; *Daily Telegraph,* October 15, 1990, HL; affirming [1990] 2 Q.B.
697; [1990] C.O.D. 443; *Times,* July 4, 1990; *Independent,* July 4, 1990;
Guardian, July 4, 1990, CA; affirming *Times,* June 16, 1990, QBD . . . . *Digested,* 91/**67**:
Applied, 93/2208: *Considered,* 90/10, 91/53, 93/2567, 95/6105

R. *v.* Secretary of State for the Environment Ex p. Islington LBC [1992] C.O.D. 67;
[1991] N.P.C. 90; *Independent,* September 6, 1991, CA . . . . *Digested,* 92/**3493**:
Applied, 00/5402

R. *v.* Secretary of State for the Environment Ex p. Kirkstall Valley Campaign Ltd; *sub
nom* R. *v.* Secretary of State for the Environment Ex p. William Morrison
Supermarket Plc [1996] 3 All E.R. 304; [1997] 1 P.L.R. 8; [1996] J.P.L. 1042;
[1996] C.O.D. 337; (1996) 160 J.P. Rep. 699; [1996] E.G.C.S. 46; (1996) 146
N.L.J. 478; [1996] N.P.C. 41; *Times,* March 20, 1996, QBD. . . . . *Digested,* 96/**4679**:
Considered, 99/3872, 00/2278: *Followed,* 99/4233

R. *v.* Secretary of State for the Environment Ex p. Leicester City Council (1988) 55 P.
& C.R. 364; [1987] J.P.L. 787, QBD . . . . *Digested,* 88/**388**:
Cited, 99/4198: *Considered,* 89/374, 90/0594, 91/3485, 92/4250

R. *v.* Secretary of State for the Environment Ex p. Nottinghamshire CC; *sub nom*
Nottinghamshire CC *v.* Secretary of State for the Environment; City of Bradford
MBC *v.* Secretary of State for the Environment [1986] A.C. 240; [1986] 2
W.L.R. 1; [1986] 1 All E.R. 199; 84 L.G.R. 305; (1986) 83 L.S.G. 359; (1985)
135 N.L.J. 1257; (1986) 130 S.J. 36, HL; reversing in part [1985] R.V.R. 165;
(1985) 82 L.S.G. 2335, CA . . . . *Digested,* 86/**27**:
Applied, 99/2643, 01/4817: *Cited,* 93/2208: *Considered,* 87/1920, 87/3190,
89/1898, 90/9, 90/2497, 90/3042, 91/63, 91/67, 92/55, 94/55, 95/67,
95/6105: *Distinguished,* 94/66

R. *v.* Secretary of State for the Environment Ex p. Oldham MBC [1998] I.C.R. 367;
Times, December 16, 1996, QBD . . . . *Digested,* 97/**3436**

R. *v.* Secretary of State for the Environment Ex p. PF Ahern (London) Ltd; *sub nom* PF
Ahern (London) Ltd *v.* Secretary of State for the Environment [1998] Env. L.R.
189; [1998] J.P.L. 351; [1997] E.G.C.S. 94, QBD . . . . *Digested,* 98/**4237**:
Considered, 99/4214

R. v. Secretary of State for the Environment Ex p. Slough BC; *sub nom* Slough BC *v.* Secretary of State for the Environment 94 L.G.R. 376; (1995) 70 P. & C.R. 560; [1995] 3 P.L.R. 28; [1995] J.P.L. 1128; [1996] C.O.D. 174; (1995) 159 L.G. Rev. 969; [1995] E.G.C.S. 95; (1995) 92(23) L.S.G. 32; (1995) 139 S.J.L.B. 130; [1995] N.P.C. 96; *Times*, May 24, 1995; *Independent*, June 14, 1995, CA; affirming [1994] E.G.C.S. 67; [1994] N.P.C. 50, QBD . . . .　*Digested*, 95/**4867**:
Applied, 96/4835, 99/4249: *Followed*, 98/4224

R. v. Secretary of State for the Environment Ex p. Tower Hamlets LBC [1993] Q.B. 632; [1993] 3 W.L.R. 32; [1993] 3 All E.R. 439; [1993] Imm. A.R. 495; (1993) 25 H.L.R. 524; [1994] C.O.D. 50; [1993] N.P.C. 65; *Times*, April 9, 1993; *Independent*, April 22, 1993, CA; reversing [1992] Imm. A.R. 389; (1992) 24 H.L.R. 594; [1992] C.O.D. 377; *Times*, April 20, 1992, QBD . . . .　*Digested*, 93/**2053**:
Applied, 98/3007: *Followed*, 98/3008

R. v. Secretary of State for the Environment Ex p. Wakefield MDC (1997) 9 Admin. L.R. 399; (1998) 75 P. & C.R. 78; *Times*, October 29, 1996, QBD . . . .　*Digested*, 96/**4702**

R. v. Secretary of State for the Environment Ex p. Walsall MBC [1997] E.G.C.S. 23; [1997] N.P.C. 25; [1998] Env. L.R. D11, QBD

R. v. Secretary of State for the Environment Ex p. Walters see R. *v.* Brent LBC Ex p. O'Malley

R. v. Secretary of State for the Environment Ex p. Ward [1984] 1 W.L.R. 834; [1984] 2 All E.R. 556; 82 L.G.R. 628; (1984) 48 P. & C.R. 212; [1984] J.P.L. 90; (1984) 128 S.J. 415, QBD . . . .　*Digested*, 84/**3438**:
Applied, 93/3894, 93/3895, 95/135, 00/2843: *Followed*, 88/2208

R. v. Secretary of State for the Environment Ex p. William Morrison Supermarket Plc see R. *v.* Secretary of State for the Environment Ex p. Kirkstall Valley Campaign Ltd

R. (on the application of Amvac Chemical UK Ltd) *v.* Secretary of State for the Environment, Food and Rural Affairs [2001] EWHC Admin 1011; [2001] N.P.C. 176, QBD (Admin Ct)

R. (on the application of Friends of the Earth Ltd) *v.* Secretary of State for the Environment, Food and Rural Affairs [2001] EWCA Civ 1847; [2001] 50 E.G.C.S. 91; [2001] N.P.C. 181, CA; affirming [2001] EWHC Admin 914; [2001] 47 E.G.C.S. 148, QBD (Admin Ct)

R. (on the application of Alconbury Developments Ltd) *v.* Secretary of State for the Environment, Transport and the Regions see R. (on the application of Holding & Barnes Plc) *v.* Secretary of State for the Environment, Transport and the Regions

R. (on the application of Anscomb) *v.* Secretary of State for the Environment, Transport and the Regions; *sub nom* Anscomb *v.* Secretary of State for the Environment, Transport and the Regions [2001] EWHC Admin 100; [2001] 2 P.L.R. 34; [2001] J.P.L. 1320 (Note); (2001) 98(8) L.S.G. 48, QBD (Admin Ct)

R. (on the application of Benham-Crosswell) *v.* Secretary of State for the Environment, Transport and the Regions; *sub nom* R. *v.* Secretary of State for the Environment, Transport and the Regions ex. p Benham-Crosswell; R. *v.* Secretary of State for the Environment, Transport and the Regions ex. p Benham Crosswell [2001] EWHC Admin 146; [2001] J.P.L. 1405; [2001] 10 E.G.C.S. 157, QBD (Admin Ct)

R. (on the application of Brandvik Kinton Ltd) *v.* Secretary of State for the Environment, Transport and the Regions; *sub nom* R. *v.* Secretary of State for the Environment, Transport and the Regions Ex p. Brandvik Kinton Ltd [2001] P.L.C.R. 19, QBD (Admin Ct) . . . .　*Digested*, 01/**4650**

R. (on the application of Campbell Court Property) *v.* Secretary of State for the Environment, Transport and the Regions; *sub nom* Campbell Court Property Ltd *v.* Secretary of State for the Environment, Transport and the Regions [2001] EWHC Admin 102; [2001] J.P.L. 1322 (Note), QBD (Admin Ct)

R. (on the application of Channel Tunnel Group Ltd) *v.* Secretary of State for the Environment, Transport and the Regions; R. (on the application of France Manche SA) *v.* Secretary of State for the Environment, Transport and the Regions [2001] EWCA Civ 1185; *Times*, August 7, 2001, CA; reversing [2000] N.P.C. 137, QBD (Admin Ct) . . . .　*Digested*, 01/**5392**

R. (on the application of Connaught Quarries Ltd) *v.* Secretary of State for the Environment, Transport and the Regions [2001] EWHC Admin 76; [2001] 4 P.L.R. 18; [2001] J.P.L. 1210 (Note), QBD (Admin Ct)

R. (on the application of CW Young Ltd) *v.* Secretary of State for the Environment, Transport and the Regions; *sub nom* CW Young (Builders Merchants) Ltd *v.* Secretary of State for the Environment, Transport and the Regions [2001] EWHC Admin 141; [2001] J.P.L. 1321 (Note), QBD (Admin Ct)

R. (on the application of Dyason) *v.* Secretary of State for the Environment, Transport and the Regions (No.3) [2001] EWHC Admin 4; [2001] J.P.L. 1109 (Note), QBD (Admin Ct)

R. (on the application of Edison First Power Ltd) v. Secretary of State for the Environment, Transport and the Regions; *sub nom* Edison First Power Ltd v. Secretary of State for the Environment, Transport and the Regions; R. (on the application of Edison First Power Ltd) v. Central Valuation Officer [2001] EWCA Civ 1096; [2001] R.A. 229; [2001] 30 E.G.C.S. 112; *Independent*, November 5, 2001 (C.S), CA; affirming [2001] R.A. 1; [2000] E.G.C.S. 142, QBD (Admin Ct) . . . .   *Digested*, 01/**4817**

R. (on the application of Edward) v. Secretary of State for the Environment, Transport and the Regions [2001] J.P.L. 997 (Note); [2001] A.C.D. 26, QBD (Admin Ct)

R. (on the application of Elmbridge BC) v. Secretary of State for the Environment, Transport and the Regions; *sub nom* Elmbridge BC v. Secretary of State for the Environment, Transport and the Regions; R. v. Secretary of State for the Environment, Transport and the Regions Ex p. Elmbridge BC; Totalfina Great Britain Ltd v. Secretary of State for the Environment, Transport and the Regions; Hadmere Ltd v. Secretary of State for the Environment, Transport and the Regions; Avalon Enterprises Ltd v. Secretary of State for the Environment, Transport and the Regions [2000] E.G.C.S. 129; [2000] N.P.C. 120, QBD (Admin Ct)

R. (on the application of First Corporate Shipping Ltd) v. Secretary of State for the Environment, Transport and the Regions (C371/98) see R. v. Secretary of State for the Environment, Transport and the Regions Ex p. First Corporate Shipping Ltd (C371/98)

R. (on the application of France Manche SA) v. Secretary of State for the Environment, Transport and the Regions see R. (on the application of Channel Tunnel Group Ltd) v. Secretary of State for the Environment, Transport and the Regions

R. (on the application of Friends Provident Life Office) v. Secretary of State for the Environment, Transport and the Regions; *sub nom* Friends Provident Life Office v. Secretary of State for the Environment, Transport and the Regions; R. (on the application of Friends Provident Life & Pensions Ltd) v. Secretary of State for Transport, Local Government and the Regions [2001] EWHC Admin 820; [2001] 44 E.G.C.S. 147; [2001] N.P.C. 152, QBD (Admin Ct)

R. (on the application of Garland) v. Secretary of State for the Environment, Transport and the Regions (2001) 3 L.G.L.R. 26, QBD (Admin Ct) . . . .   *Digested*, 01/**4370**

R. (on the application of Gloucester CC) v. Secretary of State for the Environment, Transport and the Regions; *sub nom* R. v. Secretary of State for the Environment, Transport and the Regions Ex p. Gloucestershire CC; R. (on the application of Gloucestershire CC) v. Secretary of State for the Environment, Transport and the Regions (2001) 82 P. & C.R. 15; [2001] J.P.L. 1276; [2001] A.C.D. 34; [2000] E.G.C.S. 150; [2000] N.P.C. 143, QBD (Admin Ct) . . . .   *Digested*, 01/**4703**

R. (on the application of Gloucestershire CC) v. Secretary of State for the Environment, Transport and the Regions see R. (on the application of Gloucester CC) v. Secretary of State for the Environment, Transport and the Regions

R. (on the application of Holding & Barnes Plc) v. Secretary of State for the Environment, Transport and the Regions; *sub nom* R. v. Secretary of State for the Environment, Transport and the Regions Ex p. Holdings & Barnes Plc; R. (on the application of Premier Leisure UK Ltd) v. Secretary of State for the Environment, Transport and the Regions; R. (on the application of Alconbury Developments Ltd) v. Secretary of State for the Environment, Transport and the Regions; Secretary of State for the Environment, Transport and the Regions v. Legal & General Assurance Society Ltd [2001] UKHL 23; [2001] 2 W.L.R. 1389; [2001] 2 All E.R. 929; [2001] H.R.L.R. 45; [2001] U.K.H.R.R. 728; (2001) 3 L.G.L.R. 38; (2001) 82 P. & C.R. 40; [2001] 2 P.L.R. 76; [2001] J.P.L. 920; [2001] 20 E.G.C.S. 228; (2001) 98(24) L.S.G. 45; (2001) 151 N.L.J. 727; (2001) 145 S.J.L.B. 140; [2001] N.P.C. 90; *Times*, May 10, 2001; *Independent*, June 25, 2001 (C.S); *Daily Telegraph*, May 15, 2001, HL; reversing [2001] H.R.L.R. 2; [2001] U.K.H.R.R. 270; (2001) 3 L.G.L.R. 21; [2001] 1 P.L.R. 58; [2001] 1 E.G.L.R. 33; [2001] 05 E.G. 170; [2001] J.P.L. 291; [2001] 4 E.G.C.S. 141; (2001) 151 N.L.J. 135; (2001) 145 S.J.L.B. 84; *Times*, January 24, 2001; *Independent*, January 22, 2001 (C.S), QBD (Admin Ct) . . . .   *Digested*, 01/**4761**:
   Cited, 01/**6853**

R. (on the application of O'Byrne) v. Secretary of State for the Environment, Transport and the Regions; *sub nom* O'Byrne v. Secretary of State for the Environment, Transport and the Regions; R. v. Secretary of State for the Environment, Transport and the Regions Ex p. O'Byrne [2001] EWCA Civ 499; [2001] 16 E.G.C.S. 144; (2001) 98(16) L.S.G. 36; [2001] N.P.C. 71; *Times*, April 17, 2001; *Independent*, April 10, 2001, CA; reversing (2000) 97(23) L.S.G. 46; [2000] N.P.C. 60; *Independent*, June 13, 2000, QBD . . . .   *Digested*, 01/**4215**

R. (on the application of Orange Personal Communications Services Ltd) v. Secretary of State for the Environment, Transport and the Regions see R. (on the application of Orange Personal Communications Ltd) v. Secretary of State for Trade and Industry

R. (on the application of Plymouth City Airport Ltd) *v.* Secretary of State for the Environment, Transport and the Regions; *sub nom* Plymouth City Airport Ltd *v.* Secretary of State for the Environment, Transport and the Regions; R. *v.* Plymouth City Airport Ltd; R. *v.* Secretary of State for the Environment, Transport and the Regions Ex p. Plymouth City Airport Ltd [2001] EWCA Civ 144; (2001) 82 P. & C.R. 20; (2001) 98(8) L.S.G. 48, CA; affirming (2000) 97(7) L.S.G. 42, QBD . . . . *Digested,* 01/**4681**

R. (on the application of Premier Leisure UK Ltd) *v.* Secretary of State for the Environment, Transport and the Regions see R. (on the application of Holding & Barnes Plc) *v.* Secretary of State for the Environment, Transport and the Regions

R. (on the application of Spath Holme Ltd) *v.* Secretary of State for the Environment, Transport and the Regions; *sub nom* R. *v.* Secretary of State for the Environment, Transport and the Regions Ex p. Spath Holme Ltd [2001] 2 A.C. 349; [2001] 2 W.L.R. 15; [2001] 1 All E.R. 195; (2001) 33 H.L.R. 31; [2001] 1 E.G.L.R. 129; [2000] E.G.C.S. 152; (2001) 98(8) L.S.G. 44; (2000) 150 N.L.J. 1855; (2001) 145 S.J.L.B. 39; [2000] N.P.C. 139; *Times,* December 13, 2000, HL; reversing [2000] 3 W.L.R. 141; [2000] 1 All E.R. 884; (2000) 32 H.L.R. 495; [2000] E.G.C.S. 10; (2000) 144 S.J.L.B. 100; [2000] N.P.C. 4; *Times,* February 15, 2000; *Independent,* March 6, 2000 (C.S.), CA . . . . *Digested,* 01/**4206**:
Applied, 00/**5095,** 01/**5632**

R. (on the application of Spelthorne BC) *v.* Secretary of State for the Environment, Transport and the Regions (2001) 82 P. & C.R. 10; [2001] P.L.C.R. 20, QBD (Admin Ct) . . . . *Digested,* 01/**4719**

R. (on the application of St James Homes Ltd) *v.* Secretary of State for the Environment, Transport and the Regions; *sub nom* St James Homes Ltd *v.* Secretary of State for the Environment, Transport and the Regions [2001] EWHC Admin 30; [2001] P.L.C.R. 27; [2001] J.P.L. 1110 (Note); [2001] 6 E.G.C.S. 161, QBD (Admin Ct) . *Digested,* 01/**4684**

R. (on the application of Taylor (t/a David Taylor & Sons)) *v.* Secretary of State for the Environment, Transport and the Regions see Taylor & Sons (Farms) *v.* Secretary of State for the Environment, Transport and the Regions

R. (on the application of Tesco Stores Ltd) *v.* Secretary of State for the Environment, Transport and the Regions; *sub nom* Tesco Stores Ltd *v.* Secretary of State for the Environment, Transport and the Regions (Extension of Floor Space: District Centre); R. *v.* Secretary of State for the Environment, Transport and the Regions Ex p. Tesco Stores Ltd [2001] J.P.L. 686; [2000] E.G.C.S. 117, QBD (Admin Ct) . . . . *Digested,* 01/**4763**

R. (on the application of Torridge DC) *v.* Secretary of State for the Environment, Transport and the Regions [2001] J.P.L. 1195, QBD (Admin Ct) . . . . *Digested,* 01/**4749**

R. (on the application of Trustees of the Friends of the Lake District) *v.* Secretary of State for the Environment, Transport and the Regions; *sub nom* Trustees of the Friends of the Lake District *v.* Secretary of State for the Environment, Transport and the Regions [2001] EWHC Admin 281; [2001] 15 E.G.C.S. 136; *Times,* May 17, 2001, QBD (Admin Ct) . . . . *Digested,* 01/**4725**

R. (on the application of United Kingdom Renderers Association Ltd) *v.* Secretary of State for the Environment, Transport and the Regions C/2001/2094, CA; affirming [2001] EWHC Admin 675; [2001] 36 E.G.C.S. 180; (2001) 98(34) L.S.G. 44, QBD (Admin Ct)

R. (on the application of Wainsfort Corp) *v.* Secretary of State for the Environment, Transport and the Regions; *sub nom* Wainsfort Corp *v.* Secretary of State for the Environment, Transport and the Regions (2000) 97(47) L.S.G. 41, QBD (Admin Ct)

R. (on the application of Windsor and Maidenhead RBC) *v.* Secretary of State for the Environment, Transport and the Regions; *sub nom* R. (on the application of Windsor and Maidenhead RLBC) *v.* Secretary of State for the Environment, Transport and the Regions; Windsor and Maidenhead RBC *v.* Secretary of State for the Environment, Transport and the Regions [2001] EWHC Admin 84; [2001] P.L.C.R. 30; [2001] J.P.L. 1216 (Note); (2001) 98(7) L.S.G. 42, QBD (Admin Ct) . . . . *Digested,* 01/**4652**

R. (on the application of Windsor and Maidenhead RLBC) *v.* Secretary of State for the Environment, Transport and the Regions see R. (on the application of Windsor and Maidenhead RBC) *v.* Secretary of State for the Environment, Transport and the Regions

R. *v.* Secretary of State for the Environment, Transport and the Regions Ex p. Alliance Against the Birmingham Northern Relief Road (No.1); *sub nom* Alliance against the Birmingham Northern Relief Road *v.* Secretary of State for the Environment, Transport and the Regions (No.1) [1999] Env. L.R. 447; [1999] J.P.L. 231; [1999] C.O.D. 45; [1998] N.P.C. 129, QBD . . . . *Digested,* 99/**2167**

R. *v.* Secretary of State for the Environment, Transport and the Regions Ex p. Alliance against the Birmingham Northern Relief Road (No.2); *sub nom* Alliance against the Birmingham Northern Relief Road *v.* Secretary of State for the Environment, Transport and the Regions (No.2) [1999] N.P.C. 38, CA; affirming [1999] J.P.L. 426; [1998] E.G.C.S. 146; [1998] N.P.C. 143, QBD . . . . *Digested,* 99/**4273**

R. *v.* Secretary of State for the Environment, Transport and the Regions Ex p. Bath and North East Somerset DC; *sub nom* R. *v.* Secretary of State for the Environment, Transport and the Regions Ex p. Bath and North Somerset DC; R. *v.* Bath and North Somerset DC [1999] 1 W.L.R. 1759; [1999] 4 All E.R. 418; (1999) 11 Admin. L.R. 997; [1999] 2 P.L.R. 120; [1999] J.P.L. 984; [1999] E.G.C.S. 82; (1999) 96(24) L.S.G. 38; (1999) 149 N.L.J. 930; *Times*, June 3, 1999 ; *Independent*, June 11, 1999, CA; affirming (1999) 96(8) L.S.G. 30; *Times*, January 28, 1999, QBD . . . . *Digested*, 99/**4167**

R. *v.* Secretary of State for the Environment, Transport and the Regions Ex p. Bath and North Somerset DC see R. *v.* Secretary of State for the Environment, Transport and the Regions Ex p. Bath and North East Somerset DC

R. *v.* Secretary of State for the Environment, Transport and the Regions Ex p. Batt [2001] J.P.L. 378 (Note), QBD

R. *v.* Secretary of State for the Environment, Transport and the Regions Ex p. Billson [1999] Q.B. 374; [1998] 3 W.L.R. 1240; [1998] 2 All E.R. 587; [1999] B.L.G.R. 299; (1999) 77 P. & C.R. 396; [1998] J.P.L. 883; *Times*, March 4, 1998; *Independent*, March 9, 1998 (C.S.), QBD . . . . *Digested*, 98/**2250**

R. *v.* Secretary of State for the Environment, Transport and the Regions Ex p. Brandvik Kinton Ltd see R. (on the application of Brandvik Kinton Ltd) *v.* Secretary of State for the Environment, Transport and the Regions

R. *v.* Secretary of State for the Environment, Transport and the Regions Ex p. Bury MBC [1998] 2 C.M.L.R. 787; [1998] Eu. L.R. 650; [1999] B.L.G.R. 526; *Times*, March 5, 1998, CA . . . . *Digested*, 98/**3802**

R. *v.* Secretary of State for the Environment, Transport and the Regions Ex p. Camden LBC [1998] 1 W.L.R. 615; [1998] 1 All E.R. 937; (1999) 31 H.L.R. 242; [1998] R.V.R. 199; (1998) 95(16) L.S.G. 26; (1998) 148 N.L.J. 401; (1998) 142 S.J.L.B. 110; *Times*, March 13, 1998, HL; reversing (1997) 29 H.L.R. 957, CA . . . . *Digested*, 98/**3768**

R. *v.* Secretary of State for the Environment, Transport and the Regions Ex p. Carter Commercial Developments Ltd [1999] 1 P.L.R. 1; [1999] P.L.C.R. 125; [1998] E.G.C.S. 130, QBD . . . . *Digested*, 99/**4266**

R. *v.* Secretary of State for the Environment, Transport and the Regions Ex p. Challenger [2001] Env. L.R. 12; [2000] H.R.L.R. 630; [2000] C.O.D. 448; *Times*, July 11, 2000, QBD . . . . *Digested*, 00/**3230**

R. *v.* Secretary of State for the Environment, Transport and the Regions Ex p. Croydon LBC see Croydon LBC *v.* Secretary of State for the Environment, Transport and the Regions

R. *v.* Secretary of State for the Environment, Transport and the Regions Ex p. Deanbank Investments Ltd; R. *v.* Rochdale MBC Ex p. Deanbank Investments Ltd [2001] J.P.L. 1212 (Note), QBD (Admin Ct)

R. *v.* Secretary of State for the Environment, Transport and the Regions Ex p. Dorset CC [2000] J.P.L. 396; [1999] N.P.C. 72, QBD . . . . *Digested*, 99/**2886**

R. *v.* Secretary of State for the Environment, Transport and the Regions Ex p. Eauville Ltd (2000) 80 P. & C.R. 85; [2000] 4 P.L.R. 11, QBD . . . . *Digested*, 00/**4446**

R. *v.* Secretary of State for the Environment, Transport and the Regions Ex p. Elmbridge BC see R. (on the application of Elmbridge BC) *v.* Secretary of State for the Environment, Transport and the Regions

R. *v.* Secretary of State for the Environment, Transport and the Regions Ex p. Factortame Ltd see R. *v.* Secretary of State for Transport Ex p. Factortame Ltd (No.6)

R. *v.* Secretary of State for the Environment, Transport and the Regions Ex p. First Corporate Shipping Ltd (C371/98); *sub nom* R. (on the application of First Corporate Shipping Ltd) *v.* Secretary of State for the Environment, Transport and the Regions (C371/98) [2001] All E.R. (EC) 177; [2000] E.C.R. I-9235; [2001] 1 C.M.L.R. 19; [2001] Env. L.R. 34; [2001] 4 P.L.R. 1; [2000] N.P.C. 131; *Times*, November 16, 2000, ECJ. . . . . *Digested*, 00/**2257**

R. *v.* Secretary of State for the Environment, Transport and the Regions Ex p. Forte (UK) Ltd see Forte (UK) Ltd *v.* Secretary of State for the Environment, Transport and the Regions

R. *v.* Secretary of State for the Environment, Transport and the Regions Ex p. George Harrison (Whitby) Ltd see R. (on the application of George Harrison (Whitby) Ltd) *v.* Secretary of State for the Environment, Transport and the Regions

R. *v.* Secretary of State for the Environment, Transport and the Regions Ex p. Gloucestershire CC see R. (on the application of Gloucester CC) *v.* Secretary of State for the Environment, Transport and the Regions

R. *v.* Secretary of State for the Environment, Transport and the Regions Ex p. Holdings & Barnes Plc see R. (on the application of Holding & Barnes Plc) *v.* Secretary of State for the Environment, Transport and the Regions

R. *v.* Secretary of State for the Environment, Transport and the Regions Ex p. International Air Transport Association (No.1) [1999] 1 C.M.L.R. 1287; [1999] Eu. L.R. 202, QBD . . . . *Digested*, 99/**2263**

R. *v.* Secretary of State for the Environment, Transport and the Regions Ex p. International Air Transport Association (No.2) [2000] 1 Lloyd's Rep. 242; [1999] 2 C.M.L.R. 1385; [1999] Eu. L.R. 811; [1999] C.O.D. 315; *Times*, June 3, 1999, QBD . . . . *Digested*, 99/**2264**

R. *v.* Secretary of State for the Environment, Transport and the Regions Ex p. Jarmain
see Jarmain *v.* Secretary of State for the Environment, Transport and the Regions
(No.1)

R. *v.* Secretary of State for the Environment, Transport and the Regions Ex p. Kirklees
MBC [1999] J.P.L. 882, QBD . . . .   *Digested,* 99/**4238**

R. *v.* Secretary of State for the Environment, Transport and the Regions Ex p.
Kohlerdome Corp Ltd; R. *v.* Secretary of State for the Environment, Transport and
the Regions Ex p. Whitbread Plc [1999] J.P.L. 816; [1999] E.G.C.S. 30, QBD . . .   *Digested,* 99/**4247**

R. *v.* Secretary of State for the Environment, Transport and the Regions Ex p. Locker
see Locker *v.* Secretary of State for the Environment, Transport and the Regions

R. *v.* Secretary of State for the Environment, Transport and the Regions Ex p. Maltzahn
[1998] E.G.C.S. 43, QBD

R. *v.* Secretary of State for the Environment, Transport and the Regions Ex p. Marlow
see Marlow *v.* Secretary of State for the Environment, Transport and the
Regions

R. *v.* Secretary of State for the Environment, Transport and the Regions Ex p. Marson
[1999] 1 C.M.L.R. 268; [1998] Env. L.R. 761; (1999) 77 P. & C.R. 202; [1998] 3
P.L.R. 90; [1998] J.P.L. 869; [1998] N.P.C. 81; *Times,* May 18, 1998, CA . . . . . .   *Digested,* 98/**4188**

R. *v.* Secretary of State for the Environment, Transport and the Regions Ex p. Masters
see Masters *v.* Secretary of State for the Environment, Transport and the
Regions

R. *v.* Secretary of State for the Environment, Transport and the Regions Ex p. Metson
see R. *v.* Secretary of State for the Environment, Transport and the Regions Ex p.
Standley (C293/97)

R. *v.* Secretary of State for the Environment, Transport and the Regions Ex p. Nalkin
see R. *v.* Secretary of State for the Home Department Ex p. Nalkin

R. *v.* Secretary of State for the Environment, Transport and the Regions Ex p. Next
Generation Ltd see Next Generation Clubs Ltd *v.* Secretary of State for the
Environment, Transport and the Regions

R. *v.* Secretary of State for the Environment, Transport and the Regions Ex p. North
Yorkshire CC [1999] C.O.D. 83, QBD

R. *v.* Secretary of State for the Environment, Transport and the Regions Ex p. O'Byrne
see R. (on the application of O'Byrne) *v.* Secretary of State for the Environment,
Transport and the Regions

R. *v.* Secretary of State for the Environment, Transport and the Regions Ex p. O'Byrne
(Application for Joinder); *sub nom* R. *v.* Secretary of State for the Home
Department Ex p. O'Byrne [2000] C.P. Rep. 9; *Times,* November 12, 1999, QBD .   *Digested,* 99/**449**

R. *v.* Secretary of State for the Environment, Transport and the Regions Ex p. O'Keefe
see O'Keefe *v.* Secretary of State for the Environment, Transport and the
Regions

R. *v.* Secretary of State for the Environment, Transport and the Regions Ex p. Omega
Air Ltd [2000] 2 C.M.L.R. 167; [2000] Eu. L.R. 254, QBD . . . .   *Digested,* 00/**5145**

R. *v.* Secretary of State for the Environment, Transport and the Regions Ex p. Panton
(2000) 79 P. & C.R. 485, CA. . . . .   *Digested,* 00/**4522**:
Previous proceedings, 99/4219

R. *v.* Secretary of State for the Environment, Transport and the Regions Ex p. Parry
[1998] C.O.D. 17; [1998] Env. L.R. D5, QBD

R. *v.* Secretary of State for the Environment, Transport and the Regions Ex p. Plymouth
City Airport Ltd see R. (on the application of Plymouth City Airport Ltd) *v.*
Secretary of State for the Environment, Transport and the Regions

R. *v.* Secretary of State for the Environment, Transport and the Regions Ex p. Premiere
Environment Ltd [2000] Env. L.R. 724; [2000] E.H.L.R. 246; [2000] E.G.C.S.
12; *Times,* March 15, 2000, QBD. . . . .   *Digested,* 00/**2310**

R. *v.* Secretary of State for the Environment, Transport and the Regions Ex p.
Richmondshire DC see Richmondshire DC *v.* Secretary of State for the
Environment, Transport and the Regions

R. *v.* Secretary of State for the Environment, Transport and the Regions Ex p. Rochford
DC [2000] 3 All E.R. 1018; [2000] P.L.C.R. 449; [2001] J.P.L. 111 (Note);
(2000) 97(22) L.S.G. 48; *Independent,* June 26, 2000 (C.S), QBD . . . .   *Digested,* 00/**4483**

R. *v.* Secretary of State for the Environment, Transport and the Regions Ex p. Slot
[1998] 4 P.L.R. 1; [1998] J.P.L. 692; [1998] C.O.D. 118; [1997] N.P.C. 168;
Times, December 11, 1997, CA . . . .   *Digested,* 98/**2873**

R. *v.* Secretary of State for the Environment, Transport and the Regions Ex p. Smith
[1999] J.P.L. 371, QBD . . . .   *Digested,* 99/**4218**

R. *v.* Secretary of State for the Environment, Transport and the Regions Ex p. Spath
Holme Ltd see R. (on the application of Spath Holme Ltd) *v.* Secretary of State
for the Environment, Transport and the Regions

R. *v.* Secretary of State for the Environment, Transport and the Regions Ex p. Standley
(C293/97); R. *v.* Secretary of State for the Environment, Transport and the
Regions Ex p. Metson [1999] Q.B. 1279; [1999] 3 W.L.R. 744; [1999] All E.R.
(EC) 412; [1999] E.C.R. I-2603; [1999] 2 C.M.L.R. 902; [1999] Env. L.R. 801;
Times, May 10, 1999, ECJ (5th Chamber) . . . .   *Digested,* 99/**2188**:
Previous proceedings, 97/2342

R. v. Secretary of State for the Environment, Transport and the Regions Ex p. Stevens see Stevens v. Secretary of State for the Environment, Transport and the Regions

R. v. Secretary of State for the Environment, Transport and the Regions Ex p. Tesco Stores Ltd see R. (on the application of Tesco Stores Ltd) v. Secretary of State for the Environment, Transport and the Regions

R. v. Secretary of State for the Environment, Transport and the Regions Ex p. Thomas's London Day Schools (Transport) Ltd [2000] Ed. C.R. 283; *Independent*, January 17, 2000 (C.S.), QBD . . . . *Digested*, 00/**5239**

R. v. Secretary of State for the Environment, Transport and the Regions Ex p. Walters (1998) 30 H.L.R. 328; *Times*, September 2, 1997, CA; affirming [1997] N.P.C. 41, QBD . . . . *Digested*, 97/**2701**

R. v. Secretary of State for the Environment, Transport and the Regions Ex p. Watson [1999] Env. L.R. 310; [1998] E.G.C.S. 122; (1998) 95(30) L.S.G. 26; *Times*, August 31, 1998, CA; affirming [1999] E.H.L.R. 95, QBD . . . . *Digested*, 98/**186**

R. v. Secretary of State for the Environment, Transport and the Regions Ex p. Webster [1999] J.P.L. 1113, QBD . . . . *Digested*, 00/**4529**

R. v. Secretary of State for the Environment, Transport and the Regions Ex p. West Sussex CC (1999) 77 P. & C.R. 263; [1999] P.L.C.R. 163; (1998) 95(32) L.S.G. 31; [1998] N.P.C. 133, QBD . . . . *Digested*, 99/**4274**

R. v. Secretary of State for the Environment, Transport and the Regions Ex p. Wheeler (2001) 82 P. & C.R. 1; [2000] 3 P.L.R. 98; [2000] 3 E.G.L.R. 63; [2000] 37 E.G. 156; [2001] J.P.L. 432; (2000) 97(26) L.S.G. 39; (2000) 97(29) L.S.G. 45; *Times*, August 4, 2000, QBD . . . . *Digested*, 00/**4526**

R. v. Secretary of State for the Environment, Transport and the Regions Ex p. Whitbread Plc see R. v. Secretary of State for the Environment, Transport and the Regions Ex p. Kohlerdome Corp Ltd

R. v. Secretary of State for the Environment, Transport and the Regions ex. p Benham Crosswell see R. (on the application of Benham-Crosswell) v. Secretary of State for the Environment, Transport and the Regions

R. v. Secretary of State for the Environment, Transport and the Regions ex. p Benham-Crosswell see R. (on the application of Benham-Crosswell) v. Secretary of State for the Environment, Transport and the Regions

R. (on the application of Bancoult) v. Secretary of State for the Foreign and Commonwealth Office; *sub nom* R. v. Secretary of State for the Foreign and Commonwealth Office Ex p. Bancoult; R. (on the application of Bancoult) v. Secretary of State for Foreign and Commonwealth Affairs [2001] Q.B. 1067; [2001] 2 W.L.R. 1219; [2001] A.C.D. 18; (2000) 97(47) L.S.G. 39; *Times*, November 10, 2000, QBD (Admin Ct) . . . . *Digested*, 00/**96**

R. v. Secretary of State for the Foreign and Commonwealth Office Ex p. Bancoult see R. (on the application of Bancoult) v. Secretary of State for the Foreign and Commonwealth Office

R. (on the application of Aitseguer) v. Secretary of State for the Home Department (No.2) see R. (on the application of Adan (Lul Omar)) v. Secretary of State for the Home Department

R. (on the application of Al-Hasan) v. Secretary of State for the Home Department see R. (on the application of Carroll) v. Secretary of State for the Home Department

R. (on the application of Ali (Abid)) v. Secretary of State for the Home Department see R. (on the application of Javed) v. Secretary of State for the Home Department

R. (on the application of Ali (Zulfiqar)) v. Secretary of State for the Home Department see R. (on the application of Javed) v. Secretary of State for the Home Department

R. (on the application of Altun) v. Secretary of State for the Home Department [2001] EWHC Admin 296; [2001] Imm. A.R. 570, QBD (Admin Ct)

R. (on the application of Anderson) v. Secretary of State for the Home Department; *sub nom* R. v. Secretary of State for the Home Department Ex p. Anderson; R. v. Secretary of State for the Home Department Ex p. Taylor; R. (on the application of Taylor) v. Secretary of State for the Home Department [2001] EWCA Civ 1698; (2001) 98(47) L.S.G. 27; (2001) 145 S.J.L.B. 260; *Times*, November 16, 2001; *Independent*, November 20, 2001; *Daily Telegraph*, November 20, 2001, CA; affirming [2001] EWHC Admin 181; [2001] H.R.L.R. 33; [2001] A.C.D. 84; (2001) 98(16) L.S.G. 35; *Times*, February 27, 2001, QBD (Admin Ct) . . . . *Digested*, 01/**1411**

R. (on the application of Atputharajah) v. Secretary of State for the Home Department see R. (on the application of Atputharajah) v. Immigration Appeal Tribunal

R. (on the application of Balbo B&C Auto Transporti Internazionali) v. Secretary of State for the Home Department [2001] EWHC Admin 195; [2001] 1 W.L.R. 1556; [2001] 4 All E.R. 423; (2001) 98(19) L.S.G. 37; (2001) 145 S.J.L.B. 85; *Times*, March 22, 2001; *Independent*, May 7, 2001 (C.S), QBD (Admin Ct) . . . . *Digested*, 01/**3683**

R. (on the application of Barkoci) v. Secretary of State for the Home Department (C257/99); *sub nom* R. v. Secretary of State for the Home Department Ex p. Barkoci (C257/99) [2001] All E.R. (EC) 903; [2001] E.C.R. I-6557; [2001] 3 C.M.L.R. 48; *Times*, November 13, 2001, ECJ

R. (on the application of Boafo) *v.* Secretary of State for the Home Department; *sub nom* R. *v.* Secretary of State for the Home Department Ex p. Boafo; Boafo *v.* Secretary of State for the Home Department; 2001/0437, CA; reversing [2001] EWHC Admin 782; [2001] Imm. A.R. 361, QBD . . . .   *Digested*, 01/**3672**

R. (on the application of Bouheraoua) *v.* Secretary of State for the Home Department; *sub nom* R. *v.* Secretary of State for the Home Department Ex p. Bouheraoua; R. *v.* Secretary of State for the Home Department Ex p. Kerkeb; Secretary of State for the Home Department *v.* Bouheraoua; Secretary of State for the Home Department *v.* Kerkeb; R. (on the application of Kerkeb) *v.* Secretary of State for the Home Department [2001] EWCA Civ 747; [2001] Imm. A.R. 614, CA; affirming CO/878/1998, CO/2734/1998, QBD

R. (on the application of Bulbul) *v.* Secretary of State for the Home Department see Sepet *v.* Secretary of State for the Home Department

R. (on the application of Bulger) *v.* Secretary of State for the Home Department; *sub nom* R. *v.* Secretary of State for the Home Department Ex p. Bulger; R. (on the application of Bulger) *v.* Lord Chief Justice [2001] EWHC Admin 119; [2001] 3 All E.R. 449; *Times*, March 7, 2001; *Independent*, April 9, 2001 (C.S); *Daily Telegraph*, March 13, 2001, QBD (Admin Ct) . . . .   *Digested*, 01/**89**

R. (on the application of Burgess) *v.* Secretary of State for the Home Department, *Daily Telegraph*, December 5, 2000, QBD

R. (on the application of Carroll) *v.* Secretary of State for the Home Department; *sub nom* R. *v.* Secretary of State for the Home Department Ex p. Carroll; R. (on the application of Greenfield) *v.* Secretary of State for the Home Department (No.2); R. (on the application of Al-Hasan) *v.* Secretary of State for the Home Department [2001] EWCA Civ 1224; [2001] H.R.L.R. 58; *Times*, August 16, 2001, CA; affirming [2001] EWHC Admin 110; [2001] H.R.L.R. 34, QBD (Admin Ct) . . . .   *Digested*, 01/**4571**: *Previous proceedings*, 01/4572

R. (on the application of Daly) *v.* Secretary of State for the Home Department; *sub nom* R. *v.* Secretary of State for the Home Department Ex p. Daly [2001] UKHL 26; [2001] 2 A.C. 532; [2001] 2 W.L.R. 1622; [2001] 3 All E.R. 433; [2001] H.R.L.R. 49; [2001] U.K.H.R.R. 887; [2001] A.C.D. 79; (2001) 98(26) L.S.G. 43; (2001) 145 S.J.L.B. 156; *Times*, May 25, 2001; *Daily Telegraph*, May 29, 2001, HL; reversing [1999] C.O.D. 388, CA . . . .   *Digested*, 01/**4578**: *Considered*, 01/426, 01/3660, 01/4574

R. (on the application of Davies) *v.* Secretary of State for the Home Department; *sub nom* R. *v.* Secretary of State for the Home Department Ex p. Davies *Independent*, November 23, 2000; *Daily Telegraph*, November 28, 2000, CA; affirming CO 539/98, QBD . . . .   *Digested*, 00/**4327**

R. (on the application of Farrakhan) *v.* Secretary of State for the Home Department; *sub nom* Farrakhan *v.* Secretary of State for the Home Department; C/2001/2808, CA; reversing [2001] EWHC Admin 634; [2001] EWHC Admin 781; *Daily Telegraph*, October 9, 2001, QBD (Admin Ct)

R. (on the application of Gavira) *v.* Secretary of State for the Home Department; *sub nom* Gavira *v.* Secretary of State for the Home Department; R. (on the application of Gavira) *v.* Special Adjudicator; R. (on the application of Gaviria) *v.* Secretary of State for the Home Department [2001] EWHC Admin 250; [2001] I.N.L.R. 577; *Times*, May 15, 2001, QBD (Admin Ct) . . . .   *Digested*, 01/**3598**

R. (on the application of Gaviria) *v.* Secretary of State for the Home Department see R. (on the application of Gavira) *v.* Secretary of State for the Home Department

R. (on the application of Gloszczuk) *v.* Secretary of State for the Home Department (C63/99); *sub nom* R. *v.* Secretary of State for the Home Department Ex p. Gloszczuk (C63/99) [2001] E.C.R. I-6369; [2001] 3 C.M.L.R. 46; [2001] C.E.C. 358; *Times*, November 13, 2001, ECJ . . . .   *Digested*, 01/**3674**

R. (on the application of Greenfield) *v.* Secretary of State for the Home Department (No.1); *sub nom* Greenfield *v.* Secretary of State for the Home Department [2001] EWHC Admin 129; [2001] 1 W.L.R. 1731; [2001] H.R.L.R. 35; *Times*, March 6, 2001; *Independent*, April 2, 2001 (C.S), QBD (Admin Ct) . . . .   *Digested*, 01/**4572**: *Subsequent proceedings*, 01/4571

R. (on the application of Greenfield) *v.* Secretary of State for the Home Department (No.2) see R. (on the application of Carroll) *v.* Secretary of State for the Home Department

R. (on the application of Gunn) *v.* Secretary of State for the Home Department (Recovery of Costs); *sub nom* R. *v.* Secretary of State for the Home Department Ex p. Gunn; R. (on the application of Kelly) *v.* Secretary of State for the Home Department; R. (on the application of Khan (Zahid)) *v.* Secretary of State for the Home Department [2001] EWCA Civ 891; [2001] 1 W.L.R. 1634; [2001] 3 All E.R. 481; [2001] C.P. Rep. 107; [2001] 2 Costs L.R. 263; (2001) 98(27) L.S.G. 38; (2001) 151 N.L.J. 936; (2001) 145 S.J.L.B. 160; *Times*, June 20, 2001; *Independent*, June 19, 2001; *Daily Telegraph*, June 26, 2001, CA . . . .   *Digested*, 01/**491**

R. (on the application of Harris (Darrel)) *v.* Secretary of State for the Home Department [2001] EWHC Admin 225; [2001] I.N.L.R. 584, QBD (Admin Ct)

R. (on the application of Hatim) *v.* Secretary of State for the Home Department [2001] EWHC Admin 574; [2001] Imm. A.R. 688, QBD (Admin Ct)

R. (on the application of Hirst) *v.* Secretary of State for the Home Department (Category Status) see R. *v.* Secretary of State for the Home Department Ex p. Hirst

R. (on the application of Holub) *v.* Secretary of State for the Home Department; *sub nom* Holub *v.* Secretary of State for the Home Department; R. *v.* Secretary of State for the Home Department Ex p. Holub [2001] 1 W.L.R. 1359; [2001] H.R.L.R. 24; [2001] Imm. A.R. 282; [2001] I.N.L.R. 219; [2001] E.L.R. 401; [2001] A.C.D. 31; *Times,* February 13, 2001, CA; affirming CO/3309/98, QBD . .   *Digested,* 01/**3614**

R. (on the application of Ibrahim (Ayman)) *v.* Secretary of State for the Home Department; *sub nom* Ibrahim *v.* Secretary of State for the Home Department [2001] EWCA Civ 519; [2001] Imm. A.R. 430; [2001] A.C.D. 87, CA

R. (on the application of International Transport Roth GmbH) *v.* Secretary of State for the Home Department; *sub nom* International Transport Roth GmbH *v.* Secretary of State for the Home Department; Secretary of State for the Home Department *v.* International Transport Roth GmbH; 2002/0014, CA; reversing in part *Times,* December 11, 2001; *Daily Telegraph,* December 13, 2001, QBD (Admin Ct)

R. (on the application of Isiko) *v.* Secretary of State for the Home Department; *sub nom* Secretary of State for the Home Department *v.* Isiko; R. *v.* Secretary of State for the Home Department Ex p. Isiko [2001] 1 F.L.R. 930; [2001] 1 F.C.R. 633; [2001] H.R.L.R. 15; [2001] U.K.H.R.R. 385; [2001] Imm. A.R. 291; [2001] I.N.L.R. 175; [2001] A.C.D. 39; [2001] Fam. Law 419; *Times,* February 20, 2001, CA; reversing CO/4571/99, CO/0282/00, QBD . . . .   *Digested,* 01/**3646**: *Applied,* 01/**4433**, 01/**5019**

R. (on the application of Javed) *v.* Secretary of State for the Home Department; *sub nom* R. *v.* Secretary of State for the Home Department Ex p. Ali; R. *v.* Secretary of State for the Home Department Ex p. Javed; Secretary of State for the Home Department *v.* Javed; R. (on the application of Ali (Zulfiqar)) *v.* Secretary of State for the Home Department; R. (on the application of Ali (Abid)) *v.* Secretary of State for the Home Department [2001] EWCA Civ 789; [2001] 3 W.L.R. 323; [2001] Imm. A.R. 529; [2001] I.N.L.R. 645; (2001) 98(26) L.S.G. 44; (2001) 145 S.J.L.B. 149; *Times,* May 24, 2001; *Independent,* July 16, 2001 (C.S), CA; affirming [2001] EWHC Admin 7; *Times,* February 9, 2001; *Daily Telegraph,* February 7, 2001, QBD (Admin Ct) . . . .   *Digested,* 01/**3651**

R. (on the application of Jordan) *v.* Secretary of State for the Home Department; *sub nom* R. *v.* Secretary of State for the Home Department Ex p. Jordan [2001] A.C.D. 46, QBD

R. (on the application of Kaur) *v.* Secretary of State for the Home Department (C192/99) see R. *v.* Secretary of State for the Home Department Ex p. Kaur (Manjit) (C192/99)

R. (on the application of Kelly) *v.* Secretary of State for the Home Department see R. (on the application of Gunn) *v.* Secretary of State for the Home Department (Recovery of Costs)

R. (on the application of Kerkeb) *v.* Secretary of State for the Home Department see R. (on the application of Bouheraoua) *v.* Secretary of State for the Home Department

R. (on the application of Khan (Zahid)) *v.* Secretary of State for the Home Department see R. (on the application of Gunn) *v.* Secretary of State for the Home Department (Recovery of Costs)

R. (on the application of Kolcak) *v.* Secretary of State for the Home Department see R. (on the application of Kolcak) *v.* Immigration Appellate Authority

R. (on the application of Kondova) *v.* Secretary of State for the Home Department (C235/99); *sub nom* R. *v.* Secretary of State for the Home Department Ex p. Kondova (C235/99) [2001] E.C.R. I-6427; [2001] 3 C.M.L.R. 47; *Times,* November 13, 2001, ECJ

R. (on the application of Lichniak) *v.* Secretary of State for the Home Department; *sub nom* R. *v.* Lichniak; R. *v.* Pyrah; R. (on the application of Pyrah) *v.* Secretary of State for the Home Department [2001] EWHC Admin 294; [2001] 3 W.L.R. 933; [2001] 4 All E.R. 934; [2001] H.R.L.R. 43; (2001) 98(24) L.S.G. 43; (2001) 145 S.J.L.B. 127; *Times,* May 16, 2001; *Independent,* June 11, 2001 (C.S); *Daily Telegraph,* May 15, 2001, CA (Crim Div) . . . .   *Digested,* 01/**1410**

R. (on the application of Maged) *v.* Secretary of State for the Home Department see R. (on the application of Saadi) *v.* Secretary of State for the Home Department

R. (on the application of Mahmood (Amjad)) *v.* Secretary of State for the Home Department; *sub nom* R. *v.* Secretary of State for the Home Department Ex p. Mahmood (Amjad); Mahmood (Amjad) *v.* Secretary of State for the Home Department [2001] 1 W.L.R. 840; [2001] 1 F.L.R. 756; [2001] 2 F.C.R. 63; [2001] H.R.L.R. 14; [2001] U.K.H.R.R. 307; [2001] Imm. A.R. 229; [2001] I.N.L.R. 1; (2001) 3 L.G.L.R. 23; [2001] A.C.D. 38; [2001] Fam. Law 257; *Times,* January 9, 2001; *Independent,* January 24, 2001, CA; affirming CO/254/98, QBD . . . .   *Digested,* 01/**3684**: *Applied,* 01/**3646**: *Considered,* 01/**3660**, 01/**4578**

R. (on the application of Martinez) *v.* Secretary of State for the Home Department see R. (on the application of Pearson) *v.* Secretary of State for the Home Department

R. (on the application of McCollum) *v.* Secretary of State for the Home Department; *sub nom* R. (on the application of McCollum) *v.* Home Secretary [2001] EWHC Admin 40; [2001] A.C.D. 58; *Independent*, March 12, 2001 (C.S); *Daily Telegraph*, February 20, 2001, QBD (Admin Ct)

R. (on the application of Mellor) *v.* Secretary of State for the Home Department; *sub nom* R. *v.* Secretary of State for the Home Department Ex p. Mellor [2001] EWCA Civ 472; [2001] 3 W.L.R. 533; [2001] 2 F.L.R. 1158; [2001] 2 F.C.R. 153; [2001] H.R.L.R. 38; (2001) 59 B.M.L.R. 1; [2001] Fam. Law 736; (2001) 98(22) L.S.G. 35; (2001) 145 S.J.L.B. 117; *Times*, May 1, 2001; *Independent*, April 6, 2001, CA; affirming [2000] 2 F.L.R. 951; [2000] 3 F.C.R. 148; [2000] H.R.L.R. 846; [2000] C.O.D. 497; [2000] Fam. Law 881; *Times*, September 5, 2000, QBD . . . . *Digested*, 01/**4579**:
　　　　　　　　　　　　　　　　　　　　　　　Considered, 01/1520, 01/4575

R. (on the application of Milisavljevic) *v.* Secretary of State for the Home Department see R. (on the application of Milisavljevic) *v.* Immigration Appeal Tribunal

R. (on the application of Mohammed (Rizgan)) *v.* Secretary of State for the Home Department see R. (on the application of Saadi) *v.* Secretary of State for the Home Department

R. (on the application of Montana) *v.* Secretary of State for the Home Department; *sub nom* R. *v.* Secretary of State for the Home Department Ex p. Montana; Montana *v.* Secretary of State for the Home Department [2001] 1 W.L.R. 552; [2001] 1 F.L.R. 449; [2001] 1 F.C.R. 358; [2001] H.R.L.R. 8; [2001] Imm. A.R. 381; [2001] I.N.L.R. 148; [2001] Fam. Law 94; (2001) 98(2) L.S.G. 41; *Times*, December 5, 2000; *Independent*, November 29, 2000, CA; affirming CO/1363/98, QBD . . . . *Digested*, 01/**2582**

R. (on the application of Noorkoiv) *v.* Secretary of State for the Home Department (No.2) C/01/1140, CA; reversing in part [2001] EWHC Admin 345; *Independent*, July 2, 2001 (C.S), QBD (Admin Ct)

R. (on the application of Osman (Dilshad)) *v.* Secretary of State for the Home Department see R. (on the application of Saadi) *v.* Secretary of State for the Home Department

R. (on the application of P) *v.* Secretary of State for the Home Department; *sub nom* R. *v.* Secretary of State for the Home Department Ex p. Q; R. (on the application of Q) *v.* Secretary of State for the Home Department [2001] EWCA Civ 1151; [2001] 1 W.L.R. 2002; [2001] 2 F.L.R. 1122; [2001] 3 F.C.R. 416; [2001] U.K.H.R.R. 1035; [2001] Fam. Law 803; (2001) 98(34) L.S.G. 41; (2001) 145 S.J.L.B. 203; *Times*, August 1, 2001; *Independent*, October 11, 2001; *Daily Telegraph*, July 31, 2001, CA; reversing in part [2001] EWHC Admin 357; [2001] 2 F.L.R. 383; [2001] Fam. Law 657; (2001) 98(25) L.S.G. 47; (2001) 145 S.J.L.B. 148; *Times*, June 1, 2001; *Independent*, July 9, 2001 (C.S); *Daily Telegraph*, May 29, 2001, QBD (Admin Ct) . . . . *Digested*, 01/**4575**

R. (on the application of Paulo) *v.* Secretary of State for the Home Department [2001] EWHC Admin 480; [2001] Imm. A.R. 645, QBD (Admin Ct)

R. (on the application of Pearson) *v.* Secretary of State for the Home Department; R. (on the application of Martinez) *v.* Secretary of State for the Home Department; Hirst *v.* Attorney General [2001] EWHC Admin 239; [2001] H.R.L.R. 39; (2001) 3 L.G.L.R. 48; (2001) 98(23) L.S.G. 36; *Times*, April 17, 2001; *Independent*, May 21, 2001 (C.S), QBD (Admin Ct) . . . . *Digested*, 01/**4582**

R. (on the application of Pyrah) *v.* Secretary of State for the Home Department see R. (on the application of Lichniak) *v.* Secretary of State for the Home Department

R. (on the application of Q) *v.* Secretary of State for the Home Department see R. (on the application of P) *v.* Secretary of State for the Home Department

R. (on the application of Saadi) *v.* Secretary of State for the Home Department; R. (on the application of Maged) *v.* Secretary of State for the Home Department; R. (on the application of Osman (Dilshad)) *v.* Secretary of State for the Home Department; R. (on the application of Mohammed (Rizgan)) *v.* Secretary of State for the Home Department [2001] EWCA Civ 1512; [2001] 4 All E.R. 961; (2001) 98(44) L.S.G. 35; (2001) 151 N.L.J. 1573; (2001) 145 S.J.L.B. 246; *Times*, October 22, 2001; *Independent*, October 23, 2001; *Daily Telegraph*, October 23, 2001, CA; reversing [2001] EWHC Admin 670; (2001) 151 N.L.J. 1407; *Daily Telegraph*, September 11, 2001, QBD (Admin Ct) . . . . *Digested*, 01/**3620**

R. (on the application of Samaroo) *v.* Secretary of State for the Home Department; *sub nom* R. *v.* Secretary of State for the Home Department Ex p. Samaroo; Samaroo *v.* Secretary of State for the Home Department; Sezek *v.* Secretary of State for the Home Department [2001] EWCA Civ 1139; [2001] U.K.H.R.R. 1150; (2001) 98(34) L.S.G. 40; (2001) 145 S.J.L.B. 208; *Times*, September 18, 2001, CA; affirming [2001] Imm. A.R. 324; *Daily Telegraph*, January 23, 2001, QBD (Admin Ct) . . . . *Digested*, 01/**3660**

R. (on the application of Septet) *v.* Secretary of State for the Home Department see Sepet *v.* Secretary of State for the Home Department

R. (on the application of Sezek) *v.* Secretary of State for the Home Department; *sub nom* R. *v.* Secretary of State for the Home Department Ex p. Sezek; CO/283/2000, QBD (Admin Ct) . . . . *Subsequent proceedings*, 01/3660

R. (on the application of Sezek) v. Secretary of State for the Home Department (Bail Application); *sub nom* Sezek v. Secretary of State for the Home Department (Bail Application) [2001] EWCA Civ 795; [2001] Imm. A.R. 657; [2001] I.N.L.R. 675; (2001) 98(31) L.S.G. 36; *Times*, June 20, 2001, CA . . . . *Digested*, 01/**3658**:
Subsequent proceedings, 01/3660

R. (on the application of Shah (Ahmed)) v. Secretary of State for the Home Department [2001] EWHC Admin 197; [2001] Imm. A.R. 419, QBD (Admin Ct) . . . . *Digested*, 01/**3652**

R. (on the application of Sheikh) v. Secretary of State for the Home Department; *sub nom* R. v. Secretary of State for the Home Department Ex p. Sheik; Sheikh v. Secretary of State for the Home Department; Sheik v. Secretary of State for the Home Department; R. v. Secretary of State for the Home Department Ex p. Sheikh [2001] Imm. A.R. 219; [2001] I.N.L.R. 98; [2001] A.C.D. 33; (2001) 98(6) L.S.G. 46; *Times*, December 22, 2000; *Independent*, December 12, 2000, CA; affirming *Times*, September 7, 2000, QBD . . . . *Digested*, 01/**3682**

R. (on the application of Sivakumar) v. Secretary of State for the Home Department see R. (on the application of Sivakumar) v. Immigration Appeal Tribunal

R. (on the application of Tawfick) v. Secretary of State for the Home Department see R. v. Secretary of State for the Home Department Ex p. Tawfick

R. (on the application of Taylor) v. Secretary of State for the Home Department see R. (on the application of Anderson) v. Secretary of State for the Home Department

R. (on the application of Thangarasa) v. Secretary of State for the Home Department (No.1) [2001] EWHC Admin 420, QBD (Admin Ct) . . . . *Subsequent proceed-ings*, 01/3648

R. (on the application of Thangarasa) v. Secretary of State for the Home Department (No.2) see R. (on the application of Yogathas) v. Secretary of State for the Home Department

R. (on the application of Ullah (Azad)) v. Secretary of State for the Home Department; *sub nom* R. v. Secretary of State for the Home Department Ex p. Ullah (Azad); Secretary of State for the Home Department v. Ullah (Azad) [2001] EWCA Civ 659; [2001] 3 W.L.R. 1508; [2001] Imm. A.R. 439; [2001] I.N.L.R. 542; *Times*, June 27, 2001; *Independent*, June 25, 2001 (C.S), CA; reversing [2001] Imm. A.R. 439; [2001] I.N.L.R. 74; *Times*, October 17, 2000, QBD . . . . *Digested*, 01/**3657**

R. (on the application of Westminster City Council) v. Secretary of State for the Home Department see R. (on the application of Westminster City Council) v. National Asylum Support Services

R. (on the application of Wright) v. Secretary of State for the Home Department [2001] EWHC Admin 520; [2001] U.K.H.R.R. 1399; [2001] Lloyd's Rep. Med. 478; (2001) 62 B.M.L.R. 16; [2001] A.C.D. 94; *Daily Telegraph*, June 26, 2001, QBD (Admin Ct)

R. (on the application of X) v. Secretary of State for the Home Department; *sub nom* R. v. Immigration Officer Ex p. X; X v. Secretary of State for the Home Department; R. v. Secretary of State for the Home Department Ex p. X [2001] 1 W.L.R. 740; [2001] I.N.L.R. 205; (2001) 98(8) L.S.G. 44; *Times*, January 9, 2001; *Independent*, December 14, 2000, CA; affirming (2000) 56 B.M.L.R. 180; *Times*, June 14, 2000, QBD . . . . *Digested*, 01/**3659**

R. (on the application of Yogathas) v. Secretary of State for the Home Department; R. (on the application of Thangarasa) v. Secretary of State for the Home Department (No.2) [2001] EWCA Civ 1611; *Times*, November 15, 2001, CA; affirming [2001] EWHC Admin 377; *Times*, July 25, 2001, QBD (Admin Ct) . . . . *Digested*, 01/**3648**

R. (on the application of Zeqiri) v. Secretary of State for the Home Department; *sub nom* R. v. Secretary of State for the Home Department Ex p. Zeqiri; TNS; HL; reversing [2001] EWCA Civ 342; *Times*, March 16, 2001; *Independent*, March 23, 2001, CA; reversing CO/4816/1998, QBD (Admin Ct) . . . . *Digested*, 01/**3649**:
Followed, 01/3652

R. v. Secretary of State for the Home Department and Immigration Officer Ex p. S [1998] Imm. A.R. 416, QBD . . . . *Digested*, 98/**3204**

R. v. Secretary of State for the Home Department Ex p. Kondova (C235/99) see R. (on the application of Kondova) v. Secretary of State for the Home Department (C235/99)

R. v. Secretary of State for the Home Department Ex p. A (A Juvenile); *sub nom* R. v. Home Office Ex p. A (A Juvenile) [2000] 2 A.C. 276; [2000] 2 W.L.R. 293; [2000] 1 All E.R. 651; [2000] 2 Cr. App. R. (S.) 263; (2000) 164 J.P. 141; [2000] Crim. L.R. 321; [2000] C.O.D. 209; (2000) 97(6) L.S.G. 33; (2000) 144 S.J.L.B. 82; *Times*, January 28, 2000, HL; reversing [2000] 1 Cr. App. R. (S.) 336; (2000) 164 J.P. 42; [2000] Crim. L.R. 65; *Times*, September 22, 1999, QBD . . . . *Digested*, 00/**1345**

R. v. Secretary of State for the Home Department Ex p. Adan (Hassan Hussein) see Adan (Hassan Hussein) v. Secretary of State for the Home Department

R. (on the application of Adan (Lul Omar)) *v.* Secretary of State for the Home Department; *sub nom* R. *v.* Secretary of State for the Home Department Ex p. Aitseguer (No.2); R. *v.* Secretary of State for the Home Department Ex p. Adan (Lul Omar); Secretary of State for the Home Department *v.* Aitseguer; Secretary of State for the Home Department *v.* Adan (Lul Omar); R. *v.* Secretary of Satte for the Home Department Ex p. Aitsegeur; R. *v.* Secretary of State for the Home Department Ex p. Subaskaran; R. (on the application of Aitseguer) *v.* Secretary of State for the Home Department (No.2) [2001] 2 A.C. 477; [2001] 2 W.L.R. 143; [2001] 1 All E.R. 593; [2001] Imm. A.R. 253; [2001] I.N.L.R. 44; (2001) 98(4) L.S.G. 49; (2001) 145 S.J.L.B. 15; *Times*, December 20, 2000; *Independent*, January 16, 2001, HL; affirming [1999] 3 W.L.R. 1274; [1999] 4 All E.R. 774; [1999] Imm. A.R. 521; [1999] I.N.L.R. 362; [1999] C.O.D. 480; (1999) 96(33) L.S.G. 30; *Times*, July 28, 1999 ; *Independent*, July 28, 1999, CA; reversing [1999] Imm. A.R. 114; [1999] I.N.L.R. 84; [1999] C.O.D. 156; *Times*, December 18, 1998, QBD . . . . *Digested*, 01/**3639**:
Cited, 00/3314: *Considered*, 01/3647, 01/3648: *Distinguished*, 99/3183, 01/3635: *Previous proceedings*, 99/3183

R. *v.* Secretary of State for the Home Department Ex p. Afunyah (Mary) see Afunyah (Mary) *v.* Secretary of State for the Home Department

R. *v.* Secretary of State for the Home Department Ex p. Agkurt, *Times*, March 5, 1998; *Independent*, March 2, 1998 (C.S.), QBD . . . . *Digested*, 98/**2355**

R. *v.* Secretary of State for the Home Department Ex p. Ahmad (Mariam) see Ahmad (Mariam) *v.* Secretary of State for the Home Department

R. *v.* Secretary of State for the Home Department Ex p. Ahmed (Mohammed Hussain); R. *v.* Secretary of State for the Home Department Ex p. Patel (Idris Ibrahim) [1999] Imm. A.R. 22; [1998] I.N.L.R. 570; [1999] C.O.D. 69; *Times*, October 15, 1998, CA; affirming [1998] Imm. A.R. 375; [1998] I.N.L.R. 546, QBD . . . . *Digested*, 98/**3238**:
Considered, 00/3301

R. *v.* Secretary of State for the Home Department Ex p. Ahmed (Naseer) see Ahmed (Naseer) *v.* Secretary of State for the Home Department

R. *v.* Secretary of State for the Home Department Ex p. Ahmed (Parveen) see Ahmed (Naseer) *v.* Secretary of State for the Home Department

R. *v.* Secretary of State for the Home Department Ex p. Aitsegeur (No.1); *sub nom* R. *v.* Secretary of State for the Home Department Ex p. Aitseguer [1999] I.N.L.R. 176, QBD . . . . *Digested*, 99/**3183**:
Subsequent proceedings, 99/3185

R. *v.* Secretary of State for the Home Department Ex p. Aitsegeur see R. *v.* Secretary of State for the Home Department Ex p. Aitsegeur (No.1)

R. *v.* Secretary of State for the Home Department Ex p. Aitseguer (No.2) see R. (on the application of Adan (Lul Omar)) *v.* Secretary of State for the Home Department

R. *v.* Secretary of State for the Home Department Ex p. Akdemir [1997] Imm. A.R. 498, QBD . . . . *Digested*, 98/**3229**

R. *v.* Secretary of State for the Home Department Ex p. Akhbari [2000] Imm. A.R. 165, QBD . . . . *Digested*, 00/**3301**

R. (on the application of Akhtar (T'Herah)) *v.* Secretary of State for the Home Department; *sub nom* R. *v.* Secretary of State for the Home Department Ex p. Akhtar (T'Herah) [2001] EWHC Admin 38; [2001] A.C.D. 56; *Times*, February 23, 2001, QBD . . . . *Digested*, 01/**1164**

R. *v.* Secretary of State for the Home Department Ex p. Al-Fayed (No.1) [1998] 1 W.L.R. 763; [1997] 1 All E.R. 228; [1997] I.N.L.R. 137; [1997] C.O.D. 205; *Times*, November 18, 1996; *Independent*, November 19, 1996, CA; reversing [1996] C.O.D. 302; *Times*, March 13, 1996, QBD . . . . *Digested*, 96/**3157**

R. *v.* Secretary of State for the Home Department Ex p. Al-Fayed (No.2); *sub nom* Al-Fayed *v.* Secretary of State for the Home Department [2001] Imm. A.R. 134; *Times*, September 7, 2000; *Independent*, October 13, 2000, CA; affirming *Times*, November 16, 1999, QBD. . . . . *Digested*, 00/**3367**

R. *v.* Secretary of State for the Home Department Ex p. Alabi [1997] I.N.L.R. 124; [1998] C.O.D. 103, CA. . . . . *Digested*, 98/**102**

R. *v.* Secretary of State for the Home Department Ex p. Alexander see R. *v.* Secretary of State for the Home Department Ex p. Oladehinde

R. *v.* Secretary of State for the Home Department Ex p. Alghali (Dhanniah Hahiru) see R. *v.* Immigration Appeal Tribunal Ex p. Alghali (Dhanniah Hahiru)

R. *v.* Secretary of State for the Home Department Ex p. Ali see R. (on the application of Javed) *v.* Secretary of State for the Home Department

R. *v.* Secretary of State for the Home Department Ex p. Ali [2000] Imm. A.R. 134; [2000] I.N.L.R. 89, QBD . . . . *Digested*, 00/**3363**

R. *v.* Secretary of State for the Home Department Ex p. Ali (Ifzal); *sub nom* Ali (Ifzal) *v.* Secretary of State for the Home Department [1994] Imm. A.R. 69; [1994] C.O.D. 316, CA . . . . *Digested*, 94/**2494**:
Applied, 01/3681

R. *v.* Secretary of State for the Home Department Ex p. Ali Akbar CO/1707/96, QBD . . . *Digested*, 96/**1602**:
Approved, 98/2356

R. v. Secretary of State for the Home Department Ex p. Allen (2000) 97(14) L.S.G. 43; (2000) 144 S.J.L.B. 152; *Times*, March 21, 2000; *Independent*, May 8, 2000 (C.S.), CA; reversing [2000] C.O.D. 179; *Independent*, January 31, 2000 (C.S.), QBD . . . . *Digested*, 00/**4326**:
Cited, 00/**4329**: *Distinguished*, 00/30

R. v. Secretary of State for the Home Department Ex p. Amin (Mohammed Imran) [2001] A.C.D. 11, QBD

R. v. Secretary of State for the Home Department Ex p. Amnesty International (No.1), *Times*, December 11, 1998, QBD . . . . *Digested*, 99/**2293**

R. v. Secretary of State for the Home Department Ex p. Anderson see R. (on the application of Anderson) v. Secretary of State for the Home Department

R. v. Secretary of State for the Home Department Ex p. Arthur H Cox & Co Ltd [1999] Eu. L.R. 677; (1999) 46 B.M.L.R. 144, QBD . . . . *Digested*, 99/**3642**

R. v. Secretary of State for the Home Department Ex p. Asif (Islam), *Times*, March 14, 2000, QBD . . . . *Digested*, 00/**3289**

R. v. Secretary of State for the Home Department Ex p. Asif Javed CO/2582/99, QBD . *Considered*, 00/3283

R. v. Secretary of State for the Home Department Ex p. B (Juvenile) see R. v. Secretary of State for the Home Department Ex p. J (A Juvenile)

R. v. Secretary of State for the Home Department Ex p. Bajraktari see R. v. Secretary of State for the Home Department Ex p. Jammeh

R. v. Secretary of State for the Home Department Ex p. Bani; *sub nom* R. v. Secretary of State for the Home Department Ex p. Hakimi [2000] Imm. A.R. 73, QBD . . . . *Digested*, 00/**3329**

R. v. Secretary of State for the Home Department Ex p. Barkoci (C257/99) see R. (on the application of Barkoci) v. Secretary of State for the Home Department (C257/99)

R. v. Secretary of State for the Home Department Ex p. Barrow (Buba) see Ahmed (Naseer) v. Secretary of State for the Home Department

R. v. Secretary of State for the Home Department Ex p. Beecham [1996] Imm. A.R. 87, QBD . . . . *Digested*, 96/**3276**:
Not applied, 01/591

R. v. Secretary of State for the Home Department Ex p. Befekadu [1999] Imm. A.R. 467, QBD . . . . *Digested*, 00/**3306**

R. v. Secretary of State for the Home Department Ex p. Begum (Lailun Nahar) see R. v. Secretary of State for the Home Department Ex p. Phansopkar

R. v. Secretary of State for the Home Department Ex p. Behluli; *sub nom* Behluli v. Secretary of State for the Home Department [1998] Imm. A.R. 407; [1998] I.N.L.R. 594; [1998] C.O.D. 328, CA . . . . *Digested*, 98/**3203**

R. v. Secretary of State for the Home Department Ex p. Bell [2000] Imm. A.R. 396, QBD . . . . *Digested*, 00/**3296**

R. v. Secretary of State for the Home Department Ex p. Bellache see R. v. Immigration Appeal Tribunal Ex p. Bellache (No.2)

R. v. Secretary of State for the Home Department Ex p. Berhe see Berhe v. Secretary of State for the Home Department

R. v. Secretary of State for the Home Department Ex p. Bindel [2001] Imm. A.R. 1, QBD . . . . *Digested*, 01/**3668**

R. v. Secretary of State for the Home Department Ex p. Boafo see R. (on the application of Boafo) v. Secretary of State for the Home Department

R. v. Secretary of State for the Home Department Ex p. Bostanci [1999] Imm. A.R. 411; (1999) 96(18) L.S.G. 34; *Times*, April 13, 1999, QBD . . . . *Digested*, 99/**3211**

R. v. Secretary of State for the Home Department Ex p. Bouheraoua see R. (on the application of Bouheraoua) v. Secretary of State for the Home Department

R. v. Secretary of State for the Home Department Ex p. Boybeyi [1997] Imm. A.R. 491; [1997] I.N.L.R. 130; [1997] C.O.D. 455; (1997) 94(23) L.S.G. 27; (1997) 141 S.J.L.B. 130; *Times*, June 5, 1997, CA; affirming CO/1334/96, QBD . . . . *Digested*, 97/**2869**:
Considered, 98/3196: *Followed*, 98/3190

R. v. Secretary of State for the Home Department Ex p. Briggs see R. v. Secretary of State for the Home Department Ex p. Hargreaves

R. v. Secretary of State for the Home Department Ex p. Brind [1991] 1 A.C. 696; [1991] 2 W.L.R. 588; [1991] 1 All E.R. 720; (1991) 3 Admin. L.R. 486; (1991) 141 N.L.J. 199; (1991) 135 S.J. 250; *Times*, February 8, 1991; *Independent*, February 8, 1991; *Guardian*, February 8, 1991, HL; affirming [1990] 2 W.L.R. 787; [1990] 1 All E.R. 469; [1990] C.O.D. 190; (1989) 139 N.L.J. 1751; *Times*, December 7, 1989; *Independent*, December 7, 1989; *Guardian*, December 7, 1989, CA; affirming (1989) 2 Admin. L.R. 169; [1990] C.O.D. 49; *Times*, May 30, 1989; *Independent*, June 2, 1989; *Guardian*, May 27, 1989, QBD . . . . *Digested*, 91/**71**:
Applied, 90/3072, 91/816, 92/2083, 92/2791, 93/2208, 93/3778, 94/7, 94/2504: *Considered*, 92/3, 92/4455, 93/2556, 93/2567, 93/3936, 94/55, 94/4462, 95/67, 95/3098, 00/5471: *Distinguished*, 92/2872: *Followed*, 96/3256, 96/4740, 97/2931, 98/3203, 98/3216, 01/5878: *Not followed*, 93/2174, 94/2468, 95/2713: *Referred to*, 98/5998

R. v. Secretary of State for the Home Department Ex p. Bugdaycay see Bugdaycay v. Secretary of State for the Home Department

R. v. Secretary of State for the Home Department Ex p. Bulger see R. (on the application of Bulger) v. Secretary of State for the Home Department

R. v. Secretary of State for the Home Department Ex p. Butt [1999] Imm. A.R. 341,
QBD . . . . *Digested,* 00/**3276**
R. v. Secretary of State for the Home Department Ex p. Butt (Nasir) see R. v.
Secretary of State for the Home Department Ex p. Swati
R. v. Secretary of State for the Home Department Ex p. C, *Independent,* February 22,
1999 (C.S.), QBD
R. v. Secretary of State for the Home Department Ex p. Cakabay (No.1) [1998] Imm.
A.R. 177, QBD . . . . *Digested,* 98/**3199**:
Subsequent proceedings, 98/3196
R. v. Secretary of State for the Home Department Ex p. Cakabay (No.2) see R. v.
Special Adjudicator Ex p. Secretary of State for the Home Department
R. v. Secretary of State for the Home Department Ex p. Canbolat; *sub nom* Canbolat v.
Secretary of State for the Home Department [1997] 1 W.L.R. 1569; [1998] 1
All E.R. 161; [1997] Imm. A.R. 442; [1997] I.N.L.R. 198; *Times,* May 9, 1997;
Independent, May 8, 1997, CA; affirming [1997] Imm. A.R. 281; *Times,* February
24, 1997, QBD . . . . *Digested,* 97/**2873**:
Applied, 00/3275: *Considered,* 98/3205, 99/3181, 99/3183:
Followed, 98/3208, 99/3186
R. v. Secretary of State for the Home Department Ex p. Capti (Mehmet) see R. v.
Secretary of State for the Home Department Ex p. Capti-Mehmet
R. v. Secretary of State for the Home Department Ex p. Capti-Mehmet; *sub nom* R. v.
Secretary of State for the Home Department Ex p. Capti (Mehmet) [1997]
C.O.D. 61, QBD . . . . *Distinguished,* 00/3361
R. v. Secretary of State for the Home Department Ex p. Cardoso [2000] Imm. A.R. 1,
QBD . . . . *Digested,* 00/**3370**
R. v. Secretary of State for the Home Department Ex p. Carroll see R. (on the
application of Carroll) v. Secretary of State for the Home Department
R. v. Secretary of State for the Home Department Ex p. Chahal (No.4) [2000]
H.R.L.R. 261; [2000] U.K.H.R.R. 215; *Times,* November 10, 1999, CA. . . . . . . *Digested,* 99/**3089**
R. v. Secretary of State for the Home Department Ex p. Chaumun [1999] I.N.L.R. 479,
QBD . . . . *Digested,* 00/**3288**
R. v. Secretary of State for the Home Department Ex p. Cherife [1999] Imm. A.R. 317,
QBD
R. v. Secretary of State for the Home Department Ex p. Chew see R. v. Secretary of
State for the Home Department Ex p. Popatia
R. v. Secretary of State for the Home Department Ex p. Chinoy (Nazir) (1992) 4
Admin. L.R. 457; [1991] C.O.D. 381; *Times,* April 16, 1991; *Independent,* April 22,
1991 (C.S.), QBD . . . . *Digested,* 92/**2083**:
Applied, 97/68, 00/5400
R. v. Secretary of State for the Home Department Ex p. Chiper see R. v. Secretary of
State for the Home Department Ex p. Stefan
R. v. Secretary of State for the Home Department Ex p. Chowdry (Nargis) [1998]
Imm. A.R. 241; [1998] I.N.L.R. 338; *Times,* March 3, 1998; *Independent,* March
9, 1998 (C.S.), CA; reversing CO/4078/97, QBD . . . . *Digested,* 98/**3186**
R. v. Secretary of State for the Home Department Ex p. Coulibuly [1999] Imm. A.R.
176, QBD . . . . *Digested,* 99/**3153**
R. v. Secretary of State for the Home Department Ex p. Cummings; *sub nom*
Cummings, Re [2001] EWCA Civ 45; [2001] 1 W.L.R. 822; (2001) 145 S.J.L.B.
27; *Times,* February 27, 2001; *Independent,* March 5, 2001 (C.S), CA . . . . *Digested,* 01/**4570**
R. v. Secretary of State for the Home Department Ex p. Dahmas, *Independent,*
January 24, 2000 (C.S.), CA
R. v. Secretary of State for the Home Department Ex p. Dahmas (Permission to Move
for Judicial Review) [2000] Imm. A.R. 151, QBD
R. v. Secretary of State for the Home Department Ex p. Daly see R. (on the application
of Daly) v. Secretary of State for the Home Department
R. v. Secretary of State for the Home Department Ex p. Danaei; *sub nom* R. v.
Secretary of State for the Home Department Ex p. Danaie [1998] Imm. A.R. 84;
[1998] I.N.L.R. 124; (1997) 94(47) L.S.G. 31; *Times,* January 3, 1998, CA;
affirming [1997] Imm. A.R. 366; *Times,* March 28, 1997, QBD . . . . *Digested,* 98/**3230**
R. v. Secretary of State for the Home Department Ex p. Danaie see R. v. Secretary of
State for the Home Department Ex p. Danaei
R. v. Secretary of State for the Home Department Ex p. Davies see R. (on the
application of Davies) v. Secretary of State for the Home Department
R. v. Secretary of State for the Home Department Ex p. Demiraj; R. v. Secretary of
State for the Home Department Ex p. Ethemi [1998] Imm. A.R. 147; [1998]
I.N.L.R. 451; *Times,* March 26, 1998, QBD . . . . *Digested,* 98/**3206**:
Followed, 98/3208, 99/3186
R. v. Secretary of State for the Home Department Ex p. Dinc [1999] Imm. A.R. 380;
[1999] I.N.L.R. 256; *Times,* March 29, 1999, CA; reversing [1998] I.N.L.R. 462;
[1998] C.O.D. 326; *Times,* April 23, 1998, QBD . . . . *Digested,* 99/**3194**
R. v. Secretary of State for the Home Department Ex p. Do Amaral see R. v. Secretary
of State for the Home Department Ex p. Vitale

R. *v.* Secretary of State for the Home Department Ex p. Doldur; *sub nom* Doldur *v.* Secretary of State for the Home Department [1998] Imm. A.R. 352; *Times*, April 8, 1998, CA; reversing [1997] Imm. A.R. 535, QBD . . . . *Digested*, 98/**3237**

R. *v.* Secretary of State for the Home Department Ex p. Doody; R. *v.* Secretary of State for the Home Department Ex p. Pierson; R. *v.* Secretary of State for the Home Department Ex p. Smart; R. *v.* Secretary of State for the Home Department Ex p. Pegg [1994] 1 A.C. 531; [1993] 3 W.L.R. 154; [1993] 3 All E.R. 92; (1995) 7 Admin. L.R. 1; (1993) 143 N.L.J. 991; *Times*, June 29, 1993; *Independent*, June 25, 1993, HL; affirming [1993] Q.B. 157; [1992] 3 W.L.R. 956; [1993] 1 All E.R. 151; (1993) 5 Admin. L.R. 93; [1992] C.O.D. 458; *Times*, May 8, 1992; *Independent*, May 7, 1992; *Guardian*, May 13, 1992, CA; reversing [1991] C.O.D. 256, QBD . . . . *Digested*, 93/**1213**:
Applied, 94/768, 94/3848, 95/960, 97/1335, 97/3929, 99/5437:
Considered, 93/1679, 94/44, 94/49, 94/3841, 95/42, 95/162, 95/2534, 96/1954, 96/1975, 96/4579, 96/6855, 97/1595, 97/2443, 98/4079, 00/3334, 00/4326: *Followed*, 95/81, 95/3228, 96/1953, 96/3981, 97/1626, 97/2672, 97/2678, 99/5212: *Referred to*, 95/1314

R. *v.* Secretary of State for the Home Department Ex p. Draper, *Independent*, March 20, 2000 (C.S.), QBD

R. *v.* Secretary of State for the Home Department Ex p. Duggan [1994] 3 All E.R. 277; [1994] C.O.D. 258; *Times*, December 9, 1993; *Independent*, January 28, 1994; *Guardian*, December 13, 1993, QBD . . . . *Digested*, 94/**3848**:
Cited, 00/4329: *Considered*, 97/3927: *Followed*, 97/3928

R. *v.* Secretary of State for the Home Department Ex p. Ejon [1998] I.N.L.R. 195, QBD . *Digested*, 98/**3200**:
Distinguished, 00/3296

R. *v.* Secretary of State for the Home Department Ex p. Elhasoglu; *sub nom* Elhasoglu *v.* Secretary of State for the Home Department [1997] Imm. A.R. 380, CA . . . . . *Digested*, 97/**2853**:
Distinguished, 98/3230

R. *v.* Secretary of State for the Home Department Ex p. Ellaway [1996] C.O.D. 328; *Times*, February 21, 1996; *Independent*, February 14, 1996, QBD . . . . *Digested*, 96/**2032**:
Considered, 97/3925, 98/4083

R. *v.* Secretary of State for the Home Department Ex p. Elshani; *sub nom* Berisha *v.* Secretary of State for the Home Department; Elshani *v.* Secretary of State for the Home Department [1999] Imm. A.R. 400; [1999] I.N.L.R. 265; [1999] C.O.D. 239, CA; reversing [1998] I.N.L.R. 683, QBD . . . . *Digested*, 99/**3186**

R. *v.* Secretary of State for the Home Department Ex p. Ethemi see R. *v.* Secretary of State for the Home Department Ex p. Demiraj

R. *v.* Secretary of State for the Home Department Ex p. Evans Medical Ltd (C324/93); R. *v.* Secretary of State for the Home Department Ex p. Macfarlan Smith Ltd [1995] All E.R. (E.C.) 481; [1995] E.C.R. I-563; [1996] 1 C.M.L.R. 53; [1996] 7 Med. L.R. 193; (1996) 29 B.M.L.R. 23; *Times*, May 10, 1995; *Financial Times*, April 4, 1995, ECJ . . . . *Digested*, 95/**2397**:
Considered, 99/3642

R. *v.* Secretary of State for the Home Department Ex p. Fadli see Fadli *v.* Secretary of State for the Home Department

R. *v.* Secretary of State for the Home Department Ex p. Fielding [1999] C.O.D. 525; *Times*, July 21, 1999, QBD . . . . *Digested*, 99/**4102**

R. *v.* Secretary of State for the Home Department Ex p. Fire Brigades Union [1995] 2 A.C. 513; [1995] 2 W.L.R. 464; [1995] 2 All E.R. 244; (1995) 7 Admin. L.R. 473; [1995] P.I.Q.R. P228; (1995) 145 N.L.J. 521; (1995) 139 S.J.L.B. 109; *Times*, April 6, 1995; *Independent*, April 6, 1995, HL; affirming [1995] 2 W.L.R. 1; [1995] 1 All E.R. 888; (1995) 7 Admin. L.R. 329; [1995] P.I.Q.R. P112; (1994) 144 N.L.J. 1587; *Times*, November 10, 1994; *Independent*, November 10, 1994, CA; reversing [1994] P.I.Q.R. P320; (1994) 158 L.G. Rev. 941; *Times*, May 30, 1994; *Independent*, May 24, 1994, QBD . . . . *Digested*, 95/**19**:
Applied, 99/5188: *Considered*, 01/3105

R. *v.* Secretary of State for the Home Department Ex p. Flynn [1997] 3 C.M.L.R. 888; [1995] Imm. A.R. 594; (1995) 139 S.J.L.B. 196; *Times*, July 20, 1995, CA; affirming [1995] 3 C.M.L.R. 397; [1995] C.O.D. 274; *Times*, March 23, 1995; *Independent*, March 10, 1995, QBD . . . . *Digested*, 95/**1546**:
Considered, 95/2728: *Not followed*, 99/2226

R. *v.* Secretary of State for the Home Department Ex p. Francois; *sub nom* R. *v.* Governor of Swaledale Prison Ex p. Francois [1999] 1 A.C. 43; [1998] 2 W.L.R. 530; [1998] 1 All E.R. 929; [1998] 2 Cr. App. R. (S.) 370; (1998) 95(16) L.S.G. 16; (1998) 148 N.L.J. 402; (1998) 142 S.J.L.B. 123; *Times*, March 13, 1998; *Independent*, April 23, 1998, HL; affirming [1997] 2 Cr. App. R. (S.) 359; [1997] Crim. L.R. 838; [1997] C.O.D. 347; *Times*, April 30, 1997; *Independent*, April 17, 1997, QBD . . . . *Digested*, 98/**1155**:
Considered, 97/1478, 99/1108, 99/1348: *Referred to*, 00/1148

R. *v.* Secretary of State for the Home Department Ex p. Furber [1998] 1 All E.R. 23; [1998] 1 Cr. App. R. (S.) 208; [1997] Crim. L.R. 841; [1997] C.O.D. 426; *Times*, July 11, 1997; *Independent*, July 3, 1997, QBD . . . . *Digested*, 97/**1593**:
Considered, 99/1257, 99/1268, 00/1352, 00/1355, 00/1360

R. v. Secretary of State for the Home Department Ex p. Gangadeen; *sub nom* Gangadeen v. Secretary of State for the Home Department; Khan (Khalid) v. Secretary of State for the Home Department; R. v. Secretary of State for the Home Department Ex p. Khan (Khalid) [1998] 1 F.L.R. 762; [1998] 2 F.C.R. 96; [1998] Imm. A.R. 106; [1998] I.N.L.R. 206; [1998] C.O.D. 216; [1998] Fam. Law 248; (1998) 95(1) L.S.G. 24; (1998) 142 S.J.L.B. 27; *Times*, December 12, 1997, CA. . . . . *Digested*, 98/**3215**: *Followed*, 98/3238

R. v. Secretary of State for the Home Department Ex p. Ganidagli [2001] Imm. A.R. 202, QBD . . . . *Digested*, 01/**3650**

R. v. Secretary of State for the Home Department Ex p. Garner (1999) 11 Admin. L.R. 595; (1999) 149 N.L.J. 637; *Times*, May 3, 1999, QBD . . . . *Digested*, 99/**69**

R. v. Secretary of State for the Home Department Ex p. Gashi (Besnik); *sub nom* Gashi v. Secretary of State for the Home Department (Certified Case) [1999] Imm. A.R. 415; [1999] C.O.D. 421; *Times*, March 31, 1999, CA; reversing [1999] Imm. A.R. 231; [1999] I.N.L.R. 276, QBD . . . . *Digested*, 99/**3187**: *Applied*, 01/3649: *Distinguished*, 00/3329

R. v. Secretary of State for the Home Department Ex p. Gecaj [1998] Imm. A.R. 11, QBD . . . . *Digested*, 98/**3197**

R. v. Secretary of State for the Home Department Ex p. Gilligan see R. v. Governor of Belmarsh Prison Ex p. Gilligan

R. v. Secretary of State for the Home Department Ex p. Gilmore; R. v. Secretary of State for the Home Department Ex p. Ogun [1999] Q.B. 611; [1998] 2 W.L.R. 618; [1998] 1 All E.R. 264; [1997] 2 Cr. App. R. 374; [1997] C.O.D. 365; *Times*, July 4, 1997, QBD . . . . *Digested*, 97/**2429**

R. v. Secretary of State for the Home Department Ex p. Gloszczuk (C63/99) see R. (on the application of Gloszczuk) v. Secretary of State for the Home Department (C63/99)

R. v. Secretary of State for the Home Department Ex p. Gnanavarathan see R. v. Special Adjudicator Ex p. Gnanavarathan

R. v. Secretary of State for the Home Department Ex p. Gonzalez [2001] Imm. A.R. 200, QBD . . . . *Digested*, 01/**3645**

R. v. Secretary of State for the Home Department Ex p. Green see R. v. Secretary of State for the Home Department Ex p. Hargreaves

R. v. Secretary of State for the Home Department Ex p. Gunn see R. (on the application of Gunn) v. Secretary of State for the Home Department (Recovery of Costs)

R. v. Secretary of State for the Home Department Ex p. Hakansoy [2001] Imm. A.R. 16, QBD . . . . *Digested*, 01/**3616**

R. v. Secretary of State for the Home Department Ex p. Hakimi see R. v. Secretary of State for the Home Department Ex p. Bani

R. v. Secretary of State for the Home Department Ex p. Hanuman; *sub nom* R. v. Visitor of the University of East Anglia Ex p. Hanuman [1999] Ed. C.R. 781, CA . *Digested*, 99/**1936**

R. v. Secretary of State for the Home Department Ex p. Hardial Singh see R. v. Governor of Durham Prison Ex p. Singh (Hardial)

R. v. Secretary of State for the Home Department Ex p. Hargreaves; R. v. Secretary of State for the Home Department Ex p. Briggs; R. v. Secretary of State for the Home Department Ex p. Green [1997] 1 W.L.R. 906; [1997] 1 All E.R. 397; [1997] C.O.D. 214; (1997) 94(5) L.S.G. 33; (1997) 141 S.J.L.B. 6; *Times*, December 3, 1996; *Independent*, December 11, 1996, CA; affirming [1996] C.O.D. 168; *Independent*, September 26, 1995, QBD. . . . . *Digested*, 97/**3934**: *Applied*, 99/4233: *Distinguished*, 99/2643

R. v. Secretary of State for the Home Department Ex p. Harrison [2001] A.C.D. 2, QBD (Admin Ct)

R. v. Secretary of State for the Home Department Ex p. Harrison (Miscarriage of Justice: Compensation) [1988] 3 All E.R. 86; (1988) 138 N.L.J. Rep. 187, QBD . *Digested*, 88/**7**: *Applied*, 00/5402

R. v. Secretary of State for the Home Department Ex p. Harry [1998] 1 W.L.R. 1737; [1998] 3 All E.R. 360; (1998) 43 B.M.L.R. 155; (1998) 95(22) L.S.G. 29; *Times*, May 15, 1998, QBD . . . . *Digested*, 98/**3902**

R. v. Secretary of State for the Home Department Ex p. Hepworth (Parole) [1998] C.O.D. 146, QBD

R. v. Secretary of State for the Home Department Ex p. Hepworth (Reclassification) [1996] C.O.D. 330, QBD . . . . *Considered*, 99/4106

R. v. Secretary of State for the Home Department Ex p. Herida [1998] Imm. A.R. 71, QBD . . . . *Digested*, 98/**3192**

R. v. Secretary of State for the Home Department Ex p. Hilal see Hilal v. United Kingdom (45276/99)

R. v. Secretary of State for the Home Department Ex p. Hill [1999] Q.B. 886; [1998] 3 W.L.R. 1011; [1997] 2 All E.R. 638; (1997) 147 N.L.J. 525, QBD . . . . *Digested*, 97/**2414**

R. _v._ Secretary of State for the Home Department Ex p. Hindley [2001] 1 A.C. 410;
[2000] 2 W.L.R. 730; [2000] 2 All E.R. 385; [2000] C.O.D. 173; (2000) 97(15)
L.S.G. 39; (2000) 144 S.J.L.B. 180; _Times,_ March 31, 2000, HL; affirming
[2000] Q.B. 152; [1999] 2 W.L.R. 1253; (1998) 148 N.L.J. 1673; _Times,_
November 6, 1998; _Independent,_ November 10, 1998, CA; affirming [1998] Q.B.
751; [1998] 2 W.L.R. 505; [1998] C.O.D. 171; (1998) 148 N.L.J. 49; _Times,_
December 19, 1997, QBD . . . .   _Digested,_ 00/**1349**

R. _v._ Secretary of State for the Home Department Ex p. Hirst; _sub nom_ Hirst _v._
Secretary of State for the Home Department; R. (on the application of Hirst) _v._
Secretary of State for the Home Department (Category Status) [2001] EWCA
Civ 378; (2001) 98(18) L.S.G. 45; (2001) 145 S.J.L.B. 107; _Times,_ March 22,
2001; _Independent,_ April 30, 2001 (C.S.), CA; reversing CO/3530/1999, QBD . .   _Digested,_ 01/**4576**

R. _v._ Secretary of State for the Home Department Ex p. Holub see R. (on the
application of Holub) _v._ Secretary of State for the Home Department

R. _v._ Secretary of State for the Home Department Ex p. Hoverspeed [1999] Eu. L.R.
596; [1999] I.N.L.R. 591, QBD. . . . .   _Digested,_ 99/**3191**

R. _v._ Secretary of State for the Home Department Ex p. Ibehi see Secretary of State for
the Home Department _v._ Ogilvy (Contempt of Court: Undertaking)

R. _v._ Secretary of State for the Home Department Ex p. Impower Ltd CO 539/98,
QBD. . . . .   _Digested,_ 99/**93**

R. _v._ Secretary of State for the Home Department Ex p. International Lottery in
Liechtenstein Foundation [1999] 3 C.M.L.R. 304; [1999] Eu. L.R. 905;
Independent, June 28, 1999 (C.S.), QBD . . . .   _Digested,_ 99/**588**

R. _v._ Secretary of State for the Home Department Ex p. Ionel see R. _v._ Secretary of
State for the Home Department Ex p. Stefan

R. _v._ Secretary of State for the Home Department Ex p. Ishaq (Mohammed Rauf)
[2000] Imm. A.R. 200, QBD . . . .   _Digested,_ 00/**3343**

R. _v._ Secretary of State for the Home Department Ex p. Isiko see R. (on the application
of Isiko) _v._ Secretary of State for the Home Department

R. _v._ Secretary of State for the Home Department Ex p. Isiocha [2000] Imm. A.R.
404, QBD . . . .   _Digested,_ 00/**3353**

R. _v._ Secretary of State for the Home Department Ex p. Iyadurai (No.1) [1998] Imm.
A.R. 470; [1998] I.N.L.R. 472; [1998] C.O.D. 410; _Times,_ June 16, 1998, CA;
affirming . . . .   _Digested,_ 98/**3207**:
                    Considered, 99/3183: _Explained,_ 99/3187

R. _v._ Secretary of State for the Home Department Ex p. Iyadurai (No.2) [1999] Imm.
A.R. 202, QBD . . . .   _Digested,_ 99/**3160**

R. _v._ Secretary of State for the Home Department Ex p. J (A Child) [2000] Imm. A.R.
414; [2000] I.N.L.R. 501, QBD. . . . .   _Digested,_ 00/**3344**

R. _v._ Secretary of State for the Home Department Ex p. J (A Juvenile); R. _v._ Secretary
of State for the Home Department Ex p. B (Juvenile) (1999) 96(1) L.S.G. 23;
Times, December 2, 1998, CA; affirming _Independent,_ July 20, 1998 (C.S.),
QBD . . . .   _Digested,_ 99/**1217**

R. _v._ Secretary of State for the Home Department Ex p. Jamil; R. _v._ Secretary of State
for the Home Department Ex p. Yousaf [2000] 3 All E.R. 649; [2000] I.N.L.R.
432; (2000) 97(29) L.S.G. 45; _Times,_ July 11, 2000; _Independent,_ July 31, 2000
(C.S), CA; reversing [2000] Imm. A.R. 51, QBD . . . .   _Digested,_ 00/**3295**

R. _v._ Secretary of State for the Home Department Ex p. Jammeh; R. _v._ Secretary of
State for the Home Department Ex p. Bajraktari; R. _v._ Secretary of State for the
Home Department Ex p. Rajaratnum; R. _v._ Secretary of State for the Home
Department Ex p. Patel (Idris Ibrahim) [1999] Imm. A.R. 1; [1998] I.N.L.R. 701,
CA; reversing (1998) 10 Admin. L.R. 1; _Times,_ September 11, 1997, QBD. . . . . . .   _Digested,_ 99/**3190**

R. _v._ Secretary of State for the Home Department Ex p. Javed see R. (on the
application of Javed) _v._ Secretary of State for the Home Department

R. _v._ Secretary of State for the Home Department Ex p. Jayakody [1982] 1 W.L.R.
405; [1982] 1 All E.R. 461; 125 S.J. 588; _Times,_ December 7, 1981, CA. . . . .   _Digested,_ 82/**1542**:
                    Applied, 94/2490: _Considered,_ 94/2498: _Disapproved,_ 98/3234:
                    Distinguished, 92/2412: _Referred to,_ 96/3300, 97/2929

R. _v._ Secretary of State for the Home Department Ex p. Jensath [2000] Imm. A.R.
330, QBD . . . .   _Digested,_ 00/**3321**

R. _v._ Secretary of State for the Home Department Ex p. Jeromio [2000] Imm. A.R.
604, QBD . . . .   _Digested,_ 01/**3647**

R. _v._ Secretary of State for the Home Department Ex p. Jeyeanthan; _sub nom_ R. _v._
Immigration Appeal Tribunal Ex p. Jeyeanthan; Secretary of State for the Home
Department _v._ Ravichandran; Ravichandran _v._ Secretary of State for the Home
Department [2000] 1 W.L.R. 354; [1999] 3 All E.R. 231; [2000] Imm. A.R. 10;
[1999] I.N.L.R. 241; (1999) 11 Admin. L.R. 824; [1999] C.O.D. 349; _Times,_ May
26, 1999; _Independent,_ June 8, 1999, CA; affirming [1998] Imm. A.R. 369;
[1998] I.N.L.R. 540; _Times,_ April 23, 1998, QBD . . . .   _Digested,_ 99/**3162**:
                    Applied, 01/4380: _Referred to,_ 01/4713

R. _v._ Secretary of State for the Home Department Ex p. Johnson [1999] Q.B. 1174;
[1999] 2 W.L.R. 932; [1998] 4 All E.R. 635, QBD. . . . .   _Digested,_ 98/**2356**

R. _v._ Secretary of State for the Home Department Ex p. Jordan see R. (on the
application of Jordan) _v._ Secretary of State for the Home Department

R. v. Secretary of State for the Home Department Ex p. Kabba see Kabba v. Secretary of State for the Home Department

R. v. Secretary of State for the Home Department Ex p. Kaja; *sub nom* Kaja v. Secretary of State for the Home Department [1995] Imm. A.R. 1, IAT . . . .   *Digested*, 95/**2697**:
Applied, 95/2698, 99/3147

R. v. Secretary of State for the Home Department Ex p. Kajenthra (Vallipuram) [1998] Imm. A.R. 158, QBD . . . .   *Digested*, 98/**3167**

R. v. Secretary of State for the Home Department Ex p. Karafu [2001] Imm. A.R. 26, QBD . . . .   *Digested*, 01/**3626**

R. v. Secretary of State for the Home Department Ex p. Kassim [1997] Imm. A.R. 483, QBD . . . .   *Digested*, 98/**3172**

R. v. Secretary of State for the Home Department Ex p. Kaur (Manjit) [1999] Eu. L.R. 554; [1999] C.O.D. 142, QBD . . . .   *Digested*, 99/**2226**:
Subsequent proceedings, 01/2445

R. v. Secretary of State for the Home Department Ex p. Kaur (Manjit) (C192/99); *sub nom* R. (on the application of Kaur) v. Secretary of State for the Home Department (C192/99) [2001] All E.R. (EC) 250; [2001] E.C.R. I-1237; [2001] 2 C.M.L.R. 24; [2001] I.N.L.R. 507; *Times*, March 8, 2001, ECJ . . . .   *Digested*, 01/**2445**:
Previous proceedings, 99/2226

R. v. Secretary of State for the Home Department Ex p. Kazim [2000] Imm. A.R. 400, QBD . . . .   *Digested*, 00/**3324**

R. v. Secretary of State for the Home Department Ex p. Kaziu see R. v. Uxbridge Magistrates Court Ex p. Adimi

R. v. Secretary of State for the Home Department Ex p. Kekana [1998] Imm. A.R. 136, QBD . . . .   *Digested*, 98/**3232**

R. v. Secretary of State for the Home Department Ex p. Kelso [1998] I.N.L.R. 603, QBD . . . .   *Digested*, 99/**3206**

R. v. Secretary of State for the Home Department Ex p. Kerkeb see R. (on the application of Bouheraoua) v. Secretary of State for the Home Department

R. v. Secretary of State for the Home Department Ex p. Kerrouche (No.1); *sub nom* R. v. Special Adjudicator Ex p. Kerrouche (No.1); Kerrouche v. Secretary of State for the Home Department (No.1) [1997] Imm. A.R. 610; [1998] I.N.L.R. 88, CA . . .   *Digested*, 98/**3205**:
Considered, 99/3183

R. v. Secretary of State for the Home Department Ex p. Kerrouche (No.2) [1998] Imm. A.R. 173, QBD . . . .   *Digested*, 98/**3216**

R. v. Secretary of State for the Home Department Ex p. Khaira [1998] I.N.L.R. 731, QBD . . . .   *Digested*, 99/**3195**

R. v. Secretary of State for the Home Department Ex p. Khan (Asif Mahmood); *sub nom* Khan (Asif Mahmood) v. Immigration Appeal Tribunal [1984] 1 W.L.R. 1337; [1985] 1 All E.R. 40; [1984] Imm. A.R. 68; [1984] Fam. Law 278; (1984) 81 L.S.G. 1678; (1984) 128 S.J. 580, CA . . . .   *Digested*, 85/**1702**:
Considered, 87/20, 98/2989

R. v. Secretary of State for the Home Department Ex p. Khan (Khalid) see R. v. Secretary of State for the Home Department Ex p. Gangadeen

R. v. Secretary of State for the Home Department Ex p. Khawaja; R. v. Secretary of State for the Home Department Ex p. Khera [1984] A.C. 74; [1983] 2 W.L.R. 321; [1983] 1 All E.R. 765; [1982] Imm. A.R. 139; 127 S.J. 137, HL; affirming [1982] 1 W.L.R. 625; [1982] 2 All E.R. 523; 126 S.J. 294, CA . . . .   *Digested*, 83/**1908**:
Applied, 84/1737, 90/744, 91/580, 91/2004, 91/2024, 91/2037, 92/2270, 92/2400, 93/2188, 93/2194, 94/2490, 94/2499, 94/2521, 96/606, 96/3295, 96/3305, 97/2927, 99/2167: *Approved*, 91/1956: *Considered*, 83/26, 84/1548, 84/1723, 84/1751, 85/1732, 86/1690, 86/1692, 86/1986, 87/1933, 87/1944, 87/1989, 88/23, 88/1838, 88/1853, 89/525, 90/2597, 90/2605, 91/2001, 91/2006, 91/2007, 92/2396, 92/2854, 93/2053, 93/2233, 93/2991, 94/2448, 96/3278: *Distinguished*, 85/1725, 86/1696, 88/1837, 88/1875, 00/4172, 00/5472: *Followed*, 83/1910, 96/3300, 97/2929, 00/3288: *Not followed*, 88/1882: *Referred to*, 85/1714, 86/2595, 87/1941, 87/1958, 87/2937, 88/1867

R. v. Secretary of State for the Home Department Ex p. Khera see R. v. Secretary of State for the Home Department Ex p. Khawaja

R. v. Secretary of State for the Home Department Ex p. King (Unreported, June 18, 1998), CA . . . .   *Followed*, 98/1087

R. v. Secretary of State for the Home Department Ex p. Kitaya (1998) 95(6) L.S.G. 24; *Times*, January 20, 1998, QBD . . . .   *Digested*, 98/**1355**

R. v. Secretary of State for the Home Department Ex p. Kone [1998] Imm. A.R. 291, QBD . . . .   *Digested*, 98/**3190**

R. v. Secretary of State for the Home Department Ex p. Kudaisi [2000] Imm. A.R. 46, QBD . . . .   *Digested*, 00/**3351**

R. v. Secretary of State for the Home Department Ex p. Kurumoorthy [1998] Imm. A.R. 401, QBD . . . .   *Digested*, 98/**3233**

R. v. Secretary of State for the Home Department Ex p. Launder (No.1); *sub nom* Launder, Re [1996] C.O.D. 369, DC

R. *v.* Secretary of State for the Home Department Ex p. Launder (No.2) [1997] 1 W.L.R. 839; [1997] 3 All E.R. 961; (1997) 94(24) L.S.G. 33; (1997) 147 N.L.J. 793; (1997) 141 S.J.L.B. 123; *Times,* May 26, 1997; *Independent,* June 3, 1997, HL; reversing *Times,* October 29, 1996, QBD . . . . *Digested,* 97/**2433**: *Considered,* 98/2355, 00/3392, 01/3684

R. *v.* Secretary of State for the Home Department Ex p. Launder (No.3); Launder *v.* Governor of Brixton Prison [1998] Q.B. 994; [1998] 3 W.L.R. 221; [1998] C.O.D. 301; (1998) 95(11) L.S.G. 36; (1998) 142 S.J.L.B. 101; *Times,* March 6, 1998, QBD . . . . *Digested,* 98/**2342**

R. *v.* Secretary of State for the Home Department Ex p. Lawson (Vera) [1994] Imm. A.R. 58 . . . . *Digested,* 94/**2509**: *Applied,* 99/3211

R. *v.* Secretary of State for the Home Department Ex p. Leech (No.2) [1994] Q.B. 198; [1993] 3 W.L.R. 1125; [1993] 4 All E.R. 539; (1993) 137 S.J.L.B. 173; *Times,* May 20, 1993; *Independent,* May 20, 1993, CA; reversing [1992] C.O.D. 168 . . . . *Digested,* 94/**3849**: *Applied,* 98/3899: *Considered,* 96/3219, 97/2782, 99/335

R. *v.* Secretary of State for the Home Department Ex p. M [1999] Imm. A.R. 548; [2000] C.O.D. 49, QBD . . . . *Digested,* 00/**3275**

R. *v.* Secretary of State for the Home Department Ex p. Macfarlan Smith Ltd see R. *v.* Secretary of State for the Home Department Ex p. Evans Medical Ltd (C324/93)

R. *v.* Secretary of State for the Home Department Ex p. Macit [2000] Imm. A.R. 31, QBD . . . . *Digested,* 00/**3330**

R. *v.* Secretary of State for the Home Department Ex p. Mahmood (Amjad) see R. (on the application of Mahmood (Amjad)) *v.* Secretary of State for the Home Department

R. *v.* Secretary of State for the Home Department Ex p. Mahmood (Wasted Costs Order) [1999] C.O.D. 119, QBD

R. *v.* Secretary of State for the Home Department Ex p. Main see R. *v.* Secretary of State for the Home Department Ex p. Simms

R. *v.* Secretary of State for the Home Department Ex p. Makunguru (David Nibb) [1998] Imm. A.R. 141, QBD . . . . *Digested,* 98/**3170**

R. *v.* Secretary of State for the Home Department Ex p. Malhi [1991] 1 Q.B. 194; [1990] 2 W.L.R. 933; [1990] 2 All E.R. 357; [1990] Imm. A.R. 275; (1990) 2 Admin. L.R. 839; [1990] C.O.D. 178; (1990) 134 S.J. 401; *Times,* January 4, 1990; *Independent,* February 9, 1990; *Guardian,* February 7, 1990, CA; reversing (1990) 2 Admin. L.R. 455; (1990) 87(9) L.S.G. 44; *Times,* November 8, 1989; *Guardian,* October 18, 1989, QBD . . . . *Digested,* 90/**2583**: *Applied,* 98/3222: *Approved,* 90/2585, 91/1981, 95/2720: *Distinguished,* 98/3221

R. *v.* Secretary of State for the Home Department Ex p. Mapere; *sub nom* R. *v.* Chief Immigration Officer Ex p. Mapere [2001] Imm. A.R. 89; [2001] I.N.L.R. 159, QBD . . . . *Digested,* 01/**3671**

R. *v.* Secretary of State for the Home Department Ex p. Mbandaka [1999] Ed. C.R. 656, QBD . . . . *Digested,* 99/**1799**

R. *v.* Secretary of State for the Home Department Ex p. Mbanja [1999] Imm. A.R. 508; [1999] I.N.L.R. 390; *Independent,* July 26, 1999 (C.S.), CA; affirming [1999] Imm. A.R. 63, QBD . . . . *Digested,* 99/**3189**

R. *v.* Secretary of State for the Home Department Ex p. Mbanza; *sub nom* Mbanza *v.* Secretary of State for the Home Department [1996] Imm. A.R. 136, CA . . . . *Digested,* 96/**3211**: *Followed,* 99/3179

R. *v.* Secretary of State for the Home Department Ex p. McAvoy [1998] 1 W.L.R. 790; [1998] C.O.D. 148; (1998) 95(1) L.S.G. 23; (1998) 142 S.J.L.B. 39; *Times,* December 12, 1997; *Independent,* December 12, 1997, CA . . . . *Digested,* 98/**4079**

R. *v.* Secretary of State for the Home Department Ex p. McQuire (1998) 10 Admin. L.R. 534, QBD . . . . *Digested,* 98/**2352**

R. *v.* Secretary of State for the Home Department Ex p. Mehmet; R. *v.* Secretary of State for the Home Department Ex p. O'Connor (1999) 11 Admin. L.R. 529; (1999) 163 J.P.N. 755; *Times,* February 18, 1999, QBD . . . . *Digested,* 99/**4103**

R. *v.* Secretary of State for the Home Department Ex p. Mellor see R. (on the application of Mellor) *v.* Secretary of State for the Home Department

R. *v.* Secretary of State for the Home Department Ex p. Memon [1999] Imm. A.R. 85, QBD . . . . *Digested,* 99/**3199**

R. *v.* Secretary of State for the Home Department Ex p. Mendje [2000] Imm. A.R. 353, QBD . . . . *Digested,* 00/**3298**

R. *v.* Secretary of State for the Home Department Ex p. Mersin [2000] I.N.L.R. 511, QBD . . . . *Digested,* 01/**3607**

R. *v.* Secretary of State for the Home Department Ex p. Miah (Madoris) [1998] Imm. A.R. 44, QBD . . . . *Digested,* 98/**3227**

R. *v.* Secretary of State for the Home Department Ex p. Moawad [2000] Imm. A.R. 325, QBD . . . . *Digested,* 00/**3325**

R. *v.* Secretary of State for the Home Department Ex p. Montana see R. (on the application of Montana) *v.* Secretary of State for the Home Department

R. *v.* Secretary of State for the Home Department Ex p. Mpyanguli see Kingori *v.*
Secretary of State for the Home Department

R. *v.* Secretary of State for the Home Department Ex p. Mulkerrins [1998] C.O.D. 235;
Times, February 3, 1998, CA . . . . *Digested,* 98/**4080**

R. *v.* Secretary of State for the Home Department Ex p. Musah; *sub nom* Musah *v.*
Secretary of State for the Home Department [1995] Imm. A.R. 236, CA;
affirming [1994] Imm. A.R. 395, QBD . . . . *Digested,* 96/**3265**:
Followed, 96/3298, 00/3350

R. *v.* Secretary of State for the Home Department Ex p. Nader [1998] Imm. A.R. 33,
QBD . . . . *Digested,* 98/**3180**

R. *v.* Secretary of State for the Home Department Ex p. Najem [1999] Imm. A.R. 107,
QBD . . . . *Digested,* 99/**3215**

R. *v.* Secretary of State for the Home Department Ex p. Nalkin; *sub nom* R. *v.*
Secretary of State for the Environment, Transport and the Regions Ex p. Nalkin
[2000] J.P.L. 608, QBD . . . . *Digested,* 00/**4471**

R. *v.* Secretary of State for the Home Department Ex p. Nassir (Wahid) [1999] Imm.
A.R. 250; [1999] I.N.L.R. 92; *Times*, December 11, 1998, CA . . . . *Digested,* 99/**3177**

R. *v.* Secretary of State for the Home Department Ex p. Navaratnaam see R. *v.*
Secretary of State for the Home Department Ex p. Sivakumaran

R. *v.* Secretary of State for the Home Department Ex p. Nicholas [2000] Imm. A.R.
334, QBD . . . . *Digested,* 00/**3291**

R. *v.* Secretary of State for the Home Department Ex p. Nkereuwen [1999] Imm. A.R.
267, CA . . . . *Digested,* 99/**3184**

R. *v.* Secretary of State for the Home Department Ex p. Norgren [2000] Q.B. 817;
[2000] 3 W.L.R. 181; (2000) 97(11) L.S.G. 38; (2000) 144 S.J.L.B. 127;
Independent, April 3, 2000 (C.S.), QBD

R. *v.* Secretary of State for the Home Department Ex p. O'Brien see R. *v.* Secretary of
State for the Home Department Ex p. Simms

R. *v.* Secretary of State for the Home Department Ex p. O'Byrne see R. *v.* Secretary of
State for the Environment, Transport and the Regions Ex p. O'Byrne (Application
for Joinder)

R. *v.* Secretary of State for the Home Department Ex p. O'Connor see R. *v.* Secretary
of State for the Home Department Ex p. Mehmet

R. *v.* Secretary of State for the Home Department Ex p. Ogun see R. *v.* Secretary of
State for the Home Department Ex p. Gilmore

R. *v.* Secretary of State for the Home Department Ex p. Oladehinde; R. *v.* Secretary of
State for the Home Department Ex p. Alexander [1991] 1 A.C. 254; [1990] 3
W.L.R. 797; [1990] 3 All E.R. 393; (1991) 3 Admin. L.R. 393; (1990) 140 N.L.J.
1498; (1990) 134 S.J. 1264; *Independent*, October 18, 1990, HL; affirming
[1990] 2 W.L.R. 1195; [1990] 2 All E.R. 367; (1991) 3 Admin. L.R. 23; [1990]
C.O.D. 254; (1990) 140 N.L.J. 402; *Times*, March 16, 1990; *Independent*, March
16, 1990; *Guardian*, March 16, 1990, CA; reversing *Times*, March 1, 1990, DC . . . *Digested,* 91/**1981**:
Applied, 95/2691, 98/3222: *Considered,* 96/3260: *Followed,* 96/2961:
Referred to, 92/2384

R. *v.* Secretary of State for the Home Department Ex p. Oloniluyi [1989] Imm. A.R.
135; [1989] C.O.D. 275, CA. . . . . *Digested,* 91/**2028**:
Considered, 91/2046: *Distinguished,* 91/2051, 91/2053, 91/2055, 91/2056,
92/2414, 92/2415, 01/3671

R. *v.* Secretary of State for the Home Department Ex p. Onibiyo [1996] Q.B. 768;
[1996] 2 W.L.R. 490; [1996] 2 All E.R. 901; [1996] Imm. A.R. 370; (1996)
93(17) L.S.G. 30; (1996) 140 S.J.L.B. 109; *Times*, April 2, 1996, CA; affirming
Times, January 29, 1996; *Independent*, January 24, 1996, QBD . . . . *Digested,* 96/**3242**:
Applied, 00/3296, 00/3348: *Considered,* 96/3241, 97/2866, 99/3153,
99/3177: *Followed,* 97/2865, 97/2867, 97/2869, 98/3196

R. *v.* Secretary of State for the Home Department Ex p. Orozca [1999] Imm. A.R. 225,
QBD . . . . *Digested,* 99/**3171**

R. *v.* Secretary of State for the Home Department Ex p. Oshin [2000] 1 W.L.R. 2311;
[2000] 2 All E.R. 955; *Independent*, January 17, 2000 (C.S.), QBD . . . . *Digested,* 00/**1405**

R. *v.* Secretary of State for the Home Department Ex p. Ouanes see Ouanes *v.*
Secretary of State for the Home Department

R. *v.* Secretary of State for the Home Department Ex p. Ouma [1997] Imm. A.R. 606,
QBD . . . . *Digested,* 98/**3218**

R. *v.* Secretary of State for the Home Department Ex p. Patel (Bina Rajendra) [1995]
Imm. A.R. 223, QBD . . . . *Digested,* 96/**3311**:
Considered, 98/3219: *Followed,* 97/2906

R. *v.* Secretary of State for the Home Department Ex p. Patel (Idris Ibrahim) see R. *v.*
Secretary of State for the Home Department Ex p. Ahmed (Mohammed
Hussain)

R. *v.* Secretary of State for the Home Department Ex p. Patel (Idris Ibrahim) see R. *v.*
Secretary of State for the Home Department Ex p. Jammeh

R. *v.* Secretary of State for the Home Department Ex p. Payne [1999] Imm. A.R. 489,
CA . . . . *Digested,* 00/**3348**

R. *v.* Secretary of State for the Home Department Ex p. Pegg see R. *v.* Secretary of
State for the Home Department Ex p. Doody

R. *v.* Secretary of State for the Home Department Ex p. Peries see R. *v.* Governor of
Maidstone Prison Ex p. Peries

R. *v.* Secretary of State for the Home Department Ex p. Phansopkar; R. *v.* Secretary of
State for the Home Department Ex p. Begum (Lailun Nahar) [1976] Q.B. 606;
[1975] 3 W.L.R. 322; [1975] 3 All E.R. 497; 199 S.J. 507, CA; reversing (1975)
119 S.J. 507; *Times*, April 29, 1975, QBD . . . . *Digested*, 75/**7**:
Applied, 01/3607: *Distinguished*, 75/6, 76/6, 87/1995: *Explained*, 76/16

R. *v.* Secretary of State for the Home Department Ex p. Phull; *sub nom* Phull *v.*
Secretary of State for the Home Department [1996] Imm. A.R. 72, CA . . . . *Digested*, 96/**3277**:
Applied, 01/5879: *Followed*, 96/3257, 97/2919, 00/3327

R. *v.* Secretary of State for the Home Department Ex p. Pierson see R. *v.* Secretary of
State for the Home Department Ex p. Doody

R. *v.* Secretary of State for the Home Department Ex p. Pierson; *sub nom* Pierson *v.*
Secretary of State for the Home Department [1998] A.C. 539; [1997] 3 W.L.R.
492; [1997] 3 All E.R. 577; (1997) 94(37) L.S.G. 41; (1997) 147 N.L.J. 1238;
(1997) 141 S.J.L.B. 212; *Times*, July 28, 1997; *Independent*, July 31, 1997, HL;
reversing [1996] 3 W.L.R. 547; [1996] 1 All E.R. 837; [1996] C.O.D. 362; *Times*,
December 8, 1995; *Independent*, December 12, 1995, CA; reversing [1996]
C.O.D. 255; *Times*, November 29, 1995; *Independent*, November 14, 1995, QBD .   *Digested*, 97/**1627**:
Considered, 96/1954: *Distinguished*, 98/4074

R. *v.* Secretary of State for the Home Department Ex p. Pinochet Ugarte CO/1786/99,
QBD . . . . *Digested*, 99/**2291**

R. *v.* Secretary of State for the Home Department Ex p. Polat (Unreported, November
7, 1996) . . . . *Applied*, 01/3645

R. *v.* Secretary of State for the Home Department Ex p. Popatia; R. *v.* Secretary of
State for the Home Department Ex p. Chew [2001] Imm. A.R. 46; [2000]
I.N.L.R. 587; *Times*, July 18, 2000, QBD . . . . *Digested*, 00/**3350**

R. *v.* Secretary of State for the Home Department Ex p. Probyn [1998] 1 W.L.R. 809;
[1998] 1 All E.R. 357; [1998] 1 Cr. App. R. (S.) 312; [1998] Crim. L.R. 76; *Times*,
October 30, 1997, QBD . . . . *Digested*, 97/**1654**:
Considered, 99/1184, 99/1348, 00/1153: *Joined proceedings*, 97/1477,
97/1632

R. *v.* Secretary of State for the Home Department Ex p. Propend Finance Pty Ltd see
R. *v.* Central Criminal Court Ex p. Propend Finance Property Ltd

R. *v.* Secretary of State for the Home Department Ex p. Purcell, *Times*, March 5, 1998,
QBD . . . . *Digested*, 98/**4081**

R. *v.* Secretary of State for the Home Department Ex p. Q see R. (on the application of
P) *v.* Secretary of State for the Home Department

R. *v.* Secretary of State for the Home Department Ex p. Quaquah see R. *v.* Chief
Immigration Officer Ex p. Quaquah

R. *v.* Secretary of State for the Home Department Ex p. Quaquah (Application for
Judicial Review) CO 1028/00, QBD (Admin Ct) . . . . *Previous proceedings*,
00/3290

R. *v.* Secretary of State for the Home Department Ex p. Quinn [2000] U.K.H.R.R. 386;
(1999) 96(21) L.S.G. 40; (1999) 143 S.J.L.B. 136; *Times*, April 17, 1999, QBD . . *Digested*, 99/**4107**

R. *v.* Secretary of State for the Home Department Ex p. Quinn (Refusal to Remit
Sentence) [2001] A.C.D. 45, QBD

R. *v.* Secretary of State for the Home Department Ex p. R, *Times*, November 29, 2000,
QBD . . . . *Digested*, 01/**3619**

R. *v.* Secretary of State for the Home Department Ex p. Rahman (Saidur); *sub nom*
Rahman (Saidur), Re [1998] Q.B. 136; [1997] 3 W.L.R. 990; [1997] 1 All E.R.
796; [1997] Imm. A.R. 197; [1997] C.O.D. 197; (1997) 94(4) L.S.G. 26; (1997)
141 S.J.L.B. 20; *Times*, December 24, 1996; *Independent*, January 28, 1997, CA;
affirming [1996] 4 All E.R. 945; [1996] C.O.D. 465; *Times*, July 19, 1996, QBD . . *Digested*, 97/**2927**

R. *v.* Secretary of State for the Home Department Ex p. Rajaratnum see R. *v.* Secretary
of State for the Home Department Ex p. Jammeh

R. *v.* Secretary of State for the Home Department Ex p. Rasalingan see R. *v.* Secretary
of State for the Home Department Ex p. Sivakumaran

R. *v.* Secretary of State for the Home Department Ex p. Ravichandran (No.1); *sub nom*
R. *v.* Immigration Appeal Tribunal Ex p. Sandralingam (No.1); R. *v.* Secretary of
State for the Home Department Ex p. Sandralingham (No.1); R. *v.* Immigration
Appeal Tribunal Ex p. Rajendrakumar [1996] Imm. A.R. 97; *Times*, October 30,
1995, CA . . . . *Digested*, 96/**3216**:
Applied, 98/3174: *Cited*, 99/3202: *Considered*, 96/3225, 97/2862, 98/3227,
99/3168: *Followed*, 97/2863, 00/3322

R. *v.* Secretary of State for the Home Department Ex p. Ravichandran (No.2); R. *v.*
Secretary of State for the Home Department Ex p. Sandralingham (No.2) [1996]
Imm. A.R. 418; *Times*, May 13, 1996, QBD . . . . *Digested*, 96/**3241**:
Approved, 98/3196: *Considered*, 97/2866: *Followed*, 97/2867

R. *v.* Secretary of State for the Home Department Ex p. Read (Gary John) [1989] A.C.
1014; [1988] 3 W.L.R. 948; [1988] 3 All E.R. 993; (1989) 88 Cr. App. R. 242;
(1988) 138 N.L.J. Rep. 323; (1988) 132 S.J. 1591; *Times*, November 5, 1988;
Independent, November 4, 1988; *Guardian*, November 4, 1988, HL; reversing
[1988] 2 W.L.R. 236; [1988] 1 All E.R. 759; (1988) 132 S.J. 191; *Times*,
November 2, 1987, QBD . . . .   *Digested*, 89/**1095**:
     Considered, 98/4083

R. *v.* Secretary of State for the Home Department Ex p. Rehman (Permission to Move
for Judicial Review), *Times*, July 6, 1999, CA . . . .   *Digested*, 99/**3771**

R. *v.* Secretary of State for the Home Department Ex p. Robinson [1998] Q.B. 929;
[1997] 3 W.L.R. 1162; [1997] 4 All E.R. 210; [1997] Imm. A.R. 568; [1997]
I.N.L.R. 182; (1997) 147 N.L.J. 1345; *Times*, August 1, 1997; *Independent*, July
18, 1997, CA . . . .   *Digested*, 97/**2857**:
    Applied, 99/3169, 99/3170: *Considered*, 99/3178, 99/3193, 00/3282:
     Distinguished, 00/3278, 00/3294

R. *v.* Secretary of State for the Home Department Ex p. Roomy [1999] Imm. A.R. 483,
QBD . . . .   *Digested*, 00/**3337**

R. *v.* Secretary of State for the Home Department Ex p. Roszkowski see R. (on the
application of Roszkowski) *v.* Special Adjudicator

R. *v.* Secretary of State for the Home Department Ex p. Russell, *Times*, August 31,
2000, QBD . . . .   *Digested*, 00/**4324**

R. *v.* Secretary of State for the Home Department Ex p. Sahota; *sub nom* Sahota *v.*
Secretary of State for the Home Department; Zeghraba *v.* Secretary of State for
the Home Department; Secretary of State for the Home Department *v.* Sahota;
Secretary of State for the Home Department *v.* Zeghraba; R. *v.* Secretary of State
for the Home Department Ex p. Zeghraba [1999] Q.B. 597; [1998] 2 W.L.R.
626; [1997] 3 C.M.L.R. 576; [1997] Eu. L.R. 554; [1997] 3 F.C.R. 776; [1997]
Imm. A.R. 429; (1997) 94(18) L.S.G. 31; (1997) 141 S.J.L.B. 111; *Times*, April 30,
1997; *Independent*, May 6, 1997, CA . . . .   *Digested*, 97/**2925**

R. *v.* Secretary of State for the Home Department Ex p. Salas [2001] Imm. A.R. 105,
QBD . . . .   *Digested*, 01/**3635**

R. *v.* Secretary of State for the Home Department Ex p. Saleem; *sub nom* R. *v.*
Immigration Appeal Tribunal Ex p. Saleem; Saleem *v.* Secretary of State for the
Home Department [2001] 1 W.L.R. 443; [2000] 4 All E.R. 814; [2000] Imm.
A.R. 529; [2000] I.N.L.R. 413; *Times*, June 22, 2000; *Independent*, June 23,
2000, CA; affirming [1999] I.N.L.R. 621; *Times*, November 11, 1999, QBD . . . . .   *Digested*, 00/**3281**:
     Followed, 01/3692

R. *v.* Secretary of State for the Home Department Ex p. Salem [1999] 1 A.C. 450;
[1999] 2 W.L.R. 483; [1999] 2 All E.R. 42; (1999) 11 Admin. L.R. 194; [1999]
C.O.D. 486; (1999) 96(9) L.S.G. 32; (1999) 143 S.J.L.B. 59; *Times*, February 12,
1999, HL [1999] Q.B. 805; [1999] 2 W.L.R. 1; [1998] C.O.D. 406; *Times*,
March 18, 1998, CA . . . .   *Digested*, 99/**8**

R. *v.* Secretary of State for the Home Department Ex p. Salim [2000] Imm. A.R. 6;
[1999] I.N.L.R. 628, QBD . . . .   *Digested*, 00/**3304**

R. *v.* Secretary of State for the Home Department Ex p. Salisbury CO/343/98, QBD . . .   *Digested*, 98/**4083**

R. *v.* Secretary of State for the Home Department Ex p. Samaroo see R. (on the
application of Samaroo) *v.* Secretary of State for the Home Department

R. *v.* Secretary of State for the Home Department Ex p. Sandralingham (No.1) see R. *v.*
Secretary of State for the Home Department Ex p. Ravichandran (No.1)

R. *v.* Secretary of State for the Home Department Ex p. Sandralingham (No.2) see R.
v. Secretary of State for the Home Department Ex p. Ravichandran (No.2)

R. *v.* Secretary of State for the Home Department Ex p. Sanusi; *sub nom* Sanusi *v.*
Secretary of State for the Home Department [1999] Imm. A.R. 334; [1999]
I.N.L.R. 198; [1999] C.O.D. 158; *Times*, January 6, 1999, CA . . . .   *Digested*, 99/**3188**

R. *v.* Secretary of State for the Home Department Ex p. Sasitharan [1998] Imm. A.R.
487, QBD . . . .   *Digested*, 99/**3168**

R. *v.* Secretary of State for the Home Department Ex p. Savas (Abdulnasir) (C37/98)
[2000] 1 W.L.R. 1828; [2000] All E.R. (EC) 627; [2000] E.C.R. I-2927; [2000]
3 C.M.L.R. 729; [2000] C.E.C. 624; [2000] I.N.L.R. 398; *Times*, May 23,
2000, ECJ (6th Chamber) . . . .   *Digested*, 00/**3368**

R. *v.* Secretary of State for the Home Department Ex p. Semaane [1998] Imm. A.R.
48, QBD . . . .   *Digested*, 98/**3182**

R. *v.* Secretary of State for the Home Department Ex p. Senkoy; *sub nom* Secretary of
State for the Home Department *v.* Senkoy [2001] EWCA Civ 328; [2001] Imm.
A.R. 399; [2001] I.N.L.R. 555, CA; affirming C/3789/98, QBD . . . .   *Digested*, 01/**3621**

R. *v.* Secretary of State for the Home Department Ex p. Seri [2001] Imm. A.R. 169,
QBD . . . .   *Digested*, 01/**3613**

R. *v.* Secretary of State for the Home Department Ex p. Sezek see R. (on the
application of Sezek) *v.* Secretary of State for the Home Department

R. *v.* Secretary of State for the Home Department Ex p. Shaikh [1998] Imm. A.R. 133,
QBD . . . .   *Digested*, 98/**3173**

R. *v.* Secretary of State for the Home Department Ex p. Shaw, *Times*, March 16, 2000,
QBD . . . .   *Digested*, 00/**4329**

R. *v.* Secretary of State for the Home Department Ex p. Sheikh see R. (on the application of Sheikh) *v.* Secretary of State for the Home Department

R. *v.* Secretary of State for the Home Department Ex p. Shingara (No.2); *sub nom* Shingara *v.* Secretary of State for the Home Department [1999] Imm. A.R. 257; [1999] I.N.L.R. 99, CA . . . . *Digested,* 99/**3196**:
Previous proceedings, 96/3259, 97/2913

R. *v.* Secretary of State for the Home Department Ex p. Shokar see R. *v.* Immigration Appeal Tribunal Ex p. Shokar

R. *v.* Secretary of State for the Home Department Ex p. Simba see Ahmad (Mariam) *v.* Secretary of State for the Home Department

R. *v.* Secretary of State for the Home Department Ex p. Simms; *sub nom* R. *v.* Secretary of State for the Home Department Ex p. Main; R. *v.* Secretary of State for the Home Department Ex p. O'Brien; R. *v.* Governor of Whitemoor Prison Ex p. Main [2000] 2 A.C. 115; [1999] 3 W.L.R. 328; [1999] 3 All E.R. 400; [1999] E.M.L.R. 689; 7 B.H.R.C. 411; (1999) 11 Admin. L.R. 961; [1999] C.O.D. 520; (1999) 96(30) L.S.G. 28; (1999) 149 N.L.J. 1073; (1999) 143 S.J.L.B. 212; *Times,* July 9, 1999, HL; reversing [1999] Q.B. 349; [1998] 3 W.L.R. 1169; [1998] 2 All E.R. 491; [1998] E.M.L.R. 431; (1998) 95(1) L.S.G. 23; (1998) 142 S.J.L.B. 38; *Times,* December 9, 1997; *Independent,* December 10, 1997, CA; reversing [1997] E.M.L.R. 261; [1997] C.O.D. 217; *Times,* January 17, 1997, QBD . . . . *Digested,* 99/**4105**:
Considered, 99/335, 01/4578: *Followed,* 99/4100

R. *v.* Secretary of State for the Home Department Ex p. Singh [1998] I.N.L.R. 608, CA .　*Digested,* 99/**3155**

R. *v.* Secretary of State for the Home Department Ex p. Singh (2000) (Unreported, March 3, 2000). . . . . *Applied,* 01/3640

R. *v.* Secretary of State for the Home Department Ex p. Singh (Lal) [1998] Imm. A.R. 320, QBD . . . . *Digested,* 98/**3191**:
Considered, 00/6495

R. *v.* Secretary of State for the Home Department Ex p. Singh (Manvinder) [1996] C.O.D. 476, CA; affirming [1996] Imm. A.R. 41; *Independent,* October 17, 1995, QBD . . . . *Digested,* 96/**3243**:
Applied, 01/3621: *Considered,* 98/3196

R. *v.* Secretary of State for the Home Department Ex p. Singh (Raghbir); *sub nom* Singh (Raghbir) *v.* Secretary of State for the Home Department [1996] Imm. A.R. 507, CA; affirming [1995] Imm. A.R. 447, QBD . . . . *Digested,* 97/**2911**:
Considered, 00/3352

R. *v.* Secretary of State for the Home Department Ex p. Singh (Sarbjit) [1999] Imm. A.R. 445; [1999] I.N.L.R. 632, QBD. . . . . *Digested,* 00/**3336**

R. *v.* Secretary of State for the Home Department Ex p. Singh (Tarlok) see R. *v.* Immigration Appeal Tribunal Ex p. Singh (Tarlok)

R. *v.* Secretary of State for the Home Department Ex p. Singh (Thakar) [2000] I.N.L.R. 208, QBD . . . . *Digested,* 00/**3383**

R. *v.* Secretary of State for the Home Department Ex p. Sirghi [1998] Imm. A.R. 310, QBD . . . . *Digested,* 98/**3208**

R. *v.* Secretary of State for the Home Department Ex p. Sivakumaran; R. *v.* Secretary of State for the Home Department Ex p. Vilvarajah; R. *v.* Secretary of State for the Home Department Ex p. Vanathan; R. *v.* Secretary of State for the Home Department Ex p. Rasalingan; R. *v.* Secretary of State for the Home Department Ex p. Navaratnaam [1988] A.C. 958; [1988] 1 All E.R. 193; [1988] Imm. A.R. 147; (1988) 85(6) L.S.G. 37; (1988) 132 S.J. 22, HL; reversing [1987] 3 W.L.R. 1047; (1987) 131 S.J. 1485; *Times,* October 13, 1987, CA; reversing (Unreported, September 25, 1987), QBD . . . . *Digested,* 88/**1832**:
Applied, 89/1951, 92/2443, 93/2248, 96/3209, 96/3211, 99/3170:
Considered, 88/1829, 92/2396, 95/2697, 95/2698, 96/3186, 96/3236,
00/3306, 00/3316: *Followed,* 00/6491

R. *v.* Secretary of State for the Home Department Ex p. Sivaranjan [2001] Imm. A.R. 7, QBD . . . . *Digested,* 01/**3623**

R. *v.* Secretary of State for the Home Department Ex p. Smart see R. *v.* Secretary of State for the Home Department Ex p. Doody

R. *v.* Secretary of State for the Home Department Ex p. Sorani see R. *v.* Uxbridge Magistrates Court Ex p. Adimi

R. *v.* Secretary of State for the Home Department Ex p. Sourbah [1999] Imm. A.R. 452, QBD . . . . *Digested,* 00/**3305**

R. *v.* Secretary of State for the Home Department Ex p. Stafford [1999] 2 A.C. 38; [1998] 3 W.L.R. 372; [1998] 4 All E.R. 7; (1998) 95(34) L.S.G. 31; (1998) 148 N.L.J. 1142; (1998) 142 S.J.L.B. 244; *Times,* July 24, 1998, HL; affirming [1998] 1 W.L.R. 503; (1998) 10 Admin. L.R. 385; *Times,* November 28, 1997, CA; reversing in part (1997) 147 N.L.J.1494, QBD . . . . *Digested,* 98/**4074**:
Considered, 99/1250: *Followed,* 01/1411

R. *v.* Secretary of State for the Home Department Ex p. Stefan; R. *v.* Secretary of State for the Home Department Ex p. Chiper; R. *v.* Secretary of State for the Home Department Ex p. Ionel [1995] Imm. A.R. 410, QBD . . . . *Digested,* 96/**3228**:
Considered, 98/3205: *Distinguished,* 00/3286

R. _v._ Secretary of State for the Home Department Ex p. Stewart [1999] Imm. A.R. 494, QBD . . . . _Digested,_ 00/**3361**

R. _v._ Secretary of State for the Home Department Ex p. Subaskaran see R. (on the application of Adan (Lul Omar)) _v._ Secretary of State for the Home Department

R. _v._ Secretary of State for the Home Department Ex p. Susikanth see Susikanth _v._ Secretary of State for the Home Department

R. _v._ Secretary of State for the Home Department Ex p. Swati; _sub nom_ Swati _v._ Secretary of State for the Home Department; R. _v._ Secretary of State for the Home Department Ex p. Butt (Nasir) [1986] 1 W.L.R. 477; [1986] 1 All E.R. 717; [1986] Imm. A.R. 88; (1986) 83 L.S.G. 780; (1986) 136 N.L.J. 189; (1986) 130 S.J. 186, CA . . . . _Digested,_ 86/**1711**:
Applied, 87/1997, 91/2045, 91/2048, 92/2421, 94/2509, 95/68, 95/2546, 96/3222, 96/3318, 97/2915, 00/3361, 00/3370: _Considered,_ 86/1712, 90/4428, 91/2039, 91/2048.a, 91/2050, 92/16, 93/438, 94/55, 94/2512, 95/67, 97/2921: _Distinguished,_ 96/3287: _Followed,_ 87/1990, 91/1985, 92/5891: _Referred to,_ 88/1881

R. _v._ Secretary of State for the Home Department Ex p. T see T _v._ Secretary of State for the Home Department

R. _v._ Secretary of State for the Home Department Ex p. Taore; _sub nom_ Taore _v._ Secretary of State for the Home Department [1998] Imm. A.R. 450, CA . . . . . . _Digested,_ 99/**3193**

R. _v._ Secretary of State for the Home Department Ex p. Tawfick; _sub nom_ R. (on the application of Tawfick) _v._ Secretary of State for the Home Department [2001] A.C.D. 28; (2001) 98(2) L.S.G. 40; _Times,_ December 5, 2000, QBD . . . . _Digested,_ 01/**79**

R. _v._ Secretary of State for the Home Department Ex p. Taylor see R. (on the application of Anderson) _v._ Secretary of State for the Home Department

R. _v._ Secretary of State for the Home Department Ex p. Thiruchchelvam [1999] Imm. A.R. 217, QBD . . . . _Digested,_ 99/**3157**

R. _v._ Secretary of State for the Home Department Ex p. Thompson see R. _v._ Secretary of State for the Home Department Ex p. Venables

R. _v._ Secretary of State for the Home Department Ex p. Turgut; _sub nom_ Turgut _v._ Secretary of State for the Home Department [2001] 1 All E.R. 719; [2000] H.R.L.R. 337; [2000] U.K.H.R.R. 403; [2000] Imm. A.R. 306; [2000] I.N.L.R. 292; [2001] A.C.D. 12; (2000) 97(7) L.S.G. 40; (2000) 150 N.L.J. 131; _Times,_ February 15, 2000, CA. . . . . _Digested,_ 00/**3297**:
Applied, 00/3344, 01/5879: _Considered,_ 00/3392

R. _v._ Secretary of State for the Home Department Ex p. Ullah (Azad) see R. (on the application of Ullah (Azad)) _v._ Secretary of State for the Home Department

R. _v._ Secretary of State for the Home Department Ex p. Uzun [1998] Imm. A.R. 314, QBD . . . . _Digested,_ 98/**3225**

R. _v._ Secretary of State for the Home Department Ex p. Vanathan see R. _v._ Secretary of State for the Home Department Ex p. Sivakumaran

R. _v._ Secretary of State for the Home Department Ex p. Venables; R. _v._ Secretary of State for the Home Department Ex p. Thompson [1998] A.C. 407; [1997] 3 W.L.R. 23; [1997] 3 All E.R. 97; [1997] 2 F.L.R. 471; (1997) 9 Admin. L.R. 413; [1997] Fam. Law 789; (1997) 94(34) L.S.G. 27; (1997) 147 N.L.J. 955; _Times,_ June 13, 1997; _Independent,_ June 18, 1997, HL; affirming [1997] 2 W.L.R. 67; [1997] 1 All E.R. 327; (1997) 9 Admin. L.R. 281; [1997] C.O.D. 100; _Times,_ August 7, 1996, CA; affirming [1996] C.O.D. 365; (1996) 93(18) L.S.G. 37; (1996) 146 N.L.J. 786; (1996) 140 S.J.L.B. 127; _Times,_ May 7, 1996; _Independent,_ June 10, 1996 (C.S.), QBD . . . . _Digested,_ 97/**1595**:
Applied, 97/1593, 99/781, 01/89

R. _v._ Secretary of State for the Home Department Ex p. Vijendrann CO/2503/95, QBD .   _Digested,_ 97/**2862**:
Not followed, 98/3176

R. _v._ Secretary of State for the Home Department Ex p. Vilvarajah see R. _v._ Secretary of State for the Home Department Ex p. Sivakumaran

R. _v._ Secretary of State for the Home Department Ex p. Vitale; R. _v._ Secretary of State for the Home Department Ex p. Do Amaral [1996] All E.R. (E.C.) 461; [1996] 2 C.M.L.R. 587; [1996] Imm. A.R. 275; [1996] C.O.D. 382; _Times,_ January 26, 1996, CA; affirming [1995] All E.R. (E.C.) 946; [1995] 3 C.M.L.R. 605; (1995) 145 N.L.J. 631; _Times,_ April 18, 1995, QBD . . . . _Digested,_ 96/**3164**:
Applied, 01/5879: _Considered,_ 96/5483

R. _v._ Secretary of State for the Home Department Ex p. Vladic see R. _v._ Immigration Appeal Tribunal Ex p. Secretary of State for the Home Department

R. _v._ Secretary of State for the Home Department Ex p. Walker [1998] 1 W.L.R. 809; [1998] 1 All E.R. 357; [1998] Crim. L.R. 76; _Times,_ September 2, 1997, QBD . . .   _Digested,_ 97/**1477**:
Joined proceedings, 97/1632, 97/1654

R. _v._ Secretary of State for the Home Department Ex p. Willis (2000) 97(10) L.S.G. 35; (2000) 144 S.J.L.B. 125; _Times,_ March 22, 2000, QBD . . . . _Digested,_ 00/**4325**

R. _v._ Secretary of State for the Home Department Ex p. X see R. (on the application of X) _v._ Secretary of State for the Home Department

R. _v._ Secretary of State for the Home Department Ex p. Yasun [1998] Imm. A.R. 215, QBD . . . . _Digested,_ 98/**3177**

R. *v.* Secretary of State for the Home Department Ex p. Yiadom [1998] I.N.L.R. 489;
    [1998] C.O.D. 298; *Times*, May 1, 1998, CA . . . .   *Digested,* 98/**3235**:
                                                                        Subsequent proceedings, 00/3360
R. *v.* Secretary of State for the Home Department Ex p. Yiadom (C357/98) [2001] All
    E.R. (EC) 267; [2000] E.C.R. I-9265; [2001] 2 C.M.L.R. 8; [2001] I.N.L.R. 300;
    Times, November 16, 2000, ECJ (5th Chamber) . . . .   *Digested,* 00/**3360**:
                                                                        Previous proceedings, 98/3235
R. *v.* Secretary of State for the Home Department Ex p. Yolamba [1997] Imm. A.R.
    564, QBD . . . .   *Digested,* 98/**3219**
R. *v.* Secretary of State for the Home Department Ex p. Yousaf see R. *v.* Secretary of
    State for the Home Department Ex p. Jamil
R. *v.* Secretary of State for the Home Department Ex p. Yousuf (Mohammed) [1989]
    Imm. A.R. 554. . . . .   *Digested,* 91/**2041**:
                                                                        Applied, 96/3281: *Followed,* 01/3672
R. *v.* Secretary of State for the Home Department Ex p. Z [1998] Imm. A.R. 516;
    [1999] C.O.D. 63, QBD . . . .   *Digested,* 99/**3197**
R. *v.* Secretary of State for the Home Department Ex p. Zakrocki (1997-98) 1 C.C.L.
    Rep. 374; (1996) 32 B.M.L.R. 108; [1996] C.O.D. 304; (1996) 93(16) L.S.G. 31;
    (1996) 140 S.J.L.B. 110; *Times*, April 3, 1996, QBD . . . .   *Digested,* 96/**3252**
R. *v.* Secretary of State for the Home Department Ex p. Zarycka [2000] Imm. A.R.
    431, QBD . . . .   *Digested,* 00/**3312**
R. *v.* Secretary of State for the Home Department Ex p. Zeghraba see R. *v.* Secretary
    of State for the Home Department Ex p. Sahota
R. *v.* Secretary of State for the Home Department Ex p. Zeqiri see R. (on the
    application of Zeqiri) *v.* Secretary of State for the Home Department
R. (on the application of Clarke) *v.* Secretary of State for the Transport, Local
    Government and the Regions see Clarke *v.* Secretary of State for the
    Environment, Transport and the Regions
R. (on the application of BECTU) *v.* Secretary of State for Trade and Industry (C173/99)
    see R. (on the application of Broadcasting, Entertainment, Cinematographic
    and Theatre Union) *v.* Secretary of State for Trade and Industry (C173/99)
R. (on the application of Broadcasting, Entertainment, Cinematographic and Theatre
    Union) *v.* Secretary of State for Trade and Industry (C173/99); *sub nom* R. (on
    the application of BECTU) *v.* Secretary of State for Trade and Industry (C173/99);
    R. *v.* Secretary of State for Trade and Industry Ex p. Broadcasting,
    Entertainment, Cinematographic and Theatre Union (BECTU) [2001] 1 W.L.R.
    2313; [2001] All E.R. (EC) 647; [2001] E.C.R. I-4881; [2001] 3 C.M.L.R. 7;
    [2001] C.E.C. 276; [2001] I.C.R. 1152; [2001] I.R.L.R. 559; *Times*, June 28,
    2001, ECJ (6th Chamber) . . . .   *Digested,* 01/**2218**
R. (on the application of BT3G Ltd) *v.* Secretary of State for Trade and Industry; *sub nom*
    BT3G Ltd *v.* Secretary of State for Trade and Industry; R. (on the application of
    One 2 One Personal Communications Ltd) *v.* Secretary of State for Trade and
    Industry [2001] EWCA Civ 1448; [2001] 3 C.M.L.R. 61; [2001] Eu. L.R. 822;
    (2001) 98(44) L.S.G. 35, CA; affirming [2001] Eu. L.R. 325, QBD (Admin Ct) .   *Digested,* 01/**5346**
R. (on the application of Eastaway) *v.* Secretary of State for Trade and Industry; *sub nom*
    R. *v.* Secretary of State for Trade and Industry Ex p. Eastaway [2000] 1 W.L.R.
    2222; [2001] 1 All E.R. 27; [2001] C.P. Rep. 67; [2001] A.C.D. 17; (2000)
    97(46) L.S.G. 40; (2000) 144 S.J.L.B. 282; *Times*, November 8, 2000;
    Independent, December 18, 2000 (C.S), HL [2001] B.C.C. 365, QBD . . . .   *Digested,* 01/**710**
R. (on the application of One 2 One Personal Communications Ltd) *v.* Secretary of State
    for Trade and Industry see R. (on the application of BT3G Ltd) *v.* Secretary of
    State for Trade and Industry
R. (on the application of Orange Personal Communications Ltd) *v.* Secretary of State for
    Trade and Industry; *sub nom* R. *v.* Secretary of State for Trade and Industry Ex
    p. Orange Personal Communications Services Ltd; R. (on the application of
    Orange Personal Communications Services Ltd) *v.* Secretary of State for the
    Environment, Transport and the Regions [2001] 3 C.M.L.R. 36; [2001] Eu. L.R.
    165; (2000) 97(45) L.S.G. 42; *Times*, November 15, 2000; *Independent*,
    December 4, 2000 (C.S), QBD (Admin Ct) . . . .   *Digested,* 00/**5095**
R. *v.* Secretary of State for Trade and Industry Ex p. Broadcasting, Entertainment,
    Cinematographic and Theatre Union (BECTU) see R. (on the application of
    Broadcasting, Entertainment, Cinematographic and Theatre Union) *v.* Secretary
    of State for Trade and Industry (C173/99)
R. *v.* Secretary of State for Trade and Industry Ex p. Eastaway see R. (on the
    application of Eastaway) *v.* Secretary of State for Trade and Industry
R. *v.* Secretary of State for Trade and Industry Ex p. Garman (t/a Celebration
    Fireworks) CO/3700/97, QBD . . . .   *Digested,* 98/**94**
R. *v.* Secretary of State for Trade and Industry Ex p. Greenpeace Ltd (No.1) [1998] Eu.
    L.R. 48; [1998] Env. L.R. 415; [1998] C.O.D. 59, QBD . . . .   *Digested,* 98/**2252**:
                                                                        Applied, 99/94: *Considered,* 00/2256
R. *v.* Secretary of State for Trade and Industry Ex p. Greenpeace Ltd (No.2) [2000] 2
    C.M.L.R. 94; [2000] Eu. L.R. 196; [2000] Env. L.R. 221; [2000] C.O.D. 141;
    Times, January 19, 2000, QBD . . . .   *Digested,* 00/**2256**

R. *v.* Secretary of State for Trade and Industry Ex p. Isle of Wight Council (2001) 3 L.G.L.R. 16; [2000] C.O.D. 245, QBD. . . . . *Digested,* 01/**2877**

R. *v.* Secretary of State for Trade and Industry Ex p. Langridge see Secretary of State for Trade and Industry *v.* Langridge

R. *v.* Secretary of State for Trade and Industry Ex p. McCormick [1998] B.C.C. 379; [1998] C.O.D. 160; (1998) 95(10) L.S.G. 27; *Times,* February 10, 1998; *Independent,* February 10, 1998, CA; affirming [1998] B.C.C. 381; *Independent,* January 15, 1998, QBD . . . . *Digested,* 98/**682**

R. *v.* Secretary of State for Trade and Industry Ex p. Mercury Personal Communications Ltd see Mercury Personal Communications *v.* Secretary of State for Trade and Industry

R. *v.* Secretary of State for Trade and Industry Ex p. Orange Personal Communications Services Ltd see R. (on the application of Orange Personal Communications Ltd) *v.* Secretary of State for Trade and Industry

R. *v.* Secretary of State for Trade and Industry Ex p. Thomson Holidays Ltd [2000] U.K.C.L.R. 189; [2000] E.C.C. 321; *Times,* January 12, 2000, CA; reversing CO/4178/98, QBD. . . . . *Digested,* 00/**733**

R. *v.* Secretary of State for Trade and Industry Ex p. Trades Union Congress [2001] 1 C.M.L.R. 8; *Times,* October 17, 2000, CA; affirming [2001] 1 C.M.L.R. 5; [2000] Eu. L.R. 698; [2000] I.R.L.R. 565, QBD. . . . . *Digested,* 00/**2180**

R. *v.* Secretary of State for Trade and Industry Ex p. Wolf (2000) 79 P. & C.R. 299; [1998] C.O.D. 57; (1998) 75 P. & C.R. D9, QBD . . . . *Digested,* 97/**4943**

R. *v.* Secretary of State for Transport Ex p. De Rothschild; *sub nom* De Rothschild *v.* Secretary of State for Transport [1989] 1 All E.R. 933; 87 L.G.R. 511; (1989) 57 P. & C.R. 330; [1989] 06 E.G. 123; [1988] R.V.R. 200; [1989] J.P.L. 173; *Times,* July 23, 1988; *Independent,* July 25, 1988 (C.S.), CA; affirming [1988] 1 P.L.R. 67; [1988] 20 E.G. 87; [1988] R.V.R. 200, QBD . . . . *Digested,* 90/**588**:
Applied, 99/4276: *Considered,* 92/452, 93/440, 97/4347

R. *v.* Secretary of State for Transport Ex p. Factortame Ltd (No.2) [1991] 1 A.C. 603; [1990] 3 W.L.R. 818; [1991] 1 All E.R. 70; [1991] 1 Lloyd's Rep. 10; [1990] 3 C.M.L.R. 375; (1991) 3 Admin. L.R. 333; (1990) 140 N.L.J. 1457; (1990) 134 S.J. 1189, HL. . . . . *Digested,* 91/**4032**:
Applied, 93/3263, 94/1981, 95/4734: *Considered,* 91/4030, 92/2904, 94/4, 97/4627, 98/2661, 99/5082: *Followed,* 97/5714, 00/2180:
Referred to, 95/4937

R. *v.* Secretary of State for Transport Ex p. Factortame Ltd (No.4) (C48/93) see Brasserie du Pecheur SA *v.* Germany (C46/93)

R. *v.* Secretary of State for Transport Ex p. Factortame Ltd (No.5) [2000] 1 A.C. 524; [1999] 3 W.L.R. 1062; [1999] 4 All E.R. 906; [1999] 3 C.M.L.R. 597; [2000] Eu. L.R. 40; (1999) 96(43) L.S.G. 32; [1999] N.P.C. 126; *Times,* November 3, 1999, HL; affirming [1999] 2 All E.R. 640 (Note); [1998] 3 C.M.L.R. 192; [1998] Eu. L.R. 456; [1998] C.O.D. 381; [1998] N.P.C. 68; *Times,* April 28, 1998, CA; affirming [1998] 1 All E.R. 736 (Note); [1998] 1 C.M.L.R. 1353; [1997] Eu. L.R. 475; (1998) 10 Admin. L.R. 107; *Times,* September 11, 1997, QBD. . . . . *Digested,* 99/**2259**:
Applied, 01/1092

R. *v.* Secretary of State for Transport Ex p. Factortame Ltd (No.6); *sub nom* R. *v.* Secretary of State for the Environment, Transport and the Regions Ex p. Factortame Ltd; Factortame Ltd *v.* Secretary of State for Transport (No.6) [2001] 1 W.L.R. 942; [2001] 1 C.M.L.R. 47; [2001] Eu. L.R. 207; (2001) 98(12) L.S.G. 42; (2001) 145 S.J.L.B. 19; *Times,* January 10, 2001, QBD (T&CC) . . . . *Digested,* 01/**2511**

R. *v.* Secretary of State for Transport Ex p. Moore CO 146/07, QBD . . . . *Digested,* 98/**4857**

R. (on the application of Friends Provident Life & Pensions Ltd) *v.* Secretary of State for Transport, Local Government and the Regions see R. (on the application of Friends Provident Life Office) *v.* Secretary of State for the Environment, Transport and the Regions

R. (on the application of Warwick DC) *v.* Secretary of State for Transport, Local Government and the Regions [2001] EWHC Admin 752; (2001) 98(39) L.S.G. 39, QBD (Admin Ct)

R. *v.* Secretary of State for Wales Ex p. Emery [1998] 4 All E.R. 367; [1997] E.G.C.S. 114; (1997) 94(29) L.S.G. 29; (1997) 141 S.J.L.B. 170; [1997] N.P.C. 110; *Times,* July 22, 1997, CA; affirming [1996] 4 All E.R. 1; [1996] N.P.C. 95; *Times,* June 24, 1996, QBD . . . . *Digested,* 97/**2348**

R. *v.* Secretary of State for Wales Ex p. Swansea City and County (1999) 78 P. & C.R. 317; [1999] 2 P.L.R. 14; [1999] J.P.L. 524, QBD . . . . *Digested,* 99/**4224**

R. *v.* Secretary of the Central Office of the Employment Tribunals (England and Wales) Ex p. Public Concern at Work [2000] I.R.L.R. 658; [2000] C.O.D. 302; *Times,* May 9, 2000, QBD . . . . *Digested,* 00/**40**

R. (on the application of Fleurose) *v.* Securities and Futures Authority Ltd; *sub nom* R. *v.* Securities & Futures Authority Ltd Ex p. Fleurose; Fleurose *v.* Disciplinary Appeal Tribunal of the Securities & Futures Authority Ltd; R. (on the application of Fleurose) *v.* Financial Services Authority [2001] EWCA Civ 2015, CA; affirming [2001] EWHC Admin 292; [2001] 2 All E.R. (Comm) 481; [2001] I.R.L.R. 764; [2001] A.C.D. 71; *Daily Telegraph,* May 1, 2001, QBD (Admin Ct) . . *Digested,* 01/**98**

R. *v.* Securities & Futures Authority Ltd Ex p. Fleurose see R. (on the application of
Fleurose) *v.* Securities and Futures Authority Ltd
R. *v.* Seeboard Plc Ex p. Guildford see R. *v.* Minister of Energy Ex p. Guildford
R. *v.* Sefton MBC Ex p. British Association of Shooting & Conservation Ltd [2001]
Env. L.R. 10; (2000) 2 L.G.L.R. 979; [2000] B.L.G.R. 628; [2000] C.O.D. 342;
[2000] N.P.C. 48, QBD ....   *Digested,* 01/**4316**
R. *v.* Sefton MBC Ex p. Help the Aged [1997] 4 All E.R. 532; [1997] 3 F.C.R. 573;
(1997-98) 1 C.C.L. Rep. 57; (1997) 38 B.M.L.R. 135; [1998] C.O.D. 69; *Times,*
August 23, 1997; *Independent,* October 3, 1997, CA; reversing [1997] 3 F.C.R.
392; (1997) 36 B.M.L.R. 110; [1997] C.O.D. 387; (1997) 147 N.L.J. 490; *Times,*
March 27, 1997; *Independent,* April 18, 1997, QBD ....   *Digested,* 97/**4721**:
                       Applied, 99/4622: *Considered,* 99/3052
R. (on the application of C (A Child)) *v.* Sefton MBC Independent Appeals Panel; *sub*
nom C (A Child) *v.* Sefton MBC Independent Appeals Panel [2001] E.L.R. 393,
QBD (Admin Ct) ....   *Digested,* 01/**1980**
R. *v.* Sehitoglu (Dervis); R. *v.* Ozakan (Mustafa) [1998] 1 Cr. App. R. (S.) 89, CA
(Crim Div) ....   *Digested,* 98/**1205**
R. *v.* Selby DC Ex p. Samuel Smith Old Brewery Ltd [2001] P.L.C.R. 6; [2001] J.P.L.
225 (Note), QBD ....   *Digested,* 01/**4705**
R. *v.* Selby DC Ex p. Samuel Smith Old Brewery Ltd (Permission to Move for Judicial
Review); *sub nom* R. *v.* Samuel Smith Old Brewery; (Unreported, November 29,
1999), QBD ....   *Cited,* 01/4746:
                                      Considered, 01/53
R. *v.* Selby Justices Ex p. Daltry see R. (on the application of Daltry) *v.* Selby
Magistrates Court
R. (on the application of Daltry) *v.* Selby Magistrates Court; *sub nom* R. *v.* Selby
Magistrates Court Ex p. Daltry; R. *v.* Selby Justices Ex p. Daltry (2001) 165 J.P.
89; (2001) 165 J.P.N. 685; (2000) 97(47) L.S.G. 39; *Times,* December 1,
2000; *Independent,* December 11, 2000 (C.S), QBD ....   *Digested,* 01/**4222**
R. *v.* Selby Magistrates Court Ex p. Daltry see R. (on the application of Daltry) *v.* Selby
Magistrates Court
R. *v.* Sellars (Michael) [1998] 1 Cr. App. R. (S.) 117, CA (Crim Div) ....   *Digested,* 98/**1352**
R. *v.* Serdeiro (Roberto Newton) [1996] 1 Cr. App. R. (S.) 251, CA (Crim Div) ....   *Digested,* 96/**1871**:
                                      Considered, 98/1185
R. (on the application of R) *v.* Serious Fraud Office see R. (on the application of A) *v.*
Snaresbrook Crown Court
R. *v.* Servite Houses Ex p. Goldsmith (2001) 33 H.L.R. 35; (2000) 2 L.G.L.R. 997;
[2001] B.L.G.R. 55; (2000) 3 C.C.L. Rep. 325; [2001] A.C.D. 4, QBD ....   *Digested,* 01/**5140**
R. *v.* Servite Houses Ex p. Goldsmith (Interim Relief) (2000) 3 C.C.L. Rep. 354, CA ...   *Digested,* 01/**568**
R. *v.* Serzin (Bisunas Viadas) (1995) 16 Cr. App. R. (S.) 4, CA (Crim Div) ....   *Digested,* 96/**2025**:
                                      Considered, 00/1438
R. *v.* Seth-Smith (Patrick Sidney) see Board of Trade *v.* Owen
R. *v.* Sevenoaks DC Ex p. Wickham [1998] J.P.L. 1145, QBD ....   *Considered,* 00/4529
R. *v.* Severn (Kevin) (1995) 16 Cr. App. R. (S.) 989, CA (Crim Div) ....   *Applied,* 98/1278:
                                      Considered, 98/1279
R. *v.* Sexton (Clifford John) [2000] 2 Cr. App. R. (S.) 94, CA (Crim Div) ....   *Digested,* 00/**1363**
R. *v.* Seymour-Smith (C167/97) see R. *v.* Secretary of State for Employment Ex p.
Seymour-Smith (C167/97)
R. *v.* Shafiq (Mohammed) [1998] 2 Cr. App. R. (S.) 12, CA (Crim Div) ....   *Digested,* 98/**1292**
R. *v.* Shah [1994] Crim. L.R. 125, CA. ....   *Digested,* 94/**958**:
                                  Distinguished, 98/869
R. *v.* Shahzad (Mohammed Khalid) see R. *v.* Latif (Khalid)
R. *v.* Shanahan (Thomas) see DPP *v.* Doot
R. *v.* Shannahan (Thomas) see DPP *v.* Doot
R. *v.* Shannon (John James); *sub nom* R. *v.* Alford (John James) [2001] 1 W.L.R. 51;
[2001] 1 Cr. App. R. 12; [2000] Crim. L.R. 1001; (2000) 97(40) L.S.G. 41;
(2000) 144 S.J.L.B. 257; *Times,* October 11, 2000, CA (Crim Div) ....   *Digested,* 00/**918**
R. *v.* Shanoor (Mohammed) see R. *v.* Howells (Craig)
R. *v.* Sharif (Haroon) see R. *v.* Nawaz (Mohammed)
R. *v.* Sharkey (Bernard Lee) [2000] 1 W.L.R. 160; [2000] 1 All E.R. 15; [2000] 1 Cr.
App. R. 409; [2000] 1 Cr. App. R. (S.) 541; (2000) 164 J.P. 256; [2000] Crim.
L.R. 116; (2000) 164 J.P.N. 370; (1999) 96(43) L.S.G. 32; *Times,* November
10, 1999 ; *Independent,* October 28, 1999, CA (Crim Div) ....   *Digested,* 99/**1279**:
                                      Applied, 01/1164
R. *v.* Sharman (Peter Edward) [1998] 1 Cr. App. R. 406; (1998) 162 J.P. 110; [1998] 1
F.L.R. 785; [1998] Fam. Law 315; (1998) 162 J.P.N. 187; *Times,* December 18,
1997, CA (Crim Div) ....   *Digested,* 98/**910**
R. *v.* Sharp (David Bruce) [1987] Q.B. 853; [1987] 3 W.L.R. 1; [1987] 3 All E.R. 103;
(1987) 85 Cr. App. R. 207; (1987) 151 J.P. 832; [1987] Crim. L.R. 566; (1987)
151 J.P.N. 825; (1987) 84 L.S.G. 1491; (1987) 131 S.J. 624, CA (Crim Div) .....   *Digested,* 87/**774**:
                  Considered, 88/781, 99/1020: *Followed,* 99/931
R. *v.* Sharpe (John Robin) 10 B.H.R.C. 153, Sup Ct (Can). ....   *Digested,* 01/**3473**
R. *v.* Sharpe (Sabyn John) [2000] 1 Cr. App. R. (S.) 1, CA (Crim Div) ....   *Digested,* 00/**1122**
R. *v.* Shaw (Carl William) [1998] 2 Cr. App. R. (S.) 233, CA (Crim Div) ....   *Digested,* 98/**1377**

R. *v.* Shaw (Dennis) see R. *v.* Kidd (Philip Richard)
R. *v.* Shaw (Obtaining by Deception: Incitement) [1994] Crim. L.R. 365, CA (Crim
    Div) . . . . *Digested*, 94/**836**:
                                                         Considered, 00/995
R. *v.* Shaw (William Anthony) see R. *v.* Cavanagh (James Michael)
R. *v.* Shayler (David Michael) TNS, HL; affirming [2001] EWCA Crim 1977; [2001] 1
    W.L.R. 2206; (2001) 98(40) L.S.G. 40; (2001) 145 S.J.L.B. 223; (2001) 145
    S.J.L.B. 235; *Times*, October 10, 2001; *Daily Telegraph*, October 9, 2001, CA
    (Crim Div) . . . . *Digested*, 01/**1057**
R. *v.* Shayler (James Arthur) see R. *v.* Miranda (Juan Carlos)
R. *v.* Shearn (Damien) see Attorney General's Reference (No.39 of 1998), Re
R. *v.* Sheehan (Michael); R. *v.* Moore (George Alan) [1975] 1 W.L.R. 739; [1975] 2 All
    E.R. 960; (1974) 60 Cr. App. R. 308; [1975] Crim. L.R. 339; 119 S.J. 271, CA
    (Crim Div) . . . . *Digested*, 75/**604**:
                     Applied, 83/718, 94/927: *Considered*, 75/602, 77/590, 00/1070
R. (on the application of Addinell) *v.* Sheffield City Council [2001] A.C.D. 61, QBD
    (Admin Ct)
R. *v.* Sheffield City Council Ex p. H (2000) 2 L.G.L.R. 124; [1999] Ed. C.R. 885;
    [1999] E.L.R. 511; (1999) 96(32) L.S.G. 32; *Times*, August 20, 1999, CA;
    affirming [1999] E.L.R. 242, QBD . . . . *Digested*, 99/**1838**
R. *v.* Sheffield City Council Ex p. M [2000] E.L.R. 85, QBD . . . . *Digested*, 00/**1916**
R. *v.* Sheffield Crown Court Ex p. Headley [2000] 2 Cr. App. R. 1; [2000] Crim. L.R.
    374; *Times*, November 4, 1999, QBD . . . . *Digested*, 99/**1047**:
                                                  Considered, 01/1129
R. *v.* Sheffield Housing Benefit Review Board Ex p. Smith; R. *v.* Rugby BC Housing
    Benefit Review Board Ex p. Harrison; R. *v.* Coventry DC Housing Benefit Review
    Board Ex p. Bodden (1996) 28 H.L.R. 36; 93 L.G.R. 139; *Times*, December 28,
    1994, QBD . . . . *Digested*, 95/**2601**:
                                                  Considered, 01/5028
R. (on the application of Broadhurst) *v.* Sheffield Justices [2001] R.V.R. 245;
    Independent, December 11, 2000 (C.S), QBD (Admin Ct)
R. *v.* Sheffield Justices Ex p. Foster, *Times*, November 2, 1999, QBD . . . . *Digested*, 99/**1032**
R. (on the application of DPP) *v.* Sheffield Magistrates Court; *sub nom* R. *v.* Sheffield
    Stipendiary Magistrate Ex p. DPP; R. (on the application of DPP) *v.* Sheffield
    Stipendiary Magistrate *Independent*, November 27, 2000 (C.S), QBD
R. *v.* Sheffield Magistrates Court Ex p. Ojo (2000) 164 J.P. 659; [2001] Crim. L.R. 43;
    (2000) 164 J.P.N. 665; (2000) 164 J.P.N. 743, QBD . . . . *Digested*, 00/**1031**
R. (on the application of DPP) *v.* Sheffield Stipendiary Magistrate see R. (on the
    application of DPP) *v.* Sheffield Magistrates Court
R. *v.* Sheffield Stipendiary Magistrate Ex p. DPP see R. (on the application of DPP) *v.*
    Sheffield Magistrates Court
R. *v.* Sheffield Youth Justices Ex p. M [1998] 1 F.L.R. 929; [1998] Fam. Law 315;
    Times, January 29, 1998, QBD . . . . *Digested*, 98/**1280**
R. *v.* Shephard (Hilda) [1993] A.C. 380; [1993] 2 W.L.R. 102; [1993] 1 All E.R. 225;
    (1993) 96 Cr. App. R. 345; (1993) 157 J.P. 145; [1993] Crim. L.R. 295; (1993)
    143 N.L.J. 127; (1993) 137 S.J.L.B. 12; *Times*, December 17, 1992; *Independent*,
    January 21, 1993, HL; affirming (1991) 93 Cr. App. R. 139, CA (Crim Div) . . . . . *Digested*, 93/**636**:
                     Applied, 94/675, 95/4418, 98/984, 00/914: *Considered*, 95/929, 99/990:
                                                    Followed, 97/1120
R. *v.* Shepherd (Brendan Sean) see R. *v.* Marriott (Francis Anthony)
R. *v.* Shepherd (Paul) [1998] 1 Cr. App. R. (S.) 397, CA (Crim Div) . . . . *Digested*, 98/**1395**:
                                                     Considered, 00/**1438**
R. *v.* Shepherd (Peter James) see Attorney General's Reference (Nos.14 and 24 of
    1993), Re
R. *v.* Sheppard (Robert) see Attorney General's Reference (No.6 of 1998), Re
R. *v.* Shergill (Sukdev Singh); R. *v.* Paul (Ranjit Singh); R. *v.* Sagu (Delveear); R. *v.*
    Purewal (Kulwinder Singh) [1999] 1 W.L.R. 1944; [1999] 2 All E.R. 485; [1999]
    2 Cr. App. R. (S.) 341; [1999] Crim. L.R. 591; (1999) 149 N.L.J. 334, CA (Crim
    Div) . . . . *Digested*, 99/**1106**:
                       Considered, 00/1163, 00/1170: *Referred to*, 00/1171
R. *v.* Shervill (David Anthony) (1989) 11 Cr. App. R. (S.) 284, CA (Crim Div) . . . . *Considered*, 91/1012,
                                                  92/1145, 00/1269
R. *v.* Sherwood (Ellis) see R. *v.* O'Brien (Michael Alan)
R. (on the application of Telegraph Group Plc) *v.* Sherwood; *sub nom* R. *v.* Sherwood Ex
    p. Telegraph Group Plc; Telegraph Group Plc, Ex p. [2001] EWCA Crim 1075;
    [2001] 1 W.L.R. 1983; (2001) 98(28) L.S.G. 42; (2001) 145 S.J.L.B. 159; *Times*,
    June 12, 2001, CA (Crim Div) . . . . *Digested*, 01/**1182**
R. *v.* Sherwood Ex p. Telegraph Group Plc see R. (on the application of Telegraph
    Group Plc) *v.* Sherwood
R. *v.* Shevki (Lutfiyf); R. *v.* Steele (Michael John) [2001] 2 Cr. App. R. (S.) 40; [2001]
    Crim. L.R. 153; *Times*, January 11, 2001; *Independent*, February 7, 2001 (C.S),
    CA (Crim Div) . . . . *Digested*, 01/**1242**:
                                                    Applied, 01/1241

R. *v.* Shields (David James) (1994) 15 Cr. App. R. (S.) 775, CA (Crim Div) . . . .   *Digested,* 95/**1459**:
Considered, 98/1339
R. *v.* Shields (Michael) see R. *v.* Love (JamesThomas)
R. (on the application of Criminal Injuries Compensation Appeals Panel) *v.* Shields [2001]
E.L.R. 164, QBD (Admin Ct) . . . .   *Digested,* 01/**1006**
R. *v.* Shioui (Rashid) see Attorney General's Reference (No.1 of 2000) (Unduly Lenient
Sentence), Re
R. *v.* Shivpuri (Pyare) [1987] A.C. 1; [1986] 2 W.L.R. 988; [1986] 2 All E.R. 334;
(1986) 83 Cr. App. R. 178; (1986) 150 J.P. 353; [1986] Crim. L.R. 536; (1986)
150 J.P.N. 510; (1986) 83 L.S.G. 1896; (1986) 136 N.L.J. 488; (1986) 130
S.J. 392, HL; affirming [1985] Q.B. 1029; [1985] 2 W.L.R. 29; [1985] 1 All E.R.
143; (1985) 80 Cr. App. R. 241; [1985] Crim. L.R. 43; (1984) 81 L.S.G. 3420;
(1985) 129 S.J. 31, CA (Crim Div) . . . .   *Digested,* 86/**482**:
Applied, 86/484, 00/994: *Considered,* 86/617, 87/1113, 94/3984
R. *v.* Shropshire CC Ex p. Abdullah see R. *v.* Barnet LBC Ex p. Shah (Nilish)
R. *v.* Shuck (David Philip) see R. *v.* Wright (Richard Arthur)
R. *v.* Shuker (Steven Thomas); R. *v.* Shuker (Thomas John) [1998] Crim. L.R. 906, CA
(Crim Div)
R. *v.* Shuker (Thomas John) see R. *v.* Shuker (Steven Thomas)
R. *v.* Siddique (Barbar) see Attorney General's Reference (Nos.73 and 74 of 2001), Re
R. *v.* Siggins (Frederick George) see R. *v.* Flower (Richard Arthur)
R. *v.* Silcott (Winston); R. *v.* Braithwaite; R. *v.* Raghip *Times,* December 9, 1991;
Independent, December 6, 1991; *Independent,* December 5, 1991; *Guardian,*
December 11, 1991, CA (Crim Div) . . . .   *Digested,* 91/**626**:
Considered, 94/976, 96/1343: *Not followed,* 00/5471
R. *v.* Siliavski (BoyanYossifov) [2000] 1 Cr. App. R. (S.) 23, CA (Crim Div) . . . .   *Digested,* 00/**1255**
R. *v.* Silver (Gavin Anthony); R. *v.* Gosling (Kevin David) (1982) 4 Cr. App. R. (S.) 48,
CA (Crim Div) . . . .   *Digested,* 83/**848**:
Cited, 93/1220, 95/1433: *Considered,* 87/870, 88/952, 97/1591, 99/1261
R. *v.* Silver (Michael) (1994) 15 Cr. App. R. (S.) 837, CA (Crim Div) . . . .   *Digested,* 95/**1431**:
Considered, 99/1265, 00/1366: *Referred to,* 97/1616
R. *v.* Silverman (Brian) (1983) 5 Cr. App. R. (S.) 46, CA (Crim Div) . . . .   *Digested,* 84/**834**:
Considered, 99/1186
R. *v.* Simmonds (Derek) [1999] 2 Cr. App. R. 18; [1999] 2 Cr. App. R. (S.) 218;
[1999] R.T.R. 257; [1999] Crim. L.R. 421; (1999) 96(8) L.S.G. 29; *Times,*
February 4, 1999; *Independent,* February 15, 1999 (C.S.); *Independent,* February
8, 1999 (C.S.), CA (Crim Div) . . . .   *Digested,* 99/**1318**:
Considered, 01/1225
R. *v.* Simmonds (Mark Gordon) [2001] EWCA Crim 167; [2001] 2 Cr. App. R. (S.) 70;
[2001] Crim. L.R. 326, CA (Crim Div) . . . .   *Digested,* 01/**1213**
R. *v.* Simons (Geoffrey) see R. *v.* Taylor (Derek Roy)
R. *v.* Simpson (Anthony) [1998] Crim. L.R. 481, CA (Crim Div)
R. *v.* Simpson (David); R. *v.* Fadden (Anthony); R. *v.* Dixon (Gary); R. *v.* Grant
(Stephen); R. *v.* Lillie (Lawrence); R. *v.* Allsopp (Michael) [1998] 2 Cr. App. R.
(S.) 111; [1998] Crim. L.R. 292; *Times,* January 26, 1998, CA (Crim Div) . . . . . .   *Digested,* 98/**1150**
R. *v.* Simpson (Martin) [1998] 1 Cr. App. R. (S.) 197, CA (Crim Div) . . . .   *Digested,* 98/**1401**
R. *v.* Simpson (Moira) see Attorney General's Reference (Nos.86 and 87 of 1999), Re
R. *v.* Simpson (Paul Anthony) (1981) 3 Cr. App. R. (S.) 148; [1981] Crim. L.R. 649,
CA (Crim Div) . . . .   *Digested,* 81/**525.60**:
Considered, 98/1370
R. *v.* Simsek (Muslum) see R. *v.* Kaynak (Hussein)
R. *v.* Sinclair (James); R. *v.* Johnson (Brian); R. *v.* Smith (Ian) (1998) 148 N.L.J. 1353,
CA (Crim Div)
R. *v.* Singfield; R. *v.* Gregory; (Unreported, November 23, 1999), CC (Derby) . . . .   *Cited,* 00/**916**
R. *v.* Singh (Baldev); R. *v.* Singh (Chamkaur); R. *v.* Singh (Jarnail) [2000] 1 Cr. App. R.
31; [1999] Crim. L.R. 681, CA (Crim Div) . . . .   *Digested,* 00/**1018**
R. *v.* Singh (Bhupinder) see R. *v.* Liddle (Frederick)
R. *v.* Singh (Chamkaur) see R. *v.* Singh (Baldev)
R. *v.* Singh (Daljit) [1999] 1 Cr. App. R. (S.) 490; [1999] Crim. L.R. 236; (1998)
95(45) L.S.G. 40; *Times,* November 5, 1998; *Independent,* November 12, 1998,
CA (Crim Div) . . . .   *Digested,* 98/**1227**:
Considered, 00/1255
R. *v.* Singh (Dara) [1999] 1 Cr. App. R. (S.) 445; [1999] Crim. L.R. 173; (1998)
95(42) L.S.G. 33; *Times,* October 28, 1998; *Independent,* October 20, 1998, CA
(Crim Div) . . . .   *Digested,* 98/**1157**
R. *v.* Singh (Gurphal) [1999] Crim. L.R. 582; *Times,* April 17, 1999, CA (Crim Div) . . . . .   *Digested,* 99/**945**
R. *v.* Singh (Jarnail) see R. *v.* Singh (Baldev)
R. *v.* Singh (Jasjit) [1999] 2 Cr. App. R. (S.) 160, CA (Crim Div) . . . .   *Digested,* 99/**1272**
R. *v.* Singh (Narinder) (1992) 13 Cr. App. R. (S.) 123, CA (Crim Div) . . . .   *Digested,* 93/**1246**:
Cited, 94/1410: *Considered,* 99/1287
R. *v.* Singh (Satvir) (1988) 10 Cr. App. R. (S.) 402, CA (Crim Div) . . . .   *Digested,* 90/**1290**:
Cited, 93/1139: *Considered,* 98/1191, 99/1137, 99/1148, 00/1233
R. *v.* Singleton (David) see R. *v.* Harrison (Michael John)
R. *v.* Singleton (John Paul) [1998] 1 Cr. App. R. (S.) 199, CA (Crim Div) . . . .   *Digested,* 98/**1400**

R. *v.* Sinha (Arun Kumar) [1998] Masons C.L.R. Rep. 35; [1995] Crim. L.R. 68; *Times,*
July 13, 1994; *Independent,* August 1, 1994 (C.S.), CA (Crim Div) . . . . *Digested,* 94/**1137**
R. *v.* Sissen (Henry Thomas) [2001] 1 W.L.R. 902; [2001] Crim. L.R. 232; (2001)
98(5) L.S.G. 36; (2001) 145 S.J.L.B. 14; *Times,* January 9, 2001; *Independent,*
January 29, 2001 (C.S), CA (Crim Div) . . . . *Digested,* 01/**4129**
R. *v.* Skinner (Ian Paul) see R. *v.* Skinner (Vincent Patrick)
R. *v.* Skinner (Vincent Patrick); R. *v.* Skinner (Ian Paul) (1993) 14 Cr. App. R. (S.) 115;
(1993) 137 S.J.L.B. 277, CA (Crim Div) . . . . *Digested,* 93/**1245**:
Considered, 98/1111: *Referred to,* 95/1448
R. *v.* Skittlethorpe (Stuart) see Attorney General's Reference (No.16 of 2000), Re
R. *v.* Sky (Tre) [2000] 2 Cr. App. R. (S.) 260, CA (Crim Div) . . . . *Digested,* 00/**1136**
R. *v.* Slade (Mark) see R. *v.* Preddy (John Crawford)
R. *v.* Slater (Quentin John) [1998] 2 Cr. App. R. (S.) 415, CA (Crim Div) . . . . *Digested,* 99/**1221**
R. *v.* SLC [2000] 1 Cr. App. R. (S.) 304, CA (Crim Div) . . . . *Digested,* 00/**1273**
R. *v.* Slimmings (Richard Gareth) [1999] Crim. L.R. 69, CA (Crim Div)
R. *v.* Sloan (Ian Kyle) [1998] N.I. 58, CA (Crim Div) (NI) . . . . *Digested,* 99/**5224**:
Applied, 99/5225

R. *v.* Slowey (Peter) see R. *v.* Zelzele (Behcet)
R. *v.* SM (A Juvenile) see Attorney General's Reference (Nos.53, 54, 55, 56 and 57 of
2001), Re
R. *v.* SM (A Juvenile) [2000] 1 Cr. App. R. (S.) 188, CA (Crim Div) . . . . *Digested,* 00/**1311**
R. *v.* Smethurst (John Russell) [2001] EWCA Crim 772; (2001) 165 J.P. 377; [2001]
Crim. L.R. 657; (2001) 165 J.P.N. 408; *Times,* April 13, 2001, CA (Crim Div). . . . *Digested,* 01/**1058**
R. *v.* Smith (Andrew Barry) [1998] 2 Cr. App. R. (S.) 400, CA (Crim Div) . . . . *Digested,* 99/**1101**
R. *v.* Smith (Arthur) (1981) 3 Cr. App. R. (S.) 201, CA (Crim Div) . . . . *Considered,* 98/1374
R. *v.* Smith (Brian Leonard) [1996] 1 Cr. App. R. (S.) 24, CA (Crim Div) . . . . *Considered,* 99/1356
R. *v.* Smith (Christopher) (1981) 3 Cr. App. R. (S.) 168, CA (Crim Div) . . . . *Considered,* 98/1307:
Followed, 90/1406, 91/1208: *Referred to,* 92/1394, 93/1277
R. *v.* Smith (Colin Paul) see Attorney General's Reference (Nos.65 and 66 of 2001), Re
R. *v.* Smith (Cyril) see R. *v.* Lloyd (Paul Gabriel)
R. *v.* Smith (David Brian) [1999] Env. L.R. 433; [1999] J.P.L. 270, CA (Crim Div) . . . . . *Digested,* 99/**2198**
R. *v.* Smith (David Cadman); *sub nom* R.v Cadman-Smith (David) [2001] UKHL 68;
Times, December 17, 2001; *Independent,* December 18, 2001; *Daily Telegraph,*
December 20, 2001, HL; reversing [2001] 1 Cr. App. R. (S.) 61; (2000) 164 J.P.
575; (2001) 165 J.P.N. 66; *Times,* July 26, 2000, CA (Crim Div) . . . . *Digested,* 00/**1162**
R. *v.* Smith (David Cadman) (Leave to Appeal); *sub nom* R. *v.* Cadman-Smith (David)
(Leave to Appeal) [2001] Crim. L.R. 644, CA (Crim Div)
R. *v.* Smith (David Jack) (1993) 14 Cr. App. R. (S.) 708, CA (Crim Div) . . . . *Digested,* 94/**1353**:
Considered, 98/1338
R. *v.* Smith (David James) [1998] 2 Cr. App. R. 1; *Times,* December 19, 1997, CA (Crim
Div) . . . . *Digested,* 98/**1095**
R. *v.* Smith (Eileen) (1988) 10 Cr. App. R. (S.) 120, CA (Crim Div) . . . . *Digested,* 90/**1358**:
Considered, 98/1305
R. *v.* Smith (Ian) see R. *v.* Sinclair (James)
R. *v.* Smith (Ian) [1989] 1 W.L.R. 765; [1989] 2 All E.R. 948; (1989) 89 Cr. App. R.
235; (1989) 11 Cr. App. R. (S.) 290; [1989] Crim. L.R. 752; (1989) 133 S.J. 848,
CA (Crim Div) . . . . *Digested,* 89/**987**:
Considered, 90/1034, 91/869, 98/1110: *Followed,* 97/1471
R. *v.* Smith (Joanna Gay) see Attorney General's Reference (No.3 of 2001), Re
R. *v.* Smith (Joe) [2001] 1 W.L.R. 1031; [2001] 2 Cr. App. R. 1; *Times,* December 20,
2000, CA (Crim Div) . . . . *Digested,* 01/**1185**
R. *v.* Smith (John) see R. *v.* Amlani (Chanudula)
R. *v.* Smith (Joseph Arnold) see R. *v.* Tantram (Peter John)
R. *v.* Smith (Linford) [2001] 2 Cr. App. R. (S.) 34, CA (Crim Div) . . . . *Digested,* 01/**1203**
R. *v.* Smith (Matthew Luke) [2001] 1 Cr. App. R. (S.) 66, CA (Crim Div) . . . . *Digested,* 01/**1407**
R. *v.* Smith (Morgan James) [2001] 1 A.C. 146; [2000] 3 W.L.R. 654; [2000] 4 All
E.R. 289; [2001] 1 Cr. App. R. 5; [2000] Crim. L.R. 1004; (2000) 97(37) L.S.G.
39; (2000) 150 N.L.J. 1199; (2000) 144 S.J.L.B. 251; *Times,* August 4, 2000;
Independent, October 4, 2000, HL; affirming [1999] Q.B. 1079; [1999] 2 W.L.R.
610; [1998] 4 All E.R. 387; [1999] 1 Cr. App. R. 256; (1999) 45 B.M.L.R. 146;
[1998] Crim. L.R. 896; (1998) 148 N.L.J. 1086; *Times,* July 29, 1998;
Independent, July 15, 1998, CA (Crim Div) . . . . *Digested,* 00/**986**:
Distinguished, 01/1054: *Followed,* 01/5729
R. *v.* Smith (Nicholas James) see R. *v.* Sansom (Alec James)
R. *v.* Smith (Patrick Joseph); R. *v.* Taylor (James); R. *v.* Nicholson (John); R. *v.* Johnson
(Henry) [2000] 1 All E.R. 263; [1999] 2 Cr. App. R. 238; (1999) 96(23)
L.S.G. 34; *Times,* May 31, 1999, CA (Crim Div) . . . . *Digested,* 99/**969**
R. *v.* Smith (Patrick O'Neill) (1989) 11 Cr. App. R. (S.) 55, CA (Crim Div) . . . . *Digested,* 90/**1383**:
Considered, 96/1893, 00/1254
R. *v.* Smith (Paul) [2001] 1 Cr. App. R. (S.) 67, CA (Crim Div) . . . . *Digested,* 01/**1215**
R. *v.* Smith (Peter) see Attorney General's Reference (Nos.90 and 91 of 1998), Re

R. *v.* Smith (Peter Leonard) [1998] 1 Cr. App. R. (S.) 138; [1997] Crim. L.R. 614; (1997) 94(25) L.S.G. 33; (1997) 141 S.J.L.B. 153; *Times*, June 26, 1997, CA (Crim Div) . . . .   *Digested*, 97/**1578**:
Considered, 98/1239: *Distinguished*, 00/1272

R. *v.* Smith (Richard Peter) see Attorney General's Reference (Nos.33 and 34 of 2001), Re

R. *v.* Smith (Robert) see Attorney General's Reference (No.43 of 1994), Re

R. *v.* Smith (Robert John) see Attorney General's Reference (No.47 of 1994), Re

R. *v.* Smith (Ruben); R. *v.* Fletcher (Francis Royston) [2001] EWCA Crim 1700; [2001] Crim. L.R. 833, CA (Crim Div)

R. *v.* Smith (Shevon) [2000] 1 Cr. App. R. (S.) 212, CA (Crim Div) . . . .   *Digested*, 00/**1369**

R. *v.* Smith (Wallace Duncan) (No.1) [1996] 2 B.C.L.C. 109; [1996] 2 Cr. App. R. 1; [1996] Crim. L.R. 329; (1995) 92(44) L.S.G. 31; (1996) 140 S.J.L.B. 11; *Times*, November 13, 1995; *Independent*, November 22, 1995 (C.S.), CA (Crim Div) . . .   *Digested*, 95/**1332**:
Not followed, 98/957

R. *v.* Smith (Wallace Duncan) (No.2) [1999] 2 Cr. App. R. 444; (1999) 96(23) L.S.G. 35; *Times*, May 20, 1999; *Independent*, May 28, 1999, CA (Crim Div) . . . .   *Digested*, 99/**973**

R. *v.* Smith (Wayne Anthony), *Times*, June 22, 1999, CA (Crim Div) . . . .   *Digested*, 99/**1345**

R. *v.* Smith (Wesley) [1963] 1 W.L.R. 1200; [1963] 3 All E.R. 597; 128 J.P. 13; 107 S.J. 873, CCA . . . .   *Digested*, 63/**622**:
Applied, 00/5468: *Distinguished*, 66/2603

R. *v.* Smurthwaite (Keith); R. *v.* Gill (Susan) [1994] 1 All E.R. 898; (1994) 98 Cr. App. R. 437; (1994) 158 J.P. 165; [1994] Crim. L.R. 53; (1994) 158 L.G. Rev. 92; (1993) 143 N.L.J. 1568; (1993) 137 S.J.L.B. 235; *Times*, October 5, 1993; *Guardian*, September 20, 1993, CA (Crim Div) . . . .   *Digested*, 94/**669**:
Cited, 00/916: *Considered*, 94/977, 95/921, 95/3578, 96/1455, 97/1503

R. *v.* Smyth (Paul); R. *v.* Aspinall (John); R. *v.* Aspinall (Thomas) *Times*, September 16, 1998, CA (Crim Div) . . . .   *Digested*, 98/**1048**

R. *v.* Smyth (William John) see R. *v.* Maguire (Anne Rita)

R. *v.* Smythe (Scott Lee) [2000] 1 Cr. App. R. (S.) 547, CA (Crim Div) . . . .   *Digested*, 00/**1209**

R. (on the application of A) *v.* Snaresbrook Crown Court; *sub nom* R. (on the application of R) *v.* Serious Fraud Office *Times*, July 12, 2001; *Independent*, July 30, 2001 (C.S.); *Daily Telegraph*, July 3, 2001, QBD (Admin Ct) . . . .   *Digested*, 01/**1084**

R. (on the application of Kenneally) *v.* Snaresbrook Crown Court; R. (on the application of Kenneally) *v.* Rampton Hospital Authority [2001] EWHC Admin 968; *Times*, December 17, 2001, QBD (Admin Ct)

R. *v.* Snaresbrook Crown Court Ex p. Director of the Serious Fraud Office (1998) 95(44) L.S.G. 35; (1998) 142 S.J.L.B. 263; *Times*, October 26, 1998; *Independent*, October 26, 1998 (C.S.), QBD . . . .   *Digested*, 98/**1036**

R. *v.* Snaresbrook Crown Court Ex p. Input Management Ltd (1999) 163 J.P. 533; (1999) 143 S.J.L.B. 113; *Times*, April 29, 1999; *Independent*, March 15, 1999 (C.S.), QBD . . . .   *Digested*, 99/**1002**

R. *v.* Snaresbrook Crown Court Ex p. Patel [2000] C.O.D. 255, QBD

R. *v.* Snow (Murray Franklin) (1988) 10 Cr. App. R. (S.) 93, CA (Crim Div) . . . .   *Digested*, 90/**1296**:
Considered, 97/1512, 98/1196

R. *v.* Soames-Waring (Jonathan Drew) [1999] Crim. L.R. 89; *Times*, July 20, 1998, CA (Crim Div) . . . .   *Digested*, 98/**1089**

R. *v.* Social Fund Inspector Ex p. Taylor (1998) 41 B.M.L.R. 31; [1998] C.O.D. 152; *Times*, January 20, 1998, QBD . . . .   *Digested*, 98/**4560**

R. *v.* Social Security Commissioner Ex p. Chamberlain, *Times*, August 1, 2000, QBD . . .   *Digested*, 00/**4834**

R. *v.* Socialist Worker Printers & Publishers Ltd Ex p. Attorney General [1975] Q.B. 637; [1974] 3 W.L.R. 801; [1975] 1 All E.R. 142; [1974] Crim. L.R. 711; 118 S.J. 791, DC . . . .   *Digested*, 75/**2601**:
Applied, 78/2337: *Considered*, 79/2120, 98/75

R. *v.* Soffe (Nicholas), *Times*, April 5, 2000, CA (Crim Div) . . . .   *Digested*, 00/**1064**

R. (on the application of Toth) *v.* Solicitors Disciplinary Tribunal; *sub nom* R. *v.* Solicitors Disciplinary Tribunal Ex p. Toth [2001] EWHC Admin 240; [2001] 3 All E.R. 180; (2001) 151 N.L.J. 502; *Times*, May 3, 2001, QBD (Admin Ct) . . . .   *Digested*, 01/**4270**

R. *v.* Solicitors Disciplinary Tribunal Ex p. Toth see R. (on the application of Toth) *v.* Solicitors Disciplinary Tribunal

R. *v.* Solihull BC Ex p. Berkswell Parish Council (1999) 77 P. & C.R. 312, QBD . . . .   *Digested*, 99/**4254**

R. *v.* Solihull MBC Ex p. W [1997] E.L.R. 489, QBD . . . .   *Digested*, 98/**1901**

R. *v.* Solihull MBC Housing Benefit Review Board Ex p. Simpson; *sub nom* Solihull MBC Housing Benefit Review Board *v.* Simpson [1995] 1 F.L.R. 140; [1995] 2 F.C.R. 424; (1995) 27 H.L.R. 41; 92 L.G.R. 719; [1995] Fam. Law 17; *Times*, July 19, 1994, CA; affirming (1994) 26 H.L.R. 370; [1994] C.O.D. 225; [1994] Fam. Law 380; *Times*, January 5, 1994; *Independent*, January 4, 1994, QBD . . . .   *Digested*, 95/**2598**:
Applied, 00/4824: *Considered*, 94/2355, 95/2599, 96/5447, 97/4649:
Followed, 96/5445, 97/2690

R. *v.* Somers (Mark) [1999] Crim. L.R. 744, CA (Crim Div)

R. *v.* Somerset CC Ex p. Dixon [1998] Env. L.R. 111; (1998) 75 P. & C.R. 175; [1997] J.P.L. 1030; [1997] C.O.D. 323; [1997] N.P.C. 61, QBD . . . .   *Digested*, 97/**4101**

R. *v.* Somerset CC Ex p. Fewings [1995] 1 W.L.R. 1037; [1995] 3 All E.R. 20; (1995) 7 Admin. L.R. 761; [1996] C.O.D. 76; (1995) 92(16) L.S.G. 43; (1995) 145 N.L.J. 450; (1995) 139 S.J.L.B. 88; *Times*, March 23, 1995; *Independent*, March 22, 1995, CA; affirming [1995] 1 All E.R. 513; 92 L.G.R. 674; (1994) 6 Admin. L.R. 446; [1994] C.O.D. 338; (1994) 158 L.G. Rev. 461; [1994] N.P.C. 17; *Times*, February 10, 1994; *Independent*, February 16, 1994; *Guardian*, February 14, 1994, QBD . . . . *Digested,* 95/**5406**:

Applied, 01/4335: *Considered,* 00/2212: *Followed,* 01/4316

R. *v.* Somerset CC Ex p. Harcombe (1997) 37 B.M.L.R. 1; [1998] C.O.D. 71; *Times,* May 7, 1997, QBD . . . . *Digested,* 97/**4718**

R. *v.* Somerset CC Ex p. Morris & Perry (Gurney Slade Quarry) Ltd [2000] Env. L.R. 582; (2000) 79 P. & C.R. 238; [2000] P.L.C.R. 117, QBD . . . . *Digested,* 00/**4515**

R. *v.* Somerset CC Ex p. Prospects Care Services Ltd [2000] 1 F.L.R. 636; (1999) 2 C.C.L. Rep. 161; [1999] C.O.D. 268, QBD . . . . *Digested,* 99/**2430**

R. *v.* Sood (Rajinder Kumar) [1998] 2 Cr. App. R. 355; (1999) 47 B.M.L.R. 166; [1999] Crim. L.R. 85; (1998) 148 N.L.J. 479; *Times,* March 24, 1998, CA (Crim Div) . . . . *Digested,* 98/**967**

R. (on the application of Burgess) *v.* South Bank University; *sub nom* R. *v.* South Bank University Ex p. Burgess [2001] E.L.R. 300, QBD . . . . *Digested,* 01/**1900**

R. *v.* South Bank University Ex p. Burgess see R. (on the application of Burgess) *v.* South Bank University

R. *v.* South Bank University Ex p. Coggeran [2000] I.C.R. 1342; [2001] E.L.R. 42; (2000) 97(40) L.S.G. 41; (2000) 144 S.J.L.B. 256; *Times,* September 19, 2000, CA; affirming CO/4699/1999, QBD . . . . *Digested,* 00/**2004**

R. (on the application of Secretary of State for Social Security) *v.* South Central Division Magistrates, *Daily Telegraph,* November 28, 2000, QBD

R. *v.* South Devon Magistrates Court Ex p. Hallett [2000] C.O.D. 279; *Independent,* May 8, 2000 (C.S.), QBD

R. *v.* South East Hampshire Magistrates Court Ex p. Crown Prosecution Service [1998] Crim. L.R. 422, QBD

R. *v.* South East Northumberland Magistrates Court Ex p. Knox see R. *v.* Norwich Magistrates Court Ex p. Elliott

R. *v.* South Glamorgan CC Ex p. Harding [1998] C.O.D. 243, QBD

R. *v.* South Gloucestershire Education Appeals Committee Ex p. B (A Child) [2001] E.L.R. 53, CA; affirming [2000] E.L.R. 602, QBD . . . . *Digested,* 01/**1972**

R. *v.* South Gloucestershire Education Appeals Committee Ex p. C [2000] Ed. C.R. 212; [2000] E.L.R. 220, QBD . . . . *Digested,* 00/**1921**

R. *v.* South Hams DC Ex p. Ash (2000) 32 H.L.R. 405; *Times,* May 27, 1999, QBD . . . . *Digested,* 99/**4512**

R. (on the application of Lincoln Cooperative Society Ltd) *v.* South Holland DC; *sub nom* R. *v.* South Holland DC Ex p. Lincoln Cooperative Society Ltd [2001] J.P.L. 675; [2000] E.G.C.S. 133, QBD (Admin Ct) . . . . *Digested,* 01/**4731**

R. *v.* South Holland DC Ex p. Baxter (1998) 30 H.L.R. 1069, QBD . . . . *Digested,* 99/**3049**

R. *v.* South Holland DC Ex p. Lincoln Cooperative Society Ltd see R. (on the application of Lincoln Cooperative Society Ltd) *v.* South Holland DC

R. *v.* South Norfolk CC Ex p. Pelham Homes Ltd [2001] P.L.C.R. 8; [2001] J.P.L. 230 (Note), QBD . . . . *Digested,* 01/**4748**

R. *v.* South Ribble BC Housing Benefit Review Board Ex p. Hamilton (2001) 33 H.L.R. 9; *Independent,* March 13, 2000 (C.S.), CA; affirming (2000) 32 H.L.R. 261, QBD

R. (on the application of Bozcurt) *v.* South Thames Magistrates Court see R. (on the application of Bozkurt) *v.* Thames Magistrates Court

R. *v.* South Thames Mental Health Review Tribunal Ex p. M [1998] C.O.D. 38, QBD . . . . *Cited,* 00/4173

R. *v.* South Tyneside Education Department Ex p. Cram see R. *v.* South Tyneside MBC Ex p. Cram

R. *v.* South Tyneside MBC Ex p. Cram; *sub nom* R. *v.* South Tyneside Education Department Ex p. Cram (1998) 10 Admin. L.R. 477; [1998] E.L.R. 508; [1998] C.O.D. 183; (1998) 162 J.P.N. 645; (1998) 162 J.P.N. 685, QBD . . . . *Digested,* 98/**1903**:

Applied, 01/1946

R. *v.* South West Surrey Magistrates Court Ex p. James [2000] Crim. L.R. 690, QBD

R. *v.* South Western Hospital Managers Ex p. M see R. *v.* Managers of South Western Hospital Ex p. M

R. *v.* South Worcestershire Magistrates Ex p. Lilley [1995] 1 W.L.R. 1595; [1995] 4 All E.R. 186; [1996] 1 Cr. App. R. 420; (1995) 159 J.P. 598; [1995] Crim. L.R. 954; [1996] C.O.D. 109; (1995) 92(13) L.S.G. 31; (1995) 139 S.J.L.B. 67; *Times,* February 22, 1995, QBD . . . . *Digested,* 96/**1576**:

Considered, 97/1342, 01/1198

R. *v.* South Yorkshire Police Authority Ex p. Booth, *Times,* October 10, 2000, QBD . . . . . *Digested,* 00/**4540**

R. *v.* South Yorkshire Police Authority Ex p. Chief Constable of South Yorkshire see R. *v.* DPP Ex p. Duckenfield

R. *v.* Southampton Magistrates Court Ex p. Sansome see R. *v.* Eastleigh Magistrates Court Ex p. Sansome

R. *v.* Southampton Port Authority Ex p. SPI Plc [2001] E.H.L.R. Dig. 4, QBD

R. (on the application of Seahawk Marine Foods Ltd) *v.* Southampton Port HA see Southampton Port HA *v.* Seahawk Marine Foods Ltd

R. v. Southend Borough Education Appeals Committee Ex p. Southend on Sea BC
[2000] Ed. C.R. 368, QBD . . . . *Digested,* 00/**1912**
R. (on the application of Smith) v. Southwark Crown Court [2001] 2 Cr. App. R. (S.) 35,
QBD . . . . *Digested,* 01/**1299**
R. v. Southwark Crown Court Ex p. Bowles; *sub nom* R. v. Guildford Crown Court Ex
p. DPP [1998] A.C. 641; [1998] 2 W.L.R. 715; [1998] 2 All E.R. 193; [1998] 2 Cr.
App. R. 187; [1999] Crim. L.R. 220; (1998) 95(18) L.S.G. 32; (1998) 148
N.L.J. 588; (1998) 142 S.J.L.B. 126; *Times,* April 7, 1998, HL; affirming [1998]
Q.B. 243; [1997] 2 W.L.R. 936; [1996] 4 All E.R. 961; [1997] 1 Cr. App. R. 436;
Times, October 29, 1996, QBD . . . . *Digested,* 98/**893**
R. v. Southwark Crown Court Ex p. DPP [1999] Crim. L.R. 394, QBD
R. v. Southwark Crown Court Ex p. Koncar [1998] 1 Cr. App. R. 321, QBD . . . . *Digested,* 98/**1242**
R. v. Southwark Crown Court Ex p. Screen Multimedia Ltd see R. v. Bow Street
Metropolitan Stipendiary Magistrate Ex p. Screen Multimedia Ltd
R. v. Southwark Crown Court Ex p. Sorsky Defries [1996] C.O.D. 117; *Times,* July 21,
1995; *Independent,* September 15, 1995, QBD . . . . *Digested,* 95/**1201**:
Considered, 99/900
R. (on the application of K) v. Southwark LBC; *sub nom* K v. Southwark LBC [2001]
EWCA Civ 999; (2001) 98(33) L.S.G. 31; *Times,* September 25, 2001, CA;
affirming CO/2249/00, QBD (Admin Ct) . . . . *Digested,* 01/**5132**
R. v. Southwark LBC Ex p. Anderson (2000) 32 H.L.R. 96, QBD . . . . *Digested,* 00/**3134**:
Considered, 99/3021
R. v. Southwark LBC Ex p. Bediako; R. v. Westminster City Council Ex p. Zafru (1998)
30 H.L.R. 22; *Times,* March 17, 1997, QBD . . . . *Digested,* 97/**2652**
R. v. Southwark LBC Ex p. Campisi (1999) 31 H.L.R. 560, CA . . . . *Digested,* 99/**3064**
R. v. Southwark LBC Ex p. Hong Cui (1999) 31 H.L.R. 639; (1999) 2 C.C.L. Rep. 86,
QBD . . . . *Digested,* 99/**4621**
R. v. Southwark LBC Ex p. Hughes (1998) 30 H.L.R. 1082, QBD . . . . *Digested,* 99/**3061**
R. v. Southwark LBC Ex p. Mason (2000) 32 H.L.R. 88, QBD . . . . *Digested,* 99/**3020**
R. v. Southwark LBC Ex p. Ryder (1996) 28 H.L.R. 56, QBD . . . . *Digested,* 96/**3071**:
Distinguished, 98/2998
R. v. Sowden (Clive Brian) [2000] 2 Cr. App. R. (S.) 360; [2000] Crim. L.R. 500, CA
(Crim Div) . . . . *Digested,* 00/**1175**
R. v. Sowrey (Daniel Frederick) (1994) 15 Cr. App. R. (S.) 870, CA . . . . *Digested,* 95/**1432**:
Considered, 99/1262
R. v. Spalding (Phillip Peter) (1995) 16 Cr. App. R. (S.) 803, CA (Crim Div) . . . . *Digested,* 96/**1856**:
Considered, 96/1849, 97/1509, 00/1215
R. v. Sparks (Seth Joseph); R. v. Kingsnorth (Glyn Kevin) (1995) 16 Cr. App. R. (S.)
480, CA (Crim Div) . . . . *Considered,* 98/1162,
00/1135

R. v. Spear (John); R. v. Hastie (Philip); R. v. Boyd (David Morton) [2001] EWCA Crim
2; [2001] Q.B. 804; [2001] 2 W.L.R. 1692; [2001] Crim. L.R. 485; (2001)
98(12) L.S.G. 43; (2001) 145 S.J.L.B. 38; *Times,* January 30, 2001, CMAC . . . . *Digested,* 01/**358**
R. (on the application of Chohan) v. Special Adjudicator; *sub nom* R. v. Special
Adjudicator Ex p. Chohan *Independent,* November 27, 2000 (C.S), QBD (Admin
Ct)
R. (on the application of Dhothar) v. Special Adjudicator; *sub nom* R. v. Special
Adjudicator Ex p. Dhothar [2001] Imm. A.R. 210, QBD (Admin Ct) . . . . *Digested,* 01/**3634**
R. (on the application of Gavira) v. Special Adjudicator see R. (on the application of
Gavira) v. Secretary of State for the Home Department
R. (on the application of I) v. Special Adjudicator; *sub nom* I v. Special Adjudicator; R. v.
Special Adjudicator Ex p. I [2001] EWCA Civ 1271; (2001) 98(36) L.S.G. 37;
Times, September 18, 2001, CA; reversing CO/2170/1999, QBD (Admin Ct) . . . . *Digested,* 01/**3642**
R. (on the application of Roszkowski) v. Special Adjudicator; *sub nom* R. v. Secretary of
State for the Home Department Ex p. Roszkowski; Roszkowski v. Special
Adjudicator [2001] EWCA Civ 650, CA; affirming *Times,* November 29, 2000,
QBD (Admin Ct) . . . . *Digested,* 01/**3640**
R. (on the application of Subaththeran) v. Special Adjudicator; *sub nom* R. v. Special
Adjudicator Ex p. Subaththeran [2001] EWHC Admin 12; [2001] Imm. A.R. 345,
QBD (Admin Ct) . . . . *Digested,* 01/**3630**
R. (on the application of Vallaj) v. Special Adjudicator; *sub nom* Vallaj v. Special
Adjudicator; Canaj v. Secretary of State for the Home Department [2001]
EWCA Civ 782; [2001] I.N.L.R. 342, CA; affirming [2001] I.N.L.R. 455, QBD
R. v. Special Adjudicator Ex p. Ahmad (Hanif) [1999] Imm. A.R. 390, QBD . . . . *Digested,* 00/**3308**
R. v. Special Adjudicator Ex p. B [1998] Imm. A.R. 182; [1998] I.N.L.R. 315, QBD . . . . . *Digested,* 98/**3209**:
Followed, 00/3298

R. v. Special Adjudicator Ex p. Chohan see R. (on the application of Chohan) v.
Special Adjudicator
R. v. Special Adjudicator Ex p. Demeter [2000] Imm. A.R. 424; [2000] I.N.L.R. 524,
QBD . . . . *Digested,* 00/**3277**
R. v. Special Adjudicator Ex p. Dhothar see R. (on the application of Dhothar) v.
Special Adjudicator

R. *v.* Special Adjudicator Ex p. Gnanavarathan; *sub nom* Gnanavarathan *v.* Special
Adjudicator; R. *v.* Secretary of State for the Home Department Ex p.
Gnanavarathan; R. *v.* Special Adjudicator Ex p. Norbert [1995] Imm. A.R. 64;
Independent, October 3, 1994 (C.S.), CA . . . . *Digested,* 95/**2705**:
                    Applied, 96/3198, 00/3278: *Cited,* 96/3237: *Considered,* 97/2874, 97/2876
R. *v.* Special Adjudicator Ex p. I see R. (on the application of I) *v.* Special Adjudicator
R. *v.* Special Adjudicator Ex p. John [1999] Imm. A.R. 432, QBD . . . .   *Digested,* 00/**3302**
R. *v.* Special Adjudicator Ex p. Kerrouche (No.1) see R. *v.* Secretary of State for the
Home Department Ex p. Kerrouche (No.1)
R. *v.* Special Adjudicator Ex p. Kotovas [2000] Imm. A.R. 26, QBD . . . .   *Digested,* 00/**3272**
R. *v.* Special Adjudicator Ex p. Mohammed (Mukhtar Shala) see R. *v.* Immigration
Appellate Authority Ex p. Mohammed (Mukhtar Shala)
R. *v.* Special Adjudicator Ex p. Norbert see R. *v.* Special Adjudicator Ex p.
Gnanavarathan
R. *v.* Special Adjudicator Ex p. Okonkwo [1998] Imm. A.R. 502, QBD . . . .   *Digested,* 99/**3149**
R. *v.* Special Adjudicator Ex p. Roznys [2000] Imm. A.R. 57, QBD . . . .   *Digested,* 00/**3320**
R. *v.* Special Adjudicator Ex p. Secretary of State for the Home Department; R. *v.*
Secretary of State for the Home Department Ex p. Cakabay (No.2); R. *v.*
Immigration Appellate Authority Ex p. Secretary of State for the Home
Department [1999] Imm. A.R. 176; [1998] I.N.L.R. 623; (1998) 142 S.J.L.B.
231; *Times,* July 13, 1998, CA; affirming [1998] Imm. A.R. 52; (1997) 94(44)
L.S.G. 35; *Times,* November 25, 1997; *Independent,* November 5, 1997, QBD . . .   *Digested,* 98/**3196**:
                                                            Previous proceedings, 98/3199
R. *v.* Special Adjudicator Ex p. Shokar see R. *v.* Immigration Appeal Tribunal Ex p.
Shokar
R. *v.* Special Adjudicator Ex p. Subaththeran see R. (on the application of
Subaththeran) *v.* Special Adjudicator
R. *v.* Special Adjudicator Ex p. Zaman [2000] Imm. A.R. 68, QBD . . . .   *Digested,* 00/**3328**
R. (on the application of Morgan Grenfell & Co Ltd) *v.* Special Commissioner of Income
Tax; *sub nom* R. *v.* Inland Revenue Commissioners Ex p. Morgan Grenfell & Co
Ltd; R. *v.* Special Commissioners of Income Tax Ex p. Morgan Grenfell & Co Ltd;
TNS, HL; reversing [2001] EWCA Civ 329; [2001] S.T.C. 497; [2001] S.T.I. 281;
(2001) 98(18) L.S.G. 45; [2000] N.P.C. 54; *Times,* April 17, 2001; *Independent,*
March 15, 2001, CA; affirming [2001] 1 All E.R. 535; [2000] S.T.C. 965; [2000]
S.T.I. 1609; (2000) 97(48) L.S.G. 37; (2000) 150 N.L.J. 1717; *Times,* November
22, 2000, QBD (Admin Ct) . . . .   *Digested,* 01/**5313**:
                                                            Considered, 01/5320
R. *v.* Special Commissioners of Income Tax Ex p. Inland Revenue Commissioners; R. *v.*
Inland Revenue Commissioners Ex p. Ulster Bank Ltd [2000] S.T.C. 537; 73 T.C.
209; [2000] B.T.C. 215; [2000] S.T.I. 888; *Times,* June 27, 2000, QBD . . . .   *Digested,* 00/**5064**
R. *v.* Special Commissioners of Income Tax Ex p. Morgan Grenfell & Co Ltd see R. (on
the application of Morgan Grenfell & Co Ltd) *v.* Special Commissioner of Income
Tax
R. *v.* Special Educational Needs Tribunal Ex p. F [1999] E.L.R. 417, QBD . . . .   *Digested,* 00/**1951**
R. *v.* Special Educational Needs Tribunal Ex p. KL [1997] E.L.R. 504, QBD . . . .   *Digested,* 98/**1976**
R. *v.* Special Immigration Adjudicator Ex p. T [2001] Imm. A.R. 187, QBD . . . .   *Digested,* 01/**3633**
R. *v.* Specialist Training Authority of the Medical Royal Colleges Ex p. British Medical
Association [1999] Ed. C.R. 661; (1999) 47 B.M.L.R. 95, QBD . . . .   *Digested,* 99/**2660**
R. *v.* Spence (Clinton Everton); R. *v.* Thomas (Vernon Walter) (1983) 5 Cr. App. R. (S.)
413; [1984] Crim. L.R. 372, CA (Crim Div) . . . .   *Digested,* 84/**876**:
                    Cited, 91/1146, 94/1292: *Considered,* 86/741, 86/742, 87/986, 87/988,
                            92/1445, 96/1888, 96/1889, 97/1540: *Distinguished,* 85/728, 86/842:
                                                Followed, 97/1604: *Referred to,* 00/1262
R. *v.* Spence (Colin Michael) (1999) 163 J.P. 754; [1999] R.T.R. 353; [1999] Crim.
L.R. 975; *Times,* May 24, 1999, CA (Crim Div). . . . .   *Digested,* 99/**958**
R. *v.* Spencer (Simon) see Attorney General's Reference (No.66 of 1996), Re
R. *v.* Spillman (Annette) see R. *v.* Spillman (David Stephen)
R. *v.* Spillman (David Stephen); R. *v.* Spillman (Annette) [2001] 1 Cr. App. R. (S.) 139,
CA (Crim Div) . . . .   *Digested,* 01/**1317**
R. *v.* Spinks (Gary) (1987) 9 Cr. App. R. (S.) 297; [1987] Crim. L.R. 786, CA (Crim
Div) . . . .   *Digested,* 89/**1032**:
                                                Considered, 96/1850: *Referred to,* 00/1209
R. *v.* Sporle (Sidney Frederick) see R. *v.* Andrews Weatherfoil Ltd
R. *v.* Springer (Robert) [1999] 1 Cr. App. R. (S.) 217; [1998] Crim. L.R. 912, CA (Crim
Div) . . . .   *Digested,* 99/**1131**
R. *v.* Squires (Lloyd Charles) [2000] 2 Cr. App. R. (S.) 160, CA (Crim Div) . . . .   *Digested,* 00/**1351**
R. *v.* Ssejjuko (Twaibu) [1998] 2 Cr. App. R. (S.) 262, CA (Crim Div) . . . .   *Digested,* 98/**1263**
R. *v.* St Albans and Mid Hertfordshire Magistrates Court Ex p. Kraft Jacobs Suchard
Ltd CO/390/97, QBD . . . .   *Digested,* 98/**468**
R. *v.* St Albans Crown Court Ex p. O'Donovan [2000] 1 Cr. App. R. (S.) 344, QBD . . . .   *Digested,* 00/**1204**
R. *v.* St Edmundsbury BC Ex p. Davidson [2000] J.P.L. 417; (1999) 96(27) L.S.G. 35,
QBD . . . .   *Digested,* 00/**4513**
R. *v.* St Edmundsbury BC Ex p. Sandys see R. *v.* Swansea City and County Council Ex
p. Littler

R. *v.* St Edmundsbury BC Ex p. Walton [1999] Env. L.R. 879; (1999) 11 Admin. L.R. 648; [1999] 3 P.L.R. 51; [1999] J.P.L. 805; [1999] E.G.C.S. 53; (1999) 143 S.J.L.B. 175; [1999] N.P.C. 44; *Times,* May 5, 1999; *Independent,* May 17, 1999 (C.S.), QBD . . . .   *Digested,* 99/**4234**

R. (on the application of L (A Child)) *v.* St Edward's College Independent Appeal Panel [2001] EWHC Admin 108; [2001] E.L.R. 542, QBD (Admin Ct) . . . .   *Digested,* 01/**1974**

R. *v.* St Helens Justices Ex p. Jones; R. *v.* Ealing Justices Ex p. Saleem; R. *v.* Stoke on Trent Justices Ex p. Wilby; R. *v.* Manchester City Justices Ex p. Lee; R. *v.* Greenwich Justices Ex p. Wright; R. *v.* Greenwich Justices Ex p. Davidson [1999] 2 All E.R. 73; (1999) 163 J.P. 369; (1999) 163 J.P.N. 192; *Times,* December 15, 1998, QBD . . . .   *Digested,* 99/**979**

R. (on the application of O) *v.* St James Roman Catholic Primary School Appeal Panel [2001] E.L.R. 469, QBD (Admin Ct) . . . .   *Digested,* 01/**1973**

R. *v.* St Paul's Cathedral Ex p. Williamson [1998] C.O.D. 130, QBD

R. *v.* Stables Unreported [*Ex rel.* Vine Pemberton Joss, Practice Manager, St. Paul's Chambers, 23 Park Square, Leeds] . . . .   *Digested,* 00/**3972**

R. *v.* Stacey (Glen Maurice) [1999] 2 Cr. App. R. (S.) 298, CA (Crim Div) . . . .   *Digested,* 99/**1081**

R. *v.* Stafford Crown Court Ex p. Chief Constable of Staffordshire [1999] 1 W.L.R. 398; [1998] 2 All E.R. 812; (1998) 162 J.P. 501; [1998] C.O.D. 228; *Times,* December 15, 1997, QBD . . . .   *Digested,* 98/**3764**

R. *v.* Stafford Crown Court Ex p. Shipley [1998] 1 W.L.R. 1438; [1998] 2 All E.R. 465; (1998) 162 J.P. 429; (1998) 162 J.P.N. 463; (1998) 95(2) L.S.G. 22; (1998) 142 S.J.L.B. 70; *Times,* December 29, 1997, CA; affirming [1997] C.O.D. 209, QBD . . . .   *Digested,* 98/**3765**: *Considered,* 00/4068

R. *v.* Stafford Crown Court Ex p. Wilf Gilbert (Staffordshire) Ltd; *sub nom* R. *v.* Stafford Crown Court Ex p. Wilf Gilbert (Staffs) Ltd [1999] 2 All E.R. 955; [1999] C.O.D. 262, QBD . . . .   *Digested,* 99/**375**

R. *v.* Stafford Crown Court Ex p. Wilf Gilbert (Staffs) Ltd see R. *v.* Stafford Crown Court Ex p. Wilf Gilbert (Staffordshire) Ltd

R. *v.* Stafford Justices Ex p. Customs and Excise Commissioners [1991] 2 Q.B. 339; [1990] 3 W.L.R. 656; [1991] 2 All E.R. 201; (1990) 154 J.P. 865; [1990] Crim. L.R. 742; [1990] C.O.D. 315; (1990) 154 J.P.N. 507, DC . . . .   *Digested,* 91/**864**: *Distinguished,* 94/1006: *Followed,* 00/1098

R. *v.* Stafford Prison Ex p. Bowen see R. *v.* Featherstone Prison Ex p. Bowen

R. *v.* Staffordshire CC Ex p. R [1998] Ed. C.R. 295; [1998] C.O.D. 286, QBD . . . .   *Digested,* 99/**1886**

R. *v.* Staffordshire Moorlands DC Ex p. Bartlam (1999) 77 P. & C.R. 210; [1998] P.L.C.R. 385, CA (Crim Div) . . . .   *Digested,* 99/**4258**

R. *v.* Staines Magistrates Court Ex p. DPP see R. *v.* Warley Magistrates Court Ex p. DPP

R. *v.* Staines Magistrates Court Ex p. Soper see R. *v.* Staines Magistrates Court Ex p. Westfallen

R. *v.* Staines Magistrates Court Ex p. Westfallen; R. *v.* Staines Magistrates Court Ex p. Soper; R. *v.* Swindon Magistrates Court Ex p. Nangle [1998] 1 W.L.R. 652; [1998] 4 All E.R. 210; [1998] Crim. L.R. 414, QBD . . . .   *Digested,* 98/**2353**

R. *v.* Stamford Magistrates Court Ex p. DPP [1998] C.O.D. 10, QBD

R. *v.* Stanley (Bert), *Times,* December 8, 1998; *Independent,* November 27, 1998, CA (Crim Div) . . . .   *Digested,* 99/**1012**

R. *v.* Stanley (Graham Frederick) (1987) 9 Cr. App. R. (S.) 286; [1988] Crim. L.R. 67, CA . . . .   *Digested,* 89/**1046**: *Considered,* 99/1210

R. *v.* Stapley (Douglas Peter) [2001] 1 Cr. App. R. (S.) 88, CA (Crim Div) . . . .   *Digested,* 01/**1360**

R. *v.* Stark (Rudi) see R. *v.* Le (Van Binh)

R. *v.* Steadman see R. *v.* Gummerson (James Wesley)

R. *v.* Stearn (Kennard Frederick) (1982) 4 Cr. App. R. (S.) 195, CA . . . .   *Digested,* 83/**783**: *Cited,* 89/971: *Considered,* 97/1512, 98/1196

R. *v.* Steele (Deborah) see R. *v.* Keach (Walter Stacy)

R. *v.* Steele (Melvin John) [1999] 1 Cr. App. R. (S.) 369, CA (Crim Div) . . . .   *Digested,* 99/**1164**

R. *v.* Steele (Michael John) see R. *v.* Shevki (Lutfiyf)

R. *v.* Stenhouse (James Cameron) [2000] 2 Cr. App. R. (S.) 386; *Times,* April 11, 2000, CA (Crim Div) . . . .   *Digested,* 00/**1234**

R. *v.* Stephen (Kevin Kimberley) see R. *v.* Owen (Darren Lee)

R. *v.* Stephens (Edward) see R. *v.* Dudley (Thomas)

R. *v.* Stephens (Michael) [2000] 2 Cr. App. R. (S.) 320; [2000] Crim. L.R. 402; *Times,* March 29, 2000, CA (Crim Div) . . . .   *Digested,* 00/**1350**

R. *v.* Stephens (Vivian John) see Attorney General's Reference (No.67 of 1998), Re

R. *v.* Stephenson (Alwin) [1999] 1 Cr. App. R. (S.) 177; [1998] Crim. L.R. 909, CA (Crim Div) . . . .   *Digested,* 99/**1281**

R. *v.* Stepton (Steven) [1998] 2 Cr. App. R. (S.) 319, CA (Crim Div) . . . .   *Digested,* 98/**1347**

R. *v.* Stevens (1995) 96 C.C.C. (3d) 238 . . . .   *Followed,* 99/3106

R. *v.* Stevens (Alan) [1997] 2 Cr. App. R. (S.) 180, CA (Crim Div) . . . .   *Digested,* 97/**1480**: *Considered,* 00/1177

R. v. Stevens (David) (1986) 8 Cr. App. R. (S.) 297; [1987] Crim. L.R. 139, CA (Crim Div) . . . . *Digested,* 88/**914**:
Applied, 91/1131: *Considered,* 98/1327, 00/1184
R. v. Stewart (Alexander) (1990) 12 Cr. App. R. (S.) 15, CA (Crim Div) . . . . *Digested,* 91/**1154**:
Considered, 98/1402
R. v. Stewart (Gordon Michael) [1999] Crim. L.R. 746, CA (Crim Div)
R. v. Stewart (Heather); R. v. Schofield (Barry John) [1995] 3 All E.R. 159; [1995] 1 Cr. App. R. 441; [1995] Crim. L.R. 420, CA (Crim Div) . . . . *Digested,* 95/**1272**:
Considered, 00/5466
R. v. Stewart (Livingstone) [1987] 1 W.L.R. 559; [1987] 2 All E.R. 383; (1987) 85 Cr. App. R. 66; (1987) 9 Cr. App. R. (S.) 135; [1987] Crim. L.R. 520; (1987) 84 L.S.G. 1333, CA (Crim Div) . . . . *Digested,* 87/**1015**:
Applied, 99/1274: *Considered,* 97/1530, 97/1630, 00/1370:
Followed, 99/1351: *Referred to,* 90/1208, 90/1370, 90/1371, 90/1372,
91/1126, 91/1172, 92/1351, 94/1317, 95/1387
R. v. Stewart (Mark Adam) [1999] 2 Cr. App. R. (S.) 213, CA (Crim Div) . . . . *Digested,* 99/**1324**
R. v. Stewart (Trevor Mathew) [1996] 2 Cr. App. R. (S.) 302, CA (Crim Div) . . . . *Digested,* 97/**1420**:
Considered, 98/1275, 00/1149
R. v. Stillman [1997] 144 D.L.R. (4th) 193, Sup Ct (Can) . . . . *Applied,* 99/3139
R. v. Stipendiary Magistrate for Leicestershire Ex p. Kaur; *sub nom* Kaur v. DPP (2000) 164 J.P. 127; [2000] C.O.D. 109; (2000) 164 J.P.N. 143; *Times,* October 5, 1999, QBD . . . . *Digested,* 99/**81**
R. v. Stipendiary Magistrate for Norfolk Ex p. Taylor (1997) 161 J.P. 773; [1998] Crim. L.R. 276; (1997) 161 J.P.N. 976, QBD . . . . *Digested,* 97/**1342**:
Applied, 01/1198
R. v. Stirland (William) see Stirland v. DPP
R. v. Stock (Mark Peter) see Attorney General's Reference (No.19 of 2000), Re
R. v. Stockdale (Jacqueline) (1994) 15 Cr. App. R. (S.) 48, CA (Crim Div) . . . . *Considered,* 98/1316,
98/1317
R. v. Stockton on Tees BC Ex p. W [2000] E.L.R. 93, CA. . . . . *Digested,* 00/**1920**
R. v. Stockwell (Christopher James) (1993) 97 Cr. App. R. 260; *Times,* March 11, 1993, CA (Crim Div) . . . . *Digested,* 94/**914**:
Applied, 95/932, 96/1373: *Considered,* 99/895
R. v. Stoddart (John); R. v. Duhaney (Michael) [1998] 2 Cr. App. R. 25; (1998) 162 J.P. 78; (1998) 162 J.P.N. 305; (1997) 94(46) L.S.G. 29; (1998) 142 S.J.L.B. 13; (1997) 141 S.J.L.B. 248; *Times,* December 9, 1997, CA (Crim Div) . . . . *Digested,* 98/**950**
R. v. Stoke on Trent Crown Court, Ex p. Marsden [1999] C.O.D. 114, QBD
R. v. Stoke on Trent Justices Ex p. Cawley see R. v. Oldham Justices Ex p. Cawley
R. v. Stoke on Trent Justices Ex p. Wilby see R. v. St Helens Justices Ex p. Jones
R. v. Stoke on Trent Magistrates Court Ex p. Leaf United [1998] E.H.L.R. Dig. 136, QBD
R. v. Stokes (Ellen Marie) see Attorney General's Reference (No.17 of 1998), Re
R. v. Stokes (Oliver Robert) [1998] 1 Cr. App. R. (S.) 282, CA (Crim Div) . . . . *Digested,* 98/**1369**
R. v. Stone (Gavin John) see R. v. Dewberry (Rodney Brian)
R. v. Stone (Michael James) [1998] Env. L.R. 618; [1998] Crim. L.R. 133; [1998] E.H.L.R. Dig. 135; *Times,* December 10, 1997, CA (Crim Div) . . . . *Digested,* 98/**2566**
R. v. Stone (Michael John) [2001] EWCA Crim 297; [2001] Crim. L.R. 465; (2001) 98(11) L.S.G. 43; (2001) 145 S.J.L.B. 68; *Times,* February 22, 2001, CA (Crim Div) . . . . *Digested,* 01/**1184**
R. v. Stonebank (Richard John) (Unreported, February 6, 1996), CA (Crim Div) . . . . . . *Considered,* 98/1207
R. v. Storey (Stephen David) (1984) 6 Cr. App. R. (S.) 104; [1984] Crim. L.R. 438, CA (Crim Div) . . . . *Digested,* 85/**810**:
Applied, 86/771, 86/772: *Considered,* 86/740, 87/971, 88/1018, 89/794,
89/925, 89/1101, 89/1150, 90/1054, 90/1446, 90/1478.b, 96/1749, 96/1958,
96/1959, 97/1558, 98/1275, 99/1240, 00/1310, 00/1328: *Referred to,* 87/972,
87/973, 89/1057, 90/1447, 90/1478, 90/1480, 92/1432, 93/1337
R. v. Stratford Justices Ex p. Imbert [1999] 2 Cr. App. R. 276; (1999) 163 J.P. 693; (1999) 163 J.P.N. 771; *Times,* February 25, 1999, QBD . . . . *Digested,* 99/**3131**
R. v. Stratford upon Avon DC Ex p. Lane [1998] P.L.C.R. 148; [1997] N.P.C. 172, QBD . *Digested,* 98/**4218**
R. v. Stratford upon Avon DC Housing Benefit Board Ex p. White see R. v. Stratford upon Avon Housing Benefit Review Board Ex p. White
R. v. Stratford upon Avon Housing Benefit Review Board Ex p. White; *sub nom* R. v. Stratford upon Avon DC Housing Benefit Board Ex p. White (1999) 31 H.L.R. 126; (1998) 95(21) L.S.G. 24; (1998) 142 S.J.L.B. 150; *Times,* April 23, 1998, CA; reversing (1998) 30 H.L.R. 178, QBD . . . . *Digested,* 98/**4523**
R. (on the application of DPP) v. Stratford Youth Court [2001] EWHC Admin 615; (2001) 165 J.P. 761; (2001) 165 J.P.N. 926, QBD
R. v. Stratford Youth Court Ex p. S [1998] 1 W.L.R. 1758; (1998) 162 J.P. 552; [1999] Crim. L.R. 146; (1998) 148 N.L.J. 870; *Times,* May 28, 1998, QBD . . . . *Digested,* 98/**1101**
R. v. Stratton (Simon) see R. v. Brown (Damien)
R. (on the application of Hargrave) v. Stroud DC; *sub nom* Hargrave v. Stroud DC [2001] EWHC Admin 1128; [2001] N.P.C. 180; *Times,* December 19, 2001, QBD (Admin Ct)

R. *v.* Strudwick (Kevin Vincent); R. *v.* Merry (Kathleen Anne) (1994) 99 Cr. App. R. 326; *Independent*, January 18, 1994, CA (Crim Div) . . . .   *Digested*, 95/**1205**: *Considered*, 01/975

R. *v.* Stubley see R. (on the application of Wardle) *v.* Leeds Crown Court

R. *v.* Sturdy (Michael Lewis) [1999] 1 Costs L.R. 1, Sup Ct Taxing Office . . . .   *Digested*, 00/**3975**

R. *v.* Styring (Katrina) see Attorney General's Reference (No.29 of 2001), Re

R. *v.* Suckley (George William) [2001] EWCA Crim 125; [2001] 2 Cr. App. R. (S.) 66, CA (Crim Div) . . . .   *Digested*, 01/**1319**

R. *v.* Suffolk CC Ex p. Steed; *sub nom* Steed *v.* Suffolk CC (1998) 75 P. & C.R. 102; [1997] 1 E.G.L.R. 131; [1997] 10 E.G. 146; [1996] E.G.C.S. 122; [1996] N.P.C. 117; *Times*, November 11, 1996; *Times*, August 2, 1996, CA; affirming (1995) 70 P. & C.R. 487; [1995] E.G.C.S. 80; [1995] N.P.C. 82, QBD . . . .   *Digested*, 96/**4936**: *Applied*, 97/4227: *Considered*, 00/4616: *Disapproved*, 99/4393

R. *v.* Suffolk HA Ex p. Kowlessur; *sub nom* Kowlessur *v.* Suffolk HA *Independent*, December 15, 2000, CA; affirming CO/4789/1999, QBD . . . .   *Digested*, 01/**5141**

R. *v.* Sullivan (Alan) [2000] 2 Cr. App. R. (S.) 318; [2000] Crim. L.R. 501, CA (Crim Div) . . . .   *Digested*, 00/**1264**

R. *v.* Sullman (Barry) see R. *v.* Adomako (John Asare)

R. *v.* Sunair Holidays Ltd [1973] 1 W.L.R. 1105; [1973] 2 All E.R. 1233; (1973) 57 Cr. App. R. 782; [1973] Crim. L.R. 587; 117 S.J. 429, CA (Crim Div) . . . .   *Digested*, 73/**3047**: *Applied*, 00/4619: *Considered*, 76/2472, 83/3317, 92/3887, 93/931

R. (on the application of Beresford) *v.* Sunderland City Council; *sub nom* R. *v.* Sunderland City Council Ex p. Beresford [2001] EWCA Civ 1218; [2001] 4 All E.R. 565; [2001] B.L.G.R. 469; [2001] 3 P.L.R. 120; [2001] J.P.L. 1307; [2001] 32 E.G.C.S. 86; (2001) 98(35) L.S.G. 35; (2001) 145 S.J.L.B. 203; [2001] N.P.C. 126; *Times*, August 29, 2001; *Independent*, July 31, 2001; *Daily Telegraph*, September 11, 2001, CA; affirming [2001] 1 W.L.R. 1327; (2001) 82 P. & C.R. 19; [2000] E.G.C.S. 134; *Times*, January 16, 2001; *Daily Telegraph*, November 28, 2000, QBD (Admin Ct) . . . .   *Digested*, 01/**4848**

R. *v.* Sunderland City Council Ex p. Beresford see R. (on the application of Beresford) *v.* Sunderland City Council

R. *v.* Sunders (Gurmit Singh) (Unreported, January 23, 1998), CA [*Ex rel.* Roger Turner, Barrister, Mitre Court Chambers, Temple, London, EC4Y 7BP] . . . .   *Digested*, 98/**892**

R. *v.* Sundhers (Gurmit) [1998] Crim. L.R. 497, CA (Crim Div)

R. *v.* Supreme Court Taxing Office Ex p. John Singh & Co [1997] 1 Costs L.R. 49, CA (1995) 7 Admin. L.R. 849; [1995] C.O.D. 429; *Times*, May 3, 1995, QBD . . . . .   *Digested*, 98/**1015**: *Considered*, 98/3698

R. *v.* Supremeplan Ltd [2001] 1 Cr. App. R. (S.) 71, CA (Crim Div) . . . .   *Digested*, 01/**3300**

R. *v.* Surrey CC Ex p. Bridge Court Holdings Ltd [2000] 4 P.L.R. 30; [2000] P.L.C.R. 344; (2000) 97(8) L.S.G. 38, QBD . . . .   *Digested*, 01/**4697**

R. *v.* Sussex JJ Ex p. McCarthy see R. *v.* Sussex Justices Ex p. McCarthy

R. *v.* Sussex Justices Ex p. McCarthy; *sub nom* R. *v.* Sussex JJ Ex p. McCarthy [1924] 1 K.B. 256, KBD . . . .   *Applied*, 68/3372, 75/741, 85/3432: *Considered*, 47-51/7724, 47-51/10167, 47-51/10168, 54/2011, 92/955: *Distinguished*, 93/849, 99/3796: *Followed*, 47-51/6074

R. *v.* Sussex Police Authority Ex p. Stewart [2000] I.C.R. 1122; (2000) 97(18) L.S.G. 37; (2000) 144 S.J.L.B. 219; *Times*, April 13, 2000; *Independent*, May 15, 2000 (C.S.), CA; reversing CO 4127/98, QBD . . . .   *Digested*, 00/**4544**: *Applied*, 00/4360

R. *v.* Sutcliffe (Brian) (1995) 16 Cr. App. R. (S.) 69, CA (Crim Div) . . . .   *Digested*, 96/**2091**: *Considered*, 00/1180

R. *v.* Sutcliffe (Colin) (1992) 13 Cr. App. R. (S.) 538, CA (Crim Div) . . . .   *Digested*, 93/**1142**: *Considered*, 95/1373, 96/1883, 98/1210, 99/1152

R. *v.* Sutherland (Jason) see R. *v.* Nelson (Mark Jones)

R. *v.* Sutton (Mark) [2001] EWCA Crim 291; [2001] 2 Cr. App. R. (S.) 91, CA (Crim Div) . . . .   *Digested*, 01/**1344**

R. *v.* Sutton LBC Ex p. Harrison see R. *v.* Swansea City and County Council Ex p. Littler

R. *v.* Sutton LBC Ex p. Tucker (1997-98) 1 C.C.L. Rep. 251; (1998) 40 B.M.L.R. 137; [1997] C.O.D. 144, QBD . . . .   *Digested*, 97/**4713**

R. *v.* Swaine (Robert Edward) [2001] Crim. L.R. 166; *Times*, November 1, 2000, CA (Crim Div) . . . .   *Digested*, 00/**1046**

R. *v.* Swale BC Ex p. Marchant; *sub nom* R. *v.* Swale BC Housing Benefit Review Board Ex p. Marchant; R. *v.* Housing Benefit Review Board for Swale BC Ex p. Marchant [2000] 1 F.L.R. 246; [2000] 1 F.C.R. 87; (2000) 32 H.L.R. 856; [2000] Fam. Law 87; *Times*, November 17, 1999 ; *Independent*, January 24, 2000 (C.S.), CA; affirming [1999] 1 F.L.R. 1087; [1999] 2 F.C.R. 664; (2000) 32 H.L.R. 26; [1999] Fam. Law 303; *Times*, January 21, 1999, QBD . . . .   *Digested*, 99/**4553**

R. *v.* Swale BC Ex p. Royal Society for the Protection of Birds (1990) 2 Admin. L.R. 790; [1991] 1 P.L.R. 6; [1991] J.P.L. 39; [1990] C.O.D. 263; *Times*, April 11, 1990 ; *Independent*, April 16, 1990 (C.S.), QBD . . . .   *Digested*, 92/**4368**: *Applied*, 99/4260

R. *v.* Swale BC Housing Benefit Review Board Ex p. Marchant see R. *v.* Swale BC Ex p. Marchant

R. *v.* Swallow (Mark Paul) (1985) 7 Cr. App. R. (S.) 22, CA (Crim Div) . . . . *Digested,* 86/**895**:
Considered, 91/1243, 96/1958, 00/1310

R. *v.* Swansea City and County Council Ex p. Littler; R. *v.* Sutton LBC Ex p. Harrison; R. *v.* Welwyn Hatfield DC Ex p. Nunan; R. *v.* St Edmundsbury BC Ex p. Sandys (1999) 48 B.M.L.R. 24; *Times,* September 9, 1998, CA; affirming (1998) 30 H.L.R. 800; *Times,* August 22, 1997, QBD . . . . *Digested,* 98/**4529**

R. *v.* Swansea City and County Ex p. Granada Hospitality Ltd [1999] P.L.C.R. 273, QBD . . . . *Digested,* 99/**4256**

R. *v.* Swansea City Council Ex p. D (A Child) see R. *v.* Head Teacher of Crug Glas School Ex p. D (A Child)

R. *v.* Swansea City Council Ex p. Elitestone Ltd; *sub nom* Elitestone's Application for Judicial Review, Re; Elitestone *v.* Secretary of State for Wales (1993) 66 P. & C.R. 422; [1993] 2 P.L.R. 65; [1993] 46 E.G. 181; [1993] J.P.L. 1019; [1994] C.O.D. 80; [1993] N.P.C. 74, CA; affirming 90 L.G.R. 604; (1993) 65 P. & C.R. 300; [1992] J.P.L. 1143; [1992] E.G.C.S. 72; *Times,* June 1, 1992, QBD . . . . *Digested,* 94/**4326**:
Applied, 99/4171: *Considered,* 00/4415

R. *v.* Swansea City Council Ex p. Main see Main *v.* Swansea City Council

R. *v.* Swanton (Alan) see R. *v.* Nawaz (Mohammed)

R. *v.* Sweeney (Joseph) [1998] 2 Cr. App. R. (S.) 43, CA (Crim Div) . . . . *Digested,* 98/**1265**:
Considered, 99/1198

R. *v.* Sweeting (Dawn Karen); R. *v.* Thomas (David Howard) [1999] Crim. L.R. 75, CA (Crim Div)

R. *v.* Swindell (Peter George) (1981) 3 Cr. App. R. (S.) 255; *Times,* October 9, 1981, CA . . . . *Digested,* 81/**534**:
Cited, 93/1245: *Considered,* 88/890, 98/1111

R. (on the application of S) *v.* Swindon BC; *sub nom* R. *v.* Swindon BC Ex p. S; S (Sexual Abuse Allegations: Local Authority Response), Re [2001] EWHC Admin 334; [2001] 2 F.L.R. 776; [2001] 3 F.C.R. 702; [2001] B.L.G.R. 318; [2001] Fam. Law 659; *Times,* June 27, 2001; *Independent,* June 18, 2001 (C.S.), QBD (Admin Ct) . . . . *Digested,* 01/**2550**

R. *v.* Swindon BC Ex p. S see R. (on the application of S) *v.* Swindon BC

R. *v.* Swindon Crown Court Ex p. Murray (1998) 162 J.P. 36; (1997) 161 J.P.N. 1038; *Times,* September 24, 1997, QBD . . . . *Digested,* 97/**1395**

R. *v.* Swindon Magistrates Court Ex p. Nangle see R. *v.* Staines Magistrates Court Ex p. Westfallen

R. *v.* Sylvester (Jason William) see Attorney General's Reference (No.45 of 1998), Re

R. *v.* Symonds (Jonathan Yoan) [1998] Crim. L.R. 280, CA (Crim Div)

R. *v.* T (A Juvenile) see Attorney General's Reference (Nos.52, 53, 54 and 55 of 1999), Re

R. *v.* T (Anita Grant) (A Juvenile); R. *v.* F (Suzzane) (A Juvenile) [2001] 1 Cr. App. R. (S.) 86, CA (Crim Div) . . . . *Digested,* 01/**1402**

R. *v.* T (Child Pornography); *sub nom* R. *v.* ET (Child Pornography) (1999) 163 J.P. 349; [1999] Crim. L.R. 749; (1999) 163 J.P.N. 619; *Times,* February 12, 1999, CA (Crim Div) . . . . *Digested,* 99/**948**

R. *v.* T (Craig Daniel); R. *v.* Godfrey (David Simon); R. *v.* Abdie (Gary); R. *v.* More (Jonathan); R. *v.* Love (Mark Ryan) [1999] 2 Cr. App. R. (S.) 304; [1999] Crim. L.R. 432; *Independent,* March 1, 1999 (C.S.), CA (Crim Div) . . . . *Digested,* 99/**1211**

R. *v.* T (Failure to Adduce Evidence), *Times,* June 30, 1998, CA (Crim Div) . . . . *Digested,* 98/**991**

R. *v.* T (Hardeep Singh) (A Juvenile) [1999] Crim. L.R. 842, CA (Crim Div)

R. *v.* T (James) (A Juvenile) see Attorney General's Reference (Nos.11 and 12 of 2000), Re

R. *v.* T (Jean Pierre) (A Juvenile); R. *v.* K (Anthony) (A Juvenile) [2001] 1 Cr. App. R. 32; (2001) 165 J.P. 306; [2001] Crim. L.R. 398; (2001) 98(12) L.S.G. 41; *Times,* January 11, 2001, CA (Crim Div) . . . . *Digested,* 01/**1125**

R. *v.* T (John) see Attorney General's Reference (No.77 of 1999), Re

R. *v.* T (Laurie Lee) [2000] Crim. L.R. 325, CA (Crim Div)

R. *v.* T (Leigh) (A Juvenile) see Attorney General's Reference (No.31 of 2000), Re

R. *v.* T (Marcus) (A Juvenile) [2000] 2 Cr. App. R. (S.) 155, CA (Crim Div) . . . . *Digested,* 00/**1248**

R. *v.* T (Michael John) [2000] Crim. L.R. 832, CA (Crim Div)

R. *v.* T (Michael Patrick) [1999] 1 Cr. App. R. (S.) 419; [1999] Crim. L.R. 95, CA (Crim Div) . . . . *Digested,* 99/**1352**

R. *v.* T (Nathan) (A Juvenile) see Attorney General's Reference (Nos.53, 54, 55, 56 and 57 of 2001), Re

R. *v.* T (Robert Leonard) (1994) 15 Cr. App. R. (S.) 318, CA (Crim Div) . . . . *Considered,* 00/1402

R. *v.* T (Simon William) (A Juvenile) [2000] 1 Cr. App. R. (S.) 45, CA (Crim Div) . . . . . . *Digested,* 00/**1310**

R. *v.* T (Stephen) [1999] 2 Cr. App. R. (S.) 68, CA (Crim Div) . . . . *Digested,* 99/**1098**

R. *v.* T (Timothy David) (A Juvenile) see Attorney General's Reference (Nos.35 and 37 of 1997), Re

R. *v.* Taaffe (Paul Desmond) [1984] A.C. 539; [1984] 2 W.L.R. 326; [1984] 1 All E.R. 747; (1984) 78 Cr. App. R. 301; (1984) 148 J.P. 510; [1984] Crim. L.R. 356; (1984) 81 L.S.G. 1051; (1984) 128 S.J. 203, HL; affirming [1983] 1 W.L.R. 627; [1983] 2 All E.R. 625; (1983) 77 Cr. App. R. 82; [1983] Crim. L.R. 536; (1983) 127 S.J. 377, CA (Crim Div) . . . . *Digested,* 84/**581**:
Applied, 86/617, 87/1113: *Cited,* 01/1060

R. v. Tabassum (Naveed); *sub nom* R. v. Tabassum (Navid) [2000] 2 Cr. App. R. 328; [2000] Lloyd's Rep. Med. 404; [2000] Crim. L.R. 686; (2000) 97(22) L.S.G. 43; *Times*, May 26, 2000, CA (Crim Div) . . . . *Digested*, 00/**1003**

R. v. Tabassum (Navid) see R. v. Tabassum (Naveed)

R. v. Taberer (Lee Kenneth) see R. v. McFeeley (Jason)

R. v. Tabit (Elabbes) [2000] 2 Cr. App. R. (S.) 298, CA (Crim Div) . . . . *Digested*, 00/**1277**

R. v. Tackie (Nazar) see R. v. Ofori (Noble Julius)

R. v. Tagg (Heather Susan) [2001] EWCA Crim 1230; [2001] Crim. L.R. 900; *Times*, June 14, 2001, CA (Crim Div). . . . . *Digested*, 01/**1003**

R. v. Taigel (Peter John) [1998] 1 Cr. App. R. (S.) 328, CA (Crim Div) . . . . *Digested*, 98/**1153**

R. v. Takyi (Daniel) [1998] 1 Cr. App. R. (S.) 372, CA (Crim Div) . . . . *Digested*, 98/**1321**:
Not applied, 99/1284

R. v. Tameside Magistrates Court Ex p. Coleman; R. v. Tameside Magistrates Court Ex p. Davenport (1999) 1 L.G.L.R. 72; [1999] R.V.R. 4, CA . . . . *Digested*, 99/**4304**

R. v. Tameside Magistrates Court Ex p. Davenport see R. v. Tameside Magistrates Court Ex p. Coleman

R. v. Tameside MBC Ex p. J (A Child) [2000] 1 F.L.R. 942; [2000] 1 F.C.R. 173; (2000) 3 C.C.L. Rep. 402; [2000] Fam. Law 90; *Times*, October 22, 1999, QBD . . . . *Digested*, 99/**2381**

R. v. Tan (Moira); R. v. Greaves (Brian Edwin); R. v. Greaves (Gloria Gina) [1983] Q.B. 1053; [1983] 3 W.L.R. 361; [1983] 2 All E.R. 12; (1983) 76 Cr. App. R. 300; (1983) 147 J.P. 257; [1983] Crim. L.R. 404; (1983) 127 S.J. 390, CA (Crim Div) . . . . *Digested*, 83/**610**:
Considered, 99/955: *Followed*, 96/3172

R. v. Tandridge DC Ex p. Al-Fayed [2000] E.H.L.R. 257; (2000) 80 P. & C.R. 90; [2000] 1 P.L.R. 58; [2000] J.P.L. 604; [2000] E.G.C.S. 1; [1999] N.P.C. 161; [2000] Env. L.R. D23; *Times*, February 1, 2000, CA; affirming (2000) 79 P. & C.R. 227; [1999] 1 P.L.R. 104; [1999] J.P.L. 825; [1999] E.G.C.S. 6; (1999) 96(9) L.S.G. 31; (1999) 96(4) L.S.G. 41; *Times*, January 28, 1999, QBD . . . . *Digested*, 00/**4517**

R. v. Tang Zhong see R. v. Wang Lin Hal

R. v. Tanswell (Warren) see R. v. El-Hinnachi (Samir)

R. v. Tantram (Peter John); R. v. Bibby (Darren Robert); R. v. Boid (Clive Alan); R. v. McGinty (John James); R. v. Smith (Joseph Arnold); R. v. Boid (Andrew) [2001] EWCA Crim 1364; [2001] Crim. L.R. 824; *Times*, July 20, 2001, CA (Crim Div). . . . . *Digested*, 01/**1144**

R. v. Tanyildiz (Mete) [1998] 1 Cr. App. R. (S.) 362; [1998] Crim. L.R. 228, CA (Crim Div) . . . . *Digested*, 98/**1260**

R. v. Targett (David Paul); R. v. Watkins (Bernard David) [1999] 2 Cr. App. R. (S.) 282, CA (Crim Div) . . . . *Digested*, 99/**1336**

R. v. Tarrant (James Nicholas) [1998] Crim. L.R. 342; *Times*, December 29, 1997, CA (Crim Div). . . . . *Digested*, 98/**1046**

R. v. Tavistock General Commissioners Ex p. Worth see R. v. General Commissioners of Income Tax for Tavistock Ex p. Worth

R. v. Taxing Officer Ex p. Bee-Line Roadways International Ltd, *Times*, February 11, 1982. . . . . *Digested*, 82/**2452**:
Considered, 96/736: *Distinguished*, 01/11

R. v. Taylor [1988] N.I.J.B. 88, CA (Crim Div) (NI) . . . . *Considered*, 99/5195

R. v. Taylor (Adrian Edward) [1998] 1 W.L.R. 809; [1998] 1 All E.R. 357; (1997) 161 J.P. 797; [1998] Crim. L.R. 76; (1997) 161 J.P.N. 1080; *Times*, August 11, 1997, CA (Crim Div) . . . . *Digested*, 97/**1632**:
Considered, 99/1184, 99/1231, 99/1281, 00/1192:
Joined proceedings, 97/1477, 97/1654

R. v. Taylor (Allen Robert) [1999] 2 Cr. App. R. (S.) 45, CA (Crim Div) . . . . *Digested*, 99/**1366**

R. v. Taylor (Christian Mark) [1998] Crim. L.R. 822, CA (Crim Div)

R. v. Taylor (Costs) [2000] 1 Costs L.R. 32, Sup Ct Taxing Office . . . . *Digested*, 00/**1038**

R. v. Taylor (D) see R. v. Taylor (Shaun Keith)

R. v. Taylor (David Alec) see Attorney General's Reference (No.17 of 1999), Re

R. v. Taylor (David Patrick) see R. v. Bowers (Victor John)

R. v. Taylor (Derek Roy); R. v. Roberts (David Eric); R. v. Simons (Geoffrey) [1977] 1 W.L.R. 612; [1977] 3 All E.R. 527; (1977) 64 Cr. App. R. 182; [1977] Crim. L.R. 492; 121 S.J. 239, CA (Crim Div) . . . . *Digested*, 77/**658**:
Applied, 01/1367: *Considered*, 85/853, 96/1950, 00/1383

R. v. Taylor (Elaine) see R. v. Hudson (Linda)

R. v. Taylor (Gary) [1995] Crim. L.R. 253; *Times*, August 17, 1994; *Independent*, September 12, 1994 (C.S.), CA (Crim Div) . . . . *Digested*, 94/**1062**:
Applied, 96/1424: *Considered*, 01/2524

R. v. Taylor (James) see R. v. Smith (Patrick Joseph)

R. v. Taylor (John Anthony) [1999] Crim. L.R. 77, CA (Crim Div)

R. v. Taylor (Kieron Thomas) see R. v. Curry (David Paul)

R. v. Taylor (Nicholas James); R. v. Goodman (Donald Walter) [1999] 2 Cr. App. R. 163; (1999) 163 J.P. 168; [1999] Crim. L.R. 407; (1999) 163 J.P.N. 112; (1998) 95(46) L.S.G. 33; *Times*, November 3, 1998; *Independent*, November 16, 1998 (C.S.), CA (Crim Div) . . . . *Digested*, 98/**864**

R. *v.* Taylor (Paul Simon) [2001] EWCA Crim 2263; (2001) 98(45) L.S.G. 25; (2001) 145 S.J.L.B. 252; *Times,* November 15, 2001, CA (Crim Div) . . . .   *Digested,* 01/**1193**

R. *v.* Taylor (Robert Peter) (1985) 80 Cr. App. R. 327, CA (Crim Div) . . . .   *Digested,* 85/**681**:

Applied, 00/1063: *Considered,* 99/5195: *Referred to,* 85/680, 87/680

R. *v.* Taylor (Shaun Keith); R. *v.* Harrison (J); R. *v.* Taylor (D) [1998] Crim. L.R. 582, CA (Crim Div)

R. *v.* Taylor (William Edward) (1986) 8 Cr. App. R. (S.) 450; [1987] Crim. L.R. 282, CA (Crim Div) . . . .   *Digested,* 88/**955**:

Cited, 93/1220: *Considered,* 90/1323, 91/1166, 99/1261

R. *v.* Taylor-Sabori (Sean Marc) [1999] 1 W.L.R. 858; [1999] 1 All E.R. 160; [1999] 1 Cr. App. R. 437; [1999] Masons C.L.R. 65; [1999] Crim. L.R. 322; (1998) 95(39) L.S.G. 34; (1998) 142 S.J.L.B. 259; *Times,* October 12, 1998; *Independent,* October 13, 1998, CA (Crim Div) . . . .   *Digested,* 98/**881**

R. *v.* Tebbutt (Christopher) (1988) 10 Cr. App. R. (S.) 88; (1988) 152 J.P. 321; [1988] Crim. L.R. 394; (1988) 152 J.P.N. 286, CA (Crim Div) . . . .   *Digested,* 90/**1233**:

Distinguished, 98/1336

R. *v.* Teesside Crown Court Ex p. Crown Prosecution Service see R. *v.* Bradford Crown Court Ex p. Crossling

R. *v.* Teesside Development Corp Ex p. William Morrison Supermarkets Plc see R. *v.* Teesside Development Corp Ex p. Wm Morrison Supermarkets Plc

R. *v.* Teesside Development Corp Ex p. Wm Morrison Supermarkets Plc; *sub nom* R. *v.* Teesside Development Corp Ex p. William Morrison Supermarkets Plc [1998] J.P.L. 23; [1997] N.P.C. 78, QBD . . . .   *Digested,* 97/**4125**:

Applied, 99/4225

R. (on the application of Ellison) *v.* Teesside Magistrates Court; *sub nom* R. *v.* Teesside Magistrates Court Ex p. Ellison [2001] EWHC Admin 12; (2001) 165 J.P. 355; (2001) 165 J.P.N. 426; *Times,* February 20, 2001; *Independent,* February 26, 2001 (C.S), QBD . . . .   *Digested,* 01/**12**

R. *v.* Teesside Magistrates Court Ex p. Ellison see R. (on the application of Ellison) *v.* Teesside Magistrates Court

R. *v.* Teesside Probation Committee Ex p. National Association of Probation Officers, *Independent,* November 2, 1998 (C.S.), QBD . . . .   *Digested,* 98/**4088**

R. *v.* Teixeira (Antotia de Abreu) see R. *v.* Richardson (Edward George)

R. *v.* Telli (David) see R. *v.* Middelkoop (Martin)

R. *v.* Templeton (Graham) [1996] 1 Cr. App. R. (S.) 380, CA (Crim Div) . . . .   *Digested,* 96/**1840**:

Considered, 98/1371

R. *v.* Tendring DC Ex p. Robert Leonard Estates Ltd (1998) 76 P. & C.R. 567, QBD . . . .   *Digested,* 99/**4248**

R. *v.* Terry [1996] 2 S.C.R. 207, Sup Ct (Can) . . . .   *Applied,* 99/3123:

Distinguished, 99/3139

R. (on the application of Anne) *v.* Test Valley BC [2001] EWHC Admin 1019; [2001] 48 E.G.C.S. 127, QBD (Admin Ct)

R. *v.* Test Valley BC Ex p. Peel Estates [1990] 3 P.L.R. 14; [1990] C.O.D. 215 . . . .   *Digested,* 91/**3499**:

Applied, 99/4227

R. *v.* TF (Indecent Assault: Mental Health) [2000] 2 Cr. App. R. (S.) 292, CA (Crim Div) . . . .   *Digested,* 00/**1278**

R. *v.* TH (A Juvenile) see Attorney General's Reference (Nos.59, 60 and 63 of 1998), Re

R. (on the application of Bozkurt) *v.* Thames Magistrates Court; *sub nom* Bozkurt *v.* Thames Magistrates Court; R. (on the application of Bozcurt) *v.* South Thames Magistrates Court [2001] EWHC Admin 400; *Times,* June 26, 2001; *Independent,* July 2, 2001 (C.S); *Daily Telegraph,* May 22, 2001, QBD (Admin Ct) . . . .   *Digested,* 01/**1141**

R. *v.* Thames Magistrates Court Ex p. Academy International Plc (2000) 164 J.P. 77; *Times,* June 23, 1999, QBD . . . .   *Digested,* 99/**2212**

R. *v.* Thames Magistrates Court Ex p. Horgan see R. *v.* Thames Metropolitan Stipendiary Magistrate Ex p. Horgan

R. *v.* Thames Magistrates Court Ex p. Hormoz (1999) 163 J.P. 19; [1998] Crim. L.R. 732; [1998] C.O.D. 370, QBD . . . .   *Digested,* 99/**4766**

R. *v.* Thames Magistrates Court Ex p. Ramadan [1999] 1 Cr. App. R. 386; (1999) 163 J.P. 428; (2000) 53 B.M.L.R. 49; [1999] Crim. L.R. 498; [1999] C.O.D. 19; (1999) 163 J.P.N. 212; *Independent,* October 12, 1998 (C.S.), QBD . . . .   *Digested,* 98/**1241**

R. *v.* Thames Magistrates Court Ex p. Stevens (2000) 164 J.P. 233; [2000] C.O.D. 211; (2000) 164 J.P.N. 383, QBD . . . .   *Digested,* 00/**1048**

R. *v.* Thames Metropolitan Stipendiary Magistrate Ex p. Horgan; *sub nom* R. *v.* Thames Magistrates Court Ex p. Horgan [1998] Q.B. 719; [1998] 2 W.L.R. 799; [1998] 1 All E.R. 559; [1999] B.C.C. 374; [1998] 2 B.C.L.C. 91; [1998] 2 Cr. App. R. 47; (1998) 162 J.P. 49; [1998] Crim. L.R. 344; (1998) 162 J.P.N. 121; (1997) 94(48) L.S.G. 30; (1998) 142 S.J.L.B. 14; *Times,* December 9, 1997, QBD . . . . .   *Digested,* 98/**689**

R. (on the application of Tapp) *v.* Thanet DC; *sub nom* R. *v.* Thanet DC Ex p. Tapp; R. *v.* Thanet DC Ex p. Britton [2001] EWCA Civ 559; [2001] 3 P.L.R. 52; [2001] J.P.L. 1436 (Note); [2001] 13 E.G.C.S. 151, CA; affirming (2001) 81 P. & C.R. 37; [2001] P.L.C.R. 2; [2001] J.P.L. 225 (Note); [2000] E.G.C.S. 87, QBD . . . .   *Digested,* 01/**4655**

R. *v.* Thanet DC Ex p. Britton see R. (on the application of Tapp) *v.* Thanet DC

R. *v.* Thanet DC Ex p. Tapp see R. (on the application of Tapp) *v.* Thanet DC

R. v. Thanet DC Ex p. Warren Court Hotels Ltd (2001) 33 H.L.R. 32, QBD . . . .   *Digested,* 01/**5025**
R. v. Theivendran (Sundranpillai) (1992) 13 Cr. App. R. (S.) 601, CA (Crim Div) . . . .   *Digested,* 93/**1017**:
                                   Considered, 98/1121, 98/1122: *Followed,* 97/1406
R. v. Therens [1985] 1 S.C.R. 613, Sup Ct (Can). . . . .   *Considered,* 99/3120
R. v. Thien (Vui Kiun) see R. v. Hong (Chong Kiong)
R. v. Thien (Vui Tahung) see R. v. Hong (Chong Kiong)
R. v. Thobani (Faruk Rajabali) [1998] 1 Cr. App. R. (S.) 227, CA (Crim Div) . . . .   *Digested,* 98/**1230**
R. v. Thoburn [2001] Eu. L.R. 587, MC
R. v. Thoburn (Neil Matthew) see Attorney General's Reference (No.15 of 1999), Re
R. v. Thomas (Christopher Antonio); R. v. Flannagan (Gerard) [1998] Crim. L.R. 887;
    Times, July 24, 1998, CA (Crim Div) . . . .   *Digested,* 98/**886**
R. v. Thomas (David Howard) see R. v. Sweeting (Dawn Karen)
R. v. Thomas (Derek) (1988) 10 Cr. App. R. (S.) 386, CA (Crim Div). . . . .   *Digested,* 90/**1193**:
                                         Considered, 99/1079, 00/1132
R. v. Thomas (Gerald John) see R. v. Avis (Tony)
R. v. Thomas (Heath); R. v. Richards (David Michael) [1996] 1 Cr. App. R. (S.) 208,
    CA (Crim Div) . . . .   *Digested,* 96/**1921**:
                                         Considered, 98/1407, 99/1244
R. v. Thomas (Matthew) see R. v. Cox (Francis Gerard)
R. v. Thomas (Matthew) [2000] 1 Cr. App. R. 447, CA (Crim Div) . . . .   *Digested,* 00/**1025**
R. v. Thomas (Nigel Wynn) see Attorney General's Reference (No.68 of 1999), Re
R. v. Thomas (Robert Sean) (1994) 15 Cr. App. R. (S.) 848, CA (Crim Div). . . . .   *Digested,* 95/**1466**:
                                  Considered, 97/1693, 00/1415, 01/1472
R. v. Thomas (Steven Mark) see Attorney General's Reference (No.22 of 1992), Re
R. v. Thomas (Vernon Walter) see R. v. Spence (Clinton Everton)
R. v. Thompson see R. v. Thompson (James Andrew)
R. v. Thompson (Colin David) [2001] 1 Cr. App. R. (S.) 72, CA (Crim Div) . . . .   *Digested,* 01/**1435**
R. v. Thompson (Darren) [1999] Crim. L.R. 747, CA (Crim Div)
R. v. Thompson (Emrah Joseph) [2000] 1 Cr. App. R. (S.) 85, CA (Crim Div) . . . .   *Digested,* 00/**1155**
R. v. Thompson (James Andrew); *sub nom* R. v. Thompson [1914] 2 K.B. 99, CCA . . . .   *Applied,* 60/1250,
                                          63/3265: *Considered,* 98/1032
R. v. Thompson (John William) see R. v. Eastap (Robert Leslie)
R. v. Thompson (Mark Anthony) see Attorney General's Reference (No.60 of 1999), Re
R. v. Thompson (Steven) [1997] 2 Cr. App. R. (S.) 188, CA (Crim Div) . . . .   *Digested,* 97/**1542**:
                                         Considered, 00/1244
R. v. Thompson (Tony) [1999] 2 Cr. App. R. (S.) 292, CA (Crim Div) . . . .   *Digested,* 99/**1167**:
                                         Considered, 00/1244
R. v. Thompson (Wilfrid Frank) see Attorney General's Reference (Nos.80 and 81 of
    1999), Re
R. v. Thoms (Stephen) see Attorney General's Reference (No.26 of 1997), Re
R. v. Thomson (Cameron Kirkwood) see Attorney General's Reference (Nos.37 and 38
    of 2000), Re
R. v. Thornton (Paul Anthony) see Attorney General's Reference (No.7 of 1989), Re
R. v. Thornton (Peter) [2000] 2 Cr. App. R. (S.) 47; [2000] Crim. L.R. 312, CA (Crim
    Div) . . . .   *Digested,* 00/**1298**
R. v. Thornton (Sara Elizabeth) (No.2) [1996] 1 W.L.R. 1174; [1996] 2 All E.R. 1023;
    [1996] 2 Cr. App. R. 108; [1996] Crim. L.R. 597; (1996) 93(5) L.S.G. 30;
    (1995) 145 N.L.J. 1888; (1996) 140 S.J.L.B. 38; *Times,* June 6, 1996; *Times,*
    December 14, 1995; *Independent,* December 19, 1995, CA (Crim Div) . . . .   *Digested,* 96/**1501**:
                                       Considered, 97/1618: *Followed,* 98/960
R. v. Thorogood (Michelle Deborah) [2001] 1 Cr. App. R. (S.) 68, CA (Crim Div). . . . . .   *Digested,* 01/**1102**
R. v. Thorpe (Craig Stuart), *Times,* November 2, 2000, CA (Crim Div) . . . .   *Digested,* 00/**1061**
R. v. Thorpe (Terence George) see R. v. Brewster (Alex Edward)
R. v. Threapleton (Michael) see R. v. Dearnley (Roger)
R. v. Thwaites (Stefan Peter) see R. v. Hardwicke (Joseph Philip)
R. v. Tibbs (John) [2000] 2 Cr. App. R. 309; [2001] Crim. L.R. 759; *Times,* February
    28, 2000, CA (Crim Div) . . . .   *Digested,* 00/**931**
R. v. Tidiman (Ian Lee) (1991) 12 Cr. App. R. (S.) 702, CA (Crim Div) . . . .   *Digested,* 92/**1155**:
                                         Considered, 97/1596, 00/1421
R. v. Tindall (Unreported, February 3, 1998), Crown Ct (Merthyr Tydfil) [*Ex rel.* Ieuan
    Morris, Barrister, 9 Park Place, Cardiff] . . . .   *Digested,* 98/**1212**
R. v. Tingle (James) [2001] EWCA Crim 368; [2001] 2 Cr. App. R. (S.) 83, CA (Crim
    Div) . . . .   *Digested,* 01/**1375**
R. v. Tivnan (Michael) [1999] 1 Cr. App. R. (S.) 92; [1998] Crim. L.R. 591; (1998)
    95(21) L.S.G. 36; (1998) 142 S.J.L.B. 166; *Times,* May 6, 1998; *Independent,*
    May 11, 1998 (C.S.), CA (Crim Div). . . . .   *Digested,* 98/**1179**
R. v. TM; *sub nom* R. v. M (Admissibility: Background Evidence); R. v. B; R. v. PAM
    [2000] 1 W.L.R. 421; [2000] 1 All E.R. 148; [2000] 2 Cr. App. R. 266; [1999]
    Crim. L.R. 982; *Times,* September 7, 1999 ; *Independent,* October 18, 1999
    (C.S.), CA (Crim Div) . . . .   *Digested,* 99/**870**:
                                       Considered, 01/978
R. v. Tobin (Alan) see R. v. Chisholm (John)
R. v. Todd (Unreported, March 21, 1997), CA (Crim Div) . . . .   *Distinguished,* 98/875

R. *v.* Todd (Thomas) (1990) 12 Cr. App. R. (S.) 14, CA (Crim Div) . . . . *Digested,* 91/**1006**:
Cited, 93/1321, 94/1173, 94/1390: *Considered,* 00/1123

R. *v.* Togher (Kenneth) (Appeal against Conviction); R. *v.* Doran (Brian Peter) (Appeal against Conviction); R. *v.* Parsons (Robert) (Appeal against Conviction) [2001] 3 All E.R. 463; [2001] 1 Cr. App. R. 33; [2001] Crim. L.R. 124; *Times,* November 21, 2000, CA (Crim Div) . . . . *Digested,* 00/**1026**:
Followed, 01/5877

R. *v.* Tokeley-Parry (Jonathon Aidan) [1999] Crim. L.R. 578, CA (Crim Div)

R. *v.* Tolera (Nathan) [1999] 1 Cr. App. R. 29; [1999] 1 Cr. App. R. (S.) 25; [1998] Crim. L.R. 425; *Times,* April 28, 1998, CA (Crim Div) . . . . *Digested,* 98/**1331**:
Considered, 99/1361, 00/1209, 00/1225, 01/1311

R. *v.* Tomkins (Guy Michael) see R. *v.* Love (James Thomas)

R. *v.* Tomlinson (Eric) see R. *v.* Jones (John McKinsie)

R. *v.* Toney (Damien Leonard) (1999) 96(10) L.S.G. 30; (1999) 143 S.J.L.B. 74; *Times,* March 18, 1999, CA (Crim Div) . . . . *Digested,* 99/**1346**

R. *v.* Tonnessen (Brenda Ann) [1998] 2 Cr. App. R. (S.) 328; *Times,* March 3, 1998; *Independent,* February 20, 1998, CA (Crim Div) . . . . *Digested,* 98/**1200**:
Considered, 99/1130

R. *v.* Toombs (Daren) [1997] 2 Cr. App. R. (S.) 217, CA (Crim Div) . . . . *Digested,* 97/**1671**:
Considered, 98/1367, 99/1322

R. *v.* Toomer (Martin Charles); R. *v.* Powell (Michael Edmund); R. *v.* Mould (David Frederick) [2001] 2 Cr. App. R. (S.) 8; [2001] Crim. L.R. 149; *Times,* November 21, 2000, CA (Crim Div) . . . . *Digested,* 00/**1381**:
Applied, 01/1445: *Considered,* 01/1443, 01/1446

R. *v.* Toothill (Peter Kendall) [1998] Crim. L.R. 876, CA (Crim Div)

R. *v.* Torfaen BC (amended to Monmouth DC) Ex p. Jones [1986] J.P.L. 686 . . . . *Digested,* 86/**3333**:
Distinguished, 99/4233

R. *v.* Torrington (Richard Edward) see R. *v.* Avis (Tony)

R. *v.* Tosun (Ali Yener) see R. *v.* Aziz (Kazim)

R. *v.* Totnes Licensing Justices Ex p. Chief Constable of Devon and Cornwall (1992) 156 J.P. 587; [1990] C.O.D. 404; (1992) 156 J.P.N. 538; (1992) 156 L.G. Rev. 904; *Times,* May 28, 1990, QBD . . . . *Digested,* 91/**2329**:
Cited, 00/395: *Followed,* 98/945

R. *v.* Tottenham Youth Court Ex p. Fawzy; *sub nom* R. *v.* Haringey Justices Ex p. Fawzy [1999] 1 W.L.R. 1350; [1998] 1 All E.R. 365; [1998] 1 Cr. App. R. 411; (1998) 162 J.P. 241, QBD . . . . *Digested,* 98/**1103**

R. *v.* Tovey (William Joseph) see Attorney General's Reference (No.11 of 1993), Re

R. (on the application of Inner London Probation Service) *v.* Tower Bridge Magistrates Court; *sub nom* R. *v.* Tower Bridge Magistrates Court Ex p. Inner London Probation Service [2001] EWHC Admin 401; [2001] Crim. L.R. 750; *Times,* June 26, 2001, QBD (Admin Ct) . . . . *Digested,* 01/**1440**

R. *v.* Tower Bridge Magistrates Court Ex p. Inner London Probation Service see R. (on the application of Inner London Probation Service) *v.* Tower Bridge Magistrates Court

R. *v.* Tower Hamlets Healthcare NHS Trust Ex p. B see R. (on the application of B) *v.* East London and the City Mental Health NHS Trust

R. *v.* Tower Hamlets Healthcare NHS Trust Ex p. V see R. (on the application of B) *v.* East London and the City Mental Health NHS Trust

R. (on the application of Kimvono) *v.* Tower Hamlets LBC (2001) 33 H.L.R. 78; [2001] A.C.D. 36, QBD (Admin Ct)

R. *v.* Tower Hamlets LBC Ex p. Barratt Homes Ltd [2000] J.P.L. 1050, QBD . . . . *Digested,* 00/**4441**

R. *v.* Tower Hamlets LBC Ex p. Bradford [1998] 1 F.C.R. 629; (1997) 29 H.L.R. 756; (1997-98) 1 C.C.L. Rep. 294; [1997] C.O.D. 195, QBD . . . . *Digested,* 97/**2639**:
Applied, 01/2645

R. *v.* Tower Hamlets LBC Ex p. Chetnik Developments Ltd [1988] A.C. 858; [1988] 2 W.L.R. 654; [1988] 1 All E.R. 961; 86 L.G.R. 321; [1988] R.A. 45; (1988) 138 N.L.J. Rep. 89; (1988) 132 S.J. 4621, HL; affirming [1987] 1 W.L.R. 593; 85 L.G.R. 713; [1987] 1 E.G.L.R. 180; (1987) 282 E.G. 455; [1987] R.A. 57; (1987) 151 L.G. Rev. 791; (1987) 84 L.S.G. 1058; (1987) 131 S.J. 692, CA; reversing [1985] R.V.R. 87 . . . . *Digested,* 88/**3020.1**:
Applied, 01/5940: *Considered,* 86/2759, 88/3026, 89/3186, 94/3900:
Distinguished, 89/3442, 90/2496, 90/3914, 90/3918

R. *v.* Tower Hamlets LBC Ex p. Curtis see R. *v.* Tower Hamlets LBC Ex p. Uddin

R. *v.* Tower Hamlets LBC Ex p. G (Unreported, August 18, 2000), QBD [*Ex rel.* Jon Holbrook, Barrister, 2 Garden court, London] . . . . *Digested,* 01/**3422**

R. *v.* Tower Hamlets LBC Ex p. Luck (t/a G Luck Arboricultural and Horticultural Services) (1999) 15 Const. L.J. 235; [1999] C.O.D. 294, CA . . . . *Digested,* 99/**3863**

R. *v.* Tower Hamlets LBC Ex p. Tahid see R. *v.* Tower Hamlets LBC Ex p. Uddin

R. *v.* Tower Hamlets LBC Ex p. Uddin; R. *v.* Tower Hamlets LBC Ex p. Curtis; R. *v.* Tower Hamlets LBC Ex p. Tahid (2000) 32 H.L.R. 391, QBD . . . . *Digested,* 00/**3152**

R. v. Tower Hamlets LBC Ex p. Von Goetz [1999] Q.B. 1019; [1999] 2 W.L.R. 582;
    (1999) 31 H.L.R. 669; [1999] B.L.G.R. 135; [1998] E.G.C.S. 137; (1998) 95(43)
    L.S.G. 31; (1998) 95(40) L.S.G. 37; (1998) 142 S.J.L.B. 269; (1999) 77 P. &
    C.R. D11; *Times*, October 9, 1998; *Independent*, October 19, 1998 (C.S.), CA;
    affirming (1998) 30 H.L.R. 950, QBD. . . . .   *Digested*, 98/**3050**:
                                                        Applied, 99/3733: *Followed*, 01/3418
R. v. Tower Hamlets LBC Housing Benefit Review Board Ex p. Kapur, *Times*, June 28,
    2000, QBD. . . . .   *Digested*, 00/**4831**
R. v. Towers (Richard Charles) (No.1) [1999] 2 Cr. App. R. (S.) 110, CA (Crim Div) . . . .   *Digested*, 99/**1357**
R. v. Townsend (Philip Henry); R. v. Dearsley (Simon Robert); R. v. Bretscher (Gordon
    Maxwell) [1997] 2 Cr. App. R. 540; [1998] Crim. L.R. 126, CA (Crim Div) . . . . .   *Digested*, 98/**1034**
R. v. Townsend (Scott) (1995) 16 Cr. App. R. (S.) 553; [1995] Crim. L.R. 180; *Times*,
    December 12, 1994, CA (Crim Div). . . . .   *Digested*, 94/**1284**:
                                                        Applied, 98/1260: *Considered*, 00/1289
R. v. Tozer (Kerry Anne) (1994) 15 Cr. App. R. (S.) 807, CA (Crim Div) . . . .   *Digested*, 95/**1409**:
                                                                    Considered, 00/1278
R. v. Tranter (Wayne David) (1992) 13 Cr. App. R. (S.) 515, CA (Crim Div). . . . .   *Digested*, 93/**1244**:
                                    Considered, 96/1706, 96/1710, 99/1287, 99/1288
R. v. Travell (Richard John) [1997] 1 Cr. App. R. (S.) 52, CA (Crim Div) . . . .   *Digested*, 97/**1638**:
                                                                    Considered, 00/1381
R. v. Travers (Kelvin) [1998] Crim. L.R. 655; (1997) 94(32) L.S.G. 28; *Times*, August
    13, 1997; *Independent*, July 21, 1997 (C.S.), CA (Crim Div) . . . .   *Digested*, 97/**1736**
R. v. Tredwin (Donald Roy) see R. v. Richardson (Edward George)
R. v. Trent Mental Health Review Tribunal Ex p. Secretary of State for the Home
    Department see R. v. Nottingham Mental Health Review Tribunal Ex p. Secretary
    of State for the Home Department
R. v. Trevor [1998] Crim. L.R. 652, CA (Crim Div)
R. v. Triggs (David Lawrence) [2000] 2 Cr. App. R. (S.) 179, CA (Crim Div) . . . .   *Digested*, 00/**1390**
R. (on the application of National Car Parks Ltd) v. Trinity Development Co (Banbury) Ltd
    see National Car Parks Ltd v. Trinity Development Co (Banbury) Ltd
R. v. Truro Crown Court Ex p. Adair [1997] C.O.D. 296, QBD . . . .   *Applied*, 01/1299:
                                                                    Followed, 97/1465
R. (on the application of Stevens) v. Truro Magistrates Court [2001] EWHC Admin 558;
    (2001) 98(34) L.S.G. 39; *Times*, July 27, 2001; *Independent*, November 5,
    2001 (C.S), QBD (Admin Ct). . . . .   *Digested*, 01/**1104**
R. v. Tucker (John) (1992) 13 Cr. App. R. (S.) 15; [1991] Crim. L.R. 643, CA (Crim
    Div) . . . .   *Digested*, 92/**1404**:
                                                                    Considered, 99/5227
R. v. Tucker (Lee Nigel) see R. v. Charles (Jerome) (Leave to Appeal)
R. v. Tucknott (David Neil) [2001] 1 Cr. App. R. (S.) 93; [2000] Crim. L.R. 1026, CA
    (Crim Div). . . . .   *Digested*, 01/**1496**
R. v. Tudor (Richard) [1999] 1 Cr. App. R. (S.) 197, CA (Crim Div) . . . .   *Digested*, 99/**1169**
R. v. Tuegel (Peter Johannes); R. v. Saia (Sebastiano Claudio); R. v. Martens (Gerhard
    Werner) [2000] 2 All E.R. 872; [2000] 2 Cr. App. R. 361, CA (Crim Div) . . . . . .   *Digested*, 00/**1100**:
                                                                    Applied, 01/1242
R. v. Tugwell (Mark Owen) [2001] EWCA Crim 719; [2001] 2 Cr. App. R. (S.) 113, CA
    (Crim Div). . . . .   *Digested*, 01/**1277**
R. v. Tunnicliffe (Marcus); R. v. Greenwood (Paul) [1999] 2 Cr. App. R. (S.) 88; (1999)
    96(3) L.S.G. 31; *Times*, December 16, 1998, CA (Crim Div) . . . .   *Digested*, 99/**1271**
R. v. Tunstall (Nicholas) see Attorney General's Reference (No.16 of 1998), Re
R. v. Turner (Bryan James) (1975) 61 Cr. App. R. 67; [1975] Crim. L.R. 525; [1975]
    Crim. L.R. 451; (1975) 119 S.J. 422; (1975) 119 S.J. 575, CA (Crim Div). . . . . . .   *Digested*, 75/**559**:
                    Applied, 83/649, 83/691, 84/584, 86/769: *Considered*, 76/567, 79/550,
                    83/1700, 83/2647, 84/790, 84/2254, 85/2258, 86/624, 86/747, 86/753,
                    87/1001, 87/1044, 90/1408, 92/850, 92/1394, 93/1277, 95/1338, 95/1468,
                    96/1977, 98/1213, 98/1374, 98/1375, 00/1340, 00/1352: *Explained*, 78/476:
                                            Followed, 90/1406, 91/1208, 97/1702
R. v. Turner (Frank Richard) (No.1) [1970] 2 Q.B. 321; [1970] 2 W.L.R. 1093; [1970] 2
    All E.R. 281; (1970) 54 Cr. App. R. 352; 114 S.J. 337, CA (Crim Div) . . . .   *Digested*, 70/**479**:
                    Applied, 75/717, 77/652, 78/573, 78/595.50, 78/621, 80/547,
                    90/1229, 91/794, 93/754, 99/3800: *Considered*, 84/655, 85/670, 90/1230,
                    91/1041: *Explained*, 76/541: *Followed*, 76/615, 96/1678
R. v. Turner (Graham Rodney) (1990) 12 Cr. App. R. (S.) 110, CA (Crim Div) . . . .   *Considered*, 98/1311,
                                                        99/1268: *Referred to*, 95/1446
R. v. Turner (Ian) (Application for leave) [2000] 2 Cr. App. R. (S.) 472; [2000] Crim.
    L.R. 492; *Times*, April 4, 2000, CA (Crim Div) . . . .   *Digested*, 00/**1361**
R. v. Turner (John Eric) see DPP v. Turner
R. v. Turner (Keith) (1990) 12 Cr. App. R. (S.) 570, CA (Crim Div) . . . .   *Digested*, 92/**1309**:
                                                                    Followed, 01/1484

R. v. Turner (Terence Stuart) [1975] Q.B. 834; [1975] 2 W.L.R. 56; [1975] 1 All E.R. 70; (1974) 60 Cr. App. R. 80; [1975] Crim. L.R. 98; 118 S.J. 848; *Times*, October 23, 1974, CA (Crim Div) . . . . *Digested*, 75/**562**:
　　　　　　　　　　　　Applied, 85/645, 90/826, 91/667, 95/932, 96/1373: *Considered*, 90/801,
　　　　　　　　　　　　91/666, 91/687, 93/657, 93/723, 94/698, 94/899, 94/914, 94/3835,
　　　　　　　　　　　　00/906
R. v. TW (A Juvenile) [2001] 1 Cr. App. R. (S.) 38, CA (Crim Div) . . . . *Digested*, 01/**1381**
R. v. Twisse (Michael James) [2001] 2 Cr. App. R. (S.) 9; [2001] Crim. L.R. 151; *Times*, November 30, 2000, CA (Crim Div) . . . . *Digested*, 01/**1282**:
　　　　　　　　　　　　Considered, 01/1279: *Followed*, 01/1490
R. v. Twitchell (Keith) [2000] 1 Cr. App. R. 373; [2000] Crim. L.R. 468; *Times*, November 10, 1999 ; *Independent*, November 19, 1999, CA (Crim Div) . . . . *Digested*, 99/**877**
R. v. Tyndale [1999] Crim. L.R. 320, CA (Crim Div)
R. v. Tzambazles (Christos) [1997] 1 Cr. App. R. (S.) 87, CA (Crim Div) . . . . *Digested*, 97/**1158**:
　　　　　　　　　　　　Considered, 99/1265

R. v. Uddin (Rejan) [1999] Q.B. 431; [1998] 3 W.L.R. 1000; [1998] 2 All E.R. 744; [1999] 1 Cr. App. R. 319; [1999] Crim. L.R. 987; *Times*, April 2, 1998; *Independent*, April 24, 1998, CA (Crim Div) . . . . *Digested*, 98/**959**
R. v. Ugorji (John Nwangkugi), *Independent*, July 5, 1999 (C.S.), CA (Crim Div)
R. v. Ullah (Naveed) [2000] 1 Cr. App. R. 351; [2000] Crim. L.R. 108; (1999) 96(42) L.S.G. 41; (1999) 143 S.J.L.B. 251; *Times*, November 11, 1999 ; *Independent*, November 16, 1999, CA (Crim Div) . . . . *Digested*, 99/**978**
R. v. Underhill (Gareth Paul) (1979) 1 Cr. App. R. (S.) 270, CA (Crim Div) . . . . *Cited*, 91/1063,
　　　　　　　　　　　　95/1338: *Considered*, 99/1131
R. v. Underwood (Garren Dean) [1999] Crim. L.R. 227, CA (Crim Div)
R. v. Ungruh (Helmut) [1996] 2 Cr. App. R. (S.) 205, CA (Crim Div) . . . . *Digested*, 96/**1936**:
　　　　　　　　　　　　Considered, 00/1275
R. v. United Kingdom Central Council for Nursing, Midwifery and Health Visiting Ex p. Shine [2000] C.O.D. 310, QBD
R. v. United Kingdom Central Council for Nursing, Midwifery and Health Visiting Ex p. Shine (Alternative Remedy); *sub nom* Shine v. United Kingdom Central Council for Nursing, Midwifery and Health Visiting *Independent*, October 18, 1999 (C.S.), QBD
R. v. United States Ex p. Allison see R. v. Bow Street Metropolitan Stipendiary Magistrate Ex p. United States (No.1)
R. v. University College London Ex p. Idriss [1999] Ed. C.R. 462, QBD . . . . *Digested*, 99/**1928**
R. (on the application of Persaud) v. University of Cambridge; *sub nom* R. v. University of Cambridge Ex p. Persaud [2001] EWCA Civ 534; [2001] E.L.R. 480, CA; reversing [2000] Ed. C.R. 635; [2001] E.L.R. 64, QBD . . . . *Digested*, 01/**2087**
R. v. University of Cambridge Ex p. Evans (No.1) [1998] Ed. C.R. 151; [1998] E.L.R. 515, QBD . . . . *Digested*, 98/**2008**
R. v. University of Cambridge Ex p. Evans (No.2) [1999] Ed. C.R. 556, QBD . . . . *Digested*, 99/**1930**
R. v. University of Cambridge Ex p. Persaud see R. (on the application of Persaud) v. University of Cambridge
R. v. University of Central England Ex p. Sandhu [1999] Ed. C.R. 766; [1999] E.L.R. 419, CA; affirming [1999] Ed. C.R. 594; [1999] E.L.R. 121, QBD . . . . *Digested*, 99/**1932**
R. v. University of London Ex p. Vijayatunga see R. v. HM Queen in Council Ex p. Vijayatunga
R. v. University of Nottingham Ex p. K [1998] E.L.R. 184, CA . . . . *Digested*, 98/**2009**
R. v. University of Portsmouth Ex p. Lakareber [1999] E.L.R. 135, CA . . . . *Digested*, 99/**1933**:
　　　　　　　　　　　　Considered, 01/1900
R. (on the application of M) v. University of the West of England; *sub nom* R. v. University of the West of England Ex p. M [2001] E.L.R. 458; *Independent*, February 12, 2001 (C.S), CA; affirming [2001] E.L.R. 77, QBD . . . . *Digested*, 01/**2086**
R. v. University of the West of England Ex p. M see R. (on the application of M) v. University of the West of England
R. v. Unlu (Emin) see R. v. Kolton (Grzegorz)
R. v. Unstead (Edward Thomas) see R. v. Goodwin (John Charles)
R. v. Unstead (Edward Thomas) (C3/97) see R. v. Goodwin (John Charles) (C3/97)
R. v. Upton (Anthony William) see R. v. Formosa (John)
R. v. Utting (John Benjamin) [1987] 1 W.L.R. 1375; (1988) 86 Cr. App. R. 164; [1987] Crim. L.R. 636; (1987) 84 L.S.G. 2529; (1987) 131 S.J. 1154, CA (Crim Div) . . . *Digested*, 87/**781.2**:
　　　　　　　　　　　　Distinguished, 98/952
R. v. Uxbridge Justices Ex p. Commissioner of Police of the Metropolis [1981] Q.B. 829; [1981] 3 W.L.R. 410; [1981] 3 All E.R. 129; 125 S.J. 445, CA; affirming [1981] 1 W.L.R. 112; [1981] 1 All E.R. 940; [1980] Crim. L.R. 649; 124 S.J. 828, QBD . . . . *Digested*, 81/**2104**:
　　　　　　　　　　　　Considered, 92/944, 93/2628: *Followed*, 98/945
R. v. Uxbridge Justices Ex p. Patel see R. v. Uxbridge Magistrates Court Ex p. Patel
R. v. Uxbridge Justices Ex p. Webb (1998) 162 J.P. 198; [1994] 2 C.M.L.R. 288; [1994] C.O.D. 24, QBD . . . . *Digested*, 95/**4906**

R. *v.* Uxbridge Magistrates Court Ex p. Adimi; R. *v.* Crown Prosecution Service Ex p. Sorani; R. *v.* Secretary of State for the Home Department Ex p. Sorani; R. *v.* Secretary of State for the Home Department Ex p. Kaziu [2001] Q.B. 667; [2000] 3 W.L.R. 434; [1999] 4 All E.R. 520; [1999] Imm. A.R. 560; [1999] I.N.L.R. 490; *Times*, August 12, 1999, QBD . . . . *Digested*, 99/**3164**: *Considered*, 00/3298

R. *v.* Uxbridge Magistrates Court Ex p. Henry [1994] Crim. L.R. 581; *Times*, February 24, 1994, QBD . . . . *Digested*, 95/**1040**: *Considered*, 01/1138

R. *v.* Uxbridge Magistrates Court Ex p. Patel; *sub nom* R. *v.* Uxbridge Justices Ex p. Patel; R. *v.* London City Justices Ex p. Cropper; R. *v.* London Magistrates Court Ex p. Cropper (2000) 164 J.P. 209; [2000] Crim. L.R. 383; [2000] C.O.D. 104; (2000) 97(1) L.S.G. 22; (2000) 144 S.J.L.B. 27; *Times*, December 7, 1999, QBD . . . . *Digested*, 00/**1033**

R. *v.* Uxbridge Youth Court Ex p. H (1998) 162 J.P. 327; *Times*, April 7, 1998, QBD . . . . *Digested*, 98/**1102**

R. *v.* V (Dale Anthony) (A Juvenile) [1999] 1 Cr. App. R. (S.) 220, CA (Crim Div). . . . . . . *Digested*, 99/**1214**

R. *v.* V (David Victor) see Attorney General's Reference (No.50 of 1997), Re

R. (on the application of B) *v.* Vale of Glamorgan CBC [2001] E.L.R. 529, QBD (Admin Ct) . . . . *Digested*, 01/**2042**

R. (on the application of J) *v.* Vale of Glamorgan CC; *sub nom* R. *v.* Vale of Glamorgan CC Ex p. J (A Child) [2001] EWCA Civ 593; [2001] E.L.R. 758, CA; affirming [2001] E.L.R. 223, QBD . . . . *Digested*, 01/**1984**

R. *v.* Vale of Glamorgan CC Ex p. J (A Child) see R. (on the application of J) *v.* Vale of Glamorgan CC

R. *v.* Vale of Glamorgan Council Ex p. Clements, *Times*, August 22, 2000, CA . . . . *Digested*, 00/**357**

R. *v.* Vale of Glamorgan DC Ex p. Adams [2001] J.P.L. 93, QBD . . . . *Digested*, 01/**4733**

R. *v.* Value Added Tax Tribunal Ex p. Minster Associates [1988] S.T.C. 386, QBD . . . . *Digested*, 88/**3611**: *Followed*, 98/4878

R. *v.* Van Ackeren (Michael Staneley) see R. *v.* Liddle (Frederick)

R. *v.* Van Tattenhove (Frans Willem); R. *v.* Doubtfire (Robert Henry) (No.1) [1996] 1 Cr. App. R. 408; [1996] 2 Cr. App. R. (S.) 91, CA (Crim Div) . . . . *Considered*, 00/1229

R. *v.* Vanderwell (Clive) [1998] 1 Cr. App. R. (S.) 439, CA (Crim Div) . . . . *Digested*, 98/**1121**

R. *v.* Vasilou (Panicos) [2000] Crim. L.R. 845, CA (Crim Div)

R. *v.* Veasey [1999] Crim. L.R. 158, CA (Crim Div)

R. *v.* Vehicle Inspectorate Ex p. Healy [2001] R.T.R. 17, QBD . . . . *Digested*, 01/**5425**

R. *v.* Vickers (Royston Gary) [1999] 2 Cr. App. R. (S.) 216, CA (Crim Div). . . . . *Digested*, 99/**1127**

R. *v.* Victory (Kevin) [1999] 2 Cr. App. R. (S.) 102, CA (Crim Div) . . . . *Digested*, 99/**1156**

R. *v.* Video Appeals Committee of British Board of Film Classification Ex p. British Board of Film Classification [2000] E.M.L.R. 850; [2000] C.O.D. 239; *Times*, June 7, 2000, QBD . . . . *Digested*, 00/**4034**

R. *v.* Vincent (Unreported, May 13, 1998), CA (Crim Div) . . . . *Considered*, 00/1127

R. *v.* Vincent (Christopher James) [2001] EWCA Crim 295; [2001] 1 W.L.R. 1172; [2001] 2 Cr. App. R. 10; [2001] Crim. L.R. 488; (2001) 98(14) L.S.G. 39; (2001) 145 S.J.L.B. 68; *Times*, March 13, 2001; *Independent*, March 26, 2001 (C.S), CA (Crim Div) . . . . *Digested*, 01/**1085**

R. *v.* Vincent (Dean) see R. *v.* Hewitson (James Robert)

R. *v.* Vinnicombe (Stephen Robin) see Attorney General's Reference (No.82 of 2000), Re

R. *v.* Vinson (Norman John) (1981) 3 Cr. App. R. (S.) 315; [1982] Crim. L.R. 192, CA (Crim Div). . . . . *Digested*, 82/**684.51**: *Cited*, 88/932, 92/1315, 93/1191, 96/1784: *Considered*, 90/1336, 97/1445: *Not followed*, 99/1207: *Referred to*, 88/936, 89/1050, 89/1052, 90/1337, 90/1492, 94/1288

R. *v.* Virgo (Devon) [1996] 2 Cr. App. R. (S.) 443, CA (Crim Div) . . . . *Digested*, 97/**1521**: *Considered*, 00/1226

R. *v.* Visitor of the University of East Anglia Ex p. Hanuman see R. *v.* Secretary of State for the Home Department Ex p. Hanuman

R. *v.* Vladic Ex p. Secretary of State for the Home Department see R. *v.* Immigration Appeal Tribunal Ex p. Secretary of State for the Home Department

R. *v.* W see Attorney General's Reference (No.2 of 2000), Re

R. *v.* W (Alan B) (A Juvenile) see R. *v.* Reid (Sonni Lee)

R. *v.* W (Christopher Robert) [2001] 1 Cr. App. R. (S.) 143; [2001] 1 F.C.R. 308, CA (Crim Div) . . . . *Digested*, 01/**1421**

R. *v.* W (Colin) [1999] 2 Cr. App. R. (S.) 150, CA (Crim Div). *Digested*, 99/**1207**

R. *v.* W (Dale) (A Juvenile) see R. *v.* F (Paul) (A Juvenile)

R. *v.* W (Graham) [1999] 2 Cr. App. R. 201, CA (Crim Div) . . . . *Digested*, 99/**1025**

R. *v.* W (Jeffrey Shane) [1999] 1 Cr. App. R. (S.) 268, CA (Crim Div) . . . . *Digested*, 99/**1308**

R. *v.* W (John) [1998] 2 Cr. App. R. 289, CA (Crim Div) . . . . *Digested*, 98/**908**

R. *v.* W (John Robert) see R. *v.* A (Barrie Owen)

R. *v.* W (John Thomas) [1998] 1 Cr. App. R. (S.) 24; [1997] Crim. L.R. 678, CA (Crim Div) . . . . *Digested*, 98/**1341**: *Considered*, 99/1308, 00/1394

R. *v.* W (Jonathan) (A Juvenile) [2000] 1 Cr. App. R. (S.) 488; [2000] Crim. L.R. 59, CA (Crim Div) . . . . *Digested*, 00/**1337**

R. *v.* W (Jonathan Craig); R. *v.* S (Christopher Michael) [1998] 2 Cr. App. R. (S.) 322,
  CA (Crim Div) . . . . *Digested,* 98/**1270**
R. *v.* W (Jonathan Paul) (A Juvenile) [1999] 1 Cr. App. R. (S.) 488, CA (Crim Div) . . . .   *Digested,* 99/**1226**
R. *v.* W (Lee) (A Juvenile) see Attorney General's Reference (Nos.7, 8, 9 and 10 of
  2000), Re
R. *v.* W (Leslie Edward); *sub nom* R. *v.* Wellman [1999] 2 Cr. App. R. (S.) 162; [1999]
  Crim. L.R. 343; *Times,* January 5, 1999; *Independent,* December 16, 1998, CA
  (Crim Div) . . . . *Digested,* 99/**1196**
R. *v.* W (Marc Anthony) [1998] 1 Cr. App. R. (S.) 375, CA (Crim Div) . . . .   *Digested,* 98/**1354**
R. *v.* W (Michael) (A Juvenile) see R. *v.* S (Paul) (A Juvenile)
R. *v.* W (Michael Paul) (A Juvenile) see Attorney General's Reference (No.54 of 1998),
  Re
R. *v.* W (Nathan James) see R. *v.* L (Darren Mark) (A Juvenile)
R. *v.* W (Paul) (A Juvenile) see R. *v.* S (Paul) (A Juvenile)
R. *v.* W (RL) see Attorney General's Reference (No.61 of 1998), Re
R. *v.* W (Robert) see Attorney General's Reference (No.65 of 1999), Re
R. *v.* W (Ronald Douglas); *sub nom* R. *v.* W (Sentencing: Age of Defendant) *Times,*
  October 26, 2000, CA (Crim Div) . . . . *Digested,* 00/**1399**
R. *v.* W (Sentencing: Age of Defendant) see R. *v.* W (Ronald Douglas)
R. *v.* W (Stephen) (1993) 14 Cr. App. R. (S.) 256; [1992] Crim. L.R. 905; *Times,*
  September 2, 1992, CA . . . . *Digested,* 94/**1337**:
                          Considered, 96/2046, 98/1353: *Referred to,* 97/1647
R. *v.* W (Stephen) [1999] 1 Cr. App. R. (S.) 320, CA (Crim Div) . . . .   *Digested,* 99/**1084**
R. *v.* W (Stephen Robert) [2000] 1 W.L.R. 1687; [2000] 3 All E.R. 561; [2001] 1 Cr.
  App. R. 3; [2001] 1 Cr. App. R. (S.) 8; [2000] Crim. L.R. 599; (2000) 97(21)
  L.S.G. 38; (2000) 144 S.J.L.B. 188; *Times,* April 21, 2000, CA (Crim Div) . . . . .   *Digested,* 00/**1348**
R. *v.* W (Sven Matthew) (A Juvenile); R. *v.* P (Daniel Lee) (A Juvenile) [1998] 1 Cr.
  App. R. (S.) 239, CA (Crim Div) . . . . *Digested,* 98/**1274**:
                                                      Considered, 01/1379
R. *v.* W (Tax Evasion: Prosecution) [1998] S.T.C. 550; [1998] B.T.C. 202; (1998)
  95(16) L.S.G. 24; (1998) 142 S.J.L.B. 125; *Times,* March 24, 1998; *Independent,*
  March 18, 1998, CA (Crim Div) . . . . *Digested,* 98/**990**:
                                                      Considered, 00/1098
R. *v.* W (Travis) see R. *v.* N (Anthony Norris)
R. *v.* W (Witness Reprisals) see R. *v.* H (Witness Reprisals)
R. *v.* W School Governors Ex p. H [2001] E.L.R. 192, QBD . . . .   *Digested,* 01/**1946**
R. *v.* Waddon (Graham) 99/5233/Z3, CA (Crim Div); affirming [1999] I.T.C.L.R. 422;
  [1999] Masons C.L.R. 396, Crown Ct (Southwark) . . . .   *Digested,* 00/**996**
R. *v.* Wade (Jason Nicholas) [2000] 2 Cr. App. R. (S.) 445, CA (Crim Div) . . . .   *Digested,* 01/**1433**
R. *v.* Wadland (Simon) (1994) 15 Cr. App. R. (S.) 543, CA (Crim Div) . . . .   *Digested,* 95/**1488**:
                       Considered, 95/1487: *Distinguished,* 01/1487: *Referred to,* 99/1366
R. *v.* Wagstaff (Trevor Clifford) [2000] 2 Cr. App. R. (S.) 205, CA (Crim Div) . . . .   *Digested,* 00/**1198**
R. *v.* Wainfur (Mark Andrew) [1997] 1 Cr. App. R. (S.) 43; [1996] Crim. L.R. 674, CA
  (Crim Div) . . . . *Digested,* 97/**1603**:
                                   Considered, 97/1557, 98/1286, 98/1294
R. *v.* Wainwright (Matthew Michael) [1998] Crim. L.R. 665, CA (Crim Div)
R. *v.* Wait (Delme Gareth) [1998] Crim. L.R. 68, CA (Crim Div)
R. *v.* Waite (Glen Anthony) (1992) 13 Cr. App. R. (S.) 26; [1991] Crim. L.R. 646, CA
  (Crim Div) . . . . *Digested,* 92/**1157**:
                                  Considered, 97/1475: *Referred to,* 00/1148
R. *v.* Wake (Leslie) [1999] 2 Cr. App. R. (S.) 403, CA (Crim Div) . . . .   *Digested,* 00/**1377**
R. *v.* Wakefield (Russell Eric); R. *v.* Lancashire (Darrell Andrew) *Times,* January 12,
  2001, CA (Crim Div) . . . . *Digested,* 01/**1372**
R. *v.* Wakefield DC Ex p. Warmfield Co Ltd [1998] E.G.C.S. 89, QBD
R. *v.* Wakefield Magistrates Court Ex p. Wakefield MBC [2000] E.H.L.R. 81; [2000]
  Env. L.R. D18, QBD . . . . *Digested,* 00/**2249**
R. *v.* Wakefield MBC Ex p. B see R. *v.* Wakefield MDC Ex p. G
R. (on the application of Robertson) *v.* Wakefield MDC; *sub nom* R. (on the application
  of Robertson) *v.* Electoral Registration Officer [2001] EWHC Admin 915;
  (2001) 145 S.J.L.B. 267; *Times,* November 27, 2001; *Daily Telegraph,* November
  20, 2001, QBD (Admin Ct) . . . . *Digested,* 01/**4376**
R. *v.* Wakefield MDC Ex p. G; *sub nom* G *v.* Wakefield MDC; R. *v.* Wakefield MBC Ex p.
  B [1998] 2 F.C.R. 597; [1998] C.O.D. 288; *Times,* February 10, 1998, QBD . . . .   *Digested,* 98/**1985**
R. *v.* Wakeman (Paul) [1999] 1 Cr. App. R. (S.) 222, CA (Crim Div) . . . .   *Digested,* 99/**1144**:
                                                       Considered, 00/1208
R. *v.* Walker (Andre) [1998] 2 Cr. App. R. (S.) 245, CA (Crim Div) . . . .   *Digested,* 98/**1199**
R. *v.* Walker (Colin Frederick) (1992) 13 Cr. App. R. (S.) 474, CA (Crim Div) . . . .   *Digested,* 93/**1219**:
                                     Considered, 99/1265: *Distinguished,* 97/1158
R. *v.* Walker (David) see Attorney General's Reference (No.14 of 1994), Re
R. *v.* Walker (Deborah Alison) see Attorney General's Reference (Nos.73 and 74 of
  2001), Re
R. *v.* Walker (Dominic Makarachuma) [1999] 1 Cr. App. R. (S.) 42, CA (Crim Div) . . . .   *Digested,* 99/**1282**
R. *v.* Walker (Peter Michael) [1999] 1 Cr. App. R. (S.) 121, CA (Crim Div) . . . .   *Digested,* 99/**1075**
R. *v.* Walker (Rebecca) [1998] Crim. L.R. 211, CA (Crim Div)

R. *v.* Wallace (Nadine) [2001] EWCA Crim 559; [2001] 2 Cr. App. R. (S.) 95; [2001]
    Crim. L.R. 407, CA (Crim Div) . . . .   *Digested*, 01/**1414**

R. (on the application of Transport & General Workers Union) *v.* Walsall MBC [2001]
    EWHC Admin 452; *Independent*, July 23, 2001 (C.S), QBD (Admin Ct)

R. *v.* Walsh (John); R. *v.* Nightingale (Sheila) (1993) 14 Cr. App. R. (S.) 671, CA (Crim
    Div) . . . .   *Digested*, 94/**1215**:
                              Considered, 00/1378

R. *v.* Walters [1972] Crim. L.R. 381 . . . .   *Digested*, 72/**3002**:
                              Not followed, 01/990

R. *v.* Walters (Berkeley George) [1998] 2 Cr. App. R. (S.) 167, CA (Crim Div) . . . .   *Digested*, 98/**1301**

R. *v.* Walters (Desmond Arthur) [1997] 2 Cr. App. R. (S.) 87, CA (Crim Div) . . . .   *Digested*, 97/**1585**:
                    Considered, 01/1493: *Distinguished*, 00/1175

R. *v.* Walters (Donald) (1994) 15 Cr. App. R. (S.) 690, CA (Crim Div) . . . .   *Digested*, 95/**1403**:
                              Considered, 98/1254

R. (on the application of Boxall) *v.* Waltham Forest LBC CO/3234/2000, QBD (Admin
    Ct) . . . .   *Applied*, 01/3596

R. (on the application of S) *v.* Wandsworth LBC [2001] EWHC Admin 709; *Times*,
    November 15, 2001, QBD (Admin Ct). . . . .   *Digested*, 01/**4374**

R. *v.* Wandsworth LBC Ex p. Darker Enterprises Ltd (1999) 1 L.G.L.R. 601, QBD . . . . . .   *Digested*, 99/**3853**

R. *v.* Wandsworth LBC Ex p. Dodia (1998) 30 H.L.R. 562, QBD . . . .   *Digested*, 97/**2660**

R. *v.* Wandsworth LBC Ex p. Hawthorne [1994] 1 W.L.R. 1442; [1995] 2 All E.R. 331;
    [1995] 2 F.L.R. 238; [1995] 1 F.C.R. 539; (1995) 27 H.L.R. 59; 93 L.G.R. 20;
    [1995] C.O.D. 70; [1995] Fam. Law 608; (1994) 158 L.G. Rev. 961; (1994)
    91 (37) L.S.G. 50; (1994) 138 S.J.L.B. 178; [1994] N.P.C. 107; (1994) 68 P. &
    C.R. D11; *Times*, July 14, 1994; *Independent*, July 28, 1994, CA; affirming [1994]
    C.O.D. 228 . . . .   *Digested*, 95/**2561**:
                    Applied, 99/3058: *Considered*, 97/2662

R. *v.* Wandsworth LBC Ex p. Heshmati; R. *v.* Wandsworth LBC Ex p. Lawrie [1998]
    C.O.D. 67, CA; reversing (1998) 30 H.L.R. 153, QBD.   *Digested*, 97/**2699**

R. *v.* Wandsworth LBC Ex p. Lawrie see R. *v.* Wandsworth LBC Ex p. Heshmati

R. *v.* Wandsworth LBC Ex p. M [1998] E.L.R. 424, QBD. . . . .   *Digested*, 97/**2138**

R. *v.* Wandsworth LBC Ex p. Mansoor; R. *v.* Wandsworth LBC Ex p. Wingrove [1997]
    Q.B. 953; [1996] 3 W.L.R. 282; [1996] 3 All E.R. 913; [1996] 3 F.C.R. 289;
    (1997) 29 H.L.R. 801; (1996) 160 J.P. Rep. 1020; (1996) 160 J.P.N. 786; (1996)
    140 S.J.L.B. 158; *Times*, June 7, 1996, CA . . . .   *Digested*, 96/**3059**:
                  Considered, 98/2997, 98/3004: *Followed*, 97/2654

R. *v.* Wandsworth LBC Ex p. O; *sub nom* Bhikha *v.* Leicester City Council; O *v.*
    Wandsworth LBC; R. *v.* Leicester City Council Ex p. Bhikha [2000] 1 W.L.R.
    2539; [2000] 4 All E.R. 590; (2001) 33 H.L.R. 39; [2000] B.L.G.R. 591;
    (2000) 3 C.C.L. Rep. 237; *Times*, July 18, 2000; *Independent*, June 28, 2000,
    CA . . . .   *Digested*, 00/**4895**

R. *v.* Wandsworth LBC Ex p. Wingrove see R. *v.* Wandsworth LBC Ex p. Mansoor

R. *v.* Wang Lin Hal; R. *v.* Chen Cheng; R. *v.* Li Ling Bin; R. *v.* Tang Zhong;
    199906798Y4/199906912Y4, 199906913Y4/199907138Y4, CA (Crim Div) . .   *Not applied*, 01/993

R. *v.* Ward (Adrian John) see Attorney General's Reference (No.66 of 1995), Re

R. *v.* Ward (Alan) see R. *v.* Baker (Tony) (No.1)

R. *v.* Ward (Alan John) see Attorney General's Reference (No.56 of 1999), Re

R. *v.* Ward (David) [2001] 2 Cr. App. R. (S.) 30, CA (Crim Div). . . . .   *Digested*, 01/**1318**

R. *v.* Ward (Francis) see R. *v.* El-Hinnachi (Samir)

R. *v.* Ward (Judith Theresa) [1993] 1 W.L.R. 619; [1993] 2 All E.R. 577; (1993) 96 Cr.
    App. R. 1; [1993] Crim. L.R. 312; (1992) 89(27) L.S.G. 34; (1992) 142 N.L.J.
    859; (1992) 136 S.J.L.B. 191; *Times*, June 8, 1992; *Independent*, June 5, 1992;
    Guardian, June 10, 1992, CA (Crim Div) . . . .   *Digested*, 93/**723**:
          Applied, 00/2756, 00/5464: *Considered*, 94/698, 94/872, 94/873, 94/882,
               94/899, 95/1097, 95/1102, 96/1359, 00/906: *Not followed*, 93/808,
                            94/878: *Referred to*, 95/5604

R. *v.* Ward (Mark Richard) see Attorney General's Reference (No.4 of 1998), Re

R. *v.* Ward (Michael); R. *v.* Andrews (Russell); R. *v.* Broadley (Wayne) [2001] Crim.
    L.R. 316; *Times*, February 2, 2001, CA (Crim Div) . . . .   *Digested*, 01/**976**

R. *v.* Ward (Michael Grainger) see Attorney General's Reference (Nos.14, 15 and 16 of
    1995), Re

R. *v.* Ward (Michael Grainger) (Disqualification of Company Directors); R. *v.* Howarth
    (Jeremy John) (Disqualification of Company Directors) [2001] EWCA Crim
    1648; *Times*, August 10, 2001, CA (Crim Div) . . . .   *Digested*, 01/**717**:
                       Previous proceedings, 00/3216

R. *v.* Wardenier (Robert) [1999] 1 Cr. App. R. (S.) 244, CA (Crim Div). . . . .   *Digested*, 99/**1283**

R. *v.* Wardle (Lee) see Attorney General's Reference (Nos.17 and 18 of 1996), Re

R. *v.* Warley Hospital Ex p. Barker; *sub nom* R. *v.* Managers of Warley Hospital Ex p.
    Barker [1998] C.O.D. 309, QBD

R. *v.* Warley Magistrates Court Ex p. DPP; R. *v.* Staines Magistrates Court Ex p. DPP;
R. *v.* North East Suffolk Magistrates Court Ex p. DPP; R. *v.* Lowestoft Justices Ex
p. DPP [1999] 1 W.L.R. 216; [1999] 1 All E.R. 251; [1998] 2 Cr. App. R. 307;
[1999] 1 Cr. App. R. (S.) 156; (1998) 162 J.P. 559; [1998] Crim. L.R. 684;
(1998) 162 J.P.N. 565; (1998) 95(24) L.S.G. 33; (1998) 148 N.L.J. 835; (1998)
142 S.J.L.B.165; *Times,* May 18, 1998, QBD . . . . *Digested,* 98/**1009**:
          Applied, 00/1029, 00/1030: *Distinguished,* 01/1108
R. *v.* Warneford (Timothy); R. *v.* Gibbs (Maria) [1994] Crim. L.R. 753; *Times,* May 18,
1994; *Independent,* May 9, 1994 (C.S.), CA (Crim Div) . . . . *Digested,* 94/**1112**:
                     Disapproved, 01/1046
R. *v.* Warren (Dennis Michael) see R. *v.* Jones (John McKinsie)
R. *v.* Warren (John Barry); R. *v.* Beeley (Geoffrey Terence) [1996] 1 Cr. App. R. 120;
[1996] 1 Cr. App. R. (S.) 233; [1995] Crim. L.R. 838; (1995) 139 S.J.L.B. 177;
Times, July 4, 1995; *Independent,* July 17, 1995 (C.S.), CA (Crim Div) . . . . *Digested,* 96/**1879**:
        Applied, 96/1858: *Considered,* 96/1968, 98/1190, 99/1124, 00/1229,
                           00/1231
R. *v.* Warren (Mark Stephen) see R. *v.* McCarthy (Colin Paul)
R. *v.* Warren (Robert John) see R. *v.* McCarthy (Colin Paul)
R. *v.* Warrington BC Ex p. Barrett [2000] R.V.R. 208, QBD . . . . *Digested,* 00/**10**
R. *v.* Warrington Crown Court Ex p. RBNB [2001] 1 W.L.R. 2239; [2001] 2 All E.R.
851; (2000) 164 J.P. 644; (2000) 150 N.L.J. 1492; *Times,* September 8, 2000,
CA; affirming CO/4484/98, QBD . . . . *Digested,* 00/**4066**
R. *v.* Warth (Dean Roberts) (1991) 93 Cr. App. R. 187; (1991) 12 Cr. App. R. (S.) 680,
CA (Crim Div) . . . . *Digested,* 92/**957**:
                     Followed, 99/3800
R. *v.* Warwickshire CC Ex p. Powergen Plc (1998) 75 P. & C.R. 89; [1997] 3 P.L.R. 62;
[1998] J.P.L. 131; [1998] C.O.D. 80; [1997] E.G.C.S. 127; [1997] N.P.C. 136;
Times, October 10, 1997, CA; affirming [1997] 2 P.L.R. 60; [1997] J.P.L. 843;
[1996] N.P.C.169; *Times,* January 1, 1997, QBD . . . . *Digested,* 97/**4136**
R. *v.* Waters (Carl) see R. *v.* Chisholm (John)
R. *v.* Waters (Paul Anthony) see R. *v.* Bradshaw (Wayne Martin)
R. *v.* Watkins (Bernard David) see R. *v.* Targett (David Paul)
R. *v.* Watkins (Brian) [1998] 1 Cr. App. R. (S.) 410, CA (Crim Div) . . . . *Digested,* 98/**1386**
R. *v.* Watmore (Mark) [1998] 2 Cr. App. R. (S.) 46, CA (Crim Div) . . . . *Digested,* 98/**1326**
R. *v.* Watson (Stephen David) [2000] 2 Cr. App. R. (S.) 301, CA (Crim Div) . . . . *Digested,* 00/**1431**
R. *v.* Watts (Darren Lee) [2000] 1 Cr. App. R. (S.) 460, CA (Crim Div) . . . . *Digested,* 00/**1177**
R. *v.* Watts (James Wesley) see DPP *v.* Doot
R. *v.* Watts (Julie Helen) [1998] Crim. L.R. 833, CA (Crim Div)
R. *v.* Waveney DC Ex p. Bell [2001] Env. L.R. 24; [2001] P.L.C.R. 17, QBD . . . . *Digested,* 01/**4741**
R. *v.* Waveney DC Ex p. Bowers [1983] Q.B. 238; [1982] 3 W.L.R. 661; [1982] 3 All
E.R. 727; (1981-82) 4 H.L.R. 118; 80 L.G.R. 721; (1982) 79 L.S.G. 1413; 126 S.J.
657, CA; reversing (1982) 79 L.S.G. 922; *Times,* May 25, 1982, QBD . . . . *Digested,* 82/**1467**:
     Applied, 87/1906, 88/1772, 97/2671: *Considered,* 82/1464, 94/2340,
       95/2575, 95/2576, 96/3046, 96/3047: *Followed,* 98/3018:
                     Referred to, 92/5869
R. (on the application of Barker) *v.* Waverley BC [2001] EWCA Civ 566; (2001) 98(16)
L.S.G. 36, CA; reversing [2001] A.C.D. 64, QBD
R. *v.* Wayte (William Guy) (1983) 76 Cr. App. R. 110; *Times,* March 24, 1982, CA (Crim
Div) . . . . *Digested,* 83/**659**:
        Applied, 99/3441: *Explained,* 88/845, 89/898, 90/1175
R. *v.* Wealden DC Ex p. Stratford see R. *v.* Lincolnshire CC Ex p. Atkinson
R. *v.* Wealden DC Ex p. Wales see R. *v.* Lincolnshire CC Ex p. Atkinson
R. *v.* Weaver (Tanya); R. *v.* Burton (Thomas Terry) [1998] 2 Cr. App. R. (S.) 56, CA
(Crim Div) . . . . *Digested,* 98/**1142**
R. *v.* Webb (James Albert) see R. *v.* Williams (David Omar)
R. *v.* Webb (Robert Edward) see Attorney General's Reference (Nos.86 and 87 of
1999), Re
R. *v.* Webb (Toni Elizabeth) [2001] 1 Cr. App. R. (S.) 33, CA (Crim Div) . . . . *Digested,* 01/**1452**
R. *v.* Webbe (Bernard); R. *v.* M (William Andrew) (A Juvenile); R. *v.* D (Andrew) (A
Juvenile); R. *v.* Moore (Robert John); R. *v.* White (Paul) [2001] EWCA Crim 1217;
[2001] Crim. L.R. 668; *Times,* June 13, 2001, CA (Crim Div) . . . . *Digested,* 01/**1340**
R. *v.* Weekes (Stephen) [1999] 2 Cr. App. R. 520; [1999] Crim. L.R. 907; (1999)
96(16) L.S.G. 35; (1999) 143 S.J.L.B. 106; *Times,* March 30, 1999, CA (Crim
Div) . . . . *Digested,* 99/**1060**
R. *v.* Weeks (David Alexander) [1999] 2 Cr. App. R. (S.) 16, CA (Crim Div) . . . . *Digested,* 99/**1148**
R. *v.* Weir (Michael Clive) (2000) 97(27) L.S.G. 37; *Times,* June 16, 2000, CA (Crim
Div) . . . . *Digested,* 00/**912**:
                     Applied, 00/1056
R. *v.* Weir (Michael Clive) (Extension of Time) [2001] 1 W.L.R. 421; [2001] 2 All E.R.
216; [2001] 2 Cr. App. R. 9; [2001] Crim. L.R. 656; (2001) 98(10) L.S.G. 41;
(2001) 145 S.J.L.B. 61; *Times,* February 9, 2001; *Independent,* February 14,
2001, HL. . . . . *Digested,* 01/**1099**
R. *v.* Wellman see R. *v.* W (Leslie Edward)

R. *v.* Wells (Derek) [1995] 2 Cr. App. R. 417; (1995) 159 J.P. 243; [1995] Crim. L.R. 952; (1995) 159 J.P.N. 178; *Times,* December 14, 1994; *Independent,* January 23, 1995, CA (Crim Div) . . . .   *Digested,* 96/**1612**:
                                                                             Applied, 99/1013
R. *v.* Wells (Mark) [1999] 1 Cr. App. R. (S.) 371, CA (Crim Div) . . . .   *Digested,* 99/**1355**
R. *v.* Welsby (John) [1998] 1 Cr. App. R. 197, Crown Ct (Swansea) . . . .   *Digested,* 98/**3706**
R. *v.* Welsh (Sabrina Flarita), *Times,* January 9, 2001, CA (Crim Div) . . . .   *Digested,* 01/**1419**
R. *v.* Welwyn Hatfield DC Ex p. Nunan see R. *v.* Swansea City and County Council Ex p. Littler
R. (on the application of T (A Child)) *v.* Wembley High School Head Teacher see R. (on the application of B (A Child)) *v.* Alperton Community School Head Teacher and Governing Body
R. *v.* Were (Jon Bonville) see Attorney General's Reference (No.11 of 1998), Re
R. *v.* Wernet (Robert Stewart) see Attorney General's Reference (Nos.14 and 24 of 1993), Re
R. *v.* West (Alan Robert) [2001] 1 Cr. App. R. (S.) 30, CA (Crim Div) . . . .   *Digested,* 01/**1439**
R. *v.* West (Marcus) see R. *v.* Okee (Robert)
R. *v.* West (Stewart Jonathan) see Attorney General's Reference (No.45 of 2000), Re
R. *v.* West (Thomas William Edward) [1964] 1 Q.B. 15; [1962] 3 W.L.R. 218; [1962] 2 All E.R. 624; (1962) 46 Cr. App. R. 296; (1962) 126 J.P. 352; 106 S.J. 514, CCA . . . .   *Digested,* 62/**536**:
                                  Applied, 84/9, 84/490: *Distinguished,* 98/1104
R. *v.* West (Wayne Fitzroy) [1998] 2 Cr. App. R. (S.) 310, CA (Crim Div) . . . .   *Digested,* 98/**1181**
R. *v.* West (William John) (1986) 8 Cr. App. R. (S.) 5, CA (Crim Div) . . . .   *Digested,* 87/**876**:
                                                     Considered, 98/1366
R. *v.* West Dorset DC Ex p. Searle [1999] J.P.L. 331, CA . . . .   *Digested,* 99/**4223**
R. *v.* West Dorset DC Housing Benefit Review Board Ex p. Buckerfield (2000) 32 H.L.R. 729, QBD . . . .   *Digested,* 00/**4827**
R. *v.* West London Justices Ex p. S (A Child) see R. *v.* West London Justices Ex p. S-W (A Child)
R. *v.* West London Justices Ex p. S-W (A Child); *sub nom* R. *v.* West London Justices Ex p. S (A Child) (2001) 165 J.P. 112; [2000] Crim. L.R. 926, QBD . . . .   *Digested,* 01/**1170**
R. *v.* West London Youth Court Ex p. J; *sub nom* R. *v.* West London Youth Court Ex p. N; R. *v.* Metropolitan Stipendiary Magistrate Ex p. J [2000] 1 W.L.R. 2368; [2000] 1 All E.R. 823; [1999] C.O.D. 444; (1999) 149 N.L.J. 1201; *Times,* August 2, 1999 ; *Independent,* October 11, 1999 (C.S.), QBD . . . .   *Digested,* 99/**1052**
R. *v.* West London Youth Court Ex p. M see I *v.* DPP
R. *v.* West London Youth Court Ex p. N see R. *v.* West London Youth Court Ex p. J
R. *v.* West Norfolk Justices Ex p. McMullen (1993) 157 J.P. 461; [1993] C.O.D. 25; (1993) 157 J.P.N. 250, QBD . . . .   *Digested,* 94/**750**:
                                                     Followed, 00/1082
R. *v.* West Oxfordshire DC Ex p. Pearce Homes [1986] R.V.R. 156; [1986] J.P.L. 523 . . .   *Digested,* 86/**3340**:
                                                     Applied, 99/4259
R. *v.* West Sussex CC Ex p. Cresswell (1998) 76 P. & C.R. 17, QBD . . . .   *Digested,* 98/**2856**
R. *v.* West Sussex CC Ex p. S [1999] Ed. C.R. 509; [1999] E.L.R. 40, QBD . . . .   *Digested,* 99/**1897**
R. *v.* West Sussex Registration Area Ex p. Haysport Properties Ltd see R. (on the application of Haysport Properties Ltd) *v.* West Sussex Registration Area Rent Officer
R. (on the application of Haysport Properties Ltd) *v.* West Sussex Registration Area Rent Officer; *sub nom* R. *v.* West Sussex Registration Area Rent Officer Ex p. Haysport Properties Ltd; R. *v.* West Sussex Registration Area Ex p. Haysport Properties Ltd; R. *v.* West Sussex Rent Officer Ex p. Haysport Properties Ltd [2001] EWCA Civ 237; (2001) 33 H.L.R. 71; [2001] L. & T.R. 37; [2001] 21 E.G. 168; [2001] 6 E.G.C.S. 163; (2001) 98(17) L.S.G. 37; *Times,* March 22, 2001, CA; reversing (2001) 81 P. & C.R. D5, QBD . . . .   *Digested,* 01/**4205**
R. *v.* West Sussex Registration Area Rent Officer Ex p. Haysport Properties Ltd see R. (on the application of Haysport Properties Ltd) *v.* West Sussex Registration Area Rent Officer
R. *v.* West Sussex Rent Officer Ex p. Haysport Properties Ltd see R. (on the application of Haysport Properties Ltd) *v.* West Sussex Registration Area Rent Officer
R. *v.* West Yorkshire Fire and Civil Defence Authority Ex p. Lockwood; R. *v.* West Yorkshire Fire and Civil Defence Authority Ex p. McCalman [2001] O.P.L.R. 85; *Times,* July 18, 2000; *Independent,* July 12, 2000, CA; affirming [2000] C.O.D. 123, QBD . . . .   *Digested,* 00/**4360**
R. *v.* West Yorkshire Fire and Civil Defence Authority Ex p. McCalman see R. *v.* West Yorkshire Fire and Civil Defence Authority Ex p. Lockwood
R. (on the application of Murphy) *v.* Westminster City Council see R. (on the application of Painter) *v.* Carmarthenshire CC Housing Benefit Review Board
R. *v.* Westminster City Council Ex p. A see R. *v.* Hammersmith and Fulham LBC Ex p. M
R. *v.* Westminster City Council Ex p. Al-Khorsan (2001) 33 H.L.R. 6; [1999] N.P.C. 162; *Times,* January 21, 2000, QBD . . . .   *Digested,* 00/**3135**

R. *v.* Westminster City Council Ex p. Augustin [1993] 1 W.L.R. 730; (1993) 25 H.L.R. 281; [1993] C.O.D. 316; [1993] E.G.C.S. 4, CA . . . . *Digested*, 93/**2066**: *Distinguished*, 01/568

R. *v.* Westminster City Council Ex p. Castelli (No.2); R. *v.* Westminster City Council Ex p. Tristan Garcia (No.2) (1996) 28 H.L.R. 616; (1996) 8 Admin. L.R. 435; [1996] C.O.D. 390; (1996) 140 S.J.L.B. 86; *Times*, February 27, 1996; *Independent*, February 23, 1996, CA; reversing [1996] 3 F.C.R. 383; (1996) 28 H.L.R. 125; (1995) 7 Admin. L.R. 73; (1995) 92(39) L.S.G. 28; [1995] N.P.C. 150; *Times*, October 20, 1995; *Independent*, October 11, 1995, QBD . . . . *Digested*, 96/**3058**: *Applied*, 98/3007: *Considered*, 96/5483

R. *v.* Westminster City Council Ex p. De Souza (1997) 29 H.L.R. 649, QBD . . . . *Digested*, 98/**3012**

R. *v.* Westminster City Council Ex p. Ellioua (1999) 31 H.L.R. 440, CA . . . . *Digested*, 99/**3059**

R. *v.* Westminster City Council Ex p. Ermakov [1996] 2 All E.R. 302; [1996] 2 F.C.R. 208; (1996) 28 H.L.R. 819; (1996) 8 Admin. L.R. 389; [1996] C.O.D. 391; (1996) 160 J.P. Rep. 814; (1996) 140 S.J.L.B. 23; *Times*, November 20, 1995, CA; reversing (1995) 27 H.L.R. 168; [1995] C.O.D. 123, QBD . . . . *Digested*, 95/**2568**: *Applied*, 97/3923, 01/3425: *Considered*, 97/2688, 01/95: *Distinguished*, 97/2659, 99/2167: *Followed*, 96/5448

R. *v.* Westminster City Council Ex p. Hussain (1999) 31 H.L.R. 645, QBD . . . . *Digested*, 99/**3070**

R. *v.* Westminster City Council Ex p. Jaafer (1998) 30 H.L.R. 698, QBD . . . . *Digested*, 98/**3008**

R. *v.* Westminster City Council Ex p. Legg see R. *v.* Westminster City Council Ex p. Union of Managerial and Professional Officers

R. *v.* Westminster City Council Ex p. Obeid (1997) 29 H.L.R. 389; *Times*, July 16, 1996, QBD . . . . *Digested*, 96/**3050**: *Considered*, 00/3144

R. *v.* Westminster City Council Ex p. P (1999) 31 H.L.R. 154; (1997-98) 1 C.C.L. Rep. 486; *Times*, March 31, 1998, CA . . . . *Digested*, 98/**3001**

R. *v.* Westminster City Council Ex p. Tristan Garcia (No.2) see R. *v.* Westminster City Council Ex p. Castelli (No.2)

R. *v.* Westminster City Council Ex p. Union of Managerial and Professional Officers; R. *v.* Westminster City Council Ex p. Legg (2000) 2 L.G.L.R. 961; [2000] B.L.G.R. 611; *Times*, June 13, 2000, QBD . . . . *Digested*, 00/**4112**

R. *v.* Westminster City Council Ex p. Zafru see R. *v.* Southwark LBC Ex p. Bediako

R. (on the application of Mehanne) *v.* Westminster Housing Benefit Review Board; *sub nom* Mehanne *v.* Westminster Housing Benefit Review Board; R. *v.* Westminster Housing Benefit Review Board Ex p. Mehanne [2001] UKHL 11; [2001] 1 W.L.R. 539; [2001] 2 All E.R. 690; (2001) 33 H.L.R. 46; [2001] N.P.C. 51; *Independent*, April 30, 2001 (C.S), HL; affirming [2000] 1 W.L.R. 16; [1999] 2 All E.R. 317; (2000) 32 H.L.R. 35; [1999] N.P.C. 2; *Independent*, January 11, 1999 (C.S.), CA . . . . *Digested*, 01/**5016**

R. *v.* Westminster Housing Benefit Review Board Ex p. Mehanne see R. (on the application of Mehanne) *v.* Westminster Housing Benefit Review Board

R. *v.* Westminster Housing Benefit Review Board Ex p. Monazah (2000) 32 H.L.R. 385, QBD . . . . *Digested*, 00/**4826**

R. *v.* Westminster Housing Benefit Review Board Ex p. Sier (2000) 32 H.L.R. 655, QBD . . . . *Digested*, 00/**4824**

R. *v.* WG; *sub nom* R. *v.* G (W) [2000] 1 Cr. App. R. (S.) 70, CA (Crim Div) . . . . *Digested*, 00/**1403**

R. (on the application of Bilon) *v.* WH Smith Trading Ltd see Bilon *v.* WH Smith Trading Ltd

R. *v.* Whalley (Thomas Alan) (1972) 56 Cr. App. R. 304; [1972] Crim. L.R. 324; (1972) 116 S.J. 77, CA (Crim Div) . . . . *Digested*, 72/**595**: *Considered*, 84/753, 85/693, 99/985

R. *v.* Wharton (Diamond) [2001] EWCA Crim 622; *Times*, March 27, 2001; *Independent*, May 14, 2001 (C.S), CA (Crim Div) . . . . *Digested*, 01/**1176**

R. *v.* Wharton (John David) [1998] Crim. L.R. 668, CA (Crim Div)

R. *v.* Wharton (Thomas Leslie) [2000] 2 Cr. App. R. (S.) 339, CA (Crim Div) . . . . *Digested*, 00/**1249**

R. *v.* Wheeler (Glen) see Attorney General's Reference (No.1 of 1997), Re

R. *v.* Wheeler (Ian) see Attorney General's Reference (No.1 of 1997), Re

R. *v.* Wheeler (Leslie) [2001] 1 Cr. App. R. 10; (2000) 164 J.P. 565; [2001] Crim. L.R. 744; (2001) 165 J.P.N. 66; (2000) 97(42) L.S.G. 43; *Times*, July 7, 2000, CA (Crim Div) . . . . *Digested*, 00/**930**

R. *v.* Wheeler (Paul Howard Francis) [1967] 1 W.L.R. 1531; [1967] 3 All E.R. 829; (1968) 52 Cr. App. R. 28; 132 J.P. 41; 111 S.J. 850, CA (Crim Div) . . . . *Digested*, 67/**848**: *Applied*, 73/481, 00/1065: *Considered*, 69/590, 95/1092

R. *v.* Wheeler (Stephen) see R. *v.* Lavin (Thomas)

R. *v.* Whellem (Stuart Charles) [2000] 1 Cr. App. R. (S.) 200; [1999] Crim. L.R. 1000, CA (Crim Div) . . . . *Digested*, 00/**1166**

R. *v.* Whenman (Andrew Henry) [2001] EWCA Crim 328; [2001] 2 Cr. App. R. (S.) 87, CA (Crim Div) . . . . *Digested*, 01/**1281**

R. *v.* Whicher (Desmond) see R. *v.* Jones (Fiona)

R. *v.* White (Anthony Delroy) [2001] EWCA Crim 216; [2001] 1 W.L.R. 1352; [2001] Crim. L.R. 576; *Times*, March 13, 2001; *Independent*, March 26, 2001 (C.S), CA (Crim Div) . . . . *Digested*, 01/**1065**

R. v. White (Edward) (1992) 13 Cr. App. R. (S.) 108, CA (Crim Div) . . . . *Digested*, 92/**1152**:
Considered, 98/1306, 00/1267, 00/1369
R. v. White (Eileen Veronica) [1999] 1 Cr. App. R. (S.) 325, CA (Crim Div) . . . . *Digested*, 99/**1128**
R. v. White (James Robert) see R. v. Martin (Ellis Anthony)
R. v. White (Jamie Anthony) see R. v. Bool (Christopher William)
R. v. White (Joann) 7 B.H.R.C. 120, Sup Ct (Can). . . . . *Digested*, 00/**3163**
R. v. White (Leslie James) [2001] N.I. 172, CA (Crim Div) (NI) . . . . *Digested*, 01/**5737**
R. v. White (Paul) see R. v. Webbe (Bernard)
R. v. Whitehaven Magistrates Court Ex p. Thompson [1999] C.O.D. 15, QBD
R. v. Whitehead (David) [1996] 1 Cr. App. R. (S.) 225, CA (Crim Div) . . . . *Digested*, 96/**1710**:
Considered, 99/1287
R. v. Whitehead (Patricia Anne) [1996] 1 Cr. App. R. (S.) 111; [1995] Crim. L.R. 755,
CA (Crim Div) . . . . *Digested*, 96/**1709**:
Considered, 98/1393
R. v. Whitehouse [1941] 1 W.W.R. 172, CA (BC) . . . . *Considered*, 98/956
R. v. Whitehouse (Neil) [2000] Crim. L.R. 172; (2000) 97(1) L.S.G. 22; *Times*,
December 10, 1999 ; *Independent*, December 14, 1999, CA (Crim Div) . . . . *Digested*, 00/**949**
R. v. Whitehouse (Stuart John); R. v. Morrison (James Watson) [1999] 2 Cr. App. R.
(S.) 259, CA (Crim Div) . . . . *Digested*, 99/**1362**
R. v. Whiteley (Michael) [2001] EWCA Crim 474; [2001] 2 Cr. App. R. (S.) 99, CA
(Crim Div) . . . . *Digested*, 01/**1413**
R. v. Whiteley (Paul Anthony) [2001] 2 Cr. App. R. (S.) 25, CA (Crim Div) . . . . *Digested*, 01/**1266**
R. v. Whitfield (Shaun Patrick), *Independent*, January 22, 2001 (C.S), CA (Crim Div)
R. v. Whitford (1997) 115 C.C.C. (3d) 52, CA (Alta) . . . . *Approved*, 99/3139
R. v. Whitnall (Steven John) see R. v. Karunaratne (Susantha Frederick)
R. v. Whittaker (Barrington) [1998] 1 Cr. App. R. (S.) 172, CA (Crim Div) . . . . *Digested*, 98/**1133**:
Considered, 00/1151
R. v. Whittaker (Fraud) (Unreported, August 10, 2000), CC (Burnley) [*Ex rel.* Richard
Mullan, Barrister, Sedan House, Stanley Place, Chester] . . . . *Digested*, 00/**1257**
R. v. Whittaker (Steven Alan) see Attorney General's Reference (No.32 of 1996), Re
R. v. Whitter (John) [1999] Env. L.R. D21, CA (Crim Div)
R. v. Whitton (Miriam) [1998] Crim. L.R. 492, CA (Crim Div)
R. v. Wickins (Thomas George) (1958) 42 Cr. App. R. 236, CCA. . . . . *Digested*, 58/**2988**:
Applied, 92/3792, 93/1042, 93/3502: *Considered*, 68/3456, 69/3160,
90/1091, 91/1029: *Distinguished*, 69/3177: *Explained*, 71/10303:
Not followed, 01/1265
R. v. Wickramaratne (Amitha) [1998] Crim. L.R. 565, CA (Crim Div)
R. v. Wicks (Peter Edward) [1998] A.C. 92; [1997] 2 W.L.R. 876; [1997] 2 All E.R.
801; (1997) 161 J.P. 433; (1997) 9 Admin. L.R. 349; [1997] 2 P.L.R. 97; [1997]
J.P.L. 1049; (1997) 161 J.P.N. 628; (1997) 94(35) L.S.G. 34; (1997) 147 N.L.J.
883; (1997) 141 S.J.L.B. 127; [1997] N.P.C. 85; *Times*, May 26, 1997;
Independent, June 4, 1997, HL; affirming (1996) 160 J.P. 46; 93 L.G.R. 377;
(1996) 8 Admin. L.R. 137; [1996] 1 P.L.R. 12; [1996] J.P.L. 743; (1996) 160 J.P.
Rep. 548; (1996) 160 J.P.N. 48; (1995) 92(22) L.S.G. 40; (1995) 139 S.J.L.B.
119; [1995] N.P.C. 72; *Times*, April 19, 1995; *Independent*, May 11, 1995, CA. . . . . *Digested*, 97/**4065**:
Applied, 98/3222: *Followed*, 98/4203, 01/81
R. v. Wigan MBC Ex p. Tammadge (1997-98) 1 C.C.L. Rep. 581, QBD . . . . *Digested*, 99/**4622**
R. v. Wiggan (Joy Louise), *Times*, March 22, 1999, CA (Crim Div) . . . . *Digested*, 99/**1014**
R. v. Wiggins (Jamie Mark) (2001) 165 J.P. 210; [2001] R.T.R. 3; *Times*, June 23,
2000, CA (Crim Div) . . . . *Digested*, 00/**1126**
R. v. Wijs (Eric Jan); R. v. Rae (Darryn); R. v. Donaldson (Andrew); R. v. Church
(John); R. v. Haller (Pierre Egbert) [1998] 2 Cr. App. R. 436; [1999] 1 Cr. App.
R. (S.) 181; [1998] Crim. L.R. 587; *Times*, May 21, 1998; *Independent*, June 2,
1998, CA (Crim Div) . . . . *Digested*, 98/**1182**:
Considered, 99/1123, 99/1124, 99/1125
R. v. Wild (Michael Keith) (No.1) [2001] EWCA Crim 1272; [2001] Crim. L.R. 665, CA
(Crim Div)
R. v. Wild (Michael Keith) (No.2); R. v. Jefferson (Peter John) [2001] EWCA Crim
1433; *Times*, July 4, 2001; *Independent*, June 22, 2001, CA (Crim Div) . . . . *Digested*, 01/**1443**
R. v. Wildman (Martin Geoffrey) [1998] 1 Cr. App. R. (S.) 236, CA (Crim Div) . . . . *Digested*, 98/**1234**
R. v. Wileman (Kevin) [1997] 2 Cr. App. R. (S.) 326, CA (Crim Div) . . . . *Digested*, 98/**1208**
R. v. Wilkey (David John) (1982) 4 Cr. App. R. (S.) 100, CA (Crim Div) . . . . *Digested*, 83/**769**:
Considered, 97/1401, 98/1118: *Referred to*, 89/929
R. v. Wilkins (Carl) see R. v. Baker (Janet)
R. v. Wilkins (Joseph Herbert) see R. v. Sansom (Alec James)
R. v. Wilkins (Paul Edward) (1995) 16 Cr. App. R. (S.) 49, CA (Crim Div) . . . . *Digested*, 96/**1981**:
Considered, 99/1218
R. v. Wilkinson (Edward John) (1983) 5 Cr. App. R. (S.) 105, CA (Crim Div) . . . . *Digested*, 84/**880**:
Applied, 01/1213: *Cited*, 94/1297: *Considered*, 87/1020, 89/1069, 94/3835,
94/3841, 96/1984, 96/1985, 96/1989, 96/2000, 98/1233:
Followed, 95/1428, 96/1987

R. *v.* Williams (Barry Anthony); R. *v.* Davis (Frank O'Neill) [1992] 1 W.L.R. 380; [1992] 2 All E.R. 183; (1992) 95 Cr. App. R. 1; [1992] Crim. L.R. 198; *Times*, October 23, 1991, CA (Crim Div) . . . . *Digested*, 92/**796**: *Considered*, 00/1017

R. *v.* Williams (Christopher David) [1998] Crim. L.R. 494, CA (Crim Div)

R. *v.* Williams (David Omar); R. *v.* Saunby (David); R. *v.* Ashby (Mark William); R. *v.* Schofield (John); R. *v.* Marsh (Peter James); R. *v.* Webb (James Albert); R. *v.* Leese (Henry); R. *v.* Dodds (Andrew Alistair); R. *v.* Clarkson (Lee Martin); R. *v.* English (Paul Anthony) [2001] EWCA Crim 2311; (2001) 98(38) L.S.G. 37; (2001) 145 S.J.L.B. 223; *Times*, October 8, 2001, CMAC . . . . *Digested*, 01/**366**

R. *v.* Williams (Derek Anthony); R. *v.* Dryden (Sandra Lee); R. *v.* James (Martin Sylvester) [2000] 2 Cr. App. R. (S.) 308, CA (Crim Div) . . . . *Digested*, 00/**1225**

R. *v.* Williams (Douglas William) (1992) 13 Cr. App. R. (S.) 671, CA (Crim Div) . . . . *Digested*, 93/**1197**: *Considered*, 98/1255

R. *v.* Williams (Errol) [2001] 2 Cr. App. R. (S.) 44; [2001] Crim. L.R. 242; *Times*, January 11, 2001, CA (Crim Div) . . . . *Digested*, 01/**1240**

R. *v.* Williams (Gary Ian) [2001] EWCA Crim 932; (2001) 98(19) L.S.G. 36; (2001) 145 S.J.L.B. 86; *Times*, March 30, 2001, CA (Crim Div) . . . . *Digested*, 01/**1154**

R. *v.* Williams (Gladstone) [1987] 3 All E.R. 411; (1984) 78 Cr. App. R. 276; [1984] Crim. L.R. 163; (1984) 81 L.S.G. 278, CA (Crim Div) . . . . *Digested*, 84/**504**: *Applied*, 94/1075, 96/1618: *Approved*, 86/702, 87/825: *Considered*, 87/824, 93/692, 94/1107, 00/1002, 01/1070

R. *v.* Williams (Gwilyn Lloyd) see Attorney General's Reference (No.25 of 1997), Re

R. *v.* Williams (Huw David) see Attorney General's Reference (No.92 of 1998), Re

R. *v.* Williams (John) (Life Sentence) [2001] 1 Cr. App. R. (S.) 2; [2000] Crim. L.R. 597, CA (Crim Div) . . . . *Digested*, 01/**1470**

R. *v.* Williams (Mark) [1997] 2 Cr. App. R. (S.) 221, CA (Crim Div) . . . . *Digested*, 97/**1641**: *Considered*, 99/1289

R. *v.* Williams (Meirion) (1989) 11 Cr. App. R. (S.) 152, CA (Crim Div) . . . . *Digested*, 91/**1223**: *Considered*, 92/1404, 99/5227

R. *v.* Williams (Nicholas James) [1999] 1 Cr. App. R. (S.) 105, CA (Crim Div) . . . . *Digested*, 99/**1245**

R. *v.* Williams (Paul) see R. *v.* Saunders (Kevin John)

R. *v.* Williams (Peter) see R. *v.* Barczi (Richard)

R. *v.* Williams (Richard Thomas) (1995) 16 Cr. App. R. (S.) 191, CA (Crim Div) . . . . *Digested*, 96/**2105**: *Considered*, 99/1289

R. *v.* Williams (Ronald Anthony) (1986) 8 Cr. App. R. (S.) 480, CA (Crim Div) . . . . *Digested*, 88/**980**: *Cited*, 92/1329: *Considered*, 01/1353

R. *v.* Williams (Roxanne Diane) see Attorney General's Reference (No.67 of 1999), Re

R. *v.* Williams (Roy) [2001] 1 Cr. App. R. 23; [2001] Crim. L.R. 253; *Times*, October 25, 2000, CA (Crim Div) . . . . *Digested*, 00/**1013**

R. *v.* Williams (Roy) (Confiscation and Compensation Orders) [2001] 1 Cr. App. R. (S.) 140; [2001] Crim. L.R. 54, CA (Crim Div) . . . . *Digested*, 01/**1316**

R. *v.* Williams (Thomas Richard) see R. *v.* Sansom (Alec James)

R. *v.* Williams (Timothy James) (1990) 12 Cr. App. R. (S.) 415, CA (Crim Div) . . . . *Digested*, 92/**1291**: *Considered*, 98/1109, 98/1327, 00/1184

R. *v.* Williamson (Roger) see R. *v.* Cook (Leonard)

R. *v.* Willis (Unreported, January 29, 1979), CA (Crim Div) . . . . *Considered*, 98/871

R. *v.* Willis (Peter Charles) [1975] 1 W.L.R. 292; [1975] 1 All E.R. 620; (1974) 60 Cr. App. R. 146; [1975] Crim. L.R. 177; 119 S.J. 133, CA (Crim Div) . . . . *Digested*, 75/**714**: *Applied*, 01/1217: *Considered*, 87/961, 90/1198, 90/1213, 90/1215, 91/1026, 92/1161, 93/1032, 96/1734, 97/1434, 97/1436, 98/1139, 98/1347, 99/1087, 00/1141: *Followed*, 98/1256

R. *v.* Willoughby (Lawrence Clive) [1999] 2 Cr. App. R. 82; [1999] 2 Cr. App. R. (S.) 18; [1999] Crim. L.R. 244, CA (Crim Div) . . . . *Digested*, 99/**1251**

R. *v.* Willoughby (Matthew Overton) see Attorney General's Reference (No.68 of 1997), Re

R. *v.* Wilsdon (John Patrick) [1998] 2 Cr. App. R. (S.) 361, CA (Crim Div) . . . . *Digested*, 99/**1323**

R. *v.* Wilson [1991] Crim. L.R. 838, CA (Crim Div) . . . . *Digested*, 92/**899**: *Followed*, 99/1055

R. *v.* Wilson (Edward John) (1992) 13 Cr. App. R. (S.) 397, CA (Crim Div) . . . . *Digested*, 93/**1275**: *Cited*, 97/1694: *Considered*, 96/2060, 00/1423: *Referred to*, 99/1331

R. *v.* Wilson (Godfrey) [2000] 2 Cr. App. R. (S.) 323; [2000] Crim. L.R. 503, CA (Crim Div) . . . . *Digested*, 00/**1346**

R. *v.* Wilson (Iain Malcolm) (1993) 14 Cr. App. R. (S.) 627, CA (Crim Div) . . . . *Digested*, 94/**1283**: *Considered*, 99/1298, 00/1328

R. *v.* Wilson (James) (1993) 14 Cr. App. R. (S.) 314, CA (Crim Div) . . . . *Digested*, 94/**1256**: *Considered*, 99/1152

R. *v.* Wilson (Mark Robert) see Attorney General's Reference (No.36 of 1997), Re

R. *v.* Wilson (Paul) [1998] 1 Cr. App. R. (S.) 364, CA (Crim Div) . . . . *Digested*, 98/**1192**

R. *v.* Wilson (Paul James) [1998] 2 Cr. App. R. (S.) 267, CA (Crim Div) . . . . *Digested*, 98/**1210**

R. *v.* Wilson (Tyrell) (Unreported, July 22, 1997), CA (Crim Div) . . . . *Referred to*, 00/**1281**

R. *v.* Wilson (Vernon James) (1989) 11 Cr. App. R. (S.) 20, CA (Crim Div) . . . . *Digested*, 90/**1219**: *Considered*, 99/1088

R. *v.* Wilson (William Alan) [1998] 1 Cr. App. R. (S.) 341; [1998] Crim. L.R. 73, CA
(Crim Div) . . . .   *Digested*, 98/**1398**
R. *v.* Wiltshire CC Ex p. Kaur (Lakhbir) see R. *v.* Buckinghamshire CC Ex p. Sharma
R. *v.* Wiltshire CC Ex p. Lazard Brothers & Co Ltd see R. *v.* Wiltshire CC Ex p.
Nettlecombe Ltd
R. *v.* Wiltshire CC Ex p. Nettlecombe Ltd; R. *v.* Wiltshire CC Ex p. Lazard Brothers & Co
Ltd; R. *v.* Wiltshire CC Ex p. Pelham [1998] J.P.L. 707; [1997] N.P.C. 167; *Times*,
January 13, 1998; *Times*, December 31, 1997, QBD . . . .   *Digested*, 98/**95**
R. *v.* Wiltshire CC Ex p. Pelham see R. *v.* Wiltshire CC Ex p. Nettlecombe Ltd
R. *v.* Wiltshire CC Ex p. Razazan [1997] E.L.R. 370, CA; affirming [1996] E.L.R. 220,
QBD . . . .   *Digested*, 97/**2107**:
Considered, 00/1924

R. *v.* Winchester Crown Court Ex p. B (A Minor) [1999] 1 W.L.R. 788; [1999] 4 All
E.R. 53; [2000] 1 Cr. App. R. 11; (1999) 96(5) L.S.G. 35; (1999) 143 S.J.L.B. 31;
Times, January 8, 1999, QBD . . . .   *Digested*, 99/**84**:
Considered, 99/85

R. *v.* Winchester Crown Court Ex p. Forbes see R. *v.* Manchester Crown Court Ex p.
McDonald
R. *v.* Winfield (Jeremy Vincent) [1999] 2 Cr. App. R. (S.) 116, CA (Crim Div) . . . .   *Digested*, 99/**1335**
R. *v.* Wing (David) see Attorney General's Reference (Nos.24 and 45 of 1994), Re
R. *v.* Winn (James Derrick) [1999] 1 Cr. App. R. (S.) 154, CA (Crim Div) . . . .   *Digested*, 99/**1191**:
Considered, 00/1275
R. *v.* Winn (Stephen) (1995) 16 Cr. App. R. (S.) 53, CA (Crim Div) . . . .   *Digested*, 96/**1744**:
Considered, 00/1151

R. *v.* Winston (Winston James) [1999] 1 Cr. App. R. 337; (1998) 162 J.P. 775; [1999]
Crim. L.R. 81; (1998) 162 J.P.N. 905; (1998) 95(34) L.S.G. 32; (1998) 142
S.J.L.B. 246; *Times*, July 24, 1998, CA (Crim Div) . . . .   *Digested*, 98/**951**
R. *v.* Wintle (Raymond John) (1987) 9 Cr. App. R. (S.) 262, CA (Crim Div) . . . .   *Digested*, 89/**1054**:
Considered, 98/1264

R. (on the application of McKeown) *v.* Wirral Borough Magistrates Court see R. (on the
application of DPP) *v.* Havering Magistrates Court
R. *v.* Wirral Borough Magistrates Court Ex p. McKeown see R. (on the application of
DPP) *v.* Havering Magistrates Court
R. (on the application of Jermyn) *v.* Wirral Magistrates Court; *sub nom* R. *v.* Wirral
Magistrates Court Ex p. Jermyn [2001] 1 Cr. App. R. (S.) 137; [2001] Crim. L.R.
45; *Independent*, November 27, 2000 (C.S), QBD (Admin Ct)
R. *v.* Wirral Magistrates Court Ex p. Jermyn see R. (on the application of Jermyn) *v.*
Wirral Magistrates Court
R. (on the application of B) *v.* Wirral MBC see R. *v.* Wirral MBC Ex p. B (A Child)
R. *v.* Wirral MBC Ex p. B (A Child); *sub nom* R. (on the application of B) *v.* Wirral MBC
[2001] B.L.G.R. 1; [2001] E.L.R. 266; *Daily Telegraph*, October 31, 2000, CA;
affirming [2000] B.L.G.R. 541; [2000] E.L.R. 703, QBD . . . .   *Digested*, 01/**2029**
R. *v.* Wirral MBC Ex p. Gray [1998] Env. L.R. D13, QBD
R. *v.* Wiseman Lee (Solicitors) see Wiseman Lee (Solicitors) (Wasted Costs Order)
(No.5 of 2000), Re
R. *v.* Withers (Simon) see R. *v.* Green (Wayne)
R. *v.* Withey (Michelle) (Unreported, January 5, 1999), CA (Crim Div) [*Ex rel.* Ian M
Strongman, Barrister, No 8 Chambers, Fountain Court, Steelhouse Lane,
Birmingham] . . . .   *Digested*, 99/**1179**
R. *v.* Wiwczaryk (Stephen Michael) (1980) 2 Cr. App. R. (S.) 309, CA (Crim Div) . . . . .   *Considered*, 00/1183
R. *v.* Wm Morrison Supermarkets Plc Ex p. Safeway Stores see R. *v.* Leicester City
Council Ex p. Safeway Stores Plc
R. *v.* Wokingham DC Ex p. J; *sub nom* R. *v.* Wokingham DC Ex p. SJ [1999] 2 F.L.R.
1136; [2000] 1 F.C.R. 523; [1999] C.O.D. 336; [1999] Fam. Law 807, QBD. . . .   *Digested*, 99/**2297**
R. *v.* Wokingham DC Ex p. SJ see R. *v.* Wokingham DC Ex p. J
R. *v.* Wolverhampton Justices Ex p. Uppal (1995) 159 J.P. 86; [1995] Crim. L.R. 223;
(1995) 159 J.P.N. 62; *Independent*, October 24, 1994 (C.S.), QBD. . . . .   *Applied*, 01/1091
R. *v.* Wood (Andrew Raymond) [1998] 2 Cr. App. R. (S.) 234, CA (Crim Div) . . . .   *Digested*, 98/**1360**
R. *v.* Wood (Colin John) see R. *v.* Cooney (Stephen)
R. *v.* Wood (Jane Leslie) see Attorney General's Reference (Nos.62, 63 and 64 of
1995), Re
R. *v.* Wood (Robert) [1997] 1 Cr. App. R. (S.) 347; [1996] Crim. L.R. 916, CA (Crim
Div) . . . .   *Digested*, 97/**1588**:
Applied, 99/1126
R. *v.* Wood (Saxon Swayne) see R. *v.* Booth (Stephen)
R. *v.* Wood (Thomas James); R. *v.* Mruk (Stefan Paul) (1984) 6 Cr. App. R. (S.) 139,
CA . . . .   *Digested*, 85/**817**:
Cited, 87/1040, 88/984, 94/1307: *Considered*, 96/2010, 99/1262
R. *v.* Wood (William Douglas); R. *v.* Fitzsimmons (Paul) [1998] Crim. L.R. 213, CA
(Crim Div)
R. *v.* Woodcock (Barry James) [1998] 1 Cr. App. R. (S.) 383, CA (Crim Div) . . . .   *Digested*, 98/**1258**
R. *v.* Woodhouse (Michael Charles) see R. *v.* Brewster (Alex Edward)
R. *v.* Woodliffe (Mark Alexander) [2000] 1 Cr. App. R. (S.) 330, CA (Crim Div) . . . .   *Digested*, 00/**1150**

R. *v.* Woodruff (John William); R. *v.* Hickson (William John) [1998] 1 Cr. App. R. (S.)
424, CA (Crim Div) . . . . *Digested*, 98/**1374**:
Considered, 00/1424

R. *v.* Woods (Alan) (Unreported, March 2, 2000), Crown Ct (Exeter) [*Ex rel.* Guy
Opperman, Barrister, 3 Paper Buildings, Temple, London] . . . . *Digested*, 00/**916**

R. *v.* Woods (Raymond) [1998] 2 Cr. App. R. (S.) 237, CA (Crim Div). . . . . *Digested*, 98/**1137**

R. *v.* Woodward (Paul) see Attorney General's Reference (No.21 of 2000) (Unduly
Lenient Sentence), Re

R. *v.* Woolley (Unreported, November 13, 1997), MC [*Ex rel.* Gary William Reynolds,
Barrister, Manchester House Chambers, 18-22 Bridge Street, Manchester] . . . . *Digested*, 98/**914**

R. *v.* Woollin (Stephen Leslie) [1999] 1 A.C. 82; [1998] 3 W.L.R. 382; [1998] 4 All
E.R. 103; [1999] 1 Cr. App. R. 8; [1998] Crim. L.R. 890; (1998) 95(34) L.S.G.
32; (1998) 148 N.L.J. 1178; (1998) 142 S.J.L.B. 230; (1998) 142 S.J.L.B. 248;
Times, July 23, 1998, HL; reversing [1997] 1 Cr. App. R. 97; [1997] Crim. L.R.
519; *Times*, August 12, 1996, CA (Crim Div) . . . . *Digested*, 98/**1052**:
Followed, 00/1069

R. *v.* Woolwich Crown Court Ex p. Gilligan see R. *v.* Governor of Belmarsh Prison Ex p.
Gilligan

R. *v.* Wooton (Norbert Pierre) [1998] 1 Cr. App. R. (S.) 296, CA (Crim Div) . . . . *Digested*, 98/**1308**

R. *v.* Worcester CC Ex p. SW see R. *v.* Worcester CC Ex p. W (S)

R. *v.* Worcester CC Ex p. W (S); *sub nom* R. *v.* Worcester CC Ex p. SW [2000] 3 F.C.R.
174; [2000] H.R.L.R. 702, QBD . . . . *Digested*, 00/**3250**

R. *v.* Worcester Crown Court and Birmingham Magistrates Court Ex p. Lamb (1985) 7
Cr. App. R. (S.) 44, DC . . . . *Digested*, 86/**782**:
Applied, 98/1147: *Considered*, 87/883

R. *v.* Worcester Crown Court Ex p. Norman [2000] 3 All E.R. 267; [2000] 2 Cr. App.
R. 33; (2000) 164 J.P. 201; [2000] Crim. L.R. 376; *Times*, February 17, 2000;
Independent, February 7, 2000 (C.S.), QBD . . . . *Digested*, 00/**1053**

R. *v.* Worcestershire CC Ex p. S [1999] E.L.R. 46, QBD. . . . . *Digested*, 99/**1881**

R. *v.* Worek (Peter) [1998] 2 Cr. App. R. (S.) 119, CA (Crim Div) . . . . *Digested*, 98/**1405**

R. *v.* Worthing and District Justices Ex p. Varley see R. *v.* Worthing Justices Ex p. Varley

R. *v.* Worthing Justices Ex p. Varley; *sub nom* R. *v.* Worthing and District Justices Ex p.
Varley [1998] 1 W.L.R. 819; [1998] 1 Cr. App. R. (S.) 175; (1997) 161 J.P. 748;
[1997] Crim. L.R. 688; (1997) 161 J.P.N. 817; *Times*, July 21, 1997, QBD . . . . . . *Digested*, 97/**1633**

R. *v.* Wortley (Gary) (1991) 12 Cr. App. R. (S.) 747, CA. . . . . *Cited*, 93/1183:
Considered, 01/1333

R. *v.* Wray (Andrew Simon) see R. *v.* Bisset (Ronald)

R. *v.* Wrench (Peter) [1996] 1 Cr. App. R. 340; [1996] 1 Cr. App. R. (S.) 145; [1995]
Crim. L.R. 265, CA (Crim Div) . . . . *Digested*, 96/**1566**:
Disapproved, 01/1125: *Distinguished*, 97/1428

R. *v.* Wrest (Lee Alan) (1989) 11 Cr. App. R. (S.) 83, CA (Crim Div) . . . . *Digested*, 90/**1361**:
Considered, 99/1263

R. *v.* Wrexham BC Ex p. Wall [2000] J.P.L. 32, QBD . . . . *Digested*, 00/**4467**

R. *v.* Wright (Derek) [2000] Crim. L.R. 851; *Times*, May 31, 2000, CA (Crim Div) . . . . . . *Digested*, 00/**1107**

R. *v.* Wright (Desmond Carl) (1979) 1 Cr. App. R. (S.) 82, CA (Crim Div) . . . . *Digested*, 81/**525.79**:
Considered, 99/1358

R. *v.* Wright (Ezra James) see Attorney General's Reference (No.18 of 1998), Re

R. *v.* Wright (Frederick Martin) see R. *v.* Chisholm (John)

R. *v.* Wright (Glenn Paul) [2000] Crim. L.R. 928; *Times*, May 17, 2000, CA (Crim Div) . . *Digested*, 00/**1069**

R. *v.* Wright (Lloyd George) [1999] 2 Cr. App. R. (S.) 327, CA (Crim Div) . . . . *Digested*, 99/**1090**

R. *v.* Wright (Mark Justin) [1998] 2 Cr. App. R. (S.) 333, CA (Crim Div) . . . . *Digested*, 98/**1203**

R. *v.* Wright (Raymond Eric) see R. *v.* Dickson (William Ewing)

R. *v.* Wright (Richard) [2000] 1 Cr. App. R. (S.) 109, CA (Crim Div) . . . . *Digested*, 00/**1253**

R. *v.* Wright (Richard Arthur); R. *v.* Shuck (David Philip); R. *v.* Herbert (Stevie Jefferey)
[2000] 2 Cr. App. R. (S.) 459, CA (Crim Div) [*Ex rel.* Ian Strongman, Barrister,
No. 8 Chambers, Fountain Court, Steelhouse Lane, Birmingham] . . . . *Digested*, 01/**1474**

R. *v.* Wright (Shani Ann) [2000] Crim. L.R. 510; *Times*, March 3, 2000, CA (Crim Div) . . *Digested*, 00/**1065**

R. *v.* Wyner (Ruth Avril) see R. *v.* Brock (John Terrence)

R. *v.* Wynne (Anthony Vincent) see Attorney General's Reference (No.58 of 2000), Re

R. *v.* Wyre BC Ex p. Dransfield Properties Ltd [2001] EWHC Admin 147; [2001] N.P.C.
28, QBD (Admin Ct)

R. *v.* X (Prior Acquittal) see R. *v.* Z (Prior Acquittal)

R. *v.* X (Sentencing: Confidential Information) [1999] 2 Cr. App. R. 125; [1999] 2 Cr.
App. R. (S.) 294; [1999] Crim. L.R. 678; *Times*, February 3, 1999; *Independent*,
February 9, 1999, CA (Crim Div) . . . . *Digested*, 99/**1104**

R. *v.* X (Telephone Intercepts: Admissibility of Evidence) see R. *v.* P (Telephone
Intercepts: Admissibility of Evidence)

R. *v.* X Justices Ex p. J see R. *v.* DPP Ex p. J

R. *v.* Xenofhontos (Xenophon Peter); R. *v.* Mace (Steven Terence) (1992) 13 Cr. App.
R. (S.) 580, CA (Crim Div) . . . . *Digested*, 93/**1235**:
Considered, 98/1314

R. *v.* Y (G); *sub nom* R. *v.* GY [1999] Crim. L.R. 825, CA (Crim Div)

R. *v.* Y (Jayne Alison) see Attorney General's Reference (No.24 of 2001), Re

R. *v.* Y (Paul Joseph) [2001] 1 Cr. App. R. (S.) 124, CA (Crim Div) . . . . *Digested*, 01/**1416**

R. v. Y (Sexual Offence: Complainant's Sexual History) see R. v. A (Complainant's
    Sexual History)
R. v. Y (Telephone Intercepts: Admissibility of Evidence) see R. v. P (Telephone
    Intercepts: Admissibility of Evidence)
R. v. Yala (Ngunza U Danga) [1999] 2 Cr. App. R. 1; [1999] Crim. L.R. 585, CA (Crim
    Div) .... *Digested,* 99/**944**
R. v. Yalman (Achmet) [1998] 2 Cr. App. R. 269; [1998] Crim. L.R. 569, CA (Crim
    Div) .... *Digested,* 98/**871**
R. v. Yanko (Wayne John) [1996] 1 Cr. App. R. (S.) 217, CA (Crim Div) .... *Digested,* 96/**1848**:
    Considered, 00/1182
R. v. Yazbek (Michael Said) [1998] 1 Cr. App. R. (S.) 406, CA (Crim Div) .... *Digested,* 98/**1259**
R. v. Yeardley (Peter) (Appeal against Conviction) [2000] Q.B. 374; [2000] 2 W.L.R.
    366; [2000] 2 Cr. App. R. 141; [2001] Crim. L.R. 255, CA (Crim Div) .... *Digested,* 00/**1109**
R. v. Yorganci (Metin) see R. v. Aziz (Kazim)
R. v. York Magistrates Court Ex p. Grimes (1997) 161 J.P. 550; [1998] B.P.I.R. 642;
    (1997) 161 J.P.N. 794; *Times,* June 27, 1997, QBD .... *Digested,* 97/**1532**
R. v. Yorkshire Mental Health Review Tribunal Ex p. Secretary of State for the Home
    Department see R. v. Oxford Regional Mental Health Tribunal Ex p. Secretary of
    State for the Home Department
R. v. Yorkshire Purchasing Organisation Ex p. British Educational Suppliers Association
    see R. v. Yorkshire Purchasing Organisation Ex p. British Educational Suppliers
    Ltd
R. v. Yorkshire Purchasing Organisation Ex p. British Educational Suppliers Ltd; *sub
    nom* R. v. Yorkshire Purchasing Organisation Ex p. British Educational Suppliers
    Association [1998] E.L.R. 195; [1997] C.O.D. 473; *Times,* July 10, 1997, CA;
    affirming in part [1997] C.O.D. 211, QBD...................... *Digested,* 97/**3523**:
    Considered, 98/4319
R. v. Yorkshire RHA Ex p. Gompels see R. v. Yorkshire RHA Ex p. Suri
R. v. Yorkshire RHA Ex p. Suri; R. v. Yorkshire RHA Ex p. Gompels (1996) 30 B.M.L.R.
    78; *Times,* December 5, 1995, CA; affirming [1995] 6 Med. L.R. 376; [1994]
    C.O.D. 485; *Times,* August 15, 1994, QBD..................... *Digested,* 96/**4418**:
    Applied, 95/6147: *Considered,* 99/2846
R. v. Yorkshire Water Services Ltd see Secretary of State for the Environment, Transport
    and the Regions v. Yorkshire Water Services Ltd
R. v. Young (Michelle) see R. v. Brodie (Caine)
R. v. Young (Stephen Andrew) [1995] Q.B. 324; [1995] 2 W.L.R. 430; [1995] 2 Cr.
    App. R. 379; (1995) 92(6) L.S.G. 38; (1995) 139 S.J.L.B. 32; *Times,* December
    30, 1994; *Independent,* January 16, 1995 (C.S.), CA (Crim Div) .... *Digested,* 96/**1629**:
    Distinguished, 97/1327, 99/1061
R. v. Young (Susan) [2000] 2 Cr. App. R. (S.) 248, CA (Crim Div) .... *Digested,* 00/**1223**
R. v. Z (Prior Acquittal); *sub nom* R. v. X (Prior Acquittal) [2000] 2 A.C. 483; [2000]
    3 W.L.R. 117; [2000] 3 All E.R. 385; [2000] 2 Cr. App. R. 281; (2000) 164 J.P.
    533; (2000) 164 J.P.N. 824; (2000) 97(28) L.S.G. 31; (2000) 150 N.L.J. 984;
    Times, June 23, 2000; *Independent,* June 27, 2000, HL; reversing (2000) 164
    J.P. 240; [2000] Crim. L.R. 293; (2000) 164 J.P.N. 206; (2000) 97(1) L.S.G.
    22; (2000) 144 S.J.L.B. 26; *Times,* December 14, 1999 ; *Independent,* December
    8, 1999, CA (Crim Div) .... *Digested,* 00/**924**
R. v. Z (Telephone Intercepts: Admissibility of Evidence) see R. v. P (Telephone
    Intercepts: Admissibility of Evidence)
R. v. Zafar (Mohammed); R. v. Browne (Sandra); R. v. Green (James William) [1998] 2
    Cr. App. R. (S.) 416; *Times,* May 5, 1998, CA (Crim Div) .... *Digested,* 98/**1160**
R. v. Zaman (Afraz) see Attorney General's Reference (No.46 of 1997), Re
R. v. Zelzele (Behcet); R. v. Slowey (Peter); R. v. Halil (Gursel) [2001] EWCA Crim
    1763; [2001] Crim. L.R. 830, CA (Crim Div)
R. v. Zinga (Lucifucatino) [1998] 1 Cr. App. R. (S.) 61; [1997] Crim. L.R. 904, CA
    (Crim Div).. *Digested,* 98/**1276**
R. v. Zografos (Thanassis) see R. v. Mereu (Jean-Marc)
R. v. Zundel [1992] 2 S.C.R. 731 .... *Applied,* 99/3106
R. (on the application of Reprotech (Pebsham) Ltd) v. East Sussex CC; *sub nom*
    Reprotech (Pebsham) Ltd v. East Sussex CC; East Sussex CC v. Reprotech
    (Pebsham) Ltd; R. v. East Sussex CC Ex p. Reprotech (Pebsham) Ltd; TNS, HL;
    reversing [2001] Env. L.R. 14; [2000] 1 P.L.R. 12; [2001] J.P.L. 815; [2000]
    E.G.C.S. 79; [2000] N.P.C. 67, CA; affirming [2000] Env. L.R. 381; [2000]
    J.P.L. 511; [1999] N.P.C. 109; *Times,* September 14, 1999, QBD .... *Digested,* 00/**4421**
R. (on the application of Persimmon Homes (Thames Valley) Ltd) v. North Hertfordshire
    DC; *sub nom* Persimmon Homes (Thames Valley) Ltd v. North Hertfordshire DC
    [2001] EWHC Admin 565; [2001] 1 W.L.R. 2393; [2001] 31 E.G.C.S. 102;
    (2001) 98(34) L.S.G. 41; [2001] N.P.C. 122; *Times,* September 18, 2001, QBD
    (Admin Ct) .... *Digested,* 01/**4718**
R. (on the application of George Harrison (Whitby) Ltd) v. Secretary of State for the
    Environment, Transport and the Regions; *sub nom* R. v. Secretary of State for the
    Environment, Transport and the Regions Ex p. George Harrison (Whitby) Ltd
    Daily Telegraph, November 14, 2000, QBD (Admin Ct)
R. v. Wolverhampton Deputy Recorder Ex p. DPP. see R. v. H Sherman Ltd

R.v Cadman-Smith (David) see R. *v.* Smith (David Cadman)
R.v IndependentTelevision Commission Ex p.TVDanmark 1 Ltd see R. (on the application of
TVDanmark 1 Ltd) *v.* Independent Television Commission
R.v Secretary of State for the Environment, Transport and the Regions Ex p. Framlingham
Tractors Ltd see Framlingham Tractors Ltd *v.* Secretary of State for the
Environment, Transport and the Regions
RA Securities Ltd *v.* Mercantile Credit Co Ltd [1995] 3 All E.R. 581; [1994] B.C.C.
598; [1994] 2 B.C.L.C. 721; [1994] 44 E.G. 242; [1994] N.P.C. 76, Ch D . . . . . 　*Digested*, 96/**3515**:
　　　　　　　　　　　　　　Applied, 97/3080: *Considered*, 96/3518, 98/3351
Rabaiotti 1989 Settlement, Re; *sub nom* Latour Trust Co Ltd and Latour Trustees
(Jersey) Ltds' Representation, Re [2000] W.T.L.R. 953; (1999-2000) 2
I.T.E.L.R. 763; [2001] Fam. Law 808, Royal Ct (Jer) . . . . 　*Digested*, 01/**5512**
RAC Motoring Services Ltd, Re; *sub nom* Royal Automobile Club Ltd, Re [2000] 1
B.C.L.C. 307, Ch D (Companies Ct) . . . . 　*Digested*, 00/**676**
Racal Communications Ltd, Re; *sub nom* Company (No.00996 of 1979), Re [1981]
A.C. 374; [1980] 3 W.L.R. 181; [1980] 2 All E.R. 634, HL; reversing [1980] Ch.
138; [1980] 2 W.L.R. 241; [1979] 1 All E.R. 284, CA . . . . 　*Digested*, 80/**273**:
　　　　　　Applied, 85/316, 86/91, 86/324, 92/3464: *Considered*, 87/640, 88/620:
　　　　　　　　　　　Distinguished, 92/2740: *Followed*, 01/11
Racal Communications Ltd *v.* National Enterprises Ltd see National Enterprises Ltd *v.*
Racal Communications Ltd
Racal Group Services Ltd *v.* Ashmore [1995] S.T.C. 1151; 68 T.C. 86, CA; affirming
[1994] S.T.C. 416, Ch D . . . . 　*Digested*, 96/**5784**:
　　　　　　　　　　　　　　　　　Distinguished, 98/3659
Racal Telecommunications Ltd *v.* National Union of Rail Maritime and Transport Workers
(Unreported, July 2, 1998), QBD . . . . 　*Considered*, 99/2074
Racepeak Ltd *v.* Secretary of State for the Environment, Transport and the Regions
[2001] EWHC Admin 531; (2001) 98(27) L.S.G. 41, QBD (Admin Ct)
Racial Equality Council (Cleveland) *v.* Widlinski [1998] I.C.R. 1124, EAT . . . . 　*Digested*, 99/**2090**
Racke GmbH & Co *v.* Hauptzollamt Mainz (C162/96) [1998] E.C.R. I-3655; [1998] 3
C.M.L.R. 219, ECJ . . . . 　*Followed*, 99/2226
Radcliffe *v.* McKeown (Unreported, June 7, 2000), CC (Liverpool) [*Ex rel.* Michael
Jones, Barrister, Cobden House Chambers, 19 Quay Street, Manchester] . . . . . 　*Digested*, 00/**2585**
Radford *v.* Kent CC (1998) 162 J.P. 697; (1998) 162 J.P.N. 606; *Times*, March 11,
1998, QBD . . . . 　*Digested*, 98/**1058**
Radhakrishna Hospitality Service Private Ltd *v.* EIH Ltd; Eurest SA *v.* EIH Ltd [1999] 2
Lloyd's Rep. 249, QBD . . . . 　*Digested*, 99/**711**
Radich *v.* Bank of New Zealand [2000] B.P.I.R. 783, Fed Ct (Aus) (Full Ct) . . . . 　*Digested*, 01/**3715**
Radio ABC *v.* Austria (1998) 25 E.H.R.R. 185; [1998] H.R.C.D. 9, ECHR . . . . 　*Digested*, 98/**3095**
Radio Telefis Eireann *v.* Commission of the European Communities (C241/91); *sub nom*
Magill Case (C241/91), Re; Radio Telefis Eireann *v.* Commission of the
European Communities (T69/89); Independent Television Publications Ltd *v.*
Commission of the European Communities (C242/91) [1995] All E.R. (E.C.)
416; [1995] E.C.R. I-743; [1995] 4 C.M.L.R. 718; [1995] E.M.L.R. 337; [1995]
F.S.R. 530; [1998] Masons C.L.R. Rep. 58; *Times*, April 17, 1995; *Financial Times*,
April 11, 1995, ECJ; affirming [1991] E.C.R. II-485; [1991] 4 C.M.L.R. 586;
Times, October 21, 1991, CFI (2nd Chamber) . . . . 　*Digested*, 95/**639**:
　　　　　Applied, 98/724: *Considered*, 94/3525, 01/3847: *Distinguished*, 98/3426:
　　　　　　Previous proceedings, 90/2070, 90/2123: *Referred to*, 00/702
Radio Telefis Eireann *v.* Commission of the European Communities (T69/89) see Radio
Telefis Eireann *v.* Commission of the European Communities (C241/91)
Radivojevic *v.* Secretary of State for the Home Department see Adan (Hassan
Hussein) *v.* Secretary of State for the Home Department
Radley *v.* Claremount Garments Ltd (Unreported, November 4, 1998), CC (Leeds) [*Ex
rel.* Morrish & Co Solicitors, First Floor, Oxford House, Oxford Row, Leeds] . . . . 　*Digested*, 99/**1525**
Radley-Kane (Deceased), Re see Kane *v.* Radley-Kane
Radmanovich *v.* Nedellkovic (2000-01) 3 I.T.E.L.R. 802, Sup Ct (NSW) . . . . 　*Digested*, 01/**5501**
Radomir Nicola Pachitch (Pasic)'s Application, Re see Trepca Mines Ltd (No.2), Re
Radosavljevic *v.* Rufus (Unreported, June 23, 1999), CC (Central London) [*Ex rel.* Tim
Kevan, Barrister, 1 Temple Gardens, Temple, London] . . . . 　*Digested*, 99/**2499**
Radstock Cooperative & Industrial Society *v.* Norton-Radstock Urban DC; *sub nom*
Radstock Cooperative & Industrial Society *v.* Radstock Urban DC [1968] Ch.
605; [1968] 2 W.L.R. 1214; [1968] 2 All E.R. 59; 132 J.P. 238; 66 L.G.R. 457;
112 S.J. 135, CA; affirming [1967] Ch. 1094; [1967] 3 W.L.R. 588; [1967] 2 All
E.R. 812; 131 J.P. 387; 65 L.G.R. 518, Ch D . . . . 　*Digested*, 68/**2880**:
　　　　　　　　　　　　　Doubted, 01/4547: *Followed*, 00/4287
Radstock Cooperative & Industrial Society *v.* Radstock Urban DC see Radstock
Cooperative & Industrial Society *v.* Norton-Radstock Urban DC
Rae (A Bankrupt), Re [1995] B.C.C. 102; *Times*, October 27, 1994, Ch D . . . . 　*Digested*, 95/**421**:
　　　　　　　　　　　　　Applied, 00/3442: *Followed*, 97/3013
Rae *v.* Glasgow City Council 1998 S.L.T. 292; 1997 Rep. L.R. 79; 1997 G.W.D. 18-842;
Times, April 22, 1997, OH . . . . 　*Digested*, 97/**6077**:
　　　　　　　　　　　　　　　　Referred to, 00/6426

Raeuchle v. Laimond Properties Ltd (Suspension of Possession Order) (2001) 33
     H.L.R. 10; [2000] L. & T.R. 345; (2000) 79 P. & C.R. D40, CA . . . .   *Digested*, 00/**3920**
Raffeisen Zentralbank Osterreich AG v. Five Star General Trading LLC (The Mount I) see
     Raiffeisen Zentralbank Osterreich AG v. Five Star General Trading LLC (The
     Mount I)
Rafiq v. Muse [2000] 1 F.L.R. 820; [2000] Fam. Law 396, CA . . . .   *Digested*, 00/**2543**
Rafiq (Robina) v. Secretary of State for the Home Department [1998] 1 F.C.R. 293;
     [1998] Imm. A.R. 193; [1998] I.N.L.R. 349; *Times*, January 14, 1998;
     Independent, January 16, 1998, CA . . . .   *Digested*, 98/**3217**
Raflatac Ltd v. Eade [1999] 1 Lloyd's Rep. 506; [1999] B.L.R. 261, QBD (Comm Ct)   *Digested*, 99/**787**
Rafsanjan Pistachio Producers Cooperative v. Kaufmanns Ltd, *Independent*, January 12,
     1998 (C.S.), QBD (Comm Ct) . . . .   *Digested*, 98/**851**
Rahall v. McLennan [2000] B.P.I.R. 140, QB (Alta) . . . .   *Digested*, 00/**3454**
Rahman (Saidur), Re see R. v. Secretary of State for the Home Department Ex p.
     Rahman (Saidur)
Rahman v. Arearose Ltd [2001] Q.B. 351; [2000] 3 W.L.R. 1184; (2001) 62 B.M.L.R.
     84, CA
Rahman v. Brassil (Unreported, June 12, 1998), CC (Dartford) [*Ex rel.* Julia Smyth,
     Barrister, 1 Temple Gardens, Temple, London] . . . .   *Digested*, 98/**2503**
Rahman (t/a Khayam Restaurant) v. Customs and Excise Commissioners (No.1) [1998]
     S.T.C. 826; [1998] B.T.C. 5294; [1998] B.V.C. 323; [1998] C.O.D. 487;
     Independent, June 22, 1998 (C.S.), QBD . . . .   *Digested*, 98/**4885**:
                                                       Applied, 00/**5280**: *Cited*, 00/**5370**
Rahman (t/a Khayam Restaurant) v. Customs and Excise Commissioners (No.2) [2001]
     S.T.I. 1380, Ch D; affirming [2001] B.V.C. 2266, V&DTr
Rahman v. Sterling Credit Ltd; *sub nom* Sterling Credit Ltd v. Rahman [2001] 1 W.L.R.
     496; (2001) 33 H.L.R. 63; (2000) 97(32) L.S.G. 37; (2000) 144 S.J.L.B. 243;
     [2000] N.P.C. 84; (2001) 81 P. & C.R. D4; *Times*, October 17, 2000, CA . . . . . .   *Digested*, 00/**836**
Rai v. General Medical Council (Unreported, May 14, 1984), PC (UK) . . . .   *Considered*, 00/**2718**
Raiffeisen Zentral Bank Osterreich AG v. An Feng Steel Co Ltd see Raiffeisen
     Zentralbank Osterreich AG v. Five Star General Trading LLC (The Mount I)
Raiffeisen Zentral Bank Osterreich AG v. Tranos [2001] I.L.Pr. 9, QBD (Comm Ct) . . . . .   *Digested*, 01/**807**
Raiffeisen Zentralbank Osterreich AG v. Crossseas Shipping Ltd [2000] 1 W.L.R. 1135;
     [2000] 3 All E.R. 274; [2000] 1 All E.R. (Comm) 76; [2000] Lloyd's Rep. Bank.
     108; [2000] C.L.C. 553; *Times*, February 1, 2000, CA; affirming [1999] 1 All
     E.R. (Comm.) 626; [1999] Lloyd's Rep. Bank. 164; [1999] C.L.C. 973, QBD
     (Comm Ct) . . . .   *Digested*, 00/**278**
Raiffeisen Zentralbank Osterreich AG v. Five Star General Trading LLC (The Mount I);
     sub nom Raiffeisen Zentral Bank Osterreich AG v. An Feng Steel Co Ltd;
     Raiffeisen Zentralbank Osterreich AG v. Five Star General Trading LLC (The
     Mount I) [2001] EWCA Civ 68; [2001] Q.B. 825; [2001] 2 W.L.R. 1344; [2001]
     3 All E.R. 257; [2001] 1 All E.R. (Comm) 961; [2001] 1 Lloyd's Rep. 597;
     [2001] C.L.C. 843; [2001] Lloyd's Rep. I.R. 460; (2001) 98(9) L.S.G. 38;
     (2001) 145 S.J.L.B. 45; *Times*, February 21, 2001, CA; reversing in part [2000] 1
     All E.R. (Comm) 897; [2000] 2 Lloyd's Rep. 684; [2000] C.L.C. 1359; (2000)
     97(25) L.S.G. 38; *Times*, June 21, 2000, QBD (Comm Ct) . . . .   *Digested*, 01/**811**
Raiffeisen Zentralbank Osterreich Aktiengesellschaft v. National Bank of Greece SA
     [1999] 1 Lloyd's Rep. 408; *Times*, September 25, 1998, QBD (Comm Ct) . . . . . .   *Digested*, 98/**767**
Raikes v. Raikes see Tunno, Re
Railtrack Plc v. Gojra; *sub nom* Gojra v. Railtrack Plc [1998] 1 E.G.L.R. 63; [1998] 08
     E.G. 158; [1997] E.G.C.S. 168; [1997] N.P.C. 166, CA . . . .   *Digested*, 98/**3600**
Railtrack Plc v. Ohajah [2000] E.G.C.S. 88, CA
Railtrack Plc v. Secretary of State for Transport; *sub nom* Secretary of State for
     Transport v. Railtrack Plc (1998) 76 P. & C.R. 448; [1998] 2 P.L.R. 40; [1998]
     J.P.L. 1063, QBD . . . .   *Digested*, 98/**4227**
Railtrack Plc v. Smallwood [2001] EWHC Admin 78; [2001] I.C.R. 714; (2001) 145
     S.J.L.B. 52; *Times*, February 16, 2001; *Independent*, February 26, 2001 (C.S),
     QBD (Admin Ct) . . . .   *Digested*, 01/**3317**
Railtrack Plc v. Wandsworth LBC see Wandsworth LBC v. Railtrack Plc
Rainbow Estates Ltd v. Tokenhold Ltd; *sub nom* Gaynes Park Mansion, Epping, Essex,
     Re [1999] Ch. 64; [1998] 3 W.L.R. 980; [1998] 2 All E.R. 860; [1998] L. & T.R.
     116; [1998] 2 E.G.L.R. 34; [1998] 24 E.G. 123; (1998) 95(15) L.S.G. 30;
     (1998) 142 S.J.L.B. 116; [1998] N.P.C. 33; *Times*, March 12, 1998; *Independent*,
     March 30, 1998 (C.S.); *Independent*, March 23, 1998 (C.S.), Ch D . . . .   *Digested*, 98/**3626**
Rainey (t/a First Class Taxis) v. H Rogers & Son Ltd BT/36/1999, Lands Tr (NI) . . . .   *Digested*, 00/**5611**
Rainford House Ltd (In Administrative Receivership) v. Cadogan Ltd [2001] B.L.R. 416;
     [2001] N.P.C. 39, QBD (T&CC)
Rainford-Towning (E3/98) [1999] 1 C.M.L.R. 871, EFTA . . . .   *Digested*, 99/**3621**:
                                                       Followed, 01/**2500**
Raiss v. Paimano see Paimano v. Raiss
Raja v. Lloyds TSB Bank Plc [2001] EWCA Civ 210; [2001] Lloyd's Rep. Bank. 113;
     (2001) 82 P. & C.R. 16; (2001) 98(6) L.S.G. 47; (2001) 82 P. & C.R. D3;
     Independent, March 12, 2001 (C.S), CA; affirming [2000] Lloyd's Rep. Bank.
     377; [2001] 19 E.G. 143; (2000) 97(21) L.S.G. 40; *Times*, May 16, 2000, Ch D .   *Digested*, 01/**4873**

Raja v. Rubin [2000] Ch. 274; [1999] 3 W.L.R. 606; [1999] 3 All E.R. 73; [1999] B.C.C. 579; [1999] 1 B.C.L.C 621; [1999] B.P.I.R. 575; *Times*, April 14, 1999; *Independent*, May 24, 1999 (C.S.), CA; affirming in part [1998] B.P.I.R. 647, Ch D . . . . *Digested*, 99/**3345**
Rajah v. Arogol Co Ltd; *sub nom* Arogol Co Ltd v. Rajah [2001] EWCA Civ 454; (2001) 98(21) L.S.G. 40; (2001) 82 P. & C.R. D7; *Times*, April 13, 2001, CA . . . *Digested*, 01/**4199**
Rajan v. General Medical Council [2000] Lloyd's Rep. Med. 153, PC (UK) . . . . *Digested*, 00/**2756**
Rajan Imports Ltd's Trade Mark Application (No.2013102) (1998) 21 (4) I.P.D. 21041
Rakusen v. Ellis Munday & Clarke [1912] 1 Ch. 831, CA . . . . *Applied*, 91/3372,
92/4082: *Disapproved*, 99/1: *Followed*, 95/4658, 96/3919
Rakusens Ltd v. Baser Ambalaj Plastik Sanayi Ticaret AS; *sub nom* Rakussens Ltd v. Baser Ambalaj Plastik Sanayi Ticaret AS [2001] EWCA Civ 1820; (2001) 98(42) L.S.G. 37; (2001) 145 S.J.L.B. 237; *Times*, November 9, 2001, CA . . . . *Digested*, 01/**646**
Rakussens Ltd v. Baser Ambalaj Plastik Sanayi Ticaret AS see Rakusens Ltd v. Baser Ambalaj Plastik Sanayi Ticaret AS
RALEIGH INTERNATIONAL Trade Mark [2001] R.P.C. 11, Appointed Person . . . . *Digested*, 01/**4029**
Rall v. Hume [2001] EWCA Civ 146; [2001] 3 All E.R. 248; [2001] C.P. Rep. 58; [2001] C.P.L.R. 239; (2001) 98(10) L.S.G. 44; (2001) 145 S.J.L.B. 54; *Times*, March 14, 2001; *Independent*, March 19, 2001 (C.S), CA . . . . *Digested*, 01/**443**
Rall v. Wallage (Unreported, May 8, 2000), CC (Pontefract) [*Ex rel*. Mark Henley, Barrister, 9 Woodhouse Square, Leeds] . . . . *Digested*, 00/**1679**
Ralls v. Secretary of State for the Environment, Transport and the Regions [1998] J.P.L. 444, CA. . . . . *Digested*, 98/**4186**
Ralton v. Havering College of Further and Higher Education [2001] 3 C.M.L.R. 57; [2001] I.R.L.R. 738, EAT . . . . *Digested*, 01/**2332**
Ramanathan v. Secretary of State for Foreign and Commonwealth Affairs; *sub nom* R. v. Secretary of State for Foreign and Commonwealth Affairs Ex p. Ramanathan [1999] Imm. A.R. 97, CA; affirming [1998] Imm. A.R. 437, QBD . . . . *Digested*, 99/**3201**
Ramanathan Rudra v. Abbey National Plc see Rudra v. Abbey National Plc
Ramjattan v. Trinidad and Tobago (1999) 143 S.J.L.B. 95; *Times*, April 1, 1999, PC (Trin) . *Digested*, 99/**77**
Ramnarace v. Lutchman [2001] UKPC 25; [2001] 1 W.L.R. 1651, PC (Trin) . . . . *Digested*, 01/**4892**
Ramos v. Immigration Appeal Tribunal [1989] Imm. A.R. 148, CA . . . . *Digested*, 91/**2014**:
Applied, 00/3356
Rampal v. Rampal [2001] EWCA Civ 989; [2001] 3 W.L.R. 795; [2001] 2 F.L.R. 1179; [2001] 2 F.C.R. 552; [2001] Fam. Law 731; (2001) 98(29) L.S.G. 37; (2001) 151 N.L.J. 1006; (2001) 145 S.J.L.B. 165; *Times*, July 24, 2001; *Independent*, June 29, 2001, CA [2000] 2 F.L.R. 763; [2001] 2 F.C.R. 543; [2000] Fam. Law 702, Fam Div . . . . *Digested*, 01/**2545**
Ramsay v. Rivers see Heil v. Rankin
Ramsay v. Rivers (Costs) see Heil v. Rankin (Costs)
Ramsay v. Secretary of State for the Environment, Transport and the Regions see Ramsey v. Secretary of State for the Environment, Transport and the Regions
Ramsden v. Dyson; Ramsden v. Thornton (1866) L.R. 1 H.L. 129, HL. . . . . *Applied*, 65/1487,
66/6674, 67/2196, 75/1191, 78/2901, 79/2651, 81/2732, 82/1149, 98/4367:
Considered, 47-51/3687, 74/3144, 79/1083, 80/1073, 85/1909, 87/1426,
98/123: *Distinguished*, 58/1238: *Followed*, 59/3381, 66/4174, 66/4176
Ramsden v. Thornton see Ramsden v. Dyson
Ramsey v. Hartley [1977] 1 W.L.R. 686; [1977] 2 All E.R. 673; 121 S.J. 319, CA. . . . . . . *Digested*, 77/**185**:
Applied, 80/155, 87/206: *Considered*, 99/3223
Ramsey v. Leonard Curtis (A Firm) [2001] B.P.I.R. 389, CA . . . . *Digested*, 01/**420**
Ramsey v. Secretary of State for the Environment [1991] 2 P.L.R. 112; [1991] J.P.L. 1148 . . . . *Digested*, 91/**3473**:
Followed, 99/4202
Ramsey v. Secretary of State for the Environment, Transport and the Regions; *sub nom* Ramsay v. Secretary of State for the Environment, Transport and the Regions; C/2001/0955, CA; reversing [2001] EWHC Admin 277; [2001] N.P.C. 78; *Times*, May 15, 2001, QBD (Admin Ct) . . . . *Digested*, 01/**4723**
Ramskill v. Pepper (Unreported, September 25, 1998), CC (Pontefract) [*Ex rel*. Irwin Mitchell Solicitors, Huttons Buildings, 146 West Street, Sheffield] . . . . *Digested*, 99/**2455**
Ramstead v. Queen, The [1999] 2 A.C. 92; [1999] 2 W.L.R. 698; *Times*, December 3, 1998, PC (NZ) . . . . *Digested*, 99/**1017**:
Applied, 01/1144
Rance v. Elvin (1985) 50 P. & C.R. 9, CA; reversing (1985) 49 P. & C.R. 65; (1983) 127 S.J. 732; *Times*, October 13, 1983, Ch D . . . . *Digested*, 85/**1086**:
Applied, 98/4346
Rance v. Mid-Downs HA [1991] 1 Q.B. 587; [1991] 2 W.L.R. 159; [1991] 1 All E.R. 801; [1990] 2 Med. L.R. 27; [1991] Fam. Law 24; (1990) 140 N.L.J. 325, QBD . *Digested*, 91/**2436**:
Considered, 99/5185
Rand v. East Dorset HA [2000] Lloyd's Rep. Med. 181; (2000) 56 B.M.L.R. 39, QBD . . *Digested*, 00/**4200**:
Applied, 01/4462: *Not followed*, 01/4464
Rand v. East Dorset HA (Deduction of Benefits) [2001] P.I.Q.R. Q1; [2000] Lloyd's Rep. Med. 377; *Times*, May 10, 2000, QBD . . . . *Digested*, 00/**1461**

Randall v. Plumb [1975] 1 W.L.R. 633; [1975] 1 All E.R. 734; [1975] S.T.C. 191; 50 T.C.
392; [1974] T.R. 371; (1974) 119 S.J. 188, Ch D . . . .   *Digested,* 75/**1642**:
Applied, 97/1070: *Distinguished,* 00/4922: *Explained,* 99/4665
Randall v. Raper (1858) El. Bl. & El. 84, QBD . . . .   *Applied,* 99/831
Randhawa (t/a Mill Hill Food Store) v. Customs and Excise Commissioners [2000] S.T.I.
1453, V&DTr
Random House Inc v. Rosetta Books LLC [2001] E.B.L.R. 133, US Ct
Ranger (CICB: Quantum: 1998), Re (Unreported, May 19, 1998), CICB (London) [*Ex rel.*
Michael J Mylonas-Widdall, Barrister and McMillan Williams Solicitors, 56-58
Central Parade, New Addington, Surrey] . . . .   *Digested,* 98/**1539**
Rangiora, The [2000] 1 Lloyd's Rep. 36, HC (NZ)   *Digested,* 00/**4697**
Rangoonwala v. Uddin (Unreported, March 4, 1998), CC (Romford) [*Ex rel.* Andrew
Ritchie, Barrister, 9 Gough Square, London] . . . .   *Digested,* 98/**506**
Raninen v. Finland (1998) 26 E.H.R.R. 563; [1998] H.R.C.D. 170, ECHR . . . .   *Digested,* 99/**3093**
Rank Enterprises Ltd v. Gerard [2000] 1 All E.R. (Comm) 449; [2000] 1 Lloyd's Rep.
403; [2000] C.L.C. 637; (2000) 97(6) L.S.G. 33; (2000) 144 S.J.L.B. 100;
Times, February 28, 2000, CA; reversing in part [1999] 2 All E.R. 749; [1999] 2
Lloyd's Rep. 666; [1999] C.L.C. 1726, QBD (Comm Ct) . . . .   *Digested,* 00/**4741**
Rank Leisure v. Castle Vale Housing Action Trust [2001] R.V.R. 313, Lands Tr
Ransomes Plc, Re; *sub nom* Ransomes Plc v. Winpar Holdings Ltd; Winpar Holdings
Ltd v. Ransomes Plc [2000] B.C.C. 455; [1999] 2 B.C.L.C. 591, CA; affirming
[1999] 1 B.C.L.C 775, Ch D (Companies Ct) . . . .   *Digested,* 00/**680**
Ransomes Plc v. Winpar Holdings Ltd see Ransomes Plc, Re
Rantzen v. Mirror Group Newspapers (1986) Ltd [1994] Q.B. 670; [1993] 3 W.L.R.
953; [1993] 4 All E.R. 975; (1993) 143 N.L.J. 507; *Times,* April 6, 1993;
Independent, April 1, 1993, CA . . . .   *Digested,* 93/**2579**:
Applied, 97/1768: *Approved,* 95/2647: *Considered,* 96/5673, 96/5674:
Followed, 99/1392
Rao v. Civil Aviation Authority [1994] I.R.L.R. 240, CA; affirming [1992] I.C.R. 503;
[1992] I.R.L.R. 203, EAT . . . .   *Digested,* 92/**1985**:
Applied, 95/2079: *Considered,* 96/2655, 00/2238
RAP Group Plc v. Customs and Excise Commissioners [2000] S.T.C. 980; [2000]
B.T.C. 5446; [2001] B.V.C. 65; [2000] S.T.I. 1611; (2000) 97(45) L.S.G. 42;
Times, November 16, 2000, Ch D; reversing in part [2000] B.V.C. 2352; [2000]
S.T.I. 1166, V&DTr . . . .   *Digested,* 00/**5306**
Rape Crisis Centre v. Secretary of State for the Home Department; *sub nom* Rape
Crisis Centre and Sandy Brindley, Petitioners 2000 S.C. 527; 2001 S.L.T. 389;
2000 S.C.L.R. 807; 2000 G.W.D. 25-946; *Times,* July 18, 2000, OH . . . .   *Digested,* 00/**6502**
Rape Crisis Centre and Sandy Brindley, Petitioners see Rape Crisis Centre v. Secretary of
State for the Home Department
Rapide Enterprises v. Midgley 1998 S.L.T. 504; (1997) Hous. L.R. 125; 1997 G.W.D.
25-1268; *Times,* July 30, 1997, OH . . . .   *Digested,* 97/**6093**
Rapier (Deceased), Re [1988] Q.B. 26; [1986] 3 W.L.R. 830; [1986] 3 All E.R. 726; (1986)
150 J.P.N. 605, DC . . . .   *Digested,* 86/**445**:
Considered, 89/522, 94/633, 94/635: *Distinguished,* 98/44
Rashid v. Ayub (2001) 81 P. & C.R. D17, CA
Rask v. ISS Kantineservice A/S (C209/91) [1992] E.C.R. I-5755; [1993] I.R.L.R. 133,
ECJ . . . .   *Digested,* 93/**4281**:
Applied, 94/4832, 95/2071, 00/2229, 01/2332: *Considered,* 95/2068
Rasmussen v. Denmark (A/87) (1985) 7 E.H.R.R. 371, ECHR. . . . .   *Applied,* 98/3155
Rasool v. West Midlands Passenger Transport Executive [1974] 3 All E.R. 638, QBD . . .   *Digested,* 74/**2948**:
Approved, 77/1380, 78/1428: *Followed,* 98/819
Raspin v. United News Shops Ltd [1999] I.R.L.R. 9, EAT . . . .   *Digested,* 00/**2131**
Ratcliff v. McConnell [1999] 1 W.L.R. 670; (1999) 1 L.G.L.R. 276; [1999] Ed. C.R.
523; [1999] P.I.Q.R. P170; (1999) 96(3) L.S.G. 32; (1999) 143 S.J.L.B. 53;
Times, December 3, 1998; *Independent,* December 4, 1998, CA. . . . .   *Digested,* 99/**4007**:
Applied, 99/4006: *Distinguished,* 99/3962
Ratcliffe (Deceased), Re see Holmes v. McMullan
Ratcliffe v. Plymouth and Torbay HA [1998] P.I.Q.R. P170; [1998] Lloyd's Rep. Med.
162; (1998) 42 B.M.L.R. 64, CA . . . .   *Digested,* 98/**3972**
Ratcliffe v. Sandwell MBC; Lee v. Leeds City Council; B2/2000/3589, B2/2001/
2209, CA; affirming (Unreported, November 2, 2000), CC (Birmingham) [*Ex rel.*
Tracy Lakin, Barrister, Victoria Chambers, 177 Corporation Street, Birmingham] . .   *Digested,* 01/**4203**
Rating and Valuation Commissioner v. Agrila Ltd; *sub nom* Agrila Ltd v. Rating and
Valuation Commissioner [2001] R.A. 189, CFA (HK); reversing [2000] R.A. 21,
CA (HK) . . . .   *Digested,* 01/**4835**
Rattray v. Hinds (Unreported, June 9, 2000), QBD [*Ex rel.* Richard Bendall, Barrister,
33 Bedford Row, London] . . . .   *Digested,* 00/**1615**
Raval, Re [1998] 2 F.L.R. 718; [1998] B.P.I.R. 389; [1998] Fam. Law 590, Ch D . . . . .   *Digested,* 98/**3291**
Ravenhead Brick Co v. Ruabon Brick & Terra Cotta Co (1937) 54 R.P.C. 341 . . . .   *Considered,* 94/4492,
95/4936: *Followed,* 96/5716: *Referred to,* 99/3539
Ravenocean Ltd v. Gardner [2001] N.P.C. 44, Ch D
Ravenscroft v. Jones (1864) 4 De G.J. & S. 224, CA; affirming (1864) 32 Beav. 669 . .   *Considered,* 99/4646
Ravenscroft Properties Ltd v. Hall see Ravenseft Properties Ltd v. Hall

Ravenseft Properties Ltd *v.* Hall; *sub nom* Ravenscroft Properties Ltd *v.* Hall; Kasseer *v.* Freeman; White *v.* Chubb [2001] EWCA Civ 2034; [2001] N.P.C. 188, CA

Ravichandran *v.* Secretary of State for the Home Department see R. *v.* Secretary of State for the Home Department Ex p. Jeyeanthan

Ravnsborg *v.* Sweden (A/283-B) (1994) 18 E.H.R.R. 38, ECHR . . . . *Digested*, 94/**2402**: *Considered*, 98/3146

Rawlins, Re see Cork *v.* Rawlins

Rawlins *v.* Secretary of State for the Environment see Gregory *v.* Secretary of State for the Environment

Rawlinson *v.* North Essex HA [2000] Lloyd's Rep. Med. 54, QBD . . . . *Digested*, 00/**598**

Rawson *v.* Midland Freight Services (UK) Ltd (Unreported, October 5, 1999), CC (Mansfield) [*Ex rel.* Darren Finlay, Barrister, Sovereign Chambers, 25 Park Square, Leeds] . . . . *Digested*, 00/**322**

Ray *v.* Classic FM Plc [1998] E.C.C. 488; [1999] I.T.C.L.R. 256; [1998] F.S.R. 622; (1998) 21(5) I.P.D. 21047; (1998) 95(17) L.S.G. 32; (1998) 148 N.L.J. 445; *Times*, April 8, 1998, Ch D . . . . *Digested*, 98/**3431**

Ray *v.* Fairway Motors (Barnstable) (1969) 20 P. & C.R. 261; (1968) 112 S.J. 925, CA . *Digested*, 69/**1157**: *Followed*, 00/4632

Ray *v.* Sempers see DPP *v.* Ray

Rayatt (A Bankrupt), Re [1998] 2 F.L.R. 264; [1998] B.P.I.R. 495; [1998] Fam. Law 458; *Times*, May 4, 1998, Ch D . . . . *Digested*, 98/**3282**

Raychem Corp's Patents; *sub nom* Bourns Inc *v.* Raychem Corp [1999] R.P.C. 497; (1999) 22(4) I.P.D. 22032, CA . . . . *Digested*, 99/**3519**

Raychem Corp's Patents, Re see Bourns Inc *v.* Raychem Corp (No.2)

Rayment *v.* Ministry of Defence (1999) 47 B.M.L.R. 92; *Times*, July 6, 1998, QBD . . . . . *Digested*, 98/**345**

Raymond *v.* Honey [1983] 1 A.C. 1; [1982] 2 W.L.R. 465; [1982] 1 All E.R. 756; (1982) 75 Cr. App. R. 16, HL; affirming [1981] Q.B. 874; [1981] 3 W.L.R. 218; [1981] 2 All E.R. 1084; (1981) 73 Cr. App. R. 242; *Times*, April 8, 1981, QBD . . . *Digested*, 82/**2613**: *Applied*, 88/2976, 94/735, 95/1033: *Considered*, 83/3080, 84/2762, 86/2678, 01/4582: *Distinguished*, 84/2754, 91/5481, 92/3632: *Followed*, 94/3849, 99/4104: *Referred to*, 92/6216

Raymond Construction Pte Ltd *v.* Low Yang Tong (1998) 14 Const. L.J. 136, HC (Sing). *Digested*, 98/**801**

Rayner & Keeler Ltd *v.* Courts & Co see Carl Zeiss Stiftung *v.* Rayner & Keeler Ltd (Authority to Institute Proceedings: Issue Estoppel)

Razack *v.* Osman (Unreported, March 6, 2001), MCLC [*Ex rel.* Andrew Butler, Barrister, Francis Taylor Building, Temple, London] . . . . *Digested*, 01/**4149**

Razzak *v.* Customs and Excise Commissioners [1998] B.V.C. 2061; [1997] V. & D.R. 392, V&DTr . . . . *Digested*, 00/**5312**

Razzaq *v.* Pala [1997] 1 W.L.R. 1336; [1998] B.C.C. 66; [1997] B.P.I.R. 726; [1997] 2 E.G.L.R. 53; [1997] 38 E.G. 157; [1997] E.G.C.S. 75; (1997) 94(24) L.S.G. 32; (1997) 141 S.J.L.B. 120; [1997] N.P.C. 77; *Times*, June 6, 1997, QBD . . . . *Digested*, 97/**3291**: *Applied*, 01/4154: *Followed*, 99/3264

RB (Male Patient: Sterilisation), Re see A (Mental Patient: Sterilisation), Re

RBS Leasing and Services (No.1) Ltd *v.* Customs and Excise Commissioners [2000] B.V.C. 2284; [2000] S.T.I. 958, V&DTr

RCO Support Services Ltd *v.* UNISON; Aintree Hospital Trust *v.* UNISON; A1/2000/ 2596, CA; affirming [2000] I.C.R. 1502; [2000] I.R.L.R. 624, EAT . . . . *Digested*, 00/**2226**

REACT Trade Mark [2000] R.P.C. 285, Appointed Person; affirming [1999] R.P.C. 529, TMR . . . . *Digested*, 00/**3773**

Read *v.* British Railways Board (1998) 98(1) Q.R. 6, CC (York) . . . . *Digested*, 98/**1564**

Read *v.* Brown (1889) L.R. 22 Q.B.D. 128, CA. . . . . *Applied*, 00/2130: *Distinguished*, 56/5436

Read *v.* King see King *v.* Read

Read *v.* Musicians Union (Unreported, June 1, 2000), Certification Officer [*Ex rel.* Certification Office for Trade Unions and Employers Associations, Brandon House, 180 Brandon High Street, London] . . . . *Digested*, 01/**2325**

Read *v.* Smith (Unreported, May 12, 1997), QBD [*Ex rel.* Peter Mitchell, Barrister, 29 Bedford Row, London] . . . . *Digested*, 97/**534**: *Followed*, 98/443

Reading *v.* Attorney General; *sub nom* Reading *v.* King, The; Reading's Petition of Right, Re [1951] A.C. 507; [1951] 1 All E.R. 617; [1951] 1 T.L.R. 480; 95 S.J. 155, HL; affirming [1949] 2 K.B. 232; [1949] 2 All E.R. 68; 65 T.L.R. 405, CA; affirming [1948] 2 K.B. 268; [1948] 2 All E.R. 27; [1949] L.J.R. 280; 92 S.J. 426, KBD . . . . *Digested*, 47-51/**5255**: *Applied*, 00/2132: *Considered*, 57/25, 92/1125, 93/955, 94/955: *Distinguished*, 72/483

Reading *v.* King, The see Reading *v.* Attorney General

Reading BC *v.* Ahmad (1999) 163 J.P. 451; [1999] B.L.G.R. 595; (1999) 193 J.P.N. 373; *Times*, December 4, 1998, QBD. . . . . *Digested*, 99/**4950**

Reading's Petition of Right, Re see Reading *v.* Attorney General

Ready Mixed Concrete (South East) Ltd v. Minister of Pensions and National Insurance;
Minister for Social Security v. Greenham Ready Mixed Concrete Ltd; Minister
for Social Security v. Ready Mixed Concrete (South East) Ltd [1968] 2 Q.B.
497; [1968] 2 W.L.R. 775; [1968] 1 All E.R. 433; 4 K.I.R. 132; (1967) 112 S.J. 14;
Times, December 11, 1967, QBD . . . . *Digested*, 68/**2550**:
  Applied, 77/1124, 82/1010, 01/2263, 01/2264: *Approved*, 76/871, 78/1116:
  Considered, 69/2338, 82/1011, 01/6467, 01/6468: *Followed*, 71/3945,
  76/878
Real Estate Development Co, Re [1991] B.C.L.C. 210, Ch D . . . . *Digested*, 92/**2579**:
  Applied, 97/851: *Followed*, 00/3472, 00/3499
Realkredit Danmark A/S v. York Montague Ltd [1999] C.P.L.R. 272; *Times*, February 1,
1999; *Independent*, December 2, 1998, CA . . . . *Digested*, 99/**567**
Realkredit Danmark v. Brookfield House (1999) 77 P. & C.R. D31, CA
Realm Defence Industries Ltd v. Customs and Excise Commissioners [2001] S.T.I. 182,
V&DTr
Reaper Ltd v. Merseyside Waste Authority [1998] R.V.R. 143, Lands Tr. . . . . *Digested*, 98/**4176**
Reardon Smith Line Ltd v. Hansen-Tangen (The Diana Prosperity); Hansen-Tangen v.
Sanko Steamship Co Ltd [1976] 1 W.L.R. 989; [1976] 3 All E.R. 570; [1976] 2
Lloyd's Rep. 621; 120 S.J. 719, HL; affirming [1976] 2 Lloyd's Rep. 60; 120 S.J.
329, CA . . . . *Digested*, 77/**2816**:
  Applied, 78/338, 83/2127, 92/311, 01/2287, 01/4950: *Approved*, 97/2189:
  Considered, 76/1204, 80/2458, 81/16, 86/1513, 93/2519, 94/332, 94/3430,
  98/2300: *Followed*, 76/333, 77/2668, 79/813
Reaveley v. DPP see DPP v. Charles
Reaveley v. Safeway Stores Plc [1998] P.N.L.R. 526, CA . . . . *Digested*, 98/**499**
Reavey v. Century Newspapers Ltd [2001] N.I. 187, QBD (NI) . . . . *Digested*, 01/**5744**
Rechberger v. Austria (C140/97) [1999] E.C.R. I-3499; [2000] 2 C.M.L.R. 1, ECJ . . . . *Digested*, 00/**4045**:
  Applied, 01/5581

Reckitt & Colman Products Ltd v. Borden Inc (No.3); *sub nom* Jif Lemon case [1990] 1
W.L.R. 491; [1990] 1 All E.R. 873; [1990] R.P.C. 341; (1990) 134 S.J. 784;
Times, February 9, 1990; *Independent*, March 13, 1990 (C.S.); *Guardian*,
February 13, 1990, HL; affirming [1988] F.S.R. 601; (1988) 8 Tr. L.R. 97; *Times*,
April 23, 1988; *Independent*, April 25, 1988 (C.S.); *Guardian*, April 26, 1988;
Daily Telegraph, April 28, 1988, CA; affirming [1987] F.S.R. 505, Ch D . . . . *Digested*, 90/**3465**:
  Applied, 93/3802, 00/3590: *Considered*, 94/4292, 95/4739, 96/5715:
  Distinguished, 94/4287, 95/4735: *Followed*, 96/6663: *Referred to*, 99/3593
Reckitt & Colman Products Ltd v. Richardson-Vicks Inc see Richardson-Vicks Inc's
Patent
Reckley v. Minister of Public Safety and Immigration (No.2) [1996] A.C. 527; [1996] 2
W.L.R. 281; [1996] 1 All E.R. 562; (1996) 140 S.J.L.B. 57; *Times*, February 6,
1996, PC (Bah) . . . . *Digested*, 96/**1117**:
  Not followed, 00/3201
Red Bank Manufacturing Co v. Meadows [1992] I.C.R. 204; [1992] I.R.L.R. 209, EAT . *Digested*, 92/**1949**:
  Considered, 98/2238
Red Label Fashions Ltd, Re [1999] B.C.C. 308, Ch D (Companies Ct) . . . . *Digested*, 99/**611**
Red Sea Insurance Co Ltd v. Bouygues SA [1995] 1 A.C. 190; [1994] 3 W.L.R. 926;
[1994] 3 All E.R. 749; [1995] L.R.L.R. 107; 44 Con. L.R. 116; [1995] 4 Re. L.R.
231; (1994) 91(41) L.S.G. 42; (1994) 138 S.J.L.B. 174; *Times*, July 21, 1994;
Independent, September 26, 1994 (C.S.); *Lloyd's List*, September 30, 1994, PC
(HK) . . . . *Digested*, 95/**4724**:
  Followed, 98/749
Red Sea Tankers Ltd v. Papachristidis (The Hellespont Ardent) [1997] 2 Lloyd's Rep.
547, QBD (Comm Ct) . . . . *Digested*, 98/**3949**
Redbridge LBC v. Fishman [1978] I.C.R. 569; [1978] I.R.L.R. 69; 76 L.G.R. 408, EAT . . *Digested*, 78/**1125**:
  Applied, 86/1152, 98/2239
Redbridge LBC v. Municipal Mutual Insurance Ltd [2001] Lloyd's Rep. I.R. 545;
[2001] O.P.L.R. 101, QBD (Comm Ct) . . . . *Digested*, 01/**3813**
Reddaway v. Banham [1896] A.C. 199; (1896) 13 R.P.C. 218, HL; reversing [1895] 1
Q.B. 286, CA . . . . *Applied*, 92/**4143**:
  Cited, 00/3589: *Considered*, 00/3591: *Followed*, 01/3877:
  Referred to, 93/2425
Reddy v. Lachlan [2000] Lloyd's Rep. P.N. 858, CA . . . . *Digested*, 01/**4272**
Rederi Aktienbolaget Transatlantic v. Fred Drughorn Ltd see Fred Drughorn Ltd v.
Rederiaktiebolaget Transatlantic
Redgrave v. Hurd (1881-82) L.R. 20 Ch. D. 1, CA . . . . *Applied*, 93/**3789**,
  00/5108
Rediffusion Simulation Ltd v. Link Miles Ltd [1993] F.S.R. 369, Pat Ct . . . . *Digested*, 94/**3433**:
  Applied, 97/550: *Considered*, 00/3673
Redland Aggregates Ltd v. Shepherd Hill Civil Engineering Ltd (Stay of Proceedings)
[2000] C.P. Rep. 7, CA . . . . *Digested*, 00/**591**
Redmond-Bate v. DPP (1999) 163 J.P. 789; [2000] H.R.L.R. 249; 7 B.H.R.C. 375;
[1999] Crim. L.R. 998; (1999) 163 J.P.N. 953; *Times*, July 28, 1999, QBD . . . . . *Digested*, 99/**949**:
  Approved, 00/950

Redrow Homes Ltd *v.* Bett Brothers Plc [1999] 1 A.C. 197; [1998] 2 W.L.R. 198;
[1998] 1 All E.R. 385; 1998 S.C. (H.L.) 64; 1998 S.L.T. 648; 1998 S.C.L.R. 325;
[1998] F.S.R. 345; [1998] R.P.C. 793; (1998) 21(4) I.P.D. 21034; (1998)
95(6) L.S.G. 25; (1998) 148 N.L.J. 121; (1998) 142 S.J.L.B. 79; 1998 G.W.D. 4-
160; *Times*, January 26, 1998, HL; affirming 1997 S.C. 142; 1997 S.L.T. 1125;
1997 S.C.L.R. 469; [1997] F.S.R. 828; 1997 G.W.D. 13-543; *Times*, May 2, 1997,
2 Div; reversing 1996 S.L.T. 1254, OH . . . . *Digested*, 98/**6020**:
Referred to, 98/3424

Redundant Women Employees (C173/91), Re see Commission of the European
Communities *v.* Belgium (C173/91)
Reebok International Ltd *v.* Cora SA [1999] E.T.M.R. 649, App (Brussels)
Reed *v.* Graham [1998] E.G.C.S. 166, CA
Reed *v.* Hastings Corp 62 L.G.R. 588; 190 E.G. 961; (1964) 108 S.J. 480, CA . . . . *Digested*, 64/**1710**:
Applied, 83/1815, 84/1645: *Considered*, 65/1821, 66/5722, 87/2358,
88/2193: *Followed*, 98/3038
Reed *v.* Stedman; Bull Information Systems Ltd *v.* Stedman [1999] I.R.L.R. 299, EAT . . *Digested*, 99/**2119**
Reed *v.* Sunderland HA, *Times*, October 16, 1998, CA; reversing (1998) 98(1) Q.R. 8;
(1997) 97(5/6) Q.R. 11, CC (Newcastle) . . . . *Digested*, 98/**1629**
Reed *v.* Swanlux Cleaning Services Ltd (Unreported, June 7, 1999), CC (Central
London) [*Ex rel.* Lee Evans, Barrister, Farrar's Building, Temple, London] . . . . *Digested*, 99/**566**:
Considered, 00/407

Reed Consumer Books Ltd *v.* Pomaco Ltd see MINERVA Trade Mark
REEF Trade Mark; *sub nom* South Cone Inc *v.* Bessant (t/a REEF); Bessant *v.* South
Cone Inc; A3/2001/1851, CA; reversing (2001) 24(11) I.P.D. 24072; (2001)
98(38) L.S.G. 39; [2001] E.T.M.R. CN19; *Times*, October 9, 2001, Ch D . . . . . . *Digested*, 01/**4057**
Rees *v.* Berrington (1795) 2 Ves. Jr. 540 . . . . *Applied*, 01/4877
Rees *v.* Boston BC; *sub nom* Beck Foods Ltd, Re; Boston BC *v.* Rees; Beck Foods
Ltd *v.* Boston Tax [2001] EWCA Civ 1934, CA; affirming [2001] 2 B.C.L.C. 663,
Ch D (Companies Ct)
Rees *v.* Crane [1994] 2 A.C. 173; [1994] 2 W.L.R. 476; [1994] 1 All E.R. 833; (1994)
138 S.J.L.B. 71, PC (Trin) . . . . *Digested*, 94/**493**:
Applied, 99/2297

Rees *v.* Mabco (102) Ltd (Non-Pecuniary Damages) see Heil *v.* Rankin
Rees *v.* Mabco (102) Ltd (Costs) see Heil *v.* Rankin (Costs)
Rees *v.* Mabco (102) Ltd (Quantum) (Unreported, May 17, 1999), CC (Bristol) [*Ex rel.*
Allan Gore, Barrister, Kings Bench Walk, Temple, London] . . . . *Digested*, 99/**1534**:
Considered, 01/1715: *Subsequent proceedings*, 00/1478
Rees *v.* Mabco (102) Ltd (1999) 96(4) L.S.G. 40; (1999) 143 S.J.L.B. 22; *Times*,
December 16, 1998, CA . . . . *Digested*, 99/**448**
Rees *v.* Munday [1974] 1 W.L.R. 1284; [1974] 3 All E.R. 506; (1974) 60 Cr. App. R.
20; [1974] R.T.R. 536; [1974] Crim. L.R. 561; 118 S.J. 697, DC . . . . *Digested*, 74/**3451**:
Followed, 98/4385
Rees *v.* Newbery; *sub nom* Lankesheer (Deceased), Re [1998] 1 F.L.R. 1041; [1998]
Fam. Law 320, Ch D . . . . *Digested*, 98/**4588**
Rees *v.* Palmer (Unreported, January 4, 2000), CC (Bristol) [*Ex rel.* Veale Wasbrough
Solicitors, Orchard Court, Orchard Lane, Bristol] . . . . *Digested*, 00/**1629**
Rees *v.* Sinclair [1955-95] P.N.L.R. 56; [1974] 1 N.Z.L.R. 180, CA (NZ) . . . . *Applied*, 97/3815:
Considered, 97/3832

Rees *v.* Skeret see Rees *v.* Skerrett
Rees *v.* Skerret see Rees *v.* Skerrett
Rees *v.* Skerrett; *sub nom* Rees *v.* Skeret; Rees *v.* Skerret [2001] EWCA Civ 760;
[2001] 1 W.L.R. 1541; (2001) 3 T.C.L.R. 27; [2001] 24 E.G.C.S. 162; *Times*, June
18, 2001, CA . . . . *Digested*, 01/**4482**
Rees-Davies (Personal Representatives of Rees-Davies (WR) (Deceased)) *v.* Westminster
City Council [1998] R.V.R. 219; [1998] E.G.C.S. 81, CA . . . . *Digested*, 98/**3636**
Reeves *v.* Commissioner of Police of the Metropolis [2000] 1 A.C. 360; [1999] 3
W.L.R. 363; [1999] 3 All E.R. 897; (2000) 51 B.M.L.R. 155; (1999) 96(31)
L.S.G. 41; (1999) 143 S.J.L.B. 213; *Times*, July 16, 1999 ; *Independent*, July 21,
1999, HL; reversing [1999] Q.B. 169; [1998] 2 W.L.R. 401; [1998] 2 All E.R.
381; (1998) 41 B.M.L.R. 54; (1997) 94(46) L.S.G. 29; (1997) 141 S.J.L.B. 239;
Times, November 20, 1997, CA . . . . *Digested*, 99/**4022**:
Applied, 01/4480

Reeves *v.* Thrings & Long [1996] P.N.L.R. 265; [1993] E.G.C.S. 196; [1993] N.P.C.
159, CA . . . . *Digested*, 96/**4501**:
Considered, 00/1483: *Followed*, 98/4018
Refco Capital Markets Ltd *v.* Credit Suisse First Boston Ltd; *sub nom* Genira Trade &
Finance Inc *v.* Refco Capital Markets Ltd; Refco Capital Markets Ltd *v.* CS First
Boston and Standard Bank (London) Ltd [2001] EWCA Civ 1733; *Times*,
December 7, 2001, CA; affirming1HQ/01/6564, QBD
Refco Capital Markets Ltd *v.* CS First Boston and Standard Bank (London) Ltd see
Refco Capital Markets Ltd *v.* Credit Suisse First Boston Ltd
Refco Inc *v.* Eastern Trading Co [1999] 1 Lloyd's Rep. 159, CA . . . . *Digested*, 98/**563**:
Considered, 00/490

Reference under s.48A of the Criminal Appeal (Northern Ireland) Act 1968 (No.1 of 1975),
  Re see Attorney General of Northern Ireland's Reference (No.1 of 1975), Re
Reform Party of Canada v. Attorney General of Canada (1995) 117 D.L.R. (4th) 366,
  CA (Alta) . . . .   *Applied*, 98/3094
Refugee Appeal (No.71462/99), Re [2000] I.N.L.R. 311, Refugees Status Apps
Refugee Appeal (No.71684/99), Re [2000] I.N.L.R. 165, Refugees Status Apps
Refugee Appeal (No.71427/99) [2000] I.N.L.R. 608, Refugees Status Apps
REFURBISHED TURBINE COMPONENTS/Re-establishment of rights (T281/96) [1998]
  E.P.O.R. 80, EPO (Technical Bd App)
Regal (Hastings) Ltd v. Gulliver [1967] 2 A.C. 134 (Note); [1942] 1 All E.R. 378, HL . . .   *Applied*, 52/27,
    64/3345, 65/3575, 66/11052, 69/379, 72/487, 82/3085, 83/430, 84/338,
    00/2132: *Considered*, 53/24, 72/361, 87/3552, 89/459:
    Distinguished, 67/452, 68/407: *Followed*, 54/447, 77/932, 83/990, 01/725
Regalbourne v. East Lindsey DC (1994) 6 Admin. L.R. 102; [1994] R.A. 1; [1993]
  C.O.D. 297; (1994) 158 L.G. Rev. 81; *Times*, March 16, 1993, CA; affirming
  [1992] C.O.D. 493. . . . .   *Digested*, 94/**3904**:
    Applied, 97/2132, 97/2135, 98/1962, 98/1983: *Considered*, 95/3932,
    96/676, 97/69, 97/2137
Regalian Properties Plc v. London Docklands Development Corp [1995] 1 W.L.R. 212;
  [1995] 1 All E.R. 1005; 45 Con. L.R. 37; (1995) 11 Const. L.J. 127; [1994]
  E.G.C.S. 176; (1995) 92(4) L.S.G. 34; [1994] N.P.C. 139, Ch D . . . .   *Digested*, 95/**794**:
    Distinguished, 00/2330
Regan v. Taylor [2000] E.M.L.R. 549; (2000) 150 N.L.J. 392; *Times*, March 15, 2000;
  Independent, April 17, 2000 (C.S.), CA; affirming1994 R NO. 1483, QBD . . . . . .   *Digested*, 00/**1760**
Regeling v. Bestuur van de Bedrijfsvereniging voor de Metaalnijverheid (C125/97)
  [1998] E.C.R. I-4493; [1999] 1 C.M.L.R. 1410; [1999] I.C.R. 605; [1999]
  I.R.L.R. 379; *Times*, July 20, 1998, ECJ. . . . .   *Digested*, 98/**2112**
Regenbecken (Rainwater Reservoir) (X ZR 57/96) [2000] E.P.O.R. 339, BGH (Ger) . .   *Previous proceedings*,
    00/3642
Regent Oil Co Ltd v. Inland Revenue Commissioners see Regent Oil Co Ltd v. Strick
  (Inspector of Taxes)
Regent Oil Co Ltd v. Strick (Inspector of Taxes); *sub nom* Strick (Inspector of Taxes) v.
  Regent Oil Co Ltd; Inland Revenue Commissioners v. Regent Oil Co Ltd; Regent
  Oil Co Ltd v. Inland Revenue Commissioners [1966] A.C. 295; [1965] 3 W.L.R.
  636; [1965] 3 All E.R. 174; 43 T.C. 1; (1965) 44 A.T.C. 264; [1965] T.R. 277;
  109 S.J. 633, HL; affirming [1964] 1 W.L.R. 1166; [1964] 3 All E.R. 23; (1964)
  43 A.T.C. 198; [1964] T.R. 207; 108 S.J. 500, CA; affirming [1964] 1 W.L.R. 309;
  [1964] 1 All E.R. 585; (1963) 42 A.T.C. 530; [1963] T.R. 471; 108 S.J. 54,
  Ch D . . . .   *Digested*, 65/**1937**:
    Applied, 88/534, 90/761: *Considered*, 74/482, 89/534: *Followed*, 99/4719
Regentcrest Plc (In Liquidation) v. Cohen [2001] B.C.C. 494; [2001] 2 B.C.L.C. 80,
  Ch D . . . .   *Digested*, 01/**3742**
Regeringsratten Case No (2772-1999) 2 I.T.L. Rep. 602, RR (Swe)
Regie Nationale des Usines Renault SA v. Maxicar SpA (C38/98) [2000] E.C.R. I-2973;
  [2000] E.C.D.R. 415; (2000) 23(7) I.P.D. 23050; *Times*, May 23, 2000, ECJ
  (5th Chamber) [2000] E.C.R. I-2973; [2000] E.C.D.R. 138, AGO . . . .   *Digested*, 00/**782**
Regional Aid Plans (C248/84), Re see Germany v. Commission of the European
  Communities (C248/84)
Regional Airports Ltd, Re [1999] 2 B.C.L.C. 30, Ch D . . . .   *Digested*, 99/**637**
Regional Collection Services Ltd v. Heald; *sub nom* H (In Bankruptcy), Re; H (A
  Debtor) (No.38-SD of 1997), Re [2000] B.P.I.R. 661; *Times*, May 10, 2000, CA .   *Digested*, 00/**3484**
Regione Toscana v. Commission of the European Communities (C180/97) [1997]
  E.C.R. I-5245, ECJ . . . .   *Followed*, 00/2408
Registration in Austria of a Branch of an English Company (6 Ob 124/99z), Re; *sub nom* S v.
  Companies Registrar, Graz (6 Ob 124/99z) [2001] 1 C.M.L.R. 38, OGH (A) . . . .   *Digested*, 01/**2498**
Registration in Germany of the Branch of an English Company, Re [2000] 2 C.M.L.R. 941,
  OLG (Bavaria)
Rehman (CICA: Quantum: 2001), Re [2001] 5 Q.R. 8, CICA (York) [*Ex rel.* John Worrall,
  Barrister, 10 Park Square, Leeds] . . . .   *Digested*, 01/**1574**
Rehman v. Entry Clearance Officer (Islamabad) [1998] I.N.L.R. 500, IAT . . . .   *Digested*, 99/**3198**
Rehman v. Secretary of State for the Home Department see Secretary of State for the
  Home Department v. Rehman
Reichert v. Dresdner Bank (No.1) (C115/88) [1990] E.C.R. I-27; [1990] I.L.Pr. 105;
  [1999] B.P.I.R. 941, ECJ (5th Chamber) [1989] E.C.C. 62, C d'A (Aix en
  Provence) . . . .   *Digested*, 00/**773**
Reichert v. Dresdner Bank (No.2) (C261/90) [1992] E.C.R. I-2149; [1992] I.L.Pr. 404;
  [1999] B.P.I.R. 946, ECJ (5th Chamber) [1991] I.L.Pr. 241, C d'A (Aix en
  Provence) . . . .   *Digested*, 92/**4824**:
    Considered, 01/820
Reichhold Ltd v. Wong [2000] Pens. L.R. 277, CJ (Gen Div) (Ont)

Reichhold Norway ASA v. Goldman Sachs International [2000] 1 W.L.R. 173; [2000] 2
All E.R. 679; [1999] 2 All E.R. (Comm) 174; [1999] 2 Lloyd's Rep. 567; [2000]
C.L.C. 11; *Times,* July 20, 1999, CA; affirming [1999] 1 All E.R. (Comm.) 40;
[1999] C.L.C. 486, QBD (Comm Ct) . . . .   *Digested,* 99/**546**:
Applied, 00/753
Reid (Valuation Officer) v. Barking, Havering and Brentwood Community Health Care
Trust [1997] R.A. 385, LandsTr . . . .   *Digested,* 98/**4318**
Reid v. DPP [1999] R.T.R. 357; [1998] Masons C.L.R. 269; *Times,* March 6, 1998,
QBD . . . .   *Digested,* 98/**897**
Reid v. Hamblin [2001] B.P.I.R. 929, CC (Milton Keynes)
Reid v. North West Ceilings Ltd (t/a Shopspec) [2001] Emp. L.R. 551, EAT . . . .   *Digested,* 01/**2263**
Reid (Dennis) v. Queen, The [1980] A.C. 343; [1979] 2 W.L.R. 221; [1979] 2 All E.R.
904; [1979] Crim. L.R. 179; 122 S.J. 861, PC (Jam) . . . .   *Digested,* 79/**603**:
Applied, 01/1148: *Considered,* 99/1037
Reid v. Ramlort Ltd see Thoar's Judicial Factor v. Ramlort Ltd
Reid v. Secretary of State for the Environment, Transport and the Regions [1998]
E.G.C.S. 57, QBD
Reigate v. Union Manufacturing Co (Ramsbottom) Ltd [1918] 1 K.B. 592, CA . . . .   *Applied,* 47-51/1890,
47-51/3696, 47-51/5377, 47-51/5429, 47-51/5506, 52/237, 52/1347, 60/1154,
61/56, 68/4006, 83/2064, 99/3697: *Considered,* 97/4255
Reigate and Banstead BC v. Benfield see R. (on the application of McLellan) v.
Bracknell Forest BC
Reigate and Banstead BC v. Brown see Mole Valley DC v. Smith
Reigate and Banstead BC v. Donington Investments Ltd (2000) 15 P.A.D. 216, Planning
Inspector
Reigate and Banstead BC v. Honeygrove Properties Ltd (2001) 16 P.A.D. 90, Planning
Inspector
Reinforced Earth Co v. Alviterra EC Ltd (1998) 21 (1) I.P.D. 21008, Ch D
Reinhardt v. France (22921/93); Slimane-Kaid v. France (1999) 28 E.H.R.R. 59;
[1998] H.R.C.D. 378, ECHR . . . .   *Digested,* 99/**3130**:
Referred to, 01/3533
REINSHAGEN/Electrical insulation (T1063/92) [2000] E.P.O.R. 248, EPO (Technical Bd
App) . . . .   *Digested,* 00/**3652**
Reiseburo Binder GmbH v. Finanzamt Stuttgart-Korperschaften (C116/96) [1998]
S.T.C. 604; [1997] E.C.R. I-6103; [1998] 2 C.M.L.R. 61; [1998] C.E.C. 583;
[1998] B.T.C. 5355; [1998] B.V.C. 362; *Times,* November 27, 1997, ECJ (5th
Chamber) . . . .   *Digested,* 97/**5032**
Reiss v. Woolf [1952] 2 Q.B. 557; [1952] 2 All E.R. 112; [1952] 1 T.L.R. 1606, CA;
affirming [1952] 2 All E.R. 3; [1952] 1 T.L.R. 1391; [1952] W.N. 290; 96 S.J. 378,
QBD . . . .   *Digested,* 52/**2735**:
Applied, 99/567: *Distinguished,* 00/630
Rekvenyi v. Hungary (2000) 30 E.H.R.R. 519; 6 B.H.R.C. 554, ECHR . . . .   *Digested,* 00/**3192**
Relaxion Group Plc v. Rhys-Harper see Rhys-Harper v. Relaxion Group Plc
Reliance National Insurance Co (Europe) Ltd v. Ropner Insurance Services Ltd [2001] 1
Lloyd's Rep. 477; [2001] C.P. Rep. 53; (2001) 98(4) L.S.G. 50; *Times,* January
31, 2001; *Independent,* January 15, 2001 (C.S), CA . . . .   *Digested,* 01/**667**
Reliance Water Controls Ltd v. Altecnic Ltd see Altecnic Ltd's Trade Mark Application
(No.2126884)
Remilien v. Secretary of State for Social Security see Secretary of State for Social
Security v. Remilien
Remington Products Inc's Trade Mark Application (No.1437070) (1999) 22(9) I.P.D.
22089, TMR
Remli v. France (1996) 22 E.H.R.R. 253, ECHR . . . .   *Digested,* 96/**3168**:
Considered, 98/3071
Remon v. City of London Real Property Co Ltd [1921] 1 K.B. 49, CA . . . .   *Applied,* 47-51/8528,
47-51/8831: *Considered,* 99/4386: *Distinguished,* 47-51/8850, 67/3415,
81/1322, 82/1479, 83/2120
Rendle v. Hicks (Unreported, November 17, 1997), CC (Bodmin) [*Ex rel.* Hugh Hamill,
Barrister, 12 King's Bench Walk, Temple] . . . .   *Digested,* 98/**2504**:
Considered, 99/2454: *Followed,* 98/1461
Rendlesham v. Dunne [1964] 1 Lloyd's Rep. 192; 114 L.J. 208, CC (Westminster) . . . . .   *Digested,* 64/**3223**:
Approved, 99/5404: *Considered,* 89/2059
Rendo NV v. Commission of the European Communities (T16/91 RV) [1996] E.C.R. II-
1827; [1997] 4 C.M.L.R. 453, CFI (2nd Chamber)
RENISHAW/Touch probe (T434/97) [2001] E.P.O.R. 26, EPO (Technical Bd App) . . . .   *Digested,* 01/**3914**
Renlon Ltd v. Customs and Excise Commissioners [2000] V. & D.R. 442; [2001] S.T.I.
680, V&DTr
Renshaw Birch Ltd v. Marquet [1998] B.P.I.R. 399, Ch D . . . .   *Digested,* 97/**3075**
Renton v. Hendersons Garage (Nairn) Ltd & United Dominions Trust see Renton v.
Hendersons Garage (Nairn) Ltd
Renton v. Hendersons Garage (Nairn) Ltd; *sub nom* Renton v. Hendersons Garage
(Nairn) Ltd & United Dominions Trust [1994] C.C.L.R. 29, Sh Pr . . . .   *Digested,* 95/**5564**:
Applied, 99/2513

Renwick *v.* Stanley Vickers Ltd (Unreported, February 6, 2001), CC (Middlesbrough)
    [*Ex rel.* Jeremy Freedman, Barrister, Plowden Buildings, Temple, London] . . . . . .   *Digested,* 01/**5352**
Reprotech (Pebsham) Ltd *v.* East Sussex CC see R. (on the application of Reprotech
    (Pebsham) Ltd) *v.* East Sussex CC
Request for International Judicial Assistance from the Drammen Byrett, Re (2000-01) 3
    I.T.E.L.R. 705, Grand Court (CI) . . . .   *Digested,* 01/**406**
Rescue Services on Loir-et-Cher Motorways, Re [1999] E.C.C. 238, C Concurrence (F)   *Digested,* 99/**665**
Research Triangle Institute's European Patent Application (No.90310085.7) see
    RESEARCH TRIANGLE/Amendment (T755/96)
RESEARCH TRIANGLE/Amendment (T755/96); *sub nom* Research Triangle Institute's
    European Patent Application (No.90310085.7) [2000] E.P.O.R. 391; (2000)
    23(8) I.P.D. 23063, EPO (Technical Bd App) . . . .   *Digested,* 00/**3614**
Reside *v.* North Ayrshire Council 2001 S.L.T. 6; [2000] 3 P.L.R. 86; 2000 G.W.D. 19-
    767, OH . . . .   *Digested,* 01/**6859**
Resolute Maritime Inc *v.* Nippon Kaiji Kyokai (The Skopas) [1983] 1 W.L.R. 857; [1983]
    2 All E.R. 1; [1983] 1 Lloyd's Rep. 431, QBD (Comm Ct) . . . .   *Digested,* 83/**1734**:
                                                     Cited, 01/962: *Considered,* 89/59
Resource Management Services *v.* Westminster City Council [1999] 2 C.M.L.R. 849;
    [2000] Eu. L.R. 1; (1999) 1 L.G.L.R. 893, QBD . . . .   *Digested,* 99/**839**
Restorex Ltd *v.* Customs and Excise Commissioners [1997] V. & D.R. 402, V&DTr. . . . .   *Digested,* 00/**5336**
Restormel BC *v.* Chapel Green Enterprises Ltd (1999) 14 P.A.D. 225, Planning
    Inspector
Restormel DC *v.* Kwik-Fit Properties (1998) 13 P.A.D. 296, Planning Inspector
Retail Media Ltd *v.* Secretary of State for the Environment, Transport and the Regions
    [2001] J.P.L. 1050; [2000] E.G.C.S. 111, QBD (Admin Ct) . . . .   *Digested,* 01/**4732**
Reuben *v.* Brent LBC [2000] I.C.R. 102; [2000] I.R.L.R. 176, EAT . . . .   *Digested,* 00/**2136**
Reunion Europeenne SA *v.* Spliethoffs Bevrachtingskantoor BV [1999] I.L.Pr. 613, Cass
    (F) . . . .   *Previous proceedings,*
                                                          98/769
Reunion Europeenne SA *v.* Spliethoffs Bevrachtingskantoor BV (C51/97) [2000] Q.B.
    690; [2000] 3 W.L.R. 1213; [1998] E.C.R. I-6511; [1999] C.L.C. 282; [1999]
    I.L.Pr. 205; *Times,* November 16, 1998, ECJ (3rd Chamber) . . . .   *Digested,* 98/**769**:
                                                          Followed, 01/4290
Revenko *v.* Secretary of State for the Home Department [2001] Q.B. 601; [2000] 3
    W.L.R. 1519; [2000] Imm. A.R. 610; [2000] I.N.L.R. 646; (2000) 97(39) L.S.G.
    41; *Times,* September 8, 2000, CA . . . .   *Digested,* 00/**3331**
Revill *v.* Newberry [1996] Q.B. 567; [1996] 2 W.L.R. 239; [1996] 1 All E.R. 291;
    (1995) 92(44) L.S.G. 31; (1996) 146 N.L.J. 50; (1995) 139 S.J.L.B. 244; *Times,*
    November 3, 1995; *Independent,* November 10, 1995, CA . . . .   *Digested,* 95/**3660**:
                                        Followed, 01/5349: *Referred to,* 99/4003
Revival Properties Ltd *v.* Edinburgh City Council see Edinburgh City Council *v.*
    Secretary of State for Scotland
REVLON/Nail enamel (T306/93) [2000] E.P.O.R. 575, EPO (Technical Bd App) . . . . .   *Digested,* 01/**3927**
Rewe-Zentral AG *v.* Bundesmonopolverwaltung fur Branntwein (C120/78); *sub nom*
    Cassis de Dijon [1979] E.C.R. 649; [1979] 3 C.M.L.R. 494, ECJ . . . .   *Digested,* 79/**1225**:
                      Considered, 87/2412, 88/1530: *Followed,* 97/4876, 98/3855
Rewe-Zentral AG *v.* Direktor de Landwirtschaftskammer Rheinland (C37/83) [1984]
    E.C.R. 1229; [1985] 2 C.M.L.R. 586, ECJ (5th Chamber) . . . .   *Digested,* 85/**1427**:
                                                          Followed, 00/2382
Rewe-Zentralfinanz eG *v.* Landwirtschaftskammer fur das Saarland (C33/76); Comet
    BV *v.* Produktschap voor Siergewassen (C45/76) [1976] E.C.R. 1989; [1977] 1
    C.M.L.R. 533, ECJ . . . .   *Digested,* 77/**1248**:
                            Applied, 00/2406, 00/4462: *Considered,* 95/2112
Rex Stewart Jeffries Parker Ginsberg Ltd *v.* Parker [1988] I.R.L.R. 483, CA . . . .   *Digested,* 88/**1251**:
                                          Applied, 98/2192: *Distinguished,* 98/2205
Rexworthy *v.* Secretary of State for the Environment, Transport and the Regions
    [1998] J.P.L. 864, QBD . . . .   *Digested,* 98/**4213**
Rey *v.* Graham & Oldham [2000] B.P.I.R. 354, QBD . . . .   *Digested,* 00/**4266**
Rey *v.* Switzerland [1999] 1 A.C. 54; [1998] 3 W.L.R. 1; (1998) 142 S.J.L.B. 167, PC
    (Bah) . . . .   *Digested,* 98/**2345**
Rey Banano del Pacifico CA *v.* Transportes Navieros Ecuatorianos SpA (The Isla
    Fernandina) [2000] 2 Lloyd's Rep. 15, QBD (Comm Ct) . . . .   *Digested,* 00/**4695**
Rey Soda *v.* Cassa Conguaglio Zucchero (C23/75) [1975] E.C.R. 1279; [1976] 1
    C.M.L.R. 185, ECJ . . . .   *Digested,* 76/**1029**:
                                        Considered, 79/1155
Reynard *v.* Secretary of State for Trade and Industry see Secretary of State for Trade
    and Industry *v.* Reynard
Reynolds *v.* Brent LBC see Brent LBC *v.* Reynolds
Reynolds *v.* Commissioner of Police of the Metropolis [1985] Q.B. 881; [1985] 2
    W.L.R. 93; [1984] 3 All E.R. 649; (1985) 80 Cr. App. R. 125; [1984] Crim. L.R.
    688; (1984) 81 L.S.G. 2856; (1984) 128 S.J. 736, CA . . . .   *Digested,* 84/**2533**:
                          Applied, 97/1167, 99/901: *Considered,* 99/900
Reynolds *v.* Health First Medical Group [2000] Lloyd's Rep. Med. 240, CC (Hitchin) . .   *Digested,* 00/**2777**

Reynolds v. Long Ashton Research Station (Unreported, November 1, 2000), CC (Bristol) [*Ex rel.* Matthew White, Barrister, St. John's Chambers, Small Street, Bristol] . . . . *Digested*, 01/**640**

Reynolds v. Times Newspapers Ltd [2001] 2 A.C. 127; [1999] 3 W.L.R. 1010; [1999] 4 All E.R. 609; [2000] E.M.L.R. 1; [2000] H.R.L.R. 134; 7 B.H.R.C. 289; (1999) 96(45) L.S.G. 34; (1999) 149 N.L.J. 1697; (1999) 143 S.J.L.B. 270; *Times*, October 29, 1999; *Independent*, November 3, 1999, HL; affirming [1998] 3 W.L.R. 862; [1998] 3 All E.R. 961; [1998] E.M.L.R. 723; (1998) 95(32) L.S.G. 30; (1998) 148 N.L.J. 1051; (1998) 142 S.J.L.B. 218; *Times*, July 9, 1998; *Independent*, July 14, 1998, CA . . . . *Digested*, 99/**1630**:
Applied, 99/1625, 00/1761, 00/1763, 01/1823, 01/1829, 01/1831:
Considered, 01/1824, 01/1832, 01/1834: *Followed*, 99/1626

Reynolds v. TNT (UK) Ltd (Unreported, July 8, 1998), CC (Dudley) [*Ex rel.* Jonathon Gidney, Barrister, Claremount Chambers, 26 Waterloo Road, Wolverhampton] . . *Digested*, 98/**1663**

Rezvi v. Brown Cooper [1997] 1 Costs L.R. 109, QBD . . . . *Digested*, 98/**480**

RH (A Minor) (Parental Responsibility), Re see H (A Minor) (Parental Responsibility), Re

RH (CICB: Quantum: 1998), Re (Unreported, March 11, 1998), CICB (Nottingham) [*Ex rel.* Jason Cox, Barrister, 24 The Ropewalk, Nottingham] . . . . *Digested*, 98/**1488**:
Considered, 01/1595

RH Tomlinssons (Trowbridge) Ltd v. Secretary of State for the Environment, Transport and the Regions [2000] B.C.C. 576; [1999] 2 B.C.L.C. 760; [1999] N.P.C. 110; *Times*, August 31, 1999, CA . . . . *Digested*, 99/**45**

Rheinmuhlen-Dusseldorf v. EVST (C166/73) see Firma Rheinmuhlen-Dusseldorf v. Einfuhrund Vorratsstelle fur Getreide und Futtermittel (C166/73)

Rhesa Shipping Co SA v. Edmunds (The Popi M); Rhesa Shipping Co SA v. Fenton Insurance Co Ltd [1985] 1 W.L.R. 948; [1985] 2 All E.R. 712; [1985] 2 Lloyd's Rep. 1; (1985) 82 L.S.G. 2995; (1985) 129 S.J. 503, HL; reversing [1984] 2 Lloyd's Rep. 555, CA; reversing in part [1983] 2 Lloyd's Rep. 235, QBD (Comm Ct) . . . . *Digested*, 85/**3207**:
Applied, 92/3975, 95/4534: *Distinguished*, 00/2984

Rhesa Shipping Co SA v. Fenton Insurance Co Ltd see Rhesa Shipping Co SA v. Edmunds (The Popi M)

Rhodes v. Canterbury & Thanet HA (Unreported, October 21, 1997), CC (Maidstone) [*Ex rel.* Gepp & Sons Solicitors, 58 New London Road, Chelmsford] . . . . *Digested*, 98/**515**

Rhodes v. Soor (Unreported, April 6, 1998), CC (Willesden) [*Ex rel.* Craig Moore, Barrister, Barnards Inn Chambers, 20/23 Holburn, London EC1N 2JD] . . . . *Digested*, 98/**1670**

Rhodes v. West Surrey and North East Hampshire HA [1998] Lloyd's Rep. Med. 246, CC (Aldershot & Farnham) . . . . *Digested*, 98/**3960**

Rhondda Cynon Taff CBC v. Customs and Excise Commissioners [2000] B.V.C. 2226; [2000] V. & D.R. 150; [2000] S.T.I. 837, V&DTr

Rhondda Cynon Taff CBC v. Rhondda Housing Association (2000) 15 P.A.D. 600, Planning Inspector

Rhondda Waste Disposal Ltd (In Administration), Re; *sub nom* Clark v. Environment Agency; Environment Agency v. Clark [2001] Ch. 57; [2000] 3 W.L.R. 1304; [2000] B.C.C. 653; [2000] Env. L.R. 600; [2000] 1 E.G.L.R. 113; [2000] E.G.C.S. 25; (2000) 150 N.L.J. 227; *Times*, March 2, 2000; *Independent*, April 10, 2000 (C.S.), CA; affirming (1999) 96(32) L.S.G. 32; *Times*, August 13, 1999, Ch D . . . . *Digested*, 00/**3432**

Rhone v. Stephens [1994] 2 A.C. 310; [1994] 2 W.L.R. 429; [1994] 37 E.G. 151; [1994] E.G.C.S. 50; (1994) 138 S.J.L.B. 77; [1994] N.P.C. 43; *Times*, March 18, 1994; *Independent*, March 23, 1994, HL; affirming (1994) 67 P. & C.R. 9; [1993] E.G.C.S. 3; (1993) 137 S.J.L.B. 46; [1993] N.P.C. 11; *Times*, January 21, 1993, CA . . . . *Digested*, 94/**576**:
Applied, 98/4345

Rhone Poulenc SA v. Commission of the European Communities (T1/89) [1991] E.C.R. II-867, CFI (1st Chamber) . . . . *Digested*, 92/**4712**:
Applied, 01/760

RHONE POULENC/Ester production (T427/86) [1999] E.P.O.R. 443, EPO (Technical Bd App) . . . . *Digested*, 00/**3643**

RHONE-POULENC/Taxoids (T77/97) [1998] E.P.O.R. 256, EPO (Technical Bd App)

Rhys v. Relaxation Group Plc see Rhys-Harper v. Relaxion Group Plc

Rhys-Harper v. Relaxion Group Plc; *sub nom* Rhys v. Relaxation Group Plc; Relaxion Group Plc v. Rhys-Harper [2001] EWCA Civ 634; [2001] 2 C.M.L.R. 44; [2001] I.C.R. 1176; [2001] I.R.L.R. 460; [2001] Emp. L.R. 646; (2001) 98(24) L.S.G. 43; *Times*, June 12, 2001; *Independent*, May 11, 2001; *Daily Telegraph*, May 15, 2001, CA; affirming [2000] I.R.L.R. 810, EAT . . . . *Digested*, 01/**2322**

Rialto Homes Plc v. Customs and Excise Commissioners [2000] B.V.C. 2161; [1999] V. & D.R. 477; [2000] S.T.I. 268, V&DTr . . . . *Digested*, 00/**5308**

Riaz v. Masaku [2001] L. & T.R. 22, CA [*Ex rel.* Mark Loveday, Barrister, Tanfield Chambers, Francis Taylor Building, Temple, London] . . . . *Digested*, 01/**4209**

RIB LOC/Correction of mistakes (J08/80) [1979-85] E.P.O.R. A40, EPO (Legal Bd App)
Applied, 00/3621

RIBA Publications v. Customs and Excise Commissioners [1999] B.V.C. 2201; [1999] V. & D.R. 230, V&DTr . . . . *Digested*, 00/**5354**

Ribbee v. Norrie see Ribee v. Norrie

Ribble Motor Services Ltd v. Traffic Commission for the North Western Traffic Area see Ribble Motor Services Ltd v. Traffic Commissioner for the North West Traffic Area

Ribble Motor Services Ltd v. Traffic Commissioner for the North West Traffic Area; *sub nom* Ribble Motor Services Ltd v. Traffic Commission for the North Western Traffic Area [2001] EWCA Civ 267; [2001] R.T.R. 37; (2001) 151 N.L.J. 305; *Times*, March 8, 2001; *Independent*, March 7, 2001, CA . . . . *Digested*, 01/**5384**

Ribee v. Norrie; *sub nom* Ribbee v. Norrie (2001) 33 H.L.R. 69; [2001] P.I.Q.R. P8; [2001] L. & T.R. 23; [2000] N.P.C. 116; (2001) 81 P. & C.R. D18; *Times*, November 22, 2000, CA . . . . *Digested*, 00/**4238**

Ricci Burns Ltd v. Toole [1989] 1 W.L.R. 993; [1989] 3 All E.R. 478; (1988) 138 N.L.J. Rep. 312, CA. . . . . *Digested*, 90/**3707**:
Cited, 01/572: *Not followed*, 89/3019, 90/3804

Riccio v. Ford Motor Co Ltd see Pritchard v. Ford Motor Co Ltd

Rice v. Gordon (1843) 13 Sim. 580 . . . . *Distinguished*, 00/336

Rice (t/a Garden Guardian) v. Great Yarmouth BC (2001) 3 L.G.L.R. 4; *Times*, July 26, 2000, CA . . . . *Digested*, 00/**874**

Rice v. Rice (1854) 2 Drew. 73 . . . . *Applied*, 00/4649

Rice's Application for Judicial Review, Re [1998] N.I. 265, CA (NI) . . . . *Digested*, 99/**5206**

Richard v. France [1998] H.R.C.D. 456, ECHR

Richard v. Surrey Hampshire Borders NHS Trust [1999] R.V.R. 28, Lands Tr . . . . *Digested*, 99/**4364**

Richard Cound Ltd v. BMW (GB) Ltd [1997] Eu. L.R. 301, CA; affirming in part [1997] Eu. L.R. 277, QBD (Merc Ct) . . . . *Followed*, 98/718

Richard SA v. Pavan [1998] I.L.Pr. 193, Cass (F)

Richards v. Allan [2001] W.T.L.R. 1031, Ch D

Richards v. Hampshire CC (Unreported, January 28, 2000), CC (Portsmouth) [*Ex rel.* Paul Hepher, Barrister, 2 Gray's Inn Square Chambers, 2 Gray's Inn Square, London] . . . . *Digested*, 00/**1610**

Richards v. Hopkins (Unreported, December 19, 2000), CC (Pontypool) [*Ex rel.* Palser Grossman, Solicitors, Discovery House, Scott Harbour, Cardiff Bay] . . . . *Digested*, 01/**1504**

Richards v. Jamaica 3 B.H.R.C. 339, UN HRC . . . . *Digested*, 98/**3117**

Richards v. Jones (Unreported, August 3, 1998), CC (Cardiff) [*Ex rel.* Andrew Arentsen, Barrister, 33 Park Place, Cardiff] . . . . *Digested*, 98/**1716**

Richards v. Lundy; *sub nom* Apollo Cleaning Services Ltd, Re [1999] B.C.C. 786; [2000] 1 B.C.L.C. 376, Ch D . . . . *Digested*, 99/**636**

Richards v. Prodger (Unreported, February 9, 1999), CC (Gloucester) [*Ex rel.* David Burles, Barrister, Goldsmith Building, Temple, London] . . . . *Digested*, 99/**1469**

Richards v. Richards [1984] A.C. 174; [1983] 3 W.L.R. 173; [1983] 2 All E.R. 807; (1984) 12 H.L.R. 73; (1983) 13 Fam. Law 256, HL; reversing [1983] 2 W.L.R. 633; [1983] 1 All E.R. 1017; (1983) 13 Fam. Law 84, CA . . . . *Digested*, 83/**1861**:
Applied, 83/1866, 84/1658, 85/1671, 86/1655.a, 86/1667, 87/1780, 88/1668, 94/3265, 95/3562: *Cited*, 00/2529: *Considered*, 83/1866, 84/1658, 85/1696, 85/1698, 86/1657, 87/1777, 87/1780, 88/1666, 88/1668, 93/1926, 95/2369: *Distinguished*, 83/1863, 83/1869: *Followed*, 86/1665, 94/2195: *Referred to*, 87/1773

Richards v. Somerset CC (No 2) [2001] R.V.R. 229, Lands Tr

Richards v. Somerset CC (No.1) [2001] R.V.R. 204, Lands Tr

Richards v. Whyatt [2001] 1 Q.R. 15, CC (Southampton) [*Ex rel.* Shoosmiths Solicitors, Russell House, Solent Business Park, Whiteley, Fareham] . . . . *Digested*, 01/**1725**

Richardson v. Davy Roll Co Ltd (Unreported, June 10, 1998), CC (Newcastle) [*Ex rel.* Keith Morton, Barrister, 1 Temple Gardens, Temple, London] . . . . *Digested*, 98/**1679**

Richardson (Inspector of Taxes) v. Delaney [2001] S.T.C. 1328; [2001] I.R.L.R. 663; [2001] B.T.C. 392; [2001] S.T.I. 936; (2001) 98(31) L.S.G. 37; *Times*, July 11, 2001, Ch D . . . . *Digested*, 01/**5274**

Richardson v. Desquenne et Giral UK Ltd; *sub nom* Desquenne et Giral UK Ltd v. Richardson [1999] C.P.L.R. 744; [2001] F.S.R. 1, CA . . . . *Digested*, 00/**412**:
Applied, 01/486

Richardson v. Dunning (1999) 99(3) Q.R. 6, CC (Bristol) [*Ex rel.* Helen Gower, Barrister, Old Square Chambers, Hanover House, 47 Corn Street, Bristol] . . . . . *Digested*, 99/**1475**

Richardson v. LRC Products Ltd [2000] P.I.Q.R. P164; [2000] Lloyd's Rep. Med. 280; (2001) 59 B.M.L.R. 185, QBD . . . . *Digested*, 00/**851**

Richardson v. Richardson (No.2) [1996] 2 F.L.R. 617; [1997] 2 F.C.R. 453; [1997] Fam. Law 14, CA; affirming [1994] 2 F.L.R. 1051; [1994] 2 F.C.R. 826; [1995] Fam. Law 14, Fam Div . . . . *Digested*, 97/**2477**:
Followed, 00/2533

Richardson v. Secretary of State for the Environment (1998) 75 P. & C.R. 97, QBD . . . . *Digested*, 97/**4138**

Richardson v. Solihull MBC see White v. Ealing LBC

Richardson v. Whelan [1998] I.C.R. 318; [1998] I.R.L.R. 114, EAT . . . . *Digested*, 98/**2228**:
Overruled in part, 98/2224

Richardson Development Ltd v. Birmingham City Council [1999] R.V.R. 44; [1999] J.P.L. 1001; [1999] E.G.C.S. 8, QBD . . . . *Digested*, 99/**4327**

Richardson-Vicks Inc's Patent; *sub nom* Reckitt & Colman Products Ltd *v.* Richardson-Vicks Inc [1997] R.P.C. 888; (1997) 20(8) I.P.D. 20075, CA; affirming [1995] R.P.C. 568, Pat Ct . . . .
Digested, 98/**3453**: *Referred to*, 99/3466

RICHARDSON/Nickel plating (T370/90) [1999] E.P.O.R. 293, EPO (Technical Bd App)

Richart (Inspector of Taxes) *v.* Bass Holdings Ltd see R. *v.* Inspector of Taxes Ex p. Bass Holdings Ltd

Richbell Information Services Inc, Re see Atlantic & General Investment Trust Ltd *v.* Richbell Information Services Inc

Richbell Information Services Inc *v.* Atlantic & General Investment Trust Ltd (Validation of Disposition) [1999] B.C.C. 871, Ch D . . . .
Digested, 99/**3359**: *Subsequent proceedings*, 99/3351

Richbell Strategic Holdings Ltd (In Liquidation) (No.2), Re [2001] B.C.C. 409; [2000] 2 B.C.L.C. 794; *Times*, June 14, 2000, Ch D . . . .
Digested, 00/**3462**

Richbell Strategic Holdings Ltd (No.1), Re [1997] 2 B.C.L.C. 429, Ch D (Companies Ct)
Digested, 98/**3318**

Richmond Cars Ltd *v.* Customs and Excise Commissioners [2000] V. & D.R. 388; [2001] S.T.I. 569, V&DTr

Richmond upon Thames LBC *v.* Berkeley Homes (Thames Valley) Ltd (2000) 15 P.A.D. 205, Planning Inspector

Richmond upon Thames LBC *v.* H; *sub nom* X (A Child) (Injunctions Restraining Publication), Re [2001] 1 F.C.R. 541; *Times*, October 20, 2000, Fam Div . . . .
Digested, 00/**2535**

Richmond upon Thames LBC *v.* Morton (t/a Morts Trucking Co) [2000] R.T.R. 79, QBD

Richmond Upon Thames LBC *v.* Richmond Cricket Club (1998) 13 P.A.D. 758, Planning Inspector

Richmond upon Thames LBC *v.* Secretary of State for the Environment, Transport and the Regions [2000] 2 P.L.R. 115; [2001] J.P.L. 84; [2000] E.G.C.S. 47; (2000) 97(14) L.S.G. 44, QBD

Richmond upon Thames LBC *v.* Secretary of State for the Environment, Transport and the Regions (Tree Preservation Order) [2001] EWHC Admin 205; (2001) 98(13) L.S.G. 43; (2001) 98(11) L.S.G. 45, QBD (Admin Ct)

Richmond upon Thames LBC *v.* Serrurier (2000) 15 P.A.D. 157, Planning Inspector

Richmondshire DC *v.* Chaytor Norris (2000) 15 P.A.D. 97, Planning Inspector

Richmondshire DC *v.* Secretary of State for the Environment, Transport and the Regions; *sub nom* R. *v.* Secretary of State for the Environment, Transport and the Regions Ex p. Richmondshire DC (2000) 80 P. & C.R. 302; [1999] E.G.C.S. 148; (1999) 96(48) L.S.G. 41, QBD . . . .
Digested, 00/**4439**

Rickards *v.* Jones [2000] N.P.C. 104, CA

Rickards *v.* Rickards [1990] Fam. 194; [1989] 3 W.L.R. 748; [1989] 3 All E.R. 193; [1990] 1 F.L.R. 125; [1990] F.C.R. 409; (1990) 154 J.P.N. 346; (1989) 86(41) L.S.G. 39; (1989) 139 N.L.J. 899, CA . . . .
Digested, 90/**3733**: *Considered*, 92/388, 92/389, 93/3195, 01/431

Ricketts *v.* Hurstanger Ltd [1998] C.C.L.R. 5, CC (Aldershot & Farnham) . . . .
Digested, 97/**962**: *Considered*, 99/4387: *Followed*, 98/2495, 99/2507

Ricketts *v.* Queen, The [1998] 1 W.L.R. 1016; (1998) 142 S.J.L.B. 63, PC (Jam) . . . . . .
Digested, 98/**902**

Ridehalgh *v.* Horsefield; Allen *v.* Unigate Dairies Ltd; Antonelli *v.* Wade Gery Farr; Philex Plc *v.* Golban; Roberts *v.* Coverite (Asphalters) Ltd; Watson *v.* Watson (Wasted Costs Orders) [1994] Ch. 205; [1994] 3 W.L.R. 462; [1994] 3 All E.R. 848; [1994] B.C.C. 390; [1994] 2 F.L.R. 194; [1955-95] P.N.L.R. 636; [1994] Fam. Law 560; [1994] E.G.C.S. 15; (1994) 144 N.L.J. 231; [1994] N.P.C. 7; *Times*, January 28, 1994; *Independent*, February 4, 1994, CA . . . .
Digested, 94/**3623**: *Applied*, 95/4028, 95/4030, 95/4031, 95/4034, 96/936, 96/939, 96/3524, 97/602, 99/988, 00/470, 00/471, 00/4001, 01/4516: *Approved*, 00/469: *Considered*, 94/3620, 94/3743, 95/2273, 95/4673, 96/940, 96/3899, 96/4508, 97/605, 97/607, 97/610, 97/1387, 98/497, 99/422, 99/989, 00/2466, 01/537, 01/589: *Followed*, 98/496, 98/499, 00/1043: *Previous proceedings*, 93/3176, 93/3177

Ridgway and Fairbrother *v.* National Coal Board see National Coal Board *v.* Ridgway and Fairbrother

Ridley *v.* McEwan (Unreported, November 11, 1997), CC (Portsmouth) [*Ex rel.* Thomas Roe, Barrister, Goldsmith Building, Temple, London] . . . .
Digested, 98/**431**

Ridley *v.* Taylor [1965] 1 W.L.R. 611; [1965] 2 All E.R. 51; (1965) 16 P. & C.R. 113; 109 S.J. 292, CA . . . .
Digested, 65/**3352**: *Considered*, 71/9933, 97/4262, 00/5613

Ridout *v.* TC Group [1998] I.R.L.R. 628; [1999] Disc. L.R. 8, EAT . . . .
Digested, 98/**2120**

Riepan *v.* Austria [2001] Crim. L.R. 230, ECHR

Rigby, Re (Unreported, October 9, 1997), CICB [*Ex rel.* Deborah Shield, Barrister, White Friars Chambers, 21 White Friars, Chester] . . . .
Digested, 98/**1543**

Rigby *v.* Incumbent Churchwardens of St Peter's Church (Yately) (Unreported, July 6, 1998), CC (Blackburn) [*Ex rel.* Marcus Grant, Barrister, 1 Temple Gardens, London] . . . .
Digested, 98/**337**: *Considered*, 99/326

Rigby *v.* Jayatilaka (Inspector of Taxes) [2000] S.T.C. 179; 72 T.C. 365; [2000] B.T.C. 76; [2000] S.T.I. 189; *Times*, March 21, 2000, Ch D . . . .
Digested, 00/**5052**

Rigby v. Samson (Inspector of Taxes) [1997] S.T.C. 524 (Note); 71 T.C. 153; [1997] B.T.C. 195, Ch D . . . . *Digested,* 97/**2972**

Riggs v. East Dorset HA (Unreported, October 25, 1990), QBD . . . . *Digested,* 91/**1417**: *Distinguished,* 01/1520

Riggs National Corp v. Internal Revenue Commissioner 1 I.T.L. Rep. 421, US Ct

Rignall Developments Ltd v. Halil [1988] Ch. 190; [1987] 3 W.L.R. 394; [1987] 3 All E.R. 170; (1988) 20 H.L.R. 7; (1987) 54 P. & C.R. 245; [1987] 1 E.G.L.R. 193; (1987) 282 E.G. 1414; (1987) 131 S.J. 1039, Ch D . . . . *Digested,* 87/**2108**: *Distinguished,* 00/4622

Rijksdienst voor Pensioenen v. Lustig (C244/97) [1999] All E.R. (EC) 75; [1998] E.C.R. I-8701; [1999] 1 C.M.L.R. 641, ECJ . . . . *Digested,* 99/**2277**

Rijn-Schelde-Verolme Machinefabrieken en Sheepswerven NV v. Commission of the European Communities (C223/85) [1987] E.C.R. 4617; [1989] 2 C.M.L.R. 259, ECJ . . . . *Digested,* 90/**2218**: *Distinguished,* 00/713

Riker Laboratories Inc's Patents [1997] F.S.R. 714; (1997) 20(4) I.P.D. 20031, Pat Ct. . .   *Digested,* 98/**571**

Rilett v. Greet [1999] B.P.I.R. 145, Ch D . . . . *Digested,* 99/**3339**

Riley v. Choi Chi Cui (Unreported, October 6, 2000), CC (Bury) [*Ex rel.* David Calvert, Barrister, St James' Chambers, 68 Quay Street, Manchester] . . . .   *Digested,* 01/**1738**

Riley v. Riley (Custody) (1986) 150 J.P. 439; [1986] 2 F.L.R. 429; [1987] 1 F.C.R. 65; [1987] Fam. Law 15; (1986) 150 J.P.N. 637, CA . . . . *Digested,* 87/**2489**: *Considered,* 95/3563, 96/604, 01/2666: *Disapproved,* 94/3263, 95/3561: *Not followed,* 95/3560

Rimalt v. Cartwright (1925) 132 L.T. 40 . . . . *Distinguished,* 98/370

Rimmer v. Liverpool City Council [1985] Q.B. 1; [1984] 2 W.L.R. 426; [1984] 1 All E.R. 930; (1984) 12 H.L.R. 23; 82 L.G.R. 424; (1984) 47 P. & C.R. 516; (1984) 269 E.G. 319; (1984) 81 L.S.G. 664, CA . . . . *Digested,* 84/**2300**: *Applied,* 92/3199: *Considered,* 89/2150: *Distinguished,* 00/4231: *Not applied,* 99/3735

Rimmer v. Pearson (2000) 79 P. & C.R. D21, CA

Rimron v. Khan (Unreported, December 11, 1998), CC (Preston) [*Ex rel.* Brian McCluggage, Barrister, 9 St John Street, Manchester] . . . .   *Digested,* 99/**333**

Rimsat Ltd, Re [2000] B.P.I.R. 811, US Ct

Ringeisen v. Austria (No.1) (A/13) (1979-80) 1 E.H.R.R. 455, ECHR . . . .   *Applied,* 98/3128, 98/3149: *Considered,* 96/3151

Ringway Roadmarking v. Adbruf Ltd [1998] 2 B.C.L.C. 625, QBD (OR) . . . .   *Digested,* 99/**650**

Riniker v. University College London, *Times* April 17, 1999; *Independent,* April 29, 1999, CA . . . . *Digested,* 99/**578**

Riniker v. University College London (Practice Note) [2001] 1 W.L.R. 13; [2001] 1 Costs L.R. 20, CA . . . .   *Digested,* 01/**11**

Rinner-Kuhn v. FWW Spezial-Gebaudereinigung GmbH & Co KG (C171/88) [1989] E.C.R. 2743; [1993] 2 C.M.L.R. 932; [1989] I.R.L.R. 493; *Times,* September 29, 1989, ECJ (6th Chamber) . . . . *Digested,* 90/**2203.a**: *Applied,* 94/1981, 98/2240: *Considered,* 95/2052, 96/2629: *Followed,* 96/2574, 96/5389, 96/5390

Riordan Communications Ltd v. South Buckinghamshire DC; *sub nom* Riordan Communications Ltd v. South Bucks DC (2001) 81 P. & C.R. 8; [2000] 1 P.L.R. 45; [2000] J.P.L. 594; [1999] E.G.C.S. 146; [1999] N.P.C. 150; *Times,* January 18, 2000, QBD . . . . *Digested,* 00/**4499**

Riordan Communications Ltd v. South Bucks DC see Riordan Communications Ltd v. South Buckinghamshire DC

RISAN Srl v. Comune di Ischia (C108/98) [1999] E.C.R. I-5219; [2000] 4 C.M.L.R. 657, ECJ (5th Chamber) . . . . *Digested,* 00/**2396**

Ritchie v. Burns; *sub nom* Burns Trustee v. Burns 2001 S.L.T. 1383; [2001] B.P.I.R. 666; 2000 G.W.D. 22-860, OH . . . . *Digested,* 01/**6714**

Ritchie's Car Hire Ltd v. Bailey (1958) 108 L.J. 348, CC . . . . *Digested,* 58/**2255**: *Considered,* 98/3911

Ritter v. British Steel Plc (Unreported, November 26, 1999), CC (Cardiff) [*Ex rel.* Andrew Arentsen, Barrister, 33 Park Place, Cardiff] . . . . *Digested,* 00/**1736**

Ritter v. Godfrey [1920] 2 K.B. 47, CA . . . . *Applied,* 47-51/2716, 47-51/2816, 47-51/5241, 47-51/7590, 47-51/7722, 00/5672: *Followed,* 99/5437

Rivella (UK) Ltd v. Customs and Excise Commissioners [2000] B.V.C. 2179; [2000] S.T.I. 319, V&DTr

Rivero v. Bundesanstalt fur Arbeit (C211/97) see Gomez Rivero v. Bundesanstalt fur Arbeit (C211/97)

Riverpath Properties Ltd v. Brammall, *Times,* February 16, 2000; *Independent,* March 20, 2000 (C.S.), Ch D . . . . *Digested,* 00/**572**

Rivers v. Cutting [1982] 1 W.L.R. 1146; [1982] 3 All E.R. 69; [1983] R.T.R. 105; [1982] Crim. L.R. 525; (1982) 79 L.S.G. 954; 126 S.J. 362, CA; affirming *Times,* April 22, 1982, CC (Northampton) . . . . *Digested,* 82/**2374**: *Distinguished,* 98/3978: *Followed,* 96/4966

Riverstone Meat Co Pty Ltd *v.* Lancashire Shipping Co Ltd (The Muncaster Castle)
[1961] A.C. 807; [1961] 2 W.L.R. 269; [1961] 1 All E.R. 495; [1961] 1 Lloyd's
Rep. 57; 105 S.J. 148, HL; reversing [1960] 1 Q.B. 536; [1960] 2 W.L.R. 86;
[1960] 1 All E.R. 193; [1959] 2 Lloyd's Rep. 553; 104 S.J. 50, CA; reversing
[1959] 1 Q.B. 74; [1958] 3 W.L.R. 482; [1958] 3 All E.R. 261; [1958] 2 Lloyd's
Rep. 255; 102 S.J. 656, QBD . . . . *Digested,* 61/**8222**:
Applied, 66/11173, 98/4473: *Considered,* 69/1248, 69/1258, 75/3151,
84/3200, 85/3153

Riviera Auto Service Etablissments Dalmasso SA *v.* Commission of the European
Communities (T89/96) [1999] E.C.R. II-93; [1999] 5 C.M.L.R. 31, CFI (3rd
Chamber) . . . . *Digested,* 99/**695**

Rivtow Marine *v.* Washington Iron Works (1973) 40 D.L.R. (3d) 530, Sup Ct (Can);
reversing (1972) 26 D.L.R. (3d) 559 . . . . *Digested,* 74/**2585**:
Applied, 78/706: *Not followed,* 99/3960

Rixon *v.* Chief Constable of Kent; *sub nom* Chief Constable of Kent *v.* Rixon *Times,*
April 11, 2000; *Independent,* May 22, 2000 (C.S.), CA . . . . *Digested,* 00/**4234**

Rizla Ltd's Trade Mark Application [1993] R.P.C. 365, Pat Ct; reversing [1992] F.S.R. 659,
PO . . . . *Digested,* 93/**3145**:
Applied, 00/3692, 01/4043: *Followed,* 97/3884

RJ, Re see Lincolnshire CC *v.* R-J (X Intervening)

RJ (Foster Placement), Re; *sub nom* R-J (Minors) (Fostering: Person Disqualified), Re
[1999] 1 W.L.R. 581; [1999] 1 F.L.R. 605; [1998] 3 F.C.R. 579; [1999] Fam.
Law 19; (1998) 95(39) L.S.G. 34; (1998) 148 N.L.J. 1550; (1998) 142 S.J.L.B.
259; *Times,* October 8, 1998; *Independent,* October 14, 1998, CA; reversing
[1998] 2 F.L.R. 110; [1998] Fam. Law 459, Fam Div . . . . *Digested,* 98/**2476**

RJ (Minors) (Fostering: Wardship), Re [1999] 1 F.L.R. 618; [1999] 3 F.C.R. 646; [1999]
Fam. Law 90, Fam Div . . . . *Digested,* 99/**2348**

RJB Mining (UK) Ltd *v.* National Union of Mineworkers [1997] I.R.L.R. 621, QBD . . . . . *Digested,* 98/**2157**

RJB Mining Plc *v.* Commission of the European Communities (T110/98) (No.1) [1999]
E.C.R. II-2585; [1999] 3 C.M.L.R. 445, CFI (1st Chamber) . . . . *Digested,* 00/**726**

RJB Mining Plc *v.* Commission of the European Communities (T156/98) [2001] E.C.R.
II-337; [2001] 3 C.M.L.R. 15, CFI (1st Chamber) . . . . *Digested,* 01/**788**

RJR-MacDonald Inc *v.* Attorney General of Canada [1995] 3 S.C.R. 199, Sup Ct (Can) . *Applied,* 98/3085,
00/3191

RJW Sutherland & Co *v.* Owners of the SS Thoger see Japy Freres & Co *v.* RWJ
Sutherland & Co

RL *v.* Gloucestershire CC see S *v.* Gloucestershire CC

RL *v.* Tower Hamlets LBC see S *v.* Gloucestershire CC

RM (A Person under Disability) *v.* Richards (1999) 99(1) Q.R. 6, CC (Cardiff) . . . . *Digested,* 98/**1578**

RM Broudie & Co *v.* Lord Chancellor [2000] 2 Costs L.R. 285; *Times,* July 4, 2000,
QBD . . . . *Digested,* 00/**3961**

RM Turton & Co Ltd (In Liquidation) *v.* Kerslake & Partners [2000] Lloyd's Rep. P.N.
967, CA (NZ) . . . . *Digested,* 01/**4469**

RMC Aggregates (Eastern Counties) Ltd *v.* Secretary of State for Transport, Local
Government and the Regions see RMC Eastern Aggregates (Eastern Counties)
Ltd *v.* Secretary of State for Transport, Local Government and the Regions

RMC Eastern Aggregates (Eastern Counties) Ltd *v.* Secretary of State for Transport,
Local Government and the Regions; *sub nom* RMC Aggregates (Eastern
Counties) Ltd *v.* Secretary of State for Transport, Local Government and the
Regions [2001] EWHC Admin 1006; [2001] 50 E.G.C.S. 90, QBD (Admin Ct)

RMD *v.* Switzerland (1999) 28 E.H.R.R. 224, ECHR . . . . *Digested,* 99/**3135**

RMR Housing Society *v.* Combs [1951] 1 K.B. 486; [1951] 1 All E.R. 16; [1951] 1 T.L.R.
1; 95 S.J. 44, CA . . . . *Digested,* 47-51/**8548**:
Approved, 00/3921

RNIB Properties Ltd *v.* Customs and Excise Commissioners [1999] B.V.C. 2064, V&DTr . *Digested,* 99/**5029**

Roach *v.* CSB (Moulds) Ltd [1991] I.C.R. 349; [1991] I.R.L.R. 200, EAT . . . . *Digested,* 92/**1913**:
Disapproved, 99/6047: *Doubted,* 98/2230

Roache *v.* News Group Newspapers Ltd [1998] E.M.L.R. 161; *Times,* November 23,
1992; *Independent,* December 31, 1992, CA . . . . *Digested,* 92/**3437**:
Considered, 98/442

Road Tech Computer Systems Ltd *v.* Unison Software (UK) Ltd [1996] F.S.R. 805;
(1996) 19(9) I.P.D. 19086, Ch D . . . . *Digested,* 97/**4898**:
Distinguished, 98/3426

ROAD TRAIN/Identification of real opponent (T798/93) [1998] E.P.O.R. 1, EPO (Technical
Bd App)

Roadside (Garages) Ltd *v.* Roadside Motors (Coleraine) Ltd [1999] N.I. 195, Ch D (NI) . *Digested,* 00/**5608**

Roadtech Computer Systems Ltd *v.* Mandata (Management and Data Services) Ltd
[2000] E.T.M.R. 970; [2001] E.B.L.R. 17, Ch D . . . . *Digested,* 01/**4037**

Roar Marine Ltd *v.* Bimeh Iran Insurance Co (The Daylam) [1998] 1 Lloyd's Rep. 423,
QBD (Comm Ct) . . . . *Digested,* 98/**3389**

Robb *v.* Hammersmith and Fulham LBC [1991] I.C.R. 514; [1991] I.R.L.R. 72, QBD . . . . *Digested,* 91/**1610**:
Considered, 01/2244

Robert Cort & Son Ltd v. Charman [1981] I.C.R. 816; [1981] I.R.L.R. 437, EAT . . . . . .   *Digested,* 82/**1099**:
     Applied, 82/1132: *Considered,* 82/1101, 87/1381, 00/2131:
     Not applied, 99/2145

Robert Fearon & Co Ltd v. Irish Land Commission (C182/83) [1984] E.C.R. 3677;
   [1985] 2 C.M.L.R. 228, ECJ . . . .   *Digested,* 85/**1402**:
     Applied, 00/2383

Robert Irving & Burns v. Stone [1997] C.L.C. 1593; [1998] Lloyd's Rep. I.R. 258;
   (1997) 94(41) L.S.G. 28; *Times,* October 30, 1997, CA; affirming [1997] C.L.C.
   1316, QBD (Comm Ct) . . . .   *Digested,* 97/**3143**

Robert's Golden Cod Fish Bar v. Customs and Excise Commissioners [1996] V. & D.R.
   423 (Note), V&DTr . . . .   *Digested,* 98/**4884**

ROBERTET/Deodorant compositions (T892/94) [1999] E.P.O.R. 516, EPO (Technical Bd
   App) . . . .   *Digested,* 00/**3611**

Roberts v. Bettany [2001] EWCA Civ 109; [2001] N.P.C. 45, CA

Roberts v. Chief Constable of Cheshire; *sub nom* Roberts v. Jones (Chief Constable of
   Cheshire) [1999] 1 W.L.R. 662; [1999] 2 All E.R. 326; [1999] 2 Cr. App. R.
   243; (1999) 96(7) L.S.G. 36; (1999) 149 N.L.J. 165; *Times,* January 27, 1999,
   CA . . . .   *Digested,* 99/**1038**

Roberts v. Commission of the European Communities (T25/99) [2001] E.C.R. II-1881;
   [2001] 5 C.M.L.R. 21, CFI (3rd Chamber)

Roberts v. Coverite (Asphalters) Ltd see Ridehalgh v. Horsefield

Roberts v. Customs and Excise Commissioners [1999] B.V.C. 2075, V&DTr

Roberts v. Greene King Plc [1998] Eu. L.R. 516, CC (Manchester) . . . .   *Digested,* 99/**685**

Roberts v. Johnstone [1989] Q.B. 878; [1988] 3 W.L.R. 1247; (1989) 86(5) L.S.G.
   44; (1989) 132 S.J. 1672; *Times,* April 15, 1988, CA . . . .   *Digested,* 89/**1202**:
     Applied, 94/1542, 99/1415, 00/1515, 01/1554: *Considered,* 89/1185,
     91/4896: *Referred to,* 90/1578

Roberts v. Jones (Chief Constable of Cheshire) see Roberts v. Chief Constable of
   Cheshire

Roberts v. Luton & Dunstable Hospital NHS Trust (Unreported, February 11, 2000),
   QBD [*Ex rel.* Capsticks Solicitors, 77-83 Upper Richmond Road, London] . . . . .   *Digested,* 00/**610**

Roberts v. Price [2000] C.P. Rep. 52, CA . . . .   *Digested,* 00/**619**

Roberts v. Roberts see Pettifor's Will Trusts, Re

Roberts v. Scarth (2001) 81 P. & C.R. D8, CA

Roberts v. Winbow [1999] P.I.Q.R. P77; [1999] Lloyd's Rep. Med. 31; (1999) 49
   B.M.L.R. 134; (1999) 96(4) L.S.G. 39; (1999) 143 S.J.L.B. 21; *Times,* January
   12, 1999, CA . . . .   *Digested,* 99/**468**

Roberts Petroleum Ltd v. Bernard Kenny Ltd (In Liquidation) [1983] 2 A.C. 192; [1983]
   2 W.L.R. 305; [1983] 1 All E.R. 564; [1983] Com. L.R. 564; (1983) 127 S.J.
   138, HL; reversing [1982] 1 W.L.R. 301; [1982] 1 All E.R. 685, CA . . . .   *Digested,* 83/**204**:
     Applied, 84/1691: *Considered,* 97/3002, 99/3305: *Referred to,* 84/1637,
     85/1626

Robertson v. Blackstone Franks Investment Management Ltd see Blackstone Franks
   Investment Management Ltd v. Robertson

Robertson v. Forth Road Bridge Joint Board (No.2) 1995 S.C. 364; 1996 S.L.T. 263;
   1995 S.C.L.R. 466; [1995] I.R.L.R. 251; *Times,* April 13, 1995; Scotsman, March
   8, 1995, 1 Div; affirming 1994 S.L.T. 568, OH . . . .   *Digested,* 95/**6157**:
     Applied, 00/6582: *Distinguished,* 01/5352

Robertson (Judicial Factor) v. Robertson see Thurso Building Society's Judicial Factor
   v. Robertson

Robertson Research International Ltd v. ABG Exploration BV [1999] C.P.L.R. 756;
   Times, November 3, 1999 ; *Independent,* October 29, 1999, QBD . . . .   *Digested,* 99/**387**

Robin Ellis Ltd v. Malwright Ltd [1999] C.P.L.R. 286; [1999] B.L.R. 81; (1999) 1
   T.C.L.R. 249; 68 Con. L.R. 121; (1999) 15 Const. L.J. 141, QBD (T&CC) . . . . . .   *Digested,* 99/**309**

Robins v. Goddard [1905] 1 K.B. 294, CA; reversing [1904] 2 Ch. 261, Ch D . . . .   *Considered,* 65/347,
     98/5055

Robins v. United Kingdom (1998) 26 E.H.R.R. 527; *Times,* October 24, 1997, ECHR . . . .   *Digested,* 97/**2806**

Robinson (Deceased), Re; *sub nom* Robinson (Anne) v. Robinson (Angela) [2001]
   W.T.L.R. 267, Ch D . . . .   *Digested,* 01/**5160**

Robinson v. Adair [1995] N.P.C. 30; *Times,* March 2, 1995, QBD . . . .   *Digested,* 95/**4974**:
     Applied, 98/2875

Robinson v. Brent LBC (1999) 31 H.L.R. 1015, CA . . . .   *Digested,* 00/**3139**

Robinson v. Burgess (Unreported, July 10, 2001), CC (Worksop) [*Ex rel.* Sean
   McGovern, Barrister, New Walk Chambers, 27 New Walk, Leicester] . . . .   *Digested,* 01/**521**

Robinson v. Customs and Excise Commissioners, *Times,* April 28, 2000, QBD . . . .   *Digested,* 00/**888**

Robinson v. Harman [1843-60] All E.R. Rep. 383; (1848) 1 Ex. 850, Ex Ct. . . . .   *Applied,* 92/1513,
     93/1368, 00/2131: *Considered,* 96/4483

Robinson v. Post Office [2000] I.R.L.R. 804, EAT . . . .   *Digested,* 00/**2128**

Robinson v. Queen, The see Dunkley v. Queen, The

Robinson (Anne) v. Robinson (Angela) see Robinson (Deceased), Re

Robinson v. Salford HA [1992] 3 Med. L.R. 270, QBD . . . .   *Digested,* 92/**1544**:
     Considered, 00/1464

Robinson v. Unicos Property Corp [1962] 1 W.L.R. 520; [1962] 2 All E.R. 24; 106 S.J. 193, CA . . . . *Digested*, 62 /**1766**:
Applied, 01/414: *Considered*, 69/2095
Robinson Group of Companies Ltd v. Customs and Excise Commissioners [1999] B.V.C. 2286, V&DTr
Robinson Jarvis & Rolf (A Firm) v. Cave see Cave v. Robinson Jarvis & Rolf (A Firm)
Robson v. Inland Revenue Commissioners [1998] I.R.L.R. 186, EAT . . . . *Digested*, 98/**2184**
Robson v. Safeway Plc (Unreported, June 18, 1998), CC (Newcastle) [*Ex rel.* Browell Smith & Goodyear Solicitors, Transport House, John Dobson Street, Newcastle upon Tyne] . . . . *Digested*, 98/**1653**
Roche v. Kwik Save Stores Ltd (Unreported, April 18, 2001), CC (Manchester) [*Ex rel.* Hill Dickinson, Solicitors, Pearl Assurance House, Derby Square, Liverpool] . . . . *Digested*, 01/**652**
Rochester City Council v. Kent CC; *sub nom* Rochester upon Medway City Council v. Kent CC [1998] E.G.C.S. 24; (1998) 95(15) L.S.G. 32; (1998) 142 S.J.L.B. 102; *Times*, March 5, 1998, QBD . . . . *Digested*, 98/**3845**
Rochester upon Medway City Council v. Kent CC see Rochester City Council v. Kent CC
Rochford v. Jones (Unreported, February 19, 1997), CC (Oldham) [*Ex rel.* Lace Mawer, Solicitors] . . . . *Digested*, 97/**724**:
Considered, 98/455: *Referred to*, 98/596, 99/403
Rochford DC v. McCarthy & Stone (Developments) Ltd (1999) 14 P.A.D. 11, Planning Inspector
Rock-It Cargo Ltd v. Green [1997] I.R.L.R. 581, EAT . . . . *Digested*, 98/**2204**
Rocksteady Services Ltd, Re; *sub nom* Secretary of State for Trade and Industry v. Staton [2001] C.P. Rep. 1; [2001] B.C.C. 467, CA; affirming [2001] 1 B.C.L.C. 84, Ch D (Companies Ct) . . . . *Digested*, 00/**655**
Rocky Mountain Traders Ltd v. Fellowes Manufacturing (UK) Ltd see Rocky Mountain Traders Ltd v. Hewlett Packard GmbH
Rocky Mountain Traders Ltd v. Hewlett Packard GmbH; Rocky Mountain Traders Ltd v. Fellowes Manufacturing (UK) Ltd; A3/1999/1215, CA; affirming [2000] F.S.R. 411; (2000) 23(1) I.P.D. 23002, Pat Ct . . . . *Digested*, 00/**3680**
Rodgers v. Bush (Unreported, October 30, 1997), CC (Nottingham) [*Ex rel.* Barratt, Goff & Tomlinson Solicitors, The Old Dairy, 67a Melton Road, West Bridgford, Nottingham] . . . . *Digested*, 98/**352**
Rodriguez v. Attorney General of Canada (1999) 50 B.M.L.R. 1, Sup Ct (Can)
Rodriguez v. Instituto Nacional de la Seguridad Social (INSS) (C153/97) [1998] E.C.R. I-8645; [2001] 1 C.M.L.R. 42, ECJ (5th Chamber) . . . . *Digested*, 01/**5076**
Rodriguez v. Landesversicherungsanstalt Rheinprovinz (C113/96) [1998] E.C.R. I-2461; [1999] 1 C.M.L.R. 129, ECJ (5th Chamber) . . . . *Digested*, 99/**4509**
Rodway v. Landy [2001] EWCA Civ 471; [2001] Ch. 703; [2001] 2 W.L.R. 1775; [2001] 44 E.G. 151; [2001] W.T.L.R. 755; (2001) 98(22) L.S.G. 36; (2001) 145 S.J.L.B. 116; *Times*, April 18, 2001, CA. . . . . *Digested*, 01/**4562**
Roe v. Ministry of Health; Woolley v. Ministry of Health [1954] 2 Q.B. 66; [1954] 2 W.L.R. 915; [1954] 2 All E.R. 131; 96 S.J. 319, CA; affirming [1954] 1 W.L.R. 128; 98 S.J. 30, QBD. . . . . *Digested*, 54/**2300**:
Applied, 80/1897, 81/1844: *Considered*, 65/2686, 81/1845: *Distinguished*, 98/3976
Roe v. Novak (1999) 96(3) L.S.G. 32; *Times*, December 15, 1998, CA. . . . . *Digested*, 99/**556**
Roebuck v. Mungovin [1994] 2 A.C. 224; [1994] 2 W.L.R. 290; [1994] 1 All E.R. 568; [1994] 1 Lloyd's Rep. 481; [1994] P.I.Q.R. P209; (1994) 91(13) L.S.G. 36; (1994) 144 N.L.J. 197; (1994) 138 S.J.L.B. 59; [1994] J.P.I.L. 164; *Times*, February 4, 1994; *Independent*, February 8, 1994, HL; reversing [1993] P.I.Q.R. P444; *Independent*, April 26, 1993 (C.S.), CA. . . . . *Digested*, 94/**3790**:
Applied, 98/607: *Distinguished*, 97/758: *Followed*, 96/898, 99/556: *Referred to*, 96/899, 97/763
Roedel v. Vokins Holdings Ltd (Unreported, October 14, 1997), CC (Newbury) [*Ex rel.* Pitman & Bazett, Solicitors, 34 London Road, Newbury] . . . . *Digested*, 98/**2245**
Roffey v. Care First Partnership Ltd see Care First Partnership Ltd v. Roffey
Rogan v. Woodfield Building Services Ltd (1995) 27 H.L.R. 78; [1995] 1 E.G.L.R. 72; [1995] 20 E.G. 132; [1994] E.G.C.S. 145; *Times*, August 10, 1994, CA . . . . *Digested*, 95/**3003**:
Considered, 95/3002: *Followed*, 99/3652
Roger v. Costa, CC (Watford) [*Ex rel.* Robert Kay, Barrister, Mitre Court Chambers, 199 The Strand, London]. . . . . *Digested*, 01/**60**
Roger Bullivant Ltd v. Ellis [1987] I.C.R. 464; [1987] I.R.L.R. 491; [1987] F.S.R. 172, CA . . . . *Digested*, 87/**1294**:
Applied, 00/734: *Considered*, 92/1908: *Distinguished*, 96/4556: *Referred to*, 87/1295, 88/1245, 89/1408, 99/2004
Rogers v. Bromley LBC (Unreported, April 16, 1999), CC (Bromley) [*Ex rel.* Daniel Barnett, Barrister, 2 Grays Inn Square, London] . . . . *Digested*, 99/**1570**
Rogers v. Islington LBC see Islington LBC v. Rogers
Rogers v. Lambeth LBC; *sub nom* Lambeth LBC v. Rogers (2000) 32 H.L.R. 361; [2000] B.L.G.R. 191; [2000] L. & T.R. 319; [2000] 1 E.G.L.R. 28; [2000] 03 E.G. 127; [1999] E.G.C.S. 128; (1999) 96(45) L.S.G. 33; [1999] N.P.C. 130; *Times*, November 10, 1999, CA. . . . . *Digested*, 99/**3739**

Rogers v. Parish (Scarborough) Ltd [1987] Q.B. 933; [1987] 2 W.L.R. 353; [1987] 2 All E.R. 232; [1987] R.T.R. 312; (1987) 6 Tr. L.R. 55; (1987) 84 L.S.G. 905; (1987) 131 S.J. 223, CA. . . . . *Digested*, 87/**3333**:
Applied, 87/3338, 88/3167, 98/4384: *Considered*, 88/3169, 89/3326
Rogers v. Rhys Evans (A Firm) [2000] C.P.L.R. 400, CA . . . . *Digested*, 00/**616**
Rogers v. Secretary of State for the Home Department; R. v. Lewes Justices Ex p. Secretary of State for the Home Department; R. v. Lewes Justices Ex p. Gaming Board for Great Britain [1973] A.C. 388; [1972] 3 W.L.R. 279; [1972] 2 All E.R. 1057; 116 S.J. 696, HL; affirming [1972] 1 Q.B. 232; [1971] 2 W.L.R. 1466; [1971] 2 All E.R. 1126; 115 S.J. 306, QBD . . . . *Digested*, 72/**1610**:
Applied, 75/2714, 77/3, 77/2324, 78/2324, 80/1247, 84/1373, 85/1326, 85/1998: *Considered*, 80/1256, 80/2131, 81/2142, 84/2621, 86/1519, 87/1688, 00/5392: *Distinguished*, 87/690, 88/756: *Followed*, 76/1203
Rogers v. Whitaker [1993] 4 Med. L.R. 79; (1992) 175 C.L.R. 479; [1992] A.L.M.D. 6993, HC (Aus) . . . . *Digested*, 93/**2703**:
Applied, 99/3987: *Considered*, 96/2977
Rohan Investments Ltd v. Cunningham [1999] Lloyd's Rep. I.R. 190; [1998] N.P.C. 14, CA . . . . *Digested*, 00/**3519**
Rohm & Haas Co v. Collag Ltd (No.1) [2001] EWCA Civ 1589, CA; affirming [2001] F.S.R. 28; (2001) 24(1) I.P.D. 11, Pat Ct. . . . . *Digested*, 01/**3958**
ROHM & HAAS/Power to examine (G09/91, G10/91) [1993] E.P.O.R. 485, EPO (Enlarged Bd App) . . . . *Applied*, 01/3892
ROHM/Withdrawal of a European patent application (J11/80) [1979-85] E.P.O.R. A48; [1981] O.J. E.P.O. 141, EPO (Legal Bd App) . . . . *Distinguished*, 99/3469
Roho Inc's Trade Mark Application (Nos.1577271 and 1577275) (1998) 21 (10) I.P.D. 21113, TMR
Roker House Investments Ltd v. Saunders [1997] E.G.C.S. 137, Ch D . . . . *Digested*, 98/**3959**
Roker International Properties Inc v. Couvaras [2000] 2 F.L.R. 976; [2001] 1 F.C.R. 320; [2001] Fam. Law 20, Fam Div . . . . *Digested*, 01/**2638**
Rolfe v. Midland Bank Plc see Alexander v. Midland Bank Plc
Rolfe v. Transworld Marine Agency Co NV [2000] B.P.I.R. 822, Fed Ct (Aus) (Sgl judge) . . . . *Digested*, 01/**3712**
Rolled Steel Products (Holdings) Ltd v. British Steel Corp [1986] Ch. 246; [1985] 2 W.L.R. 908; [1985] 3 All E.R. 52, CA; affirming [1982] Ch. 478; [1982] 3 W.L.R. 715; [1982] 3 All E.R. 1057, Ch D . . . . *Digested*, 85/**306**:
Applied, 95/2589, 00/2324: *Considered*, 87/321, 90/549
Rollinson v. Kimberley Clark Ltd see Rollinson v. Kimberly Clark Ltd
Rollinson v. Kimberly Clark Ltd; *sub nom* Rollinson v. Kimberley Clark Ltd [2000] C.P. Rep. 85; [1999] C.P.L.R. 581; *Times*, June 22, 1999 ; *Independent*, July 5, 1999 (C.S.), CA . . . . *Digested*, 99/**353**
Rolls Royce Ltd v. Walpole [1980] I.R.L.R. 343, EAT . . . . *Digested*, 80/**1025**:
Considered, 00/2239
Rolls Royce Plc v. Heavylift Volga Dnepr Ltd [2000] 1 All E.R. (Comm) 796; [2000] 1 Lloyd's Rep. 653; [2000] C.L.C. 1120; (2000) 97(17) L.S.G. 32; (2000) 144 S.J.L.B. 181; *Times*, April 26, 2000, QBD (Comm Ct) . . . . *Digested*, 00/**5148**
ROLLS ROYCE/Aircraft engine management system (T99/98) [2000] E.P.O.R. 116, EPO (Technical Bd App) . . . . *Digested*, 00/**3616**
Romascan v. Gurney (Unreported, January 10, 2000), MCLC [*Ex rel.* Tim Petts, Barrister, 12 King's Bench Walk, London] . . . . *Digested*, 00/**406**
Romeike & Curtice Ltd v. Newspaper Licensing Agency Ltd [1999] E.M.L.R. 142; (1998) 21 (10) I.P.D. 2111, Copyright Tr . . . . *Digested*, 99/**3444**
Romulus Trading Co Ltd v. Trustees of Henry Smith's Charity (No.1) (1990) 60 P. & C.R. 62, CA . . . . *Digested*, 90/**2777.a**:
Distinguished, 98/3609
Ron Jones (Burton on Trent) Ltd v. Hall see Jones v. Hall
Rondel v. W see Rondel v. Worsley
Rondel v. Worsley; *sub nom* Rondel v. W [1969] 1 A.C. 191; [1967] 3 W.L.R. 1666; [1967] 3 All E.R. 993; 111 S.J. 927; *Times*, November 23, 1967, HL; affirming [1967] 1 Q.B. 443; [1966] 3 W.L.R. 950; [1966] 3 All E.R. 657; 110 S.J. 810, CA; affirming [1966] 2 W.L.R. 300; [1966] 1 All E.R. 467; 110 S.J. 90; *Times*, December 22, 1965; *Guardian*, December 22, 1965, QBD . . . . *Digested*, 68/**3054**:
Applied, 77/2283: *Considered*, 74/2974, 78/2323, 79/2110, 86/2604, 87/2580, 87/3547, 88/3376, 94/3623, 99/4021: *Disapproved*, 00/4269: *Distinguished*, 68/3954, 87/2582: *Followed*, 97/3815: *Subsequent proceedings*, 67/3187
Roney v. Matthews (1975) 61 Cr. App. R. 195; [1975] R.T.R. 273; [1975] Crim. L.R. 394; (1975) 119 S.J. 613, QBD . . . . *Digested*, 75/**2950**:
Applied, 75/2942, 00/939: *Considered*, 81/2332, 82/2736
Ronfeldt v. Bundesversicherungsanstalt fur Angestellte (C227/89) [1991] E.C.R. I-323; [1993] 1 C.M.L.R. 73, ECJ (6th Chamber) . . . . *Followed*, 01/5076
Roodhill v. Medway General see First Roodhill Leasing Ltd v. Gillingham Operating Co
Rooker v. Metro Cammell Ltd (Unreported, December 5, 1997), QBD [*Ex rel.* Thompsons, Solicitors, The MacLaren Building, 35 Dale End, Birmingham] . . . . *Digested*, 98/**1622**

Rookery Investment Co *v.* Yelding [2001] N.P.C. 18, Ch D
Rookes *v.* Barnard (No.1) [1964] A.C. 1129; [1964] 2 W.L.R. 269; [1964] 1 All E.R.
367; [1964] 1 Lloyd's Rep. 28; 108 S.J. 93, HL; reversing [1963] 1 Q.B. 623;
[1962] 3 W.L.R. 260; [1962] 2 All E.R. 579; 106 S.J. 371, CA; reversing [1961]
3 W.L.R. 438; [1961] 2 All E.R. 825; 105 S.J. 530, QBD . . . . *Digested*, 64/**3703**:
Applied, 64/2120, 65/1022, 65/2254, 65/2255, 65/2260, 67/2275, 67/2276,
67/3981, 70/1143, 71/9438, 77/336, 77/1768, 78/284, 78/1822, 79/399,
84/1099, 87/1144, 94/5067, 97/3798, 98/5150, 00/5118, 01/1512:
Considered, 65/834, 65/3967, 67/3276, 69/295, 70/2739, 72/2705, 75/779,
88/1295, 93/1392, 93/1607, 96/2606, 96/3821, 97/2754:
Distinguished, 64/3702, 68/3954, 74/3867, 92/1526, 93/1598:
Explained, 79/198: *Followed*, 72/2745, 97/3286, 00/5112:
Not followed, 71/6742: *Subsequent proceedings*, 65/3115
Rooney (A Patient, by his Next Friend) *v.* Automotive Financial Group Ltd (t/a AFG
Salford) (Unreported, July 8, 1998), QBD [*Ex rel.* Gorna & Co Solicitors, Virginia
House, Cheapside, King Street, Manchester] . . . . *Digested*, 98/**605**
Rooney *v.* Black Horse Financial Services Group Ltd see Rooney *v.* Cardona (No.1)
Rooney *v.* Black Horse Life Assurance Co Ltd see Rooney *v.* Cardona (No.1)
Rooney *v.* Cardona (No.1); Rooney *v.* Black Horse Life Assurance Co Ltd; Rooney *v.*
Black Horse Financial Services Group Ltd; Rooney *v.* Lloyds Bank Plc [1999] 1
W.L.R. 1388; [1999] 1 F.L.R. 1236; [1999] B.P.I.R. 291; [1999] Fam. Law 542;
Times, March 4, 1999, CA . . . . *Digested*, 99/**3241**
Rooney *v.* Cardona (No.2) [1999] 2 F.L.R. 1148; [1999] B.P.I.R. 954; *Times*, May 24,
1999, Ch D . . . . *Digested*, 99/**3331**
Rooney *v.* Das [1999] B.P.I.R. 404, Ch D . . . . *Digested*, 99/**3319**
Rooney *v.* Lloyds Bank Plc see Rooney *v.* Cardona (No.1)
Rooney *v.* Palmer (Unreported, November 19, 1998), CC (Swindon) [*Ex rel.* Bower &
Bailey Solicitors, Cambridge House, 4 College Court, Regent Circus, Swindon,
Wiltshire] . . . . *Digested*, 99/**1473**
Rooney's Application, Re [1995] N.I. 398, CA (NI) *Applied*, 01/**5652**
Ropac Ltd *v.* Inntrepreneur Pub Co (CPC) Ltd [2001] C.P. Rep. 31; [2001] L. & T.R.
10; (2000) 97(26) L.S.G. 36; *Times*, June 21, 2000, Ch D . . . . *Digested*, 00/**629**:
Applied, 01/4161
Ropaigealach *v.* Allied Irish Bank Plc [2001] EWCA Civ 1790; [2001] 47 E.G.C.S. 146,
CA
Ropaigealach *v.* Barclays Bank Plc [2000] Q.B. 263; [1999] 3 W.L.R. 17; [1999] 4 All
E.R. 235; (2000) 32 H.L.R. 234; [1998] E.G.C.S. 189; (1999) 96(6) L.S.G. 35;
(1999) 149 N.L.J. 121; [1998] N.P.C. 167; (1999) 77 P. & C.R. D32; *Times*,
January 6, 1999; *Independent*, January 15, 1999, CA. . . . . *Digested*, 99/**4386**
Ropner *v.* Ropner see Harrison's Settlement, Re
Ropner's Settlement, Re see Harrison's Settlement, Re
Roque *v.* Lieutenant Governor of Jersey (C171/96) [1998] E.C.R. I-4607; [1998] 3
C.M.L.R. 143, ECJ
Roquette Freres SA *v.* Directeur General de la Concurrence [2001] E.C.C. 1, Cass (F)
Rosario, The (1876-77) L.R. 2 P.D. 41; (1876) 3 Asp. 334, PDAD . . . . *Considered*, 01/4935
Rose *v.* Bouchet 2000 S.L.T. (Sh Ct) 170; 1999 S.C.L.R. 1004; [1999] I.R.L.R. 463;
2001 Hous. L.R. 2; 1999 G.W.D. 20-958, Sh Pr. . . . . *Digested*, 99/**6279**
Rose *v.* McGivern [1998] 2 B.C.L.C. 593, Ch D . . . . *Digested*, 99/**633**
Rose *v.* Plenty; *sub nom* Rose *v.* Plenty and Cooperative Retail Services [1976] 1
W.L.R. 141; [1976] 1 All E.R. 97; [1976] 1 Lloyd's Rep. 263; [1975] I.C.R. 430;
[1976] I.R.L.R. 60; (1976) 18 Man. Law 148; 119 S.J. 592; *Times*, July 10, 1975,
CA . . . . *Digested*, 76/**1876**:
Applied, 84/2344: *Considered*, 01/5359
Rose *v.* Plenty and Cooperative Retail Services see Rose *v.* Plenty
Rose *v.* R. 6 B.H.R.C. 206, Sup Ct (Can) . . . . *Digested*, 99/**3138**
Rose *v.* Stavrou [2000] L. & T.R. 133; (1999) 96(25) L.S.G. 29; *Times*, June 23, 1999
; *Independent*, June 28, 1999 (C.S.), Ch D . . . . *Digested*, 99/**3670**
Rosedale Associated Manufacturers Ltd *v.* Carlton Tyre Saving Co Ltd [1960] R.P.C. 59,
CA; affirming [1959] R.P.C. 189, Ch D . . . . *Digested*, 60/**2348**:
Distinguished, 68/2921: *Referred to*, 99/3507
Rosedale (JW) Investments Ltd *v.* British Steel Plc [2001] Pens. L.R. 1, CA. . . . . *Digested*, 01/**959**
Rosen *v.* Camden Charities Trustees see Rosen *v.* Campden Charities Trustees
Rosen *v.* Campden Charities Trustees; *sub nom* Rosen *v.* Camden Charities Trustees
[2001] 3 W.L.R. 1470; [2001] 2 All E.R. 399; [2001] L. & T.R. 24; [2001] 1
E.G.L.R. 59; [2001] 10 E.G. 159; [2000] E.G.C.S. 146; (2001) 98(6) L.S.G. 45;
(2001) 81 P. & C.R. D23; *Times*, December 13, 2000; *Independent*, December
5, 2000, CA; affirming (2000) 79 P. & C.R. 33; [1999] 2 E.G.L.R. 213, Lands
Tr . . . . *Digested*, 01/**4188**
Rosenbluth International Inc's Trade Mark Application [2000] E.T.M.R. 934, OHIM (2nd Bd
App). . . . . *Digested*, 01/**4051**
ROSENLAW/Shrink Wrapping (T589/95) [2001] E.P.O.R. 45, EPO (Technical Bd App) *Digested*, 01/**3922**
Rosewood Trust Ltd *v.* Schmidt; *sub nom* Angora Trust, Re; Everest Trust, Re [2001]
W.T.L.R. 1081; (2000-01) 3 I.T.E.L.R. 734, HC (IoM) . . . . *Digested*, 01/**5506**

Rosgill Group Ltd v. Customs and Excise Commissioners [1997] 3 All E.R. 1012; [1997]
S.T.C. 811; [1997] B.T.C. 5261; [1997] B.V.C. 388; *Times*, April 30, 1997, CA . . . . *Digested*, 97/**4975**:
Applied, 99/6472: *Considered*, 01/5556: *Followed*, 00/5345
Rosingdale, Re (Unreported, December 18, 1998), CICB (York) [*Ex rel*. Simon Anderson,
Barrister, Broadway House Chambers, Broadway House, 9 Bank Street,
Bradford, West Yorkshire] . . . . *Digested*, 99/**1457**
Roskowski v. Special Adjudicator see R. (on the application of Roszkowski) v. Special
Adjudicator
Rosler v. Rottwinkel (C241/83) [1986] Q.B. 33; [1985] 3 W.L.R. 898; [1985] E.C.R.
99; [1985] 1 C.M.L.R. 806; (1985) 82 L.S.G. 3531; (1985) 129 S.J. 794, ECJ
(4th Chamber) . . . . *Digested*, 85/**1357**:
Applied, 96/1106, 96/2912: *Considered*, 00/773
Ross (A Bankrupt) (No.1), Re; *sub nom* Ross v. Jeffs [1998] B.C.C. 29; [1998] 1
B.C.L.C. 56; [1997] B.P.I.R. 735, CA . . . . *Digested*, 97/**3036**
Ross (A Bankrupt) (No.2), Re; *sub nom* Ross v. Stonewood Securities Ltd [2000]
B.P.I.R. 636; (2000) 97(21) L.S.G. 40; *Times*, May 10, 2000, CA . . . . *Digested*, 00/**3435**
Ross v. Canada 10 B.H.R.C. 219, UN HRC . . . . *Digested*, 01/**3484**
Ross v. Jeffs see Ross (A Bankrupt) (No.1), Re
Ross v. Johnston R/35/1998, Lands Tr (NI) . . . . *Digested*, 00/**5613**
Ross v. Owners of the Bowbelle; East Coast Aggregates Ltd v. Para-Pagan; Ross v.
Owners of the Marchioness [1997] 1 W.L.R. 1159; [1997] 2 Lloyd's Rep. 191;
[1998] 1 Costs L.R. 32; *Times*, April 8, 1997, CA; reversing [1997] 1 Costs L.R.
90, QBD . . . . *Digested*, 97/**541**
Ross v. Owners of the Marchioness see Ross v. Owners of the Bowbelle
Ross v. Stonewood Securities Ltd see Ross (A Bankrupt) (No.2), Re
Ross v. Telford [1997] B.C.C. 945; [1998] 1 B.C.L.C. 82; (1997) 94(28) L.S.G. 26;
Times, July 4, 1997, CA . . . . *Digested*, 97/**848**
Ross v. Wood (Unreported, May 22, 2001), CC (Lancaster) [*Ex rel*. Tom Nossiter,
Barrister, Park Lane Chambers, 19 Westgate, Leeds] . . . . *Digested*, 01/**1784**
Ross Harper & Murphy v. Banks 2000 S.C. 500; 2000 S.L.T. 699; 2000 S.C.L.R. 736;
[2000] Lloyd's Rep. P.N. 631; [2000] P.N.L.R. 631; *Times*, May 30, 2000, OH . . *Digested*, 00/**6603**
Rossendale BC v. Stateley Developments Ltd (1999) 14 P.A.D. 149, Planning Inspector
Rossendale BC v. Waldo (2001) 16 P.A.D. 70, Planning Inspector
Rosser v. Lindsay, *Times*, February 25, 1999, CA . . . . *Digested*, 99/**3958**
Rossi, Re see R. v. London County Quarter Sessions Appeals Committee Ex p. Rossi
Rossington Hall Investments Ltd v. Doncaster MBC [2001] P.L.C.R. 15, CA; reversing
(2000) 79 P. & C.R. 366; [2000] P.L.C.R. 222, QBD . . . . *Digested*, 00/**4486**
Rossiter v. Pendragon Plc; *sub nom* Rossiter v. Pengragon Plc; Crosby-Clarke v. Air
Foyle Ltd; A1/2001/0593, A1/2001/2236, CA; reversing [2001] I.C.R. 1265;
[2001] I.R.L.R. 256; [2001] Emp. L.R. 571, EAT . . . . *Digested*, 01/**2331**
Rossiter v. Pengragon Plc see Rossiter v. Pendragon Plc
Rossmeier v. Mounthooly Transport 2000 S.L.T. 208; [2000] I.L.Pr. 697; 1999 G.W.D.
35-1661; *Times*, February 7, 2000, 1 Div; reversing 1999 S.C.L.R. 236; 1999
G.W.D. 2-72, Sh Pr. . . . . *Digested*, 00/**5930**
Rossminster and Tucker, Re see R. v. Inland Revenue Commissioners Ex p. Rossminster
Ltd
Rotadata Ltd, Re [2000] B.C.C. 686; [2000] 1 B.C.L.C. 122, Ch D (Companies Ct) . . . *Digested*, 00/**692**
Rotaru v. Romania 8 B.H.R.C. 449, ECHR . . . . *Digested*, 00/**3248**
Rother DC v. Vidal (1999) 14 P.A.D. 102, Planning Inspector
Rotherham MBC v. Frank Haslam Milan & Co Ltd [1996] C.L.C. 1378; 78 B.L.R. 1; 59
Con. L.R. 33; (1996) 12 Const. L.J. 333; [1996] E.G.C.S. 59, CA . . . . *Digested*, 96/**4535**
Rotherwick's Executors v. Oxfordshire CC [2000] 2 E.G.L.R. 84, Lands Tr . . . . *Digested*, 01/**4851**
Rothmans International BV v. Commission of the European Communities (T188/97)
[1999] E.C.R. II-2463; [1999] 3 C.M.L.R. 66, CFI (1st Chamber) . . . . *Digested*, 99/**2255**
Rothmore Farms Pty Ltd (In Liquidation) v. Belgravia Pty Ltd (1999-2000) 2 I.T.E.L.R.
159, Fed Ct (Aus) (Sgl judge)
Rothschild v. Bell (A Bankrupt); *sub nom* De Rothschild v. Bell (A Bankrupt) [2000]
Q.B. 33; [1999] 2 W.L.R. 1237; [1999] 2 All E.R. 722; [1999] 1 F.L.R. 1246;
[1999] B.P.I.R. 300; (2000) 32 H.L.R. 274; [1999] L. & T.R. 320; [1999] 1
E.G.L.R. 35; [1999] 16 E.G. 155; [1999] Fam. Law 385; [1999] E.G.C.S. 27;
[1999] N.P.C. 23; (1999) 78 P. & C.R. D5; *Times*, March 10, 1999, CA . . . . *Digested*, 99/**3232**
Rothwell v. Fazel [2001] 6 Q.R. 18, CC [*Ex rel*. Paul Clark, Barrister, Exchange
Chambers, Derby Square, Liverpool] . . . . *Digested*, 01/**1731**
Rotocrop International Ltd v. Genbourne Ltd [1982] F.S.R. 241, Pat Ct . . . . *Digested*, 82/**2298**:
Considered, 98/3468
Round Imports v. Rexam Glass Barnsley Ltd (formerly PLM Redfearn Ltd) A3/2000/
6247, CA; affirming (1999) 22(7) I.P.D. 22071, Pat Ct
Rouse (CICA: Quantum: 2000), Re (Unreported, May 26, 2000), CICA (London) [*Ex rel*.
Russell Jones & Walker Solicitors, Swinton House, 324 Grays Inn Road,
London] . . . . *Digested*, 01/**1588**
Rouse v. IOOF Australia Trustees Ltd [2000] W.T.L.R. 111; (1999-2000) 2 I.T.E.L.R.
289, Sup Ct (SAus) (Full Ct) . . . . *Digested*, 00/**5269**
Roussel-Uclaf's (Clemence & Le Martret) Patent (No.1) [1987] R.P.C. 109, Pat Ct . . . . . *Digested*, 87/**2800**:
Referred to, 01/3854

Rout v. Lewis see Kudos Glass Ltd (In Liquidation), Re
Routestone Ltd v. Bird see Routestone Ltd v. Minories Finance Ltd
Routestone Ltd v. Minories Finance Ltd; Routestone Ltd v. Bird [1997] B.C.C. 180;
[1997] 1 E.G.L.R. 123; [1997] 21 E.G. 148; [1996] N.P.C. 83, Ch D . . . .   *Digested*, 97/**3855**:
         Considered, 99/3440
Routh v. Leeds City Council Unreported . . . .   *Applied*, 99/3717
Routley v. Martin [2001] 6 Q.R. 13, CC (Wolverhampton) [*Ex rel.* Andrew Granville
Stafford, Barrister, 4 King's Bench Walk, Temple, London] . . . .   *Digested*, 01/**1660**
Roux Restaurants Ltd v. Jaison Property Development Co Ltd; *sub nom* Jaison
Property Development Co Ltd v. Roux Restaurants Ltd (1997) 74 P. & C.R. 357;
[1996] E.G.C.S. 118; [1996] N.P.C. 111, CA . . . .   *Digested*, 98/**3648**
Rovenska v. General Medical Council [1998] I.C.R. 85; [1997] I.R.L.R. 367; *Times*,
December 31, 1996, CA; affirming *Independent*, September 22, 1994, EAT . . . .   *Digested*, 97/**3602**
Rowan v. Machinery Installations (South Wales) Ltd [1981] I.C.R. 386; [1981] I.R.L.R.
122, EAT . . . .   *Digested*, 81/**899**:
         Applied, 81/819, 99/2128: *Followed*, 98/2187
Rowan Companies Inc v. Lambert Eggink Offshore Transport Consultants vof (The
Gilbert Rowe) (No.1) [1998] C.L.C. 1574, CA; reversing [1997] 2 Lloyd's Rep.
218, QBD (Adm Ct) . . . .   *Digested*, 99/**4096**
Rowan Companies Inc v. Lambert Eggink Offshore Transport Consultants vof (The
Gilbert Rowe) (No.2) [1999] 2 Lloyd's Rep. 443; [1999] C.L.C. 1461, QBD
(Comm Ct) . . . .   *Digested*, 99/**460**
Rowan Timber Supplies (Scotland) Ltd v. Customs and Excise Commissioners [2000]
S.T.I. 112, V&DTr
Rowe v. Herman [1997] 1 W.L.R. 1390; 58 Con. L.R. 33; *Times*, June 9, 1997, CA . . . . .   *Digested*, 97/**3804**
Rowe v. Herman (Quantum) (Unreported, February 17, 2000), CC (Barnet) [*Ex rel.* AE
Wyeth & Co Solicitors, Bridge House, High Street, Dartford, Kent] . . . .   *Digested*, 00/**4243**
Rowe v. Matthews (2001) 33 H.L.R. 81, QBD
Rowe v. Prance [1999] 2 F.L.R. 787; [2000] W.T.L.R. 249; [1999] Fam. Law 623;
[1999] E.G.C.S. 75; (1999) 96(21) L.S.G. 41, Ch D . . . .   *Digested*, 99/**4955**
Rowe v. Rogers (Unreported, June 23, 2000), CC (Newport, Gwent) [*Ex rel.* Jane HS
Foulser McFarlane, Barrister, Temple Chambers, 32 Park Place, Cardiff] . . . . . .   *Digested*, 00/**1711**
Rowe v. Rowe see Glenister v. Rowe (Costs)
Rowe v. Swansea City and County Council (Unreported, October 11, 1999), CC
(Swansea) [*Ex rel.* Dolmans Solicitors, 17-20 Windsor Place, Cardiff] . . . .   *Digested*, 00/**4233**
Rowe v. United Kingdom [1999] Crim. L.R. 410, ECHR . . . .   *Considered*, 01/1100
Rowe v. United Kingdom; Jasper v. United Kingdom; Fitt v. United Kingdom (2000)
30 E.H.R.R. 1; 8 B.H.R.C. 325; [2000] Crim. L.R. 584; *Times*, March 1, 2000,
ECHR . . . .   *Digested*, 00/**3219**:
         Applied, 01/988: *Considered*, 00/1059, 01/989
Rowland v. Al-Fayed [2000] C.P. Rep. 35, Ch D . . . .   *Digested*, 00/**335**
Rowland v. Al-Fayed (Disclosure: Witness Statements), *Times*, July 20, 1998, Ch D . . .   *Digested*, 98/**362**
Rowland v. Divall [1923] 2 K.B. 500, CA . . . .   *Applied*, 54/2971,
         54/2972, 54/2991, 54/2993, 00/870: *Considered*, 47-51/1712
Rowland v. Gulfpac Ltd (No.1); Inoco Plc v. Gulf USA Corp (No.1) [1999] Lloyd's Rep.
Bank. 86, QBD . . . .   *Digested*, 99/**3227**
Rowland v. Jobson (Unreported, May 24, 2001), CC (Crewe) [*Ex rel.* Justin Valentine,
Barrister, Old Colony House, 6 South King Street, Manchester] . . . .   *Digested*, 01/**882**
Rowland v. Matthews (Unreported, January 2, 1997), CC (Stockport) [*Ex rel.* Andrew
Leach, Solicitor] . . . .   *Digested*, 97/**1882**:
         Considered, 98/1739
Rowland v. Turp see Performing Right Society Ltd v. Rowland
Rowland v. Vancouver College Ltd; St Thomas More Collegiate Ltd v. Burnell; Burnell v.
Christian Brothers of Ireland in Canada (In Liquidation); Christian Brothers of
Ireland in Canada (In Liquidation) v. Rowland (2000-01) 3 I.T.E.L.R. 182, Sup Ct
(BC) . . . .   *Previous proceedings*,
         01/387
Rowley v. Cerberus Software Ltd see Cerberus Software Ltd v. Rowley
Rowley v. Murphy [1964] 2 Q.B. 43; [1963] 3 W.L.R. 1061; [1964] 1 All E.R. 50; 128
J.P. 88; 107 S.J. 982, QBD . . . .   *Digested*, 64/**84**:
         Applied, 86/80: *Followed*, 98/209
Roy v. Carron Co Ltd 1967 S.L.T. (Notes) 84, 1 Div . . . .   *Digested*, 67/**4605**:
         Considered, 99/5140
Roy v. Greenline Carriers (Unreported, May 18, 1998), CC (Nottingham) [*Ex rel.*
Richard Menzies, Barrister, 8 Stone Buildings, Lincoln's Inn, London] . . . .   *Digested*, 98/**1720**
Roy v. Kensington and Chelsea and Westminster Family Practitioner Committee [1992]
1 A.C. 624; [1992] 2 W.L.R. 239; [1992] 1 All E.R. 705; [1992] I.R.L.R. 233;
(1992) 4 Admin. L.R. 649; [1992] 3 Med. L.R. 177; (1992) 142 N.L.J. 240;
(1992) 136 S.J.L.B. 63; *Times*, February 10, 1992; *Independent*, February 11,
1992, HL; affirming (1990) 2 Admin. L.R. 669; *Times*, March 27, 1990, CA;
reversing (1990) 2 Admin. L.R. 29; *Times*, March 7, 1989, QBD . . . .   *Digested*, 92/**30**:
         Applied, 97/4055, 98/98, 98/4129: *Considered*, 95/3907, 96/3087,
         96/5692: *Distinguished*, 92/2267, 96/3913, 96/5578: *Not followed*, 94/1978

Roy v. MR Pearlman Ltd 1999 S.C. 459; 2000 S.L.T. 727; 1999 S.C.L.R. 803; [1999] 2
  C.M.L.R. 1155; 1999 G.W.D. 11-486; *Times*, May 13, 1999, OH . . . .   *Digested*, 99/**5629**
Roy v. Prior [1971] A.C. 470; [1970] 3 W.L.R. 202; [1970] 2 All E.R. 729; 114 S.J.
  552, HL; reversing [1970] 1 Q.B. 283; [1969] 3 W.L.R. 365; [1969] 3 All E.R.
  1153; 113 S.J. 609, CA . . . .   *Digested*, 70/**1040**:
                        Applied, 97/4860, 99/528: *Considered*, 91/2869, 92/3499, 00/4543:
                                                                Distinguished, 71/10220
Royal & Sun Alliance Insurance Group Plc v. Customs and Excise Commissioners; *sub*
  nom Royal Sun Alliance Group Plc v. Customs and Excise Commissioners
  [2001] EWCA Civ 1476; [2001] S.T.C. 1476; [2001] S.T.I. 1345; [2001] 43
  E.G.C.S. 183; [2001] N.P.C. 142, CA; affirming [2000] S.T.C. 933; [2000] B.T.C.
  5357; [2000] B.V.C. 407; [2000] S.T.I. 1447; [2000] E.G.C.S. 106; (2000)
  97(39) L.S.G. 43; [2000] N.P.C. 99, Ch D; reversing [2000] B.V.C. 2003;
  [1999] V. & D.R. 336, V&DTr . . . .   *Digested*, 00/**5309**
Royal Automobile Club Ltd, Re see RAC Motoring Services Ltd, Re
Royal Bank v. Soundair Corp (1991) 4 O.R. (3d) 1, CA (Ont) . . . .   *Distinguished*,
                                                                                          01/3776:
                                                                               Followed, 00/3482
Royal Bank of Canada v. Lywood [1999] B.P.I.R. 968, Sup Ct (BC) . . . .   *Digested*, 00/**3451**
Royal Bank of Canada v. Woodhouse [1998] B.P.I.R. 509, CA (Ont) . . . .   *Digested*, 99/**3221**
Royal Bank of Scotland Group Plc v. Customs and Excise Commissioners (Reciprocity
  Fees) TNS, 2 Div; affirming [2001] B.V.C. 2275; [2001] S.T.I. 1041, V&DTr
Royal Bank of Scotland Group Plc v. Customs and Excise Commissioners (Time Limits)
  [2000] S.T.I. 617, V&DTr
Royal Bank of Scotland Plc v. Customs and Excise Commissioners [1999] B.V.C. 2240;
  [1999] V. & D.R. 122, V&DTr . . . .   *Digested*, 00/**5310**
Royal Bank of Scotland Plc v. Elliniko Dimosio (C311/97) see Royal Bank of Scotland
  Plc v. Greece (C311/97)
Royal Bank of Scotland Plc v. Etridge (No.1) [1997] 3 All E.R. 628; [1997] 2 F.L.R. 847;
  [1998] 1 F.C.R. 222; [1998] Fam. Law 24, CA . . . .   *Digested*, 97/**4242**:
                                                                             Not followed, 98/4358
Royal Bank of Scotland Plc v. Etridge (No.2); Barclays Bank Plc v. Coleman; Barclays
  Bank Plc v. Harris; Midland Bank Plc v. Wallace; National Westminster Bank Plc v.
  Gill; UCB Home Loans Corp Ltd v. Moore; Bank of Scotland v. Bennett;
  Kenyon-Brown v. Desmond Banks & Co (Undue Influence) (No.2) [2001] UKHL
  44; [2001] 3 W.L.R. 1021; [2001] 4 All E.R. 449; [2001] 2 All E.R. (Comm)
  1061; [2001] 2 F.L.R. 1364; [2001] 3 F.C.R. 481; [2001] Fam. Law 880; [2001]
  43 E.G.C.S. 184; (2001) 151 N.L.J. 1538; [2001] N.P.C. 147; *Times*, October 17,
  2001; *Daily Telegraph*, October 23, 2001, HL; affirming in part [1998] 4 All E.R.
  705; [1998] 2 F.L.R. 843; [1998] 3 F.C.R. 675; (1999) 31 H.L.R. 575; [1998]
  Fam. Law 665; (1998) 95(32) L.S.G. 31; (2001) 151 N.L.J. 1538; (1998) 148
  N.L.J. 1390; [1998] N.P.C. 130; (1998) 76 P. & C.R. D39; *Times*, August 17,
  1998, CA . . . .   *Digested*, 01/**4880**:
                              Applied, 00/4664, 01/4879: *Considered*, 00/2333, 01/4878:
                              Followed, 00/2334, 00/4273: *Previous proceedings*, 99/4391, 00/4273,
                                                                   00/4662: *Referred to*, 99/4030
Royal Bank of Scotland Plc v. Greece (C311/97); *sub nom* Royal Bank of Scotland Plc v.
  Elliniko Dimosio (C311/97) [2000] S.T.C. 733; [1999] E.C.R. I-2651; [1999] 2
  C.M.L.R. 973; [1999] C.E.C. 442, ECJ (5th Chamber) . . . .   *Digested*, 99/**4677**
Royal Bank of Scotland Plc v. Jennings (1998) 75 P. & C.R. 458; [1997] 1 E.G.L.R. 101;
  [1997] 19 E.G. 152; [1996] E.G.C.S. 168; [1996] N.P.C. 145, CA; affirming
  (1995) 70 P. & C.R. 459; [1995] 2 E.G.L.R. 87; [1995] 35 E.G. 140, Ch D . . . . .   *Digested*, 97/**3320**:
                                                                             Distinguished, 97/3319
Royal Bank of Scotland Plc v. Miller [2001] EWCA Civ 344; [2001] 3 W.L.R. 523, CA .   *Digested*, 01/**4875**
Royal Bank of Scotland Plc v. Sandstone Properties Ltd [1998] 2 B.C.L.C. 429; *Times*,
  March 12, 1998, QBD . . . .   *Digested*, 98/**702**
Royal Boskalis Westminster NV v. Mountain [1999] Q.B. 674; [1998] 2 W.L.R. 538;
  [1997] 2 All E.R. 929; [1997] L.R.L.R. 523, CA . . . .   *Digested*, 97/**3162**
Royal Brompton Hospital NHS Trust v. Hammond (No.1) [1999] B.L.R. 162; (2000) 2
  T.C.L.R. 92; 66 Con. L.R. 42; (1999) 15 Const. L.J. 395; (1999) 149 N.L.J. 89;
  Independent, January 25, 1999 (C.S.), QBD (T&CC) . . . .   *Digested*, 99/**1400**
Royal Brompton Hospital NHS Trust v. Hammond (No.2) 69 Con. L.R. 132, QBD
  (T&CC) . . . .   *Digested*, 01/**413**
Royal Brompton Hospital NHS Trust v. Hammond (No.3) TNS, HL; affirming 69 Con.
  L.R. 145; [2000] Lloyd's Rep. P.N. 643, CA; affirming [1999] B.L.R. 385, QBD
  (T&CC) . . . .   *Digested*, 00/**384**
Royal Brompton Hospital NHS Trust v. Hammond (No.4) [2000] B.L.R. 75; 69 Con.
  L.R. 170, QBD (T&CC) . . . .   *Digested*, 00/**814**
Royal Brompton Hospital NHS Trust v. Hammond (No.5) [2001] EWCA Civ 550; [2001]
  B.L.R. 297; [2001] Lloyd's Rep. P.N. 526; (2001) 98(23) L.S.G. 39; (2001)
  145 S.J.L.B. 118; *Times*, May 11, 2001, CA; reversing 1993-ORB-No.46, QBD
  (T&CC) . . . .   *Digested*, 01/**680**
Royal Brompton Hospital NHS Trust v. Hammond (No.6) 76 Con. L.R. 131, QBD
  (T&CC) . . . .   *Digested*, 01/**4513**

Royal Brompton Hospital NHS Trust *v.* Hammond (No.7) [2001] EWCA Civ 206; 76
Con. L.R. 148, CA . . . . *Digested*, 01/**4512**
Royal Brompton Hospital NHS Trust *v.* Hammond (No.8) [2001] EWCA Civ 778; [2001]
C.P. Rep. 90; [2001] B.L.R. 317; 76 Con. L.R. 62; *Independent*, June 13, 2001,
CA . . . . *Digested*, 01/**417**
Royal Brompton Hospital NHS Trust *v.* Watkins Gray International (UK) (2001) 3 T.C.L.R.
3, CA . . . . *Digested*, 01/**946**
Royal Brunei Airlines Sdn Bhd *v.* Philip Tan Kok Ming see Royal Brunei Airlines Sdn Bhd
v. Tan
Royal Brunei Airlines Sdn Bhd *v.* Tan; *sub nom* Royal Brunei Airlines Sdn Bhd *v.* Philip
Tan Kok Ming [1995] 2 A.C. 378; [1995] 3 W.L.R. 64; [1995] 3 All E.R. 97;
[1995] B.C.C. 899; (1995) 92(27) L.S.G. 33; (1995) 145 N.L.J. 888; [1995]
139 S.J.L.B. 146; *Times*, May 29, 1995; *Independent*, June 22, 1995, PC (Bru) . . *Digested*, 95/**2193**:
Applied, 99/294, 00/3566: *Considered*, 97/692, 97/3828, 01/721:
Followed, 95/2191, 98/4871, 99/2217, 00/2316: *Referred to*, 00/3713,
00/3768

Royal Club Liegois SA *v.* Bosman (C415/93) see Union Royale Belge des Societes de
Football Association (ASBL) *v.* Bosman (C415/93)
Royal Heritage Life Assurance Ltd *v.* Pensions Ombudsman [1999] O.P.L.R. 171, Ch D . *Digested*, 99/**4147**
Royal Institution of Chartered Surveyors *v.* Fryer FC3 99/6719/A3, CA. . . . . *Subsequent proceed-*
ings, 00/469

Royal Institution of Chartered Surveyors *v.* Wiseman Marshall see Fryer *v.* Royal
Institution of Chartered Surveyors
Royal Insurance Co Ltd *v.* Watson (Surveyor of Taxes); *sub nom* Watson (Surveyor of
Taxes) *v.* Royal Insurance Co Ltd [1897] A.C. 1, HL; affirming [1896] 1 Q.B. 41,
CA . . . . *Applied*, 00/**4928**
Royal Masonic Hospital *v.* Pensions Ombudsman [2001] 3 All E.R. 408; [2001] Pens.
L.R. 31; (2001) 98(5) L.S.G. 37; *Times*, January 31, 2001, Ch D . . . . *Digested*, 01/**4602**
Royal Midland Counties Home for Disabled People *v.* Customs and Excise
Commissioners [2001] B.T.C. 5509; [2001] B.V.C. 599; [2001] S.T.I. 967; (2001)
98(27) L.S.G. 40; *Times*, July 10, 2001, Ch D; reversing [2001] S.T.I. 745,
V&DTr. . . . . *Digested*, 01/**5624**
Royal Reinsurance Co Ltd *v.* Central Insurance Co Ltd see Gan Insurance Co Ltd *v.* Tai
Ping Insurance Co Ltd (No.1)
Royal Scholten-Honig (Holdings) Ltd *v.* Intervention Board for Agricultural Produce
(C103/77); Tunnel Refineries Ltd *v.* Intervention Board for Agricultural Produce
(C145/77); Koninklijke Scholten-Honig NV *v.* Hoofdproduktschap voor
Akkerbouwprodukten (C125/77) [1978] E.C.R. 1991; [1978] E.C.R. 2037;
[1979] 1 C.M.L.R. 675, ECJ . . . . *Digested*, 79/**1157**:
Applied, 99/144: *Distinguished*, 01/118
Royal Society for the Prevention of Cruelty to Animals *v.* Attorney General see RSPCA *v.*
Attorney General
Royal Society for the Prevention of Cruelty to Animals *v.* Attorney General (Rule Changes)
see RSPCA *v.* Attorney General (Rule Changes)
Royal Society for the Prevention of Cruelty to Animals *v.* Miller see RSPCA *v.* Miller
Royal Society for the Protection of Birds (RSPB) *v.* Croucher [1984] I.C.R. 604; [1984]
I.R.L.R. 425, EAT. . . . . *Digested*, 84/**1304**:
Applied, 97/2289: *Distinguished*, 01/2343
Royal Society for the Protection of Birds *v.* Secretary of State for Scotland; *sub nom*
RSPB, Petitioners 2000 S.L.T. 1272; 2000 S.C.L.R. 1045; [2000] 3 C.M.L.R.
1157; [2001] Env. L.R. 19; [2000] 4 P.L.R. 120; 2000 G.W.D. 26-961; *Times*,
September 12, 2000, 1 Div; reversing 2000 S.L.T. 22; [2000] 1 C.M.L.R. 449;
[2000] Eu. L.R. 481; [2000] Env. L.R. 168; [2000] 1 P.L.R. 29; 1999 G.W.D. 33-
1560; *Times*, December 14, 1999, OH . . . . *Digested*, 00/**5882**
Royal Sun Alliance Group Plc *v.* Customs and Excise Commissioners see Royal & Sun
Alliance Insurance Group Plc *v.* Customs and Excise Commissioners
Royal Trust Bank Plc *v.* Brookes Associates Finance Ltd see Royal Trust Bank Plc *v.*
National Westminster Bank Plc
Royal Trust Bank Plc *v.* National Westminster Bank Plc; Royal Trust Bank Plc *v.* Brookes
Associates Finance Ltd [1996] B.C.C. 613; [1996] 2 B.C.L.C. 699, CA;
reversing [1995] B.C.C. 128; [1996] 2 B.C.L.C. 682, Ch D . . . . *Digested*, 96/**400**:
Followed, 98/3334

Royal Wolverhampton Hospitals NHS Trust *v.* B (Medical Treatment) [2000] 1 F.L.R.
953; [2000] 2 F.C.R. 76; [2000] Fam. Law 478, Fam Div. . . . . *Digested*, 00/**2495**
Roylance *v.* General Medical Council (No.1), *Times*, January 27, 1999, PC (UK) . . . . *Digested*, 99/**2662**
Roylance *v.* General Medical Council (No.2) [2000] 1 A.C. 311; [1999] 3 W.L.R. 541;
[1999] Lloyd's Rep. Med. 139; (1999) 47 B.M.L.R. 63; (1999) 143 S.J.L.B. 183;
Times, March 26, 1999, PC (UK) . . . . *Digested*, 99/**2663**:
Considered, 01/2928

Royscot Leasing Ltd v. Customs and Excise Commissioners (C305/97); Allied Domecq Plc v. Customs and Excise Commissioners (C305/97); TC Harrison Group Ltd v. Customs and Excise Commissioners (C305/97) [2000] 1 W.L.R. 1151; [1999] All E.R. (EC) 908; [1999] S.T.C. 998; [1999] E.C.R. I-6671; [1999] 3 C.M.L.R. 485; [1999] C.E.C. 582; [1999] B.T.C. 5377; [1999] B.V.C. 419; *Times*, October 15, 1999, ECJ (6th Chamber) . . . .   *Digested*, 99/**4992**:
Considered, 01/5580

Royscot Leasing Ltd v. Customs and Excise Commissioners (Withdrawal of Reference); Allied Domecq Plc v. Customs and Excise Commissioners (Withdrawal of Reference); TC Harrison Group Ltd v. Customs and Excise Commissioners (Withdrawal of Reference) [1999] 1 C.M.L.R. 903; (1999) 11 Admin. L.R. 251; [1999] C.O.D. 136; (2000) 164 J.P.N. 2; *Times*, November 23, 1998, CA . . . . . .   *Digested*, 98/**72**

Royscot Trust Ltd v. Rogerson; *sub nom* Royscott Trust v. Maidenhead Honda Centre [1991] 2 Q.B. 297; [1991] 3 W.L.R. 57; [1991] 3 All E.R. 294; [1992] R.T.R. 99; (1992) 11 Tr. L.R. 23; [1991] C.C.L.R. 45; (1991) 141 N.L.J. 493; (1991) 135 S.J. 444; *Times*, April 3, 1991; *Independent*, April 10, 1991; *Daily Telegraph*, April 25, 1991, CA . . . .   *Digested*, 91/**1311**:
Applied, 95/2457, 96/4975, 01/965: *Cited*, 01/3844: *Considered*, 93/1398

Royscott Trust v. Maidenhead Honda Centre see Royscot Trust Ltd v. Rogerson

RP Electromechanical Enterprise Ltd v. Brewer (Unreported, February 11, 1993), CA . . .   *Followed*, 98/510

RPS Prodotti Siderurgici Srl v. Owners of the Sea Maas (The Sea Maas) [2000] 1 All E.R. 536; [1999] 1 All E.R. (Comm) 945; [1999] 2 Lloyd's Rep. 281; [1999] C.L.C. 1336; *Independent*, July 7, 1999, QBD (Adm Ct) . . . .   *Digested*, 99/**721**

RS&M Engineering Co Ltd, Re see Mond v. Hammond Suddards (No.2)

RSP Architects Planners and Engineers v. Ocean Front Pte Ltd (1998) 14 Const. L.J. 139, CA (Sing) . . . .   *Digested*, 98/**3924**

RSPB, Petitioners see Royal Society for the Protection of Birds v. Secretary of State for Scotland

RSPCA v. Attorney General; *sub nom* Royal Society for the Prevention of Cruelty to Animals v. Attorney General [2001] 3 All E.R. 530; [2001] U.K.H.R.R. 905; (2001) 98(11) L.S.G. 43; *Times*, February 13, 2001, Ch D . . . .   *Digested*, 01/**3460**

RSPCA v. Attorney General (Rule Changes); *sub nom* Royal Society for the Prevention of Cruelty to Animals v. Attorney General (Rule Changes); Ch.1998-R-6364, Ch D . . . .   *Digested*, 99/**305**

RSPCA v. Miller; *sub nom* Royal Society for the Prevention of Cruelty to Animals v. Miller [1994] Crim. L.R. 516; [1994] C.O.D. 363; *Times*, March 8, 1994, QBD . . .   *Digested*, 95/**313**:
Applied, 01/313

RTZ Pension Property Trust Ltd v. ARC Property Developments Ltd; *sub nom* RTZ Pension Property Trust Ltd v. ASFA Ltd [1999] 1 All E.R. 532; [1999] B.L.R. 23; (1998) 148 N.L.J. 1675; *Times*, November 26, 1998, CA . . . .   *Digested*, 98/**426**

RTZ Pension Property Trust Ltd v. ASFA Ltd see RTZ Pension Property Trust Ltd v. ARC Property Developments Ltd

Rubber Improvement Ltd v. Associated Newspapers Ltd see Rubber Improvement Ltd v. Daily Telegraph Ltd

Rubber Improvement Ltd v. Daily Telegraph Ltd; Rubber Improvement Ltd v. Associated Newspapers Ltd; Lewis v. Associated Newspapers Ltd; Lewis v. Daily Telegraph Ltd [1964] A.C. 234; [1963] 2 W.L.R. 1063; [1963] 2 All E.R. 151; 107 S.J. 356; *Times*, July 20, 1961, HL; affirming [1963] 1 Q.B. 340; [1962] 3 W.L.R. 50; [1962] 2 All E.R. 698; 106 S.J. 307, CA; reversing *Times*, July 22, 1961 . . . .   *Digested*, 63/**1998**:
Applied, 63/2002, 99/1623: *Considered*, 67/2278, 68/2231, 76/1601, 99/2108: *Subsequent proceedings*, 64/2130

Rubiano v. Colombia 7 B.H.R.C. 57, IA Comm HR

Rubicon Computer Systems Ltd v. United Paints Ltd (2000) 2 T.C.L.R. 453, CA . . . . . .   *Digested*, 00/**899**

Rubin v. DPP [1990] 2 Q.B. 80; [1989] 3 W.L.R. 1088; [1989] 2 All E.R. 241; (1989) 89 Cr. App. R. 44; (1989) 153 J.P. 389; [1989] R.T.R. 261; [1989] Crim. L.R. 371; [1989] C.O.D. 473; (1989) 153 J.P.N. 371; (1989) 86(5) L.S.G. 36; (1989) 139 N.L.J. 187; (1989) 133 S.J. 44; *Times*, December 29, 1988; *Independent*, January 9, 1989 (C.S.); *Daily Telegraph*, January 6, 1989, QBD . . . .   *Digested*, 89/**712**:
Applied, 01/1192

Rudra v. Abbey National Plc; *sub nom* Ramanathan Rudra v. Abbey National Plc (1998) 76 P. & C.R. 537; *Independent*, March 9, 1998 (C.S.), CA . . . .   *Digested*, 98/**318**

Rudzinske v. Poland (45223/99) (2000) 29 E.H.R.R. CD241, ECHR

Ruefach Marketing GmbH's Application (Opposition of Codemasters Ltd) [1999] E.T.M.R. 412, TMR. . . . .   *Digested*, 00/**3771**

Ruf v. Office for Harmonisation in the Internal Market (Trade Marks and Designs) (OHIM) (T146/00) [2001] E.C.R. II-1797; [2001] C.E.C. 209; [2001] E.T.M.R. 100; (2001) 24(9) I.P.D. 24061, CFI (2nd Chamber) . . . .   *Digested*, 01/**3984**

Ruff v. Royal Victoria Infirmary and Associated Hospitals NHS Trust [2001] Lloyd's Rep. Med. 530, QBD

Rugamer v. Sony Music Entertainment UK Ltd; McNicol v. Balfour Beatty Rail Maintenance Ltd [2001] I.R.L.R. 644; [2001] Emp. L.R. 1318, EAT . . . .   *Digested*, 01/**2241**

Rugby Football Union v. Secretary of State for Local Government, Transport and the Regions; *sub nom* Rugby Football Union v. Secretary of State for the Environment, Transport and the Regions [2001] EWHC Admin 927; *Times*, November 8, 2001, QBD (Admin Ct) . . . .   *Digested*, 01/**4755**

Rugby Football Union v. Secretary of State for the Environment, Transport and the Regions see Rugby Football Union v. Secretary of State for Local Government, Transport and the Regions

RUHRCHEMIE/3-(4-methyl-3-cyclohexen-1-yl) (T132/86) [2001] E.P.O.R. 5, EPO (Technical Bd App) . . . .   *Digested*, 01/**3926**

Ruiz Torija v. Spain (A/303-A) (1995) 19 E.H.R.R. 553, ECHR . . . .   *Applied*, 99/**3128**

Ruiz-Mateos v. Spain (A/262) (1993) 16 E.H.R.R. 505, ECHR . . . .   *Digested*, 94/**2406**:
Applied, 98/3121, 98/3135, 98/3136

Rumasa SA v. Multinvest (UK) see Williams & Humbert Ltd v. W&H Trade Marks (Jersey) Ltd

Rumsey v. Secretary of State for the Environment, Transport and the Regions (2001) 81 P. & C.R. 32; [2001] J.P.L. 1056, QBD (Admin Ct) . . . .   *Digested*, 01/**4736**

Runnymede BC v. Secretary of State for the Environment [1992] J.P.L. 178, QBD . . . . .   *Digested*, 92/**4247**:
Not followed, 99/4217, 01/4691

Runnymede BC v. Secretary of State for the Environment, Transport and the Regions [2000] P.L.C.R. 253; (2000) 97(1) L.S.G. 25, QBD . . . .   *Digested*, 00/**4504**

Runnymede BC v. Secretary of State for the Environment, Transport and the Regions [2001] P.L.C.R. 24; [2001] J.P.L. 843 (Note), QBD (Admin Ct) . . . .   *Digested*, 01/**4695**

Ruparel v. Awan [2001] Lloyd's Rep. P.N. 258, Ch D . . . .   *Digested*, 01/**4271**

Ruparelia v. Odedra (Unreported, May 12, 1998), CC (Leicester) [*Ex rel.* David McIlroy, Barrister, 3 Paper Buildings, Temple, London] . . . .   *Digested*, 98/**1711**

Rush v. JNR (SMD) Ltd [2000] C.P. Rep. 12, CA . . . .   *Digested*, 00/**522**

Rush v. Mobil Oil Co Ltd (1997) 97(5/6) Q.R. 10, CC (Oxford). . . . .   *Digested*, 98/**1714**

Rush & Tompkins Ltd v. Greater London Council [1989] A.C. 1280; [1988] 3 W.L.R. 939; [1988] 3 All E.R. 737; 43 B.L.R. 1; 22 Con. L.R. 114; (1988) 138 N.L.J. Rep. 315; (1988) 132 S.J. 1592, HL; reversing [1988] 2 W.L.R. 533; [1988] 1 All E.R. 549; 40 B.L.R. 53; (1988) 138 N.L.J. Rep. 22; (1988) 132 S.J. 265, CA . . .   *Digested*, 89/**1701**:
Applied, 91/2870, 94/2817, 99/309, 99/349: *Considered*, 92/106:
Distinguished, 00/337: *Followed*, 92/3288, 00/319

Rushingdale SA v. Byblos Bank SAL see Byblos Bank SAL v. Rushingdale SA

Rushiti v. Austria (28389/95) (2001) 33 E.H.R.R. 56, ECHR

Rushmer v. Countrywide Surveyors (1994) Ltd [2000] P.N.L.R. 529; [1999] E.G.C.S. 102; (1999) 96(29) L.S.G. 30, QBD (T&CC) . . . .   *Digested*, 00/**4276**

Rushton v. Gee (Unreported, November 5, 1999), CC (Salford) [*Ex rel.* Daniel Barnett, Barrister, 2 Gray's Inn Square Chambers, Gray's Inn, London] . . . .   *Digested*, 00/**1596**

Rushton v. Jervis [2000] 3 Q.R. 3, QBD [*Ex rel.* Bruce Silvester, Barrister, Devereux Chambers, Devereux Court, London]. . . . .   *Digested*, 00/**1512**

Rushton (Mary) v. Worcester City Council; Rushton (Michael) v. Worcester City Council [2001] EWCA Civ 367; [2001] 13 E.G.C.S. 149; [2001] N.P.C. 65, CA

Rushton (Michael) v. Worcester City Council see Rushton (Mary) v. Worcester City Council

Ruskin College v. Customs and Excise Commissioners [2000] S.T.I. 1553, V&DTr

Russell (Superintendent of the Royal Ulster Constabulary) v. Devine [2001] N.I. 385, CA (Crim Div) (NI)

Russell v. Dickson 1997 S.C. 269; 1998 S.L.T. 96; 1997 G.W.D. 22-1058; *Times*, June 23, 1997, OH . . . .   *Digested*, 97/**5568**

Russell v. Fulling, *Times*, June 23, 1999, Ch D . . . .   *Digested*, 99/**587**

Russell v. McAdams [2001] N.I. 157, CA (Crim Div) (NI) . . . .   *Digested*, 01/**5724**

Russell v. Nathan (1998) 98(1) Q.R. 6, QBD . . . .   *Digested*, 98/**1568**

Russell v. Pal Pak Corrugated Ltd (No.1) see Callery v. Gray (No.1)

Russell v. Pal Pak Corrugated Ltd (No.2) see Callery v. Gray (No.2)

Russell v. Russell [1998] 1 F.L.R. 936; [1999] 2 F.C.R. 137; [1998] B.P.I.R. 259; [1998] Fam. Law 313, Ch D . . . .   *Digested*, 98/**3278**:
Applied, 99/3261: *Considered*, 99/3242

Russell McVeagh McKenzie Bartleet & Co v. Tower Corp (Unreported, September 27, 1998), CA (NZ). . . . .   *Applied*, 98/**1**

Russell-Cooke Trust Co, Re see Russell-Cooke Trust Co v. Elliott (Preliminary Issue)

Russell-Cooke Trust Co v. Elliott (Preliminary Issue); *sub nom* Russell-Cooke Trust Co, Re [2001] N.P.C. 69, Ch D

Russell's Application, Re [1996] N.I. 310, QBD (NI) . . . .   *Considered*, 99/**5459**

Russian Bank for Foreign Trade, Re see Russo-Asiatic Bank, Re

Russo-Asiatic Bank, Re; *sub nom* Russian Bank for Foreign Trade, Re [1934] Ch. 720, Ch D . . . .   *Applied*, 88/**3680**:
Considered, 00/519

Rustal Trading Ltd v. Gill & Duffus SA [2000] 1 Lloyd's Rep. 14; [2000] C.L.C. 231, QBD (Comm Ct) . . . .   *Digested*, 00/**224**

Rutherford v. Wandsworth LBC (Unreported, July 17, 1998), CC (Wandsworth) [*Ex rel.* Russell-Cooke Potter Chapman Solicitors, 2 Putney Hill, Putney, London] . . . . .   *Digested*, 98/**1633**

Rutland *v.* Ferguson (Unreported, November 12, 1997), QBD [*Ex rel.* Simon Michael, Barrister, Bedford Chambers, Houghton Conquest, Bedford and Keer-Keer & Co, Hemel Hempstead] . . . . *Digested,* 98/**1643**

Rutland CC *v.* Faithfull (2001) 16 P.A.D. 31, Planning Inspector

Rutland CC *v.* Weed (1998) 13 P.A.D. 283, Planning Inspector

Rutten *v.* Cross Medical Ltd (C383/95) [1997] All E.R. (E.C.) 121; [1997] E.C.R. I-57; [1997] I.L.Pr. 199; [1997] I.C.R. 715; [1997] I.R.L.R. 249; *Times,* January 27, 1997, ECJ (6th Chamber) . . . . *Digested,* 97/**2199**: *Considered,* 00/2109

Rutter *v.* Stevenage BC (Unreported, November 17, 1998), CC (Central London) [*Ex rel.* Simon Michael, Barrister, Bedford Chambers, The Clockhouse, 2 Bedford Street, Ampthill, Bedford] . . . . *Digested,* 99/**1517**

Ruxley Electronics and Construction Ltd *v.* Forsyth; Laddingford Enclosures Ltd *v.* Forsyth [1996] A.C. 344; [1995] 3 W.L.R. 118; [1995] 3 All E.R. 268; 73 B.L.R. 1; 45 Con. L.R. 61; (1995) 14 Tr. L.R. 541; (1995) 11 Const. L.J. 381; [1995] E.G.C.S. 11; (1995) 145 N.L.J. 996; (1995) 139 S.J.L.B. 163; *Times,* July 3, 1995; *Independent,* July 12, 1995, HL; reversing [1994] 1 W.L.R. 650; [1994] 3 All E.R. 801; 66 B.L.R. 23; 36 Con. L.R. 103; (1994) 91(7) L.S.G. 31; (1994) 138 S.J.L.B. 31; *Times,* January 7, 1994, CA . . . . *Digested,* 95/**1561**: *Applied,* 01/4501: *Distinguished,* 94/215, 95/348, 95/4508: *Followed,* 96/1131

Ruxton *v.* DPP see DPP *v.* Charles

Ruxton *v.* Starrs see Starrs *v.* Ruxton

RW Miller & Co Pty Ltd *v.* Overseas Tankship (UK) Ltd see Overseas Tankship (UK) Ltd *v.* Miller Steamship Co Pty Ltd (The Wagon Mound)

RW Peak (Kings Lynn) Ltd, Re [1998] B.C.C. 596; [1998] 1 B.C.L.C. 193, Ch D (Companies Ct) . . . . *Digested,* 98/**705**

RWDSU *v.* Dolphin Delivery Ltd [1986] 2 S.C.R. 573, Sup Ct (Can) . . . . *Distinguished,* 00/3191

RWH Enterprises Ltd *v.* Portedge Ltd; *sub nom* Portedge Ltd, Re [1998] B.C.C. 556, CA; affirming [1997] B.C.C. 23, Ch D . . . . *Digested,* 98/**3320**

RWS Translations Ltd Sarl *v.* Getten [1999] E.T.M.R. 258, C d'A (Paris)

Ryan *v.* Camden LBC (1983) 8 H.L.R. 75; (1983) 13 Fam. Law 81; *Times,* December 16, 1982, CA . . . . *Digested,* 83/**2545**: *Followed,* 01/4502

Ryan *v.* Friction Dynamics Ltd [2001] C.P. Rep. 75; *Times,* June 14, 2000, Ch D . . . . . . *Digested,* 00/**490**

Ryan *v.* Imperial Brewing and Leisure see Courage Group's Pension Schemes, Re

Ryanair Ltd *v.* Commission of the European Communities (T140/95) [1998] E.C.R. II-3327; [1998] 3 C.M.L.R. 1022, CFI

Ryde International Plc *v.* London Regional Transport [2001] 1 E.G.L.R. 101; [2001] 14 E.G. 154; [2001] R.V.R. 59, Lands Tr . . . . *Digested,* 01/**4662**

Rygrange Ltd's Trade Mark Applications [2001] E.T.M.R. 78, TMR . . . . *Digested,* 01/**4025**

Ryles *v.* Chaudry [1999] Lloyd's Rep. P.N. 454, QBD (Merc Ct) . . . . *Digested,* 99/**473**

Rysaffe Trustee Co (CI) Ltd *v.* Customs and Excise Commissioners see Rysaffe Trustee Co (CI) Ltd *v.* Inland Revenue Commissioners

Rysaffe Trustee Co (CI) Ltd *v.* Inland Revenue Commissioners; *sub nom* Rysaffe Trustee Co (CI) Ltd *v.* Customs and Excise Commissioners Ch D; reversing [2001] S.T.C. (S.C.D.) 225; [2001] S.T.I. 1504, Sp Comm

Rysta Ltd's Application see Aristoc Ltd *v.* Rysta Ltd

Rytz et Cie SA *v.* Rytz Industriebau AG [2001] E.T.M.R. 32, BG (Swi)

S (A Child) (Adoption: Freeing Order), Re [2001] EWCA Civ 868; [2001] 3 F.C.R. 375, CA . . . . *Digested,* 01/**2528**

S (A Child) (Adoption: Order Made in Father's Absence), Re [2001] 2 F.C.R. 148, CA . . *Digested,* 01/**2539**

S (A Child) (Adoption Proceedings: Joinder of Father), Re see R (A Child) (Adoption: Father's Involvement), Re

S (A Child) (Change of Names: Cultural Factors), Re [2001] 2 F.L.R. 1005; [2001] 3 F.C.R. 648; [2001] Fam. Law 728, Fam Div

S (A Child) (Ex Parte Orders), Re see S (A Child) (Family Division: Without Notice Orders), Re

S (A Child) (Family Division: Without Notice Orders), Re; *sub nom* S (A Child) (Ex Parte Orders), Re [2001] 1 W.L.R. 211; [2001] 1 All E.R. 362; [2001] 1 F.L.R. 308; [2001] Fam. Law 21; *Times,* November 2, 2000, Fam Div . . . . *Digested,* 00/**2508**

S (A Child) (Residence Order: Condition), Re [2001] EWCA Civ 847; [2001] 3 F.C.R. 154, CA . . . . *Digested,* 01/**2667**

S (A Child) *v.* Birmingham HA (2001) 58 B.M.L.R. 66, QBD

S (A Child) *v.* Bloomfield (Unreported, October 7, 1999), CC (Chichester) [*Ex rel.* Tim Petts, Barrister, 12 Kings Bench Walk, Temple, London] . . . . *Digested,* 00/**1551**

S (A Child) *v.* Commissioner of Police of the Metropolis see S (A Child) *v.* Keyse

S (A Child) *v.* Countess of Chester Hospitals NHS Trust (Unreported, May 24, 2001), HC [*Ex rel.* Christopher Limb, Barrister, Young Street Chambers, 38 Young Street, Manchester] . . . . *Digested,* 01/**4454**

S (A Child) *v.* Day (Unreported, July 25, 2000), CC (Skegness) [*Ex rel.* Hodgkinsons Solicitors, The Old Manse, 14 Lumley Avenue, Skegness, Lincolnshire] . . . . *Digested,* 01/**1769**

S (A Child) *v.* Denvir [1999] N.I. 322, QBD (NI). . . . .   *Digested,* 00/**5441**

S (A Child) *v.* Department of the Environment for Northern Ireland [2000] N.I. 512, QBD (NI) . . . .   *Digested,* 01/**5901**

S (A Child) *v.* Dhillon [2001] 6 Q.R. 21, CC (Uxbridge) [*Ex rel.* Amanda Millmore, Barrister, 4 King's Bench Walk, Temple, London] . . . .   *Digested,* 01/**1777**

S (A Child) *v.* Forrester (Unreported, September 14, 1999), QBD [*Ex rel.* Philip A Butler, Barrister, Deans Court Chambers, 24 St John St, Manchester] . . . .   *Digested,* 00/**1517**

S (A Child) *v.* G see DWS (Deceased), Re

S (A Child) *v.* Keyse; *sub nom* Keyse *v.* Commissioner of Police of the Metropolis; S (A Child) *v.* Commissioner of Police of the Metropolis [2001] EWCA Civ 715; (2001) 151 N.L.J. 817, CA; reversing99/TLQ/1716, 1998 S.230, QBD

S (A Child) *v.* Thornton (Unreported, April 6, 2000), CC (Bradford) [*Ex rel.* Scott Rees & Co Solicitors, Centaur House, Gardiners Place, Skelmersdale, Lancashire] . . .   *Digested,* 00/**325**

S (A Minor) (Abduction), Re see S (Abduction: Return into Care), Re

S (A Minor) (Abduction: Access Rights), Re see S *v.* H (Abduction: Access Rights)

S (A Minor) (Abduction: Custody Rights), Re; *sub nom* S *v.* S (Child Abduction) (Child's Views) [1993] Fam. 242; [1993] 2 W.L.R. 775; [1993] 2 All E.R. 683; [1992] 2 F.L.R. 492; [1993] 1 F.C.R. 12; [1993] Fam. Law 212; (1992) 142 N.L.J. 1341; *Times,* August 4, 1992; *Independent,* July 8, 1992; *Guardian,* July 22, 1992, CA; affirming [1992] 2 F.L.R. 31; [1992] 2 F.C.R. 113, Fam Div. . . . .   *Digested,* 93/**2796**:
Applied, 97/405, 00/2443: *Considered,* 94/3146, 95/3430, 95/3431, 96/531, 98/2378: *Followed,* 99/2329

S (A Minor) (Abduction: European and Hague Conventions), Re see S (A Minor) (Abduction: European Convention), Re

S (A Minor) (Abduction: European Convention), Re; *sub nom* S (A Minor) (Abduction: European and Hague Conventions), Re; S (A Minor) (Custody: Habitual Residence), Re [1998] A.C. 750; [1997] 3 W.L.R. 597; [1997] 4 All E.R. 251; [1998] 1 F.L.R. 122; [1997] 3 F.C.R. 293; [1997] Fam. Law 782; (1997) 94(34) L.S.G. 28; (1997) 147 N.L.J. 1310; (1997) 141 S.J.L.B. 205; *Times,* July 30, 1997, HL; affirming [1997] 1 F.L.R. 958; [1997] 1 F.C.R. 588; [1997] Fam. Law 388; *Times,* January 8, 1997, CA; reversing [1996] 1 F.L.R. 660; [1996] 3 F.C.R. 115; [1996] Fam. Law 204, Fam Div. . . . .   *Digested,* 97/**398**:
Referred to, 98/4536

S (A Minor) (Adopted Child: Contact), Re; *sub nom* S (Contact: Application by Sibling), Re [1999] Fam. 283; [1999] 3 W.L.R. 504; [1999] 1 All E.R. 648; [1998] 2 F.L.R. 897; [1999] 1 F.C.R. 169; [1998] Fam. Law 581, Fam Div . . . .   *Digested,* 99/**2399**

S (A Minor) (Appeals from Principal Registry: Procedure), Re [1997] 2 F.L.R. 856; [1998] 1 F.C.R. 119; [1998] Fam. Law 22, Fam Div. . . . .   *Digested,* 98/**2398**

S (A Minor) (Change of Surname), Re [1999] 1 F.L.R. 672; [1999] 1 F.C.R. 304; [1999] Fam. Law 207; *Times,* December 29, 1998, CA . . . .   *Digested,* 99/**2374**:
Applied, 01/2572

S (A Minor) (Child Abduction: Delay), Re [1998] 1 F.L.R. 651; [1998] 1 F.C.R. 17; [1998] Fam. Law 129; (1997) 94(43) L.S.G. 30; (1997) 141 S.J.L.B. 217; *Times,* November 20, 1997, Fam Div . . . .   *Digested,* 97/**405**

S (A Minor) (Contact: Evidence), Re [1998] 1 F.L.R. 798; [1998] 3 F.C.R. 70; [1998] Fam. Law 316, CA. . . . .   *Digested,* 98/**2414**

S (A Minor) (Contact: Justices Reasons), Re [1998] 2 F.C.R. 446; (1998) 162 J.P.N. 744, Fam Div . . . .   *Digested,* 98/**2426**

S (A Minor) (Custody: Habitual Residence), Re see S (A Minor) (Abduction: European Convention), Re

S (A Minor) (Injunction to Restrain), Re see Wookey *v.* Wookey

S (A Minor) (Parental Responsibility: Jurisdiction), Re [1998] 1 W.L.R. 1701; [1998] 2 F.L.R. 921; [1999] 2 F.C.R. 27; (1998) 95(35) L.S.G. 38; (1998) 142 S.J.L.B. 248; *Times,* May 27, 1998, CA . . . .   *Digested,* 98/**2436**

S (A Minor) *v.* Calderdale MBC (Unreported, October 13, 1998), CC (Halifax) [*Ex rel.* Rhodes Thain & Collinson Solicitors, 27 Harrison Road, Halifax] . . . .   *Digested,* 99/**1563**

S (A Minor) *v.* Glynn Webb Wallpapers (Unreported, September 15, 1998), CC (Halifax) [*Ex rel.* Rhodes Thain & Collinson Solicitors, 27 Harrison Road, Halifax] . . . .   *Digested,* 99/**1610**

S (A Minor) *v.* Hearnshaw (1999) 99(5) Q.R. 5, MCLC [*Ex rel.* Thompsons Solicitors, Congress House, Great Russell Street, London] . . . .   *Digested,* 99/**1454**

S (A Minor) *v.* North Birmingham HA (1998) 40 B.M.L.R. 103, CA . . . .   *Digested,* 98/**3970**

S (A Minor) *v.* Portsmouth and South East Hampshire HA (Unreported, July 30, 1999), CA [*Ex rel.* Frank R. Moat, Barrister, 3 Pump Court, Temple, London] . . . .   *Digested,* 00/**1503**

S (A Minor) *v.* Somerset HA (1999) 99(6) Q.R. 8, QBD [*Ex rel.* Bolt Burden Solicitors, 1 Providence Place, Islington, London] . . . .   *Digested,* 99/**1546**

S (A Minor) *v.* Special Educational Needs Tribunal [1996] 1 W.L.R. 382; [1996] 2 All E.R. 286; [1996] 1 F.L.R. 663; [1996] 2 F.C.R. 292; [1996] E.L.R. 228; [1996] C.O.D. 430; [1996] Fam. Law 405; *Times,* December 18, 1995, CA; affirming [1995] 1 W.L.R. 1627; [1996] 1 All E.R. 171; [1996] 2 F.C.R. 310; [1996] E.L.R. 102; *Times,* October 5, 1995; *Independent,* September 28, 1995, QBD . . . .   *Digested,* 96/**2492**:
Applied, 97/2135, 00/1948, 01/2039

S (A Minor) (Abduction: Acquiescence), Re [1998] 2 F.L.R. 115; [1998] 3 F.C.R. 113; [1998] Fam. Law 309, CA . . . .   *Digested,* 98/**2372**

S (Abduction: Children: Separate Representation), Re [1997] 1 F.L.R. 486; [1997] 2 F.C.R. 342; [1997] Fam. Law 313, Fam Div . . . . *Digested*, 97/**394**: *Followed*, 99/2372

S (Abduction: Intolerable Situation: Beth Din), Re [2000] 1 F.L.R. 454; [2000] Fam. Law 234, Fam Div . . . . *Digested*, 00/**2448**

S (Abduction: Return into Care), Re; *sub nom* S (A Minor) (Abduction), Re [1999] 1 F.L.R. 843; [1999] 2 F.C.R. 541; [1999] Fam. Law 204, Fam Div . . . . *Digested*, 99/**2320**

S (Adoption), Re see S *v.* M (Consent: Missing Parent)

S (Adult Patient: Sterilisation: Patient's Best Interests), Re; *sub nom* SL *v.* SL; SL (Adult Patient) (Medical Treatment), Re [2001] Fam. 15; [2000] 3 W.L.R. 1288; [2000] 2 F.L.R. 389; [2000] 2 F.C.R. 452; [2000] Lloyd's Rep. Med. 339; (2000) 55 B.M.L.R. 105; [2000] Fam. Law 711; (2000) 97(24) L.S.G. 40; *Times*, May 26, 2000, CA; reversing [2000] 1 F.L.R. 465; [2000] 1 F.C.R. 361; [2000] Fam. Law 322, Fam Div. . . . . *Digested*, 00/**2779**

S (Application for Judicial Review), Re; *sub nom* R. *v.* Collins Ex p. MS; R. *v.* Collins Ex p. S [1998] 1 F.L.R. 790; [1998] 1 F.C.R. 368; [1998] C.O.D. 52; [1997] Fam. Law 790; *Independent*, July 10, 1997, CA; reversing CO4306/96, QBD . . . . *Digested*, 97/**2600**

S (Child Abduction: Acquiescence), Re [1998] 2 F.L.R. 893; [1998] Fam. Law 656, Fam Div . . . . *Digested*, 99/**2315**

S (Child Case: Intervener), Re see S (Minors) (Care: Residence: Intervener), Re

S (Children) (Care Order: Implementation of Care Plan), Re; *sub nom* W and B (Children) (Care Plan), Re; W (Children) (Care Plan), Re; W (Children) (Care Order: Adequacy of Care Plan), Re; TNS, HL; reversing in part [2001] EWCA Civ 757; [2001] 2 F.L.R. 582; [2001] 2 F.C.R. 450; [2001] H.R.L.R. 50; [2001] U.K.H.R.R. 928; [2001] Fam. Law 581; *Times*, June 7, 2001; *Independent*, June 5, 2001, CA. . . . . *Digested*, 01/**2562**

S (Children) (Foster Placement: Regulations 1991), Re [2000] 1 F.L.R. 648; [2000] Fam. Law 319, Fam Div . . . . *Digested*, 00/**2534**

S (CICB: Quantum: 1999), Re (Unreported, April 29, 1999), CICB (London) [*Ex rel*. Ex rel. Christopher Hough, Barrister, 199 Strand, London.] . . . . *Digested*, 99/**1442**

S (CICB: Quantum: 1999) (Sexual Abuse), Re (Unreported, October 20, 1999), CICB (Manchester) [*Ex rel*. Ian Huffer, Barrister, Young Street Chambers, 38 Young Street, Manchester]. . . . . *Digested*, 00/**1528**

S (CICB: Quantum: 2000), Re (Unreported, May 22, 2000), CICB (London) [*Ex rel*. Jake Harris, Pupil Barrister, Goldsmith Chambers, Temple, London] . . . . *Digested*, 00/**1534**

S (CICB: Quantum: 2000) (Burns), Re (Unreported, March 23, 2000), CICB (London) [*Ex rel*. David W Brounger, Barrister, Lamb Building, Temple, London]. . . . . *Digested*, 00/**1644**

S (Contact: Appeal), Re [2001] Fam. Law 505, Fam Div

S (Contact: Application by Sibling), Re see S (A Minor) (Adopted Child: Contact), Re

S (Contact: Indirect Contact), Re see S (Violent Parent: Indirect Contact), Re

S (Deceased), Re see DWS (Deceased), Re

S (Expert Evidence), Re [1998] Fam. Law 594, CA

S (Hospital Patient: Court's Jurisdiction) (No.1), Re [1996] Fam. 1; [1995] 3 W.L.R. 78; [1995] 3 All E.R. 290; [1995] 1 F.L.R. 1075; [1995] 3 F.C.R. 496; [1995] Fam. Law 412; (1995) 92(15) L.S.G. 40; (1995) 139 S.J.L.B. 87; *Times*, March 6, 1995; *Independent*, March 7, 1995, CA; affirming [1995] Fam. 26; [1995] 2 W.L.R. 38; [1995] 1 All E.R. 449; [1995] 1 F.L.R. 302; [1995] 1 F.C.R. 657; [1995] Fam. Law 184, Fam Div . . . . *Digested*, 95/**4105**: *Applied*, 95/4102, 96/2846: *Considered*, 00/4914

S (Leave to Remove from Jurisdiction: Securing Return from Holiday), Re [2001] 2 F.L.R. 507; [2001] Fam. Law 665, Fam Div . . . . *Digested*, 01/**2600**

S (Medical Treatment: Adult Sterilisation), Re [1998] 1 F.L.R. 944; [1999] 1 F.C.R. 277; [1998] Fam. Law 325, Fam Div . . . . *Digested*, 98/**2652**

S (Minors) (Abduction: Acquiescence), Re; *sub nom* S (Minors) (Abduction: Custody Rights), Re [1994] 1 F.L.R. 819; [1994] 2 F.C.R. 945; [1994] Fam. Law 424; *Times*, February 16, 1994; *Independent*, February 25, 1994, CA . . . . *Digested*, 95/**3430**: *Applied*, 96/536, 00/2443: *Followed*, 97/387

S (Minors) (Abduction: Custody Rights), Re see S (Minors) (Abduction: Acquiescence), Re

S (Minors) (Care: Residence: Intervener), Re; *sub nom* S (Child Case: Intervener), Re [1997] 1 F.L.R. 497; [1997] 2 F.C.R. 272; [1997] Fam. Law 232; (1997) 161 J.P.N. 458, CA . . . . *Digested*, 97/**371**: *Considered*, 00/2514

S (Minors) (Proceedings: Conflicting Interests), Re see T and E (Proceedings: Conflicting Interests), Re

S (Removal from Jurisdiction), Re [1999] 1 F.L.R. 850; [1999] Fam. Law 219, Fam Div . *Digested*, 99/**2387**

S (Sexual Abuse Allegations: Local Authority Response), Re see R. (on the application of S) *v.* Swindon BC

S (Violent Parent: Indirect Contact), Re; *sub nom* S (Contact: Indirect Contact), Re [2000] 1 F.L.R. 481; [2000] Fam. Law 239, Fam Div . . . . *Digested*, 00/**2477**

S *v.* Birmingham HA (No.1) [2001] Lloyd's Rep. Med. 382, QBD . . . . *Digested*, 01/**436**

S *v.* Bracknell Forest BC [1999] E.L.R. 51; [1999] C.O.D. 36, QBD . . . . *Digested*, 99/**1899**

S *v.* Cardiff City Council [1999] Ed. C.R. 645, QBD . . . . *Digested*, 99/**1882**

S *v.* Companies Registrar, Graz (6 Ob 124/99z) see Registration in Austria of a Branch
    of an English Company (6 Ob 124/99z), Re
S *v.* D (Rights of Audience) see D *v.* S (Rights of Audience)
S *v.* Dudley MBC [2000] Ed. C.R. 200; [2000] E.L.R. 330, QBD . . . .   *Digested*, 00/**1954**
S *v.* Dudley MBC (Costs) [2000] Ed. C.R. 410; (1999) 149 N.L.J. 1904, QBD . . . .   *Digested*, 00/**1957**
S *v.* Essex CC [2000] Ed. C.R. 471; [2000] E.L.R. 718; *Times*, May 10, 2000, QBD . . . .   *Digested*, 00/**1960**
S *v.* F (Occupation Order) [2000] 1 F.L.R. 255; [2000] 2 F.C.R. 365, Fam Div . . . .   *Digested*, 00/**2540**
S *v.* France (1990) 65 D. & R. 250, Eur Comm HR . . . .   *Applied*, 01/1525
S *v.* Gloucestershire CC; *sub nom* RL *v.* Gloucestershire CC; DS *v.* Gloucestershire CC;
    RL *v.* Tower Hamlets LBC; L *v.* Tower Hamlets LBC [2001] Fam. 313; [2001] 2
    W.L.R. 909; [2000] 3 All E.R. 346; [2000] 1 F.L.R. 825; [2000] 2 F.C.R. 345;
    (2000) 2 L.G.L.R. 848; (2000) 3 C.C.L. Rep. 294; [2000] Fam. Law 474;
    Independent, March 24, 2000, CA . . . .   *Digested*, 00/**4212**:
                Considered, 01/589
S *v.* H (Abduction: Access Rights); *sub nom* S (A Minor) (Abduction: Access Rights),
    Re [1998] Fam. 49; [1997] 3 W.L.R. 1086; [1997] 1 F.L.R. 971; [1997] 3 F.C.R.
    450; [1997] Fam. Law 470; (1997) 94(15) L.S.G. 27; (1997) 141 S.J.L.B. 64;
    Times, March 10, 1997, Fam Div . . . .   *Digested*, 97/**402**
S *v.* Hounslow LBC [2001] E.L.R. 88, QBD . . . .   *Digested*, 01/**2036**
S *v.* Italy; G *v.* Italy [2000] 2 F.L.R. 771; [2000] 3 F.C.R. 430; [2000] Fam. Law 801,
    ECHR . . . .   *Digested*, 01/**3557**
S *v.* Jija 1991 (2) S.A. 52 (E), Sup Ct (SA) . . . .   *Applied*, 98/3116
S *v.* K 3 B.H.R.C. 358, Provincial Div (SA) . . . .   *Digested*, 98/**3159**
S *v.* M (A Minor: Access Order) see Sanderson *v.* McManus
S *v.* M (Consent: Missing Parent); *sub nom* S, Petitioners; ES, Petitioner (Adoption); S
    (Adoption), Re; M *v.* S (Consent: Missing Parent) 1999 S.C. 388; 1999 S.L.T.
    571; 1999 S.C.L.R. 738; [1999] 2 F.L.R. 374; 1999 Fam. L.R. 26; [1999] Fam.
    Law 523; 1999 G.W.D. 6-286; *Times*, March 23, 1999, Ex Div . . . .   *Digested*, 99/**6056**
S *v.* M (Wasted Costs Order) [1998] 3 F.C.R. 665; *Times*, March 26, 1998, Ch D . . . . .   *Digested*, 98/**497**
S *v.* Makwanyane 1995 (3) S.A. 391 (CC), Const Ct (SA) . . . .   *Applied*, 98/2124
S *v.* Methodist Homes for the Aged (Unreported, January 10, 2000), CC (Central
    London) [*Ex rel.* Hodge Jones & Allen Solicitors, Twyman House, 31-39 Camden
    Road, London] . . . .   *Digested*, 00/**1515**
S *v.* Miller (No.1); *sub nom* S *v.* Principal Reporter (No.1) 2001 S.C. 977; 2001 S.L.T.
    531; [2001] U.K.H.R.R. 514; 2001 G.W.D. 13-458, 1 Div . . . .   *Digested*, 01/**6506**:
                Cited, 01/6507
S *v.* Newham LBC [1998] E.M.L.R. 583; [1998] 1 F.L.R. 1061; [1998] 3 F.C.R. 277;
    [1998] Fam. Law 387; (1998) 95(11) L.S.G. 35; (1998) 142 S.J.L.B. 102; *Times*,
    March 5, 1998; *Independent*, February 26, 1998, CA . . . .   *Digested*, 98/**1780**
S *v.* Principal Reporter (No.1) see S *v.* Miller (No.1)
S *v.* S (Chief Constable of West Yorkshire Intervening); *sub nom* Chief Constable of
    West Yorkshire *v.* S [1998] 1 W.L.R. 1716; [1999] 1 All E.R. 281; [1998] 2 F.L.R.
    973; [1999] 1 F.C.R. 244; [1998] Fam. Law 726; (1998) 95(35) L.S.G. 38;
    (1998) 142 S.J.L.B. 248; *Times*, August 24, 1998, CA . . . .   *Digested*, 98/**2429**
S *v.* S (Child Abduction) (Child's Views) see S (A Minor) (Abduction: Custody Rights),
    Re
S *v.* S (Damages: Sexual Abuse) (Unreported, January 12, 1998), CC (Watford) [*Ex
    rel.* Alan Saggerson, Barrister, Barnards Inn Chambers, Halton House, 20-23
    Holborn, London] . . . .   *Digested*, 98/**1510**
S *v.* S (Disclosure of Material) (No.2) see S *v.* S (Judgment in Chambers: Disclosure)
S *v.* S (Disclosure to Revenue) see S *v.* S (Judgment in Chambers: Disclosure)
S *v.* S (Financial Provision: Departing from Equality) [2001] 2 F.L.R. 246; [2001] 3
    F.C.R. 316; [2001] Fam. Law 500, Fam Div . . . .   *Digested*, 01/**2632**
S *v.* S (Financial Provision: Short marriages) [1977] Fam. 127; [1976] 3 W.L.R. 775;
    [1977] 1 All E.R. 56; (1976) 6 Fam. Law 241; (1976) 120 S.J. 780, CA . . . .   *Digested*, 77/**850**:
            Applied, 00/2519: *Considered*, 85/1052: *Distinguished*, 84/2204, 85/2210
S *v.* S (Inland Revenue: Tax Evasion) see S *v.* S (Judgment in Chambers: Disclosure)
S *v.* S (Judgment in Chambers: Disclosure); *sub nom* S *v.* S (Disclosure of Material)
    (No.2); S *v.* S (Disclosure to Revenue); S *v.* S (Inland Revenue: Tax Evasion)
    [1997] 1 W.L.R. 1621; [1997] S.T.C. 759; [1997] 2 F.L.R. 774; [1997] 3 F.C.R. 1;
    69 T.C. 313; [1997] B.T.C. 333; [1997] Fam. Law 659, Fam Div . . . .   *Digested*, 97/**4761**:
             Distinguished, 98/4707
S *v.* Swansea City and County Council [2000] E.L.R. 315, QBD . . . .   *Digested*, 00/**1961**
S *v.* Van Rensburg 1963 (2) S.A. 343 (N), Sup Ct (SA) . . . .   *Applied*, 98/3116
S *v.* Zuma 1995 (2) S.A. 642 (CC), Const Ct (SA) . . . .   *Applied*, 98/3137
S and A (Children) (Care Orders: Threshold Criteria), Re [2001] 3 F.C.R. 589, Fam Div
S and B (CICB: Quantum: 1998), Re (Unreported, September 24, 1998), CICB (York) [*Ex
    rel.* Nicola Saxton, Barrister, St Paul's Chambers, St Paul's House, 23 Park
    Square, Leeds] . . . .   *Digested*, 99/**1441**
S CC *v.* B [2000] Fam. 76; [2000] 3 W.L.R. 53; [2000] 2 F.L.R. 161; [2000] 1 F.C.R.
    536; [2000] Fam. Law 462, Fam Div . . . .   *Digested*, 00/**2465**
S Pearson & Son Ltd *v.* Dublin Corp [1907] A.C. 351, HL (UK-Irl); reversing [1907] 2
    I.R. 27, CA (UK-Irl) . . . .   *Considered*, 01/3805:
             Explained, 47-51/86, 52/35

S Settlement (2001/154), Re (2001-02) 4 I.T.E.L.R. 206, Royal Ct (Jer)

S&J Property Centres v. Customs and Excise Commissioners [2001] S.T.I. 680, V&DTr

S&T Bautrading v. Nordling [1997] 3 All E.R. 718; [1998] I.L.Pr. 151, CA . . . .   *Digested*, 97/**677**:
                                                                                                Not followed, 97/893

S-C (Mental Patient: Habeas Corpus), Re [1996] Q.B. 599; [1996] 2 W.L.R. 146; [1996] 1
    All E.R. 532; [1996] 1 F.L.R. 548; [1996] 2 F.C.R. 692; (1996) 29 B.M.L.R. 138;
    [1996] Fam. Law 210; *Times*, December 4, 1995, CA; reversing [1996] C.O.D.
    221, QBD . . . .   *Digested*, 97/**3653**:
                                                        Considered, 97/3648: *Not followed*, 98/3897

S$1.99 Private Ltd v. Lifestyle 1.99 Private Ltd [2001] F.S.R. 10, CA (Sing) . . . .   *Digested*, 01/**3877**

S, Petitioners see S v. M (Consent: Missing Parent)

SA Ateliers Reunis Caddie v. Sarl Societe Nouvelle De Presse et De Communication;
    sub nom CADDIE Trade Mark [1999] E.T.M.R. 45, Trib Gde Inst (Paris) . . . .   *Digested*, 99/**3551**

SA Diebold Courtage, Re 2 I.T.L. Rep. 365, CE (F)

SA New Building Promotion Ltd, Re 3 I.T.L. Rep. 783, CE (F)

SA Remy-Cointreau, Re (96-684) 1 I.T.L. Rep. 833, Trib Ad (F)

SA Societe LTJ Diffusion v. SA SADAS; *sub nom* SA Societe LTJ Diffusion v. Societe
    SA Sadas Vertbaudet [2001] E.T.M.R. 76, Trib Gde Inst (Paris)

SA Societe LTJ Diffusion v. Societe SA Sadas Vertbaudet see SA Societe LTJ Diffusion
    v. SA SADAS

SA Synetics, Re (96-1858) 1 I.T.L. Rep. 773, C Adm A (F)

SA Winterthur, Re (186924) 3 I.T.L. Rep. 22, CE (F)

Saab v. Saudi American Bank [1999] 1 W.L.R. 1861; [1999] 4 All E.R. 321; [1999] 2
    All E.R. (Comm) 353; [2000] B.C.C. 466; [1999] 2 B.C.L.C. 462; [1999] I.L.Pr.
    798; (1999) 96(31) L.S.G. 42; (1999) 143 S.J.L.B. 211; *Times*, July 29, 1999,
    CA; affirming [1998] 1 W.L.R. 937; [1998] 4 All E.R. 382; [1998] B.C.C. 722;
    [1998] 2 B.C.L.C. 13; *Times*, March 11, 1998, QBD . . . .   *Digested*, 99/**523**:
                                                                                                Applied, 00/486

Sabaf SpA v. MFI Furniture Centres Ltd (2001) 24(10) I.P.D. 24069, Pat Ct

Sabah Flour and Feedmills Sdn Bhd v. Comfez Ltd [1988] 2 Lloyd's Rep. 18, CA;
    affirming [1987] 2 Lloyd's Rep. 647, QBD (Comm Ct) . . . .   *Digested*, 89/**3412**:
                                                                                        Followed, 98/253, 99/4411

Sabapathee v. Mauritius [1999] 1 W.L.R. 1836, PC (Mau) . . . .   *Digested*, 00/**962**

Sabel BV v. Puma AG (C251/95); Sabel BV v. Rudolf Dassler Sport [1997] E.C.R. I-
    6191; [1998] 1 C.M.L.R. 445; [1998] C.E.C. 315; [1998] E.T.M.R. 1; [1998]
    R.P.C. 199, ECJ [1997] E.C.R. I-6191; [1997] E.T.M.R. 283, AGO . . . .   *Digested*, 98/**3512**:
                                Applied, 00/3777, 00/3778, 01/4025, 01/4036: *Considered*, 98/3501,
                                98/3509, 00/3701: *Followed*, 99/3539, 99/3541: *Referred to*, 99/3542,
                                                99/3562, 99/3568, 99/3581, 99/3587, 01/3987, 01/4024

Sabel BV v. Rudolf Dassler Sport see Sabel BV v. Puma AG (C251/95)

Sabella Ltd v. Montgomery; *sub nom* Montgomery v. Sabella Ltd (1999) 77 P. & C.R.
    431; [1998] 1 E.G.L.R. 65; [1998] 09 E.G. 153; [1997] E.G.C.S. 169; (1998) 75
    P. & C.R. D41; *Times*, December 15, 1997, CA; affirming [1997] E.G.C.S. 15, Ch D
    . . . .   *Digested*, 98/**3613**

Sabir v. Tiny Computers (Unreported, January 19, 1999), CC (Reigate) [*Ex rel.* Mary
    Ruck, Barrister, 10 King's Bench Walk, Temple, London] . . . .   *Digested*, 99/**840**

Sabri-Tabrizi v. Lothian Health Board 1998 S.C. 373; 1998 S.L.T. 607; (1998) 43
    B.M.L.R. 190; 1998 Rep. L.R. 37; 1998 G.W.D. 5-247, OH . . . .   *Digested*, 98/**6114**:
                                                                                                Applied, 01/4478

Sacco v. Chief Constable of South Wales (Unreported, May 15, 1998) . . . .

Sacer Sud-Est SA v. Directeur General de la Concurrence [2001] E.C.C. 13, Cass (F)

Sacor Maritima SA v. Repsol Petroleo SA [1998] 1 Lloyd's Rep. 518, QBD (Comm Ct) .   *Digested*, 98/**4401**

Sad Dzumhur v. Redbridge Health Care NHS Trust (Unreported, March 3, 2000) . . . . .   *Considered*, 01/2245

Saddington v. Colleys Professional Services [1999] Lloyd's Rep. P.N. 140; [1995]
    E.G.C.S. 109; [1995] N.P.C. 105; *Times*, June 22, 1995; *Independent*, July 17,
    1995 (C.S.), CA . . . .   *Digested*, 95/**3721**

Sadik v. Greece (1997) 24 E.H.R.R. 323, ECHR . . . .   *Digested*, 98/**3078**

Sadiku v. DPP [2000] R.T.R. 155; (2000) 144 S.J.L.B. 35; *Times*, December 3, 1999,
    QBD . . . .   *Digested*, 00/**988**

Saeed v. Plustrade Ltd [2001] EWCA Civ 2011, CA; affirming [2001] R.T.R. 30;
    [2000] E.G.C.S. 143; [2000] N.P.C. 134, Ch D

Saeed v. Royal Wolverhampton Hospitals NHS Trust [2001] I.C.R. 903; [2001] Lloyd's
    Rep. Med. 111; *Times*, January 17, 2001, CA; affirming [2000] Lloyd's Rep. Med.
    331, QBD . . . .   *Digested*, 01/**2892**

Safa Ltd v. Banque du Caire [2000] 2 All E.R. (Comm) 567; [2000] 2 Lloyd's Rep.
    600; [2000] Lloyd's Rep. Bank. 323; [2000] C.L.C. 1556, CA; affirming 1999
    Folio No.657, QBD (Comm Ct) . . . .   *Digested*, 00/**285**

Safety Hi-Tech Srl v. S&T Srl (C284/95) [1998] E.C.R. I-4301; [1999] 2 C.M.L.R. 515;
    Times, July 22, 1998, ECJ . . . .   *Digested*, 98/**2267**

Safeway Stores v. Secretary of State for the Environment, Transport and the Regions
    [1999] E.G.C.S. 29; (1999) 96(9) L.S.G. 34; [1999] N.P.C. 26, QBD

Safeway Stores Plc v. Burrell [1997] I.C.R. 523; [1997] I.R.L.R. 200, EAT . . . .   *Digested*, 97/**2249**:
                                                        Considered, 98/2185, 98/2186, 99/2107, 99/5280

Safeway Stores Plc v. Hachette Filipacchi Presse (Opposition) see ELLE Trade Marks
    (Opposition)

Safeway Stores Plc *v.* Hachette Filipacchi Presse (Revocation) see ELLE Trade Marks (Revocation)

Safeway Stores Plc *v.* Secretary of State for the Environment, Transport and the Regions (Leave to Appeal) (1999) 78 P. & C.R. 250, CA . . . . *Digested,* 00/**4521**

Safeway Stores Plc *v.* Tate [2001] Q.B. 1120; [2001] 2 W.L.R. 1377; [2001] 4 All E.R. 193; [2001] C.P. Rep. 56; [2001] E.M.L.R. 13; (2001) 98(8) L.S.G. 45; (2001) 145 S.J.L.B. 16; *Times,* January 25, 2001; *Independent,* February 12, 2001 (C.S.), CA . . . . *Digested,* 01/**682**: *Considered,* 01/**1827**

Saffron Walden Herts & Essex Building Society *v.* Bunbury (1999) 77 P. & C.R. D22, CA

Saga Foodstuffs Manufacturing (Pte) Ltd *v.* Best Food Pte Ltd Unreported . . . . *Considered,* 99/**3524**

Sage *v.* Maidstone BC; *sub nom* Sage *v.* Secretary of State for the Environment, Transport and the Regions [2001] EWCA Civ 1100; [2001] 3 P.L.R. 107; [2001] 27 E.G.C.S. 133; *Times,* October 23, 2001, CA; affirming [2001] J.P.L. 986; [2000] E.G.C.S. 112; *Daily Telegraph,* November 14, 2000, QBD (Admin Ct). . . . *Digested,* 01/**4698**

Sage *v.* Secretary of State for the Environment, Transport and the Regions see Sage *v.* Maidstone BC

Sage *v.* South Gloucestershire CC [1999] Ed. C.R. 420; [1998] E.L.R. 525; [1998] C.O.D. 384, QBD. . . . . *Digested,* 98/**1983**

Sagnata Investments Ltd *v.* Norwich Corp; *sub nom* Norwich Corp *v.* Sagnata Investments Ltd [1971] 2 Q.B. 614; [1971] 3 W.L.R. 133; [1971] 2 All E.R. 1441; 69 L.G.R. 471; 115 S.J. 406, CA . . . . *Digested,* 71/**5081**: *Applied,* 00/**5658**: *Considered,* 82/**1906**, 83/**3147**

Sahota *v.* Secretary of State for the Home Department see R. *v.* Secretary of State for the Home Department Ex p. Sahota

Saif Ali *v.* Sydney Mitchell & Co [1980] A.C. 198; [1978] 3 W.L.R. 849; [1978] 3 All E.R. 1033; [1955-95] P.N.L.R. 151; 122 S.J. 761, HL; reversing [1978] Q.B. 95; [1977] 3 W.L.R. 421; [1977] 3 All E.R. 744; 121 S.J. 336, CA . . . . *Digested,* 78/**2323**: *Applied,* 80/**2609**, 91/**2869**, 92/**3499**, 93/**3180**, 94/**3623**, 95/**4033**, 98/**4011**, 99/**4034**: *Considered,* 90/**3264**, 96/**3580**, 98/**4012**, 99/**4021**: *Distinguished,* 79/**2293**, 88/**2768**, 89/**3073**, 01/**42**: *Followed,* 96/**4509**, 97/**3815**, 00/**4001**: *Referred to,* 79/**2110**, 79/**2111**, 81/**2184**, 92/**3212**, 97/**3825**

Saifi *v.* Governor of Brixton Prison see R. (on the application of Saifi) *v.* Governor of Brixton Prison

Saigol *v.* Cranley Mansion Ltd (No.2) 72 Con. L.R. 54, CA. . . . . *Digested,* 01/**1539**

SAIL *v.* Farex; *sub nom* Societe Anonyme d'Intermediaries Luxembourgeois *v.* Farex Gie [1995] L.R.L.R. 116, CA. . . . . *Applied,* 01/**3805**

Sainer *v.* Clore see Clore's Settlement Trusts, Re

Sainsbury's Bank Plc's Trade Mark Application see FRESH BANKING Trade Mark

Sainsbury's Supermarkets Ltd *v.* Secretary of State for the Environment, Transport and the Regions see Bexley LBC *v.* Secretary of State for the Environment, Transport and the Regions

Saint *v.* Barking and Dagenham LBC see Barking and Dagenham LBC *v.* Saint

Saint *v.* Polygram (Britannia Music Co) Ltd (Unreported, August 1, 2000), CC (Central London) [*Ex rel.* Jonathan Loades, Barrister, 9 Gough Square, London] . . . . . . *Digested,* 01/**1689**

Saint Tropez (District and Town Council) *v.* Valais [1999] E.T.M.R. 310, Trib Gde Inst (Paris)

Saipem SpA *v.* Dredging VO2 BV (The Volvox Hollandia) (No.1); Saipem SpA *v.* Geosite Surveys Ltd [1988] 2 Lloyd's Rep. 361; [1989] E.C.C. 16; *Independent,* June 6, 1988 (C.S.); *Financial Times,* June 14, 1988, CA; reversing [1987] 2 Lloyd's Rep. 520, QBD (Comm Ct) . . . . *Digested,* 89/**378**: *Applied,* 99/**716**

Saipem SpA *v.* Geosite Surveys Ltd see Saipem SpA *v.* Dredging VO2 BV (The Volvox Hollandia) (No.1)

Sajfudinov *v.* Secretary of State for the Home Department [2001] EWCA Civ 945; [2001] Imm. A.R. 628, CA

Sakik *v.* Turkey (1998) 26 E.H.R.R. 662; [1998] I.N.L.R. 357; [1998] H.R.C.D. 107, ECHR . . . . *Digested,* 98/**3073**

Salabiaku *v.* France (A/141-A) (1991) 13 E.H.R.R. 379, ECHR. . . . . *Applied,* 00/**1169**, 00/**3229**: *Considered,* 00/**1004**, 01/**3504**

Salamander AG *v.* European Parliament (T172/98) [2000] All E.R. (EC) 754; [2000] E.C.R. II-2487; [2000] 2 C.M.L.R. 1099, CFI (3rd Chamber) . . . . *Digested,* 00/**2352**

Salamander AG *v.* Industria de Calcados Kissol Ltda [1998] E.T.M.R. 94, KKO (Fin)

Saldanha *v.* Hiross Holding AG (C122/96) [1998] All E.R. (E.C.) 238; [1997] E.C.R. I-5325; [1997] I.L.Pr. 766, ECJ (6th Chamber) . . . . *Digested,* 98/**2309**

Sale of Mobile Phones (16 Ok 22/97), Re [1999] E.C.C. 116, OGH (A)

Sale of OEM Software, Re [1998] E.C.C. 227, LG (Berlin)

Saleem *v.* Secretary of State for Social Security [2001] EWCA Civ 69; (2001) 98(10) L.S.G. 45; *Times,* March 2, 2001; *Independent,* February 26, 2001 (C.S), CA . . . *Digested,* 01/**5046**

Saleem *v.* Secretary of State for the Home Department see R. *v.* Secretary of State for the Home Department Ex p. Saleem

Saleem *v.* Siddique [2001] 6 Q.R. 4, CC (Bradford) [*Ex rel.* Jonathan Godfrey, Barrister, St Paul's Chambers, 23 Park Square, Leeds] . . . . *Digested,* 01/**1562**

Salesi *v.* Italy (A/257-E) (1998) 26 E.H.R.R. 187, ECHR . . . . *Digested,* 98/**3139**

Saleslease Ltd v. Davis [1999] 1 W.L.R. 1664; [2000] 1 All E.R. (Comm) 883; (1999) 96(17) L.S.G. 24; (1999) 143 S.J.L.B. 121; *Times*, April 15, 1999, CA . . . . *Digested, 99/4849*
Salford City Council v. Coral Racing Ltd (1998) 13 P.A.D. 348, Planning Inspector
Salgueiro da Silva Mouta v. Portugal (33290/96) [2001] 1 F.C.R. 653; (2001) 31 E.H.R.R. 47; 2001 Fam. L.R. 2, ECHR . . . . *Digested, 01/2587*
Salih v. Enfield AHA [1991] 3 All E.R. 400; [1991] 2 Med. L.R. 235; *Independent*, March 26, 1991; *Guardian*, May 2, 1991; *Daily Telegraph*, April 8, 1991, CA; reversing *Times*, December 7, 1989, QBD . . . . *Digested, 92/1797:*
                                        Considered, 00/4200: Not followed, 98/5723
Salim (Nabil Ahmed) v. Secretary of State for the Home Department [2000] Imm. A.R. 503, CA
Salisbury v. Kirklees MBC (Unreported, June 21, 2001), CC (Huddersfield) [*Ex rel.* Halliwell Landau, Solicitors, City Plaza, 2 Pinfold Street, Sheffield] . . . . *Digested, 01/4485*
Salisbury DC v. Federal Mogul (2000) 15 P.A.D. 28, Planning Inspector
Salisbury DC v. Secretary of State for the Environment [1982] J.P.L. 702 . . . . *Digested, 82/3201:*
                                        Referred to, 01/4713
Sallows v. Griffiths [2001] F.S.R. 15; (2000) 23(4) I.P.D. 23035, CA . . . . *Digested, 00/5118*
Salmet International Ltd (In Administration), Re see Spring Valley Properties Ltd v. Harris
Salmon (Deceased), Re; *sub nom* Coard v. National Westminster Bank Ltd [1981] Ch. 167; [1980] 3 W.L.R. 748; [1980] 3 All E.R. 532; 124 S.J. 813, Ch D . . . . *Digested, 80/2818:*
                   Applied, 80/2819, 81/2885, 81/2887, 99/4635: Considered, 95/5146
Salomon v. Salomon & Co Ltd; *sub nom* Broderip v. Salomon; Salomon & Co Ltd v. Salomon [1897] A.C. 22, HL; reversing [1895] 2 Ch. 323, CA . . . . *Applied, 47-51/9135,*
         62/1718, 66/1369, 77/3268, 78/271, 78/3172, 80/306, 90/538, 98/618, 01/705,
         01/944: Considered, 60/3342, 68/160, 68/2956, 69/138, 69/2956, 75/803,
         77/174, 78/2678, 81/2194, 82/3, 84/958, 87/3003, 98/2188, 00/5985:
                  Distinguished, 53/940, 74/1837: Followed, 97/2379
Salomon & Co Ltd v. Salomon see Salomon v. Salomon & Co Ltd
Salt v. Buckley (Inspector of Taxes) [2001] S.T.C. (S.C.D.) 262; [2001] S.T.I. 1526, Sp Comm
Salter Rex & Co v. Ghosh [1971] 2 Q.B. 597; [1971] 3 W.L.R. 31; [1971] 2 All E.R. 865; 115 S.J. 387, CA . . . . *Digested, 71/9150:*
       Applied, 76/2103, 83/147, 83/1238, 84/1235, 84/2614: Considered, 86/1503:
                     Distinguished, 99/5265: Followed, 83/3041
Salters Hall School Ltd (In Liquidation), Re; *sub nom* Merrygold v. Horton [1998] 1 B.C.L.C. 401; *Times*, July 11, 1997, Ch D (Companies Ct) . . . . *Digested, 97/3067*
Salvage Association v. CAP Financial Services Ltd [1995] F.S.R. 654, QBD . . . . *Digested, 95/772:*
                                  Considered, 00/870
Salvidge v. Hussein; *sub nom* Debtor (No.SD8/9 of 1998), Re [2000] B.C.C. 36; [1999] B.P.I.R. 410; *Times*, November 11, 1998, Ch D . . . . *Digested, 98/322*
Samaroo v. Secretary of State for the Home Department see R. (on the application of Samaroo) v. Secretary of State for the Home Department
Sambasivam v. Public Prosecutor, Malaya [1950] A.C. 458; 66 T.L.R. (Pt. 2) 254, PC (FMS) . . . . *Digested, 47-51/7972:*
        Applied, 83/660: Considered, 78/464: Distinguished, 64/665, 64/768,
             89/756, 90/796, 90/797, 00/924: Followed, 63/632
Sambasivam v. Secretary of State for the Home Department [2000] I.N.L.R. 105; *Times*, November 10, 1999, CA . . . . *Digested, 99/3152*
Samler v. Shaw [2000] 1 Q.R. 6, QBD [*Ex rel.* Taylor Vinters Solicitors, Merlin Place, Milton Road, Cambridge] . . . . *Digested, 99/1430*
Sampson, Re; *sub nom* Sampson's Application, Re; Sampson v. Croydon Crown Court [1987] 1 W.L.R. 194; [1987] 1 All E.R. 609; (1987) 84 Cr. App. R. 376; [1987] Crim. L.R. 570; (1987) 84 L.S.G. 825; (1987) 137 N.L.J. 169; (1987) 131 S.J. 225, HL . . . . *Digested, 87/2282:*
       Applied, 92/33, 92/39, 93/12, 93/15: Considered, 90/766, 91/613, 93/10:
                       Followed, 01/3539: Referred to, 93/11
Sampson v. Croydon Crown Court see Sampson, Re
Sampson v. Hodson-Pressinger [1981] 3 All E.R. 710; (1984) 12 H.L.R. 40; (1982) 261 E.G. 891; 125 S.J. 623, CA . . . . *Digested, 82/2268:*
                                Distinguished, 98/4044
Sampson's Application, Re see Sampson, Re
Sams v. Olley (Unreported, January 18, 1998), QBD [*Ex rel.* Gordon Exall, Barrister, 10 Park Square, Leeds] . . . . *Digested, 98/1644*
Samsonite Corp v. Vijay Sales [2000] F.S.R. 463, HC (Ind)
Samuel v. Fatih (2000) 80 P. & C.R. D45, CA
Samuel v. Secretary of State for the Environment, Transport and the Regions [1999] P.L.C.R. 356, CA; affirming (1998) 95(26) L.S.G. 32, QBD . . . . *Digested, 00/4451*
Samuels v. Coole & Haddock CCRTI 96/1182/G, CA . . . . *Digested, 97/4860:*
                                  Applied, 00/333
Samuels v. Linzi Dresses Ltd [1981] Q.B. 115; [1980] 2 W.L.R. 836; [1980] 1 All E.R. 803; 124 S.J. 187, CA . . . . *Digested, 80/2190:*
                     Applied, 80/287, 81/2201: Followed, 98/4881
San Marco Impex Italiana Srl v. Commission of the European Communities (C19/95) [1996] E.C.R. I-4435, ECJ . . . . *Followed, 00/2363*

San Remo Macaroni Co (Pty) Ltd *v.* Commissioner of Taxation 2 I.T.L. Rep. 400, Fed Ct (Aus) (Sgl judge)

San Sebastian Pty *v.* Minister Administering the Environment Planning and Assessment Act 1979 (1987) 68 A.L.R. 161; (1987) 3 Const. L.J. 212, HC (Aus) . . . . *Digested*, 87/**2588**: *Applied*, 00/4246

Sanchez Hidalgo *v.* Asociacion de Servicios Aser (C173/96); Zieman *v.* Zieman Sicherheit GmbH (C247/96) [1998] E.C.R. I-8237; [1999] I.R.L.R. 136, ECJ (5th Chamber) . . . . *Digested*, 00/**2231**: *Considered*, 01/2335

Sanchez-Reisse *v.* Switzerland (A/107) (1987) 9 E.H.R.R. 71; *Times*, November 4, 1986, ECHR . . . . *Digested*, 86/**1651**: *Applied*, 00/4322, 01/4424

Sanctuary Housing Association *v.* Baker (No.1) (1998) 30 H.L.R. 809; [1998] 1 E.G.L.R. 42; [1998] 09 E.G. 150, CA . . . . *Digested*, 98/**2984**

Sanctuary Housing Association *v.* Baker (No.2) (1999) 31 H.L.R. 746, CA . . . . *Digested*, 99/**3732**

Sanctuary Housing Association *v.* Campbell [1999] 1 W.L.R. 1279; [1999] 3 All E.R. 460; [1999] 2 F.L.R. 383; [1999] 2 F.C.R. 657; (2000) 32 H.L.R. 100; [1999] L. & T.R. 425; [1999] 2 E.G.L.R. 20; [1999] Fam. Law 449; (1999) 149 N.L.J. 521; [1999] N.P.C. 39; (1999) 78 P. & C.R. D15; *Times*, April 1, 1999, CA . . . . . . *Digested*, 99/**3740**: *Followed*, 01/4189

Sander *v.* United Kingdom (2001) 31 E.H.R.R. 44; 8 B.H.R.C. 279; [2000] Crim. L.R. 767; *Times*, May 12, 2000, ECHR . . . . *Digested*, 00/**3231**

Sanders *v.* Templar see Giles *v.* Thompson

Sanders *v.* Van der Putte (C73/77) [1977] E.C.R. 2383; [1978] 1 C.M.L.R. 331, ECJ . . . *Digested*, 78/**1297**: *Considered*, 00/773

Sanders BVBA *v.* Belgium (C47/96) see Garage Molenheide BVBA *v.* Belgium (C286/94)

Sanderson *v.* Attorney General of the Eastern Cape 3 B.H.R.C. 647, Const Ct (SA) . . . . *Digested*, 98/**3137**

Sanderson *v.* MacManus see Sanderson *v.* McManus

Sanderson *v.* McManus; *sub nom* S *v.* M (A Minor: Access Order); Sanderson *v.* MacManus 1997 S.C. (H.L.) 55; 1997 S.L.T. 629; 1997 S.C.L.R. 281; [1997] 1 F.L.R. 980; 1997 G.W.D. 6-220; *Times*, February 12, 1997, HL; affirming 1996 S.L.T. 750; 1995 S.C.L.R. 902, Ex Div; affirming 1994 S.C.L.R. 537, Sh Pr . . . . . . *Digested*, 97/**5631**: *Considered*, 01/2609, 01/6510: *Distinguished*, 01/6510

Sanderson's Trust, Re (1857) 3 Kay & J. 497 . . . . *Applied*, 78/3081, 79/2804, 99/4954

Sandford *v.* British Railways Board (Unreported, September 9, 1999), QBD [*Ex rel.* Townsends Solicitors, 42 Cricklade Street, Swindon, Wiltshire] . . . . *Digested*, 00/**1650**

Sandhu *v.* Raymond Dyers Ltd see Dataschool Ltd *v.* Sandhu

Sandilands *v.* Marsh (1819) 2 B. & Ald. 673 . . . . *Considered*, 01/4564

Sandman *v.* Panasonic UK Ltd [1998] F.S.R. 651; [1998] Masons C.L.R. 220; (1998) 21 (4) I.P.D. 21038, Ch D . . . . *Digested*, 98/**3416**: *Referred to*, 99/3493

Sandom *v.* Webb see Webb's Lease, Re

Sandoz GmbH *v.* Finanzlandesdirektion fur Wien, Niederosterreich und Burgenland (C439/97) [1999] E.C.R. I-7041; [2001] 3 C.M.L.R. 63, ECJ (6th Chamber)

Sandry *v.* Jones, *Times*, August 3, 2000, CA . . . . *Digested*, 00/**1476**

Sandvik AB *v.* KR Pfiffner (UK) Ltd (No.1) (1998) 21 (2) I.P.D. 21015, Pat Ct

Sandvik AB *v.* KR Pfiffner (UK) Ltd (No.2) [1999] Eu. L.R. 755; [2000] F.S.R. 17; (1999) 22(8) I.P.D. 22073, Pat Ct . . . . *Digested*, 99/**497**

Sanger (t/a SA Jewels) *v.* Beazley [1999] Lloyd's Rep. I.R. 424, QBD (Comm Ct)

Sanghi Polyesters (India) Ltd *v.* International Investor (KCFC) (Kuwait) [2000] 1 Lloyd's Rep. 480; [2001] C.L.C. 748, QBD (Comm Ct) . . . . *Digested*, 00/**217**

Sangwon, The [2000] 1 Lloyd's Rep. 511, CA (Sing) . . . . *Digested*, 00/**4742**

Sanjivi *v.* East Kent HA (2001) 59 B.M.L.R. 115; *Times*, December 19, 2000, QBD (Admin Ct) . . . . *Digested*, 01/**5135**

Sankar *v.* Trinidad and Tobago [1995] 1 W.L.R. 194; [1995] 1 All E.R. 236; (1995) 139 S.J.L.B. 34; *Times*, December 28, 1994; *Independent*, January 12, 1995, PC (Trin) . . . . *Digested*, 95/**1211**: *Applied*, 96/1604: *Considered*, 99/978: *Distinguished*, 96/1646

Sankey *v.* Helping Hands Group Plc [2000] C.P. Rep. 11, CA . . . . *Digested*, 00/**499**

Sankey Furniture Ltd Ex p. Harding, Re; Calorifique Ltd Ex p. Betts, Re [1995] 2 B.C.L.C. 594, Ch D . . . . *Digested*, 96/**3481**: *Considered*, 97/3868: *Distinguished*, 97/3065, 01/3767

Sansom *v.* Metcalfe Hambleton & Co 57 Con. L.R. 88; [1998] P.N.L.R. 542; [1998] 2 E.G.L.R. 103; [1998] 26 E.G. 154; [1997] E.G.C.S. 185; (1998) 95(5) L.S.G. 28; (1998) 142 S.J.L.B. 45; [1997] N.P.C. 186; *Times*, December 29, 1997, CA . . . . . . *Digested*, 98/**4007**: *Applied*, 00/4250

Santner *v.* Hoechst AG (C229/96) see Francisco Hernandez Vidal SA *v.* Perez (C127/96)

Santos *v.* Owners of the Baltic Carrier [2001] 1 Lloyd's Rep. 689; [2001] C.L.C. 990; *Independent*, April 2, 2001 (C.S), QBD (Comm Ct) . . . . *Digested*, 01/**4946**

Sanusi *v.* Secretary of State for the Home Department see R. *v.* Secretary of State for the Home Department Ex p. Sanusi

Sanwa, The and Choyang Star, The [1998] 1 Lloyd's Rep. 283, QBD (Adm Ct) . . . .   *Digested*, 98/**4417**
Sapra *v.* Secretary of State for the Environment, Transport and the Regions [2001]
    J.P.L. 1205, QBD (Admin Ct) . . . .   *Digested*, 01/**4759**
Sara Lee Household & Body Care UK Ltd *v.* Johnson Wax Ltd [2001] EWCA Civ 1609,
    CA; affirming [2001] F.S.R. 17, Pat Ct. . . . .   *Digested*, 01/**3918**
Sardegna Lines - Servizi Marittimi della Sardegna SpA *v.* Commission of the European
    Communities (C105/99) see Italy *v.* Commission of the European Communities
    (C15/98)
Sardinia Sulcis, The and Al Tawwab, The [1991] 1 Lloyd's Rep. 201; *Times*, November 21,
    1990; *Independent*, December 3, 1990 (C.S.); *Financial Times*, November 13,
    1990, CA . . . .   *Digested*, 91/**3204**:
                    Applied, 99/494: *Followed*, 96/890
Sargent *v.* Customs and Excise Commissioners [1995] 1 W.L.R. 821; [1995] S.T.C.
    398; [1995] 2 B.C.L.C. 34; (1996) 71 P. & C.R. 278; [1995] R.V.R. 168; [1995]
    E.G.C.S. 29; (1995) 92(14) L.S.G. 55; (1995) 139 S.J.L.B. 87; *Times*, February
    23, 1995; *Independent*, May 1, 1995 (C.S.), CA; affirming in part [1994] 1 W.L.R.
    235; [1994] S.T.C. 1; [1993] E.G.C.S. 182; (1994) 91(9) L.S.G. 41; [1993]
    N.P.C. 142; *Times*, November 18, 1993, Ch D . . . .   *Digested*, 95/**5106**:
              Distinguished, 96/4916: *Followed*, 99/3358
Sargent *v.* GRE (UK) Ltd [2000] Lloyd's Rep. I.R. 77; [1997] 6 Re. L.R. 281; [1997]
    P.I.Q.R. Q128; *Times*, April 25, 1997, CA . . . .   *Digested*, 97/**3122**
Sargin *v.* Turkey (A/319) see Yagci *v.* Turkey (A/319)
Sarl Mega Press *v.* Pressimage [2000] E.T.M.R. 403, C d'A (Paris)
Sarl Sygroup *v.* Societe Sylab Ypsis [2001] E.T.M.R. 109, C d'A (Paris)
Sarrio *v.* Commission of the European Communities (C291/98 P) (Application to Set
    Aside); *sub nom* Sarrio *v.* Commission of the European Communities (T334/94)
    (No.1); SCA Holding *v.* Commission of the European Communities (T327/94)
    (No.1) [1998] E.C.R. II-1439; [1998] 5 C.M.L.R. 195, CFI (3rd Chamber)
Sarrio *v.* Commission of the European Communities (T334/94) (No.1) see Sarrio *v.*
    Commission of the European Communities (C291/98 P) (Application to Set
    Aside)
Sarrio *v.* Commission of the European Communities (T334/94) (No.2) see SCA
    Holding Ltd *v.* Commission of the European Communities (C297/98 P)
Sarrio SA *v.* Kuwait Investment Authority [1999] 1 A.C. 32; [1997] 3 W.L.R. 1143;
    [1997] 4 All E.R. 929; [1998] 1 Lloyd's Rep. 129; [1998] Lloyd's Rep. Bank. 57;
    [1997] C.L.C. 1640; [1998] I.L.Pr. 319; (1997) 141 S.J.L.B. 248; *Times*,
    November 17, 1997; *Independent*, November 19, 1997, HL; reversing [1997] 1
    Lloyd's Rep. 113; [1997] C.L.C. 280; [1997] I.L.Pr. 481; *Independent*, October 3,
    1996, CA; reversing [1996] 1 Lloyd's Rep. 650; [1996] C.L.C. 211, QBD
    (Comm Ct) . . . .   *Digested*, 97/**900**:
                   Applied, 01/809: *Considered*, 00/738
Sarsfield (Inspector of Taxes) *v.* Dixons Group Plc (No.1) [1998] S.T.C. 938; 71 T.C. 121;
    [1998] B.T.C. 288; *Times*, July 20, 1998; *Independent*, July 27, 1998 (C.S.), CA;
    reversing [1997] S.T.C. 283; [1997] B.T.C. 127; (1997) 94(6) L.S.G. 28; *Times*,
    February 11, 1997; *Independent*, March 3, 1997 (C.S.), Ch D . . . .   *Digested*, 98/**4601**
Sarsfield (Inspector of Taxes) *v.* Dixons Group Plc (No.2) [1998] E.G.C.S. 116, CA . . . .   *Digested*, 98/**4603**
Sarum Properties Ltd, Re [1999] 2 E.G.L.R. 132; [1999] 17 E.G. 136; [1999] R.V.R. 90, Lands
    Tr . . . .   *Digested*, 99/**3749**
Sarwar *v.* Alam; *sub nom* Sawar *v.* Alam [2001] EWCA Civ 1401; [2001] 4 All E.R.
    541; (2001) 151 N.L.J. 1492; *Times*, October 11, 2001; *Daily Telegraph*, September
    25, 2001, CA. . . . .   *Digested*, 01/**3818**
Sasea Finance Ltd (In Liquidation), Re [1999] B.C.C. 103; [1998] 1 B.C.L.C. 559; *Times*,
    December 29, 1997, Ch D . . . .   *Digested*, 98/**483**
Sasea Finance Ltd (In Liquidation) *v.* KPMG (formerly KPMG Peat Marwick McLintock)
    (No.1) [1998] B.C.C. 216, Ch D . . . .   *Digested*, 98/**3309**
Sasea Finance Ltd (In Liquidation) *v.* KPMG (formerly KPMG Peat Marwick McLintock)
    (No.2) [2000] 1 All E.R. 676; [2000] B.C.C. 989; [2000] 1 B.C.L.C. 236;
    [2000] Lloyd's Rep. P.N. 227, CA; reversing [1999] B.C.C. 857; *Times*, August
    25, 1998, Ch D . . . .   *Digested*, 00/**4249**
SAT *v.* Eurocontrol (C364/92) see SAT Fluggesellschaft mbH *v.* European
    Organisation for the Safety of Air Navigation (Eurocontrol) (C364/92)
SAT Fluggesellschaft mbH *v.* European Organisation for the Safety of Air Navigation
    (Eurocontrol) (C364/92); *sub nom* SAT *v.* Eurocontrol (C364/92) [1994] E.C.R.
    I-43; [1994] 5 C.M.L.R. 208; *Financial Times*, January 25, 1994, ECJ . . . .   *Digested*, 94/**4772**:
                Applied, 98/717: *Considered*, 99/4990
SATAM BRANDT/Refrigeration plant (T17/86) [1989] E.P.O.R. 347, EPO (Technical Bd
    App) . . . .   *Followed*, 00/**3603**
Satam SA *v.* Minister Responsible for the Budget (C333/91) see Sofitam SA (formerly
    Satam SA) *v.* Ministre Charge du Budget (C333/91)
Satnam Investments Ltd *v.* Dunlop Heywood & Co Ltd [1999] 3 All E.R. 652; [1999] 1
    B.C.L.C 385; [1999] F.S.R. 722; [1999] Lloyd's Rep. P.N. 201; [1998] E.G.C.S.
    190; (1999) 96(2) L.S.G. 30; (1999) 96(6) L.S.G. 33; [1998] N.P.C. 169; *Times*,
    December 31, 1998, CA; reversing (1999) 96(2) L.S.G. 30; [1998] N.P.C. 169,
    Ch D . . . .   *Digested*, 99/**585**

Sauflon Pharmaceuticals Ltd v. Allergan Inc see Allergan Inc v. Sauflon Pharmaceuticals
Ltd
Saul D Harrison & Sons Plc, Re [1994] B.C.C. 475; [1995] 1 B.C.L.C. 14, CA . . . . *Digested*, 95/**2860**:
Applied, 99/5731: *Considered*, 99/646, 00/620: *Followed*, 95/615
Saunders (A Bankrupt), Re; *sub nom* Bristol and West Building Society v. Saunders;
Bearman (A Bankrupt), Re [1997] Ch. 60; [1996] 3 W.L.R. 473; [1997] 3 All
E.R. 992; [1997] B.C.C. 83; [1996] B.P.I.R. 355, Ch D . . . . *Digested*, 96/**3444**:
Followed, 98/3319
Saunders v. Adderley [1999] 1 W.L.R. 884; (1998) 142 S.J.L.B. 220; *Times*, July 20,
1998, PC (Bah) . . . . *Digested*, 98/**359**
Saunders (Executrix of the Estate of Rose Maud Gallie) v. Anglia Building Society
(formerly Northampton Town and County Building Society) (Costs); *sub nom*
Gallie v. Lee [1971] A.C. 1039; [1971] 2 W.L.R. 349; [1971] 1 All E.R. 243; 22 P.
& C.R. 300; (1970) 115 S.J. 112, HL . . . . *Digested*, 71/**9364**:
Applied, 72/2762: *Considered*, 72/2766, 99/3758
Saunders v. Hammersmith and Fulham LBC (Homelessness) (Unreported, March 18,
1999), CC (West London) [*Ex rel.* Jon Holbrook, Barrister, 2 Garden Court
Chambers, Middle Temple, London] . . . . *Digested*, 99/**3058**
Saunders v. Hammersmith and Fulham LBC (Personal Injuries: Quantum) (Unreported,
January 29, 1998), CC (Central London) [*Ex rel.* John Denniss, Barrister, 4 King's
Bench Walk, 2nd Floor, Temple, London] . . . . *Digested*, 98/**1570**
Saunders v. Punch Ltd (t/a Liberty Publishing) [1998] 1 W.L.R. 986; [1998] 1 All E.R.
234; [1998] E.M.L.R. 18; *Independent*, November 17, 1997 (C.S.), Ch D . . . . . . *Digested*, 97/**21**:
Applied, 00/14
Saunders v. Sun Life Assurance Co of Canada [1894] 1 Ch. 537, Ch D . . . . *Considered*, 00/**5608**:
Distinguished, 47-51/10335
Saunders v. United Kingdom [1997] B.C.C. 872; [1998] 1 B.C.L.C. 362; (1997) 23
E.H.R.R. 313; 2 B.H.R.C. 358; *Times*, December 18, 1996; *Independent*, January
14, 1997, ECHR; affirming *Independent*, September 30, 1994, Eur Comm HR . . . *Digested*, 97/**2816**:
Applied, 01/1047: *Considered*, 97/2818, 98/3150, 00/5473, 00/6043, 01/974,
01/6319: *Distinguished*, 00/667, 00/2300: *Followed*, 97/817, 00/3234:
Not applied, 98/682
Saunders v. Vautier (1841) 4 Beav. 115 . . . . *Applied*, 61/**6608**:
Considered, 47-51/9387, 67/410: *Distinguished*, 98/2301: *Followed*, 75/3116
Saunders v. West Glamorgan HA FC3 98/5459/1; FC3 98/6071/1; QBENF 97/1139/1,
CA . . . . *Digested*, 98/**552**:
Saunders v. Wiel [1893] 1 Q.B. 470; [1893] 10 R.P.C. 29, CA . . . . *Applied*, 00/**3696**
Savage v. Fairclough [2000] Env. L.R. 183; [1999] N.P.C. 103; [2000] E.H.L.R. Dig.
97, CA . . . . *Digested*, 00/**4289**
Savage v. J Sainsbury Ltd see J Sainsbury Ltd v. Savage
Savage v. Saxena [1998] I.C.R. 357; [1998] I.R.L.R. 182; *Times*, February 11, 1998,
EAT . . . . *Digested*, 98/**2226**
Savage v. Thomas (Unreported, January 10, 2001), CC (Chelmsford) [*Ex rel.* Richard
Menzies, Barrister, 8 Stone Buildings, Lincoln's Inn, London] . . . . *Digested*, 01/**1810**
Save and Prosper Pensions Ltd v. Homebase Ltd [2001] L. & T.R. 11, Ch D . . . . *Digested*, 01/**334**
Save & Prosper Securities Ltd v. Inland Revenue Commissioners [2000] S.T.C. (S.C.D.)
408; [2000] S.T.I. 1360, Sp Comm . . . . *Digested*, 01/**5306**
Save Britain's Heritage v. Number 1 Poultry Ltd; *sub nom* Save Britain's Heritage v.
Secretary of State for the Environment [1991] 1 W.L.R. 153; [1991] 2 All E.R. 10;
89 L.G.R. 809; (1991) 3 Admin. L.R. 437; (1991) 62 P. & C.R. 105; [1991] 3
P.L.R. 17; (1991) 155 L.G. Rev. 429; [1991] E.G.C.S. 24; (1991) 88(15) L.S.G. 31;
(1991) 135 S.J. 312; *Times*, March 1, 1991; *Independent*, March 1, 1991;
Guardian, March 1, 1991, HL; reversing (1990) 60 P. & C.R. 539; [1990] 3 P.L.R.
50; [1990] J.P.L. 831; *Times*, April 4, 1990; *Independent*, April 13, 1990;
Guardian, April 12, 1990, CA; reversing *Times*, January 5, 1990; *Independent*,
December 22, 1989, QBD . . . . *Digested*, 91/**3494**:
Applied, 92/450, 92/4157, 93/3909, 97/4090, 99/4181, 99/4267, 01/4652,
01/4747: *Cited*, 92/4319, 92/4354, 93/3810, 94/4349: *Considered*, 93/3925,
96/4734, 96/4832, 96/4836, 97/4093: *Distinguished*, 96/7151:
Followed, 95/3610, 96/4705, 96/4753, 97/4070, 98/6143, 99/6411,
00/4474, 01/4750: *Referred to*, 95/2598
Save Britain's Heritage v. Secretary of State for the Environment see Save Britain's
Heritage v. Number 1 Poultry Ltd
Save Service Stations Ltd v. Ravenseft Properties Ltd; *sub nom* Ards Autopoint, Ards
Shopping Centre, Newtownards, Re; BT/37/1996, Lands Tr (NI) . . . . *Digested*, 98/**3611**
Saver Ltd, Re [1999] B.C.C. 221, Ch D (Companies Ct) . . . . *Digested*, 99/**621**
Savile v. Roberts (1698) 1 Ld. Raym. 374 . . . . *Applied*, 47-51/**6157**,
60/1953, 61/3318, 61/5397: *Followed*, 97/4862, 98/4779
SAVILE ROW Trade Mark [1998] R.P.C. 155, TMR . . . . *Digested*, 98/**3534**
Savill v. Southend HA [1995] 1 W.L.R. 1254; [1996] 7 Med. L.R. 162; (1995) 139
S.J.L.B. 47; *Times*, December 28, 1994, CA . . . . *Digested*, 96/**676**:
Cited, 99/432: *Considered*, 97/502, 97/2137, 98/384: *Distinguished*, 97/964:
Not followed, 98/354
Saville Perfumery v. FW Woolworth & Co Ltd see Saville Perfumery v. Perfect

Saville Perfumery v. Perfect; *sub nom* Saville Perfumery v. FW Woolworth & Co Ltd
(1941) 58 R.P.C. 147 . . . . *Applied*, 67/3955:
Followed, 95/4937, 01/5881
Savills Land & Property Ltd v. Kibble [1998] E.G.C.S. 170, CA
Savings & Investment Bank Ltd (In Liquidation) v. Fincken (Statement of Claim) [2001]
EWCA Civ 1639; (2001) 98(48) L.S.G. 29; *Times*, November 15, 2001, CA;
reversing [2001] C.P. Rep. 78; (2001) 98(16) L.S.G. 35; *Times*, March 2, 2001,
Ch D . . . . *Digested*, 01/**626**
Savory v. Holland, Hannen & Cubitts (Southern) Ltd [1964] 1 W.L.R. 1158; [1964] 3
All E.R. 18; 108 S.J. 479, CA. . . . . *Digested*, 64/**2560**:
Considered, 68/175: *Distinguished*, 00/4206
Sawar v. Alam see Sarwar v. Alam
Sawoniuk v. United Kingdom [2001] Crim. L.R. 918, ECHR
Sawyer v. Ahsan [2000] I.C.R. 1; [1999] I.R.L.R. 609; (2000) 2 L.G.L.R. 884; *Times*,
September 21, 1999, EAT. . . . . *Digested*, 99/**2097**
Sawyer (Carol) v. Habgood [2001] 3 Q.R. 17, CC (Southampton) [*Ex rel.* Benjamin
Williams, Barrister, 1 Temple Gardens, Temple, London] . . . . *Digested*, 01/**1705**
Sawyer (William) v. Habgood [2001] 4 Q.R. 14, CC (Southampton) [*Ex rel.* Benjamin
Williams, Barrister, 1 Temple Gardens, Temple, London] . . . . *Digested*, 01/**1711**
Saxby v. Secretary of State for the Environment, Transport and the Regions [1998]
J.P.L. 1132; *Times*, May 18, 1998, QBD . . . . *Digested*, 98/**4231**
Saxena v. Gloor [2000] I.L.Pr. 534, Sup Ct (BC) . . . . *Digested*, 00/**788**
Sayandan v. Secretary of State for the Home Department (Unreported, March 5,
1998), IAT. . . . . *Distinguished*,
99/3169:
Followed, 99/3170
Saywell (t/a Eaton Tractor Co) v. Pope (Inspector of Taxes) [1979] S.T.C. 824; 53 T.C.
40; [1979] T.R. 229, Ch D . . . . *Digested*, 82/**1609**:
Followed, 98/4071
SB (A Child) (Care Proceedings: Children's Guardian), Re see MH (A Child) (Care
Proceedings: Children's Guardian), Re
SB SpA v. SJM Inc [2000] E.N.P.R. 177, BGH (Ger)
SBJ Stephenson Ltd v. Mandy [2000] I.R.L.R. 233; [2000] F.S.R. 286, QBD . . . . *Digested*, 00/**2116**
SBJ Stephenson Ltd v. Mandy (Interim Order) [1999] C.P.L.R. 500; *Times*, July 21,
1999, CA . . . . *Digested*, 99/**354**
SBJ Stephenson Ltd v. Mandy (Order for Costs) [2000] C.P. Rep. 64; [2000] F.S.R.
651, QBD . . . . *Digested*, 00/**423**
SC (A Minor), Re see C (A Minor) (Adoption: Freeing Order), Re
SC Rolinay Sea Star Srl v. Compania de Navigatie Maritimie Petromin SA (The
Bumbesti) see Bumbesti, The
SC Rolinay Sea Star Srl v. Owners of the Bumbesti see Bumbesti, The
SCA Holding v. Commission of the European Communites (T327/94) (No.1) see Sarrio
v. Commission of the European Communities (C291/98 P) (Application to Set
Aside)
SCA Holding Ltd v. Commission of the European Communities (C297/98 P); *sub nom*
SCA Holding Ltd v. Commission of the European Communities (T327/94)
(No.2); Sarrio v. Commission of the European Communities (T334/94) (No.2)
[2000] E.C.R. I-10101; [2001] 4 C.M.L.R. 13, ECJ (5th Chamber); affirming
SCA Holding Ltd v. Commission of the European Communities (T327/94) (No.2) see
SCA Holding Ltd v. Commission of the European Communities (C297/98 P)
Scales Trading Ltd v. Far Eastern Shipping Plc see Far Eastern Shipping Plc v. Scales
Trading Ltd
Scally v. Southern Health and Social Services Board [1992] 1 A.C. 294; [1991] 3
W.L.R. 778; [1991] 4 All E.R. 563; [1991] I.C.R. 771; [1991] I.R.L.R. 522; (1991)
141 N.L.J. 1482; (1991) 135 S.J. 172; *Times*, October 24, 1991; *Independent*,
October 25, 1991; *Financial Times*, October 30, 1991; *Guardian*, November 20,
1991, HL . . . . *Digested*, 92/**1917**:
Considered, 95/3689, 99/2012: *Followed*, 00/4216
Scammell v. Dicker; *sub nom* Dicker v. Scammell [2001] 1 W.L.R. 631; [2001] C.P.
Rep. 64; [2001] C.P.L.R. 188; (2001) 98(7) L.S.G. 41; (2001) 145 S.J.L.B. 28;
[2001] N.P.C. 1; *Times*, February 14, 2001, CA . . . . *Digested*, 01/**615**
Scandecor Development AB v. Scandecor Marketing AB [2001] UKHL 21; [2001] 2
C.M.L.R. 30; [2001] E.T.M.R. 74; (2001) 24(9) I.P.D. 24056, HL [1999] F.S.R.
26; (1999) 22(1) I.P.D. 22009; *Times*, October 7, 1998; *Independent*, October 5,
1998 (C.S.), CA; affirming [1998] F.S.R. 500; (1998) 21(7) I.P.D. 21071;
(1998) 95(12) L.S.G. 28; *Times*, March 9, 1998, Ch D . . . . *Digested*, 01/**4038**:
Applied, 01/3878
Scanfuture UK Ltd v. Bird see Scanfuture UK Ltd v. Secretary of State for Trade and
Industry
Scanfuture UK Ltd v. Secretary of State for Trade and Industry; *sub nom* Scanfuture UK
Ltd v. Bird; Link v. Secretary of State for Trade and Industry [2001] I.C.R. 1096;
[2001] I.R.L.R. 416; [2001] Emp. L.R. 590; *Times*, April 26, 2001, EAT . . . . *Digested*, 01/**2269**
Scania CV AB v. Westlye [2000] E.T.M.R. 767, Arbitration . . . . *Digested*, 01/**3875**

Scanvaegt International A/S v. Pelcombe Ltd (formerly Portals Engineering Ltd) [1998]
  F.S.R. 786; (1998) 21 (8) I.P.D. 21080, CA . . . . *Digested*, 98/**3462**:
  Referred to, 99/3518

Scapino BV v. Basic Trademark SA [2001] E.T.M.R. 27, RB (Amsterdam)
Scarborough BC v. Noble Organisation Ltd (1998) 13 P.A.D. 97, Planning Inspector
Scarborough BC v. Rural Development Association (formerly Rural Workspace and
  Housing Association) (2001) 16 P.A.D. 95, Planning Inspector
Scarborough Building Society v. Howes Percival (1998) 76 P. & C.R. D4, CA; affirming
  [1998] P.N.L.R. 395, QBD. . . . . *Digested*, 98/**4069**
Scarfe v. Adams [1981] 1 All E.R. 843; 125 S.J. 32, CA. . . . . *Digested*, 81/**2276**:
  Considered, 99/4351
Scarrott v. Straiton (Unreported, July 28, 1989), CA . . . . *Applied*, 97/538,
  97/599: *Considered*, 97/542, 98/424, 98/438, 98/453, 98/457, 99/533:
  Distinguished, 98/509: *Followed*, 94/3572, 96/699, 98/455, 98/456,
  98/460, 98/485

SCF Finance Co Ltd v. Masri (No.1); *sub nom* Masri v. SCF Finance Co Ltd (No.1)
  [1985] 1 W.L.R. 876; [1985] 2 All E.R. 747; [1985] 2 Lloyd's Rep. 206; (1985)
  82 L.S.G. 2015; (1985) 129 S.J. 450, CA. . . . . *Digested*, 85/**2676**:
  Considered, 92/3545, 99/16
Schachter v. Canada [1992] 2 S.C.R. 679, Sup Ct (Can) . . . . *Applied*, 98/3074
Schapira v. Ahronson [1998] I.L.Pr. 587; [1999] E.M.L.R. 735, CA. . . . . *Considered*, 98/748:
  Followed, 99/717

Schebsman (Deceased) Ex p. Official Receiver, Re; *sub nom* Trustee v. Cargo
  Supertintendents (London) Ltd [1944] Ch. 83; [1943] 2 All E.R. 768, CA;
  affirming in part [1943] Ch. 366, Ch D . . . . *Applied*, 47-51/2591,
  47-51/2661, 59/873: *Considered*, 59/3029, 88/2042, 98/3285:
  Distinguished, 66/1915
Scheeres v. Scheeres [1999] 1 F.L.R. 241; [1999] F.C.R. 476; [1999] Fam. Law 18, CA . *Digested*, 99/**2415**
Scheffel v. Innungskrankenkasse Vorderpfalz (C444/93) see Megner v.
  Innungskrankenkasse Vorderpfalz (C444/93)
Schellenberg v. BBC [2000] E.M.L.R. 296, QBD. . . . . *Digested*, 00/**624**
Schenk v. Switzerland (A/140) (1991) 13 E.H.R.R. 242; *Times*, August 2, 1988, ECHR . *Digested*, 88/**1810**:
  Applied, 98/3126: *Followed*, 97/2817

Schepens v. Belgium (C340/95) see Garage Molenheide BVBA v. Belgium (C286/94)
Schering AG's Application see John Wyeth & Brother Ltd's Application
Schering Agrochemicals Ltd v. Resibel NV SA (Unreported, November 26, 1992), CA. . *Distinguished*,
  98/4384:
  Referred to, 96/1248
Schering Biotech Corp's Application, Re [1993] R.P.C. 249, Pat Ct. . . . . *Referred to*, 00/3680
Schieving-Nijstad VOF v. Groeneveld (C89/99); *sub nom* VOF Schieving-Nijstad v.
  Groeneveld (C89/99) [2001] E.C.R. I-5851; [2001] 3 C.M.L.R. 44, ECJ [2000]
  I.L.Pr. 311; [2001] E.C.R. I-5851; [2001] E.T.M.R. 59, AGO . . . . *Digested*, 01/**4033**
Schiffahrtsgesellschaft MS Merkur Sky mbH & Co KG v. MS Leerort Nth Schiffahrts
  GmbH & Co KG [2001] EWCA Civ 1055; [2001] 2 Lloyd's Rep. 291, CA. . . . . . . *Digested*, 01/**4919**
Schilling v. Lenton (1988) 47 S.A.S.R. 88, Sup Ct (SAus) (Sgl judge) . . . . *Digested*, 89/**2581**:
  Considered, 00/4217
Schluter v. Hauptzollamt Lorrach (C9/73) [1973] E.C.R. 1135, ECJ. . . . . *Digested*, 74/**1376**:
  Considered, 97/1043, 98/2569
Schmautzer v. Austria (A/328-A) (1996) 21 E.H.R.R. 511, ECHR . . . . *Digested*, 96/**3123**:
  Followed, 98/3111

Schmeink & Cofreth AG & Co KG v. Finanzamt Borken (C454/98); Strobel v. Finanzamt
  Esslingen (C454/98) [2000] S.T.C. 810; [2000] E.C.R. I-6973; [2001] 1
  C.M.L.R.16; [2000] C.E.C. 687; [2000] B.T.C. 5338; [2000] B.V.C. 377; [2000]
  S.T.I. 1419, ECJ . . . . *Digested*, 00/**5311**
Schmid v. Finanzlandesdirektion fur Wien, Niederosterreich und Burgenland (C113/99)
  [2001] E.C.R. I-471; [2001] 2 C.M.L.R.13, ECJ (2nd Chamber) . . . . *Digested*, 01/**5204**
SCHMID/Etching process (T229/85) [1987] E.P.O.R. 279, EPO (Technical Bd App). . . *Considered*, 00/3636
Schmidt (Karlheinz) v. Germany (A/291-B) (1994) 18 E.H.R.R. 513, ECHR . . . . *Digested*, 95/**2666**:
  Applied, 97/2823, 98/3076
Schmidt v. Spar- und Leihkasse der Fruheren Amter Bordesholm, Keil und Cronshagen
  (C392/92) [1994] E.C.R. I-1311; [1995] 2 C.M.L.R. 331; [1995] I.C.R. 237;
  [1994] I.R.L.R. 302; *Times*, May 25, 1994, ECJ (5th Chamber) . . . . *Digested*, 95/**2071**:
  Applied, 95/2066, 95/2068, 96/2647: *Considered*, 98/2220
Schmidt & Salden GmbH v. Stichting Bill Bakers Big Band Corp see Glenn Miller
  Productions Inc v. Stichting Bill Bakers Big Band Corp
Schneider SA, Re (96-1408) 3 I.T.L. Rep. 529, C Adm A (F)
Schnitzer v. Lyons (Unreported, May 14, 2001), CC (Chelmsford) [*Ex rel*. Ford &
  Warren, Solicitors, Westgate Point, Westgate, Leeds] . . . . *Digested*, 01/**1541**
Schnoor v. Cage (Unreported, March 7, 2000), CC (Weymouth) [*Ex rel*. Amanda
  Gillett, Pupil Barrister, College Chambers, 19 Carlton Crescent, Southampton] . . *Digested*, 00/**1729**
Schnorbus v. Land Hessen (C79/99) [2000] E.C.R. I-10997; [2001] 1 C.M.L.R. 40,
  ECJ (6th Chamber). . . . . *Digested*, 01/**2285**

Schofield *v.* Chief Constable of West Yorkshire; *sub nom* Chief Constable of West
  Yorkshire *v.* Schofield [1999] I.C.R. 193; (1998) 43 B.M.L.R. 28; *Times,* May 15,
  1998, CA . . . .   *Digested,* 98/**3954**
Schofield *v.* Saunders & Taylor Ltd see Heil *v.* Rankin
Schofield *v.* Saunders & Taylor Ltd (Costs) see Heil *v.* Rankin (Costs)
Scholes Windows Ltd *v.* Magnet Ltd (No.1) [2001] EWCA Civ 532; (2001) 24(6) I.P.D.
  24036; *Times,* June 5, 2001, CA; affirming [2000] E.C.D.R. 248; [2000] F.S.R.
  432; (2000) 23(2) I.P.D. 23016, Ch D . . . .   *Digested,* 01/**3864**:
                                                                                                                        Considered, 01/3861
Scholes Windows Ltd *v.* Magnet Ltd (No.2) [2000] E.C.D.R. 266, Ch D . . . .   *Digested,* 00/**414**
Scholey *v.* Foster (Unreported, May 21, 1997), CC (Bow) [*Ex rel.* Nicholas A Peacock,
  Barrister, Ground Floor, 6 Pump Court, Temple] . . . .   *Digested,* 97/**723**:
                                                                                    Applied, 98/597: *Doubted,* 98/595
Scholler Lebensmittel GmbH & Co KG *v.* Commission of the European Communities
  (T9/93) see Langnese Iglo GmbH *v.* Commission of the European Communities
  (C279/95)
School of Finance and Management (London) Ltd *v.* Customs and Excise
  Commissioners; *sub nom* Customs and Excise Commissioners *v.* School of
  Finance and Management (London) Ltd [2001] S.T.C. 1690; [2001] S.T.I. 1663,
  Ch D; affirming [2001] B.V.C. 2284; [2001] S.T.I. 1145, V&DTr . . . .   *Digested,* 01/**5601**
Schopfer *v.* Switzerland (25405/94) (2001) 33 E.H.R.R. 34; 4 B.H.R.C. 623; [1998]
  H.R.C.D. 560, ECHR . . . .   *Digested,* 98/**3092**
Schouten *v.* Netherlands (A/304); Meldrum *v.* Netherlands (A/304) (1995) 19
  E.H.R.R. 432, ECHR . . . .   *Applied,* 98/**3119**
Schrader HS Kraftfutter GmbH & Co KG *v.* Hauptzollamt Gronau (C265/87) [1989]
  E.C.R. 2237, ECJ . . . .   *Applied,* 99/**704**
SCHRAMM/Adaptation of description (T113/92) [1999] E.P.O.R. 94, EPO (Technical Bd
  App)
Schrembri (CICB: Quantum: 1999), Re [2000] 3 Q.R. 7, CICB (London) [*Ex rel.* Hefin
  Rees, Barrister, 10 King's Bench Walk, Temple, London] . . . .   *Digested,* 00/**1621**
Schroder *v.* Deutsche Telekom AG (C50/96); *sub nom* Deutsche Telekom AG *v.*
  Schroder (C50/96); Deutsche Post AG *v.* Sievers (C270/97); Deutsche Telekom
  AG *v.* Vick (C234/96) [2000] E.C.R. I-743; [2000] I.R.L.R. 353; *Times,* March
  28, 2000, ECJ (6th Chamber) . . . .   *Digested,* 00/**2168**
Schroder Unit Trusts Ltd *v.* Inland Revenue Commissioners see M&G Securities Ltd *v.*
  Inland Revenue Commissioners
Schroll *v.* PCO Stauereibetrieb Paetz & Co Nachfolgar GmbH (C139/91) see Katsikas
  v. Konstantinidis (C132/91)
Schuldenfrei *v.* Hilton (Inspector of Taxes) [1999] S.T.C. 821; 72 T.C. 167; [1999] B.T.C.
  310; (1999) 96(33) L.S.G. 32; *Times,* August 12, 1999, CA; affirming [1998]
  S.T.C. 404; [1998] B.T.C. 156; *Times,* February 25, 1998; *Independent,* February
  23, 1998 (C.S.), Ch D . . . .   *Digested,* 99/**4653**
Schuler-Zgraggen *v.* Switzerland (A/263) [1994] 1 F.C.R. 453; (1993) 16 E.H.R.R.
  405; *Times,* October 21, 1993, ECHR . . . .   *Digested,* 95/**2667**:
                              Applied, 98/3135, 98/3145, 01/855: *Considered,* 96/3151, 01/4167:
                                                                                                Distinguished, 98/3121
Schuler-Zgraggen *v.* Switzerland (A/305-A) (1996) 21 E.H.R.R. 404, ECHR . . . .   *Digested,* 96/**3154**:
                                                                                                                        Applied, 98/3064
Schulke & Mayr UK Ltd *v.* Alkapharm UK Ltd [1999] F.S.R. 161; (1997) 20(11) I.P.D.
  20106, Ch D . . . .   *Digested,* 99/**4853**
Schultz *v.* Esso Petroleum Co Ltd [1999] 3 All E.R. 338; [1999] I.C.R. 1202; [1999]
  I.R.L.R. 488, CA . . . .   *Digested,* 99/**2051**
Schutt *v.* Germanus [2001] 6 Q.R. 11, CC (Bristol) [*Ex rel.* Matthew White, Barrister,
  St. John's Chambers, Small Street, Bristol] . . . .   *Digested,* 01/**1651**
Schutzverband gegen Unwesen in der Wirtschaft EV *v.* Warsteiner Brauerei Haus Cramer
  GmbH & Co KG (C312/98) [2000] E.C.R. I-9187; [2001] 2 C.M.L.R. 11, ECJ
  [2000] E.C.R. I-9187; [2000] E.T.M.R. 734, AGO . . . .   *Digested,* 01/**4040**
SCI (Sales Curve Interactive) Ltd *v.* Titus Sarl (A Firm) [2001] EWCA Civ 591; [2001] 2
  All E.R. (Comm) 416, CA; affirming HQ 0000480, QBD . . . .   *Digested,* 01/**936**
Scientific Investment Pension Plan (No.2), Re; *sub nom* Kemble *v.* Hicks (No.1); Trusts of
  the Scientific Investment Pension Plan, Re [1999] Ch. 53; [1998] 3 W.L.R.
  1191; [1998] 3 All E.R. 154; [1998] 2 B.C.L.C. 360; [1998] 2 F.L.R. 761; [1998]
  B.P.I.R. 410; [1998] O.P.L.R. 41; [1998] Fam. Law 582; *Times,* March 5, 1998,
  Ch D . . . .   *Digested,* 98/**3279**
Scientific Investment Pension Plan (No.3), Re; *sub nom* Kemble *v.* Hicks (No.2) [1999]
  O.P.L.R. 1; [1999] Pens. L.R. 287, Ch D . . . .   *Digested,* 00/**4383**:
                                                                                                                        Applied, 00/4359
Scindia Steamship Navigation Co Ltd Bombay *v.* Nippon Yusen Kaisha Ltd (The
  Jalagouri) see Nippon Yusen Kaisha Ltd *v.* Scindia Steam Navigation Co Ltd
  (The Jalagouri)
Scotch Premier Meat Ltd *v.* Burns [2000] I.R.L.R. 639, EAT . . . .   *Digested,* 00/**6215**
Scotch Whisky Association *v.* Compagnie Financiere Europeenne de Prises de
  Participation (C136/96) [1998] E.C.R. I-4571; [1999] 2 C.M.L.R. 229; [1998]
  E.T.M.R. 629; *Times,* August 21, 1998, ECJ (5th Chamber) . . . .   *Digested,* 98/**823**

Scotch Whisky Association *v.* Glen Kella Distillers Ltd (No.2) [1997] Eu. L.R. 455;
[1997] E.T.M.R. 470; (1997) 20(7) I.P.D. 20067; (1997) 94(16) L.S.G. 29;
(1997) 141 S.J.L.B. 91; *Times*, April 1, 1997, Ch D . . . . *Digested*, 97/**956**:
Followed, 98/3523

Scotch Whisky Association *v.* JD Vintners Ltd [1997] Eu. L.R. 446, Ch D . . . . *Digested*, 98/**3522**:
Considered, 99/3562: *Followed*, 97/956, 98/3523

Scotlife Home Loans (No.2) Ltd *v.* Melinek (1999) 78 P. & C.R. 389, CA . . . . *Digested*, 00/**4661**

Scott (Boundary Dispute), Re [2001] C.P.L.R. 5, CA . . . . *Digested*, 01/**425**

Scott (Deceased), Re; *sub nom* Widdows *v.* Friends of the Clergy Corp [1975] 1 W.L.R.
1260; [1975] 2 All E.R. 1033; 119 S.J. 508, Ch D . . . . *Digested*, 75/**3571**

Scott *v.* Associated British Ports; Swainger *v.* Associated British Ports; B3/1999/1194,
B3/1999/1195, CA; affirming1993-S-No.0387, QBD . . . . *Digested*, 99/**4006**

Scott *v.* Avery (1856) 5 H.L. Cas. 811, HL . . . . *Considered*, 47-51/448,
47-51/449, 69/3571, 84/3152, 98/761: *Distinguished*, 99/1639

Scott *v.* Cheshire CC see Scott *v.* Secretary of State for the Environment, Transport and
the Regions (Enforcement Notice)

Scott *v.* Miller (Unreported, July 24, 1998), CC (Harlow) [*Ex rel.* Richard Menzies,
Barrister, 8 Stone Buildings, Lincoln's Inn, London] . . . . *Digested*, 98/**1750**

Scott *v.* National Trust for Places of Historic Interest or Natural Beauty; *sub nom* R. *v.*
National Trust for Places of Historic Interest or Natural Beauty Ex p. Scott; Scott,
Ex p. [1998] 1 W.L.R. 226; [1998] 2 All E.R. 705; [1998] J.P.L. 465; [1998]
C.O.D. 138; *Independent*, July 21, 1997 (C.S.), QBD. *Digested*, 97/**66**:
Applied, 01/386

Scott *v.* Nucrete Buildings Ltd [1998] P.I.Q.R. Q112; [1998] Lloyd's Rep. Med. 375,
QBD . . . . *Digested*, 99/**2872**

Scott *v.* Sampson (1881-82) L.R. 8 Q.B.D. 491, QBD . . . . *Applied*, 60/1786,
61/4974: *Considered*, 61/6416, 62/1741, 01/1820: *Distinguished*, 66/7003

Scott (Otherwise Morgan) *v.* Scott [1913] A.C. 417, HL; reversing [1912] P. 241, CA;
affirming [1912] P. 4, PDAD . . . . *Applied*, 52/467,
52/494, 52/2672, 57/2235, 57/2759, 63/1807, 93/3033, 94/5047, 01/564,
01/2622: *Considered*, 53/1034, 53/2752, 63/1092, 65/203, 75/955,
76/1805, 77/1965, 79/2120, 81/2144, 83/2353, 84/866, 84/2250, 87/675,
88/692, 89/784, 92/693, 92/3139, 93/2835, 94/3282, 95/3545, 95/3959:
Distinguished, 47-51/7548: *Followed*, 58/2473, 96/2980

Scott *v.* Secretary of State for the Environment, Transport and the Regions
(Enforcement Notice); Scott *v.* Cheshire CC; C/2000/0202, C/2000/0203, CA;
affirming [2000] J.P.L. 833; [1999] N.P.C. 136, QBD . . . . *Digested*, 01/**4689**

Scott *v.* Spain (1997) 24 E.H.R.R. 391, ECHR . . . . *Digested*, 98/**3070**

Scott *v.* Swansea City and County Council [2001] 5 E.G.C.S. 167; (2001) 98(5)
L.S.G. 38, Ch D

Scott *v.* United Kingdom (34745/97) [2000] 1 F.L.R. 958; [2000] 2 F.C.R. 560;
2000 Fam. L.R. 102; [2000] Fam. Law 538, ECHR . . . . *Digested*, 00/**3238**

Scott *v.* Wakefield AHA [1997] 8 Med. L.R. 341, CA. . . . . *Digested*, 98/**3967**

Scott Wilson Kirkpatrick & Partners *v.* Ministry of Defence; Dean & Dyball Construction
Ltd *v.* Ministry of Defence [2000] B.L.R. 20; 73 Con. L.R. 52, CA . . . . *Digested*, 00/**813**

Scott, Ex p. see Scott *v.* National Trust for Places of Historic Interest or Natural Beauty

Scottish & Newcastle Plc *v.* GD Construction (St Albans) Ltd (2001) 3 T.C.L.R. 24; 80
Con. L.R. 75, QBD (T&CC) . . . . *Digested*, 01/**865**

Scottish & Newcastle Plc's Trade Mark Application [2000] E.T.M.R. 1143, OHIM
(Opposition Div) . . . . *Digested*, 01/**3988**

Scottish & Newcastle Retail Ltd *v.* Williams (Valuation Officer) see Williams (Valuation
Officer) *v.* Scottish & Newcastle Retail Ltd

Scottish Coal Co Ltd *v.* East Lothian Council; *sub nom* R. *v.* East Lothian Council Ex p.
Scottish Coal Co Ltd 2001 S.L.T. 495; [2001] 1 P.L.R. 1; 2000 G.W.D. 17-701;
Times, June 28, 2000, OH . . . . *Digested*, 00/**6625**

Scottish Eastern Investment Trust Plc *v.* Customs and Excise Commissioners [2001]
S.T.I. 257, V&DTr

Scottish Equitable Life Plc *v.* Virdee see Virdee *v.* Scottish Equitable Life Plc

Scottish Equitable Plc *v.* Derby; *sub nom* Derby *v.* Scottish Equitable Plc [2001] EWCA
Civ 369; [2001] 3 All E.R. 818; [2001] 2 All E.R. (Comm) 274; [2001] Pens.
L.R. 163; (2001) 151 N.L.J. 418; *Independent*, May 7, 2001 (C.S); *Daily
Telegraph*, March 27, 2001, CA; affirming [2000] 3 All E.R. 793; [2001] 2 All
E.R. (Comm) 119; [2000] Pens. L.R. 1, QBD. . . . . *Digested*, 01/**2440**:
Considered, 01/2434

Scottish Homes *v.* Customs and Excise Commissioners [2000] B.V.C. 2391; [2000]
S.T.I. 1311, V&DTr

Scottish Mutual Assurance Plc *v.* Jardine Public Relations Ltd [1999] E.G.C.S. 43, QBD
(T&CC) . . . . *Digested*, 99/**3747**

Scottish Nuclear Ltd *v.* Assessor for Lanarkshire [2000] R.A. 280; 2000 G.W.D. 2-79,
LVAC . . . . *Digested*, 00/**6647**

Scottish Power Plc *v.* Britoil (Exploration) Ltd (1997) 94(47) L.S.G. 30; (1997) 141
S.J.L.B. 246; *Times*, December 2, 1997, CA. . . . . *Digested*, 98/**848**:
Considered, 99/4033

Scottish Salmon Growers Association Ltd v. EFTA Surveillance Authority (E2/94) [1995] 1 C.M.L.R. 851, EFTA . . . .   *Followed*, 00/**729**

Scottish Special Housing Association v. Wimpey Construction (UK) Ltd [1986] 1 W.L.R. 995; [1986] 2 All E.R. 957; 1986 S.L.T. 559; 34 B.L.R. 1; 9 Con. L.R. 19; (1986) 2 Const. L.J. 149; (1986) 83 L.S.G. 2652; 130 S.J. 592, HL; reversing 1986 S.L.T. 173; 31 B.L.R. 17, 1 Div. . . . .   *Digested*, 86/**3613**:
Applied, 97/5721, 01/952: *Considered*, 93/309, 01/865:
Distinguished, 90/4724, 94/333, 96/1215: *Referred to*, 95/5576

ScottishTourist Board v. Customs and Excise Commissioners [2001] S.T.I. 258, V&DTr

Scotto v. Clarke see Scotto v. Petch

Scotto v. Petch; *sub nom* Sedgefield Steeplechase Co (1927) Ltd, Re; Scotto v. Clarke [2001] B.C.C. 889; *Times*, February 8, 2001, CA; affirming [2000] 2 B.C.L.C. 211; (2000) 97(6) L.S.G. 33; (2000) 144 S.J.L.B. 107; *Times*, February 16, 2000, Ch D . . . .   *Digested*, 01/**744**

Scouller v. Transport and General Workers Union (Unreported, December 21, 2000), Certification Officer [*Ex rel.* Certification Office for Trade Unions and Employers Associations, Brandon house, 180 Borough High Street, London] . . . .   *Digested*, 01/**2328**

Screeton v. East Riding DC (Unreported, April 13, 2000), CC (Kingston upon Hull) [*Ex rel*. Richard Gregory, Barrister, 24 The Ropewalk, Nottingham] . . . .   *Digested*, 00/**1691**

Scrivner v. Wojcik [2001] R.V.R. 248, QBD

Scully UK Ltd v. Lee [1998] I.R.L.R. 259, CA; affirming1997-S-No.711, QBD . . . .   *Digested*, 98/**2192**:
Distinguished, 98/727

Scutt v. Lomax (2000) 79 P. & C.R. D31, CA

SDL International Ltd v. Centre de Cooperation Internationale en Recherche Agronomique pour le Developpement [2001] C.L.C. 903; *Independent*, October 30, 2000 (C.S), Ch D . . . .   *Digested*, 01/**830**

Sea Assets Ltd v. PT Garuda Indonesia (No.1) [2000] 4 All E.R. 371; [2001] B.C.C. 294, QBD (Comm Ct) . . . .   *Digested*, 00/**486**

Sea Containers Services Ltd v. Customs and Excise Commissioners [2000] S.T.C. 82; [2000] B.T.C. 5028; [2000] B.V.C. 60, QBD; affirming [1999] B.V.C. 2214, V&DTr. . . . .   *Digested*, 00/**5343**

Sea Melody Enterprises SA v. Bulktrans (Europe) Corp (The Merak S) [2000] 1 Lloyd's Rep. 619, Local Div (SA) . . . .   *Digested*, 00/**4712**

Sea Voyager Maritime Inc v. Bielecki (t/a Hughes Hooker & Co); *sub nom* Bielecki, Re [1999] 1 All E.R. 628; [1999] B.C.C. 924; [1999] 1 B.C.L.C. 133; [1998] B.P.I.R. 655; [1999] Lloyd's Rep. I.R. 356; *Times*, October 23, 1998, Ch D . . . .   *Digested*, 98/**3354**:
Considered, 01/3787

Seabeach Shipping Ltd v. GAN Minster Insurance Co [2001] C.P. Rep. 32, QBD (Comm Ct) . . . .   *Digested*, 01/**526**

Seabridge Shipping AB v. AC Orsleff's EFTS A/S see Seabridge Shipping AB v. AC Orssleff's Eftf's A/S

Seabridge Shipping AB v. AC Orssleff's Eftf's A/S; *sub nom* Seabridge Shipping AB v. AC Orsleff's EFTS A/S [2000] 1 All E.R. (Comm) 415; [1999] 2 Lloyd's Rep. 685; [2000] C.L.C. 656, QBD (Comm Ct) . . . .   *Digested*, 00/**4728**

Seaconsar (Far East) Ltd v. Bank Markazi Jomhouri Islami Iran (Documentary Credits) [1999] 1 Lloyd's Rep. 36; [1998] C.L.C. 1543, CA; affirming [1997] 2 Lloyd's Rep. 89; [1997] C.L.C. 611, QBD (Comm Ct) . . . .   *Digested*, 98/**295**

Seaconsar (Far East) Ltd v. Bank Markazi Jomhouri Islami Iran (Service Outside Jurisdiction) [1994] 1 A.C. 438; [1993] 3 W.L.R. 756; [1993] 4 All E.R. 456; [1994] 1 Lloyd's Rep. 1; [1994] I.L.Pr. 678; (1993) 143 N.L.J. 1479; (1993) 137 S.J.L.B. 239; *Times*, October 15, 1993; *Independent*, October 20, 1993, HL; reversing [1993] 1 Lloyd's Rep. 236; *Times*, November 25, 1992, CA . . . .   *Digested*, 94/**3763**:
Applied, 95/398, 98/582: *Considered*, 95/703: *Followed*, 98/4394:
Referred to, 95/399

Seager v. Copydex Ltd (No.1) [1967] 1 W.L.R. 923; [1967] 2 All E.R. 415; 2 K.I.R. 828; [1967] F.S.R. 211; [1967] R.P.C. 349; 111 S.J. 335, CA. . . . .   *Digested*, 67/**1486**:
Applied, 72/364, 01/4265: *Considered*, 86/412, 87/1294, 88/2859, 88/2862,
89/3103, 96/1219, 96/2519: *Distinguished*, 96/4556

Seahawk Marine Foods Ltd v. Southampton Port HA see Southampton Port HA v. Seahawk Marine Foods Ltd

Seal v. Wilkinson [2000] C.P.L.R. 1, CA. . . . .   *Digested*, 00/**606**

Seale v. Maryland Estates Ltd see Martin v. Maryland Estates Ltd (Service Charges)

Sealey v. Inns of Court School of Law (Unreported, December 17, 1997), Visitors (Inns of Ct) . . . .   *Applied*, 00/1785

Seaman v. Netherclift (1876-77) L.R. 2 C.P.D. 53, CA; affirming (1875-76) L.R. 1 C.P.D. 540, CPD . . . .   *Applied*, 00/333:
Considered, 97/4860

Searles v. Cann & Hallett [1999] P.N.L.R. 494, QBD . . . .   *Digested*, 99/**4029**:
Approved, 01/4538

Sears v. Attorney General of New Zealand see De Morgan v. Director General of Social Welfare

Sears v. Sears Roebuck & Co [1993] R.P.C. 385, Ch D . . . .   *Considered*, 99/3576

Sears Tooth *v.* Payne Hicks Beach [1997] 2 F.L.R. 116; [1998] 1 F.C.R. 231; [1997]
 Fam. Law 392; (1997) 94(5) L.S.G. 32; (1997) 141 S.J.L.B. 37; *Times,* January
 24, 1997, Fam Div . . . . *Digested,* 97/**3369**
Seashore Marine SA *v.* Phoenix Assurance Plc (The Vergina) (No.2) [2001] 2 Lloyd's
 Rep. 698; [2001] C.L.C. 1441, QBD (Comm Ct)
Seashore Marine SA *v.* Phoenix Assurance Plc (The Vergina) (No.1) [2001] 2 Lloyd's
 Rep. 719, QBD (Comm Ct)
Seawind Tankers Corp *v.* Bayoil SA see Bayoil SA, Re
Sebago Inc *v.* GB Unic SA (C173/98) [2000] Ch. 558; [2000] 2 W.L.R. 1341; [1999]
 All E.R. (EC) 575; [1999] E.C.R. I-4103; [1999] 2 C.M.L.R. 1317; [1999] C.E.C.
 273; [1999] E.T.M.R. 681; [2000] R.P.C. 63; *Times,* July 7, 1999, ECJ (5th
 Chamber) [1999] E.C.R. I-4103; [1999] E.T.M.R. 467, AGO . . . . *Digested,* 99/**3547**
Sebago Inc *v.* GB-UNIC [1998] E.T.M.R. 187, Trib Comm (Brussels)
Sebanjor *v.* Brent LBC see Brent LBC *v.* Sebanjor
SECOND SKIN Trade Mark [2001] R.P.C. 30, TMR . . . . *Digested,* 01/**4028**
Secretarial Error (J32/90) [2001] E.P.O.R. 6, EPO (Technical Bd App) . . . . *Digested,* 01/**3957**
Secretary of State for Defence *v.* MacDonald see Advocate General for Scotland *v.*
 MacDonald
Secretary of State for Defence *v.* Percy [1999] 1 All E.R. 732; *Times,* May 11, 1998, Ch D
 . . . . *Digested,* 98/**4787**
Secretary of State for Defence *v.* Times Newspapers Ltd, *Independent,* May 14, 2001
 (C.S), QBD
Secretary of State for Education and Employment *v.* Bearman [1998] I.R.L.R. 431, EAT. *Digested,* 98/**2105**
Secretary of State for Education and Science *v.* Tameside MBC [1977] A.C. 1014; [1976]
 3 W.L.R. 641; [1976] 3 All E.R. 665; 120 S.J. 735, HL; affirming 120 S.J. 539,
 CA . . . . *Digested,* 76/**829**:
 Applied, 78/861, 81/1535, 82/369, 82/1453, 83/359, 83/3723, 94/4593,
 98/1901, 00/3115, 00/5397: *Considered,* 78/863, 79/198, 79/810, 87/31,
 89/3586, 94/1866, 95/1911: *Distinguished,* 90/9, 91/67, 99/4248:
 Followed, 80/1378
Secretary of State for Employment *v.* Globe Elastic Thread Co Ltd [1980] A.C. 506;
 [1979] 3 W.L.R. 143; [1979] 2 All E.R. 1077; [1979] I.C.R. 706; [1979] I.R.L.R.
 327; (1979) 123 S.J. 504, HL; reversing [1979] Q.B. 183; [1978] 3 W.L.R. 679;
 [1978] 3 All E.R. 954; [1978] I.C.R. 1041; [1978] I.R.L.R. 417; (1978) 13 I.T.R.
 540; 122 S.J. 661, CA; affirming [1978] Q.B. 86; [1977] 3 W.L.R. 293; [1978] 1
 All E.R. 987; [1978] I.C.R. 473; [1977] I.R.L.R. 233; (1977) 12 I.T.R. 402; 121
 S.J. 407, EAT . . . . *Digested,* 79/**936**:
 Applied, 87/1355, 95/2015, 96/2597, 98/2104: *Distinguished,* 78/990
Secretary of State for Employment *v.* Mann see Mann *v.* Secretary of State for Education
 and Employment
Secretary of State for Northern Ireland *v.* Hamilton; Secretary of State for Northern
 Ireland *v.* Kerr [1994] N.I. 239, QBD (NI) . . . . *Digested,* 00/**5388**
Secretary of State for Northern Ireland *v.* Kerr see Secretary of State for Northern Ireland
 v. Hamilton
Secretary of State for Scotland *v.* Hannah see Secretary of State for Scotland *v.* Wright
Secretary of State for Scotland *v.* Mann; *sub nom* Advocate General for Scotland *v.*
 Mann [2001] I.C.R. 1005; *Daily Telegraph,* December 12, 2000, EAT
Secretary of State for Scotland *v.* Revival Properties Ltd see Edinburgh City Council *v.*
 Secretary of State for Scotland
Secretary of State for Scotland *v.* Taylor see Taylor *v.* Scottish Prison Service
Secretary of State for Scotland *v.* Wright; *sub nom* Greater Glasgow Health Board *v.*
 Wright; Secretary of State for Scotland *v.* Hannah; Greater Glasgow Health
 Board *v.* Hannah [1993] 2 C.M.L.R. 257; [1991] I.R.L.R. 187, EAT . . . . *Considered,* 00/**5520**:
 Not followed, 95/2112
Secretary of State for Social Security *v.* Carter see Secretary of State for Social Security
 v. Harmon
Secretary of State for Social Security *v.* Cocks see Secretary of State for Social Security
 v. Harmon
Secretary of State for Social Security *v.* David, *Times,* January 30, 2001; *Independent,*
 February 7, 2001 (C.S), CA . . . . *Digested,* 01/**5055**
Secretary of State for Social Security *v.* Davis see Davis *v.* Secretary of State for Social
 Security
Secretary of State for Social Security *v.* Foster [2001] 1 F.C.R. 376; (2001) 165 J.P.N.
 489; *Independent,* January 22, 2001 (C.S), CA . . . . *Digested,* 01/**2558**
Secretary of State for Social Security *v.* Graham see Graham *v.* Secretary of State for
 Social Security (C92/94)
Secretary of State for Social Security *v.* Harmon; Secretary of State for Social Security *v.*
 Carter; Secretary of State for Social Security *v.* Cocks [1999] 1 W.L.R. 163;
 [1998] 2 F.L.R. 598; [1999] 1 F.C.R. 213; [1998] Fam. Law 519; (1999) 163
 J.P.N. 192; (1998) 95(25) L.S.G. 32; (1998) 142 S.J.L.B. 183; *Times,* June 10,
 1998, CA . . . . *Digested,* 98/**2395**:
 Considered, 99/4532

Secretary of State for Social Security v. Henderson; *sub nom* Henderson v. Secretary of State for Social Security [1999] 1 F.L.R. 496; [1999] 1 F.C.R. 433; [1999] Fam. Law 79; (1999) 96(1) L.S.G. 24; *Times*, December 1, 1998; *Independent*, November 24, 1998, CA . . . .   *Digested,* 98/**2397**

Secretary of State for Social Security v. M 1999 S.C. 235; 1999 S.L.T. 1046; 1999 S.C.L.R. 165; 1998 G.W.D. 39-2026; *Times*, December 31, 1998, 2 Div . . . .   *Digested,* 99/**6398**

Secretary of State for Social Security v. Remilien; *sub nom* Remilien v. Secretary of State for Social Security; R. v. Chief Adjudication Officer Ex p. Remelien; R. v. Secretary of State for Social Security Ex p. Remelien; R. v. Secretary of State for Social Security Ex p. Wolke; Chief Adjudication Officer v. Wolke [1997] 1 W.L.R. 1640; [1998] 1 All E.R. 129; [1998] 1 F.L.R. 444; [1998] 1 F.C.R. 85; [1998] I.N.L.R. 238; [1998] Fam. Law 193; (1997) 94(48) L.S.G. 30; (1998) 142 S.J.L.B. 21; *Times*, December 1, 1997, HL; reversing [1996] All E.R. (E.C.) 850; *Times*, July 12, 1996; *Independent*, July 22, 1996 (C.S.), CA . . . .   *Digested,* 98/**4539**:
                                  Considered, 00/3288: *Distinguished,* 96/5483

Secretary of State for Social Security v. Thomas (C328/91); *sub nom* Thomas v. Chief Adjudication Officer (C328/91); Morley v. Secretary of State for Social Security (C328/91); Murphy v. Secretary of State for Social Security (C328/91); Beard v. Secretary of State for Social Security (C328/91); Cooze v. Secretary of State for Social Security (C328/91) [1993] Q.B. 747; [1993] 3 W.L.R. 581; [1993] 4 All E.R. 556; [1993] E.C.R. I-1247; [1993] 3 C.M.L.R. 880; [1993] I.C.R. 673; [1993] I.R.L.R. 292; *Times*, April 5, 1993, ECJ (6th Chamber) *Times*, August 22, 1990 ; *Independent*, August 31, 1990, CA. . . . .   *Digested,* 93/**4386**:
                          Considered, 95/3641: *Followed,* 01/4604: *Referred to,* 00/4819

Secretary of State for Social Security v. Walter see Walter v. Secretary of State for Social Security

Secretary of State for the Environment v. Cambridge City Council see Cambridge City Council v. Secretary of State for the Environment

Secretary of State for the Environment v. Edwards (PG); *sub nom* Edwards (PG) v. Secretary of State for the Environment (1995) 69 P. & C.R. 607; [1994] 1 P.L.R. 62, CA; affirming (1993) 66 P. & C.R. 393; [1993] E.G.C.S. 94, QBD . . . .   *Digested,* 95/**4783**:
                                         Considered, 99/4266

Secretary of State for the Environment, Food and Rural Affairs v. Crop Protection Association UK Ltd; *sub nom* R. v. Ministry of Agriculture, Fisheries and Food Ex p. British Agrochemicals Association Ltd [2001] EWCA Civ 1656, CA; reversing [2000] 1 C.M.L.R. 826; [2000] Eu. L.R. 149; *Times*, November 16, 1999, QBD . . . .   *Digested,* 99/**180**:
                                  Previous proceedings, 99/181

Secretary of State for the Environment, Transport and the Regions v. Baylis (Gloucester) Ltd; *sub nom* Bennett Construction (UK) Ltd v. Baylis (Gloucester) Ltd; Baylis (Gloucester) Ltd v. Bennett Construction (UK) Ltd (2000) 80 P. & C.R. 324; [2000] 3 P.L.R. 61; [2000] 2 E.G.L.R. 13; [2000] 32 E.G. 92; (2000) 97(22) L.S.G. 44; *Times*, May 16, 2000, Ch D . . . .   *Digested,* 00/**3064**

Secretary of State for the Environment, Transport and the Regions v. Elsy (2000) 164 J.P. 61; [2000] R.T.R. 29; (2000) 164 J.P.N. 127; *Times*, August 25, 1999, QBD . . . .   *Digested,* 99/**4899**

Secretary of State for the Environment, Transport and the Regions v. Fletcher Estates (Harlescott) Ltd see Fletcher Estates (Harlescott) Ltd v. Secretary of State for the Environment, Transport and the Regions

Secretary of State for the Environment, Transport and the Regions v. Holt [2000] R.T.R. 309, QBD . . . .   *Digested,* 00/**928**

Secretary of State for the Environment, Transport and the Regions v. Hughes see Hughes v. Secretary of State for the Environment, Transport and the Regions

Secretary of State for the Environment, Transport and the Regions v. Legal & General Assurance Society Ltd see R. (on the application of Holding & Barnes Plc) v. Secretary of State for the Environment, Transport and the Regions

Secretary of State for the Environment, Transport and the Regions v. MJT Securities Ltd; *sub nom* MJT Securities Ltd v. Secretary of State for the Environment, Transport and the Regions; MJT Securities Ltd v. Chelmsford BC (1998) 75 P. & C.R. 188; [1997] 3 P.L.R. 43; [1998] J.P.L. 138; [1998] C.O.D. 154; [1997] E.G.C.S. 130; (1997) 147 N.L.J. 133, CA; reversing (1996) 72 P. & C.R. 342; [1997] J.P.L. 43, QBD . . . .   *Digested,* 97/**4122**

Secretary of State for the Environment, Transport and the Regions v. Newell see Fletcher Estates (Harlescott) Ltd v. Secretary of State for the Environment, Transport and the Regions

Secretary of State for the Environment, Transport and the Regions v. Redland Aggregates Ltd; R. v. Norwich City Council [1998] Env. L.R. D12, QBD

Secretary of State for the Environment, Transport and the Regions v. Skerritts of Nottingham Ltd see Skerritts of Nottingham Ltd v. Secretary of State for the Environment, Transport and the Regions (No.1)

Secretary of State for the Environment, Transport and the Regions v. Sparkes see Sparkes v. Secretary of State for the Environment, Transport and the Regions

Secretary of State for the Environment, Transport and the Regions v. Thurrock BC (No.2) see Thurrock BC v. Secretary of State for the Environment, Transport and the Regions (No.2)

Secretary of State for the Environment, Transport and the Regions v. Unicorn Consultancy
  Services Ltd [2000] N.P.C. 108, Ch D
Secretary of State for the Environment, Transport and the Regions v. Wyatt Brothers
  (Oxford) Ltd see Wyatt Bros (Oxford) Ltd v. Secretary of State for the
  Environment, Transport and the Regions
Secretary of State for the Environment, Transport and the Regions v. Yorkshire Water
  Services Ltd; *sub nom* R. v. Yorkshire Water Services Ltd [2001] EWCA Crim
  2635; *Times*, December 12, 2001, CA (Crim Div)
Secretary of State for the Foreign and Commonwealth Office v. Kier International Ltd see
  Secretary of State for the Foreign and Commonwealth Office v. Percy Thomas
  Partnership
Secretary of State for the Foreign and Commonwealth Office v. Percy Thomas
  Partnership; Secretary of State for the Foreign and Commonwealth Office v. Kier
  International Ltd 65 Con. L.R. 11, QBD (OR) . . . .   *Digested*, 00/**222**
Secretary of State for the Home Department v. Adan (Hassan Hussein) see Adan
  (Hassan Hussein) v. Secretary of State for the Home Department
Secretary of State for the Home Department v. Adan (Lul Omar) see R. (on the
  application of Adan (Lul Omar)) v. Secretary of State for the Home Department
Secretary of State for the Home Department v. Ahmed (Iftikhar) see Ahmed (Iftikhar) v.
  Secretary of State for the Home Department
Secretary of State for the Home Department v. Aitseguer see R. (on the application of
  Adan (Lul Omar)) v. Secretary of State for the Home Department
Secretary of State for the Home Department v. Ali (Shaharia) [1999] I.N.L.R. 108, IAT .   *Digested*, 99/**3150**
Secretary of State for the Home Department v. Arif; *sub nom* Arif v. Secretary of State
  for the Home Department [1999] Imm. A.R. 271; [1999] I.N.L.R. 327, CA . . . . .   *Digested*, 99/**3165**:
                                                                                       Distinguished, 01/3637
Secretary of State for the Home Department v. Bouheraoua see R. (on the application of
  Bouheraoua) v. Secretary of State for the Home Department
Secretary of State for the Home Department v. Burgess see Burgess v. Secretary of State
  for the Home Department
Secretary of State for the Home Department v. Chiver [1997] I.N.L.R. 212, IAT . . . .   *Digested*, 98/**3244**
Secretary of State for the Home Department v. International Transport Roth GmbH see R.
  (on the application of International Transport Roth GmbH) v. Secretary of State
  for the Home Department
Secretary of State for the Home Department v. Isiko see R. (on the application of Isiko) v.
  Secretary of State for the Home Department
Secretary of State for the Home Department v. Javed see R. (on the application of
  Javed) v. Secretary of State for the Home Department
Secretary of State for the Home Department v. Kacaj; *sub nom* Kacaj v. Secretary of
  State for the Home Department [2001] I.N.L.R. 354, IAT
Secretary of State for the Home Department v. Kerkeb see R. (on the application of
  Bouheraoua) v. Secretary of State for the Home Department
Secretary of State for the Home Department v. Khan (Abdul) [1999] I.N.L.R. 309, IAT .   *Digested*, 99/**3154**:
                                                                                       Disapproved, 00/3279
Secretary of State for the Home Department v. Ogilvy (Contempt of Court: Undertaking);
  R. v. Secretary of State for the Home Department Ex p. Ibehi [1998] C.O.D.
  435, QBD
Secretary of State for the Home Department v. Ouanes see Ouanes v. Secretary of State
  for the Home Department
Secretary of State for the Home Department v. Oxford Regional Mental Health Review
  Tribunal see R. v. Oxford Regional Mental Health Tribunal Ex p. Secretary of
  State for the Home Department
Secretary of State for the Home Department v. Ravichandran see R. v. Secretary of State
  for the Home Department Ex p. Jeyeanthan
Secretary of State for the Home Department v. Rehman; *sub nom* Rehman v. Secretary
  of State for the Home Department [2001] UKHL 47; [2001] 3 W.L.R. 877; 11
  B.H.R.C. 413; (2001) 98(42) L.S.G. 37; (2001) 145 S.J.L.B. 238; *Times*, October
  15, 2001; *Independent*, October 17, 2001, HL; affirming [2000] 3 W.L.R. 1240;
  [2000] 3 All E.R. 778; [2001] Imm. A.R. 30; [2000] I.N.L.R. 531; (2000)
  97(24) L.S.G. 40; *Times*, May 31, 2000; *Independent*, May 26, 2000, CA;
  reversing [1999] I.N.L.R. 517, Sp Imm App Comm . . . .   *Digested*, 01/**3662**
Secretary of State for the Home Department v. Sachithananthan [1999] I.N.L.R. 205, IAT

                                                                                       Digested, 99/**3170**:
                                                                                       Approved, 99/3178

Secretary of State for the Home Department v. Sahota see R. v. Secretary of State for the
  Home Department Ex p. Sahota
Secretary of State for the Home Department v. Senkoy see R. v. Secretary of State for
  the Home Department Ex p. Senkoy
Secretary of State for the Home Department v. Tikhonov [1998] I.N.L.R. 737, IAT . . . . .   *Digested*, 99/**3148**
Secretary of State for the Home Department v. Ullah (Azad) see R. (on the application of
  Ullah (Azad)) v. Secretary of State for the Home Department
Secretary of State for the Home Department v. Zeghraba see R. v. Secretary of State for
  the Home Department Ex p. Sahota

Secretary of State for the Home Department *v.* Zengin [2000] Imm. A.R. 518; [2001] I.N.L.R. 88, IAT . . . .   *Digested,* 01/**3608**

Secretary of State for the Home Department *v.* Ziar [1997] Imm. A.R. 456; [1997] I.N.L.R. 221, IAT . . . .   *Digested,* 97/**2834**:   *Distinguished,* 00/3308: *Doubted,* 01/3598: *Followed,* 98/3168, 00/3279

Secretary of State for the Home Department Ex p. Shah see R. *v.* Immigration Appeal Tribunal Ex p. Shah

Secretary of State for Trade and Industry *v.* Anderson see Astra Holdings Plc, Re

Secretary of State for Trade and Industry *v.* Ashcroft (No.1) [1998] Ch. 71; [1997] 3 W.L.R. 319; [1997] 3 All E.R. 86; [1997] B.C.C. 634; (1997) 94(11) L.S.G. 35; (1997) 141 S.J.L.B. 57; *Times,* March 4, 1997, CA . . . .   *Digested,* 97/**818**

Secretary of State for Trade and Industry *v.* Ashman see Blackspur Group Plc (No.2), Re

Secretary of State for Trade and Industry *v.* Aurum Marketing Ltd; *sub nom* Aurum Marketing Ltd (In Liquidation), Re [2000] 2 B.C.L.C. 645; *Times,* August 10, 2000, CA; reversing [1999] 2 B.C.L.C. 498, Ch D (Companies Ct) . . . .   *Digested,* 00/**3497**

Secretary of State for Trade and Industry *v.* Backhouse; North West Holdings Plc (In Liquidation) (Costs), Re [2001] EWCA Civ 67; [2001] 1 B.C.L.C. 468; (2001) 98(9) L.S.G. 38; (2001) 145 S.J.L.B. 53; *Times,* February 23, 2001; *Independent,* February 9, 2001, CA . . . .   *Digested,* 01/**3756**

Secretary of State for Trade and Industry *v.* Baker (No.1); *sub nom* Barings Plc (No.1), Re [1998] B.C.C. 583, Ch D (Companies Ct) . . . .   *Digested,* 98/**673**

Secretary of State for Trade and Industry *v.* Baker (No.2); *sub nom* Barings Plc (No.2), Re [1998] Ch. 356; [1998] 2 W.L.R. 667; [1998] 1 All E.R. 673; [1998] B.C.C. 888; [1998] 1 B.C.L.C. 16; *Times,* October 23, 1997; *Independent,* October 7, 1997, Ch D (Companies Ct) . . . .   *Digested,* 97/**822**

Secretary of State for Trade and Industry *v.* Baker (No.3); *sub nom* Barings Plc (No.3), Re [1999] B.C.C. 146; [1998] 1 B.C.L.C. 590, Ch D (Companies Ct) . . . .   *Digested,* 98/**664**

Secretary of State for Trade and Industry *v.* Baker (No.4); *sub nom* Barings Plc (No.4), Re [1999] 1 W.L.R. 1985; [1999] 1 All E.R. 311; [1999] B.C.C. 639; [1999] 1 B.C.L.C. 226; *Times,* July 6, 1998; *Independent,* June 11, 1998, CA; affirming *Independent,* June 9, 1998, Ch D . . . .   *Digested,* 98/**669**

Secretary of State for Trade and Industry *v.* Baker (No.5); *sub nom* Barings Plc (No.5), Re [2000] 1 W.L.R. 634; [1999] 1 All E.R. 1017; [1999] B.C.C. 960; [1999] 1 B.C.L.C. 262; (1998) 95(45) L.S.G. 38; (1998) 148 N.L.J. 1474; *Times,* October 10, 1998; *Independent,* October 9, 1998, Ch D . . . .   *Digested,* 98/**668**:   *Applied,* 01/716

Secretary of State for Trade and Industry *v.* Baker (No.6); *sub nom* Barings Plc (No.6), Re [2001] B.C.C. 273; [2000] 1 B.C.L.C. 523; *Independent,* March 9, 2000, CA; affirming [1999] 1 B.C.L.C 433, Ch D (Companies Ct) . . . .   *Digested,* 00/**660**

Secretary of State for Trade and Industry *v.* Ball; *sub nom* Landhurst Leasing Plc, Re [1999] 1 B.C.L.C 286, Ch D (Companies Ct) . . . .   *Digested,* 99/**609**:   *Followed,* 01/714

Secretary of State for Trade and Industry *v.* Barnett (Re Harbour Lane Ltd) [1998] 2 B.C.L.C. 64, Ch D (Companies Ct) . . . .   *Digested,* 98/**684**

Secretary of State for Trade and Industry *v.* Barnett (Re James Blake Ltd); *sub nom* Secretary of State for Trade and Industry, Petitioner 1998 S.L.T. 63; [1998] B.C.C. 437; 1997 G.W.D. 20-934, OH . . . .   *Digested,* 98/**6012**

Secretary of State for Trade and Industry *v.* Berry see Abermeadow Ltd (No.1), Re

Secretary of State for Trade and Industry *v.* Bottrill; *sub nom* Bottrill *v.* Secretary of State for Trade and Industry [2000] 1 All E.R. 915; [1999] B.C.C. 177; [2000] 2 B.C.L.C. 448; [1999] I.C.R. 592; [1999] I.R.L.R. 326; (1999) 96(10) L.S.G. 30; (1999) 143 S.J.L.B. 73; *Times,* February 24, 1999; *Independent,* February 17, 1999, CA; affirming [1998] I.C.R. 564; [1998] I.R.L.R. 120, EAT . . . .   *Digested,* 99/**2019**:   *Considered,* 01/2265: *Followed,* 99/2110

Secretary of State for Trade and Industry *v.* Burrows see Continental Assurance Co of London Plc (In Liquidation) (No.1), Re

Secretary of State for Trade and Industry *v.* Carter see Park House Properties Ltd, Re

Secretary of State for Trade and Industry *v.* Cash FC3 97/6278/3, CHANI 97/1631/3, CA   *Digested,* 99/**524**

Secretary of State for Trade and Industry *v.* Collins; *sub nom* TLL Realisations Ltd, Re [2000] B.C.C. 998; [2000] 2 B.C.L.C. 223; (2000) 97(2) L.S.G. 29; *Times,* January 25, 2000, CA . . . .   *Digested,* 00/**672**:   *Applied,* 01/716

Secretary of State for Trade and Industry *v.* Crane (No.2); *sub nom* Priority Stainless (UK) Ltd, Re [2001] 2 B.C.L.C. 222; (2001) 98(23) L.S.G. 40; *Times,* June 4, 2001; *Daily Telegraph,* April 24, 2001, Ch D . . . .   *Digested,* 01/**718**:   *Applied,* 01/665

Secretary of State for Trade and Industry *v.* Davies (No.2) see Blackspur Group Plc (No.2), Re

Secretary of State for Trade and Industry *v.* Davies (No.3) see Blackspur Group Plc (No.3), Re

Secretary of State for Trade and Industry *v.* Delfin International (SA) Ltd; *sub nom* Delfin International (SA) Ltd (No.2), Re [2000] 1 B.C.L.C. 71, Ch D (Companies Ct) . .   *Previous proceedings,*   99/589

Secretary of State for Trade and Industry *v.* Deverell [2001] Ch. 340; [2000] 2 W.L.R. 907; [2000] 2 All E.R. 365; [2000] B.C.C. 1057; [2000] 2 B.C.L.C. 133; (2000) 97(3) L.S.G. 35; (2000) 144 S.J.L.B. 49; *Times*, January 21, 2000; *Independent*, January 26, 2000, CA. . . . .   *Digested*, 00/**658**
Secretary of State for Trade and Industry *v.* Doe see Funtime Ltd, Re
Secretary of State for Trade and Industry *v.* Dyer see Hopes (Heathrow) Ltd, Re
Secretary of State for Trade and Industry *v.* Eastaway; *sub nom* Blackspur Group Plc, Re [2001] 1 B.C.L.C. 653, Ch D (Companies Ct) . . . .   *Digested*, 01/**3520**
Secretary of State for Trade and Industry *v.* Eastaway (Undertakings) see Blackspur Group Plc (No.3), Re
Secretary of State for Trade and Industry *v.* Ellis (No.2) see Polly Peck International Plc (In Administration) (No.3), Re
Secretary of State for Trade and Industry *v.* Forsyth; *sub nom* Helene Plc (In Liquidation), Re; Barry Artist Ltd, Re; Secretary of State for Trade and Industry *v.* Forsythe [2000] 2 B.C.L.C. 249, Ch D (Companies Ct) . . . .   *Digested*, 00/**663**
Secretary of State for Trade and Industry *v.* Forsythe see Secretary of State for Trade and Industry *v.* Forsyth
Secretary of State for Trade and Industry *v.* Glas see Senator Hanseatische Verwaltungsgesellschaft mbH, Re
Secretary of State for Trade and Industry *v.* Great Western Assurance Co SA; Secretary of State for Trade and Industry *v.* Loxley House (London) Ltd; D&L Underwriting Agencies Ltd; Company (No.007816 of 1994), Re; Company (No.007818 of 1994), Re; Company (No.007819 of 1994), Re; Company (No.007820 of 1994), Re; Company (No.007821 of 1994), Re; Company (No.007822 of 1994), Re [1997] 2 B.C.L.C. 685; [1999] Lloyd's Rep. I.R. 377; [1997] 6 Re. L.R. 197, CA .   *Digested*, 97/**3129**
Secretary of State for Trade and Industry *v.* Griffiths (No.1) see Westmid Packaging Services Ltd (No.1), Re
Secretary of State for Trade and Industry *v.* Griffiths (No.2) see Westmid Packaging Services Ltd (No.2), Re
Secretary of State for Trade and Industry *v.* Guest [1999] B.P.I.R. 587, Ch D . . . .   *Digested*, 99/**3240**
Secretary of State for Trade and Industry *v.* Hinchcliffe; *sub nom* Hinchcliffe *v.* Secretary of State for Trade and Industry [1999] B.C.C. 226; *Times*, February 2, 1998, Ch D . . . .   *Digested*, 98/**680**
Secretary of State for Trade and Industry *v.* Ivens; *sub nom* Country Farm Inns Ltd, Re [1997] B.C.C. 801; [1997] 2 B.C.L.C. 334; *Times*, September 24, 1997, CA; affirming [1997] B.C.C. 396; [1997] 2 B.C.L.C. 334, Ch D . . . .   *Digested*, 97/**820**
Secretary of State for Trade and Industry *v.* Jabble [1998] B.C.C. 39; [1998] 1 B.C.L.C. 598; (1997) 94(35) L.S.G. 33; (1997) 141 S.J.L.B. 214; *Times*, August 5, 1997, CA . . . .   *Digested*, 97/**825**
Secretary of State for Trade and Industry *v.* Jones [1999] B.C.C. 336, Ch D . . . .   *Digested*, 99/**610**
Secretary of State for Trade and Industry *v.* Kaczer see Kaytech International Plc, Re
Secretary of State for Trade and Industry *v.* Langridge; *sub nom* Cedac Ltd, Re; R. *v.* Secretary of State for Trade and Industry Ex p. Langridge [1991] Ch. 402; [1991] 2 W.L.R. 1343; [1991] 3 All E.R. 591; [1991] B.C.C. 148; [1991] B.C.L.C. 543; *Times*, March 4, 1991; *Independent*, March 11, 1991 (C.S.); *Financial Times*, February 22, 1991, CA; reversing [1990] B.C.C. 555; *Times*, May 30, 1990; *Independent*, July 3, 1990 (C.S.), Ch D . . . .   *Digested*, 91/**403**:
                  Cited, 93/374: *Considered*, 96/7085, 00/663
Secretary of State for Trade and Industry *v.* Lassman see Lassman *v.* Secretary of State for Trade and Industry
Secretary of State for Trade and Industry *v.* Lewis; *sub nom* Lewis *v.* Secretary of State for Trade and Industry [2001] 2 B.C.L.C. 597; *Times*, August 16, 2001, Ch D . . .   *Digested*, 01/**429**
Secretary of State for Trade and Industry *v.* Leyton Housing Trustees Ltd [2000] 2 B.C.L.C. 808, Ch D . . . .   *Digested*, 01/**3755**
Secretary of State for Trade and Industry *v.* Lovat (Summary Dismissal) [2000] B.C.C. 485, Sh Ct (Glasgow) . . . .   *Digested*, 01/**6274**
Secretary of State for Trade and Industry *v.* Loxley House (London) Ltd see Secretary of State for Trade and Industry *v.* Great Western Assurance Co SA
Secretary of State for Trade and Industry *v.* Lubrani (No.1); *sub nom* Amaron Ltd, Re (No.1) [1997] 2 B.C.L.C. 115, Ch D . . . .   *Digested*, 97/**814**
Secretary of State for Trade and Industry *v.* Lubrani (No.2); *sub nom* Amaron Ltd, Re (No.2) [1998] B.C.C. 264; [2001] 1 B.C.L.C. 562, Ch D (Companies Ct). . . . . . .   *Digested*, 98/**678**
Secretary of State for Trade and Industry *v.* Martin [1998] B.C.C. 184, Ch D . . . .   *Digested*, 98/**674**
Secretary of State for Trade and Industry *v.* McCormick [1998] 2 B.C.L.C. 18, Ch D . . .   *Digested*, 97/**817**
Secretary of State for Trade and Industry *v.* McTighe (No.2); *sub nom* Secretary of State for Trade and Industry *v.* McTigue [1996] 2 B.C.L.C. 477; *Times*, July 10, 1996, CA . . . .   *Digested*, 97/**806**:
                  Applied, 00/664: *Distinguished*, 01/715
Secretary of State for Trade and Industry *v.* McTigue see Secretary of State for Trade and Industry *v.* McTighe (No.2)
Secretary of State for Trade and Industry *v.* Murfitt see Cedarwood Productions Ltd, Re
Secretary of State for Trade and Industry *v.* Newstead see Cedarwood Productions Ltd, Re

Secretary of State for Trade and Industry v. North West Holdings Plc [1998] B.C.C. 997;
    [1999] 1 B.C.L.C 425, CA . . . .   *Digested, 99/**3354***
Secretary of State for Trade and Industry v. Palfreman 1995 S.L.T. 156; 1995 S.C.L.R. 172;
    [1995] B.C.C. 193; [1995] 2 B.C.L.C. 301, OH . . . .   *Digested, 95/**5547**:*
                                                                                                Considered, 98/670

Secretary of State for Trade and Industry v. Phillips see City Pram & Toy Co Ltd, Re
Secretary of State for Trade and Industry v. Pollock see Abermeadow Ltd (No.1), Re
Secretary of State for Trade and Industry v. Potier see Kaytech International Plc, Re
Secretary of State for Trade and Industry v. Prevision Sanitaria Nacional PSN Mutua de
    Seguros y Reaseguros a Prima Fija (PSN) TNS, Ch D . . . .   *Digested, 98/**3369***
Secretary of State for Trade and Industry v. Queen 1998 S.L.T. 735; [1998] B.C.C. 678;
    1997 G.W.D. 25-1238; *Times*, August 27, 1997, Ex Div . . . .   *Digested, 97/**5707***
Secretary of State for Trade and Industry v. Rayna see Cedarwood Productions Ltd, Re
Secretary of State for Trade and Industry v. Reynard; *sub nom* Reynard v. Secretary of
    State for Trade and Industry; A3/2001/1607, CA; affirming (2001) 98(27) L.S.G.
    38; *Times*, July 10, 2001, Ch D . . . .   *Digested, 01/**712***
Secretary of State for Trade and Industry v. Richardson see Sykes (Butchers) Ltd, Re
Secretary of State for Trade and Industry v. Rogers [1996] 1 W.L.R. 1569; [1996] 4 All
    E.R. 854; [1997] B.C.C. 155; [1996] 2 B.C.L.C. 513, CA . . . .   *Digested, 96/**978**:*
                                        Considered, 96/977, 97/828, 97/829, 97/831, 99/624
Secretary of State for Trade and Industry v. Rosenfield [1999] B.C.C. 413, Ch D . . . . . .   *Digested, 99/**619***
Secretary of State for Trade and Industry v. Solly see Kaytech International Plc, Re
Secretary of State for Trade and Industry v. Staton see Rocksteady Services Ltd, Re
Secretary of State for Trade and Industry v. Stephenson see Stephenson Cobbold Ltd (In
    Liquidation), Re
Secretary of State For Trade and Industry v. Tillman see Launchexcept Ltd, Re
Secretary of State for Trade and Industry v. Tjolle [1998] B.C.C. 282; [1998] 1 B.C.L.C.
    333; (1997) 94(24) L.S.G. 31; (1997) 141 S.J.L.B. 119; *Times*, May 9, 1997, Ch D
    . . . .   *Digested, 97/**811***
Secretary of State for Trade and Industry v. Travel Time (UK) Ltd; *sub nom* Company
    (No.5669 of 1998), Re [2000] B.C.C. 792; [2000] 1 B.C.L.C. 427, Ch D
    (Companies Ct) . . . .   *Digested, 00/**696***
Secretary of State for Trade and Industry v. Vane see Tech Textiles Ltd, Re
Secretary of State for Trade and Industry v. Walden [2000] I.R.L.R. 168, EAT . . . .   *Digested, 00/**2217***
Secretary of State for Trade and Industry v. Wiper see Global Info Ltd, Re
Secretary of State for Trade and Industry, Petitioner see Secretary of State for Trade and
    Industry v. Barnett (Re James Blake Ltd)
Secretary of State for Transport v. Jenkins (2000) 79 P. & C.R. 118, CA . . . .   *Digested, 00/**4435***
Secretary of State for Transport v. Nuttall (t/a Redline Coaches) see Vehicle Inspectorate
    v. Nuttall
Secretary of State for Transport v. Railtrack Plc see Railtrack Plc v. Secretary of State for
    Transport
Secretary of State for Transport v. Richards; *sub nom* Williams v. Richards (1998) 162
    J.P. 682; [1998] R.T.R. 456; *Times*, July 29, 1997; *Independent*, October 13, 1997
    (C.S.), QBD . . . .   *Digested, 97/**4769***
Secured Residential Funding Plc v. Douglas Goldberg Hendeles & Co (2000) 97(18)
    L.S.G. 38; (2000) 97(21) L.S.G. 40; (2000) 144 S.J.L.B. 218; [2000] N.P.C. 47;
    Times, April 26, 2000, CA . . . .   *Digested, 00/**2607***
Secured Residential Funding Plc v. Nationwide Anglia Building Society (Right of Suit in
    Contract) [1998] E.G.C.S. 64; [1998] N.P.C. 58, QBD
Securities and Investments Board v. Scandex Capital Management A/S [1998] 1 W.L.R.
    712; [1998] 1 All E.R. 514; (1998) 95(6) L.S.G. 24; (1998) 148 N.L.J. 85;
    (1998) 142 S.J.L.B. 63; *Times*, December 20, 1997, CA . . . .   *Digested, 98/**2545***
Security and Facilities Division v. Hayes; *sub nom* Hayes v. Security Facilities Division
    [2001] I.R.L.R. 81; *Times*, April 26, 2000, CA . . . .   *Digested, 00/**2196***
Securon (Amersham) Ltd v. Customs and Excise Commissioners [1998] V. & D.R. 286,
    V&DTr. . . . .   *Digested, 00/**4949***
Securum Finance Ltd v. Ashton (No.1); *sub nom* Ashton v. Securum Finance Ltd
    [2001] Ch. 291; [2000] 3 W.L.R. 1400; (2000) 97(27) L.S.G. 38; *Times*, July 5,
    2000; *Independent*, June 30, 2000, CA; affirming [1999] 2 All E.R. (Comm)
    331; (1999) 96(26) L.S.G. 28; (1999) 143 S.J.L.B. 182; *Times*, June 18, 1999 ;
    Independent, June 28, 1999 (C.S.), Ch D . . . .   *Digested, 00/**348**:*
                                                                                                Referred to, 01/668

Seddon v. Binions; Stork v. Binions [1978] 1 Lloyd's Rep. 381; [1978] R.T.R. 163; 122
    S.J. 34, CA . . . .   *Digested, 78/**2592**:*
                                                                                                Applied, 00/3522
Seddon v. Tekin (Unreported, August 25, 2000), CC . . . .   *Applied, 01/**889**:*
                        Cited, 01/1521: Considered, 01/890, 01/894, 01/907: Referred to, 01/892
Seder's Community Trade Mark Application [2000] E.T.M.R. 685, OHIM (Opposition Div)
                                                                                                *Digested, 00/**3745***
Sedgefield Steeplechase Co (1927) Ltd, Re see Scotto v. Petch
Sedgemoor DC v. Chase Homes (SW) Ltd (2001) 16 P.A.D. 40, Planning Inspector

Sedgwick v. Watney Combe Reid & Co Ltd; Grove v. Lloyds British Testing Co Ltd;
Turpin v. Middlesbrough Area Assessment Committee; Kaye v. Eyre Bros Ltd;
Kaye v. Burrows; Hines v. Eastern Counties Farmers Cooperative Association
Ltd; Finn v. Kerslake; Union Cold Storage Co Ltd v. Bancroft [1931] A.C. 446,
HL . . . .   *Applied,* 47-51/8302,
              57/2962, 58/593, 60/2686, 60/2689: *Considered,* 82/4217:
      Distinguished, 47-51/8300, 55/2279, 58/2839, 60/2687, 83/4838, 88/4756,
                                          00/5678: *Followed,* 47-51/8299
Sedleigh-Denfield v. O'Callagan (Trustees for St Joseph's Society for Foreign Missions)
[1940] A.C. 880; [1940] 3 All E.R. 349, HL; reversing [1939] 1 All E.R. 725, CA;
affirming [1938] 3 All E.R. 321, KBD.   *Applied,* 56/6178,
          60/2297, 66/8145, 72/1102, 79/2004, 80/2005, 80/2006, 81/2001, 82/2267,
          93/3014, 95/6164: *Considered,* 54/2302, 74/2715, 78/2201, 82/2266,
          83/2739, 87/3771, 96/7230, 00/4287: *Distinguished,* 47-51/6950,
          47-51/6972, 47-51/8784, 67/3315, 94/3405: *Explained,* 64/2727:
                                                 Followed, 88/2034
Seer Technologies Inc v. Abbas (Leave to Appeal) [2001] C.P. Rep. 51, CA . . . .   *Digested,* 01/**611**
Seer Technologies Ltd v. Abbas (No.1), *Times,* March 16, 2000; *Independent,* March 20,
2000 (C.S.), Ch D . . . .   *Digested,* 00/**54**
Seer Technologies Ltd v. Abbas (No.2) (2000) 97(7) L.S.G. 40; (2000) 144 S.J.L.B.
102, Ch D
Sefton MBC v. Kwik Fit Properties Ltd (1998) 13 P.A.D. 175, Planning Inspector
Sefton MBC v. Northern Club (1998) 13 P.A.D. 113, Planning Inspector
Sefton MBC v. Whittle (2000) 15 P.A.D. 134, Planning Inspector
Segal v. Edwards (1999-2000) 2 I.T.E.L.R. 575, HC (IoM)
SEH Holdings Ltd v. Customs and Excise Commissioners [2001] B.V.C. 2093; [2000]
S.T.I. 1770, V&DTr . . . .   *Digested,* 01/**5567**
Seifert v. Pensions Ombudsman; Lynch v. Pensions Ombudsman; Lynch v. Farrand
[1997] 4 All E.R. 947; (1998) 10 Admin. L.R. 172; [1997] O.P.L.R. 395; [1999]
Pens. L.R. 29; *Times,* October 3, 1997, CA; reversing [1997] 1 All E.R. 214;
(1997) 9 Admin. L.R. 169; *Times,* August 9, 1996, QBD . . . .   *Digested,* 97/**3996**:
                              Distinguished, 97/2535: *Followed,* 97/518
SEIKO/Image forming apparatus (T904/97) [2000] E.P.O.R. 343, EPO (Technical Bd App)
                                                 Digested, 00/**3620**
Sekisui Kaseihin Kogyo Kabushiki Kaisha v. Owens-Illinois Inc see SEKISUI/Shrinkable
sheet (T472/92)
SEKISUI/Shrinkable sheet (T472/92); *sub nom* Sekisui Kaseihin Kogyo Kabushiki
Kaisha v. Owens-Illinois Inc [1997] E.P.O.R. 432; (1997) 20(10) I.P.D. 20104,
EPO (Technical Bd App) . . . .   *Considered,* 99/3467
Selby DC v. Samuel Smith Old Brewery (Tadcaster) Ltd (2000) 80 P. & C.R. 466;
[2001] 1 E.G.L.R. 71; [2001] 01 E.G. 82; [2000] E.G.C.S. 69; (2000) 97(24)
L.S.G. 42; [2000] N.P.C. 59; (2000) 80 P. & C.R. D26, CA; affirming [1998]
E.G.C.S. 158, Ch D . . . .   *Digested,* 00/**4631**
Selcuk v. Turkey; Asker v. Turkey (1998) 26 E.H.R.R. 477; [1998] H.R.C.D. 475, ECHR . .   *Digested,* 99/**3085**
Select Service Partner Ltd v. Assessor for Glasgow [2000] R.A. 264; 1999 G.W.D. 37-
1829, LVAC. . . . .   *Digested,* 00/**6658**
Self Assessed v. Inspector of Taxes (No.2) [2000] S.T.C. (S.C.D.) 47; [2000] S.T.I. 71,
Sp Comm . . . .   *Digested,* 00/**5050**
Selfridges Ltd v. Malik [1998] I.C.R. 268; [1997] I.R.L.R. 577, EAT. . . . .   *Digested,* 98/**2225**
Seligman v. Docker [1949] Ch. 53; [1948] 2 All E.R. 887; [1949] L.J.R. 188; 92 S.J.
647, Ch D . . . .   *Digested,* 47-51/**4234**:
                                                 Followed, 98/3933
Selkent Bus Co Ltd v. Moore [1996] I.C.R. 836; [1996] I.R.L.R. 661, EAT. . . . .   *Digested,* 96/**2661**:
                                                 Applied, 00/2207
Sellars Arenascene Ltd v. Connolly see Sellers Arenascene Ltd v. Connolly (No.2)
Sellen v. Bailey [1999] R.T.R. 63, CA. . . . .   *Digested,* 99/**539**
Sellers Arenascene Ltd v. Connolly (No.2); *sub nom* Connolly v. Sellers Arenascene Ltd
(No.2); Sellars Arenascene Ltd v. Connolly [2001] EWCA Civ 184; [2001]
I.C.R. 760; [2001] I.R.L.R. 222; (2001) 98(8) L.S.G. 44; (2001) 145 S.J.L.B. 37;
Times, March 8, 2001, CA . . . .   *Digested,* 01/**2265**
Selmouni v. France (2000) 29 E.H.R.R. 403; 7 B.H.R.C. 1, ECHR . . . .   *Digested,* 00/**3260**
Selvanathan v. General Medical Council [2001] Lloyd's Rep. Med. 1; (2001) 59
B.M.L.R. 95; *Times,* October 26, 2000, PC (UK) . . . .   *Digested,* 00/**2718**
Selvanayagam v. DPP see Nicol v. DPP
Selvarajan v. Inner London Education Authority [1980] I.R.L.R. 313, EAT . . . .   *Digested,* 80/**2140**:
                                                 Approved, 00/5526
Senate Electrical Wholesalers Ltd v. Alcatel Submarine Networks Ltd (formerly STC
Submarine Systems Ltd) [1999] 2 Lloyd's Rep. 423; *Times,* June 26, 1998, CA .   *Digested,* 98/**1440**
Senator Hanseatische Verwaltungsgesellschaft mbH, Re; *sub nom* Titan Marketing
Gesellschaft, Re; Company (No.002613 of 1996), Re; Secretary of State for
Trade and Industry v. Glas [1997] 1 W.L.R. 515; [1996] 4 All E.R. 933; [1997]
B.C.C. 112; [1996] 2 B.C.L.C. 597; *Times,* July 30, 1996; *Independent,* July 30,
1996, CA; affirming [1996] 2 B.C.L.C. 562, Ch D . . . .   *Digested,* 96/**1010**:
          Considered, 97/851, 97/3098: *Followed,* 97/3960, 98/642, 99/589

Senbanjo *v.* Brent see Brent LBC *v.* Sebanjor

Sengoz *v.* Secretary of State for the Home Department [2001] EWCA Civ 1135; *Times,*
     August 13, 2001, CA . . . .   *Digested,* 01/**3596**

Senior *v.* Holdsworth Ex p. Independent Television News [1976] Q.B. 23; [1975] 2
     W.L.R. 987; [1975] 2 All E.R. 1009; 119 S.J. 393, CA . . . .   *Digested,* 75/**1393**:
                                                     Applied, 77/852: *Followed,* 98/4348

Senior Heat Treatment Ltd *v.* Bell [1997] I.R.L.R. 614, EAT . . . .   *Digested,* 98/**2187**

Senso Di Donna's Trade Mark [2001] E.T.M.R. 5, OHIM (Cancellation Div) . . . .   *Digested,* 01/**4018**

Sepet *v.* Secretary of State for the Home Department; *sub nom* R. (on the application
     of Septet) *v.* Secretary of State for the Home Department; R. (on the application
     of Bulbul) *v.* Secretary of State for the Home Department; Bulbul *v.* Secretary
     of State for the Home Department [2001] EWCA Civ 681; [2001] Imm. A.R.
     452; [2001] I.N.L.R. 376; *Times,* July 12, 2001; *Independent,* May 18, 2001, CA;
     affirming [2000] Imm. A.R. 445, IAT . . . .   *Digested,* 01/**3612**

Sepoong Engineering Construction Co Ltd *v.* Formula One Management Ltd (formerly
     Formula One Administration Ltd) [2000] 1 Lloyd's Rep. 602, QBD (Comm Ct) .   *Digested,* 00/**877**

Sepracor Inc *v.* Hoechst Marion Roussel Ltd [1999] F.S.R. 746; (1999) 22(4) I.P.D.
     22034; *Times,* March 1, 1999, Pat Ct . . . .   *Digested,* 99/**3475**

Serck Controls Ltd *v.* Drake & Schull Engineering Ltd see Serck Controls Ltd *v.* Drake &
     Scull Engineering Ltd

Serck Controls Ltd *v.* Drake & Scull Engineering Ltd; *sub nom* Serck Controls Ltd *v.*
     Drake & Schull Engineering Ltd 73 Con. L.R. 100, QBD (T&CC)

Serco Ltd *v.* Blair EAT/345/98, EAT . . . . *Distinguished,* 01/6467

Serif *v.* Greece (38178/97) (2001) 31 E.H.R.R. 20, ECHR . . . .   *Digested,* 01/**3479**

Serves *v.* France (1999) 28 E.H.R.R. 265; 3 B.H.R.C. 446; [1998] H.R.C.D. 4, ECHR . . .   *Digested,* 98/**3150**

Service Corp International Plc *v.* Channel Four Television Corp [1999] E.M.L.R. 83;
     Independent, May 14, 1998, Ch D . . . .   *Digested,* 98/**3858**

Service Motor Policies at Lloyds *v.* City Recovery Ltd CCRTF 96/1571/C, CA . . . .   *Digested,* 97/**3167**:
                                                     Cited, 00/113: *Considered,* 98/4834

Service Pour le Groupement d'Acquisitions (SGA) *v.* Commission of the European
     Communities (T189/95) [1999] E.C.R. II-3587; [2001] 4 C.M.L.R. 7, CFI (1st
     Chamber) . . . .   *Digested,* 01/**2449**

Services Sound & Vision Corp *v.* Chiltern DC see British Alcan Aluminium Plc *v.* Chiltern
     DC

Seth-Smith *v.* Worrall (Unreported, November 13, 1997), CC (Northampton) [*Ex rel.*
     The Law Partnership, City Plaza, 2 Pinfold Street, Sheffield] . . . .   *Digested,* 98/**1454**

Seven Pioneer, The [2001] 2 Lloyd's Rep. 57, HC (NZ) . . . .   *Digested,* 01/**4903**

Seven-Up Co *v.* OT Ltd (1947) 75 C.L.R. 203; [1947] A.L.R. 436; 21 A.L.J. 247, HC
     (Aus) . . . .   *Digested,*
                                                         47-51/**10378**:
                                                         Applied, 98/3521

Sevenoaks DC *v.* Bluewater Developments Ltd (2001) 16 P.A.D. 76, Planning Inspector

Sevenoaks DC *v.* Brands Hatch Leisure Group Ltd [2001] Env. L.R. 5; [2001] E.H.L.R.
     7, QBD . . . .   *Digested,* 01/**2423**

Sevenoaks DC *v.* Swanley TC (1999) 14 P.A.D. 97, Planning Inspector

Sevenoaks DC *v.* Wimpey Homes Holdings Ltd (1999) 14 P.A.D. 662, Planning
     Inspector

Sevenoaks DC *v.* Woods (2000) 15 P.A.D. 721, Planning Inspector

Sevenoaks Stationers (Retail) Ltd, Re [1991] Ch. 164; [1990] 3 W.L.R. 1165; [1991] 3 All
     E.R. 578; [1990] B.C.C. 765; [1991] B.C.L.C. 325; (1990) 134 S.J. 1367, CA;
     reversing [1990] B.C.L.C. 668, Ch D . . . .   *Digested,* 91/**401**:
                   Applied, 93/360, 00/662, 00/2243: *Cited,* 93/359, 93/374:
             Considered, 92/390, 98/670, 98/671: *Followed,* 01/712: *Referred to,* 01/706

Severn Trent Plc *v.* Dwr Cymru Cyfyngedig (Welsh Water Ltd) [2001] C.L.C. 107;
     [2001] Eu. L.R. 136, QBD (Comm Ct) . . . .   *Digested,* 01/**5635**

Severnside Siren Trust Ltd *v.* Customs and Excise Commissioners [2000] B.V.C. 2381;
     [2000] V. & D.R. 497; [2000] S.T.I. 1270, V&DTr

Severs *v.* Hunt see Hunt *v.* Severs

Sevington Properties Ltd *v.* Adams see Beegas Nominees Ltd *v.* BHP Petroleum Ltd

Sewell *v.* Harlow DC [2000] E.H.L.R. 122, CA . . . .   *Digested,* 00/**4291**

Sex Discrimination Laws (C248/83), Re; *sub nom* Commission of the European
     Communities *v.* Germany (C248/83) [1985] E.C.R. 1459; [1986] 2 C.M.L.R.
     588, ECJ . . . .   *Digested,* 86/**1457**:
                                                         Distinguished, 00/2160

Sezek *v.* Secretary of State for the Home Department see R. (on the application of
     Samaroo) *v.* Secretary of State for the Home Department

Sezek *v.* Secretary of State for the Home Department (Bail Application) see R. (on the
     application of Sezek) *v.* Secretary of State for the Home Department (Bail
     Application)

SFI Group Plc (formerly Surrey Free Inns Plc) v. Gosport BC; *sub nom* Surrey Free Inns Plc v. Gosport BC; R. v. Knightsbridge Crown Court Ex p. Cataldi [1999] Env. L.R. 750; [2000] E.H.L.R. 137; [1999] B.L.G.R. 610; [1999] E.G.C.S. 51; *Times*, April 5, 1999; *Independent*, May 3, 1999 (C.S.), CA; affirming [1999] Env. L.R. 1; [1998] E.H.L.R. 23; [1998] Crim. L.R. 578; [1998] C.O.D. 188; (1998) 95(6) L.S.G. 25; (1998) 142 S.J.L.B. 84; [1998] N.P.C. 12; *Times*, February 13, 1998, QBD . . . . *Digested*, 99/**4064**
SGAE (Spanish Authors and Editors General Society) v. Ciudad de Vigo SL (AC 2000/370) [2001] E.C.D.R. 31, Aud (Sp)
SGW Ltd v. Secretary of State for Social Security see Tullett & Tokyo Forex International Ltd v. Secretary of State for Social Security
Shabir v. Ferreh (Unreported, August 6, 2001), CC (Sheffield) [*Ex rel.* Sean D Yates, Barrister, Zenith Chambers, 10 Park Square, Leeds] . . . . *Digested*, 01/**505**
Shabpar v. Barnet LBC see R. v. Barnet LBC Ex p. Shah (Nilish)
Shade v. Compton Partnership [2000] Lloyd's Rep. P.N. 81; [2000] P.N.L.R. 218, CA . . *Digested*, 00/**536**
Shafiq v. Ahmed (Unreported, December 17, 1999), CC (Bury) [*Ex rel.* Nicholas M Siddall, Barrister, 40 King Street, Manchester] . . . . *Digested*, 00/**347**
Shah (Jitendra) v. Barnet LBC see R. v. Barnet LBC Ex p. Shah (Nilish)
Shah v. Dexion Group Ltd (Unreported, October 17, 1997), CC (Luton) [*Ex rel.* Marcus Grant, Barrister, 1 Temple Gardens, Temple] . . . . *Digested*, 98/**547**
Shah v. Kubbinga (Valuation Officer) [1999] R.V.R. 50, Lands Tr . . . . *Digested*, 99/**4338**
Shah v. Shah [2001] EWCA Civ 527; [2001] 3 W.L.R. 31; [2001] 4 All E.R. 138; *Times*, May 15, 2001; *Daily Telegraph*, April 24, 2001, CA . . . . *Digested*, 01/**2433**
Shah v. Standard Chartered Bank [1999] Q.B. 241; [1998] 3 W.L.R. 592; [1998] 4 All E.R. 155; [1998] E.M.L.R. 597; (1998) 142 S.J.L.B. 164; *Times*, May 13, 1998, CA . . . . *Digested*, 98/**1772**
Shaikh v. Bolton MBC (1998) 75 P. & C.R. 1; [1997] R.V.R. 172; [1996] E.G.C.S. 102; [1996] N.P.C. 90; (1996) 72 P. & C.R. D43; *Times*, June 11, 1996, CA . . . . *Digested*, 96/**4940**
Shaklee International v. Customs and Excise Commissioners see Customs and Excise Commissioners v. Shaklee International
Shakoor (Administratrix of the Estate of Shakoor) v. Situ (t/a Eternal Health Co) [2001] 1 W.L.R. 410; [2000] 4 All E.R. 181; (2001) 57 B.M.L.R. 178; *Independent*, May 25, 2000, QBD . . . . *Digested*, 00/**4282**
Shamoon v. Chief Constable of the Royal Ulster Constabulary [2001] I.R.L.R. 520, CA (NI) . . . . *Digested*, 01/**5771**
Shamrock Leasing Ltd v. Customs and Excise Commissioners [1999] B.V.C. 2032; [1998] V. & D.R. 323, V&DTr . . . . *Digested*, 99/**5027**
Shanaghan v. United Kingdom (37715/97), *Times*, May 18, 2001, ECHR . . . . *Joined proceedings*, 01/3575
Shanahan v. Willmott (Unreported, May 9, 2000), CC (Brentford) [*Ex rel.* Mark Lyne, Barrister, 1 Essex Court, Temple, London] . . . . *Digested*, 00/**1681**
Shanks & McEwan (Southern Waste Services) Ltd v. Environment Agency [1999] Env. L.R. 138; [1998] J.P.L. 1125; *Independent*, October 17, 1997, QBD . . . . *Digested*, 97/**2352**
Shanks & McEwan (Teesside) Ltd v. Environment Agency [1999] Q.B. 333; [1998] 2 W.L.R. 452; [1997] 2 All E.R. 332; [1997] Env. L.R. 305; [1997] J.P.L. 824; [1997] Crim. L.R. 684; *Times*, January 28, 1997, QBD . . . . *Digested*, 97/**2353**
Shanning International Ltd (In Liquidation) v. Lloyds TSB Bank Plc (formerly Lloyds Bank Plc); *sub nom* Lloyds TSB Bank Plc (formerly Lloyds Bank Plc) v. Rasheed Bank; Shanning International Ltd (In Liquidation) v. Rasheed Bank [2001] UKHL 31; [2001] 1 W.L.R. 1462; [2001] 3 C.M.L.R. 14; (2001) 98(32) L.S.G. 36; *Times*, July 2, 2001; *Daily Telegraph*, July 10, 2001, HL; affirming [2000] Lloyd's Rep. Bank. 215; [2000] 3 C.M.L.R. 450; [2000] Eu. L.R. 551; *Independent*, July 17, 2000 (C.S), CA; affirming *Times*, January 19, 2000, QBD (Comm Ct) . . . . *Digested*, 01/**4069**
Shanning International Ltd (In Liquidation) v. Rasheed Bank see Shanning International Ltd (In Liquidation) v. Lloyds TSB Bank Plc (formerly Lloyds Bank Plc)
Shannon v. Glazier [2001] 6 Q.R. 7, CC (Oxford) [*Ex rel.* Philip Goddard, Barrister, 4 King's Bench Walk, Temple, London] . . . . *Digested*, 01/**1614**
Shanshal v. Al-Kishtaini see Al-Kishtaini v. Shanshal
SHAPE INC/Divisional application [1998] E.P.O.R. 396, EPO (Technical Bd App)
Shapland v. Palmer [1999] 1 W.L.R. 2068; [1999] 3 All E.R. 50; [1999] P.I.Q.R. P249; *Times*, March 31, 1999, CA. . . . . *Digested*, 99/**475**
Shapland Inc, Re; *sub nom* Mills v. Edict Ltd [2000] B.C.C. 106; [1999] B.P.I.R. 391, Ch D . . . . *Digested*, 99/**3320**
Sharif v. Garret & Co see Sharif v. Garrett & Co
Sharif v. Garrett & Co; *sub nom* Sharif v. Garret & Co [2001] EWCA Civ 1269; (2001) 151 N.L.J. 1371, CA
Sharif v. Secretary of State for the Environment, Transport and the Regions (2000) 80 P. & C.R. 382; [2000] P.L.C.R. 243, QBD . . . . *Digested*, 00/**4445**
Sharp v. Europa Freight Corp Ltd (Unreported, September 27, 1999), CC (Sheffield) [*Ex rel.* Fancy & Jackson Solicitors, Apex House, 54-56 Park St, Camberley, Surrey] . . . . *Digested*, 00/**544**: *Considered*, 00/545: *Not followed*, 01/618

Sharp v. Griffiths (Valuation Officer) [1999] 3 E.G.L.R. 113; [1999] 47 E.G. 149; [1999]
 R.A. 265, Lands Tr . . . . *Digested*, 99/**4331**
Sharp v. Motor Insurers' Bureau see Sharp v. Pereria
Sharp v. Pereira see Sharp v. Pereira
Sharp v. Pereria; *sub nom* Sharp v. Pereira; Sharp v. Motor Insurers' Bureau [1999] 1
 W.L.R. 195; [1998] 4 All E.R. 145; [1999] R.T.R. 125; [1999] Lloyd's Rep. I.R.
 242; [1998] P.I.Q.R. Q129; *Times*, July 25, 1998; *Independent*, June 29, 1998
 (C.S.), CA . . . . *Digested*, 98/**1435**
Sharp v. Thomson; *sub nom* Sharp v. Woolwich Building Society 1997 S.C. (H.L.) 66;
 1997 S.L.T. 636; 1997 S.C.L.R. 328; [1998] B.C.C. 115; [1997] 1 B.C.L.C. 603;
 1997 G.W.D. 9-364; *Times*, March 26, 1997, HL; reversing 1995 S.C. 455; 1995
 S.L.T. 837; 1995 S.C.L.R. 683; [1995] B.C.C. 852; *Times*, July 25, 1995, 1 Div;
 affirming 1994 S.L.T. 1068, OH . . . . *Digested*, 97/**6156**:
 Applied, 00/**6511**
Sharp v. Woolwich Building Society see Sharp v. Thomson
Sharpe v. Foy (1868-69) L.R. 4 Ch. App. 35; (1868) 17 W.R. 65, CA in Chancery . . . . *Applied*, 67/**2039**:
 Considered, 98/**3021**
Sharpe v. Southend HA [1997] 8 Med. L.R. 299; *Times*, May 9, 1997, QBD . . . . *Digested*, 98/**3982**
Shaw v. Applegate [1977] 1 W.L.R. 970; [1978] 1 All E.R. 123; (1978) 35 P. & C.R.
 181; 121 S.J. 424, CA . . . . *Digested*, 77/**2485**:
 Considered, 79/1619, 99/**4856**: *Referred to*, 81/2794, 83/2787
Shaw v. Divers (Unreported, July 20, 2000), CC (Bradford) [*Ex rel.* Sean D Yates,
 Barrister, 10 Park Square, Leeds] . . . . *Digested*, 00/**1697**
Shaw v. Fraser Southwell [1999] Lloyd's Rep. P.N. 633, CA . . . . *Digested*, 99/**4031**
Shaw (Norman) v. Queen, The [2001] UKPC 26; [2001] 1 W.L.R. 1519, PC (Bze) . . . . . *Digested*, 01/**1056**
Shaw v. Sloan [1982] N.I. 393, CA (NI) . . . . *Digested*, 85/**2379**:
 Applied, 89/1533: *Considered*, 99/5146
Shaw v. Smith (1887) L.R. 18 Q.B.D. 193, CA . . . . *Applied*, 90/**3660**:
 Not applied, 99/327
Shawkat v. Nottingham City Hospital NHS Trust [2001] EWCA Civ 954; [2001]
 I.R.L.R. 555; *Independent*, June 27, 2001, CA . . . . *Digested*, 01/**2303**
Shawkat v. Nottingham City Hospital NHS Trust (Remitting) [1999] I.C.R. 780; [1999]
 I.R.L.R. 340, EAT . . . . *Digested*, 99/**2107**
Shawnee Processors Inc v. Granadex SA see Camilla Cotton Oil Co v. Granadex SA
Shea v. Drury (Valuation Officer) [2001] R.A. 263, Lands Tr . . . . *Digested*, 01/**4825**
Sheahan v. Cooper (1999-2000) 2 I.T.E.L.R. 207, Fed Ct (Aus) (Sgl judge)
Shearing v. Customs and Excise Commissioners [2001] B.V.C. 2066; [2000] S.T.I.
 1532, V&DTr
Sheath v. Secretary of State for the Environment, Transport and the Regions [2001]
 EWHC Admin 79; [2001] J.P.L. 1218 (Note); [2001] N.P.C. 31, QBD (Admin
 Ct)
Shedden v. Sheffield City Council (Unreported, May 19, 2000), CC (Sheffield) [*Ex rel.*
 Glaisyers Solicitors, 6th Floor, Manchester House, 18-20 Bridge Street,
 Manchester] . . . . *Digested*, 00/**4245**
Sheehan v. London Fire and Civil Defence Authority see Cullin v. London Fire and Civil
 Defence Authority
Sheehan v. Post Office Counters Ltd [1999] I.C.R. 734, EAT . . . . *Digested*, 99/**2046**
Sheffield (Kristina) v. United Kingdom (22885/93); Horsham v. United Kingdom
 (23390/94) [1998] 2 F.L.R. 928; [1998] 3 F.C.R. 141; (1999) 27 E.H.R.R. 163; 5
 B.H.R.C. 83; [1998] H.R.C.D. 758; [1998] Fam. Law 731; *Times*, September 4,
 1998, ECHR . . . . *Digested*, 98/**3163**
Sheffield City Council v. Hopkins [2001] EWCA Civ 1023; [2001] 26 E.G.C.S. 163;
 (2001) 98(27) L.S.G. 38; (2001) 145 S.J.L.B. 164; *Times*, July 23, 2001;
 Independent, June 21, 2001, CA . . . . *Digested*, 01/**4198**
Sheffield City Council v. Jackson [1998] 1 W.L.R. 1591; [1998] 3 All E.R. 260; (1999)
 31 H.L.R. 331; (1998) 95(24) L.S.G. 34; (1998) 142 S.J.L.B. 181; *Times*, June 22,
 1998, CA . . . . *Digested*, 98/**3059**:
 Considered, 01/958
Sheffield City Council v. Jepson (1993) 25 H.L.R. 299, CA . . . . *Digested*, 93/**2113**:
 Applied, 00/3923: *Considered*, 93/2091, 95/3043
Sheffield City Council v. Siberry [1989] I.C.R. 208; (1989) 86(10) L.S.G. 41, EAT . . . . . *Digested*, 89/**1427**:
 Not followed, 00/2158
Sheffield Corp v. Barclay [1905] A.C. 392, HL; reversing [1903] 2 K.B. 580, CA;
 reversing [1903] 1 K.B. 1, KBD . . . . *Applied*, 80/169,
 98/702
Sheik v. Secretary of State for the Home Department see R. (on the application of
 Sheikh) v. Secretary of State for the Home Department
Sheikh v. Secretary of State for the Home Department see R. (on the application of
 Sheikh) v. Secretary of State for the Home Department
Sheil v. Chamberlain (Unreported, April 3, 1991), CC (Tameside) [*Ex rel.* Rowe &
 Cohen, Solicitors] . . . . *Digested*, 91/**1405**:
 Considered, 00/1592: *Referred to*, 93/1491
Shek (t/a Golden Bowl Cafe) v. Customs and Excise Commissioners [2000] S.T.I. 841,
 V&DTr

Shelfer v. City of London Electric Lighting Co (No.1); Meux's Brewery Co v. City of
London Electric Lighting Co [1895] 1 Ch. 287, CA . . . . *Applied*, 57/3609,
61/6344, 65/3985, 67/3170, 80/2251, 84/1150, 93/4040, 94/622, 94/1763,
95/4142: *Considered*, 70/2290, 90/701, 90/3692, 91/2676, 91/2976,
92/3602, 96/1267, 00/5127: *Distinguished*, 69/2866, 69/3592, 70/2882,
81/2279, 82/2671: *Followed*, 95/3766
Shell Canada Ltd v. Queen, The 2 I.T.L. Rep. 241, Sup Ct (Can); reversing 1 I.T.L. Rep.
93, CA (Can); reversing in part
Shell Chemicals UK Ltd v. P&O Roadtanks Ltd [1995] 1 Lloyd's Rep. 297, CA; affirming
[1993] 1 Lloyd's Rep. 114, QBD (Comm Ct) . . . . *Digested*, 96/**1216**:
Disapproved, 01/949
Shell (UK) Exploration & Production v. Grampian Assessor [2000] R.A. 295, Lands Tr
(Scot). . . . . *Digested*, 00/**6646**
Shell International Chemical Co Ltd v. Commission of the European Communities
(C234/92 P) [1999] E.C.R. I-4501; [1999] 5 C.M.L.R. 1142, ECJ (6th
Chamber) . . . . *Digested*, 00/**2378**
Shell International Chemical Co Ltd v. Commission of the European Communities (T11/
89) see Huls AG v. Commission of the European Communities (C199/92 P)
Shell International Petroleum Co Ltd v. Coral Oil Co Ltd (No.1) [1999] 1 Lloyd's Rep. 72,
QBD (Comm Ct) . . . . *Digested*, 99/**733**
Shell International Petroleum Co Ltd v. Coral Oil Co Ltd (No.2) [1999] 2 Lloyd's Rep.
606, QBD (Comm Ct) . . . . *Digested*, 00/**758**
Shell Marketing (Oman) Ltd v. Owners of the Niase see Niase, The
Shell Tankers UK Ltd v. Dawson see Shell Tankers UK Ltd v. Jeromson
Shell Tankers UK Ltd v. Jeromson; *sub nom* Jeromson v. Shell Tankers UK Ltd; Dawson
v. Cherry Tree Machine Co Ltd; Cherry Tree Machine Co Ltd v. Dawson; Shell
Tankers UK Ltd v. Dawson [2001] EWCA Civ 101; [2001] I.C.R. 1223; [2001]
P.I.Q.R. P19; *Times*, March 2, 2001; *Daily Telegraph*, February 27, 2001, CA. . . . . *Digested*, 01/**4492**
Shell UK Ltd v. Enterprise Oil Plc [1999] 2 All E.R. (Comm) 87; [1999] 2 Lloyd's Rep.
456; *Times*, June 17, 1999, Ch D . . . . *Digested*, 99/**4077**
Shell UK Ltd (t/a Shell (UK) Exploration & Production) v. CLM Engineering Ltd (formerly
Land & Marine Engineering Ltd) [2000] 1 All E.R. (Comm) 940; [2000] 1
Lloyd's Rep. 612; [2000] C.L.C. 1005, QBD (Comm Ct) . . . . *Digested*, 00/**3528**
Shell-Mex and BP Ltd v. Manchester Garages [1971] 1 W.L.R. 612; [1971] 1 All E.R. 841;
115 S.J. 111, CA . . . . *Digested*, 71/**6651**:
Applied, 85/1870, 87/2176, 01/4157: *Considered*, 74/2103, 74/3833, 82/1734,
87/2252, 88/2026, 89/2145, 90/719
SHELL/Bisphenols (T1000/92) [2000] E.P.O.R. 66, EPO (Technical Bd App). . . . . *Digested*, 00/**3633**
Shenavai v. Kreischer (C266/85) [1987] E.C.R. 239; [1987] 3 C.M.L.R. 782, ECJ . . . . *Digested*, 88/**1468**:
Applied, 90/2099, 91/480, 92/3944, 94/5037, 00/284:
Considered, 89/3014, 00/739: *Followed*, 98/747: *Not applied*, 99/735
Shephard v. Wheeler [2000] W.T.L.R. 1175; *Times*, February 15, 2000, Ch D . . . . *Digested*, 00/**4907**
Shepheard v. Lamey [2001] B.P.I.R. 939, Ch D
Shepherd v. Iceland Group Plc (Unreported, May 19, 1998), CA [*Ex rel.* David
Sanderson, Barrister, 3 Paper Buildings, Temple, London, EC4Y 7EU]. . . . . *Digested*, 98/**1536**
Shepherd v. Secretary of State for the Environment, Transport and the Regions (1998)
76 P. & C.R. 74; [1998] J.P.L. 215; [1997] E.G.C.S. 134, CA . . . . *Digested*, 98/**4189**
Shepherd Construction Ltd v. Mecright Ltd [2000] B.L.R. 489, QBD (T&CC) . . . . *Digested*, 01/**862**
Shepherd Hill Civil Engineering Ltd v. Brophy Landscape see Company (No.007020 of
1996), Re
Shepherd Homes Ltd v. Sandham (No.1) [1971] Ch. 340; [1970] 3 W.L.R. 348; [1970]
3 All E.R. 402; (1970) 21 P. & C.R. 863; 114 S.J. 636, Ch D . . . . *Digested*, 70/**2293**:
Applied, 70/2436, 86/2651, 98/3628: *Considered*, 87/3022:
Distinguished, 90/2761, 90/2762
Sheppard v. McKnight (Inspector of Taxes) see McKnight (Inspector of Taxes) v.
Sheppard
Shepping v. Osada; *sub nom* Osada v. Shepping (2001) 33 H.L.R. 13; [2000] L. &
T.R. 489; [2000] 2 E.G.L.R. 38; (2000) 80 P. & C.R. D13; *Times*, March 23,
2000, CA . . . . *Digested*, 00/**3919**
Sheriff v. Klyne Tugs (Lowestoft) Ltd [1999] I.C.R. 1170; [1999] I.R.L.R. 481; (1999)
96(27) L.S.G. 34; (1999) 143 S.J.L.B. 189; *Times*, July 8, 1999, CA. . . . . *Digested*, 99/**2056**:
Applied, 01/4494: *Distinguished*, 00/575
Sherman v. Customs and Excise Commissioners (1971) 115 S.J. 657; *Times*, May 25,
1971, CA; affirming (1970) 115 S.J. 36; *Times*, November 21, 1970 . . . . *Digested*, 71/**5128**:
Followed, 00/4971
Sherman v. Customs and Excise Commissioners [2001] S.T.C. 733 (Note); [2001]
S.T.I. 74, Ch D
Sherratt v. Basildon DC, CC (Southend) [*Ex rel.* Julian Lynch, Barrister, Clarendon
Chambers, 7 Stone Buildings, Lincoln's Inn, London]. . . . . *Digested*, 01/**1671**
Sherwin v. Customs and Excise Commissioners [2000] B.V.C. 2195; [2000] S.T.I. 530,
V&D Tr
Sherwood & Casson Ltd v. Mackenzie (2000) 2 T.C.L.R. 418, QBD (T&CC) . . . . *Digested*, 01/**860**

Shetland Islands Council *v.* Local Government Boundary Commission for Scotland; Orkney Islands Council *v.* Local Government Boundary Commission for Scotland 1999 G.W.D. 6-314; *Times,* March 15, 1999, OH. . . . . *Digested,* 99/**6010**

Shetland Times Ltd *v.* Wills 1997 S.C. 316; 1997 S.L.T. 669; 1997 S.C.L.R. 160; [1997] E.M.L.R. 277; [1997-98] Info. T.L.R. 1; [1998] I.T.C.L.R. 49; [1997] F.S.R. 604; (1997) 16 Tr. L.R. 158; [1998] Masons C.L.R. 159; [1998] Masons C.L.R. Rep. 117; 1997 G.W.D. 1-5; *Times,* January 21, 1997, OH . . . . *Digested,* 97/**5742**

Shevill *v.* Presse Alliance SA (C68/93) [1995] 2 A.C. 18; [1995] 2 W.L.R. 499; [1995] All E.R. (E.C.) 289; [1995] E.C.R. I-415; [1995] I.L.Pr. 267; [1995] E.M.L.R. 543; *Times,* April 6, 1995; *Financial Times,* March 21, 1995, ECJHL; affirming [1992] 2 W.L.R. 1; [1992] 1 All E.R. 409; [1991] I.L.Pr. 568; *Times,* March 13, 1991; *Independent,* March 13, 1991; *Financial Times,* March 20, 1991, CA . . . . *Digested,* 95/**3127**:
Considered, 99/715, 99/717: *Distinguished,* 98/748: *Followed,* 01/1835:
Referred to, 97/895: *Subsequent proceedings,* 96/1083

Shevlin (t/a Trafford Heat Treatment Ltd) *v.* Trafford Park Development Corp [1998] 1 E.G.L.R. 115; [1998] 08 E.G. 161; [1998] R.V.R. 5; (1998) 95(10) L.S.G. 28, Lands Tr . . . . *Digested,* 98/**4177**

Shewu *v.* Hackney LBC (2000) 79 P. & C.R. 47; [1999] 3 E.G.L.R. 1; [2000] R.V.R. 31; [2000] J.P.L. 498; (1999) 96(31) L.S.G. 44; [1999] N.P.C. 107; *Times,* September 28, 1999, CA; affirming (1998) 76 P. & C.R. 374; [1998] 2 E.G.L.R. 232; [1998] R.V.R. 83, Lands Tr . . . . *Digested,* 99/**4195**

Shield Mark BV *v.* Kist (t/a Memex) [2000] E.T.M.R. 147, Hof (NL)

Shierson *v.* Tomlinson see NT Gallagher & Sons Ltd *v.* Howard

Shikari *v.* Malik (No.1) LTA 98/6489/1, CA . . . . *Cited,* 99/552

Shikari *v.* Malik (No.2), *Times,* May 20, 1999, CA . . . . *Digested,* 99/**550**:
Cited, 99/552

Shiloh Spinners Ltd *v.* Harding (No.1) [1973] A.C. 691; [1973] 2 W.L.R. 28; [1973] 1 All E.R. 90; 25 P. & C.R. 48; (1972) 117 S.J. 34, HL; reversing [1972] Ch. 326; [1971] 3 W.L.R. 34; [1971] 2 All E.R. 307; 22 P. & C.R. 447; 115 S.J. 248, CA. . . *Digested,* 73/**1867**:
Applied, 85/1878, 99/3290: *Considered,* 74/2023, 81/1503, 83/421,
83/3405, 84/1326, 84/1901, 84/1931, 86/1841, 87/2959, 89/2126, 89/2128,
91/2226, 97/3293, 00/2326: *Distinguished,* 00/4658

Shilton *v.* Wilmshurst (Inspector of Taxes) [1991] 1 A.C. 684; [1991] 2 W.L.R. 530; [1991] 3 All E.R. 148; [1991] S.T.C. 88; 64 T.C. 78; (1991) 135 S.J. 250; *Times,* February 13, 1991; *Independent,* February 20, 1991; *Financial Times,* February 12, 1991; *Guardian,* February 12, 1991, HL; reversing [1990] 1 W.L.R. 373; [1990] S.T.C. 55; (1990) 87(4) L.S.G. 43; (1990) 134 S.J. 50, CA; affirming [1989] 1 W.L.R. 179; [1988] S.T.C. 868; (1988) 132 S.J. 1755, Ch D . . . . *Digested,* 91/**2092**:
Applied, 93/2275, 99/4729

Shimizu (UK) Ltd *v.* Westminster City Council [1997] 1 W.L.R. 168; [1997] 1 All E.R. 481; [1997] R.V.R. 128; [1997] J.P.L. 523; (1997) 94(10) L.S.G. 31; (1997) 147 N.L.J. 218; (1997) 141 S.J.L.B. 56; [1997] N.P.C. 11; *Times,* February 11, 1997, HL; reversing (1995) 70 P. & C.R. 532; [1995] 1 E.G.L.R. 167; [1995] 23 E.G. 118; [1995] R.V.R. 105; [1996] J.P.L. 112; [1994] E.G.C.S. 205; *Independent,* February 13, 1995 (C.S.), CA; reversing [1993] R.V.R. 177, Lands Tr. . . . . *Digested,* 97/**4077**:
Considered, 01/1845

Shina *v.* Elghanian [1999] 3 E.G.L.R. 103; [1999] 48 E.G. 147, Lands Tr . . . . *Digested,* 00/**3900**

Shine *v.* United Kingdom Central Council for Nursing, Midwifery and Health Visiting see R. *v.* United Kingdom Central Council for Nursing, Midwifery and Health Visiting Ex p. Shine (Alternative Remedy)

Shingara *v.* Secretary of State for the Home Department see R. *v.* Secretary of State for the Home Department Ex p. Shingara (No.2)

Shinhan Bank Ltd *v.* Sea Containers Ltd [2000] 2 Lloyd's Rep. 406; [2000] Lloyd's Rep. Bank. 365; [2000] C.L.C. 1473, QBD (Comm Ct) . . . . *Digested,* 00/**5109**

Shipowners Mutual Protection & Indemnity Association (Luxembourg) *v.* Hodgetts [2000] 1 Lloyd's Rep. 58, Sup Ct (Qld) . . . . *Digested,* 00/**243**

Shipton *v.* Foulkes [2001] EWCA Civ 324; [2001] 3 F.C.R. 306, CA

Shire Court Residents Ltd *v.* Registrar of Companies [1995] B.C.C. 821, Ch D . . . . *Digested,* 96/**3752**:
Followed, 99/603

Shirley *v.* Caswell [2001] 1 Costs L.R. 1; [2000] Lloyd's Rep. P.N. 955; *Independent,* July 24, 2000 (C.S), CA . . . . *Digested,* 01/**460**

Shiu Wing Ltd *v.* Commissioner of Estate Duty 2 I.T.L. Rep. 794, CFA (HK); reversing 2 I.T.L. Rep. 1, CA (HK)

Shocked *v.* Goldschmidt [1998] 1 All E.R. 372; *Times,* November 4, 1994; *Independent,* December 5, 1994 (C.S.), CA . . . . *Digested,* 98/**592**:
Applied, 95/3916, 96/21, 96/4986, 00/3924: *Considered,* 97/641:
Followed, 01/441

Shogun Finance Ltd *v.* Hudson; *sub nom* Hudson *v.* Shogun Finance Ltd [2001] EWCA Civ 1000; *Times,* July 4, 2001; *Independent,* July 12, 2001, CA; affirming (Unreported, January 13, 2000), CC (Leicester) [*Ex rel.* Sunil Iyer, Barrister, 17 Main Street, Glenfield, Leicester] . . . . *Digested,* 01/**917**

Shokar *v.* Customs and Excise Commissioners [1998] V. & D.R. 301, V&DTr . . . . *Digested,* 00/**5281**

Shone *v.* Rigby (1998) 98(6) Q.R. 5, QBD . . . . *Digested,* 98/**1491**

Short *v.* Bro Taf HA [2001] 6 Q.R. 13, CC (Cardiff) [*Ex rel.* Sarah Paneth, Barrister, No. 1 Serjeants' Inn, Fleet Street, London]. . . . . *Digested*, 01/**1680**
Short *v.* Trustees of Yeovil Agricultural Society (Unreported, September 24, 1999), CC (Yeovil) [*Ex rel.* Jonathan Dingle, Barrister, South Western Chambers, 12 Middle Street, Taunton]. . . . . *Digested*, 00/**1639**
Short's Trustee *v.* Chung (No.2) 1999 S.C. 471; 1999 S.L.T. 751; 1999 S.C.L.R. 815; 1999 G.W.D. 12-537, Ex Div; affirming 1998 S.C. 105; 1998 S.L.T. 200; 1997 S.C.L.R. 1181; 1997 G.W.D. 37-1885; *Times*, May 18, 1998, OH . . . . *Digested*, 99/**5709**:
Applied, 00/**5938**
Shorter (t/a Ideal Scaffolding) *v.* Customs and Excise Commissioners [2001] S.T.I. 1392, V&D Tr
Shorters *v.* United Kingdom see McDaid *v.* United Kingdom
Shortland *v.* Northland Health Ltd (1999) 50 B.M.L.R. 255, CA (NZ) . . . . *Digested*, 00/**2782**
Showboat Entertainment Centre *v.* Owens [1984] 1 W.L.R. 384; [1984] 1 All E.R. 836; [1984] I.C.R. 65; [1984] I.R.L.R. 7; (1983) 80 L.S.G. 3002; (1984) 134 N.L.J. 37; (1984) 128 S.J. 152, EAT . . . . *Digested*, 83/**1265**:
Considered, 92/1955, 98/2180
Showerings Ltd *v.* Entam Ltd [1975] F.S.R. 45, Ch D . . . . *Digested*, 75/**3421**:
Applied, 00/496
Shraff Tip Ltd *v.* Highways Agency (No.1) [1999] 2 E.G.L.R. 205; [1999] R.V.R. 64, Lands Tr . . . . *Digested*, 99/**4194**
Shraff Tip Ltd *v.* Highways Agency (No.2) [1999] R.V.R. 322, Lands Tr . . . . *Digested*, 00/**4472**
Shraff Tip Ltd *v.* Highways Agency (No.3) [1999] 3 E.G.L.R. 224, Lands Tr . . . . *Digested*, 00/**4431**
Shredded Wheat Co Ltd *v.* Kellogg Co of Great Britain Ltd (1940) 57 R.P.C. 137, HL . . . *Referred to*, 99/3593
Shrewsbury and Atcham BC *v.* Evans (1998) 30 H.L.R. 123, CA. . . . . *Digested*, 97/**2669**
Shropshire CC *v.* Wynne [1998] C.O.D. 40; *Times*, July 22, 1997, QBD . . . . *Digested*, 97/**1252**
Shtun *v.* Zalejska [1996] 1 W.L.R. 1270; [1996] 3 All E.R. 411; *Times*, April 18, 1996, CA . . . . *Digested*, 96/**898**:
Applied, 97/760, 99/464, 00/605: *Distinguished*, 98/558: *Referred to*, 97/763
Shulem B Association Ltd's Appeal, Re [2001] 1 E.G.L.R. 105; [2001] 11 E.G. 175; [2001] N.P.C. 12, Lands Tr . . . . *Digested*, 01/**4184**
Shuttleworth *v.* Secretary of State for Trade and Industry see Dawes & Henderson (Agencies) Ltd (In Liquidation) (No.2), Re
SIAC Construction Ltd *v.* Mayo CC [1999] Eu. L.R. 535, HC (Irl) . . . . *Digested*, 99/**5078**
SIAC Construction Ltd *v.* Mayo CC (C19/00) [2001] 3 C.M.L.R. 59, ECJ (5th Chamber) . . . . *Previous proceedings*, 99/5078
SIBOLA/Packing machine (T141/89) [1998] E.P.O.R. 425, EPO (Technical Bd App)
Sicard *v.* Societe Himolla [1998] I.L.Pr. 792, Cass (F)
Sidaway *v.* Board of Governors of the Bethlem Royal Hospital [1985] A.C. 871; [1985] 2 W.L.R. 480; [1985] 1 All E.R. 643; (1985) 82 L.S.G. 1256; (1985) 135 N.L.J. 203; (1985) 129 S.J. 154, HL; affirming [1984] Q.B. 493; [1984] 2 W.L.R. 778; [1984] 1 All E.R. 1018; (1984) 81 L.S.G. 899; (1984) 128 S.J. 301, CA . . . . *Digested*, 85/**2318**:
Applied, 84/3570, 00/4194: *Considered*, 85/2651, 88/2453, 90/5498, 94/3000, 95/3622, 00/4247: *Followed*, 98/3986: *Not followed*, 87/2603
Siddell *v.* Smith Cooper & Partners; Follows *v.* Smith Cooper & Partners [1999] Lloyd's Rep. P.N. 79; [1999] P.N.L.R. 511, CA . . . . *Digested*, 99/**4013**
Siddiqui's Trade Mark Application [2001] E.T.M.R. 38, TMR. *Digested*, 01/**4060**
Sidebotham *v.* Holland [1895] 1 Q.B. 378, CA . . . . *Applied*, 47-51/**5528**:
Considered, 67/3259, 96/132, 99/2465: *Distinguished*, 58/1467
Sidhu *v.* Aerospace Composite Technology Ltd [2001] I.C.R. 167; [2000] I.R.L.R. 602; (2000) 97(25) L.S.G. 38; *Times*, June 21, 2000; *Independent*, July 17, 2000 (C.S), CA; reversing [1999] I.R.L.R. 683; [1999] Disc. L.R. 152, EAT. . . . . *Digested*, 00/**2185**
Sidhu *v.* British Airways Plc; Abnett (known as Sykes) *v.* British Airways Plc [1997] A.C. 430; [1997] 2 W.L.R. 26; [1997] 1 All E.R. 193; [1997] 2 Lloyd's Rep. 76; 1997 S.C. (H.L.) 26; 1997 S.L.T. 492; 1997 S.C.L.R. 114; (1997) 94(2) L.S.G. 26; (1996) 146 N.L.J. 1851; (1997) 141 S.J.L.B. 26; *Times*, December 13, 1996; *Independent*, December 17, 1996, HL; affirming [1995] P.I.Q.R. P427, CA . . . . . *Digested*, 97/**220**:
Applied, 97/879, 01/949: *Considered*, 00/5164: *Referred to*, 95/5499
Sidhu *v.* Memory Corp Plc (No.1) see Memory Corp Plc *v.* Sidhu (No.1)
Sidiropoulos *v.* Greece (1999) 27 E.H.R.R. 633; 4 B.H.R.C. 500; [1998] H.R.C.D. 707, ECHR . . . . *Digested*, 98/**3081**
Siebe Gorman & Co Ltd *v.* Barclays Bank Ltd; *sub nom* Siebe Gorman & Co Ltd *v.* RH McDonald Ltd [1979] 2 Lloyd's Rep. 142, Ch D . . . . *Digested*, 79/**169**:
Applied, 01/732: *Considered*, 93/2331, 00/3483
Siebe Gorman & Co Ltd *v.* RH McDonald Ltd see Siebe Gorman & Co Ltd *v.* Barclays Bank Ltd
Siegfried Demel (t/a Demotec Siegfried Demel) *v.* C&H Jefferson (No.1) (1998) 21(5) I.P.D. 21050, Pat Ct
Siegfried Demel (t/a Demotec Siegfried Demel) *v.* C&H Jefferson (No.2) [1999] F.S.R. 204; (1998) 21(8) I.P.D. 21082, Pat Ct . . . . *Digested*, 99/**3502**
Siemens AG *v.* Nold (C42/95) [1996] E.C.R. I-6017; [1997] B.C.C. 759; [1997] 1 B.C.L.C. 291; [1997] 1 C.M.L.R. 308, ECJ . . . . *Digested*, 98/**699**

Siemens AG's Application; *sub nom* XPRESSLINK Trade Mark Application, Re [1999]
 E.T.M.R. 146, Appointed Person . . . . *Digested, 99/3588*
Siemens SA v. Commission of the European Communities (C278/95 P) [1997] E.C.R.
 I-2507; [1997] C.E.C. 1267, ECJ (4th Chamber); affirming [1995] E.C.R. II-1675,
 CFI . . . . *Digested, 98/738*
SIEMENS/Contact medium (T512/89) [1998] E.P.O.R. 63, EPO (Technical Bd App)
Sierra Leone Telecommunications Co Ltd v. Barclays Bank Plc; *sub nom* Sierratel v.
 Barclays Bank Plc [1998] 2 All E.R. 820; [1998] C.L.C. 501; (1998) 95(17)
 L.S.G. 32; *Times*, February 25, 1998, QBD (Comm Ct) . . . . *Digested, 98/272*
Sierratel v. Barclays Bank Plc see Sierra Leone Telecommunications Co Ltd v. Barclays
 Bank Plc
SIG Security Services Ltd, Re; *sub nom* Official Receiver v. Bond [1998] B.C.C. 978,
 Ch D (Companies Ct) . . . . *Digested, 99/616*
Sight & Sound Education Ltd v. Books Etc Ltd [2000] L. & T.R. 146; [1999] 3 E.G.L.R.
 45; [1999] 43 E.G. 161, Ch D . . . . *Digested, 00/3886*
Signal Communications Ltd v. Office for Harmonisation in the Internal Market (Trade
 Marks and Designs) (OHIM) (T128/99); *sub nom* TELEYE Trade Mark [2001]
 C.E.C. 387, CFI (4th Chamber)
Signet Group Plc v. Hammerson UK Properties Ltd [1997] E.G.C.S. 176; (1998) 95(3)
 L.S.G. 25; (1998) 142 S.J.L.B. 70; [1997] N.P.C. 176; [1998) 75 P. & C.R. D33;
 Times, December 15, 1997, CA . . . . *Digested, 98/374*
Silberdistel Design, Re [2000] E.C.D.R. 372, BGH (Ger)
Silbers v. Southwark LBC 76 L.G.R. 421; 122 S.J. 128, CA . . . . *Digested, 78/1569*:
 Considered, 87/1879, 98/3038
Silcock v. South Ribble DC [2001] J.P.L. 500 (Note), QBD
Silcott v. Commissioner of Police of the Metropolis (1996) 8 Admin. L.R. 633; *Times*,
 July 9, 1996, CA . . . . *Digested, 96/4864*:
 Applied, 98/4784, 98/4786: Overruled in part, 00/4543
Silhouette International Schmied GmbH & Co KG v. Hartlauer Handelsgesellschaft mbH
 [1999] 3 C.M.L.R. 267, OGH (A) . . . . *Previous proceedings,*
 98/3502
Silhouette International Schmied GmbH & Co KG v. Hartlauer Handelsgesellschaft mbH
 (C355/96) [1999] Ch. 77; [1998] 3 W.L.R. 1218; [1998] All E.R. (E.C.) 769;
 [1998] E.C.R. I-4799; [1998] 2 C.M.L.R. 953; [1998] C.E.C. 676; [1998]
 E.T.M.R. 539; [1998] F.S.R. 729; (1998) 21(10) I.P.D. 21110; *Times*, July 22,
 1998, ECJ; reversing [1998] E.C.R. I-4799; [1998] E.T.M.R. 286; [1998] F.S.R.
 474, AGO . . . . *Digested, 98/3502*:
 Applied, 99/3547: Not followed, 99/3560
Silicon Graphics Inc v. Indigo Graphic Systems (UK) Ltd [1994] F.S.R. 403, Ch D . . . . *Digested, 95/4939*:
 Considered, 98/437, 01/486
Silk v. Fletcher (Inspector of Taxes) [2000] S.T.C. (S.C.D.) 565; [2000] S.T.I. 1655, Sp
 Comm . . . . *Digested, 01/5299*
Silkin v. Beaverbrook Newspapers [1958] 1 W.L.R. 743; [1958] 2 All E.R. 516; 102
 S.J. 491, QBD . . . . *Digested, 58/1859*:
 Applied, 67/2278, 68/2231, 99/1625: Approved, 91/2322
Sillifant v. Powell Duffryn Timber Ltd [1983] I.R.L.R. 91, EAT . . . . *Digested, 83/1348*:
 Applied, 88/1353, 00/2190: Considered, 91/1696, 95/2104, 96/2668
Silloth on Solway Golf Club v. Customs and Excise Commissioners see Keswick Golf
 Club v. Customs and Excise Commissioners
Silva Pontes v. Portugal (A/286-A) (1994) 18 E.H.R.R. 156, ECHR . . . . *Digested, 94/2392*:
 Applied, 98/3136: Considered, 01/3516
Silva Rocha v. Portugal (18165/91) (2001) 32 E.H.R.R. 16, ECHR
Silverburn Finance (UK) Ltd v. Salt [2001] EWCA Civ 279; [2001] 2 All E.R. (Comm)
 438; [2001] Lloyd's Rep. Bank. 119, CA . . . . *Digested, 01/693*
Silverstein, Re [1999] B.P.I.R. 813, Fed Ct (Aus) (Sgl judge) . . . . *Digested, 99/3252*
Silverton v. Goodall [1997] P.I.Q.R. P451, CA . . . . *Digested, 97/769*:
 Applied, 98/590
Silvey v. Pendragon Plc [2001] EWCA Civ 784; [2001] I.R.L.R. 685; *Daily Telegraph*,
 May 15, 2001, CA; reversing EAT/149/00, EAT . . . . *Digested, 01/2349*
Simba v. Secretary of State for the Home Department see Ahmad (Mariam) v.
 Secretary of State for the Home Department
Simister v. Fawole (Unreported, May 11, 2001), CC (Leeds) [*Ex rel.* Tom Nossiter,
 Barrister, Park Lane Chambers, 19 Westgate, Leeds] . . . . *Digested, 01/1782*
Simmenthal SpA v. Amministrazione delle Finanze dello Stato (No.3) (C70/77) [1978]
 E.C.R. 1453; [1978] 3 C.M.L.R. 670, ECJ . . . . *Digested, 79/1179*:
 Followed, 00/5360
Simmenthal SpA v. Commission of the European Communities (C92/78) [1979] E.C.R.
 777; [1978] E.C.R. 1129; [1980] 1 C.M.L.R. 25, ECJ . . . . *Digested, 79/1118*:
 Applied, 99/2278
Simmon Box (Diamonds) Ltd, Re see Cohen v. Selby
Simmonds v. Dowty Seals Ltd [1978] I.R.L.R. 211, EAT . . . . *Digested, 78/898*:
 Disapproved, 98/2239
Simmonds v. Queen, The [1998] A.C. 286; [1998] 2 W.L.R. 145; (1997) 141 S.J.L.B.
 250, PC (Jam) . . . . *Digested, 98/955*

Simmons v. Pizzey [1979] A.C. 37; [1977] 3 W.L.R. 1; [1977] 2 All E.R. 432; 75 L.G.R.
　　583; (1978) 36 P. & C.R. 36; 121 S.J. 424, HL; affirming (1976) 120 S.J. 802,
　　DC . . . . *Digested,* 77/**1520**:
　　　　　　　　　　　　Applied, 81/1314: *Considered,* 78/1569, 87/1879, 96/3104, 98/3038
Simms v. Saunders see Thirty-Eight Building Ltd (No.2), Re
Simms v. Secretary of State for the Environment, Transport and the Regions [1998]
　　P.L.C.R. 24; (1998) 75 P. & C.R. D8, QBD . . . . *Digested,* 98/**4183**
Simms v. Walls (Unreported, October 12, 1999), CC (Southampton) [*Ex rel*. Andrew
　　Lorie, Barrister, College Chambers, 19 Carlton Crescent, Southampton] . . . . *Digested,* 00/**1717**
Simon Container Machinery Ltd v. Emba Machinery AB [1998] 2 Lloyd's Rep. 429,
　　QBD (Comm Ct) . . . . *Digested,* 98/**3376**
Simple Shoes Inc v. Kabushiki Kaisha Renown Corp (2000) 23(11) I.P.D. 23097, OHIM
　　(2nd Bd App)
Simply Travel Ltd v. Customs and Excise Commissioners; *sub nom* Customs and Excise
　　Commissioners v. Simply Travel Ltd [2001] B.T.C. 5570; [2001] S.T.I. 1404, Ch
　　D; reversing [2001] S.T.I. 1166, V&DTr
Simpson v. Al Dairies Farms Ltd [2001] N.P.C. 14, CA
Simpson v. Fergus (2000) 79 P. & C.R. 398; (2000) 79 P. & C.R. D16, CA . . . . *Digested,* 00/**5125**
Simpson v. Grant (Unreported, November 15, 1999), CC (Manchester) [*Ex rel*. Betesh
　　Partnership Solicitors, P.O. Box No. 180, 2nd Floor Cardinal House, 20 St. Mary's
　　Parsonage, Manchester] . . . . *Digested,* 00/**1714**
Simpson v. Roberts, *Times,* December 21, 1984, DC . . . . *Digested,* 85/**2095**:
　　　　　　　　　　　　　Applied, 00/1047: *Considered,* 98/1037: *Followed,* 98/1038
Simpson v. United Kingdom (Unreported, December 4, 1989), ECHR . . . . *Considered,* 01/**1899**:
　　　　　　　　　　　　　　　　　　　　　　　　　　　　　　　Followed, 01/2039
Simpson's Motor Sales (London) v. Hendon Corp (No.2) [1965] 1 W.L.R. 112; [1964] 3
　　All E.R. 833; 109 S.J. 32, Ch D . . . . *Digested,* 65/**3104**:
　　　　　　　　　　　　　　　　　　　Applied, 01/457: *Previous proceedings:* 63/455
SIMSA v. Cargill International SA see Cargill International SA Antigua (Geneva Branch)
　　v. Sociedad Iberica de Molturacion SA
Simson v. Sutton (Unreported, June 3, 1999), CC (Stockport) [*Ex rel*. David Calvert,
　　Barrister, St James's Chambers, 68 Quay Street, Manchester] . . . . *Digested,* 99/**1557**
Sinclair v. British Telecommunications Plc [2001] 1 W.L.R. 38; [2000] 2 All E.R. 461;
　　[2001] 1 Costs L.R. 40; *Independent,* March 13, 2000 (C.S.), CA1998-NJ-615,
　　QBD . . . . *Digested,* 00/**431**
Sinclair v. Lockwood, CC (Birkenhead) [*Ex rel*. John Baldwin, Barrister, Oriel
　　Chambers, Liverpool] . . . . *Digested,* 01/**1647**
Sinclair v. Neighbour [1967] 2 Q.B. 279; [1967] 2 W.L.R. 1; [1966] 3 All E.R. 988; 1
　　K.I.R. 451; 110 S.J. 808, CA . . . . *Digested,* 67/**1429**:
　　　　　　　　　　　　　　　　　　　　　Applied, 00/2132: *Followed,* 96/2637
Sinclair v. Secretary of State for the Environment, Transport and the Regions (No.1)
　　[2001] J.P.L. 1000 (Note), QBD (Admin Ct)
Sinclair v. Secretary of State for Transport (1998) 75 P. & C.R. 548; [1998] 1 P.L.R. 59;
　　[1997] 2 E.G.L.R. 173; [1997] 34 E.G. 92; [1998] R.V.R. 31; [1998] J.P.L. 495,
　　Lands Tr . . . . *Digested,* 97/**4034**
Sinclair v. Sutcliffe [2001] 4 Q.R. 11, CC (Bradford) [*Ex rel*. Richard Miles, Barrister, 2
　　King's Bench Walk, London] . . . . *Digested,* 01/**1747**
Sinclair Collis Ltd v. Customs and Excise Commissioners; *sub nom* Customs and Excise
　　Commissioners v. Sinclair Collis Ltd [2001] UKHL 30; [2001] S.T.C. 989;
　　[2001] 3 C.M.L.R. 6; [2001] B.T.C. 5284; [2001] B.V.C. 378; [2001] S.T.I. 893;
　　[2001] 27 E.G.C.S. 131, HL; reversing [1999] S.T.C. 701; [1999] B.T.C. 5264;
　　[1999] B.V.C. 297; [1999] E.G.C.S. 89; [1999] N.P.C. 81, CA; affirming [1998]
　　S.T.C. 841; [1998] B.T.C. 5286; [1998] B.V.C. 335; (1998) 95(34) L.S.G. 31;
　　[1998] N.P.C. 118; *Times,* July 29, 1998; *Independent,* July 27, 1998 (C.S.),
　　QBD . . . . *Digested,* 01/**5565**
Sinclair Gardens Investments (Kensington) Ltd v. Franks (1998) 76 P. & C.R. 230;
　　[1998] R.V.R. 261, Lands Tr. . . . . *Digested,* 98/**3645**:
　　　　　　　　　　　　　　　　　　　　　　　　Applied, 98/3644, 00/3909
Sinclair Roche & Temperley v. Somatra Ltd see Somatra Ltd v. Sinclair Roche &
　　Temperley
Sindall Ltd v. Solland (2001) 3 T.C.L.R. 30; 80 Con. L.R. 152, QBD (T&CC)
Sindicato de Medicos de Asistencia Publica (SIMAP) v. Conselleria de Sanidad y
　　Consumo de la Generalidad Valenciana (C303/98) [2001] All E.R. (EC) 609;
　　[2000] E.C.R. I-7963; [2001] 3 C.M.L.R. 42; [2001] I.C.R. 1116; [2000] I.R.L.R.
　　845; *Times,* October 18, 2000, ECJ . . . . *Digested,* 00/**2716**
Sinfield v. Department of Transport (Unreported, March 2, 1998), CC (Central London)
　　[*Ex rel*. Gerard Boyle, Barrister, 1 Serjeants' Inn, Fleet Street, London] . . . . *Digested,* 98/**1666**
Singer v. Beckett; *sub nom* Continental Assurance Co of London Plc (In Liquidation),
　　Re [2001] B.P.I.R. 733, Ch D . . . . *Digested,* 01/**728**
Singer v. Isaac [2001] W.T.L.R. 1045, Ch D
Singer v. Williams (Inspector of Taxes) [1921] 1 A.C. 41, HL; affirming [1919] 2 K.B. 94,
　　CA; affirming [1918] 2 K.B. 432, KBD . . . . *Applied,* 47-51/**4228**:
　　　　　　　　　　　　　　　　　　　　　　　Considered, 69/1733, 99/4666

Singer & Friedlander Ltd *v.* John D Wood & Co [1955-95] P.N.L.R. 70; (1977) 243
E.G. 212, QBD . . . . *Digested,* 77/**2455**:
Considered, 88/2453, 92/3213, 93/2984, 93/2998, 93/2999, 94/3359:
Distinguished, 86/2232: *Followed,* 99/4057
Singh (Rajinder), Re [2000] Imm. A.R. 170, QBD . . . . *Digested,* 00/**3347**
Singh *v.* Aitken [1998] P.I.Q.R. Q37, CC (Middlesbrough) . . . . *Digested,* 98/**1421**
Singh *v.* Bhasin [2000] W.T.L.R. 275; *Times,* August 21, 1998, Ch D . . . . *Digested,* 98/**484**:
Applied, 00/429
Singh *v.* British Steel Corp [1974] I.R.L.R. 131, IT . . . . *Digested,* 74/**1326.20**:
Considered, 01/2226
Singh (Tejendra) *v.* Christie see Tejendrasingh *v.* Metsons
Singh *v.* Dhillon (Unreported, April 23, 1998), QBD [*Ex rel.* Sarah Paneth, Barrister, 1
Serjeant's Inn, Fleet Street, London] . . . . *Digested,* 98/**1642**
Singh (Jaspal) *v.* DPP (2000) 164 J.P. 82; [1999] R.T.R. 424; [1999] Crim. L.R. 914;
(2000) 164 J.P.N. 102, QBD . . . . *Digested,* 00/**1034**
Singh *v.* Eagle Star Direct (Unreported, September 2, 1998), CC (Colchester) [*Ex rel.*
Edward Lewis Solicitors and Paul McGrath, Barrister, 1 Temple Gardens, Temple,
London] . . . . *Digested,* 98/**461**
Singh *v.* General Medical Council (2000) 56 B.M.L.R. 124, PC (UK) . . . . *Digested,* 01/**2895**
Singh (Ashwini Kumar) *v.* General Medical Council (2001) 59 B.M.L.R. 106, PC (UK) . . *Digested,* 01/**2900**
Singh (Manjit) *v.* HM Advocate [2001] S.T.C. 790; 2001 J.C. 186; 2001 S.L.T. 812;
2001 S.C.C.R. 348; [2001] S.T.I. 831; 2001 G.W.D. 14-547, HCJ Appeal . . . . *Digested,* 01/**6322**
Singh *v.* Inland Revenue Board [2000] 1 W.L.R. 1421; [2000] S.T.C. 255; [2000]
B.T.C. 116; [2000] S.T.I. 234; (2000) 144 S.J.L.B. 202, PC (Trin) . . . . *Digested,* 00/**4997**
Singh *v.* Leeds City Council [1998] R.V.R. 230, Lands Tr. *Digested,* 98/**4173**
Singh *v.* M&N Contractors Ltd [2000] 4 Q.R. 7, CC (Bradford) [*Ex rel.* Ian R Millar,
Barrister, Broadway House Chambers, 9 Bank Street, Bradford] . . . . *Digested,* 00/**1699**
Singh (Amrik) *v.* Secretary of State for the Home Department [2000] Imm. A.R. 340,
CA . . . . *Digested,* 00/**3309**
Singh (Chinder) *v.* Secretary of State for the Home Department; Singh (Harjit) *v.*
Secretary of State for the Home Department; Singh (Onkar) *v.* Secretary of State
for the Home Department [1998] Imm. A.R. 551, IAT . . . . *Digested,* 99/**3166**
Singh (Dharam) *v.* Secretary of State for the Home Department [1998] Imm. A.R. 428;
[1998] I.N.L.R. 747, IAT . . . . *Digested,* 98/**3222**
Singh (Harjit) *v.* Secretary of State for the Home Department see Singh (Chinder) *v.*
Secretary of State for the Home Department
Singh (Jaswinder) *v.* Secretary of State for the Home Department (No.2) 1999 S.C.
357; *Times,* January 27, 1999, 2 Div . . . . *Digested,* 99/**6292**
Singh (Onkar) *v.* Secretary of State for the Home Department see Singh (Chinder) *v.*
Secretary of State for the Home Department
Singh (Raghbir) *v.* Secretary of State for the Home Department see R. *v.* Secretary of
State for the Home Department Ex p. Singh (Raghbir)
Singh (Tarlochan) *v.* Secretary of State for the Home Department [2000] Imm. A.R.
36, CA . . . . *Digested,* 00/**3280**
Singh *v.* United Kingdom see Hussain *v.* United Kingdom
Singh *v.* Williams (Inspector of Taxes) [2000] S.T.C. (S.C.D.) 404; [2000] S.T.I. 1240,
Sp Comm . . . . *Digested,* 01/**5247**
Single Internal Market in Electricity, Re [1999] E.C.C. 271, C Concurrence (F)
Sinochem International Oil (London) Co Ltd *v.* Fortune Oil Co Ltd [2000] 1 Lloyd's Rep.
682, QBD (Comm Ct) . . . . *Digested,* 00/**885**
Sinochem International Oil (London) Co Ltd *v.* Mobil Sales and Supply Corp (No.1)
[2000] 1 All E.R. (Comm) 474; [2000] 1 Lloyd's Rep. 339; [2000] C.L.C. 878,
CA; reversing [1999] 2 All E.R. (Comm) 522; [1999] 2 Lloyd's Rep. 769;
[2000] C.L.C. 186, QBD (Comm Ct) . . . . *Digested,* 00/**900**
Sinochem International Oil (London) Co Ltd *v.* Mobil Sales and Supply Corp (No.2)
[2000] 1 All E.R. (Comm) 758; [2000] 1 Lloyd's Rep. 670; [2000] C.L.C. 1132,
QBD (Comm Ct) . . . . *Digested,* 00/**761**
Siporex Trade SA *v.* Banque Indosuez [1986] 2 Lloyd's Rep. 146, QBD (Comm Ct) . . . . *Digested,* 86/**168**:
Applied, 01/379: *Considered,* 90/269, 91/256
Siporex Trade SA *v.* Comdel Commodities [1986] 2 Lloyd's Rep. 428, QBD (Comm Ct) . *Digested,* 87/**137**:
Considered, 99/487, 01/764
Sir Lindsay Parkinson & Co *v.* Triplan Ltd [1973] Q.B. 609; [1973] 2 W.L.R. 632; 117
S.J. 146, CA; affirming [1973] 2 All E.R. 273; (1972) 117 S.J. 36, QBD . . . . *Digested,* 73/**2632**:
Considered, 92/3442, 01/5711: *Followed,* 97/563
Sirdar *v.* Army Board (C273/97) see Sirdar *v.* Secretary of State for Defence (C273/
97)
Sirdar *v.* Secretary of State for Defence (C273/97); *sub nom* Sirdar *v.* Army Board
(C273/97) [1999] All E.R. (EC) 928; [1999] E.C.R. I-7403; [1999] 3 C.M.L.R.
559; [1999] C.E.C. 554; [2000] I.C.R. 130; [2000] I.R.L.R. 47; 7 B.H.R.C. 459;
Times, October 27, 1999, ECJ . . . . *Digested,* 99/**264**:
Followed, 00/268
Sirena Srl *v.* Eda Srl (C40/70) [1971] E.C.R. 69; [1971] C.M.L.R. 260; [1971] F.S.R.
666, ECJ . . . . *Digested,* 71/**4489**:
Applied, 98/719: *Considered,* 73/3323, 74/1462: *Followed,* 74/1535

Sirius International Insurance Corp *v.* Oriental Assurance Corp [1999] 1 All E.R. (Comm.) 699; [1999] Lloyd's Rep. I.R. 343, QBD (Comm Ct) . . . .   *Digested,* 99/**3428**

SIS (Science in Sport) Ltd *v.* Customs and Excise Commissioners [2001] S.T.I. 1002, V&DTr

SIS (Science in Sport) Ltd *v.* Customs and Excise Commissioners (No.1) [2000] B.V.C. 2277; [2000] V. & D.R. 195; [2000] S.T.I. 935, V&DTr

Sita (formerly Ebenezer Mears (Sand Producers) Ltd) *v.* Surrey CC [2001] R.V.R. 56, Lands Tr . . . .   *Digested,* 01/**4668**

Sita (GB) Ltd *v.* Burton [1998] I.C.R. 17; [1997] I.R.L.R. 501; *Times,* December 5, 1996, EAT . . . .   *Digested,* 97/**2268**

SITEPRODUCER Trade Mark see NetObjects Trade Mark Application

Sithole *v.* Thor Chemicals Holdings Ltd A2/2000/2894, CA . . . .   *Digested,* 00/**316**

Sithole *v.* Thor Chemicals Holdings Ltd (Leave to Appeal) (1999) 96(9) L.S.G. 32; *Times,* February 15, 1999, CA . . . .   *Digested,* 99/**544**

Sivakumar *v.* Secretary of State for the Home Department see R. (on the application of Sivakumar) *v.* Immigration Appeal Tribunal

Sivanentheran *v.* Immigration Appeal Tribunal see R. *v.* Immigration Appeal Tribunal Ex p. Sivanentheran

Sivieri *v.* Mills (Unreported, February 16, 1998), CC (Rawtenstall) [*Ex rel.* James Hurd, Barrister, St James's Chambers, 68 Quay Street, Manchester] . . . .   *Digested,* 98/**1719**

SJ Berwin & Co *v.* Motor Crown Petroleum Ltd see Motor Crown Petroleum Ltd *v.* SJ Berwin & Co

SJ Filhol *v.* Fairfax (Dental Equipment) [1990] R.P.C. 293, Pat Ct . . . .   *Digested,* 91/**2714**: *Considered,* 99/3518

SJY (CICB: Quantum: 1997), Re (Unreported, December 8, 1997), CICB (Nottingham) [*Ex rel.* Jeremy Janes, Barrister, King Charles House Chambers, Standard Hill, Nottingham] . . . .   *Digested,* 98/**1517**

SK Shipping Co Ltd *v.* BB Energy (Asia) Pte Ltd [2000] 1 All E.R. (Comm) 810, QBD (Comm Ct) . . . .   *Digested,* 00/**4684**

Skandarajah (Vaithialingham) *v.* Secretary of State for the Home Department see Vilvarajah (Nadarajah) *v.* Secretary of State for the Home Department

Skandia (UK) Insurance Co *v.* Chemical Bank see Banque Financiere de la Cite SA (formerly Banque Keyser Ullmann SA) *v.* Westgate Insurance Co (formerly Hodge General & Mercantile Co Ltd)

Skandia (UK) Insurance Co *v.* Credit Lyonnais Bank Nederland NV see Banque Financiere de la Cite SA (formerly Banque Keyser Ullmann SA) *v.* Westgate Insurance Co (formerly Hodge General & Mercantile Co Ltd)

Skandia International Insurance Corp *v.* NRG Victory Reinsurance Ltd see Commercial Union Assurance Co Plc *v.* NRG Victory Reinsurance Ltd

Skandia Property (UK) Ltd *v.* Thames Water Utilities Ltd [1999] B.L.R. 338; *Times,* September 7, 1999, CA; affirming 57 Con. L.R. 65, QBD (OR) . . . .   *Digested,* 99/**5038**

Skarzynski *v.* Chalford Property Co Ltd [2001] B.P.I.R. 673, Ch D   *Digested,* 01/**3737**

Skatteministeriet *v.* Aktieselskabet Forsikringsselskabet Codan (C236/97) [1998] E.C.R. I-8679; [2001] 1 C.M.L.R. 36, ECJ (6th Chamber)

Skatteministeriet *v.* Vestergaard (C55/98) [1999] E.C.R. I-7641; [2001] 3 C.M.L.R. 65, ECJ (6th Chamber)

Skeavington *v.* Bradder, *Independent,* February 28, 2000 (C.S.), CA

Skelton *v.* Lewisham and North Southwark HA [1998] Lloyd's Rep. Med. 324, QBD . . .   *Digested,* 99/**3991**

Skelton Finance Co *v.* Lawrence (1976) 120 S.J. 147 . . . .   *Digested,* 76/**1813**: *Considered,* 99/2515

Skerrits of Nottingham Ltd *v.* Secretary of State for the Environment, Transport and the Regions (No.2) see Skerritts of Nottingham Ltd *v.* Secretary of State for the Environment, Transport and the Regions (No.2)

Skerritts of Nottingham Ltd *v.* Secretary of State for the Environment, Transport and the Regions (No.1); *sub nom* Secretary of State for the Environment, Transport and the Regions *v.* Skerritts of Nottingham Ltd [2001] Q.B. 59; [2000] 3 W.L.R. 511; (2000) 80 P. & C.R. 516; [2000] 2 P.L.R. 84; [2000] J.P.L. 789; [2000] E.G.C.S. 31; (2000) 97(10) L.S.G. 38; [2000] N.P.C. 19; *Times,* March 8, 2000; *Independent,* May 8, 2000 (C.S.), CA; reversing (1999) 78 P. & C.R. 410; [1999] 2 P.L.R. 109; [1999] J.P.L. 932; [1999] E.G.C.S. 48; (1999) 96(13) L.S.G. 33; [1999] N.P.C. 37; *Times,* May 25, 1999; *Independent,* May 3, 1999 (C.S.), QBD . . . .   *Digested,* 00/**4473**

Skerritts of Nottingham Ltd *v.* Secretary of State for the Environment, Transport and the Regions (No.2); *sub nom* Skerrits of Nottingham Ltd *v.* Secretary of State for the Environment, Transport and the Regions (No.2) [2000] 2 P.L.R. 102; [2000] J.P.L. 1025; [2000] E.G.C.S. 43, CA; reversing (2000) 79 P. & C.R. 251; [1999] 4 P.L.R. 1; [2000] J.P.L. 281; *Times,* October 20, 1999, QBD . . . .   *Digested,* 00/**4415**

Skidmore *v.* Dartford and Gravesham NHS Trust A1/2001/0629, CA; reversing [2001] I.C.R. 911; [2001] Lloyd's Rep. Med. 175, EAT . . . .   *Digested,* 01/**2245**

Skills Motor Coaches Ltd *v.* Denman (C297/99); *sub nom* Criminal Proceedings against Skills Motor Coaches Ltd (C297/99) [2001] All E.R. (EC) 289; [2001] E.C.R. I-573; [2001] R.T.R. 21; [2001] 2 C.M.L.R. 3; *Times,* February 20, 2001, ECJ . . .   *Digested,* 01/**5485**

Skilton *v.* T&K Home Improvements Ltd; *sub nom* T&K Home Improvements *v.* Skilton [2000] I.C.R. 1162; [2000] I.R.L.R. 595; *Times,* April 18, 2000, CA . . . .   *Digested,* 00/**2118**

Skinner v. Farley see Farley v. Skinner (No.2)
Skipskredittforeningen v. Emperor Navigation [1998] 1 Lloyd's Rep. 66; [1997] 2
    B.C.L.C. 398; [1997] C.L.C. 1151, QBD (Comm Ct) . . . . *Digested*, 97/**2507**:
    Approved, 98/845

Skipton Building Society v. Bratley; *sub nom* Stott v. Skipton Building Society [2001]
    Q.B. 261; [2000] 3 W.L.R. 1031; [2000] 2 All E.R. 779; [2000] 1 All E.R.
    (Comm) 257; [2000] Lloyd's Rep. Bank. 34; [1999] N.P.C. 158; *Times*, January
    12, 2000, CA . . . . *Digested*, 00/**4655**
Skipton Building Society v. Collins [1998] B.P.I.R. 267, Ch D . . . . *Digested*, 98/**3352**
Skipton Building Society v. Lea Hough & Co [2000] P.N.L.R. 545, QBD (Merc Ct) . . . *Digested*, 00/**4279**
Skipton Building Society v. Sturdy Order Ltd LTA 98/7415/1, CA . . . . *Digested*, 99/**568**
Skis Rossignol SA v. Head Tyrolia Sports SA [1999] E.T.M.R. 450, Trib Gde Inst
    (Grenoble)
Skjevesland v. Geveran Trading Co Ltd (No.1) [2000] B.P.I.R. 523, Ch D . . . . *Digested*, 00/**3485**
SKM SA v. Wagner Spraytech (UK) [1982] R.P.C. 497, CA . . . . *Digested*, 83/**2775**:
    Considered, 99/3471
Skone v. Skone [1971] 1 W.L.R. 812; [1971] 2 All E.R. 582; 115 S.J. 424, HL . . . . *Digested*, 71/**3489**:
    Applied, 71/3338, 72/1001, 83/2702: *Considered*, 96/654, 01/632:
    Followed, 83/2860

Skoubo v. Teddie Thulstrup A/S; Teddie Thulstrup A/S v. Skoubo [2001] E.C.C. 9, HR
    (DK)
Skreb v. PCO Stauereibetrieb Paetz & Co Nachfolgar GmbH (C138/91) see Katsikas v.
    Konstantinidis (C132/91)
Skrenty v. Harrogate BC [1999] E.G.C.S. 127, Ch D
Skrine & Co v. Euromoney Publications Plc [2001] EWCA Civ 1479, CA; reversing in
    part [2001] E.M.L.R. 16; (2000) 97(45) L.S.G. 40; (2000) 144 S.J.L.B. 274;
    Times, November 10, 2000, QBD . . . . *Digested*, 00/**1756**
Skuse v. Granada Television Ltd [1996] E.M.L.R. 278; *Independent*, April 2, 1993, CA . . *Digested*, 93/**2584**:
    Applied, 01/1830: *Followed*, 95/3131
Skyepharma Plc v. Hyal Pharmaceutical Corp [2001] B.P.I.R. 163, CA (Ont); reversing
    [2000] B.P.I.R. 531, CJ (Gen Div) (Ont) . . . . *Digested*, 01/**3776**
Skyparks Group Plc v. Marks [2001] EWCA Civ 319; [2001] B.P.I.R. 683; [2001]
    W.T.L.R. 607, CA . . . . *Digested*, 01/**4882**
SL (Adult Patient) (Medical Treatment), Re see S (Adult Patient: Sterilisation: Patient's Best
    Interests), Re
SL v. SL see S (Adult Patient: Sterilisation: Patient's Best Interests), Re
SL Timber Systems Ltd v. Carillion Construction Ltd 2001 S.C.L.R. 935; [2001] B.L.R.
    516; 2001 G.W.D. 23-852, OH
Slaight Communications Inc v. Davidson [1989] 1 S.C.R. 1038, Sup Ct (Can) . . . . *Applied*, 98/3074
Slasor v. DPP [1999] R.T.R. 432, QBD . . . . *Digested*, 00/**936**
Slater v. Richardson [1998] N.P.C. 28, CC (Derby)
Slater v. Worthington's Cash Stores (1930) [1941] 1 K.B. 488, CA . . . . *Applied*, 01/4549:
    Distinguished, 68/2880

Slater & Co v. Sheil Land Associates Ltd see Peach Publishing Ltd v. Slater & Co
Slater Ltd v. Beacontree Income Tax General Commissioners [2001] S.T.I. 1699; *Times*,
    December 18, 2001, Ch D
Sleeman v. Highway Care Ltd, *Times*, November 3, 1999, CA . . . . *Digested*, 99/**563**
Slim v. Daily Telegraph [1968] 2 Q.B. 157; [1968] 2 W.L.R. 599; [1968] 1 All E.R. 497;
    112 S.J. 97, CA . . . . *Digested*, 68/**2231**:
    Applied, 72/2030, 95/3126: *Considered*, 97/2038, 99/1623
Slim International v. Delta Protypos Milk Industry [2000] E.T.M.R. 409, Protodikeio
    (Athens)
Slimane-Kaid v. France see Reinhardt v. France (22921/93)
Slimane-Kaid v. France (29507/95) (2001) 31 E.H.R.R. 48, ECHR . . . . *Digested*, 01/**3533**
Slinn v. Official Receiver [2000] B.P.I.R. 847, CA (Gue) . . . . *Digested*, 01/**3757**
Slocock's Will Trusts, Re [1979] 1 All E.R. 358, Ch D . . . . *Digested*, 79/**1080**:
    Applied, 00/5260: *Considered*, 89/2039: *Followed*, 90/2651
Slotz Vending Ltd & Egleton v. Avandero UK Ltd (1998) 98(2) Q.R. 6, CC (Reading) . . *Digested*, 98/**1635**
Slough BC v. Secretary of State for the Environment see R. v. Secretary of State for the
    Environment Ex p. Slough BC
Slough BC v. Thames Valley University (2001) 16 P.A.D. 104, Planning Inspector
SM Jaleel & Co Ltd's Trade Mark Application [2000] R.P.C. 471, Appointed Person . . . *Digested*, 00/**3763**
Small v. DPP [1995] R.T.R. 95; [1995] Crim. L.R. 165; (1994) 158 J.P.N. 453; *Times*,
    April 11, 1994, QBD . . . . *Digested*, 95/**4468**:
    Considered, 00/5240

Small v. Riddle (Unreported, November 3, 1998), CC (Bristol) [*Ex rel.* Lyons Davidson
    Solicitors, Victoria House, 51 Victoria Street, Bristol] . . . . *Digested*, 99/**2497**
Small v. Somerville Roberts [2000] 5 Q.R. 5, QBD [*Ex rel.* Lanyon Bowdler Solicitors,
    Brodie House, Town Centre, Telford] . . . . *Digested*, 00/**1498**
Small v. Whitehead (Unreported, July 13, 1998), CC (Swindon) [*Ex rel.* Amery-Parkes
    Solicitors, 17/18 Orchard Street, Bristol] . . . . *Digested*, 98/**1460**
Smart v. Allan see Smart v. Allen

Smart v. Allen; *sub nom* Smart v. Allan [1963] 1 Q.B. 291; [1962] 3 W.L.R. 1325; [1962] 3 All E.R. 893; 127 J.P. 35; 126 J.P. 35; 60 L.G.R. 548; 106 S.J. 881, QBD . . . . *Digested,* 62/**2723**:
                   Applied, 76/3415, 78/2598, 00/2600: *Considered,* 87/3289, 88/3129:
                                       Distinguished, 64/3225
Smart v. Royal Insurance Plc [1998] E.G.C.S. 129, QBD
Smart Cars v. Isotank (Unreported, May 16, 2000), CC (Birkenhead) [*Ex rel.* Helen M Mulholland, Barrister, 40 King Street, Manchester] . . . . *Digested,* 00/**405**
Smatt v. Rahilou [2000] E.C.C. 164, C d'A (Paris)
SMC Electronics Ltd v. Akhter Computers Ltd [2001] 1 B.C.L.C. 433, CA . . . . *Digested,* 01/**109**
SMC Engineering (Bristol) Ltd v. Fraser [2001] C.P. Rep. 76; *Times,* January 26, 2001, CA . . . . *Digested,* 01/**580**
Smeaton v. Butcher (No.1) [2000] E.M.L.R. 985; (2000) 97(22) L.S.G. 47; *Times,* May 17, 2000; *Independent,* June 19, 2000, CA . . . . *Digested,* 00/**333**
Smedvig Ltd v. Elf Exploration UK Plc (The Super Scorpio II) [1998] 2 Lloyd's Rep. 659, QBD (Comm Ct) . . . . *Digested,* 99/**4078**
Smee v. Adye QBENF 1999/0781/A2, CA; affirming(Unreported, March 29, 1999), QBD [*Ex rel.* Andrew Ritchie, Barrister, 9 Gough Square, London] . . . . *Digested,* 00/**1477**
Smerdon v. Ellis (Unreported, March 17, 1997), CC (Torquay & Ntn Abbott) [*Ex rel.* Hugh Hamill, 12 King's Bench Walk, Temple] . . . . *Digested,* 97/**960**:
               Applied, 98/2503, 98/2504: *Approved,* 97/958: *Considered,* 99/2454
Smillie v. Matsushita (UK) Ltd [2001] 6 Q.R. 11, CC (Pontypridd) [*Ex rel.* Andrew Arentsen, Barrister, 33 Park Place, Cardiff] . . . . *Digested,* 01/**1650**
Smit International (Deutschland) GmbH v. Josef Mobius Baugesellschaft GmbH & Co [2001] 2 All E.R. (Comm) 265; [2001] C.L.C. 1545, QBD (Comm Ct) . . . . *Digested,* 01/**4942**
Smith, Re; *sub nom* Smith (Samuel) v. Smith (Reginald) [1916] 1 Ch. 369, Ch D . . . . . *Distinguished,* 98/3279
Smith (CICA: Quantum: 2000), Re [2001] 4 Q.R. 9, CICA (Durham) [*Ex rel.* Robert Gilbert, Barrister, Fountain Chambers, 1 Watson Street, Middlesborough] . . . . . . *Digested,* 01/**1573**
Smith (CICB: Quantum: 2000), Re (Unreported, May 3, 2000), CICB (Durham) [*Ex rel.* Richard Power, Barrister, 6 Pump Court, Temple, London] . . . . *Digested,* 00/**1511**
Smith (Deceased), Re see Smith v. Smith (Disclaimer of Interest under Will)
Smith (Inspector of Taxes) v. Abbott; Fitzpatrick v. Inland Revenue Commissioners (No.2); Smith (Inspector of Taxes) v. Holt; Smith (Inspector of Taxes) v. Scovell; Smith (Inspector of Taxes) v. Shuttleworth; Smith (Inspector of Taxes) v. Woodhouse [1994] 1 W.L.R. 306; [1994] 1 All E.R. 673; [1994] S.T.C. 237; 1994 S.L.T. 836; 66 T.C. 407; (1994) 144 N.L.J. 270; *Times,* February 18, 1994; *Independent,* February 18, 1994; *Guardian,* February 21, 1994, HL; reversing in part [1993] 1 W.L.R. 1114; [1993] 2 All E.R. 417; [1993] S.T.C. 316; *Times,* March 18, 1993, CA; affirming [1992] 1 W.L.R. 201; [1991] S.T.C. 661; (1992) 89(3) L.S.G. 33; (1991) 135 S.J.L.B. 189; *Times,* October 23, 1991, Ch D . . . . *Digested,* 94/**5928**:
                  Followed, 99/4731: *Previous proceedings,* 93/5419
Smith v. Anderson (1880) L.R. 15 Ch. D. 247, CA . . . . *Considered,* 00/3686
Smith v. Arcadia Group Plc [2000] 1 Q.R. 7, CC (Rawtenstall) [*Ex rel.* Paul Clark, Barrister, Exchange Chambers, Pearl Assurance House, Derby Square, Liverpool] . . . . *Digested,* 99/**1471**
Smith v. Australian Securities Commission [2000] B.P.I.R. 853, Sup Ct (Vic) . . . . *Digested,* 01/**3758**
Smith v. Bank of Scotland; Mumford v. Bank of Scotland 1997 S.C. (H.L.) 111; 1997 S.L.T. 1061; 1997 S.C.L.R. 765; [1998] Lloyd's Rep. Bank. 62; [1997] 2 F.L.R. 862; (1997) Hous. L.R. 89; [1997] Fam. Law 91; [1997] N.P.C. 94; 1997 G.W.D. 21-1004; *Times,* June 23, 1997, HL; reversing 1996 S.L.T. 392; 1995 S.C.L.R. 839; [1996] 1 F.L.R. 344; [1996] Fam. Law 149; *Times,* September 29, 1995, 1 Div; affirming 1994 S.L.T. 1288; 1994 S.C.L.R. 856; *Times,* August 4, 1994; *Scotsman,* September 14, 1994, OH . . . . *Digested,* 97/**6087**:
       Applied, 99/6431, 00/6676: *Cited,* 00/6670: *Considered,* 98/6181:
              Not applied, 01/6882: *Referred to,* 00/6669, 00/6674
Smith v. Bass Plc see Hilton International Hotels (UK) Ltd v. Smith
Smith v. BeeLine Buzz Co (Unreported, July 26, 1999), CC (Dewsbury) [*Ex rel.* Tim Capstick, Barrister, 6 Park Square, Leeds] . . . . *Digested,* 99/**1574**
Smith v. Bogan & Sons Ltd (Unreported, August 8, 1997), CC (Chester) [*Ex rel.* TR Morris, Solicitor, Bartlett & Son, 16 Nicholas Street, Chester]. . . . . *Digested,* 97/**571**:
                                   Considered, 98/495
Smith v. Brothers of Charity Services Ltd see Limb v. Union Jack Removals Ltd (In Liquidation)
Smith v. Caiels see Smith v. Hughes
Smith v. Cardigan [2001] N.P.C. 108, Ch D
Smith v. Cheltenham BC see Hallam v. Avery
Smith v. Chief Constable of Kent (Unreported, September 30, 1997), CC (Maidstone) [*Ex rel.* Alistair Redford and Premelaa Jagatheeson, Barristers, Holborn Chambers, 6 Gate Street Lincoln's Inn Fields, London] . . . . *Digested,* 98/**378**
Smith v. Chief Constable of Sussex (Unreported, October 29, 1998), CC (Brighton) [*Ex rel.* Paul Ozin, Barrister, 23 Essex Street, London] . . . . *Digested,* 99/**4852**
Smith v. Cosworth Casting Processes Ltd [1998] P.I.Q.R. P192; *Times,* May 15, 1997, CA . . . . *Digested,* 97/**502**

Smith v. Cosworth Casting Processes Ltd (Practice Note) [1997] 1 W.L.R. 1538;
[1997] 4 All E.R. 840; [1997] P.I.Q.R. P227; (1997) 94(10) L.S.G. 31; (1997)
141 S.J.L.B. 66; *Times*, March 28, 1997, CA . . . . *Digested*, 97/**501**:
          Applied, 98/691: *Followed*, 99/357, 00/363

Smith v. Cottrell (Unreported, December 9, 1997), CC (Birmingham) [*Ex rel.* Jerome
Mayhew, Barrister, Goldsmith Building, Temple] . . . . *Digested*, 98/**1709**

Smith v. Customs and Excise Commissioners [2001] S.T.I. 808, V&DTr

Smith v. Director of the Serious Fraud Office see R. v. Director of the Serious Fraud
Office Ex p. Smith

Smith v. DPP (2000) 164 J.P. 96; [2000] R.T.R. 36; (1999) 96(32) L.S.G. 34; (1999)
96(34) L.S.G. 34; *Times*, July 28, 1999, QBD . . . . *Digested*, 99/**1058**

Smith (Nicholas) v. DPP [1992] R.T.R. 413 (Note), DC . . . . *Digested*, 93/**3497**:
       Applied, 98/896: *Distinguished*, 92/3799, 93/3500

Smith (Peter John) v. DPP [2001] EWHC Admin 55; (2001) 165 J.P. 432; [2001] Crim.
L.R. 735; (2001) 165 J.P.N. 820; *Independent*, March 19, 2001 (C.S), QBD
(Admin Ct)

Smith v. Ealing Hammersmith and Hounslow HA [1997] 8 Med. L.R. 290, CA . . . . *Digested*, 98/**531**

Smith (Kathleen Rose) v. East Elloe Rural DC [1956] A.C. 736; [1956] 2 W.L.R. 888;
[1956] 1 All E.R. 855; 120 J.P. 263; 54 L.G.R. 233; 6 P. & C.R. 102; 100 S.J.
282, HL; reversing in part [1955] 1 W.L.R. 380; [1955] 2 All E.R. 19; 199 J.P.
325; 53 L.G.R. 299; 5 P. & C.R. 148; 99 S.J. 235, CA . . . . *Digested*, 56/**1290**:
   Applied, 67/3805, 76/19, 94/5367: *Considered*, 90/120, 90/2829, 91/119,
    95/4800, 96/4715, 99/4244: *Distinguished*, 56/1130, 56/7545, 68/2027,
     69/1866: *Followed*, 97/4070: *Referred to*, 92/6511:
        Subsequent proceedings, 59/3215

Smith v. Eric S Bush (A Firm); Harris v. Wyre Forest DC [1990] 1 A.C. 831; [1989] 2
W.L.R. 790; [1989] 2 All E.R. 514; (1989) 21 H.L.R. 424; 87 L.G.R. 685; [1955-
95] P.N.L.R. 467; [1989] 18 E.G. 99; [1989] 17 E.G. 68; (1990) 9 Tr. L.R. 1;
(1989) 153 L.G. Rev. 984; (1989) 139 N.L.J. 576; (1989) 133 S.J. 597, HL;
affirming [1988] Q.B. 743; [1987] 3 All E.R. 179; (1987) 19 H.L.R. 287; [1987] 1
E.G.L.R. 157; (1987) 283 E.G. 56; (1987) 84 L.S.G. 3260; (1987) 137 N.L.J.
362; (1987) 131 S.J. 1423, CA . . . . *Digested*, 89/**2566**:
   Applied, 88/2422, 88/2457, 90/3258, 90/3266, 92/1547, 92/3207, 95/3718,
   01/4540, 01/4541: *Considered*, 88/2433, 88/2456, 89/2565, 90/3306,
   90/3307, 90/3315, 91/2657, 92/1553, 93/2997, 95/770, 95/2496, 96/2993,
     98/3921, 99/477: *Distinguished*, 97/3851: *Followed*, 99/4058:
          Referred to, 92/6078

Smith v. Gardner Merchant Ltd [1998] 3 All E.R. 852; [1999] I.C.R. 134; [1998]
I.R.L.R. 510; (1998) 95(32) L.S.G. 29; (1998) 142 S.J.L.B. 244; *Times*, July 23,
1998; *Independent*, July 21, 1998, CA; reversing [1996] I.R.L.R. 342, EAT . . . . *Digested*, 98/**2197**:
     Applied, 00/2206: *Explained*, 01/6475: *Followed*, 01/2315

Smith v. Greenalls Management Ltd [1998] N.P.C. 6, Ch D

Smith v. Hand [1986] R.T.R. 265, DC . . . . *Digested*, 86/**2879**:
       Considered, 00/960: *Explained*, 91/3118

Smith v. Hilton International Hotels (UK) Ltd see Hilton International Hotels (UK) Ltd v.
Smith

Smith (Inspector of Taxes) v. Holt see Smith (Inspector of Taxes) v. Abbott

Smith v. Hughes; Smith v. Caiels; Tolan v. Hughes; Tolan v. Caiels; Tolan v. Thomas;
Tolan v. Mackinnon [1960] 1 W.L.R. 830; [1960] 2 All E.R. 859; (1960) 124 J.P.
430; 104 S.J. 606, QBD . . . . *Digested*, 60/**1945**:
   Applied, 00/5244: *Considered*, 83/2613, 95/1268: *Distinguished*, 62/3099,
               62/3100

Smith v. Ian Simpson & Co [2001] Ch. 239; [2000] 3 W.L.R. 495; [2000] 3 All E.R.
434; [2000] B.P.I.R. 667; (2000) 150 N.L.J. 582; *Times*, April 24, 2000;
Independent, April 18, 2000, CA . . . . *Digested*, 00/**3436**

Smith v. Lawson (1998) 75 P. & C.R. 466; [1997] E.G.C.S. 85; [1997] N.P.C. 87, CA . . *Digested*, 98/**3593**

Smith v. Leicester HA see Smith v. Leicestershire HA

Smith v. Leicestershire HA; *sub nom* Smith v. Leicester HA [1998] Lloyd's Rep. Med.
77, CA (1997) 36 B.M.L.R. 23, QBD . . . . *Digested*, 98/**551**:
               Applied, 00/516

Smith v. Lindsay & Kirk (A Firm) (No.1) 2000 S.C. 200; 2000 S.L.T. 287; 2000 G.W.D.
1-20; *Times*, March 16, 2000, 1 Div; reversing 1998 S.L.T. 1096; 1998 S.C.L.R.
572; 1998 G.W.D. 10-508, OH . . . . *Digested*, 00/**6444**

Smith v. Linser (Unreported, August 14, 2001), CC (Chichester) [*Ex rel.* Will Noble,
Barrister, 9 Gough Square, London] . . . . *Digested*, 01/**1543**

Smith v. Linskills [1996] 1 W.L.R. 763; [1996] 2 All E.R. 353; (1996) 146 N.L.J. 209;
(1996) 140 S.J.L.B. 49; *Times*, February 7, 1996, CA; affirming [1995] 3 All E.R.
226, QBD . . . . *Digested*, 96/**4496**:
     Applied, 97/2485, 00/346: *Considered*, 96/3912, 99/350

Smith v. Littlewoods Organisation Ltd see Maloco v. Littlewoods Organisation Ltd

Smith v. Lloyds TSB Bank Plc; *sub nom* Smith v. Lloyds TSB Group Plc; Harvey Jones Ltd v. Woolwich Plc [2001] Q.B. 541; [2000] 3 W.L.R. 1725; [2001] 1 All E.R. 424; [2000] 2 All E.R. (Comm) 693; [2000] Lloyd's Rep. Bank. 334; (2000) 97(36) L.S.G. 42; (2000) 150 N.L.J. 1337; (2000) 144 S.J.L.B. 240; *Times*, September 6, 2000, CA; affirming [2000] 1 W.L.R. 1225; [2000] 1 All E.R. (Comm) 53; [2000] Lloyd's Rep. Bank. 58; *Times*, December 23, 1999, QBD . . .   *Digested*, 00/**271**
Smith v. Lloyds TSB Group Plc see Smith v. Lloyds TSB Bank Plc
Smith v. Lock (A Bankrupt) [1998] B.P.I.R. 786, Ch D . . . .   *Digested*, 99/**3235**
Smith v. Loughlin (Unreported, January 6, 2000), CC (Kingston upon Hull) [*Ex rel.* Ford & Warren Solicitors, Westgate Point, Westgate, Leeds] . . . .   *Digested*, 00/**1484**
Smith v. Manchester CC see Smith v. Manchester Corp
Smith v. Manchester Corp; *sub nom* Smith v. Manchester CC (1974) 17 K.I.R. 1; (1974) 118 S.J. 597, CA . . . .   *Digested*, 74/**843**:
    Applied, 76/684, 76/1881, 85/950: *Considered*, 96/2127, 96/2138, 98/1485:
    Distinguished, 77/798
Smith (Caroline) v. National Health Service Litigation Authority [2001] Lloyd's Rep. Med. 90, QBD . . . .   *Digested*, 01/**4457**
Smith v. P&O Bulk Shipping Ltd [1998] 2 Lloyd's Rep. 81, QBD . . . .   *Digested*, 98/**2833**
Smith v. Peter North & Partners [2001] EWCA Civ 1553; [2001] 42 E.G.C.S. 138; (2001) 98(41) L.S.G. 35, CA
Smith v. Peters (1875) L.R. 20 Eq. 511, Ct of Chancery . . . .   *Applied*, 82/419,
    82/2499, 01/3961
Smith v. Probyn (2000) 97(12) L.S.G. 44; (2000) 144 S.J.L.B. 134; *Times*, March 29, 2000, QBD . . . .   *Digested*, 00/**571**:
    Applied, 00/570
Smith v. Profile Cars (Unreported, January 12, 1999), CC (Wandsworth) [*Ex rel.* Nicholas Preston, Barrister, Bracton Chambers, Second Floor, 95a Chancery Lane, London] . . . .   *Digested*, 99/**2503**
Smith (Cleon) v. Queen, The [2001] UKPC 27; [2001] 1 W.L.R. 1533, PC (Bze) . . . . . .   *Digested*, 01/**1055**
Smith (Justis Raham) v. Queen, The [2000] 1 W.L.R. 1644, PC (Ber) . . . .   *Digested*, 00/**1022**
Smith v. Royce Properties Ltd [2001] EWCA Civ 949, CA; reversing [2000] E.G.C.S. 60; [2000] N.P.C. 54, Ch D
Smith v. Safeway Plc [1996] I.C.R. 868; [1996] I.R.L.R. 456; *Times*, March 5, 1996, CA; reversing [1995] I.C.R. 472; [1995] I.R.L.R. 132; *Times*, December 16, 1994; *Independent*, January 16, 1995 (C.S.); *Guardian*, December 30, 1994, EAT . . . . .   *Digested*, 96/**2616**:
    Distinguished, 99/2098
Smith v. Scott [1973] Ch. 314; [1972] 3 W.L.R. 783; [1972] 3 All E.R. 645; 116 S.J. 785, Ch D . . . .   *Digested*, 72/**2532**:
    Applied, 01/4197: *Considered*, 85/2496, 86/2481, 87/3771, 99/4066:
    Followed, 99/3681
Smith (Inspector of Taxes) v. Scovell see Smith (Inspector of Taxes) v. Abbott
Smith (Thomas) v. Secretary of State for the Environment, Transport and the Regions see Buckland v. Secretary of State for the Environment, Transport and the Regions
Smith (Trevor Alan) v. Secretary of State for Trade and Industry [2000] I.C.R. 69; [2000] I.R.L.R. 6; [2000] H.R.L.R. 83; *Times*, October 15, 1999, EAT . . . .   *Digested*, 99/**2110**
Smith (Inspector of Taxes) v. Shuttleworth see Smith (Inspector of Taxes) v. Abbott
Smith v. Smith (Disclaimer of Interest under Will); *sub nom* Smith (Deceased), Re [2001] 1 W.L.R. 1937; [2001] 3 All E.R. 552; [2001] W.T.L.R. 1205; (2001) 98(28) L.S.G. 43; (2001) 151 N.L.J. 784; *Times*, June 18, 2001; *Independent*, June 25, 2001 (C.S), Ch D . . . .   *Digested*, 01/**5153**
Smith v. Smith (Divorce) [1990] 1 F.L.R. 438; [1990] F.C.R. 790; [1990] Fam. Law 300, Fam Div . . . .   *Digested*, 90/**2284**:
    Followed, 00/2502
Smith (Letitia) v. Smith (Richard) [2000] 3 F.C.R. 374, CA . . . .   *Digested*, 00/**2519**
Smith (Robert) v. Smith (Daniel) (Unreported, November 4, 1997), CC (Rawtenstall) [*Ex rel.* Brian McCluggage, Barrister, 9 St John Street, Manchester] . . . .   *Digested*, 98/**1418**
Smith (Samuel) v. Smith (Reginald) see Smith, Re
Smith v. Stemler (Unreported, November 8, 2000), CC (Central London) [*Ex rel.* Michael Asher, Pupil Barrister, Francis Taylor Building, Second Floor, Temple, London] . . . .   *Digested*, 01/**2309**
Smith v. Sunseeker Leisure (Unreported, April 13, 1993), CC (Bolton) [*Ex rel.* Slatterys, Solicitors] . . . .   *Digested*, 93/**3167**:
    Cited, 00/466
Smith v. Travel West Midlands [2001] 4 Q.R. 15, CC (Altrincham) [*Ex rel.* Brown Dunne & Gray, Solicitors, Albert Buildings, 1-3 Oxford Road, Altrincham]
Smith v. UIC Insurance Co Ltd [2001] B.C.C. 11, QBD (Comm Ct) . . . .   *Digested*, 01/**507**
Smith v. United Kingdom (No.1); Grady v. United Kingdom; Beckett v. United Kingdom [1999] I.R.L.R. 734; (2000) 29 E.H.R.R. 493; (1999) 11 Admin. L.R. 879; *Times*, October 11, 1999, ECHR . . . .   *Digested*, 99/**3113**:
    Considered, 00/6485: *Previous proceedings*, 95/2663, 96/383
Smith v. United Kingdom (No.2); Grady v. United Kingdom (2001) 31 E.H.R.R. 24, ECHR . . . .   *Digested*, 01/**3580**

Smith (Jane) v. United Kingdom (25154/94) (2001) 33 E.H.R.R. 30; *Times*, January 30, 2001, ECHR. . . . . *Joined proceedings,*
01/4744
Smith v. Vauxhall Motors Ltd [1997] P.I.Q.R. P19, CA. . . . . *Digested,* 96/**732**:
Applied, 01/480: *Distinguished,* 98/459
Smith v. West Lancashire HA [1995] P.I.Q.R. P514, CA . . . . *Digested,* 95/**3169**:
Considered, 00/517: *Followed,* 97/666
Smith v. White Knight Laundry Ltd [2001] EWCA Civ 660; [2001] 3 All E.R. 862; [2001] C.P. Rep. 88; [2001] 2 B.C.L.C. 206; [2001] P.I.Q.R. P30; *Independent,* July 2, 2001 (C.S), CA; affirming (Unreported, October 22, 1999), QBD [*Ex rel.* Davies Arnold Cooper Solicitors, 6-8 Bouverie St, London] . . . . *Digested,* 01/**602**
Smith (Inspector of Taxes) v. Woodhouse see Smith (Inspector of Taxes) v. Abbott
Smith v. Zeneca (Agrochemicals) Ltd [2000] I.C.R. 800, EAT . . . . *Digested,* 00/**2207**
Smith & Nephew v. Marriott's Castle Harbour [2001] I.L.Pr. 10, CJ (Gen Div) (Ont) . . . *Digested,* 01/**803**
SMITH & NEPHEW/Wound dressing (T324/89) [1998] E.P.O.R. 374, EPO (Technical Bd App)
Smith & Williamson v. Sims Pipes [2001] B.P.I.R. 401, CA . . . . *Digested,* 01/**465**
Smith Graham (A Firm) v. Lord Chancellor's Department [1999] 2 Costs L.R. 1; (1999) 149 N.L.J. 1443; *Independent,* October 7, 1999, QBD . . . . *Digested,* 99/**3786**
Smith Hayden & Co Ltd's Application, Re (1946) 63 R.P.C. 97. . . . . *Applied,* 47-51/10363,
47-51/10364, 93/3991, 96/5721: *Considered,* 93/3990, 96/5723, 97/4897,
98/3534, 98/3539: *Followed,* 78/2957, 95/4946, 97/4899
Smith Hogg & Co Ltd v. Black Sea & Baltic General Insurance Co Ltd [1940] A.C. 997; (1940) 67 Ll. L. Rep. 253, HL; affirming [1939] 2 All E.R. 855; (1939) 64 Ll. L. Rep. 87, CA; reversing in part [1938] 4 All E.R. 383; (1938) 62 Ll. L. Rep. 70, KBD . . . . *Applied,* 61/8222,
00/591: *Considered,* 00/1939
Smith Kline & French Laboratories Ltd v. Sterling-Winthrop Group Ltd; *sub nom* Smith Kline & French Laboratories Ltd's Applications [1975] 1 W.L.R. 914; [1975] 2 All E.R. 578; [1975] F.S.R. 298; [1976] R.P.C. 511; 119 S.J. 422, HL; reversing [1974] 1 W.L.R. 861; [1974] 2 All E.R. 826; [1974] F.S.R. 455; 118 S.J. 441, CA; reversing [1973] 1 W.L.R. 1534; [1974] 1 All E.R. 529; [1973] F.S.R. 333; [1974] R.P.C. 91; 117 S.J. 648, Ch D . . . . *Digested,* 76/**2796**:
Applied, 01/5881: *Distinguished,* 85/3502, 86/3427
Smith Kline & French Laboratories Ltd's Applications see Smith Kline & French Laboratories Ltd v. Sterling-Winthrop Group Ltd
Smith (Administrator of Cosslett (Contractors) Ltd) v. Bridgend CBC; *sub nom* Cosslett (Contractors) Ltd (In Administration) (No.2), Re [2001] UKHL 58; [2001] 3 W.L.R. 1347; [2001] B.C.C. 740; 80 Con. L.R. 172; [2001] N.P.C. 161, HL; reversing [2000] B.C.C. 1155; [2000] 1 B.C.L.C. 775, CA . . . . *Digested,* 00/**3428**
Smith New Court Securities Ltd v. Citibank NA see Smith New Court Securities Ltd v. Scrimgeour Vickers (Asset Management) Ltd
Smith New Court Securities Ltd v. Scrimgeour Vickers (Asset Management) Ltd; Smith New Court Securities Ltd v. Citibank NA [1997] A.C. 254; [1996] 3 W.L.R. 1051; [1996] 4 All E.R. 769; [1997] 1 B.C.L.C. 350; (1996) 93(46) L.S.G. 28; (1996) 146 N.L.J. 1722; (1997) 141 S.J.L.B. 5; *Times,* November 22, 1996; *Independent,* November 27, 1996, HL; reversing [1994] 1 W.L.R. 1271; [1994] 4 All E.R. 225; [1994] 2 B.C.L.C. 212; (1994) 91(22) L.S.G. 32; (1994) 91(15) L.S.G. 35; (1994) 138 S.J.L.B. 77; *Times,* March 8, 1994, CA; reversing [1992] B.C.L.C. 1104; *Times,* April 7, 1992, Ch D . . . . *Digested,* 96/**996**:
Applied, 00/1452, 01/965: *Followed,* 97/3370
SmithKline Beecham Biologicals SA v. Connaught Laboratories Inc (Disclosure of Documents) [1999] 4 All E.R. 498; [1999] C.P.L.R. 505; [2000] F.S.R. 1; (2000) 51 B.M.L.R. 91; (1999) 22(10) I.P.D. 22092; *Times,* July 13, 1999 ; *Independent,* July 15, 1999, CA (1999) 22(7) I.P.D. 22062; *Times,* January 14, 1999; *Independent,* November 9, 1998 (C.S), Ch D . . . . *Digested,* 99/**339**:
Considered, 00/5491
SmithKline Beecham Biologicals SA v. Connaught Laboratories Inc (Surrender of Patent); *sub nom* Connaught Laboratories Inc's Patent (Surrender) [1999] F.S.R. 284; (1998) 21 (9) I.P.D. 21092, Pat Ct. . . . . *Digested,* 99/**3497**
SmithKline Beecham Plc v. Advertising Standards Authority see R. (on the application of SmithKline Beecham Plc) v. Advertising Standards Authority
SmithKline Beecham Plc v. Antigen Pharmaceuticals Ltd [1999] E.T.M.R. 512, HC (Irl) . *Digested,* 00/**3699**
SmithKline Beecham Plc v. Dowelhurst Ltd see Boehringer Ingelheim KG v. Swingward Ltd
SmithKline Beecham Plc v. Dowelhurst Ltd (Defence Amendments) see Glaxo Group Ltd v. Dowelhurst Ltd (Defence Amendments)
SmithKline Beecham Plc v. Dowelhurst Ltd (Infringement Action) see Glaxo Group Ltd v. Dowelhurst Ltd (Infringement Action)
Smithkline Beecham Plc v. H (A Child) see Horne-Roberts v. Smithkline Beecham Plc
SmithKline Beecham Plc's European Patent Application (No.94917637.4) see SmithKline Beecham Plc's European Patent Application (T563/97)

SmithKline Beecham Plc's European Patent Application (T563/97); *sub nom* SmithKline Beecham Plc's European Patent Application (No.94917637.4) (2000) 23(7) I.P.D. 23057, EPO (Technical Bd App)

Smithson v. Checketts (Unreported, April 3, 2000) . . . . *Cited*, 00/311:
                                                           Followed, 00/2584: *Not applied*, 01/889

Smouha Family Trust, Re; *sub nom* Detente Ltd (Matter of Representation), Re [2000] W.T.L.R. 133, Royal Ct (Jer) . . . . *Digested*, 00/**5261**

Smurthwaite v. Wilkins (1862) 11 C.B. N.S. 842 . . . . *Applied*, 01/**4948**:
                                                                                Considered, 98/4395

Smyth v. Behbehani [1999] I.L.Pr. 584; *Times*, April 9, 1999, CA. . . . . . *Digested*, 99/**734**
Smyth v. Behbehani (Disclosure) CH.1997 No.4260, Ch D . . . . *Digested*, 00/**314**
Smyth v. Ushewokunze 4 B.H.R.C. 262, Sup Ct (Zim) . . . . *Digested*, 98/**3116**
Smyth's Application for Judicial Review, Re [2001] N.I. 393, QBD (NI)
SN Group Plc v. Barclays Bank [1993] B.C.C. 506 . . . . *Digested*, 93/**2387**:
                                                                                Approved, 99/3354

Snaith and Dolding's Application, Re (1996) 71 P. & C.R. 104, LandsTr . . . . *Digested*, 96/**5007**:
                                                                                Applied, 97/4260, 98/4344

Snapes v. Aram see Hancock (Deceased), Re
Snares v. Adjudication Officer (C20/96) [1997] All E.R. (E.C.) 886; [1997] E.C.R. I-6057; [1998] 1 C.M.L.R. 897; *Times*, December 10, 1997, ECJ . . . . *Digested*, 98/**4515**:
                                                                                Applied, 98/4490

SNC Campenon Bernard SGE v. Minister for the Economy, Finance and the Budget [2000] E.C.C. 403, Cass (F)
Sneddon v. Peglers Ltd [2001] 3 Q.R. 15, CC (Doncaster) [*Ex rel.* Dermot Hughes, Barrister Paradise Square Chambers, Sheffield] . . . . *Digested*, 01/**1669**
Snell v. Beadle (otherwise Silcock) [2001] UKPC 5; [2001] 2 A.C. 304; [2001] 2 W.L.R. 1180; (2001) 145 S.J.L.B. 86, PC (Jer) . . . . *Digested*, 01/**4884**
Snellers Autos BV v. Algemeen Directeur van de Dienst Wegverkeer (C314/98) [2000] E.C.R. I-8633; [2000] 3 C.M.L.R. 1275, ECJ (6th Chamber) . . . . *Digested*, 01/**2512**
Snelling v. Evans (Unreported, April 7, 1999), CC (Leeds) [*Ex rel.* Stephen Friday, Barrister, Park Lane Chambers, Leeds] . . . . *Digested*, 99/**1602**
Snelling v. Whitehead [1998] R.T.R. 385, HL
Snelson v. Thompson [1985] R.T.R. 220, DC . . . . *Digested*, 85/**3058**:
                                                                                Considered, 00/937

Sniezek v. Bundy (Letchworth) Ltd [2000] P.I.Q.R. P213, CA . . . . *Digested*, 00/**525**
Snook v. London & West Riding Investments Ltd [1967] 2 Q.B. 786; [1967] 2 W.L.R. 1020; [1967] 1 All E.R. 518; 111 S.J. 71, CA . . . . *Digested*, 67/**1836**:
              Applied, 99/4764, 00/3879, 01/5319: *Considered*, 84/1915, 87/2162,
              88/2026, 88/2043, 89/2112, 89/2145: *Followed*, 99/2485

SNOW BRAND MILK/Sensor (T704/92) [1998] E.P.O.R. 328, EPO (Technical Bd App)
Snowden v. Secretary of State for the Environment [1980] J.P.L. 749, CA. . . . . *Digested*, 81/**2663**:
              Applied, 94/4428, 95/4833, 99/4214: *Considered*, 84/3415

Snowdonia National Park Authority v. Georgeson, *Independent*, March 16, 1998 (C.S.), QBD . . . . *Digested*, 98/**4185**
Snowdonia National Park Authority v. Kerry (2001) 16 P.A.D. 67, Planning Inspector
Snowdonia National Park Authority v. Porter (2000) 97(5) L.S.G. 36, QBD . . . . *Digested*, 00/**4450**
Snowdonia National Park Authority v. YHA (England and Wales) Ltd (2001) 16 P.A.D. 9, Planning Inspector
Sobey (A Bankrupt), Re [1999] B.P.I.R. 1009, Ch D . . . . *Digested*, 00/**3452**
Social Security Commissioners Decision (No.CI/105/1998) (Unreported, September 20, 1999), SS Comm [*Ex rel.* Desmond Rutledge, Free Representation Unit, 4th Floor, Peer House, 8-14 Verulam Street, London] . . . . *Digested*, 00/**4845**
Socialist Party v. Turkey (1999) 27 E.H.R.R. 51; [1998] H.R.C.D. 583, ECHR . . . . *Digested*, 99/**3116**:
                                                                                Applied, 01/3461

Sociedad Iberica de Molturacion SA v. Cargill International SA see Cargill International SA Antigua (Geneva Branch) v. Sociedad Iberica de Molturacion SA
Sociedade Agricola dos Arinhos v. Commission of the European Communities (T38/99) [2001] E.C.R. II-585; [2001] 2 C.M.L.R. 26, CFI (4th Chamber) . . . . *Digested*, 01/**2482**
Sociedade Independente de Comunicacao SA (SIC) v. Commission of the European Communities (T46/97) [2000] E.C.R. II-2125; [2000] 3 C.M.L.R. 987, CFI (1st Chamber) . . . . *Digested*, 01/**2447**
Societa Italiana Petroli SpA (IP) v. Borsana Srl (C2/97) [1998] E.C.R. I-8597; [2001] 1 C.M.L.R. 27, ECJ . . . . *Digested*, 01/**2506**
Societa Pastorelli Ceramiche v. Ditta Edilpoli [2001] E.C.C. 55, It Cass (I)
Societa Trasporti Castelletti Spedizioni Internazionali SpA v. Hugo Trumpy SpA [1998] I.L.Pr. 216, It Cass (I)
Societe Anonyme d'Intermediaries Luxembourgeois v. Farex Gie see SAIL v. Farex
Societe Baxter v. Premier Ministre (C254/97) [2000] All E.R. (EC) 945; [1999] E.C.R. I-4809; [2000] 2 C.M.L.R. 899; [2000] C.E.C. 707, ECJ . . . . *Digested*, 00/**4913**
Societe Centrale d'Achats des Chirurgiensdentistes Alpha GACD SA v. Micromega SA [1999] E.C.C. 267, Cass (F) . . . . *Digested*, 99/**699**
Societe Chanel v. Societe Capitolina Profumi [1999] E.C.C. 261, Cass (F). . . . . *Digested*, 99/**702**

Societe Civile Agricole Crespelle *v.* Cooperative d'Elevage du Departement de la
Mayenne (C323/93); *sub nom* Le Crespelle (C323/93) [1994] E.C.R. I-5077;
Financial Times, October 25, 1994, ECJ . . . . *Digested*, 95/**638**:
Followed, 98/725

Societe Civile Immobiliere Parodi *v.* Banque H Albert de Bary et Cie [2000] 2 C.M.L.R.
653, Cass (F) . . . . *Previous proceedings*,
98/291

Societe Civile Immobiliere Parodi *v.* Banque H Albert de Bary et Cie (C222/95) [1997]
All E.R. (E.C.) 946; [1997] E.C.R. I-3899; [1998] 1 C.M.L.R. 115; (1997)
94(34) L.S.G. 30, ECJ . . . . *Digested*, 98/**291**

Societe Commerciale des Potasses et de l'Azote (SCPA) (C30/95) see France *v.*
Commission of the European Communities (C68/94)

Societe Compagnie Gervais Danone *v.* Malnuit [2001] E.C.C. 51, Trib Gde Inst (Paris)

Societe Cooperative Providence Agricole de la Champagne *v.* Office National
Interprofessionnel des Cereales (C20/77) see Firma Albert Ruckdeschel & Co *v.*
Hauptzollamt Hamburg-St Annen (C117/76)

Societe Corsetel *v.* Director General of the INPI [2001] E.T.M.R. 82, C d'A (Paris)

Societe Critouridienne de Distribution (SOCRIDIS) *v.* Receveur Principal des Douanes
(C166/98) [1999] E.C.R. I-3791; [2000] 3 C.M.L.R. 669, ECJ (5th Chamber) . *Digested*, 00/**2382**

Societe d'Importation Edouard Leclerc-Siplec *v.* M6 Publicite SA (C412/93) see Societe
d'Importation Edouard Leclerc-Siplec *v.* TF1 Publicite SA (C412/93)

Societe d'Importation Edouard Leclerc-Siplec *v.* TF1 Publicite SA (C412/93); Societe
d'Importation Edouard Leclerc-Siplec *v.* M6 Publicite SA (C412/93) [1995] All
E.R. (E.C.) 343; [1995] E.C.R. I-179; [1995] 3 C.M.L.R. 422; [1996] E.M.L.R.
193; *Financial Times*, February 14, 1995, ECJ (6th Chamber) . . . . *Digested*, 95/**643**:
Applied, 98/728: *Followed*, 00/4165

Societe de Distribution de Mecaniques et d'Automobiles (SODIMA) (In Liquidation) *v.*
Commission of the European Communities (T190/95); Societe de Distribution
de Mecaniques et d'Automobiles (SODIMA) (In Liquidation) *v.* Commission of
the European Communities (T45/96) [1999] E.C.R. II-3617; [2001] 4 C.M.L.R.
8, CFI (1st Chamber) . . . . *Digested*, 01/**2470**

Societe de Distribution de Mecaniques et d'Automobiles (SODIMA) (In Liquidation) *v.*
Commission of the European Communities (T45/96) see Societe de Distribution
de Mecaniques et d'Automobiles (SODIMA) (In Liquidation) *v.* Commission of
the European Communities (T190/95)

Societe de Representation Textile (So Re Tex) *v.* Plauener Gardine GmbH [2000] I.L.Pr.
799, C d'A (Paris)

Societe des Etablissements J Verdier *v.* Da Silva [2001] I.L.Pr. 4, Cass (F)

Societe des Produits Nestle SA's European Patent (T343/95) (1998) 21 (12) I.P.D. 21132,
EPO (Technical Bd App)

Societe Domaines Maisons et Chateaux Sarl *v.* GIE Laurent Perrier Diffusion [2001]
E.C.C. 43, C d'A (Paris)

Societe Eram Shipping Co Ltd *v.* Compagnie International de Navigation (Security for
Costs) [2001] EWCA Civ 568; [2001] C.P. Rep. 113, CA

Societe Eram Shipping Co Ltd *v.* Compagnie Internationale de Navigation [2001] EWCA
Civ 1317; [2001] 2 All E.R. (Comm) 721; [2001] 2 Lloyd's Rep. 627; [2001]
C.P. Rep. 112; (2001) 98(36) L.S.G. 37; (2001) 151 N.L.J. 1318, CA; reversing
[2001] 1 All E.R. (Comm) 843; [2001] 2 Lloyd's Rep. 394; [2001] C.L.C. 685,
QBD (Comm Ct) . . . . *Digested*, 01/**561**:
Applied, 01/820

Societe Filtertechniek Nederland BV *v.* Hoff see Hoff *v.* Filtertechniek Nederland BV

Societe Financiere d'Investissements SPRL (SFI) *v.* Belgium (C85/97) [2000] S.T.C.
164; [1998] E.C.R. I-7447; [2000] B.T.C. 5181; [2000] B.V.C. 198, ECJ (4th
Chamber) . . . . *Digested*, 00/**5329**

Societe France Telecom *v.* Conseil de la Concurrence [2000] E.C.C. 97, Cass (F)

Societe France Touristik Service, Re (95-1188) 1 I.T.L. Rep. 857, C Adm A (F)

Societe Generale *v.* Commission of the European Communities (T34/93) [1995]
E.C.R. II-545; [1996] 4 C.M.L.R. 665, CFI (4th Chamber) . . . . *Digested*, 95/**633**:
Followed, 01/768

Societe Generale des Grandes Sources d'Eaux Minerales Francaises *v.* Bundesamt fur
Finanzen (C361/96) [1998] S.T.C. 981; [1998] E.C.R. I-3495; [1998] C.E.C.
937; [1998] B.T.C. 5466; [1999] B.V.C. 3, ECJ . . . . *Digested*, 98/**4930**:
Considered, 00/5311

Societe Generale Europeene de Presse et de Services (GEPS) Sarl *v.* D'Information et de
Documentation des Femmes et des Familles (CNIDFF) [1998] E.C.C. 406, C
d'A (Paris)

Societe Intermarbres, Re [1999] E.C.C. 254, CE (F) . . . . *Digested*, 99/**673**

Societe la Francaise des Jeux, Re [2001] E.C.C. 48, C Concurrence (F)

Societe Laboratoires Garnier et Cie SNC *v.* Societe Copar; *sub nom* Laboratoire Garnier
& Cie *v.* Copar Ste [2000] E.T.M.R. 1124, C d'A (Paris); reversing [1998]
E.T.M.R. 114, Trib Gde Inst (Paris)

Societe Levage Presentations *v.* France (1997) 24 E.H.R.R. 351, ECHR . . . . *Digested*, 98/**3112**

Societe Louis Dreyfus & Cie *v.* Commission of the European Communities (C386/96); *sub nom* Societe Louis Dreyfus & Cie *v.* Commission of the European Communities (T485/93) [1998] E.C.R. I-2309; [1999] 1 C.M.L.R. 481, ECJ; reversing [1996] E.C.R. II-1101; [1997] 1 C.M.L.R. 1008, CFI (3rd Chamber).... *Digested,* 00/**2339**:
Applied, 01/4420

Societe Louis Dreyfus & Cie *v.* Commission of the European Communities (T485/93) see Societe Louis Dreyfus & Cie *v.* Commission of the European Communities (C386/96)

Societe Maine Auto *v.* Societe Volvo Automobiles France [1998] E.C.C. 470, Cass (F)

Societe Marcel Marie *v.* Societe Henco [1998] I.L.Pr. 807, C d'A (Paris)

Societe Nationale Industrielle Aerospatiale (SNIA) *v.* Lee Kui Jak [1987] A.C. 871; [1987] 3 W.L.R. 59; [1987] 3 All E.R. 510; (1987) 84 L.S.G. 2048, PC (Bru)... *Digested,* 87/**3024**:
Applied, 97/879, 97/4597, 98/757: *Considered,* 88/1620, 89/1729, 92/3516, 93/1978, 94/3708, 96/5344, 00/747: *Distinguished,* 95/4149:
Followed, 88/2884, 89/381, 91/5405, 95/6052, 97/885

Societe Nomai *v.* Societe Iomega Corp [1998] E.C.C. 281, C d'A (Paris)

Societe Nouvelle des Usines de Pontlieue-Acieries du Temple *v.* ECSC High Authority (C42/59) [1961] E.C.R. 53; [1961] E.C.R. 103, ECJ *Applied,* 98/726

Societe Office d'Annonces *v.* Conseil de la Concurrence [2000] E.C.C. 101, Cass (F)

SOCIETE PARISIENNE/Restitutio in integrum (J05/80) [1979-85] E.P.O.R. A31, EPO (Legal Bd App) .... *Applied,* 01/3957:
Followed, 00/3618

Societe Recife *v.* Societe Recif SA [2001] E.T.M.R. 18, C d'A (Paris)

Societe Roullet Fransac Sarl *v.* V Secret Catalogue Inc [2001] E.T.M.R. 103, C d'A (Paris)

Societe SERC FUN RADIO [1999] 2 C.M.L.R. 1259, CE (F) .... *Digested,* 99/**3917**

Societe Technique de Pulverisation Step *v.* Emson Europe [1993] R.P.C. 513, CA...... *Considered,* 00/3681:
Referred to, 00/3679

Societe United Docks *v.* Mauritius; Marine Workers Union *v.* Mauritius Marine Authority [1985] A.C. 585; [1985] 2 W.L.R. 114; [1985] 1 All E.R. 864; (1984) 81 L.S.G. 3419; (1985) 129 S.J. 65, PC (Mau) .... *Digested,* 85/**185**:
Applied, 98/3108

Society of Lloyd's *v.* Colfox see Manning *v.* Society of Lloyd's

Society of Lloyd's *v.* Fraser [1998] C.L.C. 1630; [1999] Lloyd's Rep. I.R. 156, CA; affirming [1998] C.L.C. 127, QBD (Comm Ct) .... *Digested,* 99/**3405**:
Applied, 01/3823

Society of Lloyd's *v.* Jaffray [1999] 1 All E.R. (Comm) 354; [1999] C.L.C. 713; [1999] Lloyd's Rep. I.R. 182, QBD (Comm Ct) .... *Digested,* 99/**547**

Society of Lloyd's *v.* Jaffray (Costs Sharing Order) [2000] 2 All E.R. (Comm) 181; [2000] C.L.C. 725, QBD (Comm Ct) .... *Digested,* 00/**3538**

Society of Lloyd's *v.* Khan; *sub nom* Lloyd's of London *v.* Khan [1999] 1 F.L.R. 246; [1998] 3 F.C.R. 93; [1999] Fam. Law 92; (1998) 162 J.P.N. 321, QBD (Comm Ct) .... *Digested,* 98/**3386**

Society of Lloyd's *v.* Leighs; Society of Lloyd's *v.* Lyon; Society of Lloyd's *v.* Wilkinson [1997] C.L.C. 1398; [1997] 6 Re. L.R. 289; *Times,* August 11, 1997; *Independent,* October 6, 1997 (C.S.), CA; affirming [1997] C.L.C. 759, QBD.............. *Digested,* 97/**3149**:
Applied, 98/3386: *Followed,* 98/845: *Referred to,* 99/3315

Society of Lloyd's *v.* Lyon see Society of Lloyd's *v.* Leighs

Society of Lloyd's *v.* Mason see Lloyd's Society *v.* Clementson

Society of Lloyd's *v.* Morris [1993] 2 Re. L.R. 217; *Independent,* June 21, 1993 (C.S.), CA .... *Approved,* 99/3404:
Followed, 96/3591, 96/3592

Society of Lloyd's *v.* Robinson see Lord Napier and Ettrick *v.* RF Kershaw Ltd (No.2)

Society of Lloyd's *v.* Saunders [2001] I.L.Pr. 18, CJ (Gen Div) (Ont) .... *Digested,* 01/**817**

Society of Lloyd's *v.* Twinn (Gail Sally) see Society of Lloyd's *v.* Twinn (Geoffrey George)

Society of Lloyd's *v.* Twinn (Geoffrey George); Society of Lloyd's *v.* Twinn (Gail Sally) (2000) 97(15) L.S.G. 40; *Times,* April 4, 2000, CA .... *Digested,* 00/**894**

Society of Lloyd's *v.* Van Snick [2000] I.L.Pr. 805, Sup Ct (NS) .... *Digested,* 01/**544**

Society of Lloyd's *v.* Waters [2001] B.P.I.R. 698, Ch D .... *Digested,* 01/**3716**

Society of Lloyd's *v.* White (No.1) [2000] C.L.C. 961; (2000) 144 S.J.L.B. 190; *Times,* April 14, 2000, QBD (Comm Ct) .... *Digested,* 00/**755**

Society of Lloyd's *v.* Wilkinson see Society of Lloyd's *v.* Leighs

Society of Lloyd's *v.* Woodard see Lord Napier and Ettrick *v.* RF Kershaw Ltd (No.2)

Sockel GmbH *v.* Body Shop International Plc [2000] U.K.C.L.R. 262; [2000] Eu. L.R. 276, Ch D .... *Digested,* 00/**714**

Socony Mobil Oil Co Inc *v.* West of England Shipowners Mutual Insurance Association (London) Ltd (The Padre Island) (No.2) see Firma C-Trade SA *v.* Newcastle Protection and Indemnity Association (The Fanti)

Sodemare SA *v.* Lombardia (C70/95) [1997] E.C.R. I-3395; [1998] 4 C.M.L.R. 667; [1997] 3 C.M.L.R. 591; [1997] C.E.C. 1128, ECJ (1st Chamber) .... *Digested,* 98/**2325**

Soden v. British & Commonwealth Holdings Plc (In Administration) [1998] A.C. 298;
[1997] 3 W.L.R. 840; [1997] 4 All E.R. 353; [1997] B.C.C. 952; [1997] 2
B.C.L.C. 501; (1997) 94(41) L.S.G. 28; (1997) 147 N.L.J. 1546; *Times*, October
22, 1997; *Independent*, October 21, 1997, HL; affirming [1997] 2 W.L.R. 206;
[1996] 3 All E.R. 951; [1996] 2 B.C.L.C. 207; (1996) 140 S.J.L.B. 141; *Times*,
May 27, 1996; *Independent*, June 24, 1996 (C.S.), CA; affirming [1995] B.C.C.
531; [1995] 1 B.C.L.C. 686, Ch D .... *Digested*, 97/**3099**
Soderback v. Sweden [1999] 1 F.L.R. 250; (2000) 29 E.H.R.R. 95; 1999 Fam. L.R.
104; [1998] H.R.C.D. 958; [1999] Fam. Law 87, ECHR .... *Digested*, 99/**2302**
Sodifa SA v. Garage Badina Sarl [1999] E.C.C. 531, Cass (F)
Sofitam SA (formerly Satam SA) v. Ministre Charge du Budget (C333/91); *sub nom*
Satam SA v. Minister Responsible for the Budget (C333/91) [1997] S.T.C. 226;
[1993] E.C.R. I-3513; *Times*, July 22, 1993, ECJ .... *Digested*, 97/**5002**:
                                                Considered, 01/**5606**
Sogbetun v. Hackney LBC [1998] I.C.R. 1264; [1998] I.R.L.R. 676; *Times*, October 8,
1998, EAT .... *Digested*, 98/**2160**:
                     Doubted, 01/2270: *Referred to*, 99/2050
Sohio Supply Co v. Gatoil (USA) Inc [1989] 1 Lloyd's Rep. 588, CA .... *Digested*, 90/**3700**:
                                   Applied, 90/3721, 98/3400
Soils Ltd v. Bromwich (Unreported, July 1, 1998), CC (Kingston on Thames) [*Ex rel.*
Fiona Scolding, Barrister, Goldsmith Building, Temple, London] .... *Digested*, 98/**3913**
Soinco SACI v. Novokuznetsk Aluminium Plant (Appointment Of Receiver) [1998]
Q.B. 406; [1998] 2 W.L.R. 334; [1997] 3 All E.R. 523; [1997] 2 Lloyd's Rep.
330, QBD (Comm Ct) .... *Digested*, 97/**2998**
Soinco SACI v. Novokuznetsk Aluminium Plant (No.1) [1998] 2 Lloyd's Rep. 337;
[1998] C.L.C. 730; *Times*, December 29, 1997, CA; affirming1996-Folio No.1915,
QBD (Comm Ct) .... *Digested*, 98/**243**
Soinco SACI v. Novokuznetsk Aluminium Plant (No.2) [1998] 2 Lloyd's Rep. 346, CA . *Digested*, 98/**523**
Sokhal v. Ford Motor Co Ltd see Afzal v. Ford Motor Co Ltd
Sola v. La Tribune de Geneve [2000] I.L.Pr. 795, C d'A (Paris)
Solanki v. Quick Corp see Wakeman v. Quick Corp
SOLARTRON/Fluid transducer (T1149/97) [2001] E.P.O.R. 3, EPO (Technical Bd App)   *Digested*, 01/**3900**
Soleh Boneh International v. Uganda and National Housing Corp [1993] 2 Lloyd's Rep.
208; *Times*, March 18, 1993, CA .... *Digested*, 94/**3758**:
                                           Applied, 01/342
Soleimany v. Soleimany [1999] Q.B. 785; [1998] 3 W.L.R. 811; [1999] 3 All E.R. 847;
[1998] C.L.C. 779; *Times*, March 4, 1998, CA .... *Digested*, 98/**236**:
                               Applied, 01/4123: *Doubted*, 99/236
Solicitor, Re see Penna v. Law Society (Application to Set Aside Notice of Intervention)
Solicitor (Chinese Walls), Re [1999] P.N.L.R. 950, QBD (T&CC) .... *Digested*, 00/**4007**
Solicitor (CO/2504/2000), Re see Law Society v. Gilbert
Solicitor (CO/2646/99), Re, *Independent*, March 20, 2000 (C.S.), QBD
Solicitors (A Firm), Re [1992] Q.B. 959; [1992] 2 W.L.R. 809; [1992] 1 All E.R. 353; (1991)
141 N.L.J. 746; (1991) 135 S.J.L.B. 125; *Times*, June 20, 1991; *Independent*, June
26, 1991, CA .... *Digested*, 92/**4082**:
                         Considered, 00/4020: *Followed*, 95/4658, 96/3919
Solicitors (A Firm), Re [2000] 1 Lloyd's Rep. 31, QBD (Comm Ct) .... *Digested*, 00/**4008**
Solicitors (Northern Ireland) Order 1976, Re see CH, Re
Solihull BC v. Gas Council see Solihull Corp v. Gas Council
Solihull Corp v. Gas Council; *sub nom* Solihull BC v. Gas Council; Gas Council v.
Eldridge [1962] 1 W.L.R. 583; [1962] 1 All E.R. 898; 60 L.G.R. 403; [1962] R.A.
113; [1962] R.V.R. 189; 9 R.R.C. 128; 106 S.J. 306, HL; affirming [1961] 1
W.L.R. 619; [1961] 1 All E.R. 542; 125 J.P. 208; 59 L.G.R. 285; [1961] R.V.R. 118;
8 R.R.C. 13; 105 S.J. 346, CA; reversing 6 R.R.C. 348; 53 R. & I.T. 265; [1960]
J.P.L. 282, Lands Tr .... *Digested*, 62/**2576**:
                                           Applied, 98/4319
Solihull MBC v. Finn see White v. Ealing LBC
Solihull MBC v. Fischer (2001) 16 P.A.D. 92, Planning Inspector
Solihull MBC v. Special Educational Needs Tribunal see White v. Ealing LBC
Solihull MBC Housing Benefit Review Board v. Simpson see R. v. Solihull MBC Housing
Benefit Review Board Ex p. Simpson
Solihull Metropolitan BC v. Miniman (1999) 14 P.A.D. 84, Planning Inspector
Solle v. Butcher [1950] 1 K.B. 671; [1949] 2 All E.R. 1107; 66 T.L.R. (Pt. 1) 448, CA .... *Digested*, 47-51/**8914**:
              Applied, 47-51/1785, 47-51/4202, 47-51/9247, 53/3290, 66/1854, 67/623,
                             69/1819, 70/1537, 71/6632, 78/1515, 83/3888, 00/4357:
                     Considered, 58/3055, 68/3999, 70/2903: *Disapproved*, 88/449, 89/430:
                                           Distinguished, 00/121
Sollitt v. DJ Broady Ltd [2000] C.P.L.R. 259, CA .... *Digested*, 00/**355**
Solo Industries UK Ltd v. Canara Bank [2001] EWCA Civ 1059; [2001] 1 W.L.R. 1800;
[2001] 2 All E.R. (Comm) 217; [2001] 2 Lloyd's Rep. 578; [2001] Lloyd's Rep.
Bank. 346; [2001] C.L.C. 1651; (2001) 98(29) L.S.G. 37; (2001) 145 S.J.L.B.
168; *Times*, July 31, 2001; *Independent*, July 6, 2001, CA; affirming1999 Folio 13,
QBD (Comm Ct) .... *Digested*, 01/**381**

Solo Kleinmotoren GmbH *v.* Emilio Boch (C414/92) [1994] E.C.R. I-2237; [1994]
I.L.Pr. 457, ECJ (6th Chamber) . . . . *Digested,* 94/**4802**:
Considered, 98/522
Solomon Islands Plantation Ltd *v.* Inland Revenue Commissioner 1 I.T.L. Rep. 751, CA
(Sol)
Solomons *v.* Williams; *sub nom* Bankrupt (457/2001), Re [2001] B.P.I.R. 1123, Ch D
SOLUDIA/Stay of grant proceedings (J28/94) [1997] E.P.O.R. 379, EPO (Legal Bd App)
Followed, 00/3666
Solutia UK Ltd (formerly Monsanto Chemicals UK Ltd) *v.* Griffiths see Griffiths *v.* Solutia
UK Ltd
Solvalub Ltd *v.* Match Investments Ltd [1998] I.L.Pr. 419, CA (Jer)
Solvay et Cie *v.* Commission of the European Communities (27/88) [1989] E.C.R.
3355, ECJ . . . . *Followed,* 01/768
Solvay et Cie *v.* Commission of the European Communities (No.1) (T30/91) see Solvay
et Cie SA *v.* Commission of the European Communities (C287/95)
Solvay et Cie SA *v.* Commission of the European Communities (C27/88) see Orkem SA
(formerly CdF Chimie SA) *v.* Commission of the European Communities
(C374/87)
Solvay et Cie SA *v.* Commission of the European Communities (C287/95); *sub nom*
Solvay et Cie *v.* Commission of the European Communities (No.1) (T30/91); ICI
Plc *v.* Commission of the European Communities (T36/91); Solvay et Cie SA *v.*
Commission of the European Communities (T32/91) [2001] All E.R. (EC) 439;
[2000] E.C.R. I-2391; [2000] 5 C.M.L.R. 454; *Times,* April 14, 2000, ECJ (5th
Chamber) [1995] All E.R. (E.C.) 600; [1995] E.C.R. II-1775; [1996] 5 C.M.L.R.
57; [1996] C.E.C. 137; [1996] C.E.C. 196, CFI (1st Chamber) . . . . *Digested,* 00/**2370**:
Considered, 00/719: *Joined proceedings,* 00/2369
Solvay et Cie SA *v.* Commission of the European Communities (T12/89) see Huls AG *v.*
Commission of the European Communities (C199/92 P)
Solvay et Cie SA *v.* Commission of the European Communities (T32/91) see Solvay et
Cie SA *v.* Commission of the European Communities (C287/95)
Somaco Sarl *v.* Commission of the European Communities (C401/96 P) [1998] E.C.R.
I-2587; [1999] 4 C.M.L.R. 35, ECJ (5th Chamber) . . . . *Digested,* 99/**2243**
Somalia *v.* Woodhouse Drake & Carey (Suisse) SA (The Mary) [1993] Q.B. 54;
[1992] 3 W.L.R. 744; [1993] 1 All E.R. 371; [1992] 2 Lloyd's Rep. 471; *Times,*
March 23, 1992; *Financial Times,* March 24, 1992, QBD (Comm Ct) . . . . *Digested,* 92/**2629**:
Applied, 98/272: *Considered,* 98/3552, 99/723, 00/5107
Somasundaram *v.* M Julius Melchior & Co [1988] 1 W.L.R. 1394; [1989] 1 All E.R.
129; (1988) 138 N.L.J. Rep. 253; (1988) 132 S.J. 1732, CA . . . . *Digested,* 89/**3073**:
Applied, 97/3832: *Distinguished,* 98/4012: *Followed,* 96/4490
Somatra Ltd *v.* Sinclair Roche & Temperley; Sinclair Roche & Temperley *v.* Somatra Ltd
[2000] 1 W.L.R. 2453; [2000] 2 Lloyd's Rep. 673; [2000] C.P.L.R. 601;
(2000) 97(35) L.S.G. 37; *Times,* September 22, 2000, CA; reversing in part
[2000] 1 Lloyd's Rep. 311, QBD (Comm Ct) . . . . *Digested,* 00/**334**
Somerset CC *v.* Fear (1999) 14 P.A.D. 248, Planning Inspector
Somerville *v.* Attorney General of Canada (1996) 136 D.L.R. (4th) 205, CA (Alta) . . . . *Not followed,* 98/3085
Somji *v.* Cadbury Schweppes Plc see Cadbury Schweppes Plc *v.* Somji
Somwaru *v.* London Electricity (Unreported, November 29, 1994), CC (Wandsworth)
[*Ex rel.* Christopher Hough, Barrister] . . . . *Digested,* 95/**1670**:
Referred to, 98/1531
Sony Computer Entertainments Inc *v.* Tesco Stores Ltd [2000] E.T.M.R. 102, Ch D . . . . *Digested,* 00/**3706**
Sony Music Entertainment Inc *v.* Prestige Records Ltd [2000] 2 Costs L.R. 186; (2000)
23(8) I.P.D. 23061; (2000) 97(7) L.S.G. 39; (2000) 144 S.J.L.B. 106; *Times,*
March 2, 2000, Ch D . . . . *Digested,* 00/**429**
SONY WALKMAN Trade Mark [2000] E.T.M.R. 890, OGH (A)
SONY/Television receivers (T654/92) [2000] E.P.O.R. 148, EPO (Technical Bd App) . . *Digested,* 00/**3645**
Soobhan *v.* Boots (Unreported, June 20, 2001), CC (Ilford) [*Ex rel.* William Latimer-
Sayer, Barrister, Cloisters, 1 Pump Court, Temple, London] . . . . *Digested,* 01/**563**
Soobramoney *v.* Minister of Health (KwaZulu-Natal) 4 B.H.R.C. 308; (1999) 50
B.M.L.R. 224, Const Ct (SA) . . . . *Digested,* 98/**2653**
Sooklal (Narine) *v.* Trinidad and Tobago [1999] 1 W.L.R. 2011, PC (Trin) . . . . *Digested,* 00/**983**:
Considered, 00/1070
Sotgiu *v.* Deutsche Bundepost (152/73) [1974] E.C.R. 153, ECJ . . . . *Digested,* 75/**1276**:
Applied, 87/1569, 95/2773: *Considered,* 99/5272, 01/5769
Sotori *v.* Smetham (Unreported, March 17, 1998), CC (Wigan) [*Ex rel.* B.A. Varney,
Costs Negotiators, 7 Havelock Road, East Sussex] . . . . *Digested,* 98/**466**
Soules CAF *v.* Louis Dreyfus Negoce SA [2000] 2 All E.R. (Comm) 154; [2000] 2
Lloyd's Rep. 307; [2001] C.L.C. 797, QBD (Comm Ct) . . . . *Digested,* 00/**892**
Soules Caf *v.* PT Transap (Indonesia) [1999] 1 Lloyd's Rep. 917, QBD (Comm Ct) . . . . *Digested,* 99/**4413**
Soumare *v.* France [1998] H.R.C.D. 802, ECHR
Source Ltd *v.* TUV Rheinland Holding AG [1998] Q.B. 54; [1997] 3 W.L.R. 365;
[1998] I.L.Pr. 432; [1997] I.L.Pr. 514; *Times,* March 28, 1997, CA. . . . . *Digested,* 97/**898**
Souster *v.* Carman Construction Co Ltd [2000] B.P.I.R. 371, Ch D . . . . *Digested,* 00/**3494**
South *v.* Chamberlayne [2001] 43 E.G. 190; (2001) 98(38) L.S.G. 40; [2001] N.P.C.
136; *Daily Telegraph,* September 18, 2001, Ch D

South v. Phillimore Kensington Estate Trustees (Application for Disclosure) [2001] EWCA Civ 861; [2001] C.P. Rep. 96, CA. . . . . *Digested*, 01/**555**
South Africa v. Grootboom 10 B.H.R.C. 84, Const Ct (SA) . . . . *Digested*, 01/**3452**
South Africa v. Mamabolo 10 B.H.R.C. 493, Const Ct (SA) . . . . *Digested*, 01/**3471**
South African National Defence Union v. Minister of Defence 6 B.H.R.C. 574, Const Ct (SA). . . . . *Digested*, 00/**3184**
South African Supply and Cold Storage Co, Re; *sub nom* Wild v. South African Supply & Cold Storage Co [1904] 2 Ch. 268, Ch D . . . . *Applied*, 70/2715, 91/3390, 01/5183

South and East Belfast Health and Social Services Trust v. RA see KLA (An Infant) (Adoption: Freeing Order), Re
South Australia Asset Management Corp v. York Montague Ltd; United Bank of Kuwait Plc v. Prudential Property Services Ltd; Nykredit Mortgage Bank Plc v. Edward Erdman Group Ltd [1997] A.C. 191; [1996] 3 W.L.R. 87; [1996] 3 All E.R. 365; [1996] 5 Bank. L.R. 211; [1996] C.L.C. 1179; 80 B.L.R. 1; 50 Con. L.R. 153; [1996] P.N.L.R. 455; [1996] 2 E.G.L.R. 93; [1996] 27 E.G. 125; [1996] E.G.C.S. 107; (1996) 93(32) L.S.G. 33; (1996) 146 N.L.J. 956; (1996) 140 S.J.L.B. 156; [1996] N.P.C. 100; *Times*, June 24, 1996; *Independent*, July 2, 1996, HL; reversing in part [1995] E.G.C.S. 71; [1995] N.P.C. 66, QBD (Comm Ct) . . . . . . *Digested*, 96/**4519**:
Applied, 97/3846, 98/4005, 98/4027, 98/4031, 98/4384, 99/1389, 99/4053, 00/1486, 00/4249, 00/4280, 01/4504, 01/4529, 01/4532:
Considered, 97/3827, 97/3839, 98/3999, 98/4032, 98/5724, 00/4009, 00/4247, 00/4279, 01/4263: *Followed*, 98/3959, 98/3987, 99/804, 99/4018, 99/4057, 01/4528: *Not followed*, 00/4275:
Previous proceedings, 95/1834: *Referred to*, 97/4871, 98/1432
South Ayrshire Council v. Morton; *sub nom* Morton v. South Ayrshire Council; TNS, 2 Div; affirming [2001] I.R.L.R. 28, EAT
South Buckinghamshire DC v. Berkley Homes (Thames Valley) Ltd see South Buckinghamshire DC v. Secretary of State for the Environment, Transport and the Regions
South Buckinghamshire DC v. Flanagan; *sub nom* Flanagan v. South Bucks DC; B2/2001/1711, CA; affirming [2001] 4 P.L.R. 110; (2001) 98(30) L.S.G. 40, QBD
South Buckinghamshire DC v. Porter; *sub nom* South Bucks DC v. Porter; Chichester DC v. Searle; Wrexham CBC v. Berry; Hertsmere BC v. Harty [2001] EWCA Civ 1549; (2001) 98(46) L.S.G. 35; *Times*, November 9, 2001, CA . . . . *Digested*, 01/**4729**
South Buckinghamshire DC v. Secretary of State for the Environment, Transport and the Regions (1999) 78 P. & C.R. 255; [1999] J.P.L. 545; [1998] E.G.C.S. 164, QBD. . . . . *Digested*, 99/**4170**
South Buckinghamshire DC v. Secretary of State for the Environment, Transport and the Regions; South Buckinghamshire DC v. Berkley Homes (Thames Valley) Ltd [1999] P.L.C.R. 72; [1998] N.P.C. 106, QBD. . . . . *Digested*, 99/**4214**
South Buckinghamshire DC v. Secretary of State for the Environment, Transport and the Regions [2001] J.P.L. 726 (Note), QBD
South Bucks DC v. Porter see South Buckinghamshire DC v. Porter
South Cone Inc v. Bessant (t/a REEF) see REEF Trade Mark
South Durham Steel & Iron Co Ltd, Re see Dorman Long & Co Ltd, Re
South Glamorgan CC v. L and M [1996] E.L.R. 400; [1996] C.O.D. 213, QBD . . . . *Digested*, 97/**2136**:
Applied, 98/1961, 00/1948: *Distinguished*, 96/2493
South Gloucestershire Council v. Avon Turf (1998) 13 P.A.D. 135, Planning Inspector
South Gloucestershire Council v. McCracken (2000) 15 P.A.D. 662, Planning Inspector
South Gloucestershire Council v. Monyard (1999) 14 P.A.D. 109, Planning Inspector
South Gloucestershire Council v. Phillips (2001) 16 P.A.D. 101, Planning Inspector
South Hams DC v. Cunningham (1998) 13 P.A.D. 386, Planning Inspector
South Hams DC v. Rowland (1999) 14 P.A.D. 361, Planning Inspector
South Hams DC v. Thorn (1998) 13 P.A.D. 592, Planning Inspector
South Herefordshire DC v. Powell (1998) 13 P.A.D. 369, Planning Inspector
South Holland DC v. Wingland (2001) 16 P.A.D. 44, Planning Inspector
South Kesteven DC v. Mackie [2000] 1 W.L.R. 1461; [2000] 1 All E.R. 497; [2000] E.H.L.R. 87; [2000] B.L.G.R. 436; [1999] N.P.C. 119; *Times*, October 20, 1999; *Independent*, November 22, 1999 (C.S), CA. . . . . *Digested*, 99/**3847**
South Lakeland DC v. Secretary of State for the Environment [1993] J.P.L. 644; [1992] E.G.C.S. 154 . . . . *Digested*, 94/**4473**:
Considered, 00/4439
South Lanarkshire Council v. Secretary of State for Scotland (1997) 1998 S.L.T. 445; 1997 G.W.D. 19-904; *Times*, July 21, 1997, OH. . . . . *Digested*, 98/**6085**
South Lodge Imports Ltd v. Customs and Excise Commissioners [1999] V. & D.R. 411, V&DTr. . . . . *Digested*, 00/**4951**
South Molton Swimming Pool Trustees v. Customs and Excise Commissioners [2000] S.T.I. 836, V&DTr
South Northamptonshire DC v. Charles Church Developments Ltd [2000] P.L.C.R. 46, QBD. . . . . *Digested*, 00/**4443**
South Northamptonshire DC v. Wardle (1998) 13 P.A.D. 304, Planning Inspector
South Oxfordshire DC v. Greenford (2000) 15 P.A.D. 50, Planning Inspector
South Oxfordshire DC v. Jones (1998) 13 P.A.D. 438, Planning Inspector

South Oxfordshire DC v. Knight (1998) 13 P.A.D. 451, Planning Inspector
South Oxfordshire DC v. Schwarzenbach (1999) 14 P.A.D. 498, Planning Inspector
South Oxfordshire DC v. Secretary of State for the Environment, Transport and the
   Regions [2000] 2 All E.R. 667; [2000] P.L.C.R. 315; (2000) 97(2) L.S.G. 32,
   QBD . . . . *Digested*, 00/**4512**
South Oxfordshire DC v. Secretary of State for the Environment, Transport and the
   Regions (Highway Implications) [2001] J.P.L. 233 (Note), QBD
South Somerset DC v. Legal and General Property Ltd (2000) 15 P.A.D. 622, Planning
   Inspector
South Somerset DC v. Secretary of State for the Environment (1993) 66 P. & C.R. 83;
   [1993] 1 P.L.R. 80; [1993] 26 E.G. 121; [1992] E.G.C.S. 134, CA . . . . *Digested*, 93/**3927**:
                                Cited, 00/4439: *Considered*, 96/4734
South Staffordshire DC v. Stanton (1998) 13 P.A.D. 228, Planning Inspector
South Staffordshire DC v. Teddesley Boat Co (2000) 15 P.A.D. 776, Planning Inspector
South Strong Industries Sdn Bhd's Registered Design (No.2043178), Re (1998) 21(3)
   I.P.D. 21033, RDAT
South Tyneside MBC v. Jackson [1998] E.H.L.R. 249, QBD . . . . *Digested*, 99/**3907**:
                                        Considered, 97/3534
South Tyneside MBC v. Luxury Leisure (1998) 13 P.A.D. 90, Planning Inspector
South Tyneside MBC v. Smith (1998) 13 P.A.D. 396, Planning Inspector
South Tyneside MBC v. Svenska International Plc [1995] 1 All E.R. 545, QBD . . . . *Digested*, 95/**4336.A**:
                                        Considered, 00/2331
South Wales Electricity Plc v. Director General of Electricity Supply (1999) 96(44)
   L.S.G. 40; *Times*, October 28, 1999; *Independent*, December 6, 1999 (C.S.),
   Ch D . . . . *Digested*, 99/**2000**
South West Car Sales Ltd (In Liquidation), Re [1998] B.C.C. 163, Ch D . . . . *Digested*, 98/**3323**
South West Trains Ltd v. Wightman [1997] O.P.L.R. 249; *Times*, January 14, 1998, Ch D   *Digested*, 98/**4108**
South West Water Services Ltd v. International Computers Ltd [1999] B.L.R. 420;
   [1998-99] Info. T.L.R. 154; [1999] I.T.C.L.R. 439; [2001] Lloyd's Rep. P.N. 353;
   [1999] Masons C.L.R. 400, QBD (T&CC) . . . . *Digested*, 00/**870**
South West Water Services Ltd v. JFS (UK) Ltd (formerly Johnson Filtration Systems
   Ltd) see JFS (UK) Ltd (formerly Johnson Filtration Systems Ltd) v. South West
   Water Services Ltd
Southall v. Worcester City Council (Unreported, September 22, 1997), CC (Worcester)
   [*Ex rel.* Everatt & Co Solicitors, 104 High Street, Evesham, Worcestershire] . . . . *Digested*, 98/**4036**
Southampton and South West Hampshire AHA v. Marshall (No.2) see Marshall v.
   Southampton and South West Hampshire AHA (No.2)
Southampton Cargo Handling Plc v. Associated British Ports see Lotus Cars Ltd v.
   Southampton Cargo Handling Plc (The Rigoletto)
Southampton Cargo Handling Plc v. Lotus Cars Ltd (The Rigoletto) see Lotus Cars Ltd
   v. Southampton Cargo Handling Plc (The Rigoletto)
Southampton City Council v. Highwood Homes (2001) 16 P.A.D. 60, Planning
   Inspector
Southampton Container Terminals Ltd v. Hansa Schiffahrts GmbH (The Maersk
   Colombo); *sub nom* Southampton Container Terminals Ltd v. Schiffahrisgesellsch
   Hansa Australia MGH & Co; Southampton Container Terminals Ltd v. Hansa
   Schiffahrtsgesellschaft mbH [2001] EWCA Civ 717; [2001] 2 Lloyd's Rep. 275;
   (2001) 98(24) L.S.G. 43; (2001) 145 S.J.L.B. 149; *Times*, June 13, 2001, CA;
   affirming [1999] 2 Lloyd's Rep. 491; [1999] C.L.C. 1814, QBD (Adm Ct) . . . . . . *Digested*, 01/**4501**
Southampton Container Terminals Ltd v. Hansa Schiffahrisgesellschaft mbH see
   Southampton Container Terminals Ltd v. Hansa Schiffahrts GmbH (The Maersk
   Colombo)
Southampton Container Terminals Ltd v. Schiffahrisgesellsch Hansa Australia MGH &
   Co see Southampton Container Terminals Ltd v. Hansa Schiffahrts GmbH (The
   Maersk Colombo)
Southampton Port HA v. Seahawk Marine Foods Ltd; *sub nom* R. (on the application
   of Seahawk Marine Foods Ltd) v. Southampton Port HA; Seahawk Marine
   Foods Ltd v. Southampton Port HA; C/2001/0909, CA; reversing [2001]
   EWHC Admin 246; [2001] E.H.L.R. 23; *Times*, June 8, 2001, QBD (Admin Ct) . *Digested*, 01/**2846**
Southend on Sea BC v. Waite (2001) 16 P.A.D. 20, Planning Inspector
Southend United Football Club Ltd v. Customs and Excise Commissioners [1998] B.V.C.
   2010; [1997] V. & D.R. 202, V&DTr . . . . *Digested*, 98/**4883**
Southeran v. Singh (Unreported, January 7, 1998), CC (Leicester) [*Ex rel.* Rebecca
   Benstead, Barrister, Bracton Chambers, 95A Chancery Lane, London] . . . . *Digested*, 98/**1736**
Southern Equities Corp Ltd (In Liquidation), Re see England v. Smith
Southern Foundries (1926) Ltd v. Shirlaw [1940] A.C. 701, HL; affirming [1939] 2 K.B.
   206, CA . . . . *Applied*, 47-51/1755,
                47-51/10342, 56/8838, 60/1775, 68/4006, 80/190, 80/1041, 84/221, 93/2407,
                93/3588, 96/3702, 00/121: *Considered*, 70/288, 90/635, 97/4255:
                Distinguished, 47-51/4223, 47-51/4224, 52/465: *Followed*, 60/418
Southesk Trust Co Ltd v. Secretary of State for Scotland 2000 S.C. 400; 2000 S.L.T.
   680; 2000 G.W.D. 13-451; *Times*, April 26, 2000, 1 Div; affirming 1999 S.L.T.
   1131; 1999 S.C.L.R. 415; 1999 G.W.D. 10-446, OH . . . . *Digested*, 00/**5885**

Southport Corp v. Morriss [1893] 1 Q.B. 359, QBD . . . .   *Applied*, 92/3986,
                                    00/5507

Southwark LBC v. Allied Domecq Leisure Ltd [1999] E.H.L.R. 231; *Independent*,
  November 30, 1998 (C.S.), QBD . . . .   *Digested*, 99/**3852**

Southwark LBC v. B [1998] 2 F.L.R. 1095; [1999] 1 F.C.R. 550; [1998] Fam. Law
  657; (1998) 95(35) L.S.G. 38; *Times*, July 29, 1998, Fam Div . . . .   *Digested*, 98/**2411**

Southwark LBC v. Bellway Homes Ltd [2000] R.A. 437; [2000] E.G.C.S. 90, QBD . . .   *Digested*, 00/**4587**

Southwark LBC v. Bente (Unreported, December 10, 1997), CC (Lambeth) [*Ex rel.* Jon
  Holbrook, Barrister, Two Garden Court Chambers, Middle Temple, London] . . . .   *Digested*, 98/**2986**

Southwark LBC v. Camacho (Unreported, February 11, 2000), CC (Lambeth) [*Ex rel.*
  Samuel Waritay, Barrister, Arden Chambers, 27 John Street, London] . . . .   *Digested*, 00/**3930**

Southwark LBC v. Edem (Unreported, January 14, 1999), CC (Lambeth) [*Ex rel.*
  Beatrice Prevatt, Barrister, 2 Garden Court Chambers, 2 Garden Court, Middle
  Temple, London] . . . .   *Digested*, 99/**3717**

Southwark LBC v. Kennedy (Unreported, July 28, 1997), CC (Lambeth) [*Ex rel.* Dr
  Jason Williams, Barrister, 3 Dr Johnson's Buildings, Temple, London] . . . .   *Digested*, 98/**2988**

Southwark LBC v. McIntosh [2001] 47 E.G.C.S. 145; [2001] N.P.C. 162, Ch D

Southwark LBC v. Mills; *sub nom* Southwark LBC v. Tanner; Baxter v. Camden LBC
  (No.2) [2001] 1 A.C. 1; [1999] 3 W.L.R. 939; [1999] 4 All E.R. 449; [2000] Env.
  L.R. 112; (2000) 32 H.L.R. 148; [2000] B.L.G.R. 138; [2000] L. & T.R. 159;
  [1999] 3 E.G.L.R. 35; [1999] 45 E.G. 179; [1999] E.G.C.S. 122; (1999) 96(42)
  L.S.G. 41; (1999) 96(42) L.S.G. 45; (1999) 149 N.L.J. 1618; (1999) 143 S.J.L.B.
  249; [1999] N.P.C. 123; (2000) 79 P. & C.R. D13; *Times*, October 22, 1999,
  HL; affirming [2001] Ch. 1; [1999] 2 W.L.R. 409; (1999) 31 H.L.R. 187; [1999]
  B.L.G.R. 71; (1998) 10 Admin. L.R. 621; [1998] L. & T.R. 251; [1998] 3 E.G.L.R.
  46; [1998] 45 E.G. 151; (1998) 162 J.P.N. 945; [1998] E.G.C.S. 132; (1998)
  95(34) L.S.G. 31; (1998) 142 S.J.L.B. 221; [1998] N.P.C. 126; *Times*, August 20,
  1998; *Independent*, October 2, 1998, CA; reversing [1998] 3 W.L.R. 49;
  (1998) 10 Admin. L.R. 353; [1998] 2 E.G.L.R. 30; [1998] 22 E.G. 151; (1998)
  162 J.P.N. 722; [1998] E.G.C.S. 39; (1998) 95(16) L.S.G. 25; (1998) 142
  S.J.L.B. 119; [1998] N.P.C. 34; *Times*, March 11, 1998, Ch D . . . .   *Digested*, 99/**3672**:
                              Previous proceedings, 98/4044

Southwark LBC v. Morsello (1999) 14 P.A.D. 681, Planning Inspector

Southwark LBC v. Nejad [1999] 1 Costs L.R. 62; *Times*, January 28, 1999;
  Independent, February 1, 1999 (C.S.), CA . . . .   *Digested*, 99/**377**:
                                   Cited, 99/408

Southwark LBC v. Sarfo (2000) 32 H.L.R. 602; (1999) 78 P. & C.R. D41, CA;
  affirming (Unreported, December 2, 1998), CC (Lambeth) [*Ex rel.* Dominic
  Preston, Barrister and Marsons Solicitors, Arden Chambers, 27 John Street,
  London] . . . .   *Digested*, 99/**3705**:
                               Considered, 01/4166

Southwark LBC v. Simpson [1999] Env. L.R. 553; [2000] E.H.L.R. 43; (1999) 31
  H.L.R. 725, QBD . . . .   *Digested*, 99/**4065**

Southwark LBC v. St Brice see St Brice v. Southwark LBC
Southwark LBC v. Tanner see Southwark LBC v. Mills

Southwark LBC v. Tornaritis (Unreported, May 11, 1999), CC (Lambeth) [*Ex rel.*
  Chistopher Heather, Barrister, Francis Taylor Building, Temple, London] . . . .   *Digested*, 99/**3744**

Southwark LBC v. Whillier [2001] EWCA Civ 808; [2001] I.C.R. 1016; *Times*, June 29,
  2001, CA; affirming [2001] I.C.R. 142, EAT. . . . .   *Digested*, 01/**2324**

Southwick Community Association v. Customs and Excise Commissioners [2000] S.T.I.
  674, V&DTr

Southwood v. Attorney General [2000] W.T.L.R. 1199; (2000-01) 3 I.T.E.L.R. 94;
  (2000) 97(29) L.S.G. 45; (2000) 150 N.L.J. 1017; (2000) 80 P. & C.R. D34;
  Times, July 18, 2000, CA; affirming (1998) 95(43) L.S.G. 31; (1998) 95(40)
  L.S.G. 37; *Times*, October 26, 1998, Ch D . . . .   *Digested*, 00/**5254**

Southworth v. JR Birkett & Sons (Unreported, August 18, 2000), CC (Carlisle) [*Ex rel.*
  Hough Halton & Soal Solicitors, 32 Abbey Street, Carlisle] . . . .   *Digested*, 01/**1657**

Sovereign Finance Ltd v. Silver Crest Furniture Ltd (1997) 16 Tr. L.R. 370; [1997]
  C.C.L.R. 76, QBD . . . .   *Digested*, 98/**852**

Sovereign Life Assurance Co (In Liquidation) v. Dodd [1892] 2 Q.B. 573, CA; affirming
  [1892] 1 Q.B. 405, QBD . . . .   *Applied*, 01/3748:
                              Considered, 86/390

Sovereign Rubber Ltd v. Stockport MBC [2000] Env. L.R. 194; [2000] E.H.L.R. 154;
  [1999] N.P.C. 84, QBD . . . .   *Digested*, 00/**4294**

Spacek sro v. Czech Republic (26449/95) (2000) 30 E.H.R.R. 1010; 2 I.T.L. Rep. 265,
  ECHR . . . .   *Digested*, 01/**3490**

Spain v. Commission of the European Communities (C278/92) [1994] E.C.R. I-4103,
  ECJ . . . .   *Digested*, 95/**656**:
                                 Applied, 00/729

Spain v. Commission of the European Communities (C342/96) [1999] E.C.R. I-2459;
  [2000] 2 C.M.L.R. 415, ECJ (6th Chamber) . . . .   *Digested*, 00/**2415**

Spain v. Commission of the European Communities (C415/96) [1998] E.C.R. I-6993;
  [1999] 1 C.M.L.R. 304, ECJ (6th Chamber) . . . .   *Digested*, 00/**2374**

Spain v. Commission of the European Communities (C42/93); *sub nom* State Aid to
  Merco Co (C42/93), Re [1994] E.C.R. I-4175; [1995] 2 C.M.L.R. 702, ECJ . . .   *Digested*, 95/**655**:
                                                                                          Followed, 00/2415
Spain v. Council of the European Union (C36/98) [2001] E.C.R. I-779; [2001] Env.
  L.R. D10, ECJ
Spalding v. NSS Newsagents and Avery (1998) 98(1) Q.R. 7, CC (Reading) . . . .   *Digested*, 98/**1545**
SPAR Osterreichische Warenhandels AG v. Finanzlandesdirektion fur Salzburg (C318/
  96) [1998] S.T.C. 960; [1998] E.C.R. I-785, ECJ (5th Chamber) . . . .   *Digested*, 98/**4890**
Sparekassernes Datacenter (SDC) v. Skatteministeriet (C2/95) [1997] All E.R. (EC)
  610; [1997] S.T.C. 932; [1997] E.C.R. I-3017; [1997] 3 C.M.L.R. 999; [1997]
  B.T.C. 5395; [1997] B.V.C. 509, ECJ (5th Chamber) . . . .   *Digested*, 97/**4987**:
                          Applied, 98/4900: *Considered*, 00/5294: *Followed*, 98/4921
Spargo v. North Essex DHA [1997] P.I.Q.R. P235; [1997] 8 Med. L.R. 125; (1997) 37
  B.M.L.R. 99; (1997) 94(15) L.S.G. 26; (1997) 141 S.J.L.B. 90; *Times*, March 21,
  1997, CA; reversing [1996] 7 Med. L.R. 219, QBD . . . .   *Digested*, 97/**663**:
                          Applied, 01/4461: *Considered*, 97/658, 00/4197: *Followed*, 98/550, 01/603
Sparkes v. Secretary of State for the Environment, Transport and the Regions; *sub nom*
  Secretary of State for the Environment, Transport and the Regions v. Sparkes
  [2000] 3 P.L.R. 39; [2000] P.L.C.R. 279; [2000] J.P.L. 1077 (Note), QBD . . . .   *Digested*, 00/**4452**
Sparkes v. Smart [1990] 2 E.G.L.R. 245, CA . . . . *Digested*, 91/**115**:
                                                                  Applied, 97/92: *Followed*, 98/124
Sparkle Properties Ltd v. Residential Developments Ltd [1998] E.G.C.S. 68; [1998]
  N.P.C. 73, Ch D
Sparkling Mineral Water Bottle, Re [1999] E.C.C. 534, OGH (A)
Sparks v. Harland [1997] 1 W.L.R. 143; *Times*, August 9, 1996, QBD . . . . *Digested*, 96/**838**:
                                                                  Distinguished, 00/3236
Sparks v. Harris [2001] 4 Q.R. 15, CC (Bristol) [*Ex rel.* James Wilson-Smith, Barrister,
  Albion Chambers, Broad Street, Bristol] . . . .   *Digested*, 01/**1758**
Sparrow Ltd v. Inspector of Taxes (SC-289) [2001] S.T.C. (S.C.D.) 206; [2001] S.T.I.
  1502, Sp Comm
Spartan Steel & Alloys Ltd v. Martin & Co (Contractors) Ltd [1973] Q.B. 27; [1972] 3
  W.L.R. 502; [1972] 3 All E.R. 557; 14 K.I.R. 75; 116 S.J. 648, CA . . . . *Digested*, 72/**2341**:
                          Considered, 77/2009, 78/2074, 79/1864, 85/2311, 86/2270:
                          Disapproved, 78/706: *Distinguished*, 88/3409, 00/4210: *Doubted*, 82/766,
                                                                  82/4055: *Followed*, 98/1418
Sparti, The [2000] 2 Lloyd's Rep. 618, HC (HK) . . . . *Digested*, 01/**4935**
Spath Holme Ltd v. Greater Manchester and Lancashire Rent Assessment Committee
  (No.1) (1996) 28 H.L.R. 107; [1995] 2 E.G.L.R. 80; [1995] 49 E.G. 128; [1995]
  N.P.C. 138; (1996) 71 P. & C.R. D8; *Times*, August 9, 1995; *Independent*,
  August 28, 1995 (C.S.), CA; reversing (1995) 27 H.L.R. 243; *Times*, July 13,
  1994, QBD . . . .   *Digested*, 96/**3823**:
                          Considered, 96/3791, 97/3315, 97/3316: *Followed*, 98/3669, 98/3670,
                                                                                          98/3672
Spath Holme Ltd v. Greater Manchester and Lancashire Rent Assessment Committee
  (No.2); Curtis v. London Rent Assessment Committee [1999] 1 W.L.R. 1623;
  [1998] 3 All E.R. 909; [1998] 1 Costs L.R. 40; [1997] N.P.C. 173; *Times*, January
  2, 1998, QBD . . . . *Digested*, 98/**470**
Spath Holme Ltd v. North Western Rent Assessment Committee [2001] EWHC Admin
  541; [2001] 46 E.G. 181; [2001] 31 E.G.C.S. 113; [2001] N.P.C. 118; *Independent*,
  October 22, 2001 (C.S.), QBD (Admin Ct)
Spearing v. Jackson (Unreported, November 3, 1999), CC (Winchester) [*Ex rel.*
  Amanda Gillett, Pupil Barrister, College Chambers, 19 Carlton Crescent,
  Southampton] . . . . *Digested*, 00/**468**
Specht v. Netscape Communications Corp [2001] E.B.L.R. 125, US Ct
Special Trustees for Great Ormond Street Hospital for Children v. Rushin; *sub nom* Morris
  (Deceased), Re; Morris, In the estate of [2001] W.T.L.R. 1137, Ch D
Specialarbejderforbundet i Danmark v. Dansk Industri (C400/93) [1995] All E.R. (E.C.)
  577; [1995] E.C.R. I-1275; [1996] 1 C.M.L.R. 515; [1996] I.C.R. 51; [1995]
  I.R.L.R. 648; *Times*, June 23, 1995, ECJ . . . . *Digested*, 95/**2003**:
                                                                                          Applied, 01/2277
Specialist Group International Ltd v. Deakin see Deakin v. Faulding (No.2)
Spectra International Plc v. Hayesoak Ltd [1998] 1 Lloyd's Rep. 162, CA; reversing
  [1997] 1 Lloyd's Rep. 153, CC (Central London) . . . .   *Digested*, 97/**4286**
Spectra-Tech Inc's Patent Application [1999] R.P.C. 187; (1998) 21(10) I.P.D. 21106, PO   *Digested*, 99/**3469**
Spectravest Inc v. Aperknit Ltd [1988] F.S.R. 161, Ch D . . . . *Digested*, 88/**504**:
                                                                                          Not followed, 99/12
Spectros International Plc (In Voluntary Liquidation) v. Madden (Inspector of Taxes)
  [1997] S.T.C. 114; 70 T.C. 349; [1997] B.T.C. 74, Ch D . . . . *Digested*, 97/**1071**
Spectrum Investment Co v. Holmes [1981] 1 W.L.R. 221; [1981] 1 All E.R. 6; (1981) 41
  P. & C.R. 133; 125 S.J. 47, Ch D . . . . *Digested*, 81/**1495**:
                                                                  Distinguished, 98/4339
Spedition Wilhelm Rotermund GmbH v. Commission of the European Communities
  (T330/99) [2001] E.C.R. II-1619; [2001] 3 C.M.L.R. 32, CFI (2nd Chamber) . .   *Digested*, 01/**4121**

SpeechWorks Ltd v. SpeechWorks International Inc [2000] E.T.M.R. 982; 2000 G.W.D.
26-1013, OH . . . . *Digested,* 01/**6726**
Speed (A Minor) v. G&A Shipman (Unreported, May 15, 1998), CC (Skegness) [*Ex rel.*
Hodgkinsons Solicitors, The Old Manse, 14 Lumley Avenue, Skegness,
Lincolnshire] . . . . *Digested,* 98/**1671**
Speedwell Estates Ltd, Re [1999] 2 E.G.L.R. 121; [1999] 27 E.G. 128; [1999] R.V.R. 313,
Lands Tr . . . . *Digested,* 99/**3684**
Speedwell Estates Ltd v. Dalziel [2001] EWCA Civ 1277; (2001) 98(32) L.S.G. 38;
[2001] N.P.C. 133; *Times,* October 19, 2001, CA . . . . *Digested,* 01/**4182**
Speidel v. Plato Films Ltd see Plato Films Ltd v. Speidel
Speidel v. Unity Theatre Society see Plato Films Ltd v. Speidel
Speller v. Harris (Unreported, September 3, 1999), CC (Basildon) [*Ex rel.* Paul
McGrath, Barrister, 1 Temple Gardens, Temple, London] . . . . *Digested,* 99/**552**
Spence v. British Railways Board [2001] I.C.R. 232, EAT . . . . *Digested,* 01/**2346**
Spence v. United Taxis (Unreported, May 20, 1997), CC (Newcastle) [*Ex rel.* Crutes
Solicitors, 7 Osborne Terrace, Newcastle upon Tyne] . . . . *Digested,* 98/**1465**
Spence v. Wilson (No.1) 1998 S.C. 433; 1998 S.L.T. 688; 1998 G.W.D. 8-389; *Times,*
May 18, 1998, OH . . . . *Digested,* 98/**5711**:
Approved, 98/5710

Sphere Drake Insurance Plc v. Basler Versicherungs Gesellschaft; Orion Insurance Co
Plc v. Basler Versicherungs Gesellschaft [1998] Lloyd's Rep. I.R. 35, QBD
(Comm Ct) . . . . *Digested,* 98/**3411**
Spice Girls Ltd v. Aprilia World Service BV; *sub nom* Spice Girls Ltd v. Aprilla World
Service BV; A3/2000/3122, CA; reversing in part [2000] E.M.L.R. 478; *Times,*
April 5, 2000, Ch D . . . . *Digested,* 00/**891**
Spice Girls Ltd v. Aprilia World Service BV (Damages); *sub nom* Spice Girls Ltd v.
Aprilla World Service BV [2001] E.M.L.R. 8, Ch D . . . . *Digested,* 01/**965**
Spice Girls Ltd v. Aprilia World Service BV (Permission to Appeal), *Times,* September 12,
2000, Ch D . . . . *Digested,* 00/**307**
Spice Girls Ltd v. Aprilla World Service BV see Spice Girls Ltd v. Aprilia World Service
BV
Spice Girls Ltd v. Aprilla World Service BV see Spice Girls Ltd v. Aprilia World Service
BV (Damages)
Spice Girls Ltd's Application for Cancellation of Registered Designs; *sub nom* Girl Power
Toys Ltd (Registered Designs Nos.2068328, 2068329, 2068330, 2068331
and 2068332) [2000] E.C.D.R. 148; (1999) 22(12) I.P.D. 22120, Designs
Registry . . . . *Digested,* 00/**3696**
Spijker Kwasten BV v. Commission of the European Communities (C231/82) [1983]
E.C.R. 2559; [1984] 2 C.M.L.R. 284, ECJ (3rd Chamber) . . . . *Digested,* 84/**1420**:
Applied, 98/2311

Spijkers v. Gebroeders Benedik Abattoir CV (C24/85) [1986] E.C.R. 1119; [1986] 2
C.M.L.R. 296, ECJ (5th Chamber) . . . . *Digested,* 86/**1362**:
Applied, 94/2001, 94/4832, 94/5110, 95/2071, 95/2073, 99/2133, 99/6043,
00/2229, 00/2231, 00/2232: *Considered,* 95/2072, 96/2649, 97/2274,
97/2278

Spiliada Maritime Corp v. Cansulex Ltd (The Spiliada) [1987] A.C. 460; [1986] 3
W.L.R. 972; [1986] 3 All E.R. 843; [1987] 1 Lloyd's Rep. 1; [1987] E.C.C. 168;
[1987] 1 F.T.L.R. 103; (1987) 84 L.S.G. 113; (1986) 136 N.L.J. 1137; (1986) 130
S.J. 925; *Financial Times,* November 25, 1986, HL; reversing [1985] 2 Lloyd's
Rep. 116; (1985) 82 L.S.G. 1416, CA . . . . *Digested,* 87/**3135**:
Applied, 85/2597, 86/2705, 89/1722, 89/3095, 89/3394, 90/3768, 91/475,
91/476, 92/475, 93/3571, 93/5876, 94/483, 94/4040, 95/696, 96/846,
97/908, 98/4398, 99/717, 99/719, 99/750, 99/2405, 00/775, 01/815:
Considered, 81/238, 87/3095, 88/2911, 89/2725, 89/3042, 92/3072,
94/3252, 94/3256, 95/3484, 96/1089, 96/1091, 98/764:
Distinguished, 87/3024: *Explained,* 00/769: *Followed,* 91/5142, 95/690,
95/6052, 97/2453, 98/748, 98/749
Spinney's (1948) Ltd v. Royal Insurance Co Ltd [1980] 1 Lloyd's Rep. 406, QBD
(Comm Ct) . . . . *Digested,* 80/**1514**:
Applied, 82/1660: *Considered,* 91/3253, 92/3974, 01/3795
Spirit of Independence, The (formerly known as Caribia Viva, The) see Owners of The Spirit of
Independence v. Wear Dockyard Ltd
Spittle v. Bunney [1988] 1 W.L.R. 847; [1988] 3 All E.R. 1031; [1988] Fam. Law 433;
(1988) 138 N.L.J. Rep. 56; (1988) 132 S.J. 754, CA . . . . *Digested,* 88/**1056**:
Considered, 90/1561, 91/1307, 91/1308, 99/1454, 00/1451
Spolka Akcyjna PPCH's Trade Mark (III RN 5/99) [2001] E.T.M.R. 69, Sad Najwyzszy (PL)
Spooner v. British Telecommunications Plc [2000] O.P.L.R. 189; [2000] Pens. L.R. 65,
Ch D . . . . *Digested,* 00/**4357**
Sporrong and Lonnroth v. Sweden (A/52) (1983) 5 E.H.R.R. 35, ECHR . . . . *Applied,* 98/3133:
Considered, 97/2796: *Distinguished,* 98/3128
Sportoffer Ltd v. Erewash BC [1999] L. & T.R. 433; [1999] 3 E.G.L.R. 136; [1999]
E.G.C.S. 37; (1999) 96(11) L.S.G. 71, Ch D . . . . *Digested,* 99/**3671**
Sports Club v. Inspector of Taxes [2000] S.T.C. (S.C.D.) 443; [2000] S.T.I. 1364, Sp
Comm . . . . *Digested,* 01/**5249**

Sportsman v. Inland Revenue Commissioners 1 I.T.L. Rep. 237, Sp Comm

Spratley v. Universal Equipment Ltd (Unreported, September 9, 1999), CC (Kingston on Thames) [Ex rel. Morgan Cole Solicitors, Apex Plaza, Forbury Road, Reading] . . . .   *Digested*, 00/**376**

Spratt v. AT&T Automotive Services Ltd see Fleet Disposal Services Ltd, Re

Spraymiser Ltd v. Wrightway Marketing Ltd [2000] E.C.D.R. 349; (2000) 23(4) I.P.D. 23034, Ch D . . . .   *Digested*, 00/**3586**

Spring v. Guardian Assurance Plc [1995] 2 A.C. 296; [1994] 3 W.L.R. 354; [1994] 3 All E.R. 129; [1994] I.C.R. 596; [1994] I.R.L.R. 460; (1994) 91(40) L.S.G. 36; (1994) 144 N.L.J. 971; (1994) 138 S.J.L.B. 183; *Times*, July 8, 1994; *Independent*, July 12, 1994, HL; reversing [1993] 2 All E.R. 273; [1993] I.C.R. 412; [1993] I.R.L.R. 122; (1993) 12 Tr. L.R. 33; (1993) 143 N.L.J. 365; (1993) 137 S.J.L.B. 47; *Times*, December 22, 1992; *Independent*, January 26, 1993, CA; reversing [1992] I.R.L.R. 173; (1992) 11 Tr. L.R. 100; *Times*, February 10, 1992, QBD . . . .   *Digested*, 94/**1918**:
Applied, 94/1930, 94/3383, 94/3514, 95/4838, 99/2108, 00/2108:
Cited, 93/2947: *Considered*, 94/3345, 95/3652, 00/4219:
Distinguished, 98/3935: *Followed*, 01/2254

Spring v. O'Flynn [1999] E.G.C.S. 79, Ch D

Spring Form Inc v. Argos Ltd see Spring Form Inc v. Toy Brokers Ltd

Spring Form Inc v. Playhut Inc see Playhut Inc v. Spring Form Inc

Spring Form Inc v. Toy Brokers Ltd; Spring Form Inc v. Worlds Apart Ltd (Recoverability of Profits); Spring Form Inc v. Argos Ltd (2001) 24(11) I.P.D. 24073, Pat Ct

Spring Form Inc v. Worlds Apart Ltd (2001) 24(8) I.P.D. 24053, Pat Ct

Spring Form Inc v. Worlds Apart Ltd (Recoverability of Profits) see Spring Form Inc v. Toy Brokers Ltd

Spring House (Freehold) Ltd v. Mount Cook Land Ltd; *sub nom* Mount Cook Land Ltd v. Spring House (Freehold) Ltd [2001] EWCA Civ 1833; [2001] N.P.C. 182; *Independent*, December 20, 2001, CA

Spring Valley Properties Ltd v. Harris; *sub nom* Salmet International Ltd (In Administration), Re [2001] B.C.C. 796; [2001] B.P.I.R. 709, Ch D . . . .   *Digested*, 01/**3711**

Springette v. Defoe [1992] 2 F.L.R. 388; [1992] 2 F.C.R. 561; (1992) 24 H.L.R. 552; (1993) 65 P. & C.R. 1; [1992] Fam. Law 489; [1992] N.P.C. 34; *Independent*, March 24, 1992; *Guardian*, April 29, 1992, CA . . . .   *Digested*, 92/**2031**:
Considered, 96/4996, 00/3941: *Followed*, 93/1876, 95/2188, 96/2887

Springsteen v. Flute International Ltd see Masquerade Music Ltd v. Springsteen

Springsteen v. Masquerade Music Ltd see Masquerade Music Ltd v. Springsteen

Sprints Ltd v. Comptroller of Customs (Mauritius) [2000] F.S.R. 814, PC (Mau) . . . . . .   *Digested*, 00/**3786**

Sprung v. Royal Insurance (UK) Ltd [1997] C.L.C. 70; [1999] 1 Lloyd's Rep. I.R. 111, CA . . . .   *Digested*, 97/**3121**

Spurrett v. W Gimber & Sons Ltd; *sub nom* W Gimber & Sons Ltd v. Spurrett (1967) 2 I.T.R. 308, DC 1 K.I.R. 368; (1966) 1 I.T.R. 391, IT . . . .   *Digested*, 67/**1450.123**:
Considered, 72/1241, 81/910: *Not followed*, 98/2186

Spurrs v. Cronin (Unreported, September 28, 1999), CC (Willesden) [Ex rel. Graham Ludlam, Barrister, Lamb Chambers, Lamb Building, Elm Court, Temple, London].   *Digested*, 99/**2482**

SR v. Italy [1998] H.R.C.D. 461, ECHR

Srimanoharan v. Secretary of State for the Home Department, *Times*, June 29, 2000, CA . . . .   *Digested*, 00/**3282**

Srithara (Unreported, December 1, 1966), IAT . . . .   *Doubted*, 98/3195

SRJ v. DWJ see J (SR) v. J (DW)

SSC v. Sweden (46553/93) (2000) 29 E.H.R.R. CD245, ECHR

ST v. J (Transsexual: Void Marriage) see J v. ST (formerly J) (Transsexual: Ancillary Relief)

St Albans City and District Council v. Glinwell Plc (2000) 15 P.A.D. 63, Planning Inspector

St Albans City and District Council v. International Computers Ltd [1996] 4 All E.R. 481; [1997-98] Info. T.L.R. 58; [1997] F.S.R. 251; (1996) 15 Tr. L.R. 444; [1998] Masons C.L.R. Rep. 98; (1997) 20(2) I.P.D. 20020; *Times*, August 14, 1996, CA; reversing in part [1997-98] Info. T.L.R. 25; [1995] F.S.R. 686; [1998] Masons C.L.R. Rep. 19; *Times*, November 11, 1994, QBD . . . .   *Digested*, 96/**1218**

St Albans City and District Council v. Martin Grant Homes (UK) Ltd (2000) 15 P.A.D. 284, Planning Inspector

St Albans Court Ltd v. Daldorch Estates Ltd, *Times*, May 24, 1999, Ch D . . . .   *Digested*, 99/**505**

St Andrew's, Thornhaugh, Re [1976] Fam. 230; [1976] 2 W.L.R. 123; [1976] 1 All E.R. 154; (1975) 120 S.J. 80, Cons Ct (Peterborough) . . . .   *Digested*, 76/**821**:
Considered, 01/1841

St Brice v. Southwark LBC; *sub nom* Southwark LBC v. St Brice [2001] EWCA Civ 1138; (2001) 98(35) L.S.G. 34; (2001) 145 S.J.L.B. 214; [2001] N.P.C. 120; *Times*, August 6, 2001; *Independent*, November 12, 2001 (C.S), CA . . . .   *Digested*, 01/**4167**

St Dunstan's Roman Catholic Church, Southborough v. Customs and Excise Commissioners [1998] V. & D.R. 264, V&DTr . . . .   *Digested*, 00/**5368**

St Ermins Property Co Ltd v. Bello (1999) 77 P. & C.R. D29, CA

St Ermins Property Co Ltd *v.* Patel (No.1) (1998) 30 H.L.R. 462; (1998) 75 P. & C.R. 46; [1997] 2 E.G.L.R. 61; [1997] 41 E.G. 156; [1997] E.G.C.S. 83; [1997] N.P.C. 78, CA .... *Digested,* 97/**3303**

St Ermins Property Co Ltd *v.* Patel (No.2) [2001] EWCA Civ 804; [2001] L. & T.R. 38; [2001] N.P.C. 93; *Times,* July 27, 2001, CA .... *Digested,* 01/**4213**

St George's Healthcare NHS Trust *v.* S; R. *v.* Collins Ex p. S (No.1) [1998] 3 W.L.R. 936; [1998] 3 All E.R. 673; [1998] 2 F.L.R. 728; [1998] 2 F.C.R. 685; (1997-98) 1 C.C.L. Rep. 410; (1998) 44 B.M.L.R. 160; [1998] C.O.D. 396; [1998] Fam. Law 526; (1998) 95(22) L.S.G. 29; (1998) 148 N.L.J. 693; (1998) 142 S.J.L.B. 164; *Times,* May 8, 1998; *Independent,* May 12, 1998, CA .... *Digested,* 98/**2648**: *Applied,* 01/2934

St George's Healthcare NHS Trust *v.* S (Guidelines); R. *v.* Collins Ex p. S (No.2) [1999] Fam. 26; (1997-98) 1 C.C.L. Rep. 578; [1998] Fam. Law 662; *Times,* August 3, 1998, CA .... *Digested,* 98/**2647**

St Giles Hotel Ltd *v.* Microworld Technology Ltd (1998) 75 P. & C.R. 380; [1997] 2 E.G.L.R. 105; [1997] 27 E.G. 121; [1997] N.P.C. 54, CA .... *Digested,* 97/**3333**

St Gregory Offchurch, Re [2000] 1 W.L.R. 2471; [2000] 4 All E.R. 378; (2000) 97(44) L.S.G. 44; *Times,* November 8, 2000, Cons Ct (Coventry) .... *Digested,* 00/**1775**

St Helens Smelting Co *v.* Tipping (1865) 11 H.L. Cas. 642 .... *Applied,* 61/**6344**: *Considered,* 00/4293

St James Homes Ltd *v.* Secretary of State for the Environment, Transport and the Regions see R. (on the application of St James Homes Ltd) *v.* Secretary of State for the Environment, Transport and the Regions

St James's Chapel, Callow End, Re [2001] 1 W.L.R. 835, Cons Ct (Worcester) .... *Digested,* 01/**1845**

St John, Re see St John *v.* United States

St John *v.* Governor of Brixton Prison see St John *v.* United States

St John *v.* United States; *sub nom* St John *v.* Governor of Brixton Prison; St John, Re; R. (on the application of St John) *v.* Governer of Brixton Prison [2001] EWHC Admin 543; (2001) 98(35) L.S.G. 34; (2001) 145 S.J.L.B. 215; *Times,* August 10, 2001; *Independent,* November 12, 2001 (C.S), QBD (Admin Ct) .... *Digested,* 01/**2523**

St John's College School (Cambridge) *v.* Secretary of State for Social Security [2001] E.L.R. 103, QBD .... *Digested,* 01/**5008**

St Kea of Cornwall Ltd's Trade Mark (No.2001526); *sub nom* Ty Nant Spring Water Ltd's Request for Removal from the Register, Re (1998) 21(3) I.P.D. 21031, TMR

St Luke the Evangelist, Maidstone, Re [1995] Fam. 1; [1994] 3 W.L.R. 1165; [1995] 1 All E.R. 321; *Times,* October 7, 1994, Arches Ct .... *Digested,* 95/**1867**: *Applied,* 00/1775

St Martins Property Corp Ltd *v.* Sir Robert McAlpine & Sons see Linden Gardens Trust Ltd *v.* Lenesta Sludge Disposals Ltd

St Martins Property Investments Ltd *v.* CIB Properties Ltd; *sub nom* St Martins Property Ltd *v.* Citicorp Investment Bank Properties Ltd [1999] L. & T.R. 1; [1998] E.G.C.S. 161, CA; affirming [1997] E.G.C.S. 99; *Independent,* July 14, 1997 (C.S.), Ch D .... *Digested,* 97/**3318**

St Martins Property Ltd *v.* Citicorp Investment Bank Properties Ltd see St Martins Property Investments Ltd *v.* CIB Properties Ltd

St Mary the Virgin, Hurley, Re [2001] 1 W.L.R. 831; *Times,* January 26, 2001, Cons Ct (Oxford) .... *Digested,* 01/**1848**

St Mary-le-Bow, London, Re [2001] 1 W.L.R. 1507, Cons Ct (London) .... *Digested,* 01/**1843**

St Mary, Kingswinford, Re [2001] 1 W.L.R. 927, Cons Ct (Worcester) .... *Digested,* 01/**1846**

St Merryn Meat Ltd *v.* Hawkins [2001] C.P. Rep. 116; *Daily Telegraph,* July 10, 2001, Ch D

St Michaels, Orchard Portman, Re [2001] Fam. 302; [2001] 2 W.L.R. 1686, Cons Ct (Bath & Wells) .... *Digested,* 01/**1841**

St Modwen Developments Ltd *v.* Bowmer & Kirkland Ltd (1998) 14 Const. L.J. 214, QBD (OR) .... *Digested,* 98/**237**

St Paul Fire & Marine Insurance Co (UK) Ltd *v.* McConnell Dowell Constructors Ltd; *sub nom* St Paul Fire & Marine Insurance Co (UK) Ltd *v.* McDonnell Dowell Constructors Ltd [1996] 1 All E.R. 96; [1995] 2 Lloyd's Rep. 116; 74 B.L.R. 112; 45 Con. L.R. 89; [1995] 4 Re. L.R. 293; *Lloyd's List,* June 8, 1995 (I.D.), CA; affirming [1993] 2 Lloyd's Rep. 503; 67 B.L.R. 72; 37 Con. L.R. 96, QBD (Comm Ct) .... *Digested,* 95/**2895**: *Considered,* 01/3840

St Paul Fire & Marine Insurance Co (UK) Ltd *v.* McDonnell Dowell Constructors Ltd see St Paul Fire & Marine Insurance Co (UK) Ltd *v.* McConnell Dowell Constructors Ltd

St Paul's Developments Ltd *v.* Gateshead MBC [2001] P.L.C.R. 1; [2001] J.P.L. 116 (Note); [2000] E.G.C.S. 65; (2000) 97(22) L.S.G. 48, QBD .... *Digested,* 01/**4754**

St Paul's, Covent Garden, Re [1974] Fam. 1; [1973] 1 W.L.R. 464; (1972) 117 S.J. 265, Cons Ct (London) .... *Digested,* 73/**960**: *Applied,* 85/1090, 01/1841

St Petroc Minor Vicar and Parochial Church Council *v.* Customs and Excise Commissioners [2000] S.T.I. 710, V&DTr

St Thomas More Collegiate Ltd *v.* Burnell see Rowland *v.* Vancouver College Ltd

ST TRUDO Trade Mark; *sub nom* NV Konings Graanstokerij, Re [1995] F.S.R. 345;
[1995] R.P.C. 370; *Independent*, April 24, 1995 (C.S.), Ch D . . . . *Digested*, 95/**4947**:
Considered, 99/3528: *Referred to*, 99/3511, 01/4043
Staatssecretaris van Financien v. Coffeeshop Siberie vof (C158/98) [1999] All E.R.
(EC) 560; [1999] S.T.C. 742; [1999] E.C.R. I-3971; [1999] 2 C.M.L.R. 1239;
[1999] C.E.C. 314; [1999] B.T.C. 5320; [1999] B.V.C. 353; *Times*, July 8, 1999,
ECJ; reversing . . . . *Digested*, 99/**5014**
Staatssecretaris van Financien v. Heerma (C23/98) [2001] S.T.C. 1437; [2000] E.C.R.
I-419; [2000] S.T.I. 102, ECJ (6th Chamber)
Staatssecretaris van Financien v. Verkooijen (C35/98) [2000] E.C.R. I-4071; 2 I.T.L.
Rep. 727; [2000] S.T.I. 884, ECJ [2000] E.C.R. I-4071, AGO
Stabilad Ltd v. Stephens & Carter Ltd (No.1) [1999] 1 W.L.R. 1201; [1998] 4 All E.R.
129, CA . . . . *Digested*, 99/**396**
Stabilad Ltd v. Stephens & Carter Ltd (No.2) [1999] 2 All E.R. (Comm) 651, CA . . . . . *Digested*, 00/**887**
Stacey v. Babcock Power Ltd (Construction Division) [1986] Q.B. 308; [1986] 2
W.L.R. 207; [1986] I.C.R. 221; [1986] I.R.L.R. 3; (1986) 130 S.J. 71, EAT . . . . . *Digested*, 86/**1280**:
Applied, 98/2232, 98/2234: *Considered*, 97/2290
Stacey v. Player (2001) 98(10) L.S.G. 43; *Times*, February 23, 2001, Ch D . . . . *Digested*, 01/**4221**
Stadtwerke Witten GmbH v. Schade (C257/96) see Kampelmann v.
Landschaftsverband Westfalen-Lippe (C253/96)
Stafford v. Charnwood BC [1999] E.H.L.R. 438; (2000) 32 H.L.R. 289, CA. . . . . *Digested*, 00/**3126**
Stafford v. Chief Adjudication Officer; *sub nom* Chief Adjudication Officer v. Stafford;
Banks v. Chief Adjudication Officer [2001] UKHL 33; [2001] 1 W.L.R. 1411;
[2001] 4 All E.R. 62; [2001] I.C.R. 877; [2001] E.L.R. 729; (2001) 98(31)
L.S.G. 36; (2001) 145 S.J.L.B. 172; *Times*, June 29, 2001; *Independent*, July 4,
2001, HL; affirming [2000] 1 All E.R. 686; [2000] E.L.R. 6; (1999) 96(41)
L.S.G. 36; *Times*, November 9, 1999, CA. . . . . *Digested*, 01/**5040**
Stafford v. Trinidad and Tobago [1999] 1 W.L.R. 2026 (Note), PC (Trin) . . . . *Digested*, 00/**985**
Stafford BC v. Malpass (2001) 16 P.A.D. 94, Planning Inspector
Stafford BC v. Stafford (2001) 16 P.A.D. 34, Planning Inspector
Stafford BC v. Touchstone Housing Association (2000) 15 P.A.D. 478, Planning
Inspector
Stafford Engineering Services Ltd's Licence of Right (Copyright) Application [2000]
R.P.C. 797, PO. . . . . *Digested*, 01/**3854**
Stafford Land Rover v. Customs and Excise Commissioners [2000] B.V.C. 2186;
[1999] V. & D.R. 471; [2000] S.T.I. 864, V&DTr . . . . *Digested*, 00/**5291**
Staffordshire CC v. B [1998] 1 F.L.R. 261; [1999] 2 F.C.R. 333; [1998] Fam. Law 8,
Ch D . . . . *Digested*, 98/**2368**
Staffordshire CC v. Independent Energy UK Ltd (2001) 16 P.A.D. 8, Planning Inspector
Staffordshire CC v. Riley [2001] EWCA Civ 257; [2001] J.P.L. 1325 (Note); (2001)
98(9) L.S.G. 42, CA
Staffordshire Moorlands DC v. Cartwright (1992) 63 P. & C.R. 285; [1992] J.P.L. 138,
CA . . . . *Digested*, 92/**4375**:
Distinguished, 92/4352, 93/3941: *Followed*, 98/4224
Staffordshire Moorlands DC v. Goodfellow (1998) 13 P.A.D. 513, Planning Inspector
Staffordshire Moorlands DC v. St Modwen Developments Ltd (1998) 13 P.A.D. 712,
Planning Inspector
Stallinger and Kuso v. Austria (1998) 26 E.H.R.R. 81, ECHR . . . . *Digested*, 98/**3141**
Stamoulakatos v. Greece (Entitlement to Disability Pension); *sub nom* Stamoulakatos v.
Greece (No.2) [1998] H.R.C.D. 113, ECHR
Stamoulakatos v. Greece (No.2) see Stamoulakatos v. Greece (Entitlement to Disability
Pension)
Stanbury v. Lambeth LBC (1998) 75 P. & C.R. D38, CA
Standard Bank London Ltd v. Apostolakis (No.1) [2000] I.L.Pr. 766, QBD (Comm Ct) . *Digested*, 01/**816**:
Subsequent proceedings, 01/822
Standard Bank London Ltd v. Apostolakis (No.2) [2001] Lloyd's Rep. Bank. 240, QBD
(Comm Ct) . . . . *Digested*, 01/**822**:
Previous proceedings, 01/816
Standard Bank London Ltd v. Bank of Tokyo Ltd; Sudwestdeutsche Landesbank
Girozentrale v. Bank of Tokyo Ltd [1995] 2 Lloyd's Rep. 169; [1998] Masons
C.L.R. Rep. 126; *Times*, April 15, 1995, QBD. . . . . *Digested*, 95/**397**
Standard Chartered Bank v. Mehra see Standard Chartered Bank v. Pakistan National
Shipping Corp (No.2)
Standard Chartered Bank v. Pakistan National Shipping Corp (Assessment of
Damages) [2001] EWCA Civ 55; [2001] 1 All E.R. (Comm) 822; [2001] C.L.C.
825, CA; affirming [1999] 1 All E.R. (Comm.) 417; [1999] 1 Lloyd's Rep. 747;
[1999] C.L.C. 761, QBD (Comm Ct). . . . . *Digested*, 01/**1522**
Standard Chartered Bank v. Pakistan National Shipping Corp (No.1) [1998] 1 Lloyd's
Rep. 656, CA; reversing [1995] 2 Lloyd's Rep. 365, QBD (Adm Ct) . . . . *Digested*, 98/**4393**:
Considered, 00/590

Standard Chartered Bank v. Pakistan National Shipping Corp (No.2); Standard
Chartered Bank v. Mehra [2000] 1 All E.R. (Comm) 1; [2000] 1 Lloyd's Rep. 218;
[2000] Lloyd's Rep. Bank. 40; [2000] C.L.C. 133; *Times*, March 15, 2000;
Independent, December 9, 1999, CA; reversing in part [1998] 1 Lloyd's Rep.
684; *Times*, May 27, 1998, QBD (Comm Ct) . . . . *Digested*, 00/**4681**:
Applied, 01/5350: *Subsequent proceedings*, 00/5108
Standard Chartered Bank v. Pakistan National Shipping Corp (Reduction of Damages)
[2001] Q.B. 167; [2000] 3 W.L.R. 1692; [2000] 2 All E.R. (Comm) 929; [2000]
2 Lloyd's Rep. 511; [2000] Lloyd's Rep. Bank. 342; [2000] C.L.C. 1575; *Times*,
October 3, 2000, CA. . . . . *Digested*, 00/**5108**:
Previous proceedings, 98/4392
Standard Life Assurance Co v. Egan Lawson Ltd see Egan Lawson Ltd v. Standard Life
Assurance Co
Standard Life Assurance Co v. Greycoat Devonshire Square see Standard Life Co Ltd v.
Greycoat Devonshire Square Ltd
Standard Life Assurance Co v. Unipath Ltd (1998) 75 P. & C.R. 473; [1997] 2 E.G.L.R.
121; [1997] 38 E.G. 152; [1997] E.G.C.S. 69; [1997] N.P.C. 69, CA . . . . *Digested*, 97/**3319**
Standard Life Co Ltd v. Greycoat Devonshire Square Ltd; *sub nom* Standard Life
Assurance Co v. Greycoat Devonshire Square [2001] L. & T.R. 25; [2000]
E.G.C.S. 40; (2000) 97(15) L.S.G. 40; (2000) 144 S.J.L.B. 166; *Times*, April 10,
2000, Ch D . . . . *Digested*, 00/**3935**
Standard Price Lists for Chemists Products, Re [1998] E.C.C. 473, OGH (A)
Standard Tandoori Nepalese Restaurant v. Customs and Excise Commissioners (No.1)
[2000] S.T.I. 744, V&DTr
Standard Tandoori Nepalese Restaurant v. Customs and Excise Commissioners (No.2)
[2000] V. & D.R. 105; [2000] S.T.I. 1096, V&DTr
Standards Woven Fabrics Application see STANWAL Trade Mark
Standen v. Society of Lloyd's see Jones v. Society of Lloyd's
Standen Engineering Ltd v. A Spalding & Sons Ltd [1984] F.S.R. 554, Ch D . . . . *Digested*, 84/**421**:
Referred to, 00/3570
Standing v. Hill [2001] 6 Q.R. 10, CC (Birkenhead) [*Ex rel.* Michael W Halsall
Solicitors, 2 The Park, Newton-le-Willows] . . . . *Digested*, 01/**1634**
Standing v. Werrett (Unreported, March 15, 2000), CC (Pontypridd) [*Ex rel.* Andrew
Arentsen, Barrister, 33 Park Place, Cardiff] . . . . *Digested*, 00/**1688**
Standley v. Stewkesbury [1998] 2 F.L.R. 610; [1998] 3 F.C.R. 564; [1998] Fam. Law
397, CA . . . . *Digested*, 98/**2463**
Stanford v. UK, *Times*, March 8, 1994; *Guardian*, March 14, 1994, ECHR. . . . . *Digested*, 94/**2398**:
Referred to, 01/3507
Stanley v. DPP see DPP v. Jackson (Failure to Provide Specimen)
Stanley v. Ealing LBC [2000] E.H.L.R. 172; (2000) 32 H.L.R. 745; [2000] Env. L.R.
D18, QBD . . . . *Digested*, 00/**2251**
Stanley v. Saddique [1992] Q.B. 1; [1991] 2 W.L.R. 459; [1991] 1 All E.R. 529; *Times*,
May 24, 1990; *Independent*, June 8, 1990, CA . . . . *Digested*, 91/**1307**:
Applied, 98/931: *Considered*, 92/1530, 93/1394, 00/1451: *Followed*, 93/1591
Stanton v. Callaghan [2000] Q.B. 75; [1999] 2 W.L.R. 745; [1998] 4 All E.R. 961;
[1999] C.P.L.R. 31; [1999] B.L.R. 172; (1999) 1 T.C.L.R. 50; 62 Con. L.R. 1;
[1999] P.N.L.R. 116; [1998] 3 E.G.L.R. 165; [1999] 15 Const. L.J. 50; [1998]
E.G.C.S. 115; (1998) 95(28) L.S.G. 32; (1998) 95(33) L.S.G. 33; (1998) 148
N.L.J. 1355; (1998) 142 S.J.L.B. 220; [1998] N.P.C. 113; *Times*, July 25, 1998;
Independent, July 16, 1998, CA . . . . *Digested*, 98/**520**:
Applied, 01/401
STANWAL Trade Mark; *sub nom* Standards Woven Fabrics Application (1918) 35
R.P.C. 53 . . . . *Considered*, 73/**3331**:
Distinguished, 98/3533
Stanway v. Attorney General, *Times*, November 25, 1999, Ch D . . . . *Digested*, 99/**549**
Stanway v. Secretary of State for the Environment, Transport and the Regions [2001]
J.P.L. 1063, QBD (Admin Ct) . . . . *Digested*, 01/**4656**
Stanyer v. Marks [2001] 1 Q.R. 12, QBD [*Ex rel.* Gordon Catford, Barrister, Crown
Office Chambers, 1 Paper Buildings, London] . . . . *Digested*, 01/**1681**
Stapel v. Bellshore Property Investments Ltd (No.1) (Unreported, April 13, 2000), LVT
[*Ex rel.* Mark Loveday, Barrister, Francis Taylor Building, 3rd Floor, Temple,
London] . . . . *Digested*, 00/**3948**
Stapel v. Bellshore Property Investments Ltd (No.2) [2001] 20 E.G. 231, Ch D [*Ex rel.*
Mark Loveday, Barrister, Tanfield Chambers, Temple, London] . . . . *Digested*, 01/**4193**
Staples v. West Dorset DC [1995] P.I.Q.R. P439; (1995) 92(18) L.S.G. 36; (1995) 139
S.J.L.B. 117; *Times*, April 28, 1995, CA. . . . . *Digested*, 95/**4731**:
Applied, 01/4504: *Considered*, 98/3918, 01/4496
Stapley v. Gypsum Mines Ltd [1953] A.C. 663; [1953] 3 W.L.R. 279; [1953] 2 All
E.R. 478; 97 S.J. 486, HL; reversing [1952] 2 Q.B. 575; [1952] 1 All E.R. 1092,
CA . . . . *Digested*, 53/**2287**:
Applied, 54/2075, 55/1069, 55/1680, 56/5864, 61/2272, 61/3473, 66/5090,
74/2568, 00/1486: *Considered*, 69/2453, 86/973, 00/4228:
Distinguished, 54/2299, 64/2561

Stapp v. Shaftesbury Society [1982] I.R.L.R. 326, CA . . . . *Digested*, 82/**1101**:
Considered, 95/2110, 00/2131
Star News Shops v. Stafford Refrigeration Ltd [1998] 1 W.L.R. 536; [1998] 4 All E.R.
408; (1997) 94(43) L.S.G. 30; (1997) 141 S.J.L.B. 236; *Times*, November 18,
1997, CA. . . . . *Digested*, 97/**752**
Star Rider Ltd v. Inntrepreneur Pub Co [1998] 1 E.G.L.R. 53; [1998] 16 E.G. 140, Ch D . *Digested*, 98/**3660**:
Applied, 98/3680: *Considered*, 99/684: *Followed*, 99/3746
Starcevic v. West Hertfordshire HA [2001] EWCA Civ 192; (2001) 60 B.M.L.R. 221,
CA . . . . *Digested*, 01/**4458**
Stares v. Deradour (Unreported, May 24, 1999), CC (Hertford) [*Ex rel.* Andrew
Petersen, Pupil Barrister, 9 Gough Square, London] . . . . *Digested*, 99/**2468**
Stark v. Post Office [2000] I.C.R. 1013; [2000] P.I.Q.R. P105; (2000) 97(14) L.S.G.
41; (2000) 144 S.J.L.B. 150; *Times*, March 29, 2000, CA. . . . . *Digested*, 00/**2973**:
Cited, 00/2972
Starling v. Lloyds TSB Bank Plc [2000] Lloyd's Rep. Bank. 8; [2000] 1 E.G.L.R. 101;
[2000] 01 E.G. 89; [1999] E.G.C.S. 129; (1999) 96(43) L.S.G. 35; [1999]
N.P.C. 129; (2000) 79 P. & C.R. D12; *Times*, November 12, 1999, CA . . . . *Digested*, 99/**4355**
Starlite (Chandeliers) Ltd v. Customs and Excise Commissioners [1999] V. & D.R. 313,
V&DTr. . . . . *Digested*, 00/**5350**
Starmark Enterprises Ltd v. CPL Distribution Ltd [2001] EWCA Civ 1252; [2001] 32
E.G.C.S. 89; (2001) 98(38) L.S.G. 37; (2001) 98(36) L.S.G. 38; (2001) 151
N.L.J. 1440; (2001) 145 S.J.L.B. 223; [2001] N.P.C. 129; *Times*, October 2,
2001, CA; reversing [2000] 3 E.G.L.R. 37; [2000] 46 E.G. 196; [2000] E.G.C.S.
81, Ch D . . . . *Digested*, 01/**4207**
Starmer v. Bradbury, *Times*, April 11, 1994, CA . . . . *Digested*, 94/**200**:
Followed, 98/593
Starrs v. Ruxton; *sub nom* Ruxton v. Starrs 2000 J.C. 208; 2000 S.L.T. 42; 1999
S.C.C.R. 1052; [2000] H.R.L.R. 191; [2000] U.K.H.R.R. 78; 8 B.H.R.C. 1; 1999
G.W.D. 37-1793; *Times*, November 17, 1999, HCJ Appeal . . . . *Digested*, 99/**5884**:
Considered, 00/6091, 00/6095, 01/6372: *Distinguished*, 01/92, 01/358:
Followed, 00/478: *Referred to*, 00/5841
Staszewski v. Maribella Ltd (1998) 30 H.L.R. 213; [1998] 1 E.G.L.R. 34; [1998] 04
E.G. 149; [1997] E.G.C.S. 35; (1997) 94(15) L.S.G. 26; (1997) 141 S.J.L.B. 74;
[1997] N.P.C. 34; *Times*, March 28, 1997, CA . . . . *Digested*, 97/**3279**
State Aid to Merco Co (C42/93), Re see Spain v. Commission of the European
Communities (C42/93)
State Bank of India v. Sood [1997] 1 W.L.R. 1568, HL [1997] Ch. 276; [1997] 2 W.L.R.
421; [1997] 1 All E.R. 169; [1997] 6 Bank. L.R. 74; (1998) 76 P. & C.R. 47;
(1996) 93(42) L.S.G. 28; (1996) 140 S.J.L.B. 255; [1996] N.P.C. 152; *Times*,
November 7, 1996; *Independent*, December 2, 1996 (C.S.), CA . . . . *Digested*, 96/**4954**
State of Queensland v. JL Holdings Pty Ltd [1999] C.P.L.R. 1, HC (Aus) . . . . *Digested*, 99/**498**
Stathams (Wasted Costs Order), Re see Banks v. Woodhall Duckham Ltd (No.2)
STAUFFER/Cyclohexanediones (T748/89) [1999] E.P.O.R. 45, EPO (Technical Bd App)
Staunton v. Paragon Finance Plc see Paragon Finance Plc (formerly National Home
Loans Corp) v. Nash
Staveley Industries Plc (t/a El.WHS) v. Odebrecht Oil & Gas Services Ltd (2001) 98(10)
L.S.G. 46, QBD (T&CC)
Stayley Developments v. Secretary of State for the Environment, Transport and the
Regions [2001] 1 E.G.L.R. 167; [2001] R.V.R. 251; [2001] N.P.C. 10, Lands Tr . . . *Digested*, 01/**4667**
STC Submarine Systems v. Piper [1993] Pens. L.R. 185 . . . . *Considered*, 01/4631
Stead Hazel & Co v. Cooper [1933] 1 K.B. 840, KBD . . . . *Applied*, 99/3311
Steadman (CICA: Quantum: 2000), Re, CICA (Birmingham) [*Ex rel.* Anthony Verduyn,
Barrister, St. Philips Chambers, Fountain Court, Steelhouse Lane, Birmingham] . *Digested*, 01/**1611**
Steamship Mutual Underwriting Association Ltd v. Trollope & Colls (City) Ltd 33 B.L.R.
77; 6 Con. L.R. 11; (1986) 2 Const. L.J. 224, CA; affirming 11 Con. L.R. 91;
(1985) 2 Const. L.J. 75, DC . . . . *Digested*, 89/**3050**:
Applied, 90/3795, 97/3592: *Considered*, 93/3300: *Distinguished*, 97/734,
99/3944
Steane v. Chief Adjudication Officer [1996] 1 W.L.R. 1195; [1996] 4 All E.R. 83;
(1997-98) 1 C.C.L. Rep. 538; (1996) 93(37) L.S.G. 26; (1996) 140 S.J.L.B.
202; *Times*, August 8, 1996, HL; affirming (1996) 29 B.M.L.R. 87; *Times*,
December 19, 1995; *Independent*, January 8, 1996 (C.S.), CA . . . . *Digested*, 96/**5384**
Stearn v. Chief Constable of Leicester [2001] 5 Q.R. 16, CC (Leicester) [*Ex rel.* Jinder
S Boora, Barrister, Ropewalk Chambers, 24 The Ropewalk, Nottingham] . . . . . . *Digested*, 01/**1701**
Steed v. Home Office see Steed v. Secretary of State for the Home Department
Steed v. Secretary of State for the Home Department; *sub nom* Steed v. Home Office
[2000] 1 W.L.R. 1169; [2000] 3 All E.R. 226; (2000) 97(23) L.S.G. 40; *Times*,
May 26, 2000; *Independent*, July 3, 2000 (C.S), HL; affirming CCRTI 98/0272
CMS2, CA . . . . *Digested*, 00/**44**
Steed v. Suffolk CC see R. v. Suffolk CC Ex p. Steed
Steedman v. BBC [2001] EWCA Civ 1534; (2001) 98(47) L.S.G. 27; (2001) 145
S.J.L.B. 260; *Times*, December 13, 2001, CA; affirming HQ 0003940, QBD
Steedman v. Scofield [1992] 2 Lloyd's Rep. 163; *Times*, April 15, 1992, QBD (Adm Ct) . . *Digested*, 92/**3954**:
Considered, 00/5007

Steeds v. Peverel Management Services Ltd [2001] EWCA Civ 419; *Times,* May 16,
2001; *Daily Telegraph,* April 10, 2001, CA. . . . .   *Digested,* 01/**601**
Steel v. McDonald's Corp (Locus Standi) see McDonald's Corp v. Steel (No.4)
Steel v. United Kingdom (1999) 28 E.H.R.R. 603; 5 B.H.R.C. 339; [1998] Crim. L.R.
893; [1998] H.R.C.D. 872; *Times,* October 1, 1998, ECHR . . . .   *Digested,* 98/**3068**:
Distinguished, 00/3185, 01/10
Steele (Inspector of Taxes) v. European Vinyls Corp (Holdings) BV see Steele (Inspector
of Taxes) v. EVC International NV (formerly European Vinyls Corp (Holdings)
BV)
Steele (Inspector of Taxes) v. EVC International NV (formerly European Vinyls Corp
(Holdings) BV); *sub nom* Steele (Inspector of Taxes) v. European Vinyls Corp
(Holdings) BV; Steeple v. European Vinyls Corp (Holdings) BV [1996] S.T.C. 785;
69 T.C. 88, CA; affirming [1995] S.T.C. 31, Ch D . . . .   *Digested,* 96/**1291**
Steele v. Moule (Unreported, February 18, 1999), CC (Bedford) [*Ex rel.* Stuart R
Yeung, Barrister, 22 Albion Place, Northampton]. . . . .   *Digested,* 99/**326**
Steele (Marie) v. Steele (James) [2001] C.P. Rep. 106; *Times,* June 5, 2001, Ch D . . . .   *Digested,* 01/**440**
Steen v. Attorney General see Attorney General v. Punch
Steen v. Law [1964] A.C. 287; [1963] 3 W.L.R. 802; [1963] 3 All E.R. 770, PC (Aus). .   *Digested,* 63/**413**:
Considered, 01/6037

Steenhorst-Neerings v. Bestuur van de Bedrijfsvereniging voor Detailhandel,
Ambachten en Huisvrouwen (C338/91) [1993] E.C.R. I-5475; [1995] 3
C.M.L.R. 323; [1994] I.R.L.R. 244, ECJ. . . . .   *Digested,* 94/**4929**:
Applied, 95/4639, 99/5284
Steeple v. European Vinyls Corp (Holdings) BV see Steele (Inspector of Taxes) v. EVC
International NV (formerly European Vinyls Corp (Holdings) BV)
Steeples v. Lea [1998] 1 F.L.R. 138; [1998] 2 F.C.R. 144; (1998) 76 P. & C.R. 157;
[1998] Fam. Law 75, CA. . . . .   *Digested,* 97/**4269**
Stefan v. General Medical Council (No.1) [1999] 1 W.L.R. 1293; [2000] H.R.L.R. 1; 6
B.H.R.C. 487; [1999] Lloyd's Rep. Med. 90; (1999) 49 B.M.L.R. 161; (1999) 143
S.J.L.B. 112; *Times,* March 11, 1999, PC (UK) . . . .   *Digested,* 99/**2661**
Stefan v. General Medical Council (No.2) [2001] UKPC 15; (2001) 61 B.M.L.R. 143,
PC (UK)
Stefanelli v. San Marino (35396/97) (2001) 33 E.H.R.R. 16, ECHR
Stefanovic v. Carter [2001] EWCA Civ 452; [2001] P.I.Q.R. Q6, CA. . . . .   *Digested,* 01/**1533**
Stefanovic v. Carter (Quantum) [2001] 6 Q.R. 7, CC (Kingston upon Hull) [*Ex rel.*
Simon Levene, Barrister, 199 Strand, London] . . . .   *Digested,* 01/**1601**
Steibelt (Inspector of Taxes) v. Paling [1999] S.T.C. 594; 71 T.C. 376; [1999] B.T.C. 184;
(1999) 96(20) L.S.G. 40; (1999) 143 S.J.L.B. 140; *Times,* May 19, 1999, Ch D .   *Digested,* 99/**4660**
Stein v. Blake (No.1) [1996] A.C. 243; [1995] 2 W.L.R. 710; [1995] 2 All E.R. 961;
[1995] B.C.C. 543; [1995] 2 B.C.L.C. 94; (1995) 145 N.L.J. 760; *Times,* May 19,
1995; *Independent,* May 19, 1995, HL; affirming [1994] Ch. 16; [1993] 3
W.L.R. 718; [1993] 4 All E.R. 225; [1993] B.C.C. 587; [1993] B.C.L.C. 1478;
Times, May 13, 1993; *Independent,* June 14, 1993 (C.S.), CA . . . .   *Digested,* 95/**422**:
Applied, 00/3489: *Considered,* 96/682, 96/3855: *Followed,* 98/3267
Stein v. Blake (No.2) [1998] 1 All E.R. 724; [1998] B.C.C. 316; [1998] 1 B.C.L.C. 573,
CA . . . .   *Digested,* 98/**691**
Stein v. Blake (No.3) (2000) 97(43) L.S.G. 38; *Times,* October 31, 2000, Ch D . . . . . .   *Digested,* 00/**3992**
Stenhouse Australia v. Phillips [1974] A.C. 391; [1974] 2 W.L.R. 134; [1974] 1 All E.R.
117; [1974] 1 Lloyd's Rep. 1; (1973) 117 S.J. 875, PC (Aus). . . . .   *Digested,* 74/**1271**:
Applied, 98/2193: *Considered,* 91/447, 97/2257
Stennett v. Hook (Unreported, February 18, 2000), MCLC [*Ex rel.* Richard Menzies,
Barrister, 8 Stone Buildings, Lincoln's Inn, London] . . . .   *Digested,* 00/**1518**
Stent v. Monmouth DC (1987) 19 H.L.R. 269; (1987) 54 P. & C.R. 193; [1987] 1
E.G.L.R. 59; (1987) 282 E.G. 705, CA . . . .   *Digested,* 87/**2140**:
Applied, 98/3624: *Considered,* 98/3627
Stent Foundations Ltd v. Carillion Construction (Contracts) Ltd (formerly Tarmac
Construction (Contracts) Ltd); *sub nom* Stent Foundations Ltd v. Tarmac
Construction (Contracts) Ltd 78 Con. L.R. 188, CA; affirming 99/TCC/151, QBD
(T&CC)
Stent Foundations Ltd v. MJ Gleeson Group Plc [2001] B.L.R. 134; (2001) 17 Const.
L.J. 186, QBD (T&CC). . . . .   *Digested,* 01/**947**
Stent Foundations Ltd v. Tarmac Construction (Contracts) Ltd see Stent Foundations
Ltd v. Carillion Construction (Contracts) Ltd (formerly Tarmac Construction
(Contracts) Ltd)
Stephens v. Avery [1988] Ch. 449; [1988] 2 W.L.R. 1280; [1988] 2 All E.R. 477;
[1988] F.S.R. 510; (1988) 85(25) L.S.G. 45; (1988) 138 N.L.J. Rep. 69; 132
S.J. 822; *Times,* February 27, 1988; *Independent,* February 27, 1988, Ch D . . . .   *Digested,* 88/**3403**:
Applied, 01/3851: *Considered,* 01/4415: *Followed,* 97/3588
Stephenson v. FA Wellworth & Co Ltd [1997] N.I. 93, CA (NI). . . . .   *Digested,* 99/**5283**
Stephenson v. Johnson [2000] E.G.C.S. 92, CA
Stephenson Blake (Holdings) Ltd v. Streets Heaver Ltd [2001] Lloyd's Rep. P.N. 44;
[1998] Masons C.L.R. Rep. 25, QBD (OR). . . . .   *Digested,* 01/**4519**

Stephenson Cobbold Ltd (In Liquidation), Re; *sub nom* Secretary of State for Trade and
    Industry *v.* Stephenson [2001] B.C.C. 38; [2000] 2 B.C.L.C. 614, Ch D
    (Companies Ct) . . . . *Digested,* 01/**715**
Sterling Credit Ltd *v.* Rahman see Rahman *v.* Sterling Credit Ltd
Sterling Estates *v.* Pickard UK Ltd see ITM Corp Ltd (In Liquidation), Re
Sterling Fluid System Ltd's Application [1999] R.P.C. 775, PO . . . . *Digested,* 00/**3579**:
    Considered, 01/3854
Sterling Homes (Midlands) Ltd *v.* Birmingham City Council [1996] Env. L.R. 121, QBD . *Digested,* 96/**2689**:
    Applied, 00/2251: *Considered,* 00/2304: *Followed,* 97/2374
Sterling Publications Ltd *v.* Burroughs [2000] 2 Costs L.R. 155, QBD
STERLING/S (+) ibuprofen (T315/98) [2000] E.P.O.R. 401, EPO (Technical Bd App) . *Digested,* 00/**3628**
Stern *v.* Piper [1997] Q.B. 123; [1996] 3 W.L.R. 715; [1996] 3 All E.R. 385; [1996]
    E.M.L.R. 413; (1996) 93(22) L.S.G. 27; (1996) 140 S.J.L.B. 175; *Times,* May 30,
    1996; *Independent,* June 17, 1996 (C.S.), CA . . . . *Digested,* 96/**5661**:
    Considered, 99/2108: *Followed,* 98/1772
Stern Electronics Inc *v.* Kaufman; Stern Electronics Inc *v.* Omni Video Games Inc 669
    F.2d 852, US Ct . . . . *Approved,* 98/**3444**
Stern Electronics Inc *v.* Omni Video Games Inc see Stern Electronics Inc *v.* Kaufman
Sternberg *v.* Hammond see Allen *v.* Sir Alfred McAlpine & Sons Ltd
Sternberg Reed Taylor & Gill, Re (1999) 96(31) L.S.G. 35; *Times,* July 26, 1999, CA (Crim
    Div) . . . . *Digested,* 99/**988**
Stevedoring & Haulage Services Ltd *v.* Fuller [2001] EWCA Civ 651; [2001] I.R.L.R.
    627; [2001] Emp. L.R. 690, CA . . . . *Digested,* 01/**2262**
Steven (t/a City Ceramic Dental Laboratory) *v.* Customs and Excise Commissioners
    [1999] B.V.C. 2292, V&DTr
Stevens (Graham Allan)'s Patent Application (No.8721617) (1998) 21 (1) I.P.D. 21001, CA
    (1997) 20(4) I.P.D. 20034, Pat Ct
Stevens (CICA: Quantum: 2001), Re (Unreported, July 10, 2001), CICAP [*Ex rel.* John
    Bassett, Barrister, 5 Essex Court, Temple, London] . . . . *Digested,* 01/**37**
Stevens *v.* Bell; *sub nom* Airways Pension Scheme, Re; A3/2001/0721B; A3/2001/
    0722, A3/2001/0722/A, A3/2001/0722/B, CA; affirming in part [2001] Pens.
    L.R. 99, Ch D . . . . *Digested,* 01/**4594**
Stevens *v.* Gullis [2000] 1 All E.R. 527; [2001] C.P. Rep. 3; [1999] B.L.R. 394; (2000)
    2 T.C.L.R. 385; 73 Con. L.R. 42; [2000] P.N.L.R. 229; [1999] 3 E.G.L.R. 71;
    [1999] 44 E.G. 143; (2000) 16 Const. L.J. 68; *Times,* October 6, 1999;
    Independent, October 14, 1999, CA . . . . *Digested,* 99/**343**:
    Followed, 00/304
Stevens *v.* London & County Ltd (Unreported, March 16, 2000), CC (Epsom) [*Ex rel.*
    Robert Weir, Barrister, Devereux Chambers, Devereux Court, London] . . . . *Digested,* 00/**1564**
Stevens *v.* Peacock see Heath *v.* Tang
Stevens *v.* School of Oriental and African Studies, *Times,* February 2, 2001, Ch D . . . . . *Digested,* 01/**666**
Stevens *v.* Secretary of State for the Environment, Transport and the Regions; *sub nom*
    R. *v.* Secretary of State for the Environment, Transport and the Regions Ex p.
    Stevens (1998) 76 P. & C.R. 503; [1998] N.P.C. 51; *Times,* February 20, 1998,
    QBD . . . . *Digested,* 98/**2875**
Stevens *v.* Watts (Unreported, June 22, 2000), CC (Birmingham) [*Ex rel.* Taylor
    Joynson Garrett Solicitors, Carmelite, 50 Victoria Embankment, Blackfriars
    London] . . . . *Digested,* 00/**453**
Stevenson *v.* Myers (1929) 47 W.N. (N.SW.) 94, HC (Aus)   *Considered,* 99/5474
Stevenson *v.* Rogers [1999] Q.B. 1028; [1999] 2 W.L.R. 1064; [1999] 1 All E.R. 613;
    (1999) 96(2) L.S.G. 29; (1999) 149 N.L.J. 16; (1999) 143 S.J.L.B. 21; *Times,*
    December 31, 1998, CA. . . . . *Digested,* 99/**4406**
Stevenson *v.* Townsend (1998) 98(6) Q.R. 7, CC (Nottingham) . . . . *Digested,* 98/**1616**
Steventon *v.* Wales (Unreported, September 3, 1999), CC (Leicester) [*Ex rel.* Sunil Iyer,
    Barrister, Bracton Chambers, London] . . . . *Digested,* 99/**3365**
Steward (t/a GT Shooting) *v.* Customs and Excise Commissioners see Stewart (t/a GT
    Shooting) *v.* Customs and Excise Commissioners
Steward *v.* Rapley (t/a Rapley Flatt & Co) [1955-95] P.N.L.R. 451; [1989] 15 E.G.
    198; (1989) Tr. L.R. 161, CA . . . . *Digested,* 89/**1197**:
    Considered, 94/1762
Stewart *v.* Chapman [1951] 2 K.B. 792; [1951] 2 All E.R. 613; [1951] 2 T.L.R. 640; 115
    J.P. 473; 49 L.G.R. 816; 95 S.J. 641, DC . . . . *Digested,* 47-51/**9032**:
    Applied, 63/3327: *Considered,* 68/1212, 68/4065, 99/2465
Stewart *v.* Cleveland Guest (Engineering) Ltd [1996] I.C.R. 535; [1994] I.R.L.R. 440;
    Times, July 6, 1994; *Independent,* September 19, 1994 (C.S.), EAT . . . . *Digested,* 95/**2053**:
    Applied, 01/2320: *Considered,* 96/2651, 99/2098: *Followed,* 96/2607
Stewart (t/a GT Shooting) *v.* Customs and Excise Commissioners; *sub nom* Steward (t/
    a GT Shooting) *v.* Customs and Excise Commissioners [2001] EWCA Civ
    1988; [2001] S.T.I. 1774, CA; affirming [2001] S.T.I. 1122, V&DTr
Stewart *v.* DPP (Unreported, December 14, 1998), QBD. . . . . *Considered,* 01/1265
Stewart *v.* Engel [2000] B.C.C. 741; [2000] 2 B.C.L.C. 528; [2000] B.P.I.R. 383;
    [2000] Lloyd's Rep. P.N. 234; *Times,* November 19, 1999, QBD (Merc Ct) . . . . . *Digested,* 99/**3311**:
    Subsequent proceedings, 00/585

Stewart v. Engel (Permission to Amend) [2000] 1 W.L.R. 2268; [2000] 3 All E.R. 518; [2001] C.P. Rep. 9; [2001] E.C.D.R. 25; *Times*, May 26, 2000; *Independent*, June 26, 2000 (C.S), CA . . . . *Digested*, 00/**585**:
           Applied, 01/579, 01/582: *Considered*, 01/575: *Previous proceedings*, 99/3311

Stewart v. Heywood see Millar v. Dickson

Stewart (Superintendent of Police) v. Moore [1997] N.I. 218, CA (NI) . . . . *Digested*, 99/**5196**

Stewart v. Secretary of State for Scotland 1998 S.C. (H.L.) 81; 1998 S.L.T. 385; 1998 S.C.L.R. 332; 1998 G.W.D. 4-153; *Times*, January 28, 1998, HL; affirming 1996 S.C. 271; 1996 S.L.T. 1203, Ex Div; affirming 1995 S.L.T. 895, OH . . . . *Digested*, 98/**5406**

Stewart v. Welsh Office (Unreported, April 30, 1991) . . . . *Considered*, 99/3944

Stewart Chartering Ltd v. Owners of the Ship Peppy; Stewart Offshore Services (Jersey) Ltd v. Silan Maritime Co Ltd [1997] 2 Lloyd's Rep. 722, QBD (Adm Ct) . . . . *Digested*, 98/**4389**

Stewart Offshore Services (Jersey) Ltd v. Silan Maritime Co Ltd see Stewart Chartering Ltd v. Owners of the Ship Peppy

Stewart-Davies v. Sinton (Unreported, August 11, 1999), CC (Cardiff) [*Ex rel.* Andrew Arentsen, Barrister, 33 Park Place, Cardiff] . . . . *Digested*, 99/**1593**

Stichting v. Bartol (C29/91) [1992] E.C.R. I-3189; [1994] 3 C.M.L.R. 265; [1992] I.R.L.R. 366, ECJ . . . . *Digested*, 92/**4847**:
           Applied, 94/4832, 95/2071, 98/2221: *Considered*, 96/2650

Stichting Certificatie Kraanverhuurbedrijf (SCK) v. Commission of the European Communities (T213/95); Federatie van Nederlandse Kraanverhuurbedrijven (FNK) v. Commission of the European Communities (T18/96) [1997] E.C.R. II-1739; [1998] 4 C.M.L.R. 259; [1997] C.E.C. 1324, CFI (4th Chamber) . . . . *Digested*, 98/**709**

Stichting Collectieve Antennevoorziening Gouda v. Commissariaat voor de Media (C288/89) [1991] E.C.R. I-4007, ECJ . . . . *Considered*, 00/4165:
           Followed, 98/3855, 00/2397

Stichting Goed Wonen v. Staatssecretaris van Financien (C326/99) [2001] 3 C.M.L.R. 54; [2001] B.T.C. 5583, ECJ (5th Chamber)

Stichting Greenpeace Council (Greenpeace International) v. Commission of the European Communities (C321/95 P) [1998] All E.R. (E.C.) 620; [1998] E.C.R. I-1651; [1998] 3 C.M.L.R. 1; [1999] Env. L.R. 181, ECJ. *Digested*, 98/**2311**

Stichting Uitvoering Financiele Acties v. Staatssecretaris van Financien (C348/87) [1989] E.C.R. 1737; [1991] 2 C.M.L.R. 429, ECJ (4th Chamber) . . . . *Digested*, 91/**4144.a**:
           Considered, 98/4961

Stiell Ltd v. Riema Control Systems Ltd 2000 S.C. 539; 2000 S.L.T. 1102; (2001) 3 T.C.L.R. 9; 2000 G.W.D. 23-875; *Times*, June 28, 2000, Ex Div . . . . *Digested*, 00/**5977**

Stilk v. Myrick (1809) 2 Camp. 317 . . . . *Considered*, 98/974:
           Followed, 79/330

Stillwater Designs and Audio Inc's Community Trade Mark Application (B 7049) [2000] E.T.M.R. 35, OHIM (Opposition Div) . . . . *Digested*, 00/**3746**

Stimpson v. Smith [1999] Ch. 340; [1999] 1 W.L.R. 1292; [1999] 2 All E.R. 833; [1999] Lloyd's Rep. Bank. 131; (1999) 96(15) L.S.G. 29; (1999) 149 N.L.J. 414; [1999] N.P.C. 35; *Times*, March 22, 1999, CA . . . . *Digested*, 99/**284**

Stinchcombe v. Spence (Unreported, October 19, 2000), CC (Kingston upon Hull) [*Ex rel.* Haroon Rashid, Barrister, 12 Parnham Close, Radcliffe, Manchester] . . . . *Digested*, 00/**3551**

Stinton v. Motor Insurers Bureau see Stinton v. Stinton

Stinton v. Stinton; *sub nom* Stinton v. Motor Insurers Bureau [1995] R.T.R. 167; [1999] Lloyd's Rep. I.R. 305; (1995) 92(1) L.S.G. 37; *Times*, November 23, 1994, CA (Crim Div); affirming [1993] P.I.Q.R. P135; *Times*, August 5, 1992; *Independent*, August 10, 1992 (C.S), QBD . . . . *Digested*, 99/**3414**:
           Distinguished, 96/3615

Stirk v. Bridgnorth DC (1997) 73 P. & C.R. 439; [1996] E.G.C.S. 159; [1996] N.P.C. 140, CA; affirming [1995] E.G.C.S. 131; [1995] N.P.C. 134, QBD . . . . *Digested*, 97/**4071**:
           Applied, 97/4072, 99/4225, 00/4465: *Considered*, 99/4215, 99/4226:
           Distinguished, 00/4444, 00/4474: *Followed*, 98/4190

Stirland v. DPP; *sub nom* R. v. Stirland (William) [1944] A.C. 315; (1945) 30 Cr. App. R. 40, HL; affirming (1944) 29 Cr. App. R. 154, CCA . . . . *Applied*, 47-51/1985,
           47-51/2032, 47-51/2034, 47-51/2037, 47-51/2095, 47-51/2198, 47-51/2360,
           47/2037, 48/4141, 56/1825, 66/2287, 66/2357, 67/326, 67/742, 67/746, 76/531,
           83/670, 88/736, 00/926: *Considered*, 62/563, 62/609, 68/687

Stirling v. Leadenhall Residential 2 Ltd see Leadenhall Residential 2 Ltd v. Stirling

Stirling Council v. Local Government Property Commission 1998 S.L.T. 1396; 1997 G.W.D. 24-1223; *Times*, July 18, 1997, OH . . . . *Digested*, 97/**6253**

Stirling Credit Ltd v. Ford (Unreported, October 1, 1998) . . . . *Considered*, 99/4387:
           Followed, 99/2507

Stirling Estates v. Pickard UK Ltd see ITM Corp Ltd (In Liquidation), Re

Stirrup v. Foel Agricultural Cooperative Society see Stirrup's Contract, Re

Stirrup's Contract, Re; *sub nom* Stirrup v. Foel Agricultural Cooperative Society [1961] 1 W.L.R. 449; [1961] 1 All E.R. 805; 105 S.J. 206, Ch D . . . . *Digested*, 61/**3358**:
           Considered, 00/4623: *Distinguished*, 87/2189, 88/2058

Stobbart v. Ryan (Unreported, October 7, 1997), CC (Ipswich) [*Ex rel.* Tom Ranson, Solicitor, Graham & Oldham, Electric House, Lloyds Avenue, Ipswich] . . . . *Digested*, 98/**1757**

Stock (CICB: Quantum: 1998), Re (Unreported, April 24, 1998), CICB (Birmingham) [*Ex rel.* Evelyn Bugeja, Barrister, 8 Fountain Court, Steelhouse Lane, Birmingham] . . *Digested*, 98/**1640**
Stock *v.* London Underground Ltd, *Times*, August 13, 1999, CA . . . . *Digested*, 99/**3944**
Stock *v.* Stock B1/2000/0373, CA . . . . *Digested*, 01/**586**
Stock Gaylard Estate Co *v.* Rendell (Unreported, July 16, 1999), CC (Yeovil) [*Ex rel.* TM Fancourt, Barrister, Falcon Chambers, Falcon Court, London] . . . . *Digested*, 00/**3870**
Stockholm Lindopark AB *v.* Sweden (C150/99) see Sweden *v.* Stockholm Lindopark AB (C150/99)
Stockley, Re (Unreported, October 8, 1997), CC (Luton) [*Ex rel.* Benjamin Williams, Barrister, 3 Paper Buildings, 1 Alfred Street, Oxford] . . . . *Digested*, 98/**1726**
STOCKLI/Apparatus for separating disc shaped objects (T142/97) [2001] E.P.O.R. 2, EPO (Technical Bd App) . . . . *Digested*, 01/**3895**
Stockman *v.* Payne [2000] C.P. Rep. 50, QBD . . . . *Digested*, 00/**622**
Stockport MBC *v.* British Gas Plc; *sub nom* Transco Plc *v.* Stockport MBC; British Gas Plc *v.* Stockport MBC; Stockport MBC *v.* Reddish Vale Golf Club [2001] EWCA Civ 212; [2001] Env. L.R. 44; (2001) 3 L.G.L.R. 33; [2001] 9 E.G.C.S. 228; (2001) 98(9) L.S.G. 42; [2001] Env. L.R. D11; *Daily Telegraph*, March 6, 2001, CA
Stockport MBC *v.* PH Property Holdings Ltd (2001) 16 P.A.D. 73, Planning Inspector
Stockport MBC *v.* Reddish Vale Golf Club see Stockport MBC *v.* British Gas Plc
Stocks *v.* Whitgift Homes Ltd see Whitgift Homes Ltd *v.* Stocks
Stocznia Gdanska SA *v.* Latreefers Inc see Stocznia Gdanska SA *v.* Latvian Shipping Co
Stocznia Gdanska SA *v.* Latreefers Inc; *sub nom* Latreefers Inc, Re; Stocznia Gdanska SA *v.* Latvian Shipping Co (Abuse of Process) [2000] C.P.L.R. 65; [2001] B.C.C. 174; [2001] 2 B.C.L.C. 116; [2001] C.L.C. 1267; *Times*, March 15, 2000; *Independent*, February 15, 2000, CA; affirming [1999] 1 B.C.L.C. 271; *Times*, January 18, 1999, Ch D . . . . *Digested*, 00/**3472**:
Applied, 01/716: *Previous proceedings*, 99/347
Stocznia Gdanska SA *v.* Latreefers Inc (Costs: Winding Up) CH-3733 of 1998, Ch D (Companies Ct) . . . . *Digested*, 99/**417**
Stocznia Gdanska SA *v.* Latvian Shipping Co; *sub nom* Stocznia Gdanska SA *v.* Latreefers Inc [1998] 1 W.L.R. 574; [1998] 1 All E.R. 883; [1998] 1 Lloyd's Rep. 609; [1998] C.L.C. 540; (1998) 95(15) L.S.G. 33; (1998) 148 N.L.J. 330; (1998) 142 S.J.L.B. 118; *Times*, February 27, 1998, HL; reversing in part [1996] 2 Lloyd's Rep. 132; [1996] C.L.C. 1410, CA; affirming in part [1995] 2 Lloyd's Rep. 592, QBD (Comm Ct) . . . . *Digested*, 98/**861**
Stocznia Gdanska SA *v.* Latvian Shipping Co (Abuse of Process) see Stocznia Gdanska SA *v.* Latreefers Inc
Stocznia Gdanska SA *v.* Latvian Shipping Co (Abuse of Process) [1999] 3 All E.R. 822; [1999] C.L.C. 1451, QBD (Comm Ct) . . . . *Digested*, 99/**347**:
Subsequent proceedings, 00/3472
Stocznia Gdanska SA *v.* Latvian Shipping Co (Costs), *Times*, May 25, 2001, QBD . . . . . *Digested*, 01/**466**
Stocznia Gdanska SA *v.* Latvian Shipping Co (Leave to Amend Pleadings: Repudiatory Breach) [2001] 1 Lloyd's Rep. 537; [2001] C.L.C. 1290, QBD (Comm Ct) . . . . . *Digested*, 01/**944**
Stoddard International Plc *v.* William Lomas Carpets Ltd [2001] F.S.R. 44; (2001) 24(4) I.P.D. 24023; (2001) 98(14) L.S.G. 41; *Times*, February 14, 2001, Ch D . . *Digested*, 01/**3852**
Stoeckert *v.* Geddes (2000) 80 P. & C.R. D11, PC (Jam)
Stoffman *v.* Vancouver General Hospital [1990] 3 S.C.R. 483, Sup Ct (Can) . . . . *Distinguished*, 98/3074
Stoke on Trent CC *v.* Smith (Ada) [1998] C.O.D. 473, QBD
Stoke on Trent City Council *v.* B&Q (Retail) Ltd; Wolverhampton BC *v.* B&Q (Retail) Ltd; Barking and Dagenham LBC *v.* Home Charm Retail [1984] A.C. 754; [1984] 2 W.L.R. 929; [1984] 2 All E.R. 332; 82 L.G.R. 473; 128 S.J. 364; (1985) 4 Tr. L. 9, HL; affirming [1984] Ch. 1; [1983] 3 W.L.R. 78; [1983] 2 All E.R. 787; 82 L.G.R. 10; (1983) 2 Tr. L.R. 66; 127 S.J. 426, CA . . . . *Digested*, 84/**3231**:
Applied, 85/2042, 85/3431, 86/3390.c, 89/2990, 90/3704, 90/4127, 92/2904, 97/3862: *Considered*, 85/3406, 86/3390.d, 91/3463, 01/4400
Stoker *v.* Rose; *sub nom* Krzysztofowicz (Deceased), Re [2001] W.T.L.R. 883, Fam Div . . . . *Digested*, 01/**5149**
Stokes *v.* Guest Keen & Nettlefold (Bolt & Nuts) Ltd [1968] 1 W.L.R. 1776; 5 K.I.R. 401; 112 S.J. 821, Assizes . . . . *Digested*, 68/**2701**:
Applied, 99/2554: *Considered*, 84/2311, 85/2312
Stokes *v.* Peaty [2001] 6 Q.R. 21, CC (Chester) [*Ex rel.* Lees & Partners, Solicitors, St. John's Court, Vicars Lane, Chester] . . . . *Digested*, 01/**1772**
Stokke Fabrikker *v.* Playmaster of Sweden AB Ltd [1998] E.T.M.R. 395, TR (Ljungby)
Stolt Offshore Ltd *v.* Miklaszewicz see Miklaszewicz *v.* Stolt Offshore Ltd
Stone *v.* Bolton see Bolton *v.* Stone
Stone *v.* Chataway see Yorke (Deceased), Re
Stone *v.* Commissioner of Police of the Metropolis (Unreported, September 16, 1999), CC (Milton Keynes) [*Ex rel.* Giles Harrap, Barrister, 3 Pump Court, Temple, London] . . . . *Digested*, 00/**1589**
Stone (Inspector of Taxes) *v.* Hitch see Hitch *v.* Stone (Inspector of Taxes)
Stone Gemini, The *v.* [1999] 2 Lloyd's Rep. 255, Fed Ct (Aus) (Sgl judge) . . . . *Digested*, 99/**4417**

Stoneman (CICA: Quantum: 2001), Re [2001] 6 Q.R.17, CICA (London) [*Ex rel*. Rebecca Tuck, Barrister, Old Square Chambers, 1 Verulam Buildings, Gray's Inn, London] .   *Digested*, 01/**1708**

Stonor (Executor of Dickinson's Estate) *v.* Inland Revenue Commissioners [2001] S.T.C. (S.C.D.) 199; [2001] S.T.I. 1501, Sp Comm

Stora Kopparbergs Bergslags AB *v.* Commission of the European Communities (C286/98 P); *sub nom* Stora Kopparbergs Bergslags AB *v.* Commission of the European Communities (T354/94) [2000] E.C.R. I-9925; [2001] 4 C.M.L.R.12, ECJ (5th Chamber) [1998] E.C.R. II-2111; [2000] E.C.R. I-9925, AGO; reversing in part

Stora Kopparbergs Bergslags AB *v.* Commission of the European Communities (T354/94) see Stora Kopparbergs Bergslags AB *v.* Commission of the European Communities (C286/98 P)

Storage Computer Corp *v.* Hitachi Data Systems Ltd (2001) 24(10) I.P.D. 24066, Pat Ct

Storage Computer Corporation *v.* Hitachi Data Systems Ltd (Application to Strike Out) (2001) 24(10) I.P.D. 24065, Pat Ct

Storebrand Skadeforsikring AS *v.* Finanger (E1/99) [1999] 3 C.M.L.R. 863; [2000] Lloyd's Rep. I.R. 462, EFTA . . . .   *Digested*, 00/**3547**

Storehouse Properties Ltd *v.* Ocobase Ltd, *Times*, April 3, 1998, Ch D . . . .   *Digested*, 98/**3602**

Storer *v.* British Gas Plc [2000] 1 W.L.R. 1237; [2000] 2 All E.R. 440; [2000] I.C.R. 603; [2000] I.R.L.R. 495; *Times*, March 1, 2000; *Independent*, March 8, 2000, CA . . . .   *Digested*, 00/**2145**: *Considered*, 00/40

Storey *v.* Charles Church Developments Ltd; *sub nom* Storey *v.* Charles Church Developments Plc 73 Con. L.R.1; (1996) 12 Const. L.J. 206, QBD (OR) . . . . . .   *Digested*, 96/**1156**

Storey *v.* Charles Church Developments Plc see Storey *v.* Charles Church Developments Ltd

Storey *v.* Dorset Community NHS Trust (Unreported, October 18, 1999), CC (Plymouth) [*Ex rel*. Robert Weir, Barrister, Devereux Chambers, Devereux Court, London] . . . . . .   *Digested*, 00/**304**

Storey *v.* Phillips [2001] 5 Q.R. 9, CC (Croydon) [*Ex rel*. John Denniss, Barrister, 4, King's Bench Walk, Temple] . . . .   *Digested*, 01/**1565**

Storey *v.* Phillips (Costs) (Unreported, February 21, 2001), CC (Croydon) [*Ex rel*. John Denniss, Barrister, 4 King's Bench Walk, Temple, London] . . . . . .   *Digested*, 01/**504**

Storey *v.* Rae (Unreported, February 13, 1998), QBD [*Ex rel*. Frank Burton, Barrister, 12 King's Bench Walk, Temple, London] . . . .   *Digested*, 98/**1692**

Storfer *v.* Yogaratnam (1998) 98(6) Q.R. 6, CC (Reading) . . . .   *Digested*, 98/**1601**

Stork *v.* Binions see Seddon *v.* Binions

Stork Amsterdam BV *v.* Commission of the European Communities (T241/97) [2000] E.C.R. II-309; [2000] 5 C.M.L.R. 31; [2000] C.E.C. 573, CFI . . . .   *Digested*, 00/**2365**

STORK FRIESLAND/Evaporating plant (T138/85) [1998] E.P.O.R.177, EPO (Technical Bd App)

Storry *v.* Gallagher [2001] 6 Q.R. 21, CC (Leeds) [*Ex rel*. Tom Nossiter, Barrister, Park Lane Chambers, 19 Westgate, Leeds] . . . .   *Digested*, 01/**1778**

Stott (Procurator Fiscal) *v.* Brown see Brown *v.* Stott

Stott *v.* Skipton Building Society see Skipton Building Society *v.* Bratley

Stoves Ltd *v.* Baumatic Ltd (2000) 23(10) I.P.D. 23086, Pat Ct

Stovin *v.* Wise and Norfolk CC [1996] A.C. 923; [1996] 3 W.L.R. 388; [1996] 3 All E.R. 801; [1996] R.T.R. 354; (1996) 93(35) L.S.G. 33; (1996) 146 N.L.J. 1185; (1996) 140 S.J.L.B. 201; *Times*, July 26, 1996; *Independent*, July 31, 1996, HL; reversing [1994] 1 W.L.R. 1124; [1994] 3 All E.R. 467; [1994] R.T.R. 225; 92 L.G.R. 577; 159 J.P.N. 722; (1994) 91(14) L.S.G. 48; 138 S.J.L.B. 60; *Times*, March 8, 1994, CA . . . .   *Digested*, 96/**4058**: *Applied*, 97/3778, 01/4483, 01/4499: *Considered*, 97/4087: *Distinguished*, 00/4232, 01/4495: *Followed*, 99/2889

Strachan & Henshaw Ltd *v.* Stein Industrie (UK) Ltd (No.1) 63 Con. L.R.132; (1997) 13 Const. L.J. 418, QBD (OR) . . . .   *Digested*, 98/**233**

Strachan & Henshaw Ltd *v.* Stein Industrie (UK) Ltd (No.2) 87 B.L.R. 52; 63 Con. L.R. 160; (1998) 14 Const. L.J. 370, CA . . . .   *Digested*, 98/**806**

Straddlers Groups A and C *v.* Secretary of State for Health; *sub nom* Creutzfeldt-Jakob Disease Litigation (No.8), Re; CJD Litigation (No.8), Re (2000) 54 B.M.L.R. 104, QBD . . . .   *Digested*, 00/**4192**

Strainge *v.* Ho (Unreported, January 16, 1998), MCLC [*Ex rel*. Anthony Snelson, Barrister, Thomas More Chambers, 51-52 Carey Street, Lincoln's Inn, London] . .   *Digested*, 98/**1583**

Stran Greek Refineries *v.* Greece (A/301-B) (1995) 19 E.H.R.R. 293, ECHR . . . .   *Digested*, 95/**2620**: *Followed*, 01/3544

Stratford *v.* BREL see Stratford *v.* British Rail Engineering Ltd

Stratford *v.* British Rail Engineering Ltd; *sub nom* Stratford *v.* BREL; (Unreported, October 11, 1990), HC [*Ex rel*. Townsends, Solicitors] . . . .   *Digested*, 91/**1498**: *Considered*, 98/1762

Stratford *v.* Syrett [1958] 1 Q.B. 107; [1957] 3 W.L.R. 733; [1957] 3 All E.R. 363; 101 S.J. 850, CA; reversing [1957] J.P.L. 508. . . . .   *Digested*, 57/**3060**: *Considered*, 98/2988

Stratford upon Avon DC *v.* Certes Group Plc (2000) 15 P.A.D. 499, Planning Inspector

Stratford upon Avon DC v. Mercury Personal Communications (1998) 13 P.A.D. 522,
    Planning Inspector
Strathclyde RC v. Wallace; *sub nom* West Dunbartonshire Council v. Wallace [1998] 1
    W.L.R. 259; [1998] 1 All E.R. 394; 1998 S.C. (H.L.) 72; 1998 S.L.T. 421; 1998
    S.C.L.R. 340; [1998] I.C.R. 205; [1998] I.R.L.R. 146; (1998) 95(7) L.S.G. 31;
    (1998) 142 S.J.L.B. 83; 1998 G.W.D. 4-181; *Times*, January 24, 1998, HL;
    affirming 1996 S.C. 535; 1997 S.L.T. 315; 1996 S.C.L.R. 1046; [1996] I.R.L.R.
    670, 2 Div . . . . *Digested*, 98/**5807**:
                                                                    Applied, 00/**6214**
Strathclyde RC v. Zafar see Glasgow City Council v. Zafar
Strathford East Kilbride Ltd v. HLM Design Ltd 1999 S.L.T. 121; 1997 S.C.L.R. 877; 1997
    Rep. L.R. 112; 1997 G.W.D. 31-1554; *Times*, December 1, 1997, OH . . . .   *Digested*, 98/**5539**
Strathmore Building Services Ltd v. Greig (t/a Hestia Fireside Design) 2000 S.L.T. 815;
    (2001) 17 Const. L.J. 72; 2000 G.W.D. 19-735, OH . . . .   *Digested*, 01/**6293**
Stratton v. Browett (Unreported, September 2, 1999), CC (Coventry) [*Ex rel.* Paul
    Stokes, Barrister, Gough Square Chambers, 6-7 Gough Square, London] . . . . . .   *Digested*, 99/**2489**
Stratton v. Inland Revenue Commissioners see Stratton's Disclaimer, Re
Stratton's Disclaimer, Re; *sub nom* Stratton v. Inland Revenue Commissioners; Stratton's
    Executors v. Inland Revenue Commissioners [1958] Ch. 42; [1957] 3 W.L.R.
    199; [1957] 2 All E.R. 594; (1957) 36 A.T.C. 145; [1957] T.R. 161; 101 S.J. 533,
    CA; affirming [1957] Ch. 132; [1956] 3 W.L.R. 1054; [1956] 3 All E.R. 862; 49
    R. & I.T. 814; (1956) 35 A.T.C. 363; [1956] T.R. 407; 100 S.J. 928, Ch D . . . . . .   *Digested*, 57/**981**:
                                                            Considered, 69/2775, 01/5153
Stratton's Executors v. Inland Revenue Commissioners see Stratton's Disclaimer, Re
Straudley Investments Ltd v. Mount Eden Land Ltd (No.1); *sub nom* Mount Eden Land
    Ltd v. Straudley Investments Ltd (1997) 74 P. & C.R. 306; [1996] E.G.C.S. 153;
    [1996] N.P.C. 138, CA . . . .   *Digested*, 98/**3647**
Stray v. Stray [1999] 2 F.L.R. 610; [1999] Fam. Law 616, Fam Div . . . .   *Digested*, 99/**2428**
Street v. Mountford [1985] A.C. 809; [1985] 2 W.L.R. 877; [1985] 2 All E.R. 289;
    (1985) 17 H.L.R. 402; (1985) 50 P. & C.R. 258; [1985] 1 E.G.L.R. 128; (1985)
    274 E.G. 821; (1985) 82 L.S.G. 2087; (1985) 135 N.L.J. 460; (1985) 129 S.J.
    348, HL; reversing (1984) 16 H.L.R. 27; (1985) 49 P. & C.R. 324; (1984) 271
    E.G. 1153; (1984) 271 E.G. 1261; (1984) 81 L.S.G. 1844; (1984) 128 S.J. 483,
    CA . . . .   *Digested*, 85/**1893**:
                    Applied, 85/1871, 86/1931, 87/2163, 88/2042, 89/2146, 92/2290, 93/2073,
                            93/2538, 95/1979, 01/4146, 01/4157: *Cited*, 00/311: *Considered*, 86/1896,
                            86/2306, 87/2162, 87/2244, 87/2247, 87/2252, 88/66, 88/2043, 88/2047,
                            88/2061, 89/2100, 89/2148, 89/2150, 90/2809, 90/2811, 90/2813, 90/2815,
                            91/545, 91/2243, 91/2262, 92/100, 93/426, 95/3045, 96/3764, 96/3765,
                            97/3305, 99/3699: *Distinguished*, 88/2026, 89/2112, 89/2145, 92/2752,
                            98/3599: *Followed*, 86/1873, 86/1881, 99/3698, 00/2584:
                                                            Referred to, 86/1874, 87/2159, 87/2176
Streeting v. Hogg Robinson Plc [2001] 5 Q.R. 14, CC (Norwich) [*Ex rel.* Prettys,
    Solicitors, 25, Elm Street, Ipswich, Suffolk] . . . .   *Digested*, 01/**1591**
Streletz v. Germany (34044/96) (2001) 33 E.H.R.R. 31, ECHR
Stretch v. West Dorset DC (No.1) (2000) 2 L.G.L.R. 140; (1998) 10 Admin. L.R. 129;
    (1999) 77 P. & C.R. 342; [1998] 3 E.G.L.R. 62; [1998] 48 E.G. 183; (1998) 162
    J.P.N. 202; (1997) 94(46) L.S.G. 30; (1998) 75 P. & C.R. D26; *Times*,
    November 27, 1997, CA; affirming [1996] N.P.C. 66, Ch D . . . .   *Digested*, 98/**3769**
Stretch v. West Dorset DC (No.2) (2000) 2 L.G.L.R. 153; (1999) 96(21) L.S.G. 37;
    Times, May 20, 1999, CA . . . .   *Digested*, 99/**3758**
Stretton v. Stubbs, *Times*, February 28, 1905, CA . . . .   *Distinguished*, 00/337:
                                                            Not followed, 88/2956, 89/1701
Strick (Inspector of Taxes) v. Regent Oil Co Ltd see Regent Oil Co Ltd v. Strick
    (Inspector of Taxes)
Stringer v. Kordan (Unreported, August 31, 2000), CC (Birmingham) [*Ex rel.* Andrew
    Leach, Lee Crowder, Solicitors, 39 Newhall Street, Birmingham] . . . .   *Digested*, 00/**446**:
                                                                    Cited, 01/518
Stringman v. McArdle [1994] 1 W.L.R. 1653; [1994] P.I.Q.R. P230; [1994] J.P.I.L. 69;
    Times, November 19, 1993; *Independent*, December 6, 1993 (C.S.), CA . . . .   *Digested*, 94/**1482**:
                            Applied, 00/1459: *Considered*, 97/1759, 98/1437
Strix Ltd v. Otter Controls Ltd [1991] F.S.R. 354; *Independent*, February 27, 1991, CA;
    reversing [1991] F.S.R. 163, Pat Ct . . . .   *Digested*, 92/**3290**:
                            Followed, 95/3758, 98/3416, 00/3675: *Referred to*, 93/3038, 99/3497
Strobel v. Finanzamt Esslingen (C454/98) see Schmeink & Cofreth AG & Co KG v.
    Finanzamt Borken (C454/98)
Stroud v. Weir Associates (1987) 19 H.L.R. 151; [1987] 1 E.G.L.R. 191; (1987) 281 E.G.
    1198, CA . . . .   *Digested*, 87/**1893**:
                                                                    Followed, 00/893
Stroud Building Society v. Delamont [1960] 1 W.L.R. 431; [1960] 1 All E.R. 749; 104
    S.J. 329, Ch D . . . .   *Digested*, 60/**2028**:
                                                                    Applied, 71/7465, 00/3903
Stroud DC v. Davies (2001) 16 P.A.D. 14, Planning Inspector
Stroud DC v. Dickinson (2001) 16 P.A.D. 66, Planning Inspector

Stroud DC v. Management Services Ltd (1998) 13 P.A.D. 143, Planning Inspector

Strowbridge v. Customs and Excise Commissioners [2000] B.V.C. 2248; [2000] S.T.I. 900, V&DTr

Structadene v. Hackney LBC see R. (on the application of Structadene Ltd) v. Hackney LBC

Structural Concrete Ltd, Re; *sub nom* Official Receiver v. Barnes (2000) 97(26) L.S.G. 35; *Times*, July 5, 2000, Ch D .... *Digested*, 00/**664**

Structural Polymer Systems Ltd v. Brown (The Baltic Universal) [1999] C.L.C. 268; [2000] Lloyd's Rep. I.R. 64, QBD (Comm Ct)...................... *Digested*, 99/**3421**

Structures & Computers Ltd, Re; *sub nom* Structures & Computers Ltd v. Ansys Inc [1998] B.C.C. 348; [1998] 1 B.C.L.C. 292; *Times*, October 3, 1997, Ch D (Companies Ct) .... *Digested*, 97/**2997**

Structures & Computers Ltd v. Ansys Inc see Structures & Computers Ltd, Re

Struggles v. Lloyds TSB Plc [2000] E.G.C.S. 17; (2000) 97(6) L.S.G. 37, QBD (T&CC)

Stuag Bauaktiengesellschaft v. Karntner Landesregierung (C390/97) see Pelzl v. Steiermarkische Landesregierung (C338/97)

Stuart v. Ministry of Defence see Ministry of Defence v. Wheeler

Stuart-Hutcheson v. Spread Trustee Co Ltd; *sub nom* Peter Acatos No. 2 Settlement, Re (2000-01) 3 I.T.E.L.R. 683, Royal Ct (Gue)

Stubbings v. United Kingdom (22083/93 and 22095/93) [1997] 1 F.L.R. 105; [1997] 3 F.C.R. 157; (1997) 23 E.H.R.R. 213; 1 B.H.R.C. 316; [1997] Fam. Law 241; *Times*, October 24, 1996; *Independent*, October 24, 1996, ECHR .... *Digested*, 96/**3156**: *Applied*, 01/**1897**

Stubblefield v. Kemp [2001] 1 Costs L.R. 30, Ch D .... *Digested*, 01/**527**

Stumbles v. Sutton Unreported, CC (Truro) .... *Followed*, 99/2496

Stump v. Otuagomah (Unreported, March 10, 2000), CC (Lambeth) [*Ex rel.* Tim Petts, Barrister, 12 King's Bench Walk, London] .... *Digested*, 00/**2588**

Sturesson v. Sweden see Hakansson v. Sweden (A/171)

Sturge v. Bridgman see Sturges v. Bridgman

Sturges v. Bridgman; *sub nom* Sturge v. Bridgman (1879) L.R. 11 Ch. D. 852; (1879) 43 J.P. 716; (1879) 48 L.J. Ch. 785; (1879) 41 L.T. 219, CA .... *Applied*, 52/1123, 52/1124, 90/1731, 91/1508: *Considered*, 77/2146, 00/4641

Sturley v. Carmarthen Town Council (Unreported, February 5, 1998), CC (Swansea) [*Ex rel.* Leo Abse & Cohen Solicitors, 40 Churchill Way, Cardiff]............. *Digested*, 98/**1685**

Stuttard (t/a De Wynns Coffee House) v. Customs and Excise Commissioners [2000] S.T.C. 342; [2000] B.T.C. 5129; [2000] B.V.C. 159; [2000] S.T.I. 504; *Independent*, May 8, 2000 (C.S.), QBD .... *Digested*, 00/**5370**

Styranowski v. Poland [1998] H.R.C.D. 1001, ECHR..................... *Referred to*, 01/3517

Subhan v. Customs and Excise Commissioners [2001] S.T.I. 986, V&DTr

SUBIC/Anti-erosion system (T394/96) [1998] E.P.O.R. 190, EPO (Technical Bd App)

Succes de Paris Sarl v. Parfums Van Cleef et Arpels SA [1999] E.T.M.R. 869, C d'A (Paris)

Suckler Cows (C8/88), Re see Germany v. Commission of the European Communities (C8/88)

Sudbrook Trading Estate Ltd v. Eggleton [1983] 1 A.C. 444; [1982] 3 W.L.R. 315; [1982] 3 All E.R. 1; (1982) 44 P. & C.R. 153; (1983) 265 E.G. 215; (1982) 79 L.S.G. 1175; 126 S.J. 512, HL; reversing [1981] 3 W.L.R. 361; [1981] 3 All E.R. 105; (1981) 260 E.G. 1033; 125 S.J. 513, CA................. *Digested*, 82/**1776**: *Applied*, 83/2100, 84/3673, 88/2089, 95/3059, 96/3805, 97/3320, 01/5164: *Considered*, 01/956: *Distinguished*, 83/2671, 97/1145, 00/901

Sudwestdeutsche Landesbank Girozentrale v. Bank of Tokyo Ltd see Standard Bank London Ltd v. Bank of Tokyo Ltd

Suffolk CC v. C [1999] 1 F.L.R. 259; [1999] 1 F.C.R. 473 (Note); [1999] Fam. Law 13, Fam Div .... *Digested*, 99/**2355**

Suffolk CC v. Mason [1979] A.C. 705; [1979] 2 W.L.R. 571; [1979] 2 All E.R. 369; 77 L.G.R. 621; (1980) 39 P. & C.R. 20; [1979] J.P.L. 529; 123 S.J. 285, HL; affirming [1978] 1 W.L.R. 716; [1978] 2 All E.R. 618; 76 L.G.R. 569; (1979) 37 P. & C.R. 21; [1978] J.P.L. 372; 122 S.J. 349, CA; reversing [1977] J.P.L. 442; 121 S.J. 375 .... *Digested*, 79/**1362**: *Applied*, 79/1364, 00/4641

Sugar v. Venables [1998] E.M.L.R. 180, CA .... *Digested*, 98/**442**

Sugden v. Kent (Inspector of Taxes) [2001] S.T.C. (S.C.D.) 158; [2001] S.T.I. 1143, Sp Comm

Suisse Atlantique Societe d'Armement SA v. NV Rotterdamsche Kolen Centrale [1967] 1 A.C. 361; [1966] 2 W.L.R. 944; [1966] 2 All E.R. 61; [1966] 1 Lloyd's Rep. 529; 110 S.J. 367, HL; affirming [1965] 1 Lloyd's Rep. 533, CA; affirming [1965] 1 Lloyd's Rep. 166, QBD (Comm Ct)........................ *Digested*, 66/**1797**: *Applied*, 70/365, 71/1752, 74/441, 74/3529, 78/308, 78/314, 83/283, 83/3349: *Considered*, 69/490, 69/509, 70/362, 72/482, 77/378, 79/2434, 82/403, 00/899, 00/4738: *Explained*, 80/353: *Followed*, 77/377

Sulaiman v. Juffali, *Times*, November 28, 2001, Fam Div .... *Digested*, 01/**2613**

Sullivan v. Blanning [2000] C.P. Rep. 15; *Times*, October 27, 1999, CA .... *Digested*, 99/**553**

Sullivan v. Cooperative Insurance Society Ltd [1999] C.P.L.R. 487; [1999] 2 Costs L.R. 158; *Times*, May 19, 1999; *Independent*, May 18, 1999, CA .... *Digested*, 99/**414**

Sullivan *v.* Earl of Caithness [1976] Q.B. 966; [1976] 2 W.L.R. 361; [1976] 1 All E.R. 844; (1976) 62 Cr. App. R. 105; [1976] Crim. L.R. 130; (1975) 120 S.J. 8, DC. . . .   *Digested,* 76/**1252**:
Applied, 86/**1545**, 01/**1044**
Sullivan *v.* HWF Ltd (Unreported, May 23, 2001), CC (Bradford) [*Ex rel.* Sean D Yates, Barrister, 10 Park Square, Leeds] . . . .   *Digested,* 01/**3301**
Sullivan *v.* Massin-Smart (Unreported, October 7, 1997), CC (Sheffield) [*Ex rel.* James Chapman & Co, Solicitors, Canada House, Chepstow Street, Manchester] . . . .   *Digested,* 98/**1739**
Sullivan *v.* Paul (Unreported, January 27, 1998), CC (Rawtenstall) [*Ex rel.* Rollingsons Solicitors, 36 King Street, Covent Garden, London] . . . .   *Digested,* 98/**2506**
Sullivan *v.* Samuel Montagu & Co Ltd [1999] B.P.I.R. 316, Ch D . . . .   *Digested,* 99/**3324**
Sullivan *v.* West Yorkshire Passenger Transport Executive [1985] 2 All E.R. 134, CA . . . .   *Digested,* 85/**1506**:
Applied, 97/**477**, 99/**308**: *Cited,* 96/**4498**: *Distinguished,* 96/**655**
Sullivan's Application, Re [1998] N.I. 11, QBD (NI) . . . .   *Digested,* 99/**5207**
Sumitomo Corp *v.* Credit Lyonnais Rouse Ltd [2001] EWCA Civ 1152; [2001] 2 Lloyd's Rep. 517; [2001] C.P.L.R. 462; (2001) 98(34) L.S.G. 41; (2001) 145 S.J.L.B. 208; *Times,* August 15, 2001; *Independent,* October 18, 2001, CA; affirming [2001] C.P. Rep. 72; (2001) 151 N.L.J. 272, QBD (Comm Ct) . . . .   *Digested,* 01/**553**
SUMITOMO/Growth of Tulips (T430/92) [1999] E.P.O.R. 341, EPO (Technical Bd App)   *Digested,* 99/**3482**
SUMITOMO/H-shaped steels (T366/98) [2000] E.P.O.R. 512, EPO (Technical Bd App)   *Digested,* 01/**3942**
SUMITOMO/Oxygen-enriched gas (T440/92) [1998] E.P.O.R. 240, EPO (Technical Bd App)
SUMITOMO/Superconductive film (T348/94) [2001] E.P.O.R. 20, EPO (Technical Bd App) . . . .   *Digested,* 01/**3899**
Summerfield *v.* MR Goostry (A Firm) (Unreported, February 16, 2000), CC (Manchester) [*Ex rel.* Betesh Fox & Co Solicitors, 16-17 Ralli Courts, West Riverside, Manchester] . . . .   *Digested,* 00/**1663**
Summers *v.* Naylor Automatic Ltd (Unreported, February 11, 1998), CC (Nottingham) [*Ex rel.* Hopkins Hodgson Fox Solicitors, 27 Regent Street, Nottingham] . . . . . .   *Digested,* 98/**467**
Summit Financial Group Ltd *v.* Slaughter & May (A Firm), *Times,* April 2, 1999, Ch D . . .   *Digested,* 99/**4028**
Summit Property Ltd *v.* Pitmans [2001] Lloyd's Rep. P.N. 164; [2000] N.P.C. 97, Ch D .   *Digested,* 01/**4265**
Sumner *v.* Davies see Davies *v.* Sumner
Sun Alliance & London Assurance Co Ltd *v.* Pensions Ombudsman [2001] O.P.L.R. 63, Ch D
Sun Fire Office *v.* Hart (1889) L.R. 14 App. Cas. 98, PC (Wind) . . . .   *Considered,* 01/**3808**
Sun Kwong Metal Manufacturer Co Ltd *v.* Council of the European Union (T147/97) see Champion Stationery Mfg Co Ltd *v.* Council of the European Union (T147/97)
Sun Life Assurance Co of Canada *v.* Sunlife Juice Ltd (1989) 22 C.P.R. (3d) 244, HC (Ont) . . . .   *Considered,* 99/**3524**
Sun Life Assurance Plc *v.* Thales Tracs Ltd (formerly Racal Tracs Ltd) [2001] EWCA Civ 704; [2001] 1 W.L.R. 1562; [2001] L. & T.R. 39; [2001] 34 E.G. 100; [2001] 20 E.G.C.S. 230; (2001) 98(21) L.S.G. 41; (2001) 82 P. & C.R. D16; *Times,* June 25, 2001; *Independent,* July 2, 2001 (C.S), CA; reversing [2000] 1 E.G.L.R. 138; [1999] N.P.C. 154; (2000) 80 P. & C.R. D7, QBD . . . .   *Digested,* 01/**4158**
Sun Life Assurance Society Plc *v.* Tantofex (Engineers) Ltd [1999] L. & T.R. 568; [1999] 2 E.G.L.R. 135; [1999] E.G.C.S. 50, Ch D . . . .   *Digested,* 00/**3884**
Sun Microsystems Inc's Trade Mark Application [2001] R.P.C. 25, TMR . . . .   *Digested,* 01/**4043**
Sun Valley Foods Ltd *v.* Fusion Foods International Ltd see Sun Valley Foods Ltd *v.* Vincent
Sun Valley Foods Ltd *v.* Vincent; Sun Valley Foods Ltd *v.* Fusion Foods International Ltd [2000] F.S.R. 825, Ch D . . . .   *Digested,* 00/**734**
Sunday Sales of Flowers at Petrol Stations, Re [1998] E.C.C. 30, BGH (Ger)
Sunday Times *v.* United Kingdom (No.1) (A/30) (1979-80) 2 E.H.R.R. 245; (1979) 76 L.S.G. 328, ECHR . . . .   *Digested,* 80/**1385**:
Applied, 98/**3090**, 01/**3472**
Sundelta Ltd *v.* Packamist Ltd [1998] N.P.C. 1, QBD (OR)
Sunderland Association Football Club *v.* Uruguay Montevideo FC [2001] 2 All E.R. (Comm) 828, QBD . . . .   *Digested,* 01/**963**
Sunderland City Council *v.* P and C [1996] E.L.R. 283, QBD . . . .   *Digested,* 96/**2496**:
Distinguished, 00/**1954**
Sung (t/a Chinese Village) *v.* Customs and Excise Commissioners [2001] S.T.I. 1229, V&DTr
Sunrider Corp *v.* Office for Harmonisation in the Internal Market (Trade Marks and Designs) (OHIM) (T24/00) [2001] E.C.R. II-449; [2001] E.T.M.R. 56, CFI (2nd Chamber) . . . .   *Digested,* 01/**4005**
Sunrise Maritime Inc *v.* Uvisco Ltd (The Hector) [1998] 2 Lloyd's Rep. 287; [1998] C.L.C. 902, QBD (Comm Ct) . . . .   *Digested,* 98/**4397**:
Applied, 00/**4688**: *Considered,* 01/**4907**
Sunshine Porcelain Potteries Pty *v.* Nash [1961] A.C. 927; [1961] 3 W.L.R. 727; [1961] 3 All E.R. 203; 105 S.J. 646, PC (Aus) . . . .   *Digested,* 61/**9283**:
Followed, 00/**105**
Sunworld Ltd *v.* Hammersmith and Fulham LBC; R. *v.* Blackfriars Crown Court Ex p. Sunworld Ltd [2000] 1 W.L.R. 2102; [2000] 2 All E.R. 837; [2000] Crim. L.R. 593, QBD
Supperstone *v.* Auger [1999] B.P.I.R. 152, Ch D . . . .   *Digested,* 99/**3332**

Supperstone v. Greystoke see Greystoke (A Bankrupt), Re
Supperstone v. Lloyd's Names Association Working Party [1999] B.P.I.R. 832, Ch D . . — *Digested*, 99/**3237**
Supply of Photocopies of Newspaper Articles by Public Library, Re [2000] E.C.C. 237, BGH
  (Ger)
Supply of Ready Mixed Concrete (No.2), Re see Director General of Fair Trading v. Pioneer
  Concrete (UK) Ltd
Supra Medical Corp v. McGonigle [1998] I.L.Pr. 450, US Ct
Sur v. Turkey (1998) 25 E.H.R.R. CD 1, ECHR
Surdivall v. K Walker Transport (Unreported, July 17, 1998), CC (Burnley) [*Ex rel.* Barrie
  Searle, Barrister, 68 Quay Street, Manchester] . . . . — *Digested*, 98/**1597**
Surdonja v. Ealing LBC see Mohamed v. Hammersmith and Fulham LBC
Surek v. Turkey 7 B.H.R.C. 339, ECHR . . . . — *Digested*, 00/**3193**
Suriya & Douglas v. Midland Bank Plc [1999] 1 All E.R. (Comm.) 612; [1999] Lloyd's
  Rep. Bank. 103; (1999) 96(12) L.S.G. 33; *Times*, March 29, 1999, CA . . . . — *Digested*, 99/**268**
Surma News Group Ltd v. Customs and Excise Commissioners [2001] S.T.I. 1121, V&DTr
Surrey v. Manchester Health Commission (Unreported, September 10, 1997), CC
  (Manchester) [*Ex rel.* Julie Wood, Solicitor, Thompsons, Acresfield, 8 Exchange
  Street, Manchester] . . . . — *Digested*, 98/**1619**
Surrey Asset Finance Ltd v. National Westminster Bank, *Times*, November 30, 2000,
  QBD . . . . — *Digested*, 01/**377**
Surrey Breakdown Ltd v. Knight [1999] R.T.R. 84, CA . . . . — *Digested*, 98/**4834**:
                                                   Considered, 00/113
Surrey CC v. Burton Retail Ltd; *sub nom* Denard v. Burton Retail Ltd (1998) 162 J.P.
  545; (1998) 162 J.P.N. 566; *Times*, November 19, 1997, QBD . . . . — *Digested*, 97/**973**
Surrey CC v. Lamond (1999) 31 H.L.R. 1051; [1999] L. & T.R. 213; [1999] 1 E.G.L.R.
  32; [1999] 12 E.G. 170; [1998] E.G.C.S. 185; [1999] N.P.C. 1; (1999) 78 P. &
  C.R. D3; *Independent*, January 25, 1999 (C.S.), CA. . . . . — *Digested*, 99/**3736**
Surrey CC v. M (A Child); *sub nom* W v. Surrey CC [2001] EWCA Civ 691;
  Independent, June 11, 2001 (C.S), CA
Surrey CC v. P [1997] E.L.R. 516; [1997] C.O.D. 118, QBD . . . . — *Digested*, 98/**1969**
Surrey CC v. Shepperton Aggregates (1999) 14 P.A.D. 613, Planning Inspector
Surrey CC v. Verrechia [1998] J.P.L. 219, CA . . . . — *Digested*, 98/**4166**:
                              Subsequent proceedings, 99/4207
Surrey Counties (Sutton) Ltd see Waverley BC v. Kingston Estates Ltd
Surrey Free Inns Plc v. Gosport BC see SFI Group Plc (formerly Surrey Free Inns Plc) v.
  Gosport BC
Surrey Heath BC v. Grace (1998) 13 P.A.D. 363, Planning Inspector
Surrey Heath BC v. Lovell Construction Ltd 48 B.L.R. 108; 24 Con. L.R. 1; (1990) 6
  Const. L.J. 179, CA; affirming (1988) 42 B.L.R. 25; 15 Con. L.R. 68; (1988) 4
  Const. L.J. 226, QBD . . . . — *Digested*, 90/**411**:
                              Distinguished, 00/458
Surrey Heath BC v. Westcroft Park Polo & Riding Club (2001) 16 P.A.D. 103, Planning
  Inspector
Surrey Homes Ltd v. Secretary of State for the Environment, Transport and the Regions
  [2001] J.P.L. 379 (Note), QBD
Surrey Leisure Ltd, Re; *sub nom* Official Receiver v. Keam [1999] B.C.C. 847; [1999] 2
  B.C.L.C. 457; (1999) 96(32) L.S.G. 31; (1999) 143 S.J.L.B. 221; *Times*, July
  28, 1999 ; *Independent*, October 25, 1999 (C.S.), CA; affirming [1999] 1 B.C.L.C
  731; (1999) 96(6) L.S.G. 33; *Times*, January 25, 1999; *Independent*, February
  1, 1999 (C.S.), Ch D . . . . — *Digested*, 99/**618**
Surrey Police Authority v. Beckett [2001] EWCA Civ 1253; [2001] Emp. L.R. 1157;
  (2001) 151 N.L.J. 1408; *Times*, August 8, 2001, CA; affirming *Times*, July 5,
  2001, QBD . . . . — *Digested*, 01/**4777**
Surul v. Bundesanstalt fur Arbeit (C262/96) [1999] E.C.R. I-2685; [2001] 1 C.M.L.R.
  4, ECJ . . . . — *Digested*, 01/**4961**
Surzur Overseas Ltd v. Koros [1999] 2 Lloyd's Rep. 611; [1999] C.L.C. 801, CA . . . . . . — *Digested*, 99/**528**
Susikanth v. Secretary of State for the Home Department; *sub nom* R. v. Secretary of
  State for the Home Department Ex p. Susikanth; R. v. Immigration Appeal
  Tribunal Ex p. Susikanth [1998] Imm. A.R. 96; [1998] I.N.L.R. 185, CA . . . . . . — *Digested*, 98/**3187**
Suspension of Proceedings (J07/96); *sub nom* Instance's European Patent Application
  (J07/96) [2000] E.P.O.R. 1; (1998) 21(11) I.P.D. 21118, EPO (Legal Bd App) . . . — *Digested*, 00/**3666**
Sussex Investments Ltd v. Secretary of State for the Environment, Transport and the
  Regions [1998] P.L.C.R. 172; [1997] N.P.C. 190; *Times*, December 29, 1997;
  Independent, January 20, 1998, CA; affirming CO 4066-95, QBD . . . . — *Digested*, 98/**4193**
Sussex University v. Customs and Excise Commissioners [2000] B.V.C. 2074, V&DTr
Sussmann v. Germany (1998) 25 E.H.R.R. 64, ECHR . . . . — *Digested*, 98/**3135**:
                        Applied, 98/3131, 98/3136
Sutcliffe v. Big C's Marine [1998] I.C.R. 913; [1998] I.R.L.R. 428; *Times*, June 25,
  1998, EAT. . . . . — *Digested*, 98/**2161**
Sutcliffe v. Chief Constable of West Yorkshire (1995) 159 J.P. 770; [1996] R.T.R. 86;
  Times, June 5, 1995, CA . . . . — *Digested*, 95/**381**:
                        Applied, 99/4279

Sutcliffe v. Hawker Siddeley Aviation [1973] I.C.R. 560; [1973] I.R.L.R. 304; (1973)
K.I.R. 85; [1974] I.T.R. 58; [1974] I.T.R. 583, NIRC . . . . *Digested*, 73/**1187**:
Applied, 01/2295: *Considered*, 88/1291, 89/1458: *Followed*, 73/1111, 74/1217:
Not followed, 01/2234
Sutcliffe v. Heywood Williams Group Plc (Unreported, November 6, 1997), QBD [*Ex
rel*. Anthony Coombs, John Pickering & Partners Solicitors, Old Exchange
Buildings, St Ann's Passage, 29-31 King Street, Manchester] . . . . *Digested*, 98/**1624**
Sutherland (Deceased), Re see Winter v. Inland Revenue Commissioners
Sutherland v. Network Appliance Ltd [2001] I.R.L.R. 12, EAT . . . . *Digested*, 01/**6459**
Sutherland v. United Kingdom (25186/94), *Times*, April 13, 2001, ECHR . . . . *Digested*, 01/**3578**
Sutherland Shire Council v. Heyman [1955-95] P.N.L.R. 238; (1985) 60 A.L.R. 1;
(1985) 59 A.L.J.R. 564; (1986) 2 Const. L.J. 161, HC (Aus) (1985) 2 Const.
L.J. 161, CA (NSW) . . . . *Digested*, 86/**2274**:
Approved, 95/3651: *Considered*, 85/2305, 87/2580, 95/3689, 98/3951:
Followed, 90/3288, 91/2661, 98/3924
Sutherland's Estate, Re see Winter v. Inland Revenue Commissioners
Suttle v. Amec Process & Energy Ltd (Unreported, December 22, 1998), CC (Central
London) [*Ex rel*. David Levene & Co Solicitors, Ashley House, 235-239 High
Road, Wood Green, London] . . . . *Digested*, 99/**1488**
Suttle v. Simmons [1989] 2 Lloyd's Rep. 227; [1987] R.T.R. 209, PC (Ber) . . . . *Digested*, 89/**2056**:
Considered, 99/3412
Sutton (Removal of Liquidator), Re see A&C Supplies Ltd, Re
Sutton v. Ling (Unreported, July 19, 1999), CC (Ipswich) [*Ex rel*. David Barr, Barrister,
1 Temple Gardens, Temple, London] . . . . *Digested*, 99/**1550**
Sutton LBC v. Junior Tennis Centres (1998) 13 P.A.D. 211, Planning Inspector
Suzen v. Lefarth see Suzen v. Zehnacker Gebaudereinigung GmbH Krankenhausservice
(C13/95)
Suzen v. Zehnacker Gebaudereinigung GmbH Krankenhausservice (C13/95); Suzen v.
Lefarth [1997] All E.R. (E.C.) 289; [1997] E.C.R. I-1259; [1997] 1 C.M.L.R. 768;
[1997] I.C.R. 662; [1997] I.R.L.R. 255; (1997) 16 Tr. L.R. 365; *Times*, March
26, 1997, ECJ . . . . *Digested*, 97/**2278**:
Applied, 97/2270, 00/2229, 00/2231: *Considered*, 98/2220:
Distinguished, 99/2133: *Not applied*, 01/2333
Sveinbjornsdottir v. Iceland (E9/97) [1999] 1 C.M.L.R. 884, EFTA . . . . *Digested*, 99/**3620**
Svenska International Plc v. Customs and Excise Commissioners; *sub nom* Customs
and Excise Commissioners v. Svenska International Plc [1999] 1 W.L.R. 769;
[1999] 2 All E.R. 906; [1999] S.T.C. 406; [1999] B.T.C. 5171; [1999] B.V.C. 221;
(1999) 96(22) L.S.G. 35; (1999) 143 S.J.L.B. 150; *Times*, March 30, 1999, HL;
affirming [1997] S.T.C. 958; [1997] B.T.C. 5314; *Times*, July 3, 1997, CA;
reversing [1996] S.T.C. 1000, QBD . . . . *Digested*, 99/**5028**
Svenska Journalistforbundet v. Council of the European Union (T174/95) [1998] All
E.R. (E.C.) 545; [1998] E.C.R. II-2289; [1998] 3 C.M.L.R. 645; *Times*, June 22,
1998, CFI (4th Chamber) . . . . *Digested*, 98/**2327**:
Followed, 00/2393
Svensson v. Sweden see Paulsen-Medalen v. Sweden
Swaddling v. Adjudication Officer (C90/97) [1999] All E.R. (EC) 217; [1999] E.C.R. I-
1075; [1999] 2 C.M.L.R. 679; [1999] C.E.C. 184; [1999] 2 F.L.R. 184; [1999]
Fam. Law 382; *Times*, March 4, 1999, ECJ (5th Chamber) . . . . *Digested*, 99/**4565**
Swain v. Denso Marston Ltd [2000] I.C.R. 1079; [2000] P.I.Q.R. P129; *Times*, April
24, 2000, CA . . . . *Digested*, 00/**2981**
Swain v. Hillman [2001] 1 All E.R. 91; [2001] C.P. Rep. 16; [1999] C.P.L.R. 779;
[2000] P.I.Q.R. P51; *Times*, November 4, 1999 ; *Independent*, November 10,
1999, CA . . . . *Digested*, 99/**561**:
Applied, 00/1761, 01/680, 01/4855: *Cited*, 00/353: *Considered*, 01/669,
01/684
Swain v. Law Society [1983] 1 A.C. 598; [1982] 3 W.L.R. 261; [1982] 2 All E.R. 827;
(1982) 79 L.S.G. 887; 126 S.J. 464, HL; reversing [1982] 1 W.L.R. 17; [1981] 3
All E.R. 797; 125 S.J. 542; *Times*, August 4, 1981, CA; reversing in part [1980] 1
W.L.R. 1335; [1980] 3 All E.R. 615; 124 S.J. 220, Ch D . . . . *Digested*, 82/**3085**:
Applied, 98/3715: *Followed*, 99/3798
Swaine v. McClatchy, CC (Southampton) [*Ex rel*. Katherine Huyton, Barrister, College
Chambers, 19 Carlton Crescent, Southampton] . . . . *Digested*, 01/**1779**
Swainger v. Associated British Ports see Scott v. Associated British Ports
Swale Storage & Distribution Services Ltd v. Sittingbourne Paper Co Ltd (1998) 95(34)
L.S.G. 32; (1998) 142 S.J.L.B. 229; *Times*, July 30, 1998, CA . . . . *Digested*, 98/**413**
Swaledale Cleaners Ltd, Re [1968] 1 W.L.R. 1710; [1968] 3 All E.R. 619; 112 S.J. 781, CA;
affirming [1968] 1 W.L.R. 432; [1968] 1 All E.R. 1132; 112 S.J. 108, Ch D . . . . . . *Digested*, 68/**444**:
Considered, 84/331: *Followed*, 98/703
Swallow v. Dwight [2001] 1 Q.R. 9, CC (Cambridge) [*Ex rel*. Emma Smith, Barrister,
Old Square Chambers, Gray's Inn, London] . . . . *Digested*, 01/**1626**
Swallow Hotels Ltd v. Inland Revenue Commissioners [2000] S.T.C. 45; [2000] B.T.C.
8003; [1999] E.G.C.S. 151; (2000) 144 S.J.L.B. 59; *Times*, January 11, 2000,
Ch D . . . . *Digested*, 00/**5056**

Swallowfield v. Customs and Excise Commissioners see BLP Group Plc v. Customs and Excise Commissioners (C4/94)

Swan v. Bush (Unreported, December 22, 1998), CC (Cardiff) [*Ex rel.* Andrew Arentsen, Barrister, 33 Park Place, Cardiff] . . . .   *Digested,* 99/**1578**

Swan v. Secretary of State for Scotland (No.1); *sub nom* Swan, Petitioner 1998 S.C. 479; 1998 S.C.L.R. 763; [1998] 2 C.M.L.R. 1192; [1998] Env. L.R. 545; 1998 G.W.D. 11-516; *Times,* June 4, 1998, 1 Div; reversing [1998] Env. L.R. 251; 1997 G.W.D. 15-636, OH . . . .   *Digested,* 98/**5880**

Swan v. Secretary of State for Scotland (No.2) [2000] Env. L.R. 60; 1999 G.W.D. 16-761, OH . . . .   *Digested,* 00/**6229**

Swan Hill Developments Ltd v. British Waterways Board [1998] J.P.L. 153; [1997] E.G.C.S. 33; [1997] N.P.C. 29, CA; affirming [1995] E.G.C.S. 76; [1995] N.P.C. 79, Ch D . . . .   *Digested,* 97/**4225**

Swan, Petitioner see Swan v. Secretary of State for Scotland (No.1)

Swansea City and County Council v. David McLean Homes Ltd (2001) 16 P.A.D. 74, Planning Inspector

Swansea City and County Council v. Davies (2001) 165 J.P. 156; [2001] R.T.R. 6; (2001) 165 J.P.N. 143; *Times,* July 7, 2000, QBD . . . .   *Digested,* 00/**4099**

Swansea City and County Council v. Johnson [1999] Ch. 189; [1999] 2 W.L.R. 683; [1999] 1 All E.R. 863; (1999) 1 L.G.L.R. 983; [1999] O.P.L.R. 39; [1999] Pens. L.R. 187; *Times,* December 4, 1998; *Independent,* November 30, 1998 (C.S.), Ch D . . . .   *Digested,* 99/**4149**:
                                                                                    Applied, 00/4385

Swansea City and County Council v. Woodman (2001) 16 P.A.D. 29, Planning Inspector

Swaptronics Ltd, Re (1998) 95(36) L.S.G. 33; *Times,* August 17, 1998, Ch D (Companies Ct) . . . .   *Digested,* 98/**20**

Swati v. Secretary of State for the Home Department see R. v. Secretary of State for the Home Department Ex p. Swati

Swayfields Ltd v. Secretary of State for the Environment, Transport and the Regions [2001] EWHC Admin 690; (2001) 98(36) L.S.G. 38, QBD (Admin Ct)

Sweatfield Ltd, Re [1997] B.C.C. 744; [1998] B.P.I.R. 276, Ch D . . . .   *Digested,* 98/**3355**

Sweden v. Stockholm Lindopark AB (C150/99); *sub nom* Stockholm Lindopark AB v. Sweden (C150/99) [2001] S.T.C. 103; [2001] E.C.R. I-493; [2001] 2 C.M.L.R. 16; [2001] B.T.C. 5021; [2001] S.T.I. 74, ECJ (5th Chamber) . .   *Digested,* 01/**5581**

Sweeney v. Coghill (1999) 77 P. & C.R. D14, CA

Sweeney v. J&S Henderson (Concessions) Ltd [1999] I.R.L.R. 306, EAT . . . .   *Digested,* 99/**6047**

Sweeney v. National University of Ireland Co (t/a Cork University Press) [2001] E.C.D.R. 8, HC (Irl)

Sweet v. Parsley [1970] A.C. 132; [1969] 2 W.L.R. 470; [1969] 1 All E.R. 347; (1969) 53 Cr. App. R. 221; (1969) 133 J.P. 188; 113 S.J. 86, HL; reversing [1968] 2 Q.B. 418; [1968] 2 W.L.R. 1360; [1968] 2 All E.R. 337; 112 S.J. 330, DC . . . .   *Digested,* 69/**2210**:
               Applied, 70/1680, 70/1681, 75/496, 80/2684, 81/1739, 82/296, 84/631,
               84/631.2, 84/951, 85/653, 86/664, 94/1092, 00/1002: *Considered,* 69/112,
               69/845, 71/2186, 73/2990, 74/3419, 76/2369, 77/487, 77/506, 77/1417,
               83/612, 84/959, 85/656, 86/676, 87/117, 88/3111, 90/175, 90/180, 91/203,
               91/972, 94/3860, 94/4359, 95/4802: *Distinguished,* 73/606, 74/710,
                                                  91/1289: *Followed,* 70/1684, 01/1014

Sweetman v. Shepherd [2000] C.P. Rep. 56; [2000] C.P.L.R. 378; (2000) 97(14) L.S.G. 43; (2000) 144 S.J.L.B. 159; *Times,* March 29, 2000, CA . . . .   *Digested,* 00/**349**

Swift v. Dairywise Farms Ltd (No.1) [2000] 1 W.L.R. 1177; [2000] 1 All E.R. 320; [2000] B.C.C. 642; [2000] 1 B.C.L.C. 632; [1999] E.G.C.S. 137; [1999] N.P.C. 142; *Independent,* February 7, 2000 (C.S.), Ch D . . . .   *Digested,* 00/**3864**

Swift v. Dairywise Farms Ltd (No.2) [2001] EWCA Civ 145; [2001] 1 B.C.L.C. 672; [2001] 7 E.G.C.S. 159; [2001] N.P.C. 23, CA . . . .   *Digested,* 01/**3746**

Swiggs v. Nagarajan (No.1) see Nagarajan v. Agnew

Swiggs v. Nagarajan (No.2) see Nagarajan v. London Regional Transport

Swindle v. Harrison [1997] 4 All E.R. 705; [1997] P.N.L.R. 641; [1997] N.P.C. 50; *Times,* April 17, 1997, CA . . . .   *Digested,* 97/**3822**:
                                                          Cited, 00/2332: *Considered,* 01/938

Swindon BC v. McNicholas Construction Co Ltd (2000) 15 P.A.D. 413, Planning Inspector

Swingcastle Ltd v. Alastair Gibson (A Firm) [1991] 2 A.C. 223; [1991] 2 W.L.R. 1091; [1991] 2 All E.R. 353; [1955-95] P.N.L.R. 590; [1991] 17 E.G. 83; [1991] C.C.L.R. 55; [1991] E.G.C.S. 46; (1991) 141 N.L.J. 563; (1991) 135 S.J. 542; *Times,* April 19, 1991; *Independent,* May 16, 1991; *Financial Times,* April 24, 1991, HL; reversing [1990] 1 W.L.R. 1223; [1990] 3 All E.R. 463; [1990] 34 E.G. 49; [1990] C.C.L.R. 127; (1990) 140 N.L.J. 818, CA . . . .   *Digested,* 91/**1322**:
                              Considered, 96/4519: *Distinguished,* 98/1472: *Followed,* 95/3172

Swinney v. Chief Constable of Northumbria (No.1) [1997] Q.B. 464; [1996] 3 W.L.R. 968; [1996] 3 All E.R. 449; [1996] P.N.L.R. 473; (1996) 146 N.L.J. 878; *Times,* March 28, 1996, CA . . . .   *Considered,* 99/3970,
                                                                                    99/3972, 99/3982

Swinney v. Chief Constable of Northumbria (No.2) (1999) 11 Admin. L.R. 811; *Times,* May 25, 1999, QBD . . . .   *Digested,* 99/**3972**

Swintex Ltd v. Melba Products Ltd [2001] F.S.R. 4; (2000) 23(9) I.P.D. 23069, Pat Ct.   *Digested*, 01/**3879**
SWISS MISS Trade Mark; *sub nom* Hunt-Wesson Inc, Re [1998] R.P.C. 889; (1998) 21(9) I.P.D. 21099; *Times*, July 20, 1998; *Independent*, July 9, 1998, CA; reversing in part [1997] R.P.C. 219; (1997) 20(2) I.P.D. 20011, Ch D . . . .   *Digested*, 98/**3525**
Switzer v. Law (Unreported, March 26, 1998), CC (Southport) [*Ex rel.* David Knifton, Barrister, Chavasse Court Chambers, 2nd Floor, Chavasse Court, 24 Lord Street, Liverpool, L2 1TA]. . . . .   *Digested*, 98/**3624**
Switzerland Tourism v. Customs and Excise Commissioners [2001] S.T.I. 898, V&DTr
Swizzels Matlow Ltd's Three Dimensional Trade Mark Application [2000] E.T.M.R. 58; [1999] R.P.C. 879, Appointed Person. . . . .   *Digested*, 00/**3750**:
    Considered, 00/3789
Swizzels Matlow Ltd's Trade Mark Application [1998] R.P.C. 244, TMR. . . . .   *Digested*, 98/**3542**
SX Holdings Ltd v. Synchronet Ltd [2001] C.P. Rep. 43, CA
Sykes, Re (1907) 23 T.L.R. 747. . . . .   *Considered*, 01/5167
Sykes, Re [1998] B.P.I.R. 516, Sup Ct (BC) . . . .   *Digested*, 99/**3245**
Sykes (Butchers) Ltd, Re; *sub nom* Secretary of State for Trade and Industry v. Richardson [1998] B.C.C. 484; [1998] 1 B.C.L.C. 110; (1997) 94(20) L.S.G. 37; (1997) 141 S.J.L.B. 111; *Times*, May 16, 1997, Ch D (Companies Ct)   *Digested*, 98/**683**
Sykes v. Harry; Sykes v. Trustee of Harry's Estate (A Bankrupt) [2001] EWCA Civ 167; [2001] Q.B. 1014; [2001] 3 W.L.R. 62; [2001] 33 H.L.R. 80; [2001] 82 P. & C.R. 35; [2001] L. & T.R. 40; [2001] 1 E.G.L.R. 53; [2001] 17 E.G. 221; (2001) 98(14) L.S.G. 39; (2001) 145 S.J.L.B. 61; [2001] N.P.C. 26; (2001) 82 P. & C.R. D9; *Times*, February 27, 2001; *Independent*, February 7, 2001, CA . . . .   *Digested*, 01/**4163**
Sykes v. Midland Bank Executor & Trustee Co Ltd [1971] 1 Q.B. 113; [1970] 3 W.L.R. 273; [1970] 2 All E.R. 471; 114 S.J. 225, CA; reversing [1969] 2 Q.B. 518; [1969] 2 W.L.R. 1173; [1969] 2 All E.R. 1238; 113 S.J. 243, QBD . . . .   *Digested*, 70/**2710**:
    Considered, 84/3362, 85/2319, 86/2285, 90/3315, 91/2657:
    Distinguished, 84/3361, 98/4018
Sykes v. Trustee of Harry's Estate (A Bankrupt) see Sykes v. Harry
Symbian Ltd v. Christensen [2000] U.K.C.L.R. 879; [2001] I.R.L.R. 77, CA; affirming HC 2000 01767, Ch D . . . .   *Digested*, 00/**2114**
Symbol Technologies Inc v. Opticon Sensors Europe BV (No.2) [1993] R.P.C. 232, Pat Ct. . . . .   *Considered*, 01/3882
Symes v. Canada [1993] 4 S.C.R. 695, Sup Ct (Can). . . . . *Distinguished*, 98/3074
Symphony Group Plc v. Hodgson [1994] Q.B. 179; [1993] 3 W.L.R. 830; [1993] 4 All E.R. 143; (1993) 143 N.L.J. 725; (1993) 137 S.J.L.B. 134; *Times*, May 4, 1993; *Independent*, May 14, 1993, CA . . . .   *Digested*, 93/**3153**:
    Applied, 95/3994, 95/3995, 96/710, 99/389, 00/416, 00/423, 00/455,
    01/474: *Approved*, 99/749: *Considered*, 94/3623, 96/701, 97/3113, 97/3343,
    99/390, 99/391: *Followed*, 96/3464, 99/387, 99/392
Syndesmos ton en Elladi Touristikon kai Taxidiotikon Grafeion v. Ergasias (C398/95) [1997] E.C.R. I-3091; [1998] 1 C.M.L.R. 420; [1997] C.E.C. 1291, ECJ (6th Chamber) . . . .   *Digested*, 98/**2139**:
    Applied, 98/4517
Syndicat des Producteurs Independants (SPI) v. Ministere de l'Economie, des Finances et de l'Industrie (C108/00) [2001] All E.R. (EC) 564; [2001] S.T.C. 523; [2001] E.C.R. I-2361; [2001] 2 C.M.L.R. 37; [2001] B.T.C. 5146; [2001] S.T.I. 546, ECJ (5th Chamber) . . . .   *Digested*, 01/**5558**
Syndicat des Professionnels Europeens de L'Automobile (SPEA) v. Conseil National des Professions de L'Automobile (CNPA) [1998] E.C.C. 97, Cass (F)
Syndicat Francais de l'Express International (SFEI) v. Commission of the European Communities (C39/93 P) [1994] E.C.R. I-2681, ECJ (5th Chamber) . . . .   *Digested*, 94/**4797**:
    Followed, 00/2365
Syndicat Francais de l'Express International (SFEI) v. Commission of the European Communities (T77/95) see Union Francaise de l'Express (UFEX) v. Commission of the European Communities (C119/97 P)
Syndicat Francais de l'Express International (SFEI) v. La Poste (C39/94) [1996] All E.R. (EC) 685; [1996] E.C.R. I-3547; [1996] 3 C.M.L.R. 369, ECJ. . . . .   *Digested*, 96/**1068**:
    Followed, 99/2284
Synstar Computer Services (UK) Ltd v. ICL (Sorbus) Ltd [2001] C.P. Rep. 98; [2001] U.K.C.L.R. 585; (2001) 98(23) L.S.G. 40; (2001) 145 S.J.L.B. 119; *Times*, May 1, 2001, Ch D . . . .   *Digested*, 01/**442**
Syrkin v. Russia (44125/98) (2001) 29 E.H.R.R. CD254, ECHR
Systeme Europeen Promotion (SEP) Sarl v. Commission of the European Communities (T115/99) [2001] E.C.R. II-691; [2001] 5 C.M.L.R. 14, CFI (2nd Chamber) . . . .   *Digested*, 01/**2469**
Szakal, Re see R. v. Manchester Magistrates Court Ex p. Szakal
Szucs v. Austria see Werner v. Austria

T (A Child) (Abduction: Appointment of Guardian ad Litem), Re [1999] 2 F.L.R. 796; [1999] Fam. Law 613, Fam Div . . . .   *Digested*, 99/**2372**
T (A Child) v. Doncaster MBC [*Ex rel.* Frank Allen Pennington, Solicitors, 5/7 Regent Terrace, South Parade, Doncaster] . . . .   *Digested*, 01/**1703**

T (A Child) *v.* Gwynedd HA [2001] 6 Q.R. 18, QBD [*Ex rel.* Jones Maidment Wilson,
    Solicitors, 5-7 Byrom Street, Manchester] . . . .   *Digested,* 01/**1723**
T (A Child) *v.* Page [2000] 5 Q.R. 6, QBD [*Ex rel.* Bryan Thomas, Barrister, 33 Park
    Place, Cardiff] . . . .   *Digested,* 00/**1508**
T (A Minor), Re see R. *v.* East Sussex CC Ex p. Tandy
T (A Minor) (Adoption: Contact Order), Re [1995] 2 F.L.R. 251; [1995] 2 F.C.R. 537; [1995]
    Fam. Law 536; *Times,* January 13, 1995, CA . . . .   *Digested,* 96/**473**:
                                                                                                                         Applied, 99/2399

T (A Minor) (Care Order: Conditions), Re [1994] 2 F.L.R. 423; [1994] Fam. Law 558;
    (1994) 158 J.P.N. 680; (1994) 91(21) L.S.G. 40; *Times,* May 5, 1994;
    Independent, May 23, 1994 (C.S.), CA . . . .   *Digested,* 95/**3392**:
                                                                                                                         Considered, 01/2562

T (A Minor) (Change of Surname), Re [1998] 2 F.L.R. 620; [1999] 1 F.C.R. 476; [1998] Fam.
    Law 531; (1998) 95(27) L.S.G. 26; (1998) 142 S.J.L.B. 190; *Times,* June 23, 1998,
    CA . . . .   *Digested,* 98/**2431**
T (A Minor) (Contact: Non-Convention Country), Re see T (Staying Contact in Non-
    Convention Country), Re
T (A Minor) (Liver Transplant: Consent), Re see T (A Minor) (Wardship: Medical Treatment),
    Re
T (A Minor) (Wardship: Medical Treatment), Re; *sub nom* T (A Minor) (Liver Transplant:
    Consent), Re; C (A Minor) (Medical Treatment: Refusal of Parental Consent),
    Re [1997] 1 W.L.R. 242; [1997] 1 All E.R. 906; [1997] 1 F.L.R. 502; [1997] 2
    F.C.R. 363; [1997] 8 Med. L.R. 166; (1997) 35 B.M.L.R. 63; (1996) 93(42)
    L.S.G. 28; (1996) 146 N.L.J. 1577; (1996) 140 S.J.L.B. 237; *Times,* October 28,
    1996; *Independent,* October 29, 1996, CA . . . .   *Digested,* 96/**546**:
                                                                                                                         Followed, 99/2370

T (A Minor) *v.* Luton & Dunstable Hospital NHS Trust (Unreported, November 23,
    1998), QBD [*Ex rel.* Simon Michael, Barrister, Bedford Chambers, The
    Clockhouse, 2 Bedford Street, Ampthill, Bedford] . . . .   *Digested,* 99/**1545**
T (A Minor) *v.* Moloney (Unreported, April 13, 1999), CC (Nottingham) [*Ex rel.* Nelsons
    Solicitors, Pennine House, 8 Stanford Street, Nottingham] . . . .   *Digested,* 99/**1588**
T (Children) (Abduction: Child's Objections to Return), Re; *sub nom* T (Children)
    (Abduction: Custody Rights), Re [2000] 2 F.L.R. 192; [2000] 2 F.C.R. 159;
    [2000] Fam. Law 594; *Times,* April 24, 2000, CA . . . .   *Digested,* 00/**2443**
T (Children) (Abduction: Custody Rights), Re see T (Children) (Abduction: Child's
    Objections to Return), Re
T (Children) (Care Proceedings: Guardian ad Litem), Re see T and A (Children) (Risk of
    Disclosure), Re
T (Children) (Interim Care Order), Re [2001] EWCA Civ 1345; [2001] 3 F.C.R. 175, CA .   *Digested,* 01/**2565**
T (CICB: Quantum: 1998), Re (Unreported, June 2, 1998), CICB (London) [*Ex rel.* Adrian
    Roberts, Barrister, 2 Gray's Inn Square, London] . . . .   *Digested,* 99/**1437**
T (Paternity: Ordering Blood Tests), Re [2001] 2 F.L.R. 1190; [2001] 3 F.C.R. 577; [2001]
    Fam. Law 738, Fam Div
T (Staying Contact in Non-Convention Country), Re; *sub nom* T (A Minor) (Contact:
    Non-Convention Country), Re [1999] 1 F.L.R. 262; [1998] 3 F.C.R. 574; [1999]
    Fam. Law 15, Fam Div . . . .   *Digested,* 99/**2368**
T *v.* Child Support Agency [1998] 1 W.L.R. 144; [1997] 4 All E.R. 27; [1997] 2 F.L.R.
    875; [1998] 1 F.C.R. 62; [1998] Fam. Law 9, Fam Div . . . .   *Digested,* 97/**442**
T *v.* Finland (25702/94) (No.1) see K *v.* Finland (25702/94) (No.1)
T *v.* Finland (25702/94) (No.2) see K *v.* Finland (25702/94) (No.2)
T *v.* Immigration Officer see T *v.* Secretary of State for the Home Department
T *v.* North Yorkshire CC [1999] I.R.L.R. 98; (1999) 1 L.G.L.R. 61; [1999] B.L.G.R. 584;
    (1998) 10 Admin. L.R. 573; [1999] Ed. C.R. 353; [1998] E.L.R. 625; (1999) 49
    B.M.L.R. 150; (1998) 95(32) L.S.G. 29; (1998) 142 S.J.L.B. 218; *Times,*
    September 10, 1998; *Independent,* July 27, 1998 (C.S.), CA . . . .   *Digested,* 98/**2243**:
                                                                          Considered, 99/2147: *Overruled,* 01/5359

T *v.* Secretary of State for the Home Department; *sub nom* R. *v.* Secretary of State for
    the Home Department Ex p. T; T *v.* Immigration Officer [1996] A.C. 742; [1996] 2
    W.L.R. 766; [1996] 2 All E.R. 865; [1996] Imm. A.R. 443; (1996) 146 N.L.J.
    785; (1996) 140 S.J.L.B. 136; *Times,* May 23, 1996; *Independent,* June 4, 1996,
    HL; affirming [1995] 1 W.L.R. 545; [1995] 2 All E.R. 1042; [1995] Imm. A.R.
    142; *Times,* November 9, 1994; *Independent,* November 4, 1994; *Guardian,*
    November 21, 1994, CA . . . .   *Digested,* 96/**3244**:
                                                                                        Considered, 98/3205, 00/3352

T *v.* T (Child Abduction: Consent) [1999] 2 F.L.R. 912; [1999] 2 F.C.R. 2; [1999] Fam.
    Law 521, Fam Div . . . .   *Digested,* 99/**2314**
T *v.* T (Child Abduction: Non-Convention Country) [1998] 2 F.L.R. 1110; [1999] 2
    F.C.R. 70; [1998] Fam. Law 723, Fam Div . . . .   *Digested,* 99/**2336**
T *v.* T (Financial Relief: Pensions) [1998] 1 F.L.R. 1072; [1998] 2 F.C.R. 364; [1998]
    O.P.L.R. 1; [1998] Fam. Law 398, Fam Div . . . .   *Digested,* 98/**2468**:
                                                                                                                         Followed, 99/2422

T *v.* United Kingdom (24724/94); V *v.* United Kingdom (24888/94) [2000] 2 All E.R.
  1024 (Note); (2000) 30 E.H.R.R. 121; 7 B.H.R.C. 659; 12 Fed. Sent. R. 266;
  [2000] Crim. L.R. 187; *Times*, December 17, 1999, ECHR [1999] Crim. L.R. 579,
  Eur Comm HR . . . . *Digested*, 00/**3198**:
  Cited, 00/1078, 00/1331: *Considered*, 01/1410: *Referred to*, 00/1090, 00/1095
T and A (Children) (Risk of Disclosure), Re; *sub nom* T (Children) (Care Proceedings:
  Guardian ad Litem), Re [2000] 1 F.L.R. 859; [2000] 1 F.C.R. 659; [2000]
  Lloyd's Rep. P.N. 452; [2000] Fam. Law 398; (2000) 164 J.P.N. 426; (2000)
  97(3) L.S.G. 37; (2000) 144 S.J.L.B. 49; *Times*, February 1, 2000, CA. . . . . *Digested*, 00/**2469**
T and E (Proceedings: Conflicting Interests), Re; *sub nom* S (Minors) (Proceedings:
  Conflicting Interests), Re [1995] 1 F.L.R. 581; [1995] 3 F.C.R. 260; [1995] Fam.
  Law 232; *Times*, December 29, 1994, Fam Div . . . . *Digested*, 95/**3408**:
  Applied, 99/2399
T Choithram International SA *v.* Pagarani; *sub nom* Pagarani, Re [2001] 1 W.L.R. 1;
  [2001] 2 All E.R. 492; [2001] W.T.L.R. 277; (2000-01) 3 I.T.E.L.R. 254; (2001)
  145 S.J.L.B. 8; *Times*, November 30, 2000, PC (BVI); reversing (1998) 2
  O.F.L.R. 1, CA (BVI) . . . . *Digested*, 01/**5514**
T Lucas & Co Ltd *v.* Mitchell [1974] Ch. 129; [1972] 3 W.L.R. 934; [1972] 3 All E.R.
  689; 116 S.J. 711, CA; reversing [1972] 1 W.L.R. 938; [1972] 2 All E.R. 1035; 116
  S.J. 506, Ch D . . . . *Digested*, 72/**515**:
  Applied, 84/406.a, 98/2192
T Port GmbH *v.* Hauptzollamt Hamburg-Jonas (C364/95) [1998] E.C.R. I-1023;
  [1998] 3 C.M.L.R. 543, ECJ
T Port GmbH & Co KG *v.* Bundesanstalt fur Landwirtschaft und Ernahrung (C68/95)
  [1996] E.C.R. I-6065; [1997] 1 C.M.L.R. 1, ECJ . . . . *Applied*, 99/2238
T&C Hill (Haulage) *v.* Gleig (Inspector of Taxes) [2000] S.T.C. (S.C.D.) 64; [2000] S.T.I.
  163, Sp Comm . . . . *Digested*, 00/**5065**
T&D Automotive Ltd, Re see T&D Industries Plc, Re
T&D Industries Plc, Re; *sub nom* T&D Automotive Ltd, Re [2000] 1 W.L.R. 646;
  [2000] 1 All E.R. 333; [2000] B.C.C. 956; [2000] 1 B.C.L.C. 471; (1999)
  96(46) L.S.G. 37; *Times*, November 23, 1999 ; *Independent*, January 31, 2000
  (C.S.), Ch D . . . . *Digested*, 99/**3276**
T&K Home Improvements *v.* Skilton see Skilton *v.* T&K Home Improvements Ltd
T-R & W (Children) (Adoption: Expert Evidence), Re [2001] 1 F.C.R. 130, CA. . . . . *Digested*, 01/**2671**
T's Application for Judicial Review, Re [2000] N.I. 516, QBD (NI) . . . . *Digested*, 01/**5879**
TA Shipping Ltd *v.* Comet Shipping Ltd (The Agamemnon) [1998] 1 Lloyd's Rep. 675;
  [1998] C.L.C. 106, QBD (Comm Ct) . . . . *Digested*, 98/**4443**
Tabarn, Re CO 1387-97, QBD   *Digested*, 98/**44**
Tabasco Restaurant *v.* Proprietor of the Tabasco Registered Trade Mark [1998] E.T.M.R.
  100, OPM (A)
Taber *v.* MacDonald (1999) 31 H.L.R. 73, QBD . . . . *Digested*, 99/**3748**
TABO Trade Mark [2000] R.P.C. 360, Appointed Person . . . . *Digested*, 00/**3712**
Tack, Re [2000] B.P.I.R. 164, Ch D . . . . *Digested*, 00/**3438**
Tacon *v.* Monolithic Building Co see Monolithic Building Co, Re
Tadema Holdings Ltd *v.* Ferguson (2000) 32 H.L.R. 866; [1999] E.G.C.S. 138; (1999)
  96(47) L.S.G. 32; [1999] N.P.C. 144; *Times*, November 25, 1999, CA. . . . . . . *Digested*, 99/**3657**
Tadjerouni *v.* Kaderia (Unreported, May 31, 2000), CC (West London) [*Ex rel*. Moore
  & Blatch Solicitors, 64 London Road, Southampton] . . . . *Digested*, 00/**471**
Tager *v.* Westpac Banking Corp [1998] B.C.C. 73; [1997] 1 B.C.L.C. 313; [1997]
  B.P.I.R. 543; *Times*, December 24, 1996, Ch D . . . . *Digested*, 97/**3077**
Taggart *v.* Leeds City Council [1999] E.H.L.R. 185; (1999) 31 H.L.R. 693, QBD . . . . . . *Digested*, 99/**3024**
Tagro *v.* Cafane [1991] 1 W.L.R. 378; [1991] 2 All E.R. 235; (1991) 23 H.L.R. 250;
  [1991] 1 E.G.L.R. 279; [1991] E.G.C.S. 5, CA . . . . *Digested*, 91/**2291**:
  Applied, 99/3651
Tague *v.* Lancaster City Council [1999] 2 E.G.L.R. 103; [1999] 20 E.G. 156; [1998]
  R.V.R. 253, Lands Tr . . . . *Digested*, 99/**4196**
Tahir *v.* Haringey HA [1998] Lloyd's Rep. Med. 104, CA . . . . *Digested*, 98/**3966**
Tai (t/a North Bersted Chinese Takeaway) *v.* Customs and Excise Commissioners [2000]
  S.T.I. 711, V&D Tr
Tai Hing Cotton Mill Ltd *v.* Liu Chong Hing Bank Ltd (No.1) [1986] A.C. 80; [1985] 3
  W.L.R. 317; [1985] 2 All E.R. 947; [1985] 2 Lloyd's Rep. 313; [1986] F.L.R. 14;
  (1985) 82 L.S.G. 2995; (1985) 135 N.L.J. 680; (1985) 129 S.J. 503, PC (HK);
  reversing [1984] 1 Lloyd's Rep. 555, CA (HK). . . . . *Digested*, 85/**150**:
  Applied, 87/776, 88/842, 90/4101, 97/317: *Considered*, 89/2585, 93/2980,
  95/3689: *Followed*, 99/277, 01/369
Tait Consibee (Oxford) Ltd *v.* Tait [1997] 2 B.C.L.C. 349, CA . . . . *Digested*, 98/**661**:
  Applied, 01/730
Taj *v.* Ali (2001) 33 H.L.R. 26; [2000] 43 E.G. 183; (2000) 97(17) L.S.G. 36, CA . . . . . *Digested*, 00/**3932**
Taj *v.* Ali (Variation of Order) (2001) 33 H.L.R. 27, CA . . . . *Digested*, 01/**4201**
Takenaka (UK) Ltd *v.* Frankl [2001] EWCA Civ 348; [2001] E.B.L.R. 40, CA;
  affirming HQ0000328, QBD. . . . . *Digested*, 01/**1819**
Talbot, Re see Talbot *v.* Talbot
Talbot (Deceased), Re see Talbot *v.* Talbot

Talbot v. Berkshire CC [1994] Q.B. 290; [1993] 3 W.L.R. 708; [1993] 4 All E.R. 9;
[1993] R.T.R. 406; [1993] P.I.Q.R. P319; (1993) 157 L.G. Rev. 1004; (1993) 143
N.L.J. 402; *Times*, March 23, 1993, CA. . . . . *Digested*, 93/**1851**:
               Cited, 00/604: *Considered*, 95/4205, 96/773, 96/3911, 97/766, 98/2162:
              Distinguished, 99/1376, 99/5146: *Followed*, 97/491, 99/431:
                                  Referred to, 94/3773
Talbot v. Cadge see Powdrill v. Watson
Talbot v. DPP; *sub nom* Talbot v. Oxford City Magistrates Court; Talbot v. Oxford City
Justices [2000] 1 W.L.R. 1102; [2000] 2 Cr. App. R. 60; (2000) 164 J.P. 169;
[2000] Crim. L.R. 326; (2000) 164 J.P.N. 264; (2000) 97(5) L.S.G. 33; *Times*,
February 15, 2000; *Independent*, March 6, 2000 (C.S.), QBD . . . . *Digested*, 00/**1014**
Talbot v. Grundy see Powdrill v. Watson
Talbot v. Oxford City Justices see Talbot v. DPP
Talbot v. Oxford City Magistrates Court see Talbot v. DPP
Talbot v. Talbot; *sub nom* Talbot, Re; Talbot (Deceased), Re [1968] Ch. 1; [1967] 3
W.L.R. 438; [1967] 2 All E.R. 920; (1967) 111 S.J. 278, CA; affirming [1967] 1
All E.R. 601, Chancery Ct of Lancaster . . . . *Digested*, 67/**4121**:
                     Applied, 84/3673: *Distinguished*, 01/5163
Taleban v. Dunley (Unreported, June 27, 2001), CC (Chester) [*Ex rel.* David Higginson,
Solicitor, Marian Bach, Crossways Road, Pen y Cefn, Caerwys] . . . . *Digested*, 01/**29**
Tall Pines Golf & Leisure Co Ltd v. Customs and Excise Commissioners [2000] B.V.C.
2265; [2000] S.T.I. 904, V&DTr
Tallah v. Secretary of State for the Home Department [1998] I.N.L.R. 258, IAT . . . . *Digested*, 98/**5997**
Tallentire (CICB: Quantum: 1997), Re (1998) 98(1) Q.R. 6; (1997) 97(5/6) Q.R. 12, CICB
(Durham) . . . . *Digested*, 98/**1621**
Talling v. Lawrence [1999] B.P.I.R. 414, CC (Barnet) . . . . *Digested*, 99/**363**
Tamarind International Ltd v. Eastern Natural Gas (Retail) Ltd [2000] C.L.C. 1397;
[2000] Eu. L.R. 708; (2000) 97(26) L.S.G. 35; *Times*, June 27, 2000, QBD
(Comm Ct) . . . . *Digested*, 00/**118**
Tameside MBC v. Barlow Securities Group Services Ltd [2001] EWCA Civ 1; [2001]
B.L.R. 113; 75 Con. L.R. 112, CA
Tameside MBC v. Browning; *sub nom* Browning v. Tameside MBC (1998) 75 P. & C.R.
417; [1997] E.G.C.S. 38, CA. . . . . *Digested*, 98/**4197**
Tameside MBC v. Grant (2001) 98(41) L.S.G. 34; (2001) 145 S.J.L.B. 237, Fam Div
Tameside MBC v. M [2001] Fam. Law 873, CC (Manchester)
Tammer v. Estonia (41205/98) 10 B.H.R.C. 543, ECHR (2001) 29 E.H.R.R. CD257,
Eur Comm HR . . . . *Digested*, 01/**3470**
Tamworth Mouldings Ltd, Re see Ladney and Hendry's International Application, Re
Tan v. East London and City HA [1999] Lloyd's Rep. Med. 389, CC (Chelmsford) . . . . . *Digested*, 00/**531**
Tanbridge DC v. Bickers; *sub nom* Tandridge DC v. Bickers (1999) 31 H.L.R. 432;
[1999] L. & T.R. 21; [1998] 3 E.G.L.R. 31; [1998] 41 E.G. 220, CA. . . . . *Digested*, 98/**3056**
Tancic v. Times Newspapers Ltd; *sub nom* Times Newspapers Ltd v. Tancic *Times*,
January 12, 2000, CA . . . . *Digested*, 00/**1757**
Tandon v. Trustees of Spurgeons Homes [1982] A.C. 755; [1982] 2 W.L.R. 735;
[1982] 1 All E.R. 1086; (1981-82) 4 H.L.R. 1; (1982) 44 P. & C.R. 307; (1982)
263 E.G. 349; 26 S.J. 260, HL; reversing [1982] Q.B. 41; [1981] 3 W.L.R. 74;
[1981] 2 All E.R. 960; (1981) 42 P. & C.R. 34; (1981) 258 E.G. 553; 125 S.J.
201, CA . . . . *Digested*, 82/**1767**:
                                      Applied, 01/4180
Tandridge DC v. Allard (2001) 16 P.A.D. 65, Planning Inspector
Tandridge DC v. Bickers see Tanbridge DC v. Bickers
Tandridge DC v. Delaney [2000] 1 P.L.R. 11, QBD. . . . . *Digested*, 00/**4416**
Tandridge DC v. Linden Homes South East Ltd (2000) 15 P.A.D. 296, Planning
Inspector
Tandridge DC v. Owen (1998) 13 P.A.D. 650, Planning Inspector
Tandridge DC v. Redhill Aerodrome Ltd (2001) 16 P.A.D. 81, Planning Inspector
Tandridge DC v. Secretary of State for the Environment (1997) 74 P. & C.R. 159;
[1998] 1 P.L.R. 41; [1997] J.P.L. 646; [1997] E.G.C.S. 13; [1997] N.P.C. 10, CA . *Digested*, 97/**4073**
Tandridge DC v. Unicoin Homes Plc (1999) 14 P.A.D. 653, Planning Inspector
Tandridge DC v. Verrechia [2000] Q.B. 318; [1999] 3 W.L.R. 1090; [1999] 3 All E.R.
247; [1999] 3 P.L.R. 27; [2000] P.L.C.R. 1; (1999) 96(24) L.S.G. 38; *Times*,
June 16, 1999, CA; affirming [1999] P.L.C.R. 140; [1998] E.G.C.S. 32, QBD
(OR). . . . . *Digested*, 99/**4207**:
                                  Previous proceedings, 98/4166
Tandridge DC v. Wilson (1998) 13 P.A.D. 674, Planning Inspector
Tanfern Ltd v. Cameron-MacDonald [2000] 1 W.L.R. 1311; [2000] 2 All E.R. 801;
[2001] C.P. Rep. 8; [2000] 2 Costs L.R. 260; (2000) 97(24) L.S.G. 41; *Times*,
May 17, 2000; *Independent*, May 16, 2000, CA. . . . . *Digested*, 00/**358**
Tangiora v. Wellington District Legal Services Committee; *sub nom* Wellington District
Legal Services Committee v. Tangiora [2000] 1 W.L.R. 240, PC (NZ); affirming 3
B.H.R.C. 1, CA (NZ); reversing 1 B.H.R.C. 582, HC (NZ) . . . . *Digested*, 00/**3199**
Tankel v. Tankel [1999] 1 F.L.R. 676; [1999] Fam. Law 93; *Times*, April 23, 1998, Ch D . *Digested*, 98/**4873**
Tanna v. Post Office [1981] I.C.R. 374, EAT . . . . *Digested*, 81/**883**:
        Applied, 98/5133: *Considered*, 85/1220, 86/1237: *Distinguished*, 99/2046

Tanrikulu *v.* Turkey (23763/94) (2000) 30 E.H.R.R. 950, ECHR . . . . *Digested*, 01/**3573**
Taore *v.* Secretary of State for the Home Department see R. *v.* Secretary of State for
the Home Department Ex p. Taore
Tapemaze Ltd *v.* Melluish (Inspector of Taxes) [2000] S.T.C. 189; 73 T.C. 167; [2000]
B.T.C. 50; [2000] S.T.I. 160; (2000) 97(8) L.S.G. 37; *Times*, March 15, 2000,
Ch D . . . . *Digested*, 00/**4944**
Tarbuck *v.* Avon Insurance Plc [2001] 3 W.L.R. 1502; [2001] 2 All E.R. 503; [2001] 1
All E.R. (Comm) 422; [2001] B.P.I.R. 1142; (2001) 151 N.L.J. 18, QBD (Comm
Ct) . . . . *Digested*, 01/**3820**
Target Holdings Ltd *v.* Priestley [1999] Lloyd's Rep. Bank. 175; (2000) 79 P. & C.R.
305; (1999) 96(14) L.S.G. 33; (1999) 96(18) L.S.G. 34; (1999) 143 S.J.L.B.
121; [1999] N.P.C. 51, Ch D . . . . *Digested*, 99/**4358**
Target Holdings Ltd *v.* Redferns (No.1) [1996] A.C. 421; [1995] 3 W.L.R. 352; [1995] 3
All E.R. 785; (1995) 139 S.J.L.B. 195; [1995] N.P.C. 136; *Times*, July 21, 1995;
Independent, August 10, 1995; *Independent*, July 21, 1995, HL; reversing [1994]
1 W.L.R. 1089; [1994] 2 All E.R. 337; *Times*, November 24, 1993; *Independent*,
December 3, 1993, CA. . . . . *Digested*, 95/**2195**:
Applied, 00/2332: *Considered*, 96/3909, 97/3979, 99/1401, 01/729
Target Holdings Ltd *v.* Redferns (No.2) (1998) 95(41) L.S.G. 45; *Times*, October 10,
1998, Ch D . . . . *Digested*, 98/**383**
Target Home Loans Ltd *v.* Iza Ltd [2000] 1 E.G.L.R. 23; [2000] 02 E.G. 117; (2000)
97(3) L.S.G. 38, CC (Central London) . . . . *Digested*, 00/**3911**
Tarjomani *v.* Panther Securities Ltd (1983) 46 P. & C.R. 32, Ch D . . . . *Digested*, 83/**2067**:
Applied, 92/2713, 94/2764: *Considered*, 00/3894: *Followed*, 98/3061
Tarmac Heavy Building Materials UK Ltd *v.* Buckinghamshire CC see Tarmac Heavy
Building Materials UK Ltd *v.* Secretary of State for the Environment, Transport
and the Regions
Tarmac Heavy Building Materials UK Ltd *v.* Secretary of State for the Environment,
Transport and the Regions; Tarmac Heavy Building Materials UK Ltd *v.*
Buckinghamshire CC (2000) 79 P. & C.R. 260; [2000] P.L.C.R. 157; [1999]
E.G.C.S. 97; (1999) 96(28) L.S.G. 28; [1999] N.P.C. 85, QBD . . . . *Digested*, 00/**4511**
Tarr's Application, Re [1994] N.I.J.B. 163, QBD (NI) . . . . *Considered*, 99/5219
Tarrakarn Ltd *v.* Customs and Excise Commissioners [1996] V. & D.R. 516, V&DTr . . . . . *Digested*, 98/**4917**
Tarrant *v.* Ramage (The Salvital) [1998] 1 Lloyd's Rep. 185; (1997) 94(36) L.S.G. 43;
Times, July 31, 1997, QBD (Adm Ct) . . . . *Digested*, 97/**3857**
TARZAN Trade Mark [1970] F.S.R. 245, CA; affirming [1969] F.S.R. 271; [1969] R.P.C. 301,
Ch D . . . . *Digested*, 70/**2859**:
Considered, 95/4943: *Referred to*, 01/3983
Tas *v.* Turkey (24396/94) (2001) 33 E.H.R.R. 15, ECHR
Tasbian Ltd (No.2), Re [1990] B.C.C. 322; [1991] B.C.L.C. 59, CA . . . . *Digested*, 90/**474**:
Followed, 92/388, 92/389, 93/2321, 99/610
Tasci *v.* Pekalp of London Ltd [2001] I.C.R. 633; *Times*, January 17, 2001, CA . . . . *Digested*, 01/**3304**
Tasker *v.* Colley (2001) 24(3) I.P.D. 24018, Pat Ct
Tasman Discoverer, The [2001] 2 Lloyd's Rep. 665, HC (NZ)
Tasman Pulp & Paper Co Ltd *v.* Brambles JB O'Loghlen Ltd [1981] 2 N.Z.L.R. 225, HC
(NZ) . . . . *Considered*, 00/5164
Tasmanian Primary Distributors Pty Ltd, Re (1994) 13 A.C.S.R. 92, Sup Ct (Tas) (Sgl judge)
Applied, 00/3465
Taste of Bangladesh *v.* Customs and Excise Commissioners [2000] S.T.I. 554, V&DTr
TAT European Airlines SA *v.* Commission of the European Communities (T236/95)
[2000] 1 C.M.L.R. 892, CFI (2nd Chamber) . . . . *Digested*, 00/**724**
Tate *v.* Hart [1999] Lloyd's Rep. P.N. 566; [1999] P.N.L.R. 787; *Independent*, March 8,
1999 (C.S.), CA. . . . . *Digested*, 99/**425**
Tate & Lyle Industries *v.* Greater London Council [1983] 2 A.C. 509; [1983] 2 W.L.R.
649; [1983] 1 All E.R. 1159; [1983] 2 Lloyd's Rep. 117; 81 L.G.R. 4434; (1983)
46 P. & C.R. 243, HL; reversing [1982] 1 W.L.R. 970; [1982] 2 All E.R. 854; 80
L.G.R. 753, CA; reversing [1982] 1 W.L.R. 149; [1981] 3 All E.R. 716; 125 S.J.
865, QBD . . . . *Digested*, 83/**2746**:
Applied, 81/1512, 82/1743, 99/1801, 01/3800: *Considered*, 85/2311,
86/2270: *Followed*, 98/4419
Tate & Lyle Plc *v.* Commission of the European Communities (T202/98); British Sugar
Plc *v.* Commission of the European Communities (T204/98); Napier Brown Plc
v. Commission of the European Communities (T207/98) [2001] All E.R. (EC)
839; [2001] E.C.R. II-2035; [2001] 5 C.M.L.R. 22; *Times*, September 3, 2001,
CFI (4th Chamber) . . . . *Digested*, 01/**760**
Tattari *v.* Private Patients Plan Ltd [1998] I.C.R. 106; [1997] I.R.L.R. 586; (1997) 38
B.M.L.R. 24; *Times*, July 24, 1997; *Independent*, July 11, 1997, CA . . . . *Digested*, 97/**3614**:
Considered, 99/2075
Taube *v.* FX Music Ltd see Burton *v.* FX Music Ltd
Taurus Film GmbH & Co *v.* Office for the Harmonisation in the Internal Market (Trade
Marks and Designs) (OHIM) (T135/99) [2001] E.C.R. II-379; [2001] E.T.M.R.
55; (2001) 24(6) I.P.D. 24041, CFI (2nd Chamber) . . . . *Digested*, 01/**4016**
Tavita *v.* Minister of Immigration [1994] 2 N.Z.L.R. 257, CA (NZ) . . . . *Distinguished*, 98/3100

Tavoulareas *v.* Tavoulareas [1998] 2 F.L.R. 418; [1999] 1 F.C.R. 133; [1998] Fam. Law
   521, CA . . . .   *Digested,* 98/**2459**:
                                                Applied, 98/409

Tax Free Trade Mark Application, Re [1998] E.T.M.R. 193, BPG (Ger)
Tay Bok Choon *v.* Tahansan Sdn Bhd [1987] 1 W.L.R. 413; [1987] B.C.L.C. 472; (1987)
   84 L.S.G. 900; (1987) 131 S.J. 473, PC (Mal) . . . .   *Digested,* 87/**377**:
                        Applied, 97/3020: *Considered,* 00/342

Taylor, Re; *sub nom* Taylor *v.* Taylor [1961] 1 W.L.R. 9; [1961] 1 All E.R. 55; 105 S.J. 37,
   CA; affirming *Times,* February 5, 1960, Ch D . . . .   *Digested,* 61/**590**:
                        Applied, 01/2611: *Followed,* 68/1813

Taylor (Alan), Petitioner; *sub nom* Taylor *v.* Ellis & McHardy Ltd 2000 S.L.T. 1223;
   [1999] O.P.L.R. 275; 1999 G.W.D. 23-1118, 1 Div. . . . .   *Digested,* 00/**6616**

Taylor *v.* Anderton; *sub nom* Taylor *v.* Chief Constable of Greater Manchester [1995] 1
   W.L.R. 447; [1995] 2 All E.R. 420; (1995) 92(11) L.S.G. 37; (1995) 139 S.J.L.B.
   66; *Times,* January 19, 1995; *Independent,* February 28, 1995, CA . . . .   *Digested,* 95/**4123**:
                     Applied, 96/1366, 99/337: *Considered,* 97/472

Taylor *v.* Attorney General [1975] 2 N.Z.L.R. 675 . . . .   *Considered,* 79/2120,
                                                       98/75

Taylor (Patrick) *v.* Attorney General of Jamaica see Lewis *v.* Attorney General of
   Jamaica
Taylor *v.* Bath & North Somerset DC (Quantum) [2001] 3 Q.R. 15, QBD . . . .   *Digested,* 01/**1653**
Taylor *v.* Bilston Community College [2001] 6 Q.R. 24, CC (Wolverhampton) [*Ex rel.*
   Hodgkinsons, Solicitors, The Old Manse, 14 Lumley Avenue, Skegness] . . . .   *Digested,* 01/**1808**
Taylor *v.* Bolton HA (Unreported, January 14, 2000), QBD [*Ex rel.* John Whitting,
   Barrister, 1 Crown Office Row, Temple, London] . . . .   *Digested,* 00/**310**
Taylor *v.* Brock; Taylor *v.* Graham [2001] C.P. Rep. 11, CA . . . .   *Digested,* 00/**352**
Taylor *v.* Builders Accident Insurance Ltd [1997] P.I.Q.R. P247, MCLC . . . .   *Digested,* 98/**3365**:
                                              Followed, 98/3375

Taylor *v.* Chief Constable of Greater Manchester see Taylor *v.* Anderton
Taylor *v.* Cook (Unreported, August 6, 1999), CC (Oxford) [*Ex rel.* Nicholas Stanton,
   Barrister, 169 Temple Chambers, Temple Avenue, London] . . . .   *Digested,* 99/**2504**:
                    Applied, 00/1460: *Cited,* 00/2592: *Considered,* 00/2588
Taylor *v.* Cox (Inspector of Taxes) [1999] Masons C.L.R. 80, Sp Comm . . . .   *Digested,* 99/**4751**
Taylor *v.* Dickens [1998] 1 F.L.R. 806; [1998] 3 F.C.R. 455; [1998] Fam. Law 191;
   Times, November 24, 1997, Ch D . . . .   *Digested,* 97/**4736**:
                              Considered, 98/4585, 00/2321

Taylor *v.* Director of the Serious Fraud Office; *sub nom* Taylor *v.* Serious Fraud Office
   [1999] 2 A.C. 177; [1998] 3 W.L.R. 1040; [1998] 4 All E.R. 801; [1999]
   E.M.L.R. 1; *Times,* November 4, 1998; *Independent,* November 3, 1998, HL;
   affirming [1997] 4 All E.R. 887; [1998] E.M.L.R. 463; (1997) 94(36) L.S.G. 44;
   (1997) 147 N.L.J. 1309; (1997) 141 S.J.L.B. 216; *Times,* August 27, 1997;
   Independent, July 24, 1997, CA . . . .   *Digested,* 98/**1768**:
              Considered, 99/4296, 00/934, 00/2627: *Distinguished,* 99/878

Taylor *v.* East Midlands Offender Employment; *sub nom* Taylor *v.* Lowe [2000] I.R.L.R.
   760, EAT . . . .   *Digested,* 00/**2177**
Taylor *v.* Ellis [1960] Ch. 368; [1960] 2 W.L.R. 509; [1960] 1 All E.R. 549; 104 S.J.
   249, Ch D . . . .   *Digested,* 60/**2027**:
                                                Applied, 00/3903

Taylor *v.* Ellis & McHardy Ltd see Taylor (Alan), Petitioner
Taylor *v.* Gaskell (Unreported, October 9, 2000), CC (Bury) [*Ex rel.* Rowe & Cohen
   Solicitors, Quay House, Quay Street, Manchester] . . . .   *Digested,* 01/**522**:
                                               Considered, 01/521

Taylor *v.* Graham see Taylor *v.* Brock
Taylor *v.* IBC Vehicles Ltd CCRTF 98/1009/2, CA . . . .   *Digested,* 99/**1491**
Taylor *v.* Inntrepreneur Estates (CPC) Ltd (2001) 82 P. & C.R. D4, Ch D
Taylor *v.* Investors Compensation Scheme see R. *v.* Investors Compensation Scheme
   Ltd Ex p. Taylor
Taylor *v.* Ishida (Europe) Ltd (Costs) [2000] F.S.R. 224, Pat Ct . . . .   *Digested,* 00/**3672**
Taylor *v.* Ishida (Europe) Ltd; Taylor *v.* Ishida Co Ltd [2001] EWCA Civ 1092; (2001)
   24(11) I.P.D. 24070, CA; affirming (1999) 22(12) I.P.D. 22114, Ch D
Taylor *v.* Ishida Co Ltd see Taylor *v.* Ishida (Europe) Ltd
Taylor *v.* John Webster Buildings Civil Engineering [1999] I.C.R. 561, EAT . . . .   *Digested,* 99/**2135**
Taylor *v.* KD Coach Hire Ltd (Unreported, June 23, 2000), CC (Liverpool) [*Ex rel.*
   Michael W Halsall Solicitors, 2 The Parks, Newton le Willows] . . . .   *Digested,* 00/**447**
Taylor *v.* Lancashire CC [2001] EWCA Civ 174; [2001] N.P.C. 34; (2001) 82 P. & C.R.
   D5, CA
Taylor *v.* Leslie 1998 S.L.T. 1248; 1998 Rep. L.R. 110; 1998 G.W.D. 23-1184; *Times,*
   September 24, 1998, OH . . . .   *Digested,* 98/**6109**
Taylor *v.* Lowe see Taylor *v.* East Midlands Offender Employment
Taylor *v.* Marshalls Food Group Ltd (No.2) 1998 S.C. 841; 1998 S.L.T. 1022; 1998
   G.W.D. 24-1188; *Times,* September 24, 1998, 1 Div. . . . .   *Digested,* 98/**5399**
Taylor *v.* Mead [1961] 1 W.L.R. 435; [1961] 1 All E.R. 626; 125 J.P. 286; 59 L.G.R.
   202; 105 S.J. 159, DC . . . .   *Digested,* 61/**7847**:
                                      Considered, 62/2635, 98/4299

Taylor (Inspector of Taxes) v. MEPC Holdings Ltd; sub nom MEPC Holdings Ltd v. Taylor
(Inspector of Taxes) [2001] S.T.I. 834; Times, June 12, 2001; Independent, June
25, 2001 (C.S), Ch D; reversing [2000] S.T.C. (S.C.D.) 504; [2000] S.T.I. 1468,
Sp Comm . . . . *Digested, 01/5208*
Taylor v. Midland Bank Trust Co Ltd (No.1) SLJ 98/6549/7132/3, CA . . . . *Digested, 99/394*
Taylor v. Midland Bank Trust Co Ltd (No.2) (1999-2000) 2 I.T.E.L.R. 439, CA . . . . *Digested, 00/5253*
Taylor v. Pace Developments [1991] B.C.C. 406; Times, May 1, 1991, CA . . . . *Digested, 92/3427*:
Distinguished, 00/427
Taylor v. R&S Thompson (Unreported, December 1, 1994), MCLC [Ex rel. Robin
Thompson and Partners, Solicitors] . . . . *Digested, 95/1782*:
Referred to, 98/1582
Taylor v. Rajan; Fraser v. Barton [1974] Q.B. 424; [1974] 2 W.L.R. 385; [1974] 1 All
E.R. 1087; (1974) 59 Cr. App. R. 11; (1974) 59 Cr. App. R. 15; [1974] R.T.R. 304;
[1974] Crim. L.R. 188; [1974] Crim. L.R. 189; 118 S.J. 135, QBD . . . . *Digested, 74/3268*:
Applied, 85/3015, 90/1091, 91/1029, 95/1350: *Considered*, 76/2384,
77/2594, 97/1685, 99/1122: *Distinguished*, 90/3977: *Followed*, 96/5062,
96/5064, 97/1684
Taylor v. Ribby Hall Leisure Ltd [1998] 1 W.L.R. 400; [1997] 4 All E.R. 760; Times,
August 6, 1997, CA . . . . *Digested, 97/488*
Taylor v. Rover Group Ltd (Unreported, May 24, 2000), CC (Birmingham) [Ex rel.
Thompsons Solicitors, The McLaren Building, 35 Dale End, Birmingham] . . . . . *Digested, 00/575*
Taylor v. Royal Society for the Prevention of Cruelty to Animals; sub nom Taylor v.
RSPCA [2001] EWHC Admin 103; [2001] 2 Cr. App. R. 24; (2001) 165 J.P. 567;
[2001] Crim. L.R. 388; (2001) 165 J.P.N. 625, QBD (Admin Ct) . . . . *Digested, 01/313*
Taylor v. RSPCA see Taylor v. Royal Society for the Prevention of Cruelty to Animals
Taylor v. Scottish Prison Service; sub nom Secretary of State for Scotland v. Taylor;
Taylor v. Secretary of State for Scotland [2000] 3 All E.R. 90; 2000 S.C. (H.L.)
139; 2000 S.L.T. 708; [2000] I.C.R. 595; [2000] I.R.L.R. 502; 2000 G.W.D. 17-
686; Times, May 12, 2000; Independent, June 19, 2000, HL; affirming 1999
S.C. 372; 1999 S.L.T. 886; 1999 S.C.L.R. 263; [1999] I.R.L.R. 362; 1999 G.W.D.
3-156, 2 Div; affirming [1997] I.R.L.R. 608, EAT . . . . *Digested, 00/6213*
Taylor v. Secretary of State for Scotland see Taylor v. Scottish Prison Service
Taylor v. Serious Fraud Office see Taylor v. Director of the Serious Fraud Office
Taylor v. Serviceteam Ltd; Taylor v. Waltham Forest LBC [1998] P.I.Q.R. P201, CC
(Romford). . . . . *Digested, 98/372*
Taylor v. Shropshire HA (No.1) [1998] Lloyd's Rep. Med. 395, QBD . . . . *Digested, 99/4000*
Taylor v. Shropshire HA (No.2) [2000] Lloyd's Rep. Med. 96, QBD . . . . *Digested, 00/1464*
Taylor v. Smetten; sub nom Taylor v. Smetton (1882-83) L.R. 11 Q.B.D. 207, QBD . . . . . *Applied*, 73/1529,
80/1317: *Followed*, 99/589
Taylor v. Smetton see Taylor v. Smetten
Taylor v. Taylor see Taylor, Re
Taylor v. Turner (Unreported, June 30, 1998), CC (Stoke on Trent) [Ex rel. Timothy
Prudhoe, Barrister, Queens Chambers, 5 John Dalton Street, Manchester]. . . . . *Digested, 98/1738*
Taylor v. Walsall and District Property & Investment Co Ltd [1998] Env. L.R. 600;
(1998) 30 H.L.R. 1062; (1998) 95(6) L.S.G. 24; (1998) 142 S.J.L.B. 75; Times,
February 5, 1998, QBD . . . . *Digested, 98/463*
Taylor v. Waltham Forest LBC see Taylor v. Serviceteam Ltd
Taylor v. West Kent HA [1997] 8 Med. L.R. 251, QBD . . . . *Digested, 98/3979*
Taylor v. Westminster City Council (Unreported, September 23, 1998), CC (Central
London) [Ex rel. David Giles, Barrister, Verulam Chambers, Peer House, Verulam
Street, London]. . . . . *Digested, 98/4043*
Taylor & Sons (Farms) v. Secretary of State for the Environment, Transport and the
Regions; sub nom R. (on the application of Taylor (t/a David Taylor & Sons)) v.
Secretary of State for the Environment, Transport and the Regions [2001] EWCA
Civ 1254; (2001) 98(38) L.S.G. 40; [2001] N.P.C. 134; Times, October 16,
2001, CA; reversing [2001] P.L.C.R. 25; [2001] J.P.L. 996 (Note); (2001) 98(8)
L.S.G. 45; Times, January 30, 2001, QBD (Admin Ct) . . . . *Digested, 01/4721*
Taylor Clark International Ltd v. Lewis (Inspector of Taxes) [1998] S.T.C. 1259; 71 T.C.
226; [1998] B.T.C. 466; (1999) 96(1) L.S.G. 24; [1998] N.P.C. 152; Times,
December 2, 1998, CA; affirming [1997] S.T.C. 499; [1997] B.T.C. 200; Times,
March 24, 1997, Ch D; affirming [1996] S.T.C. (S.C.D.) 445, Sp Comm . . . . *Digested, 99/4666*
Taylor Fashions Ltd v. Liverpool Victoria Trustees Co Ltd; Old & Campbell Ltd v.
Liverpool Victoria Friendly Society [1982] Q.B. 133; [1981] 2 W.L.R. 576; [1981]
1 All E.R. 897; [1981] Com. L.R. 34; (1979) 251 E.G. 159, Ch D . . . . *Digested, 79/1619*:
Considered, 85/1909, 85/3647, 86/1901, 86/3551, 87/1444, 96/3694,
99/4369: *Followed*, 96/988: *Referred to*, 82/1145, 92/2054, 95/4938,
97/1056
Taylor Sinclair (Capital) Ltd (In Liquidation), Re see Knights v. Seymour Pierce Ellis Ltd
(formerly Ellis & Partners Ltd)
Taylor Woodrow Civil Engineering Ltd v. Hutchison IDH Development Ltd 75 Con. L.R. 1,
QBD (Comm Ct) . . . . *Digested, 98/228*
Taylor's Industrial Flooring v. M&H Plant Hire (Manchester) [1990] B.C.C. 44; [1990]
B.C.L.C. 216, CA. . . . . *Digested, 90/531*:
Considered, 00/4562: *Followed*, 96/1034, 97/3084

Taylor, Stileman & Underwood, Re [1891] 1 Ch. 590, CA . . . . *Followed*, 98/3719
TB *v.* JB (formerly JH) (Abduction: Grave Risk of Harm) [2001] 2 F.L.R. 515; [2001]
    2 F.C.R. 497; [2001] Fam. Law 576, CA . . . . *Digested*, 01/**2546**
TC Basbakanlik Mevzuati Ve Yayin Genel Mudurlugu *v.* Tam Bilgi Iletisim AS [2000]
    E.C.D.R. 457, AsTic Mah (Turkey)
TC Coombs & Co *v.* Inland Revenue Commissioners see R. *v.* Inland Revenue
    Commissioners Ex p. TC Coombs & Co
TC Harrison Group Ltd *v.* Customs and Excise Commissioners (C305/97) see Royscot
    Leasing Ltd *v.* Customs and Excise Commissioners (C305/97)
TC Harrison Group Ltd *v.* Customs and Excise Commissioners (Withdrawal of
    Reference) see Royscot Leasing Ltd *v.* Customs and Excise Commissioners
    (Withdrawal of Reference)
Tchoula *v.* ICTS (UK) Ltd; *sub nom* ICTS (UK) Ltd *v.* Tchoula [2000] I.C.R. 1191;
    [2000] I.R.L.R. 643, EAT . . . . *Digested*, 00/**2182**:
                                         Applied, 01/2312
Teachers Pensions Agency *v.* Hill [1998] 4 All E.R. 865; [1999] I.C.R. 435; [1998]
    O.P.L.R. 167; *Times*, July 20, 1998, Ch D . . . . *Digested*, 98/**4142**
Team Lotus Ventures Ltd's Trade Mark Application [1999] E.T.M.R. 669, TMR . . . . *Digested*, 00/**3783**
Teape *v.* Godfrey [1986] R.T.R. 213, QBD . . . . *Digested*, 86/**2885**:
                 Disapproved, 89/4901: *Distinguished*, 88/4819: *Followed*, 01/1130:
                                        Not applied, 93/3502
Tech Textiles Ltd, Re; *sub nom* Secretary of State for Trade and Industry *v.* Vane [1998] 1
    B.C.L.C. 259, Ch D (Companies Ct) . . . . *Digested*, 98/**670**
TECHMO/Powered vehicle for operation of ladles (T522/94) [1999] E.P.O.R. 75; (1998)
    21 (2) I.P.D. 21018, EPO (Technical Bd App)
TECHNICARE/Ultrasonic transducer (T04/90) [1998] E.P.O.R. 87, EPO (Technical Bd
    App)
Technograph Printed Circuits Ltd *v.* Mills & Rockley (Electronics) Ltd see Mills &
    Rockley (Electronics) Ltd *v.* Technograph Printed Circuits Ltd
TECNICA/Ski boot lining (T554/98) [2000] E.P.O.R. 475, EPO (Technical Bd App) . . . *Digested*, 01/**3887**
Teddie Thulstrup A/S *v.* Skoubo see Skoubo *v.* Teddie Thulstrup A/S
Tee *v.* Hillman see Tee *v.* Tee
Tee *v.* Tee; Tee *v.* Hillman [1999] 2 F.L.R. 613; [1999] 3 F.C.R. 409; [1999] Fam. Law
    534, CA . . . . *Digested*, 99/**2400**
Teesside Times Ltd *v.* Drury [1980] I.C.R. 338; [1980] I.R.L.R. 72; 124 S.J. 80, CA;
    affirming [1978] I.C.R. 822; (1978) 13 I.T.R. 298, EAT . . . . *Digested*, 80/**1012**:
                       Considered, 90/1949: *Followed*, 98/2215
Tehrani *v.* United Kingdom Central Council for Nursing, Midwifery and Health Visiting
    2001 S.C. 581; 2001 S.L.T. 879; [2001] I.R.L.R. 208; 2001 G.W.D. 4-165, OH . . . *Digested*, 01/**6703**
Teignbridge DC *v.* Saunders [2001] EWHC Admin 344; [2001] R.V.R. 282, QBD
    (Admin Ct)
TEIJIN/Water-repellent textile fabric (T647/91) [1998] E.P.O.R. 288, EPO (Technical Bd
    App)
Teixeira de Castro *v.* Portugal (1999) 28 E.H.R.R. 101; 4 B.H.R.C. 533; [1998] Crim.
    L.R. 751; [1998] H.R.C.D. 8, ECHR . . . . *Digested*, 98/**3122**:
            Considered, 01/992: *Distinguished*, 00/918: *Referred to*, 00/916
Tejedor Garcia *v.* Spain (1998) 26 E.H.R.R. 440; [1998] H.R.C.D. 166, ECHR . . . . *Digested*, 98/**3146**
Tejendrasingh *v.* Christie see Tejendrasingh *v.* Metsons
Tejendrasingh *v.* Ginn & Co see Tejendrasingh *v.* Metsons
Tejendrasingh *v.* Metsons; *sub nom* Tejendrasingh *v.* Christie; Singh (Tejendra) *v.*
    Christie; Tejendrasingh *v.* Ginn & Co; Tejendrasingh *v.* Pickwell [1997] E.M.L.R.
    597, CA; affirming [1995] E.M.L.R. 152; *Times*, November 11, 1993, QBD . . . . . . *Digested*, 98/**328**:
                                 Considered, 00/345
Tejendrasingh *v.* Pickwell see Tejendrasingh *v.* Metsons
Tek Corporation Provident Fund *v.* Lorentz [2001] O.P.L.R. 137, Sup Ct (SA) . . . . *Digested*, 01/**4630**
Tekin *v.* Turkey (22496/93) (2001) 31 E.H.R.R. 4; [1998] H.R.C.D. 646, ECHR . . . . *Digested*, 01/**3558**
Tekna Design Ltd *v.* Davenport Properties Ltd [2000] C.P. Rep. 63, CA . . . . *Digested*, 00/**602**
Teknek Electronics Ltd *v.* KSM International Ltd [1998] E.T.M.R. 522; 1998 G.W.D. 5-
    253, OH
Tele Danmark AS *v.* Handels- og Kontorfunktionaerernes Forbund i Danmark (C109/00)
    [2001] All E.R. (EC) 941; [2001] I.R.L.R. 853; [2001] Emp. L.R. 1389, ECJ
    (5th Chamber)
Tele-Maegleren ApS *v.* Netsource Danmark A/S [2000] E.T.M.R. 523, SH (DK)
Telecom Italia SpA *v.* Matricardi [1999] E.C.C. 206, Trib (Turin) . . . . *Digested*, 99/**693**
Telecom Securicor Cellular Radio Ltd *v.* National Assembly for Wales [2001] P.L.C.R. 23;
    [2001] J.P.L. 842 (Note), QBD (Admin Ct) . . . . *Digested*, 01/**4753**
Telecom Securicor Cellular Radio Ltd's Trade Mark Application (No.1588293/4); *sub nom*
    AFFINITY Trade Mark (1999) 22(2) I.P.D. 22018, TMR
Teleflower Services, Re [2001] E.C.C. 49, C Concurrence (F)
Telefon & Buch Verlags GmbH *v.* Office for Harmonisation in the Internal Market (Trade
    Marks and Designs) (OHIM) (T357/99) [2001] E.C.R. II-1705; [2001] 3
    C.M.L.R. 3; [2001] C.E.C. 151; [2001] E.T.M.R. 91, CFI . . . . *Digested*, 01/**4008**
Telegraph Group Plc, Ex p. see R. (on the application of Telegraph Group Plc) *v.* Sherwood

Telegraph Service Stations Ltd v. Trafford BC [2000] 3 E.G.L.R. 145; [2000] R.V.R. 356,
  Lands Tr . . . . *Digested*, 01/**4675**
TELEKOM Trade Mark; *sub nom* Alles Wird Teurer [1999] E.T.M.R. 49, KG (Berlin) . . . . . *Digested*, 99/**3548**
Telemarsicabruzzo SpA v. Circostel (C320/90); Telemarsicabruzzo SpA v. Ministerio
  delle Poste e Telecommunicazioni (C320/90) [1993] E.C.R. I-393; *Times*,
  February 10, 1993; *Financial Times*, February 12, 1993, ECJ . . . . *Digested*, 93/**4300**:
                          Applied, 98/2319: *Considered*, 97/2397
Telemarsicabruzzo SpA v. Ministerio delle Poste e Telecommunicazioni (C320/90) see
  Telemarsicabruzzo SpA v. Circostel (C320/90)
Televised News Reports, Re [1999] E.C.C. 399, BverfG (Ger)
Televising Premier League Football Matches, Re; *sub nom* Agreement between Football
  Association Premier League Ltd, Football Association Ltd, Football League Ltd
  and their respective Member Clubs, Re; Agreement relating to the Supply of
  Services facilitating the Broadcasting on Television of Premier League Football
  Matches, Re [1999] U.K.C.L.R. 258; [2000] E.M.L.R. 78; (1999) 96(32) L.S.G.
  33; *Times*, August 18, 1999, RPC . . . . *Digested*, 99/**698**
Telewest Communications Group Ltd v. Customs and Excise Commissioners [1996] V.
  & D.R. 566, V&DTr. . . . . *Digested*, 98/**4945**
TELEYE Trade Mark see Signal Communications Ltd v. Office for Harmonisation in the
  Internal Market (Trade Marks and Designs) (OHIM) (T128/99)
Telfair Shipping Corp v. Inersea Carriers SA (The Caroline P) [1985] 1 W.L.R. 553;
  [1985] 1 All E.R. 243; [1984] 2 Lloyd's Rep. 466; (1985) 82 L.S.G. 1781; (1985)
  129 S.J. 283, QBD (Comm Ct) . . . . *Digested*, 85/**2012**:
                                           Considered, 00/878
Telfner v. Austria (33501/96) [2001] Crim. L.R. 821, ECHR
Telford and Wrekin Council v. Ashley (Unreported, December 14, 2000), MC [*Ex rel.*
  John Ritson, Barrister, Clock Chambers, 78 Darlington Street, Wolverhampton,
  Staffordshire] . . . . *Digested*, 01/**1986**
Telford and Wrekin Council v. Church of Jesus Christ of Latter Day Saints (2001) 16
  P.A.D. 87, Planning Inspector
Telford and Wrekin Council v. Jordan (2001) 165 J.P. 107, QBD . . . . *Digested*, 01/**922**
Telmak Teleproducts Australia Pty Ltd v. Bond International Pty Ltd (1985) 5 I.P.R. 203 . *Considered*, 98/3418
Telstra Super Pty Ltd v. Flegeltaub [2001] Pens. L.R. 7, Sup Ct (Vic) . . . . *Digested*, 01/**4643**
Temelkowski v. McMath (Unreported, September 3, 1997), CC (Bradford) [*Ex rel.*
  Eatons Solicitors, The Old Library, 34 Darley Street, Bradford, West Yorkshire,
  BD1 3LH] . . . . *Digested*, 98/**1556**
Tempest (t/a Cesspool Sid) v. Customs and Excise Commissioners [2000] R.T.R. 227;
  Times, March 16, 2000, QBD . . . . *Digested*, 00/**4986**
Temple House Developments Ltd v. Customs and Excise Commissioners [1998] B.V.C.
  2302, V&DTr . . . . *Considered*, 01/**5619**
Templiss Properties Ltd v. Hyams [1999] E.G.C.S. 60, Ch D . . . . *Digested*, 99/**3666**
Tennant, Re [1996] 2 N.Z.L.R. 633, HC (NZ) . . . . *Followed*, 01/384
Tennant Radiant Heat v. Warrington Development Corp [1988] 1 E.G.L.R. 41; [1988] 11
  E.G. 71; (1988) 4 Const. L.J. 321, CA . . . . *Digested*, 88/**2034**:
                                           Followed, 99/786
Tennent v. Betts see Neilson v. Betts
Tennessee Secret (UK) Ltd v. Customs and Excise Commissioners [2001] S.T.I. 571,
  V&DTr
Terard Ltd v. Customs and Excise Commissioners [2001] S.T.I. 572, V&DTr
Terfenadin, Re [1998] F.S.R. 145, OLG (Munchen)
Terhoeve v. Inspecteur van de Belastingdienst Particulieren/Ondernemingen Buitenland
  (C18/95) [1999] E.C.R. I-345; [2001] 1 C.M.L.R. 12; (1999) 96(19) L.S.G. 30;
  Times, February 25, 1999, ECJ . . . . *Digested*, 99/**4547**
Termination of a Copyright Licence (4 Ob 318/98p), Re [2001] E.C.C. 7, OGH (A)
Termination of an Agency Agreement, Re (Germany) [1998] E.C.C. 249, BGH (Ger)
Terranova v. Italy (A/337-B) (Unreported, December 4, 1995), ECHR . . . . *Applied*, 98/3130
Terrazos v. Instituto Nacional de Empleo (C424/93) see Zabala Erasun v. Instituto
  Nacional de Empleo (C422/93)
Terrell v. Chatterton see Chatterton v. Terrell
Terry v. Craze see Terry v. East Sussex Coroner
Terry v. East Sussex CC [1977] 1 All E.R. 567; [1976] I.C.R. 536; [1976] I.R.L.R. 332;
  (1976) 12 I.T.R. 265; 75 L.G.R. 111, EAT . . . . *Digested*, 77/**1139**:
          Applied, 85/1252: *Approved*, 86/1284: *Considered*, 79/925:
                                           Followed, 00/2174
Terry v. East Sussex Coroner; *sub nom* Terry v. Craze [2001] EWCA Civ 1094; [2001]
  3 W.L.R. 605; (2001) 62 B.M.L.R. 61; (2001) 98(34) L.S.G. 37; *Times*, July 26,
  2001; *Independent*, October 22, 2001 (C.S), CA; affirming [2001] Q.B. 559;
  [2001] 2 W.L.R. 710; [2001] A.C.D. 27; *Times*, January 12, 2001; *Independent*,
  December 6, 2000, QBD . . . . *Digested*, 01/**28**
Terry v. Sands Farm Country House Hotel (Unreported, June 1, 2000), CC (Telford)
  [*Ex rel.* Nicholas E Starks, Barrister, St Ive's Chambers, Whittall Street,
  Birmingham] . . . . *Digested*, 00/**1643**
Terry Adams Ltd v. Bolton MBC (1997) 73 P. & C.R. 446, QBD . . . . *Digested*, 97/**4133**:
                                           Considered, 00/4528

Tertiary Institutes Allied Staff Association Inc v. Tahana (Unreported, August 14, 1997),
CA (NZ) . . . .   *Applied,* 98/3100
Terumo Kabushiki Kaisha's European Patent Application (T941/96) (2000) 23(9) I.P.D.
23071, EPO (Technical Bd App)
TERUMO/Syringe (T205/89) [1998] E.P.O.R. 247, EPO (Technical Bd App)
Tesam Distribution Ltd v. Commerzbank AG see Tesam Distribution Ltd v. Schuh Mode
Team GmbH
Tesam Distribution Ltd v. Schuh Mode Team GmbH; *sub nom* Tesam Distribution Ltd v.
Commerzbank AG [1990] I.L.Pr. 149; (1989) 86(46) L.S.G. 38; *Times,* October
24, 1989; *Independent,* October 30, 1989 (C.S.); *Financial Times,* October 27,
1989, CA . . . .   *Digested,* 89/**3015**:
Applied, 92/3285: *Not followed,* 98/583
Tesco Plc v. Crimmin (Inspector of Taxes) [1997] S.T.C. 981; 69 T.C. 510; [1997] B.T.C.
369; *Times,* June 25, 1997, Ch D . . . .   *Digested,* 97/**1069**
Tesco Plc v. Customs and Excise Commissioners [2001] B.V.C. 2416, V&DTr
Tesco Stores Ltd v. Norman Hitchcox Partnership Ltd; Clark Care Group Ltd v. Norman
Hitchcox Partnership Ltd; Maidstone Grove Ltd v. Norman Hitchcox Partnership
Ltd 56 Con. L.R. 42, QBD (OR) . . . .   *Digested,* 98/**795**
Tesco Stores Ltd v. North Norfolk DC (1999) 78 P. & C.R. 359; [1999] J.P.L. 920;
[1999] E.G.C.S. 39; (1999) 96(12) L.S.G. 35; [1999] N.P.C. 34, CA; affirming
[1998] P.L.C.R. 183, QBD . . . .   *Digested,* 00/**4498**
Tesco Stores Ltd v. Secretary of State for the Environment; Tesco Stores Ltd v. West
Oxfordshire DC; Tesco Stores Ltd v. Tarmac Provincial Properties Ltd [1995] 1
W.L.R. 759; [1995] 2 All E.R. 636; 93 L.G.R. 403; (1995) 70 P. & C.R. 184;
[1995] 2 P.L.R. 72; [1995] 2 E.G.L.R. 147; [1995] 27 E.G. 154; [1995] E.G.C.S.
82; (1995) 92(24) L.S.G. 39; (1995) 145 N.L.J. 724; (1995) 139 S.J.L.B. 145;
[1995] N.P.C. 89A; *Times,* May 13, 1995, HL; affirming (1994) 68 P. & C.R. 219;
[1994] 1 P.L.R. 97; [1994] E.G.C.S. 103; [1994] N.P.C. 80, CA; reversing
(1994) 67 P. & C.R. 216; [1993] 2 P.L.R. 108; [1994] J.P.L. 227; [1993]
E.G.C.S. 133, QBD . . . .   *Digested,* 95/**4784**:
Applied, 96/4779, 99/4215, 01/4682, 01/4731: *Considered,* 99/3049
Tesco Stores Ltd v. Secretary of State for the Environment, Transport and the Regions
(Compulsory Purchase) (2000) 80 P. & C.R. 427; [2001] J.P.L. 106 (Note),
QBD . . . .   *Digested,* 01/**4679**
Tesco Stores Ltd v. Secretary of State for the Environment, Transport and the Regions
(Extension of Floor Space: District Centre) see R. (on the application of Tesco
Stores Ltd) v. Secretary of State for the Environment, Transport and the
Regions
Tesco Stores Ltd v. Secretary of State for the Environment, Transport and the Regions
(Out of Centre Development: Conditional Planning Permission) [2001] J.P.L.
1002 (Note); (2001) 98(2) L.S.G. 42, QBD (Admin Ct)
Tesco Stores Ltd v. Tarmac Provincial Properties Ltd see Tesco Stores Ltd v. Secretary of
State for the Environment
Tesco Stores Ltd v. Ward see Ward v. Tesco Stores Ltd
Tesco Stores Ltd v. West Oxfordshire DC see Tesco Stores Ltd v. Secretary of State for
the Environment
Test Valley BC v. Cornelius-Reed (1998) 13 P.A.D. 243, Planning Inspector
Test Valley BC v. Everett (2001) 16 P.A.D. 39, Planning Inspector
Test Valley BC v. Hampshire CC [2001] J.P.L. 1319 (Note), QBD (Admin Ct)
Tetra Pak International SA v. Commission of the European Communities (C333/94); *sub*
nom Tetra Pak International SA v. Commission of the European Communities
(C333/94P); Tetra Pak International SA v. Commission of the European
Communities (T83/91) - CFI ref [1997] All E.R. (E.C.) 4; [1996] E.C.R. I-5951;
[1997] 4 C.M.L.R. 662, ECJ (5th Chamber); affirming [1994] E.C.R. II-755;
[1997] 4 C.M.L.R. 726, CFI (2nd Chamber) . . . .   *Digested,* 97/**854**:
Followed, 98/716, 01/761
Tetra Pak International SA v. Commission of the European Communities (C333/94P)
see Tetra Pak International SA v. Commission of the European Communities
(C333/94)
Tetra Pak International SA v. Commission of the European Communities (T83/91) - CFI
ref see Tetra Pak International SA v. Commission of the European Communities
(C333/94)
Tetreault-Gadoury v. Canada [1991] 2 S.C.R. 22, Sup Ct (Can) . . . .   *Applied,* 98/3074
Teward v. Inland Revenue Commissioners [2001] S.T.C. (S.C.D.) 36; [2001] S.T.I. 204,
Sp Comm . . . .   *Digested,* 01/**5248**
Tewkesbury BC v. Bryant Homes Mercia Ltd (1999) 14 P.A.D. 392, Planning Inspector
Tewkesbury BC v. Gloucester Playing Fields Association (2001) 16 P.A.D. 10, Planning
Inspector
Texaco v. North Lanarkshire Licensing Board (No.2) [2001] 18 S.L.L.P. 18, Sh Ct
(South Strathclyde) . . . .   *Digested,* 01/**6787**
Texas Electronics v. Hyundai Electronics [2000] F.S.R. 86, Pat Ct . . . .   *Digested,* 00/**3683**
Texas Instruments Inc v. Hyundai Electronics UK Ltd (1999) 22(12) I.P.D. 22116, Pat Ct
TEXAS INSTRUMENTS/Language understanding system (T236/91) [2000] E.P.O.R. 156,
EPO (Technical Bd App) . . . .   *Digested,* 00/**3640**

Texas Iron Works Inc's Patent Application; *sub nom* Nodeco Ltd *v.* Texas Iron Works Inc [2000] R.P.C. 207; (1999) 22(8) I.P.D. 22074, CA . . . . *Digested*, 00/**3676**
Texasgulf Inc *v.* Internal Revenue Commissioner 1 I.T.L. Rep. 597, US Ct
Textilwerke Deggendorg GmbH (TWD) *v.* Commission of the European Communities (C355/95P); *sub nom* Textilwerke Deggendorg GmbH (TWD) *v.* Commission of the European Communities (T244/93 and T486/93) [1997] E.C.R. I-2549; [1998] 1 C.M.L.R. 234, ECJ [1995] E.C.R. II-2265; [1996] 1 C.M.L.R. 332, CFI (3rd Chamber)
Textilwerke Deggendorg GmbH (TWD) *v.* Commission of the European Communities (T244/93 and T486/93) see Textilwerke Deggendorg GmbH (TWD) *v.* Commission of the European Communities (C355/95P)
TF 1's Involvement in Videograms, Re [2000] E.C.C. 396, C Concurrence (F)
TGA Chapman Ltd *v.* Christopher [1998] 1 W.L.R. 12; [1998] 2 All E.R. 873; [1997] C.L.C. 1306; [1998] Lloyd's Rep. I.R. 1; *Times*, July 21, 1997, CA . . . . *Digested*, 97/**3111**:
Applied, 99/3422: *Considered*, 00/413, 01/474: *Followed*, 99/388
TH Goldschmidt AG *v.* EOC Belgium NV (Amendment of Pleadings) (1999) 22(9) I.P.D. 22083, Pat Ct . . . . *Digested*, 99/**3517**
Thacker *v.* Crown Prosecution Service, *Times*, December 29, 1997, CA . . . . *Digested*, 98/**4778**
Thai Trading Co *v.* Taylor [1998] Q.B. 781; [1998] 2 W.L.R. 893; [1998] 3 All E.R. 65; [1998] 1 Costs L.R. 122; [1998] 2 F.L.R. 430; [1998] 3 F.C.R. 606; [1998] P.N.L.R. 698; [1998] Fam. Law 586; (1998) 95(15) L.S.G. 30; (1998) 142 S.J.L.B. 125; *Times*, March 6, 1998, CA . . . . *Digested*, 98/**3714**:
Considered, 98/3712, 98/3715, 01/1116: *Doubted*, 99/3798
Thakerar *v.* Pajman (Unreported, February 5, 1999), CC (Central London) [*Ex rel.* Paul Hepher, Barrister and Portner & Jaskel Solicitors, 8 Welbeck Way, London] . . . . *Digested*, 99/**1486**
Thames Launches *v.* Trinity House Corp (Deptford Strond) (No.1) [1961] Ch. 197; [1961] 2 W.L.R. 16; [1961] 1 All E.R. 26; [1960] 2 Lloyd's Rep. 407; 105 S.J. 16, Ch D . . . . *Digested*, 61/**8386**:
Applied, 71/9526: *Considered*, 99/3576
Thames Tideway Properties Ltd *v.* Serfaty & Partners [1999] 2 Lloyd's Rep. 110, CC (Central London) . . . . *Digested*, 99/**862**
Thames Water Developments Ltd *v.* Kingsalton Ltd see Kingsalton Ltd *v.* Thames Water Developments Ltd
Thames Water Utilities Ltd *v.* Oxford City Council (1999) 1 L.G.L.R. 291; [1999] 1 E.G.L.R. 167; [1998] E.G.C.S. 133; (1998) 95(31) L.S.G. 37; (1999) 77 P. & C.R. D16, Ch D . . . . *Digested*, 99/**4363**
Thames Water Utilities Ltd *v.* Reynolds [1996] I.R.L.R. 186, EAT . . . . *Digested*, 96/**2673**:
Followed, 00/2177
Thames Water Utilities Ltd *v.* Richardson [2001] E.H.L.R. 15, CA . . . . *Digested*, 01/**5634**
Thames Water Utilities Ltd *v.* Videotron Corp Ltd QBENF 1998/0981/A2, CA; reversing [1998] N.P.C. 112, QBD (OR)
Thames Water Utilities Ltd's European Patent (No.0310221) see THAMES WATER/Slow sand filter cleaning device (T443/95)
THAMES WATER/Slow sand filter cleaning device (T443/95); *sub nom* Thames Water Utilities Ltd's European Patent (No.0310221) [2001] E.P.O.R. 10; (1998) 21 (12) I.P.D. 21133, EPO (Technical Bd App) . . . . *Digested*, 01/**3947**
Thamesdown BC *v.* Goonery (Unreported, February 13, 1995), CA. . . . . *Digested*, 95/**2600**:
Not followed, 01/5021
Thamesmead Town Ltd *v.* Allotey (1998) 30 H.L.R. 1052; (2000) 79 P. & C.R. 557; [1998] 3 E.G.L.R. 97; [1998] 37 E.G. 161; (1998) 95(3) L.S.G. 26, CA . . . . *Digested*, 98/**4345**
Tharros Shipping Co Ltd *v.* Bias Shipping Ltd (The Griparion) (No.2) [1994] 1 Lloyd's Rep. 533, QBD (Comm Ct) . . . . *Digested*, 95/**4509**:
Applied, 99/504
Thayaparan, Re (Unreported, June 10, 1999), IAT . . . . *Applied*, 00/3321
Theakston *v.* Matthews, *Times*, April 13, 1998, CA . . . . *Digested*, 98/**418**
Themis FTSE Fledgling Index Trust Plc *v.* Customs and Excise Commissioners [2001] S.T.I. 810, V&DTr
Theophanous *v.* Herald & Weekly Times Ltd (1994) 182 C.L.R. 104, HC (Aus). . . . . *Applied*, 98/**3091**:
Considered, 97/2775
Therma-Tru Corp's Patent; *sub nom* Cohmor Holdings Plc *v.* Therma-Tru Corp [1997] R.P.C. 777; (1997) 20(4) I.P.D. 20033, Pat Ct. . . . . *Digested*, 98/**3458**
Thermos Ltd *v.* Aladdin Sales & Marketing Ltd [2001] EWCA Civ 667; (2001) 24(8) I.P.D. 24049, CA; affirming [2000] F.S.R. 402; (2000) 23(1) I.P.D. 23008; *Independent*, December 13, 1999 (C.S.), Pat Ct. . . . . *Digested*, 00/**3695**
Thibault *v.* Caisse Nationale d'Assurance Vieillesse des Travailleurs Salaries (C136/95) see Caisse Nationale d'Assurance Vieillesse des Travailleurs Salaries (CNAVTS) *v.* Thibault (C136/95)
Thieffry *v.* Conseil de l'Ordre des Avocats a la Cour de Paris (71/76) [1978] Q.B. 315; [1977] 3 W.L.R. 453; [1977] E.C.R. 765; [1977] 2 C.M.L.R. 373; 121 S.J. 677, ECJ . . . . *Digested*, 77/**1271**:
Applied, 01/2931
Third *v.* North East Ice & Cold Storage Co Ltd 1997 S.L.T. 1177; [1998] B.C.C. 242, OH . . . . *Digested*, 97/**5711**:
Considered, 98/694

Thirty-Eight Building Ltd (No.1), Re [1999] B.C.C. 260; [1999] 1 B.C.L.C 416; [1999]
   B.P.I.R. 620; [1999] O.P.L.R. 319; *Times*, January 14, 1999, Ch D . . . . *Digested*, 99/**3362**
Thirty-Eight Building Ltd (No.2), Re; *sub nom* Simms *v.* Saunders [2000] B.C.C. 422;
   [2000] 1 B.C.L.C. 201; [2000] B.P.I.R. 158, Ch D (Companies Ct). . . . . *Digested*, 00/**3501**
Thlimmenos *v.* Greece (34369/97) (2001) 31 E.H.R.R. 15; 9 B.H.R.C. 12, ECHR . . . . . . *Digested*, 01/**3485**
Thoar's Judicial Factor *v.* Ramlort Ltd; *sub nom* Reid *v.* Ramlort Ltd 1998 S.C. 887;
   1999 S.L.T. 1153; [1999] B.P.I.R. 133; 1998 G.W.D. 29-1504; *Times*, October 14,
   1998, Ex Div; reversing 1998 G.W.D. 20-1040, OH . . . . *Digested*, 98/**6002**
Thoburn *v.* Northumberland CC (1999) 1 L.G.L.R. 819, CA. . . . . *Digested*, 99/**2889**
Thoday *v.* Thoday [1964] P. 181; [1964] 2 W.L.R. 371; [1964] 1 All E.R. 341; 108 S.J.
   15, CA . . . . *Digested*, 64/**1129**:
               Applied, 65/100, 66/9896, 67/3912, 77/1216, 80/933, 90/2019:
                     Considered, 88/3432, 98/1981, 99/5146
Thomann *v.* Switzerland (1997) 24 E.H.R.R. 553, ECHR. . . . . *Digested*, 98/**3149**:
                     Distinguished, 98/3127
Thomas (CICA: Quantum: 2000), Re [2001] 3 Q.R. 13, CICA (Bristol) [*Ex rel.* Matthew
   White, Barrister, St. John's Chambers, Small Street, Bristol] . . . . *Digested*, 01/**1615**
Thomas *v.* Baptiste [2000] 2 A.C. 1; [1999] 3 W.L.R. 249; 6 B.H.R.C. 259; (1999)
   143 S.J.L.B. 187; *Times*, March 23, 1999, PC (Trin) . . . . *Digested*, 99/**758**:
                  Applied, 00/3201: *Distinguished*, 99/3092, 00/3172
Thomas *v.* Bradford University see Thomas *v.* University of Bradford
Thomas *v.* Brighton HA see Wells *v.* Wells
Thomas *v.* Bunn; Wilson *v.* Graham; Lea *v.* British Aerospace Plc [1991] 1 A.C. 362;
   [1991] 2 W.L.R. 27; [1991] 1 All E.R. 193; (1991) 140 N.L.J. 1789; (1991) 135
   S.J. 16; *Times*, December 17, 1990; *Independent*, December 14, 1990; *Guardian*,
   December 17, 1990, HL; reversing (Unreported, December 5, 1989), HC [*Ex rel.*
   Benussi & Powell, Solicitors] . . . . *Digested*, 91/**1312**:
                     Considered, 01/476
Thomas *v.* Chief Adjudication Officer (C328/91) see Secretary of State for Social
   Security *v.* Thomas (C328/91)
Thomas *v.* Commissioner of Police of the Metropolis [1997] Q.B. 813; [1997] 2 W.L.R.
   593; [1997] 1 All E.R. 747; *Times*, December 12, 1996; *Independent*, December
   19, 1996, CA . . . . *Digested*, 97/**455**:
                     Followed, 98/880
Thomas (Christopher) *v.* Customs and Excise Commissioners [2001] S.T.I. 1025, V&DTr
Thomas *v.* Davies (Unreported, June 13, 2000), CC (Carmarthen) [*Ex rel.* Palser
   Grossman Solicitors, Discovery House, Scott Harbour, Cardiff Bay] . . . . *Digested*, 00/**353**
Thomas *v.* F Long (Security Services) Ltd [2001] 6 Q.R. 22, CC (Aberdare) [*Ex rel.*
   Robert O'Leary, Barrister, 33 park Place, Cardiff] . . . . *Digested*, 01/**1767**
Thomas *v.* Hughes see Thomas *v.* News Group Newspapers Ltd
Thomas *v.* Kwik Save Stores Ltd, *Times*, June 27, 2000, CA . . . . *Digested*, 00/**1469**
Thomas *v.* Maxwell; *sub nom* Inquiry into Mirror Group Newspapers Plc, Re [2000]
   Ch. 194; [1999] 3 W.L.R. 583; [1999] 2 All E.R. 641; [2000] B.C.C. 217; [1999]
   1 B.C.L.C 690; (1999) 96(14) L.S.G. 31; *Times*, March 23, 1999, Ch D . . . . *Digested*, 99/**605**
Thomas *v.* National Training Partnership Ltd [1998] I.C.R. 436, EAT . . . . *Digested*, 98/**2236**:
                     Disapproved, 98/5826
Thomas *v.* News Group International Ltd see Thomas *v.* News Group Newspapers Ltd
Thomas *v.* News Group Newspapers Ltd; *sub nom* Thomas *v.* Hughes; Thomas *v.*
   News Group International Ltd [2001] EWCA Civ 1233; (2001) 98(34) L.S.G.
   43; (2001) 145 S.J.L.B. 207; *Times*, July 25, 2001; *Independent*, November 12,
   2001 (C.S); *Daily Telegraph*, July 24, 2001, CA . . . . *Digested*, 01/**4418**
Thomas *v.* Nottingham Inc Football Club [1972] Ch. 596; [1972] 2 W.L.R. 1025;
   [1972] 1 All E.R. 1176; (1971) 116 S.J. 96, Ch D . . . . *Digested*, 72/**1629**:
                     Considered, 83/1765, 99/284
Thomas *v.* Osprey Leisure Ltd (Unreported, December 8, 2000), CC (Whitehaven) [*Ex*
   rel. John Baldwin, Barrister, Oriel Chambers, 14 Water Street, Liverpool] . . . . . . *Digested*, 01/**4285**
Thomas *v.* Pearce [2000] F.S.R. 718, CA. . . . . *Digested*, 00/**3566**
Thomas *v.* Plymouth City Council [1999] R.V.R. 315, Lands Tr
Thomas *v.* South Wales Sea Fisheries Committee [2000] C.O.D. 434, QBD
Thomas *v.* Stagecoach (South) Ltd (Unreported, June 8, 1999), CC (Central London)
   [*Ex rel.* Daniel Tobin, Barrister, 46 Essex Street, London] . . . . *Digested*, 99/**1589**
Thomas (Keiron) *v.* Trinidad and Tobago, *Times*, December 15, 1997, PC (Trin) . . . . . . *Digested*, 98/**993**
Thomas *v.* Trowbridge (Unreported, August 4, 1999), CC (Oxford) [*Ex rel.* Scott Rees
   & Co Solicitors, Centaur House, Gardiners Place, Skelmersdale, Lancashire] . . . *Digested*, 99/**2480**
Thomas *v.* University of Bradford; *sub nom* Thomas *v.* Bradford University [1987] A.C.
   795; [1987] 2 W.L.R. 677; [1987] 1 All E.R. 834; [1987] I.C.R. 245; (1987) 84
   L.S.G. 980; (1987) 137 N.L.J. 220; (1987) 131 S.J. 296, HL; reversing [1986]
   Ch. 381; [1986] 2 W.L.R. 111; [1986] 1 All E.R. 217; [1986] I.C.R. 87; (1985) 129
   S.J. 890; *Times*, November 4, 1985, CA; affirming [1985] 3 W.L.R. 248; [1985]
   2 All E.R. 786; (1985) 82 L.S.G. 3083; (1985) 129 S.J. 504; *Independent*, July
   9, 1990 (C.S), Ch D . . . . *Digested*, 87/**1276**:
               Applied, 87/1275, 88/1226, 99/5290: *Considered*, 91/1577, 91/1578:
                     Disapproved, 85/3552

Thomas *v.* Watts (Unreported, March 9, 2001), CC (Birmingham) [*Ex rel.* Jamie Gamble, Barrister, 5 Fountain Court, Steelhouse Lane, Birmingham] . . . . *Digested,* 01/**907**
Thomas Bates & Son Ltd *v.* Wyndham's (Lingerie) Ltd [1981] 1 W.L.R. 505; [1981] 1 All E.R. 1077; (1981) 41 P. & C.R. 345; (1980) 257 E.G. 381; 125 S.J. 32, CA; affirming (1980) 39 P. & C.R. 517, Ch D . . . . *Digested,* 81/**1584**:
Applied, 83/417, 84/1932, 89/2136, 89/2138, 96/3756, 00/4382, 01/5510:
Cited, 95/780: *Considered,* 96/5784: *Distinguished,* 90/2833, 92/5952:
Not followed, 80/1629, 81/1574
Thomas Christy (In Liquidation), Re [1994] 2 B.C.L.C. 527, Ch D . . . . *Digested,* 95/**2857**:
Referred to, 00/346
Thomas Cook Group Ltd *v.* Air Malta Co Ltd (t/a Air Malta) [1997] 2 Lloyd's Rep. 399, QBD (Comm Ct) . . . . *Digested,* 98/**4807**
Thomas Cook Group Ltd *v.* Commission of the European Communities (T195/00) [2000] E.T.M.R. 1169 (Note), CFI
Thomas Watts & Co *v.* Smith [1998] 2 Costs L.R. 59, CA. . . . . *Digested,* 00/**402**
Thomas Witter Ltd *v.* TBP Industries Ltd [1996] 2 All E.R. 573; *Independent,* August 8, 1994 (C.S.), Ch D . . . . *Digested,* 96/**1238**:
Applied, 00/870: *Not followed,* 00/818
Thompson (Tariff Recommendation), Re; Venables (Tariff Recommendation), Re [2001] 1 All E.R. 737; [2001] 1 Cr. App. R. 25; (2000) 150 N.L.J. 1626; *Times,* October 27, 2000; *Independent,* October 31, 2000, CA (Crim Div) . . . . *Digested,* 00/**1331**:
Subsequent proceedings, 00/3198
Thompson *v.* Airtours Holidays Ltd (No.1) (Unreported, March 3, 1999), CC (Leeds) [*Ex rel.* Nelson & Co, St Andrew's House, St Andrew's Street, Leeds] . . . . *Digested,* 99/**3819**
Thompson *v.* Blake-James; *sub nom* Thomson *v.* James [1998] P.I.Q.R. P286; [1998] Lloyd's Rep. Med. 187; (1998) 41 B.M.L.R. 144, CA; reversing (1996) 31 B.M.L.R. 1, QBD . . . . *Digested,* 98/**3971**
Thompson *v.* Boulter (Unreported, November 23, 2000), CC (Weston Super Mare) [*Ex rel.* Samuel Butterfield, Barrister, Albion Chambers, Broad Street, Bristol]. . . *Digested,* 01/**1516**
Thompson *v.* Broome see Horrocks *v.* Broome
Thompson *v.* Brown Construction (Ebbw Vale) Ltd see Thompson *v.* Brown Construction Ltd (t/a George Albert Brown (Builders) & Co)
Thompson *v.* Brown Construction Ltd (t/a George Albert Brown (Builders) & Co); *sub nom* Thompson *v.* Brown Construction (Ebbw Vale) Ltd [1981] 1 W.L.R. 744; [1981] 2 All E.R. 296; 125 S.J. 377, HL. . . . . *Digested,* 81/**1618**:
Applied, 82/1848, 83/2219, 85/2016, 92/2811, 92/2812, 94/5183:
Considered, 88/2156, 91/184, 91/2348, 92/190, 99/470, 01/601:
Distinguished, 90/2960: *Followed,* 83/2210
Thompson *v.* Chappell (Unreported, July 23, 1998), CC (Ilford) [*Ex rel.* Edward Oliver & Bellis Solicitors, City House, 9 Cranbrook Road, Ilford, Essex] . . . . *Digested,* 98/**1734**
Thompson *v.* Clive Alexander & Partners 59 B.L.R. 77; 28 Con. L.R. 49; [1955-95] P.N.L.R. 603; (1992) 8 Const. L.J. 199, QBD (OR) . . . . *Digested,* 93/**293**
Thompson *v.* Commissioner of Police of the Metropolis; Hsu *v.* Commissioner of Police of the Metropolis [1998] Q.B. 498; [1997] 3 W.L.R. 403; [1997] 2 All E.R. 762; (1998) 10 Admin. L.R. 363; (1997) 147 N.L.J. 341; *Times,* February 20, 1997; *Independent,* February 28, 1997, CA . . . . *Digested,* 97/**1765**:
Applied, 98/1451, 00/5118: *Approved,* 97/4856: *Considered,* 99/5229, 01/1524: *Followed,* 99/1392
Thompson *v.* Customs and Excise Commissioners [1999] B.V.C. 2110
Thompson *v.* Department of the Environment [1986] 3 N.I.J.B. 73 . . . . *Digested,* 86/**2416**:
Considered, 99/5145
Thompson *v.* Garrandale Ltd (Unreported, July 28, 1999), CC (Nottingham) [*Ex rel.* Hopkins, Solicitors, 27 Regent Street, Nottingham]. . . . . *Digested,* 00/**528**
Thompson (Inspector of Taxes) *v.* Hart [2000] S.T.C. 381; 72 T.C. 543; [2000] B.T.C. 151; [2000] S.T.I. 544; *Times,* April 24, 2000, Ch D . . . . *Digested,* 00/**5012**
Thompson *v.* Holdsworth see Buckinghamshire Constabulary Widows and Orphans Fund Friendly Society (No.2), Re
Thompson *v.* Home Office [2001] EWCA Civ 331; *Independent,* March 16, 2001; *Daily Telegraph,* March 13, 2001, CA. . . . . *Digested,* 01/**4587**
Thompson *v.* Mersey Ferries (Unreported, February 4, 1998), CC (Liverpool) [*Ex rel.* William Waldron, Barrister, Exchange Chambers, Pearl Assurance House, Derby Square, Liverpool]. . . . . *Digested,* 98/**1628**
Thompson (Inspector of Taxes) *v.* Minzly [2001] S.T.I. 1404, Ch D
Thompson *v.* News Group International see Venables *v.* News Group International (Breach of Injunction)
Thompson *v.* News Group Newspapers Ltd see Venables *v.* News Group Newspapers Ltd
Thompson (Eversley) *v.* Queen, The [1998] A.C. 811; [1998] 2 W.L.R. 927; (1998) 142 S.J.L.B. 102, PC (StV) . . . . *Digested,* 98/**868**:
Distinguished, 98/1050
Thompson *v.* SCS Consulting Ltd [2001] I.R.L.R. 801, EAT

Thompson v. Smiths Shiprepairers (North Shields) Ltd; Mitchell v. Vickers Armstrong
Ltd; Gray v. Smiths Shiprepairers (North Shields) Ltd; Nicholson v. Smiths
Shiprepairers (North Shields) Ltd; Blacklock v. Swan Hunter Shipbuilders Ltd;
Waggott v. Swan Hunter Shipbuilders Ltd [1984] Q.B. 405; [1984] 2 W.L.R.
522; [1984] 1 All E.R. 881; [1984] I.C.R. 236; [1984] I.R.L.R. 93; (1984) 81
L.S.G. 741; (1984) 128 S.J. 225, QBD......................................   *Digested*, 84/**2307**:
           Applied, 99/2554, 01/4448: *Approved*, 00/5114: *Considered*, 98/3966:
           Followed, 84/2686
Thompson v. Spedding [1973] R.T.R. 312, CA...............................   *Digested*, 73/**2286**:
           Followed, 00/4183
Thompson v. Thompson (Financial Provision) [1991] 2 F.L.R. 530; [1992] 1 F.C.R.
368; [1992] Fam. Law 18; [1991] N.P.C. 95, CA........................   *Digested*, 92/**2085**:
           Considered, 95/2320, 95/2323, 95/2339, 96/2857, 99/3261
Thomson v. James see Thompson v. Blake-James
Thomson v. Lord Clanmorris [1900] 1 Ch. 718, CA; affirming [1899] 2 Ch. 523, Ch D   *Applied*, 47-51/10,
           47-51/8745, 47-51/8768: *Considered*, 00/519
Thomson v. RCI Europe (Unreported, February 14, 2001), CC (Manchester) [*Ex rel.*
Nicholls & Co, Solicitors, 671 Manchester Road, Denton, Manchester]........   *Digested*, 01/**4275**
Thomson Newspapers Co Ltd v. Attorney General of Canada 5 B.H.R.C. 567, Sup Ct
(Can) ....   *Digested*, 99/**3107**
Thomson Snell & Passmore v. Rose [2000] P.N.L.R. 378, CA ....   *Digested*, 00/**4262**
Thomson Tour Operations Ltd v. Birch; *sub nom* Thomson Tour Operations Ltd v.
Worcestershire CC (1999) 163 J.P. 465; *Times*, February 24, 1999; *Independent*,
February 15, 1999 (C.S.), QBD ....   *Digested*, 99/**825**
Thomson Tour Operations Ltd v. Worcestershire CC see Thomson Tour Operations Ltd v.
Birch
THOMSON/Electron tube (T953/90) [1998] E.P.O.R. 415, EPO (Technical Bd App)
Thongjai v. Queen, The; Lee Chun-Kong v. Queen, The [1998] A.C. 54; [1997] 3
W.L.R. 667; (1997) 141 S.J.L.B. 162; *Times*, August 5, 1997, PC (HK) ....   *Digested*, 97/**1094**:
           Applied, 00/907
Thor Scan, The; *sub nom* Trafalgar House Construction (Asia) Ltd v. Owners and/or
Demise Charterers of the Thor Scan [1999] 1 Lloyd's Rep. 940; [1998] 1
H.K.L.R.D. 881, CFI (HK) ....   *Digested*, 99/**746**
Thorel (Alain), Re [1999] E.C.C. 396, CE (F)
Thorgeirson v. Iceland (A/239) (1992) 14 E.H.R.R. 843; *Guardian*, July 15, 1992,
ECHR ....   *Digested*, 93/**2145**:
           Distinguished, 98/3096
Thorn EMI Electronics Ltd v. Coldicott (Inspector of Taxes) see EMI Group Electronics
Ltd v. Coldicott (Inspector of Taxes)
Thorn Materials Supply Ltd v. Customs and Excise Commissioners see Customs and
Excise Commissioners v. Thorn Materials Supply Ltd
Thorn Plc v. Customs and Excise Commissioners (Group Representative) [1998] B.V.C.
2087; [1998] V. & D.R. 80, V&DTr ....   *Digested*, 00/**5361**
Thorn Plc v. Customs and Excise Commissioners (Mobile Phones) [1998] B.V.C. 2090;
[1998] V. & D.R. 383, V&DTr ....   *Digested*, 00/**5287**
Thorn Plc v. MacDonald see MacDonald v. Thorn Plc
Thornby Farms Ltd v. Daventry DC see R. (on the application of Thornby Farms Ltd) v.
Daventry DC
Thorne v. University of London [1966] 2 Q.B. 237; [1966] 2 W.L.R. 1080; [1966] 2
All E.R. 338, CA ....   *Digested*, 66/**12308**:
           Applied, 98/2006: *Considered*, 85/3552: *Distinguished*, 86/3466
Thornton v. Andrew (t/a Hairtec) [*Ex rel.* Andrew M Jackson & Co, Solicitors, Essex
House, Manor Street, Hull] ....   *Digested*, 01/**1605**
Thornton v. Kingston upon Hull City Council [2000] 5 Q.R. 7, QBD [*Ex rel.* Andrew M
Jackson & Co Solicitors, PO Box 47, Essex House, Manor Street, Hull] ....   *Digested*, 00/**1494**
Thornton v. Shoe Lane Parking [1971] 2 Q.B. 163; [1971] 2 W.L.R. 585; [1971] 1 All
E.R. 686; [1971] 1 Lloyd's Rep. 289; [1971] R.T.R. 79; (1970) 115 S.J. 75, CA ...   *Digested*, 71/**1741**:
           Applied, 87/445, 88/430, 99/2013: *Considered*, 88/61, 92/1553, 00/5250
Thornton Springer v. NEM Insurance Co Ltd [2000] 2 All E.R. 489; [2000] 1 All E.R.
(Comm) 486; [2000] C.L.C. 975; [2000] Lloyd's Rep. I.R. 590; (2000) 97(13)
L.S.G. 42; (2000) 144 S.J.L.B. 147, QBD (Comm Ct) ....   *Digested*, 00/**3555**
Thorpe v. Chief Constable of Greater Manchester [1989] 1 W.L.R. 665; [1989] 2 All
E.R. 827; 87 L.G.R. 537; (1989) 139 N.L.J. 467; (1989) 133 S.J. 750, CA .....   *Digested*, 89/**2965**:
           Applied, 00/5516: *Considered*, 94/3670, 95/4125: *Distinguished*, 98/569
Thorpe v. Thorpe [1998] 2 F.L.R. 127; [1998] 2 F.C.R. 384; [1998] Fam. Law 320, CA .   *Digested*, 98/**1161**:
           Considered, 00/2541
Thorpe v. Weightman (Unreported, December 3, 1999), QBD [*Ex rel.* Fiona Ashworth,
Barrister, 40 King Street, Manchester] ....   *Digested*, 00/**4184**
Thrasyvoulou v. Hackney LBC (1986) 18 H.L.R. 370; (1987) 284 E.G. 511; [1984]
J.P.L. 732, CA..   *Digested*, 86/**1629**:
           Considered, 98/3038

Thrasyvoulou v. Secretary of State for the Environment; Oliver v. Secretary of State for
  the Environment [1990] 2 A.C. 273; [1990] 2 W.L.R. 1; [1990] 1 All E.R. 65; 88
  L.G.R. 217; (1990) 2 Admin. L.R. 289; (1990) 59 P. & C.R. 326; [1990] 1
  P.L.R. 69; [1990] 13 E.G. 69; (1990) 154 L.G. Rev. 192, HL; affirming [1988]
  Q.B. 809; [1988] 3 W.L.R. 1; [1988] 2 All E.R. 781; (1988) 56 P. & C.R. 259;
  [1988] 2 P.L.R. 37; [1988] 11 E.G. 83; [1988] 10 E.G. 131; [1988] J.P.L. 689;
  (1988) 152 L.G. Rev. 946; (1988) 85(17) L.S.G. 35; (1988) 138 N.L.J. Rep. 29;
  (1988) 132 S.J. 851, CA . . . .   *Digested*, 90/**4426**:
                      Applied, 90/4427, 91/3509, 97/4075, 97/4109: *Considered*, 94/4363,
                              98/1981: *Distinguished*, 92/4214, 92/4216: *Followed*, 97/4039
Three Rivers DC v. Bank of England (No.1) [1996] Q.B. 292; [1995] 3 W.L.R. 650;
  [1995] 4 All E.R. 312; *Times*, December 6, 1994; *Independent*, December 13,
  CA . . . .   *Digested*, 96/**2780**
Three Rivers DC v. Bank of England (No.2) [1996] 2 All E.R. 363; *Times*, January 8,
  1996; *Independent*, December 22, 1995, QBD (Comm Ct) . . . .   *Digested*, 96/**3928**:
                                                                                    Followed, 98/321
Three Rivers DC v. Bank of England (No.3) [2000] 2 W.L.R. 1220; [2000] 3 All E.R. 1;
  [2000] Lloyd's Rep. Bank. 235; [2000] 3 C.M.L.R. 205; [2000] Eu. L.R. 583;
  (2000) 2 L.G.L.R. 769; (2000) 97(23) L.S.G. 41; *Times*, May 19, 2000, HL;
  affirming in part [2000] 2 W.L.R. 15; [1999] 4 All E.R. 800 (Note); [1999]
  Lloyd's Rep. Bank. 283; [2000] 3 C.M.L.R. 1; [1999] Eu. L.R. 211; (1999) 1
  L.G.L.R. 645; (1999) 11 Admin. L.R. 281; (1999) 163 J.P.N. 314; *Times*,
  December 10, 1998, CA; affirming [1996] 3 All E.R. 558; [1997] 3 C.M.L.R.
  429; *Times*, April 22, 1996, QBD. . . . .   *Digested*, 00/**270**:
                                                                                   Considered, 00/5317
Three Rivers DC v. Bank of England (No.3) (Summary Judgment) [2001] UKHL 16;
  [2001] 2 All E.R. 513; [2001] Lloyd's Rep. Bank. 125; (2001) 3 L.G.L.R. 36;
  Times, March 23, 2001, HL . . . .   *Digested*, 01/**5355**:
                      Considered, 01/669: *Previous proceedings*, 99/4854
Three Rivers DC v. Bank of England (No.4) (Unreported, July 31, 1997), QBD (Comm
  Ct) . . . .   *Distinguished*, 00/620
Three Rivers DC v. Urban Forestry Tree Surgeons (2001) 16 P.A.D. 93, Planning
  Inspector
Threlfall v. Jones (Inspector of Taxes); Gallagher v. Jones (Inspector of Taxes) [1994]
  Ch. 107; [1994] 2 W.L.R. 160; [1993] S.T.C. 537; 66 T.C. 77; (1993) 90(32)
  L.S.G. 40; (1993) 137 S.J.L.B. 174; *Times*, July 1, 1993; *Independent*, July 26,
  1993, CA; reversing [1993] S.T.C. 199; *Times*, February 10, 1993, Ch D . . . .   *Digested*, 94/**2522**:
                      Approved, 99/4722: *Considered*, 94/639, 95/896, 96/3334
Threlkeld v. Northern Electric Plc (1999) 99(5) Q.R. 6, QBD [*Ex rel*. Roger Hillman,
  Barrister, Exchange Chambers, Pearl Assurance House, Derby Square,
  Liverpool] . . . .   *Digested*, 99/**1464**
Threshfield Motors Ltd v. Customs and Excise Commissioners [2000] S.T.I. 1484,
  V&DTr
Throwley Homes Ltd v. Sharratts [1998] N.P.C. 57, QBD
Thrul v. Ray (Quantum) [2000] P.I.Q.R. Q44; (1999) 99(5) Q.R. 6, QBD . . . .   *Digested*, 99/**1508**
Thurkettle v. Suffolk CC (Unreported, June 15, 1998), QBD [*Ex rel*. Browne Jacobson
  Solicitors, 44 Castle Gate, Nottingham] . . . .   *Digested*, 98/**3944**
Thurrock BC v. Fiddlers Reach Investment Ltd (1999) 14 P.A.D. 561, Planning
  Inspector
Thurrock BC v. Holding see Thurrock BC v. Secretary of State for the Environment,
  Transport and the Regions (No.1)
Thurrock BC v. Holding see Thurrock BC v. Secretary of State for the Environment,
  Transport and the Regions (No.2)
Thurrock BC v. S Walsh & Sons Ltd [1999] R.V.R. 47, QBD . . . .   *Digested*, 99/**4333**
Thurrock BC v. Secretary of State for the Environment, Transport and the Regions
  (No.1); *sub nom* Thurrock BC v. Holding [2001] C.P. Rep. 55; [2001] 1 P.L.R. 94;
  [2001] 3 E.G.C.S. 132; [2000] N.P.C. 147; *Times*, December 20, 2000, CA. . . . .   *Digested*, 01/**415**
Thurrock BC v. Secretary of State for the Environment, Transport and the Regions
  (No.2); *sub nom* Secretary of State for the Environment, Transport and the
  Regions v. Thurrock BC (No.2); Thurrock BC v. Holding; 01/0647, 01/0648, 01/
  0849, 01/0850, CA; affirming [2001] EWHC Admin 128; [2001] 3 P.L.R. 14;
  [2001] J.P.L. 1388; [2001] N.P.C. 40; *Times*, April 3, 2001, QBD (Admin Ct) . . .   *Digested*, 01/**4653**
Thurrock BC v. Southfields Gravel Co Ltd (1999) 14 P.A.D. 716, Planning Inspector
Thurso Building Society's Judicial Factor v. Robertson; *sub nom* Robertson (Judicial
  Factor) v. Robertson 2000 S.C. 547; 2001 S.L.T. 797; 2000 G.W.D. 24-904,
  OH . . . .   *Digested*, 01/**6086**
Thwaites v. B&R Pallant (Unreported, January 25, 2001), CC (Birkenhead) [*Ex rel*.
  Michael W Halsall, Solicitors, 2 The Parks, Newton-le-Willows] . . . .   *Digested*, 01/**514**
Thwaites v. United Kingdom see McDaid v. United Kingdom
Thynne v. United Kingdom (A/190); Wilson v. United Kingdom; Gunnell v. United
  Kingdom (1991) 13 E.H.R.R. 666; *Times*, December 10, 1990; *Independent*,
  November 2, 1990; *Guardian*, November 2, 1990, ECHR . . . .   *Digested*, 90/**2529**:
                      Considered, 94/3835, 94/3841, 96/3121, 01/1411, 01/4573:
                                                                                    Followed, 93/3364

Thyssen Inc v. Calypso Shipping Corp SA [2000] 2 All E.R. (Comm) 97; [2000] 2 Lloyd's Rep. 243; [2001] C.L.C. 805; 2001 A.M.C. 198; (2000) 97(27) L.S.G. 37; *Times*, August 17, 2000, QBD (Comm Ct) . . . . *Digested*, 00/**244**

Thyssen Stahl AG v. Commission of the European Communities (T141/94) [1999] E.C.R. II-347; [1999] 4 C.M.L.R. 810, CFI (2nd Chamber) . . . . *Digested*, 99/**656**

Thyssen-Bornemisza v. Thyssen-Bornemisza (1999-2000) 2 I.T.E.L.R. 467, CA (Ber)

TI v. United Kingdom [2000] I.N.L.R. 211, ECHR . . . . *Digested*, 00/**3164**

Tian Sheng No.8, The [2000] 2 Lloyd's Rep. 430, CFA (HK) . . . . *Digested*, 00/**4743**

Tibbs v. Dick [1998] 2 F.L.R. 1118; [1999] 2 F.C.R. 322; [1998] Fam. Law 588, CA . . . *Digested*, 99/**4637**

Tice v. Cartwright [1999] I.C.R. 769, EAT . . . . *Digested*, 99/**2008**

Tidman v. Aveling Marshall Ltd [1977] I.C.R. 506; [1977] I.R.L.R. 218; (1977) 12 I.T.R. 290, EAT . . . . *Digested*, 77/**1113**:
Applied, 78/1069, 82/1082, 83/1306: *Considered*, 98/2238

Tidswell v. Secretary of State for the Environment (1977) 34 P. & C.R. 152; (1976) 241 E.G. 83; [1977] J.P.L. 104, DC . . . . *Digested*, 78/**2877**:
Considered, 01/4723

Tierce Ladbroke SA v. Commission of the European Communities (C353/95 P) [1997] E.C.R. I-7007; [1998] C.E.C. 338, ECJ; affirming [1995] E.C.R. II-2537, CFI . . . *Digested*, 98/**737**

Tiernan v. Magen Insurance Co Ltd [2000] I.L.Pr. 517, QBD (Comm Ct) . . . . *Digested*, 00/**3516**

Tierney v. Mavadia (1998) 98(6) Q.R. 6, QBD . . . . *Digested*, 98/**1569**

Tietjen v. Inns (Cockermouth) Ltd [2001] 5 Q.R. 15, CC (Watford) [*Ex rel.* Greg Tee, Barrister, Guildford Chambers, Leapale Lane, Guildford] . . . . *Digested*, 01/**1700**

Tilbury v. Soundlab (UK) Ltd (1996) 96(1) Q.R. 5, CC (Kingston on Thames) [*Ex rel.* Benjamin Williams, Barrister] . . . . *Digested*, 96/**2360**:
Applied, 00/1580

Tilcon (Scotland) Ltd v. Jarvis (Scotland) Ltd 2000 S.L.T. (Sh Ct) 55; 2000 G.W.D. 11-379, Sh Pr. . . . . *Digested*, 00/**5945**:
Cited, 01/6261

Tilley v. Booker Food Service Group Ltd QBENI 98/0790/1, CA; reversing [1998] P.I.Q.R. P431, QBD . . . . *Digested*, 99/**579**

Tilley v. Wales (Inspector of Taxes); *sub nom* Wales (Inspector of Taxes) v. Tilley [1943] A.C. 386; [1943] 1 All E.R. 280, HL; reversing in part [1942] 2 K.B. 169, CA . . . *Applied*, 47-51/4782, 93/2275, 01/5247: *Considered*, 84/1800: *Distinguished*, 47-51/4783

Tilling v. Whiteman [1980] A.C. 1; [1979] 2 W.L.R. 401; [1979] 1 All E.R. 737; (1979) 38 P. & C.R. 341; (1979) 250 E.G. 51; [1979] J.P.L. 834; 123 S.J. 202, HL; reversing [1978] 3 W.L.R. 137; [1978] 3 All E.R. 1103; (1979) 37 P. & C.R. 427; (1978) 246 E.G. 1107; 122 S.J. 434, CA . . . . *Digested*, 79/**1624**:
Applied, 85/1902: *Considered*, 84/1907, 85/1884, 88/2077, 00/371, 01/440

Tillott v. Jackson (Unreported, January 26, 1999), CC (Birmingham) [*Ex rel.* Mr A Young, Barrister, St Philip's Chambers, Fountain Court, Steelhouse Lane, Birmingham] . . . . *Digested*, 99/**4365**

Tilly v. DPP see DPP v. Tilly

Tilly v. Tower Hamlets LBC Listing Officer; *sub nom* Tilly v. Valuation Officer [2001] R.V.R. 250, QBD

Tilly v. Valuation Officer see Tilly v. Tower Hamlets LBC Listing Officer

Timeload Ltd v. British Telecommunications Plc [1995] E.M.L.R. 459, CA . . . . *Digested*, 96/**1251**:
Considered, 98/525, 98/2661: *Distinguished*, 97/4849

Times Newspapers Ltd v. Chohan (Limitation Periods); *sub nom* Chohan v. Times Newspapers Ltd (Limitation Periods) [2001] EWCA Civ 964; [2001] 1 W.L.R. 1859; [2001] C.P. Rep. 100; [2001] B.P.I.R. 943; (2001) 98(30) L.S.G. 38; (2001) 145 S.J.L.B. 165; *Times*, August 1, 2001, CA; affirming [2001] 1 W.L.R. 184; [2001] 1 Costs L.R. 127; [2001] B.P.I.R. 187, Ch D . . . . *Digested*, 01/**476**

Times Newspapers Ltd v. Tancic see Tancic v. Times Newspapers Ltd

Timmins v. Gormley see Locabail (UK) Ltd v. Bayfield Properties Ltd (Leave to Appeal)

Timms v. Buchanan [2000] 1 Q.R. 7, CC (Cambridge) [*Ex rel.* Taylor Vinters Solicitors, Merlin Place, Milton Road, Cambridge] . . . . *Digested*, 99/**1481**

Timothy v. Trinidad and Tobago [2000] 1 W.L.R. 485, PC (Trin) . . . . *Digested*, 00/**907**

Timurtas v. Turkey (23531/94) (2001) 33 E.H.R.R. 6, ECHR . . . . *Digested*, 01/**3568**

Tingdene Developments Ltd v. Customs and Excise Commissioners [2000] S.T.I. 934, V&DTr

Tinker v. Tinker (No.1) [1970] P. 136; [1970] 2 W.L.R. 331; [1970] 1 All E.R. 540; 21 P. & C.R. 102; (1969) 114 S.J. 32; *Times*, December 4 1969, CA . . . . *Digested*, 70/**1245**:
Applied, 98/3315: *Distinguished*, 70/1246, 71/5503, 99/4368

Tinline v. White Cross Insurance Association Ltd [1921] 3 K.B. 327, KBD . . . . *Applied*, 47-51/**2224**, 99/5404: *Considered*, 53/3273: *Distinguished*, 70/1368, 71/6012

Tinnelly & Sons Ltd v. United Kingdom; McElduff v. United Kingdom (1999) 27 E.H.R.R. 249; 4 B.H.R.C. 393; [1998] H.R.C.D. 715; *Times*, July 16, 1998, ECHR . *Digested*, 98/**3147**:
Applied, 01/5876

Tinnion v. Fogg (Unreported, October 5, 1999), CC (Swindon) [*Ex rel.* Tim Kevan, Barrister, 1 Temple Gardens, Temple, London] . . . . *Digested*, 99/**2492**

Tinsley v. Dudley [1951] 2 K.B. 18; [1951] 1 All E.R. 252; [1951] 1 T.L.R. 315; 95 S.J. 106, CA . . . . *Digested*, 47-51/**6685**:
Applied, 57/2399: *Considered*, 66/571: *Followed*, 99/833

Tinsley v. Milligan [1994] 1 A.C. 340; [1993] 3 W.L.R. 126; [1993] 3 All E.R. 65;
  [1993] 2 F.L.R. 963; (1994) 68 P. & C.R. 412; [1993] E.G.C.S. 118; [1993]
  N.P.C. 97; *Times*, June 28, 1993; *Independent*, July 6, 1993, HL; affirming [1992]
  Ch. 310; [1992] 2 W.L.R. 508; [1992] 2 All E.R. 391; (1992) 63 P. & C.R. 152;
  (1991) 88(33) L.S.G. 32; (1991) 135 S.J.L.B. 108; [1991] N.P.C. 100; *Times*,
  August 22, 1991, CA . . . . *Digested*, 93/**1839**:
                                  Applied, 97/4730, 99/680, 99/4368: *Considered*, 95/2185, 95/3660,
                                  96/1489, 96/5554, 00/3879: *Distinguished*, 92/2045, 93/1840:
                                  Followed, 96/5000, 01/5349: *Referred to*, 94/5488
Tiny Love Ltd v. Index Ltd see Oren v. Red Box Toy Factory Ltd
Tiny Love Ltd v. Martin Yaffe International Ltd see Oren v. Red Box Toy Factory Ltd
Tiny Love Ltd v. Red Box Toy (UK) Ltd see Oren v. Red Box Toy Factory Ltd
Tiny Love Ltd v. Red Box Toy Factory Ltd see Oren v. Red Box Toy Factory Ltd
TINY PENIS Trade Mark see Ghazilian's Trade Mark Application
Tippett v. Watton (Inspector of Taxes) see Watton (Inspector of Taxes) v. Tippett
Titan International Inc, Re [1998] 1 B.C.L.C. 102, CA . . . . *Digested*, 97/**851**:
                                                                              Followed, 99/589
Titan Marketing Gesellschaft, Re see Senator Hanseatische Verwaltungsgesellschaft mbH,
  Re
Titchener v. British Railways Board; *sub nom* McGinlay v. British Railways Board
  [1983] 1 W.L.R. 1427; [1983] 3 All E.R. 770; 1984 S.L.T. 192; (1984) 81 L.S.G.
  204; (1984) 134 N.L.J. 361; (1983) 127 S.J. 825, HL; affirming 1983 S.L.T. 269,
  Ex Div; affirming 1981 S.L.T. 208, OH . . . . *Digested*, 84/**4342**:
                                        Considered, 99/4006: *Followed*, 92/6065
Titchener v. Secretary of State for Trade and Industry [2001] Emp. L.R. 1342, EAT
Titford Property Co Ltd v. Cannon Street Acceptances Ltd (Unreported, May 22, 1975),
  Ch D . . . . *Considered*, 01/683
Titterell v. Tunbridge Wells BC (1997) [1998] J.P.L. 452, CA . . . . *Digested*, 98/**4200**
Titterton v. Oates [2001] W.T.L.R. 319, Sup Ct (ACT) (Full Ct) . . . . *Digested*, 01/**5523**
Tjaskemolen (Now Named Visvliet), The (No.1); *sub nom* Profer AG v. Owners of the
  Ship Tjaskemolen (Now Named Visvliet) [1997] 2 Lloyd's Rep. 465; [1997]
  C.L.C. 521, QBD (Adm Ct). . . . . *Digested*, 98/**4390**
Tjaskemolen (Now Named Visvliet), The (No.2) [1997] 2 Lloyd's Rep. 476, QBD (Adm Ct)
                                                              Digested, 98/**4388**
TLL Realisations Ltd, Re see Secretary of State for Trade and Industry v. Collins
TNT Express Worldwide (UK) Ltd v. Brown; *sub nom* Brown v. TNT Express Worldwide
  (UK) Ltd [2001] I.C.R. 182; (2000) 97(20) L.S.G. 43; *Times*, April 18, 2000,
  CA; affirming [1999] Disc. L.R. 175, EAT . . . . *Digested*, 00/**2186**
Tobacco Prices, Re [2000] E.C.C. 406, VfGH (A)
Tobi v. Nicholas (1988) 86 Cr. App. R. 323; [1988] R.T.R. 343; [1987] Crim. L.R. 774,
  QBD . . . . *Digested*, 88/**552**:
                                        Considered, 98/1027: *Distinguished*, 97/1145
Todd v. Adams (t/a Trelawney Fishing Co) (The Maragetha Maria) A3/2001/1437, A3/
  2001/1449, CA; reversing in part [2001] 2 Lloyd's Rep. 443; [2001] C.L.C.
  1530; *Times*, August 20, 2001, QBD (Adm Ct) . . . . *Digested*, 01/**2806**
Todd v. British Midland Airways [1978] I.C.R. 959; [1978] I.R.L.R. 370; (1978) 13
  I.T.R. 553; 122 S.J. 661, CA . . . . *Digested*, 78/**1138**:
                                                    Considered, 89/1490, 99/2055
Toepfer International GmbH v. Societe Cargill France see Alfred C Toepfer International
  GmbH v. Societe Cargill France
Toff v. McDowell (1993) 25 H.L.R. 650; (1995) 69 P. & C.R. 535; [1993] E.G.C.S.
  141; [1993] N.P.C. 114, Ch D . . . . *Digested*, 94/**3409**:
                                        Considered, 01/4190: *Distinguished*, 00/3915
Togel v. Niederosterreichische Gebietskrankenkasse (C76/97) [1998] E.C.R. I-5357;
  [1998] 3 C.M.L.R. 768, ECJ
Togher v. Customs and Excise Commissioners [2001] EWCA Civ 474; *Independent*,
  May 21, 2001 (C.S), CA; reversing [1996] C.O.D. 103, QBD
Toglaci v. Secretary of State for the Home Department [1998] Imm. A.R. 38, CA . . . . . *Digested*, 98/**3223**
Tolan v. Caiels see Smith v. Hughes
Tolan v. Hughes see Smith v. Hughes
Tolan v. Mackinnon see Smith v. Hughes
Tolan v. Thomas see Smith v. Hughes
Tolhurst v. Associated Portland Cement Manufacturers (1900) Ltd; Associated
  Portland Cement Manufacturers (1900) Ltd v. Tolhurst [1903] A.C. 414, HL;
  affirming [1902] 2 K.B. 660, CA; reversing [1901] 2 K.B. 811, KBD . . . . *Applied*, 47-51/616:
                                        Considered, 98/795: *Distinguished*, 95/2974
Tollis v. Stansfield (Unreported, May 10, 1999), CC (Central London) [*Ex rel.* Dr J
  Williams, Barrister, 3 Dr Johnson's Buildings, Temple, London] . . . . *Digested*, 99/**560**
Tolsma v. Inspecteur der Omzetbelasting, Leeuwarden (C16/93) [1994] E.C.R. I-743;
  [1994] 2 C.M.L.R. 908; [1994] S.T.I. 424; *Times*, March 29, 1994, ECJ (6th
  Chamber) [1994] E.C.R. I-743, AGO . . . . *Digested*, 94/**4962**:
                                        Applied, 00/5347: *Considered*, 98/4891
Tolstoy v. Aldington see Watts v. Aldington

Tolstoy Miloslavsky *v.* United Kingdom (A/323) [1996] E.M.L.R. 152; (1995) 20
E.H.R.R. 442; *Times*, July 19, 1995; *Independent*, September 22, 1995, ECHR . . .   *Digested*, 95/**2647**:
Applied, 98/3064: *Considered*, 00/1756: *Followed*, 97/789, 00/436
Tom Wilson (Tobacco) Ltd *v.* Customs and Excise Commissioners [2000] S.T.I. 673,
V&DTr
Tom Wise Ltd *v.* Fillimore [1999] B.C.C. 129, Ch D . . . .   *Digested*, 99/**3269**
Tomkins *v.* Griffiths see Limb *v.* Union Jack Removals Ltd (In Liquidation)
Tomlinson *v.* Millins [1999] L. & T.R. 224; [1998] E.G.C.S. 178; (1998) 95(48) L.S.G.
32, Ch D
TONALITE HENNE Trade Mark [2001] R.P.C. 36, Appointed Person . . . .   *Digested*, 01/**4052**
Tonbridge and Malling BC *v.* West (1999) 14 P.A.D. 141, Planning Inspector
Tong Hwei Enterprise Co Ltd's Community Trade Mark Application [2001] E.T.M.R. 86,
OHIM (1st Bd App) . . . .   *Digested*, 01/**3996**
Toniello *v.* Top Deck Ski Ltd (1999) 96(1) L.S.G. 23; *Times*, December 7, 1998, CA . . . .   *Digested*, 99/**378**:
Considered, 99/377
Tony Mekwin Mtv & Co *v.* National Westminster Bank Plc; *sub nom* Mekwin *v.* National
Westminster Bank Plc [1998] C.C.L.R. 22, CA . . . .   *Digested*, 98/**2512**
Toogood *v.* Spyring (1834) 1 Cr. M. & R. 181 . . . .   *Applied*, 89/4549:
Considered, 98/1781
Toomey *v.* Eagle Star Insurance Co Ltd (No.2) [1995] 2 Lloyd's Rep. 88; [1995] 4 Re.
L.R. 314, QBD (Comm Ct) . . . .   *Distinguished*, 00/815
Toor *v.* Bassi [1999] E.G.C.S. 9, CA
Tootal Clothing Ltd *v.* Guinea Properties Management Ltd (1992) 64 P. & C.R. 452;
[1992] 41 E.G. 117; [1992] E.G.C.S. 80; [1992] N.P.C. 75; *Times*, June 8, 1992,
CA . . . .   *Digested*, 93/**2491**:
Considered, 94/3513: *Distinguished*, 97/1005: *Doubted*, 01/4852
Top Creative Ltd *v.* St Albans DC [1999] B.C.C. 999; [2000] 2 B.C.L.C. 379, CA . . . . .   *Digested*, 00/**652**
Topham (A Minor) *v.* Acorn Fabrics (Unreported, November 14, 1997), CC (Halifax) [*Ex
rel.* Allan Western, Solicitor, Rhodes, Thain & Collinson, Solicitors, 27 Harrison
Road, Halifax] . . . .   *Digested*, 98/**1753**
Topp *v.* London Country Bus (South West) Ltd [1993] 1 W.L.R. 976; [1993] 3 All E.R.
448; [1993] R.T.R. 279; (1993) 137 S.J.L.B. 59; *Times*, February 15, 1993, CA;
affirming [1992] R.T.R. 254; [1992] P.I.Q.R. P206; *Times*, December 3, 1991;
Independent, January 13, 1992 (C.S.), QBD . . . .   *Digested*, 93/**2934**:
Considered, 99/1535: *Distinguished*, 98/4037
Topps Co Inc *v.* Tom Hannah (Agencies) Ltd 1999 G.W.D. 40-1957; *Times*, February 14,
2000, OH . . . .   *Digested*, 00/**6519**
Toprak Enerji Sanayi AS *v.* Sale Tilney Technology Plc [1994] 1 W.L.R. 840; [1994] 3 All
E.R. 483; [1994] 1 Lloyd's Rep. 303, QBD (Comm Ct) . . . .   *Digested*, 94/**3798**:
Considered, 95/4162, 00/736: *Distinguished*, 95/4186:
Not followed, 95/4199, 96/809
TOPTOOLS Trade Mark (Unreported, May 31, 1999), OHIM (1st Bd App) . . . .   *Followed*, 00/3736
Tor Line A/B *v.* Alltrans Group of Canada Ltd (The TFL Prosperity); *sub nom* Investment
AB Torman *v.* Alltrans Group of Canada Ltd (The TFL Prosperity) [1984] 1
W.L.R. 48; [1984] 1 All E.R. 103; [1984] 1 Lloyd's Rep. 123; (1984) 81 L.S.G.
435; (1984) 134 N.L.J. 34; (1984) 128 S.J. 18, HL; reversing [1983] 2 Lloyd's
Rep. 18; (1983) 127 S.J. 409, CA; reversing [1982] 1 Lloyd's Rep. 617; [1982]
Com. L.R. 66, QBD (Comm Ct) . . . .   *Digested*, 84/**3166**:
Applied, 01/4917
Torbay Council *v.* Orange Personal Communications Ltd (1999) 14 P.A.D. 135,
Planning Inspector
Torbay DC *v.* Singh (Satnam) [1999] 2 Cr. App. R. 451; (1999) 163 J.P. 744; [2000]
F.S.R. 158; (1999) 22(9) I.P.D. 22086; (1999) 149 N.L.J. 1002; *Times*, July 5,
1999 ; *Independent*, July 5, 1999 (C.S.), QBD . . . .   *Digested*, 99/**3543**:
Followed, 01/1014
Torney's Application for Judicial Review, Re [1999] N.I. 325, QBD (NI) . . . .   *Digested*, 00/**5479**
Torridge DC *v.* Jarrad see Wyatt *v.* Jarrad
Torridge DC *v.* Plants for a Future (2000) 15 P.A.D. 712, Planning Inspector
Torvale Group Ltd, Re see Hunt *v.* Edge & Ellison Trustees Ltd
TOSHIBA/Doped regions (T631/97) [2001] E.P.O.R. 41, EPO (Technical Bd App) . . . .   *Digested*, 01/**3937**
TOSHIBA/Transistor (T378/93) [2000] E.P.O.R. 523, EPO (Technical Bd App) . . . . . .   *Digested*, 01/**3932**
Toshoku Finance UK Plc (In Liquidation), Re; *sub nom* Inland Revenue Commissioners *v.*
Kahn; Kahn *v.* Inland Revenue Commissioners; Khan *v.* Inland Revenue
Commissioners; TNS, HL; affirming [2000] 1 W.L.R. 2478; [2000] 3 All E.R.
938; [2000] S.T.C. 301; [2001] B.C.C. 373; [2000] 1 B.C.L.C. 683; [2000]
B.T.C. 96; [2000] S.T.I. 503; [2000] 97(15) L.S.G. 39; (2000) 144 S.J.L.B. 165;
Times, March 29, 2000, CA; reversing [1999] S.T.C. 922; [1999] 2 B.C.L.C.
777; [1999] B.T.C. 367, Ch D . . . .   *Digested*, 00/**3467**
Total Gas Marketing Ltd *v.* Arco British Ltd [1998] 2 Lloyd's Rep. 209; [1998] C.L.C.
1275; *Times*, June 8, 1998, HL; affirming (1998) 95(5) L.S.G. 28; (1998) 142
S.J.L.B. 47; *Times*, December 22, 1997, CA . . . .   *Digested*, 98/**4058**:
Cited, 00/4668

Total Liban SA v. Vitol Energy SA [2001] Q.B. 643; [2000] 3 W.L.R. 1142; [2000] 1 All E.R. 267; [1999] 2 All E.R. (Comm) 65; [1999] 2 Lloyd's Rep. 700; [1999] C.L.C. 1301, QBD (Comm Ct) . . . . *Digested*, 99/**831**
Total Transport Corp v. Arcadia Petroleum Ltd (The Eurus) [1998] 1 Lloyd's Rep. 351; [1998] C.L.C. 90; (1998) 95(1) L.S.G. 24; (1998) 142 S.J.L.B. 22; *Times*, December 16, 1997, CA; affirming [1996] 2 Lloyd's Rep. 408; [1996] C.L.C. 1084, QBD (Comm Ct) . . . . *Digested*, 98/**4407**
Totalfina Great Britain Ltd v. Secretary of State for the Environment, Transport and the Regions see R. (on the application of Elmbridge BC) v. Secretary of State for the Environment, Transport and the Regions
Totalise Plc v. Motley Fool Ltd [2001] EWCA Civ 1897, CA; reversing in part [2001] E.M.L.R. 29; [2001] E.B.L.R. 44; (2001) 98(19) L.S.G. 37; (2001) 151 N.L.J. 644; (2001) 145 S.J.L.B. 70; *Times*, March 15, 2001, QBD. . . . . *Digested*, 01/**1837**
Tottenham Hotspur Plc v. Ryman see Edennote Ltd, Re
Totty v. Snowden; Hewitt v. Wirral and West Cheshire Community NHS Trust [2001] EWCA Civ 1415; [2001] 4 All E.R. 577; (2001) 98(38) L.S.G. 37; (2001) 151 N.L.J. 1492; *Times*, August 10, 2001; *Independent*, October 10, 2001, CA . . . . . . *Digested*, 01/**654**
Toumia v. Evans, *Times*, April 1, 1999, CA . . . . *Digested*, 99/**4851**
Tournier v. National Provincial and Union Bank of England [1924] 1 K.B. 461, CA . . . . . . *Applied*, 70/1575, 90/251, 93/2376, 94/265, 95/388, 98/277, 99/272: *Considered*, 72/176, 72/3570, 73/142, 86/1512: *Distinguished*, 99/273
Toussaint v. Mattis [2001] C.P. Rep. 61, CA . . . . *Digested*, 00/**881**
Tower Boot Co Ltd v. Jones; *sub nom* Jones v. Tower Boot Co Ltd [1997] 2 All E.R. 406; [1997] I.C.R. 254; [1997] I.R.L.R. 168; (1997) 147 N.L.J. 60; *Times*, December 16, 1996; *Independent*, January 16, 1997, CA; reversing [1995] I.R.L.R. 529, EAT. . . . . *Digested*, 97/**2246**: *Applied*, 00/2185, 00/2211
Tower Hamlets LBC v. Azad (1998) 30 H.L.R. 241, CA. *Digested*, 98/**3043**
Tower Hamlets LBC v. Begum (Nipa) see Begum (Nipa) v. Tower Hamlets LBC
Tower Hamlets LBC v. Celestial Church of Christ (1999) 14 P.A.D. 244, Planning Inspector
Tower Hamlets LBC v. Kellum (Unreported, March 2, 2000), CC (Bow) [*Ex rel.* Jon Holbrook, Barrister, 2 Garden Court, Middle Temple, London] . . . . *Digested*, 00/**3925**
Tower Hamlets LBC v. Long (2000) 32 H.L.R. 219, CA . . . . *Digested*, 00/**13**
Tower Hamlets LBC v. Merrick [2001] EWHC Admin 799; [2001] R.V.R. 305; (2001) 98(42) L.S.G. 38, QBD (Admin Ct)
Tower Hamlets LBC v. Sherwood A3/2001/1995, CA; affirming in part [2001] N.P.C. 137, Ch D
Tower Housing Association Ltd v. Technical & General Guarantee Co Ltd 87 B.L.R. 74, QBD (OR) . . . . *Digested*, 98/**810**
Towler v. Ali (Unreported, October 14, 1999), CC (Clerkenwell) [*Ex rel.* Andrew Granville Stafford, Barrister, 4 King's Bench Walk, Temple, London] . . . . *Digested*, 00/**1693**
Town & County Factors Ltd v. Customs and Excise Commissioners; Customs and Excise Commissioners v. Town & County Factors Ltd [1998] S.T.C. 225; [1998] B.T.C. 5012; [1998] B.V.C. 30; *Independent*, February 16, 1998 (C.S.), QBD . . . . *Digested*, 98/**4891**
Town & County Factors Ltd v. Customs and Excise Commissioners (Reference to ECJ) [2000] S.T.I. 220, V&DTr
Town Shoes Ltd v. Panalpina Inc [2000] I.L.Pr. 172, Fed Ct (Can) . . . . *Digested*, 00/**751**
Townsend v. Achilleas; King v. Achilleas [2001] C.P. Rep. 45; [2000] C.P.L.R. 490; [2000] N.P.C. 79, CA . . . . *Digested*, 00/**302**
Townsend v. Customs and Excise Commissioners [2001] S.T.I. 952, V&DTr
Townsend v. Stone Toms & Partners [1981] 1 W.L.R. 1153; [1981] 2 All E.R. 690; 125 S.J. 428, CA . . . . *Digested*, 81/**2199**: *Doubted*, 99/1640
Townsend Carriers Ltd v. Pfizer Ltd (1977) 33 P. & C.R. 361; (1977) 242 E.G. 813; 121 S.J. 375, Ch D . . . . *Digested*, 78/**1790**: *Considered*, 89/2104, 89/2160, 93/2455: *Distinguished*, 85/353, 86/358, 98/3608
Townshend v. Superdrive Motoring Services Ltd CCRTI 98/1188/2, CA . . . . *Digested*, 00/**323**
Toyota (GB) Ltd v. North Yorkshire CC (1998) 162 J.P. 794; [1998] C.O.D. 248; (1998) 162 J.P.N. 905, QBD . . . . *Digested*, 98/**835**
TOYOTA/Fuel injection system (T924/91) [1999] E.P.O.R. 28, EPO (Technical Bd App)
Tozer Kemsley & Millbourn Holdings Ltd v. J Jarvis & Sons Ltd (1984) 1 Const. L.J. 79, QBD (OR). . . . . *Digested*, 85/**209**: *Applied*, 01/4511: *Considered*, 87/229, 88/2158
TP v. United Kingdom (28945/95) [2001] 2 F.L.R. 549; [2001] 2 F.C.R. 289; (2001) 3 L.G.L.R. 52; [2001] Fam. Law 590; *Times*, May 31, 2001, ECHR (2000) 2 L.G.L.R. 181, Eur Comm HR . . . . *Digested*, 01/**2571**
Tracey v. Crosville Wales Ltd; *sub nom* Crosville Wales Ltd v. Tracey [1998] A.C. 167; [1997] 3 W.L.R. 800; [1997] 4 All E.R. 449; [1997] I.C.R. 862; [1997] I.R.L.R. 691; (1997) 94(41) L.S.G. 28; (1997) 147 N.L.J. 1582; *Times*, October 20, 1997, HL; affirming [1996] I.C.R. 237; [1996] I.R.L.R. 91; *Times*, August 4, 1995; *Independent*, August 29, 1995, CA; reversing [1993] I.R.L.R. 60, EAT . . . . *Digested*, 97/**2285**
Tracey v. Heywood see Millar v. Dickson

Tracey (Alphonso) v. Queen, The [1998] 1 W.L.R. 1662; (1998) 142 S.J.L.B. 260, PC
(Jam) . . . . *Digested*, 99/**1023**
Trade Green Shipping Inc v. Securitas Bremer Allgemeine Versicherungs AG (The Trade
Green) [2001] 1 All E.R. (Comm) 1097; [2000] 2 Lloyd's Rep. 451; [2000]
C.L.C. 1268, QBD (Comm Ct) . . . . *Digested*, 00/**4687**
Tradigrain SA v. King Diamond Marine Ltd (The Spiros C); *sub nom* Tradigrain SA v.
King Diamond Shipping SA (The Spiros C) [2000] 2 All E.R. (Comm) 542;
[2000] 2 Lloyd's Rep. 319; [2000] C.L.C. 1503; *Independent*, October 9, 2000
(C.S), CA; reversing [1999] 1 All E.R. 837; [1999] 2 Lloyd's Rep. 91; [1999]
C.L.C. 1136, QBD (Comm Ct) . . . . *Digested*, 00/**4699**
Tradigrain SA v. King Diamond Shipping SA (The Spiros C) see Tradigrain SA v. King
Diamond Marine Ltd (The Spiros C)
Trading Corp of Pakistan v. Inter Continental Oceanic Enterprises Corp (The Nitsa);
National Insurance Corp v. M/S Maritime Agencies Ltd (The Sinoda) [2000] 1
Lloyd's Rep. 563, HC (Pak)
Trafalgar House Construction (Asia) Ltd v. Owners and/or Demise Charterers of the Thor
Scan see Thor Scan, The
Trafford MBC v. Alliance see Trafford MBC v. Secretary of State for the Environment,
Transport and the Regions
Trafford MBC v. Beech Housing Association (2000) 15 P.A.D. 443, Planning Inspector
Trafford MBC v. Going Places Leisure Travel Ltd (2000) 15 P.A.D. 239, Planning
Inspector
Trafford MBC v. Secretary of State for the Environment, Transport and the Regions;
Trafford MBC v. Alliance [2001] J.P.L. 114 (Note), QBD
Training in Compliance Ltd (t/a Matthew Read) v. Dewse (t/a Data Research Co) [2001]
C.P. Rep. 46, CA . . . . *Digested*, 00/**543**:
Applied, 01/673
Tramountana Armadora SA v. Atlantic Shipping Co SA (The Vorros) [1978] 2 All E.R.
870; [1978] 1 Lloyd's Rep. 391, QBD (Comm Ct) . . . . *Digested*, 78/**99**:
Applied, 80/95, 93/3159: *Considered*, 79/105, 81/90: *Explained*, 01/346
Tramp Shipping Corp v. Greenwich Marine Inc (The New Horizon) [1975] 1 W.L.R.
1042; [1975] 2 All E.R. 989; [1975] 2 Lloyd's Rep. 314; [1975] I.C.R. 261; 119
S.J. 300, CA; affirming [1974] 2 Lloyd's Rep. 210, QBD (Comm Ct) . . . . *Digested*, 75/**3166**:
Applied, 99/2074
Trane Co v. Hanjin Shipping Co Ltd (The Hanjin Marseilles) [2001] 2 Lloyd's Rep. 735,
CFI (HK)
Trans Continental Textile Recycling Ltd v. Partenreederei MS Erato [1998] I.L.Pr. 129, Fed
Ct (Can)
Trans Pacific Insurance Co (Australia) Ltd v. Grand Union Insurance Co Ltd (1989) 18
N.S.W.L.R. 675 . . . . *Applied*, 00/3532
Trans Trust SPRL v. Danubian Trading Co Ltd [1952] 2 Q.B. 297; [1952] 1 All E.R. 970;
[1952] 1 Lloyd's Rep. 348; [1952] 1 T.L.R. 1066; 96 S.J. 312, CA; reversing in
part [1952] 1 K.B. 285; [1952] 1 All E.R. 89; [1951] 2 Lloyd's Rep. 644; [1952] 1
T.L.R. 13, KBD . . . . *Digested*, 52/**3137**:
Applied, 53/3271, 95/1613, 96/3603: *Considered*, 98/4410:
Followed, 81/2015
Transag Haulage Ltd (IAR) v. Leyland DAF Finance Plc [1994] B.C.C. 356; [1994] 2
B.C.L.C. 88; (1994) 13 Tr. L.R. 361; *Times*, January 15, 1994; *Independent*,
January 31, 1994 (C.S.), Ch D . . . . *Digested*, 95/**2827**:
Applied, 00/2326
Transamerica Occidental Life Insurance Co v. Federal Insurance Co see Federal
Insurance Co v. Transamerica Occidental Life Insurance Co
Transammonia AG v. Kafco [1999] E.C.C. 176, QBD (Comm Ct)
Transco Plc (formerly BG Plc) v. O'Brien see BG Plc v. O'Brien
Transco Plc v. Stockport MBC see Stockport MBC v. British Gas Plc
Transgrain Shipping BV v. Global Transporte Oceanico SA (The Mexico 1) [1990] 1
Lloyd's Rep. 507; *Financial Times*, February 7, 1990, CA; reversing [1988] 2
Lloyd's Rep. 149, QBD (Comm Ct) . . . . *Digested*, 91/**3234**:
Applied, 01/4912: *Followed*, 97/4515
Transocean Liners Reederei GmbH v. Euxine Shipping Co Ltd (The Imvros) [1999] 1 All
E.R. (Comm) 724; [1999] 1 Lloyd's Rep. 848; [1999] C.L.C. 928, QBD (Comm
Ct) . . . . *Digested*, 99/**4433**
Transpacific Discovery SA v. Cargill International SA (The Elpa) [2001] 1 All E.R.
(Comm) 937; [2001] 2 Lloyd's Rep. 596; [2001] C.L.C. 1252, QBD (Comm
Ct) . . . . *Digested*, 01/**4906**
TRANSPAY Trade Mark [2001] R.P.C. 10, TMR. . . . . *Digested*, 01/**4058**
Transport & General Workers Union v. JR (Haulage) Ltd see Transport & General Workers
Union v. McKinnon
Transport & General Workers Union v. McKinnon; Transport & General Workers Union v.
JR (Haulage) Ltd [2001] I.C.R. 1281; [2001] I.R.L.R. 597, EAT . . . . *Digested*, 01/**6476**
Transports Frigoriphques Laurent v. Transportes Olloquiegui (Unreported, November 8,
1999), CC (Reading) [*Ex rel.* Shoosmiths, Solicitors, Regents Gate, Crown
Street, Reading, Berkshire] . . . . *Digested*, 00/**4183**

TransTec Automotive (Campsie) Ltd, Re see Ford AG-Werke AG *v.* Transtec Automotive (Campsie) Ltd
Transworld Trading, Re [1999] B.P.I.R. 628, Ch D . . . . *Digested,* 99/**3321**
Trapp *v.* Mackie [1979] 1 W.L.R. 377; [1979] 1 All E.R. 489; 1979 S.C. (H.L.) 38; 1979 S.L.T. 126; 123 S.J. 202, HL; affirming 1978 S.C. 283, 2 Div; affirming 1977 S.L.T. 194, OH . . . . *Digested,* 79/**3381**:
Applied, 84/1373, 85/1326: *Considered,* 83/2203: *Followed,* 00/2627
Trasimex Holding SA *v.* Addax BV (The Red Sea) [1999] 1 Lloyd's Rep. 28, CA; affirming [1997] 1 Lloyd's Rep. 610, QBD (Comm Ct) . . . . *Digested,* 98/**4378**
Trasporti Castelletti Spedizioni Internazionali SpA *v.* Hugo Trumpy SpA (C159/97) [1999] E.C.R. I-1597; [1999] I.L.Pr. 492, ECJ . . . . *Digested,* 99/**736**
Travel Vac SL *v.* Sanchis (C423/97) [1999] All E.R. (EC) 656; [1999] E.C.R. I-2195; [1999] 2 C.M.L.R. 1111; (1999) 96(31) L.S.G. 43, ECJ . . . . *Digested,* 99/**819**
Travell *v.* Customs and Excise Commissioners (1998) 162 J.P. 181; [1998] C.O.D. 92; *Independent,* November 4, 1997, QBD . . . . *Digested,* 97/**1741**
TRAVELPRO Trade Mark [1997] R.P.C. 864, TMR . . . . *Digested,* 98/**3535**
Travers *v.* Stych (Unreported, February 26, 1997), CC (Oxford) [*Ex rel.* Ben Williams, Barrister] . . . . *Digested,* 97/**598**:
Distinguished, 01/532
Travis *v.* British Coal Corp [1998] R.V.R. 57, Lands Tr . . . . *Digested,* 98/**3907**
Treacy, Re [1998] B.P.I.R. 528, CA (Ont) . . . . *Digested,* 99/**3230**
Treacy's Application for Judicial Review, Re [2000] N.I. 330, QBD (NI) . . . . *Digested,* 00/**5444**
Trebah Garden Trust *v.* Customs and Excise Commissioners [2000] B.V.C. 2345; [2000] S.T.I. 1165, V&DTr . . . . *Digested,* 01/**5563**
Tredget *v.* Bexley HA [1994] 5 Med. L.R. 178, CC . . . . *Distinguished,* 00/531
Treharne *v.* Brabon see Brabon, Re
Tremblay *v.* Commission of the European Communities (T224/95) [1997] E.C.R. II-2215; [1998] 4 C.M.L.R. 427, CFI (2nd Chamber)
Tremblay *v.* Commission of the European Communities (T5/93) see Bureau Europeen des Medias de l'Industrie Musicale (BEMIM) *v.* Commission of the European Communities (T114/92)
Tremblay *v.* Daigle [1989] 2 S.C.R. 530, Sup Ct (Can) . . . . *Followed,* 98/4783
Tremerton Ltd *v.* Customs and Excise Commissioners [1999] S.T.C. 1039; [1999] B.T.C. 5413; [2000] B.V.C. 3, QBD . . . . *Digested,* 00/**5303**
Treml *v.* Ernest W Gibson & Partners [1955-95] P.N.L.R. 228; (1984) 272 E.G. 68; (1984) 1 Const. L.J. 162, QBD . . . . *Digested,* 84/**242**:
Considered, 87/394: *Distinguished,* 90/1566
Trendgrove Properties Ltd *v.* Deeks (2000) 79 P. & C.R. D6, CA
Trendtex Trading Corp *v.* Credit Suisse [1982] A.C. 679; [1981] 3 W.L.R. 766; [1981] 3 All E.R. 520; [1981] Com. L.R. 262; 125 S.J. 761, HL; affirming [1980] Q.B. 629; [1980] 3 W.L.R. 367; [1980] 3 All E.R. 721; 124 S.J. 396, CA . . . . *Digested,* 81/**298**:
Applied, 89/2243, 89/2938: *Considered,* 82/397, 86/2706, 89/437, 96/2904, 97/3369, 99/3221: *Explained,* 85/2603: *Referred to,* 83/380
Trent Taverns Ltd *v.* Sykes [1999] Eu. L.R. 492; (1999) 11 Admin. L.R. 548; [1999] N.P.C. 9; *Times,* March 5, 1999, CA; affirming [1998] Eu. L.R. 571, QBD . . . . *Digested,* 99/**76**:
Applied, 01/2519
Trepca Mines Ltd (No.2), Re; *sub nom* Radomir Nicola Pachitch (Pasic)'s Application, Re [1963] Ch. 199; [1962] 3 W.L.R. 955; [1962] 3 All E.R. 351; 106 S.J. 649, CA; affirming [1962] Ch. 511; [1962] 2 W.L.R. 800; [1962] 1 All E.R. 755; 106 S.J. 175, Ch D . . . . *Digested,* 62/**2900**:
Considered, 89/437, 96/2904, 99/347
Treta (t/a The Golden Fry) *v.* Customs and Excise Commissioners [2000] S.T.I. 1436, V&DTr
Trevelyan *v.* Secretary of State for the Environment, Transport and the Regions [2001] EWCA Civ 266; [2001] 1 W.L.R. 1264; [2001] 3 All E.R. 166; [2001] 2 P.L.R. 45; (2001) 98(16) L.S.G. 32; (2001) 145 S.J.L.B. 69; [2001] N.P.C. 41; *Times,* March 15, 2001; *Independent,* March 8, 2001, CA; affirming [2000] 2 P.L.R. 49; [2000] N.P.C. 6; *Times,* March 22, 2000, QBD . . . . *Digested,* 01/**4887**
Trevis *v.* Cathey (Unreported, February 8, 2001), CC (Birmingham) [*Ex rel.* Cameron Brown, Barrister, 4 King's Bench Walk, Temple, London] . . . . *Digested,* 01/**1754**
Trevor Estate Ltd *v.* Aylwen (1999) 77 P. & C.R. D33, CA
Trew *v.* Hawes (Unreported, November 3, 1999), CC (Norwich) [*Ex rel.* Rogers & Norton Solicitors, The Old Chapel, 5-7 Willow Lane, Norwich, Norfolk] . . . . *Digested,* 00/**374**
Trewby *v.* Customs and Excise Commissioners [1976] 1 W.L.R. 932; [1976] 2 All E.R. 199; [1976] S.T.C. 122; 120 S.J. 369, DC . . . . *Digested,* 76/**2843**:
Applied, 98/4892
Tribunal Practice Notice TPN 05/2000 (TMR: Change in Practice of Appointment and Conduct of Hearings) [2001] R.P.C. 15, TMR . . . . *Digested,* 01/**3971**
Trident International Ltd *v.* Barlow see Hamlet International Plc (In Administration), Re
Triesman *v.* Ali; *sub nom* McDonagh *v.* Ali; Ali *v.* McDonagh; A1/2001/1012/EATRF, CA; reversing (2001) 151 N.L.J. 610, EAT
Trieste e Venezia Assicurazioni Genertel SpA *v.* Crowe Italia Srl [2001] E.T.M.R. 66, Trib (Rome)

Triffit Nurseries v. Salads Etcetera Ltd [2000] 1 All E.R. (Comm) 737; [2000] 2 Lloyd's
    Rep. 74; [2001] B.C.C. 457; [2000] 1 B.C.L.C. 761; *Times*, April 26, 2000;
    Independent, May 12, 2000, CA; affirming [1999] 1 All E.R. (Comm.) 110;
    [1999] 1 Lloyd's Rep. 697; [2000] B.C.C. 98; [2000] 1 B.C.L.C. 262, Ch D . . . .   *Digested*, 00/**114**
Trillium Digital Systems Inc's Trade Mark [2000] E.T.M.R. 1054 (Note), OHIM (Cancellation
    Div) . . . .   *Applied*, 01/**4009**
Trim Joint District School Board of Management v. Kelly see Board of Management of
    Trim Joint District School v. Kelly
Trimis v. Mina (2000) 2 T.C.L.R. 346, CA (NSW) . . . .   *Digested*, 00/**898**
Trinidad Oilwell Service Ltd v. Inland Revenue Board [1999] S.T.C. 1034; [1999] B.T.C.
    430, PC (Trin) . . . .   *Digested*, 00/**4915**
Trinity Mirror Plc (formerly Mirror Group Newspapers Ltd) v. Customs and Excise
    Commissioners; *sub nom* Mirror Group Newspapers Ltd v. Customs and Excise
    Commissioners [2001] EWCA Civ 65; [2001] S.T.C. 192; [2001] 2 C.M.L.R. 33;
    [2001] B.T.C. 5092; [2001] B.V.C. 167; [2001] S.T.I. 101; (2001) 98(14) L.S.G.
    40; (2001) 145 S.J.L.B. 56; *Times*, March 6, 2001, CA; affirming [2000] S.T.C.
    156; [2000] 2 C.M.L.R. 333; [2000] B.T.C. 5073; [2000] B.V.C. 119; [2000]
    S.T.I. 159; (2000) 97(8) L.S.G. 37; *Times*, March 7, 2000, QBD . . . .   *Digested*, 01/**5606**
Trio Thames v. Secretary of State for the Environment and Reading BC [1984] J.P.L.
    183 . . . .   *Digested*, 84/**3427**:
                        Considered, 99/4220: *Referred to*, 00/4419
Triomed (Proprietary) Ltd v. Beecham Group [2001] F.S.R. 34, Provincial Div (SA) . . . .   *Digested*, 01/**4026**
Trippas v. Trippas [1973] Fam. 134; [1973] 2 W.L.R. 585; [1973] 2 All E.R. 1; 117 S.J.
    204, CA . . . .   *Digested*, 73/**925.d**:
                    Applied, 75/983: *Considered*, 86/1086, 87/1755: *Disapproved*, 01/2633:
                                            Followed, 76/775

Tritonstyle Ltd's Application for Revocation (No.1301046) see ACADEMY Trade Mark
Troke v. AEP Industries (UK) Ltd [*Ex rel.* Christian Sweeney, Barrister, 3 Paper
    Buildings, 20 Lorne Park Road, Bournemouth] . . . .   *Digested*, 01/**1720**
Trollope & Colls Ltd v. North West Metropolitan Regional Hospital Board [1973] 1
    W.L.R. 601; [1973] 2 All E.R. 260; 9 B.L.R. 60; 117 S.J. 355, HL . . . .   *Digested*, 73/**270**:
                    Applied, 92/314: *Considered*, 80/17, 90/401, 96/1218, 00/4640:
                                Distinguished, 81/828: *Followed*, 80/357
Trow v. Ind Coope (West Midlands) Ltd [1967] 2 Q.B. 899; [1967] 3 W.L.R. 633;
    [1967] 2 All E.R. 900; 111 S.J. 375, CA; affirming [1966] 3 W.L.R. 1300; [1967]
    1 All E.R. 19; 110 S.J. 964, QBD . . . .   *Digested*, 67/**3259**:
                    Applied, 72/387, 73/1165, 74/1321: *Considered*, 73/1147, 96/2556:
                                Disapproved, 75/2684: *Followed*, 99/2465, 00/2568
Truk (UK) Ltd v. Tokmakidis GmbH [2000] 2 All E.R. (Comm) 594; [2000] 1 Lloyd's
    Rep. 543, QBD (Merc Ct) . . . .   *Digested*, 00/**4673**
Trummer and Mayer's Application to Register Land (C222/97), Re [1999] E.C.R. I-1661;
    [2000] 3 C.M.L.R. 1143, ECJ. . . . .   *Digested*, 01/**2485**
Trumpet Software Pty Ltd v. OzEmail Pty Ltd [1997-98] Info. T.L.R. 451, Fed Ct (Aus)
    (Sgl judge) . . . .   *Digested*, 99/**3447**
Truscott v. Truscott see Wraith v. Sheffield Forgemasters Ltd
Trusted v. Clifford Chance [2000] W.T.L.R. 1219, Ch D . . . .   *Digested*, 01/**4525**
Trustee v. Cargo Supertintendents (London) Ltd see Schebsman (Deceased) Ex p.
    Official Receiver, Re
Trustee Corp Ltd v. Nadir [2001] B.P.I.R. 541; *Independent*, January 29, 2001 (C.S), Ch
    D
Trustee Ex p. v. Kensington BC see Hone (A Bankrupt), Re
Trustee in Bankruptcy v. Bukhari [1999] B.P.I.R. 157, CA. . . . .   *Digested*, 99/**3228**
Trustee in Bankruptcy of Arthur Knapton v. Price see Claughton v. Price
Trustee of Dame Alice Owen's Foundation v. Attorney General see Master and Wardens
    of the Mystery or Art of Brewers of the City of London v. Attorney General
Trustee of the Estate of Bowe (A Bankrupt) v. Bowe [1998] 2 F.L.R. 439; [1997] B.P.I.R.
    747; [1998] Fam. Law 515, Ch D . . . .   *Digested*, 98/**3275**
Trustee of the Estate of NG v. NG see NG (A Bankrupt), Re
Trustee of the Estate of Omar (A Bankrupt) v. Omar (Diana Bridget) see Omar (A
    Bankrupt), Re
Trustee of the Property of Lord (A Bankrupt) v. Great Eastern Railway Co see Great
    Eastern Railway Co v. Lord's Trustee
Trustee of the Property of Pope v. Birmingham Midshires Building Society see Pope (A
    Bankrupt), Re
Trustee of the Property of Vickery (A Bankrupt) v. Modern Security Systems Ltd; *sub
    nom* Vickery v. Modern Security Systems Ltd [1998] 1 B.C.L.C. 428; [1998]
    B.P.I.R. 164; [1997] N.P.C. 143; *Independent*, October 27, 1997 (C.S.), CA;
    affirming [1997] B.P.I.R. 319, QBD . . . .   *Digested*, 97/**587**
Trustee Savings Bank of Wales and Border Counties v. Taylor see Barclays Bank Plc v.
    Taylor
Trustees Executors & Agency Co of New Zealand Ltd v. Price Waterhouse [2000]
    P.N.L.R. 673, CA (NZ) . . . .   *Digested*, 01/**677**
Trustees for the MacMillan Cancer Trust v. Customs and Excise Commissioners [1998]
    B.V.C. 2320; [1998] V. & D.R. 289, V&DTr. . . . .   *Digested*, 99/**4989**

Trustees of Abdul Gaffoor Trust v. Income Tax Commissioner, Colombo see Caffoor (Trustees of the Abdul Gaffoor Trust) v. Income Tax Commissioner (Colombo)

Trustees of BT Pension Scheme v. Clark (Inspector of Taxes) see Clarke (Inspector of Taxes) v. BT Pension Scheme Trustees

Trustees of Chippenham Golf Club v. North Wiltshire DC see Farrage v. North Wiltshire DC

Trustees of Henry Smith's Charity v. AWADA Trading & Promotion Services Ltd; *sub nom* Henry Smith's Charity Trustees v. AWADA Trading & Promotion Services Ltd (1984) 47 P. & C.R. 607; [1984] 1 E.G.L.R. 116; (1984) 269 E.G. 729; (1984) 81 L.S.G. 118; (1984) 128 S.J. 130, CA; reversing (1983) 46 P. & C.R. 74, Ch D
.... *Digested,* 84/**1952**:
Applied, 84/1950, 85/1935: *Considered,* 85/1918, 85/1927, 86/1913, 87/2200, 88/2075, 90/2855, 92/2726, 99/3726: *Distinguished,* 00/3914:
Followed, 91/5178, 01/4207

Trustees of Higgins (Deceased) v. Secretary of State for the Environment, Transport and the Regions (2000) 97(9) L.S.G. 44, QBD .... *Digested,* 00/**4520**

Trustees of St John's Hospital v. Keevil [2001] EWCA Civ 1730; [2001] N.P.C. 163, CA; affirming [2001] N.P.C. 21, Lands Tr

Trustees of Thames Ditton Lawn Tennis Club v. Bruce-Smith see Coppen (Trustees of Thames Ditton Lawn Tennis Club) v. Bruce-Smith

Trustees of the Castell-y-Mynach Estate v. Secretary of State for Wales; Trustees of the Castell-y-Mynach Estate v. Taff -Ely BC [1985] J.P.L. 40 .... *Digested,* 85/**3477**:
Considered, 99/4165

Trustees of the Castell-y-Mynach Estate v. Taff -Ely BC see Trustees of the Castell-y-Mynach Estate v. Secretary of State for Wales

Trustees of the Dennis Rye Pension Fund v. Sheffield City Council [1998] 1 W.L.R. 840; [1997] 4 All E.R. 747; (1998) 30 H.L.R. 645; (1998) 10 Admin. L.R. 112; (1998) 162 J.P.N. 145; *Times,* August 20, 1997, CA .... *Digested,* 97/**490**:
Applied, 98/37: *Considered,* 00/44: *Followed,* 98/92

Trustees of the Dulwich Estate's Appeal, Re (1998) 76 P. & C.R. 484; [2000] R.V.R. 242, Lands Tr .... *Digested,* 98/**3639**

Trustees of the Eyre Estate v. Saphir [1999] 2 E.G.L.R. 123; [1999] 34 E.G. 71, Lands Tr . *Digested,* 99/**3686**

Trustees of the Friends of the Lake District v. Secretary of State for the Environment, Transport and the Regions see R. (on the application of Trustees of the Friends of the Lake District) v. Secretary of State for the Environment, Transport and the Regions

Trustees of the Fussell Pension Scheme v. Hornby (Inspector of Taxes) see Venables v. Hornby (Inspector of Taxes)

Trustees of the Nell Gwynn House Maintenance Fund v. Customs and Excise Commissioners see Nell Gwynn House Maintenance Fund Trustees v. Customs and Excise Commissioners

Trustees of the Omega Group Pension Scheme v. Inland Revenue Commissioners see Trustees of the Sema Group Pension Scheme v. Inland Revenue Commissioners

Trustees of the Sema Group Pension Scheme v. Inland Revenue Commissioners; *sub nom* Inland Revenue Commissioners v. Trustees of the Sema Group Pension Scheme; Trustees of the Omega Group Pension Scheme v. Inland Revenue Commissioners; CH/2001/APP/0608, Ch D; reversing [2001] Pens. L.R. 305; [2001] S.T.C. (S.C.D.) 121; [2001] S.T.I. 1108, Sp Comm .... *Digested,* 01/**5270**

Trusthouse Forte Hotels Ltd v. Secretary of State for the Environment (1987) 53 P. & C.R. 293; [1986] 2 E.G.L.R. 185; (1986) 279 E.G. 680; [1986] J.P.L. 834, QBD .... *Digested,* 87/**3711**:
Considered, 90/4444, 97/4036, 97/4131, 01/4688: *Followed,* 94/4400

Trustor AB v. Barclays Bank Plc (2000) 97(44) L.S.G. 45; *Times,* November 22, 2000, Ch D .... *Digested,* 00/**485**

Trustor AB v. Smallbone (No.1) PTA 1999/6807/3, CA [2000] 1 All E.R. 811, Ch D .... *Digested,* 00/**79**

Trustor AB v. Smallbone (No.3) [2001] 1 W.L.R. 1177; [2001] 3 All E.R. 987; [2001] 2 B.C.L.C. 436; (2001) 98(20) L.S.G. 40; (2001) 151 N.L.J. 457; (2001) 145 S.J.L.B. 99; *Times,* March 30, 2001, Ch D .... *Digested,* 01/**705**

Trusts of the Scientific Investment Pension Plan, Re see Scientific Investment Pension Plan (No.2), Re

Truth (NZ) Ltd v. Holloway [1960] 1 W.L.R. 997; 104 S.J. 745, PC (NZ); affirming [1960] N.Z.L.R. 69, CA (NZ) .... *Digested,* 60/**1803**:
Applied, 61/6416, 79/1655: *Considered,* 98/1781

Try Build Ltd v. Blue Star Garages Ltd 66 Con. L.R. 90, QBD (T&CC) .... *Digested,* 00/**815**

Try Build Ltd v. Invicta Leisure (Tennis) Ltd 71 Con. L.R. 140, QBD (OR) .... *Digested,* 01/**864**

Trygg Hansa Insurance Co Ltd v. Equitas Ltd; *sub nom* Equitas Ltd v. Trygg Hansa Insurance Co Ltd [1998] 2 Lloyd's Rep. 439; [1998] C.L.C. 979, QBD (Comm Ct) .... *Digested,* 98/**242**:
Applied, 01/3836

Tsakos Shipping & Trading SA v. Orizon Tanker Co Ltd (The Centaurus Mar) [1998] C.L.C. 1003, QBD (Comm Ct) .... *Digested,* 98/**249**

Tsavliris Salvage (International) Ltd v. Guangdong Shantou Overseas Chinese Materials
    Marketing Co (The Pa Mar); *sub nom* Guangdong Shantou Overseas Chinese
    Materials Marketing Co v. Tsavliris Salvage (International) Ltd [1999] 1 Lloyd's
    Rep. 338, QBD (Adm Ct) . . . .   *Digested*, 99/**4489**
TSB Bank v. Camfield [1995] 1 W.L.R. 430; [1995] 1 All E.R. 951; [1995] 1 F.L.R. 751;
    [1995] 2 F.C.R. 254; (1995) 27 H.L.R. 206; (1995) 92(3) L.S.G. 37; (1995) 145
    N.L.J. 215; (1995) 139 S.J.L.B. 15; *Times*, December 7, 1994, CA . . . .   *Digested*, 95/**2447**:
                   Applied, 95/3605, 96/4974: *Considered*, 01/669: *Followed*, 96/418
TSB Bank Plc v. Harris [2000] I.R.L.R. 157, EAT . . . .   *Digested*, 00/**2108**
TSB Bank Plc v. Ladsky (No.2); *sub nom* Ladsky v. TSB Bank Plc (1997) 74 P. & C.R.
    372, CA . . . .   *Digested*, 98/**290**
TSB Bank Plc v. Marshall [1998] 2 F.L.R. 769; [1998] 3 E.G.L.R. 100; [1998] 39 E.G.
    208; [1998] Fam. Law 596, CC (Newport, IoW) . . . .   *Digested*, 98/**4356**
TSB Bank Plc v. Platts (No.1) [1997] B.P.I.R. 151, Ch D   *Digested*, 97/**3024**
TSB Bank Plc v. Platts (No.2); *sub nom* Platts v. Trustee Savings Bank Plc [1998]
    Lloyd's Rep. Bank. 163; [1998] 2 B.C.L.C. 1; [1998] B.P.I.R. 284; (1998) 95(12)
    L.S.G. 28; (1998) 142 S.J.L.B. 93; [1998] N.P.C. 23; *Times*, March 4, 1998,
    CA; affirming [1997] B.P.I.R. 302, Ch D . . . .   *Digested*, 98/**3287**:
                                                    Considered, 01/3780
TSB Bank Plc v. Robert Irving & Burns [2000] 2 All E.R. 826; [1999] Lloyd's Rep. P.N.
    956; [2000] P.N.L.R. 384, CA . . . .   *Digested*, 00/**4023**
TSB Life Ltd v. Colclough (Inspector of Taxes) see HSBC Life (UK) Ltd v. Stubbs
    (Inspector of Taxes)
TSB Private Bank International SA v. Chabra [1992] 1 W.L.R. 231; [1992] 2 All E.R. 245,
    Ch D . . . .   *Digested*, 92/**3545**:
         Applied, 01/45: *Considered*, 93/3280, 94/3738: *Distinguished*, 98/529
TSC Europe (UK) Ltd v. Massey [1999] I.R.L.R. 22, Ch D . . . .   *Digested*, 00/**2202**
Tse Wai Chun Paul v. Albert; *sub nom* Albert v. Tse Wai Chun Paul [2001] E.M.L.R. 31;
    10 B.H.R.C. 525, CFA (HK) . . . .   *Digested*, 01/**1826**:
                                                     Applied, 01/1821
Tshikangu v. Newham LBC see R. (on the application of Tshikangu) v. Newham LBC
Tsirilis v. Greece (1998) 25 E.H.R.R. 198, ECHR . . . .   *Digested*, 98/**3110**
Tuck v. Baker [1990] 32 E.G. 46, CA . . . .   *Digested*, 90/**713**:
                                                     Applied, 01/4858
Tucker, Re (Unreported, February 6, 1989), CA (Gue) . . . .   *Applied*, 01/3757
Tucker (Isle of Man), Re [1988] Fin. L.R. 323; [2000] B.P.I.R. 859, HC (IoM) . . . .   *Digested*, 88/**196**
Tucker (Jersey), Re [1988] Fin. L.R. 378; [2000] B.P.I.R. 876, Royal Ct (Jer) . . . .   *Digested*, 89/**175**
Tucker v. Allen [2001] P.N.L.R. 37; [2001] 26 E.G.C.S. 161; [2000] N.P.C. 132, QBD . . .   *Digested*, 01/**4535**
Tucker v. Granada Motorway Services Ltd [1979] 1 W.L.R. 683; [1979] 2 All E.R. 801;
    [1979] S.T.C. 393; 123 S.J. 390, HL; affirming [1979] 1 W.L.R. 87; [1979] 1 All
    E.R. 23; [1978] S.T.C. 587; [1978] T.R. 167; 122 S.J. 730, CA; affirming [1977] 1
    W.L.R. 1411; [1977] 3 All E.R. 865; [1977] S.T.C. 353; [1977] T.R. 167; 121 S.J.
    664, Ch D . . . .   *Digested*, 79/**374**:
           Applied, 91/598, 01/5201: *Considered*, 82/486, 85/462, 86/453, 88/534:
                                   Distinguished, 89/536, 90/763
Tucker v. Hutchinson (1987) 54 P. & C.R. 106, CA . . . .   *Digested*, 87/**2111**:
                                                     Applied, 98/4372
Tucker v. Secretary of State for Social Security see R. (on the application of Tucker) v.
    Secretary of State for Social Security
Tucker v. Williams see Williams v. Barclays Bank Plc
Tudor Properties Ltd v. Bolton MBC see Bolton MBC v. Tudor Properties Ltd
Tufnell, Re (1876) L.R. 3 Ch. D. 164, Ch D . . . .   *Considered*, 98/4785
Tull v. Severin [1998] I.C.R. 1037, EAT . . . .   *Digested*, 99/**2048**
Tullett & Tokyo Forex International Ltd v. Secretary of State for Social Security; Barclays
    De Zoete Wedd Services Ltd v. Secretary of State for Social Security; SGW Ltd
    v. Secretary of State for Social Security *Independent*, July 10, 2000 (C.S), QBD
Tunmore v. George (Unreported, November 11, 1998), CC (Reading) [*Ex rel.* Tim
    Kevan, Barrister, 1 Temple Gardens, Temple, London] . . . .   *Digested*, 99/**536**
Tunnel Refineries Ltd v. Council of the European Communities (124/77) see GR
    Amylum NV v. Council of the European Communities (C116/77)
Tunnel Refineries Ltd v. Intervention Board for Agricultural Produce (C145/77) see
    Royal Scholten-Honig (Holdings) Ltd v. Intervention Board for Agricultural
    Produce (C103/77)
Tunno, Re; Raikes v. Raikes (1890) L.R. 45 Ch. D. 66, Ch D
Tunstall v. Street (Unreported, November 8, 1999), CC (Central London) [*Ex rel.*
    Louise Neilson, Barrister, 9 Gough Square, London] . . . .   *Digested*, 99/**328**
Tuppen v. Microsoft Corp Ltd, *Times*, November 15, 2000, QBD . . . .   *Digested*, 00/**46**
Turberville Smith Ltd v. Turberville Smith [1998] 1 B.C.L.C. 134, QBD . . . .   *Digested*, 98/**450**
Turgut v. Secretary of State for the Home Department see R. v. Secretary of State for
    the Home Department Ex p. Turgut
Turkington v. Times Newspapers Ltd see McCartan Turkington Breen v. Times
    Newspapers Ltd

Turkiye IS Bankasi AS *v.* Bank of China [1998] 1 Lloyd's Rep. 250; [1998] C.L.C. 182;
Times, December 17, 1997, CA; affirming [1996] 2 Lloyd's Rep. 611; [1996] 5
Bank. L.R. 241; *Times*, March 8, 1996, QBD (Comm Ct) . . . . *Digested*, 98/**293**
Turnbull *v.* Rundle (Unreported, February 26, 2001), CC (Sunderland) [*Ex rel.* Sara
Robinson, Barrister, Broad Chare Chambers, Newcastle-upon-Tyne] . . . . *Digested*, 01/**905**
Turner *v.* Barclays Bank Plc [1998] 1 F.L.R. 276; [1997] 2 F.C.R. 151; [1997] Fam. Law
791, Ch D . . . . *Digested*, 97/**4244**:
Considered, 97/4232
Turner *v.* Commonwealth & British Minerals Ltd [2000] I.R.L.R. 114; *Independent*,
November 29, 1999 (C.S.), CA . . . . *Digested*, 00/**2201**
Turner *v.* Daw Unreported . . . . *Considered*, 98/455,
98/594
Turner *v.* General Motors (Australia) Pty Ltd (1929) 42 C.L.R. 352 . . . . *Considered*, 98/3497
Turner *v.* Grovit [2001] UKHL 65, HL [2000] Q.B. 345; [1999] 3 W.L.R. 794; [1999]
3 All E.R. 616; [1999] 1 All E.R. (Comm) 929; [2000] C.P. Rep. 84; [1999]
C.L.C. 1281; [1999] I.L.Pr. 656; [1999] I.C.R. 1114; [1999] I.R.L.R. 638; *Times*,
June 16, 1999, CA; reversing [1999] 1 All E.R. (Comm.) 445; *Times*, April 15,
1999, Ch D . . . . *Digested*, 99/**709**
Turner *v.* NEI Parsons Ltd (1998) 98(1) Q.R. 5, CC (Newcastle) . . . . *Digested*, 98/**1560**
Turner *v.* Owens Corning Fibreglass UK Ltd (Unreported, November 28, 1997), CC
(Chester) [*Ex rel.* Andrew Thomas, Barrister, Sedan House, Stanley Place,
Chester] . . . . *Digested*, 98/**1572**
Turner *v.* Plasplugs Ltd [1996] 2 All E.R. 939; (1996) 146 N.L.J. 370; *Times*, February
1, 1996; *Independent*, February 27, 1996, CA . . . . *Digested*, 96/**3858**:
Followed, 99/3760
Turner *v.* Royal Bank of Scotland Plc [1999] 2 All E.R. (Comm) 664; [1999] Lloyd's
Rep. Bank. 231; (1999) 96(18) L.S.G. 33; (1999) 143 S.J.L.B. 123; *Times*, April
17, 1999, CA . . . . *Digested*, 99/**272**
Turner *v.* Royal Bank of Scotland Plc (Negligent Misstatement) [2001] EWCA Civ 64;
[2001] 1 All E.R. (Comm) 1057, CA . . . . *Digested*, 01/**371**
Turner *v.* Royal Bank of Scotland Plc (Relitigation) [2000] B.P.I.R. 683, CA . . . . *Digested*, 00/**3434**:
Applied, 01/374
Turner *v.* Sefton MBC (1998) 98(1) Q.R. 7; (1997) 97(5/6) Q.R. 11, CC (Liverpool). . . . *Digested*, 98/**1546**
Turner *v.* Smith [2001] 5 Q.R. 12, CC (Hitchin) [*Ex rel.* Philip Goddard, Barrister, 4
King's Bench Walk, Temple, London] . . . . *Digested*, 01/**1752**
Turner *v.* Stevenage BC [1998] Ch. 28; [1997] 3 W.L.R. 309; [1997] 2 Lloyd's Rep.
129; (1997) 74 P. & C.R. 200; [1997] E.G.C.S. 34; (1997) 94(16) L.S.G. 29;
Times, March 27, 1997, CA; affirming [1996] 1 E.G.L.R. 23; [1996] 14 E.G. 94;
[1995] E.G.C.S. 181; [1995] N.P.C. 186; *Times*, December 7, 1995, Ch D . . . . . . *Digested*, 97/**266**
Turner *v.* Toleman (Unreported, January 15, 1999) . . . . *Applied*, 99/1395
Turner & Co *v.* O Palomo SA; *sub nom* O Palomo SA *v.* Turner & Co [2000] 1 W.L.R.
37; [1999] 4 All E.R. 353; [1999] 2 Costs L.R. 184; [1999] N.P.C. 114; *Times*,
August 30, 1999, CA . . . . *Digested*, 99/**416**
Turner & Turner *v.* Dau (Unreported, June 21, 1996), CC (Swansea) [*Ex rel.* Stefan
Lewinski, Barrister] . . . . *Digested*, 96/**666**:
Referred to, 98/596
Turner Page Music *v.* Torres Design Associates Ltd, *Times*, August 3, 1998, CA . . . . *Digested*, 98/**498**
Turner Stroud and Burley Construction Ltd *v.* Customs and Excise Commissioners
[1998] B.V.C. 2206, V&DTr. . . . . *Digested*, 98/**4978**
Turners & Growers Exporters Ltd *v.* Cornelis Verolme, The [2000] B.P.I.R. 896, HC (NZ) . . *Digested*, 01/**3760**
Turpin *v.* Middlesbrough Area Assessment Committee see Sedgwick *v.* Watney Combe
Reid & Co Ltd
Tuscany *v.* Commission of the European Communities (T81/97) [1998] E.C.R. II-2889;
[1998] 3 C.M.L.R. 1202, CFI (3rd Chamber)
TV 1000 Sverige AB *v.* Norwegian Government (C E-8/97) [1998] 3 C.M.L.R. 318,
EFTA
TVDanmark 1 Ltd *v.* Independent Television Commission see R. (on the application of
TVDanmark 1 Ltd) *v.* Independent Television Commission
TVM Ltd *v.* Commissioner of Income Tax 1 I.T.L. Rep. 296, Advance Rulings (Ind)
TW *v.* Malta (2000) 29 E.H.R.R. 185, ECHR . . . . *Digested*, 00/**3175**:
Applied, 00/6064
Twalib *v.* Greece (24294/94) (2001) 33 E.H.R.R. 24; [1998] H.R.C.D. 632, ECHR
TWD Textilwerke Deggendorf GmbH *v.* Germany (C188/92) [1994] E.C.R. I-833;
[1995] 2 C.M.L.R. 145, ECJ . . . . *Digested*, 94/**4850**:
Applied, 97/2388, 98/366, 98/726: *Considered*, 01/304
Tweed's Application for Judicial Review, Re [2001] N.I. 165, CA (NI) . . . . *Digested*, 01/**5875**
Twenty Two A Property Investments Ltd *v.* Simpson Curtis (A Firm) [2000] E.G.C.S. 140;
[2000] N.P.C. 129, CA
TWGS (A Child) *v.* JMG see DWS (Deceased), Re
Twigg Farnell *v.* Wildblood [1998] P.N.L.R. 211; (1998) 75 P. & C.R. D17, CA. . . . . *Digested*, 98/**3719**
Twinsectra Ltd *v.* Jones see Jones *v.* Twinsectra Ltd
Twinsectra Ltd *v.* Yardley TNS, HL; reversing [1999] Lloyd's Rep. Bank. 438; [2000]
Lloyd's Rep. P.N. 239; [2000] W.T.L.R. 527, CA . . . . *Digested*, 99/**294**:
Followed, 99/278

Twogates Properties Ltd v. Birmingham Midshires Building Society [1997] 2 B.C.L.C. 558; (1998) 75 P. & C.R. 386; [1997] E.G.C.S. 55, CA . . . . *Digested,* 97/**3300**
Twycross v. Hilton (Unreported, November 17, 1999), CC (Lincoln) [*Ex rel.* Andrew Stafford, Barrister, 4 King's Bench Walk, Temple, London] . . . . *Digested,* 00/**1689**
Ty Nant Spring Water Ltd v. Lemon & Co Srl [1999] E.T.M.R. 969, Trib (Napoli)
Ty Nant Spring Water Ltd v. Simon Feeney Associates Ltd (1998) 21 (6) I.P.D. 21061, Ch D
Ty Nant Spring Water Ltd's Community Trade Mark Application (R 5/1999-3) [1999] E.T.M.R. 974, OHIM (3rd Bd App) . . . . *Digested,* 00/**3718**: *Applied,* 00/3727

Ty Nant Spring Water Ltd's Request for Removal from the Register, Re see St Kea of Cornwall Ltd's Trade Mark (No. 2001526)
Ty Nant Spring Water Ltd's Trade Mark Application (No. 2162950) [1999] E.T.M.R. 981; [2000] R.P.C. 55, Appointed Person; affirming in part [1999] R.P.C. 392; (1999) 22(1) I.P.D. 22011, TMR . . . . *Digested,* 00/**3789**: *Referred to,* 01/4059

Tyagi v. BBC World Service [2001] EWCA Civ 549; [2001] I.R.L.R. 465; *Daily Telegraph,* March 20, 2001, CA . . . . *Digested,* 01/**2299**
Tyburn Productions Ltd v. Conan Doyle [1991] Ch. 75; [1990] 3 W.L.R. 167; [1990] 1 All E.R. 909; [1990] R.P.C. 185, Ch D . . . . *Digested,* 90/**609**: *Applied,* 92/4436: *Distinguished,* 99/731
Tyco European Metal Framing Ltd v. New Systems Ltd (2001) 24(5) I.P.D. 24030, Ch D
Tye v. House (1998) 76 P. & C.R. 188; [1997] 2 E.G.L.R. 171; [1997] 41 E.G. 160, Ch D
. . . . *Digested,* 97/**1004**
Tymans v. Craven (No.1) [1952] 2 Q.B. 100; [1952] 1 All E.R. 613; [1952] 1 T.L.R. 601; 96 S.J. 196, CA . . . . *Digested,* 52/**480**: *Applied,* 56/1193, 70/290: *Distinguished,* 69/399, 86/298, 87/338: *Followed,* 99/603
Tyrer v. United Kingdom (A/26) (1979-80) 2 E.H.R.R. 1, ECHR . . . . *Digested,* 79/**1173**: *Considered,* 01/1147
Tyrone v. Broadfoot (Unreported, January 16, 1998), CC (Rawtenstall) [*Ex rel.* James Hurd, Barrister, St James's Chambers, 68 Quay Street, Manchester] . . . . *Digested,* 98/**1742**
Tyrrell v. Painton (No.1) [1894] P. 151, CA . . . . *Applied,* 47-51/3872, 47-51/7915, 47-51/10960, 66/12574, 01/5165

U (A Child) v. Phillips [2001] 2 Q.R. 8, CC (Truro) [*Ex rel.* Robert McRae, Barrister, Walnut House, 63 St David's Hill, Exeter] . . . . *Digested,* 01/**1590**
U (A Minor) v. Living World Ltd (Unreported, June 15, 1998), CC (Leeds) [*Ex rel.* Jonathan Devlin, Barrister, Park Court Chambers, 40 Park Street, Leeds] . . . . . . *Digested,* 99/**1560**
U (A Minor) v. Manchester City Council (Unreported, July 6, 1999), CC (Manchester) [*Ex rel.* Hodgkinsons Solicitors, The Old Manse, 14 Lumley Avenue, Skegness, Lincolnshire] . . . . *Digested,* 99/**1569**
U v. W (Admissibility of Hansard) see U v. W (Attorney General Intervening) (No.1)
U v. W (Attorney General Intervening) (No.1); *sub nom* U v. W (Admissibility of Hansard) [1997] Eu. L.R. 342; [1997] Fam. Law 403, Fam Div . . . . *Digested,* 98/**321**
U v. W (Attorney General Intervening) (No.2) [1998] Fam. 29; [1997] 3 W.L.R. 739; [1997] 2 C.M.L.R. 431; [1997] Eu. L.R. 350; [1997] 2 F.L.R. 282; [1998] 1 F.C.R. 526; (1997) 38 B.M.L.R. 54; (1997) 141 S.J.L.B. 57; *Times,* March 4, 1997; *Independent,* April 14, 1997 (C.S.), Fam Div . . . . *Digested,* 97/**2446**
UBAF Ltd v. European American Banking Corp (The Pacific Colocotronis) [1984] Q.B. 713; [1984] 2 W.L.R. 508; [1984] 2 All E.R. 226; [1984] 1 Lloyd's Rep. 258; (1984) 81 L.S.G. 429; (1984) 128 S.J. 243, CA . . . . *Digested,* 84/**1579**: *Applied,* 01/4527
UBC Chartering Ltd v. Liepaya Shipping Co Ltd (The Liepaya) [1999] 1 Lloyd's Rep. 649, QBD (Comm Ct) . . . . *Digested,* 99/**4432**
UBS AG v. Omni Holding AG (In Liquidation) [2000] 1 W.L.R. 916; [2000] 1 All E.R. (Comm) 42; [2000] B.C.C. 593; [2000] 2 B.C.L.C. 310; [2000] I.L.Pr. 51, Ch D
. . . . *Digested,* 00/**765**
UCB Bank Plc v. Chandler (2000) 79 P. & C.R. 270; [1999] E.G.C.S. 56, CA . . . . . *Digested,* 00/**2605**
UCB Bank Plc v. David J Pinder Plc (No.1) [1998] C.L.C. 1262; [1998] P.N.L.R. 398; [1998] 2 E.G.L.R. 203; [1997] E.G.C.S. 179, QBD (OR) . . . . *Digested,* 98/**4005**
UCB Bank Plc v. David J Pinder Plc (No.2) [1998] E.G.C.S. 90, QBD (OR)
UCB Bank Plc v. Halifax (SW) Ltd (Striking Out: Want of Prosecution) [1999] Lloyd's Rep. P.N. 154, CA . . . . *Digested,* 99/**557**
UCB Bank Plc v. Hepherd Winstanley & Pugh [1999] Lloyd's Rep. P.N. 963; (1999) 96(34) L.S.G. 34; *Times,* August 25, 1999, CA . . . . *Digested,* 99/**3947**
UCB Corporate Services Ltd (formerly UCB Bank Plc) v. Clyde & Co [2000] 2 All E.R. (Comm) 257; [2000] Lloyd's Rep. P.N. 653; [2000] P.N.L.R. 841, CA. . . . . *Digested,* 00/**4281**
UCB Corporate Services Ltd (formerly UCB Bank Plc) v. Halifax (SW) Ltd (Striking Out: Breach of Rules and Orders) [1999] C.P.L.R. 691; (2000) 97(1) L.S.G. 24; (2000) 144 S.J.L.B. 25; *Times,* December 23, 1999, CA . . . . *Digested,* 00/**608**: *Applied,* 00/617: *Considered,* 00/609

UCB Corporate Services Ltd (formerly UCB Bank Plc) *v.* Halifax (SW) Ltd (In Liquidation) (Valuation) [2000] 1 E.G.L.R. 87; [2000] 16 E.G. 137; [2000] E.G.C.S. 28, CA . . . . *Digested*, 00/**4278**

UCB Home Loans Corp Ltd *v.* Carr [2000] Lloyd's Rep. P.N. 754, QBD. . . . . *Digested*, 00/**521**

UCB Home Loans Corp Ltd *v.* Moore see Royal Bank of Scotland Plc *v.* Etridge (No.2)

UCT (UK) Ltd (In Administration), Re; *sub nom* UCT (UK) Ltd *v.* Dargan [2001] 1 W.L.R. 436; [2001] 2 All E.R. 186; [2001] B.C.C. 734; [2001] 1 B.C.L.C. 443, Ch D (Companies Ct) . . . . *Digested*, 01/**3708**

UCT (UK) Ltd *v.* Dargan see UCT (UK) Ltd (In Administration), Re

Uddin *v.* Ahmed [2001] EWCA Civ 204; [2001] 3 F.C.R. 300, CA

Uecker *v.* Land Nordrhein-Westfalen (C64/96) see Land Nordrhein-Westfalen *v.* Uecker (C64/96)

Ufficio Distrettuale delle Imposte Dirette di Fiorenzuola d'Arda *v.* Comune di Carpaneto Piacentino (C231/87); Ufficio Provinciale Imposta sul Valore Aggiunto di Piacenza *v.* Comune di Rivergaro (C129/88) [1991] S.T.C. 205; [1989] E.C.R. 3233; *Times*, November 15, 1989, ECJ . . . . *Digested*, 91/**3661**: *Considered*, 01/5579, 01/5609

Ufficio Provinciale Imposta sul Valore Aggiunto di Piacenza *v.* Comune di Rivergaro (C129/88) see Ufficio Distrettuale delle Imposte Dirette di Fiorenzuola d'Arda *v.* Comune di Carpaneto Piacentino (C231/87)

UHDE/Re-establishment (T14/89) [1990] E.P.O.R. 656, EPO (Technical Bd App) . . . . . *Distinguished*, 00/**3609**

UHU Property Trust *v.* Lincoln City Council [2000] R.A. 419, QBD . . . . *Digested*, 00/**3928**

Ujima Housing Association *v.* Ansah (1998) 30 H.L.R. 831; [1997] N.P.C. 144; *Times*, November 20, 1997; *Independent*, October 23, 1997, CA. . . . . *Digested*, 97/**3251**

Ujima Housing Association *v.* Richardson (Unreported, November 29, 1995), CC [*Ex rel.* Paul Michell, Barrister] . . . . *Digested*, 96/**3771**: *Considered*, 00/3874

UK Coal Plc (formerly RJB Mining Plc) *v.* Commission of the European Communities (T12/99) [2001] E.C.R. II-2153; [2001] 3 C.M.L.R. 16, CFI . . . . *Digested*, 01/**789**

UK Digital Ltd *v.* Customs and Excise Commissioners [2001] S.T.I. 983, V&DTr

UK Safety Group Ltd *v.* Heane [1998] 2 B.C.L.C. 208, Ch D . . . . *Digested*, 98/**2113**

UK Waste Management Ltd *v.* Secretary of State for the Environment, Transport and the Regions [2000] Env. L.R. D24, QBD

UK Waste Management Ltd's Application for Judicial Review, Re see R. *v.* Department of the Environment for Northern Ireland Ex p. UK Waste Management Ltd

Ukert *v.* Interface Trustees Ltd; *sub nom* Hare Trust, Re (2001-02) 4 I.T.E.L.R. 288, Royal Ct (Jer)

Ullensaker Kommune *v.* Nille AS (E5/96) [1997] 3 C.M.L.R. 236, EFTA . . . . *Followed*, 00/3547

Ulster Bank Ltd *v.* Carter; *sub nom* Partition Acts 1868 and 1876, Re [1999] N.I. 93, Ch D (NI) . . . . *Digested*, 99/**5471**

Ulster Bank Ltd *v.* Fisher & Fisher (A Firm) [1999] N.I. 68; [1999] P.N.L.R. 794, Ch D (NI) . . . . *Digested*, 99/**5146**: *Considered*, 01/5710

Ulster Swift Ltd *v.* Fransen Transport NV see Ulster Swift Ltd *v.* Taunton Meat Haulage Ltd

Ulster Swift Ltd *v.* Taunton Meat Haulage Ltd; Ulster Swift Ltd *v.* Fransen Transport NV [1977] 1 W.L.R. 625; [1977] 3 All E.R. 641; [1977] 1 Lloyd's Rep. 346; [1977] R.T.R. 449; [1977] R.T.R. 475; 121 S.J. 169, CA; affirming [1975] 2 Lloyd's Rep. 502, QBD (Comm Ct) . . . . *Digested*, 77/**2553.a**: *Applied*, 79/235, 80/128: *Considered*, 78/204, 99/4944

Ultisol Transport Contractors Ltd *v.* Bouygues Offshore SA (No.4) see Bouygues Offshore SA *v.* Caspian Shipping Co (No.4)

Ultisol Transport Contractors Ltd *v.* Bouygues Offshore SA (No.5) see Bouygues Offshore SA *v.* Caspian Shipping Co (No.5)

Ultisol Transport Contractors Ltd *v.* Bouygues Offshore SA (Nos.1, 3, 4 and 5) see Bouygues Offshore SA *v.* Caspian Shipping Co (Nos.1, 3, 4 and 5)

ULTRA MOIST Trade Mark; *sub nom* Procter & Gamble's Trade Mark Application (ULTRA MOIST) [1999] E.T.M.R. 896, OHIM (1st Bd App) . . . . *Digested*, 00/**3722**

Ultraworth Ltd *v.* General Accident Fire & Life Assurance Corp Plc [2000] L. & T.R. 495; [2000] 2 E.G.L.R. 115; [2000] E.G.C.S. 19, QBD (T&CC) . . . . *Digested*, 01/**4191**

UMA GesmbH *v.* RM (NI 11/97) [2001] E.N.P.R. 8, BAG (Ger)

Umlauft *v.* Austria (A/328B) (1996) 22 E.H.R.R. 76, ECHR . . . . *Digested*, 96/**3119**: *Followed*, 98/3111

Umm Qarn Management Co Ltd *v.* Bunting [2001] C.P.L.R. 20, CA; reversing in part HC0000884, Ch D . . . . *Digested*, 01/**650**

Unauthorised Adaptation of Dr Zhivago (Lara's Child) (I ZR 65/96), Re [2000] E.C.C. 355, BGH (Ger)

Unauthorised Reproduction of Telephone Directories on CD ROM (I ZR 199/96), Re [2000] E.C.C. 433, BGH (Ger)

Unchained Growth III Plc *v.* Granby Village (Manchester) Management Co Ltd; Granby
    Village (Manchester) Management Co Ltd *v.* Unchained Growth III Plc [2000] 1
    W.L.R. 739; [2000] L. & T.R. 186; [1999] E.G.C.S. 116; (1999) 96(45) L.S.G.
    33; *Times*, November 4, 1999 ; *Independent*, October 21, 1999, CA;
    affirming(Unreported, October 23, 1998), QBD (T&CC) [*Ex rel.* Jeffrey Terry,
    Barrister, 8 King Street Chambers, 8 King Street, Manchester] . . . .   *Digested,* 99/**3746**
Underwood *v.* Harris (Unreported, January 31, 2000), CC (Southend) [*Ex rel.* Richard
    Roberts, Barrister, Lamb Building, Temple, London] . . . .   *Digested,* 00/**604**
Uni-Continental Holdings Ltd *v.* Eurobond Adhesives Ltd [1999] F.S.R. 263, Pat Ct . . .   *Digested,* 99/**3496**
Uniao Metalo Mecanica Lda *v.* Secretary of State for Tax Affairs (20 188) 1 I.T.L. Rep.
    136, Sup Trib Admin (P)
Unibank A/S *v.* Christensen (C260/97) [2000] 1 W.L.R. 1060; [2000] All E.R. (EC)
    374; [2000] 1 All E.R. (Comm) 859; [1999] E.C.R. I-3715; [1999] C.E.C. 656;
    [2000] I.L.Pr. 135; *Times,* June 30, 1999, ECJ (5th Chamber) [1998] I.L.Pr. 224,
    BGH (Ger) . . . .   *Digested,* 99/**727**
UNIC Centre Sarl *v.* Brent and Harrow LBC Trading Standards Service see R. *v.* Harrow
    Crown Court Ex p. UNIC Centre Sarl
UNIC Centre Sarl *v.* Harrow Crown Court see R. *v.* Harrow Crown Court Ex p. UNIC
    Centre Sarl
Unicoopjapan and Marubeni-Iida Co *v.* Ion Shipping Co (The Ion) [1971] 1 Lloyd's Rep.
    541, PDAD . . . .   *Digested,* 71/**10793**:
                                                Distinguished, 98/253
Unicorn Consultancy Services Ltd *v.* Westbrook [2000] I.R.L.R. 80, EAT . . . .   *Digested,* 00/**2227**
Unidoor *v.* Marks & Spencer Plc [1988] R.P.C. 275, Ch D . . . .   *Digested,* 89/**3691**:
                                                Considered, 98/3531
UNIFI *v.* Union Bank of Nigeria Plc [2001] I.R.L.R. 712; [2001] Pens. L.R. 239,
    Arbitration. . . . .   *Digested,* 01/**4631**
Unigate (UK) Ltd *v.* E Turner & Sons Ltd see Bellefield Computer Services Ltd *v.* E
    Turner & Sons Ltd
Unigreg Ltd *v.* Customs and Excise Commissioners [1998] 3 C.M.L.R. 128; (1999) 45
    B.M.L.R. 179; *Times,* July 27, 1998, QBD. . . . .   *Digested,* 98/**4613**
Unilever (UK) Holdings Ltd *v.* Smith (Inspector of Taxes) [2001] S.T.I. 1776, Ch D;
    affirming [2001] S.T.C. (S.C.D.) 6; [2001] S.T.I. 169, Sp Comm . . . .   *Digested,* 01/**5202**
Unilever Italia SpA *v.* Central Food SpA (C443/98) [2000] E.C.R. I-7535; [2001] 1
    C.M.L.R. 21, ECJ
Unilever NV *v.* Raisio YHTYMA OY [1999] E.T.M.R. 847, Hof (Den Haag)
Unilever NV's European Patent Application (T486/99) (2000) 23(3) I.P.D. 23019, EPO
    (Technical Bd App)
Unilever Plc *v.* Chefaro Proprietaries Ltd (Application for Expedited Appeal); Chiron
    Corp *v.* Organon Teknika Ltd (Application for Expedited Appeal); Henderson *v.*
    Merrett Syndicates Ltd (Application for Expedited Appeal); Brown *v.* KMR
    Services Ltd (Application for Expedited Appeal) [1995] 1 W.L.R. 243; [1995] 1
    All E.R. 587; (1994) 144 N.L.J. 1660; *Times,* November 28, 1994; *Independent,*
    November 24, 1994, CA. . . . .   *Digested,* 94/**3530**:
                         Considered, 01/422: *Followed,* 98/576
Unilever Plc *v.* Chefaro Proprietaries Ltd (Discovery) [1994] F.S.R. 135; *Times,* March
    29, 1993, CA. . . . .   *Digested,* 95/**4130**:
                       Followed, 95/3920, 97/3899, 00/3682
Unilever Plc *v.* Cussons (New Zealand) Pty Ltd see Cussons (New Zealand) Pty Ltd *v.*
    Unilever Plc
Unilever Plc *v.* Frisa NV [2000] F.S.R. 708; (2000) 23(4) I.P.D. 23028, Pat Ct . . . . . .   *Digested,* 00/**3667**
Unilever Plc *v.* Gillette (UK) Ltd (Joinder) [1989] R.P.C. 583; *Financial Times,* June 28,
    1989, CA . . . .   *Digested,* 89/**2805**:
                          Referred to, 93/3220, 95/4130, 99/3493
Unilever Plc *v.* Procter & Gamble Co [2000] 1 W.L.R. 2436; [2001] 1 All E.R. 783;
    [2000] F.S.R. 344; (2000) 23(1) I.P.D. 23001; (1999) 96(44) L.S.G. 40; (1999)
    143 S.J.L.B. 268; *Times,* November 4, 1999 ; *Independent,* November 5, 1999,
    CA; affirming [1999] 1 W.L.R. 1630; [1999] 2 All E.R. 691; [1999] F.S.R. 849;
    (1999) 22(5) I.P.D. 22042; (1999) 149 N.L.J. 370; *Times,* March 18, 1999, Pat
    Ct. . . . .   *Digested,* 99/**349**:
             Applied, 00/334: *Considered,* 01/397, 01/3966: *Followed,* 00/337
Unilever Plc's European Patent (No.0368680) (T742/96) see UNILEVER/Good faith
    (G02/97)
Unilever Plc's Patent Application (No.89311690.5) (G02/97) see UNILEVER/Good faith
    (G02/97)
Unilever Plc's Trade Mark Application (MISTER LONG) see MISTER LONG Trade Mark
UNILEVER/Catalyst (T626/91) [2001] E.P.O.R. 58, EPO (Technical Bd App)
UNILEVER/Emulsions (T384/94) [2000] E.P.O.R. 469, EPO (Technical Bd App) . . . . .   *Digested,* 01/**3919**
UNILEVER/Good faith (G02/97); *sub nom* Unilever Plc's Patent Application
    (No.89311690.5) (G02/97); UNILEVER/Textile (T742/96); Unilever Plc's
    European Patent (No.0368680) (T742/96) [2000] E.P.O.R. 73; (1999) 22(3)
    I.P.D. 22028, EPO (Enlarged Bd App) [1998] E.P.O.R. 100; (1997) 20(11) I.P.D.
    20112, EPO (Technical Bd App) . . . .   *Digested,* 00/**3609**
UNILEVER/Intervention (T517/97) [2001] E.P.O.R. 30, EPO (Technical Bd App) . . . . . .   *Digested,* 01/**3893**

UNILEVER/Textile (T742/96) see UNILEVER/Good faith (G02/97)

Union Camp Chemicals Ltd (t/a Arizona Chemical) v. ACE Insurance SA NV (formerly Cigna Insurance Co of Europe SA NV) [2001] C.L.C. 1609, QBD (T&CC)

Union Carbide Corp v. BP Chemicals Ltd [1999] R.P.C. 409; (1999) 22(2) I.P.D. 22012, CA; reversing in part [1998] R.P.C. 1, Pat Ct . . . . *Digested*, 99/**3480**

Union Carbide Corp v. BP Chemicals Ltd (Amendment of Statement of Claim) [1998] F.S.R. 1; (1998) 21(8) I.P.D. 21083; (1997) 20(8) I.P.D. 20077, Pat Ct . . . . *Digested*, 98/**3475**

UNION CARBIDE/Fluidised Bed Polymerisation (T379/93) [2001] E.P.O.R. 65, EPO (Technical Bd App)

Union Cold Storage Co Ltd v. Bancroft see Sedgwick v. Watney Combe Reid & Co Ltd

Union des Associations Europeennes de Football (UEFA) v. Bosman (C415/93) see Union Royale Belge des Societes de Football Association (ASBL) v. Bosman (C415/93)

Union Deutsche Lebensmittelwerke GmbH v. Commission of the European Communities (C97/85) [1987] E.C.R. 2265, ECJ . . . . *Applied*, 98/2311

Union Discount Co Ltd v. Zoller (Costs); *sub nom* Union Discount Ltd v. Union Cal Ltd [2001] EWCA Civ 1755; (2001) 151 N.L.J. 1769; (2001) 145 S.J.L.B. 276; *Times*, December 10, 2001; *Independent*, November 29, 2001, CA. . . . . *Digested*, 01/**478**

Union Discount Ltd v. Union Cal Ltd see Union Discount Co Ltd v. Zoller (Costs)

Union Europeenne de l'Artisanat et des Petites et Moyennes Entreprises (UEAPME) v. Council of the European Union (T135/96) (Application to Intervene) [1997] E.C.R. II-373; [1998] 1 C.M.L.R. 95, CFI (4th Chamber) . . . . *Digested*, 99/**2266**

Union Europeenne de l'Artisanat et des Petites et Moyennes Entreprises (UEAPME) v. Council of the European Union (T135/96) [1998] E.C.R. II-2335; [1998] 3 C.M.L.R. 385; [1998] I.R.L.R. 602, CFI (4th Chamber) . . . . *Digested*, 98/**2307**

Union Francaise de l'Express (UFEX) v. Commission of the European Communities (C119/97 P); *sub nom* Syndicat Francais de l'Express International (SFEI) v. Commission of the European Communities (T77/95) [1999] E.C.R. I-1341; [2000] 4 C.M.L.R. 268, ECJ (5th Chamber); reversing [1997] E.C.R. II-1; [1997] 5 C.M.L.R. 81, CFI (3rd Chamber) . . . . *Digested*, 00/**716**: *Distinguished*, 01/2469

Union Francaise de l'Express (UFEX) v. Commission of the European Communities (T77/95) [2000] E.C.R. II-2167; [2001] 4 C.M.L.R. 35, CFI (2nd Chamber) . . . *Digested*, 01/**2516**

Union of India v. McDonnell Douglas Corp [1993] 2 Lloyd's Rep. 48, QBD (Comm Ct) . *Digested*, 93/**175**: *Considered*, 00/239

Union Royale Belge des Societes de Football Association (ASBL) v. Bosman (C415/93); *sub nom* Royal Club Liegois SA v. Bosman (C415/93); Union des Associations Europeennes de Football (UEFA) v. Bosman (C415/93) [1996] All E.R. (EC) 97; [1995] E.C.R. I-4921; [1996] 1 C.M.L.R. 645; [1996] C.E.C. 38; *Times*, January 17, 1996, ECJ . . . . *Digested*, 96/**3149**: *Applied*, 00/2383: *Considered*, 00/2175: *Distinguished*, 00/4049

Union Syndicale-Service Public Europeen v. Council of Ministers of the European Communities (C72/74) [1975] E.C.R. 401; [1975] 2 C.M.L.R. 181, ECJ . . . . . . *Digested*, 76/**1074**: *Applied*, 98/2334

Union Transport v. Continental Lines SA; *sub nom* Cross AM Lines [1992] 1 W.L.R. 15; [1992] 1 All E.R. 161; [1992] 1 Lloyd's Rep. 229; [1992] I.L.Pr. 385; (1992) 89(2) L.S.G. 30; (1992) 136 S.J.L.B. 18; *Times*, December 16, 1991; *Independent*, January 10, 1992; *Financial Times*, December 17, 1991, HL; reversing [1991] 2 Lloyd's Rep. 48, CA. . . . . *Digested*, 92/**3944**: *Followed*, 00/3515

UNION/Food preservation (J02/94) [1998] E.P.O.R. 195, EPO (Technical Bd App) . . . *Followed*, 00/3609

Unione Calcio Sampdoria SpA v. Titan Hancocks [2000] E.T.M.R. 1017, Arbitration . . . . *Digested*, 01/**3872**

UNISON v. Westminster City Council; *sub nom* Westminster City Council v. UNISON [2001] EWCA Civ 443; [2001] I.C.R. 1046; [2001] I.R.L.R. 524; [2001] B.L.G.R. 378; (2001) 98(20) L.S.G. 41; *Times*, April 3, 2001, CA; reversing . . . *Digested*, 01/**2288**

Unisource (IV/35.830), Re; *sub nom* PTT Telecom BV Swiss PTT and Telia AB's Agreements [1998] 4 C.M.L.R. 105, CEC

Unisource NV and AT & T SA/NV's Agreements see Uniworld, Re (IV/35.738)

Unisys Corp's European Patent (No.0088538) see UNISYS/Optical memory system (T167/96)

UNISYS/Optical memory system (T167/96); *sub nom* Unisys Corp's European Patent (No.0088538) [2001] E.P.O.R. 11; (1998) 21(7) I.P.D. 21073, EPO (Technical Bd App) . . . . *Digested*, 01/**3948**

United Arab Emirates v. Abdelghafar [1995] I.C.R. 65; [1995] I.R.L.R. 243, EAT . . . . . . *Digested*, 95/**1988**: *Approved*, 99/2038

United Bank Ltd v. Hussain (t/a Burslem Filling Station) [2000] C.P.L.R. 270, CA. . . . . *Digested*, 00/**563**

United Bank of Kuwait v. Hammoud; City Trust Ltd v. Levy [1988] 1 W.L.R. 1051; [1988] 3 All E.R. 418; (1988) 138 N.L.J. Rep. 281; (1988) 132 S.J. 1388, CA; reversing (1987) 137 N.L.J. 921, DC. . . . . *Digested*, 89/**3491**: *Applied*, 01/4267: *Considered*, 01/4271: *Followed*, 99/3814

United Bank of Kuwait Plc v. Prudential Property Services Ltd see Banque Bruxelles Lambert SA v. Eagle Star Insurance Co Ltd

United Bank of Kuwait Plc v. Prudential Property Services Ltd see South Australia Asset Management Corp v. York Montague Ltd

United Bank of Kuwait Plc *v.* Prudential Property Services Ltd [1995] E.G.C.S. 190, CA;
affirming [1994] 30 E.G. 103, QBD. . . . . *Digested,* 96/**4434**:
Applied, 01/394: *Considered,* 96/4517: *Followed,* 96/4527

United City Merchants (Investments) Ltd *v.* Royal Bank of Canada (The American
Accord) [1983] 1 A.C. 168; [1982] 2 W.L.R. 1039; [1982] 2 All E.R. 720; [1982]
2 Lloyd's Rep. 1; [1982] Com. L.R. 142, HL; reversing [1982] Q.B. 208; [1981]
3 W.L.R. 242; [1981] 3 All E.R. 142; [1981] 1 Lloyd's Rep. 604; [1981] Com. L.R.
98; 125 S.J. 413, CA; affirming [1979] 1 Lloyd's Rep. 267, QBD (Comm Ct) . . . . *Digested,* 82/**215**:
Applied, 84/387, 86/394, 87/202: *Considered,* 83/358, 99/279, 00/5888:
Followed, 93/4734: *Referred to,* 81/2402, 81/2428

United Communist Party of Turkey *v.* Turkey (19392/92) (1998) 26 E.H.R.R. 121; 4
B.H.R.C. 1; [1998] H.R.C.D. 247, ECHR . . . . *Digested,* 98/**3080**:
Applied, 98/3081, 98/3093

United Dominions Corp Ltd *v.* Brian Pty Ltd (1985) 60 A.L.R. 741 . . . . *Considered,* 01/5356

United Film Distribution Ltd *v.* Chhabria [2001] EWCA Civ 416; [2001] 2 All E.R.
(Comm) 865; [2001] C.P. Rep. 84; *Times,* April 5, 2001, CA . . . . *Digested,* 01/**651**

United Food & Commercial Workers Local 1518 *v.* KMart Canada Ltd 7 B.H.R.C. 384,
Sup Ct (Can) . . . . *Digested,* 00/**3191**

United Friendly Insurance Plc *v.* Inland Revenue Commissioners [1998] S.T.C. 621;
[1998] B.T.C. 210, Ch D . . . . *Digested,* 98/**4626**

United Kingdom *v.* Commission of the European Communities (C106/96); *sub nom*
Payments to Combat Social Exclusion, Re [1998] E.C.R. I-2729; [1998] 2
C.M.L.R. 981, ECJ (1st Chamber)

United Kingdom *v.* Commission of the European Communities (C180/96) see R. *v.*
Ministry of Agriculture, Fisheries and Food Ex p. National Farmers Union (C157/
96)

United Kingdom *v.* Commission of the European Communities (C209/96) [1998]
E.C.R. I-5655; [2001] 1 C.M.L.R. 35; [1999] 1 C.M.L.R. 236, ECJ (5th
Chamber) . . . . *Digested,* 00/**170**

United Kingdom *v.* Council of the European Union (C150/94) [1998] E.C.R. I-7235;
[1999] 1 C.M.L.R. 367, ECJ (6th Chamber) . . . . *Digested,* 00/**2403**

United Kingdom Mutual Steamship Assurance Association (Bermuda) Ltd *v.* Lonestar
Drilling Nigeria Ltd see Gulf Azov Shipping Co Ltd *v.* Chief Idisi (No.2)

United Kingdom Mutual Steamship Assurance Association (Bermuda) Ltd *v.* Lonestar
Overseas Ltd see Gulf Azov Shipping Co Ltd *v.* Chief Idisi (No.2)

United Mizrahi Bank Ltd *v.* Doherty [1998] 1 W.L.R. 435; [1998] 2 All E.R. 230; *Times,*
December 15, 1997, Ch D . . . . *Digested,* 98/**526**

United Norwest Cooperatives Ltd *v.* Customs and Excise Commissioners [1999] S.T.C.
686; [1999] B.T.C. 5250; [1999] B.V.C. 283, CA; affirming [1998] S.T.C. 1065;
[1998] B.T.C. 5394; [1998] B.V.C. 448, QBD . . . . *Digested,* 99/**5022**

United Pan Europe Communications NV *v.* Deutsche Bank AG [2000] 2 B.C.L.C. 461,
CA . . . . *Digested,* 01/**372**

United Parties *v.* Minister of Justice, Legal and Parliamentary Affairs 3 B.H.R.C. 16, Sup
Ct (Zim) . . . . *Digested,* 98/**3094**

United Scientific Holdings *v.* Burnley BC; Cheapside Land Development Co *v.* Messels
Service Co [1978] A.C. 904; [1977] 2 W.L.R. 806; 75 L.G.R. 407; (1977) 33 P.
& C.R. 220; (1977) 243 E.G. 43; 121 S.J. 223, HL; reversing [1976] Ch. 128;
[1976] 2 W.L.R. 686; [1976] 2 All E.R. 220; 74 L.G.R. 316; 32 P. & C.R. 183;
(1976) 238 E.G. 487; 120 S.J. 183, CA; affirming (1974) 231 E.G. 1543, Ch D . . *Digested,* 77/**1758**:
Applied, 79/1638, 80/1637, 81/1573, 81/1580, 81/1588, 83/2126, 83/2131,
83/2138, 83/2139, 84/1947, 84/1950, 84/1951, 84/1952, 84/1956, 85/1935,
85/1937, 86/1908, 87/2202, 87/4626, 88/2075, 92/2743, 96/3814,
01/4208: *Considered,* 77/119, 77/1757, 78/101, 80/1635, 81/1582, 81/2433,
82/1801, 83/2080, 83/2128, 83/2130, 83/2132, 83/2135, 83/2137, 85/1918,
85/1920, 85/1927, 86/1913, 87/2206, 89/2151, 89/2153, 90/2855, 90/2859,
90/2861, 91/557, 91/2271, 92/2746, 93/182, 93/2462, 93/2536, 95/2965,
95/3068, 00/3914: *Distinguished,* 77/1726, 86/405, 97/3320:
Followed, 77/1759, 78/1810, 81/1585, 83/2140, 91/5178, 01/4207

United Services & Services Rendered Club (Tooting and Balham) Ltd *v.* Thorneley
(Valuation Officer) [2001] R.A. 145, LandsTr . . . . *Digested,* 01/**4827**

United States *v.* Montgomery; *sub nom* M (Restraint Order: External Confiscation
Order), Re [2001] UKHL 3; [2001] 1 W.L.R. 196; [2001] 1 All E.R. 815; (2001)
151 N.L.J. 136; *Times,* February 6, 2001; *Independent,* March 12, 2001 (C.S);
Daily Telegraph, February 7, 2001, HL; affirming [1999] 1 All E.R. 84; [1998] 2
F.L.R. 1035; *Times,* August 24, 1998; *Independent,* July 27, 1998 (C.S.), CA . . . . *Digested,* 01/**15**

United States Tobacco International Inc *v.* BBC [1998] E.M.L.R. 816; *Independent,*
March 15, 1988; *Guardian,* March 16, 1988, CA . . . . *Digested,* 88/**2124**:
Followed, 98/1769

United Wire Ltd *v.* Screen Repair Services (Scotland) Ltd [2000] 4 All E.R. 353;
[2000] E.N.P.R. 324; [2001] F.S.R. 24; [2001] R.P.C. 24; (2000) 23(12) I.P.D.
23099; *Times,* July 21, 2000; *Independent,* October 23, 2000 (C.S), HL;
affirming [2000] F.S.R. 204; (1999) 22(11) I.P.D. 22106; *Times,* August 18,
1999, CA; reversing (1997) 20(12) I.P.D. 20121; *Times,* August 20, 1997, Ch D . *Digested,* 00/**3674**

Unity FR 165 Ltd *v.* Ministry of Agriculture, Fisheries and Food, *Times,* January 20, 1999, QBD . . . . *Digested,* 99/**2564**

Universal Bulk Carriers Pte Ltd *v.* Andre et Cie SA; *sub nom* Andre et Cie SA *v.* Universal Bulk Carriers Ltd [2001] EWCA Civ 588; [2001] 2 All E.R. (Comm) 510; [2001] 2 Lloyd's Rep. 65, CA; affirming [2000] 1 Lloyd's Rep. 459; [2001] C.L.C. 1179, QBD (Comm Ct) . . . . *Digested,* 01/**4911**

Universal Cargo Carriers Corp *v.* Citati (No.1) [1957] 1 W.L.R. 979; [1957] 3 All E.R. 234; [1957] 2 Lloyd's Rep. 191; 101 S.J. 762, CA; affirming [1957] 2 Q.B. 401; [1957] 2 W.L.R. 713; [1957] 2 All E.R. 70; [1957] 1 Lloyd's Rep. 174; (1957) 101 S.J. 320, QBD . . . . *Digested,* 57/**130**:
Applied, 61/8255, 62/2838, 79/2449, 81/2403: *Considered,* 72/3202, 73/3109, 86/1259, 00/870: *Followed,* 99/5791

Universal Corp *v.* Five Ways Properties [1979] 1 All E.R. 552; (1979) 38 P. & C.R. 687; (1978) 250 E.G. 447; 123 S.J. 33, CA; reversing [1978] 3 All E.R. 1131, Ch D . . *Digested,* 79/**2775**:
Applied, 80/2800, 84/2951: *Considered,* 01/4854

Universal Cycles Plc *v.* Grangebriar Ltd [2000] C.P.L.R. 42, CA . . . . *Digested,* 00/**398**:
Considered, 01/470

Universal General Insurance Co (UGIC) *v.* Group Josi Reinsurance Co SA (C412/98); *sub nom* Group Josi Reinsurance Co SA *v.* Compagnie d'Assurances Universal General Insurance Co (UGIC) (C412/98); Group Josi Reinsurance Co SA *v.* Universal General Insurance Co (UGIC) [2001] Q.B. 68; [2000] 3 W.L.R. 1625; [2000] All E.R. (EC) 653; [2000] 2 All E.R. (Comm) 467; [2000] E.C.R. I-5925; [2001] C.L.C. 893; [2000] C.E.C. 462; [2000] I.L.Pr. 549; [2001] Lloyd's Rep. I.R. 483; *Times,* August 9, 2000, ECJ (6th Chamber) [1999] I.L.Pr. 351, C d'A (Versailles) . . . . *Digested,* 00/**774**

Universal Thermosensors Ltd *v.* Hibben [1992] 1 W.L.R. 840; [1992] 3 All E.R. 257; [1992] F.S.R. 361; (1992) 142 N.L.J. 195; *Times,* February 12, 1992; *Independent,* February 12, 1992; *Guardian,* March 20, 1992, Ch D . . . . *Digested,* 92/**1910**:
Applied, 00/2200: *Considered,* 94/3706, 95/4173

Universities Superannuation Scheme Ltd *v.* Marks & Spencer Plc [1999] L. & T.R. 237; [1999] 1 E.G.L.R. 13; [1999] 04 E.G. 158; [1998] E.G.C.S. 168, CA; reversing1997 No.Ch.UNO-1909, Ch D . . . . *Digested,* 99/**3745**

Universities Superannuation Scheme Ltd *v.* Royal Insurance (UK) Ltd [2000] 1 All E.R. (Comm) 266; [2000] Lloyd's Rep. I.R. 524, QBD (Comm Ct) . . . . *Digested,* 00/**529**

University College (Oxford) *v.* Durdy; *sub nom* Master and Fellows of University College (Oxford) *v.* Durdy [1982] Ch. 413; [1982] 3 W.L.R. 94; [1982] 1 All E.R. 1108; (1982) 43 P. & C.R. 399; (1982) 262 E.G. 338, CA . . . . *Digested,* 82/**27**:
Distinguished, 00/3886

University College London Hospitals NHS Trust *v.* UNISON [1999] I.C.R. 204; [1999] I.R.L.R. 31; (1998) 95(41) L.S.G. 45; (1998) 142 S.J.L.B. 270; *Times,* October 15, 1998; *Independent,* October 16, 1998, CA . . . . *Digested,* 98/**2159**

University Court of the University of Glasgow *v.* William Whitfield and John Laing (Construction) Ltd see University of Glasgow *v.* William Whitfield

University of Bath *v.* Customs and Excise Commissioners [1996] B.V.C. 2909, V&DTr . . *Applied,* 01/5619:
Considered, 01/5618

University of Cambridge Local Examination Syndicate *v.* Customs and Excise Commissioners [1997] V. & D.R. 245, V&DTr . . . . *Digested,* 98/**4954**

University of Glasgow *v.* John Laing (Construction) Ltd see University of Glasgow *v.* William Whitfield

University of Glasgow *v.* William Whitfield; *sub nom* University Court of the University of Glasgow *v.* William Whitfield and John Laing (Construction) Ltd; University of Glasgow *v.* John Laing (Construction) Ltd 42 B.L.R. 66; (1989) 5 Const. L.J. 73, QBD . . . . *Digested,* 89/**2539**:
Considered, 98/795

University of Huddersfield *v.* Customs and Excise Commissioners [2001] S.T.I. 1118, V&DTr

University of Liverpool *v.* Customs and Excise Commissioners [2001] B.V.C. 2088; [2000] S.T.I. 1769, V&DTr. . . . . *Digested,* 01/**5584**

University of Nottingham *v.* Eyett (No.1) [1999] 2 All E.R. 437; [1999] I.C.R. 721; [1999] I.R.L.R. 87; [1999] E.L.R. 141; [1999] O.P.L.R. 55; [1999] Pens. L.R. 17; (1999) 96(1) L.S.G. 24; *Times,* December 3, 1998; *Independent,* December 7, 1998 (C.S.), Ch D . . . . *Digested,* 99/**2012**

University of Nottingham *v.* Eyett (No.2) [1999] 1 W.L.R. 594; [1999] 2 All E.R. 445; [1999] Pens. L.R. 25; *Times,* December 3, 1998, Ch D . . . . *Digested,* 99/**373**:
Followed, 99/4154

University of Nottingham *v.* Fishel [2000] I.C.R. 1462; [2000] I.R.L.R. 471; [2001] R.P.C. 22; [2000] Ed. C.R. 505; [2000] E.L.R. 385; (2001) 24(2) I.P.D. 24009; *Times,* March 31, 2000, QBD . . . . *Digested,* 00/**2113**

University of Nottingham *v.* Fishel (Amendment of Defence) (Unreported, July 22, 1999), QBD [*Ex rel.* Daniel Lightman, Barrister, Serle Court Chambers, 13 Old Square, Lincoln's Inn, London] . . . . *Digested,* 00/**387**

University of Reading *v.* Customs and Excise Commissioners [1998] B.V.C. 2163; [1998] V. & D.R. 27, V&DTr . . . . *Digested,* 98/**4882**

University of Sussex v. Customs and Excise Commissioners [2001] S.T.C. 1495; [2001] S.T.I. 1346; (2001) 98(42) L.S.G. 37, Ch D; reversing [2001] B.V.C. 2003; [2000] S.T.I. 1351, V&DTr

University of Victoria v. British Columbia see McConnell (Deceased), Re

University of Wales College, Newport v. Customs and Excise Commissioners; Allt-Yr-Yn and Caerleon Enterprises & Services Ltd v. Customs and Excise Commissioners [1998] B.V.C. 2082; [1997] V. & D.R. 417, V&DTr. . . . . *Digested,* 00/**5283**

University of Westminster v. President of the Lands Tribunal see University of Westminster's Application, Re

University of Westminster's Application, Re; *sub nom* University of Westminster v. President of the Lands Tribunal [1998] 3 All E.R. 1014; (1999) 78 P. & C.R. 82; [1999] R.V.R. 8; [1998] E.G.C.S. 118; (1998) 95(33) L.S.G. 33; (1998) 142 S.J.L.B. 245; [1998] N.P.C. 120; (1998) 76 P. & C.R. D44; *Times,* September 1, 1998; *Independent,* July 22, 1998, CA; affirming (1997) 74 P. & C.R. 86; [1997] 1 E.G.L.R. 191; [1997] 22 E.G. 147, Lands Tr . . . . *Digested,* 98/**4342**

UNIVERSITY PATENTS/Herpes simplex virus (T377/95) [1999] E.P.O.R. 211; (1998) 21 (11) I.P.D. 21120, EPO (Technical Bd App). . . . . *Digested,* 00/**3623**:
Subsequent proceedings, 01/3956

UNIVERSITY PATENTS/Six-month period (G03/98) [2001] E.P.O.R. 33, EPO (Enlarged Bd App) . . . . *Digested,* 01/**3956**:
Previous proceedings, 00/3623

Uniworld, Re (IV/35.738); *sub nom* Unisource NV and AT & T SA/NV's Agreements [1998] 4 C.M.L.R. 145, CEC

Unterweser Reederei GmbH v. Zapata Offshore Co (The Chaparral) [1968] 2 Lloyd's Rep. 158, CA. . . . . *Digested,* 68/**3187**:
Followed, 98/771

UOC Corp (No.1), Re see Alipour v. Ary

UOC Corp (No.2), Re; *sub nom* Alipour v. UOC Corp (No.2) [1998] B.C.C. 191; [1997] 2 B.C.L.C. 569, Ch D (Companies Ct) . . . . *Digested,* 98/**3305**

Upjohn Ltd v. Licensing Authority (C120/97) [1999] 1 W.L.R. 927; [1999] E.C.R. I-223; [1999] 1 C.M.L.R. 825; [2000] C.E.C. 648; (2000) 51 B.M.L.R. 206; (1999) 96(19) L.S.G. 30; *Times,* January 26, 1999, ECJ . . . . *Digested,* 99/**2696**

Upjohn SA, Danmark v. Paranova A/S (C379/97) see Pharmacia & Upjohn SA (formerly Upjohn SA) v. Paranova A/S (C379/97)

Uprichard v. Fife Council 2000 S.C.L.R. 949; [2001] Env. L.R. 8; 2000 G.W.D. 14-514, OH . . . . *Digested,* 01/**6856**

UPS Europe SA v. Commission of the European Communities (T127/98) [1999] All E.R. (EC) 794; [1999] E.C.R. II-2633; [2000] 4 C.M.L.R. 94; [1999] C.E.C. 506, CFI (4th Chamber) . . . . *Digested,* 00/**2367**

UPS Ltd v. Lewis, *Independent,* February 23, 1998 (C.S.), CA; affirming (Unreported, July 28, 1997), DR (Leeds) [*Ex rel.* District Judge SJ Greenwood, Newland, Drax, Selby] . . . . *Digested,* 98/**369**

Upton v. Burbridge (Unreported, December 22, 2000), CC (Leicester) [*Ex rel.* Charles Crow, Barrister, 5 Fountain Court, Steelhouse Lane, Birmingham] . . . . *Digested,* 01/**881**

Upton v. Taylor [1999] B.P.I.R. 168, Ch D . . . . *Digested,* 99/**3333**

Uratemp Ventures Ltd v. Carrell see Uratemp Ventures Ltd v. Collins

Uratemp Ventures Ltd v. Collins; Uratemp Ventures Ltd v. Carrell [2001] UKHL 43; [2001] 3 W.L.R. 806; (2001) 33 H.L.R. 85; 2001 Hous. L.R. 133; [2001] 43 E.G.C.S. 186; (2001) 98(41) L.S.G. 35; [2001] N.P.C. 145; *Times,* October 18, 2001; *Independent,* December 3, 2001; *Daily Telegraph,* October 16, 2001, HL; reversing (2001) 33 H.L.R. 4; [2000] L. & T.R. 369; [2000] 1 E.G.L.R. 156; (2000) 97(1) L.S.G. 23; [1999] N.P.C. 153; (2000) 79 P. & C.R. D18; *Times,* December 10, 1999, CA . . . . *Digested,* 01/**4148**

Urdd Gobaith Cymru v. Customs and Excise Commissioners [1997] V. & D.R. 273, V&DTr. . . . . *Digested,* 98/**4981**

US Ring Binder Corp v. Council of the European Union (T147/97) see Champion Stationery Mfg Co Ltd v. Council of the European Union (T147/97)

USA Detergents Inc's Application [1998] E.T.M.R. 562, OHIM (1st Bd App)

USF Ltd (t/a USF Memcor) v. Aqua Technology Hanson NV/SA [2001] 1 All E.R. (Comm) 856, QBD (Comm Ct) . . . . *Digested,* 01/**802**

Uslusow v. Secretary of State for the Home Department see Hersi v. Secretary of State for the Home Department

Uter v. Williams (Unreported, October 21, 1999), CC (Bristol) [*Ex rel.* Christopher Taylor, Barrister, Queen Square Chambers, 56 Queen Square, Bristol] . . . . *Digested,* 00/**1616**

Utley v. Parker [2000] 3 Q.R. 5, CC (Sheffield) [*Ex rel.* Andrew Hogan, Barrister, 24 The Ropewalk, Nottingham] . . . . *Digested,* 00/**1573**

Uttlesford DC v. Berisford Property Developments Ltd (2000) 15 P.A.D. 422, Planning Inspector

Uttlesford DC v. Seers (2000) 15 P.A.D. 728, Planning Inspector

UVG Ambulances Ltd v. Auto Conversions Ltd [2000] E.C.D.R. 479; 2000 G.W.D. 22-866, OH . . . . *Digested,* 01/**6724**

UYB Ltd v. British Railways Board (2000) 97(43) L.S.G. 37; (2000) 97(42) L.S.G. 45; (2001) 81 P. & C.R. D19; *Times,* November 15, 2000, CA . . . . *Digested,* 00/**319**

UYCF Ltd (formerly Night Trunkers (London) Ltd) *v.* Forrester; *sub nom* Forrester *v.* UYCF Ltd [2001] 3 E.G.C.S.131; [2000] N.P.C.141, CA

V (A Child) (Contact: Domestic Violence), Re see L (A Child) (Contact: Domestic Violence), Re

V (A Child) (Jurisdiction: Habitual Residence), Re; *sub nom* VP (Loss of Child's Habitual Residence), Re [2001] 1 F.L.R. 253; [2001] 1 F.C.R. 712; [2000] Fam. Law 874, Fam Div.. *Digested*, 01/**2658**

V (A Child) *v.* Williams [2001] 3 Q.R. 12, CC (Birmingham) [*Ex rel.* Stephen Garner, Barrister, No 8 Chambers, Fountain Court, Steelhouse Lane, Birmingham].......... *Digested*, 01/**1597**

V (Minors) (Sexual Abuse: Disclosure), Re see L (Minors) (Sexual Abuse: Disclosure), Re

V *v.* C [2001] EWCA Civ 1509; (2001) 98(43) L.S.G. 34; (2001) 145 S.J.L.B. 243; *Times*, November 1, 2001, CA... *Digested*, 01/**638**

V *v.* United Kingdom (24888/94) see T *v.* United Kingdom (24724/94)

V *v.* V (Ancillary Relief: Power to Order Child Maintenance) [2001] 2 F.L.R. 799; [2001] Fam. Law 649; *Times*, August 16, 2001, Fam Div.................. *Digested*, 01/**2636**

V and W (Minors), Re see L (Minors) (Sexual Abuse: Disclosure), Re

V-B (Abduction: Rights of Custody), Re; B (A Minor), Re [1999] 2 F.L.R. 192; [1999] 2 F.C.R. 371; [1999] Fam. Law 372, CA............................... *Digested*, 99/**2334**

Vaassen-Gobbels *v.* Beambtenfonds Voor Het Mijnbedrijf (C61/65) [1966] E.C.R. 261; [1966] E.C.R. 377; [1966] C.M.L.R. 508, ECJ......................... *Digested*, 67/**1563**:
Applied, 98/2320

Vacco *v.* Quill (1999) 50 B.M.L.R.119, US Ct

Vacher *v.* France (1997) 24 E.H.R.R. 482, ECHR .... *Digested*, 98/**3143**

Vadera *v.* Shaw (1999) 45 B.M.L.R.162, CA................................. *Digested*, 99/**3988**

Vadher *v.* Weisgard [1998] B.P.I.R. 295, Ch D .... *Digested*, 98/**3349**

VAG-Handlerbeirat eV *v.* SYD-Consult (C41/96) [1997] E.C.R. I-3123; [1997] 5 C.M.L.R. 537; [1997] C.E.C. 1226, ECJ (6th Chamber).................... *Digested*, 98/**743**

Vale do Rio Doce Navegacao SA *v.* Ocean Freighters Corp see Allied Marine Transport *v.* Vale do Rio Doce Navegacao SA (The Leonidas D)

Vale do Rio doce Navegacao SA *v.* Shanghai Bao Steel Ocean Shipping Co Ltd (t/a Bao Steel Ocean Shipping Co); *sub nom* Vale do Rio doce Navegacao SA *v.* Shanghai Bao Steel Ocean Shipping Co Ltd (t/a Baosteel Ocean Shipping Co) [2000] 2 All E.R. (Comm) 70; [2000] 2 Lloyd's Rep. 1; [2000] C.L.C. 1200; *Times*, May 16, 2000, QBD (Comm Ct)................................. *Digested*, 00/**240**

Vale do Rio doce Navegacao SA *v.* Shanghai Bao Steel Ocean Shipping Co Ltd (t/a Baosteel Ocean Shipping Co) see Vale do Rio doce Navegacao SA *v.* Shanghai Bao Steel Ocean Shipping Co Ltd (t/a Bao Steel Ocean Shipping Co)

Vale of Glamorgan CBC *v.* Cottrell Park Golf Club Ltd (2001) 16 P.A.D. 33, Planning Inspector

Vale of Glamorgan Council *v.* BJ Skip Hire Ltd (2000) 15 P.A.D.126, Planning Inspector

Vale of Glamorgan Council *v.* Green Circle Sustainable Developments Ltd (1999) 14 P.A.D. 602, Planning Inspector

Vale of White Horse DC *v.* Cox (2000) 15 P.A.D. 458, Planning Inspector

Vale of White Horse DC *v.* Discovery Properties (1999) 14 P.A.D. 588, Planning Inspector

Valente *v.* Fazenda Publica (C393/98) see Ministerio Publico *v.* Fazenda Publica (C393/98)

Valente's Application for Judicial Review, Re [1998] N.I. 341, QBD (NI)............. *Digested*, 99/**5213**

Valentine *v.* Valentine see Valentine's Settlement, Re

Valentine's Settlement, Re; *sub nom* Valentine *v.* Valentine [1965] Ch. 831; [1965] 2 W.L.R. 1015; [1965] 2 All E.R. 226; 109 S.J. 237, CA; affirming [1965] Ch. 226; [1964] 3 W.L.R. 768; [1964] 3 All E.R. 174; 108 S.J. 582, Ch D .... *Digested*, 65/**3556**:
Applied, 67/1991, 00/2436: *Followed*, 96/467

Valenzuela Contreras *v.* Spain (1999) 28 E.H.R.R. 483; [1998] H.R.C.D. 744, ECHR ... *Digested*, 00/**3252**

Valigeria Roncato SpA's Community Trade Mark Application (R164/1998-1) [2000] E.T.M.R. 46, OHIM (1st Bd App).. *Digested*, 00/**3733**

Vallaj *v.* Special Adjudicator see R. (on the application of Vallaj) *v.* Special Adjudicator

VALMET/Glide shoe (T92/92) [2000] E.P.O.R. 566, EPO (Technical Bd App) .... *Digested*, 01/**3921**

Valsamis *v.* Greece (1997) 24 E.H.R.R. 294; [1998] E.L.R. 430, ECHR .... *Digested*, 97/**2787**

Valucci Designs Ltd (t/a Hugo Hog's) Trade Mark Application (No.2061604) see LOADED Trade Mark

Value Added Tax on Postal Transport (C107/84), Re; *sub nom* Commission of the European Communities *v.* Germany (C107/84); VAT on Postal Transport, Re (C107/84) [1985] E.C.R. 2655; [1986] 2 C.M.L.R. 177, ECJ .... *Digested*, 86/**1494**:
Followed, 01/761

Van Boeckel *v.* Customs and Excise Commissioners [1981] 2 All E.R. 505; [1981] S.T.C. 290; [1980] T.R. 477, QBD................................. *Digested*, 81/**2839**:
Applied, 90/4578, 94/4561, 00/5280: *Approved*, 96/5865:
Considered, 87/3798, 98/4884, 98/4885, 98/4888: *Followed*, 90/4577, 96/5907: *Referred to*, 95/5011, 95/5022

Van Cant (Remi) v. Rijksdienst voor Pensioenen (C154/92) [1993] E.C.R. I-3811;
   [1994] I.R.L.R. 38; *Financial Times*, July 13, 1993, ECJ (6th Chamber) . . . .   *Digested*, 93/**4385**:
                                   Applied, 98/2155: *Followed*, 01/4604

van de Laan (C383/97), Re see Criminal Proceedings against Van der Laan (C383/97)
Van den Bergh Foods Ltd v. Commission of the European Communities (T65/98R)
   [1998] E.C.R. II-2641; [1998] 5 C.M.L.R. 475, CFI
Van den Berghs Ltd (Inspector of Taxes) v. Clark [1935] A.C. 431; 19 T.C. 390, HL . . . . .   *Applied*, 65/1921,
           81/343, 01/5284: *Considered*, 65/1922, 95/882: *Distinguished*, 55/1284,
                                       58/1539, 58/3860
Van den Boogaard v. Laumen (C220/95) [1997] Q.B. 759; [1997] All E.R. (E.C.) 517;
   [1997] E.C.R. I-1147; [1997] I.L.Pr. 278; [1997] 2 F.L.R. 399; [1997] 3 F.C.R.
   493; [1997] Fam. Law 599; *Times*, March 26, 1997, ECJ (5th Chamber) . . . . . .   *Digested*, 97/**2454**:
                                   Considered, 98/2470
Van der Leer v. Netherlands (A/170) (1990) 12 E.H.R.R. 567; *Times*, March 2, 1990,
   ECHR . . . .   *Digested*, 90/**2528**:
                       Considered, 96/3132, 98/3146, 01/3564
Van der Wal v. Commission of the European Communities (C174/98); *sub nom* Van der
   Wal v. Commission of the European Communities (T83/96); Van der Wal v.
   Commission of the European Communities (C189/98) [2000] E.C.R. I-1; *Times*,
   February 22, 2000, ECJ; reversing [1998] All E.R. (E.C.) 289; [1998] E.C.R. II-
   545; [1998] 4 C.M.L.R. 954; [1998] C.E.C. 395, CFI (4th Chamber) . . . .   *Digested*, 00/**2395**
Van der Wal v. Commission of the European Communities (C189/98) see Van der Wal v.
   Commission of the European Communities (C174/98)
Van der Wal v. Commission of the European Communities (T83/96) see Van der Wal v.
   Commission of the European Communities (C174/98)
Van der Woude v. Stichting Beatrixoord (C222/98) [2000] E.C.R. I-7111; [2001] 4
   C.M.L.R. 2, ECJ (6th Chamber) . . . .   *Digested*, 01/**2446**
Van Dooselaere v. Holt Cargo Systems Inc [1999] I.L.Pr. 634; 1999 A.M.C. 1486, CA
   (Can) . . . .   *Digested*, 00/**4722**
Van Droogenbroeck v. Belgium (A/50) (1982) 4 E.H.R.R. 443, ECHR . . . .   *Followed*, 98/3073
Van Geyseghem v. Belgium (26103/95) (2001) 32 E.H.R.R. 24, ECHR
Van Leuven v. Belgium (A/43) see Le Compte v. Belgium (A/43)
Van Mechelen v. Netherlands (Art.50) [1998] H.R.C.D. 46, ECHR
Van Mechelen v. Netherlands (Art.6) (1998) 25 E.H.R.R. 647; 2 B.H.R.C. 486, ECHR . .   *Digested*, 97/**2815**:
                                       Applied, 01/6323
Van Orshoven v. Belgium (20122/92) (1998) 26 E.H.R.R. 55, ECHR . . . .   *Digested*, 98/**3142**:
                                       Applied, 99/3127
Van Oudenhoven v. Griffin Inns Ltd [2000] 1 W.L.R. 1413; [2000] P.I.Q.R. Q276;
   (2000) 97(19) L.S.G. 42; (2000) 144 S.J.L.B. 214; *Times*, April 10, 2000, CA . .   *Digested*, 00/**1470**
Van Raalte v. Netherlands (1997) 24 E.H.R.R. 503, ECHR . . . .   *Digested*, 98/**3076**
Van Rijs (Hendrik) v. HM Advocate (No.3) see Hoekstra v. HM Advocate (No.3)
Van Rijs (Hendrik) v. HM Advocate (No.5) see Hoekstra v. HM Advocate (No.5)
Van Rijs (Jan) v. HM Advocate (No.3) see Hoekstra v. HM Advocate (No.3)
Van Rijs (Jan) v. HM Advocate (No.5) see Hoekstra v. HM Advocate (No.5)
Van Rijs (Ronny) v. HM Advocate (No.3) see Hoekstra v. HM Advocate (No.3)
Van Rijs (Ronny) v. HM Advocate (No.5) see Hoekstra v. HM Advocate (No.5)
Van Rooij v. Dagelijks bestuur van het waterschap de Dommel (C231/97); *sub nom*
   Van Rooj v. Dagelijks bestuur van het water schap de Dommel (C231/97)
   [1999] E.C.R. I-6355; [2000] Env. L.R. D16; *Times*, October 15, 1999, ECJ (6th
   Chamber) . . . .   *Digested*, 99/**5044**
Van Rooj v. Dagelijks bestuur van het water schap de Dommel (C231/97) see Van
   Rooij v. Dagelijks bestuur van het waterschap de Dommel (C231/97)
Van Stillevoldt (CM) BV v. EL Carriers Inc [1983] 1 W.L.R. 207; [1983] 1 All E.R. 699,
   CA . . . .   *Digested*, 83/**2864**:
                     Applied, 91/2778: *Considered*, 88/2009: *Followed*, 99/394:
                                    Not followed, 85/2590
Van Uden Maritime BV (t/a Van Uden Africa Line) v. Kommanditgesellschaft in Firma
   Deco-Line (C391/95) [1999] Q.B. 1225; [1999] 2 W.L.R. 1181; [1999] All E.R.
   (E.C.) 258; [1999] 1 All E.R. (Comm.) 385; [1998] E.C.R. I-7091; [1999] I.L.Pr.
   73; *Times*, December 1, 1998, ECJ [1996] I.L.Pr. 269, HR (NL) . . . .   *Digested*, 99/**739**
Van Vlimmeren v. Netherlands (25989/94) [2001] R.V.R. 34, ECHR . . . .   *Digested*, 01/**3524**
Vanbraekel v. Alliance Nationale des Mutualites Chretiennes (ANMC) (C368/98); *sub*
   nom Vanbraekel v. Alliance Nationale des Mutualities Chretiennes (ANMC)
   (C368/98) [2001] E.C.R. I-5363; *Times*, September 4, 2001, ECJ . . . .   *Digested*, 01/**5134**
Vanbraekel v. Alliance Nationale des Mutualities Chretiennes (ANMC) (C368/98) see
   Vanbraekel v. Alliance Nationale des Mutualites Chretiennes (ANMC) (C368/
   98)
Vandeleur v. Sloane [1919] I.R. 116, CA (UK-Irl) . . . .   *Distinguished*, 00/4615
Vandepitte v. Preferred Accident Insurance Co of New York see Vandepitte v. Preferred
   Accident Insurance Corp of New York

Vandepitte v. Preferred Accident Insurance Corp of New York; *sub nom* Vandepitte v. Preferred Accident Insurance Co of New York [1933] A.C. 70; (1932) 44 Ll. L. Rep. 41, PC (Can) . . . . *Applied,* 59/**873**:
Overruled, 00/**3531**

Vandermolen v. Toma (1982-83) 9 H.L.R. 91, CA . . . . *Digested,* 83/**227.u**:
Applied, 00/**3932**

Vango v. Kettering General Hospital NHS Trust (Unreported, August 26, 1998), CC (Central London) [*Ex rel.* Anthony Snelson, Barrister, Thomas More Chambers, 51-52 Carey Street, Lincoln's Inn, London and Douglas-Mann & Co Solicitors] . *Digested,* 98/**1574**

Vanilla Accumulation Ltd, Re, *Times,* February 24, 1998, Ch D . . . . *Digested,* 98/**642**

Vanneck v. Sluggett (Unreported, August 18, 1999), CC (Yeovil) [*Ex rel.* Adrian Posta, Barrister, South Western Chambers, 12 Middle Street, Taunton] . . . . *Digested,* 00/**1700**

Varey v. United Kingdom (26662/95), *Times,* January 30, 2001, ECHR . . . . *Digested,* 01/**4707**

Varia v. Ihezue (Unreported, December 17, 1999), CC (Watford) [*Ex rel.* Ben Maltz, Barrister, 1 Essex Court, Temple, London] . . . . *Digested,* 00/**462**:
Distinguished, 01/**532**

Varley v. Coppard (1871-72) L.R. 7 C.P. 505, CCP . . . . *Applied,* 00/**3929**

Varsani v. Jesani (Cy Pres) [1999] Ch. 219; [1999] 1 W.L.R. 255; [1998] 3 All E.R. 273; [1998] N.P.C. 63, CA. . . . . *Digested,* 98/**310**

Vasilescu v. Romania (1999) 28 E.H.R.R. 241; 4 B.H.R.C. 653; [1998] H.R.C.D. 563, ECHR . . . . *Digested,* 98/**3151**

VAT on Advertising, Re see Commission of the European Communities v. France (C68/92)

VAT on Postal Transport, Re (C107/84) see Value Added Tax on Postal Transport (C107/84), Re

VAT Rates on Wine (C356/85), Re; *sub nom* Commission of the European Communities v. Belgium (C356/85) [1987] E.C.R. 3299; [1988] 3 C.M.L.R. 277, ECJ . . . . . . *Digested,* 90/**2237**:
Followed, 00/2382

Vaughan v. BT Whelan (Unreported, September 15, 1998), CC (Southampton) [*Ex rel.* Benjamin Williams, Barrister, Oxford Chambers, 1 Alfred Street, Oxford] . . . . *Digested,* 98/**1700**

Vautier's Estate, Re (2000-01) 3 I.T.E.L.R. 566, Royal Ct (Jer)

Vax Appliances Ltd v. Hoover Plc (No.1) [1990] R.P.C. 656, Ch D . . . . *Digested,* 91/**2704**:
Applied, 96/1266: *Considered,* 95/3790: *Followed,* 98/401:
Referred to, 92/581

VCS Car Park Management Ltd v. Regional Railways North East Ltd; *sub nom* VCS Carpark Management Ltd v. Regional Railways North East Ltd [2001] Ch. 121; [2000] 3 W.L.R. 370; [2000] 1 All E.R. 403; [2000] 1 E.G.L.R. 57; [2000] 05 E.G. 145; [1999] E.G.C.S. 136; (2000) 97(4) L.S.G. 33; (2000) 144 S.J.L.B. 50; (2000) 79 P. & C.R. D20; *Times,* January 11, 2000, CA . . . . *Digested,* 00/**3891**

VCS Carpark Management Ltd v. Regional Railways North East Ltd see VCS Car Park Management Ltd v. Regional Railways North East Ltd

Veba Oil Supply & Trading GmbH v. Petrotrade Inc (The Robin); *sub nom* Veba Oil Supply & Trading Ltd v. Petrotrade Inc (The Robin) [2001] EWCA Civ 1832, CA; affirming [2001] 1 All E.R. (Comm) 1051; [2001] 2 Lloyd's Rep. 731, QBD (Comm Ct)

Veba Oil Supply & Trading Ltd v. Petrotrade Inc (The Robin) see Veba Oil Supply & Trading GmbH v. Petrotrade Inc (The Robin)

Veedfald v. Arhus Amtskommune (C203/99) [2001] E.C.R. I-3569; *Times,* June 4, 2001, ECJ (5th Chamber) . . . . *Digested,* 01/**919**

Vehicle Inspectorate v. Anelay; *sub nom* Browne v. Anelay [1998] R.T.R. 279; [1997] C.O.D. 408; *Times,* June 10, 1997, QBD . . . . *Digested,* 97/**4365**

Vehicle Inspectorate v. Arriva (West Sussex) Ltd [2001] A.C.D. 95, QBD

Vehicle Inspectorate v. Bruce Cook Road Planing Ltd [1999] 1 W.L.R. 1907; [1999] 4 All E.R. 761; [2000] R.T.R. 90; (1999) 96(42) L.S.G. 42; (1999) 143 S.J.L.B. 249; *Times,* October 26, 1999, HL; affirming *Times,* March 23, 1998, QBD . . . . . *Digested,* 99/**4947**:
Followed, 98/4861

Vehicle Inspectorate v. Cantabrica Coach Holdings Ltd; *sub nom* Cantabrica Coach Holdings Ltd v. Vehicle Inspectorate [2001] UKHL 60; [2001] 1 W.L.R. 2288; (2001) 145 S.J.L.B. 275; *Times,* November 28, 2001, HL; affirming (2000) 164 J.P. 593; [2000] R.T.R. 286; (2000) 97(18) L.S.G. 37; *Times,* April 13, 2000, QBD. . . . . *Digested,* 01/**5489**

Vehicle Inspectorate v. Dukes Transport Ltd see Birkett v. Vehicle Inspectorate

Vehicle Inspectorate v. Norman; *sub nom* Wing v. Norman; Wing v. Crouch [1999] R.T.R. 366, QBD . . . . *Digested,* 99/**4946**

Vehicle Inspectorate v. Nuttall; *sub nom* Secretary of State for Transport v. Nuttall (t/a Redline Coaches); Wing v. Nuttall; Nuttall v. Vehicle Inspectorate [1999] 1 W.L.R. 629; [1999] 3 All E.R. 833; [1999] R.T.R. 264; [1999] I.R.L.R. 656; [1999] Crim. L.R. 674; (1999) 96(16) L.S.G. 36; (1999) 149 N.L.J. 521; (1999) 143 S.J.L.B. 111; *Times,* March 19, 1999; *Independent,* March 24, 1999, HL; reversing (1997) 161 J.P. 701; [1998] R.T.R. 321; (1997) 94(18) L.S.G. 31; (1997) 141 S.J.L.B. 98; *Times,* April 30, 1997, QBD. . . . . *Digested,* 99/**4945**

Vehicle Inspectorate v. Richard Read Transport Ltd [1998] R.T.R. 288, QBD . . . . . . *Digested,* 98/**4823**

Vehicle Inspectorate v. Sam Anderson (Newhouse) Ltd [2001] EWHC Admin 893; *Times,* November 15, 2001, QBD (Admin Ct) . . . . *Digested,* 01/**5490**

Vehicle Inspectorate v. Southern Coaches Ltd (2000) 164 J.P. 492; [2000] R.T.R. 165; [2000] 2 C.M.L.R. 887; [2000] Crim. L.R. 595; *Times*, February 23, 2000; *Independent*, February 14, 2000 (C.S.), QBD . . . . *Digested*, 00/**5153**

Vehicle Inspectorate v. TD&C Kelly Ltd; *sub nom* Wing v. TD&C Kelly Ltd [1998] R.T.R. 297; [1997] C.O.D. 225; *Times*, January 3, 1997, QBD . . . . *Digested*, 97/**4320**

Vehicle Inspectorate v. York Pullman Ltd [2001] EWHC Admin 113; [2001] R.T.R. 18, QBD . . . . *Digested*, 01/**5441**

Vellino v. Chief Constable of Greater Manchester [2001] EWCA Civ 1249; (2001) 151 N.L.J. 1441; *Times*, August 9, 2001, CA . . . . *Digested*, 01/**4478**

Velos Group Ltd v. Harbour Insurance Services Ltd [1997] 2 Lloyd's Rep. 461, CC (Central London) . . . . *Digested*, 98/**3387**: *Considered*, 98/3361

Venables (Tariff Recommendation), Re see Thompson (Tariff Recommendation), Re

Venables v. Hornby (Inspector of Taxes); *sub nom* Trustees of the Fussell Pension Scheme v. Hornby (Inspector of Taxes) [2001] S.T.C. 1221; [2001] Pens. L.R. 227; [2001] B.T.C. 229; [2001] S.T.I. 940; (2001) 98(31) L.S.G. 36; (2001) 145 S.J.L.B. 159; *Times*, July 11, 2001, Ch D; reversing [2001] Pens. L.R. 17; [2000] S.T.C. (S.C.D.) 579; [2000] S.T.I. 1677, Sp Comm . . . . *Digested*, 01/**5263**

Venables v. MGN Ltd see Venables v. Mirror Group Newspapers Ltd

Venables v. Mirror Group Newspapers Ltd; *sub nom* Venables v. MGN Ltd *Times*, December 9, 1998, CA; reversing 1996-V-No.376, QBD. . . . . *Digested*, 99/**571**

Venables v. News Group International (Breach of Injunction); *sub nom* Attorney General v. Greater Manchester Newspapers Ltd; Thompson v. News Group International (2001) 145 S.J.L.B. 279; *Times*, December 7, 2001; *Daily Telegraph*, December 13, 2001, QBD

Venables v. News Group Newspapers Ltd; Thompson v. News Group Newspapers Ltd [2001] Fam. 430; [2001] 2 W.L.R. 1038; [2001] 1 All E.R. 908; [2001] E.M.L.R. 10; [2001] 1 F.L.R. 791; [2001] H.R.L.R. 19; [2001] U.K.H.R.R. 628; 9 B.H.R.C. 587; [2001] Fam. Law 258; (2001) 98(12) L.S.G. 41; (2001) 151 N.L.J. 57; (2001) 145 S.J.L.B. 43; *Times*, January 16, 2001; *Independent*, January 17, 2001; *Daily Telegraph*, January 16, 2001, Fam Div . . . . *Digested*, 01/**3476**: *Applied*, 01/3577: *Considered*, 01/4415

Venezuela, The [1980] 1 Lloyd's Rep. 393, QBD (Adm Ct) . . . . *Digested*, 80/**2431**: *Considered*, 98/582

Vennootschap Onder Firma Senta Aromatic Marketing's Application [1999] E.T.M.R. 429, OHIM (2nd Bd App) . . . . *Considered*, 00/3789

Ventouris v. Mountain (The Italia Express) (No.2) [1992] 1 W.L.R. 887; [1992] 3 All E.R. 414; [1992] 2 Lloyd's Rep. 216; *Financial Times*, January 14, 1992, CA; reversing in part *Financial Times*, December 20, 1991, QBD . . . . *Digested*, 92/**2060**: *Followed*, 99/3381

Verast v. Belgium 1 I.T.L. Rep. 435, App (Liege)

Verband des SB-Grosshandels eV v. Commission of the European Communities (C26/76) see Metro SB-Grossmarkte GmbH & Co KG v. Commission of the European Communities (C26/76)

Verbond Van Nederlandse Ondernemingen v. Inspecteur der Invoerrechten en Accijnzen (C51/76); *sub nom* Federation of Dutch Industries v. Inspector of Customs and Excise (C51/76) [1977] E.C.R. 113; [1977] 1 C.M.L.R. 413, ECJ . . . . *Digested*, 77/**1359**: *Applied*, 01/5594

Verbraucherschutzverein EV v. Sektkellerei GC Kessler GmbH & Co (C303/97) [1999] E.C.R. I-513; [1999] 1 C.M.L.R. 756; [1999] E.T.M.R. 269, ECJ (5th Chamber) . *Digested*, 00/**3698**

Verby Print for Advertising Ltd, Re; *sub nom* Verby Print for Advertising Ltd v. Secretary of State for Trade and Industry; Fine v. Secretary of State for Trade and Industry [1998] B.C.C. 652; [1998] 2 B.C.L.C. 23, Ch D (Companies Ct) . . . . *Digested*, 98/**671**

Verby Print for Advertising Ltd v. Secretary of State for Trade and Industry see Verby Print for Advertising Ltd, Re

Verderame v. Commercial Union Assurance Co Plc [1992] B.C.L.C. 793; [2000] Lloyd's Rep. P.N. 557; [1955-95] P.N.L.R. 612; *Times*, April 2, 1992; *Independent*, May 25, 1992 (C.S), CA . . . . *Digested*, 92/**2604**

Vere v. Minter (1914) 49 L.J. 129 . . . . *Considered*, 99/4177

Verein fur Konsumenteninformation v. Osterreichische Kreditversicherungs AG (C364/96) [1999] All E.R. (EC) 183; [1998] E.C.R. I-2949; [1999] 1 C.M.L.R. 1430; *Times*, May 18, 1998, ECJ (5th Chamber) . . . . *Digested*, 98/**3738**

Verein Gegen Unwesen in Handel und Gewerbe Koln eV v. Mars GmbH (C470/93) [1995] E.C.R. I-1923; [1995] 3 C.M.L.R. 1, ECJ (5th Chamber) . . . . *Digested*, 95/**737**: *Followed*, 97/4876, 01/2489

Vereinigte Familiapress Zeitungsverlags- und Vertriebs GmbH v. Bauer Verlag (C368/95) [1997] E.C.R. I-3689; [1997] 3 C.M.L.R. 1329, ECJ . . . . *Distinguished*, 00/2397

Vereniging Dorpsbelang Hees v. Directeur van de Dienst Milieu en Water van de Provincie Gelderland (C419/97) see ARCO Chemie Nederland Ltd v. Minister van Volkshuisvesting, Ruimtelijke Ordening en Milieubeheer (C418/97)

Vereniging Happy Family Rustenburgerstraat v. Inspecteur der Omzetbelasting (C289/86) see Mol v. Inspecteur der Invoerrechten en Accijnzen (C269/86)

Vereniging van Groothandel in Bloemkwekerijprodukten *v.* Commission of the European
    Communities (T77/94); *sub nom* VGB *v.* Commission of the European
    Communities (T77/94); Vereniging van Groothandelaren in
    Bloemkwekerijprodukten *v.* Commission of the European Communities (T77/94)
    [1997] All E.R. (E.C.) 828; [1997] E.C.R. II-759; [1997] 5 C.M.L.R. 812, CFI
    (2nd Chamber) . . . . *Digested,* 98/**2314**
Vereniging van Groothandelaren in Bloemkwekerijprodukten *v.* Commission of the
    European Communities (T77/94) see Vereniging van Groothandel in
    Bloemkwekerijprodukten *v.* Commission of the European Communities (T77/
    94)
Verify International NV's Community Trade Mark Application [2000] E.T.M.R. 716, OHIM
    (Opposition Div) . . . . *Digested,* 00/**3776**
Verjee *v.* CIBC Bank & Trust Co (Channel Islands) Ltd [2001] Lloyd's Rep. Bank. 279;
    [2001] B.P.I.R. 1149, Ch D . . . . *Digested,* 01/**374**
Verkan & Co Ltd *v.* Byland Close (Winchmore Hill) Ltd [1998] 2 E.G.L.R. 139; [1998]
    28 E.G. 118; [1998] R.V.R. 255, Lands Tr . . . . *Digested,* 98/**3644**:
                                                                                                Applied, 98/3643
Vermaat (t/a Cotton Productions) *v.* Boncrest Ltd (No.1) [2001] F.S.R. 5; (2000) 23(8)
    I.P.D. 23062; (2000) 97(25) L.S.G. 40; (2000) 144 S.J.L.B. 255; *Times,* June
    23, 2000, Ch D . . . . *Digested,* 00/**3572**
Vermaat (t/a Cotton Productions) *v.* Boncrest Ltd (No.2) (2001) 24(7) I.P.D. 24048,
    Ch D
Vermeulen *v.* Belgium (19075/91) (2001) 32 E.H.R.R. 15, ECHR . . . . *Applied,* 98/3125,
                                                    98/3142, 99/3127: *Distinguished,* 00/2375
Vermuelen *v.* Pennington see Pardoe *v.* Pennington
VERMUELEN-HOLLANDIA/Vehicle open roof (T43/98) [2001] E.P.O.R. 37, EPO
    (Technical Bd App) . . . . *Digested,* 01/**3933**
Vernillo *v.* France (A/198) (1991) 13 E.H.R.R. 880, ECHR . . . . *Followed,* 01/3544
Vernon *v.* Bosley (No.1) [1997] 1 All E.R. 577; [1997] R.T.R. 1; [1998] 1 F.L.R. 297;
    [1997] P.I.Q.R. P255; [1997] 35 B.M.L.R. 135; [1997] Fam. Law 476; (1996)
    146 N.L.J. 589; *Times,* April 4, 1996, CA . . . . *Digested,* 96/**2156**
Vernon *v.* Bosley (No.2) [1999] Q.B. 18; [1997] 3 W.L.R. 683; [1997] 1 All E.R. 614;
    [1997] R.T.R. 275; [1998] 1 F.L.R. 304; [1997] P.I.Q.R. P326; (1997) 35
    B.M.L.R. 174; [1997] Fam. Law 476; (1997) 94(4) L.S.G. 26; (1997) 147 N.L.J.
    89; (1997) 141 S.J.L.B. 27; *Times,* December 19, 1996; *Independent,* January
    21, 1997, CA . . . . *Digested,* 97/**456**
Vernon *v.* United Kingdom (38753/97) (2001) 29 E.H.R.R. CD264, ECHR
Verrall, Re; *sub nom* National Trust for Places of Historic Interest or Natural Beauty *v.*
    Attorney General [1916] 1 Ch. 100, Ch D . . . . *Followed,* 01/384
Versicherungs AG *v.* Fortuna Co Inc see Allianz Versicherungs AG *v.* Fortuna Co Inc
    (The Baltic Universal)
Vesta Fire Insurance Co *v.* New Cap Reinsurance Corp Ltd [2000] B.P.I.R. 916, US Ct
Veznedaroglu *v.* Turkey (32357/96) (2001) 33 E.H.R.R. 59, ECHR (2001) 29 E.H.R.R.
    CD269, Eur Comm HR
VGB *v.* Commission of the European Communities (T77/94) see Vereniging van
    Groothandel in Bloemkwekerijprodukten *v.* Commission of the European
    Communities (T77/94)
Vgt Verein gegen Tierfabriken *v.* Switzerland (24699/94) 10 B.H.R.C. 473, ECHR . . . . . . *Digested,* 01/**3462**
VH *v.* Belgium (RC006G4-1) 3 I.T.L. Rep. 83, Cass (B)
VHE Construction Plc *v.* RBSTB Trust Co Ltd [2000] B.L.R. 187; (2000) 2 T.C.L.R.
    278; 70 Con. L.R. 51; *Independent,* February 28, 2000 (C.S.), QBD (T&CC) . . . *Digested,* 00/**806**
Vicary *v.* British Telecommunications Plc [1999] I.R.L.R. 680, EAT . . . . *Digested,* 00/**2125**:
                                                                                                Applied, 01/2242
Vickers Shipbuilding & Engineering Ltd *v.* Cape Contracts Plc see VSEL Ltd *v.* Cape
    Contracts Plc
Vickery *v.* Modern Security Systems Ltd see Trustee of the Property of Vickery (A
    Bankrupt) *v.* Modern Security Systems Ltd
Vickneswaran *v.* Immigration Appeal Tribunal see R. *v.* Immigration Appeal Tribunal Ex
    p. Vickneswaran
VICOM/Computer-related invention (T208/84) [1987] E.P.O.R. 74, EPO (Technical Bd
    App) . . . . *Considered,* 96/4570,
                                                                                                97/3915, 99/3488
Victor Chandler International Ltd *v.* Customs and Excise Commissioners [2000] 1
    W.L.R. 1296; [2000] 2 All E.R. 315; (2000) 97(11) L.S.G. 36; (2000) 150 N.L.J.
    341; (2000) 144 S.J.L.B. 127; *Times,* March 8, 2000; *Independent,* March 10,
    2000, CA; reversing [1999] 1 W.L.R. 2160; [2000] 1 All E.R. 160; (1999) 96(31)
    L.S.G. 42; (1999) 143 S.J.L.B. 219; *Times,* August 17, 1999 ; *Independent,*
    October 4, 1999, Ch D . . . . *Digested,* 00/**4147**
Victoria Film A/S *v.* Riksskatteverket (C134/97); *sub nom* Victoria Film A/S's Reference
    (C134/97), Re [1998] E.C.R. I-7023; [1999] 1 C.M.L.R. 279; [2000] E.C.D.R.
    519, ECJ (6th Chamber) . . . . *Digested,* 00/**2381**
Victoria Film A/S's Reference (C134/97), Re see Victoria Film A/S *v.* Riksskatteverket
    (C134/97)

Video Box Office v. GST Holdings, *Times*, April 3, 1990, CA. . . . . *Digested*, 90/**3593**:
                      Considered, 99/533: *Followed*, 98/445: *Referred to*, 97/569

Vidler v. UNISON [1999] I.C.R. 746, EAT . . . . *Digested*, 99/**574**

Vidranyi v. Commission of the European Communities (C283/90 P) [1991] E.C.R. I-4339

Vigon v. DPP (1998) 162 J.P. 115; [1998] Crim. L.R. 289; (1998) 162 J.P.N. 88; *Times*, December 9, 1997, QBD. . . . . *Digested*, 98/**970**

Viking Property Co Ltd v. Rawlinson (Unreported, June 11, 1999), CC (Shoreditch) [*Ex rel*. Jon Holbrook, Barrister, 2 Garden Court Chambers, 2 Garden Court, Middle Temple, London] . . . . *Digested*, 99/**3714**

Villa Denizcilik Sanayi Ve Ticaret AS v. Longen SA (The Villa) [1998] 1 Lloyd's Rep. 195, QBD (Comm Ct) . . . . *Digested*, 98/**247**

Village Cay Marina Ltd v. Acland [1998] B.C.C. 417; [1998] 2 B.C.L.C. 327, PC (BVI) . . *Digested*, 98/**3313**

Village of Euclid, Ohio v. Ambler Realty Co; *sub nom* Euclid, Ohio v. Ambler Realty Co 272 U.S. 365, US Ct . . . . *Applied*, 00/**4408**

Villaswan Ltd (In Receivership) v. Sheraton Caltrust (Blythswood) Ltd (In Liquidation) 1999 S.C.L.R. 199; [2000] B.C.C. 188; 1998 G.W.D. 39-2017; *Times*, January 27, 1999, OH . . . . *Digested*, 99/**6304**

Villella v. MFI Furniture Centres Ltd [1999] I.R.L.R. 468, QBD . . . . *Digested*, 99/**2013**

Villers v. Equitas Ltd see Barclays Plc v. Villers

Villers v. Lovells (formerly Lovell White Durrant) see Barclays Plc v. Villers

Villiers v. Villiers [1994] 1 W.L.R. 493; [1994] 2 All E.R. 149; [1994] 1 F.L.R. 647; [1994] 2 F.C.R. 702; [1994] Fam. Law 317; (1994) 144 N.L.J. 159; *Independent*, December 27, 1993 (C.S.), CA . . . . *Digested*, 94/**3553**:
                      Considered, 01/19

Vilvarajah (Nadarajah) v. Secretary of State for the Home Department; Skandarajah (Vaithialingham) v. Secretary of State for the Home Department [1990] Imm. A.R. 457, CA. . . . . *Digested*, 91/**1971**:
          Applied, 00/3298: *Considered*, 01/3658: *Distinguished*, 99/3206

Vincent v. CUC Software International SA [2001] E.C.C. 21, C d'A (Versailles)

Vincent v. Restormel BC (Unreported, July 27, 2000), CC (Truro) [*Ex rel*. Veitch Penny Solicitors, 1 Manor Court, Dix's Field, Exeter, Devon] . . . . *Digested*, 01/**4496**

Vincent v. Slaymaker (1810) 12 East 372 . . . . *Considered*, 00/4024

Vine v. National Dock Labour Board [1957] A.C. 488; [1957] 2 W.L.R. 106; [1956] 3 All E.R. 939; [1956] 2 Lloyd's Rep. 567; 101 S.J. 86, HL; reversing in part [1956] 1 Q.B. 658; [1956] 2 W.L.R. 311; [1956] 1 All E.R. 1; [1955] 2 Lloyd's Rep. 531; 100 S.J. 73, CA . . . . *Digested*, 57/**1264**:
         Applied, 66/12184, 67/3973, 73/1164, 74/1350, 84/14: *Considered*, 65/951,
              86/1084, 00/5396: *Distinguished*, 58/2124, 62/1131, 98/2242:
                      Subsequent proceedings, 58/1200

Vine v. Waltham Forest LBC [2000] 1 W.L.R. 2383; [2000] 4 All E.R. 169; [2000] R.T.R. 270; [2000] B.L.G.R. 481; (2000) 97(18) L.S.G. 37; *Times*, April 12, 2000; *Independent*, May 22, 2000 (C.S.), CA . . . . *Digested*, 00/**5250**

Vinmar International Ltd v. Theresa Navigation SA [2001] 2 All E.R. (Comm) 243; [2001] 2 Lloyd's Rep. 1; [2001] C.L.C. 1035, QBD (Comm Ct) . . . . *Digested*, 01/**4899**

Vinos v. Marks & Spencer Plc [2001] 3 All E.R. 784; [2001] C.P. Rep. 12; [2000] C.P.L.R. 570; *Independent*, July 17, 2000 (C.S), CA . . . . *Applied*, 00/535,
                   01/641, 01/645: *Considered*, 01/643, 01/644

Virdee v. Scottish Equitable Life Plc; *sub nom* Scottish Equitable Life Plc v. Virdee [1999] 1 F.L.R. 863; [1999] Fam. Law 218; (1999) 77 P. & C.R. D24; *Independent*, November 30, 1998 (C.S.), CA . . . . *Digested*, 99/**4402**

Virdi v. Law Society CHANI 1999/1185/A3, CA; affirming (1999) 96(29) L.S.G. 29; (1999) 143 S.J.L.B. 198; *Times*, July 20, 1999, Ch D . . . . *Digested*, 00/**4030**

Virgin Cinema Properties Ltd v. Secretary of State for the Environment, Transport and the Regions [1998] 2 P.L.R. 24; [1998] P.L.C.R. 1; [1997] E.G.C.S. 135; [1997] N.P.C. 139; *Independent*, October 20, 1997 (C.S.), QBD. . . . . *Digested*, 97/**4127**:
                       Applied, 99/4256, 00/4504

Virgin Enterprises Ltd v. One in a Million Ltd see British Telecommunications Plc v. One in a Million Ltd

Virgin Interactive Entertainment (Europe) Ltd v. Bluewall Ltd [1998] Masons C.L.R. Rep. 83, Ch D . . . . *Digested*, 96/**1217**

Virgin Retail Ltd v. Phonographic Performance Ltd; *sub nom* Phonographic Performance Ltd v. Virgin Retail Ltd [2001] E.M.L.R. 6; (2000) 23(11) I.P.D. 23094, Ch D; affirming [2000] E.M.L.R. 323; (2000) 23(2) I.P.D. 23015, Copyright Tr. . . . . *Digested*, 00/**3581**

Virk v. Gan Life Holdings Plc [2000] Lloyd's Rep. I.R. 159; (2000) 52 B.M.L.R. 207, CA . . . . *Digested*, 00/**530**

Visa International (US) v. Editions Jibena [1998] E.T.M.R. 580, Cass (F)

Visa International Service Association's Community Trade Mark Application [2000] E.T.M.R. 263, OHIM (1st Bd App). . . . . *Digested*, 00/**3729**

VISA Striped Device Application, Re [1998] E.T.M.R. 118, BPG (Ger)

Viscido v. Ente Poste Italiane (C52/97) [1998] All E.R. (E.C.) 857; [1998] E.C.R. I-2629; [1998] 3 C.M.L.R. 184, ECJ . . . . *Digested*, 98/**2130**

VISCOSUD/Mechanical expander lubricants (T460/87) [2000] E.P.O.R. 45, EPO
(Technical Bd App) . . . . *Digested*, 00/**3647**
Viscount Chelsea v. Hirshorn [1998] 2 E.G.L.R. 90; [1998] 20 E.G. 130, CC (West
London) . . . . *Digested*, 98/**3656**
Viscount Chelsea v. Morris; Cadogan Estates Ltd v. Morris; Earl Cadogan v. Morris
(1999) 31 H.L.R. 732; (1999) 77 P. & C.R. 336; [1999] L. & T.R. 154; [1999] 1
E.G.L.R. 59; [1999] 04 E.G. 155; [1998] E.G.C.S. 156; (1998) 95(45) L.S.G.
40; (1999) 143 S.J.L.B. 11; [1998] N.P.C. 146; (1999) 77 P. & C.R. D13; *Times*,
November 24, 1998; *Independent*, November 23, 1998 (C.S.), CA; reversing
[1997] 2 E.G.L.R. 100; [1997] 46 E.G. 159, CC (West London) . . . . *Digested*, 98/**3657**:
Considered, 01/**4158**
Vishaka v. Rajasthan 3 B.H.R.C. 261, Sup Ct (Ind) . . . . *Digested*, 98/**2201**
Visible Information Packaged Systems Ltd v. Squarepoint (London) Ltd [2000] 2
E.G.L.R. 93, Lands Tr . . . . *Digested*, 01/**4178**
Vision Express Ltd v. Customs and Excise Commissioners [2001] S.T.I. 252, V&DTr
Vision Express (UK) Ltd v. Wilson (1997) [1998] B.C.C. 173, Ch D . . . . *Digested*, 98/**706**
Visionhire Ltd v. Britel Fund Trustees Ltd 1991 S.L.T. 883; 1992 S.C.L.R. 236; [1992] 1
E.G.L.R. 128, 1 Div; affirming 1991 S.L.T. 347; 1991 S.C.L.R. 92, OH . . . . *Digested*, 91/**5178**:
Applied, 98/6038: *Followed*, 99/3726
Viskase Ltd v. Paul Kiefal GmbH [1999] 1 W.L.R. 1305; [1999] 3 All E.R. 362; [1999]
1 All E.R. (Comm.) 641; [1999] C.L.C. 957; [2000] I.L.Pr. 29; *Times*, March 30,
1999, CA . . . . *Digested*, 99/**751**
Vista Maritime Inc v. Sesa Goa [1997] C.L.C. 1600, QBD (Comm Ct) . . . . *Digested*, 98/**357**
Visx Inc v. Nidek Co Ltd (No.1) (1998) 21(6) I.P.D. 21057, Pat Ct
Visx Inc v. Nidek Co Ltd (No.2) [1999] F.S.R. 91; (1998) 21(9) I.P.D. 21094, CA
Visx Inc v. Nidek Co Ltd (No.3) (1998) 21(9) I.P.D. 21095, Pat Ct
Visx Inc v. Nidek Co Ltd (No.4) [1999] F.S.R. 405; (1998) 21(12) I.P.D. 21126, Pat Ct. . *Digested*, 99/**3478**
Vita Food Products Inc v. Unus Shipping Co Ltd (In Liquidation) [1939] A.C. 277;
(1939) 63 Ll. L. Rep. 21, PC (Can) . . . . *Applied*, 47-51/**438**,
47-51/9502, 56/1347, 56/1351, 56/1388, 56/8303, 61/1433, 68/475:
Considered, 82/2849: *Disapproved*, 59/474: *Followed*, 98/771
Vitara Foods Ltd, Re [1999] B.C.C. 315, Ch D . . . . *Digested*, 99/**352**
Vitek, Re 8 B.H.R.C. 265, NS CR (CZ)
Viticultural Products, Re [2000] E.C.C. 479, BGH (Ger)
Vitol Energy (Bermuda) Ltd v. Pisco Shipping Co Ltd [1998] 1 Lloyd's Rep. 509;
[1998] C.L.C. 362, CA . . . . *Digested*, 98/**587**
Vlaams Gewest (Flemish Region) v. Commission of the European Communities (T214/
95) [1998] E.C.R. II-717, CFI . . . . *Followed*, 00/**2408**
Vlaamse Televisie Maatschappij NV v. Commission of the European Communities
(T266/97) [1999] E.C.R. II-2329; [2000] 4 C.M.L.R. 1171, CFI (1st Chamber) . . *Digested*, 00/**728**
Vlaar v. BV City Garage JC Polderman en Zonen [2001] E.C.C. 45, RB (NL)
Vladic v. Secretary of State for the Home Department see R. v. Immigration Appeal
Tribunal Ex p. Secretary of State for the Home Department
VN Legetoj A/S v. Patentankenaevnet [2001] E.T.M.R. 50, SH (DK)
VNU Business Publications BV v. Monster Board BV [2000] E.T.M.R. 111, RB (Den
Haag)
Voaden v. Champion (The Baltic Surveyor and the Timbuktu) A3/2000/3519/A-C, CA;
reversing in part [2001] 1 Lloyd's Rep. 739, QBD. . . . . *Digested*, 01/**1538**
Vocam Europe Ltd, Re [1998] B.C.C. 396, Ch D (Companies Ct). . . . . *Digested*, 98/**696**
Vodafone Cellular Ltd v. Shaw (Inspector of Taxes) [1997] S.T.C. 734; 69 T.C. 376;
[1997] B.T.C. 247; (1997) 141 S.J.L.B. 93; *Times*, March 31, 1997, CA; reversing
[1995] S.T.C. 353; [1995] S.T.I. 219; (1995) 92(10) L.S.G. 39; *Times*, February 8,
1995; *Independent*, March 20, 1995 (C.S.), Ch D . . . . *Digested*, 97/**1062**:
Applied, 00/4932, 00/4934, 00/4935: *Considered*, 98/4630
Vodafone Group Plc v. Orange Personal Communications Services Ltd [1997] E.M.L.R.
84; [1997-98] Info. T.L.R. 8; [1997] F.S.R. 34; (1996) 19(10) I.P.D. 19091;
Times, August 31, 1996, Ch D . . . . *Digested*, 96/**5705**:
Considered, 98/3511: *Followed*, 99/3535
Vodden v. Gayton [2001] P.I.Q.R. P4, QBD . . . . *Digested*, 01/**4503**
VOEST ALPINE/Re-establishment of opponent (G01/86) [1987] E.P.O.R. 388, EPO
(Enlarged Bd App) . . . . *Distinguished*, 00/**3617**
VOF Schieving-Nijstad v. Groeneveld (C89/99) see Schieving-Nijstad VOF v.
Groeneveld (C89/99)
Vogelaar v. Callaghan (2000) 16 Const. L.J. 221, Sup Ct (Irl) . . . . *Digested*, 01/**335**
Vogt v. Germany (A/323) (1996) 21 E.H.R.R. 205; [1996] E.L.R. 232; *Times*,
November 1, 1995, ECHR . . . . *Digested*, 95/**2643**:
Applied, 98/3082, 98/3084, 99/3110
Voisin v. Matheson Securities (CI) Ltd (1999-2000) 2 I.T.E.L.R. 907, CA (Jer)
Voisine v. France (27362/95) (2001) 33 E.H.R.R. 23, ECHR
VOITH/Re-establishment (T99/96) [2000] E.P.O.R. 458, EPO (Technical Bd App). . . . *Digested*, 00/**3610**
Vokes v. Bear [1974] I.C.R. 1; [1973] I.R.L.R. 363; (1973) 15 K.I.R. 302; [1974] I.T.R.
85, NIRC. . . . . *Digested*, 74/**1338**:
Applied, 77/1172, 78/1160, 98/2238: *Considered*, 76/993:
Not followed, 86/1221

Vokes v. Evans (1932) 49 R.P.C. 140 . . . .   *Applied*, 01/4034

Volkswagen AG v. Commission of the European Communities (T143/96) see Freistaat Sachsen v. Commission of the European Communities (T132/96)

Volkswagen AG v. Commission of the European Communities (T62/98) [2000] E.C.R. II-2707; [2000] 5 C.M.L.R. 853, CFI . . . .   *Digested*, 01/**775**

Volkswagen AG's Community Trade Mark Application [2000] E.T.M.R. 320, OHIM (Opposition Div) . . . .   *Digested*, 00/**3749**

Volkswagen Leasing GmbH's Community Trade Mark (No.525824) [2001] E.T.M.R. 101, OHIM (Cancellation Div)

Voller v. Lloyds Bank Plc see Lloyds Bank Plc v. Voller

Voluntary Purchasing Group Inc v. Insurco International Ltd [1994-95] C.I.L.R. 84, Grand Court (CI) . . . .   *Applied*, 01/406

Volvo Ltd v. DS Larm Ltd [2000] E.T.M.R. 299, HD (Swe)

Von Colson v. Land Nordrhein-Westfahlen (C14/83); Harz v. Deutsche Tradax GmbH (C79/83) [1984] E.C.R. 1891; [1986] 2 C.M.L.R. 430, ECJ . . . .   *Digested*, 86/**1455**:
           Considered, 88/1325: *Distinguished*, 00/5529: *Followed*, 97/2218

Von Hoffmann v. Finanzamt Trier (C145/96) [1997] All E.R. (E.C.) 852; [1997] S.T.C. 1321; [1997] E.C.R. I-4857; [1998] 1 C.M.L.R. 99; [1997] C.E.C. 1209; [1997] B.T.C. 5448; [1997] B.V.C. 562; *Times*, November 10, 1997, ECJ (6th Chamber) .   *Digested*, 97/**5018**

Von Horn v. Cinnamond (C163/95) [1998] Q.B. 214; [1998] 2 W.L.R. 104; [1997] All E.R. (E.C.) 913; [1997] E.C.R. I-5451; [1997] I.L.Pr. 784; *Times*, November 26, 1997, ECJ (6th Chamber) . . . .   *Digested*, 97/**903**:
           Not applied, 98/760

Von Rocks, The [1998] 2 Lloyd's Rep. 198, Sup Ct (Irl) . . . .   *Considered*, 01/5269

Von Starck v. Queen, The [2000] 1 W.L.R. 1270; *Times*, March 16, 2000, PC (Jam) . . . .   *Digested*, 00/**1101**

Vorarlberg Online, Re (4 OB 15/00 K) [2001] E.C.D.R. 30, OGH (A)

Vosnoc Ltd v. Transglobal Projects Ltd [1998] 1 W.L.R. 101; [1998] 2 All E.R. 990; [1998] 1 Lloyd's Rep. 711; [1997] C.L.C. 1345; (1997) 94(34) L.S.G. 28; (1997) 141 S.J.L.B. 215; *Times*, August 27, 1997, QBD (Comm Ct) . . . .   *Digested*, 97/**273**:
       Disapproved, 99/4455: *Distinguished*, 98/245: *Not followed*, 99/242, 99/4456

Vougioukas v. Idrima Koinonikon Asphalisseon (C443/93) [1995] E.C.R. I-4033; [1996] I.C.R. 913, ECJ. . . . .   *Digested*, 96/**5442**:
           Followed, 00/4818

Vowles v. Jervis [2001] 6 Q.R. 10, CC (Gloucester) [*Ex rel*. Andrew Granville Stafford, Barrister, 4 King's Bench Walk, Temple, London] . . . .   *Digested*, 01/**1636**

Vowles v. Miller (1810) 3 Taunt. 137. . . . .   *Followed*, 99/4352

VP (Loss of Child's Habitual Residence), Re see V (A Child) (Jurisdiction: Habitual Residence), Re

VPL Research Inc's European Patent Application (J26/95) see VPL/Bankruptcy (J26/95)

VPL/Bankruptcy (J26/95); *sub nom* VPL Research Inc's European Patent Application (J26/95) [2000] E.P.O.R. 270; (1999) 22(8) I.P.D. 22080, EPO (Legal Bd App). . . . .   *Digested*, 00/**3659**

Vranken SA v. Champagne H Germain et Fils SA [1998] E.T.M.R. 390, C d'A (Paris)

Vriend v. Alberta 4 B.H.R.C. 140, Sup Ct (Can) . . . .   *Digested*, 98/**3160**

Vroege v. NCIV Instituut voor Volkshuisvesting BV (C57/93); Vroege v. Stichting Pensioenfonds NCIV; Fisscher v. Voorhuis Hengelo BV (C128/93); Fisscher v. Stichting Bedrijfspensioenfonds voor de Detailhandel (C128/93) [1995] All E.R. (E.C.) 193; [1994] E.C.R. I-4541; [1995] 1 C.M.L.R. 881; [1995] I.C.R. 635; [1994] I.R.L.R. 651; *Times*, December 7, 1994; *Financial Times*, October 4, 1994, ECJ . . . .   *Digested*, 95/**2000**:
       Considered, 98/4134: *Referred to*, 97/2214, 97/3983

Vroege v. Stichting Pensioenfonds NCIV see Vroege v. NCIV Instituut voor Volkshuisvesting BV (C57/93)

VSEL Ltd v. Cape Contracts Plc; *sub nom* Vickers Shipbuilding & Engineering Ltd v. Cape Contracts Plc [1998] P.I.Q.R. P207, QBD . . . .   *Digested*, 98/**338**

VT (CICA: Quantum: 2001), Re, CICA (Birmingham) [*Ex rel*. Jeffrey Jupp, Barrister, 36 Bedford Row, London] . . . .   *Digested*, 01/**1586**

VT4 Ltd v. Vlaamse Gemeenschap (C56/96) [1997] E.C.R. I-3143; [1997] 3 C.M.L.R. 1225; [1997] C.E.C. 1309; [1999] E.M.L.R. 102, ECJ (6th Chamber) . . . .   *Digested*, 98/**3883**

VTI Fertasco (UK) Ltd v. Customs and Excise Commissioners [2000] V. & D.R. 110, V&DTr

Vulgar v. Customs and Excise Commissioners [1976] V.A.T.T.R. 197, VAT Tr . . . .   *Digested*, 77/**3131.26**:
           Applied, 94/4596: *Considered*, 98/4937

Vuong v. Hoang (Unreported, January 11, 1999), Fam Div [*Ex rel*. Tom Cosgrove, Barrister, 2-3 Gray's Inn Square, Gray's Inn, London] . . . .   *Digested*, 99/**3734**

Vzao Sojuzplodimport's Community Trade Mark Application [2000] E.T.M.R. 618, OHIM (Opposition Div) . . . .   *Digested*, 00/**3752**

W (A Child) (Change of Name), Re see W (A Child) (Illegitimate Child: Change of Surname), Re

W (A Child) (CICB: Quantum: 1999), Re (Unreported, July 28, 1999), CICB (Manchester) [*Ex rel*. Rhodes, Thain & Collinson Solicitors, 27 Harrison Road, Halifax] . . . . . .   *Digested*, 00/**1752**

W (A Child) (Contact Application: Procedure), Re; *sub nom* W (A Child) (Contact: Leave
    to Apply), Re [2000] 1 F.L.R. 263; [2000] 1 F.C.R. 185; [2000] Fam. Law 82;
    Times, October 12, 1999, Fam Div . . . .   *Digested*, 99/**2369**
W (A Child) (Contact: Leave to Apply), Re see W (A Child) (Contact Application:
    Procedure), Re
W (A Child) (Illegitimate Child: Change of Surname), Re; *sub nom* W (A Child) (Change
    of Name), Re; A (A Child) (Change of Name), Re; B (Children) (Change of
    Name), Re [2001] Fam. 1; [2000] 2 W.L.R. 258; [1999] 2 F.L.R. 930; [1999] 3
    F.C.R. 337; [1999] Fam. Law 688; (1999) 96(33) L.S.G. 29; *Times*, August 5,
    1999, CA . . . .   *Digested*, 99/**2375**
W (A Child) (Parental Contact: Prohibition), Re; *sub nom* W (A Child) (Section 34(2)
    Orders), Re [2000] Fam. 130; [2000] 2 W.L.R. 1276; [2000] 1 F.L.R. 502;
    [2000] 1 F.C.R. 752; [2000] Fam. Law 235; (2000) 97(3) L.S.G. 36; *Times*,
    January 21, 2000 ; *Independent*, February 21, 2000 (C.S.), CA . . . .   *Digested*, 00/**2482**
W (A Child) (Section 34(2) Orders), Re see W (A Child) (Parental Contact: Prohibition), Re
W (A Child) *v.* Banks [*Ex rel*. Amanda Millmore, Barrister, 4 King's Bench Walk, Temple,
    London] . . . .   *Digested*, 01/**1732**
W (A Child) *v.* Classic Cuts (Unreported, October 7, 1999), CC (Kingston upon Hull)
    [*Ex rel*. Paul W Miller, Barrister, Wilberforce Chambers, 7 Bishop Lane, Hull] . . . .   *Digested*, 00/**1552**
W (A Child) *v.* EJ Eagle [2001] 6 Q.R. 7, CC (Manchester) [*Ex rel*. David Calvert,
    Barrister, St James Chambers, 68 Quay Street, Manchester] . . . .   *Digested*, 01/**1552**
W (A Child) *v.* Kerry (Unreported, November 24, 1999), CC (Norwich) [*Ex rel*. Anthony
    Bate, Barrister, East Anglian Chambers, 57 London Street, Norwich] . . . .   *Digested*, 00/**1535**
W (A Child) *v.* Marchwood Motorways Ltd [2001] 6 Q.R. 6, CC (Southampton) [*Ex
    rel*. Stuart McKechnie, Barrister, 199 Strand, London] . . . .   *Digested*, 01/**1603**
W (A Child) *v.* Metcalfe (Unreported, January 16, 2001), CC (Birmingham) [*Ex rel*.
    Stephen Garner, Barrister, 8 Fountain Court, Birmingham] . . . .   *Digested*, 01/**1781**
W (A Child) *v.* Northern General Hospital NHS Trust see Heil *v.* Rankin
W (A Child) *v.* Northern General Hospital NHS Trust (Costs) see Heil *v.* Rankin (Costs)
W (A Child) *v.* Northern General Hospital NHS Trust (Structured Settlements) [2000] 1
    W.L.R. 1404; [2000] P.I.Q.R. Q284; [2000] Lloyd's Rep. Med. 234; (2000)
    97(19) L.S.G. 42; (2000) 144 S.J.L.B. 213; *Times*, April 10, 2000; *Independent*,
    May 15, 2000 (C.S.), CA . . . .   *Digested*, 00/**1492**:
                                                         Applied, 01/1546: *Previous proceedings*, 00/1478
W (A Minor) (Adoption Details: Disclosure), Re [1998] 2 F.L.R. 625; [1999] 2 F.C.R. 283;
    [1998] Fam. Law 513; (1998) 95(21) L.S.G. 36; (1998) 142 S.J.L.B. 158; *Times*,
    May 21, 1998, Fam Div . . . .   *Digested*, 98/**2364**
W (A Minor) (Adoption: Homosexual Adopter), Re [1998] Fam. 58; [1997] 3 W.L.R. 768;
    [1997] 3 All E.R. 620; [1997] 2 F.L.R. 406; [1997] Fam. Law 597; (1997) 94(24)
    L.S.G. 32; (1997) 141 S.J.L.B. 137; *Times*, May 21, 1997; *Independent*, June 9,
    1997 (C.S.), Fam Div . . . .   *Digested*, 97/**354**
W (A Minor) (Care Proceedings: Assessment), Re see W (Assessment of Child), Re
W (A Minor) (Contact Orders: Medical Reports), Re; *sub nom* W (Contact: Parent's
    Delusional Beliefs), Re [1999] 1 F.L.R. 1263; [1999] Fam. Law 298, CA;
    reversing . . . .   *Digested*, 99/**2366**
W (A Minor) (Secure Accommodation Order), Re; *sub nom* W *v.* North Yorkshire CC
    [1993] 1 F.L.R. 692; [1993] 1 F.C.R. 693; [1993] Fam. Law 345; (1993) 157
    J.P.N. 249; *Times*, February 8, 1993 . . . .   *Digested*, 94/**3268**:
                                                               Applied, 01/2533
W (A Minor) (Secure Accommodation Order: Attendance at Court), Re [1994] 2 F.L.R.
    1092; [1994] 3 F.C.R. 248; [1995] Fam. Law 19; (1994) 158 J.P.N. 731; *Times*, July
    13, 1994; *Independent*, July 18, 1994 (C.S.), Fam Div . . . .   *Digested*, 94/**3266**:
                                                               Applied, 99/2395
W (A Minor) (Staying Contact), Re [1998] 2 F.L.R. 450; [1998] 2 F.C.R. 453, CA . . . .   *Digested*, 98/**2415**
W (A Minor) (Unmarried Father), Re see W (Minors) (Abduction: Father's Rights), Re
W (A Minor) *v.* Gloucestershire CC (Unreported, September 10, 1999), CC
    (Cheltenham) [*Ex rel*. Davis Gregory Solicitors, 25 Rodney Road, Cheltenham,
    Gloucestershire] . . . .   *Digested*, 00/**1614**
W (A Patient), Re [1999] P.I.Q.R. Q143, CP . . . .   *Digested*, 00/**3512**
W (Adoption: Homosexual Adopter), Re [1997] 3 F.C.R. 650, Fam Div . . . .   *Digested*, 98/**2361**
W (Adoption: Parental Agreement), Re see H(B) (An Infant), Re
W (An Infant), Re [1971] A.C. 682; [1971] 2 W.L.R. 1011; [1971] 2 All E.R. 49; 115 S.J. 286,
    HL; reversing [1970] 2 Q.B. 589; [1970] 3 W.L.R. 175; [1970] 3 All E.R. 990; 114 S.J.
    433, CA . . . .   *Digested*, 71/**5831**:
                        Applied, 73/2142, 76/1751, 76/1752, 76/1753, 76/1755, 77/1919, 77/1920,
                          88/2304, 89/2416: *Considered*, 74/2360, 75/2142, 75/2148, 76/1746,
                  85/2203, 85/2204, 86/2158, 88/2301, 96/468, 97/352, 98/2365, 00/2430:
             Disapproved, 70/1327: *Distinguished*, 94/3141: *Followed*, 76/1748, 83/2424,
                                                               87/2526
W (Assessment of Child), Re; *sub nom* W (A Minor) (Care Proceedings: Assessment),
    Re [1998] 2 F.L.R. 130; [1998] 1 F.C.R. 287; [1998] Fam. Law 318, CA. . . . . . .   *Digested*, 98/**2400**
W (Children) (Care Order: Adequacy of Care Plan), Re see S (Children) (Care Order:
    Implementation of Care Plan), Re
W (Children) (Care Plan), Re see S (Children) (Care Order: Implementation of Care Plan), Re

W (Children) (Threshold Criteria: Parental Concessions), Re [2001] 1 F.C.R. 139, CA
W (Children) v. Legal Services Commission see R. v. Legal Aid Board Ex p. W
(Children)
W (CICA: Quantum: 2000), Re [2001] 2 Q.R. 12, CICAP [*Ex rel.* Paul Hepher, Barrister, 2
Gray's Inn Chambers, 2 Gray's Inn Square, London] . . . .   *Digested,* 01/**1709**
W (CICA: Quantum: 2001), Re [2001] 5 Q.R. 10, CICAP [*Ex rel.* Linda Sweeney, Barrister,
24A St John Street Chambers, Manchester] . . . .   *Digested,* 01/**1584**
W (CICB: Quantum: 1999), Re (Unreported, July 22, 1999), CICB (Plymouth) [*Ex rel.*
James Rees, Barrister, 2 King's Bench Walk, Temple, London] . . . .   *Digested,* 99/**1503**
W (CICB: Quantum: 1999), Re (Unreported, June 7, 1999), CICB (London) [*Ex rel.* Graham
Watson, Barrister, Pump Court Chambers, 31 Southgate Street, Winchester] . . .   *Digested,* 00/**1523**
W (CICB: Quantum: 1999), Re (1999) 99(3) Q.R. 4, CICB (London) [*Ex rel.* Reynolds,
Parry-Jones & Crawford Solicitors, 10 Easton Street, High Wycombe, Bucks] . .   *Digested,* 99/**1428**
W (CICB: Quantum: 2000), Re (Unreported, November 4, 1999), CICB (Manchester) [*Ex
rel.* Rowlands Solicitors, 3 York Street, Manchester] . . . .   *Digested,* 00/**1654**
W (Contact: Parent's Delusional Beliefs), Re see W (A Minor) (Contact Orders: Medical
Reports), Re
W (Disclosure to Police), Re see W (Minors) (Social Worker: Disclosure), Re
W (Enduring Power of Attorney), Re [2001] Ch. 609; [2001] 2 W.L.R. 957; [2001] 4 All E.R.
88; [2001] 1 F.L.R. 832; [2001] Fam. Law 262; (2001) 98(4) L.S.G. 50; (2001) 145
S.J.L.B. 16; *Times,* January 10, 2001, CA; affirming [2000] Ch. 343; [2000] 3
W.L.R. 45; [2000] 1 All E.R. 175; [1999] 2 F.L.R. 1163; [2000] W.T.L.R. 19;
[1999] Fam. Law 699, Ch D . . . .   *Digested,* 01/**5162**
W (Ex Parte Orders), Re see W v. H (Family Division: Without Notice Orders)
W (Exclusion: Statement of Evidence), Re; *sub nom* W v. A Local Authority (Exclusion
Requirement); W v. Middlesbrough BC (Exclusion Order: Evidence) [2000] 2
F.L.R. 666; [2000] 2 F.C.R. 662; [2000] Fam. Law 705; *Times,* August 8, 2000,
Fam Div . . . .   *Digested,* 00/**2467**
W (Minors) (Abduction: Father's Rights), Re; *sub nom* W (A Minor) (Unmarried Father),
Re; B (A Minor) (Unmarried Father), Re; B (A Minor) (Abduction: Father's
Rights), Re [1999] Fam. 1; [1998] 3 W.L.R. 1372; [1998] 2 F.L.R. 146; [1998] 2
F.C.R. 549; [1998] Fam. Law 452; (1998) 95(21) L.S.G. 24; (1998) 142
S.J.L.B. 131; *Times,* April 9, 1998, Fam Div . . . .   *Digested,* 98/**2385**:
      Approved, 99/2327
W (Minors) (Custody), Re see H (B) (An Infant), Re
W (Minors) (Residence Order), Re [1999] 1 F.L.R. 869; [1998] 1 F.C.R. 75; [1999] Fam. Law
220, CA . . . .   *Digested,* 98/**2439**
W (Minors) (Social Worker: Disclosure), Re; *sub nom* W (Disclosure to Police), Re
[1999] 1 W.L.R. 205; [1998] 2 All E.R. 801; [1998] 2 F.L.R. 135; [1998] 2 F.C.R.
405; [1998] Fam. Law 387; (1998) 142 S.J.L.B. 132; *Times,* April 8, 1998, CA . .   *Digested,* 98/**2389**
W (Residence), Re [1999] 2 F.L.R. 390; [1999] 3 F.C.R. 274; [1999] Fam. Law 454, CA
      Digested, 99/**2392**
W v. A Local Authority (Exclusion Requirement) see W (Exclusion: Statement of
Evidence), Re
W v. B see R. (on the application of L (A Child)) v. J School Governors
W v. Commissioner of Police of the Metropolis [2000] 1 W.L.R. 1607; [2000] 4 All
E.R. 934; [2000] I.C.R. 1064; [2000] I.R.L.R. 720; [2001] P.I.Q.R. P6; (2000)
97(39) L.S.G. 42; (2000) 144 S.J.L.B. 248; *Times,* August 1, 2000;
Independent, November 6, 2000 (C.S), HL; reversing [1997] I.C.R. 1073; [1997]
I.R.L.R. 589; *Times,* July 21, 1997, CA; affirming [1995] I.C.R. 510; [1995]
I.R.L.R. 531, EAT . . . .   *Digested,* 00/**4229**:
      Applied, 00/2211
W v. Essex CC [2001] 2 A.C. 592; [2000] 2 W.L.R. 601; [2000] 2 All E.R. 237;
[2000] 1 F.L.R. 657; [2000] 1 F.C.R. 568; [2000] B.L.G.R. 281; (2000) 53
B.M.L.R. 1; [2000] Fam. Law 476; (2000) 164 J.P.N. 464; (2000) 97(13) L.S.G.
44; (2000) 144 S.J.L.B. 147; *Times,* March 17, 2000, HL; reversing in part
[1999] Fam. 90; [1998] 3 W.L.R. 534; [1998] 3 All E.R. 111; [1998] 2 F.L.R.
278; [1998] 2 F.C.R. 269; [1998] P.I.Q.R. P346; [1998] Fam. Law 455; (1998)
95(20) L.S.G. 33; *Times,* April 9, 1998, CA; affirming [1997] 2 F.L.R. 535;
[1998] 2 F.C.R. 232; [1997] Fam. Law 720; (1997) 161 J.P.N. 1158; *Times,* July
16, 1997, QBD . . . .   *Digested,* 00/**4213**
W v. Gloucestershire CC [2001] EWHC Admin 481; (2001) 98(29) L.S.G. 39; *Times,*
August 20, 2001; *Independent,* July 30, 2001 (C.S), QBD (Admin Ct) . . . .   *Digested,* 01/**2028**
W (A Patient: Multiple Injuries) v. Grey (Unreported, January 12, 2000), QBD [*Ex rel.*
Hough Halton & Soal Solicitors, 32 Abbey Street, Carlisle] . . . .   *Digested,* 01/**1557**
W v. H (Ex Parte Injunctions) see W v. H (Family Division: Without Notice Orders)
W v. H (Family Division: Without Notice Orders); *sub nom* W v. H (Ex Parte
Injunctions); W (Ex Parte Orders), Re [2001] 1 All E.R. 300; [2000] 2 F.L.R. 927;
[2000] 3 F.C.R. 481; [2000] Fam. Law 811, Fam Div . . . .   *Digested,* 01/**2623**
W v. Hardman, CC (Leeds) [*Ex rel.* Hartley & Worstenholme, Solicitors, 20 Bank
Street, Castleford] . . . .   *Digested,* 01/**4452**
W v. Middlesbrough BC (Exclusion Order: Evidence) see W (Exclusion: Statement of
Evidence), Re
W v. North Yorkshire CC see W (A Minor) (Secure Accommodation Order), Re

W *v.* Preston [2001] 4 Q.R. 10, CC (Portsmouth) [*Ex rel.* Frank Moat, Barrister, Pump Court Chambers, 3 Pump Court, Temple, London] . . . . *Digested,* 01/**1592**

W *v.* Secretary of State for Scotland 1999 S.C. 412; 1999 S.L.T. 640; 1999 S.C.L.R. 481; 1999 G.W.D. 11-518; *Times*, April 21, 1999, 2 Div; affirming 1998 S.L.T. 841; 1998 S.C.L.R. 221; 1997 G.W.D. 40-2101, OH . . . . *Digested,* 99/**6361**

W *v.* Special Educational Needs Tribunal, *Times*, December 12, 2000, CA; reversing CO/ 1861/00, QBD . . . . *Digested,* 01/**2038**:
Distinguished, 01/2018

W *v.* Surrey CC see Surrey CC *v.* M (A Child)

W *v.* United Kingdom (A/121) (1988) 10 E.H.R.R. 29, ECHR . . . . *Applied,* 98/3104

W *v.* W (Ancillary Relief: Practice) [2000] Fam. Law 473; *Times*, March 15, 2000, Fam Div . . . . *Digested,* 00/**2522**

W *v.* W (Decree Absolute) [1998] 2 F.L.R. 326; [1998] 2 F.C.R. 304; [1998] Fam. Law 457; (1998) 142 S.J.L.B. 148; *Times*, March 31, 1998, Fam Div . . . . *Digested,* 98/**2446**

W *v.* W (Divorce: Behaviour of the Respondent) [1998] N.I. 207, Fam Div . . . . *Digested,* 99/**5305**

W *v.* W (Financial Provision: Company Shares) B1/2001/1387, CA; reversing [2001] Fam. Law 656, Fam Div

W *v.* W (Nullity: Gender); *sub nom* W *v.* W (Physical Inter-sex) [2001] Fam. 111; [2001] 2 W.L.R. 674; [2001] 1 F.L.R. 324; (2001) 58 B.M.L.R. 15; [2001] Fam. Law 104; *Times*, October 31, 2000, Fam Div. . . . . *Digested,* 00/**2538**

W *v.* W (Physical Inter-sex) see W *v.* W (Nullity: Gender)

W and B (Children) (Care Plan), Re see S (Children) (Care Order: Implementation of Care Plan), Re

W BC *v.* AK see K (A Child) (Secure Accommodation Order: Right to Liberty), Re

W BC *v.* DK see K (A Child) (Secure Accommodation Order: Right to Liberty), Re

W Beus GmbH & Co *v.* Hauptzollamt Munchen Landsbergerstrasse (C5/67) [1968] E.C.R. 125; [1968] C.M.L.R. 131, ECJ . . . . *Digested,* 68/**1473**:
Followed, 00/3808

W Devis & Sons Ltd *v.* Atkins [1977] A.C. 931; [1977] 3 W.L.R. 214; 8 B.L.R. 57; [1977] I.C.R. 662; [1977] I.R.L.R. 314; (1978) 13 I.T.R. 71; 121 S.J. 512, HL; affirming [1977] 2 W.L.R. 70; [1977] 2 All E.R. 321; [1977] I.C.R. 377; [1976] I.R.L.R. 428; (1976) 12 I.T.R. 12; 121 S.J. 52, CA; affirming [1976] 1 W.L.R. 393; [1976] 2 All E.R. 822; [1976] I.C.R. 196; [1976] I.R.L.R. 16; (1976) 10 I.T.R. 15; 120 S.J. 62, QBD. . . . . *Digested,* 77/**1160**:
Applied, 76/991, 78/1059, 81/951, 81/972, 85/1270, 88/1353, 93/1815:
Considered, 76/986, 77/1137, 79/1017, 97/2290: *Distinguished,* 76/979, 84/1310, 85/1238, 86/1280, 86/1285, 98/2232

W Gimber & Sons Ltd *v.* Spurrett see Spurrett *v.* W Gimber & Sons Ltd

W Lamb Ltd (t/a Premier Pump & Tank Co) *v.* J Jarvis & Sons Plc 60 Con. L.R. 1, QBD . *Digested,* 99/**786**:
Distinguished, 00/458

W Weddel & Co *v.* Tepper [1980] I.C.R. 286; [1980] I.R.L.R. 96; 124 S.J. 80, CA . . . . . *Digested,* 80/**1005**:
Applied, 83/1339: *Considered,* 84/1312: *Followed,* 00/2237

W&G du Cros Ltd's Application, Re; *sub nom* W&G Trade Mark; Du Cross Application, Re (1913) 30 R.P.C. 660 . . . . *Applied,* 67/3958,
01/4031: *Considered,* 95/4945, 98/3534: *Doubted,* 99/3567

W&G Trade Mark see W&G du Cros Ltd's Application, Re

W-R *v.* Solihull MBC [1999] E.L.R. 528, QBD . . . . *Digested,* 00/**1955**

W's Application, Re [1998] N.I. 219, CA (NI); affirming [1998] N.I. 19, QBD (NI) . . . . . . *Digested,* 99/**5188**

W(N) (An Infant), Re see H(B) (An Infant), Re

WA Armstrong & Sons Ltd *v.* Borrill [2000] I.C.R. 367, EAT. *Digested,* 00/**2192**

Wabl *v.* Austria (24773/94) (2001) 31 E.H.R.R. 51, ECHR . . . . *Digested,* 01/**3469**

Wachauf *v.* Bundesamt fur Ernahrung und Forstwirtschaft (C5/88) see Wachauf *v.* Germany (C5/88)

Wachauf *v.* Germany (C5/88); *sub nom* Wachauf *v.* Bundesamt fur Ernahrung und Forstwirtschaft (C5/88) [1989] E.C.R. 2609; [1991] 1 C.M.L.R. 328, ECJ (3rd Chamber) . . . . *Digested,* 91/**3730**:
Applied, 95/219: *Considered,* 91/50, 92/107, 92/108: *Followed,* 00/2382

WACKERS Trade Mark [1999] R.P.C. 453, TMR . . . . *Digested,* 99/**3580**

Waddell *v.* Kensington and Chelsea RLBC see R. *v.* Kensington and Chelsea RLBC Ex p. Waddell

Waddon *v.* Whitecroft-Scovill Ltd [1988] 1 W.L.R. 309; [1988] 1 All E.R. 996; (1988) 85(11) L.S.G. 43; (1988) 132 S.J. 263, HL . . . . *Digested,* 88/**2961**:
Applied, 91/2981: *Considered,* 00/594: *Followed,* 99/531

Wade *v.* Chief Constable of West Yorkshire, *Times*, September 9, 1998, CA . . . . *Digested,* 98/**2199**

Wadey *v.* Surrey CC see Wisely *v.* John Fulton (Plumbers) Ltd (No.2)

Wadey *v.* Surrey CC [1999] 1 W.L.R. 1614; [1999] 2 All E.R. 334; [1999] P.I.Q.R. Q128; (1999) 96(4) L.S.G. 38; (1999) 143 S.J.L.B. 20; *Times*, January 8, 1999; *Independent*, December 17, 1998, CA. . . . . *Digested,* 99/**1387**:
Subsequent proceedings, 00/6160

Wadham Kenning Motor Group Ltd *v.* Brighton and Hove Council CO/3155/97, QBD . . *Digested,* 98/**4385**

Wadham Stringer Commercials (London) Ltd *v.* Brown [1983] I.R.L.R. 46, EAT . . . . . . *Digested,* 83/**1203**:
Applied, 01/2341

Wadman *v.* Dick [1998] 3 F.C.R. 9; [1999] Fam. Law 17, CA (Jer)

Wadsworth v. Gillespie (Unreported, November 9, 1978), HC [*Ex rel.* Robert S Smith, Barrister] . . . . *Digested,* 78/**2534**:
Distinguished, 85/2978, 98/3913
Wagamama Ltd v. City Centre Restaurants Plc [1997] Eu. L.R. 313; [1996] E.T.M.R. 23; [1995] F.S.R. 713, Ch D . . . . *Digested,* 96/**5716**:
Considered, 96/5712, 98/3537: *Referred to,* 99/3539
Waggott v. Swan Hunter Shipbuilders Ltd see Thompson v. Smiths Shiprepairers (North Shields) Ltd
Waghorn v. George Wimpey & Co Ltd [1969] 1 W.L.R. 1764; [1970] 1 All E.R. 474; 113 S.J. 671, QBD . . . . *Digested,* 69/**2448**:
Considered, 97/690: *Followed,* 00/579
Wagner v. Wright (Unreported, December 1, 1998), CC (Trowbridge) [*Ex rel.* Tim Kevan, Barrister, 1 Temple Gardens, Temple, London] . . . . *Digested,* 99/**3794**
Wagon Finance Ltd v. Customs and Excise Commissioners [2000] B.V.C. 2125; [2000] S.T.I. 75, V&DTr
Wagstaff v. Department of the Environment, Transport and the Regions [1999] 2 E.G.L.R. 108; [1999] 21 E.G. 137; [1999] R.V.R. 325, LandsTr . . . . *Digested,* 99/**4187**
Wahda Bank v. Arab Bank Plc [1998] C.L.C. 689, QBD (Comm Ct) . . . . *Digested,* 98/**302**
Wahl v. Attorney General (1932) 147 L.T. 382 . . . . *Applied,* 74/1816,
01/5258: *Distinguished,* 72/429
Wailes v. Stapleton Construction and Commercial Services Ltd; Wailes v. Unum Ltd [1997] 2 Lloyd's Rep. 112, QBD . . . . *Digested,* 97/**3114**:
Applied, 99/504
Wailes v. Unum Ltd see Wailes v. Stapleton Construction and Commercial Services Ltd
Wain v. F Sherwood & Sons Transport Ltd [1999] P.I.Q.R. P159; (1998) 95(25) L.S.G. 32; (1998) 142 S.J.L.B. 187; *Times,* July 16, 1998; *Independent,* June 15, 1998 (C.S.), CA . . . . *Digested,* 98/**80**
Wainsfort Corp v. Secretary of State for the Environment, Transport and the Regions see R. (on the application of Wainsfort Corp) v. Secretary of State for the Environment, Transport and the Regions
Waite v. Germany (26083/94) (2000) 30 E.H.R.R. 261; 6 B.H.R.C. 499, ECHR . . . . *Digested,* 99/**3134**
Waite v. Throup (Unreported, May 22, 1998), CC (Bury) [*Ex rel.* Mendelsons Solicitors, 81 King Street, Manchester] . . . . *Digested,* 98/**398**
Waitomo Wools (NZ) Ltd v. Nelsons (NZ) Ltd [1974] 1 N.Z.L.R. 484 . . . . *Considered,* 98/3338
Wake v. Page see Wake v. Wylie
Wake v. Wylie; *sub nom* Wylie v. Wake; Wake v. Page [2001] R.T.R. 20; [2001] P.I.Q.R. P13; *Times,* February 9, 2001, CA . . . . *Digested,* 01/**622**
Wakefield v. Child Support Officer see Wakefield v. Secretary of State for Social Security
Wakefield v. Secretary of State for Social Security; *sub nom* Wakefield v. Child Support Officer [2000] 1 F.L.R. 510; [2000] 1 F.C.R. 761; [2000] Fam. Law 312; (2000) 97(8) L.S.G. 37; *Times,* February 29, 2000, CA . . . . *Digested,* 00/**2456**
Wakefield (City) MBC v. Bass Leisure Retail (2001) 16 P.A.D. 47, Planning Inspector
Wakefield MBC v. Carney (2001) 16 P.A.D. 25, Planning Inspector
Wakefield MDC v. Stockdale's Riding School and Livery (1998) 13 P.A.D. 217, Planning Inspector
Wakefield (Tower Hill Trinity Square) Trust v. Janson Green Properties Ltd [1998] E.G.C.S. 95; [1998] N.P.C. 104; *Times,* July 20, 1998 . . . . *Digested,* 98/**3675**
Wakeland-Jones v. Chief Constable of Devon and Cornwall (Unreported, November 5, 1999), CC (Taunton) [*Ex rel.* James Hassall, Barrister, Southernhay Chambers, 33 Southernhay East, Exeter] . . . . *Digested,* 00/**510**
Wakelin v. Read [2000] O.P.L.R. 277; [2000] Pens. L.R. 319; *Times,* April 10, 2000, CA; reversing [1998] O.P.L.R. 147, Ch D . . . . *Digested,* 00/**4393**
Wakeling v. Marley Building Materials (Unreported, March 6, 2000), CC (Central London) [*Ex rel.* Alastair Sharp, Barrister, Lamb Chambers, Lamb Building, Temple, London] . . . . *Digested,* 00/**4812**
Wakeman v. Quick Corp; Solanki v. Quick Corp; Mitchell v. Quick Corp [1999] I.R.L.R. 424, CA . . . . *Digested,* 99/**2095**
Walchester v. Chief Constable of Staffordshire (Unreported, December 4, 1998), CC (Stoke on Trent) [*Ex rel.* Adam Farrer, Barrister, 4 Fountain Court, Steelhouse Lane, Birmingham, West Midlands] . . . . *Digested,* 99/**1548**
Wale v. London Underground Ltd (Unreported, October 30, 1998), CC (Central London) [*Ex rel.* Jackaman Smith & Mulley, Solicitors, Oak House, 7 Northgate Street, Ipswich, Suffolk] . . . . *Digested,* 00/**1598**
Wales (Inspector of Taxes) v. Tilley see Tilley v. Wales (Inspector of Taxes)
Walji v. Mount Cook Land Ltd [2000] N.P.C. 148; (2001) 81 P. & C.R. D24, CA
Walker, Re [1999] N.I. 84, QBD (NI) . . . . *Digested,* 99/**5474**
Walker (Albert Johnston), Re [2000] B.P.I.R. 930, HC (Ont) . . . . *Digested,* 01/**3722**
Walker v. Badcock (1998) 30 H.L.R. 513; [1997] 2 E.G.L.R. 163; [1997] 42 E.G. 180, CA . . . . *Digested,* 98/**3662**
Walker v. Boyle; *sub nom* Boyle v. Walker [1982] 1 W.L.R. 495; [1982] 1 All E.R. 634; (1982) 44 P. & C.R. 20; (1982) 261 E.G. 1090; (1982) 79 L.S.G. 954; 125 S.J. 724, Ch D . . . . *Digested,* 82/**2669**:
Considered, 88/1710, 98/4372: *Distinguished,* 87/465, 90/650

Walker (Inspector of Taxes) v. Centaur Clothes Group Ltd; *sub nom* Centaur Clothes Group Ltd v. Walker (Inspector of Taxes) [2000] 1 W.L.R. 799; [2000] 2 All E.R. 589; [2000] S.T.C. 324; 72 T.C. 379; [2000] B.T.C. 121; [2000] S.T.I. 581; (2000) 97(16) L.S.G. 42; (2000) 144 S.J.L.B. 188; *Times*, April 7, 2000, HL; reversing [1998] S.T.C. 814; [1998] B.T.C. 277; (1998) 95(34) L.S.G. 31; *Times*, July 25, 1998, CA; affirming [1997] S.T.C. 72; [1997] B.T.C. 45, Ch D; reversing [1996] S.T.C. (S.C.D.) 222, Sp Comm . . . . *Digested*, 00/**4912**: *Applied*, 00/820

Walker v. Chief Constable of the West Midlands see Hunter v. Chief Constable of the West Midlands

Walker v. Customs and Excise Commissioners see Craddock v. Customs and Excise Commissioners

Walker v. D (A Child) see D (A Child) v. Walker

Walker v. Geo H Medlicott & Son [1999] 1 W.L.R. 727; [1999] 1 All E.R. 685; [1999] 1 F.L.R. 1095; [1999] Lloyd's Rep. P.N. 20; [1999] P.N.L.R. 531; [1999] Fam. Law 214; (1999) 96(1) L.S.G. 24; [1998] N.P.C.156; *Times*, November 25, 1998, CA . . . . *Digested*, 98/**4584**: *Distinguished*, 99/4045

Walker v. Higgit see Walker v. Home Office

Walker v. Hocking (Bankruptcy: Disposal of Property) [1998] B.P.I.R. 789, Ch D . . . . . *Digested*, 99/**3258**

Walker v. Home Office; Walker v. Higgit; LTA 1998/5625/2, LTA 1998/5626/2, CA. . . . *Digested*, 99/**4104**

Walker v. Josiah Wedgwood & Sons Ltd [1978] I.C.R. 744; [1978] I.R.L.R. 105; (1978) 13 I.T.R. 271, EAT. . . . . *Digested*, 78/**904**: *Applied*, 98/2102: *Followed*, 97/2206

Walker v. Midland Fox Ltd (Unreported, October 21, 1996), CC (Leicester) [*Ex rel.* Irwin Mitchell, Solicitors] . . . . *Digested*, 97/**595**: *Cited*, 01/518

Walker v. Miricki [2000] 4 Q.R. 4, CC (Chesterfield) [*Ex rel.* Richard Gregory, Barrister, 24 The Ropewalk, Nottingham] . . . . *Digested*, 00/**1522**

Walker v. Northumberland CC [1995] 1 All E.R. 737; [1995] I.C.R. 702; [1995] I.R.L.R. 35; [1995] P.I.Q.R. P521; (1994) 144 N.L.J. 1659; *Times*, November 24, 1994; *Independent*, November 18, 1994, QBD . . . . *Digested*, 95/**3659**: *Considered*, 01/4502

Walker v. Rome; *sub nom* Walker v. Rowe [1999] 2 All E.R. (Comm) 961; [2000] 1 Lloyd's Rep. 116; [2000] C.L.C. 265; *Independent*, January 24, 2000 (C.S.), QBD (Comm Ct) . . . . *Digested*, 00/**231**

Walker v. Rowe see Walker v. Rome

Walker v. Seed Crushers (Scotland) Ltd see Wheelan v. Seed Crushers (Scotland) Ltd (No.1)

Walker v. Smith (Inspector of Taxes) [1999] S.T.C. 605; 72 T.C. 447; [1999] B.T.C. 209, Ch D . . . . *Digested*, 99/**4699**

Walker v. Standard Chartered Bank [1998] N.P.C. 29, Ch D

Walker v. Stones [2001] Q.B. 902; [2001] 2 W.L.R. 623; [2000] 4 All E.R. 412; [2001] B.C.C. 757; [2000] Lloyd's Rep. P.N. 864; [2000] W.T.L.R. 975; (1999-2000) 2 I.T.E.L.R. 848; (2000) 97(35) L.S.G. 36; *Times*, September 26, 2000; *Independent*, July 27, 2000, CA; reversing in part [2000] W.T.L.R. 79, Ch D . . . *Digested*, 00/**5268**

Walker v. United Kingdom (34979/97) (2001) 29 E.H.R.R. CD276, ECHR

Walker v. Warrington BC (Unreported, January 23, 2001), CC (Manchester) [*Ex rel.* Glaisyers, Solicitors, Manchester House, 18-20 Bridge Street, Manchester] . . . . . *Digested*, 01/**482**

Walker v. Worth (Unreported, August 20, 1999), CC (Birkenhead) [*Ex rel.* David A Tubby & Co Solicitors, Alexander House, 2a Aughton Street, Ormskirk, Lancs] . *Digested*, 00/**2586**

Walker Cain Ltd v. McCaughey see Courage Ltd v. Crehan (No.1)

Walker Morris (A Firm) v. Khalastchi [2001] 1 B.C.L.C. 1, Ch D (Companies Ct) . . . . . . *Digested*, 01/**3751**

Walker's Executors v. Inland Revenue Commissioners [2001] S.T.C. (S.C.D.) 86; [2001] W.T.L.R. 773; [2001] S.T.I. 734, Sp Comm. . . . . *Digested*, 01/**5279**

Walkers Snack Foods Ltd v. Coventry City Council [1998] 3 All E.R. 163; [1998] E.H.L.R. 260; *Times*, April 9, 1998, QBD . . . . *Digested*, 98/**2587**

Walkes (A Minor) v. Oxley (1998) 98(6) Q.R. 4, CC (Croydon) . . . . *Digested*, 98/**1715**

Walkin v. South Manchester HA [1995] 1 W.L.R. 1543; [1995] 4 All E.R. 132; [1996] 7 Med. L.R. 211; *Times*, July 3, 1995, CA . . . . *Digested*, 96/**833**: *Considered*, 98/541: *Followed*, 98/549

Walkinshaw v. Diniz (Amendment to Particulars of Claim) A3/2001/0465, A3/2001/0465/A, A3/2001/0465/B, CA; affirming [2001] 1 Lloyd's Rep. 632, QBD (Comm Ct) . . . . *Previous proceedings*, 00/861

Walkinshaw v. Diniz (Stay of Proceedings) [2000] 2 All E.R. (Comm) 237, QBD (Comm Ct) . . . . *Digested*, 00/**861**

Walkley v. Precision Forgings Ltd [1979] 1 W.L.R. 606; [1979] 2 All E.R. 548; 123 S.J. 548, HL; reversing [1978] 1 W.L.R. 1228; [1979] 1 All E.R. 102; 122 S.J. 645, CA . . . . *Digested*, 79/**1665**: *Applied*, 80/1676, 82/1848, 83/2219, 89/2698, 95/3175: *Considered*, 80/1682, 81/1618, 98/686: *Distinguished*, 82/1853, 89/2277, 92/413, 95/6098, 98/545: *Followed*, 93/2607, 97/653: *Not applied*, 99/475

Wall *v.* Lefever [1998] 1 F.C.R. 605; *Times*, August 1, 1997, CA . . . .   *Digested*, 97/**603**:
                      Applied, 00/469: *Followed*, 98/496
Wall *v.* Rose (1998) 162 J.P. 38; (1997) 161 J.P.N. 1118, QBD . . . .   *Digested*, 97/**953**
Wall *v.* Standard Telephones & Cables Ltd (No.1) see Alexander *v.* Standard Telephones
     & Cables Ltd (No.1)
Wall *v.* Standard Telephones & Cables Ltd (No.2) see Alexander *v.* Standard
     Telephones & Cables Ltd (No.2)
Wallace *v.* Brian Gale & Associates; *sub nom* Wallace *v.* Gale & Associates [1998] 2
     Costs L.R. 53; [1998] 1 F.L.R. 1091; [1998] Fam. Law 400; *Times*, March 5,
     1998, CA; affirming 53 Con. L.R. 103; [1997] 2 Costs L.R. 15; *Times*, March 31,
     1997, QBD (OR) . . . .   *Digested*, 98/**452**
Wallace *v.* British Telecommunications Plc, CC (Preston) [*Ex rel.* David Wilby Q.C.,
     Barrister, Park Lane Chambers, 19 Westgate, Leeds] . . . .   *Digested*, 01/**661**
Wallace *v.* Ford Motor Co Ltd see Boyle *v.* Ford Motor Co Ltd
Wallace *v.* Gale & Associates see Wallace *v.* Brian Gale & Associates
Wallace *v.* Jeremy Roberts & Co QBEN1 98/1252/1, CA. . . . .   *Digested*, 99/**3951**
Wallace *v.* Korean Air Unreported, US Ct . . . .   *Considered*, 01/5385
Wallace *v.* Manchester City Council (1998) 30 H.L.R. 1111; [1998] L. & T.R. 279;
     [1998] 3 E.G.L.R. 38; [1998] 41 E.G. 223; [1998] E.G.C.S. 114; [1998] N.P.C.
     115; *Times*, July 23, 1998; *Independent*, July 17, 1998, CA . . . .   *Digested*, 98/**3678**:
                      Considered, 99/3674, 00/4290
Wallace *v.* Newton [1982] 1 W.L.R. 375; 126 S.J. 101; *Times*, December 8, 1981, QBD . .   *Digested*, 82/**842**:
                      Considered, 00/205
Wallace *v.* Paterson 2001 S.C.L.R. 521; 2001 Rep. L.R. 65; [2001] 5 Q.R. 18; 2001
     G.W.D. 1-48, OH . . . .   *Digested*, 01/**6421**
Wallace *v.* Richards (Leicester) see Baker *v.* Market Harborough Industrial Cooperative
     Society
Wallace *v.* Shoa Leasing (Singapore) PTE Ltd; *sub nom* Japan Leasing (Europe) Plc,
     Re [1999] B.P.I.R. 911; [2000] W.T.L.R. 301, Ch D . . . .   *Digested*, 00/**3433**
Wallace Smith Trust Co Ltd (In Liquidation) *v.* Deloitte Haskins & Sells [1997] 1 W.L.R.
     257; [1996] 4 All E.R. 403; [1997] B.C.C. 29; *Times*, July 12, 1996, CA . . . . . .   *Digested*, 96/**1361**:
                Applied, 99/337: *Considered*, 98/340: *Followed*, 97/472
Wallbank *v.* Aston Cantlow and Wilmcote with Billesley Parochial Church Council see
     Aston Cantlow and Wilmcote with Billesley Parochial Church Council *v.*
     Wallbank
Wallcite Ltd *v.* Ferrishurst Ltd; Ferrishurst Ltd *v.* Wallcite Ltd [1999] Ch. 355; [1999] 2
     W.L.R. 667; [1999] 1 All E.R. 977; [1999] 1 E.G.L.R. 85; [1999] 05 E.G. 161;
     [1998] E.G.C.S. 175; (1999) 96(4) L.S.G. 39; (1998) 95(47) L.S.G. 30; (1999)
     143 S.J.L.B. 54; [1998] N.P.C. 157; (1999) 77 P. & C.R. D20; *Times*, December
     8, 1998, CA. . . . .   *Digested*, 99/**4395**
Waller *v.* AB (A firm) (Unreported, July 19, 2000), QBD [*Ex rel.* Hugh Potter & Co
     Solicitors, 14-32 Hewitt Street, Manchester] . . . .   *Digested*, 01/**4522**
Wallersteiner *v.* Moir (No.2); *sub nom* Moir *v.* Wallersteiner (No.2) [1975] Q.B. 373;
     [1975] Q.B. 508 (Note); [1975] 2 W.L.R. 389; [1975] 1 All E.R. 849; 119 S.J. 97,
     CA . . . .   *Digested*, 75/**2602**:
       Applied, 94/2086, 94/3556, 94/3911, 95/2203, 95/3836, 96/4149:
       Considered, 78/2402, 87/334, 89/437, 98/481, 98/482, 01/481, 01/3803:
       Distinguished, 84/388, 86/316, 91/2853: *Followed*, 92/3525
Wallis *v.* Hands [1893] 2 Ch. 75, Ch D . . . .   *Applied*, 47-51/5626,
       47-51/8895, 98/3650: *Distinguished*, 56/4728, 56/4753, 56/4755
Wallis Fashion Group Ltd *v.* CGU Life Assurance Ltd; *sub nom* Wallis Fashion Group Ltd
     v. General Accident Life Assurance Ltd (2001) 81 P. & C.R. 28; [2000] L. &
     T.R. 520; [2000] 2 E.G.L.R. 49; [2000] E.G.C.S. 45; (2000) 80 P. & C.R. D31,
     Ch D
Wallis Fashion Group Ltd *v.* General Accident Life Assurance Ltd see Wallis Fashion
     Group Ltd *v.* CGU Life Assurance Ltd
Walls Meat Co Ltd *v.* Khan [1979] I.C.R. 52; [1978] I.R.L.R. 499; 122 S.J. 759, CA;
     affirming [1978] I.R.L.R. 74; (1977) 12 I.T.R. 497, EAT . . . .   *Digested*, 79/**979**:
       Applied, 97/2294: *Considered*, 84/1238, 99/2051, 99/2146, 01/2307:
                    Followed, 80/999, 89/4302
Walmsley *v.* Acid Jazz Records Ltd [2001] E.C.D.R. 4, Ch D . . . .   *Digested*, 01/**3855**
Walsall MBC *v.* West Midlands Probation Committee see West Midlands Probation
     Committee *v.* Secretary of State for the Environment, Transport and the Regions
Walsh *v.* Customs and Excise Commissioners [2001] EWHC Admin 426; (2001) 165
     J.P. 677; (2001) 98(29) L.S.G. 37; *Times*, July 4, 2001, QBD (Admin Ct) . . . . . .   *Digested*, 01/**1138**
Walsh *v.* Ervin [1952] V.L.R. 361 . . . .   *Applied*, 01/3800
Walsh *v.* Gwynedd HA (Unreported, April 27, 1998), CC (Llangefni) [*Ex rel.* Nigel
     Spencer Ley, Barrister, Farrar's Building, Temple, London] . . . .   *Digested*, 98/**3977**
Walsh *v.* Misseldine [2000] C.P. Rep. 74; [2000] C.P.L.R. 201, CA. . . . .   *Digested*, 00/**618**
Walsh *v.* William Morrison Supermarkets Ltd see Walsh *v.* Wm Morrison Supermarkets
     Ltd

Walsh v. Wm Morrison Supermarkets Ltd; *sub nom* Walsh v. William Morrison
Supermarkets Ltd; (Unreported, September 30, 1997), CC (Worcester) [*Ex rel.*
DL Green, Parkinson Wright, Solicitors, Haswell House, St Nicholas Street,
Worcester] . . . .   *Digested,* 98/**1571**
Walter v. Barbeito [2001] 3 Q.R. 14, CC (Bournemouth) [*Ex rel.* Blake Lapthorn,
Solicitors, Kings Court, 21 Brunswick Place, Southampton, Hampshire] . . . .   *Digested,* 01/**1617**
Walter v. Secretary of State for Social Security; *sub nom* Secretary of State for Social
Security v. Walter [2001] EWCA Civ 1913; *Times,* December 13, 2001;
Independent, December 14, 2001, CA
Walter v. Selfe (1851) 4 De G. & Sm. 315 . . . .   *Applied,* 61/**6344,**
68/3139: *Considered,* 00/**4290**
Walter L Jacob & Co Ltd, Re (1989) 5 B.C.C. 244; [1989] B.C.L.C. 345; [1989] P.C.C. 47,
CA; reversing (1987) 3 B.C.C. 532, DC . . . .   *Digested,* 89/**350:**
Applied, 96/3552: *Followed,* 99/589
Walters v. Webb (1869-70) L.R. 5 Ch. App. 531, CA in Chancery; affirming (1869-70)
L.R. 9 Eq. 83, Ct of Chancery. . . . .   *Distinguished,* 00/**4615**
Walters v. Welsh Development Agency [2001] R.V.R. 93, Lands Tr . . . .   *Digested,* 01/**4666**
Waltham Forest Community Based Housing Association v. Fanning see Fanning v.
Waltham Forest Community Based Housing Association
Waltham Forest LBC v. Inner London Hotels Ltd (2001) 16 P.A.D. 99, Planning
Inspector
Walton v. Gallagher see Walton v. Miller
Walton v. Inland Revenue Commissioners [1996] S.T.C. 68; [1996] 1 E.G.L.R. 159;
[1996] R.V.R. 55; [1995] E.G.C.S. 191; *Times,* December 11, 1995, CA; affirming
[1994] 38 E.G. 161; [1994] R.V.R. 217, Lands Tr . . . .   *Digested,* 96/**5569:**
Applied, 00/3873
Walton v. Magna Carta Polo (Unreported, March 8, 2000), CC (Staines) [*Ex rel.*
Benjamin Williams, Barrister, 1 Temple Gardens, Temple, London] . . . .   *Digested,* 00/**1694**
Walton v. Miller; *sub nom* Walton v. Gallagher 1999 S.L.T. 1137; [2000] E.H.L.R. Dig.
274; 1999 G.W.D. 20-914, HCJ Appeal. . . . .   *Digested,* 99/**5651**
Walton v. Sedgefield BC [1999] J.P.L. 541; (1998) 95(45) L.S.G. 42, QBD. . . . .   *Digested,* 99/**4205**
Wandsworth LBC v. A [2000] 1 W.L.R. 1246; (2001) 3 L.G.L.R. 3; [2000] B.L.G.R. 81;
[2000] Ed. C.R. 167; [2000] E.L.R. 257; (2000) 97(3) L.S.G. 35; (2000) 144
S.J.L.B. 47; *Times,* January 28, 2000 ; *Independent,* January 21, 2000, CA . . . .   *Digested,* 00/**5126**
Wandsworth LBC v. D'Silva [1998] I.R.L.R. 193, CA. . . . .   *Digested,* 98/**2110**
Wandsworth LBC v. Griffin [2000] 2 E.G.L.R. 105; [2000] 26 E.G. 147; [2001] R.V.R.
45, Lands Tr. . . . .   *Digested,* 00/**3947**
Wandsworth LBC v. Lloyd, *Times,* January 6, 1998, QBD . . . .   *Digested,* 98/**2859**
Wandsworth LBC v. London Concrete Ltd (1999) 14 P.A.D. 435, Planning Inspector
Wandsworth LBC v. Mills & Allen Ltd (1998) 76 P. & C.R. 214; [1997] N.P.C. 137;
Independent, October 20, 1997 (C.S.), QBD . . . .   *Digested,* 97/**4025**
Wandsworth LBC v. Osei Bonsu see Osei Bonsu v. Wandsworth LBC
Wandsworth LBC v. Railtrack Plc; *sub nom* Railtrack Plc v. Wandsworth LBC [2001]
EWCA Civ 1236; [2001] B.L.G.R. 544; [2001] 32 E.G.C.S. 88; (2001) 98(37)
L.S.G. 38; (2001) 145 S.J.L.B. 219; [2001] N.P.C. 131; *Times,* August 2, 2001;
Daily Telegraph, September 4, 2001, CA; affirming [2001] 1 W.L.R. 368; [2001]
B.L.R. 160; [2001] Env. L.R. 23; [2001] E.H.L.R. 4; [2000] E.G.C.S. 104;
(2000) 97(42) L.S.G. 43; (2000) 144 S.J.L.B. 255; *Times,* October 12, 2000,
QBD . . . .   *Digested,* 01/**4549**
Wandsworth LBC v. Winder (No.1) [1985] A.C. 461; [1984] 3 W.L.R. 1254; [1984] 3
All E.R. 976; (1985) 17 H.L.R. 196; 83 L.G.R. 143; (1985) 82 L.S.G. 201; (1985)
135 N.L.J. 381; (1984) 128 S.J. 838, HL; affirming [1984] 3 W.L.R. 563;
[1984] 3 All E.R. 83; (1984) 15 H.L.R. 1; 82 L.G.R. 509; (1984) 81 L.S.G. 1684;
(1984) 128 S.J. 384, CA . . . .   *Digested,* 85/**9:**
Applied, 87/678, 88/593, 92/30, 92/79, 99/4749: *Considered,* 84/1344,
87/2378, 87/3052, 87/3097, 88/3432, 96/3087, 97/2691:
Distinguished, 87/3609.a, 88/1, 88/2211, 88/2226, 89/35, 92/394, 93/2048:
Followed, 00/5126: *Referred to,* 87/2385
Wandsworth LBC's Planning Application, Re (2000) 15 P.A.D. 120, Planning Inspector
Wannop & Fox (A Firm) v. Middleton (Unreported, December 17, 1999), CC
(Chichester) [*Ex rel.* Harveys Solicitors, 96 Station Road, Liss, Hampshire] . . . .   *Digested,* 00/**4024**
Waple v. Surrey CC [1998] 1 W.L.R. 860; [1998] 1 All E.R. 624; [1998] E.M.L.R. 503;
[1998] 2 F.L.R. 630; [1998] 2 F.C.R. 611; [1998] Fam. Law 517; (1998) 95(5)
L.S.G. 29; (1998) 142 S.J.L.B. 46; *Times,* December 29, 1997, CA; reversing
[1997] 2 All E.R. 836, QBD . . . .   *Digested,* 98/**1779**
War Memorial Hostel Committee of the Presbyterian Church in Ireland v. Commissioner of
Valuation for Northern Ireland [2001] R.A. 166, Lands Tr (NI) . . . .   *Digested,* 01/**5939**
Warburton v. Wyre Waste Management, CC (Blackpool) [*Ex rel.* John G Baldwin,
Barrister, Oriel Chambers, 14 Water Street, Liverpool] . . . .   *Digested,* 01/**895**
Warby v. Perkins (Unreported, October 29, 1997), CC (Luton) [*Ex rel.* Geoffrey Mott,
Barrister, Gray's Inn Chambers, Gray's Inn] . . . .   *Digested,* 98/**1588**
Ward v. Aitken see Oasis Merchandising Services Ltd (In Liquidation), Re
Ward v. Barking and Dagenham LBC [2000] E.H.L.R. 263; [1999] Crim. L.R. 920,
QBD . . . .   *Digested,* 00/**1047**

Ward v. Brunt [2000] W.T.L.R. 731; [2000] N.P.C. 50, Ch D . . . . *Digested*, 01/**5154**
Ward v. Cape Contracts Ltd see Ward v. Newalls Insulation Co Ltd
Ward v. Chief Constable of the Royal Ulster Constabulary [2000] N.I. 543, QBD (NI) . . *Digested*, 01/**6045**
Ward v. Chief Constable of the West Midlands, *Times*, December 15, 1997, CA . . . . *Digested*, 98/**4776**
Ward v. Customs and Excise Commissioners [1999] B.V.C. 2024, V&DTr . . . . *Digested*, 99/**5003**
Ward v. Guinness Mahon & Co Ltd; Koppel v. Guinness Mahon & Co Ltd; Evans v.
    Guinness Mahon & Co Ltd [1996] 1 W.L.R. 895; [1996] 4 All E.R. 112; [1996]
    C.L.C. 1199, CA . . . . *Considered*, 98/427
Ward v. Hertfordshire CC [1970] 1 W.L.R. 356; [1970] 1 All E.R. 535; 68 L.G.R. 151;
    (1969) 114 S.J. 87; *Times*, December 19, 1969, CA; reversing [1969] 1 W.L.R.
    790; [1969] 2 All E.R. 807; 67 L.G.R. 418; 113 S.J. 343; *Times*, March 15, 1969,
    QBD . . . . *Digested*, 69/**2473**:
                                      Distinguished, 98/3991
Ward v. Hillingdon LBC see R. (on the application of Ward) v. Hillingdon LBC
Ward v. Kingston upon Hull City Council [1993] R.A. 71 . . . . *Digested*, 93/**2636**:
                                      Considered, 98/4308
Ward v. Lewis [1955] 1 W.L.R. 9; [1955] 1 All E.R. 55; 99 S.J. 27, CA . . . . *Digested*, 55/**1541**:
                                      Considered, 00/5106
Ward v. Newalls Insulation Co Ltd; Ward v. Cape Contracts Ltd [1998] 1 W.L.R. 1722;
    [1998] 2 All E.R. 690; [1998] P.I.Q.R. Q41; (1998) 95(15) L.S.G. 32; (1998)
    142 S.J.L.B. 103; *Times*, March 5, 1998, CA . . . . *Digested*, 98/**1442**
Ward v. Newalls Insulation Co Ltd (Quantum) (Unreported, February 19, 1998), CA
    [*Ex rel.* Irwin Mitchell Solicitors, St Peter's House, Hartshead, Sheffield] . . . . *Digested*, 98/**1623**
Ward v. Ritz Hotel (London) Ltd [1992] P.I.Q.R. P315, CA . . . . *Digested*, 93/**2975**:
                              Distinguished, 99/4004
Ward v. Sabherwal (t/a Nath Bros, Fashion Wholesale & Retail) [2000] N.I. 551, QBD
    (NI) . . . . *Digested*, 01/**5712**
Ward v. Taylor see Leigh v. Taylor
Ward v. Tesco Stores Ltd; *sub nom* Tesco Stores Ltd v. Ward [1976] 1 W.L.R. 810;
    [1976] 1 All E.R. 219; [1976] I.R.L.R. 92; 120 S.J. 555, CA . . . . *Digested*, 76/**1866**:
                  Considered, 00/4241: *Distinguished*, 89/2547
Ward v. United Kingdom see McDaid v. United Kingdom
Ward of Court (Withholding Medical Treatment), Re (1999) 50 B.M.L.R. 140, Sup Ct (Irl)
                                        Digested, 00/**2962**
Wardens and Commonalty of the Mystery of Mercers of the City of London v. New
    Hampshire Insurance Co Ltd; *sub nom* Mercers Co v. New Hampshire Insurance
    Co Ltd [1992] 1 W.L.R. 792; [1992] 3 All E.R. 57; [1992] 2 Lloyd's Rep. 365;
    60 B.L.R. 26; 29 Con. L.R. 30; (1993) 9 Const. L.J. 66; *Financial Times*, June 4,
    1992, CA; affirming in part [1991] 1 W.L.R. 1173; [1991] 4 All E.R. 542; [1992]
    1 Lloyd's Rep. 431; (1991) 7 Const. L.J. 130; (1991) 135 S.J. 541; *Times*, March
    22, 1991, QBD (Comm Ct) . . . . *Digested*, 92/**3520**:
                                        Followed, 99/1411
Wardlaw v. Bonnington Castings Ltd see Bonnington Castings Ltd v. Wardlaw
Wards Construction (Medway) Ltd v. Kent CC [1999] B.L.G.R. 675; [1999] 2 P.L.R. 61;
    [1999] J.P.L. 738; [1999] E.G.C.S. 18; [1999] N.P.C. 16; *Times*, March 3, 1999;
    Independent, February 22, 1999 (C.S.), CA; reversing [1997] E.G.C.S. 67;
    [1997] N.P.C. 74, QBD . . . . *Digested*, 99/**4193**
Warlow v. Harrison (1858) 1 El. & El. 295 . . . . *Distinguished*,
                                              77/2505,
                          78/2501: *Followed*, 00/860
Warman International Ltd's Three Dimensional Trade Mark Application [2000] E.T.M.R.
    1159, OHIM (1st Bd App) . . . . *Digested*, 01/**3998**
Warner (A Minor), Re (1998) 98(1) Q.R. 5; (1997) 97(5/6) Q.R. 9, CICB (York) . . . . . . *Digested*, 98/**1561**
Warner v. Adnet Ltd [1998] I.C.R. 1056; [1998] I.R.L.R. 394; (1998) 98(1) Q.R. 5;
    Times, March 12, 1998, CA . . . . *Digested*, 98/**2219**
Warner v. Gestetner (Unreported, December 17, 1987), DC . . . . *Applied*, 98/3423:
                                        Referred to, 95/774
Warner Brothers Inc v. Christiansen (158/86) [1988] E.C.R. 2605; [1990] 3 C.M.L.R.
    684; [1991] F.S.R. 161; *Times*, June 1, 1988, ECJ . . . . *Digested*, 92/**4719**:
                        Considered, 92/580, 97/3892, 99/3451
Warren v. Carson (Valuation Officer) [2001] R.V.R. 35, LandsTr . . . . *Digested*, 01/**4831**
Warren v. Uttlesford DC [1997] J.P.L. 1130; [1997] C.O.D. 483; [1997] N.P.C. 102,
    CA; affirming [1997] J.P.L. 562; [1996] E.G.C.S. 131, QBD . . . . *Digested*, 97/**4092**:
                                        Applied, 00/4486
Warren v. Warren (1834) 1 Cr. & M. 250 . . . . *Distinguished*, 01/1825
Warriner v. Smith (Unreported, January 11, 1999), CC (Chester) [*Ex rel.* Dominic
    Adamson, Barrister, 1 Temple Gardens, Temple] . . . . *Digested*, 99/**533**
Warrington BC v. Hull; *sub nom* Cheshire CC v. Hull [1999] Env. L.R. 869; (1999)
    96(17) L.S.G. 26, CA . . . . *Digested*, 00/**4484**
Warrington BC v. Warrington Community Health Care NHS Trust (2001) 16 P.A.D. 51,
    Planning Inspector
Warrington BC v. Warrington Discount Bikes (1998) 13 P.A.D. 339, Planning Inspector
Warrington BC v. Wilcon Homes (NW) Ltd (2001) 16 P.A.D. 19, Planning Inspector
Warsame v. Entry Clearance Officer (Nairobi) [2000] Imm. A.R. 155, CA . . . . *Digested*, 00/**3364**

Warsame v. Hounslow LBC [2000] 1 W.L.R. 696; (2000) 32 H.L.R. 335; (1999) 96(28) L.S.G. 26; (1999) 143 S.J.L.B. 197; *Times*, July 21, 1999 ; *Independent*, July 2, 1999, CA . . . .   *Digested*, 99/**3047**

Warsame v. Secretary of State for the Home Department see Hersi v. Secretary of State for the Home Department

Warsteiner Brauerei Haus GmbH & Co KG's Application (Opposition of Brauerei Beck GmbH & Co) [1999] E.T.M.R. 225, OHIM (Opposition Div). . . . .   *Digested*, 99/**3534**

Warwick DC v. Freeman (1995) 27 H.L.R. 616, CA . . . .   *Digested*, 96/**3087**:
Applied, 97/2691: *Considered*, 00/4828: *Distinguished*, 99/4555

Warwick Motor Auctions v. Bennett (Unreported, October 14, 1996), CC (Warwick) [*Ex rel*. Anthony Verduyn, Barrister] . . . .   *Digested*, 97/**1815**:
Cited, 00/1484: *Followed*, 01/1543

Warwick Rural DC v. Miller-Mead; *sub nom* Miller-Mead v. Warwick Rural DC [1962] Ch. 441; [1962] 2 W.L.R. 284; [1962] 1 All E.R. 212; 126 J.P. 143; 60 L.G.R. 29; 105 S.J. 1124; *Times*, December 21, 1961, CA; affirming [1961] Ch. 590; [1961] 3 W.L.R. 737; [1961] 3 All E.R. 542; 125 J.P. 640; 59 L.G.R. 436; 105 S.J. 707, Ch D . . . .   *Digested*, 62/**2542**:
Applied, 70/1531, 83/3469: *Considered*, 01/4730

Warwickshire CC's Applications, Re (1999) 14 P.A.D. 449, Planning Inspector

Washington v. Glucksberg (1999) 50 B.M.L.R. 65, US Ct

Wasiuk v. Auto Travel Ltd (Unreported, July 20, 1999), CC (Chester) [*Ex rel*. Nigel Brockley, Barrister, Bracton Chambers, 95a Chancery Lane, London] . . . .   *Digested*, 99/**1567**

Watchtower Investments Ltd v. Payne [2001] EWCA Civ 1159; (2001) 98(35) L.S.G. 32; *Times*, August 22, 2001, CA . . . .   *Digested*, 01/**911**

Waterford Wedgwood Plc v. David Nagli Ltd [1998] F.S.R. 92, Ch D . . . .   *Digested*, 98/**3508**

Waterford Wedgwood Plc v. David Nagli Ltd (In Liquidation) (Costs) [1999] 3 All E.R. 185; (1998) 148 N.L.J. 1881; *Times*, January 4, 1999, Ch D . . . .   *Digested*, 99/**3759**

Waterford Wedgwood Plc v. David Nagli Ltd (Third Party Notice) [1998] C.L.C. 1011; [1999] I.L.Pr. 9; *Times*, May 13, 1998, Ch D . . . .   *Digested*, 98/**751**

Waterlow & Sons Ltd v. Banco de Portugal see Banco de Portugal v. Waterlow & Sons Ltd

Waters v. Iqbal (No.2) (Unreported, August 9, 1999), CC (Milton Keynes) [*Ex rel*. Marc Willems, Barrister, Cobden House Chambers, 19 Quay Street, Manchester] . . . .   *Digested*, 99/**2481**

Waters v. Maguire [1999] Lloyd's Rep. P.N. 855, QBD . . . .   *Digested*, 99/**3791**

Waters v. Thomson Holidays Ltd (Unreported, April 11, 2000), CC (Bow) [*Ex rel*. Matthew Chapman, Barrister, Barnards Inn Chambers, Halton House, 20/23 Holborn, London] . . . .   *Digested*, 00/**879**

Waters v. Welsh Development Agency [2001] 1 E.G.L.R. 185, Lands Tr. . . . .   *Digested*, 01/**4670**

Waters Corp v. Hewlett Packard GmbH see Hewlett Packard GmbH v. Waters Corp

Wates Building Group Ltd v. Jones 59 Con. L.R. 97, CA . . . .   *Digested*, 98/**856**

Watford (A Minor) v. Tesco Stores Ltd (Unreported, May 7, 1998), CC (Uxbridge) [*Ex rel*. The Woodbridge Partnership Solicitors, Windsor House, 42 Windsor Street, Uxbridge, Middlesex] . . . .   *Digested*, 98/**1672**

Watford and District Old People's Housing Association Ltd (t/a Watford Help in the Home Service) v. Customs and Excise Commissioners [1998] B.V.C. 2351, V&DTr . . . .   *Digested*, 99/**4987**

Watford BC v. Colne Bridge Investments Ltd (2000) 15 P.A.D. 641, Planning Inspector

Watford BC v. Simpson (2000) 32 H.L.R. 901; (2000) 80 P. & C.R. D37, CA . . . .   *Digested*, 01/**4202**

Watford Electronics Ltd v. Sanderson CFL Ltd [2001] EWCA Civ 317; [2001] 1 All E.R. (Comm) 696; [2001] B.L.R. 143; (2001) 3 T.C.L.R. 14; (2001) 98(18) L.S.G. 44; *Times*, March 9, 2001, CA; reversing [2000] 2 All E.R. (Comm) 984, QBD (T&CC) . . . .   *Digested*, 01/**953**

Watkins v. Olafson [1989] 2 S.C.R. 750, Sup Ct (Can) . . . .   *Applied*, 98/4783

Watkins v. Pauls Industrial Services, CC (Cardiff) [*Ex rel*. Andrew Arentsen, Barrister, 33 Park Place, Cardiff] . . . .   *Digested*, 01/**1724**

Watkins v. Rover Group Ltd (Unreported, May 1, 1998), CC (Swindon) [*Ex rel*. Bond Pearce Solicitors, Darwin House, Southernhay Gardens, Exeter] . . . .   *Digested*, 99/**462**

Watkins v. Toms [1998] 1 W.L.R. 1376; [1998] 2 All E.R. 534; [1998] P.I.Q.R. P299, CA . . . .   *Digested*, 98/**609**:
Followed, 97/740

Watkinson v. Chief Constable of the West Midlands (Unreported, December 8, 1999), CC (Leicester) [*Ex rel*. Nicholas George, Barrister, 27 New Walk, Leicester] . . . .   *Digested*, 00/**1672**

Watson (CICB: Quantum: 1998), Re (Unreported, June 3, 1998), CICB (London) [*Ex rel*. Jonathan Ashworth, Bar School Student, Inner Temple, London] . . . .   *Digested*, 98/**1533**

Watson (Deceased), Re [1999] 1 F.L.R. 878; [1999] 3 F.C.R. 595; [1999] Fam. Law 211; (1999) 96(2) L.S.G. 28; (1999) 143 S.J.L.B. 51; *Times*, December 31, 1998, Ch D . . . .   *Digested*, 99/**4636**

Watson v. British Boxing Board of Control Ltd [2001] Q.B. 1134; [2001] 2 W.L.R. 1256; [2001] P.I.Q.R. P16; (2001) 98(12) L.S.G. 44; (2001) 145 S.J.L.B. 31; *Times*, February 2, 2001; *Independent*, January 11, 2001; *Daily Telegraph*, January 16, 2001, CA; affirming [2000] E.C.C. 141; (1999) 96(39) L.S.G. 38; (1999) 143 S.J.L.B. 235; *Times*, October 12, 1999, QBD . . . .   *Digested*, 01/**4468**

Watson v. First Choice Holidays & Flights Ltd; Aparta Hotels Caledonia SA v. Watson [2001] EWCA Civ 972; [2001] 2 Lloyd's Rep. 339, CAQB/2000/APP/0031B, QBD . . . .   *Digested,* 01/**4290**

Watson v. Gray, *Times,* November 26, 1998, QBD . . . .   *Digested,* 98/**3952**

Watson v. Gray (Quantum) (1999) 99(4) Q.R. 5, QBD [*Ex rel.* Craig Moore, Barrister, Barnards Inn Chambers, Halton House, 20/23 Holborn, London] . . . .   *Digested,* 99/**1510**

Watson v. James Robinson Fibres Ltd (Unreported, August 25, 1999), CC (Birkenhead) [*Ex rel.* Scott Rees & Co Solicitors, Centaur House, Gardiners Place, Skelmersdale, Lancashire] . . . .   *Digested,* 99/**2486**

Watson v. Lambeth LBC (Unreported, December 7, 1999), CC (Wandsworth) [*Ex rel.* David Carter, Barrister, Arden Chambers, 27 John Street, London] . . . .   *Digested,* 00/**3140**

Watson v. National Children's Home; *sub nom* Chambers (Deceased), Re [2001] W.T.L.R. 1375; (1995) 92(37) L.S.G. 24; *Times,* October 31, 1995, Ch D . . . . . .   *Digested,* 95/**5144**

Watson v. Rhonnda Cynon Taff CBC [2001] EWHC Admin 913; (2001) 98(44) L.S.G. 37, QBD (Admin Ct)

Watson (Surveyor of Taxes) v. Royal Insurance Co Ltd see Royal Insurance Co Ltd v. Watson (Surveyor of Taxes)

Watson v. Warwickshire CC (Unreported, March 22, 2001), CC (Stoke on Trent) [*Ex rel.* Pickerings, Solicitors, 9 Colehill, Tamworth, Staffordshire] . . . .   *Digested,* 01/**3302**

Watson (Wasted Costs Orders) see Ridehalgh v. Horsefield

Watson v. Woodhouse QBENI 1998/1384/1, CA . . . .   *Digested,* 99/**548**

Watt (A Minor) v. Asda Stores Ltd (1998) 98(3) Q.R. 6, CC (Liverpool) . . . .   *Digested,* 98/**1548**

Watt v. Kesteven CC [1955] 1 Q.B. 408; [1955] 2 W.L.R. 499; [1955] 1 All E.R. 473; 119 J.P. 220; 53 L.G.R. 254; 99 S.J. 149, CA; affirming [1954] 3 W.L.R. 729; [1954] 3 All E.R. 441; 119 J.P. 37; 52 L.G.R. 539; 98 S.J. 806, QBD . . . .   *Digested,* 55/**911**:
    Applied, 56/2984, 57/1175, 66/4256, 70/847, 88/3703, 88/4199:
    Distinguished, 98/1972: *Followed,* 71/3831

Watton v. News Group Newspapers Ltd see Mapp v. News Group Newspapers Ltd

Watton (Inspector of Taxes) v. Tippett; *sub nom* Tippett v. Watton (Inspector of Taxes) [1997] S.T.C. 893; 69 T.C. 491; [1997] B.T.C. 338; *Times,* June 27, 1997; *Independent,* June 9, 1997 (C.S.), CA; affirming [1996] S.T.C. 101; (1996) 93(2) L.S.G. 29; *Times,* December 21, 1995, Ch D; reversing [1995] S.T.C. 17, Sp Comm . . . .   *Digested,* 97/**339**

Watts v. Aldington; Tolstoy v. Aldington [1999] L. & T.R. 578; *Times,* December 16, 1993; *Independent,* January 25, 1994, CA . . . .   *Digested,* 94/**2882**:
    Applied, 98/3351: *Considered,* 00/3884: *Followed,* 99/4400

Watts v. Morrow [1991] 1 W.L.R. 1421; [1991] 4 All E.R. 937; 54 B.L.R. 86; 26 Con. L.R. 98; (1991) 23 H.L.R. 608; [1991] 2 E.G.L.R. 152; [1991] 43 E.G. 121; (1992) 8 Const. L.J. 73; [1991] E.G.C.S. 88; (1992) 89(14) L.S.G. 33; (1991) 141 N.L.J. 1331; [1991] N.P.C. 98; *Independent,* August 20, 1991; *Guardian,* September 4, 1991, CA; reversing 24 Con. L.R. 125; [1991] 15 E.G. 113; [1991] 14 E.G. 111; *Independent,* November 19, 1990 (C.S.), QBD (OR) . . . .   *Digested,* 92/**1548**:
    Applied, 94/1762, 94/3395, 95/1565, 95/3706, 96/1211, 96/1882, 96/4499,
    96/4518, 00/1480, 00/1485, 00/4276: *Considered,* 92/1514, 94/1445,
    97/3839, 97/6307, 98/2106, 01/4539: *Followed,* 93/1386, 96/4514, 99/1375

Watts v. Savills [1998] E.G.C.S. 99; (1998) 95(25) L.S.G. 34, CA; reversing [1996] E.G.C.S. 203, QBD

Watts v. Silwood Crane Hire Ltd (Unreported, July 1, 1998), CC (Dartford) [*Ex rel.* Peter Skelton, Barrister, 35 Essex Street, Temple, London] . . . .   *Digested,* 99/**2017**

Watts v. Times Newspapers Ltd [1997] Q.B. 650; [1996] 2 W.L.R. 427; [1996] 1 All E.R. 152; [1996] E.M.L.R. 1; *Times,* September 22, 1995, CA . . . .   *Digested,* 95/**3133**:
    Applied, 99/1629: *Considered,* 98/1782, 00/1760

Waugh v. Morris (1872-73) L.R. 8 Q.B. 202, QBD . . . .   *Considered,* 01/743:
    Distinguished, 63/1578

Waveney DC v. Jones (2001) 33 H.L.R. 3; (1999) 96(48) L.S.G. 40; [1999] N.P.C. 151; *Times,* December 22, 1999 ; *Independent,* December 10, 1999, CA . . . .   *Digested,* 00/**4828**

Waverley BC v. Castles (2000) 15 P.A.D. 331, Planning Inspector

Waverley BC v. Kingston Estates Ltd; Surrey Counties (Sutton) Ltd (1998) 13 P.A.D. 666, Planning Inspector

Waverley BC v. Lawson (1998) 13 P.A.D. 399, Planning Inspector

Wawrznczyk v. Chief Constable of Staffordshire see Wawrzynczyk v. Chief Constable of Staffordshire

Wawrzynczyk v. Chief Constable of Staffordshire; *sub nom* Wawrznczyk v. Chief Constable of Staffordshire (2000) 97(12) L.S.G. 40; (2000) 144 S.J.L.B. 133; *Times,* March 16, 2000, QBD . . . .   *Digested,* 00/**999**

Waxed Papers Ltd, Re [1937] 2 All E.R. 481, CA . . . .   *Applied,* 00/683

Wayling v. Jones [1995] 2 F.L.R. 1029; [1996] 2 F.C.R. 41; (1995) 69 P. & C.R. 170; [1996] Fam. Law 88; [1993] E.G.C.S. 153; *Independent,* August 2, 1993 (C.S.), CA . . . .   *Digested,* 94/**2108**:
    Considered, 01/4859

Wayte v. Slocombe (Unreported, June 15, 1994), CA . . . .   *Considered,* 00/351

WC Wentworth v. JC Lloyd Unreported . . . .   *Applied,* 01/3901

Wealand v. CLC Contractors Ltd see Wealands v. CLC Contractors Ltd

Wealands v. CLC Contractors Ltd; *sub nom* Wealand v. CLC Contractors Ltd [2000] 1
All E.R. (Comm) 30; [1999] 2 Lloyd's Rep. 739; [1999] C.L.C. 1821; [1999]
B.L.R. 401; (2000) 2 T.C.L.R. 367; 74 Con. L.R. 1; *Times*, October 5, 1999; *Times*,
November 16, 1999, CA; affirming [1998] C.L.C. 808, QBD (Comm Ct) . . . . . . *Digested,* 99/**234**
Wealden DC v. Birling Gap Cliff Protection Association (2001) 16 P.A.D. 86, Planning
Inspector
Wealden DC v. Krushandal [1999] J.P.L. 174, CA . . . . *Digested,* 99/**4175**
Wear Ironmongers Ltd v. Baird (Inspector of Taxes) see Joseph Carter & Sons Ltd v.
Baird (Inspector of Taxes)
Weatherill v. LloydsTSB Bank Plc [2000] C.P.L.R. 584, CA . . . . *Digested,* 01/**13**
Weathersfield Ltd (t/a Van & Truck Rentals) v. Sargent [1999] I.C.R. 425; [1999] I.R.L.R.
94; [1999] Disc. L.R. 290; (1999) 96(5) L.S.G. 35; (1999) 143 S.J.L.B. 39;
Times, December 31, 1998, CA; affirming [1998] I.C.R. 198; [1998] I.R.L.R. 14,
EAT . . . . *Digested,* 99/**2091**:
Distinguished, 00/2184

Webb, Re see Criminal Proceedings against Webb (C279/80)
Webb v. Barclays Bank Plc; Webb v. Portsmouth Hospitals NHS Trust [2001] EWCA
Civ 1141; [2001] Lloyd's Rep. Med. 500, CA1999 W 25, QBD
Webb v. Chief Constable of Merseyside; *sub nom* Porter v. Chief Constable of
Merseyside; Chief Constable of Merseyside v. Porter [2000] Q.B. 427; [2000] 2
W.L.R. 546; [2000] 1 All E.R. 209; (1999) 96(47) L.S.G. 33; (2000) 144
S.J.L.B. 9; *Times*, December 1, 1999, CA . . . . *Digested,* 00/**4546**:
Followed, 01/4789

Webb v. EMO Air Cargo (UK) Ltd (C32/93) [1994] Q.B. 718; [1994] 4 All E.R. 115;
[1994] E.C.R. I-3567; [1994] 2 C.M.L.R. 729; [1994] I.C.R. 770; [1994] I.R.L.R.
482; (1994) 144 N.L.J. 1278; *Times*, July 15, 1994; *Financial Times*, July 19,
1994; *Guardian*, July 23, 1994, ECJ (5th Chamber) [1993] 1 W.L.R. 49; [1992]
4 All E.R. 929; [1993] 1 C.M.L.R. 259; [1993] I.C.R. 175; [1993] I.R.L.R. 27;
(1992) 142 N.L.J. 1720; (1993) 137 S.J.L.B. 48; *Times*, December 3, 1992, HL
[1992] 2 All E.R. 43; [1992] 1 C.M.L.R. 793; [1992] I.C.R. 445; [1992] I.R.L.R.
116; (1992) 89(10) L.S.G. 33; (1992) 142 N.L.J. 16; (1992) 136 S.J.L.B. 32;
Times, December 30, 1991; *Independent*, January 22, 1992; *Guardian*, January 8,
1992, CA; affirming [1990] I.C.R. 442; [1990] I.R.L.R. 124, EAT . . . . *Digested,* 94/**4825**:
Applied, 92/1971, 92/1972, 93/1771, 96/2623, 96/6958, 97/2239, 97/5227,
99/5283: *Considered,* 94/1984, 96/2611, 96/2620, 00/6215:
Followed, 00/5528, 01/2317

Webb v. EMO Air Cargo (UK) Ltd (No.2) [1995] 1 W.L.R. 1454; [1995] 4 All E.R. 577;
[1996] 2 C.M.L.R. 990; [1995] I.C.R. 1021; [1995] I.R.L.R. 645; *Times*,
October 20, 1995; *Independent*, October 26, 1995, HL . . . . *Digested,* 96/**2622**:
Applied, 96/2623, 98/2194: *Considered,* 96/2617, 96/2628, 97/2237:
Distinguished, 00/2004: *Followed,* 96/2621: *Referred to,* 96/2615
Webb v. Pollmount Ltd [1966] Ch. 584; [1966] 2 W.L.R. 543; [1966] 1 All E.R. 481;
109 S.J. 1029, Ch D . . . . *Digested,* 66/**6733**:
Considered, 84/2952, 85/3607, 96/4995, 99/4395: *Distinguished,* 74/3131,
77/1685
Webb v. Portsmouth Hospitals NHS Trust see Webb v. Barclays Bank Plc
Webb v. Sandown Sports Club Ltd [2000] E.G.C.S. 13, Ch D
Webb v. Secretary of State for the Environment and Salisbury DC (1996) 71 P. & C.R.
411; [1995] E.G.C.S. 147, QBD . . . . *Digested,* 96/**4741**:
Considered, 98/4213
Webb v. Webb [1992] I.L.Pr. 374; [1992] E.G.C.S. 34; [1992] N.P.C. 30; *Financial
Times*, March 11, 1992, CA [1991] 1 W.L.R. 1410; [1992] 1 All E.R. 17; [1992]
I.L.Pr. 362, Ch D . . . . *Digested,* 92/**472**:
Considered, 98/768
Webb (George Lawrence) v. Webb (Lawrence Desmond) (C294/92) [1994] Q.B. 696;
[1994] 3 W.L.R. 801; [1994] 3 All E.R. 911; [1994] E.C.R. I-1717; [1994] I.L.Pr.
389; [1994] N.P.C. 97; *Times*, June 27, 1994, ECJ . . . . *Digested,* 94/**4798**:
Applied, 00/3490, 01/3736
Webb Plant Hire v. Customs and Excise Commissioners [1998] B.V.C. 4015, V&DTr
Webb's Lease, Re; *sub nom* Sandom v. Webb [1951] Ch. 808; [1951] 2 All E.R. 131;
[1951] 2 T.L.R. 530; 95 S.J. 367, CA; reversing [1951] Ch. 142; [1950] 2 All E.R.
828; 66 T.L.R. (Pt. 2) 743; 94 S.J. 704, Ch D . . . . *Digested,* 47-51/**3227**:
Applied, 62/1707, 99/4397, 01/4867: *Considered,* 70/823, 00/4640
Webber v. Bruton (Unreported, October 6, 1997), QBD [*Ex rel.* Allan Gore, Dan
Brennan Q.C. 12 King's Bench Walk, instructed by Barratt, Goff and Tomlinson,
Nottingham] . . . . *Digested,* 98/**1490**
Webber v. DPP [1998] R.T.R. 111; *Times*, December 20, 1995; *Independent*, January 1,
1996 (C.S.), QBD . . . . *Digested,* 96/**5056**
Weber v. Jolly Hotels [1999] I.L.Pr. 169, US Ct
Webster, Re (1998) 98(3) Q.R. 6, CICB (York) . . . . *Digested,* 98/**1544**
Webster v. Cooper & Burnett [2000] Lloyd's Rep. P.N. 167; [2000] P.N.L.R. 240, CA . . *Digested,* 00/**4235**
Webster v. James Chapman & Co [1989] 3 All E.R. 939, Ch D . . . . *Digested,* 90/**3656**:
Considered, 01/3851
Webster v. Official Receiver see Migration Services International Ltd, Re

Webster v. United Kingdom (A/44) see Young v. United Kingdom (A/44)
Webster Communications International Ltd v. Customs and Excise Commissioners
    [1997] V. & D.R. 173, V&DTr . . . . *Digested*, 98/**4915**
Weddel & Co BV v. Commission of the European Communities (C354/87) [1990]
    E.C.R. I-3847, ECJ . . . . *Distinguished*, 99/2260
Weddell v. JA Pearce & Major (A Firm) [1988] Ch. 26; [1987] 3 W.L.R. 592; [1987] 3
    All E.R. 624; (1988) 85(32) L.S.G. 33; (1987) 131 S.J. 1120, Ch D . . . . *Digested*, 87/**206**:
                                    Applied, 96/1287: *Considered*, 98/3451
Weekes v. Isebor (Unreported, April 7, 1998), CC (Shoreditch) [*Ex rel*. Robert Jan
    Temminnk, Barrister, 35 Essex Street, Temple, London] . . . . *Digested*, 98/**1606**
Weeks v. Dillamore (Unreported, October 26, 2000), CC (Birmingham) [*Ex rel*. David
    McHugh, Barrister, Bracton Chambers, 8 Bell Yard, London] . . . . *Digested*, 01/**545**
Weeks v. Magill see Porter v. Magill
Wegmann v. Elsevier Science Ltd [1999] I.L.Pr. 379, Cass (F)
Wehmeyer v. Wehmeyer [2001] 2 F.L.R. 84; [2001] B.P.I.R. 548; [2001] Fam. Law
    493, Ch D . . . . *Digested*, 01/**3733**
Wehrs v. Hauptzollamt Luneburg (C264/90) [1992] E.C.R. I-6285, ECJ (3rd
    Chamber) . . . . *Digested*, 93/**4223**:
                                                        Distinguished, 00/2373
Wein & Co Handelsges mbH v. Oberosterreichische Landesregierung (C437/97) see
    Evangelischer Krankenhausverein Wien v. Abgabenberufungskommission Wien
    (C437/97)
Weinberger (A Minor) v. Jacobs (Unreported, January 15, 1998), CC (Luton) [*Ex rel*.
    Matthew Arnold & Baldwin Solicitors, 20 Station Road, Watford, Hartfordshire] . *Digested*, 98/**1695**
Weir and Higgins Application, Re [1988] N.I. 338; [1988] 10 N.I.J.B. 1, CA (NI); reversing
    [1986] 16 N.I.J.B. 46 . . . . *Digested*, 89/**2715**:
                                                        Followed, 99/5206
Weise's European Patent Application (No.89913155.1) (1998) 21 (9) I.P.D. 21100
Weiss, Re; *sub nom* Weiss v. Germany [2000] Crim. L.R. 484; *Independent*, February
    7, 2000 (C.S.), QBD
Weiss v. Germany see Weiss, Re
Welch v. O'Leary (Unreported, August 17, 1998), CC (Croydon) [*Ex rel*. Tim Kevan,
    Barrister, 1 Temple Gardens, Temple, London] . . . . *Digested*, 98/**3911**
Welch v. United Kingdom (A/307-A) (1995) 20 E.H.R.R. 247; *Times*, February 15,
    1995, ECHR . . . . *Digested*, 95/**2650**:
                         Applied, 00/1169: *Considered*, 01/1062, 01/6327
Weldon v. GRE Linked Life Assurance Ltd [2000] 2 All E.R. (Comm) 914, QBD . . . . *Digested*, 01/**4490**
Weldon v. Home Office see R. v. Deputy Governor of Parkhurst Prison Ex p. Weldon
Weldon Plant Ltd v. Commission for the New Towns [2001] 1 All E.R. (Comm) 264;
    [2000] B.L.R. 496; (2000) 2 T.C.L.R. 785; 77 Con. L.R. 1, QBD (T&CC) . . . . . . *Digested*, 01/**343**
Wellcome Foundation Ltd (Hitchings) Application, Re v. [1983] F.S.R. 593, CA (NZ);
    reversing [1980] R.P.C. 305, Sup Ct (NZ); reversing [1978] F.S.R. 51, PO (NZ) . *Digested*, 83/**2785**:
                                                 Considered, 01/3965
Wellcome Trust Ltd v. Hamad; *sub nom* Wellcome Trust Ltd v. Hammad; Ebied v.
    Hopkins; Church Commissioners for England v. Baines [1998] Q.B. 638; [1998]
    2 W.L.R. 156; [1998] 1 All E.R. 657; (1998) 30 H.L.R. 629; [1998] L. & T.R.
    130; [1998] 1 E.G.L.R. 73; [1998] 02 E.G. 121; *Times*, October 13, 1997, CA . . . . *Digested*, 97/**3334**:
                                                Applied, 98/3682
Wellcome Trust Ltd v. Hammad see Wellcome Trust Ltd v. Hamad
Wellcome Trust Ltd v. Romines [1999] 3 E.G.L.R. 229, Lands Tr . . . . *Digested*, 00/**3909**:
                                                Applied, 00/3898
Weller v. Dunbar (Unreported, January 27, 1984), CA . . . . *Considered*, 98/322
Wellingborough BC v. Ascott (1999) 14 P.A.D. 8, Planning Inspector
Wellingborough BC v. Bailey (1998) 13 P.A.D. 633, Planning Inspector
Wellington District Legal Services Committee v. Tangiora see Tangiora v. Wellington
    District Legal Services Committee
Wells v. Barnsley MBC see Leeds City Council v. Carr
Wells v. Bedfordshire CC see Wells v. Secretary of State for the Environment, Transport
    and the Regions
Wells v. Bournemouth BC [2000] R.V.R. 335, Lands Tr . . . . *Digested*, 01/**3400**
Wells v. First National Commercial Bank [1998] P.N.L.R. 552, CA . . . . *Digested*, 98/**3927**
Wells v. Hall (Unreported, March 13, 2001), CC (Macclesfield) [*Ex rel*. Silverbeck
    Rymer, Solicitors, Heywoods Building, 5 Brunswick Street, Liverpool] . . . . *Digested*, 01/**494**
Wells v. Minister of Housing and Local Government [1967] 1 W.L.R. 1000; [1967] 2
    All E.R. 1041; 131 J.P. 431; 65 L.G.R. 408; 18 P. & C.R. 401; 111 S.J. 519, CA;
    affirming 65 L.G.R. 43; 110 S.J. 889, DC . . . . *Digested*, 67/**3843**:
      Applied, 70/2781, 71/5852, 73/3254, 74/3765, 77/2985, 78/2904, 80/2665:
              Distinguished, 72/3362: *Followed*, 97/4063, 99/4235, 00/4421
Wells v. Secretary of State for the Environment, Transport and the Regions; *sub nom*
    Wells v. Bedfordshire CC [2001] EWHC Admin 227; [2001] J.P.L. 1438 (Note);
    [2001] 14 E.G.C.S. 147; (2001) 98(14) L.S.G. 42, QBD (Admin Ct)

Wells v. Wells; Thomas v. Brighton HA; Page v. Sheerness Steel Co Plc [1999] 1 A.C. 345; [1998] 3 W.L.R. 329; [1998] 3 All E.R. 481; [1998] I.R.L.R. 536; [1998] 2 F.L.R. 507; [1998] P.I.Q.R. Q56; (1998) 43 B.M.L.R. 99; [1998] Fam. Law 593; (1998) 95(35) L.S.G. 35; (1998) 148 N.L.J. 1087; (1998) 142 S.J.L.B. 245; *Times*, July 20, 1998; *Independent*, July 27, 1998 (C.S.), HL; reversing [1997] 1 W.L.R. 652; [1997] 1 All E.R. 673; [1997] P.I.Q.R. Q1; (1997) 37 B.M.L.R. 111; (1996) 93(40) L.S.G. 25; (1996) 140 S.J.L.B. 239; *Times*, October 24, 1996; *Independent*, November 13, 1996, CA; reversing [1996] P.I.Q.R. Q62, QBD . . . . *Digested*, 98/**1446**:
Applied, 98/1478, 98/1573, 00/1479, 00/1503, 01/1546: *Cited*, 00/1489, 00/6430: *Considered*, 98/1474, 99/1397, 99/5671: *Distinguished*, 00/1470, 01/6222: *Followed*, 97/1833, 99/1422, 99/5950, 99/5972, 99/5974, 00/1464, 00/1490, 00/1492, 00/5905, 00/6161, 00/6164
Wells v. West Hertfordshire HA TNS, QBD [*Ex rel.* Andrew Ritchie, Barrister, 9 Gough Square, London] . . . . *Digested*, 00/**2982**
Wells v. West Hertfordshire HA (Quantum) [2000] 6 Q.R. 7, QBD [*Ex rel.* Andrew Ritchie, Barrister, 9 Gough Square, London] . . . . *Digested*, 00/**1594**
Wells, In the Estate of see Wintle v. Nye (No.2)
Welsby v. Brelec Installations Ltd (In Liquidation); *sub nom* Brelec Installations Ltd, Re [2001] B.C.C. 421; [2000] 2 B.C.L.C. 576; [2001] B.P.I.R. 210; (2000) 97(20) L.S.G. 43; *Times*, April 18, 2000, Ch D . . . . *Digested*, 00/**3491**
Welsh v. Greenwich LBC (2001) 33 H.L.R. 40; (2001) 81 P. & C.R. 12; [2001] L. & T.R. 12; [2000] 3 E.G.L.R. 41; [2000] 49 E.G. 118; [2000] E.G.C.S. 84; (2000) 97(28) L.S.G. 32; (2000) 97(27) L.S.G. 40; *Times*, August 4, 2000, CA; affirming (Unreported, January 7, 1999), CC (Woolwich) [*Ex rel.* William Geldart, Barrister, 6 King's Bench Walk, Temple, London] . . . . *Digested*, 00/**3937**
Welsh v. MacBryde Homes Plc (Unreported, December 11, 1998), CC (Liverpool) [*Ex rel.* Paul Simpson, Barrister, First National Chambers, 24 Fenwick Street, Liverpool] . . . . *Digested*, 99/**788**
Welsh Development Agency v. Carmarthenshire CC (2000) 80 P. & C.R. 192; [2000] J.P.L. 692; [1999] E.G.C.S. 119, CA . . . . *Digested*, 00/**4474**
Welsh Development Agency v. Redpath Dorman Long Ltd [1994] 1 W.L.R. 1409; [1994] 4 All E.R. 10; 67 B.L.R. 1; 38 Con. L.R. 106; (1994) 10 Const. L.J. 325; (1994) 91(21) L.S.G. 42; (1994) 138 S.J.L.B. 87; *Times*, April 4, 1994; *Independent*, May 2, 1994 (C.S.), CA . . . . *Digested*, 95/**4191**:
Applied, 97/1047: *Considered*, 96/859, 97/2719, 99/481: *Distinguished*, 96/820, 99/542
Welthgrove BV v. Staatssecretaris van Financien (C102/00) [2001] E.C.R. I-5679; [2001] 3 C.M.L.R. 43, ECJ (1st Chamber)
Wenborn & Co, Re [1905] 1 Ch. 413, Ch D . . . . *Considered*, 01/**507**
Wendy Fair Markets Ltd v. Secretary of State for the Environment; Huggett v. Secretary of State for the Environment; Bello v. Secretary of State for the Environment [1996] J.P.L. 649; (1995) 159 L.G. Rev. 769; (1995) 139 S.J.L.B. 93; *Times*, March 1, 1995, CA [1995] E.G.C.S. 17, QBD . . . . *Digested*, 96/**4728**:
Followed, 99/45
Wenham v. Bexley (Unreported, July 15, 1999), CC (Central London) [*Ex rel.* Andrew Ritchie, Barrister, 9 Gough Square, London] . . . . *Digested*, 99/**2879**
Wenlock v. Moloney [1965] 1 W.L.R. 1238; [1965] 2 All E.R. 871; 109 S.J. 496, CA . . . . *Digested*, 65/**3232**:
Considered, 81/1251, 82/285, 94/3445, 95/861, 95/4938: *Distinguished*, 75/2568: *Followed*, 98/3416: *Subsequent proceedings*, 68/186
Wentwalk Ltd v. Customs and Excise Commissioners see Granton Marketing Ltd v. Customs and Excise Commissioners
Werner v. Austria; Szucs v. Austria (1998) 26 E.H.R.R. 310; [1998] H.R.C.D. 85, ECHR . *Digested*, 98/**3121**
Wesley v. Cobb (Deceased) (Unreported, January 19, 2000), CC (Altrincham) [*Ex rel.* Myers Lister Price, Solicitors, 376 Palatine Road, Northenden, Manchester] . . . . *Digested*, 00/**1558**
Wesley Jessen Corp v. Coopervision Ltd; *sub nom* Ciba Vision UK Ltd v. Coopervision Ltd (2001) 24(10) I.P.D. 24067; (2001) 98(31) L.S.G. 37; *Times*, July 31, 2001, Pat Ct . . . . *Digested*, 01/**3882**
West (A Minor) v. Kerr (Unreported, August 10, 1998), CC (Leicester) [*Ex rel.* Stuart R Yeung, Barrister, 22 Albion Place, Northampton] . . . . *Digested*, 98/**1496**
West v. Blanchet [2000] 1 B.C.L.C. 795; *Times*, February 9, 2000, Ch D . . . . *Digested*, 00/**687**
West (Inspector of Taxes) v. Crossland see West (Inspector of Taxes) v. O'Neill
West (Inspector of Taxes) v. O'Neill; West (Inspector of Taxes) v. Crossland [1999] S.T.C. 147; 71 T.C. 314; [1999] B.T.C. 32; *Times*, February 9, 1999, Ch D . . . . *Digested*, 99/**4712**
West v. Sharp (2000) 79 P. & C.R. 327; (1999) 96(19) L.S.G. 29; (1999) 78 P. & C.R. D31, CA . . . . *Digested*, 00/**4638**
West Berkshire DC v. Keeps Care Children's Home (2000) 15 P.A.D. 18, Planning Inspector
West Berkshire DC v. Langdon (2000) 15 P.A.D. 325, Planning Inspector
West Bowers Farm Products v. Essex CC (1985) 50 P. & C.R. 368; [1985] 1 E.G.L.R. 271; [1985] R.V.R. 176; [1985] J.P.L. 857, CA . . . . *Digested*, 86/**3326**:
Considered, 01/4659

West Bromwich Building Society v. Mander Hadley & Co [1998] C.L.C. 814; [1998]
   N.P.C. 30; *Times*, March 9, 1998; *Independent*, March 10, 1998, CA;
   reversing CH-1995-W-No.7967, Ch D . . . .   *Digested*, 98/**559**
West Central Halifax Partnership Ltd v. Customs and Excise Commissioners [2000]
   B.V.C. 2295; [2000] S.T.I. 960, V&DTr
West Cheshire Caravan Co Ltd v. Ellesmere Port BC [1976] 1 E.G.L.R. 143; (1975) 237
   E.G. 573; [1976] J.P.L. 235, DC . . . .   *Digested*, 76/**2689**:
                              Distinguished, 00/4512: *Followed*, 96/4740
West Cumberland Iron and Steel Co, Re (1889) L.R. 40 Ch. D. 361, Ch D . . . .   *Followed*, 99/3361
West Devon BC v. Customs and Excise Commissioners; *sub nom* West Devon DC v.
   Customs and Excise Commissioners [2001] S.T.C. 1282; [2001] B.T.C. 5463;
   [2001] B.V.C. 525; [2001] S.T.I. 1106; (2001) 98(38) L.S.G. 39, Ch D [2001]
   S.T.I. 985, V&DTr . . . .   *Digested*, 01/**5579**
West Devon BC v. Wigens (1998) 13 P.A.D. 393, Planning Inspector
West Devon DC v. Customs and Excise Commissioners see West Devon BC v. Customs
   and Excise Commissioners
West Dorset DC v. AG Jessopp Ltd (1998) 13 P.A.D. 11, Planning Inspector
West Dunbartonshire Council v. Wallace see Strathclyde RC v. Wallace
West Glamorgan CC v. Confrey; *sub nom* West Glamorgan CC v. Special Educational
   Needs Tribunal [1998] E.L.R. 121; [1997] C.O.D. 34, QBD . . . .   *Digested*, 98/**1982**
West Glamorgan CC v. Special Educational Needs Tribunal see West Glamorgan CC v.
   Confrey
West Herts College v. Customs and Excise Commissioners see Customs and Excise
   Commissioners v. West Herts College
West Kent College v. Richardson [1999] I.C.R. 511, EAT . . . .   *Digested*, 99/**2104**
West Kent Housing Association Ltd v. Davies (1999) 31 H.L.R. 415; [1998] E.G.C.S.
   103, CA . . . .   *Digested*, 99/**3708**:
                                        Applied, 00/3923
West Lancashire DC v. Autism Initiatives (2001) 16 P.A.D. 77, Planning Inspector
West Lancashire DC v. J Rothwell and Son Ltd (1998) 13 P.A.D. 41, Planning Inspector
West Lancashire DC v. Pincock (2001) 16 P.A.D. 57, Planning Inspector
West Lancashire DC v. Secretary of State for the Environment, Transport and the
   Regions [1998] J.P.L. 1086; [1998] E.G.C.S. 33; (1998) 95(9) L.S.G. 30, QBD .   *Digested*, 98/**4184**
West Lancashire DC v. Secretary of State for the Environment, Transport and the
   Regions [1999] J.P.L. 890, CA . . . .   *Digested*, 99/**4206**
West Middlesex Golf Club Ltd v. Ealing LBC (1994) 68 P. & C.R. 461; [1993] E.G.C.S.
   136; [1993] N.P.C. 109, Ch D . . . .   *Digested*, 95/**832**:
                               Followed, 97/3307, 98/3769
West Midland Baptist (Trust) Association Inc v. Birmingham Corp see Birmingham Corp
   v. West Midland Baptist (Trust) Association Inc
West Midland Cooperative Society v. Tipton [1986] A.C. 536; [1986] 2 W.L.R. 306;
   [1986] 1 All E.R. 513; [1986] I.C.R. 192; [1986] I.R.L.R. 112; (1986) 83 L.S.G.
   780; (1986) 136 N.L.J. 163; (1986) 130 S.J. 143, HL; reversing [1985] I.C.R.
   444; [1985] I.R.L.R. 116; (1985) 82 L.S.G. 2009, CA; reversing [1983] I.R.L.R.
   276, EAT . . . .   *Digested*, 86/**1285**:
                Applied, 86/1283, 87/1407, 89/1500: *Approved*, 94/2017:
                      Considered, 87/1319, 91/1696: *Distinguished*, 98/2232
West Midlands Passenger Transport Executive v. Singh [1988] 1 W.L.R. 730; [1988] 2
   All E.R. 873; [1988] I.C.R. 614; [1988] I.R.L.R. 186; (1988) 132 S.J. 933, CA . .   *Digested*, 88/**1296**:
                         Applied, 00/5516: *Considered*, 89/1432, 90/1910
West Midlands Probation Committee v. Secretary of State for the Environment,
   Transport and the Regions; *sub nom* Walsall MBC v. West Midlands Probation
   Committee (1998) 10 Admin. L.R. 297; (1998) 76 P. & C.R. 589; [1998] J.P.L.
   388; [1997] N.P.C. 157; *Times*, December 1, 1997; *Independent*, November 13,
   1997, CA; affirming [1997] J.P.L. 323; [1996] N.P.C. 135; *Times*, October 18,
   1996, QBD; affirming (1996) 11 P.A.D. 167, Planning Inspector . . . .   *Digested*, 97/**4097**
West Norwood Cemetery (No.1), Re [1994] Fam. 210; [1994] 3 W.L.R. 820; [1995] 1 All
   E.R. 387; *Times*, April 11, 1994, Cons Ct (Southwark) . . . .   *Digested*, 94/**1790**
West Norwood Cemetery (No.2), Re [1998] Fam. 84; [1998] 3 W.L.R. 128; [1998] 1 All E.R.
   606, Cons Ct (Southwark) . . . .   *Digested*, 98/**1787**
West of England Ship Owners Mutual Protection and Indemnity Association (Luxembourg)
   v. Hellenic Industrial Development Bank SA [1999] 1 Lloyd's Rep. 93; [1998]
   C.L.C. 1431, QBD (Comm Ct) . . . .   *Digested*, 99/**4462**
West of England Shipowners Mutual Insurance Association (Luxembourg) v. Cristal Ltd
   (The Glacier Bay) [1996] 1 Lloyd's Rep. 370; [1996] C.L.C. 240; *Times*,
   October 26, 1995; *Independent*, November 1, 1995, CA; reversing [1995] 1
   Lloyd's Rep. 560; *Lloyd's List*, March 15, 1995, QBD (Comm Ct) . . . .   *Digested*, 96/**5373**:
                                        Considered, 98/3405
West Oxfordshire DC v. Secretary of State for the Environment (1988) 56 P. & C.R.
   434; [1988] 1 P.L.R. 73; [1988] J.P.L. 324, QBD . . . .   *Digested*, 89/**3553**:
                                   Considered, 95/4770, 01/4690
West Riding CC v. Huddersfield Corp [1957] 1 Q.B. 540; [1957] 2 W.L.R. 428; [1957]
   1 All E.R. 669; 121 J.P. 219; 55 L.G.R. 153; 101 S.J. 209, QBD . . . .   *Digested*, 57/**2025**:
                                        Applied, 01/3784

West Sussex CC *v.* Secretary of State for the Environment, Transport and the Regions [1999] P.L.C.R. 365, CA . . . . *Digested*, 00/**4527**
West Sussex Properties Ltd *v.* Chichester DC; *sub nom* Chichester DC *v.* West Sussex Properties Ltd [2000] N.P.C. 74, CA
West Wiltshire DC *v.* Hocken (1998) 13 P.A.D. 266, Planning Inspector
West Wiltshire DC *v.* Pertwood Partners (1999) 14 P.A.D. 649, Planning Inspector
West Wiltshire DC *v.* Snelgrove (1998) 30 H.L.R. 57; [1997] C.O.D. 452, QBD . . . . *Digested*, 97/**3290**
Westacre Investments Inc *v.* Jugoimport SPDR Holding Co Ltd [2000] Q.B. 288; [1999] 3 W.L.R. 811; [1999] 3 All E.R. 864; [1999] 1 All E.R. (Comm) 865; [1999] 2 Lloyd's Rep. 65; [1999] C.L.C. 1176; [1999] B.L.R. 279; *Times*, May 25, 1999; *Independent*, May 25, 1999, CA; affirming [1999] Q.B. 740; [1998] 3 W.L.R. 770; [1998] 4 All E.R. 570; [1998] 2 Lloyd's Rep. 111; [1998] C.L.C. 409, QBD (Comm Ct) . . . . *Digested*, 99/**236**:
Applied, 99/230

Westbourne Galleries, Re see Ebrahimi *v.* Westbourne Galleries Ltd
Westbury *v.* Sampson [2001] EWCA Civ 407; [2001] 2 F.C.R. 210; (2001) 98(20) L.S.G. 44, CA . . . . *Digested*, 01/**4533**
Westbury Settlement, Re (2000-01) 3 I.T.E.L.R. 699, Royal Ct (Jer)
Westdeutsche Landesbank Girozentrale *v.* Islington LBC; Kleinwort Benson Ltd *v.* Sandwell BC [1996] A.C. 669; [1996] 2 W.L.R. 802; [1996] 2 All E.R. 961; [1996] 5 Bank. L.R. 341; [1996] C.L.C. 990; (1996) 160 J.P. Rep. 1130; (1996) 146 N.L.J. 877; (1996) 140 S.J.L.B. 136; *Times*, May 30, 1996, HL; reversing [1994] 1 W.L.R. 938; [1994] 4 All E.R. 890; 92 L.G.R. 405; (1994) 158 L.G. Rev. 981; (1994) 91(8) L.S.G. 29; (1994) 138 S.J.L.B. 26; *Times*, December 30, 1993; *Independent*, January 5, 1994, CA; affirming 91 L.G.R. 323; *Times*, February 23, 1993 . . . . *Digested*, 96/**4149**:
Applied, 98/304, 00/2320: *Considered*, 97/712, 98/1433:
Distinguished, 95/4151: *Followed*, 98/231, 99/278
Westerman *v.* Travel Promotions Ltd (Unreported, November 26, 1999), CC (Stafford) [*Ex rel.* Matthew Chapman, Barrister, Barnard's Inn Chambers, Halton House, 20-23 Holborn, London] . . . . *Digested*, 00/**4042**
Western Digital Corp *v.* British Airways Plc [2001] Q.B. 733; [2000] 3 W.L.R. 1855; [2001] 1 All E.R. 109; [2000] 2 All E.R. (Comm) 647; [2000] 2 Lloyd's Rep. 142; [2000] C.L.C. 1276; (2000) 144 S.J.L.B. 273; *Times*, June 28, 2000; *Independent*, July 10, 2000 (C.S), CA; reversing in part [1999] 2 All E.R. (Comm) 270; [1999] 2 Lloyd's Rep. 380; [1999] C.L.C. 1681; *Times*, July 23, 1999, QBD (Comm Ct) . . . . *Digested*, 00/**5164**:
Considered, 01/930
Western Excavating (ECC) Ltd *v.* Sharp [1978] Q.B. 761; [1978] 2 W.L.R. 344; [1978] 1 All E.R. 713; [1978] I.C.R. 221; (1978) 13 I.T.R. 132; (1987) 121 S.J. 814; *Times*, November 16, 1977, CA; reversing [1978] I.R.L.R. 27, EAT . . . . *Digested*, 78/**900**:
Applied, 78/891, 78/893, 78/904, 79/838, 80/892, 81/981, 82/1097, 84/1194, 88/1247, 90/1929, 01/2234: *Considered*, 80/883, 80/1008, 81/807, 81/808, 86/1261, 88/1291, 89/1458, 99/2030: *Distinguished*, 79/846:
Explained, 80/893
Western Fish Products Ltd *v.* Penwith DC [1981] 2 All E.R. 204; 77 L.G.R. 185; (1979) 38 P. & C.R. 7; [1978] J.P.L. 623; 122 S.J. 471, CA . . . . *Digested*, 81/**2732**:
Applied, 81/2683, 93/3858: *Cited*, 93/3848: *Considered*, 94/4470, 96/4767:
Distinguished, 88/3432, 98/4159: *Followed*, 97/4063, 99/4203, 00/4421
Western Intelligence Ltd *v.* KDO Label Printing Machines Ltd (In Administrative Receivership) [1998] B.C.C. 472; *Times*, July 15, 1998, Ch D . . . . *Digested*, 98/**3317**
Western Steamship Co Ltd *v.* NV Koninklijke Rotterdamsche Lloyd (The Empire Jamaica) see NV Koninklijke Rotterdamsche Lloyd *v.* Western Steamship Co Ltd (The Empire Jamaica)
Western Trust & Savings Ltd *v.* Clive Travers & Co [1997] P.N.L.R. 295; (1998) 75 P. & C.R. 200, CA. . . . . *Digested*, 97/**3827**
Western Trust & Savings Ltd *v.* Strutt & Parker [1999] P.N.L.R. 154; [1998] 3 E.G.L.R. 89; [1998] 44 E.G. 208; [1998] E.G.C.S. 121; [1998] N.P.C. 116; *Times*, September 17, 1998, CA. . . . . *Digested*, 98/**4034**
Westinghouse Electric Corp and Duquesne Light Co, Re (1977) 16 O.R. (2d) 273, HC (Ont)
Applied, 00/330
Westlake *v.* JP Cave & Co [1998] N.P.C. 3, QBD
Westley *v.* Hertfordshire CC (1998) 76 P. & C.R. 518; [1998] 2 P.L.R. 72; [1998] J.P.L. 947; [1998] N.P.C. 24; *Times*, March 5, 1998, QBD . . . . *Digested*, 98/**2874**
Westlowe Storage & Distribution Ltd (In Liquidation), Re [2000] B.C.C. 851; [2000] 2 B.C.L.C. 590; *Independent*, November 29, 1999 (C.S.), Ch D . . . . *Digested*, 00/**3470**
Westmaze Ltd (In Administrative Receivership), Re [1999] B.C.C. 441; *Times*, July 15, 1998, Ch D . . . . *Digested*, 98/**3334**
Westmid Packaging Services Ltd (No.1), Re; *sub nom* Secretary of State for Trade and Industry *v.* Griffiths (No.1) [1995] B.C.C. 203, Ch D . . . . *Digested*, 96/**979**
Westmid Packaging Services Ltd (No.2), Re; *sub nom* Secretary of State for Trade and Industry *v.* Griffiths (No.2) [1998] 2 All E.R. 124; [1998] B.C.C. 836; [1998] 2 B.C.L.C. 646; *Times*, December 29, 1997; *Independent*, January 13, 1998, CA . . *Digested*, 98/**663**:
Applied, 00/656

Westminister City Council v. Flatford Ltd (2000) 15 P.A.D. 68, Planning Inspector

Westminster Bank Ltd v. Beverley BC see Westminster Bank Ltd v. Minister of Housing and Local Government

Westminster Bank Ltd v. Beverley Corp see Westminster Bank Ltd v. Minister of Housing and Local Government

Westminster Bank Ltd v. Minister of Housing and Local Government; *sub nom* Westminster Bank Ltd v. Beverley BC; Westminster Bank Ltd v. Beverley Corp [1971] A.C. 508; [1970] 2 W.L.R. 645; [1970] 1 All E.R. 734; (1969) 21 P. & C.R. 379; 114 S.J. 190, HL; affirming [1969] 1 Q.B. 499; [1968] 3 W.L.R. 671; [1968] 2 All E.R. 1199; 132 J.P. 468; 66 L.G.R. 687; 19 P. & C.R. 644; 112 S.J. 585, CA; reversing [1968] 2 W.L.R. 1080; [1968] 2 All E.R. 104; 132 J.P. 291; 19 P. & C.R. 399; [1968] R.V.R. 186; 112 S.J. 215, QBD . . . . *Digested,* 70/**2780**:
Applied, 70/2778, 72/3364, 75/3335, 00/4408: *Considered,* 89/3643, 90/4452: *Followed,* 71/10949, 95/6080

Westminster City Council v. Bass Taverns Ltd (1999) 14 P.A.D. 336, Planning Inspector

Westminster City Council v. Blenheim Leisure (Restaurants) Ltd (No.1); *sub nom* Blenheim Leisure (Restaurants) Ltd v. Westminster City Council (No.1); Westminster City Council v. Langer (No.1); Westminster City Council v. Cura (No.1) [1999] E.H.L.R. Dig. 203, QBD

Westminster City Council v. Blenheim Leisure (Restaurants) Ltd (No.2); Westminster City Council v. Langer (No.2); Westminster City Council v. Cura (No.2) (1999) 163 J.P. 401; *Times,* February 24, 1999; *Independent,* March 1, 1999 (C.S.), QBD . . . . *Digested,* 99/**955**

Westminster City Council v. City Cruises Plc (2001) 16 P.A.D. 36, Planning Inspector

Westminster City Council v. Clarke [1992] 2 A.C. 288; [1992] 2 W.L.R. 229; [1992] 1 All E.R. 695; (1992) 24 H.L.R. 360; 90 L.G.R. 210; (1992) 156 L.G. Rev. 681; [1992] E.G.C.S. 13; (1992) 142 N.L.J. 196; (1992) 136 S.J.L.B. 82; [1992] N.P.C. 18; *Times,* February 13, 1992; *Independent,* February 7, 1992; *Guardian,* February 12, 1992, HL; reversing (1991) 23 H.L.R. 506; 89 L.G.R. 917; [1991] E.G.C.S. 35; *Times,* March 25, 1991; *Independent,* March 29, 1991; *Daily Telegraph,* April 1, 1991, CA. . . . . *Digested,* 92/**2290**:
Followed, 98/3664, 00/3878

Westminster City Council v. Crown Estate (2001) 16 P.A.D. 100, Planning Inspector

Westminster City Council v. Cura (No.1) see Westminster City Council v. Blenheim Leisure (Restaurants) Ltd (No.1)

Westminster City Council v. Cura (No.2) see Westminster City Council v. Blenheim Leisure (Restaurants) Ltd (No.2)

Westminster City Council v. Football Association (1998) 13 P.A.D. 170, Planning Inspector

Westminster City Council v. Great Portland Estates Plc; *sub nom* Great Portland Estates Plc v. Westminster City Council [1985] A.C. 661; [1984] 3 W.L.R. 1035; [1984] 3 All E.R. 744; (1985) 50 P. & C.R. 34; [1985] J.P.L. 108; (1984) 81 L.S.G. 3501; (1984) 128 S.J. 784, HL; reversing (1985) 49 P. & C.R. 20; [1984] J.P.L. 510, CA . . . . *Digested,* 84/**3413**:
Applied, 92/450, 94/4320, 95/4767, 01/4683, 01/4762:
Considered, 85/3437, 90/4428, 90/4475, 91/3561, 92/4277, 93/3938, 97/4090, 98/4213, 00/5658, 01/4708: *Distinguished,* 92/4264:
Followed, 96/2760, 97/2357, 97/4070, 01/4733: *Referred to,* 84/3442, 93/3947

Westminster City Council v. Haywood (No.1) [1998] Ch. 377; [1997] 3 W.L.R. 641; [1997] 2 All E.R. 84; [1998] I.C.R. 920; (1997) 9 Admin. L.R. 489; [1997] O.P.L.R. 61; *Times,* February 12, 1997; *Independent,* February 12, 1997, CA; reversing [1996] 3 W.L.R. 563; [1996] 2 All E.R. 467; [1996] O.P.L.R. 95; [1996] C.O.D. 408; *Times,* March 12, 1996, Ch D . . . . *Digested,* 97/**4010**:
Followed, 96/4660

Westminster City Council v. Haywood (No.2) [2000] 2 All E.R. 634; [2000] I.C.R. 827; [2000] B.L.G.R. 526; [2000] O.P.L.R. 175; [2000] Pens. L.R. 235; (2000) 97(5) L.S.G. 34; (2000) 144 S.J.L.B. 58; *Times,* March 10, 2000; *Times,* January 26, 2000 ; *Independent,* February 21, 2000 (C.S.), Ch D . . . . *Digested,* 00/**105**

Westminster City Council v. Langer (No.1) see Westminster City Council v. Blenheim Leisure (Restaurants) Ltd (No.1)

Westminster City Council v. Langer (No.2) see Westminster City Council v. Blenheim Leisure (Restaurants) Ltd (No.2)

Westminster City Council v. Mendoza; *sub nom* R. v. Horseferry Road Magistrates Court Ex p. Rezouali; Westminster City Council v. Rezouali [2001] EWCA Civ 216; [2001] E.H.L.R. 16; [2001] N.P.C. 56; *Times,* March 22, 2001; *Daily Telegraph,* March 6, 2001, CA; affirming in part *Times,* April 12, 2000, QBD . . . . *Digested,* 01/**4380**

Westminster City Council v. Miller Developments Ltd see Westminster City Council v. Secretary of State for the Environment

Westminster City Council v. Moran (1999) 77 P. & C.R. 294; [1998] 4 P.L.R. 79; [1999] J.P.L. 41; *Times,* October 14, 1998; *Independent,* June 22, 1998 (C.S.), QBD . . . . *Digested,* 98/**4155**

Westminster City Council v. National Asylum Support Service see R. (on the application of Westminster City Council) v. National Asylum Support Services

Westminster City Council v. Parkin see Parkins v. Westminster City Council (Appeal against Bankruptcy)

Westminster City Council v. Reform Club Secretary (2001) 16 P.A.D. 98, Planning Inspector

Westminster City Council v. Rezouali see Westminster City Council v. Mendoza

Westminster City Council v. Secretary of State for the Environment; Westminster City Council v. Miller Developments Ltd [1991] 2 P.L.R. 44; [1992] J.P.L. 24, QBD . . *Digested, 92/4343: Considered, 99/4173*

Westminster City Council v. Southern Railway Co Ltd; *sub nom* Westminster Corp v. Southern Railway Co Ltd; Kent Valuation Committee v. Southern Railway Co Ltd [1936] A.C. 511; [1936] 2 All E.R. 322; 34 L.G.R. 313, HL . . . . *Applied, 47-51/8291,* 47-51/8292, 47-51/8316, 47-51/8317, 55/2275, 65/3332, 66/10227, 66/10256, 75/2762, 78/216, 79/244, 98/4319, 01/4820: *Considered,* 66/10233, 66/14375, 73/2778, 73/3933, 88/2997, 88/3011, 88/3029: *Distinguished,* 99/4333: *Followed,* 60/3938, 61/7437, 99/4335

Westminster City Council v. Tomlin [1989] 1 W.L.R. 1287; [1990] 1 All E.R. 920; (1990) 154 J.P. 165; 88 L.G.R. 29; [1990] R.A. 79; [1989] C.O.D. 235; (1990) 154 J.P.N. 140; (1990) 154 L.G. Rev. 156; (1989) 133 S.J. 1033, CA; affirming (1989) 153 J.P. 247; [1988] R.V.R. 196; (1989) 153 L.G. Rev. 267; *Times,* August 25, 1988, QBD . . . . *Digested, 90/3913: Applied, 01/4820*

Westminster City Council v. UNISON see UNISON v. Westminster City Council

Westminster City Council v. Wingrove [1991] 1 Q.B. 652; [1991] 2 W.L.R. 708; [1991] 4 All E.R. 691; (1991) 92 Cr. App. R. 179; (1991) 155 J.P. 303; [1991] Crim. L.R. 43; [1991] C.O.D. 85; (1990) 154 J.P.N. 754, QBD . . . . *Digested, 91/725: Applied, 00/1037*

Westminster Corp v. Southern Railway Co Ltd see Westminster City Council v. Southern Railway Co Ltd

Westminster Property Management Ltd (No.1), Re; *sub nom* Official Receiver v. Stern (No.1) [2000] 1 W.L.R. 2230; [2001] 1 All E.R. 633; [2001] B.C.C. 121; [2000] 2 B.C.L.C. 396; [2000] U.K.H.R.R. 332; *Independent,* February 10, 2000, CA; affirming [2001] 1 All E.R. 633; [2000] Eu. L.R. 342; (2000) 97(5) L.S.G. 33; (2000) 150 N.L.J. 21; (2000) 144 S.J.L.B. 80; *Times,* January 19, 2000, Ch D (Companies Ct) . . . . *Digested, 00/665*

Westminster Property Management Ltd (No.2), Re; *sub nom* Official Receiver v. Stern (No.2) [2001] EWCA Civ 111, CA; affirming [2001] B.C.C. 305, Ch D (Companies Ct) . . . . *Digested, 01/716*

Westmoquette v. Dean (Unreported, April 3, 1998), QBD [*Ex rel.* Gerard Martin, Barrister, Exchange Chambers, Pearl Assurance House, Derby Square, Liverpool] . . . . *Digested, 98/1477*

Westmoreland Investments Ltd v. MacNiven (Inspector of Taxes) see Macniven (Inspector of Taxes) v. Westmoreland Investments Ltd

Weston v. Inland Revenue Commissioners [2000] S.T.C. 1064; [2000] B.T.C. 8041; [2001] W.T.L.R. 1217; [2000] S.T.I. 1635; (2001) 98(2) L.S.G. 41; [2000] N.P.C. 126; *Times,* November 29, 2000, Ch D . . . . *Digested, 01/5283*

Weston v. Law Society (1998) 95(31) L.S.G. 35; (1998) 142 S.J.L.B. 250; *Times,* July 15, 1998, QBD . . . . *Digested, 98/3723*

Westside Nominees Ltd v. Bolton MBC (2001) 81 P. & C.R. 11; [2000] L. & T.R. 533; [2000] E.G.C.S. 20, Ch D . . . . *Digested, 01/4159*

Weth v. Attorney General (No.1) [2001] EWCA Civ 263, CA; affirming [2001] W.T.L.R. 155, Ch D

Weth v. Attorney General (No.2) [1999] 1 W.L.R. 686; [2001] W.T.L.R. 183; (1998) 95(41) L.S.G. 45; (1998) 142 S.J.L.B. 271; *Times,* October 12, 1998; *Independent,* October 15, 1998, CA . . . . *Digested, 98/311*

Wetherall v. Harrison [1976] Q.B. 773; [1976] 2 W.L.R. 168; [1976] 1 All E.R. 241; [1976] R.T.R. 125; [1976] Crim. L.R. 54; 119 S.J. 848, QBD . . . . *Digested, 76/1690: Applied,* 80/931, 82/2781: *Followed,* 99/1018

WEYERSHAEUSER/Cellulose (T727/95) [2001] E.P.O.R. 35, EPO (Technical Bd App) . *Digested, 01/3912*

Weyl Beef Products BV v. Commission of the European Communities (T197/97); Groninger Vleeshandel BV v. Commission of the European Communities (T198/97) [2001] E.C.R. II-303; [2001] 2 C.M.L.R. 22, CFI (4th Chamber) . . . . *Digested, 01/786*

Weymouth and Portland BC v. Simpson (Unreported, September 10, 1999), QBD [*Ex rel.* Pip Punwar, Barrister, Francis Taylor Building, Temple, London] . . . . *Digested, 00/3958*

WGS v. United Kingdom [2000] B.C.C. 719, ECHR . . . . *Digested, 00/666*

WH Martin Ltd v. Feldbinder Spezialfahrzeugwerke GmbH; *sub nom* WH Martin Ltd v. Spezialfahrzeugwerke GmbH [1998] I.L.Pr. 794, CA . . . . *Digested, 98/747*

WH Martin Ltd v. Spezialfahrzeugwerke GmbH see WH Martin Ltd v. Feldbinder Spezialfahrzeugwerke GmbH

WH Smith Ltd v. Colman (t/a Cherished Domains) [2001] F.S.R. 9, CA . . . . *Digested, 01/397*

WH Smith Ltd v. Customs and Excise Commissioners [2000] B.V.C. 2237; [2000] S.T.I. 839, V&DTr

WH Tolley & Son Ltd v. Secretary of State for the Environment; WH Tolley & Son Ltd v. Torridge DC (1998) 75 P. & C.R. 533, QBD . . . . *Digested, 98/4216*

WH Tolley & Son Ltd v. Torridge DC see WH Tolley & Son Ltd v. Secretary of State for the Environment

Whaley v. Lord Watson of Invergowrie; *sub nom* Whalley v. Lord Watson of Invergowrie 2000 S.C. 340; 2000 S.L.T. 475; 2000 S.C.L.R. 279; 2000 G.W.D. 8-272; *Times*, March 21, 2000, 1 Div; affirming in part 2000 S.C. 125; 1999 G.W.D. 39-1882, OH . . . . *Digested*, 00/**5975**

Whalley v. Lord Watson of Invergowrie see Whaley v. Lord Watson of Invergowrie

Whalley v. Roberts & Roberts [1955-95] P.N.L.R. 506; [1990] 06 E.G. 104, QBD . . . . . *Digested*, 90/**3305**

Wharf v. Bildwell Insulations Ltd 1988-N-16, QBD . . . . *Digested*, 99/**2047**

Wharmby v. Customs and Excise Commissioners [2000] S.T.I. 672, V&DTr

Wheat v. E Lacon & Co Ltd [1966] A.C. 552; [1966] 2 W.L.R. 581; [1966] 1 All E.R. 582; [1966] R.A. 193; [1966] R.V.R. 223; 110 S.J. 149, HL; affirming [1966] 1 Q.B. 335; [1965] 3 W.L.R. 142; [1965] 2 All E.R. 700; 109 S.J. 334, CA . . . . . . *Digested*, 66/**8132**:
Applied, 71/7847, 93/2976, 01/4503: *Approved*, 66/10256:
Considered, 70/1191, 75/2006, 75/2342, 76/1649, 93/2688, 99/4003, 00/4240

Wheatley v. Credit Suisse see Israel-British Bank Ltd (In Liquidation), Re

Wheatley v. Drillsafe Ltd [2001] R.P.C. 7; *Times*, July 25, 2000, CA; reversing in part (1999) 22(5) I.P.D. 22044, Pat Ct . . . . *Digested*, 00/**3639**

Wheatley v. Wheatley [1999] 2 F.L.R. 205; [1999] B.P.I.R. 431; [1999] Fam. Law 375, QBD [*Ex rel.* Timothy VR Hanson, Barrister, St Phillips Chambers, Fountain Court, Steelhouse Lane, Birmingham] . . . . *Digested*, 99/**3261**

Wheelan v. Seed Crushers (Scotland) Ltd (No.1); *sub nom* Walker v. Seed Crushers (Scotland) Ltd 1998 S.L.T. 1308; 1998 S.C.C.R. 293; [1998] Env. L.R. 586; 1998 G.W.D. 13-671, HCJ Appeal; reversing 1997 G.W.D. 32-1630, Sh Ct . . . . *Digested*, 98/**5829**

Wheeldon v. Burrows (1879) L.R. 12 Ch. D. 31; [1874-90] All E.R. Rep. 669; (1879) 48 L.J. Ch. 853; (1879) 41 L.T. 327, CA . . . . *Applied*, 69/1153,
69/1158, 00/4631: *Considered*, 70/823, 72/1109, 77/333, 81/743, 83/224, 87/1231, 88/1181, 88/2088, 95/3740, 00/4640: *Distinguished*, 68/1313:
Followed, 47-51/3227, 93/3007: *Not followed*, 66/4174, 66/4176

Wheeldon v. Wheeldon [1998] 1 F.L.R. 463; [1997] 3 F.C.R. 769; [1997] Fam. Law 602, CA . . . . *Digested*, 98/**2449**

Wheeler v. Le Marchant (1881) L.R. 17 Ch. D. 675, CA . . . . *Applied*, 55/2119,
82/2552: *Considered*, 63/2767: *Followed*, 69/2838, 98/355

Wheeler v. Mercer [1957] A.C. 416; [1956] 3 W.L.R. 841; [1956] 3 All E.R. 631; 100 S.J. 836, HL; reversing [1956] 1 Q.B. 274; [1955] 3 W.L.R. 714; [1955] 3 All E.R. 455; 99 S.J. 794, CA . . . . *Digested*, 56/**4861**:
Applied, 75/1884, 99/3669: *Considered*, 70/1526, 91/2218:
Distinguished, 86/1838

Wheeler v. Patel [1987] I.C.R. 631; [1987] I.R.L.R. 211; (1987) 84 L.S.G. 1240, EAT . . . *Digested*, 87/**1416**:
Applied, 89/1507: *Considered*, 98/2213

Wheeler v. Smith [2001] 6 Q.R. 12, CC (Oxford) [*Ex rel.* Amanda Millmore, Barrister, 4 King's Bench Walk, Temple, London] . . . . *Digested*, 01/**1656**

Whelan Group (Ennis) Ltd v. Clare CC [2001] 3 C.M.L.R. 31, HC (Irl)

Whelan's Application, Re [1990] N.I. 348, CA (NI) . . . . *Digested*, 94/**4983**:
Applied, 99/5221

Whidbourne v. Troth see Worldhams Park Golf Course Ltd, Re

Whiddett v. Phillips (1999) 99(5) Q.R. 7, CC (Hertford) [*Ex rel.* Andrew Granville Stafford, Barrister, 4 King's Bench Walk, Temple, London] . . . . *Digested*, 99/**1582**

Whiffen v. Milham Ford Girls School; Whiffen v. Oxfordshire CC [2001] EWCA Civ 385; [2001] I.C.R. 1023; [2001] I.R.L.R. 468; [2001] Emp. L.R. 541; [2001] B.L.G.R. 309; (2001) 98(23) L.S.G. 36; *Times*, April 3, 2001, CA . . . . *Digested*, 01/**2321**

Whiffen v. Oxfordshire CC see Whiffen v. Milham Ford Girls School

Whinmoor Estates Ltd v. Merseyside and Cheshire Rent Assessment Committee see Queensway Housing Association Ltd v. Chiltern, Thames and Eastern Rent Assessment Committee

Whirlpool Corp v. Camco Inc [2001] F.S.R. 46, Sup Ct (Can)

WHIRLPOOL Trade Mark [1997] F.S.R. 905, Sup Ct (Ind) . . . . *Digested*, 98/**3521**

Whistler International Ltd v. Kawasaki Kisen Kaisha Ltd (The Hill Harmony); Kawasaki Kisen Kaisha Ltd v. Tokai Shipping Co Ltd of Tokyo [2001] 1 A.C. 638; [2000] 3 W.L.R. 1954; [2001] 1 All E.R. 403; [2001] 1 All E.R. (Comm) 76; [2001] 1 Lloyd's Rep. 147; [2001] C.L.C. 502; (2001) 98(7) L.S.G. 41; (2000) 150 N.L.J. 1856; (2001) 145 S.J.L.B. 6; *Times*, December 8, 2000; *Independent*, December 13, 2000, HL; reversing [2000] Q.B. 241; [1999] 3 W.L.R. 724; [1999] 4 All E.R. 199; [1999] 2 All E.R. (Comm) 1; [1999] 2 Lloyd's Rep. 209; [1999] C.L.C. 1254; (1999) 96(23) L.S.G. 35; *Times*, May 25, 1999, CA; affirming [1999] Q.B. 72; [1998] 3 W.L.R. 184; [1998] 4 All E.R. 286; [1998] 2 Lloyd's Rep. 367; [1998] C.L.C. 794; (1998) 95(11) L.S.G. 34; (1998) 142 S.J.L.B. 94; *Times*, March 5, 1998, QBD (Comm Ct) . . . . *Digested*, 01/**4915**

Whiston v. Whiston [1995] Fam. 198; [1995] 3 W.L.R. 405; [1998] 1 All E.R. 423; [1995] 2 F.L.R. 268; [1995] 2 F.C.R. 496; [1995] Fam. Law 549; *Times*, April 15, 1995; *Independent*, May 8, 1995 (C.S.), CA; reversing [1994] 2 F.L.R. 906; [1994] 2 F.C.R. 529; [1994] Fam. Law 620, Fam Div . . . . *Digested*, 96/**2852**:
Applied, 01/2544: *Considered*, 01/2545: *Distinguished*, 96/2896

Whitbread (Habeas Corpus: Compulsory Admission), Re; *sub nom* Whitbread *v.* Kingston and District NHS Trust; AW, Re; Whitbread (Mental Patient: Habeas Corpus), Re (1998) 39 B.M.L.R. 94; (1997) 94(27) L.S.G. 23; (1997) 141 S.J.L.B. 152; *Times*, July 14, 1997, CA; affirming [1997] C.O.D. 269, QBD . . . . . . *Digested*, 97/**3651**

Whitbread (Habeas Corpus: Continued Detention), Re [1999] C.O.D. 370, QBD . . . . . . *Digested*, 99/**3936**

Whitbread (Mental Patient: Habeas Corpus), Re see Whitbread (Habeas Corpus: Compulsory Admission), Re

Whitbread *v.* Kingston and District NHS Trust see Whitbread (Habeas Corpus: Compulsory Admission), Re

Whitbread Plc *v.* Falla [2001] Eu. L.R. 150; [2000] E.G.C.S. 136; [2000] N.P.C. 123, Ch D . . . . *Digested*, 01/**2519**

Whitbread Plc (t/a Whitbread Medway Inns) *v.* Hall [2001] EWCA Civ 268; [2001] I.C.R. 699; [2001] I.R.L.R. 275; (2001) 145 S.J.L.B. 77; *Times*, March 15, 2001, CA . . . . *Digested*, 01/**2344**

Whitbread Plc *v.* UCB Corporate Services Ltd [2000] 3 E.G.L.R. 60; [2000] 35 E.G. 136; [2000] E.G.C.S. 77; (2000) 97(26) L.S.G. 35; *Times*, June 22, 2000, CA . . *Digested*, 00/**2624**

White (Deceased), Re; *sub nom* White *v.* Minnis [2001] Ch. 393; [2000] 3 W.L.R. 855; [2000] 3 All E.R. 618; [2000] W.T.L.R. 755; (2000) 97(21) L.S.G. 41; (2000) 150 N.L.J. 682; *Times*, May 10, 2000; *Independent*, June 12, 2000 (C.S), CA; reversing [1999] 1 W.L.R. 2079; [1999] 2 All E.R. 663; *Times*, January 18, 1999, Ch D . . . . *Digested*, 00/**4319**

White *v.* Aldridge (President of the Special Educational Needs Tribunal); *sub nom* Ealing LBC *v.* White; White *v.* Ealing LBC (Striking out of Second Appeal) (1999) 1 L.G.L.R. 501; [1999] Ed. C.R. 612; [1999] E.L.R. 150; *Independent*, December 14, 1998 (C.S.), CA; reversing [1999] Ed. C.R. 488; [1999] E.L.R. 58, QBD . . . . *Digested*, 99/**1901**

Applied, 99/1880: *Considered*, 00/1950: *Distinguished*, 01/2037: *Previous proceedings*, 98/1977

White *v.* Brunton [1984] Q.B. 570; [1984] 3 W.L.R. 105; [1984] 2 All E.R. 606; (1984) 81 L.S.G. 1685; (1984) 128 S.J. 434, CA . . . . *Digested*, 84/**2614**:

Applied, 92/3387: *Considered*, 86/1503, 96/819: *Distinguished*, 99/5265

White *v.* Chief Constable of South Yorkshire see Frost *v.* Chief Constable of South Yorkshire

White *v.* Chubb see Ravenseft Properties Ltd *v.* Hall

White *v.* Cubitt [1930] 1 K.B. 443, KBD . . . . *Applied*, 00/**5244**

White *v.* Customs and Excise Commissioners [1998] B.V.C. 2167, V&DTr . . . . *Digested*, 98/**4909**

White *v.* Ealing LBC; Richardson *v.* Solihull MBC; Hereford and Worcester CC *v.* Lane; Solihull MBC *v.* Finn; Solihull MBC *v.* Special Educational Needs Tribunal [1999] 1 F.C.R. 356; [1998] Ed. C.R. 308; [1998] E.L.R. 319; (1998) 42 B.M.L.R. 182; *Times*, April 10, 1998, CA; affirming [1998] 1 F.C.R. 344; [1998] E.L.R. 203; *Times*, August 1, 1997, QBD . . . . *Digested*, 98/**1977**:

Considered, 98/1961, 98/1979: *Subsequent proceedings*, 98/1981

White *v.* Ealing LBC (Striking out of Second Appeal) see White *v.* Aldridge (President of the Special Educational Needs Tribunal)

White *v.* Holbrook Precision Castings Ltd [1985] I.R.L.R. 215, CA . . . . *Digested*, 85/**2312**:

Considered, 98/2842

White *v.* Jones [1995] 2 A.C. 207; [1995] 2 W.L.R. 187; [1995] 1 All E.R. 691; [1995] 3 F.C.R. 51; (1995) 145 N.L.J. 251; (1995) 139 S.J.L.B. 83; [1995] N.P.C. 31; *Times*, February 17, 1995; *Independent*, February 17, 1995, HL; affirming [1993] 3 W.L.R. 730; [1993] 3 All E.R. 481; (1993) 90(23) L.S.G. 43; (1993) 143 N.L.J. 473; [1993] N.P.C. 37; *Times*, March 9, 1993; *Independent*, March 5, 1993, CA . . *Digested*, 95/**3701**:

Applied, 98/4593, 98/4595, 01/4507, 01/4524, 01/4538: *Considered*, 94/3335, 95/3689, 96/4484, 97/331, 97/692, 97/3830, 98/3921, 98/3927, 98/3931, 98/3951, 98/4019, 00/4219, 00/4225, 01/4487, 01/4525: *Distinguished*, 97/3833, 98/4584, 99/3400, 99/4050: *Followed*, 97/3834, 98/4021, 00/4253, 00/4259, 01/4534, 01/4537: *Referred to*, 95/5841

White *v.* London Fire and Civil Defence Authority see Cullin *v.* London Fire and Civil Defence Authority

White *v.* Minnis see White (Deceased), Re

White *v.* Port of London Authority [2001] 3 Q.R. 19, QBD [*Ex rel*. Trevor Davies, Barrister, 9 Gough Square, London] . . . . *Digested*, 01/**1716**

White (Kory) *v.* Queen, The [1999] 1 A.C. 210; [1998] 3 W.L.R. 992; [1999] 1 Cr. App. R. 153; (1998) 142 S.J.L.B. 260; *Times*, September 25, 1998, PC (Jam) . . . . *Digested*, 98/**879**

White *v.* Reflecting Roadstuds [1991] I.C.R. 733; [1991] I.R.L.R. 331, EAT . . . . *Digested*, 91/**1613**:

Applied, 98/5827: *Considered*, 98/2107

White *v.* South London Transport Ltd [1998] I.C.R. 293, EAT . . . . *Digested*, 98/**2234**

White *v.* Weston [1968] 2 Q.B. 647; [1968] 2 W.L.R. 1459; [1968] 2 All E.R. 842; 112 S.J. 217, CA . . . . *Digested*, 68/**618**:

Considered, 94/3759: *Distinguished*, 68/617, 69/576: *Not followed*, 98/417

White *v.* White see Evans *v.* Motor Insurers Bureau

White v. White [2001] UKHL 9; [2001] 1 W.L.R. 481; [2001] 2 All E.R. 43; [2001] 1 All E.R. (Comm) 1105; [2001] 1 Lloyd's Rep. 679; [2001] R.T.R. 25; [2001] 2 C.M.L.R. 1; [2001] Lloyd's Rep. I.R. 493; [2001] P.I.Q.R. P20; (2001) 98(15) L.S.G. 33; (2001) 151 N.L.J. 350; (2001) 145 S.J.L.B. 67; *Times*, March 6, 2001; *Independent*, April 30, 2001 (C.S), HL . . . . *Digested*, 01/**3828**

White (Pamela) v. White (Martin) [2001] 1 A.C. 596; [2000] 3 W.L.R. 1571; [2001] 1 All E.R. 1; [2000] 2 F.L.R. 981; [2000] 3 F.C.R. 555; [2001] Fam. Law 12; (2000) 97(43) L.S.G. 38; (2000) 150 N.L.J. 1716; (2000) 144 S.J.L.B. 266; [2000] N.P.C. 111; *Times*, October 31, 2000; *Independent*, November 1, 2000; *Daily Telegraph*, November 7, 2000, HL; affirming [1999] Fam. 304; [1999] 2 W.L.R. 1213; [1998] 4 All E.R. 659; [1998] 2 F.L.R. 310; [1998] 3 F.C.R. 45; [1998] Fam. Law 522; *Times*, July 13, 1998; *Independent*, June 29, 1998 (C.S.), CA . . . . *Digested*, 00/**2530**:
Applied, 01/2634, 01/5156: *Considered*, 01/2632, 01/2635, 01/2639:
Followed, 01/2633

White Property Co Ltd v. Birse Construction Ltd [1999] E.G.C.S. 147, QBD

White Sea & Onega Shipping Co Ltd v. International Transport Workers Federation (The Amur-2528 and The Pyalma) [2001] 1 Lloyd's Rep. 421, QBD (Comm Ct) . . . . . *Digested*, 01/**4930**

White Swan Ltd v. Chodiev 1997-W-No.895, QBD (Comm Ct) . . . . *Digested*, 98/**588**

White's Application for Judicial Review, Re [2000] N.I. 432, QBD (NI) . . . . *Digested*, 01/**5651**

Whitechurch v. Royal Pharmaceutical Society of Great Britain (1998) 41 B.M.L.R. 46, QBD . . . . *Digested*, 98/**2820**

Whitecross Wire & Iron Co Ltd v. Savill (1881-82) L.R. 8 Q.B.D. 653, CA . . . . *Considered*, 00/**4687**

Whitehead, Re see R. v. Leeds Crown Court Ex p. Whitehead (No.2)

Whitehead v. Alexander (Unreported, August 4, 1999), CC (Epsom) [*Ex rel.* Charles Foster, Barrister, 6 Pump Court, Temple, London] . . . . *Digested*, 00/**205**

Whitehead (Patrick Whitehead Partnership) v. Jenks & Cattell Engineering Ltd [1999] Eu. L.R. 827, QBD . . . . *Digested*, 00/**117**

Whitehead v. Leeds/Bradford International Airport Ltd [1999] R.V.R. 241, Lands Tr . . . . *Digested*, 00/**4424**

Whitehill v. Bradford [1952] Ch. 236; [1952] 1 All E.R. 115; [1952] 1 T.L.R. 66; 96 S.J. 42, CA; affirming [1951] 2 T.L.R. 946, Ch D . . . . *Digested*, 52/**2271**:
Applied, 86/3399: *Considered*, 69/1287, 69/3522: *Followed*, 98/4024

Whitehouse v. Charles A Blatchford & Sons Ltd [2000] I.C.R. 542; [1999] I.R.L.R. 492, CA . . . . *Digested*, 99/**2131**

Whitehouse v. Fellowes (1861) 10 C.B. N.S. 765 . . . . *Considered*, 99/**4067**

Whitehouse v. Jordan [1981] 1 W.L.R. 246; [1981] 1 All E.R. 267; 125 S.J. 167, HL; affirming [1980] 1 All E.R. 650, CA . . . . *Digested*, 81/**1844**:
Applied, 81/1857, 83/2547, 83/2548, 84/2324, 01/393:
Considered, 83/2558, 88/2453, 93/3612, 96/4446

Whitehouse v. Smith (Michael) see Bajwa v. British Airways Plc

Whiteley, Re see Learoyd v. Whiteley

Whiteley v. Learoyd see Learoyd v. Whiteley

Whiteley v. Picton (Unreported, December 19, 1997), CC (Aldershot & Farnham) [*Ex rel.* Lloyd Sefton-Smith, Barrister, Bridewell Chambers, Bridewell Place, London, EC4V 6AP] . . . . *Digested*, 98/**456**:
Considered, 98/453, 98/457: *Distinguished*, 98/424

Whiteminster Estates Ltd v. Hodges Menswear Ltd (1974) 232 E.G. 715 . . . . *Digested*, 75/**1849**:
Followed, 99/3671

Whiteside v. Whiteside [1950] Ch. 65; [1949] 2 All E.R. 913; 66 T.L.R. (Pt. 1) 126; [1949] T.R. 457, CA; affirming [1949] Ch. 448; [1949] 1 All E.R. 755, Ch D . . . *Digested*, 47-51/**9380**:
Applied, 94/643: *Considered*, 75/1313, 75/3131, 76/2508, 89/2039, 96/5784, 98/4873: *Distinguished*, 72/2909, 86/2203, 90/2681:
Explained, 79/1080: *Referred to*, 00/5261

Whitewater Leisure Management Ltd v. Barnes [2000] I.C.R. 1049; [2000] I.R.L.R. 456, EAT . . . . *Digested*, 00/**2232**:
Applied, 01/2333

Whiteways Contractors (Sussex) Ltd v. Impresa Castelli Construction UK Ltd 75 Con. L.R. 92; (2000) 16 Const. L.J. 453, QBD (T&CC)

Whitfield v. DPP [1998] Crim. L.R. 349, QBD

Whitfield v. Faulkner (Unreported, August 19, 1998), CC (Rawtenstall) [*Ex rel.* James Chapman & Co Solicitors, 76 King Street, Manchester] . . . . *Digested*, 98/**457**

Whitfield v. North Durham HA [1995] P.I.Q.R. P361; [1995] 6 Med. L.R. 32, CA. . . . . . *Considered*, 99/470, 99/475

Whitford v. Alstons Furniture (Unreported, August 29, 2001), CC (Central London) [*Ex rel.* Adam Dawson, Barrister, 199 Strand, London] . . . . *Digested*, 01/**1514**

Whitgift Homes Ltd v. Stocks; *sub nom* Stocks v. Whitgift Homes Ltd [2001] EWCA Civ 1732; [2001] 48 E.G.C.S. 130; [2001] N.P.C. 169, CA

Whitley v. Challis [1892] 1 Ch. 64, CA . . . . *Applied*, 72/**2205**:
Followed, 98/3310

Whitley & Sons v. Secretary of State for Wales (1992) 64 P. & C.R. 296; [1992] 3 P.L.R. 72; [1992] J.P.L. 856; [1992] E.G.C.S. 46; [1992] N.P.C. 45; *Times*, April 2, 1992, CA; affirming (1990) 60 P. & C.R. 185; [1990] 2 P.L.R. 44; [1990] J.P.L. 678; *Times*, October 24, 1989, QBD . . . . *Digested*, 93/**3941**:
Applied, 00/4452: *Considered*, 96/4755, 99/4259, 00/4510

Whitmore *v.* Humphries (1871-72) L.R. 7 C.P. 1, CCP . . . . *Applied*, 01/**4844**:
Explained, 74/**2089**

Whittaker *v.* Farley (Unreported, March 2, 2000), CC (Bury) [*Ex rel.* DLA Solicitors,
101 Barbirolli Square, Manchester] . . . . *Digested*, 00/**492**
Whittaker *v.* Gallagher (1998) 98(2) Q.R. 7, CC (Rawtenstall) . . . . *Digested*, 98/**1747**
Whittaker *v.* Inland Revenue Commissioners [2001] S.T.C. (S.C.D.) 61 (Note); [2001]
S.T.I. 634, Sp Comm . . . . *Digested*, 01/**5178**
Whittal *v.* Kirby [1947] K.B. 194; [1946] 2 All E.R. 552; 62 T.L.R. 696; 111 J.P. 1;
[1947] L.J.R. 234; 175 L.T. 449; 90 S.J. 571, KBD. . . . . *Digested*, 47-51/**9056**:
Applied, 47-51/2333, 47-51/9049, 47-51/9059, 47-51/9062, 47-51/9066,
47-51/9068, 47-51/9074, 47-51/9867, 54/2936, 54/2940, 57/3151,
58/2988, 69/3177, 75/2980, 86/2881, 86/2911, 93/1042, 01/1265:
Considered, 72/2998, 90/1091, 91/1029: *Distinguished*, 71/10303:
Followed, 68/3450

Whitworth Street Estates (Manchester) Ltd *v.* James Miller & Partners Ltd; *sub nom*
James Miller & Partners Ltd *v.* Whitworth Street Estates (Manchester) Ltd
[1970] A.C. 583; [1970] 2 W.L.R. 728; [1970] 1 All E.R. 796; [1970] 1 Lloyd's
Rep. 269; 114 S.J. 225, HL; reversing [1969] 1 W.L.R. 377; [1969] 2 All E.R.
210; 113 S.J. 126, CA . . . . *Digested*, 70/**326**:
Applied, 73/396, 74/390, 75/356, 82/94, 01/2287: *Considered*, 72/475,
82/2.u, 87/156: *Followed*, 86/361

Whixall Old Burial Ground, Re [2001] 1 W.L.R. 995; [2001] 2 All E.R. 348, Cons Ct
(Lichfield) . . . . *Digested*, 01/**1842**
Whybro *v.* Seymour [1998] P.I.Q.R. P130, CA . . . . *Digested*, 98/**607**
Whybrow *v.* Kentish Bus & Coach Co Ltd (Unreported, August 2, 1998), CC
(Dartford) [*Ex rel.* Easthams Solicitors, Tenth Floor, Leon House, 233 High
Street, Croydon] . . . . *Digested*, 99/**419**
Whyte *v.* Redland Aggregates Ltd QBENF 96/0963, CA . . . . *Digested*, 98/**3989**
Wicken *v.* Wicken [1999] Fam. 224; [1999] 2 W.L.R. 1166; [1999] 1 F.L.R. 293;
[1999] 1 F.C.R. 109; [1999] Fam. Law 16, Fam Div . . . . *Digested*, 99/**2436**
Wickes Plc's Trade Mark Application [1998] R.P.C. 698, TMR . . . . *Digested*, 99/**3584**
Wickman Machine Tool Sales Ltd *v.* L Schuler AG see L Schuler AG *v.* Wickman Machine
Tool Sales Ltd
Wicks *v.* Wicks [1999] Fam. 65; [1998] 3 W.L.R. 277; [1998] 1 All E.R. 977; [1998] 1
F.L.R. 470; [1998] 1 F.C.R. 466; [1998] Fam. Law 311; (1998) 95(5) L.S.G. 29;
(1998) 142 S.J.L.B. 76; *Times*, December 29, 1997, CA . . . . *Digested*, 98/**2467**
Widdicombe *v.* Longcombe Software Ltd [1998] I.C.R. 710, EAT . . . . *Digested*, 98/**2241**
Widdows *v.* Friends of the Clergy Corp see Scott (Deceased), Re
Widdowson *v.* Newgate Meat Corp [1998] P.I.Q.R. P138; (1997) 94(47) L.S.G. 31;
(1998) 142 S.J.L.B. 22; *Times*, December 4, 1997, CA . . . . *Digested*, 98/**3912**
Widnell Group *v.* Customs and Excise Commissioners [1998] B.V.C. 2030; [1997] V. &
D.R. 145, V&DTr . . . . *Digested*, 98/**4878**
Wiener SI GmbH *v.* Hauptzollamt Emmerich (C338/95) [1997] E.C.R. I-6495; [1998]
1 C.M.L.R. 1110, ECJ
Wiener Stadtische Allgemeine Versicherungs AG *v.* Tiroler Landesregierung (C344/97)
see Pelzl *v.* Steiermarkische Landesregierung (C338/97)
Wienerworld Ltd *v.* Vision Video Ltd [1998] F.S.R. 832, Ch D . . . . *Digested*, 97/**1031**
Wierzbicki *v.* Secretary of State for the Home Department [2001] EWCA Civ 830;
[2001] Imm. A.R. 602, CA
Wigan MBC *v.* Holden (1999) 14 P.A.D. 556, Planning Inspector
Wiggett Construction Ltd *v.* Customs and Excise Commissioners; *sub nom* Customs
and Excise Commissioners *v.* Wiggett Construction Ltd [2001] S.T.C. 933;
[2001] B.T.C. 5564; [2001] S.T.I. 836; [2001] 22 E.G.C.S. 152; *Times*, June 7,
2001, Ch D; affirming [2001] B.V.C. 2159; [2001] S.T.I. 679, V&DTr . . . . *Digested*, 01/**5585**
Wiggin Alloys *v.* Jenkins [1981] I.R.L.R. 275, EAT . . . . *Digested*, 81/**958**:
Considered, 00/2148
Wiggins *v.* Richard Read (Transport) Ltd, *Times*, January 14, 1999, CA. . . . . *Digested*, 99/**389**
Wiggins *v.* Secretary of State for the Environment, Transport and the Regions [2001]
P.L.C.R. 22; [2001] J.P.L. 1001 (Note); [2001] N.P.C. 3, QBD (Admin Ct) . . . . . *Digested*, 01/**4699**
Wiggins *v.* Thornton (Unreported, July 7, 1999), CC (Medway) [*Ex rel.* Tim Petts,
Barrister, 12 King's Bench Walk, London] . . . . *Digested*, 99/**2461**
WIGGINS TEAPE/Legitimate expectation (T690/93) [2001] E.P.O.R. 23, EPO (Technical
Bd App) . . . . *Digested*, 01/**3898**
Wigginton & Milner Ltd *v.* Winster Engineering Ltd [1978] 1 W.L.R. 1462; [1978] 3 All
E.R. 436; (1978) 36 P. & C.R. 203; 122 S.J. 826, CA . . . . *Digested*, 78/**2500**:
Applied, 83/2090, 84/1153, 87/1236: *Considered*, 82/2661, 88/2088,
99/4351: *Followed*, 93/527, 96/4932
Wight *v.* Olswang (No.1) (1998-99) 1 I.T.E.L.R. 783; *Times*, May 18, 1999;
Independent, May 24, 1999, CA; reversing [1998] N.P.C. 111; *Times*, September
17, 1998, Ch D . . . . *Digested*, 99/**4960**
Wight *v.* Olswang (No.2) [2001] C.P. Rep. 54; [2001] Lloyd's Rep. P.N. 269; [2001]
W.T.L.R. 291; (2000-01) 3 I.T.E.L.R. 352, CA; reversing [2000] Lloyd's Rep. P.N.
662; [2000] W.T.L.R. 783; (1999-2000) 2 I.T.E.L.R. 689; (2000) 97(18) L.S.G.
37; *Times*, April 18, 2000, Ch D . . . . *Digested*, 01/**681**

Wijsenbeek (C378/97), Re; *sub nom* Criminal Proceedings against Wijsenbeek (C378/97) [1999] E.C.R. I-6207; [2001] 2 C.M.L.R. 53; [2000] I.N.L.R. 336; *Times*, October 12, 1999, ECJ . . . .   *Digested*, 99/**2257**

Wilcock, Re (Unreported, January 15, 1999), CICB (Nottingham) [*Ex rel*. Elizabeth Hodgson, Barrister, Ropewalk Chambers, 24 The Ropewalk, Nottingham] . . . . .   *Digested*, 99/**1549**

Wilcox *v*. East Riding of Yorkshire DC (Unreported, April 22, 1998), CC (Kingston upon Hull) [*Ex rel*. Langleys Solicitors, Queens House, Micklegate, York] . . . . . .   *Digested*, 98/**2858**

WILD CHILD Trade Mark [1998] R.P.C. 455, Appointed Person . . . .   *Digested*, 98/**3531**:
                       Considered, 99/3590: *Followed*, 99/3528: *Referred to*, 99/3568

Wild *v*. South African Supply & Cold Storage Co see South African Supply and Cold Storage Co, Re

Wildman *v*. DPP [2001] EWHC Admin 14; (2001) 165 J.P. 453; [2001] Crim. L.R. 565; (2001) 165 J.P.N. 290; *Times*, February 8, 2001; *Independent*, March 5, 2001 (C.S), QBD . . . .   *Digested*, 01/**1128**:
                                          Cited, 01/1106

Wildtree Hotels Ltd *v*. Harrow LBC [2001] 2 A.C. 1; [2000] 3 W.L.R. 165; [2000] 3 All E.R. 289; [2000] B.L.G.R. 547; (2001) 81 P. & C.R. 9; [2000] 2 E.G.L.R. 5; [2000] R.V.R. 235; [2000] E.G.C.S. 80; (2000) 97(28) L.S.G. 31; (2000) 150 N.L.J. 984; [2000] N.P.C. 71; (2001) 81 P. & C.R. D9; *Times*, June 27, 2000; *Independent*, July 31, 2000 (C.S), HL; reversing in part [1999] Q.B. 634; [1998] 3 W.L.R. 1318; [1998] 3 All E.R. 638; [1998] 3 E.G.L.R. 133; [1998] R.V.R. 288; [1999] J.P.L. 136; (1998) 95(27) L.S.G. 26; (1998) 95(24) L.S.G. 35; (1998) 142 S.J.L.B. 195; [1998] N.P.C. 103; *Times*, June 22, 1998, CA . . . . . .   *Digested*, 00/**4293**

Wiles *v*. Bedfordshire CC (Unreported, February 12, 2001), CC (Luton) [*Ex rel*. Edwin Buckett, Barrister, 9 Gough Square, London] . . . .   *Digested*, 01/**3305**

Wilhelm *v*. Hickson see Earl *v*. Wilhelm

Wilhelm Kaimann's Trade Mark Application (No.20457617); *sub nom* KAIMANN Trade Mark (1999) 22(10) I.P.D. 22102, TMR

Wilkes *v*. Coal Authority [1998] R.V.R. 204; [1998] E.G.C.S. 65; (1998) 95(17) L.S.G. 33, CA

Wilkie *v*. Oxford Radcliffe Hospital NHS Trust (Unreported, January 9, 1997), CC (Central London) [*Ex rel*. Anthony Snelson, Barrister, Thomas More Chambers, 51-52 Carey Street, Lincoln's Inn, London] . . . .   *Digested*, 98/**1573**

Wilkin *v*. Goldthorpe [1998] E.L.R. 345, QBD . . . .   *Digested*, 98/**1980**

Wilkins *v*. Gowrings Food Services (Unreported, August 12, 1999), CC (Plymouth) [*Ex rel*. Bond Pearce Solicitors, Ballard House, West Hoe Road, Plymouth] . . . .   *Digested*, 99/**2483**

Wilkins *v*. Horrowitz [1990] 2 E.G.L.R. 217; [1990] 29 E.G. 57, Lands Tr . . . .   *Applied*, 01/4375:
                                        Followed, 91/2245

Wilkins *v*. Press Construction see Wilkins *v*. William Press Ltd

Wilkins *v*. William Press Ltd; *sub nom* Wilkins *v*. Press Construction [2001] 3 Q.R. 19, QBD [*Ex rel*. Andrew Hogarth, Barrister, 12 Kings Bench Walk, Temple, London] .   *Digested*, 01/**1718**

Wilkinson *v*. Chief Adjudication Officer [2000] 2 F.C.R. 82, CA . . . .   *Digested*, 00/**4839**

Wilkinson *v*. Crown Prosecution Service; *sub nom* Wilkinson *v*. DPP (1998) 162 J.P. 591; [1998] Crim. L.R. 743; [1998] C.O.D. 367; (1998) 162 J.P.N. 625, QBD . . .   *Digested*, 98/**873**

Wilkinson *v*. DPP see Wilkinson *v*. Crown Prosecution Service

Wilkinson *v*. Inland Revenue Commissioners; *sub nom* Debtor *v*. Inland Revenue Commissioners [1998] B.P.I.R. 418; 68 T.C. 157, Ch D . . . .   *Digested*, 97/**3020**

Wilkinson *v*. Jones (1998) 98(2) Q.R. 4, QBD . . . .   *Digested*, 98/**1479**

Wille *v*. Liechtenstein (2000) 30 E.H.R.R. 558; 8 B.H.R.C. 69, ECHR . . . .   *Digested*, 00/**3189**

Willerby Manor Hotels Ltd *v*. Customs and Excise Commissioners [2000] S.T.I. 1407, V&DTr

William Brandt's Sons & Co *v*. Dunlop Rubber Co Ltd [1905] A.C. 454, HL; reversing [1904] 1 K.B. 387, CA . . . .   *Applied*, 56/3778,
                       91/2601: *Considered*, 01/2430

William Cook Estates Ltd *v*. Secretary of State for the Environment, Transport and the Regions [1998] P.L.C.R. 393; *Times*, May 11, 1998, CA; reversing (1998) 76 P. & C.R. 79; [1998] P.L.C.R. 70; [1997] E.G.C.S. 110, QBD . . . .   *Digested*, 98/**4222**

William Cook Plc *v*. Commission of the European Communities (C198/91) [1993] E.C.R. I-2487; [1993] 3 C.M.L.R. 206; *Financial Times*, May 25, 1993, ECJ . . . .   *Digested*, 93/**4392**:
                               Applied, 98/735, 98/2311

William Grant & Sons International Ltd *v*. Marie Brizard et Roger International SA (France) [2000] I.L. Pr. 774, Cass (F)

William Grant & Sons Ltd *v*. Glen Catrine Bonded Warehouse Ltd (No.2) 1999 G.W.D. 15-714; *Times*, May 11, 1999, OH . . . .   *Digested*, 99/**6314**

William Hill (Southern) Ltd *v*. Cabras Ltd (1987) 54 P. & C.R. 42; [1987] 1 E.G.L.R. 37; (1987) 281 E.G. 309, CA; affirming [1985] 2 E.G.L.R. 62; (1985) 275 E.G. 149 .   *Digested*, 87/**1231**:
                                   Applied, 01/4857

William Hill (Football) Ltd *v*. Ladbroke (Football) Ltd see Ladbroke (Football) Ltd *v*. William Hill (Football) Ltd

William Hill Organisation Ltd *v*. Tucker [1999] I.C.R. 291; [1998] I.R.L.R. 313; (1998) 95(20) L.S.G. 33; (1998) 142 S.J.L.B. 140; *Times*, April 8, 1998, CA . . . .   *Digested*, 98/**2125**

William Lacey (Hounslow) Ltd *v*. Davis [1957] 1 W.L.R. 932; [1957] 2 All E.R. 712; 101 S.J. 629, QBD . . . .   *Digested*, 57/**356**:
                                   Considered, 00/2330

William Morrison Supermarkets Plc v. Secretary of State for the Environment, Transport and the Regions see Wm Morrison Supermarkets Plc v. Secretary of State for the Environment, Transport and the Regions

William Sindall Plc v. Cambridgeshire CC [1994] 1 W.L.R. 1016; [1994] 3 All E.R. 932; 92 L.G.R. 121; [1993] E.G.C.S. 105; [1993] N.P.C. 82; *Times*, June 8, 1993, CA . . *Digested*, 94/**572**:
Distinguished, 00/121: *Followed*, 00/818

Williams (A Bankrupt), Re see Judd v. Williams

Williams (James) (Deceased), Re (1999-2000) 2 I.T.E.L.R. 313, US Ct

Williams v. Barclays Bank Plc; *sub nom* Williams v. Williams; Tucker v. Williams [1988] Q.B. 161; [1987] 3 W.L.R. 790; [1987] 3 All E.R. 257; [1988] 1 F.L.R. 455; [1987] 2 F.T.L.R. 393; [1987] Fin. L.R. 361; [1988] Fam. Law 204; (1987) 84 L.S.G. 2455; (1987) 131 S.J. 1214, CA . . . . *Digested*, 87/**1674**:
Applied, 94/3797, 95/4226: *Considered*, 00/308

Williams v. Bedwellty Justices see R. v. Bedwellty Justices Ex p. Williams

Williams v. Blaenau Gwent BC (No.2) [1999] 2 E.G.L.R. 195, Lands Tr . . . . *Digested*, 00/**4433**

Williams v. BOC Gases Ltd [2000] I.C.R. 1181; [2000] P.I.Q.R. Q253; *Times*, April 5, 2000, CA . . . . *Digested*, 00/**1488**

Williams v. Bowen (Unreported, February 12, 1998), CC (Swansea) [*Ex rel.* Harriet Edmondson, Pupil Barrister, 30 Park Place, Cardiff, Glamorgan] . . . . *Digested*, 98/**1724**

Williams v. Butcher (1998) 98(2) Q.R. 7, CC (Blackwood) . . . . *Digested*, 98/**1648**

Williams v. Caterpillar (Peterlee) Ltd (Unreported, January 11, 2000), CC (Sunderland) [*Ex rel.* Craig Moore, Barrister, Park Lane Chambers, 19 Westgate, Leeds] . . . . . *Digested*, 00/**1676**

Williams v. Clarkson (1999) 99(2) Q.R. 7, CC (Central London) [*Ex rel.* David Barr, Barrister, 1 Temple Gardens, Temple, London] . . . . *Digested*, 99/**1490**

Williams v. Compair Maxam [1982] I.C.R. 156; [1982] I.R.L.R. 83, EAT . . . . *Digested*, 82/**1121**:
Applied, 83/1339, 90/1927, 98/2238: *Considered*, 83/1340, 85/1225, 85/1268, 86/1225: *Distinguished*, 83/1280, 85/1266: *Referred to*, 85/1198, 86/1227, 86/1265

Williams v. Concrete Pump Hire Sales and Service (Unreported, February 20, 2001), CC (Bristol) [*Ex rel.* James Hassall, Barrister, Guildhall Chambers, 22-26 Broad Street, Bristol] . . . . *Digested*, 01/**569**

Williams v. Cowell (t/a The Stables) (No.1) [2000] 1 W.L.R. 187; [2000] I.C.R. 85; (1999) 96(31) L.S.G. 38; *Times*, August 12, 1999 ; *Independent*, July 29, 1999, CA . . . . *Digested*, 99/**2040**

Williams v. Dolin (Unreported, May 18, 2000), CC (Shoreditch) [*Ex rel.* Marcus Grant, Barrister, 1 Temple Gardens, Temple, London] . . . . *Digested*, 00/**450**

Williams v. Doyle (Unreported, June 17, 1998), CC (Cardiff) [*Ex rel.* Peter Brooks, Barrister, Loosemores Solicitors, Alliance House, 18-19 High Street, Cardiff] . . . *Digested*, 99/**1431**

Williams (Alan Davis) v. DPP [1991] 1 W.L.R. 1160; [1991] 3 All E.R. 651; (1991) 93 Cr. App. R. 319; (1992) 156 J.P. 804; [1991] R.T.R. 214; [1991] C.O.D. 500; (1991) 141 N.L.J. 564; (1991) 135 S.J. 508; *Times*, March 26, 1991; *Independent*, April 15, 1991 (C.S.), QBD . . . . *Digested*, 92/**685**:
Applied, 93/700: *Considered*, 98/1027

Williams v. First Choice Holidays and Flights Ltd (Unreported, April 2, 2001), CC (Warrington) [*Ex rel.* Matthew Chapman, Barrister, No.1 Serjeants' Inn, London] . *Digested*, 01/**4282**

Williams v. Fisher (Unreported, March 13, 1998), CC (Brighton) [*Ex rel.* Michael Fullerton, Barrister, 9 Old Steine, Brighton] . . . . *Digested*, 98/**1579**

Williams v. Greatrex [1957] 1 W.L.R. 31; [1956] 3 All E.R. 705; 101 S.J. 43, CA . . . . *Digested*, 56/**9054**:
Followed, 99/4369

Williams v. Gregory (Valuation Officer) [1998] R.V.R. 139, Lands Tr . . . . *Digested*, 98/**4329**

Williams v. Inland Revenue Commissioners [2001] S.T.C. (S.C.D.) 35 (Note); [2001] S.T.I. 203, Sp Comm . . . . *Digested*, 01/**5267**

Williams v. Inspector of Taxes see Locabail (UK) Ltd v. Bayfield Properties Ltd (Leave to Appeal)

Williams v. Kaye Presteigne Ltd [2000] 6 Q.R. 8, CC (Derby) [*Ex rel.* Karl Hirst, Barrister, 5 Fountain Court, Steelhouse Lane, Birmingham] . . . . *Digested*, 00/**1606**

Williams v. King (Unreported, September 1, 2000), CC (Cardiff) [*Ex rel.* Andrew Arentsen, Barrister, 33 Park Place, Cardiff] . . . . *Digested*, 01/**1688**

Williams v. Macardle (No.2) (Unreported, June 5, 2000), CC (Romford) [*Ex rel.* Timothy Petts, Barrister, 12 Kings Bench Walk, London] . . . . *Digested*, 01/**678**

Williams v. Mendham (Unreported, January 6, 1998), CC (Watford) [*Ex rel.* Rebecca Bensted, Barrister, 95A Chancery Lane, London] . . . . *Digested*, 98/**438**

Williams v. Natural Life Health Foods Ltd [1998] 1 W.L.R. 830; [1998] 2 All E.R. 577; [1998] B.C.C. 428; [1998] 1 B.C.L.C. 689; (1998) 17 Tr. L.R. 152; (1998) 95(21) L.S.G. 37; (1998) 148 N.L.J. 657; (1998) 142 S.J.L.B. 166; *Times*, May 1, 1998, HL; reversing [1997] B.C.C. 605; [1997] 1 B.C.L.C. 131; *Times*, January 9, 1997; *Independent*, December 13, 1996, CA; affirming [1996] B.C.C. 376; [1996] 1 B.C.L.C. 288; (1996) 140 S.J.L.B. 43; *Independent*, January 18, 1996, QBD . . . *Digested*, 98/**3920**:
Applied, 99/4014, 99/4019, 00/4218: *Cited*, 99/3311: *Followed*, 99/4405

Williams v. Outline Design Ltd (Unreported, August 8, 1999), CC (Newport, Gwent) [*Ex rel.* Eversheds Solicitors, Fitzallan House, Fitzallan Road, Cardiff] . . . . *Digested*, 99/**3979**

Williams v. R. 6 B.H.R.C. 189, Sup Ct (Can) . . . . *Digested*, 99/**3140**

Williams v. Richards see Secretary of State for Transport v. Richards

Williams v. Roffey Bros & Nicholls (Contractors) Ltd [1991] 1 Q.B. 1; [1990] 2 W.L.R.
  1153; [1990] 1 All E.R. 512; 48 B.L.R. 69; (1991) 10 Tr. L.R. 12; (1990) 87(12)
  L.S.G. 36; (1989) 139 N.L.J. 1712, CA . . . .   *Digested*, 90/**629**:
                                              Applied, 98/3376: *Distinguished*, 94/537, 95/763
Williams (Valuation Officer) v. Scottish & Newcastle Retail Ltd; *sub nom* Scottish &
  Newcastle Retail Ltd v. Williams (Valuation Officer); Allied Domecq Retailing Ltd
  v. Williams (Valuation Officer) [2001] EWCA Civ 185; [2001] 1 E.G.L.R. 157;
  [2001] R.A. 41; [2001] 9 E.G.C.S. 227; (2001) 98(19) L.S.G. 37; [2001] N.P.C.
  46; *Times*, March 6, 2001; *Independent*, February 21, 2001, CA; affirming
  [2000] 2 E.G.L.R. 171; [2000] R.A. 119, Lands Tr. . . . .   *Digested*, 01/**4833**:
                                                                                                Applied, 01/4834
Williams v. Southwark LBC (2001) 33 H.L.R. 22; [2000] B.L.G.R. 646; [2000]
  E.G.C.S. 44; (2000) 97(16) L.S.G. 40; (2000) 144 S.J.L.B. 167; *Times*, April 5,
  2000, Ch D . . . .   *Digested*, 00/**3918**
Williams v. Thompson (Unreported, July 4, 2000), CC (Altrincham) [*Ex rel*. David
  Calvert, Barrister, 68 Quay Street, Manchester] . . . .   *Digested*, 00/**1709**
Williams v. Tower Hamlets LBC (Unreported, April 27, 2000), CA [*Ex rel*. Jon
  Holbrook, Barrister, 2 Garden Court, Middle Temple, London] . . . .   *Digested*, 00/**3149**
Williams v. Travel Promotions Ltd (t/a Voyages Jules Verne), *Times*, March 9, 1998, CA . .   *Digested*, 98/**3742**
Williams v. Welsh Rugby Union [1999] Eu. L.R. 195, QBD.   *Digested*, 99/**545**
Williams v. Williams see Williams v. Barclays Bank Plc
Williams v. Williams (Unreported, July 16, 1998), Ch D [*Ex rel*. Graham Sellers, Barrister
  and Richard Hall, Barrister, 14 Castle Street, Liverpool] . . . .   *Digested*, 99/**4095**
Williams v. Williams (Recovery of Vehicle Hire Charges) (Unreported, August 28,
  1998), CC (Central London) [*Ex rel*. David McIlroy, Barrister, 3 Paper Buildings,
  Temple, London] . . . .   *Digested*, 99/**2462**
Williams & Glyn's Bank Ltd v. Barnes [1981] Com. L.R. 205, HC. . . . .   *Digested*, 82/**184**:
                                                                                                Considered, 01/683

Williams & Glyn's Bank Ltd v. Boland; Williams & Glyn's Bank Ltd v. Brown [1981] A.C.
  487; [1980] 3 W.L.R. 138; [1980] 2 All E.R. 408; (1980) 40 P. & C.R. 451; 124
  S.J. 443, HL; affirming [1979] Ch. 312; [1979] 2 W.L.R. 550; [1979] 2 All E.R.
  697; (1979) 38 P. & C.R. 622; 123 S.J. 183, CA; reversing (1978) 36 P. & C.R.
  448; (1980) 77 L.S.G. 1242; (1980) 130 N.L.J. 896; (1979) 129 N.L.J. 1159,
  Ch D . . . .   *Digested*, 80/**1847**:
                      Applied, 81/1494, 81/1495, 83/2057, 84/2952, 85/3607, 86/1817, 86/2231,
                                87/470, 87/2109, 88/480, 88/491, 89/468: *Considered*, 82/1709, 85/2269,
                                                                   99/4395: *Distinguished*, 87/2540
Williams & Glyn's Bank Ltd v. Brown see Williams & Glyn's Bank Ltd v. Boland
Williams & Glyn's Bank Ltd v. Customs and Excise Commissioners [1974] V.A.T.T.R. 262,
  VAT Tr. . . . .   *Digested*, 75/**3504.14**:
                                                      Applied, 91/3643, 95/5045: *Considered*, 01/5289
Williams & Humbert Ltd v. W&H Trade Marks (Jersey) Ltd; Rumasa SA v. Multinvest
  (UK) [1986] A.C. 368; [1986] 2 W.L.R. 24; [1986] 1 All E.R. 129; (1986) 83
  L.S.G. 362; (1986) 136 N.L.J. 15, HL; affirming [1985] 3 W.L.R. 501; [1985] 2
  All E.R. 619; (1986) 83 L.S.G. 37, CA; affirming [1985] 2 All E.R. 208; (1985)
  129 S.J. 573, Ch D . . . .   *Digested*, 86/**363**:
                               Cited, 93/3037: *Considered*, 85/1508, 86/1512, 88/1605, 89/1715, 98/303:
                                                                                          Followed, 93/3789
Williams Ltd's Application (1917) 34 R.P.C. 197 . . . .   *Referred to*, 99/3593
Williams Will Trust, Re see Harrison's Settlement, Re
Williamson, Re see Marsh & McLennan Companies UK Ltd v. Pensions Ombudsman
Williamson v. East London and City HA [1998] Lloyd's Rep. Med. 6; (1998) 41
  B.M.L.R. 85, Ch D . . . .   *Digested*, 98/**3980**
Williamson v. Secretary of State for Education and Employment see R. (on the
  application of Williamson) v. Secretary of State for Education and Employment
Williamson's Application for Judicial Review, Re [2000] N.I. 281, CA (NI) . . . .   *Digested*, 00/**5397**
Willingale v. Globalgrange Ltd; *sub nom* Willingale v. Global Grange Ltd (2001) 33
  H.L.R. 17; (2000) 80 P. & C.R. 448; [2000] L. & T.R. 549; [2000] 2 E.G.L.R.
  55; [2000] 18 E.G. 152; (2000) 97(12) L.S.G. 44; (2000) 80 P. & C.R. D12;
  Times, March 29, 2000; *Independent*, April 17, 2000 (C.S.), CA . . . .   *Digested*, 00/**3899**
Willingham v. Kimberley Clark Ltd see Afzal v. Ford Motor Co Ltd
Willis v. McLaughlin & Harvey Plc (In Administrative Receivership and Liquidation)
  [1996] N.I. 427; [1998] Eu. L.R. 22, CA (NI) . . . .   *Digested*, 98/**2213**
Willis v. Quality Heating Services PTA+A 2000/5687/A2, CA . . . .   *Digested*, 00/**583**
Willis Application, Re (1998) 76 P. & C.R. 97; [1997] 2 E.G.L.R. 185; [1997] 28 E.G. 137;
  [1998] J.P.L. 497, Lands Tr. . . . .   *Digested*, 97/**4259**
Willmott v. Barber (1881) L.R. 17 Ch. D. 772, CA; affirming in part (1880) L.R. 15 Ch.
  D. 96, Ch D . . . .   *Applied*, 65/3356,
                            75/1191, 80/1073: *Considered*, 73/413, 86/1301, 98/123, 99/4856:
                                   Distinguished, 97/983: *Explained*, 77/2485: *Followed*, 59/3381, 66/4174,
                                                                                                   66/4176
Willows v. Craggs (t/a Wellingore Garages) (Unreported, December 23, 1998), CC
  (Lincoln) [*Ex rel*. Langleys Solicitors, Newport House, Doddington Road
  Business Park, Lincoln] . . . .   *Digested*, 99/**2855**

Wills *v.* Corfe Joinery Ltd (In Liquidation); *sub nom* Corfe Joinery Ltd (In Liquidation),
Re [1997] B.C.C. 511; [1998] 2 B.C.L.C. 75; [1997] B.P.I.R. 611; (1997) 94(7)
L.S.G. 29; *Times*, January 21, 1997, Ch D (Companies Ct) . . . . *Digested*, 97/**3049**:
Applied, 99/3294

Wills *v.* Martin (TF) (Roof Contractors) Ltd see Wills *v.* TF Martin (Roof Contractors)
Ltd

Wills *v.* TF Martin (Roof Contractors) Ltd; *sub nom* Wills *v.* Martin (TF) (Roof
Contractors) Ltd [1972] 1 Lloyd's Rep. 541; [1972] R.T.R. 368; 116 S.J. 145,
QBD . . . . *Digested*, 72/**3081**:
Applied, 72/3082: *Considered*, 99/4070

Willson *v.* Greene [1971] 1 W.L.R. 635; [1971] 1 All E.R. 1098; (1971) 22 P. & C.R.
697; (1970) 115 S.J. 206, Ch D . . . . *Digested*, 71/**9887**:
Applied, 72/2906: *Considered*, 99/4351: *Distinguished*, 87/1236

Willson *v.* Ministry of Defence [1991] 1 All E.R. 638; [1991] I.C.R. 595, QBD . . . . *Digested*, 91/**1323**:
Considered, 01/1712

Wilmott Trading Ltd (No.1), Re; *sub nom* Henry *v.* Environment Agency (No.1) [2000]
Env. L.R. 42; [1999] B.P.I.R. 1021; (1999) 96(18) L.S.G. 34; *Times*, April 28,
1999; *Independent*, May 10, 1999 (C.S.), Ch D (Companies Ct) . . . . *Digested*, 99/**3279**

Wilmott Trading Ltd (No.2), Re; *sub nom* Henry *v.* Environment Agency (No.2) [2000]
B.C.C. 321; [1999] 2 B.C.L.C. 541; [2000] Env. L.R. 54; (1999) 96(25) L.S.G.
29; *Times*, June 17, 1999 ; *Independent*, June 21, 1999 (C.S.), Ch D (Companies
Ct) . . . . *Digested*, 99/**3263**

Wilsher *v.* Essex AHA [1988] A.C. 1074; [1988] 2 W.L.R. 557; [1988] 1 All E.R. 871;
(1988) 138 N.L.J. Rep. 78; (1988) 132 S.J. 418, HL; affirming [1987] Q.B. 730;
[1987] 2 W.L.R. 425; [1986] 3 All E.R. 801; (1986) 83 L.S.G. 2661; (1986)
136 N.L.J. 1061; (1986) 130 S.J. 749; *Times*, August 6, 1986, CA . . . . *Digested*, 88/**2415**:
Applied, 90/3279, 91/2654, 96/4468: *Considered*, 98/1501, 00/5114:
Referred to, 90/2956

Wilson, Re (Unreported, April 13, 1992), CICB (Leeds) [*Ex rel.* Philip Hamer & Co.,
Solicitors] . . . . *Digested*, 93/**1591**

Wilson *v.* Associated Newspapers Ltd see Associated Newspapers Ltd *v.* Wilson

Wilson *v.* Australia [2000] B.P.I.R. 207, Fed Ct (Aus) (Sgl judge) . . . . *Digested*, 00/**3453**

Wilson *v.* Best Travel Ltd [1993] 1 All E.R. 353, QBD . . . . *Digested*, 93/**494**:
Applied, 99/4005, 00/4041: *Distinguished*, 00/4038: *Followed*, 01/4281,
01/4453

Wilson *v.* Burne (1888) L.R. 24 Ir. 14, CA (UK-Irl) . . . . *Applied*, 01/4186

Wilson *v.* Chief Constable of Lancashire, *Daily Telegraph*, December 5, 2000, CA

Wilson *v.* Christie see Christie *v.* Wilson

Wilson (t/a Mountain View Hotel) *v.* Customs and Excise Commissioners [2000] S.T.I.
552, V&DTr

Wilson *v.* De Keyser Ltd see De Keyser Ltd *v.* Wilson

Wilson *v.* Ethicon Ltd [2000] I.R.L.R. 4, EAT . . . . *Digested*, 00/**6219**

Wilson *v.* First County Trust Ltd (No.1); *sub nom* Wilson *v.* First National Trust Ltd
(No.1) [2001] Q.B. 407; [2001] 2 W.L.R. 302; [2001] H.R.L.R. 7; (2001) 98(3)
L.S.G. 42; (2000) 144 S.J.L.B. 288; *Times*, December 6, 2000, CA . . . . *Digested*, 01/**879**

Wilson *v.* First County Trust Ltd (No.2) [2001] EWCA Civ 633; [2001] 3 W.L.R. 42;
[2001] 3 All E.R. 229; [2001] 2 All E.R. (Comm) 134; [2001] E.C.C. 37; [2001]
H.R.L.R. 44; [2001] U.K.H.R.R. 1175; (2001) 98(24) L.S.G. 44; (2001) 145
S.J.L.B. 125; *Times*, May 16, 2001; *Independent*, May 8, 2001; *Daily Telegraph*,
May 8, 2001, CA . . . . *Digested*, 01/**909**:
Applied, 01/2315: *Considered*, 01/100, 01/3504

Wilson *v.* First National Trust Ltd (No.1) see Wilson *v.* First County Trust Ltd (No.1)

Wilson *v.* Fylde Borough Transport (Unreported, June 22, 1998), CA [*Ex rel.*
Weightmans Solicitors, Richmond House, 1 Rumford Place, Liverpool] . . . . *Digested*, 98/**351**

Wilson *v.* Graham see Thomas *v.* Bunn

Wilson *v.* Hall [*Ex rel.* Andrew Granville Stafford, Barrister, 4 King's Bench Walk, Temple,
London] . . . . *Digested*, 01/**1702**

Wilson *v.* Housing Corp [1998] I.C.R. 151; [1997] I.R.L.R. 346; *Times*, December 18,
1996, QBD

Wilson *v.* Layne 7 B.H.R.C. 274, US Ct

Wilson *v.* Le Fevre Wood & Royle 66 Con. L.R. 74; [1996] P.N.L.R. 107; *Independent*,
October 12, 1995, CA . . . . *Digested*, 96/**824**

Wilson *v.* Liverpool Corp [1971] 1 W.L.R. 302; [1971] 1 All E.R. 628; (1971) 22 P. &
C.R. 282; (1970) 114 S.J. 932, CA . . . . *Digested*, 71/**8984**:
Applied, 79/303, 89/365: *Considered*, 90/582, 92/439, 00/4426:
Distinguished, 81/2629

Wilson *v.* Martin's Executors [1993] 1 E.G.L.R. 178; [1993] 24 E.G. 119, CA . . . . *Digested*, 94/**567**:
Considered, 99/4348

Wilson *v.* Maynard Shipbuilding Consultants AB [1978] Q.B. 665; [1978] 2 W.L.R.
466; [1978] 2 All E.R. 78; [1978] I.C.R. 376; [1977] I.R.L.R. 491; (1978) 13 I.T.R.
23; 121 S.J. 792, CA; reversing [1976] I.R.L.R. 384; (1976) 11 I.T.R. 303, EAT . . . *Digested*, 78/**981**:
Applied, 78/1138: *Considered*, 89/1490, 99/2055

Wilson *v.* Mid Glamorgan CC see Bajwa *v.* British Airways Plc

Wilson v. Nithsdale DC 1992 S.L.T. 1131, OH. . . . .   *Digested*, 92/**5869**:
                       Applied, 97/6114, 98/3018: *Considered*, 96/3046, 96/3047
Wilson v. Post Office [2000] I.R.L.R. 834, CA . . . .   *Digested*, 01/**2340**
Wilson v. Rickett Cockerell & Co Ltd [1954] 1 Q.B. 598; [1954] 2 W.L.R. 629; [1954]
  1 All E.R. 868; 98 S.J. 233, CA. . . . .   *Digested*, 54/**2979**:
                                      Considered, 01/939
Wilson v. Sacred Heart Roman Catholic Primary School, Carlton, Governors [1998] 1
  F.L.R. 663; [1998] E.L.R. 637; [1998] P.I.Q.R. P145; [1998] Fam. Law 249;
  Times, November 28, 1997, CA. . . . .   *Digested*, 98/**3948**
Wilson v. Secretary of State for the Environment, Transport and the Regions; Froggatt
  v. Secretary of State for the Environment, Transport and the Regions (1998)
  95(2) L.S.G. 24; [1997] N.P.C. 189, QBD
Wilson v. Shayshutt [2001] 6 Q.R. 14, CC (North Shields) [*Ex rel.* Peter Freeman,
  Barrister, Farrar's Building, Temple, London] . . . .   *Digested*, 01/**1666**
Wilson v. South Kesteven DC [2001] 1 W.L.R. 387; [2000] 4 All E.R. 577; (2001) 81
  P. & C.R. 24; [2000] R.A. 371; *Times*, October 17, 2000; *Independent*, July 19,
  2000, CA . . . .   *Digested*, 00/**4582**
Wilson v. St Helens BC; *sub nom* British Fuels Ltd v. Baxendale; Meade v. British Fuels
  Ltd; Baxendale v. British Fuels Ltd [1999] 2 A.C. 52; [1998] 3 W.L.R. 1070;
  [1998] 4 All E.R. 609; [1999] 1 C.M.L.R. 918; [1998] I.C.R. 1141; [1998] I.R.L.R.
  706; (1999) 1 L.G.L.R. 123; [1999] B.L.G.R. 255; *Times*, October 30, 1998;
  Independent, November 5, 1998, HL; affirming [1997] 3 C.M.L.R. 1267; [1998]
  I.C.R. 387; [1997] I.R.L.R. 505; (1997) 94(33) L.S.G. 26; (1997) 147 N.L.J.
  1150; (1997) 141 S.J.L.B. 176; *Times*, July 18, 1997, CA; reversing [1996] I.C.R.
  711; [1996] I.R.L.R. 320; *Times*, April 10, 1996, EAT . . . .   *Digested*, 98/**2218**:
                 Applied, 01/2332: *Considered*, 98/2212, 98/2222:
                      Previous proceedings, 96/2594: *Referred to*, 96/2594
Wilson v. Stone [1998] 2 E.G.L.R. 155; [1998] 26 E.G. 153, LVT. . . . .   *Digested*, 98/**3625**
Wilson v. United Counties Bank Ltd [1920] A.C. 102, HL . . . .   *Applied*, 98/4384,
       99/4485: *Considered*, 87/3338, 88/3167, 98/3285: *Distinguished*, 85/1282:
                    Followed, 96/401: *Referred to*, 94/3445, 95/861
Wilson v. United Kingdom see Thynne v. United Kingdom (A/190)
Wilson v. Webster [1998] 1 F.L.R. 1097; [1998] 2 F.C.R. 575; [1998] Fam. Law 391;
  (1998) 95(16) L.S.G. 23; *Times*, March 5, 1998, CA . . . .   *Digested*, 98/**11**
Wilson v. West Sussex CC [1963] 2 Q.B. 764; [1963] 2 W.L.R. 669; [1963] 1 All E.R.
  751; 127 J.P. 243; 61 L.G.R. 287; (1963) 14 P. & C.R. 301; [1963] R.V.R. 278; 107
  S.J. 114, CA; affirming (1962) 13 P. & C.R. 310, Lands Tr . . . .   *Digested*, 63/**3358**:
               Applied, 69/3470, 99/4249: *Considered*, 70/2775, 88/3539, 89/3632,
                                   97/4094: *Followed*, 68/3830
Wilson Barca (A Firm) v. Goulden see Goulden v. Wilson Barca (A Firm)
Wilton-Davies v. Kirk [1997] B.C.C. 770; [1998] 1 B.C.L.C. 274, Ch D . . . .   *Digested*, 98/**692**
Wiltshire v. Warwick DC (Unreported, May 11, 1998), CC (Warwick) [*Ex rel.* Dominic
  Boothroyd, Barrister, Gower Chambers, 57 Walter Road, Swansea, SA1 5PZ] . .   *Digested*, 98/**1647**
Wily v. Fuller (2000-01) 3 I.T.E.L.R. 321, Fed Ct (Aus) (Sgl judge) . . . .   *Digested*, 01/**3740**
Wily v. St George Partnership Banking Ltd [1999] B.P.I.R. 1030, Fed Ct (Aus) (Full
  Ct) . . . .   *Digested*, 00/**3502**
Wimbledon and Merton Democratic Club Society Ltd, Re, *Times*, January 7, 1999, Ch D   *Digested*, 99/**2510**
Wincanton Ltd v. Cranny [2000] I.R.L.R. 716, CA . . . .   *Digested*, 00/**2200**
Wincanton Ltd v. P&O Trans European Ltd [2001] EWCA Civ 227; [2001] C.L.C. 962,
  CA . . . .   *Digested*, 01/**932**
Wincanton Rural DC v. Parsons [1905] 2 K.B. 34, KBD . . . .   *Applied*, 01/5633
Winchester City Council v. Davies (2000) 15 P.A.D. 251, Planning Inspector
Winchester City Council v. Flemons (2000) 15 P.A.D. 292, Planning Inspector
Winchester City Council v. Portman Building Society (1999) 14 P.A.D. 181, Planning
  Inspector
Winchester Commodities Group Ltd v. RD Black & Co [2000] B.C.C. 310, QBD . . . . . .   *Digested*, 00/**4026**
Winding Up of the Christian Brothers of Ireland in Canada, Re (2000-01) 3 I.T.E.L.R. 34, CA
  (Ont) . . . .   *Digested*, 01/**387**
Window v. Customs and Excise Commissioners [2001] B.V.C. 2299; [2001] S.T.I.
  1164; [2001] S.T.I. 1218, V&DTr. . . . .   *Digested*, 01/**5569**
Windpark Groothusen GmbH & Co Betriebs KG v. Commission of the European
  Communities (C48/96 P); *sub nom* Windpark Groothusen GmbH & Co Betriebs
  KG v. Commission of the European Communities (T109/94) [1998] E.C.R. I-
  2873; [1999] 1 C.M.L.R. 199, ECJ (3rd Chamber) [1995] E.C.R. II-3007, CFI . . .   *Digested*, 96/**2687**
Windpark Groothusen GmbH & Co Betriebs KG v. Commission of the European
  Communities (T109/94) see Windpark Groothusen GmbH & Co Betriebs KG v.
  Commission of the European Communities (C48/96 P)
Windsor and Maidenhead RBC v. Amalgamated Berkshire Holdings Ltd (1999) 14
  P.A.D. 699, Planning Inspector
Windsor and Maidenhead RBC v. Century 2000 Enterprises Ltd (1999) 14 P.A.D. 26,
  Planning Inspector
Windsor and Maidenhead RBC v. Harpoon Louie's (Windsor) Ltd (1998) 13 P.A.D. 741,
  Planning Inspector

Windsor and Maidenhead RBC v. Secretary of State for the Environment, Transport and the Regions see R. (on the application of Windsor and Maidenhead RBC) v. Secretary of State for the Environment, Transport and the Regions

Windsurfing Chiemsee Produktions und Vertriebs GmbH v. Attenberger (C109/97) see Windsurfing Chiemsee Produktions und Vertriebs GmbH v. Boots und Segelzubehor Walter Huber (C108/97)

Windsurfing Chiemsee Produktions und Vertriebs GmbH v. Boots und Segelzubehor Walter Huber (C108/97); Windsurfing Chiemsee Produktions und Vertriebs GmbH v. Attenberger (C109/97) [2000] Ch. 523; [2000] 2 W.L.R. 205; [1999] E.C.R. I-2779; [1999] E.T.M.R. 585; *Times*, May 18, 1999, ECJ . . . . *Digested*, 99/**3530**:
Applied, 00/3705, 00/3718: *Considered*, 00/3724, 00/3758

Windsurfing International Inc v. Tabur Marine (Great Britain) Ltd [1985] R.P.C. 59, CA. . *Applied*, 92/3291, 92/3319, 93/3041, 95/3758, 95/3777, 95/3778, 96/4568, 97/3902, 98/3477, 99/3506, 99/3519, 00/3639, 01/3902: *Considered*, 94/2766, 01/3963: *Followed*, 96/4543, 97/3901, 00/3678, 01/3967: *Referred to*, 94/3438, 99/3480, 99/3514

Wing v. Crouch see Vehicle Inspectorate v. Norman

Wing v. Norman see Vehicle Inspectorate v. Norman

Wing v. Nuttall see Vehicle Inspectorate v. Nuttall

Wing v. TD&C Kelly Ltd see Vehicle Inspectorate v. TD&C Kelly Ltd

Wingrove v. Employment Service (Unreported, April 5, 2000), CC (Northampton) [*Ex rel.* DLA & Partners Solicitors, Fountain Precinct, Balm Green, Sheffield] . . . . . . *Digested*, 01/**4471**

Wingrove v. United Kingdom (1997) 24 E.H.R.R. 1; 1 B.H.R.C. 509; *Times*, December 5, 1996; *Independent*, November 28, 1996, ECHR . . . . *Digested*, 96/**3143**:
Referred to, 01/3479

Wingrove v. Wingrove (1886) L.R. 11 P.D. 81, PDAD . . . . *Considered*, 98/4021

Winkworth v. Christie Manson & Woods Ltd [1980] Ch. 496; [1980] 2 W.L.R. 937; [1980] 1 All E.R. 1121; *Times*, November 20, 1979, Ch D . . . . *Digested*, 80/**318**:
Considered, 01/813

Winn v. Townend; Kwiatkowski v. Townend (1998) 98(6) Q.R. 6, CC (York) . . . . *Digested*, 98/**1612**

Winnipeg Child and Family Services (Northwest Area) v. G 3 B.H.R.C. 611, Sup Ct (Can) *Digested*, 98/**4783**

Winpar Holdings Ltd v. Joseph Holt Group Plc; *sub nom* Joseph Holt Plc, Re [2001] EWCA Civ 770; [2001] 2 B.C.L.C. 604; (2001) 98(28) L.S.G. 42; *Times*, May 24, 2001, CA; affirming (2000) 97(44) L.S.G. 44; *Times*, November 14, 2000, Ch D . . . . *Digested*, 01/**751**

Winpar Holdings Ltd v. Ransomes Plc see Ransomes Plc, Re

Winstanley v. Laithwaite (Unreported, February 2, 1998), CC (Altrincham) [*Ex rel.* Jonathan Thompson, Barrister, 8 King Street, Manchester] . . . . *Digested*, 98/**1699**

Winstanley v. Winstanley (No.1) (1999-2000) 2 I.T.E.L.R. 269, CA

Winstanley v. Winstanley (No.2) [2001] EWCA Civ 460; [2001] B.P.I.R. 720, CA . . . . . *Digested*, 01/**583**

Winter v. Cotton (Unreported, May 3, 1984), CC (Gravesend) [*Ex rel.* David Phillips, Barrister] . . . . *Digested*, 85/**2978**:
Distinguished, 98/3913

Winter v. Inland Revenue Commissioners; *sub nom* Sutherland (Deceased), Re; Sutherland's Estate, Re [1963] A.C. 235; [1961] 3 W.L.R. 1062; [1961] 3 All E.R. 855; (1961) 40 A.T.C. 361; [1961] T.R. 349; 105 S.J. 929, HL; reversing [1960] Ch. 611; [1960] 3 W.L.R. 47; [1960] 3 All E.R. 270; (1961) 40 A.T.C. 318; [1961] T.R. 329; 104 S.J. 134; reversing [1960] Ch. 134; [1959] 3 W.L.R. 543; [1959] 2 All E.R. 682; 52 R. & I.T. 644; (1959) 38 A.T.C. 212; [1959] T.R. 193; 102 S.J. 563, Ch D . . . . *Digested*, 61/**2417**:
Applied, 67/497, 00/6276: *Considered*, 98/3271

Winter Maritime Ltd v. Maritime Oil Trading Ltd see Winter Maritime Ltd v. North End Oil Ltd (The Winter)

Winter Maritime Ltd v. North End Oil Ltd (The Winter); Winter Maritime Ltd v. Maritime Oil Trading Ltd [2000] 2 Lloyd's Rep. 298, QBD (Comm Ct) . . . . *Digested*, 00/**776**

Winterson v. Hogarth [2000] E.T.M.R. 783, Arbitration . . . . *Digested*, 01/**3873**

Winterthur Life UK Ltd v. Customs and Excise Commissioners (No.1) [1999] B.V.C. 2093, V&DTr

Winterwerp v. Netherlands (A/33) (1979-80) 2 E.H.R.R. 387, ECHR . . . . *Digested*, 81/**1089**:
Distinguished, 00/3171

Winther Brown & Co Ltd v. Anglo Group Plc see Anglo Group Plc v. Winther Browne & Co Ltd

Wintle v. Nye (No.2); *sub nom* Wells, In the Estate of [1959] 1 W.L.R. 284; [1959] 1 All E.R. 552; *Times*, December 19, 1958, HL; reversing *Times*, December 17, 1957, CA; reversing *Times*, May 21, 1957, PDAD . . . . *Digested*, 59/**3451**:
Applied, 80/1263, 01/5167: *Considered*, 65/1611, 66/4999, 66/5003, 73/3494: *Followed*, 01/5169

Wire TV Ltd v. CableTel (UK) Ltd [1998] C.L.C. 244, Ch D . . . . *Digested*, 98/**3878**

Wirral BC v. Evans see Wirral MBC v. Evans

Wirral MBC v. Evans; *sub nom* Wirral BC v. Evans (2001) 3 L.G.L.R. 30; [2001] O.P.L.R. 73; *Times*, February 20, 2001, Ch D . . . . *Digested*, 01/**4613**

Wirtschaftsvereinigung Stahl (IV/36.069), Re [1998] 4 C.M.L.R. 450, CEC . . . . *Overruled*, 01/782

Wirtschaftsvereinigung Stahl v. Commission of the European Communities (T16/98) [2001] E.C.R. II-1217; [2001] 5 C.M.L.R. 9, CFI . . . .   *Digested*, 01/**782**
WisdomToothbrushes Ltd'sTrade Mark Application (No.2008229) see Oral-B Laboratories Trade Mark Application (No.1589316)
Wise Finance Ltd v. Braymist Ltd see Braymist Ltd v. Wise Finance Co Ltd
Wisely v. John Fulton (Plumbers) Ltd (No.2); Wadey v. Surrey CC [2000] 1 W.L.R. 820; [2000] 2 All E.R. 545; 2000 S.C. (H.L.) 95; 2000 S.L.T. 494; 2000 S.C.L.R. 693; [2000] P.I.Q.R. Q306; (2000) 97(22) L.S.G. 43; (2000) 144 S.J.L.B. 197; 2000 G.W.D. 13-487; *Times*, April 7, 2000, HL; affirming 1998 S.C. 910; 1998 S.L.T. 1026; 1998 S.C.L.R. 954; 1998 Rep. L.R. 103; 1998 G.W.D. 26-1332; *Times*, December 2, 1998, 1 Div 1998 G.W.D. 20-1034, OH . . . .   *Digested*, 00/**6160**:
           Considered, 99/1387: *Previous proceedings*, 99/1387
Wiseman v. Borneman [1971] A.C. 297; [1969] 3 W.L.R. 706; [1969] 3 All E.R. 275; 45 T.C. 540; [1969] T.R. 279; 113 S.J. 838, HL; affirming [1968] Ch. 429; [1968] 2 W.L.R. 320; [1967] 3 All E.R. 1045; (1967) 46 A.T.C. 237; [1967] T.R. 415; 111 S.J. 892, CA; affirming [1968] Ch. 334; [1967] 3 W.L.R. 1372; [1967] 3 All E.R. 546; (1967) 46 A.T.C. 439; 111 S.J. 606, Ch D . . . .   *Digested*, 69/**1748**:
      Applied, 68/3703, 88/165, 89/147, 00/1787: *Considered*, 70/1690, 74/1851,
      79/15, 81/108, 86/2017, 87/3162, 88/2234, 89/37, 96/4753, 00/5063:
                                   Followed, 78/1681
Wiseman Lee (Solicitors) (Wasted Costs Order) (No.5 of 2000), Re; *sub nom* R. v. Wiseman Lee (Solicitors) [2001] EWCA Crim 707; (2001) 145 S.J.L.B. 119; *Times*, April 5, 2001, CA (Crim Div) . . . .   *Digested*, 01/**540**
Wisepark Ltd, Re [1994] B.C.C. 221, Ch D (Companies Ct) . . . .   *Digested*, 94/**2628**:
                                   Distinguished, 98/3271
Wiszniewski v. Central Manchester HA; *sub nom* Wisniewski v. Central Manchester HA [1998] P.I.Q.R. P324; [1998] Lloyd's Rep. Med. 223, CA; affirming [1996] 7 Med. L.R. 248, QBD . . . .   *Digested*, 98/**3961**:
                                   Applied, 00/3517
Withers v. Perry Chain Co Ltd [1961] 1 W.L.R. 1314; [1961] 3 All E.R. 676; 59 L.G.R. 496; 105 S.J. 648, CA . . . .   *Digested*, 61/**5938**:
      Considered, 68/1355, 84/2311, 85/2312, 98/2842: *Followed*, 97/2617
Witley & District Mens Club v. Mackay [2001] I.R.L.R. 595, EAT . . . .   *Digested*, 01/**2286**
Witt v. British Coal Corp (Unreported, June 22, 1998), CC (Doncaster) [*Ex rel.* Nabarro Nathanson Solicitors, 1 South Quay, Victoria Quays, Wharf Street, Sheffield] . . . .   *Digested*, 98/**546**
Witzemann v. Munich Central Tax Office (C343/89) [1993] S.T.C. 108; [1990] E.C.R. I-4477; (1991) 135 S.J. 84, ECJ . . . .   *Digested*, 91/**3868**:
                                   Considered, 98/4636
WJ Alan & Co Ltd v. El Nasr Export & Import Co [1972] 2 Q.B. 189; [1972] 2 W.L.R. 800; [1972] 2 All E.R. 127; [1972] 1 Lloyd's Rep. 313; 116 S.J. 139, CA; reversing [1971] 1 Lloyd's Rep. 401; *Times*, December 22, 1970, QBD (Comm Ct) . . . .   *Digested*, 72/**3138**:
      Applied, 75/179, 79/2379, 98/3440: *Considered*, 77/167, 80/2372, 93/2526,
                         95/2533, 96/3781: *Doubted*, 80/1064
Wm Morrison Supermarkets Plc v. Secretary of State for the Environment, Transport and the Regions; *sub nom* William Morrison Supermarkets Plc v. Secretary of State for the Environment, Transport and the Regions [2000] J.P.L. 1139; (2000) 97(19) L.S.G. 45; [2000] N.P.C. 46, QBD . . . .   *Digested*, 01/**4686**
WM Nelson Cladding Ltd v. Murray Williamson (Builders) Ltd 1995 S.L.T. (Sh Ct) 86; (2000) 16 Const. L.J. 75, Sh Ct (Tayside) . . . .   *Digested*, 95/**5486**
Wm Wrigley Jr Co v. Office for Harmonisation in the Internal Market (Trade Marks and Designs) (OHIM) (T193/99) [2001] E.C.R. II-417; [2001] E.T.M.R. 58; (2001) 24(5) I.P.D. 24033, CFI (2nd Chamber) . . . .   *Digested*, 01/**3994**
Wm Wrigley Jr Co's Trade Mark Application [1999] E.T.M.R. 214, OHIM (3rd Bd App) . .   *Digested*, 99/**3531**:
                          Applied, 01/5881: *Followed*, 00/3718
WMC Resources Ltd v. Leighton Contractors Proprietory Ltd (2000) 2 T.C.L.R. 1, Sup Ct (WA) (Full Ct); reversing (1999) 15 Const. L.J. 488, Sup Ct (WA) (Sgl judge) . . . .   *Digested*, 00/**237**
WN v. Staatssecretaris van Financien (C420/98) [2001] S.T.C. 974; [2000] E.C.R. I-2847; [2001] B.T.C. 366; 2 I.T.L. Rep. 685; [2000] S.T.I. 638; *Times*, April 19, 2000, ECJ . . . .   *Digested*, 00/**4963**
Woe v. Playforth see Wroe v. Playforth
Wojcik v. Poland (26757/95) (2001) 29 E.H.R.R. CD84, ECHR
Wokingham DC v. Costco UK Ltd (2001) 16 P.A.D. 97, Planning Inspector
Wolfs v. Office National des Pensions (ONP) (C154/96) [1998] E.C.R. I-6173; [2000] 3 C.M.L.R. 1414, ECJ (6th Chamber) . . . .   *Digested*, 01/**4604**
Wolsey Theatre Co Ltd, Re [2001] B.C.C. 486, Ch D
Wolstencroft v. Bolton MBC (Unreported, November 5, 1997), CC (Bolton) [*Ex rel.* Forbes & Partners Solicitors, Marsden House, 28-32 Wellington Street, St John's, Blackburn] . . . .   *Digested*, 98/**472**
Woltmann (t/a Trans-ex-Import) v. Hauptzollamt Potsdam (C86/97) [1999] E.C.R. I-1041, ECJ (6th Chamber) . . . .   *Applied*, 01/**4121**:
                                   Followed, 00/2349

Wolverhampton and Dudley Breweries Plc *v.* Customs and Excise Commissioners
    [1990] V.A.T.T.R. 131, VAT Tr (Manchester) . . . . *Digested*, 92/**4516**:
                                            Disapproved, 98/4907
Wolverhampton BC *v.* B&Q (Retail) Ltd see Stoke on Trent City Council *v.* B&Q
    (Retail) Ltd
Wolverhampton Citizens Advice Bureau *v.* Customs and Excise Commissioners [2000]
    B.V.C. 2198; [2000] S.T.I. 555, V&DTr
Wolverhampton MBC *v.* Wolverhampton Lawn Tennis and Squash Club (1999) 14
    P.A.D. 232, Planning Inspector
Wong (t/a Hing Hung Restaurant) *v.* Customs and Excise Commissioners [2001] S.T.I.
    984, V&DTr
Wong *v.* Parkside Health NHS Trust [2001] EWCA Civ 1721; (2001) 145 S.J.L.B. 276;
    Times, December 7, 2001; *Independent*, November 27, 2001, CA. . . . . *Digested*, 01/**5353**
Wong *v.* Vizards [1997] 2 Costs L.R. 46, QBD . . . . *Digested*, 98/**3725**
Woningen *v.* Netherlands (1997) 24 E.H.R.R. 456, ECHR . . . . *Digested*, 98/**3120**
Wood *v.* Bentall Simplex Ltd [1992] P.I.Q.R. P332; *Times*, March 3, 1992, CA . . . . *Digested*, 93/**1394**:
                                            Considered, 01/1528
Wood *v.* Blackpool BC [2001] 6 Q.R. 23, CC (Preston) [*Ex rel.* Hodgkinsons,
    Solicitors, The Old Manse, 14 Lumley Avenue, Skegness] . . . . *Digested*, 01/**1801**
Wood *v.* Customs and Excise Commissioners [2001] S.T.I. 1277, V&DTr
Wood *v.* Gahlings, *Times*, November 29, 1996, CA . . . . *Digested*, 97/**640**:
                                            Considered, 01/655
Wood *v.* Intervention Board for Agricultural Produce see J&SA Wood (A Firm) *v.*
    Intervention Board for Agricultural Produce
Wood *v.* Secretary of State for the Environment, Transport and the Regions [2001]
    EWHC Admin 35; [2001] J.P.L. 1111 (Note), QBD (Admin Ct) . . . . *Digested*, 01/**4737**
Wood *v.* Sibley (Unreported, April 17, 2000), CC (Exeter) [*Ex rel.* Tim Petts, Barrister,
    12 King's Bench Walk, London] . . . . *Digested*, 00/**2580**
Wood *v.* Smith [1993] Ch. 90; [1992] 3 W.L.R. 583; [1992] 3 All E.R. 556; (1992)
    136 S.J.L.B. 99; *Times*, March 4, 1992, CA; affirming [1991] 3 W.L.R. 514;
    [1991] 2 All E.R. 939; *Times*, July 10, 1990, Ch D . . . . *Digested*, 92/**4591**:
                             Applied, 99/4647: *Considered*, 94/4668
Wood *v.* West Dorset General Hospital NHS Trust [1998] Lloyd's Rep. Med. 258, CA . . *Digested*, 98/**617**
Wood *v.* William Ball Ltd [1999] I.C.R. 277; [1999] I.R.L.R. 773, EAT . . . . *Digested*, 00/**2158**
Wood *v.* York City Council [1978] I.C.R. 840; [1978] I.R.L.R. 228; 122 S.J. 192, CA. . . . *Digested*, 78/**908**:
                            Applied, 99/2140: *Considered*, 80/956, 83/1281
Wood Floor Studio Ltd *v.* Customs and Excise Commissioners [2001] S.T.I. 881, V&DTr
Wood Group Heavy Industrial Turbines Ltd *v.* Crossan [1998] I.R.L.R. 680, EAT . . . . . . *Digested*, 99/**6044**
Wood Pulp Cartel (C89/85), Re see Ahlstrom (A) OY *v.* Commission of the European
    Communities (C89/85)
Wood-Robinson *v.* Secretary of State for the Environment, Transport and the Regions
    [1998] J.P.L. 976, QBD . . . . *Digested*, 98/**4239**
Woodall *v.* Stockton on Tees BC [1999] R.V.R. 156, Lands Tr . . . . *Digested*, 99/**4191**
Woodard *v.* North Somerset DC [1998] 1 F.L.R. 950; [1999] 2 F.C.R. 132; [1998]
    Fam. Law 323, Fam Div. . . . . *Digested*, 98/**2390**:
                                      Applied, 98/2391, 01/5135
Woodburn *v.* BCH Prestige (Unreported, November 4, 1999), CC (Manchester) [*Ex rel.*
    NDH Edwards, Barrister, 8 King Street Chambers, Manchester] . . . . *Digested*, 00/**2568**:
                                            Followed, 00/2577
Woodbury (Valuation Officer) *v.* Toby Restaurants Ltd [1998] R.A. 315, Lands Tr . . . . . . *Digested*, 98/**4327**
Woodchester Equipment (Leasing) Ltd *v.* British Association of Canned and Preserved
    Foods Importers and Distributors Ltd [1995] C.C.L.R. 51, CA . . . . *Digested*, 96/**1193**:
                                            Applied, 98/2491
Woodchester Lease Management Services Ltd *v.* Swain & Co; *sub nom* Worcester
    Lease Management Services Ltd *v.* Swain & Co [1999] 1 W.L.R. 263; [1999]
    C.C.L.R. 8; (1998) 95(32) L.S.G. 29; (1998) 142 S.J.L.B. 221; *Times*, August 29,
    1998; *Independent*, July 20, 1998 (C.S.), CA . . . . *Digested*, 98/**2496**
Woodcock *v.* Living Connection (Unreported, November 28, 1997), CC (Watford) [*Ex
    rel.* DA Pears, Barrister, Francis Taylor Building, Temple, London] . . . . *Digested*, 98/**568**
Woodford & Ackroyd *v.* Burgess [2000] C.P. Rep. 79; [1999] Lloyd's Rep. P.N. 231;
    Times, February 1, 1999; *Independent*, February 1, 1999 (C.S.), CA . . . . *Digested*, 99/**308**
Woodgate *v.* Stafantos (Unreported, February 18, 1997), CC (Swindon) [*Ex rel.* Susan
    Chan, Barrister] . . . . *Digested*, 97/**591**:
                                              Cited, 00/462
Woodhall *v.* Inland Revenue Commissioners [2000] S.T.C. (S.C.D.) 558; [2001]
    W.T.L.R. 475; [2000] S.T.I. 1653, Sp Comm . . . . *Digested*, 01/**5282**
Woodhouse *v.* Nigerian Produce Marketing Co Ltd see Woodhouse AC Israel Cocoa
    SA *v.* Nigerian Produce Marketing Co Ltd

Woodhouse AC Israel Cocoa SA v. Nigerian Produce Marketing Co Ltd; *sub nom*
Woodhouse v. Nigerian Produce Marketing Co Ltd [1972] A.C. 741; [1972] 2
W.L.R. 1090; [1972] 2 All E.R. 271; [1972] 1 Lloyd's Rep. 439; 116 S.J. 329, HL;
affirming [1971] 2 Q.B. 23; [1971] 2 W.L.R. 272; [1971] 1 All E.R. 665; [1971] 1
Lloyd's Rep. 25; (1970) 115 S.J. 56; *Times*, November 25, 1970, CA; reversing
[1970] 2 All E.R. 124; [1970] 1 Lloyd's Rep. 295, QBD (Comm Ct) . . . .   *Digested*, 72/**495**:
                     Applied, 77/2669: *Considered*, 80/2791, 82/421, 92/3611, 95/1264:
                                                 Followed, 01/931
Woodhouse & Co Ltd v. Woodhouse (1914) 30 T.L.R. 559, CA . . . .   *Applied*, 00/671
Woodings v. Customs and Excise Commissioners [2000] B.V.C. 2032; [1999] V. &
D.R. 294, V&DTr . . . .   *Digested*, 00/**5369**
Woodridge Ltd v. Downie (1998) 76 P. & C.R. 239; [1997] 2 E.G.L.R. 193; [1997] 36
E.G. 169; (1997) 161 J.P.N. 860, Lands Tr . . . .   *Digested*, 97/**3280**
Woodroffes (Musical Instruments) Ltd, Re [1986] Ch. 366; [1985] 3 W.L.R. 543; [1985] 2
All E.R. 908; [1985] P.C.C. 318; (1985) 82 L.S.G. 3170; (1985) 129 S.J. 589, Ch D
                                                 Digested, 85/**281**:
           Cited, 00/3471: *Considered*, 95/2826: *Distinguished*, 93/2390:
                                                 Followed, 93/2331
Woodrow v. Albany Uninsured Loss Recoveries Ltd (Unreported, May 3, 2001), CC
(Shoreditch) [*Ex rel.* Nigel Ffitch, Barrister, Phoenix Chambers, Gray's Inn,
London] . . . .   *Digested*, 01/**3817**
Woodrow v. Chalk Catering Ltd 1998-W-No.00360, QBD . . . .   *Digested*, 99/**569**
Woods v. Chaleff 99/6196/1, CA . . . .   *Digested*, 99/**500**
Woods v. WM Car Services (Peterborough) Ltd [1982] Com. L.R. 208; [1982] I.C.R.
693; [1982] I.R.L.R. 413, CA; affirming [1981] I.C.R. 666; [1981] I.R.L.R. 347,
EAT . . . .   *Digested*, 83/**1204**:
                          Applied, 91/1612, 91/2725: *Considered*, 99/838
Woods Hardwick Ltd v. Chiltern Air Conditioning Ltd [2001] B.L.R. 23, QBD (T&CC) .   *Digested*, 01/**853**
Woodward v. Finch [1999] C.P.L.R. 699, CA. . . . .   *Digested*, 00/**627**
Wookey v. Wookey; S (A Minor) (Injunction to Restrain), Re [1991] Fam. 121; [1991] 3
W.L.R. 135; [1991] 3 All E.R. 365; [1991] 2 F.L.R. 319; [1991] F.C.R. 811; *Times*,
April 2, 1991; *Daily Telegraph*, April 22, 1991, CA . . . .   *Digested*, 92/**3513**:
                              Applied, 99/2437: *Considered*, 96/928
Woolgar v. Chief Constable of Sussex [2000] 1 W.L.R. 25; [1999] 3 All E.R. 604;
(2000) 2 L.G.L.R. 340; [1999] Lloyd's Rep. Med. 335; (1999) 50 B.M.L.R. 296;
(1999) 96(23) L.S.G. 33; (1999) 149 N.L.J. 857; (1999) 143 S.J.L.B. 195;
Times, May 28, 1999, CA . . . .   *Digested*, 99/**4296**
Woolley v. Ministry of Health see Roe v. Ministry of Health
Woolls v. Powling, *Times*, March 9, 1999, CA . . . .   *Digested*, 99/**4351**
Woolwich Building Society v. Fineberg [1998] P.N.L.R. 216, CA . . . .   *Digested*, 98/**501**
Woolwich Building Society (formerly Woolwich Equitable Building Society) v. Inland
Revenue Commissioners [1993] A.C. 70; [1992] 3 W.L.R. 366; [1992] 3 All E.R.
737; [1992] S.T.C. 657; (1993) 5 Admin. L.R. 265; 65 T.C. 265; (1992) 142
N.L.J. 1196; (1992) 136 S.J.L.B. 230; *Times*, July 22, 1992; *Independent*, August
13, 1992; *Guardian*, August 19, 1992, HL; affirming [1991] 3 W.L.R. 790; [1991]
4 All E.R. 577; [1991] S.T.C. 364; (1991) 135 S.J.L.B. 46; *Times*, May 27, 1991,
CA; reversing [1989] 1 W.L.R. 137; [1989] S.T.C. 111; (1989) 133 S.J. 291, QBD .   *Digested*, 92/**2508**:
          Applied, 94/4567: *Considered*, 94/3900, 94/6018, 95/5586, 95/6118:
                     Distinguished, 96/5578, 01/5024: *Followed*, 97/1735
Woolwich Plc v. Davidson (Inspector of Taxes) [2000] S.T.C. (S.C.D.) 302; [2000]
S.T.I. 1006, Sp Comm. . . . .   *Digested*, 00/**4935**
Woolwich Plc v. Gomm; *sub nom* Gomm v. Woolwich Plc (2000) 79 P. & C.R. 61;
(1999) 96(34) L.S.G. 33; [1999] N.P.C. 100; (1999) 78 P. & C.R. D45; *Times*,
September 21, 1999; *Independent*, November 8, 1999 (C.S.), CA . . . .   *Digested*, 99/**4389**
Woolwich Plc v. Le Foe see Le Foe v. Le Foe
Wootton v. Central Land Board [1957] 1 W.L.R. 424; [1957] 1 All E.R. 441; 121 J.P.
137; 55 L.G.R. 84; 8 P. & C.R. 121; 101 S.J. 188, CA; reversing (1956) 6 P. & C.R.
177, Lands Tr . . . .   *Digested*, 57/**3474.16**:
                                                 Considered, 99/4188
Worby v. Rosser [1999] Lloyd's Rep. P.N. 972; [2000] P.N.L.R. 140; (1999-2000) 2
I.T.E.L.R. 59; (1999) 96(24) L.S.G. 39; *Times*, June 9, 1999, CA . . . .   *Digested*, 99/**4050**:
                                                 Considered, 01/4534
Worcester City Council v. Connell (2001) 16 P.A.D. 5, Planning Inspector
Worcester Lease Management Services Ltd v. Swain & Co see Woodchester Lease
Management Services Ltd v. Swain & Co
Worcestershire CC v. Newar see Hereford and Worcester CC v. Newman
Workers Compensation Board v. Amchem Products Inc [1993] I.L.Pr. 689, Sup Ct
(Can) . . . .   *Considered*, 01/803
Workman v. Cowper [1961] 2 Q.B. 143; [1961] 2 W.L.R. 386; [1961] 1 All E.R. 683;
(1961) 125 J.P. 254; 105 S.J. 130, QBD . . . .   *Digested*, 61/**248**:
                                                 Referred to, 00/186
Worksop Tarmacadam Co Ltd v. Hannaby 66 Con. L.R. 105, CA
Workvale Ltd (In Dissolution), Re see Workvale Ltd (No.2), Re

Workvale Ltd (No.2), Re; *sub nom* Workvale Ltd (In Dissolution), Re [1992] 1 W.L.R.
416; [1992] 2 All E.R. 627; [1992] B.C.C. 349; [1992] B.C.L.C. 544; (1992)
89(14) L.S.G. 28, CA; affirming [1991] 1 W.L.R. 294; [1991] B.C.C. 109; [1991]
B.C.L.C. 531, Ch D . . . . *Digested,* 92/**413**:
Applied, 94/412, 01/602: *Considered,* 00/519
World Wide Fund for Nature (formerly World Wildlife Fund) *v.* World Wrestling Federation
Entertainment Inc; *sub nom* WWF *v.* World Wrestling Federation Entertainment
Inc; 2001/2214, CA; affirming (2001) 24(12) I.P.D. 24079; *Times,* November 13,
2001, Ch D . . . . *Digested,* 01/**3978**
World Wildlife Fund (WWF) *v.* Autonome Provinz Bozen (C435/97) [1999] E.C.R. I-
5613; [2000] 1 C.M.L.R. 149; [2000] 2 P.L.R. 1; [2000] Env. L.R. D14; *Times,*
October 12, 1999, ECJ (6th Chamber) . . . . *Digested,* 99/**2162**:
Applied, 01/4700: *Cited,* 00/4458
Worldcom International *v.* Home Communications Ltd 1988-W-572, QBD . . . . *Digested,* 99/**436**
Worldhams Park Golf Course Ltd, Re; *sub nom* Whidbourne *v.* Troth [1998] 1 B.C.L.C.
554, Ch D (Companies Ct) . . . . *Digested,* 98/**3331**
Worldpro Software Ltd *v.* Desi Ltd; Desi Ltd *v.* Worldpro Software Ltd; Desi Ltd *v.*
Spreckley [1997-98] Info. T.L.R. 279, Ch D . . . . *Digested,* 98/**3440**
Worldwide Corp Ltd *v.* GPT Ltd LTA 98/7526/3, CA . . . . *Digested,* 99/**499**:
Considered, 99/3517: *Referred to,* 99/497
Worldwide Corp Ltd *v.* Marconi Communications Ltd (formerly GPT Ltd) (Stay of
Costs Order) LTA 99/5076/3, CA . . . . *Digested,* 99/**386**
Worldwide Corp Ltd *v.* Marconi Communications Ltd (formerly GPT Ltd) (1999)
96(28) L.S.G. 25; *Times,* July 7, 1999, CA. . . . . *Digested,* 99/**3790**
Worm *v.* Austria (1998) 25 E.H.R.R. 454; 3 B.H.R.C. 180, ECHR . . . . *Digested,* 98/**3090**:
Applied, 01/3474
Wormell *v.* RHM Agricultural (East) Ltd [1987] 1 W.L.R. 1091; [1987] 3 All E.R. 75;
(1987) 84 L.S.G. 2197; (1987) 131 S.J. 1085, CA; reversing [1986] 1 W.L.R.
336; [1986] 1 All E.R. 769; (1986) 83 L.S.G. 786; (1985) 129 S.J. 166, QBD . . . *Digested,* 87/**3327**:
Applied, 98/4384
Worrall *v.* British Railways Board QBENI 1998/0885/1, CA. *Digested,* 99/**1413**
Worrall *v.* Chief Constable of Merseyside see Calveley *v.* Chief Constable of
Merseyside
Worrall *v.* Powergen Plc [1999] P.I.Q.R. Q103; [1999] Lloyd's Rep. Med. 177; (1999)
96(6) L.S.G. 34; (1999) 99(2) Q.R. 8; *Times,* February 10, 1999, QBD . . . . *Digested,* 99/**1619**
Worsley *v.* Tambrands Ltd [2000] P.I.Q.R. P95, QBD . . . . *Previous proceedings,*
00/548
Worsley *v.* Tambrands Ltd (Preliminary Hearing) [2000] C.P. Rep. 43; (1999) 96(48)
L.S.G. 40; *Times,* February 11, 2000, CA . . . . *Digested,* 00/**548**
WORTH Trade Marks [1998] R.P.C. 875, TMR . . . . *Digested,* 99/**3557**
Wotton *v.* Flagg [1998] C.C.L.R. 63, CC (Plymouth) . . . . *Digested,* 97/**959**:
Considered, 99/2454: *Disapproved,* 98/2500: *Followed,* 98/2501:
Not followed, 98/2503, 98/2504, 00/2568
WR *v.* Austria (26602/95) (2001) 31 E.H.R.R. 43, ECHR . . . . *Digested,* 01/**3527**
Wraith *v.* Sheffield Forgemasters Ltd; Truscott *v.* Truscott [1998] 1 W.L.R. 132; [1998]
1 All E.R. 82; [1997] 2 Costs L.R. 74; [1998] 1 F.L.R. 265; [1998] 1 F.C.R. 270;
[1998] Fam. Law 74; *Times,* October 15, 1997, CA; reversing [1996] 1 W.L.R.
617; [1996] 2 All E.R. 527; [1997] 1 Costs L.R. 23; (1996) 146 N.L.J. 590;
(1996) 140 S.J.L.B. 64; *Times,* February 20, 1996, QBD . . . . *Digested,* 97/**540**:
Distinguished, 01/524: *Followed,* 99/414, 99/415
Wrekin DC *v.* Evans (1998) 13 P.A.D. 279, Planning Inspector
Wren (t/a Blue and White Car Services) *v.* Customs and Excise Commissioners [2001]
S.T.I. 769, V&DTr
Wrexham CBC *v.* Berry see South Buckinghamshire DC *v.* Porter
Wright *v.* Atlas Wright (Europe) Ltd; *sub nom* Atlas Wright (Europe) Ltd *v.* Wright
[1999] B.C.C. 163; [1999] 2 B.C.L.C. 301; (1999) 96(8) L.S.G. 29; *Times,*
February 3, 1999, CA. . . . . *Digested,* 99/**607**
Wright *v.* Bennett (No.1) [1948] 1 K.B. 601; [1948] 1 All E.R. 411; 64 T.L.R. 149;
[1948] L.J.R. 1019; 92 S.J. 167, CA; reversing in part [1947] K.B. 828; [1947] 2
All E.R. 61; (1947) 63 T.L.R. 328; [1948] L.J.R 282, KBD . . . . *Digested,* 47-51/**7615**:
Applied, 01/4176
Wright *v.* British Railways Board [1983] 2 A.C. 773; [1983] 3 W.L.R. 211; [1983] 2 All
E.R. 698, HL . . . . *Digested,* 83/**1063**:
Applied, 00/1489: *Considered,* 85/958, 86/989, 88/1172, 89/1202:
Distinguished, 84/1004, 85/942: *Followed,* 94/5333
Wright *v.* Cherrytree Finance Ltd [2001] EWCA Civ 449; [2001] 2 All E.R. (Comm)
877; (2001) 82 P. & C.R. D10, CA
Wright *v.* Customs and Excise Commissioners [1999] 1 Cr. App. R. 69; (1998) 162
J.P. 207; *Times,* February 23, 1998, QBD. . . . . *Digested,* 98/**3574**
Wright *v.* Holman (Unreported, June 16, 1994), CC (Wolverhampton) [*Ex rel.* Sue
Thompson, Solicitor] . . . . *Digested,* 94/**3604**:
Applied, 97/567: *Considered,* 95/3973: *Disapproved,* 98/398:
Doubted, 98/399

Wright v. Macadam [1949] 2 K.B. 744; [1949] 2 All E.R. 565; 93 S.J. 646, CA . . . . *Digested*, 47-51/**5446**:
Applied, 47-51/5444, 47-51/5445, 64/1199, 70/824, 84/1153, 00/4629:
Approved, 66/4174, 66/4176: *Considered*, 72/2907
Wright v. Manchester City Council (Unreported, December 14, 1999), CC (Altrincham)
[*Ex rel.* Colemans Solicitors, Elisabeth House, 16 St Peter's Square,
Manchester] . . . . *Digested*, 00/**424**
Wright v. Marina Developments Ltd (Unreported, January 5, 1998), CC
(Southampton) [*Ex rel.* Daniel Barnett, Barrister, 2 Gray's Inn Square Chambers,
London] . . . . *Digested*, 98/**1698**
Wright v. Nicholson [1970] 1 W.L.R. 142; [1970] 1 All E.R. 12; (1970) 54 Cr. App. R.
38; (1969) 113 S.J. 939, DC. . . . . *Digested*, 70/**1651**:
Applied, 73/2083: *Considered*, 98/4385: *Disapproved*, 86/539:
Explained, 73/470
Wright v. Official Receiver [2001] B.P.I.R. 196, CC (Medway). . . . . *Digested*, 01/**3730**
Wright v. Sanderson (1884) L.R. 9 P.D. 149, CA. . . . . *Applied*, 99/4647
Wright v. Scottbridge Construction Ltd [2001] I.R.L.R. 589, EAT . . . . *Digested*, 01/**6472**
Wright v. South Buckinghamshire NHS Trust [2001] 6 Q.R. 7, QBD [*Ex rel.* Henmans
Solicitors, 116 St Aldates, Oxford] . . . . *Digested*, 01/**1610**
Wright's Application (No.1), Re [1996] N.I. 83, QBD (NI)
Wright's Application (No.2), Re [1997] N.I. 318, QBD (NI) . . . . *Digested*, 99/**5221**
Wrightson Ltd v. Fletcher Challenge Nominees Ltd; *sub nom* Fletcher Challenge
Nominees Ltd v. Wrightson Ltd [2001] UKPC 23; [2001] Pens. L.R. 207, PC
(NZ); affirming [1999] Pens. L.R. 355, CA (NZ); reversing [1999] Pens. L.R.
317, HC (NZ). . . . . *Digested*, 01/**4629**
WRM Group Ltd v. Wood [1998] C.L.C. 189, CA . . . . *Digested*, 98/**845**
Wroe (t/a Telepower) v. Exmos Cover Ltd [2000] 1 E.G.L.R. 66; [2000] 15 E.G. 155;
[2000] E.G.C.S. 22; (2000) 97(8) L.S.G. 36; [2000] N.P.C. 12; (2000) 80 P. &
C.R. D1; *Times*, March 14, 2000, CA . . . . *Digested*, 00/**3890**
Wroe v. Playforth; *sub nom* Woe v. Playforth (1998) 98(2) Q.R. 6, CC (Doncaster). . . . *Digested*, 98/**1718**
Wrotham Park Estate Co Ltd v. Parkside Homes Ltd [1974] 1 W.L.R. 798; [1974] 2 All
E.R. 321; (1974) 27 P. & C.R. 296; (1973) 118 S.J. 420, Ch D . . . . *Digested*, 74/**3130**:
Applied, 75/1017: *Considered*, 86/2827, 87/1227, 88/2729, 93/427, 93/1368,
95/2968, 95/3766, 98/4341: *Distinguished*, 86/2824, 87/3654:
Explained, 88/3269, 89/3422
Wrotham Park Settled Estates v. Hertsmere BC [1993] 2 E.G.L.R. 15; [1993] 27 E.G.
124; [1993] R.V.R. 56; [1994] J.P.L. 832; [1993] N.P.C. 48; *Independent*, April
12, 1993 (C.S.), CA; affirming (1991) 62 P. & C.R. 652; [1991] 22 E.G. 135;
[1991] 21 E.G. 123; [1991] R.V.R. 107; [1992] J.P.L. 75, Lands Tr . . . . *Digested*, 93/**427**:
Applied, 99/4363
WT Lamb & Sons v. Rider [1948] 2 K.B. 331; [1948] 2 All E.R. 402; 64 T.L.R. 530;
[1949] L.J.R. 258; 92 S.J. 556, CA . . . . *Digested*, 47-51/**7678**:
Approved, 98/539: *Considered*, 88/2155
WT Ramsay Ltd v. Inland Revenue Commissioners; Eilbeck (Inspector of Taxes) v.
Rawling [1982] A.C. 300; [1981] 2 W.L.R. 449; [1981] 1 All E.R. 865; [1981]
S.T.C. 174; 54 T.C. 101; [1982] T.R. 123; 125 S.J. 220, HL; affirming [1979] 1
W.L.R. 974; [1979] 3 All E.R. 213; [1979] S.T.C. 582; 123 S.J. 456, CA; affirming
[1978] 1 W.L.R. 1313; [1978] 2 All E.R. 321; 8 B.L.R. 169; [1978] T.R. 113; 122
S.J. 249, Ch D . . . . *Digested*, 81/**1385**:
Applied, 82/1576, 83/1980, 84/270, 85/3364, 85/3407, 86/258, 86/2203,
86/3204, 88/257, 91/2090, 92/2518, 95/876, 96/1310, 97/2975, 97/2979,
00/4942, 00/5043, 01/5237: *Cited*, 97/1073: *Considered*, 85/1909, 86/262,
87/274, 87/2036, 90/2685, 90/3943.a, 91/2115, 92/611, 92/2505, 96/428,
96/3958, 00/4916, 01/5199: *Distinguished*, 82/1582, 83/1955, 87/270,
87/282, 92/2519, 95/2750, 98/4631, 99/4709: *Not applied*, 98/4627:
Referred to, 82/485, 85/456, 95/527
Wuidart v. Laiterie Cooperative Eupenoise Societe Cooperative (C267/88) [1990]
E.C.R. I-435, ECJ . . . . *Followed*, 00/2403
Wunsche Handelsgesellschaft International mbH v. Tai Ping Insurance Co Ltd [1998] 2
Lloyd's Rep. 8; [1998] C.L.C. 851, CA . . . . *Digested*, 98/**3378**
Wurttembergische AG Versicherungs Beteiligungsgesellschaft v. Home Insurance Co
(No.2) [1999] 1 All E.R. (Comm.) 535; [1999] Lloyd's Rep. I.R. 397;
Independent, March 22, 1999 (C.S.), CA . . . . *Digested*, 99/**455**
WWF v. World Wrestling Federation Entertainment Inc see World Wide Fund for Nature
(formerly World Wildlife Fund) v. World Wrestling Federation Entertainment Inc
WWF Denmark v. Den Bla Avis A/S [1999] E.T.M.R. 300, SH (DK)
WWF UK (World Wide Fund for Nature) v. Commission of the European Communities
(T105/95) [1997] All E.R. (E.C.) 300; [1997] E.C.R. II-313; [1997] 2 C.M.L.R.
55; [1997] Env. L.R. 242; *Times*, March 26, 1997, CFI (4th Chamber) . . . . *Digested*, 97/**2386**:
Applied, 99/2239
WWF UK Ltd v. Scottish Natural Heritage see WWF UK Ltd v. Secretary of State for
Scotland
WWF UK Ltd v. Secretary of State for Scotland; *sub nom* WWF UK Ltd v. Scottish
Natural Heritage [1999] 1 C.M.L.R. 1021; [1999] Env. L.R. 632; 1998 G.W.D. 37-
1936; *Times*, November 20, 1998, OH . . . . *Digested*, 98/**5830**

Wyatt *v.* Jarrad; *sub nom* Torridge DC *v.* Jarrad [1998] 2 P.L.R. 81; [1998] J.P.L. 954;
Times, April 13, 1998; *Independent*, March 16, 1998 (C.S.), QBD . . . .　*Digested, 98/**4154***
Wyatt Bros (Oxford) Ltd *v.* Secretary of State for the Environment, Transport and the
Regions; *sub nom* Secretary of State for the Environment, Transport and the
Regions *v.* Wyatt Brothers (Oxford) Ltd [2001] EWCA Civ 1560; (2001) 98(43)
L.S.G. 35, CA; reversing [2001] P.L.C.R. 10, QBD. . . . .　*Digested, 01/**4654***
Wychavon DC *v.* McWilliams (1998) 13 P.A.D. 129, Planning Inspector
Wychavon DC *v.* Secretary of State for the Environment, Transport and the Regions
[2001] J.P.L. 495 (Note), QBD
Wychavon DC *v.* Smith (Siting of Caravans) see Buckland *v.* Secretary of State for the
Environment, Transport and the Regions
Wychavon DC *v.* Westbury Homes (Holdings) Ltd [2001] P.L.C.R. 13; [2000] J.P.L.
1305 (Note), Ch D . . . .　*Digested, 01/**4758***
Wycombe DC *v.* Batt (Extension of Hangar) (2000) 15 P.A.D. 271, Planning Inspector
Wylie *v.* Wake see Wake *v.* Wylie
Wyndham Rather Ltd *v.* Eagle Star & British Dominions Insurance Co Ltd (1925) 21 Ll.
L. Rep. 214, CA . . . .　*Followed, 98/3366*
Wynn Realisations Ltd *v.* Vogue Holdings Inc [1999] S.T.C. 524; [1999] B.T.C. 5224;
[1999] B.V.C. 245, CA . . . .　*Digested, 99/**4968***
Wynne *v.* United Kingdom (A/294-A) (1995) 19 E.H.R.R. 333; *Times*, July 27, 1994;
Independent, September 26, 1994 (C.S.); *Guardian*, July 25, 1994, ECHR . . . . . .　*Digested, 95/**2617***:
Applied, 01/6836: *Followed*, 01/1411

X (A Child) (Injunctions Restraining Publication), Re see Richmond upon Thames LBC *v.* H
X (A Child) (Parental Responsibility Agreement: Child in Care), Re see X (Children) (Care
Proceedings: Parental Responsibility), Re
X (A Child) *v.* Woollcombe Yonge (A Firm); *sub nom* X (An Infant) *v.* Woollcombe Yonge
(A Firm) [2001] Lloyd's Rep. P.N. 274; [2001] W.T.L.R. 301, Ch D . . . .　*Digested, 01/**4534***
X (Adult Patient: Sterilisation), Re; *sub nom* X (Adult Sterilisation), Re [1998] 2 F.L.R.
1124; [1999] 3 F.C.R. 426; [1998] Fam. Law 737, Fam Div . . . .　*Digested, 99/**2682***
X (Adult Sterilisation), Re see X (Adult Patient: Sterilisation), Re
X (An Infant) *v.* Woollcombe Yonge (A Firm) see X (A Child) *v.* Woollcombe Yonge (A
Firm)
X (Children) (Care Proceedings: Parental Responsibility), Re; *sub nom* X (A Child)
(Parental Responsibility Agreement: Child in Care), Re [2000] Fam. 156; [2000]
2 W.L.R. 1031; [2000] 2 All E.R. 66; [2000] 1 F.L.R. 517; [2000] 1 F.C.R. 379;
[2000] Fam. Law 244; (2000) 97(1) L.S.G. 23; (2000) 144 S.J.L.B. 25; *Times*,
January 19, 2000; *Independent*, January 12, 2000, Fam Div . . . .　*Digested, 00/**2483***
X (CICB: Quantum: 1998), Re (Unreported, September 23, 1998), CICB (London) [*Ex rel.*
Miss E.A. Gumbel, Barrister, 199 Strand, London] . . . .　*Digested, 99/**1447***
X (Disclosure of Information), Re [2001] 2 F.L.R. 440; [2001] Fam. Law 586, Fam Div.　*Digested, 01/**2568***
X (Leave to Remove from Jurisdiction: No Order Principle), Re [2001] 2 F.L.R. 118; [2001] 2
F.C.R. 398, Fam Div . . . .　*Digested, 01/**2609***:
Doubted, 01/2597

X (Minors) *v.* Bedfordshire CC; M (A Minor) *v.* Newham LBC; E (A Minor) *v.* Dorset
CC; Christmas *v.* Hampshire CC (Duty of Care); Keating *v.* Bromley LBC (No.2)
[1995] 2 A.C. 633; [1995] 3 W.L.R. 152; [1995] 3 All E.R. 353; [1995] 2 F.L.R.
276; [1995] 3 F.C.R. 337; 94 L.G.R. 313; (1995) 7 Admin. L.R. 705; [1995]
Fam. Law 537; (1996) 160 L.G. Rev. 103; (1996) 160 L.G. Rev. 123; (1995) 145
N.L.J. 993; *Times*, June 30, 1995; *Independent*, June 30, 1995, HL; affirming
[1994] 2 W.L.R. 554; [1994] 4 All E.R. 602; [1994] 1 F.L.R. 431; 92 L.G.R. 427;
[1994] Fam. Law 434; (1994) 144 N.L.J. 357; *Times*, March 3, 1994;
Independent, February 24, 1994; *Guardian*, February 28, 1994, CA; affirming
[1993] 2 F.L.R. 575; [1994] P.I.Q.R. P515; [1993] Fam. Law 575; (1993) 143
N.L.J. 1783; *Times*, November 24, 1993; *Independent*, December 23, 1993,
QBD . . . .　*Digested, 95/**3452***:
Applied, 98/2570, 98/3935, 98/3944, 98/3945, 99/1765, 99/1889,
99/3968, 99/5435, 00/5662, 01/4470: *Considered*, 96/4140, 96/4441,
97/2692, 97/2879, 97/3775, 98/3931, 98/3937, 98/3942, 99/5434:
Distinguished, 99/3966: *Doubted*, 00/1947: *Followed*, 96/3913, 97/424,
97/2142, 97/4087, 97/4860, 98/1965, 99/3967:
Previous proceedings, 94/1878, 95/1927: *Subsequent proceedings*, 98/3943
X (Non-Accidental Injury: Expert Evidence), Re [2001] 2 F.L.R. 90; [2001] Fam. Law 497,
Fam Div . . . .　*Digested, 01/**400***
X *v.* A [2000] 1 All E.R. 490; [2000] Env. L.R. 104; [2000] 1 E.G.L.R. 19; [2000] 01
E.G. 94; [2000] W.T.L.R. 11; (1999) 96(39) L.S.G. 38; *Times*, October 6, 1999,
Ch D . . . .　*Digested, 99/**4962***
X *v.* Argentina 6 B.H.R.C. 314, IA Comm HR
X *v.* Benjy's Group Ltd (Unreported, June 6, 2001), MC [*Ex rel.* Simon Brindle,
Barrister, 199 Strand, London] . . . .　*Digested, 01/**1192***
X *v.* Commissioner of Police of the Metropolis [1985] 1 W.L.R. 420; [1985] 1 All E.R.
890; [1985] Crim. L.R. 324; (1985) 82 L.S.G. 1165; (1985) 129 S.J. 187, Ch D .　*Digested, 85/**2564***:
Considered, 01/4581

X *v.* Criminal Injuries Compensation Board; *sub nom* D *v.* Criminal Injuries
Compensation Board 1999 S.C.L.R. 1066; 1999 G.W.D. 23-1079; *Times*, July 5,
1999, OH   *Digested*, 99/**5615**
X *v.* Dempster [1999] 1 F.L.R. 894; [1999] 3 F.C.R. 757; [1999] Fam. Law 300, Fam
Div . . . .   *Digested*, 99/**18**
X *v.* General Medical Council see R. (on the application of X) *v.* General Medical
Council
X *v.* Inland Revenue Commissioners (SC-281) see Ben Nevis *v.* Inland Revenue
Commissioners (SC-281)
X *v.* Netherlands (A/91); Y *v.* Netherlands (A/91) (1986) 8 E.H.R.R. 235, ECHR . . . . . .   *Considered*, 98/3154:
                                                                              Followed, 01/3467
X *v.* Secretary of State for the Home Department see R. (on the application of X) *v.*
Secretary of State for the Home Department
X *v.* Switzerland (1978) 12 D. & R. 241, Eur Comm HR . . . .   *Applied*, 00/**3243**
X *v.* United Kingdom (1975) 2 D. & R. 105, Eur Comm HR . . . .   *Applied*, 00/**3243**
X *v.* United Kingdom (Detention of a Mental Patient) (1982) 4 E.H.R.R. 188, ECHR . . . .   *Applied*, 99/**3094**
X *v.* Y (Enduring Powers of Attorney) see E (Enduring Power of Attorney), Re
X (HA) *v.* Y [1988] 2 All E.R. 648; [1988] R.P.C. 379; (1987) 137 N.L.J. 1062, QBD . . .   *Digested*, 88/**2859**:
                                                                              Considered, 01/1828
X *v.* Z Ltd [1998] I.C.R. 43; *Times*, April 18, 1997, CA . . . .   *Digested*, 97/**2228**
X AB *v.* Riksskatteverket (C200/98) [1999] E.C.R. I-8261; [2000] 3 C.M.L.R. 1337; 2
I.T.L. Rep. 302, ECJ . . . .   *Digested*, 01/**2499**
X and Y, Re [2000] N.I. 68, QBD (NI) . . . .   *Digested*, 00/**5484**
X BV (35398), Re 3 I.T.L. Rep. 466, HR (NL)
X GmbH (32709), Re 1 I.T.L. Rep. 839, HR (NL)
X Ltd, Re (2001) 98(23) L.S.G. 36; *Times*, June 5, 2001, Ch D . . . .   *Digested*, 01/**735**
X Ltd *v.* Morgan Grampian (Publishers) Ltd [1991] 1 A.C. 1; [1990] 2 W.L.R. 1000;
[1990] 2 All E.R. 1; (1990) 87(17) L.S.G. 28; (1990) 140 N.L.J. 553; (1990) 134
S.J. 546, HL; affirming [1990] 2 W.L.R. 421; [1990] 1 All E.R. 616; (1990) 140
N.L.J. 17; (1990) 134 S.J. 861, CA . . . .   *Digested*, 90/**3581**:
            Applied, 97/2780, 99/16: *Considered*, 96/3145: *Followed*, 96/23
X v Inland Revenue Commissioners (SC-282) [2001] S.T.C. (S.C.D.) 152; [2001] S.T.I. 1111,
Sp Comm
X, Y and Z *v.* United Kingdom [1997] 2 F.L.R. 892; [1997] 3 F.C.R. 341; (1997) 24
E.H.R.R. 143; (1998) 39 B.M.L.R. 128; [1997] Fam. Law 605; (1997) 94(17)
L.S.G. 25; *Times*, April 23, 1997; *Independent*, April 24, 1997, ECHR . . . .   *Digested*, 97/**2822**
X/Polysuccinate esters (G01/89 and G02/89) [1991] E.P.O.R. 239, EPO (Enlarged Bd
App) . . . .   *Followed*, 00/**3597**
X/Same Invention (G02/98), Re [1999] E.P.O.R. 503, EPO (President)
XE Trade Mark [2000] R.P.C. 405, Appointed Person . . . .   *Digested*, 00/**3780**
XEROX/Gas laser (T59/82) [1998] E.P.O.R. 157, EPO (Technical Bd App)
XEROX/High addressability image generator (T216/97) [1999] E.P.O.R. 111, EPO
(Technical Bd App)
XL Insurance Ltd *v.* Owens Corning [2001] 1 All E.R. (Comm) 530; [2000] 2 Lloyd's
Rep. 500; [2001] C.P. Rep. 22; [2001] C.L.C. 914, QBD (Comm Ct) . . . .   *Digested*, 00/**786**
XN Corp Ltd *v.* Point of Sale Ltd [2001] I.L.Pr. 35, Ch D . . . .   *Digested*, 01/**815**
XPRESSLINK Trade Mark Application, Re see Siemens AG's Application
XTC Trade Mark [1998] E.T.M.R. 268, OGH (A)
XXX/Notice of appeal (J16/94) [1998] E.P.O.R. 49, EPO (Legal Bd App)
Xydhias *v.* Xydhias [1999] 2 All E.R. 386; [1999] 1 F.L.R. 683; [1999] 1 F.C.R. 289;
[1999] Fam. Law 301; (1999) 96(6) L.S.G. 34; (1999) 149 N.L.J. 52; *Times*,
January 13, 1999; *Independent*, January 21, 1999, CA . . . .   *Digested*, 99/**2416**
Xylum Corp *v.* Gorog (1998) 21 (1) I.P.D. 21004, Pat Ct

Y (Children) (Matrimonial Home: Vacation), Re see Y (Children) (Occupation Order), Re
Y (Children) (Occupation Order), Re; *sub nom* Y (Children) (Matrimonial Home:
Vacation), Re [2000] 2 F.C.R. 470, CA . . . .   *Digested*, 00/**2547**
Y *v.* Netherlands (A/91) see X *v.* Netherlands (A/91)
Y *v.* United Kingdom (A/247-A) (1994) 17 E.H.R.R. 238, ECHR . . . .   *Digested*, 94/**2378**:
                                                                              Considered, 01/1147
Y's Application, Re 2 I.T.L. Rep. 66, Advance Rulings (Ind)
Yachia *v.* Levi (1999-2000) 2 I.T.E.L.R. 398, Royal Ct (Jer)
Yagci *v.* Turkey (A/319); Sargin *v.* Turkey (A/319) (1995) 20 E.H.R.R. 505; *Times*, June
26, 1995, ECHR . . . .   *Digested*, 96/**3134**:
                                                      Considered, 97/2771: *Followed*, 98/3073
Yahiaoui *v.* France (30962/96) (2001) 33 E.H.R.R. 17, ECHR
Yahoo! Inc *v.* Akash Arora [1999] F.S.R. 931, HC (Ind) . . . .   *Digested*, 00/**3591**
Yakult Honsha Kabushiki Kaisha *v.* Danone Nederland BV [1998] E.T.M.R. 465, RB (Den
Haag)
Yakult Honsha KK's Trade Mark Application (Nos.1260017 and 1560018) see Kabushiki
Kaisha Yakult Honsha's Trade Mark Application (Nos.1260017 and 1560018)
Yamaha-Kemble Music (UK) Ltd *v.* ARC Properties Ltd [1990] 1 E.G.L.R. 261 . . . .   *Digested*, 91/**2214**:
                                                                              Distinguished, 98/3598

Yamaichi International Europe Ltd *v.* Anthony 1999 Folio No.JC-0578, QBD . . . .   *Digested*, 99/**345**
Yamanouchi Pharmaceuticals Co Ltd *v.* Comptroller-General of Patents, Designs and
     Trade Marks (C110/95) [1997] E.C.R. I-3251; [1997] 3 C.M.L.R. 749; [1997]
     R.P.C. 844; (1998) 41 B.M.L.R. 99, ECJ (6th Chamber) . . . .   *Digested*, 98/**3480**
Yang (CICA: Quantum: 2000), Re [2001] 3 Q.R. 11, CICA (London) [*Ex rel.* David
     Edwards, Barrister, 7, Harrington Street Chambers, Liverpool] . . . .   *Digested*, 01/**1595**
Yankwood Ltd *v.* Havering LBC [1998] E.G.C.S. 75, Ch D . . . .   *Digested*, 99/**3695**
Yarburgh Childrens Trust *v.* Customs and Excise Commissioners; *sub nom* Customs and
     Excise Commissioners *v.* Yarburgh Children's Trust [2001] B.T.C. 5651; [2001]
     S.T.I. 1661; [2001] N.P.C. 173, Ch D; affirming [2001] B.V.C. 2307; [2001] S.T.I.
     1170, V&DTr
Yasa *v.* Turkey (1999) 28 E.H.R.R. 408; [1998] H.R.C.D. 828, ECHR . . . .   *Digested*, 99/**3143**
Yasin, The [1979] 2 Lloyd's Rep. 45, QBD (Comm Ct) . . . .   *Digested*, 79/**2472**:
                                 Considered, 99/793: *Distinguished*, 85/1788, 86/1787
Yasuda Fire & Marine Insurance Co of Europe Ltd *v.* Lloyd's Underwriting Syndicate
     No.229 [1998] C.L.C. 330; [1998] Lloyd's Rep. I.R. 285; (1998) 95(7) L.S.G.
     32; *Times*, January 24, 1998, QBD (Comm Ct)   *Subsequent proceed-*
                                              ings, 98/3403
Yasuda Fire & Marine Insurance Co of Europe Ltd *v.* Lloyd's Underwriting Syndicate
     No.229 (CA) see Denby *v.* English & Scottish Maritime Insurance Co Ltd
Yates *v.* John Smedley Ltd (Unreported, June 13, 2000), CC (York) [*Ex rel.* Morrish &
     Co Solicitors, First Floor, Oxford House, Oxford Row, Leeds] . . . .   *Digested*, 00/**1733**
Yates *v.* Yates see Yates Settlement Trust, Re
Yates Building Co Ltd *v.* RJ Pulleyn & Sons (York) Ltd (1975) 237 E.G. 183; 119 S.J.
     370, CA; reversing (1973) 229 E.G. 1597, Ch D . . . .   *Digested*, 75/**388**:
              Applied, 98/3440: *Distinguished*, 95/6072, 96/7107: *Followed*, 95/6071
Yates Property Corp *v.* Boland [1999] Lloyd's Rep. P.N. 459, Fed Ct (Aus) (Full Ct) . . .   *Digested*, 99/**4026**
Yates Settlement Trust, Re; *sub nom* Yates *v.* Yates; Yates Settlement Trusts, Re [1954] 1
     W.L.R. 564; [1954] 1 All E.R. 619; 98 S.J. 213, CA . . . .   *Digested*, 54/**2492**:
                                        Applied, 77/1009: *Considered*, 99/24
Yates Settlement Trusts, Re see Yates Settlement Trust, Re
Yau *v.* Customs and Excise Commissioners see Han (t/a Murdishaw Supper Bar) *v.*
     Customs and Excise Commissioners
Yaxley *v.* Gotts; *sub nom* Yaxley *v.* Gott [2000] Ch. 162; [1999] 3 W.L.R. 1217; [2000]
     1 All E.R. 711; [1999] 2 F.L.R. 941; (2000) 32 H.L.R. 547; (2000) 79 P. & C.R.
     91; [1999] 2 E.G.L.R. 181; [1999] Fam. Law 700; [1999] E.G.C.S. 92; (1999)
     96(28) L.S.G. 25; (1999) 143 S.J.L.B. 198; [1999] N.P.C. 76; (1999) 78 P. &
     C.R. D33; *Times*, July 8, 1999 ; *Independent*, July 6, 1999, CA . . . .   *Digested*, 99/**848**:
                                            Distinguished, 00/4670
Yeates *v.* Secretary of State for the Environment, Transport and the Regions [2001]
     EWHC Admin 34; [2001] P.L.C.R. 28; [2001] J.P.L. 1211 (Note), QBD (Admin
     Ct)
Yelocagi *v.* Secretary of State for the Home Department (2000) 97(23) L.S.G. 40;
     Times, May 31, 2000, CA. . . . .   *Digested*, 00/**3273**
Yenula Properties Ltd *v.* Naidu; *sub nom* Naidu *v.* Yenula Properties Ltd; B2/2001/1739,
     CA; affirming [2001] 31 E.G.C.S. 100; [2001] N.P.C. 119; *Times*, August 1, 2001;
     Independent, November 12, 2001 (C.S), Ch D . . . .   *Digested*, 01/**4144**
YES Trade Mark (I ZB 16/97) [2000] E.T.M.R. 883, BGH (Ger); reversing [1998] E.T.M.R.
     386, BPG (Ger)
Yeshurun Hebrew Congregation *v.* Customs and Excise Commissioners [2000] S.T.I.
     833, V&DTr
Yeung *v.* Customs and Excise Commissioners [2001] S.T.I. 260, V&DTr
Yildiz *v.* Secretary of State for Social Security [2001] EWCA Civ 309; *Independent*,
     March 9, 2001, CA . . . .   *Digested*, 01/**5038**
Yip *v.* Eckah (Unreported, November 17, 1999), CC (Brentford) [*Ex rel.* Patrick
     McMorrow, Barrister, 169 Temple Chambers, Temple Avenue, London] . . . .   *Digested*, 00/**3552**:
                                             Applied, 01/3819: *Followed*, 01/3830
York *v.* Casey (1999) 31 H.L.R. 209; [1998] 2 E.G.L.R. 25; [1998] 30 E.G. 110; [1998]
     E.G.C.S. 26, CA. . . . .   *Digested*, 98/**3598**:
                                        Applied, 00/5612: *Considered*, 99/3654
Yorke (Deceased), Re; *sub nom* Stone *v.* Chataway [1997] 4 All E.R. 907; (1997)
     94(33) L.S.G. 26; *Times*, August 11, 1997, Ch D . . . .   *Digested*, 97/**4724**:
                                        Applied, 01/625
Yorkshire Bank Plc *v.* Hall; Hall *v.* Yorkshire Bank Plc [1999] 1 W.L.R. 1713; [1999] 1 All
     E.R. 879; (1999) 78 P. & C.R. 136; *Times*, January 14, 1999; *Independent*,
     January 11, 1999 (C.S.), CA . . . .   *Digested*, 99/**439**
Yorkshire Bank Plc *v.* Lloyds Bank Plc [1999] 1 All E.R. (Comm) 154; [1999] Lloyd's
     Rep. Bank. 191; *Times*, May 12, 1999, QBD . . . .   *Digested*, 99/**277**
Yorkshire Building Society *v.* United Kingdom see National & Provincial Building
     Society *v.* United Kingdom
Yorkshire Cooperatives Ltd *v.* Customs and Excise Commissioners [1999] B.V.C. 2098,
     V&DTr
Yorkshire Cooperatives Ltd *v.* Customs and Excise Commissioners (Reference to ECJ)
     [2000] S.T.I. 109, V&DTr

Yorkshire Dales National Park Authority v. Wood (1999) 14 P.A.D. 293, Planning Inspector

Yorkshire Metropolitan Properties Ltd v. Cooperative Retail Services Ltd [2001] L. & T.R. 26; [1997] E.G.C.S. 57; [1997] N.P.C. 60, Ch D . . . . *Digested,* 01/**4195**

Yorkshire Traction Co Ltd v. Secretary of State for Transport (1998) 75 P. & C.R. 437; [1997] 2 E.G.L.R. 28; [1997] 36 E.G. 165; [1997] R.V.R. 150; [1997] E.G.C.S. 5; [1997] N.P.C. 6, CA; affirming [1996] E.G.C.S. 13; [1996] N.P.C. 13, QBD . . . . . *Digested,* 97/**4347**

Yorkshire Traction Co Ltd v. Vehicle Inspectorate [2001] EWHC Admin 190; [2001] R.T.R. 34; *Times,* March 15, 2001, QBD (Admin Ct) . . . . *Digested,* 01/**5401**

Yorkshire Water Authority v. Sir Alfred McAlpine & Son (Northern) Ltd 32 B.L.R. 114, QBD . . . . *Digested,* 86/**220**:
Considered, 99/235

Yorkshire Water Services Ltd v. Sun Alliance and London Insurance Plc (No.2) [1998] Env. L.R. 204, QBD (OR) . . . . *Digested,* 98/**3367**

Yorkshire Woolcombers Association Ltd, Re see Illingworth v. Houldsworth

Youell v. Bland Welch & Co Ltd (No.1) [1992] 2 Lloyd's Rep. 127, CA; affirming [1990] 2 Lloyd's Rep. 423, QBD (Comm Ct) . . . . *Digested,* 92/**2621**:
Applied, 00/3541: *Considered,* 01/3840

Youell v. Bland Welch & Co Ltd (No.2) [1990] 2 Lloyd's Rep. 431, QBD (Comm Ct) . . . *Digested,* 91/**3288**:
Applied, 00/4252

Youell v. Kara Mara Shipping Co Ltd [2000] 2 Lloyd's Rep. 102; [2000] C.L.C. 1058; [2001] I.L.Pr. 34; [2001] Lloyd's Rep. I.R. 553; *Times,* April 10, 2000, QBD (Comm Ct) . . . . *Digested,* 00/**759**

Young v. Betts see Neilson v. Betts

Young v. Black [2001] 6 Q.R. 4, CC (Stockport) [*Ex rel.* John Parr, Barrister, 8 King Street, Manchester]. . . . . *Digested,* 01/**1561**

Young v. Bristol Aeroplane Co Ltd [1946] A.C. 163; (1946) 79 Ll. L. Rep. 35, HL; affirming [1944] K.B. 718; (1945) 78 Ll. L. Rep. 6, CA. . . . . *Applied,* 47-51/2724,
47-51/3047, 47-51/7361, 47-51/7864, 47-51/7882, 47-51/11049, 52/847, 55/351, 55/2193, 56/5868, 56/6105, 56/6138, 56/6957, 57/3680, 75/1906, 77/1527, 84/186, 84/366, 84/602, 85/471, 85/568, 85/2704, 89/2893, 90/3733, 01/814: *Considered,* 47-51/7868, 53/3472, 67/547, 68/496, 68/647, 68/3317, 73/3458, 74/3952, 75/2657, 78/1590, 86/743, 87/994, 89/631, 90/1522: *Distinguished,* 47-51/7869, 47-51/7874, 47-51/8551, 47-51/9934: *Followed,* 54/1531, 54/1583, 59/1052

Young v. Carr Fasteners Ltd [1979] I.C.R. 844; [1979] I.R.L.R. 420, EAT. . . . . *Digested,* 80/**987**:
Considered, 01/4631

Young v. Charles Church (Southern) Ltd (1998) 39 B.M.L.R. 146; *Times,* May 1, 1997, CA; reversing (1997) 33 B.M.L.R. 101, QBD . . . . *Digested,* 97/**2616**

Young v. Chief Constable of Northumbria (Unreported, January 20, 1998), QBD [*Ex rel.* Crutes Solicitors, 7 Osborne Terrace, Newcastle upon Tyne] . . . . *Digested,* 99/**476**

Young (t/a Michael Graham Chartered Surveyors) v. JR Smart (Builders) Ltd (Counterclaim) QBENI 99/0742/1, CA . . . . *Digested,* 00/**456**

Young v. National Power Plc; *sub nom* National Power Plc v. Young [2001] 2 All E.R. 339; [2001] I.C.R. 328; [2001] I.R.L.R. 32; (2000) 97(46) L.S.G. 39; *Times,* November 23, 2000; *Independent,* November 14, 2000, CA; affirming [2000] I.C.R. 78, EAT . . . . *Digested,* 00/**2166**

Young (Inspector of Taxes) v. Pearce; Young (Inspector of Taxes) v. Scrutton [1996] S.T.C. 743; 70 T.C. 331, Ch D . . . . *Digested,* 98/**4683**

Young v. Prudent [2001] 6 Q.R. 14, CC (Southend) [*Ex rel.* David McHugh, Barrister, Bracton Chambers, 95a Chancery Lane, London]. . . . . *Digested,* 01/**1663**

Young v. Robson Rhodes (A Firm) [1999] 3 All E.R. 524; [1999] Lloyd's Rep. P.N. 641; *Times,* May 11, 1999, Ch D . . . . *Digested,* 99/**2**

Young (Inspector of Taxes) v. Scrutton see Young (Inspector of Taxes) v. Pearce

Young v. Sealey [1949] Ch. 278; [1949] 1 All E.R. 92; [1949] L.J.R. 529; 93 S.J. 58, Ch D . . . . *Digested,* 47-51/**4322**:
Considered, 68/1212, 68/4065, 01/5517

Young v. Sun Alliance and London Insurance Ltd [1977] 1 W.L.R. 104; [1976] 3 All E.R. 561; [1976] 2 Lloyd's Rep. 189; 120 S.J. 469, CA . . . . *Digested,* 76/**1468**:
Considered, 00/3519

Young v. United Kingdom (A/44); James v. United Kingdom (A/44); Webster v. United Kingdom (A/44) [1982] E.C.C. 264; [1981] I.R.L.R. 408; (1982) 4 E.H.R.R. 38, ECHR; affirming [1980] E.C.C. 332; (1981) 3 E.H.R.R. 20, Eur Comm HR . . . . . *Referred to,* 01/3466

Young v. Young (Costs: Order Nisi) [1998] 2 F.L.R. 1131; [1999] 3 F.C.R. 36; [1998] Fam. Law 660; *Independent,* July 20, 1998 (C.S.), CA . . . . *Digested,* 98/**409**

Your Move v. Dunbar (Unreported, June 21, 2000), CC (Canterbury) [*Ex rel.* Holly Pelham, Barrister, Plowden Buildings, Temple, London] . . . . *Digested,* 01/**112**

Yousfi v. Secretary of State for the Home Department [1998] I.N.L.R. 136, IAT . . . . *Digested,* 98/**3242**:
Doubted, 99/3175

Yrityspankki Skop Oyj v. Reinikka [2000] I.L.Pr. 122, CJ (Gen Div) (Ont) . . . . *Digested,* 00/**781**

Yu Long Shan: Guangzhou Maritime Group Co v. Dry Bulk SA 1997 (2) S.A. 454 (D), Local Div (SA) . . . . *Applied,* 00/4712

Yudt v. Leonard Ross & Craig; Goodeve-Docker v. Leonard Ross & Craig; Kantor v.
   Leonard Ross & Craig; Kedem v. Leonard Ross & Craig *Independent*, October
   12, 1998 (C.S.); *Independent*, October 5, 1998 (C.S.), Ch D . . . .   *Digested*, 98/**3928**
Yugoslavia v. Croatia [2000] I.L.Pr. 591, Cass (F)
Yuill Developments Ltd v. Darlington BC see Alfred McAlpine Homes Northumbria Ltd
   v. Darlington BC
Yukong Line Ltd of Korea v. Rendsburg Investments Corp of Liberia (The Rialto) [1998]
   1 W.L.R. 294; [1998] 4 All E.R. 82; [1998] 1 Lloyd's Rep. 322; [1998] B.C.C.
   870; [1998] 2 B.C.L.C. 485; (1997) 94(39) L.S.G. 39; (1997) 141 S.J.L.B. 212;
   Times, October 30, 1997, QBD (Comm Ct) . . . .   *Digested*, 97/**3044**
Yukong Line Ltd of Korea v. Rendsburg Investments Corp of Liberia (The Rialto)
   (Injunctive Relief) [2001] 2 Lloyd's Rep. 113, CA . . . .   *Digested*, 01/**45**
Yule v. South Lanarkshire Council (No.1) 1998 S.L.T. 490; (1997-98) 1 C.C.L. Rep. 571;
   1998 G.W.D. 9-476; *Times*, May 18, 1998, OH . . . .   *Digested*, 98/**6199**
Yule v. South Lanarkshire Council (No.2) 2001 S.C. 203; 2000 S.L.T. 1249; 2001
   S.C.L.R. 26; 2000 G.W.D. 27-1066, Ex Div; affirming 1999 S.C.L.R. 985; (1999)
   2 C.C.L. Rep. 394; 1999 G.W.D. 18-859, OH . . . .   *Digested*, 00/**6693**
Yunghanns v. Candoora No 19 Pty Ltd (No.1) (1999-2000) 2 I.T.E.L.R. 589, Sup Ct
   (Vic)
Yunghanns v. Candoora No 19 Pty Ltd (No.2) (2000-01) 3 I.T.E.L.R. 154, Sup Ct (Vic)
Yusuf v. Aberplace [1984] I.C.R. 850; (1984) 81 L.S.G. 2381, EAT . . . .   *Digested*, 85/**1271**:
   Not followed, 00/2136
Yuta Bondarovskaya, The [1998] 2 Lloyd's Rep. 357, QBD (Adm Ct) . . . .   *Digested*, 98/**4414**
Yves Saint Laurent Parfums SA v. Javico International (C306/96); *sub nom* Javico
   International v. Yves Saint Laurent Parfums SA (C306/96) [1999] Q.B. 477;
   [1998] 3 W.L.R. 1200; [1998] E.C.R. I-1983; [1998] 5 C.M.L.R. 172; [1998]
   C.E.C. 813, ECJ . . . .   *Digested*, 98/**715**

Z (A Child) v. Greater Manchester Police Authority (Unreported, November 16, 1999),
   CC (Skegness) [*Ex rel.* Hodgkinsons Solicitors, The Old Manse, 14 Lumley
   Avenue, Skegness, Lincolnshire] . . . .   *Digested*, 00/**1668**
Z (A Minor) (Freedom of Publication), Re; *sub nom* Z (A Minor) (Identification:
   Restrictions on Publication), Re [1997] Fam. 1; [1996] 2 W.L.R. 88; [1995] 4 All
   E.R. 961; [1996] 1 F.L.R. 191; [1996] 2 F.C.R. 164; [1996] Fam. Law 90, CA. . . .   *Digested*, 96/**547**:
   Followed, 00/4162
Z (A Minor) (Identification: Restrictions on Publication), Re see Z (A Minor) (Freedom of
   Publication), Re
Z (Abduction: Non-Convention Country), Re [1999] 1 F.L.R. 1270; [1999] 1 F.C.R. 251;
   [1999] Fam. Law 373, Fam Div . . . .   *Digested*, 99/**2333**
Z (CICB: Quantum: 1997), Re (Unreported, November 3, 1997), CICB (London) [*Ex rel.*
   Baljinder Uppal, Barrister, College Chambers, Southampton] . . . .   *Digested*, 98/**1515**
Z (Medical Treatment: Hysterectomy), Re see ZM and OS (Sterilisation: Patient's Best
   Interests), Re
Z v. Finland (1998) 25 E.H.R.R. 371; (1999) 45 B.M.L.R. 107, ECHR . . . .   *Digested*, 98/**3104**:
   Considered, 98/3105

Z v. United Kingdom (29392/95) [2001] 2 F.L.R. 612; [2001] 2 F.C.R. 246; 10
   B.H.R.C. 384; (2001) 3 L.G.L.R. 51; [2001] Fam. Law 583; *Times*, May 31, 2001,
   ECHR [2000] 2 F.C.R. 245; (2000) 2 L.G.L.R. 212, Eur Comm HR . . . .   *Digested*, 01/**3459**
Z and A (Children) (Contact: Supervision Order), Re [2000] 2 F.L.R. 406; [2000] Fam.
   Law 700, Fam Div . . . .   *Digested*, 00/**2479**
Z CC v. R see R (A Child) (Adoption: Duty to Investigate), Re
Zabala Erasun v. Instituto Nacional de Empleo (C422/93); *sub nom* Zabala v. Instituto
   Nacional de Empleo (C422/93); Carillo v. Instituto Nacional de Empleo (C423/
   93); Terrazos v. Instituto Nacional de Empleo (C424/93) [1995] All E.R. (E.C.)
   758; [1995] E.C.R. I-1567; [1996] 1 C.M.L.R. 861, ECJ (4th Chamber) . . . .   *Digested*, 96/**2796**:
   Applied, 98/2318
Zachow v. Land Nordrhein-Westfalen (C312/94) see Hoever v. Land Nordrhein-
   Westfalen (C245/94)
Zafar v. Glasgow City Council see Glasgow City Council v. Zafar
Zair v. Eastern Health and Social Services Board [1999] I.L.Pr. 823, CA . . . .   *Digested*, 00/**566**
Zaitz v. Secretary of State for the Home Department [2000] I.N.L.R. 346, CA. . . . .   *Digested*, 00/**3286**
Zakay v. Zakay [1998] 3 F.C.R. 35; [1999] Fam. Law 82, Sup Ct (Gib) . . . .   *Digested*, 98/**343**
Zaman v. Secretary of State for the Environment, Transport and the Regions (2000) 32
   H.L.R. 734, QBD . . . .   *Digested*, 00/**4425**
Zambia Steel & Building Supplies Ltd v. James Clark & Eaton Ltd [1986] 2 Lloyd's Rep.
   225; *Financial Times*, August 15, 1986, CA . . . .   *Digested*, 87/**155**:
                                        Applied, 98/239: *Considered*, 00/812
Zana v. Turkey (1999) 27 E.H.R.R. 667; 4 B.H.R.C. 241; [1998] H.R.C.D. 95, ECHR . . . .   *Digested*, 98/**3113**:
                                        Applied, 99/3111: *Distinguished*, 98/3093
Zander v. Sweden (A/279-B) (1994) 18 E.H.R.R. 175, ECHR . . . .   *Digested*, 94/**2389**:
                                        Applied, 98/3118, 99/3119

Zandfarid v. Bank of Credit and Commerce International SA (In Liquidation); *sub nom*
    Zandfarid, Re [1996] 1 W.L.R. 1420; [1997] 1 F.L.R. 274; [1997] 1 F.C.R. 78;
    [1996] B.P.I.R. 501; [1996] N.P.C. 40, Ch D . . . .   *Digested*, 96/**3448**:
    Followed, 01/4839
Zanella SNC's Community Trade Mark Application (B.42053) [2000] E.T.M.R. 69, OHIM
    (Opposition Div)
Zannier SA v. Minister for the Economy, Finance and the Budget [1999] E.C.C. 390,
    Cass (F)
Zanzibar v. British Aerospace (Lancaster House) Ltd [2000] 1 W.L.R. 2333; [2000]
    C.L.C. 735; *Times*, March 28, 2000, QBD (Comm Ct) . . . .   *Digested*, 00/**890**
Zaventem Airport Landing Fees, Re; *sub nom* British Midland v. Belgium [1996] 4
    C.M.L.R. 232, CEC   *Applied*, 98/719
Zealander v. Blitz Corp Ltd (Unreported, October 13, 1999), CC (Stockport) [*Ex rel.*
    Thorneycroft & Co Solicitors, Bridge Street Mills, Bridge Street, Macclesfield,
    Cheshire] . . . .   *Digested*, 00/**459**
Zealander v. Laing Homes Ltd (2000) 2 T.C.L.R. 724, QBD (T&CC) . . . .   *Digested*, 01/**970**
Zeghraba v. Secretary of State for the Home Department see R. v. Secretary of State
    for the Home Department Ex p. Sahota
Zegluga Polska SA v. TR Shipping Ltd (No.2) [1998] 2 Lloyd's Rep. 341, CA . . . .   *Digested*, 98/**4474**
Zelger v. Salinitri (C129/83) [1984] E.C.R. 2397; [1985] 3 C.M.L.R. 366, ECJ (4th
    Chamber) . . . .   *Digested*, 85/**1380**:
    Applied, 92/3534, 93/3569, 01/5419
Zelouf v. Republic National Bank of New York [1999] 2 All E.R. (Comm) 215; [1999]
    Lloyd's Rep. Bank. 270; [1999] C.L.C. 1227, QBD (Comm Ct) . . . .   *Digested*, 99/**267**
Zenziper Grains and Feed Stuffs v. Bulk Trading Corp Ltd see Bulk Trading Corp Ltd v.
    Zenziper Grains and Feed Stuffs
Zero Gee Enterprises Trust v. Internal Revenue Commissioner see Lund v. Internal
    Revenue Commissioner
Zero-rating (C416/85), Re see Commission of the European Communities v. United
    Kingdom (C416/85)
Zero-rating for Earthquake Victims (C203/87), Re see Commission of the European
    Communities v. Italy (C203/87)
Zeus Tradition Marine Ltd v. Bell (The Zeus V) [2000] 2 All E.R. (Comm) 769; [2000] 2
    Lloyd's Rep. 587; [2000] C.L.C. 1705, CA; reversing [1999] 1 Lloyd's Rep. 703;
    [1999] C.L.C. 391, QBD (Comm Ct) . . . .   *Digested*, 00/**3541**:
    Followed, 99/3408
Zezza v. Villa Gina SpA (1999-2000) 2 I.T.E.L.R. 701, Trib (Rome)
ZI Pompey Industrie v. Ecu-Line NV [2000] I.L.Pr. 600, Fed Ct (Can) . . . .   *Subsequent proceed-*
    ings, 00/**4685**
ZI Pompey Industrie v. Ecu-Line NV (Appeal) [2000] I.L.Pr. 608, Fed Ct (Can) . . . .   *Digested*, 00/**4685**
Zielinski v. France (24846/94) (2001) 31 E.H.R.R. 19, ECHR . . . .   *Digested*, 01/**3544**
Zielinski Baker & Partners Ltd v. Customs and Excise Commissioners see Customs and
    Excise Commissioners v. Zielinski Baker & Partners Ltd
Zieman v. Zieman Sicherheit GmbH (C247/96) see Sanchez Hidalgo v. Asociacion de
    Servicios Aser (C173/96)
Ziliotto v. Reuter [2001] E.C.C. 14, Cass (F)
Zimbler v. Miller (Unreported, November 27, 2000), CA [*Ex rel.* Brian D Cummins,
    Barrister, Bridewell Chambers, 2 Bridewell Place, London] . . . .   *Digested*, 01/**674**
Zimmermann Logo (4 Ob 73/99k), Re [2001] E.C.D.R. CN1, OGH (A)
Zincroft Civil Engineering Ltd v. Sphere Drake Insurance Plc, *Times*, December 13, 1996,
    CA . . . .   *Digested*, 97/**458**:
    Distinguished, 01/655
Zino Davidoff SA v. A&G Imports Ltd (C414/99); *sub nom* Levi Strauss & Co v. Tesco
    Plc (C415/99); Levi Strauss & Co v. Costco Wholesale UK Ltd (C416/99); Levi
    Strauss & Co v. Tesco Stores Ltd (C415/99) [2001] E.C.R. I-8691; *Times*,
    November 23, 2001; *Daily Telegraph*, November 27, 2001, ECJ [2001] E.T.M.R.
    67; [2001] R.P.C. 44, AGO . . . .   *Digested*, 01/**4032**:
    Previous proceedings, 00/3702
Zino Davidoff SA v. A&G Imports Ltd (No.1) [2000] Ch. 127; [1999] 3 W.L.R. 849;
    [1999] 3 All E.R. 711; [1999] 2 C.M.L.R. 1056; [1999] E.T.M.R. 700; [1999]
    I.T.C.L.R. 392; [1999] R.P.C. 631; (1999) 22(8) I.P.D. 22078; *Times*, May 24,
    1999, Ch D . . . .   *Digested*, 99/**3560**
Zino Davidoff SA v. A&G Imports Ltd (No.2) [2000] 2 C.M.L.R. 750, Ch D . . . .   *Digested*, 00/**3702**
Zino Davidoff SA v. M&S Toiletries Ltd (No.1) 2000 S.L.T. 683; [2000] 2 C.M.L.R.
    735; [2000] E.T.M.R. 622; 2000 G.W.D. 14-550, OH . . . .   *Digested*, 00/**6522**
Zino Davidoff SA v. M&S Toiletries Ltd (No.2) [2001] E.T.M.R. 10; 2000 G.W.D. 27-
    1067, OH . . . .   *Digested*, 01/**6727**
Zino Davidoff SA v. M&S Toiletries Ltd (No.3) 2001 G.W.D. 3-135; [2001] E.T.M.R.
    CN7, OH
Zionmor v. Islington LBC (1998) 30 H.L.R. 822; (1998) 75 P. & C.R. D11, CA . . . .   *Digested*, 98/**3061**
ZIPPO Trade Mark; *sub nom* DDM Italia SpA v. Zippo Manufacturing Co [1999] R.P.C.
    173; (1999) 22(2) I.P.D. 22017, TMR . . . .   *Digested*, 99/**3544**
Zirceram Ltd (In Liquidation), Re; *sub nom* J Paterson Brodie & Son v. Zirceram Ltd (In
    Liquidation) [2000] B.C.C. 1048; [2000] 1 B.C.L.C. 751, Ch D (Companies Ct) .   *Digested*, 00/**3507**

ZJAH AG *v.* WB GmbH & Co (X ZR 85/94) [2001] E.N.P.R. 3, BGH (Ger)

ZM and OS (Sterilisation: Patient's Best Interests), Re; *sub nom* Z (Medical Treatment: Hysterectomy), Re [2000] 1 F.L.R. 523; [2000] 1 F.C.R. 274; (2000) 53 B.M.L.R. 53; [2000] Fam. Law 321, Fam Div . . . .   *Digested,* 00/**2781**

Zoan *v.* Rouamba [2000] 1 W.L.R. 1509; [2000] 2 All E.R. 620; [2000] C.C.L.R. 18; (2000) 150 N.L.J. 99; *Times,* March 7, 2000, CA [*Ex rel.* Tim Kevan, Barrister, 1 Temple Gardens, Temple, London] . . . .   *Digested,* 00/**2589**:
Cited, 00/2564

Zockoll Group Ltd *v.* Mercury Communications Ltd (No.1) [1998] F.S.R. 354, CA; affirming97 Z 1815, Ch D . . . .   *Digested,* 98/**525**

Zockoll Group Ltd *v.* Mercury Communications Ltd (No.2) [1999] E.M.L.R. 385; [1998] I.T.C.L.R. 104, CA . . . .   *Digested,* 98/**4772**

Zockoll Group Ltd *v.* Telecom Eireann [1998-99] Info. T.L.R. 349, QBD . . . .   *Digested,* 01/**940**

Zolele *v.* Secretary of State for the Home Department [1999] I.N.L.R. 422, IAT . . . .   *Digested,* 00/**3279**

Zoological Society of London *v.* Customs and Excise Commissioners see Customs and Excise Commissioners *v.* Zoological Society of London

Zubaida (t/a Elley's Enterprises) *v.* Hargreaves [2000] Lloyd's Rep. P.N. 771; [1955-95] P.N.L.R. 665; [1995] 1 E.G.L.R. 127; [1995] 09 E.G. 320, CA; affirming [1993] 43 E.G. 111, QBD . . . .   *Digested,* 95/**3714**

Zubani *v.* Italy (14025/88) (2001) 32 E.H.R.R. 14, ECHR

Zuckerfabrik Franken GmbH *v.* Hauptzollamt Wurzburg (C121/83) [1984] E.C.R. 2039, ECJ . . . .   *Followed,* 00/2349

Zuckerfabrik Soest GmbH *v.* Hauptzollamt Paderborn (C92/89) see Zuckerfabrik Suderdithmarschen AG *v.* Hauptzollamt Itzehoe (C143/88)

Zuckerfabrik Suderdithmarschen AG *v.* Hauptzollamt Itzehoe (C143/88); Zuckerfabrik Soest GmbH *v.* Hauptzollamt Paderborn (C92/89) [1991] E.C.R. I-415; [1993] 3 C.M.L.R. 1; (1991) 135 S.J.L.B. 6; *Times,* March 27, 1991, ECJ . . . .   *Digested,* 91/**4051**:
Considered, 96/222, 01/2462: *Referred to,* 00/2356

ZUMBACH/Cross Section Measurement (T186/97) [1999] E.P.O.R. 483, EPO (Technical Bd App) . . . .   *Digested,* 00/**3618**

Zumtobel *v.* Austria (A/268-A) (1994) 17 E.H.R.R. 116, ECHR . . . .   *Digested,* 94/**2393**:
Applied, 98/3128, 01/4761: *Distinguished,* 98/3121

Zurstrassen *v.* Administration des Contributions Directes (C87/99) [2001] S.T.C. 1102; [2000] E.C.R. I-3337; [2001] 3 C.M.L.R. 66; [2000] S.T.I. 1510, ECJ . . . .   *Digested,* 01/**5244**

Zwebner *v.* Mortgage Corp Plc [1998] P.N.L.R. 769; [1998] E.G.C.S. 104, CA; reversing in part [1997] P.N.L.R. 504; [1997] N.P.C. 42, Ch D . . . .   *Digested,* 99/**4036**:
Distinguished, 99/3807

ZYX Music GmbH *v.* King [1997] 2 All E.R. 129; [1997] E.C.C. 477; [1997] E.M.L.R. 319; (1997) 20(6) I.P.D. 20056, CA; affirming [1995] 3 All E.R. 1; [1996] E.C.C. 314; [1995] E.M.L.R. 281; [1995] F.S.R. 566, Ch D . . . .   *Digested,* 97/**1048**:
Considered, 98/3424

SCOTTISH CASE CITATOR

This section contains:

(a) **Details of cases decided or judicially considered in the Scottish courts during 1998-2001.**

(b) **References to English Cases judicially considered in Scotland during 1998-2001.**

Scottish cases published in English Law Reports are included in both the English and Scottish sections.

Figures appearing in bold type indicate the main substantive paragraph.

1st Indian Cavalry Club Ltd *v.* Customs and Excise Commissioners [1998] S.T.C. 293; 1998 S.C. 126; 1998 S.L.T. 554; 1998 S.C.L.R. 47; [1998] B.T.C. 5030; [1998] B.V.C. 58; 1997 G.W.D. 38-1976, Ex Div . . . . *Digested,* 98/**6218**

A *v.* Criminal Injuries Compensation Board 1998 G.W.D. 15-732, OH
A *v.* G 1996 S.L.T. (Sh Ct) 123; 1997 S.C.L.R. 186, Sh Pr; reversing 1996 S.C.L.R. 787, Sh Ct . . . . *Digested,* 96/**6615**:
Overruled, 00/6261
A *v.* M 1999 Fam. L.R. 42, Sh Ct . . . . *Digested,* 99/**6063**
A *v.* Scottish Ministers; D *v.* Scottish Ministers; R *v.* Scottish Ministers [2001] UKPC D5; 2001 S.L.T. 1331; 2001 G.W.D. 33-1312; *Times,* October 29, 2001; *Independent,* December 17, 2001 (C.S), PC (Sc); affirming 2001 S.C. 1; 2000 S.L.T. 873; [2000] H.R.L.R. 450; [2000] U.K.H.R.R. 439; 8 B.H.R.C. 590; 2000 G.W.D. 22-864; *Times,* June 21, 2000, 1 Div . . . . *Digested,* 01/**6707**
A *v.* Tayside Fire Board 2000 S.C. 232; 2000 S.L.T. 1307; 2000 G.W.D. 5-174, OH . . . . . *Digested,* 00/**5836**
A Gordon & Co Ltd *v.* Ritchie 2001 G.W.D. 36-1394, Sh Ct (Grampian)
A's Curator Bonis *v.* Criminal Injuries Compensation Board see P's Curator Bonis *v.* Criminal Injuries Compensation Board
Aannamaersbedrijf PK Kraaijveld BV *v.* Gedeputeerde Staten van Zuid-Holland (C72/95) [1997] All E.R. (E.C.) 134; [1996] E.C.R. I-5403; [1997] 3 C.M.L.R. 1; [1997] Env. L.R. 265, ECJ . . . . *Digested,* 97/**2319**:
Applied, 01/4700: *Followed,* 99/2161
AB *v.* CD 2000 Fam. L.R. 91; 2000 G.W.D. 24-900, OH . . . . *Digested,* 00/**5961**
Abacus Trustees (Guernsey) Ltd *v.* Stewart 1999 G.W.D. 12-539, OH
ABB Power Construction Ltd *v.* Norwest Holst Engineering Ltd (2000) 2 T.C.L.R. 831; 77 Con. L.R. 20; (2001) 17 Const. L.J. 246, QBD (T&CC) . . . . *Digested,* 01/**859**:
Followed, 01/6287
Abbey National Plc *v.* Arthur (No.1) 1998 G.W.D. 11-560, 2 Div
Abbey National Plc *v.* Arthur (No.2) 2000 S.L.T. 103; 1999 G.W.D. 34-1640, Ex Div . . . *Digested,* 00/**6673**
Abbey National Plc *v.* Arthur (No.3) 2001 G.W.D. 37-1400, Ex Div
Abbott *v.* Forest Hills Trossachs Club; *sub nom* Abott *v.* Forest Hill Trossachs Club 2001 S.L.T. (Sh Ct) 155; 2000 G.W.D. 40-1478, Sh Pr . . . . *Digested,* 01/**6300**
Abdadou *v.* Secretary of State for the Home Department 1998 S.C. 504; 1999 S.L.T. 229, OH . . . . *Digested,* 98/**5998**
Abdelnagip *v.* Lees 1999 G.W.D. 4-226, HCJ Appeal
Abdulaziz *v.* United Kingdom (A/94); Cabales *v.* United Kingdom (9473/81); Balkandali *v.* United Kingdom (9474/81) (1985) 7 E.H.R.R. 471, ECHR; affirming in part (1984) 6 E.H.R.R. 28, Eur Comm HR . . . . *Applied,* 90/5327,
94/5927, 95/2724, 98/3154, 98/3229: *Followed,* 98/3218, 01/3616:
Referred to, 98/5998
Aberdeen Bon Accord Loyal Orange Lodge 701 *v.* Aberdeen City Council 2001 G.W.D. 30-1213, Sh Ct (Grampian)
Aberdeen City Council *v.* Bredero Aberdeen Centre Ltd 1998 S.C. 269; 1997 G.W.D. 38-1924, 1 Div . . . . *Digested,* 98/**5431**
Aberdeen City Council *v.* Clark 1999 S.L.T. 613; 1998 G.W.D. 26-1339, Ex Div . . . . *Digested,* 99/**6325**
Aberdeen City Council *v.* J see J *v.* Aberdeen City Council
Aberdeen City Council *v.* Local Government Boundary Commission for Scotland 1998 S.L.T. 613; 1997 G.W.D. 5-212, OH . . . . *Digested,* 98/**5771**:
Applied, 99/6010: *Distinguished,* 99/5626
Aberdeen City Council *v.* R 2000 G.W.D. 27-1024, Sh Ct (Grampian)
Aberdeen City Council *v.* W 2000 G.W.D. 32-1241, Sh Pr

Aberdeen City Council v. WA Fairhurst 2000 S.C.L.R. 392; 1999 G.W.D. 31-1493, OH . .   *Digested*, 00/**5918**
Aberdeen Water Technologists v. Henderson 2000 G.W.D. 20-783, Sh Ct
Aberdeenshire CC v. Lord Glentanar 1999 S.L.T. 1456 (Note), OH
Aberdeenshire Council v. Booth for Better Service 2001 G.W.D. 12-406, Sh Ct (Grampian)
Aberdein Considine & Co v. Edwards 2001 G.W.D. 4-167, Sh Ct (Grampian)
Aberdyce Joinery v. Ali 2000 G.W.D. 1-9, Sh Ct
Abitibi-Consolidated Inc v. North British Newsprint Ltd; *sub nom* Abitibi-Price Ltd v. North British Newsprint Ltd 1998 G.W.D. 8-360, 2 Div; affirming 1997 G.W.D. 16-715, OH
Abitibi-Price Ltd v. North British Newsprint Ltd see Abitibi-Consolidated Inc v. North British Newsprint Ltd
Abott v. Forest Hill Trossachs Club see Abbott v. Forest Hills Trossachs Club
AC Drysdale Ltd v. Menzies 1998 G.W.D. 17-839, Sh Ct
Accountant in Bankruptcy v. Halifax Plc; *sub nom* Accountant of Court v. Halifax Plc 1999 S.C.L.R. 1135; 1999 G.W.D. 24-1166, OH . . . .   *Digested*, 00/**6504**
Accountant in Bankruptcy v. Nottay see Nottay's Trustee v. Nottay
Accountant of Court v. Halifax Plc see Accountant in Bankruptcy v. Halifax Plc
Accounting Secretarial and Personnel Ltd v. Halford 2000 G.W.D. 27-1038, OH
Accounting Secretarial and Personnel Ltd v. Power 2000 G.W.D. 27-1039, OH
Acharki v. HM Advocate 1999 G.W.D. 17-805, HCJ Appeal
Ackerman v. Blackburn (No.1); *sub nom* Ackerman v. Logan's Executors (No.1) 2001 Fam. L.R. 90; 2001 G.W.D. 18-701, Ex Div; affirming 2000 Fam. L.R. 35; 2000 G.W.D. 4-151, OH. . . . .   *Digested*, 00/**6283**: *Referred to*, 00/6284
Ackerman v. Blackburn (No.2); *sub nom* Ackerman v. Logan's Executors (No.2) 2001 G.W.D. 35-1346, Ex Div
Ackerman v. Logan's Executors (No.1) see Ackerman v. Blackburn (No.1)
Ackerman v. Logan's Executors (No.2) see Ackerman v. Blackburn (No.2)
Adair v. David Colville & Sons Ltd 1926 S.C. (H.L.) 51; 1926 S.L.T. 590, HL . . . .   *Applied*, 93/**5676**: *Distinguished*, 94/6150: *Followed*, 99/5618
Adam v. Friel 1998 G.W.D. 19-981, HCJ Appeal
Adam v. Wadbister Offshore Ltd see Wadbister Offshore Ltd v. Adam
Adam Associates (Strathclyde) Ltd (In Receivership) v. CGU Insurance Plc 2001 S.L.T. (Sh Ct) 18; 2000 G.W.D. 25-931, Sh Pr . . . .   *Digested*, 01/**6214**
Adams v. Glasgow City Council 2000 Hous. L.R. 3, Sh Ct (Glasgow). . . . .   *Digested*, 00/**6602**
Adams v. Heywood (Sentencing) 2000 G.W.D. 8-284, HCJ Appeal
Adams v. Higson (Sentencing) 1998 G.W.D. 13-666, HCJ Appeal
Adams v. HM Advocate (Sentencing) 2000 G.W.D. 29-1137, HCJ Appeal
Adams (John) v. HM Advocate 1999 J.C. 139; 1999 S.C.C.R. 188; 1999 G.W.D. 6-293, HCJ Appeal . . . .   *Digested*, 99/**5816**
Adams v. Reith 1998 G.W.D. 20-1024, HCJ Appeal
Adams v. South Lanarkshire Council 2001 G.W.D. 38-1442, OH
Adams v. Young [2001] N.P.C. 38; 2001 G.W.D. 3-127, OH
Adamson v. HM Advocate (Sentencing) 1998 G.W.D. 32-1660, HCJ Appeal
Adamson (Stuart) v. HM Advocate; *sub nom* HM Advocate v. Adamson (Stuart) 2000 J.C. 165; 2000 S.L.T. 1405; 1999 S.C.C.R. 994; 1999 G.W.D. 35-1690, HCJ Appeal; reversing 1999 S.L.T. (Sh Ct) 37; 1999 G.W.D. 4-191, Sh Ct (Tayside). . .   *Digested*, 00/**6132**
Adamson v. Houston 2000 G.W.D. 38-1428, HCJ
Adamson v. Lothian Health Board 2000 Rep. L.R. 44, OH . . . .   *Digested*, 00/**6175**
Adan (Hassan Hussein) v. Secretary of State for the Home Department; *sub nom* Secretary of State for the Home Department v. Adan (Hassan Hussein); R. v. Secretary of State for the Home Department Ex p. Adan (Hassan Hussein); Nooh v. Secretary of State for the Home Department; Lazarevic v. Secretary of State for the Home Department; Radivojevic v. Secretary of State for the Home Department [1999] 1 A.C. 293; [1998] 2 W.L.R. 702; [1998] 2 All E.R. 453; [1998] Imm. A.R. 338; [1998] I.N.L.R. 325; (1998) 95(18) L.S.G. 33; (1998) 148 N.L.J. 552; (1998) 142 S.J.L.B. 139; *Times*, April 6, 1998, HL; reversing [1997] 1 W.L.R. 1107; [1997] 2 All E.R. 723; 2 B.H.R.C. 65; [1997] Imm. A.R. 251; [1997] I.N.L.R. 1; *Times*, March 7, 1997; *Independent*, March 12, 1997, CA . .   *Digested*, 98/**3241**: *Applied*, 99/3183: *Considered*, 00/3319: *Followed*, 00/6491, 01/3639: *Not followed*, 01/3694
Adrami v. Glasgow City Licensing Board 2000 S.C.L.R. 639; [2000] 16 S.L.L.P. 7; 2000 G.W.D. 10-366, Ex Div . . . .   *Digested*, 00/**6565**
Advocate General for Scotland v. John D Reid Joinery Ltd see Customs and Excise Commissioners v. John D Reid Joinery Ltd
Advocate General for Scotland v. MacDonald; *sub nom* Secretary of State for Defence v. MacDonald; MacDonald v. Ministry of Defence 2001 S.L.T. 819; 2001 S.C.L.R. 795; [2001] I.R.L.R. 431; 2001 G.W.D. 19-731, Ex Div; reversing [2001] 1 All E.R. 620; [2001] I.C.R. 1; [2000] I.R.L.R. 748; [2001] H.R.L.R. 5; *Independent*, November 27, 2000 (C.S), EAT . . . .   *Digested*, 01/**6475**: *Considered*, 01/2315
Advocate General for Scotland v. Mann see Secretary of State for Scotland v. Mann
AETC Ltd v. Steel 2001 G.W.D. 26-1003, OH

AF Drysdale Ltd v. Menzies 1998 G.W.D. 32-1667, Sh Pr
Afzal v. Vannet 1999 G.W.D. 26-1264, HCJ Appeal
AGA Estate Agencies, Re [1986] P.C.C. 358; *Times*, June 4, 1986, Ch D . . . . *Digested*, 87/**338**:
                                            Applied, 98/5521: *Considered*, 00/5956
Agar v. HM Advocate (Misdirection) 2000 G.W.D. 12-421, HCJ Appeal
Agar v. HM Advocate (Sentencing) 2000 G.W.D. 26-985, HCJ Appeal
AGE Ltd v. Brown see Age Ltd v. Kwik Save Stores Ltd
Age Ltd v. Kwik Save Stores Ltd; *sub nom* AGE Ltd v. Brown 2001 S.C. 144; 2001
    S.L.T. 841; 2000 G.W.D. 27-1018, OH . . . . *Digested*, 01/**6751**
Aggarwall v. Crowe 1998 G.W.D. 6-289, HCJ Appeal
Agnew v. Brown (Sentencing) 2000 G.W.D. 19-757, HCJ Appeal
Agnew v. Scott Lithgow Ltd (No.1) 2001 S.C. 516; 2001 S.L.T. 876; 2001 Rep. L.R.
    45; 2001 G.W.D. 1-70, OH. . . . . *Digested*, 01/**6251**
Ahmad (Munir), Petitioner see Ahmad (Munir) v. Secretary of State for the Home
    Department
Ahmad (Munir) v. Secretary of State for the Home Department; *sub nom* Ahmad
    (Munir), Petitioner 2001 S.L.T. 282; 2000 S.C.L.R. 796; 2000 G.W.D. 15-613,
    OH . . . . *Digested*, 00/**6495**
Ahmed (Nisar), Petitioner; *sub nom* Ahmed (Nisar) v. Secretary of State for the Home
    Department 2000 S.C.L.R. 761; 2000 G.W.D. 12-433, OH . . . . *Digested*, 00/**6500**
Ahmed v. Clydesdale Bank Plc 2001 S.L.T. 423; 2000 G.W.D. 27-1037, OH
Ahmed v. Craigen 2001 G.W.D. 31-1241, HCJ Appeal
Ahmed v. Glasgow City Council 2000 S.L.T. (Sh Ct) 153; 2000 Rep. L.R. 130; 2000
    G.W.D. 26-1004, Sh Pr; affirming 2000 G.W.D. 12-440, Sh Ct . . . . *Digested*, 00/**6588**
Ahmed v. McFadyen 1999 G.W.D. 18-857, HCJ Appeal
Ahmed v. McLeod 1998 J.C. 242; 1999 S.L.T. 762; 1998 S.C.C.R. 486; [2000] R.T.R.
    201; 1998 G.W.D. 27-1391, HCJ Appeal . . . . *Digested*, 98/**5695**:
                                        Followed, 00/1201
Ahmed (Mahmood) v. North Lanarkshire Council 1999 S.L.T. 1064; 1999 S.C.L.R. 585;
    [1999] 14 S.L.L.P. 7; 1999 G.W.D. 6-313, Ex Div . . . . *Digested*, 99/**6348**
Ahmed (Nasim) v. Secretary of State for the Home Department 2001 S.C. 705; 2001
    S.C.L.R. 623; 2001 G.W.D. 10-365, OH . . . . *Digested*, 01/**6712**
Ahmed (Nisar) v. Secretary of State for the Home Department see Ahmed (Nisar),
    Petitioner
Ahmed (Saleem) v. Secretary of State for the Home Department 2001 S.L.T. 1347;
    2000 G.W.D. 13-496, OH
Aiken v. Board of Management of Aberdeen College 2001 G.W.D. 10-370, Ex Div;
    affirming 2000 G.W.D. 2-74, Sh Ct
Ailsa Craig Fishing Co Ltd v. Malvern Fishing Co Ltd (The Strathallan); Malvern Fishing
    Co Ltd v. Ailsa Craig Fishing Co Ltd (The Strathallan) [1983] 1 W.L.R. 964;
    [1983] 1 All E.R. 101; [1983] 1 Lloyd's Rep. 183 (Note); 1982 S.C. (H.L.) 14; 1982
    S.L.T. 377; (1983) 80 L.S.G. 2516; (1983) 127 S.J. 508, HL; affirming 1981
    S.L.T. 130, 1 Div . . . . *Digested*, 83/**3440**:
                         Applied, 83/3314, 95/5569, 00/895: *Considered*, 82/403
Aird (Kirsty) v. Vannet 1999 J.C. 205; 2000 S.L.T. 435; 1999 S.C.C.R. 322; 1999
    G.W.D. 14-662, HCJ Appeal . . . . *Digested*, 99/**5959**
Airlie v. Edinburgh DC [1996] I.R.L.R. 516, EAT . . . . *Digested*, 96/**2521**:
                                  Distinguished, 98/5827, 99/6027
Airnes v. Chief Constable of Strathclyde 1998 S.L.T. (Sh Ct) 15; 1998 Rep. L.R. 19;
    1997 G.W.D. 34-1704, Sh Pr; affirming 1997 Rep. L.R. (Quantum) 10, Sh Ct
    (Glasgow) . . . . *Digested*, 98/**5438**
Aitchison v. Ruxton 1999 G.W.D. 16-738, HCJ Appeal
Aitken v. Aitken 1978 S.C. 297; 1978 S.L.T. 183, 1 Div . . . . *Digested*, 78/**3148**:
                                Approved, 85/3731: *Considered*, 00/6261
Aitken v. Independent Insurance Co Ltd 2001 S.L.T. 376; 2001 G.W.D. 2-101, OH . . . . . *Digested*, 01/**6720**
Aitken's Trustee v. Aitken see Kerr v. Aitken
Akbar v. Crichton 1999 G.W.D. 29-1356, Sh Ct
Akhtal v. Vannet (Sentencing) 1998 G.W.D. 12-623, HCJ Appeal
Akhtar v. Secretary of State for the Home Department; *sub nom* Akhtar, Petitioner
    2001 S.L.T. 1239; 2000 G.W.D. 13-495, OH
Akhtar v. Vannet 1999 G.W.D. 11-526, HCJ Appeal
Akhtar, Petitioner see Akhtar v. Secretary of State for the Home Department
Al-Megrahi v. HM Advocate (No.2) see HM Advocate v. Al-Megrahi (No.2)
Al-Megrahi v. HM Advocate (No.3) see HM Advocate v. Al-Megrahi (No.3)
Al-Megrahi v. HM Advocate (No.5) see HM Advocate v. Al-Megrahi (No.5)
Al-Megrahi v. Times Newspapers Ltd; *sub nom* Megrahi v. Times Newspapers Ltd
    2000 J.C. 22; 1999 S.C.C.R. 824; 1999 G.W.D. 29-1367, HCJ . . . . *Digested*, 00/**6031**
Alba Tools Ltd v. Buchanan 1999 G.W.D. 34-1614, OH
Albatown Ltd v. Credential Group Ltd 2001 G.W.D. 27-1102, OH
Albon v. Inland Revenue Commissioners [1998] S.T.C. 1181; 1998 S.C. 934; 1999 S.L.T.
    814; 71 T.C. 174; [1999] B.T.C. 138; 1998 G.W.D. 28-1441, Ex Div . . . . *Digested*, 99/**6458**
Albyn Housing Society Ltd v. Taylor Woodrow Homes Ltd 1985 S.C. 104; 1985 S.L.T.
    309, Ex Div. . . . . *Digested*, 85/**3689**:
                                        Considered, 01/6293

Alcock v. Chief Constable of South Yorkshire; *sub nom* Jones v. Wright; Penk v. Wright; Jones v. Chief Constable of South Yorkshire; Copoc v. Chief Constable of South Yorkshire [1992] 1 A.C. 310; [1991] 3 W.L.R. 1057; [1991] 4 All E.R. 907; [1992] P.I.Q.R. P1; (1992) 89(3) L.S.G. 34; (1991) 141 N.L.J. 166; (1992) 136 S.J.L.B. 9; *Times,* November 29, 1991; *Independent,* November 29, 1991; *Guardian,* December 11, 1991, HL; affirming [1991] 3 All E.R. 88; *Times,* May 6, 1991; *Independent,* May 10, 1991; *Guardian,* May 9, 1991, CA; affirming [1991] 2 W.L.R. 814; [1991] 1 All E.R. 353; (1990) 140 N.L.J. 1717, QBD . . . .   *Digested,* 92/**3250**:
Applied, 92/3253, 93/2972, 95/6157, 98/3938, 00/531, 01/5352, 01/6665:
Considered, 95/3682, 97/2615, 98/4035, 99/4059, 00/4213, 00/4220, 00/6598

Alex Lawrie Factors Ltd v. Mitchell Engineering Ltd 2001 S.L.T. (Sh Ct) 93; 2000 G.W.D. 36-1352, Sh Ct (Glasgow)
Alexander v. HM Advocate (Sentencing) 2001 G.W.D. 30-1181, HCJ Appeal
Alexander v. Lees 1998 G.W.D. 19-995, HCJ Appeal
Alexander v. McGlennan 1999 G.W.D. 13-594, HCJ Appeal
Alexander v. Royal Hotel (Caithness) Ltd; *sub nom* Alexander v. Taylor 2001 S.L.T. 17; [2001] 1 E.G.L.R. 6; [2001] 16 E.G. 148; 2000 G.W.D. 33-1258, Ex Div . . . .   *Digested,* 01/**6737**
Alexander v. Taylor see Alexander v. Royal Hotel (Caithness) Ltd
Alexandra v. Murphy 2000 S.L.T. (Sh Ct) 44; 2000 S.C.L.R. 200; 2000 G.W.D. 4-153, Sh Pr . . . .   *Digested,* 00/**5923**
Alexandra Hotel (Ballater) Ltd v. Scottish Hydro Electric Plc 1998 S.L.T. 668; 1997 G.W.D. 27-1385, OH . . . .   *Digested,* 98/**5803**
Alford v. West Bromwich Building Society see Investors Compensation Scheme Ltd v. West Bromwich Building Society (No.1)
Ali (Liaqat), Petitioner see Ali (Liaqat) v. Secretary of State for the Home Department
Ali v. Ali (Financial Provision); *sub nom* Ali, Petitioner 1999 S.L.T. 943; 1999 Fam. L.R. 18; 1998 G.W.D. 40-2033, Ex Div; reversing 1998 G.W.D. 23-1150, OH . . . .   *Digested,* 99/**6078**
Ali v. Ali (No.1) 1999 G.W.D. 34-1638, OH
Ali v. Ali (No.2) 2001 S.C. 618; 2001 S.L.T. 602; 2001 S.C.L.R. 485; 2001 G.W.D. 5-179, Ex Div . . . .   *Digested,* 01/**6516**
Ali v. Ali (No.3) 2001 G.W.D. 38-1430, OH
Ali v. HM Advocate (Sentencing) 2000 G.W.D. 4-122, HCJ Appeal
Ali v. Khosla 2001 S.C.L.R. 1072; 2001 G.W.D. 25-917, Ex Div
Ali (Liaqat) v. Secretary of State for the Home Department; *sub nom* Ali (Liaqat), Petitioner 2000 S.C.L.R. 783; 2000 G.W.D. 16-669, OH . . . .   *Digested,* 00/**6494**
Ali (Rafaqat) v. Secretary of State for the Home Department 1999 S.C.L.R. 555; 1999 G.W.D. 7-348, OH . . . .   *Digested,* 99/**6290**
Ali, Petitioner see Ali v. Ali (Financial Provision)
Allan v. Gilchrist 1999 G.W.D. 18-840, HCJ Appeal
Allan v. Greater Glasgow Health Board 1998 S.L.T. 580; (1993) 17 B.M.L.R. 135, OH . .   *Digested,* 98/**5720**:
Followed, 98/6115

Allan v. Heywood (Sentencing) 1998 G.W.D. 19-970, HCJ Appeal
Allan v. Heywood (Sentencing: Further Offence) 1999 G.W.D. 30-1419, HCJ Appeal
Allan v. HM Advocate (Sentencing) 2000 G.W.D. 4-134, HCJ Appeal
Allan v. HM Advocate (Sentencing) 2001 G.W.D. 26-1037, HCJ Appeal
Allan (Thomas Reid) v. HM Advocate 2000 J.C. 75; 1999 S.C.C.R. 923; 1999 G.W.D. 31-1465, HCJ Appeal . . . .   *Digested,* 00/**6056**:
Distinguished, 01/6359

Allan v. McFadyen (Sentencing) 2000 G.W.D. 8-303, HCJ Appeal
Allan v. Napier 1999 G.W.D. 29-1364, HCJ Appeal
Allan v. Scott 1972 S.C. 59; 1972 S.L.T. 45, 2 Div; affirming 1971 S.L.T. (Notes) 49, OH .   *Digested,* 72/**3716**:
Considered, 85/1038, 00/6165

Allan v. Vannet (Sentencing) 1998 G.W.D. 16-827, HCJ Appeal
Allen v. Allen 1998 G.W.D. 7-314, Sh Pr
Allerdyce v. HM Advocate 1998 G.W.D. 12-589, HCJ Appeal
Alliance & Leicester Building Society v. Macgregor see Alliance & Leicester Building Society v. Murray's Trustee
Alliance & Leicester Building Society v. Murray's Trustee; *sub nom* Alliance & Leicester Building Society v. Macgregor 1995 S.L.T. (Sh Ct) 77; 1994 S.C.L.R. 19, Sh Ct (Tayside). . . . .   *Digested,* 94/**5915**:
Not followed, 98/6179, 01/6883

Allied Domecq Retailing Ltd v. Glasgow City Licensing Board [1999] 14 S.L.L.P. 12; 1999 G.W.D. 8-403, Sh Ct. . . . .   *Digested,* 00/**6564**
Allied Domecq Spirits & Wine Ltd v. Murray McDavid Ltd 1998 S.C. 354; 1999 S.L.T. 157; [1998] E.T.M.R. 61; [1997] F.S.R. 864; 1997 G.W.D. 35-1816; *Times,* December 9, 1997, OH. . . . .   *Digested,* 98/**6021**
Allied London & Scottish Properties Plc v. Riverbrae Construction Ltd 2000 S.L.T. 981; [1999] B.L.R. 346; (2000) 2 T.C.L.R. 398; 68 Con. L.R. 79; 1999 G.W.D. 27-1265; *Times,* November 11, 1999, OH . . . .   *Digested,* 99/**5781**
Allison v. HM Advocate 2001 G.W.D. 40-1512, HCJ Appeal
Allseas UK Ltd v. Greenpeace Ltd 2001 S.C. 844; 2001 G.W.D. 13-464, OH
Alpine House Ltd v. Links 1990 S.L.T. (Sh. Ct.) 87, Sh Pr . . . .   *Digested,* 90/**5873**:
Not followed, 99/5721

Alvis *v.* Harrison 1991 S.L.T. 64; (1991) 62 P. & C.R. 10, HL; reversing 1989 S.C. 136; 1989 S.L.T. 746, 2 Div . . . . *Digested*, 91/**5109**: *Applied*, 99/6239
Ambion Homes Ltd *v.* Friel (Sentencing) 1998 G.W.D. 9-460, HCJ Appeal
Ambrose *v.* O'Donnell 1999 G.W.D. 8-375, HCJ Appeal
Ameen *v.* Hunter 2000 S.L.T. 954; 2000 Rep. L.R. 34; 2000 G.W.D. 5-208, OH . . . . . . *Digested*, 00/**6581**
Amin *v.* Amin 2000 S.L.T. (Sh Ct) 115; 2000 Fam. L.R. 114; 2000 G.W.D. 25-942, Sh Pr . . . . *Digested*, 00/**6272**
Amin *v.* Secretary of State for the Home Department 2000 G.W.D. 15-614, OH
Ampliflaire Ltd *v.* Secretary of State for Scotland 1999 S.L.T. 937; 1998 S.C.L.R. 565; 1998 G.W.D. 8-405, Ex Div . . . . *Digested*, 98/**6141**
AMT, Petitioners see T, Petitioner
Anderson (Neil Gordon), Petitioner 1998 S.L.T. 101; 1997 S.C.C.R. 734; 1997 G.W.D. 36-1835, HCJ Appeal. . . . . *Digested*, 98/**6051**
Anderson *v.* Angiolini (Sentencing) 2001 G.W.D. 30-1186, HCJ Appeal
Anderson *v.* Bamber 1998 G.W.D. 1-56, HCJ Appeal
Anderson *v.* Carnegie (Sentencing) 1998 G.W.D. 2-72, HCJ Appeal
Anderson *v.* Colley 1998 G.W.D. 31-1626, HCJ Appeal
Anderson *v.* Commercial Union Assurance Co Plc (No.1) 1998 S.C. 197; 1998 S.L.T. 826; 1997 G.W.D. 29-1486, 2 Div. . . . . *Digested*, 98/**6014**
Anderson *v.* Commercial Union Assurance Co Plc (No.2) 1998 G.W.D. 30-1537, Sh Ct
Anderson *v.* Crowe 1998 G.W.D. 39-2010, HCJ Appeal
Anderson (Steven) *v.* Douglas 1998 S.L.T. 379; 1997 S.C.C.R. 632; 1997 G.W.D. 32-1611, HCJ Appeal . . . . *Digested*, 97/**5775**
Anderson *v.* Dundee City Council 2000 S.L.T. (Sh Ct) 134; 1999 S.C.L.R. 518; 1999 Hous. L.R. 82; [2000] E.H.L.R. Dig. 96; 1999 G.W.D. 1-52, Sh Ct (Tayside) . . . . *Digested*, 99/**6379**
Anderson *v.* Fisher 1999 G.W.D. 36-1768, OH
Anderson *v.* Forth Valley Health Board 1998 S.L.T. 588; 1998 S.C.L.R. 97; (1998) 44 B.M.L.R. 108; 1998 Rep. L.R. 3; 1997 G.W.D. 39-2016, OH . . . . *Digested*, 98/**6115**: *Applied*, 00/1464: *Considered*, 00/4200
Anderson *v.* Higson 2001 S.L.T. 1035; 2001 G.W.D. 10-325, HCJ Appeal. . . . . *Digested*, 01/**6324**
Anderson *v.* HM Advocate (Sentencing) 1998 G.W.D. 2-76, HCJ Appeal
Anderson *v.* HM Advocate (Sentencing) 1998 G.W.D. 35-1794, HCJ Appeal
Anderson *v.* HM Advocate (Sentencing) 2000 G.W.D. 8-281, HCJ Appeal
Anderson (Graham Ivor) *v.* HM Advocate 1998 S.L.T. 532; 1998 S.C.C.R. 196; 1998 G.W.D. 9-450, HCJ Appeal . . . . *Digested*, 98/**5698**
Anderson (James McAulay) *v.* HM Advocate 1996 J.C. 29; 1996 S.L.T. 155, HCJ Appeal . . . . *Digested*, 96/**6764**: *Distinguished*, 00/6091: *Referred to*, 97/5804
Anderson (James Stewart) *v.* HM Advocate 2001 S.L.T. 1265; 2001 S.C.C.R. 738; 2001 G.W.D. 27-1090, HCJ Appeal. . . . . *Digested*, 01/**6310**
Anderson (John James) *v.* HM Advocate 1996 J.C. 138; 1996 S.C.C.R. 487, HCJ Appeal . . . . *Digested*, 96/**6757**: *Considered*, 98/5596
Anderson *v.* Hogg 2001 G.W.D. 40-1501, Ex Div; reversing in part 2000 S.L.T. 634; 2000 G.W.D. 6-217, OH . . . . *Digested*, 00/**5959**
Anderson *v.* Howdle (Sentencing) 1998 G.W.D. 25-1279, HCJ Appeal
Anderson *v.* Howdle (Sentencing) 2001 G.W.D. 2-90, HCJ Appeal
Anderson *v.* Kennedy 1999 G.W.D. 28-1336, HCJ Appeal
Anderson *v.* Lothian Health Board 1996 S.C.L.R. 1068; 1996 Rep. L.R. 88, OH . . . . *Digested*, 97/**6081**: *Considered*, 00/6423
Anderson (Lee John) *v.* McGlennan 1998 S.C.C.R. 552; 1997 G.W.D. 32-1649, HCJ Appeal . . . . *Digested*, 98/**5673**
Anderson *v.* O'Donnell (Sentencing) 2000 G.W.D. 13-485, HCJ Appeal
Anderson *v.* Perth and Kinross Council 2000 S.C.L.R. 987, Sh Pr . . . . *Digested*, 01/**6416**
Anderson *v.* Pringle of Scotland Ltd 1998 S.L.T. 754; [1998] I.R.L.R. 64; 1997 G.W.D. 40-2033; *Times*, May 18, 1998, OH . . . . *Digested*, 98/**5814**: *Considered*, 99/6033
Anderson *v.* Secretary of State for Scotland 1999 S.L.T. 515; 1998 Rep. L.R. 115; 1998 G.W.D. 25-1272, OH . . . . *Digested*, 98/**5747**
Anderson *v.* Secretary of State for Work and Pensions; *sub nom* Anderson, Petitioner 2001 G.W.D. 39-1445, OH
Anderson *v.* Trotter 1998 S.C. 925; 1999 S.L.T. 442; 1998 G.W.D. 28-1438, 2 Div . . . . . *Digested*, 99/**6230**
Anderson *v.* Vannet 1998 G.W.D. 19-1000, HCJ Appeal
Anderson *v.* Wheelan 1998 G.W.D. 38-1981, HCJ Appeal
Anderson *v.* Williamson 1997 S.L.T. (Land Ct) 46; 1997 S.L.C.R. 23, Land Ct . . . . *Digested*, 98/**6028**
Anderson's Trustees *v.* Skinner 1871 S.L.R. 325, 1 Div . . . . *Distinguished*, 98/5462

Anderson, Petitioner see Anderson *v.* Secretary of State for Work and Pensions
Andrew *v.* Carnegie (Sentencing) 2000 G.W.D. 19-758, HCJ Appeal
Andrew *v.* HM Advocate 2000 S.L.T. 402; 1999 G.W.D. 32-1517, HCJ Appeal. . . . . *Digested*, 00/**6044**
Andrew *v.* O'Donnell 2001 G.W.D. 31-1243, HCJ Appeal
Andrew Bryan & Co Ltd *v.* DF Storage & Distribution Ltd 1999 G.W.D. 34-1612, OH
Angiolini *v.* Brown (Sentencing) 2001 G.W.D. 21-799, Sh Ct (Grampian)

Angiolini *v.* Duguid 2001 G.W.D. 29-1158, Sh Ct (Grampian)
Anglia Television Ltd *v.* Reed [1972] 1 Q.B. 60; [1971] 3 W.L.R. 528; [1971] 3 All E.R.
    690; 115 S.J. 723, CA . . . . *Digested,* 71/**1735**:
                    Applied, 95/772: *Distinguished,* 78/303, 83/439: *Explained,* 84/371:
                                                    Followed, 96/1235, 99/6443
Angus *v.* HM Advocate (1905) 8 F. (J.) 10, HCJ Appeal . . . . *Not followed,* 00/6036
Angus *v.* HM Advocate (Sentencing) 1999 G.W.D. 25-1188, HCJ Appeal
Angus Council *v.* Advocate General for Scotland 2000 G.W.D. 26-959, OH
Angus Council *v.* C 2000 S.L.T. 761; 1998 G.W.D. 23-1148, OH . . . . *Digested,* 00/**6248**
Anisminic Ltd *v.* Foreign Compensation Commission (No.2) [1969] 2 A.C. 147; [1969]
    2 W.L.R. 163; [1969] 1 All E.R. 208; (1968) 113 S.J. 55; *Times,* December 18,
    1968, HL; reversing [1968] 2 Q.B. 862; [1967] 3 W.L.R. 382; [1967] 3 All E.R.
    986; 111 S.J. 374, CA; reversing [1969] 2 A.C. 223, QBD . . . . *Digested,* 69/**1866**:
                    Applied, 70/2778, 74/3742, 78/2324, 79/19, 80/1639, 84/447, 92/2435,
                    93/2167, 96/4839, 00/5979, 01/81: *Considered,* 68/1909, 70/2436,
                    84/3464.A, 84/3483, 85/2791, 85/3415, 86/950, 88/2417, 88/3418,
                    89/3626, 90/4424, 94/1896, 96/2508: *Distinguished,* 76/19, 92/2740,
                    92/3464, 94/5367: *Explained,* 80/273: *Not applied,* 92/163, 93/63:
                                                                    Referred to, 92/6511
Annable *v.* Southern Derbyshire HA see Heil *v.* Rankin
Annandale and Hartfell Peerage Claim see Earldom of Annandale and Hartfell
Anthony *v.* Anthony 1999 S.C. 494; 1999 G.W.D. 12-531, Ex Div . . . . *Digested,* 99/**6072**
Anthony *v.* Brabbs 1998 S.C. 894; 1998 S.L.T. 1137; 1998 S.C.L.R. 982; 1998 Rep.
    L.R. 123; 1998 G.W.D. 28-1437, 1 Div . . . . *Digested,* 98/**5716**
Anthony *v.* McFadyen 2000 G.W.D. 13-466, HCJ Appeal
Antonio *v.* Secretary of State for the Home Department 1998 G.W.D. 15-770, OH
AR *v.* Reporter for Aberdeen Local Authority see R, Petitioner
Arbuckle *v.* Scottish Power Plc 2000 G.W.D. 10-358, 2 Div
Archbold *v.* HM Advocate 1998 G.W.D. 20-1023, HCJ Appeal
Archer *v.* Secretary of State for the Home Department 2001 G.W.D. 36-1391, OH
Arenson *v.* Arenson see Arenson *v.* Casson Beckman Rutley & Co
Arenson *v.* Casson Beckman Rutley & Co; *sub nom* Arenson *v.* Arenson [1977] A.C.
    405; [1975] 3 W.L.R. 815; [1975] 3 All E.R. 901; [1976] 1 Lloyd's Rep. 179; 119
    S.J. 810, HL; reversing [1973] Ch. 346; [1973] 2 W.L.R. 553; [1973] 2 All E.R.
    235; [1973] 2 Lloyd's Rep. 104; 117 S.J. 247, CA; affirming [1972] 1 W.L.R. 1196;
    [1972] 2 All E.R. 939, Ch D . . . . *Digested,* 75/**2318**:
                    Applied, 75/1889, 76/1533, 84/2337, 85/2315, 97/2485:
                    Considered, 83/336, 87/2209, 92/2740: *Referred to,* 01/6751
Argos Distributors Ltd *v.* Customs and Excise Commissioners (C288/94) [1997] Q.B.
    499; [1997] 2 W.L.R. 477; [1996] S.T.C. 1359; [1996] E.C.R. I-5311; [1996] 3
    C.M.L.R. 569; [1996] C.E.C. 963; [1997] B.V.C. 64; *Times,* November 18, 1996;
    Independent, November 25, 1996 (C.S.), ECJ (6th Chamber) . . . . *Digested,* 96/**5909**:
                    Applied, 99/6472: *Distinguished,* 00/5364, 01/5614: *Followed,* 97/4980:
                                    Joined proceedings, 96/5908: *Referred to,* 00/5317
Argus Care Ltd *v.* Balmoral Nursing Homes Ltd 2001 G.W.D. 29-1155, Sh Ct
    (Grampian)
Argyll Arms (McManus) Ltd *v.* Lorn, Mid-Argyll, Kintyre and Islay Divisional Licensing
    Board 1988 S.L.T. 290; 1988 S.C.L.R. 241; *Times,* March 9, 1988, OH . . . . *Digested,* 88/**4399**:
                                                                    Followed, 98/6067
Argyll Training Ltd *v.* Sinclair [2000] I.R.L.R. 630, EAT
Armia Ltd *v.* Daejan Developments Ltd 1979 S.C. (H.L.) 56; 1979 S.L.T. 147, HL;
    reversing 1978 S.C. 152, 1 Div; affirming 1977 S.L.T. (Notes) 49, OH . . . . *Digested,* 79/**3117**:
                    Applied, 89/3854, 96/6570, 00/6467: *Followed,* 91/5346, 93/5383
Armit (Mark James) *v.* O'Donnell 1999 J.C. 289; 1999 S.L.T. 1035; 1999 G.W.D. 24-
    1129, HCJ Appeal . . . . *Digested,* 99/**5809**
Armit *v.* Ruxton 1998 G.W.D. 26-1305, HCJ Appeal
Armitage *v.* West Bromwich Building Society see Investors Compensation Scheme Ltd
    v. West Bromwich Building Society (No.1)
Armitt *v.* Clark 1999 G.W.D. 24-1133, HCJ Appeal
Armstrong *v.* HM Advocate 1998 G.W.D. 39-2013, HCJ Appeal
Arnot *v.* McFadyen see Arnott (Neil Paterson) *v.* McFadyen
Arnott *v.* Bristol-Myers Co Ltd 1998 S.L.T. 110; 1997 Rep. L.R. 46; 1997 G.W.D. 13-
    568, OH . . . . *Digested,* 97/**5927**:
                                                                    Approved, 98/5707
Arnott (Neil Paterson) *v.* McFadyen; *sub nom* Arnot *v.* McFadyen 2001 G.W.D. 40-
    1508, HCJ Appeal
Arthur *v.* Brown (Sentencing) 2000 S.C.C.R. 94; 2000 G.W.D. 4-140, HCJ Appeal . . . . *Digested,* 00/**6144**
Arthur *v.* Carnegie 1998 G.W.D. 23-1168, HCJ Appeal
Arthur *v.* HM Advocate 1993 J.C. 57; 1994 S.L.T. 244; 1993 S.C.C.R. 130, HCJ Appeal . *Digested,* 94/**5678**:
                                            Applied, 99/6300: *Followed,* 99/6303
Arthur *v.* SMT Sales & Service Co Ltd (No.1) 1998 S.C. 525; 1998 S.L.T. 1446; 1998
    G.W.D. 10-477, 2 Div . . . . *Digested,* 98/**6005**
Arthur *v.* SMT Sales & Service Co Ltd (No.2) 1999 S.C. 109; 1999 S.L.T. 783; 1998
    G.W.D. 35-1776, 1 Div; reversing 1998 G.W.D. 22-1108, OH . . . . *Digested,* 99/**6300**

Artico *v.* Italy (A/37) (1981) 3 E.H.R.R. 1, ECHR. . . . . *Considered*, 01/3534,
                                                                              01/6760

Arundale *v.* HM Advocate (Sentencing) 2000 G.W.D. 5-190, HCJ Appeal

ASA International Ltd *v.* Nelson 1999 S.L.T. (Sh Ct) 44; 1998 S.C.L.R. 1123; 1998
  G.W.D. 35-1775, Sh Pr. . . . . *Digested*, 99/**5710**

ASDA Stores Ltd *v.* Secretary of State for Scotland 1999 S.L.T. 503; 1998 S.C.L.R.
  246; [1998] P.L.C.R. 233; 1998 G.W.D. 3-146, Ex Div; reversing 1997 S.L.T.
  1286; 1997 S.C.L.R. 661; 1997 G.W.D. 10-439, OH . . . . *Digested*, 98/**6151**:
                                         Applied, 99/4266: *Distinguished*, 01/6855

Asghar *v.* HM Advocate 1999 G.W.D. 2-96, HCJ Appeal

Ashraf *v.* Friel (Sentencing) 1998 G.W.D. 9-453, HCJ Appeal

Ashton *v.* HM Advocate 1999 G.W.D. 20-924, HCJ Appeal

Asif *v.* Secretary of State for the Home Department 2001 G.W.D. 40-1525, Ex Div;
  affirming 1999 S.L.T. 890; 1999 S.C.L.R. 427; 1999 G.W.D. 6-311, OH . . . . *Digested*, 99/**6291**:
                                                        Approved, 00/6491

Aslam *v.* Gallagher 1999 G.W.D. 24-1145, HCJ Appeal

Aslam *v.* HM Advocate 2000 J.C. 325; 2000 S.C.C.R. 243; 2000 G.W.D. 7-251, HCJ
  Appeal . . . . *Digested*, 00/**6049**

Aspin *v.* Estill (Inspector of Taxes) [1987] S.T.C. 723; 60 T.C. 549; (1988) 132 S.J.
  266, CA; affirming [1986] S.T.C. 323, Ch D . . . . *Digested*, 88/**1898**:
                                                          Applied, 99/6458

Aspinall *v.* HM Advocate 2001 G.W.D. 14-546, HCJ Appeal

Assessor for Glasgow *v.* Ron Wood Greetings Cards [2000] R.A. 271; 1999 G.W.D. 38-
  1868, LVAC . . . . *Digested*, 00/**6661**

Assessor for Highland and Western Isles Valuation Joint Board *v.* A; *sub nom* Assessor for
  Highland and Western Isles Valuation Joint Board's Appeal (No.1), Re; Assessor
  for Highland and Western Isles Valuation Joint Board *v.* Fraser 2001 S.C. 473;
  [2001] R.V.R. 32; 2001 G.W.D. 1-72, 1 Div . . . . *Digested*, 01/**6871**

Assessor for Highland and Western Isles Valuation Joint Board *v.* Fraser see Assessor for
  Highland and Western Isles Valuation Joint Board *v.* A

Assessor for Highland and Western Isles Valuation Joint Board *v.* Macleod; *sub nom*
  Assessor for Highland and Western Isles Valuation Joint Board's Appeal (No.2),
  Re 2001 S.C. 476; 2001 S.L.T. 483; [2001] R.V.R. 33; 2001 G.W.D. 1-71, 1 Div . . *Digested*, 01/**6872**

Assessor for Highland and Western Isles Valuation Joint Board's Appeal (No.1), Re see
  Assessor for Highland and Western Isles Valuation Joint Board *v.* A

Assessor for Highland and Western Isles Valuation Joint Board's Appeal (No.2), Re see
  Assessor for Highland and Western Isles Valuation Joint Board *v.* Macleod

Assessor for Lothian Region *v.* Heriot Watt University 1998 S.C. 736; 1998 G.W.D. 21-
  1096, LVAC. . . . . *Digested*, 98/**6087**

Assessor for Lothian Region *v.* Livingston Development Corp 1984 S.L.T. 42, LVAC . . . *Digested*, 84/**4484**:
                                                         Distinguished, 00/6665

Assessor for Tayside Joint Valuation Board *v.* Joseph Johnston & Sons Ltd 2000 S.L.T.
  308; [2000] R.A. 258; 1999 G.W.D. 37-1828, LVAC

Assuranceforeningen Skuld *v.* International Oil Pollution Compensation Fund
  (Documentary Evidence) 1999 G.W.D. 28-1309, OH

Assuranceforeningen Skuld *v.* International Oil Pollution Compensation Fund
  (Expenses) 2001 G.W.D. 12-438, OH

Assuranceforeningen Skuld *v.* International Oil Pollution Compensation Fund (No.1)
  2000 S.L.T. 1333; 1999 G.W.D. 16-766; *Times,* June 14, 1999, OH. . . . . *Digested*, 99/**6442**

Assuranceforeningen Skuld *v.* International Oil Pollution Compensation Fund (No.2)
  2000 S.L.T. 1348; 2000 G.W.D. 21-839, OH . . . . *Digested*, 01/**6869**

Assuranceforeningen Skuld *v.* International Oil Pollution Compensation Fund (No.3);
  sub nom Shetland Seafarms Ltd *v.* International Oil Pollution Compensation
  Fund (No.5) 2000 S.L.T. 1352; 2000 G.W.D. 24-905, OH . . . . *Digested*, 01/**6240**

Assuranceforeningen Skuld *v.* International Oil Pollution Compensation Fund
  (Procedure: Proof) 1999 G.W.D. 35-1662, OH

Assuranceforeningen Skuld *v.* International Oil Pollution Compensation Fund (Proof of
  Damage) 2001 G.W.D. 7-289, OH

Atlas Appointments Ltd *v.* Tinsley (No.2) 1997 S.C. 200; 1998 S.L.T. 395; 1997
  S.C.L.R. 482; 1997 G.W.D. 15-640, 1 Div; reversing 1996 S.C.L.R. 476, OH . . . . *Digested*, 97/**5666**:
                                                         Followed, 98/5466

Atlas Hydraulic Loaders Ltd *v.* Seabon Ltd 1998 S.L.T. (Sh Ct) 6; 1997 G.W.D. 15-683,
  Sh Ct (North Strathclyde) . . . . *Digested*, 98/**5470**

Atlas Investments Ltd *v.* Glasgow City Council 2001 G.W.D. 13-456, OH

Attorney General *v.* Channel 4 Television see Attorney General *v.* Channel Four
  Television Co Ltd

Attorney General *v.* Channel Four Television Co Ltd; *sub nom* Attorney General *v.*
  Channel 4 Television [1988] Crim. L.R. 237, CA . . . . *Digested*, 88/**666**:
                                                         Not followed, 00/6031

Attorney General v. Guardian Newspapers Ltd (No.2); Attorney General v. Observer
   Ltd (No.2); Attorney General v. Times Newspapers Ltd (No.2) [1990] 1 A.C. 109;
   [1988] 3 W.L.R. 776; [1988] 3 All E.R. 545; [1989] 2 F.S.R. 181; (1988)
   85(42) L.S.G. 45; (1988) 138 N.L.J. Rep. 296; (1988) 132 S.J. 1496; *Times*,
   October 14, 1988; *Independent*, October 14, 1988, HL; affirming [1988] 2 W.L.R.
   805; (1988) 138 N.L.J. Rep. 47; (1988) 132 S.J. 566, CA; affirming *Times*,
   December 22, 1987, Ch D . . . .   *Digested*, 89/**3103**:
                                 Applied, 89/2900, 89/4740, 90/3099, 92/2791: *Considered*, 96/1219,
                                                              99/5990, 01/1057: *Followed*, 97/2040
Attorney General v. Observer Ltd (No.2) see Attorney General v. Guardian Newspapers
   Ltd (No.2)
Attorney General v. Times Newspapers Ltd (No.2) see Attorney General v. Guardian
   Newspapers Ltd (No.2)
Aubrey Investments Ltd v. DS Crawford Ltd (In Receivership) 1998 S.L.T. 628; 1997
   G.W.D. 25-1273; *Times*, July 30, 1997, OH . . . .   *Digested*, 98/**6032**
Aubrey Investments Ltd v. DSC (Realisations) Ltd (In Receivership) 1999 S.C. 21; 2000
   S.L.T. 183; 1998 G.W.D. 31-1623, OH . . . .   *Digested*, 99/**6323**
Auld v. Herron 1969 J.C. 4, HCJ Appeal . . . .   *Digested*, 71/**12672**:
                                                                              Applied, 98/5674
Austin (Malcolm Russell) v. Fraser 1998 S.L.T. 106; 1997 S.C.C.R. 775; 1997 G.W.D.
   38-1929, HCJ Appeal . . . .   *Digested*, 98/**5566**
Aventis Pharma AB v. Paranova Lakemedel AB [2001] E.T.M.R. 60, TR (Stockholm) . . .   *Considered*, 01/6728
Axis West Developments Ltd v. Chartwell Land Investments Ltd 1999 S.L.T. 1416; 1999
   G.W.D. 32-1551, HL; affirming 1998 G.W.D. 13-674, 1 Div; reversing 1997
   G.W.D. 2-62, OH . . . .   *Digested*, 99/**6240**
Azapovic (13611) (Unreported), IAT   *Followed*, 98/5997
Aziz (Mohammed Shahid) v. HM Advocate 1999 S.L.T. 451; 1998 S.C.C.R. 736; 1998
   G.W.D. 39-2005, HCJ Appeal . . . .   *Digested*, 99/**5921**

B (A Juvenile) v. HM Advocate (Sentencing) 2001 G.W.D. 13-493, HCJ Appeal
B v. B (Interim Aliment) 1999 Fam. L.R. 74; 1998 G.W.D. 38-1970, OH . . . .   *Digested*, 99/**6077**
B v. B (Settlement prior to Proof) 1998 G.W.D. 18-929, OH . . . .   *Previous proceedings*,
                                                                                 98/5849
B v. B (Sist) 1998 S.L.T. 1245; 1998 G.W.D. 15-740, OH . . . .   *Digested*, 98/**5849**
B v. HM Advocate (Evidence: Indecent Assault) 2000 S.C.C.R. 407; 2000 G.W.D. 9-
   324, HCJ Appeal. . . . .   *Digested*, 00/**6019**
B v. HM Advocate (Sentencing) 2001 S.C.C.R. 876; 2001 G.W.D. 31-1240, HCJ
   Appeal
B v. L (No.1) see Brixey v. Lynas (No.1)
B (IW) v. Ruxton 1998 S.L.T. 1282; 1998 S.C.C.R. 440; 1998 G.W.D. 24-1191, HCJ
   Appeal . . . .   *Digested*, 98/**5629**
B and B v. C see FB and AB, Petitioners
B&Q Plc v. Central Scotland Assessor [2000] R.A. 205, Lands Tr (Scot) . . . .   *Digested*, 00/**6665**
B's Curator Bonis, Noter 1996 S.L.T. (Sh Ct) 27; 1995 S.C.L.R. 671, Sh Pr . . . .   *Digested*, 95/**6464**:
                                                                              Approved, 98/5464
Babcock Rosyth Defence Ltd v. Grootcon (UK) Ltd 1998 S.L.T. 1143; 1997 G.W.D. 19-
   864, OH . . . .   *Digested*, 98/**5537**
Baigent v. BBC; Baigent v. McCulloch (Damages); Baigent v. O'Hare (Damages) 2001
   S.C. 281; 2001 S.L.T. 427; 2001 S.C.L.R. 869; 2001 Rep. L.R. 15; 2000 G.W.D.
   35-1339, Ex Div; affirming 1999 S.C.L.R. 787; 1999 G.W.D. 10-474; *Times*, May
   5, 1999, OH. . . . .   *Digested*, 01/**6414**:
                                                                 Previous proceedings, 97/5973
Baigent v. McCulloch; Baigent v. O'Hare 1998 S.L.T. 780; 1997 Rep. L.R. 107; 1997
   G.W.D. 16-737, OH. . . . .   *Digested*, 97/**5973**:
                                                                 Subsequent proceedings, 99/5991
Baigent v. McCulloch (Damages) see Baigent v. BBC
Baigent v. O'Hare see Baigent v. McCulloch
Baigent v. O'Hare (Damages) see Baigent v. BBC
Baigrie v. HM Advocate 2001 G.W.D. 26-1028, HCJ Appeal
Baikie v. HM Advocate (Sentencing) 2000 S.C.C.R. 119; 2000 G.W.D. 4-137, HCJ
   Appeal . . . .   *Digested*, 00/**6147**
Bailey v. Ayr Engineering & Constructional Co Ltd [1959] 1 Q.B. 183; [1958] 2 W.L.R.
   882; [1958] 2 All E.R. 222; 102 S.J. 363, CA . . . .   *Digested*, 58/**350**:
                                 Applied, 66/1095, 66/12790, 67/4181: *Distinguished*, 98/5937
Bailey v. Bailey 2001 Fam. L.R. 133; 2001 G.W.D. 29-1148, Sh Pr
Bailey v. HM Advocate (Sentencing) 2001 G.W.D. 12-421, HCJ Appeal
Bailey v. McFadyen 1999 G.W.D. 16-740, HCJ Appeal
Baillie v. Crowe (Sentencing) 1998 G.W.D. 32-1661, HCJ Appeal
Baillie Lite Ltd v. Glasgow City Council 1999 S.C. 606; 2001 S.C.L.R. 331; [1999] 3
   P.L.R. 64; 1999 G.W.D. 18-849, OH . . . .   *Digested*, 99/**6402**
Baillie Marshall Ltd (In Liquidation) v. Avian Communications Ltd 2000 G.W.D. 27-1057,
   OH
Bain v. Allan (1884) 11 R. 650, 1 Div . . . .   *Applied*, 99/6301

Bain v. Bain 2001 G.W.D. 32-1270, OH
Bain v. HM Advocate (Sentencing) 1999 G.W.D. 17-778, HCJ Appeal
Bain (Robert Malcolm) v. HM Advocate 1999 S.C.C.R. 424; 1999 G.W.D. 20-931, HCJ
    Appeal   *Digested,* 99/**5918**
Bain (Robert Malcolm) v. HM Advocate (Sentencing) 1999 G.W.D. 20-945, HCJ
    Appeal
Bain (Ronald James) v. McNaughtan; *sub nom* Bain (Ronald James) v. Wilson 1999
    S.L.T. 410; 1998 S.C.C.R. 454; 1998 G.W.D. 26-1318, HCJ Appeal . . . .   *Digested,* 98/**5674**
Bain (Ronald James) v. Wilson see Bain (Ronald James) v. McNaughtan
Bains v. HM Advocate 1999 G.W.D. 13-608, HCJ Appeal
Baird v. Black 2000 G.W.D. 27-1062, Sh Ct (Lothian)
Baird v. Drumpellier & Mount Vernon Estates Ltd (No.1) 2000 S.C. 103; 1999 G.W.D.
    39-1896, OH . . . .   *Digested,* 00/**6437**
Baird v. Drumpellier & Mount Vernon Estates Ltd (No.2) 2000 G.W.D. 12-427, OH
Baird v. Earl of Rosebery (1776) Mor. Dic. 14019, IH . . . .   *Followed,* 99/6298
Baird v. HM Advocate (Sentencing) 1998 G.W.D. 24-1207, HCJ Appeal
Baird v. HM Advocate (Sentencing) 2001 G.W.D. 1-44, HCJ Appeal
Baird v. McFadyen (Sentencing) 2000 G.W.D. 13-474, HCJ Appeal
Bairstow v. Bairstow 2000 G.W.D. 17-688, Sh Ct
Baker v. Birmingham City Council see R. v. Birmingham City Council Ex p. Ireland
Baker v. MacLeod (Sentencing) 1998 G.W.D. 11-540, HCJ Appeal
Baker v. Willoughby [1970] A.C. 467; [1970] 2 W.L.R. 50; [1969] 3 All E.R. 1528; 7
    K.I.R. 457; 114 S.J. 15, HL; reversing [1969] 2 W.L.R. 489; [1969] 2 All E.R. 549;
    6 K.I.R. 5; (1968) 113 S.J. 37; *Times,* December 11, 1968, CA; reversing [1969]
    1 Q.B. 38; [1968] 2 W.L.R. 1138; [1968] 2 All E.R. 236; 112 S.J. 234, QBD . . . .   *Digested,* 70/**1862**:
          Applied, 71/3255, 72/2531, 76/2671, 00/6163: *Cited,* 00/1482:
          Considered, 70/599, 70/737: *Distinguished,* 78/718, 80/1885:
          Doubted, 81/1835: *Followed,* 77/2011, 79/683, 98/6103
Balfour v. Carnegie (Sentencing) 1998 G.W.D. 9-447, HCJ Appeal
Balgowan Trustees, Petitioners see Winning, Petitioners
Balkandali v. United Kingdom (9474/81) see Abdulaziz v. United Kingdom (A/94)
Ballantyne v. Crowe 1998 G.W.D. 18-940, HCJ Appeal
Ballantyne v. Gilchrist 1999 G.W.D. 24-1135, HCJ Appeal
Ballast Plc v. Burrell Co (Construction Management) Ltd 2001 S.L.T. 1039; 2001
    S.C.L.R. 837; [2001] B.L.R. 529; 2001 G.W.D. 22-826; *Times,* October 9, 2001,
    OH . . . .   *Digested,* 01/**6288**
Balloch v. HM Advocate 1977 S.C. 23; 1977 S.L.T. (Notes) 29, HCJ Appeal . . . .   *Digested,* 77/**3304**:
          Followed, 91/4546: *Overruled,* 00/5996: *Referred to,* 95/5729
Balmoral Group Ltd v. Rae, *Times,* January 25, 2000, EAT . . . .   *Digested,* 00/**6218**
Bank of Ireland v. Bass Brewers Ltd (No.1) 2000 G.W.D. 20-786, OH
Bank of Ireland v. Bass Brewers Ltd (No.2) 2000 G.W.D. 28-1077, OH
Bank of Ireland v. Morton 2000 G.W.D. 14-522, Sh Pr
Bank of Scotland v. Brunswick Developments (1987) Ltd (No.2) 1999 S.C. (H.L.) 53;
    1999 S.L.T. 716; 2000 S.C.L.R. 30; 1999 G.W.D. 15-687; *Times,* May 5, 1999, HL;
    reversing 1997 S.C. 226; 1998 S.L.T. 439; 1997 S.C.L.R. 498; 1997 G.W.D. 16-
    716, 1 Div; affirming 1997 S.L.T. 48, OH . . . .   *Digested,* 99/**5726**
Bank of Scotland v. Dunedin Property Investment Co Ltd (No.1) 1998 S.C. 657; 1999
    S.L.T. 470; 1998 S.C.L.R. 531; 1998 G.W.D. 18-887; *Times,* September 24, 1998,
    1 Div; reversing 1997 G.W.D. 17-761; *Times,* May 16, 1997, OH . . . .   *Digested,* 98/**5864**
Bank of Scotland v. Dunedin Property Investment Co Ltd (No.2) 1999 S.C.L.R. 1039;
    1999 G.W.D. 25-1182, OH . . . .   *Digested,* 00/**6288**
Bank of Scotland v. Fuller Peiser 2001 G.W.D. 37-1411, OH
Bank of Scotland v. Junior 1999 S.C.L.R. 284; 1999 G.W.D. 4-171, Ex Div . . . .   *Digested,* 99/**5795**
Bank of Scotland v. Macleod Paxton Woolard & Co 1998 S.L.T. 258; 1997 G.W.D. 19-
    860, OH . . . .   *Digested,* 98/**5432**
Bank of Scotland v. Millward 1999 S.L.T. 901; 1998 S.C.L.R. 577; 1998 G.W.D. 18-932,
    Ex Div . . . .   *Digested,* 98/**6177**
Bank of Scotland v. Mitchell 2001 G.W.D. 39-1447, Sh Ct (Tayside)
Bank of Scotland v. Reid 2000 G.W.D. 22-858, OH
Bank of Scotland Cashflow Finance v. Suffolk Carpet Weavers 2001 G.W.D. 27-1108, Sh
    Ct (Glasgow)
Banks v. Vannet 1998 G.W.D. 36-1853, HCJ Appeal
Banna v. Delicato 1999 S.L.T. (Sh Ct) 84; 1999 Rep. L.R. 89; 1998 G.W.D. 34-1758,
    Sh Ct (Lothian) . . . .   *Digested,* 99/**6229**:
          Followed, 99/6222
Bannatyne's Health Club v. Aberdeen City Licensing Board 2000 S.L.T. (Sh Ct) 187;
    [2000] 17 S.L.L.P. 15; 2000 G.W.D. 28-1099, Sh Ct (Grampian) . . . .   *Digested,* 01/**6777**
Bannerman Co Ltd v. Cromarty Firth Port Authority 2000 G.W.D. 11-400, Sh Pr
Bannon v. HM Advocate 1999 G.W.D. 31-1486, HCJ Appeal
Bantop Ltd v. Glasgow District Licensing Board 1990 S.L.T. 366; 1989 S.C.L.R. 731,
    OH . . . .   *Digested,* 90/**5334**:
          Followed, 01/6783
Barbara v. HM Advocate (Sentencing) 2001 G.W.D. 6-207, HCJ Appeal

Barber v. NCR (Manufacturing) [1993] I.R.L.R. 95, EAT . . . . *Digested*, 93/**1746**:
Distinguished, 98/**5807**

Barbour v. Grieve 2001 G.W.D. 2-81, Sh Pr
Barbour v. Walkingshaw 1998 G.W.D. 8-361, HCJ Appeal
Barclay v. HM Advocate (Sentencing) 2001 G.W.D. 32-1282, HCJ Appeal
Barclay v. Morris 1998 S.C. 74; 1997 G.W.D. 36-1826, OH . . . . *Digested*, 98/**5449**
Barclay v. Renfrewshire Council 2001 S.L.T. 647; 2001 G.W.D. 13-510, Ex Div . . . . *Digested*, 01/**6792**
Barclays Bank Ltd v. McGreish 1983 S.L.T. 344, OH . . . . *Digested*, 83/**4442**:
Doubted, 99/**6298**: *Overruled*, 00/**6508**

Barclays Bank Plc v. O'Brien [1994] 1 A.C. 180; [1993] 3 W.L.R. 786; [1993] 4 All E.R.
417; [1994] 1 F.L.R. 1; [1994] 1 F.C.R. 357; (1994) 26 H.L.R. 75; (1994) 13 Tr.
L.R. 165; [1994] C.C.L.R. 94; [1994] Fam. Law 78; [1993] E.G.C.S. 169; (1993)
143 N.L.J. 1511; (1993) 137 S.J.L.B. 240; [1993] N.P.C. 135; *Times*, October
22, 1993; *Independent*, October 22, 1993, HL; affirming [1993] Q.B. 109; [1992]
3 W.L.R. 593; [1992] 4 All E.R. 983; [1993] 1 F.L.R. 124; [1993] 1 F.C.R. 97;
(1993) 66 P. & C.R. 135; (1992) 11 Tr. L.R. 153; [1992] C.C.L.R. 37; [1993] Fam.
Law 62; (1992) 89(27) L.S.G. 34; (1992) 142 N.L.J. 1040; (1992) 136 S.J.L.B.
175; [1992] N.P.C. 74; *Times*, June 3, 1992; *Independent*, June 17, 1992;
Financial Times, June 10, 1992, CA . . . . *Digested*, 94/**3300**:
Applied, 94/3291, 94/3294, 94/3299, 95/2443, 95/2451, 96/419, 98/4363,
99/6431, 01/4878, 01/4880: *Cited*, 98/305, 00/4662, 01/2653:
Considered, 94/276, 94/2246, 95/2196, 95/2444, 95/2446, 95/2448,
95/2449, 95/2452, 95/4659, 96/411, 96/4967, 96/4970, 97/4232,
97/4240, 97/4244, 99/3715, 99/4377, 00/2333, 00/4664, 00/6670, 01/669:
Disapproved, 97/6087: *Distinguished*, 94/5914: *Explained*, 98/4358:
Followed, 97/4238, 99/4390, 00/4273: *Not followed*, 94/5881, 95/5982,
96/6577: *Referred to*, 94/3290, 95/2447, 99/310

Barker v. HM Advocate (Sentencing) 1999 G.W.D. 10-463, HCJ Appeal
Barnes v. Carnegie (Sentencing) 2000 G.W.D. 8-290, HCJ Appeal
Barnes v. Higson (Sentencing) 2001 G.W.D. 1-46, HCJ Appeal
Barnes v. HM Advocate 1998 G.W.D. 40-2061, HCJ Appeal
Barnes (Craig Brown) v. HM Advocate 2001 J.C. 61; 2000 S.C.C.R. 995; 2000 G.W.D.
35-1330, HCJ Appeal . . . . *Digested*, 01/**6312**
Barnes v. McGlennan 1999 G.W.D. 33-1604, HCJ Appeal
Barns-Graham v. Ballance 2000 Hous. L.R. 11, Sh Ct (Tayside) . . . . *Digested*, 00/**6537**
Barns-Graham v. Boyd 1998 Hous. L.R. 39, Sh Ct . . . . *Digested*, 98/**6041**
Barns-Graham v. McQueen 2000 Hous. L.R. 7, Sh Ct (Tayside) . . . . *Digested*, 00/**6536**
Barr v. HM Advocate (Sentencing) 2001 G.W.D. 12-427, HCJ Appeal
Barr (David) v. HM Advocate 1999 G.W.D. 11-501, HCJ Appeal
Barr (Samuel Ferguson) v. HM Advocate 1999 S.C.C.R. 13; 1999 G.W.D. 3-132, HCJ
Appeal . . . . *Digested*, 99/**5859**
Barr & Stroud Ltd v. West of Scotland Water Authority [1998] Env. L.R. D5, OH
Barr Ltd v. Law Mining Ltd 80 Con. L.R. 135; 2001 G.W.D. 21-787, OH
Barr's Trustees v. Crofters Sharing in Oldshoremore Common Grazings see MacKenzie
v. Barr's Trustees
Barrett v. Donnelly 1999 G.W.D. 25-1186, HCJ Appeal
Barrett v. HM Advocate 1998 G.W.D. 40-2049, HCJ Appeal
Barrie v. Glasgow City Council 2000 Rep. L.R. 46, OH . . . . *Digested*, 00/**6422**
Barron v. HM Advocate (Sentencing) 1999 G.W.D. 40-1939, HCJ Appeal
Barron v. McFadyen 1999 G.W.D. 35-1671, HCJ Appeal
Barrs v. British Wool Marketing Board 1957 S.C. 72; 1957 S.L.T. 153, 1 Div . . . . *Digested*, 57/**3764**:
Applied, 98/6071: *Considered*, 92/5290: *Followed*, 89/3919
Barry v. News Group Newspapers Ltd see Clinton v. News Group Newspapers Ltd
Barry v. Sutherland (Damages) 2001 G.W.D. 38-1431, OH
Bartraham v. Vannet (Sentencing) 2000 G.W.D. 8-306, HCJ Appeal
Basingstoke and Deane BC v. Host Group [1988] 1 W.L.R. 348; [1988] 1 All E.R. 824;
(1988) 56 P. & C.R. 31; (1987) 284 E.G. 1587; (1988) 85(6) L.S.G. 37; (1988)
132 S.J. 158, CA; reversing [1986] 2 E.G.L.R. 107; (1986) 279 E.G. 505, Ch D . *Digested*, 88/**2069**:
Applied, 92/2722, 92/2730, 92/2739: *Approved*, 99/6325:
Considered, 88/2074, 89/2183, 90/180, 90/2857, 90/2886, 91/203,
91/2268, 91/2269, 92/2721, 92/2735, 92/2738, 92/2740, 93/2524,
93/2531, 96/3805: *Referred to*, 90/2791
Bass Brewers Ltd v. Independent Insurance Co Ltd 2001 G.W.D. 37-1409, Ex Div
Bass Taverns Ltd v. Secretary of State for Scotland 2000 S.L.T. 775; 1999 G.W.D. 30-
1442, Ex Div . . . . *Digested*, 00/**6623**
Batchelor (Peter) v. Brown 1999 S.C.C.R. 661; 1999 G.W.D. 25-1204, HCJ Appeal . . . . *Digested*, 00/**6134**
Batchelor v. HM Advocate (Sentencing) 2000 G.W.D. 34-1315, HCJ Appeal
Batchelor v. Vannet 1998 G.W.D. 25-1259, HCJ Appeal
Bates v. Spiers 1999 G.W.D. 11-507, HCJ Appeal
Bathgate v. British Telecommunications Plc 2000 G.W.D. 40-1502, OH
Baxter v. Carnegie (Sentencing) 1998 G.W.D. 11-548, HCJ Appeal
Baxter v. Carnegie (Sentencing) 1999 G.W.D. 22-1061, HCJ Appeal
Baxter v. Central Fife Divisional Licensing Board [1999] 14 S.L.L.P. 32, Sh Ct . . . . *Digested*, 00/**6562**
Baxter v. Freshbake Frozen Foods Ltd 2001 G.W.D. 3-138, OH

Baxter (James Patrick) *v.* HM Advocate 1998 J.C. 219; 1998 S.L.T. 414; 1997 S.C.C.R.
    437; 1997 G.W.D. 21-1006, HCJ Appeal . . . . *Digested,* 97/**5792**
Baxter Clark & Paul *v.* Tulloch Construction Group Ltd 1999 G.W.D. 37-1789, OH
BBC Scotland *v.* Souster 2001 S.C. 458; [2001] I.R.L.R. 150; 2000 G.W.D. 40-1490,
    Ex Div. . . . . *Digested,* 01/**6473**
BBC, Petitioners (No.1) 2000 J.C. 419; 2000 S.L.T. 845; 2000 G.W.D. 11-383; *Times,* April
    11, 2000, HCJ. . . . . *Digested,* 00/**6117**
BBC, Petitioners (No.2) 2000 J.C. 521; 2000 S.L.T. 860; 2000 G.W.D. 15-584; [2000]
    H.R.L.R. 423; 2000 G.W.D. 15-584; *Times,* June 13, 2000, HCJ Appeal . . . . *Digested,* 00/**6116**
BBC, Petitioners (No.3) 2001 S.C.C.R. 440; 2001 G.W.D. 17-671, HCJ Appeal
BBW Leisure Ltd *v.* Edinburgh City Licensing Board 2001 S.L.T. (Sh Ct) 26; 2000
    G.W.D. 38-1436, Sh Ct (Lothian) . . . . *Digested,* 01/**6776**
Beagan *v.* Vannet 1999 G.W.D. 23-1100, HCJ Appeal
Beagrie *v.* HM Advocate (Sentencing) 2000 G.W.D. 4-133, HCJ Appeal
Beasley *v.* Fife Health Board 2001 G.W.D. 32-1300, OH
Beaton *v.* Cain 2000 S.L.T. 920; 2000 G.W.D. 22-844, OH. . . . . *Digested,* 00/**5906**
Beaton *v.* McGlennan 1999 G.W.D. 7-333, HCJ Appeal
Beattie *v.* Hingston 1998 G.W.D. 15-742, HCJ Appeal
Beattie *v.* Hingston (Sentencing) 1999 G.W.D. 32-1542, HCJ Appeal
Beattie (Scott Alexander Henderson) *v.* Hingston 1999 S.L.T. 362; 1998 G.W.D. 37-
    1895, HCJ Appeal. . . . . *Digested,* 99/**5872**
Beattie *v.* L see L *v.* L
Beck *v.* Lees 1998 G.W.D. 18-901, HCJ Appeal
Beck *v.* United Closures & Plastics Plc 2001 S.L.T. 1299; 2001 Rep. L.R. 91; 2001
    G.W.D. 22-842, OH. . . . . *Digested,* 01/**6662**
Beckett *v.* United Kingdom see Smith *v.* United Kingdom (No.1)
Beecham Group Plc *v.* Munro Wholesale Medical Supplies Ltd [2001] E.T.M.R. 29;
    2001 G.W.D. 1-67, OH . . . . *Digested,* 01/**6728**
Beechwood Development Co (Scotland) Ltd *v.* Mitchell (t/a Discovery Land Surveys)
    2001 S.L.T. 1214; 2001 S.C.L.R. 725; 2001 G.W.D. 6-224, OH . . . . *Digested,* 01/**6290**
Beedie *v.* Summers 2001 G.W.D. 13-515, Sh Ct (Grampian)
Beedie *v.* Wheelan 1999 G.W.D. 27-1305, HCJ Appeal
Beggs *v.* HM Advocate (Preliminary Diet) 2001 S.C.C.R. 836, HCJ Appeal
Beggs *v.* Motherwell Bridge Fabricators Ltd 1998 S.L.T. 1215; 1997 S.C.L.R. 1019; 1997
    Rep. L.R. 87; 1997 G.W.D. 25-1275, OH . . . . *Digested,* 97/**6072**
Beglan *v.* HM Advocate 2001 G.W.D. 10-341, HCJ Appeal
Belcher Food Products Ltd *v.* Miller & Black 1999 S.L.T. 142; 1998 G.W.D. 16-775, OH. . *Digested,* 99/**5784**
Belgian International Insurance Group SA *v.* McNicoll 1999 G.W.D. 22-1065, 2 Div;
    reversing 1999 G.W.D. 13-622, OH
Bell *v.* Bell's Trustee (No.1) 2000 G.W.D. 20-815, Ex Div
Bell *v.* Bell's Trustee (No.2) 2001 G.W.D. 26-1050, Ex Div
Bell *v.* Fulton's Curator ad Litem 1998 G.W.D. 37-1929, OH
Bell *v.* HM Advocate 1998 G.W.D. 19-960, HCJ Appeal
Bell *v.* HM Advocate (Sentencing) 2000 G.W.D. 39-1451, HCJ Appeal
Bell *v.* Lees (Sentencing) 1998 G.W.D. 32-1680, HCJ Appeal
Bell *v.* McMillan (No.1) 2001 G.W.D. 2-95, Ex Div; affirming 1999 S.L.T. 947, OH . . . . . . *Digested,* 99/**6302**
Bell *v.* McMillan (No.2) 1999 G.W.D. 6-290, 2 Div
Bell *v.* Ruxton (Sentencing) 1998 G.W.D. 12-621, HCJ Appeal
Bell's Curator Bonis, Noter 1998 S.C. 365; 1999 S.L.T. 33; 1998 G.W.D. 5-232, OH . . . . *Digested,* 98/**6211**
Bellgrade Ltd *v.* McGlennan 2000 S.L.T. 14; 1999 S.C.C.R. 820; 1999 G.W.D. 28-1343,
    HCJ Appeal . . . . *Digested,* 00/**6306**
Bellmill Ltd *v.* Wight 2001 G.W.D. 14-539, Sh Ct (Grampian)
Bennett (Gary John) *v.* HM Advocate 1998 S.L.T. 1258; 1998 S.C.C.R. 23; 1998 G.W.D.
    3-108, HCJ Appeal . . . . *Digested,* 98/**5600**
Bennett (Paul James) *v.* HM Advocate 1995 S.L.T. 510; 1994 S.C.C.R. 902, HCJ
    Appeal . . . . *Digested,* 95/**5744**:
                                               Considered, 98/2353
Bennett *v.* J Lamont & Sons 2000 S.L.T. 17; 2000 Rep. L.R. 2; 1999 G.W.D. 31-1501,
    OH . . . . *Digested,* 00/**6586**
Bennett *v.* Wallace 1998 S.C. 457; 1998 S.L.T. 1165; 1998 S.C.L.R. 757; 1998 G.W.D. 9-
    470, 2 Div. . . . . *Digested,* 98/**6120**
Bennie *v.* HM Advocate (Sentencing) 1998 G.W.D. 10-498, HCJ Appeal
Benson *v.* Scottish Lion Engineering Ltd; *sub nom* Benson's Executor *v.* Scottish Lion
    Engineering Ltd; TNS, 2 Div; affirming 2001 G.W.D. 36-1355, OH
Benson's Executor *v.* Scottish Lion Engineering Ltd see Benson *v.* Scottish Lion
    Engineering Ltd
Bentley *v.* Eurosales (UK) Ltd 2001 G.W.D. 27-1074, Sh Ct (Lothian)
Beresford *v.* Ritchie (Sentencing) 2001 G.W.D. 6-202, HCJ Appeal
Bernard *v.* Stott 2001 G.W.D. 32-1277, HCJ Appeal
Bernhardt *v.* Abrahams 1912 S.C. 748, 1 Div . . . . *Applied,* 00/**6179**
Berry *v.* HM Advocate 1998 G.W.D. 20-1054, HCJ Appeal
Besler *v.* Ritchie (Sentencing) 2000 G.W.D. 13-507, HCJ Appeal

Beta Computers (Europe) Ltd v. Adobe Systems (Europe) Ltd 1996 S.L.T. 604; [1996]
    C.L.C. 821; [1997-98] Info. T.L.R. 73; [1996] F.S.R. 367; [1998] Masons C.L.R.
    Rep.104, OH . . . . *Digested*, 96/**6703**
Bethel v. Carnegie 1999 G.W.D. 35-1670, HCJ Appeal
Bett (Robert John) v. Brown; *sub nom* Bett v. Hamilton 1998 J.C. 1; 1997 S.L.T. 1310;
    1997 S.C.C.R. 621; 1997 G.W.D. 27-1353, HCJ Appeal . . . . *Digested*, 97/**5796**
Bett v. Hamilton see Bett (Robert John) v. Brown
Bett v. Lees (Sentencing) 1998 G.W.D. 20-1025, HCJ Appeal
Bett (Andrew Rae) v. Lees 1998 S.L.T. 1069; 1998 S.C.C.R. 554; 1998 G.W.D. 28-1401,
    HCJ Appeal . . . . *Digested*, 98/**5555**
Bett Properties Ltd v. Scottish Ministers 2001 S.C. 238; 2001 S.L.T. 1131; 2001 S.C.L.R.
    223; 2000 G.W.D. 29-1160, OH . . . . *Digested*, 01/**6855**
Bevan Investments Ltd v. Blackhall & Struthers (No.2) 11 B.L.R. 78; [1978] 2 N.Z.L.R.
    97, CA (NZ) . . . . *Digested*, 80/**188**:
    Distinguished, 00/6597
Beveridge v. Crowe 1998 G.W.D. 28-1402, HCJ Appeal
Beveridge v. HM Advocate (Sentencing) 2000 G.W.D. 20-792, HCJ Appeal
Beveridge v. McGlennan (Sentencing) 1998 G.W.D. 7-330, HCJ Appeal
Beveridge v. O'Donnell 1999 G.W.D. 38-1847, HCJ Appeal
Beveridge & Kellas WS v. Abercromby (No.2) 1999 S.C.L.R. 533; 1999 G.W.D. 15-683,
    Sh Ct . . . . *Digested*, 99/**6332**:
    Not followed, 00/6540
BG Hamilton Ltd v. Ready Mixed Concrete (Scotland) Ltd 1999 S.L.T. 524; 1998
    G.W.D. 35-1819, OH . . . . *Digested*, 99/**6326**
Bhattacharjee v. Secretary of State for the Home Department 1999 G.W.D. 28-1346,
    OH
Bhatti v. Secretary of State for the Home Department 1999 G.W.D. 9-433, OH
Bhoyrub v. Cadzow 1999 S.C.L.R. 539; 1999 G.W.D. 9-411, Sh Ct . . . . *Digested*, 99/**5789**
Bhutta v. Secretary of State for the Home Department 2000 G.W.D. 15-615, OH
Bieniwoski v. Ruxton 1997 S.L.T. 1173; 1997 G.W.D. 23-1143, HCJ Appeal. . . . . *Digested*, 97/**5822**:
    Distinguished, 98/5624
Biggart v. Fraser (Sentencing) 1998 G.W.D. 32-1682, HCJ Appeal
Biggins (Daniel James) v. Stott 1999 J.C. 298; 1999 S.L.T. 1037; 1999 S.C.C.R. 595;
    1999 G.W.D. 24-1136, HCJ Appeal. . . . . *Digested*, 99/**5824**
Biggs v. Somerset CC [1996] 2 C.M.L.R. 292; [1996] I.C.R. 364; [1996] I.R.L.R. 203;
    (1996) 146 N.L.J. 174; (1996) 140 S.J.L.B. 59; *Times*, January 29, 1996;
    Independent, February 1, 1996, CA; affirming [1995] I.C.R. 811; [1995] I.R.L.R.
    452; *Times*, July 17, 1995, EAT . . . . *Digested*, 96/**2577**:
    Applied, 97/2241, 98/2236, 98/5826: *Approved*, 96/2578:
    Distinguished, 98/2195: *Referred to*, 96/2625, 97/2266
Bilka-Kaufhaus GmbH v. Weber von Hartz (C170/84) [1986] E.C.R. 1607; [1986] 2
    C.M.L.R. 701; [1987] I.C.R. 110; [1986] I.R.L.R. 317, ECJ . . . . *Digested*, 87/**1633**:
    Applied, 86/1190, 87/1325, 89/1626, 91/4077, 91/4078, 94/1981, 95/2048,
    98/2240: *Approved*, 98/5807: *Considered*, 95/2052, 96/2629, 97/2214
Bilton v. Fastnet Highlands Ltd 1998 S.L.T. 1323; 1997 G.W.D. 28-1443; *Times*,
    November 20, 1997, OH. . . . . *Digested*, 97/**6084**
Binks v. Department of the Environment [1975] R.T.R. 318; [1975] Crim. L.R. 244;
    (1975) 119 S.J. 304, QBD . . . . *Digested*, 75/**3038**:
    Applied, 78/2537, 98/5591
Binnie v. Rederij Theodoro BV 1993 S.C. 71; 1992 G.W.D. 34-2013, 1 Div . . . . *Digested*, 96/**7224**:
    Applied, 99/6364
Birkett v. Kennedy 1998 G.W.D. 40-2057, HCJ Appeal
Birrell v. HM Advocate 1999 G.W.D. 17-771, HCJ Appeal
Birse v. HM Advocate; *sub nom* Birse v. MacNeill 2000 J.C. 503; 2000 S.L.T. 869;
    2000 S.C.C.R. 505; 2000 G.W.D. 16-649; *Times*, June 28, 2000, HCJ Appeal . . *Digested*, 00/**6125**
Birse v. MacNeill see Birse v. HM Advocate
Bishop v. Vannet (Sentencing) 1998 G.W.D. 32-1644, HCJ Appeal
Bissell v. Crowe 1998 G.W.D. 17-851, HCJ Appeal
Bisset v. Aberdeen Magistrates (1898) 1 F. (Ct. of Sess.) 87, 2 Div . . . . *Considered*, 00/6527
Bisset v. Standard Property Investment Plc 1999 G.W.D. 26-1253, OH
Bissett v. Russell 1998 G.W.D. 38-1964, HCJ Appeal
Black v. Braer Corp 1999 S.L.T. 1401; 1998 G.W.D. 29-1523; *Times*, October 12, 1998,
    OH . . . . *Digested*, 98/**5834**
Black v. Higson (Sentencing) 1998 G.W.D. 12-622, HCJ Appeal
Black v. Higson (Sentencing) 2001 G.W.D. 6-249, HCJ Appeal
Black v. HM Advocate 1998 G.W.D. 34-1745, HCJ Appeal
Black v. Lees (Sentencing) 1998 G.W.D. 7-352, HCJ Appeal
Black v. MacLeod 1999 G.W.D. 26-1219, Sh Pr
Black v. McCallum (1924) 40 Sh. Ct. Rep. 108. . . . . *Disapproved*, 01/6500
Black v. Neizer 1999 G.W.D. 13-609, HCJ Appeal
Black v. Scott Lithgow Ltd 1990 S.C. 322; 1990 S.L.T. 612, 1 Div . . . . *Digested*, 90/**5812**:
    Followed, 01/6333
Black v. Somerfield Stores Ltd 1998 S.L.T. 1315; 1998 G.W.D. 24-1189, OH . . . . *Digested*, 98/**5477**
Black v. Wrangler (UK) Ltd 2000 G.W.D. 12-441, OH

Blackfriars (Scotland) Ltd v. Laurie see Blackfriars (Scotland) Ltd v. Shetland Salmon Co's Trustee

Blackfriars (Scotland) Ltd v. Shetland Salmon Co's Trustee; *sub nom* Blackfriars (Scotland) Ltd v. Laurie 2001 S.L.T. 315; 2000 S.C.L.R. 385, OH . . . . *Digested*, 00/**5951**

Blacklock v. HM Advocate (Sentencing) 1998 G.W.D. 7-328, HCJ Appeal

Blackwood v. Gilchrist 1999 G.W.D. 33-1571, HCJ Appeal

Blair v. Carnegie (Sentencing) 1998 G.W.D. 9-461, HCJ Appeal

Blair v. Carnegie (Sentencing) 2001 G.W.D. 20-768, HCJ Appeal

Blair (Patricia Elaine) v. Carnegie see Cowan (Paul Matthew) v. HM Advocate

Blair v. Craigen 1999 G.W.D. 17-818, HCJ Appeal

Blair v. HM Advocate 1999 G.W.D. 3-146, HCJ Appeal

Blair v. Reith (Sentencing) 1998 G.W.D. 12-618, HCJ Appeal

Blake v. Heywood 1998 G.W.D. 17-859, HCJ Appeal

Blake v. Lothian Health Board 1993 S.L.T. 1248, OH . . . . *Digested*, 93/**5500**: *Followed*, 98/5480

Blane v. HM Advocate 1991 S.C.C.R. 576, HCJ Appeal . . . . *Digested*, 91/**4772**: *Applied*, 97/5790: *Followed*, 94/5673: *Overruled in part*, 00/6036

Blaney (Peter) v. HM Advocate (Sentencing) 2001 S.C.C.R. 858; 2001 G.W.D. 30-1191, HCJ Appeal

Blissgrange Ltd v. John G McGregor (Contractors) Ltd 1987 G.W.D. 19-707 . . . . *Considered*, 01/6292

Blue Circle Industries Plc v. Scottish Ministers 2001 G.W.D. 29-1174, OH

Blues v. Lees 1998 G.W.D. 25-1249, HCJ Appeal

Blusins Ltd v. Dundee City Licensing Board 2001 S.L.T. (Sh Ct) 176; 2000 G.W.D. 40-1500, Sh Ct (Tayside)

Blyszczak v. GEC Marconi Avionics Ltd 1996 S.L.T. (Sh Ct) 54, Sh Pr . . . . *Digested*, 96/**7346**: *Followed*, 99/5719

Blyth & Blyth Ltd v. Carillion Construction Ltd 79 Con. L.R. 142; 2001 G.W.D. 13-473, OH

Blythswood Investments (Scotland) Ltd v. Clydesdale Electrical Stores Ltd (in Receivership) 1995 S.L.T. 150; *Times*, October 20, 1994, OH . . . . *Digested*, 95/**6063**: *Followed*, 97/6176, 98/6032

Boal v. Secretary of State for Social Security 1998 S.C. 207; 1998 S.L.T. 639; 1997 G.W.D. 30-1547, 2 Div . . . . *Digested*, 98/**6190**

BOCM Silcock Ltd v. Hunter 1976 S.L.T. 217, 1 Div . . . . *Digested*, 76/**3117**: *Considered*, 99/6431

Boehringer Ingelheim KG v. Dowelhurst Ltd (Infringement Action) see Glaxo Group Ltd v. Dowelhurst Ltd (Infringement Action)

Boehringer Ingelheim KG v. Swingward Ltd (Infringement Action) see Glaxo Group Ltd v. Dowelhurst Ltd (Infringement Action)

Bogan's Curator Bonis v. Graham; *sub nom* MacDonald v. Graham 1992 S.C.L.R. 920, OH . . . . *Digested*, 94/**6009**: *Distinguished*, 98/5462

Bogie (t/a Oakbank Services) v. Forestry Commission 2001 G.W.D. 38-1432, OH

Bollan v. HM Advocate (Sentencing) 2001 G.W.D. 13-482, HCJ Appeal

Bonar v. HM Advocate 1999 G.W.D. 21-1005, HCJ Appeal

Boncza-Tomaszewksi v. HM Advocate; *sub nom* Fraser (George) v. HM Advocate 2000 J.C. 586; 2001 S.L.T. 336; 2000 S.C.C.R. 657; 2000 G.W.D. 25-933, HCJ Appeal . . . . *Digested*, 00/**5999**

Bond v. Brown (Sentencing) 2001 G.W.D. 1-77, HCJ Appeal

Bondway Properties Ltd v. Edinburgh City Council 1999 S.L.T. 127; 1998 S.C.L.R. 225; 1997 G.W.D. 40-2031, OH . . . . *Digested*, 98/**6148**

Bonini v. HM Advocate 1999 G.W.D. 17-815, HCJ Appeal

Bonnar v. Friel 1998 G.W.D. 26-1343, HCJ Appeal

Booker Aquaculture Ltd (t/a Marine Harvest McConnell) v. Scottish Ministers (By Order Hearing); *sub nom* Booker Aquaculture Ltd (t/a Marine Harvest McConnell) v. Secretary of State for Scotland (By Order Hearing) 1999 G.W.D. 36-1770, 1 Div

Booker Aquaculture Ltd (t/a Marine Harvest McConnell) v. Secretary of State for Scotland (By Order Hearing) see Booker Aquaculture Ltd (t/a Marine Harvest McConnell) v. Scottish Ministers (By Order Hearing)

Booker Aquaculture Ltd (t/a Marine Harvest McConnell) v. Secretary of State for Scotland (Judicial Review) 2000 S.C. 9; [2000] U.K.H.R.R. 1; 1999 G.W.D. 30-1435, 1 Div; reversing [1999] 1 C.M.L.R. 35; [1999] Eu. L.R. 54; 1998 G.W.D. 21-1089; *Times*, September 24, 1998, OH . . . . *Digested*, 00/**6301**

Booker Aquaculture Ltd (t/a Marine Harvest McConnell) v. Secretary of State for Scotland (Reference to ECJ) [2000] Eu. L.R. 449, 1 Div . . . . *Digested*, 01/**6501**

Boots the Chemist Ltd v. Ayrshire and Arran Primary Care NHS Trust 2001 S.C. 479; 2001 S.L.T. 594; 2001 G.W.D. 1-58, Ex Div; affirming 2000 G.W.D. 16-665, OH . *Digested*, 01/**6660**

Boots the Chemist Ltd v. GA Estates Ltd 1993 S.L.T. 136; 1992 S.C.L.R. 859, 2 Div; affirming Scotsman, July 4, 1991, OH . . . . *Digested*, 93/**5153**: *Applied*, 94/5713: *Followed*, 01/6416

Boots the Chemists Ltd v. Secretary of State for Scotland 2000 G.W.D. 1-18, OH

Borders RC v. Roxburgh DC 1989 S.L.T. 837, OH . . . . *Digested*, 89/**3877**: *Distinguished*, 01/6826: *Referred to*, 92/5249

Borgers v. Belgium (A/214) (1993) 15 E.H.R.R. 92, ECHR . . . . *Digested*, 93/**2128**:
Applied, 97/2803, 98/3142: *Distinguished*, 00/**6100**
Borrowman v. West Lothian Council [1998] R.V.R. 53, Lands Tr. . . . . *Digested*, 98/**6137**
Borve and Annishader Township v. Macleod 2001 S.L.C.R. 160, Land Ct (Div Ct)
Bottomley v. HM Advocate (Sentencing) 1999 G.W.D. 5-247, HCJ Appeal
Bouju v. Lees 1998 G.W.D. 28-1429, HCJ Appeal
Boulting v. Elias 1990 S.C. 135; 1990 S.L.T. 596, 1 Div. . . . . *Digested*, 90/**5619**:
Distinguished, 98/**5996**
Bourib v. Secretary of State for the Home Department 2000 G.W.D. 33-1294, OH
Boutineau v. Glasgow City Council 1998 Hous. L.R. 121, Sh Pr . . . . *Digested*, 99/**6265**
Bouygues UK Ltd v. Dahl-Jensen UK Ltd [2001] 1 All E.R. (Comm) 1041; [2001]
    C.L.C. 927; [2000] B.L.R. 522; (2001) 3 T.C.L.R. 2; 73 Con. L.R. 135; (2000)
    97(35) L.S.G. 36; *Times*, August 17, 2000, CA; affirming [2000] B.L.R. 49;
    (2000) 2 T.C.L.R. 308; 70 Con. L.R. 41; *Independent*, February 7, 2000 (C.S.),
    QBD (T&CC) . . . . *Digested*, 00/**3489**:
Followed, 01/6289
Bow Farm Housing Association v. Kelly 1998 Hous. L.R. 98, Sh Pr . . . . *Digested*, 98/**5986**
Bowden v. HM Advocate 1999 G.W.D. 35-1693, HCJ Appeal
Bowen v. Lees (Sentencing) 1998 G.W.D. 14-708, HCJ Appeal
Bowers v. Kennedy 2000 S.C. 555; 2000 S.L.T. 1006; 2000 G.W.D. 24-911; *Times*,
    July 27, 2000, 1 Div. . . . . *Digested*, 00/**6641**:
Considered, 01/6677, 01/6738
Bowie v. HM Advocate (Sentencing) 2000 G.W.D. 19-750, HCJ Appeal
Bowman v. Guthrie 1998 S.L.T. (Land Ct) 2; 1997 S.L.C.R. 40, Land Ct . . . . *Digested*, 98/**6030**
Bowman v. HM Advocate 1999 G.W.D. 16-757, HCJ Appeal
Boyack v. HM Advocate 1998 G.W.D. 34-1750, HCJ Appeal
Boyce v. British Airways Plc (Unreported, July 31, 1997), EAT . . . . *Followed*, 98/**5811**:
Subsequent proceedings, 01/6474
Boyce v. Cape Contracts Ltd 1998 S.L.T. 889; 1997 G.W.D. 31-1550, OH . . . . *Digested*, 98/**5467**
Boyce v. HM Advocate 1999 G.W.D. 5-243, HCJ Appeal
Boyce v. Sherrie 1998 S.L.T. 611; 1998 Rep. L.R. 60; 1998 G.W.D. 9-428, OH . . . . *Digested*, 98/**5453**
Boyd v. Crowe 1998 G.W.D. 21-1101, HCJ Appeal
Boyd v. Dyer 2001 G.W.D. 10-335, HCJ Appeal
Boyd v. HM Advocate (Sentencing) 2000 G.W.D. 8-313, HCJ Appeal
Boyd (John) v. HM Advocate; Moffat (Graeme William) v. HM Advocate 2001 J.C. 53;
    2000 S.L.T. 1358; 2000 S.C.C.R. 962; 2000 G.W.D. 35-1337, HCJ Appeal . . . . *Digested*, 01/**6357**
Boyd v. Howdle (Sentencing) 1998 G.W.D. 32-1681, HCJ Appeal
Boyd v. Kennedy 2001 G.W.D. 25-989, HCJ Appeal
Boyd v. Lanarkshire Health Board 2000 G.W.D. 9-341, OH
Boyd v. Spiers 1998 G.W.D. 30-1555, HCJ Appeal
Boyd v. Vannet 2000 G.W.D. 26-974, HCJ Appeal
Boyd v. Walkingshaw 1998 G.W.D. 30-1559, HCJ Appeal
Boyes v. Macleod (No.1) 1997 S.L.T. 1348; 1997 G.W.D. 21-1007, HCJ Appeal . . . . *Digested*, 98/**5612**
Boyes v. Macleod (No.2) 1998 S.L.T. 1129; 1998 S.C.C.R. 373; 1998 G.W.D. 18-894,
    HCJ Appeal . . . . *Digested*, 98/**5623**
Boyle v. Boyle's Executor 1999 S.C. 479; 1999 G.W.D. 12-584, OH . . . . *Digested*, 99/**6454**
Boyle v. Castlemilk East Housing Cooperative Ltd (No.1) 1998 S.L.T. 56; 1997 Hous.
    L.R. 58; 1997 G.W.D. 15-634; *Times*, May 16, 1997, OH . . . . *Digested*, 97/**6115**
Boyle v. Castlemilk East Housing Cooperative Ltd (No.2) 1999 S.L.T. 74; 1998 Hous.
    L.R. 33; 1998 G.W.D. 11-561, OH . . . . *Digested*, 98/**5974**
Boyle v. HM Advocate 2001 G.W.D. 37-1404, HCJ Appeal
Boyle v. HM Advocate (Sentencing) 1998 G.W.D. 28-1413, HCJ Appeal
Boyle v. HM Advocate (Sentencing) 1998 G.W.D. 26-1313, HCJ Appeal
Boyle (Peter) v. HM Advocate 1995 S.L.T. 162; *Scotsman*, January 12, 1995, HCJ
    Appeal . . . . *Digested*, 95/**5660**:
Distinguished, 95/5661: *Overruled*, 00/6064
Boyle v. McGlennan (Sentencing) 1999 G.W.D. 28-1337, HCJ Appeal
Boyle v. McGlennan (Sentencing) 2000 G.W.D. 20-820, HCJ Appeal
Boyle (William) v. Ritchie 1999 S.C.C.R. 278; 1999 G.W.D. 13-593, HCJ Appeal . . . . . . *Digested*, 99/**5846**
Boyle v. Vannet 1998 G.W.D. 25-1257, HCJ Appeal
BP Exploration Operating Co Ltd v. Chevron Shipping Co; *sub nom* BP Exploration
    Operating Co Ltd v. Chevron Transport (Scotland); BP Exploration Operating Co
    Ltd v. Chevron Tankers (Bermuda) Ltd; BP Exploration Operating Co Ltd v.
    Chevron Transport Corp [2001] UKHL 50; [2001] 3 W.L.R. 949; 2001 S.L.T.
    1394; 2001 S.C.L.R. 1029; (2001) 98(45) L.S.G. 26; (2001) 145 S.J.L.B. 244;
    2001 G.W.D. 33-1316; *Times*, October 19, 2001; *Independent*, December 3, 2001,
    HL; reversing 2000 S.L.T. 1374; 2000 S.C.L.R. 580; 2000 G.W.D. 14-559, 1
    Div; reversing in part 2000 S.L.T. 201; 1999 S.C.L.R. 438; 1999 G.W.D. 7-355;
    Times, May 6, 1999, OH . . . . *Digested*, 01/**6865**
BP Exploration Operating Co Ltd v. Chevron Tankers (Bermuda) Ltd see BP Exploration
    Operating Co Ltd v. Chevron Shipping Co
BP Exploration Operating Co Ltd v. Chevron Transport (Scotland) see BP Exploration
    Operating Co Ltd v. Chevron Shipping Co

BP Exploration Operating Co Ltd *v.* Chevron Transport Corp see BP Exploration
    Operating Co Ltd *v.* Chevron Shipping Co
BPCC Purnell Ltd *v.* Webb Unreported, EAT . . . . *Not followed,* 98/5827
Bracey *v.* Munro (Sentencing) 1998 G.W.D. 3-122, HCJ Appeal
Bradford *v.* Vannet (Sentencing) 1999 G.W.D. 35-1701, HCJ Appeal
Bradford *v.* Vannet (Sentencing) 1999 G.W.D. 7-329, HCJ Appeal
Bradford & Bingley Building Society *v.* Thorntons Plc 1998 G.W.D. 40-2071, OH
Bradley *v.* Vannet 1998 G.W.D. 27-1379, HCJ Appeal
Brady *v.* National Coal Board 1999 S.C. 621; 1999 G.W.D. 22-1070, 2 Div
Brady *v.* Neilsons 1999 G.W.D. 4-209, OH
Brailsford *v.* Webster 1999 G.W.D. 20-969, HCJ Appeal
Braithwaite *v.* Bank of Scotland 1999 S.L.T. 25; 1997 G.W.D. 40-2037, OH . . . . *Digested,* 99/**6431**
Brannigan (Alexandrina), Petitioner 1999 S.L.T. 679; 1999 S.C.C.R. 274; 1999 G.W.D. 11-
    514, HCJ Appeal . . . . *Digested,* 99/**6339**
Brannigan *v.* McGlennan 2000 S.C.C.R. 12; 1999 G.W.D. 35-1718, HCJ Appeal. . . . . . . *Digested,* 00/**6073**
Brash *v.* East of Scotland Water Authority 1998 G.W.D. 39-1989, Sh Pr
Bratty *v.* Attorney General of Northern Ireland [1963] A.C. 386; [1961] 3 W.L.R. 965;
    [1961] 3 All E.R. 523; (1962) 46 Cr. App. R. 1; 105 S.J. 865, HL. . . . . *Digested,* 61/**1839**:
                  Applied, 61/7782, 63/748, 68/3422, 74/654, 81/2346, 91/903:
        Cited, 00/6026: *Considered,* 73/558, 83/618, 87/3266, 88/3071, 91/902,
                93/925, 94/3944: *Followed,* 80/431: *Not applied,* 62/667
Breach *v.* Hingston 1998 G.W.D. 30-1551, HCJ Appeal
Breadalbane's Case see Campbell *v.* Campbell
Breen *v.* HM Advocate (Sentencing) 2000 G.W.D. 20-802, HCJ Appeal
Breen *v.* McGlennan (Sentencing) 1998 G.W.D. 14-714, HCJ Appeal
Bremner *v.* Bremner 1998 S.L.T. 844; 1998 S.C.L.R. 561; 1998 G.W.D. 10-507, Ex Div . . *Digested,* 98/**5474**
Bremner *v.* Bremner (Financial Provision) 2000 S.C.L.R. 912, Sh Pr . . . . *Digested,* 01/**6517**
Bremner *v.* HM Advocate 1998 G.W.D. 22-1116, HCJ Appeal
Brennan *v.* Clark 2000 Rep. L.R. 89; 2000 G.W.D. 17-684, Sh Ct . . . . *Digested,* 00/**6159**
Brennan *v.* HM Advocate 1977 J.C. 38; 1977 S.L.T. 151, HCJ Appeal . . . . *Digested,* 77/**3325**:
                  Applied, 92/5532, 92/5533: *Followed,* 00/6026: *Not followed,* 93/4752,
                                    94/5678
Brennan *v.* Vannet (Sentencing) 2000 G.W.D. 14-528, HCJ Appeal
Brewster *v.* Friel (Sentencing) 1998 G.W.D. 1-54, HCJ Appeal
Brewster *v.* Tayside Primary Care NHS Trust 2001 G.W.D. 16-643, OH
Bridon International Ltd *v.* Deep Water Recovery & Exploration Ltd 2000 G.W.D. 33-
    1264, OH
Briggs *v.* South Eastern Recovery III Plc 1999 G.W.D. 31-1453, OH
Brightside Kilpatrick Engineering Services *v.* Mitchell Construction (1973) Ltd [1975] 2
    Lloyd's Rep. 493; 1 B.L.R. 62, CA . . . . *Digested,* 76/**208**:
                  Distinguished, 98/5537: *Followed,* 95/5488
Brinded *v.* Crowe 1998 G.W.D. 36-1870, HCJ Appeal
Bristol and West Building Society *v.* Aitken Nairn WS 1999 S.C. 678; 2000 S.L.T. 763;
    2000 S.C.L.R. 47; 1999 G.W.D. 26-1258, 2 Div; reversing 1999 S.L.T. 43; 1998
    S.C.L.R. 465; 1998 G.W.D. 16-817, OH . . . . *Digested,* 00/**6596**
Bristol and West Building Society *v.* Rollo Steven & Bond 1998 S.L.T. 9; 1997 G.W.D.
    22-1096, OH. . . . . *Digested,* 98/**5724**
Britannia Building Society *v.* Clarke 2001 S.L.T. 1355; 2001 G.W.D. 18-710, OH . . . . *Digested,* 01/**6868**
Britel Fund Trustees Ltd *v.* Scottish and Southern Energy Plc 2001 G.W.D. 34-1334, OH
British Airways Plc *v.* Boyce 2001 S.C. 510; [2001] I.R.L.R. 157; 2000 G.W.D. 40-1489,
    Ex Div. . . . . *Digested,* 01/**6474**
British Linen Asset Finance Ltd *v.* Ridgeway 1999 G.W.D. 2-78, Sh Pr
British Telecommunications Plc *v.* James Thomson & Sons (Engineers) Ltd [1999] 1
    W.L.R. 9; [1999] 2 All E.R. 241; 1999 S.C. (H.L.) 9; 1999 S.L.T. 224; 1999
    S.C.L.R. 126; [1999] B.L.R. 35; (1999) 1 T.C.L.R. 1; 61 Con. L.R. 1; [1999] 1
    Lloyd's Rep. I.R. 105; [1999] Lloyd's Rep. I.R. 105; (1999) 96(4) L.S.G. 40;
    (1999) 143 S.J.L.B. 28; [1998] N.P.C. 161; 1999 G.W.D. 1-47; *Times,* December
    11, 1998, HL; reversing 1997 S.C. 59; 1997 S.L.T. 767; 1997 S.C.L.R. 228; 82
    B.L.R. 1; 54 Con. L.R. 108; [1997] 6 Re. L.R. 325; 1997 Rep. L.R. 23; (1997) 13
    Const. L.J. 332; 1997 G.W.D. 3-77; *Times,* January 28, 1997, 2 Div; affirming
    49 Con. L.R. 163, OH . . . . *Digested,* 99/**5783**:
                                      Applied, 01/4469
British Waterways Board *v.* Moore & Mulheron Contracts Ltd 1998 G.W.D. 11-569, Sh
    Ct
British Waterways Board, Petitioners 2001 G.W.D. 25-916, OH
Brixey *v.* Lynas (No.1); *sub nom* B *v.* L (No.1) 1997 S.C. (H.L.) 1; 1996 S.L.T. 908; 1996
    S.C.L.R. 856; [1996] 2 F.L.R. 499; [1997] 1 F.C.R. 220; [1997] Fam. Law 10,
    HL; affirming 1994 S.C. 606; 1994 S.L.T. 847, 1 Div . . . . *Digested,* 96/**6616**:
                                      Applied, 99/6068
Broadway *v.* Clydesdale Bank Plc (No.1) 2000 G.W.D. 19-763; *Times,* September 12,
    2000, OH . . . . *Digested,* 00/**6676**
Broadway *v.* Clydesdale Bank Plc (No.2) 2001 G.W.D. 14-552, OH
Brock *v.* Clark 1999 G.W.D. 20-932, HCJ Appeal
Brocklehurst *v.* HM Advocate (Sentencing) 1998 G.W.D. 15-756, HCJ Appeal

Broderip v. Salomon see Salomon v. Salomon & Co Ltd
Brodie v. Gilchrist (Sentencing) 2000 G.W.D. 9-345, HCJ Appeal
Brodie v. HM Advocate (Sentencing) 2001 G.W.D. 13-490, HCJ Appeal
Brodie v. Ker 1952 S.C. 216; 1952 S.L.T. 226, IH (Ct of 7 judges) . . . .   *Digested*, 52/**4161**:
      Applied, 82/3399, 82/4319: *Followed*, 95/6137, 96/6675, 01/6737
Brolly v. Bank of Scotland 2001 G.W.D. 11-380, Sh Pr
Bromham v. Highland RC 1997 S.L.T. 1137; 1997 Rep. L.R. 101; 1997 G.W.D. 25-1235,
   OH . . . .   *Digested*, 97/**5694**:
                                                   Considered, 98/5453
Brooks v. Civil Aviation Authority 2000 S.C. 565; 2000 S.L.T. 1386; [2000] O.P.L.R.
   365; 2000 G.W.D. 24-918; *Times*, July 28, 2000, 1 Div . . . .   *Digested*, 00/**6620**
Brooks v. Lind 2000 G.W.D. 8-307, Ex Div; reversing 1997 Rep. L.R. 83; 1997 G.W.D.
   13-570; *Times*, March 26, 1997, OH . . . .   *Digested*, 97/**5972**
Brouwer v. McLeod 1999 G.W.D. 6-296, HCJ Appeal
Brown v. Carnegie 1998 G.W.D. 31-1605, HCJ Appeal
Brown v. Clark 2001 G.W.D. 10-336, HCJ Appeal
Brown v. Douglas (Sentencing) 1998 G.W.D. 8-414, HCJ Appeal
Brown v. East and Midlothian NHS Trust 2000 S.L.T. 342; 2000 Rep. L.R. 10; 1999
   G.W.D. 40-1962, OH . . . .   *Digested*, 00/**6428**
Brown v. Edinburgh City Council 1999 S.L.T. (Sh Ct) 43; 1998 S.C.L.R. 1150; 1998
   Rep. L.R. 136; 1998 G.W.D. 32-1675, Sh Ct (Lothian) . . . .   *Digested*, 99/**6366**
Brown v. Edinburgh Magistrates 1907 S.C. 256, 1 Div . . . .   *Applied*, 99/6035
Brown v. Glen (Robert Doran) 1998 J.C. 4; 1998 S.L.T. 115; 1997 S.C.C.R. 636; 1997
   G.W.D. 27-1355, HCJ Appeal . . . .   *Digested*, 97/**5836**
Brown v. Higson (Sentencing) 2001 G.W.D. 16-617, HCJ Appeal
Brown v. Higson (Sentencing) 2001 G.W.D. 27-1091, HCJ Appeal
Brown (James) v. Higson 2000 S.L.T. 994; 2000 G.W.D. 14-562, HCJ Appeal . . . .   *Digested*, 00/**6033**
Brown v. HM Advocate (Misdirection) 1998 G.W.D. 12-590, HCJ Appeal
Brown v. HM Advocate (Sentencing) 1998 G.W.D. 10-494, HCJ Appeal
Brown v. HM Advocate (Sentencing) 1998 G.W.D. 18-919, HCJ Appeal
Brown v. HM Advocate (Sentencing) 1998 G.W.D. 24-1214, HCJ Appeal
Brown v. HM Advocate (Sentencing) 1998 G.W.D. 29-1481, HCJ Appeal
Brown v. HM Advocate (Sentencing) 1998 G.W.D. 3-120, HCJ Appeal
Brown v. HM Advocate (Sentencing) 1999 G.W.D. 30-1429, HCJ Appeal
Brown v. HM Advocate (Sentencing) 1999 G.W.D. 36-1766, HCJ Appeal
Brown v. HM Advocate (Sentencing) 1999 G.W.D. 20-950, HCJ Appeal
Brown v. HM Advocate (Sentencing) 2000 G.W.D. 8-294, HCJ Appeal
Brown v. HM Advocate (Sentencing) 2000 G.W.D. 15-596, HCJ
Brown v. HM Advocate (Sentencing) 2000 S.C.C.R. 736; 2000 G.W.D. 29-1152, HCJ
   Appeal . . . .   *Digested*, 01/**6410**
Brown v. HM Advocate (Sentencing) 2001 G.W.D. 28-1133, HCJ Appeal
Brown (David) v. HM Advocate 1998 S.L.T. 971; 1998 G.W.D. 13-640, HCJ Appeal . . . .   *Digested*, 98/**5597**
Brown (Frank Innes) v. HM Advocate 1998 J.C. 201; 1998 S.L.T. 1169; 1998 S.C.C.R.
   356; 1998 G.W.D. 18-899, HCJ Appeal . . . .   *Digested*, 98/**5645**
Brown (John) v. HM Advocate 1999 S.L.T. 1369; 1998 S.C.C.R. 461; 1998 G.W.D. 27-
   1358, HCJ Appeal. . . . .   *Digested*, 98/**5593**
Brown v. Hutchison 2001 G.W.D. 12-435, HCJ Appeal
Brown (Paul Allison) v. Kennedy 1999 S.C.C.R. 574; 1999 G.W.D. 24-1141, HCJ Appeal   *Digested*, 99/**5840**
Brown v. McLeod 1999 G.W.D. 26-1263, HCJ Appeal
Brown v. Millar 2000 G.W.D. 37-1385, HCJ Appeal
Brown v. Miller (Sentencing) 1998 G.W.D. 2-79, HCJ Appeal
Brown v. Prosser 1999 G.W.D. 33-1594, OH
Brown v. Reith (Sentencing) 1998 G.W.D. 11-580, HCJ Appeal
Brown v. Scottish Border Springs Ltd 2001 G.W.D. 23-851, OH
Brown v. Selfridge (Allan) 2000 J.C. 9; 2000 S.L.T. 437; 1999 S.C.C.R. 809; 1999
   G.W.D. 28-1323, HCJ Appeal. . . . .   *Digested*, 00/**6082**
Brown v. South Lanarkshire Council 2001 G.W.D. 12-402, Ex Div; affirming 2001
   Hous. L.R. 34; 2001 G.W.D. 6-189, OH . . . .   *Digested*, 01/**6693**
Brown v. Spiers 1998 G.W.D. 19-978, HCJ Appeal
Brown v. Stott; *sub nom* Stott (Procurator Fiscal) v. Brown [2001] 2 W.L.R. 817;
   [2001] 2 All E.R. 97; 2001 S.C. (P.C.) 43; 2001 S.L.T. 59; 2001 S.C.C.R. 62;
   [2001] R.T.R. 11; [2001] H.R.L.R. 9; [2001] U.K.H.R.R. 333; 11 B.H.R.C. 179;
   (2001) 3 L.G.L.R. 24; (2001) 145 S.J.L.B. 100; 2000 G.W.D. 40-1513; *Times*,
   December 6, 2000; *Independent*, February 7, 2001 (C.S), PC (Sc); reversing
   2000 J.C. 328; 2000 S.L.T. 379; 2000 S.C.C.R. 314; [2000] R.T.R. 394; [2000]
   U.K.H.R.R. 239; 2000 G.W.D. 6-237; *Times*, February 14, 2000, HCJ Appeal . . .   *Digested*, 01/**6319**:
                                Applied, 01/972: *Considered*, 01/1237, 01/5291
Brown v. Vannet (Sentencing) 1998 G.W.D. 31-1587, HCJ Appeal
Brown v. Vannet (Sentencing) 1999 G.W.D. 7-360, HCJ Appeal
Brown (Carolyn) v. Vannet 1999 S.L.T. 932; 1999 S.C.C.R. 458; 1999 G.W.D. 19-873,
   HCJ Appeal . . . .   *Digested*, 99/**5888**
Brown v. Wilson (Sentencing) 1998 G.W.D. 32-1653, HCJ Appeal
Brown & Tawse Steelstock Ltd v. Heywood 2001 G.W.D. 30-1190, HCJ Appeal
Bruce v. HM Advocate 1999 G.W.D. 15-707, HCJ Appeal

Bruce v. Kordula 2001 S.L.T. 983; 2001 G.W.D. 17-662, OH. . . . . *Digested,* 01/**6210**
Bruce (Allan) v. Macleod 1998 S.L.T. 173; 1997 G.W.D. 37-1888, HCJ Appeal . . . . *Digested,* 98/**5665**
Bruce (Hans) v. McLeod 1998 S.C.C.R. 733; 1998 G.W.D. 40-2044, HCJ Appeal. . . . . *Digested,* 99/**5835**
Bruce v. Modern Homes Investment Co Ltd 1978 S.L.T. (Lands Tr.) 34, Lands Tr (Scot). . *Digested,* 78/**3389**:
　　　　　　　　　　　　　　　　　　　　　　　　　　　　　　　　　Approved, 99/6230
Bruce v. Stott 2001 G.W.D. 6-247, HCJ Appeal
Bruce v. Wiggins Teape (Stationery) Ltd [1994] I.R.L.R. 536, EAT. . . . . *Digested,* 95/**2120**:
　　　　　　　　　　　　　　　　　　　　　　　　　　　　　　　Distinguished, 98/5827
Brunton v. HM Advocate (Sentencing) 2001 S.C.C.R. 689; 2001 G.W.D. 28-1146, HCJ
　　Appeal
Bryan v. United Kingdom (A/335-A) (1996) 21 E.H.R.R. 342; [1996] 1 P.L.R. 47;
　　[1996] 2 E.G.L.R. 123; [1996] 28 E.G. 137; *Times,* December 8, 1995, ECHR . . . *Digested,* 96/**4707**:
　　　　　　　　　　　　Applied, 98/3120, 01/4761: *Considered,* 01/855: *Distinguished,* 00/5841,
　　　　　　　　　　　　　　　　　　　　　　　　　　　　　　　　　　　01/2269
Bryant Homes (Scotland) Ltd v. Secretary of State for Scotland 2000 G.W.D. 25-925,
　　Ex Div
Bryant Homes (Scotland) Ltd v. Secretary of State for Scotland (Costs) 2001 G.W.D.
　　19-738, Ex Div
Bryce v. Brown (Sentencing) 2001 G.W.D. 19-726, HCJ Appeal
Bryce v. HM Advocate (Sentencing) 1999 G.W.D. 36-1745, HCJ Appeal
Bryce v. McKirdy 1999 S.L.T. 988; 1999 G.W.D. 5-271, OH. . . . . *Digested,* 99/**6365**
Bryce (Robert Kenneth) v. Normand 1997 S.L.T. 1351, HCJ Appeal. . . . . *Digested,* 98/**5575**
Bryce v. Vannet (Sentencing) 1998 G.W.D. 13-667, HCJ Appeal
Bryden v. HM Advocate 1998 G.W.D. 37-1909, HCJ Appeal
Bryson v. BT Rolatruc Ltd 1998 G.W.D. 35-1824, OH
Bryson v. HM Advocate 1998 G.W.D. 17-863, HCJ Appeal
BSS Group Plc v. Huntly Plumbing, Heating & Electrical; Italian Distribution Co v. Pizza
　　& Pasta 1998 S.C.L.R. 979, Sh Ct　　　　　　　　　　　　　　　　　　　　*Digested,* 98/**6006**
Buchan v. Buchan 2001 Fam. L.R. 48; 2001 G.W.D. 6-226, Sh Ct (Grampian) . . . . *Digested,* 01/**6522**
Buchan v. Higson (Sentencing) 1999 G.W.D. 12-579, HCJ Appeal
Buchan v. HM Advocate (Sentencing) 1998 G.W.D. 3-117, HCJ Appeal
Buchan v. HM Advocate (Sentencing) 1998 G.W.D. 39-2012, HCJ Appeal
Buchan v. HM Advocate (Sentencing) 1999 G.W.D. 34-1629, HCJ Appeal
Buchan v. North Lanarkshire Council 2000 Hous. L.R. 98; 2000 G.W.D. 21-835, Sh Ct. *Digested,* 00/**6461**
Buchan v. Secretary of State for Employment; Ivey v. Secretary of State for
　　Employment [1997] B.C.C. 145; [1997] I.R.L.R. 80, EAT. . . . . *Digested,* 97/**2251**:
　　　　　　　　　Considered, 98/5812, 99/2019, 99/2100: *Disapproved,* 98/2188:
　　　　　　　　　　　　　　　　　　　　　　　　　　　　　Referred to, 99/2110
Buchan v. Stott (Sentencing) 2000 G.W.D. 4-169, HCJ Appeal
Buchan v. West Lothian Council 2001 S.L.T. 1452; 2001 G.W.D. 24-880, OH
Buchanan v. Alba Diagnostics Ltd 2001 S.C.L.R. 307; [2001] R.P.C. 43; 2001 G.W.D.
　　6-234, 1 Div; affirming [2000] R.P.C. 367; 1999 G.W.D. 24-1170, OH . . . . *Digested,* 01/**6725**
Buchanan v. Dillon 2001 G.W.D. 17-663, Sh Ct (Grampian)
Buchanan v. Drummond Miller, WS 1999 G.W.D. 12-570, OH
Buchanan (Scott John) v. HM Advocate 1998 S.L.T. 13; 1997 S.C.C.R. 441; 1997 G.W.D.
　　20-942, HCJ Appeal. . . . . *Digested,* 97/**5865**
Buchanan v. Lees (Sentencing) 1998 G.W.D. 6-281, HCJ Appeal
Buchanan v. Mason 2001 Rep. L.R. 67; [2001] 5 Q.R. 19, OH. . . . . *Digested,* 01/**6425**
Buchanan v. McLean see McLean v. Buchanan
Buchanan v. Vannet (Sentencing) 1998 G.W.D. 15-743, HCJ Appeal
Buckley v. Ritchie (Sentencing) 1999 G.W.D. 40-1949, HCJ Appeal
Budge v. Donald; *sub nom* Donald & Budge (A Firm) v. Donald; TNS, Sh Pr; reversing
　　2001 G.W.D. 28-1124, Sh Ct (Grampian)
Budge v. Forrest-Jones 2000 S.L.T. (Land Ct) 19; 2000 S.L.C.R. 34; 2000 G.W.D. 31-
　　1235, Land Ct (Full Ct) . . . . *Digested,* 01/**6747**
Buglass v. Stott 2001 S.C.C.R. 692; 2001 G.W.D. 25-980, HCJ Appeal
Bullock (Gary John) v. HM Advocate 1999 J.C. 260; 1999 S.L.T. 1319; 1999 S.C.C.R.
　　492; 1999 G.W.D. 20-930, HCJ Appeal . . . . *Digested,* 99/**5914**
Bunkate v. Netherlands (A/248-B) (1995) 19 E.H.R.R. 477, ECHR . . . . *Digested,* 95/**2637**:
　　　　　　　　　　　　　　　　　　　　　　　　　　　　　　Distinguished, 00/6090
Buntin v. Ruxton 2000 G.W.D. 29-1117, HCJ Appeal
Burke v. Royal Infirmary of Edinburgh NHS Trust 1999 S.L.T. 539; 1998 Rep. L.R. 87;
　　1998 G.W.D. 20-1045; *Times,* June 8, 1998, OH . . . . *Digested,* 98/**5718**:
　　　　　　　　　　　　　　　　　　　　　　　　　　　　　　Considered, 00/6169
Burn (Geoffrey Keith) v. Miller see Burn, Petitioner
Burn Stewart Distillers Plc v. Assessor for Lanarkshire Valuation Joint Board [2001] R.A.
　　110; 2001 G.W.D. 20-780, Lands Tr (Scot) . . . . *Digested,* 01/**6877**
Burn, Petitioner; *sub nom* Burn (Geoffrey Keith) v. Miller; McQuilken v. Procurator
　　Fiscal 2000 J.C. 403; 2000 S.L.T. 538; 2000 S.C.C.R. 384; 2000 G.W.D. 12-
　　418, HCJ Appeal. . . . . *Digested,* 00/**6064**
Burnett v. Higson 2000 G.W.D. 8-314, HCJ Appeal
Burnett v. Smith 1990 J.C. 119; 1990 S.L.T. 537; 1989 S.C.C.R. 628, HCJ Appeal . . . . *Digested,* 90/**5748**:
　　　　　　　　　　　　　　　　　　　　　Applied, 93/5770: *Considered,* 00/6008

Burnett's Trustee *v.* Grainger TNS, Ex Div; reversing 2000 S.L.T. (Sh Ct) 116; 2000
    G.W.D. 28-1093, Sh Pr... *Digested,* 00/**6511**
Burns *v.* Gilchirst 1999 G.W.D. 27-1292, HCJ Appeal
Burns *v.* HM Advocate (Procedure: Delay) 2001 G.W.D. 19-722, HCJ Appeal
Burns *v.* HM Advocate (Sentencing) 1998 G.W.D. 7-350, HCJ Appeal
Burns *v.* HM Advocate (Sentencing) 1998 G.W.D. 36-1858, HCJ Appeal
Burns *v.* HM Advocate (Sentencing) 1998 S.C.C.R. 281; 1998 G.W.D. 12-597, HCJ
    Appeal... *Digested,* 98/**5671**
Burns *v.* HM Advocate (Sentencing) 2001 G.W.D. 39-1455, HCJ Appeal
Burns *v.* Munro 1998 G.W.D. 18-924, HCJ Appeal
Burns Trustee *v.* Burns see Ritchie *v.* Burns
Burnside *v.* Siwek 2000 G.W.D. 39-1463, Sh Ct (Grampian)
Burnside Kemp Fraser *v.* Robb 1999 G.W.D. 34-1610, OH
Burnside Kemp Fraser *v.* Siwek 2000 G.W.D. 16-664, Sh Ct
Burnside Kemp Fraser *v.* Stirton 2000 G.W.D. 40-1499, OH
Burrell *v.* McFadyen (Sentencing) 2001 G.W.D. 16-613, HCJ Appeal
Burt *v.* HM Advocate (Sentencing) 2001 G.W.D. 24-897, HCJ Appeal
Burton Allton & Johnson Ltd *v.* Peck [1975] I.C.R. 193; [1975] I.R.L.R. 87, QBD...... *Digested,* 75/**1141**:
                                                              Applied, 00/6215: *Distinguished,* 84/1214, 85/1150
Bush *v.* Bush 2000 S.L.T. (Sh Ct) 22; 1999 G.W.D. 39-1894, Sh Ct (North
    Strathclyde) .... *Digested,* 00/**6436**
Butler *v.* Stott 1999 G.W.D. 14-669, HCJ Appeal
Buttercase *v.* Russell 1999 G.W.D. 21-992, HCJ Appeal
Bye *v.* Bye (Change of Circumstances) 1999 G.W.D. 33-1591, Sh Pr
Bye *v.* Bye (Valuation of Business) 1998 G.W.D. 32-1668, OH
Byrne *v.* HM Advocate (No.1) 1999 G.W.D. 18-822, HCJ Appeal
Byrne *v.* HM Advocate (No.2) 2000 J.C. 155; 2000 S.L.T. 233; 2000 S.C.C.R. 77;
    1999 G.W.D. 40-1912, HCJ Appeal .... *Digested,* 00/**6036**

C (A Juvenile) *v.* HM Advocate (Sentencing) 1999 G.W.D. 3-138, HCJ Appeal
C (A Juvenile) *v.* HM Advocate (Sentencing) 2000 G.W.D. 9-335, HCJ Appeal
C (A Minor) (Abduction: Rights of Custody Abroad), Re see C *v.* C (A Minor) (Abduction:
    Rights of Custody Abroad)
C *v.* C 1999 G.W.D. 35-1711, OH
C *v.* C (A Minor) (Abduction: Rights of Custody Abroad); *sub nom* C (A Minor)
    (Abduction: Rights of Custody Abroad), Re [1989] 1 W.L.R. 654; [1989] 2 All
    E.R. 465; [1989] 1 F.L.R. 403; [1989] F.C.R. 197; [1989] Fam. Law 228; (1989)
    153 J.P.N. 236; (1989) 133 S.J. 660; *Times,* December 19, 1988; *Independent,*
    January 2, 1989 (C.S.), CA... *Digested,* 89/**2437**:
                         Applied, 89/2491, 90/3155, 91/2522, 91/2527, 93/2789:
                        Considered, 95/3431, 95/3436, 95/3448, 96/534, 97/402:
              Distinguished, 94/3151, 95/5533: *Followed,* 94/5440, 98/2383, 98/5842
C *v.* Criminal Injuries Compensation Board see C, Petitioner
C *v.* Greater Glasgow Community and Mental Health Service NHS Trust 1998 S.C.L.R.
    214, Sh Ct.. *Digested,* 98/**6098**
C *v.* HM Advocate (Sentencing) 1998 G.W.D. 17-849, HCJ Appeal
C *v.* HM Advocate (Sentencing) 1998 G.W.D. 40-2060, HCJ Appeal
C *v.* Ruxton (Sentencing) 1998 G.W.D. 3-151, HCJ Appeal
C *v.* Scottish Legal Aid Board 1999 S.L.T. (Sh Ct) 48, Sh Ct (Lothian) .... *Digested,* 99/**6334**
C Czarnikow Ltd *v.* Koufos (The Heron II) see Koufos *v.* C Czarnikow Ltd (The Heron
    II)
C&C Joinery Services *v.* Lakeside Design and Club Refurbishment Specialists Ltd 1999
    G.W.D. 26-1224, Sh Pr
C, Petitioner; *sub nom* C *v.* Criminal Injuries Compensation Board 1999 S.C. 551; 1999
    S.C.L.R. 992; 1999 G.W.D. 21-985; *Times,* June 3, 1999, OH .... *Digested,* 99/**5614**
Cabales *v.* United Kingdom (9473/81) see Abdulaziz *v.* United Kingdom (A/94)
Caddies *v.* McLeod 1999 G.W.D. 26-1259, HCJ Appeal
Cadoux *v.* Central RC 1986 S.L.T. 117; [1986] I.R.L.R. 131, OH .... *Digested,* 86/**1174**:
                                                  Distinguished, 99/6027
Cahill *v.* Cahill 1998 S.L.T. (Sh Ct) 96; 1998 G.W.D. 11-556, Sh Pr................. *Digested,* 99/**6073**
Cahill's Judicial Factor *v.* Cahill (No.1) 2001 G.W.D. 24-884, Ex Div
Cahill's Judicial Factor *v.* Cahill (No.2) 2001 G.W.D. 31-1252, 1 Div
Cahill's Judicial Factor *v.* Smith 1998 G.W.D. 36-1846, OH
Caird *v.* HM Advocate (Sentencing) 1998 G.W.D. 12-603, HCJ Appeal
Caird Energy Plc *v.* Royal Bank of Scotland Plc see Cairn Energy Plc *v.* Royal Bank of
    Scotland Plc
Cairn Energy Plc *v.* Royal Bank of Scotland Plc; *sub nom* Caird Energy Plc *v.* Royal
    Bank of Scotland Plc 2000 S.C. 325; 2000 S.L.T. 1098; 2000 G.W.D. 7-240,
    OH... *Digested,* 00/**5888**
Cairns *v.* HM Advocate (Corroboration) 1999 G.W.D. 35-1667, HCJ Appeal
Cairns *v.* HM Advocate (Drug Offences) 1999 G.W.D. 1-15, HCJ Appeal
Cairns *v.* HM Advocate (Onus of Proof) 1998 G.W.D. 29-1466, HCJ Appeal
Cairns *v.* HM Advocate (Sentencing) 1998 G.W.D. 10-497, HCJ Appeal

Cairns *v.* HM Advocate (Sentencing) 1998 G.W.D. 32-1659, HCJ Appeal
Cairns *v.* HM Advocate (Sentencing) 1999 G.W.D. 2-97, HCJ Appeal
Cairns *v.* HM Advocate (Sentencing) 1999 G.W.D. 17-780, HCJ Appeal
Cairns (Peter John) *v.* HM Advocate 1999 S.L.T. 1072; 1999 S.C.C.R. 552; 1999 G.W.D.
   22-1044, HCJ Appeal . . . . *Digested,* 99/**5904**
Cairns *v.* Howdle 2000 S.C.C.R. 742; 2000 G.W.D. 29-1113, HCJ Appeal . . . . *Digested,* 01/**6309**
Cairns *v.* Howdle (Sentencing) 1999 G.W.D. 10-478, HCJ Appeal
Cairns *v.* Torq Partnership Ltd 2000 G.W.D. 15-575, Sh Pr
Cala Homes (South) Ltd *v.* Alfred McAlpine Homes East Ltd (No.2) [1996] F.S.R. 36;
   (1996) 19(5) I.P.D. 19042; *Independent,* October 30, 1995 (C.S.), Ch D . . . . . . *Digested,* 95/**850**:
                            Considered, 97/5741: *Not followed,* 96/6707: *Overruled,* 98/6020
Cala Management Ltd *v.* Scottish Ministers 2001 S.L.T. 1219; 2001 G.W.D. 24-910, Ex
   Div . . . . *Digested,* 01/**6851**
Calder *v.* HM Advocate (Sentencing) 1998 G.W.D. 28-1412, HCJ Appeal
Calder *v.* HM Advocate (Sentencing) 1998 G.W.D. 36-1863, HCJ Appeal
Caldwell *v.* Normand 1994 S.L.T. 489; 1993 S.C.C.R. 624, HCJ Appeal . . . . *Digested,* 93/**5064**:
                                 Applied, 95/5755, 96/6745, 97/5777, 98/5398
Caledonia Bureau Investment & Property *v.* Caffrey [1998] I.C.R. 603; [1998] I.R.L.R.
   110, EAT . . . . *Digested,* 98/**5825**
Caledonia North Sea Ltd *v.* British Telecommunications Plc see Caledonia North Sea Ltd
   v. London Bridge Engineering Ltd
Caledonia North Sea Ltd *v.* BT Plc see Caledonia North Sea Ltd *v.* London Bridge
   Engineering Ltd
Caledonia North Sea Ltd *v.* London Bridge Engineering Ltd; *sub nom* Caledonia North
   Sea Ltd *v.* British Telecommunications Plc; Caledonia North Sea Ltd *v.* BT Plc;
   Caledonia North Sea Ltd *v.* Norton (No.2) Ltd (In Liquidation); TNS, HL;
   affirming 2000 S.L.T. 1123; [2000] Lloyd's Rep. I.R. 249; 2000 G.W.D. 3-84;
   Times, February 8, 2000, 1 Div . . . . *Digested,* 00/**6517**
Caledonia North Sea Ltd *v.* Norton (No.2) Ltd (In Liquidation) see Caledonia North Sea
   Ltd *v.* London Bridge Engineering Ltd
Caledonia Subsea Ltd *v.* Micoperi Srl; *sub nom* Caledonia Subsea Ltd *v.* Microperi Srl
   2001 S.C. 716; 2001 S.L.T. 1186; 2001 S.C.L.R. 634; 2001 G.W.D. 10-366, OH . . *Digested,* 01/**6278**
Caledonia Subsea Ltd *v.* Microperi Srl see Caledonia Subsea Ltd *v.* Micoperi Srl
Caledonian Heritable Ltd *v.* Canyon Investments Ltd (No.1) 2001 G.W.D. 1-62, OH
Callaghan *v.* Glasgow City Council; *sub nom* Callagan *v.* Glasgow City Council [2001]
   I.R.L.R. 724, EAT . . . . *Digested,* 01/**6463**
Callaghan *v.* HM Advocate 1999 G.W.D. 5-237, HCJ Appeal
Callaghan *v.* Southern General Hospital NHS Trust 2000 S.L.T. 1059; 2001 S.C.L.R.
   168; 2000 Rep. L.R. 114; 2000 G.W.D. 24-915, OH . . . . *Digested,* 00/**6169**
Callan (David James) *v.* HM Advocate 1999 S.L.T. 1102; 1999 S.C.C.R. 57; 1999 G.W.D.
   6-298, HCJ Appeal . . . . *Digested,* 99/**5894**
Calvin *v.* Carr [1980] A.C. 574; [1979] 2 W.L.R. 755; [1979] 2 All E.R. 440; 123 S.J.
   112, PC (Aus) . . . . *Digested,* 79/**14**:
             Applied, 80/315, 80/2904, 89/1500: *Considered,* 87/3162, 95/3252,
          00/6628: *Distinguished,* 97/63: *Followed,* 91/43, 93/31: *Referred to,* 81/108
Cambridge Bionutritional Ltd *v.* VDC Plc 2000 G.W.D. 6-230, Sh Ct
Cameron *v.* Abbey Life Assurance Co Ltd 1999 G.W.D. 1-42, Sh Ct
Cameron *v.* Cameron; *sub nom* Fitzsimmons *v.* Cameron 2001 G.W.D. 39-1479, Sh Pr
Cameron *v.* Carr (No.1) see Cameron *v.* Carr's Curator ad Litem
Cameron *v.* Carr's Curator ad Litem; *sub nom* Cameron *v.* Carr (No.1) 1998 S.L.T. (Sh
   Ct) 22; 1997 S.C.L.R. 1164; 1997 G.W.D. 36-1823, Sh Ct (North Strathclyde) . . . *Digested,* 98/**5461**
Cameron (Kieran) *v.* Higson 2001 S.C.C.R. 344; 2001 G.W.D. 17-686, HCJ Appeal
Cameron *v.* HM Advocate 1991 J.C. 251; 1988 S.L.T. 169; 1987 S.C.C.R. 608, HCJ
   Appeal . . . . *Digested,* 88/**3925**:
          Applied, 88/3926, 90/4892, 93/4942, 98/5559: *Followed,* 92/5429,
                                       00/6059
Cameron *v.* HM Advocate 2000 G.W.D. 8-277, HCJ Appeal
Cameron *v.* HM Advocate (Sentencing) 1999 G.W.D. 17-801, HCJ Appeal
Cameron (Hugh William) *v.* HM Advocate see Muirhead (George Alexander) *v.* HM
   Advocate
Cameron (John Edward) *v.* HM Advocate 1999 S.C.C.R. 198; 1999 G.W.D. 6-304, HCJ
   Appeal . . . . *Digested,* 99/**5941**
Cameron (John Paul) *v.* HM Advocate 1999 S.C.C.R. 476; 1999 G.W.D. 18-825, HCJ
   Appeal . . . . *Digested,* 99/**5917**
Cameron *v.* Kvaerner Govan Ltd (Personal Injury) 2001 Rep. L.R. 52; 2000 G.W.D. 40-
   1508, OH
Cameron *v.* MacLeod (Sentencing) 1998 G.W.D. 13-689, HCJ Appeal
Cameron (Allan Gordon) *v.* Maguire 1999 J.C. 63; 1999 S.L.T. 883; 1999 S.C.C.R. 44;
   1999 G.W.D. 2-82, HCJ Appeal . . . . *Digested,* 99/**5833**
Cameron *v.* McFadyen 2001 G.W.D. 25-983, HCJ Appeal
Cameron *v.* Stenhouse 1998 G.W.D. 24-1230, Sh Ct
Cameron *v.* Vannet (Sentencing) 1998 G.W.D. 11-551, HCJ Appeal
Cameron & Waterston *v.* Muir & Sons (1861) 23 D. 535, 1 Div . . . . *Distinguished,*
                                         98/5469

Cameron (Scotland) Ltd *v.* Melville Dundas Ltd 2001 S.C.L.R. 691; 2001 G.W.D. 9-312,
      OH
Campbell (Caroline), Petitioner 1990 J.C. 128; 1990 S.L.T. 875; 1989 S.C.C.R. 722, HCJ
      Appeal . . . .   *Digested,* 90/**4895**:
                                                                                                        Doubted, 98/5601, 98/5604
Campbell *v.* Bamber 1998 G.W.D. 30-1572, HCJ Appeal
Campbell *v.* Campbell; *sub nom* Breadalbane's Case (1866-69) L.R. 1 Sc. 182; (1867)
      5 M. (H.L.) 115, HL . . . .   *Considered,* 74/1069:
                                                                                                         Followed, 00/6283
Campbell *v.* Edinburgh City Council 1999 S.L.T. 1009; 1998 G.W.D. 17-877, OH . . . .   *Digested,* 99/**6407**
Campbell *v.* Friel (Sentencing) 1998 G.W.D. 1-20, HCJ Appeal
Campbell *v.* Gilchrist (Sentencing) 2000 G.W.D. 29-1154, HCJ Appeal
Campbell *v.* Hamilton 1998 G.W.D. 17-853, HCJ Appeal
Campbell *v.* Heywood (Sentencing) 1998 G.W.D. 28-1433, HCJ Appeal
Campbell *v.* Heywood (Sentencing) 1999 G.W.D. 27-1298, HCJ Appeal
Campbell *v.* HM Advocate (Sentencing) 1998 G.W.D. 9-451, HCJ Appeal
Campbell *v.* HM Advocate (Sentencing) 1998 G.W.D. 20-1030, HCJ Appeal
Campbell *v.* HM Advocate (Sentencing) 1998 G.W.D. 22-1144, HCJ Appeal
Campbell *v.* HM Advocate (Sentencing) 1998 G.W.D. 30-1549, HCJ Appeal
Campbell *v.* HM Advocate (Sentencing) 1998 G.W.D. 31-1602, HCJ Appeal
Campbell (Austin Allen) *v.* HM Advocate; *sub nom* Campbell *v.* Spiers 1999 J.C. 147;
      1999 S.L.T. 399; 1998 G.W.D. 36-1854, HCJ Appeal. . . . .   *Digested,* 99/**5911**
Campbell (Colin Bryson) *v.* HM Advocate; *sub nom* Campbell *v.* Ritchie 1999 S.C.C.R.
      914; 1999 G.W.D. 31-1467, HCJ Appeal . . . .   *Digested,* 00/**6108**
Campbell (Duncan McNeil) *v.* HM Advocate 1992 J.C. 6; 1993 S.L.T. 245; 1992
      S.C.C.R. 35, HCJ Appeal . . . .   *Digested,* 92/**5367**:
                                                                                      Applied, 01/6315: *Followed,* 96/6714
Campbell (James John) *v.* HM Advocate 1998 S.C.C.R. 111; 1998 G.W.D. 7-344, HCJ
      Appeal . . . .   *Digested,* 98/**5650**
Campbell (Thomas) *v.* HM Advocate 1998 J.C. 130; 1998 S.L.T. 923; 1998 S.C.C.R.
      214; 1998 G.W.D. 9-437, HCJ Appeal. . . . .   *Digested,* 98/**5561**:
                                                                                                         Applied, 99/5857
Campbell *v.* James Walker Insulation Ltd 1988 S.L.T. 263; 1988 S.C.L.R. 161, 2 Div . . . .   *Digested,* 88/**4667**:
                                                                                                       Considered, 01/6244
Campbell *v.* Lees (Sentencing) 1998 G.W.D. 15-744, HCJ Appeal
Campbell *v.* McGlennan (Sentencing) 1998 G.W.D. 2-78, HCJ Appeal
Campbell *v.* Munro 1998 G.W.D. 30-1561, HCJ Appeal
Campbell *v.* North Lanarkshire Council 2000 S.C.L.R. 373, OH . . . .   *Digested,* 00/**6598**
Campbell *v.* Ritchie see Campbell (Colin Bryson) *v.* HM Advocate
Campbell *v.* Spiers see Campbell (Austin Allen) *v.* HM Advocate
Campbell *v.* Stott (Compensation Order) 2001 S.L.T. 112; 2001 S.C.C.R. 10; 2000
      G.W.D. 37-1397, HCJ Appeal . . . .   *Digested,* 01/**6397**
Campbell *v.* Stott (Sentencing) 1999 G.W.D. 27-1304, HCJ Appeal
Campbell *v.* Vannet (Sentencing) 1998 G.W.D. 6-298, HCJ Appeal
Campbell *v.* Vannet (Sentencing) 1998 G.W.D. 9-475, HCJ Appeal
Campbell (Craig) *v.* Vannet 1998 S.C.C.R. 207; 1998 G.W.D. 9-433, HCJ Appeal. . . . . . .   *Digested,* 98/**5563**
Campbell (Sharon) *v.* Vannet 1997 S.C.C.R. 787; 1997 G.W.D. 40-2039, HCJ Appeal. . .   *Digested,* 98/**5603**
Campbell & Smith Construction Group Ltd *v.* Greenwood [2001] I.R.L.R. 588, EAT . . .   *Digested,* 01/**6478**
Campbell-Birkett *v.* Vannet 1999 S.L.T. 865; 1998 G.W.D. 26-1348, HCJ Appeal . . . . . .   *Digested,* 99/**5813**
Campsie Spring Scotland Ltd *v.* Assessor for Dunbartonshire, Argyll and Bute Valuation
      Joint Board [2000] R.A. 401, Lands Tr (Scot) . . . .   *Digested,* 00/**6664**
Canada Steamship Lines Ltd *v.* King, The [1952] A.C. 192; [1952] 1 All E.R. 305;
      [1952] 1 Lloyd's Rep. 1; [1952] 1 T.L.R. 261; 96 S.J. 72, HL . . . .   *Digested,* 52/**610**:
                            Applied, 55/1174, 55/3036, 71/9949, 74/296, 74/447, 74/4063, 75/273,
                                 76/2987, 78/339, 78/3186, 80/359, 82/2909, 88/461, 90/636, 93/499,
                                          94/540, 95/778, 96/1216, 99/836, 01/947: *Cited,* 99/3311:
                                 Considered, 68/2647, 72/489, 73/407, 79/2344, 81/304, 81/3603, 97/937,
                            00/895, 00/5991: *Followed,* 94/4078, 96/5302: *Referred to,* 95/5571
Candlish *v.* Candlish 2001 Fam. L.R. 45; 2000 G.W.D. 40-1492, OH
Cannon (Kevin Barry) *v.* HM Advocate (No.1) 1999 S.L.T. 358; 1998 S.C.C.R. 579;
      1998 G.W.D. 28-1407, HCJ Appeal . . . .   *Digested,* 98/**5615**
Cannon (Kevin Barry) *v.* HM Advocate (No.2) 2000 S.L.T. 779; 1999 G.W.D. 34-1620,
      HCJ Appeal . . . .   *Digested,* 00/**6021**
Cansco International Plc *v.* North of Scotland Water Authority 1999 S.C.L.R. 494, Sh Ct   *Digested,* 99/**6378**
Cant *v.* Eastern Scottish Omnibuses Ltd 1998 G.W.D. 32-1677, Sh Ct
Cantone Ltd *v.* McGlennan 2000 J.C. 359; 2000 S.C.C.R. 347; 2000 G.W.D. 7-252,
      HCJ Appeal . . . .   *Digested,* 00/**6105**
Cantwell *v.* Criminal Injuries Compensation Board [2001] UKHL 36; 2001 S.L.T. 966;
      2001 G.W.D. 24-879; *Times,* July 16, 2001, HL; reversing 2000 S.C. 407; 2000
      S.L.T. 956; 2000 G.W.D. 7-238, 1 Div; reversing 1998 G.W.D. 28-1395, OH. . . . .   *Digested,* 01/**6413**

Caparo Industries Plc *v.* Dickman [1990] 2 A.C. 605; [1990] 2 W.L.R. 358; [1990] 1
All E.R. 568; [1990] B.C.C. 164; [1990] B.C.L.C. 273; [1990] E.C.C. 313; [1955-
95] P.N.L.R. 523; (1990) 87(12) L.S.G. 42; (1990) 140 N.L.J. 248; (1990) 134
S.J. 494; *Times*, February 12, 1990; *Independent*, February 16, 1990; *Financial
Times*, February 13, 1990; *Guardian*, February 15, 1990; *Daily Telegraph*, February
15, 1990, HL; reversing [1989] Q.B. 653; [1989] 2 W.L.R. 316; [1989] 1 All
E.R. 798; (1989) 5 B.C.C. 105; [1989] B.C.L.C. 154; [1989] P.C.C. 125; (1988)
138 N.L.J. Rep. 289; (1989) 133 S.J. 221; *Times*, August 8, 1988; *Independent*,
August 10, 1988; *Financial Times*, August 5, 1988; *Daily Telegraph*, August 26,
1988, CA; reversing in part (1988) 4 B.C.C. 144; [1988] B.C.L.C. 387, QBD. . . .   *Digested*, 90/**3266**:
    Applied, 89/2540, 90/3254, 90/3265, 91/2650, 91/2652, 92/1915,
    92/2605, 92/3201, 93/2953, 93/2982, 94/3335, 94/3352, 94/3365,
    95/3668, 95/3686, 95/3701, 95/4519, 95/4730, 96/4440, 96/4484,
    97/331, 97/3778, 97/3816, 98/3997, 99/3956, 99/3963, 99/3966, 99/4025,
    99/5435, 00/679, 00/4201, 00/4246, 00/4249, 00/6162, 00/6586, 01/1509,
    01/1989, 01/4462, 01/4464, 01/4541: *Cited*, 00/4218: *Considered*, 89/2538,
    90/3315, 91/2657, 93/2044, 93/2958, 93/2983, 93/2997, 94/3345,
    95/3452, 95/3652, 98/3921, 98/3951, 98/3999, 99/3953, 00/4205,
    01/550: *Distinguished*, 91/2653: *Followed*, 90/3281, 93/5553, 97/424,
    97/4087, 98/3930, 98/3987, 99/3959, 99/4015, 00/4219, 00/4224,
    01/4470: *Referred to*, 92/6078, 94/6386, 95/5841, 99/4023
Capital Copiers (Edinburgh) Ltd *v.* Dawson 1998 G.W.D. 27-1385, OH
Cardle *v.* Gilchrist 1999 G.W.D. 35-1672, HCJ Appeal
Carlin *v.* Trainor Alston 1998 G.W.D. 39-2020, OH
Carlin *v.* Vannet 1999 G.W.D. 8-377, HCJ Appeal
Carlyle *v.* Lees 1998 G.W.D. 18-950, HCJ Appeal
Carmichael *v.* Bearsden and District Rifle & Pistol Club 2000 S.L.T. (Sh Ct) 49; 2000
   Rep. L.R. 55; 2000 G.W.D. 13-457, Sh Pr . . . .   *Digested*, 00/**5952**
Carmichael *v.* Marks & Spencer Plc 1996 S.L.T. 1167; 1995 S.C.C.R. 781, HCJ Appeal . .   *Digested*, 96/**7023**:
    Followed, 99/5885
Carnall *v.* HM Advocate 2001 G.W.D. 39-1453, HCJ Appeal
Carnegie *v.* Findlay 2000 S.C.C.R. 873, Sh Ct (North Strathclyde) . . . .   *Digested*, 01/**6316**
Carnegie *v.* Lord Advocate (No.1) 1998 S.L.T. 872; 1997 Rep. L.R. 128; 1997 G.W.D.
   31-1587, OH . . . .   *Digested*, 98/**5480**
Carnegie *v.* Lord Advocate (No.2) 1999 S.L.T. 521; 1998 G.W.D. 38-1951, OH . . . .   *Digested*, 99/**5691**:
    Not followed, 00/5929
Carnegie *v.* Lord Advocate (No.3) 2001 S.C. 802; 2001 G.W.D. 13-512, Ex Div;
   reversing 2000 S.L.T. 806; 2000 S.C.L.R. 868; 2000 Rep. L.R. 31; 2000 G.W.D.
   3-106, OH. . . . .   *Digested*, 00/**5929**
Carnegie *v.* McKechnie (William) 1999 S.L.T. 536; 1999 G.W.D. 7-319, Ex Div
Carnie *v.* HM Advocate (Sentencing) 1998 G.W.D. 5-228, HCJ Appeal
Carnie *v.* McGlennan 1999 G.W.D. 14-668, HCJ Appeal
Carr *v.* HM Advocate (Sentencing) 2000 G.W.D. 8-282, HCJ Appeal
Carr *v.* McFadyen (Sentencing) 1999 G.W.D. 40-1944, HCJ Appeal
Carr *v.* Secretary of State for Scotland 1998 S.C.L.R. 160, OH . . . .   *Digested*, 98/**6123**
Carr *v.* Stott 1998 G.W.D. 23-1161, HCJ Appeal
Carracher *v.* Friel 1998 G.W.D. 27-1394, HCJ Appeal
Carrick *v.* MacDonald 1999 G.W.D. 15-676, Sh Ct
Carrigan *v.* HM Advocate (Sentencing) 2001 G.W.D. 26-1039, HCJ Appeal
Carroll *v.* Carnegie 1999 G.W.D. 32-1543, HCJ Appeal
Carroll *v.* HM Advocate (Sentencing) 1998 G.W.D. 11-545, HCJ Appeal
Carroll *v.* HM Advocate (Sentencing) 1999 G.W.D. 11-500, HCJ Appeal
Carroll (John McFarlane) *v.* HM Advocate 1999 J.C. 302; 1999 S.L.T. 1185; 1999
   S.C.C.R. 617, HCJ Appeal . . . .   *Digested*, 99/**5912**
Carroll (Patrick) *v.* Vannet 1998 S.C.C.R. 577; 1998 G.W.D. 29-1518, HCJ Appeal . . . . .   *Digested*, 98/**5691**
Carruthers *v.* Pryadarshani 1999 Hous. L.R. 13, Sh Pr . . . .   *Digested*, 99/**5675**
Carruthers *v.* Vannet 1999 G.W.D. 11-508, HCJ Appeal
Carson *v.* Higson (Sentencing) 2001 G.W.D. 12-428, HCJ Appeal
Carson *v.* McGlennan 2000 J.C. 580; 2000 S.L.T. 810; 2000 S.C.C.R. 631; 2000
   G.W.D. 15-582, HCJ Appeal . . . .   *Digested*, 00/**6006**
Carson *v.* Reith 2001 G.W.D. 25-985, HCJ Appeal
Carstairs *v.* Hamilton 1997 J.C. 168; 1998 S.L.T. 220; 1997 S.C.C.R. 311; 1997 G.W.D.
   15-695, HCJ Appeal. . . . .   *Digested*, 97/**6401**
Carswell *v.* Howdle 2000 G.W.D. 18-705, HCJ Appeal
Cartmill *v.* Heywood 2000 S.L.T. 799; 1999 G.W.D. 22-1075, HCJ Appeal. . . . .   *Digested*, 01/**6330**
Cartwright (Nigel Mark) *v.* HM Advocate (Sentencing) 2001 S.L.T. 1163; 2001 S.C.C.R.
   695; 2001 G.W.D. 23-860, HCJ Appeal . . . .   *Digested*, 01/**6408**
Casola *v.* HM Advocate (Sentencing) 1998 G.W.D. 16-801, HCJ Appeal
Cassidy *v.* Brown 1999 G.W.D. 27-1302, HCJ Appeal
Cassidy *v.* HM Advocate (Sentencing) 1999 G.W.D. 6-301, HCJ Appeal
Cassidy (Barbara) *v.* HM Advocate (Sentencing) 2000 G.W.D. 13-482, HCJ Appeal
Cassidy *v.* Howdle (Sentencing) 2001 G.W.D. 1-40, HCJ Appeal
Cassidy *v.* Spiers (Sentencing) 1999 G.W.D. 10-465, HCJ Appeal
Cassidy *v.* Vannet (Sentencing) 1999 G.W.D. 18-831, HCJ Appeal

Cassidy v. Vannet (Sentencing) 1999 G.W.D. 14-636, HCJ Appeal

Castelvecchi v. HM Advocate 1998 G.W.D. 22-1113, HCJ Appeal

Castle View Services Ltd v. Howes; *sub nom* Howes v. Castle View Services Ltd 2000
S.C. 419; 2000 S.L.T. 696; 2000 G.W.D. 10-357, 1 Div . . . . *Digested*, 00/**6220**

Castlemilk East Housing Cooperative Ltd v. Nixon 2000 Hous. L.R. 133, Sh Pr . . . . *Digested*, 01/**6267**

Castleton Homes Ltd v. Eastern Motor Co Ltd 1998 S.L.T. (Sh Ct) 51; 1998 G.W.D. 7-
317, Sh Pr . . . . *Digested*, 98/**5487**

Cathcart v. Arnold Clark Ltd 2001 G.W.D. 7-252, OH

Cathcart v. HM Advocate 1999 G.W.D. 5-241, HCJ Appeal

Cathcart v. Stott (Sentencing) 2000 G.W.D. 4-164, HCJ Appeal

Catholic Care Consortium Ltd v. Customs and Excise Commissioners [2001] B.V.C.
2381, V&DTr . . . . *Digested*, 01/**6922**

Catleugh v. Caradon Everest Ltd 1999 G.W.D. 32-1554, OH

Catscratch Ltd v. Glasgow City Licensing Board (No.1); *sub nom* Catscratch Ltd,
Petitioners 2001 S.C. 218; 2001 S.L.T. 344; 2001 S.C.L.R. 209; [2000] 17
S.L.L.P. 7; 2000 G.W.D. 28-1098, OH . . . . *Digested*, 01/**6782**

Catscratch Ltd v. Glasgow City Licensing Board (No.2) 2001 S.C.L.R. 817; [2001]
U.K.H.R.R. 1309; [2001] 20 S.L.L.P. 10; 2001 G.W.D. 19-748, OH

Catscratch Ltd, Petitioners see Catscratch Ltd v. Glasgow City Licensing Board (No.1)

Cattanach v. Heywood (Sentencing) 1998 G.W.D. 2-80, HCJ Appeal

Catterson v. Davidson 2000 S.L.T. (Sh Ct) 51; 2000 G.W.D. 8-269, Sh Pr . . . . *Digested*, 00/**5934**

Caughie v. O'Donnell 1998 G.W.D. 19-976, HCJ Appeal

Caven v. Cumming 1998 S.L.T. 768; 1998 S.C.C.R. 313, HCJ Appeal . . . . *Digested*, 98/**5618**

Cavendish Pharmacies Ltd v. Stephensons Ltd 1998 S.L.T. (Sh Ct) 66; 1998 G.W.D. 10-
480, Sh Pr . . . . *Digested*, 98/**5495**

Cawkwell v. East Calder District Homing Society Social Club 2000 Rep. L.R. 115;
2000 G.W.D. 23-877, OH . . . . *Digested*, 00/**6172**

Cay's Trustee v. Cay 1998 S.C. 780; 1999 S.L.T. 321; 1998 S.C.L.R. 456; 1998 G.W.D.
14-722, 2 Div; affirming 1997 S.C.L.R. 556; 1997 G.W.D. 4-162, OH . . . . *Digested*, 98/**6001**

Centriforce Engineering Ltd v. Bank of Scotland 1993 S.L.T. 190; 1993 S.C.L.R. 165;
Times, December 23, 1992, OH . . . . *Digested*, 93/**4734**:
Applied, 99/5793: Distinguished, 94/5488

Ceylon Motor Insurance Association v. Thambugala [1953] A.C. 584; [1953] 3 W.L.R.
486; [1953] 2 All E.R. 870; [1953] 2 Lloyd's Rep. 289; 97 S.J. 555, PC (Cey) . . *Digested*, 53/**3227**:
Considered, 89/2055, 90/3754, 95/6309, 98/6019

Chalmers v. Chalmers (Music School Expenses) (No.1) 2001 G.W.D. 16-586, Sh Ct
(Grampian)

Chalmers (John) v. HM Advocate 1954 J.C. 66; 1954 S.L.T. 177, HCJ Appeal . . . . *Digested*, 54/**3688**:
Approved, 74/4121, 74/4243, 75/1416: Distinguished, 58/3662, 58/3671:
Followed, 62/3275, 63/3045, 00/5996

Chalmers v. Strathclyde Fire Board 1999 G.W.D. 14-657, OH

Chan v. To 1999 G.W.D. 23-1082, Sh Pr

Chandler v. Crofters Commission 1998 S.L.T. (Land Ct) 27; 1997 S.L.C.R. 51; 1998
G.W.D. 12-629, Land Ct . . . . *Digested*, 98/**6027**

Chant v. HM Advocate 2001 G.W.D. 14-540, HCJ Appeal

Chao v. British Traders & Shippers Ltd (No.1) see Kwei Tek Chao (t/a Zung Fu Co) v.
British Traders & Shippers Ltd (No.1)

Chappell v. Friel 1997 S.L.T. 1325; 1997 G.W.D. 1-6, HCJ . . . . *Digested*, 98/**5398**

Charcuterie Continental v. Lintec Laminations Ltd 1998 G.W.D. 10-484, Sh Pr

Charles Brand Ltd v. Orkney Islands Council 2001 S.C. 545; 2001 S.L.T. 698; 2001
G.W.D. 4-150, Ex Div . . . . *Digested*, 01/**6291**

Charterhouse Square Finance Co Ltd v. A&J Menswear 1998 S.L.T. 720; 1997 G.W.D.
40-2098, OH . . . . *Digested*, 98/**6038**

Chartwell Land Investments Ltd v. Amec Construction Scotland Ltd 2001 S.L.T. 732;
2001 G.W.D. 11-379, OH . . . . *Digested*, 01/**6269**

Chauncy v. Higson (Sentencing) 2001 G.W.D. 12-450, HCJ Appeal

Cheltenham & Gloucester Plc v. Royal & Sun Alliance Insurance Co see Cheltenham &
Gloucester Plc v. Sun Alliance and London Insurance Plc

Cheltenham & Gloucester Plc v. Sun Alliance and London Insurance Plc; *sub nom*
Cheltenham & Gloucester Plc v. Royal & Sun Alliance Insurance Co 2001 S.C.
965; 2001 S.L.T. 1151; 2001 S.C.L.R. 670; 2001 G.W.D. 19-746, 1 Div; reversing
2001 S.L.T. 347; 2000 G.W.D. 32-1253, OH . . . . *Digested*, 01/**6723**

Chen v. Secretary of State for the Home Department 2001 S.L.T. 703; 2001 G.W.D. 14-
556, OH . . . . *Digested*, 01/**6711**

Cheyne v. Hingston 1998 G.W.D. 17-881, HCJ Appeal

Chief Adjudication Officer v. Combe 1997 S.C. 297; 1998 S.L.T. 15; 1997 G.W.D. 25-
1291, 2 Div . . . . *Digested*, 98/**6193**

Chief Adjudication Officer v. Eggleton (Unreported, March 17, 1995), CA . . . . *Distinguished*,
00/**6687**

Chief Adjudication Officer v. Faulds [2000] 1 W.L.R. 1035; [2000] 2 All E.R. 961; 2000
S.C. (H.L.) 116; 2000 S.L.T. 712; 2000 S.C.L.R. 713; [2000] I.C.R. 1297;
(2000) 97(22) L.S.G. 46; 2000 G.W.D. 17-703; *Times*, May 16, 2000;
Independent, June 19, 2000, HL; affirming 1998 S.L.T. 1203; 1998 S.C.L.R. 719;
1998 G.W.D. 22-1145, Ex Div . . . . *Digested*, 00/**4846**:
Considered, 00/4845
Chief Constable of Gwent v. Dash [1986] R.T.R. 41; [1985] Crim. L.R. 674, QBD . . . . . . *Digested*, 86/**2969**:
Applied, 92/3789: *Followed*, 99/5870
Chisholm v. HM Advocate (Sentencing) 2001 G.W.D. 31-1259, HCJ Appeal
Chittick v. Fraser 1997 S.L.T. 1300; 1997 G.W.D. 13-546, HCJ Appeal . . . . *Digested*, 98/**5562**
Chmylowskyj v. Reith (Sentencing) 2001 G.W.D. 20-767, HCJ Appeal
Chohan v. HM Advocate 1998 G.W.D. 34-1739, HCJ Appeal
Chow v. Lees 1997 J.C. 137; 1998 S.L.T. 5; 1997 S.C.C.R. 253; 1997 G.W.D. 11-453,
HCJ Appeal . . . . *Digested*, 97/**5852**
Chowdry (Sodagar), Petitioner (No.1); *sub nom* Chowdry v. Social Security Appeal
Tribunal 1999 S.L.T. 697; 1998 S.C.L.R. 375; 1997 G.W.D. 40-2030, OH . . . . *Digested*, 98/**6196**
Chowdry (Sodagar), Petitioner (No.2); *sub nom* Chowdry (Sodagar) v. Secretary of
State for Social Security 2000 S.C.L.R. 663; 2000 G.W.D. 13-512, OH . . . . *Digested*, 00/**6687**
Chowdry (Sodagar) v. Secretary of State for Social Security see Chowdry (Sodagar),
Petitioner (No.2)
Chowdry v. Social Security Appeal Tribunal see Chowdry (Sodagar), Petitioner (No.1)
Christie v. Aberdeen City Council Licensing Committee 2001 S.L.T. (Sh Ct) 167; 2001
G.W.D. 29-1171, Sh Ct (Grampian) . . . . *Digested*, 01/**6791**
Christie v. Heywood 1999 G.W.D. 35-1687, HCJ Appeal
Christie Owen & Davis Plc v. King 1998 S.C.L.R. 786; 1998 G.W.D. 22-1103, 2 Div 1998
S.C.L.R. 149, Sh Pr . . . . *Digested*, 98/**5421**
Church v. HM Advocate (No.2) 1996 S.L.T. 383, HCJ Appeal . . . . *Digested*, 96/**6715**:
Considered, 96/6717: *Followed*, 00/6059, 00/6061
Church Commissioners for England v. Scor (UK) Co Ltd 1998 G.W.D. 20-1041, OH
City & County Investments (Scotland) Ltd v. McIver 1998 S.L.T. 541; 1997 G.W.D. 6-
248, OH . . . . *Digested*, 98/**5945**
City Inn Ltd v. Shepherd Construction Ltd 2001 S.C.L.R. 961; 2001 G.W.D. 26-999, OH
City of Glasgow DC v. Zafar see Glasgow City Council v. Zafar
City Petroleum Co Ltd v. City of Edinburgh Licensing Board [1998] 10 S.L.L.P. 20, Sh
Ct. . . . . *Digested*, 98/**6076**
Clackmannanshire Council v. Tullis Plastics Ltd 2001 G.W.D. 16-654, OH
Clampett v. Stott 2001 S.C.C.R. 860; 2001 G.W.D. 33-1307, HCJ Appeal
Clancy v. Caird (No.1) 2000 S.C. 441; 2000 S.L.T. 546; 2000 S.C.L.R. 526; [2000]
H.R.L.R. 557; [2000] U.K.H.R.R. 509; 2000 G.W.D. 13-455; *Times*, May 9,
2000, Ex Div 2000 G.W.D. 1-4, OH . . . . *Digested*, 00/**478**
Clancy v. Caird (No.2) 2000 G.W.D. 18-716, OH
Clancy v. HM Advocate 1998 G.W.D. 36-1864, HCJ Appeal
Clark v. Gallagher 1999 G.W.D. 25-1185, HCJ Appeal
Clark v. HM Advocate (Sentencing) 1998 G.W.D. 29-1471, HCJ Appeal
Clark v. HM Advocate (Sentencing) 1999 G.W.D. 13-602, HCJ Appeal
Clark v. HM Advocate (Sentencing) 1999 G.W.D. 5-249, HCJ Appeal
Clark v. HM Advocate (Sentencing) 1999 G.W.D. 10-457, HCJ Appeal
Clark v. HM Advocate (Sentencing) 1999 G.W.D. 1-20, HCJ Appeal
Clark v. HM Advocate (Sentencing) 1999 G.W.D. 35-1682, HCJ Appeal
Clark v. HM Advocate (Sentencing) 2000 G.W.D. 19-746, HCJ Appeal
Clark (Carolyne) v. HM Advocate (Misdirection) 2000 J.C. 637; 2000 S.L.T. 1107;
2000 S.C.C.R. 767; 2000 G.W.D. 26-979, HCJ Appeal . . . . *Digested*, 00/**6119**
Clark v. Kelly 2001 J.C. 16; 2000 S.L.T. 1038; 2000 S.C.C.R. 821; 2000 G.W.D. 27-
1041, HCJ Appeal . . . . *Digested*, 00/**6100**
Clark v. Maersk Co Ltd 2000 S.L.T. (Sh Ct) 9; 1999 G.W.D. 32-1556, Sh Pr . . . . *Digested*, 00/**6590**
Clark v. McKay (Sentencing) 1998 G.W.D. 13-649, HCJ Appeal
Clark v. North Ayrshire Licensing Board 1998 G.W.D. 8-396, OH
Clark v. Novacold Ltd see Clark v. TDG Ltd (t/a Novacold Ltd)
Clark v. Secretary of State for Social Security 1998 S.C. 263; 1997 G.W.D. 37-1923, Ex
Div . . . . *Digested*, 98/**6192**
Clark v. Shepherd & Wedderburn 2000 G.W.D. 5-207, OH
Clark v. Syme 1957 J.C. 1; 1957 S.L.T. 32, HCJ Appeal . . . . *Digested*, 57/**3889**:
Followed, 01/6334

Clark v. TDG Ltd (t/a Novacold Ltd); *sub nom* Clark v. Novacold Ltd [1999] 2 All E.R.
977; [1999] I.C.R. 951; [1999] I.R.L.R. 318; [1999] Disc. L.R. 240; (1999) 48
B.M.L.R. 1; *Times*, April 1, 1999, CA; reversing [1998] I.C.R. 1044; [1998] I.R.L.R.
420; [1999] Disc. L.R. 22; (1998) 42 B.M.L.R. 101; *Times*, June 11, 1998, EAT . . *Digested*, 99/**2022**:
Applied, 99/2024, 01/2239, 01/2240, 01/6461: *Followed*, 00/2127
Clarke v. Edinburgh and District Tramways Co Ltd 1919 S.C. (H.L.) 35; (1919) 1
S.L.T.247, HL. . . . . *Applied*, 01/6217
Clarke v. Fennoscandia Ltd (No.1) 1998 S.C. 465; 1998 S.L.T. 1014; 1998 S.C.L.R.
568; 1998 G.W.D. 10-479, 2 Div; affirming 1998 G.W.D. 4-158, OH . . . . *Digested*, 98/**5532**
Clarke v. Fennoscandia Ltd (No.2) 2001 S.L.T. 1311; 2000 G.W.D. 11-377, OH
Clarke v. Heywood 1998 G.W.D. 30-1573, HCJ Appeal

Class 98 Ltd v. Hogg 2001 G.W.D. 1-61, OH
Classic House Developments Ltd v. Gd Lodge & Partners 1998 G.W.D. 7-351, OH
Clegg v. Clegg 1999 S.C.L.R. 773, Sh Ct . . . . *Digested*, 99/**6330**
Cleishman v. Carnegie (Sentencing) 1999 G.W.D. 36-1764, HCJ Appeal
Cleland v. Campbell 1998 S.L.T. 642; 1998 Rep. L.R. 30; 1998 G.W.D. 1-34, OH . . . . . . *Digested*, 98/**5712**
Clelland v. HM Advocate (Sentencing) 1998 G.W.D. 27-1366, HCJ Appeal
Clelland (Derek George) v. HM Advocate 1999 S.L.T. 1071; 1999 G.W.D. 16-739, HCJ
    Appeal . . . . *Digested*, 99/**5811**
Clelland v. McGlennan 1999 G.W.D. 27-1279, HCJ Appeal
Clements (Keith Richard) v. HM Advocate 1991 J.C. 62; 1991 S.L.T. 388; 1991 S.C.C.R.
    266, HCJ Appeal . . . . *Digested*, 91/**4777**:
                                                                                      Considered, 98/5558
Clements v. Macleod 2000 S.C.L.R. 803; 2000 G.W.D. 17-676, OH . . . . *Digested*, 00/**5902**
Clifford v. HM Advocate 1998 G.W.D. 35-1830, HCJ Appeal
Clifford Finance Ltd v. Hughes 2000 S.L.T. (Sh Ct) 19; 1999 G.W.D. 35-1659, Sh Pr . . . *Digested*, 00/**5926**
Clinton v. HM Advocate (Sentencing) 2001 G.W.D. 30-1207, HCJ Appeal
Clinton v. News Group Newspapers Ltd; Barry v. News Group Newspapers Ltd 1999
    S.C. 367; 1999 S.L.T. 590; 1999 G.W.D. 2-66; *Times*, March 22, 1999, OH . . . . . *Digested*, 99/**5657**
Clowes Developments (Scotland) Ltd v. Whannel; *sub nom* Clowes Developments
    (Scotland) Ltd v. Whannell 2001 G.W.D. 25-970, Sh Ct (Lothian)
Clowes Developments (Scotland) Ltd v. Whannell see Clowes Developments
    (Scotland) Ltd v. Whannel
Cloy v. TM Adams & Sons 2000 S.L.T. (Sh Ct) 39; 1999 G.W.D. 19-908, Sh Pr . . . . *Digested*, 00/**6448**
Clyde Solway Consortium v. Scottish Ministers; *sub nom* Clyde Solway Consortium,
    Petitioners 2001 S.C. 553; 2001 S.L.T. 1455; 2001 S.C.L.R. 279; 2001 G.W.D. 10-
    324, Ex Div; affirming 2001 G.W.D. 3-106, OH . . . . *Digested*, 01/**6299**
Clyde Solway Consortium, Petitioners see Clyde Solway Consortium v. Scottish Ministers
Clydebank DC v. Sweeney 1998 Hous. L.R. 84, Sh Ct
Clydebank Football Club Ltd v. Steedman 2000 G.W.D. 31-1217, OH
Clydesdale Bank Plc v. Adamson 2001 G.W.D. 27-1082, Sh Ct (South Strathclyde)
Clydesdale Bank Plc v. Aitken 2001 G.W.D. 24-882, Sh Pr; affirming 2001 G.W.D. 11-
    377, Sh Ct (Grampian)
Clydesdale Bank Plc v. Davidson 1998 S.C. (H.L.) 51; 1998 S.L.T. 522; 1998 S.C.L.R.
    278; [1997] N.P.C. 182; 1998 G.W.D. 1-41; *Times*, December 20, 1997, HL;
    affirming 1996 S.L.T. 437, 2 Div; affirming 1994 S.C.L.R. 828, Sh Pr . . . . *Digested*, 98/**6031**
Clydesdale Bank Plc v. Grantly Developments (Sequestration) 2000 S.L.T. 1369; 2000
    S.C.L.R. 771; 2000 G.W.D. 15-617, OH . . . . *Digested*, 00/**6507**:
                                                                               Distinguished, 00/6516
Clydesdale Bank Plc v. Mclay Collier & Partners 1998 S.L.T. 1102; 1998 G.W.D. 23-1155,
    OH . . . . *Digested*, 98/**5542**
Clydesdale Bank Plc v. Mowbray 2000 S.C. 151; 1999 G.W.D. 40-1951, Ex Div;
    affirming in part 1998 G.W.D. 34-1757, OH . . . . *Digested*, 00/**5915**
Clydesdale Bank Plc v. Spencer 2001 G.W.D. 17-667, OH
Coates v. Lothian RC 1999 Fam. L.R. 8, Sh Ct (Lothian)
Cochrane (John Wallace) v. Heywood 1998 S.L.T. 1127; 1998 S.C.C.R. 331; 1998
    G.W.D. 13-662, HCJ Appeal . . . . *Digested*, 98/**5660**
Cochrane v. HM Advocate (Assault) 2001 S.C.C.R. 655; 2001 G.W.D. 21-791, HCJ
    Appeal
Cochrane v. HM Advocate (Misuse of Drugs) 1999 G.W.D. 20-927, HCJ Appeal
Cochrane v. HM Advocate (Sentencing) 1999 G.W.D. 5-250, HCJ Appeal
Cochrane (John) v. HM Advocate see Mills (Kenneth Anthony Paton) v. HM Advocate
    (No.2)
Cochrane v. Vannet (Sentencing) 1999 G.W.D. 40-1933, HCJ Appeal
Cockburn v. Chief Adjudication Officer; Secretary of State for Social Security v.
    Halliday; Secretary of State for Social Security v. Fairey [1997] 1 W.L.R. 799;
    [1997] 3 All E.R. 844; (1997) 94(24) L.S.G. 32; (1997) 147 N.L.J. 794; (1997)
    141 S.J.L.B. 122; *Times*, May 26, 1997, HL; affirming (1997) 33 B.M.L.R. 47;
    Times, July 30, 1996, CA . . . . *Digested*, 97/**4625**:
                                                                                    Considered, 01/6893
Codona v. Higson 2001 G.W.D. 1-75, HCJ Appeal
Codona v. Showmen's Guild of Great Britain 2001 G.W.D. 18-689, OH
Coe v. HM Advocate (Sentencing) 2001 G.W.D. 26-1040, HCJ Appeal
Cole v. Crowe 1998 G.W.D. 38-1958, HCJ Appeal
Cole v. Lonie 2001 S.C. 610; 2001 S.L.T. 608; 2001 G.W.D. 5-184, Ex Div; reversing
    1999 S.C.L.R. 952; 1999 G.W.D. 15-720, Sh Pr; affirming 1999 G.W.D. 2-106, Sh
    Ct . . . . *Digested*, 01/**6866**
Coleman v. HM Advocate (Sentencing) 1998 G.W.D. 7-346, HCJ Appeal
Coleman (Henry George William) v. HM Advocate 1999 S.L.T. 1261; 1999 S.C.C.R. 87;
    1999 G.W.D. 7-325; 1998 G.W.D. 35-1782, HCJ Appeal . . . . *Digested*, 99/**5902**
Colgan v. McDonald 1999 S.C.C.R. 901; 1999 G.W.D. 33-1602, HCJ Appeal . . . . *Digested*, 00/**6154**
Coll v. HM Advocate 1999 G.W.D. 30-1420, HCJ Appeal
Coll v. Russell; *sub nom* Coll v. Victoria Infirmary NHS Trust 1999 S.C.L.R. 862; 1999
    Rep. L.R. 114; 1999 G.W.D. 18-847, OH. . . . . *Digested*, 99/**5698**
Coll v. Victoria Infirmary NHS Trust see Coll v. Russell

Coll, Petitioner 1977 J.C. 29; 1977 S.L.T. 58, HCJ Appeal . . . . *Digested*, 77/**3310**:
Referred to, 01/6305

Colley *v.* Celtic Pacific Ship Management (Overseas) Ltd 2001 S.L.T. 320; 2000
G.W.D. 33-1260, OH . . . . *Digested*, 01/**6268**

Collie *v.* Donald 1999 S.C.L.R. 420; 1999 G.W.D. 4-215, OH . . . . *Digested*, 99/**6387**

Collier *v.* Walkinshaw 1998 G.W.D. 18-939, HCJ Appeal

Collins *v.* HM Advocate (Misdirection) 1999 G.W.D. 15-703, HCJ Appeal

Collins *v.* HM Advocate (Sentencing) 1999 G.W.D. 19-882, HCJ Appeal

Collins *v.* Lees (Sentencing) 1999 G.W.D. 7-327, HCJ Appeal

Color Steels Ltd *v.* Presscut Metals Ltd 1998 G.W.D. 39-1990, Sh Ct

Colquhoun *v.* Brooks (1889) L.R. 14 App. Cas. 493; 2 T.C. 490, HL; affirming (1888)
L.R. 21 Q.B.D. 52, CA; reversing (1887) L.R. 19 Q.B.D. 400, QBD . . . . *Applied*, 70/1308,
71/5739, 77/1600, 77/2482, 78/1685, 99/6458: *Followed*, 53/1710, 53/1917

Colvilles Ltd *v.* Devine see Devine *v.* Colvilles Ltd

Commercial Aluminium Windows Ltd *v.* Cumbernauld Development Corp 1987 S.L.T.
(Sh. Ct.) 91, Sh Pr . . . . *Digested*, 87/**4053**:
Applied, 01/6220: *Followed*, 89/3931

Commission for Racial Equality *v.* Dutton [1989] Q.B. 783; [1989] 2 W.L.R. 17; [1989]
1 All E.R. 306; [1989] I.R.L.R. 8; (1989) 133 S.J. 19; *Times*, July 29, 1988;
Independent, August 3, 1988; *Guardian*, August 18, 1988, CA . . . . *Digested*, 89/**267**:
Considered, 91/1656, 92/1958: *Referred to*, 01/6878

Commonwealth War Graves Commission, Petitioners (Unreported, May 6, 1961), CS . . *Applied*, 01/6500

Compagnie Commerciale Andre SA *v.* Artibell Shipping Co Ltd (No.1) 1999 S.L.T. 1051;
1999 S.C.L.R. 349; 1999 G.W.D. 5-264, OH . . . . *Digested*, 99/**5734**

Compagnie Commerciale Andre SA *v.* Artibell Shipping Co Ltd (No.2) 2001 S.C. 653;
2001 G.W.D. 8-307, OH . . . . *Digested*, 01/**6918**

Compaq Computer Manufacturing Ltd *v.* Circle International Ltd 2001 S.C. 331; 2001
S.L.T. 368; 2000 G.W.D. 36-1346, OH . . . . *Digested*, 01/**6733**

Condon *v.* HM Advocate (Sentencing) 1998 G.W.D. 12-592, HCJ Appeal

Conn *v.* Conn 2001 G.W.D. 2-80, Sh Ct (Grampian)

Connell *v.* HM Advocate 1999 G.W.D. 10-456, HCJ Appeal

Connell *v.* Mitchell 1909 S.C. (J.) 13; (1908) 5 Adam 641; (1908) 16 S.L.T.669, HCJ
Appeal . . . . *Followed*, 52/3882,
98/5662: *Not applied*, 99/5952

Connellan *v.* HM Advocate 2001 G.W.D. 28-1132, HCJ Appeal

Connelly *v.* Gilchrist 1999 G.W.D. 24-1128, HCJ Appeal

Connelly *v.* HM Advocate 1990 J.C. 349; 1991 S.L.T. 397; 1990 S.C.C.R. 504, HCJ
Appeal . . . . *Digested*, 90/**4945**:
Applied, 94/5636, 95/5654: *Considered*, 01/6335: *Followed*, 92/5510

Connelly *v.* Lanarkshire Health Board 1999 S.C. 364; 1999 G.W.D. 3-122, 2 Div . . . . . . *Digested*, 99/**5676**

Connelly *v.* New Hampshire Insurance Co Ltd 1997 S.L.T. 1341; 1997 S.C.L.R. 459;
[1997] 6 Re. L.R. 367; 1997 G.W.D. 18-840, OH . . . . *Digested*, 97/**6171**:
Approved, 98/6194

Connolly *v.* Friel 1998 G.W.D. 20-1047, HCJ Appeal

Connolly *v.* Tasker see Heil *v.* Rankin

Connor *v.* Secretary of State for Scotland 2000 Rep. L.R. 18; 2000 G.W.D. 1-29; *Times*,
March 22, 2000, OH . . . . *Digested*, 00/**6585**

Conti *v.* AIP Private Bank Ltd (formerly Ueberseebank AG); *sub nom* Conti, Petitioner
2000 S.C. 240; 2000 S.L.T. 1015; [2000] B.C.C. 172; 2000 G.W.D. 3-83; *Times*,
March 15, 2000, Ex Div; reversing 1999 S.L.T. 580; *Times*, October 12, 1998,
OH . . . . *Digested*, 00/**5956**

Conti, Petitioner see Conti *v.* AIP Private Bank Ltd (formerly Ueberseebank AG)

Conway *v.* Gilchrist (Sentencing) 2001 G.W.D. 32-1289, HCJ Appeal

Conway *v.* Glasgow City Council 2001 S.L.T. 1472 (Note); 2001 S.C.L.R. 546, Ex Div;
reversing 1999 S.L.T. (Sh Ct) 102; 1999 S.C.L.R. 1058; 1999 Hous. L.R. 67; 1999
G.W.D. 22-1064, Sh Pr; reversing 1999 S.C.L.R. 248, Sh Ct (Glasgow) . . . . *Digested*, 01/**6683**

Conway *v.* Vannet 1999 G.W.D. 18-851, HCJ Appeal

Conway *v.* Wood 2001 G.W.D. 38-1426, Sh Ct (Tayside)

Cook *v.* Crowe (Sentencing) 1998 G.W.D. 9-444, HCJ Appeal

Cook (Craig Garry) *v.* HM Advocate; *sub nom* HM Advocate *v.* Cook (Craig Garry)
2001 S.L.T. (Sh Ct) 53; 2000 S.C.C.R. 922; 2000 G.W.D. 29-1118, Sh Ct
(Tayside) . . . . *Digested*, 01/**6366**

Cook *v.* Jessop 1990 J.C. 286; 1991 S.L.T. 132; 1990 S.C.C.R. 211, HCJ Appeal . . . . . . *Digested*, 90/**4920**:
Applied, 98/5617

Cook *v.* Lees 1999 G.W.D. 5-255, HCJ Appeal

Cook *v.* Paxton 1910 S.L.R. 7 . . . . *Considered*, 01/6683

Cook *v.* Renfrewshire DC 1998 Hous. L.R. 14, Lands Tr . . . . *Digested*, 98/**5988**:
Considered, 98/5989

Cook *v.* Wyvern Structures Ltd (In Liquidation); *sub nom* Durie *v.* Wyvern Structures
Ltd 2001 S.L.T. 1212; 2001 S.C.L.R. 188; 2000 Rep. L.R. 136; 2000 G.W.D. 28-
1102, OH. . . . . *Digested*, 01/**6812**

Coomer *v.* Fraser 2000 G.W.D. 8-317, HCJ Appeal

Cooney *v.* Dumfries and Galloway Council 2001 G.W.D. 13-466, Ex Div

Cooney *v.* HM Advocate 1999 G.W.D. 28-1322, HCJ Appeal

Cooper v. HM Advocate (Sentencing) 1998 G.W.D. 10-490, HCJ Appeal
Cooper v. HM Advocate (Sentencing) 2000 G.W.D. 8-295, HCJ Appeal
Cooper v. HM Advocate (Sentencing) 2000 G.W.D. 15-587, HCJ
Cooper v. Secretary of State for Scotland 2000 S.L.T. 138; 1999 G.W.D. 38-1866, OH . .   *Digested,* 00/**6628**
Cooperative Insurance Society Ltd v. Halfords Ltd (No.1) 1998 S.L.T. 90; 1997 S.C.L.R.
   719; 1997 G.W.D. 17-798, OH   *Digested,* 97/**6184**
Cooperative Insurance Society Ltd v. Halfords Ltd (No.2) 1998 S.C. 212; 1999 S.L.T.
   685; 1998 S.C.L.R. 11, OH . . . .   *Digested,* 98/**6035**
Cooperative Wholesale Society Ltd v. Ravenseft Properties Ltd (No.1) 2001 G.W.D. 24-
   905, OH
Copeland v. Lord Wimborne 1912 S.C. 355; (1912) 1 S.L.T.97, 2 Div . . . .   *Distinguished,*
                      98/5493
Copoc v. Chief Constable of South Yorkshire see Alcock v. Chief Constable of South
   Yorkshire
Cormack v. HM Advocate 1998 G.W.D. 18-904, HCJ Appeal
Cormack v. National House Building Council 1998 S.L.T. 1051; 1997 G.W.D. 24-1218,
   OH . . . .   *Digested,* 98/**5540**
Corral v. Friel (Sentencing) 1998 G.W.D. 15-764, HCJ Appeal
Corrigal v. Vannet 1999 G.W.D. 9-421, HCJ Appeal
Cosar Ltd v. UPS Ltd 1999 S.L.T. 259; 1998 G.W.D. 30-1535, OH . . . .   *Digested,* 99/**5790**
Cosgrove v. Caesar & Howie [2001] I.R.L.R. 653, EAT . . . .   *Digested,* 01/**6461**
Cosmopolitan Investments Ltd v. New Hearts Ltd see New Hearts Ltd v. Cosmopolitan
   Investments Ltd
Coulter v. HM Advocate see Montgomery v. HM Advocate
Council of the Law Society of Scotland v. McIntyre 1999 G.W.D. 20-960, Ex Div
Counting House (Scotland) Ltd v. Bill Hay Ltd 2000 G.W.D. 23-880, Sh Ct
County Properties Ltd v. Scottish Ministers 2001 S.L.T. 1125; [2001] 4 P.L.R. 122; 2001
   G.W.D. 26-1068, Ex Div; reversing 2000 S.L.T. 965; [2000] H.R.L.R. 677;
   [2000] 4 P.L.R. 83; [2001] J.P.L. 170; 2000 G.W.D. 26-1007; *Times,* September
   19, 2000, OH . . . .   *Digested,* 01/**6853**
Courage Group's Pension Schemes, Re; Ryan v. Imperial Brewing and Leisure [1987] 1
   W.L.R. 495; [1987] 1 All E.R. 528; [1987] 1 F.T.L.R. 210; (1987) 84 L.S.G.
   1573; (1987) 131 S.J. 507; *Times,* December 22, 1986; *Financial Times,*
   December 16, 1986, Ch D . . . .   *Digested,* 87/**2822**:
                  Applied, 00/6616: *Considered,* 91/2726: *Distinguished,* 01/4628
Coutts Trustees v. Coutts; *sub nom* Sharp v. Coutts 1998 S.C. 798; 1998 S.C.L.R. 729;
   1998 G.W.D. 22-1137, 1 Div; reversing 1996 S.C.L.R. 1026, Sh Pr . . . .   *Digested,* 98/**6000**
Cowan v. Hamilton 1998 G.W.D. 19-964, HCJ Appeal
Cowan v. HM Advocate 2001 G.W.D. 18-692, HCJ Appeal
Cowan v. HM Advocate (Sentencing) 1998 G.W.D. 27-1375, HCJ Appeal
Cowan (Paul Matthew) v. HM Advocate; Rennie (Jennifer Margaret) v. Kennedy; Blair
   (Patricia Elaine) v. Carnegie; Simpson (Alan Robert) v. Vannet 1999 J.C. 248;
   1999 S.C.C.R. 400; 1999 G.W.D. 17-796, HCJ Appeal . . . .   *Digested,* 99/**5933**:
                    Followed, 00/6150
Cowan v. Jeffrey Associates 1998 S.C. 496; 1999 S.L.T. 757; 1998 S.C.L.R. 619; 1998
   G.W.D. 13-675, OH . . . .   *Digested,* 98/**6015**
Cowan v. O'Donnell 1998 G.W.D. 26-1350, HCJ Appeal
Cowan v. Toffolo Jackson & Co Ltd 1998 S.L.T. 1000; 1997 Rep. L.R. 40; 1997 G.W.D.
   6-252, OH . . . .   *Digested,* 98/**5483**
Cowan v. Vannet 1998 G.W.D. 20-1031, HCJ Appeal
Cowell v. Beaton 2001 S.L.C.R. 65, Land Ct (Full Ct)
Cowie v. Atlantic Drilling Co Ltd 1995 S.C. 288; 1995 S.L.T. 1151; 1995 S.C.L.R. 335, 1
   Div; affirming 1994 G.W.D. 29-1755, OH . . . .   *Digested,* 95/**5844**:
                 Applied, 98/5712: *Followed,* 95/5845
Cowie v. HM Advocate (Sentencing) 2001 G.W.D. 30-1193, HCJ Appeal
Cowie v. Walsh 1999 G.W.D. 15-686, Sh Ct
Cox (Peter), Petitioner see Cox and Griffiths, Petitioners
Cox and Griffiths, Petitioners; *sub nom* Cox (Peter), Petitioner 1998 J.C. 267; 1998
   S.L.T. 1172; 1998 S.C.C.R. 561; 1998 G.W.D. 28-1400, HCJ Appeal . . . .   *Digested,* 98/**5396**
Coyle v. Glasgow City Council 1998 S.C. 370; 1998 S.L.T. 453; 1997 G.W.D. 29-1491,
   1 Div . . . .   *Digested,* 98/**6209**
Coyle v. Higson 2001 S.L.T. 1161; 2001 S.C.C.R. 548; 2001 G.W.D. 24-886, HCJ
   Appeal . . . .   *Digested,* 01/**6317**
Coyle v. HM Advocate (Sentencing) 1999 G.W.D. 37-1816, HCJ Appeal
CR Smith Glaziers (Dunfermline) Ltd v. Customs and Excise Commissioners; *sub nom*
   CR Smith Glaziers (Dunfermline) Ltd v. Edinburgh VAT and Duties Tribunal [2001]
   S.T.C. 770; 2001 S.C. 646; [2001] S.T.I. 830; 2001 G.W.D. 7-290, Ex Div;
   affirming [2000] B.V.C. 2146; [2000] S.T.I. 264, V&DTr . . . .   *Digested,* 01/**6920**
CR Smith Glaziers (Dunfermline) Ltd v. Edinburgh VAT and Duties Tribunal see CR Smith
   Glaziers (Dunfermline) Ltd v. Customs and Excise Commissioners
Crabb v. HM Advocate 1999 G.W.D. 20-940, HCJ Appeal
Crabbie v. HM Advocate (Sentencing) 2000 G.W.D. 33-1297, HCJ Appeal
Craib v. Craib 2001 G.W.D. 14-549, Sh Ct (Grampian)
Craig v. Carnegie 1998 G.W.D. 33-1711, HCJ Appeal

Craig v. Crowe (Sentencing) 1998 G.W.D. 1-30, HCJ Appeal
Craig v. HM Advocate (Sentencing) 1998 G.W.D. 16-797, HCJ Appeal
Craig v. HM Advocate (Sentencing) 1998 G.W.D. 22-1127, HCJ Appeal
Craig v. HM Advocate (Sentencing) 2000 G.W.D. 34-1313, HCJ Appeal
Craig v. Hogg (1896) 24 R. 6; (1896) 4 S.L.T. 94, 2 Div . . . . *Distinguished,*
95/6465,
96/7232: Followed, 99/5687

Craig v. Rough 1998 G.W.D. 15-771, Ex Div
Craig v. Strathclyde RC 1998 Hous. L.R. 104, Sh Ct . . . . *Digested, 98/5975*
Craig v. Vannet (Sentencing) 1999 G.W.D. 8-391, HCJ Appeal
Craig v. Vannet (Sentencing) 1999 G.W.D. 1-33, HCJ Appeal
Craiglaw Developments Ltd v. Gordon Wilson & Co 1997 S.C. 356; 1998 S.L.T. 1046;
1997 S.C.L.R. 1157; [1998] B.C.C. 530; 1997 G.W.D. 21-1050; *Times,* September
11, 1997, Ex Div . . . . *Digested, 97/6162*
Craik v. Howdle 1998 G.W.D. 31-1629, HCJ Appeal
Cramer v. Argyll and Clyde Health Board 1998 Hous. L.R. 119, Sh Pr
Cranston v. Lees 1998 S.C.C.R. 435; 1998 G.W.D. 24-1237, HCJ Appeal . . . . *Digested, 98/5692*
Cranston v. Reith 1999 G.W.D. 33-1584, HCJ Appeal
Crawford v. Gilchrist (Sentencing) 2000 G.W.D. 3-91, HCJ Appeal
Crawford v. HM Advocate (Sentencing) 2000 G.W.D. 14-529, HCJ Appeal
Crawford (David) v. HM Advocate 1999 S.L.T. 1381; 1999 S.C.C.R. 674; 1999 G.W.D.
28-1326, HCJ Appeal . . . . *Digested, 00/6113:*
Distinguished, 00/6054
Crawford (Thomas Cooper) v. O'Donnell 1999 S.C.C.R. 39; 1999 G.W.D. 1-56, HCJ
Appeal . . . . *Digested, 99/5844*
Crawford v. Renfrewshire Council 2001 Rep. L.R. 50; 2000 G.W.D. 40-1476, OH
Crawford v. Ritchie 1999 G.W.D. 21-999, HCJ Appeal
Crawford v. Strathclyde RC 1999 Fam. L.R. 119, Sh Ct . . . . *Digested, 00/6189*
Crawford's Trustee v. Crawford; *sub nom* Hall v. Crawford; TNS, Ex Div; affirming 2001
S.L.T. (Sh Ct) 101; 2000 G.W.D. 31-1232, Sh Pr; reversing 2000 G.W.D. 10-362,
Sh Ct
Crean v. Vannet 1998 G.W.D. 31-1589, HCJ Appeal
Creasey v. Creasey (Divorce: Adultery) 1931 S.C. 374; 1931 S.L.T. 55, 1 Div . . . . *Considered, 99/5990*
Creston Land and Estates Plc v. Brown 2000 S.C. 320; 2000 G.W.D. 6-212, OH . . . . . . *Digested, 00/5950*
Crichton v. Burrell 1951 S.C. 107; 1951 J.C. 107; 1951 S.L.T. 365, HCJ Appeal . . . . *Digested, 47-51/4432:*
Applied, 98/5581: Considered, 89/3259: Distinguished, 52/3088, 52/4483
Crichton v. HM Advocate (Sentencing) 1999 G.W.D. 20-926, HCJ Appeal
Crighton v. Crighton's Trustee 1999 S.L.T. (Sh Ct) 113; 1999 S.C.L.R. 16; 1999 G.W.D. 1-
2, Sh Pr. . . . . *Digested, 99/6299*
Crofters Commission v. Scottish Ministers 2001 S.L.C.R. 82; 2001 G.W.D. 31-1267,
Land Ct (Full Ct)
Crofters Commission v. Westminster (Liverpool) Trust Co 2000 S.L.C.R. 115, Land Ct
(Full Ct) . . . . *Digested, 01/6741*
Crofters Sharing in Oldshoremore Common Grazings v. Barr's Trustees see MacKenzie v.
Barr's Trustees
Crombie v. Clark (Procurator Fiscal); *sub nom* Crombie v. Guild 2001 S.L.T. 635; 2001
S.C.C.R. 231; 2001 G.W.D. 10-340, HCJ Appeal
Crombie v. Guild see Crombie v. Clark (Procurator Fiscal)
Crombie v. HM Advocate (Sentencing) 2001 G.W.D. 25-947, HCJ Appeal
Crombie v. HM Advocate (Sentencing) 2001 G.W.D. 25-948, HCJ Appeal
Crooks v. Haddow 2000 S.C.L.R. 755; 2000 G.W.D. 10-367, 2 Div . . . . *Digested, 00/6593*
Crooks v. Lawford Kidd & Co 1999 G.W.D. 14-651, OH
Cropper v. Chief Constable of Dumfries and Galloway 1998 S.L.T. 548; 1997 G.W.D.
22-1106, 1 Div . . . . *Digested, 98/6158*
Cross v. Highland and Islands Enterprise see Cross v. Highlands and Islands Enterprise
Cross v. Highlands and Islands Enterprise; *sub nom* Cross v. Highland and Islands
Enterprise; Macdonald v. Highlands and Islands Enterprise 2001 S.L.T. 1060;
2001 S.C.L.R. 547; [2001] Eu. L.R. 256; [2001] I.R.L.R. 336; 2001 Rep. L.R.
26; 2000 G.W.D. 40-1506, OH. . . . . *Digested, 01/6665*
Crossan v. Douglas 1998 G.W.D. 4-156, HCJ Appeal
Crossan v. HM Advocate 1999 G.W.D. 19-898, HCJ Appeal
Crossley v. HM Advocate 1999 G.W.D. 25-1202, HCJ Appeal
Crowe v. French 2000 S.C.L.R. 832; 2000 G.W.D. 13-498, OH . . . . *Digested, 00/6170*
Crowe v. HM Advocate 2000 G.W.D. 19-737, HCJ Appeal
Crowe v. Waugh (William) 1999 J.C. 292; 1999 S.L.T. 1181; 1999 S.C.C.R. 610, HCJ
Appeal . . . . *Digested, 99/5836*
Crown Estate Commissioners v. John Mowlem & Co Ltd 70 B.L.R. 1; 40 Con. L.R. 36;
(1994) 10 Const. L.J. 311, CA . . . . *Digested, 95/491:*
Applied, 01/876: Distinguished, 99/5784
Cruickshank Botanic Gardens Trustees v. Jamieson 2001 G.W.D. 19-735, OH
Cruikshank v. Lees (Sentencing) 1999 G.W.D. 11-523, HCJ Appeal
Crummock (Scotland) Ltd v. HM Advocate 2000 J.C. 408; 2000 S.L.T. 677; 2000
S.C.C.R. 453; 2000 G.W.D. 12-420; *Times,* May 9, 2000, HCJ Appeal . . . . *Digested, 00/6087*
Cuffe v. Carnegie 1999 G.W.D. 25-1205, HCJ Appeal

Cullen *v.* Cullen 2000 S.C. 396; 2000 S.L.T. 540; 2000 S.C.L.R. 491; 2000 G.W.D. 12-
  437, IH (Ct of 5 judges) . . . .   *Digested,* 00/**6543**
Cullen *v.* North Lanarkshire Council 1998 S.C. 451; 1998 S.L.T. 847; 1998 S.C.L.R.
  408; 1998 Rep. L.R. 26; 1998 G.W.D. 8-400, 2 Div; reversing 1996 S.C.L.R.
  1109; 1996 Rep. L.R. 87, OH . . . .   *Digested,* 98/**5939**:
                                                                                                           Considered, 00/6423
Cullinane *v.* British Rema Manufacturing Co Ltd [1954] 1 Q.B. 292; [1953] 3 W.L.R.
  923; [1953] 2 All E.R. 1257; 97 S.J. 811, CA . . . .   *Digested,* 53/**935**:
                                          Applied, 78/303: *Explained,* 84/371: *Followed,* 99/6443
Cullington *v.* HM Advocate (Indecent Assault) 1999 G.W.D. 28-1314, HCJ Appeal
Cullington *v.* HM Advocate (Sentencing) 1999 G.W.D. 26-1244, HCJ Appeal
Culloch *v.* Gilchrist 2000 S.C.C.R. 25; 1999 G.W.D. 34-1621, HCJ Appeal. . . . .   *Digested,* 00/**6020**
Cumming *v.* Deas 1998 S.L.T. 832; 1997 S.C.L.R. 1176, OH . . . .   *Digested,* 98/**5462**
Cumming *v.* Mayen Holdings Ltd 2000 G.W.D. 13-459, Sh Ct
Cumpstie *v.* Liquidator of Piershill PictureTheatre Co Ltd see Cumpstie *v.* Waterston
Cumpstie *v.* Waterston; *sub nom* Cumpstie *v.* Liquidator of Piershill Picture Theatre Co
  Ltd 1933 S.C. 1; 1933 S.L.T. 10, 2 Div 1933 S.L.T. 89, OH . . . .   *Considered,* 98/5493
Cunniff *v.* Cunniff 1999 S.C. 537; 1999 S.L.T. 992; 1999 Fam. L.R. 46; 1999 G.W.D. 12-
  562, Ex Div. . . . .   *Digested,* 99/**6075**
Cunningham *v.* Cunningham 2001 Fam. L.R. 12; 2000 G.W.D. 36-1362, OH . . . .   *Digested,* 01/**6519**
Cunningham *v.* Fearghas McKay Association Ltd 1999 G.W.D. 3-124, Sh Ct
Cunningham *v.* HM Advocate 1998 G.W.D. 23-1166, HCJ Appeal
Cunningham *v.* Lees 1998 G.W.D. 35-1838, HCJ Appeal
Cunningham *v.* McGlennan (Sentencing) 2000 G.W.D. 13-481, HCJ Appeal
Cunningham *v.* Western Automobile Co Ltd 1998 G.W.D. 28-1446, Sh Ct
Curley *v.* Fraser 1997 S.C.C.R. 705; 1997 G.W.D. 39-1983, HCJ Appeal . . . .   *Digested,* 98/**5647**
Curley (Grant Ploughman) *v.* HM Advocate 1999 S.C.C.R. 467; 1999 G.W.D. 19-870,
  HCJ Appeal . . . .   *Digested,* 99/**5821**
Curran *v.* Heywood (Sentencing) 2000 G.W.D. 39-1453, HCJ Appeal
Curran *v.* Lees 1998 G.W.D. 34-1741, HCJ Appeal
Curran *v.* Lord Advocate 1999 S.L.T. 332; 1998 G.W.D. 24-1222, OH . . . .   *Digested,* 99/**6011**
Curran *v.* Wheelan 1999 G.W.D. 19-903, HCJ Appeal
Currie *v.* Clamp; *sub nom* Currie *v.* Clamp's Executor 2001 S.C.L.R. 504; 2001 Rep.
  L.R. 87; 2001 G.W.D. 9-319, OH . . . .   *Digested,* 01/**6816**
Currie *v.* Clamp's Executor see Currie *v.* Clamp
Currie *v.* Crowe (Sentencing) 1998 G.W.D. 9-474, HCJ Appeal
Currie *v.* ERDC Ltd 1999 G.W.D. 2-105, Sh Ct
Currie *v.* HM Advocate 1999 G.W.D. 5-248, HCJ Appeal
Currie *v.* O'Donnell (Sentencing) 2001 G.W.D. 16-625, HCJ Appeal
Currie *v.* Strathclyde Regional Council Fire Brigade 1999 S.L.T. 62; 1998 Rep. L.R. 41;
  1998 G.W.D. 7-318, OH . . . .   *Digested,* 98/**5457**
Cusak *v.* HM Advocate 1998 G.W.D. 20-1021, HCJ Appeal
Cusick *v.* Brown (Sentencing) 2000 G.W.D. 33-1287, HCJ Appeal
Cussick (Barry) *v.* HM Advocate 2001 S.L.T. 1316; 2001 S.C.C.R. 683; 2001 G.W.D. 21-
  796, HCJ Appeal . . . .   *Digested,* 01/**6392**
Customs and Excise Commissioners *v.* John D Reid Joinery Ltd; *sub nom* Advocate
  General for Scotland *v.* John D Reid Joinery Ltd 2001 S.L.T. 588; 2000 G.W.D.
  31-1213, OH . . . .   *Digested,* 01/**6220**
Customs and Excise Commissioners *v.* Kingscrest Associates Ltd see Kingscrest
  Associates Ltd *v.* Customs and Excise Commissioners
Customs and Excise Commissioners *v.* McConnachie 1999 S.C.L.R. 762; [1999] V. &
  D.R. 59; 1999 G.W.D. 13-616, 2 Div . . . .   *Digested,* 99/**6457**
Customs and Excise Commissioners *v.* Morrison's Academy Boarding Houses
  Association [1978] S.T.C. 1; 1977 S.C. 279; 1977 S.L.T. 197, 1 Div . . . .   *Digested,* 77/**3812**:
                             Applied, 79/2743, 95/5121: *Considered,* 01/5579: *Distinguished,* 98/6219
Customs and Excise Commissioners *v.* Zaoui 2001 S.C. 448; 2001 S.L.T. 201; 2000
  G.W.D. 40-1498, Ex Div; reversing 2000 S.L.T. (Sh Ct) 197; 2000 G.W.D. 25-
  949, Sh Pr . . . .   *Digested,* 01/**6717**
Cuthbertson *v.* Merchiston Castle School 2001 S.L.T. (Sh Ct) 13; 2000 G.W.D. 15-
  628, Sh Pr. . . . .   *Digested,* 01/**6818**
CWW Logistics Ltd *v.* Ronald EAT/774/98, EAT . . . .   *Digested,* 99/**6043**
Czajkowski *v.* Vannet (Sentencing) 2000 G.W.D. 14-525, HCJ Appeal

D (Minors) (Adoption Reports: Confidentiality), Re [1996] A.C. 593; [1995] 3 W.L.R. 483;
  [1995] 4 All E.R. 385; [1995] 2 F.L.R. 687; [1996] 1 F.C.R. 205; [1996] Fam. Law 8;
  (1995) 145 N.L.J. 1612, HL; reversing [1995] 1 W.L.R. 356; [1995] 1 F.L.R. 631;
  (1995) 139 S.J.L.B. 13; *Times,* December 8, 1994; *Independent,* December 6,
  1994; *Guardian,* December 5, 1994, CA . . . .   *Digested,* 96/**474**:
                                Applied, 96/508, 97/356, 99/2360, 99/6065, 00/2534:
                                                                                   Distinguished, 99/6064
D *v.* B (Parent and Child: Access: Rights under Hague Convention) 1999 G.W.D. 12-
  528, OH

D v. Criminal Injuries Compensation Board see X v. Criminal Injuries Compensation
    Board
D v. D 1998 S.C. 259; 1997 G.W.D. 37-1881, 2 Div . . . .   *Digested,* 98/**5846**
D v. D (Parent and Child: Residence) 2001 S.L.T. 1104; 2001 Fam. L.R. 66; 2001
    G.W.D. 22-823, 1 Div; reversing 2001 G.W.D. 15-565, OH . . . .   *Digested,* 01/**6513**
D v. HM Advocate (Sentencing) 2001 G.W.D. 31-1242, HCJ Appeal
D v. Scottish Ministers see A v. Scottish Ministers
D Cameron & Son v. McLeod 1999 G.W.D. 20-918, Sh Pr
D McEwing & Sons v. Renfrew CC 1960 S.C. 53; 1960 S.L.T. 140; (1959) 11 P. & C.R.
    306, 1 Div . . . .   *Digested,* 60/**3426**:
            Followed, 99/**6443**
D's Curator Bonis, Noter 1998 S.L.T. 2; 1997 G.W.D. 13-538, OH . . . .   *Digested,* 98/**5464**
D, Petitioner 2001 G.W.D. 14-535, OH
Dailey Petroleum Services Corp v. Pioneer Oil Tools Ltd 1994 S.L.T. 757, OH . . . .   *Digested,* 94/**6085**:
            Overruled, 98/**5451**
Dailly v. Friel 1999 G.W.D. 10-452, HCJ Appeal
Dailly v. HM Advocate (Sentencing) 2000 G.W.D. 9-328, HCJ Appeal
Dalgleish v. Lees (Sentencing) 1998 G.W.D. 10-503, HCJ Appeal
Dalglish v. National Westminster Bank Plc 2001 S.L.T. (Sh Ct) 124; 2001 G.W.D. 3-112,
    Sh Ct (Glasgow) . . . .   *Digested,* 01/**6296**
Dalson v. Tayside Health Board 1998 S.L.T. 1304; 1998 Rep. L.R. 40; 1998 G.W.D. 1-
    52, OH . . . .   *Digested,* 98/**5489**
Daly v. Lees (Sentencing) 1998 G.W.D. 11-532, HCJ Appeal
Daly (James Anthony) v. Vannet 1999 S.C.C.R. 346; 1999 G.W.D. 16-737, HCJ Appeal .   *Digested,* 99/**5797**
Danskin v. HM Advocate 2001 G.W.D. 26-1025, HCJ Appeal
Darrie v. Duncan 2001 S.L.T. 941; 2001 Fam. L.R. 80; 2000 G.W.D. 36-1367, OH . . . . . .   *Digested,* 01/**6825**
Datelock Ltd v. Bain 1998 S.L.T. 381; 1998 S.C.L.R. 209; 1997 G.W.D. 36-1872, OH . . .   *Digested,* 98/**6067**
David Wilson Construction Ltd v. Newbattle Properties Ltd 1998 G.W.D. 40-2040, OH
Davidson v. City Electrical Factors Ltd [1998] I.C.R. 443; [1998] I.R.L.R. 108, EAT . . . .   *Digested,* 98/**5826**
Davidson v. Heywood (Sentencing) 2000 G.W.D. 19-769, HCJ Appeal
Davidson v. Higson 1999 G.W.D. 27-1299, HCJ Appeal
Davidson v. Reith (Sentencing) 1998 G.W.D. 13-651, HCJ Appeal
Davidson v. Scottish Ministers; *sub nom* Scott v. Scottish Ministers; Scott, Petitioner;
    TNS, Ex Div; affirming 2001 G.W.D. 35-1341, OH
Davidson v. Smith 1998 G.W.D. 1-1, 2 Div
Davidson v. Vannet (Sentencing) 1998 G.W.D. 14-709, HCJ Appeal
Davidson v. Wiseman 2001 G.W.D. 9-317, Sh Ct (Grampian)
Davie (James Pennycook) v. Edinburgh Corp (No.2); *sub nom* Davie v. Edinburgh
    Magistrates 1953 S.C. 34; 1953 S.L.T. 54, 1 Div . . . .   *Digested,* 53/**4145**:
            Applied, 97/5959, 98/6102: *Considered,* 66/13144
Davie v. Edinburgh Magistrates see Davie (James Pennycook) v. Edinburgh Corp
    (No.2)
Davie v. McLeod 1999 G.W.D. 6-300, HCJ Appeal
Davie v. Scottish Homes (Unreported, February 28, 1995), Lands Tr (Scot) . . . .   *Not followed,* 98/**5982**
Davie (or Stuart) v. Stuart see Stuart v. Stuart (Divorce: Financial Provision)
Davies v. HM Advocate (Misdirection: Self Defence) 2000 G.W.D. 20-789, HCJ
    Appeal
Davies v. HM Advocate (Sentencing) 2000 G.W.D. 29-1134, HCJ Appeal
Davies v. Levi Strauss (UK) Ltd 2001 G.W.D. 7-271, OH
Davies v. Massey Ferguson Perkins [1986] I.C.R. 580, QBD . . . .   *Digested,* 86/**1539**:
            Applied, 98/5938
Davies v. MJ Wyatt (Decorators) Ltd [2000] I.R.L.R. 759; *Times,* October 24, 2000,
    EAT . . . .   *Digested,* 00/**2198**:
            Followed, 01/6471
Dawes v. McLeod 1999 G.W.D. 2-109, HCJ Appeal
Dawson (Neil Grant) v. Dickson; *sub nom* Dawson (Neil Grant) v. McKay 1999 J.C.
    315; 1999 S.L.T. 1328; 1999 S.C.C.R. 698; 1999 G.W.D. 28-1353, HCJ Appeal . .   *Digested,* 00/**6035**
Dawson v. Higson (Sentencing) 2001 G.W.D. 13-491, HCJ Appeal
Dawson (Neil Grant) v. McKay see Dawson (Neil Grant) v. Dickson
Dawson v. Ritchie (Sentencing) 1998 S.L.T. 807; 1998 G.W.D. 11-575, HCJ Appeal . . . .   *Digested,* 98/**5569**
Dawson v. Scottish Power Plc 1999 S.L.T. 672; 1998 G.W.D. 38-1975, OH . . . .   *Digested,* 99/**6368**
De Gernier v. Heywood (Sentencing) 1998 G.W.D. 15-746, HCJ Appeal
De La Rue International Ltd v. Scottish Power Plc 2000 G.W.D. 34-1325, OH
De Montfort Insurance Co Plc v. Lafferty 1997 S.C. 335; 1998 S.L.T. 535; 1997 S.C.L.R.
    622; 1997 G.W.D. 4-140, OH . . . .   *Digested,* 97/**5722**
De Sykes v. HM Advocate 1998 G.W.D. 22-1130, HCJ Appeal
Dean (Raymond) v. HM Advocate see McAnea (Thomas) v. HM Advocate
Deans v. Colley 1999 G.W.D. 3-148, HCJ Appeal
Debidin v. Chief Constable of the Northern Constabulary 2001 G.W.D. 25-975, Sh Pr
Deen-Koroma v. Immigration Appeal Tribunal see R. v. Immigration Appeal Tribunal Ex
    p. Deen-Koroma
Degnan v. HM Advocate 2001 S.L.T. 1233; 2001 S.C.C.R. 810; 2001 G.W.D. 27-1087,
    HCJ Appeal . . . .   *Digested,* 01/**6383**
Dehn v. Dehn 1998 G.W.D. 2-59, OH

Deighan *v.* MacLeod 1959 J.C. 25; 1960 S.L.T. 2; [1961] Crim. L.R. 711, HCJ Appeal. . .   *Digested*, 61/**1736**:
                                                                       Applied, 00/6044: *Followed*, 91/4687
Dekker (Stephen Alexander), Fatal Accident Inquiry 2000 S.C.L.R. 1087, Sh Ct (South
    Strathclyde) . . . . *Digested*, 01/**6333**
Delaney *v.* RJ Staples (t/a De Montfort Recruitment) [1992] 1 A.C. 687; [1992] 2
    W.L.R. 451; [1992] 1 All E.R. 944; [1992] I.C.R. 483; [1992] I.R.L.R. 191; (1992)
    142 N.L.J. 384; *Times*, March 16, 1992; *Independent*, March 13, 1992, HL;
    affirming [1991] 2 Q.B. 47; [1991] 2 W.L.R. 627; [1991] 1 All E.R. 609; [1991]
    I.C.R. 331; [1991] I.R.L.R. 112; (1991) 141 N.L.J. 581, CA; reversing in part
    [1990] I.C.R. 364; [1990] I.R.L.R. 86; (1990) 87(10) L.S.G. 35, EAT. . . . .   *Digested*, 92/**2028**:
                     Applied, 95/1981, 95/2040, 97/2294, 98/2208, 98/2245:
              Considered, 00/2247, 01/5274: *Distinguished*, 96/2675, 98/5827:
                      Followed, 99/2017: *Not followed*, 90/1985, 91/1709
Delcourt *v.* Belgium (A/11) (1979-80) 1 E.H.R.R. 355, ECHR . . . .   *Applied*, 98/3112,
                               98/3122, 98/3142, 98/3143: *Considered*, 00/6100
Delikes Ltd *v.* Scottish & Newcastle Plc 2000 S.L.T. (Sh Ct) 67; 2000 G.W.D. 5-182,
    Sh Pr; affirming 2000 S.C.L.R. 163, Sh Ct . . . .   *Digested*, 00/**5987**
Dempsey *v.* Brown 1999 G.W.D. 22-1035, HCJ Appeal
Dempsey *v.* HM Advocate 1995 J.C. 84; 1996 S.L.T. 289; 1995 S.C.C.R. 431, HCJ
    Appeal . . . .   *Digested*, 95/**5722**:
                                              Distinguished, 00/6054
Dempsey *v.* HM Advocate (Sentencing) 2001 G.W.D. 1-36, HCJ Appeal
Dempster *v.* Crowe (Sentencing) 1998 G.W.D. 2-84, HCJ Appeal
Dempster *v.* McFadyen (Sentencing) 2000 G.W.D. 29-1132, HCJ Appeal
Dempster *v.* Ruxton (Sentencing) 1999 G.W.D. 1-24, HCJ Appeal
Denholm *v.* O'Donnell (Sentencing) 2001 G.W.D. 36-1372, HCJ Appeal
Denney *v.* HM Advocate (Sentencing) 2001 G.W.D. 25-954, HCJ Appeal
Dennis Walton Construction *v.* McKay (t/a Cuemasters) 1999 S.L.T. (Sh Ct) 39; 1999
    S.C.L.R. 373; 1999 G.W.D. 6-289, Sh Pr . . . .   *Digested*, 99/**5714**
Dennison *v.* HM Advocate 1999 G.W.D. 31-1483, HCJ Appeal
Denny *v.* Carnegie (Sentencing) 2001 G.W.D. 26-1030, HCJ Appeal
Denny *v.* Walkingshaw (Sentencing) 1998 G.W.D. 6-299, HCJ Appeal
Denovan *v.* Blue Triangle (Glasgow) Housing Association Ltd 1999 Hous. L.R. 97, Sh
    Ct . . . .   *Digested*, 99/**6261**
Derwent Coachworks *v.* Kirby [1995] I.C.R. 48; [1994] I.R.L.R. 639, EAT. . . . .   *Digested*, 95/**2080**:
                      Applied, 98/5821: *Considered*, 96/2607: *Disapproved*, 97/2283
Devaney *v.* Yarrow Shipbuilders Ltd 1999 S.L.T. 561; 1999 G.W.D. 1-49, OH . . . . . .   *Digested*, 99/**5669**
Devine *v.* Colvilles Ltd; *sub nom* Colvilles Ltd *v.* Devine [1969] 1 W.L.R. 475; [1969] 2
    All E.R. 53; 1969 S.C. (H.L.) 67; 1969 S.L.T. 154; 6 K.I.R. 333; 113 S.J. 287, HL;
    affirming 1968 S.L.T. 294, 2 Div; affirming 1967 S.L.T. 89, OH . . . .   *Digested*, 72/**2402**:
                             Applied, 00/6599: *Distinguished*, 95/6162
Devine *v.* HM Advocate (Sentencing) 2001 G.W.D. 21-800, HCJ Appeal
Devlin *v.* HM Advocate (Sentencing) 2000 G.W.D. 4-125, HCJ Appeal
Devlin *v.* MacGregor 2001 G.W.D. 3-125, OH
Devos Gebroeder NV *v.* Sunderland Sportswear Ltd (No.2) 1990 S.C. 291; 1990 S.L.T.
    473; 1990 S.C.L.R. 466, 1 Div; affirming 1989 S.L.T. 382; 1989 S.C.L.R. 302,
    OH . . . .   *Digested*, 90/**5636**:
                        Applied, 94/5764: *Distinguished*, 01/6869: *Followed*, 91/5462
Dewar *v.* Munro 1998 G.W.D. 40-2082, HCJ Appeal
Dewar *v.* Strathclyde RC 1984 S.C. 102; 1985 S.L.T. 114, 2 Div . . . .   *Digested*, 85/**3731**:
                              Considered, 96/6615: *Distinguished*, 95/5525, 00/6261
Dewar *v.* Winton 1999 S.C.L.R. 1014; 1999 G.W.D. 20-916, Ex Div . . . .   *Digested*, 00/**5893**
DI, Petitioner see I, Petitioner
Diamond (James Thomason) *v.* HM Advocate (No.1) 1999 S.L.T. 973, HCJ Appeal . . . .   *Digested*, 99/**5903**
Diamond (James Thomason) *v.* HM Advocate (No.2) 1999 J.C. 244; 1999 S.L.T. 1001;
    1999 S.C.C.R. 411; 1999 G.W.D. 15-689, HCJ Appeal . . . .   *Digested*, 99/**5800**
Diaz *v.* Diaz 1999 S.C.L.R. 329, Sh Ct . . . .   *Digested*, 99/**5716**
Dibben *v.* Ruxton (Sentencing) 2000 G.W.D. 30-1205, HCJ Appeal
Dible *v.* Morton Fraser Partnership 2001 Fam. L.R. 84; 2000 G.W.D. 28-1097, OH . . . . .   *Digested*, 01/**6823**
Dick *v.* Higson (Sentencing) 2001 G.W.D. 21-807, HCJ Appeal
Dick *v.* McFadyen 2001 G.W.D. 30-1177, HCJ Appeal
Dickie *v.* HM Advocate 1999 G.W.D. 2-87, HCJ Appeal
Dickie *v.* Vannet (Sentencing) 2000 G.W.D. 33-1282, HCJ Appeal
Dickson (Alan), Petitioner (Sentencing); *sub nom* Dickson (Alan) *v.* HM Advocate
    (Sentencing) 2000 S.C.C.R. 617; 2000 G.W.D. 13-478, HCJ Appeal . . . .   *Digested*, 00/**6143**
Dickson (Robert) *v.* Crowe 1998 S.L.T. 1065; 1998 S.C.C.R. 406; 1998 G.W.D. 20-
    1010, HCJ Appeal . . . .   *Digested*, 98/**5646**
Dickson *v.* Grant (Sentencing) 2001 G.W.D. 4-154, Sh Ct (Grampian)
Dickson *v.* HM Advocate (Unreported, October 23, 1980), HCJ Appeal . . . .   *Distinguished*,
                                                      00/6060
Dickson *v.* HM Advocate (Sentencing) 1998 G.W.D. 15-755, HCJ Appeal
Dickson *v.* HM Advocate (Sentencing) 1998 G.W.D. 29-1486, HCJ Appeal
Dickson (Alan) *v.* HM Advocate (Sentencing) see Dickson (Alan), Petitioner
    (Sentencing)

Dickson (Annie Mulvey) *v.* HM Advocate 2001 J.C. 203; 2001 S.L.T. 674; 2001
   S.C.C.R. 397; 2001 G.W.D. 16-595, HCJ Appeal
Dickson *v.* Main (Sentencing) 2001 G.W.D. 4-155, Sh Ct (Grampian)
Dickson *v.* McFadyen (Sentencing) 2000 G.W.D. 3-99, HCJ Appeal
Dickson *v.* Munro 1998 G.W.D. 35-1842, HCJ Appeal
Dickson *v.* Purcell 2001 G.W.D. 7-288, Sh Ct (Grampian)
Dickson *v.* Ross 2001 G.W.D. 21-783, Sh Ct (Grampian)
Dickson *v.* Stott (Sentencing) 1998 G.W.D. 7-353, HCJ Appeal
Digby Brown *v.* Ackerman 2001 G.W.D. 40-1526, Ex Div; affirming 2001 G.W.D. 21-
   812, OH
Dignall *v.* HM Advocate 1998 G.W.D. 26-1323, HCJ Appeal
Dignon *v.* Irving 2001 S.C. 310; 2001 S.L.T. 32; 2000 G.W.D. 36-1366, 1 Div; affirming
   1999 S.C.L.R. 601, Sh Ct . . . .   *Digested,* 01/**6721**
Dilworth *v.* Lovat Highland Estates Ltd 1999 G.W.D. 38-1840, OH
Dimanna *v.* Crowe 1999 G.W.D. 1-30, HCJ Appeal
Dimond *v.* Lovell [2000] 2 W.L.R. 1121; [2000] 2 All E.R. 897; [2000] R.T.R. 243;
   [2000] C.C.L.R. 57; 2000 Rep. L.R. 62; (2000) 97(22) L.S.G. 47; (2000) 150
   N.L.J. 740; *Times,* May 12, 2000; *Independent,* May 17, 2000, HL; affirming
   [2000] Q.B. 216; [1999] 3 W.L.R. 561; [1999] 3 All E.R. 1; [1999] R.T.R. 297;
   [1999] C.C.L.R. 46; (1999) 96(21) L.S.G. 40; (1999) 149 N.L.J. 681; (1999)
   143 S.J.L.B. 181; *Times,* May 3, 1999, CA; reversing(Unreported, May 1, 1998),
   CC (Sheffield) . . . .   *Digested,* 00/**2566**:
              Applied, 99/2470, 99/2471, 99/2475, 99/2478, 99/2481, 00/2570, 00/2587,
              01/881, 01/900, 01/1527: *Cited,* 99/2458, 99/2461, 99/2476, 99/2499,
              00/425, 00/2574, 00/2580, 00/2592, 00/2593, 01/896, 01/899, 01/3830:
              Considered, 99/532, 99/2453, 99/2454, 99/2459, 99/2460, 99/2466,
              99/2467, 99/2468, 99/2496, 00/311, 01/885, 01/888, 01/890, 01/898:
              Distinguished, 99/535, 99/2452, 99/2482, 99/2491, 99/2504, 00/2578,
              00/2585, 00/2597, 01/893, 01/894: *Followed,* 99/2463, 99/2489, 00/2565,
              00/2577, 00/2579, 01/657, 01/887, 01/901: *Referred to,* 99/2451, 99/2464,
              99/2465, 99/2472, 99/2473, 99/2474, 99/2483, 99/2485, 99/2487,
              99/2490, 00/2562, 00/2589, 01/1542
Dinan *v.* Dennett 2001 S.L.C.R. 55, Land Ct (Full Ct); affirming 1999 S.L.C.R. 70,
   Land Ct (Div Ct) . . . .   *Digested,* 00/**6534**
Dingley *v.* Chief Constable of Strathclyde (No.1) 2000 S.C. (H.L.) 77; 2000 S.C.L.R.
   309; (2000) 55 B.M.L.R. 1; 2000 G.W.D. 11-401, HL; affirming 1998 S.C. 548;
   1998 G.W.D. 13-677, 1 Div; reversing 1997 S.L.T. 880; 1997 Rep. L.R. (Quantum)
   1, OH . . . .   *Digested,* 00/**6579**
Dingwall *v.* Ruxton see Mackay (Alexander Munro) *v.* Ruxton
Dingwall-Fordyce *v.* Dingwall-Fordyce 2001 G.W.D. 18-702, Sh Ct (Grampian)
Dinnen *v.* HM Advocate 1999 G.W.D. 20-934, HCJ Appeal
Dirom *v.* Howdle 1995 S.L.T. 1016; 1995 S.C.C.R. 368, HCJ Appeal . . . .   *Digested,* 95/**5687**:
              Applied, 00/6091
Discovery Communications Inc *v.* Discovery FM Ltd 2000 S.C. 69; 2000 S.L.T. 212;
   [2000] E.T.M.R. 516; 1999 G.W.D. 35-1722; *Times,* January 25, 2000, Ex Div;
   reversing 1999 G.W.D. 35-1723, OH . . . .   *Digested,* 00/**6521**
Disotto *v.* Lees 1998 G.W.D. 18-917, HCJ Appeal
Divers *v.* Vannet 1998 G.W.D. 25-1280, HCJ Appeal
Dixon *v.* Van der Wetering 2000 G.W.D. 12-409, OH
Dobbie *v.* Fife Council [1998] R.V.R. 119; 1998 Hous. L.R. 48, Lands Tr . . . .   *Digested,* 98/**5947**
Dobbs *v.* HM Advocate 1999 G.W.D. 25-1191, HCJ Appeal
Dobell *v.* Munro 1998 G.W.D. 18-908, HCJ Appeal
Docherty *v.* Carnegie 1999 G.W.D. 21-1022, HCJ Appeal
Docherty *v.* Edinburgh City Council 2000 S.C. 598; 2001 S.L.T. 291; 2000 G.W.D. 26-
   1003, Ex Div; affirming [2000] 15 S.L.L.P. 10; 1999 G.W.D. 37-1824, OH . . . . . .   *Digested,* 01/**6790**
Docherty *v.* HM Advocate (Delay) 2000 J.C. 307; 2000 S.L.T. 1312; 2000 S.C.C.R.
   717; 2000 G.W.D. 8-275, HCJ Appeal . . . .   *Digested,* 00/**6084**
Docherty *v.* HM Advocate (Sentencing) 1999 G.W.D. 35-1692, HCJ Appeal
Docherty *v.* HM Advocate (Sentencing) 2000 S.C.C.R. 106; 2000 G.W.D. 3-97, HCJ
   Appeal . . . .   *Digested,* 00/**6138**
Docherty *v.* HM Advocate (Sentencing) 2000 G.W.D. 15-599, HCJ
Docherty *v.* HM Advocate (Sentencing) 2001 G.W.D. 25-929, HCJ Appeal
Docherty (Andrew) *v.* HM Advocate 1987 J.C. 81; 1987 S.L.T. 784; 1987 S.C.C.R. 418,
   HCJ Appeal . . . .   *Digested,* 87/**4119**:
             Applied, 92/5416: *Considered,* 92/5496: *Not applied,* 00/6023
Docherty (David) *v.* HM Advocate 1997 J.C. 196; 1998 S.L.T. 278; 1997 S.C.C.R. 345;
   1997 G.W.D. 15-663, HCJ Appeal . . . .   *Digested,* 97/**5866**
Docherty *v.* Leitch 1998 S.L.T. 374; 1997 S.C.L.R. 847; [1997] 8 S.L.L.P. 13; 1997
   G.W.D. 24-1220, OH . . . .   *Digested,* 97/**6224**
Docherty *v.* MacLeod (Sentencing) 1998 G.W.D. 13-691, HCJ Appeal
Docherty *v.* McGlennan (Sentencing) 1998 G.W.D. 4-176, HCJ Appeal
Docherty *v.* McGlennan (Sentencing) 1999 G.W.D. 17-776, HCJ Appeal
Docherty *v.* Mcglynn (No.1) 1983 S.C. 202; 1983 S.L.T. 645, 1 Div . . . .   *Digested,* 83/**3977**:
             Applied, 98/5461

Docherty v. Watt (Sentencing) 2000 G.W.D. 34-1304, HCJ Appeal
Dodds v. HM Advocate 1998 G.W.D. 29-1491, HCJ Appeal
Dodson v. HM Advocate (Sentencing) 2000 G.W.D. 6-225, HCJ Appeal
Doherty v. Carnegie (Sentencing) 2001 G.W.D. 16-633, HCJ Appeal
Doherty v. Jaymarke Developments (Prospecthill) Ltd 2001 S.L.T. (Sh Ct) 75; 2001
    G.W.D. 4-149, Sh Pr; affirming 2001 S.L.T. (Sh Ct) 6; 2000 G.W.D. 26-971, Sh Ct
    (Grampian) . . . .   *Digested,* 01/**6277**
Doherty v. McDonald 1999 G.W.D. 32-1536, HCJ Appeal
Doherty v. Vannet 1999 G.W.D. 19-911, HCJ Appeal
Dolan (Gwen Margaret) v. McLeod 1999 J.C. 32; 1998 S.C.C.R. 653; 1998 G.W.D. 37-
    1941, HCJ Appeal . . . .   *Digested,* 99/**5939**
Dollar Land (Cumbernauld) Ltd v. CIN Properties Ltd 1998 S.C. (H.L.) 90; 1998 S.L.T.
    992; 1998 S.C.L.R. 929; [1998] 3 E.G.L.R. 79; [1998] 51 E.G. 83; 1998 G.W.D.
    25-1268; *Times,* August 24, 1998, HL; affirming 1996 S.C. 331; 1997 S.L.T. 260;
    1996 S.C.L.R. 697, Ex Div; affirming 1996 S.L.T. 186; *Times,* April 21, 1995, OH .   *Digested,* 98/**6034**:
                                                                                           Followed, 00/6634
Dolphin Packaging Materials Ltd, Noters 1999 S.C.L.R. 1099, Sh Ct . . . .   *Digested,* 00/**6515**
Donald v. Hutchinson 2000 S.L.T. 963; 2000 G.W.D. 21-834, OH. . . . .   *Digested,* 00/**6446**
Donald v. McGlennan (Sentencing) 1998 G.W.D. 6-275, HCJ Appeal
Donald v. Ritchie 2001 G.W.D. 27-1114, HCJ Appeal
Donald & Budge (A Firm) v. Donald see Budge v. Donald
Donaldson (John) v. Brown 1998 J.C. 31; 1998 S.L.T. 1007; 1997 S.C.C.R. 689; 1997
    G.W.D. 36-1836, HCJ Appeal . . . .   *Digested,* 98/**5619**
Donaldson v. Craigen; *sub nom* Donaldson v. Gallacher 2000 S.L.T. 622; 2000
    S.C.C.R. 14; 1999 G.W.D. 31-1460, HCJ Appeal . . . .   *Digested,* 00/**6016**
Donaldson v. Ferguson 1998 G.W.D. 24-1227, Sh Ct
Donaldson v. Gallacher see Donaldson v. Craigen
Donaldson v. Lothian Health Board 1998 S.L.T. 416; 1998 S.C.L.R. 188; 1997 Rep. L.R.
    (Quantum) 32; 1997 G.W.D. 31-1551, OH . . . .   *Digested,* 98/**5745**
Donaldson v. Vannet 1999 G.W.D. 3-150, HCJ Appeal
Donaldson (James) v. Vannet 1998 S.L.T. 957; 1998 S.C.C.R. 421; 1998 G.W.D. 20-
    1006, HCJ Appeal. . . . .   *Digested,* 98/**5574**
Donlon v. Colonial Mutual Group (UK Holdings) Ltd 1998 S.C. 244; 1997 S.C.L.R.
    1088, Ex Div . . . .   *Digested,* 98/**5804**
Donnachie v. Carnegie 1999 G.W.D. 32-1535, HCJ Appeal
Donnachie v. Happit Ltd 2001 G.W.D. 40-1520, OH
Donnelly v. Carmichael 1995 J.C. 215; 1996 S.L.T. 153, HCJ Appeal . . . .   *Digested,* 96/**6728**:
                                                                                           Distinguished, 99/5820
Donnelly v. Clark (Sentencing) 2001 G.W.D. 16-618, HCJ Appeal
Donnelly v. HM Advocate (Sentencing) 2001 G.W.D. 31-1233, HCJ Appeal
Donnelly (Alexander Bain) v. HM Advocate 1999 J.C. 276; 1999 S.C.C.R. 508; 1999
    G.W.D. 21-993, HCJ Appeal. . . . .   *Digested,* 99/**5930**
Donnelly (Brian) v. HM Advocate 2000 S.C.C.R. 861, HCJ Appeal. . . . .   *Digested,* 01/**6391**
Donnelly v. Stott 1999 G.W.D. 14-642, HCJ Appeal
Donnelly v. Stott (Sentencing) 2000 G.W.D. 4-147, HCJ Appeal
Donnett v. HM Advocate (Sentencing) 2000 G.W.D. 19-775, HCJ Appeal
Donofrio v. Burrell 2000 S.L.T. 1051; 2000 S.C.L.R. 465; 1999 Fam. L.R. 141; 1999
    G.W.D. 26-1218, Ex Div . . . .   *Digested,* 00/**6255**
Donoghue v. Donoghue 2000 G.W.D. 15-608, Sh Ct
Doonan v. DHL International (UK) Ltd 1999 G.W.D. 5-272, OH
Doorson v. Netherlands (1996) 22 E.H.R.R. 330, ECHR . . . .   *Digested,* 96/**3124**:
                                                                            Applied, 01/6323: *Considered,* 97/2815
Doran v. Gilchrist 1999 G.W.D. 17-793, HCJ Appeal
Doran v. HM Advocate (Sentencing) 2000 G.W.D. 4-124, HCJ Appeal
Doris v. Vannet (Sentencing) 2000 G.W.D. 15-602, HCJ
Dornan v. Brown 1999 G.W.D. 22-1063, HCJ Appeal
Dorris v. McFadyen (Sentencing) 2000 G.W.D. 19-778, HCJ Appeal
Dosoo v. Dosoo (No.1) 1999 S.L.T. (Sh Ct) 86; 1999 S.C.L.R. 905; 1999 Fam. L.R.
    80; 1999 G.W.D. 13-586, Sh Ct (Lothian) . . . .   *Digested,* 99/**6064**:
                                                                                           Considered, 99/6065
Dosoo v. Dosoo (No.2) 1999 Fam. L.R. 130; 1999 G.W.D. 40-1907, Sh Ct. . . . .   *Digested,* 00/**6264**
Dougall v. Duke of Argyll; *sub nom* Duke of Argyll v. John Campbell 1949 S.L.C.R.
    App. 195, Land Ct (Full Ct) . . . .   *Applied,* 00/**6532**
Dougan v. Dougan 1998 S.L.T. (Sh Ct) 27; 1998 G.W.D. 4-182, Sh Ct (Lothian) . . . . . .   *Digested,* 98/**5854**
Dougan v. Lanarkshire Acute Hospitals NHS Trust 2001 G.W.D. 13-516, OH
Dougbar Properties Ltd v. Keeper of the Registers of Scotland 1999 S.C. 513; 1999
    S.C.L.R. 458; 1999 G.W.D. 9-432, OH . . . .   *Digested,* 99/**6235**
Douglas v. Glasgow DC 1996 S.L.T. 713, 2 Div . . . .   *Digested,* 96/**7154**:
                                                                                           Followed, 98/6210
Douglas v. HM Advocate 2000 G.W.D. 37-1388, HCJ Appeal
Douglas v. HM Advocate (Sentencing) 1998 G.W.D. 28-1428, HCJ Appeal
Douglas v. HM Advocate (Sentencing) 1999 G.W.D. 4-182, HCJ Appeal
Douglas (Stephen Austin) v. HM Advocate 1997 S.C.C.R. 671; 1997 G.W.D. 35-1753,
    HCJ Appeal . . . .   *Digested,* 98/**5656**

Douglas v. Ireland 2001 Fam. L.R. 42; 2000 G.W.D. 38-1427, OH

Douglas (Christopher Paul) v. Lees; *sub nom* Douglas (Christopher Paul) v. McFadyen 2000 J.C. 17; 2000 S.L.T. 399; 1999 S.C.C.R. 884; 1999 G.W.D. 31-1461, HCJ Appeal . . . . *Digested*, 00/**6038**

Douglas (Christopher Paul) v. McFadyen see Douglas (Christopher Paul) v. Lees

Douglas v. Ogilvie see Douglas v. Stuart Wyse Ogilvie Estates Ltd

Douglas v. Stuart Wyse Ogilvie Estates Ltd; *sub nom* Douglas v. Ogilvie 2001 S.L.T. 689; 2000 G.W.D. 25-953, OH

Dove v. Scottish Ministers 2001 G.W.D. 40-1519, OH

Dow v. HM Advocate (Sentencing) 1998 G.W.D. 7-341, HCJ Appeal

Dow v. HM Advocate (Sentencing) 1998 G.W.D. 28-1421, HCJ Appeal

Dowling & Rutter v. Abacus Frozen Foods Ltd (No.1) 2000 G.W.D. 12-412; *Times*, April 26, 2000, OH . . . . *Digested*, 00/**5986**

Dowling & Rutter v. Abacus Frozen Foods Ltd (No.2) 2001 G.W.D. 1-19, OH. . . . . *Previous proceedings*, 00/5986

Downie v. Chief Constable of Strathclyde 1998 S.L.T. 8; 1997 S.C.L.R. 603; 1997 Rep. L.R. (Quantum) 16; 1997 G.W.D. 19-910, OH . . . . *Digested*, 97/**5966**

Downie v. Fife Council 2001 S.C. 793; 2001 S.L.T. 669; 2001 G.W.D. 13-513, OH

Downie v. HM Advocate (Sentencing) 2000 G.W.D. 20-806, HCJ Appeal

Downie (Carole Anne) v. HM Advocate 1999 S.C.C.R. 375; 1999 G.W.D. 16-752, HCJ Appeal . . . . *Digested*, 99/**5927**

Doyle (James McKay Meek) v. Ruxton 1999 S.L.T. 487; 1998 S.C.C.R. 467; 1998 G.W.D. 26-1291, HCJ Appeal . . . . *Digested*, 98/**5590**

DP v. SM see HM Advocate v. P

DPP v. Doot; *sub nom* R. v. Doot (Robert Leroy); R. v. Shanahan (Thomas); R. v. Watts (James Wesley); R. v. Fay (Michael Augustus); R. v. Loving (Jeffrey Richard); R. v. Shannahan (Thomas); DPP v. Shanahan (Thomas); DPP v. Watts (James Wesley); DPP v. Fay (Michael Augustus); DPP v. Loving (Jeffrey Richard) [1973] A.C. 807; [1973] 2 W.L.R. 532; [1973] 1 All E.R. 940; (1973) 57 Cr. App. R. 600; [1973] Crim. L.R. 292; 117 S.J. 266, HL; reversing [1973] 1 Q.B. 73; [1973] Q.B. 73; [1972] 3 W.L.R. 33; [1972] 2 All E.R. 1046; (1973) 57 Cr. App. R. 13; [1972] Crim. L.R. 500; 116 S.J. 445, CA (Crim Div) . . . . *Digested*, 73/**493**: *Applied*, 83/613, 84/580, 89/854: *Considered*, 73/491, 82/686, 83/574, 83/607, 88/801, 91/914, 93/930: *Followed*, 96/1473, 00/6029

DPP v. Fay (Michael Augustus) see DPP v. Doot

DPP v. Loving (Jeffrey Richard) see DPP v. Doot

DPP v. Shanahan (Thomas) see DPP v. Doot

DPP v. Watkins (Steven) [1989] Q.B. 821; [1989] 2 W.L.R. 966; [1989] 1 All E.R. 1126; (1989) 89 Cr. App. R. 112; (1990) 154 J.P. 370; [1989] R.T.R. 324; [1989] Crim. L.R. 453; (1990) 154 J.P.N. 266; (1989) 139 N.L.J. 365; (1989) 133 S.J. 514; *Times*, March 3, 1989; *Independent*, March 13 (C.S.); *Independent*, March 10, 1989; *Guardian*, March 3, 1989; *Daily Telegraph*, March 13, 1989, QBD. . . . . *Digested*, 89/**3259**: *Applied*, 94/3968, 95/4410, 98/5581: *Considered*, 94/986, 95/1246, 95/2955

DPP v. Watts (James Wesley) see DPP v. Doot

Drake and Scull Engineering Ltd v. NG Bailey Ltd 2000 G.W.D. 14-520, OH

Dramgate Ltd v. Tyne Dock Engineering Ltd 2000 S.C. 43; 1999 S.L.T. 1392; 1999 G.W.D. 31-1452, Ex Div; affirming 1999 S.C.L.R. 1; 1998 G.W.D. 31-1580, OH . . . *Digested*, 00/**5900**

Drew v. Rowan 2001 G.W.D. 34-1321, OH

Drummond v. Crowe 1998 G.W.D. 35-1840, HCJ Appeal

Drummond v. HM Advocate (Sentencing) 2000 G.W.D. 20-807, HCJ Appeal

Drummond v. Hunter 1948 J.C. 109; 1948 S.L.T. 526; 1948 S.L.T. (Notes) 57, HCJ Appeal . . . . *Digested*, 48/**4156**: *Followed*, 93/5473, 00/6270

Drummond v. Munro (Sentencing) 1998 G.W.D. 12-600, HCJ Appeal

Drummond v. Ritchie (Sentencing) 1998 G.W.D. 2-69, HCJ Appeal

Drummond, Petitioner 1998 S.L.T. 757; 1998 S.C.C.R. 42; 1998 G.W.D. 2-63, HCJ Appeal . . . . *Digested*, 98/**5648**

Drury v. HM Advocate 2001 S.L.T. 1013; 2001 S.C.C.R. 583; 2001 G.W.D. 26-1027, HCJ Appeal . . . . *Digested*, 01/**6336**

DSQ Property Co Ltd v. Lotus Cars Ltd [1987] 1 W.L.R. 127; [1987] B.C.L.C. 60; [1987] P.C.C. 157; (1987) 84 L.S.G. 735; (1987) 131 S.J. 195, Ch D . . . . *Digested*, 87/**2953**: *Applied*, 97/6031: *Approved*, 01/6242

DTL Gas Supplies Ltd v. Protan SRL 1999 S.L.T. 397; 1998 S.C.L.R. 990; 1998 G.W.D. 31-1578, 1 Div . . . . *Digested*, 98/**5501**

DTZ Debenham Thorpe v. I Henderson Transport Services 1995 S.C. 282; 1995 S.L.T. 553; 1995 S.C.L.R. 345, 1 Div . . . . *Digested*, 95/**6364**: *Followed*, 98/5510

Duckwari Plc (No.2), Re; *sub nom* Duckwari Plc *v.* Offerventure Ltd (No.2) [1999] Ch. 253; [1998] 3 W.L.R. 913; [1999] B.C.C. 11; [1998] 2 B.C.L.C. 315; (1998) 95(22) L.S.G. 28; (1998) 95(20) L.S.G. 36; (1998) 142 S.J.L.B. 163; *Times*, May 18, 1998, CA; reversing [1997] Ch. 201; [1997] 2 W.L.R. 48; [1997] B.C.C. 45; [1997] 2 B.C.L.C. 729; *Times*, July 23, 1996, Ch D . . . .   *Digested, 98/***685***: Applied, 00/5955*

Duckwari Plc *v.* Offerventure Ltd (No.2) see Duckwari Plc (No.2), Re
Duff *v.* East Dunbartonshire Council 1999 G.W.D. 22-1072, OH
Duff *v.* HM Advocate (Sentencing) 2001 G.W.D. 24-896, HCJ Appeal
Duff (Craig Charles) *v.* Stott 1999 S.C.C.R. 455; 1999 G.W.D. 21-1001, HCJ Appeal . . .   *Digested, 99/***5940***
Duffin *v.* HM Advocate 2000 J.C. 316; 2000 S.C.C.R. 224; 2000 G.W.D. 7-249, HCJ Appeal . . . .   *Digested, 00/***6014***
Duffy *v.* Donnelly (Sentencing) 1999 G.W.D. 12-544, HCJ Appeal
Duffy *v.* HM Advocate (Sentencing) 1998 G.W.D. 18-915, HCJ Appeal
Duffy *v.* HM Advocate (Sentencing) 1998 G.W.D. 16-781, HCJ Appeal
Duffy *v.* HM Advocate (Sentencing) 2001 G.W.D. 36-1373, HCJ Appeal
Duffy (Anthony) *v.* HM Advocate see Howitt (Alan John) *v.* HM Advocate
Duffy (Anthony) *v.* HM Advocate (Preliminary Appeal against Conviction) 2000 S.L.T. 441; 1999 G.W.D. 37-1791, HCJ . . . .   *Digested, 00/***6055***
Duffy (Anthony) *v.* HM Advocate (Sentencing) 2000 G.W.D. 8-291, HCJ Appeal
Duffy *v.* Lanarkshire Health Board 2001 G.W.D. 10-368, Ex Div; affirming 1999 S.L.T. 906; 1998 S.C.L.R. 1142; 1998 Rep. L.R. 119; 1998 G.W.D. 29-1507, OH . . . . . .   *Digested, 98/***5753***
Duffy *v.* Mairs 1998 S.L.T. 433; 1997 S.C.L.R. 590; 1997 Rep. L.R. (Quantum) 3; 1997 G.W.D. 7-288, OH . . . .   *Digested, 97/***6303***
Duffy *v.* McFadyen (Sentencing) 2000 G.W.D. 30-1172, HCJ Appeal
Duffy *v.* Mcglennan 1998 G.W.D. 19-998, HCJ Appeal
Duffy *v.* Secretary of State for Scotland 1999 S.L.T. 1372, OH . . . .   *Digested, 00/***6133***: Considered, 01/6398*

Duggan *v.* HM Advocate 1999 G.W.D. 28-1331, HCJ Appeal
Duke *v.* HM Advocate 2001 G.W.D. 21-795, HCJ Appeal
Duke *v.* HM Advocate (Sentencing) 1999 G.W.D. 37-1796, HCJ Appeal
Duke of Argyll *v.* Duchess of Argyll (No.2) 1962 S.C. (H.L.) 88; 1962 S.L.T. 333, HL; reversing 1962 S.C. 140; 1962 S.L.T. (Notes) 25, 1 Div . . . .   *Digested, 62/***3638***: Considered, 99/5990*

Duke of Argyll *v.* John Campbell see Dougall *v.* Duke of Argyll
Dukes *v.* McKay 2001 G.W.D. 7-258, Sh Ct (Grampian)
Dumbarton DC *v.* McLaughlin 2000 Hous. L.R. 16, Sh Ct (North Strathclyde) . . . .   *Digested, 00/***6438***
Dumfries and Galloway Council *v.* Scottish Ministers 2000 G.W.D. 27-1019, OH
Dumfries and Galloway Council *v.* W 2001 G.W.D. 14-533, Sh Ct (South Strathclyde)
Duncan *v.* British Coal Corp see Frost *v.* Chief Constable of South Yorkshire
Duncan *v.* Duncan 2000 G.W.D. 21-827, OH
Duncan *v.* Duncan 2000 G.W.D. 26-1012, OH
Duncan *v.* HM Advocate (Sentencing) 2000 G.W.D. 5-193, HCJ Appeal
Duncan *v.* Mckay 1998 G.W.D. 20-1050, HCJ Appeal
Duncan *v.* Strathclyde RC 1998 G.W.D. 35-1825, OH
Duncan *v.* Strathclyde RC (Preliminary Procedure) 1998 Rep. L.R. 62; 1998 G.W.D. 13-632, OH . . . .   *Digested, 98/***6108***
Duncanson *v.* South Ayrshire Council 1999 S.L.T. 519; 1998 S.C.L.R. 1015; 1999 Rep. L.R. 35; 1998 G.W.D. 36-1882, OH . . . .   *Digested, 99/***6221***
Dundas *v.* Kennedy (Sentencing) 2000 G.W.D. 30-1203, HCJ Appeal
Dundee City Council *v.* Bailey 1998 Hous. L.R. 93, Sh Ct . . . .   *Digested, 98/***5511***
Dundee City Council *v.* G 2000 Fam. L.R. 22, Sh Pr. . . . .   *Digested, 00/***6249***
Dundee City Council, Petitioners 1999 Fam. L.R. 13; 1998 G.W.D. 9-465, OH . . . .   *Digested, 99/***5999***
Dundee United Football Co Ltd *v.* Scottish Football Association 1998 S.L.T. 1244; 1998 G.W.D. 9-420, OH . . . .   *Digested, 98/***5413***
Dunn *v.* David A Hall Ltd (No.2) 1998 G.W.D. 21-1093, OH
Dunn *v.* McKay (Sentencing) 1998 G.W.D. 11-570, HCJ Appeal
Dunn *v.* Rigblast Energy Services Ltd 1999 S.L.T. 531; 1999 G.W.D. 1-8, OH . . . .   *Digested, 99/***5671***
Dunsmuir *v.* Stott 1999 G.W.D. 27-1270, HCJ Appeal
Durie *v.* Wyvern Structures Ltd see Cook *v.* Wyvern Structures Ltd (In Liquidation)
Duthie *v.* MacFish Ltd 2001 S.L.T. 833; 2001 S.C.L.R. 175; 2000 Rep. L.R. 103; 2000 G.W.D. 25-941, OH . . . .   *Digested, 00/***6165***
Duthie *v.* Watson 1997 Hous. L.R. 129, Lands Tr . . . .   *Digested, 98/***6042***
Dyce *v.* Aitchison 1985 S.L.T. 512, HCJ Appeal . . . .   *Digested, 85/***3931***: Applied, 99/5926*

Dyer *v.* Alternative Welding Services Ltd 2001 G.W.D. 32-1291, Sh Ct
Dyer *v.* Craiglaw Developments Ltd 1999 S.L.T. 1228; 1998 G.W.D. 39-2015, OH . . . . . .   *Digested, 99/***5687***
Dyer *v.* HM Advocate (Sentencing) 2001 G.W.D. 24-894, HCJ Appeal
Dyer *v.* O'Neill 2001 G.W.D. 16-593, Sh Ct (Lothian)
Dyer *v.* Stirling Water Seafield Ltd 2001 G.W.D. 27-1098, Sh Ct (Lothian)
Dyer *v.* Watson; *sub nom* HM Advocate *v.* K (A Juvenile); K (A Juvenile) *v.* HM Advocate; No. 1 of 2001, PC (Sc); reversing 2001 S.L.T. 751; 2001 S.C.C.R. 430; 2001 G.W.D. 14-544, HCJ Appeal . . . .   *Digested, 01/***6370***: Previous proceedings, 01/6368*

Dyker *v.* Napier (Sentencing) 2001 G.W.D. 25-927, HCJ Appeal
Dysart Peerage Case (1880-81) L.R. 6 App. Cas. 489, CA. . . . .   *Followed*, 98/5860

E (James) *v.* HM Advocate 2001 J.C. 115; 2001 S.C.C.R. 36, HCJ Appeal . . . .   *Digested*, 01/**6345**
Eadie Cairns *v.* Programmed Maintenance Painting Ltd 1987 S.L.T. 777, Ex Div . . . .   *Digested*, 87/**4892**:
              Distinguished, 92/6395, 99/5706: *Followed*, 97/5969:
                         Not followed, 94/6298
Ealing LBC *v.* Race Relations Board [1972] A.C. 342; [1972] 2 W.L.R. 71; [1972] 1 All
 E.R. 105; 70 L.G.R. 219; (1971) 116 S.J. 60; *Times,* December 17, 1971, HL;
 reversing [1971] 1 Q.B. 309; [1970] 3 W.L.R. 921; [1971] 1 All E.R. 424; 68
 L.G.R. 807; (1970) 114 S.J. 807, QBD. . . . .   *Digested*, 72/**28**:
         Applied, 76/939, 01/1065: *Considered*, 82/980, 98/5811: *Followed*, 87/3203
Earldom of Annandale and Hartfell; *sub nom* Annandale and Hartfell Peerage Claim
 [1986] A.C. 319; [1986] 2 W.L.R. 43; [1985] 3 All E.R. 577; 1986 S.L.T. (Lyon
 Ct.) 18, HL . . . .   *Digested*, 86/**4387**:
                          Referred to, 00/5970
Easson *v.* Dundee Teaching Hospitals NHS Trust 2000 S.L.T. 345; 2000 Rep. L.R. 7;
 1999 G.W.D. 40-1961, OH . . . .   *Digested*, 00/**6425**
Easson *v.* McFadyen (Sentencing) 2001 G.W.D. 12-413, HCJ Appeal
East Ayrshire Council *v.* Tait 1999 S.C.L.R. 566, Sh Ct . . . .   *Digested*, 99/**6275**
East Dunbartonshire Council *v.* Cameron 2000 Hous. L.R. 126, Sh Pr . . . .   *Digested*, 01/**6697**
East Dunbartonshire Council *v.* Mactaggart & Mickel Ltd see East Dunbartonshire
 Council *v.* Secretary of State for Scotland
East Dunbartonshire Council *v.* Secretary of State for Scotland; *sub nom* East
 Dunbartonshire Council *v.* Mactaggart & Mickel Ltd 1999 S.L.T. 1088; 1999
 S.C.L.R. 396; [1999] 1 P.L.R. 53; 1998 G.W.D. 40-2079, Ex Div . . . .   *Digested*, 99/**6410**:
                          Followed, 00/4499
East Lothian Council *v.* A; *sub nom* East Lothian Council *v.* M; East Lothian Council *v.*
 MA 2001 G.W.D. 31-1226, Ex Div
East Lothian Council *v.* Lumsden 2001 G.W.D. 11-397, OH
East Lothian Council *v.* M see East Lothian Council *v.* A
East Lothian Council *v.* MA see East Lothian Council *v.* A
East of Scotland Water Authority *v.* Livingstone; *sub nom* Livingstone *v.* East of Scotland
 Water Authority 1999 S.C. 65; 1999 S.L.T. 869; 1998 S.C.L.R. 1049; 1998
 Hous. L.R. 124; 1998 G.W.D. 36-1881, 1 Div; affirming 1997 S.L.T. (Lands Tr) 28;
 1998 Hous. L.R. 58, Lands Tr (Scot) . . . .   *Digested*, 99/**6272**:
              Considered, 00/6466: *Followed*, 00/6467, 01/6698
East of Scotland Water Authority *v.* Logan 2000 S.L.T. 28; 1999 G.W.D. 34-1653, Ex Div   *Digested*, 00/**6710**
East Staffordshire BC *v.* Fairless [1999] Env. L.R. 525; [1999] E.H.L.R. 128; (1999) 31
 H.L.R. 677; [1998] E.G.C.S. 140; (1998) 95(41) L.S.G. 46; *Times*, October 26,
 1998; *Independent*, October 19, 1998 (C.S.), QBD. . . . .   *Digested*, 98/**4049**:
                          Followed, 00/6602
Eaton *v.* West Lothian NHS Trust 1999 G.W.D. 23-1114, OH
Eaton Ltd *v.* King see King *v.* Eaton Ltd (No.2)
Eckle *v.* Germany (A/51) (1983) 5 E.H.R.R. 1, ECHR. . . . .   *Applied*, 98/3132,
        98/3150, 99/3130, 00/6074, 00/6090: *Considered*, 00/6083
Economic Documentation & Information Centre Ltd *v.* Aberdeenshire Council 2000
 G.W.D. 13-464, Sh Ct
Eddie *v.* Alpa Srl 2000 S.L.T. 1062; 2000 G.W.D. 11-397, OH. . . . .   *Digested*, 00/**5963**
Edgar *v.* HM Advocate (Sentencing) 2001 G.W.D. 39-1456, HCJ Appeal
Edinburgh City Council *v.* A 1999 G.W.D. 37-1785, Sh Ct (Lothian)
Edinburgh City Council *v.* Allan 1999 Hous. L.R. 3, Sh Ct . . . .   *Digested*, 99/**6273**
Edinburgh City Council *v.* Aslam 1999 Hous. L.R. 124; 1999 G.W.D. 35-1666, Sh Ct . . .   *Digested*, 00/**5982**
Edinburgh City Council *v.* B 1999 S.C.L.R. 694; 1999 Fam. L.R. 54; 1999 G.W.D. 13-
 585, Ex Div. . . . .   *Digested*, 99/**6057**
Edinburgh City Council *v.* Brown [1999] I.R.L.R. 208, EAT . . . .   *Digested*, 99/**6027**
Edinburgh City Council *v.* D 2001 S.L.T. (Sh Ct) 135; 2000 G.W.D. 31-1212, Sh Ct
 (Lothian)
Edinburgh City Council *v.* H 2000 G.W.D. 24-898, Sh Ct
Edinburgh City Council *v.* H (A Child) 2001 S.L.T. (Sh Ct) 51; 2000 G.W.D. 27-1027, Sh
 Ct (Lothian)
Edinburgh City Council *v.* J 1998 G.W.D. 40-2030, Sh Ct
Edinburgh City Council *v.* M 1996 S.L.T. (Sh Ct) 112; 1996 S.C.L.R. 779, Sh Pr . . . .   *Digested*, 96/**6603**:
                         Considered, 01/6514
Edinburgh City Council *v.* Rapley 2000 S.C. 78; [2000] O.P.L.R. 67; 1999 G.W.D. 39-
 1873, Ex Div . . . .   *Digested*, 00/**5899**
Edinburgh City Council *v.* S 2000 S.L.T. (Sh Ct) 147; 2000 S.C.L.R. 605; 1999 G.W.D.
 35-1655, Sh Ct (Lothian) . . . .   *Digested*, 00/**6247**
Edinburgh City Council *v.* Scottish Ministers 2001 S.C. 957; 2001 S.C.L.R. 891; 2001
 G.W.D. 18-709, 1 Div

Edinburgh City Council v. Secretary of State for Scotland; Revival Properties Ltd v.
Edinburgh City Council; Secretary of State for Scotland v. Revival Properties Ltd
[1997] 1 W.L.R. 1447; [1998] 1 All E.R. 174; 1998 S.C. (H.L.) 33; 1998 S.L.T.
120; 1997 S.C.L.R. 1112; [1997] 3 P.L.R. 71; [1998] J.P.L. 224; [1997] E.G.C.S.
140; (1997) 94(42) L.S.G. 31; (1997) 141 S.J.L.B. 228; [1997] N.P.C. 146; 1997
G.W.D. 33-1693; *Times*, October 31, 1997, HL; affirming in part 1996 S.C.L.R.
600, 2 Div. . . . .   *Digested*, 97/**6350**:
            Applied, 99/4178: *Considered*, 99/4218, 01/4743: *Followed*, 97/4116, 99/6411
Edinburgh City Council v. Swann 2001 S.L.T. (Sh Ct) 161; 2000 Hous. L.R. 123; 2000
G.W.D. 26-969, Sh Pr . . . .   *Digested*, 01/**6265**
Edinburgh Grain Ltd (In Liquidation) v. Marshall Food Group Ltd 1999 S.L.T. 15; 1997
G.W.D. 35-1746, OH . . . .   *Digested*, 99/**5791**
Edmond v. Miller 1998 G.W.D. 31-1630, HCJ Appeal
Edmond v. Reith (Continuation of Appeal) 1999 G.W.D. 14-635, HCJ Appeal
Edmond v. Reith (Social Inquiry Report) 1999 G.W.D. 40-1924, HCJ Appeal
Edmonds v. Donnelly (Sentencing) 2001 G.W.D. 19-727, HCJ Appeal
Edward v. Scottish Ministers 2001 S.C.L.R. 338; 2000 G.W.D. 11-403, OH
Edwards (Inspector of Taxes) v. Bairstow; Edwards (Inspector of Taxes) v. Harrison
[1956] A.C. 14; [1955] 3 W.L.R. 410; [1955] 3 All E.R. 48; 48 R. & I.T. 534; 36
T.C. 207; (1955) 34 A.T.C. 198; [1955] T.R. 209; (1955) 99 S.J. 558, HL;
reversing (1954) 47 R. & I.T. 340; (1954) 33 A.T.C. 131; [1954] T.R. 155, CA;
affirming 46 R. & I.T. 177; (1954) 33 A.T.C. 58; [1954] T.R. 65, QBD. . . . .   *Digested*, 55/**1287**:
            Applied, 56/4272, 59/1529, 62/1506, 66/6053, 67/1949, 71/999, 71/3949,
            74/319, 76/250, 77/2446, 81/1419, 82/476, 82/1617, 82/1647, 83/1225,
            83/1976, 84/460, 89/125, 89/3189, 90/754, 90/2675, 92/3364, 93/2274,
            94/262, 95/391, 95/876, 98/2137, 98/2140, 98/4622, 99/3066, 99/6471:
            Considered, 74/485, 74/1816, 74/1834, 74/1873, 74/2097, 81/2812, 81/3710,
            82/3282, 83/3412, 84/3218, 84/3253, 87/3193, 90/1864, 91/2373, 92/164,
            93/332, 93/3778, 94/7, 94/357, 94/639, 95/155, 95/896, 95/5020,
            98/4604, 99/4660, 99/4663: *Distinguished*, 56/4853
Edwards v. Butlins Ltd 1998 S.L.T. 500; 1997 G.W.D. 21-1052, 2 Div; reversing 1996
S.L.T. 1354, OH . . . .   *Digested*, 98/**5936**
Edwards v. Edwards 2001 G.W.D. 6-228, Sh Ct (Grampian)
Edwards (Inspector of Taxes) v. Harrison see Edwards (Inspector of Taxes) v. Bairstow
Edwards v. HM Advocate (Sentencing) 1998 G.W.D. 7-348, HCJ Appeal
Edwards (Peter Alan) v. Wheelan 1999 S.L.T. 917; 1998 S.C.C.R. 689; 1998 G.W.D. 37-
1938, HCJ Appeal. . . . .   *Digested*, 99/**5957**
EE Caledonia Ltd v. London Bridge Engineering Ltd (No.1); *sub nom* Elf Enterprise
Caledonia Ltd v. London Bridge Engineering Ltd (No.1) 1997 G.W.D. 33-1658;
Times, November 28, 1997, OH . . . .   *Digested*, 98/**5708**
EE Caledonia Ltd v. London Bridge Engineering Ltd (No.2); *sub nom* Elf Enterprise
(Caledonia) Ltd v. London Bridge Engineering Ltd (No.2) 1998 G.W.D. 2-86,
OH
Egginton v. Heywood (Sentencing) 2001 G.W.D. 12-431, HCJ Appeal
ELCAP v. Milne's Executor 1999 S.L.T. 58; 1998 G.W.D. 6-263, OH . . . .   *Digested*, 99/**5792**
Elder v. Cameron 2000 S.C. 331; 2000 G.W.D. 10-350, 2 Div.   *Digested*, 00/**5947**
Elf Enterprise Caledonia Ltd v. London Bridge Engineering Ltd (No.1) see EE Caledonia
Ltd v. London Bridge Engineering Ltd (No.1)
Elf Enterprise (Caledonia) Ltd v. London Bridge Engineering Ltd (No.2) see EE
Caledonia Ltd v. London Bridge Engineering Ltd (No.2)
Eli Lilly & Co v. Dowelhurst Ltd (Infringement Action) see Glaxo Group Ltd v.
Dowelhurst Ltd (Infringement Action)
Elitestone Ltd v. Davies see Elitestone Ltd v. Morris
Elitestone Ltd v. Morris; Elitestone Ltd v. Davies [1997] 1 W.L.R. 687; [1997] 2 All E.R.
513; (1998) 30 H.L.R. 266; [1997] 2 E.G.L.R. 115; [1997] 27 E.G. 116; [1997]
E.G.C.S. 62; (1997) 94(19) L.S.G. 25; (1997) 147 N.L.J. 721; (1997) 141 S.J.L.B.
113; [1997] N.P.C. 66; *Times*, May 7, 1997, HL; reversing (1997) 73 P. & C.R.
259; [1995] N.P.C. 142, CA. . . . .   *Digested*, 97/**3304**:
            Applied, 00/3880: *Distinguished*, 00/6537
Ellingham v. HM Advocate (Sentencing) 2001 G.W.D. 26-1047, HCJ Appeal
Ellingham v. McGlennan (Sentencing) 2000 G.W.D. 14-543, HCJ Appeal
Ellington v. HM Advocate 1999 G.W.D. 17-775, HCJ Appeal
Elliot v. HM Advocate 1999 G.W.D. 19-879, HCJ Appeal
Elliott v. Combustion Engineering Ltd 1997 S.C. 126; 1998 S.L.T. 253; 1997 S.C.L.R.
1144; 1997 G.W.D. 13-542, Ex Div . . . .   *Digested*, 97/**5723**
Elliott v. McFadyen (Sentencing) 2001 G.W.D. 1-28, HCJ Appeal
Elliott v. Reith 1999 G.W.D. 33-1603, HCJ Appeal
Elliott v. Vannet 1999 G.W.D. 22-1033, HCJ Appeal
Ellis v. HM Advocate 2001 G.W.D. 28-1128, HCJ Appeal
Ellis v. Lees 1998 G.W.D. 23-1170, HCJ Appeal
Ellis v. Stott 1999 G.W.D. 22-1054, HCJ Appeal
Elmford Ltd v. Glasgow City Council 2001 S.C. 267; 2001 S.L.T. 725; 2000 G.W.D. 29-
1157, OH . . . .   *Digested*, 01/**6681**
Elrick v. Higson (Sentencing) 1998 G.W.D. 11-577, HCJ Appeal

Elsby v. McFadyen 2000 S.C.C.R. 97; 1999 G.W.D. 40-1964, HCJ Appeal . . . .   *Digested*, 00/**6041**
Elsholz v. Germany [2000] 2 F.L.R. 486; [2000] 3 F.C.R. 385; [2000] Fam. Law 800,
    ECHR . . . .   *Digested*, 01/**3556**:
                                             Followed, 01/6510
Emeh v. Kensington and Chelsea and Westminster AHA [1985] Q.B. 1012; [1985] 2
    W.L.R. 233; [1984] 3 All E.R. 1044; (1984) 81 L.S.G. 2856; (1984) 128 S.J.
    705, CA . . . .   *Digested*, 85/**2322**:
                   Applied, 93/1416, 96/833, 00/1464: *Considered*, 86/422: *Followed*, 98/6116:
                                           Overruled, 00/4200
Emslie v. HM Advocate 1999 G.W.D. 7-338, HCJ Appeal
Enfield LBC v. Local Government Boundary Commission for England [1979] 3 All E.R.
    747; 78 L.G.R. 49, HL; affirming [1979] 1 All E.R. 950; 77 L.G.R. 119, CA;
    affirming [1978] 2 All E.R. 1073, QBD. . . . .   *Digested*, 79/**1679**:
                                             Approved, 98/5771
English v. North Lanarkshire Council 1999 S.C.L.R. 310; [1999] Eu. L.R. 701; 1999
    Rep. L.R. 53; 1999 G.W.D. 7-351, OH . . . .   *Digested*, 99/**6226**
Enriquez v. Urquhart 2001 S.L.T. 1320; 2001 G.W.D. 26-1051, HCJ Appeal . . . .   *Digested*, 01/**6536**
Eraker v. HM Advocate 1998 S.L.T. 499; 1997 G.W.D. 5-183, HCJ Appeal . . . .   *Digested*, 98/**5639**
Erskine v. Miller (Sentencing) 1998 G.W.D. 15-749, HCJ Appeal
Erven Warnink BV v. J Townend & Sons (Hull) Ltd (No.1) [1979] A.C. 731; [1979] 3
    W.L.R. 68; [1979] 2 All E.R. 927; [1979] F.S.R. 397; [1980] R.P.C. 31; 123 S.J.
    47, HL; reversing [1978] F.S.R. 473, CA; reversing [1978] F.S.R. 1, Ch D . . . . . .   *Digested*, 79/**2690**:
                  Applied, 80/2728, 84/3531, 94/4293, 95/4938, 95/6459, 98/3523:
                 Considered, 82/3263, 82/4426, 84/3534, 84/3536, 90/4319, 96/3637,
                   96/3638: *Followed*, 99/6314: *Referred to*, 93/3803, 94/4290, 97/4902
ES, Petitioner (Adoption) see S v. M (Consent: Missing Parent)
ES, Petitioner (Local Authority Care) see S v. Stirling Council (Local Authority Care)
Esk Frozen Foods Ltd v. New Hampshire Insurance Co Ltd 1998 S.L.T. 899; 1998
    G.W.D. 1-40, OH . . . .   *Digested*, 98/**6018**
Esmail v. Bank of Scotland (No.1) 1999 S.L.T. 1289; 1999 G.W.D. 22-1026, OH . . . .   *Digested*, 99/**5631**
Esmail v. Bank of Scotland (No.2) 2001 G.W.D. 39-1448, OH
Esso Petroleum Co Ltd v. Gardener 1998 G.W.D. 39-1994, OH
Esson v. HM Advocate 1998 G.W.D. 27-1373, HCJ Appeal
Ettinger v. McFadyen 2000 J.C. 583; 2000 S.C.C.R. 653; 2000 G.W.D. 22-851, HCJ
    Appeal . . . .   *Digested*, 00/**6099**
Euan Wallace & Partners v. Westscot Homes Plc 2000 S.L.T. 327; 1999 G.W.D. 17-806,
    OH . . . .   *Digested*, 00/**5988**
Eunson v. Braer Corp 1999 S.L.T. 1405; 1998 G.W.D. 29-1524, OH . . . .   *Digested*, 00/**6681**
Euro Properties Scotland Ltd v. Alam 2000 G.W.D. 23-896, OH
Eurocopy Rentals Ltd v. Streamline Shipping Agencies Ltd 2001 G.W.D. 28-1121, Sh Pr
European and International Investments Inc v. McLaren Building Services Ltd 2001 S.C.
    745; 2001 G.W.D. 12-405, OH . . . .   *Digested*, 01/**6294**
Europools Ltd v. Clydeside Steel Fabrications Ltd 2001 S.L.T. (Sh Ct) 91; 2001 G.W.D.
    5-178, Sh Pr
Evans v. Argus Healthcare (Glenesk) Ltd 2001 S.C.L.R. 117; 2001 G.W.D. 2-96, OH . . . .   *Digested*, 01/**6673**
Evans v. Chief Constable of Central Scotland Police 2001 G.W.D. 16-642, Sh Pr
Evans v. HM Advocate (Sentencing) 2000 G.W.D. 13-472, HCJ Appeal
Evans v. Howdle 1999 G.W.D. 26-1246, HCJ Appeal
Evans v. Lees 1998 G.W.D. 17-858, HCJ Appeal
Evans v. Reith (Sentencing) 1998 G.W.D. 6-295, HCJ Appeal
Ewen v. Hutchison 2001 G.W.D. 13-525, HCJ Appeal
Ewing v. Orr Ewing (No.2) see Ewing's Trustees v. Ewing
Ewing's Trustees v. Ewing; *sub nom* Ewing v. Orr Ewing (No.2) (1884-85) L.R. 10 App.
    Cas. 453; (1885) 13 R. (H.L.) 1, HL; reversing in part (1884) 11 R. 600, 1 Div . . .   *Applied*, 70/3588:
                                           Considered, 99/6396
Express & Echo Publications Ltd v. Tanton [1999] I.C.R. 693; [1999] I.R.L.R. 367;
    (1999) 96(14) L.S.G. 31; *Times*, April 7, 1999; *Independent* April 19, 1999 (C.S.),
    CA . . . .   *Digested*, 99/**2045**:
                                           Distinguished, 01/6468
Express Newspapers Plc, Petitioners 1999 J.C. 176; 1999 S.L.T. 644; 1999 S.C.C.R. 262;
    1999 G.W.D. 11-494, HCJ Appeal. . . . .   *Digested*, 99/**5856**:
                                  Previous proceedings, 98/5397

F (R) (An Infant), Re [1970] 1 Q.B. 385; [1969] 3 W.L.R. 853; [1969] 3 All E.R. 1101; 113 S.J.
    835, CA . . . .   *Digested*, 69/**1755**:
                                           Considered, 99/6056
F v. Constanda 1999 S.C. 125; 1999 S.L.T. 421; 1998 G.W.D. 36-1844, Ex Div . . . .   *Digested*, 99/**5610**
F v. F (Expenses: Motion for Increase) 2000 S.L.T. (Sh Ct) 106; 2000 Fam. L.R. 53;
    2000 G.W.D. 7-266, Sh Ct (Tayside). . . . .   *Digested*, 00/**6540**
F v. General Teaching Council for Scotland; *sub nom* F, Appellant 2001 G.W.D. 35-
    1343, 2 Div

F (A Parent) *v.* Kennedy (Reporter to the Children's Panel) (No.1) 1992 S.C. 28; 1993
    S.L.T. 1277; 1992 S.C.L.R. 139, 2 Div. . . . .   *Digested,* 92/**5729**:
                                                                      Considered, 01/6217
F Brown Plc *v.* Tarmac Construction (Contracts) Ltd 2000 G.W.D. 7-246, OH
F, Appellant see F *v.* General Teaching Council for Scotland
Fairbairn *v.* Fairbairn 1998 G.W.D. 23-1149, Sh Ct
Fairbairn *v.* Vayro 2001 S.L.T. 1167; 2000 G.W.D. 22-843, OH . . . .   *Digested,* 01/**6227**
Fairlie *v.* Perth and Kinross Healthcare NHS Trust 2001 G.W.D. 13-468, OH
Falconer *v.* HM Advocate 1998 G.W.D. 27-1377, HCJ Appeal
Falconer *v.* South Ayrshire Council (No.1) 2001 G.W.D. 10-321, OH
Falconer *v.* South Ayrshire Council (No.2) 2001 G.W.D. 22-820, OH
Falkirk Council *v.* Whyte [1997] I.R.L.R. 560, EAT . . . .   *Digested,* 98/**5819**
Fallimento la Pantofola D'Oro SpA *v.* Blane Leisure Ltd see La Pantofola D'Oro SpA *v.*
    Blane Leisure Ltd (No.2)
Farkan *v.* Immigration and Nationality Department 1999 G.W.D. 39-1897, OH
Farley *v.* HM Advocate 1998 G.W.D. 38-1967, HCJ Appeal
Farquhar *v.* HM Advocate 2000 G.W.D. 6-223, HCJ Appeal
Farquharson *v.* Vannet 1998 G.W.D. 35-1790, HCJ Appeal
Farrell (Paul Michael) *v.* HM Advocate 2001 S.C.C.R. 720; 2001 G.W.D. 26-1016, HCJ
    Appeal
Farrer *v.* Lothian Health Board 1999 G.W.D. 14-653, OH
Faulds *v.* HM Advocate 2000 G.W.D. 23-883, HCJ Appeal
Fay (Edmund Louis) *v.* HM Advocate 1989 S.L.T. 758; 1989 S.C.C.R. 373, HCJ Appeal.   *Digested,* 89/**4077**:
                                             Distinguished, 01/6392: *Referred to,* 95/5725
Fay *v.* Vannet 1998 J.C. 186; 1998 S.L.T. 1099; 1998 S.C.C.R. 327; 1998 G.W.D. 13-
    646, HCJ Appeal . . . .   *Digested,* 98/**5630**
FB and AB, Petitioners; *sub nom* B and B *v.* C 1999 Fam. L.R. 2; 1998 G.W.D. 29-1457,
    2 Div. . . . .   *Digested,* 99/**6059**
Feely *v.* HM Advocate 2000 G.W.D. 12-422, HCJ Appeal
Fellowes *v.* Friel (Sentencing) 1998 G.W.D. 15-758, HCJ Appeal
Fenning *v.* HM Advocate 1985 J.C. 76; 1985 S.L.T. 540, HCJ Appeal . . . .   *Digested,* 85/**3949**:
                                                     Considered, 98/5634
Fenwick *v.* Valentine 1994 S.L.T. 485; 1993 S.C.C.R. 892, HCJ Appeal . . . .   *Digested,* 93/**4989**:
                                         Applied, 99/5886: *Referred to,* 95/5693
Ferguson *v.* Crofters Commission 1999 S.L.C.R. 77, Land Ct (Full Ct). . . . .   *Digested,* 00/**6529**:
                                                        Applied, 00/6528
Ferguson *v.* Duncan 1998 G.W.D. 9-471, OH
Ferguson *v.* Hellinga 1977 S.L.C.R. App. 100, Land Ct (Div Ct). . . . .   *Considered,* 99/6319
Ferguson *v.* HM Advocate (Sentencing) 2000 G.W.D. 22-852, HCJ Appeal
Ferguson *v.* HM Advocate (Sentencing) 2001 G.W.D. 39-1460, HCJ Appeal
Ferguson (Raymond) *v.* HM Advocate 2000 S.C.C.R. 954; 2000 G.W.D. 32-1249,
    HCJ . . . .   *Digested,* 01/**6388**
Ferguson *v.* McFadyen 1999 G.W.D. 22-1051, HCJ Appeal
Ferguson *v.* McGlennan 1999 G.W.D. 2-90, HCJ Appeal
Ferguson *v.* Stringfellow 1999 G.W.D. 9-436, OH
Ferguson *v.* Wheelan 1999 G.W.D. 32-1557, HCJ Appeal
Ferguson & Menzies Ltd *v.* JW Soils Suppliers Ltd 1999 S.L.T. (Sh Ct) 20; 1998
    S.C.L.R. 1042, Sh Pr . . . .   *Digested,* 99/**5718**
Ferguson Shipbuilders Ltd *v.* Voith Hydro GmbH & Co KG 2000 S.L.T. 229; 1999
    G.W.D. 31-1500, OH . . . .   *Digested,* 00/**5962**
Ferns *v.* Hendron 2001 G.W.D. 33-1303, OH
Ferrari *v.* Zucconi 2001 G.W.D. 16-587, Sh Ct (Grampian) [*Ex rel.* Peterkins, Solicitors,
    100 Union Street, Aberdeen] . . . .   *Digested,* 01/**6261**
Ferrier *v.* McKay (Sentencing) 1998 G.W.D. 11-578, HCJ Appeal
Ferries *v.* Higson 1999 G.W.D. 22-1031, HCJ Appeal
Fforde *v.* Mckinnon 1998 S.C. 110; 1998 S.L.T. 902; 1997 S.C.L.R. 1129; 1997 G.W.D.
    39-1978, 2 Div . . . .   *Digested,* 98/**5423**
FH Bertling Ltd *v.* Tube Developments Ltd [1999] 2 Lloyd's Rep. 55; 1998 G.W.D. 39-
    1998, OH . . . .   *Digested,* 99/**5630**
Findlay *v.* Gilchrist (Sentencing) 2000 G.W.D. 39-1448, HCJ Appeal
Findlay *v.* HM Advocate (Sentencing) 1999 G.W.D. 40-1937, HCJ Appeal
Findlay *v.* Ruxton 1998 G.W.D. 40-2029, HCJ Appeal
Findlay *v.* Vannet (Sentencing) 2000 G.W.D. 33-1279, HCJ Appeal
Findlay (Alan Alexander) *v.* Walkingshaw 1998 S.C.C.R. 181; 1998 G.W.D. 8-410, HCJ
    Appeal . . . .   *Digested,* 98/**5686**
Finegan *v.* Heywood 2000 J.C. 444; 2000 S.L.T. 905; 2000 S.C.C.R. 460; 2000
    G.W.D. 15-633; *Times,* May 10, 2000, HCJ Appeal . . . .   *Digested,* 00/**6026**
Finlay (Barry Thomas) *v.* HM Advocate; *sub nom* HM Advocate *v.* Finlay (Barry
    Thomas) 1998 S.L.T. 1235; 1998 G.W.D. 8-364, HCJ Appeal; affirming 1998
    S.C.C.R. 103; 1998 G.W.D. 5-206, HCJ . . . .   *Digested,* 98/**5598**
Finlay *v.* Stott (Sentencing) 2001 G.W.D. 12-429, HCJ Appeal
Finlayson *v.* McFadyen (Sentencing) 2000 G.W.D. 39-1469, HCJ Appeal
Finlayson *v.* Stornoway Trust 2000 S.L.C.R. 158, Land Ct (Full Ct) . . . .   *Digested,* 01/**6745**
Finlayson *v.* Turnbull (No.3) 2001 G.W.D. 37-1412, OH

Finlayson v. Vannet 1999 G.W.D. 18-838, HCJ Appeal
Finn v. Vannet 1998 G.W.D. 31-1614, HCJ Appeal
Finnie v. HM Advocate (Sentencing) 1999 G.W.D. 12-551, HCJ Appeal
Finnigan v. HM Advocate 1998 G.W.D. 24-1212, HCJ Appeal
Finnon v. Brown 2000 G.W.D. 29-1161, HCJ Appeal
Fire Brigades Union v. Fraser [1998] I.R.L.R. 697; 1998 G.W.D. 21-1086, Ex Div;
   reversing [1997] I.R.L.R. 671, EAT . . . .   *Digested*, 99/**6042**
Firma Mund & Fester v. Firma Hatrex International Transport (6 W 53/92) see Mund &
   Fester v. Hatrex Internationaal Transport (C398/92)
First National Bank Plc v. Bank of Scotland 1999 S.L.T. (Sh Ct) 10, Sh Ct (Lothian) . . . .   *Digested*, 99/**6367**
First Quench Retailing Ltd v. McLeod 2001 S.L.T. 372; 2001 S.C.C.R. 154; [2001] 19
   S.L.L.P. 17; 2001 G.W.D. 1-68, HCJ Appeal . . . .   *Digested*, 01/**6789**
Fisher v. Gilchrist 1999 G.W.D. 14-666, HCJ Appeal
Fitchett v. McFadyen (Sentencing) 2000 G.W.D. 34-1312, HCJ Appeal
Fitzgerald v. Higson see Fitzgerald v. Vannet
Fitzgerald v. Lloyd Williams see Fitzgerald v. Williams
Fitzgerald v. Vannet; *sub nom* Fitzgerald v. Higson 2000 J.C. 413; 2000 S.C.C.R. 422;
   2000 G.W.D. 10-354, HCJ Appeal . . . .   *Digested*, 00/**6098**
Fitzgerald v. Williams; *sub nom* Fitzgerald v. Lloyd Williams; O'Regan v. Williams [1996]
   Q.B. 657; [1996] 2 W.L.R. 447; [1996] 2 All E.R. 171; [1996] C.L.C. 646; [1996]
   I.L.Pr. 275; *Times*, January 3, 1996; *Independent*, February 12, 1996 (C.S.), CA . .   *Digested*, 96/**726**:
                                    Applied, 00/439: *Distinguished*, 99/5701: *Followed*, 96/731
Fitzpatrick v. Coal Authority 2001 G.W.D. 7-282, Lands Tr (Scot)
Fitzpatrick v. Reith 1998 G.W.D. 19-977, HCJ Appeal
Fitzsimmons v. Cameron see Cameron v. Cameron
Flanagan v. HM Advocate (Sentencing) 1999 G.W.D. 36-1759, HCJ Appeal
Flanigan v. Napier 1999 G.W.D. 14-637, HCJ Appeal
Flaws v. International Oil Pollution Compensation Fund 2001 G.W.D. 40-1505, Ex Div;
   affirming 2001 S.L.T. 897; 2001 G.W.D. 10-331, OH . . . .   *Digested*, 01/**6298**
Fleming v. Colley 2000 G.W.D. 13-504, HCJ Appeal
Fleming v. Hingston (Sentencing) 1999 G.W.D. 12-578, HCJ Appeal
Fleming v. HM Advocate (Sentencing) 1998 G.W.D. 5-225, HCJ Appeal
Fleming v. HM Advocate (Sentencing) 1998 G.W.D. 17-857, HCJ Appeal
Fleming (Christopher Paul) v. Munro 1998 S.L.T. 144; 1997 S.C.C.R. 527; 1997 G.W.D.
   24-1196, HCJ Appeal . . . .   *Digested*, 97/**5888**
Fleming v. Secretary of State for Trade and Industry; *sub nom* Fleming v. Xaniar Ltd (In
   Liquidation) 1998 S.C. 8; 1998 S.L.T. 703; [1997] I.R.L.R. 682; 1997 G.W.D. 31-
   1582, 1 Div . . . .   *Digested*, 98/**5812**:
                                      Followed, 98/2188
Fleming v. Stirling Council 2001 S.L.T. 123; 2000 S.C.L.R. 779; 2000 Rep. L.R. 52;
   2000 G.W.D. 13-499, OH . . . .   *Digested*, 00/**6424**
Fleming v. Stott 1999 G.W.D. 14-643, HCJ Appeal
Fleming v. Xaniar Ltd (In Liquidation) see Fleming v. Secretary of State for Trade and
   Industry
Fleming's Trustee v. Fleming; *sub nom* Jackson v. Fleming 2000 S.C. 206; 2000 S.L.T.
   406; 2000 G.W.D. 2-61, Ex Div; affirming 1998 S.C.L.R. 1070; 1998 G.W.D. 38-
   1972, Sh Ct . . . .   *Digested*, 00/**6508**
Flockhart v. GA Properties Ltd 2001 G.W.D. 37-1410, OH
Floor Coverings International (UK) Ltd v. Brown 2000 G.W.D. 16-671, Sh Ct
Flynn v. Hamilton 1998 G.W.D. 27-1369, HCJ Appeal
FMC Corp v. Russell 1999 S.L.T. 99; 1998 G.W.D. 11-521, OH . . . .   *Digested*, 99/**5733**
Foley v. HM Advocate (Sentencing) 2001 G.W.D. 2-91, HCJ Appeal
Follen (Gary) v. HM Advocate [2001] UKPC D2; [2001] 1 W.L.R. 1668; 2001 S.C.
   (P.C.) 105; 2001 S.L.T. 774; 2001 S.C.C.R. 255; 2001 G.W.D. 12-409, PC (Sc) . .   *Digested*, 01/**6352**
Forbes v. Cawdor Estate Trustees; *sub nom* Forbes v. Duke of Roxburghe 1999 S.L.T.
   1283; 1999 G.W.D. 16-759, OH. . . . .   *Digested*, 99/**6029**
Forbes v. Duke of Roxburghe see Forbes v. Cawdor Estate Trustees
Ford v. HM Advocate 2001 G.W.D. 34-1325, HCJ
Ford v. McFadyen 2001 G.W.D. 31-1261, HCJ Appeal
Forest Property Trust v. Lindsay 1998 G.W.D. 31-1581, Sh Ct
Forkgen v. Stott 1999 G.W.D. 16-746, HCJ Appeal
Forman v. Forman 2001 G.W.D. 8-296, Sh Ct (Grampian)
Forrest v. Cooperative Wholesale Society Ltd 2001 S.L.T. (Sh Ct) 59; 2000 G.W.D. 18-
   721, Sh Ct (Glasgow)
Forrest v. Hendry 2000 S.C. 110; 1999 G.W.D. 39-1880, OH . . . .   *Digested*, 00/**5938**
Forrest-Lloyd v. Clydesdale Bank Plc 1999 S.L.T. (Sh Ct) 34; 1998 G.W.D. 34-1762,
   Sh Pr . . . .   *Digested*, 99/**6306**
Forrester v. Munro 1998 G.W.D. 25-1278, HCJ Appeal
Forrestor v. HM Advocate 2001 G.W.D. 19-723, HCJ Appeal
Forsyth v. HM Advocate 2000 S.C.C.R. 400; 2000 G.W.D. 9-321, HCJ Appeal. . . . . . .   *Digested*, 00/**6002**
Forsyth v. Miller 1998 G.W.D. 18-951, HCJ Appeal
Forsyth v. Royal Bank of Scotland Plc 2000 S.L.T. 1295; 2000 S.C.L.R. 61, OH . . . . . .   *Digested*, 00/**6669**:
                                      Followed, 00/6674
Forsyth v. Walker 1998 G.W.D. 19-966, HCJ Appeal

Foskett v. McClymont 1998 S.C. 96; 1998 S.L.T. 892; 1998 Rep. L.R. 13; 1997 G.W.D.
   36-1818, OH . . . . *Digested,* 98/**5430**
Foss v. Harbottle (1843) 2 Hare 461 . . . . *Applied,* 56/1149,
                  63/411, 64/465, 77/299, 78/241, 78/366: *Cited,* 01/6300: *Considered,* 68/445,
                  81/251, 82/330, 82/331, 85/3514, 85/3534, 91/414, 94/421, 96/1213,
                  96/5732: *Distinguished,* 63/397, 66/1409, 71/11770, 72/3459
Foster v. HM Advocate 1998 G.W.D. 20-1018, HCJ Appeal
Fourman v. Fourman 1998 G.W.D. 32-1638, Sh Ct
Fowler v. HM Advocate (Sentencing) 1998 G.W.D. 11-572, HCJ Appeal
Fowler v. Kelvin Central Buses Ltd 1998 G.W.D. 2-60, OH
Fox v. Glasgow City Council 2001 Rep. L.R. 59; 2001 G.W.D. 3-131, Sh Ct (Glasgow) . .   *Digested,* 01/**6820**
Fox v. HM Advocate 1998 G.W.D. 24-1215, HCJ Appeal
Fox (Richard John) v. HM Advocate 1998 J.C. 94; 1998 S.L.T. 335; 1998 S.C.C.R. 115;
   1998 G.W.D. 7-322, HCJ Appeal . . . .   *Digested,* 98/**5564**
Foy v. HM Advocate (Sentencing) 1998 G.W.D. 14-717, HCJ Appeal
Foy v. Howdle (Sentencing) 1998 G.W.D. 13-683, HCJ Appeal
Foy v. Monklands & Bellshill Hospital NHS Trust 2001 Rep. L.R. 130 (Note); 2001
   G.W.D. 17-684, OH
Frail v. Lees 1998 G.W.D. 27-1380, HCJ Appeal
Frame v. Fraioli 1998 G.W.D. 34-1736, OH
Framgord Ltd v. International Oil Pollution Compensation Fund 1999 G.W.D. 4-169, OH
Francois v. Secretary of State for the Home Department 1999 S.L.T. 79, OH . . . .   *Digested,* 99/**6287**
Franklin v. Chief Constable of Grampian Police 2001 Rep. L.R. 79; 2001 G.W.D. 19-
   752, OH . . . .   *Digested,* 01/**6815**
Frape v. Emreco International Ltd 2001 S.C.L.R. 997; 2001 G.W.D. 26-993, OH
Fraser v. BN Furman (Productions) Ltd [1967] 1 W.L.R. 898; [1967] 3 All E.R. 57;
   [1967] 2 Lloyd's Rep. 1; 2 K.I.R. 483; (1967) 111 S.J. 471, CA . . . .   *Digested,* 67/**2037**:
                  Applied, 79/1501, 94/2661, 94/2702, 94/2703, 99/6308:
                  Considered, 69/1828, 73/1695, 73/3756, 74/1882, 75/1882, 97/6167:
                  Followed, 89/2051, 98/6016
Fraser v. Greater Glasgow Health Board 1997 S.L.T. 554; 1996 S.C.L.R. 1108; 1996
   Rep. L.R. 58, OH . . . .   *Digested,* 97/**5933**:
                  Considered, 00/6424: *Not followed,* 99/3974
Fraser v. Higson 1998 G.W.D. 19-993, HCJ Appeal
Fraser v. Hingston 1998 G.W.D. 20-1014, HCJ Appeal
Fraser v. HM Advocate (Sentencing) 1998 G.W.D. 26-1302, HCJ Appeal
Fraser v. HM Advocate (Sentencing) 1998 G.W.D. 30-1570, HCJ Appeal
Fraser v. HM Advocate (Sentencing) 2001 G.W.D. 21-803, HCJ Appeal
Fraser (Celia Jane) v. HM Advocate 2000 S.C.C.R. 755; 2000 G.W.D. 26-978, HCJ
   Appeal . . . .   *Digested,* 01/**6390**
Fraser (George) v. HM Advocate see Boncza-Tomaszewksi v. HM Advocate
Fraser v. MacDonald (Sentencing) 2000 G.W.D. 29-1129, HCJ Appeal
Fraser v. McGlennan (Sentencing) 1998 G.W.D. 4-163, HCJ Appeal
Fraser v. Miller (Sentencing) 1998 G.W.D. 8-412, HCJ Appeal
Fraser v. Munro (Sentencing) 1998 G.W.D. 6-279, HCJ Appeal
Fraser v. Professional Golfers Association; *sub nom* Fraser, Petitioner 1999 S.C.L.R.
   1032; 1999 G.W.D. 22-1025, OH . . . .   *Digested,* 00/**5832**
Fraser v. Ruxton 1999 G.W.D. 27-1269, HCJ Appeal
Fraser v. Scott 2000 G.W.D. 32-1250, Sh Ct
Fraser v. Spencer 2001 S.L.C.R. 116, Land Ct (Div Ct)
Fraser v. State Hospitals Board for Scotland 2001 S.L.T. 1051; 2001 S.C.C.R. 357;
   2000 Rep. L.R. 94; 2000 G.W.D. 25-952; *Times,* September 12, 2000, OH . . . .   *Digested,* 00/**6582**
Fraser v. Vannet (Sentencing) 1999 G.W.D. 4-225, HCJ Appeal
Fraser Trading Co v. Bank of Scotland Plc 2000 G.W.D. 40-1475, Ex Div; affirming 1999
   G.W.D. 18-820, OH
Fraser, Petitioner see Fraser v. Professional Golfers Association
Freebairn v. Chief Constable of Strathclyde 1999 S.L.T. 520; 1998 S.C.L.R. 1013; 1998
   G.W.D. 30-1569, OH . . . .   *Digested,* 98/**5737**
Freeburn v. Crowe 1998 G.W.D. 27-1371, HCJ Appeal
Freeman & Lockyer v. Buckhurst Park Properties (Mangal) Ltd [1964] 2 Q.B. 480;
   [1964] 2 W.L.R. 618; [1964] 1 All E.R. 630; 108 S.J. 96, CA . . . .   *Digested,* 64/**444**:
                  Applied, 72/525, 73/420, 74/30, 77/2890, 84/27, 85/21, 94/554, 95/775:
                  Considered, 67/33, 72/1649, 80/14, 83/202, 00/4024:
                  Distinguished, 94/362: *Followed,* 94/5374, 01/6105
Freeport Leisure Plc v. West Lothian Council 1999 S.C. 215; 1999 S.L.T. 452; 1998
   G.W.D. 38-1977, 2 Div; affirming 1998 G.W.D. 28-1450, OH . . . .   *Digested,* 99/**6409**
French v. Kerr McGee Oil (UK) Plc (No.1) 1999 G.W.D. 2-79, OH
French v. Kerr McGee Oil (UK) Plc (No.2) 2000 G.W.D. 5-181, OH
Frew v. HM Advocate (Sentencing) 2000 G.W.D. 19-751, HCJ Appeal
Friedrich v. Friedrich 78 F.3d 1060, US Ct . . . .   *Approved,* 97/387:
                  Followed, 98/5842
Friel v. Carnegie 1999 G.W.D. 30-1410, HCJ Appeal
Friel (Paul Patrick Peter) v. HM Advocate 1998 S.L.T. 1327; 1998 S.C.C.R. 47; 1998
   G.W.D. 2-65, HCJ . . . .   *Digested,* 98/**5634**

Friel *v.* Scott (John) 2000 J.C. 86; 1999 S.L.T. 1384; 1999 G.W.D. 30-1413, HCJ
Appeal . . . . *Digested,* 00/**6037**
Friel *v.* Thorley 1997 S.C.C.R. 694, Sh Ct . . . . *Digested,* 98/**5554**
Frost *v.* Chief Constable of South Yorkshire; White *v.* Chief Constable of South
Yorkshire; Duncan *v.* British Coal Corp [1999] 2 A.C. 455; [1998] 3 W.L.R.
1509; [1999] 1 All E.R. 1; [1999] I.C.R. 216; [1999] I.R.L.R. 110; (1999) 45
B.M.L.R. 1; (1999) 96(2) L.S.G. 28; (1998) 148 N.L.J. 1844; (1999) 143
S.J.L.B. 51; *Times,* December 4, 1998; *Independent,* December 9, 1998, HL;
reversing [1998] Q.B. 254; [1997] 3 W.L.R. 1194; [1997] 1 All E.R. 540; [1997]
I.R.L.R. 173; (1997) 33 B.M.L.R. 108; (1996) 146 N.L.J. 1651; *Times,* November
6, 1996; *Independent,* November 5, 1996, CA; reversing *Times,* July 3, 1995,
QBD . . . . *Digested,* 99/**4059**:
Applied, 01/4462: *Considered,* 97/2615, 00/4213, 00/4220:
Followed, 99/3980: *Referred to,* 00/6598
Frost (Stephen John Charles) *v.* McGlennan 1998 J.C. 263; 1998 S.L.T. 1284; 1998
S.C.C.R. 573; 1998 G.W.D. 26-1296, HCJ. . . . . *Digested,* 98/**5624**
Frost *v.* Unity Trust Bank Plc (No.1) [1998] B.P.I.R. 459, 1 Div . . . . *Digested,* 98/**6013**
Frost *v.* Unity Trust Bank Plc (No.2) 1999 S.C. 402; 1999 G.W.D. 8-397, Ex Div 1997
S.L.T. 1358; 1997 G.W.D. 16-705, OH . . . . *Digested,* 99/**5690**
Frost *v.* Unity Trust Bank Plc (No.3) 2000 S.L.T. 952; 2000 S.C.L.R. 171; 1999 G.W.D.
20-954, OH . . . . *Digested,* 00/**5914**
Frost *v.* Unity Trust Bank Plc (No.4) 2000 G.W.D. 23-888, OH
Frost *v.* Unity Trust Bank Plc (No.5) 2000 G.W.D. 32-1251, OH
Froud *v.* HM Advocate (Sentencing) 1999 G.W.D. 37-1808, HCJ Appeal
Fugaccia *v.* Mcleod 1998 G.W.D. 34-1752, HCJ Appeal
Fugro-Udi Ltd *v.* Angiolini 2001 G.W.D. 16-645, HCJ Appeal
Fullarton Computer Industries Ltd *v.* Central Arbitration Committee [2001] I.R.L.R. 752;
2001 G.W.D. 23-864, OH
Fulton *v.* Fulton 1998 S.L.T. 1262; 2000 Fam. L.R. 8; 1998 G.W.D. 15-768, OH. . . . . *Digested,* 98/**5857**
Fulton (Stewart Farquharson) *v.* HM Advocate 2000 J.C. 62; 1999 S.L.T. 1423; 1999
S.C.C.R. 851; 1999 G.W.D. 30-1406, HCJ Appeal . . . . *Digested,* 00/**6003**
Furber *v.* Furber (No.1) 1999 S.L.T. (Sh Ct) 26; 1999 S.C.L.R. 145; 1998 Fam. L.R.
108, Sh Pr. . . . . *Digested,* 99/**5693**:
Not followed, 99/5692
Furber *v.* Furber (No.2) 1999 S.L.T. (Sh Ct) 67; 1999 S.C.L.R. 1152; 1999 G.W.D. 19-
866, Sh Pr . . . . *Digested,* 99/**5694**:
Not followed, 00/5923
Futter *v.* Bryceland 2000 G.W.D. 9-339, OH
Fyfe (Edward Irvine) *v.* HM Advocate 1998 S.L.T. 195; 1997 S.C.C.R. 602; 1997 G.W.D.
28-1407, HCJ Appeal . . . . *Digested,* 97/**5763**
Fyfe (Kevin) *v.* HM Advocate 1998 S.L.T. 682; 1997 S.C.C.R. 755, HCJ Appeal. . . . . . . *Digested,* 98/**5699**
Fyfe *v.* Walker (Sentencing) 1998 G.W.D. 16-828, HCJ Appeal

G *v.* G 1999 Fam. L.R. 30; 1999 G.W.D. 10-447, Sh Pr . . . . *Digested,* 99/**6067**
G *v.* G (Divorce: Transfer of Joint Tenancy) 2001 Fam. L.R. 99; 2001 Hous. L.R. 99;
2001 G.W.D. 17-677, Sh Ct (Grampian)
G *v.* Glasgow City Council 2001 G.W.D. 25-965, OH
G *v.* H 1999 G.W.D. 24-1125, Sh Ct
G *v.* HM Advocate 1998 G.W.D. 26-1325, HCJ Appeal
G *v.* M; *sub nom* G, Petitioners 1999 S.C. 439; 1999 S.C.L.R. 648; 1999 Fam. L.R. 64;
1999 G.W.D. 12-529, 2 Div. . . . . *Digested,* 99/**6058**
G *v.* Scanlon 1999 S.C. 226; 1999 S.L.T. 707; 2000 S.C.L.R. 1; 1999 G.W.D. 8-365, Ex
Div . . . . *Digested,* 99/**6071**
G *v.* Templeton 1998 S.C.L.R. 180, Sh Pr . . . . *Digested,* 98/**5850**
G *v.* United Kingdom (Children: Right of Contact) (32346/96) [2001] 1 F.L.R. 153;
[2000] 3 F.C.R. 193; (2001) 33 E.H.R.R. 1; 2001 Fam. L.R. 103; [2000] Fam.
Law 880; *Times,* November 1, 2000, ECHR . . . . *Digested,* 00/**3232**
G Dunlop & Sons, Noter 2000 G.W.D. 35-1328, OH
G&H Construction (Aberdeen) Ltd *v.* Cargill 2000 G.W.D. 16-635, Sh Ct
G&S Properties *v.* Francis 2001 S.L.T. 934; 2001 S.C.L.R. 827; 2001 G.W.D. 21-782, Ex
Div . . . . *Digested,* 01/**6104**
G&S Properties *v.* Henderson 1999 G.W.D. 6-283, OH
G, Petitioners see G *v.* M
GA Estates Ltd *v.* Caviapen Trustees Ltd (No.1) 1993 S.L.T. 1037, OH . . . . *Digested,* 93/**4761**:
Applied, 01/6826
Gaelic Assignments Ltd *v.* Sharp; *sub nom* Gaelic Assignments Ltd *v.* Sharpe 2001
S.L.T. 914; 2001 G.W.D. 5-175, OH . . . . *Digested,* 01/**6722**
Gaelic Assignments Ltd *v.* Sharpe see Gaelic Assignments Ltd *v.* Sharp
Gaffney *v.* Kennedy 1998 G.W.D. 40-2063, HCJ Appeal
Gailey *v.* Gailey 2001 G.W.D. 40-1493, Ex Div
Gair (Walter) *v.* HM Advocate (Sentencing) 2001 G.W.D. 36-1384, HCJ Appeal
Gala Leisure Ltd *v.* Glasgow Licensing Board [2000] 15 S.L.L.P. 16; 1999 G.W.D. 33-
1561, OH. . . . . *Digested,* 00/**6555**

Galbraith *v.* Gilchrist 2001 G.W.D. 31-1231, HCJ Appeal
Galbraith (Kim Louise) *v.* HM Advocate (No.1) 2001 S.L.T. 465; 2000 S.C.C.R. 935;
    2000 G.W.D. 31-1223, HCJ Appeal . . . .   *Digested,* 01/**6328**
Galbraith (Kim Louise) *v.* HM Advocate (No.2) 2001 G.W.D. 20-759, HCJ Appeal
Galbraith (Kim Louise) *v.* HM Advocate (No.3) 2001 S.L.T. 953; 2001 S.C.C.R. 551;
    2001 G.W.D. 25-924, HCJ . . . .   *Digested,* 01/**6335**
Galbraith *v.* MacLeod (Sentencing) 1998 G.W.D. 16-779, HCJ Appeal
Galbraith *v.* Vannet (Sentencing) 1998 G.W.D. 5-215, HCJ Appeal
Galbraith's Curator ad Litem *v.* Stewart (No.2) 1998 S.L.T. 1305; 1998 Rep. L.R. 64;
    1998 G.W.D. 8-398, OH . . . .   *Digested,* 98/**6107**
Gallacher (Paul) *v.* Carnegie 1997 S.C.C.R. 667; 1997 G.W.D. 35-1813, HCJ Appeal   . . .   *Digested,* 98/**5688**
Gallacher *v.* Heywood (Sentencing) 2001 G.W.D. 1-27, HCJ Appeal
Gallacher *v.* HM Advocate 1999 G.W.D. 13-603, HCJ Appeal
Gallacher *v.* Lanarkshire Health Board 1999 S.L.T. 166; 1998 S.C.L.R. 592; 1998 Rep.
    L.R. 97; 1998 G.W.D. 16-805, OH . . . .   *Digested,* 98/**5742**
Gallacher *v.* McGlennan 1999 G.W.D. 18-842, HCJ Appeal
Gallacher *v.* Score (Sentencing) 2001 G.W.D. 17-674, Sh Ct (Tayside)
Gallacher *v.* Stirling Council 2001 S.L.T. 94; 2000 Hous. L.R. 52; 2000 G.W.D. 17-691,
    OH . . . .   *Digested,* 00/**6455**
Gallagher *v.* Dick see Miller *v.* Dick (William)
Gallagher *v.* Ferns 1998 S.L.T. (Sh Ct) 79; 1998 G.W.D. 4-186, Sh Pr . . . .   *Digested,* 98/**6178**
Gallagher *v.* HM Advocate 1998 G.W.D. 28-1408, HCJ Appeal
Gallagher *v.* HM Advocate (Sentencing) 2001 G.W.D. 25-932, HCJ Appeal
Gallagher (John) *v.* HM Advocate 2000 S.C.C.R. 634; 2000 G.W.D. 15-580, HCJ . . . .   *Digested,* 00/**6004**
Gallagher *v.* Lanarkshire Health Board 2001 G.W.D. 21-817, OH
Gallagher *v.* McGlennan 1999 G.W.D. 35-1680, HCJ Appeal
Gallagher *v.* Vannet 1998 G.W.D. 20-1022, HCJ Appeal
Galloway *v.* Clark 2001 S.C.C.R. 734; 2001 G.W.D. 26-1018, HCJ Appeal
Galloway *v.* Glasgow City Council 2001 Hous. L.R. 59; 2001 G.W.D. 16-647, Sh Ct
    (Glasgow) . . . .   *Digested,* 01/**6695**
Galloway (or Hunter) *v.* Hanley see Hunter *v.* Hanley
Galloway *v.* Heywood 1998 G.W.D. 28-1416, HCJ Appeal
Galt *v.* Watt (Sentencing) 2001 G.W.D. 21-801, HCJ Appeal
Gamble *v.* Unison Scotland 1998 S.L.T. (Sh Ct) 5; 1997 S.C.L.R. 803; 1997 G.W.D. 15-
    639, Sh Pr . . . .   *Digested,* 97/**5651**
Gammie *v.* Crofters Commission 1999 S.L.C.R. 49, Land Ct . . . .   *Digested,* 99/**6320**
Gannon *v.* HM Advocate 2000 G.W.D. 24-907, HCJ Appeal
Garden *v.* HM Advocate (Sentencing) 2001 G.W.D. 12-417, HCJ Appeal
Garden (Philip George) *v.* HM Advocate 1999 S.L.T. 1352; 1999 G.W.D. 19-875, HCJ
    Appeal . . . .   *Digested,* 00/**6111**
Gardiner *v.* HM Advocate (Sentencing) 1999 G.W.D. 16-763, HCJ Appeal
Gardiner *v.* Jacques Vert Plc 2001 G.W.D. 38-1433, OH
Gardiner *v.* Munro (Sentencing) 1998 G.W.D. 6-278, HCJ Appeal
Gardner *v.* MacNeal 2001 Hous. L.R. 8; 2000 G.W.D. 38-1430, Ex Div . . . .   *Digested,* 01/**6675**
Garfoot *v.* HM Advocate 1998 G.W.D. 20-1027, HCJ Appeal
Garrow *v.* HM Advocate 2000 S.C.C.R. 772; 2000 G.W.D. 26-975, HCJ Appeal . . . . . .   *Digested,* 01/**6359**:
                                   Applied, 01/6349
Garrow (Ian) *v.* HM Advocate 1999 J.C. 209; 1999 S.L.T. 1202; 1999 S.C.C.R. 282;
    1999 G.W.D. 11-497, HCJ Appeal . . . .   *Digested,* 99/**5852**
Gasparini *v.* HM Advocate 1998 G.W.D. 26-1315, HCJ Appeal
Gate *v.* Reith (Sentencing) 1998 G.W.D. 2-96, HCJ Appeal
Gatti *v.* Lees (Sentencing) 1998 G.W.D. 4-193, HCJ Appeal
Gaul *v.* Deerey 2000 S.C.L.R. 407; 1999 G.W.D. 33-1593, OH . . . .   *Digested,* 00/**6697**
Gauld *v.* HM Advocate (Sentencing) 1998 G.W.D. 3-113, HCJ Appeal
Gault *v.* Gault 2000 G.W.D. 40-1474, Sh Ct (Grampian)
Gawthorpe *v.* Stewart 2000 G.W.D. 39-1461, OH
Gayne *v.* Vannet 2000 J.C. 51; 1999 S.L.T. 1292; 2000 S.C.C.R. 5; 1999 G.W.D. 30-
    1415, HCJ Appeal . . . .   *Digested,* 99/**5913**:
                                   Considered, 00/6089
GB & AM Anderson *v.* White 2000 S.L.T. 37; 1998 G.W.D. 33-1721, OH . . . .   *Digested,* 00/**6601**
Geddes *v.* Dickson 2001 J.C. 69; 2000 S.C.C.R. 1007; 2000 G.W.D. 35-1335, HCJ
    Appeal . . . .   *Digested,* 01/**6338**
Geddes *v.* HM Advocate 1999 G.W.D. 27-1277, HCJ Appeal
Gellatly *v.* Heywood 1997 J.C. 171; 1998 S.L.T. 287; 1997 S.C.C.R. 300; 1997 G.W.D.
    12-499, HCJ Appeal . . . .   *Digested,* 97/**5840**
Gemmell *v.* Bank of Scotland 1998 S.C.L.R. 144, Sh Ct . . . .   *Digested,* 98/**6101**
Gentles *v.* HM Advocate 1998 G.W.D. 34-1747, HCJ Appeal
George *v.* George C Peebles & Son 1998 S.L.T. 685; 1998 G.W.D. 8-388; 1998 G.W.D.
    8-401, OH . . . .   *Digested,* 98/**5709**:
                                   Overruled, 98/5710
George *v.* HM Advocate 1998 G.W.D. 18-911, HCJ Appeal
George *v.* Vannet 1999 G.W.D. 18-856, HCJ Appeal
George Martin (Builders) Ltd *v.* Jamal; *sub nom* Martin (George) Builders Ltd *v.* Jamal
    2001 S.L.T. (Sh Ct) 119; 2000 G.W.D. 25-924, Sh Ct (Tayside) . . . .   *Digested,* 01/**6258**

Gerry v. Higson (Sentencing) 2001 G.W.D. 25-951, HCJ Appeal
Gibb v. HM Advocate (Sentencing) 1998 G.W.D. 14-705, HCJ Appeal
Gibb v. HM Advocate (Sentencing) 2001 G.W.D. 18-698, HCJ Appeal
Gibbs v. Ruxton 2000 J.C. 258; 2000 S.L.T. 310; 2000 S.C.C.R. 136; 2000 G.W.D. 1-15, HCJ Appeal . . . . *Digested*, 00/**6095**
Gibbs Palmer (Holdings) Ltd v. Gibbs Palmer (Midland) Ltd 1999 G.W.D. 36-1730, OH
Gibney v. HM Advocate (Sentencing) 2001 G.W.D. 16-631, HCJ Appeal
Gibson v. Chief Constable of Strathclyde see Gibson v. Orr
Gibson v. Gilchrist 1999 G.W.D. 26-1262, HCJ Appeal
Gibson v. HM Advocate (Sentencing) 1998 G.W.D. 33-1697, HCJ Appeal
Gibson v. HM Advocate (Sentencing) 1998 G.W.D. 9-441, HCJ Appeal
Gibson v. HM Advocate (Sentencing) 1998 G.W.D. 36-1859, HCJ Appeal
Gibson (David Blair) v. HM Advocate 2001 J.C. 125; 2001 S.L.T. 591; 2001 S.C.C.R. 51; 2001 G.W.D. 3-117, HCJ Appeal . . . . *Digested*, 01/**6361**
Gibson v. McAndrew Wormald & Co Ltd 1998 S.L.T. 562; 1997 G.W.D. 39-1979, OH . . *Digested*, 98/**5456**
Gibson v. O'Donnell (Sentencing) 1998 G.W.D. 12-596, HCJ Appeal
Gibson v. Orr; *sub nom* Gibson v. Chief Constable of Strathclyde 1999 S.C. 420; 1999 S.C.L.R. 661; 1999 Rep. L.R. 78; 1999 G.W.D. 11-520; *Times*, May 11, 1999, OH . . *Digested*, 99/**6370**
Gibson v. Pickfords Removals Ltd 2000 Rep. L.R. 90; 2000 G.W.D. 15-627, OH . . . . . . *Digested*, 00/**6167**
Gibson, Petitioner (Medical Records) 1984 S.L.T. 61, OH . . . . *Digested*, 85/**4081**:
Considered, 99/5990
Gibson, Petitioner (Sentencing) 1998 G.W.D. 29-1515, HCJ Appeal
Giff v. Carnegie (Sentencing) 1998 G.W.D. 11-539, HCJ Appeal
Giff v. Munro 1998 G.W.D. 23-1163, HCJ Appeal
Gilbert v. Buchanan 1998 S.L.T. 303; 1997 S.C.C.R. 642, HCJ Appeal . . . . *Digested*, 97/**5885**
Gilbride v. Blythswood Shipbuilding Co Ltd 2001 G.W.D. 23-849, OH
Gilchrist v. McCaul (Sentencing) 2000 G.W.D. 36-1359, Sh Ct (North Strathclyde)
Gilchrist v. Scott 2000 S.C.C.R. 28, HCJ Appeal . . . . *Digested*, 00/**6096**
Gilchrist v. Vannet (Sentencing) 1998 G.W.D. 4-177, HCJ Appeal
Gilday v. HM Advocate (Sentencing) 2000 G.W.D. 13-479, HCJ Appeal
Gilday v. Miller; *sub nom* Gilday v. Ritchie 2000 J.C. 133; 2000 S.C.C.R. 53; 1999 G.W.D. 32-1528, HCJ Appeal . . . . *Digested*, 00/**6103**
Gilday v. Ritchie see Gilday v. Miller
Gilfillan v. HM Advocate (Sentencing) 2000 G.W.D. 34-1317, HCJ Appeal
Gilfillan v. Lees 1999 G.W.D. 21-988, HCJ Appeal
Gillan v. Normand see Gillan v. Vannet
Gillan v. Vannet; *sub nom* Gillan v. Normand 1997 S.L.T. 1299; 1997 G.W.D. 11-474, HCJ Appeal . . . . *Digested*, 98/**5701**
Gillanders v. Westminster Motor Insurance Association Ltd 2000 G.W.D. 10-364, Sh Ct
Gillespie (Kevin) v. Brown 1999 S.L.T. 1115; 1999 G.W.D. 22-1036, HCJ Appeal . . . . . . *Digested*, 99/**5823**
Gillespie v. HM Advocate (Sentencing) 2001 G.W.D. 16-607, HCJ Appeal
Gillies v. British Railways Board 1998 G.W.D. 31-1624, OH
Gillies v. HM Advocate (Sentencing) 2000 G.W.D. 4-160, HCJ Appeal
Gillies v. Vannet 1999 G.W.D. 9-417, HCJ Appeal
Gillingham v. HM Advocate (Sentencing) 1998 G.W.D. 2-74, HCJ Appeal
Gillingham v. HM Advocate (Sentencing) 1999 G.W.D. 7-340, HCJ Appeal
Gillon v. Friel 1998 G.W.D. 40-2058, HCJ Appeal
Gillon v. HM Advocate 1998 G.W.D. 20-1017, HCJ Appeal
Gilmartin v. HM Advocate (Sentencing) 1998 G.W.D. 14-713, HCJ Appeal
Gilmour v. HM Advocate (Sentencing) 1998 G.W.D. 12-601, HCJ Appeal
Gilmour (Joseph Gary) v. HM Advocate (Evidence) 1994 S.C.C.R. 133, HCJ Appeal . . . *Digested*, 94/**5535**:
Referred to, 00/6013
Gilmour (Raymond) v. HM Advocate 1982 S.C.C.R. 590, HCJ Appeal . . . . *Digested*, 83/**4191**:
Applied, 00/6044
Gilmour v. Master of Lovat 1979 S.L.T. (Land Ct.) 2, Land Ct . . . . *Digested*, 79/**3456**:
Considered, 99/6319
Girvan v. Girvan 1988 S.L.T. 866; 1988 S.C.L.R. 493, 1 Div . . . . *Digested*, 88/**3771**:
Applied, 98/5847: *Distinguished*, 00/6266
Girvan v. Inverness Farmers Dairy (No.2) 1998 S.C. (H.L.) 1; 1998 S.L.T. 21; 1998 S.C.L.R. 72; 1997 G.W.D. 37-1883; *Times*, December 15, 1997, HL; affirming 1996 S.C. 134; 1996 S.L.T. 631, Ex Div . . . . *Digested*, 98/**5478**
Gizzi v. Tudhope 1983 S.L.T. 214; 1982 S.C.C.R. 442, HCJ Appeal . . . . *Digested*, 83/**4403**:
Doubted, 99/5833
GJ Van Der Bent BV v. Young & McMillan Plc; *sub nom* GJ Van Der Bent BV v. Young & MacMillan Plc 2000 S.L.T. (Sh Ct) 74; 2000 G.W.D. 14-560, Sh Pr . . . . *Digested*, 00/**6636**
Glancy v. HM Advocate 2001 S.C.C.R. 385; 2001 G.W.D. 15-578, HCJ Appeal . . . . *Digested*, 01/**6386**
Glancy (Alan James) v. Lees; *sub nom* Glancy v. McFadyen 1999 S.C.C.R. 726; 1999 G.W.D. 29-1366, HCJ Appeal . . . . *Digested*, 00/**6022**
Glancy v. McFadyen see Glancy (Alan James) v. Lees
Glasgow and Newcastle and Middlesborough Steam Shipping Co v. Watson (1873) 1 R. 189, 1 Div . . . . *Followed*, 01/6298
Glasgow City Council v. Al-Abassi 2001 Hous. L.R. 23; 2001 G.W.D. 8-298, Sh Ct (Glasgow) . . . . *Digested*, 01/**6696**
Glasgow City Council v. B 2000 S.L.T. (Sh Ct) 167, Sh Ct (Glasgow) . . . . *Digested*, 01/**6512**

Glasgow City Council *v.* Cannell 2000 S.L.T. 1023; 1999 S.C.L.R. 385; 1998 G.W.D.
33-1722, OH . . . . *Digested,* 99/**6405**
Glasgow City Council *v.* Caststop Ltd 2001 G.W.D. 28-1137, OH
Glasgow City Council *v.* Cavanagh 1999 Hous. L.R. 7, Sh Ct . . . . *Digested,* 99/**6274**
Glasgow City Council *v.* Collins 1998 Hous. L.R. 23, Sh Ct. *Digested,* 98/**5990**
Glasgow City Council *v.* Customs and Excise Commissioners (No.1) [1998] B.V.C.
2239, V&DTr . . . . *Digested,* 98/**6219**
Glasgow City Council *v.* Customs and Excise Commissioners (No.2) [2000] B.V.C.
2363; [2000] S.T.I. 1216, V&DTr . . . . *Digested,* 01/**6921**
Glasgow City Council *v.* Kelly 1999 S.C.L.R. 168, Sh Pr . . . . *Digested,* 99/**5723**
Glasgow City Council *v.* Lockhart 1997 Hous. L.R. 99, Sh Ct . . . . *Digested,* 97/**6129**:
Applied, 00/**6460**
Glasgow City Council *v.* Logan 1999 Hous. L.R. 15, Sh Pr . . . . *Digested,* 99/**5722**
Glasgow City Council *v.* M (Assumption of Parental Rights) 1998 S.L.T. 1413; 1998
G.W.D. 11-519, Ex Div. . . . . *Digested,* 99/**6082**
Glasgow City Council *v.* M (Relevant Persons) 1999 S.L.T. 989; 1999 S.C.L.R. 746;
1999 Fam. L.R. 34; 1999 G.W.D. 9-409, Ex Div. . . . . *Digested,* 99/**6081**
Glasgow City Council *v.* M (Transfer of Parental Rights: Jurisdiction) 2001 S.C. 415;
2001 S.L.T. 396; 2001 G.W.D. 3-107, Ex Div; reversing 2000 G.W.D. 26-962, Sh
Ct (Glasgow) . . . . *Digested,* 01/**6511**
Glasgow City Council *v.* Marshall [2000] 1 W.L.R. 333; [2000] 1 All E.R. 641; 2000
S.C. (H.L.) 67; 2000 S.L.T. 429; 2000 S.C.L.R. 889; [2000] I.C.R. 196; [2000]
I.R.L.R. 272; (2000) 2 L.G.L.R. 679; [2000] B.L.G.R. 229; (2000) 97(7) L.S.G.
39; (2000) 144 S.J.L.B. 101; *Times,* February 8, 2000 ; *Independent,* March 27,
2000 (C.S.), HL; affirming 1998 S.C. 274; 1998 S.L.T. 799; 1998 S.C.L.R. 33;
1997 G.W.D. 40-2089, 1 Div. . . . . *Digested,* 00/**6214**
Glasgow City Council *v.* McAlinden 2001 Hous. L.R. 110, Sh Pr
Glasgow City Council *v.* Murray 1998 Hous. L.R. 27, Sh Pr; affirming 1997 Hous. L.R.
105, Sh Ct. . . . . *Digested,* 98/**5505**
Glasgow City Council *v.* Peart 1999 Hous. L.R. 117; 1999 G.W.D. 29-1390, OH . . . . *Digested,* 00/**6445**
Glasgow City Council *v.* Rankin 2001 S.C.L.R. 876; 2001 Hous. L.R. 12; 2000 G.W.D.
37-1378, Sh Pr . . . . *Digested,* 01/**6266**
Glasgow City Council *v.* Torrance 2000 S.L.T. (Sh Ct) 32; 1999 Hous. L.R. 120; 1999
G.W.D. 35-1709, Sh Pr. . . . . *Digested,* 00/**6538**
Glasgow City Council *v.* Zafar; *sub nom* City of Glasgow DC *v.* Zafar; Strathclyde RC *v.*
Zafar; Zafar *v.* Glasgow City Council [1997] 1 W.L.R. 1659; [1998] 2 All E.R.
953; 1998 S.C. (H.L.) 27; 1998 S.L.T. 135; [1998] I.C.R. 120; [1998] I.R.L.R. 36;
(1997) 94(48) L.S.G. 29; (1998) 142 S.J.L.B. 30; *Times,* December 8, 1997,
HL; affirming 1996 S.C. 502; 1997 S.L.T. 281; 1996 S.C.L.R. 1084; [1997]
I.R.L.R. 229, 2 Div. . . . . *Digested,* 98/**5810**:
Cited, 00/2183: *Considered,* 01/2301, 01/2320
Glasgow City Council, Applicants 2001 S.L.T. (Sh Ct) 85; 2001 G.W.D. 3-108, Sh Ct
(Glasgow)
Glasgow City Council, Petitioners 1998 G.W.D. 29-1459, Sh Ct
Glasgow DC *v.* Everson 1998 Hous. L.R. 56, Sh Ct . . . . *Digested,* 98/**5991**
Glasgow DC *v.* Girvan 1998 S.C. 363; 1998 S.L.T. 1004; 1997 G.W.D. 22-1103, Ex Div. . *Digested,* 98/**6210**
Glasgow DC *v.* Mullin 1998 Hous. L.R. 89, Sh Ct
Glasgow DC *v.* Secretary of State for Scotland 1998 S.L.T. 283; 1997 S.C.L.R. 417;
1997 G.W.D. 4-169, 2 Div. . . . . *Digested,* 97/**6327**
Glasgow District Licensing Board *v.* Din 1995 S.C. 244; 1996 S.L.T. 363; 1995 S.C.L.R.
290, Ex Div. . . . . *Digested,* 96/**7150**:
Applied, 97/6227, 00/6565: *Considered,* 98/6074: *Distinguished,* 96/7151
Glasgow West Housing Association Ltd *v.* Siddique 1997 S.C. 375; 1998 S.L.T. 1081;
1997 G.W.D. 25-1231, 1 Div . . . . *Digested,* 98/**5419**
Glasper *v.* Rodger 1996 S.L.T. 44, 1 Div . . . . *Digested,* 96/**6667**:
Cited, 96/7335, 97/5682: *Distinguished,* 01/6868
Glaxo Group Ltd *v.* Dowelhurst Ltd (Infringement Action); Boehringer Ingelheim KG *v.*
Dowelhurst Ltd (Infringement Action); SmithKline Beecham Plc *v.* Dowelhurst
Ltd (Infringement Action); Eli Lilly & Co *v.* Dowelhurst Ltd (Infringement Action);
Boehringer Ingelheim KG *v.* Swingward Ltd (Infringement Action); Glaxo Group
Ltd *v.* Swingward Ltd (Infringement Action) [2000] 2 C.M.L.R. 571; [2000]
E.T.M.R. 415; [2000] F.S.R. 529; (2000) 55 B.M.L.R. 157; (2000) 23(6) I.P.D.
23046; *Times,* March 14, 2000, Pat Ct . . . . *Digested,* 00/**3703**:
Applied, 01/4034: *Considered,* 01/6728: *Subsequent proceedings,* 01/2480
Glaxo Group Ltd *v.* Swingward Ltd (Infringement Action) see Glaxo Group Ltd *v.*
Dowelhurst Ltd (Infringement Action)
Glen *v.* HM Advocate (Sentencing) 2001 G.W.D. 12-418, HCJ Appeal
Glen Builders (Scotland) Ltd *v.* Doig 1999 S.C.L.R. 900, Sh Pr. . . . . *Digested,* 00/**5940**
Glennie (Dean) *v.* HM Advocate 2001 S.L.T. 903; 2001 S.C.C.R. 423; 2001 G.W.D. 16-
597, HCJ Appeal. . . . . *Digested,* 01/**6354**
Global Marine Drilling Co *v.* Triton Holdings Ltd (The Sovereign Explorer) (No.1) 1999
G.W.D. 39-1905, OH
Global Marine Drilling Co *v.* Triton Holdings Ltd (The Sovereign Explorer) (No.2) [2001]
1 Lloyd's Rep. 60; 2000 G.W.D. 5-210, OH

Globe (Aberdeen) Ltd v. North of Scotland Water Authority 2000 S.C. 392; 2000 S.L.T. 674; 2000 G.W.D. 11-402, Ex Div . . . . *Digested, 00/6600*

Glover v. Deighan 1992 S.L.T. (Sh. Ct.) 88; 1992 S.C.L.R. 718, Sh Pr . . . . *Digested, 92/5773:*
Considered, 94/5852: Followed, 01/6246

Gold v. Brown 1999 G.W.D. 23-1103, HCJ Appeal

Gold v. McGlennan (Sentencing) 2000 G.W.D. 20-819, HCJ Appeal

Goldie v. HM Advocate (Sentencing) 1999 G.W.D. 36-1737, HCJ Appeal

Goldie v. Houston (Sentencing) 1999 G.W.D. 8-385, HCJ Appeal

Goodwillie & Hunter v. Mitchell 1999 G.W.D. 13-588, Sh Ct

Goodwin v. Friel (Sentencing) 1998 G.W.D. 7-354, HCJ Appeal

Gordon v. Glasgow Corp (Unreported, June 26, 1923), 1 Div . . . . *Followed, 01/6820*

Gordon v. HM Advocate 1999 G.W.D. 1-37, HCJ Appeal

Gordon v. HM Advocate (Sentencing) 2001 G.W.D. 36-1374, HCJ Appeal

Gordon v. Howdle (Sentencing) 1998 G.W.D. 1-26, HCJ Appeal

Gordon v. Lees (Sentencing) 1999 G.W.D. 12-580, HCJ Appeal

Gordon v. McFadyen (Careless Driving) 1999 G.W.D. 18-850, HCJ Appeal

Gordon v. McFadyen (Theft) (Sentencing) 2000 G.W.D. 9-334, HCJ Appeal

Gordon v. Russell 1999 S.L.T. 897; 1999 G.W.D. 9-442, HCJ Appeal . . . . *Digested, 99/5956*

Gordon Coutts Thomson (A Firm) v. Council of the Law Society of Scotland (No.1) 1999 S.C.L.R. 823; 1999 G.W.D. 11-515; *Times*, May 13, 1999, Ex Div . . . . *Digested, 99/6341*

Gordon Coutts Thomson (A Firm) v. Council of the Law Society of Scotland (No.2) 2001 S.C.L.R. 61; 2000 G.W.D. 28-1095, Ex Div . . . . *Digested, 01/6772*

Gordon Leslie Ltd v. General Accident Fire & Life Assurance Corp Plc 1998 S.L.T. 391; 1997 S.C.L.R. 550; 1997 G.W.D. 2-65, OH . . . . *Digested, 97/6167:*
Applied, 99/6308

Gorman v. Carnegie 1999 G.W.D. 25-1206, HCJ Appeal

Gorman v. Friel 1998 G.W.D. 30-1542, HCJ Appeal

Gorrie v. Ciba Geigy Ltd 1996 G.W.D. 28-1685, OH . . . . *Referred to, 00/5918*

Gorrie v. Heywood 1998 G.W.D. 29-1479, HCJ Appeal

Gorrie v. Marist Bros 2001 G.W.D. 39-1484, Sh Pr

Goudie v. Mulholland 2000 S.C. 61; 2000 S.L.T. 303; 1999 G.W.D. 39-1876, 1 Div . . . . . *Digested, 00/5925*

Gourlay v. Angiolini 2001 G.W.D. 30-1220, HCJ Appeal

Gourlay v. Assistant Chief Constable of Lothian and Borders Police 2001 G.W.D. 6-237, OH

Gourlay v. Higson (Sentencing) 1999 G.W.D. 40-1946, HCJ Appeal

Gourlay v. HM Advocate (Sentencing) 1999 G.W.D. 25-1198, HCJ Appeal

Gourlay (Pamela Ann) v. HM Advocate (Appeal against Conviction) 2001 G.W.D. 10-343, HCJ Appeal

Gourlay (Pamela Ann) v. HM Advocate (Sentencing) 2001 G.W.D. 33-1308, HCJ Appeal

Govanhill Housing Association Ltd v. Palmer 1998 S.L.T. 887; 1997 Hous. L.R. 133; 1997 G.W.D. 30-1531, OH . . . . *Digested, 98/5987*

Govell v. HM Advocate 1999 G.W.D. 7-322, HCJ Appeal

Govens v. O'Donnell 1999 G.W.D. 25-1183, HCJ Appeal

Governors of the Peabody Donation Fund v. Grant (1982) 264 E.G. 925, CA . . . . *Digested, 83/2145:*
Applied, 00/6462, 00/6463: Considered, 87/2240

Gowans v. Teneco (Polbeth Packaging) Ltd 2000 G.W.D. 34-1301, OH

Gracey v. Sykes 1994 S.C.L.R. 909, Sh Pr . . . . *Digested, 94/6290:*
Cited, 01/6261: Followed, 95/6374

Grady v. McFadyen 1999 G.W.D. 22-1060, HCJ Appeal

Grady v. United Kingdom see Smith v. United Kingdom (No.1)

Graham v. Bell 2000 G.W.D. 13-502, OH

Graham v. Hawick Common Riding Committee 1998 S.L.T. (Sh Ct) 42; 1997 S.C.L.R. 917; 1997 G.W.D. 36-1867, Sh Pr . . . . *Digested, 98/5996*

Graham v. HM Advocate 1999 G.W.D. 24-1157, HCJ Appeal

Graham v. HM Advocate (Sentencing) 2000 G.W.D. 29-1140, HCJ Appeal

Graham v. Kennedy (Sentencing) 2001 G.W.D. 6-221, HCJ Appeal

Graham v. Marshall Food Group Ltd 1998 S.L.T. 1448; 1998 S.C.L.R. 1146; 1998 Rep. L.R. 140; 1998 G.W.D. 32-1676, OH . . . . *Digested, 99/5979*

Graham v. Northern Joint Police Board 2000 S.L.T. (Land Ct) 7; 2000 Hous. L.R. 74; 2000 G.W.D. 18-720, Lands Tr (Scot) . . . . *Digested, 00/6467*

Graham v. Redman 1999 G.W.D. 25-1187, HCJ Appeal

Graham v. Stott 1999 G.W.D. 16-756, HCJ Appeal

Graham v. Ubiquitous Chip 1999 Rep. L.R. 75, OH . . . . *Digested, 99/5982*

Graham v. Wilson-Clarke 1962 S.L.C.R. 35; 1963 S.L.T. (Sh. Ct.) 2; (1963) 79 Sh. Ct. Rep. 113, Sh Ct (Grampian) . . . . *Digested, 63/3649:*
Overruled, 01/6737

Graham (Preservation) Ltd v. Douglas 2001 S.L.T. (Sh Ct) 142; 2001 G.W.D. 8-295, Sh Pr . . . . *Digested, 01/6243*

Grahame v. Secretary of State for Scotland 1951 S.C. 368; 1951 S.L.T. 312; 1951 S.L.C.R. 35, 1 Div . . . . *Digested, 47-51/4362:*
Applied, 00/5938

Grampian Joint Police Board v. Pearson 2001 S.C. 772; 2001 S.L.T. 734; 2001 G.W.D. 12-439, 1 Div; affirming 2001 S.L.T. 90; 2000 G.W.D. 15-610, OH . . . . *Digested, 01/6674*

Grampian RC v. R 2000 S.L.T. 116; 1999 G.W.D. 31-1450, Ex Div. . . . .   *Digested,* 00/**6246**
Grampian Valuation Joint Board Assessor v. Macdonald 2001 S.C.L.R. 686; 2001 G.W.D.
    20-779, OH
Granger (Joseph), Petitioner 2001 J.C. 183; 2001 S.L.T. 1095; 2001 S.C.C.R. 337; 2001
    G.W.D. 13-477, HCJ . . . .   *Digested,* 01/**6358**:
                                     Previous proceedings, 90/2557
Granger v. United Kingdom (A/174) (1990) 12 E.H.R.R. 469; *Times,* March 29, 1990;
    Independent, May 14, 1990 (C.S.); *Guardian,* May 10, 1990, ECHR . . . .   *Digested,* 90/**2557**:
                                    Subsequent proceedings, 01/6358
Granite Properties v. Edinburgh City Council 2001 G.W.D. 28-1115, Sh Ct (Lothian)
Grant v. Airdrie Magistrates; *sub nom* Grant v. Provost, Magistrates and Councillors of
    Airdrie 1939 S.C. 738; 1939 S.L.T. 559, 1 Div. . . . .   *Applied,* 99/5677:
                                        Followed, 00/5900
Grant v. Brown (Sentencing) 2000 G.W.D. 3-101, HCJ Appeal
Grant v. Chief Constable of Grampian Police 2001 Rep. L.R. 74; 2001 G.W.D. 15-583,
    OH . . . .   *Digested,* 01/**6814**
Grant v. Grant 2000 G.W.D. 5-177, Sh Pr
Grant (Paul) v. HM Advocate 1998 S.C.C.R. 113; 1998 G.W.D. 7-329, HCJ Appeal. . . . .   *Digested,* 98/**5657**
Grant v. Macdonald 1998 S.L.T. (Sh Ct) 76, Sh Ct (Grampian) . . . .   *Digested,* 98/**5490**
Grant v. Provost, Magistrates and Councillors of Airdrie see Grant v. Airdrie
    Magistrates
Grant (otherwise White) v. White see White v. White
Grant (William) & Sons Ltd v. Glen Catrine Bonded Warehouse Ltd see William Grant &
    Sons Ltd v. Glen Catrine Bonded Warehouse Ltd (No.3)
Grant's Executors v. Grant 1999 G.W.D. 36-1772, OH
Grantly Developments v. Clydesdale Bank Plc (Interim Interdict) 2000 G.W.D. 6-213,
    OH
Grantly Developments v. Clydesdale Bank Plc (Recall of Sequestration) 2001 G.W.D.
    36-1393, OH
Grassie v. MacLaren 2000 S.L.T. 944; 1999 Rep. L.R. 93; 1999 G.W.D. 14-655, OH. . . .   *Digested,* 99/**5973**
Graves v. Russell (Sentencing) 1998 G.W.D. 6-274, HCJ Appeal
Gray v. Binny (1879) 7 R. 332, 1 Div . . . .   *Applied,* 00/**6697**
Gray v. Boyd 1996 S.L.T. 60; 1995 S.C.L.R. 1075, 2 Div; affirming 1994 S.C.L.R. 923,
    Sh Ct (Glasgow). . . . .   *Digested,* 96/**6662**:
                          Followed, 98/5487, 01/6225
Gray v. Braer Corp [1999] 2 Lloyd's Rep. 541; 1999 S.L.T. 1410; 1999 S.C.L.R. 336;
    1999 G.W.D. 5-279; *Times,* March 10, 1999, OH . . . .   *Digested,* 99/**6421**
Gray v. Clark 1999 G.W.D. 15-694, HCJ Appeal
Gray v. Criminal Injuries Compensation Board 1999 S.C. 137; 1999 S.L.T. 425; 1999
    S.C.L.R. 191; 1998 G.W.D. 37-1892, 2 Div; affirming 1993 S.L.T. 28; 1992
    S.C.L.R. 777; *Scotsman,* May 28, 1992, OH . . . .   *Digested,* 99/**5613**:
                                  Followed, 93/5068
Gray v. Fortune 2000 S.L.T. (Sh Ct) 91; 2000 S.C.L.R. 178, Sh Pr. . . . .   *Digested,* 00/**5948**
Gray v. Gray 1999 Fam. L.R. 135; 1999 G.W.D. 33-1590, OH. . . . .   *Digested,* 00/**6278**
Gray v. Gray 1999 G.W.D. 38-1852, Sh Pr
Gray v. Gray 2001 S.C.L.R. 681; 2001 G.W.D. 21-811, Sh Ct (Tayside)
Gray v. HM Advocate (Sentencing) 1998 G.W.D. 29-1492, HCJ Appeal
Gray v. HM Advocate (Sentencing) 2001 G.W.D. 28-1134, HCJ Appeal
Gray (James) v. HM Advocate 1999 S.L.T. 528; 1999 S.C.C.R. 24; 1999 G.W.D. 1-17,
    HCJ Appeal . . . .   *Digested,* 99/**5915**
Gray v. Lanarkshire Health Board (No.2) 1998 S.L.T. 1378; 1998 S.C.L.R. 396; 1998
    G.W.D. 5-237, OH. . . . .   *Digested,* 98/**5468**
Gray v. Urquhart 2001 G.W.D. 25-977, HCJ Appeal
Gray v. Vannet 1998 G.W.D. 35-1834, HCJ Appeal
Greater Glasgow Health Board v. Baxter Clark & Paul 1990 S.C. 237; 1992 S.L.T. 35,
    OH . . . .   *Digested,* 92/**6209**:
        Approved, 96/6667: *Cited,* 96/7335, 97/5682: *Considered,* 96/6666:
                                  Distinguished, 00/6638
Green v. Gill 1999 G.W.D. 32-1508, OH
Green v. Lord Advocate 1918 S.C. 667, 2 Div. . . . .   *Distinguished,* 01/6771
Green v. Vannet (No.2) 1998 G.W.D. 21-1076, HCJ Appeal
Greer v. Gilchrist 2000 G.W.D. 33-1270, HCJ Appeal
Greer v. HM Advocate 1999 G.W.D. 9-424, HCJ Appeal
Greer v. McFadyen (Sentencing) 2000 G.W.D. 3-90, HCJ Appeal
Greig v. Gilchrist 2001 G.W.D. 13-524, HCJ Appeal
Greig v. Higson (Sentencing) 2001 G.W.D. 10-356, HCJ Appeal
Greig v. Vannet (Sentencing) 1998 G.W.D. 6-282, HCJ Appeal
Grierson v. Harvey 2001 Rep. L.R. 84; 2001 G.W.D. 10-372, Sh Ct (South Strathclyde) .   *Digested,* 01/**6810**
Grieve v. Hillary 1987 S.C.C.R. 317, HCJ Appeal. . . . .   *Digested,* 87/**5210**:
                                  Distinguished, 98/5590
Griffin v. HM Advocate (Sentencing) 1998 G.W.D. 32-1654, HCJ Appeal
Griffin v. Lees 1998 G.W.D. 18-949, HCJ Appeal
Griffith and Powdrill, Petitioners 1998 G.W.D. 40-2037, OH
Grimes v. Hamilton 1998 G.W.D. 25-1247, HCJ Appeal

Grogan (Violet Cairnie Williamson) *v.* Heywood 1999 S.C.C.R. 705; 1999 G.W.D. 28-
  1317, HCJ Appeal . . . . *Digested*, 00/**6027**
Grunwald *v.* Hughes 1965 S.L.T. 209, 2 Div; affirming 1964 S.L.T. 94, OH . . . . *Digested*, 65/**4552**:
  Applied, 98/5542: *Followed*, 90/5711, 93/5652
Guild *v.* HM Advocate (Sentencing) 2000 G.W.D. 19-741, HCJ Appeal
Gunn *v.* Carnegie 2000 G.W.D. 9-346, HCJ Appeal
Gunn *v.* Newman 2001 S.L.T. 776; 2001 G.W.D. 12-403, 1 Div 2001 S.C. 525; 2001
  Rep. L.R. 40; 2001 G.W.D. 1-14, OH . . . . *Digested*, 01/**6228**
Guthrie *v.* Bowman (No.1) 1998 S.L.T. (Land Ct) 5; 1997 S.L.C.R. 71, Land Ct. . . . . *Digested*, 98/**6025**
Guthrie *v.* Bowman (No.2) 1998 S.L.T. (Land Ct) 7; 1997 S.L.C.R. 80, Land Ct. . . . . *Digested*, 98/**6026**
Guthrie *v.* Scottish Environmental Protection Agency [1998] Env. L.R. 128; 1997
  G.W.D. 6-244, OH . . . . *Digested*, 97/**6022**
GW Tait & Sons SSC *v.* Taylor 2001 G.W.D. 33-1320, OH

H *v.* H (Contact Order: Views of Child) 2000 Fam. L.R. 73; 2000 G.W.D. 11-376, Sh Pr . *Digested*, 00/**6262**
H *v.* Harkness 1998 S.C. 287; 1998 S.L.T. 1431; 1998 G.W.D. 12-584, Ex Div . . . . *Digested*, 98/**5851**:
  Followed, 00/6270
H *v.* HM Advocate 1999 G.W.D. 25-1193, HCJ Appeal
H *v.* Kennedy 1999 S.C.L.R. 961; 1992 G.W.D. 6-270, 1 Div . . . . *Applied*, 95/5525
H *v.* M (Unmarried Father: Residence Order) 2000 S.L.T. (Sh Ct) 88; 2000 Fam. L.R.
  70; 2000 G.W.D. 14-518, Sh Pr . . . . *Digested*, 00/**6267**
H *v.* Petrie; *sub nom* H *v.* Taylor 2000 S.L.T. (Sh Ct) 145; 1999 G.W.D. 34-1608, Sh Ct
  (Lothian) . . . . *Digested*, 00/**6268**
H *v.* Stark 1999 G.W.D. 17-767, Sh Ct
H *v.* Taylor see H *v.* Petrie
Ha You Zhu *v.* Secretary of State for the Home Department; *sub nom* Zhu *v.* Secretary
  of State for the Home Department 1998 S.L.T. 1251, OH . . . . *Digested*, 98/**5999**
Hackett *v.* HM Advocate (Sentencing) 2001 G.W.D. 1-32, HCJ Appeal
Hain (Nicholas Thomas) *v.* Ruxton 1999 J.C. 166; 1999 S.L.T. 789; 1999 S.C.C.R. 243;
  1999 G.W.D. 9-440, HCJ Appeal . . . . *Digested*, 99/**5831**
Hake *v.* HM Advocate 1999 G.W.D. 22-1047, HCJ Appeal
Hakim *v.* Secretary of State for the Home Department 2001 S.C. 789; 2001 S.L.T. 639;
  2001 G.W.D. 13-506, Ex Div. . . . . *Digested*, 01/**6710**
Halbert *v.* British Airports Authority Plc 1998 G.W.D. 27-1356, OH
Hale *v.* HM Advocate (Sentencing) 1999 G.W.D. 37-1800, HCJ Appeal
Halfpenny *v.* IGE Medical Systems Ltd [2001] I.C.R. 73; [2001] I.R.L.R. 96; (2001) 58
  B.M.L.R. 1; (2001) 98(7) L.S.G. 39; *Times*, December 19, 2000; *Independent*,
  February 12, 2001 (C.S), HL; reversing [1999] I.C.R. 834; [1999] I.R.L.R. 177;
  [1999] Disc. L.R. 265; [1999] 1 F.L.R. 944; (2000) 52 B.M.L.R. 153; (1999)
  96(5) L.S.G. 36; (1999) 143 S.J.L.B. 38; *Times*, January 4, 1999, CA; reversing
  [1997] I.C.R. 1007; [1998] I.R.L.R. 10, EAT . . . . *Digested*, 01/**2318**:
  Considered, 98/5825
Halifax Plc *v.* Gorman's Trustee 2000 S.L.T. 1409; 2000 G.W.D. 8-312, OH . . . . *Digested*, 01/**6883**
Hall *v.* Crawford see Crawford's Trustee *v.* Crawford
Hall *v.* Edinburgh City Council 1999 S.L.T. 744; 1998 G.W.D. 37-1935, OH . . . . *Digested*, 99/**6224**:
  Considered, 00/6423
Hall *v.* Gamut Technologies Ltd 1999 S.L.T. 1276, OH . . . . *Digested*, 99/**5731**
Hall *v.* Hall 2001 G.W.D. 38-1429, Sh Ct (Grampian)
Hall *v.* HM Advocate (Sentencing) 2000 G.W.D. 33-1278, HCJ Appeal
Hall (Alexander Grant) *v.* HM Advocate (No.1) 1998 S.C.C.R. 525; 1998 G.W.D. 28-
  1403, HCJ Appeal. . . . . *Digested*, 98/**5560**
Hall (Alexander Grant) *v.* HM Advocate (No.2) 1999 S.C.C.R. 130; 1999 G.W.D. 8-379,
  HCJ Appeal . . . . *Digested*, 99/**5860**
Hall *v.* Kingston upon Hull City Council see R. *v.* Birmingham City Council Ex p. Ireland
Hall *v.* Webster 1999 G.W.D. 20-968, HCJ Appeal
Hall, Petitioner (Minority Shareholders) 1999 G.W.D. 1-11, OH
Halleron *v.* Vannet 2000 S.C.C.R. 50; 1999 G.W.D. 36-1754, HCJ Appeal . . . . *Digested*, 00/**6139**
Halliday (Paul William) *v.* HM Advocate 1999 S.L.T. 485; 1998 S.C.C.R. 509; 1998
  G.W.D. 26-1292, HCJ Appeal. . . . . *Digested*, 98/**5584**
Hamam (14918) Unreported, IAT . . . . *Doubted*, 98/5997
Hambros Bank Ltd *v.* Lloyds Bank Plc 1999 S.L.T. 649; 1998 G.W.D. 10-511, OH . . . . . . *Digested*, 99/**6433**
Hambros Bank Ltd *v.* Lloyds Bank Plc (Preliminary Procedure) 1999 S.L.T. 49; 1997
  S.C.L.R. 1104; 1997 G.W.D. 37-1915, OH. . . . . *Digested*, 98/**6180**
Hamid *v.* Glasgow City Licensing Board 2001 S.C. 398; 2001 S.L.T. 193; 2001 S.C.L.R.
  252; [2001] 18 S.L.L.P. 8; 2000 G.W.D. 37-1410, Ex Div . . . . *Digested*, 01/**6788**
Hamill *v.* HM Advocate (Sentencing) 2000 G.W.D. 13-480, HCJ Appeal
Hamill (James Joseph) *v.* HM Advocate; *sub nom* HM Advocate *v.* Hamill (James
  Joseph) 1999 S.L.T. 963; 1999 S.C.C.R. 384, HCJ Appeal; affirming 1999 J.C.
  190; 1998 S.L.T. 1260; 1998 S.C.C.R. 164; 1998 G.W.D. 11-529, HCJ . . . . *Digested*, 99/**5804**
Hamill *v.* Vannet 1998 G.W.D. 23-1169, HCJ Appeal
Hamilton *v.* Allied Domecq Plc 2001 S.C. 829; 2001 G.W.D. 13-517, OH
Hamilton *v.* Brown 1999 G.W.D. 23-1105, HCJ Appeal
Hamilton *v.* Hamilton 1998 S.C.L.R. 773, Sh Ct . . . . *Digested*, 98/**5508**

Hamilton (Ryan Paul James) *v.* Heywood 1998 S.L.T. 133; 1997 S.C.C.R. 783; 1997
    G.W.D. 38-1941, HCJ Appeal . . . .   *Digested,* 98/**5659**
Hamilton *v.* HM Advocate (Sentencing) 2000 G.W.D. 4-142, HCJ Appeal
Hamilton *v.* HM Advocate (Sentencing) 2001 G.W.D. 1-39, HCJ Appeal
Hamilton *v.* Houston (Sentencing) 1998 G.W.D. 2-97, HCJ Appeal
Hamilton *v.* Rodwell (No.1) 1998 S.C.L.R. 418; 1998 G.W.D. 3-134, OH. . . . .   *Digested,* 98/**5956**:
                                                                                                  Approved, 00/6444
Hamilton *v.* Rodwell (No.2) 1999 G.W.D. 35-1706, OH
Hamilton *v.* Ruxton (Procurator Fiscal) 2001 S.L.T. 351; 2001 S.C.C.R. 1; 2000 G.W.D.
    29-1163, HCJ Appeal . . . .   *Digested,* 01/**6406**
Hamilton *v.* Stirling Council 1998 Hous. L.R. 11, LandsTr (Scot) . . . .   *Digested,* 98/**5989**
Hamilton *v.* Vannet 1999 G.W.D. 8-406, HCJ Appeal
Hamilton *v.* Vannet (Sentencing) 1998 G.W.D. 13-663, HCJ Appeal
Hamilton *v.* Wahla 1999 Rep. L.R. 118; 1999 G.W.D. 25-1217, Sh Ct . . . .   *Digested,* 99/**6381**
Hamilton *v.* Watt (Sentencing) 2000 G.W.D. 30-1209, HCJ Appeal
Hamilton Academical Football Club Ltd *v.* Flayest Ltd 1997 G.W.D. 2-45, OH . . . .   *Doubted,* 98/5477
Hammerton-Boyes *v.* Higson 1999 G.W.D. 33-1601, HCJ Appeal
Hammond *v.* Bristow Helicopters Ltd see King *v.* Bristow Helicopters Ltd
Hampden Park Ltd *v.* Dow 2001 S.C.L.R. 951; 2001 G.W.D. 28-1116, OH
Handels-og Kontorfunktionaerernes Forbund i Danmark *v.* Dansk Arbejdsgiverforening
    Ex p. Danfoss A/S (C109/88); *sub nom* Union of Clerical and Commercial
    Employees *v.* Danish Employers Association Ex p. Danfoss A/S (C109/88)
    [1989] E.C.R. 3199; [1991] 1 C.M.L.R. 8; [1991] I.C.R. 74; [1989] I.R.L.R. 532;
    Times, October 28, 1989, ECJ . . . .   *Digested,* 91/**4078**:
                                                          Applied, 96/6958: *Considered,* 98/5825
Handley *v.* HM Advocate (Sentencing) 1999 G.W.D. 40-1942, HCJ Appeal
Handley (Jane Smith) *v.* HM Advocate; *sub nom* Handley *v.* Howdle 1998 S.L.T. 1104;
    1998 S.C.C.R. 584; 1998 G.W.D. 28-1409, HCJ Appeal . . . .   *Digested,* 98/**5633**
Handley *v.* Howdle see Handley (Jane Smith) *v.* HM Advocate
Handley *v.* Pirie 1976 J.C. 65; 1977 S.L.T. 30, HCJ Appeal . . . .   *Digested,* 77/**3327**:
                                                          Applied, 99/5892: *Overruled,* 00/6104
Hanif *v.* Secretary of State for the Home Department 1999 S.C. 337; 1999 S.L.T. 858;
    1999 S.C.L.R. 48; 1999 G.W.D. 1-39, Ex Div . . . .   *Digested,* 99/**6289**:
                                                                                                  Distinguished, 00/6492
Hanlin *v.* McFadyen 2000 S.C.C.R. 428; 2000 G.W.D. 14-523, HCJ Appeal . . . .   *Digested,* 00/**6097**
Hanlon *v.* HM Advocate (Sentencing) 1998 G.W.D. 14-706, HCJ Appeal
Hanlon *v.* HM Advocate (Sentencing) 2000 G.W.D. 4-131, HCJ Appeal
Hanlon *v.* Vannet (Sentencing) 2000 G.W.D. 4-139, HCJ Appeal
Hannah *v.* Scotrail 2001 G.W.D. 4-151, Sh Ct (Glasgow)
Hannah *v.* Scottish Daily Record and Sunday Mail Ltd 2000 S.L.T. 673; 2000 G.W.D.
    2-50, OH . . . .   *Digested,* 00/**6177**
Hannah *v.* Vannet 1999 G.W.D. 29-1380, HCJ Appeal
Hannan *v.* Henderson (1879) 7 R. 380, 1 Div . . . .   *Distinguished,* 91/5173,
                                                          92/5950: *Referred to,* 98/6034
Hannigan *v.* Hutchison 1999 G.W.D. 23-1119, HCJ Appeal
Hanratty *v.* Vannet (Sentencing) 1998 G.W.D. 1-23, HCJ Appeal
Hanton *v.* HM Advocate (Sentencing) 1998 G.W.D. 5-220, HCJ Appeal
Hardie *v.* Edinburgh City Council 2000 S.L.T. 130; 1999 G.W.D. 37-1780; *Times,*
    February 16, 2000, OH . . . .   *Digested,* 00/**6205**
Hardie *v.* Keller Colcrete Ltd 1999 G.W.D. 35-1715, OH
Hardie *v.* Reith 1999 G.W.D. 33-1577, HCJ Appeal
Hardie *v.* Walker 1948 S.C. 674; 1949 S.L.T. 13; 1948 S.L.T. (Notes) 47, 1 Div. . . . .   *Digested,* 49/**4664**:
                                                                                                  Followed, 01/6542
Hardie Polymers Ltd *v.* Polymerland Ltd 2001 G.W.D. 35-1338, OH
Harding *v.* Joy Manufacturing Holdings Ltd; *sub nom* Joy Manufacturing Holdings Ltd
    and Pension & Life Assurance Scheme Trustees, Petitioners 2000 S.L.T. 843;
    [2001] O.P.L.R. 235; 1999 G.W.D. 7-353; *Independent,* April 21, 1999, 1 Div. . . .   *Digested,* 99/**6396**
Harkins *v.* HM Advocate (Sentencing) 1999 G.W.D. 36-1750, HCJ Appeal
Harkins (Angela) *v.* HM Advocate 1998 S.C.C.R. 603; 1998 G.W.D. 31-1604, HCJ
    Appeal . . . .   *Digested,* 98/**5700**
Harlow *v.* HM Advocate 1998 G.W.D. 24-1198, HCJ Appeal
Harper *v.* Gilchrist 2001 G.W.D. 23-877, HCJ Appeal
Harper *v.* Heywood 1998 S.L.T. 644; 1998 G.W.D. 3-110, HCJ Appeal. . . . .   *Digested,* 98/**5628**
Harper *v.* Higson (Sentencing) 2000 G.W.D. 37-1396, HCJ Appeal
Harper *v.* Lees (Sentencing) 1998 G.W.D. 12-617, HCJ Appeal
Harper *v.* Tayside University Hospitals NHS Trust 2001 G.W.D. 1-50, OH
Harrier *v.* McLeod 1999 G.W.D. 21-983, HCJ Appeal
Harrington *v.* Link Motor Policies at Lloyd's; *sub nom* Harrington *v.* Pinkey [1989] 2
    Lloyd's Rep. 310; [1989] R.T.R. 345; *Times,* May 12, 1989, CA . . . .   *Digested,* 90/**3754**:
                                                          Considered, 95/6309, 98/6019
Harrington *v.* Pinkey see Harrington *v.* Link Motor Policies at Lloyd's
Harris *v.* Fyfe 1998 G.W.D. 30-1528, Ex Div
Harris *v.* Heywood (Sentencing) 2001 G.W.D. 36-1369, HCJ Appeal
Harris *v.* HM Advocate (Sentencing) 1998 G.W.D. 10-500, HCJ Appeal

Harrison v. DM Hall (A Firm) 2001 G.W.D. 33-1314, OH
Harrison v. HM Advocate 1993 S.C.C.R. 1087, HCJ Appeal . . . . *Digested,* 94/**5637**:
Applied, 98/5637: *Distinguished,* 00/6110
Harrison v. HM Advocate (Sentencing) 1999 G.W.D. 24-1153, HCJ Appeal
Harrison (John) v. HM Advocate 2000 S.L.T. 2; 1999 G.W.D. 18-824, HCJ Appeal . . . . *Digested,* 00/**6118**
Harrison v. Walkingshaw 1998 G.W.D. 31-1610, HCJ Appeal
Harrison v. West of Scotland Kart Club 2001 S.C. 367; 2001 S.L.T. 1171; 2001 Rep. L.R.
2; 2000 G.W.D. 38-1422, OH . . . . *Digested,* 01/**6813**
Harrup v. Bayley (1856) 25 L.J. M.C. 107, CA . . . . *Applied,* 98/5521
Hart v. Hingston (Sentencing) 2001 G.W.D. 16-620, HCJ Appeal
Harvey v. HM Advocate (Sentencing) 2000 G.W.D. 20-799, HCJ Appeal
Harvey v. Mactaggart & Mickel Ltd (No.1); *sub nom* Mactaggart & Mickel Ltd v.
Harvey 2000 S.C. 137; 2000 S.L.T. 318; 1999 S.L.C.R. 1; 1999 G.W.D. 40-1906,
Ex Div; reversing 1998 S.L.T. (Land Ct) 20; 1998 S.L.C.R. 1; 1998 G.W.D. 12-
582, Land Ct . . . . *Digested,* 00/**5871**
Harvey v. Mactaggart & Mickel Ltd (No.2) 1999 S.L.C.R. 21, Land Ct . . . . *Digested,* 99/**5636**
Hasson (Alan Guthrahan) v. HM Advocate 1971 J.C. 35; 1971 S.L.T. 199, HCJ . . . . *Digested,* 71/**12653**:
Considered, 98/5607
Hastie v. Higson 1999 G.W.D. 26-1240, HCJ Appeal
Hastie v. HM Advocate 2001 G.W.D. 17-672, HCJ Appeal
Hatfield v. Hiscock [1998] C.C.L.R. 68, CC (Southampton) . . . . *Digested,* 98/**2501**:
Approved, 01/898: *Considered,* 99/2454: *Distinguished,* 99/2500, 99/5789:
Not followed, 00/2568
Haughan v. Haughan (No.2); *sub nom* Haugan v. Haugan (No.2) 2001 G.W.D. 16-641,
OH
Haughian v. HM Advocate 1998 G.W.D. 15-741, HCJ Appeal
Hawkins v. Northern Marine Management Ltd 1998 S.L.T. 1107; 1997 G.W.D. 17-760,
OH . . . . *Digested,* 98/**5546**
Hay v. Edinburgh City Council 1998 G.W.D. 13-679, OH
Hay v. Hay 2000 S.L.T. (Sh Ct) 95; 2000 Fam. L.R. 65; 2000 G.W.D. 13-452, Sh Ct
(Grampian) . . . . *Digested,* 00/**6260**
Hay (Gordon Scott Stuart) v. HM Advocate 1999 S.L.T. 867; 1998 S.C.C.R. 634; 1998
G.W.D. 35-1780, HCJ Appeal . . . . *Digested,* 99/**5805**
Hay v. Perry 2001 G.W.D. 36-1389, HCJ Appeal
Hay v. Secretary of State for Scotland 1998 S.L.T. 436; 1997 S.C.L.R. 1185; 1997 Rep.
L.R. (Quantum) 12; 1997 G.W.D. 20-985, OH . . . . *Digested,* 97/**5931**:
Considered, 00/6169
Hay v. Stott (Sentencing) 2001 G.W.D. 13-480, HCJ Appeal
Hay v. Vannet (Sentencing) 2000 G.W.D. 13-483, HCJ Appeal
Hayden v. Hingston 1998 G.W.D. 35-1772, HCJ Appeal
Haylock v. Dow 2001 G.W.D. 19-719, OH
Hays Personnel Services Ltd v. Meston Reid & Co 2001 G.W.D. 1-18, Sh Ct (Grampian)
Hazlett v. HM Advocate 1999 G.W.D. 19-896, HCJ Appeal
Hazlett v. McFadyen (Sentencing) 2000 G.W.D. 4-162, HCJ Appeal
Heafey v. Craigen (Sentencing) 2001 G.W.D. 16-615, HCJ Appeal
Healey v. Vannet 1999 G.W.D. 31-1456, HCJ Appeal
Healy v. HM Advocate (Sentencing) 1998 G.W.D. 5-209, HCJ Appeal
Healy (Elizabeth Kirwan) v. HM Advocate 1990 S.C.C.R. 110, HCJ Appeal . . . . *Digested,* 90/**4908**:
Applied, 93/5003, 96/6774, 97/5822, 98/5624
Healy v. Vannet 2000 S.C.C.R. 35, HCJ Appeal . . . . *Digested,* 00/**6013**
Heather Isle Meats Ltd v. Intervention Board Executive Agency 2001 G.W.D. 35-1337,
OH
Hedley v. Drilltech Services (North Sea) Ltd 1999 S.C.L.R. 777, Sh Pr . . . . *Digested,* 99/**5713**
Heenan v. Dillon 1999 S.L.T. (Sh Ct) 32; 1999 S.C.L.R. 547; 1999 Fam. L.R. 62; 1999
G.W.D. 8-369, Sh Ct (Lothian) . . . . *Digested,* 99/**5692**:
Considered, 99/5694: *Followed,* 00/5923
Heeremac vof v. Munro 1999 S.L.T. 492; 1999 S.C.C.R. 48; 1998 G.W.D. 40-2045,
HCJ Appeal . . . . *Digested,* 99/**5885**
Heggie v. Uniroyal Englebert Tyres Ltd 2000 S.L.T. 227; [1999] I.R.L.R. 802; 1999
G.W.D. 30-1432, 2 Div; reversing [1998] I.R.L.R. 425, EAT . . . . *Digested,* 00/**6217**
Heil v. Rankin; Rees v. Mabco (102) Ltd (Non-Pecuniary Damages); Schofield v.
Saunders & Taylor Ltd; Ramsay v. Rivers; Kent v. Griffiths (Non-Pecuniary
Damages); W (A Child) v. Northern General Hospital NHS Trust; Annable v.
Southern Derbyshire HA; Connolly v. Tasker [2001] Q.B. 272; [2000] 2 W.L.R.
1173; [2000] 3 All E.R. 138; [2000] I.R.L.R. 334; [2000] P.I.Q.R. Q187; [2000]
Lloyd's Rep. Med. 203; (2000) 97(14) L.S.G. 41; (2000) 150 N.L.J. 464;
(2000) 144 S.J.L.B. 157; *Times,* March 24, 2000; *Independent,* March 28, 2000,
CA . . . . *Digested,* 00/**1478**:
Considered, 00/1529, 00/6165, 01/612, 01/1585, 01/6421:
Followed, 00/1495, 00/1500, 00/1511, 00/1644, 00/1733:
Previous proceedings, 99/1534, 00/4203: *Subsequent proceedings,* 00/1492
Hemming v. HM Advocate 1997 J.C. 140; 1998 S.L.T. 213; 1997 S.C.C.R. 257, HCJ . . . . *Digested,* 97/**5808**:
Approved, 98/5607
Hemphill v. HM Advocate 2001 S.C.C.R. 361; 2001 G.W.D. 15-575, HCJ Appeal . . . . . . *Digested,* 01/**6349**

Henderson v. Adamson 1998 S.C.L.R. 365, Sh Pr . . . .   *Digested,* 98/**5844**
Henderson v. Alexander 1998 G.W.D. 3-105, OH
Henderson v. Argyll & Bute Council 1998 S.L.T. 1224; 1998 S.C.L.R. 1; 1997 G.W.D.
    28-1446, OH. . . . .   *Digested,* 98/**6149**:
                                                Distinguished, 01/6855
Henderson v. Barden 2001 Hous. L.R. 113; 2001 G.W.D. 7-264, LandsTr (Scot)
Henderson v. Hamilton 1995 S.L.T. 968; 1995 S.C.C.R. 413, HCJ Appeal . . . .   *Digested,* 95/**6281**:
                                                Distinguished, 00/6153
Henderson v. Henderson [1843-60] All E.R. Rep. 378; (1843) 67 E.R. 313; (1843) 3
    Hare 100, Ct of Chancery. . . . .   *Applied,* 65/100,
            67/1498, 91/1736, 97/461, 97/997, 98/80, 98/2162, 98/2163, 98/3454,
            99/3313, 99/4025, 00/5111, 01/4678: *Considered,* 75/2463, 84/2704,
            88/2920, 89/1534, 93/3308, 94/3285, 94/3746, 95/3894, 96/1105,
            98/244, 98/518, 98/618, 98/4067, 99/620, 00/604, 00/785, 01/410,
            01/6474: *Distinguished,* 47-51/3681, 99/549, 99/4384, 00/349, 00/2605:
            Followed, 99/3952, 00/2322: *Not applied,* 99/1376, 99/3732:
                                            Referred to, 99/4014
Henderson v. Henderson 2000 S.L.T. (Sh Ct) 6; 1999 G.W.D. 31-1494, Sh Pr . . . .   *Digested,* 00/**5920**
Henderson v. HM Advocate (Sentencing) 1998 G.W.D. 5-249, HCJ Appeal
Henderson v. HM Advocate (Sentencing) 1999 G.W.D. 18-843, HCJ Appeal
Henderson v. Munro (Sentencing) 1998 G.W.D. 8-372, HCJ Appeal
Henderson v. Stott (Sentencing) 1998 G.W.D. 32-1652, HCJ Appeal
Henderson v. Walker 1998 G.W.D. 38-1980, HCJ Appeal
Henderson v. Webster 1999 G.W.D. 18-853, HCJ Appeal
Hendrie v. Heywood (Sentencing) 2001 G.W.D. 10-355, HCJ Appeal
Hendrie v. Ruxton 1999 G.W.D. 20-920, HCJ Appeal
Hendry v. Craigen (Sentencing) 2001 G.W.D. 19-728, HCJ Appeal
Hendry v. HM Advocate (Sentencing) 1999 G.W.D. 21-1004, HCJ Appeal
Hendry v. HM Advocate (Sentencing) 2001 G.W.D. 12-414, HCJ Appeal
Hendry v. HM Advocate (Sentencing) 2001 G.W.D. 25-931, HCJ Appeal
Hendry (Steven Joseph) v. HM Advocate 1987 J.C. 63; 1988 S.L.T. 25; 1987 S.C.C.R.
    394, HCJ Appeal . . . .   *Digested,* 87/**4200**:
                                            Applied, 00/6017
Hendry (William) v. HM Advocate 2001 J.C. 122; 2001 S.C.C.R. 59; 2001 G.W.D. 2-88,
    HCJ Appeal . . . .   *Digested,* 01/**6364**
Hendry v. Walkingshaw (Sentencing) 1998 G.W.D. 3-128, HCJ Appeal
Henry v. Carnegie 1999 G.W.D. 17-803, HCJ Appeal
Henry v. Chief Constable of Tayside 1998 G.W.D. 26-1342, OH
Hepburn v. Brown; *sub nom* Hepburn v. Vannet 1998 J.C. 63; 1997 S.C.C.R. 698; 1997
    G.W.D. 36-1839, HCJ Appeal . . . .   *Digested,* 98/**5556**
Hepburn (Andrew Kirkpatrick) v. Howdle 1998 J.C. 204; 1998 S.L.T. 808; 1998
    S.C.C.R. 363; 1998 G.W.D. 18-910, HCJ Appeal . . . .   *Digested,* 98/**5670**
Hepburn v. Vannet see Hepburn v. Brown
Herd v. HM Advocate see Herd (Alan) v. Vannet
Herd v. Lees 1998 G.W.D. 34-1767, HCJ Appeal
Herd (Alan) v. Vannet; *sub nom* Herd v. HM Advocate 1999 S.L.T. 927; 1999 S.C.C.R.
    315; 1999 G.W.D. 13-599, HCJ Appeal. . . . .   *Digested,* 99/**5922**
Heritable Reversionary Co Ltd v. Millar [1892] A.C. 598; (1892) 19 R. 43, HL. . . . .   *Applied,* 94/5460:
                                   Distinguished, 95/5549: *Referred to,* 00/6511
Heritage Fisheries Ltd v. Duke of Roxburghe 2000 S.L.T. 800; 1999 G.W.D. 24-1161, 1
    Div. . . . .   *Digested,* 01/**6542**
Heron v. Lees 1998 G.W.D. 37-1911, HCJ Appeal
Herries v. Heath (Scotland) Ltd 1998 G.W.D. 21-1056, Ex Div
Hewit v. Williamson 1999 S.L.T. 313; 1998 S.C.L.R. 601; 1998 G.W.D. 10-510, OH . . . . .   *Digested,* 98/**6181**
Hewitt v. Hingston (Sentencing) 1998 G.W.D. 4-192, HCJ Appeal
Heywood, Petitioner 1998 S.L.T. 1417; 1998 S.C.C.R. 335; 1998 G.W.D. 13-639, HCJ
    Appeal . . . .   *Digested,* 98/**5613**
HG Robertson (A Firm) v. Murray International Metals Ltd 1988 S.L.T. 747; 1988
    S.C.L.R. 574, OH. . . . .   *Digested,* 88/**4728**:
                          Approved, 93/5688: *Followed,* 00/6636
Higgins v. Donnelly (Sentencing) 1999 G.W.D. 4-183, HCJ Appeal
Higgins (Graham Alexander) v. HM Advocate 1990 S.C.C.R. 268, HCJ Appeal . . . .   *Digested,* 90/**4899**:
                         Considered, 93/4970: *Disapproved,* 98/5607
Higgins v. Miller (Sentencing) 1998 G.W.D. 12-604, HCJ Appeal
Higgins v. North Lanarkshire Council 2001 S.L.T. (Lands Tr) 2; 2000 G.W.D. 31-1236,
    LandsTr (Scot)
Higgins v. Ritchie (Sentencing) 2001 G.W.D. 36-1366, HCJ Appeal
Highland and Universal Properties Ltd v. Safeway Properties Ltd (No.2) 2000 S.C. 297;
    2000 S.L.T. 414; [2000] 3 E.G.L.R. 110; 2000 G.W.D. 6-231; *Times,* March 22,
    2000, 1 Div; reversing in part 1998 G.W.D. 3-136, OH . . . .   *Digested,* 00/**6526**
Highland Council v. MacKenzie 2000 S.L.C.R. 75, Land Ct (Div Ct) . . . .   *Digested,* 01/**6743**
Highland Primary Care NHS Trust v. Thomson 1999 S.L.T. (Land Ct) 10; 1999 S.L.C.R.
    32, Land Ct. . . . .   *Digested,* 00/**6531**

Higson *v.* Aberdeen City Council 1999 S.C.C.R. 708; 1999 G.W.D. 28-1349, HCJ
　　Appeal . . . . *Digested,* 00/**6572**
Higson *v.* Boyle 2001 S.L.T. (Sh Ct) 49; 2000 G.W.D. 36-1358, Sh Ct (Glasgow)
Higson *v.* Morrison 2001 G.W.D. 16-600, Sh Ct (Glasgow)
Hill *v.* CA Parsons & Co [1972] Ch. 305; [1971] 3 W.L.R. 995; [1971] 3 All E.R. 1345;
　　115 S.J. 868, CA . . . . *Digested,* 72/**1192**:
　　　　　　　　　　Applied, 72/1253, 73/2659, 84/1202, 85/1181: *Considered,* 98/5814,
　　　　　　　　　　　　　　　　　　　　　　　01/2244: *Distinguished,* 74/1350, 75/1095
Hill *v.* Council of the Law Society of Scotland 2000 S.C. 582; 2000 S.L.T. 1389; 2000
　　G.W.D. 26-1001, Ex Div; affirming 1999 G.W.D. 14-650, Sh Ct . . . . *Digested,* 01/**6771**
Hill *v.* General Accident Fire & Life Assurance Corp Plc (No.1) 1999 S.L.T. 1157; 1998
　　S.C.L.R. 1031; [1998] I.R.L.R. 641; 1998 G.W.D. 31-1622, OH . . . . *Digested,* 98/**5813**:
　　　　　　　　　　　　　　　　　　　　　　　　　　　　　　　　Followed, 99/6029
Hill *v.* General Accident Fire & Life Assurance Corp Plc (No.2) 1999 S.L.T. 1281, OH . . . 　*Digested,* 99/**6026**
Hill *v.* HM Advocate (Sentencing) 1998 G.W.D. 34-1743, HCJ Appeal
Hill *v.* HM Advocate (Sentencing) 1998 G.W.D. 4-183, HCJ Appeal
Hill *v.* Wildfowl Trust (Holdings) Ltd (No.2) 1998 S.L.T. (Sh Ct) 89, Sh Ct (South
　　Strathclyde) . . . . *Digested,* 99/**5634**
Hill *v.* Wilson 1998 S.C. 81; 1998 S.L.T. 69; 1998 Rep. L.R. 9; 1997 G.W.D. 35-1743, 1
　　Div; affirming 1997 G.W.D. 17-756, OH . . . . *Digested,* 98/**5719**
Hillhouse *v.* South Ayrshire Council 2000 G.W.D. 31-1240, OH
Hillis *v.* Vannet (Sentencing) 1998 G.W.D. 12-595, HCJ Appeal
Hilson *v.* Gallagher 1999 G.W.D. 30-1408, HCJ Appeal
Hiram Walker & Sons Inc *v.* Drambuie Liqueur Co 1998 S.L.T. 771; 1997 G.W.D. 7-261,
　　OH . . . . *Digested,* 98/**5547**
Hislop *v.* Dickson Motors (Forres) Ltd 1978 S.L.T. (Notes) 73, OH . . . . *Digested,* 78/**3189**:
　　　　　　　　　　　　　　　　　　　　　　　　　　　　　　　　　Considered, 00/5988

Hlakula *v.* HM Advocate (Sentencing) 1999 G.W.D. 37-1802, HCJ Appeal
HM Advocate *v.* Adamson (Stuart) see Adamson (Stuart) *v.* HM Advocate
HM Advocate *v.* Al-Megrahi (No.1); *sub nom* HM Advocate *v.* Megrahi (No.1) 2000
　　J.C. 555; 2000 S.L.T. 1393; 2000 S.C.C.R. 177; 2000 G.W.D. 5-183, HCJ . . . . . *Digested,* 00/**6029**
HM Advocate *v.* Al-Megrahi (No.2); *sub nom* Megrahi *v.* HM Advocate (No.2); HM
　　Advocate *v.* Megrahi (No.2); Al-Megrahi *v.* HM Advocate (No.2) 2000 S.L.T.
　　1399; 2000 S.C.C.R. 1003; 2000 G.W.D. 33-1266, HCJ . . . . *Digested,* 01/**6305**
HM Advocate *v.* Al-Megrahi (No.3); *sub nom* Megrahi *v.* HM Advocate (No.3); HM
　　Advocate *v.* Megrahi (No.3); Al-Megrahi *v.* HM Advocate (No.3) 2000 S.L.T.
　　1401; 2000 G.W.D. 33-1265, HCJ . . . . *Digested,* 01/**6303**
HM Advocate *v.* Al-Megrahi (No.4); *sub nom* HM Advocate *v.* Megrahi (No.4); Megrahi
　　v. HM Advocate (No.4) 2001 G.W.D. 5-177, HCJ
HM Advocate *v.* Al-Megrahi (No.5); *sub nom* Megrahi *v.* HM Advocate (No.5); Al-
　　Megrahi *v.* HM Advocate (No.5) 2001 S.L.T. 1473; 2001 S.C.C.R. 701; 2001
　　G.W.D. 26-1014, HCJ Appeal
HM Advocate *v.* Allan (Steven George) (Sentencing) 2000 S.C.C.R. 219; 2000 G.W.D.
　　9-331, HCJ Appeal . . . . *Digested,* 00/**6137**
HM Advocate *v.* Ashrif 1988 S.L.T. 567; 1988 S.C.C.R. 197, HCJ Appeal . . . . *Digested,* 88/**3944**:
　　　　　　　　　　　　　　　　　　　　　　　　　　　　　　　　　Considered, 01/6314

HM Advocate *v.* Bain (David) 2001 S.C.C.R. 461; 2001 G.W.D. 18-693, HCJ Appeal
HM Advocate *v.* Beggs (No.1) 2001 S.C.C.R. 869; 2001 G.W.D. 34-1330, HCJ
HM Advocate *v.* Beggs (No.2) 2001 S.C.C.R. 879; 2001 G.W.D. 34-1327, HCJ
HM Advocate *v.* Beggs (No.3) 2001 S.C.C.R. 891; 2001 G.W.D. 38-1421, HCJ
HM Advocate *v.* Bell (Jamie) 2001 G.W.D. 13-472, Ex Div
HM Advocate *v.* Biggar 1999 G.W.D. 8-383, HCJ
HM Advocate *v.* Boland Construction (Scotland) Ltd 2001 G.W.D. 4-162, Sh Ct
　　(Lothian)
HM Advocate *v.* Boyd Unreported, HCJ Appeal . . . . *Disapproved,* 00/6036
HM Advocate *v.* Brand (Gilbert Donaldson) 1998 S.L.T. 486; 1998 S.C.C.R. 71; 1998
　　G.W.D. 4-174, HCJ Appeal . . . . *Digested,* 98/**5697**
HM Advocate *v.* Briody (Sentencing) 2000 G.W.D. 29-1138, HCJ Appeal
HM Advocate *v.* Brown (William Cunningham) 1969 J.C. 72; 1970 S.L.T. 121, HCJ. . . . . *Digested,* 70/**3068**:
　　　　　　　　　　　　　　　　　　　　　　Applied, 98/5567: *Distinguished,* 89/3998
HM Advocate *v.* Burns (Thomas Fowler) (Sentencing) 2001 J.C. 1; 2000 S.L.T. 1242;
　　2000 S.C.C.R. 884; 2000 G.W.D. 26-983, HCJ . . . . *Digested,* 00/**6142**
HM Advocate *v.* Campbell (Devolution Issues: Procedure) 1999 S.C.C.R. 980; 1999
　　G.W.D. 34-1622, HCJ . . . . *Digested,* 00/**6070**
HM Advocate *v.* Campbell (Sentencing) 2000 G.W.D. 27-1043, HCJ
HM Advocate *v.* Carnall 1999 S.C.C.R. 904; 1999 G.W.D. 31-1485, HCJ Appeal . . . . . . *Digested,* 00/**6146**
HM Advocate *v.* Carpenter (Jennifer Jane Evans) 1999 S.L.T. 1273; 1998 S.C.C.R. 706;
　　1998 G.W.D. 37-1906, HCJ Appeal . . . . *Digested,* 99/**5942**
HM Advocate *v.* Caulfield (Robert Gilmore) 1999 S.L.T. 1003; 1999 S.C.C.R. 542; 1999
　　G.W.D. 19-872, HCJ Appeal. . . . . *Digested,* 99/**5853**
HM Advocate *v.* Chapman 1999 G.W.D. 26-1228, Sh Ct
HM Advocate *v.* Cook (Craig Garry) see Cook (Craig Garry) *v.* HM Advocate
HM Advocate *v.* Cook (Sentencing) 2000 G.W.D. 21-829, Sh Ct (South Strathclyde)
HM Advocate *v.* Danskin 2000 S.C.C.R. 101, Sh Ct . . . . *Digested,* 00/**6030**

HM Advocate v. Davidson (Craig) 1999 S.C.C.R. 729; 1999 G.W.D. 28-1335, HCJ
Appeal . . . . *Digested*, 00/**6158**
HM Advocate v. Dickson (Annie Mulvey); *sub nom* HM Advocate v. Gourlay (Annie
Mulvey) 2000 J.C. 93; 1999 S.C.C.R. 859; 1999 G.W.D. 31-1466, HCJ Appeal. . *Digested*, 00/**6069**
HM Advocate v. Dodwell 2001 G.W.D. 32-1274, HCJ Appeal
HM Advocate v. Donaldson (George) 1998 S.L.T. 877; 1997 S.C.C.R. 738; 1997 G.W.D.
36-1859, HCJ Appeal . . . . *Digested*, 98/**5653**
HM Advocate v. DP see HM Advocate v. P
HM Advocate v. Drain (John Friel) (Sentencing); HM Advocate v. Thom (Alastair
Scott) (Sentencing) 2000 S.C.C.R. 256; 2000 G.W.D. 7-256, HCJ Appeal . . . . *Digested*, 00/**6128**
HM Advocate v. Duff 1999 G.W.D. 31-1491, HCJ
HM Advocate v. Duff (Richard Alexander) 1999 S.C.C.R. 193; 1999 G.W.D. 6-306,
HCJ Appeal . . . . *Digested*, 99/**5961**
HM Advocate v. Express Newspapers Plc 1999 S.L.T. 838; 1998 S.C.C.R. 471; 1998
G.W.D. 27-1357, HCJ . . . . *Digested*, 98/**5397**:
Subsequent proceedings, 99/5856
HM Advocate v. Finlay (Barry Thomas) see Finlay (Barry Thomas) v. HM Advocate
HM Advocate v. Foley 1999 G.W.D. 17-788, HCJ Appeal
HM Advocate v. Forrest (George Henderson) 1998 S.C.C.R. 153; 1998 G.W.D. 8-378,
HCJ Appeal . . . . *Digested*, 98/**5682**
HM Advocate v. Fraser (Nat Gordon) 2000 S.C.C.R. 412, HCJ. . . . . *Digested*, 00/**6093**
HM Advocate v. Gourlay (Annie Mulvey) see HM Advocate v. Dickson (Annie Mulvey)
HM Advocate v. Graham 1999 G.W.D. 26-1235, HCJ Appeal
HM Advocate v. Grimmond (David) 2001 S.C.C.R. 708; 2001 G.W.D. 27-1083, HCJ
HM Advocate v. H (James) 2000 J.C. 552; 2000 S.L.T. 1321; 2000 S.C.C.R. 644;
2000 G.W.D. 17-682, HCJ Appeal . . . . *Digested*, 00/**6088**
HM Advocate v. Halley (Sentencing) 2000 G.W.D. 31-1226, Sh Ct (South Strathclyde)
HM Advocate v. Hamill (James Joseph) see Hamill (James Joseph) v. HM Advocate
HM Advocate v. Hemphill (John) 2001 S.C.C.R. 816; 2001 G.W.D. 28-1127, HCJ
Appeal
HM Advocate v. Heron (James Lamb) 1998 S.C.C.R. 449; 1998 G.W.D. 26-1299, HCJ
Appeal . . . . *Digested*, 98/**5655**
HM Advocate v. Hodgson (Robert) 1998 S.C.C.R. 320; 1998 G.W.D. 15-761, HCJ
Appeal . . . . *Digested*, 98/**5654**
HM Advocate v. Jenkinson (Darren John) 2001 G.W.D. 33-1305, HCJ
HM Advocate v. K (A Juvenile) see Dyer v. Watson
HM Advocate v. Kiernan (Gordon) 2001 S.C.C.R. 129, HCJ . . . . *Digested*, 01/**6332**
HM Advocate v. Lee (Paul James) 1996 S.L.T. 568; 1996 S.C.C.R. 205, HCJ Appeal . . *Digested*, 96/**6849**:
Applied, 98/5651: *Considered*, 96/6843
HM Advocate v. Little (William Maxwell) 1999 S.L.T. 1145; 1999 S.C.C.R. 625, HCJ . . . *Digested*, 99/**5867**
HM Advocate v. Mac Mowat; *sub nom* HM Advocate v. MacMowat 2001 S.L.T. 738;
2001 S.C.C.R. 242; 2001 G.W.D. 12-408, HCJ . . . . *Digested*, 01/**6302**
HM Advocate v. MacMowat see HM Advocate v. Mac Mowat
HM Advocate v. Mason (Sentencing) 2001 G.W.D. 29-1159, HCJ
HM Advocate v. McCann 1999 G.W.D. 32-1525, Sh Ct . . . . *Disapproved*, 00/6071
HM Advocate v. McDonald (Charles) 1928 J.C. 42, HCJ . . . . *Disapproved*, 99/5896
HM Advocate v. McGinlay (McGregor) 1983 S.L.T. 562, HCJ Appeal. . . . . *Digested*, 83/**4078**:
Distinguished, 97/5763, 00/6017: *Explained*, 87/4200
HM Advocate v. McGinlay (Michael) 1999 S.L.T. 1297; 1999 S.C.C.R. 779; 1999 G.W.D.
29-1372, HCJ Appeal . . . . *Digested*, 00/**6052**
HM Advocate v. McGinn (Sentencing) 1999 G.W.D. 12-553, HCJ Appeal
HM Advocate v. McGlinchey (Martin); HM Advocate v. Renicks (Ryan James) 2000
J.C. 564; 2000 S.L.T. 995; 2000 S.C.C.R. 593; 2000 G.W.D. 23-882, HCJ
Appeal . . . . *Digested*, 00/**6090**
HM Advocate v. McGowan (Sentencing) 2001 G.W.D. 26-1043, HCJ Appeal
HM Advocate v. McIntosh (Robert) (No.1); *sub nom* McIntosh, Petitioner; McIntosh
(Robert) v. HM Advocate [2001] UKPC D1; [2001] 3 W.L.R. 107; [2001] 2 All
E.R. 638; 2001 S.C. (P.C.) 89; 2001 S.L.T. 304; 2001 S.C.C.R. 191; [2001] 2 Cr.
App. R. 27; [2001] H.R.L.R. 20; [2001] U.K.H.R.R. 463; (2001) 98(11) L.S.G.
43; (2001) 145 S.J.L.B. 83; 2001 G.W.D. 6-206; *Times*, February 8, 2001;
Independent, February 16, 2001, PC (UK); reversing 2001 J.C. 78; 2000 S.L.T.
1280; 2000 S.C.C.R. 1017; [2000] U.K.H.R.R. 751; 2000 G.W.D. 33-1284; *Times*,
October 31, 2000, HCJ Appeal; reversing 2000 S.L.T. 1233; 2000 G.W.D. 25-
937, HCJ . . . . *Digested*, 01/**6327**
HM Advocate v. McKinlay (Alexander Malcolm) 1998 S.C.C.R. 201; 1998 G.W.D. 9-
442, HCJ Appeal . . . . *Digested*, 98/**5651**
HM Advocate v. McLean 2001 S.L.T. 189; 2000 S.C.C.R. 987; 2000 G.W.D. 38-1441,
HCJ . . . . *Digested*, 01/**6306**
HM Advocate v. McNally (Scott) 1999 S.L.T. 1377; 1999 S.C.C.R. 565, HCJ Appeal . . . *Digested*, 99/**5854**
HM Advocate v. McSalley (Sentencing) 2000 J.C. 485; 2000 S.L.T. 1235; 2000
G.W.D. 16-653, HCJ Appeal . . . . *Digested*, 00/**6131**
HM Advocate v. Megrahi (No.1) see HM Advocate v. Al-Megrahi (No.1)
HM Advocate v. Megrahi (No.2) see HM Advocate v. Al-Megrahi (No.2)
HM Advocate v. Megrahi (No.3) see HM Advocate v. Al-Megrahi (No.3)

HM Advocate *v.* Megrahi (No.4) see HM Advocate *v.* Al-Megrahi (No.4)

HM Advocate *v.* Meikleham (Iain John William) 1999 S.C.C.R. 621, HCJ . . . .   *Digested,* 99/**5873**

HM Advocate *v.* Millard (Sentencing) 2000 G.W.D. 25-939, HCJ Appeal

HM Advocate *v.* Montgomery (David Shields) see Montgomery *v.* HM Advocate

HM Advocate *v.* Montgomery (David Shields) (Amendment of Minute) 2000 J.C. 111;
2000 S.L.T. 122; 1999 S.C.C.R. 959; 1999 G.W.D. 32-1522, HCJ Appeal . . . . . .   *Digested,* 00/**6068**:
Subsequent proceedings, 01/6371

HM Advocate *v.* Muir (David McLaren) 1998 J.C. 20; 1998 S.L.T. 1296; 1997 S.C.C.R.
677; 1997 G.W.D. 35-1750, HCJ. . . . .   *Digested,* 98/**5601**

HM Advocate *v.* Nairn (Michael Alexander) 2000 S.L.T. (Sh Ct) 176; 2000 S.C.C.R.
943; 2000 G.W.D. 31-1224, Sh Ct (Tayside) . . . .   *Digested,* 01/**6353**

HM Advocate *v.* Nulty 2000 S.L.T. 528; 2000 S.C.C.R. 431; 2000 G.W.D. 11-385, HCJ .   *Digested,* 00/**5998**

HM Advocate *v.* P; *sub nom* HM Advocate *v.* DP; DP *v.* SM; HM Advocate *v.* SM 2001
S.L.T. 924; 2001 S.C.C.R. 210; 2001 G.W.D. 7-255, HCJ . . . .   *Digested,* 01/**6351**

HM Advocate *v.* Palmers Ltd 1998 G.W.D. 13-672, Sh Ct

HM Advocate *v.* Paterson (Mark Alexander) (Sentencing) 2000 S.C.C.R. 309; 2000
G.W.D. 7-255, HCJ Appeal. . . . .   *Digested,* 00/**6129**

HM Advocate *v.* Penders 1996 J.C. 107; 1996 S.C.C.R. 404, HCJ . . . .   *Digested,* 96/**6711**

HM Advocate *v.* R 2001 S.L.T. 1366; 2001 S.C.C.R. 915; 2001 G.W.D. 32-1275, HCJ
Appeal . . . .   *Digested,* 01/**6365**

HM Advocate *v.* Rae 1992 S.C.C.R. 1. . . . .   *Digested,* 92/**5524**:
Disapproved, 00/6125

HM Advocate *v.* Renicks 1999 S.L.T. 407; 1998 S.C.C.R. 417, HCJ Appeal. . . . .   *Digested,* 98/**5605**

HM Advocate *v.* Renicks (Ryan James) see HM Advocate *v.* McGlinchey (Martin)

HM Advocate *v.* Robb (Bryan) 2000 J.C. 127; 1999 S.C.C.R. 971; 1999 G.W.D. 32-
1524, HCJ Appeal. . . . .   *Digested,* 00/**6071**

HM Advocate *v.* Roose (Andrew Roy) 1999 S.C.C.R. 259, HCJ . . . .   *Digested,* 99/**5847**

HM Advocate *v.* Sands (Andrew) 2001 S.L.T. 1323; 2001 S.C.C.R. 786; 2001 G.W.D.
26-1017, HCJ Appeal . . . .   *Digested,* 01/**6346**

HM Advocate *v.* Savage (John Henry) 1923 J.C. 49; 1923 S.L.T. 659, HCJ . . . .   *Applied,* 94/5636:
Considered, 01/6335: *Followed,* 90/4945, 92/5510

HM Advocate *v.* Scotsman Publications Ltd 1999 S.L.T. 466; 1999 S.C.C.R. 163; 1998
G.W.D. 21-1060, HCJ Appeal. . . . .   *Digested,* 99/**5827**

HM Advocate *v.* Scottish Media Newspapers Ltd 2000 S.L.T. 331; 1999 S.C.C.R. 599,
HCJ Appeal . . . .   *Digested,* 99/**5826**

HM Advocate *v.* Simpson (Alexander Hastings) 1952 J.C. 1; 1952 S.L.T. 85, HCJ
Appeal . . . .   *Digested,* 52/**3891**:
Applied, 00/6119

HM Advocate *v.* SM see HM Advocate *v.* P

HM Advocate *v.* Smith (David) 1999 S.L.T. 909; 1998 S.C.C.R. 637; 1998 G.W.D. 36-
1871, HCJ Appeal . . . .   *Digested,* 99/**5925**

HM Advocate *v.* Smith (Iain Gary) 1994 J.C. 21; 1994 S.L.T. 683; 1993 S.C.C.R. 987,
HCJ Appeal . . . .   *Digested,* 94/**5556**:
Approved, 00/6050

HM Advocate *v.* Smith (Peter Thomson) 2000 S.C.C.R. 910, HCJ Appeal . . . .   *Digested,* 01/**6323**

HM Advocate *v.* Swift (James Aloysius) 1984 J.C. 83; 1985 S.L.T. 26; 1984 S.C.C.R.
216, HCJ Appeal. . . . .   *Digested,* 84/**3906**:
Applied, 88/3921, 97/5801, 98/5594: *Considered,* 97/5862:
Followed, 97/5803, 01/6344: *Referred to,* 92/5423, 93/4935

HM Advocate *v.* Thom (Alastair Scott) (Sentencing) see HM Advocate *v.* Drain (John
Friel) (Sentencing)

HM Advocate *v.* Todd (George M) see HM Advocate *v.* Young (Alexander)

HM Advocate *v.* Touati 2001 S.L.T. 1195; 2001 S.C.C.R. 392; 2001 G.W.D. 15-576, HCJ
Appeal . . . .   *Digested,* 01/**6382**

HM Advocate *v.* Wales see HM Advocate *v.* Wilson

HM Advocate *v.* Wallace (Kevin Ian James) 1999 S.L.T. 1134; 1999 S.C.C.R. 309; 1999
G.W.D. 12-549, HCJ Appeal. . . . .   *Digested,* 99/**5943**

HM Advocate *v.* Welsh (Gary) 1988 S.L.T. 402, HCJ . . . .   *Digested,* 88/**3987**:
Distinguished, 98/5645

HM Advocate *v.* Wheldon (Ian Adam) 1999 J.C. 5; 1998 S.C.C.R. 710; 1998 G.W.D. 37-
1905, HCJ Appeal. . . . .   *Digested,* 99/**5937**

HM Advocate *v.* Willoughby 2000 S.C.C.R. 73; 1999 G.W.D. 37-1792, HCJ . . . .   *Digested,* 00/**6050**

HM Advocate *v.* Wilson; *sub nom* HM Advocate *v.* Wales; Wilson *v.* HM Advocate;
Wales *v.* HM Advocate 2001 S.C.C.R. 633, HCJ Appeal; reversing 2001 G.W.D.
26-1010, HCJ

HM Advocate *v.* Witherington (1881) 8 R. (J.) 41, HCJ Appeal . . . .   *Distinguished,*
00/6029

HM Advocate *v.* Workman 2000 J.C. 383, HCJ Appeal . . . .   *Digested,* 00/**6085**

HM Advocate *v.* Wright (Karen Halliday) (otherwise Skilbeck) 2001 S.C.C.R. 509;
2001 G.W.D. 19-721, HCJ Appeal

HM Advocate *v.* Young (Alexander); HM Advocate *v.* Todd (George M) 1932 S.L.T.
465, HCJ Appeal . . . .   *Considered,* 84/3858:
Distinguished, 00/6078

HM Advocate, Complainer 2000 J.C. 365; 2000 S.L.T. 653; 2000 S.C.C.R. 439; 2000
    G.W.D. 10-353, HCJ Appeal. . . . .   *Digested*, 00/**6080**
HM Advocate, Petitioner (Bail) 1998 G.W.D. 23-1158, HCJ Appeal
HM Advocate, Petitioner (Indecent Exposure) 1998 G.W.D. 20-1007, HCJ Appeal
Hodge v. Higson (Sentencing) 2001 G.W.D. 18-699, HCJ Appeal
Hodge v. HM Advocate (Sentencing) 1998 G.W.D. 3-112, HCJ Appeal
Hodge (James Boyce) v. McFadyen 2000 S.C.C.R. 648; 2000 G.W.D. 22-846, HCJ
    Appeal . . . .   *Digested*, 00/**6024**
Hodgson v. Fraser 2001 G.W.D. 24-914, HCJ Appeal
Hoekstra v. HM Advocate (No.1); Van Rijs (Jan) v. HM Advocate (No.1); Van Rijs
    (Ronny) v. HM Advocate (No.1); Van Rijs (Hendrik) v. HM Advocate (No.1) 2000
    S.C.C.R. 263; 2000 G.W.D. 6-221, HCJ Appeal . . . .   *Digested*, 00/**6054**
Hoekstra v. HM Advocate (No.2); Van Rijs (Jan) v. HM Advocate (No.2); Van Rijs
    (Ronny) v. HM Advocate (No.2); Van Rijs (Hendrik) v. HM Advocate (No.2)
    2000 J.C. 387; 2000 S.L.T. 602; 2000 G.W.D. 11-382, HCJ Appeal . . . .   *Digested*, 00/**6063**
Hoekstra v. HM Advocate (No.3); Van Rijs (Jan) v. HM Advocate (No.3); Van Rijs
    (Ronny) v. HM Advocate (No.3); Van Rijs (Hendrik) v. HM Advocate (No.3)
    2000 J.C. 391; 2000 S.L.T. 605; 2000 S.C.C.R. 367; [2000] H.R.L.R. 410;
    [2000] U.K.H.R.R. 578; 2000 G.W.D. 12-417; *Times*, April 14, 2000, HCJ
    Appeal . . . .   *Digested*, 00/**6092**:
                                               Followed, 01/6249
Hoekstra v. HM Advocate (No.4); Van Rijs (Jan) v. HM Advocate (No.4); Van Rijs
    (Ronny) v. HM Advocate (No.4); Van Rijs (Hendrik) v. HM Advocate (No.4)
    2000 J.C. 599; 2000 S.C.C.R. 676; 2000 G.W.D. 22-849, HCJ Appeal . . . .   *Digested*, 00/**6107**
Hoekstra v. HM Advocate (No.5); Van Rijs (Jan) v. HM Advocate (No.5); Van Rijs
    (Ronny) v. HM Advocate (No.5); Van Rijs (Hendrik) v. HM Advocate (No.5)
    [2001] 1 A.C. 216; [2000] 3 W.L.R. 1817; 2001 S.C. (P.C.) 37; 2001 S.L.T. 28;
    2000 S.C.C.R. 1121; (2000) 144 S.J.L.B. 272; 2000 G.W.D. 40-1486; *Times*,
    October 31, 2000, PC (Sc) . . . .   *Digested*, 00/**6057**
Hoekstra v. HM Advocate (No.6); Van Rijs (Jan) v. HM Advocate (No.6); Van Rijs
    (Ronny) v. HM Advocate (No.6); Van Rijs (Hendrik) v. HM Advocate (No.6)
    2001 J.C. 131; 2001 S.L.T. 632; 2001 S.C.C.R. 121; 2001 G.W.D. 3-115, HCJ
    Appeal . . . .   *Digested*, 01/**6347**
Hogg v. Angiolini (Sentencing) 2001 G.W.D. 13-488, HCJ Appeal
Hogg v. Carrigan see Hogg v. Carrigan's Executrix
Hogg v. Carrigan's Executrix; *sub nom* Hogg v. Carrigan 2001 S.C. 542; 2001 S.L.T.
    444; 2001 Rep. L.R. 60; 2001 G.W.D. 3-122, OH . . . .   *Digested*, 01/**6415**
Hogg (Steven Kenneth) v. HM Advocate 1999 J.C. 142; 1999 S.L.T. 371; 1998 S.C.C.R.
    338; 1998 G.W.D. 13-638, HCJ Appeal . . . .   *Digested*, 98/**5611**
Hogg v. Inverclyde Council 1998 G.W.D. 12-583, Sh Ct
Hogg v. MacNeill 2001 S.L.T. 873; 2001 S.C.C.R. 134; 2000 G.W.D. 40-1514, HCJ
    Appeal
Hogg v. Motherwell DC 2001 G.W.D. 40-1495, 2 Div
Hogg v. Normand 1992 S.L.T. 736; 1992 S.C.C.R. 26, HCJ Appeal . . . .   *Digested*, 92/**5483**:
                Applied, 96/6799, 98/5629: *Distinguished*, 96/6802: *Followed*, 97/5855
Hogg v. Stott 1998 G.W.D. 35-1836, HCJ Appeal
Hoggan's Curator ad Litem v. Cowan 2000 G.W.D. 27-1050, Sh Ct (Lothian)
Holliday v. Higson (Sentencing) 2000 G.W.D. 37-1415, HCJ Appeal
Holmes v. Secretary of State for Scotland 1999 S.L.T. 706; 1998 G.W.D. 27-1351, OH. . .   *Digested*, 99/**6390**
Home Office v. Dorset Yacht Co Ltd [1970] A.C. 1004; [1970] 2 W.L.R. 1140; [1970] 2
    All E.R. 294; [1970] 1 Lloyd's Rep. 453; 114 S.J. 375, HL; affirming [1969] 2
    Q.B. 412; [1969] 2 W.L.R. 1008; [1969] 2 All E.R. 564; 113 S.J. 227, CA;
    affirming 113 S.J. 57; *Times*, December 20, 1968, QBD. . . . .   *Digested*, 70/**1849**:
                    Applied, 71/7843, 72/1104, 72/2352, 72/2532, 77/2030, 78/2068, 78/3250,
                    78/3606, 79/1865, 81/1859, 81/3409, 82/4055, 83/2531, 84/2298,
                    95/3730: *Approved*, 73/2308: *Considered*, 79/1866, 82/2126, 82/4057,
                    83/2538, 85/3549, 86/4338, 87/2580, 87/2597, 87/4737, 88/2435,
                    89/1286, 95/3452, 95/3681: *Distinguished*, 83/2746, 87/2857, 93/2958,
                    94/3384, 98/3938: *Followed*, 00/6585: *Referred to*, 72/2528, 73/2306,
                    75/2324, 79/1884
Homecare Contracts (Scotland) Ltd v. Scottish Midland Cooperative Society Ltd 1999
    G.W.D. 23-1111, Sh Pr
Homer Burgess Ltd v. Chirex (Annan) Ltd 2000 S.L.T. 277; [2000] B.L.R. 124; 71 Con.
    L.R. 245; 1999 G.W.D. 38-1843; 1999 G.W.D. 38-1844; *Times*, January 25,
    2000, OH . . . .   *Digested*, 00/**5979**:
                                               Followed, 01/859
Hood v. Anchor Line (Henderson Bros) Ltd [1918] A.C. 837; 1918 S.C. (H.L.) 143;
    (1918) 2 S.L.T. 118, HL; affirming 1918 S.C. 27, 2 Div . . . .   *Considered*, 68/519:
                                               Followed, 00/5989
Hood v. Vannet 1999 G.W.D. 21-1000, HCJ Appeal
Hooke v. Glasgow see Hooke, Noter
Hooke, Noter; *sub nom* Hooke v. Glasgow 2000 S.L.T. 1028; 2000 S.C.L.R. 936; 2000
    G.W.D. 25-947, Ex Div . . . .   *Digested*, 00/**6509**
Hooks v. McFadyen 1999 G.W.D. 20-949, HCJ Appeal

Horlick's Trustees v. O'Hara 2001 S.L.C.R. 125, Land Ct (Div Ct)
Horn v. Clark 1999 G.W.D. 23-1121, HCJ Appeal
Horsburgh v. Howdle (Sentencing) 2000 G.W.D. 30-1170, HCJ Appeal
Hosie v. Heywood 1999 G.W.D. 38-1848, HCJ Appeal
Hosie v. Higson 1998 G.W.D. 38-1960, HCJ Appeal
Hosie v. Vannet 1999 G.W.D. 20-966, HCJ Appeal
Houghton v. HM Advocate 1999 G.W.D. 17-789, HCJ Appeal
Houghton v. Reith 2000 G.W.D. 14-566, HCJ Appeal
Houston v. Carnegie 1999 G.W.D. 36-1777, HCJ Appeal
Houston (David) v. Carnegie; *sub nom* Houston v. Macdonald 2000 S.L.T. 333; 1999
    S.C.C.R. 605, HCJ Appeal. . . . . *Digested*, 99/**5798**
Houston v. Macdonald see Houston (David) v. Carnegie
Houston v. Vannet (Sentencing) 1998 G.W.D. 12-620, HCJ Appeal
Howarth v. Friel 1998 G.W.D. 25-1281, HCJ Appeal
Howatson v. Walker (Sentencing) 1998 G.W.D. 16-825, HCJ Appeal
Howdle v. O'Connor 1998 S.L.T. 94; 1997 G.W.D. 15-694, HCJ Appeal . . . . *Digested*, 98/**5589**
Howells v. Munro 1998 G.W.D. 37-1915, HCJ Appeal
Howes v. Castle View Services Ltd see Castle View Services Ltd v. Howes
Howes v. Crombie 2001 S.C.L.R. 921; 2001 Rep. L.R. 98; 2001 G.W.D. 23-873, OH
Howgate Shopping Centre Ltd v. Pinwise Ltd 2001 G.W.D. 28-1142, OH
Howie v. HM Advocate 1999 G.W.D. 17-795, HCJ Appeal
Howitt (Alan John) v. HM Advocate; Duffy (Anthony) v. HM Advocate 2000 J.C. 284;
    2000 S.L.T. 449; 2000 S.C.C.R. 195; 2000 G.W.D. 1-13, HCJ Appeal . . . .   *Digested*, 00/**6078**:
                                            Referred to, 00/6055
Howitt (Alan John) v. HM Advocate (Sentencing) 2000 G.W.D. 8-287, HCJ Appeal
Hoy v. HM Advocate see Hoy v. McFadyen
Hoy (Derek Gavin) v. HM Advocate 1999 G.W.D. 12-542, HCJ Appeal
Hoy (Sean) v. HM Advocate (Retrial) 1998 S.C.C.R. 8; 1998 G.W.D. 1-9, HCJ Appeal . .   *Digested*, 98/**5568**
Hoy v. McFadyen; *sub nom* Hoy v. HM Advocate 2000 J.C. 313; 2000 S.L.T. 1060;
    2000 S.C.C.R. 875; 2000 G.W.D. 8-315, HCJ Appeal . . . .   *Digested*, 00/**6153**
HSBC Gibbs Ltd v. Torrance 1999 G.W.D. 3-127, 2 Div; affirming 1999 G.W.D. 3-126, OH
Hudson v. HM Advocate 1998 G.W.D. 40-2066, HCJ Appeal
Hugh Macrae & Co (Builders) Ltd v. Secretary of State for Scotland 1999 G.W.D. 28-
    1350; 1999 G.W.D. 24-1173, OH
Hughes v. Friel (Sentencing) 1998 G.W.D. 1-24, HCJ Appeal
Hughes v. HM Advocate (Sentencing) 1999 G.W.D. 13-613, HCJ Appeal
Hughes v. HM Advocate (Sentencing) 1999 G.W.D. 31-1473, HCJ Appeal
Hughes (Brian Andrew) v. HM Advocate 2001 G.W.D. 15-572, HCJ Appeal
Hughes (David Alexander) v. HM Advocate 2000 S.C.C.R. 250; 2000 G.W.D. 9-327,
    HCJ Appeal . . . . *Digested*, 00/**6112**
Hughes (Ryan Iain) v. HM Advocate; Steedman v. HM Advocate 1997 J.C. 151; 1998
    S.L.T. 48; 1997 S.C.C.R. 277; 1997 G.W.D. 11-454, HCJ Appeal . . . . *Digested*, 97/**5868**
Hughes v. Lees (Sentencing) 1998 G.W.D. 32-1655, HCJ Appeal
Hughes (Russell McDonald) v. Lord Advocate [1963] A.C. 837; [1963] 2 W.L.R. 779;
    [1963] 1 All E.R. 705; 1963 S.C. 31; 1963 S.C. (H.L.) 31; 1963 S.L.T. 150; (1963)
    107 S.J. 232, HL; reversing 1961 S.C. 310; 1962 S.L.T. 90, 1 Div . . . .   *Digested*, 63/**4056**:
                      Applied, 64/2500, 66/8175, 66/8283, 67/1197, 67/2675, 70/744, 75/933,
                          75/2288, 80/1904, 83/3962, 87/2614, 98/3988, 98/6107:
                Considered, 69/2412, 90/3285, 96/4427, 00/4239: *Distinguished*, 64/2499:
                                         Followed, 84/4347, 85/4437
Hughes v. Vannet 1999 G.W.D. 21-1002, HCJ Appeal
Hull v. Walkingshaw (Sentencing) 1998 G.W.D. 4-175, HCJ Appeal
Humphrey v. HM Advocate (Sentencing) 2000 G.W.D. 4-136, HCJ Appeal
Humphries v. Elmegirab 1998 S.C.L.R. 783, Sh Ct . . . . *Digested*, 98/**5714**
Hunt v. HM Advocate (Sentencing) 1998 G.W.D. 15-762, HCJ Appeal
Hunter v. Canary Wharf Ltd; *sub nom* Hunter v. London Docklands Development Corp
    [1997] A.C. 655; [1997] 2 W.L.R. 684; [1997] 2 All E.R. 426; [1997] C.L.C.
    1045; 84 B.L.R. 1; 54 Con. L.R. 12; [1997] Env. L.R. 488; [1997] 2 F.L.R. 342;
    (1998) 30 H.L.R. 409; [1997] Fam. Law 601; [1997] E.G.C.S. 59; (1997) 94(19)
    L.S.G. 25; (1997) 147 N.L.J. 634; (1997) 141 S.J.L.B. 108; [1997] N.P.C. 64;
    Times, April 25, 1997; *Independent*, May 2, 1997, HL; affirming [1996] 2 W.L.R.
    348; [1996] 1 All E.R. 482; [1996] C.L.C. 197; 75 B.L.R. 27; 47 Con. L.R. 136;
    [1996] Env. L.R. 138; (1996) 28 H.L.R. 383; [1995] E.G.C.S. 153; (1995)
    92(39) L.S.G. 28; (1995) 145 N.L.J. 1645; (1995) 139 S.J.L.B. 214; [1995]
    N.P.C. 155; *Times*, October 13, 1995; *Independent*, October 19, 1995, CA;
    affirming in part *Independent*, January 23, 1995 (C.S.); *Independent*, December
    20, 1994, QBD . . . . *Digested*, 97/**3865**:
                Applied, 01/3800: *Considered*, 99/4067: *Distinguished*, 00/4297:
                                Followed, 98/4040, 99/3681
Hunter v. Gallagher 1999 G.W.D. 30-1445, HCJ Appeal

Hunter v. Hanley; *sub nom* Galloway (or Hunter) v. Hanley 1955 S.C. 200; 1955 S.L.T.
213; [1955-95] P.N.L.R. 1, 1 Div; reversing 1954 S.L.T. 303, OH . . . . *Digested*, 55/**3451**:
Applied, 83/2548, 83/2576, 83/3962, 84/2322, 90/3264, 97/6302,
00/6588: *Considered*, 86/3608, 89/2558: *Distinguished*, 00/6585:
Followed, 90/5498: *Not applied*, 88/4930, 89/3935, 89/4195:
Referred to, 00/6603
Hunter v. Higson (Sentencing) 2001 G.W.D. 16-604, HCJ Appeal
Hunter v. HM Advocate (Sentencing) 2001 G.W.D. 13-485, HCJ Appeal
Hunter v. HM Advocate (Sentencing) 2001 G.W.D. 25-938, HCJ Appeal
Hunter (Gary John) v. HM Advocate; *sub nom* Silverman (Brian) v. HM Advocate 1999
J.C. 117; 1999 S.C.C.R. 72, HCJ Appeal . . . . *Digested*, 99/**5893**
Hunter (Thomas) v. HM Advocate 1999 G.W.D. 11-490; 1999 G.W.D. 11-505, HCJ
Appeal
Hunter (Duncan John) v. Hunter (Jill Caroline) 1999 S.C. 1; 1998 S.L.T. 1152; 1997
S.C.L.R. 962; 1997 G.W.D. 28-1445, OH . . . . *Digested*, 98/**6121**
Hunter v. Lees 1998 G.W.D. 37-1944, HCJ Appeal
Hunter v. London Docklands Development Corp see Hunter v. Canary Wharf Ltd
Hunter v. Moffat's Trustees 1999 G.W.D. 11-488, OH
Hunter v. Perth and Kinross Council 2001 S.C.L.R. 856; 2001 Rep. L.R. 95 (Note);
2001 G.W.D. 25-974, OH
Hunter v. Secretary of State for Scotland 1998 S.C. 446; 1998 S.C.L.R. 446, Ex Div . . . *Digested*, 98/**6147**
Hunter v. Vannet (Sentencing) 1998 G.W.D. 6-269, HCJ Appeal
Hunter v. Vannet (Sentencing) 2000 S.C.C.R. 131; 2000 G.W.D. 4-141, HCJ Appeal . . . . *Digested*, 00/**6145**
Hurley v. Reith 1998 G.W.D. 31-1606, HCJ Appeal
Hurley v. William Muir (Bond 9) Ltd 2000 G.W.D. 4-158, OH
Hurst Fuels Ltd v. Dundonald House Ltd; *sub nom* Mackinnon, Noter 1999 S.C.L.R.
767; 1999 G.W.D. 13-619, 2 Div . . . . *Digested*, 99/**5681**
Husband (Brian) v. Russell 1998 S.L.T. 377; 1997 S.C.C.R. 592; 1997 G.W.D. 27-1378,
HCJ Appeal . . . . *Digested*, 97/**6398**
Hussman Manufacturing Ltd v. Weir [1998] I.R.L.R. 288; (1998) 95(31) L.S.G. 34, EAT   *Digested*, 98/**5827**
Hutcheson v. HM Advocate (Sentencing) 2001 S.C.C.R. 43; 2000 G.W.D. 39-1450,
HCJ Appeal . . . . *Digested*, 01/**6394**
Hutchison v. Clark (Sentencing) 2001 G.W.D. 36-1375, HCJ Appeal
Hutchison v. Clydeport Operations Ltd 1998 S.C. 336; 1998 S.L.T. 765; 1998 G.W.D.
4-197, Ex Div; affirming 1997 G.W.D. 12-535, OH . . . . *Digested*, 98/**6188**
Hutchison v. HM Advocate (Sentencing) 2001 G.W.D. 26-1041, HCJ Appeal
Hutchison (David John) v. HM Advocate 1998 S.L.T. 679; 1997 S.C.C.R. 726; 1998
G.W.D. 1-12, HCJ Appeal . . . . *Digested*, 98/**5567**
Hutchison v. Lees 1998 G.W.D. 28-1399, HCJ Appeal
Hutchison v. Munro (Sentencing) 1998 G.W.D. 3-118, HCJ Appeal
Hutchison v. Vannet (Sentencing) 1998 G.W.D. 2-66, HCJ Appeal
Hutton v. Coal Authority 2001 S.L.C.R. 1, Land Ct (Full Ct)
Hutton v. Heywood 1998 G.W.D. 20-1011, HCJ Appeal
Hutton v. Higson 1999 G.W.D. 29-1397, HCJ Appeal
Huwaish v. Vannet 1999 G.W.D. 22-1067, HCJ Appeal
Huxtable v. Fraser (Sentencing) 1998 G.W.D. 11-573, HCJ Appeal
Huxtable v. Vannet 1999 G.W.D. 18-839, HCJ Appeal
Hydro Seafood GSP Ltd v. Scottish Ministers 2000 G.W.D. 7-260, OH
Hynd v. McGlennan 2000 S.C.C.R. 231; 2000 G.W.D. 7-253, HCJ Appeal . . . . *Digested*, 00/**6106**

I, Petitioner; *sub nom* DI, Petitioner 1999 Fam. L.R. 126; 1999 G.W.D. 21-972, OH . . . . . *Digested*, 00/**6253**
Ian Gordon Commercials v. Richmond Light Transport 1998 S.L.T. (Sh Ct) 69; 1998
G.W.D. 7-311, Sh Pr . . . . *Digested*, 98/**5507**
Ideal Services Scotland Ltd v. Premier Glass Packaging Ltd 1999 S.L.T. 134; 1998
G.W.D. 7-321, OH . . . . *Digested*, 99/**5794**
Imbrioscia v. Switzerland (A/275) (1994) 17 E.H.R.R. 441, ECHR . . . . *Digested*, 94/**2407**:
Applied, 00/3223: *Considered*, 98/3146, 01/6760: *Followed*, 97/2817
Imlach v. Perry 1998 G.W.D. 38-1963, HCJ Appeal
Imlay v. Heywood (Sentencing) 1998 G.W.D. 6-265, HCJ Appeal
Imrie v. Comhairle nan Eilean Siar see Imrie, Petitioner
Imrie v. Western Isles Council see Imrie, Petitioner
Imrie, Petitioner; *sub nom* Imrie v. Comhairle nan Eilean Siar; Imrie v. Western Isles
Council 2000 S.C.L.R. 364; 1999 G.W.D. 28-1341, OH . . . . *Digested*, 00/**6195**
Inayat v. Secretary of State for the Home Department 2001 G.W.D. 37-1407, OH
Inderhaug v. Grampian RC 1999 Fam. L.R. 119, Sh Ct . . . . *Digested*, 00/**6190**
Ingle v. Ingle's Trustee 1999 S.L.T. 650; 1998 G.W.D. 22-1110, 2 Div; affirming 1997
S.L.T. 160, OH . . . . *Digested*, 99/**5618**
Inglis v. Buttery & Co (1878) 5 R. (H.L.) 87, HL . . . . *Applied*, 00/**6437**
Inglis v. Inglis 1999 S.L.T. (Sh Ct) 59; 1998 G.W.D. 26-1335, Sh Ct (Lothian) . . . . *Digested*, 99/**6076**
Inglis v. Lees 1998 G.W.D. 29-1467, HCJ Appeal
Inglis v. National Bank of Scotland Ltd (No.2) 1911 S.C. 6, 1 Div . . . . *Followed*, 00/**5940**
Inglis (Alexander) & Son Ltd v. Forth Ports Plc 2000 G.W.D. 27-1035, OH
Ingram v. HM Advocate 1999 G.W.D. 16-743, HCJ Appeal

Ingram v. HM Advocate (Sentencing) 1998 G.W.D. 21-1064, HCJ Appeal
Ingram v. Ingram 2001 G.W.D. 29-1165, Sh Ct (Grampian)
Ingram v. McLeod 1999 G.W.D. 33-1599, HCJ Appeal
Inkson v. McKay 1999 G.W.D. 3-152, HCJ Appeal
Inland Revenue Commissioners v. Aberdeen Milk Co Ltd [1999] S.T.C. 787; 2000
    S.C.L.R. 37; 73 T.C. 563; [1999] B.T.C. 378; 1999 G.W.D. 24-1127, Ex Div . . . . .   *Digested*, 99/**6456**
Inland Revenue Commissioners v. Fraser 1942 S.C. 493; 1942 S.L.T. 280, 1 Div . . . .   *Applied*, 55/417,
    55/1287, 99/6471: *Considered*, 54/1555: *Not followed*, 53/1693
Inland Revenue Commissioners v. Macdonald 1998 G.W.D. 26-1287, Sh Ct
Inland Revenue Commissioners v. McIntosh see Inland Revenue Commissioners v.
    McMillan's Curator Bonis
Inland Revenue Commissioners v. McMillan's Curator Bonis; *sub nom* Inland Revenue
    Commissioners v. McIntosh 1956 S.C. 142; 1956 S.L.T. 67; (1955) 49 R. & I.T.
    137; 36 T.C. 334; (1955) 34 A.T.C. 345; [1955] T.R. 333, 1 Div . . . .   *Digested*, 56/**11283**:
    Considered, 98/5464
Inland Revenue Commissioners v. Shepherd 2001 G.W.D. 25-968, OH
Innes v. Howdle (Sentencing) 2001 G.W.D. 25-930, HCJ Appeal
Institute of Chartered Accountants of Scotland v. Kay 2001 S.L.T. 1449; 2001 S.C.L.R.
    1086; 2001 G.W.D. 27-1079, OH
Institute of Chartered Accountants of Scotland v. Martin 1998 G.W.D. 26-1286, 1 Div
Interfoto Picture Library Ltd v. Stiletto Visual Programmes Ltd [1989] Q.B. 433; [1988]
    2 W.L.R. 615; [1988] 1 All E.R. 348; (1988) 7 Tr. L.R. 187; (1988) 85(9) L.S.G.
    45; (1987) 137 N.L.J. 1159; [1988] 132 S.J. 460, CA . . . .   *Digested*, 88/**430**:
    Applied, 00/5989, 01/955: *Considered*, 88/61, 95/4501, 99/1801, 00/876,
    00/4710
International Computers Ltd v. Eccleson 2000 G.W.D. 28-1074, OH
Inverdale Ltd v. Secretary of State for Scotland 2000 G.W.D. 22-870, 1 Div
Inverness Seafield Development Co Ltd v. Mackintosh 2001 S.C. 406; 2001 S.L.T. 118;
    2000 G.W.D. 38-1431, 1 Div; reversing 1999 G.W.D. 31-1497, OH . . . .   *Digested*, 01/**6677**
Inverness Taxi Owners and Drivers Association v. Highland Council 1999 S.L.T. 1316;
    1999 G.W.D. 10-445; *Times*, May 5, 1999, OH . . . .   *Digested*, 99/**5626**
Investors Compensation Scheme Ltd v. Hopkin & Sons see Investors Compensation
    Scheme Ltd v. West Bromwich Building Society (No.1)
Investors Compensation Scheme Ltd v. West Bromwich Building Society (No.1);
    Investors Compensation Scheme Ltd v. Hopkin & Sons; Alford v. West
    Bromwich Building Society; Armitage v. West Bromwich Building Society [1998]
    1 W.L.R. 896; [1998] 1 All E.R. 98; [1998] 1 B.C.L.C. 531; [1997] C.L.C. 1243;
    [1997] P.N.L.R. 541; (1997) 147 N.L.J. 989; *Times*, June 24, 1997, HL; reversing
    [1998] 1 B.C.L.C. 521; [1997] C.L.C. 363; [1997] P.N.L.R. 166; [1997] N.P.C.
    104; *Times*, November 8, 1996, CA; affirming [1998] 1 B.C.L.C. 493; [1997]
    C.L.C. 348; *Times*, October 10, 1996, Ch D . . . .   *Digested*, 97/**2537**:
    Applied, 99/852, 99/3420, 99/5795, 00/900, 01/375, 01/959, 01/4272,
    01/4950, 01/5508: *Cited*, 99/2489: *Considered*, 99/2480, 00/878, 00/3686,
    00/5932, 01/2430: *Followed*, 98/807, 00/2173
Iomega Corp v. Myrica (UK) Ltd (No.1) 1999 S.L.T. 793; 1997 G.W.D. 39-1980, OH . . .   *Digested*, 99/**5663**
Iomega Corp v. Myrica (UK) Ltd (No.2); *sub nom* Iomega Corp, Petitioners 1998 S.C.
    637; 1999 S.L.T. 796; 1998 S.C.L.R. 475; 1998 G.W.D. 16-774; *Times*, May 28,
    1998, 1 Div . . . .   *Digested*, 98/**5451**
Iomega Corp, Petitioners see Iomega Corp v. Myrica (UK) Ltd (No.2)
IPCC Ltd v. Caledonian Quarry Products Ltd 2000 G.W.D. 36-1353, OH
Iqbal v. Vannet (Sentencing) 1998 G.W.D. 4-413, HCJ Appeal
Irani v. Southampton and South West Hampshire HA [1985] I.C.R. 590; [1985]
    I.R.L.R. 203; (1985) 82 L.S.G. 1167, Ch D . . . .   *Digested*, 85/**1181**:
    Considered, 90/1858, 98/5814: *Distinguished*, 91/1622
Ireland v. Birmingham City Council see R. v. Birmingham City Council Ex p. Ireland
Ireland v. Dunfermline DC 1998 S.L.T. 321; 1997 Rep. L.R. 62; 1997 G.W.D. 10-405,
    OH . . . .   *Digested*, 97/**5691**
Ireland Alloys Ltd v. Buchanan see Ireland Alloys Ltd v. Dingwall
Ireland Alloys Ltd v. Dingwall; *sub nom* Ireland Alloys Ltd v. Buchanan 1999 S.L.T. 267;
    1998 G.W.D. 13-635, OH . . . .   *Digested*, 99/**5730**
Irvine v. Balmoral Hotel Edinburgh Ltd 1999 Rep. L.R. 41; 1998 G.W.D. 38-1952, OH . . .   *Digested*, 99/**5668**
Irvine v. Friel 1998 G.W.D. 26-1349, HCJ Appeal
Irvine (George Lees) v. HM Advocate 2000 J.C. 321; 2000 S.C.C.R. 234; 2000 G.W.D.
    5-186, HCJ Appeal . . . .   *Digested*, 00/**6114**
Irving v. Hiddleston 1998 S.C. 759; 1998 S.L.T. 912; 1998 S.C.L.R. 350; 1998 G.W.D.
    7-320, OH . . . .   *Digested*, 98/**5715**
Irving v. Irving 1998 S.C.L.R. 373, Sh Pr . . . .   *Digested*, 98/**5499**
Irzikevikius v. Secretary of State for the Home Department 2001 G.W.D. 25-967, Ex
    Div
Islam (Mujahid) v. Heywood 1999 S.C.C.R. 68; 1999 G.W.D. 4-199, HCJ Appeal . . . . .   *Digested*, 99/**5960**
Italian Bank Ltd v. Olivieri 1938 S.L.T. (Sh. Ct.) 27, Sh Ct (North Strathclyde) . . . .   *Approved*, 99/6431
Italian Distribution Co v. Pizza & Pasta see BSS Group Plc v. Huntly Plumbing, Heating
    & Electrical
Itelsor Ltd v. Smith 2001 Hous. L.R. 120; 2001 G.W.D. 7-260, Lands Tr (Scot)

Ivey v. Secretary of State for Employment see Buchan v. Secretary of State for Employment

Ivory & Sime Trustlink Ltd v. Customs and Excise Commissioners [1998] S.T.C. 597; 1998 S.C. 774; 1998 S.C.L.R. 968; [1998] B.T.C. 5173; [1998] B.V.C. 191; 1998 G.W.D. 14-731, 1 Div . . . . *Digested,* 98/**6216**

Izatt v. Robertson (1842) 2 D. 476, 1 Div . . . . *Followed,* 00/5951

J v. Aberdeen City Council; *sub nom* Aberdeen City Council v. J 1999 S.C. 404; 1999 S.L.T. 953; 1999 Fam. L.R. 75; 1999 G.W.D. 16-728, 2 Div . . . . *Digested,* 99/**6055**

J v. Caldwell 2001 S.L.T. (Sh Ct) 164; 2001 Fam. L.R. 54; 2001 G.W.D. 10-326, Sh Ct (South Strathclyde) . . . . *Digested,* 01/**6505**

J v. HM Advocate 1998 G.W.D. 29-1508, HCJ Appeal

J Kelly & Sons Ltd v. Meat & Livestock Commission 2001 S.C.L.R. 1093; 2001 G.W.D. 26-994, OH

J Sainsbury Plc v. Secretary of State for Scotland 1997 S.L.T. 1391; 1997 G.W.D. 14-629, Ex Div . . . . *Digested,* 98/**6143**

J Sykes & Sons (Fish Merchants) Ltd v. Grieve 2001 G.W.D. 23-866, Sh Pr

Jabbo v. McFadyen 1999 G.W.D. 34-1648, HCJ Appeal

Jack (James Geddes) v. HM Advocate 1999 S.L.T. 749; 1999 S.C.C.R. 296; 1999 G.W.D. 14-629, HCJ Appeal . . . . *Digested,* 99/**5806**

Jack v. McIntyre's Executors 1999 S.L.T. 85; 1998 G.W.D. 1-49, OH . . . . *Digested,* 99/**6333**

Jack v. O'Donnell 2001 G.W.D. 30-1187, HCJ Appeal

Jack Allen (Sales & Service) Ltd v. Smith 1999 S.L.T. 820; [1999] I.R.L.R. 19; 1998 G.W.D. 38-1957, OH . . . . *Digested,* 99/**6031**

Jackson v. Fleming see Fleming's Trustee v. Fleming

Jackson v. Friel 1998 G.W.D. 31-1612, HCJ Appeal

Jackson v. Heywood 1998 G.W.D. 17-879, HCJ Appeal

Jackson (John) v. HM Advocate 1998 S.C.C.R. 539; 1998 G.W.D. 33-1695, HCJ Appeal . . . . *Digested,* 98/**5680**

Jackson v. Jackson 2000 S.C.L.R. 81; 1999 Fam. L.R. 108, OH . . . . *Digested,* 00/**6275**

Jackson (Matthew) v. McFadyen (Procurator Fiscal) 2001 S.C.C.R. 224, HCJ Appeal . *Digested,* 01/**6395**

Jacques v. Oxfordshire CC 66 L.G.R. 440, Assizes (Oxford) . . . . *Digested,* 68/**2727**: *Followed,* 80/861: *Referred to,* 00/6588

Jahov v. Reith 1999 G.W.D. 10-480, HCJ Appeal

Jalloh v. Secretary of State for the Home Department; *sub nom* Jalloh, Petitioner 2001 G.W.D. 36-1392, OH

Jalloh, Petitioner see Jalloh v. Secretary of State for the Home Department

James Aitken & Sons (Meat Producers) Ltd v. Edinburgh DC 1990 S.L.T. 241; 1989 S.C.L.R. 674, OH . . . . *Digested,* 90/**5943**: *Distinguished,* 01/6855: *Followed,* 90/5944

James Callander & Sons Ltd v. Gallagher 1999 S.C.C.R. 788; 1999 G.W.D. 32-1550, HCJ Appeal . . . . *Digested,* 00/**6427**

James Cardno (Shopfitters) Ltd v. Royal Bank of Scotland Plc 2001 G.W.D. 20-756, Sh Pr

James Howden & Co Ltd v. Taylor Woodrow Property Co Ltd 1998 S.C. 853; 1999 S.L.T. 841; 1998 S.C.L.R. 903; 1998 G.W.D. 27-1386, Ex Div; affirming 1997 G.W.D. 32-1637; *Times,* December 8, 1997, OH . . . . *Digested,* 98/**5550**

James Scott Ltd v. Apollo Engineering Ltd 2000 S.C. 228; 2000 S.L.T. 1262; 2000 G.W.D. 5-180, OH . . . . *Digested,* 00/**5980**

James Sim (Building and Civil Engineering) Ltd v. Douglas Dickson (Property Management) Ltd 1998 G.W.D. 7-308, 1 Div

James Strang Ltd v. Vannet 1998 G.W.D. 16-808, HCJ Appeal

Jamieson v. Cradock 2001 G.W.D. 29-1151, Sh Ct (Grampian)

Jamieson v. Criminal Injuries Compensation Board 1999 G.W.D. 38-1846, OH

Jamieson v. Higgins 1998 Rep. L.R. 23 (Note), OH . . . . *Digested,* 98/**5735**

Jamieson v. Higson 2001 G.W.D. 35-1342, HCJ Appeal

Jamieson v. HM Advocate (Sentencing) 1998 G.W.D. 16-793, HCJ Appeal

Jamieson v. HM Advocate (Sentencing) 2001 G.W.D. 36-1386, HCJ Appeal

Jamieson v. Jamieson [1952] A.C. 525; [1952] 1 All E.R. 875; 1952 S.C. (H.L.) 44; 1952 S.L.T. 257; [1952] 1 T.L.R. 833; 116 J.P. 226, HL; reversing 1951 S.C. 286; 1951 S.L.T. 174, 1 Div . . . . *Digested,* 52/**4378**: *Applied,* 52/984, 54/950, 54/951, 54/3721, 55/782, 55/788, 56/2542, 57/1025, 60/951, 62/911, 62/921, 94/6087, 95/6163, 00/6599: *Considered,* 73/886, 73/3632, 94/6150: *Distinguished,* 54/943: *Followed,* 01/6252

Jamieson v. McGlennan (Sentencing) 1999 G.W.D. 36-1763, HCJ Appeal

Jamil v. Secretary of State for the Home Department 1999 G.W.D. 27-1293, OH

Japan Leasing (Europe) Plc v. Hastings see Japan Leasing (Europe) Plc v. Weir's Trustee (No.1)

Japan Leasing (Europe) Plc v. Weir's Trustee (No.1); *sub nom* Japan Leasing (Europe) Plc v. Hastings 1998 S.L.T. 224; 1997 S.C.L.R. 519; 1997 G.W.D. 16-706, 1 Div . . *Digested,* 97/**5648**

Japan Leasing (Europe) Plc v. Weir's Trustee (No.2) 1998 S.C. 543; 1998 S.L.T. 973; 1998 G.W.D. 13-631, 2 Div . . . . *Digested,* 98/**5434**

Jardine (Robert) v. Crowe 1999 J.C. 59; 1999 S.L.T. 1023; 1999 S.C.C.R. 52; 1999
G.W.D. 3-161, HCJ Appeal . . . . *Digested*, 99/**5883**
Jardine v. Howdle 1997 J.C. 163; 1998 S.L.T. 142; 1997 S.C.C.R. 294; 1997 G.W.D. 14-
583, HCJ Appeal . . . . *Digested*, 97/**5754**
Jardine v. Lord Advocate see Sellwood's Curator Bonis v. Lord Advocate
Jardine v. Vannet 1998 G.W.D. 18-947, HCJ Appeal
Jardine v. Webster (Sentencing) 1998 G.W.D. 5-210, HCJ Appeal
Jarvie v. HM Advocate (Sentencing) 1998 G.W.D. 10-502, HCJ Appeal
Jeffrey v. Dixon 1983 S.L.C.R. 69, Land Ct (Div Ct) . . . . *Digested*, 84/**4662**:
Applied, 00/6532

Jeffrey v. HM Advocate (Sentencing) 1998 G.W.D. 10-499, HCJ Appeal
Jelks v. MacLeod 1998 G.W.D. 21-1098, HCJ Appeal
Jenkins v. Allied Ironfounders Ltd [1970] 1 W.L.R. 304; [1969] 3 All E.R. 1609; 1970
S.C. (H.L.) 37; 1970 S.L.T. 46; 8 K.I.R. 801; 114 S.J. 71, HL; affirming 1969 S.C.
139; 1969 S.L.T. 185, 1 Div; reversing 1968 S.L.T. (Notes) 68, OH . . . . *Digested*, 70/**1076**:
Applied, 78/1458: *Distinguished*, 97/6076: *Followed*, 01/6663
Jenkins v. HM Advocate 1999 G.W.D. 19-904, HCJ Appeal
Jenkins v. Kingsgate (Clothing Productions) Ltd (C96/80) [1981] 1 W.L.R. 972;
[1981] E.C.R. 911; [1981] 2 C.M.L.R. 24; [1981] I.C.R. 592; [1981] I.R.L.R. 228;
125 S.J. 442, ECJ [1981] 1 W.L.R. 1485; [1980] 1 C.M.L.R. 81; [1981] I.C.R.
715; [1980] I.R.L.R. 6; 125 S.J. 587; *Times*, November 15, 1979, EAT . . . . *Digested*, 81/**1157**:
Applied, 81/847, 82/1071, 86/1190, 87/1325, 91/1635, 94/5096, 98/2240:
Considered, 83/2635, 84/1225, 86/1458, 87/1633, 87/4409, 95/2052,
96/2550, 96/2629: *Distinguished*, 98/5807

Jenkins v. Maersk Co Ltd 2001 G.W.D. 27-1111, OH
Jenkins & Marr v. Harris 2000 G.W.D. 17-681, Sh Ct
Jenners of Edinburgh v. Norris 2001 S.C.L.R. 516; 2001 G.W.D. 12-404, Sh Pr . . . . *Digested*, 01/**6263**
Jensen v. Dickson 1999 G.W.D. 35-1700, HCJ Appeal
JG Martin Plant Hire Ltd v. MacDonald 1996 S.L.T. 1192, 2 Div . . . . *Digested*, 96/**6664**:
Distinguished, 01/6869
Jimmy Nicks Property Co Ltd's Application [1999] E.T.M.R. 445, Appointed Person . . . *Digested*, 00/**6524**
JK Investments Ltd v. Heywood 1998 G.W.D. 1-36, HCJ Appeal
Joe Walker (Capital Business) Ltd v. Stuart 1999 G.W.D. 3-128, OH
Johannesburg Municipal Council v. D Stewart & Co (1902) Ltd 1909 S.C. (H.L.) 53,
HL . . . . *Applied*, 99/6035
Johannesen v. O'Donnell 1999 G.W.D. 17-799, HCJ Appeal
John (Helen) v. O'Donnell 1999 J.C. 336; 2000 S.L.T. 11; 1999 S.C.C.R. 802; 1999
G.W.D. 31-1463, HCJ Appeal . . . . *Digested*, 00/**6047**
John Davidson (Pipes) Ltd v. First Engineering Ltd 2001 S.C.L.R. 73; 2000 G.W.D. 37-
1382, OH . . . . *Digested*, 01/**6105**
John Lewis Plc v. Siwek 1998 S.C. 875; 1998 G.W.D. 29-1461, Ex Div . . . . *Digested*, 99/**6086**
Johnson v. Gilchrist 1999 G.W.D. 29-1389, HCJ Appeal
Johnson v. HM Advocate (Sentencing) 2001 G.W.D. 6-220, HCJ Appeal
Johnson v. McGlennan 1998 G.W.D. 35-1805, HCJ Appeal
Johnson v. Taylor Bros & Co Ltd [1920] A.C. 144; (1919) 1 Ll. L. Rep. 183, HL . . . . *Applied*, 47-51/7856,
52/3210, 61/1426, 74/3035: *Referred to*, 00/5963

Johnston v. Angiolini 2001 G.W.D. 31-1223, HCJ Appeal
Johnston v. Ayrshire and Arran Health Board 1998 G.W.D. 40-2078, OH
Johnston v. Clark (No.2) 1998 S.L.T. 139; 1997 Rep. L.R. 73; 1997 G.W.D. 16-712, OH . . *Digested*, 97/**5687**
Johnston v. Gilchrist 1999 G.W.D. 22-1032, HCJ Appeal
Johnston v. Hamilton (Sentencing) 1998 G.W.D. 5-229, HCJ Appeal
Johnston v. Heywood 1998 G.W.D. 39-2007, HCJ Appeal
Johnston v. HM Advocate 1999 G.W.D. 37-1809, HCJ Appeal
Johnston v. HM Advocate (Sentencing) 2000 G.W.D. 16-657, HCJ Appeal
Johnston (Derek) v. HM Advocate 1993 J.C. 187; 1994 S.L.T. 300; 1993 S.C.C.R. 693,
HCJ Appeal . . . . *Digested*, 93/**4889**:
Applied, 99/5805
Johnston (Steven Alexander Robert) v. HM Advocate 1998 S.L.T. 788; 1997 S.C.C.R.
568; 1997 G.W.D. 26-1314, HCJ Appeal . . . . *Digested*, 97/**5864**
Johnston v. Johnston (Common Property: Division or Sale) 1999 G.W.D. 7-347, OH
Johnston v. JT Inglis & Sons Ltd 2000 G.W.D. 1-6, OH
Johnston v. Lees 1998 G.W.D. 23-1164, HCJ Appeal
Johnston v. MacFarlane's Trustees 1986 S.C. 298; 1987 S.L.T. 593; 1987 S.C.L.R. 104,
2 Div; reversing in part 1985 S.L.T. 339, OH . . . . *Digested*, 87/**5217**:
Distinguished, 98/5423
Johnston v. Maguire (Sentencing) 2001 G.W.D. 11-387, HCJ Appeal
Johnston v. McFadyen (Sentencing) 2001 G.W.D. 6-209, HCJ Appeal
Johnston v. McGlennan 1998 G.W.D. 19-980, HCJ Appeal
Johnston v. Reith 1998 G.W.D. 21-1066, HCJ Appeal
Johnston v. WH Brown Construction (Dundee) Ltd 2000 S.L.T. 791; 2000 S.C.L.R.
792; [2000] B.L.R. 243; 69 Con. L.R. 100; 2000 G.W.D. 14-521; *Times*, June 7,
2000, 1 Div; affirming 2000 S.L.T. 223; 1999 S.C.L.R. 1145; 68 Con. L.R. 70;
1999 G.W.D. 23-1088; *Times*, November 11, 1999, OH . . . . *Digested*, 00/**5981**
Johnstone v. Douglas (Sentencing) 1998 G.W.D. 13-665, HCJ Appeal

Johnstone v. HM Advocate (Evidence) 1999 G.W.D. 7-323, HCJ Appeal
Johnstone v. HM Advocate (Sentencing) 1999 G.W.D. 20-941, HCJ Appeal
Johnstone v. McFadyen 1999 G.W.D. 34-1649, HCJ Appeal
Joint Liquidators of Automatic Oil Tools Ltd, Noters 2001 S.L.T. 279; 2000 G.W.D. 6-228, OH . . . . *Digested,* 01/**6718**
Jolly v. Howdle 1998 G.W.D. 24-1236, HCJ Appeal
Jones v. Carnegie (Sentencing) 2001 G.W.D. 10-354, HCJ Appeal
Jones v. Chief Constable of South Yorkshire see Alcock v. Chief Constable of South Yorkshire
Jones v. Department of Employment [1989] Q.B. 1; [1988] 2 W.L.R. 493; [1988] 1 All E.R. 725; (1988) 85(4) L.S.G. 35; (1987) 137 N.L.J. 1182; (1988) 132 S.J. 128, CA . . . . *Digested,* 88/**2438**:
Followed, 89/259, 90/5493, 00/6686
Jones v. HM Advocate (Sentencing) 1998 G.W.D. 40-2084, HCJ Appeal
Jones (Frederick John) v. HM Advocate 1992 S.L.T. 115; 1991 S.C.C.R. 290, HCJ Appeal . . . . *Digested,* 91/**4740**:
Applied, 98/5641: *Distinguished,* 92/5521
Jones v. Kippen Campbell & Burt 1998 G.W.D. 11-562, 2 Div; affirming 1997 G.W.D. 27-1377, OH
Jones v. Post Office; *sub nom* Post Office v. Jones [2001] EWCA Civ 558; [2001] I.C.R. 805; [2001] I.R.L.R. 384; [2001] Emp. L.R. 527; *Times,* June 5, 2001; *Independent,* April 26, 2001, CA; affirming [2000] I.C.R. 388, EAT . . . . *Digested,* 01/**2236**:
Applied, 01/6463

Jones v. Wright see Alcock v. Chief Constable of South Yorkshire
Joop! GmbH v. M&S Toiletries Ltd, *Times,* June 14, 2000, OH . . . . *Digested,* 00/**6523**
Joshi v. Joshi 1998 G.W.D. 8-357, OH
Joy Manufacturing Holdings Ltd and Pension & Life Assurance Scheme Trustees, Petitioners see Harding v. Joy Manufacturing Holdings Ltd
JR Thomson 's Trustees v. Clydesdale Bank Ltd see Thomson v. Clydesdale Bank Ltd
Judge v. HM Advocate 1998 G.W.D. 34-1738; 1998 G.W.D. 34-1749, HCJ Appeal

K (A Juvenile) v. HM Advocate (PC (Sc)) see Dyer v. Watson
K (A Juvenile) v. HM Advocate 2001 S.L.T. 1261; 2001 S.C.C.R. 621; 2001 G.W.D. 16-599, HCJ Appeal . . . . *Digested,* 01/**6368**
K v. Craig; *sub nom* K, Petitioner 1999 S.C. (H.L.) 1; 1999 S.L.T. 219; 1999 S.C.L.R. 67; 1998 G.W.D. 40-2074; *Times,* December 7, 1998, HL; affirming 1997 S.C. 327; 1997 S.L.T. 748; 1997 S.C.L.R. 566; 1997 G.W.D. 11-482; *Times,* May 2, 1997, 1 Div; affirming 1997 S.C.L.R. 384, OH . . . . *Digested,* 99/**6362**
K v. HM Advocate (Sentencing) 1998 G.W.D. 30-1553, HCJ Appeal
K v. HM Advocate (Sentencing) 1999 G.W.D. 3-139, HCJ Appeal
K, Petitioner see K v. Craig
Kabalu v. HM Advocate (No.1) 1999 S.C.C.R. 348; 1999 G.W.D. 15-697, HCJ Appeal . . *Digested,* 99/**5822**
Kabalu v. HM Advocate (No.2) 1999 G.W.D. 15-704, HCJ Appeal
Kaddouri v. McLeod 1999 G.W.D. 34-1651, HCJ Appeal
Kane v. Argyll and Clyde Health Board 1999 S.L.T. 823; 1999 G.W.D. 1-46, Ex Div; affirming 1997 S.L.T. 965; 1997 G.W.D. 8-342, OH . . . . *Digested,* 99/**5695**
Kane v. HM Advocate 1998 G.W.D. 27-1370, HCJ Appeal
Kane v. Ruxton 2000 G.W.D. 18-710, HCJ Appeal
Kang v. Secretary of State for the Home Department 1998 G.W.D. 1-39, OH
Karl Construction (Scotland) Ltd v. Sweeney Civil Engineering (Scotland) Ltd TNS, Ex Div; affirming 2001 S.C.L.R. 95; 2001 G.W.D. 1-17, OH . . . . *Digested,* 01/**6289**
Karling (Richard Wilhelm) v. HM Advocate 1999 S.C.C.R. 359, HCJ Appeal . . . . *Digested,* 99/**5861**
Kaur v. Singh (No.1) 1999 S.C. 180; 1999 S.L.T. 412; 1998 S.C.L.R. 849; 1998 G.W.D. 24-1226, 1 Div; affirming 1998 S.C. 233; 1997 S.C.L.R. 1075; 1997 G.W.D. 37-1914, OH . . . . *Digested,* 98/**5951**
Kaur v. Singh (No.2) 2000 S.L.T. 1323; 2000 G.W.D. 25-943, Ex Div; affirming 2000 S.C.L.R. 187; 1999 Hous. L.R. 76; 1999 G.W.D. 24-1163, OH . . . . *Digested,* 00/**6439**
Kay v. HM Advocate (Sentencing) 2001 G.W.D. 24-891, HCJ Appeal
Kay v. Lees (Sentencing) 1998 G.W.D. 13-686, HCJ Appeal
Kazmi v. Secretary of State for the Home Department 2000 G.W.D. 18-717, Ex Div
Keane v. Walker Contracts (Scotland) Ltd 1999 G.W.D. 9-410, OH
Kearney v. HM Advocate 1999 G.W.D. 2-94, HCJ Appeal
Kearney (Brian Arthur) v. HM Advocate 1998 S.C.C.R. 52; 1998 G.W.D. 5-203, HCJ Appeal . . . . *Digested,* 98/**5572**
Kearney v. Vannet 2000 G.W.D. 9-325, HCJ Appeal
Kearns (Owen McLeod) v. HM Advocate 1999 J.C. 124; 1999 S.C.C.R. 141; 1999 G.W.D. 6-299, HCJ Appeal . . . . *Digested,* 99/**5900**
Keavney (Kevin) v. HM Advocate 1999 J.C. 240; 1999 S.L.T. 1030; 1999 G.W.D. 16-744, HCJ Appeal . . . . *Digested,* 99/**5901**
Keddie v. Woodside Building Services Ltd 1998 G.W.D. 33-1714, 1 Div
Keegan v. Friel see Keegan (Kevin Michael) v. Gilchrist
Keegan (Kevin Michael) v. Gilchrist; *sub nom* Keegan v. Friel 1999 J.C. 185; 1999 S.L.T. 1111; 1999 S.C.C.R. 378; 1999 G.W.D. 15-698, HCJ Appeal . . . . *Digested,* 99/**5864**

Keegan v. McFadyen 2001 G.W.D. 10-333, HCJ Appeal
Keegan v. Vannet 1999 G.W.D. 35-1675, HCJ Appeal
Keenan v. Aberdeen Slating Co Ltd 2000 S.C. 81; 2000 S.L.T. 1259; 1999 G.W.D. 36-
    1774, 2 Div . . . . *Digested*, 00/**6434**
Keenan v. McFadyen 1999 G.W.D. 18-828, HCJ Appeal
Keenan v. Sega Amusements Europe Ltd 2001 G.W.D. 40-1506, Sh Ct (Grampian)
Keeper of the Registers of Scotland v. MRS Hamilton Ltd see MRS Hamilton Ltd v.
    Keeper of the Registers of Scotland (No.4)
Keeper of the Registers of Scotland v. MRS Hamilton Ltd (Expenses) see MRS Hamilton
    Ltd v. Keeper of the Registers of Scotland (No.3)
Keith v. Houston 1999 G.W.D. 25-1192, HCJ Appeal
Keith v. McLeod 1999 G.W.D. 9-429, HCJ Appeal
Keith v. Napier 2001 G.W.D. 31-1258, HCJ Appeal
Keizer v. HM Advocate (Sentencing) 2000 G.W.D. 9-333, HCJ Appeal
Kellock v. HM Advocate (Sentencing) 2001 S.C.C.R. 267; 2001 G.W.D. 12-448, HCJ
    Appeal . . . . *Digested*, 01/**6405**
Kelly v. Dumfries and Galloway RC 1999 Fam. L.R. 119, Sh Ct . . . . *Digested*, 00/**6192**
Kelly v. First Engineering Ltd 1999 S.C.L.R. 1025; 1999 Rep. L.R. 106; 1999 G.W.D. 21-
    1016, OH . . . . *Digested*, 99/**6225**
Kelly v. HM Advocate (Sentencing) 1998 G.W.D. 17-862, HCJ Appeal
Kelly v. HM Advocate (Sentencing) 1998 G.W.D. 18-922, HCJ Appeal
Kelly v. HM Advocate (Sentencing) 1999 G.W.D. 7-336, HCJ Appeal
Kelly v. HM Advocate (Sentencing) 1999 G.W.D. 15-711, HCJ Appeal
Kelly v. HM Advocate (Sentencing) 1999 G.W.D. 20-948, HCJ Appeal
Kelly v. HM Advocate (Sentencing) 1999 G.W.D. 2-93, HCJ Appeal
Kelly v. HM Advocate (Sentencing) 2001 G.W.D. 6-210, HCJ Appeal
Kelly v. HM Advocate (Sentencing) 2001 G.W.D. 16-619, HCJ Appeal
Kelly (Charles Patrick Tully) v. HM Advocate 1999 J.C. 35; 1999 S.L.T. 1117; 1998
    S.C.C.R. 660; 1998 G.W.D. 36-1852, HCJ Appeal. . . . . *Digested*, 99/**5817**
Kelly (Francis Kevin) v. HM Advocate (Sentencing) 2001 J.C. 12; 2000 S.C.C.R. 815;
    2000 G.W.D. 27-1042, HCJ Appeal . . . . *Digested*, 01/**6400**
Kelly (Peter David) v. HM Advocate 2001 S.C.C.R. 534; 2001 G.W.D. 20-762, HCJ
    Appeal
Kelly v. McLeod 1999 G.W.D. 2-110, HCJ Appeal
Kelly v. Mussen 2000 G.W.D. 24-914, OH
Kelly v. O'Donnell (Sentencing) 1999 G.W.D. 1-23, HCJ Appeal
Kelly (Christopher) v. Vannet 1999 J.C. 109; 2000 S.L.T. 75; 1999 S.C.C.R. 169; 1999
    G.W.D. 4-175, HCJ Appeal . . . . *Digested*, 99/**5818**
Kelly v. Watt (Sentencing) 2000 G.W.D. 33-1290, HCJ Appeal
Kelso (Alan) v. Brown; *sub nom* Kelso v. Vannet (Sentencing) 1998 S.L.T. 921; 1998
    S.C.C.R. 278; 1998 G.W.D. 11-574, HCJ Appeal . . . . *Digested*, 98/**5581**:
    Considered, 01/6330

Kelso v. Vannet (Sentencing) see Kelso (Alan) v. Brown
Kelvin International Services v. Walker 1999 G.W.D. 24-1158, 1 Div
Kelvinside Community Council v. Glasgow District Licensing Board 1990 S.L.T. 725;
    1990 S.C.L.R. 110, 2 Div . . . . *Digested*, 90/**5337**:
    Followed, 97/6224, 01/6782
Kemp v. Ling (Unreported, March 26, 1998), CC (Thanet) [*Ex rel.* Tim Kevan, Barrister,
    1 Temple Gardens, Temple, London] . . . . *Digested*, 98/**2502**:
    Considered, 99/2454: *Followed*, 99/5789
Kemp v. Secretary of State for Scotland 2000 S.L.T. 471; 2000 S.C.L.R. 10; 1999 Rep.
    L.R. 110; 1999 G.W.D. 14-648, OH . . . . *Digested*, 99/**6252**
Kendal v. Davies 2001 S.C.L.R. 140; 2000 Rep. L.R. 126; 2000 G.W.D. 27-1046, OH . . . *Digested*, 01/**6418**
Kennan v. Kennedy 1999 G.W.D. 27-1287, HCJ Appeal
Kennedy v. Forrest-Jones 2001 S.L.T. 630; 2001 G.W.D. 1-16, OH . . . . *Digested*, 01/**6230**
Kennedy v. H 1988 S.C. 114; 1988 S.L.T. 586, 1 Div. . . . . *Digested*, 88/**3782**:
    Applied, 98/5853
Kennedy v. HM Advocate 1999 G.W.D. 15-691, HCJ Appeal
Kennedy v. Kennedy 2000 G.W.D. 40-1491, Sh Pr
Kennedy v. Kershaw 2000 S.L.C.R. 1, Land Ct (Full Ct); affirming 1999 S.L.C.R. 125,
    Land Ct (Div Ct) . . . . *Digested*, 01/**6738**
Kennedy v. Lees (Sentencing) 1998 G.W.D. 5-213, HCJ Appeal
Kennedy v. Steinberg; *sub nom* Rowan v. Steinberg 1998 S.C. 379; 1997 S.L.T. 1204;
    1997 S.C.L.R. 595; [1997] 8 Med. L.R. 30; 1997 Rep. L.R. (Quantum) 5; 1997
    G.W.D. 7-287, OH . . . . *Digested*, 97/**6302**
Kenny v. HM Advocate 1999 G.W.D. 27-1286, HCJ Appeal
Kent v. Griffiths (Non-Pecuniary Damages) see Heil v. Rankin
Kent v. Stott (Sentencing) 2001 G.W.D. 39-1486, HCJ Appeal
Keogh v. Watt 2000 S.C.C.R. 443, HCJ Appeal . . . . *Digested*, 00/**6155**
Keough v. Gilchrist (Sentencing) 2000 G.W.D. 13-509, HCJ Appeal
Kerr (David), Petitioner; *sub nom* Kerr (David) v. HM Advocate *Times*, July 4, 2000,
    HCJ Appeal . . . . *Digested*, 00/**6065**
Kerr v. Aitken; *sub nom* Aitken's Trustee v. Aitken [2000] B.P.I.R. 278; 1999 G.W.D.
    39-1898, OH . . . . *Digested*, 00/**6506**

Kerr (Henry) *v.* Carnegie 1998 J.C. 88; 1998 S.L.T. 1010; 1998 S.C.C.R. 168; 1998 G.W.D. 8-368, HCJ Appeal . . . .   *Digested,* 98/**5616**:
                                   Applied, 98/5611
Kerr *v.* Higson (Sentencing) 2000 G.W.D. 30-1186, HCJ Appeal
Kerr *v.* HM Advocate 2001 G.W.D. 10-332, HCJ Appeal
Kerr *v.* HM Advocate (Sentencing) 1999 G.W.D. 19-897, HCJ Appeal
Kerr *v.* HM Advocate (Sentencing) 1999 G.W.D. 32-1532, HCJ Appeal
Kerr (David) *v.* HM Advocate see Kerr (David), Petitioner
Kerr (Henry) *v.* HM Advocate 1999 S.C.C.R. 28; 1999 G.W.D. 1-18, HCJ Appeal . . . . . .   *Digested,* 99/**5916**
Kerr (John Dundee) *v.* HM Advocate 1999 S.L.T. 1359; 1999 S.C.C.R. 763; 1999 G.W.D. 29-1377, HCJ Appeal . . . .   *Digested,* 00/**6115**
Kerr (John) *v.* HM Advocate 1958 J.C. 14; 1958 S.L.T. 82, HCJ Appeal . . . .   *Digested,* 58/**3660**:
                         Distinguished, 91/4558: *Referred to,* 01/6305
Kerr *v.* Lees 1998 G.W.D. 30-1544, HCJ Appeal
Kerr *v.* McKenzie 2001 G.W.D. 3-133, Sh Ct (Glasgow)
Kerr *v.* Vannet (Sentencing) 1999 G.W.D. 5-256, HCJ Appeal
Kerr *v.* Vannet (Sentencing) 1999 G.W.D. 33-1583, HCJ Appeal
Kerr *v.* Vannet (Sentencing) 2000 G.W.D. 4-138, HCJ Appeal
Kerr (Ronald Smith) *v.* Vannet 1999 J.C. 51; 1999 S.L.T. 369; 1998 S.C.C.R. 698; 1998 G.W.D. 39-2003, HCJ Appeal . . . .   *Digested,* 99/**5886**
Kerrigan *v.* HM Advocate 1999 G.W.D. 3-135, HCJ Appeal
Kerrigan *v.* McGlennan 1999 G.W.D. 9-439, HCJ Appeal
Kerry Foods Ltd *v.* Creber [2000] I.C.R. 556; [2000] I.R.L.R. 10, EAT . . . .   *Digested,* 00/**2223**:
                                     Considered, 01/6476
Kershaw *v.* Wilcon Homes Ltd 2001 G.W.D. 24-885, Sh Ct (Lothian)
Kettrick *v.* HM Advocate 2001 G.W.D. 19-725, HCJ Appeal
Key Housing Association Ltd *v.* Cameron 1999 Hous. L.R. 47, Sh Ct. . . . .   *Digested,* 99/**6269**
Khalil *v.* Secretary of State for the Home Department 2001 G.W.D. 38-1439, OH
Khan *v.* HM Advocate (Sentencing) 1999 G.W.D. 36-1734, HCJ Appeal
Khan *v.* Secretary of State for the Home Department 2001 G.W.D. 38-1437, 2 Div
Kidd *v.* Higson (Sentencing) 2000 G.W.D. 30-1178, HCJ Appeal
Kidd *v.* HM Advocate 2000 J.C. 509; 2000 S.L.T. 1068; 2000 S.C.C.R. 513; 2000 G.W.D. 16-645, HCJ Appeal . . . .   *Digested,* 00/**6059**
Kidd *v.* Vannet (Sentencing) 1998 G.W.D. 32-1646, HCJ Appeal
Kiely (Anthony) *v.* HM Advocate 1990 J.C. 264; 1990 S.L.T. 847, HCJ Appeal . . . .   *Digested,* 90/**4907**:
                                     Considered, 01/6383
Kieran *v.* HM Advocate 1999 G.W.D. 27-1273, HCJ Appeal
Kilminster *v.* Higson 1998 G.W.D. 35-1833, HCJ Appeal
Kilna *v.* Higson 2001 G.W.D. 23-855, HCJ Appeal
Kilpatrick *v.* Gilchrist 2001 G.W.D. 30-1196, HCJ Appeal
Kilpatrick *v.* Webster 2001 G.W.D. 6-250, HCJ Appeal
Kilpatrick, Petitioner (1881) 8 R. 592, CS . . . .   *Applied,* 01/6500
Kim *v.* Secretary of State for the Home Department 2000 S.L.T. 249; 2000 G.W.D. 3-103, OH . . . .   *Digested,* 00/**6501**
Kinani *v.* HM Advocate (Sentencing) 2001 G.W.D. 6-212, HCJ Appeal
Kinara Estate Trustees *v.* Campbell 1999 Hous. L.R. 55, Sh Ct . . . .   *Digested,* 99/**6271**
King *v.* Bristow Helicopters Ltd; *sub nom* Hammond *v.* Bristow Helicopters Ltd; Morris *v.* KLM Royal Dutch Airlines; TNS, HL; reversing [2001] 1 Lloyd's Rep. 95; 2001 S.C. 54; 2001 S.L.T. 126; 2001 S.C.L.R. 393; 2000 G.W.D. 25-923; *Times,* October 25, 2000, 1 Div; reversing 1999 S.L.T. 919; 1998 G.W.D. 40-2028, OH .   *Digested,* 00/**6704**:
                       Not followed, 01/5385: *Previous proceedings,* 01/5385
King *v.* Carron Phoenix Ltd 1999 Rep. L.R. 51; 1999 G.W.D. 9-437, OH . . . .   *Digested,* 99/**6223**
King *v.* Donnelly 2001 G.W.D. 26-1035, HCJ Appeal
King *v.* East Ayrshire Council 1998 S.C. 182; 1998 S.L.T. 1287; 1997 G.W.D. 30-1528; *Times,* November 3, 1997, 1 Div. . . . .   *Digested,* 97/**5986**:
                                   Applied, 00/5833
King *v.* Eaton Ltd (No.2); *sub nom* Eaton Ltd *v.* King 1999 S.L.T. 656; 1998 S.C.L.R. 1017; [1998] I.R.L.R. 686; 1998 G.W.D. 27-1381, 2 Div . . . .   *Digested,* 99/**6048**
King *v.* Great Britain China Centre [1992] I.C.R. 516; [1991] I.R.L.R. 513; *Times,* October 30, 1991; *Independent,* October 22, 1991; *Guardian,* October 16, 1991, CA . . . .   *Digested,* 92/**1959**:
               Applied, 97/2239, 97/6011, 98/5810, 98/5817, 01/2296:
                       Considered, 01/2298: *Followed,* 97/2247, 97/2248
King (John Ian) *v.* HM Advocate 1999 J.C. 226; 1999 S.L.T. 604; 1999 S.C.C.R. 330; 1999 G.W.D. 13-598, HCJ Appeal . . . .   *Digested,* 99/**5919**
King *v.* Lamont 2001 G.W.D. 25-922, OH
King *v.* T Tunnock Ltd 2000 S.C. 424; 2000 S.L.T. 744; [2001] E.C.C. 6; [2000] Eu. L.R. 531; [2000] I.R.L.R. 569; 2000 G.W.D. 12-408; *Times,* May 12, 2000, Ex Div; reversing (Unreported, December 24, 1997), Sh Pr; affirming 1996 S.C.L.R. 742, Sh Ct . . . .   *Digested,* 00/**5846**
Kingori *v.* Secretary of State for the Home Department; *sub nom* R. *v.* Secretary of State for the Home Department Ex p. Mpyanguli [1994] Imm. A.R. 539, CA . . .   *Digested,* 95/**2695**:
        Applied, 95/2696, 96/3200: *Considered,* 96/3197: *Followed,* 99/6287

Kingscrest Associates Ltd *v.* Customs and Excise Commissioners; *sub nom* Kingscrest
    Residential Care Homes *v.* Customs and Excise Commissioners; Customs and
    Excise Commissioners *v.* Kingscrest Associates Ltd; CH/2001/APP/010500, Ch
    D; affirming [2001] B.V.C. 2326; [2001] S.T.I. 1066, V&DTr . . . . *Distinguished*, 01/**6922**
Kingscrest Residential Care Homes *v.* Customs and Excise Commissioners see
    Kingscrest Associates Ltd *v.* Customs and Excise Commissioners
Kinnaird *v.* Higson 2001 S.C.C.R. 427; 2001 G.W.D. 16-592, HCJ Appeal
Kinnear *v.* HM Advocate (Sentencing) 2001 G.W.D. 1-29, HCJ Appeal
Kinnon (William McGraw Robb) *v.* HM Advocate 1998 S.L.T. 1056; 1997 S.C.C.R. 552;
    1997 G.W.D. 26-1311, HCJ Appeal . . . . *Digested*, 97/**5755**
Kinross *v.* Sterling Precast Ltd 2001 Rep. L.R. 131 (Note); 2001 G.W.D. 32-1297, OH
Kippen *v.* McLeod 2000 G.W.D. 14-563, HCJ Appeal
Kirk *v.* Fife Council 2001 G.W.D. 36-1398, OH
Kirk *v.* Kennedy (Sentencing) 2001 S.C.C.R. 31; 2000 G.W.D. 39-1454, HCJ Appeal. . . *Digested*, 01/**6403**
Kirk *v.* O'Donnell (Sentencing) 2000 G.W.D. 19-773, HCJ Appeal
Kirk Care Housing Association *v.* Clugston 2000 Hous. L.R. 106, Sh Ct (North
    Strathclyde) . . . . *Digested*, 00/**6460**
Kirkby *v.* Sutherland 2001 G.W.D. 9-315, Sh Ct (Grampian)
Kirkpatrick *v.* Dumfries and Galloway Council 2001 S.C.L.R. 261, Sh Ct (South
    Strathclyde) . . . . *Digested*, 01/**6821**
Kirkpatrick *v.* HM Advocate 1998 G.W.D. 37-1908, HCJ Appeal
Kirmani, Petitioner see Sharif, Petitioner
Kivlin *v.* HM Advocate (Sentencing) 2001 G.W.D. 39-1458, HCJ Appeal
Klawikowski *v.* MacLeod (Sentencing) 2000 G.W.D. 19-779, HCJ Appeal
Knapdale (Nominees) Ltd *v.* Donald 2001 S.L.T. 617; 2000 S.C.L.R. 1013; 2000 G.W.D.
    19-730; *Times*, August 22, 2000, OH . . . . *Digested*, 00/**5850**
Knight *v.* Crofters Commission 1999 S.L.C.R. 102, Land Ct (Full Ct) . . . . *Digested*, 00/**6528**
Knights *v.* Gilchrist (Sentencing) 2001 G.W.D. 25-950, HCJ Appeal
Knowes Housing Association Ltd *v.* Millar 2001 S.L.T. 1326; 2001 S.C.L.R. 1090; 2001
    Hous. L.R. 106; 2001 G.W.D. 26-1064, Ex Div . . . . *Digested*, 01/**6699**
Kostovski *v.* Netherlands (A/166) (1990) 12 E.H.R.R. 434; *Times*, November 22, 1989,
    ECHR . . . . *Digested*, 90/**2539**:
                                    Applied, 01/6323: *Distinguished*, 96/3124
Koufos *v.* C Czarnikow Ltd (The Heron II); *sub nom* C Czarnikow Ltd *v.* Koufos (The
    Heron II) [1969] 1 A.C. 350; [1967] 3 W.L.R. 1491; [1967] 3 All E.R. 686;
    [1967] 2 Lloyd's Rep. 457; 111 S.J. 848, HL; affirming [1966] 2 Q.B. 695; [1966]
    2 W.L.R. 1397; [1966] 2 All E.R. 593; [1966] 1 Lloyd's Rep. 595, CA; reversing
    [1966] 1 Lloyd's Rep. 259; 110 S.J. 287, QBD (Comm Ct) . . . . *Digested*, 67/**3623**:
                    Applied, 70/924, 77/2881, 78/2821, 85/198, 87/1130, 88/1165, 96/3566,
                    97/6093, 99/5790: *Approved*, 66/3146: *Considered*, 67/3605, 68/1013,
                                    69/3226, 72/990, 73/2306, 75/2324, 94/5413
Kraus's Administrators *v.* Sullivan 1998 S.L.T. 963; 1997 G.W.D. 20-931, OH . . . . *Digested*, 98/**5488**
Kriba *v.* Secretary of State for the Home Department 1998 S.L.T. 1113; 1997 G.W.D. 20-
    983; *Times*, July 18, 1997, OH . . . . *Digested*, 97/**6137**
Krol *v.* HM Advocate 1999 G.W.D. 20-947, HCJ Appeal
Kublin *v.* Fotheringham (No.1) 2000 G.W.D. 17-699, Sh Pr
Kublin *v.* Fotheringham (No.2) 2001 G.W.D. 29-1153, Sh Pr; reversing 2000 G.W.D.
    39-1466, Sh Ct (Grampian)
Kuma *v.* Secretary of State for the Home Department 1999 S.C.L.R. 148; 1998 G.W.D.
    32-1670, OH . . . . *Digested*, 99/**6293**
Kumar *v.* Secretary of State for the Home Department 1998 G.W.D. 15-769, OH
Kuzub *v.* Kuzub 1999 S.C.L.R. 902, Sh Ct . . . . *Digested*, 00/**6259**
KV Agriculture *v.* Armstrong 1998 S.L.T. (Sh Ct) 40; 1998 S.C.L.R. 169; 1998 G.W.D.
    3-104, Sh Pr . . . . *Digested*, 98/**5512**:
                                                                    Followed, 00/5948
Kvaerner Construction (Regions) Ltd *v.* Kirkpatrick & Partners Consulting Engineers Ltd
    1999 S.C. 291; 1999 S.L.T. 1120; 1999 S.C.L.R. 40; 1998 G.W.D. 40-2038, Ex
    Div; affirming 1998 G.W.D. 11-522, OH . . . . *Digested*, 99/**5965**
Kwei Tek Chao (t/a Zung Fu Co) *v.* British Traders & Shippers Ltd (No.1); *sub nom* Chao
    v. British Traders & Shippers Ltd (No.1) [1954] 2 Q.B. 459; [1954] 2 W.L.R.
    365; [1954] 1 All E.R. 779; [1954] 1 Lloyd's Rep. 16; 98 S.J. 163, QBD . . . . *Digested*, 54/**2993**:
                    Applied, 91/1868: *Followed*, 67/3527: *Referred to*, 00/5963
Kwik Save Stores Ltd *v.* Greaves [1997] I.C.R. 629; [1997] I.R.L.R. 268, EAT . . . . *Digested*, 97/**2236**:
                    Considered, 98/5825: *Followed*, 98/2168: *Subsequent proceedings*, 98/2172
Kwik Save Stores Ltd *v.* Secretary of State for Scotland 1999 S.L.T. 193; 1997 G.W.D.
    29-1457, OH . . . . *Digested*, 99/**5786**
Kwik-Fit (GB) Ltd *v.* Customs and Excise Commissioners [1998] S.T.C. 159; 1998 S.C.
    139; 1999 S.L.T. 301; [1998] B.T.C. 5042; [1998] B.V.C. 48; 1997 G.W.D. 38-
    1977, Ex Div . . . . *Digested*, 98/**6217**
Kyle *v.* Craigen 1999 G.W.D. 34-1634, HCJ Appeal

L *v.* L 1998 S.L.T. 672; 1997 S.C.L.R. 866; 1997 G.W.D. 30-1501, 1 Div; affirming 1996
    S.L.T. 767; 1996 S.C.L.R. 11, OH . . . . *Digested*, 98/**5439**:
    Applied, 98/5440: *Overruled*, 01/6217
L *v.* L; *sub nom* Beattie *v.* L 2000 S.L.T. (Sh Ct) 12; 1999 G.W.D. 38-1839, Sh Ct
    (Lothian) . . . . *Digested*, 00/**5960**
L, Petitioners (No.3) 1996 S.L.T. 928, 1 Div . . . . *Digested*, 96/**7129**:
    Followed, 01/6758
La Pantofola D'Oro SpA *v.* Blane Leisure Ltd (No.1) 2000 S.L.T. 105; 1999 G.W.D. 37-
    1784, OH . . . . *Digested*, 00/**5887**
La Pantofola D'Oro SpA *v.* Blane Leisure Ltd (No.2); *sub nom* Fallimento la Pantofola
    D'Oro SpA *v.* Blane Leisure Ltd 2000 S.L.T. 1264; 2000 G.W.D. 20-811, OH . . . . *Digested*, 01/**6242**
Lacy *v.* Reith 1999 G.W.D. 26-1261, HCJ Appeal
Lady Taylor *v.* Brunton 1998 S.L.T. (Sh Ct) 72; 1998 G.W.D. 14-723, Sh Pr . . . . *Digested*, 98/**6203**
Lafarge Redland Aggregates Ltd *v.* Scottish Ministers 2001 S.C. 298; 2000 S.L.T. 1361;
    [2001] Env. L.R. 27; [2000] 4 P.L.R. 151; [2000] N.P.C. 109; 2000 G.W.D. 34-
    1322, OH . . . . *Digested*, 01/**6854**
Laidlaw *v.* Midlothian Council 2001 G.W.D. 13-509, Sh Ct (Lothian)
Laidman *v.* Dickson (Sentencing) 2000 G.W.D. 3-109, HCJ Appeal
Laing (Gary Frederick) *v.* Heywood 1998 S.C.C.R. 458; 1998 G.W.D. 25-1252, HCJ
    Appeal . . . . *Digested*, 98/**5672**
Laing *v.* Keeper of the Registers of Scotland see Short's Trustee *v.* Keeper of the
    Registers of Scotland
Laing *v.* Macleod 1998 G.W.D. 18-938, HCJ Appeal
Laing *v.* Scottish Arts Council 2001 S.C. 493; 2001 S.L.T. 298; 2001 S.C.L.R. 86;
    2001 G.W.D. 1-54, Ex Div; reversing 2000 S.L.T. 338; 1999 G.W.D. 38-1851,
    OH . . . . *Digested*, 01/**6244**
Laing *v.* Thistle Hotels Plc (No.1) 2001 G.W.D. 13-499, OH
Laing *v.* Thistle Hotels Plc (No.2) 2001 G.W.D. 35-1344, OH
Laird *v.* AK Stoddart Ltd [2001] I.R.L.R. 591, EAT . . . . *Digested*, 01/**6471**
Laird *v.* HM Advocate (Sentencing) 1999 G.W.D. 4-184, HCJ Appeal
Laird *v.* Vannet 1999 G.W.D. 40-1918, HCJ Appeal
Laird, Applicant 1973 S.L.T. (Land Ct.) 4, Land Ct . . . . *Digested*, 73/**3996**:
    Not followed, 00/6531
Lakin Ltd *v.* Secretary of State for Scotland 1988 S.L.T. 780, 2 Div . . . . *Digested*, 88/**5014**:
    Considered, 97/6352: *Distinguished*, 98/6151, 99/4266: *Referred to*, 94/5934
Lamarra *v.* Miller 1998 G.W.D. 22-1119, HCJ Appeal
Lamb *v.* HM Advocate 1998 G.W.D. 37-1912, HCJ Appeal
Lamb & Gardiner Ltd *v.* Perth and Kinross District Licensing Board [1998] 10 S.L.L.P.
    23, Sh Ct . . . . *Digested*, 98/**6079**
Lambe *v.* HM Advocate (Sentencing) 1999 G.W.D. 36-1747, HCJ Appeal
Lamont *v.* Crofters Commission 2001 S.L.C.R. 7, Land Ct (Full Ct)
Lamont *v.* Russell 1998 G.W.D. 26-1310, HCJ Appeal
Lamont *v.* Walkingshaw (Sentencing) 1999 G.W.D. 4-202, HCJ Appeal
Landcatch Ltd *v.* Braer Corp see Landcatch Ltd *v.* International Oil Pollution
    Compensation Fund
Landcatch Ltd *v.* Gilbert Gilkes 1990 S.L.T. 688, OH . . . . *Digested*, 90/**5489**:
    Applied, 98/6113
Landcatch Ltd *v.* International Oil Pollution Compensation Fund; Landcatch Ltd *v.*
    Braer Corp [1999] 2 Lloyd's Rep. 316; 1999 S.L.T. 1208; 1999 S.C.L.R. 709;
    1999 G.W.D. 20-962; *Times*, June 14, 1999, 2 Div; affirming [1998] 2 Lloyd's
    Rep. 552; [1998] E.C.C. 314; 1998 G.W.D. 12-614; *Times*, March 6, 1998, OH . . . *Digested*, 99/**6445**:
    Followed, 99/6447
Landell *v.* Landell (1841) 3 D. 819, 2 Div . . . . *Applied*, 47-51/2542,
    50/4681, 47-51/3846: *Considered*, 91/4866, 98/5478
Lander *v.* Premier Pict Petroleum Ltd 1997 S.L.T. 1361; [1998] B.C.C. 248; 1997 G.W.D.
    17-759, OH . . . . *Digested*, 98/**5524**
Lang *v.* HM Advocate (Sentencing) 1998 G.W.D. 16-778, HCJ Appeal
Langan *v.* O'Donnell 1998 G.W.D. 38-1978, HCJ Appeal
Langford *v.* Brown (Sentencing) 2001 G.W.D. 6-216, HCJ Appeal
Lappin *v.* O'Donnell 2001 J.C. 137; 2001 S.C.C.R. 219; 2001 G.W.D. 8-305, HCJ
    Appeal . . . . *Digested*, 01/**6407**
Larg *v.* Moore 2001 S.L.T. (Sh Ct) 147; 2000 G.W.D. 31-1220, Sh Ct (Tayside)
Larkin *v.* Friel (Sentencing) 1998 G.W.D. 7-349, HCJ Appeal
Latham *v.* HM Advocate see Latham (John) *v.* Vannet
Latham (John) *v.* Vannet; *sub nom* Latham *v.* HM Advocate 1999 S.C.C.R. 119; 1999
    G.W.D. 5-239, HCJ Appeal . . . . *Digested*, 99/**5842**
Latter *v.* Latter 1990 S.L.T. 805, OH . . . . *Digested*, 90/**5114**:
    Not followed, 93/5223, 99/6074
Latto *v.* Vannet 1998 S.L.T. 711; 1997 S.C.C.R. 721; 1997 G.W.D. 34-1714, HCJ Appeal . . *Digested*, 98/**5625**
Lauchlan *v.* HM Advocate (Sentencing) 2001 G.W.D. 40-1516, HCJ Appeal
Lauder *v.* Briggs 1999 S.C. 453, OH . . . . *Digested*, 99/**6453**
Lavelle *v.* Lavelle 2001 G.W.D. 4-144, Sh Ct (Tayside)
Lavery *v.* Walkingshaw 1998 G.W.D. 30-1558, HCJ Appeal
Law *v.* Lees 1998 G.W.D. 33-1707, HCJ Appeal

LAW Construction Co Ltd *v.* LAW Holdings Ltd 1998 G.W.D. 17-875, OH
Law Hospital NHS Trust *v.* Lord Advocate 1996 S.C. 301; 1996 S.L.T. 848; [1996] 2
     F.L.R. 407; (1998) 39 B.M.L.R. 166; [1996] Fam. Law 670; *Times,* May 20,
     1996, IH (Ct of 5 judges) . . . .   *Digested,* 97/**6070**
Law Hospital NHS Trust *v.* Rush [2001] I.R.L.R. 611; 2001 G.W.D. 21-810, Ex Div;
     affirming EAT/842/99, EAT
Lawrence *v.* Vannet 1998 G.W.D. 40-2041, HCJ Appeal
Lawrie *v.* HM Advocate (Sentencing) 2000 G.W.D. 28-1081, HCJ Appeal
Lawrie (Jeanie) *v.* Muir 1950 J.C. 19; 1950 S.L.T. 37; 1949 S.L.T. (Notes) 58, HCJ
     Appeal . . . .   *Digested,* 47-51/**2075**:
                Applied, 47-51/2076, 47-51/4013, 01/6303: *Considered,* 94/5508:
                                                     Referred to, 01/6385
Lawson *v.* Dickson (Sentencing) 2001 G.W.D. 24-899, HCJ Appeal
Lawson *v.* Lawson 1996 S.L.T. (Sh Ct) 83, Sh Pr . . . .   *Digested,* 96/**6913**:
                                                Distinguished, 00/6276
Lawson *v.* Lothian Health Board 1999 G.W.D. 17-811, OH
Lawson *v.* McHugh 1998 Rep. L.R. 138; 1998 G.W.D. 31-1618, Sh Ct . . . .   *Digested,* 99/**5975**
Lawson *v.* Scotdem Ltd 2000 S.L.T. 543 (Note); 1999 Rep. L.R. 100; 1999 G.W.D. 8-
     393, OH . . . .   *Digested,* 99/**5976**
Lawson *v.* Vannet (Sentencing) 2000 G.W.D. 29-1131, HCJ Appeal
Lazarevic *v.* Secretary of State for the Home Department see Adan (Hassan Hussein)
     v. Secretary of State for the Home Department
Leaper *v.* Leaper 1998 S.L.T. 659; 1997 S.C.L.R. 757; 1997 G.W.D. 25-1237, OH . . . . . .   *Digested,* 97/**6052**
Learmonth *v.* Learmonth 1995 S.C.L.R. 768, Sh Pr . . . .   *Digested,* 95/**6093**:
                                                Not followed, 00/6541
Learmonth *v.* Lees 1998 G.W.D. 21-1067, HCJ Appeal
Learmonth Property Investment Co Ltd *v.* Jopp Management Services Ltd 2001 G.W.D.
     8-301, Sh Pr
Ledger *v.* MacGregor Energy Services Ltd 2000 G.W.D. 39-1464, Ex Div
Lee *v.* McFadyen (Sentencing) 2000 G.W.D. 13-484, HCJ Appeal
Leebody *v.* Liddle 2000 S.C.L.R. 495; 2000 Rep. L.R. 59; 2000 G.W.D. 16-663, OH . .   *Digested,* 00/**6168**
Leeds & Holbeck Building Society *v.* Alex Morison & Co (No.1) 1999 G.W.D. 9-434, OH
Leeds & Holbeck Building Society *v.* Alex Morison & Co (No.2) 2001 S.C.L.R. 41;
     [2001] P.N.L.R. 13; 2000 G.W.D. 30-1194, OH . . . .   *Digested,* 01/**6822**
Lees *v.* Brown (Sentencing) 1998 G.W.D. 1-14, Sh Ct
Lees *v.* Dougan 1998 G.W.D. 11-526, Sh Ct
Lees *v.* Laftavi 1998 G.W.D. 17-865, HCJ Appeal
Lees *v.* McCann (Sentencing) 1998 G.W.D. 9-445, Sh Ct
Lees *v.* McLachlan 1998 G.W.D. 35-1789, Sh Ct
Lees *v.* Neal 1998 G.W.D. 22-1120, Sh Ct
Lees *v.* Reith (Sentencing) 1998 G.W.D. 6-297, HCJ Appeal
Lees *v.* Ritchie (Sentencing) 1998 G.W.D. 6-271, HCJ Appeal
Lees *v.* Rys 1998 G.W.D. 28-1431, Sh Ct
Lees *v.* Taylor (Sentencing) 1998 G.W.D. 3-111, Sh Ct
Lees, Petitioner see Lord Advocate, Petitioner (Shameless Indecency)
Lefevre *v.* City of Aberdeen Licensing Board [2000] 16 S.L.L.P. 15; 2000 G.W.D. 15-
     622, Sh Ct . . . .   *Digested,* 00/**6561**
Legal & General Assurance Society Ltd *v.* Tesco Stores Ltd 2001 G.W.D. 18-707, OH
Leitch *v.* Donnelly (Sentencing) 2000 G.W.D. 30-1184, HCJ Appeal
Lennox *v.* McGlennan 1999 G.W.D. 21-1020, HCJ Appeal
Lenting *v.* Bristow Helicopters Ltd 1998 S.L.T. 664; 1997 G.W.D. 25-1264, 1 Div . . . . . .   *Digested,* 98/**5815**
Leonard *v.* HM Advocate (Sentencing) 2000 G.W.D. 20-824, HCJ Appeal
Leonard *v.* Strathclyde Buses Ltd 1999 S.C. 57; 1999 S.L.T. 734; [1998] I.R.L.R. 693;
     1998 G.W.D. 31-1621, 2 Div . . . .   *Digested,* 99/**6045**:
                                                Followed, 00/6218
Leslie *v.* HM Advocate 1999 G.W.D. 18-827, HCJ Appeal
Leslie *v.* Secretary of State for Scotland 1999 Rep. L.R. 39; 1999 G.W.D. 4-212, OH . . .   *Digested,* 99/**6371**
Leslie *v.* Watt (Sentencing) 2001 G.W.D. 21-819, HCJ Appeal
Letton *v.* HM Advocate 1998 G.W.D. 25-1258, HCJ Appeal
Levine *v.* Morris [1970] 1 W.L.R. 71; [1970] 1 All E.R. 144; [1970] 1 Lloyd's Rep. 7;
     (1969) 113 S.J. 798; *Times,* October 10 1969, CA . . . .   *Digested,* 70/**1867**:
                               Applied, 01/6817: *Distinguished,* 00/4232
Leys *v.* Higson 1999 G.W.D. 34-1626, HCJ Appeal
Liangsiriprasert *v.* United States [1991] 1 A.C. 225; [1990] 3 W.L.R. 606; [1990] 2 All
     E.R. 866; (1991) 92 Cr. App. R. 77; (1990) 134 S.J. 1123, PC (HK) . . . .   *Digested,* 91/**1743**:
                          Applied, 90/948, 91/820, 00/952: *Considered,* 97/2441:
                             Distinguished, 91/4777: *Followed,* 00/6029
Liddell *v.* Inland Revenue Commissioners 72 T.C. 62; 1997 G.W.D. 26-1344, OH . . . . . .   *Digested,* 00/**6699**
Liddell *v.* Vannet 1999 G.W.D. 20-953, HCJ Appeal
Lightbody *v.* Upper Clyde Shipbuilders Ltd 1998 S.L.T. 884; 1998 S.C.L.R. 597; 1998
     Rep. L.R. 95; 1998 G.W.D. 17-873, OH . . . .   *Digested,* 98/**5743**
Lightways (Contractors) Ltd *v.* Associated Holdings Ltd 2000 S.C. 262; 2000 S.L.T.
     1093; [2000] I.R.L.R. 247; 2000 G.W.D. 5-199, 2 Div . . . .   *Digested,* 00/**6216**

Linden Gardens Trust Ltd *v.* Lenesta Sludge Disposals Ltd; St Martins Property Corp
    Ltd *v.* Sir Robert McAlpine & Sons [1994] 1 A.C. 85; [1993] 3 W.L.R. 408;
    [1993] 3 All E.R. 417; 63 B.L.R. 1; 36 Con. L.R. 1; [1993] E.G.C.S. 139; (1993)
    143 N.L.J. 1152; (1993) 137 S.J.L.B. 183; *Times*, July 23, 1993; *Independent*,
    July 30, 1993, HL; reversing in part 57 B.L.R. 57; 30 Con. L.R. 1; (1992) 8 Const.
    L.J. 180; *Times*, February 27, 1992; *Independent*, March 6, 1992; *Financial
    Times*, February 20, 1992, CA; reversing 52 B.L.R. 93; 25 Con. L.R. 28; [1991]
    E.G.C.S. 11, QBD . . . . *Digested*, 93/**303**:
                      Applied, 94/319, 95/487, 95/3701, 98/809, 99/832: *Cited*, 99/1417:
                          Considered, 94/549, 95/771, 95/4162, 99/440, 00/864: *Followed*, 98/401,
                                                00/859, 00/5980
Lindie *v.* Friel (Sentencing) 1998 G.W.D. 21-1099, HCJ Appeal
Lindie *v.* Friel (Sentencing) 1998 G.W.D. 32-1651, HCJ Appeal
Lindop *v.* Stewart Noble & Sons Ltd; *sub nom* Lindop *v.* Stuart Noble & Sons Ltd
    1999 S.C.L.R. 889; [2000] B.C.C. 747; 1999 G.W.D. 23-1112, 2 Div; affirming
    1998 S.C.L.R. 648; [1999] B.C.C. 616; *Times*, June 25, 1998, OH . . . . *Digested*, 00/**6514**
Lindop *v.* Stuart Noble & Sons Ltd see Lindop *v.* Stewart Noble & Sons Ltd
Lindsay *v.* Gilchrist 1999 G.W.D. 24-1144, HCJ Appeal
Lindsay *v.* Glasgow DC 1998 Hous. L.R. 4, Sh Ct. . . . . *Digested*, 98/**5973**
Lindsay *v.* HM Advocate 1998 G.W.D. 27-1374, HCJ Appeal
Lindsay *v.* McFadyen 1999 G.W.D. 34-1652, HCJ Appeal
Lindsay *v.* McLeod (Sentencing) 1999 G.W.D. 7-326, HCJ Appeal
Lindsay *v.* McLeod (Sentencing) 1999 G.W.D. 34-1646, HCJ Appeal
Lindsay *v.* Walker 1998 G.W.D. 35-1829, HCJ Appeal
Lindsay *v.* Watt (Sentencing) 2000 G.W.D. 33-1291, HCJ Appeal
Lindsay Plant Ltd *v.* Norwest Holst Group Plc 2000 S.C. 93; 1999 G.W.D. 38-1845, OH   *Digested*, 00/**5991**
Linton *v.* HM Advocate (Sentencing) 1998 G.W.D. 7-333, HCJ Appeal
Linton *v.* HM Advocate (Sentencing) 1999 G.W.D. 37-1811, HCJ Appeal
Liquidators of the Western Bank of Scotland *v.* Douglas (1860) 22 D. 447, 2 Div . . . . . .   *Applied*, 98/**5445**:
                                                 Followed, 96/6663
Lister *v.* Lees 1994 S.L.T. 1328; 1993 S.C.C.R. 548, HCJ Appeal . . . .   *Digested*, 94/**5661**:
                                                 Applied, 99/5836
Lithgow Factoring Ltd (t/a Inver Salmon) *v.* Nordvik Salmon Farms Ltd 1999 S.L.T. 106;
    1998 S.C.L.R. 496; 1998 G.W.D. 16-833, OH . . . . *Digested*, 98/**6182**
Lithoprint (Scotland) Ltd *v.* Summit Leasing Ltd 1998 G.W.D. 38-1956, OH
Little (Cheryl), Petitioner 2001 G.W.D. 30-1179, Sh Ct (Tayside)
Little *v.* East Ayrshire Council 1998 S.C.L.R. 520; 1998 G.W.D. 18-885, OH . . . .   *Digested*, 98/**5481**
Little *v.* East Ayrshire Licensing Board [1998] 11 S.L.L.P. 8, Sh Ct. . . . .   *Digested*, 98/**6069**
Little *v.* Friel (Sentencing) 1998 G.W.D. 1-33, HCJ Appeal
Littlejohn (Victoria Hilary) *v.* McLeod 1999 J.C. 333; [2000] E.H.L.R. Dig. 272; 1999
    G.W.D. 30-1402, HCJ Appeal
Livie *v.* Livie 1999 G.W.D. 34-1639, Sh Ct
Living Design (Home Improvements) Ltd, Petitioners (Restrictive Covenant: Interim
    Interdict) 1999 G.W.D. 10-450, OH
Livingstone *v.* East of Scotland Water Authority see East of Scotland Water Authority *v.*
    Livingstone
Lloyd *v.* McMahon [1987] A.C. 625; [1987] 2 W.L.R. 821; [1987] 1 All E.R. 1118; 85
    L.G.R. 545; [1987] R.V.R. 58; [1987] 84 L.S.G. 1240; (1987) 137 N.L.J. 265;
    (1987) 131 S.J. 409, HL; affirming 85 L.G.R. 348; [1986] R.V.R. 188, CA . . . . . .   *Digested*, 87/**3162**:
                     Applied, 94/66, 00/538: *Considered*, 93/1679, 93/3757, 94/44, 94/3835,
                            94/4226, 94/6012, 95/162, 95/3252, 95/4668, 00/6628
Lloyd *v.* Thompson 2001 S.L.T. (Sh Ct) 127; 2001 G.W.D. 14-536, Sh Pr . . . .   *Digested*, 01/**6254**
Lochcarron John Buchan Ltd *v.* Macrae 1999 S.L.C.R. 88, Land Ct   *Digested*, 99/**6316**
Lock *v.* Edinburgh City Council 2001 S.L.T. (Lands Tr) 19; 2000 G.W.D. 31-1237, Lands
    Tr (Scot)
Lockhart *v.* Bamber 1999 G.W.D. 34-1630, HCJ Appeal
Lockhart *v.* Deighan 1985 S.L.T. 549, HCJ Appeal . . . .   *Digested*, 85/**4714**:
                              Distinguished, 88/4827, 99/5831
Logan *v.* Falkirk and District Royal Infirmary NHS Trust 1999 G.W.D. 30-1431, OH
Logan *v.* HM Advocate 1999 G.W.D. 21-987, HCJ Appeal
Logan *v.* HM Advocate (Sentencing) 2001 G.W.D. 26-1033, HCJ Appeal
Logan *v.* McGlennan (Sentencing) 1999 G.W.D. 2-89, HCJ Appeal
Logan (Rachel) *v.* McGlennan 1999 J.C. 285; 1999 S.L.T. 1179; 1999 S.C.C.R. 584;
    1999 G.W.D. 22-1040, HCJ Appeal . . . . *Digested*, 99/**5934**
Logan *v.* Strathclyde Fire Board 1999 Rep. L.R. 97, OH . . . .   *Digested*, 99/**5974**:
                              Not followed, 99/5973
Logie *v.* Heywood 1999 G.W.D. 35-1669, HCJ Appeal
Logue *v.* Vannet 1998 G.W.D. 19-999, HCJ Appeal
Lomax *v.* Lees (Sentencing) 1999 G.W.D. 12-552, HCJ Appeal
Lomond Assured Properties Ltd *v.* McGrigor Donald 2000 S.L.T. 797; 1999 S.C.L.R.
    568; 1999 G.W.D. 11-512, OH . . . . *Digested*, 99/**5969**

London and Clydeside Estates Ltd v. Aberdeen DC [1980] 1 W.L.R. 182; [1979] 3 All
E.R. 876; 1980 S.C. (H.L.) 1; 1980 S.L.T. 81; (1980) 39 P. & C.R. 549; (1979)
253 E.G. 1011; 124 S.J. 100, HL; reversing 1979 S.L.T. 221, 2 Div; affirming in part
1977 S.L.T. 162, OH . . . . *Digested*, 80/**2904**:
Applied, 85/3463, 92/6121, 95/4375: *Considered*, 78/3000, 85/2919,
85/3401, 85/3415, 86/2159, 87/2319, 96/2689, 96/4652:
Followed, 82/4414, 83/3648, 00/6438
Long (John Patrick) v. HM Advocate 1984 S.C.C.R. 161, HCJ Appeal . . . . *Digested*, 84/**3832**:
Not followed, 98/5606

Longden v. British Coal Corp [1998] A.C. 653; [1997] 3 W.L.R. 1336; [1998] 1 All
E.R. 289; [1998] I.C.R. 26; [1998] I.R.L.R. 29; [1998] P.I.Q.R. Q11; [1998]
O.P.L.R. 223; (1998) 95(1) L.S.G. 25; (1997) 147 N.L.J. 1774; (1998) 142
S.J.L.B. 28; *Times*, November 28, 1997, HL; affirming in part [1995] I.C.R. 957;
[1995] I.R.L.R. 642; [1995] P.I.Q.R. Q48; (1995) 92(15) L.S.G. 40; (1995) 139
S.J.L.B. 88; *Times*, April 14, 1995, CA . . . . *Digested*, 98/**1468**:
Applied, 98/1692: *Followed*, 99/5973
Longmuir (Derek) v. HM Advocate 2000 J.C. 378; 2000 S.C.C.R. 447; 2000 G.W.D.
11-381, HCJ Appeal . . . . *Digested*, 00/**6039**:
Applied, 01/6403

Longstaff v. HM Advocate 1999 G.W.D. 17-794, HCJ Appeal
Lonie v. HM Advocate 1999 G.W.D. 35-1695, HCJ Appeal
Lord Advocate v. Leukaemia and Cancer Children's Fund 1998 G.W.D. 14-692, OH
Lord Advocate v. Ruffle 1979 S.C. 371; 1979 S.L.T. 212, OH . . . . *Digested*, 79/**2901**:
Considered, 98/6218

Lord Advocate v. Scotsman Publications Ltd [1990] 1 A.C. 812; [1989] 3 W.L.R. 358;
[1989] 2 All E.R. 852; 1989 S.C. (H.L.) 122; 1989 S.L.T. 705; [1989] 1 F.S.R.
580; (1989) 86(38) L.S.G. 32; (1989) 139 N.L.J. 971; *Times*, July 7, 1989;
Independent, July 7, 1989; *Guardian*, July 7, 1989, HL; affirming 1988 S.L.T. 490;
[1989] 1 F.S.R. 310; *Times*, April 25, 1988, 2 Div; affirming [1989] 1 F.S.R. 291;
Times, March 9, 1988; *Independent*, March 8, 1988, OH . . . . *Digested*, 89/**4740**:
Considered, 96/1121: *Distinguished*, 99/5703: *Referred to*, 92/5715
Lord Advocate v. Tursi 1998 S.L.T. 1035; 1997 S.C.L.R. 264; 1997 G.W.D. 6-254, OH. . . *Digested*, 97/**6173**
Lord Advocate v. Williams of Chirnside 2000 S.L.T. (Lyon Ct) 3, Lyon Ct. . . . . *Digested*, 00/**5969**
Lord Advocate's Reference (No.1of 2000), Re 2001 J.C.143; 2001 S.L.T. 507; 2001 S.C.C.R.
296; 2001 G.W.D. 13-475, HCJ Appeal . . . . *Digested*, 01/**6334**
Lord Advocate, Petitioner (Evidence: Foreign Proceedings) 1998 S.C. 87; 1998 S.L.T. 835;
1997 G.W.D. 37-1882; *Times*, May 28, 1998, Ex Div. . . . . *Digested*, 98/**5531**
Lord Advocate, Petitioner (Shameless Indecency); *sub nom* Lees, Petitioner 1998 J.C.
209; 1999 S.L.T. 405; 1998 S.C.C.R. 401, HCJ Appeal . . . . *Digested*, 98/**5696**
Lord Gray's Motion, Re [2000] 2 W.L.R. 664; 2000 S.C. (H.L.) 46; 2000 S.L.T.1337; *Times*,
November 12, 1999, HL . . . . *Digested*, 99/**5768**
Lorimar v. Normand 1997 S.C. 230; 1997 S.L.T. 1277; 1997 S.C.C.R. 582; 1997 G.W.D.
27-1358, HCJ Appeal . . . . *Digested*, 97/**5816**:
Applied, 00/6081

Lothian Borders and Angus Cooperative Society Ltd v. Scottish Borders Council [1999]
2 P.L.R. 19; 1999 G.W.D. 6-316; *Times*, March 10, 1999, OH . . . . *Digested*, 99/**6408**
Lothian RC v. A 1992 S.L.T. 858; 1992 S.C.L.R. 376, 1 Div . . . . *Digested*, 92/**5263**:
Applied, 94/5425, 00/6246
Loudon v. McFadyen (Sentencing) 2001 G.W.D. 16-612, HCJ Appeal
Loudonhill Contracts Ltd v. John Mowlem Construction Ltd; *sub nom* Loundonhill
Contracts Ltd v. John Mowlem Construction Ltd 2000 S.C.L.R. 1111; (2001) 3
T.C.L.R. 23; 80 Con. L.R. 1; 2000 G.W.D. 25-930, 1 Div . . . . *Digested*, 01/**6292**
Loughlin v. London Midland & Scottish Contractors Ltd 1999 G.W.D. 20-917, OH
Loughlin v. Peters 1998 S.C.L.R. 371, Sh Pr . . . . *Digested*, 98/**5509**
Loughran v. Lanarkshire Acute Hospitals NHS Trust 2000 Rep. L.R. 58 (Note); 2000
G.W.D. 14-555, OH . . . . *Digested*, 00/**6592**:
Considered, 01/6218
Loundonhill Contracts Ltd v. John Mowlem Construction Ltd see Loudonhill Contracts
Ltd v. John Mowlem Construction Ltd
Lousada & Co Ltd v. JE Lesser (Properties) Ltd 1990 S.C. 178; 1990 S.L.T. 823, 2 Div . . *Digested*, 90/**5365**:
Applied, 00/6467: *Followed*, 93/5383
Love v. Brown (Insurance Certificate) 1999 G.W.D. 30-1444, HCJ Appeal
Love (Philip Andrew) v. Brown 2000 S.C.C.R. 931; 2000 G.W.D. 33-1268, HCJ Appeal . . *Digested*, 01/**6380**
Love v. HM Advocate 2000 J.C. 1; 1999 S.C.C.R. 783; 1999 G.W.D. 30-1409, HCJ
Appeal . . . . *Digested*, 00/**6007**
Love, Petitioner 1998 J.C. 85; 1998 S.L.T. 461; 1998 S.C.C.R. 161; 1998 G.W.D. 11-528, HCJ
Appeal . . . . *Digested*, 98/**5604**
Low v. Adams 2000 G.W.D. 40-1510, Sh Ct (Grampian)
Low v. McLeod (Sentencing) 2000 G.W.D. 8-305, HCJ Appeal
Lowe v. Grampian Health Board 1998 S.L.T. 731; 1997 Rep. L.R. 94; 1997 G.W.D. 24-
1222, OH . . . . *Digested*, 97/**5674**
Lowe v. Hamilton (Sentencing) 1998 G.W.D. 15-747, HCJ Appeal
Lowe v. Munro 1998 G.W.D. 40-2055, HCJ Appeal
Lowey v. Walkingshaw (Sentencing) 1998 G.W.D. 32-1679, HCJ Appeal

Lucas's Executors *v.* Demarco; *sub nom* Lurie *v.* Demarco 1968 S.L.T. 89; 1967 S.L.T.
   (Notes) 110, 1 Div . . . . *Digested*, 68/**4413**:
                                                     Followed, 97/6176, 98/6032
Ludi *v.* Switzerland (A/238) (1993) 15 E.H.R.R. 173; *Times*, August 13, 1992; *Guardian*,
   July 15, 1992, ECHR. . . . . *Digested*, 93/**2139**:
                       Applied, 01/6323: *Considered*, 97/2766: *Distinguished*, 98/3122
Lumsden *v.* HM Advocate (Sentencing) 1998 G.W.D. 29-1476, HCJ Appeal
Lumsden *v.* HM Advocate (Sentencing) 1999 G.W.D. 17-774, HCJ Appeal
Lumsden *v.* MacNeill 1998 G.W.D. 37-1899, HCJ Appeal
Lurie *v.* Demarco see Lucas's Executors *v.* Demarco
Lusk *v.* HM Advocate (Sentencing) 1999 G.W.D. 10-458, HCJ Appeal
Lusk *v.* Kennedy 1999 G.W.D. 26-1247, HCJ Appeal
Luss Estates Co *v.* GB Garman & Co 1999 G.W.D. 38-1864, 2 Div; affirming 1999
   G.W.D. 23-1117, OH
Lutea Trustees Ltd *v.* Orbis Trustees Guernsey Ltd 1997 S.C. 255; 1998 S.L.T. 471; 1997
   S.C.L.R. 735; 1997 G.W.D. 19-927, 2 Div. . . . . *Digested*, 97/**6456**
Lutton *v.* Wheelan (Sentencing) 1998 G.W.D. 2-83, HCJ Appeal
Luxton *v.* Crowe (Sentencing) 1999 G.W.D. 4-185, HCJ Appeal
Lyall *v.* Carnegy (1900) 2 F. (Ct. of Sess.) 423, CS   *Followed*, 01/6542
Lyall *v.* HM Advocate (Sentencing) 2001 G.W.D. 31-1260, HCJ Appeal
Lye *v.* McFadyen (Sentencing) 2000 G.W.D. 39-1467, HCJ Appeal
Lyle *v.* HM Advocate 2001 G.W.D. 26-1022, HCJ Appeal
Lyle *v.* HM Advocate (Sentencing) 1998 G.W.D. 21-1082, HCJ Appeal
Lynch *v.* Gilchrist 1999 G.W.D. 27-1272, HCJ Appeal
Lynn *v.* McFadyen 1999 G.W.D. 24-1142, HCJ Appeal
Lynn *v.* McGlennan (Sentencing) 2000 G.W.D. 37-1401, HCJ Appeal
Lyons Laing *v.* Land 2001 S.L.T. 1246 (Note); 2000 G.W.D. 38-1423, Ex Div
Lyttle *v.* HM Advocate (Sentencing) 2001 G.W.D. 39-1470, HCJ Appeal

M (A Juvenile) *v.* HM Advocate (Sentencing) 1998 G.W.D. 18-905, HCJ Appeal
M *v.* Caldwell 2001 S.L.T. (Sh Ct) 106; 2001 Fam. L.R. 76; 2000 G.W.D. 38-1418, Sh
    Ct (South Strathclyde)
M *v.* Clark 2000 G.W.D. 33-1272, HCJ Appeal
M *v.* Constanda 1999 S.C. 348; 1999 S.L.T. 494; 1999 S.C.L.R. 108; 1999 G.W.D. 1-3,
   Ex Div. . . . . *Digested*, 99/**6070**
M *v.* HM Advocate (Restriction Order) 1998 G.W.D. 24-1231, HCJ Appeal
M *v.* HM Advocate (Sentencing) 1998 G.W.D. 26-1327, HCJ Appeal
M *v.* HM Advocate (Sentencing) 1999 G.W.D. 7-341, HCJ Appeal
M *v.* HM Advocate (Sentencing) 2001 G.W.D. 26-1038, HCJ Appeal
M *v.* M 2001 Fam. L.R. 131; 2001 G.W.D. 35-1340, Ex Div
M *v.* M (Residence Order) 2000 Fam. L.R. 84; 2000 G.W.D. 21-826, OH . . . . *Digested*, 00/**6265**
M *v.* S (Consent: Missing Parent) see S *v.* M (Consent: Missing Parent)
M, Petitioner 2000 G.W.D. 32-1242, OH
M, Petitioner 2001 G.W.D. 19-715, Sh Ct (Grampian)
Maan (Habib), Petitioner see Maan (Habib) *v.* HM Advocate
Maan (Habib) *v.* HM Advocate; *sub nom* Maan (Habib), Petitioner 2001 S.L.T. 408;
   2001 S.C.C.R. 172; 2001 G.W.D. 6-194, HCJ . . . . *Digested*, 01/**6314**
McAdam *v.* McAdam (Divorce: Financial Provision) 1999 G.W.D. 40-1954, OH
McAdam *v.* Wood 2001 G.W.D. 35-1354, OH
McAlease *v.* Stott (Sentencing) 2000 G.W.D. 4-165, HCJ Appeal
McAlinden *v.* Ruxton (Sentencing) 1998 G.W.D. 8-381, HCJ Appeal
McAllan *v.* HM Advocate (No.1) 1999 G.W.D. 18-826, HCJ Appeal
McAllan *v.* HM Advocate (No.2) 1999 G.W.D. 18-836, HCJ Appeal
McAllister *v.* Donnelly 1999 G.W.D. 22-1057, HCJ Appeal
McAllister *v.* East Dunbartonshire Licensing Board 1998 S.C. 748; 1998 S.L.T. 713, 2
   Div . . . . *Digested*, 98/**6068**
McAllister *v.* ICI Plc 1997 S.L.T. 351; 1996 Rep. L.R. 136, OH . . . . *Digested*, 97/**5926**:
                                         Approved, 99/5968: *Followed*, 98/5705
McAllister *v.* McGlennan (Sentencing) 1999 G.W.D. 12-582, HCJ Appeal
McAllister *v.* MacKechnie 2000 G.W.D. 38-1421, OH
McAllister *v.* Queens Cross Housing Association Ltd 2001 Hous. L.R. 143; 2001
   G.W.D. 38-1441, Lands Tr (Scot)
McAlonan *v.* HM Advocate (Sentencing) 2001 G.W.D. 39-1474, HCJ Appeal
McAloon *v.* Lord Advocate 1999 G.W.D. 29-1393, OH
McAloon *v.* Ruxton 1998 G.W.D. 13-636, HCJ Appeal
Macalpin *v.* Duke of Hamilton's Trustees 1914 S.L.C.R. 74, Land Ct . . . . *Not followed*, 98/6029
McAlpine *v.* Spiers (Sentencing) 1998 G.W.D. 16-785, HCJ Appeal
McAlpine *v.* Vannet 1999 G.W.D. 23-1096, HCJ Appeal
McAnea (Thomas) *v.* HM Advocate; Dean (Raymond) *v.* HM Advocate; McGregor
   (John Joseph) *v.* HM Advocate; McGinnis (Dennis) *v.* HM Advocate 2000 J.C.
   641; 2001 S.L.T. 12; 2000 S.C.C.R. 779; 2000 G.W.D. 26-981, HCJ Appeal . . . . *Digested*, 01/**6385**
McArdle *v.* Vannet (Sentencing) 1998 G.W.D. 16-822, HCJ Appeal

McArthur (Thomas Frederick) *v.* HM Advocate 2000 S.L.T. 694; 1999 G.W.D. 28-1327,
HCJ Appeal . . . . *Digested,* 00/**6120**
McArthur *v.* Lees 1998 G.W.D. 19-973, HCJ Appeal
McArthur *v.* McArthur's Trustee; *sub nom* McArthur's Trustee *v.* McArthur; McNeill *v.*
McArthur 1997 S.L.T. 926; 1997 S.C.L.R. 252; 1997 G.W.D. 5-175, Ex Div . . . . . *Digested,* 97/**5650**:
Distinguished, 98/5497
McArthur *v.* McFadyen 1999 G.W.D. 21-1008, HCJ Appeal
McArthur *v.* McLeod (Sentencing) 2000 G.W.D. 33-1286, HCJ Appeal
MacArthur *v.* MacNeill 1986 J.C. 182; 1987 S.L.T. 299; 1986 S.C.C.R. 552, HCJ
Appeal . . . . *Digested,* 87/**4163**:
Distinguished, 93/4989, 99/5886
MacArthur *v.* Tenth Duke of Argyll's Trustees 2000 S.L.C.R. 94, Land Ct (Full Ct) . . . . . *Digested,* 01/**6742**
McArthur's Trustee *v.* McArthur see McArthur *v.* McArthur's Trustee
MacAskill *v.* HM Advocate (Sentencing) 2001 G.W.D. 16-606, HCJ Appeal
Macaskill *v.* Nicol 1943 S.C. 17; 1943 S.L.T. 147, 2 Div . . . . *Applied,* 94/6149:
Considered, 97/5647: *Followed,* 88/4667: *Overruled,* 98/5493
MacAuley *v.* Bamber 1998 G.W.D. 8-356, HCJ Appeal
McAuley *v.* HM Advocate 1946 J.C. 8; 1946 S.L.T. 50, HCJ Appeal . . . . *Applied,* 55/532,
55/3080: *Considered,* 00/6055: *Distinguished,* 92/5440: *Overruled,* 00/6078
McAuley *v.* McLeod 1998 G.W.D. 37-1918, HCJ Appeal
Macaura *v.* Northern Assurance Co Ltd [1925] A.C. 619, HL . . . . *Applied,* 98/6015
McAvoy *v.* Friel 1998 S.L.T. 480; 1997 G.W.D. 40-2074, HCJ Appeal . . . . *Digested,* 98/**5668**
McAvoy *v.* Glasgow DC 1993 S.L.T. 859; 1993 S.C.L.R. 393, OH . . . . *Digested,* 93/**5283**:
Followed, 99/5658
McAvoy (Thomas) *v.* HM Advocate 1991 J.C. 16; 1992 S.L.T. 46; 1991 S.C.C.R. 123,
HCJ Appeal . . . . *Digested,* 91/**4744**:
Applied, 96/6811, 99/5901: *Distinguished,* 97/5765: *Referred to,* 93/5019,
95/5715
McAvoy *v.* Vannet (Sentencing) 1999 G.W.D. 40-1963, HCJ Appeal
McBain *v.* Viscount Reidhaven 1991 S.L.C.R. 74, Land Ct (Div Ct) . . . . *Digested,* 91/**5698**:
Considered, 99/6319
McBeath *v.* Halliday 2000 Rep. L.R. 38; 2000 G.W.D. 2-75, OH . . . . *Digested,* 00/**6429**
McBeth *v.* Dickson (Sentencing) 1999 G.W.D. 36-1739, HCJ Appeal
McBlain *v.* Dolan 1998 S.L.T. 512; [2001] Lloyd's Rep. I.R. 309, OH . . . . *Digested,* 98/**6019**:
Considered, 01/622
McBlain *v.* HM Advocate 1999 G.W.D. 11-510, HCJ Appeal.
McBratney *v.* Redman (Sentencing) 1998 G.W.D. 1-15, HCJ Appeal
McBrearty (Thomas John) *v.* HM Advocate 1999 S.L.T. 1333; 1999 S.C.C.R. 122; 1999
G.W.D. 5-244, HCJ Appeal . . . . *Digested,* 99/**5907**
McBride *v.* Vannet (Sentencing) 1999 G.W.D. 26-1230, HCJ Appeal
McBride *v.* Vannet (Sentencing) 1998 G.W.D. 8-416, HCJ Appeal
McC *v.* HM Advocate (Sentencing) 2001 S.C.C.R. 576; 2001 G.W.D. 25-953, HCJ
Appeal
McCabe *v.* Heywood (Sentencing) 1998 G.W.D. 15-760, HCJ Appeal
McCadden (Patrick) *v.* HM Advocate 1985 J.C. 98; 1986 S.L.T. 138; 1985 S.C.C.R.
282, HCJ Appeal . . . . *Digested,* 86/**3832**:
Applied, 97/5818, 99/5875: *Considered,* 87/4183, 87/4185, 88/4018,
99/5832: *Followed,* 94/5639
McCafferty (Colin) *v.* McCafferty (William Muir) 2000 S.C.L.R. 256; 1999 G.W.D. 37-
1827, Sh Ct. . . . . *Digested,* 00/**6634**
Mccafferty *v.* Secretary of State for Scotland 1998 S.C.L.R. 379; 1998 G.W.D. 3-144,
OH . . . . *Digested,* 98/**6117**
McCaig Butler Computing Ltd *v.* Campbell Lee Computer Services Ltd 1999 G.W.D.
39-1884, Sh Pr; reversing 1999 G.W.D. 29-1360, Sh Ct
McCaillie *v.* Watt (Sentencing) 2000 G.W.D. 30-1204, HCJ Appeal
McCairns *v.* HM Advocate 1998 G.W.D. 22-1129, HCJ Appeal
McCall *v.* Dumfries and Galloway Rugby Football Club 1999 S.C.L.R. 977, Sh Ct . . . . . *Digested,* 00/**5896**
McCall *v.* Hamilton (Sentencing) 1998 G.W.D. 11-553, HCJ Appeal
McCall (Marc) *v.* Vannet (Sentencing) 1997 S.C.C.R. 778; 1998 G.W.D. 1-28, HCJ
Appeal . . . . *Digested,* 98/**5669**
McCall's Entertainments (Ayr) Ltd *v.* South Ayrshire Council (No.1) 1998 S.L.T. 1403;
1998 G.W.D. 1-47, OH . . . . *Digested,* 99/**6324**
McCall's Entertainments (Ayr) Ltd *v.* South Ayrshire Council (No.2) 1998 S.L.T. 1421;
1998 G.W.D. 19-988, OH . . . . *Digested,* 99/**6327**
McCallum (Andrew William) *v.* Brown 2000 J.C. 6; 2000 S.L.T. 97; 1999 S.C.C.R. 806;
1999 G.W.D. 32-1553, HCJ Appeal . . . . *Digested,* 00/**6568**
McCallum *v.* HM Advocate 1999 G.W.D. 14-634, HCJ Appeal
Mccallum *v.* Paterson (No.2) 1969 S.C. 85; 1969 S.L.T. 177, 1 Div . . . . *Digested,* 69/**3921**:
Considered, 91/4866: *Disapproved,* 98/5478
McCallum *v.* S&D Properties (Commercial) Ltd 2000 Rep. L.R. 24; 2000 G.W.D. 1-32,
OH . . . . *Digested,* 00/**6591**

McCandless *v.* General Medical Council [1996] 1 W.L.R. 167; [1996] 7 Med. L.R. 379; (1996) 30 B.M.L.R. 53; (1996) 93(5) L.S.G. 31; (1996) 140 S.J.L.B. 28; *Times,* December 12, 1995, PC (UK) . . . .   *Digested,* 96/**4187**: *Followed,* 00/6401

McCann *v.* Chief Constable of Strathclyde 1998 G.W.D. 22-1136, Sh Ct

McCann *v.* Kennedy (Sentencing) 2000 G.W.D. 37-1394, HCJ Appeal

McCann *v.* Scottish Media Newspapers Ltd 2000 S.L.T. 256; 1999 S.C.L.R. 636; 1999 G.W.D. 10-473, OH   *Digested,* 99/**5989**

McCarron (George Wallace) *v.* HM Advocate 2001 J.C. 199; 2001 S.L.T. 866; 2001 S.C.C.R. 419; 2001 G.W.D. 16-598, HCJ Appeal . . . .   *Digested,* 01/**6378**

McCarthy *v.* McFadyen (Sentencing) 2000 G.W.D. 37-1393, HCJ Appeal

McCarthy's Executors *v.* McCafferty 2000 G.W.D. 14-549, Sh Pr

McCartney *v.* Buchanan 1999 G.W.D. 9-416, HCJ Appeal

McCartney *v.* HM Advocate 1998 S.L.T. 160; 1997 S.C.C.R. 644; 1997 G.W.D. 32-1625, HCJ Appeal. . . . .   *Digested,* 97/**5907**

McCaskill *v.* HM Advocate 1998 G.W.D. 34-1740, HCJ Appeal

McCaw *v.* Lees 1998 G.W.D. 24-1204, HCJ Appeal

McClure *v.* McGlennan 2000 G.W.D. 8-316, HCJ Appeal

McClure, Applicant see Munro, Applicant

McCluskey *v.* HM Advocate (Sentencing) 1998 G.W.D. 5-218, HCJ Appeal

McCluskey *v.* Wallace 1998 S.C. 711; 1998 S.L.T. 1357; 1998 Rep. L.R. 86; 1998 G.W.D. 20-1005, 2 Div   *Digested,* 98/**6103**

McClymont *v.* Vannet (Sentencing) 2000 G.W.D. 16-660, HCJ Appeal

McColl *v.* HM Advocate 1998 G.W.D. 34-1753, HCJ Appeal

McColl *v.* Russell 2001 G.W.D. 11-384, HCJ Appeal

McConachie *v.* Macleod 1998 G.W.D. 26-1328, HCJ Appeal

McConnell *v.* Ayrshire and Arran Health Board 2001 Rep. L.R. 85; 2001 G.W.D. 7-280, OH. . . . .   *Digested,* 01/**6218**

McConnell *v.* British Shipbuilders 2000 G.W.D. 21-836, OH

McCorkindale *v.* McGlennan (Sentencing) 2001 G.W.D. 1-31, HCJ Appeal

McCormack *v.* CSC Forest Products Ltd 2001 G.W.D. 40-1499, OH

MacCormack *v.* Heywood 1999 G.W.D. 1-31, HCJ Appeal

McCrae *v.* Henderson 1999 G.W.D. 33-1580, HCJ Appeal

McCreaddie *v.* HM Advocate 1999 G.W.D. 16-742, HCJ Appeal

McCreadie *v.* Stott (Sentencing) 2000 G.W.D. 19-756, HCJ Appeal

McCready *v.* Walkingshaw 1998 G.W.D. 35-1791, HCJ Appeal

McCredie *v.* Kennedy (Sentencing) 2000 G.W.D. 5-194, HCJ Appeal

McCrindle *v.* McGlennan (Sentencing) 1998 G.W.D. 11-531, HCJ Appeal

McCrindle *v.* Sandilands 1980 S.L.T. (Notes) 12, OH . . . .   *Digested,* 80/**3478**: *Distinguished,* 00/5932

McCrory *v.* Walkingshaw (Sentencing) 1999 G.W.D. 4-222, HCJ Appeal

McCrudden *v.* Heywood 1998 G.W.D. 25-1245, HCJ Appeal

McCue *v.* Scottish Daily Record & Sunday Mail Ltd (No.1) 1998 S.C. 811; 1998 S.L.T. 983; 1998 S.C.L.R. 742; 1998 G.W.D. 23-1153, IH (Ct of 5 judges) . . . .   *Digested,* 98/**5493**: *Considered,* 99/5680: *Distinguished,* 00/5940

McCue *v.* Scottish Daily Record & Sunday Mail Ltd (No.2) 1999 S.C. 332; 1999 S.L.T. 558; 1999 S.C.L.R. 380; 1999 G.W.D. 4-203, 2 Div; reversing 1998 G.W.D. 8-392, OH . . . .   *Digested,* 99/**5682**

McCue *v.* Scottish Daily Record & Sunday Mail Ltd (No.3) 1999 G.W.D. 32-1547, OH

McCue *v.* Scottish Daily Record & Sunday Mail Ltd (No.4) 2000 Rep. L.R. 133; 2000 G.W.D. 28-1084, OH . . . .   *Digested,* 01/**6430**

McCulloch (Stewart) *v.* HM Advocate 2001 J.C. 100; 2001 S.L.T. 113; 2000 S.C.C.R. 1115; 2000 G.W.D. 36-1357, HCJ Appeal . . . .   *Digested,* 01/**6343**

McCulloch (Stewart) *v.* HM Advocate (Sentencing) 2000 G.W.D. 13-470, HC

McCulloch *v.* McGlennan (Sentencing) 1999 G.W.D. 36-1757, HCJ Appeal

McCulloch *v.* Riach 1999 S.C.L.R. 159, Sh Pr. . . . .   *Digested,* 99/**5712**

McCulloch *v.* Vannet (Sentencing) 2000 G.W.D. 8-300, HCJ Appeal

McCutcheon *v.* David MacBrayne Ltd [1964] 1 W.L.R. 125; [1964] 1 All E.R. 430; [1964] 1 Lloyd's Rep. 16; 1964 S.C. (H.L.) 28; 1964 S.L.T. 66; 108 S.J. 93, HL; reversing [1963] 1 Lloyd's Rep. 123; 1962 S.C. 506; 1963 S.L.T. 30; 1962 S.L.T. (Notes) 98, 2 Div; affirming [1962] 1 Lloyd's Rep. 303; 1962 S.L.T. 231, OH. . . .   *Digested,* 64/**4455**: *Applied,* 68/3526, 69/510, 70/369, 71/1741, 73/404, 74/442, 01/4261: *Considered,* 78/340, 90/4800, 91/4514, 92/1553: *Disapproved,* 72/470: *Distinguished,* 79/2431, 87/430: *Doubted,* 65/3517, 66/10837: *Followed,* 00/5989

McCutcheon *v.* HM Advocate 2001 G.W.D. 18-694, HCJ Appeal

McCutcheon (George) *v.* HM Advocate 2001 G.W.D. 40-1507, HCJ Appeal

McCutcheon (George) *v.* HM Advocate (Interim Hearing) 2001 G.W.D. 1-22, HCJ Appeal

McDade *v.* Carnegie 2001 G.W.D. 32-1281, HCJ Appeal

McDade (Richard Carlyle) *v.* HM Advocate 1998 S.L.T. 68; 1997 S.C.C.R. 731; 1997 G.W.D. 34-1727, HCJ Appeal . . . .   *Digested,* 98/**5679**

McDermott (William) *v.* HM Advocate 2000 J.C. 299; 2000 S.L.T. 366; 2000 S.C.C.R. 208; 2000 G.W.D. 2-45, HCJ Appeal. . . . .   *Digested,* 00/**6066**

McDermott v. HM Advocate (No.1) 1998 G.W.D. 37-1893, HCJ Appeal
McDermott v. HM Advocate (No.2) 1999 G.W.D. 5-251, HCJ Appeal
McDermott v. Miller 1998 G.W.D. 17-868, HCJ Appeal
Mcdiarmid v. Friel 1998 G.W.D. 40-2051, HCJ Appeal
McDonagh v. Reith (Sentencing) 2001 G.W.D. 6-203, HCJ Appeal
Macdonald v. Brough 2001 G.W.D. 39-1450, OH
McDonald v. Chambers 2000 S.L.T. 454; 2000 Rep. L.R. 38; 2000 G.W.D. 2-48, OH . .   *Digested*, 00/**6163**
MacDonald v. Chief Constable of the Northern Constabulary 1999 G.W.D. 36-1726, Sh Pr
McDonald v. Council of Saint Andrew's Ambulance Association 1999 G.W.D. 3-112, OH
MacDonald v. Federation International de Football Association 1999 S.L.T. 1129; 1999 S.C.L.R. 59; 1999 G.W.D. 1-48; *Times*, January 7, 1999, OH . . . .   *Digested*, 99/**6369**
McDonald v. Friel 1998 G.W.D. 20-1048, HCJ Appeal
MacDonald v. Graham see Bogan's Curator Bonis v. Graham
McDonald v. Grampian RC 1999 Fam. L.R. 119, Sh Ct   *Digested*, 00/**6191**
McDonald v. Heywood 2001 G.W.D. 40-1515, HCJ Appeal
Macdonald v. Highlands and Islands Enterprise see Cross v. Highlands and Islands Enterprise
MacDonald v. Hingston 1999 G.W.D. 14-663, HCJ Appeal
MacDonald (James Scott) v. HM Advocate 1998 S.L.T. 37; 1997 S.C.C.R. 116; 1997 G.W.D. 3-80, HCJ Appeal . . . .   *Digested*, 97/**5766**
Macdonald (Robert Grant) v. HM Advocate 1999 S.L.T. 533; 1999 S.C.C.R. 146; 1999 G.W.D. 6-291, HCJ Appeal. . . . .   *Digested*, 99/**5803**
MacDonald v. HM Advocate 1998 G.W.D. 24-1208, HCJ Appeal
McDonald v. HM Advocate (Sentencing) 1999 G.W.D. 3-145, HCJ Appeal
McDonald v. HM Advocate (Sentencing) 1998 G.W.D. 10-489, HCJ Appeal
McDonald v. HM Advocate (Sentencing) 2001 G.W.D. 30-1198, HCJ Appeal
MacDonald v. Howdle 2001 G.W.D. 31-1263, HCJ Appeal
McDonald v. Hutchison 1999 G.W.D. 19-886, HCJ Appeal
McDonald v. Kwok 1999 S.L.T. 593; 1999 G.W.D. 3-125, OH . . . .   *Digested*, 99/**5665**
McDonald v. Lees (Sentencing) 1998 G.W.D. 2-85, HCJ Appeal
McDonald v. Lees (Sentencing) 1998 G.W.D. 8-411, HCJ Appeal
MacDonald v. Lord Advocate 2000 S.L.T. 691; 1999 G.W.D. 8-395, OH . . . .   *Digested*, 00/**6208**
McDonald v. McFadyen 1999 G.W.D. 34-1627, HCJ Appeal
MacDonald v. MacNab (No.1) 2000 S.L.C.R. 133, Land Ct (Full Ct) . . . .   *Digested*, 01/**6739**
MacDonald v. MacNab (No.2) 2000 S.L.C.R. 145, Land Ct (Full Ct) . . . .   *Digested*, 01/**6749**
MacDonald v. Ministry of Defence see Advocate General for Scotland v. MacDonald
MacDonald v. Moray Council 1998 G.W.D. 16-819, OH
McDonald v. Ritchie (Sentencing) 2000 G.W.D. 30-1202, HCJ Appeal
McDonald v. Salmond 1999 S.C. 396; 1999 S.L.T. 1238; 1999 S.C.L.R. 561, OH . . . . . .   *Digested*, 99/**5689**
McDonald v. Vannet (Sentencing) 1999 G.W.D. 10-467, HCJ Appeal
McDonald v. Vannet (Sentencing) 1998 G.W.D. 22-1135, HCJ Appeal
Macdonald v. Western Isles Licensing Board 2001 S.C. 628; [2001] 19 S.L.L.P. 12; 2001 G.W.D. 7-279, OH . . . .   *Digested*, 01/**6784**
McDonald v. Wilson 1998 G.W.D. 21-1075, HCJ Appeal
McDonald's Trustee v. Aberdeen City Council 2000 S.C. 185; 2000 S.L.T. 985; 2000 Hous. L.R. 30; 2000 G.W.D. 1-24, Ex Div . . . .   *Digested*, 00/**6465**
MacDonald's Trustees v. Cunningham 1998 S.L.T. (Sh Ct) 12; 1997 S.C.L.R. 986; 1997 Hous. L.R. 117; 1997 G.W.D. 32-1638, Sh Pr . . . .   *Digested*, 97/**6180**
McDonnell (Stuart) v. HM Advocate 1998 J.C. 228; 1998 S.L.T. 897; 1997 S.C.C.R. 760, HCJ Appeal . . . .   *Digested*, 98/**5552**
MacDonnell v. MacDonnell 2001 S.C. 877; 2001 S.L.T. 757; 2001 Fam. L.R. 61; 2001 G.W.D. 15-580, Ex Div. . . . .   *Digested*, 01/**6518**
MacDougal v. Yuk-Sun Ho 1985 S.C.C.R. 199, HCJ Appeal . . . .   *Digested*, 85/**3994**:
                                                 Distinguished, 00/6047
McDougall v. Dochree 1992 J.C. 154; 1992 S.L.T. 624; 1992 S.C.C.R. 531, HCJ Appeal .   *Digested*, 92/**5535**:
                                                  Applied, 98/5575
McDougall v. HM Advocate 1999 G.W.D. 27-1276, HCJ Appeal
MacDougall v. MacNeil 2001 S.L.C.R. 166, Land Ct (Full Ct)
McDougall v. Tawse 2001 G.W.D. 29-1164, Sh Ct (Grampian)
McDougall v. Vannet (Sentencing) 1998 G.W.D. 32-1663, HCJ Appeal
MacDowall v. Cunninghame DC 1987 S.C. 217; 1987 S.L.T. 662; 1987 S.C.L.R. 587, 2 Div. . . . .   *Digested*, 87/**4693**:
                             Considered, 01/6793: *Distinguished*, 92/6352
McDowall (Fraser Symington) v. HM Advocate 1998 J.C. 194; 1999 S.L.T. 243; 1998 S.C.C.R. 343; 1998 G.W.D. 14-701, HCJ Appeal . . . .   *Digested*, 98/**5580**
McDowall v. HM Advocate (Sentencing) 1998 G.W.D. 29-1482, HCJ Appeal
McDowell v. McGlennan 2001 G.W.D. 25-984, HCJ Appeal
McDyer v. Celtic Football & Athletic Co Ltd (No.1) 2000 S.C. 379; 2000 S.L.T. 736; 2000 S.C.L.R. 643; 2000 G.W.D. 10-369, 1 Div; reversing 1999 S.L.T. 2; 1997 Rep. L.R. 117; 1997 G.W.D. 30-1536, OH . . . .   *Digested*, 00/**6599**
McDyer v. Celtic Football & Athletic Co Ltd (No.2) 2001 S.L.T. 1387; 2001 S.C.L.R. 879; 2001 G.W.D. 6-233, OH . . . .   *Digested*, 01/**6427**

McDyre v. Ruxton (Sentencing) 1998 G.W.D. 13-661, HCJ Appeal
McEachern v. HM Advocate (Sentencing) 1998 G.W.D. 10-501, HCJ Appeal
McEleny (Patrick) v. Carnegie 1998 S.C.C.R. 15; 1998 G.W.D. 2-81, HCJ Appeal . . . . . .   *Digested*, 98/**5658**:
            Previous proceedings, 97/5909
McErlean v. J&B Scotland Ltd 1999 G.W.D. 18-848, Ex Div; affirming 1997 S.L.T.
    1326; 1997 Rep. L.R. 29; 1997 G.W.D. 6-253, OH . . . .   *Digested*, 97/**6075**
McEvoy v. Lees 1998 G.W.D. 23-1171, HCJ Appeal
McEwan v. Higson 2001 S.C.C.R. 579; 2001 G.W.D. 25-982, HCJ Appeal
McEwan v. Maguire 1999 G.W.D. 27-1290, HCJ Appeal
McEwan v. Miller 1999 G.W.D. 3-116, HCJ Appeal
McEwan v. Reith 1998 G.W.D. 37-1917, HCJ Appeal
McEwan v. Vannet 2000 G.W.D. 15-581, HCJ
McEwen v. McEwen 2001 S.L.T. (Sh Ct) 8; 2000 Fam. L.R. 116; 2000 G.W.D. 29-1111,
    Sh Pr . . . .   *Digested*, 00/**6266**
McFadyen v. Annan 1992 J.C. 53; 1992 S.L.T. 163; 1992 S.C.C.R. 186; *Times*, February
    11, 1992, HCJ Appeal . . . .   *Digested*, 92/**5466**:
       Applied, 92/5467, 94/5574, 95/5666, 97/5826, 00/6086:
       Considered, 95/5680, 00/6089: *Referred to*, 94/5610
McFadyen v. Clarke 1999 G.W.D. 19-890, Sh Ct
McFadyen v. Excel Scientech (Europe) Co Ltd 1999 G.W.D. 19-912, Sh Ct
McFadyen v. Gatley 2000 S.L.T. (Sh Ct) 41; 2000 S.C.C.R. 123; 1999 G.W.D. 39-1892,
    Sh Ct (Lothian) . . . .   *Digested*, 00/**6245**
McFadyen v. McGlennan (Sentencing) 1998 G.W.D. 9-452, HCJ Appeal
McFadyen v. Todd (Brian) 1999 S.C.C.R. 463, HCJ Appeal . . . .   *Digested*, 99/**5932**
McFadyen v. University of Edinburgh 1999 G.W.D. 7-344, Sh Ct (Lothian)
McFall v. West Dumbartonshire Council 1999 S.L.T. 775; 1998 S.C.L.R. 1009; 1998
    G.W.D. 29-1510, OH . . . .   *Digested*, 98/**5736**
MacFarlane v. Falfield Investments Ltd 1998 S.L.T. 145, 1 Div; affirming 1997 S.L.T. 518;
    1996 S.C.L.R. 826, OH . . . .   *Digested*, 97/**5583**
MacFarlane v. Falkirk Council 2000 S.L.T. (Sh Ct) 29; 1999 G.W.D. 37-1788, Sh Pr . . . .   *Digested*, 00/**5946**
MacFarlane v. Glasgow City Council [2001] I.R.L.R. 7, EAT . . . .   *Digested*, 01/**6468**
McFarlane v. HM Advocate 2001 G.W.D. 11-386, HCJ Appeal
McFarlane v. HM Advocate (Sentencing) 1999 G.W.D. 4-186, HCJ Appeal
McFarlane v. HM Advocate (Sentencing) 1998 G.W.D. 22-1134, HCJ Appeal
McFarlane v. Tayside Health Board; *sub nom* Macfarlane v. Tayside Health Board
    [2000] 2 A.C. 59; [1999] 3 W.L.R. 1301; [1999] 4 All E.R. 961; 2000 S.C. (H.L.)
    1; 2000 S.L.T. 154; 2000 S.C.L.R. 105; [2000] 1 F.C.R. 102; [2000] P.I.Q.R.
    Q101; [2000] Lloyd's Rep. Med. 1; (2000) 52 B.M.L.R. 1; (1999) 149 N.L.J.
    1868; 1999 G.W.D. 39-1888; *Times*, November 26, 1999 ; *Independent*,
    December 3, 1999, HL; reversing in part 1998 S.C. 389; 1998 S.L.T. 307; 1998
    S.C.L.R. 126; (1998) 44 B.M.L.R. 140; 1998 G.W.D. 4-180; *Times*, May 8, 1998, 2
    Div; reversing 1997 S.L.T. 211; 1996 Rep. L.R. 159; *Times*, November 11, 1996,
    OH . . . .   *Digested*, 00/**6162**:
       Applied, 01/4462, 01/6412: *Cited*, 00/2777: *Considered*, 00/4200, 01/4463:
       Distinguished, 01/1508, 01/4464: *Followed*, 01/1509: *Not followed*, 98/6115
McFarlane v. Vannet (Sentencing) 1999 G.W.D. 7-342, HCJ Appeal
McFarlane v. Vannet (Sentencing) 2000 G.W.D. 20-822, HCJ Appeal
Macfie's Executor v. Cunningham 2001 G.W.D. 7-251, OH
McGarry v. Dickson 1999 G.W.D. 17-816, HCJ Appeal
McGarry v. HM Advocate 1999 G.W.D. 33-1575, HCJ Appeal
McGeachy v. Henderson 1998 G.W.D. 31-1632, HCJ Appeal
McGeechan v. Higson 2000 G.W.D. 39-1445, HCJ Appeal
McGeechan v. McFadyen 1999 G.W.D. 26-1234, HCJ Appeal
McGettigan, Petitioner 1996 S.L.T. 76; 1995 S.C.C.R. 480, HCJ Appeal . . . .   *Digested*, 95/**5673**:
             Distinguished, 98/6051
McGhee v. McGhee 1998 G.W.D. 22-1105, Sh Ct
McGhee v. Spiers (Sentencing) 2000 G.W.D. 5-189, HCJ Appeal
McGhee v. Vannet (Sentencing) 1999 G.W.D. 36-1756, HCJ Appeal
Mcghie v. Dunedin Property Investment Co Ltd 1998 G.W.D. 39-2019, OH
McGibbon v. Sanchez 1998 G.W.D. 15-736, Sh Pr
McGibbon v. Vannet 1999 G.W.D. 21-989, HCJ Appeal
McGiffen v. Hamilton 1998 G.W.D. 26-1304, HCJ Appeal
McGilchrist v. McGilchrist 1998 S.L.T. (Sh Ct) 2; 1997 S.C.L.R. 800; 1997 G.W.D. 15-
    638, Sh Ct (North Strathclyde) . . . .   *Digested*, 97/**5614**
McGill (David Alexander) v. HM Advocate 2000 S.C.C.R. 253; 2000 G.W.D. 9-322,
    HCJ Appeal . . . .   *Digested*, 00/**6015**
McGill v. HM Advocate (Procedure) 2001 S.C.C.R. 28; 2000 G.W.D. 37-1389, HCJ
    Appeal . . . .   *Digested*, 01/**6308**
McGill v. HM Advocate (Sentencing) 1998 G.W.D. 30-1550, HCJ Appeal
MacGillivray v. Napier (Sentencing) 2001 G.W.D. 12-449, HCJ Appeal
McGinley v. HM Advocate 1998 G.W.D. 21-1059, HCJ Appeal
McGinley (Michael) v. HM Advocate 2001 S.L.T. 198; 2001 S.C.C.R. 47; 2000 G.W.D.
    39-1446, HCJ Appeal . . . .   *Digested*, 01/**6360**
McGinnes v. HM Advocate 1998 G.W.D. 18-897, HCJ Appeal

McGinnis (Dennis) *v.* HM Advocate see McAnea (Thomas) *v.* HM Advocate
McGinty *v.* HM Advocate 1985 S.L.T. 25; 1984 S.C.C.R. 176, HCJ Appeal. . . . .   *Digested,* 85/**3901**:
                                            Followed, 01/6344: *Referred to,* 89/4023
McGinty (John Thomas) *v.* HM Advocate (No.1) 2000 J.C. 277; 2000 S.C.C.R. 393;
    2000 G.W.D. 1-10, HCJ Appeal . . . .   *Digested,* 00/**6062**
McGinty (John Thomas) *v.* HM Advocate (No.2) (Sentencing) 2000 G.W.D. 14-538,
    HCJ Appeal
McGinty *v.* MacNeill 1999 G.W.D. 9-426, HCJ Appeal
McGivern *v.* HM Advocate 1999 G.W.D. 29-1383, HCJ Appeal
McGlashan *v.* Donnelly 1998 G.W.D. 35-1796, HCJ Appeal
McGlennan *v.* McKinnon (Sentencing) 1998 S.L.T. 494; 1998 S.C.C.R. 285; 1998
    G.W.D. 13-660, HCJ Appeal. . . . .   *Digested,* 98/**5662**
McGlone *v.* Friel 1998 G.W.D. 29-1490, HCJ Appeal
McGonagall *v.* HM Advocate 1998 G.W.D. 28-1411, HCJ Appeal
McGonigal *v.* Taylor 2001 S.C.L.R. 1070, Sh Pr
McGonnigle (Adam James) *v.* Vannet 1999 J.C. 129; 1999 S.C.C.R. 152; 1999 G.W.D. 6-
    305, HCJ Appeal . . . .   *Digested,* 99/**5936**
McGovern *v.* Lees (Sentencing) 1998 G.W.D. 13-664, HCJ Appeal
McGowan *v.* HM Advocate (Sentencing) 2000 G.W.D. 20-790, HCJ Appeal
McGowan *v.* Joint Receivers of Clyde Shaw Ltd see McGowan *v.* Readman
McGowan *v.* McLeod (Sentencing) 2000 G.W.D. 19-760, HCJ Appeal
McGowan *v.* Readman; *sub nom* McGowan *v.* Joint Receivers of Clyde Shaw Ltd
    2000 S.C.L.R. 898; 2000 G.W.D. 10-355, OH . . . .   *Digested,* 01/**6460**
McGowan *v.* Ritchie 1998 S.L.T. 324; 1997 S.C.C.R. 322; 1997 G.W.D. 15-657, HCJ
    Appeal. . . . .   *Digested,* 97/**5823**
McGrandles *v.* HM Advocate (Sentencing) 1998 G.W.D. 10-486, HCJ Appeal
McGrath *v.* McGrath 1999 S.L.T. (Sh Ct) 90; 1999 S.C.L.R. 1121; 1999 Fam. L.R. 83;
    1999 G.W.D. 20-915, Sh Pr . . . .   *Digested,* 99/**6065**
McGrath *v.* Ritchie 2001 G.W.D. 31-1248, HCJ Appeal
McGregor *v.* D (Francis) 1977 S.C. 330; 1977 S.L.T. 182, 1 Div . . . .   *Digested,* 77/**3239**:
                        Applied, 95/5516: *Considered,* 96/6612, 99/5610: *Followed,* 95/5524
McGregor *v.* Donnelly 1998 G.W.D. 25-1282, HCJ Appeal
MacGregor *v.* Donnelly (Sentencing) 1999 G.W.D. 40-1925, HCJ Appeal
McGregor *v.* Friel 1998 G.W.D. 23-1167, HCJ Appeal
McGregor *v.* Gilchrist 1999 G.W.D. 24-1137, HCJ Appeal
McGregor *v.* H 1983 S.L.T. 626, 1 Div . . . .   *Digested,* 83/**3981**:
                      Distinguished, 95/5517, 99/6070: *Followed,* 92/5277, 93/4784, 93/4785
MacGregor *v.* HM Advocate 1998 G.W.D. 28-1430, HCJ Appeal
McGregor *v.* HM Advocate (Sentencing) 2001 G.W.D. 16-629, HCJ Appeal
McGregor *v.* HM Advocate (Sentencing) 2001 G.W.D. 26-1042, HCJ Appeal
McGregor *v.* HM Advocate (Sentencing) 2001 G.W.D. 36-1368, HCJ Appeal
McGregor (John Joseph) *v.* HM Advocate see McAnea (Thomas) *v.* HM Advocate
McGregor *v.* Howdle 1998 G.W.D. 17-866, HCJ Appeal
McGregor *v.* Hutchison 1999 S.C.L.R. 506, Sh Pr . . . .   *Digested,* 99/**5719**
McGregor *v.* Intercity East Coast Ltd 1998 S.C. 440, 1 Div . . . .   *Digested,* 98/**5824**
McGregor *v.* Napier (Sentencing) 2000 G.W.D. 4-170, HCJ Appeal
MacGregor *v.* South Lanarkshire Council 2001 S.C. 502; 2001 S.L.T. 233; 2001 G.W.D.
    1-73, OH . . . .   *Digested,* 01/**6904**
McGregor *v.* Vannet 1999 G.W.D. 23-1092, HCJ Appeal
Mcgregor *v.* Webster's Executors 1976 S.L.T. 29, 1 Div . . . .   *Digested,* 75/**3736**:
                                                Disapproved, 98/5478
McGregor (Paul), Petitioner 1999 S.L.T. 676; 1999 S.C.C.R. 225; 1999 G.W.D. 10-468, HCJ
    Appeal. . . . .   *Digested,* 99/**5963**
McGregor Construction Ltd *v.* DIFSL Reorganisation Ltd 2000 G.W.D. 22-845, OH
McGroarty *v.* Lloyds Bowmaker Ltd 1999 G.W.D. 4-170, Sh Ct (Lothian)
McGrogan *v.* HM Advocate 1999 G.W.D. 9-422, HCJ Appeal
McGrory *v.* Clark 2001 G.W.D. 13-520, HCJ Appeal
McGuckian *v.* O'Donnell see McGuckin *v.* O'Donnell
McGuckin *v.* O'Donnell; *sub nom* McGuckian *v.* O'Donnell 2000 J.C. 629; 2001 S.L.T.
    768; 2000 G.W.D. 26-1010, HCJ Appeal
McGugan *v.* McGlennan 1999 G.W.D. 2-99, HCJ Appeal
McGuigan *v.* Lees 1998 G.W.D. 9-436, HCJ Appeal
McGuire (James) *v.* HM Advocate 2000 S.C.C.R. 896, HCJ Appeal. . . . .   *Digested,* 01/**6342**
McGuire *v.* Spiers (Sentencing) 2001 G.W.D. 29-1161, HCJ Appeal
McGuire *v.* Watt (Sentencing) 2000 G.W.D. 33-1283, HCJ Appeal
McGurk *v.* Donnelly 1999 G.W.D. 24-1139, HCJ Appeal
McHarg *v.* HM Advocate (Sentencing) 1998 G.W.D. 5-217, HCJ Appeal
McHarg Houston & Mcfarlane *v.* Newman (Unreported, August 1, 1983), Sh Pr . . . . . .   *Not followed,* 98/**5715**
McHenry *v.* McCaskey 1998 G.W.D. 31-1583, Sh Ct
McHugh *v.* Hamilton 1998 G.W.D. 34-1768, HCJ Appeal
McHugh *v.* McHugh 2001 Fam. L.R. 30; 2001 G.W.D. 1-56, OH . . . .   *Digested,* 01/**6520**
McIlraith *v.* Vannet (Sentencing) 1998 G.W.D. 3-121, HCJ Appeal
McIlroy *v.* HM Advocate (Sentencing) 2001 G.W.D. 20-769, HCJ Appeal
McIlroy *v.* Vannet 1998 G.W.D. 35-1792, HCJ Appeal

McIlvride v. HM Advocate (No.1) 1999 S.C.C.R. 429; 1999 G.W.D. 19-874, HCJ Appeal . . . .   *Digested*, 99/**5898**
McIlvride v. HM Advocate (No.2) 2001 G.W.D. 2-87, HCJ Appeal
McIlwaine v. Higson 2000 G.W.D. 31-1211, HCJ Appeal
McIlwham v. Secretary of State for Scotland 1989 S.L.T. 167, OH . . . .   *Digested*, 89/**4747**:
    Doubted, 98/5477

McInally v. HM Advocate 2000 G.W.D. 33-1267, HCJ Appeal
McInally v. HM Advocate (Sentencing) 1998 G.W.D. 29-1470, HCJ Appeal
McInnes v. HM Advocate (Sentencing) 1999 G.W.D. 37-1817, HCJ Appeal
McInnes v. Kirkforthar Brick Co Ltd 1998 S.L.T. 568; 1998 Rep. L.R. 57; 1998 G.W.D. 7-319, OH . . . .   *Digested*, 98/**5455**
McInnes v. Vannet (Sentencing) 1999 G.W.D. 13-611, HCJ Appeal
McInnes v. Vannet (Sentencing) 1998 G.W.D. 32-1664, HCJ Appeal
McIntosh v. Aberdeenshire Council 1999 S.L.T. 93; 1998 S.C.L.R. 435; 1998 G.W.D. 6-255, OH . . . .   *Digested*, 98/**5410**
McIntosh v. Alam 1998 S.L.T. (Sh Ct) 19; 1997 S.C.L.R. 1171; 1997 Hous. L.R. 141; 1997 G.W.D. 36-1829, Sh Ct (North Strathclyde) . . . .   *Digested*, 98/**5958**
MacIntosh v. Findlay 2000 S.C.L.R. 751, OH . . . .   *Digested*, 00/**5904**
McIntosh v. Findlay 2001 Rep. L.R. 66; [2001] 5 Q.R. 19, OH . . . .   *Digested*, 01/**6428**
Macintosh v. HM Advocate (Sentencing) 1999 G.W.D. 40-1938, HCJ Appeal
McIntosh v. HM Advocate (Sentencing) 1998 G.W.D. 21-1080, HCJ Appeal
Mcintosh (Andrew Neil) v. HM Advocate (No.1) 1997 S.L.T. 1315; 1997 S.C.C.R. 389, HCJ Appeal . . . .   *Digested*, 97/**5872**:
    Applied, 00/6062
McIntosh (Robert) v. HM Advocate see HM Advocate v. McIntosh (Robert) (No.1)
McIntosh v. Napier 1999 G.W.D. 23-1102, HCJ Appeal
McIntosh v. Scottish Borders Council 2001 G.W.D. 14-561, OH
McIntosh v. Stott see Mackintosh (Ross) v. Stott
McIntosh v. Vannet (Sentencing) 2000 G.W.D. 5-195, HCJ Appeal
McIntosh, Petitioner see HM Advocate v. McIntosh (Robert) (No.1)
McIntyre v. Clark; *sub nom* McIntyre v. Munro 1999 S.C.C.R. 239; 1999 G.W.D. 9-419, HCJ Appeal . . . .   *Digested*, 99/**5923**
McIntyre v. Clark (Sentencing) 1999 G.W.D. 23-1104, HCJ Appeal
McIntyre v. Council of the Law Society of Scotland 2001 G.W.D. 35-1350, Ex Div
MacIntyre v. Crofters Commission 2001 S.L.T. 929; 2001 G.W.D. 13-527, OH . . . .   *Digested*, 01/**6744**
McIntyre v. Hingston 1998 G.W.D. 17-878, HCJ Appeal
McIntyre v. HM Advocate 2001 G.W.D. 26-1026, HCJ Appeal
McIntyre v. HM Advocate (Sentencing) 1999 G.W.D. 37-1814, HCJ Appeal
McIntyre v. HM Advocate (Sentencing) 2000 G.W.D. 20-803, HCJ Appeal
McIntyre v. HM Advocate (Sentencing) 1998 G.W.D. 40-2083, HCJ Appeal
McIntyre (William Richard) v. HM Advocate; *sub nom* Townsley (Edward Newlands) v. HM Advocate 1999 J.C. 232; 1999 S.L.T. 374; 1998 S.C.C.R. 379; 1998 G.W.D. 18-892, HCJ Appeal . . . .   *Digested*, 98/**5610**
McIntyre v. Munro see McIntyre v. Clark
McIntyre v. Vannet 1999 G.W.D. 21-984, HCJ Appeal
McIsaac v. HM Advocate 1998 G.W.D. 22-1123, HCJ Appeal
MacIver v. J&A Gardner Ltd 2001 S.L.T. 585; 2000 G.W.D. 26-1005, OH . . . .   *Digested*, 01/**6666**
McKay v. Carnegie 2001 G.W.D. 36-1399, HCJ Appeal
McKay (t/a House of Hair Fashion) v. Cranna 1999 S.C.L.R. 170, Sh Ct. . . . .   *Digested*, 99/**6030**
McKay v. Dundee City Council 2000 S.L.T. (Sh Ct) 191, Sh Ct (Tayside)
McKay v. Dundee DC 1996 S.L.T. (Lands Tr) 9, Lands Tr (Scot) . . . .   *Digested*, 96/**7077**:
    Followed, 00/6466
McKay v. Friel 1998 G.W.D. 23-1186, HCJ Appeal
Mackay v. Gaylor 2001 G.W.D. 1-59, Sh Pr
McKay v. Glasgow City Council 1998 S.L.T. 579; 1998 S.C.L.R. 202; 1998 Rep. L.R. 23 (Note); 1998 G.W.D. 1-5, OH . . . .   *Digested*, 98/**5740**
Mackay (Elizabeth Lazenby) v. Heywood 1998 S.C.C.R. 210; 1998 G.W.D. 10-485, HCJ Appeal . . . .   *Digested*, 98/**5576**
Mackay v. HM Advocate (Evidence) 1998 G.W.D. 36-1851, HCJ Appeal
McKay (John McIntosh) v. HM Advocate see McLay (John McIntosh) v. HM Advocate
MacKay (Mark David Joseph) v. HM Advocate 1998 J.C. 47; 1998 S.L.T. 751; 1997 S.C.C.R. 743; 1997 G.W.D. 36-1838, HCJ Appeal . . . .   *Digested*, 98/**5642**
McKay (Ronald) v. HM Advocate (Sentencing) 2001 S.C.C.R. 341; 2001 G.W.D. 16-627, HCJ Appeal. . . . .   *Digested*, 01/**6401**
McKay (Uisdean) v. HM Advocate; *sub nom* Scottish Legal Aid Board, Applicants 1999 S.C. 670; 1999 S.C.C.R. 679, HCJ Appeal . . . .   *Digested*, 00/**6544**
Mackay v. Lothian Health Board 2001 S.L.T. 581; 2000 Rep. L.R. 82; 2000 G.W.D. 15-625, OH . . . .   *Digested*, 00/**6635**
McKay v. McFadyen 2001 G.W.D. 30-1215, HCJ Appeal
Mackay v. McGlennan (Sentencing) 1998 G.W.D. 11-541, HCJ Appeal
MacKay v. Napier 2001 G.W.D. 31-1264, HCJ Appeal

Mackay (Alexander Munro) *v.* Ruxton; Dingwall *v.* Ruxton 1998 J.C. 51; 1997 S.C.C.R.
  790; 1998 G.W.D. 1-11, HCJ Appeal . . . . *Digested*, 98/**5626**:
                                                                                 Applied, 98/5622
MacKay *v.* Scottish and Southern Energy Plc 2000 G.W.D. 12-444, Sh Ct
Mackay *v.* Scottish Hydro Electric Plc 2000 S.C. 87; 1999 G.W.D. 36-1769, 1 Div . . . . . *Digested*, 00/**6179**
MacKay *v.* Vannet (Sentencing) 1998 G.W.D. 1-55, HCJ Appeal
McKay *v.* Vannet (Sentencing) 2000 G.W.D. 3-92, HCJ Appeal
Mackay, Petitioner; *sub nom* Rosewell Nurses Endowment Fund 1955 S.C. 361; 1955
  S.L.T. 305, 1 Div. . . . . *Digested*, 55/**3767**:
                                                                             Distinguished, 99/6468
Mackay Decorators (Perth) Ltd *v.* Miller EAT/782/98, EAT. . . . . *Digested*, 99/**6034**
McKeand *v.* Dorian 2001 G.W.D. 37-1401, Ex Div; affirming 2000 G.W.D. 15-578, OH
McKechnie *v.* MacDiarmid 1919 S.L.C.R. App. 49, Land Ct (Div Ct) . . . . *Referred to*, 00/6532
McKee *v.* Brown 2001 S.C.C.R. 6; 2000 G.W.D. 34-1302, HCJ Appeal . . . . *Digested*, 01/**6384**
McKee *v.* MacDonald 1995 S.L.T. 1342; 1995 S.C.C.R. 513, HCJ Appeal. . . . . *Digested*, 95/**5781**:
                                                                             Distinguished, 99/5842
McKellar *v.* HM Advocate (Sentencing) 1999 G.W.D. 40-1948, HCJ Appeal
McKeller *v.* Aberdeen City Council 2001 S.C. 729; 2001 S.L.T. 662; 2001 G.W.D. 11-
  393, OH
McKellican *v.* Walker (Sentencing) 1998 G.W.D. 13-669, HCJ Appeal
McKelvie *v.* HM Advocate 1997 S.L.T. 758, HCJ Appeal. . . . . *Digested*, 97/**5790**:
                                                                               Overruled, 00/6036
McKendrick (Archibald Samuel) *v.* HM Advocate 1999 S.C.C.R. 33, HCJ Appeal . . . . . *Digested*, 99/**5948**
McKenna *v.* Chief Constable of Strathclyde see McKenna *v.* Sharp
McKenna *v.* Greater Glasgow Health Board 2000 Rep. L.R. 16 (Note); 1999 G.W.D.
  39-1901, OH . . . . *Digested*, 00/**6430**
McKenna *v.* HM Advocate (Sentencing) 1999 G.W.D. 40-1936, HCJ Appeal
McKenna *v.* HM Advocate (Sentencing) 1998 G.W.D. 27-1364, HCJ Appeal
McKenna (Michael) *v.* HM Advocate 2000 J.C. 291; 2000 S.L.T. 508; 2000 S.C.C.R.
  159; 2000 G.W.D. 2-41, HCJ Appeal . . . . *Digested*, 00/**5994**
McKenna *v.* Sharp; *sub nom* McKenna *v.* Chief Constable of Strathclyde 1998 S.C.
  297; 1998 S.L.T. 1161; 1998 Rep. L.R. 71; 1998 G.W.D. 13-670, OH . . . . *Digested*, 98/**5707**
MacKenzie *v.* Barr's Trustees; *sub nom* Crofters Sharing in Oldshoremore Common
  Grazings *v.* Barr's Trustees; Barr's Trustees *v.* Crofters Sharing in Oldshoremore
  Common Grazings 1993 S.C. 472; 1993 S.L.T. 1228; 1993 S.C.L.R. 658; 1993
  S.L.C.R. 56, IH (Ct of 5 judges); reversing in part 1991 S.L.C.R. 121, Land Ct (Full
  Ct) . . . . *Digested*, 93/**5893**:
                                                                             Distinguished, 01/6743
Mackenzie *v.* Employment Appeal Tribunal (Scotland) see MacKenzie, Petitioner
McKenzie *v.* Friel 1998 G.W.D. 13-676, HCJ Appeal
Mackenzie *v.* Hardy 1999 S.L.C.R. 63, Land Ct . . . . *Digested*, 99/**6318**
Mackenzie *v.* HD Fraser & Sons 2001 S.L.T. 116; 2001 Rep. L.R. 21; 2000 G.W.D. 37-
  1406, OH . . . . *Digested*, 01/**6426**
MacKenzie *v.* HM Advocate (Procedure) 1999 G.W.D. 31-1470, HCJ Appeal
MacKenzie *v.* HM Advocate (Sentencing) 1998 G.W.D. 4-165, HCJ Appeal
McKenzie *v.* HM Advocate 1986 S.L.T. 389; 1986 S.C.C.R. 94, HCJ . . . . *Digested*, 89/**3837**:
                                                              Applied, 95/5739: *Considered*, 96/6823, 98/5639
McKenzie *v.* HM Advocate (Misdirection) 1999 G.W.D. 6-297, HCJ Appeal
McKenzie *v.* HM Advocate (Sentencing) 1999 G.W.D. 32-1540, HCJ Appeal
McKenzie *v.* HM Advocate (Sentencing) 1999 G.W.D. 31-1475, HCJ Appeal
McKenzie *v.* Law Society of Scotland 2000 S.L.T. 836; 1999 G.W.D. 26-1254, Ex Div . . *Digested*, 00/**6551**
Mackenzie *v.* Redman (Sentencing) 1998 G.W.D. 15-748, HCJ Appeal
McKenzie *v.* Skeen 1983 S.L.T. 121, HCJ Appeal . . . . *Digested*, 83/**4132**:
                                                              Applied, 96/6814: *Approved*, 99/5832
McKenzie *v.* Sykes 2000 G.W.D. 16-638, Sh Ct
MacKenzie (Ian Gordon) *v.* Vannet 1999 J.C. 44; 1999 G.W.D. 1-16, HCJ Appeal . . . . . . *Digested*, 99/**5838**
McKenzie *v.* Watt (Sentencing) 2000 G.W.D. 30-1171, HCJ Appeal
Mackenzie's Trustee, Noter see Roy's Trustee, Noter
MacKenzie, Petitioner; *sub nom* Mackenzie *v.* Employment Appeal Tribunal (Scotland)
  2000 S.C. 1; 1999 S.C.L.R. 1085; 1999 G.W.D. 31-1492, OH . . . . *Digested*, 00/**6210**
McKeown *v.* Lord Advocate 2001 G.W.D. 3-137, OH
McKernon (Robert Graham) *v.* McGlennan 1999 S.C.C.R. 255; 1999 G.W.D. 11-493,
  HCJ Appeal . . . . *Digested*, 99/**5837**:
                                                                             Distinguished, 00/6010
McKerrol *v.* McGlennan 1999 G.W.D. 13-600, HCJ Appeal
McKerron *v.* Crowe 1998 G.W.D. 31-1590, HCJ Appeal
McKew *v.* Holland & Hannen & Cubitts (Scotland) Ltd [1969] 3 All E.R. 1621; 1970
  S.C. (H.L.) 20; 1970 S.L.T. 68; 8 K.I.R. 921, HL; affirming 1969 S.C. 14; 1969
  S.L.T. 101; 1968 S.L.T. (Notes) 99, 2 Div; affirming 1968 S.L.T. 12, OH . . . . *Digested*, 70/**612**:
                                                              Applied, 84/2342, 85/2322, 98/6114: *Considered*, 92/3216
McKie *v.* HM Advocate (Sentencing) 2001 G.W.D. 30-1201, HCJ Appeal
McKillop *v.* Aberdeen Harbour Board 2000 G.W.D. 32-1257, Sh Ct

McKim v. Carnegie (Sentencing); *sub nom* McKimm v. Carnegie (Sentencing) 2000
J.C. 453; 2000 S.L.T. 755; 2000 S.C.C.R. 466; 2000 G.W.D. 14-540, HCJ
Appeal . . . .   *Digested*, 00/**6150**
McKimm v. Carnegie (Sentencing) see McKim v. Carnegie (Sentencing)
McKinlay v. HM Advocate (Sentencing) 2001 G.W.D. 12-426, HCJ Appeal
McKinney v. Chief Constable of Strathclyde 2000 G.W.D. 24-919, 1 Div
McKinney v. Chief Constable of Strathclyde 1998 S.L.T. (Sh Ct) 80; 1998 Rep. L.R. 81;
1998 G.W.D. 18-936, Sh Pr . . . .   *Digested*, 98/**6154**
MacKinnon v. Argyll and Bute Council 2001 S.L.T. 1275; 2000 G.W.D. 11-371, OH . . . . .   *Digested*, 01/**6096**
McKinnon v. O'Donnell (Sentencing) 2001 G.W.D. 25-961, HCJ Appeal
Mackinnon, Noter see Hurst Fuels Ltd v. Dundonald House Ltd
MacKintosh v. Forbes 1999 S.L.C.R. 155, Land Ct (Full Ct) . . . .   *Digested*, 00/**6530**
Mackintosh (Ross) v. Stott; *sub nom* McIntosh v. Stott 1999 S.C.C.R. 291; 1999
G.W.D. 13-597, HCJ Appeal . . . .   *Digested*, 99/**5882**
McKirdy (Maxwell Neil) v. Ruxton 1999 S.L.T. 1206; 1999 S.C.C.R. 372; 1999 G.W.D.
13-620, HCJ Appeal . . . .   *Digested*, 99/**5834**
McKnight v. Clydeside Buses Ltd 1999 S.L.T. 1167; 1999 S.C.L.R. 272; 1999 Rep. L.R.
61; 1999 G.W.D. 4-213, OH . . . .   *Digested*, 99/**6373**
McLachlan v. Bowie 2000 G.W.D. 17-697, OH
McLachlan v. HM Advocate 1999 G.W.D. 14-641, HCJ Appeal
Maclachlan v. Maclachlan 1998 S.L.T. 693; 1997 G.W.D. 8-339, OH . . . .   *Digested*, 98/**5855**
McLachlan v. Vannet 1999 G.W.D. 20-939, HCJ Appeal
Maclaine v. Houston (Sentencing) 1998 G.W.D. 4-196, HCJ Appeal
McLanachan's Judicial Factor, Noter (No.1) 1998 G.W.D. 15-739, 2 Div; affirming 1998
G.W.D. 5-201, OH
McLanachan's Judicial Factor, Noter (No.2) 1999 G.W.D. 19-861, Ex Div; affirming 1999
G.W.D. 8-368, OH
McLaren v. Caldwell's Paper Mill Co Ltd 1973 S.L.T. 158, 2 Div . . . .   *Digested*, 73/**3682**:
                                                                                                        Considered, 98/5439
McLaren v. HM Advocate (Sentencing) 2001 G.W.D. 39-1469, HCJ Appeal
McLaren v. Munro (Sentencing) 1999 G.W.D. 10-469, HCJ Appeal
McLaughlan (Donna Jane) v. HM Advocate 1996 S.L.T. 304, HCJ Appeal . . . .   *Digested*, 96/**6820**:
                                                                                                        Distinguished, 99/5912
McLaughlin v. Allied Irish Bank 2001 S.C. 485; 2001 S.L.T. 403; 2001 G.W.D. 1-1, Ex
Div . . . .   *Digested*, 01/**6213**
McLaughlin v. East and Midlothian NHS Trust 2001 S.L.T. 387; 2000 S.C.L.R. 1108;
2000 Rep. L.R. 87; 2000 G.W.D. 17-696, OH . . . .   *Digested*, 00/**5935**
McLaughlin v. McLaughlin 2001 G.W.D. 5-181, Sh Ct (Tayside)
McLaughlin v. Shaw 2000 S.L.T. 794; 2000 G.W.D. 18-708, OH . . . .   *Digested*, 00/**5903**
McLay v. Bennett 1998 G.W.D. 16-810, Sh Ct
McLay v. HM Advocate (Sentencing) 2000 G.W.D. 8-283, HCJ Appeal
McLay (John McIntosh) v. HM Advocate; *sub nom* McLay (Jon McIntosh) v. HM
Advocate; McKay (John McIntosh) v. HM Advocate 2000 J.C. 536; 2000 S.L.T.
1076; 2000 S.C.C.R. 579; 2000 G.W.D. 16-646, HCJ Appeal . . . .   *Digested*, 00/**6061**
McLay (Jon McIntosh) v. HM Advocate see McLay (John McIntosh) v. HM Advocate
Maclay & Co Ltd v. Clark 1997 S.C. 293; 1998 S.L.T. 64; 1997 G.W.D. 23-1175, 1 Div . . .   *Digested*, 98/**5822**
McLean v. Buchanan; *sub nom* Buchanan v. McLean [2001] UKPC D3; [2001] 1
W.L.R. 2425; 2001 S.L.T. 780; 2001 S.C.C.R. 475; [2001] H.R.L.R. 51; [2001]
U.K.H.R.R. 793; (2001) 98(28) L.S.G. 44; (2001) 145 S.J.L.B. 158; 2001 G.W.D.
19-720; *Times*, June 4, 2001, PC (Sc); affirming 2000 J.C. 603; 2000 S.L.T.
928; 2000 S.C.C.R. 682; [2000] U.K.H.R.R. 598; 2000 G.W.D. 22-850; *Times*,
August 11, 2000, HCJ Appeal . . . .   *Digested*, 01/**6760**
MacLean v. Caledonian MacBrayne Ltd 1999 G.W.D. 35-1713, Ex Div; affirming 2000
S.C. 74; 2000 S.C.L.R. 625; 1999 G.W.D. 5-269, OH . . . .   *Digested*, 00/**6578**
MacLean v. DG MacSween Trust see MacLean v. MacSween's Trust
McLean v. Dorman see McLean v. Dornan
McLean v. Dornan; *sub nom* McLean v. Dorman 2001 S.L.T. (Sh Ct) 97; 2001 Fam.
L.R. 58; 2001 G.W.D. 13-460, Sh Pr; reversing 2001 G.W.D. 4-145, Sh Ct (South
Strathclyde) . . . .   *Digested*, 01/**6514**
Maclean v. Glasgow City Council 1999 S.L.T. 11; 1997 S.C.L.R. 1049, OH . . . .   *Digested*, 98/**5516**
McLean v. Henderson 1998 G.W.D. 31-1628, HCJ Appeal
MacLean v. Higson 1998 G.W.D. 30-1552, HCJ Appeal
McLean v. Higson (Sentencing) 2000 G.W.D. 34-1324, HCJ Appeal
McLean (Fraser) v. Higson 2000 S.C.C.R. 764, HCJ Appeal . . . .   *Digested*, 01/**6326**
MacLean v. Hingston (Sentencing) 1998 G.W.D. 14-715, HCJ Appeal
McLean v. HM Advocate 2001 G.W.D. 32-1273, HCJ Appeal
McLean v. HM Advocate (Devolution Issue) 2000 J.C. 140; 2000 S.C.C.R. 112;
[2000] U.K.H.R.R. 73; 1999 G.W.D. 36-1738, HCJ Appeal . . . .   *Digested*, 00/**6079**
McLean v. HM Advocate (Sentencing) 2000 S.L.T. 299; 1999 G.W.D. 36-1732, HCJ
Appeal
McLean v. HM Advocate (Sentencing) 1999 G.W.D. 17-779, HCJ Appeal
McLean v. HM Advocate (Sentencing) 1999 G.W.D. 22-1056, HCJ Appeal
McLean v. HM Advocate (Sentencing) 1999 G.W.D. 37-1831, HCJ Appeal
McLean v. HM Advocate (Sentencing) 1998 G.W.D. 15-757, HCJ Appeal

McLean v. HM Advocate (Sentencing) 1998 G.W.D. 32-1640, HCJ Appeal
McLean v. HM Advocate (Sentencing) 2000 G.W.D. 29-1142, HCJ Appeal
McLean v. HM Advocate (Sentencing) 2001 G.W.D. 36-1378, HCJ Appeal
McLean (Ronald) v. HM Advocate 2001 S.L.T. 1096; 2001 S.C.C.R. 526; 2001 G.W.D.
    19-724, HCJ Appeal . . . . *Digested,* 01/**6355**
MacLean v. Lothian and Borders Fire Brigade 1999 S.L.T. 702; 1998 S.C.L.R. 1004;
    1999 Rep. L.R. 45; 1998 G.W.D. 29-1499, OH . . . . *Digested,* 98/**5749**
Maclean v. McDonald (Sentencing) 1999 G.W.D. 4-198, HCJ Appeal
MacLean v. MacLean 2001 Fam. L.R. 118, OH
MacLean v. MacLeod 1998 G.W.D. 20-1052, HCJ Appeal
McLean v. MacLeod (Sentencing) 1998 G.W.D. 12-619, HCJ Appeal
MacLean v. MacSween's Trust; *sub nom* MacLean v. DG MacSween Trust 2001 S.L.T.
    (Land Ct) 39; 2001 S.L.C.R. 36; 2001 G.W.D. 31-1268, Land Ct
Mclean v. Marwhirn Developments Ltd 1976 S.L.T. (Notes) 47, 1 Div. . . . . *Digested,* 76/**3333**:
    Approved, 99/6240

McLean v. Scottish Power Plc 2000 G.W.D. 4-157, OH
McLean v. Walkingshaw 1998 G.W.D. 25-1242, HCJ Appeal
MacLean v. Wheelan 1999 G.W.D. 19-887, HCJ Appeal
McLean's Administrators, Noters 1999 G.W.D. 19-891, OH
MacLeay v. HM Advocate 2000 G.W.D. 8-278, HCJ Appeal
Macleay v. HM Advocate (Sentencing) 2000 G.W.D. 29-1148, HCJ Appeal
McLeish v. McFadyen 2001 G.W.D. 23-856, HCJ Appeal
McLellan v. HM Advocate (Sentencing) 1999 G.W.D. 14-633, HCJ Appeal
McLellan v. HM Advocate (Sentencing) 1998 G.W.D. 25-1254, HCJ Appeal
McLellan v. HM Advocate (Sentencing) 1998 G.W.D. 18-920, HCJ Appeal
MacLellan v. Lees (Sentencing) 1998 G.W.D. 9-440, HCJ Appeal
McLelland v. Greater Glasgow Health Board 2001 S.L.T. 446; 2001 G.W.D. 10-357, Ex
    Div; affirming in part 1999 S.C. 305; 1999 S.L.T. 543; 1998 S.C.L.R. 1081; 1999
    Rep. L.R. 1; 1998 G.W.D. 34-1754; *Times,* October 14, 1998, OH . . . . *Digested,* 01/**6412**
McLennan v. HM Advocate (Sentencing) 1999 G.W.D. 40-1920, HCJ Appeal
McLeod (Alistair), Petitioner see McLeod (Alistair) v. HM Advocate (No.2)
McLeod v. Aberdeen City Council 1999 G.W.D. 23-1115, OH
MacLeod v. Alexander 2000 Hous. L.R. 136, Sh Ct (North Strathclyde) . . . . *Digested,* 01/**6754**
McLeod v. Boyce (Sentencing) 2000 G.W.D. 39-1455, Sh Ct (Tayside)
McLeod v. British Railways Board 2001 S.C. 534; 2001 S.L.T. 238; 2001 S.C.L.R. 110;
    2001 Rep. L.R. 54; 2001 G.W.D. 1-12, 1 Div; affirming 2000 Rep. L.R. 58, OH . . . *Digested,* 01/**6250**
McLeod v. Heywood (Sentencing) 2000 G.W.D. 29-1164, HCJ Appeal
MacLeod (Guenther Robert) v. Hingston 1999 S.C.C.R. 717, HCJ Appeal. . . . . *Digested,* 00/**6102**
Macleod v. HM Advocate (Sentencing) 1998 G.W.D. 11-535, HCJ Appeal
McLeod v. HM Advocate 1998 G.W.D. 37-1913, HCJ Appeal
McLeod v. HM Advocate (Sentencing) 1999 G.W.D. 37-1810, HCJ Appeal
McLeod v. HM Advocate (Sentencing) 1998 G.W.D. 14-716, HCJ Appeal
McLeod v. HM Advocate (Sentencing) 2001 G.W.D. 6-215, HCJ Appeal
McLeod v. HM Advocate (Sentencing) 2001 G.W.D. 21-805, HCJ Appeal
McLeod (Alistair) v. HM Advocate (No.1) 1997 J.C. 212; 1998 S.L.T. 60; 1997 S.C.C.R.
    423; 1997 G.W.D. 20-941, HCJ Appeal. . . . . *Digested,* 97/**5827**
McLeod (Alistair) v. HM Advocate (No.2); *sub nom* McLeod (Alistair), Petitioner 1998
    J.C. 67; 1998 S.L.T. 233; 1998 S.C.C.R. 77; 1998 G.W.D. 4-161, HCJ Appeal. . . . *Digested,* 98/**5607**:
    Applied, 01/6347: *Considered,* 01/6314
Macleod v. Lothian Health Board 1999 S.L.T. 163; 1997 G.W.D. 36-1874, OH . . . . *Digested,* 99/**5623**
McLeod v. MacDougall 1989 S.L.T. 151; 1988 S.C.C.R. 519, HCJ Appeal . . . . *Digested,* 89/**4911**:
    Distinguished, 99/5939: *Referred to,* 93/5761
McLeod v. Miller (Sentencing) 1998 G.W.D. 12-594, HCJ Appeal
MacLeod v. New Hampshire Insurance Co Ltd 1998 S.L.T. 1191; 1997 G.W.D. 29-1487,
    OH . . . . *Digested,* 98/**6017**
McLeod v. Ruxton (Sentencing) 1998 G.W.D. 32-1662, HCJ Appeal
MacLeod v. Spiers 1999 G.W.D. 21-980, HCJ Appeal
McLeod v. Tiffney 1994 J.C. 77; 1994 S.L.T. 531; 1994 S.C.C.R. 169, HCJ Appeal . . . . . *Digested,* 94/**5613**:
    Applied, 95/5702: *Distinguished,* 95/5700, 96/6790, 98/5623
McLeod v. Vannet 1999 G.W.D. 2-108, HCJ Appeal
McLernan v. Ash 2001 G.W.D. 10-374, OH
McLintock v. Wheelan (Sentencing) 2000 G.W.D. 8-304, HCJ Appeal
McLoughlin v. O'Brian [1983] 1 A.C. 410; [1982] 2 W.L.R. 982; [1982] 2 All E.R. 298;
    [1982] R.T.R. 209; (1982) 79 L.S.G. 922; 126 S.J. 347, HL; reversing [1981]
    Q.B. 599; [1981] 2 W.L.R. 1014; [1981] 1 All E.R. 809; 125 S.J. 169, CA. . . . . . . *Digested,* 82/**2153**:
    Applied, 84/2330, 87/2857, 91/2670, 91/2671, 92/3250, 92/3251, 95/6157:
    Considered, 83/2609, 84/2342, 85/2322, 85/2326, 86/1069, 87/2580,
    87/2608, 88/6, 90/1571, 90/3727, 91/2512, 00/4213, 00/4220:
    Distinguished, 98/5723
McMahon v. HM Advocate 1998 G.W.D. 28-1427, HCJ Appeal
McMahon v. Lees 1993 S.L.T. 593, HCJ Appeal . . . . *Digested,* 93/**5100**:
    Distinguished, 99/5926
McMail v. HM Advocate 1998 G.W.D. 25-1253, HCJ Appeal
McMains v. HM Advocate 1999 G.W.D. 32-1538, HCJ Appeal

McManus v. O'Donnell (Sentencing) 2000 G.W.D. 37-1398, HCJ Appeal
McManus Executrix v. Babcock Energy Ltd 1999 S.C. 569; 2000 S.L.T. 655; 2000
    S.C.L.R. 426; 1999 G.W.D. 21-1013, OH . . . . *Digested,* 99/**5985**
McMaster (Ross Charles) v. HM Advocate 2001 S.C.C.R. 517, HCJ Appeal
McMenemy v. HM Advocate 1998 G.W.D. 25-1248, HCJ Appeal
McMichael v. United Kingdom (A/308) [1995] 2 F.C.R. 718; (1995) 20 E.H.R.R. 205;
    [1995] Fam. Law 478; *Times,* March 2, 1995, ECHR . . . . *Applied,* 97/2803,
                                          99/6065: *Distinguished,* 99/6064
McMillan v. Higson (Sentencing) 2001 G.W.D. 16-605, HCJ Appeal
McMillan v. HM Advocate 1999 G.W.D. 29-1378, HCJ Appeal
McMillan v. Houston 2001 G.W.D. 22-828, HCJ Appeal
McMillan v. Russell (Sentencing) 2001 G.W.D. 1-37, HCJ Appeal
McMillan v. Spiers 1999 G.W.D. 17-782, HCJ Appeal
McMillan v. Vannet 1998 G.W.D. 30-1556, HCJ Appeal
McMorrow v. Vannet 1998 S.L.T. 1171; 1998 G.W.D. 18-952, HCJ Appeal. . . . . *Digested,* 98/**5591**
McMullan v. Glasgow City Council 1998 G.W.D. 17-874, OH
McMullan v. Lees (Sentencing) 1998 G.W.D. 16-823, HCJ Appeal
McMullen v. Mackenzie 1999 S.L.T. 203; 1998 S.L.T. 1445; 1998 S.C.L.R. 587; 1998
    Rep. L.R. 67; 1998 G.W.D. 9-469, OH . . . . *Digested,* 98/**5754**
McMurray v. Safeway Stores Plc 2000 S.L.T. 1033; 2000 G.W.D. 25-928, OH . . . . *Digested,* 00/**5931**
McNab (Caroline) v. HM Advocate 2000 J.C. 80; 2000 S.L.T. 99; 1999 S.C.C.R. 930;
    1999 G.W.D. 32-1520, HCJ Appeal . . . . *Digested,* 00/**6067**
McNab v. Vannet (Sentencing) 1998 G.W.D. 1-29, HCJ Appeal
McNally v. Higson (Sentencing) 2000 G.W.D. 39-1468, HCJ Appeal
McNaughton v. Friel 1999 G.W.D. 21-986, HCJ Appeal
MacNaughton v. MacNaughton (Expenses: Taxation) 1949 S.C. 42; 1949 S.L.T. 10;
    1948 S.L.T. (Notes) 85, 1 Div . . . . *Digested,* 49/**4629**:
                                           Followed, 99/5689
Macnaughton v. Macnaughton's Trustees 1953 S.C. 387; 1953 S.L.T. 240, 2 Div . . . . . . *Digested,* 53/**4489**:
                                         Considered, 98/5880
McNaughton v. Michelin Tyre Plc 2001 S.L.T. (Sh Ct) 67; 2001 G.W.D. 4-173, Sh Ct
    (Tayside)
McNaughton v. Miller 1999 G.W.D. 8-374, HCJ Appeal
McNee v. Ruxton (Cross Examination) 1997 J.C. 160; 1998 S.L.T. 140; 1997 S.C.C.R.
    291; 1997 G.W.D. 13-545, HCJ Appeal . . . . *Digested,* 97/**5752**
McNee v. Ruxton (Police Powers) 1999 G.W.D. 28-1354, HCJ Appeal
McNeil v. McGlennan 1999 G.W.D. 27-1284, HCJ Appeal
McNeilage (Alan Scott), Petitioner; *sub nom* McNeilage v. HM Advocate 1999 S.C.C.R.
    471; 1999 G.W.D. 18-821, HCJ Appeal . . . . *Digested,* 99/**5828**
McNeilage v. HM Advocate see McNeilage (Alan Scott), Petitioner
McNeill v. HM Advocate 1998 G.W.D. 20-1012, HCJ Appeal
McNeill v. McArthur see McArthur v. McArthur's Trustee
MacNeill v. Sutherland 1998 S.C.C.R. 474; [1999] E.H.L.R. 44; 1998 G.W.D. 27-1383,
    HCJ Appeal; reversing [1998] E.H.L.R. Dig. 279, Sh Ct . . . . *Digested,* 98/**5878**
McNeillie v. HM Advocate 1999 G.W.D. 25-1201, HCJ Appeal
MacNeish v. Lees (Sentencing) 1998 G.W.D. 2-99, HCJ Appeal
McNelis v. HM Advocate (Sentencing) 2001 G.W.D. 39-1457, HCJ Appeal
McNicol v. Strathclyde Buses Ltd 1999 G.W.D. 20-963, OH
McNicoll v. Walter Davidson & Sons Ltd 2000 S.L.T. (Sh Ct) 16; 1999 G.W.D. 38-
    1867, Sh Ct (Tayside) . . . . *Digested,* 00/**6633**
McNiven v. Munro (Sentencing) 1999 G.W.D. 7-361, HCJ Appeal
McNulty v. Crowe 1998 G.W.D. 19-969, HCJ Appeal
McNulty v. Gilchrist 1999 G.W.D. 19-905, HCJ Appeal
McNulty v. Marshalls Food Group Ltd 1999 S.C. 195; 1999 Rep. L.R. 17 (Note); 1998
    G.W.D. 36-1875; *Times,* January 7, 1999, OH. . . . . *Digested,* 99/**5972**
McPake v. Lees (Sentencing) 1998 S.C.C.R. 184; 1998 G.W.D. 9-473, HCJ Appeal. . . . *Digested,* 98/**5687**
McPhail v. HM Advocate 1999 G.W.D. 30-1424, HCJ Appeal
MacPhee v. Angiolini (Sentencing) 2001 G.W.D. 6-213, HCJ Appeal
McPhee v. Heatherwick 1977 S.L.T. (Sh. Ct.) 46, Sh Ct (Glasgow) . . . . *Digested,* 77/**3752**:
                                Followed, 98/5715: *Not followed,* 93/5849
McPhee v. HM Advocate (Sentencing) 2001 G.W.D. 30-1194, HCJ Appeal
McPhee (William McAllister) v. HM Advocate 2001 S.C.C.R. 674; 2001 G.W.D. 21-789,
    HCJ Appeal
McPhee v. McDonald (Sentencing) 1998 G.W.D. 4-164, HCJ Appeal
McPhee v. Maguire 2001 S.L.T. 1217; 2001 S.C.C.R. 715; 2001 G.W.D. 24-912, HCJ
    Appeal . . . . *Digested,* 01/**6331**
McPhee v. North Lanarkshire Council 1998 S.L.T. 1317; 1998 G.W.D. 25-1238, OH . . . . *Digested,* 98/**5411**
MacPherson v. Gilchrist (Sentencing) 2000 J.C. 463; 2000 S.C.C.R. 477; 2000
    G.W.D. 16-659, HCJ Appeal . . . . *Digested,* 00/**6157**
McPherson v. HM Advocate (Sentencing) 1998 G.W.D. 3-124, HCJ Appeal
McPherson (Adrian Stewart) v. HM Advocate 1999 S.L.T. 1374; 1999 G.W.D. 19-900,
    HCJ Appeal . . . . *Digested,* 00/**6151**
McPherson v. Mutch 2001 G.W.D. 40-1498, Sh Ct (Grampian)
McPherson v. Perth and Kinross Council 2001 G.W.D. 4-171, OH

McPherson *v.* Rathgael Centre for Children and Young People [1990] N.I. 370; [1991] I.R.L.R. 206, CA (NI) . . . . *Digested,* 94/**5096**:
Overruled, 98/5807
MacPherson *v.* Secretary of State for Scotland 1985 S.L.T. 134; [1985] J.P.L. 788, 1 Div . . . . *Digested,* 85/**4892**:
Considered, 00/4455
McPike *v.* Lees (Sentencing) 1998 G.W.D. 6-283, HCJ Appeal
McPike *v.* Watt (Sentencing) 2001 G.W.D. 16-634, HCJ Appeal
McQuade *v.* Vannet (Plea in Bar of Trial) 2000 S.C.C.R. 18; 1999 G.W.D. 34-1623, HCJ Appeal . . . . *Digested,* 00/**6086**
McQuade *v.* Vannet (Shoplifting) (Sentencing) 2000 G.W.D. 13-486, HCJ Appeal
McQuarrie *v.* Durant 1999 Hous. L.R. 114, Sh Pr; reversing 1998 Hous. L.R. 105, Sh Ct . *Digested,* 00/**5933**
McQuat *v.* HM Advocate 1999 G.W.D. 21-990, HCJ Appeal
McQueen *v.* Glasgow Garden Festival (1988) Ltd 1995 S.L.T. 211, OH . . . . *Digested,* 95/**6162**:
Distinguished, 00/6599
MacQueen (James Findlay) *v.* Hingston 1998 S.L.T. 573; 1997 S.C.C.R. 561; 1997 G.W.D. 27-1357, HCJ Appeal . . . . *Digested,* 97/**6108**
McQueen *v.* HM Advocate 1999 G.W.D. 31-1477, HCJ Appeal
McQuilken *v.* Procurator Fiscal see Burn, Petitioner
McQuillan *v.* HM Advocate 1998 G.W.D. 20-1019, HCJ Appeal
MacRae *v.* HM Advocate (Sentencing) 1999 G.W.D. 36-1744, HCJ Appeal
McRae *v.* HM Advocate 1998 G.W.D. 40-2053, HCJ Appeal
McRae *v.* Lees 1999 G.W.D. 14-671, HCJ Appeal
Macrae *v.* Redman (Sentencing) 1998 G.W.D. 15-750, HCJ Appeal
McSeveney *v.* HM Advocate 1999 G.W.D. 30-1421, HCJ Appeal
McShane *v.* McFadyen 2001 G.W.D. 21-792, HCJ Appeal
McShannon *v.* Crowe 1998 G.W.D. 20-1015, HCJ Appeal
McSheehy *v.* MacMillan 1993 S.L.T. (Sh Ct) 10; 1992 S.C.L.R. 603, Sh Ct (Glasgow) . . *Digested,* 93/**5849**:
Not followed, 98/5715
McSherry *v.* Friel (Sentencing) 1998 G.W.D. 8-384, HCJ Appeal
McTaggart *v.* Brown (Sentencing) 2000 G.W.D. 20-809, HCJ Appeal
McTaggart *v.* McGlennan 2001 G.W.D. 30-1219, HCJ Appeal
Mactaggart & Mickel Ltd *v.* Harvey see Harvey *v.* Mactaggart & Mickel Ltd (No.1)
McTavish *v.* HM Advocate 1999 G.W.D. 19-913, HCJ Appeal
McTear *v.* Imperial Tobacco Ltd 2001 G.W.D. 34-1322, OH
McTighe *v.* East and Midlothian NHS Trust 1998 S.L.T. 969; 1998 S.C.L.R. 203; 1998 Rep. L.R. 21; 1997 G.W.D. 40-2102, OH . . . . *Digested,* 98/**5741**
McVey *v.* Friel 1996 S.C.C.R. 768, HCJ Appeal . . . . *Digested,* 97/**5789**:
Distinguished, 98/5587
McVey *v.* HM Advocate (Sentencing) 1999 G.W.D. 40-1928, HCJ Appeal
McWilliams *v.* Gallacher 1999 G.W.D. 21-979, HCJ Appeal
McWilliams *v.* HM Advocate (Sentencing) 2001 G.W.D. 31-1246, HCJ Appeal
Macari *v.* Celtic Football & Athletic Co Ltd 1999 S.C. 628; 2000 S.L.T. 80; 2000 S.C.L.R. 209; [1999] I.R.L.R. 787; 1999 G.W.D. 25-1208, 1 Div; affirming 1999 S.L.T. 138; 1998 G.W.D. 10-506, OH . . . . *Digested,* 00/**6221**
Macey-Lillie *v.* Lanarkshire Health Board 2001 S.L.T. 215; 2000 Rep. L.R. 109; 2000 G.W.D. 19-761; *Times,* June 28, 2000, OH . . . . *Digested,* 00/**6161**
Mack *v.* HM Advocate (Evidence) 1999 G.W.D. 15-695, HCJ Appeal
Mack *v.* HM Advocate (Sentencing) 1999 G.W.D. 15-705, HCJ Appeal
Mack (James Alexander) *v.* HM Advocate 1999 S.L.T. 1163; 1999 S.C.C.R. 181; 1999 G.W.D. 11-499, HCJ Appeal . . . . *Digested,* 99/**5906**
Mackie *v.* Dundee City Council 2001 Rep. L.R. 62; 2001 G.W.D. 11-398, Sh Ct (Grampian) . . . . *Digested,* 01/**6664**
Mackie *v.* East Ayrshire Council 2000 G.W.D. 33-1262, OH
Mackie *v.* Grampian RC 1999 Fam. L.R. 119, Sh Ct . . . . *Digested,* 00/**6193**
Mackie *v.* Higson (Sentencing) 2000 G.W.D. 30-1181, HCJ Appeal
Mackie *v.* HM Advocate 2001 G.W.D. 26-1009, HCJ Appeal
Mackie *v.* HM Advocate (Sentencing) 1999 G.W.D. 21-1003, HCJ Appeal
Mackie *v.* HM Advocate (Sentencing) 2000 G.W.D. 29-1145, HCJ Appeal
Mackie (Thorold) *v.* HM Advocate 1994 J.C. 132; 1995 S.L.T. 110; 1994 S.C.C.R. 277; *Times,* March 30, 1994, HCJ Appeal. . . . . *Digested,* 94/**5521**:
Disapproved, 98/5564
Mackin *v.* Mackin 1991 S.L.T. (Sh. Ct.) 22; 1990 S.C.L.R. 728, Sh Pr . . . . *Digested,* 91/**4932**:
Distinguished, 00/6276
Mackland *v.* Yarrow Shipbuilders Ltd 1998 S.L.T. 955; 1998 S.C.L.R. 589; 1998 Rep. L.R. 92; 1998 G.W.D. 16-804, OH. . . . . *Digested,* 98/**5734**
Maher *v.* HM Advocate 1999 G.W.D. 31-1471, HCJ Appeal
Maher *v.* HM Advocate (Sentencing) 2001 G.W.D. 13-521, HCJ Appeal
Mahmood *v.* West Dunbartonshire Licensing Board 1998 S.C.L.R. 843, Ex Div . . . . *Digested,* 98/**6071**:
Followed, 00/6562
Mahmood *v.* West Lothian Licensing Board 1998 S.C. 162; 1998 S.L.T. 304; 1998 S.C.L.R. 413; 1998 G.W.D. 1-50, 2 Div . . . . *Digested,* 98/**6073**
Maich *v.* HM Advocate (Sentencing) 1998 G.W.D. 5-250, HCJ Appeal
Maillie *v.* Swanney 2000 S.L.T. 464; 2000 G.W.D. 6-233, OH. . . . . *Digested,* 00/**6604**

Main v. Carnegie 1998 G.W.D. 38-1968, HCJ Appeal
Main (Derek) v. HM Advocate 1999 S.L.T. 881; 1998 S.C.C.R. 694; 1998 G.W.D. 38-
     1959, HCJ Appeal . . . .   *Digested,* 99/**5855**
Main v. Russell 1999 G.W.D. 13-592, HCJ Appeal
Mair (Bryan), Petitioner 2001 G.W.D. 14-543, Sh Ct (South Strathclyde)
Mair v. McKay 1998 G.W.D. 37-1902, HCJ Appeal
Mair v. Wood 1948 S.C. 83; 1948 S.L.T. 326; 1948 S.L.T. (Notes) 4, 1 Div . . . .   *Digested,* 48/**4623**:
                                                                   Followed, 84/4379, 00/5952
Malcolm v. Park Lane Motors Ltd (No.2) 1998 S.L.T. 1252; 1998 S.C.L.R. 152; 1997
     G.W.D. 34-1705, OH . . . .   *Digested,* 98/**5506**
Malcolm v. Ritchie 1999 G.W.D. 26-1233, HCJ Appeal
Maley v. Daylay Foods Ltd 1998 S.C. 324; 1998 G.W.D. 3-106, 2 Div; affirming 1997
     S.L.T. 1267; 1997 G.W.D. 3-114, OH . . . .   *Digested,* 98/**5494**
Mallinson v. Ethicon Ltd 2000 S.C.L.R. 150; 1999 G.W.D. 15-710, Sh Pr . . . .   *Digested,* 00/**5922**
Mallison (Thomas) v. HM Advocate 1987 S.C.C.R. 320, HCJ Appeal . . . .   *Digested,* 87/**4149**:
                                                                     Considered, 98/5599
Mallows v. HM Advocate (Sentencing) 2001 G.W.D. 39-1464, HCJ Appeal
Malone v. HM Advocate 1998 G.W.D. 31-1613, HCJ Appeal
Malpas v. Fife Council 1999 S.L.T. 499; 1999 S.C.L.R. 550; 1999 G.W.D. 6-308, OH . . .   *Digested,* 99/**5688**
Malvern Fishing Co Ltd v. Ailsa Craig Fishing Co Ltd (The Strathallan) see Ailsa Craig
     Fishing Co Ltd v. Malvern Fishing Co Ltd (The Strathallan)
Manchester & County Bank Ltd v. Moore (1908) 16 S.L.T. 595, 2 Div . . . .   *Distinguished,*
                                                                             98/5497
Mandla (Sewa Singh) v. Dowell Lee [1983] 2 A.C. 548; [1983] 2 W.L.R. 620; [1983]
     1 All E.R. 1062; [1983] I.C.R. 385; [1983] I.R.L.R. 209; (1983) 127 S.J. 242,
     HL; reversing [1983] Q.B. 1; [1982] 3 W.L.R. 932; [1982] 3 All E.R. 1108; [1983]
     I.R.L.R. 17; 126 S.J. 726, CA . . . .   *Digested,* 83/**1163**:
               Applied, 86/1212, 87/1353, 88/275, 89/267, 98/5811, 01/1065:
                         Considered, 84/1669, 85/3550, 91/1656, 92/1958
Maneely v. Stott 1999 G.W.D. 9-441, HCJ Appeal
Mann v. Clark (Sentencing) 2001 G.W.D. 12-425, HCJ Appeal
Mann v. Higson (Sentencing) 2000 G.W.D. 3-93, HCJ Appeal
Mann v. Sinclair (1879) 6 R. 1078, 1 Div . . . .   *Followed,* 00/**6508**
Mannering v. Vannet 1999 G.W.D. 14-673, HCJ Appeal
Manson v. HM Advocate 1998 G.W.D. 24-1209, HCJ Appeal
Manson v. McFadyen 2000 G.W.D. 14-564, HCJ Appeal
Manson v. Skinner TNS, 2 Div; reversing 2000 S.L.T. (Sh Ct) 161; 2000 Rep. L.R. 28;
     2000 G.W.D. 4-149, Sh Pr; reversing in part 1999 G.W.D. 25-1209, Sh Ct
     (Lothian) . . . .   *Digested,* 00/**5919**
Marckx v. Belgium (A/31) (1979-80) 2 E.H.R.R. 330, ECHR . . . .   *Applied,* 00/**6142**
Marco's Leisure v. West Lothian District Licensing Board 1994 S.L.T. 129, OH . . . .   *Digested,* 93/**4695**:
                                                                   Distinguished, 98/5880
Marelic v. Marelic 2000 G.W.D. 16-636, Sh Ct
Maresq (t/a La Belle Angele) v. Edinburgh Licensing Board 2001 S.C. 126; 2001 S.L.T.
     801; 2001 S.C.L.R. 199; [2000] 17 S.L.L.P. 10; 2000 G.W.D. 31-1239, OH . . . . .   *Digested,* 01/**6783**
Marie Brizard et Roger International SA v. William Grant & Sons Ltd (No.1); *sub nom*
     Marie Brizzard et Roger International SA, Petitioner 2001 G.W.D. 33-1302, OH
Marie Brizzard et Roger International SA, Petitioner see Marie Brizard et Roger International
     SA v. William Grant & Sons Ltd (No.1)
Marinello v. Chief Constable of Lothian and Borders 1997 S.L.T. (Sh Ct) 93, Sh Ct
     (Lothian) . . . .   *Digested,* 98/**6080**
Maris Ltd v. Mitchell 2000 G.W.D. 16-639, Sh Ct
Marks v. McFadyen (Sentencing) 1999 G.W.D. 40-1941, HCJ Appeal
Marks & Spencer Plc v. Customs and Excise Commissioners (No.1) [2000] S.T.C. 16;
     [2000] 1 C.M.L.R. 256; [2000] Eu. L.R. 293; [2000] B.T.C. 5003; [2000]
     B.V.C. 35; [2000] S.T.I. 22; *Times,* January 19, 2000, CA; reversing in part [1999]
     S.T.C. 205; [1999] 1 C.M.L.R. 1152; [1999] Eu. L.R. 450; [1999] B.T.C. 5073;
     [1999] B.V.C. 107; *Times,* January 19, 1999, QBD; affirming [1997] V. & D.R. 85,
     V&DTr . . . .   *Digested,* 00/**5317**:
                       Considered, 00/4462: *Distinguished,* 01/6921:
                                        Previous proceedings, 98/4926, 00/5360
Mars Pension Trustees Ltd v. County Properties & Developments Ltd 1999 S.C. 267;
     2000 S.L.T. 581; 1999 S.C.L.R. 117; 1999 G.W.D. 1-44, Ex Div; reversing in part
     1999 S.C. 10; 1998 G.W.D. 30-1567, OH . . . .   *Digested,* 99/**6322**
Marsden v. Craighelen Lawn Tennis and Squash Club 1999 G.W.D. 37-1820, Sh Ct
Marsh v. Baxendale 1994 S.C. 157; 1995 S.L.T. 198; 1994 S.C.L.R. 239, 1 Div; affirming
     1995 S.L.T. 195, OH . . . .   *Digested,* 95/**5931**:
                                                           Followed, 96/6635: *Overruled,* 98/5493
Marsh v. Marsh 2001 G.W.D. 36-1358, Sh Pr; affirming 2001 Fam. L.R. 96; 2001
     G.W.D. 14-538, Sh Ct (Grampian)
Marshall v. HM Advocate 1998 G.W.D. 22-1128, HCJ Appeal
Marshall v. Lees 1998 G.W.D. 33-1724, HCJ Appeal

Marshall (Steven) v. McLeod 1998 S.L.T. 1199; 1998 S.C.C.R. 317; 1998 G.W.D. 12-
625, HCJ Appeal . . . .   *Digested*, 98/**5693**:
Applied, 99/**5956**

Marshall v. Marshall 1999 G.W.D. 32-1509, OH
Marshall v. Ritchie see Millar v. Dickson
Marshall v. Stott 1999 G.W.D. 34-1631, HCJ Appeal
Martin v. Clark 2001 G.W.D. 6-240, HCJ Appeal
Martin v. HM Advocate 1998 G.W.D. 8-369, HCJ Appeal
Martin v. HM Advocate 2001 G.W.D. 3-118, HCJ Appeal
Martin v. HM Advocate (Sentencing) 1999 G.W.D. 36-1760, HCJ Appeal
Martin v. HM Advocate (Sentencing) 2001 G.W.D. 32-1279, HCJ Appeal
Martin v. Scottish Coal Co Ltd 1998 G.W.D. 40-2077, OH
Martin v. United Kingdom 1999 S.C.C.R. 941, ECHR
Martin v. Vannet (Sentencing) 1998 G.W.D. 13-650, HCJ Appeal
Martin v. Watt (Sentencing) 2000 G.W.D. 30-1183, HCJ Appeal
Martin (George) Builders Ltd v. Jamal see George Martin (Builders) Ltd v. Jamal
Mason v. Grampian University Hospitals NHS Trust 2000 G.W.D. 14-554, Sh Ct
Mason v. HM Advocate (No.1) 2000 J.C. 626; 2000 S.L.T. 1004; 2000 S.C.C.R. 710;
2000 G.W.D. 23-881, HCJ Appeal . . . .   *Digested*, 00/**6023**

Mason v. HM Advocate (No.2) (Sentencing) 2000 G.W.D. 25-938, HCJ Appeal
Mason v. Lees (Sentencing) 1998 G.W.D. 32-1643, HCJ Appeal
Mason v. McFadyen (Sentencing) 2000 G.W.D. 9-329, HCJ Appeal
Mason v. McGlennan 1999 G.W.D. 34-1635, HCJ Appeal
Mason v. Stott 1999 G.W.D. 20-923, HCJ Appeal
Masse v. Lord Advocate 1999 Rep. L.R. 75, OH . . . .   *Digested*, 99/**5977**
Massey v. Howdle 1998 G.W.D. 27-1352, HCJ Appeal
Massey v. Paterson 2000 G.W.D. 35-1342, Sh Ct (Grampian)
Masson v. Masson 2001 S.C.L.R. 501, Sh Ct (Grampian) . . . .   *Digested*, 01/**6239**
Masson v. Masson (Assessment of Liability) (No.1) 2001 Fam. L.R. 138; 2001 G.W.D.
29-1169, Sh Pr; reversing 2001 G.W.D. 16-655, Sh Ct (Grampian)
Masson v. Masson (Assessment of Liability) (No.2) 2001 Fam. L.R. 142; 2001 G.W.D.
39-1482, Sh Ct (Grampian)
Masterton v. Health Centre Kirkliston 2000 G.W.D. 6-232, OH
Masterton v. Thomas Smith & Sons (Kirkoswald) Ltd 1998 S.L.T. 699; 1997 G.W.D.
24-1215, OH . . . .   *Digested*, 98/**5469**
Mather v. British Telecommunications Plc 2001 S.L.T. 325; 2000 G.W.D. 20-816, OH . . .   *Digested*, 01/**6252**
Matheson v. Dickson (Sentencing) 2000 G.W.D. 4-132, HCJ Appeal
Matheson v. MacDonald (Sentencing) 2001 G.W.D. 36-1385, HCJ Appeal
Mathieson v. Customs and Excise Commissioners [1999] S.T.C. 835; [1999] B.T.C.
5310; [1999] B.V.C. 343; 1999 G.W.D. 18-860; *Times*, June 17, 1999, OH . . . . . .   *Digested*, 99/**6471**
Matthew v. Council of the Law Society of Scotland 1998 S.C. 306; 1998 S.L.T. 759;
1998 G.W.D. 3-139, Ex Div. . . . .   *Digested*, 98/**6057**
Matthew v. HM Advocate 1999 G.W.D. 2-88, HCJ Appeal
Matthew v. HM Advocate 1998 G.W.D. 5-204, HCJ Appeal
Matthewson v. Scottish Ministers 2001 G.W.D. 23-875; *Times*, October 24, 2001, OH . .   *Digested*, 01/**6833**
Matts (Elizabeth) v. Cumming 1999 J.C. 171; 2000 S.L.T. 220; 1999 S.C.C.R. 249; 1999
G.W.D. 10-454, HCJ Appeal . . . .   *Digested*, 99/**5601**
Matznick v. Matznick 1998 S.L.T. 636; 1997 G.W.D. 27-1345, OH . . . .   *Digested*, 98/**5471**
Maund v. Julia Arredamenti SpA 2001 G.W.D. 38-1417, OH
Mavor v. McFadyen (Sentencing) 2000 G.W.D. 30-1182, HCJ Appeal
Maxi Construction Management Ltd v. Morton Rolls Ltd 2001 G.W.D. 26-1001, OH
Maxtone v. HM Advocate (Sentencing) 2001 G.W.D. 36-1380, HCJ Appeal
Maxwell v. HM Advocate 1999 G.W.D. 13-614, HCJ Appeal
Maxwell (Janette Carruthers) v. HM Advocate (Sentencing) 2000 G.W.D. 6-224, HCJ
Appeal
Maxwell (John Hill) v. HM Advocate 1980 J.C. 40; 1980 S.L.T. 241, HCJ Appeal. . . . . .   *Digested*, 80/**2958**:
Distinguished, 00/6029

Maxwell v. O'Donnell (Sentencing) 1998 G.W.D. 5-251, HCJ Appeal
Maypark Properties Ltd v. Stirrat; *sub nom* Maypark Properties Ltd v. Stirrit 2001 S.L.T.
(Sh Ct) 171; 2001 Rep. L.R. 9; 2000 G.W.D. 37-1412, Sh Pr . . . .   *Digested*, 01/**6419**
Maypark Properties Ltd v. Stirrit see Maypark Properties Ltd v. Stirrat
Meaney v. McFadyen (Sentencing) 2001 G.W.D. 16-636, HCJ Appeal
Mearns v. Glasgow City Council 2001 Hous. L.R. 130; 2001 G.W.D. 28-1140, Sh Pr
Mearns v. McFadyen 2001 J.C. 51; 2001 S.C.C.R. 25; 2000 G.W.D. 37-1384, HCJ
Appeal . . . .   *Digested*, 01/**6321**
Mearns v. Smedvig Ltd 1999 S.C. 243; 1999 S.L.T. 585; 1999 Rep. L.R. 22; 1999
G.W.D. 1-4, OH . . . .   *Digested*, 99/**5702**:
Followed, 00/5931

Meek v. HM Advocate see Meek v. Vannet
Meek v. Strathclyde RC 2001 G.W.D. 27-1109, OH
Meek v. Vannet; *sub nom* Meek v. HM Advocate 2000 S.C.C.R. 192; 2000 G.W.D. 9-
323, HCJ Appeal . . . .   *Digested*, 00/**6018**
Megrahi v. HM Advocate (No.2) see HM Advocate v. Al-Megrahi (No.2)
Megrahi v. HM Advocate (No.3) see HM Advocate v. Al-Megrahi (No.3)

Megrahi v. HM Advocate (No.4) see HM Advocate v. Al-Megrahi (No.4)
Megrahi v. HM Advocate (No.5) see HM Advocate v. Al-Megrahi (No.5)
Megrahi v. Times Newspapers Ltd see Al-Megrahi v. Times Newspapers Ltd
Meichan v. HM Advocate 1998 G.W.D. 26-1322, HCJ Appeal
Meikle v. HM Advocate (Sentencing) 2000 G.W.D. 14-539, HCJ Appeal
Meiklejohn v. HM Advocate (Sentencing) 1998 G.W.D. 2-68, HCJ Appeal
Mejury v. Renfrewshire Council 2001 S.C. 426; 2000 G.W.D. 40-1501, Ex Div
Meldrum v. Crolla 2001 G.W.D. 13-469, OH
Meldrum v. Lees 1999 G.W.D. 10-481, HCJ Appeal
Melley v. HM Advocate 1999 G.W.D. 31-1478, HCJ Appeal
Mellors v. HM Advocate 1999 S.C.C.R. 869; 1999 G.W.D. 32-1530, HCJ Appeal . . . . . .   *Digested*, 00/**6060**
Melville v. HM Advocate 1999 G.W.D. 35-1679, HCJ Appeal
Menzies v. Clark (Sentencing) 2001 G.W.D. 12-412, HCJ Appeal
Menzies v. Lloyds 2001 G.W.D. 26-1002, Sh Ct (Lothian)
Menzies v. McLeod 1999 G.W.D. 1-57, HCJ Appeal
Mercedes-Benz Finance Ltd v. Clydesdale Bank Plc 1997 S.L.T. 905; 1996 S.C.L.R.
    1005; [1998] Lloyd's Rep. Bank. 249; [1997] C.L.C. 81; *Times*, September 16,
    1996, OH . . . .   *Digested*, 96/**6576**
Mercer v. Heart of Midlothian Plc 2001 S.L.T. 945; 2001 S.C.L.R. 701; 2001 G.W.D. 19-
    717, OH . . . .   *Digested*, 01/**6275**
Methven v. Methven 1999 S.L.T. (Sh Ct) 117; 1999 G.W.D. 28-1342, Sh Ct (North
    Strathclyde) . . . .   *Digested*, 00/**6279**
Michael v. Carruthers 1998 S.L.T. 1179; 1997 S.C.L.R. 1005; 1997 G.W.D. 22-1097, OH. .   *Digested*, 98/**5946**
Michie (Gordon) v. Gilchrist 2000 S.C.C.R. 627; 2000 G.W.D. 18-727, HCJ Appeal . . . .   *Digested*, 00/**6011**
Michie v. Higson (Sentencing) 1999 G.W.D. 40-1945, HCJ Appeal
Michie v. McLeod 1999 G.W.D. 23-1089, HCJ Appeal
Micro Leisure Ltd v. County Properties & Developments Ltd (No.1) 1999 S.C. 501;
    1999 S.L.T. 1307; 1999 G.W.D. 7-320, OH . . . .   *Digested*, 99/**5728**
Micro Leisure Ltd v. County Properties & Developments Ltd (No.2) 1999 S.L.T. 1428;
    [2000] B.C.C. 872; 1999 G.W.D. 33-1570; *Times*, January 12, 2000, OH . . . . .   *Digested*, 00/**5955**
Middleton v. Dundee City Council 2001 S.L.T. 287; 2000 G.W.D. 25-950, Ex Div . . . . .   *Digested*, 01/**6793**
Middleton v. HM Advocate (Sentencing) 2000 G.W.D. 20-808, HCJ Appeal
Middleton v. Napier 1997 S.C.C.R. 669; 1997 G.W.D. 35-1808, HCJ Appeal . . . .   *Digested*, 98/**5689**
Midlothian Council v. Roxburgh 1999 Hous. L.R. 50, Sh Pr. . . . .   *Digested*, 99/**5724**
Mikhailitchenko v. Normand 1993 S.L.T. 1138; 1993 S.C.C.R. 56, HCJ Appeal . . . .   *Digested*, 93/**4997**:
    Distinguished, 99/5888
Miklasewicz v. Stolt Offshore Ltd see Miklaszewicz v. Stolt Offshore Ltd
Miklaszewicz v. Stolt Offshore Ltd; *sub nom* Stolt Offshore Ltd v. Miklaszewicz;
    Miklasewicz v. Stolt Offshore Ltd; Stolt Offshore Ltd v. Miklasewicz; TNS, Ex
    Div; affirming [2001] I.R.L.R. 656; *Independent*, July 9, 2001 (C.S), EAT . . . . .   *Digested*, 01/**6477**:
    Applied, 01/2348
Millar v. Criminal Injuries Compensation Board see P's Curator Bonis v. Criminal Injuries
    Compensation Board
Millar v. Dickson; Stewart v. Heywood; Payne v. Heywood; Tracey v. Heywood;
    Marshall v. Ritchie [2001] UKPC D4; 2001 S.L.T. 988; 2001 S.C.C.R. 741; [2001]
    H.R.L.R. 59; [2001] U.K.H.R.R. 999; 2001 G.W.D. 26-1015; *Times*, July 27,
    2001, PC (Sc); reversing 2000 J.C. 648; 2000 S.L.T. 1111; 2000 S.C.C.R. 793;
    [2000] U.K.H.R.R. 776; 2000 G.W.D. 27-1040, HCJ Appeal . . . .   *Digested*, 01/**6372**
Millar v. HM Advocate (Sentencing) 1998 G.W.D. 24-1195, HCJ Appeal
Millar v. HM Advocate (Sentencing) 1998 G.W.D. 29-1494, HCJ Appeal
Millar v. Houston (Sentencing) 1998 G.W.D. 11-579, HCJ Appeal
Millar v. Ritchie (Sentencing) 1998 G.W.D. 13-655, HCJ Appeal
Millard v. Grampian Joint Fire Board 2001 S.L.T. 653; 2000 G.W.D. 2-55, OH
Millard v. McFadyen (No.1) 1999 G.W.D. 21-1006, HCJ Appeal
Millard v. McFadyen (No.2) 1999 G.W.D. 29-1385, HCJ Appeal
Miller v. Brown (Sentencing) 2001 G.W.D. 16-626, HCJ Appeal
Miller v. Clerical Medical Investment Group Ltd 2001 S.C.L.R. 990; 2001 G.W.D. 25-
    973, OH
Miller v. Council of the Law Society of Scotland 2000 S.L.T. 513; 2000 S.C.L.R. 849;
    2000 G.W.D. 1-25; *Times*, March 22, 2000, OH . . . .   *Digested*, 00/**6552**
Miller v. Dick (William); *sub nom* Gallagher v. Dick 2000 J.C. 71; 1999 S.C.C.R. 919;
    1999 G.W.D. 32-1558, HCJ Appeal . . . .   *Digested*, 00/**6008**
Miller v. HM Advocate (Sentencing) 1998 G.W.D. 33-1703, HCJ Appeal
Miller v. HM Advocate (Sentencing) 2001 G.W.D. 12-424, HCJ Appeal
Miller (Robert) v. HM Advocate 1998 S.L.T. 571; 1997 S.C.C.R. 748; 1997 G.W.D. 36-
    1831, HCJ Appeal . . . .   *Digested*, 98/**5557**
Miller v. McGlennan 1999 G.W.D. 23-1101, HCJ Appeal
Miller v. Miller 2000 Fam. L.R. 19, Sh Ct (South Strathclyde) . . . .   *Digested*, 00/**6277**
Miller v. Muirhead (1893) 21 R. 658, 2 Div. . . . .   *Considered*, 81/3242:
    Followed, 01/6725
Miller v. O'Donnell (Sentencing) 2000 G.W.D. 30-1201, HCJ Appeal
Miller v. Perth and Kinross Council 2001 G.W.D. 40-1530, OH
Miller v. Spiers 1998 G.W.D. 21-1063, HCJ Appeal
Miller v. Stott 1999 G.W.D. 17-777, HCJ Appeal

Miller v. Vannet (Sentencing) 1998 G.W.D. 11-552, HCJ Appeal
Miller v. Walker (Sentencing) 1998 G.W.D. 12-624, HCJ Appeal
Miller Group Ltd v. Scottish Coal Co Ltd 1998 G.W.D. 40-2039, 2 Div; reversing 1998
    G.W.D. 2-62, OH
Miller Homes Ltd v. Frame 2001 S.L.T. 459; 2000 G.W.D. 11-388, OH . . . .   *Digested,* 01/**6676**
Miller Homes Ltd v. West of Scotland Water Authority 1999 S.L.T. 149; 1998 G.W.D. 22-
    1146, OH. . . . .   *Digested,* 99/**6474**
Milligan v. Higson 2001 G.W.D. 6-238, HCJ Appeal
Milligan v. HM Advocate (Sentencing) 2001 G.W.D. 12-416, HCJ Appeal
Milligan v. HM Advocate (Sentencing) 2001 G.W.D. 25-939, HCJ Appeal
Milligan v. Houston (Sentencing) 2000 G.W.D. 3-114, HCJ Appeal
Milligan v. Wilson 1998 G.W.D. 30-1533, Sh Ct
Milloy v. HM Advocate (Sentencing) 1998 G.W.D. 10-487, HCJ Appeal
Millport Burgh, Petitioners 1974 S.L.T. (Notes) 23, OH . . . .   *Digested,* 74/**4058**:
                                                                                                              Applied, 99/6301
Mills (Kenneth Anthony Paton) v. HM Advocate (Fresh Evidence) 2001 G.W.D. 20-760,
    HCJ Appeal
Mills (Kenneth Anthony Paton) v. HM Advocate (No.1) 1999 J.C. 216; 1999 S.L.T. 680;
    1999 S.C.C.R. 202; 1999 G.W.D. 11-495, HCJ Appeal . . . .   *Digested,* 99/**5857**
Mills (Kenneth Anthony Paton) v. HM Advocate (No.2); Cochrane (John) v. HM
    Advocate 2001 S.L.T. 1359; 2001 S.C.C.R. 821; 2001 G.W.D. 31-1228, HCJ
    Appeal . . . .   *Digested,* 01/**6369**
Milmor Properties Ltd v. W and T Investment Co Ltd 2000 S.L.T. (Sh Ct) 2; 1999
    G.W.D. 36-1727, Sh Pr; affirming 1999 S.C.L.R. 910, Sh Ct . . . .   *Digested,* 00/**5939**
Milnbank Housing Association Ltd v. Page & Park (No.1) 2000 G.W.D. 12-410, OH
Milnbank Housing Association Ltd v. Page & Park (No.2) 2001 G.W.D. 40-1532, OH
Milne (Gavin William), Petitioner see Shaw (Robert French), Petitioner
Milne v. Duguid (No.1) 1999 S.C.L.R. 512, Sh Ct . . . .   *Digested,* 99/**5970**
Milne v. Duguid (No.2) 2000 G.W.D. 20-817, Sh Ct
Milne v. HM Advocate (Sentencing) 1998 G.W.D. 12-593, HCJ Appeal
Milne v. HM Advocate (Sentencing) 1998 G.W.D. 17-848, HCJ Appeal
Milne v. HM Advocate (Sentencing) 1999 G.W.D. 24-1152, HCJ Appeal
Milne v. HM Advocate (Sentencing) 1999 G.W.D. 37-1806, HCJ Appeal
Milne v. HM Advocate (Sentencing) 2000 G.W.D. 18-715, HCJ Appeal
Milne v. McKay (Sentencing) 1998 G.W.D. 7-355, HCJ Appeal
Milne v. Moores Rowland 2000 G.W.D. 2-69, OH
Milne v. Napier 2001 G.W.D. 31-1232, HCJ Appeal
Milne v. William Cowie Partnership 2000 G.W.D. 21-837, OH
Milroy v. HM Advocate (Sentencing) 1998 G.W.D. 32-1641, HCJ Appeal
Milton (Kenneth William) v. McLeod 1999 S.C.C.R. 210; 1999 G.W.D. 6-295, HCJ
    Appeal . . . .   *Digested,* 99/**5891**
Minevco Ltd v. Barratt Southern Ltd 2000 S.L.T. 790; 2000 G.W.D. 12-435, 2 Div;
    affirming 1999 G.W.D. 5-266, OH . . . .   *Digested,* 00/**6535**
Mining Scotland Ltd v. Fyfe 1999 S.L.T. (Land Ct) 6; 1999 S.L.C.R. 22; 1999 G.W.D.
    32-1505, Land Ct . . . .   *Digested,* 00/**5848**
Mirfin v. Dickson 2001 G.W.D. 11-400, HCJ Appeal
Mitchell v. Campbeltown Shipyard Ltd 1998 G.W.D. 12-616, OH
Mitchell v. H; *sub nom* Mitchell v. S 2000 S.C. 334; 2000 S.L.T. 524; 2000 Fam. L.R.
    50; 2000 G.W.D. 7-241, 2 Div. . . . .   *Digested,* 00/**6269**
Mitchell v. HM Advocate 1998 G.W.D. 9-435, HCJ Appeal
Mitchell v. HM Advocate 2000 G.W.D. 2-43, HCJ Appeal
Mitchell v. HM Advocate (Sentencing) 1998 G.W.D. 24-1219, HCJ Appeal
Mitchell v. HM Advocate (Sentencing) 1999 G.W.D. 37-1801, HCJ Appeal
Mitchell (Alexander Todd) v. HM Advocate 2001 S.C.C.R. 110; 2001 G.W.D. 2-89, HCJ
    Appeal . . . .   *Digested,* 01/**6363**
Mitchell v. Inverclyde DC 1998 S.L.T. 1157; 1998 S.C.L.R. 191; 1997 Rep. L.R.
    (Quantum) 29; 1997 G.W.D. 31-1593, OH . . . .   *Digested,* 98/**5744**
Mitchell v. Laing 1998 S.C. 342; 1998 S.L.T. 203; 1998 S.C.L.R. 266; 1997 G.W.D. 40-
    2035; *Times,* January 28, 1998, 1 Div . . . .   *Digested,* 98/**5703**
Mitchell v. Ritchie 1999 G.W.D. 11-513, HCJ Appeal
Mitchell v. S see Mitchell v. H
Mitchell (John) v. Vannet 1999 S.L.T. 934; 1999 S.C.C.R. 547; 1999 G.W.D. 20-928,
    HCJ Appeal . . . .   *Digested,* 99/**5892**:
                                                                                                              Overruled, 00/6104
Mitre Pensions Ltd v. Pensions Ombudsman [2000] O.P.L.R. 349; 2000 G.W.D. 22-
    868, Ex Div
Mitsui Babcock Energy Services Ltd v. Foster Wheeler Energia OY 2001 S.L.T. 1158;
    2001 G.W.D. 21-785, OH . . . .   *Digested,* 01/**6287**
Moar v. Redman 1999 G.W.D. 10-477, HCJ Appeal
Modern Housing Ltd v. Love 1998 S.L.T. 1188; 1997 G.W.D. 27-1346, OH . . . .   *Digested,* 98/**5466**
Moffat v. HM Advocate (Sentencing) 1998 G.W.D. 5-221, HCJ Appeal
Moffat v. HM Advocate (Sentencing) 1999 G.W.D. 26-1243, HCJ Appeal
Moffat (Graeme William) v. HM Advocate see Boyd (John) v. HM Advocate
Moffat v. Longmuir 2001 S.C. 137; 2001 S.L.T. 108; 2000 G.W.D. 27-1061, Ex Div . . . . .   *Digested,* 01/**6829**

Moffat v. McFadyen 1999 G.W.D. 22-1038, HCJ Appeal
Moffat v. McFadyen (Sentencing) 2001 G.W.D. 13-522, HCJ Appeal
Moffat v. McGlennan 1998 G.W.D. 31-1603, HCJ Appeal
Moffat v. News Group Newspapers Ltd 1999 S.C. 664; 2000 S.C.L.R. 346; 1999
    G.W.D. 24-1126, OH . . . .   *Digested*, 00/**5913**
Moffat v. West Highland Publishing Co Ltd 2000 S.L.T. 335; 1999 G.W.D. 33-1586,
    OH . . . .   *Digested*, 00/**6176**
Mohammed v. Glasgow Licensing Board 1998 S.C. 415; 1999 S.L.T. 87; 1998 S.C.L.R.
    426; [1998] 9 S.L.L.P. 12; 1998 G.W.D. 5-244, Ex Div; reversing [1997] 6
    S.L.L.P. 14, Sh Ct. . . . .   *Digested*, 98/**6074**
Moir v. Hutchison (Sentencing) 2001 G.W.D. 30-1221, HCJ Appeal
Moir v. Hutchison (Sentencing) 2001 G.W.D. 31-1266, HCJ Appeal
Moles v. Miller 1998 G.W.D. 22-1133, HCJ Appeal
Molfino v. Lees (Sentencing) 1999 G.W.D. 12-581, HCJ Appeal
Monaghan v. HM Advocate (Sentencing) 1999 G.W.D. 35-1685, HCJ Appeal
Monaghan v. HM Advocate (Sentencing) 2000 G.W.D. 15-597, HCJ
Moncrieff v. Jamieson 1999 G.W.D. 26-1220, Sh Pr
Monklands DC v. Gallagher 2000 Hous. L.R. 112, Sh Ct (South Strathclyde) . . . .   *Digested*, 00/**6463**
Monklands DC v. Johnstone 1987 S.C.L.R. 480, Sh Ct (South Strathclyde) . . . .   *Digested*, 87/**4640**:
                                                                                                                                        Not followed, 00/5939
Monson v. Higson (Sentencing); *sub nom* Monson v. HM Advocate (Sentencing)
    2000 S.C.C.R. 751; 2000 G.W.D. 29-1127, HCJ Appeal . . . .   *Digested*, 01/**6396**
Monson v. HM Advocate (Sentencing) see Monson v. Higson (Sentencing)
Montagu Evans (A Firm) v. Young 2000 S.L.T. 1083; 2000 G.W.D. 24-912; *Times*,
    September 19, 2000, OH . . . .   *Digested*, 00/**5927**
Montague (Paul Patrick Thomas) v. Vannet 1999 S.C.C.R. 588; 1999 G.W.D. 22-1034,
    HCJ Appeal . . . .   *Digested*, 99/**5820**
Monterosso v. HM Advocate see Monterosso v. Secretary of State for the Home
    Department
Monterosso v. Secretary of State for the Home Department; *sub nom* Monterosso v.
    HM Advocate 2001 S.C. 291; 2000 S.C.C.R. 974; 2000 G.W.D. 33-1295, OH . . .   *Digested*, 01/**6348**
Montgomery (Andrina) v. Cumming 1999 S.C.C.R. 178; 1999 G.W.D. 5-258, HCJ
    Appeal . . . .   *Digested*, 99/**5997**
Montgomery v. Donnelly 1998 G.W.D. 33-1702, HCJ Appeal
Montgomery v. HM Advocate; *sub nom* HM Advocate v. Montgomery (David Shields);
    Coulter v. HM Advocate [2001] 2 W.L.R. 779; 2001 S.C. (P.C.) 1; 2001 S.L.T.
    37; 2000 S.C.C.R. 1044; [2001] U.K.H.R.R. 124; 9 B.H.R.C. 641; 2000 G.W.D.
    40-1487; *Times*, December 6, 2000, PC (Sc) . . . .   *Digested*, 01/**6371**:
                                                                                                                                        Previous proceedings, 00/6068
Montgomery v. HM Advocate (Sentencing) 1998 G.W.D. 9-455, HCJ Appeal
Montgomery v. Houston 1999 G.W.D. 28-1325, HCJ Appeal
Montgomery v. RGC (Offshore) Ltd 2000 G.W.D. 1-17, OH
Montgomery v. Vannet (Sentencing) 1998 G.W.D. 10-491, HCJ Appeal
Montgomery Litho Ltd v. Maxwell 2000 S.C. 56; 1999 S.L.T. 1431; 2000 S.C.L.R. 101;
    1999 G.W.D. 34-1617, Ex Div; reversing 1999 S.C.L.R. 115; 1999 G.W.D. 19-869,
    Sh Pr . . . .   *Digested*, 00/**5989**
Montieth v. Cape Insulation Ltd 1998 S.C. 903; 1999 S.L.T. 116; 1998 G.W.D. 29-1496,
    Ex Div; affirming 1998 S.L.T. 456; 1998 S.C.L.R. 940; 1997 Rep. L.R. 133; 1997
    G.W.D. 28-1431, OH . . . .   *Digested*, 99/**5968**
Moodie v. Dempster 1931 S.C. 553; 1931 S.L.T. 324, 1 Div . . . .   *Distinguished*,
                                                                                                                                        98/5462
Moohan v. HM Advocate 1999 G.W.D. 7-335, HCJ Appeal
Mooney v. Carnegie (Sentencing) 2000 G.W.D. 3-89, HCJ Appeal
Mooney v. Glasgow City Council 2000 G.W.D. 12-443, Sh Ct
Moore v. HM Advocate (Sentencing) 2000 G.W.D. 14-530, HCJ Appeal
Moore v. HM Advocate (Sentencing) 2000 G.W.D. 29-1147, HCJ Appeal
Moore (Anthony James Irvine) v. HM Advocate see Salmon (Donald) v. HM Advocate
Moore v. Piretta PTA Ltd [1999] 1 All E.R. 174; [1998] C.L.C. 992; [1998] E.C.C. 392;
    [1999] Eu. L.R. 32; (1998) 17 Tr. L.R. 161; *Times*, May 11, 1998, QBD . . . .   *Digested*, 98/**113**:
                                                                                                                                        Followed, 99/5629
Moore, Petitioner 2001 S.L.T. (Sh Ct) 111; 2001 G.W.D. 10-320, Sh Pr . . . .   *Digested*, 01/**6094**
Moran v. Heywood (Sentencing) 1999 G.W.D. 12-556, HCJ Appeal
Moran's Executors v. Shenstone Properties Ltd 2001 Hous. L.R. 124; 2001 G.W.D. 7-
    262, Lands Tr (Scot)
Moray Estates Development Co v. Butler 1999 S.L.T. 1338; 1999 S.C.L.R. 447; 1999
    G.W.D. 8-364, OH . . . .   *Digested*, 99/**5635**
Moreman v. Donnelly (Sentencing) 1999 G.W.D. 4-219, HCJ Appeal
Morgan v. HM Advocate (Sentencing) 1998 G.W.D. 34-1742, HCJ Appeal
Morgan v. HM Advocate (Sentencing) 2001 G.W.D. 1-35, HCJ Appeal
Morgan v. McFadyen (Evidence) 2001 J.C. 58; 2000 G.W.D. 32-1245, HCJ Appeal . . .   *Digested*, 01/**6340**
Morgan v. McFadyen (Sentencing) 2000 G.W.D. 33-1298, HCJ Appeal
Morgan v. Morgan 1998 S.C.L.R. 681, Sh Pr . . . .   *Digested*, 98/**5845**
Morgan v. Morgan 2000 Hous. L.R. 90, Sh Pr . . . .   *Digested*, 00/**6273**

Morgan Moore Engineering Ltd *v.* Engineering Construction Industry Training Board 1999 S.L.T. 1303, OH . . . . *Digested,* 00/**6211**

Morley *v.* Campbell 1998 S.L.T. 325; 1997 S.C.L.R. 813; 1997 Rep. L.R. (Quantum) 14; 1997 G.W.D. 18-844, OH . . . . *Digested,* 97/**5934**

Morning *v.* HM Advocate (Sentencing) 2001 G.W.D. 6-197, HCJ Appeal

Morran *v.* Glasgow Council of Tenants Associations 1997 S.C. 279; 1997 S.L.T. 1133; 1997 S.C.L.R. 841; [1998] I.R.L.R. 67; 1997 G.W.D. 20-977, 1 Div . . . . *Digested,* 97/**6006**

Morris *v.* Donnelly 1998 G.W.D. 31-1615, HCJ Appeal

Morris *v.* Highland Spring Ltd 1998 G.W.D. 40-2034, OH

Morris *v.* HM Advocate (Sentencing) 2000 G.W.D. 29-1124, HCJ Appeal

Morris *v.* KLM Royal Dutch Airlines see King *v.* Bristow Helicopters Ltd

Morris *v.* Lees 1999 G.W.D. 4-224, HCJ Appeal

Morrison *v.* Aberdeen City Council 2001 S.C.L.R. 1067; 2001 G.W.D. 22-840, Sh Ct (Grampian)

Morrison *v.* HM Advocate (Evidence) 1990 J.C. 299; 1991 S.L.T. 57; 1990 S.C.C.R. 235, HCJ Appeal . . . . *Digested,* 91/**4552**:
Applied, 97/5751, 99/5905: *Considered,* 92/5504, 95/5729, 96/6807:
Distinguished, 93/4963, 96/6709: *Followed,* 91/4740, 94/5630, 97/5867:
Not applied, 96/6731: *Not followed,* 00/6114: *Referred to,* 92/5506, 94/5634, 95/5732

Morrison *v.* HM Advocate (Sentencing) 1998 G.W.D. 18-937, HCJ Appeal

Morrison *v.* HM Advocate (Sentencing) 2000 G.W.D. 29-1144, HCJ Appeal

Morrison *v.* HM Advocate (Sentencing) 2001 G.W.D. 39-1466, HCJ Appeal

Morrison *v.* McKay 1999 G.W.D. 14-670, HCJ Appeal

Morrison *v.* O'Donnell 2001 S.C.C.R. 272; 2001 G.W.D. 14-541, HCJ Appeal . . . . *Digested,* 01/**6320**

Morrison *v.* Showmen's Guild of Great Britain 1998 G.W.D. 19-958, OH

Morrison *v.* Vannet (Sentencing) 1998 G.W.D. 4-172, HCJ Appeal

Morrison-Low *v.* Paterson (No.2) 2000 S.L.T. 624; 1999 G.W.D. 36-1724, Ex Div; affirming 1998 S.L.T. 564; 1998 G.W.D. 7-307, OH. *Digested,* 00/**5847**

Morrow *v.* Houston 1999 G.W.D. 8-378, HCJ Appeal

Morston Assets Ltd *v.* Edinburgh City Council 2001 S.L.T. 613; 2001 G.W.D. 8-291, OH . *Digested,* 01/**6103**

Mortgage Corp Ltd *v.* Mitchells Roberton 1997 S.L.T. 1305; 1997 G.W.D. 19-901, OH. . . *Digested,* 98/**6056**

Mortimer *v.* Safeway Plc 1998 S.C. 520; 1998 S.L.T. 885; 1998 Rep. L.R. 84; 1998 G.W.D. 16-816, OH . . . . *Digested,* 98/**5938**

Morton *v.* Knaggs 1999 G.W.D. 13-624, OH

Morton (David Robert) *v.* Munro 1998 S.C.C.R. 178; 1998 G.W.D. 8-415, HCJ Appeal. . *Digested,* 98/**5694**

Morton *v.* South Ayrshire Council see South Ayrshire Council *v.* Morton

Moscrop, Petitioner 1999 G.W.D. 16-758, HCJ Appeal

Moss *v.* Elphick [1910] 1 K.B. 846, CA; affirming [1910] 1 K.B. 465, KBD . . . . *Applied,* 88/2672:
Disapproved, 00/6604

Moss *v.* Howdle 1997 J.C. 123; 1997 S.L.T. 782; 1997 S.C.C.R. 215; 1997 G.W.D. 8-304, HCJ Appeal . . . . *Digested,* 97/**6417**:
Followed, 01/6334

Moss Bros Group Plc *v.* Scottish Mutual Assurance Plc 2001 S.C. 779; 2001 S.L.T. 641; 2001 G.W.D. 12-440, OH . . . . *Digested,* 01/**6678**

Moss's Empires *v.* Glasgow Assessor 1917 S.C. (H.L.) 1, HL . . . . *Considered,* 00/5836

Motorola Ltd *v.* Davidson [2001] I.R.L.R. 4, EAT . . . . *Digested,* 01/**6467**

Mowat (Paul Anthony) *v.* HM Advocate 1999 S.C.C.R. 688, HCJ Appeal . . . . *Digested,* 00/**6109**

Mowat *v.* Kerr 1977 S.L.T. (Sh. Ct.) 62, Sh Pr . . . . *Digested,* 77/**3738**:
Followed, 98/5507: *Not followed,* 89/4946

Mowat *v.* MJ Rennie Joiners (Aberdeen) Ltd 2000 G.W.D. 23-878, Sh Ct

Mowat *v.* Ross 2001 G.W.D. 26-1005, Sh Ct (Grampian)

Mowatt *v.* Mowatt 1999 G.W.D. 19-864, Sh Pr

Mowbray *v.* Crowe 1993 J.C. 212; 1994 S.L.T. 445; 1993 S.C.C.R. 730, HCJ Appeal . . . *Digested,* 93/**5001**:
Distinguished, 96/6790, 98/5623

Mowbray *v.* DC Thomson & Co Ltd 1996 S.C. 197; 1996 S.L.T. 846, 1 Div . . . . *Digested,* 96/**6635**:
Overruled, 98/5493

Mowbray (John Renton) *v.* Valentine (Sequestration) 1998 S.C. 424; 1998 S.L.T. 1440; 1998 S.C.L.R. 305; 1998 G.W.D. 9-423, OH . . . . *Digested,* 98/**6004**

Mowles *v.* HM Advocate 1998 G.W.D. 26-1314, HCJ Appeal

Moyes *v.* Clark 1999 G.W.D. 27-1297, HCJ Appeal

MRS Hamilton Ltd *v.* Baxter 1998 S.L.T. 1075; 1997 Hous. L.R. 85; 1997 G.W.D. 19-898, OH . . . . *Digested,* 97/**6091**

MRS Hamilton Ltd *v.* Keeper of the Registers of Scotland (No.1) 1999 S.L.T. 829; 1998 G.W.D. 25-1267, OH . . . . *Digested,* 99/**6233**:
Disapproved, 00/6440

MRS Hamilton Ltd *v.* Keeper of the Registers of Scotland (No.2) 1999 S.L.T. 840; 1998 G.W.D. 26-1336, OH . . . . *Digested,* 99/**6234**

MRS Hamilton Ltd *v.* Keeper of the Registers of Scotland (No.3); *sub nom* Keeper of the Registers of Scotland *v.* MRS Hamilton Ltd (Expenses) 1999 S.C. 116; 1999 S.L.T. 855; 1998 G.W.D. 35-1813, Ex Div. . . . . *Digested,* 99/**5685**

MRS Hamilton Ltd *v.* Keeper of the Registers of Scotland (No.4); *sub nom* Keeper of the Registers of Scotland *v.* MRS Hamilton Ltd 2000 S.C. 271; 2000 S.L.T. 352; 2000 G.W.D. 5-203, 1 Div . . . . *Digested,* 00/**6440**

MT *v.* DT; *sub nom* T *v.* T 2001 S.C. 337; 2000 S.L.T. 1442; 2000 S.C.L.R. 1057; 2000 Fam. L.R. 125; 2000 G.W.D. 37-1376, IH (Ct of 5 judges)................. *Digested*, 01/**6217**

MT *v.* DT (Admissibility of Child Statement); *sub nom* T *v.* T (Admissibility of Child Statement) 2000 G.W.D. 25-927, 1 Div

MTM Construction Ltd *v.* William Reid Engineering Ltd 1998 S.L.T. 211; 1997 S.C.L.R. 778; 1997 Rep. L.R. 27; 1997 G.W.D. 7-260; *Times*, April 22, 1997, OH .... *Digested*, 97/**6073**

Muir *v.* Grampian Health Board 2000 G.W.D. 12-442, OH...................... *Considered*, 01/6218

Muir *v.* Houston 2001 G.W.D. 38-1424, HCJ Appeal

Muir *v.* Lees 1999 G.W.D. 13-591, HCJ Appeal

Muir *v.* McGlennan 1999 G.W.D. 3-158, HCJ Appeal

Muir *v.* Vannet 1998 G.W.D. 30-1574, HCJ Appeal

Muirhead *v.* HM Advocate (Sentencing) 1998 G.W.D. 39-2011, HCJ Appeal

Muirhead (George Alexander) *v.* HM Advocate; *sub nom* Cameron (Hugh William) *v.* HM Advocate 1999 S.L.T. 1231; 1999 S.C.C.R. 11; 1999 G.W.D. 4-176, HCJ Appeal .... *Digested*, 99/**5863**

Muirhead (George Alexander) *v.* HM Advocate (Sentencing) 1999 G.W.D. 2-92, HCJ Appeal

Muirhead *v.* Vannet (Sentencing) 2000 G.W.D. 30-1177, HCJ Appeal

Mulenga *v.* HM Advocate (Sentencing) 2000 G.W.D. 19-749, HCJ Appeal

Mulhern *v.* Vannet 1998 G.W.D. 17-882, HCJ Appeal

Mulholland *v.* HM Advocate 1998 G.W.D. 40-2050, HCJ Appeal

Mullen *v.* HM Advocate (Sentencing) 2001 G.W.D. 13-489, HCJ Appeal

Mulligan *v.* Houston (Sentencing) 1998 G.W.D. 32-1656, HCJ Appeal

Mulroy *v.* Bott (Sentencing) 2000 G.W.D. 37-1402, HCJ Appeal

Mulvanny *v.* HM Advocate (Sentencing) 1999 G.W.D. 27-1275, HCJ Appeal

Mulvanny *v.* HM Advocate (Sentencing) 2000 G.W.D. 22-853, HCJ Appeal

Mumford *v.* Bank of Scotland see Smith *v.* Bank of Scotland

Mund & Fester *v.* Hatrex Internationaal Transport (C398/92); *sub nom* Firma Mund & Fester *v.* Firma Hatrex International Transport (6 W 53/92) [1994] E.C.R. I-467; [1994] I.L.Pr. 264; *Times*, March 29, 1994; *Financial Times*, February 22, 1994; ECJ (6th Chamber) [1993] I.L.Pr. 593, OLG (Hamburg) .... *Digested*, 94/**4799**: *Considered*, 99/5701: *Followed*, 96/726

Munir *v.* Lees 1999 G.W.D. 8-408, HCJ Appeal

Munro *v.* Clark 2001 G.W.D. 23-858, HCJ Appeal

Munro *v.* George 2001 G.W.D. 23-843, OH

Munro *v.* HM Advocate (Sentencing) 1998 G.W.D. 16-782, HCJ Appeal

Munro *v.* HM Advocate (Sentencing) 1998 G.W.D. 24-1213, HCJ Appeal

Munro (Graham) *v.* HM Advocate 1999 J.C. 257; 2000 S.L.T. 950; 1999 G.W.D. 17-773, HCJ Appeal .... *Digested*, 99/**5802**

Munro, Applicant; *sub nom* McClure, Applicant 2000 S.C.L.R. 920, Sh Ct (Glasgow).. *Digested*, 01/**6758**

Muqit *v.* General Medical Council 2000 S.L.T. 943; 1999 S.C.L.R. 924; 1999 G.W.D. 14-654, OH .... *Digested*, 00/**6401**

Murdoch *v.* Friel 1998 G.W.D. 18-926, HCJ Appeal

Murdoch *v.* Glasgow City Council 1998 Hous. L.R. 30, Sh Ct.................... *Digested*, 98/**5984**

Murdoch *v.* Vannet (Sentencing) 1998 G.W.D. 8-380, HCJ Appeal

Murison *v.* Rattray 1998 Rep. L.R. 94, Sh Ct .... *Digested*, 98/**5706**

Murley *v.* Murley 1995 S.C.L.R. 1138, OH .... *Digested*, 96/**6911**: *Not followed*, 00/6274

Murphy *v.* HM Advocate (Sentencing) 2001 G.W.D. 25-958, HCJ Appeal

Murphy (Michael) *v.* HM Advocate see Valentine (Alan) *v.* HM Advocate

Murphy (Thomas) *v.* HM Advocate see Valentine (Alan) *v.* HM Advocate

Murphy *v.* Madden 2000 G.W.D. 13-460, Sh Pr

Murphy *v.* Oilfield Material Management Ltd 2001 G.W.D. 13-500, Sh Ct (Grampian)

Murphy *v.* Ritchie (Sentencing) 2000 G.W.D. 14-542, HCJ Appeal

Murphy *v.* Vannet (Sentencing) 1999 G.W.D. 4-188, HCJ Appeal

Murray *v.* Edinburgh DC 1981 S.L.T. 253, OH .... *Digested*, 81/**3405**: *Applied*, 00/5935: *Followed*, 00/6591

Murray *v.* Gilchrist (Sentencing) 2001 G.W.D. 6-241, HCJ Appeal

Murray (Neil Grant) *v.* HM Advocate; Simpson (Steven) *v.* HM Advocate 2000 J.C. 102; 1999 S.C.C.R. 946; 1999 G.W.D. 32-1541, HCJ Appeal .... *Digested*, 00/**6148**: *Followed*, 00/6149

Murray (Roger Geoffrey) *v.* HM Advocate 2001 S.L.T. 435; 2001 S.C.C.R. 114; 2000 G.W.D. 40-1512, HCJ Appeal

Murray (William Morton) *v.* HM Advocate 2000 S.L.T. 439; 2000 S.C.C.R. 1; 1999 G.W.D. 31-1469; 1999 G.W.D. 29-1373, HCJ Appeal .... *Digested*, 00/**6110**

Murray *v.* Howdle 1998 G.W.D. 25-1246, HCJ Appeal

Murray *v.* Lees 1998 G.W.D. 27-1361, HCJ Appeal

Murray *v.* MacNeill (Sentencing) 2000 G.W.D. 3-113, HCJ Appeal

Murray *v.* National Association of Round Tables of Great Britain and Ireland 2001 G.W.D. 38-1444, Ex Div; affirming 2000 G.W.D. 32-1256, Sh Ct

Murray *v.* Seath 1939 S.L.T. 348, OH .... *Applied*, 01/6740

Murray *v.* United Kingdom (Right to Silence) (1996) 22 E.H.R.R. 29; *Times*, February
    9, 1996; *Independent*, March 1, 1996, ECHR . . . . *Digested*, 96/**1516**:
                Applied, 00/3228: *Considered*, 98/3150, 00/6043: *Distinguished*, 00/6070,
                                              00/6071
Murray *v.* Vannet 1999 G.W.D. 29-1368, HCJ Appeal
Murray *v.* Vannet (Sentencing) 1998 G.W.D. 11-536, HCJ Appeal
Murray *v.* Vannet (Sentencing) 1998 G.W.D. 28-1425, HCJ Appeal
Myles *v.* Heywood 2001 G.W.D. 28-1117, Sh Ct (Tayside)
Myles *v.* Secretary of State for Transport 2000 G.W.D. 17-702, Sh Ct
Myles J Callaghan Ltd (In Receivership) *v.* Glasgow DC 1987 S.C. 171; 1988 S.L.T. 227;
    1987 S.C.L.R. 627; (1987) 3 B.C.C. 337, OH . . . . *Digested*, 88/**3818**:
                                              Applied, 98/6009

Namli *v.* Namli 1998 G.W.D. 27-1353, Ex Div; affirming 1997 G.W.D. 35-1741, OH
Napier *v.* Dyer 2001 S.L.T. 1298; 2001 G.W.D. 24-888, HCJ Appeal . . . . *Digested*, 01/**6393**
Napier *v.* Scottish Ministers 2001 G.W.D. 23-876; *Times*, November 15, 2001, OH . . . . . *Digested*, 01/**6834**
Nassaris *v.* Children's Hearing Reporter (Unreported, November 5, 1998), Sh Pr . . . . . . *Cited*, 00/6552
National Children's Home and Orphanage Trustees *v.* Stirrat Park Hogg 2001 S.C. 324;
    2001 S.L.T. 469; 2000 G.W.D. 35-1329, OH . . . . *Digested*, 01/**6679**
National Express Group Plc *v.* Campbell 2000 G.W.D. 37-1381, OH
National Trust for Scotland *v.* Macrae 2000 S.L.T. (Land Ct) 27; 2000 S.L.C.R. 56;
    2000 G.W.D. 31-1233, Land Ct (Full Ct) . . . . *Digested*, 01/**6748**
National Westminster Bank Plc *v.* WJ Elrick & Co 1991 S.L.T. 709; 1991 S.C.L.R. 621, OH   *Digested*, 91/**4417**:
                          Applied, 00/6507: *Distinguished*, 00/6516
Naylor *v.* Greenacres Curling Ltd 2001 S.L.T. 1092; 2001 G.W.D. 23-854, OH
Nazimudden, Petitioner see Sattar *v.* Secretary of State for the Home Department
Nazir *v.* Secretary of State for the Home Department 2001 G.W.D. 33-1311, OH
Neil *v.* HM Advocate 1998 G.W.D. 18-903, HCJ Appeal
Neil *v.* Stott 1999 G.W.D. 23-1091, HCJ Appeal
Neill *v.* HM Advocate 1998 G.W.D. 31-1586, HCJ Appeal
Neilson *v.* Brown 1999 G.W.D. 24-1138, HCJ Appeal
Neilson (David William) *v.* HM Advocate (Sentencing) 1989 S.C.C.R. 527, HCJ Appeal   *Digested*, 90/**5007**:
                                    Considered, 91/4819, 98/5657
Neilson *v.* Scottish Homes 1999 S.L.T. (Sh Ct) 2; 1998 Hous. L.R. 52; 1998 G.W.D. 6-
    286, Sh Pr . . . . *Digested*, 98/**5976**
Nelson *v.* Carnegie (Sentencing) 1999 G.W.D. 36-1755, HCJ Appeal
Nelson (John Holmes) *v.* HM Advocate 1994 J.C. 94; 1994 S.L.T. 389; 1994 S.C.C.R.
    192, HCJ Appeal. . . . . *Digested*, 94/**5509**:
                                              Applied, 99/5800
Nelson *v.* Williamson 2000 G.W.D. 2-35, Sh Ct
Ness (David William), Petitioner 1999 S.L.T. 214; 1998 S.C.C.R. 589; 1998 G.W.D. 28-1442,
    HCJ Appeal . . . . *Digested*, 98/**6055**
Ness *v.* Lees (Sentencing) 1998 G.W.D. 10-488, HCJ Appeal
Ness *v.* Stott 1999 G.W.D. 10-464, HCJ Appeal
Ness Training Ltd *v.* Triage Central Ltd 2001 G.W.D. 27-1075, OH
Network Housing Association Ltd *v.* Westminster City Council [1995] Env. L.R. 176;
    (1995) 27 H.L.R. 189; 93 L.G.R. 280; [1994] E.G.C.S. 173; *Times*, November 8,
    1994; *Independent*, November 7, 1994 (C.S.), QBD . . . . *Digested*, 96/**2745**:
               Considered, 96/2744, 00/2304: *Distinguished*, 96/2746: *Followed*, 00/6602
New Hearts Ltd *v.* Cosmopolitan Investments Ltd; *sub nom* Cosmopolitan Investments
    Ltd *v.* New Hearts Ltd [1997] 2 B.C.L.C. 249, OH . . . . *Digested*, 98/**5526**
New Timbiqui Gold Mines Ltd, Re [1961] Ch. 319; [1961] 2 W.L.R. 344; [1961] 1 All E.R. 865;
    105 S.J. 206, Ch D . . . . *Digested*, 61/**1167**:
                  Applied, 98/5521: *Considered*, 00/5956: *Followed*, 86/298, 87/338
Newall *v.* McFadyen 2001 G.W.D. 40-1514, HCJ Appeal
Newberry *v.* Simmonds [1961] 2 Q.B. 345; [1961] 2 W.L.R. 675; [1961] 2 All E.R.
    318; 125 J.P. 409; 59 L.G.R. 309; 105 S.J. 324, QBD . . . . *Digested*, 61/**7908**:
              Applied, 98/5591: *Considered*, 87/3289, 88/3129: *Distinguished*, 62/2723:
                                  Not followed, 61/7909, 62/3771
Newcastle Building Society *v.* Paterson Robertson & Graham 2001 S.C. 734; 2001
    S.C.L.R. 737; [2001] P.N.L.R. 36; [2001] N.P.C. 63; 2001 G.W.D. 12-446, OH . . *Digested*, 01/**6819**
Newcombe *v.* Walkingshaw (Sentencing) 1998 G.W.D. 15-753, HCJ Appeal
Newlands *v.* McLeod 2001 G.W.D. 2-84, HCJ Appeal
Newman *v.* HM Advocate 1999 G.W.D. 24-1151, HCJ Appeal
Newton *v.* Newton 1925 S.C. 715; 1925 S.L.T. 476, 2 Div . . . . *Distinguished*,
                                              00/6634
Newtongrange Branch of the Scottish National Party, Petitioners 1999 G.W.D. 35-1663, OH
Nguyen *v.* Searchnet Associates Ltd 2000 S.L.T. (Sh Ct) 83; 1999 S.C.L.R. 1075;
    [1999] 3 C.M.L.R. 413; 1999 G.W.D. 23-1106, Sh Pr . . . . *Digested*, 99/**5680**
Nicholas *v.* HM Advocate (Sentencing) 2000 G.W.D. 34-1307, HCJ Appeal
Nicholls *v.* Angus Council 1997 S.C.L.R. 941, Sh Ct . . . . *Digested*, 98/**6081**
Nicholson *v.* HM Advocate (Sentencing) 1999 G.W.D. 23-1095, HCJ Appeal
Nicholson *v.* HM Advocate (Sentencing) 1999 G.W.D. 35-1696, HCJ Appeal

Nicholson v. HM Advocate (Sentencing) 2001 G.W.D. 1-41, HCJ Appeal
Nicholson (Robert William) v. Westwater (Sentencing) 1995 S.L.T. 1018; 1995 S.C.C.R.
    428, HCJ Appeal . . . . *Digested,* 95/**6317**:
                                                      Followed, 00/6152

Nicol v. Advocate General for Scotland 2001 G.W.D. 25-963, OH
Nicol v. Higson (Sentencing) 1998 G.W.D. 1-31, HCJ Appeal
Nicol v. HM Advocate (Sentencing) 2000 J.C. 497; 2000 S.L.T. 811; 2000 S.C.C.R.
    499; 2000 G.W.D. 16-656, HCJ Appeal . . . . *Digested,* 00/**6149**
Nicol v. Lees (Sentencing) 1998 G.W.D. 11-549, HCJ Appeal
Nicol v. Lowe 1990 J.C. 107; 1990 S.L.T. 543; 1989 S.C.C.R. 675, HCJ Appeal . . . . *Digested,* 90/**4996**:
                                                      Approved, 99/5864

Nicol v. Nicol 2001 G.W.D. 23-865, Sh Pr
Nicol v. Scottish Power Plc 1998 S.L.T. 822; 1997 S.C.L.R. 1191; 1997 Rep. L.R.
    (Quantum) 19; 1997 G.W.D. 28-1432, OH. . . . . *Digested,* 97/**5953**
Nicol v. Shetland Islands Council 2001 G.W.D. 7-274, Lands Tr (Scot)
Nicol v. Walkingshaw 1998 G.W.D. 33-1706, HCJ Appeal
Nicoll v. Chief Constable of Tayside 1999 G.W.D. 32-1549, Sh Ct
Nicolson (Alan) v. HM Advocate 2001 S.C.C.R. 13; 2000 G.W.D. 29-1119, HCJ Appeal . *Digested,* 01/**6304**
Nicolson v. Tait & Peterson 2001 S.C.L.R. 766; 2001 G.W.D. 19-753, OH
Nigel Lowe & Associates v. John Mowlem Construction Plc 1999 S.L.T. 1298; 1998
    G.W.D. 35-1828, OH . . . . *Digested,* 00/**5990**
Nimmo v. British Railways Board 1999 S.L.T. 778; 1999 Rep. L.R. 30; 1998 G.W.D. 32-
    1674, OH . . . . *Digested,* 99/**5700**
Nimmo v. Secretary of State for Scotland 2000 Rep. L.R. 14, OH . . . . *Digested,* 00/**6173**
Nisbet v. Brown (Sentencing) 2000 G.W.D. 15-598, HCJ
Nisbet v. Crowe 1998 G.W.D. 36-1861, HCJ Appeal
Nisbet v. HM Advocate (Sentencing) 1998 G.W.D. 16-791, HCJ Appeal
Niven v. Heywood 1999 G.W.D. 15-722, HCJ Appeal
NJ&J Macfarlane (Developments) Ltd v. MacSween's Trustees 1999 S.L.T. 619; 1998
    G.W.D. 34-1760, OH . . . . *Digested,* 99/**6238**
Noble v. Crofters Sharing in Breakish Common Grazings 1999 S.L.C.R. 82, Land Ct . . . *Digested,* 99/**6317**
Noble v. De Boer 2001 G.W.D. 11-396, Sh Ct (Grampian)
Noble v. Glasgow City Council; *sub nom* Noble, Petitioner 2001 S.L.T. 2; 2000 Hous.
    L.R. 38; 2000 G.W.D. 4-115, OH. . . . . *Digested,* 00/**5833**
Noble v. Osprey Trawlers Ltd 1998 S.C. 835; 1998 G.W.D. 24-1223, Ex Div . . . . *Digested,* 99/**6028**
Noble v. Vannet 1998 G.W.D. 40-2086, HCJ Appeal
Noble's Trustees v. Economic Forestry (Scotland) Ltd 1988 S.L.T. 662, OH . . . . *Digested,* 88/**4578**:
                                            Applied, 01/6826: *Followed,* 93/4761

Noble, Petitioner see Noble v. Glasgow City Council
Nooh v. Secretary of State for the Home Department see Adan (Hassan Hussein) v.
    Secretary of State for the Home Department
Norman v. Lovie 1998 G.W.D. 26-1337, Sh Ct
Normand v. Donnelly 1994 S.L.T. 62; 1993 S.C.C.R. 639, HCJ Appeal . . . . *Digested,* 93/**5084**:
                                            Considered, 99/5841

Norquay v. HM Advocate (Sentencing) 1998 G.W.D. 5-226, HCJ Appeal
North Anderson Cars Ltd v. Customs and Excise Commissioners [1999] S.T.C. 902;
    2000 S.C. 37; 2000 S.L.T. 619; 2000 S.C.L.R. 273; [1999] B.T.C. 5335; [1999]
    B.V.C. 389; 1999 G.W.D. 30-1446, 2 Div; affirming [1998] B.V.C. 2174; [1998]
    V. & D.R. 11, V&DTr. . . . . *Digested,* 99/**6472**
                                            Applied, 00/5886
North British Railway v. Brown Gordon & Co (1857) 19 D. 840, 1 Div . . . . *Digested,* 00/**6640**
North East Fife DC v. Nisbet 2000 S.C.L.R. 413; 2000 G.W.D. 9-342, 2 Div . . . .
North Lanarkshire Council v. British Telecommunications Plc; *sub nom* North
    Lanarkshire Council v. BT Plc 2000 G.W.D. 27-1030, OH
North Lanarkshire Council v. BT Plc see North Lanarkshire Council v. British
    Telecommunications Plc
North Lanarkshire Council v. C 1998 S.C. 528; 1999 S.L.T. 238; 1998 G.W.D. 14-693, 2
    Div . . . . *Digested,* 98/**5861**
North Lanarkshire Council v. Local Government Property Commission (No.1) 1998
    G.W.D. 11-565, 1 Div; reversing 1998 G.W.D. 5-246, OH
North Lanarkshire Council v. Local Government Property Commission (No.2) 1998
    G.W.D. 22-1141, OH
North Uist Estate Trust 1990 v. Morrison 2000 S.L.C.R. 120, Land Ct (Div Ct) . . . . *Digested,* 01/**6746**
Northern Joint Police Board v. Power [1997] I.R.L.R. 610, EAT. *Digested,* 98/**5811**:
                                            Considered, 01/6473

Norwest Holst Construction Ltd v. Dumfries and Galloway Council 1999 S.C.L.R. 915;
    1999 G.W.D. 13-589, 2 Div . . . . *Digested,* 00/**5978**
Norwich Union Life Insurance Society v. Svenska Handelsbanken see Norwich Union
    Life Insurance Society v. Tanap Investments VK Ltd (In Liquidation) (No.3)
Norwich Union Life Insurance Society v. Tanap Investments VK Ltd (In Liquidation)
    (No.1) 1998 S.L.T. 623; 1997 G.W.D. 24-1183, OH. . . . . *Digested,* 98/**5446**
Norwich Union Life Insurance Society v. Tanap Investments VK Ltd (In Liquidation)
    (No.3); Norwich Union Life Insurance Society v. Svenska Handelsbanken 2000
    S.C. 515; 2000 S.L.T. 819; 2000 S.C.L.R. 1034; 2000 G.W.D. 19-736, Ex Div;
    affirming 1999 S.L.T. 204; 1998 S.C.L.R. 627; 1998 G.W.D. 14-700, OH . . . . *Digested,* 00/**5992**

Norwood v. HM Advocate (Sentencing) 1998 G.W.D. 5-219, HCJ Appeal
Nothard v. Lees 1998 G.W.D. 26-1344, HCJ Appeal
Nottay's Trustee v. Nottay; *sub nom* Accountant in Bankruptcy v. Nottay 2001 S.L.T.
  769; 2000 G.W.D. 28-1091, OH
Nova Glaze Replacement Windows Ltd v. Clark Thomson & Co 2001 S.C. 815; 2001
  G.W.D. 13-508, OH
Novacold v. Fridge Freight (Fyvie) Ltd (In Receivership) 1999 S.C.L.R. 409, Sh Pr . . . .   *Digested*, 99/**6321**
Nwokoye v. Secretary of State for the Home Department; *sub nom* Nwokoye,
  Petitioner 2001 S.C.L.R. 909; 2001 G.W.D. 22-835, OH
Nwokoye, Petitioner see Nwokoye v. Secretary of State for the Home Department
NWS Trust Ltd v. Siwek 1998 G.W.D. 19-959, 1 Div
Nykredit Mortgage Bank Plc v. Edward Erdman Group Ltd see South Australia Asset
  Management Corp v. York Montague Ltd

O'Brien v. Duke of Argyll's Trustees 1999 S.L.T. (Sh Ct) 88; 1999 G.W.D. 13-623, Sh Ct
  (North Strathclyde) . . . .   *Digested*, 99/**6222**
O'Brien v. HM Advocate 1999 G.W.D. 31-1476, HCJ Appeal
O'Brien (Alan) v. HM Advocate 2001 S.L.T. 1101; 2001 S.C.C.R. 542; 2001 G.W.D. 20-
  761, HCJ Appeal . . . .   *Digested*, 01/**6362**
O'Brien v. McCreadie (Senga Miller) 1994 S.C.C.R. 516, HCJ Appeal . . . .   *Digested*, 94/**5538**:
                                                                                              Referred to, 00/6018
O'Brien (Darren) v. Ruxton 1999 S.C.C.R. 217; 1999 G.W.D. 8-382, HCJ Appeal . . . . . .   *Digested*, 99/**5890**
O'Brien's Curator Bonis v. British Steel Plc 1991 S.C. 315; 1991 S.L.T. 477; 1991 S.C.L.R.
  831, 1 Div; reversing in part 1990 S.C.L.R. 566; Scotsman, March 14, 1990, OH .   *Digested*, 91/**4906**:
          Followed, 94/5753, 96/6881: *Not followed*, 98/5743, 99/5972, 99/5974
O'Connor v. Atlantis Fisheries Ltd 1998 S.L.T. (Sh Ct) 61; 1998 S.C.L.R. 401; 1998
  G.W.D. 8-359, Sh Pr . . . .   *Digested*, 98/**6010**
O'Doherty v. Renfrewshire Council 1997 S.C. 238; 1998 S.L.T. 327; 1997 S.C.L.R. 821;
  [1997] 7 S.L.L.P. 6; 1997 G.W.D. 14-625, Ex Div . . . .   *Digested*, 97/**6216**
O'Donnell v. Fife Council 2001 G.W.D. 1-74, OH
O'Hagan v. Rea 2001 S.L.T. (Sh Ct) 30; 2001 G.W.D. 2-94, Sh Ct (South Strathclyde) . .   *Digested*, 01/**6440**
O'Hara v. Central SMT Co Ltd 1941 S.C. 363; 1941 S.L.T. 202, 1 Div . . . .   *Applied*, 52/752,
          52/754, 52/2798, 71/4587: *Considered*, 00/4217: *Distinguished*, 48/4584,
          57/4189, 98/5564: *Followed*, 47-51/2502, 47-51/6908, 47/2502, 50/4686,
                                                                          50/5313, 66/13332
O'Hare v. HM Advocate (Sentencing) 2001 G.W.D. 29-1160, HCJ Appeal
O'Neil v. McGlennan 1999 G.W.D. 27-1288, HCJ Appeal
O'Neill v. Brown (Sentencing) 2000 G.W.D. 8-298, HCJ Appeal
O'Neill v. Crowe (Sentencing) 1998 G.W.D. 4-171, HCJ Appeal
O'Neill v. Higson (Sentencing) 2001 G.W.D. 29-1156, HCJ Appeal
O'Neill v. HM Advocate (Sentencing) 1998 G.W.D. 16-795, HCJ Appeal
O'Neill v. HM Advocate (Sentencing) 1999 G.W.D. 35-1720, HCJ Appeal
O'Neill (John) v. HM Advocate 1999 S.L.T. 958; 1999 S.C.C.R. 300; 1999 G.W.D. 16-
  754, HCJ Appeal . . . .   *Digested*, 99/**5949**:
                                                                              Distinguished, 00/6148
O'Neill (Thomas) v. HM Advocate; Pugh (Justin St John) v. HM Advocate 1999 J.C. 1;
  1999 S.L.T. 364; 1998 S.C.C.R. 644; 1998 G.W.D. 37-1910, HCJ Appeal . . . . . .   *Digested*, 99/**5950**
O'Neill v. Stott 1999 G.W.D. 23-1090, HCJ Appeal
O'Neill v. Wilson 1983 J.C. 42; 1983 S.L.T. 573; 1983 S.C.C.R. 265, HCJ Appeal . . . . . .   *Digested*, 83/**4158**:
                                                                              Considered, 98/5623
O'Pray v. HM Advocate (Sentencing) 2000 G.W.D. 19-748, HCJ Appeal
O'Regan v. Williams see Fitzgerald v. Williams
O'Reilly v. Carnegie 1999 G.W.D. 13-607, HCJ Appeal
O'Reilly v. Lees (Sentencing) 1998 G.W.D. 9-448, HCJ Appeal
O'Rourke v. HM Advocate 1998 G.W.D. 29-1474, HCJ Appeal
O'Sullivan v. O'Sullivan 2001 S.C.L.R. 696; 2001 G.W.D. 13-462, Sh Pr
Oakes v. Angiolini (Sentencing) 2001 G.W.D. 39-1446, HCJ Appeal
Oakes v. McFadyen 1999 G.W.D. 28-1312, HCJ Appeal
Oates v. Vannet 1998 G.W.D. 35-1797, HCJ Appeal
OBC Caspian Ltd v. Thorp 1998 S.L.T. 653; 1997 S.C.L.R. 946; 1997 G.W.D. 25-1239,
  OH . . . .   *Digested*, 98/**5523**
Oceaneering International Services Ltd v. Offshore Project Management Support
  Services Ltd 1999 S.L.T. 1045; 1998 G.W.D. 17-841, OH . . . .   *Digested*, 99/**5707**
Official Receiver v. Jacob see Walter L Jacob & Co Ltd, Re
Oghonoghor v. Secretary of State for the Home Department 1995 S.L.T. 733, OH . . . . .   *Digested*, 95/**5923**:
                                                                              Followed, 00/6501
Ogilvie (Glen Stewart), Petitioner see Ogilvie (Glen Stewart) v. HM Advocate (No.1)
Ogilvie v. Heywood 2001 G.W.D. 18-695, HCJ Appeal
Ogilvie (Alan Joseph) v. HM Advocate (Sentencing) 2001 S.L.T. 1391; 2001 S.C.C.R.
  792; 2001 G.W.D. 26-1046, HCJ Appeal . . . .   *Digested*, 01/**6402**
Ogilvie (Glen Stewart) v. HM Advocate (No.1); *sub nom* Ogilvie (Glen Stewart),
  Petitioner 1998 J.C. 125; 1998 S.L.T. 1339; 1998 S.C.C.R. 187; 1998 G.W.D. 9-
  438, HCJ Appeal . . . .   *Digested*, 98/**5606**

Ogilvie (Glen Stewart) v. HM Advocate (No.2) 1999 S.L.T. 1068; 1999 G.W.D. 14-632,
    HCJ Appeal . . . .   *Digested*, 99/**5899**
Oliver v. Brown & Root McDermott Fabricators Ltd (t/a Barmac) 2000 S.C.L.R. 628,
    OH . . . .   *Digested*, 00/**6171**
Oliver & Son Ltd, Petitioners 1999 S.C. 656; 1999 S.L.T. 1039; 2000 S.C.L.R. 599; 1999
    G.W.D. 25-1179, 1 Div 1999 G.W.D. 22-1028, OH . . . .   *Digested*, 99/**5703**
Onifade v. Secretary of State for Social Security 1999 S.C.L.R. 836; 1999 G.W.D. 17-
    819, Sh Ct . . . .   *Digested*, 00/**6686**
Onyicke v. Heywood (Sentencing) 2000 G.W.D. 19-743, HCJ Appeal
Optical Express (Gyle) Ltd v. Marks & Spencer Plc 2000 S.L.T. 644; 2000 G.W.D. 7-
    264, OH . . . .   *Digested*, 00/**6527**
Orkney Islands Council v. Charles Brand Ltd; *sub nom* Orkney Islands Council,
    Petitioners 2001 G.W.D. 29-1152, OH
Orkney Islands Council v. Local Government Boundary Commission for Scotland see
    Shetland Islands Council v. Local Government Boundary Commission for
    Scotland
Orkney Islands Council, Petitioners see Orkney Islands Council v. Charles Brand Ltd
Orme v. Ruxton 1999 S.C.C.R. 344; 1999 G.W.D. 15-700, HCJ Appeal . . . .   *Digested*, 99/**5839**
Ormiston v. HM Advocate 2000 G.W.D. 37-1390, HCJ Appeal
Orr v. Carnegie (Sentencing) 2001 G.W.D. 12-419, HCJ Appeal
Orr v. Carnegie (Sentencing: Backdating) 1998 G.W.D. 1-27, HCJ Appeal
Orr v. McGlennan (Sentencing) 1998 G.W.D. 4-173, HCJ Appeal
Orrock v. Griffiths (Sentencing) 2001 G.W.D. 39-1471, HCJ Appeal
Orru v. HM Advocate 1998 S.C.C.R. 59; 1998 G.W.D. 5-235, HCJ Appeal . . . .   *Digested*, 98/**6205**
Orttewell v. Gilchrist (No.1) 1998 S.L.T. (Sh Ct) 63; 1998 S.C.L.R. 451; 1998 G.W.D. 9-
    466, Sh Pr . . . .   *Digested*, 98/**6048**:
                                                                                                                Referred to, 00/6543
Orttewell v. Gilchrist (No.2) 2001 G.W.D. 28-1136, Sh Pr
Osborne v. BBC 2000 S.C. 29; 2000 S.L.T. 150; 2000 S.C.L.R. 401; 1999 G.W.D. 30-
    1404, Ex Div . . . .   *Digested*, 00/**5924**
Osborne v. HM Advocate (Sentencing) 2001 G.W.D. 39-1467, HCJ Appeal
Osborne v. Matthan (No.1) 1997 S.C. 29; 1997 S.L.T. 811; 1997 S.C.L.R. 154, 1 Div. . . . .   *Digested*, 97/**5634**:
                                                                                                                Considered, 98/5848
Osborne v. Matthan (No.2) 1998 G.W.D. 9-424, Ex Div
Osborne v. Matthan (No.3) 1998 S.C. 682; 1998 S.L.T. 1264; 1998 S.C.L.R. 691; 1998
    G.W.D. 19-955, 1 Div . . . .   *Digested*, 98/**5848**:
                                                                                                                Followed, 00/6256
Osborne & Hunter Ltd v. Hardie Caldwell (No.1) 1999 S.L.T. 153; 1998 G.W.D. 28-1449,
    2 Div; reversing 1998 S.L.T. 420, OH . . . .   *Digested*, 99/**6420**
Osborne & Hunter Ltd v. Hardie Caldwell (No.2) 2001 G.W.D. 4-174, OH
Overwaele, Petitioner see Van Overwaele v. Hacking & Paterson
Oyeneyin v. Oyeneyin 1999 G.W.D. 38-1836, Sh Ct

P v. Aberdeen City Council 2001 Fam. L.R. 127; 2001 G.W.D. 25-919, Ex Div
P v. HM Advocate (Sentencing) 1998 G.W.D. 7-347, HCJ Appeal
P v. P 1999 S.C.L.R. 679, Sh Ct. . . . .   *Digested*, 99/**6069**
P v. P (Contact: Supervision) 2000 S.L.T. 781; 2000 S.C.L.R. 477; 2000 Fam. L.R. 26;
    2000 G.W.D. 10-349, Ex Div . . . .   *Digested*, 00/**6261**
P v. S 2001 G.W.D. 19-714, Ex Div
P&O Property Holdings Ltd v. Glasgow City Council 2000 S.L.T. 444; 1999 S.C.L.R.
    216; [2000] R.A. 447; 1998 G.W.D. 40-2080, OH . . . .   *Digested*, 99/**6428**
P&O Scottish Ferries Ltd v. Braer Corp [1999] 2 Lloyd's Rep. 535; 1999 S.C.L.R. 540;
    1999 G.W.D. 4-227; *Times*, March 10, 1999, OH. . . . .   *Digested*, 99/**6446**
P's Curator Bonis v. Criminal Injuries Compensation Board; *sub nom* A's Curator Bonis
    v. Criminal Injuries Compensation Board; Millar v. Criminal Injuries Compensation
    Board 1997 S.L.T. 1180; 1997 S.C.L.R. 69; (1998) 44 B.M.L.R. 70; 1997 Rep.
    L.R. 3; *Times*, January 24, 1997, OH . . . .   *Digested*, 97/**5783**
Pacetta v. Clydesdale Bank Plc 2000 G.W.D. 38-1437, OH
Pae v. HM Advocate (Sentencing) 1998 G.W.D. 7-338, HCJ Appeal
Pagan v. Miller Group Ltd 2001 G.W.D. 38-1428, OH
Page v. Sheerness Steel Co Plc see Wells v. Wells
Page v. Smith [1996] A.C. 155; [1995] 2 W.L.R. 644; [1995] 2 All E.R. 736; [1995] 2
    Lloyd's Rep. 95; [1995] R.T.R. 210; [1995] P.I.Q.R. P329; (1995) 92(23) L.S.G.
    33; (1995) 145 N.L.J. 723; (1995) 139 S.J.L.B. 173; *Times*, May 12, 1995;
    Independent, May 12, 1995; *Lloyd's List*, May 25, 1995 (I.D.), HL; reversing
    [1994] 4 All E.R. 522; [1994] R.T.R. 293; [1995] P.I.Q.R. P58; (1994) 144
    N.L.J. 756; *Times*, May 4, 1994, CA; reversing [1993] P.I.Q.R. Q55, QBD . . . .   *Digested*, 95/**3682**:
         Applied, 99/3978, 00/6582: *Considered*, 96/4426, 96/4478, 96/4862,
                            98/3954, 98/3981, 99/4059, 00/4220, 00/6598: *Followed*, 99/3980
Paini v. McGlennan 1999 G.W.D. 36-1740, HCJ Appeal
Palmer v. Forsyth 1999 S.L.T. (Sh Ct) 93, Sh Ct (Tayside). . . . .   *Digested*, 00/**6435**
Palmer v. Heywood (Sentencing) 2000 G.W.D. 15-601, HCJ
Park v. Lothian Health Board 1998 G.W.D. 19-990, OH

Park v. Park 2000 S.L.T. (Sh Ct) 65; 2000 G.W.D. 14-517, Sh Pr . . . . *Digested*, 00/**6257**
Parker v. HM Advocate (Sentencing) 1998 G.W.D. 24-1202, HCJ Appeal
Parker v. HM Advocate (Sentencing) 2001 G.W.D. 12-451, HCJ Appeal
Parker v. Lees 1998 G.W.D. 28-1454, HCJ Appeal
Parker v. Secretary of State for Scotland 1998 S.L.T. 299; 1997 S.C.L.R. 829; 1997
    G.W.D. 14-628, 2 Div . . . . *Digested*, 98/**6136**
Parkes v. Secretary of State for Scotland 1998 G.W.D. 6-292, 1 Div
Parks v. West Lothian NHS Trust 1998 S.C.L.R. 201; 1997 G.W.D. 35-1794, OH . . . . *Digested*, 98/**5752**
Parratt v. Ceiling Decor Ltd (No.1) 1998 S.C. 179; 1999 S.L.T. 53; 1998 S.C.L.R. 557;
    1998 G.W.D. 2-87, OH . . . . *Digested*, 98/**5472**
Parratt v. Ceiling Decor Ltd (No.2) 1998 G.W.D. 13-673, OH
Parry v. Cleaver [1970] A.C. 1; [1969] 2 W.L.R. 821; [1969] 1 All E.R. 555; [1969] 1
    Lloyd's Rep. 183; 6 K.I.R. 265; 113 S.J. 147, HL; reversing [1968] 1 Q.B. 195;
    [1967] 3 W.L.R. 739; [1967] 2 All E.R. 1168; 2 K.I.R. 844; 111 S.J. 415, CA . . . . . *Digested*, 69/**906**:
                      Applied, 69/917, 69/919, 71/3207, 72/836, 73/729, 73/740, 74/814, 75/3217,
                      76/677, 76/2517, 79/2472, 84/1004, 85/942, 85/3398, 86/350, 87/1220,
                      88/1069, 89/1285, 92/2029, 94/2039, 01/6413: *Considered*, 72/826,
                      72/834, 78/788, 80/630, 82/894, 83/1272, 86/981, 87/394, 87/1161,
                      88/1070, 96/1218, 96/4527, 96/6896, 98/2099, 99/810, 00/5816:
                      Disapproved, 78/719: *Distinguished*, 95/1613, 96/3603, 99/3410:
                      Followed, 77/773, 90/5070, 91/1327, 98/1468, 99/3411, 00/1488
Partnership of MFV Ocean Quest v. Finning Ltd 2000 S.L.T. (Sh Ct) 157; 1999 S.C.L.R.
    1105; 1999 G.W.D. 15-684, Sh Pr . . . . *Digested*, 00/**5932**
Pascoe-Watson v. Brock's Executor 1998 S.L.T. 40; 1997 G.W.D. 4-159, OH . . . . *Digested*, 97/**6450**
Paterson v. Butler 2001 G.W.D. 40-1527, OH
Paterson v. Crowe 1998 G.W.D. 29-1519, HCJ Appeal
Paterson v. George Wimpey & Co Ltd 1999 S.L.T. 577; 1998 Rep. L.R. 132; 1998
    G.W.D. 28-1452, OH . . . . *Digested*, 99/**6417**
Paterson v. Higson 1998 G.W.D. 17-842, HCJ Appeal
Paterson v. HM Advocate 1999 G.W.D. 17-817, HCJ Appeal
Paterson v. HM Advocate (Sentencing) 2000 G.W.D. 33-1288, HCJ Appeal
Paterson (Alexander) v. HM Advocate 1998 J.C. 183; 1998 S.L.T. 117; 1997 S.C.C.R.
    707; 1997 G.W.D. 34-1710, HCJ Appeal . . . . *Digested*, 98/**5573**
Paterson (John) v. HM Advocate 2000 S.L.T. 833; 1999 S.C.C.R. 750; 1999 G.W.D.
    30-1407, HCJ Appeal . . . . *Digested*, 00/**6000**
Paterson v. Lees (Sentencing) 1998 G.W.D. 32-1683, HCJ Appeal
Paterson (Tate Wilson) v. Lees 1999 J.C. 159; 1999 S.C.C.R. 231; 1999 G.W.D. 9-414,
    HCJ Appeal . . . . *Digested*, 99/**5848**
Paterson v. Ogilvy 1957 J.C. 42; 1957 S.L.T. 354, HCJ Appeal . . . . *Digested*, 57/**4320**:
                      Applied, 98/5582
Paterson v. Paterson 2001 G.W.D. 38-1416, Sh Ct (Grampian)
Paterson, Petitioner 2000 S.C. 574; 2001 S.L.T. 869; 2001 S.C.L.R. 134; 2000 G.W.D. 25-
    932, OH . . . . *Digested*, 01/**6500**
Paton v. Clark 1999 G.W.D. 32-1533, HCJ Appeal
Paton v. HM Advocate 1999 G.W.D. 26-1249, HCJ Appeal
Paton (Glen Christie) v. HM Advocate (Sentencing) 2001 G.W.D. 36-1383, HCJ Appeal
Paton v. Houston (Sentencing) 2000 G.W.D. 20-797, HCJ Appeal
Paton v. Loffland Brothers North Sea Inc 1994 S.L.T. 784, OH . . . . *Digested*, 94/**6008**:
                      Followed, 98/5482
Paton v. Ritchie 2000 J.C. 271; 2000 S.L.T. 239; 2000 S.C.C.R. 151; 1999 G.W.D. 39-
    1886, HCJ Appeal . . . . *Digested*, 00/**6121**
Paton v. Sarwar 2001 G.W.D. 38-1427, Ex Div; affirming 2000 G.W.D. 36-1361, OH
Paton v. Tube Developments Ltd 2001 Rep. L.R. 132 (Note); 2001 G.W.D. 19-751, OH
Patterson v. Donnelly 1999 G.W.D. 5-238, HCJ Appeal
Patterson (Ronald Thomas) v. Gilchrist 1999 S.C.C.R. 419, HCJ Appeal . . . . *Digested*, 99/**5938**
Patterson v. HM Advocate (Hearsay Evidence) 2000 J.C. 137; 2000 S.L.T. 302; 1999
    G.W.D. 34-1619, HCJ Appeal . . . . *Digested*, 00/**5995**
Patterson v. HM Advocate (Sentencing) 1999 G.W.D. 35-1719, HCJ Appeal
Patterson v. Howdle 1999 J.C. 56; 1999 S.C.C.R. 41; 1999 G.W.D. 3-117, HCJ Appeal . . *Digested*, 99/**5801**
Patterson v. Menzies 2001 S.C.L.R. 266; 2001 G.W.D. 1-5, OH . . . . *Digested*, 01/**6247**
Pattison v. Fitzgerald (1823) 2 S. 536, 2 Div . . . . *Distinguished*, 99/5703
Patton v. Vannet 1999 G.W.D. 36-1735, HCJ Appeal
Paul v. Ogilvy 2001 S.L.T. 171; 2000 G.W.D. 5-176, OH . . . . *Digested*, 01/**6420**
Paxton (Nicholas John) v. HM Advocate 2000 J.C. 56; 2000 S.L.T. 771; 1999 S.C.C.R.
    895; 1999 G.W.D. 31-1459, HCJ Appeal . . . . *Digested*, 00/**6017**
Payne v. Heywood see Millar v. Dickson
Payne v. HM Advocate 1998 G.W.D. 26-1309, HCJ Appeal
Peace v. Edinburgh City Council 1999 S.L.T. 712; 1999 S.C.L.R. 593; [1999] I.R.L.R.
    417; 1999 G.W.D. 8-394, OH . . . . *Digested*, 99/**6033**
Peachey v. Friel 1998 G.W.D. 26-1317, HCJ Appeal
Peacock v. Sutton 1999 S.L.T. (Sh Ct) 69; 1998 G.W.D. 15-766, Sh Pr. . . . . *Digested*, 99/**5684**
Pearson v. Crowe 1994 S.L.T. 378, HCJ Appeal . . . . *Digested*, 94/**5609**:
                      Followed, 00/6105

Pearson v. Educational Institute of Scotland 1997 S.C. 245; 1998 S.L.T. 189; 1997
   G.W.D. 18-812, 2 Div; affirming 1997 S.C.L.R. 933; 1997 G.W.D. 2-47, OH . . . . .   *Digested,* 98/**5448**
Pearson v. Gilchrist (Sentencing) 2000 G.W.D. 37-1404, HCJ Appeal
Pearson v. Hickman 2001 G.W.D. 7-286, 1 Div
Pearson v. O'Donnell (Sentencing) 1998 G.W.D. 4-190, HCJ Appeal
Pearson v. Pearson 1999 S.L.T. 1364; 1999 G.W.D. 32-1507, Ex Div. . . . .   *Digested,* 00/**6256**
Peden v. Lothian Region Transport 2001 S.L.T. 985; 2001 S.C.L.R. 1078; 2001 G.W.D.
   27-1081, OH . . . .   *Digested,* 01/**6253**
Peebles v. Bowman (formerly Peebles) 2001 S.C.L.R. 712; 2001 Fam. L.R. 101; 2001
   G.W.D. 19-732, OH
Peebles v. Brown; *sub nom* Peebles v. Crowe 2000 J.C. 548; 2000 G.W.D. 16-673,
   HCJ Appeal . . . .   *Digested,* 00/**6034**
Peebles v. Crowe see Peebles v. Brown
Peel's Trustees v. Drummond 1936 S.C. 786; 1936 S.L.T. 467, 1 Div . . . .   *Applied,* 00/6616
Penk v. Wright see Alcock v. Chief Constable of South Yorkshire
Penman v. A&S Scaffolding see Penman v. Smillie
Penman v. Blue Cap Logistics Ltd 1999 S.L.T. 1246; 1999 Rep. L.R. 91; 1999 G.W.D.
   12-536, OH . . . .   *Digested,* 99/**6364**:
                                                                                                            Not followed, 00/6581
Penman v. Higson (Sentencing) 2000 G.W.D. 33-1276, HCJ Appeal
Penman (Andrew Walker) v. HM Advocate 1999 S.C.C.R. 740, HCJ Appeal . . . .   *Digested,* 00/**6136**
Penman v. McFadyen (Sentencing) 2000 G.W.D. 19-774, HCJ Appeal
Penman v. Smillie; *sub nom* Penman v. A&S Scaffolding 1998 S.L.T. 966; 1997 Rep.
   L.R. 125; 1997 G.W.D. 32-1607, OH . . . .   *Digested,* 98/**5937**
Penman v. Spiers 1999 S.L.T. 490; 1998 S.C.C.R. 514; 1998 G.W.D. 27-1359, HCJ
   Appeal . . . .   *Digested,* 98/**5627**
Penman v. Stott 2001 S.C.C.R. 911; 2001 G.W.D. 36-1363, HCJ Appeal
Pennycuick v. Lees 1992 S.L.T. 763; 1992 S.C.C.R. 160, HCJ Appeal. . . . .   *Digested,* 92/**5364**:
                                                                                                            Applied, 99/5807
Pentland v. Munro 1998 G.W.D. 19-954, HCJ Appeal
Peralta v. Carnegie 1999 G.W.D. 11-503, HCJ Appeal
Percy v. Board of National Mission of the Church of Scotland 2001 S.C. 757; 2001
   S.L.T. 497; 2001 G.W.D. 12-434, 1 Div
Percy (David) v. HM Advocate 1998 S.L.T. 333; 1997 G.W.D. 28-1411, HCJ Appeal . . . .   *Digested,* 98/**5641**:
                                                                                                            Explained, 99/5896
Perendes v. Sim 1998 S.L.T. 1382; 1998 G.W.D. 15-735, OH . . . .   *Digested,* 99/**6061**
Perera v. Civil Service Commission (No.1) [1980] I.C.R. 699; [1980] I.R.L.R. 233, EAT .   *Digested,* 81/**875**:
                                                                                                            Disapproved, 98/5819
Perkins v. McFadyen (Sentencing) 2001 S.C.C.R. 264; 2001 G.W.D. 6-214, HCJ
   Appeal . . . .   *Digested,* 01/**6399**
Perrie v. Heywood 1998 G.W.D. 33-1694, HCJ Appeal
Perrie v. Munro 1998 G.W.D. 19-986, HCJ Appeal
Perry v. West 2000 J.C. 122; 2000 S.L.T. 363; 2000 S.C.C.R. 43; 1999 G.W.D. 33-
   1592, HCJ Appeal. . . . .   *Digested,* 00/**6307**
Perth and Kinross Council v. Roy 1999 Hous. L.R. 10, Sh Pr   *Digested,* 99/**6276**
Perth and Kinross Council v. Secretary of State for Scotland 1999 S.C. 144; 1999 S.L.T.
   1095; 1998 G.W.D. 38-1976, 2 Div. . . . .   *Digested,* 99/**6411**
Perth City Wall Ltd v. Smart Events Ltd 2001 G.W.D. 23-871, OH
Pervez v. Clark 2001 S.C.C.R. 138; 2000 G.W.D. 40-1515, HCJ Appeal
Peterhead Snooker Co Ltd v. Strachan 2001 G.W.D. 20-777, Sh Ct (Grampian)
Peters v. HM Advocate 1999 G.W.D. 29-1379, HCJ Appeal
Petire v. HM Advocate 1998 G.W.D. 11-530, HCJ Appeal
Petro v. Heywood 1999 G.W.D. 9-420, HCJ Appeal
Pettie v. Thomson Pettie Tube Products Ltd 2001 S.C. 431; 2001 S.L.T. 473; 2000
   G.W.D. 40-1479, OH
Pettigrew v. Inverclyde Council 1999 Hous. L.R. 31, Sh Ct . . . .   *Digested,* 99/**6380**
Phillips v. HM Advocate 1999 G.W.D. 27-1278, HCJ Appeal
Phillips v. Kvaerner Govan Ltd 2001 G.W.D. 40-1497, 2 Div
Phillips v. McFadyen 1999 G.W.D. 20-944, HCJ Appeal
Phillips v. Strathclyde Joint Police Board 2001 S.L.T. 1271; 2001 G.W.D. 26-1069, OH. . .   *Digested,* 01/**6864**
Piacentini v. McGlennan (Sentencing) 2001 G.W.D. 10-350, HCJ Appeal
Pickering v. HM Advocate (Sentencing) 1998 G.W.D. 7-337, HCJ Appeal
Pickthall v. HM Advocate 1998 G.W.D. 29-1465, HCJ Appeal
Pickthall (Neil) v. HM Advocate 1998 S.L.T. 1117; 1997 S.C.C.R. 586; 1997 G.W.D. 27-
   1360, HCJ Appeal. . . . .   *Digested,* 97/**5867**
Pietryea v. Strathclyde RC 1998 S.L.T. 184; 1997 Rep. L.R. 74; 1997 G.W.D. 16-711, OH. .   *Digested,* 97/**5690**
PIK Facilities Ltd v. Lord Advocate 1997 S.C.L.R. 855; 1997 G.W.D. 27-1374, OH. . . . . .   *Digested,* 98/**6036**
Pinkerton v. Pinkerton 1986 S.L.T. 672, OH . . . .   *Digested,* 86/**4199**:
                                                                   Distinguished, 94/5964, 96/7114, 98/6031
Pinochet Ugarte (No.2), Re see R. v. Bow Street Metropolitan Stipendiary Magistrate Ex
   p. Pinochet Ugarte (No.2)
Pinytek v. Secretary of State for the Home Department 2000 S.C. 158; 2000 G.W.D. 1-
   22, Ex Div. . . . .   *Digested,* 00/**6492**

Pioneer Aggregates (UK) Ltd v. Secretary of State for the Environment [1985] A.C. 132;
   [1984] 3 W.L.R. 32; [1984] 2 All E.R. 358; 82 L.G.R. 488; (1984) 48 P. &
   C.R. 95; (1984) 272 E.G. 425; [1984] J.P.L. 651; (1984) 81 L.S.G. 2148; (1984)
   128 S.J. 416, HL; affirming 82 L.G.R. 112; (1983) 267 E.G. 941; [1983] J.P.L.
   733, CA; affirming (1983) 46 P. & C.R. 113; [1982] J.P.L. 371, QBD . . . . *Digested*, 84/**3465**:
                                    Applied, 85/3476, 86/3348, 92/4357, 00/4515: *Approved*, 99/4255:
                   Considered, 89/3569, 90/3917, 90/4435, 91/3457, 92/4272, 92/4373,
                      93/3956, 95/4770, 98/6136: *Distinguished*, 86/3337, 87/3710:
                                    Followed, 88/3517, 89/3553
Pioneer Seafood Ltd v. Braer Corp 1999 S.C.L.R. 1126; [2000] B.C.C. 680; 1999
   G.W.D. 20-956, OH . . . . *Digested*, 00/**5916**
Pipetronix (UK) Ltd v. Zijlstra (No.1) 2001 G.W.D. 12-407, Sh Ct (Grampian)
Pipetronix (UK) Ltd v. Zijlstra (No.2) 2001 G.W.D. 18-700, Sh Ct (Grampian)
Pirie v. HM Advocate 1998 G.W.D. 17-856, HCJ Appeal
Pithie v. Clark 2001 G.W.D. 25-946, HCJ Appeal
Pizzey v. Vannet (Sentencing) 2000 G.W.D. 13-510, HCJ Appeal
Platt (Raymond) v. HM Advocate 2000 J.C. 468; 2001 S.L.T. 87; 2000 S.C.C.R. 620;
   2000 G.W.D. 16-643, HCJ Appeal . . . . *Digested*, 00/**5997**
Platt v. Vannet (Sentencing) 1998 G.W.D. 9-462, HCJ Appeal
Plews v. Plaisted (No.2) 1997 S.L.T. 1371; 1997 G.W.D. 27-1373, OH . . . . *Digested*, 98/**6016**
Ploetner v. Ploetner 1997 S.C.L.R. 998, Sh Ct . . . . *Digested*, 98/**5944**
Pole v. Heywood 1999 G.W.D. 8-407, HCJ Appeal
Polkey v. AE Dayton Services Ltd; *sub nom* Polkey v. Edmund Walker (Holdings) Ltd
   [1988] A.C. 344; [1987] 3 W.L.R. 1153; [1987] 3 All E.R. 974; [1988] I.C.R. 142;
   [1987] I.R.L.R. 503; (1987) 137 N.L.J. 1109; (1988) 138 N.L.J. Rep. 33;
   (1987) 131 S.J. 1624, HL; reversing [1987] 1 W.L.R. 1147; [1987] 1 All E.R. 984;
   [1987] I.C.R. 301; [1987] I.R.L.R. 13; (1987) 84 L.S.G. 2690; (1987) 131 S.J.
   1062, CA . . . . *Digested*, 88/**1353**:
               Applied, 89/1500, 90/1927, 92/1985, 96/2655, 98/2238, 99/2115, 99/2135,
           00/2190: *Considered*, 86/1266, 89/1440, 90/1895, 92/1946, 92/1988,
               94/2022, 94/2025, 94/2026, 95/2079, 95/2098, 96/2664, 97/2283,
                      01/2313: *Explained*, 99/6048: *Referred to*, 91/1704
Polkey v. Edmund Walker (Holdings) Ltd see Polkey v. AE Dayton Services Ltd
Polkinghorne v. Lees 1999 G.W.D. 14-674, HCJ Appeal
Pollard v. Munro 1998 G.W.D. 19-965, HCJ Appeal
Pollock v. Bell; *sub nom* Pollock v. Ishoka 2001 Rep. L.R. 132 (Note); 2001 G.W.D. 21-
   816, Sh Ct (Grampian)
Pollock (Mark) v. HM Advocate 1998 S.L.T. 880; 1998 G.W.D. 13-637, HCJ Appeal . . . *Digested*, 98/**5585**
Pollock v. Ishoka see Pollock v. Bell
Pont v. McFadyen 2001 G.W.D. 18-711, HCJ Appeal
Pool v. Howdle (Sentencing) 2000 G.W.D. 4-130, HCJ Appeal
Porte v. Vannet 1998 G.W.D. 39-2000, HCJ Appeal
Porteous v. Lees 1999 G.W.D. 14-675, HCJ Appeal
Porteous v. Stott 1999 G.W.D. 27-1289, HCJ Appeal
Porter v. HM Advocate (Sentencing) 1998 G.W.D. 3-126, HCJ Appeal
Porter v. HM Advocate (Sentencing) 1998 G.W.D. 34-1748, HCJ Appeal
Porter v. Kennedy 2001 G.W.D. 16-661, HCJ Appeal
Porter, Petitioners 2000 G.W.D. 2-46, HCJ
Porterfield v. Spiers (Sentencing) 1998 G.W.D. 16-796, HCJ Appeal
Post Office v. Jones see Jones v. Post Office
Post Office v. Norwich Union Fire Insurance Society Ltd [1967] 2 Q.B. 363; [1967] 2
   W.L.R. 709; [1967] 1 All E.R. 577; [1967] 1 Lloyd's Rep. 216; 111 S.J. 71, CA;
   reversing [1966] 2 Lloyd's Rep. 499; 116 N.L.J. 1544; 110 S.J. 867; *Times*,
   November 9, 1966, QBD . . . . *Digested*, 67/**2038**:
               Applied, 98/6113: *Approved*, 89/2064: *Considered*, 69/1825, 74/1887,
                      74/1904, 84/3152, 85/2013, 94/2067, 94/2607, 96/3508
Pothul v. Vannet 1999 G.W.D. 28-1330, HCJ Appeal
Potter (Mark Anthony), Petitioner 1999 G.W.D. 12-569, HCJ Appeal
Potter v. Vannet 1999 G.W.D. 33-1582, HCJ Appeal
Pottinger v. Hay 1928 S.L.C.R. 14, Land Ct (Full Ct) . . . . *Referred to*, 01/**6747**
Potts v. McNulty 2000 S.L.T. 1269; 2000 Rep. L.R. 72; 2000 G.W.D. 15-574, OH . . . . . *Digested*, 00/**5907**
Powell v. Brown & Root Ltd 2001 G.W.D. 30-1212, Sh Ct (Grampian)
Powell v. Ritchie (Sentencing) 2001 G.W.D. 20-766, HCJ Appeal
Powrie Castle Properties Ltd v. Dundee City Council 2001 S.C.L.R. 146, Sh Pr . . . . *Digested*, 01/**6826**
Prenty v. Vannet (Sentencing) 1998 G.W.D. 16-829, HCJ Appeal
Presslie v. Cochrane McGregor Group Ltd (No.3) 1998 G.W.D. 35-1810, OH
Presslie v. Cochrane McGregor Group Ltd (No.4) 1999 S.L.T. 1242; 1999 G.W.D. 12-
   559, OH . . . . *Digested*, 99/**5686**
Preston v. Douglas 1998 G.W.D. 24-1194, HCJ Appeal
Preston v. McFadyen 1999 G.W.D. 33-1576, HCJ Appeal
Pringle v. Houston 1998 G.W.D. 40-2062, HCJ Appeal
Pringle's Executor v. Pringle (Assignation in Security) 1999 G.W.D. 37-1832, 2 Div
Proctor v. Munro 1999 G.W.D. 10-483, HCJ Appeal

Project Consultancy Group *v.* Trustees of the Gray Trust [1999] B.L.R. 377; (2000) 2
T.C.L.R. 72; 65 Con. L.R. 146, QBD (T&CC) . . . .   *Digested*, 00/**807**:
Applied, 00/5979
Property Selection & Investment Trust Ltd *v.* United Friendly Insurance Plc 1999 S.L.T.
975; 1998 S.C.L.R. 792; 1998 G.W.D. 25-1264, OH . . . .   *Digested*, 98/**5948**
Property Selection & Investment Trust Ltd *v.* United Friendly Insurance Plc (Preliminary
Proceedings) 1998 S.C.L.R. 314, OH . . . .   *Digested*, 98/**5949**
Prosoft Resources Ltd *v.* Griffiths 1999 S.L.T. 1255; 2000 S.C.L.R. 157; 1999 G.W.D. 16-
735, OH . . . .   *Digested*, 99/**6032**
Provan *v.* HM Advocate 1998 G.W.D. 29-1464, HCJ Appeal
Provan *v.* Swan 2001 G.W.D. 22-822, OH
Pryce *v.* Gilchrist 1999 G.W.D. 23-1120, HCJ Appeal
PTOA Ltd *v.* Renfrew DC 1997 S.L.T. 1112, OH . . . .   *Digested*, 97/**6230**:
Not followed, 99/5626

Pugh *v.* Higson 1999 G.W.D. 13-605, HCJ Appeal
Pugh *v.* HM Advocate 1999 G.W.D. 5-253, HCJ Appeal
Pugh (Justin St John) *v.* HM Advocate see O'Neill (Thomas) *v.* HM Advocate
Pullar *v.* United Kingdom 1996 S.C.C.R. 755; (1996) 22 E.H.R.R. 391; *Times*, June 24,
1996, ECHR . . . .   *Digested*, 96/**3169**:
Considered, 01/6371
Purdie *v.* Dryburgh 2000 S.C. 497; 2000 G.W.D. 17-695, Ex Div; affirming 1999 Rep.
L.R. 68, Sh Pr . . . .   *Digested*, 00/**6597**
Purdie *v.* Higson (Sentencing) 2001 G.W.D. 6-196, HCJ Appeal
Purves *v.* HM Advocate 1999 G.W.D. 25-1200, HCJ Appeal

Q, Petitioner 2000 G.W.D. 15-570, OH
Quantrill *v.* Higson 1999 G.W.D. 32-1539, HCJ Appeal
Quantum Claims Compensation Specialists Ltd *v.* Powell 1998 S.C. 316; 1998 S.L.T.
228; 1998 S.C.C.R. 173; 1998 G.W.D. 3-137; *Times*, February 26, 1998, Ex Div;
affirming 1997 S.C.L.R. 242, Sh Pr . . . .   *Digested*, 98/**5548**
Quantum Glass Ltd *v.* Spowart 2001 G.W.D. 1-7, OH
Quarantelli *v.* Forbes 2000 G.W.D. 2-67, Sh Ct
Quigley *v.* Munro 1999 G.W.D. 3-147, HCJ Appeal
Quilty *v.* Windsor 1999 S.L.T. 346; 1998 G.W.D. 29-1501, OH . . . .   *Digested*, 99/**5990**
Quinn *v.* Calder Industrial Materials Ltd [1996] I.R.L.R. 126, EAT   *Followed*, 01/**6460**
Quinn *v.* Cunningham 1956 J.C. 22; 1956 S.L.T. 55, HCJ Appeal . . . .   *Digested*, 56/**12853**:
Applied, 83/4077, 99/5833: *Overruled in part*, 93/5087
Quinn *v.* McGinty 1999 S.L.T. (Sh Ct) 27; 1998 Rep. L.R. 107; 1998 G.W.D. 23-1185,
Sh Pr . . . .   *Digested*, 98/**5805**
Quinn *v.* Normand (No.1) 1998 G.W.D. 8-409, HCJ Appeal
Quinn *v.* Normand (No.2) 1998 G.W.D. 8-408, HCJ Appeal
Quinn *v.* Schwarzkopf Ltd [2001] I.R.L.R. 67, EAT . . . .   *Digested*, 01/**6462**:
Not followed, 01/6463

R (Children) *v.* Grant 2000 S.L.T. 372; 2000 Fam. L.R. 2; 2000 G.W.D. 4-118, Ex Div. . .   *Digested*, 00/**6270**
R *v.* HM Advocate (Sentencing) 1999 G.W.D. 40-1940, HCJ Appeal
R (Norman Charles) *v.* HM Advocate 2000 J.C. 368; 2000 S.L.T. 1315; 2000 S.C.C.R.
354; [2000] H.R.L.R. 389; 2000 G.W.D. 8-276; *Times*, April 14, 2000, HCJ
Appeal . . . .   *Digested*, 00/**6122**
R *v.* R see Robertson *v.* Robertson (No.1)
R *v.* R (Interim Contact with Child) 2000 G.W.D. 2-36, Sh Pr
R *v.* Scottish Ministers see A *v.* Scottish Ministers
R *v.* Secretary of State for Scotland [1999] 2 A.C. 512; [1999] 2 W.L.R. 28; [1999] 1
All E.R. 481; 1999 S.C. (H.L.) 17; 1999 S.L.T. 279; 1999 S.C.L.R. 74; (1999)
96(4) L.S.G. 37; 1998 G.W.D. 40-2075; *Times*, December 7, 1998; *Independent*,
December 8, 1998, HL; reversing 1998 S.C. 49; 1998 S.L.T. 162; 1997 S.C.L.R.
1056; 1997 G.W.D. 35-1793, 2 Div; reversing 1997 S.L.T. 555, OH . . . .   *Digested*, 99/**6363**:
Applied, 00/4174: *Considered*, 99/6361, 00/6472
R *v.* Templeton see R, Petitioner
R *v.* Walker see R, Petitioner
R Peter & Co Ltd *v.* Pancake Place Ltd 1993 S.L.T. 322, OH . . . .   *Digested*, 93/**5688**:
Followed, 00/6636
R, Petitioner; *sub nom* AR *v.* Reporter for Aberdeen Local Authority; R *v.* Templeton; R
v. Walker 1999 S.C. 380; 1999 S.L.T. 1233; 1999 S.C.L.R. 341; 1999 Fam. L.R.
20; 1999 G.W.D. 4-163, Ex Div . . . .   *Digested*, 99/**5660**
R. *v.* A (Joinder of Appropriate Minister) [2001] 1 W.L.R. 789; *Times*, March 21, 2001;
Independent, March 27, 2001, HL . . . .   *Digested*, 01/**3535**:
Followed, 01/6228: *Subsequent proceedings*, 01/977
R. *v.* Bartle Ex p. Pinochet Ugarte (No.2) see R. *v.* Bow Street Metropolitan
Stipendiary Magistrate Ex p. Pinochet Ugarte (No.2)

R. *v.* BBC Ex p. Lavelle [1983] 1 W.L.R. 23; [1983] 1 All E.R. 241; [1983] I.C.R. 99; [1982] I.R.L.R. 404; (1983) 133 N.L.J. 133; (1982) 126 S.J.L.B. 836, QBD . . . . *Digested,* 83/**15**: *Approved,* 83/2943: *Considered,* 85/2672, 87/6, 89/12: *Not applied,* 00/5836: *Referred to,* 85/1147, 86/1176

R. *v.* Bentley (Derek) [2001] 1 Cr. App. R. 21; [1999] Crim. L.R. 330; *Times,* July 31, 1998, CA (Crim Div) . . . . *Digested,* 98/**1051**: *Applied,* 00/1023, 00/5999: *Referred to,* 01/79

R. *v.* Birmingham City Council Ex p. Ireland; *sub nom* Hall *v.* Kingston upon Hull City Council; Ireland *v.* Birmingham City Council; Baker *v.* Birmingham City Council; R. *v.* Kingston City Council Ex p. Hall; R. *v.* Kingston City Council Ex p. Baker [1999] 2 All E.R. 609; (2000) 164 J.P. 9; [1999] E.H.L.R. 243; (1999) 31 H.L.R. 1079; [1999] B.L.G.R. 184; (1999) 163 J.P.N. 894; [1999] E.G.C.S. 4; (1999) 149 N.L.J. 122; [1999] N.P.C. 5; [1999] Env. L.R. D19; *Times,* February 9, 1999, QBD . . . . *Digested,* 99/**2214**: *Applied,* 00/2274: *Followed,* 00/6602

R. *v.* Bow Street Metropolitan Stipendiary Magistrate Ex p. Pinochet Ugarte (No.2); *sub nom* Pinochet Ugarte (No.2), Re; R. *v.* Evans Ex p. Pinochet Ugarte (No.2); R. *v.* Bartle Ex p. Pinochet Ugarte (No.2) [2000] 1 A.C. 119; [1999] 2 W.L.R. 272; [1999] 1 All E.R. 577; 6 B.H.R.C. 1; (1999) 11 Admin. L.R. 57; (1999) 96(6) L.S.G. 33; (1999) 149 N.L.J. 88; *Times,* January 18, 1999; *Independent,* January 19, 1999, HL . . . . *Digested,* 99/**39**: *Applied,* 99/38: *Considered,* 00/4140, 00/6092, 01/6705

R. *v.* Bowden (Jonathan) [2001] Q.B. 88; [2000] 2 W.L.R. 1083; [2000] 2 All E.R. 418; [2000] 1 Cr. App. R. 438; [2000] 2 Cr. App. R. (S.) 26; [2000] Crim. L.R. 381; (1999) 96(47) L.S.G. 29; (2000) 144 S.J.L.B. 5; *Times,* November 19, 1999 ; *Independent,* November 26, 1999, CA (Crim Div) . . . . *Digested,* 99/**947**: *Applied,* 00/993, 01/1450: *Followed,* 00/6039

R. *v.* BP Oil Grangemouth Refinery Ltd see Reid *v.* BP Grangemouth Refinery Ltd

R. *v.* Brophy (Edward Manning) [1982] A.C. 476; [1981] 3 W.L.R. 103; [1981] 2 All E.R. 705; (1981) 73 Cr. App. R. 287; [1981] Crim. L.R. 831; 125 S.J. 479, HL (NI); reversing [1980] 4 N.I.J.B., Crown Ct (Belfast) . . . . *Digested,* 81/**1890**: *Applied,* 00/5996

R. *v.* Canons Park Mental Health Review Tribunal Ex p. A [1995] Q.B. 60; [1994] 3 W.L.R. 630; [1994] 2 All E.R. 659; [1994] C.O.D. 480; (1994) 91(22) L.S.G. 33; (1994) 138 S.J.L.B. 75; *Times,* March 2, 1994, CA; reversing [1994] 1 All E.R. 481; [1994] C.O.D. 125; *Times,* August 24, 1993; *Independent,* September 1, 1993, QBD . . . . *Digested,* 94/**3066**: *Disapproved,* 00/4174: *Distinguished,* 98/6097: *Followed,* 97/6265

R. *v.* Cousins; R. *v.* Narwani; (Unreported, August 1, 1994), Crown Ct (Inner London) [*Ex rel.* Barry Phillips, Barrister] . . . . *Digested,* 94/**1435**: *Approved,* 98/6205

R. *v.* Cross (Patrick Vernon) [1973] Q.B. 937; [1973] 2 W.L.R. 1049; [1973] 2 All E.R. 920; (1973) 57 Cr. App. R. 660; [1973] Crim. L.R. 433; 117 S.J. 464, CA (Crim Div) . . . . *Digested,* 73/**594**: *Applied,* 89/584: *Distinguished,* 76/544, 77/488, 01/6385

R. *v.* Devon CC Ex p. Baker; R. *v.* Durham CC Ex p. Curtis ; R. *v.* Devon CC Ex p. Ruxton [1995] 1 All E.R. 73; 91 L.G.R. 479; (1994) 6 Admin. L.R. 113; [1993] C.O.D. 253; *Times,* January 21, 1993; *Independent,* February 22, 1993 (C.S.), CA; affirming [1993] C.O.D. 138; *Times,* October 20, 1992, QBD . . . . *Digested,* 95/**88**: *Applied,* 95/3252, 95/3272, 96/5526: *Considered,* 95/68, 95/2546, 01/6790: *Followed,* 97/4713: *Referred to,* 98/3001

R. *v.* Devon CC Ex p. Ruxton see R. *v.* Devon CC Ex p. Baker

R. *v.* Doot (Robert Leroy) see DPP *v.* Doot

R. *v.* Durham CC Ex p. Curtis see R. *v.* Devon CC Ex p. Baker

R. *v.* East Lothian Council Ex p. Scottish Coal Co Ltd see Scottish Coal Co Ltd *v.* East Lothian Council

R. *v.* Evans Ex p. Pinochet Ugarte (No.2) see R. *v.* Bow Street Metropolitan Stipendiary Magistrate Ex p. Pinochet Ugarte (No.2)

R. *v.* Fay (Michael Augustus) see DPP *v.* Doot

R. *v.* Graham-Kerr (John) [1988] 1 W.L.R. 1098; (1989) 88 Cr. App. R. 302; (1989) 153 J.P. 171; (1989) 153 J.P.N. 170; (1988) 132 S.J. 1299, CA (Crim Div) . . . . . . *Digested,* 89/**836**: *Applied,* 99/5835, 01/1058

R. *v.* Immigration Appeal Tribunal Ex p. Deen-Koroma; *sub nom* Deen-Koroma *v.* Immigration Appeal Tribunal [1997] Imm. A.R. 242, CA. . . . . *Digested,* 97/**2829**: *Considered,* 00/6495

R. *v.* Immigration Appeal Tribunal Ex p. Zaman [1982] Imm. A.R. 61, QBD . . . . *Digested,* 84/**1753**: *Applied,* 99/6289

R. *v.* Kent (Michael Peter) [1983] 1 W.L.R. 794; [1983] 3 All E.R. 1; (1983) 77 Cr. App. R. 120; (1983) 5 Cr. App. R. (S.) 171; [1983] R.T.R. 393; [1983] Crim. L.R. 553; (1983) 127 S.J. 394, CA (Crim Div) . . . . *Digested,* 83/**3288**: *Applied,* 83/913, 84/934, 85/3012, 86/2916, 98/5695

R. *v.* Kingston City Council Ex p. Baker see R. *v.* Birmingham City Council Ex p. Ireland

R. *v.* Kingston City Council Ex p. Hall see R. *v.* Birmingham City Council Ex p. Ireland

R. *v.* L (Young Offender: Time in Custody on Remand) see R. *v.* M (Young Offender:
Time in Custody on Remand)

R. *v.* Loving (Jeffrey Richard) see DPP *v.* Doot

R. *v.* M (Discretionary Life Sentence) see R. *v.* M (Young Offender: Time in Custody
on Remand)

R. *v.* M (Young Offender: Time in Custody on Remand); *sub nom* R. *v.* M
(Discretionary Life Sentence); R. *v.* L (Young Offender: Time in Custody on
Remand) [1999] 1 W.L.R. 485; [1998] 2 All E.R. 939; [1999] 1 Cr. App. R. (S.)
6; [1998] Crim. L.R. 512; *Times*, April 7, 1998, CA (Crim Div) . . . .   *Digested,* 98/**1269**:
Applied, 99/5949, 00/1356, 01/1353, 01/1439: *Considered,* 99/1079,
99/1248, 99/1255, 99/1268, 00/1351, 00/1352, 00/1354, 00/1355, 00/1360,
01/1298: *Followed,* 99/1241, 99/1252, 99/1257

R. *v.* McNamara (James) (1988) 87 Cr. App. R. 246; (1988) 152 J.P. 390; [1988]
Crim. L.R. 440; (1988) 152 J.P.N. 350; (1988) 132 S.J. 300; *Times,* February 16,
1988, CA (Crim Div) . . . .   *Digested,* 89/**823**:
Considered, 97/1223, 99/5832: *Distinguished,* 90/2339: *Followed,* 99/926

R. *v.* Mental Health Review Tribunal Ex p. Clatworthy [1985] 3 All E.R. 699, QBD . . . . .   *Digested,* 86/**2140**:
Applied, 91/2030: *Followed,* 98/6098

R. *v.* Narwani see R. *v.* Cousins

R. *v.* Secretary of State for Employment Ex p. Seymour-Smith (No.1) [1997] 1 W.L.R.
473; [1997] 2 All E.R. 273; [1997] 2 C.M.L.R. 904; [1997] I.C.R. 371; [1997]
I.R.L.R. 315; (1997) 147 N.L.J. 414; *Times,* March 14, 1997, HL; reversing [1996]
All E.R. (E.C.) 1; [1995] I.C.R. 889; [1995] I.R.L.R. 464; *Times,* August 3, 1995;
Independent, August 8, 1995, CA; reversing [1994] I.R.L.R. 448; [1994] C.O.D.
474, QBD . . . .   *Digested,* 97/**2265**:
Applied, 97/2262, 98/2240: *Considered,* 96/2540, 98/2236:
Referred to, 97/5233, 98/5826

R. *v.* Secretary of State for the Environment Ex p. Haringey LBC 92 L.G.R. 538;
[1994] C.O.D. 518; (1995) 159 L.G. Rev. 21; *Times,* March 2, 1994, CA . . . .   *Digested,* 94/**2946**:
Followed, 97/6242, 98/6085

R. (on the application of Alconbury Developments Ltd) *v.* Secretary of State for the
Environment, Transport and the Regions see R. (on the application of Holding &
Barnes Plc) *v.* Secretary of State for the Environment, Transport and the
Regions

R. (on the application of Holding & Barnes Plc) *v.* Secretary of State for the Environment,
Transport and the Regions; *sub nom* R. *v.* Secretary of State for the
Environment, Transport and the Regions Ex p. Holdings & Barnes Plc; R. (on the
application of Premier Leisure UK Ltd) *v.* Secretary of State for the
Environment, Transport and the Regions; R. (on the application of Alconbury
Developments Ltd) *v.* Secretary of State for the Environment, Transport and the
Regions; Secretary of State for the Environment, Transport and the Regions *v.*
Legal & General Assurance Society Ltd [2001] UKHL 23; [2001] 2 W.L.R. 1389;
[2001] 2 All E.R. 929; [2001] H.R.L.R. 45; [2001] U.K.H.R.R. 728; (2001) 3
L.G.L.R. 38; (2001) 82 P. & C.R. 40; [2001] 2 P.L.R. 76; [2001] J.P.L. 920;
[2001] 20 E.G.C.S. 228; (2001) 98(24) L.S.G. 45; (2001) 151 N.L.J. 727;
(2001) 145 S.J.L.B. 140; [2001] N.P.C. 90; *Times,* May 10, 2001; *Independent,*
June 25, 2001 (C.S); *Daily Telegraph,* May 15, 2001, HL; reversing [2001]
H.R.L.R. 2; [2001] U.K.H.R.R. 270; (2001) 3 L.G.L.R. 21; [2001] 1 P.L.R. 58;
[2001] 1 E.G.L.R. 33; [2001] 05 E.G. 170; [2001] J.P.L. 291; [2001] 4 E.G.C.S.
141; (2001) 151 N.L.J. 135; (2001) 145 S.J.L.B. 84; *Times,* January 24, 2001;
Independent, January 22, 2001 (C.S), QBD (Admin Ct) . . . .   *Digested,* 01/**4761**:
Cited, 01/6853

R. (on the application of Premier Leisure UK Ltd) *v.* Secretary of State for the
Environment, Transport and the Regions see R. (on the application of Holding &
Barnes Plc) *v.* Secretary of State for the Environment, Transport and the
Regions

R. *v.* Secretary of State for the Environment, Transport and the Regions Ex p. Holdings
& Barnes Plc see R. (on the application of Holding & Barnes Plc) *v.* Secretary of
State for the Environment, Transport and the Regions

R. *v.* Secretary of State for the Home Department Ex p. Adan (Hassan Hussein) see
Adan (Hassan Hussein) *v.* Secretary of State for the Home Department

R. *v.* Secretary of State for the Home Department Ex p. Brind [1991] 1 A.C. 696;
[1991] 2 W.L.R. 588; [1991] 1 All E.R. 720; (1991) 3 Admin. L.R. 486; (1991)
141 N.L.J. 199; (1991) 135 S.J. 250; *Times,* February 8, 1991; *Independent,*
February 8, 1991; *Guardian,* February 8, 1991, HL; affirming [1990] 2 W.L.R. 787;
[1990] 1 All E.R. 469; [1990] C.O.D. 190; (1989) 139 N.L.J. 1751; *Times,*
December 7, 1989; *Independent,* December 7, 1989; *Guardian,* December 7,
1989, CA; affirming (1989) 2 Admin. L.R. 169; [1990] C.O.D. 49; *Times,* May 30,
1989; *Independent,* June 2, 1989; *Guardian,* May 27, 1989, QBD . . . .   *Digested,* 91/**71**:
Applied, 90/3072, 91/816, 92/2083, 92/2791, 93/2208, 93/3778, 94/7,
94/2504: *Considered,* 92/3, 92/4455, 93/2556, 93/2567, 93/3936, 94/55,
94/4462, 95/67, 95/3098, 00/5471: *Distinguished,* 92/2872:
Followed, 96/3256, 96/4740, 97/2931, 98/3203, 98/3216, 01/5878:
Not followed, 93/2174, 94/2468, 95/2713: *Referred to,* 98/5998

R. *v.* Secretary of State for the Home Department Ex p. Mpyanguli see Kingori *v.*
    Secretary of State for the Home Department
R. *v.* Secretary of State for the Home Department Ex p. Navaratnaam see R. *v.*
    Secretary of State for the Home Department Ex p. Sivakumaran
R. *v.* Secretary of State for the Home Department Ex p. Ogunshakin [1997] Imm. A.R.
    159, QBD . . . . *Digested,* 97/**2831**:
                                                 Distinguished, 99/6288
R. *v.* Secretary of State for the Home Department Ex p. Rasalingan see R. *v.* Secretary
    of State for the Home Department Ex p. Sivakumaran
R. *v.* Secretary of State for the Home Department Ex p. Singh (Lal) [1998] Imm. A.R.
    320, QBD . . . . *Digested,* 98/**3191**:
                                                 Considered, 00/6495
R. *v.* Secretary of State for the Home Department Ex p. Sivakumaran; R. *v.* Secretary
    of State for the Home Department Ex p. Vilvarajah; R. *v.* Secretary of State for the
    Home Department Ex p. Vanathan; R. *v.* Secretary of State for the Home
    Department Ex p. Rasalingan; R. *v.* Secretary of State for the Home Department
    Ex p. Navaratnaam [1988] A.C. 958; [1988] 1 All E.R. 193; [1988] Imm. A.R.
    147; (1988) 85(6) L.S.G. 37; (1988) 132 S.J. 22, HL; reversing [1987] 3 W.L.R.
    1047; (1987) 131 S.J. 1485; *Times,* October 13, 1987, CA; reversing (Unreported,
    September 25, 1987), QBD . . . . *Digested,* 88/**1832**:
                   Applied, 89/1951, 92/2443, 93/2248, 96/3209, 96/3211, 99/3170:
           Considered, 88/1829, 92/2396, 95/2697, 95/2698, 96/3186, 96/3236,
                               00/3306, 00/3316: *Followed,* 00/6491
R. *v.* Secretary of State for the Home Department Ex p. Vanathan see R. *v.* Secretary of
    State for the Home Department Ex p. Sivakumaran
R. *v.* Secretary of State for the Home Department Ex p. Vilvarajah see R. *v.* Secretary of
    State for the Home Department Ex p. Sivakumaran
R. *v.* Sevenoaks DC Ex p. Terry [1985] 3 All E.R. 226; [1984] J.P.L. 420, QBD . . . . *Digested,* 85/**3459**:
                   Applied, 90/4349, 94/4418, 94/4469: *Considered,* 86/2017:
                                  Followed, 85/3458, 99/6408

R. *v.* Shanahan (Thomas) see DPP *v.* Doot
R. *v.* Shannahan (Thomas) see DPP *v.* Doot
R. *v.* Watts (James Wesley) see DPP *v.* Doot
Radivojevic *v.* Secretary of State for the Home Department see Adan (Hassan
    Hussein) *v.* Secretary of State for the Home Department
Rae *v.* Blackrock International Ltd 2001 G.W.D. 1-49, OH
Rae *v.* Broad 2000 G.W.D. 40-1504, OH
Rae *v.* Chief Constable of Strathclyde 1998 Rep. L.R. 63; 1998 G.W.D. 8-406, OH . . . . *Digested,* 98/**5440**
Rae *v.* Glasgow City Council 1998 S.L.T. 292; 1997 Rep. L.R. 79; 1997 G.W.D. 18-842;
    Times, April 22, 1997, OH . . . . *Digested,* 97/**6077**:
                                                  Referred to, 00/6426
Rae *v.* Lees 1998 G.W.D. 24-1234, HCJ Appeal
Rae *v.* Scottish Power Plc 2001 G.W.D. 36-1397, OH
Rae *v.* Strathclyde Joint Police Board 1999 S.C.L.R. 793; 1999 G.W.D. 12-571, OH . . . . . *Digested,* 00/**6426**
Rafferty *v.* HM Advocate 1998 G.W.D. 29-1463, HCJ Appeal
Rafferty *v.* Secretary of State for Scotland 1998 G.W.D. 16-818, OH
Raiker *v.* Raiker 1998 G.W.D. 32-1636, Sh Ct
Rainey *v.* Greater Glasgow Health Board [1987] A.C. 224; [1986] 3 W.L.R. 1017;
    [1987] 1 All E.R. 65; 1987 S.C. (H.L.) 1; 1987 S.L.T. 146; [1987] 2 C.M.L.R. 11;
    [1987] I.C.R. 129; [1987] I.R.L.R. 26; (1987) 84 L.S.G. 188; (1986) 136 N.L.J.
    1161; (1986) 130 S.J. 954, HL; affirming 1985 S.L.T. 518; [1985] I.R.L.R. 414, 1
    Div; affirming [1984] I.R.L.R. 88; (1984) 134 N.L.J. 360, EAT . . . . *Digested,* 87/**4409**:
               Applied, 98/5807: *Considered,* 87/1326, 88/1274, 89/1431, 96/2550:
                                         Referred to, 88/1323
Ralston *v.* Crowe 1999 G.W.D. 8-389, HCJ Appeal
Ramage (Stuart Robert) *v.* HM Advocate 1999 S.C.C.R. 592; 1999 G.W.D. 25-1199,
    HCJ Appeal . . . . *Digested,* 99/**5953**
Ramage *v.* Matthew 1998 S.C. 167; 1998 S.L.T. 383; 1998 G.W.D. 2-91, HCJ Appeal . . . *Digested,* 98/**6058**
Ramage *v.* Stott 1998 G.W.D. 17-843, HCJ Appeal
Ramsay *v.* HM Advocate 1999 G.W.D. 30-1426, HCJ Appeal
Ramsay *v.* Rivers see Heil *v.* Rankin
Ramsay *v.* Timbmet Woyka Ltd 2001 G.W.D. 4-161, OH
Ramsay *v.* Vannet 1999 G.W.D. 27-1271, HCJ Appeal
Ranaldi *v.* City of Edinburgh DC see Ranaldi *v.* Edinburgh City Council
Ranaldi *v.* Edinburgh City Council; *sub nom* Ranaldi *v.* City of Edinburgh DC 2000
    S.L.T. 297; 2000 S.C.L.R. 368; [2000] 15 S.L.L.P. 6; 1999 G.W.D. 25-1213, 2
    Div . . . . *Digested,* 00/**4069**
Rankin *v.* HM Advocate (Sentencing) 2001 G.W.D. 31-1238, HCJ Appeal
Rankin *v.* McGlennan 2001 G.W.D. 32-1286, HCJ Appeal
Rankin *v.* Wilson Terris & Co 2001 G.W.D. 7-277, OH
Rankin's Trustee *v.* HC Somerville & Russell; *sub nom* Robinson *v.* HC Somerville &
    Russell 1999 S.C. 166; 1999 S.L.T. 65; 1998 S.C.L.R. 292; 1998 G.W.D. 7-309,
    OH . . . . *Digested,* 98/**6003**
Rannie *v.* Higson (Sentencing) 2000 G.W.D. 30-1169, HCJ Appeal

Rape Crisis Centre v. Secretary of State for the Home Department; *sub nom* Rape
   Crisis Centre and Sandy Brindley, Petitioners 2000 S.C. 527; 2001 S.L.T. 389;
   2000 S.C.L.R. 807; 2000 G.W.D. 25-946; *Times,* July 18, 2000, OH . . . .   *Digested,* 00/**6502**
Rape Crisis Centre and Sandy Brindley, Petitioners see Rape Crisis Centre v. Secretary of
   State for the Home Department
Rapide Enterprises v. Midgley 1998 S.L.T. 504; (1997) Hous. L.R. 125; 1997 G.W.D.
   25-1268; *Times,* July 30, 1997, OH . . . .   *Digested,* 97/**6093**
Rashid v. Anwar 1998 G.W.D. 25-1241, Sh Ct
Rattray v. Anderson 1998 G.W.D. 1-7, OH
Rattray v. Higson 1998 G.W.D. 19-953, HCJ Appeal
Rattray v. Petrie 1999 G.W.D. 39-1872, Sh Pr
Ravenseft Properties v. Assessor for Strathclyde Region 1991 S.C. 266, LVAC . . . .   *Digested,* 94/**6182**:
                                                                                       Distinguished, 00/6665
Rawes v. Watt 2001 G.W.D. 10-334, HCJ Appeal
Rawlinson v. Initial Property Maintenance Ltd 1998 S.L.T. (Sh Ct) 54; 1998 Rep. L.R.
   17; 1997 G.W.D. 35-1742, Sh Ct (Glasgow) . . . .   *Digested,* 98/**5484**
Razaq v. HM Advocate 1998 G.W.D. 27-1372, HCJ Appeal
Razzle Dazzle Ltd v. Vannet (Sentencing) 1998 G.W.D. 12-602, HCJ Appeal
Redbrae Ltd v. Glasgow Licensing Board 1998 G.W.D. 28-1445, OH
Redfern v. British Waterways Board 1999 G.W.D. 1-5, OH
Redmond v. HM Advocate (Sentencing) 2001 G.W.D. 6-200, HCJ Appeal
Redpath Dorman Long Ltd v. Tarmac Construction Ltd 1982 S.C. 14; 1982 S.L.T. 442,
   OH . . . .   *Digested,* 82/**3420**:
                                                                                       Approved, 01/6293

Redrow Homes Ltd v. Bett Brothers Plc [1999] 1 A.C. 197; [1998] 2 W.L.R. 198;
   [1998] 1 All E.R. 385; 1998 S.C. (H.L.) 64; 1998 S.L.T. 648; 1998 S.C.L.R. 325;
   [1998] F.S.R. 345; [1998] R.P.C. 793; (1998) 21(4) I.P.D. 21034; (1998)
   95(6) L.S.G. 25; (1998) 148 N.L.J. 121; (1998) 142 S.J.L.B. 79; 1998 G.W.D. 4-
   160; *Times,* January 26, 1998, HL; affirming 1997 S.C. 142; 1997 S.L.T. 1125;
   1997 S.C.L.R. 469; [1997] F.S.R. 828; 1997 G.W.D. 13-543; *Times,* May 2, 1997,
   2 Div; reversing 1996 S.L.T. 1254, OH . . . .   *Digested,* 98/**6020**:
                                                                                       Referred to, 98/3424

Rees v. Mabco (102) Ltd (Non-Pecuniary Damages) see Heil v. Rankin
Reganne v. Secretary of State for the Home Department 1998 G.W.D. 32-1669, OH
Reid (Philip Edward Strachan), Petitioner 1999 S.L.T. 212; 1998 S.C.C.R. 430; 1998 G.W.D.
   23-1180, HCJ Appeal . . . .   *Digested,* 98/**6054**
Reid v. Aberdeen City Council 2000 G.W.D. 37-1413, Sh Ct (Grampian)
Reid v. Anderson 2000 G.W.D. 13-511, HCJ Appeal
Reid v. BP Grangemouth Refinery Ltd; *sub nom* R. v. BP Oil Grangemouth Refinery
   Ltd 2001 G.W.D. 16-589, OH
Reid v. Buchanan 2000 S.C.C.R. 747; 2000 G.W.D. 29-1116, HCJ Appeal . . . .   *Digested,* 01/**6315**
Reid v. Cardno 2001 G.W.D. 9-308, Sh Pr; affirming 2000 G.W.D. 27-1026, Sh Ct
   (Grampian)
Reid v. Gilchrist 2001 G.W.D. 40-1513, HCJ Appeal
Reid v. Higgins 1998 G.W.D. 18-942, HCJ Appeal
Reid v. HM Advocate 1984 S.L.T. 391; 1984 S.C.C.R. 153, HCJ Appeal . . . .   *Digested,* 84/**3919**:
                                                                                Followed, 91/4663, 91/4664, 98/5611
Reid v. HM Advocate (Identification) 2001 G.W.D. 40-1511, HCJ Appeal
Reid v. HM Advocate (Misdirection) 1999 G.W.D. 26-1229, HCJ Appeal
Reid v. HM Advocate (Murder) 1999 G.W.D. 19-871, HCJ Appeal
Reid v. HM Advocate (Sentencing) 1998 G.W.D. 16-790, HCJ Appeal
Reid v. HM Advocate (Sentencing) 1998 G.W.D. 17-847, HCJ Appeal
Reid v. HM Advocate (Sentencing) 1998 G.W.D. 22-1114, HCJ Appeal
Reid v. HM Advocate (Sentencing) 1999 G.W.D. 5-252, HCJ Appeal
Reid v. HM Advocate (Sentencing) 2000 G.W.D. 33-1280, HCJ Appeal
Reid (Colin Turnbull) v. HM Advocate 1999 J.C. 320; 1999 S.L.T. 1257; 1999 S.C.C.R.
   769; 1999 G.W.D. 29-1362, HCJ Appeal . . . .   *Digested,* 99/**5896**
Reid (David James) v. HM Advocate 1999 S.L.T. 1414; 1999 G.W.D. 20-919, HCJ
   Appeal . . . .   *Digested,* 00/**6001**
Reid (Lindsey) v. HM Advocate 1999 J.C. 54; 1999 S.L.T. 1275; 1999 S.C.C.R. 19; 1999
   G.W.D. 2-84, HCJ Appeal . . . .   *Digested,* 99/**5843**
Reid v. MacDonald 1998 G.W.D. 31-1598, HCJ Appeal
Reid v. McCabe's Executor 1998 S.L.T. 531; 1998 G.W.D. 8-417, OH . . . .   *Digested,* 98/**6202**
Reid v. Morison (1892) 20 R. 510, CS . . . .   *Followed,* 01/6725
Reid v. Ramlort Ltd see Thoar's Judicial Factor v. Ramlort Ltd
Reid v. Ruxton 1999 G.W.D. 36-1765, HCJ Appeal
Reid v. Ski Independence 1999 S.L.T. (Sh Ct) 62; 1998 G.W.D. 31-1576, Sh Ct
   (Lothian) . . . .   *Digested,* 99/**6462**
Reid v. Walkingshaw 1998 G.W.D. 26-1316, HCJ Appeal
Reid Furniture Co Ltd v. Coll 1999 S.L.T. (Sh Ct) 23; 1998 S.C.L.R. 1129; 1998 G.W.D.
   38-1954, Sh Pr . . . .   *Digested,* 99/**5721**
Reilly v. Heywood (Sentencing: Assault) 2001 G.W.D. 12-415, HCJ Appeal
Reilly v. Heywood (Sentencing: Theft) 1998 G.W.D. 8-382, HCJ Appeal
Reilly v. HM Advocate (Sentencing) 1998 G.W.D. 3-125, HCJ Appeal

Reilly (Elizabeth Liddle) *v.* HM Advocate 2000 J.C. 632; 2000 S.L.T. 1330; 2000
S.C.C.R. 879; 2000 G.W.D. 26-977, HCJ Appeal . . . . *Digested,* 00/**6083**
Reith *v.* Bates (Ross Stan) 1998 J.C. 224; 1999 S.L.T. 380; 1998 S.C.C.R. 426; 1998
G.W.D. 20-1008, HCJ Appeal . . . . *Digested,* 98/**5631**
Reitze *v.* Strathclyde RC 1999 S.C. 614; 2000 S.L.T. 593; 1999 G.W.D. 17-810, 2 Div . . . *Digested,* 00/**6584**
Remnant Kings (East) *v.* McKeon 1998 G.W.D. 38-1973, OH
Renfrew *v.* HM Advocate (Sentencing) 1998 G.W.D. 3-129, HCJ Appeal
Renfrew DC *v.* AB Leisure (Renfrew) Ltd 1988 S.L.T. 635; 1988 S.C.L.R. 512, 2 Div . . . *Digested,* 88/**4424**:
Applied, 98/6040
Renfrewshire Council *v.* McGinlay 2001 S.L.T. (Sh Ct) 79; 2001 G.W.D. 2-102, Sh Ct
(North Strathclyde) . . . . *Digested,* 01/**6753**
Rennie *v.* HM Advocate 2001 G.W.D. 21-793, HCJ Appeal
Rennie *v.* HM Advocate (Sentencing) 1999 G.W.D. 29-1388, HCJ Appeal
Rennie (Charles McDonald) *v.* HM Advocate 1998 S.C.C.R. 191; 1998 G.W.D. 8-365,
HCJ Appeal . . . . *Digested,* 98/**5599**
Rennie (Jennifer Margaret) *v.* Kennedy see Cowan (Paul Matthew) *v.* HM Advocate
Rennie *v.* Webster 1999 G.W.D. 7-330, HCJ Appeal
Renyana-Stahl Anstalt *v.* MacGregor; *sub nom* Reyana-Stahl Anstalt *v.* MacGregor
2001 S.L.T. 1247; 2001 G.W.D. 13-502, OH . . . . *Digested,* 01/**6670**
Reside *v.* North Ayrshire Council 2001 S.L.T. 6; [2000] 3 P.L.R. 86; 2000 G.W.D. 19-
767, OH . . . . *Digested,* 01/**6859**
Retail Parks Investments Ltd *v.* Royal Bank of Scotland Plc (No.2) 1996 S.C. 227; 1996
S.L.T. 669; *Times,* April 22, 1996, Ex Div; affirming 1996 S.L.T. 52, OH . . . . *Digested,* 96/**7110**:
Considered, 97/6185: *Followed,* 98/6035
Revie *v.* HM Advocate 2000 G.W.D. 33-1273, HCJ Appeal
Revival Properties Ltd *v.* Edinburgh City Council see Edinburgh City Council *v.*
Secretary of State for Scotland
Reyana-Stahl Anstalt *v.* MacGregor see Renyana-Stahl Anstalt *v.* MacGregor
Reynolds *v.* Vannet (Sentencing) 2000 G.W.D. 4-163, HCJ Appeal
Rhind *v.* McFadyen 2001 G.W.D. 25-988, HCJ Appeal
Rhinds *v.* Vannet 1998 G.W.D. 29-1489, HCJ Appeal
Rhins District Committee of Wigtownshire CC *v.* Cuninghame (1917) 2 S.L.T.169, OH . . *Considered,* 00/6640
RHM Bakeries (Scotland) Ltd *v.* Strathclyde RC 1985 S.L.T. 214; *Times,* January 29,
1985, HL; reversing 1985 S.L.T. 3, 2 Div . . . . *Digested,* 85/**4458**:
Considered, 88/4575, 95/6164, 96/7230, 00/6600: *Followed,* 95/6162
Riaviz *v.* Howdle 1996 S.L.T. 747; 1996 S.C.C.R. 20, HCJ Appeal . . . . *Digested,* 96/**6744**:
Applied, 99/5934
Rice *v.* HM Advocate (Sentencing) 2000 G.W.D. 39-1456, HCJ Appeal
Richards & Wallington (Earthmoving) Ltd *v.* Whatlings Ltd 1982 S.L.T. 66, OH . . . . *Digested,* 82/**4120**:
Distinguished, 98/5466: *Followed,* 93/5629
Richardson *v.* Gilchrist 1999 G.W.D. 19-895, HCJ Appeal
Richardson *v.* HM Advocate (Sentencing) 1999 G.W.D. 36-1752, HCJ Appeal
Richardson *v.* Pitt-Stanley [1995] Q.B. 123; [1995] 2 W.L.R. 26; [1995] 1 All E.R. 460;
[1995] I.C.R. 303; [1994] P.I.Q.R. P496; *Times,* August 11, 1994; *Independent,*
September 6, 1994, CA . . . . *Digested,* 95/**2901**:
Not followed, 98/5805
Richardson *v.* Quercus Ltd 1999 S.C. 278; 1999 S.L.T. 596; 1999 S.C.L.R. 133; 1999
G.W.D. 5-273, Ex Div; affirming 1997 S.C.L.R. 815; 1997 G.W.D. 17-804, OH . . . *Digested,* 99/**6419**
Richmond *v.* HM Advocate 1998 G.W.D. 36-1872, HCJ Appeal
Richmond Securities Ltd *v.* Weatherhead UK Ltd 1998 G.W.D. 1-45, OH
Riddell *v.* McLeod 1998 G.W.D. 33-1726, HCJ Appeal
Riddicks *v.* HM Advocate 1998 G.W.D. 37-1914, HCJ Appeal
Ridge *v.* Baldwin (No.1) [1964] A.C. 40; [1963] 2 W.L.R. 935; [1963] 2 All E.R. 66;
127 J.P. 251; 127 J.P. 295; 61 L.G.R. 369; 37 A.L.J. 140; 234 L.T. 423; 113 L.J.
716; 107 S.J. 313, HL; reversing [1963] 1 Q.B. 539; [1962] 2 W.L.R. 716; [1962]
1 All E.R. 834; 126 J.P. 196; 60 L.G.R. 229; 106 S.J. 111, CA; affirming [1961] 2
W.L.R. 1054; [1961] 2 All E.R. 523; 125 J.P. 422; 59 L.G.R. 327; 105 S.J. 384,
QBD . . . . *Digested,* 63/**2667**:
Applied, 63/2164, 64/2322, 65/12, 65/951, 67/242, 68/93, 68/297, 69/81,
70/286, 71/29, 71/6934, 78/1551, 78/2429, 79/1371, 79/2195, 82/1106,
84/14, 85/3081, 97/3387: *Considered,* 66/6, 71/3866, 71/12835, 77/3072,
80/9, 84/1202, 85/1181, 85/3145, 86/2017, 98/5814: *Followed,* 77/956
Rigby *v.* McFadyen 1999 G.W.D. 22-1050, HCJ Appeal
Riggins *v.* HM Advocate (Sentencing) 1998 G.W.D. 11-537, HCJ Appeal
Riley (Hector) *v.* HM Advocate 1999 J.C. 308; 1999 S.L.T. 1076; 1999 S.C.C.R. 644,
HCJ Appeal . . . . *Digested,* 99/**5952**
Rimmer (Roy William) *v.* HM Advocate 2001 G.W.D. 33-1306, HCJ Appeal
Ringland *v.* Walkingshaw 1998 G.W.D. 35-1832, HCJ Appeal
Rintoul *v.* Reith 1998 G.W.D. 38-1985, HCJ Appeal
Rippin Group Ltd *v.* IPT Interpipe SA 1995 S.C. 302; 1995 S.L.T. 831, 2 Div . . . . *Digested,* 95/**6195**:
Applied, 00/5977
Risky Business Ltd *v.* Glasgow City Licensing Board 2000 S.L.T. 923; [2000] 16
S.L.L.P. 9; 2000 G.W.D. 22-862, Ex Div . . . . *Digested,* 00/**6560**

Ritchie *v.* Bainbridge 2000 J.C. 458; 2000 S.L.T. 909; 2000 S.C.C.R. 472; 2000
    G.W.D. 16-672, HCJ Appeal . . . .   *Digested,* 00/**6140**
Ritchie *v.* Burns; *sub nom* Burns Trustee *v.* Burns 2001 S.L.T. 1383; [2001] B.P.I.R. 666;
    2000 G.W.D. 22-860, OH . . . .   *Digested,* 01/**6714**
Ritchie *v.* Dickie 1999 S.C. 593; 1999 S.C.L.R. 939; 1999 G.W.D. 15-712, OH . . . .   *Digested,* 99/**6301**
Ritchie *v.* EFT Industrial Ltd; *sub nom* Ritchie and Readman (Joint Receivers of
    Madame Foods Ltd) *v.* EFT Industrial Ltd 1998 S.L.T. (Sh Ct) 11; 1997 S.C.L.R.
    955; 1997 G.W.D. 28-1400, Sh Ct (Lothian) . . . .   *Digested,* 98/**6009**
Ritchie *v.* Howdle 1999 G.W.D. 31-1503, HCJ Appeal
Ritchie *v.* Secretary of State for Scotland 1999 S.L.T. 55; 1998 G.W.D. 3-102, OH . . . . .   *Digested,* 99/**5620**
Ritchie *v.* Urquhart 1998 G.W.D. 37-1937, HCJ Appeal
Ritchie *v.* Vannet 1998 G.W.D. 35-1841, HCJ Appeal
Ritchie and Readman (Joint Receivers of Madame Foods Ltd) *v.* EFT Industrial Ltd see
    Ritchie *v.* EFT Industrial Ltd
Roach *v.* CSB (Moulds) Ltd [1991] I.C.R. 349; [1991] I.R.L.R. 200, EAT . . . .   *Digested,* 92/**1913**:
                                                                              Disapproved, 99/6047: *Doubted,* 98/2230
Robb *v.* Dundee City Council TNS, Ex Div; affirming 2001 Hous. L.R. 42, Sh Pr. . . . .   *Digested,* 01/**6827**
Robb *v.* HM Advocate 1999 G.W.D. 27-1291, HCJ Appeal
Robb (David Gordon) *v.* HM Advocate 1999 J.C. 223; 1999 G.W.D. 15-688, HCJ
    Appeal . . . .   *Digested,* 99/**5874**
Robb *v.* Webster (Sentencing) 1999 G.W.D. 40-1932, HCJ Appeal
Robbie the Pict *v.* Hingston (No.1) 1998 S.L.T. 1196; 1997 G.W.D. 39-1982, HCJ Appeal   *Digested,* 98/**5621**
Robbie the Pict *v.* Hingston (No.2) 1998 S.L.T. 1201; 1998 G.W.D. 2-89, HCJ Appeal . .   *Digested,* 98/**5620**
Robbie the Pict *v.* MacDonald 2001 G.W.D. 20-764, HCJ Appeal
Robbie the Pict *v.* Miller Civil Engineering Ltd 2001 S.C.L.R. 1103; 2001 G.W.D. 26-
    1053, Ex Div; affirming 1999 S.C.L.R. 749; 1999 G.W.D. 12-566, OH . . . .   *Digested,* 99/**6254**
Robbins *v.* HM Advocate (Sentencing) 1998 G.W.D. 3-123, HCJ Appeal
Robbins *v.* O'Donnell (Sentencing) 1998 G.W.D. 32-1684, HCJ Appeal
Robert Barry & Co *v.* Doyle 1998 S.L.T. 1238; 1998 G.W.D. 6-262, OH . . . .   *Digested,* 98/**5420**
Roberton *v.* Roberton 1999 S.L.T. 38; 1998 G.W.D. 12-606, 1 Div . . . .   *Digested,* 99/**6080**
Roberts *v.* British Railways Board 1998 S.C.L.R. 577; 1998 Rep. L.R. 84; 1998 G.W.D.
    16-814, OH. . . . .   *Digested,* 98/**5441**
Roberts *v.* Hamilton (Sentencing) 1998 G.W.D. 1-25, HCJ Appeal
Roberts *v.* John Johnston & Son 1999 S.L.T. 728; 1998 S.C.L.R. 996; 1998 Rep. L.R.
    112; 1998 G.W.D. 25-1271, OH . . . .   *Digested,* 98/**5750**
Robertson *v.* Anderson 2001 G.W.D. 17-669, OH
Robertson *v.* Fife Council 2001 S.C. 849; 2001 S.L.T. 708; 2001 G.W.D. 13-528, 1 Div;
    affirming 2000 S.L.T. 1226; 2000 G.W.D. 4-172, OH . . . .   *Digested,* 01/**6903**
Robertson *v.* Gallagher 1999 G.W.D. 27-1280, HCJ Appeal
Robertson *v.* Heywood 1999 G.W.D. 3-143, HCJ Appeal
Robertson *v.* Higson 1999 G.W.D. 14-640, HCJ Appeal
Robertson *v.* Higson (Sentencing) 2001 G.W.D. 27-1113, HCJ Appeal
Robertson *v.* Hingston 1999 G.W.D. 24-1165, HCJ Appeal
Robertson *v.* HM Advocate (Sentencing) 1998 G.W.D. 7-340, HCJ Appeal
Robertson *v.* HM Advocate (Sentencing) 2001 G.W.D. 21-806, HCJ Appeal
Robertson (James Mark) *v.* HM Advocate 1997 S.C.C.R. 534; 1997 G.W.D. 24-1188,
    HCJ Appeal . . . .   *Digested,* 97/**5875**:
                                                                              Disapproved, 99/5949
Robertson (Kenneth) *v.* HM Advocate 1998 J.C. 213; 1998 S.L.T. 1352; 1998 S.C.C.R.
    390; 1998 G.W.D. 18-898, HCJ Appeal . . . .   *Digested,* 98/**5640**
Robertson *v.* J Sidney Smith Ltd 1999 G.W.D. 4-214, OH
Robertson *v.* Kennedy (Sentencing) 2001 G.W.D. 27-1095, HCJ Appeal
Robertson *v.* MacDonald see Robertson (Colin James) *v.* Perry
Robertson *v.* MacLeod (Sentencing) 1998 G.W.D. 6-305, HCJ Appeal
Robertson *v.* MacNeill (Sentencing) 2000 G.W.D. 19-768, HCJ Appeal
Robertson *v.* McGlennan 1998 G.W.D. 40-2087, HCJ Appeal
Robertson (Colin James) *v.* Perry; *sub nom* Robertson *v.* MacDonald 1998 S.C.C.R.
    599; 1998 G.W.D. 33-1705, HCJ Appeal . . . .   *Digested,* 98/**5675**
Robertson *v.* Robertson (International Child Abduction) 1998 S.L.T. 468; 1997 G.W.D.
    21-1000, 2 Div . . . .   *Digested,* 98/**5841**
Robertson *v.* Robertson (No.1); *sub nom* R *v.* R 2000 Fam. L.R. 43; 1999 G.W.D. 40-
    1952, OH . . . .   *Digested,* 00/**6282**
Robertson *v.* Robertson (No.2) 2001 G.W.D. 11-389, OH
Robertson (Judicial Factor) *v.* Robertson see Thurso Building Society's Judicial Factor
    v. Robertson
Robertson *v.* Secretary of State for Scotland 1999 G.W.D. 26-1251, Sh Ct
Robertson *v.* Sharp 2001 G.W.D. 29-1150, Sh Ct (Grampian)
Robertson *v.* Smith 2000 S.C. 591; 2000 S.L.T. 1012; 2000 Rep. L.R. 100; 2000
    G.W.D. 27-1032, Ex Div; affirming 1999 S.C.L.R. 1117; 1999 G.W.D. 19-868, OH .   *Digested,* 00/**5905**
Robertson *v.* Vannet (Sentencing) 2000 G.W.D. 3-112, HCJ Appeal
Robertson *v.* Vannet (Sentencing) 2000 G.W.D. 4-146, HCJ Appeal
Robertson (Charles) *v.* Vannet 1999 S.L.T. 1081; 1998 S.C.C.R. 669; 1998 G.W.D. 36-
    1865, HCJ Appeal. . . . .   *Digested,* 99/**5946**
Robertson *v.* Williamson 2001 S.L.C.R. 18, Land Ct (Div Ct)

Robin v. Vannet (Sentencing) 1998 G.W.D. 16-787, HCJ Appeal
Robinson v. Buchanan (Sentencing) 1998 G.W.D. 32-1657, HCJ Appeal
Robinson v. HC Somerville & Russell see Rankin's Trustee v. HC Somerville & Russell
Robinson v. McFadyen 1999 G.W.D. 22-1055, HCJ Appeal
Robson v. Higson 1998 G.W.D. 25-1244, HCJ Appeal
Robson (Ian) v. Spiers 1999 S.L.T. 1141; 1999 G.W.D. 25-1184, HCJ Appeal . . . .   *Digested,* 99/**5829**
Roche v. Clark 1999 G.W.D. 32-1506, HCJ Appeal
Rodden (George Fisher) v. HM Advocate 1995 S.L.T. 185; 1994 S.C.C.R. 841, HCJ
   Appeal . . . .   *Digested,* 95/**5723**:
                             Disapproved, 99/**5832**: *Explained,* 98/**5558**
Rodger v. Crowe 1998 G.W.D. 23-1159, HCJ Appeal
Rodger v. HM Advocate 1999 G.W.D. 40-1914, HCJ Appeal
Rodger v. Spiers 2001 G.W.D. 31-1247, HCJ Appeal
Rodgers v. British Steel Plc 1990 S.L.T. 642, OH . . . .   *Digested,* 90/**5600**:
                             Distinguished, 98/**5489**
Rodgers v. HM Advocate (Sentencing) 1998 G.W.D. 2-67, HCJ Appeal
Rodgers v. HM Advocate (Sentencing) 1999 G.W.D. 37-1812, HCJ Appeal
Rodgers v. Lees (Sentencing) 1998 G.W.D. 6-296, HCJ Appeal
Rodgers v. McGlennan 1998 G.W.D. 30-1562, HCJ Appeal
Rodwell v. Edinburgh City Council 2001 G.W.D. 2-82, OH
Rogers v. HM Advocate (Sentencing) 2001 G.W.D. 39-1473, HCJ Appeal
Rogerson Roofing Ltd v. Hall & Tawse Scotland Ltd 2000 S.C. 249; 2000 G.W.D. 4-
   116, 1 Div. . . . .   *Digested,* 00/**5886**
Rolland v. Lees 1999 G.W.D. 9-444, HCJ Appeal
Roney v. Heywood 1998 G.W.D. 18-945, HCJ Appeal
Rooney v. Guinness Plc 1999 S.L.T. 700; 1998 S.C.L.R. 995; 1998 Rep. L.R. 96; 1998
   G.W.D. 21-1094, OH . . . .   *Digested,* 98/**5729**
Rooney v. Hingston 1998 G.W.D. 22-1112, HCJ Appeal
Rorrison v. West Lothian College; *sub nom* Rorrison v. West Lothian Council 2000
   S.C.L.R. 245; 1999 Rep. L.R. 102; 1999 G.W.D. 27-1296, OH . . . .   *Digested,* 99/**6038**
Rorrison v. West Lothian Council see Rorrison v. West Lothian College
Rose v. Bouchet 2000 S.L.T. (Sh Ct) 170; 1999 S.C.L.R. 1004; [1999] I.R.L.R. 463;
   2001 Hous. L.R. 2; 1999 G.W.D. 20-958, Sh Pr. . . . .   *Digested,* 99/**6279**
Rose v. McGlennan (Sentencing) 2001 G.W.D. 36-1371, HCJ Appeal
Rose v. Rose 1998 S.L.T. (Sh Ct) 56; 1998 G.W.D. 11-557, Sh Pr . . . .   *Digested,* 98/**5856**
Rose's Trustees v. Rose 1993 S.L.T. (Sh Ct) 85, Sh Pr . . . .   *Digested,* 93/**5294**:
                             Not followed, 98/5470
Roselli v. Vannet 1998 J.C. 13; 1998 S.L.T. 706; 1997 S.C.C.R. 655; 1997 G.W.D. 32-
   1613, HCJ Appeal . . . .   *Digested,* 97/**5848**
Roseweir v. Ritchie (Sentencing) 2001 G.W.D. 16-660, HCJ Appeal
Rosewell Nurses Endowment Fund see Mackay, Petitioner
Rosgill Group Ltd v. Customs and Excise Commissioners [1997] 3 All E.R. 1012; [1997]
   S.T.C. 811; [1997] B.T.C. 5261; [1997] B.V.C. 388; *Times,* April 30, 1997, CA . . . .   *Digested,* 97/**4975**:
              Applied, 99/6472: *Considered,* 01/5556: *Followed,* 00/5345
Ross v. Dundee City Council 2000 S.L.T. (Land Ct) 2; 2000 Hous. L.R. 84; 2000
   G.W.D. 18-719, Lands Tr (Scot) . . . .   *Digested,* 00/**6466**
Ross v. Fife Health Care NHS Trust 2000 S.C.L.R. 620; 2000 G.W.D. 13-456, 1 Div;
   reversing 1999 Rep. L.R. 75, OH . . . .   *Digested,* 00/**5928**
Ross v. Gallacher (Sentencing) 2000 G.W.D. 15-593, HCJ
Ross v. Hingston 1998 G.W.D. 33-1723, HCJ Appeal
Ross v. HJ Banks & Co Ltd see Stuart's Trustee v. HJ Banks & Co Ltd
Ross v. HM Advocate 1999 G.W.D. 30-1422, HCJ Appeal
Ross (Crawford David) v. HM Advocate 1998 S.L.T. 1313; 1998 S.C.C.R. 359; 1998
   G.W.D. 18-891, HCJ Appeal. . . . .   *Digested,* 98/**5586**
Ross (Robert) v. HM Advocate 1991 J.C. 210; 1991 S.L.T. 564; 1991 S.C.C.R. 823, HCJ
   Appeal . . . .   *Digested,* 91/**4754**:
           Applied, 92/5531, 92/5533, 93/5055: *Considered,* 96/6835:
                             Distinguished, 00/6026
Ross (Scott Andrew) v. HM Advocate (Sentencing) 2001 G.W.D. 30-1197, HCJ Appeal
Ross (Stephen Jonathon) v. HM Advocate 1998 S.C.C.R. 445; 1998 G.W.D. 24-1192,
   HCJ Appeal . . . .   *Digested,* 98/**5637**
Ross v. Lees 1998 G.W.D. 33-1710, HCJ Appeal
Ross v. McFadyen 2001 G.W.D. 25-987, HCJ Appeal
Ross v. Neizer (Sentencing) 1998 G.W.D. 3-149, HCJ Appeal
Ross v. Reith 1999 G.W.D. 19-910, HCJ Appeal
Ross v. Ross 1999 S.C.L.R. 1112; 1999 G.W.D. 19-863, Sh Pr . . . .   *Digested,* 00/**5943**
Ross v. Ross 1999 S.L.C.R. 956, Land Ct (Full Ct); affirming 1997 S.L.C.R. 123, Land
   Ct (Div Ct) . . . .   *Digested,* 99/**6315**
Ross v. Walker (Sentencing) 1998 G.W.D. 6-266, HCJ Appeal
Ross v. Wilson 1998 G.W.D. 21-1097, HCJ Appeal
Ross & Bonnyman Ltd v. Hawson Garner Ltd 2001 S.L.T. (Sh Ct) 134; 2001 G.W.D. 25-
   921, Sh Ct (Tayside) . . . .   *Digested,* 01/**6259**
Ross & Bonnyman Ltd v. Small 2001 S.C.L.R. 900; 2001 G.W.D. 20-770, OH
Ross & Fullerton Ltd v. Carnegie 2000 G.W.D. 30-1191, HCJ Appeal

Ross Harper & Murphy v. Banks 2000 S.C. 500; 2000 S.L.T. 699; 2000 S.C.L.R. 736;
    [2000] Lloyd's Rep. P.N. 631; [2000] P.N.L.R. 631; *Times,* May 30, 2000, OH . .   *Digested,* 00/**6603**
Ross Harper & Murphy v. Banks (Leave to Reclaim) 2000 G.W.D. 20-782, OH
Rossmeier v. Mounthooly Transport 2000 S.L.T. 208; [2000] I.L.Pr. 697; 1999 G.W.D.
    35-1661; *Times,* February 7, 2000, 1 Div; reversing 1999 S.C.L.R. 236; 1999
    G.W.D. 2-72, Sh Pr. . . . .   *Digested,* 00/**5930**
Roulston v. Friel 1998 G.W.D. 19-979, HCJ Appeal
Rowan v. HM Advocate see Rowan, Petitioners (No.2)
Rowan v. Steinberg see Kennedy v. Steinberg
Rowan, Petitioners (No.2); *sub nom* Rowan v. HM Advocate 1998 S.L.T. 53; 1997
    G.W.D. 12-512, HCJ. . . . .   *Digested,* 98/**5667**
Rowe v. Lees 1998 G.W.D. 30-1546, HCJ Appeal
Rowley v. McFadyen (Sentencing) 2001 G.W.D. 26-1029, HCJ Appeal
Roxburgh DC v. Collins 1991 S.L.T. (Sh. Ct.) 49; 1991 S.C.L.R. 575, Sh Pr . . . .   *Digested,* 91/**5195**:
                                                                                          Distinguished, 00/6537
Roy v. MR Pearlman Ltd 1999 S.C. 459; 2000 S.L.T. 727; 1999 S.C.L.R. 803; [1999] 2
    C.M.L.R. 1155; 1999 G.W.D. 11-486; *Times,* May 13, 1999, OH . . . .   *Digested,* 99/**5629**
Roy's Trustee, Noter; *sub nom* Wright, Noter; Mackenzie's Trustee, Noter 2000 S.L.T. (Sh
    Ct) 77; 2000 S.C.L.R. 1105; 2000 G.W.D. 15-621, Sh Ct (Tayside) . . . .   *Digested,* 00/**6510**
Royal Air Force Association Club v. Dumfries and Galloway Council 2001 S.C.L.R. 1;
    2000 G.W.D. 14-516, OH . . . .   *Digested,* 01/**6875**
Royal & Sun Alliance Insurance v. Wyman-Gordon Ltd 2001 S.L.T. 1305; 2001 G.W.D.
    31-1251, OH . . . .   *Digested,* 01/**6669**
Royal Assurance Plc v. Scottish Equitable Plc 2001 G.W.D. 10-329, OH
Royal Bank of Scotland Plc v. Bird 1999 G.W.D. 4-172, Sh Ct
Royal Bank of Scotland Plc v. Blake Unreported. . . . .   *Distinguished,* 98/6013
Royal Bank of Scotland Plc v. Boyle 1999 Hous. L.R. 63, Sh Pr; reversing 1999 Hous.
    L.R. 43, Sh Ct . . . .   *Digested,* 99/**6270**
Royal Bank of Scotland Plc v. Clark 2000 S.L.T. (Sh Ct) 101; 2000 S.C.L.R. 193; 2000
    G.W.D. 2-40, Sh Ct (South Strathclyde) . . . .   *Digested,* 00/**6670**
Royal Bank of Scotland Plc v. Customs and Excise Commissioners [1999] B.V.C. 2240;
    [1999] V. & D.R. 122, V&DTr. . . . .   *Digested,* 00/**5310**
Royal Bank of Scotland Plc v. Forbes 1987 S.C. 99; 1988 S.L.T. 73; 1987 S.C.L.R. 294,
    OH . . . .   *Digested,* 88/**3747**:
                            Considered, 91/4417: *Followed,* 92/5245, 00/6516: *Not followed,* 89/4234,
                                                                                                  91/4418
Royal Bank of Scotland Plc v. Harper Macleod 1999 S.L.T. (Sh Ct) 99; 1999 S.C.L.R.
    781; 1999 G.W.D. 16-733, Sh Pr . . . .   *Digested,* 99/**5705**
Royal Bank of Scotland Plc v. Holmes 1999 S.L.T. 563; 1999 S.C.L.R. 297; 1999 G.W.D.
    5-234, OH . . . .   *Digested,* 99/**5793**
Royal Bank of Scotland Plc v. Home 2001 S.C. 224; 2000 G.W.D. 29-1109, OH. . . . . . .   *Digested,* 01/**6867**
Royal Bank of Scotland Plc v. Kinnear 2001 G.W.D. 3-124, Sh Pr
Royal Bank of Scotland Plc v. Lamb's Trustee 1998 G.W.D. 36-1880, OH
Royal Bank of Scotland Plc v. MacGregor 1998 S.C.L.R. 923, OH . . . .   *Digested,* 98/**6179**
Royal Bank of Scotland Plc v. Malcolm (No.1) 1998 S.L.T. 331; 1997 G.W.D. 23-1134, 1
    Div . . . .   *Digested,* 98/**5498**
Royal Bank of Scotland Plc v. Malcolm (No.2) 1999 S.C.L.R. 854; 1999 G.W.D. 16-734,
    2 Div. . . . .   *Digested,* 00/**5892**
Royal Bank of Scotland Plc v. Shanks 1998 S.L.T. 355, OH . . . .   *Digested,* 98/**5433**
Royal Bank of Scotland Plc v. Tominey 2001 G.W.D. 18-690, Ex Div
Royal Bank of Scotland Plc v. Wilson 2001 S.L.T. (Sh Ct) 2; 2000 G.W.D. 17-689, Sh Ct
    (Lothian) . . . .   *Digested,* 01/**6882**
Royal Life Insurance Ltd v. Douglas 1998 S.C.L.R. 405, Sh Pr . . . .   *Digested,* 98/**5510**
Royal Society for the Protection of Birds v. Secretary of State for Scotland; *sub nom*
    RSPB, Petitioners 2000 S.L.T. 1272; 2000 S.C.L.R. 1045; [2000] 3 C.M.L.R.
    1157; [2001] Env. L.R. 19; [2000] 4 P.L.R. 120; 2000 G.W.D. 26-961; *Times,*
    September 12, 2000, 1 Div; reversing 2000 S.L.T. 22; [2000] 1 C.M.L.R. 449;
    [2000] Eu. L.R. 481; [2000] Env. L.R. 168; [2000] 1 P.L.R. 29; 1999 G.W.D. 33-
    1560; *Times,* December 14, 1999, OH . . . .   *Digested,* 00/**5882**
RSPB, Petitioners see Royal Society for the Protection of Birds v. Secretary of State for
    Scotland
Rubislaw Land Co Ltd v. Aberdeen Construction Group Ltd 1999 G.W.D. 14-647, OH
Ruddle v. Secretary of State for Scotland 1999 G.W.D. 29-1395, Sh Ct
Rumney v. HM Advocate 1998 G.W.D. 33-1699, HCJ Appeal
Rush v. William Sommerville & Sons Ltd 1997 Rep. L.R. 135, Sh Ct . . . .   *Digested,* 98/**5935**
Rush's Trustee v. Rush 1998 G.W.D. 33-1690, OH
Rushberry v. Vannet 1998 G.W.D. 20-1051, HCJ Appeal
Russell v. Cleland 1885 S.L.R. 211, 2 Div . . . .   *Distinguished,*
                                                                                                     98/6201
Russell v. Dickson 1997 S.C. 269; 1998 S.L.T. 96; 1997 G.W.D. 22-1058; *Times,* June
    23, 1997, OH. . . . .   *Digested,* 97/**5568**
Russell v. Higson (Sentencing) 2001 G.W.D. 6-223, HCJ Appeal
Russell v. HM Advocate (Sentencing) 1999 G.W.D. 19-880, HCJ Appeal
Russell v. HM Advocate (Sentencing) 1999 G.W.D. 2-91, HCJ Appeal

Russell v. Russell 1999 S.L.T. (Sh Ct) 97; 1999 S.C.L.R. 936; 1999 G.W.D. 15-719, Sh
Pr . . . . *Digested*, 00/**6541**
Russo v. Hardey 2000 G.W.D. 27-1049, Ex Div; affirming 1997 G.W.D. 6-246, OH
Russo v. Russo 1998 S.L.T. (Sh Ct) 32; 1997 S.C.L.R. 1035; 1997 G.W.D. 32-1656, Sh
Pr . . . . *Digested*, 98/**6201**
Russo v. Russo (Expenses) 1999 G.W.D. 38-1850, OH
Rutherford (James George Neville) v. HM Advocate 1998 J.C. 34; 1998 S.L.T. 740;
1997 S.C.C.R. 711; 1997 G.W.D. 35-1749, HCJ Appeal . . . . *Digested*, 98/**5638**
Rutherford v. Virtue 1993 S.C.L.R. 886, Sh Ct . . . . *Digested*, 94/**6315**:
Considered, 00/5939
Ruxton v. Borland 2000 G.W.D. 9-326, HCJ Appeal . . . . *Subsequent proceed-
ings*, 00/6104
Ruxton v. Borland (Procedural Issues) 2000 J.C. 475; 2000 S.L.T. 612; 2000 S.C.C.R.
484; 2000 G.W.D. 14-524, HCJ Appeal . . . . *Digested*, 00/**6104**
Ruxton v. Lang (Fiona Marjorie) 1998 S.C.C.R. 1, Sh Ct . . . . *Digested*, 98/**5583**
Ruxton v. Starrs see Starrs v. Ruxton
Ryan v. HM Advocate 1998 G.W.D. 29-1488, HCJ Appeal
Ryan (Mary) v. HM Advocate 1999 J.C. 325; 2000 S.L.T. 4; 1999 S.C.C.R. 792; 1999
G.W.D. 30-1416, HCJ Appeal . . . . *Digested*, 00/**6053**
Ryan v. Imperial Brewing and Leisure see Courage Group's Pension Schemes, Re
Ryan v. Ritchie 1999 G.W.D. 24-1160, HCJ Appeal

S (Adoption), Re see S v. M (Consent: Missing Parent)
S v. Edinburgh City Council see Shiels v. Edinburgh City Council
S v. HM Advocate see Steele v. HM Advocate
S v. HM Advocate (Indecent Conduct) 2001 S.C.C.R. 276; 2001 G.W.D. 10-337, HCJ
Appeal . . . . *Digested*, 01/**6379**
S v. HM Advocate (Sentencing) 1999 G.W.D. 40-1930, HCJ Appeal
S v. HM Advocate (Sentencing) 2001 G.W.D. 16-623, HCJ Appeal
S v. Lynch 1997 S.L.T. 1377; 1997 S.C.L.R. 971; 1997 G.W.D. 30-1500, 1 Div . . . . *Digested*, 98/**5853**
S v. M (A Minor: Access Order) see Sanderson v. McManus
S v. M (Consent: Missing Parent); *sub nom* S, Petitioners; ES, Petitioner (Adoption); S
(Adoption), Re; M v. S (Consent: Missing Parent) 1999 S.C. 388; 1999 S.L.T.
571; 1999 S.C.L.R. 738; [1999] 2 F.L.R. 374; 1999 Fam. L.R. 26; [1999] Fam.
Law 523; 1999 G.W.D. 6-286; *Times*, March 23, 1999, Ex Div . . . . *Digested*, 99/**6056**
S v. Miller (No.1); *sub nom* S v. Principal Reporter (No.1) 2001 S.C. 977; 2001 S.L.T.
531; [2001] U.K.H.R.R. 514; 2001 G.W.D. 13-458, 1 Div . . . . *Digested*, 01/**6506**:
Cited, 01/6507
S v. Miller (No.2); *sub nom* S v. Principal Reporter (No.2) 2001 S.L.T. 1304; 2001
G.W.D. 26-995, 1 Div . . . . *Digested*, 01/**6507**
S v. Principal Reporter (No.1) see S v. Miller (No.1)
S v. Principal Reporter (No.2) see S v. Miller (No.2)
S v. Stirling Council (Local Authority Care); *sub nom* ES, Petitioner (Local Authority
Care) 2000 S.L.T. 979; 1999 Hous. L.R. 73; 1999 G.W.D. 25-1216, OH . . . . *Digested*, 99/**6066**
S v. Wright 2001 G.W.D. 25-920, Ex Div
S, Petitioners see S v. M (Consent: Missing Parent)
Sabri-Tabrizi v. Lothian Health Board 1998 S.C. 373; 1998 S.L.T. 607; (1998) 43
B.M.L.R. 190; 1998 Rep. L.R. 37; 1998 G.W.D. 5-247, OH . . . . *Digested*, 98/**6114**
Saddiq v. Brown 1999 G.W.D. 28-1348, HCJ Appeal
Saddiq v. Crowe [1999] 12 S.L.L.P. 21; 1998 G.W.D. 35-1822, HCJ Appeal . . . . *Digested*, 99/**5962**
Sadiq v. Higson (Sentencing) 2001 G.W.D. 32-1287, HCJ Appeal
Saeed v. Waheed 1996 S.L.T. (Sh Ct) 39; 1995 S.C.L.R. 504, Sh Pr . . . . *Digested*, 95/**5841**:
Not followed, 98/5539
Safeway Stores Plc v. Glasgow City Licensing Board 2001 S.L.T. 1115; [2001] 20
S.L.L.P. 16; 2001 G.W.D. 24-907, Ex Div . . . . *Digested*, 01/**6786**
Sahota v. HM Advocate 2000 G.W.D. 39-1447, HCJ Appeal
Saini v. Secretary of State for the Home Department 2001 S.C. 951; 2001 G.W.D. 13-
507, Ex Div; reversing 1999 S.L.T. 1249; 1999 G.W.D. 12-567, OH . . . . *Digested*, 99/**6294**
Salih v. Enfield AHA [1991] 3 All E.R. 400; [1991] 2 Med. L.R. 235; *Independent*,
March 26, 1991; *Guardian*, May 2, 1991; *Daily Telegraph*, April 8, 1991, CA;
reversing *Times*, December 7, 1989, QBD . . . . *Digested*, 92/**1797**:
Considered, 00/4200: *Not followed*, 98/5723
Salmon (Donald) v. HM Advocate; Moore (Anthony James Irvine) v. HM Advocate
1999 J.C. 67; 1999 S.L.T. 169; 1998 S.C.C.R. 740; 1998 G.W.D. 39-2002, HCJ
Appeal . . . . *Digested*, 99/**5832**:
Considered, 01/6387
Salomon v. Salomon & Co Ltd; *sub nom* Broderip v. Salomon; Salomon & Co Ltd v.
Salomon [1897] A.C. 22, HL; reversing [1895] 2 Ch. 323, CA . . . . *Applied*, 47-51/9135,
62/1718, 66/1369, 77/3268, 78/271, 78/3172, 80/306, 90/538, 98/618, 01/705,
01/944: *Considered*, 60/3342, 68/160, 68/2956, 69/138, 69/2956, 75/803,
77/174, 78/2678, 81/2194, 83/923, 84/958, 87/3003, 98/2188, 00/5985:
Distinguished, 53/940, 74/1837: *Followed*, 97/2379
Salomon & Co Ltd v. Salomon see Salomon v. Salomon & Co Ltd

Saltire Press Ltd, Re see Saltire Press Ltd v. AB
Saltire Press Ltd v. AB; *sub nom* Saltire Press Ltd, Re; Saltire Press Ltd v. Boyd 1998
    S.C. 718; 1999 S.L.T. 438; 1998 S.C.L.R. 836; 1998 G.W.D. 20-1036, 1 Div. . . . .   *Digested*, 98/**5820**
Saltire Press Ltd v. Boyd see Saltire Press Ltd v. AB
Samson v. Heywood 1998 G.W.D. 21-1083, HCJ Appeal
Samson v. Ruxton 1998 G.W.D. 33-1704, HCJ Appeal
Samuel Smith Old Brewery (Tadcaster) v. Edinburgh City Council (No.1) 2000 G.W.D.
    15-632, OH
Samuel Smith Old Brewery (Tadcaster) v. Edinburgh City Council (No.2) 2001 S.L.T.
    977; 2000 G.W.D. 36-1369, OH
Samushanga v. Higson (Sentencing) 2001 G.W.D. 39-1490, HCJ Appeal
Sanderson (Robert Ross) v. HM Advocate 1999 S.L.T. 1033; 1999 G.W.D. 23-1093,
    HCJ Appeal . . . .   *Digested*, 99/**5909**
Sanderson v. MacManus see Sanderson v. McManus
Sanderson v. McManus; *sub nom* S v. M (A Minor: Access Order); Sanderson v.
    MacManus 1997 S.C. (H.L.) 55; 1997 S.L.T. 629; 1997 S.C.L.R. 281; [1997] 1
    F.L.R. 980; 1997 G.W.D. 6-220; *Times*, February 12, 1997, HL; affirming 1996
    S.L.T. 750; 1995 S.C.L.R. 902, Ex Div; affirming 1994 S.C.L.R. 537, Sh Pr . . . .   *Digested*, 97/**5631**:
              Considered, 01/2609, 01/6510: *Distinguished*, 01/6510
Sandison v. Graham Begg Ltd 2001 S.C. 821; 2001 S.L.T. 1352; 2001 Rep. L.R. 70;
    2001 G.W.D. 13-470, OH . . . .   *Digested*, 01/**6229**
Sangeelee v. Smith 1997 S.L.T. (Sh Ct) 97; 1997 S.C.L.R. 977; 1997 G.W.D. 28-1391,
    Sh Pr . . . .   *Digested*, 98/**5847**
Santini v. HM Advocate (Misdirection) 2000 S.C.C.R. 726; 2000 G.W.D. 16-647, HCJ
    Appeal . . . .   *Digested*, 01/**6389**
Santini v. HM Advocate (Sentencing) 2000 G.W.D. 23-886, HCJ Appeal
Sargent v. Dewar see Sargent v. Secretary of State for Scotland
Sargent v. Secretary of State for Scotland; *sub nom* Sargent v. Dewar 2001 S.C.L.R.
    190; 2000 Rep. L.R. 118; 2000 G.W.D. 28-1089, OH . . . .   *Digested*, 01/**6817**
Sarwar v. News Group Newspapers Ltd 1999 S.L.T. 327; 1998 G.W.D. 21-1085, OH . . .   *Digested*, 99/**5988**
Sattar v. Higson 2001 G.W.D. 25-978, HCJ Appeal
Sattar v. Secretary of State for the Home Department; *sub nom* Sattar, Petitioner;
    Nazimudden, Petitioner 2001 S.C.L.R. 748; 2001 G.W.D. 18-704, OH
Sattar, Petitioner see Sattar v. Secretary of State for the Home Department
Saul D Harrison & Sons Plc, Re [1994] B.C.C. 475; [1995] 1 B.C.L.C. 14, CA . . . . . .   *Digested*, 95/**2860**:
            Applied, 99/5731: *Considered*, 99/646, 00/620: *Followed*, 95/615
Saunders v. Royal Insurance Plc 1999 S.L.T. 358; 1998 S.C.L.R. 1118; 1998 G.W.D. 32-
    1672, OH . . . .   *Digested*, 99/**6309**
Saunders v. Royal Insurance Plc (Judicial Review) see Saunders, Petitioner
Saunders v. United Kingdom [1997] B.C.C. 872; [1998] 1 B.C.L.C. 362; (1997) 23
    E.H.R.R. 313; 2 B.H.R.C. 358; *Times*, December 18, 1996; *Independent*, January
    14, 1997, ECHR; affirming *Independent*, September 30, 1994, Eur Comm HR . . .   *Digested*, 97/**2816**:
           Applied, 01/1047: *Considered*, 97/2818, 98/3150, 00/5473, 00/6043, 01/974,
           01/6319: *Distinguished*, 00/667, 00/2300: *Followed*, 97/817, 00/3234:
                                    Not applied, 98/682
Saunders, Petitioner; *sub nom* Saunders v. Royal Insurance Plc (Judicial Review) 1999
    S.C. 564; 2000 S.L.T. 597; 1999 S.C.L.R. 1131; 1999 G.W.D. 23-1078, OH . . . . .   *Digested*, 99/**5619**
Save Britain's Heritage v. Number 1 Poultry Ltd; *sub nom* Save Britain's Heritage v.
    Secretary of State for the Environment [1991] 1 W.L.R. 153; [1991] 2 All E.R. 10;
    89 L.G.R. 809; (1991) 3 Admin. L.R. 437; (1991) 62 P. & C.R. 105; [1991] 3
    P.L.R. 17; (1991) 155 L.G. Rev. 429; [1991] E.G.C.S. 24; (1991) 88(15) L.S.G. 31;
    (1991) 135 S.J. 312; *Times*, March 1, 1991; *Independent*, March 1, 1991;
    Guardian, March 1, 1991, HL; reversing (1990) 60 P. & C.R. 539; [1990] 3 P.L.R.
    50; [1990] J.P.L. 831; *Times*, April 4, 1990; *Independent*, April 13, 1990;
    Guardian, April 12, 1990, CA; reversing *Times*, January 5, 1990; *Independent*,
    December 22, 1989, QBD . . . .   *Digested*, 91/**3494**:
        Applied, 92/450, 92/4157, 93/3909, 97/4090, 99/4181, 99/4267, 01/4652,
        01/4747: *Cited*, 92/4319, 92/4354, 93/3810, 94/4349: *Considered*, 93/3925,
           96/4734, 96/4832, 96/4836, 97/4093: *Distinguished*, 96/7151:
        Followed, 95/3610, 96/4705, 96/4753, 97/4070, 98/6143, 99/6411,
                    00/4474, 01/4750: *Referred to*, 95/2598
Save Britain's Heritage v. Secretary of State for the Environment see Save Britain's
    Heritage v. Number 1 Poultry Ltd
Sayer v. British Railways Board 1998 G.W.D. 2-61, OH
Scanlon v. Spiers 1999 G.W.D. 18-832, HCJ Appeal
Scherrer v. Dumfries and Galloway Council 2000 Hous. L.R. 42, Lands Tr (Scot) . . . . . .   *Digested*, 00/**6468**
Schofield v. Saunders & Taylor Ltd see Heil v. Rankin
Scobie v. Morefield Rhue and Ardmair Crofters 2001 S.L.C.R. 100, Land Ct (Div Ct)
Scotch Premier Meat Ltd v. Burns [2000] I.R.L.R. 639, EAT . . . .   *Digested*, 00/**6215**
Scotland v. Spiers 1998 G.W.D. 19-982, HCJ Appeal
Scott v. Adam 1998 G.W.D. 33-1693, HCJ Appeal
Scott v. Chief Constable of Strathclyde 1999 S.L.T. (Sh Ct) 66; 1999 G.W.D. 5-232,
    Sh Pr . . . .   *Digested*, 99/**5720**
Scott v. Crowe see Scott (David) v. Friel

Scott v. Fraser (Sentencing) 1998 G.W.D. 11-533, HCJ Appeal
Scott (David) v. Friel; *sub nom* Scott v. Crowe 1999 S.L.T. 930; 1999 S.C.C.R. 415;
    1999 G.W.D. 17-772, HCJ Appeal . . . . *Digested*, 99/**5850**
Scott v. Glasgow DC 1999 Rep. L.R. 122, OH
Scott v. Heywood (Sentencing) 2000 G.W.D. 4-135, HCJ Appeal
Scott v. HM Advocate 1999 G.W.D. 36-1761, HCJ Appeal
Scott v. Lees (Sentencing) 1998 G.W.D. 1-13, HCJ Appeal
Scott v. Lees (Sentencing) 1998 G.W.D. 14-728, HCJ Appeal
Scott v. Lothian RC 1999 Rep. L.R. 15; 1998 G.W.D. 33-1719, OH . . . . *Digested*, 99/**6374**
Scott v. McFadyen (Breach of Peace) 1999 G.W.D. 33-1579, HCJ Appeal
Scott v. McFadyen (Sentencing) 1999 G.W.D. 40-1947, HCJ Appeal
Scott v. McGlennan (Sentencing) 2000 G.W.D. 4-166, HCJ Appeal
Scott v. Robertson 2001 G.W.D. 7-261, Lands Tr (Scot)
Scott v. Scottish Ministers see Davidson v. Scottish Ministers
Scott, Petitioner see Davidson v. Scottish Ministers
Scottish Coal Co Ltd v. East Lothian Council; *sub nom* R. v. East Lothian Council Ex p.
    Scottish Coal Co Ltd 2001 S.L.T. 495; [2001] 1 P.L.R. 1; 2000 G.W.D. 17-701;
    Times, June 28, 2000, OH . . . . *Digested*, 00/**6625**
Scottish Criminal Cases Review Commission v. HM Advocate 2001 J.C. 36; 2001 S.L.T.
    905; 2000 S.C.C.R. 842; 2000 G.W.D. 28-1080, HCJ . . . . *Digested*, 01/**6374**
Scottish Criminal Cases Review Commission, Petitioners 2001 S.L.T. 1198; 2001 S.C.C.R.
    775; 2001 G.W.D. 27-1088, HCJ . . . . *Digested*, 01/**6375**
Scottish Daily Record & Sunday Mail Ltd v. News Group Newspapers Ltd 1998 S.L.T.
    1411; 1998 G.W.D. 12-585, 1 Div; reversing 1998 G.W.D. 9-427, OH . . . . *Digested*, 99/**6311**
Scottish Daily Record & Sunday Mail Ltd, Petitioners 1999 S.L.T. 624; 1998 S.C.C.R. 626;
    1998 G.W.D. 35-1785, HCJ Appeal . . . . *Digested*, 99/**5825**
Scottish Enterprise v. MacGeachy 2001 G.W.D. 9-314, 1 Div
Scottish Equitable Plc v. Miller Construction Ltd 2001 G.W.D. 28-1119, Ex Div
Scottish Football League v. Smith 1998 S.L.T. 606; 1998 G.W.D. 1-4, OH . . . . *Digested*, 98/**6062**
Scottish Homes v. Fairbairn 2000 Hous. L.R. 114, Sh Ct (Glasgow) . . . . *Digested*, 00/**6462**
Scottish Housebuilders Association Ltd v. Scottish Ministers see SHBA Ltd v. Scottish
    Ministers
Scottish Legal Aid Board, Applicants see McKay (Uisdean) v. HM Advocate
Scottish Life Assurance Co v. Agfa-Gevaert Ltd 1998 S.C. 171; 1998 S.L.T. 481; 1998
    S.C.L.R. 238; 1998 G.W.D. 1-48, Ex Div; affirming 1997 S.L.T. 1200; 1997 G.W.D.
    4-164; *Times*, January 8, 1997, OH . . . . *Digested*, 98/**6037**
Scottish Lion Engineering Ltd v. Benson (Restoration to Register of Companies) 2001
    S.L.T. 1037; 2001 G.W.D. 21-784, OH . . . . *Digested*, 01/**6273**
Scottish Ministers v. Drummond's Trustees see Scottish Ministers v. Trustees of the
    Drummond Trust
Scottish Ministers v. Trustees of the Diamond Trust see Scottish Ministers v. Trustees of
    the Drummond Trust
Scottish Ministers v. Trustees of the Drummond Trust; *sub nom* Scottish Ministers v.
    Trustees of the Diamond Trust; Scottish Ministers v. Drummond's Trustees 2001
    S.L.T. 665; 2001 S.C.L.R. 495; 2001 G.W.D. 12-444, OH
Scottish National Party v. Scottish Television Plc 1998 S.L.T. 1395; 1997 G.W.D. 20-932,
    OH . . . . *Digested*, 99/**6459**
Scottish Nuclear Ltd v. Assessor for Lanarkshire [2000] R.A. 280; 2000 G.W.D. 2-79,
    LVAC . . . . *Digested*, 00/**6647**
Scottish Old People's Welfare Council, Petitioners 1987 S.L.T. 179, OH. . . . . *Digested*, 87/**5156**:
                                 Applied, 94/6126, 96/6684: *Considered*, 89/3865, 00/6505:
                                               Distinguished, 97/6230, 99/5626
Scottish Power Plc v. Kvaerner Construction (Regions) Ltd 1999 S.L.T. 721; 1998
    G.W.D. 14-698, OH . . . . *Digested*, 99/**5782**
Scottish Provident Institution v. Shore 2001 G.W.D. 25-972, OH
Scottish Tourist Board v. Deanpark Ltd 1998 S.L.T. 1121; 1998 G.W.D. 3-135, OH . . . . . . *Digested*, 98/**6040**
Scrimgeour v. HM Advocate (Sentencing) 1998 G.W.D. 7-326, HCJ Appeal
Scrimgeour v. Scrimgeour 1988 S.L.T. 590, OH . . . . *Digested*, 88/**4640**:
                                Considered, 00/6436: *Distinguished*, 89/4724
Scrimshaw v. Stott 1998 G.W.D. 23-1165, HCJ Appeal
Sea Breeze Properties Ltd v. Bio-Medical Systems Ltd 1998 S.L.T. 319; 1997 G.W.D. 8-
    341, OH . . . . *Digested*, 98/**6033**
Seamless Roofing v. Smith 2000 S.C.L.R. 1102; 2000 G.W.D. 14-519, Sh Pr . . . . *Digested*, 01/**6264**
Sears Properties Netherlands BV v. Coal Pension Properties Ltd 2001 S.L.T. 761; 2000
    S.C.L.R. 1002; 2000 G.W.D. 14-551, OH. . . . . *Digested*, 01/**6752**
Seaton v. HM Advocate 1999 G.W.D. 14-664, HCJ Appeal
Secretary of State for Defence v. MacDonald see Advocate General for Scotland v.
    MacDonald
Secretary of State for Scotland v. Associated Asphalt Ltd 2000 G.W.D. 8-273, OH
Secretary of State for Scotland v. Highland Council 1998 S.L.T. 222; 1997 G.W.D. 19-
    907, OH . . . . *Digested*, 98/**6140**
Secretary of State for Scotland v. Mann; *sub nom* Advocate General for Scotland v.
    Mann [2001] I.C.R. 1005; *Daily Telegraph*, December 12, 2000, EAT

Secretary of State for Scotland v. Ramage 1952 S.L.C.R. 29, Land Ct (Full Ct) . . . . *Digested*, 52/**4532**:
　　　　　　　　　　　　　　　　　　　　Followed, 62/3812: *Not followed*, 98/6029
Secretary of State for Scotland v. Revival Properties Ltd see Edinburgh City Council v.
　　Secretary of State for Scotland
Secretary of State for Scotland v. Taylor see Taylor v. Scottish Prison Service
Secretary of State for Social Security v. Ainslie 2000 S.L.T. (Sh Ct) 35; 1999 G.W.D. 36-
　　1778, Sh Pr . . . . *Digested*, 00/**6685**
Secretary of State for Social Security v. Fairey see Cockburn v. Chief Adjudication
　　Officer
Secretary of State for Social Security v. Halliday see Cockburn v. Chief Adjudication
　　Officer
Secretary of State for Social Security v. M 1999 S.C. 235; 1999 S.L.T. 1046; 1999
　　S.C.L.R. 165; 1998 G.W.D. 39-2026; *Times*, December 31, 1998, 2 Div . . . . *Digested*, 99/**6398**
Secretary of State for the Environment, Transport and the Regions v. Legal & General
　　Assurance Society Ltd see R. (on the application of Holding & Barnes Plc) v.
　　Secretary of State for the Environment, Transport and the Regions
Secretary of State for the Home Department v. Adan (Hassan Hussein) see Adan
　　(Hassan Hussein) v. Secretary of State for the Home Department
Secretary of State for Trade and Industry v. Barnett (Re James Blake Ltd); *sub nom*
　　Secretary of State for Trade and Industry, Petitioner 1998 S.L.T. 63; [1998] B.C.C.
　　437; 1997 G.W.D. 20-934, OH . . . . *Digested*, 98/**6012**
Secretary of State for Trade and Industry v. Burn 1998 S.L.T. 1009, OH . . . . *Digested*, 98/**6011**
Secretary of State for Trade and Industry v. Campleman 1999 S.L.T. 787; 1998 G.W.D. 38-
　　1955, OH . . . . *Digested*, 99/**5729**
Secretary of State for Trade and Industry v. Hasta International Ltd 1998 S.L.T. 73, OH . . *Digested*, 98/**5519**
Secretary of State for Trade and Industry v. Josolyne 1990 S.L.T. (Sh. Ct.) 48; 1990
　　S.C.L.R. 32, Sh Pr . . . . *Digested*, 90/**4471**:
　　　　　　　　　　　　　　　　　　　　Followed, 94/5458, 95/6129, 99/5729
Secretary of State for Trade and Industry v. Lovat (Summary Dismissal) [2000] B.C.C.
　　485, Sh Ct (Glasgow) . . . . *Digested*, 01/**6274**
Secretary of State for Trade and Industry v. Mitchell 2001 S.L.T. 658; 2000 G.W.D. 37-
　　1379, OH
Secretary of State for Trade and Industry v. Normand 1994 S.L.T. 1249; 1994 S.C.L.R.
　　930; [1995] B.C.C. 158; [1995] 2 B.C.L.C. 297, OH . . . . *Digested*, 94/**5458**:
　　　　　　　　　　　　　　　　　　　　　　　　　　　Followed, 99/5729
Secretary of State for Trade and Industry v. Palfreman 1995 S.L.T. 156; 1995 S.C.L.R. 172;
　　[1995] B.C.C. 193; [1995] 2 B.C.L.C. 301, OH . . . . *Digested*, 95/**5547**:
　　　　　　　　　　　　　　　　　　　　　　　　　　　Considered, 98/670
Secretary of State for Trade and Industry v. Queen 1998 S.L.T. 735; [1998] B.C.C. 678;
　　1997 G.W.D. 25-1238; *Times*, August 27, 1997, Ex Div . . . . *Digested*, 97/**5707**
Secretary of State for Trade and Industry v. Ross 1998 G.W.D. 37-1890, OH
Secretary of State for Trade and Industry, Petitioner see Secretary of State for Trade and
　　Industry v. Barnett (Re James Blake Ltd)
Seils v. HM Advocate 1997 J.C. 176; 1998 S.L.T. 296; 1997 S.C.C.R. 518; 1997 G.W.D.
　　27-1359, HCJ Appeal . . . . *Digested*, 97/**5768**
Select Service Partner Ltd v. Assessor for Glasgow [2000] R.A. 264; 1999 G.W.D. 37-
　　1829, LVAC . . . . *Digested*, 00/**6658**
Sellwood's Curator Bonis v. Lord Advocate; *sub nom* Jardine v. Lord Advocate 1998
　　S.L.T. 1438; 1998 Rep. L.R. 47; 1998 G.W.D. 5-245, OH . . . . *Digested*, 98/**5482**
Semple v. Black 2000 S.C.L.R. 1098, Sh Pr . . . . *Digested*, 01/**6246**
Semple v. States Hospitals Board for Scotland 1998 G.W.D. 40-2035, Sh Ct
Semple Cochrane Plc v. Hughes 2001 S.L.T. 1121; 2001 S.C.L.R. 1081; 2001 G.W.D. 27-
　　1078, OH . . . . *Digested*, 01/**6223**
Semple Cochrane Plc v. P&O Cruises (UK) Ltd 2000 G.W.D. 30-1193, OH
Semple Fraser WS v. Quayle 2001 G.W.D. 16-653, Sh Ct (Glasgow)
Senior v. Munro 1998 G.W.D. 25-1260, HCJ Appeal
Senna-Cheribbo v. Wood 1999 S.C. 328; 1999 G.W.D. 4-162, Ex Div . . . . *Digested*, 99/**6068**
Shah v. MacLeod 1998 G.W.D. 20-1053, HCJ Appeal
Shah v. Secretary of State for the Home Department 2000 G.W.D. 26-997, Ex Div
Shand v. Higson 1999 G.W.D. 10-470, HCJ Appeal
Shankly v. Higson 2001 G.W.D. 10-342, HCJ Appeal
Shanks v. Gray 1977 S.L.T. (Notes) 26, 2 Div . . . . *Digested*, 77/**3334**:
　　　　　　　　　　　　　　　　　　　　　　　　Distinguished, 99/6443
Shanks v. Heywood (Sentencing) 2000 G.W.D. 14-544, HCJ Appeal
Shanks v. Lees 1998 G.W.D. 28-1417, HCJ Appeal
Shannon v. Crowe (Sentencing) 1998 G.W.D. 6-276, HCJ Appeal
Sharif v. Singh (t/a India Gate Tandoori Restaurant); *sub nom* Shariff v. Singh (t/a India
　　Gate Tandoori Restaurant) 2000 S.L.T. (Sh Ct) 188; 2000 G.W.D. 28-1070, Sh
　　Pr . . . . *Digested*, 01/**6256**
Sharif, Petitioner; *sub nom* Shariff v. Hamid; Kirmani, Petitioner 2000 S.L.T. 294; 2000
　　S.C.L.R. 351; 1999 G.W.D. 25-1176, OH
Shariff v. Hamid see Sharif, Petitioner
Shariff v. Singh (t/a India Gate Tandoori Restaurant) see Sharif v. Singh (t/a India Gate
　　Tandoori Restaurant)

Sharkey (John Jamieson) *v.* HM Advocate 2001 S.C.C.R. 290; 2001 G.W.D. 13-478, HCJ Appeal . . . . *Digested,* 01/**6387**

Sharp *v.* Avery & Kerwood [1938] 4 All E.R. 85, CA . . . . *Distinguished,* 99/6373

Sharp *v.* Coutts see Coutts Trustees *v.* Coutts

Sharp *v.* Henderson 1999 G.W.D. 29-1359, OH

Sharp *v.* Thomson; *sub nom* Sharp *v.* Woolwich Building Society 1997 S.C. (H.L.) 66; 1997 S.L.T. 636; 1997 S.C.L.R. 328; [1998] B.C.C. 115; [1997] 1 B.C.L.C. 603; 1997 G.W.D. 9-364; *Times,* March 26, 1997, HL; reversing 1995 S.C. 455; 1995 S.L.T. 837; 1995 S.C.L.R. 683; [1995] B.C.C. 852; *Times,* July 25, 1995, 1 Div; affirming 1994 S.L.T. 1068, OH . . . . *Digested,* 97/**6156**: *Applied,* 00/6511

Sharp *v.* Woolwich Building Society see Sharp *v.* Thomson

Sharpe *v.* HM Advocate 1999 G.W.D. 35-1694, HCJ Appeal

Sharples *v.* Ruxton (Sentencing) 1998 G.W.D. 16-799, HCJ Appeal

Shaw (Robert French), Petitioner; Milne (Gavin William), Petitioner 1999 S.L.T. 215; 1998 S.C.C.R. 672; 1998 G.W.D. 37-1930, HCJ Appeal . . . . *Digested,* 99/**6338**

Shaw (Dylan Latimer) *v.* Colley 1998 S.L.T. 17; 1997 S.C.C.R. 597; 1997 G.W.D. 27-1356, HCJ Appeal . . . . *Digested,* 97/**5842**

Shaw *v.* HM Advocate (Sentencing) 1998 G.W.D. 7-324, HCJ Appeal

Shaw *v.* McDonald 2001 G.W.D. 24-911, HCJ Appeal

SHBA Ltd *v.* Scottish Ministers; *sub nom* Scottish Housebuilders Association Ltd *v.* Scottish Ministers 2001 G.W.D. 40-1531, OH

Shearer *v.* Hingston (Sentencing) 2000 G.W.D. 15-594, HCJ

Shell (UK) Exploration & Production *v.* Grampian Assessor [2000] R.A. 295, Lands Tr (Scot) . . . . *Digested,* 00/**6646**

Sheltered Housing Management Ltd *v.* Aitken 1998 S.C. 150; 1998 S.L.T. 515; 1998 S.C.L.R. 59; 1997 G.W.D. 38-1925, Ex Div . . . . *Digested,* 98/**5497**

Shepherd *v.* Heywood 2000 G.W.D. 19-762, HCJ Appeal

Shepherd *v.* HM Advocate 1999 G.W.D. 31-1479, HCJ Appeal

Shepherd *v.* McDonald 1999 G.W.D. 22-1066, HCJ Appeal

Shepherd *v.* Scottish Ministers 2001 G.W.D. 15-570, OH

Shepherd *v.* Watt (Sentencing) 2001 G.W.D. 13-479, HCJ Appeal

Sheppard *v.* Kennedy 1999 G.W.D. 1-59, HCJ Appeal

Sheridan *v.* HM Advocate (Sentencing) 1998 G.W.D. 32-1642, HCJ Appeal

Sherlock *v.* Stillwater Clinic 260 N.W.2d 169, US Ct . . . . *Considered,* 98/5720

Shetland Islands Council *v.* Local Government Boundary Commission for Scotland; Orkney Islands Council *v.* Local Government Boundary Commission for Scotland 1999 G.W.D. 6-314; *Times,* March 15, 1999, OH . . . . *Digested,* 99/**6010**

Shetland Norse Preserving Co Ltd *v.* Braer Corp 1999 G.W.D. 21-978, OH

Shetland Sea Farms Ltd *v.* Assuranceforeningen Skuld see Shetland Seafarms Ltd *v.* Assuranceforeningen Skuld

Shetland Seafarms Ltd *v.* Assuranceforeningen Skuld; *sub nom* Shetland Sea Farms Ltd *v.* Assuranceforeningen Skuld 2001 G.W.D. 24-915, OH

Shetland Seafarms Ltd *v.* Braer Corp 1999 S.L.T. 1189; 1998 G.W.D. 31-1635, OH . . . . . *Digested,* 99/**6443**

Shetland Seafarms Ltd *v.* International Oil Pollution Compensation Fund (No.5) see Assuranceforeningen Skuld *v.* International Oil Pollution Compensation Fund (No.3)

Shetland Times Ltd *v.* Wills 1997 S.C. 316; 1997 S.L.T. 669; 1997 S.C.L.R. 160; [1997] E.M.L.R. 277; [1997-98] Info. T.L.R. 1; [1998] I.T.C.L.R. 49; [1997] F.S.R. 604; (1997) 16 Tr. L.R. 158; [1998] Masons C.L.R. 159; [1998] Masons C.L.R. Rep. 117; 1997 G.W.D. 1-5; *Times,* January 21, 1997, OH . . . . *Digested,* 97/**5742**

Shevlin *v.* Vannet (Sentencing) 1998 G.W.D. 6-300, HCJ Appeal

Shields (Alan Michael) *v.* Donnelly 2000 J.C. 46; 2000 S.L.T. 147; 1999 S.C.C.R. 890; 1999 G.W.D. 30-1417, HCJ Appeal . . . . *Digested,* 00/**6101**

Shiels *v.* Edinburgh City Council; *sub nom* S *v.* Edinburgh City Council 1999 Fam. L.R. 92; 1999 G.W.D. 21-1014, Sh Pr; affirming 1999 Fam. L.R. 86, Sh Ct . . . . *Digested,* 99/**5998**

Shilliday *v.* Smith 1998 S.C. 725; 1998 S.L.T. 976; 1998 S.C.L.R. 502; 1998 G.W.D. 16-821, 1 Div . . . . *Digested,* 98/**6215**

Shingleston *v.* Kennedy 1999 G.W.D. 17-802, HCJ Appeal

Shishmanian et Cie *v.* Loudon Valley Manufacturing Co Ltd 1998 G.W.D. 33-1692, OH

Shone (Andrew James) *v.* HM Advocate 1999 S.C.C.R. 486; 1999 G.W.D. 21-1018, HCJ Appeal . . . . *Digested,* 99/**5955**

Shoprite Group Plc *v.* Kwik Save Stores Ltd 1999 G.W.D. 5-233, Ex Div; reversing 1997 G.W.D. 18-813, OH

Shorrock Ltd *v.* Tarmac Construction Ltd 1998 G.W.D. 4-159, OH

Short's Trustee *v.* Chung (No.1) 1991 S.L.T. 472; 1991 S.C.L.R. 629, 2 Div . . . . *Digested,* 91/**4415**: *Considered,* 96/7035: *Followed,* 93/4825, 97/6154, 98/6001

Short's Trustee *v.* Chung (No.2) 1999 S.C. 471; 1999 S.L.T. 751; 1999 S.C.L.R. 815; 1999 G.W.D. 12-537, Ex Div; affirming 1998 S.C. 105; 1998 S.L.T. 200; 1997 S.C.L.R. 1181; 1997 G.W.D. 37-1885; *Times,* May 18, 1998, OH . . . . *Digested,* 99/**5709**: *Applied,* 00/5938

Short's Trustee v. Keeper of the Registers of Scotland; *sub nom* Laing v. Keeper of the
    Registers of Scotland 1996 S.L.T. 166; 1996 S.C.L.R. 571; *Times,* December 26,
    1995, HL; affirming 1994 S.L.T. 65; 1994 S.C.L.R. 135, 1 Div; affirming 1993
    S.L.T. 1291; 1993 S.C.L.R. 242, OH . . . .   *Digested,* 96/**7035**:
                                    Considered, 98/5496: *Subsequent proceedings,* 99/5709
Shovlin (Stephen) v. HM Advocate 1999 S.C.C.R. 421; 1999 G.W.D. 19-881, HCJ
    Appeal . . . .   *Digested,* 99/**5931**
Siddiqi v. HM Advocate 1998 J.C. 190; 1999 S.L.T. 111; 1998 S.C.C.R. 368, HCJ
    Appeal . . . .   *Digested,* 98/**5596**
Sigourney v. General Teaching Council for Scotland 2000 G.W.D. 2-53, 1 Div
Silver v. Higson 1998 G.W.D. 21-1073, HCJ Appeal
Silverman v. HM Advocate (Sentencing) 2001 G.W.D. 36-1376, HCJ Appeal
Silverman (Brian) v. HM Advocate see Hunter (Gary John) v. HM Advocate
Silverscreen Print Plc v. Watters 1999 G.W.D. 8-399, OH
Sim v. HM Advocate 1996 S.C.C.R. 77, HCJ Appeal. . . . .   *Digested,* 96/**6814**:
                                                                                                        Considered, 99/5832
Sim v. HM Advocate (Sentencing) 1999 G.W.D. 35-1678, HCJ Appeal
Sim v. Napier 1999 G.W.D. 18-834, HCJ Appeal
Simmons v. British Steel Plc 2001 Rep. L.R. 82; 2001 G.W.D. 8-303, OH . . . .   *Digested,* 01/**6663**
Simpson v. Crowe 1999 G.W.D. 3-144, HCJ Appeal
Simpson v. Donnelly (Sentencing) 1998 G.W.D. 15-759, HCJ Appeal
Simpson v. HM Advocate 2001 G.W.D. 16-603, HCJ Appeal
Simpson v. HM Advocate (Sentencing) 1998 G.W.D. 5-214, HCJ Appeal
Simpson v. HM Advocate (Sentencing) 2001 G.W.D. 10-349, HCJ Appeal
Simpson (Steven) v. HM Advocate see Murray (Neil Grant) v. HM Advocate
Simpson v. Lees 1998 G.W.D. 35-1803, HCJ Appeal
Simpson v. McKay (Sentencing) 1998 G.W.D. 15-763, HCJ Appeal
Simpson v. O'Donnell (Sentencing) 1998 G.W.D. 4-191, HCJ Appeal
Simpson v. Transocean Offshore (UK) Inc 2001 G.W.D. 35-1351, Sh Pr; reversing in
    part 2001 G.W.D. 17-682, Sh Ct (Grampian)
Simpson v. Urquhart (Sentencing) 2001 G.W.D. 36-1377, HCJ Appeal
Simpson v. Vannet (Sentencing) 1998 G.W.D. 36-1862, HCJ Appeal
Simpson (Alan Robert) v. Vannet see Cowan (Paul Matthew) v. HM Advocate
Simpson v. Wilson 1999 G.W.D. 1-27, HCJ Appeal
Simrad Ltd v. Scott [1997] I.R.L.R. 147, EAT . . . .   *Digested,* 97/**6014**:
                                                                                                        Considered, 99/6045
Sinclair v. Clan Line Steamers Ltd 2001 G.W.D. 4-172, Sh Ct (Grampian)
Sinclair v. Clark 1962 J.C. 57; 1962 S.L.T. 307; [1962] Crim. L.R. 777, HCJ Appeal. . . . .   *Digested,* 62/**3759**:
                                    Applied, 78/2599.a, 79/2353, 99/5809: *Explained,* 92/5401
Sinclair v. Heywood 1998 G.W.D. 36-1888, HCJ Appeal
Sinclair v. HM Advocate 1998 G.W.D. 40-2046, HCJ Appeal
Sinclair v. Lees (Sentencing) 1998 G.W.D. 13-668, HCJ Appeal
Sinclair v. MacDougall Estates Ltd 1994 S.L.T. 76, OH . . . .   *Digested,* 94/**6161**:
                                                                                                        Approved, 01/6866
Sinclair v. RD Fire Protection Ltd 2000 G.W.D. 4-121, OH
Singh (Gurdial), Petitioner 2000 S.C.L.R. 236; 1999 G.W.D. 25-1212, OH . . . .   *Digested,* 00/**6497**
Singh (Jijar), Petitioner see Singh (Jijar) v. Secretary of State for the Home Department
Singh v. Gallacher 2001 G.W.D. 13-529, HCJ Appeal
Singh v. Glasgow Licensing Board 1998 S.C. 830; 1998 S.C.L.R. 865; 1998 G.W.D.
    24-1229, 2 Div . . . .   *Digested,* 98/**6075**
Singh (Manjit) v. HM Advocate [2001] S.T.C. 790; 2001 J.C. 186; 2001 S.L.T. 812;
    2001 S.C.C.R. 348; [2001] S.T.I. 831; 2001 G.W.D. 14-547, HCJ Appeal. . . . . . .   *Digested,* 01/**6322**
Singh v. Lees (Sentencing) 1998 G.W.D. 16-831, HCJ Appeal
Singh (Harjinder) v. Secretary of State for Scotland 2000 G.W.D. 25-945, OH
Singh v. Secretary of State for the Home Department (Asylum: Credibility) 1999
    G.W.D. 29-1392, OH
Singh v. Secretary of State for the Home Department (Asylum: Material Evidence)
    1999 G.W.D. 35-1707, Ex Div; affirming 1998 G.W.D. 28-1440, OH
Singh v. Secretary of State for the Home Department (Asylum: Reasons) 1998 G.W.D.
    40-2070, OH
Singh v. Secretary of State for the Home Department (Leave to Remain) 1999 G.W.D.
    38-1856, OH
Singh (Amrik) v. Secretary of State for the Home Department 2000 G.W.D. 23-895,
    OH
Singh (Charanjit) v. Secretary of State for the Home Department Unreported, IAT . . . . .   *Referred to,* 00/**6498**
Singh (Charanjit) v. Secretary of State for the Home Department 2001 G.W.D. 32-1296,
    OH
Singh (Daljit) v. Secretary of State for the Home Department 2000 S.C. 219; 2000
    S.L.T. 243; 2000 G.W.D. 2-63, 1 Div . . . .   *Digested,* 00/**6491**
Singh (Gurjit) v. Secretary of State for the Home Department (No.1) 2000 S.L.T. 533;
    2000 S.C.L.R. 655; 2000 G.W.D. 12-431, OH . . . .   *Digested,* 00/**6493**
Singh (Gurjit) v. Secretary of State for the Home Department (No.2) 2001 S.C.L.R.
    776; 2001 G.W.D. 19-745, OH

Singh (Jasvir) v. Secretary of State for the Home Department 2000 G.W.D. 27-1056, 1 Div

Singh (Jasvir) v. Secretary of State for the Home Department (Continued Appeal) 2001 G.W.D. 26-1060, 1 Div

Singh (Jaswinder) v. Secretary of State for the Home Department (No.1) 1998 S.L.T. 1370; 1997 G.W.D. 40-2095, OH . . . . *Digested*, 99/**6288**

Singh (Jaswinder) v. Secretary of State for the Home Department (No.2) 1999 S.C. 357; *Times*, January 27, 1999, 2 Div . . . . *Digested*, 99/**6292**

Singh (Jijar) v. Secretary of State for the Home Department; *sub nom* Singh (Jijar), Petitioner 2000 G.W.D. 23-893, OH

Singh (Joga) v. Secretary of State for the Home Department 2000 G.W.D. 28-1075, OH

Singh (Kulwinder) v. Secretary of State for the Home Department 2000 S.C. 288, OH . *Digested*, 00/**6496**

Singh (Major) v. Secretary of State for the Home Department 2000 S.C.L.R. 610; 2000 G.W.D. 11-395, OH . . . . *Digested*, 00/**6498**

Singh (Ramel) v. Secretary of State for the Home Department 2000 G.W.D. 26-999, OH

Singh v. Singh 1998 S.C. 68; 1998 S.L.T. 1084; 1997 G.W.D. 34-1703, Ex Div; reversing 1997 G.W.D. 20-930, OH. . . . . *Digested*, 98/**5843**

Singh v. Vannet (Sentencing) 1998 G.W.D. 30-1560, HCJ Appeal

Singh v. Vannet (Sentencing) 1999 G.W.D. 18-854, HCJ Appeal

Singh v. Vannet (Sentencing) 2000 G.W.D. 20-798, HCJ Appeal

Singh (Pauiter Pal) v. Vannet 1999 S.L.T. 985; 1998 S.C.C.R. 679; 1998 G.W.D. 36-1855, HCJ Appeal. . . . . *Digested*, 99/**5889**: *Distinguished*, 00/6099

Singh, Petitioner 1999 G.W.D. 14-649, OH

Skead (Cameron) v. HM Advocate 1999 S.L.T. 1357; 1999 S.C.C.R. 669; 1999 G.W.D. 27-1268, HCJ Appeal . . . . *Digested*, 00/**6051**

Skelton v. Higson (Sentencing) 2001 G.W.D. 40-1517, HCJ Appeal

Skene v. Miller 1998 G.W.D. 31-1601, HCJ Appeal

Skerries Salmon Ltd v. Braer Corp 1999 S.L.T. 1196; 1999 S.C.L.R. 225; 1999 G.W.D. 1-63, OH . . . . *Digested*, 99/**6447**

Skinner v. Aberdeen City Council 2001 Rep. L.R. 118; 2001 G.W.D. 16-657, OH

Skinner v. MacLeod (Sentencing) 1998 G.W.D. 2-100, HCJ Appeal

Skinnider v. McFadyen 1999 G.W.D. 19-894, HCJ Appeal

Skirving v. Russell 1999 G.W.D. 15-701, HCJ Appeal

SL Timber Systems Ltd v. Carillion Construction Ltd 2001 S.C.L.R. 935; [2001] B.L.R. 516; 2001 G.W.D. 23-852, OH

Slater v. Fife Primary Care NHS Trust 2000 G.W.D. 19-765, OH

Slater (Oscar) v. HM Advocate 1928 J.C. 94; 1928 S.L.T. 602, HCJ Appeal . . . . *Considered*, 98/5607

Slater v. Vannet 1997 J.C. 226; 1998 S.L.T. 112; 1997 S.C.C.R. 578; 1997 G.W.D. 28-1406, HCJ Appeal. . . . . *Digested*, 97/**5764**: *Distinguished*, 99/5821

Sleigh v. Reith 2001 G.W.D. 25-981, HCJ Appeal

Slessor v. Wilson 1998 G.W.D. 30-1541, HCJ Appeal

Sloan v. HM Advocate 1998 G.W.D. 24-1200, HCJ Appeal

Sloss v. HM Advocate 1998 G.W.D. 22-1124, HCJ Appeal

Smillie v. Gallacher (Sentencing) 2001 G.W.D. 25-952, HCJ Appeal

Smith (Elizabeth Anne), Petitioner; *sub nom* Smith (Elizabeth Anne) v. Smith (John Matthew) 1999 S.L.T. (Sh Ct) 5; 1998 S.C.L.R. 818; 1998 G.W.D. 26-1341, Sh Ct (South Strathclyde) . . . . *Digested*, 98/**6122**

Smith v. Aberdeen City Council 2001 Hous. L.R. 17; 2001 Hous. L.R. 93; 2001 G.W.D. 7-276, Lands Tr (Scot) . . . . *Digested*, 01/**6698**

Smith v. Advocate General for Scotland 2001 G.W.D. 3-139, OH

Smith v. Bank of Scotland; Mumford v. Bank of Scotland 1997 S.C. (H.L.) 111; 1997 S.L.T. 1061; 1997 S.C.C.R. 765; [1998] Lloyd's Rep. Bank. 62; [1997] 2 F.L.R. 862; (1997) Hous. L.R. 89; [1997] Fam. Law 791; [1997] N.P.C. 94; 1997 G.W.D. 21-1004; *Times*, June 23, 1997, HL; reversing 1996 S.L.T. 392; 1995 S.C.L.R. 839; [1996] 1 F.L.R. 344; [1996] Fam. Law 149; *Times*, September 29, 1995, 1 Div; affirming 1994 S.L.T. 1288; 1994 S.C.L.R. 856; *Times*, August 4, 1994; Scotsman, September 14, 1994, OH . . . . *Digested*, 97/**6087**: *Applied*, 99/6431, 00/6676: *Cited*, 00/6670: *Considered*, 98/6181: *Not applied*, 01/6882: *Referred to*, 00/6669, 00/6674

Smith v. Braer Corp 1999 G.W.D. 21-1023, OH

Smith v. Donnelly 2001 S.L.T. 1007; 2001 S.C.C.R. 800; 2001 G.W.D. 26-1011, HCJ Appeal . . . . *Digested*, 01/**6702**

Smith v. Donnelly (Sentencing) 2001 G.W.D. 32-1284, HCJ Appeal

Smith v. Dundee City Council 2001 Hous. L.R. 78; 2001 G.W.D. 20-778, Lands Tr (Scot)

Smith v. Forsyth 2001 G.W.D. 27-1110, Sh Ct (Grampian)

Smith v. Gardner Merchant Ltd [1998] 3 All E.R. 852; [1999] I.C.R. 134; [1998] I.R.L.R. 510; (1998) 95(32) L.S.G. 29; (1998) 142 S.J.L.B. 244; *Times*, July 23, 1998; *Independent*, July 21, 1998, CA; reversing [1996] I.R.L.R. 342, EAT . . . . *Digested*, 98/**2197**: *Applied*, 00/2206: *Explained*, 01/6475: *Followed*, 01/2315

Smith *v.* Gilchrist (Sentencing) 2000 G.W.D. 37-1392, HCJ Appeal
Smith *v.* Gordon & Smyth 2001 G.W.D. 26-1066, OH
Smith *v.* Hamilton 1998 G.W.D. 29-1487, HCJ Appeal
Smith *v.* Heywood (Sentencing) 2000 G.W.D. 20-796, HCJ Appeal
Smith *v.* Higson (Sentencing) 1998 G.W.D. 16-824, HCJ Appeal
Smith *v.* Higson (Sentencing) 1998 G.W.D. 31-1608, HCJ Appeal
Smith *v.* Higson (Sentencing) 1999 G.W.D. 40-1917, HCJ Appeal
Smith *v.* Higson (Sentencing) 2000 G.W.D. 19-777, HCJ Appeal
Smith *v.* Hingston 2000 G.W.D. 2-62, HCJ Appeal
Smith *v.* HM Advocate (Delay) 2000 S.C.C.R. 926; 2000 G.W.D. 30-1168, HCJ
    Appeal . . . . *Digested,* 01/**6367**
Smith *v.* HM Advocate (Sentencing) 1998 G.W.D. 20-1029, HCJ Appeal
Smith *v.* HM Advocate (Sentencing) 1999 G.W.D. 37-1799, HCJ Appeal
Smith *v.* HM Advocate (Sentencing) 2000 G.W.D. 14-526, HCJ Appeal
Smith *v.* HM Advocate (Sentencing) 2000 G.W.D. 14-541, HCJ Appeal
Smith *v.* HM Advocate (Sentencing) 2000 G.W.D. 36-1360, HCJ Appeal
Smith *v.* HM Advocate (Sentencing) 2001 G.W.D. 13-484, HCJ Appeal
Smith *v.* HM Advocate (Sentencing) 2001 G.W.D. 13-494, HCJ Appeal
Smith *v.* HM Advocate (Sentencing) 2001 G.W.D. 13-495, HCJ Appeal
Smith *v.* HM Advocate (Sentencing) 2001 G.W.D. 36-1367, HCJ Appeal
Smith *v.* HM Advocate (Sentencing) 2001 G.W.D. 31-1239, HCJ Appeal
Smith (Andrew) *v.* HM Advocate 2001 S.L.T. 438; 2001 S.C.C.R. 143; 2001 G.W.D. 3-
    116, HCJ Appeal . . . . *Digested,* 01/**6307**
Smith (James) *v.* HM Advocate 1952 J.C. 66; 1952 S.L.T. 286, HCJ Appeal . . . . *Digested,* 52/**3862**:
    Considered, 98/5607
Smith (Peter Cockburn) *v.* HM Advocate 1999 G.W.D. 14-630, HCJ Appeal
Smith *v.* Kennedy 2000 G.W.D. 37-1414, HCJ Appeal
Smith *v.* Lees 1998 G.W.D. 33-1725, HCJ Appeal
Smith *v.* Lindsay & Kirk (A Firm) (No.1) 2000 S.C. 200; 2000 S.L.T. 287; 2000 G.W.D.
    1-20; *Times,* March 16, 2000, 1 Div; reversing 1998 S.L.T. 1096; 1998 S.C.L.R.
    572; 1998 G.W.D. 10-508, OH . . . . *Digested,* 00/**6444**
Smith *v.* Lindsay & Kirk (A Firm) (No.2) 2001 G.W.D. 10-362, OH
Smith *v.* McFadyen (Sentencing) 2000 G.W.D. 37-1403, HCJ Appeal
Smith *v.* Murray 1990 S.L.C.R. 90, Land Ct (Div Ct) . . . . *Digested,* 91/**5707**:
    Applied, 01/6738
Smith *v.* Redman 1998 G.W.D. 14-724, HCJ Appeal
Smith *v.* Reith 1999 G.W.D. 8-387, HCJ Appeal
Smith *v.* Ruxton 1999 G.W.D. 1-60, HCJ Appeal
Smith *v.* Shaw & McInnes Ltd 2001 G.W.D. 14-558, OH
Smith *v.* Smith 1998 G.W.D. 5-248, OH
Smith *v.* Smith 2001 G.W.D. 20-771, Sh Ct (Grampian)
Smith (Elizabeth Anne) *v.* Smith (John Matthew) see Smith (Elizabeth Anne), Petitioner
Smith *v.* South Ayrshire Hospitals NHS Trust 2000 G.W.D. 28-1076, OH
Smith *v.* South Wales Switchgear Co Ltd [1978] 1 W.L.R. 165; [1978] 1 All E.R. 18;
    1978 S.C. (H.L.) 1; 1978 S.L.T. 21; 8 B.L.R. 1; 122 S.J. 61, HL; reversing 1977 S.C.
    93; 1977 S.L.T. (Notes) 37, 2 Div; affirming 1976 S.L.T. (Notes) 42, OH . . . . *Digested,* 80/**359**:
    Applied, 83/4038, 93/499, 96/1216, 98/5546: *Considered,* 92/1553:
    Followed, 86/223, 94/4078, 96/5302
Smith *v.* Spiers 1998 G.W.D. 18-948, HCJ Appeal
Smith *v.* United Kingdom (No.1); Grady *v.* United Kingdom; Beckett *v.* United Kingdom
    [1999] I.R.L.R. 734; (2000) 29 E.H.R.R. 493; (1999) 11 Admin. L.R. 879; *Times,*
    October 11, 1999, ECHR . . . . *Digested,* 99/**3113**:
    Considered, 00/6485: *Previous proceedings,* 95/2663, 96/383
Smith *v.* Unum Ltd 2001 S.L.T. 184; 2000 G.W.D. 13-497, OH . . . . *Digested,* 01/**6719**
Smith *v.* Vannet 1999 G.W.D. 4-223, HCJ Appeal
Smith (Bernard Connolly) *v.* Vannet 1999 S.L.T. 435; 1998 S.C.C.R. 410; 1998 G.W.D.
    23-1157, HCJ Appeal. . . . . *Digested,* 98/**5587**
Smith Maritime Ltd *v.* Miller Methil Ltd 2001 G.W.D. 36-1359, Sh Ct (Grampian)
Smith's Executors *v.* Upper Clyde Shipbuilders Ltd (In Liquidation) 1999 G.W.D. 33-
    1597, OH
Smitheman *v.* Lees (Sentencing); *sub nom* Smithman *v.* Lees (Sentencing) 1998
    S.C.C.R. 108; 1998 G.W.D. 6-277, HCJ Appeal . . . . *Digested,* 98/**5681**
SmithKline Beecham Plc *v.* Dowelhurst Ltd (Infringement Action) see Glaxo Group Ltd
    v. Dowelhurst Ltd (Infringement Action)
Smithman *v.* Lees (Sentencing) see Smitheman *v.* Lees (Sentencing)
Smiths Gore *v.* Reilly (t/a Booth and Reilly Consulting Engineers) 2001 S.C.L.R. 661;
    2001 G.W.D. 17-687, Sh Pr
Smyth *v.* HM Advocate 1999 G.W.D. 35-1698, HCJ Appeal
Smyth *v.* HM Advocate (Sentencing) 2000 G.W.D. 34-1314, HCJ Appeal
Smyth *v.* Lees 1998 G.W.D. 37-1898, HCJ Appeal
Sneddon *v.* Forth Valley Health Board 2001 G.W.D. 18-708, OH
Sneddon *v.* HM Advocate 1998 G.W.D. 22-1131, HCJ Appeal
Sneddon *v.* Munro 1998 G.W.D. 37-1916, HCJ Appeal
Sneddon *v.* West Dunbartonshire Council 1998 G.W.D. 34-1766, Sh Ct

Societe General SA v. LloydsTSB Bank Plc 1999 G.W.D. 37-1822, 2 Div
Sodden v. Prudential Assurance Co Ltd 1999 S.C.L.R. 367; 1999 G.W.D. 6-312, 2 Div;
    affirming 1997 G.W.D. 28-1440, OH . . . .   *Digested*, 99/**6305**
Soderback v. Sweden [1999] 1 F.L.R. 250; (2000) 29 E.H.R.R. 95; 1999 Fam. L.R.
    104; [1998] H.R.C.D. 958; [1999] Fam. Law 87, ECHR . . . .   *Digested*, 99/**2302**
Sohal v. Glasgow City Licensing Board [1999] 13 S.L.L.P. 12, Sh Ct . . . .   *Digested*, 99/**6349**:
    Followed, 00/6562
Sokha v. Secretary of State for the Home Office 1992 S.L.T. 1049, OH . . . .   *Digested*, 91/**5142**:
    Considered, 99/6290
Sood Enterprises Ltd v. Glasgow City Licensing Board 1999 S.L.T. (Sh Ct) 51; [1999]
    12 S.L.L.P. 14; 1998 G.W.D. 33-1718, Sh Ct (Glasgow) . . . .   *Digested*, 99/**6350**
Soriani v. Cluckie 2001 G.W.D. 28-1138, Sh Ct (South Strathclyde)
Souter v. Andrew 1999 S.L.C.R. 52, Land Ct (Div Ct) . . . .   *Digested*, 00/**6533**
Souter v. McKay 1999 G.W.D. 11-509, HCJ Appeal
Souter v. McLeod 1999 S.L.T. 1006; 1999 G.W.D. 24-1132, HCJ Appeal . . . .   *Digested*, 99/**5812**
South Australia Asset Management Corp v. York Montague Ltd; United Bank of Kuwait
    Plc v. Prudential Property Services Ltd; Nykredit Mortgage Bank Plc v. Edward
    Erdman Group Ltd [1997] A.C. 191; [1996] 3 W.L.R. 87; [1996] 3 All E.R. 365;
    [1996] 5 Bank. L.R. 211; [1996] C.L.C. 1179; 80 B.L.R. 1; 50 Con. L.R. 153;
    [1996] P.N.L.R. 455; [1996] 2 E.G.L.R. 93; [1996] 27 E.G. 125; [1996] E.G.C.S.
    107; (1996) 93(32) L.S.G. 33; (1996) 146 N.L.J. 956; (1996) 140 S.J.L.B.
    156; [1996] N.P.C. 100; *Times*, June 24, 1996; *Independent*, July 2, 1996, HL;
    reversing in part [1995] E.G.C.S. 71; [1995] N.P.C. 66, QBD (Comm Ct) . . . . . .   *Digested*, 96/**4519**:
    Applied, 97/3846, 98/4005, 98/4027, 98/4031, 98/4384, 99/1389,
    99/4053, 00/1486, 00/4249, 00/4280, 01/4504, 01/4529, 01/4532:
    Considered, 97/3827, 97/3839, 98/3999, 98/4032, 98/5724, 00/4009,
    00/4247, 00/4279, 01/2511, 01/4263: *Followed*, 98/3959, 98/3987, 99/804,
    99/4018, 99/4057, 01/4528: *Not followed*, 00/4275:
    Previous proceedings, 95/1834: *Referred to*, 97/4871, 98/1432
South Ayrshire Council v. Morton; *sub nom* Morton v. South Ayrshire Council; TNS, 2
    Div; affirming [2001] I.R.L.R. 28, EAT
South Lanarkshire Council v. Lord Advocate 2001 G.W.D. 29-1154, 1 Div
South Lanarkshire Council v. Secretary of State for Scotland (1997) 1998 S.L.T. 445;
    1997 G.W.D. 19-904; *Times*, July 21, 1997, OH . . . .   *Digested*, 98/**6085**
Southesk Trust Co Ltd v. Secretary of State for Scotland 2000 S.C. 400; 2000 S.L.T.
    680; 2000 G.W.D. 13-451; *Times*, April 26, 2000, 1 Div; affirming 1999 S.L.T.
    1131; 1999 S.C.L.R. 415; 1999 G.W.D. 10-446, OH . . . .   *Digested*, 00/**5885**
Southwark LBC v. Ince (1989) 153 J.P. 597; (1989) 21 H.L.R. 504; [1989] C.O.D.
    549; (1989) 153 L.G. Rev. 831, QBD . . . .   *Digested*, 90/**2512**:
    Followed, 00/6602
Spalding v. McFadyen (Sentencing) 2001 G.W.D. 12-453, HCJ Appeal
Spears v. HM Advocate 1998 G.W.D. 28-1398, HCJ Appeal
SpeechWorks Ltd v. SpeechWorks International Inc [2000] E.T.M.R. 982; 2000 G.W.D.
    26-1013, OH . . . .   *Digested*, 01/**6726**
Speedie v. HM Advocate (Sentencing) 2001 G.W.D. 6-199, HCJ Appeal
Speirs v. Crawford & Son 2001 G.W.D. 19-750, Sh Ct (Grampian)
Spence v. Ayrshire and Arran Health Board see Urquhart v. Ayrshire and Arran Health
    Board
Spence v. McFadyen 2001 G.W.D. 23-878, HCJ Appeal
Spence v. Murray (Alford) Ltd 2001 G.W.D. 7-265, Sh Ct (Grampian)
Spence v. Wilson (No.1) 1998 S.C. 433; 1998 S.L.T. 688; 1998 G.W.D. 8-389; *Times*,
    May 18, 1998, OH . . . .   *Digested*, 98/**5711**:
    Approved, 98/5710
Spence v. Wilson (No.2) 1998 S.L.T. 959; 1998 Rep. L.R. 51; 1998 G.W.D. 20-1038,
    OH . . . .   *Digested*, 98/**5473**
Spencer v. Carnegie (Sentencing) 1999 G.W.D. 40-1934, HCJ Appeal
Spencer v. Vannet 1999 G.W.D. 27-1301, HCJ Appeal
Spiers v. GM Mining Ltd (No.1) 2000 G.W.D. 5-200, Sh Ct
Spiers v. GM Mining Ltd (No.2) 2000 G.W.D. 5-201, Sh Ct
Spijkers v. Gebroeders Benedik Abattoir CV (C24/85) [1986] E.C.R. 1119; [1986] 2
    C.M.L.R. 296, ECJ (5th Chamber) . . . .   *Digested*, 86/**1362**:
    Applied, 94/2001, 94/4832, 94/5110, 95/2071, 95/2073, 99/2133, 99/6043,
    00/2229, 00/2231, 00/2232: *Considered*, 95/2072, 96/2649, 97/2274,
    97/2278
Sportstune Motor Co Ltd v. Sarwar 2001 G.W.D. 7-259, Lands Tr (Scot)
Sproat v. South West Services (Galloway) Ltd 2000 G.W.D. 37-1416, OH
Sproul v. Vannet 1998 G.W.D. 19-967, HCJ Appeal
Sproull (Jason Robert) v. McGlennan 1999 J.C. 105; 1999 S.L.T. 402; 1999 S.C.C.R.
    63; 1999 G.W.D. 3-140, HCJ Appeal. . . . .   *Digested*, 99/**5926**
Spurway v. Morrod 2001 G.W.D. 36-1395, OH
Squire v. HM Advocate 1998 G.W.D. 28-1410, HCJ Appeal
St Johnstone Football Club Ltd v. Scottish Football Association Ltd 1965 S.L.T. 171, OH   *Digested*, 65/**4163**:
    Distinguished, 00/5832

St Martins Property Corp Ltd *v.* Sir Robert McAlpine & Sons see Linden Gardens Trust
    Ltd *v.* Lenesta Sludge Disposals Ltd
St Silas Church Vestry *v.* Trustees of St Silas Church; *sub nom* Vestry of St Silas Church
    v. Trustees of St Silas Church 1945 S.C. 110, 2 Div . . . . *Considered*, 99/6468
Staite *v.* Vannet 1998 G.W.D. 31-1611, HCJ Appeal
Standard Commercial Property Securities Ltd *v.* Glasgow City Council 2001 S.C. 177;
    2000 G.W.D. 27-1033, OH . . . . *Digested*, 01/**6849**
Stangoe *v.* Terex Equipment Ltd 2001 G.W.D. 40-1529, OH
Stannifer Developments Ltd *v.* Clydeport Properties Ltd 2000 G.W.D. 6-236, OH
Stannifer Developments Ltd *v.* Glasgow Development Agency (No.1) 1999 S.L.T. 430;
    1998 G.W.D. 2-57, OH . . . . *Digested*, 99/**5617**
Stannifer Developments Ltd *v.* Glasgow Development Agency (No.2) 1999 S.C. 156;
    1999 S.L.T. 459; 1998 S.C.L.R. 1132; 1998 G.W.D. 38-1946, 2 Div; affirming
    1998 S.C.L.R. 870; 1998 G.W.D. 26-1283, OH . . . . *Digested*, 99/**5625**
Stansfield *v.* Findlay 1998 S.L.T. 784; 1997 G.W.D. 26-1331, 1 Div . . . . *Digested*, 98/**5959**
Star Fire and Burglary Insurance Co Ltd *v.* C Davidson & Sons Ltd (1902) 10 S.L.T.282,
    2 Div. . . . . *Distinguished*, 01/6240
Stark *v.* HM Advocate 1999 G.W.D. 13-601, HCJ Appeal
Stark *v.* McGlennan (Sentencing) 2000 G.W.D. 19-771, HCJ Appeal
Starr *v.* Starr; *sub nom* Starr, Petitioner 1999 S.L.T. 335; 1998 S.C.L.R. 775; 1998
    G.W.D. 17-837, OH. . . . . *Digested*, 98/**5842**
Starr, Petitioner see Starr *v.* Starr
Starrs *v.* Ruxton; *sub nom* Ruxton *v.* Starrs 2000 J.C. 208; 2000 S.L.T. 42; 1999
    S.C.C.R. 1052; [2000] H.R.L.R. 191; [2000] U.K.H.R.R. 78; 8 B.H.R.C. 1; 1999
    G.W.D. 37-1793; *Times*, November 17, 1999, HCJ Appeal . . . . *Digested*, 99/**5884**:
              Considered, 00/6091, 00/6095, 01/6372: *Distinguished*, 01/92, 01/358:
                        Followed, 00/478: *Referred to*, 00/5841
Stead *v.* HM Advocate (Sentencing) 2001 G.W.D. 1-24, HCJ Appeal
Steedman *v.* HM Advocate see Hughes (Ryan Iain) *v.* HM Advocate
Steel *v.* Begg Cousland & Co Ltd 1999 S.L.T. (Sh Ct) 74; 1998 G.W.D. 21-1092, Sh Ct
    (Glasgow) . . . . *Digested*, 99/**5699**
Steel Aviation Services Ltd *v.* H Allan & Son Ltd (No.2) 1998 G.W.D. 21-1058, OH
Steele *v.* Brown 1999 G.W.D. 20-952, HCJ Appeal
Steele *v.* HM Advocate; *sub nom* S *v.* HM Advocate 1998 G.W.D. 26-1326, HCJ
    Appeal
Steelmek Marine and General Engineers Trust *v.* Shetland Sea Farms Ltd see Steelmek
    Marine and General Engineers Trust *v.* Shetland Seafarms Ltd
Steelmek Marine and General Engineers Trust *v.* Shetland Seafarms Ltd; *sub nom*
    Steelmek Marine and General Engineers Trust *v.* Shetland Sea Farms Ltd 1999
    S.L.T. (Sh Ct) 30; 1999 S.C.L.R. 735; 1999 G.W.D. 4-164, Sh Pr. . . . . *Digested*, 99/**5706**
Stenton (Leslie George) *v.* HM Advocate 1998 J.C. 278; 1999 S.L.T. 255; 1998
    S.C.C.R. 594; 1998 G.W.D. 28-1406, HCJ Appeal. . . . . *Digested*, 98/**5594**
Stephen *v.* City of Aberdeen Licensing Board 1999 S.C.L.R. 909, Sh Ct . . . . *Digested*, 00/**6563**
Stephen *v.* Dickson 1999 G.W.D. 33-1578, HCJ Appeal
Stephen *v.* HM Advocate (Sentencing) 2001 G.W.D. 24-898, HCJ Appeal
Stephen (William Gavin) *v.* McKay 1998 S.L.T. 280; 1997 S.C.C.R. 444; [1997] 8
    S.L.L.P. 22; 1997 G.W.D. 21-1024, HCJ Appeal. . . . . *Digested*, 97/**5902**
Stephen *v.* McLeod 2001 G.W.D. 11-385, HCJ Appeal
Stephen *v.* North of Scotland Water Authority (No.1) 1999 S.L.T. 342; 1998 G.W.D. 28-
    1448, OH . . . . *Digested*, 99/**5696**
Stephen *v.* North of Scotland Water Authority (No.2) 2000 G.W.D. 1-28, OH
Stephenson *v.* Higson (Sentencing) 2001 G.W.D. 27-1092, HCJ Appeal
Steven *v.* McFadyen 1999 G.W.D. 19-907, HCJ Appeal
Stevens *v.* Hamilton 1998 G.W.D. 24-1210, HCJ Appeal
Stevens (Andrew) *v.* HM Advocate 2001 S.C.C.R. 948; 2001 G.W.D. 36-1361, HCJ
Stevenson *v.* Chief Constable of Strathclyde 1998 Rep. L.R. 136; 1998 G.W.D. 18-935,
    Sh Ct . . . . *Digested*, 99/**5658**
Stevenson *v.* Lord Advocate 1998 S.C. 825; 1999 S.L.T. 382; 1998 G.W.D. 24-1224, 1
    Div; affirming 1997 G.W.D. 29-1482; *Times*, November 20, 1997, OH . . . . *Digested*, 99/**6397**
Stevenson *v.* Miller 1999 G.W.D. 14-667, HCJ Appeal
Stevenson *v.* Vannet (Sentencing) 2000 G.W.D. 29-1123, HCJ Appeal
Stevenson-Hamilton's Executors *v.* McStay (No.1) 1999 S.L.T. 1175; 1999 S.C.L.R. 488;
    1999 G.W.D. 12-565, OH . . . . *Digested*, 99/**6236**
Stevenson-Hamilton's Executors *v.* McStay (No.2); *sub nom* Stevenson-Hamilton's
    Trustees *v.* McStay 2001 S.L.T. 694; 2000 G.W.D. 22-872, OH . . . . *Digested*, 01/**6870**
Stevenson-Hamilton's Trustees *v.* McStay see Stevenson-Hamilton's Executors *v.*
    McStay (No.2)
Stewart *v.* Advocate General for Scotland 2001 S.C.L.R. 11; 2000 G.W.D. 21-840, 1 Div
Stewart *v.* Brown see Stewart (Patrick) *v.* Crowe
Stewart *v.* Carnegie (Sentencing) 2001 G.W.D. 1-33, HCJ Appeal
Stewart (Patrick) *v.* Crowe; *sub nom* Stewart *v.* Brown 1999 S.L.T. 899; 1999 S.C.C.R.
    327; 1999 G.W.D. 15-723, HCJ Appeal. . . . . *Digested*, 99/**5870**
Stewart *v.* Greenock Harbour Trustees (1868) 6 M. 95, 1 Div. . . . . *Applied*, 00/**5937**
Stewart *v.* Heywood see Millar *v.* Dickson

Stewart v. Heywood (Sentencing) 1998 G.W.D. 8-383, HCJ Appeal
Stewart v. Heywood (Sentencing) 1999 G.W.D. 26-1242, HCJ Appeal
Stewart v. Heywood (Sentencing) 2000 G.W.D. 14-536, HCJ Appeal
Stewart v. Heywood (Sentencing) 2001 G.W.D. 10-352, HCJ Appeal
Stewart v. Higson (Sentencing) 1998 G.W.D. 13-682, HCJ Appeal
Stewart v. Higson (Sentencing) 2001 G.W.D. 21-808, HCJ Appeal
Stewart v. HM Advocate (Sentencing) 1998 G.W.D. 20-1020, HCJ Appeal
Stewart v. HM Advocate (Sentencing) 1998 G.W.D. 33-1701, HCJ Appeal
Stewart v. HM Advocate (Sentencing) 1998 G.W.D. 28-1436, HCJ Appeal
Stewart v. HM Advocate (Sentencing) 2001 G.W.D. 21-802, HCJ Appeal
Stewart v. HM Advocate (Sentencing) 2001 G.W.D. 24-892, HCJ Appeal
Stewart (James Lumsden) v. HM Advocate 1980 J.C. 103; 1980 S.L.T. 245, HCJ
    Appeal . . . . *Digested*, 80/**3030**:
                           Applied, 90/4947, 99/5906: *Distinguished*, 86/3882, 89/3837
Stewart v. Kennedy 2001 G.W.D. 25-940, HCJ Appeal
Stewart v. McGlennan 1999 G.W.D. 18-837, HCJ Appeal
Stewart v. North Lanarkshire Council (Damages) 1998 S.L.T. 419; 1998 S.C.L.R. 195;
    1997 Rep. L.R. (Quantum) 34; 1997 G.W.D. 32-1642, OH . . . . *Digested*, 98/**5738**
Stewart v. North Lanarkshire Council (Employers Liability) 1997 Rep. L.R. 138; 1997
    G.W.D. 32-1642, OH . . . . *Digested*, 98/**5942**
Stewart v. Obertelli 1999 S.L.C.R. 104, Land Ct . . . . *Digested*, 99/**5633**
Stewart v. Perth and Kinross DC (No.2) 2001 S.C. 229; 2000 G.W.D. 28-1068, OH . . . *Digested*, 01/**6781**
Stewart v. Perth and Kinross DC (No.3) 2001 G.W.D. 21-813, OH
Stewart v. Ryden Residential Ltd 1999 G.W.D. 12-576, OH
Stewart (John) v. Scottish Ministers; *sub nom* Stewart (John) v. Secretary of State for
    Scotland 2001 S.C. 884; 2001 S.L.T. 856; 2001 G.W.D. 13-519, Ex Div; affirming
    2000 S.C. 255; 2000 S.L.T. 348; 2000 G.W.D. 4-159, OH . . . . *Digested*, 01/**6835**
Stewart v. Secretary of State for Scotland 1998 S.C. (H.L.) 81; 1998 S.L.T. 385; 1998
    S.C.L.R. 332; 1998 G.W.D. 4-153; *Times*, January 28, 1998, HL; affirming 1996
    S.C. 271; 1996 S.L.T. 1203, Ex Div; affirming 1995 S.L.T. 895, OH . . . . *Digested*, 98/**5406**
Stewart (John) v. Secretary of State for Scotland see Stewart (John) v. Scottish
    Ministers
Stewart v. Secretary of State for Social Security 2000 S.L.T. 826, 1 Div. . . . . *Digested*, 01/**6893**
Stewart v. Stewart 2001 S.L.T. (Sh Ct) 114; 2001 Fam. L.R. 72; 2001 G.W.D. 22-831,
    Sh Ct (North Strathclyde) . . . . *Digested*, 01/**6521**
Stewart v. Vannet 1998 G.W.D. 19-1001, HCJ Appeal
Stewart v. Walkingshaw 1998 G.W.D. 35-1795, HCJ Appeal
Stewart Buchanan Gauges Ltd v. BEC Ltd 2001 G.W.D. 3-126, OH
Stewart Milne Homes Ltd v. Secretary of State for Scotland 2000 G.W.D. 18-725, Ex
    Div
Stiell Facilities Ltd v. Sir Robert McAlpine Ltd 2001 S.L.T. 1229; 2001 G.W.D. 27-1077,
    OH . . . . *Digested*, 01/**6221**
Stiell Ltd v. Riema Control Systems Ltd 2000 S.C. 539; 2000 S.L.T. 1102; (2001) 3
    T.C.L.R. 9; 2000 G.W.D. 23-875; *Times*, June 28, 2000, Ex Div . . . . *Digested*, 00/**5977**
Stillie v. Crowe (Sentencing) 1998 G.W.D. 14-720, HCJ Appeal
Stipanovski v. Vannet 1999 G.W.D. 5-277, HCJ Appeal
Stirling v. McFadyen 2000 S.C.C.R. 239; 2000 G.W.D. 8-274, HCJ Appeal . . . . *Digested*, 00/**6005**
Stirling v. Norwest Holst Ltd (No.2) 1998 S.L.T. 1359; 1997 S.C.L.R. 1196; 1997 Rep.
    L.R. (Quantum) 23; 1997 G.W.D. 30-1527, OH . . . . *Digested*, 98/**5751**:
                                                      Considered, 98/5749
Stirling Council v. Local Government Property Commission 1998 S.L.T. 1396; 1997
    G.W.D. 24-1223; *Times*, July 18, 1997, OH . . . . *Digested*, 97/**6253**
Stirling Council, Petitioners 2000 G.W.D. 18-722, OH
Stirrat v. Edinburgh City Council 1999 S.L.T. 274; 1998 S.C.L.R. 971; 1998 G.W.D. 23-
    1182, OH. . . . . *Digested*, 98/**6088**
Stirrat Park Hogg v. Glasgow City Council 1998 G.W.D. 3-141, OH
Stoddart v. Farstad Shipping Ltd 1998 G.W.D. 3-131, OH
Stoddart v. Hingston (Sentencing) 1998 G.W.D. 11-534, HCJ Appeal
Stokes v. Reith 1998 G.W.D. 38-1969, HCJ Appeal
Stokes v. Spiers (Sentencing) 1998 G.W.D. 12-591, HCJ Appeal
Stokes v. Stokes 1999 S.C.L.R. 327, Sh Pr . . . . *Digested*, 99/**6062**
Stolt Offshore Ltd v. Miklaszewicz see Miklaszewicz v. Stolt Offshore Ltd
Stott (Procurator Fiscal) v. Brown see Brown v. Stott
Stott v. Minogue 2001 S.L.T. (Sh Ct) 25; 2000 G.W.D. 37-1386, Sh Ct (Tayside) . . . . . . *Digested*, 01/**6705**
Stott v. Willox 1998 S.L.T. (Land Ct) 34; 1997 S.L.C.R. 165, Land Ct . . . . *Digested*, 98/**5479**
Stout v. Wilson (Sentencing) 1998 G.W.D. 13-659, HCJ Appeal
Strachan v. Highland Council 1999 G.W.D. 38-1863, Sh Pr
Strachan v. HM Advocate 1999 G.W.D. 3-137, HCJ Appeal
Strachan v. Scottish Boatowners Mutual Insurance Association 2001 G.W.D. 19-754,
    OH
Strachan v. Strathmore Glazing 1998 G.W.D. 36-1884, OH
Strain v. Friel (Sentencing) 1998 G.W.D. 19-983, HCJ Appeal
Strain v. Friel (Sentencing) 1999 G.W.D. 4-189, HCJ Appeal
Strang v. Le Brusq 2001 Rep. L.R. 52, OH . . . . *Digested*, 01/**64**

Strathclyde Joint Police Board v. Elderslie Estates Ltd 2001 G.W.D. 27-1101, Lands Tr (Scot)

Strathclyde Joint Police Board v. Prestwick International Airport Ltd 1998 S.C. 490; 1998 G.W.D. 11-524, 2 Div; reversing 1997 G.W.D. 24-1184, OH . . . . *Digested, 98/6207*

Strathclyde RC v. Border Engineering Contractors Ltd 1998 S.L.T. 175; 1997 S.C.L.R. 100, OH . . . . *Digested, 97/5683*

Strathclyde RC v. Wallace; *sub nom* West Dunbartonshire Council v. Wallace [1998] 1 W.L.R. 259; [1998] 1 All E.R. 394; 1998 S.C. (H.L.) 72; 1998 S.L.T. 421; 1998 S.C.L.R. 340; [1998] I.C.R. 205; [1998] I.R.L.R. 146; (1998) 95(7) L.S.G. 31; (1998) 142 S.J.L.B. 83; 1998 G.W.D. 4-181; *Times,* January 24, 1998, HL; affirming 1996 S.C. 535; 1997 S.L.T. 315; 1996 S.C.L.R. 1046; [1996] I.R.L.R. 670, 2 Div. . . . . *Digested, 98/5807*: *Applied, 00/6214*

Strathclyde RC v. Zafar see Glasgow City Council v. Zafar

Strathford East Kilbride Ltd v. HLM Design Ltd 1999 S.L.T. 121; 1997 S.C.L.R. 877; 1997 Rep. L.R. 112; 1997 G.W.D. 31-1554; *Times,* December 1, 1997, OH . . . . *Digested, 98/5539*

Strathmore Building Services Ltd v. Greig (t/a Hestia Fireside Design) 2000 S.L.T. 815; (2001) 17 Const. L.J. 72; 2000 G.W.D. 19-735, OH. . . . . *Digested, 01/6293*

Strathtay Retail Ltd v. Perth and Kinross Licensing Board 1998 S.C.L.R. 1115; [1998] 11 S.L.L.P. 20, Sh Ct . . . . *Digested, 98/6072*

Strong v. Craig Associates 2000 G.W.D. 22-871, OH

Stroud v. HM Advocate 1999 G.W.D. 17-783, HCJ Appeal

Struebel v. Kennedy 2000 G.W.D. 14-561, HCJ Appeal

Struthers v. Struthers (Residence Order) 2000 G.W.D. 39-1443, Sh Ct (Grampian)

Stuart v. Angiolioni (Sentencing) 2000 G.W.D. 39-1470, HCJ Appeal

Stuart v. McGlennan 1998 G.W.D. 33-1727, HCJ Appeal

Stuart v. Stuart (Divorce: Financial Provision); *sub nom* Davie (or Stuart) v. Stuart 2001 S.L.T. (Sh Ct) 20; 2001 S.C.L.R. 215; 2000 Fam. L.R. 109; 2000 G.W.D. 28-1086, Sh Pr. . . . . *Digested, 00/6276*

Stuart v. Urquhart 1999 G.W.D. 22-1046, HCJ Appeal

Stuart's Trustee v. HJ Banks & Co Ltd; *sub nom* Ross v. HJ Banks & Co Ltd 1998 S.C.L.R. 1109, Sh Pr. . . . . *Digested, 99/6297*

Sturzenegger, Petitioner 2000 S.L.T. (Lyon Ct) 2, Lyon Ct . . . . *Digested, 00/5970*

Stuurman v. HM Advocate 1980 S.L.T. (Notes) 95, HCJ Appeal . . . . *Digested, 80/3011*: *Applied,* 92/5466, 93/4968, 93/4969: *Considered,* 01/6371: *Distinguished,* 97/5827

Style Financial Services Ltd v. Bank of Scotland (No.2) 1998 S.L.T. 851; 1997 S.C.L.R. 633; 1997 G.W.D. 7-255, OH . . . . *Digested, 97/5578*

Sullivan v. MacLeod (Sentencing) 1998 G.W.D. 29-1521, HCJ Appeal

Sullivan (Craig Alexander) v. McLeod 1998 S.L.T. 552; 1997 S.C.C.R. 764, HCJ Appeal   *Digested, 98/5664*

Summers v. Crichton 2000 G.W.D. 40-1495, OH

Summit Lease Finance (No.2) Ltd v. Lithoprint (Scotland) Ltd 1999 G.W.D. 27-1266, OH

Sunley v. McFadyen 2001 G.W.D. 29-1176, HCJ Appeal

Super (Tom) Printing and Supplies Ltd v. South Lanarkshire Council (No.1) see Tom Super Printing and Supplies Ltd v. South Lanarkshire Council (No.1)

Super (Tom) Printing and Supplies Ltd v. South Lanarkshire Council (No.2) see Tom Super Printing and Supplies Ltd v. South Lanarkshire Council (No.2)

Supreme Grand Chapter of Scotland, Order of the Eastern Star v. Shirkie 1998 S.C.L.R. 771, Sh Ct. . . . . *Digested, 98/5465*

Sureweld (UK) Ltd v. DS Baddeley (Engineering) Ltd 1987 S.C.L.R. 332, Sh Pr . . . . . . *Digested, 87/5124*: *Not followed, 99/5721*

Sutherland (Deceased), Re see Winter v. Inland Revenue Commissioners

Sutherland v. Barry (Retention of Rent) 2001 G.W.D. 38-1431, OH

Sutherland v. HM Advocate (Sentencing) 1998 G.W.D. 16-789, HCJ Appeal

Sutherland v. HM Advocate (Sentencing) 2001 G.W.D. 25-944, HCJ Appeal

Sutherland v. Inland Revenue Commissioners; *sub nom* Sutherland v. Lord Advocate 1999 S.C. 104; 1999 S.L.T. 944; 1998 G.W.D. 35-1814, 1 Div . . . . *Digested, 99/6303*

Sutherland v. Lord Advocate see Sutherland v. Inland Revenue Commissioners

Sutherland v. MacKenzie 1999 S.L.T. (Land Ct) 2; 1999 S.L.C.R. 70, Land Ct . . . . *Digested, 99/6319*

Sutherland v. MacLeod 2000 S.L.C.R. 18, Land Ct (Div Ct) . . . . *Digested, 01/6740*

Sutherland (Ian David) v. McGlennan 1999 S.C.C.R. 652, HCJ Appeal. . . . . *Digested, 99/5858*

Sutherland v. Network Appliance Ltd [2001] I.R.L.R. 12, EAT. . . . . *Digested, 01/6459*

Sutherland Estates v. Sutherland 1998 S.L.T. (Land Ct) 37; 1997 S.L.C.R. 144; 1998 G.W.D. 12-630, Land Ct. . . . . *Digested, 98/6029*

Sutherland's Estate, Re see Winter v. Inland Revenue Commissioners

Suttie v. HM Advocate (Sentencing) 2000 G.W.D. 4-145, HCJ Appeal

Swan v. Andrew Minto & Son 1998 Rep. L.R. 42, Sh Ct. . . . . *Digested, 98/6105*

Swan v. Secretary of State for Scotland (No.1); *sub nom* Swan, Petitioner 1998 S.C. 479; 1998 S.C.L.R. 763; [1998] 2 C.M.L.R. 1192; [1998] Env. L.R. 545; 1998 G.W.D. 11-516; *Times,* June 4, 1998, 1 Div; reversing [1998] Env. L.R. 251; 1997 G.W.D. 15-636, OH . . . . *Digested, 98/5880*

Swan v. Secretary of State for Scotland (No.2) [2000] Env. L.R. 60; 1999 G.W.D. 16-761, OH . . . . *Digested, 00/6229*

Swan, Petitioner see Swan v. Secretary of State for Scotland (No.1)
Swankie (Arthur Thomas) v. HM Advocate 1999 J.C. 40; 1999 S.L.T. 1225; 1999
    S.C.C.R. 1; 1999 G.W.D. 2-86, HCJ Appeal . . . .   *Digested*, 99/**5875**
Swankie v. Wilson 1999 G.W.D. 3-115, HCJ Appeal
Sweeney v. Carnegie (Sentencing) 2000 G.W.D. 33-1277, HCJ Appeal
Sweeney v. J&S Henderson (Concessions) Ltd [1999] I.R.L.R. 306, EAT. . . . .   *Digested*, 99/**6047**
Sweeney v. MacKenzie Construction Ltd 1998 S.C. 879; 1998 S.L.T. 1385; 1998
    S.C.L.R. 947; 1998 Rep. L.R. 128; 1998 G.W.D. 27-1388, 2 Div; reversing 1997
    S.C.L.R. 613; 1997 Rep. L.R. 35; 1997 G.W.D. 4-167, OH . . . .   *Digested*, 98/**5941**
Sweeney v. McLeod 1999 G.W.D. 19-899, HCJ Appeal
Sweeney v. Vannet 1999 G.W.D. 29-1399, HCJ Appeal
Swift v. Gilchrist 2001 G.W.D. 39-1452, HCJ Appeal
Swift v. MacNeill (Sentencing) 2000 G.W.D. 30-1200, HCJ Appeal
Swilken Ltd v. Applecraft Ltd 2000 G.W.D. 40-1483, OH
Swinton v. Reith (Sentencing) 2001 G.W.D. 6-195, HCJ Appeal
Symmers v. Lees; *sub nom* Symmers v. McFadyen 2000 J.C. 149; 2000 S.L.T. 507;
    2000 S.C.C.R. 66; 1999 G.W.D. 35-1717, HCJ Appeal . . . .   *Digested*, 00/**6040**
Symmers v. McFadyen see Symmers v. Lees

T v. A (Parental Rights) 2001 S.C.L.R. 647; 2001 G.W.D. 15-567, Sh Pr
T v. T see MT v. DT
T v. T (Admissibility of Child Statement) see MT v. DT (Admissibility of Child
    Statement)
T&I Consultants v. Cullion 1998 Hous. L.R. 9, LandsTr . . . .   *Digested*, 98/**5950**
T, Petitioner; *sub nom* AMT, Petitioners 1997 S.L.T. 724; 1996 S.C.L.R. 897; [1997]
    Fam. Law 8; [1997] Fam. Law 225; *Times*, August 20, 1996, 1 Div . . . .   *Digested*, 96/**6596**:
                                                                                                Applied, 00/6485
Taggart v. Friel 1999 G.W.D. 8-388, HCJ Appeal
Tailors of Aberdeen v. Coutts (1840) 1 Rob. 296, HL . . . .   *Distinguished*,
                                                                                                00/**6438**:
                                                                                          Referred to, 92/5853
Tait v. Abernethy (No.1) 1984 S.L.C.R. 19, Land Ct (Div Ct) . . . .   *Digested*, 85/**4833**:
                                                                                          Referred to, 00/6532
Tait v. Diamond Offshore Drilling (UK) Ltd 2001 G.W.D. 1-15, OH
Tait v. Fischer see Tate v. Fischer
Tait v. Heywood 1998 G.W.D. 17-861, HCJ Appeal
Tait v. HM Advocate (Sentencing) 1998 G.W.D. 22-1121, HCJ Appeal
Tait v. HM Advocate (Sentencing) 1999 G.W.D. 31-1482, HCJ Appeal
Tait v. HM Advocate (Sentencing) 2001 G.W.D. 39-1468, HCJ Appeal
Tait v. Main 1989 S.L.T. (Sh. Ct.) 81; 1989 S.C.L.R. 106, Sh Pr . . . .   *Digested*, 89/**4946**:
                                                                                          Considered, 98/5507
Tallah v. Secretary of State for the Home Department [1998] I.N.L.R. 258, IAT . . . .   *Digested*, 98/**5997**
Tams v. HM Advocate (Sentencing) 2001 G.W.D. 16-630, HCJ Appeal
Tannoch v. Glasgow City Council 2000 Hous. L.R. 64, Sh Ct . . . .   *Digested*, 00/**6469**
Tannock v. McGlennan 1998 G.W.D. 35-1835, HCJ Appeal
Tant v. HM Advocate (Sentencing) 2001 G.W.D. 6-205, HCJ Appeal
Tarmac Econowaste Ltd v. Assessor for Lothian Region 1991 S.L.T. 77, OH . . . .   *Digested*, 91/**5502**:
                                                              Applied, 01/6096: *Referred to*, 92/6511
Tarran v. Ferguson 2001 G.W.D. 24-883, Sh Ct (Tayside)
Tasker v. HM Advocate 1999 G.W.D. 12-545, HCJ Appeal
Tasker v. Munro 1998 G.W.D. 27-1362, HCJ Appeal
Tate v. Fischer; *sub nom* Tait v. Fischer 1998 S.L.T. 1419; 1998 Rep. L.R. 54; 1998
    G.W.D. 14-696, 2 Div; affirming 1997 Rep. L.R. (Quantum) 17, OH. . . . .   *Digested*, 98/**5717**
Tattersall v. HM Advocate 1998 G.W.D. 40-2048, HCJ Appeal
Taupo Totara Timber Co v. Rowe [1978] A.C. 537; [1977] 3 W.L.R. 466; [1977] 3 All
    E.R. 123; 121 S.J. 692, PC (NZ) . . . .   *Digested*, 77/**288**:
                                                     Applied, 79/342: *Followed*, 98/5524: *Referred to*, 80/1612
Taylor (Alan), Petitioner; *sub nom* Taylor v. Ellis & McHardy Ltd 2000 S.L.T. 1223;
    [1999] O.P.L.R. 275; 1999 G.W.D. 23-1118, 1 Div . . . .   *Digested*, 00/**6616**
Taylor v. Confederation Management Ltd 1998 G.W.D. 6-285, Sh Ct
Taylor v. Ellis & McHardy Ltd see Taylor (Alan), Petitioner
Taylor v. Glasgow City Council TNS, Ex Div; reversing 2000 S.L.T. 670; 1999 Fam. L.R.
    124; 1999 G.W.D. 30-1440, OH . . . .   *Digested*, 00/**6423**:
                                                                                                Followed, 00/6425
Taylor v. HM Advocate 2001 G.W.D. 16-602, HCJ Appeal
Taylor v. HM Advocate (Sentencing) 1998 G.W.D. 16-800, HCJ Appeal
Taylor v. HM Advocate (Sentencing) 1998 G.W.D. 28-1415, HCJ Appeal
Taylor v. HM Advocate (Sentencing) 1999 G.W.D. 1-22, HCJ Appeal
Taylor v. HM Advocate (Sentencing) 1999 G.W.D. 29-1382, HCJ Appeal
Taylor v. HM Advocate (Sentencing) 1999 G.W.D. 25-1196, HCJ Appeal
Taylor v. Kennedy (Sentencing) 2001 G.W.D. 19-729, HCJ Appeal
Taylor v. Leslie 1998 S.L.T. 1248; 1998 Rep. L.R. 110; 1998 G.W.D. 23-1184; *Times*,
    September 24, 1998, OH . . . .   *Digested*, 98/**6109**

Taylor *v.* Marshalls Food Group Ltd (No.1) 1998 S.L.T. 869; 1997 S.C.L.R. 815; 1997
    Rep. L.R. (Quantum) 11; 1997 G.W.D. 18-836, OH . . . .   *Digested,* 97/**5958**
Taylor *v.* Marshalls Food Group Ltd (No.2) 1998 S.C. 841; 1998 S.L.T. 1022; 1998
    G.W.D. 24-1188; *Times,* September 24, 1998, 1 Div.   *Digested,* 98/**5399**
Taylor *v.* Marshalls Food Group Ltd (No.3) 1999 S.L.T. 629; 1998 G.W.D. 39-2014, OH .   *Digested,* 99/**5678**
Taylor *v.* McGlennan 1998 G.W.D. 21-1061, HCJ Appeal
Taylor *v.* O'Donnell 1998 G.W.D. 18-902, HCJ Appeal
Taylor *v.* Reith (Sentencing) 1998 G.W.D. 8-385, HCJ Appeal
Taylor *v.* Scottish Prison Service; *sub nom* Secretary of State for Scotland *v.* Taylor;
    Taylor *v.* Secretary of State for Scotland [2000] 3 All E.R. 90; 2000 S.C. (H.L.)
    139; 2000 S.L.T. 708; [2000] I.C.R. 595; [2000] I.R.L.R. 502; 2000 G.W.D. 17-
    686; *Times,* May 12, 2000; *Independent,* June 19, 2000, HL; affirming 1999
    S.C. 372; 1999 S.L.T. 886; 1999 S.C.L.R. 263; [1999] I.R.L.R. 362; 1999 G.W.D.
    3-156, 2 Div; affirming [1997] I.R.L.R. 608, EAT. . . . .   *Digested,* 00/**6213**
Taylor *v.* Secretary of State for Scotland *see* Taylor *v.* Scottish Prison Service
Taylor *v.* Smith 2000 Rep. L.R. 75; 2000 G.W.D. 14-556, OH . . . .   *Digested,* 00/**6577**
Taylor *v.* Taylor 2000 S.L.T. 1419; 2001 S.C.L.R. 16; 2000 Fam. L.R. 78; 2000 G.W.D.
    20-813, Ex Div . . . .   *Digested,* 00/**6280**
TC Industrial Plant Pty Ltd *v.* Robert's Queensland Pty Ltd (1964) 37 A.L.J.R. 239, HC
    (Aus) . . . .   *Followed,* 99/6443
Tehrani *v.* United Kingdom Central Council for Nursing, Midwifery and Health Visiting
    2001 S.C. 581; 2001 S.L.T. 879; [2001] I.R.L.R. 208; 2001 G.W.D. 4-165, OH . . .   *Digested,* 01/**6703**
Teknek Electronics Ltd *v.* KSM International Ltd [1998] E.T.M.R. 522; 1998 G.W.D. 5-
    253, OH
Telfer *v.* HM Advocate 1999 G.W.D. 34-1624, HCJ Appeal
Telford *v.* Ruxton (Sentencing) 2000 G.W.D. 19-754, HCJ Appeal
Temperley *v.* Watt 2001 G.W.D. 16-658, HCJ Appeal
Templeton (Robert) *v.* Crowe 1999 J.C. 47; 1999 S.C.C.R. 7; 1999 G.W.D. 1-62, HCJ
    Appeal . . . .   *Digested,* 99/**5815**
Templeton *v.* E 1998 S.C.L.R. 672, Sh Pr . . . .   *Digested,* 98/**5852**
Tenbey *v.* Stolt Comex Seaway Ltd; *sub nom* Tenby *v.* Stolt Comex Seaway Ltd 2001
    S.C. 638; 2001 S.L.T. 418; 2001 G.W.D. 7-254, OH . . . .   *Digested,* 01/**6224**
Tenby *v.* Stolt Comex Seaway Ltd *see* Tenbey *v.* Stolt Comex Seaway Ltd
Tennent Caledonian Breweries Ltd *v.* Gearty 1980 S.L.T. (Sh. Ct.) 71, Sh Pr . . . .   *Digested,* 80/**3602**:
                                              Distinguished, 00/5939: *Followed,* 94/6315
Tennie (Maxwell Andrew) *v.* Munro 1999 S.C.C.R. 70; 1999 G.W.D. 4-201, HCJ Appeal   *Digested,* 99/**5964**
Terras *v.* HM Advocate 1999 G.W.D. 3-149, HCJ Appeal
Tesco Stores Ltd *v.* Keeper of the Registers of Scotland 2001 S.L.T. (Lands Tr) 23; 2001
    G.W.D. 19-736, Lands Tr (Scot)
Tetsall *v.* HM Advocate (Sentencing) 1998 G.W.D. 7-323, HCJ Appeal
Tewnion's Trustee, Noter 2000 S.L.T. (Sh Ct) 37; 1999 G.W.D. 38-1858, Sh Ct (Grampian)
    . . . .   *Digested,* 00/**6512**
Texaco Ltd *v.* Glasgow Licensing Board 1999 S.C. 131; 1999 S.C.L.R. 184; [1999] 12
    S.L.L.P. 9; 1998 G.W.D. 37-1932, Ex Div . . . .   *Digested,* 99/**6351**
Texaco Ltd *v.* North Lanarkshire Licensing Board (No.1) 1998 S.C. 409; 1998 S.L.T.
    726; 1998 S.C.L.R. 809; [1998] 10 S.L.L.P. 9; 1998 G.W.D. 5-241, Ex Div . . . . .   *Digested,* 98/**6077**
Texaco Ltd *v.* North Lanarkshire Licensing Board (No.2) [2001] 18 S.L.L.P. 18, Sh Ct
    (South Strathclyde) . . . .   *Digested,* 01/**6787**
Texaco Ltd *v.* West Fife Divisional Licensing Board 1998 S.C. 470; 1998 S.L.T. 1059;
    1998 S.C.L.R. 826; [1998] 10 S.L.L.P. 14; 1998 G.W.D. 11-563, 2 Div . . . .   *Digested,* 98/**6078**:
                                                     Applied, 98/6076
Thain *v.* Aberdeenshire Council 2000 G.W.D. 25-951, Sh Ct
Thain *v.* Anniesland Trade Centre 1997 S.L.T. (Sh Ct) 102; 1997 S.C.L.R. 991; 1997
    G.W.D. 32-1654, Sh Pr. . . . .   *Digested,* 98/**6183**
Thain *v.* Fishers Services (Aberfeldy) Ltd 2001 S.L.T. 1237; 2001 G.W.D. 30-1205, OH . .   *Digested,* 01/**6417**
Thake *v.* Maurice [1986] Q.B. 644; [1986] 2 W.L.R. 337; [1986] 1 All E.R. 479;
    (1986) 83 L.S.G. 123; (1986) 136 N.L.J. 92, CA; affirming [1985] 2 W.L.R. 215;
    [1984] 2 All E.R. 513; (1985) 82 L.S.G. 871; (1985) 129 S.J. 86, QBD . . . .   *Digested,* 86/**422**:
                       Applied, 93/1416, 96/833: *Considered,* 84/2342, 85/2322, 88/1174,
                                                   98/5720: *Distinguished,* 88/489
Third *v.* North East Ice & Cold Storage Co Ltd 1997 S.L.T. 1177; [1998] B.C.C. 242,
    OH . . . .   *Digested,* 97/**5711**:
                                              Considered, 98/694
Third *v.* North East Ice & Cold Storage Co Ltd (Expenses) 1999 G.W.D. 26-1248, OH
Thistle *v.* Thistle Telecom Ltd 1998 G.W.D. 19-987, OH
Thistle Communications *v.* Thistle Telecom Ltd 2000 S.L.T. 262, OH . . . .   *Digested,* 00/**6518**
Thoar's Judicial Factor *v.* Ramlort Ltd; *sub nom* Reid *v.* Ramlort Ltd 1998 S.C. 887;
    1999 S.L.T. 1153; [1999] B.P.I.R. 133; 1998 G.W.D. 29-1504; *Times,* October 14,
    1998, Ex Div; reversing 1998 G.W.D. 20-1040, OH . . . .   *Digested,* 98/**6002**
Thomas *v.* Brighton HA *see* Wells *v.* Wells
Thomas *v.* Gilchrist (Sentencing) 2000 G.W.D. 29-1133, HCJ Appeal
Thomas *v.* Heywood 1999 G.W.D. 10-471, HCJ Appeal

Thomas v. HM Advocate; Waddell v. HM Advocate 1997 J.C. 35; 1997 S.L.T. 849; 1997 S.C.C.R. 77; 1996 G.W.D. 40-2286, HCJ Appeal . . . .   *Digested*, 97/**5916**: *Applied*, 98/5679

Thomas v. HM Advocate 2001 G.W.D. 24-913, HCJ Appeal

Thomas v. National Training Partnership Ltd [1998] I.C.R. 436, EAT . . . .   *Digested*, 98/**2236**: *Disapproved*, 98/5826

Thomas v. Thomas; *sub nom* Watt v. Thomas [1947] A.C. 484; [1947] 1 All E.R. 582; 1947 S.C. (H.L.) 45; 1948 S.L.T. 2; 1947 S.L.T. (Notes) 53; 63 T.L.R. 314; [1948] L.J.R. 515; 176 L.T. 498, HL; reversing 1946 S.C. 81; 1946 S.L.T. 63, 2 Div . . . . .   *Digested*, 48/**4277**: *Applied*, 47-51/2723, 47-51/2829, 47-51/2837, 47-51/5995, 47-51/7495, 47-51/9902, 47-51/10957, 52/987, 55/2078, 59/431, 70/3157, 76/338, 97/5959, 98/5439, 98/6102, 01/6217: *Considered*, 74/1069, 91/5082, 94/3280, 94/3439: *Distinguished*, 89/5013, 90/4099: *Followed*, 86/4416, 88/4930: *Not applied*, 47-51/3869

Thomas Menzies (Builders) Ltd v. Anderson & Menzies 1998 S.L.T. 794; 1997 G.W.D. 26-1338, OH . . . .   *Digested*, 98/**5491**

Thomas Muir (Haulage) Ltd v. Secretary of State for the Environment, Transport and the Regions 1999 S.C. 86; 1999 S.L.T. 666; 1998 G.W.D. 34-1771, IH (Ct of 5 judges) . . . .   *Digested*, 99/**6463**

Thompson (Andrew) v. Crowe 2000 J.C. 173; 1999 S.L.T. 1434; 1999 S.C.C.R. 1003; 1999 G.W.D. 37-1790, HCJ Appeal. . . . .   *Digested*, 00/**5996**

Thompson (Andrew) v. Crowe (Preliminary Procedure) 1999 G.W.D. 10-455, HCJ Appeal

Thompson v. HM Advocate 2001 G.W.D. 3-119, HCJ Appeal

Thompson v. HM Advocate (Sentencing) 1999 G.W.D. 7-332, HCJ Appeal

Thompson v. HM Advocate (Sentencing) 1999 G.W.D. 35-1697, HCJ Appeal

Thompson v. HM Advocate (Sentencing) 1999 G.W.D. 37-1805, HCJ Appeal

Thomson (Blair Russell), Petitioner see Thomson v. Principal Reporter of the Scottish Children's Reporter Administration

Thomson v. BP Fuels Marketing Ltd 2000 G.W.D. 27-1048, Sh Ct (Lothian)

Thomson v. Chief Constable of Grampian Police 2000 G.W.D. 28-1087, Sh Ct (Grampian)

Thomson v. Chief Constable of Grampian Police (Medical Certificates) 2001 S.C. 443; 2001 S.L.T. 480; 2000 G.W.D. 40-1473, OH

Thomson v. Clydesdale Bank Ltd; *sub nom* JR Thomson 's Trustees v. Clydesdale Bank Ltd [1893] A.C. 282; (1893) 20 R. (H.L.) 50; (1893) 1 S.L.T.111, HL; affirming (1891) 18 R. 282, 2 Div . . . .   *Applied*, 75/160, 97/5578, 98/5432

Thomson v. Cooperative Bank Plc (No.1) 1999 S.L.T. 701; 1998 G.W.D. 26-1333, Ex Div . . . .   *Digested*, 99/**5679**

Thomson v. Cooperative Bank Plc (No.2) 1999 G.W.D. 28-1347, OH

Thomson v. Coutts 2001 G.W.D. 25-923, Sh Ct (Grampian)

Thomson v. Crowe 1998 G.W.D. 35-1804, HCJ Appeal

Thomson v. HM Advocate 2001 S.C.C.R. 162; 2001 G.W.D. 4-153, HCJ Appeal . . . . . .   *Digested*, 01/**6318**

Thomson v. HM Advocate (Sentencing) 1998 G.W.D. 31-1609, HCJ Appeal

Thomson v. HM Advocate (Sentencing) 1999 G.W.D. 21-1009, HCJ Appeal

Thomson v. HM Advocate (Sentencing) 1999 G.W.D. 25-1189, HCJ Appeal

Thomson v. HM Advocate (Sentencing) 1999 G.W.D. 15-708, HCJ Appeal

Thomson (Douglas Iain) v. HM Advocate 1998 S.C.C.R. 56; 1998 G.W.D. 5-207, HCJ Appeal . . . .   *Digested*, 98/**5565**

Thomson (Kenneth William) v. HM Advocate 1999 S.L.T. 913; 1998 S.C.C.R. 683; 1998 G.W.D. 37-1896, HCJ Appeal. . . . .   *Digested*, 99/**5905**

Thomson (Lawrence McKenzie) v. HM Advocate 1998 S.C.C.R. 657; 1998 G.W.D. 6-1260, 1856, HCJ Appeal. . . . .   *Digested*, 99/**5895**

Thomson (Niall Ferguson) v. HM Advocate 1999 S.C.C.R. 640; 1999 S.L.T. 364; 1997 HCJ Appeal . . . .   *Digested*, 99/**5947**

Thomson (William Brown) v. HM Advocate 1997 J.C.D. 15-630, OH S.C.C.R. 121; 1997 G.W.D. 5-184, HCJ Appeal; Reporter Administration . . . .   *Digested*, 97/**5817**

Thomson v. Kvaerner Govan Ltd 1998 G.W.D. 8 . . . 848; 1998 S.L.T. 1066; *sub* . . . . .   *Digested*, 01/**6811**

Thomson v. Lothian Health Board 2001 S.C.C.R. 38; 1999 G.W.D. 31-1502, HCJ

Thomson v. Principal Reporter of the G.W.D. 35-1341, Ex Div; affirming 2000 . . . . .   *Digested*, 98/**5663**
nom Thomson (Blair Russ . . . S.C.L.R. 898; 1998 (radings) 2000 G.W.D. 19-732, OH . . . .   *Digested*, 00/**6072**

Thomson v. Ritchie 200 . . . y Default) 2000 G.W.D. 24-903, OH Appeal . . . G.W.D. 5-198, 2 Div

Thomson v. P01 G.W.D. 23-874, 1 Div
GW.1999 G.W.D. 1-55, Sh Ct (Grampian)
Thom . . . 1999 G.W.D. 10-479, HCJ Appeal
T . . . ire Building Society (No.1) 1998 G.W.D. 14-694, OH

Thomson v. Yorkshire Building Society (No.2) 1998 G.W.D. 14-695, OH
Thomson Pettie Tube Products Ltd v. Hogg (No.1) 2000 G.W.D. 27-1036, OH
Thomson Pettie Tube Products Ltd v. Hogg (No.2) 2001 G.W.D. 15-568, OH
Thomson's Judicial Factor v. Reid 2000 G.W.D. 1-33, Sh Ct
Thomson, Petitioner 1999 G.W.D. 23-1087, 1 Div . . . . *Previous proceedings,* 99/6341

Thomson, Petitioner (Sentencing) 2000 G.W.D. 8-289, HCJ Appeal
Thorne (Adrian Paul) v. Stott 2000 J.C. 13; 2000 S.L.T. 113; 1999 S.C.C.R. 815; 1999
  G.W.D. 28-1332, HCJ Appeal . . . . *Digested,* 00/**6135**
Thurso Building Society's Judicial Factor v. Robertson; *sub nom* Robertson (Judicial
  Factor) v. Robertson 2000 S.C. 547; 2001 S.L.T. 797; 2000 G.W.D. 24-904,
  OH . . . . *Digested,* 01/**6086**
Tierney v. HM Advocate 1999 G.W.D. 22-1062, HCJ Appeal
Tilcon (Scotland) Ltd v. Jarvis (Scotland) Ltd 2000 S.L.T. (Sh Ct) 55; 2000 G.W.D. 11-
  379, Sh Pr. . . . . *Digested,* 00/**5945**: *Cited,* 01/6261
Tinlin v. Accountant in Bankruptcy 2000 S.L.T. (Sh Ct) 57; 1999 G.W.D. 2-103, Sh Ct
  (Lothian) . . . . *Digested,* 00/**6505**
Tinlin's Trustee v. Tinlin 1998 G.W.D. 29-1503, Sh Ct
TJ Ross (Joiners) Ltd v. High Range Developments Ltd 2000 S.C.L.R. 161, Sh Ct . . . . . *Digested,* 00/**6513**
Tod v. HM Advocate (Sentencing) 1998 G.W.D. 3-150, HCJ Appeal
Tod's Trustees, Petitioners 1999 S.L.T. 308; 1998 G.W.D. 5-254, Ex Div . . . . *Digested,* 99/**6469**
Todd v. British Railways Board 1998 G.W.D. 11-568, OH
Todd v. HM Advocate 1999 G.W.D. 31-1484, HCJ Appeal
Todd v. Scottish Qualifications Authority 2001 G.W.D. 23-862, OH
Todd v. Todd 1966 S.L.T. 50; 1965 S.L.T. (Notes) 25, 1 Div. *Digested,* 66/**13387**:
  Applied, 93/5478: *Followed,* 98/6048: *Referred to,* 00/6543
Todd v. Vannet 1998 G.W.D. 19-963, HCJ Appeal
Tods Murray WS v. Arakin Ltd 2001 S.C. 840; 2001 S.L.T. 1193; 2001 G.W.D. 13-463, Ex
  Div; affirming 2000 S.L.T. 758; 2000 S.C.L.R. 804; 2000 G.W.D. 18-707, OH . . . *Digested,* 01/**6219**
Tollcross Housing Association v. Carmichael 2000 Hous. L.R. 50, Sh Pr . . . . *Digested,* 00/**6452**
Tolmie v. HM Advocate 1998 S.L.T. 508; 1997 G.W.D. 26-1312, HCJ Appeal . . . . *Digested,* 98/**5559**
Tom Super Printing and Supplies Ltd v. South Lanarkshire Council (No.1); *sub nom*
  Super (Tom) Printing and Supplies Ltd v. South Lanarkshire Council (No.1) 1999
  G.W.D. 31-1496, OH
Tom Super Printing and Supplies Ltd v. South Lanarkshire Council (No.2); *sub nom*
  Super (Tom) Printing and Supplies Ltd v. South Lanarkshire Council (No.2) 1999
  G.W.D. 38-1853, OH
Took v. HM Advocate 1989 S.L.T. 425; 1988 S.C.C.R. 495, HCJ Appeal . . . . *Digested,* 88/**3982**:
  Applied, 00/6123: *Followed,* 91/4737
Topek (Bur) Ltd v. HM Advocate 1998 S.C.C.R. 352; 1998 G.W.D. 17-871, HCJ Appeal . *Digested,* 98/**5943**
Topps Co Inc v. Tom Hannah (Agencies) Ltd 1999 G.W.D. 40-1957; *Times,* February 14,
  2000, OH . . . . *Digested,* 00/**6519**
Tor Corporate AS v. China National Star Petroleum Corp 2001 S.C. 314; 2001 S.C.L.R.
  465; 2000 G.W.D. 35-1326, Ex Div; affirming 2000 G.W.D. 26-963, OH . . . . . . *Digested,* 01/**6222**
Torbet (Alexander James) v. HM Advocate 1999 S.L.T. 113; 1998 S.C.C.R. 546; 1998
  G.W.D. 28-1423, HCJ Appeal. . . . . *Digested,* 98/**5677**
Torliefson v. Buchanan 1998 G.W.D. 17-867, HCJ Appeal
Torres v. HM Advocate 1998 S.L.T. 811; 1997 S.C.C.R. 491; 1997 G.W.D. 21-1008, HCJ
  Appeal . . . . *Digested,* 97/**5744**
Tough v. SPS (Hold. . . Ltd 1999 G.W.D. 2-77, OH
Toumi v. Crossan 200. . Ltd 1999 G.W.D. 2-77, OH
Towler v. Higson 1998 G. . . 8-294, Sh Ct (South Strathclyde)
Towns v. HM Advocate 199. . 726, HCJ Appeal
Townsley v. HM Advocate 199. . 1-1074, HCJ Appeal
Townsley (Edward Newlands) v. . . 7-1274, HCJ Appeal
  Advocate
Townsley v. McGlennan (Sentencing) . . . . ate see McIntyre (William Richard) v. HM
Townsley (Albert) v. McGlennan 1998 S. . .
Tracey v. Heywood see Millar v. Dickson
Trade Development Bank v. Warriner & Mason . . 342, HCJ Appeal
  223, 1 Div; affirming 1980 S.L.T. 49, OH . . . . C.C.R. 752, HCJ Appeal . . . . *Digested,* 98/**5683**
Transport & General Workers Union v. JR (Haulage) Ltd. . . . 80 S.C. 74; 1980 S.L.T.
  Union v. McKinnon . . . . *Digested,* 80/**3536**:
Transport & General Workers Union v. McKinnon; Transport . . . *nsidered,* 96/7101: *Followed,* 00/6527
  JR (Haulage) Ltd [2001] I.C.R. 1281; [2001] I.R.L.R. 59. . . ral Workers
Tremble v. HM Advocate 1998 G.W.D. 33-1696, HCJ Appeal
Trent v. HM Advocate 1998 G.W.D. 24-1190, HCJ Appeal
Triplis, Petitioner 1998 S.L.T. 186; 1997 S.C.C.R. 398; 1997 G.W.D. 25-12. . . . . *Digested,* 01/**6476**
Trotter (James Alexander) v. HM Advocate 2001 S.L.T. 296; 2000 S.C.C.R. . . .
  G.W.D. 32-1246, HCJ Appeal. . . . . **994** 97/**6050**

Trotter *v.* Trotter 2001 S.L.T. (Sh Ct) 42; 2000 Fam. L.R. 94; 2000 G.W.D. 12-425, Sh
     Pr . . . . *Digested,* 00/**6274**
Trusthouse Forte (UK) Ltd *v.* Perth and Kinross DC 1990 S.L.T. 737; 1991 S.C.L.R. 1, OH   *Digested,* 90/**5944**:
                                                    Distinguished, 01/**6855**
Tudhope *v.* Gough 1982 S.C.C.R. 157, Sh Ct (Glasgow) . . . . *Digested,* 82/**3611**:
                                                    Approved, 98/**5630**
Tudhope *v.* McKee 1988 S.L.T. 153, HCJ Appeal . . . . *Digested,* 88/**4018**:
                                       Considered, 98/**5558**, 99/**5832**
Tulewicz *v.* Munro 1999 G.W.D. 11-491, HCJ Appeal
Tullis Russell & Co Ltd *v.* Eadie Industries Ltd 2001 G.W.D. 28-1122, OH
Tulloch Construction Group Ltd *v.* Raigmore Hospital NHS Trust 1999 G.W.D. 35-1665,
     Sh Pr
Tulloch, Petitioner 1999 G.W.D. 31-1490, HCJ Appeal
Turnbull *v.* Ruxton 1999 G.W.D. 24-1154, HCJ Appeal
Turnbull *v.* TSB Scotland Plc 1999 S.C. 121; 1999 S.L.T. 1028; 1998 G.W.D. 35-1808, 2
     Div . . . . *Digested,* 99/**5656**
Turner *v.* Heywood 1998 G.W.D. 38-1961, HCJ Appeal
Turner *v.* Lees 1998 G.W.D. 26-1347, HCJ Appeal
Turner *v.* Secretary of State for Social Security 1999 G.W.D. 32-1504, OH . . . . *Followed,* 00/**6687**
Turnock *v.* HM Advocate 1998 G.W.D. 25-1243, HCJ Appeal
TW *v.* Malta (2000) 29 E.H.R.R. 185, ECHR . . . . *Digested,* 00/**3175**:
                                                   Applied, 00/**6064**
TW Scott (Painting Contractors) Ltd *v.* Higson (Sentencing) 2000 G.W.D. 29-1136,
     HCJ Appeal
TWL Incorporated Ltd *v.* Technology Leasing Ltd 2000 G.W.D. 13-463, Sh Pr
Twycross *v.* Spiers (Sentencing) 2001 G.W.D. 16-614, HCJ Appeal
Tyldesley *v.* TML Plastics Ltd [1996] I.C.R. 356; [1996] I.R.L.R. 395, EAT . . . . *Digested,* 96/**2550**:
                            Applied, 97/**6009**: *Approved,* 98/**5807**

Ucak *v.* HM Advocate 1998 J.C. 283; 1999 S.L.T. 392; 1998 S.C.C.R. 517; 1998
     G.W.D. 26-1295, HCJ Appeal. . . . . *Digested,* 98/**5609**
UCB Bank Ltd *v.* Hire Foulis Ltd (In Liquidation) 1999 S.C. 250; 1999 S.L.T. 950; 1999
     S.C.L.R. 35; 1998 G.W.D. 40-2069, Ex Div. . . . . *Digested,* 99/**6432**
UCB Bank Plc *v.* Dundas & Wilson, CS (No.2) 1990 S.C. 377; 1991 S.L.T. 90; 1990
     S.C.L.R. 827, 1 Div; affirming 1990 S.C.L.R. 371, OH . . . . *Digested,* 91/**4997**:
                                  Considered, 98/**5469**: *Followed,* 95/**5935**
Udale *v.* Bloomsbury AHA [1983] 1 W.L.R. 1098, QBD . . . . *Digested,* 84/**1005**:
              Considered, 98/**5720**: *Distinguished,* 86/**1070**: *Doubted,* 84/**2342**, 85/**2322**
Ul-Haq *v.* Secretary of State for the Home Department 1999 G.W.D. 1-40, OH
Ulhaq *v.* McFadyen (Sentencing) 2000 G.W.D. 34-1309, HCJ Appeal
Unilodge Services Ltd *v.* University of Dundee 2001 S.C.L.R. 1008; 2001 G.W.D. 28-
     1143, OH
Union of Clerical and Commercial Employees *v.* Danish Employers Association Ex p.
     Danfoss A/S (C109/88) see Handels-og Kontorfunktionaererernes Forbund i
     Danmark *v.* Dansk Arbejdsgiverforening Ex p. Danfoss A/S (C109/88)
United Bank of Kuwait Plc *v.* Prudential Property Services Ltd see South Australia Asset
     Management Corp *v.* York Montague Ltd
Unity Trust Bank Plc *v.* Frost (No.1) 2001 S.C.L.R. 344; 2001 G.W.D. 6-190, Ex Div;
     affirming in part 2000 G.W.D. 2-37, OH . . . . *Digested,* 01/**6225**
Unity Trust Bank Plc *v.* Frost (No.2) 2001 S.C.L.R. 350; 2001 G.W.D. 6-188, Ex Div . . . . *Digested,* 01/**6249**
Universal Cargo Carriers Corp *v.* Citati (No.1) [1957] 1 W.L.R. 979; [1957] 3 All E.R.
     234; [1957] 2 Lloyd's Rep. 191; 101 S.J. 762, CA; affirming [1957] 2 Q.B. 401;
     [1957] 2 W.L.R. 713; [1957] 2 All E.R. 70; [1957] 1 Lloyd's Rep. 174; (1957) 101
     S.J. 320, QBD . . . . *Digested,* 57/**130**:
         Applied, 61/**8255**, 62/**2838**, 79/**2449**, 81/**2403**: *Considered,* 72/**3202**,
                            73/**3109**, 86/**1259**, 00/**870**: *Followed,* 99/**5791**
University of Strathclyde *v.* Walker Technical Resources Ltd 2000 G.W.D. 15-577, Sh Ct
Unsworth *v.* Friel 1999 G.W.D. 13-612, HCJ Appeal
Upland Developments Ltd *v.* Web Shop (Aviemore) Ltd 1998 G.W.D. 16-773, 2 Div;
     affirming 1997 G.W.D. 22-1057, OH
Uprichard *v.* Fife Council 2000 S.C.L.R. 949; [2001] Env. L.R. 8; 2000 G.W.D. 14-514,
     OH . . . . *Digested,* 01/**6856**
Uratemp Ventures Ltd *v.* Carrell see Uratemp Ventures Ltd *v.* Collins
Uratemp Ventures Ltd *v.* Collins; Uratemp Ventures Ltd *v.* Carrell [2001] UKHL 43;
     [2001] 3 W.L.R. 806; (2001) 33 H.L.R. 85; 2001 Hous. L.R. 133; [2001] 43
     E.G.C.S. 186; (2001) 98(41) L.S.G. 35; [2001] N.P.C. 145; *Times,* October 18,
     2001; *Independent,* December 3, 2001; *Daily Telegraph,* October 16, 2001, HL;
     reversing (2001) 33 H.L.R. 4; [2000] L. & T.R. 369; [2000] 1 E.G.L.R. 156;
     (2000) 97(1) L.S.G. 23; [1999] N.P.C. 153; (2000) 79 P. & C.R. D18; *Times,*
     December 10, 1999, CA . . . . *Digested,* 01/**4148**
Urquhart *v.* Ayrshire and Arran Health Board; *sub nom* Spence *v.* Ayrshire and Arran
     Health Board 2000 S.L.T. 829; 2000 G.W.D. 20-812, OH . . . . *Digested,* 01/**6245**

Urquhart *v.* Biwater Industries Ltd 1998 S.L.T. 576; 1998 S.C.L.R. 198; 1997 G.W.D. 36-1875, OH . . . . *Digested,* 98/**5739**
Urquhart *v.* Coakley Bus Co Ltd 2000 G.W.D. 27-1047, Sh Ct (South Strathclyde)
Urquhart *v.* Higson 1998 G.W.D. 18-889, HCJ Appeal
Urquhart *v.* HM Advocate see Urquhart *v.* Lees
Urquhart *v.* Lees; *sub nom* Urquhart *v.* HM Advocate 2000 S.L.T. 1109; 1999 G.W.D. 29-1400, HCJ Appeal . . . . *Digested,* 00/**6152**
Urquhart *v.* Sweeney 2001 G.W.D. 22-824, Ex Div
Usai *v.* Russell 2000 J.C. 144; 2000 S.C.C.R. 57; 1999 G.W.D. 32-1519, HCJ Appeal . . . *Digested,* 00/**6046**
UVG Ambulances Ltd *v.* Auto Conversions Ltd [2000] E.C.D.R. 479; 2000 G.W.D. 22-866, OH . . . . *Digested,* 01/**6724**

Valentine *v.* Dickson 1999 G.W.D. 30-1443, HCJ Appeal
Valentine (Alan) *v.* HM Advocate; Wells (Philip) *v.* HM Advocate; Murphy (Thomas) *v.* HM Advocate; Murphy (Michael) *v.* HM Advocate 2001 S.C.C.R. 727; 2001 G.W.D. 25-925, HCJ Appeal
Valentine *v.* Valentine 2001 G.W.D. 31-1250, Sh Ct (Grampian)
Van Lierop *v.* McLeod 2000 S.L.T. 291; 1999 S.C.C.R. 577; 1999 G.W.D. 22-1030, HCJ Appeal . . . . *Digested,* 99/**5808**
Van Mechelen *v.* Netherlands (Art.6) (1998) 25 E.H.R.R. 647; 2 B.H.R.C. 486, ECHR . . *Digested,* 97/**2815**: *Applied,* 01/6323
Van Overwaele *v.* Hacking & Paterson; *sub nom* Overwaele, Petitioner 2001 S.C.L.R. 1098; 2001 G.W.D. 26-1063, Ex Div; affirming 2000 G.W.D. 37-1408, OH
Van Rijs (Hendrik) *v.* HM Advocate (No.1) see Hoekstra *v.* HM Advocate (No.1)
Van Rijs (Hendrik) *v.* HM Advocate (No.2) see Hoekstra *v.* HM Advocate (No.2)
Van Rijs (Hendrik) *v.* HM Advocate (No.3) see Hoekstra *v.* HM Advocate (No.3)
Van Rijs (Hendrik) *v.* HM Advocate (No.4) see Hoekstra *v.* HM Advocate (No.4)
Van Rijs (Hendrik) *v.* HM Advocate (No.5) see Hoekstra *v.* HM Advocate (No.5)
Van Rijs (Hendrik) *v.* HM Advocate (No.6) see Hoekstra *v.* HM Advocate (No.6)
Van Rijs (Jan) *v.* HM Advocate (No.1) see Hoekstra *v.* HM Advocate (No.1)
Van Rijs (Jan) *v.* HM Advocate (No.2) see Hoekstra *v.* HM Advocate (No.2)
Van Rijs (Jan) *v.* HM Advocate (No.3) see Hoekstra *v.* HM Advocate (No.3)
Van Rijs (Jan) *v.* HM Advocate (No.4) see Hoekstra *v.* HM Advocate (No.4)
Van Rijs (Jan) *v.* HM Advocate (No.5) see Hoekstra *v.* HM Advocate (No.5)
Van Rijs (Jan) *v.* HM Advocate (No.6) see Hoekstra *v.* HM Advocate (No.6)
Van Rijs (Ronny) *v.* HM Advocate (No.1) see Hoekstra *v.* HM Advocate (No.1)
Van Rijs (Ronny) *v.* HM Advocate (No.2) see Hoekstra *v.* HM Advocate (No.2)
Van Rijs (Ronny) *v.* HM Advocate (No.3) see Hoekstra *v.* HM Advocate (No.3)
Van Rijs (Ronny) *v.* HM Advocate (No.4) see Hoekstra *v.* HM Advocate (No.4)
Van Rijs (Ronny) *v.* HM Advocate (No.5) see Hoekstra *v.* HM Advocate (No.5)
Van Rijs (Ronny) *v.* HM Advocate (No.6) see Hoekstra *v.* HM Advocate (No.6)
Vance *v.* HM Advocate (Sentencing) 1998 G.W.D. 16-803, HCJ Appeal
Vance *v.* Vannet (Sentencing) 1998 G.W.D. 16-780, HCJ Appeal
Vannet *v.* Burns (Paul Joseph) 1999 S.L.T. 340; 1998 S.C.C.R. 414; 1998 G.W.D. 23-1187, HCJ Appeal . . . . *Digested,* 98/**5582**
Vannet *v.* Hamilton (James) 1999 S.C.C.R. 558, Sh Ct. . . . . *Digested,* 99/**5741**
Vannet *v.* Milligan (Scott) 1998 S.L.T. 1018; 1998 S.C.C.R. 305; 1998 G.W.D. 13-644, HCJ Appeal . . . . *Digested,* 98/**5622**
Vannet *v.* Taylor (Stephen) 1998 S.L.T. 1436; 1998 S.C.C.R. 30; 1998 G.W.D. 3-107, HCJ Appeal . . . . *Digested,* 98/**5570**
Varey *v.* Scottish Ministers 2001 S.C. 162; 2000 S.L.T. 1432; 2000 G.W.D. 27-1064, OH . . . . *Digested,* 01/**6836**
Varney (Scotland) Ltd *v.* Lanark Burgh 1974 S.C. 245; 1976 S.L.T. 46, 2 Div; reversing 1974 S.L.T. 80; 1973 S.L.T. (Notes) 82, OH . . . . *Digested,* 76/**2991**: *Considered,* 77/3294, 90/4820: *Followed,* 01/6753
Vass *v.* McFadyen 1999 G.W.D. 20-964, HCJ Appeal
Vass *v.* McFadyen (Fines: Disqualification) 2000 G.W.D. 14-565, HCJ Appeal
Vaughan *v.* Greater Glasgow Passenger Transport Executive 1984 S.C. 32; 1984 S.L.T. 44, 1 Div; reversing 1983 S.L.T. 200, OH . . . . *Digested,* 84/**3992**: *Applied,* 98/5716: *Considered,* 93/5165
Vaughan *v.* HM Advocate 1979 S.L.T. 49, HCJ Appeal . . . . *Digested,* 79/**2922**: *Followed,* 88/4003: *Referred to,* 99/5843
Vaughan *v.* McFadyen (Sentencing) 2001 G.W.D. 36-1379, HCJ Appeal
Velzian *v.* Adam (No.1) 1998 G.W.D. 29-1469, HCJ Appeal
Velzian *v.* Adam (No.2) 1998 G.W.D. 31-1585, HCJ Appeal
Venters *v.* HM Advocate 1999 S.L.T. 1345; 1999 S.C.C.R. 441; 1999 G.W.D. 18-823, HCJ Appeal . . . . *Digested,* 99/**5910**
Vestry of St Silas Church *v.* Trustees of St Silas Church see St Silas Church Vestry *v.* Trustees of St Silas Church
Victoria's (Licence) Ltd *v.* Glasgow Licensing Board [1998] 11 S.L.L.P. 15, Sh Ct. . . . . . *Digested,* 98/**6070**
Video Stop Ltd *v.* Peterhead Snooker Co Ltd 2000 G.W.D. 33-1296, Sh Ct (Grampian)

Villaswan Ltd (In Receivership) *v.* Sheraton Caltrust (Blythswood) Ltd (In Liquidation)
    1999 S.C.L.R. 199; [2000] B.C.C. 188; 1998 G.W.D. 39-2017; *Times*, January 27,
    1999, OH .... *Digested,* 99/**6304**
Vincent *v.* HM Advocate (Sentencing) 2000 G.W.D. 20-801, HCJ Appeal
Visionhire Ltd *v.* Britel Fund Trustees Ltd 1991 S.L.T. 883; 1992 S.C.L.R. 236; [1992] 1
    E.G.L.R. 128, 1 Div; affirming 1991 S.L.T. 347; 1991 S.C.L.R. 92, OH .... *Digested,* 91/**5178**:
                                      Applied, 98/6038: *Followed,* 99/3726
Vosilius *v.* Vosilius 2000 S.C.L.R. 679; 2000 Fam. L.R. 58; 2000 G.W.D. 14-547, OH ... *Digested,* 00/**6284**

W (A Child) *v.* Northern General Hospital NHS Trust see Heil *v.* Rankin
W (A Juvenile) *v.* O'Donnell (Sentencing) 2000 G.W.D. 19-742, HCJ Appeal
W *v.* B (Paternity: Parental Rights) 2000 G.W.D. 30-1166, Sh Ct
W *v.* Clark 1999 S.C.C.R. 775; 1999 G.W.D. 30-1403, HCJ Appeal .... *Digested,* 00/**6028**
W *v.* Criminal Injuries Compensation Board see W, Petitioner
W *v.* Schaffer 2001 S.L.T. (Sh Ct) 86; 2000 G.W.D. 36-1348, Sh Pr
W *v.* Secretary of State for Scotland 1999 S.C. 412; 1999 S.L.T. 640; 1999 S.C.L.R.
    481; 1999 G.W.D. 11-518; *Times*, April 21, 1999, 2 Div; affirming 1998 S.L.T. 841;
    1998 S.C.L.R. 221; 1997 G.W.D. 40-2101, OH .... *Digested,* 99/**6361**
W&J Burness, WS *v.* Smith 1998 S.C. 1; 1997 G.W.D. 30-1502, Ex Div .... *Digested,* 98/**5504**
W, Petitioner; *sub nom* W *v.* Criminal Injuries Compensation Board 1999 S.C.L.R. 921;
    1999 G.W.D. 14-631, OH .... *Digested,* 00/**5817**
Wackett *v.* Colley 2001 G.W.D. 6-243, HCJ Appeal
Wadbister Offshore Ltd *v.* Adam; *sub nom* Adam *v.* Wadbister Offshore Ltd 1998 J.C.
    56; 1998 S.L.T. 1230; 1998 S.C.C.R. 33; 1998 G.W.D. 3-109, HCJ Appeal. ..... *Digested,* 98/**5617**
Waddell *v.* HM Advocate see Thomas *v.* HM Advocate
Waddell *v.* Watt (Sentencing) 2001 G.W.D. 13-487, HCJ Appeal
Wadey *v.* Surrey CC (HL) see Wisely *v.* John Fulton (Plumbers) Ltd (No.2)
Wadey *v.* Surrey CC [1999] 1 W.L.R. 1614; [1999] 2 All E.R. 334; [1999] P.I.Q.R.
    Q128; (1999) 96(4) L.S.G. 38; (1999) 143 S.J.L.B. 20; *Times*, January 8, 1999;
    Independent, December 17, 1998, CA. .... *Digested,* 99/**1387**:
                                   Subsequent proceedings, 00/6160
Wales *v.* HM Advocate see HM Advocate *v.* Wilson
Walker *v.* Aberdeen City Council; *sub nom* Walker *v.* Aberdeen DC 1998 S.L.T. 427;
    1997 S.C.L.R. 425; 1997 G.W.D. 4-170, OH. .... *Digested,* 97/**6347**
Walker *v.* Aberdeen DC see Walker *v.* Aberdeen City Council
Walker *v.* Hendry 1925 S.C. 855; 1925 S.L.T. 592, 2 Div .... *Distinguished,*
                                            98/5423
Walker *v.* Higson (Sentencing) 1998 G.W.D. 6-301, HCJ Appeal
Walker (Scott Barry) *v.* Higson 1998 S.L.T. 131; 1997 S.C.C.R. 767; 1997 G.W.D. 37-
    1920, HCJ Appeal. .... *Digested,* 98/**5614**
Walker *v.* HM Advocate (Sentencing) 2000 G.W.D. 11-386, HCJ Appeal
Walker *v.* HM Advocate (Sentencing) 2001 G.W.D. 16-624, HCJ Appeal
Walker *v.* HM Advocate (Sentencing) 2001 G.W.D. 25-949, HCJ Appeal
Walker (Stuart Douglas) *v.* HM Advocate 1999 S.L.T. 1388; 1999 S.C.C.R. 986; 1999
    G.W.D. 32-1526, HCJ Appeal. .... *Digested,* 00/**6077**
Walker *v.* Hunter (1853) 16 D. 226, 1 Div .... *Applied,* 93/5626:
                                   Distinguished, 98/5466
Walker *v.* Moncur 2001 Rep. L.R. 67; [2001] 5 Q.R. 19, OH. .... *Digested,* 01/**6424**
Walker *v.* Roberts 1998 S.L.T. 1133; 1998 G.W.D. 14-721, OH .... *Digested,* 98/**5860**
Walker *v.* Seed Crushers (Scotland) Ltd see Wheelan *v.* Seed Crushers (Scotland) Ltd
    (No.1)
Walker *v.* Tidewater Cyprus Ltd 2001 G.W.D. 39-1477, Sh Ct (Grampian)
Wall *v.* HM Advocate (Sentencing) 1998 G.W.D. 7-332, HCJ Appeal
Wallace *v.* Dundee City Council 2000 S.L.T. (Sh Ct) 60; 2000 G.W.D. 2-52, Sh Ct
    (Tayside) .... *Digested,* 00/**6194**
Wallace *v.* Friel (No.1) 1998 G.W.D. 8-377, HCJ Appeal
Wallace *v.* Friel (No.2) 1998 G.W.D. 21-1068, HCJ Appeal
Wallace *v.* Hamilton 1998 G.W.D. 30-1543, HCJ Appeal
Wallace *v.* HM Advocate 1999 G.W.D. 7-328, HCJ Appeal
Wallace *v.* Howdle 1999 G.W.D. 34-1645, HCJ Appeal
Wallace *v.* Paterson 2001 S.C.L.R. 521; 2001 Rep. L.R. 65; [2001] 5 Q.R. 18; 2001
    G.W.D. 1-48, OH .... *Digested,* 01/**6421**
Wallace (James Douglas) *v.* Ruxton 1999 S.L.T. 447; 1998 S.C.C.R. 701; 1998 G.W.D.
    40-2042, HCJ Appeal. .... *Digested,* 99/**5841**:
                                   Applied, 00/6010
Wallace *v.* Stott 1999 G.W.D. 16-736, HCJ Appeal
Wallace *v.* Vannet 1999 G.W.D. 20-933, HCJ Appeal
Wallis *v.* Wallis (Divorce: Financial Provision) 1993 S.C. (H.L.) 49; 1993 S.L.T. 1348;
    1993 S.C.L.R. 800; [1993] E.G.C.S. 148; *Times*, August 5, 1993, HL; affirming
    1992 S.L.T. 676; 1993 S.C.L.R. 7; Scotsman, June 10, 1992, 1 Div; reversing 1991
    S.C.L.R. 192, Sh Ct (Tayside) .... *Digested,* 94/**2186**:
               Considered, 01/6823: *Followed,* 94/5782: *Referred to,* 95/5878

Walls v. Heywood 2000 S.L.T. 841; 2000 S.C.C.R. 21; 1999 G.W.D. 31-1468, HCJ
Appeal . . . .   *Digested*, 00/**6081**
Walls v. Maguire 1998 G.W.D. 18-943, HCJ Appeal
Walls v. McFadyen 2001 G.W.D. 31-1245, HCJ Appeal
Walsh v. Heywood (Sentencing) 2000 G.W.D. 15-591, HCJ
Walsh v. HM Advocate (Sentencing) 2001 G.W.D. 6-222, HCJ Appeal
Walsh v. McFadyen 2001 S.C.C.R. 864; 2001 G.W.D. 31-1227, HCJ Appeal
Walter L Jacob & Co Ltd, Re; *sub nom* Official Receiver v. Jacob [1993] B.C.C. 512,
Ch D (Companies Ct) . . . .   *Digested*, 94/**403**:
                                                                                          Followed, 99/5729
Walton v. Gallagher see Walton v. Miller
Walton v. Higgins 1998 G.W.D. 18-916, HCJ Appeal
Walton v. Miller; *sub nom* Walton v. Gallagher 1999 S.L.T. 1137; [2000] E.H.L.R. Dig.
274; 1999 G.W.D. 20-914, HCJ Appeal. . . . .   *Digested*, 99/**5651**
Walton Bros v. Glasgow Magistrates (1876) 3 R. 1130, 1 Div . . . .   *Considered*, 01/6677
Wanderers World Ltd v. Marco's Leisure Ltd 2000 S.L.T. (Sh Ct) 79; 1999 S.C.L.R. 930;
1999 G.W.D. 15-678, Sh Pr . . . .   *Digested*, 00/**5944**
Wands v. Fife Council 1998 G.W.D. 3-145, OH
Ward v. Brown (Sentencing) 2000 S.L.T. 1355; 2000 S.C.C.R. 947; 2000 G.W.D. 31-
1228, HCJ Appeal . . . .   *Digested*, 01/**6409**
Ward (William) v. Crowe 1999 J.C. 151; 1999 S.L.T. 1106; 1999 S.C.C.R. 219; 1999
G.W.D. 9-415, HCJ Appeal . . . .   *Digested*, 99/**5862**
Ward v. Dundee City Council 1999 S.L.T. (Sh Ct) 56, Sh Ct (Tayside) . . . .   *Digested*, 99/**6467**
Ward v. HM Advocate 1999 G.W.D. 25-1197, HCJ Appeal
Ward v. Scotrail Railways Ltd 1999 S.C. 255; 1999 G.W.D. 1-53, OH . . . .   *Digested*, 99/**6037**
Ward v. Spiers 1998 G.W.D. 34-1770, HCJ Appeal
Wardhaugh v. HM Advocate (Sentencing) 2001 G.W.D. 6-198, HCJ Appeal
Wardlaw v. Fife Health Board 2000 S.C.L.R. 840, OH . . . .   *Digested*, 00/**6166**
Wardrop v. HM Advocate 2000 G.W.D. 33-1274, HCJ Appeal
Wardrop v. Vannet (Sentencing) 1998 G.W.D. 13-684, HCJ Appeal
Wark v. HM Advocate (Sentencing) 2001 G.W.D. 24-889, HCJ Appeal
Warnes (Thomas Alfred) v. HM Advocate 2001 J.C. 110; 2001 S.L.T. 34; 2000 S.C.C.R.
1127; 2000 G.W.D. 36-1356, HCJ Appeal.   *Digested*, 01/**6344**
Warnes v. Lees 1998 G.W.D. 20-1049, HCJ Appeal
Warren v. Bruce 2001 G.W.D. 13-461, Sh Pr
Waste Systems International Inc v. Eurocare Environmental Services Ltd 1999 S.L.T. 198;
1998 G.W.D. 6-260, OH. . . . .   *Digested*, 99/**6310**
Waterson v. McGlennan 1999 G.W.D. 12-555, HCJ Appeal
Watkins v. HM Advocate 1998 G.W.D. 17-844, HCJ Appeal
Watret v. HM Advocate (Sentencing) 2000 G.W.D. 16-650, HCJ Appeal
Watson v. Bogue (No.1) 2000 S.L.T. (Sh Ct) 125; 1998 S.C.L.R. 512; 1998 G.W.D. 18-
930, Sh Pr; reversing 1998 G.W.D. 5-239, Sh Ct . . . .   *Digested*, 98/**6176**
Watson v. Bogue (No.2) 2000 S.L.T. (Sh Ct) 129; 1998 G.W.D. 35-1827, Sh Ct
(Lothian) . . . .   *Digested*, 00/**6594**
Watson v. Higson 2001 G.W.D. 37-1415, HCJ Appeal
Watson v. HM Advocate 1998 G.W.D. 17-846, HCJ Appeal
Watson v. HM Advocate (Sentencing) 1998 G.W.D. 17-864, HCJ Appeal
Watson v. HM Advocate (Sentencing) 1999 G.W.D. 36-1751, HCJ Appeal
Watson v. HM Advocate (Sentencing) 1999 G.W.D. 22-1059, HCJ Appeal
Watson v. HM Advocate (Sentencing) 2000 G.W.D. 15-588, HCJ
Watson v. HM Advocate (Sentencing) 2001 G.W.D. 25-941, HCJ Appeal
Watson v. HM Advocate (Sentencing) 2001 G.W.D. 31-1237, HCJ Appeal
Watson v. Jamieson 1998 S.L.T. 180; 1997 G.W.D. 4-131, OH . . . .   *Digested*, 97/**5616**
Watson v. MacDonald 1998 G.W.D. 17-845, HCJ Appeal
Watson v. McGlennan (Sentencing) 1998 G.W.D. 6-306, HCJ Appeal
Watson v. Vannet 1999 G.W.D. 4-197, HCJ Appeal
Watson (Mark Steven) v. Vannet 1999 S.C.C.R. 722; 1999 G.W.D. 29-1365, HCJ Appeal   *Digested*, 00/**6010**
Watson v. Walker 1998 G.W.D. 36-1885, HCJ Appeal
Watson v. Watson 1998 G.W.D. 11-520, 2 Div
Watson v. Watson (Additional Proof) 1998 G.W.D. 27-1354, 2 Div
Watson v. Watson (Divorce: Adultery) 1934 S.C. 374; 1934 S.L.T. 275, 2 Div . . . .   *Considered*, 99/5990
Watson Building Services Ltd v. Harrison 2001 S.L.T. 846; 2001 G.W.D. 11-381, OH . . . .   *Digested*, 01/**6286**
Watt (David Cuthbertson) v. Annan 1978 J.C. 84; 1978 S.L.T. 198, HCJ Appeal . . . .   *Digested*, 78/**3235**:
                                                                   Considered, 00/6046, 01/6338: *Referred to*, 95/5788
Watt v. Fairfield Shipbuilding & Engineering Co Ltd 1999 S.L.T. 1084; 1998 G.W.D. 39-
2016, OH . . . .   *Digested*, 99/**6220**
Watt v. HM Advocate (Sentencing) 1998 G.W.D. 2-75, HCJ Appeal
Watt v. Lees 1998 G.W.D. 19-968, HCJ Appeal
Watt v. Lord Advocate 1979 S.C. 120; 1979 S.L.T. 137, 1 Div; reversing 1977 S.L.T. 130,
OH . . . .   *Digested*, 79/**2815**:
                                           Applied, 97/6043, 00/5979: *Considered*, 83/3600, 84/3344
Watt v. Scottish Daily Record and Sunday Mail Ltd 1998 G.W.D. 16-807, OH
Watt v. Thomas see Thomas v. Thomas
Watt's Trustee v. SPS (Holdings) Ltd 2000 S.C. 371; 2000 G.W.D. 9-319, 2 Div . . . .   *Digested*, 00/**5985**

Watts v. McFadyen (Sentencing) 2000 G.W.D. 19-740, HCJ Appeal
Waydale Ltd v. DHL Holdings (UK) Ltd (No.2) 2000 S.C. 172; 2001 S.L.T. 207; 2000
    G.W.D. 1-7, Ex Div; affirming 1999 S.L.T. 631; 1999 S.C.L.R. 23; 1998 G.W.D. 40-
    2036, OH . . . . *Digested,* 00/**5937**
Waydale Ltd v. DHL Holdings (UK) Ltd (No.3) 2001 S.L.T. 224; 2000 G.W.D. 38-1434,
    OH . . . . *Digested,* 01/**6750**
Weatherseal Holdings Ltd v. Stewart 1998 G.W.D. 30-1538, Sh Ct
Webb v. BP Petroleum Development Ltd 1988 S.L.T. 775; 1988 S.C.L.R. 450, OH . . . . . *Followed,* 98/5483
Webb (Eli) v. HM Advocate 1927 J.C. 93; 1927 S.L.T. 631, HCJ Appeal . . . . *Considered,* 99/5919
Webb (John) v. HM Advocate 1996 J.C. 166; 1997 S.L.T. 170; 1996 S.C.C.R. 530, HCJ
    Appeal . . . . *Digested,* 96/**6811**:
                                           Distinguished, 99/5901

Webley (Don Lee) v. McFadyen 2001 G.W.D. 36-1364, HCJ Appeal
Webster v. HM Advocate (Sentencing) 1998 G.W.D. 14-712, HCJ Appeal
Webster v. HM Advocate (Sentencing) 1998 G.W.D. 10-496, HCJ Appeal
Weeks v. United Kingdom (A/114) (1988) 10 E.H.R.R. 293; *Times,* March 5, 1987,
    ECHR . . . . *Digested,* 89/**1916**:
                             Considered, 94/3833, 96/3121: *Referred to,* 01/6836
Weight v. HM Advocate (Sentencing) 1998 G.W.D. 16-794, HCJ Appeal
Weir v. Carnegie (Sentencing) 1998 G.W.D. 3-116, HCJ Appeal
Weir v. East of Scotland Water Authority 2001 S.L.T. 1205; 2000 G.W.D. 39-1472, OH . . *Digested,* 01/**6924**
Weir v. Inland Revenue Commissioners 1998 G.W.D. 3-133, OH
Weir v. Wyper 1992 S.L.T. 579; 1992 S.C.L.R. 483, OH . . . . *Digested,* 92/**6068**:
                                              Followed, 98/6109

Weldon v. Friel (Sentencing) 1998 G.W.D. 7-331, HCJ Appeal
Welikanna v. Welikanna 2000 Fam. L.R. 121; 2000 G.W.D. 23-890, Sh Pr . . . . *Digested,* 00/**6258**
Wells v. Hay 1999 Rep. L.R. 44, OH . . . . *Digested,* 99/**5986**
Wells (Philip) v. HM Advocate see Valentine (Alan) v. HM Advocate
Wells v. Stenhouse 2000 G.W.D. 21-828, OH
Wells v. Wells; Thomas v. Brighton HA; Page v. Sheerness Steel Co Plc [1999] 1 A.C.
    345; [1998] 3 W.L.R. 329; [1998] 3 All E.R. 481; [1998] I.R.L.R. 536; [1998] 2
    F.L.R. 507; [1998] P.I.Q.R. Q56; (1998) 43 B.M.L.R. 99; [1998] Fam. Law
    593; (1998) 95(35) L.S.G. 35; (1998) 148 N.L.J. 1087; (1998) 142 S.J.L.B.
    245; *Times,* July 20, 1998; *Independent,* July 27, 1998 (C.S.), HL; reversing
    [1997] 1 W.L.R. 652; [1997] 1 All E.R. 673; [1997] P.I.Q.R. Q1; (1997) 37
    B.M.L.R. 111; (1996) 93(40) L.S.G. 25; (1996) 140 S.J.L.B. 239; *Times,* October
    24, 1996; *Independent,* November 13, 1996, CA; reversing [1996] P.I.Q.R. Q62,
    QBD . . . . *Digested,* 98/**1446**:
                  Applied, 98/1478, 98/1573, 00/1479, 00/1503, 01/1546: *Cited,* 00/1489,
             00/6430: *Considered,* 98/1474, 99/1397, 99/5671: *Distinguished,* 00/1470,
             01/6222: *Followed,* 97/1833, 99/1422, 99/5950, 99/5972, 99/5974,
                        00/1464, 00/1490, 00/1492, 00/5905, 00/6161, 00/6164
Welsh v. Lees 1998 G.W.D. 24-1196, HCJ Appeal
Welsh v. McFadyen (Sentencing) 2000 G.W.D. 30-1208, HCJ Appeal
Welsh v. McGlennan 1999 G.W.D. 18-833, HCJ Appeal
Welsh v. Wheelan 2001 G.W.D. 6-239, HCJ Appeal
Wescol Structures Ltd v. Miller Construction Ltd 1998 G.W.D. 18-886, OH
West v. Colley 2001 J.C. 104; 2001 S.L.T. 220; 2000 G.W.D. 36-1364, HCJ Appeal . . . . *Digested,* 01/**6535**
West v. Heywood (Sentencing) 1998 G.W.D. 14-729, HCJ Appeal
West v. Scottish Prison Service; *sub nom* West v. Secretary of State for Scotland 1992
    S.C. 385; 1992 S.L.T. 636; 1992 S.C.L.R. 504; *Times,* June 11, 1992; Scotsman,
    May 5, 1992, 1 Div; affirming 1991 S.C.L.R. 795, OH . . . . *Digested,* 92/**5191**:
                   Applied, 94/5369, 95/5443, 97/5714, 97/6043, 97/6359:
          Considered, 00/6205: *Explained,* 93/4730: *Followed,* 95/5442, 00/5832:
                                        Referred to, 95/5889

West v. Secretary of State for Scotland see West v. Scottish Prison Service
West Dunbartonshire Council v. Harvie 1998 S.C. 789; 1998 S.C.L.R. 639; 1998 G.W.D.
    16-813, Ex Div; affirming 1997 S.L.T. 979, OH . . . . *Digested,* 98/**6082**
West Dunbartonshire Council v. McGougan 1998 Hous. L.R. 15; 1998 G.W.D. 2-94, Sh
    Ct . . . . *Digested,* 98/**5993**
West Dunbartonshire Council v. Wallace see Strathclyde RC v. Wallace
West End Business Centre Ltd v. Magregor Neil Partnership 1998 G.W.D. 35-1818, Sh
    Ct
West Errol Trust's Trustees v. Lawrie (Motion Hearing) 1999 S.C.L.R. 624, Sh Ct . . . . . . *Digested,* 99/**5717**
West Errol Trust's Trustees v. Lawrie (Notice to Quit) 2000 S.L.T. 911; 1998 G.W.D. 22-
    1104, 1 Div. . . . . *Digested,* 00/**5849**
Westcott v. Houston (Sentencing) 1998 G.W.D. 3-152, HCJ Appeal
Westerhall Farms v. Scottish Ministers 2001 G.W.D. 14-537, OH
Weston v. HM Advocate (Sentencing) (No.1) 1999 G.W.D. 14-639, HCJ Appeal
Weston v. HM Advocate (Sentencing) (No.2) 2000 G.W.D. 29-1141, HCJ Appeal
Weston v. Ritchie (Sentencing) 2000 G.W.D. 20-795, HCJ Appeal

Whaley *v.* Lord Watson of Invergowrie; *sub nom* Whalley *v.* Lord Watson of Invergowrie 2000 S.C. 340; 2000 S.L.T. 475; 2000 S.C.L.R. 279; 2000 G.W.D. 8-272; *Times,* March 21, 2000, 1 Div; affirming in part 2000 S.C. 125; 1999 G.W.D. 39-1882, OH . . . .   *Digested,* 00/**5975**
Whalley *v.* Lord Watson of Invergowrie see Whaley *v.* Lord Watson of Invergowrie
Whan *v.* Kennedy 1999 G.W.D. 1-21, HCJ Appeal
Wheelan *v.* Seed Crushers (Scotland) Ltd (No.1); *sub nom* Walker *v.* Seed Crushers (Scotland) Ltd 1998 S.L.T. 1308; 1998 S.C.C.R. 293; [1998] Env. L.R. 586; 1998 G.W.D. 13-671, HCJ Appeal; reversing 1997 G.W.D. 32-1630, Sh Ct . . . .   *Digested,* 98/**5829**
Wheelan *v.* Seed Crushers (Scotland) Ltd (No.2) 1999 G.W.D. 9-428, Sh Ct
White *v.* Chief Constable of South Yorkshire see Frost *v.* Chief Constable of South Yorkshire
White *v.* Ferguson 2000 S.L.T. (Sh Ct) 179, Sh Ct (Lothian) . . . .   *Digested,* 01/**6878**
White *v.* HM Advocate (Sentencing) 1999 G.W.D. 21-997, HCJ Appeal
White *v.* HM Advocate (Sentencing) 2000 G.W.D. 20-805, HCJ Appeal
White *v.* McLeod 1999 G.W.D. 8-372, HCJ Appeal
White *v.* Reflecting Roadstuds [1991] I.C.R. 733; [1991] I.R.L.R. 331, EAT . . . .   *Digested,* 91/**1613**:
Applied, 98/5827: *Considered,* 98/2107
White (Chad Vernal) *v.* Ruxton 1998 S.L.T. 105; 1997 S.C.C.R. 771, HCJ Appeal . . . . . .   *Digested,* 98/**5643**
White *v.* Vannet 1999 G.W.D. 20-935, HCJ Appeal
White *v.* White; *sub nom* Grant (otherwise White) *v.* White 2001 S.C. 689; 2001 S.L.T. 485; 2001 S.C.L.R. 607; 2001 Fam. L.R. 21; 2001 G.W.D. 10-327, 1 Div; reversing 1999 S.L.T. (Sh Ct) 106; 1999 G.W.D. 28-1308, Sh Pr . . . .   *Digested,* 01/**6510**:
Not followed, 00/6267
Whiteford *v.* HM Advocate (Sentencing) 2001 G.W.D. 30-1192, HCJ Appeal
Whiting *v.* Lees 1999 G.W.D. 3-160, HCJ Appeal
Whittome *v.* Whittome (No.1) 1994 S.L.T. 114; 1993 S.C.L.R. 137, OH. . . . .   *Digested,* 93/**5223**:
Followed, 99/6074
Whyte *v.* Barbour (Sentencing) 2000 G.W.D. 29-1162, HCJ Appeal
Whyte *v.* Higson 1998 G.W.D. 19-992, HCJ Appeal
Whyte *v.* HM Advocate 2000 S.L.T. 544; 1999 G.W.D. 16-745, HCJ Appeal . . . .   *Digested,* 00/**6123**
Whyte *v.* HM Advocate (Sentencing) 1998 G.W.D. 22-1125, HCJ Appeal
Whyte *v.* Nestle (UK) Ltd 1998 S.L.T. 1071; 1997 S.C.L.R. 598; 1997 Rep. L.R. 7; 1997 G.W.D. 13-569, OH . . . .   *Digested,* 97/**5950**
Wichary *v.* Fraser 1998 G.W.D. 8-363, HCJ Appeal
Wightman (David Alexander) *v.* Lees 2000 S.L.T. 111; 1999 S.C.C.R. 664; 1999 G.W.D. 27-1267, HCJ Appeal . . . .   *Digested,* 00/**6025**
Wigley *v.* British Vinegars [1964] A.C. 307; [1962] 3 W.L.R. 731; [1962] 3 All E.R. 161; 61 L.G.R. 1; 106 S.J. 609, HL; affirming [1961] 1 W.L.R. 1261; [1961] 3 All E.R. 418; 105 S.J. 666, CA . . . .   *Digested,* 62/**1264**:
Applied, 71/7931, 71/12717, 71/13048, 98/5938: *Followed,* 67/370
Wilkes *v.* HM Advocate 2001 S.L.T. 1268; 2001 G.W.D. 26-1024, HCJ Appeal . . . .   *Digested,* 01/**6356**
Wilkie *v.* Direct Line Insurance Plc (No.1) 2000 G.W.D. 30-1197, OH
Wilkie *v.* Direct Line Insurance Plc (No.2) 2001 S.C.L.R. 1018; 2001 G.W.D. 29-1175, OH
Wilkie *v.* McFadyen (Sentencing) 2000 G.W.D. 3-111, HCJ Appeal
Wilkins *v.* Carnegie 1999 G.W.D. 20-951, HCJ Appeal
Will (Alasdair Taylor) *v.* McDonald; *sub nom* Will (Alasdair Taylor) *v.* MacDonald 1999 J.C. 135; 1999 S.C.C.R. 159, HCJ Appeal . . . .   *Digested,* 99/**5600**
William Dow (Potatoes) Ltd *v.* Dow 2001 S.L.T. (Sh Ct) 37; 2001 G.W.D. 7-256, Sh Pr .   *Digested,* 01/**6241**
William Grant & Sons International Ltd *v.* Marie Brizard Espana SA 1998 S.C. 536, OH .   *Digested,* 98/**5530**:
Considered, 00/5927
William Grant & Sons Ltd *v.* Glen Catrine Bonded Warehouse Ltd (No.2) 1999 G.W.D. 15-714; *Times,* May 11, 1999, OH. . . . .   *Digested,* 99/**6314**
William Grant & Sons Ltd *v.* Glen Catrine Bonded Warehouse Ltd (No.3); *sub nom* Grant (William) & Sons Ltd *v.* Glen Catrine Bonded Warehouse Ltd 2001 S.C. 901; 2001 S.L.T. 1419; 2001 G.W.D. 17-680, 1 Div; affirming 1999 G.W.D. 33-1596, OH
William Grant & Sons (Distillers) Ltd *v.* Stuart 1998 S.C. 741; 1998 S.L.T. 1210; 1998 G.W.D. 23-1174, 2 Div . . . .   *Digested,* 98/**5823**
William Miller Plumbing Contractors Ltd *v.* James Lumsden Ltd 2000 S.C. 595; 2000 S.L.T. 1425; 2000 G.W.D. 26-968, Ex Div . . . .   *Digested,* 01/**6260**
Williams *v.* Clark 2001 S.C.C.R. 505; 2001 G.W.D. 20-758, HCJ Appeal
Williams *v.* Crowe 1998 G.W.D. 37-1940, HCJ Appeal
Williams *v.* Farne Salmon & Trout Ltd 1998 S.L.T. 1329; 1998 Rep. L.R. 32; 1998 G.W.D. 4-187, OH . . . .   *Digested,* 98/**5940**
Williams (Olufemi David) *v.* Friel 1999 J.C. 28; 1999 S.L.T. 366; 1998 S.C.C.R. 649; 1998 G.W.D. 36-1849, HCJ Appeal . . . .   *Digested,* 99/**5807**
Williams *v.* Scottish Ministers (Sentencing) 2001 S.C. 153; 2000 S.L.T. 1427; 2000 G.W.D. 26-984, OH . . . .   *Digested,* 01/**6398**
Williams *v.* Walkingshaw (Sentencing) 1998 G.W.D. 1-32, HCJ Appeal
Williamson *v.* Hingston 1999 G.W.D. 4-220, HCJ Appeal
Williamson *v.* HM Advocate (Sentencing) 1998 G.W.D. 10-492, HCJ Appeal
Williamson *v.* HM Advocate (Sentencing) 1998 G.W.D. 24-1199, HCJ Appeal

Williamson v. HM Advocate (Sentencing) 2001 G.W.D. 30-1183, HCJ Appeal
Williamson v. HM Advocate (Sentencing) 2001 G.W.D. 39-1462, HCJ Appeal
Williamson v. Howdle 1999 G.W.D. 29-1371, HCJ Appeal
Williamson v. McFadyen 1999 G.W.D. 21-1019, HCJ Appeal
Williamson v. Vannet 1998 G.W.D. 37-1919, HCJ Appeal
Wilson v. British Railways Board 1998 G.W.D. 24-1233, OH
Wilson v. Carr 1998 G.W.D. 29-1460, Ex Div
Wilson v. Chief Constable of Lothian and Borders 1999 G.W.D. 2-107, OH
Wilson v. Ethicon Ltd [2000] I.R.L.R. 4, EAT . . . .   *Digested*, 00/**6219**
Wilson v. Gallacher (Amphetamines) (Sentencing) 2000 G.W.D. 37-1400, HCJ Appeal
Wilson v. Gallacher (Indecent Assault) (Sentencing) 2000 G.W.D. 19-753, HCJ Appeal
Wilson (Fraser Ian) v. Heywood 1999 S.L.T. 915; 1998 S.C.C.R. 686; 1998 G.W.D. 40-
    2085, HCJ Appeal . . . .   *Digested*, 99/**5958**
Wilson v. Higson (Sentencing) 2001 G.W.D. 25-943, HCJ Appeal
Wilson v. HM Advocate see HM Advocate v. Wilson
Wilson v. HM Advocate 2000 G.W.D. 13-469, HCJ Appeal
Wilson v. HM Advocate (Sentencing) 1998 G.W.D. 29-1468, HCJ Appeal
Wilson v. HM Advocate (Sentencing) 1999 G.W.D. 16-747, HCJ Appeal
Wilson v. HM Advocate (Sentencing) 1999 G.W.D. 23-1099, HCJ Appeal
Wilson v. HM Advocate (Sentencing) 2001 G.W.D. 26-1031, HCJ Appeal
Wilson v. HM Advocate (Sentencing) 2001 G.W.D. 25-959, HCJ Appeal
Wilson (Alexander Thomas) v. HM Advocate 2001 S.L.T. 1149; 2001 S.L.T. 1203; 2001
    S.C.C.R. 455; 2001 G.W.D. 15-571, HCJ Appeal . . . .   *Digested*, 01/**6311**
Wilson (Diane) v. HM Advocate 1998 S.C.C.R. 437; 1998 G.W.D. 25-1256, HCJ
    Appeal . . . .   *Digested*, 98/**5676**
Wilson (James McLean) v. HM Advocate 1997 S.C.C.R. 674; 1997 G.W.D. 35-1767,
    HCJ Appeal . . . .   *Digested*, 98/**5661**
Wilson v. Independent Broadcasting Authority 1979 S.C. 351; 1979 S.L.T. 279, OH . . . .   *Digested*, 79/**3481**:
                                            Distinguished, 00/5975: *Followed*, 88/4986
Wilson v. Inverclyde Council 2001 G.W.D. 3-129, OH
Wilson v. Keeper of the Registers of Scotland 2000 S.L.T. 267; 1999 S.C.L.R. 872;
    1999 G.W.D. 25-1211, Ex Div . . . .   *Digested*, 00/**6441**
Wilson v. Lees 1999 G.W.D. 7-356, HCJ Appeal
Wilson v. McFadyen 1999 G.W.D. 35-1676, HCJ Appeal
Wilson v. McGlennan 1998 G.W.D. 21-1100, HCJ Appeal
Wilson v. Midlothian Council 2001 Rep. L.R. 127; 2001 G.W.D. 30-1214, Sh Pr
Wilson v. Munro (Sentencing) 1998 G.W.D. 32-1645, HCJ Appeal
Wilson v. Nithsdale DC 1992 S.L.T. 1131, OH . . . .   *Digested*, 92/**5869**:
                      Applied, 97/6114, 98/3018: *Considered*, 96/3046, 96/3047
Wilson v. Norwich Union Fire Insurance Society Ltd (No.1) 1999 S.L.T. 1139; 2000
    S.C.L.R. 184, 2 Div . . . .   *Digested*, 99/**6308**
Wilson v. Norwich Union Fire Insurance Society Ltd (No.2) 2001 G.W.D. 11-394, Sh Ct
    (Grampian)
Wilson v. Pyeroy Ltd 2000 S.L.T. 1087; 2000 S.C.L.R. 448; 1999 Rep. L.R. 138; 1999
    G.W.D. 34-1637, OH . . . .   *Digested*, 00/**6164**
Wilson v. Rolls Royce Plc 1998 S.L.T. 247; 1997 Rep. L.R. 64; 1997 G.W.D. 12-531, OH .   *Digested*, 97/**6080**
Wilson v. Smith 1997 S.L.T. (Sh Ct) 91, Sh Ct (Grampian). . . . .   *Digested*, 98/**5588**
Wilson v. Stott 2001 G.W.D. 25-937, HCJ Appeal
Wilson v. Vannet 2000 J.C. 152; 2000 S.L.T. 600; 2000 S.C.C.R. 70; 1998 G.W.D. 19-
    1003, HCJ Appeal. . . . .   *Digested*, 00/**6124**
Wilson v. Walkingshaw (Sentencing) 1998 G.W.D. 6-302, HCJ Appeal
Wilson v. Watt 2000 G.W.D. 34-1323, HCJ Appeal
Wilson (James Jenkinson) v. Webster 1999 S.C.C.R. 747; 1999 G.W.D. 27-1300, HCJ
    Appeal . . . .   *Digested*, 00/**6009**
Wilson v. Wilson (Appeal without Leave) 2001 S.L.T. (Sh Ct) 55; 2001 G.W.D. 1-2, Sh
    Pr . . . .   *Digested*, 01/**6255**
Wilson (Hazel) v. Wilson (Stewart James) 1999 S.L.T. 249; 1998 S.C.L.R. 1103; 1998
    G.W.D. 23-1177, OH. . . . .   *Digested*, 99/**6074**
Wimpey Homes Holdings Ltd v. Collins 1999 S.L.T. (Sh Ct) 16; 1998 G.W.D. 8-395, Sh
    Pr . . . .   *Digested*, 99/**6239**
Wincentzen v. Monklands DC 1988 S.C. 329; 1988 S.L.T. 847; 1989 S.C.L.R. 190, 1
    Div; affirming 1987 S.C. 310; 1988 S.L.T. 259; 1988 S.C.L.R. 712, OH . . . .   *Digested*, 88/**4365**:
                                          Distinguished, 98/6193
Winchcole v. Vannet 1998 G.W.D. 30-1540, HCJ Appeal
Wingate v. HM Advocate 1999 G.W.D. 35-1699, HCJ Appeal
Winning v. Napier Son & Co Ltd 1963 S.C. 293; 1963 S.L.T. 43, 1 Div . . . .   *Digested*, 63/**4117**:
                                          Distinguished, 98/5493
Winning, Petitioners; *sub nom* Balgowan Trustees, Petitioners 1999 S.C. 51; 1999 S.L.T.
    817; 1998 G.W.D. 29-1526, OH. . . . .   *Digested*, 99/**6468**

Winter *v.* Inland Revenue Commissioners; *sub nom* Sutherland (Deceased), Re; Sutherland's Estate, Re [1963] A.C. 235; [1961] 3 W.L.R. 1062; [1961] 3 All E.R. 855; (1961) 40 A.T.C. 361; [1961] T.R. 349; 105 S.J. 929, HL; reversing [1960] Ch. 611; [1960] 3 W.L.R. 47; [1960] 3 All E.R. 270; (1961) 40 A.T.C. 318; [1961] T.R. 329; 104 S.J. 684, CA; reversing [1960] Ch. 134; [1959] 3 W.L.R. 543; [1959] 2 All E.R. 682; 52 R. & I.T. 644; (1959) 38 A.T.C. 212; [1959] T.R. 193; 102 S.J. 563, Ch D .... *Digested,* 61/**2417**:
Applied, 67/497, 00/6276: *Considered,* 98/3271

Winters *v.* Ruxton 1999 G.W.D. 28-1307, HCJ Appeal

Winterwerp *v.* Netherlands (A/47) (1982) 4 E.H.R.R. 228, ECHR .... *Considered,* 01/6707

Wirral BC *v.* Currys Group Plc 1998 S.L.T. 463; 1997 S.C.L.R. 805; 1997 G.W.D. 19-900, OH .... *Digested,* 97/**6181**

Wisely *v.* John Fulton (Plumbers) Ltd (No.1) 1998 Rep. L.R. 91; 1998 G.W.D. 19-991, OH .... *Digested,* 98/**5748**

Wisely *v.* John Fulton (Plumbers) Ltd (No.2); Wadey *v.* Surrey CC [2000] 1 W.L.R. 820; [2000] 2 All E.R. 545; 2000 S.C. (H.L.) 95; 2000 S.L.T. 494; 2000 S.C.L.R. 693; [2000] P.I.Q.R. Q306; (2000) 97(22) L.S.G. 43; (2000) 144 S.J.L.B. 197; 2000 G.W.D. 13-487; *Times,* April 7, 2000, HL; affirming 1998 S.C. 910; 1998 S.L.T. 1026; 1998 S.C.L.R. 954; 1998 Rep. L.R. 103; 1998 G.W.D. 26-1332; *Times,* December 2, 1998, 1 Div 1998 G.W.D. 20-1034, OH .... *Digested,* 00/**6160**:
Considered, 99/1387: *Previous proceedings,* 99/1387

Wishart (Mark) *v.* Miller 1998 S.C.C.R. 21; 1998 G.W.D. 2-98, HCJ Appeal .... *Digested,* 98/**5690**

Wishart Arch Defenders Loyal Orange Lodge 404 *v.* Angus Council 2001 G.W.D. 31-1256, Sh Ct (Tayside)

WM Nelson Cladding Ltd *v.* Murray Williamson (Builders) Ltd 1995 S.L.T. (Sh Ct) 86; (2000) 16 Const. L.J. 75, Sh Ct (Tayside). .... *Digested,* 95/**5486**

Wong Kam-Ming *v.* Queen, The [1980] A.C. 247; [1979] 2 W.L.R. 81; [1979] 1 All E.R. 939; (1979) 69 Cr. App. R. 47; [1979] Crim. L.R. 168; 123 S.J. 47, PC (HK) .... *Digested,* 79/**442**:
Applied, 81/1890, 91/628, 00/5996: *Considered,* 87/560:
Distinguished, 96/1908

Wood *v.* HM Advocate (Sentencing) 1998 G.W.D. 5-211, HCJ Appeal
Wood *v.* HM Advocate (Sentencing) 2000 G.W.D. 20-823, HCJ Appeal
Wood Group Heavy Industrial Turbines Ltd *v.* Crossan [1998] I.R.L.R. 680, EAT ...... *Digested,* 99/**6044**
Woodland Trust *v.* MacMillan 2001 G.W.D. 34-1332, OH
Woods *v.* HM Advocate 1999 G.W.D. 19-893, HCJ Appeal
Woodward *v.* Chief Constable of Fife 1998 S.L.T. 1342; 1998 Rep. L.R. 74; 1998 G.W.D. 16-820, OH .... *Digested,* 98/**6155**
Woodward *v.* Ruxton (Sentencing) 2000 G.W.D. 3-94, HCJ Appeal
Woolard *v.* Reith 2001 G.W.D. 25-986, HCJ Appeal
Woolley *v.* Strachan 1997 S.L.T. (Sh Ct) 88; 1997 S.C.L.R. 976; 1997 G.W.D. 28-1389, Sh Pr .... *Digested,* 98/**5840**
Wordie Property Co Ltd *v.* Secretary of State for Scotland 1984 S.L.T. 345, 1 Div...... *Digested,* 84/**4735**:
Applied, 89/5083, 92/5890, 93/5939, 96/7151, 97/6113:
Considered, 00/6491, 00/6500: *Followed,* 97/6144, 99/6411:
Referred to, 93/5937

Wormold *v.* Walkingshaw (Sentencing) 1998 G.W.D. 8-407, HCJ Appeal
Wotherspoon (William) *v.* HM Advocate (No.1) 1999 S.L.T. 664; 1998 S.C.C.R. 615; 1998 G.W.D. 35-1786, HCJ Appeal .... *Digested,* 99/**5819**
Wotherspoon (William) *v.* HM Advocate (No.2) 1999 G.W.D. 33-1574, HCJ Appeal
Wray *v.* Associated Newspapers Ltd 2000 S.L.T. 869; 2000 S.C.L.R. 819; 2000 Rep. L.R. 59 (Note); 2000 G.W.D. 15-606, OH .... *Digested,* 00/**6178**
Wright *v.* Cotias Investments Inc 2001 S.L.T. 353; 2000 S.C.L.R. 324; 2000 G.W.D. 13-465, OH .... *Digested,* 00/**6674**
Wright *v.* Eurospares (Continental Parts) Ltd 2001 G.W.D. 34-1324, Sh Ct (Grampian)
Wright *v.* HM Advocate (Sentencing) 1998 G.W.D. 5-223, HCJ Appeal
Wright *v.* HM Advocate (Sentencing) 1999 G.W.D. 7-337, HCJ Appeal
Wright *v.* HM Advocate (Sentencing) 2000 G.W.D. 34-1306, HCJ Appeal
Wright (Trevor Rush) *v.* HM Advocate 2000 S.L.T. 1020; 2000 S.C.C.R. 638; 2000 G.W.D. 17-683, HCJ Appeal.. *Digested,* 00/**6012**
Wright *v.* McGlennan 2001 G.W.D. 25-928, HCJ Appeal
Wright *v.* Reith (Sentencing) 1998 G.W.D. 4-194, HCJ Appeal
Wright *v.* Scottbridge Construction Ltd [2001] I.R.L.R. 589, EAT .... *Digested,* 01/**6472**
Wright *v.* Vannet 1998 G.W.D. 37-1942, HCJ Appeal
Wright *v.* Vannet (Sentencing) 2000 G.W.D. 4-148, HCJ Appeal
Wright *v.* Vannet (Sentencing) 2000 G.W.D. 30-1176, HCJ Appeal
Wright *v.* Wright 1999 G.W.D. 3-119, Sh Ct
Wright, Noter see Roy's Trustee, Noter
WWF UK Ltd *v.* Scottish Natural Heritage see WWF UK Ltd *v.* Secretary of State for Scotland
WWF UK Ltd *v.* Secretary of State for Scotland; *sub nom* WWF UK Ltd *v.* Scottish Natural Heritage [1999] 1 C.M.L.R. 1021; [1999] Env. L.R. 632; 1998 G.W.D. 37-1936; *Times,* November 20, 1998, OH .... *Digested,* 98/**5830**
Wylie *v.* Corrigan 1999 S.C. 97; 1999 S.L.T. 739; 1999 S.C.L.R. 177; 1998 G.W.D. 34-1731, Ex Div .... *Digested,* 99/**5661**

Wylie v. Friel 2001 G.W.D. 15-584, OH
Wyllie v. Reith 2001 G.W.D. 30-1202, HCJ Appeal
Wyness v. HM Advocate (Sentencing) 2000 G.W.D. 15-589, HCJ
Wyness v. Lockhart 1992 S.C.C.R. 808, HCJ Appeal . . . .   *Digested*, 93/**5056**:
                                                        Distinguished, 98/5574

Wynne v. Napier (Sentencing) 2001 G.W.D. 16-637, HCJ Appeal
Wynne v. United Kingdom (A/294-A) (1995) 19 E.H.R.R. 333; *Times*, July 27, 1994;
    Independent, September 26, 1994 (C.S.); *Guardian*, July 25, 1994, ECHR . . . . . .   *Digested*, 95/**2617**:
                                          Applied, 01/6836: *Followed*, 01/1411

X v. Austria (2742/66) Unreported, Eur Comm HR . . . .   *Referred to*, 01/6357
X v. Criminal Injuries Compensation Board; *sub nom* D v. Criminal Injuries
   Compensation Board 1999 S.C.L.R. 1066; 1999 G.W.D. 23-1079; *Times*, July 5,
   1999, OH . . . .   *Digested*, 99/**5615**

Yarrow Shipbuilders Ltd v. Normand 1995 S.L.T. 1215; 1995 S.C.C.R. 224, HCJ Appeal .   *Digested*, 95/**5692**:
                                          Distinguished, 98/5618
Yates v. HM Advocate 1977 S.L.T. (Notes) 42, HCJ Appeal . . . .   *Digested*, 77/**3321**:
                Affirmed, 97/5761: *Applied*, 88/3893, 99/5824: *Distinguished*, 86/3976
Yip v. HM Advocate (Sentencing) 2000 G.W.D. 8-280, HCJ Appeal
Yoker Housing Association Ltd v. McGurn Logan Duncan & Opfer (No.1) 1998 S.L.T.
   1334; 1998 S.C.L.R. 388; 1998 G.W.D. 6-258, OH . . . .   *Digested*, 98/**5445**
Yoker Housing Association Ltd v. McGurn Logan Duncan & Opfer (No.2) 1998 G.W.D.
   26-1288, OH
Young v. Archibald 1999 G.W.D. 4-205, OH
Young (Steven James) v. Barbour 2001 G.W.D. 39-1488, HCJ Appeal
Young v. Blue Star Line Ltd 1998 S.L.T. 109; 1997 G.W.D. 4-156, OH . . . .   *Digested*, 97/**6032**
Young v. Friel (Sentencing) 1998 G.W.D. 9-443, HCJ Appeal
Young v. Glasgow Tramway & Omnibus Co Ltd (1882) 10 R. 242; 1882 S.L.R. 169, 1
   Div . . . .   *Considered*,
                                          47-51/2542,
                          50/4681, 98/5478: *Followed*, 89/4764
Young v. HM Advocate 1999 G.W.D. 30-1425, HCJ Appeal
Young (John William) v. Lees 1998 S.C.C.R. 558; 1998 G.W.D. 28-1404, HCJ Appeal . .   *Digested*, 98/**5652**
Young v. McDowall 2001 S.C.L.R. 155, OH . . . .   *Digested*, 01/**6423**
Young v. McFadyen (Sentencing) 2001 G.W.D. 6-219, HCJ Appeal
Young v. Ormiston 1936 S.L.T. 79, OH . . . .   *Considered*, 98/**5716**:
                                          Doubted, 83/4254, 84/3992
Young v. Scottish Coal (Deep Mining) Co Ltd 2001 Rep. L.R. 107; 2001 G.W.D. 24-
   902, OH
Young v. Walkingshaw 1998 G.W.D. 20-1028, HCJ Appeal
Young v. West 2000 G.W.D. 7-262, Sh Pr
Young's Executors v. Peebles 1997 S.C. 309; 1997 S.L.T. 286, IH (Ct of 5 judges) . . . . .   *Digested*, 97/**5647**:
                                          Followed, 98/5493
Younger v. HM Advocate (Sentencing) 2000 G.W.D. 13-473, HCJ Appeal
Youngson v. Higson (Sentencing) 2000 S.L.T. 1441; 2000 G.W.D. 29-1125, HCJ
   Appeal . . . .   *Digested*, 00/**6130**
Yule v. Houston (Sentencing) 1998 G.W.D. 13-688, HCJ Appeal
Yule v. South Lanarkshire Council (No.1) 1998 S.L.T. 490; (1997-98) 1 C.C.L. Rep. 571;
   1998 G.W.D. 9-476; *Times*, May 18, 1998, OH . . . .   *Digested*, 98/**6199**
Yule v. South Lanarkshire Council (No.2) 2001 S.C. 203; 2000 S.L.T. 1249; 2001
   S.C.L.R. 26; 2000 G.W.D. 27-1066, Ex Div; affirming 1999 S.C.L.R. 985; (1999)
   2 C.C.L. Rep. 394; 1999 G.W.D. 18-859, OH . . . .   *Digested*, 00/**6693**
Yule v. Vannet (Sentencing) 2000 G.W.D. 3-102, HCJ Appeal

Zafar (Rashid), Petitioner; *sub nom* Zafar v. Glasgow City Council (EAT Appeal
   Procedure) 2001 S.C.L.R. 474; 2001 G.W.D. 1-52, OH . . . .   *Digested*, 01/**6466**
Zafar v. Glasgow City Council see Glasgow City Council v. Zafar
Zafar v. Glasgow City Council (EAT Appeal Procedure) see Zafar (Rashid), Petitioner
Zhu v. Secretary of State for the Home Department see Ha You Zhu v. Secretary of
   State for the Home Department
Zino Davidoff SA v. M&S Toiletries Ltd (No.1) 2000 S.L.T. 683; [2000] 2 C.M.L.R.
   735; [2000] E.T.M.R. 622; 2000 G.W.D. 14-550, OH . . . .   *Digested*, 00/**6522**
Zino Davidoff SA v. M&S Toiletries Ltd (No.2) [2001] E.T.M.R. 10; 2000 G.W.D. 27-
   1067, OH . . . .   *Digested*, 01/**6727**
Zino Davidoff SA v. M&S Toiletries Ltd (No.3) 2001 G.W.D. 3-135; [2001] E.T.M.R.
   CN7, OH

PART III

SHIPS' NAMES INDEX

Boucraa,The [1994] 1 A.C. 486; [1994] 2 W.L.R. 39; [1994] 1 All E.R. 20; [1994] 1 Lloyd's
Rep. 251; (1994) 138 S.J.L.B. 19; *Times*, December 20, 1993; *Independent*,
January 19, 1994, HL; reversing [1993] 3 W.L.R. 266; [1993] 3 All E.R. 686;
[1993] 2 Lloyd's Rep. 149; [1993] N.P.C. 64; *Times*, April 16, 1993, CA . . . . *Digested*, 94/**221**:
Applied, 95/2038, 96/3566: *Considered*, 93/1081, 94/1211, 97/82, 97/1075:
Followed, 99/5471, 00/105
Bowbelle,The (Interest on Taxed Costs) [1997] 1 W.L.R. 1159; [1997] 2 Lloyd's Rep. 191;
[1998] 1 Costs L.R. 32; *Times*, April 8, 1997, CA; reversing [1997] 1 Costs L.R.
90, QBD . . . . *Digested*, 97/**541**
Brij,The [2001] 1 Lloyd's Rep. 431, CFI (HK) . . . . *Digested*, 01/**4898**
Bukhta Russkaya,The [1997] 2 Lloyd's Rep. 744, QBD (Comm Ct) . . . . *Digested*, 98/**4412**
Bunga Seroja,The [1999] 1 Lloyd's Rep. 512; 1999 A.M.C. 427, HC (Aus); affirming [1994] 1
Lloyd's Rep. 455, Sup Ct (NSW) . . . . *Digested*, 99/**4420**

Cape Don,The [2000] 1 Lloyd's Rep. 388, Fed Ct (Aus) (Sgl judge) . . . . *Digested*, 00/**752**
Capricorn 1,The [1998] 2 Lloyd's Rep. 379, QBD (Comm Ct) . . . . *Digested*, 98/**230**
Carbonnade,The [2000] 1 W.L.R. 2068; [2001] 1 All E.R. 626; [2001] 1 All E.R. (Comm)
847; [2000] 1 Lloyd's Rep. 359; [2000] C.L.C. 784; [2000] I.C.R. 1024; (2000)
97(12) L.S.G. 39; (2000) 144 S.J.L.B. 135; *Times*, March 21, 2000, QBD (Adm
Ct) . . . . *Digested*, 00/**4706**
Caribia Viva,The [1999] 1 Lloyd's Rep. 43; [1999] C.L.C. 87, QBD (Adm Ct) . . . . *Digested*, 99/**4479**
Caroline P,The [1985] 1 W.L.R. 553; [1985] 1 All E.R. 243; [1984] 2 Lloyd's Rep. 466;
(1985) 82 L.S.G. 1781; (1985) 129 S.J. 283, QBD (Comm Ct) . . . . *Digested*, 85/**2012**:
Considered, 00/878
Carslogie,The [1952] A.C. 292; [1952] 1 All E.R. 20; [1951] 2 Lloyd's Rep. 441; [1951] 2
T.L.R. 1099; 95 S.J. 801, HL; reversing [1951] P. 167; (1950) 84 Ll. L. Rep. 399; 66
T.L.R. (Pt. 2) 683; 94 S.J. 594, CA; reversing (1950) 84 Ll. L. Rep. 148; [1950] W.N.
388, PDAD . . . . *Digested*, 47-51/**10521**:
Considered, 61/2345, 94/1442, 98/3914: *Distinguished*, 58/882
Catherine Helen,The [1998] 3 All E.R. 714; [1998] 2 Lloyd's Rep. 511; [1998] C.L.C. 1310;
Times, July 25, 1998, QBD (Comm Ct) . . . . *Digested*, 98/**252**
Centaurus Mar,The [1998] C.L.C. 1003, QBD (Comm Ct) . . . . *Digested*, 98/**249**
Chaparral,The [1968] 2 Lloyd's Rep. 158, CA . . . . *Digested*, 68/**3187**:
Followed, 98/771
Chevron North America,The [2001] UKHL 50; [2001] 3 W.L.R. 949; 2001 S.L.T. 1394; 2001
S.C.L.R. 1029; (2001) 98(45) L.S.G. 26; (2001) 145 S.J.L.B. 244; 2001 G.W.D. 33-
1316; *Times*, October 19, 2001; *Independent*, December 3, 2001, HL; reversing
2000 S.L.T. 1374; 2000 S.C.L.R. 580; 2000 G.W.D. 14-559, 1 Div; reversing in
part 2000 S.L.T. 201; 1999 S.C.L.R. 438; 1999 G.W.D. 7-355; *Times*, May 6,
1999, OH . . . . *Digested*, 01/**6865**
Chitral,The [2000] 1 All E.R. (Comm) 932; [2000] 1 Lloyd's Rep. 529; [2000] C.L.C. 1021,
QBD (Comm Ct) . . . . *Digested*, 00/**4683**
Choyang Star,The [1998] 1 Lloyd's Rep. 283, QBD (Adm Ct) . . . . *Digested*, 98/**4417**
Christiansborg,The (1885) L.R. 10 P.D. 141, CA . . . . *Applied*, 47-51/**7898.a**,
55/2200, 60/2579, 00/4712: *Distinguished*, 68/3618, 69/2922:
Followed, 67/3239
Clipper Sao Luis,The [2000] 1 All E.R. (Comm) 920; [2000] 1 Lloyd's Rep. 645; [2001]
C.L.C. 762, QBD (Comm Ct) . . . . *Digested*, 00/**4696**
Contship Success,The [2000] 1 All E.R. (Comm) 905; [2000] 1 Lloyd's Rep. 627; [2000]
C.L.C. 1181, CA; affirming [1998] 2 Lloyd's Rep. 488; [1998] C.L.C. 1495, QBD
(Adm Ct) . . . . *Digested*, 00/**4707**
Cornelis Verolme,The [2000] B.P.I.R. 896, HC (NZ) . . . . *Digested*, 01/**3760**

David Agmashenebeli,The [2001] C.L.C. 942, QBD (Adm Ct) . . . . *Digested*, 01/**398**
Daylam,The [1998] 1 Lloyd's Rep. 423, QBD (Comm Ct) . . . . *Digested*, 98/**3389**
Delos,The [2001] 1 All E.R. (Comm) 763; [2001] 1 Lloyd's Rep. 703, QBD (Comm Ct) . *Digested*, 01/**344**
Delphine,The [2001] 2 Lloyd's Rep. 542; (2001) 151 N.L.J. 694, QBD (Comm Ct) . . . . *Digested*, 01/**3824**
Demosthenes V,The (No.2) [1982] 1 Lloyd's Rep. 282, QBD (Comm Ct) . . . . *Digested*, 82/**2871**:
Considered, 00/4711
Derbyshire,The [1988] A.C. 276; [1987] 3 W.L.R. 1181; [1987] 3 All E.R. 1068; [1988] 1
Lloyd's Rep. 109; [1988] I.C.R. 67; [1988] F.T.L.R. 217; (1988) 85(3) L.S.G. 36;
(1987) 137 N.L.J. 1157; (1987) 131 S.J. 1658, HL; reversing [1987] 2 W.L.R. 1098;
[1987] 1 All E.R. 932; [1987] 1 Lloyd's Rep. 411; [1987] I.C.R. 619; [1987] 1 F.T.L.R.
353; (1987) 84 L.S.G. 743; (1987) 131 S.J. 166, CA; reversing [1986] 1 W.L.R. 751;
[1986] 2 All E.R. 65; [1986] 1 Lloyd's Rep. 418; (1986) 83 L.S.G. 1399; (1986) 130
S.J. 447, QBD (Adm Ct) . . . . *Digested*, 88/**1258**:
Applied, 93/2016: *Considered*, 92/4179, 98/2832
Derbyshire,The, *Times*, October 28, 1999, QBD (Adm Ct) . . . . *Digested*, 99/**4410**

Halki, The [1998] 1 W.L.R. 726; [1998] 2 All E.R. 23; [1998] 1 Lloyd's Rep. 465; [1998]
    C.L.C. 583; (1998) 142 S.J.L.B. 44; [1998] N.P.C. 4; *Times*, January 19, 1998;
    Independent, January 12, 1998 (C.S.), CA; affirming [1997] 1 W.L.R. 1268;
    [1997] 3 All E.R. 833; [1998] 1 Lloyd's Rep. 49; (1997) 94(28) L.S.G. 26;
    (1997) 141 S.J.L.B. 172; *Times*, October 13, 1997, QBD (Adm Ct) . . . .   *Digested*, 98/**246**:
                                                                                              Followed, 00/227
Hamtun, The [1999] 1 All E.R. (Comm.) 587; [1999] 1 Lloyd's Rep. 883, QBD (Adm Ct)   *Digested*, 99/**4472**
Hanjin Madras, The [2001] EWCA Civ 1278; [2001] 2 All E.R. (Comm) 805; [2001] 2
    Lloyd's Rep. 419, CA; affirming [2000] 1 All E.R. (Comm) 870; [2000] 1 Lloyd's
    Rep. 282; [2000] C.L.C. 772, QBD (Adm Ct) . . . .   *Digested*, 00/**4709**
Hanjin Marseilles, The [2001] 2 Lloyd's Rep. 735, CFI (HK)
Happy Day, The [2001] 1 All E.R. (Comm) 659; [2001] 1 Lloyd's Rep. 754; [2001] C.L.C.
    813; *Times*, February 22, 2001, QBD (Comm Ct) . . . .   *Digested*, 01/**4912**
Happy Fellow, The [1998] 1 Lloyd's Rep. 13; [1997] C.L.C. 1391; [1998] I.L.Pr. 440, CA;
    affirming [1997] 1 Lloyd's Rep. 130; [1997] C.L.C. 567, QBD (Adm Ct) . . . .   *Digested*, 98/**773**:
                                                                                              Considered, 00/738
Happy Ranger, The A3/2001/1695, CA; reversing [2001] 2 Lloyd's Rep. 530, QBD (Comm
    Ct)
Hawk, The [1999] 1 Lloyd's Rep. 176, QBD (Comm Ct) . . . .   *Digested*, 99/**4453**:
                                                                                              Applied, 01/4906
Hector, The [1998] 2 Lloyd's Rep. 287; [1998] C.L.C. 902, QBD (Comm Ct) . . . .   *Digested*, 98/**4397**:
                                                            Applied, 00/4688: *Considered*, 01/4907
Hellespont Ardent, The [1997] 2 Lloyd's Rep. 547, QBD (Comm Ct) . . . .   *Digested*, 98/**3949**
Herceg Novi, The [1998] 4 All E.R. 238; [1998] 2 Lloyd's Rep. 454; [1998] C.L.C. 1487;
    Times, July 30, 1998, CA; reversing [1998] 1 Lloyd's Rep. 167, QBD (Adm Ct) . .   *Digested*, 98/**4422**
Hermosa, The [1982] 1 Lloyd's Rep. 570; *Times*, March 4, 1982, CA; affirming [1980] 1
    Lloyd's Rep. 638, QBD (Comm Ct) . . . .   *Digested*, 82/**2877**:
                                                                                              Applied, 00/870

Hill Harmony, The [2001] 1 A.C. 638; [2000] 3 W.L.R. 1954; [2001] 1 All E.R. 403; [2001] 1
    All E.R. (Comm) 76; [2001] 1 Lloyd's Rep. 147; [2001] C.L.C. 502; (2001) 98(7)
    L.S.G. 41; (2000) 150 N.L.J. 1856; (2001) 145 S.J.L.B. 6; *Times*, December 8,
    2000; *Independent*, December 13, 2000, HL; reversing [2000] Q.B. 241; [1999]
    3 W.L.R. 724; [1999] 4 All E.R. 199; [1999] 2 All E.R. (Comm) 1; [1999] 2
    Lloyd's Rep. 209; [1999] C.L.C. 1254; (1999) 96(23) L.S.G. 35; *Times*, May 25,
    1999, CA; affirming [1999] Q.B. 72; [1998] 3 W.L.R. 184; [1998] 4 All E.R.
    286; [1998] 2 Lloyd's Rep. 367; [1998] C.L.C. 794; (1998) 95(11) L.S.G. 34;
    (1998) 142 S.J.L.B. 94; *Times*, March 5, 1998, QBD (Comm Ct) . . . .   *Digested*, 01/**4915**
Holstencruiser, The [1992] 2 Lloyd's Rep. 378, QBD (Comm Ct) . . . .   *Digested*, 93/**3591**:
                                                                                              Considered, 01/4906
Honam Jade, The [1991] 1 Lloyd's Rep. 38, CA . . . .   *Digested*, 91/**508**:
                                                                                              Applied, 00/4684
Hongkong Fir, The [1962] 2 Q.B. 26; [1962] 2 W.L.R. 474; [1962] 1 All E.R. 474; [1961] 2
    Lloyd's Rep. 478; (1961) 106 S.J. 35, CA; affirming [1961] 2 W.L.R. 716; [1961] 2 All
    E.R. 257; [1961] 1 Lloyd's Rep. 159; 105 S.J. 347, QBD (Comm Ct) . . . .   *Digested*, 62/**2838**:
                                Applied, 71/1838, 75/3041, 78/2636, 79/2387, 99/3700, 00/874, 00/899:
                                Considered, 67/1833, 68/1777, 69/490, 70/362, 74/3426, 80/2393, 99/838,
                                00/3532: *Distinguished*, 66/1818, 83/262: *Explained*, 81/2433
Hontestroom, The [1927] A.C. 37; (1926) 25 Ll. L. Rep. 377, HL; reversing (1925) 22 Ll. L.
    Rep. 458, CA; reversing (1925) 21 Ll. L. Rep. 359, PDAD . . . .   *Applied*, 47-51/2829,
                                47-51/2837, 47-51/5995, 47-51/7495, 47-51/9902, 59/431, 71/11754, 76/338,
                                80/1897, 81/1844, 01/4261: *Distinguished*, 56/8238
Huntingdon, The [1974] 1 W.L.R. 505; [1974] 2 All E.R. 97; [1974] 1 Lloyd's Rep. 520; (1974)
    59 Cr. App. R. 131; 118 S.J. 478, HL; affirming [1973] 1 W.L.R. 1373; [1973] 3 All E.R.
    849; [1974] 1 Lloyd's Rep. 8; (1974) 58 Cr. App. R. 68; [1973] Crim. L.R. 575; 117 S.J.
    712, CA (Crim Div) . . . .   *Digested*, 74/**3626**:
                                Considered, 99/5209: *Distinguished*, 91/5046: *Followed*, 83/4180

I Congreso del Partido, The [1983] 1 A.C. 244; [1981] 3 W.L.R. 328; [1981] 2 All E.R. 1064;
    [1981] 2 Lloyd's Rep. 367; [1981] Com. L.R. 190; 125 S.J. 528, HL; reversing [1981]
    1 All E.R. 1092; [1980] 1 Lloyd's Rep. 23, CA; affirming [1978] Q.B. 500; [1977] 3
    W.L.R. 778; [1978] 1 All E.R. 1169; [1977] 1 Lloyd's Rep. 536, QBD (Adm Ct) . .   *Digested*, 81/**285**:
                                Applied, 82/1045, 83/1345, 94/3720, 95/2940, 01/376: *Considered*, 84/349,
                                94/3720, 95/2940, 95/2944: *Followed*, 80/328, 81/284
Ikariada, The [1999] 2 All E.R. (Comm) 257; [1999] 2 Lloyd's Rep. 365; [1999] C.L.C. 1713,
    QBD (Comm Ct) . . . .   *Digested*, 99/**4416**
Ikarian Reefer, The (No.1) [1995] 1 Lloyd's Rep. 455, CA; reversing [1993] 2 Lloyd's Rep. 68;
    [1993] F.S.R. 563; [1993] 37 E.G. 158; *Times*, March 5, 1993, QBD (Comm Ct) .   *Digested*, 96/**3609**:
                                Considered, 94/3167, 95/3419, 99/343, 00/3517

Ikarian Reefer, The (No.2) [2000] 1 W.L.R. 603; [2000] 1 All E.R. 37; [1999] 2 All E.R.
  (Comm) 673; [2000] 1 Lloyd's Rep. 129; [2000] C.P. Rep. 13; [2000] C.L.C. 22;
  [2000] 1 Costs L.R. 37; [2000] I.L.Pr. 490; [2000] Lloyd's Rep. I.R. 230; (1999)
  96(41) L.S.G. 35; (1999) 96(42) L.S.G. 40; (1999) 149 N.L.J. 1561; (1999) 143
  S.J.L.B. 255; *Times*, October 15, 1999; *Independent*, October 20, 1999;
  Independent, November 22, 1999 (C.S.), CA; affirming [1999] 2 Lloyd's Rep.
  621, QBD (Comm Ct) .... *Digested*, 99/**749**:
                                                                     Considered, 00/455

Illustrious Colocotronis, The [1984] Q.B. 713; [1984] 2 W.L.R. 508; [1984] 2 All E.R. 226;
  [1984] 1 Lloyd's Rep. 258; (1984) 81 L.S.G. 429; (1984) 128 S.J. 243, CA .... *Digested*, 84/**1579**:
                                                                     Applied, 01/4527

Imvros, The [1999] 1 All E.R. (Comm) 724; [1999] 1 Lloyd's Rep. 848; [1999] C.L.C. 928,
  QBD (Comm Ct) .... *Digested*, 99/**4433**

Indian Endurance, The (No.2) [1998] A.C. 878; [1997] 3 W.L.R. 818; [1997] 4 All E.R. 380;
  [1998] 1 Lloyd's Rep. 1; [1997] C.L.C. 1581; [1998] I.L.Pr. 511; (1997) 94(43) L.S.G.
  29; (1997) 147 N.L.J. 1581; (1997) 141 S.J.L.B. 230; *Times*, October 23, 1997, HL;
  affirming [1997] 2 W.L.R. 538; [1996] 3 All E.R. 641; [1996] 2 Lloyd's Rep. 12;
  [1996] C.L.C. 1548; *Times*, May 1, 1996, CA; reversing [1994] 2 Lloyd's Rep.
  331; *Times*, June 9, 1994, QBD (Adm Ct) .... *Digested*, 97/**875**:
                                                                     Applied, 00/2320

Indian Grace, The (No.2) [1998] A.C. 878; [1997] 3 W.L.R. 818; [1997] 4 All E.R. 380;
  [1998] 1 Lloyd's Rep. 1; [1997] C.L.C. 1581; [1998] I.L.Pr. 511; (1997) 94(43) L.S.G.
  29; (1997) 147 N.L.J. 1581; (1997) 141 S.J.L.B. 230; *Times*, October 23, 1997, HL;
  affirming [1997] 2 W.L.R. 538; [1996] 3 All E.R. 641; [1996] 2 Lloyd's Rep. 12;
  [1996] C.L.C. 1548; *Times*, May 1, 1996, CA; reversing [1994] 2 Lloyd's Rep.
  331; *Times*, June 9, 1994, QBD (Adm Ct) .... *Digested*, 97/**875**:
                                                                     Applied, 00/2320

Ines, The (No.1) [1993] 2 Lloyd's Rep. 492, QBD (Comm Ct) .... *Digested*, 94/**3764**:
                                                                     Disapproved, 98/4394

Ines, The (No.2) [1995] 2 Lloyd's Rep. 144, QBD (Comm Ct) .... *Considered*, 98/582:
                                                                     Followed, 97/4494

Ira, The [1998] Q.B. 43; [1996] 3 W.L.R. 849; [1996] 2 Lloyd's Rep. 274; [1996] 2 B.C.L.C.
  626; [1996] C.L.C. 1564; *Times*, May 1, 1996; *Lloyd's List*, June 5, 1996, CA. .... *Digested*, 96/**2782**

Iran Abad, The [1999] 1 Lloyd's Rep. 818, QBD (Adm Ct) .... *Digested*, 99/**4439**

Irina Zharkikh, The [2001] 2 Lloyd's Rep. 319, HC (NZ) .... *Digested*, 01/**4905**

Irini A, The (No.1) [1999] 1 Lloyd's Rep. 196, QBD (Comm Ct) .... *Digested*, 99/**4478**

Irini A, The (No.2) [1999] 1 Lloyd's Rep. 189, QBD (Comm Ct) .... *Digested*, 99/**4426**

Irish Rowan, The [1991] 2 Q.B. 206; [1990] 2 W.L.R. 117; [1989] 3 All E.R. 853; [1989] 2
  Lloyd's Rep. 144; (1990) 87(5) L.S.G. 39; (1990) 134 S.J. 426; *Times*, May 5, 1989,
  CA .... *Digested*, 90/**3768**:
            Considered, 90/3744, 91/2921, 00/3516: *Distinguished*, 91/2188, 92/3976

Isla Fernandina, The [2000] 2 Lloyd's Rep. 15, QBD (Comm Ct) .... *Digested*, 00/**4695**

Italia Express, The (No.2) [1992] 1 W.L.R. 887; [1992] 3 All E.R. 414; [1992] 2 Lloyd's Rep.
  216; *Financial Times*, January 14, 1992, CA; reversing in part *Financial Times*,
  December 20, 1991, QBD. .... *Digested*, 92/**2060**:
                                                                     Followed, 99/3381

Jalagouri, The [2000] 1 All E.R. (Comm) 700; [2000] 1 Lloyd's Rep. 515; [2000] C.L.C.
  1051; *Independent*, April 7, 2000, CA; affirming [1999] 1 Lloyd's Rep. 903;
  [1998] C.L.C. 1054, QBD (Comm Ct) .... *Digested*, 00/**4703**

Jay Bola, The [1992] Q.B. 907; [1992] 2 W.L.R. 898; [1992] 3 All E.R. 329; [1992] 2 Lloyd's
  Rep. 62; (1992) 136 S.J.L.B. 52; *Times*, February 26, 1992, QBD (Comm Ct) ... *Digested*, 92/**3628**:
            Applied, 92/3927, 96/5316: *Considered*, 98/587: *Followed*, 93/3324, 98/762

Joint Frost, The [1998] 1 Lloyd's Rep. 310, QBD (Comm Ct) .... *Digested*, 98/**3388**

Kalliopi A, The [1988] 2 Lloyd's Rep. 101; [1988] 2 F.T.L.R. 73, CA; reversing [1987] 2 Lloyd's
  Rep. 263; [1987] 1 F.T.L.R. 399, QBD (Comm Ct)..................... *Digested*, 89/**3406**:
                                            Applied, 92/3934, 92/3946, 00/4698

Kalma, The [1999] 2 All E.R. (Comm) 761; [1999] 2 Lloyd's Rep. 374; [1999] C.L.C. 1398,
  QBD (Comm Ct) .... *Digested*, 99/**4435**

Kapitan Sakharov, The [2000] 2 Lloyd's Rep. 255; [2000] C.L.C. 933, CA .... *Digested*, 00/**4686**

Kapitan Shvetsov, The [1998] 1 Lloyd's Rep. 199, CA (HK) .... *Digested*, 98/**774**

KH Enterprise, The [1994] 2 A.C. 324; [1994] 3 W.L.R. 1; [1994] 2 All E.R. 250; [1994] 1
  Lloyd's Rep. 593; (1994) 91(18) L.S.G. 37; (1994) 138 S.J.L.B. 85; *Times*, March
  29, 1994, PC (HK)... *Digested*, 94/**255**:
                                            Distinguished, 96/5298, 00/4678

Kommunar, The (No.1) [1997] 1 Lloyd's Rep. 1; [1996] C.L.C. 1919; *Times*, July 9, 1996,
  QBD (Adm Ct) .... *Digested*, 96/**5289**:
                                                                     Applied, 00/4740

Kommunar, The (No.3) [1997] 1 Lloyd's Rep. 22, QBD (Adm Ct) .... *Digested*, 97/**4489**:
                                                                     Distinguished, 00/3472

Koningin Juliana, The [1975] 2 Lloyd's Rep. 111, HL; reversing [1974] 2 Lloyd's Rep. 353, CA;
    reversing [1973] 2 Lloyd's Rep. 308, QBD (Adm Ct) . . . .   *Digested*, 75/**3186**:
                   Applied, 96/5321: *Considered*, 00/4705

Krapan J, The [1999] 1 Lloyd's Rep. 688, QBD (Comm Ct) . . . .   *Digested*, 99/**244**

Kribi, The [2001] 1 Lloyd's Rep. 76; [2001] C.L.C. 148; *Times*, November 28, 2000, QBD
    (Comm Ct) . . . .   *Digested*, 01/**808**

Ksenia Zharkikh, The [2001] 2 Lloyd's Rep. 319, HC (NZ) . . . .   *Digested*, 01/**4905**

Kumanovo, The [1998] 2 Lloyd's Rep. 301; *Times*, February 5, 1998, QBD (Adm Ct) . . .   *Digested*, 98/**4419**

Kyriaki, The [1992] 1 Lloyd's Rep. 484; *Financial Times*, May 24, 1991, QBD (Comm Ct) .   *Digested*, 92/**3976**:
                                        Applied, 01/642

La Pintada, The (No.1) [1985] A.C. 104; [1984] 3 W.L.R. 10; [1984] 2 All E.R. 773; [1984] 2
    Lloyd's Rep. 9; [1984] C.I.L.L. 110; (1984) 81 L.S.G. 1999; (1984) 128 S.J. 414, HL;
    reversing [1983] 1 Lloyd's Rep. 37; [1982] Com. L.R. 250; *Times*, November 1,
    1982, QBD (Comm Ct) . . . .   *Digested*, 84/**123**:
            Applied, 84/120, 85/3160: *Cited*, 00/1453: *Considered*, 84/2346, 86/2760,
                         87/2429, 97/3839, 98/1433: *Followed*, 98/231

Leerort, The [2001] EWCA Civ 1055; [2001] 2 Lloyd's Rep. 291, CA . . . .   *Digested*, 01/**4919**

Lefthero, The [1992] 2 Lloyd's Rep. 109; *Financial Times*, April 15, 1992, CA; affirming
    [1991] 2 Lloyd's Rep. 599, QBD (Comm Ct) . . . .   *Digested*, 92/**3946**:
                                          Applied, 00/4698

Lendoudis Evangelos II, The (Unseaworthiness) [2001] 2 Lloyd's Rep. 304; [2001] C.L.C.
    1598, QBD (Comm Ct) . . . .   *Digested*, 01/**4953**

Lendoudis Evangelos II, The (Wrongful Detention) [1997] 1 Lloyd's Rep. 404; [1997] C.L.C.
    432; *Independent*, December 16, 1996 (C.S.), QBD (Comm Ct) . . . .   *Digested*, 97/**4594**:
                                          Applied, 01/4917

Leonidas, The [2001] 1 All E.R. (Comm) 392; [2001] 1 Lloyd's Rep. 533; [2001] C.L.C.
    1800, QBD (Comm Ct) . . . .   *Previous proceedings*,
                                          98/3324

Leonidas D, The [1985] 1 W.L.R. 925; [1985] 2 All E.R. 796; [1985] 2 Lloyd's Rep. 18; (1985)
    82 L.S.G. 2160; (1985) 129 S.J. 431, CA; reversing [1984] 1 W.L.R. 1; [1983] 3 All
    E.R. 737; [1983] 2 Lloyd's Rep. 411; (1983) 127 S.J. 729, QBD (Comm Ct) . . . .   *Digested*, 85/**110**:
            Applied, 84/94, 87/133: *Considered*, 86/90, 87/147: *Distinguished*, 98/3675

Liepaya, The [1999] 1 Lloyd's Rep. 649, QBD (Comm Ct) . . . .   *Digested*, 99/**4432**

Lipa, The [2001] 2 Lloyd's Rep. 17, QBD (Comm Ct) . . . .   *Digested*, 01/**4917**

Litsion Pride, The [1985] 1 Lloyd's Rep. 437; (1984) 134 N.L.J. 887, QBD (Comm Ct) . .   *Digested*, 85/**3208**:
            Considered, 95/4533: *Not followed*, 90/4101, 96/3572, 01/3825:
                                          Referred to, 97/3152

London Corp, The [1935] P. 70; (1935) 51 Ll. L. Rep. 67, CA; affirming (1934) 50 Ll. L. Rep.
    14, PDAD . . . .   *Applied*, 67/1021:
                                          Followed, 99/2504

Lorfri, The [1979] A.C. 757; [1978] 3 W.L.R. 991; [1979] 1 All E.R. 307; [1979] 1 Lloyd's Rep.
    201; 122 S.J. 843, HL; affirming in part [1978] Q.B. 927; [1978] 3 W.L.R. 309; [1978]
    3 All E.R. 1066; 1978] 2 Lloyd's Rep. 132; 122 S.J. 347, CA; reversing [1978] 1 Lloyd's
    Rep. 581, QBD (Comm Ct) . . . .   *Digested*, 79/**2452**:
            Applied, 79/342, 80/1627, 80/2457, 81/2484, 94/4062, 01/941:
            Considered, 79/100, 79/156, 80/2460, 85/259, 85/2604, 85/3203, 93/2495,
            94/2797, 97/3366: *Distinguished*, 80/2792, 82/2925, 83/3413:
                                          Referred to, 80/99

Lucy, The [1983] 1 Lloyd's Rep. 188, QBD (Comm Ct) . . . .   *Digested*, 83/**1726**:
                                          Followed, 00/818

Lutra II, The [2000] 1 W.L.R. 2068; [2001] 1 All E.R. 450; [2000] 1 All E.R. (Comm) 847;
    [2000] 1 Lloyd's Rep. 359; [2000] C.L.C. 784; [2000] I.C.R. 1024; (2000) 97(12)
    L.S.G. 39; (2000) 144 S.J.L.B. 135; *Times*, March 21, 2000, QBD (Adm Ct) . . . .   *Digested*, 00/**4706**

Lydia Flag, The [1998] 2 Lloyd's Rep. 652, QBD (Comm Ct) . . . .   *Digested*, 99/**3407**

Maciej Rataj, The [1999] Q.B. 515; [1999] 2 W.L.R. 181; [1995] All E.R. (E.C.) 229; [1995] 1
    Lloyd's Rep. 302; [1994] E.C.R. I-5439; [1995] I.L.Pr. 81; *Times*, December 28,
    1994; *Financial Times*, December 13, 1994, ECJ [1992] 2 Lloyd's Rep. 552;
    [1995] I.L.Pr. 114; *Lloyd's List*, September 27, 1991, CA; affirming [1991] 2
    Lloyd's Rep. 458, QBD (Adm Ct) . . . .   *Digested*, 95/**704**:
            Applied, 96/7098, 99/732, 00/738, 00/776: *Considered*, 97/900, 99/715,
                                     00/5442: *Followed*, 96/1089

Maersk Colombo, The [2001] EWCA Civ 717; [2001] 2 Lloyd's Rep. 275; (2001) 98(24)
    L.S.G. 43; (2001) 145 S.J.L.B. 149; *Times*, June 13, 2001, CA; affirming [1999] 2
    Lloyd's Rep. 491; [1999] C.L.C. 1814, QBD (Adm Ct) . . . .   *Digested*, 01/**4501**

Maira,The (No.3) [1990] 1 A.C. 637; [1989] 3 W.L.R.1330; [1990] 1 All E.R. 78; [1990] 1
    Lloyd's Rep. 225; [1988] 2 F.T.L.R. 9; [1988] Fin. L.R. 249; [1990] C.C.L.R. 18;
    (1990) 87(4) L.S.G. 33; (1989) 139 N.L.J. 1711; (1990) 134 S.J. 261; *Times*,
    December 1, 1989; *Independent*, December 6, 1989; *Financial Times*, December
    5, 1989, HL; reversing [1989] 3 W.L.R. 185; [1989] 1 All E.R. 213; [1988] 2
    Lloyd's Rep. 126; (1989) 133 S.J. 817; *Times*, March 5, 1988; *Independent*,
    March 3, 1988; *Financial Times*, May 16, 1988, CA. . . . . *Digested*, 90/**267**:
                        Applied, 90/4101, 00/2603: *Distinguished*, 00/2624
Maragetha Maria, The A3/2001/1437, A3/2001/1449, CA; reversing in part [2001] 2
    Lloyd's Rep. 443; [2001] C.L.C.1530; *Times*, August 20, 2001, QBD (Adm Ct) .   *Digested*, 01/**2806**
Marble Islands,The (No.1) [1983] 1 A.C. 244; [1981] 3 W.L.R. 328; [1981] 2 All E.R.1064;
    [1981] 2 Lloyd's Rep. 367; [1981] Com. L.R.190;125 S.J. 528, HL; reversing [1981]
    1 All E.R.1092; [1980] 1 Lloyd's Rep. 23, CA; affirming [1978] Q.B. 500; [1977] 3
    W.L.R. 778; [1978] 1 All E.R. 1169; [1977] 1 Lloyd's Rep. 536, QBD (Adm Ct) . .   *Digested*, 81/**285**:
          Applied, 82/1045, 83/1345, 94/3720, 95/2940, 01/376: *Considered*, 84/349,
                       94/3720, 95/2940, 95/2944: *Followed*, 80/328, 81/284
Marel,The [1994] 1 Lloyd's Rep. 624, CA; affirming [1992] 1 Lloyd's Rep. 402, QBD (Comm
    Ct) . . . . *Digested*, 95/**4534**:
                                Applied, 00/4724
Mareva AS, The [1977] 1 Lloyd's Rep. 368, QBD (Comm Ct) . . . . *Digested*, 77/**2757**:
                Applied, 98/4408, 00/4703: *Referred to*, 78/2705
Margaretha Maria, The A3/2001/1437, A3/2001/1449, CA; reversing in part [2001] 2
    Lloyd's Rep. 443; [2001] C.L.C. 1530; *Times*, August 20, 2001, QBD (Adm Ct) .   *Digested*, 01/**2806**
Mary,The [1993] Q.B. 54; [1992] 3 W.L.R. 744; [1993] 1 All E.R. 371; [1992] 2 Lloyd's Rep.
    471; *Times*, March 23, 1992; *Financial Times*, March 24, 1992, QBD (Comm Ct) .   *Digested*, 92/**2629**:
                Applied, 98/272: *Considered*, 98/3552, 99/723, 00/5107
Massira,The [1998] 2 Lloyd's Rep. 301; *Times*, February 5, 1998, QBD (Adm Ct) . . . . .   *Digested*, 98/**4419**
Mata K,The [1998] 2 Lloyd's Rep. 614; [1998] C.L.C. 1300, QBD (Comm Ct) . . . .   *Digested*, 99/**4415**
Merawi,The [1999] 1 Lloyd's Rep. 818, QBD (Adm Ct) . . . .   *Digested*, 99/**4439**
Mercandian Continent, The [2001] EWCA Civ 1275; [2001] 2 Lloyd's Rep. 563; [2001]
    C.L.C. 1836; [2001] Lloyd's Rep. I.R. 802; *Times*, September 3, 2001, CA;
    affirming [2000] 2 All E.R. (Comm) 731; [2000] 2 Lloyd's Rep. 357; [2000]
    C.L.C. 1425; [2000] Lloyd's Rep. I.R. 694; (2000) 97(29) L.S.G. 45; *Times*,
    August 8, 2000, QBD (Comm Ct) . . . . *Digested*, 01/**3827**
MessiniakiTolmi,The [1984] 1 Lloyd's Rep. 266; (1984) 128 S.J. 265, CA; reversing [1983]
    1 Lloyd's Rep. 666, QBD (Comm Ct) . . . . *Digested*, 84/**351**:
                                 Applied, 00/768
Metagama, The (1928) 30 Ll. L. Rep. 132; 1928 S.C. 21, OH . . . . *Considered*, 98/3914
Mexico 1,The [1990] 1 Lloyd's Rep. 507; *Financial Times*, February 7, 1990, CA; reversing
    [1988] 2 Lloyd's Rep.149, QBD (Comm Ct) . . . . *Digested*, 91/**3234**:
                      Applied, 01/4912: *Followed*, 97/4515
Michael,The [1979] 2 Lloyd's Rep. 1, CA; affirming [1979] 1 Lloyd's Rep. 55, QBD (Comm
    Ct) . . . . *Digested*, 79/**2471**:
                                  Applied, 01/3825
Mihalis Angelos,The [1971] 1 Q.B.164; [1970] 3 W.L.R. 601; [1970] 3 All E.R.125; [1970] 2
    Lloyd's Rep. 43; 114 S.J. 548, CA; reversing [1970] 2 W.L.R. 907; [1970] 1 All E.R.
    673; [1970] 1 Lloyd's Rep. 118, QBD (Comm Ct) . . . . *Digested*, 70/**357**:
                  Considered, 76/2547: *Followed*, 98/811, 00/4702
Milasan,The [2000] 2 All E.R. (Comm) 803; [2000] 2 Lloyd's Rep. 458, QBD (Comm Ct)
                                      Digested, 00/**4724**
Mineral Dampier, The [2001] EWCA Civ 1278; [2001] 2 All E.R. (Comm) 805; [2001] 2
    Lloyd's Rep. 419, CA; affirming [2000] 1 All E.R. (Comm) 870; [2000] 1 Lloyd's Rep.
    282; [2000] C.L.C. 772, QBD (Adm Ct). . . . . *Digested*, 00/**4709**
Ming Galaxy,The [1998] 4 All E.R. 238; [1998] 2 Lloyd's Rep. 454; [1998] C.L.C.1487;
    Times, July 30, 1998, CA; reversing [1998] 1 Lloyd's Rep. 167, QBD (Adm Ct) . .   *Digested*, 98/**4422**
Miss Jay Jay, The [1987] 1 Lloyd's Rep. 32; [1987] F.T.L.R. 14; [1987] Fin. L.R. 120, CA;
    affirming [1985] 1 Lloyd's Rep. 264, QBD (Comm Ct). . . . . *Digested*, 87/**3409**:
                                  Applied, 00/3557
Montan,The [1985] 1 W.L.R. 625; [1985] 1 All E.R. 520; [1985] 1 Lloyd's Rep.189; (1985)
    82 L.S.G.1329; (1985) 129 S.J. 219, CA; affirming [1984] 1 Lloyd's Rep. 389, QBD
    (Comm Ct) . . . . *Digested*, 85/**104**:
           Applied, 01/416: *Considered*, 85/105, 87/3093, 91/199
Moorcock,The (1889) L.R.14 P.D. 64; [1886-90] All E.R. Rep. 530, CA; affirming (1888)
    L.R. 13 P.D. 157, PDAD. . . . . *Applied*, 83/2064,
         93/2407: *Considered*, 76/1532, 86/421, 98/2492: *Distinguished*, 80/1643:
                Doubted, 47-51/1756: *Referred to*, 84/1935, 85/1929
Mosconici, The [2001] 2 Lloyd's Rep. 313, QBD (Comm Ct) . . . . *Digested*, 01/**4936**
Mount I,The [2001] EWCA Civ 68; [2001] Q.B. 825; [2001] 2 W.L.R.1344; [2001] 3 All
    E.R. 257; [2001] 1 All E.R. (Comm) 961; [2001] 1 Lloyd's Rep. 597; [2001] C.L.C.
    843; [2001] Lloyd's Rep. I.R. 460; (2001) 98(9) L.S.G. 38; (2001) 145 S.J.L.B. 45;
    Times, February 21, 2001, CA; reversing in part [2000] 1 All E.R. (Comm) 897;
    [2000] 2 Lloyd's Rep. 684; [2000] C.L.C. 1359; (2000) 97(25) L.S.G. 38;
    Times, June 21, 2000, QBD (Comm Ct) . . . . *Digested*, 01/**811**

Vrontados, The [1982] 2 Lloyd's Rep. 241; (1982) 79 L.S.G. 954; 126 S.J. 331, CA . . . .   *Digested,* 82/**2597**:
Applied, 86/2725: *Considered,* 98/586: *Referred to,* 84/2745

Wagon Mound, The (No.1) [1961] A.C. 388; [1961] 2 W.L.R. 126; [1961] 1 All E.R. 404;
[1961] 1 Lloyd's Rep. 1; 105 S.J. 85, PC (Aus); reversing [1959] 2 Lloyd's Rep. 697,
CA (NSW); affirming [1958] 1 Lloyd's Rep. 575, Sup Ct (NSW). . . . .   *Digested,* 61/**2343**:
Applied, 64/2499, 66/8175, 67/1198, 67/2675, 67/2676, 68/2673, 68/4511,
73/2320, 80/1904, 81/1855, 83/2555: *Approved,* 66/8283, 67/1197:
Considered, 63/969, 64/1004, 67/4282, 68/1201, 68/2640, 68/3227,
68/4233, 69/2412, 69/2435, 70/1849, 74/3704, 75/2343, 78/2074,
82/2126, 86/1069, 95/3682, 98/3914, 00/4239: *Distinguished,* 61/2348,
62/860, 62/862, 62/3311, 64/2500, 66/3445: *Followed,* 66/9533, 67/3114,
69/966, 69/1054
Wagon Mound, The (No.2) [1967] 1 A.C. 617; [1966] 3 W.L.R. 498; [1966] 2 All E.R. 709;
[1966] 1 Lloyd's Rep. 657; 110 S.J. 447, PC (Aus); reversing [1963] 1 Lloyd's Rep.
402, Sup Ct (NSW). . . . .   *Digested,* 66/**3445**:
Applied, 67/2676, 80/1904, 81/1855: *Considered,* 73/2318, 76/1858,
82/4057, 85/2496, 86/2481, 87/2597, 87/4737, 93/1828, 94/3410, 98/3914,
01/4548: *Distinguished,* 83/257: *Referred to,* 92/6076
White Rose, The [1922] 2 K.B. 249; (1922) 11 Ll. L. Rep. 170, KBD . . . .   *Considered,* 96/3555,
98/1461
Windfall, The [1998] 2 Lloyd's Rep. 664, QBD (Comm Ct) . . . .   *Digested,* 99/**4485**
Winnie Rigg, The [1999] Q.B. 1119; [1999] 2 W.L.R. 489; [1998] 2 Lloyd's Rep. 675; (1998)
95(33) L.S.G. 34; (1998) 142 S.J.L.B. 228; *Times,* September 1, 1998;
Independent, October 5, 1998 (C.S.), QBD . . . .   *Digested,* 98/**4428**
Winter, The [2000] 2 Lloyd's Rep. 298, QBD (Comm Ct) . . . .   *Digested,* 00/**776**
World Renown, The [1992] 2 Lloyd's Rep. 115, CA; affirming [1991] 2 Lloyd's Rep. 251, QBD
(Comm Ct) . . . .   *Digested,* 92/**3941**:
Considered, 01/4910
World Symphony, The [1992] 2 Lloyd's Rep. 115, CA; affirming [1991] 2 Lloyd's Rep. 251,
QBD (Comm Ct) . . . .   *Digested,* 92/**3941**:
Considered, 01/4910

Yasin, The [1979] 2 Lloyd's Rep. 45, QBD (Comm Ct) . . . .   *Digested,* 79/**2472**:
Considered, 99/793: *Distinguished,* 85/1788, 86/1787
Yellow Star, The [2000] 2 Lloyd's Rep. 637, CC (Central London) . . . .   *Digested,* 01/**4916**
Yuta Bondarovskaya, The [1998] 2 Lloyd's Rep. 357, QBD (Adm Ct) . . . .   *Digested,* 98/**4414**

Zeus V, The [2000] 2 All E.R. (Comm) 769; [2000] 2 Lloyd's Rep. 587; [2000] C.L.C. 1705,
CA; reversing [1999] 1 Lloyd's Rep. 703; [1999] C.L.C. 391, QBD (Comm Ct) . .   *Digested,* 00/**3541**:
Followed, 99/3408
Zinovia, The [1984] 2 Lloyd's Rep. 264, QBD (Comm Ct) . . . .   *Digested,* 84/**3175**:
Applied, 01/3824